PETERSON'S GUIDE TO
TWO-YEAR COLLEGES
1997

TWENTY-SEVENTH EDITION

Peterson's
Princeton, New Jersey

Visit Peterson's Education Center on the Internet (World Wide Web) at http://www.petersons.com

The colleges and universities represented in this book recognize that federal laws, where applicable, require compliance with Title IX (Education Amendments of 1972), Title VII (Civil Rights Act of 1964), and Section 504 of the Rehabilitation Act of 1973 as amended, prohibiting discrimination on the basis of sex, race, color, handicap, or national or ethnic origin in their educational programs and activities, including admissions and employment.

Editorial inquiries concerning this book should be addressed to the editor at Peterson's, 202 Carnegie Center, P.O. Box 2123, Princeton, New Jersey 08543-2123 (609-243-9111).

Copyright © 1996 by Peterson's

Previous editions published as *Peterson's Annual Guide to Undergraduate Study,* © 1970, 1971, 1972, 1973, 1974, 1975, 1976, 1977, 1978, 1979, 1980, 1981, 1982, and as *Peterson's Guide to Two-Year Colleges,* © 1983, 1984, 1985, 1986, 1987, 1988, 1989, 1990, 1991, 1992, 1993, 1994, 1995

All rights reserved. No part of this book may be reproduced, stored in a retrieval system, or transmitted, in any form or by any means—electronic, mechanical, photocopying, recording, or otherwise—except for citations of data for scholarly or reference purposes with full acknowledgment of title, edition, and publisher and written notification to Peterson's prior to such use.

ISSN 0894-9328
ISBN 1-56079-605-7

Printed in the United States of America

10 9 8 7 6 5 4 3 2 1

Contents

Introduction	iv
What You'll Need to Know	1
What You Need to Know About Two-Year Colleges	2
Fifteen Frequently Asked Questions About Transferring	5
Returning to School: A Guide for Adult Students	8
Paying for Your College Education	11
Surviving Standardized Tests	16
How to Use the Information in This Book	19
Quick-Reference College Search Indexes	27
State-by-State Summary Table	28
What Majors Are Offered Where	
Associate Degree Programs at Two-Year Colleges	49
Associate Degree Programs at Four-Year Colleges	133
Recent Institutional Changes	148
College Profiles and Special Announcements	149
In-Depth Descriptions of the Colleges	687
Index to Colleges and Universities	833

INTRODUCTION

For nearly thirty years, Peterson's has provided students, parents, guidance counselors, and researchers with the most comprehensive, up-to-date information on undergraduate institutions in the United States and Canada. During that time, the college admission process and undergraduate education have changed dramatically, and *Peterson's Guide to Two-Year Colleges* has responded to those changes. The data published in this guide, obtained directly from the colleges themselves and updated annually, are completely accurate and current, and the information and guidance offered reflect trends as they emerge.

The 1990s have seen the number of traditional college-age students dwindling and colleges worried that their enrollments will shrink as a result. Many colleges, especially two-year colleges, now have many older or part-time students. And yet, while colleges are getting more concerned about keeping enrollments up, students seem to be getting more, not less, nervous about choosing and getting into the right college. That's where *Peterson's Guide to Two-Year Colleges* can help. This guide gives students the information they need to make important decisions and to approach college in general and the admission process in particular without fear. Opportunities abound for students, and this guide can help readers find out about them in a number of ways:

- **For information about particular colleges,** turn to the section called College Profiles and Special Announcements. In this section colleges are listed alphabetically and state-by-state, and profiles contain information on all aspects of college life, from admission and transferring to graduation. In addition, for some colleges, narratives are included in the In-Depth Descriptions of the Colleges section, which follows the College Profiles. These descriptions provide greater detail and cover more of the student life and campus atmosphere aspects of the institutions.

- **For colleges that have specific characteristics you're looking for,** turn to the Quick-Reference Indexes, beginning on page 27. In these indexes you can look up colleges by state or by major. When you've noted which colleges have the features you're looking for, just flip to the College Profiles or In-Depth Descriptions for more information.

- **To find out more about a two-year college education,** just turn the page. Helpful articles give up-to-the-minute information on the advantages a two-year college has to offer, the transfer process, how adult students can survive their return to school, understanding financial aid, and surviving standardized tests (including SAT I and ACT test dates).

If you still have questions after you've read and thought about what you find in this guide, or if it has raised new concerns, you may want to consult other resources. Peterson's publishes a wide range of books and software on everything from SAT preparation to getting scholarships to preparing for life as a college freshman. You can find these and other reference sources at your local bookstore, library, or high school guidance office. In addition, Peterson's offers access to the data in the *Guide to Two-Year Colleges* through Apple e-World, CompuServe, Dialog, Dow Jones News/Retrieval, the Microsoft Network, and the Internet at http://www.petersons.com.

As you refine your list of colleges, you will want to contact the colleges directly and visit some campuses. Admission staff members are more than happy to answer questions, address specific problems, and help in any way they can. Whatever your aim in looking at colleges, the staff at Peterson's hopes you will be successful and that this guide will help you get the information you need.

Joseph G. Emanski
Editor

Michael Gilbey
Data Editor

WHAT YOU'LL NEED TO KNOW

What You Need to Know About Two-Year Colleges   2
    What two-year colleges have to offer, by David R. Pierce,
    President, American Association of Community Colleges.

Fifteen Frequently Asked Questions About Transferring   5
    Important information for students exploring the transfer
    process, by Muriel M. Shishkoff.

Returning to School: A Guide for Adult Students   8
    Coping mechanisms and survival tips for adults who have
    made the decision to return to school, by Sandra Cook, Ph.D.,
    Associate Dean, Mundelein College of Loyola University
    Chicago.

Paying for Your College Education   11
    What types of financial aid are given? What are the sources?
    Who is eligible?

Surviving Standardized Tests   16
    Information about American College Testing's ACT and the
    College Board's SAT I and Subject Tests, including the test
    dates for 1996–97.

How to Use the Information in This Book   19
    An explanation of the different college descriptions in this
    book, including special terms, criteria for inclusion, and how
    Peterson's brings this information together.

Peterson's Guide to Two-Year Colleges 1997

What You Need to Know About Two-Year Colleges

by David R. Pierce, President, American Association of Community Colleges

A Brief Overview

Two-year colleges—better known as community colleges—are often called "the people's colleges." With their open-door policies (admission is open to individuals with a high school diploma or its equivalent), community colleges provide access to higher education for millions of Americans who might otherwise be excluded from higher education. Community college students are diverse, of all ages, races, and economic backgrounds. While many community college students enroll full-time, an equally large number attend on a part-time basis so that they can fulfill employment and family commitments as they advance their education.

Today there are nearly 1,200 community colleges in the United States. They enroll more than 5 million credit students, representing almost half of all undergraduates in the United States. Nearly 55 percent of all first-time freshmen begin their higher education in a community college.

Community colleges can also be referred to as either technical or junior colleges, and they may either be under public or independent control. What unites these two-year colleges is that they are regionally accredited, postsecondary institutions, whose highest credential awarded is the associate degree. With few exceptions, community colleges offer a comprehensive curriculum, which includes transfer, technical, and continuing education programs.

Important Factors in a Community College Education

The student who attends a community college can count on receiving quality instruction in a supportive learning community. This setting frees the student to pursue his or her own goals, nurture special talents, explore new fields of learning, and develop the capacity for lifelong learning.

From the student's perspective, four characteristics capture the essence of community colleges:

- First, they are community-based institutions that work in close partnership with high schools, community groups, and employers in extending high-quality programs at convenient times and places.
- Second, community colleges are cost effective. Annual tuition and fees at public community colleges average approximately half those at public four-year colleges and less than 15% of private four-year institutions. In addition, since most community colleges are generally close to their students' homes, these students can also save a significant amount of money on the room, board, and transportation expenses traditionally associated with a college education.
- Third, they provide a caring environment, with faculty members who are expert instructors, known for excellent teaching and for meeting students at the point of their individual needs, regardless of age, sex, race, current job status, or previous academic preparation. Community colleges join a strong curriculum to a broad range of counseling and career services intended to assist students in making the most of their education opportunities.
- Fourth, many offer comprehensive programs, including transfer curricula in such liberal arts programs as chemistry, psychology, and business management, that lead directly to a baccalaureate degree and career programs that prepare students for employment or assist those already employed to upgrade their skills. For those students who need to strengthen their academic skills, community colleges also offer a wide range of developmental programs in mathematics, languages, and learning skills, designed to prepare the student for success in college studies.

Getting to Know Your Two-Year College

The first step in determining the quality of a community college is to check the status of its accreditation. The colleges listed in this guide, for example, all meet the rigorous accreditation standards set by regional accrediting associations. (See the explanation on page 32 for further information on accreditation.) Once you have established that a community college is appropriately accredited, find out as much as you can about the programs and services it has to offer. Much of that information can be found in this book or in materials the college provides. However, the best way to learn about your college is to visit in person.

During a campus visit be prepared to ask a lot of questions. Talk to students, faculty members, administrators, and counselors about the college and its programs, particularly those in which you have a special interest. Ask about available certificates and associate degrees. Don't be shy. Do what you can to dig below the surface. Ask college officials about the transfer rate to four-year colleges. If a college emphasizes student services, find out what particular assistance is offered, such as educational or career guidance. Colleges are eager to provide you with the information you need to make informed decisions.

COMMUNITY COLLEGES CAN SAVE YOU MONEY

If you are able to live at home while you attend college, you will certainly save money on room and board, but it does cost something to commute. Many two-year colleges can now offer you instruction in your own home through cable television or public broadcast stations or through home study courses that can save both time and money. Look into all your options, and be sure to add up all the costs of attending various colleges before deciding which is best for you.

FINANCIAL AID

Many students who attend community colleges are eligible for a range of financial aid programs, including Federal Pell Grants, Perkins and Stafford Loans, state aid, and on-campus jobs. The article in this book entitled "Paying for Your College Education" provides detailed information on the options for financing your college education. Your high school counselor or the financial aid officer at a community college will also be able to help you. It is in your interest to apply for financial aid months in advance of the date you intend to start your college program, so find out early what assistance is available to you. While many community colleges are able to help students who make a last-minute decision to attend college, either through short-term loans or emergency grants, if you are considering entering college and think you might need financial aid, it is best to find out as much as you can as early as you can.

WORKING AND GOING TO SCHOOL

Many two-year college students maintain full-time or part-time employment while they earn their degrees. Over the past decades, a steadily growing number of students have chosen to attend community colleges while they fulfill family and employment responsibilities. To enable these students to balance the demands of home, work, and school, most community colleges offer classes at night and on weekends.

For the full-time student, the usual length of time it takes to obtain an associate degree is two years. However, your length of study will depend on the course load you take: the fewer credits you earn each term, the longer it will take you to earn a degree. To assist you in moving more quickly to your degree, many community colleges now award credit through examination or for experience gained through relevant life experience. Be certain to find out the credit options that are available to you at the college in which you are interested. You may discover that it will take less time to earn a degree than you might have first thought.

PREPARATION FOR TRANSFER

Studies have repeatedly shown students who first attend a community college and then transfer to a four-year college or university do as well academically as the students who entered the four-year institutions as freshmen. Most community colleges have agreements with nearby four-year institutions to make transfer of credits easier. If you are thinking of transferring, be sure to meet with a counselor or faculty adviser before choosing your courses. You will want to map out a course of study with transfer in mind. Make sure you also find out the credit-transfer requirements of the four-year institution you might want to attend.

NEW CAREER OPPORTUNITIES

Community colleges realize that many entering students are not sure about the field in which they want to focus their studies or the career they would like to pursue. Often, students discover fields and careers they never knew existed. Community colleges have the resources to help students identify areas of career interest and to set challenging occupational goals.

Once a career goal is set, the student can be confident that his or her community college will provide job-relevant, quality occupation and technical education. About half the students who take courses for credit at community colleges do so to prepare for employment or to acquire or upgrade skills for their current job. Especially helpful in charting a career path is the assistance of a counselor or a faculty adviser, who can discuss job opportunities in your chosen field and help you map out your course of study.

In addition, since community colleges have close ties to their communities, they are in constant touch with leaders in business, industry, organized labor, and public life. Community colleges work with these individuals and their organizations to prepare students for direct entry into the world of work. For example, some community colleges have established partnerships with local businesses and industries to provide specialized training programs. Some also provide the academic portion of apprenticeship training, while others offer extensive job-shadowing and cooperative education opportunities. Be sure to examine all the career-preparation opportunities offered by the community colleges in which you are interested.

ATTENDING A TWO-YEAR COLLEGE IN ANOTHER REGION

Although many community colleges serve a specific county or district, they are committed (to the extent of their ability) to the goal of equal educational opportunity without regard to economic status, race, creed, color, sex, or national origin. Independent two-year colleges recruit from a much broader geographical area—throughout the United States and, increasingly, around the world.

What You Need to Know About Two-Year Colleges

Although some community colleges do provide on-campus housing for their students, most do not. However, even if on-campus housing is not available, most colleges do have housing referral services.

Advantages at a Glance

- *A Caring Environment.* Faculty members at two-year colleges are known for their excellent teaching and for meeting students at the point of their individual needs.
- *Convenience and Accessibility.* Most two-year colleges are community based, making higher education accessible for all qualified citizens in their service area.
- *Reasonable Cost.* Community colleges are generally quite affordable and work with students to identify sources of financial need as needed.
- *Variety of Associate Degree Programs.* University transfer, occupational-technical fields, and lifelong learning are all components of the typical community college curriculum.
- *Community Partnerships.* Because of their close links to the communities they serve, many two-year colleges establish arrangements with local agencies and employers that provide experience and job opportunities for students both before and after graduation.

Of course, these are generalizations. There is tremendous variety among community colleges, and you would be advised to do careful research about the offerings and environment at any community college you would consider attending. Try to visit at least one two-year college as you investigate postsecondary education. You may find, as did more than half of all entering college freshmen last year, that a community college can offer you the relevant, affordable, and quality education for which you are looking.

Fifteen Frequently Asked Questions About Transferring

by Muriel M. Shishkoff

Among the students attending two-year colleges are a large number who began their higher education knowing they would eventually transfer to a four-year school to obtain their bachelor's degree. There are many reasons why students are going this route. Upon graduating from high school, some simply do not have definite career goals. Although they don't want to put their education on hold, they prefer not to pay exorbitant amounts in tuition while trying to "find themselves." As the cost of a university education escalates—even in public institutions—the option of spending the freshman and sophomore years at a two-year college looks attractive to many students. Others attend a two-year college because they are unable to meet the initial entrance standards—a specified grade point average (GPA), standardized test scores, or knowledge of specific academic subjects—required by the four-year school of their choice. Many such students praise the community college system for giving them the chance to be, academically speaking, "born again." In addition, students from other countries often find that they can adapt more easily to language and cultural changes at a two-year school before transferring to a larger, more diverse four-year college.

If your plan is to attend a two-year college with the ultimate goal of transferring to a four-year school, you will be pleased to know that the increased importance of the community college route to a bachelor's degree is recognized by all segments of higher education. As a result, many two-year schools have revised their course outlines and established new courses in order to comply with the programs and curricular offerings of the universities. Institutional improvements to make transferring easier have also proliferated at both the two- and four-year levels. The generous transfer policies of the Pennsylvania, New York, and Florida state university systems, among others, reflect this attitude; these systems accept *all* credits from students who have graduated from accredited community colleges.

If you are interested in moving from a two-year college to a four-year school, the sooner you make up your mind that you are going to make the switch the better position you will be in to transfer successfully (that is, without having wasted valuable time and credits). The ideal point at which to make such a decision is *before* you register for classes at your two-year school; a counselor can help you plan your course work with an eye toward fulfilling the requirements needed for your major course of study.

Naturally, it is not always possible to plan your transferring strategy that far in advance, but keep in mind that the key to a successful transfer is *preparation,* and preparation takes time—time to think through your objectives and time to plan the right classes to begin work at that school.

As students face the prospect of transferring from a two-year to a four-year school, many thoughts and concerns about this complicated and often frustrating process race through their minds. Here are answers to a few of the questions that are most frequently asked by transferring students.

Q Does every college and university accept transfer students?

A Most four-year institutions accept transfer students, but some do so more enthusiastically than others. Graduating from a community college is an advantage at, for example, Arizona State University and the University of Massachusetts at Boston; both accept more community college transfer students than traditional freshmen. At the State University of New York at Albany, graduates of two-year transfer programs within the State University of New York System are given priority for upper-division (i.e., junior- and senior-level) vacancies.

Schools offering undergraduate work at the upper division only, such as Metropolitan State University in St. Paul, Minnesota, are especially receptive to transfer applications. On the other hand, some schools accept only a few transfer students; others refuse entrance to sophomores or those in their final year. Princeton University requires an "excellent academic record and particularly compelling reasons to transfer." Check an individual college's profiles in *Peterson's Guide to Four-Year Colleges*—or the catalogs of several colleges—for their transfer requirements before you make your final choice of school.

Fifteen Frequently Asked Questions About Transferring

Q Do students who go directly from high school to a four-year college do better academically than transfer students from community colleges?

A On the contrary: some institutions report that transfers from two-year schools who persevere until graduation do *better* than those who started as freshmen.

Q Why is it so important that my two-year college be accredited?

A Four-year colleges and universities accept transfer credit only from schools formally recognized by a regional, national, or professional educational agency. This accreditation signifies that an institution or program of study meets or exceeds a minimum level of educational quality necessary for meeting stated educational objectives.

Q After enrolling at a four-year school, may I still make up necessary courses at a community college?

A Some institutions restrict credit after transfer to their own facilities. Others allow students to take a limited number of transfer courses after matriculation, depending on the subject matter. A few provide opportunities for cross-registration or dual enrollment, which means taking classes on more than one campus.

Q What do I need to do to transfer?

A First, send for your high school and college transcripts. Having chosen the school you wish to transfer to, check its admission requirements against your transcripts. If you find that you are admissible, file an application as early as possible before the deadline. Part of the process will be asking your former schools to send *official transcripts* to the admission office, i.e., not the copies you used in determining your admissibility.

Plan your transfer program with the head of your new department as soon as you have decided to transfer. Determine the recommended general education pattern and necessary preparation for your major. At your present school, take the courses you will need to meet transfer requirements for the new one.

Q What qualifies me for admission as a transfer student?

A Admission requirements for most four-year institutions vary. Depending on the reputation or popularity of the school and program you wish to enter, requirements may be quite selective and competitive. Usually you will need to show satisfactory test scores, an academic record up to a certain standard, and completion of specific subject matter.

Transfer students can be eligible to enter a four-year school in a number of ways: by having been eligible for admission directly upon graduation from high school, by making up shortcomings in grades (or in subject matter not covered in high school) at a community college, or by satisfactory completion of necessary courses or credit hours at another postsecondary institution. Ordinarily, students coming from a community college or from another four-year institution must meet or exceed the receiving institution's standards for freshmen and show appropriate college-level course work taken since high school. Students who did not graduate from high school can present proof of proficiency through results on the General Educational Development test.

Q Are exceptions ever made for students who don't meet all the requirements for transfer?

A Extenuating circumstances, such as disability, low family income, refugee or veteran status, or athletic talent, may permit the special enrollment of students who would not otherwise be eligible but who demonstrate the potential for academic success. Consult the appropriate office—the Educational Opportunity Program, the disabled students' office, the athletic department, or the academic dean—to see whether an exception can be made in your case.

Q How far in advance do I need to apply for transfer?

A Some schools have a rolling admission policy, which means that they process transfer applications as they are received, all year long. With other schools, you must apply during the priority filing period, which can be up to a year before you wish to enter. Check the date with the admission office at your prospective campus or in *Peterson's Guide to Four-Year Colleges.*

Fifteen Frequently Asked Questions About Transferring

Q: Is it possible to transfer courses from several different institutions?

A: Institutions ordinarily accept the courses that they consider transferable, regardless of the number of accredited schools involved. However, there is the danger of exceeding the maximum number of credit hours that can be transferred from all other schools or earned through credit by examination, extension courses, or correspondence courses. The limit placed on transfer credits varies from school to school, so read the catalog carefully to avoid taking courses you won't be able to use. To avoid duplicating courses, keep attendance at different campuses to a minimum.

Q: What is involved in transferring from a semester system to a quarter or trimester system?

A: In the semester system, the academic calendar is divided into two equal parts. The quarter system is more aptly named trimester, since the academic calendar is divided into three equal terms (not counting a summer session). To convert semester units into quarter units or credit hours, simply multiply the semester units by one and a half. Conversely, multiply quarter units by two thirds to come up with semester units. If you are used to a semester system of fifteen- to sixteen-week courses, the ten-week courses of the quarter system may seem to fly by.

Q: Why might a course be approved for transfer credit by one four-year school but not by another?

A: The beauty of postsecondary education in the United States lies in its variety. Entrance policies and graduation requirements are designed to reflect and serve each institution's mission. Because institutional policies vary so widely, schools may interpret the subject matter of a course from quite different points of view. Given that the granting of transfer credit indicates that a course is viewed as being, in effect, parallel to one offered by the receiving institution, it is easy to see how this might be the case at one university and not another.

Q: Must I take a foreign language to transfer?

A: Foreign language proficiency is often required for admission to a four-year institution; such proficiency also often figures in certain majors or in the general education pattern. At Princeton University, for example, where foreign language proficiency is a graduation requirement, all students must demonstrate it by the end of their junior year.

However, at the University of Southern California and other schools, the foreign language competence necessary for admission can be certified before entrance. Often two or three years of a single language in high school will do the trick. Find out if scores received on Advanced Placement examinations, placement examinations given by the foreign language department, or Subject Tests will be accepted in lieu of college course work.

Q: Will the school to which I'm transferring accept pass/no pass, pass/fail, or credit/no credit grades in lieu of letter grades?

A: Usually a limit is placed on the number of these courses you can transfer, and there may be other restrictions as well. If you want to use other-than-letter grades for the fulfillment of general education requirements or lower-division (freshman and sophomore) preparation for the major, check with the receiving institution.

Q: Which is more important for transfer—my grade point average or my course completion pattern?

A: Some schools believe that your past grades indicate academic potential and overshadow prior preparation for a specific degree program. Others require completion of certain introductory courses before transfer to prepare you for upper-division work in your major. In any case, appropriate course selection will cut down the time to graduation and increase your chances of making a successful transfer.

Q: What happens to my credits if I change majors?

A: If you change majors after admission, your transferable course credit should remain fairly intact. However, because you may need extra or different preparation for your new major, some of the courses you've taken may now be useful only as electives. The need for additional lower-level preparation may mean your staying longer at your new school than you originally planned. On the other hand, you may already have taken courses that count toward your new major as part of the university's general education pattern.

Excerpted from Transferring Made Easy: A Guide to Changing Colleges Successfully *by Muriel M. Shishkoff. Copyright 1991 by Muriel M. Shishkoff (published by Peterson's Guides).*

Returning to School: A Guide for Adult Students

by Sandra Cook, Ph.D., Associate Dean, Mundelein College of Loyola University Chicago

Many adults think about returning to school for a long time without taking any action. One purpose of this article is to help the "thinkers" finally make some decisions by examining what is keeping them from action. Another purpose is to describe not only some of the difficulties and obstacles that adult students may face when returning to school but also tactics for coping with them.

If you have been thinking about going back to college... and thinking about it... and thinking about it, believing you are the only person your age contemplating college, you should know that approximately 6 million adult students are currently enrolled in higher education institutions. This number represents 45 percent of total higher education enrollments. And the majority of adult students are enrolled at two-year colleges.

There are many reasons why adult students choose to attend a two-year college. Studies have shown that the three most important criteria that adult students consider when choosing a college are location, cost, and availability of the major or program desired. Most two-year colleges are public institutions that serve a geographic district, making them readily accessible to the community (and they usually have plenty of parking spaces, another criterion that ranks reasonably high in terms of importance). Costs at most two-year colleges are far less than at other types of higher education institutions. For many students who plan to pursue a bachelor's degree, completing their first two years of college at a community college is an affordable means to that end. If you are interested in an academic program that will transfer to a four-year institution, most two-year colleges offer the "general education" courses that compose most freshman and sophomore years. If you are interested in a vocational or technical program, two-year colleges excel in providing this type of training.

Uncertainty, Choice, and Support

There are three different "stages" in the process of adults returning to school. The first stage is *uncertainty*. Do I really want to go back to school? What will my friends or family think? Can I compete with those 18-year-old whiz kids? Am I too old? The second stage is *choice*. Once the decision to return has been made, you must choose where you will attend. There are many criteria to use in making this decision. The third stage is *support*. You have just added another role to your already-too-busy life. There are, however, strategies that will help you accomplish your goals—perhaps not without struggle but with grace and humor. Let's look at each of these stages.

Uncertainty

WHY are you thinking about returning to school? Is it to:
- fulfill a dream that had to be delayed?
- become more educationally well rounded?
- fill an intellectual void in your life?

These reasons focus on *personal growth*.

If you are returning to school to:
- meet people and make friends
- attain and enjoy higher social status and prestige among friends, relatives, and associates
- understand/study a cultural heritage, or
- have a medium in which to exchange ideas,

you are interested in *social and cultural opportunities*.

If you are like most adult students, you want to:
- qualify for a new occupation
- enter or reenter the job market
- increase earnings potential, or
- qualify for a more challenging position in the same field of work.

You are seeking *career growth*.

Understanding the reason(s) why you want to go back to school is an important step in setting your educational goal(s) and will help you to establish some criteria in selecting a college. However, don't delay your decision because you haven't been able to clearly define your motives. Many times these aren't clear until you have already begun the process, and they may change as you move through your college experience. Whatever your reasons, the benefits to you personally and to society in general are overwhelmingly positive.

Assuming that you agree that additional education will be of benefit to you, what is it that keeps you from returning to school? You may have a litany of excuses running through your mind:

I don't have time.
I can't afford it.
I'm too old to learn.

My friends will think I'm crazy.

The teachers will be younger than I.

My family can't survive without me to take care of them every minute.

I'll be *(fill in the blank)* years old when I finish.

I'm afraid.

I don't know what to expect.

And that is just what these are—*excuses*. You can make school, like anything else in your life, a priority or not. If you really want to return, you can. The more you understand your motivation for returning to school and the more you understand what excuses are keeping you from taking action, the easier your task will be.

If you think you don't have time: The best way to decide how attending class and studying can fit into your schedule is to keep track of what you do with your time each day for several weeks. Completing a standard time-management grid (each day is plotted out by the half hour) is helpful for visualizing how your time is spent. For each 3-credit-hour class you take, you will need to find 3 hours for class plus 6 to 9 hours for reading-studying-library time. This study time should be spaced evenly throughout the week, not loaded up on one day. It is not possible to learn or retain the material that way. When you examine your grid, see where there are activities that could be replaced with school and study time. You may decide to give up your bowling league or some time in front of the TV. Try not to give up sleeping, and don't cut out every moment of free time. There are also a number of smaller ways to divert time to school. Here are some suggestions that have come from adults who have returned to school:

- Enroll in a time-management workshop. It helps you rethink how you use your time. We all have only 24 hours in a day, and we need to make the best use of them.
- Don't think you have to take more than one course at a time. You may eventually want to work up to taking more, but consider starting with one. (It's more than you're taking now!)
- If you have a family, start assigning those household chores that you think only you can do "correctly" to them—and don't redo what they do.
- Rethink whether some tasks really need to be done as often as you think—or by you.
- Use your lunch hour or commuting time for reading.

If you think you can't afford it: As mentioned earlier, two-year colleges are extremely affordable. If you cannot afford the tuition, look into the various financial aid options. Most federal and state funds are available to full- and part-time students. Loans are also available. While many people prefer not to accumulate a debt for school, these same people will think nothing of taking out a loan to buy a car. After five or six years, which is the better investment? Adult students who work should look into whether their company has a tuition-reimbursement policy. There are also an increasing number of private scholarships, available through foundations, service organizations, and clubs, that are focused on adult learners. Your public library is an excellent source for reference materials regarding financial aid. A college or university financial aid adviser is also an excellent resource.

If you think you are too old to learn: This is pure myth. As a matter of fact, there have been a number of studies that show adult learners performing as well as or better than traditional-age students.

If you are afraid your friends will think you're crazy: Who cares? Maybe they will, maybe they won't. Usually they will admire your courage and be just a little jealous of your ambition (although they'll never tell you that). Follow *your* dreams, not theirs.

If you are concerned because the teachers or students will be younger than you: Don't be. The age differences that may be apparent in other settings evaporate in the classroom. If anything, an adult in the classroom strikes fear into the hearts of some 18-year-olds because adults have been known to be prepared, ask questions, be truly motivated, and be there to learn!

If you think your family will have a difficult time surviving while you are in school: If you have done everything for them up to now, they might struggle. Consider this an opportunity to help them become independent, more self-sufficient people. Husbands have been known to learn to cook, kids have been known to do laundry, and wives have painted the garage when a family member returns to school. Your family can only make you feel guilty if you let them. You are not abandoning them; you are becoming an educational role model. When you are happy and working toward your goals, everyone benefits. Admittedly, it sometimes takes time for them to realize this. For single parents there are schools that have begun to offer support groups, child care, and cooperative babysitting.

If you're appalled at the thought of being *(fill in the blank)* years old when you graduate in X years: How old will you be in X years if you don't go back to school?

If you are afraid or don't know what to expect: Know that these are natural feelings when one encounters any new situation. Adult students find that their fears usually dissipate once they begin classes. Fear of trying is usually the biggest roadblock to the reentry process.

No doubt you have dreamed up a few more reasons for not making the decision to return to school. Keep in mind that what you are doing is making up excuses, and you are using these excuses to release you from the obligation to make a decision about your life. The thought of returning to college can be scary. Anytime anyone ventures into unknown territory there is a risk—and risks are scary. But taking risks is also a necessary component of personal and professional growth. It is your life, and you alone are responsible for making the decisions that determine its course. Education is an investment in your future.

Choice

Once you have decided to go back to school, your next task is to decide *where* to go. If your educational goals are well defined (e.g., you want to pursue a degree in order to change careers), then your task is a bit easier. But even if your educational goals are still evolving, don't deter your return. Many students who enter higher education with a specific major in mind change that major at least once.

Returning to School

Most students who attend a public two-year college choose the community college in the district in which they live. This is generally the closest and least expensive option if the school offers the programs you want. If you are planning to begin your education at a two-year college and then transfer to a four-year school, there are distinct advantages to choosing your four-year school early. Many community and four-year colleges have "articulation" agreements that designate what credits from the two-year school will transfer to the four-year college and how. Some four-year institutions accept an associate degree as equivalent to the freshman and sophomore years regardless of the courses you have taken. Some four-year schools accept two-year college work only on a course-by-course basis. If you can identify which school you will transfer to, you can know in advance *exactly* how your two-year credits will apply. This can prevent an unexpected loss of credit or time. You can use the strategies outlined below not only to help you choose your two-year college but also to help you identify early which four-year school you will transfer to.

Each institution of higher education is distinctive. Your goal in choosing a college is to come up with the best student-institution fit—matching your needs with the offerings and characteristics of the school. The first step in choosing a college is to determine what criteria are most important to you in attaining your educational goals. It was mentioned earlier that location, cost, and program availability are the three main factors that influenced an adult student's college choice. In considering location, don't forget that some colleges have conveniently located branch campuses. In considering cost, remember to explore your financial aid options before ruling out an institution because of its tuition. Program availability should include not only the major in which you are interested but also whether classes in that major are available when you can take them.

Determining what criteria are important in a college selection decision can seem daunting. It need not be. Some considerations beyond location, cost, and programs are:

- Does the school have a commitment to adult students and offer appropriate services such as child care, tutoring, and advising?
- Are classes offered when you can take them?
- Are there academic options for adults such as credit for life or work experience, credit by examination (including CLEP and PEP), credit for military service, or accelerated programs?
- Is the faculty sensitive to the needs of adult learners?

Once you determine which (if any) criteria are vital in your choice of an institution, you can begin to narrow your choices. There are myriad ways for you to locate the information you desire. This guide and its companion, *Peterson's Guide to Four-Year Colleges*, are excellent sources of information. Many urban newspapers publish a "School Guide" several times a year in which colleges and universities advertise to an adult student market. Consider also talking with current or former students about an institution. In addition, schools themselves publish catalogs, class schedules, and promotional materials that contain much of the information you need, and they are yours for the asking. Many colleges sponsor information sessions and open houses that allow you to visit the campus and ask questions. An appointment with an adviser is a good way to assess the fit between you and the institution. Be sure to bring your questions (write them down as you think of them so you won't miss any) with you to your interview.

Support

Once you have made the decision to return to school and have chosen the institution that best meets your needs, take some additional steps to ensure your success during your crucial first semester. Take advantage of institutional support and build some social support systems of your own. Here are some ways of doing just that:

- Plan to participate in any orientation programs. These serve the threefold purpose of providing you with a great deal of important information, familiarizing you with the campus and its facilities, and giving you the opportunity to meet and begin networking with other students.
- Take steps to deal with any academic weaknesses. Take mathematics and writing placement tests if you have reason to believe you may need some extra help in these areas. It is not uncommon for adult students to need a math refresher course or a program to help alleviate math anxiety. Ignoring a weakness won't make it go away.
- Look into adult reentry programs. Many institutions offer study-skills, textbook-reading, test-taking, and time-management workshops to help adult students.
- You may find that you need to develop a new support system. Your friends or family may not share your enthusiasm for your new endeavor nor understand the trauma of a first test or oral report. This can cause a sense of isolation that can affect your academic success. You can build new support networks by joining an adult student organization, making a point of meeting other adult students through workshops, or actively seeking out a "study buddy" in each class—that invaluable friend who shares and understands your experience.
- You can incorporate your new status as "student" into your family life. Doing your homework with your children at a designated "homework time" is a valuable family activity and reinforces the importance of education.
- Make sure you take a reasonable course load in your first semester. It is far better to have some extra time on your hands and succeed magnificently than to spend the entire semester on the brink of a breakdown. Also, whenever possible, try to focus your first courses not only on requirements but also in areas of personal interest.
- There may be times that test your limits—midterm slump, the exam from hell, an unreasonable professor, a class that cures insomnia, family problems. Faculty, advisers, and student affairs personnel are there to help you—let them.

After completing your first semester, you will probably look back in wonder at why you thought going back to school was so imposing. Certainly it's not without its occasional exasperations. But, as with life, keeping things in perspective and maintaining your sense of humor make the difference between just coping and succeeding brilliantly.

Paying for Your College Education

One important reason students choose to attend two-year colleges is economics. Tuition at two-year colleges is generally lower and many students live at home, thus keeping room and board expenses to a minimum. Many two-year college students are older students, some with families of their own, who attend school part-time and continue working full-time to try to meet their college expenses.

Still, the expenses of attending even a community college can be considerable and are increasing each year at a rate faster than most other products and services. This is where financial aid comes in. Financial aid is money made available by the government and other sources to help students who otherwise would be unable to attend college. Almost $40 billion in aid is given or loaned to students each year, and about half of the college students in this country receive some sort of aid. Most of this aid is distributed to students because neither they nor their families have the necessary resources on their own. This kind of aid is referred to as need-based aid.

Another form of aid, called merit-based aid, is awarded to students who may or may not have need, but who display a particular talent, show extraordinary promise, or are members of groups that are underrepresented in college. Few community or junior colleges award much in the way of merit-based aid, but virtually every two-year college awards need-based aid to students who qualify.

Types and Sources of Financial Aid

There are three types of aid: scholarships (also known as grants or gift aid); loans; and student employment. Scholarships and grants are outright gifts and do not have to be repaid. Loans must be repaid, with interest, usually after graduation. Student jobs can be arranged for a student during the academic year with the wages going toward the college expenses.

Almost all of the aid available to two-year college students is from the federal government, which has six large financial aid programs. Two of these are grants—the Federal Pell Grant and the Federal Supplemental Educational Opportunity Grant (FSEOG). Three are loan programs—the Federal Perkins Loan, the Federal Family of Education Loans, and the William Ford Federal Direct Loan. The sixth program is a student employment program called Federal Work-Study.

A second source of aid is state governments. Nearly every state provides aid for students attending college in that state. Almost all state aid programs feature scholarships and grants, although a few states also have loan and work-study programs.

Federal Financial Aid Programs at a Glance

Name of Program	Type of Program	Maximum Award Per Year
Federal Pell Grant	Need-based grant	$2,300
Federal Supplemental Educational Opportunity Grant (FSEOG)	Need-based grant	$4,000
Federal Work-Study	Part-time job	no maximum
Federal Perkins Loan	Need-based loan	$3,000 (undergraduate)
Federal Stafford Loan Federal Direct Loan (Subsidized)	Need-based student loans	$2,625 (first year)
Federal Stafford Loan Federal Direct Loan (Unsubsidized)	Non-need-based student loans	$2,625 (first year, dependent student)
Federal PLUS Loan	Non-need-based parent loan	Up to the cost of education

A third source of aid is private sources, such as foundations, corporations, civic associations, unions, fraternal organizations, and religious groups that award scholarships and grants to students. Most of these are not based strictly on need, although the amount of the scholarship may vary depending upon your need. The competition for these scholarships can be quite stiff, but the reward is well worth it. You should also keep in mind that many companies also offer tuition reimbursement to employees and their dependents. The personnel or human resources department at your or your parents' place of employment can tell you whether the company offers this benefit and who is eligible.

Finally, many colleges offer scholarships and/or grants to students out of their own funds or through local foundations. This aid is called institutional aid. Junior and county or community colleges, particularly those that are state-supported, usually have very little institutional aid available for students. Sometimes a student must apply separately for these funds, and sometimes they are awarded along with all the other sources. Later in this article, we'll discuss the process of applying for financial aid.

Eligibility for Financial Aid

Most of the financial aid that two-year college students receive is based on need. To see whether you have need, the first thing you must determine is the total cost of attending

Peterson's Guide to Two-Year Colleges 1997

Paying for Your College Education

college. The listings in this book will tell you of how much each college charges for tuition and fees. To determine the total cost of your education for the year, add in your expected room and board expenses, that is, the amount you will spend on food and rent or dorm charges for the 9 months you will be attending school (if you will be living at home, add in about $1800), an amount for books and supplies you will need to buy (about $500 to $600 per year for most full-time students), and a reasonable amount for all other expenses you will have during the year. These expenses include such things as transportation, utilities, entertainment, and childcare. Most colleges will be able to give you an idea of how much you should plan to spend on these items for the year. The total of all your expenses is your total cost of attendance.

The next step in determining your eligibility for financial aid is to determine how much you can afford to pay toward your total cost of education. This process is called, appropriately, "need analysis" and is based your family's income, assets, size of family, etc. A formula has been devised by the U.S. Congress that takes into account these and a few other criteria. The end result of this need analysis is your "expected family contribution" (EFC) and represents the amount you and your family should be able to contribute toward your educational expenses.

Who's in Your Family: Dependent or Independent

The basic principle of government financial aid is that the primary responsibility for paying college expenses resides with the family. So, in determining your expected family contribution, you will first need to know who makes up your "family." That will tell you whose income is counted when the need analysis is done. If you are financially dependent upon your parents, then their income and assets, as well as yours, are counted toward the family contribution. But if you are considered independent of your parents, only your income (and your spouse if you're married) counts in the calculation. There are strict rules for determining whether you are independent (see the definition in the sidebar in the next column). If there are extraordinary circumstances, the financial aid administrator at the college you will be attending has the authority to change this. Such a change, however, often requires extensive documentation of the extraordinary situation.

If you are a dependent student, use the table that appears on the next page to help you estimate your Expected Family Contribution. If you are independent, you can use the following quick calculation to estimate your family contribution:

Take your total family income (yours and your spouse's income) for the previous year, subtract all state and federal taxes you paid (including FICA), subtract another $3000 ($6000 if you are married), and divide the result in half. If your family income is less than $50,000, this figure is your estimated Expected Family Contribution. If your income is greater than $50,000, add 35 percent (12 percent if you have children) of your total assets (bank accounts, stocks, etc.). This result is your estimated Expected Family Contribution.

In order to be considered independent for financial aid, you must meet any one of the following:
- You must be at least 24 years old, or
- You must be a veteran of the U.S. Armed Forces, or
- You must be married, or
- You must be an orphan or a ward of the court (or were a ward of the court until you were 18 years old), or
- You have legal dependents other than a spouse.

If you meet any one of these conditions, you are considered independent and only your income (and your spouse's if you are married) counts toward your family contribution.

Determining Your Need

Now that you know how much your education will cost and the amount you and your family will be expected to contribute toward your college expenses, you can determine your eligibility for financial aid. Simply subtract your calculated expected family contribution from the total cost of attending a college and the result is the amount you will need to attend that college. It is also the total amount of need-based financial aid you will be eligible for at that college. Since each college will have a different cost, depending on the tuition and fees charged, your need at each college will differ.

Applying for Financial Aid

Now that you have determined that you have a financial need, you'll want to apply for financial aid to meet that need. The process for applying for aid is a simple one for most two-year college students. For those students who are also applying to four-year colleges, the process may be a bit more complicated and we suggest you contact the colleges themselves to make sure you are proceeding correctly.

For most two-year colleges there is just one application that every student must use to apply for financial aid: the Free Application for Federal Student Aid (FAFSA). This is a four-page application available in high school guidance offices, college financial aid offices, state education department offices, many local libraries, the U.S. Department of Education, and even the local office of your congressional representative. It is also available on computer diskette, called FAFSA Express. You can get either the paper application or computer diskette by calling the U.S. Department of Education at 1-800-433-3243. The FAFSA that students use to apply for aid in the 1997–98

Paying for Your College Education

year (typically September 1997 through June 1998) will first become available in November or December of 1996. However, you may not complete it until after January 1, 1997. Make sure you and your parents (if appropriate) have signed your completed FAFSA, and send it to the processing center in the envelope provided. Do not send any additional materials, but do make a copy of what you filled out.

The processing center only enters the data into a computer that runs the federal methodology of need analysis to calculate your family contribution. It then distributes the information to the colleges and agencies you listed on the FAFSA. The actual determination of need and the awarding of aid is handled by the college financial aid office.

It's generally recommended that you complete the FAFSA as soon after January 1, 1997 as possible, but if it is much later, even fall of 1997, it's not too late to qualify for financial aid. If, for example, you did not decide to go to college until just before classes began, or will be attending only the spring 1998 semester, you can still complete the FAFSA and be eligible for many federal and state financial aid programs. If you had completed a FAFSA for 1997–98 but did not list the two-year college you are now considering, you should not complete a second FAFSA. You should, however, call or visit the financial aid office at the two-year college and ask them how they want you to proceed.

FAFSA Express

The U.S. Department of Education has recently begun using an electronic version of the FAFSA. To use this program you

Approximate Expected Family Contribution for 1996–97

ASSETS ▼	FAMILY SIZE	$20,000	30,000	40,000	50,000	60,000	70,000	80,000	90,000	100,000
$20,000	3	$400	2,000	3,800	6,700	9,900	12,500	15,500	18,500	21,500
	4	0	1,300	2,900	5,300	8,300	11,300	14,200	17,200	20,200
	5	0	700	2,200	4,200	6,800	10,100	13,100	16,100	19,100
	6	0	0	1,500	3,300	5,200	8,800	11,700	14,700	17,400
$30,000	3	$400	2,000	3,800	6,700	9,900	12,500	15,500	18,500	21,500
	4	0	1,300	2,900	5,300	8,300	11,300	14,200	17,200	20,200
	5	0	700	2,200	4,200	6,800	10,100	13,100	16,100	19,100
	6	0	0	1,500	3,300	5,200	8,800	11,700	14,700	17,400
$40,000	3	$400	2,000	3,800	6,800	10,000	12,600	15,600	18,600	21,600
	4	0	1,300	2,900	5,400	8,400	11,400	14,300	17,300	20,300
	5	0	700	2,200	4,300	6,900	10,200	13,200	16,200	19,200
	6	0	0	1,500	3,400	5,300	8,900	11,800	14,800	17,500
$50,000	3	$400	2,000	3,800	7,300	10,500	13,200	16,200	19,100	22,100
	4	0	1,300	2,900	5,900	9,000	11,900	14,900	18,000	20,900
	5	0	700	2,200	4,800	7,500	10,800	13,700	16,700	19,700
	6	0	0	1,500	3,700	5,800	9,400	12,400	15,400	18,100
$60,000	3	$400	2,000	3,800	7,900	11,100	13,700	16,700	19,700	22,700
	4	0	1,300	2,900	6,500	9,500	12,500	15,500	18,500	21,400
	5	0	700	2,200	5,200	8,000	11,300	14,300	17,300	20,300
	6	0	0	1,500	4,100	6,400	10,000	13,000	16,000	18,600
$70,000	3	$400	2,000	3,800	8,500	11,700	14,300	17,300	20,300	23,300
	4	0	1,300	2,900	7,000	10,100	13,000	16,000	19,000	22,000
	5	0	700	2,200	5,700	8,600	11,900	14,900	17,900	20,800
	6	0	0	1,500	4,500	6,900	10,600	13,500	16,500	19,200
$80,000	3	$400	2,000	3,800	9,000	12,200	14,900	17,800	21,800	23,800
	4	0	1,300	2,900	7,600	10,700	13,600	16,600	19,600	22,600
	5	0	700	2,200	6,300	9,200	12,400	15,400	18,400	21,400
	6	0	0	1,500	4,900	7,500	11,100	14,100	17,100	19,700
$90,000	3	$400	2,000	3,800	9,600	12,800	15,400	18,400	21,400	24,400
	4	0	1,300	2,900	8,200	11,200	14,200	17,200	20,200	23,100
	5	0	700	2,200	6,900	9,700	13,000	16,000	19,000	22,000
	6	0	0	1,500	5,400	8,100	11,700	14,700	17,700	20,300
$100,000	3	$400	2,000	3,800	10,200	13,400	16,000	19,000	22,000	25,000
	4	0	1,300	2,900	8,800	11,800	14,700	17,700	20,700	23,700
	5	0	700	2,200	7,400	10,300	13,600	16,600	19,500	22,500
	6	0	0	1,500	6,000	8,600	11,200	15,200	18,200	20,900

Peterson's Guide to Two-Year Colleges 1997

Paying for Your College Education

must have an IBM-compatible PC with a hard disk and 3 1/2" floppy drive. The computer must have at least a 486 33MHz processor, 8 megabytes of RAM and 10 megabytes free on the hard disk, Windows 3.1 or later, and a 1200 baud Hayes-compatible modem to transmit the data. The computer should also have a printer since and you and your parents must sign and send in a hard copy of a Signature Page.

WHAT HAPPENS AFTER YOU SUBMIT THE FAFSA

About two to four weeks after you send in your completed FAFSA, either electronically using FAFSA Express, or hard copy through the mail, you will receive a Student Aid Report (SAR) that shows the information you reported and your calculated expected family contribution. This is the chance you have to make any corrections in the information you reported, and the SAR contains instructions on how to make corrections.

At the time you receive the SAR, the college(s) you specified should also receive the information. The financial aid office may request additional information from you or may ask you to provide documentation verifying the information you reported on the FAFSA. For example, they may ask you for a copy of your (and your parents') income tax return or official forms verifying any untaxed income you or your parents received (e.g., social security, disability, or welfare benefits).

Once the financial aid office is satisfied that the information is correct and they have determined you have need, they can make you a financial aid offer. Many colleges like to be able to make this offer in the spring prior to the fall enrollment so that students have an opportunity to make their plans, but many others wait until summer.

YOUR FINANCIAL AID OFFER

If you have need, a college will typically offer a combination of the three types of assistance to meet that need: scholarship/grant, loan, and work-study. You may accept all or part of the financial aid offer, which is usually made with the idea that you will be attending full-time. If you plan on attending less than full-time, you should contact the financial aid office. It is quite possible your award will be less, partly because colleges recognize that, as a part-time student, you will have more opportunity to earn money. In addition, your total costs will likely decrease.

If you are awarded Federal Work-Study, the amount you are awarded, plus the total of any unmet need and your family contribution, is the total you are allowed to earn for the year. If you already have a job, chances are it will pay more than a Federal Work-Study job or a job on campus, so you'll want to talk with your employer about working part-time to attend school.

If you earn more on your job than the amount you are awarded in Federal Work-Study and receive other need-based aid, there is a possibility you will receive more than

LOWER YOUR COLLEGE EXPENSES

If your resources don't meet your need, use these tips to lower your expenses:

1. Live in your parents' home or share an apartment with a roommate or two.
2. Limit long-distance telephone calls and turn down utilities at night and when you're not at home.
3. Use public transportation if possible. Owning, operating, and insuring a car can be very expensive. If you own a car, consider carpooling.
4. Bring your lunch to school rather than eating out.
5. Cook your meals rather than eating out. Even low-cost fast food is more expensive than cooking a meal, and a home-cooked meal is likely to be much more nutritious.
6. If possible, buy used books rather than new ones, and sell some of your books back to the college bookstore if you no longer need them.
7. Avoid using credit cards if possible. If you must, be sure to pay off the balance each month. If you don't, you are borrowing money at high rates, and you will be paying interest on every purchase from the day that the purchase is made.
8. Plan your budget for the academic year. The financial aid office will likely have brochures and literature to help you plan, as well as other hints on lowering your costs.

the total cost of attending college for the year. In this case, a good idea may be to turn down some of the loan portion of your financial aid offer so that when you complete your schooling you will owe less.

One thing you need to keep in mind is that the student budget used to establish eligibility for financial aid is based on averages. It may not reflect your actual expenses. Student budgets usually reflect most expenses for categories of students (for example, single students living in their parents' home, single parents living in an apartment or house near campus, etc.). But if you have expenses that are not included, you should talk with someone in the financial aid office about making a budget adjustment. Often, students are permitted to earn or borrow more in order to meet expenses not normally counted in the student budget. On occasion, more grant money is awarded. More often than not, however, if a budget adjustment is made, students are awarded more loan or work-study money or are allowed to earn more in their own jobs.

IF YOUR FAMILY OR JOB SITUATION CHANGES

Because a family contribution is based on the previous year's income, many two-year college students find they do not qualify for need-based aid (or not enough to pay their full

Paying for Your College Education

expenses). This is particularly true of older students who were working full-time last year but are no longer doing so, or will not be during the academic year, and students whose families are currently experiencing financial difficulties. If this is your situation, you should speak to a counselor in the financial aid office about making an adjustment in your family contribution need analysis. Financial aid administrators are allowed to make changes to any of the elements that go into a need analysis or to the calculated expected family contribution if there are conditions that merit a change. A loss of a job or a change in the family makeup are examples of those conditions.

IF YOU STILL DON'T QUALIFY FOR NEED-BASED AID

If you still do not qualify for need-based aid but feel you don't have the resources necessary to pay for college, you still have many options available.

First, there are two loan programs for which need is not a consideration. These two programs are the Unsubsidized Federal Stafford Loan and the Unsubsidized Federal Direct Loan. There is also a non-need-based loan program for parents of dependent children called the Federal PLUS Loan. If you or your parents are interested in borrowing through one of these programs, you should check with the financial aid office for more information. For many students, borrowing to pay for their college education can be an excellent investment in their future. At the same time, you want to be sure that you don't overburden yourself when it comes to paying back the loans. Before you take out a student loan, the financial aid office will have you go through a counseling session to make sure that you know the terms of the loan and understand the ramifications of borrowing. If you can do without, it is often suggested that you postpone student loans until you absolutely need them.

A second option if you don't qualify for aid is to search for scholarships that are not based on need. But be wary of scholarship search agencies that promise to find you scholarships and ask you to pay a fee. Often, you can find out about scholarships in the library or from the financial aid office for free. Also, you still have to apply for them, and sometimes they are extremely competitive, awarding aid to just a handful of students out of thousands of applicants. The old rule, "if it sounds too good to be true, it probably is" definitely applies to the scholarship search companies. When they claim billions of dollars of aid go unused, most are referring to potential employer tuition contributions that go unused because the employees don't go to school so they don't take advantage of tuition benefits.

Another option you might have if you don't qualify for need-based aid is to work more hours or find a job if you do not already have one. You will probably be on your own when it comes to finding summer work, but the student employment office at your college should be able to help you with a school-year job, either on- or off-campus. Many colleges have vacancies remaining after they have placed aid students in their work-study jobs.

Surviving Standardized Tests

What Are Standardized Tests?

Colleges and universities in the United States use tests to evaluate applicants for admission or to place them in courses. The tests that are most frequently used by colleges are American College Testing's ACT Assessment Program, commonly known as the ACT, and the College Board SAT Program. Both programs offer the tests at designated testing centers located at high schools and colleges throughout the United States and U.S. territories, and both also have testing centers in various countries throughout the world. The ACT program examines approximately 1.6 million students annually; in 1993–94, approximately 2.7 million SAT Program tests were administered.

Both services offer, upon request, special accommodations for students with documented visual, hearing, physical, or learning disabilities. Examples of special accommodations include tests in Braille or large print, and aids, including a reader, recorder, magnifying glass, or sign language interpreter. Additional testing time may be allowed in some instances. Please contact the appropriate testing program or your guidance counselor for details on how to request special accommodations.

Some colleges may require that students take the tests by a certain date. For further information students should contact their secondary school adviser. Here is a brief description of each testing program.

College Board SAT Program

The SAT Program consists of the SAT I: Reasoning Test and the SAT II: Subject Tests. The SAT I is a three-hour test, primarily multiple-choice, that measures verbal and mathematical abilities. The verbal sections test vocabulary, verbal reasoning, and critical reading skills. Emphasis is placed on reading passages, which are 400–850 words in length. Some reading passages are paired; the second opposes, supports, or in some way complements the point of view expressed in the first. The mathematics sections test students' ability to solve problems involving arithmetic, algebra, and geometry. They include questions that require students to produce their own responses rather than choose from four or five answer choices. Also, students may use caluculators on the SAT I mathematics sections.

The SAT II: Subject Tests are one-hour tests, primarily multiple-choice, in specific subjects that measure students' knowledge of these subjects and their ability to apply the knowledge. Tests offered during 1995–96 include Writing, Literature, Math Level I, Math Level IC, Math Level IIC, Biology, Chemistry, Physics, American History and Social Studies, World History, French (reading only), German (reading only), Modern Hebrew, Italian, Latin, Spanish (reading only), and Foreign Language Tests with Listening in German, Spanish, Japanese, French, and Chinese. The Mathematics Level IC and IIC tests require the use of a scientific calculator. Beginning in November 1995, the English Language Proficiency Test (ELPT) will be introduced.

SAT Program scores are sent automatically to each student who has taken the test. Students may request that they be reported to their high schools or to the colleges to which they are applying. If they choose the Score Choice Option, students may review their SAT II: Subject Test scores and decide whether they want them to appear on their cumulative score record.

New Scoring Scale as of April 1995

For all test dates on or after April 1, 1995, students, guidance counselors, and colleges and universities will receive scores that have been placed on a new, "recentered" SAT I score scale. Over the years, the average score on the

---

1996–97 ACT and SAT Test Dates

ACT Program
October 26, 1996
December 14, 1996
February 8, 1997
April 12, 1997
June 14, 1997

All test dates fall on a Saturday. Due to the special requirements of legislation in effect in New York State, a February test date is not scheduled in that state. For the same reasons, fees for students testing in that state will be higher on all test dates. Tests are also given on the Sundays following the Saturday test dates, but only for students who cannot take the test on Saturday because of religious reasons. The basic ACT registration fee for 1995–96 was $18 ($21 in New York State and Florida).

SAT Program
October 12, 1996 (SAT I and SAT II)
November 2, 1996 (SAT I, SAT II, and
Language Tests with Listening*)
December 7, 1996 (SAT I and SAT II)
January 25, 1997 (SAT I and SAT II)
March 15, 1997 (SAT I only)
May 3, 1997 (SAT I and SAT II)
June 7, 1997 (SAT I and SAT II)

*Language Tests with Listening (including ELPT) are offered only at this administration and only at some test centers in the U.S. and Puerto Rico. See the *Registration Bulletin* for details.

For the 1995–96 academic year, the basic fee for the SAT I: Reasoning Test was $21 and the basic fee for the SAT II: Subject Tests was $13 plus $4 per Subject Test. Fee waivers are available to juniors and seniors who cannot afford test fees.

SAT has moved away from 500—the midpoint of the 200-to-800 scale. This change will reestablish the average score near the midpoint of the scale. In addition, it will realign the verbal and math scores so that a student with a score of 450 on each test can conclude that his or her math and verbal skills are equal. The previous scales showed the average verbal score to be about 425 and the average math score to be about 475, which made comparison between the two much more difficult. This new system is also designed to help reflect more accurately the diversity of students now taking the test and continuing their education in college.

Using the SAT I Score Conversion Chart

During this year of transition, it is likely that you will come across some information with the old scores and some with the new. For instance, you may receive some college literature that reports average verbal and math SAT scores for entering students based on the original scale. You will want to know how your verbal and math recentered scores compare with these. To find out, simply look up your score in the "New" column of the chart on this page. This score will line up with the original score in the "Old" column of the chart. For example, if you received a recentered score of **560** on your verbal test, it would be equivalent to an original score of **480**. If you look at these scores at face value, you will be comparing apples and oranges. By using the chart, you will gain a much better sense of how the old and new scores relate to one another. Keep in mind that all conversions should be considered approximate and that when actual scores are calculated, very precise formulae are used to generate a scaled score from a raw or formula score. It's also important to remember that even though recentered scores may appear to be "higher," it does not translate to improved performance.

Interpreting the Data in This Guide

In the College Profiles and Special Announcements section of this guide, the percentage of students admitted with verbal and math SAT I scores above 500 has been reported in the highlights section at the beginning of each college's profile. Please note that this percentage is based on *original scores and not based on the recentered scale,* due to the fact that the new information was unavailable at the time of publication. However, by using the Conversion Chart you will gain a better sense of whether or not your scores fit in with a particular college's admission patterns.

ACT ASSESSMENT PROGRAM

The ACT Assessment Program is a comprehensive data collection, processing, and reporting service designed to assist in educational and career planning by students, high schools, and postsecondary institutions. The ACT Assessment instrument consists of four academic tests, taken under timed conditions, and a Student Profile Section and Interest Inventory, completed when students register for the ACT.

The academic tests cover four areas—English, mathematics, reading, and science reasoning. They are designed to assess the student's educational development and readiness to handle college-level work. For all four tests the minimum standard score is 1 and the maximum is 36. The composite score is the average of the four standard scores; it, too, has a range of 1–36. In 1995 the mean composite score for college-bound graduating seniors who took the ACT was 20.8; about two thirds of these students had composite scores between 12 and 22.

The Student Profile Section requests information about each student's admission and enrollment plans, academic and

SAT I SCORE EQUIVALENCE CHART

\multicolumn{6}{c	}{Verbal}	\multicolumn{6}{c}{Math}
Old	New	Old	New	Old	New	Old	New	Old	New	Old	New
790	800	590	660	390	470	790	800	590	600	390	430
780	800	580	650	380	460	780	800	580	590	380	430
770	800	570	640	370	450	770	780	570	580	370	420
760	800	560	630	360	440	760	770	560	570	360	410
750	800	550	620	350	430	750	760	550	560	350	400
740	800	540	610	340	420	740	740	540	560	340	390
730	800	530	600	330	410	730	730	530	550	330	380
720	790	520	600	320	400	720	720	520	540	320	370
710	780	510	590	310	390	710	700	510	530	310	350
700	760	500	580	300	380	700	690	500	520	300	340
690	750	490	570	290	370	690	680	490	520	290	330
680	740	**480**	**560**	280	360	680	670	480	510	280	310
670	730	470	550	270	350	670	660	470	500	270	300
660	720	460	540	260	340	660	650	460	490	260	280
650	710	450	530	250	330	650	650	450	480	250	260
640	700	440	520	240	310	640	640	440	480	240	240
630	690	430	510	230	300	630	630	430	470	230	220
620	680	420	500	220	290	620	620	420	460	220	200
610	670	410	490	210	270	610	610	410	450	210	200
600	670	400	480	200	230	600	600	400	440	200	200

Reprinted with permission by the College Board.

out-of-class high school achievements and aspirations, and high school course work. The student is also asked to supply biographical data and self-reported high school grades in the four subject-matter areas covered by the academic tests.

The ACT Interest Inventory is designed to measure six major dimensions of student interests. Results are used to compare the student's interests with those of college-bound students who later majored in each of a wide variety of areas. Inventory results are also used to help students compare their work-activity preferences with work activities that characterize specific families of jobs.

Because the information resulting from the ACT Assessment Program is used in a variety of educational settings, American College Testing prepares three reports for each student: the Student Report, the High School Report, and the College Report. It provides one copy of the Student Report, consisting of an easy-to-understand, personalized narrative report and the student guide *Using Your ACT Assessment Results*, for each student and one copy of the High School Report for the counselor's use. Both reports are sent to the student's high school, except after the June test date, when the Student Report is sent directly to the student's home address. The College Report is sent to the colleges the student designates.

Early in the school year, American College Testing sends to high schools across the country registration packets containing all the information a student needs to register for the ACT Assessment. High school guidance offices also receive a supply of *Preparing for the ACT Assessment*, a booklet that contains a complete practice test, an answer key, and general information about preparing for the test. Students can pick up a copy free of charge at their guidance office.

Students should contact their secondary school counselor for full information about the SAT and ACT programs.

How To Use the Information in This Book

Peterson's Guide to Two-Year Colleges 1997 contains a wealth of information for anyone interested in colleges offering associate degrees. This section details the criteria that institutions must meet to be included in this guide and provides information about research procedures used by Peterson's Guides.

In addition, this section gives readers an overview of the various databased components of the book and presents explanatory material to help them interpret the data it contains.

How Schools Get into the Guide

Peterson's Guide to Two-Year Colleges 1997 covers accredited institutions in the United States and U.S. territories that award the associate degree as their most popular undergraduate offering (a few also offer bachelor's, master's, or doctoral degrees). The term "two-year college" is the commonly used designation for institutions that grant the associate, since two years is the normal duration of the traditional associate degree program. However, some programs may be completed in one year, others require three years, and, of course, part-time programs may take a considerably longer period. Therefore, "two-year college" should be understood as a conventional term that accurately describes most of the institutions included in this guide but which should not be taken literally in all cases. Also included are some non-degree-granting institutions, usually branch campuses of a multicampus system, that offer the equivalent of the first two years of a bachelor's degree, transferable to a bachelor's-degree-granting institution.

To be included in this guide, an institution must have full accreditation or candidate-for-accreditation (preaccreditation) status granted by an institutional or specialized accrediting body recognized by the U.S. Department of Education. Recognized institutional accrediting bodies, which consider each institution as a whole, are the following: the six regional associations of schools and colleges (Middle States, New England, North Central, Northwest, Southern, and Western), each of which is responsible for a specified portion of the United States and its territories; the Accrediting Association of Bible Colleges (AABC); the Accrediting Council for Independent Colleges and Schools (ACICS); the Accrediting Commission of Career Schools/Colleges of Technology; the Distance Education and Training Council (DETC); the American Academy for Liberal Education (AALE); the Council on Occupational Education (COE); and the Transnational Association of Christian Schools (TRACS). Program registration by the New York State Board of Regents is considered to be the equivalent of institutional accreditation, since the Board requires that all programs offered by an institution meet its standards before recognition is granted. This guide also includes institutions outside the United States and its territories that are accredited by recognized U.S. accrediting bodies. There are recognized specialized accrediting bodies in over forty different fields, each of which is authorized to accredit specific programs in its particular field. This can serve as the equivalent of institutional accreditation for specialized institutions that offer programs in one field only (schools of art, music, optometry, theology, etc.). For a full explanation of the accrediting process and complete information on recognized accrediting bodies, the reader should refer to *Peterson's Register of Higher Education*.

Research Procedures

The data contained in the college indexes and college profiles were collected between fall 1995 and spring 1996 through Peterson's Annual Survey of Undergraduate Institutions. Questionnaires were sent to the more than 1,500 colleges that meet the criteria for inclusion outlined above. All data included in this edition have been submitted by officials (usually admission and financial aid officers, registrars, or institutional research personnel) at the schools themselves. In addition, the great majority of institutions that submitted data were contacted directly by Peterson's editorial staff to verify unusual figures, resolve discrepancies, and obtain additional data. All usable information received in time for publication has been included. The omission of any particular item from an index or profile listing signifies that the item is either not applicable to that institution or that data were not available. Because of the comprehensive editorial review that takes place in our offices and because all material comes directly from college officials, we have every reason to believe that the information presented in this guide is accurate. However, students should check with a specific college at the time of

How to Use the Information in This Book

application to verify such information as tuition and fees and application deadlines, which may have changed since the publication of this volume.

STATE-BY-STATE SUMMARY TABLE

This geographically arranged index lists colleges by name and city under the state, territory, or country in which they are located. Areas are listed in the following order: United States (the fifty states and the District of Columbia), U.S. territories (American Samoa, Federated States of Micronesia, Guam, the Marshall Islands, Northern Mariana Islands, Palau Island, and Puerto Rico), and other countries (Republic of Panama and Switzerland); the institutions in these countries are included because they are accredited by recognized U.S. accrediting bodies—see the section on How Schools Get into the Guide.

The index contains basic information that will enable the reader to classify each institution quickly according to broad characteristics. An asterisk (*) after an institution's name denotes that a Special Announcement is included in the college's profile, and a dagger (†) indicates that an institution has one or more entries in the In-Depth Descriptions of the Colleges section.

Degrees Awarded (Column 1)

C = *college transfer associate degree:* the degree awarded after a "university-parallel" program, equivalent to the first two years of a bachelor's degree.

T = *terminal associate degree:* the degree resulting from a one- to three-year program providing training for a specific occupation.

B = *bachelor's degree* (baccalaureate): the degree resulting from a liberal arts, science, professional, or preprofessional program normally lasting four years, although in some cases an accelerated program can be completed in three years.

M = *master's degree:* the first graduate (postbaccalaureate) degree in the liberal arts and sciences and certain professional fields, usually requiring one to two years of full-time study.

D = *doctoral degree* (doctorate): the highest degree awarded in research-oriented academic disciplines, usually requiring from three to six years of full-time study beyond the baccalaureate and intended as preparation for university-level teaching and research.

F = *first professional degree*: the degree required to be academically qualified to practice in certain professions, such as law and medicine, having as a prerequisite at least two years of college credit and usually requiring a total of at least six years of study including prior college-level work.

Institutional Control (Column 2)

Private institutions are designated as one of the following:
  Ind = *independent* (nonprofit)
  Ind-R = *independent-religious:* sponsored by or affiliated with a certain religious group or having a nondenominational or interdenominational religious orientation.
  Prop = *proprietary* (profit-making)

Public institutions are designated by the source of funding, as follows:
  Fed = *federal*
  State
  Comm = *commonwealth* (Puerto Rico)
  Terr = *territory* (U.S. territories)
  County
  Dist = *district:* an administrative unit of public education, often having boundaries different from units of local government.
  City
  St & Loc = *state and local:* "local" may refer to county, district, or city.
  St-R = *state-related:* funded primarily by the state but administratively autonomous.

Student Body (Column 3)

Men = *men only* (100% of student body)

Prim M = *primarily men*

Women = *women only* (100% of student body)

Prim W = *primarily women*

Coed = *coeducational*

Undergraduate Enrollment (Column 4)

The figure shown represents the actual number of full-time and part-time students enrolled in undergraduate degree programs as of fall 1995.

Enrollment Percentages (Columns 5–9)

Figures are shown for the percentages of the fall 1995 undergraduate enrollment made up of students attending part-time (column 5), students receiving some form of need-based financial aid (column 6), and students 25 years of age or older (column 7). Also listed are the percentage of fall 1994 freshmen who returned for the fall 1995 term (column 8) and the percentage of 1994–95 graduates who completed a college-transfer associate program and went directly on to four-year colleges (column 9).

For columns 10 through 19, the following letter codes are used: Y—yes; N—no; R—recommended; S—for some.

Peterson's Guide to Two-Year Colleges 1997

How to Use the Information in This Book

Admission Policies (Columns 10–13)

The information in these columns shows whether the college has an open admission policy (column 10) whereby virtually all applicants are accepted without regard to standardized test scores, grade average, or class rank; whether a high school equivalency certificate is accepted in place of a high school diploma for admission consideration (column 11); and whether a high school transcript (column 12) or one or more entrance tests (column 13) are required as part of the application process. In columns 12 and 13, the combination of the codes R and S indicates that a high school transcript and/or entrance tests are recommended for all applicants *and* required for some.

Financial Aid (Columns 14–16)

These columns show which colleges offer the following types of financial aid: college-administered scholarships (column 14), which may be need-based or non-need awards; loans (column 15), either short-term or low-interest long-term; and part-time jobs (column 16) on or off campus, including those offered through the federal government's Federal Work-Study Program. For full definitions of these and other sources of financial aid, see the explanation of the Financial Aid section of the College Profiles below and Paying for Your College Education in the What You'll Need to Know section.

Services and Facilities (Columns 17–19)

These columns show which colleges offer the following: career counseling (column 17) on either an individual or group basis; job placement services (column 18) for individual students; and college-owned or -operated housing facilities (column 19) for noncommuting students.

Sports (Column 20)

This figure indicates the number of sports that a college offers at the intramural and/or intercollegiate levels.

Majors (Column 21)

This figure indicates the number of major fields of study in which a college offers degree programs. See the College Profiles section for a complete list of majors for each college.

ASSOCIATE DEGREE PROGRAMS AT TWO-YEAR COLLEGES

This index presents approximately 350 undergraduate major fields of study that two-year colleges' responses to Peterson's Annual Survey of Undergraduate Institutions indicate are currently offered most widely. (The Liberal Arts/General Studies category indicates a general program with no specified major.) The majors appear in alphabetical order, each followed by an alphabetical list of the schools that offer a program in that field.

The names of the major areas represent their most widely used designations. However, many institutions use different terms for the same or similar areas. Readers should refer to a college's catalog or to its In-Depth Description in this book for the college's exact terminology. In addition, while the term "major" is used in this guide, some colleges may use other terms, such as concentration, program of study, or field.

ASSOCIATE DEGREE PROGRAMS AT FOUR-YEAR COLLEGES

This index presents approximately 310 undergraduate major fields of study that four-year colleges offer at the associate degree level, in addition to a bachelor's degree program and, in some cases, graduate programs. Since they are classified as four-year colleges, these institutions are not included in the other indexes and profile listings of this volume. They are listed here for the reader's convenience because they offer programs equivalent to those of the two-year colleges covered by this guide. For full information on the colleges in this index, the reader should consult the companion volume to this guide, *Peterson's Guide to Four-Year Colleges 1997*.

COLLEGE PROFILES AND SPECIAL ANNOUNCEMENTS

The College Profiles contain basic data in capsule form for quick review. The following outline of the profile format shows the section headings and the items that each section covers. Any item that does not apply to a particular college or for which no information was supplied is omitted from that college's profile. The Special Announcements, which appear at the beginning of some institutions' profiles, have been written by those colleges that wished to supplement the profile data with additional timely, important information. In addition, each college that has one or more descriptive messages in the guide will have a cross-reference referring the reader directly to the pages containing more information about that institution in the In-Depth Descriptions of the Colleges section.

Profile Highlights

The profile highlights feature important information for quick reference. Abbreviations that occur include UG—undergraduate, N/R—not reported, N/App—not applicable, and N/Avail—not available.

How to Use the Information in This Book

General

Institutional control: See explanation under State-by-State Summary Table.

Institutional type: Each institution is classified as one of the following:

Two-year college: Awards associate degrees.

Primarily two-year college: Awards baccalaureate degrees but the vast majority of students are enrolled in two-year programs.

In addition, either of the above types may be designated as specialized, indicating that degrees are offered in one field only, such as art or music.

Student body: See explanation under State-by-State Summary Table.

System affiliation: The name of a formal administrative grouping of institutions, either private or public, such as a state university system, of which the college is a part, or the name of a single institution with which the college is administratively affiliated.

Degrees awarded: See explanation under State-by-State Summary Table.

Founding date: If the year an institution was chartered differs from the year when instruction actually began, the earlier date is given.

Campus setting: Designated as *urban* (located within a major city), *suburban* (a residential area within commuting distance of a major city), *small town* (a small but compactly settled area not within commuting distance of a major city), or *rural* (a remote and sparsely populated area). The phrase *easy access to . . .* indicates that the campus is within an hour's drive of a major metropolitan area with a population of over 500,000.

Endowment: The total dollar value of donations to the institution or the multicampus educational system of which the institution is a part.

Total research spending 1994–95: Total dollar value of all funds expended for activities specifically organized to produce research outcomes and commissioned by an agency either external to the institution or separately budgeted by an organizational unit within the institution.

Educational spending 1994–95: Dollar value of average expenditure per undergraduate student for all instructional divisions of an institution. Includes general academic instruction, academic remediation, adult education, tutoring, and vocational and technical instruction. Does not include expenditures for academic administration.

Faculty: The number of full-time and part-time faculty members as of fall 1995, the percentage of the full-time faculty holding doctoral/first professional/terminal degrees, and the school's estimate of the ratio of matriculated undergraduate students to faculty members teaching undergraduate courses.

Notable Alumni: Lists the institution's notable alumni and their occupations.

Enrollment Profile

The fall 1995 enrollment is listed, followed by the number of states and U.S. territories, including the District of Columbia and Puerto Rico (or, for Canadian institutions, provinces and territories), and other countries from which undergraduates come. Percentages are given of undergraduates who are men, women, part-time students, state (or province or territory) residents, living on campus, transfer students, need-based financial aid recipients, non-need-based financial aid recipients, international students, 25 or older, Native American (Indian, Eskimo, Polynesian), Hispanic, African American, and Asian American.

Fields chosen: The percentages of students pursuing degree programs in the following fields of study: agriculture, architecture, area and ethnic studies, biological and life sciences, business management and administrative services, communications and journalism, computer and information sciences, education, engineering and applied sciences, English language/literature/letters, fine arts, foreign language and literature, health professions and related sciences, interdisciplinary studies, liberal arts/general studies, library and information studies, mathematics, military science, natural resource sciences, performing arts, philosophy, physical sciences, predentistry, prelaw, premed, prevet, psychology, social sciences, theology/religion, and vocational and home economics.

Most popular recent majors: The 1995 graduating class's highest-enrolled majors.

First-Year Class

Figures are given for the number of first-year students who enrolled in fall 1995, the number of students who applied for fall 1995 admission, the percentage of those accepted, and the percentage of those accepted who enrolled. Freshman enrollment statistics include the percentages of freshmen from the top 10 percent, top 25 percent, and top half of their secondary school classes, as well as the number of 1995 freshmen who were National Merit Scholars, National Black Merit Scholars, Westinghouse recipients, class presidents, valedictorians, and student government officers.

Academic Program

Core: A program requiring the distribution of an undergraduate's degree credits between several subject areas.

Curriculum: A brief description of the focus of the institution's course of instruction.

Calendar: Most colleges indicate one of the following—*4-1-4, 4-4-1,* or a similar arrangement (two terms of equal length plus an abbreviated winter or spring term, with the numbers referring to months); *semesters; trimesters; quarters; 3-3* (three courses for each of three terms); *modular* (the academic year is divided into small blocks of time; courses of varying lengths are assembled according to individual programs); or *standard year* (for most Canadian institutions).

Courses and class size: The number of under-graduate courses offered in the 1995–96 academic year and the average class size for core undergraduate courses.

Academic offerings include:

Academic remediation for entering students: Remedial courses or special help for accepted students with deficiencies in their college-preparatory education.

English as a second language: English courses for students whose native language is not English.

Services for LD students: Special help for learning-disabled students with resolvable difficulties, such as dyslexia.

Advanced Placement: Credit toward a degree awarded for acceptable scores on some or all College Board Advanced Placement tests.

Self-designed majors: Students may design their own program of study based on individual interests.

Freshman Honors College: A separate academic program for talented freshmen.

Tutorials: Undergraduates can arrange for special in-depth academic assignments (not for remediation) working with faculty one-on-one or in small groups.

Honors program: Unusually challenging academic program for superior students.

Summer session for credit: Summer courses through which students may make up degree work or accelerate their program.

Part-time degree programs: Students may earn a degree without having to attend classes full-time; part-time degree programs may be offered for students attending regular-session classes (daytime) or evening, weekend, or summer classes.

External degree programs: Students may earn a degree through a program that (1) requires no more than 25% of the degree credit to be earned through campus-located instruction, (2) grants credit for documented extra-institutional and experiential learning, and (3) emphasizes off-campus self-directed study.

Adult/continuing education programs: Courses offered for nontraditional students who are currently working or are returning to formal education.

Cooperative (co-op) education programs: Formal arrangement with off-campus employers allowing students to combine work and study in order to gain degree-related experience, usually extending the time required to complete a degree.

Internships: College-arranged work experience for which student earns academic credit.

Off-campus study: Formal exchange or consortium arrangement under which students may take courses at other institutions for credit.

Study abroad: Students may enroll for credit in a foreign study program sponsored by the college. Percentage of students participating is given.

ROTC: Army, Navy, or Air Force Reserve Officers' Training Corps programs offered either on campus or at a cooperating host institution.

General Degree Requirements

Course load and distribution requirements that students must meet in order to complete a degree program include any or all of the following: a minimum number of total courses or credits for an associate or a bachelor's degree; a minimum amount of course work or equivalent proficiency in mathematics, science, a foreign language; and a computer course, internship, or senior project required either of all students or of students majoring in certain specified fields.

Majors

This section lists the major fields of study offered by the college.

Library

This section lists the name of the main library; the number of other libraries on campus; numbers of books, microform titles, periodicals, CD-ROMs, on-line bibliographic services, records/tapes/CDs; and the 1994–95 acquisition expenditure.

Computers on Campus

This paragraph includes the number of on-campus computer terminals and PCs available for general student use and their locations; PC requirement for entering students; the 1994–95 academic computing expenditure; campuswide computer network, and a listing of network assistance and services, including e-mail; access to the main academic computer, computer labs, and software; and other on-line services.

Noteworthy Research Facilities

This section lists prominent institution-owned or institution-operated campus facilities that provide special research resources for undergraduates.

College Life

Information on college life indicates if the college has a preterm college orientation session of two days or more to prepare new students for college life, a drama-theater group, a choral group, a marching band, a student-run campus newspaper, or a student-run radio station. The percentage of students that voted in the last campus election is noted. Information on campus organizations lists the number of clubs and organizations open to all students, the types of social organizations (national and local fraternities and sororities, eating clubs, etc.) on campus, as well as the percentages of eligible undergraduate men and women who are members of the social organizations. Listings of the five most popular student organizations and the three major annual campus events follow. Information on student services indicates which of the following are provided by the college: availability of legal services, a health clinic, personal-psychological counseling, and a women's center. This section concludes with a list of campus safety measures, including 24-hour emergency response devices (telephones and alarms) and patrols by trained security personnel, student patrols, late-night transport-escort service, and controlled dormitory access (key, security card, etc.).

Housing

This section contains information on the number of college-owned or -operated housing spaces for undergraduates and the number of those spaces occupied during the 1995–96 academic year; the institution's policy toward freshman applicants for college housing; whether students are permitted to live off campus or are required to live on campus for a specified period; whether freshmen-only, coed, single-sex, and international student housing options are available; and whether resident assistants live in dorms. The phrase *college housing not available* indicates that no college-owned or -operated housing facilities are provided for undergraduates and that noncommuting students must therefore arrange for their own accommodations.

Athletics

Membership in one or more of the following athletic associations is indicated by their initials.

NCAA: National Collegiate Athletic Association
NAIA: National Association of Intercollegiate Athletics
NCCAA: National Christian Athletic Association
NSCAA: National Small College Athletic Association
NJCAA: National Junior College Athletic Association
CIAU: Canadian Interuniversity Athletic Union

The overall NCAA division in which all or most intercollegiate teams compete is designated by a roman numeral I, II, or III. All teams that do not compete in this division are listed as exceptions. (Men's Division I football is listed as I-A or I-AA.)

Sports offered by the college are divided into two groups: *intercollegiate* (*M* or *W* following the name of each sport indicates that it is offered for men or women) and *intramural*. An *s* in parentheses following an *M* or *W* for an intercollegiate sport indicates that athletic scholarships (or grants-in-aid) are offered for men or women in that sport, and a *c* indicates a club team as opposed to a varsity team. The name, title, and telephone number of the college's athletics director are also listed.

Career Planning

This paragraph includes numbers of full- and part-time placement office staff; the 1994–95 career center operating expenditure; the career center director's name, title, and telephone number; a listing of career center services, including job fairs, résumé preparation, résumé referral, career counseling, careers library, job bank, and job interviews; the class year by which undergraduates must register for career services; and number of organizations, corporations, government agencies, and nonprofit organizations that recruited on campus during the 1994–95 academic year.

After Graduation

This section lists the percentage of the class of 1995 that had job offers within six months of graduation and the percentage of the class of 1995 that went directly to four-year colleges.

Expenses

If provided by the institution, the one-time application fee is listed. Costs are given for the 1996–97 academic year (or estimated for the 1996–97 academic year) or for the 1995–96 academic year if 1996–97 figures were not yet available. Annual expenses may be expressed as a comprehensive fee (including full-time tuition, mandatory fees, and college room and board) or may be given as separate figures for full-time tuition, fees, room and board, or room only. For public institutions where tuition differs according to residence, separate figures are given for area or state residents and for nonresidents. Part-time tuition is expressed in terms of a per-unit rate (per credit, per semester hour, etc.) as specified by the institution.

The tuition structure at some institutions is complex in that freshmen and sophomores may be charged a different rate from that for juniors and seniors, a professional or vocational division may have a different fee structure from the liberal arts division of the same institution, or part-time tuition may be prorated on a sliding scale according to the number of credit hours taken. In all of these cases, the maximum and minimum figures are given along with an explanation of the basis for the variable rate. For colleges that report that room and board costs vary according to the type of accommodation and meal plan, the figures given are for the most common room arrangement and a full meal plan, or the lowest figures are given, followed by the notation *minimum*. If no college-owned or -operated housing facilities are offered, the phrase *college housing not available* will appear in the Housing section of the profile.

A college may offer a *guaranteed tuition plan* whereby a student's tuition does not increase for the entire term of enrollment, from entrance to graduation.

Financial Aid

Information on college-administered aid for all 1995–96 undergraduates includes the types of aid offered and, where applicable, the number of each type awarded and the average dollar amount per award.

Scholarships: Awards for which the college chooses the recipient and uses funds under its control, broken down into need-based and non-need scholarships.

Loans: Broken down into short-term loans from college funds and low-interest long-term loans from college funds and from external sources, such as the government-sponsored Federal Perkins Loan program.

Federal Work-Study: A federal program that enables students to earn money by working on or off campus in public or private nonprofit organizations.

Part-time jobs: On-campus work provided by the college apart from Federal Work-Study.

The information in this section is limited to *college-administered* aid for which the college determines the recipient and amount of each award. It does not cover awards from public and private sources that a student may use to help pay college costs. The largest single source of such outside aid is the Federal Pell Grant program, for which students apply directly to the government.

Data on financial aid awarded to eligible freshmen who enrolled full-time in fall 1995 includes the dollar amount of the average financial aid "package" received by eligible freshmen, and the average percentage of need covered by this aid package.

The supporting data that a student may have to submit in applying for financial aid are grouped into three categories: required for all, required for some, and acceptable (may be submitted in lieu of a required form). The types of supporting data most commonly required are the following:

AFSSA-CSX: CSX Technology's Application for Federal and State Student Aid

CSS Financial Aid PROFILE: The College Scholarship Service's supplementary financial aid form.

FAFSA: The federal government's Free Application for Federal Student Aid

FARE: Financial Aid Report of Eligibility

Financial Aid Transcript: A record of aid previously received for college study, required of transfer applicants

GAPSFAS: Graduate and Professional School Financial Aid Service form

Institutional form: A college's own financial aid application form

SINGLEFILE Form of United Student Aid Funds

State form: A state government aid application form, such as the Student Aid Application for California (SAAC), Illinois State Scholarship Commission form (ISSC), Tuition Assistance Program form (TAP) for New York, or Pennsylvania Higher Education Assistance Agency form (PHEAA)

The college's financial aid application deadline may be given as a specific date; continuous processing up to a specific date or until all available aid has been awarded; or a priority date rather than a strict deadline, meaning that students are encouraged to apply by that date in order to have the best chance of obtaining aid.

Tuition payment plans that may be offered to undergraduates include tuition prepayment, installment, and deferred payment. A tuition prepayment plan gives a student the option of locking in the current tuition rate for the entire term of enrollment by paying the full amount in advance rather than year by year. Colleges that offer such a prepayment plan may also help the student to arrange financing.

The availability of full or partial undergraduate tuition waivers to minority students, children of alumni, employees or children of employees, adult students, and senior citizens may be listed.

The financial aid applicant notification date is given either as a specific date or as continuous.

If the level of financial aid awarded to freshmen is guaranteed to remain at the same level throughout their undergraduate years of study, the policy is noted.

The dollar amount representing the average indebtedness of graduates who were recipients of undergraduate financial aid is given.

Applying

Admission policies and options include the following:

Open admission: Virtually all applicants are accepted without regard to standardized test scores, grade average, or class rank. A college may indicate that open admission is limited to a certain category of applicants, such as state residents, or does not apply to certain selective programs, such as those in allied health professions.

Preferential admission: First consideration is given to qualified applicants from specified geographical, religious, or other groups based on institutional support or control.

Early entrance: Highly qualified students may matriculate before graduating from high school.

Early decision: Students apply early, are notified of acceptance or rejection well in advance of the usual notification date, and agree to accept an offer of admission.

Early action: The same as early decision except that applicants are not obligated to accept an offer of admission.

Deferred entrance: An accepted student may postpone entrance in order to travel, work, or study elsewhere for a specified period.

Midyear entrance: Students may apply for entrance between terms after the start of the academic year.

Application requirements are grouped into three categories: required for all, recommended, and required for some. They may include an essay, standardized test scores, a high school transcript, a minimum high school grade point average (expressed as a number on a scale of 0 to 4.0, where 4.0 equals A, 3.0 equals B, etc.), three or four years of high school mathematics or science, some high school foreign language, letters of recommendation, an interview on campus or with local alumni, and, for certain types of schools or programs, special requirements such as a musical audition or an art portfolio. The most commonly required standardized tests are American College Testing's ACT and College Board's SAT I and SAT II Subject Tests, including the SAT II: Writing Test (see Surviving Standardized Tests). In addition to the ACT and SAT I, the following standardized entrance and placement examinations are referred to by their initials:

ABLE: Adult Basic Learning Examination

ACT ASSET: ACT Assessment of Skills for Successful Entry and Transfer

ACT PEP: ACT Proficiency Examination Program

CAT: California Achievement Tests

CELT: Comprehensive English Language Test

CPAt: Career Programs Assessment

CPT: Computerized Placement Test

DAT: Differential Aptitude Test

MAPS: Multiple Assessment Program Service

MMPI: Minnesota Multiphasic Personality Inventory

PAA: Prueba de Aptitud Académica (Spanish-language version of the SAT I)

PSAT: Preliminary Scholastic Assessment Test

SCAT: Scholastic College Aptitude Test

SRA: Scientific Research Association (administers verbal, arithmetical, and achievement tests)

TABE: Test of Adult Basic Education

TASP: Texas Academic Skills Program

TOEFL: Test of English as a Foreign Language (for international students whose native language is not English)

WPCT: Washington Pre-College Test

These and other standardized tests may be used for selective admission, as a basis for counseling or course placement, or for both purposes, as indicated in the profile.

How to Use the Information in This Book

Admission application deadlines and dates for notification of acceptance or rejection are given either as specific dates or as *rolling* and *continuous*. Rolling means that applications are processed as they are received, and qualified students are accepted as long as there are openings. Continuous notification means that applicants are notified of acceptance or rejection as applications are processed up until the date indicated or the actual beginning of classes. The application deadline and the notification date for nonresidents are given if they differ from the dates for state residents. Early decision and early action application deadlines and notification dates are also indicated when relevant.

Applying/Transfer

This section includes application requirements, the college's own assessment of entrance difficulty (see explanation under How Hard Is It to Get In?), application deadline, notification date, and transfer services contact name, title, and phone number. Requirements for transfers may include a college transcript and a minimum college grade point average (expressed as a number on a scale of 0 to 4.0, where 4.0 equals A, 3.0 equals B, etc.).

Contact

The name, title, mailing address, and telephone number of the person to contact for further information are given at the end of the profile. Toll-free telephone numbers may also be included. The admission office fax number and e-mail address, if available, are listed provided the school wanted it printed for the use of prospective students. Lastly, if a college admissions video or electronic viewbook is available, it is noted at the end of the paragraph.

Additional Information

Each college that has one or more descriptive messages in the guide will have a cross-reference appended to the profile, referring the reader directly to the pages containing more information about that institution in the In-Depth Descriptions of the Colleges section.

Quick-Reference College Search Indexes

State-by-State Summary Table   28
A quick state-by-state way to compare institutions by a variety of characteristics, including enrollment, application requirements, types of financial aid available, and numbers of sports and majors offered.

What Majors Are Offered Where
Alphabetical listings of majors, showing the two-year and four-year colleges that offer each one.

    Associate Degree Programs at Two-Year Colleges   49

    Associate Degree Programs at Four-Year Colleges   133

STATE-BY-STATE SUMMARY TABLE

This index includes the names and locations of accredited two-year colleges in the United States and U.S. territories and shows institutions' responses to our 1996 Survey of Undergraduate Institutions. If an institution submitted incomplete or no data, one or more columns opposite the institution's name is blank. An asterisk after the school name denotes a Special Announcement following the college's profile, and a dagger indicates that the institution has one or more entries in the In-Depth Descriptions of the Colleges section.

Y—Yes; N—No; R—Recommended; S—For Some

Column headers (angled):
- Degrees Awarded: Transfer Associate (C), Terminal Associate (T), Bachelor's (B), Master's (M), Doctorate (D), First Professional (F)
- Institutional Control: Independent, Independent-Religious, Proprietary, Federal, State, Province, Commonwealth, Territory, County, District, City, State and Local, State-Related
- Student Body: Men, Primarily Men, Women, Primarily Women, Coeducational
- Undergraduate Enrollment Fall 1995
- Percent Attending Part-Time
- Percent Receiving Need-Based Financial Aid
- Percent 25 Years of Age or Older
- Percent of Grads Going on to 4-Year Colleges
- Freshman Retention Rate
- High School Equivalency Certificate Accepted
- High School Transcript Required
- Open Admissions
- Entrance Test(s) Required
- College Scholarships Available
- Loans Available
- Part-Time Jobs Available
- Career Counseling Services Available
- Job Placement Services Available
- College Housing Available
- Number of Sports Offered
- Number of Majors Offered

UNITED STATES

Alabama

Institution	Location	Deg	Ctrl	Body	Enr	PT	NBA	25+	Grad	Ret	HSE	HST	OA	ET	CS	Ln	PT	CC	JP	CH	Sp	Maj
Alabama Aviation and Technical College	Ozark	C,T	State	Prim M	293	16		55	60		Y	Y		Y	Y	Y	Y	Y	Y	Y	0	4
Alabama Southern Community College	Monroeville	C,T	State	Coed	1,800	36		36			Y	Y	Y	Y			Y	Y	Y	N	2	36
Alabama Southern Community College	Thomasville	C,T	State	Coed	1,225	18					Y	Y	Y	Y				Y	Y	N	3	27
Bessemer State Technical College	Bessemer	T	State	Coed	1,840	56	8	63			N	Y	Y	Y	Y	Y	Y	Y	Y	N	0	12
Bevill State Community College	Sumiton	C,T	State	Coed	4,597	46		43			Y	Y		Y			Y	Y	Y	N	8	21
Bishop State Community College	Mobile	C,T	State	Coed	4,127	45	46	57			Y	Y	Y	Y		Y		Y	Y	N	3	25
Central Alabama Community College	Alexander City	C,T	State	Coed	1,917	65		43		33	Y	Y	Y	Y			Y	Y	Y	N	5	11
Chattahoochee Valley State Community College	Phenix City	C,T	State	Coed	2,101	43		51	42	18	Y	Y		Y			Y	Y	Y	N	5	33
Community College of the Air Force	Maxwell Air Force Base	T	Fed	Coed	410,100	0	0	82			Y	Y		Y					Y		15	65
Douglas MacArthur State Technical College	Opp	T	State	Coed	630	19	66	58			Y	Y	Y	Y			Y	Y	Y	N	0	12
Draughons Junior College	Montgomery		Prop	Coed	209	21	90	70			N	Y		Y	Y	Y	Y	Y	Y	N	0	7
Enterprise State Junior College	Enterprise	C,T	State	Coed	1,822	41		21			Y	Y		Y				Y	Y	N	7	28
Gadsden State Community College	Gadsden	C,T	State	Coed	6,243	50	22	47	68		Y	Y		S	Y		Y	Y	Y	Y	7	38
George Corley Wallace State Community College	Selma	C,T	State	Coed	1,847	35		31	45	25	Y	Y		S			Y	Y	Y	N	6	22
George C Wallace State Community College	Dothan	C,T	State	Coed	4,000	52		43			Y	Y		S			Y	Y	Y	N	4	25
Harry M Ayers State Technical College	Anniston	C,T	State	Coed	800	32		51			Y	Y		Y			Y	Y	Y	N	0	4
Herzing College of Business and Technology	Birmingham	T	Prop	Coed	425	15		70			N	Y					Y	Y	Y	N	0	8
ITT Technical Institute	Birmingham	C,T	Prop	Coed	133	0					N	Y		Y			Y	Y	Y	N	0	2
James H Faulkner State Community College	Bay Minette	C,T	State	Coed	3,042	40	32	39	40	72	Y	Y		Y	R		Y	Y	Y	Y	8	16
Jefferson Davis Community College	Brewton	C,T	State	Coed	1,600	30		30			Y	Y		Y			Y	Y	Y	N	7	19
Jefferson State Community College	Birmingham	C,T	State	Coed	6,749	59	18	46			Y	Y	S	R	Y			Y	Y	N	8	36
J F Drake State Technical College	Huntsville	C	State	Coed	688	30					Y			Y			Y	Y	Y	N	0	7
John C Calhoun State Community College	Decatur	C,T	State	Coed	7,514	57	24	46	38		Y	Y		Y			Y	Y	Y	N	3	52
John M Patterson State Technical College	Montgomery	T	State	Coed	1,066	46		52			Y			S	Y		Y	Y	Y	N	0	15
Lawson State Community College	Birmingham	C,T	State	Coed	1,892	23	80	45	43	2	Y	Y		Y			Y	Y	Y	N	6	31
Lurleen B Wallace State Junior College	Andalusia	C,T	State	Coed	1,147	34		39			Y	Y		S	Y		Y	Y	Y	N	5	6
Marion Military Institute	Marion	C,T	Ind	Coed	220	0	96	0	75	100	N	Y		Y			Y	Y	Y	Y	14	3
Northeast Alabama State Community College	Rainsville	C,T	State	Coed	1,589	37	40	40	60	30	Y	Y		Y			Y	Y	Y	Y	0	16
Northwest-Shoals Community College	Muscle Shoals	C,T	State	Coed	4,545	43		43			Y	Y		Y				Y	Y	Y	6	23
Reid State Technical College	Evergreen	T	State	Coed	833	42	46	55			Y	Y		Y			Y	Y	Y	N	0	9
Shelton State Community College	Tuscaloosa	C,T	State	Coed	6,000	56		37	47		Y	Y		Y			Y	Y	Y	N	5	32
Snead State Community College	Boaz	C,T	State	Coed	1,708	28		28			Y	Y	Y	Y			Y	Y	Y	Y	5	8
Southern Union State Community College	Wadley	C,T	State	Coed	6,499	54	50	33			Y	Y		Y			Y	Y	Y	Y	6	6
Trenholm State Technical College	Montgomery	T	State	Coed	767	39	71	86		19	Y	Y	Y	Y			Y	Y	Y	Y	2	10
UAB Walker College	Jasper	C,T	State	Coed	957	45		38		85	Y		Y	R,S	Y		Y	Y	Y	Y	7	8
Virginia College at Birmingham	Birmingham	T	Prop	Coed	500						N	Y		Y	Y		Y	Y	Y	N	0	7
Virginia College at Huntsville	Huntsville	T	Prop	Coed	250						N	Y		Y	Y		Y			N	0	
Wallace State Community College	Hanceville	C,T	State	Coed	5,824	42		41		79	Y	Y		Y	R,S	Y		Y	Y	Y	9	59

Alaska

Charter College	Anchorage	C,T	Prop	Coed								Y			Y		Y	Y		N	0	5
U of Alaska Anchorage, Kenai Peninsula College	Soldotna	C,T	State	Coed	1,658	78		76				Y	R		Y	Y	Y	Y		N	0	8
U of Alaska Anchorage, Kodiak College	Kodiak	C,T	State	Coed	948	90	5	83				Y			R	Y		Y	Y	N	0	3
U of Alaska Anchorage, Matanuska-Susitna College	Palmer	C,T	State	Coed	1,654	82	60	82		25	Y			R	Y	Y	Y	Y		N	0	8
U of Alaska, Prince William Sound Comm College	Valdez	C,T	State	Coed	1,508	86		76			Y				Y	Y	Y	Y	Y	Y	0	4
U of Alaska Southeast, Ketchikan Campus	Ketchikan	C,T	St & Loc	Coed	95	35		46	50	90	Y	Y		R	Y	Y	Y	Y	Y	Y	0	8
U of Alaska Southeast, Sitka Campus	Sitka	C,T	State	Coed	1,470	51		65		40		Y		R	Y		Y	Y		Y	0	6

Arizona

Academy of Business College	Phoenix	T	Prop	Coed	240	0					N	Y	Y							N	0	5
Apollo College–Phoenix, Inc	Phoenix		Prop		85							Y		Y	S						0	3
Apollo College–Tri-City, Inc	Mesa	C,T	Prop	Coed		0	40	50			Y			Y	S	Y	Y				0	
Apollo College–Tucson, Inc	Tucson	C,T	Prop	Coed	320		90				N			Y	S		Y				0	
Apollo College–Westside, Inc	Phoenix	C,T	Prop	Coed	68	0	40	65			Y			Y	Y		Y				0	
Arizona Western College	Yuma	C,T	St & Loc	Coed	5,837	72	75	53		32	Y	Y			S	Y	Y	Y	Y	Y	10	45
Central Arizona College	Coolidge	C,T	County	Coed	14,724																	
Chandler-Gilbert Community College	Chandler	C,T	Dist	Coed	3,500	75		42	83	95	Y							Y		N	0	6
Chaparral Career College	Tucson	C,T	Prop	Coed	363	0		50			Y						Y			N	0	7
Cochise College*†	Douglas	C,T	St & Loc	Coed	1,204	49		42			Y	Y			Y		Y	Y	Y	Y	10	38
Cochise College	Sierra Vista	C,T	St & Loc	Coed	2,614	74		67			Y	Y			Y		Y	Y	Y	N	10	37
Coconino County Community College	Flagstaff	C,T	State	Coed	1,991	88		36			Y			S			Y	Y	Y	N	0	8
Eastern Arizona College	Thatcher	C,T	St & Loc	Coed	2,269	39	10	35			Y				Y		Y	Y	Y	Y	10	48
Gateway Community College	Phoenix	C,T	St & Loc	Coed	6,804	91		75		3	Y	Y	S		Y		Y	Y	Y	N	0	26
Glendale Community College	Glendale	C,T	St & Loc	Coed	16,235	74		53			Y				Y		Y	Y	Y	N	13	64

Peterson's Guide to Two-Year Colleges 1997

State-by-State Summary Table
Arizona–California

This index includes the names and locations of accredited two-year colleges in the United States and U.S. territories and shows institutions' responses to our 1996 Survey of Undergraduate Institutions. If an institution submitted incomplete or no data, one or more columns opposite the institution's name is blank. An asterisk after the school name denotes a Special Announcement following the college's profile, and a dagger indicates that the institution has one or more entries in the In-Depth Descriptions of the Colleges section.

Y—Yes; N—No; R—Recommended; S—For Some

Institution	Location	Degrees Awarded	Institutional Control	Student Body	Undergraduate Enrollment Fall 1995	% Attending Part Time	% Receiving Need-Based Financial Aid	% 25 Years of Age or Older	% Grads Going on to 4-Year Colleges	Freshman Retention Rate	HS Equivalency Cert Accepted	HS Transcript Required	Open Admissions	Entrance Test(s) Required	College Scholarships	Part-Time Jobs	Loans	Career Counseling	Job Placement	College Housing	# Sports	# Majors
ITT Technical Institute	Phoenix	T,B	Prop	Coed	264	0		39			N	Y		Y	Y	Y	Y	Y	Y	N	3	4
ITT Technical Institute	Tucson	C,T	Prop	Coed	212	0		50			N	Y		Y	Y	Y	Y	Y	Y	N	0	2
Lamson Junior College	Mesa	C,T	Prop	Coed	73	0		40			N	Y	Y	Y	Y	Y	Y	Y	Y	N	0	6
Mesa Community College	Mesa	C,T	St & Loc	Coed	22,302	72		44	45		Y					Y	Y	Y	Y	N	11	36
Mohave Community College	Kingman	C,T	State	Coed	5,681	88	22	72	3		Y	Y	S	R	Y	Y	Y	Y	Y	N	6	19
Navajo Community College†	Tsaile	C,T	Fed	Coed	1,767	54		63			Y	Y	Y					Y	Y	Y	2	14
Northland Pioneer College	Holbrook	C,T	St & Loc	Coed	4,779	85	15	77			Y				Y	Y	Y	Y	Y	Y	1	19
Paradise Valley Community College	Phoenix	C,T	St & Loc	Coed	5,574	80		56			Y					Y	Y	Y	Y	N	3	6
Paralegal Institute, Inc	Phoenix	T	Prop		600																0	1
Phoenix College	Phoenix			Coed	11,266																	
Pima Community College†	Tucson	C,T	State	Coed	27,960	74		50		16	Y			R	Y		Y	Y	Y	N	15	75
Pima Medical Institute	Mesa																					
Pima Medical Institute	Tucson																					
Rio Salado Community College	Phoenix	C,T	St & Loc	Coed	8,754	96		59	14		Y			S	Y	Y	Y	Y	Y	N	0	14
Scottsdale Community College	Scottsdale	C,T	St & Loc	Coed	9,765	75					Y	Y			Y	Y	Y	Y	Y	N	11	25
South Mountain Community College	Phoenix	C,T	St & Loc	Coed	2,423	72	40	40	25	17	Y	Y			Y	Y	Y	Y	Y	N	8	19
Yavapai College	Prescott	C,T	St & Loc	Coed	6,297	80	20	67		80	Y			R	Y	Y	Y	Y	Y	Y	5	24

Arkansas

Institution	Location	Degrees	Control	Body	Enroll	PT	NBFA	25+	Grads	Ret	HSEq	HST	Open	Ent	Sch	PT Jobs	Loans	Career	Job	Hous	Sport	Maj
Arkansas State University–Beebe Branch	Beebe	C	State	Coed	1,999	33		38			Y	Y		Y	Y	Y				Y	9	16
Black River Technical College	Pocahontas	C,T	State	Coed	1,189						Y	Y	Y	Y	Y	Y				N	0	2
Cossatot Technical College	DeQueen	C	State	Coed	800						Y		R	Y							0	3
East Arkansas Community College	Forrest City	C,T	State	Coed	1,333	44		47	47	54	Y	Y	Y			Y	Y	Y	Y	N	0	8
Garland County Community College	Hot Springs	C,T	St & Loc	Coed	1,988	58	48	55	58		Y	Y	Y		Y	Y	Y	Y	Y	N	7	34
ITT Technical Institute	Little Rock	T	Prop	Coed	138	0		36			N	Y		Y	Y	Y	Y	Y	Y	N	0	2
Mississippi County Community College	Blytheville	C,T	State	Coed	2,114	58		45			Y	Y	R		R	Y	Y	Y	Y	N	0	11
North Arkansas Community/Technical College	Harrison	C,T	St & Loc	Coed	1,482	39		45	44		Y				Y	Y	Y	Y	Y	N	9	12
NorthWest Arkansas Community College	Bentonville	C,T	St & Loc	Coed	2,245	71	16	42	27		Y	Y	R		Y	Y	Y	Y	Y	N	0	15
Ouachita Technical College	Malvern	T	State	Coed	568						Y		Y	S						N	0	7
Ozarka Technical College	Melbourne	C,T	State	Coed	453	60	33	45	40	40	Y					Y		Y	Y	N	0	7
Petit Jean Technical College	Morrilton	C,T	State	Coed	651	40	44		50		Y							Y	Y	N	0	17
Phillips County Community College	Helena	C,T	St & Loc	Coed	1,520	47		45		80	Y				Y	Y	Y	Y	Y	N	5	31
Pines Technical College	Pine Bluff	C,T	State	Coed	1,231							Y	Y							N	0	7
Pulaski Technical College	North Little Rock	C	State	Coed	1,412						Y	Y		Y				Y		N	0	4
Red River Technical College	Hope	C	State	Coed	920	53	50	46			Y		Y	R						N	0	5
Rich Mountain Community College	Mena	C,T	St & Loc	Coed	758	60		50		75	Y			R						N	0	9
Shorter College	North Little Rock	C,T	Ind-R	Coed	264	35		50	75	50	Y	Y	Y							Y	2	17
South Arkansas Community College	El Dorado	C,T	State	Coed	1,000	55		46			Y				Y	Y	Y	Y	Y	N	4	11
Southern Arkansas University Tech	Camden	C,T	State	Coed	1,197	54		55			Y			Y	Y	Y	Y	Y	Y	N	6	16
Westark Community College	Fort Smith	C,T	St & Loc	Coed	5,323	55	29	43		47	Y	Y		R	Y	Y	Y	Y	Y	N	7	24

California

Institution	Location	Degrees	Control	Body	Enroll	PT	NBFA	25+	Grads	Ret	HSEq	HST	Open	Ent	Sch	PT Jobs	Loans	Career	Job	Hous	Sport	Maj
Allan Hancock College	Santa Maria	C,T	St & Loc	Coed	7,403	71		51			Y	Y		S	Y	Y	Y	Y	Y	N	10	45
American Academy of Dramatic Arts/West†	Pasadena	C,T	Ind	Coed	208	0	39	21	77		N	Y	Y	R	Y	Y	Y	Y	Y	N	0	1
American River College	Sacramento	C,T	Dist	Coed	19,695	77		50			Y	Y		R,S	Y	Y	Y	Y	Y	N	9	54
Antelope Valley College	Lancaster	C,T	St & Loc	Coed	9,027	75		53			Y	Y	Y			Y	Y	Y	Y	N	14	51
Bakersfield College	Bakersfield	C,T	St & Loc	Coed	12,000	74					Y	Y			Y	Y	Y	Y	Y	N	12	64
Barstow College	Barstow	C,T	St & Loc	Coed	2,632	76		66			Y	Y				Y	Y	Y	Y	N	4	33
Brooks College	Long Beach	T	Prop	Coed	720	0		3			N	Y	Y	Y	Y	Y	Y	Y	Y	N	0	4
Butte College	Oroville	C,T	Dist	Coed	11,900	60		53			Y	Y	S		Y	Y	Y	Y	Y	N	9	55
Cabrillo College	Aptos	C,T	Dist	Coed	11,805	72		50			Y	Y	S		Y	Y	Y	Y	Y	N	16	39
Cañada College	Redwood City	C,T	Dist	Coed	5,261	75	7	61			Y	Y				Y	Y	Y	Y	N	6	62
Cerritos College	Norwalk	C,T	St & Loc	Coed	22,068	77		46			Y	Y			R	Y	Y	Y	Y	N	13	67
Cerro Coso Community College	Ridgecrest	C,T	State	Coed	5,564	88		70			Y	Y	R			Y	Y	Y	Y	N	6	28
Chabot College	Hayward	C,T	State	Coed	13,285	79	20	47		85	Y	Y				Y	Y	Y	Y	N	21	91
Chaffey College	Rancho Cucamonga	C,T	Dist	Coed	12,651	72		42			Y	Y				Y	Y	Y	Y	N	10	63
Citrus College	Glendora	C,T	St & Loc	Coed	10,448	71		45			Y	Y		S		Y	Y	Y	Y	N	11	30
City College of San Francisco	San Francisco	C,T	St & Loc	Coed		76		56			Y	Y				Y	Y	Y	Y	N	16	72
Coastline Community College	Fountain Valley	C	St & Loc	Coed	11,950	92		82			Y			S		Y	Y	Y	Y	N	0	1
College of Alameda	Alameda	C,T	St & Loc	Coed	4,858	73		44	61		Y	Y				Y	Y	Y	Y	N	7	30
College of Marin	Kentfield	C,T	St & Loc	Coed	8,845	77		50			Y	Y				Y	Y	Y	Y	N	10	57
College of Oceaneering	Wilmington	C	Prop	Prim M	230	0	95	40			Y	Y				Y	Y	Y	Y	N	0	1
College of San Mateo	San Mateo	C,T	St & Loc	Coed	11,506	71		51			Y					Y	Y	Y	Y	N	6	62
College of the Canyons	Santa Clarita	C,T	St & Loc	Coed	6,123	70		43		65	Y		R			Y	Y	Y	Y	N	10	44
College of the Desert	Palm Desert	C,T	St & Loc	Coed	9,638	80		60	55		Y					Y	Y	Y	Y	N	14	59
College of the Redwoods	Eureka	C,T	St & Loc	Coed	6,968	67		52			Y					Y	Y	Y	Y	Y	7	21
College of the Sequoias	Visalia	C,T	St & Loc	Coed	8,721	53	22	40			Y					Y	Y	Y	Y	N	13	72
College of the Siskiyous*	Weed	C,T	St & Loc	Coed	2,888	68	45	63	55	15	Y					Y	Y	Y	Y	Y	11	35
Columbia College	Sonora	C,T	St & Loc	Coed	2,644	52		68		91	Y	Y	S	Y		Y	Y	Y	Y	N	3	32
Compton Community College	Compton	C,T	St & Loc	Coed	5,700																	
Contra Costa College	San Pablo	C	St & Loc	Coed	9,000	79		54			Y			R		Y	Y	Y	Y	N	8	46
Cosumnes River College	Sacramento	C,T	Dist	Coed	11,245	77	11	52			Y			R		Y	Y	Y	Y	N	11	63
Crafton Hills College	Yucaipa	C,T	St & Loc	Coed	5,041	72	11	47			Y					Y	Y	Y	Y	N	10	39
Cuesta College	San Luis Obispo	C,T	Dist	Coed	7,800	56	18	33			Y	Y				Y	Y	Y	Y	N	10	43
Cuyamaca College	El Cajon	C,T	State	Coed	4,469	86		63			Y			Y		Y	Y	Y	Y	N	1	18
Cypress College	Cypress	C,T	St & Loc	Coed	14,350	65		45			Y			R		Y	Y	Y	Y	N	10	53
De Anza College	Cupertino	C,T	St & Loc	Coed	23,497	67		52	31	13	Y					Y	Y	Y	Y	N	18	58
Deep Springs College	Deep Springs	C	Ind	Men	25	0		0		92	N	Y		Y						Y	0	1
Diablo Valley College	Pleasant Hill	C	St & Loc	Coed	21,000	70					Y					Y	Y	Y	Y	N	10	1
Don Bosco Technical Institute	Rosemead	C,T	Ind-R	Men	950			0		85	Y	Y			S			Y	Y	N	7	8
D-Q University	Davis	C,T	Ind	Coed	466	45		50			Y	Y		Y			Y	Y	Y	Y	8	9

Peterson's Guide to Two-Year Colleges 1997

State-by-State Summary Table
California

This index includes the names and locations of accredited two-year colleges in the United States and U.S. territories and shows institutions' responses to our 1996 Survey of Undergraduate Institutions. If an institution submitted incomplete or no data, one or more columns opposite the institution's name is blank. An asterisk after the school name denotes a Special Announcement following the college's profile, and a dagger indicates that the institution has one or more entries in the In-Depth Descriptions of the Colleges section.

Y—Yes; N—No; R—Recommended; S—For Some

Institution	Location	Degrees Awarded	Institutional Control	Student Body	Undergraduate Enrollment Fall 1995	Percent Attending Part-Time	Percent Receiving Need-Based Financial Aid	Percent 25 Years of Age or Older	Percent of Grads Going on to 4-Year Colleges	Freshman Retention Rate	Open Admissions	High School Equivalency Certificate Accepted	High School Transcript Required	Entrance Test(s) Required	College Scholarships Available	Loans Available	Part-Time Jobs Available	Career Counseling Available	Job Placement Services Available	College Housing Available	Number of Sports Offered	Number of Majors Offered
East Los Angeles College	Monterey Park	C,T	St & Loc	Coed	15,100	68		60		15	Y	Y			Y	Y	Y	Y	N	5	60
El Camino College	Torrance	C	Dist	Coed	21,860	77		45			Y	Y	Y		Y	Y	Y	Y	N	14	73
Evergreen Valley College	San Jose	C,T	St & Loc	Coed	9,002	80		52			Y	Y			Y	Y	Y	Y	N	6	21
Fashion Inst of Design & Merchandising, LA Campus*†	Los Angeles	C	Prop	Coed	3,038	18		27	55		N	Y	Y	R	Y	Y	Y	Y	N	0	10
Fashion Inst of Design & Merchandising, SD Campus	San Diego	C	Prop	Coed	300	10		27	55	18		Y	Y			Y	Y	Y	N	0	7
Fashion Inst of Design & Merchandising, SF Campus	San Francisco	C	Prop	Coed	1,690	18		13			N	Y	Y	R	Y	Y	Y	Y	N	0	7
Feather River Community College District	Quincy	C,T	St & Loc	Coed	1,200	86		68			Y	Y		R		Y	Y	Y	N	2	13
Foothill College	Los Altos Hills	C,T	St & Loc	Coed	15,500	78		67			Y			R		Y	Y	Y	N	13	66
Fresno City College	Fresno	C,T	Dist	Coed	17,099	69	80	46	48	85	Y	Y		R	Y	Y	Y	Y	N	16	86
Fullerton College	Fullerton	C,T	St & Loc	Coed	18,007	49		40			Y				Y	Y	Y	Y	N	10	67
Gavilan College	Gilroy	C,T	St & Loc	Coed	4,029	63		40			Y	Y	S		Y		Y	Y	N	9	39
Glendale Community College	Glendale	C,T			15,337																
Golden West College	Huntington Beach	C,T	St & Loc	Coed	12,415	68		44	82	80	Y	Y	R	S	Y	Y	Y	Y	N	13	35
Grossmont College	El Cajon	C,T	St & Loc	Coed	14,500	64		38			Y	Y		R	Y	Y	Y	Y	N	11	55
Hartnell College	Salinas	C,T	Dist	Coed	7,500	70					Y	Y	S	R	Y	Y	Y	Y	N	9	45
Heald Business College	Concord	T	Ind	Coed	472	0		30			N	Y		Y	Y	Y	Y	Y	N	0	6
Heald Business College	Fresno	C,T	Ind	Coed	500	1		20			N	Y	Y	Y		Y	Y	Y	N	0	5
Heald Business College	Hayward	C,T	Ind	Coed	500	5		30			Y	Y				Y	Y	Y	N	0	5
Heald Business College	Oakland	C,T	Ind	Coed	300																
Heald Business College	Rancho Cordova	T	Ind	Coed	600	5		20			N	Y	Y	S	Y	Y	Y	Y	N	0	6
Heald Business College	Salinas																				
Heald Business College	San Francisco	C,T	Ind	Coed	600	21		34			N	Y	Y	Y	Y	Y	Y	Y	N	0	7
Heald Business College	San Jose	T	Ind		304								Y							0	
Heald Business College	Santa Rosa	T	Ind		210																
Heald Business College	Stockton																				
Heald Institute of Technology	Hayward	T	Ind		349							Y								0	
Heald Institute of Technology	Martinez	T	Ind	Coed	430	0		70			N	Y	Y		Y	Y	Y	Y	N	0	2
Heald Institute of Technology	Milpitas	T	Ind	Coed	470	5	80	50	85		N	Y	Y		Y	Y	Y	Y	N	0	3
Heald Institute of Technology	Sacramento																				
Heald Institute of Technology	San Francisco	T	Ind	Prim M	400	0	33	70			N	Y	Y	R	Y	Y	Y	Y	N	0	1
Imperial Valley College	Imperial	C,T	St & Loc	Coed	5,696	54					Y	Y	R,S		Y	Y	Y	Y	N	6	40
Irvine Valley College	Irvine	C	St & Loc	Coed	10,300	80		55			Y				Y	Y	Y	Y	N	5	21
ITT Technical Institute	Anaheim	C,T,B	Prop	Coed	702	0		24			N	Y			Y	Y	Y	Y	N	0	2
ITT Technical Institute	Carson	T	Prop	Coed	467	0		30			N	Y		Y	Y	Y	Y	Y	N	0	2
ITT Technical Institute	Oxnard	C,T	Prop	Coed	294						N	Y	Y	Y	Y	Y	Y	Y	N	0	2
ITT Technical Institute	Sacramento	T,B	Prop	Coed	419			40			N	Y			Y	Y	Y	Y	N	2	2
ITT Technical Institute	San Bernardino	T,B	Prop	Coed	511	0		20			N	Y			Y	Y	Y	Y	N	0	3
ITT Technical Institute	San Diego	T,B	Prop	Coed	663	0		37			N	Y		Y	Y	Y	Y	Y	N	0	3
ITT Technical Institute	Van Nuys	T	Prop	Coed	410	0		80			N	Y	Y		Y	Y	Y	Y	N	0	2
ITT Technical Institute	West Covina	T,B	Prop	Coed	681	0		30			N	Y			Y	Y	Y	Y	N	0	4
Kelsey Jenney College	San Diego	T	Ind	Coed	900	10		20		15	Y	Y	Y		Y	Y	Y	Y	N	0	11
Kings River Community College	Reedley	C,T	St & Loc	Coed	6,278	56		53			Y	Y	Y	R	Y	Y	Y	Y	Y	8	33
Lake Tahoe Community College	South Lake Tahoe	C,T	St & Loc	Coed	2,700	89		71			Y	Y			Y	Y	Y	Y	N	2	26
Laney College	Oakland	C,T	St & Loc	Coed	10,454	71		57	71		Y	Y				Y	Y	Y	N	4	42
Las Positas College	Livermore	C,T	State	Coed	5,600	83		52			Y	Y	R			Y	Y	Y	N	7	23
Lassen College	Susanville	C,T	St & Loc	Coed	2,951	67		58			Y	Y	R	R	Y	Y	Y	Y	Y	18	48
Long Beach City College	Long Beach	C,T	State	Coed	24,000	89		61		20	Y	Y	R		Y	Y	Y	Y	N	17	73
Los Angeles City College	Los Angeles	C,T	Dist	Coed	15,217	66		62			Y				Y	Y	Y	Y	N	16	68
Los Angeles Harbor College	Wilmington	C,T	St & Loc	Coed	7,603	73		49							Y	Y	Y	Y	N	5	26
Los Angeles Mission College	Sylmar	C,T	St & Loc	Coed	6,027	73		55			Y	Y			Y	Y	Y	Y	N	4	39
Los Angeles Pierce College	Woodland Hills	C,T	St & Loc	Coed	18,212	70		48			Y	Y			Y	Y	Y	Y	N	19	46
Los Angeles Southwest College	Los Angeles	C,T	St & Loc	Coed	5,802	77		63			Y	Y				Y	Y	Y	N	9	30
Los Angeles Trade-Technical College	Los Angeles	C,T	St & Loc	Coed	13,373	64		57			Y	Y	R		Y	Y	Y	Y	N	4	37
Los Angeles Valley College	Van Nuys	C,T	St & Loc	Coed	17,768	77		48			Y			R		Y	Y	Y	N	16	61
Los Medanos College	Pittsburg	C,T	Dist	Coed	7,311	76		53			Y	Y		S	Y	Y	Y	Y	N	6	27
Maric College of Medical Careers	San Diego	C	Prop	Coed	1,100		80	60					Y		S	Y		Y	N	0	2
Marymount College, Palos Verdes, California	Rancho Palos Verdes	C	Ind-R	Coed	852	30	40	20	70	92	N	Y	Y		Y	Y	Y	Y	Y	9	1
Mendocino College	Ukiah	C,T	St & Loc	Coed	3,400	76		60		10	Y			R	R	Y	Y	Y	N	4	33
Merced College	Merced	C,T	St & Loc	Coed	6,327	47		42		80	Y	Y		R		Y	Y	Y	N	14	58
Merritt College	Oakland	C,T	St & Loc	Coed	5,123	74		55	60		Y				Y	Y	Y	Y	N	7	34
MiraCosta College	Oceanside	C	State	Coed	8,038	72		46			Y	Y			Y	Y	Y	Y	N	5	46
Mission College	Santa Clara	C,T	St & Loc	Coed	8,750	79		64			Y					Y	Y	Y	N	3	22
Modesto Junior College	Modesto	C	St & Loc	Coed	14,774	76		58			Y	Y	R			Y	Y	Y	N	14	97
Monterey Peninsula College	Monterey	C,T	State	Coed	8,300	82					Y	Y				Y	Y	Y	N	10	72
Moorpark College†	Moorpark	C,T	County	Coed	10,226	60		42			Y	S			Y		Y	Y	N	10	44
Mt San Antonio College	Walnut	C,T	Dist	Coed	32,000	67		38			Y			R	Y	Y	Y	Y	N	13	72
Mt San Jacinto College	San Jacinto	C,T	St & Loc	Coed	5,627	72		46			Y	Y		Y		Y	Y	Y	N	6	21
Napa Valley College	Napa	C,T	St & Loc	Coed	7,000	72		44			Y	Y		S		Y	Y	Y	N	21	37
Ohlone College	Fremont	C,T	St & Loc	Coed	8,400	71		49			Y	Y			S	Y	Y	Y	N	8	39
Orange Coast College	Costa Mesa	C,T	St & Loc	Coed	22,009	66		42	62	10	Y	Y		R	Y	Y	Y	Y	N	13	62
Oxnard College†	Oxnard	C	County	Coed	5,073	79		62			Y	Y				Y	Y	Y	N	3	43
Palomar College	San Marcos	C	St & Loc	Coed	22,945	62		3	46		Y	Y		S	Y	Y	Y	Y	N	12	89
Palo Verde College	Blythe	C,T	St & Loc	Coed	1,200	44		88			Y			R			Y	Y	N	0	23
Pasadena City College	Pasadena	C,T	St & Loc	Coed	21,756	70	19	37			Y	Y				Y	Y	Y	N	11	106
Phillips Junior College	Van Nuys	C,T	Prop	Coed	600																
Phillips Junior College, Condie Campus	Campbell	C,T	Prop	Coed		0		80			N	Y			Y	Y	Y	Y	N	0	15
Porterville College	Porterville	C,T	State	Coed	2,651	59	52				Y					Y	Y	Y	N	5	35
Queen of the Holy Rosary College	Mission San Jose	C,T	Ind-R	Prim W	224	95				100	Y	Y						Y	N	0	1
Rancho Santiago College	Santa Ana	C,T	State	Coed	20,714	81		63			Y	Y				Y	Y	Y	N	13	83
Rio Hondo College	Whittier	C,T	St & Loc	Coed	14,500	78		40			Y				R	Y	Y	Y	N	13	5
Riverside Community College	Riverside	T	St & Loc	Coed	20,000	77		50			Y					Y	Y	Y	N	15	43
Sacramento City College	Sacramento	C,T	St & Loc	Coed	16,039	69	21	50			Y					Y	Y	Y	N	19	46
Saddleback College	Mission Viejo	C	St & Loc	Coed	16,917	60	10	52	65	60	Y				Y	Y	Y	Y	N	11	84

This index includes the names and locations of accredited two-year colleges in the United States and U.S. territories and shows institutions' responses to our 1996 Survey of Undergraduate Institutions. If an institution submitted incomplete or no data, one or more columns opposite the institution's name is blank. An asterisk after the school name denotes a Special Announcement following the college's profile, and a dagger indicates that the institution has one or more entries in the In-Depth Descriptions of the Colleges section.

Y—Yes; N—No; R—Recommended; S—For Some

Institution	Location	Degrees Awarded (Transfer Associate (C), Terminal Associate (T), Bachelor's (B), Master's (M), Doctoral (D), First Professional (F))	Institutional Control (Independent, Independent-Religious, Proprietary, Federal, State, Province, Commonwealth, Territory, County, District, City, State and Local, State-Related)	Student Body (Men, Primarily Men, Women, Primarily Women, Coeducational)	Undergraduate Enrollment Fall 1995	Percent Attending Part-Time	Percent Receiving Need-Based Financial Aid	Percent 25 Years of Age or Older	Freshman Retention Rate	Percent of Grads Going on to 4-Year Colleges	Open Admissions	High School Equivalency Certificate Accepted	High School Transcript Required	Entrance Test(s) Required	College Scholarships Available	Loans Available	Part-Time Jobs Available	Career Counseling Available	Job Placement Services Available	College Housing Available	Number of Sports Offered	Number of Majors Offered
Salvation Army College for Officer Training	Rancho Palos Verdes	C,T	Ind-R	Coed								N								Y	0	
San Bernardino Valley College	San Bernardino	C,T	St & Loc	Coed	10,673	70		55			Y	Y		Y	Y	Y	Y	Y	Y	N	9	66
San Diego City College	San Diego	C,T	St & Loc	Coed	12,616	48		63			Y	Y	S		Y	Y	Y	Y	Y	N	16	71
San Diego Mesa College	San Diego	C,T	Dist	Coed	22,677	83		48			Y			R	Y	Y	Y	Y	Y	N	15	57
San Diego Miramar College	San Diego	C	St & Loc	Coed	8,935	88	6	57			Y	Y			Y	Y	Y	Y		N	1	39
San Francisco College of Mortuary Science	San Francisco	T	Ind	Coed	65	0		50			Y	Y				Y	Y	Y	Y	N	0	1
San Joaquin Delta College	Stockton	C	Dist	Coed	17,860	67		49			Y				Y	Y	Y	Y	Y	N	14	87
San Joaquin Valley College	Visalia	C	Ind		425						N		Y	Y						N	0	
San Jose City College	San Jose	C,T	Dist	Coed	10,044	83		56		12	Y	Y		S	Y	Y	Y	Y	Y	N	9	29
Santa Barbara City College	Santa Barbara	T	Dist	Coed	11,288	58		34	63		Y	Y	R		Y	Y	Y	Y	Y	N	10	63
Santa Monica College†	Santa Monica	C,T	St & Loc	Coed	22,127	70		41		20	Y	S			Y	Y	Y	Y	Y	N	10	62
Santa Rosa Junior College	Santa Rosa	C,T	St & Loc	Coed	21,651	69		60			Y	Y			Y	Y	Y	Y	Y	Y	13	61
Shasta College	Redding	C,T	St & Loc	Coed	11,152	77		60			Y	Y	Y	Y	Y	Y	Y	Y	Y	Y	9	44
Sierra College	Rocklin	C,T	State	Coed	13,567	71	15	46			Y	Y		Y	Y	Y	Y	Y		Y	16	52
Skyline College	San Bruno	C,T	County	Coed	8,104	74		46			Y	Y		R	Y	Y	Y	Y	Y	N	8	46
Solano Community College	Suisun City	C	St & Loc	Coed	9,909	72		51			Y	Y		R	Y	Y		Y	Y	N	7	49
Southwestern College	Chula Vista	C,T	St & Loc	Coed	15,498	66	8	50			Y	Y			Y	Y	Y	Y	Y	N	10	83
Taft College	Taft	C,T	St & Loc	Coed	532	40		47			Y	Y			Y	Y	Y	Y	Y	Y	4	23
Ventura College†	Ventura	C,T	St & Loc	Coed	10,083	72		47			Y	Y	Y	S	Y	Y	Y	Y	Y	N	10	41
Victor Valley College	Victorville	C,T	State	Coed	8,000	80		60			Y	Y			Y	Y	Y	Y	Y	N	9	28
Vista Community College	Berkeley	C,T	St & Loc	Coed	3,171	81		63	48		Y				Y		Y	Y		N	0	11
West Hills Community College	Coalinga	C,T	State	Coed	2,810	24		48	46	14	Y			R	Y	Y	Y	Y	Y	Y	4	29
West Los Angeles College	Culver City	C,T	St & Loc	Coed	7,400	78		76			Y		R		Y	Y	Y	Y	Y	N	4	46
West Valley College	Saratoga	C,T	St & Loc	Coed	14,224	69		58			Y				Y	Y	Y	Y	Y	N	12	40
Yuba College*	Marysville	C,T	St & Loc	Coed	9,860	70		54			Y	Y	Y		Y	Y	Y	Y	Y	Y	12	59
Colorado																						
Aims Community College	Greeley	C,T	Dist	Coed	6,958	70		59			Y				Y	Y	Y	Y	Y	N	2	18
Arapahoe Community College	Littleton	C,T	State	Coed	7,346	75		61		16	Y	Y	R	Y	Y	Y	Y	Y	Y	N	9	38
Bel-Rea Institute of Animal Technology†	Denver	T	Prop	Coed	325	4		25			N	Y		R	Y	Y	Y	Y	Y	N	0	2
Blair Junior College	Colorado Springs	C,T	Prop	Coed	290			69			N	Y	Y	Y	Y	Y	Y	Y	Y	N	1	9
Colorado Institute of Art	Denver	T	Prop	Coed	1,478	0	80	28	65		N	Y	Y		Y	Y	Y	Y	Y	Y	0	11
Colorado Mountn Coll, Alpine Cmps†	Steamboat Springs	C,T	Dist	Coed	1,262	64		50		57	Y	Y	S	R	Y	Y	Y	Y	Y	Y	5	20
Colorado Mountn Coll, Roaring Fork Cmps-Spring Valley Ctr*†	Glenwood Springs	C,T	Dist	Coed	868	56		51		57	Y	Y	S	R	Y	Y	Y	Y	Y	Y	6	24
Colorado Mountn Coll, Timberline Cmps†	Leadville	C,T	Dist	Coed	576	76		62		57	Y	Y	S	R	Y	Y	Y	Y	Y	Y	5	24
Colorado Northwestern Community College	Rangely	C,T	Dist	Coed	555	21	53	41	51	61	Y	S	R	R	Y	Y	Y	Y	Y	Y	11	20
Community College of Aurora	Aurora	C,T	State	Coed	4,670	84		68		20	Y	Y		R	Y	Y	Y	Y	Y	N	0	17
Community College of Denver	Denver	C,T	State	Coed	11,897	68		51			Y		R	R	Y	Y	Y	Y	Y	N	23	29
Denver Automotive and Diesel College	Denver	T	Prop	Coed	388		90	20			N	Y			Y	Y	Y	Y	Y	N	0	1
Front Range Community College	Westminster	C,T	State	Coed	11,471	72		60			Y			Y	Y	Y	Y	Y	Y	N	2	31
ITT Technical Institute	Aurora	T,B	Prop	Coed	287	0		31	70	68	N	Y	Y	Y	Y	Y	Y	Y	Y	N	0	2
Johnson & Wales University	Vail	T	Ind	Coed	39			50			N	Y	Y	R	Y	Y	Y	Y		N	0	1
Lamar Community College	Lamar	C,T	State	Coed	701	44	79	43	50	64	Y	Y		R	Y	Y	Y	Y		Y	5	48
Morgan Community College	Fort Morgan	C,T	State	Coed	997	67		56			Y		Y		Y	Y	Y	Y	Y	N	0	10
Northeastern Junior College	Sterling	C,T	St & Loc	Coed	2,734	25	60	16		75	Y	Y	Y	S	Y	Y	Y	Y	Y	Y	11	69
Otero Junior College	La Junta	C,T	State	Coed	1,000	35	70	52		36	Y	Y	R	R	Y		Y	Y	Y	Y	4	30
Parks Junior College	Denver	T	Prop	Coed	400	2		30			N	Y		Y	Y	Y	Y	Y	Y	N	0	16
Pikes Peak Community College	Colorado Springs	C,T	State	Coed	6,615	64		58			Y			R	Y	Y	Y	Y	Y	N	4	49
Pima Medical Institute	Denver	T	Prop		450								Y		Y	Y				N	0	2
PPI Health Careers School	Colorado Springs	T	Prop	Prim W							Y				Y	Y	Y			N	0	2
Pueblo College of Business and Technology	Pueblo	T	Prop	Coed	200								Y								0	5
Pueblo Community College	Pueblo	C,T	State	Coed	4,127	58	57	62			Y	Y		S	Y	Y	Y	Y	Y	N	0	34
Red Rocks Community College	Lakewood	C,T	State	Coed	6,939	76		69			Y				Y	Y	Y	Y	Y	N	1	41
Trinidad State Junior College	Trinidad	C,T	State	Coed	2,142	28		26			Y	Y		R,S	Y	Y	Y	Y	Y	Y	13	41
Connecticut																						
Asnuntuck Community-Technical College	Enfield	C,T	State	Coed	2,051	85		87		75	Y	Y			Y	Y	Y	Y	Y	N	0	12
Briarwood College†	Southington	C,T	Prop	Coed	541	45	83	37		11	N	Y	Y		Y	Y	Y	Y	Y	Y	5	22
Capital Community Technical College	Hartford	C,T	State	Coed	2,900	79		67			Y	Y		S	Y	Y	Y	Y	Y	N	0	19
Gateway Community-Technical College	New Haven	C,T	State	Coed	4,843	75	22	60		40	Y	Y	Y		Y	Y	Y	Y	Y	N	5	31
Housatonic Community-Technical College	Bridgeport	C,T	State	Coed	2,654	84		54			Y	Y	Y	S	Y		Y	Y	Y	N	1	24
Katharine Gibbs School	Norwalk	T	Prop	Prim W	350	0		10			N	Y	Y	Y	Y	Y	Y	Y	Y	N	0	3
Manchester Community-Technical College	Manchester	C,T	State	Coed	5,400	72					Y	Y	Y		Y	Y	Y	Y		N	3	30
Middlesex Community– Technical College	Middletown	C,T	State	Coed	2,785	75		60			Y	Y			Y	Y	Y	Y	Y	N	0	26
Mitchell College†	New London	C,T	Ind	Coed	509	20	60	7	65	90	N	Y	Y	S	Y	Y	Y	Y	Y	Y	11	33
Naugatuck Valley Community–Technical College	Waterbury	C,T	State	Coed	5,533	69	38	54	65	30	Y	Y	Y	S	Y	Y	Y	Y	Y	N	3	45
Northwestern Connecticut Community-Technical Coll	Winsted	C,T	State	Coed	2,116	78	13	62		30	Y	Y			Y	Y	Y	Y	Y	N	0	37
Norwalk Community-Technical College	Norwalk	C,T	State	Coed	5,352	78		55		40	Y	Y		R	Y	Y	Y	Y	Y	N	5	34
Quinebaug Valley Community-Technical College	Danielson	C,T	State	Coed	1,120	73		62			Y	Y			Y	Y	Y	Y		N	2	12
St Vincent's College	Bridgeport	C	Ind	Coed	212	60	61	58			N	Y	Y	S	Y	Y	Y	Y		Y	0	2
Swiss Hospitality Institute "Cesar Ritz"*†	Washington	C,T	Prop	Coed	100	1	67	31	94	40	N	Y	Y	R	Y	Y	Y	Y	Y	Y	0	1
Three Rivers Community-Technical College	Norwich	C,T	State	Coed	3,977	76	24	61		45	Y	Y	R	Y	Y	Y	Y	Y		N	4	42
Tunxis Community Technical College	Farmington	C,T	State	Coed	3,675	77	40	65			Y	Y	Y	S	Y	Y	Y	Y		N	0	23
Delaware																						
Delaware Tech & Comm Coll, Jack F Owens Cmps	Georgetown	T	State	Coed	3,251	56	40	54	42		Y				Y	Y	Y	Y	Y	N	3	33
Delaware Tech & Comm Coll, Stanton/Wilmington Cmps	Newark	T	State	Coed	6,552	66		50	37		Y				Y	Y	Y	Y	Y	N	5	29
Delaware Tech & Comm Coll, Terry Cmps	Dover	T	State	Coed	1,861	71	40	56	25		Y				Y	Y	Y	Y	Y	N	1	26

Peterson's Guide to Two-Year Colleges 1997

31

This index includes the names and locations of accredited two-year colleges in the United States and U.S. territories and shows institutions' responses to our 1996 Survey of Undergraduate Institutions. If an institution submitted incomplete or no data, one or more columns opposite the institution's name is blank. An asterisk after the school name denotes a Special Announcement following the college's profile, and a dagger indicates that the institution has one or more entries in the In-Depth Descriptions of the Colleges section.

Y—Yes; N—No; R—Recommended; S—For Some

		Degrees Awarded: Certificate (C), Transfer Associate (T), Terminal Associate (T), Bachelor's (B), Master's (M), Doctoral (D), First Professional (F)	Institutional Control: Independent, Independent-Religious, Proprietary, Federal, State, Province, Commonwealth, Territory, County, District, City, State and Local, State-Related	Student Body: Men, Primarily Men, Women, Primarily Women, Coeducational	Undergraduate Enrollment Fall 1995	Percent Attending Part-Time	Percent Receiving Need-Based Financial Aid	Percent 25 Years of Age or Older	Freshman Retention Rate	Percent of Grads Going on to 4-Year Colleges	Open Admissions	High School Equivalency Certificate Accepted	High School Transcript Required	Entrance Test(s) Required	College Scholarships Available	Loans Available	Part-Time Jobs Available	Career Counseling Available	Job Placement Services Available	College Housing Available	Number of Sports Offered	Number of Majors Offered
Florida																						
American Flyers College	Fort Lauderdale	C	Prop	Coed	50						Y	N		R	Y			Y		Y	0	1
Art Institute of Fort Lauderdale*†	Fort Lauderdale	C,T,B	Prop	Coed	1,950	0		12			N	Y		R	Y	Y	Y	Y	Y	Y	0	18
ATI Health Education Center	Miami	C,T	Prop	Coed	300	0		50			N	Y	Y	Y	Y	Y		Y	Y	N	0	2
Brevard Community College	Cocoa	C,T	State	Coed	14,341	69		57		70	Y	Y	Y	S	Y	Y	Y	Y	Y	N	11	70
Broward Community College	Fort Lauderdale	C,T	State	Coed	24,600	78		29		39	Y	Y			Y	Y	Y	Y	Y	N	6	49
Central Florida Community College	Ocala	C,T	St & Loc	Coed	6,068	59					Y	Y	Y		Y	Y	Y	Y	Y	N	5	25
Chipola Junior College	Marianna	C,T	State	Coed	2,273	58			38	35	Y	Y			Y	Y	Y	Y	Y	Y	3	15
Daytona Beach Community College	Daytona Beach	C,T	State	Coed	12,001	63	30	52			Y	Y	Y	Y	Y	Y	Y	Y	Y	N	10	90
Edison Community College	Fort Myers	C,T	St & Loc	Coed	9,836	68		43		70	Y	Y		Y	Y	Y	Y	Y	Y	N	2	25
Education America–Tampa Tech Inst Campus	Tampa	C,B	Prop	Coed	1,150	0		32			Y	Y	Y		Y	Y		Y	Y	N	0	4
Flagler Career Institute	Jacksonville	T	Prop	Coed	214	50						Y	Y	Y						N	0	1
Florida College	Temple Terrace	C	Ind	Coed	378	2	21	1			N	Y	Y	Y	Y	Y	Y	Y		Y	6	1
Florida Community College at Jacksonville	Jacksonville	C,T	State	Coed	19,211	67		64		81	Y	Y		R	Y	Y	Y	Y	Y	N	13	50
Florida Hospital College of Health Sciences	Orlando	T	Ind										Y	Y						Y	0	
Florida Keys Community College	Key West	C,T	State	Coed	2,200	71	10	57			Y	Y		S	Y	Y	Y	Y	Y	N	0	15
Florida National College	Hialeah	C,T	Prop	Coed	1,100	0	85				Y		Y	Y	Y		Y	Y	Y	N	0	20
Full Sail Center for the Recording Arts	Winter Park	T	Prop	Coed	754	0		29		10	Y	Y	Y			Y		Y	Y	N	0	2
Gulf Coast Community College	Panama City	C,T	State	Coed	5,865	65		42		68	Y	Y	Y	Y	Y	Y	Y	Y		N	4	75
Hillsborough Community College	Tampa	C,T	State	Coed	19,189	72	18	44			Y	Y	Y	Y	Y	Y	Y	Y	Y	N	5	37
Indian River Community College	Fort Pierce	C,T	State	Coed	6,919	68		51			Y	Y		Y	Y	Y	Y	Y	Y	N	7	72
Institute of Career Education	West Palm Beach	T	Prop	Coed	180	35		85	98		N	Y	Y		Y	Y		Y	Y	N	0	8
International Fine Arts College*†	Miami	T	Prop	Coed	790	0	70	5		15	N	Y	Y		Y	Y	Y	Y	Y	Y	0	5
ITT Technical Institute	Fort Lauderdale	T	Prop	Coed	386	0					N	Y		Y	Y	Y	Y	Y	Y	N	0	1
ITT Technical Institute	Jacksonville	T,B	Prop	Coed	417	0	97	30			N	Y			Y	Y	Y	Y	Y	N	0	2
ITT Technical Institute	Tampa	C,T,B	Prop	Coed	582	0		27	77	45	N	Y			Y	Y	Y	Y	Y	N	0	2
Keiser College of Technology	Daytona Beach	C,T	Prop	Coed	196						Y		Y	Y	Y	Y	Y	Y	Y	N	0	7
Keiser College of Technology†	Fort Lauderdale	C,T	Prop	Coed	700		88	70		35	N	Y	Y	R	Y	Y	Y	Y	Y	N	0	3
Keiser College of Technology	Melbourne	C,T	Prop		428	0					N		Y							N	0	
Keiser College of Technology	Sarasota	T	Prop	Coed	120							Y								N	0	5
Keiser College of Technology	Tallahassee																					
Lake City Community College	Lake City	C,T	State	Coed	2,700	47		48	50	35	Y	Y		Y	Y	Y	Y	Y	Y	Y	3	26
Lake-Sumter Community College	Leesburg	C,T	St & Loc	Coed	2,700	69		52			Y	Y	Y	Y	Y	Y	Y	Y	Y	N	10	23
Manatee Community College	Bradenton	C,T	State	Coed	7,605	61		45		77	Y	Y		Y	Y	Y	Y	Y	Y	N	6	21
Miami-Dade Community College*†	Miami	C,T	St & Loc	Coed	51,019	67		43	79	78	Y	Y		Y	Y	Y	Y	Y	Y	N	15	132
National Institute for Paralegal Arts and Sciences	Boca Raton	C,T	Prop	Coed							Y	Y									0	1
National School of Technology, Inc	North Miami Beach	T	Prop	Coed	800	60		90			Y		Y		Y	Y	Y	Y	Y	N	0	3
New England Inst of Tech & Florida Culinary Inst	West Palm Beach	T	Prop	Coed	945	0		40			Y	Y	Y		Y	Y	Y	Y	Y	N	0	8
North Florida Community College	Madison	C	State	Coed	1,003	58	55	26	14	68	Y	Y	Y	Y	Y	Y	Y	Y		N	5	1
Okaloosa-Walton Community College	Niceville	C,T	St & Loc	Coed	5,820	88	34	55	36		Y	Y		Y	Y	Y	Y	Y	Y	N	15	49
Palm Beach Community College	Lake Worth	C,T	State	Coed	16,717	69		45		90	Y	Y			Y		Y	Y	Y	Y	9	62
Pasco-Hernando Community College	Dade City	C,T	State	Coed	5,242	78		46			Y	Y	S	S	Y		Y	Y		N	9	14
Pensacola Junior College	Pensacola	C,T	State	Coed	12,000	71		50			Y	Y			Y	Y	Y	Y	Y	N	17	64
Peoples College	Kissimmee	C	Prop	Coed	380	100		98			Y	Y						Y		N	0	3
Phillips Junior College of Business	Melbourne	T	Prop	Coed	525																	
Polk Community College	Winter Haven	C,T	State	Coed	6,000	65		55			Y	Y	Y	R	Y	Y	Y	Y	Y	N	4	67
Prospect Hall	Hollywood	T	Prop	Coed	200	5			80		N	Y	Y	R	Y	Y		Y	Y	N	0	9
St Johns River Community College	Palatka	C,T	State	Coed	3,500	60		41			Y	Y	Y		Y		Y	Y	Y	N	4	17
St Petersburg Junior College	St Petersburg	C	St & Loc	Coed	19,207	69		49			Y	Y	Y		Y	Y	Y	Y		N	5	35
Santa Fe Community College	Gainesville	C,T	St & Loc	Coed	12,286	51		35		89	Y	Y		Y	Y	Y	Y	Y	Y	N	4	37
Seminole Community College	Sanford	C,T	St & Loc	Coed	6,522	64		43			Y	Y		Y	Y	Y	Y	Y	Y	N	9	29
South College	West Palm Beach	C,T	Prop		350						Y		Y	Y						N	0	8
Southern College	Orlando	C	Prop	Coed	500	31		65		15	N	Y	Y	Y	Y	Y	Y	Y	Y	N	0	8
South Florida Community College	Avon Park	C,T	State	Coed	1,530						Y	Y	Y	Y	Y	Y	Y	Y	Y	N	5	19
Southwest Florida College of Business	Fort Meyers	T	Ind	Coed	220				70		Y	Y	R		Y		Y	Y	Y	N	0	7
Tallahassee Community College	Tallahassee	C,T	St & Loc	Coed	10,084	52		25	79		Y	Y		Y	Y	Y	Y	Y	Y	N	12	17
Valencia Community College	Orlando	C,T	State	Coed	24,121	68		41		73	Y	Y	Y	R	Y	Y	Y	Y		N	6	30
Ward Stone College	Miami	T	Prop	Coed	500						N	Y	Y	Y							0	7
Webster College	Fort Pierce																					
Webster College	Gainesville																					
Webster College	New Port Richey																					
Webster College	Ocala	T	Prop	Prim W	224	0	90	70	65		Y	Y	Y		Y			Y	Y	N	0	7
Georgia																						
Abraham Baldwin Agricultural College	Tifton	C,T	State	Coed	2,592	32		31	50		Y	Y	Y	Y	Y	Y	Y	Y	Y	Y	8	55
Andrew College	Cuthbert	C	Ind-R	Coed	305	5	65	3		96	N	Y	Y	Y	Y	Y	Y	Y		Y	18	39
Art Institute of Atlanta	Atlanta	T,B	Prop	Coed	1,408	18		50			N	Y	Y		Y	Y	Y	Y	Y	Y	0	6
Athens Area Technical Institute	Athens	C,T	State	Coed	1,653	48	30	40			Y	Y	Y	Y	Y		Y	Y	Y	N	0	27
Atlanta Metropolitan College	Atlanta	C,T	State	Coed	1,811	48		38	23		N	Y	Y	Y	Y		Y	Y	Y	N	3	51
Augusta Technical Institute	Augusta	T	State	Coed	2,325	44	41				N	Y	Y	Y	Y		Y	Y	Y	N	0	39
Bainbridge College	Bainbridge	C,T	State	Coed	1,180	54		40	70	30	Y	Y		S	Y	Y	Y	Y	Y	N	3	35
Bauder College	Atlanta	C	Prop	Prim W	500	0			70	2	N	Y			Y	Y	Y	Y	Y	Y	0	4
Brunswick College	Brunswick	C,T	State	Coed	2,085	58		48			Y	Y	Y	Y	Y	Y	Y	Y	Y	N	3	47
Chattahoochee Technical Institute	Marietta	T	State	Coed	1,930	65					Y	Y	S	S	Y		Y	Y	Y	N	0	13
Columbus Technical Institute	Columbus	T	State		1,964								Y	Y							0	3
Dalton College	Dalton	C,T	State	Coed	3,172	54		33			Y	Y		S	Y	Y	Y	Y	Y	N	8	48
Darton College	Albany	C,T	State	Coed	2,635	52	30	41	25	80	N				Y	Y	Y	Y	Y	N	9	55
DeKalb College	Decatur	C,T	State	Coed	16,073	65		41			N	Y	Y	Y	Y		Y	Y	Y	N	6	38
DeKalb Technical Institute	Clarkston	T	State		4,347						Y	Y			Y						0	13
East Georgia College	Swainsboro	C,T	State	Coed	905	21	44	4	50	85	N	Y	Y	S	Y	Y	Y	Y		N	10	23
Emory University, Oxford College	Oxford	C	Ind-R	Coed	600	1		0	85	99	N	Y	Y	Y	Y	Y	Y			Y	15	1

This index includes the names and locations of accredited two-year colleges in the United States and U.S. territories and shows institutions' responses to our 1996 Survey of Undergraduate Institutions. If an institution submitted incomplete or no data, one or more columns opposite the institution's name is blank. An asterisk after the school name denotes a Special Announcement following the college's profile, and a dagger indicates that the institution has one or more entries in the In-Depth Descriptions of the Colleges section.

Y—Yes; N—No; R—Recommended; S—For Some

Institution	Location	Degrees Awarded: Transfer Associate (C), Terminal Associate (T), Bachelor's (B), Master's (M), Doctoral (D), First Professional (F)	Institutional Control: Independent, Independent-Religious, Proprietary, Federal, State, Province, Commonwealth, Territory, County, District, City, State and Local, State-Related	Student Body: Men, Primarily Men, Women, Primarily Women, Coeducational	Undergraduate Enrollment Fall 1995	Percent Attending Part-Time	Percent Receiving Need-Based Financial Aid	Percent 25 Years of Age or Older	Freshman Retention Rate	Percent of Grads Going on to 4-Year Colleges	Open Admissions	High School Equivalency Certificate Accepted	High School Transcript Required	Entrance Test(s) Required	College Scholarships Available	Loans Available	Part-Time Jobs Available	Career Counseling Available	Job Placement Services Available	College Housing Available	Number of Sports Offered	Number of Majors Offered
Floyd College	Rome	C,T	State	Coed	3,048	47			36	39	Y	Y	Y	S	Y	Y	Y	Y		N	5	22
Gainesville College	Gainesville	C,T	State	Coed	2,646	40		26	78	80	Y	Y		Y	Y	Y	Y	Y	Y	N	10	46
Georgia Military College	Milledgeville	C,T	St & Loc	Coed	3,495	61	70	27			N	Y	Y	R,S	Y		Y	Y		Y	9	11
Gordon College	Barnesville	C,T	State	Coed	2,204	38	44	26	60	50	Y	Y		Y	Y	Y	Y	Y		Y	10	22
Gupton-Jones College of Funeral Service	Decatur	T	Ind	Coed	325			20			Y	Y				Y		Y	Y	N	0	1
Gwinnett Technical Institute	Lawrenceville	T	State	Coed	4,000	66		62					Y	Y	Y	Y	Y			N	0	25
Herzing College of Business and Technology	Atlanta	T	Prop	Coed	400	0		30		20	N	Y	Y	Y	Y	Y	Y	Y	Y	N	0	11
Macon College	Macon	C	State	Coed	4,500	64		49	60			Y	Y	Y	Y	Y	Y	Y	Y	N	6	52
Macon Technical Institute	Macon																					
Meadows College of Business	Columbus	T	Prop	Coed	260	0		42			Y	Y	Y	S	Y	Y	Y	Y	Y	N	2	6
Middle Georgia College*	Cochran	C,T	State	Coed	2,049	42		23			N	Y	Y	Y	Y	Y	Y	Y		Y	7	74
Savannah Technical Institute	Savannah	T	State		2,022									Y							0	
South College	Savannah	C,T,B	Prop	Coed	308	33		68			N	Y		R	Y	Y	Y	Y	Y	N	0	7
South Georgia College	Douglas	C,T	State	Coed	1,171	38	38	33			N	Y		S	Y	Y	Y	Y		Y	8	40
Thomas Technical Institute	Thomasville	T	State	Coed	998						Y			Y							0	
Truett-McConnell College*	Cleveland	C,T	Ind-R	Coed	1,957	12	45	5		97	N	Y		Y	Y	Y	Y			Y	9	3
Waycross College	Waycross	C,T	State	Coed	885	35		43			Y	Y		S	Y	Y	Y	Y	Y	N	8	41
Young Harris College	Young Harris	C	Ind-R	Coed	519	1		1		93	N	Y	Y	Y	Y	Y	Y	Y		Y	12	32
Hawaii																						
Hawaii Tokai International College	Honolulu	C	Ind	Coed	84	0		15			Y	Y	R								0	1
Heald Business College	Honolulu	T	Ind	Coed	650	2					Y	Y	Y	Y		Y		Y	Y	N	0	10
University of Hawaii–Hawaii Community College	Hilo	C	State	Coed	2,800	59	30	64			Y				Y	Y	Y			Y	0	19
University of Hawaii–Honolulu Community College	Honolulu	C,T	State	Coed	4,717	71	13	43	54		Y	Y			Y	Y	Y	Y	Y	N	0	22
University of Hawaii–Kapiolani Community College	Honolulu	C,T	State	Coed	7,283	64	9	40			Y	Y			Y	Y	Y	Y	Y	N	2	17
University of Hawaii–Kauai Community College	Lihue	C	State	Coed	1,143	49		37	66		Y	Y			Y	Y	Y	Y	Y	N	3	11
University of Hawaii–Leeward Community College	Pearl City	C,T	State	Coed	6,330	55		36			Y	Y	S	S	Y	Y	Y	Y	Y	N	5	12
University of Hawaii–Maui Community College	Kahului	C,T	State	Coed	2,759	66		45			Y		S	Y	Y	Y	Y	Y	Y	Y	5	17
University of Hawaii–Windward Community College	Kaneohe	C,T	State	Coed	1,666	64		43			Y				Y	Y	Y	Y	Y	N	0	5
Idaho																						
College of Southern Idaho	Twin Falls	C,T	St & Loc	Coed	4,342	50		52	55		Y	Y	Y	S	Y	Y	Y	Y	Y	Y	10	49
Eastern Idaho Technical College	Idaho Falls	T	State	Coed	365	14	81	44			Y	Y	Y	Y	Y	Y	Y	Y	Y	N	0	14
ITT Technical Institute	Boise	T	Prop	Coed	339						N	Y		Y	Y	Y	Y		Y	N	0	2
North Idaho College	Coeur d'Alene	C,T	St & Loc	Coed	3,312	41		36			Y	Y	S	R,S	Y	Y	Y	Y	Y	Y	17	63
Ricks College	Rexburg	C,T	Ind-R	Coed	7,956	3	60	2		90	N	Y	Y	Y	Y	Y	Y	Y	Y	Y	19	114
Illinois																						
American Academy of Art	Chicago	T	Prop	Coed	392	17	68	47			N	Y			Y	Y	Y	Y	Y	N	0	9
Belleville Area College	Belleville	C,T	Dist	Coed	15,267	74		60			Y	Y		S	Y	Y	Y	Y	Y	N	8	41
Black Hawk College	Kewanee	C,T	St & Loc	Coed	765	45		36			Y	Y	Y	Y	Y		Y	Y	Y	N	2	14
Black Hawk College	Moline	C,T	St & Loc	Coed	6,335	57		63			Y		Y	S	Y	Y	Y	Y	Y	N	10	70
Carl Sandburg College	Galesburg	C,T	St & Loc	Coed	3,000	78				63	Y	Y	Y		Y	Y	Y	Y	Y	N	3	20
Chicago College of Commerce	Chicago	T	Prop	Prim W	292	60		79			Y	Y			Y	Y		Y	Y	N	0	3
City Colls of Chicago, Harold Washington Coll	Chicago	C,T	St & Loc	Coed	7,745	77		61			Y	Y		R	Y	Y	Y	Y	Y	N	0	61
City Colls of Chicago, Harry S Truman Coll	Chicago	C,T	St & Loc	Coed	4,620	64		70			Y	Y		Y	Y	Y	Y	Y	Y	N	6	24
City Colls of Chicago, Kennedy-King Coll	Chicago	C,T	St & Loc	Coed	2,539	61		61			Y			R	Y	Y	Y	Y	Y	N	3	33
City Colls of Chicago, Malcolm X Coll	Chicago	C,T	St & Loc	Coed	3,480	69		41	80		Y	Y	Y	S	Y	Y	Y	Y	Y	N	4	24
City Colls of Chicago, Olive-Harvey Coll	Chicago	C,T	St & Loc	Coed	3,419	63	70	45			Y	Y		Y	Y	Y	Y	Y	Y	N	8	27
City Colls of Chicago, Richard J Daley Coll	Chicago	C,T	St & Loc	Coed	4,679	63		54			Y	Y		R,S	Y	Y	Y	Y	Y	N	0	39
City Colls of Chicago, Wilbur Wright Coll	Chicago	C,T	St & Loc	Coed	6,949	69		43	43	52	Y	Y	R	Y	Y	Y	Y	Y	Y	N	9	27
College of DuPage	Glen Ellyn	C,T	St & Loc	Coed	33,920	72		48		72	Y			R	Y	Y	Y	Y	Y	N	14	84
College of Lake County	Grayslake	C,T	Dist	Coed	14,865	81		60			Y	Y	R	R	Y	Y	Y	Y	Y	N	12	43
Danville Area Community College	Danville	C,T	St & Loc	Coed		58		52			Y	Y	Y		Y	Y	Y	Y	Y	N	7	53
Elgin Community College	Elgin	C,T	St & Loc	Coed	8,589	75		53	91		Y	Y		R	Y	Y	Y	Y	Y	N	7	48
Gem City College	Quincy	T	Prop	Coed	250	10		40			Y	Y				Y		Y	Y	N	0	11
Heartland Community College	Bloomington	C,T	Dist	Coed	2,769	74		33		94	Y		R	R	Y		Y	Y	Y	N	0	16
Highland Community College	Freeport	C,T	St & Loc	Coed	2,663	63		58	75	82	Y	Y		R	Y	Y	Y	Y	Y	N	6	39
Illinois Central College	East Peoria	C,T	St & Loc	Coed	11,680	69	12	55		89	Y		Y	S	Y	Y	Y	Y	Y	N	8	38
Illinois Eastern Comm Colls, Frontier Comm Coll	Fairfield	C,T	St & Loc	Coed	1,904	91	24	71			Y	Y	Y	Y	Y	Y	Y	Y	Y	N	0	6
Illinois Eastern Comm Colls, Lincoln Trail Coll	Robinson	C,T	St & Loc	Coed	1,127	54	44	53			Y	Y	Y	Y	Y	Y	Y	Y	Y	N	3	17
Illinois Eastern Comm Colls, Olney Central Coll	Olney	C,T	St & Loc	Coed	1,486	45	52	47			Y	Y	Y	Y	Y	Y	Y	Y	Y	N	2	14
Illinois Eastern Comm Colls, Wabash Valley Coll	Mount Carmel	C,T	St & Loc	Coed	2,023	67	34	67			Y	Y	Y	Y	Y	Y	Y	Y	Y	N	5	16
Illinois Valley Community College	Oglesby	C,T	Dist	Coed	4,281	64		6			Y	N	Y	R	Y	Y	Y	Y	Y	N	5	25
ITT Technical Institute	Hoffman Estates	T,B	Prop	Coed	470	0		30			N	Y			Y	Y	Y	Y	Y	N	0	2
ITT Technical Institute	Matteson	C,T	Prop	Coed	331	0		10	70		N	Y		Y	Y	Y	Y	Y	Y	N	0	
John A Logan College	Carterville	C,T	St & Loc	Coed	4,897	42		37			Y	Y	Y	Y	Y	Y	Y	Y	Y	N	6	50
John Wood Community College	Quincy	C,T	Dist	Coed	2,300	62		59			Y	Y	Y	Y	Y	Y	Y	Y	Y	N	7	66
Joliet Junior College	Joliet	C,T	St & Loc	Coed	10,417	70		51		85	Y	Y	Y	R	Y	Y	Y	Y	Y	N	4	54
Kankakee Community College	Kankakee	C,T	St & Loc	Coed	3,776	67		25			Y	Y	Y	R,S	Y		Y	Y	Y	N	7	26
Kaskaskia College	Centralia	C,T	St & Loc	Coed	2,916	52		45	59		Y	Y	Y	R,S	Y	Y	Y	Y	Y	N	4	22
Kishwaukee College	Malta	C,T	St & Loc	Coed	3,690	52		51	67	60	Y	Y	S		Y	Y	Y	Y	Y	N	6	47
Lake Land College	Mattoon	C,T	St & Loc	Coed	4,734	55	27	48			Y	Y		R,S	Y	Y	Y	Y	Y	N	7	53
Lewis and Clark Community College	Godfrey	C,T	Dist	Coed	5,303	71		49			Y	Y	R		Y	Y	Y	Y	Y	N	7	36
Lexington College	Chicago	C,T	Ind	Women	44	9	73	20		7	Y	Y	Y		Y		Y	Y	Y	Y	0	5
Lincoln College†	Lincoln	C	Ind	Coed	570	11		6	72	83	N	Y	Y	Y	Y	Y	Y	Y	Y	Y	17	1
Lincoln College†	Normal	C,T	Ind	Coed	600	45	75	25		87	N	Y	Y	S	Y	Y		Y	Y	Y	10	29
Lincoln Land Community College	Springfield	C,T	Dist	Coed	11,016	75		50			Y		R	R	Y	Y	Y	Y	Y	N	6	68
MacCormac Junior College†	Chicago	C,T	Ind	Coed	569	28		20	78	20	N	Y	Y	Y	Y	Y	Y	Y	Y	N	4	15

Peterson's Guide to Two-Year Colleges 1997
33

State-by-State Summary Table
Illinois–Iowa

This index includes the names and locations of accredited two-year colleges in the United States and U.S. territories and shows institutions' responses to our 1996 Survey of Undergraduate Institutions. If an institution submitted incomplete or no data, one or more columns opposite the institution's name is blank. An asterisk after the school name denotes a Special Announcement following the college's profile, and a dagger indicates that the institution has one or more entries in the In-Depth Descriptions of the Colleges section.

Y—Yes; N—No; R—Recommended; S—For Some

Institution	City	Degrees Awarded (Transfer Associate (C), Terminal Associate (T), Bachelor's (B), Master's (M), Doctoral (D), First Professional (F))	Institutional Control (Independent, Independent-Religious, Proprietary, Federal, State, Province, Commonwealth, Territory, County, District, City, State and Local, State-Related)	Student Body (Men, Primarily Men, Women, Primarily Women, Coeducational)	Undergraduate Enrollment Fall 1995	Percent Attending Part-Time	Percent Receiving Need-Based Financial Aid	Percent 25 Years of Age or Older	Freshman Retention Rate	Percent of Grads Going on to 4-Year Colleges	Open Admissions	High School Equivalency Certificate Accepted	High School Transcript Required	Entrance Test(s) Required	College Scholarships Available	Loans Available	Part-Time Jobs Available	Career Counseling Available	Job Placement Services Available	College Housing Available	Number of Sports Offered	Number of Majors Offered
McHenry County College	Crystal Lake	C,T	St & Loc	Coed	4,933	74	5	53			Y		Y	R	Y	Y	Y	Y	Y	N	6	17
Midstate College	Peoria	T	Prop	Coed	284	29		36			N	Y	Y		Y	Y	Y	Y	Y	N	0	15
Moraine Valley Community College	Palos Hills	C,T	St & Loc	Coed	12,813	63	24	40	69	78	Y	Y	Y	Y	Y	Y	Y		Y	N	8	57
Morrison Institute of Technology*	Morrison	C,T	Ind	Coed	173	0	73	20	82	6	Y	Y	Y	R	Y	Y	Y	Y	Y	Y	11	11
Morton College	Cicero	C,T	St & Loc	Coed	4,050	81	16	53	37		Y	Y	Y	R	Y	Y	Y	Y		N	11	20
Northwestern Business College†	Chicago	C,T	Prop	Coed	610	58		21			N	Y	Y	Y	Y	Y		Y	Y	N	0	16
Oakton Community College	Des Plaines	C,T	Dist	Coed	10,976	73		46			Y	Y	Y	R	Y	Y	Y	Y	Y	N	12	28
Parkland College	Champaign	C,T	Dist	Coed	8,403	57	60	49			Y	Y	R	S	Y	Y	Y	Y	Y	N	9	68
Prairie State College	Chicago Heights	C,T	St & Loc	Coed	5,000	76		53			Y	Y	Y		Y	Y	Y	Y	Y	N	2	34
Rend Lake College	Ina	C,T	State	Coed	3,759	77	46	55			Y	Y	Y	Y	Y	Y	Y	Y	Y	N	5	21
Richland Community College	Decatur	C,T	Dist	Coed	3,384	61	33	48	30	60	Y	Y	Y		Y	Y	Y	Y	Y	N	0	21
Robert Morris College*†	Chicago	C,T,B	Ind	Coed	3,100	5		15	75		N	Y	Y		Y	Y	Y	Y	Y	N	5	15
Rock Valley College	Rockford	C,T	Dist	Coed	8,936	76		54	36		Y	Y	Y	S	Y	Y	Y	Y	Y	N	8	42
Saint Augustine College	Chicago	C,T	Ind	Coed	1,345	6	97	67	45		Y				Y	Y	Y	Y	Y	N	2	8
Sauk Valley Community College	Dixon	C,T	Dist	Coed	2,635	60		50			Y		R	Y	Y	Y	Y	Y	Y	N	6	41
Shawnee Community College	Ullin	C,T	St & Loc	Coed	2,288	68		54		60	Y	Y	Y	Y	Y	Y	Y	Y	Y	N	9	25
Southeastern Illinois College	Harrisburg	C,T	State	Coed	3,382	69		40			Y	Y	Y	Y	Y	Y	Y	Y	Y	N	2	25
South Suburban College	South Holland	C,T	St & Loc	Coed	6,185	67	27	49		61	Y	Y	Y	Y	Y		Y	Y	Y	N	9	56
Spoon River College	Canton	C,T	State	Coed	1,950	49		50		75	Y	Y	Y	R	Y	Y	Y	Y		N	6	40
Springfield College in Illinois	Springfield	C	Ind-R	Coed	465	29		24		86	N	Y		Y	Y	Y	Y	Y		Y	5	13
State Community College of East St Louis	East St Louis	C,T	State	Coed	1,268	56		59			Y	Y		S	Y	Y	Y	Y	Y	N	3	31
Triton College	River Grove	C,T	State	Coed	12,050	68		48		68	Y	Y	Y	R	Y	Y	Y	Y	Y	N	10	86
Waubonsee Community College	Sugar Grove	C,T	Dist	Coed	7,460	79		54		85	Y	Y	R	R	Y		Y	Y	Y	N	11	49
William Rainey Harper College	Palatine	C,T	St & Loc	Coed	13,744	69		49	63	67	Y	Y	Y	S	Y	Y	Y	Y	Y	N	18	69
Indiana																						
Ancilla College	Donaldson	C,T	Ind-R	Coed	709	63		58		60	Y	Y	S	S	Y	Y	Y	Y		N	5	7
Commonwealth Business College	LaPorte	C,T	Prop	Coed	115	59		44			N	Y	Y	Y		Y		Y	Y	N	0	7
Commonwealth Business College	Merrillville	T	Prop	Coed	180	19		40			N	Y	Y	Y		Y		Y	Y	N	0	9
Holy Cross College*	Notre Dame	C	Ind-R	Coed	445	9	50	6		85	N	Y	Y	Y	Y	Y	Y	Y		N	3	1
Indiana Business College†	Indianapolis	C,T	Prop	Coed	1,700	25		35	82		N	Y	Y		Y	Y	Y	Y	Y	N	0	11
International Business College	Fort Wayne	T	Prop	Prim W	512	29		21			N	Y	Y		Y	Y	Y	Y	Y	Y	0	9
ITT Technical Institute	Evansville	C,T	Prop	Coed	300	0		20		10	N	Y	Y	Y	Y	Y	Y	Y	Y	N	0	2
ITT Technical Institute	Fort Wayne	T,B	Prop	Coed	767						N	Y			Y	Y	Y	Y	Y	N	0	6
ITT Technical Institute	Indianapolis	T,B	Prop	Coed	860	0		12			N	Y			Y	Y	Y	Y	Y	N	2	8
Ivy Tech State Coll–Central Indiana	Indianapolis	C,T	State	Coed	5,428	79		64			Y	Y	Y	Y	Y	Y	Y	Y	Y	N	0	34
Ivy Tech State Coll–Columbus	Columbus	C,T	State	Coed	2,849	74		65			Y	Y	Y	Y	Y	Y	Y	Y	Y	N	0	20
Ivy Tech State Coll–Eastcentral	Muncie	C,T	State	Coed	2,140	58		60			Y	Y	Y	Y	Y	Y	Y	Y	Y	N	0	23
Ivy Tech State Coll–Kokomo	Kokomo	C,T	State	Coed	1,570	76		66			Y	Y	Y	Y	Y	Y	Y	Y	Y	N	0	23
Ivy Tech State Coll–Lafayette	Lafayette	C,T	State	Coed	2,187	68		51			Y	Y	Y	Y	Y	Y	Y	Y	Y	N	0	21
Ivy Tech State Coll–Northcentral	South Bend	C,T	State	Coed	2,787	78		70			Y	Y	Y	Y	Y	Y	Y	Y	Y	N	3	26
Ivy Tech State Coll–Northeast	Fort Wayne	C,T	State	Coed	3,411	76		63			Y	Y	Y	Y	Y	Y	Y	Y	Y	N	0	28
Ivy Tech State Coll–Northwest	Gary	C,T	State	Coed	2,570	65		56			Y	Y	Y	Y	Y		Y	Y	Y	N	2	26
Ivy Tech State Coll–Southcentral	Sellersburg	C,T	State	Coed	1,890	73		61			Y	Y	Y	Y	Y	Y	Y	Y	Y	N	0	20
Ivy Tech State Coll–Southeast	Madison	C,T	State	Coed	866	67		66			Y	Y	Y	Y	Y	Y	Y	Y	Y	N	1	11
Ivy Tech State Coll–Southwest	Evansville	C,T	State	Coed	2,795	75		63		1	Y	Y	Y	Y	Y	Y	Y	Y	Y	N	0	19
Ivy Tech State Coll–Wabash Valley	Terre Haute	C,T	State	Coed	2,447	55		50			Y	Y	Y	Y	Y	Y	Y	Y	Y	N	3	28
Ivy Tech State Coll–Whitewater	Richmond	C,T	State	Coed	1,028	74		63			Y	Y	Y	Y	Y	Y	Y	Y	Y	N	0	18
Lincoln Technical Institute	Indianapolis	T	Prop	Coed	400	0		25			N	Y	Y		Y	Y	Y	Y	Y	N	0	2
Lutheran College of Health Professions	Fort Wayne	C,B	Ind-R	Prim W	649	59	55	53	84		N	Y	Y	Y	Y			Y		Y	0	6
Michiana College	South Bend	T	Prop	Coed	325	34		58		10	N	Y			Y	Y	Y	Y	Y	N	0	11
Mid-America College of Funeral Service	Jeffersonville	T	Ind	Prim M	141	0		13			Y	Y	Y			Y		Y	Y	N	0	1
Vincennes University	Vincennes	C,T	State	Coed	6,500	25		5			Y	Y	Y	R,S	Y	Y	Y	Y	Y	Y	16	134
Vincennes University–Jasper Center	Jasper	C,T	State	Coed	1,206	77	30	50			Y	Y	Y	S	Y	Y	Y	Y		N	0	19
Iowa																						
American Institute of Business	Des Moines	T	Ind	Coed	916	22		11	72		Y	Y	Y	R	Y	Y	Y	Y	Y	Y	5	13
American Institute of Commerce	Davenport	T	Prop	Coed	482	39		44	70		N	Y	Y	Y	Y		Y	Y	Y	N	0	13
Clinton Community College	Clinton	C,T	State	Coed	1,125	50		50			Y		Y	R	Y	Y	Y	Y	Y	N	9	38
Des Moines Area Community College	Ankeny	C,T	St & Loc	Coed	10,287	58		46			Y	Y	S	Y	Y	Y	Y	Y	Y	N	5	43
Ellsworth Community College	Iowa Falls	C,T	St & Loc	Coed	850	21		30	60	90	Y	Y	Y	R,S	Y	Y	Y	Y	Y	Y	14	45
Hamilton Business College	Cedar Rapids	T	Prop	Prim W	353	30	80	83	80		N		Y	Y	Y		Y	Y	Y	N	0	9
Hawkeye Community College	Waterloo	C,T	St & Loc	Coed	3,530	30	81	33			Y	Y	Y	S	Y	Y	Y	Y	Y	N	10	50
Indian Hills Community College	Ottumwa	C,T	St & Loc	Coed	3,292	28		32		45	Y	Y	S		Y	Y	Y	Y		Y	10	25
Iowa Central Community College	Fort Dodge	C,T	St & Loc	Coed	2,627	50	60	43		45	Y	Y	R,S	Y	Y	Y	Y	Y	Y	Y	10	38
Iowa Lakes Community College	Estherville	C,T	St & Loc	Coed	2,068	16		12		60	Y	Y	Y	S	Y	Y	Y	Y	Y	Y	12	87
Iowa Western Community College	Council Bluffs	C,T	Dist	Coed	3,638	51		36	55	72	Y	Y	Y	S	Y	Y	Y	Y	Y	Y	6	42
Kirkwood Community College	Cedar Rapids	C,T	St & Loc	Coed	10,025	46		40			Y	Y	Y	Y	Y	Y	Y	Y	Y	N	10	110
Marshalltown Community College	Marshalltown	C,T	Dist	Coed	1,248	39	55	34		80	Y	Y	Y	R	Y	Y	Y	Y	Y	N	6	22
Muscatine Community College	Muscatine	C,T	State	Coed	1,250	50		49			Y		Y	Y	Y	Y	Y	Y	Y	N	5	28
Northeast Iowa Community College, Calmar Campus	Calmar	C,T	St & Loc	Coed	900	23		38			Y	Y	Y	Y	Y	Y	Y	Y	Y	N	9	13
Northeast Iowa Community College, Peosta Campus	Peosta	C,T	St & Loc	Coed	1,700	35		27			Y	Y	Y	Y	Y	Y	Y	Y	Y	N	11	30
North Iowa Area Community College	Mason City	C,T	St & Loc	Coed	2,771	36		30		50	Y	Y	Y		Y	Y	Y	Y	Y	Y	8	24
Northwest Iowa Community College	Sheldon	C,T	State	Coed	684	32		25			Y		Y	Y	Y	Y	Y	Y	Y	Y	9	30
Scott Community College	Bettendorf	C,T	St & Loc	Coed	4,000	50					Y	Y	R	Y	Y	Y	Y	Y	Y	N	0	49
Southeastern Community College, North Campus	West Burlington	C,T	St & Loc	Coed	1,791	34		34	50		Y	Y		Y	Y	Y	Y	Y		Y	7	29
Southeastern Community College, South Campus	Keokuk	C,T	St & Loc	Coed	599	40					Y	Y	R,S	Y	Y	Y	Y	Y		N	5	7
Southwestern Community College	Creston	C,T	State	Coed	1,211	44	82	40		85	Y	Y	R,S	Y	Y		Y	Y	Y	Y	5	38
Waldorf College*	Forest City	C,B	Ind-R	Coed	588	10	96	11	69	86	N	Y	Y	Y	Y	Y	Y	Y		Y	10	55
Western Iowa Tech Community College	Sioux City	C,T	State	Coed	3,000	1		28			Y	Y	Y	Y	Y	Y	Y	Y	Y	N	4	21

34

Peterson's Guide to Two-Year Colleges 1997

State-by-State Summary Table
Kansas–Maine

This index includes the names and locations of accredited two-year colleges in the United States and U.S. territories and shows institutions' responses to our 1996 Survey of Undergraduate Institutions. If an institution submitted incomplete or no data, one or more columns opposite the institution's name is blank. An asterisk after the school name denotes a Special Announcement following the college's profile, and a dagger indicates that the institution has one or more entries in the In-Depth Descriptions of the Colleges section.

Y—Yes; N—No; R—Recommended; S—For Some

Institution	Location	Degrees Awarded	Institutional Control	Student Body	Undergrad Enroll Fall 1995	% Attend P-T	% Rec Need Aid	% 25+	% to 4-Yr	Fresh Retn	HS Equiv Cert	Open Adm	HS Transcript	Entr Test Req	Coll Schol	Part-Time Jobs	Loans	Job Place	Career Couns	Coll Hous	Part-Time Sports	Majors

Kansas

Allen County Community College	Iola	C,T	St & Loc	Coed	1,689	69		62				Y	Y		Y	R,S	Y		Y	Y	Y	11	85
Barton County Community College	Great Bend	C,T	St & Loc	Coed	10,000	80		65				Y	Y				Y	Y	Y	Y	Y	11	59
The Brown Mackie College	Salina	C,T	Prop	Coed	611	2		34	50	15	Y	Y	Y	Y		Y	Y	Y	Y	Y	N	4	7
The Brown Mackie College-Olathe Campus	Olathe	T	Prop	Coed	300	2	95				Y	Y	Y	Y			Y	Y	Y	Y	N	0	4
Butler County Community College	El Dorado	C,T	St & Loc	Coed	7,931	70		50					Y	R,S	Y		Y	Y	Y	Y	Y	11	69
Central College	McPherson	C,T,B	Ind-R	Coed	323	6		3		70	N	Y	Y	Y		Y	Y	Y		Y		9	71
Cloud County Community College	Concordia	C,T	St & Loc	Coed	3,112	78		67		78	Y	Y	Y	Y		Y	Y	Y		Y		9	29
Coffeyville Community College	Coffeyville	C,T	St & Loc	Coed	2,380	55		40			Y		Y	R		Y	Y	Y		Y		14	67
Colby Community College*	Colby	C,T	St & Loc	Coed	1,150	30		9	83	60	Y		Y	R			Y	Y		Y	Y	15	77
Cowley County Comm Coll and Voc-Tech School	Arkansas City	C,T	St & Loc	Coed	3,054	57		46		46	Y		Y	R,S			Y	Y			Y	7	42
Dodge City Community College	Dodge City	C,T	St & Loc	Coed	2,676	62		67		92	Y	Y	Y	Y		Y	Y	Y	Y	Y	Y	11	74
Donnelly College	Kansas City	C,T	Ind-R	Coed	409	28		55		66	Y	Y	R			Y	Y	Y	Y	Y	N	0	20
Fort Scott Community College	Fort Scott	C,T	St & Loc	Coed	1,651	48	8	40	82		Y	Y		S		Y	Y	Y	Y	Y	Y	12	37
Garden City Community College	Garden City	C,T	Dist	Coed	2,204	66	31	52		60	Y	Y	R	R		Y	Y	Y	Y	Y	Y	12	60
Haskell Indian Nations University	Lawrence	C,T,B	Fed	Coed	809	5		1			N	Y	Y	Y		Y	Y	Y	Y	Y		8	9
Hesston College	Hesston	C,T	Ind-R	Coed	472	15	65		69	65	Y		Y	R		Y	Y	Y	Y	Y		9	10
Highland Community College	Highland	C,T	St & Loc	Coed	2,654	61		31			Y	Y	Y	Y		Y	Y	Y	Y	Y	Y	6	69
Hutchinson Community College and Area Vocational School	Hutchinson	C,T	St & Loc	Coed	3,621	63		54			Y	Y	Y	R	R,S	Y	Y	Y	Y	Y	Y	13	92
Independence Community College	Independence	C,T	State	Coed	1,848	65		54			Y	Y	Y	R		Y	Y	Y	Y		Y	7	43
Johnson County Community College	Overland Park	C,T	St & Loc	Coed	15,477	70		44			Y	Y	S			Y	Y	Y	Y	Y	N	8	45
Kansas City Kansas Community College	Kansas City	C,T	St & Loc	Coed	6,000	70		53		40	Y		Y	Y		Y	Y	Y	Y	Y	N	8	85
Labette Community College	Parsons	C,T	St & Loc	Coed	2,598	68		40		30	Y	Y	R			Y					Y	5	33
Neosho County Community College	Chanute	C,T	St & Loc	Coed	1,666	60		58		60	Y			R		Y	Y	Y		Y		6	24
Pratt Comm Coll and Area Voc Sch	Pratt	C,T	Dist	Coed	1,349	60		36	55		Y	Y		R		Y	Y	Y				10	57
Seward County Community College	Liberal	C,T	St & Loc	Coed	1,899	68		72	61	67		Y		R		Y	Y	Y	Y	Y	Y	4	45

Kentucky

Draughons Junior College	Bowling Green	C		Prop	Prim W	160						Y	Y									0	5
Fugazzi College	Lexington	T	Prop	Coed	202	3		25			Y	Y	Y			Y	Y	Y	Y	Y	N	0	8
Institute of Electronic Technology	Paducah	T	Prop	Prim M	149	0		38			Y	Y	Y				Y	Y	Y	Y	N	0	6
ITT Technical Institute	Louisville																						
Kentucky College of Business	Danville	T	Prop		92						Y	Y	Y									0	
Kentucky College of Business	Florence	T	Prop		85						Y	Y	Y									0	
Kentucky College of Business	Lexington	C,T	Prop	Coed	119	30					Y	Y	Y			Y	Y	Y	Y	Y	N	0	6
Kentucky College of Business	Louisville	T	Prop		155						Y	Y	Y								N	0	
Kentucky College of Business	Pikeville	T	Prop		88						Y	Y	Y									0	
Kentucky College of Business	Richmond	T	Prop		140						Y	Y	Y									0	
Louisville Technical Institute	Louisville	T	Prop	Coed	488	4		40			N	Y	Y	S		Y	Y	Y	Y	Y	Y	3	13
Owensboro Community College	Owensboro	C,T	State	Coed	2,614	58		52		49	Y	Y	Y	Y		Y	Y	Y	Y	Y	N	1	10
Owensboro Junior College of Business	Owensboro	C	Prop	Coed	175	5		35	90		N	Y		S		Y	Y	Y	Y	Y	N	0	6
RETS Electronic Institute	Louisville	T	Prop	Coed	300	0						Y		Y			Y	Y	Y	Y		0	1
St Catharine College	St Catharine	C,T	Ind-R	Coed	442	37	87	39	93	80	Y	Y	S	S		Y	Y	Y	Y		Y	8	51
Southern Ohio College, Northern Kentucky Campus	Fort Mitchell	C	Prop	Coed	215	9		42		10	N	Y	Y	Y		Y		Y	Y	Y	N	0	6
U of Kentucky, Ashland Community College	Ashland	C,T	State	Coed	2,560	42	40	44		40	Y	Y	Y		S	Y	Y	Y	Y	Y	N	8	9
U of Kentucky, Elizabethtown Community College	Elizabethtown	C,T	State	Coed	3,766	61		52			Y	Y	Y	Y		Y	Y	Y	Y	Y	N	6	10
U of Kentucky, Hazard Community College	Hazard	C	State	Coed	1,690	37		39			Y	Y	Y			Y		Y	Y	Y	N	1	10
U of Kentucky, Henderson Community College	Henderson	C,T	State	Coed	1,396	54		34			Y	Y				Y	Y	Y	Y	Y	N	4	9
U of Kentucky, Hopkinsville Community College	Hopkinsville	C,T	State	Coed	2,898	75	60	51			Y	Y				Y	Y	Y	Y	Y	N	4	13
U of Kentucky, Jefferson Community College	Louisville	C,T	State	Coed	9,273	71		54			Y	Y				Y	Y	Y	Y	Y	N	0	48
U of Kentucky, Lexington Community College	Lexington	C,T	State	Coed	5,225	44		39			Y	Y				Y		Y	Y	Y	N	11	14
U of Kentucky, Madisonville Community College	Madisonville	C,T	State	Coed	2,533	60					Y	Y				Y		Y	Y	Y	N	5	16
U of Kentucky, Maysville Community College	Maysville	C,T	State	Coed	1,409	59		52		42	Y					Y		Y	Y	Y	N	0	7
U of Kentucky, Paducah Community College	Paducah	C,T	State	Coed	2,833	53		52	48		Y	Y	Y	S	S	Y	Y	Y	Y	Y	N	3	11
U of Kentucky, Prestonsburg Community College	Prestonsburg	C,T	State	Coed	2,798	37	75	40	34	35	Y	Y		Y		Y	Y	Y	Y	Y	N	9	6
U of Kentucky, Somerset Community College	Somerset	C,T	State	Coed	2,647	45		45			Y	Y				Y		Y	Y	Y	N	4	6
U of Kentucky, Southeast Community College	Cumberland	C,T	State	Coed	2,466	35		30		60	Y	Y				Y	Y	Y	Y	Y	N	4	8

Louisiana

Bossier Parish Community College	Bossier City	C,T	St & Loc	Coed	4,687	50					Y	Y	Y	S		Y	Y	Y	Y	Y	N	10	14
Cumberland School of Technology	Baton Rouge	C	Prop	Coed	32				85		N	Y	Y	R		Y	Y		Y	Y		0	2
Delgado Community College	New Orleans	C,T	State	Coed	13,937	57		44	45		Y	Y				Y	Y	Y	Y	Y	N	6	44
Elaine P Nunez Community College	Chalmette	C,T	State	Coed	1,521	64	50	57	28		Y	Y	S	R		Y	Y	Y	Y	Y	N	4	20
Louisiana State University at Alexandria	Alexandria	C,T	State	Coed	2,546	58		49			Y	Y	Y	Y		Y	Y	Y	Y	Y	N	7	7
Louisiana State University at Eunice	Eunice	C,T	State	Coed	2,861	54		50		40	Y	Y	Y	R,S	Y	Y	Y	Y	Y	Y	N	5	10
Our Lady of the Lake College	Baton Rouge	C,T	Ind-R	Coed	768	65	10	65			Y	Y	Y	S		Y	Y		Y		N	0	5
Phillips Junior College	New Orleans	C,T	Prop	Coed	300																		
Southern U at Shreveport–Bossier City Campus	Shreveport	C,T	State	Coed	1,202	13	95	42		25	Y	Y	Y	Y		Y	Y	Y	Y	Y	N	3	31

Maine

Andover College*	Portland	T	Prop	Coed	2,158	4		60	89	3	Y	Y	Y			Y	Y	Y	Y	Y	N	0	10
Beal College	Bangor	T	Prop	Coed	455	28		59		3	Y	Y	Y			Y						0	11
Casco Bay College†	Portland	C,T	Prop	Coed	350	20		10	85	10	Y	Y	Y			Y	Y	Y	Y	Y	Y	12	12
Central Maine Medical Center School of Nursing	Lewiston	T		Ind	84	12		75	75			Y	Y								Y	0	1
Central Maine Technical College	Auburn	T	State	Coed	962	40		32			N	Y	Y	Y		Y	Y	Y	Y	Y	N	13	17
Eastern Maine Technical College	Bangor	C,T	State	Coed	750	7		26			N	Y			S		Y	Y	Y	Y	N	11	17
Kennebec Valley Technical College	Fairfield	T	State	Coed	701	82		40				Y	Y	Y	Y	Y	Y	Y	Y	Y	N	0	18
Mid-State College*	Auburn	C,T	Prop	Coed	513	64		72			Y	Y	Y				Y	Y				10	8

Peterson's Guide to Two-Year Colleges 1997

35

State-by-State Summary Table
Maine–Michigan

		Degrees Awarded	Institutional Control	Student Body	Undergraduate Enrollment Fall 1995	Percent Attending Part-Time	Percent Receiving Need-Based Financial Aid	Percent of Grads Going on to 4-Year Colleges	Percent 25 Years of Age or Older	Freshman Retention Rate	High School Equivalency Certificate Accepted	Open Admissions	High School Transcript Accepted	Entrance Test(s) Required	College Scholarships Required	Loans Available	Part-Time Jobs Available	Career Counseling Services Available	College Housing Available	Job Placement Services Available	Number of Sports Offered	Number of Majors Offered
Northern Maine Technical College	Presque Isle	T	St-R	Coed	620	23		10			Y	Y		Y		Y	Y	Y	Y	Y	11	17
Southern Maine Technical College	South Portland	C,T	State	Coed	2,524	20	60	40	71	15	N	Y	Y	S	R	Y	Y	Y	N	Y	9	47
University of Maine at Augusta	Augusta	C,T,B	State	Coed	6,123	77	66	60			N	Y	Y	R		Y	Y	Y	N		9	19
Washington County Technical College	Calais	C,T	State	Coed	380						Y	Y	Y						Y		0	4

Maryland

Allegany Community College	Cumberland	C,T	St & Loc	Coed	2,844	44	70	41		50	Y	Y		S		Y	Y	Y	N		9	37
Anne Arundel Community College	Arnold	C,T	St & Loc	Coed	11,890	72		50	18		Y	Y		R		Y	Y	Y	N	Y	12	66
Baltimore City Community College	Baltimore	C,T	State	Coed	5,970	70		70			Y		Y			Y	Y	Y	N		4	31
Baltimore International Culinary College†	Baltimore	C	Ind	Coed	776	6		40			N	Y		R		Y	Y	Y	Y		0	3
Carroll Community College	Westminster	C	St & Loc	Coed	2,532	67		32			Y					Y	Y	Y	N		0	0
Catonsville Community College	Catonsville	C,T	County	Coed	10,240	72		52			Y	Y		S		Y	Y	Y	N		14	71
Cecil Community College	North East	C,T	County	Coed	1,055	71	22	43	57		Y	Y	Y			Y	Y	Y	N		9	24
Charles County Community College	La Plata	C,T	St & Loc	Coed	6,077	75		66	44	43	Y	Y	R	S		Y	Y	Y	N	Y	7	17
Chesapeake College	Wye Mills	C,T	St & Loc	Coed	2,068	75		55		45	Y	Y				Y	Y	Y	N		6	30
Dundalk Community College	Baltimore	C,T	County	Coed	3,203	82		68			Y	Y		Y		Y	Y	Y	N		7	23
Essex Community College	Baltimore	C,T	St & Loc	Coed	9,252	71	30	50			Y					Y	Y	Y	N	Y	10	44
Frederick Community College	Frederick	C,T	St & Loc	Coed	4,378	69		60	66	39	Y					Y	Y	Y	N		4	41
Garrett Community College	McHenry	C,T	St & Loc	Coed	722	47	85	44					Y		R	Y	Y	Y	Y		10	22
Hagerstown Business College	Hagerstown	T	Prop	Prim W	517	42	63	47			Y	Y				Y	Y	Y	Y		0	12
Hagerstown Junior College	Hagerstown	C,T	County	Coed	3,026	64	30	55		65	Y	Y	Y	S		Y	Y	Y	N		9	23
Harford Community College	Bel Air	C,T	St & Loc	Coed	4,957	74		54	59	45	Y					Y	Y	Y	N		7	51
Howard Community College	Columbia	C,T	St & Loc	Coed	5,130	74	25	77	37		Y	Y	Y	S	S	Y	Y	Y	N	Y	7	42
Maryland College of Art and Design	Silver Spring	C	Ind	Coed	80	25	25	35	95	80	N	Y	Y	R		Y	Y	Y	N		0	7
Montgomery College–Germantown Campus	Germantown	C,T	St & Loc	Coed	3,896	78	5	62	62		Y	Y				Y	Y	Y	N		8	21
Montgomery College–Rockville Campus	Rockville	C,T	St & Loc	Coed	13,144	66		43	62		Y	Y				Y	Y	Y	N		12	53
Montgomery College–Takoma Park Campus	Takoma Park	C,T	St & Loc	Coed	4,471	76		57	62		Y	Y				Y	Y	Y	N		7	30
Prince George's Community College	Largo	C,T	County	Coed	12,050	76		54		77	Y		Y	S		Y	Y	Y	N		8	33
Wor-Wic Community College	Salisbury	C,T	St & Loc	Coed	1,963	82		50			Y	Y	R	S		Y	Y	Y	N		0	13

Massachusetts

Aquinas College at Milton	Milton	C,T	Ind-R	Women	140	5		30		18	N	Y	Y			Y	Y	Y	N		0	10
Aquinas College at Newton†	Newton	C,T	Ind-R	Women	225	8				30	N	Y	Y			Y	Y	Y	N		0	9
Bay Path College*†	Longmeadow	C,T,B	Ind	Women	599	25	82	19	80	48	N	Y	Y			Y	Y	Y	Y	Y	15	18
Bay State College*†	Boston	T	Ind	Coed	674	0	80	5	53		N	Y	Y			Y	Y	Y	Y		0	14
Berkshire Community College	Pittsfield	C,T	State	Coed	2,388	62		55		66	Y	Y	Y			Y	Y	Y	N		5	41
Bristol Community College	Fall River	C,T	State	Coed	5,223	26				20	Y			S		Y	Y	Y	N		0	33
Bunker Hill Community College	Boston	C,T	State	Coed.	6,002	63		41			Y		Y			Y	Y	Y	N		6	30
Cape Cod Community College	West Barnstable	C,T	State	Coed	3,640	53		54			Y					Y	Y	Y	N		5	33
Dean College*†	Franklin	C,T	Ind	Coed	1,950	44	65	1		90	N	Y	Y	R		Y	Y	Y	Y	Y	15	36
Endicott College*	Beverly	C,T,B,M	Ind	Coed	802	3	74	14	77		N	Y	Y	R,S		Y	Y	Y	Y		10	45
Fisher College*†	Boston	C,T	Ind	Women	420	1				50	N	Y	Y			Y	Y	Y	Y		1	15
Franklin Institute of Boston†	Boston	T	Ind	Prim M	302	1		20			N	Y	Y	R		Y	Y	Y	N		3	10
Greenfield Community College	Greenfield	C,T	State	Coed	1,863	38		48		50	Y		Y	S	S	Y	Y	Y	N		4	29
Holyoke Community College	Holyoke	C,T	State	Coed	3,558	32	35	35		45	Y			S		Y	Y	Y	N		7	40
ITT Technical Institute	Framingham	C	Prop	Coed	267					6	N	Y	Y	Y		Y	Y	Y	N		0	2
Katharine Gibbs School	Boston	T	Ind	Prim W	450	32		35			N	Y	Y			Y	Y	Y	N		0	5
Labouré College*	Boston	C,T	Ind-R	Coed	548	60		40		25	N	Y				Y	Y	Y	N		0	5
Lasell College*†	Newton	C,T,B	Ind	Women	700	18	77	7	70	90	N	Y	Y	R		Y	Y	Y	Y	Y	6	24
Marian Court College	Swampscott	C	Ind-R	Prim W	220	28	79	38	70	20	N	Y	Y			Y	Y	Y	N		0	10
Massachusetts Bay Community College	Wellesley Hills	C,T	State	Coed	5,252	58	21	57	46		Y		Y			Y	Y	Y	N		4	58
Massasoit Community College	Brockton	C,T	State	Coed	5,602	50	34	45		32	Y					Y	Y	Y	N		5	30
Middlesex Community College	Bedford	C,T	State	Coed	5,984	56	30	48	51	38	Y		Y			Y	Y	Y	N		3	30
Mount Ida College†	Newton Centre	C,T,B	Ind	Coed	2,008	21	75	8	94	50	Y			R		Y	Y	Y	Y	Y	16	50
Mount Wachusett Community College	Gardner	C,T	State	Coed	1,900	39		42		25	Y					Y	Y	Y	N		0	23
Newbury College*†	Brookline	C,T,B	Ind	Coed	1,088	4	75	24	67	24	N	Y	Y	R		Y	Y	Y	Y		9	29
The New England Banking Institute	Boston	T,B	Ind	Coed	1,744	100		81		45	N	Y					Y		N		0	6
Northern Essex Community College	Haverhill	C,T	State	Coed	6,359	60	50	46		50	Y	Y				Y	Y	Y	N		11	46
North Shore Community College	Danvers	C,T	State	Coed	5,163	67		79		79	Y	Y	S			Y	Y	Y	N		5	36
Quincy College	Quincy	C,T	City	Coed		43		45			Y	Y	Y			Y	Y	Y	N		0	32
Quinsigamond Community College	Worcester	C,T	State	Coed	4,680	62		47	80	40	N	Y				Y	Y	Y	N		11	24
Roxbury Community College	Roxbury Crossing	C,T	State	Coed	3,000	43		75			Y			Y		Y	Y	Y	N		4	21
St Hyacinth College and Seminary	Granby		Ind-R	Prim M	40						N	Y		Y		Y	Y		N		8	1
Springfield Technical Community College	Springfield	C,T	State	Coed	6,084	59		64	51	25	Y		Y	S		Y	Y	Y	N		8	60

Michigan

Alpena Community College	Alpena	C,T	St & Loc	Coed	1,866	58		57	60	35	Y	Y	Y	S		Y	Y	Y	Y	N	8	20
Baker College of Jackson	Jackson	C,T	Ind	Coed	461	34		26			Y	Y				Y	Y	Y	N		0	10
Bay de Noc Community College	Escanaba	C,T	County	Coed	2,229	44	63	62		60	Y					Y	Y	Y	Y		6	37
Bay Mills Community College	Brimley	C	Dist		180	10					Y		Y						Y		0	11
Charles Stewart Mott Community College	Flint	C,T	Dist	Coed	9,754	73		49			Y			R		Y	Y	Y	N		5	45
Delta College	University Center	C,T	Dist	Coed	10,446	67		43			Y	Y				Y	Y	Y	N		10	76
Glen Oaks Community College	Centreville	C,T	St & Loc	Coed	1,190	63		47			Y			Y		Y		Y	N		0	23
Gogebic Community College	Ironwood	C,T	St & Loc	Coed	1,399	51	43	46			Y			R		Y	Y	Y	Y		9	35
Grand Rapids Community College	Grand Rapids	C,T	Dist	Coed	13,934	68		24			Y	Y		Y	R,S	Y	Y	Y	N		14	48
Great Lakes Junior College of Business	Saginaw	C,T	Ind	Coed	1,606	74		70		6	Y	Y	Y			Y	Y	Y	N		0	15
Henry Ford Community College	Dearborn	C,T	Dist	Coed	13,300	76	22	44			Y			R	R	Y	Y	Y	N		12	52
Highland Park Community College	Highland Park	C,T	St & Loc	Coed		49		50			Y					Y	Y	Y	N		3	23
Jackson Community College	Jackson	C,T	County	Coed	7,100	73		55			Y				R	Y	Y	Y	N		9	30
Kalamazoo Valley Community College	Kalamazoo	C,T	St & Loc	Coed	11,027	76		43			Y					Y	Y	Y	N		6	34

This index includes the names and locations of accredited two-year colleges in the United States and U.S. territories and shows institutions' responses to our 1996 Survey of Undergraduate Institutions. If an institution submitted incomplete or no data, one or more columns opposite the institution's name is blank. An asterisk after the school name denotes a Special Announcement following the college's profile, and a dagger indicates that the institution has one or more entries in the In-Depth Descriptions of the Colleges section.

Y—Yes; N—No; R—Recommended; S—For Some

		Degrees Awarded: Transfer Associate (C), Terminal Associate (T), Bachelor's (B), Master's (M), Doctoral (D), First Professional (F)	Institutional Control: Independent, Independent-Religious, Proprietary, Federal, State, Province, Commonwealth, Territory, County, District, City, State and Local, State-Related	Student Body: Men, Primarily Men, Women, Primarily Women, Coeducational	Undergraduate Enrollment Fall 1995	Percent Attending Part-Time	Percent Receiving Need-Based Financial Aid	Percent 25 Years of Age or Older	Freshman Retention Rate	Percent of Grads Going on to 4-Year Colleges	Open Admissions	High School Equivalency Certificate Accepted	High School Transcript Required	Entrance Test(s) Required	College Scholarships Available	Loans Available	Part-Time Jobs Available	Career Counseling Available	Job Placement Services Available	College Housing Available	Number of Sports Offered	Number of Majors Offered
Kellogg Community College	Battle Creek	C,T	St & Loc	Coed	9,012	73	40	51	54	63	Y	Y		S	Y	Y	Y	Y	Y	N	11	72
Kirtland Community College	Roscommon	C,T	Dist	Coed	1,352	65		45			Y	Y		Y	Y	Y	Y	Y	Y	N	0	23
Lake Michigan College	Benton Harbor	C,T	Dist	Coed	3,260	75	28	56			Y	Y	Y	Y	Y	Y	Y	Y	Y	N	3	54
Lansing Community College	Lansing	C,T	St & Loc	Coed	16,404	75					Y	Y		Y	Y	Y	Y	Y	Y	N	4	106
Lewis College of Business	Detroit	C,T	Ind	Coed	191	39			32		Y	Y	Y		Y	Y	Y	Y	Y	N	1	11
Macomb Community College	Warren	C,T	Dist	Coed	24,500	76		47			Y				Y	Y	Y	Y	Y	N	15	61
Mid Michigan Community College	Harrison	C,T	St & Loc	Coed	3,304	60		63			Y	Y	R		Y	Y	Y	Y	Y	N	0	41
Monroe County Community College	Monroe	C,T	County	Coed	3,923	72	42	44			Y	Y	Y	Y	Y	Y	Y	Y	Y	N	0	40
Montcalm Community College	Sidney	C,T	St & Loc	Coed	1,753	74		56	42		Y	Y	Y	Y	Y	Y	Y	Y	Y	N	10	25
Muskegon Community College	Muskegon	C,T	St & Loc	Coed	5,169	57		52			Y	Y			Y	Y	Y	Y	Y	N	6	45
North Central Michigan College	Petoskey	C,T	County	Coed	2,032	71	45	55	71	85	Y			R	Y	Y	Y	Y		Y	6	15
Northwestern Michigan College	Traverse City	C,T	St & Loc	Coed	3,937	63		42		50	Y	Y		Y	Y	Y	Y	Y	Y	Y	6	35
Oakland Community College	Bloomfield Hills	C,T	St & Loc	Coed	26,144	79		51			Y	Y			Y	Y	Y	Y	Y	N	12	79
St Clair County Community College	Port Huron	C,T	County	Coed	4,264	69	32	45			Y	Y		S	Y	Y	Y	Y	Y	N	4	37
Schoolcraft College	Livonia	C,T	Dist	Coed	9,393	75	11	45		65	Y	Y			Y	Y	Y	Y	Y	N	5	40
Southwestern Michigan College	Dowagiac	C,T	St & Loc	Coed	2,551	67		48	65		Y	Y	Y	R	Y	Y	Y	Y	Y	N	19	37
Suomi College*†	Hancock	C,T,B	Ind-R	Coed	336	11	92	32	52		N	Y			Y	Y	Y	Y	Y	Y	8	25
Washtenaw Community College*	Ann Arbor	C,T	St & Loc	Coed	10,224	81		38	82	89	Y	Y			Y	Y	Y	Y	Y	N	0	56
Wayne County Community College†	Detroit	C,T	St & Loc	Coed	10,792	70		74			Y	Y		Y	Y	Y	Y	Y	Y	N	0	34
West Shore Community College	Scottville	C,T	Dist	Coed	1,617	65	40	43			Y		R,S	R,S	Y	Y	Y	Y	Y	N	6	42
Minnesota																						
Alexandria Technical College	Alexandria	C,T	State	Coed	1,630	13	85	26	68		N	Y	Y	S	Y	Y	Y	Y	Y	N	7	37
Anoka-Ramsey Community College*	Coon Rapids	C,T	State	Coed	4,449	60		40			Y	Y		R,S	Y	Y	Y	Y	Y	N	15	19
Austin Community College	Austin	C,T	State	Coed	1,420	56	70	50		55	Y	Y	Y	Y	Y	Y	Y	Y	Y	N	6	11
Bethany Lutheran College*	Mankato	C	Ind-R	Coed	387	2	75	1		87	N	Y		Y	Y	Y	Y	Y		Y	6	1
Brown Institute	Minneapolis	C,T	Prop	Coed	1,300	0					N	Y	Y	Y	Y	Y	Y	Y	Y	N	0	10
Central Lakes College	Brainerd	C,T	State	Coed	1,961	52	50	45			Y	Y		R	Y	Y	Y	Y		N	8	10
College of St Catherine–Minneapolis†	Minneapolis	C,T,M	Ind-R	Coed	1,085	78	75	63			N	Y	Y	R	Y	Y	Y	Y		Y	0	11
Dunwoody Institute	Minneapolis	C,T	Ind	Coed	1,191						Y	Y	R								0	12
Fergus Falls Community College	Fergus Falls	C,T	State	Coed	1,299	49		36		70	Y	Y	Y	R	Y	Y	Y	Y	Y	N	14	13
Fond du Lac Tribal and Community College	Cloquet	C,T	State	Coed	833	65		84			Y	Y		Y	Y	Y	Y			N	0	3
Hibbing Community College	Hibbing	C,T	State	Coed	1,042	51		38			Y	Y	Y	R	Y	Y	Y	Y	Y	N	12	14
Inver Hills Community College	Inver Grove Heights	C,T	State	Coed	5,161	67	50	50			Y	Y	R	S	Y	Y	Y	Y	Y	N	9	29
Itasca Community College	Grand Rapids	C,T	State	Coed	1,138	31		36	49	80	Y	Y	Y	R	Y	Y	Y	Y		N	10	17
Lakeland Medical-Dental Academy	Minneapolis																					
Lakewood Community College	White Bear Lake	C,T	State	Coed	5,290	64		49			Y	Y		R	Y	Y	Y	Y	Y	N	10	13
Lowthian College	Minneapolis	T	Prop	Coed	118	24	64	31	53	15	N	Y		Y	Y	Y	Y	Y	Y	N	0	3
Medical Institute of Minnesota*	Bloomington	C,T	Prop	Coed	650	30		50			N	Y	Y	Y	Y	Y	Y	Y	Y	N	0	8
Mesabi Community College	Virginia	C,T	State	Coed	1,009	42		32		80	Y	Y		R	Y	Y	Y	Y	Y	Y	12	9
Minneapolis Community College	Minneapolis	C,T	State	Coed	4,224	55		50			Y	Y	Y		Y	Y	Y	Y		N	3	13
Minnesota Riverland Technical College	Rochester	C,T	State	Coed							Y	Y	Y	R							0	1
NEI College of Technology	Columbia Heights	C,T	Ind	Coed	468	37	82	37	88	10	N	Y	Y	Y	Y	Y	Y	Y	Y	N	3	13
Normandale Community College	Bloomington	C,T	State	Coed	7,718	55		41			Y	Y	S	S	Y	Y	Y	Y	Y	N	15	26
Northeast Metro Technical College	White Bear Lake	C,T	State	Coed	1,800	40		65	36		Y		Y		Y		Y			N	0	6
North Hennepin Community College	Minneapolis	C,T	State	Coed	5,527	64		46	65	60	Y	Y	S		Y	Y	Y	Y	Y	N	9	21
Northland Community and Technical College	Thief River Falls	C,T	State	Coed	1,150	32		32	67	52	Y	Y	Y	R	Y	Y	Y	Y	Y	Y	10	36
Northwest Technical Institute	Eden Prairie	C,T	Prop	Coed	180	0		10	85		Y	Y	Y		Y	Y		Y	Y	N	0	1
Pine Technical College	Pine City	C	State	Coed	700	53	92	60	75		Y	Y	Y	Y				Y	Y		0	1
Rainy River Community College	International Falls	C,T	State	Coed	760	53		45	56	62	Y	Y	Y	Y	Y	Y	Y	Y	Y	Y	10	10
Rasmussen College Eagan	Eagan	T	Prop	Prim W	438	34	77	39			N	Y	Y	Y	Y	Y	Y	Y	Y	N	0	9
Rasmussen College Mankato	Mankato	T	Prop	Prim W	280	20	85	40	75	1	N	Y	Y	Y	Y	Y	Y	Y	Y	N	0	15
Rasmussen College Minnetonka	Minnetonka	T	Prop	Coed	375	33	22	80	80		N	Y	Y		Y	Y		Y	Y	N	0	8
Rasmussen College St Cloud	St Cloud	C,T	Prop	Prim W	198	27	97	35	32	1	N	Y	Y	Y	Y	Y	Y	Y	Y	N	0	9
Rochester Community College	Rochester	C,T	State	Coed	3,593	47	60	41			Y	Y		R	Y	Y	Y	Y	Y	N	10	20
St Cloud Technical College	St Cloud	T	State	Coed	2,431	41		47	80		Y	Y	Y	Y	Y	Y	Y	Y	Y	N	3	30
St Paul Technical College	St Paul	T	St-R	Coed	3,401	27		50			Y	Y			Y	Y	Y	Y	Y	N	0	11
Southwestern Technical College	Granite Falls	T	State	Coed	450						Y		Y	Y	Y	Y	Y	Y		N	4	17
Vermilion Community College	Ely	C,T	State	Coed	735	13		18			Y	Y	Y	R	Y	Y	Y	Y	Y	Y	11	74
Willmar Community College	Willmar	C,T	State	Coed	1,318	39	81	28			Y	Y	Y	R,S	Y	Y	Y	Y	Y	N	9	51
Willmar Technical College	Willmar	T	State	Coed	1,340	34		36	65		Y	Y	Y		Y	Y	Y	Y	Y	N	9	28
Worthington Community College	Worthington	C,T	State	Coed	882	49		39		40	Y	Y	Y	Y	Y	Y	Y	Y	Y	N	9	8
Mississippi																						
Coahoma Community College	Clarksdale	C,T	St & Loc	Coed	940	50		10	75		Y	Y	Y	Y	Y	Y	Y	Y	Y	Y	2	23
Copiah-Lincoln Community College	Wesson	C,T	St & Loc	Coed	1,805	19		26			Y	Y			Y	Y	Y	Y	Y	Y	8	34
Copiah-Lincoln Community College–Natchez Campus	Natchez	C,T	St & Loc	Coed	655	40		50			Y	Y	Y	Y	Y	Y	Y	Y		N	1	11
East Central Community College	Decatur	C,T	St & Loc	Coed	1,699	30		31	55		Y	Y	Y	Y	Y	Y	Y	Y		Y	8	41
East Mississippi Community College	Scooba	C,T	St & Loc	Coed	1,535	40		8			Y	Y	Y	Y	Y	Y	Y			Y	6	42
Hinds Community College	Raymond	C,T	St & Loc	Coed	10,743	28	66	43			Y	Y	Y		Y	Y	Y	Y	Y	Y	9	54
Holmes Community College	Goodman	C,T	St & Loc	Coed	2,553	47	65		75	65	N	Y	Y	Y	Y	Y	Y	Y	Y	Y	8	26
Itawamba Community College	Fulton	C,T	St & Loc	Coed	3,500	35		8			Y	Y	Y	Y	Y	Y	Y	Y	Y	Y	6	56
Jones County Junior College	Ellisville	C,T	St & Loc	Coed	4,430	22		28			Y	Y	Y	Y	Y	Y	Y	Y		Y	8	31
Mary Holmes College	West Point	C,T	Ind-R	Coed	375	6	90	10		80	Y	Y	Y		Y	Y	Y	Y		Y	10	18
Meridian Community College	Meridian	C,T	St & Loc	Coed	2,928	39		43		75	Y	Y	Y	Y	Y	Y	Y	Y	Y	Y	8	34
Mississippi Delta Community College	Moorhead	C,T	Dist	Coed	2,403	8		5	80	98	N	Y	Y	S	Y		Y	Y	Y	Y	7	42
Mississippi Gulf Coast Community College	Perkinston	C,T	Dist	Coed	9,858	39		43	50		Y	Y	Y	S	Y	Y	Y	Y	Y	Y	8	38
Northeast Mississippi Community College	Booneville	C,T	State	Coed	3,000	9		20	80		Y	Y		S	Y	Y	Y	Y	Y	Y	10	105
Northwest Mississippi Community College	Senatobia	C,T	St & Loc	Coed	4,200	31			40		Y	Y	Y	Y	Y	Y	Y	Y		Y	7	53
Pearl River Community College	Poplarville	C,T	St & Loc	Coed	2,575	28		27			Y	Y	Y	Y	Y	Y	Y	Y	Y	Y	9	9
Phillips Junior College of Jackson	Jackson	T	Prop	Coed	275																	

Peterson's Guide to Two-Year Colleges 1997
37

State-by-State Summary Table
Mississippi–New Hampshire

This index includes the names and locations of accredited two-year colleges in the United States and U.S. territories and shows institutions' responses to our 1996 Survey of Undergraduate Institutions. If an institution submitted incomplete or no data, one or more columns opposite the institution's name is blank. An asterisk after the school name denotes a Special Announcement following the college's profile, and a dagger indicates that the institution has one or more entries in the In-Depth Descriptions of the Colleges section.

Y—Yes; N—No; R—Recommended; S—For Some

Institution	Location	Degrees Awarded	Institutional Control	Student Body	Undergrad Enroll Fall 1995	% Attend P-T	% Need-Based Aid	% 25 or Older	Fresh Retention	% to 4-Yr	Open Adm	HS Equiv Accept	HS Transcript Req	Entrance Tests Req	Coll Schol Avail	Part-Time Jobs	Loans Avail	Career Counsel	Job Placement	Coll Housing	Sports	Majors
Southwest Mississippi Community College	Summit	C,T	Dist	Coed	1,650	24		31	70		Y	Y	Y	S	Y	Y	Y	Y	Y	4	35
Wood College	Mathiston	C	Ind-R	Coed	1,500	33		25		83	N	Y	Y	Y	Y	Y	Y	Y	Y	7	8

Missouri

Cottey College	Nevada	C	Ind	Women	329	1	59	2		94	N	Y	Y	Y	Y	Y	Y	Y	Y	9	2
Crowder College	Neosho	C,T	St & Loc	Coed	1,698	57		45			Y	Y	Y	Y	Y	Y	Y	Y	5	30
East Central College	Union	C,T	Dist	Coed	2,990	53	24	42	75	85	Y	Y	Y	R	Y	Y	Y	Y	N	6	75
ITT Technical Institute	Earth City	C,T,B	Prop	Coed	539	0		25			N	Y	Y	Y	Y	Y	Y	Y	N	0	2
Jefferson College	Hillsboro	C,T	St & Loc	Coed	3,783	54		50	65		Y	Y	Y	Y	Y	Y	Y	Y	N	5	57
Jewish Hospital Coll of Nursing and Allied Health	St Louis	C,B	Ind	Prim W	470	45	75	70			Y	Y	Y	Y	Y	Y	Y	Y	3	3
Kemper Military Junior College	Boonville	C	Ind	Coed	202	13		8	35	81	N	Y	Y	Y	Y	Y	Y	Y	Y	12	15
Longview Community College	Lee's Summit	C,T	St & Loc	Coed	8,388	69	16	50	45	61	Y	Y	Y		Y	Y	Y	Y	N	4	28
Maple Woods Community College	Kansas City	C,T	St & Loc	Coed	4,572	69	18	45	45	63	Y	Y	Y		Y	Y	Y	Y	N	3	23
Mineral Area College	Park Hills	C,T	Dist	Coed	2,388	55	47	42	65	28	Y	Y	Y		Y	Y	Y	Y	N	4	30
Moberly Area Community College	Moberly	C,T	St & Loc	Coed	2,014	44		44	40		Y	Y	Y	R,S	Y	Y	Y	Y	Y	1	29
North Central Missouri College	Trenton	C,T	Dist	Coed	1,093	59		33			Y	Y	Y	R,S	Y	Y	Y	Y	Y	5	17
Ozarks Technical Community College	Springfield	C,T	Dist	Coed	3,507	60	40	55	60		Y	Y	Y	Y	Y	Y	Y	Y	N	0	20
Penn Valley Community College	Kansas City	C,T	St & Loc	Coed	4,432	73	29	49	45	61	Y	Y	Y	Y	Y	Y	Y	Y	N	2	36
Phillips Junior College of Springfield	Springfield	T	Prop	Coed	360	5		60			Y	Y	Y	Y	Y	Y	Y	Y	N	0	7
Ranken Technical College	St Louis	T	Ind	Coed	700	0		25	80		N	Y	Y	R		Y	Y	Y	N	0	9
Saint Charles County Community College	St Peters	C,T	State	Coed	4,590	72	22	46		52	Y	Y	S	S	Y	Y	Y	Y	N	6	21
St Louis Community College at Florissant Valley	St Louis	C,T	Dist	Coed	8,160	70		48	37	26	Y	Y	Y	R	Y	Y	Y	Y	N	7	49
St Louis Community College at Forest Park	St Louis	C,T	Dist	Coed	8,197	76		62			Y	Y			Y	Y	Y	Y	N	5	44
St Louis Community College at Meramec	Kirkwood	C,T	Dist	Coed	13,211	65		42	50	43	Y	Y	S	S	Y	Y	Y	Y	N	7	45
Sanford-Brown College	Des Peres	T	Prop	Coed	410	0	85	75			Y	Y	Y	Y		Y	Y	Y	N	1	8
Sanford-Brown College	Hazelwood	T	Prop	Coed	348	0					N	Y	Y	Y			Y	Y		1	7
Sanford-Brown College	North Kansas City	T	Prop	Coed	277						N	Y		S	Y		Y	Y		0	2
Sanford-Brown College	St Charles	C,T	Prop	Coed		2	80	60	75		N	Y	Y	S	Y	Y	Y	Y	Y	1	8
Southwest Missouri State University–West Plains	West Plains	C,T	State	Coed	1,018						Y		Y	Y	Y	Y				0	10
State Fair Community College	Sedalia	C,T	Dist	Coed	2,277	57		52			Y	Y	Y		Y	Y	Y	Y	N	2	28
Three Rivers Community College	Poplar Bluff	C,T	State	Coed	3,000	46		49		40	Y	Y	Y	R	Y	Y	Y	Y	N	4	18
Wentworth Military Academy and Junior College*	Lexington	C	Ind	Coed	247	35	95	30		82	N	Y	Y	R		Y	Y		Y	10	1

Montana

Blackfeet Community College	Browning	C,T	Ind	Coed	428	60		73			Y		Y		Y	Y	Y	Y	N	10	7
Dawson Community College	Glendive	C,T	St & Loc	Coed	535	33	75	24		60	Y	Y	Y	R	Y	Y	Y	Y	Y	7	10
Dull Knife Memorial College	Lame Deer	C	Ind	Coed	328	80		60		50	Y	Y	Y			Y	Y	Y	N	2	4
Flathead Valley Community College	Kalispell	C,T	St & Loc	Coed	1,116	32		65			Y	Y	Y		Y	Y	Y	Y	N	8	13
Fort Belknap College	Harlem	C	Ind	Coed	438	58		60				Y	Y		Y			Y	N	3	10
Fort Peck Community College	Poplar	C,T	Ind	Coed	425	33		80			Y	Y		Y	Y		Y		N	0	14
Helena Coll of Tech of The U of Montana	Helena	T	State	Coed	634						Y	Y					Y	Y	N	2	13
Little Big Horn College	Crow Agency	C,T	Ind	Coed	295	25		50			Y		Y			Y	Y	Y	N	1	7
Miles Community College	Miles City	C,T	St & Loc	Coed	560	26	95	26	68	96	Y	Y	Y	S	Y	Y	Y	Y	Y	16	14
Montana State U Coll of Tech-Great Falls	Great Falls	T	State	Coed	961	33	80				Y	Y	Y	Y		Y	Y	Y	N	0	19
Salish Kootenai College	Pablo	C,T,B	Ind	Coed	750	50		48			Y	Y	Y		Y	Y	Y	Y	N	8	15
Stone Child College	Box Elder	C	Ind	Coed	247						Y	Y	Y		Y					0	4

Nebraska

Central Community College–Grand Island Campus	Grand Island	C,T	St & Loc	Coed	1,602	92		82			Y	S	Y	R	Y	Y	Y	Y	N	4	23
Central Community College–Hastings Campus	Hastings	C,T	St & Loc	Coed	1,629	84		82			Y	S	Y	S	Y	Y	Y	Y	Y	7	40
Central Community College–Platte Campus	Columbus	C,T	St & Loc	Coed	1,511	84		82		7	Y	S	S	S	Y	Y	Y	Y	N	7	53
Gateway College	Omaha	C,T	Prop	Coed	350	20		45			N	Y	Y	Y	Y	Y	Y	Y	N	0	7
ITT Technical Institute	Omaha	T	Prop	Coed	203						N	Y	Y	Y	Y	Y	Y	Y	N	0	2
Lincoln School of Commerce	Lincoln	C,T	Prop	Coed	450	7		40	70	10	N	Y	Y	Y	Y	Y	Y	Y	Y	3	10
McCook Community College	McCook	C,T	St & Loc	Coed	951	61			50		Y	Y	Y	Y	Y	Y	Y	Y	Y	6	6
Metropolitan Community College	Omaha	C,T	St & Loc	Coed	10,686	73		65		6	Y	Y	R		Y	Y	Y	Y	N	4	47
Mid-Plains Community College	North Platte	C,T	Dist	Coed	1,824	63		20	61	45	Y	Y	Y		Y	Y	Y	Y	Y	4	53
Nebraska College of Business	Omaha	T	Prop	Coed	310	0		60			N	Y	Y	Y	Y	Y	Y	Y	N	0	8
Nebraska College of Technical Agriculture	Curtis	C,T	State	Coed	294	1	70	26	80	12	Y	Y	Y	Y	Y	Y	Y	Y	Y	6	10
Nebraska Indian Community College	Winnebago	C,T	Ind	Coed	253	45		80			Y		Y		Y		Y	Y	N	7	16
Northeast Community College	Norfolk	C,T	St & Loc	Coed	3,413	55		15		60	Y		R	R	Y	Y	Y	Y	Y	9	50
Omaha College of Health Careers	Omaha	C	Prop	Coed	225	0		15		25	N	Y	Y		Y	Y	Y	Y	N	0	4
Southeast Community College, Beatrice Campus	Beatrice	C,T	Dist	Coed	920	36		40	90	80	Y	Y	Y	R	Y	Y	Y	Y	Y	3	24
Southeast Community College, Lincoln Campus	Lincoln	C,T	Dist	Coed	4,555	65	60	50	50	50	Y	Y	Y	S	Y	Y	Y	Y	N	5	24
Southeast Community College, Milford Campus	Milford	T	Dist	Coed	920	3		20			Y	Y	Y	Y	Y	Y	Y	Y	Y	12	30
Spencer School of Business	Grand Island	C,T	Prop	Prim W	136	1	100	17			N	Y	Y	R	Y	Y	Y	Y	Y	4	12
Western Nebraska Community College	Scottsbluff	C,T	St & Loc	Coed	2,291	33	76	54	65	62	Y	Y			Y	Y	Y	Y	Y	8	50

Nevada

Community College of Southern Nevada*	North Las Vegas	C	State	Coed	20,417	87		60	49		Y	Y			Y	Y	Y	Y	N	6	79
Great Basin College	Elko	C,T	State	Coed	3,000	83		60			Y	Y			Y	Y	Y	Y	N	3	19
Truckee Meadows Community College	Reno	C,T	State	Coed	8,346	84	10	64	50		Y	Y		R	Y	Y	Y	Y	N	0	43
Western Nevada Community College	Carson City	C,T	State	Coed	4,498	91		60			Y	Y		R		Y	Y	Y	N	0	23

New Hampshire

Castle College*	Windham	C,T	Ind	Coed	267	16	86	35	78	14	N	Y	Y		Y	Y	Y	Y	N	0	13
Hesser College†	Manchester	C,T	Prop	Coed	3,000	19		25	72	40	N	Y	Y	Y	Y	Y	Y	Y	Y	8	37
McIntosh College†	Dover	C	Prop	Coed	1,050	43		65	90		Y	Y		R	Y	Y	Y	Y	Y	1	13

This index includes the names and locations of accredited two-year colleges in the United States and U.S. territories and shows institutions' responses to our 1996 Survey of Undergraduate Institutions. If an institution submitted incomplete or no data, one or more columns opposite the institution's name is blank. An asterisk after the school name denotes a Special Announcement following the college's profile, and a dagger indicates that the institution has one or more entries in the In-Depth Descriptions of the Colleges section.

Y—Yes; N—No; R—Recommended; S—For Some

Institution	Location	Degrees Awarded: Transfer Associate (C), Terminal Associate (T), Bachelor's (B), Master's (M), Doctoral (D), First Professional (F)	Institutional Control: Independent, Independent-Religious, Proprietary, Federal, State, Province, Commonwealth, Territory, County, District, City, State and Local, State-Related	Student Body: Men, Primarily Men, Women, Primarily Women, Coeducational	Undergraduate Enrollment Fall 1995	Percent Attending Part-Time	Percent Receiving Need-Based Financial Aid	Percent 25 Years of Age or Older	Freshman Retention Rate	Percent of Grads Going on to 4-Year Colleges	Open Admissions	High School Equivalency Certificate Accepted	High School Transcript Required	Entrance Test(s) Required	College Scholarships Available	Loans Available	Part-Time Jobs Available	Career Counseling Available	Job Placement Services Available	College Housing Available	Number of Sports Offered	Number of Majors Offered
New Hampshire Technical College	Berlin	C,T	State	Coed		28		18			N	Y			Y		Y	Y	Y	N	7	18
New Hampshire Technical College	Claremont	T	State	Coed	519	38		70			N	Y	Y	Y	Y	Y	Y	Y	Y	N	2	12
New Hampshire Technical College	Laconia	C,T	State	Coed	900	25		50	70	11	N	Y	Y	R,S	Y	Y	Y	Y	Y	N	8	16
New Hampshire Technical College	Manchester	C,T	State	Coed	676	35		35	61	9	N	Y	Y	S	Y	Y	Y	Y	Y	N	9	22
New Hampshire Technical College	Nashua	C,T	State	Coed	542	17		23			N	Y	Y	Y	Y	Y	Y	Y	Y	N	10	22
New Hampshire Technical College	Stratham																					
New Hampshire Technical Institute†	Concord	C	State	Coed	1,413	30	45	70		20	N	Y	Y	R	Y	Y	Y	Y	Y	Y	9	20
White Pines College†	Chester	C,T	Ind	Coed	55	5	85	35	85	100	N	Y	Y	R	Y	Y	Y	Y	Y	Y	4	10
New Jersey																						
Assumption College for Sisters	Mendham	C	Ind-R	Women	32	50	100	37	87	100		Y	Y	R	Y			Y		Y	0	2
Atlantic Community College†	Mays Landing	C,T	County	Coed	6,004	68		48			Y	Y	S	Y	Y	Y	Y	Y	Y	N	4	39
Bergen Community College*†	Paramus	C,T	County	Coed	13,207	59		43	80		Y	Y			Y	Y	Y	Y	Y	N	10	52
Berkeley College†	West Paterson	C,T	Prop	Coed	1,572	21		30			N	Y	Y		Y	Y	Y	Y	Y	Y	0	11
Brookdale Community College	Lincroft	C,T	County	Coed	12,446	62	8	48	61	72	Y	Y	Y		Y	Y	Y	Y	Y	N	8	43
Burlington County College	Pemberton	C,T	County	Coed	6,433	65		52		60	Y	Y		Y	Y	Y	Y	Y	Y	N	9	50
Camden County College	Blackwood	C,T	St & Loc	Coed	13,068	61	24	39			Y	Y	S		Y	Y	Y	Y	Y	N	4	41
County College of Morris	Randolph	C,T	County	Coed	9,342	55		41	65		Y		Y	Y	Y	Y	Y	Y	Y	N	12	47
Cumberland County College	Vineland	C,T	St & Loc	Coed	2,484	58		50			Y	Y	Y		Y	Y	Y	Y	Y	N	0	37
DeVry Technical Institute	Woodbridge	T	Prop	Coed	2,536	34	80	45			N	Y	Y	Y	Y	Y	Y	Y	Y	N	0	4
Essex County College	Newark	C,T	County	Coed	8,952	47		54			Y	Y	Y	Y	Y	Y	Y	Y	Y	N	6	40
Fairleigh Dickinson U, Edward Williams College	Hackensack	C	Ind	Coed	746	30	34	9	57	90	N	Y		Y	Y	Y	Y	Y	Y	Y	8	1
Gloucester County College	Sewell	C,T	County	Coed	5,047	58	20	48			Y	Y	Y	S	Y		Y	Y	Y	N	9	32
Hudson County Community College	Jersey City	C,T	St & Loc	Coed	4,249	38	46	50		13	Y	Y	Y	Y	Y	Y	Y	Y	Y	N	9	21
Katharine Gibbs School	Montclair	C,T	Prop	Coed	400							Y	Y	Y		Y	Y			N	0	1
Mercer County Community College	Trenton	C,T	St & Loc	Coed	6,936	60		48	61	64	Y		Y	R	Y	Y	Y	Y	Y	N	8	63
Middlesex County College*†	Edison	C,T	County	Coed	12,500	47	22	44			Y	Y			Y	Y	Y	Y	Y	N	12	82
Ocean County College	Toms River	C,T	County	Coed	8,122	57		41		65	Y	Y		S	Y		Y	Y	Y	N	10	26
Passaic County Community College	Paterson	C,T	County	Coed	3,642	70	48	54	53		Y				Y	Y	Y	Y	Y	N	4	20
Raritan Valley Community College	Somerville	C,T	County	Coed	5,555	58		49		65	Y	Y	Y		Y	Y	Y	Y	Y	N	10	54
Salem Community College	Carneys Point	C,T	County	Coed	1,228	62		49			Y	Y	R	Y	Y	Y	Y	Y	Y	N	4	40
Sussex County Community College	Newton	C,T	St & Loc	Coed	2,293	62	67	50	65		Y				Y	Y	Y	Y	Y		4	23
Union County College	Cranford	C,T	St & Loc	Coed	10,046	56	26	52		44	Y	Y		R	Y	Y	Y	Y	Y	N	8	41
Warren County Community College	Washington	C,T	St & Loc	Coed	1,619	77		57			Y			Y	Y	Y	Y	Y	Y	N	6	11
New Mexico																						
Albuquerque Technical Vocational Institute	Albuquerque	C,T	State	Coed	15,021	73		57			Y	Y	S					Y	Y	N	0	25
Clovis Community College	Clovis	C,T	State	Coed	3,920						Y	Y	Y		Y	Y				N	0	27
Doña Ana Branch Community College	Las Cruces	T	St & Loc	Coed	3,768	65		46			Y	Y	Y	R	Y	Y	Y	Y	Y	Y	0	22
Eastern New Mexico University–Roswell	Roswell	C,T	State	Coed	2,536	55		50			Y	Y	Y	R	Y	Y	Y	Y	Y	Y	5	20
Institute of American Indian Arts	Santa Fe	C	Fed	Coed	240	22	70	51	89	25	N	Y	Y		Y		Y	Y	Y	Y	11	11
Luna Vocational Technical Institute	Las Vegas																					
New Mexico Junior College	Hobbs	C,T	St & Loc	Coed	2,752	57		52	81	67	Y	Y			Y	Y	Y	Y	Y	Y	13	54
New Mexico Military Institute*†	Roswell	C	State	Prim M	460	0		0	100	87	N	Y	Y	Y	Y	Y	Y	Y		Y	19	28
New Mexico State University–Alamogordo	Alamogordo	C,T	State	Coed	2,300	79		69	59		Y	Y	Y		Y	Y	Y	Y	Y	N	2	10
New Mexico State University–Carlsbad	Carlsbad	C,T	State	Coed	1,151	61	2	70		12	Y	Y	Y	R,S	Y	Y	Y	Y	Y	N	0	16
New Mexico State University–Grants	Grants	C,T	State	Coed	700	62					Y	Y	Y							N	0	9
Northern New Mexico Community College	Española																					
Parks College	Albuquerque	C,T	Prop	Coed	289	5	85	20	95	5	Y		Y	Y	Y	Y	Y	Y	Y	N	0	4
Pima Medical Institute	Albuquerque	C,T	Prop	Coed	125							Y	S	Y	Y		Y				0	4
San Juan College	Farmington	C,T	County	Coed	4,500	68		61			Y	Y	Y		Y	Y	Y	Y	Y	N	14	59
Santa Fe Community College	Santa Fe	C,T	St & Loc	Coed		49		78			Y	Y	Y		Y	Y	Y	Y	Y	N	0	30
Southwestern Indian Polytechnic Institute	Albuquerque	C,T	Fed	Coed	638		70	35	60		Y			Y	Y			Y	Y	Y	1	16
University of New Mexico–Gallup Branch	Gallup	C,T,B	State	Coed	3,000	66		50		10	Y			S	Y	Y	Y	Y	Y	N	0	30
University of New Mexico–Los Alamos Branch	Los Alamos	C,T	State	Coed	1,023	85		40			Y	Y		S	Y	Y	Y	Y	Y	N	0	14
University of New Mexico–Valencia Campus	Los Lunas	C,T	State	Coed	1,440	59		76		50	Y	Y		S	Y		Y	Y	Y	N	0	14
New York																						
Adirondack Community College*	Queensbury	C,T	St & Loc	Coed	3,602	53	49	46	75	80	Y	Y	Y	R	Y	Y	Y	Y	Y	N	13	35
American Acad McAllister Inst of Funeral Service	New York	T	Ind	Coed	173	5		97			Y	Y	Y			Y		Y		N	0	1
American Academy of Dramatic Arts†	New York	T	Ind	Coed	201	0	50	26			N	Y	S	R	Y	Y	Y	Y	Y	N	0	1
Berkeley College†	New York	C,T	Prop	Coed	1,007	18		5			N	Y	Y		Y	Y	Y	Y	Y	N	0	11
Berkeley College†	White Plains	C,T	Prop	Coed	494			4	55		N	Y	Y		Y	Y	Y	Y	Y	Y	0	18
Borough of Manhattan Comm Coll of City U of NY	New York	C,T	St & Loc	Coed	16,334	53		47	63	45	Y	Y			Y	Y	Y	Y	Y	N	7	28
Bramson ORT Technical Institute	Forest Hills	T	Ind	Coed	1,200	10		80			Y	Y	Y		Y	Y	Y	Y	Y	N	0	15
Briarcliffe–The Coll for Business & Tech	Woodbury	C,T	Prop	Coed	1,243	19		49		20	N	Y	Y		Y	Y	Y	Y	Y	N	2	7
Bronx Comm Coll of City U of NY	Bronx	C,T	St & Loc	Coed	8,450	47					Y	Y	Y		Y	Y	Y	Y	Y	N	6	27
Broome Community College	Binghamton	C,T	St & Loc	Coed	5,986	41		48		38	Y	Y			Y	Y	Y	Y	Y	N	12	29
Bryant and Stratton Business Inst	Albany	C	Prop	Coed	537	14	93	49	57		N	Y	Y	Y	Y	Y	Y	Y	Y	N	1	10
Bryant and Stratton Business Inst	Buffalo	C	Prop	Coed	673	11	99	44			N	Y	Y	Y	Y	Y	Y	Y	Y	N	0	11
Bryant and Stratton Business Inst	Cicero	C	Prop	Coed	678	22		40			N	Y	Y	Y	Y	Y	Y	Y	Y	N	0	8
Bryant and Stratton Business Inst	Lackawanna	C	Prop	Coed	427	23		54			N	Y	Y	Y	Y	Y	Y	Y	Y	N	0	7
Bryant and Stratton Business Inst	Rochester	C	Prop	Coed	314	3	97	30			N	Y	Y	Y	Y	Y	Y	Y	Y	N	3	14
Bryant and Stratton Business Inst	Rochester	C	Prop	Coed	718	25		68			N	Y	Y	Y	Y	Y	Y	Y	Y	N	0	15
Bryant and Stratton Business Inst	Syracuse	C	Prop	Coed	587	13		60	60	7	N	Y	Y	Y	Y		Y	Y	Y	Y	0	10
Bryant and Stratton Business Inst, E Hills Campus	Williamsville	C	Prop	Coed	550	11		30			N	Y	Y	Y	Y	Y	Y	Y	Y	N	1	14
Cath Med Ctr of Brooklyn & Queens Sch of Nursing	Woodhaven	T	Ind	Coed	85	65		56	96		N	Y		Y	Y			Y		N	0	1
Cayuga County Community College	Auburn	C,T	St & Loc	Coed	2,751	51			56		Y	Y	Y		Y	Y	Y	Y	Y	N	9	28
Cazenovia College*†	Cazenovia	C,T,B	Ind	Coed	851	3	87	6	53	70	N	Y	Y	R	Y	Y	Y	Y	Y	Y	13	22
Central City Business Institute	Syracuse	C,T	Prop	Coed	326	15	75	25		12	N	Y	Y	Y	Y	Y	Y	Y	Y	N	4	11

Peterson's Guide to Two-Year Colleges 1997
39

This index includes the names and locations of accredited two-year colleges in the United States and U.S. territories and shows institutions' responses to our 1996 Survey of Undergraduate Institutions. If an institution submitted incomplete or no data, one or more columns opposite the institution's name is blank. An asterisk after the school name denotes a Special Announcement following the college's profile, and a dagger indicates that the institution has one or more entries in the In-Depth Descriptions of the Colleges section.

Y—Yes; N—No; R—Recommended; S—For Some

		Degrees Awarded: Transfer Associate (C), Terminal Associate (T), Bachelor's (B), Master's (M), Doctoral (D), First Professional (F)	Institutional Control: Independent, Independent-Religious, Proprietary, Federal, State, Province, Commonwealth, Territory, County, District, City, State and Local, State-Related	Student Body: Men, Primarily Men, Women, Primarily Women, Coeducational	Undergraduate Enrollment Fall 1995	Percent Attending Part-Time	Percent Receiving Need-Based Financial Aid	Percent 25 Years of Age or Older	Freshman Retention Rate	Percent of Grads Going on to 4-Year Colleges	Open Admissions	High School Equivalency Certificate Accepted	High School Transcript Required	Entrance Test(s) Required	College Scholarships Available	Loans Available	Part-Time Jobs Available	Career Counseling Available	Job Placement Services Available	College Housing Available	Number of Sports Offered	Number of Majors Offered
Clinton Community College	Plattsburgh	C,T	St & Loc	Coed	1,662	42		40			Y	Y			Y	Y	Y	Y	Y	N	12	13
Cochran School of Nursing	Yonkers	T	State	Prim W	142			68	89		N	Y			Y	Y	Y	Y		N	0	1
Columbia-Greene Community College	Hudson	C,T	St & Loc	Coed	1,711	48	80	56		75	Y			Y	Y		Y	Y	Y	N	13	20
Corning Community College	Corning	C,T	St & Loc	Coed	3,295	33	70	40	67	66	Y	Y		S	Y	Y	Y	Y	Y	N	15	29
Culinary Institute of America	Hyde Park	T,B	Ind	Coed	2,000	0	85	43			N	Y		R	Y	Y	Y	Y	Y	Y	7	1
Dutchess Community College	Poughkeepsie	C,T	St & Loc	Coed	6,284	56		48		40	Y	Y		R	Y	Y	Y	Y	Y	N	10	32
Erie Community College, City Campus	Buffalo	C,T	St & Loc	Coed	3,112	33		49		30	Y	Y		Y	Y	Y	Y	Y	Y	N	12	30
Erie Community College, North Campus	Williamsville	C,T	St & Loc	Coed	6,434	45				32	Y	Y		Y	Y	Y	Y	Y	Y	N	12	34
Erie Community College, South Campus	Orchard Park	C,T	St & Loc	Coed	3,391	43		37		32	Y	Y		Y	Y		Y	Y	Y	N	13	25
Eugenio María de Hostos Comm Coll of City U of NY	Bronx	C,T	St & Loc	Coed	4,953	22		68	65		Y	Y	Y		Y		Y	Y		N	0	15
Finger Lakes Community College	Canandaigua	C,T	St & Loc	Coed	3,848	47		24	59		Y	Y			Y	Y	Y	Y	Y	N	7	54
Fiorello H LaGuardia Comm Coll of City U of NY*	Long Island City	C,T	St & Loc	Coed	10,675	38	43	47		49	Y	Y	Y		Y	Y	Y	Y	Y	N	9	34
Fulton-Montgomery Community College	Johnstown	C,T	St & Loc	Coed	1,726	39		40		47	Y				Y	Y	Y			N	10	45
Genesee Community College	Batavia	C,T	St & Loc	Coed	4,346	47		42			Y	Y		Y	Y	Y	Y	Y	Y	Y	15	34
Helene Fuld Coll of Nursing of North General Hosp	New York	C,T	Ind	Coed	202	60		93			N	Y	Y	Y	Y	Y		Y		N	0	1
Herkimer County Community College	Herkimer	C,T	St & Loc	Coed	2,445	24		28	60	70	Y	Y	Y		Y	Y	Y	Y	Y	N	12	48
Hudson Valley Community College	Troy	C,T	St & Loc	Coed	10,102	17		35		37	Y	Y	Y	R,S	Y	Y	Y	Y	Y	N	16	42
Institute of Design and Construction	Brooklyn	C	Ind	Coed	246	50		66	60	20	Y	Y	Y			Y		Y	Y	N	0	4
Interboro Institute	New York	C,T	Prop	Coed	1,147	3	90	20	32		N		R	Y	Y	Y	Y	Y	Y	N	1	8
Jamestown Business College	Jamestown	T	Prop	Coed	315	0	93	33	76		N	Y	Y		Y	Y	Y	Y	Y	N	9	7
Jamestown Community College	Jamestown	C,T	St & Loc	Coed	3,660	47		49		82	Y	Y			Y	Y	Y	Y	Y	N	12	19
Jefferson Community College	Watertown	C,T	St & Loc	Coed	3,200	36		48		53	N	Y	Y		Y	Y	Y	Y	Y	N	10	29
Katharine Gibbs School	Melville	C	Prop	Prim W	430	0					N	Y	Y	S	Y	Y	Y	Y	Y	N	0	2
Katharine Gibbs School	New York																					
Kingsborough Comm Coll of City U of NY	Brooklyn	C,T	St & Loc	Coed	15,464	52		17	65	70	Y	Y	Y		Y	Y	Y	Y	Y	N	11	29
Long Island College Hospital School of Nursing	Brooklyn	C,T	Ind	Coed	185	67		81			N	Y	Y	Y	Y	Y	Y			N	0	1
Maria College*†	Albany	C,T	Ind	Coed	829	57	46	65	67	14	N	Y	Y	Y	Y	Y	Y	Y	Y	N	0	8
Mater Dei College*†	Ogdensburg	C,T	Ind-R	Coed	394	5	75	47		19	N	Y	Y	R,S	Y	Y	Y	Y	Y	Y	5	13
Mohawk Valley Community College	Utica	C,T	St & Loc	Coed	6,328	12		37		45	Y	Y			Y	Y	Y	Y	Y	Y	16	69
Monroe College	Bronx	C,T	Prop	Coed	2,625	2		37		26	N				Y	Y	Y	Y	Y	N	3	6
Monroe College	New Rochelle	C,T	Prop	Coed	562	1	70	29		26	N				Y	Y	Y	Y	Y	N	3	6
Monroe Community College	Rochester	C,T	St & Loc	Coed	13,730	47				59	Y	Y	Y		Y	Y	Y	Y	Y	N	18	63
Nassau Community College	Garden City	C,T	St & Loc	Coed	21,975	45		32	70	65	Y	Y	Y		Y	Y	Y	Y	Y	N	13	46
New York City Tech Coll of the City U of NY	Brooklyn	C,T,B	St & Loc	Coed		42		45			Y	Y	Y		Y	Y	Y	Y	Y	N	3	34
Niagara County Community College	Sanborn	C,T	St & Loc	Coed	5,361	40	46	42	56	56	Y	Y	Y	R	Y	Y	Y	Y	Y	N	20	30
North Country Community College	Saranac Lake	C,T	St & Loc	Coed	1,148	19		41		39	Y	Y	Y	R	Y	Y	Y	Y	Y	N	15	14
Olean Business Institute	Olean	T	Prop	Coed	173	5	80	50			N	Y	Y		Y	Y		Y	Y	N	3	6
Onondaga Community College	Syracuse	C,T	St & Loc	Coed	7,400	50		45			Y	Y		R	Y	Y	Y	Y	Y	N	7	46
Orange County Community College	Middletown	C,T	St & Loc	Coed	5,853	55		44	78	62	Y	Y			Y	Y	Y	Y	Y	N	8	37
Paul Smith's College*†	Paul Smiths	C,T	Ind	Coed	771	3		1		25	N	Y	Y	Y	Y	Y	Y	Y	Y	Y	13	16
Phillips Beth Israel School of Nursing	New York	C	Ind	Coed	140	55	85	75	90	15	N	Y	Y	Y	Y	Y		Y		N	0	1
Plaza Business Institute	Jackson Heights																					
Queensborough Comm Coll of City U of NY	Bayside	C,T	St & Loc	Coed	12,000	58		39		58	Y	Y			Y	Y	Y	Y	Y	N	19	19
Rochester Business Institute	Rochester	T	Prop	Coed	300	5		45			N	Y		Y	Y		Y	Y	Y	N	2	6
Rockland Community College	Suffern	C,T	St & Loc	Coed	7,240	52		43		50	Y			R	Y	Y	Y	Y	Y	N	14	38
Sage Junior College of Albany*†	Albany	C,T	Ind	Coed	655	9	85	10		61	N	Y	Y	S	Y	Y	Y	Y	Y	Y	3	21
Schenectady County Community College	Schenectady	C,T	St & Loc	Coed	3,692	52	75	50	75	70	Y	Y		R	Y	Y	Y	Y	Y	N	6	28
Simmons Institute of Funeral Service	Syracuse	T	Prop	Coed	74						N				Y					N	0	1
State U of NY Coll of A&T at Cobleskill†	Cobleskill	C,T,B	State	Coed	2,410	8		10	65	95	N	Y	Y	R	Y	Y	Y	Y	Y	Y	18	45
State U of NY Coll of A&T at Morrisville†	Morrisville	C,T	State	Coed	2,890	18		23	45	44	N	Y			Y	Y	Y	Y	Y	Y	15	66
State U of NY Coll of Environ Sci & For Ranger Sch†	Wanakena	T	State	Coed	48	0		10		31	N	Y		S	Y	Y	Y	Y	Y	Y	0	1
State U of NY Coll of Technology at Alfred	Alfred	C,T,B	State	Coed	3,319	6		17	93	38	N	Y	Y	R	Y	Y	Y	Y	Y	Y	19	52
State U of NY Coll of Technology at Canton*†	Canton	C,T	State	Coed	2,004	16		26	45	81	N	Y		R,S	Y	Y	Y	Y	Y	Y	15	43
State U of NY Coll of Technology at Delhi	Delhi	C,T	State	Coed	2,098	7	68	15	72	82	N	Y	Y	R	Y	Y	Y	Y	Y	Y	14	36
State U of NY Coll of Technology at Farmingdale†	Farmingdale	C,T,B	State	Coed	6,209	46	60	28	80	50	N	Y	Y	R	Y		Y	Y	Y	Y	18	38
Stenotype Academy	New York	T	Prop	Coed	800	22		35			Y	Y	Y		Y	Y		Y	Y	N	0	2
Suffolk County Comm College–Ammerman Cmps	Selden	C,T	St & Loc	Coed	13,154	53		37		60	Y	Y		R,S	Y	Y	Y	Y	Y	N	9	50
Suffolk County Comm Coll–Eastern Cmps	Riverhead	C,T	St & Loc	Coed	2,680	68		51		75	Y	Y		R,S	Y	Y	Y	Y	Y	N	10	19
Suffolk County Comm Coll–Western Cmps	Brentwood	C,T	St & Loc	Coed	6,097	70		46	60	60	Y	Y		R,S	Y	Y	Y	Y	Y	N	6	18
Sullivan County Community College*	Loch Sheldrake	C,T	St & Loc	Coed	2,085	33		43		48	Y	Y	Y	R	Y	Y	Y	Y	Y	N	13	52
Taylor Business Institute	New York	C,T	Prop	Coed	525	0		20			N	Y	Y	Y	Y	Y	Y	Y	Y	N	0	4
Technical Career Institutes	New York	T	Prop	Coed	3,300	30			52		Y	Y			Y	Y	Y	Y	Y	N	0	4
Tompkins Cortland Community College	Dryden	C,T	St & Loc	Coed	2,754	48	88	51		59	Y			S	Y	Y	Y	Y	Y	N	14	29
Trocaire College*	Buffalo	C,T	Ind	Coed	1,044	50	80	64		8	N	Y	Y	S	Y	Y	Y	Y	Y	N	0	15
Ulster County Community College	Stone Ridge	C,T	St & Loc	Coed	2,642	50		47	46	48	Y	Y			Y	Y	Y	Y	Y	N	13	28
U of the State of NY, Regents College†	Albany	C,T,B	Ind	Coed	19,443	100		94			Y				Y					N	0	36
Utica School of Commerce	Utica	C,T	Prop	Coed	605	19		29			N	Y	Y	Y	Y	Y		Y	Y	N	4	7
Villa Maria College of Buffalo	Buffalo	C,T	Ind-R	Coed	312	27	65	44	61	48	N	Y		Y	Y	Y	Y	Y	Y	N	0	12
Westchester Business Institute	White Plains	C,T	Prop	Coed	975	6		45			N	Y		R	Y		Y	Y	Y	N	0	10
Westchester Community College	Valhalla	C,T	St & Loc	Coed	16,914	59	29	46	46	63	Y	Y		R	Y	Y	Y	Y	Y	N	16	55
Wood Tobe–Coburn School	New York	T	Prop	Women	223	0		1			N	Y	Y	S	Y	Y	Y	Y	Y	N	0	5
North Carolina																						
Alamance Community College	Graham	C,T	State	Coed	3,340	64		50	63		Y	Y	Y		Y	Y	Y	Y	Y	N	5	40
Anson Community College	Polkton	C,T	State	Coed	1,379	59		65			Y	Y	Y	R	Y	Y	Y	Y	Y	N	0	25
Asheville-Buncombe Technical Community College	Asheville	C,T	State	Coed	4,021	65		52			Y	Y	R	Y	Y	Y	Y	Y	Y	N	0	24
Beaufort County Community College	Washington	C,T	State	Coed	1,154	48		57		75	Y	Y	Y	Y	Y	Y	Y	Y	Y	N	0	18
Bladen Community College	Dublin	C,T	St & Loc	Coed	692	44	31	42		65	Y	Y	Y	Y	Y	Y	Y	Y	Y	N	4	6
Blue Ridge Community College	Flat Rock	C,T	St & Loc	Coed	2,529	60		61			Y	Y	Y		Y	Y	Y	Y	Y	N	0	23
Brevard College*†	Brevard	C,B	Ind-R	Coed	636	7	60	3		93	N	Y	Y	Y	Y	Y	Y	Y	Y	Y	20	131
Brunswick Community College	Supply	C,T	State	Coed	829	51		79			Y	Y	Y	S	Y		Y	Y	Y	N	4	13
Caldwell Comm Coll and Tech Inst	Hudson	C,T	State	Coed	3,162	56		36	15		Y	Y			Y	Y	Y	Y	Y	N	4	19

State-by-State Summary Table
North Carolina–Ohio

This index includes the names and locations of accredited two-year colleges in the United States and U.S. territories and shows institutions' responses to our 1996 Survey of Undergraduate Institutions. If an institution submitted incomplete or no data, one or more columns opposite the institution's name is blank. An asterisk after the school name denotes a Special Announcement following the college's profile, and a dagger indicates that the institution has one or more entries in the In-Depth Descriptions of the Colleges section.

Column legend (diagonal headers): Degrees Awarded — Bachelor's (B), Associate (A), Transfer Associate (T), Terminal Associate (T), Certificate (C), Master's (M), Doctoral (D), First Professional (F); Institutional Control — Federal, State, Province, County, District, City, State and Local, Independent, Independent-Religious, Commonwealth, Proprietary; Student Body — Men, Primarily Men, Women, Primarily Women, Coeducational; Undergraduate Enrollment Fall 1995; Percent Receiving Need-Based Financial Aid; Percent Attending Part-Time; Percent of Grads Going on to 4-Year Colleges; Percent 25 Years of Age or Older; Freshman Retention Rate; High School Equivalency Certificate Accepted; Open Admissions; Entrance Tests Required; High School Transcript Required; College Scholarships Available; Loans Available; Part-Time Jobs Available; Career Counseling Available; Job Placement Services Available; College Housing Available; Number of Sports Offered; Number of Majors Offered. Y—Yes; N—No; R—Recommended; S—For Some.

College	City	Degrees	Control	Student Body	Enroll	%Aid	%PT	%4yr	%25+	Retn	HSE	OA	Ent	HST	Sch	Loan	PT	Car	Job	Hsg	Sp	Maj
Cape Fear Community College	Wilmington	C,T	State	Coed	3,700	50	16	40		85	Y	Y	Y		Y	Y	Y	Y	Y	N	6	23
Carteret Community College	Morehead City	C,T	State	Coed	1,428	59		53			Y	Y	Y	R	Y	Y	Y	Y	Y	N	2	15
Catawba Valley Community College	Hickory	C,T	St & Loc	Coed	3,499	74		54		60	Y	Y			Y	Y	Y	Y	Y	N	3	26
Cecils Junior College of Business	Asheville	C	Prop		150	35		80			Y		Y	Y	Y	Y	Y	Y	Y	N	0	4
Central Carolina Community College	Sanford	C,T	St & Loc	Coed	3,140	52		52	26		Y	Y		Y	Y	Y	Y	Y	Y	N	6	28
Central Piedmont Community College	Charlotte	C,T	St & Loc	Coed	15,614	70		62		29	Y		Y		Y	Y	Y	Y	Y	N	7	71
Cleveland Community College	Shelby	C,T	State	Coed	1,873	67		75			Y	Y				Y		Y	Y	N	2	13
Coastal Carolina Community College	Jacksonville	C,T	St & Loc	Coed	3,491	46		50			Y	Y			Y	Y	Y	Y	Y	N	10	28
College of The Albemarle	Elizabeth City	C,T	State	Coed	1,894	55	31	56		84	Y	Y	Y	R	Y	Y	Y	Y	Y	N	9	19
Craven Community College	New Bern	C,T	State	Coed	2,254	45	25	54	51		Y	Y	R		Y	Y	Y	Y	Y	N	3	20
Davidson County Community College	Lexington	C,T	St & Loc	Coed	2,301	52	51	35		67	Y	Y			Y	Y	Y	Y	Y	N	2	22
Durham Technical Community College	Durham	C,T	State	Coed	4,694	70		64			Y	Y	Y		Y	Y	Y	Y	Y	N	1	34
Edgecombe Community College	Tarboro	C,T	St & Loc	Coed	1,978	61	55	65	82	65	Y	Y	Y	R	Y	Y	Y	Y	Y	N	5	24
Fayetteville Technical Community College	Fayetteville	C,T	State	Coed	7,118	50		58	63		Y	Y			Y	Y	Y	Y	Y	N	2	37
Forsyth Technical Community College	Winston-Salem	C,T	State	Coed	4,895	66		51			Y	Y	Y	R	Y	Y	Y	Y	Y	N	3	40
Gaston College	Dallas	C,T	St & Loc	Coed	4,046	53	72	55		28	Y	Y	S		Y	Y	Y	Y	Y	N	0	28
Guilford Technical Community College	Jamestown	C,T	St & Loc	Coed	6,647	64		44		50	Y	Y	Y	Y	Y	Y	Y	Y	Y	N	0	39
Halifax Community College	Weldon	C	St & Loc	Coed	1,360	46					Y	Y			Y	Y	Y	Y	Y	N	0	16
Haywood Community College	Clyde	C,T	St & Loc	Coed	1,322	47	20	45			Y	Y			Y	Y	Y	Y	Y	N	5	23
Isothermal Community College	Spindale	C,T	State	Coed	1,747	75		49			Y	Y	Y		Y	Y	Y	Y	Y	N	6	36
James Sprunt Community College	Kenansville	C,T	State	Coed	1,021	48		56	56	90	Y	Y			Y	Y	Y	Y	Y	N	1	17
Johnston Community College	Smithfield	C,T	State	Coed	2,655	48		46			Y	Y		S	Y	Y	Y	Y	Y	N	4	15
Lenoir Community College	Kinston	C,T	State	Coed	2,069	47					Y	Y			Y	Y	Y	Y	Y	N	5	45
Louisburg College	Louisburg	C,T	Ind-R	Coed	560	2	50	5	59	90	N	Y	Y	Y	Y	Y	Y	Y	Y	Y	9	5
Louise Harkey Sch of Nurs–Cabarrus Memorial Hosp	Concord	T	Ind	Prim W	139	23	47	45	98		N	Y	Y	Y	Y		Y	Y	Y	N	0	1
Martin Community College	Williamston	C,T	State	Coed	702	39	40	51		50	Y	Y			Y	Y	Y	Y	Y	N	3	10
Mayland Community College	Spruce Pine	C	St & Loc	Coed	798	60		46	62		Y	Y			Y	Y	Y	Y	Y	N	0	18
McDowell Technical Community College	Marion	C,T	State	Coed	939	54			72	60	Y	Y	S	S	Y	Y	Y	Y	Y	N	4	20
Mitchell Community College	Statesville	C,T	State	Coed	1,550	50		30			Y	Y		Y	Y	Y	Y	Y	Y	N	6	15
Montgomery Community College	Troy	C,T	State	Coed	551	41	58	63	49		Y	Y	Y	Y	Y	Y	Y	Y	Y	N	3	14
Nash Community College	Rocky Mount	C,T	State	Coed	1,880	63		45		90	Y	Y			Y	Y	Y	Y	Y	N	0	15
Pamlico Community College	Grantsboro	T	State	Coed	205	43		56			Y	Y			Y	Y	Y	Y	Y	N	2	10
Peace College	Raleigh	C,B	Ind-R	Women	424	4	44	1			N	N	Y	Y	Y	Y	Y	Y	Y	Y	8	6
Piedmont Community College	Roxboro	C,T	State	Coed	600	61					Y	Y	Y		Y	Y	Y	Y	Y	N	1	12
Pitt Community College	Greenville	C,T	St & Loc	Coed	4,712	53		37			Y	Y			Y	Y	Y	Y	Y	N	4	29
Randolph Community College	Asheboro	C,T	State	Coed	1,343	51		47	40	70	Y	Y	Y	R	Y	Y	Y	Y	Y	N	0	18
Richmond Community College	Hamlet	C,T	State	Coed	1,146	47		55	40		Y	Y			Y	Y	Y	Y	Y	N	0	12
Roanoke-Chowan Community College	Ahoskie	C,T	State	Coed	855	47		73			Y	Y		Y	Y	Y	Y	Y	Y	N	2	15
Robeson Community College	Lumberton	C,T	State	Coed	1,322	50				82	Y	Y			Y	Y	Y	Y	Y	N	0	12
Rockingham Community College	Wentworth	C,T	State	Coed	1,907	49		53			Y	Y		S	Y	Y	Y	Y	Y	N	7	29
Rowan-Cabarrus Community College	Salisbury	C,T	State	Coed	3,500	45		55		95	Y	Y	Y		Y	Y	Y	Y	Y	N	0	28
Saint Mary's College	Raleigh	C	Ind-R	Women	136	4	65	0	80	99	N	N	Y	Y	Y	Y	Y	Y	Y	Y	8	1
Sampson Community College	Clinton	C,T	St & Loc	Coed	993	50		55		23	Y	Y			Y	Y	Y	Y	Y	N	3	10
Sandhills Community College	Pinehurst	C,T	St & Loc	Coed	2,396	43	40	39	45	69	Y	Y		S	Y	Y	Y	Y	Y	N	7	44
Southeastern Baptist Theological Seminary	Wake Forest	C,T,M,D,F	Ind-R	Coed	142	20	75	100	95		Y		Y		Y	Y	Y	Y	Y	Y	8	3
Southeastern Community College	Whiteville	C,T	State	Coed	1,750	40	40	45	45		Y	Y		S	Y	Y	Y	Y	Y	N	1	17
Southwestern Community College	Sylva	C,T	State	Coed	1,517	48	60	46			Y	Y			Y	Y	Y	Y	Y	N	0	22
Stanly Community College	Albemarle	C,T	State	Coed	1,660	57		55			Y	Y			Y	Y	Y	Y	Y	N	0	16
Surry Community College	Dobson	C,T	State	Coed	3,036	35		60	75	90	Y	Y			Y	Y	Y	Y	Y	N	6	23
Tri-County Community College	Murphy	C,T	State	Coed	919	63		62		40	Y	Y		S	Y	Y	Y	Y	Y	N	0	9
Vance-Granville Community College	Henderson	C,T	State	Coed	2,434	52	55	52	72	92	Y	Y		S	Y	Y	Y	Y	Y	N	5	33
Wake Technical Community College	Raleigh	C,T	St & Loc	Coed	7,340	63		56		100	Y	Y	Y		Y	Y	Y	Y	Y	N	0	42
Wayne Community College	Goldsboro	C,T	St & Loc	Coed	2,639	34	95	44		25	Y	Y		S	Y	Y	Y	Y	Y	N	7	31
Western Piedmont Community College	Morganton	C,T	State	Coed	2,562	63					Y	Y			Y	Y	Y	Y	Y	N	2	26
Wilkes Community College	Wilkesboro	C,T	State	Coed	2,178	55	60	50	50	71	Y	Y			Y	Y	Y	Y	Y	N	7	24
Wilson Technical Community College	Wilson	C,T	State	Coed	1,416	53	27	57			Y	Y	Y		Y	Y	Y	Y	Y	N	0	18

North Dakota

College	City	Degrees	Control	Student Body	Enroll	%Aid	%PT	%4yr	%25+	Retn	HSE	OA	Ent	HST	Sch	Loan	PT	Car	Job	Hsg	Sp	Maj
Bismarck State College	Bismarck	C,T	State	Coed	2,313	31	66	30			Y	Y	S	S	Y	Y	Y	Y	Y	Y	7	43
Fort Berthold Community College	New Town	C	Ind	Coed	423	52		57		42	Y	Y			Y		Y	Y	Y	N	6	16
Little Hoop Community College	Fort Totten	C	Fed	Coed	120	41		50		10	Y	Y					Y	Y	Y	N	4	19
North Dakota State College of Science	Wahpeton	C,T	State	Coed	2,492	9		17		85	Y		Y	Y	Y	Y	Y	Y	Y	Y	7	42
North Dakota State University–Bottineau	Bottineau	C,T	State	Coed	356	6	65	14		58	Y	Y	Y	Y	Y	Y	Y	Y	Y	Y	10	37
Standing Rock College	Fort Yates	C,T	Ind	Coed	204	19		40		40	Y	Y			Y		Y	Y	Y	N	1	6
Turtle Mountain Community College	Belcourt	C	Ind	Coed	404	44		75			Y	Y	Y	Y	Y		Y	Y	Y	N	4	27
United Tribes Technical College	Bismarck	C,T	Fed	Coed	250	0			80		Y	Y		R	Y	Y	Y	Y	Y	Y	3	7
University of North Dakota–Lake Region	Devils Lake	C,T	State	Coed	723	45		39			Y	Y			Y	Y	Y	Y	Y	Y	5	20
University of North Dakota–Williston	Williston	C,T	State	Coed	919	28	65	40	90	80	Y	Y	S		Y	Y	Y	Y	Y	Y	6	8

Ohio

College	City	Degrees	Control	Student Body	Enroll	%Aid	%PT	%4yr	%25+	Retn	HSE	OA	Ent	HST	Sch	Loan	PT	Car	Job	Hsg	Sp	Maj
Antonelli College	Cincinnati	T	Prop	Coed	175	0		20	95		Y	Y			Y	Y	Y	Y	Y	N	0	5
Belmont Technical College	St Clairsville	T	State	Coed	1,694	34		55	31		Y	Y		Y	Y		Y	Y	Y	N	0	18
Bowling Green State University–Firelands Coll	Huron	C,T,B	State	Coed	1,379	48	55	47	63		Y	Y	Y	S	Y	Y	Y	Y	Y	N	6	27
Bradford School	Columbus	C	Prop	Prim W	214	0		0	70		N	Y	S		Y	Y	Y	Y	Y	N	0	8
Bryant and Stratton Coll	Parma	C	Prop	Coed	493	28		45	54	10	N	Y	Y		Y	Y	Y	Y	Y	N	1	11
Bryant and Stratton Coll	Richmond Heights	C	Prop	Coed	234	43				3	N	Y	Y		Y	Y	Y	Y	Y	N	0	5
Central Ohio Technical College	Newark	T	State	Coed	1,664	55		81			Y	Y		Y	Y	Y	Y	Y	Y	Y	12	18
Chatfield College	St Martin	C	Ind	Coed	226	68	65	86	42	41	Y	Y		Y	Y		Y	Y	Y	N	0	5
Cincinnati State Technical and Community College	Cincinnati	C,T	State	Coed	5,790	55		41		8	Y	Y			Y	Y	Y	Y	Y	N	2	46
Clark State Community College	Springfield	C,T	State	Coed	2,746	63					Y	Y	Y	R	Y	Y	Y	Y	Y	N	4	36
Cleveland Institute of Electronics	Cleveland	T	Prop	Prim M	2,300	100		87			Y	Y				Y				N	0	1

Peterson's Guide to Two-Year Colleges 1997

State-by-State Summary Table
Ohio–Oregon

This index includes the names and locations of accredited two-year colleges in the United States and U.S. territories and shows institutions' responses to our 1996 Survey of Undergraduate Institutions. If an institution submitted incomplete or no data, one or more columns opposite the institution's name is blank. An asterisk after the school name denotes a Special Announcement following the college's profile, and a dagger indicates that the institution has one or more entries in the In-Depth Descriptions of the Colleges section.

Y—Yes; N—No; R—Recommended; S—For Some

		Degrees Awarded: Transfer Associate (C), Terminal Associate (T), Bachelor's (B), Master's (M), Doctoral (D), First Professional (F)	Institutional Control: Independent, Independent-Religious, Proprietary, Federal, State, Province, Commonwealth, Territory, County, District, City, State and Local, State-Related	Student Body: Men, Primarily Men, Women, Primarily Women, Coeducational	Undergraduate Enrollment Fall 1995	Percent Attending Part-Time	Percent Receiving Need-Based Financial Aid	Percent 25 Years of Age or Older	Freshman Retention Rate	Percent of Grads Going on to 4-Year Colleges	Open Admissions	High School Equivalency Certificate Accepted	High School Transcript Required	Entrance Test(s) Required	College Scholarships Available	Loans Available	Part-Time Jobs Available	Career Counseling Available	Job Placement Services Available	College Housing Available	Number of Sports Offered	Number of Majors Offered
Columbus State Community College†	Columbus	C,T	State	Coed	16,500	63	34	48		28	Y	Y	Y	Y	Y	Y	Y	Y	Y	N	11	63
Cuyahoga Community College, Eastern Campus	Highland Hills	C,T	St & Loc	Coed	5,382	73	20	65	43		Y	Y	S		Y	Y	Y	Y	Y	N	5	18
Cuyahoga Community College, Metropolitan Campus	Cleveland	C,T	St & Loc	Coed	6,015	57	41	64	44		Y	Y	S		Y	Y	Y	Y	Y	N	11	35
Cuyahoga Community College, Western Campus	Parma	C,T	St & Loc	Coed	12,228	71	39	52	59		Y	Y	S		Y	Y	Y	Y	Y	N	8	29
Davis College	Toledo	T	Prop	Coed	466	50	75	70	70	10	N	Y	Y	Y	Y	Y	Y	Y	Y	N	0	15
Edison State Community College	Piqua	C,T	State	Coed	3,297	69		53			Y	Y		S			Y	Y	Y	N	4	36
ETI Technical College	Niles	T	Prop	Coed	246			70			N	Y		Y	Y	Y		Y	Y	N	0	4
Hocking College	Nelsonville	T	State	Coed	6,200	29	51	48			Y	Y	Y	S	Y	Y	Y	Y	Y	Y	10	44
ITT Technical Institute	Dayton	T	Prop	Coed	547	0		22			N	Y		Y	Y	Y	Y		Y	N	0	5
ITT Technical Institute	Youngstown	T	Prop	Coed	269	0					N	Y		Y	Y	Y	Y	Y	Y	N	0	4
Jefferson Community College	Steubenville	C,T	St & Loc	Coed	1,437	47		54	48		Y	Y		S	Y	Y	Y	Y	Y	N	3	28
Kent State University, Ashtabula Campus	Ashtabula	C,T	State	Coed	1,100	52	75	40	75		Y	Y		Y	Y	Y	Y	Y	Y	N	0	22
Kent State University, East Liverpool Campus	East Liverpool	C,T	State	Coed	817	49	71	51	62	50	Y	Y		R,S	Y	Y	Y	Y	Y	N	6	11
Kent State University, Geauga Campus	Burton	C	State	Coed	474	60		55		65	Y	Y	Y	R	Y	Y	Y	Y		N	1	9
Kent State University, Salem Campus	Salem	C,T	State	Coed	924	52		47			Y	Y		R,S	Y	Y	Y	Y	Y	N	10	11
Kent State University, Stark Campus	Canton	C	State	Coed	2,464	46	30				Y	Y	Y	Y	Y	Y	Y	Y		N	9	5
Kent State University, Trumbull Campus	Warren	C,T	State	Coed	1,918	60		54			Y	Y	Y	Y	Y	Y	Y	Y	Y	N	5	16
Kent State University, Tuscarawas Campus	New Philadelphia	C,T	State	Coed	1,133	49	65	43	50	80	Y	Y		S	Y	Y	Y	Y	Y	N	3	13
Kettering College of Medical Arts	Kettering	C,T	Ind-R	Coed	599	51		47	88		N	Y	Y	Y	Y	Y	Y	Y		Y	3	9
Lakeland Community College	Kirtland	C,T	St & Loc	Coed	8,515	72	19	53	74		Y	Y	Y	S	Y	Y	Y	Y	Y	N	7	33
Lima Technical College*	Lima	C,T	State	Coed	2,591	50	60	54		12	Y	Y			Y	Y	Y	Y	Y	N	11	32
Lorain County Community College	Elyria	C,T	St & Loc	Coed	7,047	66		54	68	80	Y	Y	S	R,S	Y	Y	Y	Y	Y	N	5	58
Marion Technical College	Marion	C,T	St-R	Coed	1,800	57		65			Y	Y	Y	S	Y	Y	Y	Y	Y	N	7	18
Mercy College of Northwest Ohio	Toledo	C,T	Ind	Coed							N	Y	S	Y						Y	0	2
Miami-Jacobs College	Dayton	T	Prop	Prim W	410	23		48			N	Y	Y	Y	Y	Y	Y	Y	Y	N	0	7
Miami University–Hamilton Campus	Hamilton	C,T	State	Coed	2,324	61		38			Y	Y	Y	S	Y	Y	Y	Y	Y	N	10	14
Miami University–Middletown Campus	Middletown	C,T	State	Coed	2,296	55		40	65		Y	Y	Y	Y	Y	Y	Y	Y	Y	N	13	48
Muskingum Area Technical College	Zanesville	T	St & Loc	Coed	2,135	65		45			Y	Y	Y	Y	Y	Y	Y	Y	Y	N	4	21
North Central Technical College	Mansfield	T	State	Coed	2,601	57	56	60			Y	Y	S	Y	Y	Y	Y	Y	Y	N	7	28
Northwestern College	Lima	C	Ind	Coed	1,800	11		14		40	Y	Y	Y	R	Y		Y	Y	Y	Y	5	9
Northwest State Community College	Archbold	C,T	State	Coed	1,991	68		52	58		Y	Y	Y	Y	Y	Y	Y	Y	Y	N	3	23
Ohio Institute of Photography and Technology	Dayton	T	Prop	Coed	373	19	78	23	75		N	Y		Y	Y	Y	Y	Y	Y	N	0	3
Ohio State U Agricultural Technical Institute	Wooster	T	State	Coed	783	14		26	65		Y	Y			Y	Y	Y	Y	Y	Y	5	21
Ohio University–Southern Campus	Ironton	C,T,B	State	Coed	2,102	45		56			Y	Y		R	Y		Y			N	6	5
Owens Community College	Findlay	C,T	State	Coed	1,767	67		50			Y	Y	Y	R,S	Y	Y	Y	Y	Y	N	10	36
Owens Community College	Toledo	C,T	State	Coed	9,682	66		48			Y	Y	Y	R,S	Y	Y	Y	Y	Y	N	11	51
Professional Skills Institute	Toledo	T	Prop	Prim W	120	8		60			Y	Y	Y	Y				Y	Y	N	0	1
RETS Tech Center	Centerville	C,T	Prop	Coed	443	0	85	50	70		Y	Y		Y	Y	Y		Y	Y	N	0	10
Sawyer College of Business	Cleveland	C	Prop	Prim W	212	0					N	Y	Y		Y	Y		Y	Y	N	0	8
Sawyer College of Business	Cleveland Heights	T	Prop	Prim W	223	5		50			N	Y	Y	Y	Y	Y	Y	Y	Y	N	0	5
Sinclair Community College	Dayton	C,T	St & Loc	Coed	19,817	69	32	60			Y	Y		S	Y	Y	Y	Y	Y	N	9	71
Southern Ohio College, Cincinnati Campus	Cincinnati	T	Prop	Coed	440	18		65			N	Y		Y	Y	Y	Y	Y	Y	N	0	10
Southern Ohio College, Northeast Campus	Akron	T	Prop	Coed	300	40	67	70		9	N	Y		Y	Y	Y	Y	Y	Y	N	0	5
Southern State Community College	Hillsboro	C,T	State	Coed	1,468	49		48	42		Y	Y	Y	R,S	Y	Y	Y	Y	Y	N	9	17
Southwestern College of Business	Cincinnati	T	Prop	Coed	190	6					N	Y		S	Y	Y		Y	Y	N	0	11
Southwestern College of Business	Cincinnati	C,T	Prop	Coed	252	4	95	41			N	Y		S	Y	Y		Y	Y	N	0	5
Southwestern College of Business	Dayton	T	Prop	Coed	200	1					N	Y		S	Y	Y	Y	Y	Y	N	0	5
Southwestern College of Business	Middletown	T	Prop	Coed	187	10		75				Y	Y					Y	Y	N	0	4
Stark Technical College	Canton	T	St & Loc	Coed	4,164	61		62			Y	Y	Y	R	Y		Y	Y	Y	N	7	32
Terra State Community College	Fremont	C,T	State	Coed	2,628	56		50			Y	Y		Y	Y	Y	Y	Y	Y	N	8	36
The University of Akron–Wayne College	Orrville	C,T	State	Coed	1,458	56		61			Y	Y		R,S	Y	Y	Y	Y	Y	N	4	10
University of Cincinnati Clermont College	Batavia	C,T	State	Coed	1,997	54		50			Y	Y	Y	R,S	Y	Y	Y	Y	Y	N	6	19
University of Cincinnati Raymond Walters College	Cincinnati	C,T	State	Coed	2,838	61	45	55	52		Y	Y	Y	R,S	Y	Y	Y	Y	Y	N	14	37
Virginia Marti College of Fashion and Art†	Lakewood	T	Prop	Coed	200	37		40			N	Y		Y	Y	Y	Y	Y	Y	N	0	5
Washington State Community College	Marietta	C,T	State	Coed	2,019	46		51	67	90	Y	Y	R,S	Y	Y		Y	Y	Y	N	3	29
West Side Institute of Technology	Cleveland	C,T	Prop	Prim M	14																	
Wright State University, Lake Campus	Celina	C,T	State	Coed	650	52	46	52			Y	Y	Y	Y	Y	Y	Y	Y	Y	N	3	31
Oklahoma																						
Bacone College	Muskogee	C,T	Ind-R	Coed	386	30		50		80	Y	Y	Y	Y	Y	Y	Y	Y	Y	Y	9	13
Carl Albert State College	Poteau	C,T	State	Coed	1,933	60					Y	Y	Y	Y	Y	Y	Y	Y	Y	Y	4	25
Connors State College	Warner	C,T	State	Coed	2,317	35		45			Y		S	S	Y	Y	Y	Y		Y	6	36
Eastern Oklahoma State College	Wilburton	C,T	State	Coed	2,474	43		31		80	Y	Y	Y	Y	Y	Y	Y	Y	Y	Y	10	50
Murray State College	Tishomingo	C,T	State	Coed	1,701	44					Y		Y	Y	Y	Y	Y	Y	Y	Y	8	31
National Ed Ctr–Spartan Sch of Aeronautics Cmps	Tulsa	T	Prop	Prim M	1,110			32		2	Y	Y	Y	Y	Y	Y	Y	Y	Y	N	8	7
Northeastern Oklahoma A&M College	Miami	C,T	State	Coed	2,200	25		35	50	70	Y	Y	Y	Y	Y	Y	Y	Y	Y	Y	6	63
Northern Oklahoma College	Tonkawa	C,T	State	Coed	2,350	44		40	75		Y	Y	Y	Y	Y	Y	Y	Y		Y	9	17
Oklahoma City Community College	Oklahoma City	C,T	State	Coed	10,586	68	27	50	28	30	Y	Y		S	Y	Y	Y	Y	Y	N	11	44
Oklahoma State University, Oklahoma City	Oklahoma City	C,T	State	Coed	4,357	70		80		30	Y	Y		S	Y	Y	Y	Y	Y	N	1	34
Oklahoma State U, Okmulgee	Okmulgee	T	State	Coed	2,188	30	70	40	48		Y		Y	Y	Y	Y	Y	Y	Y	Y	4	31
Redlands Community College	El Reno	C,T	State	Coed	1,901	51	47	37	63	54	Y	Y	Y	Y	Y	Y	Y	Y	Y	N	2	63
Rogers State College	Claremore	C,T	State	Coed	3,204	64		58			Y	Y	Y	Y	Y	Y	Y	Y	Y	Y	1	38
Rose State College	Midwest City	C,T	St & Loc	Coed	9,083	68		60	36		Y	Y	Y	R	Y	Y	Y	Y	Y	N	7	41
St Gregory's College	Shawnee	C,T	Ind-R	Coed	335	26		16	41	91	N	Y	Y	Y	Y	Y	Y	Y		Y	14	19
Seminole Junior College	Seminole	C,T	State	Coed	1,700	38		42			Y	Y		S	Y	Y	Y	Y		Y	2	13
Southwestern Oklahoma State University at Sayre	Sayre	C,T	St & Loc	Coed	623	35	75	45		75	Y	Y	Y	Y	Y	Y	Y	Y	Y	N	5	8
Tulsa Junior College	Tulsa	C,T	State	Coed	21,147	78		50			Y	Y		Y	Y	Y	Y	Y	Y	N	10	114
Western Oklahoma State College	Altus	C,T	State	Coed	1,718	45		50			Y		Y	S	Y	Y	Y	Y		N	6	36
Oregon																						
Blue Mountain Community College	Pendleton	C,T	St & Loc	Coed	3,808	71		59			Y	Y	Y	Y	Y	Y		Y	Y	N	7	21

This index includes the names and locations of accredited two-year colleges in the United States and U.S. territories and shows institutions' responses to our 1996 Survey of Undergraduate Institutions. If an institution submitted incomplete or no data, one or more columns opposite the institution's name is blank. An asterisk after the school name denotes a Special Announcement following the college's profile, and a dagger indicates that the institution has one or more entries in the In-Depth Descriptions of the Colleges section.

Y—Yes; N—No; R—Recommended; S—For Some

		Degrees Awarded (Transfer Associate (C), Terminal Associate (T), Bachelor's (B), Master's (M), Doctoral (D), First Professional (F))	Institutional Control (Independent, Independent-Religious, Proprietary, Federal, State, Province, Commonwealth, Territory, County, District, City, State and Local, State-Related)	Student Body (Men, Primarily Men, Women, Primarily Women, Coeducational)	Undergraduate Enrollment Fall 1995	Percent Attending Part-Time	Percent Receiving Need-Based Financial Aid	Percent 25 Years of Age or Older	Freshman Retention Rate	Percent of Grads Going on to 4-Year Colleges	Open Admissions	High School Equivalency Certificate Accepted	High School Transcript Required	Entrance Test(s) Required	College Scholarships Available	Loans Available	Part-Time Jobs Available	Job Placement Services Available	Career Counseling Available	College Housing Available	Number of Sports Offered	Number of Majors Offered
Central Oregon Community College*	Bend	C,T	Dist	Coed	3,240	62	36	53		50	Y	Y	R		Y	Y	Y	Y	Y	Y	16	44
Chemeketa Community College	Salem	C,T	St & Loc	Coed	9,784	80	50	61			Y	Y		S	Y	Y	Y	Y	Y	N	7	78
Clackamas Community College	Oregon City	C,T	Dist	Coed	6,933	69		51	50		Y	Y	R	R	Y	Y	Y	Y	Y	N	8	45
Clatsop Community College	Astoria	C	County	Coed	2,474	83		66			Y			Y	Y	Y	Y	Y		N	6	12
ITT Technical Institute	Portland	T,B	Prop	Coed	498	0		31		3	N	Y			Y	Y	Y	Y	Y	N	3	4
Lane Community College	Eugene	C,T	St & Loc	Coed	9,533	59	26	51			Y	Y			Y	Y	Y	Y	Y	N	15	39
Linn-Benton Community College	Albany	C,T	St & Loc	Coed	5,453	61		57			Y			Y	Y	Y	Y	Y	Y	N	4	38
Mt Hood Community College	Gresham	C,T	St & Loc	Coed	7,171	70	25	56			Y	Y		S	Y	Y	Y	Y	Y	N	18	42
Oregon Polytechnic Institute	Portland	T	Prop	Coed	200	1		65			Y	Y	Y	Y	Y	Y	Y	Y	Y	N	0	3
Portland Community College	Portland	C,T	St & Loc	Coed	22,840	68		67			Y				Y	Y	Y	Y	Y	N	15	53
Rogue Community College	Grants Pass	C,T	St & Loc	Coed	1,804	60	70	57	43		Y				Y	Y	Y	Y	Y	N	5	21
Southwestern Oregon Community College	Coos Bay	C,T	St & Loc	Coed	1,534	51		46			Y	Y	S		Y	Y	Y	Y		N	6	21
Treasure Valley Community College	Ontario	C,T	St & Loc	Coed	2,348	75		45	65		Y	Y			Y	Y	Y	Y	Y	Y	4	41
Umpqua Community College	Roseburg	C,T	St & Loc	Coed	2,100	40	56			35	Y	Y	R		Y	Y	Y	Y	Y	N	4	55
Pennsylvania																						
Allentown Business School	Allentown	C,T	Prop	Coed	1,000	0		20			Y	Y		S	Y	Y		Y	Y	N	0	8
American Institute of Design	Philadelphia	T	Prop	Coed	350	5		10			N	Y	R		Y	Y	Y	Y	Y	N	2	5
Antonelli Institute	Erdenheim	C,T	Prop	Coed	200	5	65	17	82		Y	Y	Y		Y	Y	Y	Y	Y	Y	0	4
The Art Institute of Philadelphia*†	Philadelphia	C,T	Prop	Coed	1,700	2		5				Y	Y		Y	Y	Y	Y	Y	Y	0	8
Art Institute of Pittsburgh*	Pittsburgh	C,T	Prop	Coed	2,100	0					Y	Y	Y		Y	Y		Y	Y	Y	0	25
Berean Institute	Philadelphia	T	Ind	Coed	319	20		25			Y	Y	Y		Y	Y	Y	Y	Y	N	1	7
Bradley Academy for the Visual Arts†	York	T	Prop	Coed	266	5	35	18	73		N	Y	Y		Y	Y	Y	Y	Y	N	0	8
Bucks County Community College	Newtown	C,T	County	Coed	9,500	72		49		90	Y	Y			Y	Y	Y	Y	Y	N	15	60
Butler County Community College	Butler	C,T	County	Coed	3,133	52	50	40	65		Y	Y			Y	Y	Y	Y	Y	N	11	43
Cambria-Rowe Business College	Johnstown	C,T	Prop	Coed	235	1		40		2	N	Y	Y		Y	Y	Y	Y	Y	N	0	5
Central Pennsylvania Business School	Summerdale	C,T	Prop	Coed	574	11		3	67	4	Y	Y	Y	S	Y	Y	Y	Y	Y	Y	7	17
CHI Institute	Southampton	T	Prop	Coed	550	33		50			N	Y	S			Y		Y	Y	N	0	5
CHI Institute, RETS Campus	Broomall	C,T	Prop	Coed	440	0		30			N	Y	Y	Y		Y	Y	Y	Y	N	0	1
Churchman Business School	Easton	C,T	Prop	Coed	205	3		1			N	Y	Y			Y		Y	Y	N	0	6
Comm Coll of Allegheny County Allegheny Campus*†	Pittsburgh	C,T	County	Coed	5,701	56		45	45	28	Y	Y	R		Y	Y	Y	Y	Y	N	7	81
Comm Coll of Allegheny County Boyce Campus†	Monroeville	C,T	County	Coed	3,725	61		55	45	28	Y	Y	R		Y		Y	Y	Y	N	4	51
Comm Coll of Allegheny County North Campus†	Pittsburgh	C,T	County	Coed	4,374	71		50	45	28	Y	Y	R		Y	Y	Y	Y	Y	N	11	52
Comm Coll of Allegheny County South Campus†	West Mifflin	C,T	County	Coed	4,567	61		40	45	28	Y	Y	R		Y	Y	Y	Y	Y	N	9	117
Community College of Beaver County	Monaca	C,T	State	Coed	2,497	49		56		59	Y	Y	R	S	Y	Y	Y	Y	Y	N	7	34
Community College of Philadelphia	Philadelphia	C,T	St & Loc	Coed	18,713	71	38	53			Y	Y	S		Y	Y	Y	Y	Y	N	8	54
Dean Institute of Technology	Pittsburgh	T	Prop	Coed	200	36	90	15		2	Y	Y			Y	Y		Y	Y	N	0	2
Delaware County Community College*†	Media	C,T	St & Loc	Coed	9,807	68	20	48	54	71	Y	Y	Y		Y	Y	Y	Y	Y	N	9	35
DuBois Business College	DuBois	T	Prop	Prim W	230	1		40	82		N	Y	Y		Y	Y		Y	Y	N	2	5
Duff's Business Institute	Pittsburgh	C,T	Prop	Prim W	600	15		40		10	N	Y		Y	Y	Y	Y	Y	Y	N	1	10
Electronic Institute	Middletown	C,T	Ind	Coed	109	0		14	82		N	Y	Y		Y	Y		Y	Y	N	0	2
Electronic Institutes	Pittsburgh	C,T	Ind	Prim M	113	0		25	75		N	Y	Y		Y	Y		Y	Y	N	0	3
Erie Business Center, Main	Erie	T	Prop	Coed	353	4		20	40	5	N	Y	Y	Y	Y	Y	Y	Y	Y	Y	0	12
Erie Business Center South	New Castle	C,T	Prop	Coed	80	2			80		N	Y		R		Y	Y	Y	Y	N	4	10
Harcum College*†	Bryn Mawr	C,T	Ind	Prim W	661	29	51	23		37	N	Y	Y	S	Y	Y	Y	Y	Y	Y	4	24
Harrisburg Area Community College	Harrisburg	C,T	St & Loc	Coed	10,726	63		47		73	Y	Y	Y	S	Y	Y	Y	Y	Y	N	11	66
Hussian School of Art	Philadelphia	T	Prop	Coed	130	3		2			N	Y	Y		Y	Y	Y	Y	Y	N	0	2
ICM School of Business	Pittsburgh	C,T	Prop	Coed	493	0		45			N	Y	Y	Y	Y	Y	Y	Y	Y	N	0	13
ICS Center for Degree Studies	Scranton	T	Prop	Coed				80			Y	Y	Y							N	0	11
Johnson Technical Institute	Scranton	T	Ind	Prim M	308	3		11	78		N	Y	Y	R	Y	Y	Y	Y	Y	Y	6	13
Keystone College*†	La Plume	C,T	Ind	Coed	875	44	54	41	54		N	Y		R	Y	Y	Y	Y	Y	Y	14	29
Lackawanna Junior College	Scranton	C	Ind	Coed	740	35		43		80	Y	Y	Y	R	Y		Y	Y	Y	N	7	13
Lansdale School of Business	North Wales	T	Prop	Coed	350	60		50	90		N	Y				Y		Y	Y	N	0	10
Lehigh Carbon Community College	Schnecksville	C,T	St & Loc	Coed	4,397	55		54	75	53	Y	Y	S		Y	Y	Y	Y	Y	N	18	46
Lincoln Technical Institute	Allentown	T	Prop	Coed	650	0					Y	Y	Y		Y	Y	Y	Y	Y	N	0	2
Lincoln Technical Institute	Philadelphia	T	Prop	Prim M	200						Y	Y	Y		Y	Y	Y	Y	Y	N	0	2
Luzerne County Community College	Nanticoke	C,T	County	Coed	6,407	62	60	51		40	Y	Y	R		Y	Y	Y	Y	Y	N	9	56
Manor Junior College*†	Jenkintown	C,T	Ind-R	Coed	659	23		14		54	N	Y	Y	S	Y	Y	Y	Y	Y	Y	3	25
McCann School of Business	Mahanoy City	C,T	Prop	Coed	205	32		36	93		N	Y	Y		Y	Y		Y	Y	N	0	6
McCarrie Schools of Health Sci and Tech	Philadelphia	T	Prop	Coed	427			30			N	Y			Y	Y		Y	Y	N	0	6
Median School of Allied Health Careers	Pittsburgh	T	Prop	Coed	83	0	84	37			N	Y	Y	Y	Y	Y	Y	Y	Y	N	0	1
Montgomery County Community College	Blue Bell	C,T	County	Coed	8,751	71	18	47	50		Y	Y			Y	Y	Y	Y	Y	N	14	43
Newport Business Institute	Lower Burrell	T	Prop	Coed	215	1		25		4	Y	Y	Y		Y	Y		Y	Y	N	0	12
Northampton County Area Community College	Bethlehem	C,T	St & Loc	Coed	5,857	64	40	48	58	56	Y	Y	Y		Y	Y	Y	Y	Y	Y	9	41
Peirce College*†	Philadelphia	C,T	Ind	Coed	1,154	32	75	35		25	N	Y		R	Y	Y	Y	Y	Y	Y	0	9
Penn Commercial, Inc	Washington	C	Prop	Coed	230	4		50	95		Y	Y	Y		Y	Y		Y	Y	N	0	5
Pennco Tech	Bristol	C,T	Prop	Coed		0					N	Y			Y	Y	Y	Y	Y	N	0	4
Pennsylvania College of Technology*†	Williamsport	C,T,B	St-R	Coed	4,729	24		35	63		Y	Y	Y	S	Y	Y	Y	Y	Y	N	18	60
Pennsylvania Institute of Technology	Media	C,T	Ind	Coed	540	40		16			Y	Y	Y	R	Y	Y	Y	Y	Y	N	1	12
Penn State U Abington-Ogontz Campus	Abington	T	St-R	Coed	3,149	38		25	78		N	Y	Y	Y	Y	Y	Y	Y	Y	N	13	7
Penn State U Allentown Campus	Fogelsville	T	St-R	Coed	583	24		13	78		N	Y	Y	Y	Y	Y	Y	Y	Y	N	8	1
Penn State U Altoona Campus	Altoona	T	St-R	Coed	2,895	12		14	78		N	Y	Y	Y	Y	Y	Y	Y	Y	Y	7	10
Penn State U Beaver Campus	Monaca	T	St-R	Coed	836	8		6	78		N	Y	Y	Y	Y	Y	Y	Y	Y	Y	12	9
Penn State U Berks Campus	Reading	T	St-R	Coed	1,708	19		14	78		N	Y	Y	Y	Y	Y	Y	Y	Y	Y	8	9
Penn State U Delaware County Campus	Media	C,T,B	St-R	Coed	1,531	27		20	78		N	Y		Y	Y	Y	Y	Y	Y	N	10	3
Penn State U DuBois Campus	DuBois	T	St-R	Coed	915	27		32	78		N	Y	Y	Y	Y	Y	Y	Y	Y	N	7	12
Penn State U Fayette Campus	Uniontown	T	St-R	Coed	994	28		33	78		N	Y	Y	Y	Y	Y	Y	Y	Y	N	9	9
Penn State U Hazleton Campus	Hazleton	T	St-R	Coed	1,314	8		7	78		N	Y	Y	Y	Y	Y	Y	Y	Y	Y	11	10
Penn State U McKeesport Campus	McKeesport	T	St-R	Coed	876	21		21	78		N	Y	Y	Y	Y	Y	Y	Y	Y	Y	13	9
Penn State U Mont Alto Campus	Mont Alto	T	St-R	Coed	1,127	22		23	78		N	Y	Y	Y	Y	Y	Y	Y	Y	Y	4	8
Penn State U New Kensington Campus	New Kensington	T	St-R	Coed	980	35		36	78		N	Y	Y	Y	Y	Y	Y	Y	Y	N	6	11
Penn State U Schuylkill Campus	Schuylkill Haven	T	St-R	Coed	1,040	31		24	78		N	Y	Y	Y	Y	Y	Y	Y	Y	Y	12	11

This index includes the names and locations of accredited two-year colleges in the United States and U.S. territories and shows institutions' responses to our 1996 Survey of Undergraduate Institutions. If an institution submitted incomplete or no data, one or more columns opposite the institution's name is blank. An asterisk after the school name denotes a Special Announcement following the college's profile, and a dagger indicates that the institution has one or more entries in the In-Depth Descriptions of the Colleges section.

Y—Yes; N—No; R—Recommended; S—For Some

Institution	Location	Degrees Awarded: Transfer Associate (C), Terminal Associate (T), Bachelor's (B), Master's (M), Doctoral (D), First Professional (F)	Institutional Control: Independent, Independent-Religious, Proprietary, Federal, State, Province, Commonwealth, Territory, County, District, City, State and Local, State-Related	Student Body: Men, Primarily Men, Women, Primarily Women, Coeducational	Undergraduate Enrollment Fall 1995	Percent Attending Part-Time	Percent Receiving Need-Based Financial Aid	Percent 25 Years of Age or Older	Freshman Retention Rate	Percent of Grads Going on to 4-Year Colleges	Open Admissions	High School Equivalency Certificate Accepted	High School Transcript Required	Entrance Test(s) Required	College Scholarships Available	Loans Available	Part-Time Jobs Available	Career Counseling Available	Job Placement Services Available	College Housing Available	Number of Sports Offered	Number of Majors Offered
Penn State U Shenango Campus	Sharon	T	St-R	Coed	976	44		52	78		N	Y	Y	Y	Y	Y	Y	Y	Y	N	6	11
Penn State U Wilkes-Barre Campus	Lehman	T	St-R	Coed	777	21		18	78		N	Y	Y	Y	Y	Y	Y	Y	Y	N	6	8
Penn State U Worthington Scranton Campus	Dunmore	T	St-R	Coed	1,115	23		21	78		N	Y	Y	Y	Y	Y	Y	Y	Y	N	8	6
Penn State U York Campus	York	T	St-R	Coed	1,896	55		46	78		N	Y	Y	Y	Y	Y	Y	Y	Y	N	9	8
Penn Technical Institute	Pittsburgh	C,T	Prop	Prim M	150	20					N	Y			Y	Y			Y	N	0	1
Pittsburgh Institute of Aeronautics	Pittsburgh	C,T	Ind	Prim M	350	0		45			Y	Y			Y	Y		Y	Y	N	0	3
Pittsburgh Institute of Mortuary Science, Inc	Pittsburgh	C,T	Ind	Coed	130	4		50	25		Y		Y		Y	Y	Y	Y	Y	N	0	1
Pittsburgh Technical Institute	Pittsburgh	T	Prop	Coed	657	0	75	8	93		N	Y	Y	R	Y	Y	Y	Y	Y	N	3	7
Reading Area Community College	Reading	C,T	County	Coed	3,000	73		56	52		Y	Y			Y	Y	Y	Y	Y	N	4	58
Remington Education Center–Vale Campus	Blairsville	C,T	Ind	Prim M	298	0		30			N	Y	Y		Y	Y	Y	Y	Y	Y	0	1
Thaddeus Stevens State School of Technology	Lancaster	T	State	Prim M	427	0	20	25		15	N	Y		Y	Y	Y	Y	Y	Y	Y	14	15
Thompson Institute	Harrisburg	T	Prop	Coed	400	18		25	80		Y	Y	Y		Y	Y	Y	Y	Y	Y	4	7
Triangle Tech, Inc	Pittsburgh	T	Prop	Coed	360	0					N	Y			Y	Y	Y	Y	Y	N	0	5
Triangle Tech, Inc–DuBois School	DuBois	T	Prop	Prim M	325	0		18			N	Y			Y	Y	Y	Y	Y	N	0	4
Triangle Tech, Inc–Erie School	Erie	C,T	Prop	Prim M	215	0		40		2	Y	Y	Y	Y	Y	Y	Y	Y		N	5	4
Triangle Tech, Inc–Greensburg Center	Greensburg	T	Prop	Coed	225	1		20			N	Y			Y	Y	Y	Y	Y	N	0	4
University of Pittsburgh–Titusville	Titusville	C,T	St-R	Coed	299	20	80	30			N	Y	Y	Y	Y	Y	Y	Y	Y	Y	14	6
Valley Forge Military College*†	Wayne	C	Ind	Men	182	0		1	70	96	N	Y	Y	Y	Y	Y	Y	Y		Y	10	5
Welder Training and Testing Institute	Allentown	T	Prop	Prim M	300	31					N	Y		Y	Y	Y		Y	Y	N	0	1
Westmoreland County Community College	Youngwood	C,T	County	Coed	6,026	55		55	60		Y	Y			Y		Y	Y	Y	N	12	55
The Williamson Free School of Mechanical Trades	Media	T	Ind	Men	254	0		0			N	Y		Y				Y	Y	Y	12	7
Williamsport School of Commerce	Williamsport	T	Prop	Prim W	134	1					N	Y				Y		Y	Y	N	0	4
Rhode Island																						
Community College of Rhode Island	Warwick	C,T	State	Coed	12,184	62		55			Y	Y			Y	Y	Y	Y	Y	N	14	46
New England Institute of Technology	Warwick	C,T,B	Ind	Coed	2,354			36			Y	Y	Y		Y	Y	Y	Y	Y	N	0	20
South Carolina																						
Aiken Technical College	Aiken	C,T	St & Loc	Coed	2,258	57	30	49	51	30	Y	Y	Y	S	Y	Y	Y	Y	Y	N	3	17
Central Carolina Technical College	Sumter	C,T	State	Coed	2,189	54	80	47		10	Y	S	Y	S	Y	Y	Y	Y	Y	N	0	14
Chesterfield-Marlboro Technical College	Cheraw	C,T	St & Loc	Coed	1,030	67	26	50		14	Y	Y	Y	Y	Y	Y	Y	Y	Y	Y	0	12
Columbia Junior College of Business	Columbia	T	Prop	Coed	400	21	60	14			Y	Y	Y	R	Y	Y	Y	Y	Y	Y	0	9
Denmark Technical College	Denmark	C	State	Coed	842	24	98	20		10	Y	Y	Y	Y	Y	Y	Y	Y	Y	Y	5	7
Florence-Darlington Technical College	Florence	C,T	State	Coed	3,125	53		38			Y	Y	S	S	Y	Y	Y	Y	Y	N	0	27
Forrest Junior College	Anderson	T	Prop		104																0	
Greenville Technical College	Greenville	C,T	State	Coed	8,734	56	31	42			Y	Y		R	Y	Y	Y	Y	Y	N	3	39
Horry-Georgetown Technical College	Conway	C,T	St & Loc	Coed	3,194	37				10	Y	Y	S	Y	Y	Y	Y	Y	Y	N	1	20
Midlands Technical College	Columbia	C,T	St & Loc	Coed	9,834	58		46			N	Y	R	Y	Y	Y	Y	Y	Y	N	4	29
Nielsen Electronics Institute	Charleston	T	Prop	Coed	260	0		29			N	Y		R	Y			Y	Y	Y	1	1
Orangeburg-Calhoun Technical College	Orangeburg	C,T	St & Loc	Coed	1,768	43	65	37	54		Y	Y		R	Y		Y	Y	Y	N	6	29
Piedmont Technical College	Greenwood	C,T	State	Coed	3,148	52		44		10	Y	Y	Y		Y	Y	Y	Y	Y	N	3	32
Spartanburg Methodist College	Spartanburg	C,T	Ind-R	Coed	878	18		1		91	N	Y		Y	Y	Y	Y	Y	Y	Y	10	6
Spartanburg Technical College	Spartanburg	C,T	State	Coed	2,500	50		41			Y	Y	Y	Y	Y		Y	Y	Y	N	0	18
Technical College of the Lowcountry	Beaufort	C,T	State	Coed	1,600																	
Tri-County Technical College	Pendleton	C,T	State	Coed	3,179	51	30	52			Y	Y		S	Y	Y	Y	Y	Y	N	0	22
Trident Technical College	Charleston	C,T	St & Loc	Coed	9,110	65	50	50			Y	Y		Y	Y	Y	Y	Y	Y	N	0	34
U of South Carolina at Beaufort	Beaufort	C	State	Coed	1,223	65		50			Y	Y	Y	S	Y	Y	Y	Y	Y	N	4	2
U of South Carolina at Lancaster	Lancaster	C,T	State	Coed	1,153	62		37		42	Y	Y	Y	Y	Y	Y	Y	Y		N	7	7
U of South Carolina at Sumter	Sumter	C,T	State	Coed	1,396	48	69	41	40	68	N	Y	Y	Y	Y	Y	Y	Y		N	11	2
U of South Carolina at Union	Union	C	State	Coed	400	44		48			Y		Y	Y	Y	Y	Y			N	0	2
U of South Carolina Salkehatchie Regional Cmps	Allendale	C	State	Coed	908	54		32	42	60	Y	Y	Y	Y	Y	Y	Y	Y		N	5	3
Williamsburg Technical College	Kingstree	C,T	State	Coed	625	77		60	42	23	Y	Y		Y	Y		Y	Y	Y	N	6	5
York Technical College	Rock Hill	C,T	State	Coed	3,342	57	46	47			Y	Y		Y	Y		Y	Y	Y	N	0	27
South Dakota																						
Central Indian Bible College	Mobridge	C,T	Ind-R	Coed	25		100	95				Y	Y		Y	Y	Y			Y	0	1
Kilian Community College	Sioux Falls	C,T	Ind	Coed	202	64	90	62		10	Y	Y	Y		Y	Y	Y	Y	Y	N	0	13
Lake Area Vocational-Technical Institute	Watertown	C,T	State	Coed	1,044				90		N		Y	S	Y	Y	Y	Y	Y	N	0	23
Mitchell Technical Institute	Mitchell	C	Dist	Coed							N		Y	Y							0	2
Nettleton Career College	Sioux Falls	T	Prop	Coed	134	9	78	30			N	Y	Y	Y	Y	Y	Y	Y	Y	N	0	9
Sisseton-Wahpeton Community College	Sisseton	C,T	Fed	Coed	224	25		75	73		Y	Y	Y	R	Y	Y	Y	Y	Y	N	0	13
Southeast Technical Institute	Sioux Falls	C	State	Coed	2,581						N	Y									0	4
Western Dakota Technical Institute	Rapid City	T	State	Coed	842	17	72	38	68	4	Y		Y	Y	Y	Y	Y	Y	Y	N	0	12
Tennessee																						
American Academy of Nutrition	Knoxville	C	Prop	Coed	150	91		87			Y		S								0	1
Aquinas College	Nashville	C,T	Ind-R	Coed	408	56		41			N	Y	Y	Y	Y	Y	Y	Y	Y	N	2	3
Chattanooga State Technical Community College	Chattanooga	C,T	State	Coed	8,676	63		50			Y	Y	Y	S	Y	Y	Y	Y	Y	N	5	66
Cleveland State Community College	Cleveland	C,T	State	Coed	3,670	59	30	48	55	30	Y	Y	Y	S	Y	Y	Y	Y	Y	N	8	14
Columbia State Community College	Columbia	C,T	State	Coed	3,755	54		38	41		Y	Y	Y	S	Y	Y	Y	Y	Y	N	6	36
Cumberland School of Technology	Cookeville	C	Prop	Coed	47				95		N	Y	Y	R	Y	Y		Y	Y		0	2
Draughons Junior College	Clarksville	T	Prop	Coed	300						Y	Y	Y	R							0	
Draughons Junior College	Nashville	C,T	Prop	Coed	440	20		50	65		Y	Y	Y	R	Y	Y	Y	Y	Y	N	0	12
Dyersburg State Community College	Dyersburg	C,T	State	Coed	2,079	44		39	49		Y	Y	Y	S	Y	Y	Y	Y	Y	N	2	5
Fugazzi College	Nashville	T	Prop		150							Y								N	0	
Hiwassee College	Madisonville	C,T	Ind-R	Coed	479	31	80	13	58	90	N	Y	Y	Y	Y	Y	Y	Y		Y	9	67
ITT Technical Institute	Knoxville	T,B	Prop	Coed	364						N	Y						Y	Y	N	0	1
ITT Technical Institute	Memphis	T	Prop	Coed	170	0		28			N	Y	Y	Y			Y	Y	Y	N	0	2
ITT Technical Institute	Nashville	C,T,B	Prop	Coed	475	0		29			N	Y	Y	Y	Y	Y	Y	Y	Y	N	0	2

This index includes the names and locations of accredited two-year colleges in the United States and U.S. territories and shows institutions' responses to our 1996 Survey of Undergraduate Institutions. If an institution submitted incomplete or no data, one or more columns opposite the institution's name is blank. An asterisk after the school name denotes a Special Announcement following the college's profile, and a dagger indicates that the institution has one or more entries in the In-Depth Descriptions of the Colleges section.

Y—Yes; N—No; R—Recommended; S—For Some

Institution	Location	Degrees Awarded: Transfer Associate (C), Terminal Associate (T), Bachelor's (B), Master's (M), Doctoral (D), First Professional (F)	Institutional Control: Independent, Independent-Religious, Proprietary, Federal, State, Province, Commonwealth, Territory, County, District, City, State and Local, State-Related	Student Body: Men, Primarily Men, Women, Primarily Women, Coeducational	Undergraduate Enrollment Fall 1995	Percent Attending Part-Time	Percent Receiving Need-Based Financial Aid	Percent 25 Years of Age or Older	Freshman Retention Rate	Percent of Grads Going on to 4-Year Colleges	Open Admissions	High School Equivalency Certificate Accepted	High School Transcript Required	Entrance Test(s) Required	College Scholarships Available	Loans Available	Part-Time Jobs Available	Career Counseling Available	Job Placement Services Available	College Housing Available	Number of Sports Offered	Number of Majors Offered
Jackson State Community College	Jackson	C,T	State	Coed	3,438	55	32	46		80	Y	Y	S	S	Y		Y	Y	Y	N	5	51
John A Gupton College	Nashville	C	Ind	Coed	78	0					N	Y	Y	Y		Y		Y	Y	N	0	1
Knoxville Business College	Knoxville	C,T	Prop	Coed	711	5		60	62	9	N	Y	Y	R	Y	Y	Y	Y	Y	N	0	11
Mid-America Baptist Theological Seminary	Germantown																					
Motlow State Community College	Tullahoma	C,T	State	Coed	3,129	48		43			Y	Y	Y	S	Y	Y	Y	Y	Y	N	5	36
Nashville State Technical Institute	Nashville	T	State	Coed	6,386	81		71			Y	Y	Y	Y	Y	Y	Y	Y	Y	N	2	17
Northeast State Technical Community College	Blountville	C,T	State	Coed	3,488	50		40	62	85	Y	Y	Y	Y	Y	Y	Y	Y	Y	N	0	17
Pellissippi State Technical Community College	Knoxville	C,T	State	Coed	7,468	52	28	41		45	Y	Y	Y	R,S	Y	Y	Y	Y	Y	N	6	27
Roane State Community College	Harriman	C,T	State	Coed	5,803	50		52			Y	Y	Y	S	Y	Y	Y	Y	Y	N	4	37
Shelby State Community College	Memphis	C	State	Coed	6,350	52	63	46			Y	Y	Y	S	Y	Y	Y	Y	Y	N	3	16
State Technical Institute at Memphis	Memphis	T	State	Coed	10,569	74	16	66	50		Y	Y			Y		Y	Y	Y	N	0	23
Tennessee Institute of Electronics	Knoxville	T	Prop	Coed	90	30		20			Y	Y	S			Y			Y	N	0	4
Volunteer State Community College	Gallatin	C,T	State	Coed	6,583	58	34	48	48		Y	Y	Y	S	Y	Y	Y	Y	Y	N	3	13
Walters State Community College	Morristown	C,T	State	Coed	5,824	56		45	75	85	Y	Y		Y	Y	Y	Y	Y	Y	N	1	18
Watkins Institute of Interior Design	Nashville	C	Ind	Coed							Y	Y	Y		Y		Y			N	0	5
Texas																						
Alvin Community College	Alvin	C,T	St & Loc	Coed	3,864	63		48			Y	Y			Y	Y	Y	Y	Y	N	4	30
Amarillo College	Amarillo																					
Angelina College	Lufkin	C,T	St & Loc	Coed	3,984	50		58	35		Y	Y	Y	Y	Y	Y	Y	Y	Y	Y	11	54
Art Institute of Dallas*†	Dallas	T	Prop	Coed	1,200	0		5			Y	Y	Y	Y	Y	Y	Y	Y	Y	Y	0	7
The Art Institute of Houston	Houston	C,T	Prop	Coed	1,189	0	85		89		N	Y	Y	R	Y	Y	Y	Y	Y	Y	0	8
Austin Community College	Austin	C,T	Dist	Coed	25,275	75		28			Y	Y	R	R	Y	Y	Y	Y	Y	N	5	70
Bee County College	Beeville	C,T	County	Coed	2,417	43	48	45			Y	Y	Y	S	Y		Y	Y	Y	Y	11	55
Blinn College	Brenham	C,T	St & Loc	Coed	9,165	48		18	34	55	Y	Y	Y	S	Y	Y	Y	Y		Y	9	28
Brazosport College	Lake Jackson	C,T	St & Loc	Coed	3,104	73		48			Y	Y			Y	Y	Y	Y	Y	N	5	49
Brookhaven College	Farmers Branch	C,T	County	Coed	9,060	75		52			Y			R,S	Y	Y	Y	Y	Y	N	10	16
Cedar Valley College	Lancaster	C,T	State	Coed	3,136	74					Y	Y	R	R	Y	Y	Y	Y	Y	N	3	8
Central Texas College	Killeen	C,T	St & Loc	Coed	8,600	70		55			Y	Y	Y	R	Y	Y	Y	Y	Y	Y	11	92
Cisco Junior College	Cisco	C,T	St & Loc	Coed	2,553	44		45	45		Y	Y		R	Y	Y	Y	Y		Y	6	35
Clarendon College	Clarendon	C,T	St & Loc	Coed	811	44		43			Y	Y	Y	Y	Y	Y	Y	Y	Y	Y	7	14
The College of Saint Thomas More	Fort Worth	C,T	Ind-R	Coed	15						Y	Y	Y	Y	Y					N	0	4
College of the Mainland	Texas City	C,T	St & Loc	Coed	3,564	70		60			Y	Y		S	Y	Y	Y	Y	Y	N	7	18
Collin County Community College	McKinney	C,T	St & Loc	Coed	10,300	69	35	48		36	Y	Y	Y	S	Y	Y		Y	Y	N	8	63
Commonwealth Institute of Funeral Service	Houston	T	Ind	Coed	130			30			N	Y	Y			Y		Y	Y	N	0	1
Computer Career Center	El Paso	C	Prop	Coed	230						Y	Y		R							0	1
Dallas Institute of Funeral Service	Dallas	C,T	Ind	Coed	225						Y	Y									0	1
Del Mar College	Corpus Christi	C,T	St & Loc	Coed	10,757	66		68			Y	Y		Y	Y	Y	Y	Y	Y	N	14	78
Eastfield College	Mesquite	C,T	St & Loc	Coed	8,458	71		51			Y	Y			Y	Y	Y	Y	Y	N	7	17
El Centro College	Dallas	C,T	County	Coed	4,593	74	32	51	47	34	Y	Y	Y	R	Y	Y	Y	Y	Y	N	3	31
El Paso Community College	El Paso	C,T	County	Coed	22,264	55		48		39	Y		R	R	Y	Y	Y	Y	Y	N	9	64
Frank Phillips College	Borger	C,T	St & Loc	Coed	1,108	25		45			Y	Y	Y	Y	Y	Y	Y	Y	Y	Y	4	60
Galveston College	Galveston	C,T	St & Loc	Coed	2,218	71		50			Y	Y	S	Y	Y	Y	Y	Y	Y	N	5	28
Grayson County College	Denison	C,T	St & Loc	Coed	3,286	67		53			Y	Y		R,S	Y	Y	Y	Y		Y	3	50
Hill College of the Hill Junior College District	Hillsboro	C,T	Dist	Coed	2,500	40		40		60	Y	Y		R	Y	Y	Y	Y	Y	Y	6	83
Houston Community College System	Houston	C,T	St & Loc	Coed	39,541	73		61	37	22	Y	Y		R,S	Y	Y	Y	Y	Y	N	12	56
Howard College	Big Spring	C,T	St & Loc	Coed	2,400	57		26	75		Y	Y	Y	S	Y	Y	Y	Y	Y	Y	6	37
ITT Technical Institute	Arlington	T	Prop	Coed	336	0		72			N	Y		Y	Y	Y		Y	Y	N	0	2
ITT Technical Institute	Austin	T	Prop	Coed	465			30			N	Y	Y	Y	Y		Y	Y	Y	N	0	2
ITT Technical Institute	Garland	T	Prop	Coed	379						N	Y	Y	Y	Y	Y	Y	Y	Y	N	0	2
ITT Technical Institute	Houston	C,T	Prop	Coed	316	0	82	22		7	N	Y	S		Y	Y	Y	Y	Y	N	3	2
ITT Technical Institute	Houston	T	Prop	Coed	600	0		44			N	Y		Y	Y	Y	Y	Y	Y	N	0	3
ITT Technical Institute	San Antonio	C	Prop	Coed	464						N	Y	Y	Y				Y	Y	N	0	2
Jacksonville College	Jacksonville	C,T	Ind-R	Coed	325	19		20		85	Y	Y		Y	Y	Y		Y		Y	4	2
KD Studio	Dallas	T	Prop	Coed		0		24	49	4	Y	Y	Y					Y		N	0	1
Kilgore College	Kilgore																					
Kingwood College	Kingwood	C,T	St & Loc	Coed	3,400	66		57			Y	Y		R	Y	Y		Y		N	0	8
Lamar University–Orange	Orange	C,T	State	Coed	1,489	60			42		Y	Y	Y	R	Y	Y	Y	Y		N	0	15
Lamar University–Port Arthur	Port Arthur	C,T	State	Coed	2,233	59	36	45			Y	Y	Y		Y	Y	Y	Y	Y	N	0	20
Laredo Community College	Laredo	C,T	St & Loc	Coed	6,919	57			59		Y		Y		Y	Y	Y	Y	Y	Y	8	23
Lee College	Baytown	C,T	Dist	Coed	5,753	64		52		5	Y		S	S	Y	Y	Y	Y	Y	N	8	37
Lon Morris College	Jacksonville	C	Ind-R	Coed	350	4		4			N	Y	Y	Y	Y	Y	Y	Y		Y	8	51
McLennan Community College	Waco	C,T	County	Coed	5,561	54		55			Y	Y	Y	S	Y	Y	Y	Y	Y	N	7	29
Midland College	Midland	C,T	St & Loc	Coed	3,763	65	42	55	65	80	Y	Y	Y	Y	Y	Y	Y	Y	Y	N	7	62
Miss Wade's Fashion Merchandising College	Dallas	C	Prop	Coed	226	0	85	27	65	35	N	Y	Y		Y	Y	Y	Y	Y	Y	0	5
Montgomery College	Conroe	C,T	St & Loc	Coed	3,196		20		75		Y	Y			Y	Y	Y	Y		N	0	18
Mountain View College	Dallas	C,T	County	Coed	6,027	70		40			Y	Y	S	R	Y	Y	Y	Y	Y	N	5	16
Navarro College	Corsicana	C,T	St & Loc	Coed	3,211	47		35			Y	Y		R	Y	Y	Y	Y	Y	Y	9	56
North Central Texas College	Gainesville	C,T	County	Coed	4,133	74	25	49	40		Y	Y		R,S	Y	Y	Y	Y		Y	9	30
Northeast Texas Community College	Mount Pleasant	C,T	St & Loc	Coed	1,952	54		48			Y	Y		S	Y	Y	Y	Y	Y	Y	5	17
North Harris College	Houston	C,T	St & Loc	Coed	3,080	70		48			Y	Y	Y	Y	Y	Y	Y	Y	Y	N	8	41
North Lake College	Irving	C,T	County	Coed	6,400	75		53			Y	Y	R		Y	Y	Y	Y	Y	N	4	16
Odessa College	Odessa	C,T	St & Loc	Coed	4,679	67	20	44	48	42	Y	Y			Y	Y	Y	Y	Y	Y	12	56
Palo Alto College	San Antonio	C,T	St & Loc	Coed	7,499	70		46			Y	Y	Y	Y	Y	Y	Y	Y	Y	N	0	38
Panola College	Carthage																					
Paris Junior College	Paris	C,T	St & Loc	Coed	2,450	50		41			Y	Y	Y	R,S	Y		Y	Y	Y	Y	7	22
Ranger College	Ranger	C,T	St-R	Coed	856	30	38				Y	Y		R	Y	Y	Y	Y	Y	Y	7	6
Richland College	Dallas	C,T	St & Loc	Coed	13,391	73		47			Y		S	R	Y	Y	Y	Y	Y	N	12	16
St Philip's College	San Antonio	C,T	Dist	Coed	72,128	66		58			Y	Y	Y	R	Y	Y	Y	Y	Y	N	0	61
San Antonio College	San Antonio	C,T	St & Loc	Coed	21,238	64		54			Y	Y		S	Y	Y	Y	Y	Y	N	9	33
San Jacinto College–Central Campus	Pasadena	C,T	St & Loc	Coed		67		48			Y	Y	Y	R,S	Y	Y	Y	Y	Y	N	7	85
San Jacinto College–North Campus	Houston	C,T	St & Loc	Coed	4,211	69		39			Y	Y			Y	Y	Y	Y	Y	N	5	42

Peterson's Guide to Two-Year Colleges 1997
45

This index includes the names and locations of accredited two-year colleges in the United States and U.S. territories and shows institutions' responses to our 1996 Survey of Undergraduate Institutions. If an institution submitted incomplete or no data, one or more columns opposite the institution's name is blank. An asterisk after the school name denotes a Special Announcement following the college's profile, and a dagger indicates that the institution has one or more entries in the In-Depth Descriptions of the Colleges section.

Y—Yes; N—No; R—Recommended; S—For Some

		Degrees Awarded Transfer Associate (C), Terminal Associate (T), Bachelor's (B), Master's (M), Doctoral (D), First Professional (F)	**Institutional Control** Independent, Independent-Religious, Proprietary, Federal, State, Province, Commonwealth, Territory, County, District, City, State and Local, State-Related	**Student Body** Men, Primarily Men, Women, Primarily Women, Coeducational	**Undergraduate Enrollment Fall 1995**	Percent Attending Part-Time	Percent Receiving Need-Based Financial Aid	Percent 25 Years of Age or Older	Freshman Retention Rate	Percent of Grads Going on to 4-Year Colleges	Open Admissions	High School Equivalency Certificate Accepted	High School Transcript Required	Entrance Test(s) Required	College Scholarships Available	Loans Available	Part-Time Jobs Available	Career Counseling Available	Job Placement Services Available	College Housing Available	Number of Sports Offered	Number of Majors Offered
San Jacinto College–South Campus	Houston	C,T	St & Loc	Coed	5,411	75		50			Y	Y			Y	Y	Y	Y	Y	N	10	38
South Plains College	Levelland	C,T	St & Loc	Coed	5,703	47	40	45		90	Y	Y		R	Y	Y	Y	Y	Y	Y	9	59
SouthWest Collegiate Institute for the Deaf	Big Spring	C,T	State	Coed	100	7		21		10	Y		Y	Y	Y	Y	Y	Y	Y	Y	6	32
Southwest Texas Junior College	Uvalde	C,T	St & Loc	Coed	3,256	35					Y	Y			Y	Y	Y	Y	Y	Y	7	14
Tarrant County Junior College	Fort Worth	C,T	County	Coed	26,584	72	8	48	41	65	Y			Y	Y	Y	Y	Y	Y	N	5	43
Temple College	Temple	C,T	Dist	Coed	2,450	60		54			Y		S	S	Y	Y	Y	Y	Y	Y	6	20
Texarkana College	Texarkana	C,T	St & Loc	Coed	4,038	59		42		25	Y	Y		S	Y		Y	Y	Y	N	7	32
Texas Southmost College	Brownsville	C,T	Dist	Coed	6,564	47		32			Y	Y		Y	Y	Y	Y	Y	Y	N	12	27
Texas State Tech Coll	Sweetwater	T	State	Coed	860	24	77	50	33		Y	Y	Y	Y	Y	Y	Y	Y	Y	Y	4	11
Texas State Tech Coll–Harlingen Campus	Harlingen	T	State	Coed	3,056	44	78	29	16		Y	Y	Y		Y	Y	Y	Y	Y	Y	13	23
Texas State Tech Coll–Waco/Marshall Campus	Waco	C,T	State	Coed	3,313	20		36			Y	Y	Y	Y	Y	Y	Y	Y	Y	Y	7	28
Tomball College	Tomball	C,T	St & Loc	Coed	3,641	65		46	56	77	Y	Y	Y	R	Y	Y	Y	Y		N	0	18
Trinity Valley Community College	Athens	C,T	St & Loc	Coed	4,786	68		51			Y	Y		Y	Y	Y	Y	Y	Y	Y	5	54
Tyler Junior College	Tyler	C,T	St & Loc	Coed	7,984	31		38			Y	S		R	Y	Y	Y	Y	Y	Y	9	53
Vernon Regional Junior College	Vernon	C,T	St & Loc	Coed	1,721	64		43			Y	Y		Y	Y		Y	Y	Y	Y	8	19
Victoria College	Victoria	C,T	County	Coed	3,643	61		49			Y	Y		Y	Y	Y		Y	Y	N	2	12
Weatherford College	Weatherford	C,T	St & Loc	Coed	2,277	50		56	46		Y	Y		Y	Y	Y	Y	Y	Y	Y	3	13
Western Texas College	Snyder	C,T	St & Loc	Coed	1,200	54		45			Y	Y	Y	Y	Y	Y	Y	Y	Y	Y	11	22
Wharton County Junior College	Wharton	C,T	St & Loc	Coed	3,720	40		38			Y	Y	Y	Y	Y	Y	Y	Y	Y	Y	2	29
Utah																						
College of Eastern Utah	Price	C,T	State	Coed	3,067	51		36	30		Y	Y			Y	Y	Y	Y	Y	Y	7	15
Dixie College	St George	C,T	State	Coed	2,902	23		16	43		Y	Y	Y		Y	Y	Y	Y	Y	Y	8	86
ITT Technical Institute	Murray	T,B	Prop	Coed	540	0		48			N	Y			Y	Y	Y	Y	Y	N	0	3
LDS Business College	Salt Lake City	C,T	Ind-R	Coed	830	23	50	28			Y	Y	Y		Y		Y	Y	Y	Y	0	13
Phillips Junior College	Salt Lake City	T	Prop	Coed	275							Y	Y	R						N	0	7
Salt Lake Community College	Salt Lake City	C,T	State	Coed	19,568	63		39			Y			Y	Y	Y	Y	Y	Y	N	14	73
Snow College	Ephraim	C	State	Coed	2,491	31		10	42		Y	Y	Y	Y	Y	Y	Y	Y		Y	11	67
Stevens Henager College	Ogden	T	Prop	Coed	175	43		50			Y	Y	Y	R	Y	Y	Y	Y	Y	N	0	5
Utah Valley State College	Orem	C,T,B	State	Coed	14,041	55		23	47		Y		R	R	Y	Y	Y	Y	Y	N	14	34
Vermont																						
Champlain College†	Burlington	C,T,B	Ind	Coed	2,085	39	61	32	77	30	N	Y	Y	R	Y	Y	Y	Y	Y	Y	6	26
Community College of Vermont	Waterbury	C,T	State	Coed	3,024	89	85	75			Y	Y			Y	Y	Y	Y		N	0	14
Landmark College	Putney	C,T	Ind	Coed	240	0	40	12		100	N	Y			Y	Y	Y	Y		Y	16	1
New England Culinary Institute*	Montpelier	T,B	Prop	Coed	450	0		53			N	Y	Y	R	Y	Y	Y	Y	Y	Y	0	2
Sterling College	Craftsbury Common	C,T	Ind	Coed	82	0	70	7			N	Y	Y	R	Y	Y	Y	Y	Y	Y	4	7
Vermont Technical College*†	Randolph Center	C,T,B	State	Coed	746	9	62	25	67	23	N	Y	Y	Y	Y	Y	Y	Y	Y	Y	19	23
Woodbury College	Montpelier	C	Ind	Coed	140	20	95	100	95	20	Y	Y	Y		Y		Y			N	0	2
Virginia																						
Blue Ridge Community College	Weyers Cave	C,T	State	Coed	2,736	81	2	56		86	Y	Y		R	Y	Y	Y	Y	Y	N	4	14
Central Virginia Community College	Lynchburg	C,T	State	Coed	4,038	77		42			Y			Y	Y	Y	Y	Y	Y	N	2	24
Commonwealth College, Hampton	Hampton	T	Prop	Coed	272																	
Commonwealth College, Richmond	Richmond	T	Prop	Coed	453																	
Commonwealth College, Virginia Beach	Virginia Beach	T	Prop	Coed	358																	
Comm Hospital Roanoke Valley–Coll of Health Scis	Roanoke	C,T,B	Ind	Coed	561	54		66			N	Y	Y	Y	Y	Y	Y	Y	Y	Y	0	7
Dabney S Lancaster Community College	Clifton Forge	C,T	State	Coed	1,722	65		59		60	Y	Y		Y	Y	Y	Y	Y	Y	N	9	17
Danville Community College	Danville	C,T	State	Coed	3,869	75		56			Y	Y	Y	S	Y	Y	Y	Y	Y	N	5	9
Eastern Shore Community College	Melfa	C,T	State	Coed	684	65		45		50	Y	Y	Y		Y	Y	Y	Y	Y	N	2	7
ECPI College of Technology	Hampton	T	Prop	Coed	285	40	80	64			N	Y			Y	Y	Y	Y	Y	N	0	18
ECPI College of Technology	Virginia Beach	T	Prop	Coed	720	48	78	72			N	Y			Y	Y	Y	Y	Y	N	0	22
ECPI Computer Institute	Richmond	T	Prop	Coed	450	37	76	52			N	Y			Y	Y	Y	Y	Y	N	0	20
ECPI Computer Institute	Roanoke	T	Prop	Coed	180	35	74	49			N	Y			Y	Y	Y	Y	Y	N	0	18
Germanna Community College	Locust Grove	C,T	State	Coed	2,596	69	25	53		80	Y	Y	S		Y	Y	Y	Y	Y	N	6	10
ITT Technical Institute	Norfolk	T	Prop	Coed	266																	
Johnson & Wales University	Norfolk	T	Ind	Coed	538	1	95	37			N		Y	S	Y	Y	Y	Y	Y	Y	0	1
John Tyler Community College	Chester	C,T	State	Coed	5,367	81	22	64	50		Y	Y	R		Y	Y	Y	Y		N	4	16
J Sargeant Reynolds Community College	Richmond	C,T	State	Coed	9,160	80		67			Y		Y		Y		Y	Y	Y	N	3	35
Lord Fairfax Community College	Middletown	C,T	State	Coed	3,292	74		59			Y		R		Y	Y	Y	Y	Y	N	3	15
Mountain Empire Community College	Big Stone Gap	C,T	State	Coed	2,700	58		30	60	90	Y	Y	Y		Y		Y	Y	Y	N	4	35
National Business College	Bluefield	T	Prop	Coed	165	18		25			Y	Y	Y		Y	Y	Y	Y	Y	N	0	9
National Business College	Bristol	T	Prop	Coed	81	29	93	40			Y	Y	Y		Y	Y	Y	Y	Y	N	0	2
National Business College	Charlottesville	T	Prop	Coed	99	18		25			Y	Y	Y		Y	Y	Y	Y	Y	N	0	8
National Business College	Danville	T	Prop	Coed	158	18	70	30			Y	Y	Y		Y	Y	Y	Y	Y	N	0	10
National Business College	Harrisonburg	T	Prop	Coed	86	18		25			Y	Y	Y		Y	Y	Y	Y	Y	N	0	9
National Business College	Lynchburg	T	Prop	Coed	106	7		50			Y	Y	Y		Y	Y	Y	Y	Y	N	0	9
National Business College	Martinsville	T	Prop	Coed	148	5		25			Y	Y	Y		Y	Y	Y	Y	Y	N	0	7
National Business College	Roanoke	C,T,B	Prop	Coed	362	55	70	30			Y	Y		R	Y	Y	Y	Y	Y	Y	0	12
New River Community College	Dublin	C,T	State	Coed	1,554	58		45		75	Y	Y	S		Y	Y	Y	Y	Y	N	9	27
Northern Virginia Community College	Annandale	C,T	State	Coed	38,084	75		57			Y	S	S		Y	Y	Y	Y	Y	N	5	58
Patrick Henry Community College	Martinsville	C,T	State	Coed	2,800	69		52			Y	Y	Y		Y	Y	Y	Y	Y	N	4	11
Paul D Camp Community College	Franklin	C,T	State	Coed	1,629	82	46	55	62		Y	Y	Y		Y		Y	Y	Y	N	3	6
Piedmont Virginia Community College	Charlottesville	C,T	State	Coed	4,436	81		60			Y	Y	S		Y	Y	Y	Y	Y	N	4	18
Rappahannock Community College	Glenns	C,T	St-R	Coed	2,129	81		68			Y			Y	Y	Y	Y	Y	Y	N	5	9
Richard Bland Coll of the Coll of William and Mary	Petersburg	C	State	Coed	1,205	30		20	50	88	N	Y	Y	R	Y	Y	Y	Y	Y	N	6	3
Southside Virginia Community College	Alberta	C,T	State	Coed	1,697	76	52	53			Y	Y	Y	S	Y	Y	Y	Y	Y	N	5	12
Southwest Virginia Community College	Richlands	C,T	State	Coed	4,235	61		57			Y	Y	Y	Y	Y	Y	Y	Y	Y	N	5	18
Thomas Nelson Community College	Hampton	C,T	State	Coed	7,192	73	33	62			Y	Y	Y	R	Y	Y	Y	Y	Y	N	5	28
Tidewater Community College	Portsmouth	C,T	State	Coed	16,780	72		60		65	Y				Y	Y	Y	Y	Y	N	2	22

46 *Peterson's Guide to Two-Year Colleges 1997*

This index includes the names and locations of accredited two-year colleges in the United States and U.S. territories and shows institutions' responses to our 1996 Survey of Undergraduate Institutions. If an institution submitted incomplete or no data, one or more columns opposite the institution's name is blank. An asterisk after the school name denotes a Special Announcement following the college's profile, and a dagger indicates that the institution has one or more entries in the In-Depth Descriptions of the Colleges section.

Y—Yes; N—No; R—Recommended; S—For Some

Institution	Location	**Degrees Awarded** Transfer Associate (C), Terminal Associate (T), Bachelor's (B), Master's (M), Doctoral (D), First Professional (F)	**Institutional Control** Independent, Independent-Religious, Proprietary, Federal, State, Province, Commonwealth, Territory, County, District, City, State and Local, State-Related	**Student Body** Men, Primarily Men, Women, Primarily Women, Coeducational	**Undergraduate Enrollment Fall 1995**	Percent Attending Part-Time	Percent Receiving Need-Based Financial Aid	Percent 25 Years of Age or Older	Freshman Retention Rate	Percent of Grads Going on to 4-Year Colleges	Open Admissions	High School Equivalency Certificate Accepted	High School Transcript Required	Entrance Test(s) Required	College Scholarships Available	Loans Available	Part-Time Jobs Available	Career Counseling Available	Job Placement Services Available	College Housing Available	Number of Sports Offered	Number of Majors Offered
Virginia College	Salem	T	Prop	Coed	80						N	Y	Y	Y	Y	Y	Y			N	0	3
Virginia Highlands Community College	Abingdon	C,T	State	Coed	1,891	53	75	52		65	Y	Y	Y	R,S	Y		Y	Y	Y	N	6	19
Virginia Western Community College	Roanoke	C,T	State	Coed	6,845	75		64			Y		Y	R	Y	Y	Y	Y	Y	N	1	25
Wytheville Community College	Wytheville	C,T	State	Coed	2,600	60		58			Y		Y		Y	Y	Y	Y	Y	N	6	22
Washington																						
Art Institute of Seattle	Seattle	T	Prop	Coed	1,965	6		26			Y	Y		R	Y	Y	Y	Y	Y	Y	0	13
Bellevue Community College	Bellevue	C,T	State	Coed	10,099	47		47			Y	Y			Y	Y	Y	Y	Y	N	10	18
Big Bend Community College	Moses Lake	C,T	State	Coed	1,872	46		46			Y	Y	S		Y	Y	Y	Y		Y	6	21
Centralia College	Centralia	C,T	State	Coed	1,800	5		69			Y	Y		Y	Y	Y	Y	Y	Y	N	3	43
Clark College	Vancouver	C,T	State	Coed	10,300	50		50		50	Y	Y		Y	Y	Y	Y	Y	Y	N	6	91
Columbia Basin College	Pasco	C,T	State	Coed	6,580	53		50		30	Y	Y	Y	S	Y	Y	Y	Y	Y	N	8	21
Edmonds Community College	Lynnwood	C,T	St & Loc	Coed	9,194	58		66			Y			S	Y	Y	Y	Y	Y	Y	8	39
Everett Community College	Everett	C,T	State	Coed	7,788	54		52			Y	Y	R		Y	Y	Y	Y	Y	N	4	77
Grays Harbor College	Aberdeen	C,T	State	Coed	2,815	23	85	29			Y	Y		Y	Y		Y	Y	Y	N	6	45
Green River Community College	Auburn	C,T	State	Coed	8,000	69		51			Y		S	Y	Y	Y	Y	Y	Y	N	10	37
Highline Community College	Des Moines	C,T	State	Coed	7,271	42	60	50			Y	Y		R	Y	Y	Y	Y	Y	N	6	39
ITT Technical Institute	Seattle	T,B	Prop	Coed	484	0		36			N	Y			Y	Y	Y	Y	Y	N	0	2
ITT Technical Institute	Spokane	T	Prop	Coed	241	0					N	Y		Y	Y	Y	Y	Y	Y	N	1	2
Lake Washington Technical College	Kirkland	C	Dist	Coed	2,787			64			Y	Y	S	Y	Y		Y	Y		N	0	12
Lower Columbia College	Longview	C,T	State	Coed	4,081	40		50			Y		R		Y	Y	Y	Y	Y	N	5	55
North Seattle Community College	Seattle	C,T	State	Coed	8,199	76		73		40	Y				Y	Y	Y	Y	Y	N	6	31
Northwest Indian College	Bellingham	C,T	Fed	Coed	1,500	40	90	75		40	Y		Y	Y	Y		Y	Y	Y	N	3	11
Olympic College	Bremerton	C,T	State	Coed	7,470	52		75			Y	Y			Y	Y	Y	Y	Y	N	4	28
Peninsula College	Port Angeles	C,T	State	Coed	3,550	67		72	67		Y		S	Y	Y	Y	Y	Y	Y	Y	5	13
Phillips Junior College of Spokane	Spokane	C	Prop	Coed	256																	
Pierce College	Tacoma	C,T	State	Coed	10,294	44		56			Y	Y			Y	Y	Y	Y	Y	N	5	21
Pima Medical Institute	Seattle																					
Renton Technical College	Renton	T	State	Coed	810	93		78	70	1	Y			Y	Y	Y	Y	Y	Y	N	0	19
Seattle Central Community College	Seattle	C,T	State	Coed	10,333	51		63			Y	Y			Y	Y	Y	Y		N	6	26
Shoreline Community College	Seattle	C,T	State	Coed	8,575	47	12	45			Y			S	Y	Y	Y	Y	Y	N	15	54
Skagit Valley College	Mount Vernon	C,T	State	Coed	7,200	54		68			Y	Y	Y	Y	Y	Y	Y	Y	Y	N	7	60
South Puget Sound Community College	Olympia	C,T	State	Coed	5,195	53	100	62		32	Y	Y		R	Y	Y	Y	Y	Y	N	3	29
South Seattle Community College	Seattle	C,T	State	Coed	3,892	54		68			Y				Y	Y	Y	Y		N	0	27
Spokane Community College	Spokane	C,T	State	Coed	5,000	14	40	56			Y	Y	R	Y	Y	Y	Y	Y	Y	N	13	56
Spokane Falls Community College	Spokane	C,T	State	Coed	5,300	22	23	55			Y	Y	R	R	Y	Y	Y	Y	Y	N	12	28
Tacoma Community College	Tacoma	C,T	State	Coed	5,461	34	40	53			Y	Y		S	Y	Y	Y	Y	Y	N	11	62
Walla Walla Community College	Walla Walla	C,T	State	Coed	4,772	50		48	53	53	Y	Y	R	Y	Y	Y	Y	Y	Y	N	12	32
Wenatchee Valley College	Wenatchee	C,T	St & Loc	Coed	3,764	39	50	58			Y	Y		Y	Y	Y	Y	Y	Y	Y	11	34
Whatcom Community College	Bellingham	C,T	State	Coed	2,621	47	32	31			Y	Y		Y	Y	Y	Y	Y		N	0	14
Yakima Valley Community College	Yakima	C,T	State	Coed	4,290	41		50			Y	Y	R,S	Y	Y	Y	Y	Y	Y	Y	8	38
West Virginia																						
Huntington Junior College of Business	Huntington	T	Prop	Coed	475	2		40			Y	Y	Y		Y	Y	Y	Y	Y	N	0	11
National Ed Ctr–National Inst of Tech Campus	Cross Lanes	C	Prop	Coed	380	0		10			N	Y	Y		Y	Y		Y	Y	N	0	2
Ohio Valley College	Parkersburg	C,T,B	Ind-R	Coed	314	7		2			N	Y		Y	Y	Y	Y	Y	Y	Y	9	22
Potomac State College of West Virginia University†	Keyser	C,T	State	Coed	1,163	32		16	40		Y	Y	Y	Y	Y	Y	Y	Y	Y	Y	7	48
Southern West Virginia Comm and Tech Coll	Mount Gay	C,T	State	Coed	3,097	45		80			Y	Y		Y	Y		Y	Y	Y	N	0	14
Webster College	Fairmont	C,T	Prop	Coed	204																	
West Virginia Career College	Charleston	T	Prop	Prim W	200	2		40			Y	Y			Y	Y	Y	Y	Y	N	0	8
West Virginia Career College	Morgantown	T	Prop	Coed	200	0		70		5	Y	Y	Y		Y	Y		Y	Y	N	0	3
West Virginia Northern Community College	Wheeling	C,T	State	Coed	2,720	61	46	62			Y	Y	S	S	Y	Y	Y	Y	Y	N	12	22
West Virginia University at Parkersburg	Parkersburg	C,T,B	State	Coed	3,600	48		46		20	Y	Y	S	Y	Y	Y	Y	Y	Y	N	10	22
Wisconsin																						
Blackhawk Technical College	Janesville	C,T	Dist	Coed	3,000	61		60			Y	Y	Y		Y	Y	Y	Y	Y	N	0	16
Chippewa Valley Technical College	Eau Claire	T	Dist	Coed	3,800	10		50		10	Y	Y	Y		Y	Y	Y	Y	Y	N	8	41
Fox Valley Technical College	Appleton	C,T	St & Loc	Coed	6,370	35		54			Y	Y		Y	Y	Y	Y	Y	Y	N	8	35
Gateway Technical College	Kenosha	T	St & Loc	Coed	10,568																	
Herzing College of Technology	Madison	C	Prop	Prim M	350	0		33	60	5	N	Y	Y		Y	Y	Y	Y	Y	N	0	3
ITT Technical Institute	Greenfield	T	Prop	Coed	418						N	Y		Y	Y	Y	Y	Y	Y	N	0	2
Lac Courte Oreilles Ojibwa Community College	Hayward	C,T	Fed	Coed	488	40		68			Y	Y			Y		Y	Y	Y	N	3	8
Lakeshore Technical College	Cleveland	C,T	St & Loc	Coed	2,400	70		55			Y	Y	S	Y	Y	Y	Y	Y	Y	N	3	28
Madison Area Technical College	Madison	C,T	Dist	Coed	19,050	65	25	50	37		Y	Y	S	S	Y	Y	Y	Y	Y	N	9	47
Madison Junior College of Business†	Madison	T	Ind	Coed	99	31		28	50		Y	Y	Y	R	Y	Y	Y	Y	Y	N	0	7
Mid-State Technical College	Wisconsin Rapids	T	St & Loc	Coed	3,104	64		51			Y	Y	Y	Y	Y	Y	Y	Y	Y	N	9	22
Milwaukee Area Technical College	Milwaukee	C,T	Dist	Coed	23,099	74		61			Y	Y	Y	Y	Y	Y	Y	Y	Y	N	12	67
Moraine Park Technical College	Fond du Lac	C,T	St & Loc	Coed	6,670	83		57			Y	Y	Y	Y	Y	Y	Y	Y	Y	N	3	22
Nicolet Area Technical College	Rhinelander	C,T	St & Loc	Coed	1,433	64		64			Y	Y	Y	Y	Y	Y	Y	Y	Y	N	2	22
Northcentral Technical College	Wausau	C,T	Dist	Coed	3,500	67		55			Y	Y	Y	S	Y	Y	Y	Y	Y	N	10	25
Northeast Wisconsin Technical College	Green Bay	T	St & Loc	Coed	8,594																	
Southwest Wisconsin Technical College	Fennimore	T	St & Loc	Coed	3,870	79	70	54	75		Y	Y	Y	Y	Y	Y	Y	Y	Y	N	4	24
Stratton College	Milwaukee	C	Prop	Coed	754	42		41	70	2	N	Y	Y	Y	Y	Y	Y	Y	Y	N	0	13
U of Wisconsin Center–Baraboo/Sauk County	Baraboo	C,T	State	Coed	395	33		30	40	80	N	Y	Y	Y	Y	Y	Y	Y		N	8	1
U of Wisconsin Center–Barron County	Rice Lake	C	State	Coed	518	29		25		92	N	Y	Y	Y	Y	Y	Y	Y		N	11	2
U of Wisconsin Center–Fond du Lac	Fond du Lac	C	State	Coed	550	33		27			N	Y	Y	Y	Y		Y	Y		N	8	1
U of Wisconsin Center–Fox Valley	Menasha	C	State	Coed	1,250	55		40	60		N	Y	Y		Y		Y	Y		N	5	1
U of Wisconsin Center–Manitowoc County	Manitowoc	C	State	Coed	500	30		23	45	80	N	Y			Y	Y	Y	Y		N	4	1
U of Wisconsin Center–Marathon County	Wausau	C	State	Coed	1,011	30	44	26		96	N	Y		Y	Y	Y	Y	Y		Y	19	20
U of Wisconsin Center–Marinette County	Marinette	T	State	Coed	373	37		32		90	Y	Y	Y	Y	Y	Y	Y	Y		N	4	5

Peterson's Guide to Two-Year Colleges 1997
47

State-by-State Summary Table
Wisconsin–Switzerland

This index includes the names and locations of accredited two-year colleges in the United States and U.S. territories and shows institutions' responses to our 1996 Survey of Undergraduate Institutions. If an institution submitted incomplete or no data, one or more columns opposite the institution's name is blank. An asterisk after the school name denotes a Special Announcement following the college's profile, and a dagger indicates that the institution has one or more entries in the In-Depth Descriptions of the Colleges section.

Column legend: Y—Yes; N—No; R—Recommended; S—For Some

Columns: Degrees Awarded (Bachelor's (B), Master's (M), Doctoral (D), First Professional (F), Transfer Associate (C), Terminal Associate (T), State Related); Institutional Control (Federal, Independent, Independent-Religious, Proprietary, County, District, City, State and Local, State, Province, Commonwealth, Territory, Primarily Men, Primarily Women, Coeducational); Student Body; Undergraduate Enrollment Fall 1995; Percent Attending Part-Time; Percent Receiving Need-Based Financial Aid; Percent 25 Years of Age or Older; Percent of Grade Going on to 4-Year Colleges; Freshman Retention Rate; High School Equivalency Open Admissions; High School Transcript Accepted; Entrance Test(s) Required; College Scholarships Required; Career Counseling Available; Part-Time Jobs Available; Loans Available; Job Placement Services Available; College Housing Available; Number of Sports Offered; Number of Majors Offered

Institution	City	Degrees	Control	Student Body	Enroll	PT%	Aid%	25+	4yr	Ret	HSEq	Open	Trans	Test	Schol	Career	PT Jobs	Loans	JobPl	Hous	Sports	Majors
U of Wisconsin Center–Marshfield/Wood County	Marshfield	C	State	Coed	579	35		25			N	Y	Y	Y		Y	Y	Y	Y	Y	N	11	1
U of Wisconsin Center–Richland	Richland Center	C	State	Coed	375	20	60	25	45	65	N	Y	Y	Y	Y	Y	Y	Y	Y	Y	10	2
U of Wisconsin Center–Rock County	Janesville	C,T	State	Coed	875	51		34			N	Y	Y	Y	Y	Y	Y	Y	Y	N	4	1
U of Wisconsin Center–Sheboygan County	Sheboygan	C	State	Coed	458	43		34	71		Y	Y	Y	Y		Y	Y	Y	Y	N	6	1
U of Wisconsin Center–Washington County	West Bend	C	State	Coed	670	36		24		90	Y	Y	R		Y	Y	Y	Y	Y	N	7	1
U of Wisconsin Center–Waukesha County	Waukesha	C	State	Coed	1,681	44		41			Y	Y	Y	Y	Y	Y	Y	Y	Y	N	9	1
Waukesha County Technical College	Pewaukee	T	St & Loc	Coed	4,700	65		90				Y		Y	S	Y	Y	Y	Y	N	9	15
Western Wisconsin Technical College	La Crosse	T	Dist	Coed	4,458	60	63	52				Y	Y			Y	Y	Y	Y	Y	3	50
Wisconsin Indianhead Tech Coll, Ashland Cmps	Ashland	T	Dist	Coed	474	30		50				Y		S	Y	Y	Y	Y	Y	N	0	7
Wisconsin Indianhead Tech Coll, New Richmond Cmps	New Richmond	T	Dist	Coed	1,300	54		55				Y		Y	Y	Y	Y	Y	Y	N	0	8
Wisconsin Indianhead Tech Coll, Rice Lake Cmps	Rice Lake	T	Dist	Coed	1,136	32		52				Y			Y	Y	Y	Y	Y	N	7	13
Wisconsin Indianhead Tech Coll, Superior Cmps	Superior	C	Dist	Coed	800	34		55						Y	Y	Y	Y	Y	Y	N	0	8

Wyoming

Institution	City	Degrees	Control	Student Body	Enroll	PT%	Aid%	25+	4yr	Ret	HSEq	Open	Trans	Test	Schol	Career	PT Jobs	Loans	JobPl	Hous	Sports	Majors
Casper College	Casper	C,T	Dist	Coed	3,743	20		38	50		Y	Y	Y	R,S	Y	Y	Y	Y	Y	Y	18	87
Central Wyoming College	Riverton	C,T	St & Loc	Coed	1,510	56	44	55	69		Y	Y	Y	R		Y	Y	Y	Y	Y	10	43
Eastern Wyoming College	Torrington	C,T	St & Loc	Coed	1,766	71		55		80	Y	Y				Y	Y	Y	Y	Y	11	47
Laramie County Community College	Cheyenne	C,T	County	Coed	4,282	71		60	36		Y	Y	Y			Y	Y	Y	Y	Y	9	49
Northwest College	Powell	C,T	St & Loc	Coed	2,000	34	40	37		59	Y	Y	Y	S		Y	Y	Y	Y	Y	23	85
Sheridan College	Sheridan	C,T	St & Loc	Coed	2,555	57		55			Y	Y	R,S	R		Y	Y	Y	Y	Y	8	34
Western Wyoming Community College	Rock Springs	C,T	St & Loc	Coed	3,094	61		64		42		Y				Y	Y	Y	Y	Y	13	57
Wyoming Technical Institute	Laramie	T	Prop	Prim M	600	0	85				Y	Y	Y			Y		Y	Y	Y	4	1

US TERRITORIES

American Samoa

Institution	City	Degrees	Control	Student Body	Enroll																	
American Samoa Community College	Pago Pago																					

Federated States of Micronesia

Institution	City	Degrees	Control	Student Body	Enroll	PT%	Aid%	25+	4yr	Ret	HSEq	Open	Trans	Test	Schol	Career	PT Jobs	Loans	JobPl	Hous	Sports	Majors
College of Micronesia–FSM	Kolonia Pohnpei		Terr	Coed	853	15	100	3			N	Y	Y	Y	Y	Y	Y	Y	Y	Y	5	8

Guam

Institution	City	Degrees	Control	Student Body	Enroll																	
Guam Community College	Guam Main Facility	C,T	Terr	Coed	723																	

Marshall Islands

College of the Marshall Islands	Majuro

Northern Mariana Islands

Institution	City	Degrees	Control	Student Body	Enroll	PT%	Aid%	25+	4yr	Ret	HSEq	Open	Trans	Test	Schol	Career	PT Jobs	Loans	JobPl	Hous	Sports	Majors
Northern Marianas College	Saipan	C,T	Comm	Coed	954	49	13	36				Y		Y		Y		Y	Y	N	8	13

Palau Island

Institution	City	Degrees	Control	Student Body	Enroll	PT%	Aid%	25+	4yr	Ret	HSEq	Open	Trans	Test	Schol	Career	PT Jobs	Loans	JobPl	Hous	Sports	Majors
Palau Community College	Koror	C,T	Terr	Coed	367	4		8	58		Y		Y			Y	Y	Y	Y	Y	11	10

Puerto Rico

Institution	City	Degrees	Control	Student Body	Enroll	PT%	Aid%	25+	4yr	Ret	HSEq	Open	Trans	Test	Schol	Career	PT Jobs	Loans	JobPl	Hous	Sports	Majors
Huertas Junior College	Caguas	T	Prop	Coed	2,220	34			55		N	Y				Y		Y	Y	Y	N	0	6
Instituto Comercial de Puerto Rico Junior College	Hato Rey																					
Instituto Técnico Comercial Junior College	Río Piedras																					
Inter American U of PR, Guayama Campus	Guayama	T,B	Ind	Coed	1,304	25					N	Y		Y		Y	Y			Y	N	9	10
Ramírez College of Business and Technology	San Juan	C,T	Prop	Coed	1,364	0		24			Y	Y				Y			Y	Y	N	0	4
Technological College of Municipality of San Juan	Hato Rey	C	City	Coed	946	13					N	Y		Y	Y			Y	Y	Y	N	6	8
U of Puerto Rico, Carolina Regional College	Carolina																					
U of Puerto Rico, Colegio Regional de la Montaña	Utuado																					

OTHER COUNTRIES

Republic of Panama

Institution	City	Degrees	Control	Student Body	Enroll	PT%	Aid%	25+	4yr	Ret	HSEq	Open	Trans	Test	Schol	Career	PT Jobs	Loans	JobPl	Hous	Sports	Majors
Panama Canal College	Balboa	C,T	Fed	Coed	878	86		39	7		Y	Y			Y			Y	Y		N	13	9

Switzerland

Institution	City	Degrees	Control	Student Body	Enroll	PT%	Aid%	25+	4yr	Ret	HSEq	Open	Trans	Test	Schol	Career	PT Jobs	Loans	JobPl	Hous	Sports	Majors
Schiller International University	Engelberg	C,T	Ind	Coed	57	2					N	Y				Y	Y		Y		Y	4	2

Associate Degree Programs at Two-Year Colleges

ACCOUNTING
Abraham Baldwin Ag Coll (GA)
Acad of Business Coll (AZ)
Adirondack Comm Coll (NY)
Aiken Tech Coll (SC)
Aims Comm Coll (CO)
Alabama Southern Comm Coll, Monroeville (AL)
Alamance Comm Coll (NC)
Albuquerque Tech Vocational Inst (NM)
Alexandria Tech Coll (MN)
Allan Hancock Coll (CA)
Allegany Comm Coll (MD)
Allen County Comm Coll (KS)
Allentown Business Sch (PA)
Alpena Comm Coll (MI)
Alvin Comm Coll (TX)
American Inst of Business (IA)
American Inst of Commerce (IA)
American River Coll (CA)
Andover Coll (ME)
Angelina Coll (TX)
Anne Arundel Comm Coll (MD)
Anoka-Ramsey Comm Coll (MN)
Anson Comm Coll (NC)
Aquinas Coll at Milton (MA)
Aquinas Coll at Newton (MA)
Arapahoe Comm Coll (CO)
Asheville-Buncombe Tech Comm Coll (NC)
Asnuntuck Comm-Tech Coll (CT)
Athens Area Tech Inst (GA)
Atlanta Metropolitan Coll (GA)
Atlantic Comm Coll (NJ)
Augusta Tech Inst (GA)
Austin Comm Coll (TX)
Bainbridge Coll (GA)
Baker Coll of Jackson (MI)
Bakersfield Coll (CA)
Baltimore City Comm Coll (MD)
Barstow Coll (CA)
Bay de Noc Comm Coll (MI)
Bay State Coll (MA)
Beal Coll (ME)
Beaufort County Comm Coll (NC)
Bee County Coll (TX)
Belleville Area Coll (IL)
Bellevue Comm Coll (WA)
Belmont Tech Coll (OH)
Berean Inst (PA)
Bergen Comm Coll (NJ)
Berkeley Coll (NJ)
Berkeley Coll, New York (NY)
Berkeley Coll, White Plains (NY)
Berkshire Comm Coll (MA)
Bessemer State Tech Coll (AL)
Bevill State Comm Coll (AL)
Big Bend Comm Coll (WA)
Bishop State Comm Coll (AL)
Black Hawk Coll, Moline (IL)
Blackhawk Tech Coll (WI)
Blair Jr Coll (CO)
Blue Mountain Comm Coll (OR)
Blue Ridge Comm Coll (VA)
Borough of Manhattan Comm Coll of City U of NY (NY)

Bowling Green State University–Firelands Coll (OH)
Bradford Sch (OH)
Bramson ORT Tech Inst (NY)
Brevard Coll (NC)
Brevard Comm Coll (FL)
Briarwood Coll (CT)
Bristol Comm Coll (MA)
Bronx Comm Coll of City U of NY (NY)
Brookdale Comm Coll (NJ)
Brookhaven Coll (TX)
Broome Comm Coll (NY)
Broward Comm Coll (FL)
The Brown Mackie Coll (KS)
The Brown Mackie Coll-Olathe Cmps (KS)
Brunswick Coll (GA)
Bryant and Stratton Business Inst, Albany (NY)
Bryant and Stratton Business Inst, Buffalo (NY)
Bryant and Stratton Business Inst, Cicero (NY)
Bryant and Stratton Business Inst, Lackawanna (NY)
Bryant and Stratton Business Inst, Rochester (NY)
Bryant and Stratton Business Inst, Rochester (NY)
Bryant and Stratton Business Inst, Syracuse (NY)
Bryant and Stratton Business Inst, E Hills Cmps, Williamsville (NY)
Bryant and Stratton Coll, Parma (OH)
Bryant and Stratton Coll, Richmond Heights (OH)
Bucks County Comm Coll (PA)
Bunker Hill Comm Coll (MA)
Burlington County Coll (NJ)
Butler County Comm Coll (KS)
Butler County Comm Coll (PA)
Butte Coll (CA)
Cabrillo Coll (CA)
Caldwell Comm Coll and Tech Inst (NC)
Cambria-Rowe Business Coll (PA)
Camden County Coll (NJ)
Cañada Coll (CA)
Cape Cod Comm Coll (MA)
Cape Fear Comm Coll (NC)
Capital Comm Tech Coll (CT)
Carl Albert State Coll (OK)
Carl Sandburg Coll (IL)
Casco Bay Coll (ME)
Casper Coll (WY)
Castle Coll (NH)
Catawba Valley Comm Coll (NC)
Catonsville Comm Coll (MD)
Cayuga County Comm Coll (NY)
Cecil Comm Coll (MD)
Cedar Valley Coll (TX)
Central Carolina Comm Coll (NC)
Central Carolina Tech Coll (SC)
Central City Business Inst (NY)
Central Coll (KS)

Central Comm College–Grand Island Cmps (NE)
Central Comm College–Hastings Cmps (NE)
Central Comm College–Platte Cmps (NE)
Central Florida Comm Coll (FL)
Central Lakes Coll (MN)
Central Ohio Tech Coll (OH)
Central Oregon Comm Coll (OR)
Central Pennsylvania Business Sch (PA)
Central Piedmont Comm Coll (NC)
Central Virginia Comm Coll (VA)
Central Wyoming Coll (WY)
Cerritos Coll (CA)
Chabot Coll (CA)
Chaffey Coll (CA)
Champlain Coll (VT)
Chandler-Gilbert Comm Coll (AZ)
Chaparral Career Coll (AZ)
Charles County Comm Coll (MD)
Charles Stewart Mott Comm Coll (MI)
Charter Coll (AK)
Chattahoochee Tech Inst (GA)
Chattahoochee Valley State Comm Coll (AL)
Chattanooga State Tech Comm Coll (TN)
Chemeketa Comm Coll (OR)
Chesapeake Coll (MD)
Chesterfield-Marlboro Tech Coll (SC)
Chipola Jr Coll (FL)
Chippewa Valley Tech Coll (WI)
Churchman Business Sch (PA)
Cincinnati State Tech and Comm Coll (OH)
Cisco Jr Coll (TX)
City Coll of San Francisco (CA)
City Colls of Chicago, Harold Washington Coll (IL)
City Colls of Chicago, Harry S Truman Coll (IL)
City Colls of Chicago, Kennedy-King Coll (IL)
City Colls of Chicago, Malcolm X Coll (IL)
City Colls of Chicago, Olive-Harvey Coll (IL)
City Colls of Chicago, Richard J Daley Coll (IL)
City Colls of Chicago, Wilbur Wright Coll (IL)
Clackamas Comm Coll (OR)
Clark Coll (WA)
Clark State Comm Coll (OH)
Clatsop Comm Coll (OR)
Cleveland Comm Coll (NC)
Cleveland State Comm Coll (TN)
Clinton Comm Coll (IA)
Clinton Comm Coll (NY)
Clovis Comm Coll (NM)
Coahoma Comm Coll (MS)
Coastal Carolina Comm Coll (NC)

Coconino County Comm Coll (AZ)
Coffeyville Comm Coll (KS)
Colby Comm Coll (KS)
Coll of Alameda (CA)
Coll of DuPage (IL)
Coll of Lake County (IL)
Coll of Marin (CA)
Coll of Micronesia–FSM (FM)
Coll of San Mateo (CA)
Coll of Southern Idaho (ID)
Coll of the Canyons (CA)
Coll of the Mainland (TX)
Coll of the Sequoias (CA)
Coll of the Siskiyous (CA)
Collin County Comm Coll (TX)
Colorado Mountn Coll, Alpine Cmps (CO)
Colorado Mountn Coll, Roaring Fork Cmps-Spring Valley Ctr (CO)
Colorado Mountn Coll, Timberline Cmps (CO)
Columbia-Greene Comm Coll (NY)
Columbia Jr Coll of Business (SC)
Columbia State Comm Coll (TN)
Columbus State Comm Coll (OH)
Columbus Tech Inst (GA)
Commonwealth Business Coll, LaPorte (IN)
Commonwealth Business Coll, Merrillville (IN)
Comm Coll of Allegheny County Allegheny Cmps (PA)
Comm Coll of Allegheny County Boyce Cmps (PA)
Comm Coll of Allegheny County North Cmps (PA)
Comm Coll of Allegheny County South Cmps (PA)
Comm Coll of Aurora (CO)
Comm Coll of Beaver County (PA)
Comm Coll of Denver (CO)
Comm Coll of Philadelphia (PA)
Comm Coll of Rhode Island (RI)
Comm Coll of Southern Nevada (NV)
Comm Coll of the Air Force (AL)
Comm Coll of Vermont (VT)
Computer Career Ctr (TX)
Connors State Coll (OK)
Copiah-Lincoln Comm Coll (MS)
Corning Comm Coll (NY)
Cosumnes River Coll (CA)
County Coll of Morris (NJ)
Cowley County Comm Coll and Voc-Tech Sch (KS)
Crafton Hills Coll (CA)
Craven Comm Coll (NC)
Cumberland County Coll (NJ)
Cuyahoga Comm Coll, Eastern Cmps (OH)
Cuyahoga Comm Coll, Metropolitan Cmps (OH)
Cuyahoga Comm Coll, Western Cmps (OH)
Cuyamaca Coll (CA)
Cypress Coll (CA)

Dalton Coll (GA)
Danville Area Comm Coll (IL)
Danville Comm Coll (VA)
Darton Coll (GA)
Davidson County Comm Coll (NC)
Davis Coll (OH)
Daytona Beach Comm Coll (FL)
Dean Coll (MA)
De Anza Coll (CA)
DeKalb Coll (GA)
DeKalb Tech Inst (GA)
Delaware County Comm Coll (PA)
Delaware Tech & Comm Coll, Jack F Owens Cmps (DE)
Delaware Tech & Comm Coll, Stanton/Wilmington Cmps (DE)
Delaware Tech & Comm Coll, Terry Cmps (DE)
Delgado Comm Coll (LA)
Del Mar Coll (TX)
Delta Coll (MI)
Des Moines Area Comm Coll (IA)
Dixie Coll (UT)
Dodge City Comm Coll (KS)
Donnelly Coll (KS)
Douglas MacArthur State Tech Coll (AL)
Draughons Jr Coll (AL)
Draughons Jr Coll (KY)
Draughons Jr Coll, Nashville (TN)
DuBois Business Coll (PA)
Duff's Business Inst (PA)
Dundalk Comm Coll (MD)
Durham Tech Comm Coll (NC)
Dutchess Comm Coll (NY)
East Central Coll (MO)
East Central Comm Coll (MS)
Eastern Idaho Tech Coll (ID)
Eastern Oklahoma State Coll (OK)
Eastern Wyoming Coll (WY)
Eastfield Coll (TX)
East Los Angeles Coll (CA)
East Mississippi Comm Coll (MS)
ECPI Coll of Tech, Hampton (VA)
ECPI Coll of Tech, Virginia Beach (VA)
ECPI Computer Inst, Richmond (VA)
ECPI Computer Inst, Roanoke (VA)
Edgecombe Comm Coll (NC)
Edison Comm Coll (FL)
Edison State Comm Coll (OH)
Edmonds Comm Coll (WA)
Elaine P Nunez Comm Coll (LA)
El Camino Coll (CA)
El Centro Coll (TX)
Elgin Comm Coll (IL)
Ellsworth Comm Coll (IA)
El Paso Comm Coll (TX)
Erie Business Ctr, Main (PA)
Erie Business Ctr South (PA)
Essex Comm Coll (MD)
Essex County Coll (NJ)
Eugenio María de Hostos Comm Coll of City U of NY (NY)

Everett Comm Coll (WA)
Fayetteville Tech Comm Coll (NC)
Feather River Comm Coll District (CA)
Finger Lakes Comm Coll (NY)
Fiorello H LaGuardia Comm Coll of City U of NY (NY)
Fisher Coll (MA)
Florence-Darlington Tech Coll (SC)
Florida Comm Coll at Jacksonville (FL)
Florida National Coll (FL)
Foothill Coll (CA)
Forsyth Tech Comm Coll (NC)
Fort Berthold Comm Coll (ND)
Fort Scott Comm Coll (KS)
Fox Valley Tech Coll (WI)
Frank Phillips Coll (TX)
Frederick Comm Coll (MD)
Fresno City Coll (CA)
Front Range Comm Coll (CO)
Fullerton Coll (CA)
Fulton-Montgomery Comm Coll (NY)
Gainesville Coll (GA)
Garden City Comm Coll (KS)
Garland County Comm Coll (AR)
Gaston Coll (NC)
Gateway Comm Coll (AZ)
Gateway Comm-Tech Coll (CT)
Gavilan Coll (CA)
Gem City Coll (IL)
Genesee Comm Coll (NY)
George Corley Wallace State Comm Coll, Selma (AL)
George C Wallace State Comm Coll, Dothan (AL)
Germanna Comm Coll (VA)
Glendale Comm Coll (AZ)
Gloucester County Coll (NJ)
Gogebic Comm Coll (MI)
Golden West Coll (CA)
Grand Rapids Comm Coll (MI)
Grays Harbor Coll (WA)
Grayson County Coll (TX)
Great Basin Coll (NV)
Great Lakes Jr Coll of Business (MI)
Greenfield Comm Coll (MA)
Green River Comm Coll (WA)
Greenville Tech Coll (SC)
Grossmont Coll (CA)
Guilford Tech Comm Coll (NC)
Gulf Coast Comm Coll (FL)
Gwinnett Tech Inst (GA)
Hagerstown Business Coll (MD)
Hagerstown Jr Coll (MD)
Hamilton Business Coll (IA)
Harford Comm Coll (MD)
Harrisburg Area Comm Coll (PA)
Haskell Indian Nations U (KS)
Hawkeye Comm Coll (IA)
Heald Business Coll, Concord (CA)
Heald Business Coll, Fresno (CA)
Heald Business Coll, Hayward (CA)

Peterson's Guide to Two-Year Colleges 1997

Associate Degree Programs at Two-Year Colleges

Accounting

Heald Business Coll, Rancho Cordova (CA)
Heald Business Coll, San Francisco (CA)
Heald Business Coll (HI)
Helena Coll of Tech of The U of Montana (MT)
Henry Ford Comm Coll (MI)
Herkimer County Comm Coll (NY)
Herzing Coll of Business and Tech (GA)
Hesser Coll (NH)
Hibbing Comm Coll (MN)
Highland Comm Coll (IL)
Highland Comm Coll (KS)
Highland Park Comm Coll (MI)
Highline Comm Coll (WA)
Hill Coll of the Hill Jr Coll District (TX)
Hillsborough Comm Coll (FL)
Hinds Comm Coll (MS)
Hiwassee Coll (TN)
Hocking Coll (OH)
Holyoke Comm Coll (MA)
Housatonic Comm-Tech Coll (CT)
Houston Comm Coll System (TX)
Howard Coll (TX)
Howard Comm Coll (MD)
Hudson County Comm Coll (NJ)
Hudson Valley Comm Coll (NY)
Huertas Jr Coll (PR)
Huntington Jr Coll of Business (WV)
Hutchinson Comm Coll and Area Vocational Sch (KS)
ICM Sch of Business (PA)
ICS Ctr for Degree Studies (PA)
Illinois Central Coll (IL)
Illinois Eastern Comm Colls, Olney Central Coll (IL)
Illinois Valley Comm Coll (IL)
Imperial Valley Coll (CA)
Independence Comm Coll (KS)
Indiana Business Coll (IN)
Indian River Comm Coll (FL)
Inst of Career Education (FL)
Inter American U of PR, Guayama Cmps (PR)
Interboro Inst (NY)
International Business Coll (IN)
Inver Hills Comm Coll (MN)
Iowa Central Comm Coll (IA)
Iowa Lakes Comm Coll (IA)
Iowa Western Comm Coll (IA)
Irvine Valley Coll (CA)
Itasca Comm Coll (MN)
Itawamba Comm Coll (MS)
ITT Tech Inst, Youngstown (OH)
Ivy Tech State Coll–Central Indiana (IN)
Ivy Tech State Coll–Columbus (IN)
Ivy Tech State Coll–Eastcentral (IN)
Ivy Tech State Coll–Kokomo (IN)
Ivy Tech State Coll–Lafayette (IN)
Ivy Tech State Coll–Northcentral (IN)
Ivy Tech State Coll–Northeast (IN)
Ivy Tech State Coll–Northwest (IN)
Ivy Tech State Coll–Southcentral (IN)
Ivy Tech State Coll–Southeast (IN)
Ivy Tech State Coll–Southwest (IN)
Ivy Tech State Coll–Wabash Valley (IN)
Ivy Tech State Coll–Whitewater (IN)
Jackson Comm Coll (MI)
Jackson State Comm Coll (TN)
James Sprunt Comm Coll (NC)
Jamestown Business Coll (NY)
Jamestown Comm Coll (NY)
Jefferson Coll (MO)
Jefferson Comm Coll (NY)
Jefferson Comm Coll (OH)
Jefferson State Comm Coll (AL)
J F Drake State Tech Coll (AL)
John A Logan Coll (IL)
John C Calhoun State Comm Coll (AL)
Johnson County Comm Coll (KS)
Johnston Comm Coll (NC)
John Tyler Comm Coll (VA)
John Wood Comm Coll (IL)
Joliet Jr Coll (IL)
Jones County Jr Coll (MS)
J Sargeant Reynolds Comm Coll (VA)
Kalamazoo Valley Comm Coll (MI)
Kankakee Comm Coll (IL)
Kansas City Kansas Comm Coll (KS)
Kaskaskia Coll (IL)
Keiser Coll of Tech, Daytona Beach (FL)
Keiser Coll of Tech, Sarasota (FL)
Kellogg Comm Coll (MI)
Kelsey Jenney Coll (CA)
Kent State U, Ashtabula Cmps (OH)
Kent State U, East Liverpool Cmps (OH)
Kent State U, Geauga Cmps (OH)
Kent State U, Salem Cmps (OH)
Kent State U, Trumbull Cmps (OH)
Kent State U, Tuscarawas Cmps (OH)
Kentucky Coll of Business, Lexington (KY)
Keystone Coll (PA)
Kilian Comm Coll (SD)
Kingsborough Comm Coll of City U of NY (NY)
Kings River Comm Coll (CA)
Kingwood Coll (TX)
Kirkwood Comm Coll (IA)
Kirtland Comm Coll (MI)
Knoxville Business Coll (TN)
Labette Comm Coll (KS)
Lackawanna Jr Coll (PA)
Lake Area Vocational-Tech Inst (SD)
Lake City Comm Coll (FL)
Lake Land Coll (IL)
Lakeland Comm Coll (OH)
Lake Michigan Coll (MI)
Lakeshore Tech Coll (WI)
Lake Tahoe Comm Coll (CA)
Lake Washington Tech Coll (WA)
Lakewood Comm Coll (MN)
Lamar Comm Coll (CO)
Lamar University–Orange (TX)
Lamar University–Port Arthur (TX)
Lamson Jr Coll, Mesa (AZ)
Lane Comm Coll (OR)
Laney Coll (CA)
Lansdale Sch of Business (PA)
Lansing Comm Coll (MI)
Laramie County Comm Coll (WY)
Las Positas Coll (CA)
Lassen Coll (CA)
Lawson State Comm Coll (AL)
LDS Business Coll (UT)
Lee Coll (TX)
Lehigh Carbon Comm Coll (PA)
Lenoir Comm Coll (NC)
Lewis and Clark Comm Coll (IL)
Lewis Coll of Business (MI)
Lima Tech Coll (OH)
Lincoln Coll, Normal (IL)
Lincoln Land Comm Coll (IL)
Lincoln Sch of Commerce (NE)
Linn-Benton Comm Coll (OR)
Little Hoop Comm Coll (ND)
Long Beach City Coll (CA)
Longview Comm Coll (MO)
Lon Morris Coll (TX)
Lorain County Comm Coll (OH)
Lord Fairfax Comm Coll (VA)
Los Angeles City Coll (CA)
Los Angeles Harbor Coll (CA)
Los Angeles Mission Coll (CA)
Los Angeles Pierce Coll (CA)
Los Angeles Southwest Coll (CA)
Los Angeles Trade-Tech Coll (CA)
Los Angeles Valley Coll (CA)
Los Medanos Coll (CA)
Lower Columbia Coll (WA)
Luzerne County Comm Coll (PA)
MacCormac Jr Coll (IL)
Macomb Comm Coll (MI)
Macon Coll (GA)
Madison Area Tech Coll (WI)
Madison Jr Coll of Business (WI)
Manatee Comm Coll (FL)
Manchester Comm-Tech Coll (CT)
Manor Jr Coll (PA)
Maple Woods Comm Coll (MO)
Maria Coll (NY)
Marian Court Coll (MA)
Marion Tech Coll (OH)
Marshalltown Comm Coll (IA)
Martin Comm Coll (NC)
Mary Holmes Coll (MS)
Massachusetts Bay Comm Coll (MA)
Massasoit Comm Coll (MA)
Mater Dei Coll (NY)
Mayland Comm Coll (NC)
McCann Sch of Business (PA)
McDowell Tech Comm Coll (NC)
McHenry County Coll (IL)
McIntosh Coll (NH)
McLennan Comm Coll (TX)
Meadows Coll of Business (GA)
Mendocino Coll (CA)
Merced Coll (CA)
Mercer County Comm Coll (NJ)
Merritt Coll (CA)
Mesa Comm Coll (AZ)
Metropolitan Comm Coll (NE)
Miami-Dade Comm Coll (FL)
Miami-Jacobs Coll (OH)
Miami University–Hamilton Cmps (OH)
Miami University–Middletown Cmps (OH)
Michiana Coll (IN)
Middle Georgia Coll (GA)
Middlesex Comm Coll (MA)
Middlesex Community–Tech Coll (CT)
Middlesex County Coll (NJ)
Midland Coll (TX)
Midlands Tech Coll (SC)
Mid Michigan Comm Coll (MI)
Mid-Plains Comm Coll (NE)
Midstate Coll (IL)
Mid-State Coll (ME)
Mid-State Tech Coll (WI)
Milwaukee Area Tech Coll (WI)
Minneapolis Comm Coll (MN)
MiraCosta Coll (CA)
Mission Coll (CA)
Mississippi Delta Comm Coll (MS)
Mississippi Gulf Coast Comm Coll (MS)
Mitchell Coll (CT)
Mitchell Comm Coll (NC)
Mitchell Tech Inst (SD)
Moberly Area Comm Coll (MO)
Modesto Jr Coll (CA)
Mohave Comm Coll (AZ)
Mohawk Valley Comm Coll (NY)
Monroe Coll, Bronx (NY)
Monroe Coll, New Rochelle (NY)
Monroe Comm Coll (NY)
Monroe County Comm Coll (MI)
Montana State U Coll of Tech-Great Falls (MT)
Montcalm Comm Coll (MI)
Monterey Peninsula Coll (CA)
Montgomery Coll (TX)
Montgomery College–Germantown Cmps (MD)
Montgomery College–Rockville Cmps (MD)
Montgomery College–Takoma Park Cmps (MD)
Montgomery Comm Coll (NC)
Montgomery County Comm Coll (PA)
Moorpark Coll (CA)
Moraine Park Tech Coll (WI)
Morgan Comm Coll (CO)
Morton Coll (IL)
Motlow State Comm Coll (TN)
Mountain Empire Comm Coll (VA)
Mountain View Coll (TX)
Mt Hood Comm Coll (OR)
Mount Ida Coll (MA)
Mt San Antonio Coll (CA)
Mount Wachusett Comm Coll (MA)
Muscatine Comm Coll (IA)
Muskegon Comm Coll (MI)
Muskingum Area Tech Coll (OH)
Napa Valley Coll (CA)
Nash Comm Coll (NC)
Nashville State Tech Inst (TN)
Nassau Comm Coll (NY)
National Business Coll, Bluefield (VA)
National Business Coll, Charlottesville (VA)
National Business Coll, Danville (VA)
National Business Coll, Harrisonburg (VA)
National Business Coll, Lynchburg (VA)
National Business Coll, Martinsville (VA)
National Business Coll, Roanoke (VA)
Naugatuck Valley Community–Tech Coll (CT)
Navarro Coll (TX)
Nebraska Coll of Business (NE)
Neosho County Comm Coll (KS)
Nettleton Career Coll (SD)
Newbury Coll (MA)
The New England Banking Inst (MA)
New Hampshire Tech Coll, Berlin (NH)
New Hampshire Tech Coll, Claremont (NH)
New Hampshire Tech Coll, Laconia (NH)
New Hampshire Tech Coll, Manchester (NH)
New Hampshire Tech Coll, Nashua (NH)
New Hampshire Tech Inst (NH)
New Mexico Jr Coll (NM)
New Mexico Military Inst (NM)
Newport Business Inst (PA)
New River Comm Coll (VA)
New York City Tech Coll of the City U of NY (NY)
Niagara County Comm Coll (NY)
Nicolet Area Tech Coll (WI)
Normandale Comm Coll (MN)
Northampton County Area Comm Coll (PA)
North Central Michigan Coll (MI)
North Central Missouri Coll (MO)
North Central Tech Coll (OH)
Northcentral Tech Coll (WI)
North Dakota State Coll of Science (ND)
Northeast Comm Coll (NE)
Northeastern Jr Coll (CO)
Northeastern Oklahoma A&M Coll (OK)
Northeast Iowa Comm Coll, Calmar Cmps (IA)
Northeast Iowa Comm Coll, Peosta Cmps (IA)
Northeast Mississippi Comm Coll (MS)
Northeast State Tech Comm Coll (TN)
Northeast Texas Comm Coll (TX)
Northern Essex Comm Coll (MA)
Northern Maine Tech Coll (ME)
Northern Marianas Coll (MP)
Northern Oklahoma Coll (OK)
Northern Virginia Comm Coll (VA)
North Harris Coll (TX)
North Hennepin Comm Coll (MN)
North Iowa Area Comm Coll (IA)
North Lake Coll (TX)
Northland Comm and Tech Coll (MN)
Northland Pioneer Coll (AZ)
North Seattle Comm Coll (WA)
North Shore Comm Coll (MA)
NorthWest Arkansas Comm Coll (AR)
Northwest Coll (WY)
Northwestern Business Coll (IL)
Northwestern Coll (OH)
Northwestern Connecticut Comm-Tech Coll (CT)
Northwestern Michigan Coll (MI)
Northwest Iowa Comm Coll (IA)
Northwest Mississippi Comm Coll (MS)
Northwest-Shoals Comm Coll (AL)
Northwest State Comm Coll (OH)
Norwalk Comm-Tech Coll (CT)
Oakland Comm Coll (MI)
Oakton Comm Coll (IL)
Ocean County Coll (NJ)
Odessa Coll (TX)
Ohio Valley Coll (WV)
Ohlone Coll (CA)
Okaloosa-Walton Comm Coll (FL)
Oklahoma City Comm Coll (OK)
Oklahoma State U, Oklahoma City (OK)
Oklahoma State U, Okmulgee (OK)
Olean Business Inst (NY)
Olympic Coll (WA)
Onondaga Comm Coll (NY)
Orangeburg-Calhoun Tech Coll (SC)
Orange Coast Coll (CA)
Orange County Comm Coll (NY)
Ouachita Tech Coll (AR)
Owensboro Comm Coll (KY)
Owens Comm Coll, Findlay (OH)
Owens Comm Coll, Toledo (OH)
Oxnard Coll (CA)
Ozarks Tech Comm Coll (MO)
Palau Comm Coll (PW)
Palm Beach Comm Coll (FL)
Palomar Coll (CA)
Palo Verde Coll (CA)
Pamlico Comm Coll (NC)
Paradise Valley Comm Coll (AZ)
Parkland Coll (IL)
Parks Coll (NM)
Parks Jr Coll (CO)
Pasadena City Coll (CA)
Passaic County Comm Coll (NJ)
Patrick Henry Comm Coll (VA)
Peirce Coll (PA)
Pellissippi State Tech Comm Coll (TN)
Peninsula Coll (WA)
Pennsylvania Coll of Tech (PA)
Penn Valley Comm Coll (MO)
Pensacola Jr Coll (FL)
Phillips Jr Coll (UT)
Phillips Jr Coll, Condie Cmps (CA)
Phillips Jr Coll of Springfield (MO)
Piedmont Comm Coll (NC)
Piedmont Tech Coll (SC)
Piedmont Virginia Comm Coll (VA)
Pierce Coll (WA)
Pikes Peak Comm Coll (CO)
Pima Comm Coll (AZ)
Pitt Comm Coll (NC)
Portland Comm Coll (OR)
Potomac State Coll of West Virginia U (WV)
Pratt Comm Coll and Area Voc Sch (KS)
Prince George's Comm Coll (MD)
Prospect Hall (FL)
Pueblo Comm Coll (CO)
Queensborough Comm Coll of City U of NY (NY)
Quincy Coll (MA)
Quinebaug Valley Comm-Tech Coll (CT)
Quinsigamond Comm Coll (MA)
Rainy River Comm Coll (MN)
Ramírez Coll of Business and Tech (PR)
Rancho Santiago Coll (CA)
Randolph Comm Coll (NC)
Rappahannock Comm Coll (VA)
Raritan Valley Comm Coll (NJ)
Rasmussen Coll Eagan (MN)
Rasmussen Coll Mankato (MN)
Rasmussen Coll Minnetonka (MN)
Rasmussen Coll St Cloud (MN)
Reading Area Comm Coll (PA)
Redlands Comm Coll (OK)
Red Rocks Comm Coll (CO)
Rend Lake Coll (IL)
Renton Tech Coll (WA)
Richland Coll (TX)
Richland Comm Coll (IL)
Richmond Comm Coll (NC)
Ricks Coll (ID)
Rio Salado Comm Coll (AZ)
Riverside Comm Coll (CA)
Roane State Comm Coll (TN)
Robeson Comm Coll (NC)
Rochester Business Inst (NY)
Rockingham Comm Coll (NC)
Rockland Comm Coll (NY)
Rock Valley Coll (IL)
Rogers State Coll (OK)
Rogue Comm Coll (OR)
Rose State Coll (OK)
Rowan-Cabarrus Comm Coll (NC)
Roxbury Comm Coll (MA)
Sacramento City Coll (CA)
Saddleback Coll (CA)
Sage Jr Coll of Albany (NY)
Saint Augustine Coll (IL)
St Catharine Coll (KY)
Saint Charles County Comm Coll (MO)
St Clair County Comm Coll (MI)
St Cloud Tech Coll (MN)
St Louis Comm Coll at Florissant Valley (MO)
St Louis Comm Coll at Forest Park (MO)
St Louis Comm Coll at Meramec (MO)
St Paul Tech Coll (MN)
St Petersburg Jr Coll (FL)
St Philip's Coll (TX)
Salem Comm Coll (NJ)
Salt Lake Comm Coll (UT)
Sampson Comm Coll (NC)
San Bernardino Valley Coll (CA)
Sandhills Comm Coll (NC)
San Diego City Coll (CA)
San Diego Mesa Coll (CA)
San Diego Miramar Coll (CA)
Sanford-Brown Coll, Des Peres (MO)
Sanford-Brown Coll, Hazelwood (MO)
Sanford-Brown Coll, St Charles (MO)
San Jacinto College–Central Cmps (TX)
San Jacinto College–North Cmps (TX)
San Jacinto College–South Cmps (TX)
San Joaquin Delta Coll (CA)
San Jose City Coll (CA)
San Juan Coll (NM)
Santa Fe Comm Coll (FL)
Santa Fe Comm Coll (NM)
Santa Monica Coll (CA)
Sauk Valley Comm Coll (IL)
Sawyer Coll of Business, Cleveland (OH)

Associate Degree Programs at Two-Year Colleges
Accounting–Agricultural Business

Sawyer Coll of Business, Cleveland Heights (OH)
Schenectady County Comm Coll (NY)
Schoolcraft Coll (MI)
Scott Comm Coll (IA)
Scottsdale Comm Coll (AZ)
Seattle Central Comm Coll (WA)
Seminole Comm Coll (FL)
Seminole Jr Coll (OK)
Seward County Comm Coll (KS)
Shasta Coll (CA)
Shawnee Comm Coll (IL)
Shelby State Comm Coll (TN)
Shoreline Comm Coll (WA)
Sierra Coll (CA)
Sinclair Comm Coll (OH)
Sisseton-Wahpeton Comm Coll (SD)
Skagit Valley Coll (WA)
Skyline Coll (CA)
Snow Coll (UT)
Solano Comm Coll (CA)
South Arkansas Comm Coll (AR)
South Coll (FL)
South Coll (GA)
Southeast Comm Coll, Beatrice Cmps (NE)
Southeast Comm Coll, Lincoln Cmps (NE)
Southeastern Comm Coll, North Cmps, West Burlington (IA)
Southeastern Illinois Coll (IL)
Southern Coll (FL)
Southern Ohio Coll, Northeast Cmps (OH)
Southern Ohio Coll, Northern Kentucky Cmps (KY)
Southern State Comm Coll (OH)
Southern U at Shreveport–Bossier City Cmps (LA)
Southern West Virginia Comm and Tech Coll (WV)
South Florida Comm Coll (FL)
South Georgia Coll (GA)
South Plains Coll (TX)
South Puget Sound Comm Coll (WA)
South Seattle Comm Coll (WA)
South Suburban Coll (IL)
SouthWest Collegiate Inst for the Deaf (TX)
Southwestern Coll (CA)
Southwestern Coll of Business, Cincinnati (OH)
Southwestern Coll of Business, Cincinnati (OH)
Southwestern Coll of Business, Dayton (OH)
Southwestern Comm Coll (IA)
Southwestern Comm Coll (NC)
Southwestern Indian Polytechnic Inst (NM)
Southwestern Michigan Coll (MI)
Southwestern Oregon Comm Coll (OR)
Southwestern Tech Coll (MN)
Southwest Florida Coll of Business (FL)
Southwest Mississippi Comm Coll (MS)
Southwest Missouri State University– West Plains (MO)
Southwest Virginia Comm Coll (VA)
Southwest Wisconsin Tech Coll (WI)
Spartanburg Tech Coll (SC)
Spencer Sch of Business (NE)
Spokane Comm Coll (WA)
Spokane Falls Comm Coll (WA)
Spoon River Coll (IL)
Springfield Tech Comm Coll (MA)
Stanly Comm Coll (NC)
Stark Tech Coll (OH)
State Comm Coll of East St Louis (IL)
State Fair Comm Coll (MO)
State Tech Inst at Memphis (TN)

State U of NY Coll of A&T at Cobleskill (NY)
State U of NY Coll of A&T at Morrisville (NY)
State U of NY Coll of Tech at Alfred (NY)
State U of NY Coll of Tech at Canton (NY)
State U of NY Coll of Tech at Delhi (NY)
State U of NY Coll of Tech at Farmingdale (NY)
Stevens Henager Coll (UT)
Stratton Coll (WI)
Suffolk County Comm College–Ammerman Cmps (NY)
Suffolk County Comm Coll–Eastern Cmps (NY)
Suffolk County Comm Coll–Western Cmps (NY)
Sullivan County Comm Coll (NY)
Surry Comm Coll (NC)
Sussex County Comm Coll (NJ)
Tacoma Comm Coll (WA)
Taft Coll (CA)
Tarrant County Jr Coll (TX)
Taylor Business Inst (NY)
Tech Coll of Municipality of San Juan (PR)
Terra State Comm Coll (OH)
Texas Southmost Coll (TX)
Texas State Tech Coll (TX)
Thomas Nelson Comm Coll (VA)
Thompson Inst (PA)
Three Rivers Comm Coll (MO)
Three Rivers Comm-Tech Coll (CT)
Tidewater Comm Coll (VA)
Tomball Coll (TX)
Tompkins Cortland Comm Coll (NY)
Trenholm State Tech Coll (AL)
Tri-County Comm Coll (NC)
Tri-County Tech Coll (SC)
Trident Tech Coll (SC)
Trinidad State Jr Coll (CO)
Trinity Valley Comm Coll (TX)
Triton Coll (IL)
Trocaire Coll (NY)
Truckee Meadows Comm Coll (NV)
Tulsa Jr Coll (OK)
Tunxis Comm Tech Coll (CT)
Tyler Jr Coll (TX)
Ulster County Comm Coll (NY)
Umpqua Comm Coll (OR)
Union County Coll (NJ)
The U of Akron–Wayne Coll (OH)
U of Alaska Anchorage, Matanuska-Susitna Coll (AK)
U of Cincinnati Clermont Coll (OH)
U of Cincinnati Raymond Walters Coll (OH)
U of Hawaii–Hawaii Comm Coll (HI)
U of Hawaii–Kapiolani Comm Coll (HI)
U of Hawaii–Kauai Comm Coll (HI)
U of Hawaii–Leeward Comm Coll (HI)
U of Hawaii–Maui Comm Coll (HI)
U of Hawaii–Windward Comm Coll (HI)
U of Kentucky, Ashland Comm Coll (KY)
U of Kentucky, Jefferson Comm Coll (KY)
U of Kentucky, Lexington Comm Coll (KY)
U of Kentucky, Madisonville Comm Coll (KY)
U of Kentucky, Paducah Comm Coll (KY)
U of Kentucky, Prestonsburg Comm Coll (KY)
U of Kentucky, Somerset Comm Coll (KY)
U of Maine at Augusta (ME)
U of New Mexico–Gallup Branch (NM)
U of New Mexico–Los Alamos Branch (NM)

U of Pittsburgh–Titusville (PA)
U of Wisconsin Center–Marinette County (WI)
Utah Valley State Coll (UT)
Utica Sch of Commerce (NY)
Valencia Comm Coll (FL)
Vance-Granville Comm Coll (NC)
Ventura Coll (CA)
Vermilion Comm Coll (MN)
Vermont Tech Coll (VT)
Vernon Regional Jr Coll (TX)
Victoria Coll (TX)
Vincennes U (IN)
Vincennes University–Jasper Ctr (IN)
Virginia Highlands Comm Coll (VA)
Virginia Western Comm Coll (VA)
Vista Comm Coll (CA)
Wake Tech Comm Coll (NC)
Waldorf Coll (IA)
Wallace State Comm Coll (AL)
Walla Walla Comm Coll (WA)
Warren County Comm Coll (NJ)
Washington State Comm Coll (OH)
Washtenaw Comm Coll (MI)
Waubonsee Comm Coll (IL)
Waukesha County Tech Coll (WI)
Waycross Coll (GA)
Wayne Comm Coll (NC)
Wayne County Comm Coll (MI)
Webster Coll, Ocala (FL)
Wenatchee Valley Coll (WA)
Westark Comm Coll (AR)
Westchester Business Inst (NY)
Westchester Comm Coll (NY)
Western Dakota Tech Inst (SD)
Western Iowa Tech Comm Coll (IA)
Western Nebraska Comm Coll, Scottsbluff (NE)
Western Nevada Comm Coll (NV)
Western Oklahoma State Coll (OK)
Western Piedmont Comm Coll (NC)
Western Texas Coll (TX)
Western Wisconsin Tech Coll (WI)
Western Wyoming Comm Coll (WY)
West Hills Comm Coll (CA)
West Los Angeles Coll (CA)
Westmoreland County Comm Coll (PA)
West Shore Comm Coll (MI)
West Valley Coll (CA)
West Virginia Career Coll, Charleston (WV)
West Virginia Career Coll, Morgantown (WV)
West Virginia Northern Comm Coll (WV)
West Virginia U at Parkersburg (WV)
Whatcom Comm Coll (WA)
Wilkes Comm Coll (NC)
William Rainey Harper Coll (IL)
Willmar Comm Coll (MN)
Willmar Tech Coll (MN)
Wilson Tech Comm Coll (NC)
Wisconsin Indianhead Tech Coll, Ashland Cmps (WI)
Wisconsin Indianhead Tech Coll, New Richmond Cmps (WI)
Wisconsin Indianhead Tech Coll, Rice Lake Cmps (WI)
Wisconsin Indianhead Tech Coll, Superior Cmps (WI)
Wood Tobe–Coburn Sch (NY)
Wor-Wic Comm Coll (MD)
Wright State U, Lake Cmps (OH)
Wytheville Comm Coll (VA)
Yakima Valley Comm Coll (WA)
Yavapai Coll (AZ)
York Tech Coll (SC)
Yuba Coll (CA)

ACTUARIAL SCIENCE
Harrisburg Area Comm Coll (PA)
Vincennes U (IN)

ADVERTISING
Allen County Comm Coll (KS)
American Acad of Art (IL)
American River Coll (CA)
Art Inst of Pittsburgh (PA)
Bradley Acad for the Visual Arts (PA)
Brown Inst (MN)
Butler County Comm Coll (KS)
Central Piedmont Comm Coll (NC)
Chabot Coll (CA)
Chattanooga State Tech Comm Coll (TN)
Collin County Comm Coll (TX)
Comm Coll of Allegheny County South Cmps (PA)
Cosumnes River Coll (CA)
County Coll of Morris (NJ)
Cypress Coll (CA)
Daytona Beach Comm Coll (FL)
Eastern Arizona Coll (AZ)
El Camino Coll (CA)
Erie Business Ctr South (PA)
Glendale Comm Coll (AZ)
Grossmont Coll (CA)
Gulf Coast Comm Coll (FL)
Highland Comm Coll (KS)
Hussian Sch of Art (PA)
Hutchinson Comm Coll and Area Vocational Sch (KS)
Jackson Comm Coll (MI)
Lansing Comm Coll (MI)
Long Beach City Coll (CA)
Los Angeles City Coll (CA)
Los Angeles Valley Coll (CA)
Massasoit Comm Coll (MA)
Middlesex County Coll (NJ)
Mississippi Delta Comm Coll (MS)
Mississippi Gulf Coast Comm Coll (MS)
Mohawk Valley Comm Coll (NY)
Montgomery College–Rockville Cmps (MD)
Mount Ida Coll (MA)
Mt San Antonio Coll (CA)
Muskegon Comm Coll (MI)
Northwestern Business Coll (IL)
Palomar Coll (CA)
Parkland Coll (IL)
Pasadena City Coll (CA)
Pennsylvania Coll of Tech (PA)
Ricks Coll (ID)
Rockland Comm Coll (NY)
Sacramento City Coll (CA)
St Clair County Comm Coll (MI)
St Cloud Tech Coll (MN)
St Louis Comm Coll at Meramec (MO)
South Plains Coll (TX)
South Suburban Coll (IL)
Southwest Mississippi Comm Coll (MS)
Three Rivers Comm-Tech Coll (CT)
Tidewater Comm Coll (VA)
Triton Coll (IL)
Tulsa Jr Coll (OK)
Vincennes U (IN)
White Pines Coll (NH)
Yuba Coll (CA)

AEROSPACE ENGINEERING
Prince George's Comm Coll (MD)

AEROSPACE SCIENCES
Alvin Comm Coll (TX)
Comm Coll of Beaver County (PA)
Comm Coll of the Air Force (AL)
Delaware Tech & Comm Coll, Terry Cmps (DE)
Foothill Coll (CA)
Lee Coll (TX)
Miami-Dade Comm Coll (FL)

National Ed Ctr–Spartan Sch of Aeronautics Cmps (OK)
Northland Comm and Tech Coll (MN)
Orange Coast Coll (CA)
San Bernardino Valley Coll (CA)
San Jacinto College–Central Cmps (TX)
State U of NY Coll of Tech at Farmingdale (NY)

AFRICAN STUDIES
Los Angeles Southwest Coll (CA)
Pasadena City Coll (CA)
Sinclair Comm Coll (OH)
Solano Comm Coll (CA)
Southwestern Coll (CA)

AGRICULTURAL BUSINESS
Abraham Baldwin Ag Coll (GA)
Alabama Southern Comm Coll, Thomasville (AL)
Allen County Comm Coll (KS)
Angelina Coll (TX)
Arizona Western Coll (AZ)
Bakersfield Coll (CA)
Bismarck State Coll (ND)
Black Hawk Coll, Kewanee (IL)
Blue Mountain Comm Coll (OR)
Butler County Comm Coll (KS)
Butte Coll (CA)
Carl Albert State Coll (OK)
Carl Sandburg Coll (IL)
Casper Coll (WY)
Central Coll (KS)
Central Comm College–Hastings Cmps (NE)
Central Comm College–Platte Cmps (NE)
Central Wyoming Coll (WY)
Chattahoochee Valley State Comm Coll (AL)
Chippewa Valley Tech Coll (WI)
Cisco Jr Coll (TX)
City Coll of San Francisco (CA)
Clark State Comm Coll (OH)
Cloud County Comm Coll (KS)
Clovis Comm Coll (NM)
Coffeyville Comm Coll (KS)
Colby Comm Coll (KS)
Coll of Southern Idaho (ID)
Coll of the Desert (CA)
Coll of the Redwoods (CA)
Coll of the Sequoias (CA)
Columbia Basin Coll (WA)
Columbia State Comm Coll (TN)
Cosumnes River Coll (CA)
County Coll of Morris (NJ)
Crowder Coll (MO)
Cumberland County Coll (NJ)
Danville Area Comm Coll (IL)
Dawson Comm Coll (MT)
Delaware Tech & Comm Coll, Jack F Owens Cmps (DE)
Delta Coll (MI)
Des Moines Area Comm Coll (IA)
Dodge City Comm Coll (KS)
Eastern Arizona Coll (AZ)
Eastern Oklahoma State Coll (OK)
Eastern Wyoming Coll (WY)
Ellsworth Comm Coll (IA)
Enterprise State Jr Coll (AL)
Fort Scott Comm Coll (KS)
Fox Valley Tech Coll (WI)
Frank Phillips Coll (TX)
Frederick Comm Coll (MD)
Fresno City Coll (CA)
Garden City Comm Coll (KS)
Glendale Comm Coll (AZ)
Grayson County Coll (TX)
Hartnell Coll (CA)
Hawkeye Comm Coll (IA)
Highland Comm Coll (IL)
Highland Comm Coll (KS)
Hill Coll of the Hill Jr Coll District (TX)
Hinds Comm Coll (MS)
Hiwassee Coll (TN)

Hutchinson Comm Coll and Area Vocational Sch (KS)
Illinois Central Coll (IL)
Illinois Eastern Comm Colls, Wabash Valley Coll (IL)
Illinois Valley Comm Coll (IL)
Imperial Valley Coll (CA)
Indian River Comm Coll (FL)
Iowa Western Comm Coll (IA)
Itawamba Comm Coll (MS)
James Sprunt Comm Coll (NC)
John Wood Comm Coll (IL)
Joliet Jr Coll (IL)
J Sargeant Reynolds Comm Coll (VA)
Kankakee Comm Coll (IL)
Kansas City Kansas Comm Coll (KS)
Kaskaskia Coll (IL)
Kings River Comm Coll (CA)
Kirkwood Comm Coll (IA)
Kishwaukee Coll (IL)
Lake Area Vocational-Tech Inst (SD)
Lake Land Coll (IL)
Lamar Comm Coll (CO)
Laramie County Comm Coll (WY)
Lassen Coll (CA)
Lenoir Comm Coll (NC)
Lewis and Clark Comm Coll (IL)
Lincoln Land Comm Coll (IL)
Linn-Benton Comm Coll (OR)
Lord Fairfax Comm Coll (VA)
Los Angeles Pierce Coll (CA)
Merced Coll (CA)
Mesa Comm Coll (AZ)
Milwaukee Area Tech Coll (WI)
Mississippi Delta Comm Coll (MS)
Mississippi Gulf Coast Comm Coll (MS)
Modesto Jr Coll (CA)
Mt San Antonio Coll (CA)
Muscatine Comm Coll (IA)
Nebraska Coll of Tech Agriculture (NE)
North Central Missouri Coll (MO)
North Dakota State Coll of Science (ND)
Northeast Comm Coll (NE)
Northeastern Jr Coll (CO)
Northeastern Oklahoma A&M Coll (OK)
Northeast Iowa Comm Coll, Calmar Cmps (IA)
Northeast Iowa Comm Coll, Peosta Cmps (IA)
Northern Maine Tech Coll (ME)
Northern Marianas Coll (MP)
Northern Oklahoma Coll (OK)
North Iowa Area Comm Coll (IA)
Northwest Coll (WY)
Northwest Iowa Comm Coll (IA)
Ohio State U Ag Tech Inst (OH)
Otero Jr Coll (CO)
Owens Comm Coll, Findlay (OH)
Owens Comm Coll, Toledo (OH)
Oxnard Coll (CA)
Parkland Coll (IL)
Penn State U Abington-Ogontz Cmps (PA)
Penn State U Altoona Cmps (PA)
Penn State U Beaver Cmps (PA)
Penn State U Berks Cmps (PA)
Penn State U Delaware County Cmps (PA)
Penn State U DuBois Cmps (PA)
Penn State U Fayette Cmps (PA)
Penn State U Hazleton Cmps (PA)
Penn State U McKeesport Cmps (PA)
Penn State U Mont Alto Cmps (PA)
Penn State U New Kensington Cmps (PA)

# Associate Degree Programs at Two-Year Colleges
Agricultural Business–Aircraft and Missile Maintenance

Penn State U Schuylkill Cmps (PA)
Penn State U Shenango Cmps (PA)
Penn State U Wilkes-Barre Cmps (PA)
Penn State U Worthington Scranton Cmps (PA)
Penn State U York Cmps (PA)
Pensacola Jr Coll (FL)
Phillips County Comm Coll (AR)
Potomac State Coll of West Virginia U (WV)
Pratt Comm Coll and Area Voc Sch (KS)
Redlands Comm Coll (OK)
Rend Lake Coll (IL)
Richland Comm Coll (IL)
Ricks Coll (ID)
Rogers State Coll (OK)
St Catharine Coll (KY)
St Clair County Comm Coll (MI)
San Joaquin Delta Coll (CA)
Santa Rosa Jr Coll (CA)
Shasta Coll (CA)
Shawnee Comm Coll (IL)
Sheridan Coll (WY)
Snow Coll (UT)
Southeast Comm Coll, Beatrice Cmps (NE)
Southeastern Comm Coll, North Cmps, West Burlington (IA)
South Florida Comm Coll (FL)
South Georgia Coll (GA)
Spokane Comm Coll (WA)
State Fair Comm Coll (MO)
State U of NY Coll of A&T at Cobleskill (NY)
State U of NY Coll of A&T at Morrisville (NY)
State U of NY Coll of Tech at Alfred (NY)
Surry Comm Coll (NC)
Three Rivers Comm Coll (MO)
Treasure Valley Comm Coll (OR)
Tulsa Jr Coll (OK)
Tyler Jr Coll (TX)
U of North Dakota–Lake Region (ND)
Ventura Coll (CA)
Vermilion Comm Coll (MN)
Vermont Tech Coll (VT)
Vincennes U (IN)
Walla Walla Comm Coll (WA)
Weatherford Coll (TX)
Western Dakota Tech Inst (SD)
Western Iowa Tech Comm Coll (IA)
Western Oklahoma State Coll (OK)
Western Wisconsin Tech Coll (WI)
West Hills Comm Coll (CA)
Willmar Comm Coll (MN)
Willmar Tech Coll (MN)
Wisconsin Indianhead Tech Coll, Rice Lake Cmps (WI)
Worthington Comm Coll (MN)
Yakima Valley Comm Coll (WA)
Yuba Coll (CA)

AGRICULTURAL ECONOMICS
Abraham Baldwin Ag Coll (GA)
Butte Coll (CA)
Central Comm College–Platte Cmps (NE)
Chattahoochee Valley State Comm Coll (AL)
Coffeyville Comm Coll (KS)
Colby Comm Coll (KS)
Dodge City Comm Coll (KS)
Eastern Oklahoma State Coll (OK)
Fort Scott Comm Coll (KS)
Frank Phillips Coll (TX)
Garden City Comm Coll (KS)
Highland Comm Coll (KS)
Hill Coll of the Hill Jr Coll District (TX)
Lassen Coll (CA)
Mississippi Delta Comm Coll (MS)
Modesto Jr Coll (CA)

Northeastern Jr Coll (CO)
Northeastern Oklahoma A&M Coll (OK)
Northeast Iowa Comm Coll, Peosta Cmps (IA)
North Iowa Area Comm Coll (IA)
Northwest Coll (WY)
Northwest Mississippi Comm Coll (MS)
Ohio State U Ag Tech Inst (OH)
Potomac State Coll of West Virginia U (WV)
Pratt Comm Coll and Area Voc Sch (KS)
Redlands Comm Coll (OK)
Ricks Coll (ID)
Snow Coll (UT)
South Plains Coll (TX)
State U of NY Coll of A&T at Cobleskill (NY)
Tyler Jr Coll (TX)
Vermilion Comm Coll (MN)

AGRICULTURAL EDUCATION
Allen County Comm Coll (KS)
Central Comm College–Platte Cmps (NE)
Clark Coll (WA)
Coffeyville Comm Coll (KS)
Colby Comm Coll (KS)
Coll of the Sequoias (CA)
Connors State Coll (OK)
Eastern Oklahoma State Coll (OK)
Eastern Wyoming Coll (WY)
Fort Scott Comm Coll (KS)
Frank Phillips Coll (TX)
Grayson County Coll (TX)
Highland Comm Coll (KS)
Joliet Jr Coll (IL)
Kirkwood Comm Coll (IA)
Lamar Comm Coll (CO)
Laramie County Comm Coll (WY)
Linn-Benton Comm Coll (OR)
Murray State Coll (OK)
Northeastern Jr Coll (CO)
Northeast Mississippi Comm Coll (MS)
Northwest Coll (WY)
Northwest-Shoals Comm Coll (AL)
Potomac State Coll of West Virginia U (WV)
Pratt Comm Coll and Area Voc Sch (KS)
Redlands Comm Coll (OK)
Sheridan Coll (WY)
Spoon River Coll (IL)
State U of NY Coll of A&T at Cobleskill (NY)
Trinity Valley Comm Coll (TX)
Tyler Jr Coll (TX)
Vermilion Comm Coll (MN)
Victor Valley Coll (CA)
Western Texas Coll (TX)

AGRICULTURAL SCIENCES
Abraham Baldwin Ag Coll (GA)
Alabama Southern Comm Coll, Thomasville (AL)
Allen County Comm Coll (KS)
Andrew Coll (GA)
Angelina Coll (TX)
Antelope Valley Coll (CA)
Arkansas State University–Beebe Branch (AR)
Atlanta Metropolitan Coll (GA)
Bainbridge Coll (GA)
Barton County Comm Coll (KS)
Bee County Coll (TX)
Black Hawk Coll, Kewanee (IL)
Blinn Coll (TX)
Brevard Coll (NC)
Brunswick Coll (GA)
Butler County Comm Coll (KS)
Butte Coll (CA)
Casper Coll (WY)
Central Texas Coll (TX)
Central Wyoming Coll (WY)
Cerritos Coll (CA)
Chattahoochee Valley State Comm Coll (AL)

Chemeketa Comm Coll (OR)
Chipola Jr Coll (FL)
Cisco Jr Coll (TX)
Clarendon Coll (TX)
Clark Coll (WA)
Clark State Comm Coll (OH)
Cochise Coll, Douglas (AZ)
Coffeyville Comm Coll (KS)
Colby Comm Coll (KS)
Coll of Micronesia–FSM (FM)
Coll of Southern Idaho (ID)
Coll of the Sequoias (CA)
Cowley County Comm Coll and Voc-Tech Sch (KS)
Crowder Coll (MO)
Cumberland County Coll (NJ)
Dalton Coll (GA)
Danville Area Comm Coll (IL)
Darton Coll (GA)
Daytona Beach Comm Coll (FL)
Delta Coll (MI)
Dixie Coll (UT)
D-Q U (CA)
Eastern Arizona Coll (AZ)
East Georgia Coll (GA)
Finger Lakes Comm Coll (NY)
Fort Scott Comm Coll (KS)
Frederick Comm Coll (MD)
Fullerton Coll (CA)
Gainesville Coll (GA)
Garden City Comm Coll (KS)
Gordon Coll (GA)
Grayson County Coll (TX)
Highland Comm Coll (KS)
Hill Coll of the Hill Jr Coll District (TX)
Holmes Comm Coll (MS)
Horry-Georgetown Tech Coll (SC)
Houston Comm Coll System (TX)
Howard Coll (TX)
Illinois Valley Comm Coll (IL)
Imperial Valley Coll (CA)
John A Logan Coll (IL)
John C Calhoun State Comm Coll (AL)
John Wood Comm Coll (IL)
Jones County Jr Coll (MS)
Kankakee Comm Coll (IL)
Kings River Comm Coll (CA)
Kirkwood Comm Coll (IA)
Kishwaukee Coll (IL)
Lake Land Coll (IL)
Lakeshore Tech Coll (WI)
Lamar Comm Coll (CO)
Laramie County Comm Coll (WY)
Lassen Coll (CA)
Lenoir Comm Coll (NC)
Lewis and Clark Comm Coll (IL)
Lincoln Land Comm Coll (IL)
Linn-Benton Comm Coll (OR)
Los Angeles Pierce Coll (CA)
Macon Coll (GA)
Merced Coll (CA)
Miami-Dade Comm Coll (FL)
Middle Georgia Coll (GA)
Mid-Plains Comm Coll (NE)
Mitchell Comm Coll (NC)
Modesto Jr Coll (CA)
Moorpark Coll (CA)
Moraine Park Tech Coll (WI)
Mt San Antonio Coll (CA)
Murray State Coll (OK)
Napa Valley Coll (CA)
New Mexico Jr Coll (NM)
Northeastern Jr Coll (CO)
Northeast Mississippi Comm Coll (MS)
Northeast Texas Comm Coll (TX)
Northern Marianas Coll (MP)
North Idaho Coll (ID)
Northwest Coll (WY)
Northwest Mississippi Comm Coll (MS)
Ohio State U Ag Tech Inst (OH)
Orangeburg-Calhoun Tech Coll (SC)
Palau Comm Coll (PW)
Palo Alto Coll (TX)
Palo Verde Coll (CA)
Parkland Coll (IL)
Pensacola Jr Coll (FL)
Potomac State Coll of West Virginia U (WV)
Pratt Comm Coll and Area Voc Sch (KS)
Rancho Santiago Coll (CA)

Redlands Comm Coll (OK)
Ricks Coll (ID)
Robeson Comm Coll (NC)
St Catharine Coll (KY)
St Clair County Comm Coll (MI)
San Joaquin Delta Coll (CA)
Santa Rosa Jr Coll (CA)
Seward County Comm Coll (KS)
Shawnee Comm Coll (IL)
Sheridan Coll (WY)
Skagit Valley Coll (WA)
Snow Coll (UT)
Southeast Comm Coll, Beatrice Cmps (NE)
South Georgia Coll (GA)
South Plains Coll (TX)
Southwestern Comm Coll (IA)
Southwest Wisconsin Tech Coll (WI)
State Fair Comm Coll (MO)
State U of NY Coll of A&T at Cobleskill (NY)
State U of NY Coll of A&T at Morrisville (NY)
State U of NY Coll of Tech at Alfred (NY)
Sterling Coll (VT)
Surry Comm Coll (NC)
Texarkana Coll (TX)
Treasure Valley Comm Coll (OR)
Tulsa Jr Coll (OK)
Tyler Jr Coll (TX)
Umpqua Comm Coll (OR)
U of Hawaii–Hawaii Comm Coll (HI)
U of New Mexico–Valencia Cmps (NM)
U of North Dakota–Lake Region (ND)
U of Wisconsin Center–Marathon County (WI)
Vernon Regional Jr Coll (TX)
Wallace State Comm Coll (AL)
Walla Walla Comm Coll (WA)
Waycross Coll (GA)
Wayne Comm Coll (NC)
Western Texas Coll (TX)
Wharton County Jr Coll (TX)
Worthington Comm Coll (MN)
Yakima Valley Comm Coll (WA)
Young Harris Coll (GA)
Yuba Coll (CA)

AGRICULTURAL TECHNOLOGIES
Abraham Baldwin Ag Coll (GA)
Aims Comm Coll (CO)
Allen County Comm Coll (KS)
Arizona Western Coll (AZ)
Beaufort County Comm Coll (NC)
Black Hawk Coll, Kewanee (IL)
Butler County Comm Coll (KS)
Carl Sandburg Coll (IL)
Casper Coll (WY)
Central Comm College–Hastings Cmps (NE)
Central Texas Coll (TX)
Central Wyoming Coll (WY)
Clark State Comm Coll (OH)
Coahoma Comm Coll (MS)
Coffeyville Comm Coll (KS)
Colby Comm Coll (KS)
Coll of the Sequoias (CA)
Columbia Basin Coll (WA)
Connors State Coll (OK)
Cosumnes River Coll (CA)
Cowley County Comm Coll and Voc-Tech Sch (KS)
Cuesta Coll (CA)
Cuyahoga Comm Coll, Eastern Cmps (OH)
Del Mar Coll (TX)
Delta Coll (MI)
Dodge City Comm Coll (KS)
Eastern Idaho Tech Coll (ID)
Eastern Wyoming Coll (WY)
Fort Peck Comm Coll (MT)
Fort Scott Comm Coll (KS)
Frank Phillips Coll (TX)
Garden City Comm Coll (KS)
Garrett Comm Coll (MD)
George C Wallace State Comm Coll, Dothan (AL)
Hawkeye Comm Coll (IA)

Highland Comm Coll (IL)
Hutchinson Comm Coll and Area Vocational Sch (KS)
Illinois Central Coll (IL)
Illinois Eastern Comm Colls, Wabash Valley Coll (IL)
Imperial Valley Coll (CA)
Indian Hills Comm Coll (IA)
Jefferson State Comm Coll (AL)
John Wood Comm Coll (IL)
Kishwaukee Coll (IL)
Lake Land Coll (IL)
Lane Comm Coll (OR)
Lassen Coll (CA)
Lincoln Land Comm Coll (IL)
Longview Comm Coll (MO)
Madison Area Tech Coll (WI)
Mesa Comm Coll (AZ)
Miles Comm Coll (MT)
Mississippi County Comm Coll (AR)
Mitchell Tech Inst (SD)
Mt San Antonio Coll (CA)
Navarro Coll (TX)
Nebraska Coll of Tech Agriculture (NE)
Northcentral Tech Coll (WI)
North Central Texas Coll (TX)
North Dakota State Coll of Science (ND)
Northeast Comm Coll (NE)
Northeastern Jr Coll (CO)
Northeast Iowa Comm Coll, Peosta Cmps (IA)
Northern Marianas Coll (MP)
North Iowa Area Comm Coll (IA)
Northwest Coll (WY)
Northwest Iowa Comm Coll (IA)
Ohio State U Ag Tech Inst (OH)
Oxnard Coll (CA)
Paris Jr Coll (TX)
Parkland Coll (IL)
Potomac State Coll of West Virginia U (WV)
Pratt Comm Coll and Area Voc Sch (KS)
Redlands Comm Coll (OK)
Rend Lake Coll (IL)
St Clair County Comm Coll (MI)
San Joaquin Delta Coll (CA)
Shasta Coll (CA)
Sierra Coll (CA)
Skagit Valley Coll (WA)
Southeast Comm Coll, Beatrice Cmps (NE)
Southeastern Illinois Coll (IL)
Southern State Comm Coll (OH)
South Florida Comm Coll (FL)
Southwest Texas Jr Coll (TX)
Southwest Wisconsin Tech Coll (WI)
Spokane Comm Coll (WA)
Spoon River Coll (IL)
State Fair Comm Coll (MO)
State U of NY Coll of A&T at Cobleskill (NY)
State U of NY Coll of A&T at Morrisville (NY)
Surry Comm Coll (NC)
Three Rivers Comm Coll (MO)
Treasure Valley Comm Coll (OR)
U of Hawaii–Maui Comm Coll (HI)
U of North Dakota–Lake Region (ND)
U of North Dakota–Williston (ND)
Vincennes U (IN)
Walla Walla Comm Coll (WA)
Walters State Comm Coll (TN)
Wenatchee Valley Coll (WA)
Western Iowa Tech Comm Coll (IA)
Western Wisconsin Tech Coll (WI)
West Hills Comm Coll (CA)
Worthington Comm Coll (MN)
Yakima Valley Comm Coll (WA)
Yuba Coll (CA)

AGRONOMY/SOIL AND CROP SCIENCES
Allen County Comm Coll (KS)

Blue Mountain Comm Coll (OR)
Butte Coll (CA)
Central Comm College–Platte Cmps (NE)
Central Texas Coll (TX)
Chipola Jr Coll (FL)
Colby Comm Coll (KS)
Coll of the Redwoods (CA)
Cosumnes River Coll (CA)
Cowley County Comm Coll and Voc-Tech Sch (KS)
Dodge City Comm Coll (KS)
Eastern Oklahoma State Coll (OK)
East Mississippi Comm Coll (MS)
Fort Scott Comm Coll (KS)
Frank Phillips Coll (TX)
Hartnell Coll (CA)
Hawkeye Comm Coll (IA)
Highland Comm Coll (KS)
Jackson State Comm Coll (TN)
Kings River Comm Coll (CA)
Kirkwood Comm Coll (IA)
Lamar Comm Coll (CO)
Lassen Coll (CA)
Los Angeles Pierce Coll (CA)
Merced Coll (CA)
Mesa Comm Coll (AZ)
Modesto Jr Coll (CA)
Moorpark Coll (CA)
Mt San Antonio Coll (CA)
Nebraska Coll of Tech Agriculture (NE)
Northeast Comm Coll (NE)
Northeastern Jr Coll (CO)
Northeastern Oklahoma A&M Coll (OK)
Northeast Mississippi Comm Coll (MS)
North Iowa Area Comm Coll (IA)
Northwest Coll (WY)
Ohio State U Ag Tech Inst (OH)
Potomac State Coll of West Virginia U (WV)
Ricks Coll (ID)
Shawnee Comm Coll (IL)
Sierra Coll (CA)
Snow Coll (UT)
Southeast Comm Coll, Beatrice Cmps (NE)
Southeastern Comm Coll, North Cmps, West Burlington (IA)
Southern Maine Tech Coll (ME)
South Plains Coll (TX)
Spokane Comm Coll (WA)
State U of NY Coll of A&T at Cobleskill (NY)
State U of NY Coll of A&T at Morrisville (NY)
Treasure Valley Comm Coll (OR)
Ventura Coll (CA)
Vermilion Comm Coll (MN)
West Hills Comm Coll (CA)
Willmar Tech Coll (MN)
Yakima Valley Comm Coll (WA)
Yuba Coll (CA)

AIRCRAFT AND MISSILE MAINTENANCE
Alabama Aviation and Tech Coll (AL)
Belleville Area Coll (IL)
Big Bend Comm Coll (WA)
Chandler-Gilbert Comm Coll (AZ)
City Coll of San Francisco (CA)
Cochise Coll, Douglas (AZ)
Coll of San Mateo (CA)
Colorado Northwestern Comm Coll (CO)
Columbus State Comm Coll (OH)
Comm Coll of Denver (CO)
Comm Coll of the Air Force (AL)
Cowley County Comm Coll and Voc-Tech Sch (KS)
Delgado Comm Coll (LA)
Dixie Coll (UT)
Enterprise State Jr Coll (AL)
Florence-Darlington Tech Coll (SC)
Greenville Tech Coll (SC)

Associate Degree Programs at Two-Year Colleges
Aircraft and Missile Maintenance–Architectural Technologies

Guilford Tech Comm Coll (NC)
Hawkeye Comm Coll (IA)
Heartland Comm Coll (IL)
Helena Coll of Tech of The U of Montana (MT)
Ivy Tech State Coll–Wabash Valley (IN)
Lincoln Land Comm Coll (IL)
Merced Coll (CA)
Mohawk Valley Comm Coll (NY)
Mt San Antonio Coll (CA)
Northwest Mississippi Comm Coll (MS)
Oklahoma City Comm Coll (OK)
Parkland Coll (IL)
Pima Comm Coll (AZ)
Pittsburgh Inst of Aeronautics (PA)
Pratt Comm Coll and Area Voc Sch (KS)
Sacramento City Coll (CA)
St Philip's Coll (TX)
Salt Lake Comm Coll (UT)
San Diego Miramar Coll (CA)
Solano Comm Coll (CA)
South Seattle Comm Coll (WA)
Texas State Tech Coll–Harlingen Cmps (TX)
Tomball Coll (TX)
Trident Tech Coll (SC)
Vincennes U (IN)
West Los Angeles Coll (CA)

AIR TRAFFIC CONTROL
Catonsville Comm Coll (MD)
Comm Coll of Beaver County (PA)
Comm Coll of the Air Force (AL)
Cuyamaca Coll (CA)
Green River Comm Coll (WA)
Inver Hills Comm Coll (MN)
Mt San Antonio Coll (CA)
Southwestern Coll (CA)

AMERICAN STUDIES
Anne Arundel Comm Coll (MD)
Bucks County Comm Coll (PA)
Cosumnes River Coll (CA)
El Camino Coll (CA)
Everett Comm Coll (WA)
Foothill Coll (CA)
Greenfield Comm Coll (MA)
Holyoke Comm Coll (MA)
Los Angeles City Coll (CA)
Miami-Dade Comm Coll (FL)
Mississippi Delta Comm Coll (MS)
Naugatuck Valley Community–Tech Coll (CT)
Palomar Coll (CA)
Paul Smith's Coll (NY)
Redlands Comm Coll (OK)
Saddleback Coll (CA)
Santa Fe Comm Coll (NM)
Tulsa Jr Coll (OK)

ANATOMY
Brevard Coll (NC)
Cañada Coll (CA)
Clark Coll (WA)
Frank Phillips Coll (TX)
Modesto Jr Coll (CA)
Northeastern Jr Coll (CO)
San Jacinto College–Central Cmps (TX)

ANIMAL SCIENCES
Abraham Baldwin Ag Coll (GA)
Alamance Comm Coll (NC)
Allen County Comm Coll (KS)
Antelope Valley Coll (CA)
Arkansas State University–Beebe Branch (AR)
Bakersfield Coll (CA)
Berkshire Comm Coll (MA)
Blue Mountain Comm Coll (OR)
Butte Coll (CA)
Camden County Coll (NJ)
Casper Coll (WY)
Central Texas Coll (TX)
Central Wyoming Coll (WY)
Coffeyville Comm Coll (KS)
Colby Comm Coll (KS)
Coll of the Sequoias (CA)
Connors State Coll (OK)
Cosumnes River Coll (CA)
Dodge City Comm Coll (KS)
Eastern Oklahoma State Coll (OK)
Eastern Wyoming Coll (WY)
Fort Scott Comm Coll (KS)
Harcum Coll (PA)
Hartnell Coll (CA)
Hawkeye Comm Coll (IA)
Highland Comm Coll (KS)
Hill Coll of the Hill Jr Coll District (TX)
Hiwassee Coll (TN)
James Sprunt Comm Coll (NC)
John Wood Comm Coll (IL)
Kings River Comm Coll (CA)
Kirkwood Comm Coll (IA)
Lamar Comm Coll (CO)
Linn-Benton Comm Coll (OR)
Los Angeles Pierce Coll (CA)
Manor Jr Coll (PA)
Mendocino Coll (CA)
Merced Coll (CA)
Modesto Jr Coll (CA)
Moorpark Coll (CA)
Mount Ida Coll (MA)
Mt San Antonio Coll (CA)
Murray State Coll (OK)
Nebraska Coll of Tech Agriculture (NE)
Niagara County Comm Coll (NY)
Northeastern Jr Coll (CO)
Northeastern Oklahoma A&M Coll (OK)
North Iowa Area Comm Coll (IA)
Northwest Coll (WY)
Ohio State U Ag Tech Inst (OH)
Orange Coast Coll (CA)
Potomac State Coll of West Virginia U (WV)
Redlands Comm Coll (OK)
Ricks Coll (ID)
St Catharine Coll (KY)
San Joaquin Delta Coll (CA)
Santa Rosa Jr Coll (CA)
Shasta Coll (CA)
Shawnee Comm Coll (IL)
Sierra Coll (CA)
Snow Coll (UT)
Southeast Comm Coll, Beatrice Cmps (NE)
South Georgia Coll (GA)
State U of NY Coll of A&T at Cobleskill (NY)
State U of NY Coll of A&T at Morrisville (NY)
State U of NY Coll of Tech at Alfred (NY)
Trinity Valley Comm Coll (TX)
Ventura Coll (CA)
West Hills Comm Coll (CA)
Yakima Valley Comm Coll (WA)
Yuba Coll (CA)

ANTHROPOLOGY
Atlanta Metropolitan Coll (GA)
Bakersfield Coll (CA)
Barton County Comm Coll (KS)
Black Hawk Coll, Moline (IL)
Cañada Coll (CA)
Casper Coll (WY)
Cerritos Coll (CA)
Chaffey Coll (CA)
Clackamas Comm Coll (OR)
Cochise Coll, Douglas (AZ)
Cochise Coll, Sierra Vista (AZ)
Coll of Alameda (CA)
Coll of Southern Idaho (ID)
Coll of the Desert (CA)
Collin County Comm Coll (TX)
Columbia Coll (CA)
Comm Coll of Allegheny County North Cmps (PA)
Comm Coll of Allegheny County South Cmps (PA)
Comm Coll of Southern Nevada (NV)
Contra Costa Coll (CA)
Crafton Hills Coll (CA)
Cypress Coll (CA)
Darton Coll (GA)
Daytona Beach Comm Coll (FL)
East Central Coll (MO)
Eastern Arizona Coll (AZ)
East Georgia Coll (GA)
East Los Angeles Coll (CA)
El Camino Coll (CA)
Essex Comm Coll (MD)
Everett Comm Coll (WA)
Foothill Coll (CA)
Fresno City Coll (CA)
Fullerton Coll (CA)
Gainesville Coll (GA)
Gulf Coast Comm Coll (FL)
Hartnell Coll (CA)
Imperial Valley Coll (CA)
Indian River Comm Coll (FL)
Kellogg Comm Coll (MI)
Laramie County Comm Coll (WY)
Los Medanos Coll (CA)
Lower Columbia Coll (WA)
Miami-Dade Comm Coll (FL)
Miami University–Middletown Cmps (OH)
Modesto Jr Coll (CA)
Monterey Peninsula Coll (CA)
Muskegon Comm Coll (MI)
North Idaho Coll (ID)
Oxnard Coll (CA)
Palomar Coll (CA)
Pasadena City Coll (CA)
Pikes Peak Comm Coll (CO)
Pima Comm Coll (AZ)
Rancho Santiago Coll (CA)
Saddleback Coll (CA)
San Bernardino Valley Coll (CA)
San Diego City Coll (CA)
San Diego Mesa Coll (CA)
San Diego Miramar Coll (CA)
San Jacinto College–Central Cmps (TX)
San Joaquin Delta Coll (CA)
San Juan Coll (NM)
Santa Barbara City Coll (CA)
Santa Monica Coll (CA)
Santa Rosa Jr Coll (CA)
Sauk Valley Comm Coll (IL)
Skagit Valley Coll (WA)
Skyline Coll (CA)
Southwestern Coll (CA)
Tacoma Comm Coll (WA)
Triton Coll (IL)
Umpqua Comm Coll (OR)
Vincennes U (IN)
Western Nebraska Comm Coll, Scottsbluff (NE)
Western Wyoming Comm Coll (WY)
West Los Angeles Coll (CA)

APPLIED ART
Allan Hancock Coll (CA)
American Acad of Art (IL)
Anne Arundel Comm Coll (MD)
Art Inst of Fort Lauderdale (FL)
Art Inst of Pittsburgh (PA)
Barton County Comm Coll (KS)
Bee County Coll (TX)
Brevard Coll (NC)
Bristol Comm Coll (MA)
Brookdale Comm Coll (NJ)
Burlington County Coll (NJ)
Butte Coll (CA)
Camden County Coll (NJ)
Casper Coll (WY)
Catonsville Comm Coll (MD)
Centralia Coll (WA)
Central Piedmont Comm Coll (NC)
Chattanooga State Tech Comm Coll (TN)
Cincinnati State Tech and Comm Coll (OH)
Coffeyville Comm Coll (KS)
Colby Comm Coll (KS)
Coll of Marin (CA)
Comm Coll of Allegheny County South Cmps (PA)
Cosumnes River Coll (CA)
Cuesta Coll (CA)
Cypress Coll (CA)
DeKalb Coll (GA)
Del Mar Coll (TX)
Delta Coll (MI)
Edison Comm Coll (FL)
Evergreen Valley Coll (CA)
Harcum Coll (PA)
Henry Ford Comm Coll (MI)
Hill Coll of the Hill Jr Coll District (TX)
Howard Comm Coll (MD)
Iowa Lakes Comm Coll (IA)
Jefferson Davis Comm Coll (AL)
Jones County Jr Coll (MS)
Kingsborough Comm Coll of City U of NY (NY)
Kirkwood Comm Coll (IA)
Lassen Coll (CA)
Lincoln Coll, Normal (IL)
Lon Morris Coll (TX)
Los Angeles City Coll (CA)
Maryland Coll of Art and Design (MD)
Merced Coll (CA)
Middle Georgia Coll (GA)
Middlesex Community- Tech Coll (CT)
Middlesex County Coll (NJ)
Mississippi Delta Comm Coll (MS)
Montcalm Comm Coll (MI)
Mount Ida Coll (MA)
Muskegon Comm Coll (MI)
Nassau Comm Coll (NY)
Northern Virginia Comm Coll (VA)
Northwest Mississippi Comm Coll (MS)
Odessa Coll (TX)
Oklahoma City Comm Coll (OK)
Palomar Coll (CA)
Parkland Coll (IL)
Pima Comm Coll (AZ)
Porterville Coll (CA)
Pratt Comm Coll and Area Voc Sch (KS)
Redlands Comm Coll (OK)
Rockland Comm Coll (NY)
St Johns River Comm Coll (FL)
San Diego Mesa Coll (CA)
Santa Rosa Jr Coll (CA)
Sinclair Comm Coll (OH)
Skyline Coll (CA)
Southwestern Michigan Coll (MI)
Tomball Coll (TX)
Tunxis Comm Tech Coll (CT)
U of Maine at Augusta (ME)
U of New Mexico–Los Alamos Branch (NM)
Washtenaw Comm Coll (MI)
Wenatchee Valley Coll (WA)
Westchester Comm Coll (NY)
Willmar Comm Coll (MN)

APPLIED MATHEMATICS
Chabot Coll (CA)
Middle Georgia Coll (GA)
Mid-Plains Comm Coll (NE)
Muskegon Comm Coll (MI)
Northeastern Jr Coll (CO)
San Diego Miramar Coll (CA)
State Comm Coll of East St Louis (IL)
State U of NY Coll of A&T at Cobleskill (NY)
State U of NY Coll of Tech at Farmingdale (NY)
U of Kentucky, Jefferson Comm Coll (KY)

ARCHAEOLOGY
Black Hawk Coll, Moline (IL)
East Central Coll (MO)
Fresno City Coll (CA)
Gulf Coast Comm Coll (FL)
Palomar Coll (CA)
Pima Comm Coll (AZ)
Vincennes U (IN)

ARCHITECTURAL TECHNOLOGIES
Albuquerque Tech Vocational Inst (NM)
Allan Hancock Coll (CA)
American Inst of Design (PA)
Anne Arundel Comm Coll (MD)
Anoka-Ramsey Comm Coll (MN)
Arapahoe Comm Coll (CO)
Broward Comm Coll (FL)
Burlington County Coll (NJ)
Butler County Comm Coll (PA)
Cañada Coll (CA)
Capital Comm Tech Coll (CT)
Catawba Valley Comm Coll (NC)
Catonsville Comm Coll (MD)
Central Coll (KS)
Central Comm College–Hastings Cmps (NE)
Central Piedmont Comm Coll (NC)
Cerritos Coll (CA)
Chabot Coll (CA)
Charles Stewart Mott Comm Coll (MI)
Chesapeake Coll (MD)
Chippewa Valley Tech Coll (WI)
Cincinnati State Tech and Comm Coll (OH)
City Colls of Chicago, Harold Washington Coll (IL)
City Colls of Chicago, Kennedy-King Coll (IL)
City Colls of Chicago, Olive-Harvey Coll (IL)
City Colls of Chicago, Richard J Daley Coll (IL)
City Colls of Chicago, Wilbur Wright Coll (IL)
Clinton Comm Coll (IA)
Coastal Carolina Comm Coll (NC)
Coll of DuPage (IL)
Coll of Lake County (IL)
Coll of Marin (CA)
Coll of San Mateo (CA)
Coll of the Desert (CA)
Coll of the Mainland (TX)
Coll of the Redwoods (CA)
Coll of the Sequoias (CA)
Columbus State Comm Coll (OH)
Comm Coll of Allegheny County South Cmps (PA)
Comm Coll of Beaver County (PA)
Comm Coll of Philadelphia (PA)
Cosumnes River Coll (CA)
Cuyahoga Comm Coll, Metropolitan Cmps (OH)
Cuyamaca Coll (CA)
Daytona Beach Comm Coll (FL)
Delaware County Comm Coll (PA)
Delaware Tech & Comm Coll, Jack F Owens Cmps (DE)
Delaware Tech & Comm Coll, Stanton/Wilmington Cmps (DE)
Delaware Tech & Comm Coll, Terry Cmps (DE)
Delgado Comm Coll (LA)
Del Mar Coll (TX)
Delta Coll (MI)
Dixie Coll (UT)
Doña Ana Branch Comm Coll (NM)
Dutchess Comm Coll (NY)
East Los Angeles Coll (CA)
El Camino Coll (CA)
El Paso Comm Coll (TX)
Erie Comm Coll, South Cmps (NY)
Essex County Coll (NJ)
Everett Comm Coll (WA)
Fayetteville Tech Comm Coll (NC)
Florida Comm Coll at Jacksonville (FL)
Forsyth Tech Comm Coll (NC)
Fort Scott Comm Coll (KS)
Franklin Inst of Boston (MA)
Fresno City Coll (CA)
Front Range Comm Coll (CO)
Fullerton Coll (CA)
Gaston Coll (NC)
Golden West Coll (CA)
Grand Rapids Comm Coll (MI)
Greenville Tech Coll (SC)
Guilford Tech Comm Coll (NC)
Harrisburg Area Comm Coll (PA)
Hawkeye Comm Coll (IA)
Hillsborough Comm Coll (FL)
Illinois Central Coll (IL)
Inst of Design and Construction (NY)
Iowa Western Comm Coll (IA)
ITT Tech Inst, Fort Wayne (IN)
ITT Tech Inst, Indianapolis (IN)
ITT Tech Inst, Dayton (OH)
Ivy Tech State Coll–Central Indiana (IN)
Ivy Tech State Coll–Columbus (IN)
Ivy Tech State Coll–Kokomo (IN)
Ivy Tech State Coll–Lafayette (IN)
Ivy Tech State Coll–Northcentral (IN)
Ivy Tech State Coll–Northeast (IN)
Ivy Tech State Coll–Southcentral (IN)
Ivy Tech State Coll–Wabash Valley (IN)
Jefferson Coll (MO)
Jefferson State Comm Coll (AL)
Johnson Tech Inst (PA)
John Tyler Comm Coll (VA)
Lake Land Coll (IL)
Lamar University–Orange (TX)
Laney Coll (CA)
Lansing Comm Coll (MI)
Lincoln Land Comm Coll (IL)
Long Beach City Coll (CA)
Los Angeles City Coll (CA)
Los Angeles Harbor Coll (CA)
Los Angeles Pierce Coll (CA)
Los Angeles Trade-Tech Coll (CA)
Louisville Tech Inst (KY)
Luzerne County Comm Coll (PA)
Macomb Comm Coll (MI)
Madison Area Tech Coll (WI)
Massasoit Comm Coll (MA)
Mayland Comm Coll (NC)
Mercer County Comm Coll (NJ)
Merritt Coll (CA)
Metropolitan Comm Coll (NE)
Miami-Dade Comm Coll (FL)
Midlands Tech Coll (SC)
Monroe County Comm Coll (MI)
Montgomery College–Rockville Cmps (MD)
Morrison Inst of Tech (IL)
Mountain Empire Comm Coll (VA)
Mt Hood Comm Coll (OR)
Mt San Antonio Coll (CA)
Nash Comm Coll (NC)
Nashville State Tech Inst (TN)
New Hampshire Tech Inst (NH)
New River Comm Coll (VA)
New York City Tech Coll of the City U of NY (NY)
Normandale Comm Coll (MN)
Northampton County Area Comm Coll (PA)
Northcentral Tech Coll (WI)
North Dakota State Coll of Science (ND)
Northeast Iowa Comm Coll, Peosta Cmps (IA)
Northern Virginia Comm Coll (VA)
Norwalk Comm-Tech Coll (CT)
Oakland Comm Coll (MI)
Oakton Comm Coll (IL)
Oklahoma State U, Oklahoma City (OK)
Oklahoma State U, Okmulgee (OK)
Onondaga Comm Coll (NY)
Orange Coast Coll (CA)
Orange County Comm Coll (NY)
Otero Jr Coll (CO)
Owens Comm Coll, Toledo (OH)
Palo Alto Coll (TX)
Pasadena City Coll (CA)
Pennsylvania Coll of Tech (PA)
Pennsylvania Inst of Tech (PA)
Penn State U Worthington Scranton Cmps (PA)
Pikes Peak Comm Coll (CO)
Pitt Comm Coll (NC)
Rancho Santiago Coll (CA)
Rend Lake Coll (IL)

Peterson's Guide to Two-Year Colleges 1997
53

Associate Degree Programs at Two-Year Colleges
Architectural Technologies–Art/Fine Arts

Ricks Coll (ID)
Roanoke-Chowan Comm Coll (NC)
Roxbury Comm Coll (MA)
Saddleback Coll (CA)
St Clair County Comm Coll (MI)
St Louis Comm Coll at Meramec (MO)
St Petersburg Jr Coll (FL)
St Philip's Coll (TX)
Salem Comm Coll (NJ)
Salt Lake Comm Coll (UT)
San Bernardino Valley Coll (CA)
Sandhills Comm Coll (NC)
San Diego Mesa Coll (CA)
Santa Monica Coll (CA)
Seminole Comm Coll (FL)
Sinclair Comm Coll (OH)
Southeast Comm Coll, Milford Cmps (NE)
Southern Maine Tech Coll (ME)
South Suburban Coll (IL)
Southwestern Coll (CA)
Southwestern Michigan Coll (MI)
Spartanburg Tech Coll (SC)
Spokane Comm Coll (WA)
Springfield Tech Comm Coll (MA)
Stark Tech Coll (OH)
State Tech Inst at Memphis (TN)
State U of NY Coll of A&T at Morrisville (NY)
State U of NY Coll of Tech at Alfred (NY)
State U of NY Coll of Tech at Delhi (NY)
State U of NY Coll of Tech at Farmingdale (NY)
Tarrant County Jr Coll (TX)
Terra State Comm Coll (OH)
Thaddeus Stevens State Sch of Tech (PA)
Thomas Nelson Comm Coll (VA)
Three Rivers Comm-Tech Coll (CT)
Triangle Tech, Inc, Pittsburgh (PA)
Triangle Tech, Inc–Erie Sch (PA)
Triangle Tech, Inc–Greensburg Ctr (PA)
Truckee Meadows Comm Coll (NV)
Union County Coll (NJ)
U of Hawaii–Honolulu Comm Coll (HI)
U of Kentucky, Lexington Comm Coll (KY)
U of Maine at Augusta (ME)
Ventura Coll (CA)
Vermilion Comm Coll (MN)
Vincennes U (IN)
Virginia Western Comm Coll (VA)
Wake Tech Comm Coll (NC)
Washtenaw Comm Coll (MI)
Western Iowa Tech Comm Coll (IA)
Westmoreland County Comm Coll (PA)
William Rainey Harper Coll (IL)
Wisconsin Indianhead Tech Coll, Rice Lake Cmps (WI)
Yavapai Coll (AZ)

ART EDUCATION

Allen County Comm Coll (KS)
Angelina Coll (TX)
Bakersfield Coll (CA)
Bay de Noc Comm Coll (MI)
Bee County Coll (TX)
Brazosport Coll (TX)
Brevard Coll (NC)
Butler County Comm Coll (KS)
Cañada Coll (CA)
Carl Albert State Coll (OK)
Central Coll (KS)
Central Comm College–Platte Cmps (NE)
Chattahoochee Valley State Comm Coll (AL)
Clarendon Coll (TX)
Coll of the Siskiyous (CA)
Comm Coll of Allegheny County South Cmps (PA)
Connors State Coll (OK)
Copiah-Lincoln Comm Coll (MS)
Del Mar Coll (TX)
Delta Coll (MI)
East Central Comm Coll (MS)
Eastern Arizona Coll (AZ)
Eastern Oklahoma State Coll (OK)
Eastern Wyoming Coll (WY)
Ellsworth Comm Coll (IA)
Essex Comm Coll (MD)
Frank Phillips Coll (TX)
Gainesville Coll (GA)
Grayson County Coll (TX)
Halifax Comm Coll (NC)
Hill Coll of the Hill Jr Coll District (TX)
Independence Comm Coll (KS)
Iowa Lakes Comm Coll (IA)
Itawamba Comm Coll (MS)
John A Logan Coll (IL)
John C Calhoun State Comm Coll (AL)
Jones County Jr Coll (MS)
Kansas City Kansas Comm Coll (KS)
Kellogg Comm Coll (MI)
Kirkwood Comm Coll (IA)
Lake-Sumter Comm Coll (FL)
Lincoln Coll, Normal (IL)
Lincoln Land Comm Coll (IL)
Lon Morris Coll (TX)
Los Angeles Mission Coll (CA)
McLennan Comm Coll (TX)
Miami-Dade Comm Coll (FL)
Middle Georgia Coll (GA)
Midland Coll (TX)
Mid-Plains Comm Coll (NE)
Mississippi Delta Comm Coll (MS)
Mississippi Gulf Coast Comm Coll (MS)
Modesto Jr Coll (CA)
Montgomery College–Rockville Cmps (MD)
Muskegon Comm Coll (MI)
New Mexico Jr Coll (NM)
Northeast Comm Coll (NE)
Northeastern Jr Coll (CO)
Northeastern Oklahoma A&M Coll (OK)
Northeast Mississippi Comm Coll (MS)
Northern Virginia Comm Coll (VA)
North Harris Coll (TX)
Northwest Coll (WY)
Ohio Valley Coll (WV)
Oxnard Coll (CA)
Palomar Coll (CA)
Pensacola Jr Coll (FL)
Prairie State Coll (IL)
Pratt Comm Coll and Area Voc Sch (KS)
Roane State Comm Coll (TN)
St Catharine Coll (KY)
Shelton State Comm Coll (AL)
Southwestern Comm Coll (IA)
Trinidad State Jr Coll (CO)
Tulsa Jr Coll (OK)
Umpqua Comm Coll (OR)
U of Kentucky, Jefferson Comm Coll (KY)
Vermilion Comm Coll (MN)
Vincennes U (IN)
Waldorf Coll (IA)
Wallace State Comm Coll (AL)
Walters State Comm Coll (TN)
Western Nebraska Comm Coll, Scottsbluff (NE)
Western Oklahoma State Coll (OK)
Western Texas Coll (TX)
Young Harris Coll (GA)

ART/FINE ARTS

Abraham Baldwin Ag Coll (GA)
Alabama Southern Comm Coll, Monroeville (AL)
Alabama Southern Comm Coll, Thomasville (AL)
Allan Hancock Coll (CA)
Allegany Comm Coll (MD)
Allen County Comm Coll (KS)
Alvin Comm Coll (TX)
American Acad of Art (IL)
American River Coll (CA)
Andrew Coll (GA)
Angelina Coll (TX)
Anne Arundel Comm Coll (MD)
Antelope Valley Coll (CA)
Arizona Western Coll (AZ)
The Art Inst of Houston (TX)
Asnuntuck Comm-Tech Coll (CT)
Atlanta Metropolitan Coll (GA)
Austin Comm Coll (TX)
Bacone Coll (OK)
Bainbridge Coll (GA)
Barstow Coll (CA)
Barton County Comm Coll (KS)
Bee County Coll (TX)
Bergen Comm Coll (NJ)
Berkshire Comm Coll (MA)
Black Hawk Coll, Moline (IL)
Blue Ridge Comm Coll (NC)
Bradley Acad for the Visual Arts (PA)
Brazosport Coll (TX)
Brevard Coll (NC)
Brevard Comm Coll (FL)
Bristol Comm Coll (MA)
Bronx Comm Coll of City U of NY (NY)
Brookdale Comm Coll (NJ)
Brunswick Coll (GA)
Bucks County Comm Coll (PA)
Burlington County Coll (NJ)
Butler County Comm Coll (KS)
Butte Coll (CA)
Camden County Coll (NJ)
Cañada Coll (CA)
Cape Cod Comm Coll (MA)
Casper Coll (WY)
Catonsville Comm Coll (MD)
Central Coll (KS)
Central Comm College–Platte Cmps (NE)
Centralia Coll (WA)
Central Oregon Comm Coll (OR)
Central Piedmont Comm Coll (NC)
Central Texas Coll (TX)
Central Wyoming Coll (WY)
Cerritos Coll (CA)
Cerro Coso Comm Coll (CA)
Chabot Coll (CA)
Chaffey Coll (CA)
Charles Stewart Mott Comm Coll (MI)
Chesapeake Coll (MD)
Chipola Jr Coll (FL)
Cincinnati State Tech and Comm Coll (OH)
Citrus Coll (CA)
City Coll of San Francisco (CA)
City Colls of Chicago, Harold Washington Coll (IL)
City Colls of Chicago, Harry S Truman Coll (IL)
City Colls of Chicago, Malcolm X Coll (IL)
City Colls of Chicago, Olive-Harvey Coll (IL)
City Colls of Chicago, Richard J Daley Coll (IL)
City Colls of Chicago, Wilbur Wright Coll (IL)
Clackamas Comm Coll (OR)
Clarendon Coll (TX)
Clark Coll (WA)
Clinton Comm Coll (IA)
Cloud County Comm Coll (KS)
Clovis Comm Coll (NM)
Coahoma Comm Coll (MS)
Coastal Carolina Comm Coll (NC)
Cochise Coll, Douglas (AZ)
Cochise Coll, Sierra Vista (AZ)
Coffeyville Comm Coll (KS)
Colby Comm Coll (KS)
Coll of Alameda (CA)
Coll of Marin (CA)
Coll of San Mateo (CA)
Coll of Southern Idaho (ID)
Coll of The Albemarle (NC)
Coll of the Canyons (CA)
Coll of the Desert (CA)
Coll of the Sequoias (CA)
Collin County Comm Coll (TX)
Colorado Inst of Art (CO)
Colorado Mountn Coll, Roaring Fork Cmps-Spring Valley Ctr (CO)
Colorado Mountn Coll, Timberline Cmps (CO)
Columbia Coll (CA)
Columbia-Greene Comm Coll (NY)
Columbia State Comm Coll (TN)
Comm Coll of Allegheny County Allegheny Cmps (PA)
Comm Coll of Allegheny County Boyce Cmps (PA)
Comm Coll of Allegheny County North Cmps (PA)
Comm Coll of Allegheny County South Cmps (PA)
Comm Coll of Philadelphia (PA)
Comm Coll of Rhode Island (RI)
Comm Coll of Southern Nevada (NV)
Contra Costa Coll (CA)
Cosumnes River Coll (CA)
County Coll of Morris (NJ)
Cowley County Comm Coll and Voc-Tech Sch (KS)
Crafton Hills Coll (CA)
Crowder Coll (MO)
Cuesta Coll (CA)
Cypress Coll (CA)
Danville Area Comm Coll (IL)
Darton Coll (GA)
Daytona Beach Comm Coll (FL)
Dean Coll (MA)
De Anza Coll (CA)
DeKalb Coll (GA)
Delgado Comm Coll (LA)
Del Mar Coll (TX)
Dixie Coll (UT)
Dodge City Comm Coll (KS)
D-Q U (CA)
East Central Coll (MO)
East Central Comm Coll (MS)
Eastern Arizona Coll (AZ)
Eastern Oklahoma State Coll (OK)
East Georgia Coll (GA)
East Los Angeles Coll (CA)
East Mississippi Comm Coll (MS)
Edison Comm Coll (FL)
Edison State Comm Coll (OH)
El Camino Coll (CA)
Elgin Comm Coll (IL)
Ellsworth Comm Coll (IA)
El Paso Comm Coll (TX)
Essex Comm Coll (MD)
Essex County Coll (NJ)
Everett Comm Coll (WA)
Florida Keys Comm Coll (FL)
Floyd Coll (GA)
Foothill Coll (CA)
Frank Phillips Coll (TX)
Frederick Comm Coll (MD)
Fresno City Coll (CA)
Fullerton Coll (CA)
Fulton-Montgomery Comm Coll (NY)
Gainesville Coll (GA)
Galveston Coll (TX)
Garland County Comm Coll (AR)
Garrett Comm Coll (MD)
Gaston Coll (NC)
Gavilan Coll (CA)
Glendale Comm Coll (AZ)
Golden West Coll (CA)
Gordon Coll (GA)
Grand Rapids Comm Coll (MI)
Grays Harbor Coll (WA)
Grayson County Coll (TX)
Great Basin Coll (NV)
Greenfield Comm Coll (MA)
Gulf Coast Comm Coll (FL)
Harford Comm Coll (MD)
Harrisburg Area Comm Coll (PA)
Hartnell Coll (CA)
Henry Ford Comm Coll (MI)
Herkimer County Comm Coll (NY)
Highland Comm Coll (IL)
Highland Comm Coll (KS)
Highline Comm Coll (WA)
Hill Coll of the Hill Jr Coll District (TX)
Hiwassee Coll (TN)
Holyoke Comm Coll (MA)
Housatonic Comm-Tech Coll (CT)
Houston Comm Coll System (TX)
Howard Coll (TX)
Howard Comm Coll (MD)
Hutchinson Comm Coll and Area Vocational Sch (KS)
Illinois Eastern Comm Colls, Lincoln Trail Coll (IL)
Illinois Eastern Comm Colls, Wabash Valley Coll (IL)
Imperial Valley Coll (CA)
Inst of American Indian Arts (NM)
Iowa Lakes Comm Coll (IA)
Irvine Valley Coll (CA)
Itawamba Comm Coll (MS)
Jackson State Comm Coll (TN)
Jefferson Coll (MO)
John A Logan Coll (IL)
John Wood Comm Coll (IL)
Joliet Jr Coll (IL)
Kankakee Comm Coll (IL)
Kansas City Kansas Comm Coll (KS)
Kellogg Comm Coll (MI)
Kent State U, Stark Cmps (OH)
Keystone Coll (PA)
Kingsborough Comm Coll of City U of NY (NY)
Kings River Comm Coll (CA)
Kirkwood Comm Coll (IA)
Kirtland Comm Coll (MI)
Kishwaukee Coll (IL)
Labette Comm Coll (KS)
Lake Michigan Coll (MI)
Lake Tahoe Comm Coll (CA)
Lamar Comm Coll (CO)
Laney Coll (CA)
Lansing Comm Coll (MI)
Laramie County Comm Coll (WY)
Lassen Coll (CA)
Lee Coll (TX)
Lenoir Comm Coll (NC)
Lewis and Clark Comm Coll (IL)
Lincoln Land Comm Coll (IL)
Linn-Benton Comm Coll (OR)
Little Hoop Comm Coll (ND)
Long Beach City Coll (CA)
Lon Morris Coll (TX)
Lorain County Comm Coll (OH)
Los Angeles City Coll (CA)
Los Angeles Pierce Coll (CA)
Los Angeles Valley Coll (CA)
Los Medanos Coll (CA)
Lower Columbia Coll (WA)
Macon Coll (GA)
Manchester Comm-Tech Coll (CT)
Maryland Coll of Art and Design (MD)
Mendocino Coll (CA)
Merced Coll (CA)
Mercer County Comm Coll (NJ)
Mesa Comm Coll (AZ)
Miami-Dade Comm Coll (FL)
Miami University–Middletown Cmps (OH)
Middle Georgia Coll (GA)
Middlesex Comm Coll (MA)
Middlesex Community– Tech Coll (CT)
Middlesex County Coll (NJ)
Midland Coll (TX)
Mid Michigan Comm Coll (MI)
Mineral Area Coll (MO)
MiraCosta Coll (CA)
Mission Coll (CA)
Mississippi Gulf Coast Comm Coll (MS)
Mitchell Comm Coll (NC)
Moberly Area Comm Coll (MO)
Modesto Jr Coll (CA)
Mohave Comm Coll (AZ)
Mohawk Valley Comm Coll (NY)
Monroe Comm Coll (NY)
Monroe County Comm Coll (MI)
Monterey Peninsula Coll (CA)
Montgomery College–Germantown Cmps (MD)
Montgomery College–Takoma Park Cmps (MD)
Montgomery County Comm Coll (PA)
Moorpark Coll (CA)
Morton Coll (IL)
Mount Ida Coll (MA)
Mt San Jacinto Coll (CA)
Mount Wachusett Comm Coll (MA)
Murray State Coll (OK)
Muskegon Comm Coll (MI)
Napa Valley Coll (CA)
Nassau Comm Coll (NY)
Navajo Comm Coll (AZ)
Navarro Coll (TX)
New Mexico Jr Coll (NM)
New Mexico Military Inst (NM)
Niagara County Comm Coll (NY)
Northampton County Area Comm Coll (PA)
Northeastern Jr Coll (CO)
Northeastern Oklahoma A&M Coll (OK)
Northeast Mississippi Comm Coll (MS)
Northern Virginia Comm Coll (VA)
North Harris Coll (TX)
North Idaho Coll (ID)
North Seattle Comm Coll (WA)
Northwest Coll (WY)
Northwestern Connecticut Comm-Tech Coll (CT)
Northwest Indian Coll (WA)
Northwest Mississippi Comm Coll (MS)
Norwalk Comm-Tech Coll (CT)
Oakland Comm Coll (MI)
Odessa Coll (TX)
Ohlone Coll (CA)
Okaloosa-Walton Comm Coll (FL)
Oklahoma City Comm Coll (OK)
Olympic Coll (WA)
Onondaga Comm Coll (NY)
Orangeburg-Calhoun Tech Coll (SC)
Palm Beach Comm Coll (FL)
Palo Alto Coll (TX)
Palomar Coll (CA)
Paris Jr Coll (TX)
Parkland Coll (IL)
Pasadena City Coll (CA)
Pensacola Jr Coll (FL)
Phillips County Comm Coll (AR)
Piedmont Tech Coll (SC)
Piedmont Virginia Comm Coll (VA)
Pikes Peak Comm Coll (CO)
Pima Comm Coll (AZ)
Polk Comm Coll (FL)
Porterville Coll (CA)
Prairie State Coll (IL)
Pratt Comm Coll and Area Voc Sch (KS)
Prince George's Comm Coll (MD)
Queensborough Comm Coll of City U of NY (NY)
Quinebaug Valley Comm-Tech Coll (CT)
Quinsigamond Comm Coll (MA)
Rancho Santiago Coll (CA)
Raritan Valley Comm Coll (NJ)
Redlands Comm Coll (OK)
Red Rocks Comm Coll (CO)
Ricks Coll (ID)
Riverside Comm Coll (CA)
Roane State Comm Coll (TN)
Rockingham Comm Coll (NC)
Rockland Comm Coll (NY)
Rogers State Coll (OK)
Rose State Coll (OK)
Roxbury Comm Coll (MA)
Sacramento City Coll (CA)
Saddleback Coll (CA)
Sage Jr Coll of Albany (NY)
St Catharine Coll (KY)
St Clair County Comm Coll (MI)
St Gregory's Coll (OK)
St Johns River Comm Coll (FL)
St Louis Comm Coll at Florissant Valley (MO)
St Louis Comm Coll at Forest Park (MO)

Associate Degree Programs at Two-Year Colleges
Art/Fine Arts–Automotive Technologies

St Louis Comm Coll at Meramec (MO)
St Philip's Coll (TX)
Salt Lake Comm Coll (UT)
San Bernardino Valley Coll (CA)
Sandhills Comm Coll (NC)
San Diego City Coll (CA)
San Diego Mesa Coll (CA)
San Diego Miramar Coll (CA)
San Jacinto College–Central Cmps (TX)
San Jacinto College–North Cmps (TX)
San Jacinto College–South Cmps (TX)
San Joaquin Delta Coll (CA)
San Juan Coll (NM)
Santa Barbara City Coll (CA)
Santa Monica Coll (CA)
Santa Rosa Jr Coll (CA)
Sauk Valley Comm Coll (IL)
Schoolcraft Coll (MI)
Scott Comm Coll (IA)
Seminole Jr Coll (OK)
Seward County Comm Coll (KS)
Shasta Coll (CA)
Sheridan Coll (WY)
Sierra Coll (CA)
Sinclair Comm Coll (OH)
Skagit Valley Coll (WA)
Skyline Coll (CA)
Snow Coll (UT)
Solano Comm Coll (CA)
Southeast Comm Coll, Beatrice Cmps (NE)
Southeastern Comm Coll (NC)
Southern U at Shreveport–Bossier City Cmps (LA)
South Mountain Comm Coll (AZ)
South Plains Coll (TX)
South Suburban Coll (IL)
SouthWest Collegiate Inst for the Deaf (TX)
Southwestern Coll (CA)
Southwestern Comm Coll (IA)
Spokane Falls Comm Coll (WA)
Spoon River Coll (IL)
Springfield Coll in Illinois (IL)
Springfield Tech Comm Coll (MA)
State Fair Comm Coll (MO)
Suffolk County Comm College–Ammerman Cmps (NY)
Sussex County Comm Coll (NJ)
Tacoma Comm Coll (WA)
Taft Coll (CA)
Temple Coll (TX)
Texarkana Coll (TX)
Texas Southmost Coll (TX)
Thomas Nelson Comm Coll (VA)
Three Rivers Comm-Tech Coll (CT)
Tidewater Comm Coll (VA)
Treasure Valley Comm Coll (OR)
Trinity Valley Comm Coll (TX)
Triton Coll (IL)
Tulsa Jr Coll (OK)
Tunxis Comm Tech Coll (CT)
Turtle Mountain Comm Coll (ND)
Tyler Jr Coll (TX)
Umpqua Comm Coll (OR)
Union County Coll (NJ)
U of Kentucky, Jefferson Comm Coll (KY)
U of New Mexico–Gallup Branch (NM)
U of Wisconsin Center–Marathon County (WI)
Vermilion Comm Coll (MN)
Vernon Regional Jr Coll (TX)
Victor Valley Coll (CA)
Villa Maria Coll of Buffalo (NY)
Vincennes U (IN)
Virginia Western Comm Coll (VA)
Vista Comm Coll (CA)
Waldorf Coll (IA)
Walters State Comm Coll (TN)
Watkins Inst of Interior Design (TN)
Waubonsee Comm Coll (IL)
Westark Comm Coll (AR)
Westchester Comm Coll (NY)
Western Piedmont Comm Coll (NC)
Western Texas Coll (TX)
Western Wyoming Comm Coll (WY)
West Hills Comm Coll (CA)
West Los Angeles Coll (CA)
West Shore Comm Coll (MI)
West Valley Coll (CA)
Wharton County Jr Coll (TX)
White Pines Coll (NH)
William Rainey Harper Coll (IL)
Willmar Comm Coll (MN)
Yavapai Coll (AZ)
Young Harris Coll (GA)
Yuba Coll (CA)

ART HISTORY

Brevard Coll (NC)
Cañada Coll (CA)
Del Mar Coll (TX)
El Camino Coll (CA)
Foothill Coll (CA)
Grossmont Coll (CA)
Hill Coll of the Hill Jr Coll District (TX)
Iowa Lakes Comm Coll (IA)
Kansas City Kansas Comm Coll (KS)
Lincoln Land Comm Coll (IL)
Little Hoop Comm Coll (ND)
Lon Morris Coll (TX)
Mercer County Comm Coll (NJ)
Modesto Jr Coll (CA)
Monterey Peninsula Coll (CA)
Montgomery College–Rockville Cmps (MD)
Muskegon Comm Coll (MI)
Northern Virginia Comm Coll (VA)
Palm Beach Comm Coll (FL)
Pasadena City Coll (CA)
Polk Comm Coll (FL)
Prairie State Coll (IL)
Rogue Comm Coll (OR)
St Catharine Coll (KY)
Skagit Valley Coll (WA)
Skyline Coll (CA)
Umpqua Comm Coll (OR)
Vermilion Comm Coll (MN)
White Pines Coll (NH)

ARTS ADMINISTRATION

Brevard Coll (NC)
Cuesta Coll (CA)
Kellogg Comm Coll (MI)
Palomar Coll (CA)

ART THERAPY

Burlington County Coll (NJ)

ASIAN/ORIENTAL STUDIES

City Coll of San Francisco (CA)
Cypress Coll (CA)
East Los Angeles Coll (CA)
El Camino Coll (CA)
Laney Coll (CA)
Miami-Dade Comm Coll (FL)
Pima Comm Coll (AZ)

ASTRONOMY

Anne Arundel Comm Coll (MD)
Austin Comm Coll (TX)
Crafton Hills Coll (CA)
Daytona Beach Comm Coll (FL)
El Camino Coll (CA)
Fullerton Coll (CA)
Iowa Lakes Comm Coll (IA)
Modesto Jr Coll (CA)
North Idaho Coll (ID)
Palomar Coll (CA)
Pasadena City Coll (CA)
Polk Comm Coll (FL)
Saddleback Coll (CA)
San Bernardino Valley Coll (CA)
Santa Monica Coll (CA)
Santa Rosa Jr Coll (CA)
Southwestern Coll (CA)

ATHLETIC TRAINING

Dean Coll (MA)
Dodge City Comm Coll (KS)
Essex Comm Coll (MD)
Fort Scott Comm Coll (KS)
Garden City Comm Coll (KS)
Independence Comm Coll (KS)
Mitchell Coll (CT)
New Mexico Jr Coll (NM)
Northland Comm and Tech Coll (MN)
Odessa Coll (TX)
Orange Coast Coll (CA)
Pratt Comm Coll and Area Voc Sch (KS)
Santa Monica Coll (CA)
Seward County Comm Coll (KS)
Vincennes U (IN)

ATMOSPHERIC SCIENCES

Everett Comm Coll (WA)

AUDIO ENGINEERING

Art Inst of Pittsburgh (PA)
Art Inst of Seattle (WA)
Brown Inst (MN)
Full Sail Ctr for the Recording Arts (FL)
Harford Comm Coll (MD)
Houston Comm Coll System (TX)
Nassau Comm Coll (NY)
San Jacinto College–Central Cmps (TX)
Shoreline Comm Coll (WA)
Southern Ohio Coll, Cincinnati Cmps (OH)
South Plains Coll (TX)
Texas State Tech Coll–Waco/Marshall Cmps (TX)

AUTOMOTIVE TECHNOLOGIES

Aims Comm Coll (CO)
Alamance Comm Coll (NC)
Alexandria Tech Coll (MN)
Allan Hancock Coll (CA)
Allegany Comm Coll (MD)
Alpena Comm Coll (MI)
American River Coll (CA)
Angelina Coll (TX)
Anoka-Ramsey Comm Coll (MN)
Anson Comm Coll (NC)
Antelope Valley Coll (CA)
Arapahoe Comm Coll (CO)
Arizona Western Coll (AZ)
Asheville-Buncombe Tech Comm Coll (NC)
Athens Area Tech Inst (GA)
Austin Comm Coll (TX)
Bainbridge Coll (GA)
Bakersfield Coll (CA)
Barstow Coll (CA)
Barton County Comm Coll (KS)
Bay de Noc Comm Coll (MI)
Beaufort County Comm Coll (NC)
Bee County Coll (TX)
Bergen Comm Coll (NJ)
Bessemer State Tech Coll (AL)
Big Bend Comm Coll (WA)
Bismarck State Coll (ND)
Black Hawk Coll, Kewanee (IL)
Black Hawk Coll, Moline (IL)
Blue Mountain Comm Coll (OR)
Blue Ridge Comm Coll (VA)
Brazosport Coll (TX)
Brookdale Comm Coll (NJ)
Brookhaven Coll (TX)
Broward Comm Coll (FL)
Burlington County Coll (NJ)
Butler County Comm Coll (KS)
Butte Coll (CA)
Camden County Coll (NJ)
Cape Fear Comm Coll (NC)
Carl Sandburg Coll (IL)
Casper Coll (WY)
Catonsville Comm Coll (MD)
Cedar Valley Coll (TX)
Central Carolina Comm Coll (NC)
Central Carolina Tech Coll (SC)
Central Coll (KS)
Central Comm College–Grand Island Cmps (NE)
Central Comm College–Hastings Cmps (NE)
Central Comm College–Platte Cmps (NE)
Central Maine Tech Coll (ME)
Central Oregon Comm Coll (OR)
Central Piedmont Comm Coll (NC)
Central Texas Coll (TX)
Central Wyoming Coll (WY)
Cerritos Coll (CA)
Cerro Coso Comm Coll (CA)
Chabot Coll (CA)
Chaffey Coll (CA)
Charles Stewart Mott Comm Coll (MI)
Chattahoochee Tech Inst (GA)
Chattanooga State Tech Comm Coll (TN)
Chemeketa Comm Coll (OR)
Chippewa Valley Tech Coll (WI)
Cincinnati State Tech and Comm Coll (OH)
Cisco Jr Coll (TX)
Citrus Coll (CA)
City Coll of San Francisco (CA)
City Colls of Chicago, Harold Washington Coll (IL)
City Colls of Chicago, Kennedy-King Coll (IL)
Clackamas Comm Coll (OR)
Clarendon Coll (TX)
Clark Coll (WA)
Clatsop Comm Coll (OR)
Clovis Comm Coll (NM)
Coffeyville Comm Coll (KS)
Coll of Alameda (CA)
Coll of DuPage (IL)
Coll of Eastern Utah (UT)
Coll of Lake County (IL)
Coll of Marin (CA)
Coll of Southern Idaho (ID)
Coll of the Desert (CA)
Coll of the Mainland (TX)
Coll of the Redwoods (CA)
Coll of the Sequoias (CA)
Coll of the Siskiyous (CA)
Columbia Basin Coll (WA)
Columbia Coll (CA)
Columbia-Greene Comm Coll (NY)
Columbus State Comm Coll (OH)
Comm Coll of Allegheny County North Cmps (PA)
Comm Coll of Allegheny County South Cmps (PA)
Comm Coll of Aurora (CO)
Comm Coll of Denver (CO)
Comm Coll of Philadelphia (PA)
Comm Coll of Southern Nevada (NV)
Comm Coll of the Air Force (AL)
Contra Costa Coll (CA)
Corning Comm Coll (NY)
Cosumnes River Coll (CA)
Cowley County Comm Coll and Voc-Tech Sch (KS)
Crowder Coll (MO)
Cuesta Coll (CA)
Cuyahoga Comm Coll, Western Cmps (OH)
Cuyamaca Coll (CA)
Cypress Coll (CA)
Danville Area Comm Coll (IL)
Dawson Comm Coll (MT)
Daytona Beach Comm Coll (FL)
De Anza Coll (CA)
DeKalb Coll (GA)
DeKalb Tech Inst (GA)
Delaware Tech & Comm Coll, Jack F Owens Cmps (DE)
Delgado Comm Coll (LA)
Del Mar Coll (TX)
Delta Coll (MI)
Denmark Tech Coll (SC)
Denver Automotive and Diesel Coll (CO)
Des Moines Area Comm Coll (IA)
Dixie Coll (UT)
Dodge City Comm Coll (KS)
Doña Ana Branch Comm Coll (NM)
Don Bosco Tech Inst (CA)
Douglas MacArthur State Tech Coll (AL)
Dunwoody Inst (MN)
Durham Tech Comm Coll (NC)
East Central Coll (MO)
Eastern Arizona Coll (AZ)
Eastern Idaho Tech Coll (ID)
Eastern Maine Tech Coll (ME)
Eastern New Mexico University–Roswell (NM)
Eastfield Coll (TX)
East Los Angeles Coll (CA)
East Mississippi Comm Coll (MS)
El Camino Coll (CA)
Elgin Comm Coll (IL)
El Paso Comm Coll (TX)
Enterprise State Jr Coll (AL)
Erie Comm Coll, North Cmps (NY)
Erie Comm Coll, South Cmps (NY)
Everett Comm Coll (WA)
Evergreen Valley Coll (CA)
Fayetteville Tech Comm Coll (NC)
Florence-Darlington Tech Coll (SC)
Florida Comm Coll at Jacksonville (FL)
Floyd Coll (GA)
Forsyth Tech Comm Coll (NC)
Fort Peck Comm Coll (MT)
Fox Valley Tech Coll (WI)
Franklin Inst of Boston (MA)
Fresno City Coll (CA)
Front Range Comm Coll (CO)
Fullerton Coll (CA)
Fulton-Montgomery Comm Coll (NY)
Gainesville Coll (GA)
Garden City Comm Coll (KS)
Gaston Coll (NC)
Gateway Comm Coll (AZ)
Gateway Comm-Tech Coll (CT)
Gavilan Coll (CA)
George C Wallace State Comm Coll, Dothan (AL)
Glendale Comm Coll (AZ)
Glen Oaks Comm Coll (MI)
Gloucester County Coll (NJ)
Gogebic Comm Coll (MI)
Golden West Coll (CA)
Grand Rapids Comm Coll (MI)
Grays Harbor Coll (WA)
Grayson County Coll (TX)
Great Basin Coll (NV)
Green River Comm Coll (WA)
Greenville Tech Coll (SC)
Guilford Tech Comm Coll (NC)
Gwinnett Tech Inst (GA)
Harford Comm Coll (MD)
Harrisburg Area Comm Coll (PA)
Hartnell Coll (CA)
Hawkeye Comm Coll (IA)
Haywood Comm Coll (NC)
Helena Coll of Tech of The U of Montana (MT)
Henry Ford Comm Coll (MI)
Highland Comm Coll (IL)
Highland Comm Coll (KS)
Highland Park Comm Coll (MI)
Hill Coll of the Hill Jr Coll District (TX)
Hillsborough Comm Coll (FL)
Hocking Coll (OH)
Howard Coll (TX)
Hudson Valley Comm Coll (NY)
Hutchinson Comm Coll and Area Vocational Sch (KS)
Illinois Central Coll (IL)
Illinois Eastern Comm Colls, Olney Central Coll (IL)
Illinois Valley Comm Coll (IL)
Imperial Valley Coll (CA)
Indian Hills Comm Coll (IA)
Indian River Comm Coll (FL)
Inver Hills Comm Coll (MN)
Iowa Central Comm Coll (IA)
Iowa Western Comm Coll (IA)
Isothermal Comm Coll (NC)
ITT Tech Inst, Fort Wayne (IN)
Ivy Tech State Coll–Central Indiana (IN)
Ivy Tech State Coll–Columbus (IN)
Ivy Tech State Coll–Eastcentral (IN)
Ivy Tech State Coll–Kokomo (IN)
Ivy Tech State Coll–Lafayette (IN)
Ivy Tech State Coll–Northcentral (IN)
Ivy Tech State Coll–Northeast (IN)
Ivy Tech State Coll–Northwest (IN)
Ivy Tech State Coll–Southcentral (IN)
Ivy Tech State Coll–Southeast (IN)
Ivy Tech State Coll–Southwest (IN)
Ivy Tech State Coll–Wabash Valley (IN)
Ivy Tech State Coll–Whitewater (IN)
Jackson Comm Coll (MI)
Jefferson Coll (MO)
John A Logan Coll (IL)
John C Calhoun State Comm Coll (AL)
John M Patterson State Tech Coll (AL)
Johnson County Comm Coll (KS)
Johnson Tech Inst (PA)
John Tyler Comm Coll (VA)
John Wood Comm Coll (IL)
Joliet Jr Coll (IL)
J Sargeant Reynolds Comm Coll (VA)
Kalamazoo Valley Comm Coll (MI)
Kankakee Comm Coll (IL)
Kansas City Kansas Comm Coll (KS)
Kaskaskia Coll (IL)
Kent State U, Trumbull Cmps (OH)
Kings River Comm Coll (CA)
Kirkwood Comm Coll (IA)
Kirtland Comm Coll (MI)
Kishwaukee Coll (IL)
Lake Area Vocational-Tech Inst (SD)
Lake Land Coll (IL)
Lakeshore Tech Coll (WI)
Lake Washington Tech Coll (WA)
Lamar University–Port Arthur (TX)
Lane Comm Coll (OR)
Lansing Comm Coll (MI)
Laramie County Comm Coll (WY)
Las Positas Coll (CA)
Lassen Coll (CA)
Lehigh Carbon Comm Coll (PA)
Lewis and Clark Comm Coll (IL)
Lincoln Land Comm Coll (IL)
Lincoln Tech Inst (IN)
Lincoln Tech Inst, Philadelphia (PA)
Linn-Benton Comm Coll (OR)
Long Beach City Coll (CA)
Longview Comm Coll (MO)
Los Angeles Harbor Coll (CA)
Los Angeles Pierce Coll (CA)
Los Angeles Trade-Tech Coll (CA)
Lower Columbia Coll (WA)
Luzerne County Comm Coll (PA)
Macomb Comm Coll (MI)
Madison Area Tech Coll (WI)
Manatee Comm Coll (FL)
Martin Comm Coll (NC)
Massachusetts Bay Comm Coll (MA)
Massasoit Comm Coll (MA)
McDowell Tech Comm Coll (NC)
McHenry County Coll (IL)
Mendocino Coll (CA)
Merced Coll (CA)
Mercer County Comm Coll (NJ)
Mesa Comm Coll (AZ)
Metropolitan Comm Coll (NE)
Middlesex Comm Coll (MA)
Middlesex County Coll (NJ)
Midland Coll (TX)

Peterson's Guide to Two-Year Colleges 1997
55

Associate Degree Programs at Two-Year Colleges
Automotive Technologies–Behavioral Sciences

Mid Michigan Comm Coll (MI)
Mid-Plains Comm Coll (NE)
Miles Comm Coll (MT)
Milwaukee Area Tech Coll (WI)
MiraCosta Coll (CA)
Mississippi Gulf Coast Comm Coll (MS)
Mitchell Comm Coll (NC)
Modesto Jr Coll (CA)
Mohave Comm Coll (AZ)
Monroe Comm Coll (NY)
Monroe County Comm Coll (MI)
Montana State U Coll of Tech-Great Falls (MT)
Montcalm Comm Coll (MI)
Monterey Peninsula Coll (CA)
Montgomery College–Rockville Cmps (MD)
Montgomery Comm Coll (NC)
Montgomery County Comm Coll (PA)
Moorpark Coll (CA)
Moraine Park Tech Coll (WI)
Moraine Valley Comm Coll (IL)
Morgan Comm Coll (CO)
Morton Coll (IL)
Mt Hood Comm Coll (OR)
Mt San Jacinto Coll (CA)
Mount Wachusett Comm Coll (MA)
Muskegon Comm Coll (MI)
Muskingum Area Tech Coll (OH)
Nashville State Tech Inst (TN)
Naugatuck Valley Community–Tech Coll (CT)
New England Inst of Tech (RI)
New England Inst of Tech & Florida Culinary Inst (FL)
New Hampshire Tech Coll, Berlin (NH)
New Hampshire Tech Coll, Laconia (NH)
New Hampshire Tech Coll, Manchester (NH)
New Hampshire Tech Coll, Nashua (NH)
New Mexico Jr Coll (NM)
New River Comm Coll (VA)
New York City Tech Coll of the City U of NY (NY)
Nicolet Area Tech Coll (WI)
Northampton County Area Comm Coll (PA)
North Arkansas Comm/Tech Coll (AR)
North Central Missouri Coll (MO)
Northcentral Tech Coll (WI)
North Central Texas Coll (TX)
North Dakota State Coll of Science (ND)
Northeast Comm Coll (NE)
Northeastern Jr Coll (CO)
Northeastern Oklahoma A&M Coll (OK)
Northeast Iowa Comm Coll, Peosta Cmps (IA)
Northeast State Tech Comm Coll (TN)
Northeast Texas Comm Coll (TX)
Northern Maine Tech Coll (ME)
Northern Virginia Comm Coll (VA)
North Harris Coll (TX)
North Hennepin Comm Coll (MN)
North Idaho Coll (ID)
North Iowa Area Comm Coll (IA)
Northland Comm and Tech Coll (MN)
Northwestern Coll (OH)
Northwestern Michigan Coll (MI)
Northwest Iowa Comm Coll (IA)
Northwest Mississippi Comm Coll (MS)
Oakland Comm Coll (MI)
Oakton Comm Coll (IL)
Odessa Coll (TX)
Okaloosa-Walton Comm Coll (FL)
Oklahoma City Comm Coll (OK)
Oklahoma State U, Okmulgee (OK)
Olympic Coll (WA)
Onondaga Comm Coll (NY)
Orangeburg-Calhoun Tech Coll (SC)
Otero Jr Coll (CO)
Ouachita Tech Coll (AR)
Owens Comm Coll, Findlay (OH)
Owens Comm Coll, Toledo (OH)
Oxnard Coll (CA)
Ozarka Tech Coll (AR)
Ozarks Tech Comm Coll (MO)
Palau Comm Coll (PW)
Palomar Coll (CA)
Palo Verde Coll (CA)
Pamlico Comm Coll (NC)
Parkland Coll (IL)
Pasadena City Coll (CA)
Pellissippi State Tech Comm Coll (TN)
Peninsula Coll (WA)
Pennco Tech (PA)
Pennsylvania Coll of Tech (PA)
Pensacola Jr Coll (FL)
Petit Jean Tech Coll (AR)
Phillips County Comm Coll (AR)
Piedmont Tech Coll (SC)
Piedmont Virginia Comm Coll (VA)
Pikes Peak Comm Coll (CO)
Pima Comm Coll (AZ)
Pines Tech Coll (AR)
Pitt Comm Coll (NC)
Porterville Coll (CA)
Portland Comm Coll (OR)
Prairie State Coll (IL)
Pratt Comm Coll and Area Voc Sch (KS)
Pueblo Comm Coll (CO)
Quinsigamond Comm Coll (MA)
Rancho Santiago Coll (CA)
Randolph Comm Coll (NC)
Ranger Coll (TX)
Ranken Tech Coll (MO)
Raritan Valley Comm Coll (NJ)
Red Rocks Comm Coll (CO)
Remington Education Center–Vale Cmps (PA)
Rend Lake Coll (IL)
Renton Tech Coll (WA)
Richland Comm Coll (IL)
Rich Mountain Comm Coll (AR)
Ricks Coll (ID)
Riverside Comm Coll (CA)
Roanoke-Chowan Comm Coll (NC)
Rockland Comm Coll (NY)
Rock Valley Coll (IL)
Rogue Comm Coll (OR)
Rowan-Cabarrus Comm Coll (NC)
Saddleback Coll (CA)
St Cloud Tech Coll (MN)
St Louis Comm Coll at Forest Park (MO)
St Philip's Coll (TX)
Salt Lake Comm Coll (UT)
San Bernardino Valley Coll (CA)
Sandhills Comm Coll (NC)
San Diego City Coll (CA)
San Diego Miramar Coll (CA)
San Jacinto College–Central Cmps (TX)
San Jacinto College–North Cmps (TX)
San Jacinto College–South Cmps (TX)
San Joaquin Delta Coll (CA)
San Juan Coll (NM)
Santa Barbara City Coll (CA)
Santa Fe Comm Coll (FL)
Santa Monica Coll (CA)
Santa Rosa Jr Coll (CA)
Scott Comm Coll (IA)
Seminole Comm Coll (FL)
Shasta Coll (CA)
Shawnee Comm Coll (IL)
Shelton State Comm Coll (AL)
Sheridan Coll (WY)
Shoreline Comm Coll (WA)
Sierra Coll (CA)
Sinclair Comm Coll (OH)
Skagit Valley Coll (WA)
Skyline Coll (CA)
Snow Coll (UT)
Solano Comm Coll (CA)
South Arkansas Comm Coll (AR)
Southeast Comm Coll, Lincoln Cmps (NE)
Southeast Comm Coll, Milford Cmps (NE)
Southeastern Comm Coll, North Cmps, West Burlington (IA)
Southeastern Illinois Coll (IL)
Southern Maine Tech Coll (ME)
Southern West Virginia Comm and Tech Coll (WV)
South Plains Coll (TX)
South Puget Sound Comm Coll (WA)
South Seattle Comm Coll (WA)
SouthWest Collegiate Inst for the Deaf (TX)
Southwestern Coll (CA)
Southwestern Comm Coll (NC)
Southwestern Michigan Coll (MI)
Southwestern Oregon Comm Coll (OR)
Southwestern Tech Coll (MN)
Southwest Mississippi Comm Coll (MS)
Southwest Texas Jr Coll (TX)
Southwest Wisconsin Tech Coll (WI)
Spartanburg Tech Coll (SC)
Spokane Comm Coll (WA)
Spoon River Coll (IL)
Springfield Tech Comm Coll (MA)
Stark Tech Coll (OH)
State Fair Comm Coll (MO)
State Tech Inst at Memphis (TN)
State U of NY Coll of A&T at Cobleskill (NY)
State U of NY Coll of A&T at Morrisville (NY)
State U of NY Coll of Tech at Alfred (NY)
State U of NY Coll of Tech at Canton (NY)
State U of NY Coll of Tech at Delhi (NY)
State U of NY Coll of Tech at Farmingdale (NY)
Suffolk County Comm College–Ammerman Cmps (NY)
Surry Comm Coll (NC)
Taft Coll (CA)
Tarrant County Jr Coll (TX)
Temple Coll (TX)
Terra State Comm Coll (OH)
Texarkana Coll (TX)
Texas Southmost Coll (TX)
Texas State Tech Coll–Waco/Marshall Cmps (TX)
Thaddeus Stevens State Sch of Tech (PA)
Thomas Nelson Comm Coll (VA)
Tidewater Comm Coll (VA)
Tri-County Comm Coll (NC)
Trident Tech Coll (SC)
Trinidad State Jr Coll (CO)
Trinity Valley Comm Coll (TX)
Triton Coll (IL)
Truckee Meadows Comm Coll (NV)
Tulsa Jr Coll (OK)
Umpqua Comm Coll (OR)
United Tribes Tech Coll (ND)
U of Cincinnati Raymond Walters Coll (OH)
U of Hawaii–Hawaii Comm Coll (HI)
U of Hawaii–Honolulu Comm Coll (HI)
U of Hawaii–Kauai Comm Coll (HI)
U of Hawaii–Leeward Comm Coll (HI)
U of Hawaii–Maui Comm Coll (HI)
U of Hawaii–Windward Comm Coll (HI)
U of Kentucky, Jefferson Comm Coll (KY)
U of New Mexico–Gallup Branch (NM)
U of North Dakota–Lake Region (ND)
U of North Dakota–Williston (ND)
Utah Valley State Coll (UT)
Vance-Granville Comm Coll (NC)
Ventura Coll (CA)
Vernon Regional Jr Coll (TX)
Victor Valley Coll (CA)
Vincennes U (IN)
Virginia Western Comm Coll (VA)
Wallace State Comm Coll (AL)
Walla Walla Comm Coll (WA)
Washington County Tech Coll (ME)
Washington State Comm Coll (OH)
Washtenaw Comm Coll (MI)
Waubonsee Comm Coll (IL)
Waycross Coll (GA)
Wayne Comm Coll (NC)
Wayne County Comm Coll (MI)
Wenatchee Valley Coll (WA)
Westark Comm Coll (AR)
Westchester Comm Coll (NY)
Western Dakota Tech Inst (SD)
Western Iowa Tech Comm Coll (IA)
Western Nebraska Comm Coll, Scottsbluff (NE)
Western Nevada Comm Coll (NV)
Western Texas Coll (TX)
Western Wisconsin Tech Coll (WI)
Western Wyoming Comm Coll (WY)
West Hills Comm Coll (CA)
West Shore Comm Coll (MI)
West Virginia U at Parkersburg (WV)
Wharton County Jr Coll (TX)
Wilkes Comm Coll (NC)
Willmar Tech Coll (MN)
Wyoming Tech Inst (WY)
Yakima Valley Comm Coll (WA)
Yavapai Coll (AZ)
York Tech Coll (SC)
Yuba Coll (CA)

AVIATION ADMINISTRATION

Broward Comm Coll (FL)
Catonsville Comm Coll (MD)
Central Texas Coll (TX)
Chattanooga State Tech Comm Coll (TN)
Comm Coll of Allegheny County Allegheny Cmps (PA)
Comm Coll of the Air Force (AL)
Cuyamaca Coll (CA)
Cypress Coll (CA)
Davis Coll (OH)
Delaware Tech & Comm Coll, Terry Cmps (DE)
Dixie Coll (UT)
Florida Comm Coll at Jacksonville (FL)
Green River Comm Coll (WA)
Guilford Tech Comm Coll (NC)
Gulf Coast Comm Coll (FL)
Inver Hills Comm Coll (MN)
Iowa Central Comm Coll (IA)
Iowa Lakes Comm Coll (IA)
Lehigh Carbon Comm Coll (PA)
Lenoir Comm Coll (NC)
Lincoln Land Comm Coll (IL)
Luzerne County Comm Coll (PA)
Mercer County Comm Coll (NJ)
Meridian Comm Coll (MS)
Miami-Dade Comm Coll (FL)
Middle Georgia Coll (GA)
Midstate Coll (IL)
Mountain View Coll (TX)
New Hampshire Tech Coll, Laconia (NH)
Northland Comm and Tech Coll (MN)
Palo Alto Coll (TX)
Palomar Coll (CA)
Pasadena City Coll (CA)
Rio Salado Comm Coll (AZ)
St Catharine Coll (KY)
St Petersburg Jr Coll (FL)
San Diego Mesa Coll (CA)
Sinclair Comm Coll (OH)
Southwestern Coll (CA)
Vermilion Comm Coll (MN)
Western Oklahoma State Coll (OK)

AVIATION TECHNOLOGY

Aims Comm Coll (CO)
Alabama Aviation and Tech Coll (AL)
Alexandria Tech Coll (MN)
American Flyers Coll (FL)
Atlanta Metropolitan Coll (GA)
Belleville Area Coll (IL)
Big Bend Comm Coll (WA)
Broward Comm Coll (FL)
Catonsville Comm Coll (MD)
Central Coll (KS)
Central Texas Coll (TX)
Chandler-Gilbert Comm Coll (AZ)
Chattanooga State Tech Comm Coll (TN)
Chesapeake Coll (MD)
Cincinnati State Tech and Comm Coll (OH)
City Coll of San Francisco (CA)
City Colls of Chicago, Richard J Daley Coll (IL)
Cloud County Comm Coll (KS)
Clovis Comm Coll (NM)
Cochise Coll, Douglas (AZ)
Coll of Alameda (CA)
Coll of San Mateo (CA)
Colorado Northwestern Comm Coll (CO)
Columbus State Comm Coll (OH)
Comm Coll of Allegheny County Allegheny Cmps (PA)
Comm Coll of Beaver County (PA)
Comm Coll of the Air Force (AL)
Cumberland County Coll (NJ)
Cuyahoga Comm Coll, Western Cmps (OH)
Delaware Tech & Comm Coll, Terry Cmps (DE)
Delta Coll (MI)
Dixie Coll (UT)
Eastern New Mexico University–Roswell (NM)
East Mississippi Comm Coll (MS)
Edison State Comm Coll (OH)
Enterprise State Jr Coll (AL)
Everett Comm Coll (WA)
Florida Comm Coll at Jacksonville (FL)
Foothill Coll (CA)
Frederick Comm Coll (MD)
Fresno City Coll (CA)
Gateway Comm-Tech Coll (CT)
Gavilan Coll (CA)
Green River Comm Coll (WA)
Greenville Tech Coll (SC)
Guilford Tech Comm Coll (NC)
Hawkeye Comm Coll (IA)
Hesston Coll (KS)
Housatonic Comm-Tech Coll (CT)
Indian Hills Comm Coll (IA)
Iowa Western Comm Coll (IA)
Jackson Comm Coll (MI)
Johnson County Comm Coll (KS)
Kings River Comm Coll (CA)
Lake Area Vocational-Tech Inst (SD)
Lane Comm Coll (OR)
Lansing Comm Coll (MI)
Lee Coll (TX)
Lehigh Carbon Comm Coll (PA)
Lenoir Comm Coll (NC)
Long Beach City Coll (CA)
Los Angeles Mission Coll (CA)
Luzerne County Comm Coll (PA)
Macomb Comm Coll (MI)
Maple Woods Comm Coll (MO)
Mercer County Comm Coll (NJ)
Miami-Dade Comm Coll (FL)
Midland Coll (TX)
Mountain View Coll (TX)
Mt Hood Comm Coll (OR)
Mt San Antonio Coll (CA)
National Ed Ctr–Spartan Sch of Aeronautics Cmps (OK)
Navarro Coll (TX)
NEI Coll of Tech (MN)
New Hampshire Tech Coll, Nashua (NH)
Northern Virginia Comm Coll (VA)
Northland Comm and Tech Coll (MN)
North Shore Comm Coll (MA)
Northwestern Michigan Coll (MI)
Oakland Comm Coll (MI)
Okaloosa-Walton Comm Coll (FL)
Oklahoma City Comm Coll (OK)
Oklahoma State U, Oklahoma City (OK)
Oklahoma State U, Okmulgee (OK)
Orange Coast Coll (CA)
Palo Alto Coll (TX)
Palomar Coll (CA)
Pasadena City Coll (CA)
Pennsylvania Coll of Tech (PA)
Pikes Peak Comm Coll (CO)
Pittsburgh Inst of Aeronautics (PA)
Portland Comm Coll (OR)
Pratt Comm Coll and Area Voc Sch (KS)
Quinebaug Valley Comm-Tech Coll (CT)
Rock Valley Coll (IL)
Rogers State Coll (OK)
Rose State Coll (OK)
Sacramento City Coll (CA)
St Catharine Coll (KY)
St Philip's Coll (TX)
Salt Lake Comm Coll (UT)
San Diego Miramar Coll (CA)
San Jacinto College–Central Cmps (TX)
San Juan Coll (NM)
Santa Rosa Jr Coll (CA)
Scott Comm Coll (IA)
Shasta Coll (CA)
Solano Comm Coll (CA)
Southern Arkansas U Tech (AR)
Southern U at Shreveport–Bossier City Cmps (LA)
South Seattle Comm Coll (WA)
South Suburban Coll (IL)
Southwestern Coll (CA)
Southwestern Michigan Coll (MI)
Southwest Texas Jr Coll (TX)
Spokane Comm Coll (WA)
State U of NY Coll of Tech at Farmingdale (NY)
Tarrant County Jr Coll (TX)
Texas State Tech Coll–Waco/Marshall Cmps (TX)
Three Rivers Comm-Tech Coll (CT)
Tulsa Jr Coll (OK)
U of Cincinnati Clermont Coll (OH)
U of Hawaii–Honolulu Comm Coll (HI)
U of North Dakota–Lake Region (ND)
Utah Valley State Coll (UT)
Vincennes U (IN)
Wallace State Comm Coll (AL)
Wayne Comm Coll (NC)
Wayne County Comm Coll (MI)
Western Nebraska Comm Coll, Scottsbluff (NE)
West Los Angeles Coll (CA)

BEHAVIORAL SCIENCES

Allen County Comm Coll (KS)
Anne Arundel Comm Coll (MD)
Brevard Coll (NC)
Bunker Hill Comm Coll (MA)
Butler County Comm Coll (KS)
Casper Coll (WY)
Central Coll (KS)

Associate Degree Programs at Two-Year Colleges
Behavioral Sciences–Biology/Biological Sciences

Central Comm College–Platte Cmps (NE)
Central Texas Coll (TX)
Chabot Coll (CA)
Citrus Coll (CA)
Cloud County Comm Coll (KS)
Cochise Coll, Douglas (AZ)
Cochise Coll, Sierra Vista (AZ)
Coffeyville Comm Coll (KS)
Colby Comm Coll (KS)
Coll of Marin (CA)
Coll of Southern Idaho (ID)
Colorado Mountn Coll, Alpine Cmps (CO)
Colorado Mountn Coll, Roaring Fork Cmps-Spring Valley Ctr (CO)
Colorado Mountn Coll, Timberline Cmps (CO)
Comm Coll of Allegheny County Allegheny Cmps (PA)
Comm Coll of Allegheny County Boyce Cmps (PA)
Comm Coll of Allegheny County North Cmps (PA)
Comm Coll of Allegheny County South Cmps (PA)
Comm Coll of Southern Nevada (NV)
Daytona Beach Comm Coll (FL)
De Anza Coll (CA)
DeKalb Coll (GA)
Dodge City Comm Coll (KS)
East Central Comm Coll (MS)
Fulton-Montgomery Comm Coll (NY)
Galveston Coll (TX)
Garrett Comm Coll (MD)
Gordon Coll (GA)
Greenfield Comm Coll (MA)
Harford Comm Coll (MD)
Highline Comm Coll (WA)
Hill Coll of the Hill Jr Coll District (TX)
Howard Coll (TX)
Imperial Valley Coll (CA)
Iowa Lakes Comm Coll (IA)
Irvine Valley Coll (CA)
Labette Comm Coll (KS)
Lamar Comm Coll (CO)
Lincoln Coll, Normal (IL)
Lincoln Land Comm Coll (IL)
Los Angeles Southwest Coll (CA)
Los Medanos Coll (CA)
Macomb Comm Coll (MI)
Miami-Dade Comm Coll (FL)
Middle Georgia Coll (GA)
Midland Coll (TX)
Mid-Plains Comm Coll (NE)
MiraCosta Coll (CA)
Mississippi Delta Comm Coll (MS)
Moberly Area Comm Coll (MO)
Monroe Comm Coll (NY)
Moorpark Coll (CA)
Mt San Jacinto Coll (CA)
Napa Valley Coll (CA)
Northwestern Connecticut Comm-Tech Coll (CT)
Ohio Valley Coll (WV)
Orange Coast Coll (CA)
Owens Comm Coll, Findlay (OH)
Owens Comm Coll, Toledo (OH)
Oxnard Coll (CA)
Palo Verde Coll (CA)
Pueblo Comm Coll (CO)
Quincy Coll (MA)
Reading Area Comm Coll (PA)
Redlands Comm Coll (OK)
Riverside Comm Coll (CA)
San Diego City Coll (CA)
San Jacinto College–Central Cmps (TX)
San Jacinto College–South Cmps (TX)
San Joaquin Delta Coll (CA)
Scott Comm Coll (IA)
Seminole Jr Coll (OK)
Shorter Coll (AR)
Springfield Tech Comm Coll (MA)
Sullivan County Comm Coll (NY)
Tacoma Comm Coll (WA)
Tyler Jr Coll (TX)
Umpqua Comm Coll (OR)
U of Wisconsin Center–Marathon County (WI)
Vincennes U (IN)
Vincennes University–Jasper Ctr (IN)
Waldorf Coll (IA)
Western Oklahoma State Coll (OK)
West Shore Comm Coll (MI)
Wharton County Jr Coll (TX)

BIBLICAL LANGUAGES
Ohio Valley Coll (WV)

BIBLICAL STUDIES
Brevard Coll (NC)
Central Coll (KS)
Central Indian Bible Coll (SD)
Hesston Coll (KS)
Hiwassee Coll (TN)
Lon Morris Coll (TX)
Northeast Mississippi Comm Coll (MS)
Ohio Valley Coll (WV)
St Catharine Coll (KY)
San Jacinto College–Central Cmps (TX)
Waldorf Coll (IA)

BIOCHEMICAL TECHNOLOGY
Comm Coll of Allegheny County Allegheny Cmps (PA)
De Anza Coll (CA)
Lansing Comm Coll (MI)
Mid Michigan Comm Coll (MI)
Southwestern Michigan Coll (MI)
U of Cincinnati Raymond Walters Coll (OH)

BIOLOGY/BIOLOGICAL SCIENCES
Abraham Baldwin Ag Coll (GA)
Alabama Southern Comm Coll, Monroeville (AL)
Alabama Southern Comm Coll, Thomasville (AL)
Allan Hancock Coll (CA)
Allegany Comm Coll (MD)
Allen County Comm Coll (KS)
Alpena Comm Coll (MI)
Alvin Comm Coll (TX)
Andrew Coll (GA)
Angelina Coll (TX)
Anne Arundel Comm Coll (MD)
Antelope Valley Coll (CA)
Arizona Western Coll (AZ)
Arkansas State University–Beebe Branch (AR)
Atlanta Metropolitan Coll (GA)
Atlantic Comm Coll (NJ)
Austin Comm Coll (TX)
Bainbridge Coll (GA)
Bakersfield Coll (CA)
Barton County Comm Coll (KS)
Bee County Coll (TX)
Bergen Comm Coll (NJ)
Berkshire Comm Coll (MA)
Bismarck State Coll (ND)
Black Hawk Coll, Moline (IL)
Blinn Coll (TX)
Brazosport Coll (TX)
Brevard Coll (NC)
Brevard Comm Coll (FL)
Bronx Comm Coll of City U of NY (NY)
Brunswick Coll (GA)
Bucks County Comm Coll (PA)
Burlington County Coll (NJ)
Butler County Comm Coll (KS)
Butler County Comm Coll (PA)
Butte Coll (CA)
Cañada Coll (CA)
Carl Albert State Coll (OK)
Casper Coll (WY)
Central Coll (KS)
Central Comm College–Grand Island Cmps (NE)
Central Comm College–Hastings Cmps (NE)
Central Comm College–Platte Cmps (NE)
Centralia Coll (WA)
Central Piedmont Comm Coll (NC)
Central Texas Coll (TX)
Central Wyoming Coll (WY)
Cerritos Coll (CA)
Chabot Coll (CA)
Chaffey Coll (CA)
Charles County Comm Coll (MD)
Charles Stewart Mott Comm Coll (MI)
Chattahoochee Valley State Comm Coll (AL)
Chattanooga State Tech Comm Coll (TN)
Cisco Jr Coll (TX)
Citrus Coll (CA)
City Colls of Chicago, Harold Washington Coll (IL)
City Colls of Chicago, Kennedy-King Coll (IL)
City Colls of Chicago, Olive-Harvey Coll (IL)
Clackamas Comm Coll (OR)
Clark Coll (WA)
Clinton Comm Coll (IA)
Cloud County Comm Coll (KS)
Coahoma Comm Coll (MS)
Cochise Coll, Douglas (AZ)
Cochise Coll, Sierra Vista (AZ)
Coffeyville Comm Coll (KS)
Colby Comm Coll (KS)
Coll of Alameda (CA)
Coll of DuPage (IL)
Coll of Marin (CA)
Coll of San Mateo (CA)
Coll of Southern Idaho (ID)
Coll of the Canyons (CA)
Coll of the Desert (CA)
Coll of the Sequoias (CA)
Coll of the Siskiyous (CA)
Collin County Comm Coll (TX)
Colorado Mountn Coll, Alpine Cmps (CO)
Colorado Mountn Coll, Roaring Fork Cmps-Spring Valley Ctr (CO)
Colorado Mountn Coll, Timberline Cmps (CO)
Columbia Coll (CA)
Columbia State Comm Coll (TN)
Comm Coll of Allegheny County Allegheny Cmps (PA)
Comm Coll of Allegheny County South Cmps (PA)
Comm Coll of Beaver County (PA)
Comm Coll of Southern Nevada (NV)
Connors State Coll (OK)
Contra Costa Coll (CA)
Copiah-Lincoln Comm Coll (MS)
Cosumnes River Coll (CA)
County Coll of Morris (NJ)
Crafton Hills Coll (CA)
Crowder Coll (MO)
Cuesta Coll (CA)
Cypress Coll (CA)
Dalton Coll (GA)
Danville Area Comm Coll (IL)
Darton Coll (GA)
Daytona Beach Comm Coll (FL)
De Anza Coll (CA)
Del Mar Coll (TX)
Delta Coll (MI)
Dixie Coll (UT)
Dodge City Comm Coll (KS)
East Central Coll (MO)
East Central Comm Coll (MS)
Eastern Arizona Coll (AZ)
Eastern Oklahoma State Coll (OK)
Eastern Wyoming Coll (WY)
East Georgia Coll (GA)
East Los Angeles Coll (CA)
East Mississippi Comm Coll (MS)
El Camino Coll (CA)
Ellsworth Comm Coll (IA)
El Paso Comm Coll (TX)
Essex Comm Coll (MD)
Essex County Coll (NJ)
Everett Comm Coll (WA)
Feather River Comm Coll District (CA)
Finger Lakes Comm Coll (NY)
Foothill Coll (CA)
Frank Phillips Coll (TX)
Frederick Comm Coll (MD)
Fresno City Coll (CA)
Front Range Comm Coll (CO)
Fullerton Coll (CA)
Fulton-Montgomery Comm Coll (NY)
Gainesville Coll (GA)
Garrett Comm Coll (MD)
Gavilan Coll (CA)
Glendale Comm Coll (AZ)
Gloucester County Coll (NJ)
Gogebic Comm Coll (MI)
Golden West Coll (CA)
Gordon Coll (GA)
Grays Harbor Coll (WA)
Grayson County Coll (TX)
Grossmont Coll (CA)
Gulf Coast Comm Coll (FL)
Hagerstown Jr Coll (MD)
Harford Comm Coll (MD)
Harrisburg Area Comm Coll (PA)
Hawkeye Comm Coll (IA)
Herkimer County Comm Coll (NY)
Highland Comm Coll (KS)
Hill Coll of the Hill Jr Coll District (TX)
Hinds Comm Coll (MS)
Hiwassee Coll (TN)
Holmes Comm Coll (MS)
Holyoke Comm Coll (MA)
Howard Coll (TX)
Hutchinson Comm Coll and Area Vocational Sch (KS)
Illinois Eastern Comm Colls, Lincoln Trail Coll (IL)
Independence Comm Coll (KS)
Indian River Comm Coll (FL)
Iowa Lakes Comm Coll (IA)
Irvine Valley Coll (CA)
Itawamba Comm Coll (MS)
Jackson State Comm Coll (TN)
Jefferson Davis Comm Coll (AL)
John A Logan Coll (IL)
John C Calhoun State Comm Coll (AL)
John Wood Comm Coll (IL)
Joliet Jr Coll (IL)
Jones County Jr Coll (MS)
J Sargeant Reynolds Comm Coll (VA)
Kalamazoo Valley Comm Coll (MI)
Kansas City Kansas Comm Coll (KS)
Kellogg Comm Coll (MI)
Kemper Military Jr Coll (MO)
Keystone Coll (PA)
Kingsborough Comm Coll of City U of NY (NY)
Kings River Comm Coll (CA)
Kirkwood Comm Coll (IA)
Kishwaukee Coll (IL)
Labette Comm Coll (KS)
Lake Land Coll (IL)
Lake Michigan Coll (MI)
Lamar Comm Coll (CO)
Lansing Comm Coll (MI)
Laramie County Comm Coll (WY)
Lassen Coll (CA)
Lee Coll (TX)
Lewis and Clark Comm Coll (IL)
Lincoln Land Comm Coll (IL)
Linn-Benton Comm Coll (OR)
Long Beach City Coll (CA)
Longview Comm Coll (MO)
Lon Morris Coll (TX)
Lorain County Comm Coll (OH)
Los Angeles City Coll (CA)
Los Angeles Harbor Coll (CA)
Los Angeles Mission Coll (CA)
Los Angeles Valley Coll (CA)
Los Medanos Coll (CA)
Lower Columbia Coll (WA)
Macon Coll (GA)
Maple Woods Comm Coll (MO)
Mendocino Coll (CA)
Mercer County Comm Coll (NJ)
Mesa Comm Coll (AZ)
Miami-Dade Comm Coll (FL)
Middle Georgia Coll (GA)
Middlesex County Coll (NJ)
Midland Coll (TX)
Mid Michigan Comm Coll (MI)
Mid-Plains Comm Coll (NE)
MiraCosta Coll (CA)
Mississippi Delta Comm Coll (MS)
Mitchell Coll (CT)
Moberly Area Comm Coll (MO)
Modesto Jr Coll (CA)
Mohawk Valley Comm Coll (NY)
Monroe Comm Coll (NY)
Monroe County Comm Coll (MI)
Monterey Peninsula Coll (CA)
Montgomery College–Rockville Cmps (MD)
Montgomery College–Takoma Park Cmps (MD)
Montgomery County Comm Coll (PA)
Moorpark Coll (CA)
Motlow State Comm Coll (TN)
Mountain Empire Comm Coll (VA)
Muscatine Comm Coll (IA)
Navarro Coll (TX)
New Mexico Jr Coll (NM)
New Mexico Military Inst (NM)
Niagara County Comm Coll (NY)
Northampton County Area Comm Coll (PA)
North Dakota State University–Bottineau (ND)
Northeast Comm Coll (NE)
Northeastern Jr Coll (CO)
Northeast Mississippi Comm Coll (MS)
North Idaho Coll (ID)
Northwest Coll (WY)
Northwestern Connecticut Comm-Tech Coll (CT)
Odessa Coll (TX)
Ohlone Coll (CA)
Okaloosa-Walton Comm Coll (FL)
Oklahoma City Comm Coll (OK)
Orange County Comm Coll (NY)
Otero Jr Coll (CO)
Owens Comm Coll, Findlay (OH)
Owens Comm Coll, Toledo (OH)
Oxnard Coll (CA)
Palm Beach Comm Coll (FL)
Palo Alto Coll (TX)
Palomar Coll (CA)
Palo Verde Coll (CA)
Panama Canal Coll (Republic of Panama)
Parkland Coll (IL)
Pasadena City Coll (CA)
Pennsylvania Coll of Tech (PA)
Penn State U Altoona Cmps (PA)
Penn State U Beaver Cmps (PA)
Penn State U DuBois Cmps (PA)
Penn State U McKeesport Cmps (PA)
Penn State U New Kensington Cmps (PA)
Penn State U Schuylkill Cmps (PA)
Penn State U Shenango Cmps (PA)
Penn Valley Comm Coll (MO)
Pensacola Jr Coll (FL)
Phillips County Comm Coll (AR)
Pikes Peak Comm Coll (CO)
Pima Comm Coll (AZ)
Polk Comm Coll (FL)
Porterville Coll (CA)
Potomac State Coll of West Virginia U (WV)
Pratt Comm Coll and Area Voc Sch (KS)
Rancho Santiago Coll (CA)
Raritan Valley Comm Coll (NJ)
Reading Area Comm Coll (PA)
Redlands Comm Coll (OK)
Red Rocks Comm Coll (CO)
Ricks Coll (ID)
Roane State Comm Coll (TN)
Rogers State Coll (OK)
Rose State Coll (OK)
Roxbury Comm Coll (MA)
Saddleback Coll (CA)
St Catharine Coll (KY)
St Gregory's Coll (OK)
St Louis Comm Coll at Forest Park (MO)
St Philip's Coll (TX)
Salem Comm Coll (NJ)
Salt Lake Comm Coll (UT)
San Bernardino Valley Coll (CA)
San Diego City Coll (CA)
San Diego Mesa Coll (CA)
San Diego Miramar Coll (CA)
San Jacinto College–Central Cmps (TX)
San Jacinto College–South Cmps (TX)
San Joaquin Delta Coll (CA)
San Juan Coll (NM)
Santa Barbara City Coll (CA)
Santa Fe Comm Coll (NM)
Santa Monica Coll (CA)
Santa Rosa Jr Coll (CA)
Sauk Valley Comm Coll (IL)
Seminole Jr Coll (OK)
Seward County Comm Coll (KS)
Shelton State Comm Coll (AL)
Sheridan Coll (WY)
Sierra Coll (CA)
Skagit Valley Coll (WA)
Skyline Coll (CA)
Snow Coll (UT)
Solano Comm Coll (CA)
Southeast Comm Coll, Beatrice Cmps (NE)
Southern U at Shreveport–Bossier City Cmps (LA)
South Georgia Coll (GA)
South Mountain Comm Coll (AZ)
South Plains Coll (TX)
SouthWest Collegiate Inst for the Deaf (TX)
Southwestern Coll (CA)
Southwestern Michigan Coll (MI)
Southwest Mississippi Comm Coll (MS)
Southwest Missouri State University– West Plains (MO)
Spoon River Coll (IL)
State Comm Coll of East St Louis (IL)
State U of NY Coll of A&T at Cobleskill (NY)
State U of NY Coll of A&T at Morrisville (NY)
State U of NY Coll of Tech at Canton (NY)
Suffolk County Comm College–Ammerman Cmps (NY)
Sullivan County Comm Coll (NY)
Sussex County Comm Coll (NJ)
Tacoma Comm Coll (WA)
Taft Coll (CA)
Texarkana Coll (TX)
Treasure Valley Comm Coll (OR)
Trinidad State Jr Coll (CO)
Trinity Valley Comm Coll (TX)
Triton Coll (IL)
Tulsa Jr Coll (OK)
Turtle Mountain Comm Coll (ND)
Umpqua Comm Coll (OR)
Union County Coll (NJ)
U of Cincinnati Raymond Walters Coll (OH)
U of Kentucky, Jefferson Comm Coll (KY)
U of Wisconsin Center–Marathon County (WI)
Vermilion Comm Coll (MN)
Victor Valley Coll (CA)
Vincennes U (IN)
Waldorf Coll (IA)
Warren County Comm Coll (NJ)

Peterson's Guide to Two-Year Colleges 1997
57

Washington State Comm Coll (OH)
Washtenaw Comm Coll (MI)
Waubonsee Comm Coll (IL)
Waycross Coll (GA)
Wenatchee Valley Coll (WA)
Western Nebraska Comm Coll, Scottsbluff (NE)
Western Nevada Comm Coll (NV)
Western Oklahoma State Coll (OK)
Western Wyoming Comm Coll (WY)
West Hills Comm Coll (CA)
West Los Angeles Coll (CA)
West Valley Coll (CA)
Wharton County Jr Coll (TX)
William Rainey Harper Coll (IL)
Wright State U, Lake Cmps (OH)
Young Harris Coll (GA)
Yuba Coll (CA)

BIOMEDICAL TECHNOLOGIES

Alabama Southern Comm Coll, Monroeville (AL)
Alamance Comm Coll (NC)
Berkshire Comm Coll (MA)
Brevard Comm Coll (FL)
Caldwell Comm Coll and Tech Inst (NC)
Cerritos Coll (CA)
Chattahoochee Tech Inst (GA)
Cincinnati State Tech and Comm Coll (OH)
Comm Coll of Philadelphia (PA)
Comm Coll of the Air Force (AL)
County Coll of Morris (NJ)
Delaware County Comm Coll (PA)
Delaware Tech & Comm Coll, Stanton/Wilmington Cmps (DE)
Delgado Comm Coll (LA)
Des Moines Area Comm Coll (IA)
ECPI Coll of Tech, Virginia Beach (VA)
ECPI Computer Inst, Roanoke (VA)
Erie Comm Coll, South Cmps (NY)
Florida Comm Coll at Jacksonville (FL)
Gateway Comm-Tech Coll (CT)
George Corley Wallace State Comm Coll, Selma (AL)
Great Lakes Jr Coll of Business (MI)
Hillsborough Comm Coll (FL)
Howard Comm Coll (MD)
Ivy Tech State Coll–Eastcentral (IN)
Jefferson State Comm Coll (AL)
John C Calhoun State Comm Coll (AL)
Johnson County Comm Coll (KS)
Johnson Tech Inst (PA)
Kansas City Kansas Comm Coll (KS)
Kettering Coll of Medical Arts (OH)
Lansing Comm Coll (MI)
Lehigh Carbon Comm Coll (PA)
Milwaukee Area Tech Coll (WI)
Muskegon Comm Coll (MI)
Napa Valley Coll (CA)
Normandale Comm Coll (MN)
North Central Tech Coll (OH)
Oakton Comm Coll (IL)
Owens Comm Coll, Findlay (OH)
Owens Comm Coll, Toledo (OH)
Penn State U Abington-Ogontz Cmps (PA)
Penn State U Altoona Cmps (PA)
Penn State U Beaver Cmps (PA)
Penn State U Berks Cmps (PA)
Penn State U DuBois Cmps (PA)
Penn State U Fayette Cmps (PA)
Penn State U Hazleton Cmps (PA)
Penn State U McKeesport Cmps (PA)
Penn State U New Kensington Cmps (PA)
Penn State U Schuylkill Cmps (PA)
Penn State U Shenango Cmps (PA)
Penn State U Wilkes-Barre Cmps (PA)
Penn State U York Cmps (PA)
Pensacola Jr Coll (FL)
St Louis Comm Coll at Forest Park (MO)
St Philip's Coll (TX)
Santa Barbara City Coll (CA)
Santa Fe Comm Coll (FL)
Schoolcraft Coll (MI)
South Suburban Coll (IL)
Spokane Comm Coll (WA)
Springfield Tech Comm Coll (MA)
Stanly Comm Coll (NC)
Stark Tech Coll (OH)
State Tech Inst at Memphis (TN)
State U of NY Coll of Tech at Farmingdale (NY)
Texas State Tech Coll–Harlingen Cmps (TX)
Texas State Tech Coll–Waco/Marshall Cmps (TX)
U of Kentucky, Madisonville Comm Coll (KY)
Westchester Comm Coll (NY)
Western Wisconsin Tech Coll (WI)

BIOTECHNOLOGY

Alamance Comm Coll (NC)
Athens Area Tech Inst (GA)
Central Comm College–Hastings Cmps (NE)
Coll of San Mateo (CA)
Contra Costa Coll (CA)
De Anza Coll (CA)
Ellsworth Comm Coll (IA)
Finger Lakes Comm Coll (NY)
Indian Hills Comm Coll (IA)
Kirkwood Comm Coll (IA)
Lake Area Vocational-Tech Inst (SD)
Madison Area Tech Coll (WI)
Massachusetts Bay Comm Coll (MA)
Middlesex Comm Coll (MA)
Middlesex Community–Tech Coll (CT)
Middlesex County Coll (NJ)
Mid Michigan Comm Coll (MI)
Monroe Comm Coll (NY)
Montgomery Coll (TX)
Muskegon Comm Coll (MI)
North Harris Coll (TX)
North Shore Comm Coll (MA)
Portland Comm Coll (OR)
San Diego Miramar Coll (CA)
Seattle Central Comm Coll (WA)
Shoreline Comm Coll (WA)
Southeast Comm Coll, Beatrice Cmps (NE)
Springfield Tech Comm Coll (MA)
State U of NY Coll of A&T at Morrisville (NY)
State U of NY Coll of Tech at Alfred (NY)
Vermont Tech Coll (VT)
Vista Comm Coll (CA)

BLACK/ AFRICAN-AMERICAN STUDIES

Bronx Comm Coll of City U of NY (NY)
City Coll of San Francisco (CA)
City Colls of Chicago, Olive-Harvey Coll (IL)
Coll of Alameda (CA)
Contra Costa Coll (CA)
El Camino Coll (CA)
Fresno City Coll (CA)
Laney Coll (CA)
Los Angeles City Coll (CA)
Los Angeles Harbor Coll (CA)
Los Angeles Valley Coll (CA)
Merritt Coll (CA)
Nassau Comm Coll (NY)
Pasadena City Coll (CA)
Rancho Santiago Coll (CA)
St Louis Comm Coll at Forest Park (MO)
San Diego City Coll (CA)
San Diego Mesa Coll (CA)
Santa Barbara City Coll (CA)
Solano Comm Coll (CA)
Southwestern Coll (CA)
Yuba Coll (CA)

BOTANY/PLANT SCIENCES

Anne Arundel Comm Coll (MD)
Arizona Western Coll (AZ)
Brevard Coll (NC)
Casper Coll (WY)
Cerritos Coll (CA)
Chemeketa Comm Coll (OR)
City Coll of San Francisco (CA)
Coffeyville Comm Coll (KS)
Coll of the Siskiyous (CA)
Comm Coll of Allegheny County South Cmps (PA)
Dixie Coll (UT)
East Central Coll (MO)
El Camino Coll (CA)
Everett Comm Coll (WA)
Foothill Coll (CA)
Frank Phillips Coll (TX)
Grays Harbor Coll (WA)
Hill Coll of the Hill Jr Coll District (TX)
Iowa Lakes Comm Coll (IA)
Lassen Coll (CA)
Lon Morris Coll (TX)
Mercer County Comm Coll (NJ)
Miami University–Middletown Cmps (OH)
Mid-Plains Comm Coll (NE)
Modesto Jr Coll (CA)
North Dakota State University–Bottineau (ND)
Northeastern Oklahoma A&M Coll (OK)
North Idaho Coll (ID)
Northwest Coll (WY)
Ohio State U Ag Tech Inst (OH)
Palm Beach Comm Coll (FL)
Polk Comm Coll (FL)
Rancho Santiago Coll (CA)
Redlands Comm Coll (OK)
Ricks Coll (ID)
St Gregory's Coll (OK)
San Bernardino Valley Coll (CA)
San Jacinto College–Central Cmps (TX)
San Joaquin Delta Coll (CA)
Santa Rosa Jr Coll (CA)
Snow Coll (UT)
Southern Maine Tech Coll (ME)
Southwestern Coll (CA)
Spoon River Coll (IL)
State U of NY Coll of A&T at Cobleskill (NY)
Tacoma Comm Coll (WA)
Tulsa Jr Coll (OK)

BROADCASTING

Adirondack Comm Coll (NY)
American Inst of Commerce (IA)
Anne Arundel Comm Coll (MD)
Arizona Western Coll (AZ)
Bakersfield Coll (CA)
Beal Coll (ME)
Bergen Comm Coll (NJ)
Black Hawk Coll, Moline (IL)
Blue Mountain Comm Coll (OR)
Brevard Coll (NC)
Briarwood Coll (CT)
Brown Inst (MN)
Bucks County Comm Coll (PA)
Cayuga County Comm Coll (NY)
Central Comm College–Hastings Cmps (NE)
Centralia Coll (WA)
Central Texas Coll (TX)
Central Wyoming Coll (WY)
Chabot Coll (CA)
Chaffey Coll (CA)
Chattanooga State Tech Comm Coll (TN)
City Coll of San Francisco (CA)
City Colls of Chicago, Kennedy-King Coll (IL)
Cloud County Comm Coll (KS)
Coffeyville Comm Coll (KS)
Colby Comm Coll (KS)
Coll of San Mateo (CA)
Comm Coll of Allegheny County Boyce Cmps (PA)
Cosumnes River Coll (CA)
County Coll of Morris (NJ)
Cumberland County Coll (NJ)
Dean Coll (MA)
DeKalb Coll (GA)
Delta Coll (MI)
Dodge City Comm Coll (KS)
Draughons Jr Coll, Nashville (TN)
El Paso Comm Coll (TX)
Finger Lakes Comm Coll (NY)
Frank Phillips Coll (TX)
Fugazzi Coll (KY)
Gadsden State Comm Coll (AL)
Gaston Coll (NC)
Green River Comm Coll (WA)
Gulf Coast Comm Coll (FL)
Harford Comm Coll (MD)
Herkimer County Comm Coll (NY)
Hesser Coll (NH)
Hocking Coll (OH)
Hutchinson Comm Coll and Area Vocational Sch (KS)
Iowa Central Comm Coll (IA)
Isothermal Comm Coll (NC)
Jackson State Comm Coll (TN)
Kellogg Comm Coll (MI)
Kingsborough Comm Coll of City U of NY (NY)
Kirkwood Comm Coll (IA)
Lake Land Coll (IL)
Lake-Sumter Comm Coll (FL)
Lane Comm Coll (OR)
Laney Coll (CA)
Lansing Comm Coll (MI)
Lehigh Carbon Comm Coll (PA)
Lewis and Clark Comm Coll (IL)
Los Angeles City Coll (CA)
Los Angeles Valley Coll (CA)
Luzerne County Comm Coll (PA)
Meridian Comm Coll (MS)
Miami-Dade Comm Coll (FL)
Middlesex Community–Tech Coll (CT)
Milwaukee Area Tech Coll (WI)
Moorpark Coll (CA)
Mt Hood Comm Coll (OR)
Mount Wachusett Comm Coll (MA)
Navarro Coll (TX)
Northeast Comm Coll (NE)
Northeastern Oklahoma A&M Coll (OK)
Northeast Mississippi Comm Coll (MS)
Northern Oklahoma Coll (OK)
Northland Comm and Tech Coll (MN)
Northwest Mississippi Comm Coll (MS)
Ocean County Coll (NJ)
Ohlone Coll (CA)
Oklahoma City Comm Coll (OK)
Parkland Coll (IL)
Pasadena City Coll (CA)
Pennsylvania Coll of Tech (PA)
Pikes Peak Comm Coll (CO)
Polk Comm Coll (FL)
Pratt Comm Coll and Area Voc Sch (KS)
Pueblo Comm Coll (CO)
Ricks Coll (ID)
Rogers State Coll (OK)
Rose State Coll (OK)
St Clair County Comm Coll (MI)
St Louis Comm Coll at Florissant Valley (MO)
St Louis Comm Coll at Meramec (MO)
San Joaquin Delta Coll (CA)
Santa Monica Coll (CA)
Schoolcraft Coll (MI)
Southeast Comm Coll, Beatrice Cmps (NE)
Suffolk County Comm College–Ammerman Cmps (NY)
Sullivan County Comm Coll (NY)
Sussex County Comm Coll (NJ)
Trident Tech Coll (SC)
U of Alaska, Prince William Sound Comm Coll (AK)
Vincennes U (IN)
White Pines Coll (NH)
Willmar Comm Coll (MN)
Yakima Valley Comm Coll (WA)

BUSINESS ADMINISTRATION/ COMMERCE/ MANAGEMENT

Abraham Baldwin Ag Coll (GA)
Adirondack Comm Coll (NY)
Aiken Tech Coll (SC)
Alabama Southern Comm Coll, Monroeville (AL)
Alabama Southern Comm Coll, Thomasville (AL)
Alamance Comm Coll (NC)
Albuquerque Tech Vocational Inst (NM)
Allan Hancock Coll (CA)
Allegany Comm Coll (MD)
Allen County Comm Coll (KS)
Allentown Business Sch (PA)
Alpena Comm Coll (MI)
Alvin Comm Coll (TX)
American Inst of Business (IA)
American Inst of Commerce (IA)
American River Coll (CA)
Ancilla Coll (IN)
Andover Coll (ME)
Andrew Coll (GA)
Angelina Coll (TX)
Anne Arundel Comm Coll (MD)
Anoka-Ramsey Comm Coll (MN)
Anson Comm Coll (NC)
Antelope Valley Coll (CA)
Aquinas Coll at Milton (MA)
Aquinas Coll at Newton (MA)
Arapahoe Comm Coll (CO)
Arizona Western Coll (AZ)
Arkansas State University–Beebe Branch (AR)
Asheville-Buncombe Tech Comm Coll (NC)
Asnuntuck Comm-Tech Coll (CT)
Atlanta Metropolitan Coll (GA)
Atlantic Comm Coll (NJ)
Austin Comm Coll (MN)
Austin Comm Coll (TX)
Bacone Coll (OK)
Bainbridge Coll (GA)
Baker Coll of Jackson (MI)
Bakersfield Coll (CA)
Baltimore City Comm Coll (MD)
Barstow Coll (CA)
Barton County Comm Coll (KS)
Bauder Coll (GA)
Bay de Noc Comm Coll (MI)
Bay Mills Comm Coll (MI)
Bay State Coll (MA)
Beal Coll (ME)
Beaufort County Comm Coll (NC)
Bee County Coll (TX)
Belleville Area Coll (IL)
Bellevue Comm Coll (WA)
Belmont Tech Coll (OH)
Bergen Comm Coll (NJ)
Berkeley Coll (NJ)
Berkeley Coll, New York (NY)
Berkeley Coll, White Plains (NY)
Berkshire Comm Coll (MA)
Bevill State Comm Coll (AL)
Big Bend Comm Coll (WA)
Bishop State Comm Coll (AL)
Bismarck State Coll (ND)
Blackfeet Comm Coll (MT)
Black Hawk Coll, Kewanee (IL)
Black Hawk Coll, Moline (IL)
Bladen Comm Coll (NC)
Blair Jr Coll (CO)
Blinn Coll (TX)
Blue Mountain Comm Coll (OR)
Blue Ridge Comm Coll (NC)
Blue Ridge Comm Coll (VA)
Borough of Manhattan Comm Coll of City U of NY (NY)
Bossier Parish Comm Coll (LA)
Bowling Green State University–Firelands Coll (OH)
Bramson ORT Tech Inst (NY)
Brazosport Coll (TX)
Brevard Coll (NC)
Brevard Comm Coll (FL)
Briarcliffe–The Coll for Business & Tech (NY)
Briarwood Coll (CT)
Bristol Comm Coll (MA)
Bronx Comm Coll of City U of NY (NY)
Brookdale Comm Coll (NJ)
Brookhaven Coll (TX)
Broome Comm Coll (NY)
Broward Comm Coll (FL)
Brown Inst (MN)
The Brown Mackie Coll (KS)
The Brown Mackie Coll-Olathe Cmps (KS)
Brunswick Coll (GA)
Brunswick Comm Coll (NC)
Bryant and Stratton Business Inst, Albany (NY)
Bryant and Stratton Business Inst, Buffalo (NY)
Bryant and Stratton Business Inst, Cicero (NY)
Bryant and Stratton Business Inst, Lackawanna (NY)
Bryant and Stratton Business Inst, Rochester (NY)
Bryant and Stratton Business Inst, Rochester (NY)
Bryant and Stratton Business Inst, Syracuse (NY)
Bryant and Stratton Business Inst, E Hills Cmps, Williamsville (NY)
Bryant and Stratton Coll, Parma (OH)
Bryant and Stratton Coll, Richmond Heights (OH)
Bucks County Comm Coll (PA)
Bunker Hill Comm Coll (MA)
Burlington County Coll (NJ)
Butler County Comm Coll (KS)
Butler County Comm Coll (PA)
Cabrillo Coll (CA)
Caldwell Comm Coll and Tech Inst (NC)
Cambria-Rowe Business Coll (PA)
Camden County Coll (NJ)
Cañada Coll (CA)
Cape Cod Comm Coll (MA)
Cape Fear Comm Coll (NC)
Capital Comm Tech Coll (CT)
Carl Albert State Coll (OK)
Carl Sandburg Coll (IL)
Carteret Comm Coll (NC)
Casco Bay Coll (ME)
Casper Coll (WY)
Castle Coll (NH)
Catawba Valley Comm Coll (NC)
Catonsville Comm Coll (MD)
Cayuga County Comm Coll (NY)
Cecil Comm Coll (MD)
Cecils Jr Coll of Business (NC)
Central Alabama Comm Coll (AL)
Central Carolina Comm Coll (NC)
Central Carolina Tech Coll (SC)
Central City Business Inst (NY)

Associate Degree Programs at Two-Year Colleges
Business Administration/Commerce/Management

Central Coll (KS)
Central Comm College–Grand Island Cmps (NE)
Central Comm College–Hastings Cmps (NE)
Central Comm College–Platte Cmps (NE)
Central Florida Comm Coll (FL)
Centralia Coll (WA)
Central Lakes Coll (MN)
Central Maine Tech Coll (ME)
Central Ohio Tech Coll (OH)
Central Oregon Comm Coll (OR)
Central Pennsylvania Business Sch (PA)
Central Piedmont Comm Coll (NC)
Central Texas Coll (TX)
Central Virginia Comm Coll (VA)
Central Wyoming Coll (WY)
Cerritos Coll (CA)
Cerro Coso Comm Coll (CA)
Chabot Coll (CA)
Chaffey Coll (CA)
Champlain Coll (VT)
Chaparral Career Coll (AZ)
Charles County Comm Coll (MD)
Charles Stewart Mott Comm Coll (MI)
Chatfield Coll (OH)
Chattahoochee Tech Inst (GA)
Chattahoochee Valley State Comm Coll (AL)
Chattanooga State Tech Comm Coll (TN)
Chemeketa Comm Coll (OR)
Chesapeake Coll (MD)
Chesterfield-Marlboro Tech Coll (SC)
Chipola Jr Coll (FL)
Churchman Business Sch (PA)
Cincinnati State Tech and Comm Coll (OH)
Cisco Jr Coll (TX)
Citrus Coll (CA)
City Coll of San Francisco (CA)
City Colls of Chicago, Harold Washington Coll (IL)
City Colls of Chicago, Harry S Truman Coll (IL)
City Colls of Chicago, Kennedy-King Coll (IL)
City Colls of Chicago, Malcolm X Coll (IL)
City Colls of Chicago, Olive-Harvey Coll (IL)
City Colls of Chicago, Richard J Daley Coll (IL)
City Colls of Chicago, Wilbur Wright Coll (IL)
Clackamas Comm Coll (OR)
Clarendon Coll (TX)
Clark Coll (WA)
Clark State Comm Coll (OH)
Clatsop Comm Coll (OR)
Cleveland Comm Coll (NC)
Cleveland State Comm Coll (TN)
Clinton Comm Coll (IA)
Clinton Comm Coll (NY)
Cloud County Comm Coll (KS)
Clovis Comm Coll (NM)
Coahoma Comm Coll (MS)
Coastal Carolina Comm Coll (NC)
Cochise Coll, Douglas (AZ)
Cochise Coll, Sierra Vista (AZ)
Coconino County Comm Coll (AZ)
Coffeyville Comm Coll (KS)
Colby Comm Coll (KS)
Coll of Alameda (CA)
Coll of DuPage (IL)
Coll of Eastern Utah (UT)
Coll of Lake County (IL)
Coll of Marin (CA)
Coll of Micronesia–FSM (FM)
Coll of San Mateo (CA)
Coll of The Albemarle (NC)
Coll of the Canyons (CA)
Coll of the Desert (CA)
Coll of the Mainland (TX)
Coll of the Redwoods (CA)
Coll of the Sequoias (CA)
Coll of the Siskiyous (CA)
Collin County Comm Coll (TX)
Colorado Mountn Coll, Alpine Cmps (CO)
Colorado Mountn Coll, Roaring Fork Cmps-Spring Valley Ctr (CO)
Colorado Mountn Coll, Timberline Cmps (CO)
Colorado Northwestern Comm Coll (CO)
Columbia Coll (CA)
Columbia-Greene Comm Coll (NY)
Columbia Jr Coll of Business (SC)
Columbus State Comm Coll (OH)
Commonwealth Business Coll, LaPorte (IN)
Commonwealth Business Coll, Merrillville (IN)
Comm Coll of Allegheny County Allegheny Cmps (PA)
Comm Coll of Allegheny County Boyce Cmps (PA)
Comm Coll of Allegheny County North Cmps (PA)
Comm Coll of Allegheny County South Cmps (PA)
Comm Coll of Aurora (CO)
Comm Coll of Beaver County (PA)
Comm Coll of Denver (CO)
Comm Coll of Philadelphia (PA)
Comm Coll of Rhode Island (RI)
Comm Coll of Southern Nevada (NV)
Comm Coll of the Air Force (AL)
Comm Coll of Vermont (VT)
Connors State Coll (OK)
Contra Costa Coll (CA)
Copiah-Lincoln Comm Coll (MS)
Corning Comm Coll (NY)
Cossatot Tech Coll (AR)
Cosumnes River Coll (CA)
County Coll of Morris (NJ)
Cowley County Comm Coll and Voc-Tech Sch (KS)
Crafton Hills Coll (CA)
Craven Comm Coll (NC)
Crowder Coll (MO)
Cuesta Coll (CA)
Cumberland County Coll (NJ)
Cuyahoga Comm Coll, Eastern Cmps (OH)
Cuyahoga Comm Coll, Metropolitan Cmps (OH)
Cuyahoga Comm Coll, Western Cmps (OH)
Cuyamaca Coll (CA)
Cypress Coll (CA)
Dabney S Lancaster Comm Coll (VA)
Dalton Coll (GA)
Danville Area Comm Coll (IL)
Danville Comm Coll (VA)
Darton Coll (GA)
Davidson County Comm Coll (NC)
Davis Coll (OH)
Dawson Comm Coll (MT)
Daytona Beach Comm Coll (FL)
Dean Coll (MA)
De Anza Coll (CA)
DeKalb Coll (GA)
Delaware County Comm Coll (PA)
Delaware Tech & Comm Coll, Jack F Owens Cmps (DE)
Delaware Tech & Comm Coll, Stanton/Wilmington Cmps (DE)
Delaware Tech & Comm Coll, Terry Cmps (DE)
Delgado Comm Coll (LA)
Del Mar Coll (TX)
Delta Coll (MI)
Denmark Tech Coll (SC)
Des Moines Area Comm Coll (IA)
Dixie Coll (UT)
Dodge City Comm Coll (KS)
Doña Ana Branch Comm Coll (NM)
Donnelly Coll (KS)
D-Q U (CA)
Draughons Jr Coll (AL)
Draughons Jr Coll (KY)
Draughons Jr Coll, Nashville (TN)
Duff's Business Inst (PA)
Dundalk Comm Coll (MD)
Durham Tech Comm Coll (NC)
Dutchess Comm Coll (NY)
Dyersburg State Comm Coll (TN)
East Arkansas Comm Coll (AR)
East Central Coll (MO)
East Central Comm Coll (MS)
Eastern Arizona Coll (AZ)
Eastern Maine Tech Coll (ME)
Eastern New Mexico University–Roswell (NM)
Eastern Oklahoma State Coll (OK)
Eastern Shore Comm Coll (VA)
Eastern Wyoming Coll (WY)
Eastfield Coll (TX)
East Georgia Coll (GA)
East Los Angeles Coll (CA)
East Mississippi Comm Coll (MS)
Edgecombe Comm Coll (NC)
Edison Comm Coll (FL)
Edison State Comm Coll (OH)
Edmonds Comm Coll (WA)
Education America–Tampa Tech Inst Cmps (FL)
Elaine P Nunez Comm Coll (LA)
El Camino Coll (CA)
Elgin Comm Coll (IL)
Ellsworth Comm Coll (IA)
El Paso Comm Coll (TX)
Enterprise State Jr Coll (AL)
Erie Business Ctr, Main (PA)
Erie Business Ctr South (PA)
Erie Comm Coll, City Cmps (NY)
Erie Comm Coll, North Cmps (NY)
Erie Comm Coll, South Cmps (NY)
Essex Comm Coll (MD)
Essex County Coll (NJ)
Eugenio María de Hostos Comm Coll of City U of NY (NY)
Everett Comm Coll (WA)
Evergreen Valley Coll (CA)
Fayetteville Tech Comm Coll (NC)
Feather River Comm Coll District (CA)
Fergus Falls Comm Coll (MN)
Finger Lakes Comm Coll (NY)
Fiorello H LaGuardia Comm Coll of City U of NY (NY)
Fisher Coll (MA)
Flathead Valley Comm Coll (MT)
Florence-Darlington Tech Coll (SC)
Florida Comm Coll at Jacksonville (FL)
Florida Keys Comm Coll (FL)
Florida National Coll (FL)
Floyd Coll (GA)
Foothill Coll (CA)
Forsyth Tech Comm Coll (NC)
Fort Belknap Coll (MT)
Fort Berthold Comm Coll (ND)
Fort Peck Comm Coll (MT)
Fort Scott Comm Coll (KS)
Frank Phillips Coll (TX)
Frederick Comm Coll (MD)
Fresno City Coll (CA)
Front Range Comm Coll (CO)
Fugazzi Coll (KY)
Fullerton Coll (CA)
Fulton-Montgomery Comm Coll (NY)
Gadsden State Comm Coll (AL)
Gainesville Coll (GA)
Galveston Coll (TX)
Garden City Comm Coll (KS)
Garland County Comm Coll (AR)
Garrett Comm Coll (MD)
Gaston Coll (NC)
Gateway Comm Coll (AZ)
Gateway Comm-Tech Coll (CT)
Gavilan Coll (CA)
Gem City Coll (IL)
Genesee Comm Coll (NY)
George Corley Wallace State Comm Coll, Selma (AL)
George C Wallace State Comm Coll, Dothan (AL)
Georgia Military Coll (GA)
Germanna Comm Coll (VA)
Glendale Comm Coll (AZ)
Glen Oaks Comm Coll (MI)
Gloucester County Coll (NJ)
Gogebic Comm Coll (MI)
Golden West Coll (CA)
Gordon Coll (GA)
Grand Rapids Comm Coll (MI)
Grays Harbor Coll (WA)
Grayson County Coll (TX)
Great Basin Coll (NV)
Great Lakes Jr Coll of Business (MI)
Greenfield Comm Coll (MA)
Green River Comm Coll (WA)
Greenville Tech Coll (SC)
Grossmont Coll (CA)
Guilford Tech Comm Coll (NC)
Gulf Coast Comm Coll (FL)
Hagerstown Business Coll (MD)
Hagerstown Jr Coll (MD)
Halifax Comm Coll (NC)
Hamilton Business Coll (IA)
Harcum Coll (PA)
Harford Comm Coll (MD)
Harrisburg Area Comm Coll (PA)
Hartnell Coll (CA)
Haskell Indian Nations U (KS)
Hawkeye Comm Coll (IA)
Haywood Comm Coll (NC)
Heald Business Coll (HI)
Heartland Comm Coll (IL)
Henry Ford Comm Coll (MI)
Herkimer County Comm Coll (NY)
Herzing Coll of Business and Tech (GA)
Hesser Coll (NH)
Hesston Coll (KS)
Hibbing Comm Coll (MN)
Highland Comm Coll (IL)
Highland Comm Coll (KS)
Highline Comm Coll (WA)
Hill Coll of the Hill Jr Coll District (TX)
Hillsborough Comm Coll (FL)
Hiwassee Coll (TN)
Hocking Coll (OH)
Holmes Comm Coll (MS)
Holyoke Comm Coll (MA)
Horry-Georgetown Tech Coll (SC)
Housatonic Comm-Tech Coll (CT)
Houston Comm Coll System (TX)
Howard Coll (TX)
Howard Comm Coll (MD)
Hudson County Comm Coll (NJ)
Hudson Valley Comm Coll (NY)
Huertas Jr Coll (PR)
Huntington Jr Coll of Business (WV)
Hutchinson Comm Coll and Area Vocational Sch (KS)
ICM Sch of Business (PA)
ICS Ctr for Degree Studies (PA)
Illinois Central Coll (IL)
Illinois Eastern Comm Colls, Wabash Valley Coll (IL)
Illinois Valley Comm Coll (IL)
Imperial Valley Coll (CA)
Independence Comm Coll (KS)
Indiana Business Coll (IN)
Indian Hills Comm Coll (IA)
Indian River Comm Coll (FL)
Inst of Career Education (FL)
Inter American U of PR, Guayama Cmps (PR)
Interboro Inst (NY)
International Business Coll (IN)
Inver Hills Comm Coll (MN)
Iowa Central Comm Coll (IA)
Iowa Lakes Comm Coll (IA)
Iowa Western Comm Coll (IA)
Irvine Valley Coll (CA)
Isothermal Comm Coll (NC)
Itasca Comm Coll (MN)
Itawamba Comm Coll (MS)
ITT Tech Inst, Youngstown (OH)
Ivy Tech State Coll–Central Indiana (IN)
Ivy Tech State Coll–Columbus (IN)
Ivy Tech State Coll–Eastcentral (IN)
Ivy Tech State Coll–Kokomo (IN)
Ivy Tech State Coll–Lafayette (IN)
Ivy Tech State Coll–Northcentral (IN)
Ivy Tech State Coll–Northeast (IN)
Ivy Tech State Coll–Northwest (IN)
Ivy Tech State Coll–Southcentral (IN)
Ivy Tech State Coll–Southeast (IN)
Ivy Tech State Coll–Southwest (IN)
Ivy Tech State Coll–Wabash Valley (IN)
Ivy Tech State Coll–Whitewater (IN)
Jackson Comm Coll (MI)
Jackson State Comm Coll (TN)
James Sprunt Comm Coll (NC)
Jamestown Business Coll (NY)
Jamestown Comm Coll (NY)
Jefferson Coll (MO)
Jefferson Comm Coll (NY)
Jefferson Comm Coll (OH)
Jefferson Davis Comm Coll (AL)
Jefferson State Comm Coll (AL)
John A Logan Coll (IL)
John C Calhoun State Comm Coll (AL)
Johnson County Comm Coll (KS)
Johnston Comm Coll (NC)
John Tyler Comm Coll (VA)
John Wood Comm Coll (IL)
Joliet Jr Coll (IL)
Jones County Jr Coll (MS)
J Sargeant Reynolds Comm Coll (VA)
Kalamazoo Valley Comm Coll (MI)
Kankakee Comm Coll (IL)
Kansas City Kansas Comm Coll (KS)
Kaskaskia Coll (IL)
Katharine Gibbs Sch (MA)
Keiser Coll of Tech, Daytona Beach (FL)
Keiser Coll of Tech, Fort Lauderdale (FL)
Keiser Coll of Tech, Sarasota (FL)
Kellogg Comm Coll (MI)
Kelsey Jenney Coll (CA)
Kemper Military Jr Coll (MO)
Kennebec Valley Tech Coll (ME)
Kent State U, Ashtabula Cmps (OH)
Kent State U, East Liverpool Cmps (OH)
Kent State U, Geauga Cmps (OH)
Kent State U, Salem Cmps (OH)
Kent State U, Stark Cmps (OH)
Kent State U, Trumbull Cmps (OH)
Kent State U, Tuscarawas Cmps (OH)
Kentucky Coll of Business, Lexington (KY)
Keystone Coll (PA)
Kilian Comm Coll (SD)
Kingsborough Comm Coll of City U of NY (NY)
Kings River Comm Coll (CA)
Kingwood Coll (TX)
Kirkwood Comm Coll (IA)
Kirtland Comm Coll (MI)
Kishwaukee Coll (IL)
Knoxville Business Coll (TN)
Labette Comm Coll (KS)
Lac Courte Oreilles Ojibwa Comm Coll (WI)
Lackawanna Jr Coll (PA)
Lake City Comm Coll (FL)
Lake Land Coll (IL)
Lakeland Comm Coll (OH)
Lake Michigan Coll (MI)
Lake-Sumter Comm Coll (FL)
Lake Tahoe Comm Coll (CA)
Lakewood Comm Coll (MN)
Lamar Comm Coll (CO)
Lamar University–Orange (TX)
Lamson Jr Coll, Mesa (AZ)
Lane Comm Coll (OR)
Laney Coll (CA)
Lansing Comm Coll (MI)
Laramie County Comm Coll (WY)
Las Positas Coll (CA)
Lassen Coll (CA)
Lawson State Comm Coll (AL)
LDS Business Coll (UT)
Lee Coll (TX)
Lehigh Carbon Comm Coll (PA)
Lenoir Comm Coll (NC)
Lewis and Clark Comm Coll (IL)
Lewis Coll of Business (MI)
Lima Tech Coll (OH)
Lincoln Land Comm Coll (IL)
Lincoln Sch of Commerce (NE)
Linn-Benton Comm Coll (OR)
Little Big Horn Coll (MT)
Little Hoop Comm Coll (ND)
Long Beach City Coll (CA)
Longview Comm Coll (MO)
Lon Morris Coll (TX)
Lorain County Comm Coll (OH)
Lord Fairfax Comm Coll (VA)
Los Angeles City Coll (CA)
Los Angeles Harbor Coll (CA)
Los Angeles Mission Coll (CA)
Los Angeles Pierce Coll (CA)
Los Angeles Trade-Tech Coll (CA)
Los Angeles Valley Coll (CA)
Los Medanos Coll (CA)
Louisburg Coll (NC)
Louisiana State U at Alexandria (LA)
Louisiana State U at Eunice (LA)
Lower Columbia Coll (WA)
Lurleen B Wallace State Jr Coll (AL)
Luzerne County Comm Coll (PA)
MacCormac Jr Coll (IL)
Macomb Comm Coll (MI)
Macon Coll (GA)
Madison Area Tech Coll (WI)
Madison Jr Coll of Business (WI)
Manatee Comm Coll (FL)
Manchester Comm-Tech Coll (CT)
Manor Jr Coll (PA)
Maple Woods Comm Coll (MO)
Maria Coll (NY)
Marian Court Coll (MA)
Marion Tech Coll (OH)
Marshalltown Comm Coll (IA)
Martin Comm Coll (NC)
Mary Holmes Coll (MS)
Massachusetts Bay Comm Coll (MA)
Massasoit Comm Coll (MA)
Mater Dei Coll (NY)
Mayland Comm Coll (NC)
McCann Sch of Business (PA)
McDowell Tech Comm Coll (NC)
McIntosh Coll (NH)
McLennan Comm Coll (TX)
Mendocino Coll (CA)
Merced Coll (CA)
Mercer County Comm Coll (NJ)
Meridian Comm Coll (MS)
Merritt Coll (CA)
Mesa Comm Coll (AZ)
Metropolitan Comm Coll (NE)
Miami-Dade Comm Coll (FL)
Miami-Jacobs Coll (OH)
Miami University–Hamilton Cmps (OH)

Peterson's Guide to Two-Year Colleges 1997
59

Associate Degree Programs at Two-Year Colleges
Business Administration/Commerce/Management

Miami University–Middletown Cmps (OH)
Michiana Coll (IN)
Middle Georgia Coll (GA)
Middlesex Comm Coll (MA)
Middlesex Community–Tech Coll (CT)
Middlesex County Coll (NJ)
Midland Coll (TX)
Midlands Tech Coll (SC)
Mid Michigan Comm Coll (MI)
Mid-Plains Comm Coll (NE)
Midstate Coll (IL)
Mid-State Coll (ME)
Mid-State Tech Coll (WI)
Miles Comm Coll (MT)
Milwaukee Area Tech Coll (WI)
Mineral Area Coll (MO)
Minneapolis Comm Coll (MN)
MiraCosta Coll (CA)
Mission Coll (CA)
Mississippi County Comm Coll (AR)
Mississippi Delta Comm Coll (MS)
Mississippi Gulf Coast Comm Coll (MS)
Miss Wade's Fashion Merchandising Coll (TX)
Mitchell Coll (CT)
Mitchell Comm Coll (NC)
Moberly Area Comm Coll (MO)
Modesto Jr Coll (CA)
Mohave Comm Coll (AZ)
Mohawk Valley Comm Coll (NY)
Monroe Coll, Bronx (NY)
Monroe Coll, New Rochelle (NY)
Monroe Comm Coll (NY)
Monroe County Comm Coll (MI)
Montana State U Coll of Tech-Great Falls (MT)
Montcalm Comm Coll (MI)
Monterey Peninsula Coll (CA)
Montgomery Coll (TX)
Montgomery College–Germantown Cmps (MD)
Montgomery College–Rockville Cmps (MD)
Montgomery College–Takoma Park Cmps (MD)
Montgomery Comm Coll (NC)
Montgomery County Comm Coll (PA)
Moorpark Coll (CA)
Moraine Valley Comm Coll (IL)
Morgan Comm Coll (CO)
Morton Coll (IL)
Motlow State Comm Coll (TN)
Mountain Empire Comm Coll (VA)
Mt Hood Comm Coll (OR)
Mount Ida Coll (MA)
Mt San Antonio Coll (CA)
Mt San Jacinto Coll (CA)
Mount Wachusett Comm Coll (MA)
Murray State Coll (OK)
Muscatine Comm Coll (IA)
Muskegon Comm Coll (MI)
Muskingum Area Tech Coll (OH)
Napa Valley Coll (CA)
Nash Comm Coll (NC)
Nashville State Tech Inst (TN)
Nassau Comm Coll (NY)
National Business Coll, Bluefield (VA)
National Business Coll, Charlottesville (VA)
National Business Coll, Danville (VA)
National Business Coll, Harrisonburg (VA)
National Business Coll, Lynchburg (VA)
National Business Coll, Martinsville (VA)
National Business Coll, Roanoke (VA)
Naugatuck Valley Community–Tech Coll (CT)
Navajo Comm Coll (AZ)
Navarro Coll (TX)
Nebraska Coll of Business (NE)
Nebraska Indian Comm Coll (NE)

Neosho County Comm Coll (KS)
Nettleton Career Coll (SD)
Newbury Coll (MA)
The New England Banking Inst (MA)
New Hampshire Tech Coll, Berlin (NH)
New Hampshire Tech Coll, Claremont (NH)
New Hampshire Tech Coll, Laconia (NH)
New Hampshire Tech Coll, Nashua (NH)
New Hampshire Tech Inst (NH)
New Mexico Jr Coll (NM)
New Mexico Military Inst (NM)
New Mexico State University–Alamogordo (NM)
New Mexico State University–Carlsbad (NM)
New Mexico State University–Grants (NM)
Newport Business Inst (PA)
New River Comm Coll (VA)
Niagara County Comm Coll (NY)
Nicolet Area Tech Coll (WI)
Normandale Comm Coll (MN)
Northampton County Area Comm Coll (PA)
North Arkansas Comm/Tech Coll (AR)
North Central Michigan Coll (MI)
North Central Missouri Coll (MO)
North Central Tech Coll (OH)
Northcentral Tech Coll (WI)
North Central Texas Coll (TX)
North Country Comm Coll (NY)
North Dakota State University–Bottineau (ND)
Northeast Alabama State Comm Coll (AL)
Northeast Comm Coll (NE)
Northeastern Jr Coll (CO)
Northeastern Oklahoma A&M Coll (OK)
Northeast Iowa Comm Coll, Peosta Cmps (IA)
Northeast Mississippi Comm Coll (MS)
Northern Essex Comm Coll (MA)
Northern Maine Tech Coll (ME)
Northern Marianas Coll (MP)
Northern Oklahoma Coll (OK)
Northern Virginia Comm Coll (VA)
North Harris Coll (TX)
North Hennepin Comm Coll (MN)
North Idaho Coll (ID)
North Iowa Area Comm Coll (IA)
North Lake Coll (TX)
Northland Comm and Tech Coll (MN)
Northland Pioneer Coll (AZ)
North Seattle Comm Coll (WA)
North Shore Comm Coll (MA)
NorthWest Arkansas Comm Coll (AR)
Northwest Coll (WY)
Northwestern Business Coll (IL)
Northwestern Coll (OH)
Northwestern Connecticut Comm-Tech Coll (CT)
Northwestern Michigan Coll (MI)
Northwest Indian Coll (WA)
Northwest Mississippi Comm Coll (MS)
Northwest-Shoals Comm Coll (AL)
Northwest State Comm Coll (OH)
Norwalk Comm-Tech Coll (CT)
Oakland Comm Coll (MI)
Oakton Comm Coll (IL)
Ocean County Coll (NJ)
Odessa Coll (TX)
Ohio Valley Coll (WV)
Ohlone Coll (CA)

Okaloosa-Walton Comm Coll (FL)
Oklahoma City Comm Coll (OK)
Oklahoma State U, Oklahoma City (OK)
Oklahoma State U, Okmulgee (OK)
Olean Business Inst (NY)
Onondaga Comm Coll (NY)
Orangeburg-Calhoun Tech Coll (SC)
Orange Coast Coll (CA)
Orange County Comm Coll (NY)
Otero Jr Coll (CO)
Owensboro Comm Coll (KY)
Owensboro Jr Coll of Business (KY)
Owens Comm Coll, Findlay (OH)
Owens Comm Coll, Toledo (OH)
Oxnard Coll (CA)
Ozarks Tech Comm Coll (MO)
Palm Beach Comm Coll (FL)
Palo Alto Coll (TX)
Palomar Coll (CA)
Palo Verde Coll (CA)
Pamlico Comm Coll (NC)
Panama Canal Coll (Republic of Panama)
Paradise Valley Comm Coll (AZ)
Paris Jr Coll (TX)
Parkland Coll (IL)
Parks Coll (NM)
Parks Jr Coll (CO)
Pasadena City Coll (CA)
Pasco-Hernando Comm Coll (FL)
Passaic County Comm Coll (NJ)
Patrick Henry Comm Coll (VA)
Paul D Camp Comm Coll (VA)
Paul Smith's Coll (NY)
Pearl River Comm Coll (MS)
Peirce Coll (PA)
Pellissippi State Tech Comm Coll (TN)
Peninsula Coll (WA)
Penn Commercial, Inc (PA)
Pennsylvania Coll of Tech (PA)
Penn State U Abington-Ogontz Cmps (PA)
Penn State U Altoona Cmps (PA)
Penn State U Berks Cmps (PA)
Penn State U Delaware County Cmps (PA)
Penn State U DuBois Cmps (PA)
Penn State U Fayette Cmps (PA)
Penn State U Hazleton Cmps (PA)
Penn State U McKeesport Cmps (PA)
Penn State U Mont Alto Cmps (PA)
Penn State U New Kensington Cmps (PA)
Penn State U Schuylkill Cmps (PA)
Penn State U Shenango Cmps (PA)
Penn State U Wilkes-Barre Cmps (PA)
Penn State U Worthington Scranton Cmps (PA)
Penn State U York Cmps (PA)
Penn Valley Comm Coll (MO)
Pensacola Jr Coll (FL)
Phillips County Comm Coll (AR)
Phillips Jr Coll (UT)
Phillips Jr Coll, Condie Cmps (CA)
Phillips Jr Coll of Springfield (MO)
Piedmont Comm Coll (NC)
Piedmont Tech Coll (SC)
Piedmont Virginia Comm Coll (VA)
Pierce Coll (WA)
Pikes Peak Comm Coll (CO)
Pima Comm Coll (AZ)
Pines Tech Coll (AR)

Pitt Comm Coll (NC)
Pittsburgh Tech Inst (PA)
Polk Comm Coll (FL)
Porterville Coll (CA)
Portland Comm Coll (OR)
Potomac State Coll of West Virginia U (WV)
Prairie State Coll (IL)
Pratt Comm Coll and Area Voc Sch (KS)
Prince George's Comm Coll (MD)
Prospect Hall (FL)
Pueblo Comm Coll (CO)
Queensborough Comm Coll of City U of NY (NY)
Quincy Coll (MA)
Quinebaug Valley Comm-Tech Coll (CT)
Quinsigamond Comm Coll (MA)
Rainy River Comm Coll (MN)
Ramírez Coll of Business and Tech (PR)
Rancho Santiago Coll (CA)
Randolph Comm Coll (NC)
Rappahannock Comm Coll (VA)
Raritan Valley Comm Coll (NJ)
Rasmussen Coll Eagan (MN)
Rasmussen Coll Mankato (MN)
Rasmussen Coll Minnetonka (MN)
Rasmussen Coll St Cloud (MN)
Reading Area Comm Coll (PA)
Redlands Comm Coll (OK)
Red River Tech Coll (AR)
Red Rocks Comm Coll (CO)
Rend Lake Coll (IL)
Renton Tech Coll (WA)
Richard Bland Coll of the Coll of William and Mary (VA)
Richland Coll (TX)
Richland Comm Coll (IL)
Richmond Comm Coll (NC)
Rich Mountain Comm Coll (AR)
Ricks Coll (ID)
Rio Salado Comm Coll (AZ)
Riverside Comm Coll (CA)
Roane State Comm Coll (TN)
Roanoke-Chowan Comm Coll (NC)
Robeson Comm Coll (NC)
Rochester Comm Coll (MN)
Rockingham Comm Coll (NC)
Rockland Comm Coll (NY)
Rock Valley Coll (IL)
Rogers State Coll (OK)
Rogue Comm Coll (OR)
Rose State Coll (OK)
Rowan-Cabarrus Comm Coll (NC)
Roxbury Comm Coll (MA)
Sacramento City Coll (CA)
Saddleback Coll (CA)
Sage Jr Coll of Albany (NY)
Saint Augustine Coll (IL)
St Catharine Coll (KY)
Saint Charles County Comm Coll (MO)
St Clair County Comm Coll (MI)
St Cloud Tech Coll (MN)
St Gregory's Coll (OK)
St Johns River Comm Coll (FL)
St Louis Comm Coll at Florissant Valley (MO)
St Louis Comm Coll at Forest Park (MO)
St Louis Comm Coll at Meramec (MO)
St Petersburg Jr Coll (FL)
St Philip's Coll (TX)
Salem Comm Coll (NJ)
Salt Lake Comm Coll (UT)
Sampson Comm Coll (NC)
San Antonio Coll (TX)
San Bernardino Valley Coll (CA)
Sandhills Comm Coll (NC)
San Diego City Coll (CA)
San Diego Mesa Coll (CA)
San Diego Miramar Coll (CA)
Sanford-Brown Coll, Hazelwood (MO)
Sanford-Brown Coll, St Charles (MO)

San Jacinto College–Central Cmps (TX)
San Jacinto College–North Cmps (TX)
San Jacinto College–South Cmps (TX)
San Joaquin Delta Coll (CA)
San Jose City Coll (CA)
San Juan Coll (NM)
Santa Barbara City Coll (CA)
Santa Fe Comm Coll (FL)
Santa Fe Comm Coll (NM)
Santa Monica Coll (CA)
Santa Rosa Jr Coll (CA)
Sauk Valley Comm Coll (IL)
Sawyer Coll of Business, Cleveland (OH)
Sawyer Coll of Business, Cleveland Heights (OH)
Schenectady County Comm Coll (NY)
Schoolcraft Coll (MI)
Scott Comm Coll (IA)
Scottsdale Comm Coll (AZ)
Seminole Comm Coll (FL)
Seminole Jr Coll (OK)
Seward County Comm Coll (KS)
Shasta Coll (CA)
Shawnee Comm Coll (IL)
Shelby State Comm Coll (TN)
Shelton State Comm Coll (AL)
Sheridan Coll (WY)
Shoreline Comm Coll (WA)
Shorter Coll (AR)
Sierra Coll (CA)
Sinclair Comm Coll (OH)
Sisseton-Wahpeton Comm Coll (SD)
Skagit Valley Coll (WA)
Skyline Coll (CA)
Snead State Comm Coll (AL)
Snow Coll (UT)
Solano Comm Coll (CA)
South Coll (FL)
South Coll (GA)
Southeast Comm Coll, Beatrice Cmps (NE)
Southeast Comm Coll, Lincoln Cmps (NE)
Southeastern Comm Coll (NC)
Southeastern Comm Coll, North Cmps, West Burlington (IA)
Southeastern Comm Coll, South Cmps, Keokuk (IA)
Southeastern Illinois Coll (IL)
Southeast Tech Inst (SD)
Southern Arkansas U Tech (AR)
Southern Coll (FL)
Southern Maine Tech Coll (ME)
Southern Ohio Coll, Cincinnati Cmps (OH)
Southern Ohio Coll, Northeast Cmps (OH)
Southern Ohio Coll, Northern Kentucky Cmps (KY)
Southern State Comm Coll (OH)
Southern Union State Comm Coll (AL)
Southern U at Shreveport–Bossier City Cmps (LA)
Southern West Virginia Comm and Tech Coll (WV)
South Florida Comm Coll (FL)
South Georgia Coll (GA)
South Mountain Comm Coll (AZ)
South Plains Coll (TX)
South Puget Sound Comm Coll (WA)
South Seattle Comm Coll (WA)
Southside Virginia Comm Coll (VA)
South Suburban Coll (IL)
Southwestern Coll (CA)
Southwestern Coll of Business, Cincinnati (OH)
Southwestern Coll of Business, Cincinnati (OH)
Southwestern Coll of Business, Dayton (OH)
Southwestern Coll of Business, Middletown (OH)
Southwestern Comm Coll (IA)
Southwestern Comm Coll (NC)

Southwestern Indian Polytechnic Inst (NM)
Southwestern Michigan Coll (MI)
Southwestern Oklahoma State U at Sayre (OK)
Southwestern Oregon Comm Coll (OR)
Southwestern Tech Coll (MN)
Southwest Florida Coll of Business (FL)
Southwest Mississippi Comm Coll (MS)
Southwest Missouri State University–West Plains (MO)
Southwest Texas Jr Coll (TX)
Southwest Virginia Comm Coll (VA)
Spartanburg Tech Coll (SC)
Spencer Sch of Business (NE)
Spokane Comm Coll (WA)
Spokane Falls Comm Coll (WA)
Spoon River Coll (IL)
Springfield Coll in Illinois (IL)
Springfield Tech Comm Coll (MA)
Stanly Comm Coll (NC)
Stark Tech Coll (OH)
State Comm Coll of East St Louis (IL)
State Fair Comm Coll (MO)
State Tech Inst at Memphis (TN)
State U of NY Coll of A&T at Cobleskill (NY)
State U of NY Coll of A&T at Morrisville (NY)
State U of NY Coll of Tech at Alfred (NY)
State U of NY Coll of Tech at Canton (NY)
State U of NY Coll of Tech at Delhi (NY)
State U of NY Coll of Tech at Farmingdale (NY)
Stone Child Coll (MT)
Stratton Coll (WI)
Suffolk County Comm College–Ammerman Cmps (NY)
Suffolk County Comm Coll–Eastern Cmps (NY)
Suffolk County Comm Coll–Western Cmps (NY)
Sullivan County Comm Coll (NY)
Surry Comm Coll (NC)
Sussex County Comm Coll (NJ)
Tacoma Comm Coll (WA)
Taft Coll (CA)
Tallahassee Comm Coll (FL)
Tarrant County Jr Coll (TX)
Taylor Business Inst (NY)
Temple Coll (TX)
Terra State Comm Coll (OH)
Texarkana Coll (TX)
Texas Southmost Coll (TX)
Thomas Nelson Comm Coll (VA)
Thompson Inst (PA)
Three Rivers Comm Coll (MO)
Three Rivers Comm-Tech Coll (CT)
Tidewater Comm Coll (VA)
Tomball Coll (TX)
Tompkins Cortland Comm Coll (NY)
Treasure Valley Comm Coll (OR)
Tri-County Comm Coll (NC)
Tri-County Tech Coll (SC)
Trident Tech Coll (SC)
Trinidad State Jr Coll (CO)
Trinity Valley Comm Coll (TX)
Triton Coll (IL)
Trocaire Coll (NY)
Truckee Meadows Comm Coll (NV)
Truett-McConnell Coll (GA)
Tulsa Jr Coll (OK)
Tunxis Comm Tech Coll (CT)
Turtle Mountain Comm Coll (ND)
Tyler Jr Coll (TX)
UAB Walker Coll (AL)
Ulster County Comm Coll (NY)
Umpqua Comm Coll (OR)
Union County Coll (NJ)

Associate Degree Programs at Two-Year Colleges
Business Administration/Commerce/Management–Carpentry

United Tribes Tech Coll (ND)
The U of Akron–Wayne Coll (OH)
U of Alaska Anchorage, Kenai Peninsula Coll (AK)
U of Alaska Anchorage, Kodiak Coll (AK)
U of Alaska Anchorage, Matanuska-Susitna Coll (AK)
U of Alaska Southeast, Ketchikan Cmps (AK)
U of Alaska Southeast, Sitka Cmps (AK)
U of Cincinnati Clermont Coll (OH)
U of Cincinnati Raymond Walters Coll (OH)
U of Hawaii–Leeward Comm Coll (HI)
U of Kentucky, Ashland Comm Coll (KY)
U of Kentucky, Elizabethtown Comm Coll (KY)
U of Kentucky, Hazard Comm Coll (KY)
U of Kentucky, Henderson Comm Coll (KY)
U of Kentucky, Hopkinsville Comm Coll (KY)
U of Kentucky, Jefferson Comm Coll (KY)
U of Kentucky, Lexington Comm Coll (KY)
U of Kentucky, Madisonville Comm Coll (KY)
U of Kentucky, Maysville Comm Coll (KY)
U of Kentucky, Paducah Comm Coll (KY)
U of Kentucky, Prestonsburg Comm Coll (KY)
U of Kentucky, Somerset Comm Coll (KY)
U of Kentucky, Southeast Comm Coll (KY)
U of Maine at Augusta (ME)
U of New Mexico–Gallup Branch (NM)
U of New Mexico–Los Alamos Branch (NM)
U of New Mexico–Valencia Cmps (NM)
U of North Dakota–Lake Region (ND)
U of Pittsburgh–Titusville (PA)
U of South Carolina at Lancaster (SC)
U of Wisconsin Center–Marathon County (WI)
U of Wisconsin Center–Marinette County (WI)
Utah Valley State Coll (UT)
Utica Sch of Commerce (NY)
Valencia Comm Coll (FL)
Valley Forge Military Coll (PA)
Vance-Granville Comm Coll (NC)
Ventura Coll (CA)
Vermilion Comm Coll (MN)
Vermont Tech Coll (VT)
Vernon Regional Jr Coll (TX)
Victoria Coll (TX)
Victor Valley Coll (CA)
Villa Maria Coll of Buffalo (NY)
Vincennes U (IN)
Vincennes University–Jasper Ctr (IN)
Virginia Highlands Comm Coll (VA)
Virginia Western Comm Coll (VA)
Vista Comm Coll (CA)
Volunteer State Comm Coll (TN)
Wake Tech Comm Coll (NC)
Waldorf Coll (IA)
Wallace State Comm Coll (AL)
Walla Walla Comm Coll (WA)
Walters State Comm Coll (TN)
Ward Stone Coll (FL)
Warren County Comm Coll (NJ)
Washington State Comm Coll (OH)
Washtenaw Comm Coll (MI)
Waubonsee Comm Coll (IL)
Waukesha County Tech Coll (WI)
Waycross Coll (GA)
Wayne Comm Coll (NC)
Wayne County Comm Coll (MI)
Weatherford Coll (TX)
Webster Coll, Ocala (FL)
Wenatchee Valley Coll (WA)
Westark Comm Coll (AR)
Westchester Business Inst (NY)
Westchester Comm Coll (NY)
Western Dakota Tech Inst (SD)
Western Iowa Tech Comm Coll (IA)
Western Nebraska Comm Coll, Scottsbluff (NE)
Western Nevada Comm Coll (NV)
Western Oklahoma State Coll (OK)
Western Piedmont Comm Coll (NC)
Western Texas Coll (TX)
Western Wisconsin Tech Coll (WI)
Western Wyoming Comm Coll (WY)
West Hills Comm Coll (CA)
West Los Angeles Coll (CA)
Westmoreland County Comm Coll (PA)
West Shore Comm Coll (MI)
West Valley Coll (CA)
West Virginia Career Coll, Charleston (WV)
West Virginia Career Coll, Morgantown (WV)
West Virginia Northern Comm Coll (WV)
West Virginia U at Parkersburg (WV)
Wharton County Jr Coll (TX)
Whatcom Comm Coll (WA)
Wilkes Comm Coll (NC)
William Rainey Harper Coll (IL)
Williamsburg Tech Coll (SC)
Williamsport Sch of Commerce (PA)
Willmar Comm Coll (MN)
Wilson Tech Comm Coll (NC)
Wisconsin Indianhead Tech Coll, Ashland Cmps (WI)
Wisconsin Indianhead Tech Coll, New Richmond Cmps (WI)
Wood Coll (MS)
Worthington Comm Coll (MN)
Wor-Wic Comm Coll (MD)
Wright State U, Lake Cmps (OH)
Wytheville Comm Coll (VA)
Yakima Valley Comm Coll (WA)
Yavapai Coll (AZ)
York Tech Coll (SC)
Young Harris Coll (GA)
Yuba Coll (CA)

BUSINESS ECONOMICS

Anne Arundel Comm Coll (MD)
Brevard Coll (NC)
Central Coll (KS)
Central Texas Coll (TX)
Chabot Coll (CA)
Clarendon Coll (TX)
Coahoma Comm Coll (MS)
Colby Comm Coll (KS)
Coll of the Desert (CA)
Darton Coll (GA)
DeKalb Coll (GA)
Frank Phillips Coll (TX)
Hill Coll of the Hill Jr Coll District (TX)
Joliet Jr Coll (IL)
Lincoln Coll, Normal (IL)
Los Medanos Coll (CA)
Miami University–Middletown Cmps (OH)
Morgan Comm Coll (CO)
Northeast Mississippi Comm Coll (MS)
Olympic Coll (WA)
Palomar Coll (CA)
Potomac State Coll of West Virginia U (WV)
St Catharine Coll (KY)
San Joaquin Delta Coll (CA)
Tacoma Comm Coll (WA)
Vermilion Comm Coll (MN)

BUSINESS EDUCATION

Alabama Southern Comm Coll, Monroeville (AL)
Allegany Comm Coll (MD)
Allen County Comm Coll (KS)
Andrew Coll (GA)
Atlanta Metropolitan Coll (GA)
Bacone Coll (OK)
Bainbridge Coll (GA)
Belleville Area Coll (IL)
Bismarck State Coll (ND)
Black Hawk Coll, Kewanee (IL)
Bramson ORT Tech Inst (NY)
Brevard Coll (NC)
Bristol Comm Coll (MA)
Bronx Comm Coll of City U of NY (NY)
Burlington County Coll (NJ)
Butler County Comm Coll (KS)
Butte Coll (CA)
Carl Albert State Coll (OK)
Casco Bay Coll (ME)
Casper Coll (WY)
Central Coll (KS)
Centralia Coll (WA)
Central Wyoming Coll (WY)
Chabot Coll (CA)
Chaffey Coll (CA)
Charles Stewart Mott Comm Coll (MI)
Chattahoochee Valley State Comm Coll (AL)
Chippewa Valley Tech Coll (WI)
Cisco Jr Coll (TX)
Clarendon Coll (TX)
Clark Coll (WA)
Coastal Carolina Comm Coll (NC)
Coffeyville Comm Coll (KS)
Colby Comm Coll (KS)
Coll of Alameda (CA)
Coll of Southern Idaho (ID)
Columbia State Comm Coll (TN)
Comm Coll of Allegheny County South Cmps (PA)
Comm Coll of Philadelphia (PA)
Dalton Coll (GA)
Darton Coll (GA)
DeKalb Coll (GA)
Delta Coll (MI)
Eastern Arizona Coll (AZ)
Eastern Oklahoma State Coll (OK)
Eastern Wyoming Coll (WY)
East Georgia Coll (GA)
East Mississippi Comm Coll (MS)
Essex County Coll (NJ)
Frank Phillips Coll (TX)
Gainesville Coll (GA)
George Corley Wallace State Comm Coll, Selma (AL)
Green River Comm Coll (WA)
Gulf Coast Comm Coll (FL)
Halifax Comm Coll (NC)
Harrisburg Area Comm Coll (PA)
Heald Business Coll, San Francisco (CA)
Herzing Coll of Business and Tech (GA)
Hesston Coll (KS)
Highland Comm Coll (KS)
Hiwassee Coll (TN)
Holmes Comm Coll (MS)
Holyoke Comm Coll (MA)
Independence Comm Coll (KS)
Iowa Central Comm Coll (IA)
Isothermal Comm Coll (NC)
James Sprunt Comm Coll (NC)
Jefferson Coll (MO)
John A Logan Coll (IL)
John C Calhoun State Comm Coll (AL)
Kirkwood Comm Coll (IA)
Lamar Comm Coll (CO)
Lawson State Comm Coll (AL)
Lincoln Coll, Normal (IL)
Little Hoop Comm Coll (ND)
Macon Coll (GA)
Madison Area Tech Coll (WI)
Mary Holmes Coll (MS)
Merritt Coll (CA)
Middle Georgia Coll (GA)
Middlesex Comm Coll (MA)
Mid-Plains Comm Coll (NE)
Mississippi Gulf Coast Comm Coll (MS)
Montgomery College–Germantown Cmps (MD)
Montgomery College–Takoma Park Cmps (MD)
Morgan Comm Coll (CO)
Mountain Empire Comm Coll (VA)
Mt Hood Comm Coll (OR)
Mt San Antonio Coll (CA)
Murray State Coll (OK)
New Mexico Jr Coll (NM)
North Dakota State University–Bottineau (ND)
Northeast Comm Coll (NE)
Northeastern Jr Coll (CO)
Northeast Mississippi Comm Coll (MS)
Northern Essex Comm Coll (MA)
North Idaho Coll (ID)
Northland Pioneer Coll (AZ)
Northwest Coll (WY)
Palau Comm Coll (PW)
Palomar Coll (CA)
Paris Jr Coll (TX)
Parkland Coll (IL)
Pasadena City Coll (CA)
Phillips County Comm Coll (AR)
Porterville Coll (CA)
Pratt Comm Coll and Area Voc Sch (KS)
Prince George's Comm Coll (MD)
Reading Area Comm Coll (PA)
Ricks Coll (ID)
Rio Hondo Coll (CA)
Roane State Comm Coll (TN)
St Catharine Coll (KY)
San Juan Coll (NM)
Shelton State Comm Coll (AL)
Shorter Coll (AR)
Snow Coll (UT)
South Georgia Coll (GA)
SouthWest Collegiate Inst for the Deaf (TX)
Southwestern Indian Polytechnic Inst (NM)
Southwest Mississippi Comm Coll (MS)
Spoon River Coll (IL)
Trinity Valley Comm Coll (TX)
Tulsa Jr Coll (OK)
U of Kentucky, Jefferson Comm Coll (KY)
Vincennes U (IN)
Vincennes University–Jasper Ctr (IN)
Wallace State Comm Coll (AL)
Waycross Coll (GA)

BUSINESS MACHINE TECHNOLOGIES

Alamance Comm Coll (NC)
Alexandria Tech Coll (MN)
Athens Area Tech Inst (GA)
Barstow Coll (CA)
Bay de Noc Comm Coll (MI)
Black Hawk Coll, Kewanee (IL)
Bramson ORT Tech Inst (NY)
Butler County Comm Coll (KS)
Cabrillo Coll (CA)
Cañada Coll (CA)
Castle Coll (NH)
Centralia Coll (WA)
Central Oregon Comm Coll (OR)
Central Piedmont Comm Coll (NC)
Central Wyoming Coll (WY)
Cerro Coso Comm Coll (CA)
Chabot Coll (CA)
Coffeyville Comm Coll (KS)
Comm Coll of Allegheny County South Cmps (PA)
DeKalb Coll (GA)
Dutchess Comm Coll (NY)
ECPI Coll of Tech, Virginia Beach (VA)
ECPI Computer Inst, Richmond (VA)
Fiorello H LaGuardia Comm Coll of City U of NY (NY)
Florida Keys Comm Coll (FL)
Frank Phillips Coll (TX)
Great Basin Coll (NV)
Hamilton Business Coll (IA)
Hartnell Coll (CA)
Henry Ford Comm Coll (MI)
Herzing Coll of Business and Tech (AL)
Herzing Coll of Business and Tech (GA)
Iowa Lakes Comm Coll (IA)
Irvine Valley Coll (CA)
Lassen Coll (CA)
Lon Morris Coll (TX)
Los Angeles Valley Coll (CA)
Miami University–Middletown Cmps (OH)
Mississippi Delta Comm Coll (MS)
Moberly Area Comm Coll (MO)
Moorpark Coll (CA)
Moraine Valley Comm Coll (IL)
Muscatine Comm Coll (IA)
Muskegon Comm Coll (MI)
Neosho County Comm Coll (KS)
North Seattle Comm Coll (WA)
Northwestern Michigan Coll (MI)
Ohio State U Ag Tech Inst (OH)
Orange Coast Coll (CA)
Ozarks Tech Comm Coll (MO)
Palo Alto Coll (TX)
Palomar Coll (CA)
Pellissippi State Tech Comm Coll (TN)
Rockingham Comm Coll (NC)
St Catharine Coll (KY)
San Antonio Coll (TX)
Shoreline Comm Coll (WA)
Solano Comm Coll (CA)
Southern Maine Tech Coll (ME)
Southern Ohio Coll, Northeast Cmps (OH)
Stevens Henager Coll (UT)
U of New Mexico–Gallup Branch (NM)
Ventura Coll (CA)
Washtenaw Comm Coll (MI)
West Shore Comm Coll (MI)

CANADIAN STUDIES

Massachusetts Bay Comm Coll (MA)

CARPENTRY

Alamance Comm Coll (NC)
Alexandria Tech Coll (MN)
American River Coll (CA)
Anson Comm Coll (NC)
Bakersfield Coll (CA)
Belleville Area Coll (IL)
Bishop State Comm Coll (AL)
Bismarck State Coll (ND)
Blue Ridge Comm Coll (NC)
Brazosport Coll (TX)
Butler County Comm Coll (KS)
Cape Fear Comm Coll (NC)
Casper Coll (WY)
Cecil Comm Coll (MD)
Central Coll (KS)
Central Comm College–Hastings Cmps (NE)
Coffeyville Comm Coll (KS)
Coll of Eastern Utah (UT)
Coll of the Sequoias (CA)
Columbia Basin Coll (WA)
Comm Coll of Aurora (CO)
Delaware Tech & Comm Coll, Jack F Owens Cmps (DE)
Delgado Comm Coll (LA)
Delta Coll (MI)
Dixie Coll (UT)
Douglas MacArthur State Tech Coll (AL)
Durham Tech Comm Coll (NC)
East Central Comm Coll (MS)
Eastern Maine Tech Coll (ME)
Fayetteville Tech Comm Coll (NC)
Forsyth Tech Comm Coll (NC)
Fort Berthold Comm Coll (ND)
Fresno City Coll (CA)
Fullerton Coll (CA)
Fulton-Montgomery Comm Coll (NY)
Gadsden State Comm Coll (AL)
Garden City Comm Coll (KS)
Gateway Comm Coll (AZ)
George C Wallace State Comm Coll, Dothan (AL)
Grays Harbor Coll (WA)
Green River Comm Coll (WA)
Hartnell Coll (CA)
Helena Coll of Tech of The U of Montana (MT)
Highland Comm Coll (KS)
Hinds Comm Coll (MS)
Hutchinson Comm Coll and Area Vocational Sch (KS)
Illinois Valley Comm Coll (IL)
Iowa Central Comm Coll (IA)
Ivy Tech State Coll–Eastcentral (IN)
Ivy Tech State Coll–Kokomo (IN)
Ivy Tech State Coll–Northeast (IN)
Ivy Tech State Coll–Wabash Valley (IN)
Ivy Tech State Coll–Whitewater (IN)
John C Calhoun State Comm Coll (AL)
John M Patterson State Tech Coll (AL)
Johnson Tech Inst (PA)
Kansas City Kansas Comm Coll (KS)
Lac Courte Oreilles Ojibwa Comm Coll (WI)
Lake Area Vocational-Tech Inst (SD)
Laney Coll (CA)
Lansing Comm Coll (MI)
Laramie County Comm Coll (WY)
Lassen Coll (CA)
Lawson State Comm Coll (AL)
Lincoln Land Comm Coll (IL)
Little Big Horn Coll (MT)
Little Hoop Comm Coll (ND)
Long Beach City Coll (CA)
Los Angeles Trade-Tech Coll (CA)
Merced Coll (CA)
Mid-Plains Comm Coll (NE)
Nebraska Indian Comm Coll (NE)
Neosho County Comm Coll (KS)
New England Inst of Tech (RI)
New Mexico Jr Coll (NM)
Northeast Comm Coll (NE)
Northeast Iowa Comm Coll, Peosta Cmps (IA)
Northeast Mississippi Comm Coll (MS)
Northern Maine Tech Coll (ME)
North Idaho Coll (ID)
North Lake Coll (TX)
Northwest Iowa Comm Coll (IA)
Northwest Mississippi Comm Coll (MS)
Olympic Coll (WA)
Palau Comm Coll (PW)
Palomar Coll (CA)
Pasadena City Coll (CA)
Piedmont Tech Coll (SC)
Porterville Coll (CA)
Portland Comm Coll (OR)
Pratt Comm Coll and Area Voc Sch (KS)
Rancho Santiago Coll (CA)
Ranken Tech Coll (MO)
Red Rocks Comm Coll (CO)
Reid State Tech Coll (AL)
Rich Mountain Comm Coll (AR)
Ricks Coll (ID)
Rockingham Comm Coll (NC)
Saddleback Coll (CA)
St Cloud Tech Coll (MN)
St Philip's Coll (TX)
Salish Kootenai Coll (MT)
Salt Lake Comm Coll (UT)
San Diego City Coll (CA)
San Jacinto College–North Cmps (TX)
San Joaquin Delta Coll (CA)
San Juan Coll (NM)
Seattle Central Comm Coll (WA)

Peterson's Guide to Two-Year Colleges 1997
61

Associate Degree Programs at Two-Year Colleges
Carpentry–Child Care/Child and Family Studies

Shasta Coll (CA)
Sierra Coll (CA)
Sisseton-Wahpeton Comm Coll (SD)
Snow Coll (UT)
Southeast Comm Coll, Milford Cmps (NE)
Southern Maine Tech Coll (ME)
South Plains Coll (TX)
SouthWest Collegiate Inst for the Deaf (TX)
Southwestern Comm Coll (IA)
Southwest Mississippi Comm Coll (MS)
Spokane Comm Coll (WA)
State U of NY Coll of Tech at Alfred (NY)
State U of NY Coll of Tech at Canton (NY)
State U of NY Coll of Tech at Delhi (NY)
Surry Comm Coll (NC)
Thaddeus Stevens State Sch of Tech (PA)
Triangle Tech, Inc–DuBois Sch (PA)
Trinidad State Jr Coll (CO)
Truckee Meadows Comm Coll (NV)
U of Hawaii–Hawaii Comm Coll (HI)
U of Hawaii–Honolulu Comm Coll (HI)
U of Hawaii–Kauai Comm Coll (HI)
U of Hawaii–Maui Comm Coll (HI)
Utah Valley State Coll (UT)
Vance-Granville Comm Coll (NC)
Wallace State Comm Coll (AL)
Walla Walla Comm Coll (WA)
Wenatchee Valley Coll (WA)
Western Wisconsin Tech Coll (WI)
The Williamson Free Sch of Mech Trades (PA)
Willmar Tech Coll (MN)
Yavapai Coll (AZ)

CARTOGRAPHY
Alexandria Tech Coll (MN)
Cabrillo Coll (CA)
Montgomery College–Rockville Cmps (MD)
National Sch of Tech, Inc (FL)

CERAMIC ART AND DESIGN
Allen County Comm Coll (KS)
Art Inst of Pittsburgh (PA)
Brevard Coll (NC)
Butler County Comm Coll (KS)
Cabrillo Coll (CA)
Casper Coll (WY)
Chaffey Coll (CA)
City Colls of Chicago, Harold Washington Coll (IL)
Colby Comm Coll (KS)
Coll of the Siskiyous (CA)
Garden City Comm Coll (KS)
Garland County Comm Coll (AR)
Gavilan Coll (CA)
Grossmont Coll (CA)
Haywood Comm Coll (NC)
Henry Ford Comm Coll (MI)
Hill Coll of the Hill Jr Coll District (TX)
Inst of American Indian Arts (NM)
Iowa Lakes Comm Coll (IA)
Kansas City Kansas Comm Coll (KS)
Kirkwood Comm Coll (IA)
Laney Coll (CA)
Lassen Coll (CA)
Los Angeles City Coll (CA)
Los Angeles Valley Coll (CA)
Mercer County Comm Coll (NJ)
Mohave Comm Coll (AZ)
Monterey Peninsula Coll (CA)
Northwest Coll (WY)
Oakland Comm Coll (MI)
Palm Beach Comm Coll (FL)
Palomar Coll (CA)
Pasadena City Coll (CA)
Polk Comm Coll (FL)
St Catharine Coll (KY)
Ventura Coll (CA)

CERAMIC SCIENCES
Hocking Coll (OH)
Pasadena City Coll (CA)

CHEMICAL ENGINEERING TECHNOLOGY
Alpena Comm Coll (MI)
Arizona Western Coll (AZ)
Belleville Area Coll (IL)
Bishop State Comm Coll (AL)
Bismarck State Coll (ND)
Brazosport Coll (TX)
Brevard Coll (NC)
Broome Comm Coll (NY)
Bucks County Comm Coll (PA)
Burlington County Coll (NJ)
Cape Fear Comm Coll (NC)
Capital Comm Tech Coll (CT)
Catonsville Comm Coll (MD)
Chattanooga State Tech Comm Coll (TN)
City Coll of San Francisco (CA)
City Colls of Chicago, Harry S Truman Coll (IL)
Clark Coll (WA)
Coll of Lake County (IL)
Comm Coll of Allegheny County Allegheny Cmps (PA)
Comm Coll of Allegheny County South Cmps (PA)
Comm Coll of Philadelphia (PA)
Comm Coll of Rhode Island (RI)
Corning Comm Coll (NY)
County Coll of Morris (NJ)
Delaware Tech & Comm Coll, Jack F Owens Cmps (DE)
Delaware Tech & Comm Coll, Stanton/Wilmington Cmps (DE)
Delta Coll (MI)
Dixie Coll (UT)
Erie Comm Coll, North Cmps (NY)
Essex County Coll (NJ)
Finger Lakes Comm Coll (NY)
Florence-Darlington Tech Coll (SC)
Gloucester County Coll (NJ)
Hudson Valley Comm Coll (NY)
Iowa Lakes Comm Coll (IA)
ITT Tech Inst, Indianapolis (IN)
ITT Tech Inst, Houston (TX)
Kellogg Comm Coll (MI)
Lansing Comm Coll (MI)
Los Angeles Trade-Tech Coll (CA)
Lower Columbia Coll (WA)
Mary Holmes Coll (MS)
Massachusetts Bay Comm Coll (MA)
Miami University–Middletown Cmps (OH)
Milwaukee Area Tech Coll (WI)
Mississippi Gulf Coast Comm Coll (MS)
Mohawk Valley Comm Coll (NY)
Monroe Comm Coll (NY)
Muskegon Comm Coll (MI)
Naugatuck Valley Community–Tech Coll (CT)
New York City Tech Coll of the City U of NY (NY)
Northampton County Area Comm Coll (PA)
Pellissippi State Tech Comm Coll (TN)
Ricks Coll (ID)
Saddleback Coll (CA)
St Louis Comm Coll at Florissant Valley (MO)
San Bernardino Valley Coll (CA)
San Juan Coll (NM)
Schenectady County Comm Coll (NY)
Shoreline Comm Coll (WA)
South Suburban Coll (IL)
Southwestern Michigan Coll (MI)
State Tech Inst at Memphis (TN)
State U of NY Coll of Tech at Alfred (NY)
Texas State Tech Coll–Harlingen Cmps (TX)
Texas State Tech Coll–Waco/Marshall Cmps (TX)
Trident Tech Coll (SC)
U of Kentucky, Jefferson Comm Coll (KY)
Washington State Comm Coll (OH)
Westchester Comm Coll (NY)
West Virginia U at Parkersburg (WV)

CHEMISTRY
Abraham Baldwin Ag Coll (GA)
Alabama Southern Comm Coll, Monroeville (AL)
Alabama Southern Comm Coll, Thomasville (AL)
Allan Hancock Coll (CA)
Allegany Comm Coll (MD)
Allen County Comm Coll (KS)
Alpena Comm Coll (MI)
Andrew Coll (GA)
Angelina Coll (TX)
Anne Arundel Comm Coll (MD)
Antelope Valley Coll (CA)
Arizona Western Coll (AZ)
Atlanta Metropolitan Coll (GA)
Atlantic Comm Coll (NJ)
Austin Comm Coll (TX)
Bainbridge Coll (GA)
Bakersfield Coll (CA)
Barton County Comm Coll (KS)
Bee County Coll (TX)
Bergen Comm Coll (NJ)
Bismarck State Coll (ND)
Black Hawk Coll, Moline (IL)
Blinn Coll (TX)
Brazosport Coll (TX)
Brevard Coll (NC)
Brevard Comm Coll (FL)
Bronx Comm Coll of City U of NY (NY)
Brookdale Comm Coll (NJ)
Brunswick Coll (GA)
Bucks County Comm Coll (PA)
Burlington County Coll (NJ)
Butler County Comm Coll (KS)
Cañada Coll (CA)
Casper Coll (WY)
Centralia Coll (WA)
Central Texas Coll (TX)
Cerritos Coll (CA)
Chabot Coll (CA)
Chaffey Coll (CA)
Charles Stewart Mott Comm Coll (MI)
Chattahoochee Valley State Comm Coll (AL)
Chattanooga State Tech Comm Coll (TN)
Chemeketa Comm Coll (OR)
Cisco Jr Coll (TX)
City Coll of San Francisco (CA)
City Colls of Chicago, Harold Washington Coll (IL)
City Colls of Chicago, Kennedy-King Coll (IL)
City Colls of Chicago, Olive-Harvey Coll (IL)
Clackamas Comm Coll (OR)
Clark Coll (WA)
Clinton Comm Coll (IA)
Coahoma Comm Coll (MS)
Cochise Coll, Douglas (AZ)
Cochise Coll, Sierra Vista (AZ)
Coffeyville Comm Coll (KS)
Colby Comm Coll (KS)
Coll of Marin (CA)
Coll of San Mateo (CA)
Coll of Southern Idaho (ID)
Coll of the Canyons (CA)
Coll of the Desert (CA)
Coll of the Sequoias (CA)
Collin County Comm Coll (TX)
Columbia Coll (CA)
Columbia State Comm Coll (TN)
Comm Coll of Allegheny County Allegheny Cmps (PA)
Comm Coll of Allegheny County Boyce Cmps (PA)
Comm Coll of Allegheny County South Cmps (PA)
Comm Coll of Southern Nevada (NV)
Connors State Coll (OK)
Contra Costa Coll (CA)
Copiah-Lincoln Comm Coll (MS)
County Coll of Morris (NJ)
Cowley County Comm Coll and Voc-Tech Sch (KS)
Crafton Hills Coll (CA)
Cuesta Coll (CA)
Cypress Coll (CA)
Dalton Coll (GA)
Darton Coll (GA)
Daytona Beach Comm Coll (FL)
DeKalb Coll (GA)
Del Mar Coll (TX)
Delta Coll (MI)
Dixie Coll (UT)
Dodge City Comm Coll (KS)
East Central Coll (MO)
East Central Comm Coll (MS)
Eastern Arizona Coll (AZ)
Eastern Idaho Tech Coll (ID)
Eastern Oklahoma State Coll (OK)
Eastern Wyoming Coll (WY)
East Georgia Coll (GA)
East Los Angeles Coll (CA)
East Mississippi Comm Coll (MS)
El Camino Coll (CA)
El Paso Comm Coll (TX)
Essex Comm Coll (MD)
Essex County Coll (NJ)
Everett Comm Coll (WA)
Finger Lakes Comm Coll (NY)
Foothill Coll (CA)
Frank Phillips Coll (TX)
Frederick Comm Coll (MD)
Fullerton Coll (CA)
Gainesville Coll (GA)
Gavilan Coll (CA)
Glendale Comm Coll (AZ)
Gloucester County Coll (NJ)
Grays Harbor Coll (WA)
Grayson County Coll (TX)
Grossmont Coll (CA)
Gulf Coast Comm Coll (FL)
Hagerstown Jr Coll (MD)
Harford Comm Coll (MD)
Harrisburg Area Comm Coll (PA)
Herkimer County Comm Coll (NY)
Highland Comm Coll (IL)
Highland Comm Coll (KS)
Hill Coll of the Hill Jr Coll District (TX)
Hiwassee Coll (TN)
Holyoke Comm Coll (MA)
Howard Coll (TX)
Hudson Valley Comm Coll (NY)
Hutchinson Comm Coll and Area Vocational Sch (KS)
Independence Comm Coll (KS)
Indian River Comm Coll (FL)
Inter American U of PR, Guayama Cmps (PR)
Iowa Lakes Comm Coll (IA)
Itawamba Comm Coll (MS)
Jackson State Comm Coll (TN)
John A Logan Coll (IL)
John C Calhoun State Comm Coll (AL)
John Wood Comm Coll (IL)
Joliet Jr Coll (IL)
Jones County Jr Coll (MS)
Kansas City Kansas Comm Coll (KS)
Kellogg Comm Coll (MI)
Keystone Coll (PA)
Kingsborough Comm Coll of City U of NY (NY)
Kishwaukee Coll (IL)
Labette Comm Coll (KS)
Lake Michigan Coll (MI)
Laramie County Comm Coll (WY)
Lassen Coll (CA)
Lee Coll (TX)
Lincoln Land Comm Coll (IL)
Little Hoop Comm Coll (ND)
Longview Comm Coll (MO)
Lon Morris Coll (TX)
Lorain County Comm Coll (OH)
Los Angeles City Coll (CA)
Los Angeles Mission Coll (CA)
Los Medanos Coll (CA)
Lower Columbia Coll (WA)
Macon Coll (GA)
Maple Woods Comm Coll (MO)
Massachusetts Bay Comm Coll (MA)
Mercer County Comm Coll (NJ)
Miami-Dade Comm Coll (FL)
Miami University–Middletown Cmps (OH)
Middle Georgia Coll (GA)
Middlesex County Coll (NJ)
Midland Coll (TX)
Mid Michigan Comm Coll (MI)
Mid-Plains Comm Coll (NE)
MiraCosta Coll (CA)
Modesto Jr Coll (CA)
Mohawk Valley Comm Coll (NY)
Monroe Comm Coll (NY)
Monterey Peninsula Coll (CA)
Montgomery County Comm Coll (PA)
Moorpark Coll (CA)
Mountain Empire Comm Coll (VA)
Murray State Coll (OK)
Muscatine Comm Coll (IA)
Navarro Coll (TX)
New Mexico Jr Coll (NM)
New Mexico Military Inst (NM)
Niagara County Comm Coll (NY)
Northampton County Area Comm Coll (PA)
Northeast Comm Coll (NE)
Northeastern Oklahoma A&M Coll (OK)
Northeast Mississippi Comm Coll (MS)
Northeast State Tech Comm Coll (TN)
North Idaho Coll (ID)
Northwest Coll (WY)
Odessa Coll (TX)
Okaloosa-Walton Comm Coll (FL)
Oklahoma City Comm Coll (OK)
Palm Beach Comm Coll (FL)
Palo Alto Coll (TX)
Palomar Coll (CA)
Pasadena City Coll (CA)
Penn Valley Comm Coll (MO)
Pensacola Jr Coll (FL)
Phillips County Comm Coll (AR)
Pikes Peak Comm Coll (CO)
Pima Comm Coll (AZ)
Polk Comm Coll (FL)
Potomac State Coll of West Virginia U (WV)
Pratt Comm Coll and Area Voc Sch (KS)
Rancho Santiago Coll (CA)
Raritan Valley Comm Coll (NJ)
Reading Area Comm Coll (PA)
Redlands Comm Coll (OK)
Red Rocks Comm Coll (CO)
Ricks Coll (ID)
Roane State Comm Coll (TN)
Rogers State Coll (OK)
Rose State Coll (OK)
Saddleback Coll (CA)
St Catharine Coll (KY)
St Gregory's Coll (OK)
St Philip's Coll (TX)
Salem Comm Coll (NJ)
San Bernardino Valley Coll (CA)
San Diego Mesa Coll (CA)
San Diego Miramar Coll (CA)
San Jacinto College–Central Cmps (TX)
San Jacinto College–North Cmps (TX)
San Jacinto College–South Cmps (TX)
San Joaquin Delta Coll (CA)
San Juan Coll (NM)
Santa Barbara City Coll (CA)
Santa Fe Comm Coll (NM)
Santa Monica Coll (CA)
Santa Rosa Jr Coll (CA)
Sauk Valley Comm Coll (IL)
Seward County Comm Coll (KS)
Shelton State Comm Coll (AL)
Sierra Coll (CA)
Skagit Valley Coll (WA)
Skyline Coll (CA)
Snow Coll (UT)
Solano Comm Coll (CA)
Southern U at Shreveport–Bossier City Cmps (LA)
South Georgia Coll (GA)
South Mountain Comm Coll (AZ)
South Plains Coll (TX)
South Suburban Coll (IL)
SouthWest Collegiate Inst for the Deaf (TX)
Southwestern Coll (CA)
Southwest Mississippi Comm Coll (MS)
Southwest Missouri State University– West Plains (MO)
Spoon River Coll (IL)
State Comm Coll of East St Louis (IL)
State U of NY Coll of A&T at Cobleskill (NY)
State U of NY Coll of A&T at Morrisville (NY)
State U of NY Coll of Tech at Canton (NY)
Suffolk County Comm College–Ammerman Cmps (NY)
Sussex County Comm Coll (NJ)
Tacoma Comm Coll (WA)
Terra State Comm Coll (OH)
Texarkana Coll (TX)
Treasure Valley Comm Coll (OR)
Trinidad State Jr Coll (CO)
Trinity Valley Comm Coll (TX)
Triton Coll (IL)
Tulsa Jr Coll (OK)
Umpqua Comm Coll (OR)
U of Cincinnati Raymond Walters Coll (OH)
U of Kentucky, Jefferson Comm Coll (KY)
Vermilion Comm Coll (MN)
Vincennes U (IN)
Waldorf Coll (IA)
Waubonsee Comm Coll (IL)
Waycross Coll (GA)
Wenatchee Valley Coll (WA)
Western Nebraska Comm Coll, Scottsbluff (NE)
Western Wyoming Comm Coll (WY)
West Hills Comm Coll (CA)
West Los Angeles Coll (CA)
West Valley Coll (CA)
Wharton County Jr Coll (TX)
Wright State U, Lake Cmps (OH)
Young Harris Coll (GA)
Yuba Coll (CA)

CHILD CARE/CHILD AND FAMILY STUDIES
Abraham Baldwin Ag Coll (GA)
Aims Comm Coll (CO)
Alamance Comm Coll (NC)
Alexandria Tech Coll (MN)
Allen County Comm Coll (KS)
Alvin Comm Coll (TX)
American River Coll (CA)
Angelina Coll (TX)
Aquinas Coll at Newton (MA)
Asheville-Buncombe Tech Comm Coll (NC)
Athens Area Tech Inst (GA)
Atlantic Comm Coll (NJ)
Augusta Tech Inst (GA)
Austin Comm Coll (MN)
Bakersfield Coll (CA)
Barstow Coll (CA)
Barton County Comm Coll (KS)
Bee County Coll (TX)
Belleville Area Coll (IL)
Bishop State Comm Coll (AL)
Black Hawk Coll, Moline (IL)
Blue Ridge Comm Coll (NC)

Associate Degree Programs at Two-Year Colleges
Child Care/Child and Family Studies–City/Community/Regional Planning

Borough of Manhattan Comm Coll of City U of NY (NY)
Brazosport Coll (TX)
Brevard Comm Coll (FL)
Briarwood Coll (CT)
Bristol Comm Coll (MA)
Bronx Comm Coll of City U of NY (NY)
Brookhaven Coll (TX)
Broome Comm Coll (NY)
Broward Comm Coll (FL)
Bucks County Comm Coll (PA)
Butler County Comm Coll (KS)
Cabrillo Coll (CA)
Casco Bay Coll (ME)
Central Carolina Comm Coll (NC)
Central Coll (KS)
Central Comm College–Grand Island Cmps (NE)
Central Comm College–Hastings Cmps (NE)
Central Comm College–Platte Cmps (NE)
Central Florida Comm Coll (FL)
Centralia Coll (WA)
Central Pennsylvania Business Sch (PA)
Central Piedmont Comm Coll (NC)
Central Texas Coll (TX)
Chaffey Coll (CA)
Chattahoochee Valley State Comm Coll (AL)
Chattanooga State Tech Comm Coll (TN)
Chemeketa Comm Coll (OR)
Chippewa Valley Tech Coll (WI)
Cisco Jr Coll (TX)
City Colls of Chicago, Harold Washington Coll (IL)
City Colls of Chicago, Kennedy-King Coll (IL)
City Colls of Chicago, Richard J Daley Coll (IL)
Clarendon Coll (TX)
Clark Coll (WA)
Cloud County Comm Coll (KS)
Coastal Carolina Comm Coll (NC)
Colby Comm Coll (KS)
Coll of DuPage (IL)
Coll of Eastern Utah (UT)
Coll of Southern Idaho (ID)
Coll of the Canyons (CA)
Coll of the Mainland (TX)
Collin County Comm Coll (TX)
Colorado Mountn Coll, Timberline Cmps (CO)
Columbus State Comm Coll (OH)
Comm Coll of Allegheny County Allegheny Cmps (PA)
Comm Coll of Allegheny County South Cmps (PA)
Comm Coll of Denver (CO)
Comm Coll of Southern Nevada (NV)
Comm Coll of Vermont (VT)
Connors State Coll (OK)
Copiah-Lincoln Comm Coll (MS)
Corning Comm Coll (NY)
Cosumnes River Coll (CA)
Cowley County Comm Coll and Voc-Tech Sch (KS)
Cuesta Coll (CA)
Danville Area Comm Coll (IL)
Daytona Beach Comm Coll (FL)
Dean Coll (MA)
De Anza Coll (CA)
DeKalb Coll (GA)
Del Mar Coll (TX)
Delta Coll (MI)
Des Moines Area Comm Coll (IA)
Dixie Coll (UT)
Dodge City Comm Coll (KS)
Durham Tech Comm Coll (NC)
Dutchess Comm Coll (NY)
Eastern Arizona Coll (AZ)
Eastern New Mexico University–Roswell (NM)
Eastern Wyoming Coll (WY)
East Los Angeles Coll (CA)
Elgin Comm Coll (IL)
Ellsworth Comm Coll (IA)
El Paso Comm Coll (TX)
Enterprise State Jr Coll (AL)
Erie Comm Coll, City Cmps (NY)
Everett Comm Coll (WA)
Florida Comm Coll at Jacksonville (FL)
Forsyth Tech Comm Coll (NC)
Fox Valley Tech Coll (WI)
Frederick Comm Coll (MD)
Front Range Comm Coll (CO)
Gainesville Coll (GA)
Garden City Comm Coll (KS)
Garland County Comm Coll (AR)
Gaston Coll (NC)
Gavilan Coll (CA)
Gogebic Comm Coll (MI)
Grand Rapids Comm Coll (MI)
Grays Harbor Coll (WA)
Great Basin Coll (NV)
Grossmont Coll (CA)
Guilford Tech Comm Coll (NC)
Harford Comm Coll (MD)
Hartnell Coll (CA)
Hawkeye Comm Coll (IA)
Heartland Comm Coll (IL)
Herkimer County Comm Coll (NY)
Highland Comm Coll (IL)
Highland Park Comm Coll (MI)
Hill Coll of the Hill Jr Coll District (TX)
Hillsborough Comm Coll (FL)
Hiwassee Coll (TN)
Holmes Comm Coll (MS)
Housatonic Comm-Tech Coll (CT)
Houston Comm Coll System (TX)
Howard Coll (TX)
Howard Comm Coll (MD)
Hudson County Comm Coll (NJ)
Hutchinson Comm Coll and Area Vocational Sch (KS)
Illinois Eastern Comm Colls, Wabash Valley Coll (IL)
Illinois Valley Comm Coll (IL)
Independence Comm Coll (KS)
Indian Hills Comm Coll (IA)
Indian River Comm Coll (FL)
Inver Hills Comm Coll (MN)
Iowa Central Comm Coll (IA)
Iowa Lakes Comm Coll (IA)
Iowa Western Comm Coll (IA)
Itasca Comm Coll (MN)
Ivy Tech State Coll–Central Indiana (IN)
Ivy Tech State Coll–Eastcentral (IN)
Ivy Tech State Coll–Northeast (IN)
Ivy Tech State Coll–Whitewater (IN)
Jefferson Coll (MO)
Johnston Comm Coll (NC)
John Wood Comm Coll (IL)
Jones County Jr Coll (MS)
Kankakee Comm Coll (IL)
Kansas City Kansas Comm Coll (KS)
Kaskaskia Coll (IL)
Kellogg Comm Coll (MI)
Keystone Coll (PA)
Kirkwood Comm Coll (IA)
Kishwaukee Coll (IL)
Labette Comm Coll (KS)
Lake Land Coll (IL)
Lakeshore Tech Coll (WI)
Lake Washington Tech Coll (WA)
Lamar University–Port Arthur (TX)
Lane Comm Coll (OR)
Lansing Comm Coll (MI)
Laramie County Comm Coll (WY)
Laredo Comm Coll (TX)
Lewis and Clark Comm Coll (IL)
Lima Tech Coll (OH)
Lincoln Land Comm Coll (IL)
Los Angeles City Coll (CA)
Los Angeles Southwest Coll (CA)
Los Angeles Valley Coll (CA)
Lower Columbia Coll (WA)
Macomb Comm Coll (MI)
Madison Area Tech Coll (WI)
Manor Jr Coll (PA)
Marshalltown Comm Coll (IA)
Mary Holmes Coll (MS)
Massasoit Comm Coll (MA)
McCook Comm Coll (NE)
McDowell Tech Comm Coll (NC)
McHenry County Coll (IL)
Mendocino Coll (CA)
Merritt Coll (CA)
Mesa Comm Coll (AZ)
Metropolitan Comm Coll (NE)
Miami-Dade Comm Coll (FL)
Middlesex County Coll (NJ)
Midland Coll (TX)
Mid Michigan Comm Coll (MI)
Milwaukee Area Tech Coll (WI)
Minneapolis Comm Coll (MN)
Mitchell Coll (CT)
Moberly Area Comm Coll (MO)
Modesto Jr Coll (CA)
Mohawk Valley Comm Coll (NY)
Monroe County Comm Coll (MI)
Montcalm Comm Coll (MI)
Monterey Peninsula Coll (CA)
Montgomery College–Germantown Cmps (MD)
Montgomery College–Rockville Cmps (MD)
Montgomery College–Takoma Park Cmps (MD)
Moraine Valley Comm Coll (IL)
Mount Ida Coll (MA)
Mt San Antonio Coll (CA)
Mount Wachusett Comm Coll (MA)
Murray State Coll (OK)
Muscatine Comm Coll (IA)
Muskegon Comm Coll (MI)
Napa Valley Coll (CA)
Nassau Comm Coll (NY)
New Hampshire Tech Coll, Nashua (NH)
New River Comm Coll (VA)
Nicolet Area Tech Coll (WI)
North Central Tech Coll (OH)
Northeast Comm Coll (NE)
Northeastern Jr Coll (CO)
Northeastern Oklahoma A&M Coll (OK)
Northeast Iowa Comm Coll, Peosta Cmps (IA)
Northeast Mississippi Comm Coll (MS)
North Harris Coll (TX)
Northland Comm and Tech Coll (MN)
Northland Pioneer Coll (AZ)
North Seattle Comm Coll (WA)
North Shore Comm Coll (MA)
Northwestern Connecticut Comm-Tech Coll (CT)
Northwest Mississippi Comm Coll (MS)
Northwest-Shoals Comm Coll (AL)
Northwest State Comm Coll (OH)
Oakland Comm Coll (MI)
Odessa Coll (TX)
Ohlone Coll (CA)
Okaloosa-Walton Comm Coll (FL)
Oklahoma City Comm Coll (OK)
Orange County Comm Coll (NY)
Otero Jr Coll (CO)
Owens Comm Coll, Findlay (OH)
Owens Comm Coll, Toledo (OH)
Oxnard Coll (CA)
Palomar Coll (CA)
Peninsula Coll (WA)
Pensacola Jr Coll (FL)
Petit Jean Tech Coll (AR)
Piedmont Tech Coll (SC)
Pima Comm Coll (AZ)
Porterville Coll (CA)
Portland Comm Coll (OR)
Prairie State Coll (IL)
Pratt Comm Coll and Area Voc Sch (KS)
Rancho Santiago Coll (CA)
Raritan Valley Comm Coll (NJ)
Rasmussen Coll Eagan (MN)
Rasmussen Coll Mankato (MN)
Rasmussen Coll Minnetonka (MN)
Reading Area Comm Coll (PA)
Redlands Comm Coll (OK)
Reid State Tech Coll (AL)
Richland Comm Coll (IL)
Ricks Coll (ID)
Rockingham Comm Coll (NC)
Rock Valley Coll (IL)
Rogue Comm Coll (OR)
Rowan-Cabarrus Comm Coll (NC)
Saddleback Coll (CA)
Sage Jr Coll of Albany (NY)
Saint Charles County Comm Coll (MO)
St Clair County Comm Coll (MI)
St Cloud Tech Coll (MN)
St Louis Comm Coll at Florissant Valley (MO)
St Louis Comm Coll at Forest Park (MO)
St Louis Comm Coll at Meramec (MO)
St Paul Tech Coll (MN)
Salish Kootenai Coll (MT)
Salt Lake Comm Coll (UT)
San Antonio Coll (TX)
Sandhills Comm Coll (NC)
San Jacinto College–Central Cmps (TX)
San Jacinto College–North Cmps (TX)
San Joaquin Delta Coll (CA)
San Jose City Coll (CA)
San Juan Coll (NM)
Santa Fe Comm Coll (FL)
Sauk Valley Comm Coll (IL)
Schoolcraft Coll (MI)
Seminole Comm Coll (FL)
Seward County Comm Coll (KS)
Shawnee Comm Coll (IL)
Shoreline Comm Coll (WA)
Sinclair Comm Coll (OH)
Skagit Valley Coll (WA)
Snow Coll (UT)
Southeast Comm Coll, Lincoln Cmps (NE)
Southeastern Comm Coll, North Cmps, West Burlington (IA)
Southeastern Illinois Coll (IL)
Southern Maine Tech Coll (ME)
Southern U at Shreveport–Bossier City Cmps (LA)
South Plains Coll (TX)
South Suburban Coll (IL)
SouthWest Collegiate Inst for the Deaf (TX)
Southwestern Oregon Comm Coll (OR)
Southwestern Tech Coll (MN)
Southwest Wisconsin Tech Coll (WI)
Spokane Falls Comm Coll (WA)
Spoon River Coll (IL)
State Comm Coll of East St Louis (IL)
Suffolk County Comm College–Ammerman Cmps (NY)
Sullivan County Comm Coll (NY)
Terra State Comm Coll (OH)
Texas Southmost Coll (TX)
Tri-County Tech Coll (SC)
Trinity Valley Comm Coll (TX)
Truckee Meadows Comm Coll (NV)
Tulsa Jr Coll (OK)
Umpqua Comm Coll (OR)
U of Kentucky, Jefferson Comm Coll (KY)
U of North Dakota–Lake Region (ND)
Utah Valley State Coll (UT)
Vance-Granville Comm Coll (NC)
Vernon Regional Jr Coll (TX)
Victor Valley Coll (CA)
Vincennes U (IN)
Virginia Western Comm Coll (VA)
Wake Tech Comm Coll (NC)
Waldorf Coll (IA)
Wallace State Comm Coll (AL)
Walla Walla Comm Coll (WA)
Walters State Comm Coll (TN)
Washtenaw Comm Coll (MI)
Wayne County Comm Coll (MI)
Westchester Comm Coll (NY)
Western Nevada Comm Coll (NV)
Western Oklahoma State Coll (OK)
Western Wisconsin Tech Coll (WI)
West Hills Comm Coll (CA)
Westmoreland County Comm Coll (PA)
West Shore Comm Coll (MI)
White Pines Coll (NH)
William Rainey Harper Coll (IL)
Willmar Comm Coll (MN)
Yakima Valley Comm Coll (WA)
Yuba Coll (CA)

CHILD PSYCHOLOGY/ CHILD DEVELOPMENT

Albuquerque Tech Vocational Inst (NM)
Angelina Coll (TX)
Antelope Valley Coll (CA)
Arizona Western Coll (AZ)
Atlanta Metropolitan Coll (GA)
Austin Comm Coll (TX)
Bee County Coll (TX)
Blinn Coll (TX)
Brevard Coll (NC)
Brookhaven Coll (TX)
Carl Sandburg Coll (IL)
Central Coll (KS)
Central Lakes Coll (MN)
Cerro Coso Comm Coll (CA)
Chaffey Coll (CA)
Chatfield Coll (OH)
Chemeketa Comm Coll (OR)
Cisco Jr Coll (TX)
City Coll of San Francisco (CA)
City Colls of Chicago, Harold Washington Coll (IL)
City Colls of Chicago, Harry S Truman Coll (IL)
City Colls of Chicago, Malcolm X Coll (IL)
City Colls of Chicago, Olive-Harvey Coll (IL)
City Colls of Chicago, Richard J Daley Coll (IL)
Coll of the Canyons (CA)
Coll of the Sequoias (CA)
Collin County Comm Coll (TX)
Columbia Coll (CA)
Columbus State Comm Coll (OH)
Comm Coll of Allegheny County Allegheny Cmps (PA)
Comm Coll of Allegheny County North Cmps (PA)
Comm Coll of Allegheny County South Cmps (PA)
Comm Coll of Rhode Island (RI)
Comm Coll of Vermont (VT)
Connors State Coll (OK)
Cuyamaca Coll (CA)
De Anza Coll (CA)
Dundalk Comm Coll (MD)
Eastern New Mexico University–Roswell (NM)
Eastern Wyoming Coll (WY)
Eastfield Coll (TX)
East Los Angeles Coll (CA)
Ellsworth Comm Coll (IA)
Fiorello H LaGuardia Comm Coll of City U of NY (NY)
Flathead Valley Comm Coll (MT)
Foothill Coll (CA)
Frank Phillips Coll (TX)
Fresno City Coll (CA)
Fullerton Coll (CA)
Fulton-Montgomery Comm Coll (NY)
Garden City Comm Coll (KS)
Gavilan Coll (CA)
Great Basin Coll (NV)
Grossmont Coll (CA)
Gulf Coast Comm Coll (FL)
Hartnell Coll (CA)
Hill Coll of the Hill Jr Coll District (TX)
Hinds Comm Coll (MS)
Hiwassee Coll (TN)
Illinois Central Coll (IL)
Iowa Lakes Comm Coll (IA)
Itawamba Comm Coll (MS)
Ivy Tech State Coll–Whitewater (IN)
Jefferson Comm Coll (OH)
Jefferson State Comm Coll (AL)
John Tyler Comm Coll (VA)
Joliet Jr Coll (IL)
Kings River Comm Coll (CA)
Kirkwood Comm Coll (IA)
Lake Area Vocational-Tech Inst (SD)
Lakewood Comm Coll (MN)
Laramie County Comm Coll (WY)
Little Hoop Comm Coll (ND)
Long Beach City Coll (CA)
Los Angeles City Coll (CA)
Los Angeles Harbor Coll (CA)
Los Angeles Mission Coll (CA)
Los Angeles Southwest Coll (CA)
Los Angeles Valley Coll (CA)
Los Medanos Coll (CA)
Manatee Comm Coll (FL)
McLennan Comm Coll (TX)
Mendocino Coll (CA)
Merced Coll (CA)
Meridian Comm Coll (MS)
Midland Coll (TX)
MiraCosta Coll (CA)
Mississippi Delta Comm Coll (MS)
Mitchell Coll (CT)
Mount Ida Coll (MA)
Muskegon Comm Coll (MI)
Muskingum Area Tech Coll (OH)
Navarro Coll (TX)
Normandale Comm Coll (MN)
Northeast Mississippi Comm Coll (MS)
North Idaho Coll (ID)
Palomar Coll (CA)
Palo Verde Coll (CA)
Parkland Coll (IL)
Pasadena City Coll (CA)
Pitt Comm Coll (NC)
Prairie State Coll (IL)
Redlands Comm Coll (OK)
Rochester Comm Coll (MN)
Rockland Comm Coll (NY)
Rose State Coll (OK)
Saddleback Coll (CA)
St Gregory's Coll (OK)
St Louis Comm Coll at Forest Park (MO)
San Antonio Coll (TX)
San Bernardino Valley Coll (CA)
San Diego City Coll (CA)
San Diego Mesa Coll (CA)
San Diego Miramar Coll (CA)
San Jacinto College–Central Cmps (TX)
San Joaquin Delta Coll (CA)
Santa Monica Coll (CA)
Santa Rosa Jr Coll (CA)
Schoolcraft Coll (MI)
South Plains Coll (TX)
Southwestern Coll (CA)
State Comm Coll of East St Louis (IL)
Tarrant County Jr Coll (TX)
Trinity Valley Comm Coll (TX)
Tyler Jr Coll (TX)
United Tribes Tech Coll (ND)
Waldorf Coll (IA)
Waycross Coll (GA)
West Los Angeles Coll (CA)
Willmar Comm Coll (MN)
York Tech Coll (SC)

CHINESE

Glendale Comm Coll (AZ)

CITY/COMMUNITY/ REGIONAL PLANNING

D-Q U (CA)
Montgomery College–Rockville Cmps (MD)
Woodbury Coll (VT)

CIVIL ENGINEERING TECHNOLOGY

Allan Hancock Coll (CA)
Antelope Valley Coll (CA)
Asheville-Buncombe Tech Comm Coll (NC)
Belmont Tech Coll (OH)
Big Bend Comm Coll (WA)
Blue Mountain Comm Coll (OR)
Brevard Comm Coll (FL)
Bristol Comm Coll (MA)
Broome Comm Coll (NY)
Broward Comm Coll (FL)
Burlington County Coll (NJ)
Butler County Comm Coll (KS)
Butler County Comm Coll (PA)
Butte Coll (CA)
Capital Comm Tech Coll (CT)
Catonsville Comm Coll (MD)
Central Carolina Tech Coll (SC)
Centralia Coll (WA)
Central Maine Tech Coll (ME)
Central Oregon Comm Coll (OR)
Central Piedmont Comm Coll (NC)
Central Texas Coll (TX)
Central Virginia Comm Coll (VA)
Chabot Coll (CA)
Chattanooga State Tech Comm Coll (TN)
Chemeketa Comm Coll (OR)
Chippewa Valley Tech Coll (WI)
Cincinnati State Tech and Comm Coll (OH)
City Coll of San Francisco (CA)
Clark Coll (WA)
Clark State Comm Coll (OH)
Coll of Lake County (IL)
Coll of the Siskiyous (CA)
Columbus State Comm Coll (OH)
Comm Coll of Allegheny County Boyce Cmps (PA)
Comm Coll of Allegheny County South Cmps (PA)
Comm Coll of the Air Force (AL)
Copiah-Lincoln Comm Coll (MS)
Daytona Beach Comm Coll (FL)
Delaware Tech & Comm Coll, Jack F Owens Cmps (DE)
Delaware Tech & Comm Coll, Stanton/Wilmington Cmps (DE)
Delaware Tech & Comm Coll, Terry Cmps (DE)
Delgado Comm Coll (LA)
Dunwoody Inst (MN)
East Los Angeles Coll (CA)
Edison State Comm Coll (OH)
Erie Comm Coll, North Cmps (NY)
Everett Comm Coll (WA)
Fayetteville Tech Comm Coll (NC)
Florence-Darlington Tech Coll (SC)
Florida Comm Coll at Jacksonville (FL)
Franklin Inst of Boston (MA)
Fresno City Coll (CA)
Fullerton Coll (CA)
Gadsden State Comm Coll (AL)
Gaston Coll (NC)
Gloucester County Coll (NJ)
Guilford Tech Comm Coll (NC)
Gulf Coast Comm Coll (FL)
Hawkeye Comm Coll (IA)
Hill Coll of the Hill Jr Coll District (TX)
Hinds Comm Coll (MS)
Horry-Georgetown Tech Coll (SC)
Houston Comm Coll System (TX)
Hudson Valley Comm Coll (NY)
ICS Ctr for Degree Studies (PA)
Independence Comm Coll (KS)
Indian River Comm Coll (FL)
Iowa Western Comm Coll (IA)
Itawamba Comm Coll (MS)
Jefferson Coll (MO)
Jefferson State Comm Coll (AL)
Johnson County Comm Coll (KS)
J Sargeant Reynolds Comm Coll (VA)
Lake Land Coll (IL)
Lakeland Comm Coll (OH)
Lansing Comm Coll (MI)
Laramie County Comm Coll (WY)
Lincoln Land Comm Coll (IL)
Lorain County Comm Coll (OH)
Lord Fairfax Comm Coll (VA)
Los Angeles Valley Coll (CA)
Macomb Comm Coll (MI)
Madison Area Tech Coll (WI)
Manatee Comm Coll (FL)
Massasoit Comm Coll (MA)
Mercer County Comm Coll (NJ)
Metropolitan Comm Coll (NE)
Miami-Dade Comm Coll (FL)
Middlesex County Coll (NJ)
Midlands Tech Coll (SC)
Mid-State Tech Coll (WI)
Milwaukee Area Tech Coll (WI)
Mineral Area Coll (MO)
Mississippi Delta Comm Coll (MS)
Mohawk Valley Comm Coll (NY)
Monroe Comm Coll (NY)
Montgomery College–Rockville Cmps (MD)
Moraine Park Tech Coll (WI)
Morrison Inst of Tech (IL)
Mt Hood Comm Coll (OR)
Mt San Antonio Coll (CA)
Nashville State Tech Inst (TN)
Nassau Comm Coll (NY)
New Mexico Military Inst (NM)
New York City Tech Coll of the City U of NY (NY)
North Dakota State Coll of Science (ND)
Northeast Mississippi Comm Coll (MS)
Northern Essex Comm Coll (MA)
Northern Virginia Comm Coll (VA)
Northwest Mississippi Comm Coll (MS)
Norwalk Comm-Tech Coll (CT)
Ocean County Coll (NJ)
Oklahoma State U, Oklahoma City (OK)
Olympic Coll (WA)
Owens Comm Coll, Findlay (OH)
Owens Comm Coll, Toledo (OH)
Pasadena City Coll (CA)
Pellissippi State Tech Comm Coll (TN)
Peninsula Coll (WA)
Pennsylvania Coll of Tech (PA)
Pennsylvania Inst of Tech (PA)
Pensacola Jr Coll (FL)
Polk Comm Coll (FL)
Portland Comm Coll (OR)
Potomac State Coll of West Virginia U (WV)
Pueblo Comm Coll (CO)
Renton Tech Coll (WA)
Ricks Coll (ID)
Rochester Comm Coll (MN)
St Cloud Tech Coll (MN)
St Louis Comm Coll at Florissant Valley (MO)
Salt Lake Comm Coll (UT)
San Antonio Coll (TX)
San Bernardino Valley Coll (CA)
Sandhills Comm Coll (NC)
San Joaquin Delta Coll (CA)
San Juan Coll (NM)
Santa Rosa Jr Coll (CA)
Seminole Comm Coll (FL)
Shasta Coll (CA)
Shoreline Comm Coll (WA)
Sinclair Comm Coll (OH)
Skagit Valley Coll (WA)
Southeast Comm Coll, Milford Cmps (NE)
Southwestern Indian Polytechnic Inst (NM)
Spartanburg Tech Coll (SC)
Spokane Comm Coll (WA)
Springfield Tech Comm Coll (MA)
Stark Tech Coll (OH)
State Tech Inst at Memphis (TN)
State U of NY Coll of Tech at Alfred (NY)
State U of NY Coll of Tech at Canton (NY)
Suffolk County Comm College–Ammerman Cmps (NY)
Tallahassee Comm Coll (FL)
Three Rivers Comm-Tech Coll (CT)
Trident Tech Coll (SC)
Trinidad State Jr Coll (CO)
Umpqua Comm Coll (OR)
Union County Coll (NJ)
U of Kentucky, Jefferson Comm Coll (KY)
Valencia Comm Coll (FL)
Ventura Coll (CA)
Vermont Tech Coll (VT)
Vincennes U (IN)
Virginia Western Comm Coll (VA)
Wake Tech Comm Coll (NC)
Walla Walla Comm Coll (WA)
Westchester Comm Coll (NY)
Western Piedmont Comm Coll (NC)
Wytheville Comm Coll (VA)
Yakima Valley Comm Coll (WA)
York Tech Coll (SC)

CLASSICS

The Coll of Saint Thomas More (TX)
Foothill Coll (CA)
John Wood Comm Coll (IL)

COMMERCIAL ART

Alamance Comm Coll (NC)
Allen County Comm Coll (KS)
American Acad of Art (IL)
Antonelli Coll (OH)
Antonelli Inst (PA)
Arapahoe Comm Coll (CO)
Art Inst of Atlanta (GA)
Art Inst of Dallas (TX)
Art Inst of Fort Lauderdale (FL)
The Art Inst of Houston (TX)
The Art Inst of Philadelphia (PA)
Art Inst of Pittsburgh (PA)
Art Inst of Seattle (WA)
Atlanta Metropolitan Coll (GA)
Austin Comm Coll (TX)
Bee County Coll (TX)
Bergen Comm Coll (NJ)
Bismarck State Coll (ND)
Black Hawk Coll, Moline (IL)
Bradley Acad for the Visual Arts (PA)
Brevard Coll (NC)
Brevard Comm Coll (FL)
Brookhaven Coll (TX)
Brown Inst (MN)
Bryant and Stratton Business Inst, Rochester (NY)
Bryant and Stratton Business Inst, E Hills Cmps, Williamsville (NY)
Butler County Comm Coll (KS)
Butte Coll (CA)
Casper Coll (WY)
Catonsville Comm Coll (MD)
Central Comm College–Hastings Cmps (NE)
Central Comm College–Platte Cmps (NE)
Centralia Coll (WA)
Central Piedmont Comm Coll (NC)
Central Texas Coll (TX)
Central Virginia Comm Coll (VA)
Chabot Coll (CA)
Chatfield Coll (OH)
Chattanooga State Tech Comm Coll (TN)
City Colls of Chicago, Harold Washington Coll (IL)
City Colls of Chicago, Kennedy-King Coll (IL)
City Colls of Chicago, Wilbur Wright Coll (IL)
Clark Coll (WA)
Clark State Comm Coll (OH)
Colby Comm Coll (KS)
Coll of DuPage (IL)
Coll of San Mateo (CA)
Coll of Southern Idaho (ID)
Coll of the Sequoias (CA)
Collin County Comm Coll (TX)
Colorado Inst of Art (CO)
Colorado Mountn Coll, Roaring Fork Cmps-Spring Valley Ctr (CO)
Comm Coll of Allegheny County Allegheny Cmps (PA)
Comm Coll of Allegheny County South Cmps (PA)
Comm Coll of Denver (CO)
Cuyahoga Comm Coll, Eastern Cmps (OH)
Cuyahoga Comm Coll, Western Cmps (OH)
Delgado Comm Coll (LA)
Des Moines Area Comm Coll (IA)
Dutchess Comm Coll (NY)
East Central Coll (MO)
Eastern Arizona Coll (AZ)
Edison State Comm Coll (OH)
Education America–Tampa Tech Inst Cmps (FL)
Ellsworth Comm Coll (IA)
El Paso Comm Coll (TX)
Everett Comm Coll (WA)
Fashion Inst of Design & Merchandising, LA Cmps (CA)
Fashion Inst of Design & Merchandising, SD Cmps (CA)
Fashion Inst of Design & Merchandising, SF Cmps (CA)
Fayetteville Tech Comm Coll (NC)
Finger Lakes Comm Coll (NY)
Garland County Comm Coll (AR)
Genesee Comm Coll (NY)
Gogebic Comm Coll (MI)
Guilford Tech Comm Coll (NC)
Halifax Comm Coll (NC)
Harford Comm Coll (MD)
Harrisburg Area Comm Coll (PA)
Hawkeye Comm Coll (IA)
Henry Ford Comm Coll (MI)
Highland Comm Coll (KS)
Hill Coll of the Hill Jr Coll District (TX)
Hinds Comm Coll (MS)
Holyoke Comm Coll (MA)
Houston Comm Coll System (TX)
Hutchinson Comm Coll and Area Vocational Sch (KS)
Illinois Central Coll (IL)
International Fine Arts Coll (FL)
Iowa Lakes Comm Coll (IA)
Isothermal Comm Coll (NC)
Ivy Tech State Coll–Columbus (IN)
Ivy Tech State Coll–Northcentral (IN)
Ivy Tech State Coll–Southcentral (IN)
Ivy Tech State Coll–Southwest (IN)
James H Faulkner State Comm Coll (AL)
James Sprunt Comm Coll (NC)
John C Calhoun State Comm Coll (AL)
Johnson County Comm Coll (KS)
Johnston Comm Coll (NC)
Kansas City Kansas Comm Coll (KS)
Kellogg Comm Coll (MI)
Labette Comm Coll (KS)
Laney Coll (CA)
Lansing Comm Coll (MI)
Lassen Coll (CA)
Lon Morris Coll (TX)
Los Angeles Pierce Coll (CA)
Los Angeles Trade-Tech Coll (CA)
Los Angeles Valley Coll (CA)
Luzerne County Comm Coll (PA)
Macomb Comm Coll (MI)
Madison Area Tech Coll (WI)
Maryland Coll of Art and Design (MD)
Massasoit Comm Coll (MA)
McDowell Tech Comm Coll (NC)
Mercer County Comm Coll (NJ)
Metropolitan Comm Coll (NE)
Miami-Dade Comm Coll (FL)
Middle Georgia Coll (GA)
Middlesex Community–Tech Coll (CT)
Middlesex County Coll (NJ)
Midland Coll (TX)
Milwaukee Area Tech Coll (WI)
Mission Coll (CA)
Mississippi Delta Comm Coll (MS)
Mohawk Valley Comm Coll (NY)
Monroe Comm Coll (NY)
Montgomery College–Rockville Cmps (MD)
Moorpark Coll (CA)
Mt Hood Comm Coll (OR)
Mount Ida Coll (MA)
Mt San Antonio Coll (CA)
Nassau Comm Coll (NY)
Navarro Coll (TX)
New Hampshire Tech Coll, Manchester (NH)
New York City Tech Coll of the City U of NY (NY)
Northampton County Area Comm Coll (PA)
Northeast Mississippi Comm Coll (MS)
Northern Essex Comm Coll (MA)
Northern Virginia Comm Coll (VA)
North Hennepin Comm Coll (MN)
North Idaho Coll (ID)
Northwest Coll (WY)
Northwestern Connecticut Comm-Tech Coll (CT)
Northwestern Michigan Coll (MI)
Northwest Mississippi Comm Coll (MS)
Oakland Comm Coll (MI)
Oklahoma City Comm Coll (OK)
Oklahoma State U, Okmulgee (OK)
Omaha Coll of Health Careers (NE)
Orange Coast Coll (CA)
Palm Beach Comm Coll (FL)
Palomar Coll (CA)
Parkland Coll (IL)
Pellissippi State Tech Comm Coll (TN)
Penn Valley Comm Coll (MO)
Pikes Peak Comm Coll (CO)
Pima Comm Coll (AZ)
Pitt Comm Coll (NC)
Pittsburgh Tech Inst (PA)
Porterville Coll (CA)
Pratt Comm Coll and Area Voc Sch (KS)
Rancho Santiago Coll (CA)
Randolph Comm Coll (NC)
Raritan Valley Comm Coll (NJ)
Redlands Comm Coll (OK)
Ricks Coll (ID)
Riverside Comm Coll (CA)
Rockland Comm Coll (NY)
Saddleback Coll (CA)
Saint Charles County Comm Coll (MO)
St Clair County Comm Coll (MI)
St Johns River Comm Coll (FL)
St Louis Comm Coll at Florissant Valley (MO)
St Louis Comm Coll at Forest Park (MO)
Salt Lake Comm Coll (UT)
San Antonio Coll (TX)
San Bernardino Valley Coll (CA)
San Diego City Coll (CA)
San Jacinto College–Central Cmps (TX)
San Jacinto College–South Cmps (TX)
Schoolcraft Coll (MI)
Seattle Central Comm Coll (WA)
Shasta Coll (CA)
Shoreline Comm Coll (WA)
Sinclair Comm Coll (OH)
Solano Comm Coll (CA)
Southeast Comm Coll, Milford Cmps (NE)
South Plains Coll (TX)
Southwestern Comm Coll (NC)
Southwestern Michigan Coll (MI)
Springfield Tech Comm Coll (MA)
Sullivan County Comm Coll (NY)
Texas State Tech Coll–Waco/Marshall Cmps (TX)
Thomas Nelson Comm Coll (VA)
Treasure Valley Comm Coll (OR)
Trident Tech Coll (SC)
Trinidad State Jr Coll (CO)
Tunxis Comm Tech Coll (CT)
U of Cincinnati Raymond Walters Coll (OH)
U of Hawaii–Honolulu Comm Coll (HI)
U of Kentucky, Jefferson Comm Coll (KY)
Utah Valley State Coll (UT)
Ventura Coll (CA)
Vincennes U (IN)
Virginia Marti Coll of Fashion and Art (OH)
Virginia Western Comm Coll (VA)
Waldorf Coll (IA)
Washtenaw Comm Coll (MI)
Wenatchee Valley Coll (WA)
Western Oklahoma State Coll (OK)
Western Wisconsin Tech Coll (WI)
Westmoreland County Comm Coll (PA)
Yavapai Coll (AZ)

COMMUNICATION

Adirondack Comm Coll (NY)
Allegany Comm Coll (MD)
Allen County Comm Coll (KS)
Andrew Coll (GA)
Anne Arundel Comm Coll (MD)
Art Inst of Pittsburgh (PA)
Asnuntuck Comm-Tech Coll (CT)
Austin Comm Coll (TX)
Bergen Comm Coll (NJ)
Blinn Coll (TX)
Borough of Manhattan Comm Coll of City U of NY (NY)
Brevard Coll (NC)
Briarwood Coll (CT)
Bristol Comm Coll (MA)
Brookdale Comm Coll (NJ)
Bucks County Comm Coll (PA)
Butler County Comm Coll (KS)
Butler County Comm Coll (PA)
Camden County Coll (NJ)
Casper Coll (WY)
Catonsville Comm Coll (MD)
Central Coll (KS)
Central Comm College–Grand Island Cmps (NE)
Central Comm College–Hastings Cmps (NE)
Central Comm College–Platte Cmps (NE)
Centralia Coll (WA)
Central Pennsylvania Business Sch (PA)
Central Texas Coll (TX)
Chabot Coll (CA)
Champlain Coll (VT)
Chattanooga State Tech Comm Coll (TN)
Chipola Jr Coll (FL)

City Colls of Chicago, Richard J Daley Coll (IL)
Clark Coll (WA)
Clinton Comm Coll (IA)
Cochise Coll, Douglas (AZ)
Cochise Coll, Sierra Vista (AZ)
Coffeyville Comm Coll (KS)
Coll of DuPage (IL)
Coll of Marin (CA)
Coll of the Desert (CA)
Coll of the Sequoias (CA)
Columbia State Comm Coll (TN)
Comm Coll of Allegheny County Allegheny Cmps (PA)
Comm Coll of Allegheny County Boyce Cmps (PA)
Comm Coll of Allegheny County South Cmps (PA)
Comm Coll of Southern Nevada (NV)
Comm Coll of the Air Force (AL)
Cosumnes River Coll (CA)
County Coll of Morris (NJ)
Crowder Coll (MO)
Cuesta Coll (CA)
Daytona Beach Comm Coll (FL)
Dean Coll (MA)
De Anza Coll (CA)
Dixie Coll (UT)
Dodge City Comm Coll (KS)
Dutchess Comm Coll (NY)
East Central Coll (MO)
Eastern Wyoming Coll (WY)
El Paso Comm Coll (TX)
Enterprise State Jr Coll (AL)
Everett Comm Coll (WA)
Finger Lakes Comm Coll (NY)
Fisher Coll (MA)
Foothill Coll (CA)
Frederick Comm Coll (MD)
Fullerton Coll (CA)
Fulton-Montgomery Comm Coll (NY)
Genesee Comm Coll (NY)
Georgia Military Coll (GA)
Glendale Comm Coll (AZ)
Grand Rapids Comm Coll (MI)
Greenfield Comm Coll (MA)
Grossmont Coll (CA)
Gulf Coast Comm Coll (FL)
Hagerstown Jr Coll (MD)
Harford Comm Coll (MD)
Harrisburg Area Comm Coll (PA)
Henry Ford Comm Coll (MI)
Hesser Coll (NH)
Hill Coll of the Hill Jr Coll District (TX)
Hinds Comm Coll (MS)
Hiwassee Coll (TN)
Holyoke Comm Coll (MA)
Houston Comm Coll System (TX)
Iowa Central Comm Coll (IA)
Iowa Lakes Comm Coll (IA)
Ivy Tech State Coll–Northcentral (IN)
Jackson State Comm Coll (TN)
Jamestown Comm Coll (NY)
John Wood Comm Coll (IL)
Kellogg Comm Coll (MI)
Keystone Coll (PA)
Kirkwood Comm Coll (IA)
Lamar Comm Coll (CO)
Lamar University–Orange (TX)
Lansing Comm Coll (MI)
Laramie County Comm Coll (WY)
Lassen Coll (CA)
Lee Coll (TX)
Lincoln Land Comm Coll (IL)
Lon Morris Coll (TX)
Lorain County Comm Coll (OH)
Los Angeles City Coll (CA)
Los Angeles Valley Coll (CA)
Macon Coll (GA)
Manchester Comm-Tech Coll (CT)
Mary Holmes Coll (MS)
Massachusetts Bay Comm Coll (MA)
Massasoit Comm Coll (MA)
Mercer County Comm Coll (NJ)
Miami-Dade Comm Coll (FL)
Miami University–Middletown Cmps (OH)
Middlesex Comm Coll (MA)
Middlesex Community–Tech Coll (CT)
Midland Coll (TX)
Mineral Area Coll (MO)
Monroe Comm Coll (NY)
Monroe County Comm Coll (MI)
Monterey Peninsula Coll (CA)
Montgomery College–Rockville Cmps (MD)
Montgomery County Comm Coll (PA)
Mount Ida Coll (MA)
Nassau Comm Coll (NY)
Newbury Coll (MA)
Niagara County Comm Coll (NY)
Northeast Comm Coll (NE)
Northeast Mississippi Comm Coll (MS)
North Idaho Coll (ID)
Northland Comm and Tech Coll (MN)
Northwest Coll (WY)
Norwalk Comm-Tech Coll (CT)
Oakland Comm Coll (MI)
Ohio Valley Coll (WV)
Ohlone Coll (CA)
Oklahoma City Comm Coll (OK)
Palm Beach Comm Coll (FL)
Palomar Coll (CA)
Parkland Coll (IL)
Pasadena City Coll (CA)
Pennsylvania Coll of Tech (PA)
Pensacola Jr Coll (FL)
Pikes Peak Comm Coll (CO)
Pima Comm Coll (AZ)
Polk Comm Coll (FL)
Pratt Comm Coll and Area Voc Sch (KS)
Quincy Coll (MA)
Raritan Valley Comm Coll (NJ)
Redlands Comm Coll (OK)
Red Rocks Comm Coll (CO)
Ricks Coll (ID)
Rockland Comm Coll (NY)
Sacramento City Coll (CA)
Sage Jr Coll of Albany (NY)
St Clair County Comm Coll (MI)
St Louis Comm Coll at Florissant Valley (MO)
St Louis Comm Coll at Forest Park (MO)
Salem Comm Coll (NJ)
Salt Lake Comm Coll (UT)
San Diego Miramar Coll (CA)
San Jacinto College–Central Cmps (TX)
San Juan Coll (NM)
Santa Barbara City Coll (CA)
Santa Fe Comm Coll (NM)
Santa Monica Coll (CA)
Santa Rosa Jr Coll (CA)
Scott Comm Coll (IA)
Seward County Comm Coll (KS)
Sierra Coll (CA)
Sinclair Comm Coll (OH)
Snow Coll (UT)
South Georgia Coll (GA)
South Mountain Comm Coll (AZ)
South Plains Coll (TX)
Spokane Falls Comm Coll (WA)
Spoon River Coll (IL)
State Fair Comm Coll (MO)
Sullivan County Comm Coll (NY)
Tompkins Cortland Comm Coll (NY)
Treasure Valley Comm Coll (OR)
Triton Coll (IL)
Tulsa Jr Coll (OK)
Ulster County Comm Coll (NY)
Union County Coll (NJ)
U of Kentucky, Henderson Comm Coll (KY)
U of Kentucky, Jefferson Comm Coll (KY)
U of Kentucky, Paducah Comm Coll (KY)
U of New Mexico–Gallup Branch (NM)
U of Wisconsin Center–Marathon County (WI)
Vermilion Comm Coll (MN)
Vincennes U (IN)
Waldorf Coll (IA)
Waubonsee Comm Coll (IL)
Westchester Comm Coll (NY)
Western Texas Coll (TX)
Western Wisconsin Tech Coll (WI)
Western Wyoming Comm Coll (WY)
West Shore Comm Coll (MI)
White Pines Coll (NH)
Willmar Comm Coll (MN)
Wright State U, Lake Cmps (OH)
Wytheville Comm Coll (VA)
Yuba Coll (CA)

COMMUNICATION EQUIPMENT TECHNOLOGY

Alexandria Tech Coll (MN)
Allegany Comm Coll (MD)
Anne Arundel Comm Coll (MD)
Art Inst of Pittsburgh (PA)
Athens Area Tech Inst (GA)
Brown Inst (MN)
Bunker Hill Comm Coll (MA)
Burlington County Coll (NJ)
Cayuga County Comm Coll (NY)
Central Texas Coll (TX)
Chemeketa Comm Coll (OR)
Cleveland Comm Coll (NC)
Coffeyville Comm Coll (KS)
Coll of DuPage (IL)
Comm Coll of Allegheny County South Cmps (PA)
Comm Coll of Beaver County (PA)
Comm Coll of Philadelphia (PA)
Comm Coll of the Air Force (AL)
Dodge City Comm Coll (KS)
Dundalk Comm Coll (MD)
ECPI Coll of Tech, Hampton (VA)
ECPI Coll of Tech, Virginia Beach (VA)
ECPI Computer Inst, Richmond (VA)
ECPI Computer Inst, Roanoke (VA)
Erie Comm Coll, South Cmps (NY)
Inst of Electronic Tech (KY)
Ivy Tech State Coll–Northcentral (IN)
John Wood Comm Coll (IL)
Kirkwood Comm Coll (IA)
Lansing Comm Coll (MI)
Lassen Coll (CA)
Macomb Comm Coll (MI)
Madison Area Tech Coll (WI)
Milwaukee Area Tech Coll (WI)
Mohawk Valley Comm Coll (NY)
Montgomery County Comm Coll (PA)
Moraine Valley Comm Coll (IL)
Napa Valley Coll (CA)
National Ed Ctr–Spartan Sch of Aeronautics Cmps (OK)
NEI Coll of Tech (MN)
Newbury Coll (MA)
North Dakota State Coll of Science (ND)
North Lake Coll (TX)
North Seattle Comm Coll (WA)
Northwestern Connecticut Comm-Tech Coll (CT)
Orange Coast Coll (CA)
Parkland Coll (IL)
Pasadena City Coll (CA)
Pensacola Jr Coll (FL)
Pima Comm Coll (AZ)
Ranken Tech Coll (MO)
Reading Area Comm Coll (PA)
Renton Tech Coll (WA)
St Philip's Coll (TX)
Santa Fe Comm Coll (FL)
Santa Fe Comm Coll (NM)
Southern Maine Tech Coll (ME)
Southern West Virginia Comm and Tech Coll (WV)
South Puget Sound Comm Coll (WA)
Southwestern Coll (CA)
Tennessee Inst of Electronics (TN)
Vincennes U (IN)
Western Nebraska Comm Coll, Scottsbluff (NE)

COMMUNITY SERVICES

Borough of Manhattan Comm Coll of City U of NY (NY)
Brevard Coll (NC)
Bunker Hill Comm Coll (MA)
Coll of the Sequoias (CA)
Comm Coll of Allegheny County North Cmps (PA)
Comm Coll of Philadelphia (PA)
Comm Coll of Vermont (VT)
Crafton Hills Coll (CA)
Cumberland County Coll (NJ)
Dean Coll (MA)
Del Mar Coll (TX)
Edison State Comm Coll (OH)
Edmonds Comm Coll (WA)
Iowa Central Comm Coll (IA)
Joliet Jr Coll (IL)
J Sargeant Reynolds Comm Coll (VA)
Lamar Comm Coll (CO)
Lane Comm Coll (OR)
Marshalltown Comm Coll (IA)
Mercer County Comm Coll (NJ)
Merritt Coll (CA)
Mohawk Valley Comm Coll (NY)
New Hampshire Tech Coll, Manchester (NH)
New River Comm Coll (VA)
Ocean County Coll (NJ)
Piedmont Comm Coll (NC)
Redlands Comm Coll (OK)
Salem Comm Coll (NJ)
State Comm Coll of East St Louis (IL)
Suffolk County Comm College–Ammerman Cmps (NY)
Ulster County Comm Coll (NY)
Waldorf Coll (IA)
Willmar Comm Coll (MN)

COMPUTER GRAPHICS

American Acad of Art (IL)
Art Inst of Dallas (TX)
Art Inst of Pittsburgh (PA)
Art Inst of Seattle (WA)
Belleville Area Coll (IL)
Bessemer State Tech Coll (AL)
Bradley Acad for the Visual Arts (PA)
Brevard Coll (NC)
Catonsville Comm Coll (MD)
Cecil Comm Coll (MD)
Central Oregon Comm Coll (OR)
Coll of Eastern Utah (UT)
Coll of the Sequoias (CA)
Colorado Inst of Art (CO)
Corning Comm Coll (NY)
Cowley County Comm Coll and Voc-Tech Sch (KS)
Elgin Comm Coll (IL)
Evergreen Valley Coll (CA)
Gadsden State Comm Coll (AL)
Garden City Comm Coll (KS)
Garland County Comm Coll (AR)
Gateway Comm-Tech Coll (CT)
Glendale Comm Coll (AZ)
Gloucester County Coll (NJ)
Gogebic Comm Coll (MI)
Howard Comm Coll (MD)
International Fine Arts Coll (FL)
Kingwood Coll (TX)
Lansing Comm Coll (MI)
Lincoln Coll, Normal (IL)
Linn-Benton Comm Coll (OR)
Maryland Coll of Art and Design (MD)
Massachusetts Bay Comm Coll (MA)
Mercer County Comm Coll (NJ)
Miami-Dade Comm Coll (FL)
Middlesex County Coll (NJ)
Montgomery Coll (TX)
Moraine Valley Comm Coll (IL)
Morrison Inst of Tech (IL)
Navarro Coll (TX)
New Mexico Jr Coll (NM)
Northwestern Connecticut Comm-Tech Coll (CT)
Ohio Inst of Photography and Tech (OH)
Oklahoma State U, Okmulgee (OK)
Orange Coast Coll (CA)
Parkland Coll (IL)
Pima Comm Coll (AZ)
Pittsburgh Tech Inst (PA)
Pueblo Comm Coll (CO)
Queensborough Comm Coll of City U of NY (NY)
Salt Lake Comm Coll (UT)
Schoolcraft Coll (MI)
Shoreline Comm Coll (WA)
Southern Arkansas U Tech (AR)
State U of NY Coll of Tech at Alfred (NY)
Tomball Coll (TX)
Tompkins Cortland Comm Coll (NY)
Triton Coll (IL)
U of Cincinnati Clermont Coll (OH)
U of New Mexico–Gallup Branch (NM)
Wake Tech Comm Coll (NC)
Washtenaw Comm Coll (MI)
Westmoreland County Comm Coll (PA)
West Shore Comm Coll (MI)
Yakima Valley Comm Coll (WA)

COMPUTER INFORMATION SYSTEMS

Aims Comm Coll (CO)
Alabama Southern Comm Coll, Thomasville (AL)
Alexandria Tech Coll (MN)
Allan Hancock Coll (CA)
Allen County Comm Coll (KS)
Anne Arundel Comm Coll (MD)
Aquinas Coll at Milton (MA)
Arapahoe Comm Coll (CO)
Arizona Western Coll (AZ)
Arkansas State University–Beebe Branch (AR)
Atlanta Metropolitan Coll (GA)
Atlantic Comm Coll (NJ)
Augusta Tech Inst (GA)
Austin Comm Coll (TX)
Bainbridge Coll (GA)
Baker Coll of Jackson (MI)
Bakersfield Coll (CA)
Baltimore City Comm Coll (MD)
Barton County Comm Coll (KS)
Bay Mills Comm Coll (MI)
Belleville Area Coll (IL)
Bellevue Comm Coll (WA)
Berkshire Comm Coll (MA)
Bishop State Comm Coll (AL)
Blue Ridge Comm Coll (VA)
Bossier Parish Comm Coll (LA)
Bramson ORT Tech Inst (NY)
Brazosport Coll (TX)
Brevard Coll (NC)
Briarcliffe–The Coll for Business & Tech (NY)
Brookhaven Coll (TX)
Broward Comm Coll (FL)
Brown Inst (MN)
Bryant and Stratton Business Inst, Albany (NY)
Bryant and Stratton Business Inst, Rochester (NY)
Bryant and Stratton Business Inst, Rochester (NY)
Bucks County Comm Coll (PA)
Butler County Comm Coll (PA)
Cañada Coll (CA)
Cape Cod Comm Coll (MA)
Casco Bay Coll (ME)
Catonsville Comm Coll (MD)
Cayuga County Comm Coll (NY)
Central Alabama Comm Coll (AL)
Central Comm College–Grand Island Cmps (NE)
Central Comm College–Hastings Cmps (NE)
Central Oregon Comm Coll (OR)
Central Pennsylvania Business Sch (PA)
Central Texas Coll (TX)
Central Virginia Comm Coll (VA)
Central Wyoming Coll (WY)
Chabot Coll (CA)
Chaffey Coll (CA)
Champlain Coll (VT)
Charles Stewart Mott Comm Coll (MI)
Chattahoochee Valley State Comm Coll (AL)
Chattanooga State Tech Comm Coll (TN)
Cincinnati State Tech and Comm Coll (OH)
City Colls of Chicago, Harry S Truman Coll (IL)
Clark Coll (WA)
Clark State Comm Coll (OH)
Cleveland State Comm Coll (TN)
Clovis Comm Coll (NM)
Cochise Coll, Douglas (AZ)
Cochise Coll, Sierra Vista (AZ)
Coconino County Comm Coll (AZ)
Coffeyville Comm Coll (KS)
Coll of Alameda (CA)
Coll of DuPage (IL)
Coll of Lake County (IL)
Coll of Marin (CA)
Coll of San Mateo (CA)
Coll of the Canyons (CA)
Coll of the Sequoias (CA)
Collin County Comm Coll (TX)
Colorado Northwestern Comm Coll (CO)
Columbia-Greene Comm Coll (NY)
Columbia Jr Coll of Business (SC)
Columbia State Comm Coll (TN)
Comm Coll of Allegheny County Allegheny Cmps (PA)
Comm Coll of Allegheny County Boyce Cmps (PA)
Comm Coll of Allegheny County North Cmps (PA)
Comm Coll of Allegheny County South Cmps (PA)
Comm Coll of Aurora (CO)
Comm Coll of Beaver County (PA)
Comm Coll of Southern Nevada (NV)
Corning Comm Coll (NY)
Cosumnes River Coll (CA)
County Coll of Morris (NJ)
Craven Comm Coll (NC)
Cumberland County Coll (NJ)
Dabney S Lancaster Comm Coll (VA)
Danville Area Comm Coll (IL)
Daytona Beach Comm Coll (FL)
Dean Coll (MA)
De Anza Coll (CA)
Delaware County Comm Coll (PA)
Delgado Comm Coll (LA)
Del Mar Coll (TX)
Delta Coll (MI)
DeVry Tech Inst (NJ)
Dixie Coll (UT)
Dodge City Comm Coll (KS)
Draughons Jr Coll (AL)
Draughons Jr Coll (KY)
Draughons Jr Coll, Nashville (TN)
Dundalk Comm Coll (MD)
Dunwoody Inst (MN)
Dutchess Comm Coll (NY)
East Central Coll (MO)
Eastern Arizona Coll (AZ)
Eastern New Mexico University–Roswell (NM)

Eastfield Coll (TX)
ECPI Coll of Tech, Hampton (VA)
ECPI Coll of Tech, Virginia Beach (VA)
ECPI Computer Inst, Richmond (VA)
ECPI Computer Inst, Roanoke (VA)
Edmonds Comm Coll (WA)
Elaine P Nunez Comm Coll (LA)
El Centro Coll (TX)
Erie Business Ctr, Main (PA)
Erie Comm Coll, City Cmps (NY)
Erie Comm Coll, North Cmps (NY)
Erie Comm Coll, South Cmps (NY)
Essex Comm Coll (MD)
Essex County Coll (NJ)
Evergreen Valley Coll (CA)
Fiorello H LaGuardia Comm Coll of City U of NY (NY)
Florida Comm Coll at Jacksonville (FL)
Floyd Coll (GA)
Fort Berthold Comm Coll (ND)
Front Range Comm Coll (CO)
Fullerton Coll (CA)
Fulton-Montgomery Comm Coll (NY)
Garden City Comm Coll (KS)
Garland County Comm Coll (AR)
Gateway Coll (NE)
Gavilan Coll (CA)
Gem City Coll (IL)
Genesee Comm Coll (NY)
Glendale Comm Coll (AZ)
Gloucester County Coll (NJ)
Grand Rapids Comm Coll (MI)
Great Basin Coll (NV)
Greenfield Comm Coll (MA)
Green River Comm Coll (WA)
Grossmont Coll (CA)
Guilford Tech Comm Coll (NC)
Hagerstown Business Coll (MD)
Hagerstown Jr Coll (MD)
Hamilton Business Coll (IA)
Harcum Coll (PA)
Harford Comm Coll (MD)
Harrisburg Area Comm Coll (PA)
Haskell Indian Nations U (KS)
Heald Business Coll, Concord (CA)
Heald Business Coll, Fresno (CA)
Heald Business Coll, San Francisco (CA)
Heald Business Coll (HI)
Heartland Comm Coll (IL)
Henry Ford Comm Coll (MI)
Herkimer County Comm Coll (NY)
Herzing Coll of Business and Tech (AL)
Herzing Coll of Business and Tech (GA)
Hesser Coll (NH)
Highland Comm Coll (KS)
Hill Coll of the Hill Jr Coll District (TX)
Hillsborough Comm Coll (FL)
Holyoke Comm Coll (MA)
Illinois Eastern Comm Colls, Frontier Comm Coll (IL)
Imperial Valley Coll (CA)
Indian River Comm Coll (FL)
Inst of Career Education (FL)
Ivy Tech State Coll–Central Indiana (IN)
Ivy Tech State Coll–Columbus (IN)
Ivy Tech State Coll–Eastcentral (IN)
Ivy Tech State Coll–Kokomo (IN)
Ivy Tech State Coll–Lafayette (IN)
Ivy Tech State Coll–Northcentral (IN)
Ivy Tech State Coll–Northeast (IN)
Ivy Tech State Coll–Northwest (IN)
Ivy Tech State Coll–Southcentral (IN)
Ivy Tech State Coll–Southeast (IN)
Ivy Tech State Coll–Southwest (IN)
Ivy Tech State Coll–Wabash Valley (IN)
Ivy Tech State Coll–Whitewater (IN)
Jamestown Comm Coll (NY)
Jefferson Coll (MO)
Jefferson Comm Coll (NY)
J F Drake State Tech Coll (AL)
John A Logan Coll (IL)
John C Calhoun State Comm Coll (AL)
John M Patterson State Tech Coll (AL)
John Tyler Comm Coll (VA)
John Wood Comm Coll (IL)
Joliet Jr Coll (IL)
Kalamazoo Valley Comm Coll (MI)
Kansas City Kansas Comm Coll (KS)
Kaskaskia Coll (IL)
Keiser Coll of Tech, Sarasota (FL)
Kellogg Comm Coll (MI)
Kelsey Jenney Coll (CA)
Keystone Coll (PA)
Kings River Comm Coll (CA)
Kirtland Comm Coll (MI)
Knoxville Business Coll (TN)
Lackawanna Jr Coll (PA)
Lakeland Comm Coll (OH)
Lamar Comm Coll (CO)
Lamar University–Orange (TX)
Lamson Jr Coll, Mesa (AZ)
Laney Coll (CA)
Lansing Comm Coll (MI)
Laramie County Comm Coll (WY)
Laredo Comm Coll (TX)
Las Positas Coll (CA)
Lawson State Comm Coll (AL)
LDS Business Coll (UT)
Lee Coll (TX)
Lehigh Carbon Comm Coll (PA)
Lewis Coll of Business (MI)
Lincoln Coll, Normal (IL)
Lorain County Comm Coll (OH)
Lord Fairfax Comm Coll (VA)
Los Angeles Harbor Coll (CA)
Los Angeles Trade-Tech Coll (CA)
Los Angeles Valley Coll (CA)
Lower Columbia Coll (WA)
Macomb Comm Coll (MI)
Macon Coll (GA)
Manatee Comm Coll (FL)
Martin Comm Coll (NC)
Massachusetts Bay Comm Coll (MA)
Massasoit Comm Coll (MA)
McHenry County Coll (IL)
McIntosh Coll (NH)
McLennan Comm Coll (TX)
Mendocino Coll (CA)
Mercer County Comm Coll (NJ)
Merritt Coll (CA)
Miami-Dade Comm Coll (FL)
Miami University–Middletown Cmps (OH)
Middlesex County Coll (NJ)
Mid Michigan Comm Coll (MI)
Midstate Coll (IL)
Milwaukee Area Tech Coll (WI)
MiraCosta Coll (CA)
Mission Coll (CA)
Mitchell Coll (CT)
Moberly Area Comm Coll (MO)
Mohawk Valley Comm Coll (NY)
Monroe Comm Coll (NY)
Montana State U Coll of Tech-Great Falls (MT)
Monterey Peninsula Coll (CA)
Montgomery Coll (TX)
Montgomery County Comm Coll (PA)
Moorpark Coll (CA)
Moraine Valley Comm Coll (IL)
Motlow State Comm Coll (TN)
Mountain Empire Comm Coll (VA)
Mountain View Coll (TX)
Mount Wachusett Comm Coll (MA)
Murray State Coll (OK)
Muskegon Comm Coll (MI)
Nashville State Tech Inst (TN)
Naugatuck Valley Community–Tech Coll (CT)
Navajo Comm Coll (AZ)
NEI Coll of Tech (MN)
Neosho County Comm Coll (KS)
Nettleton Career Coll (SD)
Newbury Coll (MA)
New England Inst of Tech (RI)
New Hampshire Tech Coll, Nashua (NH)
New Hampshire Tech Inst (NH)
New Mexico State University–Carlsbad (NM)
New River Comm Coll (VA)
Northampton County Area Comm Coll (PA)
North Central Tech Coll (OH)
Northcentral Tech Coll (WI)
North Central Texas Coll (TX)
Northeast Alabama State Comm Coll (AL)
Northeast Iowa Comm Coll, Peosta Cmps (IA)
Northeast Mississippi Comm Coll (MS)
Northeast Texas Comm Coll (TX)
Northern Oklahoma Coll (OK)
Northern Virginia Comm Coll (VA)
North Lake Coll (TX)
North Shore Comm Coll (MA)
Northwest Coll (WY)
Northwestern Connecticut Comm-Tech Coll (CT)
Northwestern Michigan Coll (MI)
Northwest-Shoals Comm Coll (AL)
Norwalk Comm-Tech Coll (CT)
Oakland Comm Coll (MI)
Odessa Coll (TX)
Oklahoma State U, Okmulgee (OK)
Olympic Coll (WA)
Onondaga Comm Coll (NY)
Orange Coast Coll (CA)
Orange County Comm Coll (NY)
Ouachita Tech Coll (AR)
Owensboro Comm Coll (KY)
Oxnard Coll (CA)
Ozarks Tech Comm Coll (MO)
Palo Alto Coll (TX)
Palomar Coll (CA)
Paris Jr Coll (TX)
Parkland Coll (IL)
Pasadena City Coll (CA)
Passaic County Comm Coll (NJ)
Peirce Coll (PA)
Pennsylvania Coll of Tech (PA)
Pensacola Jr Coll (FL)
Petit Jean Tech Coll (AR)
Phillips Jr Coll (UT)
Pierce Coll (WA)
Pikes Peak Comm Coll (CO)
Portland Comm Coll (OR)
Prairie State Coll (IL)
Prince George's Comm Coll (MD)
Pueblo Comm Coll (CO)
Pulaski Tech Coll (AR)
Queensborough Comm Coll of City U of NY (NY)
Quinsigamond Comm Coll (MA)
Rancho Santiago Coll (CA)
Rappahannock Comm Coll (VA)
Raritan Valley Comm Coll (NJ)
Reading Area Comm Coll (PA)
Redlands Comm Coll (OK)
Richland Comm Coll (IL)
Ricks Coll (ID)
Riverside Comm Coll (CA)
Rockingham Comm Coll (NC)
Rose State Coll (OK)
Roxbury Comm Coll (MA)
Saddleback Coll (CA)
Sage Jr Coll of Albany (NY)
St Catharine Coll (KY)
St Clair County Comm Coll (MI)
St Louis Comm Coll at Florissant Valley (MO)
St Louis Comm Coll at Meramec (MO)
St Petersburg Jr Coll (FL)
St Philip's Coll (TX)
Salem Comm Coll (NJ)
Salt Lake Comm Coll (UT)
San Diego Miramar Coll (CA)
San Jacinto College–North Cmps (TX)
San Jacinto College–South Cmps (TX)
Santa Barbara City Coll (CA)
Santa Fe Comm Coll (FL)
Santa Fe Comm Coll (NM)
Santa Monica Coll (CA)
Schoolcraft Coll (MI)
Scottsdale Comm Coll (AZ)
Seminole Comm Coll (FL)
Shawnee Comm Coll (IL)
Sheridan Coll (WY)
Shoreline Comm Coll (WA)
Sierra Coll (CA)
Sinclair Comm Coll (OH)
Sisseton-Wahpeton Comm Coll (SD)
Snow Coll (UT)
South Arkansas Comm Coll (AR)
South Coll (FL)
South Coll (GA)
Southeastern Comm Coll, North Cmps, West Burlington (IA)
Southeastern Comm Coll, South Cmps, Keokuk (IA)
Southeastern Illinois Coll (IL)
Southern Maine Tech Coll (ME)
Southern Union State Comm Coll (AL)
Southern West Virginia Comm and Tech Coll (WV)
South Georgia Coll (GA)
South Mountain Comm Coll (AZ)
South Puget Sound Comm Coll (WA)
Southside Virginia Comm Coll (VA)
South Suburban Coll (IL)
Southwestern Coll (CA)
Southwestern Coll of Business, Cincinnati (OH)
Southwestern Comm Coll (NC)
Southwestern Michigan Coll (MI)
Southwestern Oregon Comm Coll (OR)
Southwestern Tech Coll (MN)
Southwest Florida Coll of Business (FL)
Southwest Virginia Comm Coll (VA)
Spencer Sch of Business (NE)
Spokane Falls Comm Coll (WA)
Springfield Tech Comm Coll (MA)
State Fair Comm Coll (MO)
State Tech Inst at Memphis (TN)
State U of NY Coll of A&T at Cobleskill (NY)
State U of NY Coll of A&T at Morrisville (NY)
State U of NY Coll of Tech at Alfred (NY)
State U of NY Coll of Tech at Canton (NY)
State U of NY Coll of Tech at Delhi (NY)
State U of NY Coll of Tech at Farmingdale (NY)
Suffolk County Comm College–Ammerman Cmps (NY)
Sullivan County Comm Coll (NY)
Sussex County Comm Coll (NJ)
Tacoma Comm Coll (WA)
Terra State Comm Coll (OH)
Thomas Nelson Comm Coll (VA)
Tomball Coll (TX)
Tompkins Cortland Comm Coll (NY)
Trenholm State Tech Coll (AL)
Trinidad State Jr Coll (CO)
Triton Coll (IL)
Truckee Meadows Comm Coll (NV)
Tulsa Jr Coll (OK)
Tunxis Comm Tech Coll (CT)
Ulster County Comm Coll (NY)
Union County Coll (NJ)
U of Cincinnati Clermont Coll (OH)
U of Cincinnati Raymond Walters Coll (OH)
U of Kentucky, Ashland Comm Coll (KY)
U of Kentucky, Elizabethtown Comm Coll (KY)
U of Kentucky, Lexington Comm Coll (KY)
U of Kentucky, Madisonville Comm Coll (KY)
U of Kentucky, Paducah Comm Coll (KY)
U of Kentucky, Prestonsburg Comm Coll (KY)
U of Kentucky, Somerset Comm Coll (KY)
U of Maine at Augusta (ME)
U of New Mexico–Valencia Cmps (NM)
Utah Valley State Coll (UT)
Utica Sch of Commerce (NY)
Ventura Coll (CA)
Victoria Coll (TX)
Victor Valley Coll (CA)
Vincennes U (IN)
Virginia Coll (VA)
Virginia Highlands Comm Coll (VA)
Vista Comm Coll (CA)
Waldorf Coll (IA)
Warren County Comm Coll (NJ)
Washtenaw Comm Coll (MI)
Waubonsee Comm Coll (IL)
Wayne Comm Coll (NC)
Weatherford Coll (TX)
Westark Comm Coll (AR)
Westchester Business Inst (NY)
Westchester Comm Coll (NY)
Western Nevada Comm Coll (NV)
Western Wyoming Comm Coll (WY)
West Hills Comm Coll (CA)
Westmoreland County Comm Coll (PA)
West Valley Coll (CA)
West Virginia Northern Comm Coll (WV)
William Rainey Harper Coll (IL)
Willmar Comm Coll (MN)
Wisconsin Indianhead Tech Coll, Rice Lake Cmps (WI)
Wytheville Comm Coll (VA)
Yavapai Coll (AZ)

COMPUTER MANAGEMENT

American Inst of Business (IA)
Anne Arundel Comm Coll (MD)
Berkeley Coll, White Plains (NY)
Bramson ORT Tech Inst (NY)
Brevard Coll (NC)
Bryant and Stratton Business Inst, Lackawanna (NY)
Bryant and Stratton Business Inst, Rochester (NY)
Bryant and Stratton Business Inst, Rochester (NY)
Bryant and Stratton Coll, Parma (OH)
Catonsville Comm Coll (MD)
Cayuga County Comm Coll (NY)
City Colls of Chicago, Malcolm X Coll (IL)
Comm Coll of Allegheny County North Cmps (PA)
Comm Coll of Allegheny County South Cmps (PA)
Cossatot Tech Coll (AR)
Cosumnes River Coll (CA)
Delta Coll (MI)
DuBois Business Coll (PA)
ECPI Coll of Tech, Hampton (VA)
ECPI Coll of Tech, Virginia Beach (VA)
ECPI Computer Inst, Richmond (VA)
Grossmont Coll (CA)
Herzing Coll of Business and Tech (GA)
Hesser Coll (NH)
ICM Sch of Business (PA)
James H Faulkner State Comm Coll (AL)
Knoxville Business Coll (TN)
Lamar Comm Coll (CO)
Lansing Comm Coll (MI)
Lewis Coll of Business (MI)
Lincoln Coll, Normal (IL)
McIntosh Coll (NH)
Michiana Coll (IN)
Miles Comm Coll (MT)
Montana State U Coll of Tech-Great Falls (MT)
Moraine Valley Comm Coll (IL)
National Business Coll, Harrisonburg (VA)
New Hampshire Tech Coll, Claremont (NH)
North Central Texas Coll (TX)
Northeast Mississippi Comm Coll (MS)
Otero Jr Coll (CO)
Palo Alto Coll (TX)
Parks Coll (NM)
Phillips Jr Coll, Condie Cmps (CA)
Pittsburgh Tech Inst (PA)
Prince George's Comm Coll (MD)
Prospect Hall (FL)
Shasta Coll (CA)
Southern Maine Tech Coll (ME)
Southwest Wisconsin Tech Coll (WI)
Thompson Inst (PA)
Tri-County Comm Coll (NC)
Tulsa Jr Coll (OK)
Vermilion Comm Coll (MN)
Villa Maria Coll of Buffalo (NY)
Vincennes U (IN)
William Rainey Harper Coll (IL)
Willmar Comm Coll (MN)

COMPUTER PROGRAMMING

Abraham Baldwin Ag Coll (GA)
Alabama Southern Comm Coll, Monroeville (AL)
Alamance Comm Coll (NC)
Albuquerque Tech Vocational Inst (NM)
Alexandria Tech Coll (MN)
Allegany Comm Coll (MD)
Allen County Comm Coll (KS)
Alvin Comm Coll (TX)
American Inst of Commerce (IA)
American River Coll (CA)
Andover Coll (ME)
Angelina Coll (TX)
Anne Arundel Comm Coll (MD)
Antelope Valley Coll (CA)
Arapahoe Comm Coll (CO)
Asheville-Buncombe Tech Comm Coll (NC)
Asnuntuck Comm-Tech Coll (CT)
Athens Area Tech Inst (GA)
Atlantic Comm Coll (NJ)
Augusta Tech Inst (GA)
Austin Comm Coll (TX)
Beaufort County Comm Coll (NC)
Belmont Tech Coll (OH)
Bergen Comm Coll (NJ)
Big Bend Comm Coll (WA)
Black Hawk Coll, Moline (IL)
Blackhawk Tech Coll (WI)
Bladen Comm Coll (NC)
Blair Jr Coll (CO)
Blue Ridge Comm Coll (NC)
Borough of Manhattan Comm Coll of City U of NY (NY)
Bowling Green State University–Firelands Coll (OH)

Associate Degree Programs at Two-Year Colleges
Computer Programming–Computer Science

Bradford Sch (OH)
Bramson ORT Tech Inst (NY)
Brevard Coll (NC)
Brevard Comm Coll (FL)
Bristol Comm Coll (MA)
Brookdale Comm Coll (NJ)
Broward Comm Coll (FL)
Brown Inst (MN)
Brunswick Comm Coll (NC)
Bryant and Stratton Business Inst, Buffalo (NY)
Bryant and Stratton Business Inst, Cicero (NY)
Bryant and Stratton Business Inst, Rochester (NY)
Bryant and Stratton Business Inst, Rochester (NY)
Bryant and Stratton Business Inst, Syracuse (NY)
Bryant and Stratton Business Inst, E Hills Cmps, Williamsville (NY)
Bryant and Stratton Coll, Parma (OH)
Bucks County Comm Coll (PA)
Bunker Hill Comm Coll (MA)
Burlington County Coll (NJ)
Butler County Comm Coll (KS)
Butler County Comm Coll (PA)
Cabrillo Coll (CA)
Camden County Coll (NJ)
Cañada Coll (CA)
Casper Coll (WY)
Catawba Valley Comm Coll (NC)
Catonsville Comm Coll (MD)
Cayuga County Comm Coll (NY)
Cecil Comm Coll (MD)
Central Alabama Comm Coll (AL)
Central Carolina Comm Coll (NC)
Central Coll (KS)
Central Comm College–Grand Island Cmps (NE)
Central Comm College–Hastings Cmps (NE)
Central Florida Comm Coll (FL)
Central Ohio Tech Coll (OH)
Central Piedmont Comm Coll (NC)
Central Texas Coll (TX)
Cerritos Coll (CA)
Champlain Coll (VT)
Chaparral Career Coll (AZ)
Charles County Comm Coll (MD)
Chattahoochee Tech Inst (GA)
Chattanooga State Tech Comm Coll (TN)
Chemeketa Comm Coll (OR)
Chesapeake Coll (MD)
Chesterfield-Marlboro Tech Coll (SC)
Cincinnati State Tech and Comm Coll (OH)
Cisco Jr Coll (TX)
City Coll of San Francisco (CA)
Clark Coll (WA)
Clark State Comm Coll (OH)
Clinton Comm Coll (IA)
Clovis Comm Coll (NM)
Coahoma Comm Coll (MS)
Coastal Carolina Comm Coll (NC)
Cochise Coll, Douglas (AZ)
Cochise Coll, Sierra Vista (AZ)
Coffeyville Comm Coll (KS)
Colby Comm Coll (KS)
Coll of Lake County (IL)
Coll of The Albemarle (NC)
Coll of the Sequoias (CA)
Coll of the Siskiyous (CA)
Collin County Comm Coll (TX)
Columbus State Comm Coll (OH)
Comm Coll of Allegheny County Allegheny Cmps (PA)
Comm Coll of Allegheny County North Cmps (PA)
Comm Coll of Allegheny County South Cmps (PA)
Comm Coll of Beaver County (PA)

Comm Coll of Denver (CO)
Comm Coll of Rhode Island (RI)
Comm Coll of Southern Nevada (NV)
Connors State Coll (OK)
Contra Costa Coll (CA)
Copiah-Lincoln Comm Coll (MS)
Cosumnes River Coll (CA)
Craven Comm Coll (NC)
Dabney S Lancaster Comm Coll (VA)
Dalton Coll (GA)
Danville Area Comm Coll (IL)
Danville Comm Coll (VA)
Darton Coll (GA)
Davidson County Comm Coll (NC)
Daytona Beach Comm Coll (FL)
DeKalb Coll (GA)
DeKalb Tech Inst (GA)
Delaware County Comm Coll (PA)
Delaware Tech & Comm Coll, Jack F Owens Cmps (DE)
Delaware Tech & Comm Coll, Terry Cmps (DE)
Del Mar Coll (TX)
Delta Coll (MI)
Des Moines Area Comm Coll (IA)
Dodge City Comm Coll (KS)
Douglas MacArthur State Tech Coll (AL)
Draughons Jr Coll, Nashville (TN)
Duff's Business Inst (PA)
Durham Tech Comm Coll (NC)
East Central Coll (MO)
Eastern Wyoming Coll (WY)
Eastfield Coll (TX)
East Los Angeles Coll (CA)
ECPI Coll of Tech, Virginia Beach (VA)
ECPI Computer Inst, Richmond (VA)
Edgecombe Comm Coll (NC)
Edison State Comm Coll (OH)
El Centro Coll (TX)
Elgin Comm Coll (IL)
El Paso Comm Coll (TX)
Essex County Coll (NJ)
ETI Tech Coll, Niles (OH)
Fayetteville Tech Comm Coll (NC)
Fiorello H LaGuardia Comm Coll of City U of NY (NY)
Florida Comm Coll at Jacksonville (FL)
Florida Keys Comm Coll (FL)
Florida National Coll (FL)
Floyd Coll (GA)
Fox Valley Tech Coll (WI)
Frank Phillips Coll (TX)
Fugazzi Coll (KY)
Garden City Comm Coll (KS)
Gaston Coll (NC)
Gateway Coll (NE)
Gavilan Coll (CA)
George Corley Wallace State Comm Coll, Selma (AL)
Gloucester County Coll (NJ)
Grand Rapids Comm Coll (MI)
Great Lakes Jr Coll of Business (MI)
Greenfield Comm Coll (MA)
Greenville Tech Coll (SC)
Grossmont Coll (CA)
Guilford Tech Comm Coll (NC)
Gulf Coast Comm Coll (FL)
Gwinnett Tech Inst (GA)
Harrisburg Area Comm Coll (PA)
Heartland Comm Coll (IL)
Helena Coll of Tech of The U of Montana (MT)
Herkimer County Comm Coll (NY)
Herzing Coll of Business and Tech (AL)
Hesser Coll (NH)
Hill Coll of the Hill Jr Coll District (TX)
Hillsborough Comm Coll (FL)
Hinds Comm Coll (MS)
Hiwassee Coll (TN)
Hocking Coll (OH)
Howard Coll (TX)

Howard Comm Coll (MD)
Huntington Jr Coll of Business (WV)
Hutchinson Comm Coll and Area Vocational Sch (KS)
ICM Sch of Business (PA)
Illinois Eastern Comm Colls, Lincoln Trail Coll (IL)
Illinois Valley Comm Coll (IL)
Indian Hills Comm Coll (IA)
Indian River Comm Coll (FL)
International Business Coll (IN)
Inver Hills Comm Coll (MN)
Iowa Lakes Comm Coll (IA)
Iowa Western Comm Coll (IA)
Isothermal Comm Coll (NC)
Ivy Tech State Coll–Central Indiana (IN)
Ivy Tech State Coll–Columbus (IN)
Ivy Tech State Coll–Eastcentral (IN)
Ivy Tech State Coll–Kokomo (IN)
Ivy Tech State Coll–Lafayette (IN)
Ivy Tech State Coll–Northwest (IN)
Ivy Tech State Coll–Southcentral (IN)
Ivy Tech State Coll–Southeast (IN)
Ivy Tech State Coll–Southwest (IN)
Ivy Tech State Coll–Wabash Valley (IN)
Ivy Tech State Coll–Whitewater (IN)
Jackson State Comm Coll (TN)
Jefferson Coll (MO)
Jefferson State Comm Coll (AL)
Johnston Comm Coll (NC)
John Wood Comm Coll (IL)
J Sargeant Reynolds Comm Coll (VA)
Kalamazoo Valley Comm Coll (MI)
Kansas City Kansas Comm Coll (KS)
Kellogg Comm Coll (MI)
Kent State U, Geauga Cmps (OH)
Kingsborough Comm Coll of City U of NY (NY)
Kirkwood Comm Coll (IA)
Lake Area Vocational-Tech Inst (SD)
Lake City Comm Coll (FL)
Lake Michigan Coll (MI)
Lamar Comm Coll (CO)
Lamar University–Port Arthur (TX)
Lane Comm Coll (OR)
Laney Coll (CA)
Lansing Comm Coll (MI)
Laredo Comm Coll (TX)
Lehigh Carbon Comm Coll (PA)
Lenoir Comm Coll (NC)
Lewis and Clark Comm Coll (IL)
Lewis Coll of Business (MI)
Lima Tech Coll (OH)
Lincoln Coll, Normal (IL)
Lincoln Land Comm Coll (IL)
Lincoln Sch of Commerce (NE)
Linn-Benton Comm Coll (OR)
Long Beach City Coll (CA)
Longview Comm Coll (MO)
Lorain County Comm Coll (OH)
Los Angeles City Coll (CA)
Los Angeles Mission Coll (CA)
Los Angeles Pierce Coll (CA)
Los Angeles Trade-Tech Coll (CA)
Los Angeles Valley Coll (CA)
Louisiana State U at Eunice (LA)
Lower Columbia Coll (WA)
Lurleen B Wallace State Jr Coll (AL)
Macon Coll (GA)
Madison Area Tech Coll (WI)
Madison Jr Coll of Business (WI)
Manatee Comm Coll (FL)
Maple Woods Comm Coll (MO)

Massachusetts Bay Comm Coll (MA)
Mayland Comm Coll (NC)
McDowell Tech Comm Coll (NC)
Mercer County Comm Coll (NJ)
Merritt Coll (CA)
Metropolitan Comm Coll (NE)
Miami-Dade Comm Coll (FL)
Michiana Coll (IN)
Middlesex Comm Coll (MA)
Middlesex Community–Tech Coll (CT)
Middlesex County Coll (NJ)
Midland Coll (TX)
Mid-Plains Comm Coll (NE)
Milwaukee Area Tech Coll (WI)
Minneapolis Comm Coll (MN)
Mohawk Valley Comm Coll (NY)
Montgomery Coll (TX)
Moraine Park Tech Coll (WI)
Moraine Valley Comm Coll (IL)
Motlow State Comm Coll (TN)
Mountain View Coll (TX)
Mount Ida Coll (MA)
National Business Coll, Danville (VA)
National Sch of Tech, Inc (FL)
Naugatuck Valley Community–Tech Coll (CT)
Navarro Coll (TX)
Nebraska Coll of Business (NE)
Newbury Coll (MA)
New England Inst of Tech & Florida Culinary Inst (FL)
New Mexico Jr Coll (NM)
New Mexico Military Inst (NM)
Newport Business Inst (PA)
North Central Michigan Coll (MI)
North Central Tech Coll (OH)
North Central Texas Coll (TX)
North Dakota State Coll of Science (ND)
North Dakota State University–Bottineau (ND)
Northeast Comm Coll (NE)
Northeastern Oklahoma A&M Coll (OK)
Northeast Iowa Comm Coll, Peosta Cmps (IA)
Northeast Mississippi Comm Coll (MS)
Northeast State Tech Comm Coll (TN)
Northern Essex Comm Coll (MA)
Northern Maine Tech Coll (ME)
North Idaho Coll (ID)
North Lake Coll (TX)
North Seattle Comm Coll (WA)
North Shore Comm Coll (MA)
NorthWest Arkansas Comm Coll (AR)
Northwestern Business Coll (IL)
Northwestern Connecticut Comm-Tech Coll (CT)
Northwestern Michigan Coll (MI)
Northwest Iowa Comm Coll (IA)
Northwest State Comm Coll (OH)
Oakland Comm Coll (MI)
Oakton Comm Coll (IL)
Ohlone Coll (CA)
Okaloosa-Walton Comm Coll (FL)
Oklahoma State U, Oklahoma City (OK)
Orange Coast Coll (CA)
Orange County Comm Coll (NY)
Oregon Polytechnic Inst (OR)
Otero Jr Coll (CO)
Owens Comm Coll, Findlay (OH)
Owens Comm Coll, Toledo (OH)
Palm Beach Comm Coll (FL)
Parkland Coll (IL)
Parks Jr Coll (CO)
Pasadena City Coll (CA)

Pasco-Hernando Comm Coll (FL)
Patrick Henry Comm Coll (VA)
Pellissippi State Tech Comm Coll (TN)
Pennco Tech (PA)
Peoples Coll (FL)
Phillips County Comm Coll (AR)
Phillips Jr Coll, Condie Cmps (CA)
Piedmont Comm Coll (NC)
Piedmont Tech Coll (SC)
Piedmont Virginia Comm Coll (VA)
Pierce Coll (WA)
Pima Comm Coll (AZ)
Pitt Comm Coll (NC)
Pittsburgh Tech Inst (PA)
Portland Comm Coll (OR)
Potomac State Coll of West Virginia U (WV)
Prairie State Coll (IL)
Prince George's Comm Coll (MD)
Prospect Hall (FL)
Queensborough Comm Coll of City U of NY (NY)
Quincy Coll (MA)
Quinsigamond Comm Coll (MA)
Randolph Comm Coll (NC)
Raritan Valley Comm Coll (NJ)
Reading Area Comm Coll (PA)
Redlands Comm Coll (OK)
Red Rocks Comm Coll (CO)
RETS Tech Ctr (OH)
Richland Coll (TX)
Ricks Coll (ID)
Riverside Comm Coll (CA)
Roanoke-Chowan Comm Coll (NC)
Robeson Comm Coll (NC)
Rockland Comm Coll (NY)
Rogers State Coll (OK)
Rowan-Cabarrus Comm Coll (NC)
Saddleback Coll (CA)
St Cloud Tech Coll (MN)
St Johns River Comm Coll (FL)
St Louis Comm Coll at Florissant Valley (MO)
St Louis Comm Coll at Meramec (MO)
St Paul Tech Coll (MN)
St Petersburg Jr Coll (FL)
Salt Lake Comm Coll (UT)
Sampson Comm Coll (NC)
San Antonio Coll (TX)
Sandhills Comm Coll (NC)
Sanford-Brown Coll, Hazelwood (MO)
Sanford-Brown Coll, St Charles (MO)
San Jacinto College–Central Cmps (TX)
San Joaquin Delta Coll (CA)
Santa Fe Comm Coll (FL)
Santa Fe Comm Coll (NM)
Santa Monica Coll (CA)
Sawyer Coll of Business, Cleveland (OH)
Schoolcraft Coll (MI)
Scott Comm Coll (IA)
Seminole Comm Coll (FL)
Seward County Comm Coll (KS)
Shorter Coll (AR)
Skyline Coll (CA)
Solano Comm Coll (CA)
Southeast Comm Coll, Milford Cmps (NE)
Southeastern Comm Coll, North Cmps, West Burlington (IA)
Southern Arkansas U Tech (AR)
Southern Coll (FL)
Southern State Comm Coll (OH)
South Florida Comm Coll (FL)
South Georgia Coll (GA)
South Plains Coll (TX)
South Puget Sound Comm Coll (WA)
South Seattle Comm Coll (WA)
SouthWest Collegiate Inst for the Deaf (TX)

Southwestern Coll (CA)
Southwestern Coll of Business, Cincinnati (OH)
Southwestern Comm Coll (IA)
Southwestern Michigan Coll (MI)
Southwestern Oklahoma State U at Sayre (OK)
Southwest Wisconsin Tech Coll (WI)
Spokane Comm Coll (WA)
Stanly Comm Coll (NC)
Stark Tech Coll (OH)
State Comm Coll of East St Louis (IL)
State U of NY Coll of A&T at Cobleskill (NY)
State U of NY Coll of A&T at Morrisville (NY)
State U of NY Coll of Tech at Farmingdale (NY)
Stratton Coll (WI)
Suffolk County Comm College–Ammerman Cmps (NY)
Tallahassee Comm Coll (FL)
Tarrant County Jr Coll (TX)
Tech Coll of Municipality of San Juan (PR)
Temple Coll (TX)
Texarkana Coll (TX)
Texas State Tech Coll (TX)
Texas State Tech Coll–Waco/Marshall Cmps (TX)
Thompson Inst (PA)
Three Rivers Comm-Tech Coll (CT)
Tidewater Comm Coll (VA)
Tomball Coll (TX)
Tri-County Tech Coll (SC)
Truckee Meadows Comm Coll (NV)
Tulsa Jr Coll (OK)
U of Cincinnati Clermont Coll (OH)
U of Cincinnati Raymond Walters Coll (OH)
U of Kentucky, Jefferson Comm Coll (KY)
U of New Mexico–Los Alamos Branch (NM)
Valencia Comm Coll (FL)
Vance-Granville Comm Coll (NC)
Vincennes U (IN)
Vincennes University–Jasper Ctr (IN)
Wake Tech Comm Coll (NC)
Waldorf Coll (IA)
Wallace State Comm Coll (AL)
Walla Walla Comm Coll (WA)
Washtenaw Comm Coll (MI)
Wayne Comm Coll (NC)
Weatherford Coll (TX)
Westark Comm Coll (AR)
Westchester Business Inst (NY)
Western Iowa Tech Comm Coll (IA)
Western Nebraska Comm Coll, Scottsbluff (NE)
Western Piedmont Comm Coll (NC)
Western Wisconsin Tech Coll (WI)
Western Wyoming Comm Coll (WY)
West Los Angeles Coll (CA)
West Shore Comm Coll (MI)
Wilkes Comm Coll (NC)
William Rainey Harper Coll (IL)
Wilson Tech Comm Coll (NC)
Wisconsin Indianhead Tech Coll, New Richmond Cmps (WI)
Wisconsin Indianhead Tech Coll, Superior Cmps (WI)
Wood Tobe–Coburn Sch (NY)
Wor-Wic Comm Coll (MD)
York Tech Coll (SC)

COMPUTER SCIENCE
Abraham Baldwin Ag Coll (GA)
Adirondack Comm Coll (NY)
Alabama Southern Comm Coll, Monroeville (AL)
Alabama Southern Comm Coll, Thomasville (AL)
Allan Hancock Coll (CA)
Allegany Comm Coll (MD)

Peterson's Guide to Two-Year Colleges 1997

67

Associate Degree Programs at Two-Year Colleges
Computer Science

Allen County Comm Coll (KS)
Ancilla Coll (IN)
Andover Coll (ME)
Angelina Coll (TX)
Anne Arundel Comm Coll (MD)
Antelope Valley Coll (CA)
Arapahoe Comm Coll (CO)
Arizona Western Coll (AZ)
Asnuntuck Comm-Tech Coll (CT)
Atlanta Metropolitan Coll (GA)
Austin Comm Coll (TX)
Bacone Coll (OK)
Bakersfield Coll (CA)
Baltimore City Comm Coll (MD)
Barstow Coll (CA)
Barton County Comm Coll (KS)
Bee County Coll (TX)
Berean Inst (PA)
Bergen Comm Coll (NJ)
Berkshire Comm Coll (MA)
Bessemer State Tech Coll (AL)
Big Bend Comm Coll (WA)
Bismarck State Coll (ND)
Black Hawk Coll, Moline (IL)
Blair Jr Coll (CO)
Blinn Coll (TX)
Bramson ORT Tech Inst (NY)
Brevard Coll (NC)
Brevard Comm Coll (FL)
Bronx Comm Coll of City U of NY (NY)
Brookdale Comm Coll (NJ)
Broome Comm Coll (NY)
Broward Comm Coll (FL)
Brunswick Coll (GA)
Bryant and Stratton Coll, Parma (OH)
Bucks County Comm Coll (PA)
Bunker Hill Comm Coll (MA)
Burlington County Coll (NJ)
Butler County Comm Coll (KS)
Cabrillo Coll (CA)
Cañada Coll (CA)
Cape Cod Comm Coll (MA)
Carl Albert State Coll (OK)
Casper Coll (WY)
Catawba Valley Comm Coll (NC)
Catonsville Comm Coll (MD)
Cayuga County Comm Coll (NY)
Central Alabama Comm Coll (AL)
Central Coll (KS)
Central Oregon Comm Coll (OR)
Central Piedmont Comm Coll (NC)
Central Texas Coll (TX)
Central Wyoming Coll (WY)
Cerritos Coll (CA)
Cerro Coso Comm Coll (CA)
Chabot Coll (CA)
Charter Coll (AK)
Chattanooga State Tech Comm Coll (TN)
Chemeketa Comm Coll (OR)
Chesapeake Coll (MD)
Chesterfield-Marlboro Tech Coll (SC)
Chipola Jr Coll (FL)
Cisco Jr Coll (TX)
Citrus Coll (CA)
City Coll of San Francisco (CA)
City Colls of Chicago, Harold Washington Coll (IL)
Clackamas Comm Coll (OR)
Clark Coll (WA)
Clinton Comm Coll (IA)
Coahoma Comm Coll (MS)
Cochise Coll, Douglas (AZ)
Cochise Coll, Sierra Vista (AZ)
Coffeyville Comm Coll (KS)
Colby Comm Coll (KS)
Coll of DuPage (IL)
Coll of Marin (CA)
Coll of San Mateo (CA)
Coll of Southern Idaho (ID)
Coll of the Canyons (CA)
Coll of the Desert (CA)
Coll of the Mainland (TX)
Coll of the Sequoias (CA)
Coll of the Siskiyous (CA)

Collin County Comm Coll (TX)
Columbia Basin Coll (WA)
Columbia Coll (CA)
Columbia-Greene Comm Coll (NY)
Columbus State Comm Coll (OH)
Commonwealth Business Coll, Merrillville (IN)
Comm Coll of Allegheny County Allegheny Cmps (PA)
Comm Coll of Allegheny County Boyce Cmps (PA)
Comm Coll of Allegheny County North Cmps (PA)
Comm Coll of Allegheny County South Cmps (PA)
Comm Coll of Denver (CO)
Comm Coll of Philadelphia (PA)
Comm Coll of Rhode Island (RI)
Comm Coll of Southern Nevada (NV)
Comm Coll of Vermont (VT)
Connors State Coll (OK)
Contra Costa Coll (CA)
Corning Comm Coll (NY)
Crafton Hills Coll (CA)
Crowder Coll (MO)
Cuesta Coll (CA)
Cypress Coll (CA)
Dalton Coll (GA)
Darton Coll (GA)
Daytona Beach Comm Coll (FL)
Dean Coll (MA)
De Anza Coll (CA)
DeKalb Coll (GA)
Delaware County Comm Coll (PA)
Delgado Comm Coll (LA)
Del Mar Coll (TX)
Delta Coll (MI)
Dixie Coll (UT)
Dodge City Comm Coll (KS)
Donnelly Coll (KS)
Douglas MacArthur State Tech Coll (AL)
D-Q U (CA)
Draughons Jr Coll, Nashville (TN)
Dutchess Comm Coll (NY)
East Central Coll (MO)
East Central Comm Coll (MS)
Eastern Arizona Coll (AZ)
Eastern New Mexico University–Roswell (NM)
Eastern Oklahoma State Coll (OK)
Eastern Wyoming Coll (WY)
East Mississippi Comm Coll (MS)
ECPI Coll of Tech, Hampton (VA)
ECPI Coll of Tech, Virginia Beach (VA)
ECPI Computer Inst, Richmond (VA)
ECPI Computer Inst, Roanoke (VA)
Edison Comm Coll (FL)
Edison State Comm Coll (OH)
Elaine P Nunez Comm Coll (LA)
El Centro Coll (TX)
Enterprise State Jr Coll (AL)
Erie Business Ctr, Main (PA)
Erie Business Ctr South (PA)
Erie Comm Coll, City Cmps (NY)
Erie Comm Coll, North Cmps (NY)
Essex Comm Coll (MD)
Essex County Coll (NJ)
Everett Comm Coll (WA)
Finger Lakes Comm Coll (NY)
Fiorello H LaGuardia Comm Coll of City U of NY (NY)
Florida National Coll (FL)
Foothill Coll (CA)
Forsyth Tech Comm Coll (NC)
Fort Peck Comm Coll (MT)
Fort Scott Comm Coll (KS)
Franklin Inst of Boston (MA)
Frank Phillips Coll (TX)
Fullerton Coll (CA)
Fulton-Montgomery Comm Coll (NY)

Gadsden State Comm Coll (AL)
Gainesville Coll (GA)
Galveston Coll (TX)
Garden City Comm Coll (KS)
Gateway Coll (NE)
Gavilan Coll (CA)
Gem City Coll (IL)
George Corley Wallace State Comm Coll, Selma (AL)
George C Wallace State Comm Coll, Dothan (AL)
Gloucester County Coll (NJ)
Gogebic Comm Coll (MI)
Gordon Coll (GA)
Grand Rapids Comm Coll (MI)
Grayson County Coll (TX)
Grossmont Coll (CA)
Gulf Coast Comm Coll (FL)
Gwinnett Tech Inst (GA)
Hagerstown Jr Coll (MD)
Harford Comm Coll (MD)
Harrisburg Area Comm Coll (PA)
Hartnell Coll (CA)
Heald Business Coll, Hayward (CA)
Heald Business Coll, Rancho Cordova (CA)
Heartland Comm Coll (IL)
Henry Ford Comm Coll (MI)
Herkimer County Comm Coll (NY)
Herzing Coll of Business and Tech (AL)
Hesser Coll (NH)
Hesston Coll (KS)
Highland Comm Coll (IL)
Highland Comm Coll (KS)
Highland Park Comm Coll (MI)
Hill Coll of the Hill Jr Coll District (TX)
Hiwassee Coll (TN)
Hocking Coll (OH)
Holmes Comm Coll (MS)
Houston Comm Coll System (TX)
Howard Coll (TX)
Howard Comm Coll (MD)
Hudson County Comm Coll (NJ)
Huertas Jr Coll (PR)
Huntington Jr Coll of Business (WV)
Hutchinson Comm Coll and Area Vocational Sch (KS)
ICM Sch of Business (PA)
ICS Ctr for Degree Studies (PA)
Indian River Comm Coll (FL)
Inter American U of PR, Guayama Cmps (PR)
Iowa Central Comm Coll (IA)
Iowa Lakes Comm Coll (IA)
Isothermal Comm Coll (NC)
Itawamba Comm Coll (MS)
ITT Tech Inst, Phoenix (AZ)
Jackson State Comm Coll (TN)
James H Faulkner State Comm Coll (AL)
Jamestown Comm Coll (NY)
Jefferson Comm Coll (NY)
Jefferson State Comm Coll (AL)
John A Logan Coll (IL)
Johnson County Comm Coll (KS)
John Wood Comm Coll (IL)
Kansas City Kansas Comm Coll (KS)
Kelsey Jenney Coll (CA)
Kilian Comm Coll (SD)
Kingsborough Comm Coll of City U of NY (NY)
Kings River Comm Coll (CA)
Kirkwood Comm Coll (IA)
Knoxville Business Coll (TN)
Labette Comm Coll (KS)
Lac Courte Oreilles Ojibwa Comm Coll (WI)
Lake Land Coll (IL)
Lake Michigan Coll (MI)
Lake-Sumter Comm Coll (FL)
Lake Tahoe Comm Coll (CA)
Lamar Comm Coll (CO)
Lamar University–Orange (TX)
Laramie County Comm Coll (WY)
Las Positas Coll (CA)
Lassen Coll (CA)

Lehigh Carbon Comm Coll (PA)
Lewis Coll of Business (MI)
Lincoln Coll, Normal (IL)
Lincoln Land Comm Coll (IL)
Linn-Benton Comm Coll (OR)
Little Big Horn Coll (MT)
Little Hoop Comm Coll (ND)
Longview Comm Coll (MO)
Lon Morris Coll (TX)
Lorain County Comm Coll (OH)
Los Angeles Pierce Coll (CA)
Los Angeles Southwest Coll (CA)
Louisiana State U at Alexandria (LA)
Lower Columbia Coll (WA)
Lurleen B Wallace State Jr Coll (AL)
Luzerne County Comm Coll (PA)
Macon Coll (GA)
Maple Woods Comm Coll (MO)
Marshalltown Comm Coll (IA)
Mary Holmes Coll (MS)
Massachusetts Bay Comm Coll (MA)
McCann Sch of Business (PA)
McIntosh Coll (NH)
Meadows Coll of Business (GA)
Merced Coll (CA)
Mercer County Comm Coll (NJ)
Miami-Dade Comm Coll (FL)
Miami University–Middletown Cmps (OH)
Middle Georgia Coll (GA)
Middlesex Comm Coll (MA)
Middlesex County Coll (NJ)
Midland Coll (TX)
Mid Michigan Comm Coll (MI)
Midstate Coll (IL)
Mid-State Coll (ME)
Milwaukee Area Tech Coll (WI)
Mississippi Gulf Coast Comm Coll (MS)
Mitchell Comm Coll (NC)
Modesto Jr Coll (CA)
Mohave Comm Coll (AZ)
Mohawk Valley Comm Coll (NY)
Monroe Coll, Bronx (NY)
Monroe Coll, New Rochelle (NY)
Monroe Comm Coll (NY)
Monterey Peninsula Coll (CA)
Montgomery College–Germantown Cmps (MD)
Montgomery College–Rockville Cmps (MD)
Montgomery College–Takoma Park Cmps (MD)
Montgomery Comm Coll (NC)
Montgomery County Comm Coll (PA)
Moorpark Coll (CA)
Moraine Valley Comm Coll (IL)
Motlow State Comm Coll (TN)
Mt San Antonio Coll (CA)
Mt San Jacinto Coll (CA)
Murray State Coll (OK)
Muscatine Comm Coll (IA)
Napa Valley Coll (CA)
Nassau Comm Coll (NY)
National Business Coll, Bluefield (VA)
National Business Coll, Bristol (VA)
National Business Coll, Charlottesville (VA)
National Business Coll, Danville (VA)
National Business Coll, Lynchburg (VA)
National Business Coll, Martinsville (VA)
National Business Coll, Roanoke (VA)
Navajo Comm Coll (AZ)
Navarro Coll (TX)
Nebraska Indian Comm Coll (NE)
Neosho County Comm Coll (KS)
The New England Banking Inst (MA)
New Mexico Jr Coll (NM)

New Mexico Military Inst (NM)
New Mexico State University–Carlsbad (NM)
Niagara County Comm Coll (NY)
Nicolet Area Tech Coll (WI)
Northampton County Area Comm Coll (PA)
North Central Texas Coll (TX)
North Dakota State Coll of Science (ND)
North Dakota State University–Bottineau (ND)
Northeast Alabama State Comm Coll (AL)
Northeastern Jr Coll (CO)
Northeastern Oklahoma A&M Coll (OK)
Northeast Mississippi Comm Coll (MS)
Northeast Texas Comm Coll (TX)
Northern Essex Comm Coll (MA)
Northern Oklahoma Coll (OK)
Northern Virginia Comm Coll (VA)
North Harris Coll (TX)
North Idaho Coll (ID)
North Iowa Area Comm Coll (IA)
Northland Comm and Tech Coll (MN)
Northland Pioneer Coll (AZ)
North Seattle Comm Coll (WA)
North Shore Comm Coll (MA)
Northwest Coll (WY)
Northwestern Business Coll (IL)
Northwestern Connecticut Comm-Tech Coll (CT)
Northwest Iowa Comm Coll (IA)
Northwest Mississippi Comm Coll (MS)
Northwest-Shoals Comm Coll (AL)
Oakland Comm Coll (MI)
Oakton Comm Coll (IL)
Ocean County Coll (NJ)
Odessa Coll (TX)
Ohio University–Southern Cmps (OH)
Ohio Valley Coll (WV)
Ohlone Coll (CA)
Okaloosa-Walton Comm Coll (FL)
Oklahoma City Comm Coll (OK)
Oklahoma State U, Oklahoma City (OK)
Onondaga Comm Coll (NY)
Orange County Comm Coll (NY)
Owensboro Jr Coll of Business (KY)
Palm Beach Comm Coll (FL)
Palo Alto Coll (TX)
Panama Canal Coll (Republic of Panama)
Parkland Coll (IL)
Parks Jr Coll (CO)
Pasadena City Coll (CA)
Pellissippi State Tech Comm Coll (TN)
Pennsylvania Coll of Tech (PA)
Penn State U New Kensington Cmps (PA)
Penn State U Schuylkill Cmps (PA)
Penn State U York Cmps (PA)
Penn Valley Comm Coll (MO)
Pensacola Jr Coll (FL)
Phillips Jr Coll, Condie Cmps (CA)
Pikes Peak Comm Coll (CO)
Pima Comm Coll (AZ)
Polk Comm Coll (FL)
Porterville Coll (CA)
Potomac State Coll of West Virginia U (WV)
Prince George's Comm Coll (MD)
Pueblo Coll of Business and Tech (CO)
Quincy Coll (MA)
Rancho Santiago Coll (CA)
Randolph Comm Coll (NC)
Raritan Valley Comm Coll (NJ)

Reading Area Comm Coll (PA)
Redlands Comm Coll (OK)
Red Rocks Comm Coll (CO)
Renton Tech Coll (WA)
RETS Tech Ctr (OH)
Ricks Coll (ID)
Roane State Comm Coll (TN)
Rochester Comm Coll (MN)
Rock Valley Coll (IL)
Rogers State Coll (OK)
Rogue Comm Coll (OR)
Sacramento City Coll (CA)
Saddleback Coll (CA)
Saint Charles County Comm Coll (MO)
St Louis Comm Coll at Florissant Valley (MO)
St Louis Comm Coll at Forest Park (MO)
St Louis Comm Coll at Meramec (MO)
Salish Kootenai Coll (MT)
Salt Lake Comm Coll (UT)
San Bernardino Valley Coll (CA)
San Diego Mesa Coll (CA)
Sanford-Brown Coll, Des Peres (MO)
San Jacinto College–Central Cmps (TX)
San Jacinto College–North Cmps (TX)
San Jacinto College–South Cmps (TX)
San Joaquin Delta Coll (CA)
San Jose City Coll (CA)
San Juan Coll (NM)
Santa Barbara City Coll (CA)
Santa Fe Comm Coll (NM)
Schenectady County Comm Coll (NY)
Schoolcraft Coll (MI)
Scott Comm Coll (IA)
Seminole Jr Coll (OK)
Seward County Comm Coll (KS)
Shasta Coll (CA)
Shelton State Comm Coll (AL)
Shorter Coll (AR)
Sierra Coll (CA)
Skagit Valley Coll (WA)
Skyline Coll (CA)
Snow Coll (UT)
Southeast Comm Coll, Beatrice Cmps (NE)
Southern Ohio Coll, Cincinnati Cmps (OH)
Southern Ohio Coll, Northeast Cmps (OH)
Southern Ohio Coll, Northern Kentucky Cmps (KY)
Southern U at Shreveport–Bossier City Cmps (LA)
South Georgia Coll (GA)
South Plains Coll (TX)
SouthWest Collegiate Inst for the Deaf (TX)
Southwestern Coll (CA)
Southwestern Coll of Business, Cincinnati (OH)
Southwestern Coll of Business, Cincinnati (OH)
Southwestern Coll of Business, Dayton (OH)
Southwestern Coll of Business, Middletown (OH)
Southwestern Indian Polytechnic Inst (NM)
Southwest Mississippi Comm Coll (MS)
Springfield Coll in Illinois (IL)
State Comm Coll of East St Louis (IL)
State Tech Inst at Memphis (TN)
State U of NY Coll of A&T at Cobleskill (NY)
State U of NY Coll of A&T at Morrisville (NY)
State U of NY Coll of Tech at Alfred (NY)
State U of NY Coll of Tech at Farmingdale (NY)
Stone Child Coll (MT)
Suffolk County Comm College–Ammerman Cmps (NY)
Tacoma Comm Coll (WA)
Taft Coll (CA)
Tarrant County Jr Coll (TX)
Temple Coll (TX)
Texarkana Coll (TX)

Texas State Tech Coll–Harlingen Cmps (TX)
Texas State Tech Coll–Waco/Marshall Cmps (TX)
Thomas Nelson Comm Coll (VA)
Tompkins Cortland Comm Coll (NY)
Treasure Valley Comm Coll (OR)
Trinidad State Jr Coll (CO)
Trinity Valley Comm Coll (TX)
Triton Coll (IL)
Tulsa Jr Coll (OK)
Turtle Mountain Comm Coll (ND)
Tyler Jr Coll (TX)
Ulster County Comm Coll (NY)
Umpqua Comm Coll (OR)
Union County Coll (NJ)
The U of Akron–Wayne Coll (OH)
U of Cincinnati Raymond Walters Coll (OH)
U of Hawaii–Leeward Comm Coll (HI)
U of Kentucky, Jefferson Comm Coll (KY)
U of New Mexico–Los Alamos Branch (NM)
U of New Mexico–Valencia Cmps (NM)
U of Wisconsin Center–Marathon County (WI)
Vermilion Comm Coll (MN)
Victor Valley Coll (CA)
Vincennes U (IN)
Virginia Western Comm Coll (VA)
Waldorf Coll (IA)
Wallace State Comm Coll (AL)
Walla Walla Comm Coll (WA)
Walters State Comm Coll (TN)
Washtenaw Comm Coll (MI)
Waycross Coll (GA)
Wayne County Comm Coll (MI)
Westark Comm Coll (AR)
Westchester Comm Coll (NY)
Western Nebraska Comm Coll, Scottsbluff (NE)
Western Texas Coll (TX)
Westmoreland County Comm Coll (PA)
Wharton County Jr Coll (TX)
Whatcom Comm Coll (WA)
Wilkes Comm Coll (NC)
William Rainey Harper Coll (IL)
Yakima Valley Comm Coll (WA)
Yuba Coll (CA)

COMPUTER TECHNOLOGIES

Abraham Baldwin Ag Coll (GA)
Acad of Business Coll (AZ)
Aiken Tech Coll (SC)
Alabama Southern Comm Coll, Monroeville (AL)
Alamance Comm Coll (NC)
Alexandria Tech Coll (MN)
Allan Hancock Coll (CA)
Allegany Comm Coll (MD)
Allen County Comm Coll (KS)
Alvin Comm Coll (TX)
American River Coll (CA)
Angelina Coll (TX)
Anne Arundel Comm Coll (MD)
Anson Comm Coll (NC)
Antelope Valley Coll (CA)
Antonelli Coll (OH)
Arkansas State University–Beebe Branch (AR)
Atlantic Comm Coll (NJ)
Beaufort County Comm Coll (NC)
Bee County Coll (TX)
Belmont Tech Coll (OH)
Bergen Comm Coll (NJ)
Berkeley Coll, White Plains (NY)
Bevill State Comm Coll (AL)
Bishop State Comm Coll (AL)
Black Hawk Coll, Moline (IL)
Blue Ridge Comm Coll (VA)
Bowling Green State University–Firelands Coll (OH)
Bramson ORT Tech Inst (NY)
Brazosport Coll (TX)
Brevard Coll (NC)
Brevard Comm Coll (FL)
Briarcliffe–The Coll for Business & Tech (NY)
Bristol Comm Coll (MA)
Broward Comm Coll (FL)
Bryant and Stratton Coll, Richmond Heights (OH)
Bucks County Comm Coll (PA)
Bunker Hill Comm Coll (MA)
Butler County Comm Coll (PA)
Camden County Coll (NJ)
Cañada Coll (CA)
Cape Fear Comm Coll (NC)
Capital Comm Tech Coll (CT)
Carteret Comm Coll (NC)
Casper Coll (WY)
Catawba Valley Comm Coll (NC)
Catonsville Comm Coll (MD)
Cecil Comm Coll (MD)
Central Carolina Tech Coll (SC)
Central Comm College–Platte Cmps (NE)
Central Oregon Comm Coll (OR)
Central Piedmont Comm Coll (NC)
Central Texas Coll (TX)
Cerro Coso Comm Coll (CA)
Chabot Coll (CA)
Chandler-Gilbert Comm Coll (AZ)
Charles County Comm Coll (MD)
Charles Stewart Mott Comm Coll (MI)
Charter Coll (AK)
Chattahoochee Tech Inst (GA)
Chattanooga State Tech Comm Coll (TN)
Chemeketa Comm Coll (OR)
Chesapeake Coll (MD)
CHI Inst (PA)
Chippewa Valley Tech Coll (WI)
Cincinnati State Tech and Comm Coll (OH)
City Colls of Chicago, Olive-Harvey Coll (IL)
Cleveland Comm Coll (NC)
Clinton Comm Coll (IA)
Coastal Carolina Comm Coll (NC)
Coll of DuPage (IL)
Coll of Lake County (IL)
Coll of The Albemarle (NC)
Coll of the Sequoias (CA)
Colorado Mountn Coll, Alpine Cmps (CO)
Colorado Mountn Coll, Roaring Fork Cmps-Spring Valley Ctr (CO)
Colorado Mountn Coll, Timberline Cmps (CO)
Colorado Northwestern Comm Coll (CO)
Columbus State Comm Coll (OH)
Comm Coll of Allegheny County North Cmps (PA)
Comm Coll of Allegheny County South Cmps (PA)
Comm Coll of Philadelphia (PA)
Comm Coll of Southern Nevada (NV)
Comm Coll of the Air Force (AL)
Corning Comm Coll (NY)
Cowley County Comm Coll and Voc-Tech Sch (KS)
Craven Comm Coll (NC)
Cuesta Coll (CA)
Cuyahoga Comm Coll, Eastern Cmps (OH)
Cuyahoga Comm Coll, Metropolitan Cmps (OH)
Cuyahoga Comm Coll, Western Cmps (OH)
Cuyamaca Coll (CA)
Dalton Coll (GA)
Davidson County Comm Coll (NC)
Davis Coll (OH)
Dawson Comm Coll (MT)
DeKalb Coll (GA)
DeKalb Tech Inst (GA)
Delaware County Comm Coll (PA)
Delaware Tech & Comm Coll, Terry Cmps (DE)
Denmark Tech Coll (SC)
Des Moines Area Comm Coll (IA)
Doña Ana Branch Comm Coll (NM)
Durham Tech Comm Coll (NC)
East Arkansas Comm Coll (AR)
Eastern Idaho Tech Coll (ID)
Eastern Oklahoma State Coll (OK)
East Los Angeles Coll (CA)
East Mississippi Comm Coll (MS)
ECPI Coll of Tech, Hampton (VA)
ECPI Coll of Tech, Virginia Beach (VA)
ECPI Computer Inst, Roanoke (VA)
Edgecombe Comm Coll (NC)
Edmonds Comm Coll (WA)
Education America–Tampa Tech Inst Cmps (FL)
Elaine P Nunez Comm Coll (LA)
Electronic Inst, Middletown (PA)
Electronic Institutes, Pittsburgh (PA)
Erie Comm Coll, South Cmps (NY)
Finger Lakes Comm Coll (NY)
Fiorello H LaGuardia Comm Coll of City U of NY (NY)
Flathead Valley Comm Coll (MT)
Florence-Darlington Tech Coll (SC)
Florida Comm Coll at Jacksonville (FL)
Florida Keys Comm Coll (FL)
Foothill Coll (CA)
Forsyth Tech Comm Coll (NC)
Fort Belknap Coll (MT)
Franklin Inst of Boston (MA)
Frank Phillips Coll (TX)
Frederick Comm Coll (MD)
Fugazzi Coll (KY)
Fulton-Montgomery Comm Coll (NY)
Garden City Comm Coll (KS)
Garland County Comm Coll (AR)
Gateway Coll (NE)
Gateway Comm-Tech Coll (CT)
Genesee Comm Coll (NY)
Glendale Comm Coll (AZ)
Gloucester County Coll (NJ)
Gogebic Comm Coll (MI)
Grand Rapids Comm Coll (MI)
Grayson County Coll (TX)
Great Basin Coll (NV)
Greenville Tech Coll (SC)
Harrisburg Area Comm Coll (PA)
Haskell Indian Nations U (KS)
Hawkeye Comm Coll (IA)
Haywood Comm Coll (NC)
Heald Inst of Tech, Martinez (CA)
Heald Inst of Tech, Milpitas (CA)
Helena Coll of Tech of The U of Montana (MT)
Herzing Coll of Business and Tech (GA)
Herzing Coll of Tech (WI)
Hesser Coll (NH)
Highline Comm Coll (WA)
Hillsborough Comm Coll (FL)
Hiwassee Coll (TN)
Hocking Coll (OH)
Horry-Georgetown Tech Coll (SC)
Howard Comm Coll (MD)
Hudson County Comm Coll (NJ)
Hutchinson Comm Coll and Area Vocational Sch (KS)
ICM Sch of Business (PA)
Indian Hills Comm Coll (IA)
Indian River Comm Coll (FL)
Inst of Electronic Tech (KY)
International Business Coll (IN)
Inver Hills Comm Coll (MN)
Irvine Valley Coll (CA)
Itawamba Comm Coll (MS)
James Sprunt Comm Coll (NC)
Jamestown Comm Coll (NY)
Johnson County Comm Coll (KS)
Kankakee Comm Coll (IL)
Kansas City Kansas Comm Coll (KS)
Keiser Coll of Tech, Fort Lauderdale (FL)
Kellogg Comm Coll (MI)
Kent State U, Ashtabula Cmps (OH)
Kent State U, East Liverpool Cmps (OH)
Kent State U, Geauga Cmps (OH)
Kent State U, Salem Cmps (OH)
Kent State U, Trumbull Cmps (OH)
Kent State U, Tuscarawas Cmps (OH)
Kilian Comm Coll (SD)
Kingwood Coll (TX)
Lakeshore Tech Coll (WI)
Lake-Sumter Comm Coll (FL)
Lake Washington Tech Coll (WA)
Lamar Comm Coll (CO)
Lamar University–Port Arthur (TX)
Lane Comm Coll (OR)
Lansdale Sch of Business (PA)
Lansing Comm Coll (MI)
Lehigh Carbon Comm Coll (PA)
Lorain County Comm Coll (OH)
Lord Fairfax Comm Coll (VA)
Los Angeles City Coll (CA)
Los Angeles Harbor Coll (CA)
Los Angeles Pierce Coll (CA)
Los Angeles Trade-Tech Coll (CA)
Louisville Tech Inst (KY)
Lower Columbia Coll (WA)
Luzerne County Comm Coll (PA)
Macomb Comm Coll (MI)
Macon Coll (GA)
Madison Area Tech Coll (WI)
Massachusetts Bay Comm Coll (MA)
McLennan Comm Coll (TX)
Merced Coll (CA)
Mercer County Comm Coll (NJ)
Meridian Comm Coll (MS)
Merritt Coll (CA)
Miami University–Hamilton Cmps (OH)
Miami University–Middletown Cmps (OH)
Middlesex Comm Coll (MA)
Middlesex County Coll (NJ)
Midlands Tech Coll (SC)
Mid-State Tech Coll (WI)
Minneapolis Comm Coll (MN)
MiraCosta Coll (CA)
Mission Coll (CA)
Mississippi County Comm Coll (AR)
Mississippi Delta Comm Coll (MS)
Mississippi Gulf Coast Comm Coll (MS)
Monroe Comm Coll (NY)
Monroe County Comm Coll (MI)
Montana State U Coll of Tech-Great Falls (MT)
Monterey Peninsula Coll (CA)
Montgomery Coll (TX)
Montgomery College–Rockville Cmps (MD)
Moraine Park Tech Coll (WI)
Moraine Valley Comm Coll (IL)
Morrison Inst of Tech (IL)
Motlow State Comm Coll (TN)
Mt Hood Comm Coll (OR)
Mt San Antonio Coll (CA)
Nashville State Tech Inst (TN)
Nebraska Coll of Business (NE)
NEI Coll of Tech (MN)
New England Inst of Tech (RI)
New Hampshire Tech Coll, Berlin (NH)
New Hampshire Tech Coll, Claremont (NH)
New Hampshire Tech Coll, Laconia (NH)
New Hampshire Tech Coll, Nashua (NH)
New River Comm Coll (VA)
North Central Missouri Coll (MO)
North Central Texas Coll (TX)
North Dakota State Coll of Science (ND)
North Dakota State University–Bottineau (ND)
Northeastern Jr Coll (CO)
Northeast Iowa Comm Coll, Calmar Cmps (IA)
Northeast Metro Tech Coll (MN)
Northern Essex Comm Coll (MA)
Northern Maine Tech Coll (ME)
Northland Comm and Tech Coll (MN)
North Seattle Comm Coll (WA)
North Shore Comm Coll (MA)
Northwestern Coll (OH)
Northwestern Connecticut Comm-Tech Coll (CT)
Northwestern Michigan Coll (MI)
Northwest Mississippi Comm Coll (MS)
Northwest State Comm Coll (OH)
Norwalk Comm-Tech Coll (CT)
Oakland Comm Coll (MI)
Oklahoma City Comm Coll (OK)
Oklahoma State U, Oklahoma City (OK)
Onondaga Comm Coll (NY)
Orangeburg-Calhoun Tech Coll (SC)
Orange Coast Coll (CA)
Orange County Comm Coll (NY)
Owens Comm Coll, Toledo (OH)
Palo Alto Coll (TX)
Pamlico Comm Coll (NC)
Paris Jr Coll (TX)
Parkland Coll (IL)
Pasadena City Coll (CA)
Pellissippi State Tech Comm Coll (TN)
Pennsylvania Coll of Tech (PA)
Pennsylvania Inst of Tech (PA)
Penn State U Altoona Cmps (PA)
Phillips Jr Coll, Condie Cmps (CA)
Pikes Peak Comm Coll (CO)
Portland Comm Coll (OR)
Potomac State Coll of West Virginia U (WV)
Prince George's Comm Coll (MD)
Queensborough Comm Coll of City U of NY (NY)
Quinsigamond Comm Coll (MA)
Randolph Comm Coll (NC)
Ranger Coll (TX)
Ranken Tech Coll (MO)
Red Rocks Comm Coll (CO)
RETS Tech Ctr (OH)
Roane State Comm Coll (TN)
Rock Valley Coll (IL)
Rogers State Coll (OK)
Roxbury Comm Coll (MA)
St Catharine Coll (KY)
St Louis Comm Coll at Florissant Valley (MO)
Salem Comm Coll (NJ)
Salt Lake Comm Coll (UT)
San Antonio Coll (TX)
San Bernardino Valley Coll (CA)
Sandhills Comm Coll (NC)
San Diego City Coll (CA)
San Joaquin Delta Coll (CA)
San Jose City Coll (CA)
Santa Fe Comm Coll (FL)
Schoolcraft Coll (MI)
Seminole Comm Coll (FL)
Sierra Coll (CA)
Skagit Valley Coll (WA)
Snead State Comm Coll (AL)
Southeast Comm Coll, Lincoln Cmps (NE)
Southeast Comm Coll, Milford Cmps (NE)
Southeastern Comm Coll (NC)
Southern Maine Tech Coll (ME)
Southern State Comm Coll (OH)
South Plains Coll (TX)
South Seattle Comm Coll (WA)
Southwestern Coll (CA)
Southwestern Comm Coll (NC)
Southwest Texas Jr Coll (TX)
Spartanburg Tech Coll (SC)
Spencer Sch of Business (NE)
Springfield Tech Comm Coll (MA)
Stark Tech Coll (OH)
State Fair Comm Coll (MO)
State Tech Inst at Memphis (TN)
State U of NY Coll of A&T at Cobleskill (NY)
State U of NY Coll of A&T at Morrisville (NY)
State U of NY Coll of Tech at Alfred (NY)
Stratton Coll (WI)
Suffolk County Comm College–Ammerman Cmps (NY)
Sullivan County Comm Coll (NY)
Tacoma Comm Coll (WA)
Tech Career Institutes (NY)
Tennessee Inst of Electronics (TN)
Texas State Tech Coll (TX)
Texas State Tech Coll–Harlingen Cmps (TX)
Texas State Tech Coll–Waco/Marshall Cmps (TX)
Three Rivers Comm Coll (MO)
Three Rivers Comm-Tech Coll (CT)
Tri-County Tech Coll (SC)
Trident Tech Coll (SC)
Triton Coll (IL)
Truckee Meadows Comm Coll (NV)
Tulsa Jr Coll (OK)
Tyler Jr Coll (TX)
Umpqua Comm Coll (OR)
The U of Akron–Wayne Coll (OH)
U of Alaska Southeast, Sitka Cmps (AK)
U of Cincinnati Raymond Walters Coll (OH)
U of Kentucky, Southeast Comm Coll (KY)
U of New Mexico–Gallup Branch (NM)
U of New Mexico–Los Alamos Branch (NM)
U of North Dakota–Lake Region (ND)
Vance-Granville Comm Coll (NC)
Vermilion Comm Coll (MN)
Vermont Tech Coll (VT)
Vernon Regional Jr Coll (TX)
Vincennes U (IN)
Wake Tech Comm Coll (NC)
Walla Walla Comm Coll (WA)
Washington State Comm Coll (OH)
Western Nebraska Comm Coll, Scottsbluff (NE)
Western Piedmont Comm Coll (NC)
Western Texas Coll (TX)
Western Wisconsin Tech Coll (WI)
Westmoreland County Comm Coll (PA)
West Shore Comm Coll (MI)
Whatcom Comm Coll (WA)
William Rainey Harper Coll (IL)

Associate Degree Programs at Two-Year Colleges
Computer Technologies–Corrections

Yakima Valley Comm Coll (WA)
York Tech Coll (SC)

CONSERVATION

Berkshire Comm Coll (MA)
Brevard Coll (NC)
Ellsworth Comm Coll (IA)
Finger Lakes Comm Coll (NY)
Fox Valley Tech Coll (WI)
Fulton-Montgomery Comm Coll (NY)
Grayson County Coll (TX)
Herkimer County Comm Coll (NY)
Highland Comm Coll (KS)
Iowa Lakes Comm Coll (IA)
Joliet Jr Coll (IL)
Kirkwood Comm Coll (IA)
Murray State Coll (OK)
Muscatine Comm Coll (IA)
Nebraska Coll of Tech Agriculture (NE)
New Hampshire Tech Coll, Berlin (NH)
North Dakota State University–Bottineau (ND)
State U of NY Coll of A&T at Morrisville (NY)
Vermilion Comm Coll (MN)
Vincennes U (IN)

CONSTRUCTION MANAGEMENT

Allen County Comm Coll (KS)
Arapahoe Comm Coll (CO)
Atlantic Comm Coll (NJ)
Belleville Area Coll (IL)
Broward Comm Coll (FL)
Cabrillo Coll (CA)
Cape Cod Comm Coll (MA)
Catonsville Comm Coll (MD)
City Coll of San Francisco (CA)
Coll of the Desert (CA)
Columbus State Comm Coll (OH)
Comm Coll of Allegheny County South Cmps (PA)
Comm Coll of Southern Nevada (NV)
Comm Coll of the Air Force (AL)
Cosumnes River Coll (CA)
Delaware Tech & Comm Coll, Jack F Owens Cmps (DE)
Delaware Tech & Comm Coll, Terry Cmps (DE)
Delgado Comm Coll (LA)
Delta Coll (MI)
Durham Tech Comm Coll (NC)
Edison State Comm Coll (OH)
Edmonds Comm Coll (WA)
El Paso Comm Coll (TX)
Frederick Comm Coll (MD)
Fresno City Coll (CA)
Gwinnett Tech Inst (GA)
Hesser Coll (NH)
Jefferson State Comm Coll (AL)
Laney Coll (CA)
Massachusetts Bay Comm Coll (MA)
Montgomery College–Rockville Cmps (MD)
Mt San Antonio Coll (CA)
Northeast Iowa Comm Coll, Peosta Cmps (IA)
North Hennepin Comm Coll (MN)
Oklahoma State U, Oklahoma City (OK)
Palm Beach Comm Coll (FL)
Paris Jr Coll (TX)
Piedmont Tech Coll (SC)
Piedmont Virginia Comm Coll (VA)
Rend Lake Coll (IL)
Santa Rosa Jr Coll (CA)
Seminole Comm Coll (FL)
Sierra Coll (CA)
Snow Coll (UT)
Southeastern Comm Coll, North Cmps, West Burlington (IA)
State Comm Coll of East St Louis (IL)
State U of NY Coll of Tech at Delhi (NY)
Terra State Comm Coll (OH)
Triton Coll (IL)
U of New Mexico–Valencia Cmps (NM)
Utah Valley State Coll (UT)
Vermont Tech Coll (VT)
Vincennes U (IN)
Washtenaw Comm Coll (MI)

CONSTRUCTION TECHNOLOGIES

Albuquerque Tech Vocational Inst (NM)
Allen County Comm Coll (KS)
American River Coll (CA)
Anson Comm Coll (NC)
Antelope Valley Coll (CA)
Austin Comm Coll (TX)
Bay de Noc Comm Coll (MI)
Bessemer State Tech Coll (AL)
Brazosport Coll (TX)
Brevard Comm Coll (FL)
Butler County Comm Coll (KS)
Butte Coll (CA)
Casper Coll (WY)
Catonsville Comm Coll (MD)
Cecil Comm Coll (MD)
Central Coll (KS)
Central Comm College–Hastings Cmps (NE)
Central Maine Tech Coll (ME)
Central Texas Coll (TX)
Charles Stewart Mott Comm Coll (MI)
Chemeketa Comm Coll (OR)
Chippewa Valley Tech Coll (WI)
Cincinnati State Tech and Comm Coll (OH)
Cisco Jr Coll (TX)
Clackamas Comm Coll (OR)
Clark Coll (WA)
Cleveland State Comm Coll (TN)
Clovis Comm Coll (NM)
Coffeyville Comm Coll (KS)
Coll of Eastern Utah (UT)
Coll of Lake County (IL)
Coll of San Mateo (CA)
Coll of the Redwoods (CA)
Coll of the Sequoias (CA)
Columbus State Comm Coll (OH)
Comm Coll of Allegheny County North Cmps (PA)
Comm Coll of Allegheny County South Cmps (PA)
Comm Coll of Philadelphia (PA)
Comm Coll of Southern Nevada (NV)
Cosumnes River Coll (CA)
Crowder Coll (MO)
Cuesta Coll (CA)
Cuyamaca Coll (CA)
Daytona Beach Comm Coll (FL)
Delaware County Comm Coll (PA)
Delaware Tech & Comm Coll, Terry Cmps (DE)
Delta Coll (MI)
Dixie Coll (UT)
Dodge City Comm Coll (KS)
Don Bosco Tech Inst (CA)
Durham Tech Comm Coll (NC)
Dutchess Comm Coll (NY)
East Central Coll (MO)
Eastern Maine Tech Coll (ME)
Edmonds Comm Coll (WA)
El Camino Coll (CA)
Erie Comm Coll, North Cmps (NY)
Florida Comm Coll at Jacksonville (FL)
Forsyth Tech Comm Coll (NC)
Fort Peck Comm Coll (MT)
Fresno City Coll (CA)
Fullerton Coll (CA)
Fulton-Montgomery Comm Coll (NY)
Garden City Comm Coll (KS)
Gateway Comm Coll (AZ)
Gogebic Comm Coll (MI)
Green River Comm Coll (WA)
Greenville Tech Coll (SC)
Gulf Coast Comm Coll (FL)
Harrisburg Area Comm Coll (PA)
Hartnell Coll (CA)
Henry Ford Comm Coll (MI)
Herkimer County Comm Coll (NY)
Highland Comm Coll (KS)
Hillsborough Comm Coll (FL)
Houston Comm Coll System (TX)
Hudson Valley Comm Coll (NY)
Hutchinson Comm Coll and Area Vocational Sch (KS)
Inst of Design and Construction (NY)
Inver Hills Comm Coll (MN)
Itawamba Comm Coll (MS)
Ivy Tech State Coll–Eastcentral (IN)
Ivy Tech State Coll–Kokomo (IN)
Ivy Tech State Coll–Northeast (IN)
Ivy Tech State Coll–Southcentral (IN)
Ivy Tech State Coll–Wabash Valley (IN)
Ivy Tech State Coll–Whitewater (IN)
John M Patterson State Tech Coll (AL)
Johnson Tech Inst (PA)
Joliet Jr Coll (IL)
J Sargeant Reynolds Comm Coll (VA)
Kirkwood Comm Coll (IA)
Lane Comm Coll (OR)
Lansing Comm Coll (MI)
Laramie County Comm Coll (WY)
Laredo Comm Coll (TX)
Lassen Coll (CA)
Lincoln Land Comm Coll (IL)
Los Angeles Pierce Coll (CA)
Los Angeles Trade-Tech Coll (CA)
Macomb Comm Coll (MI)
Manatee Comm Coll (FL)
McDowell Tech Comm Coll (NC)
Merced Coll (CA)
Mercer County Comm Coll (NJ)
Meridian Comm Coll (MS)
Metropolitan Comm Coll (NE)
Miami-Dade Comm Coll (FL)
Middlesex County Coll (NJ)
Mid-Plains Comm Coll (NE)
Milwaukee Area Tech Coll (WI)
Mineral Area Coll (MO)
Mississippi Delta Comm Coll (MS)
Modesto Jr Coll (CA)
Monroe Comm Coll (NY)
Morrison Inst of Tech (IL)
Neosho County Comm Coll (KS)
New England Inst of Tech (RI)
New Hampshire Tech Coll, Manchester (NH)
New Mexico Jr Coll (NM)
New York City Tech Coll of the City U of NY (NY)
North Central Missouri Coll (MO)
North Dakota State Coll of Science (ND)
Northeast Comm Coll (NE)
Northeastern Oklahoma A&M Coll (OK)
Northeast Iowa Comm Coll, Calmar Cmps (IA)
Northeast Iowa Comm Coll, Peosta Cmps (IA)
Northern Oklahoma Coll (OK)
Northern Virginia Comm Coll (VA)
North Lake Coll (TX)
Northland Pioneer Coll (AZ)
Northwest Indian Coll (WA)
Northwest Iowa Comm Coll (IA)
Norwalk Comm-Tech Coll (CT)
Ocean County Coll (NJ)
Odessa Coll (TX)
Ohio State U Ag Tech Inst (OH)
Okaloosa-Walton Comm Coll (FL)
Oklahoma State U, Oklahoma City (OK)
Oklahoma State U, Okmulgee (OK)
Onondaga Comm Coll (NY)
Orange Coast Coll (CA)
Orange County Comm Coll (NY)
Ozarks Tech Comm Coll (MO)
Palau Comm Coll (PW)
Palomar Coll (CA)
Parkland Coll (IL)
Pasadena City Coll (CA)
Pasco-Hernando Comm Coll (FL)
Pellissippi State Tech Comm Coll (TN)
Pennsylvania Coll of Tech (PA)
Pensacola Jr Coll (FL)
Pima Comm Coll (AZ)
Portland Comm Coll (OR)
Pratt Comm Coll and Area Voc Sch (KS)
Raritan Valley Comm Coll (NJ)
Redlands Comm Coll (OK)
Reid State Tech Coll (AL)
Rend Lake Coll (IL)
Richland Comm Coll (IL)
Ricks Coll (ID)
Riverside Comm Coll (CA)
Roanoke-Chowan Comm Coll (NC)
Rockingham Comm Coll (NC)
Rock Valley Coll (IL)
Saddleback Coll (CA)
St Cloud Tech Coll (MN)
St Louis Comm Coll at Florissant Valley (MO)
St Petersburg Jr Coll (FL)
St Philip's Coll (TX)
Salt Lake Comm Coll (UT)
San Diego Mesa Coll (CA)
San Jacinto College–North Cmps (TX)
San Joaquin Delta Coll (CA)
San Jose City Coll (CA)
Santa Fe Comm Coll (FL)
Santa Fe Comm Coll (NM)
Santa Monica Coll (CA)
Santa Rosa Jr Coll (CA)
Seminole Comm Coll (FL)
Shasta Coll (CA)
Sierra Coll (CA)
Skagit Valley Coll (WA)
Snow Coll (UT)
Southeast Comm Coll, Milford Cmps (NE)
Southeastern Comm Coll, North Cmps, West Burlington (IA)
Southern Maine Tech Coll (ME)
South Florida Comm Coll (FL)
South Suburban Coll (IL)
Southwestern Coll (CA)
Southwest Mississippi Comm Coll (MS)
Spokane Comm Coll (WA)
Stark Tech Coll (OH)
State Fair Comm Coll (MO)
State U of NY Coll of A&T at Morrisville (NY)
State U of NY Coll of Tech at Alfred (NY)
State U of NY Coll of Tech at Canton (NY)
State U of NY Coll of Tech at Delhi (NY)
State U of NY Coll of Tech at Farmingdale (NY)
Suffolk County Comm College–Ammerman Cmps (NY)
Surry Comm Coll (NC)
Tarrant County Jr Coll (TX)
Texas Southmost Coll (TX)
Texas State Tech Coll–Harlingen Cmps (TX)
Thaddeus Stevens State Sch of Tech (PA)
Three Rivers Comm Coll (MO)
Tompkins Cortland Comm Coll (NY)
Trenholm State Tech Coll (AL)
Trinidad State Jr Coll (CO)
Triton Coll (IL)
Truckee Meadows Comm Coll (NV)
Tulsa Jr Coll (OK)
U of Hawaii–Maui Comm Coll (HI)
U of New Mexico–Gallup Branch (NM)
U of New Mexico–Valencia Cmps (NM)
Utah Valley State Coll (UT)
Valencia Comm Coll (FL)
Vance-Granville Comm Coll (NC)
Ventura Coll (CA)
Victor Valley Coll (CA)
Vincennes U (IN)
Wallace State Comm Coll (AL)
Washington County Tech Coll (ME)
Western Iowa Tech Comm Coll (IA)
Western Oklahoma State Coll (OK)
Western Wyoming Comm Coll (WY)
Wilkes Comm Coll (NC)
The Williamson Free Sch of Mech Trades (PA)

CONSUMER SERVICES

Bryant and Stratton Business Inst, Rochester (NY)
City Coll of San Francisco (CA)
Dixie Coll (UT)
Guilford Tech Comm Coll (NC)
Los Angeles Mission Coll (CA)
Ohlone Coll (CA)
Rio Salado Comm Coll (AZ)
Rockingham Comm Coll (NC)
Saddleback Coll (CA)
San Diego City Coll (CA)
San Diego Mesa Coll (CA)
Southwestern Tech Coll (MN)

CORRECTIONS

Adirondack Comm Coll (NY)
Alamance Comm Coll (NC)
Alexandria Tech Coll (MN)
Alvin Comm Coll (TX)
Anne Arundel Comm Coll (MD)
Atlantic Comm Coll (NJ)
Austin Comm Coll (MN)
Bakersfield Coll (CA)
Baltimore City Comm Coll (MD)
Belmont Tech Coll (OH)
Bossier Parish Comm Coll (LA)
Brevard Comm Coll (FL)
Broward Comm Coll (FL)
Bucks County Comm Coll (PA)
Casper Coll (WY)
Catonsville Comm Coll (MD)
Cayuga County Comm Coll (NY)
Central Carolina Comm Coll (NC)
Central Ohio Tech Coll (OH)
Central Texas Coll (TX)
Chabot Coll (CA)
Chaffey Coll (CA)
Charles Stewart Mott Comm Coll (MI)
Chattahoochee Tech Inst (GA)
Chemeketa Comm Coll (OR)
Chesapeake Coll (MD)
City Colls of Chicago, Harold Washington Coll (IL)
Clark Coll (WA)
Clark State Comm Coll (OH)
Coll of DuPage (IL)
Coll of Marin (CA)
Coll of the Sequoias (CA)
Colorado Northwestern Comm Coll (CO)
Columbus State Comm Coll (OH)
Comm Coll of Allegheny County Allegheny Cmps (PA)
Comm Coll of Allegheny County South Cmps (PA)
Comm Coll of Rhode Island (RI)
Comm Coll of Southern Nevada (NV)
Cowley County Comm Coll and Voc-Tech Sch (KS)
Cumberland County Coll (NJ)
Darton Coll (GA)
Davidson County Comm Coll (NC)
Daytona Beach Comm Coll (FL)
Dean Coll (MA)
De Anza Coll (CA)
Delaware Tech & Comm Coll, Stanton/Wilmington Cmps (DE)
Delaware Tech & Comm Coll, Terry Cmps (DE)
Delta Coll (MI)
Des Moines Area Comm Coll (IA)
Eastern Oklahoma State Coll (OK)
Ellsworth Comm Coll (IA)
El Paso Comm Coll (TX)
Fresno City Coll (CA)
Gavilan Coll (CA)
Gogebic Comm Coll (MI)
Grand Rapids Comm Coll (MI)
Grossmont Coll (CA)
Guilford Tech Comm Coll (NC)
Gulf Coast Comm Coll (FL)
Halifax Comm Coll (NC)
Hawkeye Comm Coll (IA)
Henry Ford Comm Coll (MI)
Herkimer County Comm Coll (NY)
Hesser Coll (NH)
Hillsborough Comm Coll (FL)
Hocking Coll (OH)
Hutchinson Comm Coll and Area Vocational Sch (KS)
Indian River Comm Coll (FL)
Jackson Comm Coll (MI)
Jefferson Comm Coll (OH)
John C Calhoun State Comm Coll (AL)
Joliet Jr Coll (IL)
Kansas City Kansas Comm Coll (KS)
Kellogg Comm Coll (MI)
Kirkwood Comm Coll (IA)
Kirtland Comm Coll (MI)
Lake City Comm Coll (FL)
Lakeland Comm Coll (OH)
Lake Michigan Coll (MI)
Lansing Comm Coll (MI)
Lima Tech Coll (OH)
Lincoln Coll, Normal (IL)
Lincoln Land Comm Coll (IL)
Longview Comm Coll (MO)
Lorain County Comm Coll (OH)
Los Angeles City Coll (CA)
Macon Coll (GA)
Massasoit Comm Coll (MA)
Mercer County Comm Coll (NJ)
Middlesex County Coll (NJ)
Mid-State Tech Coll (WI)
Modesto Jr Coll (CA)
Monroe Comm Coll (NY)
Montcalm Comm Coll (MI)
Monterey Peninsula Coll (CA)
Montgomery College–Rockville Cmps (MD)
Moraine Park Tech Coll (WI)
Mountain Empire Comm Coll (VA)
Mt San Antonio Coll (CA)
Mount Wachusett Comm Coll (MA)
Napa Valley Coll (CA)
Navarro Coll (TX)
Northeast Comm Coll (NE)
Northeastern Jr Coll (CO)
Northern Virginia Comm Coll (VA)
Oakland Comm Coll (MI)
Olympic Coll (WA)
Parkland Coll (IL)
Penn Valley Comm Coll (MO)
Pima Comm Coll (AZ)
Pitt Comm Coll (NC)
Polk Comm Coll (FL)
Pueblo Comm Coll (CO)
Rancho Santiago Coll (CA)
Redlands Comm Coll (OK)
Rio Salado Comm Coll (AZ)
Roane State Comm Coll (TN)

70

Peterson's Guide to Two-Year Colleges 1997

Associate Degree Programs at Two-Year Colleges
Corrections–Criminal Justice

St Clair County Comm Coll (MI)
St Louis Comm Coll at Florissant Valley (MO)
St Louis Comm Coll at Meramec (MO)
St Petersburg Jr Coll (FL)
San Antonio Coll (TX)
San Bernardino Valley Coll (CA)
San Diego Miramar Coll (CA)
San Jacinto College–North Cmps (TX)
San Joaquin Delta Coll (CA)
Santa Fe Comm Coll (FL)
Santa Fe Comm Coll (NM)
Sauk Valley Comm Coll (IL)
Schoolcraft Coll (MI)
Shoreline Comm Coll (WA)
Sierra Coll (CA)
Sinclair Comm Coll (OH)
Southeastern Illinois Coll (IL)
Southwestern Coll (CA)
Spokane Comm Coll (WA)
State U of NY Coll of Tech at Canton (NY)
Sullivan County Comm Coll (NY)
Three Rivers Comm-Tech Coll (CT)
Trinidad State Jr Coll (CO)
Trinity Valley Comm Coll (TX)
Truckee Meadows Comm Coll (NV)
Tulsa Jr Coll (OK)
Tunxis Comm Tech Coll (CT)
U of New Mexico–Gallup Branch (NM)
Vance-Granville Comm Coll (NC)
Vincennes U (IN)
Walla Walla Comm Coll (WA)
Washtenaw Comm Coll (MI)
Wayne Comm Coll (NC)
Weatherford Coll (TX)
Westchester Comm Coll (NY)
Western Nevada Comm Coll (NV)
Western Oklahoma State Coll (OK)
Western Texas Coll (TX)
West Shore Comm Coll (MI)
Wor-Wic Comm Coll (MD)
Wytheville Comm Coll (VA)
Yuba Coll (CA)

COSMETOLOGY

Alamance Comm Coll (NC)
Allan Hancock Coll (CA)
Anson Comm Coll (NC)
Athens Area Tech Inst (GA)
Bakersfield Coll (CA)
Barton County Comm Coll (KS)
Bee County Coll (TX)
Bishop State Comm Coll (AL)
Black Hawk Coll, Moline (IL)
Blue Ridge Comm Coll (NC)
Brevard Comm Coll (FL)
Brunswick Comm Coll (NC)
Butte Coll (CA)
Carl Sandburg Coll (IL)
Central Texas Coll (TX)
Cerritos Coll (CA)
Cisco Jr Coll (TX)
Citrus Coll (CA)
Coastal Carolina Comm Coll (NC)
Coll of Eastern Utah (UT)
Coll of San Mateo (CA)
Coll of the Mainland (TX)
Coll of the Sequoias (CA)
Coll of the Siskiyous (CA)
Copiah-Lincoln Comm Coll (MS)
Cowley County Comm Coll and Voc-Tech Sch (KS)
Daytona Beach Comm Coll (FL)
Del Mar Coll (TX)
Dodge City Comm Coll (KS)
Douglas MacArthur State Tech Coll (AL)
East Central Comm Coll (MS)
Eastern Arizona Coll (AZ)
Eastern Wyoming Coll (WY)
East Mississippi Comm Coll (MS)
El Camino Coll (CA)
Everett Comm Coll (WA)
Fayetteville Tech Comm Coll (NC)
Fort Scott Comm Coll (KS)
Frank Phillips Coll (TX)
Fresno City Coll (CA)
Fullerton Coll (CA)
Garden City Comm Coll (KS)
Gavilan Coll (CA)
Gem City Coll (IL)
Gogebic Comm Coll (MI)
Golden West Coll (CA)
Grayson County Coll (TX)
Haywood Comm Coll (NC)
Hill Coll of the Hill Jr Coll District (TX)
Howard Coll (TX)
Illinois Eastern Comm Colls, Olney Central Coll (IL)
Illinois Eastern Comm Colls, Wabash Valley Coll (IL)
Independence Comm Coll (KS)
Indian River Comm Coll (FL)
Isothermal Comm Coll (NC)
Ivy Tech State Coll–Northcentral (IN)
John A Logan Coll (IL)
John C Calhoun State Comm Coll (AL)
John M Patterson State Tech Coll (AL)
John Wood Comm Coll (IL)
Kansas City Kansas Comm Coll (KS)
Kirtland Comm Coll (MI)
Lake Area Vocational-Tech Inst (SD)
Lamar Comm Coll (CO)
Lamar University–Port Arthur (TX)
Laney Coll (CA)
Lassen Coll (CA)
Lawson State Comm Coll (AL)
Lenoir Comm Coll (NC)
Los Angeles Trade-Tech Coll (CA)
McDowell Tech Comm Coll (NC)
MiraCosta Coll (CA)
Montcalm Comm Coll (MI)
Mt Hood Comm Coll (OR)
Napa Valley Coll (CA)
Nash Comm Coll (NC)
New Mexico Jr Coll (NM)
Northeastern Jr Coll (CO)
Northeast Texas Comm Coll (TX)
North Harris Coll (TX)
Northland Comm and Tech Coll (MN)
Northland Pioneer Coll (AZ)
Northwest Mississippi Comm Coll (MS)
Oakland Comm Coll (MI)
Odessa Coll (TX)
Olympic Coll (WA)
Paris Jr Coll (TX)
Pasadena City Coll (CA)
Phillips County Comm Coll (AR)
Rancho Santiago Coll (CA)
Reid State Tech Coll (AL)
Riverside Comm Coll (CA)
Roanoke-Chowan Comm Coll (NC)
Rockingham Comm Coll (NC)
Sacramento City Coll (CA)
Saddleback Coll (CA)
Salt Lake Comm Coll (UT)
Sandhills Comm Coll (NC)
San Diego City Coll (CA)
San Jacinto College–Central Cmps (TX)
San Jacinto College–North Cmps (TX)
San Jacinto College–South Cmps (TX)
San Jose City Coll (CA)
Santa Monica Coll (CA)
Sawyer Coll of Business, Cleveland (OH)
Seattle Central Comm Coll (WA)
Shawnee Comm Coll (IL)
Shelton State Comm Coll (AL)
Shoreline Comm Coll (WA)
Skyline Coll (CA)
Solano Comm Coll (CA)
Southeastern Comm Coll (NC)
Southeastern Comm Coll, North Cmps, West Burlington (IA)
Southeastern Comm Coll, South Cmps, Keokuk (IA)
South Plains Coll (TX)
South Seattle Comm Coll (WA)
South Suburban Coll (IL)
Southwestern Comm Coll (NC)
Southwest Mississippi Comm Coll (MS)
Southwest Texas Jr Coll (TX)
Southwest Wisconsin Tech Coll (WI)
Spokane Comm Coll (WA)
Springfield Tech Comm Coll (MA)
Texarkana Coll (TX)
Trinidad State Jr Coll (CO)
Trinity Valley Comm Coll (TX)
Umpqua Comm Coll (OR)
U of Hawaii–Honolulu Comm Coll (HI)
U of New Mexico–Gallup Branch (NM)
Vance-Granville Comm Coll (NC)
Vernon Regional Jr Coll (TX)
Vincennes U (IN)
Wallace State Comm Coll (AL)
Walla Walla Comm Coll (WA)
Waycross Coll (GA)
Weatherford Coll (TX)
Western Nebraska Comm Coll, Scottsbluff (NE)
Willmar Tech Coll (MN)
Wisconsin Indianhead Tech Coll, Rice Lake Cmps (WI)
Yuba Coll (CA)

COURT REPORTING

Albuquerque Tech Vocational Inst (NM)
Alvin Comm Coll (TX)
American Inst of Business (IA)
American Inst of Commerce (IA)
Aquinas Coll at Milton (MA)
Berean Inst (PA)
The Brown Mackie Coll (KS)
The Brown Mackie Coll-Olathe Cmps (KS)
Bryant and Stratton Business Inst, Buffalo (NY)
Butte Coll (CA)
Central City Business Inst (NY)
Central Pennsylvania Business Sch (PA)
Cerritos Coll (CA)
Chaffey Coll (CA)
Chicago Coll of Commerce (IL)
City Coll of San Francisco (CA)
Clark State Comm Coll (OH)
Coll of Marin (CA)
Comm Coll of Allegheny County Allegheny Cmps (PA)
Comm Coll of Southern Nevada (NV)
Cuyahoga Comm Coll, Metropolitan Cmps (OH)
Cuyahoga Comm Coll, Western Cmps (OH)
Cypress Coll (CA)
Daytona Beach Comm Coll (FL)
Del Mar Coll (TX)
Duff's Business Inst (PA)
Edmonds Comm Coll (WA)
El Paso Comm Coll (TX)
Gadsden State Comm Coll (AL)
Gateway Comm Coll (AZ)
Gogebic Comm Coll (MI)
Great Lakes Jr Coll of Business (MI)
Green River Comm Coll (WA)
Hagerstown Business Coll (MD)
Herkimer County Comm Coll (NY)
Houston Comm Coll System (TX)
Huntington Jr Coll of Business (WV)
Illinois Central Coll (IL)
Illinois Eastern Comm Colls, Wabash Valley Coll (IL)
Inst of Career Education (FL)
James H Faulkner State Comm Coll (AL)
Kelsey Jenney Coll (CA)
Lakeshore Tech Coll (WI)
Lansing Comm Coll (MI)
Lenoir Comm Coll (NC)
Lewis and Clark Comm Coll (IL)
Lincoln Sch of Commerce (NE)
MacCormac Jr Coll (IL)
Madison Area Tech Coll (WI)
Manor Jr Coll (PA)
Massachusetts Bay Comm Coll (MA)
Massasoit Comm Coll (MA)
Mater Dei Coll (NY)
Miami-Dade Comm Coll (FL)
Midlands Tech Coll (SC)
Midstate Coll (IL)
Mississippi Gulf Coast Comm Coll (MS)
Oakland Comm Coll (MI)
Peirce Coll (PA)
Pensacola Jr Coll (FL)
Rancho Santiago Coll (CA)
Rasmussen Coll Eagan (MN)
Rasmussen Coll Minnetonka (MN)
Rasmussen Coll St Cloud (MN)
Rogers State Coll (OK)
Rose State Coll (OK)
St Louis Comm Coll at Meramec (MO)
San Antonio Coll (TX)
San Diego City Coll (CA)
South Suburban Coll (IL)
Southwest Florida Coll of Business (FL)
Springfield Tech Comm Coll (MA)
Stark Tech Coll (OH)
State Fair Comm Coll (MO)
State U of NY Coll of Tech at Alfred (NY)
Stenotype Acad (NY)
Triton Coll (IL)
U of Cincinnati Clermont Coll (OH)
Ward Stone Coll (FL)
Wayne County Comm Coll (MI)
West Valley Coll (CA)
Wisconsin Indianhead Tech Coll, New Richmond Cmps (WI)

CREATIVE WRITING

Barstow Coll (CA)
Brevard Coll (NC)
Comm Coll of Allegheny County South Cmps (PA)
Foothill Coll (CA)
Grossmont Coll (CA)
Inst of American Indian Arts (NM)
Irvine Valley Coll (CA)
Kirtland Comm Coll (MI)
Lon Morris Coll (TX)
Polk Comm Coll (FL)
St Louis Comm Coll at Meramec (MO)
San Jacinto College–Central Cmps (TX)
Tulsa Jr Coll (OK)

CRIMINAL JUSTICE

Abraham Baldwin Ag Coll (GA)
Adirondack Comm Coll (NY)
Aims Comm Coll (CO)
Alabama Southern Comm Coll, Thomasville (AL)
Alamance Comm Coll (NC)
Albuquerque Tech Vocational Inst (NM)
Alexandria Tech Coll (MN)
Allegany Comm Coll (MD)
Allen County Comm Coll (KS)
Ancilla Coll (IN)
Andover Coll (ME)
Angelina Coll (TX)
Anne Arundel Comm Coll (MD)
Anson Comm Coll (NC)
Antelope Valley Coll (CA)
Arapahoe Comm Coll (CO)
Arizona Western Coll (AZ)
Atlanta Metropolitan Coll (GA)
Atlantic Comm Coll (NJ)
Austin Comm Coll (TX)
Bainbridge Coll (GA)
Bakersfield Coll (CA)
Barton County Comm Coll (KS)
Bay de Noc Comm Coll (MI)
Bee County Coll (TX)
Belleville Area Coll (IL)
Bellevue Comm Coll (WA)
Bergen Comm Coll (NJ)
Berkshire Comm Coll (MA)
Bishop State Comm Coll (AL)
Bismarck State Coll (ND)
Blinn Coll (TX)
Blue Mountain Comm Coll (OR)
Bowling Green State University–Firelands Coll (OH)
Brazosport Coll (TX)
Brevard Comm Coll (FL)
Briarwood Coll (CT)
Bristol Comm Coll (MA)
Brookdale Comm Coll (NJ)
Broome Comm Coll (NY)
Broward Comm Coll (FL)
The Brown Mackie Coll (KS)
Brunswick Coll (GA)
Bucks County Comm Coll (PA)
Bunker Hill Comm Coll (MA)
Burlington County Coll (NJ)
Butler County Comm Coll (KS)
Butte Coll (CA)
Camden County Coll (NJ)
Cape Cod Comm Coll (MA)
Cape Fear Comm Coll (NC)
Carl Sandburg Coll (IL)
Carteret Comm Coll (NC)
Casper Coll (WY)
Catonsville Comm Coll (MD)
Cayuga County Comm Coll (NY)
Cecil Comm Coll (MD)
Central Carolina Comm Coll (NC)
Central Carolina Tech Coll (SC)
Central Coll (KS)
Central Florida Comm Coll (FL)
Central Ohio Tech Coll (OH)
Central Oregon Comm Coll (OR)
Central Piedmont Comm Coll (NC)
Central Texas Coll (TX)
Central Virginia Comm Coll (VA)
Central Wyoming Coll (WY)
Cerro Coso Comm Coll (CA)
Chabot Coll (CA)
Champlain Coll (VT)
Charles Stewart Mott Comm Coll (MI)
Chattahoochee Valley State Comm Coll (AL)
Chattanooga State Tech Comm Coll (TN)
Chemeketa Comm Coll (OR)
Chesapeake Coll (MD)
Citrus Coll (CA)
City Coll of San Francisco (CA)
City Colls of Chicago, Harold Washington Coll (IL)
Clackamas Comm Coll (OR)
Clark Coll (WA)
Clark State Comm Coll (OH)
Clatsop Comm Coll (OR)
Cleveland Comm Coll (NC)
Clinton Comm Coll (IA)
Clinton Comm Coll (NY)
Cloud County Comm Coll (KS)
Clovis Comm Coll (NM)
Coahoma Comm Coll (MS)
Coastal Carolina Comm Coll (NC)
Cochise Coll, Douglas (AZ)
Cochise Coll, Sierra Vista (AZ)
Coconino County Comm Coll (AZ)
Colby Comm Coll (KS)
Coll of DuPage (IL)
Coll of Lake County (IL)
Coll of Southern Idaho (ID)
Coll of The Albemarle (NC)
Coll of the Canyons (CA)
Coll of the Desert (CA)
Coll of the Mainland (TX)
Coll of the Redwoods (CA)
Coll of the Sequoias (CA)
Coll of the Siskiyous (CA)
Collin County Comm Coll (TX)
Colorado Mountn Coll, Roaring Fork Cmps-Spring Valley Ctr (CO)
Colorado Northwestern Comm Coll (CO)
Columbia-Greene Comm Coll (NY)
Comm Coll of Allegheny County Boyce Cmps (PA)
Comm Coll of Allegheny County South Cmps (PA)
Comm Coll of Aurora (CO)
Comm Coll of Beaver County (PA)
Comm Coll of Philadelphia (PA)
Comm Coll of Southern Nevada (NV)
Comm Coll of the Air Force (AL)
Connors State Coll (OK)
Contra Costa Coll (CA)
Corning Comm Coll (NY)
Cosumnes River Coll (CA)
County Coll of Morris (NJ)
Cowley County Comm Coll and Voc-Tech Sch (KS)
Crafton Hills Coll (CA)
Craven Comm Coll (NC)
Dabney S Lancaster Comm Coll (VA)
Dalton Coll (GA)
Danville Area Comm Coll (IL)
Darton Coll (GA)
Davidson County Comm Coll (NC)
Daytona Beach Comm Coll (FL)
Dean Coll (MA)
De Anza Coll (CA)
Delaware County Comm Coll (PA)
Delaware Tech & Comm Coll, Jack F Owens Cmps (DE)
Delaware Tech & Comm Coll, Stanton/Wilmington Cmps (DE)
Delaware Tech & Comm Coll, Terry Cmps (DE)
Delgado Comm Coll (LA)
Del Mar Coll (TX)
Delta Coll (MI)
Denmark Tech Coll (SC)
Des Moines Area Comm Coll (IA)
Dixie Coll (UT)
Dodge City Comm Coll (KS)
Durham Tech Comm Coll (NC)
Dutchess Comm Coll (NY)
East Arkansas Comm Coll (AR)
East Central Coll (MO)
Eastern Arizona Coll (AZ)
Eastern New Mexico University–Roswell (NM)
Eastern Wyoming Coll (WY)
East Georgia Coll (GA)
East Los Angeles Coll (CA)
East Mississippi Comm Coll (MS)
Edgecombe Comm Coll (NC)
Edison Comm Coll (FL)
Edison State Comm Coll (OH)
El Centro Coll (TX)
Elgin Comm Coll (IL)
Ellsworth Comm Coll (IA)
Enterprise State Jr Coll (AL)
Erie Comm Coll, City Cmps (NY)
Erie Comm Coll, North Cmps (NY)
Essex Comm Coll (MD)
Essex County Coll (NJ)
Everett Comm Coll (WA)
Evergreen Valley Coll (CA)
Fayetteville Tech Comm Coll (NC)
Feather River Comm Coll District (CA)
Finger Lakes Comm Coll (NY)
Fisher Coll (MA)

Associate Degree Programs at Two-Year Colleges
Criminal Justice–Culinary Arts

Flathead Valley Comm Coll (MT)
Florence-Darlington Tech Coll (SC)
Florida Comm Coll at Jacksonville (FL)
Forsyth Tech Comm Coll (NC)
Fort Peck Comm Coll (MT)
Fort Scott Comm Coll (KS)
Fox Valley Tech Coll (WI)
Frederick Comm Coll (MD)
Fresno City Coll (CA)
Fulton-Montgomery Comm Coll (NY)
Gadsden State Comm Coll (AL)
Gainesville Coll (GA)
Garden City Comm Coll (KS)
Garland County Comm Coll (AR)
Gaston Coll (NC)
Gavilan Coll (CA)
Genesee Comm Coll (NY)
George Corley Wallace State Comm Coll, Selma (AL)
George C Wallace State Comm Coll, Dothan (AL)
Georgia Military Coll (GA)
Glendale Comm Coll (AZ)
Gogebic Comm Coll (MI)
Golden West Coll (CA)
Grand Rapids Comm Coll (MI)
Grays Harbor Coll (WA)
Grayson County Coll (TX)
Great Basin Coll (NV)
Greenfield Comm Coll (MA)
Green River Comm Coll (WA)
Greenville Tech Coll (SC)
Grossmont Coll (CA)
Guilford Tech Comm Coll (NC)
Gulf Coast Comm Coll (FL)
Harford Comm Coll (MD)
Harrisburg Area Comm Coll (PA)
Hartnell Coll (CA)
Hawkeye Comm Coll (IA)
Haywood Comm Coll (NC)
Henry Ford Comm Coll (MI)
Herkimer County Comm Coll (NY)
Hesser Coll (NH)
Highland Comm Coll (IL)
Highland Comm Coll (KS)
Highland Park Comm Coll (MI)
Highline Comm Coll (WA)
Hill Coll of the Hill Jr Coll District (TX)
Hillsborough Comm Coll (FL)
Hinds Comm Coll (MS)
Hocking Coll (OH)
Horry-Georgetown Tech Coll (SC)
Housatonic Comm-Tech Coll (CT)
Houston Comm Coll System (TX)
Howard Comm Coll (MD)
Hudson County Comm Coll (NJ)
Hudson Valley Comm Coll (NY)
Illinois Valley Comm Coll (IL)
Imperial Valley Coll (CA)
Indian Hills Comm Coll (IA)
Indian River Comm Coll (FL)
Iowa Lakes Comm Coll (IA)
Iowa Western Comm Coll (IA)
Irvine Valley Coll (CA)
Isothermal Comm Coll (NC)
Ivy Tech State Coll–Central Indiana (IN)
Jackson Comm Coll (MI)
James Sprunt Comm Coll (NC)
Jamestown Comm Coll (NY)
Jefferson Coll (MO)
Jefferson Comm Coll (NY)
Jefferson State Comm Coll (AL)
John A Logan Coll (IL)
John C Calhoun State Comm Coll (AL)
Johnson County Comm Coll (KS)
Kansas City Kansas Comm Coll (KS)
Kaskaskia Coll (IL)
Kellogg Comm Coll (MI)
Kent State U, East Liverpool Cmps (OH)
Kent State U, Trumbull Cmps (OH)
Keystone Coll (PA)
Kilian Comm Coll (SD)
Kirkwood Comm Coll (IA)
Kirtland Comm Coll (MI)
Labette Comm Coll (KS)
Lackawanna Jr Coll (PA)
Lake City Comm Coll (FL)
Lakeland Comm Coll (OH)
Lake Michigan Coll (MI)
Lake-Sumter Comm Coll (FL)
Lake Tahoe Comm Coll (CA)
Lamar University–Port Arthur (TX)
Lane Comm Coll (OR)
Lansing Comm Coll (MI)
Laramie County Comm Coll (WY)
Lawson State Comm Coll (AL)
Lee Coll (TX)
Lehigh Carbon Comm Coll (PA)
Lenoir Comm Coll (NC)
Lewis and Clark Comm Coll (IL)
Lincoln Land Comm Coll (IL)
Linn-Benton Comm Coll (OR)
Long Beach City Coll (CA)
Longview Comm Coll (MO)
Los Angeles City Coll (CA)
Los Angeles Southwest Coll (CA)
Los Angeles Valley Coll (CA)
Louisiana State U at Eunice (LA)
Luzerne County Comm Coll (PA)
Macomb Comm Coll (MI)
Macon Coll (GA)
Manatee Comm Coll (FL)
Manchester Comm-Tech Coll (CT)
Maple Woods Comm Coll (MO)
Massachusetts Bay Comm Coll (MA)
Massasoit Comm Coll (MA)
Mater Dei Coll (NY)
Mayland Comm Coll (NC)
McDowell Tech Comm Coll (NC)
McHenry County Coll (IL)
McIntosh Coll (NH)
McLennan Comm Coll (TX)
Mendocino Coll (CA)
Mercer County Comm Coll (NJ)
Mesa Comm Coll (AZ)
Miami-Dade Comm Coll (FL)
Middle Georgia Coll (GA)
Middlesex Comm Coll (MA)
Middlesex County Coll (NJ)
Midland Coll (TX)
Midlands Tech Coll (SC)
Mid Michigan Comm Coll (MI)
Mid-Plains Comm Coll (NE)
Milwaukee Area Tech Coll (WI)
Mineral Area Coll (MO)
MiraCosta Coll (CA)
Mississippi County Comm Coll (AR)
Mississippi Delta Comm Coll (MS)
Mississippi Gulf Coast Comm Coll (MS)
Mitchell Coll (CT)
Mitchell Comm Coll (NC)
Modesto Jr Coll (CA)
Mohawk Valley Comm Coll (NY)
Monroe Comm Coll (NY)
Montcalm Comm Coll (MI)
Monterey Peninsula Coll (CA)
Montgomery Coll (TX)
Montgomery College–Rockville Cmps (MD)
Montgomery Comm Coll (NC)
Montgomery County Comm Coll (PA)
Moraine Valley Comm Coll (IL)
Mountain Empire Comm Coll (VA)
Mount Ida Coll (MA)
Mount Wachusett Comm Coll (MA)
Muskegon Comm Coll (MI)
Muskingum Area Tech Coll (OH)
Napa Valley Coll (CA)
Nassau Comm Coll (NY)
Naugatuck Valley Community–Tech Coll (CT)
Navarro Coll (TX)
Nebraska Indian Comm Coll (NE)
Neosho County Comm Coll (KS)
Newbury Coll (MA)
New Hampshire Tech Inst (NH)
New Mexico Military Inst (NM)
New Mexico State University–Carlsbad (NM)
New Mexico State University–Grants (NM)
New River Comm Coll (VA)
Niagara County Comm Coll (NY)
Northampton County Area Comm Coll (PA)
North Central Michigan Coll (MI)
North Central Missouri Coll (MO)
North Central Tech Coll (OH)
North Central Texas Coll (TX)
North Country Comm Coll (NY)
Northeast Comm Coll (NE)
Northeastern Oklahoma A&M Coll (OK)
Northeast Mississippi Comm Coll (MS)
Northeast Texas Comm Coll (TX)
Northern Essex Comm Coll (MA)
Northern Oklahoma Coll (OK)
North Harris Coll (TX)
North Idaho Coll (ID)
Northland Comm and Tech Coll (MN)
Northland Pioneer Coll (AZ)
North Shore Comm Coll (MA)
NorthWest Arkansas Comm Coll (AR)
Northwestern Connecticut Comm-Tech Coll (CT)
Northwestern Michigan Coll (MI)
Northwest-Shoals Comm Coll (AL)
Northwest State Comm Coll (OH)
Norwalk Comm-Tech Coll (CT)
Oakland Comm Coll (MI)
Ocean County Coll (NJ)
Odessa Coll (TX)
Ohlone Coll (CA)
Okaloosa-Walton Comm Coll (FL)
Olympic Coll (WA)
Onondaga Comm Coll (NY)
Orangeburg-Calhoun Tech Coll (SC)
Orange County Comm Coll (NY)
Palm Beach Comm Coll (FL)
Palomar Coll (CA)
Palo Verde Coll (CA)
Parkland Coll (IL)
Pasadena City Coll (CA)
Pasco-Hernando Comm Coll (FL)
Passaic County Comm Coll (NJ)
Paul D Camp Comm Coll (VA)
Peninsula Coll (WA)
Penn Valley Comm Coll (MO)
Pensacola Jr Coll (FL)
Piedmont Tech Coll (SC)
Piedmont Virginia Comm Coll (VA)
Pierce Coll (WA)
Pikes Peak Comm Coll (CO)
Pima Comm Coll (AZ)
Pitt Comm Coll (NC)
Polk Comm Coll (FL)
Porterville Coll (CA)
Portland Comm Coll (OR)
Prairie State Coll (IL)
Prince George's Comm Coll (MD)
Pueblo Comm Coll (CO)
Quincy Coll (MA)
Quinsigamond Comm Coll (MA)
Rancho Santiago Coll (CA)
Randolph Comm Coll (NC)
Raritan Valley Comm Coll (NJ)
Redlands Comm Coll (OK)
Red Rocks Comm Coll (CO)
Rend Lake Coll (IL)
Richmond Comm Coll (NC)
Ricks Coll (ID)
Rio Hondo Coll (CA)
Riverside Comm Coll (CA)
Roane State Comm Coll (TN)
Roanoke-Chowan Comm Coll (NC)
Rockingham Comm Coll (NC)
Rockland Comm Coll (NY)
Rock Valley Coll (IL)
Rogers State Coll (OK)
Rogue Comm Coll (OR)
Rose State Coll (OK)
Rowan-Cabarrus Comm Coll (NC)
Sacramento City Coll (CA)
St Catharine Coll (KY)
Saint Charles County Comm Coll (MO)
St Clair County Comm Coll (MI)
St Johns River Comm Coll (FL)
St Louis Comm Coll at Florissant Valley (MO)
St Louis Comm Coll at Forest Park (MO)
St Louis Comm Coll at Meramec (MO)
Salem Comm Coll (NJ)
Salt Lake Comm Coll (UT)
Sampson Comm Coll (NC)
San Antonio Coll (TX)
Sandhills Comm Coll (NC)
San Diego Miramar Coll (CA)
San Jacinto College–Central Cmps (TX)
San Jacinto College–North Cmps (TX)
San Jose City Coll (CA)
Santa Barbara City Coll (CA)
Santa Fe Comm Coll (FL)
Santa Fe Comm Coll (NM)
Santa Monica Coll (CA)
Santa Rosa Jr Coll (CA)
Sauk Valley Comm Coll (IL)
Schenectady County Comm Coll (NY)
Schoolcraft Coll (MI)
Scott Comm Coll (IA)
Scottsdale Comm Coll (AZ)
Seminole Comm Coll (FL)
Shasta Coll (CA)
Shelby State Comm Coll (TN)
Sheridan Coll (WY)
Shoreline Comm Coll (WA)
Sierra Coll (CA)
Sinclair Comm Coll (OH)
Skyline Coll (CA)
Snead State Comm Coll (AL)
Snow Coll (UT)
Solano Comm Coll (CA)
Southeastern Comm Coll (NC)
Southeastern Comm Coll, North Cmps, West Burlington (IA)
Southern Maine Tech Coll (ME)
Southern West Virginia Comm and Tech Coll (WV)
South Florida Comm Coll (FL)
South Georgia Coll (GA)
South Plains Coll (TX)
Southside Virginia Comm Coll (VA)
South Suburban Coll (IL)
Southwestern Coll (CA)
Southwestern Oregon Comm Coll (OR)
Southwest Texas Jr Coll (TX)
Spartanburg Methodist Coll (SC)
Spoon River Coll (IL)
Springfield Tech Comm Coll (MA)
Stanly Comm Coll (NC)
State Fair Comm Coll (MO)
State U of NY Coll of Tech at Canton (NY)
State U of NY Coll of Tech at Farmingdale (NY)
Suffolk County Comm College–Ammerman Cmps (NY)
Suffolk County Comm Coll–Eastern Cmps (NY)
Suffolk County Comm Coll–Western Cmps (NY)
Sullivan County Comm Coll (NY)
Surry Comm Coll (NC)
Sussex County Comm Coll (NJ)
Tacoma Comm Coll (WA)
Taft Coll (CA)
Tallahassee Comm Coll (FL)
Tarrant County Jr Coll (TX)
Temple Coll (TX)
Texarkana Coll (TX)
Texas Southmost Coll (TX)
Three Rivers Comm Coll (MO)
Three Rivers Comm-Tech Coll (CT)
Tomball Coll (TX)
Tompkins Cortland Comm Coll (NY)
Treasure Valley Comm Coll (OR)
Tri-County Tech Coll (SC)
Trident Tech Coll (SC)
Trinity Valley Comm Coll (TX)
Triton Coll (IL)
Truckee Meadows Comm Coll (NV)
Tulsa Jr Coll (OK)
Tunxis Comm Tech Coll (CT)
Tyler Jr Coll (TX)
Ulster County Comm Coll (NY)
Umpqua Comm Coll (OR)
Union County Coll (NJ)
United Tribes Tech Coll (ND)
U of Cincinnati Clermont Coll (OH)
U of Hawaii–Hawaii Comm Coll (HI)
U of Hawaii–Maui Comm Coll (HI)
U of Maine at Augusta (ME)
U of New Mexico–Gallup Branch (NM)
U of New Mexico–Valencia Cmps (NM)
U of South Carolina at Lancaster (SC)
Valencia Comm Coll (FL)
Valley Forge Military Coll (PA)
Vance-Granville Comm Coll (NC)
Ventura Coll (CA)
Vermilion Comm Coll (MN)
Vernon Regional Jr Coll (TX)
Vincennes U (IN)
Virginia Western Comm Coll (VA)
Wake Tech Comm Coll (NC)
Wallace State Comm Coll (AL)
Walla Walla Comm Coll (WA)
Walters State Comm Coll (TN)
Warren County Comm Coll (NJ)
Washtenaw Comm Coll (MI)
Waubonsee Comm Coll (IL)
Waycross Coll (GA)
Wayne Comm Coll (NC)
Wayne County Comm Coll (MI)
Weatherford Coll (TX)
Westchester Comm Coll (NY)
Western Nebraska Comm Coll, Scottsbluff (NE)
Western Nevada Comm Coll (NV)
Western Piedmont Comm Coll (NC)
Western Texas Coll (TX)
Western Wyoming Comm Coll (WY)
West Hills Comm Coll (CA)
West Los Angeles Coll (CA)
Westmoreland County Comm Coll (PA)
West Shore Comm Coll (MI)
West Valley Coll (CA)
West Virginia Northern Comm Coll (WV)
West Virginia U at Parkersburg (WV)
Wharton County Jr Coll (TX)
Wilkes Comm Coll (NC)
William Rainey Harper Coll (IL)
Willmar Comm Coll (MN)
Wilson Tech Comm Coll (NC)
Wor-Wic Comm Coll (MD)
Wytheville Comm Coll (VA)
Yakima Valley Comm Coll (WA)
Young Harris Coll (GA)
Yuba Coll (CA)

CRIMINOLOGY

Albuquerque Tech Vocational Inst (NM)
Butler County Comm Coll (PA)
Daytona Beach Comm Coll (FL)
Gulf Coast Comm Coll (FL)
Northland Comm and Tech Coll (MN)
Pensacola Jr Coll (FL)

CULINARY ARTS

Adirondack Comm Coll (NY)
Albuquerque Tech Vocational Inst (NM)
Alexandria Tech Coll (MN)
American River Coll (CA)
Art Inst of Atlanta (GA)
Art Inst of Fort Lauderdale (FL)
The Art Inst of Houston (TX)
Art Inst of Seattle (WA)
Asheville-Buncombe Tech Comm Coll (NC)
Atlantic Comm Coll (NJ)
Baltimore International Culinary Coll (MD)
Berkshire Comm Coll (MA)
Bishop State Comm Coll (AL)
Black Hawk Coll, Moline (IL)
Bucks County Comm Coll (PA)
Bunker Hill Comm Coll (MA)
Central Oregon Comm Coll (OR)
Central Piedmont Comm Coll (NC)
Charles Stewart Mott Comm Coll (MI)
Chippewa Valley Tech Coll (WI)
Cincinnati State Tech and Comm Coll (OH)
Clark Coll (WA)
Clinton Comm Coll (IA)
Coll of DuPage (IL)
Coll of Southern Idaho (ID)
Coll of the Desert (CA)
Coll of the Sequoias (CA)
Colorado Inst of Art (CO)
Colorado Mountn Coll, Roaring Fork Cmps-Spring Valley Ctr (CO)
Columbia Coll (CA)
Columbus State Comm Coll (OH)
Comm Coll of Allegheny County Allegheny Cmps (PA)
Comm Coll of Beaver County (PA)
Comm Coll of Philadelphia (PA)
Comm Coll of Southern Nevada (NV)
Contra Costa Coll (CA)
Culinary Inst of America (NY)
Cuyahoga Comm Coll, Metropolitan Cmps (OH)
Cypress Coll (CA)
Daytona Beach Comm Coll (FL)
Delgado Comm Coll (LA)
Del Mar Coll (TX)
Des Moines Area Comm Coll (IA)
Edmonds Comm Coll (WA)
Elaine P Nunez Comm Coll (LA)
El Camino Coll (CA)
El Centro Coll (TX)
Elgin Comm Coll (IL)
Erie Comm Coll, City Cmps (NY)
Florida Comm Coll at Jacksonville (FL)
Fox Valley Tech Coll (WI)
Galveston Coll (TX)
Grand Rapids Comm Coll (MI)
Guilford Tech Comm Coll (NC)
Gulf Coast Comm Coll (FL)
Harrisburg Area Comm Coll (PA)
Henry Ford Comm Coll (MI)
Hibbing Comm Coll (MN)
Hocking Coll (OH)

Associate Degree Programs at Two-Year Colleges
Culinary Arts–Data Processing

Horry-Georgetown Tech Coll (SC)
Hudson County Comm Coll (NJ)
Iowa Western Comm Coll (IA)
Ivy Tech State Coll–Central Indiana (IN)
Ivy Tech State Coll–Northeast (IN)
Ivy Tech State Coll–Northwest (IN)
James H Faulkner State Comm Coll (AL)
Jefferson Comm Coll (NY)
Jefferson State Comm Coll (AL)
Johnson & Wales U (CO)
Johnson & Wales U (VA)
Johnson County Comm Coll (KS)
Joliet Jr Coll (IL)
Keystone Coll (PA)
Kirkwood Comm Coll (IA)
Lane Comm Coll (OR)
Laney Coll (CA)
Lexington Coll (IL)
Linn-Benton Comm Coll (OR)
Los Angeles Mission Coll (CA)
Los Angeles Trade-Tech Coll (CA)
Luzerne County Comm Coll (PA)
Macomb Comm Coll (MI)
Madison Area Tech Coll (WI)
Manchester Comm-Tech Coll (CT)
Massasoit Comm Coll (MA)
Metropolitan Comm Coll (NE)
Middlesex County Coll (NJ)
Milwaukee Area Tech Coll (WI)
Monroe County Comm Coll (MI)
Moraine Valley Comm Coll (IL)
Newbury Coll (MA)
New England Culinary Inst (VT)
New England Inst of Tech & Florida Culinary Inst (FL)
New Hampshire Tech Coll, Berlin (NH)
Niagara County Comm Coll (NY)
Nicolet Area Tech Coll (WI)
North Dakota State Coll of Science (ND)
North Idaho Coll (ID)
North Seattle Comm Coll (WA)
Northwestern Michigan Coll (MI)
Oakland Comm Coll (MI)
Odessa Coll (TX)
Oklahoma State U, Okmulgee (OK)
Onondaga Comm Coll (NY)
Orange Coast Coll (CA)
Oxnard Coll (CA)
Ozarka Tech Coll (AR)
Paul Smith's Coll (NY)
Pennsylvania Coll of Tech (PA)
Penn Valley Comm Coll (MO)
Pensacola Jr Coll (FL)
Pima Comm Coll (AZ)
Pueblo Comm Coll (CO)
Rend Lake Coll (IL)
Renton Tech Coll (WA)
St Cloud Tech Coll (MN)
St Louis Comm Coll at Forest Park (MO)
St Philip's Coll (TX)
Salt Lake Comm Coll (UT)
Sandhills Comm Coll (NC)
San Jacinto College–North Cmps (TX)
San Joaquin Delta Coll (CA)
Santa Fe Comm Coll (NM)
Santa Rosa Jr Coll (CA)
Schenectady County Comm Coll (NY)
Schoolcraft Coll (MI)
Scott Comm Coll (IA)
Scottsdale Comm Coll (AZ)
Seattle Central Comm Coll (WA)
Shasta Coll (CA)
Sinclair Comm Coll (OH)
Skagit Valley Coll (WA)
Southeast Comm Coll, Lincoln Cmps (NE)
Southern Maine Tech Coll (ME)
South Florida Comm Coll (FL)
South Puget Sound Comm Coll (WA)
South Seattle Comm Coll (WA)
Southwestern Indian Polytechnic Inst (NM)
Spokane Comm Coll (WA)
State U of NY Coll of A&T at Cobleskill (NY)
State U of NY Coll of Tech at Alfred (NY)
State U of NY Coll of Tech at Delhi (NY)
Sullivan County Comm Coll (NY)
Texas State Tech Coll–Waco/Marshall Cmps (TX)
Trident Tech Coll (SC)
Triton Coll (IL)
Truckee Meadows Comm Coll (NV)
U of Hawaii–Kapiolani Comm Coll (HI)
U of Hawaii–Kauai Comm Coll (HI)
U of Kentucky, Jefferson Comm Coll (KY)
Vincennes U (IN)
Wake Tech Comm Coll (NC)
Washtenaw Comm Coll (MI)
Wayne County Comm Coll (MI)
Westchester Comm Coll (NY)
Westmoreland County Comm Coll (PA)
West Virginia Northern Comm Coll (WV)
William Rainey Harper Coll (IL)

CYTOTECHNOLOGY
Allen County Comm Coll (KS)
Barton County Comm Coll (KS)
Butler County Comm Coll (KS)
Highland Comm Coll (KS)
Hutchinson Comm Coll and Area Vocational Sch (KS)
Keystone Coll (PA)
Manor Jr Coll (PA)
UAB Walker Coll (AL)

DAIRY SCIENCES
Chippewa Valley Tech Coll (WI)
Cisco Jr Coll (TX)
Coll of the Sequoias (CA)
Highland Comm Coll (KS)
Hill Coll of the Hill Jr Coll District (TX)
Hiwassee Coll (TN)
Lakeshore Tech Coll (WI)
Modesto Jr Coll (CA)
Mt San Antonio Coll (CA)
Northeastern Oklahoma A&M Coll (OK)
Northeast Iowa Comm Coll, Calmar Cmps (IA)
Northeast Mississippi Comm Coll (MS)
Northeast Texas Comm Coll (TX)
Ohio State U Ag Tech Inst (OH)
Ricks Coll (ID)
Southwest Wisconsin Tech Coll (WI)
State U of NY Coll of A&T at Cobleskill (NY)
State U of NY Coll of A&T at Morrisville (NY)
State U of NY Coll of Tech at Alfred (NY)
Vermont Tech Coll (VT)

DANCE
Allan Hancock Coll (CA)
Bergen Comm Coll (NJ)
Borough of Manhattan Comm Coll of City U of NY (NY)
Brevard Coll (NC)
Cañada Coll (CA)
Central Piedmont Comm Coll (NC)
Chaffey Coll (CA)
Coll of Marin (CA)
County Coll of Morris (NJ)
Cypress Coll (CA)
Daytona Beach Comm Coll (FL)
Dean Coll (MA)
De Anza Coll (CA)
Dixie Coll (UT)
Essex Comm Coll (MD)
Fresno City Coll (CA)
Fullerton Coll (CA)
Grossmont Coll (CA)
Lake Tahoe Comm Coll (CA)
Laney Coll (CA)
Long Beach City Coll (CA)
Lon Morris Coll (TX)
Mercer County Comm Coll (NJ)
Miami-Dade Comm Coll (FL)
Middlesex County Coll (NJ)
Midland Coll (TX)
MiraCosta Coll (CA)
Monterey Peninsula Coll (CA)
Montgomery College–Rockville Cmps (MD)
Mt San Jacinto Coll (CA)
Navarro Coll (TX)
Northern Essex Comm Coll (MA)
Orange Coast Coll (CA)
Palomar Coll (CA)
Pikes Peak Comm Coll (CO)
Rancho Santiago Coll (CA)
Ricks Coll (ID)
St Catharine Coll (KY)
St Johns River Comm Coll (FL)
San Joaquin Delta Coll (CA)
San Juan Coll (NM)
Santa Monica Coll (CA)
Sinclair Comm Coll (OH)
Snow Coll (UT)
Southwestern Coll (CA)
Trinity Valley Comm Coll (TX)
Westchester Comm Coll (NY)
Western Wyoming Comm Coll (WY)

DATA PROCESSING
Abraham Baldwin Ag Coll (GA)
Adirondack Comm Coll (NY)
Allegany Comm Coll (MD)
Allen County Comm Coll (KS)
Alpena Comm Coll (MI)
American River Coll (CA)
Angelina Coll (TX)
Anne Arundel Comm Coll (MD)
Anson Comm Coll (NC)
Antelope Valley Coll (CA)
Atlanta Metropolitan Coll (GA)
Bainbridge Coll (GA)
Baker Coll of Jackson (MI)
Bakersfield Coll (CA)
Baltimore City Comm Coll (MD)
Bee County Coll (TX)
Belleville Area Coll (IL)
Bellevue Comm Coll (WA)
Berkeley Coll, White Plains (NY)
Berkshire Comm Coll (MA)
Bevill State Comm Coll (AL)
Big Bend Comm Coll (WA)
Bishop State Comm Coll (AL)
Black Hawk Coll, Moline (IL)
Blackhawk Tech Coll (WI)
Black River Tech Coll (AR)
Blue Ridge Comm Coll (NC)
Borough of Manhattan Comm Coll of City U of NY (NY)
Bossier Parish Comm Coll (LA)
Brevard Comm Coll (FL)
Bronx Comm Coll of City U of NY (NY)
Broome Comm Coll (NY)
Broward Comm Coll (FL)
Brunswick Coll (GA)
Bryant and Stratton Business Inst, E Hills Cmps, Williamsville (NY)
Bucks County Comm Coll (PA)
Burlington County Coll (NJ)
Butler County Comm Coll (KS)
Butler County Comm Coll (PA)
Butte Coll (CA)
Cabrillo Coll (CA)
Caldwell Comm Coll and Tech Inst (NC)
Camden County Coll (NJ)
Cañada Coll (CA)
Capital Comm Tech Coll (CT)
Carl Sandburg Coll (IL)
Casper Coll (WY)
Castle Coll (NH)
Catawba Valley Comm Coll (NC)
Catonsville Comm Coll (MD)
Cayuga County Comm Coll (NY)
Cecil Comm Coll (MD)
Central City Business Inst (NY)
Central Coll (KS)
Central Comm College–Grand Island Cmps (NE)
Central Comm College–Hastings Cmps (NE)
Central Comm College–Platte Cmps (NE)
Central Piedmont Comm Coll (NC)
Central Texas Coll (TX)
Central Virginia Comm Coll (VA)
Central Wyoming Coll (WY)
Cerritos Coll (CA)
Cerro Coso Comm Coll (CA)
Chabot Coll (CA)
Champlain Coll (VT)
Charles County Comm Coll (MD)
Chattahoochee Tech Inst (GA)
Chattahoochee Valley State Comm Coll (AL)
Chattanooga State Tech Comm Coll (TN)
Chemeketa Comm Coll (OR)
Chesapeake Coll (MD)
Chesterfield-Marlboro Tech Coll (SC)
Chippewa Valley Tech Coll (WI)
Cincinnati State Tech and Comm Coll (OH)
Cisco Jr Coll (TX)
Citrus Coll (CA)
City Colls of Chicago, Harold Washington Coll (IL)
City Colls of Chicago, Kennedy-King Coll (IL)
City Colls of Chicago, Malcolm X Coll (IL)
City Colls of Chicago, Olive-Harvey Coll (IL)
City Colls of Chicago, Richard J Daley Coll (IL)
City Colls of Chicago, Wilbur Wright Coll (IL)
Clark Coll (WA)
Clatsop Comm Coll (OR)
Colby Comm Coll (KS)
Coll of Lake County (IL)
Coll of Marin (CA)
Coll of the Siskiyous (CA)
Collin County Comm Coll (TX)
Columbia-Greene Comm Coll (NY)
Columbia Jr Coll of Business (SC)
Columbus State Comm Coll (OH)
Comm Coll of Allegheny County Allegheny Cmps (PA)
Comm Coll of Allegheny County Boyce Cmps (PA)
Comm Coll of Allegheny County North Cmps (PA)
Comm Coll of Allegheny County South Cmps (PA)
Comm Coll of Beaver County (PA)
Comm Coll of Philadelphia (PA)
Comm Coll of Southern Nevada (NV)
Connors State Coll (OK)
Copiah-Lincoln Comm Coll (MS)
Cuesta Coll (CA)
Cypress Coll (CA)
Dabney S Lancaster Comm Coll (VA)
Danville Area Comm Coll (IL)
Darton Coll (GA)
Davidson County Comm Coll (NC)
Davis Coll (OH)
DeKalb Coll (GA)
Delaware Tech & Comm Coll, Jack F Owens Cmps (DE)
Delaware Tech & Comm Coll, Stanton/Wilmington Cmps (DE)
Delaware Tech & Comm Coll, Terry Cmps (DE)
Delta Coll (MI)
Des Moines Area Comm Coll (IA)
Dodge City Comm Coll (KS)
Donnelly Coll (KS)
Durham Tech Comm Coll (NC)
East Central Coll (MO)
East Central Comm Coll (MS)
East Los Angeles Coll (CA)
ECPI Coll of Tech, Virginia Beach (VA)
ECPI Computer Inst, Richmond (VA)
Edgecombe Comm Coll (NC)
Edison State Comm Coll (OH)
El Camino Coll (CA)
El Centro Coll (TX)
Elgin Comm Coll (IL)
Ellsworth Comm Coll (IA)
Erie Comm Coll, City Cmps (NY)
Essex County Coll (NJ)
Eugenio María de Hostos Comm Coll of City U of NY (NY)
Everett Comm Coll (WA)
Evergreen Valley Coll (CA)
Finger Lakes Comm Coll (NY)
Fiorello H LaGuardia Comm Coll of City U of NY (NY)
Florida National Coll (FL)
Forsyth Tech Comm Coll (NC)
Fort Belknap Coll (MT)
Frank Phillips Coll (TX)
Frederick Comm Coll (MD)
Fresno City Coll (CA)
Fulton-Montgomery Comm Coll (NY)
Garland County Comm Coll (AR)
Gateway Comm-Tech Coll (CT)
George C Wallace State Comm Coll, Dothan (AL)
Germanna Comm Coll (VA)
Glendale Comm Coll (AZ)
Gloucester County Coll (NJ)
Gogebic Comm Coll (MI)
Grand Rapids Comm Coll (MI)
Grays Harbor Coll (WA)
Great Lakes Jr Coll of Business (MI)
Hagerstown Business Coll (MD)
Hamilton Business Coll (IA)
Harrisburg Area Comm Coll (PA)
Hartnell Coll (CA)
Heald Business Coll, Concord (CA)
Heald Business Coll, Rancho Cordova (CA)
Heald Business Coll, San Francisco (CA)
Henry Ford Comm Coll (MI)
Herkimer County Comm Coll (NY)
Herzing Coll of Business and Tech (AL)
Herzing Coll of Business and Tech (GA)
Highland Comm Coll (IL)
Highland Comm Coll (KS)
Highland Park Comm Coll (MI)
Highline Comm Coll (WA)
Hill Coll of the Hill Jr Coll District (TX)
Hillsborough Comm Coll (FL)
Hinds Comm Coll (MS)
Hiwassee Coll (TN)
Hocking Coll (OH)
Holmes Comm Coll (MS)
Housatonic Comm-Tech Coll (CT)
Howard Comm Coll (MD)
Hudson County Comm Coll (NJ)
Hudson Valley Comm Coll (NY)
Hutchinson Comm Coll and Area Vocational Sch (KS)
Illinois Central Coll (IL)
Illinois Eastern Comm Colls, Lincoln Trail Coll (IL)
Illinois Valley Comm Coll (IL)
Imperial Valley Coll (CA)
Independence Comm Coll (KS)
Iowa Central Comm Coll (IA)
Iowa Lakes Comm Coll (IA)
Irvine Valley Coll (CA)
Itawamba Comm Coll (MS)
Ivy Tech State Coll–Northeast (IN)
Jackson Comm Coll (MI)
Jackson State Comm Coll (TN)
Jefferson Coll (MO)
Jefferson Comm Coll (OH)
John A Logan Coll (IL)
Johnson County Comm Coll (KS)
Jones County Jr Coll (MS)
J Sargeant Reynolds Comm Coll (VA)
Kalamazoo Valley Comm Coll (MI)
Kansas City Kansas Comm Coll (KS)
Kellogg Comm Coll (MI)
Kent State U, East Liverpool Cmps (OH)
Kent State U, Geauga Cmps (OH)
Kingsborough Comm Coll of City U of NY (NY)
Kingwood Coll (TX)
Kirkwood Comm Coll (IA)
Kishwaukee Coll (IL)
Labette Comm Coll (KS)
Lake Land Coll (IL)
Lakeland Comm Coll (OH)
Lake Michigan Coll (MI)
Lakeshore Tech Coll (WI)
Lakewood Comm Coll (MN)
Lamar Comm Coll (CO)
Lamar University–Orange (TX)
Lansdale Sch of Business (PA)
Lansing Comm Coll (MI)
Laredo Comm Coll (TX)
Lee Coll (TX)
Lewis and Clark Comm Coll (IL)
Lewis Coll of Business (MI)
Lincoln Coll, Normal (IL)
Lincoln Land Comm Coll (IL)
Long Beach City Coll (CA)
Longview Comm Coll (MO)
Los Angeles City Coll (CA)
Los Angeles Harbor Coll (CA)
Los Angeles Pierce Coll (CA)
Los Angeles Southwest Coll (CA)
Los Angeles Trade-Tech Coll (CA)
Los Angeles Valley Coll (CA)
Lower Columbia Coll (WA)
Luzerne County Comm Coll (PA)
Macon Coll (GA)
Madison Area Tech Coll (WI)
Manchester Comm-Tech Coll (CT)
Maple Woods Comm Coll (MO)
Marian Court Coll (MA)
Marion Tech Coll (OH)
Mendocino Coll (CA)
Merced Coll (CA)
Mercer County Comm Coll (NJ)
Meridian Comm Coll (MS)
Mesa Comm Coll (AZ)
Miami-Dade Comm Coll (FL)
Michiana Coll (IN)
Middle Georgia Coll (GA)
Midland Coll (TX)
Midlands Tech Coll (SC)
Mid Michigan Comm Coll (MI)
Mid-Plains Comm Coll (NE)
Mid-State Tech Coll (WI)
Milwaukee Area Tech Coll (WI)
Mississippi County Comm Coll (AR)
Mississippi Delta Comm Coll (MS)
Mitchell Comm Coll (NC)
Moberly Area Comm Coll (MO)

Associate Degree Programs at Two-Year Colleges
Data Processing–Dental Services

Mohawk Valley Comm Coll (NY)
Monroe Comm Coll (NY)
Monroe County Comm Coll (MI)
Montcalm Comm Coll (MI)
Monterey Peninsula Coll (CA)
Montgomery College–Germantown Cmps (MD)
Montgomery College–Rockville Cmps (MD)
Montgomery College–Takoma Park Cmps (MD)
Montgomery County Comm Coll (PA)
Moorpark Coll (CA)
Moraine Park Tech Coll (WI)
Moraine Valley Comm Coll (IL)
Morton Coll (IL)
Mount Ida Coll (MA)
Mt San Antonio Coll (CA)
Mount Wachusett Comm Coll (MA)
Muskegon Comm Coll (MI)
Muskingum Area Tech Coll (OH)
Napa Valley Coll (CA)
Nashville State Tech Inst (TN)
Nassau Comm Coll (NY)
National Business Coll, Bluefield (VA)
National Business Coll, Harrisonburg (VA)
Navarro Coll (TX)
Nettleton Career Coll (SD)
New Mexico Jr Coll (NM)
New Mexico State University–Alamogordo (NM)
New Mexico State University–Grants (NM)
Newport Business Inst (PA)
New York City Tech Coll of the City U of NY (NY)
Nicolet Area Tech Coll (WI)
Northampton County Area Comm Coll (PA)
North Arkansas Comm/Tech Coll (AR)
North Central Michigan Coll (MI)
North Central Missouri Coll (MO)
North Central Texas Coll (TX)
Northeast Comm Coll (NE)
Northeastern Jr Coll (CO)
Northeast Iowa Comm Coll, Peosta Cmps (IA)
Northeast Mississippi Comm Coll (MS)
Northeast State Tech Comm Coll (TN)
Northern Essex Comm Coll (MA)
Northern Maine Tech Coll (ME)
Northern Marianas Coll (MP)
North Harris Coll (TX)
North Lake Coll (TX)
Northland Pioneer Coll (AZ)
North Seattle Comm Coll (WA)
NorthWest Arkansas Comm Coll (AR)
Northwestern Business Coll (IL)
Northwestern Michigan Coll (MI)
Northwest Mississippi Comm Coll (MS)
Norwalk Comm-Tech Coll (CT)
Oakton Comm Coll (IL)
Odessa Coll (TX)
Oklahoma State U, Oklahoma City (OK)
Onondaga Comm Coll (NY)
Orange Coast Coll (CA)
Orange County Comm Coll (NY)
Otero Jr Coll (CO)
Owensboro Comm Coll (KY)
Owensboro Jr Coll of Business (KY)
Palm Beach Comm Coll (FL)
Panama Canal Coll (Republic of Panama)
Parkland Coll (IL)
Parks Jr Coll (CO)
Pasadena City Coll (CA)
Patrick Henry Comm Coll (VA)
Paul D Camp Comm Coll (VA)
Pellissippi State Tech Comm Coll (TN)
Peninsula Coll (WA)
Penn Valley Comm Coll (MO)
Phillips County Comm Coll (AR)
Phillips Jr Coll, Condie Cmps (CA)
Phillips Jr Coll of Springfield (MO)
Piedmont Virginia Comm Coll (VA)
Polk Comm Coll (FL)
Potomac State Coll of West Virginia U (WV)
Quinsigamond Comm Coll (MA)
Randolph Comm Coll (NC)
Raritan Valley Comm Coll (NJ)
Rasmussen Coll Mankato (MN)
Reading Area Comm Coll (PA)
Richland Coll (TX)
Richmond Comm Coll (NC)
Rich Mountain Comm Coll (AR)
Ricks Coll (ID)
Riverside Comm Coll (CA)
Rochester Business Inst (NY)
Rockland Comm Coll (NY)
Rock Valley Coll (IL)
Rowan-Cabarrus Comm Coll (NC)
Sacramento City Coll (CA)
St Cloud Tech Coll (MN)
St Louis Comm Coll at Florissant Valley (MO)
St Louis Comm Coll at Forest Park (MO)
St Philip's Coll (TX)
Salt Lake Comm Coll (UT)
San Antonio Coll (TX)
San Bernardino Valley Coll (CA)
Sandhills Comm Coll (NC)
San Diego City Coll (CA)
San Diego Mesa Coll (CA)
Sanford-Brown Coll, St Charles (MO)
San Jacinto College–Central Cmps (TX)
San Jacinto College–North Cmps (TX)
San Jacinto College–South Cmps (TX)
San Jose City Coll (CA)
San Juan Coll (NM)
Santa Fe Comm Coll (FL)
Santa Monica Coll (CA)
Sauk Valley Comm Coll (IL)
Sawyer Coll of Business, Cleveland (OH)
Sawyer Coll of Business, Cleveland Heights (OH)
Schenectady County Comm Coll (NY)
Seminole Comm Coll (FL)
Seward County Comm Coll (KS)
Shelton State Comm Coll (AL)
Skyline Coll (CA)
Southeast Comm Coll, Milford Cmps (NE)
Southern Coll (FL)
South Plains Coll (TX)
South Puget Sound Comm Coll (WA)
South Suburban Coll (IL)
Southwestern Indian Polytechnic Inst (NM)
Southwestern Michigan Coll (MI)
Southwest Texas Jr Coll (TX)
Southwest Wisconsin Tech Coll (WI)
Spokane Comm Coll (WA)
Spoon River Coll (IL)
Springfield Tech Comm Coll (MA)
State Comm Coll of East St Louis (IL)
State Tech Inst at Memphis (TN)
State U of NY Coll of A&T at Cobleskill (NY)
State U of NY Coll of A&T at Morrisville (NY)
State U of NY Coll of Tech at Alfred (NY)
State U of NY Coll of Tech at Farmingdale (NY)
Stratton Coll (WI)
Suffolk County Comm College–Ammerman Cmps (NY)
Suffolk County Comm Coll–Western Cmps (NY)
Sullivan County Comm Coll (NY)
Tacoma Comm Coll (WA)
Taft Coll (CA)
Tallahassee Comm Coll (FL)
Temple Coll (TX)
Texarkana Coll (TX)
Texas Southmost Coll (TX)
Texas State Tech Coll–Harlingen Cmps (TX)
Three Rivers Comm-Tech Coll (CT)
Tidewater Comm Coll (VA)
Tri-County Tech Coll (SC)
Trinidad State Jr Coll (CO)
Trinity Valley Comm Coll (TX)
Triton Coll (IL)
Truckee Meadows Comm Coll (NV)
Tulsa Jr Coll (OK)
Tunxis Comm Tech Coll (CT)
Ulster County Comm Coll (NY)
Union County Coll (NJ)
The U of Akron–Wayne Coll (OH)
U of Hawaii–Hawaii Comm Coll (HI)
U of Hawaii–Kapiolani Comm Coll (HI)
U of Kentucky, Hazard Comm Coll (KY)
U of Kentucky, Henderson Comm Coll (KY)
U of Kentucky, Jefferson Comm Coll (KY)
U of Kentucky, Southeast Comm Coll (KY)
U of North Dakota–Lake Region (ND)
Utica Sch of Commerce (NY)
Vance-Granville Comm Coll (NC)
Vermilion Comm Coll (MN)
Virginia Highlands Comm Coll (VA)
Virginia Western Comm Coll (VA)
Wake Tech Comm Coll (NC)
Waldorf Coll (IA)
Walla Walla Comm Coll (WA)
Warren County Comm Coll (NJ)
Washington State Comm Coll (OH)
Washtenaw Comm Coll (MI)
Waukesha County Tech Coll (WI)
Wayne County Comm Coll (MI)
Webster Coll, Ocala (FL)
Westchester Business Inst (NY)
Westchester Comm Coll (NY)
Western Oklahoma State Coll (OK)
Western Wisconsin Tech Coll (WI)
Western Wyoming Comm Coll (WY)
West Los Angeles Coll (CA)
Westmoreland County Comm Coll (PA)
West Shore Comm Coll (MI)
West Valley Coll (CA)
West Virginia Career Coll, Charleston (WV)
West Virginia Northern Comm Coll (WV)
West Virginia U at Parkersburg (WV)
Wharton County Jr Coll (TX)
William Rainey Harper Coll (IL)
Willmar Comm Coll (MN)

DEAF INTERPRETER TRAINING

Allen County Comm Coll (KS)
American River Coll (CA)
Austin Comm Coll (TX)
Bishop State Comm Coll (AL)
Catonsville Comm Coll (MD)
Central Piedmont Comm Coll (NC)
Charles Stewart Mott Comm Coll (MI)
Chattanooga State Tech Comm Coll (TN)
Coll of St Catherine–Minneapolis (MN)
Coll of the Sequoias (CA)
Collin County Comm Coll (TX)
Columbus State Comm Coll (OH)
Comm Coll of Allegheny County North Cmps (PA)
Comm Coll of Philadelphia (PA)
Comm Coll of Southern Nevada (NV)
DeKalb Coll (GA)
Eastfield Coll (TX)
El Paso Comm Coll (TX)
Floyd Coll (GA)
Front Range Comm Coll (CO)
Golden West Coll (CA)
Hillsborough Comm Coll (FL)
Houston Comm Coll System (TX)
Inver Hills Comm Coll (MN)
Iowa Western Comm Coll (IA)
John A Logan Coll (IL)
Johnson County Comm Coll (KS)
Lansing Comm Coll (MI)
Los Angeles Pierce Coll (CA)
Los Angeles Southwest Coll (CA)
McLennan Comm Coll (TX)
Miami-Dade Comm Coll (FL)
Mt San Antonio Coll (CA)
Nassau Comm Coll (NY)
New River Comm Coll (VA)
Northcentral Tech Coll (WI)
Northern Essex Comm Coll (MA)
Northwestern Connecticut Comm-Tech Coll (CT)
Ohlone Coll (CA)
Oklahoma State U, Oklahoma City (OK)
Palomar Coll (CA)
Pasadena City Coll (CA)
Pima Comm Coll (AZ)
Portland Comm Coll (OR)
Riverside Comm Coll (CA)
St Louis Comm Coll at Florissant Valley (MO)
St Paul Tech Coll (MN)
Salt Lake Comm Coll (UT)
Scott Comm Coll (IA)
Seattle Central Comm Coll (WA)
Sinclair Comm Coll (OH)
South Puget Sound Comm Coll (WA)
SouthWest Collegiate Inst for the Deaf (TX)
Spokane Falls Comm Coll (WA)
Suffolk County Comm College–Ammerman Cmps (NY)
Tarrant County Jr Coll (TX)
Terra State Comm Coll (OH)
Tulsa Jr Coll (OK)
Tyler Jr Coll (TX)
Union County Coll (NJ)
Vincennes U (IN)
Vista Comm Coll (CA)
Waubonsee Comm Coll (IL)
William Rainey Harper Coll (IL)
Wilson Tech Comm Coll (NC)

DENTAL SERVICES

Alamance Comm Coll (NC)
Allan Hancock Coll (CA)
Allegany Comm Coll (MD)
Andrew Coll (GA)
Asheville-Buncombe Tech Comm Coll (NC)
Atlanta Metropolitan Coll (GA)
Bakersfield Coll (CA)
Baltimore City Comm Coll (MD)
Bee County Coll (TX)
Bergen Comm Coll (NJ)
Black Hawk Coll, Moline (IL)
Brevard Comm Coll (FL)
Briarwood Coll (CT)
Bristol Comm Coll (MA)
Broome Comm Coll (NY)
Broward Comm Coll (FL)
Brunswick Coll (GA)
Cabrillo Coll (CA)
Camden County Coll (NJ)
Cape Cod Comm Coll (MA)
Central Comm College–Hastings Cmps (NE)
Central Florida Comm Coll (FL)
Central Piedmont Comm Coll (NC)
Cerritos Coll (CA)
Chabot Coll (CA)
Charles Stewart Mott Comm Coll (MI)
Chattanooga State Tech Comm Coll (TN)
Chemeketa Comm Coll (OR)
Chippewa Valley Tech Coll (WI)
Citrus Coll (CA)
City Coll of San Francisco (CA)
City Colls of Chicago, Olive-Harvey Coll (IL)
City Colls of Chicago, Richard J Daley Coll (IL)
Clark Coll (WA)
Coastal Carolina Comm Coll (NC)
Coll of Alameda (CA)
Coll of Marin (CA)
Coll of San Mateo (CA)
Colorado Northwestern Comm Coll (CO)
Columbia State Comm Coll (TN)
Comm Coll of Philadelphia (PA)
Comm Coll of Rhode Island (RI)
Comm Coll of Southern Nevada (NV)
Comm Coll of the Air Force (AL)
Contra Costa Coll (CA)
Cuyahoga Comm Coll, Metropolitan Cmps (OH)
Cypress Coll (CA)
Dalton Coll (GA)
Darton Coll (GA)
DeKalb Coll (GA)
Delaware Tech & Comm Coll, Stanton/Wilmington Cmps (DE)
Delgado Comm Coll (LA)
Del Mar Coll (TX)
Delta Coll (MI)
Des Moines Area Comm Coll (IA)
Dixie Coll (UT)
Dodge City Comm Coll (KS)
Durham Tech Comm Coll (NC)
Edison Comm Coll (FL)
Elgin Comm Coll (IL)
El Paso Comm Coll (TX)
Erie Comm Coll, North Cmps (NY)
Erie Comm Coll, South Cmps (NY)
Essex County Coll (NJ)
Eugenio María de Hostos Comm Coll of City U of NY (NY)
Fayetteville Tech Comm Coll (NC)
Florence-Darlington Tech Coll (SC)
Florida Comm Coll at Jacksonville (FL)
Florida National Coll (FL)
Floyd Coll (GA)
Foothill Coll (CA)
Fresno City Coll (CA)
Gainesville Coll (GA)
Grand Rapids Comm Coll (MI)
Greenville Tech Coll (SC)
Guilford Tech Comm Coll (NC)
Gulf Coast Comm Coll (FL)
Gwinnett Tech Inst (GA)
Harcum Coll (PA)
Harrisburg Area Comm Coll (PA)
Hawkeye Comm Coll (IA)
Highland Comm Coll (KS)
Highline Comm Coll (WA)
Hinds Comm Coll (MS)
Hiwassee Coll (TN)
Howard Coll (TX)
Hudson Valley Comm Coll (NY)
Huertas Jr Coll (PR)
Huntington Jr Coll of Business (WV)
Hutchinson Comm Coll and Area Vocational Sch (KS)
Illinois Central Coll (IL)
Indian River Comm Coll (FL)
James H Faulkner State Comm Coll (AL)
Jefferson Comm Coll (OH)
John A Logan Coll (IL)
John C Calhoun State Comm Coll (AL)
Johnson County Comm Coll (KS)
J Sargeant Reynolds Comm Coll (VA)
Kalamazoo Valley Comm Coll (MI)
Kellogg Comm Coll (MI)
Kings River Comm Coll (CA)
Lake Area Vocational-Tech Inst (SD)
Lake Land Coll (IL)
Lakeland Comm Coll (OH)
Lake Michigan Coll (MI)
Lakeshore Tech Coll (WI)
Lake Washington Tech Coll (WA)
Lane Comm Coll (OR)
Lansing Comm Coll (MI)
Laramie County Comm Coll (WY)
Lewis and Clark Comm Coll (IL)
Lima Tech Coll (OH)
Long Beach City Coll (CA)
Los Angeles City Coll (CA)
Luzerne County Comm Coll (PA)
Macon Coll (GA)
Madison Area Tech Coll (WI)
Manor Jr Coll (PA)
Marshalltown Comm Coll (IA)
Massasoit Comm Coll (MA)
McCarrie Schools of Health Sci and Tech (PA)
Merced Coll (CA)
Meridian Comm Coll (MS)
Miami-Dade Comm Coll (FL)
Middlesex Comm Coll (MA)
Middlesex County Coll (NJ)
Midlands Tech Coll (SC)
Mid-Plains Comm Coll (NE)
Milwaukee Area Tech Coll (WI)
Minnesota Riverland Tech Coll (MN)
Modesto Jr Coll (CA)
Monroe Comm Coll (NY)
Montana State U Coll of Tech-Great Falls (MT)
Monterey Peninsula Coll (CA)
Montgomery College–Takoma Park Cmps (MD)
Montgomery County Comm Coll (PA)
Morton Coll (IL)
Mt Hood Comm Coll (OR)
Mount Ida Coll (MA)
Navarro Coll (TX)
New Hampshire Tech Inst (NH)
New York City Tech Coll of the City U of NY (NY)
Normandale Comm Coll (MN)
Northampton County Area Comm Coll (PA)
Northcentral Tech Coll (WI)
North Dakota State Coll of Science (ND)
Northeast Mississippi Comm Coll (MS)
Northern Virginia Comm Coll (VA)
Northwestern Michigan Coll (MI)
Northwest Mississippi Comm Coll (MS)
Oakland Comm Coll (MI)
Onondaga Comm Coll (NY)
Orange Coast Coll (CA)
Orange County Comm Coll (NY)
Owens Comm Coll, Toledo (OH)
Ozarks Tech Comm Coll (MO)
Palm Beach Comm Coll (FL)
Palomar Coll (CA)
Parkland Coll (IL)
Pasadena City Coll (CA)
Pasco-Hernando Comm Coll (FL)

Associate Degree Programs at Two-Year Colleges
Dental Services–Drafting and Design

Pennsylvania Coll of Tech (PA)
Pensacola Jr Coll (FL)
Pierce Coll (WA)
Pikes Peak Comm Coll (CO)
Pima Comm Coll (AZ)
Portland Comm Coll (OR)
Prairie State Coll (IL)
Pueblo Comm Coll (CO)
Quinsigamond Comm Coll (MA)
Ramírez Coll of Business and Tech (PR)
Rancho Santiago Coll (CA)
Reading Area Comm Coll (PA)
Ricks Coll (ID)
Rio Hondo Coll (CA)
Riverside Comm Coll (CA)
Roane State Comm Coll (TN)
Rochester Comm Coll (MN)
Rogers State Coll (OK)
Rose State Coll (OK)
Sacramento City Coll (CA)
St Cloud Tech Coll (MN)
St Louis Comm Coll at Forest Park (MO)
St Petersburg Jr Coll (FL)
Salish Kootenai Coll (MT)
Salt Lake Comm Coll (UT)
San Antonio Coll (TX)
San Bernardino Valley Coll (CA)
San Diego Mesa Coll (CA)
San Jose City Coll (CA)
Santa Barbara City Coll (CA)
Santa Fe Comm Coll (FL)
Santa Monica Coll (CA)
Santa Rosa Jr Coll (CA)
Sheridan Coll (WY)
Shoreline Comm Coll (WA)
Sinclair Comm Coll (OH)
Southern Coll (FL)
South Puget Sound Comm Coll (WA)
SouthWest Collegiate Inst for the Deaf (TX)
Spokane Comm Coll (WA)
Springfield Tech Comm Coll (MA)
State U of NY Coll of Tech at Farmingdale (NY)
Taft Coll (CA)
Tallahassee Comm Coll (FL)
Tarrant County Jr Coll (TX)
Temple Coll (TX)
Texas State Tech Coll–Harlingen Cmps (TX)
Texas State Tech Coll–Waco/Marshall Cmps (TX)
Trenholm State Tech Coll (AL)
Trident Tech Coll (SC)
Truckee Meadows Comm Coll (NV)
Tulsa Jr Coll (OK)
Tunxis Comm Tech Coll (CT)
Tyler Jr Coll (TX)
U of Cincinnati Raymond Walters Coll (OH)
U of Kentucky, Elizabethtown Comm Coll (KY)
U of Kentucky, Lexington Comm Coll (KY)
U of Kentucky, Maysville Comm Coll (KY)
Valencia Comm Coll (FL)
Vincennes U (IN)
Virginia Western Comm Coll (VA)
Volunteer State Comm Coll (TN)
Wake Tech Comm Coll (NC)
Wallace State Comm Coll (AL)
Washtenaw Comm Coll (MI)
Waycross Coll (GA)
Wayne Comm Coll (NC)
Wayne County Comm Coll (MI)
West Los Angeles Coll (CA)
Westmoreland County Comm Coll (PA)
Wharton County Jr Coll (TX)
Wilkes Comm Coll (NC)
William Rainey Harper Coll (IL)
Wytheville Comm Coll (VA)
Yakima Valley Comm Coll (WA)
York Tech Coll (SC)

DIETETICS

Alexandria Tech Coll (MN)
Bakersfield Coll (CA)
Baltimore City Comm Coll (MD)
Briarwood Coll (CT)
Bucks County Comm Coll (PA)
Camden County Coll (NJ)
Central Coll (KS)
Central Comm College–Hastings Cmps (NE)
Chaffey Coll (CA)
Cincinnati State Tech and Comm Coll (OH)
City Coll of San Francisco (CA)
City Colls of Chicago, Malcolm X Coll (IL)
Columbus State Comm Coll (OH)
Comm Coll of Allegheny County Allegheny Cmps (PA)
Comm Coll of Philadelphia (PA)
Delgado Comm Coll (LA)
Delta Coll (MI)
Dutchess Comm Coll (NY)
El Paso Comm Coll (TX)
Erie Comm Coll, North Cmps (NY)
Fiorello H LaGuardia Comm Coll of City U of NY (NY)
Florida Comm Coll at Jacksonville (FL)
Fresno City Coll (CA)
Front Range Comm Coll (CO)
Gateway Comm-Tech Coll (CT)
Genesee Comm Coll (NY)
Grossmont Coll (CA)
Harrisburg Area Comm Coll (PA)
Hinds Comm Coll (MS)
Hocking Coll (OH)
Houston Comm Coll System (TX)
John Wood Comm Coll (IL)
Labouré Coll (MA)
Lake Michigan Coll (MI)
Lakewood Comm Coll (MN)
Lawson State Comm Coll (AL)
Lexington Coll (IL)
Lima Tech Coll (OH)
Long Beach City Coll (CA)
Los Angeles City Coll (CA)
Madison Area Tech Coll (WI)
Merced Coll (CA)
Miami-Dade Comm Coll (FL)
Middlesex County Coll (NJ)
Milwaukee Area Tech Coll (WI)
Mohawk Valley Comm Coll (NY)
Montgomery College–Rockville Cmps (MD)
Normandale Comm Coll (MN)
Northeast Metro Tech Coll (MN)
Oakland Comm Coll (MI)
Okaloosa-Walton Comm Coll (FL)
Oklahoma State U, Okmulgee (OK)
Orange Coast Coll (CA)
Owens Comm Coll, Toledo (OH)
Pensacola Jr Coll (FL)
Portland Comm Coll (OR)
Ricks Coll (ID)
Rockland Comm Coll (NY)
St Louis Comm Coll at Florissant Valley (MO)
San Jacinto College–Central Cmps (TX)
San Jacinto College–North Cmps (TX)
Shelby State Comm Coll (TN)
Shoreline Comm Coll (WA)
Sinclair Comm Coll (OH)
Southeast Comm Coll, Lincoln Cmps (NE)
Southern Maine Tech Coll (ME)
South Plains Coll (TX)
Spokane Comm Coll (WA)
State U of NY Coll of A&T at Morrisville (NY)
Suffolk County Comm Coll–Eastern Cmps (NY)
Tarrant County Jr Coll (TX)
U of Cincinnati Raymond Walters Coll (OH)
Vincennes U (IN)
Wayne County Comm Coll (MI)
Westchester Comm Coll (NY)
Westmoreland County Comm Coll (PA)
William Rainey Harper Coll (IL)

DRAFTING AND DESIGN

Adirondack Comm Coll (NY)
Alamance Comm Coll (NC)
Albuquerque Tech Vocational Inst (NM)
Allen County Comm Coll (KS)
Alpena Comm Coll (MI)
Alvin Comm Coll (TX)
American Inst of Design (PA)
American River Coll (CA)
Angelina Coll (TX)
Anson Comm Coll (NC)
Arapahoe Comm Coll (CO)
Arizona Western Coll (AZ)
Arkansas State University–Beebe Branch (AR)
The Art Inst of Houston (TX)
Art Inst of Pittsburgh (PA)
Asheville-Buncombe Tech Comm Coll (NC)
Athens Area Tech Inst (GA)
Austin Comm Coll (TX)
Bainbridge Coll (GA)
Baltimore City Comm Coll (MD)
Barstow Coll (CA)
Barton County Comm Coll (KS)
Bay de Noc Comm Coll (MI)
Beaufort County Comm Coll (NC)
Bee County Coll (TX)
Belleville Area Coll (IL)
Bergen Comm Coll (NJ)
Bessemer State Tech Coll (AL)
Black Hawk Coll, Moline (IL)
Blue Mountain Comm Coll (OR)
Blue Ridge Comm Coll (NC)
Blue Ridge Comm Coll (VA)
Bossier Parish Comm Coll (LA)
Brazosport Coll (TX)
Brevard Comm Coll (FL)
Brookdale Comm Coll (NJ)
Brunswick Coll (GA)
Bucks County Comm Coll (PA)
Burlington County Coll (NJ)
Butler County Comm Coll (KS)
Butler County Comm Coll (PA)
Butte Coll (CA)
Cabrillo Coll (CA)
Caldwell Comm Coll and Tech Inst (NC)
Cape Fear Comm Coll (NC)
Carl Sandburg Coll (IL)
Casper Coll (WY)
Catawba Valley Comm Coll (NC)
Catonsville Comm Coll (MD)
Cayuga County Comm Coll (NY)
Central Alabama Comm Coll (AL)
Central Carolina Comm Coll (NC)
Central Coll (KS)
Central Comm College–Grand Island Cmps (NE)
Central Comm College–Hastings Cmps (NE)
Central Comm College–Platte Cmps (NE)
Central Florida Comm Coll (FL)
Central Maine Tech Coll (ME)
Central Ohio Tech Coll (OH)
Central Oregon Comm Coll (OR)
Central Piedmont Comm Coll (NC)
Central Texas Coll (TX)
Central Virginia Comm Coll (VA)
Cerritos Coll (CA)
Cerro Coso Comm Coll (CA)
Chaffey Coll (CA)
Charles Stewart Mott Comm Coll (MI)
Chattanooga State Tech Comm Coll (TN)
Chemeketa Comm Coll (OR)
Chippewa Valley Tech Coll (WI)
Cisco Jr Coll (TX)
Citrus Coll (CA)
City Colls of Chicago, Harold Washington Coll (IL)
City Colls of Chicago, Harry S Truman Coll (IL)
City Colls of Chicago, Richard J Daley Coll (IL)
Clackamas Comm Coll (OR)
Clark State Comm Coll (OH)
Clinton Comm Coll (IA)
Cloud County Comm Coll (KS)
Coahoma Comm Coll (MS)
Cochise Coll, Douglas (AZ)
Cochise Coll, Sierra Vista (AZ)
Coffeyville Comm Coll (KS)
Coll of DuPage (IL)
Coll of Lake County (IL)
Coll of San Mateo (CA)
Coll of Southern Idaho (ID)
Coll of the Canyons (CA)
Coll of the Desert (CA)
Coll of the Mainland (TX)
Coll of the Redwoods (CA)
Coll of the Sequoias (CA)
Collin County Comm Coll (TX)
Comm Coll of Allegheny County Boyce Cmps (PA)
Comm Coll of Allegheny County North Cmps (PA)
Comm Coll of Allegheny County South Cmps (PA)
Comm Coll of Beaver County (PA)
Comm Coll of Denver (CO)
Comm Coll of Philadelphia (PA)
Comm Coll of Southern Nevada (NV)
Connors State Coll (OK)
Contra Costa Coll (CA)
Copiah-Lincoln Comm Coll (MS)
Corning Comm Coll (NY)
Cosumnes River Coll (CA)
County Coll of Morris (NJ)
Cowley County Comm Coll and Voc-Tech Sch (KS)
Craven Comm Coll (NC)
Crowder Coll (MO)
Cumberland County Coll (NJ)
Cuyamaca Coll (CA)
Dabney S Lancaster Comm Coll (VA)
Dalton Coll (GA)
Danville Area Comm Coll (IL)
Daytona Beach Comm Coll (FL)
Dean Inst of Tech (PA)
DeKalb Tech Inst (GA)
Delaware County Comm Coll (PA)
Delaware Tech & Comm Coll, Jack F Owens Cmps (DE)
Delaware Tech & Comm Coll, Stanton/Wilmington Cmps (DE)
Delaware Tech & Comm Coll, Terry Cmps (DE)
Del Mar Coll (TX)
Delta Coll (MI)
Des Moines Area Comm Coll (IA)
Dixie Coll (UT)
Doña Ana Branch Comm Coll (NM)
Don Bosco Tech Inst (CA)
Donnelly Coll (KS)
Douglas MacArthur State Tech Coll (AL)
Dunwoody Inst (MN)
Durham Tech Comm Coll (NC)
East Arkansas Comm Coll (AR)
East Central Coll (MO)
East Central Comm Coll (MS)
Eastern Arizona Coll (AZ)
Eastern New Mexico University–Roswell (NM)
Eastfield Coll (TX)
East Los Angeles Coll (CA)
East Mississippi Comm Coll (MS)
Edison Comm Coll (FL)
Edison State Comm Coll (OH)
Elaine P Nunez Comm Coll (LA)
El Camino Coll (CA)
El Centro Coll (TX)
Elgin Comm Coll (IL)
El Paso Comm Coll (TX)
Erie Comm Coll, South Cmps (NY)
Essex Comm Coll (MD)
Everett Comm Coll (WA)
Evergreen Valley Coll (CA)
Finger Lakes Comm Coll (NY)
Florence-Darlington Tech Coll (SC)
Florida Comm Coll at Jacksonville (FL)
Forsyth Tech Comm Coll (NC)
Fort Scott Comm Coll (KS)
Fox Valley Tech Coll (WI)
Franklin Inst of Boston (MA)
Frederick Comm Coll (MD)
Fresno City Coll (CA)
Front Range Comm Coll (CO)
Fullerton Coll (CA)
Gadsden State Comm Coll (AL)
Garden City Comm Coll (KS)
Gaston Coll (NC)
Gateway Coll (NE)
Gavilan Coll (CA)
Genesee Comm Coll (NY)
George Corley Wallace State Comm Coll, Selma (AL)
George C Wallace State Comm Coll, Dothan (AL)
Glendale Comm Coll (AZ)
Gloucester County Coll (NJ)
Gogebic Comm Coll (MI)
Golden West Coll (CA)
Grand Rapids Comm Coll (MI)
Grayson County Coll (TX)
Green River Comm Coll (WA)
Greenville Tech Coll (SC)
Guilford Tech Comm Coll (NC)
Gulf Coast Comm Coll (FL)
Gwinnett Tech Inst (GA)
Harford Comm Coll (MD)
Harry M Ayers State Tech Coll (AL)
Hartnell Coll (CA)
Hawkeye Comm Coll (IA)
Heartland Comm Coll (IL)
Henry Ford Comm Coll (MI)
Herkimer County Comm Coll (NY)
Herzing Coll of Tech (WI)
Hibbing Comm Coll (MN)
Highland Comm Coll (IL)
Highland Comm Coll (KS)
Highland Park Comm Coll (MI)
Highline Comm Coll (WA)
Hill Coll of the Hill Jr Coll District (TX)
Hinds Comm Coll (MS)
Hiwassee Coll (TN)
Hocking Coll (OH)
Holmes Comm Coll (MS)
Houston Comm Coll System (TX)
Howard Coll (TX)
Howard Comm Coll (MD)
Hutchinson Comm Coll and Area Vocational Sch (KS)
Illinois Eastern Comm Colls, Lincoln Trail Coll (IL)
Illinois Valley Comm Coll (IL)
Independence Comm Coll (KS)
Indian Hills Comm Coll (IA)
Indian River Comm Coll (FL)
Inst of Design and Construction (NY)
Iowa Central Comm Coll (IA)
Iowa Lakes Comm Coll (IA)
Isothermal Comm Coll (NC)
Itawamba Comm Coll (MS)
ITT Tech Inst (AL)
ITT Tech Inst, Phoenix (AZ)
ITT Tech Inst, Tucson (AZ)
ITT Tech Inst (AR)
ITT Tech Inst, Anaheim (CA)
ITT Tech Inst, Carson (CA)
ITT Tech Inst, Oxnard (CA)
ITT Tech Inst, Sacramento (CA)
ITT Tech Inst, San Bernardino (CA)
ITT Tech Inst, San Diego (CA)
ITT Tech Inst, Van Nuys (CA)
ITT Tech Inst, West Covina (CA)
ITT Tech Inst (CO)
ITT Tech Inst, Jacksonville (FL)
ITT Tech Inst, Tampa (FL)
ITT Tech Inst (ID)
ITT Tech Inst, Hoffman Estates (IL)
ITT Tech Inst, Indianapolis (IN)
ITT Tech Inst (MA)
ITT Tech Inst (MO)
ITT Tech Inst (NE)
ITT Tech Inst, Dayton (OH)
ITT Tech Inst, Youngstown (OH)
ITT Tech Inst (OR)
ITT Tech Inst, Memphis (TN)
ITT Tech Inst, Nashville (TN)
ITT Tech Inst, Arlington (TX)
ITT Tech Inst, Austin (TX)
ITT Tech Inst, Garland (TX)
ITT Tech Inst, Houston (TX)
ITT Tech Inst, Houston (TX)
ITT Tech Inst, San Antonio (TX)
ITT Tech Inst (UT)
ITT Tech Inst, Seattle (WA)
ITT Tech Inst, Spokane (WA)
ITT Tech Inst (WI)
Ivy Tech State Coll–Central Indiana (IN)
Ivy Tech State Coll–Columbus (IN)
Ivy Tech State Coll–Eastcentral (IN)
Ivy Tech State Coll–Kokomo (IN)
Ivy Tech State Coll–Lafayette (IN)
Ivy Tech State Coll–Northcentral (IN)
Ivy Tech State Coll–Northeast (IN)
Ivy Tech State Coll–Northwest (IN)
Ivy Tech State Coll–Southcentral (IN)
Ivy Tech State Coll–Southwest (IN)
Ivy Tech State Coll–Wabash Valley (IN)
Jackson Comm Coll (MI)
Jefferson Coll (MO)
Jefferson Comm Coll (OH)
J F Drake State Tech Coll (AL)
John A Logan Coll (IL)
John C Calhoun State Comm Coll (AL)
John M Patterson State Tech Coll (AL)
Johnson County Comm Coll (KS)
Johnson Tech Inst (PA)
John Wood Comm Coll (IL)
Jones County Jr Coll (MS)
Kalamazoo Valley Comm Coll (MI)
Kansas City Kansas Comm Coll (KS)
Kaskaskia Coll (IL)
Kellogg Comm Coll (MI)
Kirkwood Comm Coll (IA)
Kirtland Comm Coll (MI)
Kishwaukee Coll (IL)
Labette Comm Coll (KS)
Lake Area Vocational-Tech Inst (SD)
Lake Land Coll (IL)
Lake Michigan Coll (MI)
Lakeshore Tech Coll (WI)
Lake Washington Tech Coll (WA)
Lane Comm Coll (OR)
Lansing Comm Coll (MI)
Las Positas Coll (CA)
Lassen Coll (CA)
Lawson State Comm Coll (AL)
Lee Coll (TX)
Lehigh Carbon Comm Coll (PA)
Lenoir Comm Coll (NC)
Lewis and Clark Comm Coll (IL)
Lima Tech Coll (OH)
Lincoln Land Comm Coll (IL)

Peterson's Guide to Two-Year Colleges 1997
75

Associate Degree Programs at Two-Year Colleges
Drafting and Design–Early Childhood Education

Lincoln Tech Inst (IN)
Lincoln Tech Inst, Allentown (PA)
Lincoln Tech Inst, Philadelphia (PA)
Linn-Benton Comm Coll (OR)
Long Beach City Coll (CA)
Longview Comm Coll (MO)
Lorain County Comm Coll (OH)
Los Angeles City Coll (CA)
Los Angeles Harbor Coll (CA)
Los Angeles Pierce Coll (CA)
Los Angeles Southwest Coll (CA)
Los Angeles Trade-Tech Coll (CA)
Los Angeles Valley Coll (CA)
Los Medanos Coll (CA)
Louisville Tech Inst (KY)
Lower Columbia Coll (WA)
Luzerne County Comm Coll (PA)
Macomb Comm Coll (MI)
Manatee Comm Coll (FL)
Marion Tech Coll (OH)
Marshalltown Comm Coll (IA)
Massachusetts Bay Comm Coll (MA)
Mercer County Comm Coll (NJ)
Meridian Comm Coll (MS)
Mesa Comm Coll (AZ)
Metropolitan Comm Coll (NE)
Miami-Dade Comm Coll (FL)
Middle Georgia Coll (GA)
Middlesex Comm Coll (MA)
Middlesex County Coll (NJ)
Midland Coll (TX)
Mid Michigan Comm Coll (MI)
Mid-Plains Comm Coll (NE)
Mid-State Tech Coll (WI)
Milwaukee Area Tech Coll (WI)
Mineral Area Coll (MO)
MiraCosta Coll (CA)
Mission Coll (CA)
Mississippi Delta Comm Coll (MS)
Mississippi Gulf Coast Comm Coll (MS)
Mitchell Comm Coll (NC)
Mohawk Valley Comm Coll (NY)
Monroe County Comm Coll (MI)
Montcalm Comm Coll (MI)
Monterey Peninsula Coll (CA)
Montgomery Coll (TX)
Montgomery College–Germantown Cmps (MD)
Montgomery County Comm Coll (PA)
Moraine Park Tech Coll (WI)
Moraine Valley Comm Coll (IL)
Morrison Inst of Tech (IL)
Morton Coll (IL)
Mountain Empire Comm Coll (VA)
Mountain View Coll (TX)
Mt San Antonio Coll (CA)
Murray State Coll (OK)
Muskegon Comm Coll (MI)
Napa Valley Coll (CA)
Naugatuck Valley Community–Tech Coll (CT)
Navarro Coll (TX)
New England Inst of Tech (RI)
New England Inst of Tech & Florida Culinary Inst (FL)
New Hampshire Tech Coll, Berlin (NH)
New Hampshire Tech Coll, Manchester (NH)
New Hampshire Tech Coll, Nashua (NH)
New Mexico Jr Coll (NM)
New River Comm Coll (VA)
New York City Tech Coll of the City U of NY (NY)
Niagara County Comm Coll (NY)
Normandale Comm Coll (MN)
Northampton County Area Comm Coll (PA)
North Central Michigan Coll (MI)
North Central Missouri Coll (MO)
North Central Tech Coll (OH)
Northcentral Tech Coll (WI)
North Central Texas Coll (TX)

North Dakota State Coll of Science (ND)
Northeast Comm Coll (NE)
Northeastern Oklahoma A&M Coll (OK)
Northeast Iowa Comm Coll, Peosta Cmps (IA)
Northeast Mississippi Comm Coll (MS)
Northeast State Tech Comm Coll (TN)
Northern Maine Tech Coll (ME)
Northern Oklahoma Coll (OK)
North Harris Coll (TX)
North Idaho Coll (ID)
Northland Comm and Tech Coll (MN)
North Seattle Comm Coll (WA)
Northwest Coll (WY)
Northwestern Michigan Coll (MI)
Northwest Iowa Comm Coll (IA)
Northwest Mississippi Comm Coll (MS)
Northwest-Shoals Comm Coll (AL)
Northwest State Comm Coll (OH)
Northwest Tech Inst (MN)
Oakland Comm Coll (MI)
Odessa Coll (TX)
Ohlone Coll (CA)
Okaloosa-Walton Comm Coll (FL)
Oklahoma City Comm Coll (OK)
Oklahoma State U, Oklahoma City (OK)
Oklahoma State U, Okmulgee (OK)
Olympic Coll (WA)
Onondaga Comm Coll (NY)
Orangeburg-Calhoun Tech Coll (SC)
Orange Coast Coll (CA)
Orange County Comm Coll (NY)
Oregon Polytechnic Inst (OR)
Owens Comm Coll, Findlay (OH)
Owens Comm Coll, Toledo (OH)
Palm Beach Comm Coll (FL)
Palomar Coll (CA)
Paris Jr Coll (TX)
Pasadena City Coll (CA)
Pearl River Comm Coll (MS)
Pellissippi State Tech Comm Coll (TN)
Pennco Tech (PA)
Pennsylvania Coll of Tech (PA)
Pennsylvania Inst of Tech (PA)
Pensacola Jr Coll (FL)
Petit Jean Tech Coll (AR)
Phillips County Comm Coll (AR)
Piedmont Tech Coll (SC)
Pima Comm Coll (AZ)
Pines Tech Coll (AR)
Pittsburgh Tech Inst (PA)
Polk Comm Coll (FL)
Porterville Coll (CA)
Portland Comm Coll (OR)
Prairie State Coll (IL)
Prince George's Comm Coll (MD)
Pulaski Tech Coll (AR)
Queensborough Comm Coll of City U of NY (NY)
Rancho Santiago Coll (CA)
Raritan Valley Comm Coll (NJ)
Redlands Comm Coll (OK)
Red Rocks Comm Coll (CO)
Richland Comm Coll (IL)
Ricks Coll (ID)
Riverside Comm Coll (CA)
Rockland Comm Coll (NY)
Rock Valley Coll (IL)
Rose State Coll (OK)
Rowan-Cabarrus Comm Coll (NC)
Roxbury Comm Coll (MA)
Sacramento City Coll (CA)
Saddleback Coll (CA)
Saint Charles County Comm Coll (MO)
St Clair County Comm Coll (MI)

St Cloud Tech Coll (MN)
St Philip's Coll (TX)
Salem Comm Coll (NJ)
Salt Lake Comm Coll (UT)
San Antonio Coll (TX)
San Bernardino Valley Coll (CA)
San Diego City Coll (CA)
San Jacinto College–Central Cmps (TX)
San Jacinto College–North Cmps (TX)
San Jacinto College–South Cmps (TX)
San Joaquin Delta Coll (CA)
San Jose City Coll (CA)
San Juan Coll (NM)
Santa Barbara City Coll (CA)
Santa Fe Comm Coll (FL)
Santa Fe Comm Coll (NM)
Santa Monica Coll (CA)
Sauk Valley Comm Coll (IL)
Schoolcraft Coll (MI)
Scott Comm Coll (IA)
Seattle Central Comm Coll (WA)
Seminole Comm Coll (FL)
Shasta Coll (CA)
Shelton State Comm Coll (AL)
Sheridan Coll (WY)
Shoreline Comm Coll (WA)
Sierra Coll (CA)
Sinclair Comm Coll (OH)
Solano Comm Coll (CA)
Southeast Comm Coll, Lincoln Cmps (NE)
Southeast Comm Coll, Milford Cmps (NE)
Southeastern Comm Coll, North Cmps, West Burlington (IA)
Southern Maine Tech Coll (ME)
Southern State Comm Coll (OH)
Southern West Virginia Comm and Tech Coll (WV)
South Florida Comm Coll (FL)
South Plains Coll (TX)
South Puget Sound Comm Coll (WA)
South Seattle Comm Coll (WA)
Southside Virginia Comm Coll (VA)
South Suburban Coll (IL)
SouthWest Collegiate Inst for the Deaf (TX)
Southwestern Coll (CA)
Southwestern Comm Coll (IA)
Southwestern Indian Polytechnic Inst (NM)
Southwestern Michigan Coll (MI)
Southwestern Tech Coll (MN)
Southwest Missouri State University–West Plains (MO)
Southwest Virginia Comm Coll (VA)
Southwest Wisconsin Tech Coll (WI)
Spokane Comm Coll (WA)
Springfield Tech Comm Coll (MA)
Stanly Comm Coll (NC)
Stark Tech Coll (OH)
State U of NY Coll of A&T at Morrisville (NY)
State U of NY Coll of Tech at Alfred (NY)
State U of NY Coll of Tech at Delhi (NY)
Suffolk County Comm College–Ammerman Cmps (NY)
Surry Comm Coll (NC)
Taft Coll (CA)
Tarrant County Jr Coll (TX)
Temple Coll (TX)
Terra State Comm Coll (OH)
Texarkana Coll (TX)
Texas Southmost Coll (TX)
Texas State Tech Coll (TX)
Texas State Tech Coll–Harlingen Cmps (TX)
Texas State Tech Coll–Waco/Marshall Cmps (TX)
Thaddeus Stevens State Sch of Tech (PA)
Thomas Nelson Comm Coll (VA)

Thompson Inst (PA)
Three Rivers Comm-Tech Coll (CT)
Tidewater Comm Coll (VA)
Treasure Valley Comm Coll (OR)
Triangle Tech, Inc, Pittsburgh (PA)
Triangle Tech, Inc–DuBois Sch (PA)
Triangle Tech, Inc–Erie Sch (PA)
Triangle Tech, Inc–Greensburg Ctr (PA)
Tri-County Tech Coll (SC)
Trinidad State Jr Coll (CO)
Trinity Valley Comm Coll (TX)
Triton Coll (IL)
Truckee Meadows Comm Coll (NV)
Tulsa Jr Coll (OK)
Tyler Jr Coll (TX)
Ulster County Comm Coll (NY)
U of Hawaii–Hawaii Comm Coll (HI)
U of Hawaii–Honolulu Comm Coll (HI)
U of Hawaii–Leeward Comm Coll (HI)
Utah Valley State Coll (UT)
Valencia Comm Coll (FL)
Ventura Coll (CA)
Vernon Regional Jr Coll (TX)
Victoria Coll (TX)
Vincennes U (IN)
Virginia Coll at Birmingham (AL)
Virginia Highlands Comm Coll (VA)
Wake Tech Comm Coll (NC)
Wallace State Comm Coll (AL)
Washington State Comm Coll (OH)
Washtenaw Comm Coll (MI)
Waubonsee Comm Coll (IL)
Waukesha County Tech Coll (WI)
Waycross Coll (GA)
Wayne Comm Coll (NC)
Wayne County Comm Coll (MI)
Weatherford Coll (TX)
Westark Comm Coll (AR)
Western Dakota Tech Inst (SD)
Western Iowa Tech Comm Coll (IA)
Western Nevada Comm Coll (NV)
Western Oklahoma State Coll (OK)
Western Piedmont Comm Coll (NC)
Western Wisconsin Tech Coll (WI)
West Los Angeles Coll (CA)
Westmoreland County Comm Coll (PA)
West Valley Coll (CA)
West Virginia U at Parkersburg (WV)
Wharton County Jr Coll (TX)
Wilkes Comm Coll (NC)
William Rainey Harper Coll (IL)
Willmar Comm Coll (MN)
Willmar Tech Coll (MN)
Wilson Tech Comm Coll (NC)
Wright State U, Lake Cmps (OH)
Wytheville Comm Coll (VA)
Yavapai Coll (AZ)
York Tech Coll (SC)

DRAMA THERAPY
Brevard Coll (NC)
Collin County Comm Coll (TX)
Indian River Comm Coll (FL)
Miami-Dade Comm Coll (FL)

DRUG AND ALCOHOL/SUBSTANCE ABUSE COUNSELING
Asnuntuck Comm-Tech Coll (CT)
Capital Comm Tech Coll (CT)
Castle Coll (NH)
Central Texas Coll (TX)
Chemeketa Comm Coll (OR)

Clark Coll (WA)
Cleveland State Comm Coll (TN)
Coll of DuPage (IL)
Coll of Lake County (IL)
Coll of St Catherine–Minneapolis (MN)
Coll of San Mateo (CA)
Columbus State Comm Coll (OH)
Comm Coll of Rhode Island (RI)
Danville Area Comm Coll (IL)
Dawson Comm Coll (MT)
Eastfield Coll (TX)
Edmonds Comm Coll (WA)
Elgin Comm Coll (IL)
Ellsworth Comm Coll (IA)
Florida Comm Coll at Jacksonville (FL)
Fresno City Coll (CA)
Gadsden State Comm Coll (AL)
Gateway Comm-Tech Coll (CT)
Genesee Comm Coll (NY)
Grays Harbor Coll (WA)
Housatonic Comm-Tech Coll (CT)
Howard Coll (TX)
Howard Comm Coll (MD)
Iowa Western Comm Coll (IA)
Lac Courte Oreilles Ojibwa Comm Coll (WI)
Lamar University–Port Arthur (TX)
Lane Comm Coll (OR)
Lansing Comm Coll (MI)
Lee Coll (TX)
Lower Columbia Coll (WA)
Mater Dei Coll (NY)
Mesabi Comm Coll (MN)
Middlesex Community–Tech Coll (CT)
Milwaukee Area Tech Coll (WI)
Minneapolis Comm Coll (MN)
Mohawk Valley Comm Coll (NY)
Moraine Valley Comm Coll (IL)
Naugatuck Valley Community–Tech Coll (CT)
Nebraska Indian Comm Coll (NE)
Northern Virginia Comm Coll (VA)
Northland Comm and Tech Coll (MN)
North Shore Comm Coll (MA)
Northwestern Connecticut Comm-Tech Coll (CT)
Norwalk Comm-Tech Coll (CT)
Odessa Coll (TX)
Oklahoma State U, Oklahoma City (OK)
Pierce Coll (WA)
Pima Comm Coll (AZ)
Quinebaug Valley Comm-Tech Coll (CT)
Rio Salado Comm Coll (AZ)
Rogers State Coll (OK)
Rogue Comm Coll (OR)
Saddleback Coll (CA)
Sage Jr Coll of Albany (NY)
Sandhills Comm Coll (NC)
San Juan Coll (NM)
Seattle Central Comm Coll (WA)
Shoreline Comm Coll (WA)
Sisseton-Wahpeton Comm Coll (SD)
Southeastern Comm Coll, North Cmps, West Burlington (IA)
Spokane Falls Comm Coll (WA)
Suffolk County Comm Coll–Western Cmps (NY)
Sullivan County Comm Coll (NY)
Tacoma Comm Coll (WA)
Texarkana Coll (TX)
Texas Southmost Coll (TX)
Three Rivers Comm-Tech Coll (CT)
Triton Coll (IL)
Truckee Meadows Comm Coll (NV)
Tunxis Comm Tech Coll (CT)
Washtenaw Comm Coll (MI)
Wenatchee Valley Coll (WA)
Westchester Comm Coll (NY)

Willmar Comm Coll (MN)
Yakima Valley Comm Coll (WA)

EARLY CHILDHOOD EDUCATION
Abraham Baldwin Ag Coll (GA)
Aims Comm Coll (CO)
Alabama Southern Comm Coll, Monroeville (AL)
Alamance Comm Coll (NC)
Allan Hancock Coll (CA)
Allen County Comm Coll (KS)
American River Coll (CA)
Anne Arundel Comm Coll (MD)
Antelope Valley Coll (CA)
Aquinas Coll at Newton (MA)
Atlanta Metropolitan Coll (GA)
Bainbridge Coll (GA)
Baltimore City Comm Coll (MD)
Barstow Coll (CA)
Bay de Noc Comm Coll (MI)
Bay State Coll (MA)
Beaufort County Comm Coll (NC)
Bellevue Comm Coll (WA)
Bergen Comm Coll (NJ)
Bishop State Comm Coll (AL)
Blackfeet Comm Coll (MT)
Borough of Manhattan Comm Coll of City U of NY (NY)
Brazosport Coll (TX)
Brevard Coll (NC)
Brevard Comm Coll (FL)
Brookdale Comm Coll (NJ)
Broward Comm Coll (FL)
Bucks County Comm Coll (PA)
Burlington County Coll (NJ)
Butler County Comm Coll (KS)
Butler County Comm Coll (PA)
Butte Coll (CA)
Cabrillo Coll (CA)
Camden County Coll (NJ)
Cañada Coll (CA)
Cape Cod Comm Coll (MA)
Cape Fear Comm Coll (NC)
Capital Comm Tech Coll (CT)
Carl Albert State Coll (OK)
Casper Coll (WY)
Castle Coll (NH)
Catonsville Comm Coll (MD)
Cayuga County Comm Coll (NY)
Cecil Comm Coll (MD)
Central Carolina Comm Coll (NC)
Central Coll (KS)
Centralia Coll (WA)
Central Ohio Tech Coll (OH)
Central Piedmont Comm Coll (NC)
Central Virginia Comm Coll (VA)
Cerritos Coll (CA)
Cerro Coso Comm Coll (CA)
Chabot Coll (CA)
Chaffey Coll (CA)
Champlain Coll (VT)
Charles County Comm Coll (MD)
Chattanooga State Tech Comm Coll (TN)
Chemeketa Comm Coll (OR)
Chesapeake Coll (MD)
Cisco Jr Coll (TX)
City Colls of Chicago, Harold Washington Coll (IL)
City Colls of Chicago, Kennedy-King Coll (IL)
City Colls of Chicago, Malcolm X Coll (IL)
City Colls of Chicago, Olive-Harvey Coll (IL)
Clark Coll (WA)
Clark State Comm Coll (OH)
Coahoma Comm Coll (MS)
Colby Comm Coll (KS)
Coll of DuPage (IL)
Coll of Eastern Utah (UT)
Coll of Marin (CA)
Coll of St Catherine–Minneapolis (MN)
Coll of the Canyons (CA)
Coll of the Desert (CA)
Coll of the Redwoods (CA)
Coll of the Sequoias (CA)

76 Peterson's Guide to Two-Year Colleges 1997

Associate Degree Programs at Two-Year Colleges
Early Childhood Education–Economics

Collin County Comm Coll (TX)
Colorado Mountn Coll, Timberline Cmps (CO)
Columbia Basin Coll (WA)
Columbus State Comm Coll (OH)
Comm Coll of Allegheny County Allegheny Cmps (PA)
Comm Coll of Allegheny County North Cmps (PA)
Comm Coll of Allegheny County South Cmps (PA)
Comm Coll of Aurora (CO)
Comm Coll of Denver (CO)
Comm Coll of Philadelphia (PA)
Comm Coll of Rhode Island (RI)
Comm Coll of Southern Nevada (NV)
Contra Costa Coll (CA)
Corning Comm Coll (NY)
Cosumnes River Coll (CA)
Craven Comm Coll (NC)
Cuesta Coll (CA)
Cumberland County Coll (NJ)
Cuyahoga Comm Coll, Eastern Cmps (OH)
Cuyahoga Comm Coll, Metropolitan Cmps (OH)
Cuyahoga Comm Coll, Western Cmps (OH)
Dalton Coll (GA)
Danville Area Comm Coll (IL)
Darton Coll (GA)
Daytona Beach Comm Coll (FL)
Dean Coll (MA)
DeKalb Coll (GA)
Delaware County Comm Coll (PA)
Delaware Tech & Comm Coll, Terry Cmps (DE)
Delgado Comm Coll (LA)
Del Mar Coll (TX)
Dixie Coll (UT)
Donnelly Coll (KS)
Dundalk Comm Coll (MD)
Durham Tech Comm Coll (NC)
Dutchess Comm Coll (NY)
East Central Comm Coll (MS)
Eastfield Coll (TX)
Edgecombe Comm Coll (NC)
Edison State Comm Coll (OH)
Edmonds Comm Coll (WA)
Elaine P Nunez Comm Coll (LA)
El Camino Coll (CA)
Ellsworth Comm Coll (IA)
Enterprise State Jr Coll (AL)
Essex Comm Coll (MD)
Essex County Coll (NJ)
Eugenio María de Hostos Comm Coll of City U of NY (NY)
Everett Comm Coll (WA)
Fayetteville Tech Comm Coll (NC)
Finger Lakes Comm Coll (NY)
Fiorello H LaGuardia Comm Coll of City U of NY (NY)
Fisher Coll (MA)
Forsyth Tech Comm Coll (NC)
Fort Belknap Coll (MT)
Fort Berthold Comm Coll (ND)
Fort Peck Comm Coll (MT)
Frederick Comm Coll (MD)
Front Range Comm Coll (CO)
Fullerton Coll (CA)
Fulton-Montgomery Comm Coll (NY)
Gadsden State Comm Coll (AL)
Gainesville Coll (GA)
Gaston Coll (NC)
Gateway Comm-Tech Coll (CT)
Gavilan Coll (CA)
Genesee Comm Coll (NY)
Glendale Comm Coll (AZ)
Gogebic Comm Coll (MI)
Grays Harbor Coll (WA)
Greenfield Comm Coll (MA)
Green River Comm Coll (WA)
Guilford Tech Comm Coll (NC)
Hagerstown Jr Coll (MD)
Harcum Coll (PA)
Harford Comm Coll (MD)
Harrisburg Area Comm Coll (PA)
Hartnell Coll (CA)
Heartland Comm Coll (IL)
Herkimer County Comm Coll (NY)
Hesser Coll (NH)
Hesston Coll (KS)
Highland Comm Coll (IL)
Highline Comm Coll (WA)
Hiwassee Coll (TN)
Holyoke Comm Coll (MA)
Howard Comm Coll (MD)
Hudson Valley Comm Coll (NY)
Hutchinson Comm Coll and Area Vocational Sch (KS)
Imperial Valley Coll (CA)
Independence Comm Coll (KS)
Indian River Comm Coll (FL)
Isothermal Comm Coll (NC)
Itasca Comm Coll (MN)
Itawamba Comm Coll (MS)
James Sprunt Comm Coll (NC)
Jefferson Coll (MO)
Jefferson Comm Coll (NY)
John A Logan Coll (IL)
Johnston Comm Coll (NC)
Kansas City Kansas Comm Coll (KS)
Kent State U, Ashtabula Cmps (OH)
Kent State U, Salem Cmps (OH)
Keystone Coll (PA)
Kingsborough Comm Coll of City U of NY (NY)
Kirkwood Comm Coll (IA)
Labette Comm Coll (KS)
Lakeland Comm Coll (OH)
Lake Tahoe Comm Coll (CA)
Lane Comm Coll (OR)
Lansing Comm Coll (MI)
Laramie County Comm Coll (WY)
Las Positas Coll (CA)
Lassen Coll (CA)
Lehigh Carbon Comm Coll (PA)
Lewis and Clark Comm Coll (IL)
Long Beach City Coll (CA)
Lorain County Comm Coll (OH)
Los Angeles Southwest Coll (CA)
Los Angeles Valley Coll (CA)
Lower Columbia Coll (WA)
Luzerne County Comm Coll (PA)
Macomb Comm Coll (MI)
Manchester Comm-Tech Coll (CT)
Manor Jr Coll (PA)
Maria Coll (NY)
Mary Holmes Coll (MS)
Massachusetts Bay Comm Coll (MA)
Massasoit Comm Coll (MA)
Mater Dei Coll (NY)
Mayland Comm Coll (NC)
McLennan Comm Coll (TX)
Merced Coll (CA)
Merritt Coll (CA)
Metropolitan Comm Coll (NE)
Miami-Dade Comm Coll (FL)
Miami University–Middletown Cmps (OH)
Middlesex Comm Coll (MA)
Middlesex County Coll (NJ)
Mid-Plains Comm Coll (NE)
MiraCosta Coll (CA)
Mississippi Gulf Coast Comm Coll (MS)
Mitchell Coll (CT)
Monterey Peninsula Coll (CA)
Montgomery College–Rockville Cmps (MD)
Montgomery Comm Coll (NC)
Montgomery County Comm Coll (PA)
Moorpark Coll (CA)
Motlow State Comm Coll (TN)
Mt Hood Comm Coll (OR)
Mount Ida Coll (MA)
Mt San Antonio Coll (CA)
Mt San Jacinto Coll (CA)
Napa Valley Coll (CA)
Nash Comm Coll (NC)
Nassau Comm Coll (NY)
Naugatuck Valley Community–Tech Coll (CT)
Nebraska Indian Comm Coll (NE)
New Hampshire Tech Coll, Laconia (NH)
New Hampshire Tech Coll, Manchester (NH)
New Hampshire Tech Coll, Nashua (NH)
New Hampshire Tech Inst (NH)
Nicolet Area Tech Coll (WI)
Northampton County Area Comm Coll (PA)
North Central Tech Coll (OH)
Northeastern Jr Coll (CO)
Northeast Mississippi Comm Coll (MS)
Northern Essex Comm Coll (MA)
Northern Virginia Comm Coll (VA)
Northland Pioneer Coll (AZ)
North Seattle Comm Coll (WA)
North Shore Comm Coll (MA)
Northwest Coll (WY)
Northwestern Connecticut Comm-Tech Coll (CT)
Northwest Indian Coll (WA)
Northwest State Comm Coll (OH)
Norwalk Comm-Tech Coll (CT)
Oakland Comm Coll (MI)
Oakton Comm Coll (IL)
Odessa Coll (TX)
Ohlone Coll (CA)
Okaloosa-Walton Comm Coll (FL)
Olympic Coll (WA)
Onondaga Comm Coll (NY)
Orange Coast Coll (CA)
Otero Jr Coll (CO)
Owens Comm Coll, Findlay (OH)
Owens Comm Coll, Toledo (OH)
Oxnard Coll (CA)
Ozarks Tech Comm Coll (MO)
Palm Beach Comm Coll (FL)
Palomar Coll (CA)
Palo Verde Coll (CA)
Parkland Coll (IL)
Pasadena City Coll (CA)
Passaic County Comm Coll (NJ)
Pennsylvania Coll of Tech (PA)
Penn Valley Comm Coll (MO)
Pensacola Jr Coll (FL)
Pierce Coll (WA)
Pikes Peak Comm Coll (CO)
Pima Comm Coll (AZ)
Pitt Comm Coll (NC)
Potomac State Coll of West Virginia U (WV)
Prairie State Coll (IL)
Pratt Comm Coll and Area Voc Sch (KS)
Prince George's Comm Coll (MD)
Pueblo Comm Coll (CO)
Quincy Coll (MA)
Quinsigamond Comm Coll (MA)
Rancho Santiago Coll (CA)
Raritan Valley Comm Coll (NJ)
Reading Area Comm Coll (PA)
Redlands Comm Coll (OK)
Ricks Coll (ID)
Riverside Comm Coll (CA)
Roane State Comm Coll (TN)
Roanoke-Chowan Comm Coll (NC)
Rose State Coll (OK)
Rowan-Cabarrus Comm Coll (NC)
Roxbury Comm Coll (MA)
Sacramento City Coll (CA)
Saddleback Coll (CA)
Saint Augustine Coll (IL)
St Catharine Coll (KY)
St Cloud Tech Coll (MN)
St Gregory's Coll (OK)
St Petersburg Jr Coll (FL)
Salem Comm Coll (NJ)
Salish Kootenai Coll (MT)
Salt Lake Comm Coll (UT)
Sandhills Comm Coll (NC)
San Jacinto College–Central Cmps (TX)
San Jacinto College–North Cmps (TX)
San Joaquin Delta Coll (CA)
San Jose City Coll (CA)
San Juan Coll (NM)
Santa Barbara City Coll (CA)
Santa Fe Comm Coll (FL)
Santa Fe Comm Coll (NM)
Santa Monica Coll (CA)
Schoolcraft Coll (MI)
Scottsdale Comm Coll (AZ)
Seattle Central Comm Coll (WA)
Shasta Coll (CA)
Shelby State Comm Coll (TN)
Shelton State Comm Coll (AL)
Shoreline Comm Coll (WA)
Shorter Coll (AR)
Sierra Coll (CA)
Sinclair Comm Coll (OH)
Sisseton-Wahpeton Comm Coll (SD)
Snow Coll (UT)
Solano Comm Coll (CA)
Southeastern Comm Coll (NC)
Southern Maine Tech Coll (ME)
Southern State Comm Coll (OH)
Southern U at Shreveport–Bossier City Cmps (LA)
South Georgia Coll (GA)
South Puget Sound Comm Coll (WA)
South Suburban Coll (IL)
Southwestern Coll (CA)
Southwestern Comm Coll (NC)
Southwestern Michigan Coll (MI)
Southwestern Oregon Comm Coll (OR)
Spokane Falls Comm Coll (WA)
Spoon River Coll (IL)
Springfield Tech Comm Coll (MA)
Stanly Comm Coll (NC)
Stark Tech Coll (OH)
State U of NY Coll of A&T at Cobleskill (NY)
State U of NY Coll of Tech at Canton (NY)
Suffolk County Comm College–Ammerman Cmps (NY)
Suffolk County Comm Coll–Eastern Cmps (NY)
Suffolk County Comm Coll–Western Cmps (NY)
Sullivan County Comm Coll (NY)
Taft Coll (CA)
Terra State Comm Coll (OH)
Thomas Nelson Comm Coll (VA)
Three Rivers Comm-Tech Coll (CT)
Tidewater Comm Coll (VA)
Trident Tech Coll (SC)
Trinidad State Jr Coll (CO)
Trinity Valley Comm Coll (TX)
Triton Coll (IL)
Trocaire Coll (NY)
Truckee Meadows Comm Coll (NV)
Turtle Mountain Comm Coll (ND)
Umpqua Comm Coll (OR)
Union County Coll (NJ)
United Tribes Tech Coll (ND)
U of Hawaii–Hawaii Comm Coll (HI)
U of Hawaii–Honolulu Comm Coll (HI)
U of Hawaii–Kauai Comm Coll (HI)
U of Kentucky, Hopkinsville Comm Coll (KY)
U of Kentucky, Jefferson Comm Coll (KY)
U of New Mexico–Gallup Branch (NM)
Utah Valley State Coll (UT)
Vance-Granville Comm Coll (NC)
Ventura Coll (CA)
Vermilion Comm Coll (MN)
Victor Valley Coll (CA)
Villa Maria Coll of Buffalo (NY)
Vincennes U (IN)
Virginia Western Comm Coll (VA)
Wake Tech Comm Coll (NC)
Waldorf Coll (IA)
Wallace State Comm Coll (AL)
Walla Walla Comm Coll (WA)
Washington State Comm Coll (OH)
Waubonsee Comm Coll (IL)
Wayne Comm Coll (NC)
Wenatchee Valley Coll (WA)
Western Iowa Tech Comm Coll (IA)
Western Nebraska Comm Coll, Scottsbluff (NE)
West Hills Comm Coll (CA)
West Valley Coll (CA)
Whatcom Comm Coll (WA)
Wilkes Comm Coll (NC)
William Rainey Harper Coll (IL)
Wilson Tech Comm Coll (NC)
Yakima Valley Comm Coll (WA)
Yuba Coll (CA)

EARTH SCIENCE

Black Hawk Coll, Moline (IL)
Brevard Coll (NC)
Casper Coll (WY)
City Colls of Chicago, Olive-Harvey Coll (IL)
Colby Comm Coll (KS)
Columbia Coll (CA)
Comm Coll of Allegheny County South Cmps (PA)
Everett Comm Coll (WA)
Glendale Comm Coll (AZ)
Iowa Lakes Comm Coll (IA)
Lower Columbia Coll (WA)
Modesto Jr Coll (CA)
Navajo Comm Coll (AZ)
Rock Valley Coll (IL)
Santa Barbara City Coll (CA)
Skagit Valley Coll (WA)
Snow Coll (UT)
Southwestern Coll (CA)
Tacoma Comm Coll (WA)
Trinity Valley Comm Coll (TX)
Tulsa Jr Coll (OK)
Vermilion Comm Coll (MN)
Vincennes U (IN)
Waubonsee Comm Coll (IL)

ECOLOGY

Abraham Baldwin Ag Coll (GA)
Berkshire Comm Coll (MA)
Brevard Coll (NC)
Burlington County Coll (NJ)
Casper Coll (WY)
Chabot Coll (CA)
Coll of Marin (CA)
Colorado Mountn Coll, Timberline Cmps (CO)
Comm Coll of the Air Force (AL)
East Central Coll (MO)
Everett Comm Coll (WA)
Grays Harbor Coll (WA)
Iowa Lakes Comm Coll (IA)
Joliet Jr Coll (IL)
Milwaukee Area Tech Coll (WI)
Mitchell Coll (CT)
North Dakota State University–Bottineau (ND)
Northwest Coll (WY)
Paul Smith's Coll (NY)
Ricks Coll (ID)
Southwestern Coll (CA)
State U of NY Coll of Tech at Canton (NY)
Sterling Coll (VT)
Tulsa Jr Coll (OK)
Vermilion Comm Coll (MN)

ECONOMICS

Alabama Southern Comm Coll, Monroeville (AL)
Allen County Comm Coll (KS)
Anne Arundel Comm Coll (MD)
Antelope Valley Coll (CA)
Atlanta Metropolitan Coll (GA)
Austin Comm Coll (TX)
Bakersfield Coll (CA)
Barstow Coll (CA)
Barton County Comm Coll (KS)
Bay de Noc Comm Coll (MI)
Bee County Coll (TX)
Bergen Comm Coll (NJ)
Black Hawk Coll, Moline (IL)
Brevard Coll (NC)
Brevard Comm Coll (FL)
Brunswick Coll (GA)
Cañada Coll (CA)
Casper Coll (WY)
Central Coll (KS)
Central Comm College–Platte Cmps (NE)
Central Wyoming Coll (WY)
Cerritos Coll (CA)
Chabot Coll (CA)
Chaffey Coll (CA)
Chemeketa Comm Coll (OR)
Clackamas Comm Coll (OR)
Clark Coll (WA)
Clinton Comm Coll (IA)
Coahoma Comm Coll (MS)
Coffeyville Comm Coll (KS)
Coll of the Desert (CA)
Collin County Comm Coll (TX)
Columbia State Comm Coll (TN)
Comm Coll of Allegheny County Allegheny Cmps (PA)
Comm Coll of Allegheny County North Cmps (PA)
Comm Coll of Allegheny County South Cmps (PA)
Comm Coll of Southern Nevada (NV)
Copiah-Lincoln Comm Coll (MS)
Crafton Hills Coll (CA)
Cypress Coll (CA)
Dalton Coll (GA)
Darton Coll (GA)
Daytona Beach Comm Coll (FL)
De Anza Coll (CA)
DeKalb Coll (GA)
Dixie Coll (UT)
East Central Coll (MO)
East Central Comm Coll (MS)
Eastern Oklahoma State Coll (OK)
Eastern Wyoming Coll (WY)
East Mississippi Comm Coll (MS)
El Camino Coll (CA)
Ellsworth Comm Coll (IA)
Essex Comm Coll (MD)
Everett Comm Coll (WA)
Foothill Coll (CA)
Frank Phillips Coll (TX)
Fullerton Coll (CA)
Glendale Comm Coll (AZ)
Grossmont Coll (CA)
Gulf Coast Comm Coll (FL)
Hartnell Coll (CA)
Hill Coll of the Hill Jr Coll District (TX)
Hinds Comm Coll (MS)
Hiwassee Coll (TN)
Hutchinson Comm Coll and Area Vocational Sch (KS)
Indian River Comm Coll (FL)
Iowa Lakes Comm Coll (IA)
Itawamba Comm Coll (MS)
Jackson State Comm Coll (TN)
John Wood Comm Coll (IL)
Jones County Jr Coll (MS)
Kansas City Kansas Comm Coll (KS)
Kemper Military Jr Coll (MO)
Kent State U, Geauga Cmps (OH)
Lake Land Coll (IL)
Lake Michigan Coll (MI)
Laramie County Comm Coll (WY)
Lincoln Coll, Normal (IL)
Lincoln Land Comm Coll (IL)
Linn-Benton Comm Coll (OR)
Lon Morris Coll (TX)
Los Angeles Mission Coll (CA)
Los Angeles Southwest Coll (CA)
Los Angeles Valley Coll (CA)
Lower Columbia Coll (WA)
Macon Coll (GA)
Marshalltown Comm Coll (IA)
Merritt Coll (CA)

Peterson's Guide to Two-Year Colleges 1997
77

Associate Degree Programs at Two-Year Colleges
Economics–Electrical and Electronics Technologies

Miami-Dade Comm Coll (FL)
Miami University–Middletown Cmps (OH)
Mississippi Delta Comm Coll (MS)
Modesto Jr Coll (CA)
Monterey Peninsula Coll (CA)
Motlow State Comm Coll (TN)
Muscatine Comm Coll (IA)
Muskegon Comm Coll (MI)
New Mexico Military Inst (NM)
Northeastern Jr Coll (CO)
Northeastern Oklahoma A&M Coll (OK)
Northeast Mississippi Comm Coll (MS)
Northwest Coll (WY)
Oxnard Coll (CA)
Palm Beach Comm Coll (FL)
Palo Alto Coll (TX)
Palomar Coll (CA)
Palo Verde Coll (CA)
Parks Jr Coll (CO)
Pasadena City Coll (CA)
Polk Comm Coll (FL)
Potomac State Coll of West Virginia U (WV)
Rancho Santiago Coll (CA)
Redlands Comm Coll (OK)
Red Rocks Comm Coll (CO)
Ricks Coll (ID)
Saddleback Coll (CA)
San Bernardino Valley Coll (CA)
San Jacinto College–Central Cmps (TX)
San Jacinto College–North Cmps (TX)
San Joaquin Delta Coll (CA)
Santa Barbara City Coll (CA)
Santa Monica Coll (CA)
Santa Rosa Jr Coll (CA)
Sauk Valley Comm Coll (IL)
Sawyer Coll of Business, Cleveland (OH)
Seward County Comm Coll (KS)
Skagit Valley Coll (WA)
Skyline Coll (CA)
Snow Coll (UT)
SouthWest Collegiate Inst for the Deaf (TX)
Southwestern Coll (CA)
Southwestern Comm Coll (IA)
State Comm Coll of East St Louis (IL)
Tacoma Comm Coll (WA)
Treasure Valley Comm Coll (OR)
Triton Coll (IL)
Tulsa Jr Coll (OK)
Umpqua Comm Coll (OR)
U of Cincinnati Raymond Walters Coll (OH)
U of Kentucky, Jefferson Comm Coll (KY)
Vermilion Comm Coll (MN)
Vincennes U (IN)
Waubonsee Comm Coll (IL)
Wenatchee Valley Coll (WA)
Western Nebraska Comm Coll, Scottsbluff (NE)
Western Oklahoma State Coll (OK)
West Los Angeles Coll (CA)
West Valley Coll (CA)

EDUCATION
Abraham Baldwin Ag Coll (GA)
Alabama Southern Comm Coll, Monroeville (AL)
Alabama Southern Comm Coll, Thomasville (AL)
Allegany Comm Coll (MD)
Allen County Comm Coll (KS)
Ancilla Coll (IN)
Andrew Coll (GA)
Anne Arundel Comm Coll (MD)
Arizona Western Coll (AZ)
Atlantic Comm Coll (NJ)
Bainbridge Coll (GA)
Barstow Coll (CA)
Barton County Comm Coll (KS)
Bay de Noc Comm Coll (MI)
Bee County Coll (TX)
Bergen Comm Coll (NJ)
Bevill State Comm Coll (AL)
Bismarck State Coll (ND)
Black Hawk Coll, Moline (IL)
Bowling Green State University–Firelands Coll (OH)
Brazosport Coll (TX)
Brevard Coll (NC)
Brevard Comm Coll (FL)
Brookdale Comm Coll (NJ)
Brunswick Coll (GA)
Bucks County Comm Coll (PA)
Butler County Comm Coll (PA)
Cañada Coll (CA)
Cape Cod Comm Coll (MA)
Casper Coll (WY)
Catonsville Comm Coll (MD)
Cecil Comm Coll (MD)
Central Carolina Comm Coll (NC)
Central Coll (KS)
Central Comm College–Platte Cmps (NE)
Central Florida Comm Coll (FL)
Central Oregon Comm Coll (OR)
Central Texas Coll (TX)
Central Virginia Comm Coll (VA)
Central Wyoming Coll (WY)
Chabot Coll (CA)
Charles County Comm Coll (MD)
Chemeketa Comm Coll (OR)
Chipola Jr Coll (FL)
Cisco Jr Coll (TX)
City Colls of Chicago, Harry S Truman Coll (IL)
City Colls of Chicago, Kennedy-King Coll (IL)
City Colls of Chicago, Richard J Daley Coll (IL)
Clackamas Comm Coll (OR)
Clarendon Coll (TX)
Clark Coll (WA)
Clinton Comm Coll (IA)
Cloud County Comm Coll (KS)
Cochise Coll, Douglas (AZ)
Cochise Coll, Sierra Vista (AZ)
Coffeyville Comm Coll (KS)
Colby Comm Coll (KS)
Coll of DuPage (IL)
Coll of Micronesia–FSM (FM)
Coll of Southern Idaho (ID)
Coll of the Desert (CA)
Collin County Comm Coll (TX)
Comm Coll of Allegheny County Allegheny Cmps (PA)
Comm Coll of Allegheny County Boyce Cmps (PA)
Comm Coll of Allegheny County North Cmps (PA)
Comm Coll of Allegheny County South Cmps (PA)
Comm Coll of Beaver County (PA)
Comm Coll of Philadelphia (PA)
Comm Coll of Rhode Island (RI)
Comm Coll of Vermont (VT)
Connors State Coll (OK)
Copiah-Lincoln Comm Coll (MS)
Cowley County Comm Coll and Voc-Tech Sch (KS)
Crowder Coll (MO)
Cumberland County Coll (NJ)
Dabney S Lancaster Comm Coll (VA)
Dalton Coll (GA)
Danville Area Comm Coll (IL)
Danville Comm Coll (VA)
Darton Coll (GA)
Daytona Beach Comm Coll (FL)
Del Mar Coll (TX)
Des Moines Area Comm Coll (IA)
Dixie Coll (UT)
Dodge City Comm Coll (KS)
Donnelly Coll (KS)
East Central Coll (MO)
East Central Comm Coll (MS)
Eastern Arizona Coll (AZ)
Eastern Oklahoma State Coll (OK)
Eastern Shore Comm Coll (VA)
Eastern Wyoming Coll (WY)
East Georgia Coll (GA)
East Mississippi Comm Coll (MS)
Ellsworth Comm Coll (IA)
El Paso Comm Coll (TX)
Enterprise State Jr Coll (AL)
Essex County Coll (NJ)
Everett Comm Coll (WA)
Fiorello H LaGuardia Comm Coll of City U of NY (NY)
Fort Scott Comm Coll (KS)
Frank Phillips Coll (TX)
Frederick Comm Coll (MD)
Gainesville Coll (GA)
Galveston Coll (TX)
Garden City Comm Coll (KS)
Garland County Comm Coll (AR)
Garrett Comm Coll (MD)
Genesee Comm Coll (NY)
Germanna Comm Coll (VA)
Glendale Comm Coll (AZ)
Gloucester County Coll (NJ)
Gogebic Comm Coll (MI)
Gordon Coll (GA)
Grays Harbor Coll (WA)
Grayson County Coll (TX)
Greenfield Comm Coll (MA)
Gulf Coast Comm Coll (FL)
Hagerstown Jr Coll (MD)
Halifax Comm Coll (NC)
Harford Comm Coll (MD)
Harrisburg Area Comm Coll (PA)
Hawkeye Comm Coll (IA)
Highland Comm Coll (IL)
Highland Comm Coll (KS)
Highline Comm Coll (WA)
Hill Coll of the Hill Jr Coll District (TX)
Hiwassee Coll (TN)
Howard Comm Coll (MD)
Hutchinson Comm Coll and Area Vocational Sch (KS)
Illinois Eastern Comm Colls, Lincoln Trail Coll (IL)
Illinois Valley Comm Coll (IL)
Indian River Comm Coll (FL)
Iowa Central Comm Coll (IA)
Iowa Lakes Comm Coll (IA)
Isothermal Comm Coll (NC)
Itawamba Comm Coll (MS)
Jackson State Comm Coll (TN)
James Sprunt Comm Coll (NC)
Jefferson Coll (MO)
Jefferson Davis Comm Coll (AL)
John A Logan Coll (IL)
John C Calhoun State Comm Coll (AL)
John Wood Comm Coll (IL)
Joliet Jr Coll (IL)
Jones County Jr Coll (MS)
J Sargeant Reynolds Comm Coll (VA)
Kalamazoo Valley Comm Coll (MI)
Kansas City Kansas Comm Coll (KS)
Kellogg Comm Coll (MI)
Kennebec Valley Tech Coll (ME)
Kent State U, Stark Cmps (OH)
Kirkwood Comm Coll (IA)
Kishwaukee Coll (IL)
Labette Comm Coll (KS)
Lackawanna Jr Coll (PA)
Lake City Comm Coll (FL)
Lake Michigan Coll (MI)
Lansing Comm Coll (MI)
Laramie County Comm Coll (WY)
Las Positas Coll (CA)
Lawson State Comm Coll (AL)
Lehigh Carbon Comm Coll (PA)
Lincoln Coll, Normal (IL)
Lincoln Land Comm Coll (IL)
Linn-Benton Comm Coll (OR)
Lon Morris Coll (TX)
Lorain County Comm Coll (OH)
Lord Fairfax Comm Coll (VA)
Los Angeles Southwest Coll (CA)
Louisiana State U at Alexandria (LA)
Lower Columbia Coll (WA)
Luzerne County Comm Coll (PA)
Macon Coll (GA)
Manor Jr Coll (PA)
Mary Holmes Coll (MS)
Mercer County Comm Coll (NJ)
Miami-Dade Comm Coll (FL)
Miami University–Middletown Cmps (OH)
Middle Georgia Coll (GA)
Middlesex County Coll (NJ)
Mid-Plains Comm Coll (NE)
Mineral Area Coll (MO)
Mississippi Delta Comm Coll (MS)
Mississippi Gulf Coast Comm Coll (MS)
Moberly Area Comm Coll (MO)
Montgomery College–Germantown Cmps (MD)
Montgomery College–Rockville Cmps (MD)
Montgomery College–Takoma Park Cmps (MD)
Montgomery County Comm Coll (PA)
Moraine Valley Comm Coll (IL)
Motlow State Comm Coll (TN)
Mountain Empire Comm Coll (VA)
Mount Ida Coll (MA)
Muscatine Comm Coll (IA)
Muskegon Comm Coll (MI)
Navarro Coll (TX)
Nebraska Indian Comm Coll (NE)
New Mexico Jr Coll (NM)
New Mexico State University–Carlsbad (NM)
New Mexico State University–Grants (NM)
New River Comm Coll (VA)
Northampton County Area Comm Coll (PA)
North Dakota State University–Bottineau (ND)
Northeast Comm Coll (NE)
Northeastern Jr Coll (CO)
Northeast Mississippi Comm Coll (MS)
Northern Essex Comm Coll (MA)
Northern Marianas Coll (MP)
North Harris Coll (TX)
North Idaho Coll (ID)
NorthWest Arkansas Comm Coll (AR)
Northwest Coll (WY)
Northwest Indian Coll (WA)
Northwest Mississippi Comm Coll (MS)
Northwest-Shoals Comm Coll (AL)
Odessa Coll (TX)
Ohio Valley Coll (WV)
Okaloosa-Walton Comm Coll (FL)
Otero Jr Coll (CO)
Palm Beach Comm Coll (FL)
Palo Alto Coll (TX)
Palo Verde Coll (CA)
Paris Jr Coll (TX)
Parkland Coll (IL)
Patrick Henry Comm Coll (VA)
Paul D Camp Comm Coll (VA)
Pensacola Jr Coll (FL)
Phillips County Comm Coll (AR)
Piedmont Virginia Comm Coll (VA)
Pikes Peak Comm Coll (CO)
Pima Comm Coll (AZ)
Polk Comm Coll (FL)
Porterville Coll (CA)
Potomac State Coll of West Virginia U (WV)
Pratt Comm Coll and Area Voc Sch (KS)
Prince George's Comm Coll (MD)
Raritan Valley Comm Coll (NJ)
Reading Area Comm Coll (PA)
Redlands Comm Coll (OK)
Ricks Coll (ID)
Roane State Comm Coll (TN)
Roanoke-Chowan Comm Coll (NC)
Robeson Comm Coll (NC)
St Catharine Coll (KY)
St Louis Comm Coll at Meramec (MO)
Salem Comm Coll (NJ)
Salt Lake Comm Coll (UT)
San Juan Coll (NM)
Santa Fe Comm Coll (FL)
Sauk Valley Comm Coll (IL)
Schenectady County Comm Coll (NY)
Scott Comm Coll (IA)
Seward County Comm Coll (KS)
Shelton State Comm Coll (AL)
Sheridan Coll (WY)
Shoreline Comm Coll (WA)
Shorter Coll (AR)
Sinclair Comm Coll (OH)
Skagit Valley Coll (WA)
Snow Coll (UT)
Southeast Comm Coll, Beatrice Cmps (NE)
South Florida Comm Coll (FL)
South Georgia Coll (GA)
South Plains Coll (TX)
Southside Virginia Comm Coll (VA)
SouthWest Collegiate Inst for the Deaf (TX)
Southwestern Comm Coll (IA)
Southwestern Michigan Coll (MI)
Southwest Mississippi Comm Coll (MS)
Southwest Texas Jr Coll (TX)
Southwest Virginia Comm Coll (VA)
Spoon River Coll (IL)
Springfield Coll in Illinois (IL)
Standing Rock Coll (ND)
State Comm Coll of East St Louis (IL)
Sullivan County Comm Coll (NY)
Tacoma Comm Coll (WA)
Three Rivers Comm Coll (MO)
Tidewater Comm Coll (VA)
Treasure Valley Comm Coll (OR)
Trinidad State Jr Coll (CO)
Trinity Valley Comm Coll (TX)
Triton Coll (IL)
Tulsa Jr Coll (OK)
Umpqua Comm Coll (OR)
Union County Coll (NJ)
U of Cincinnati Raymond Walters Coll (OH)
U of Kentucky, Jefferson Comm Coll (KY)
U of New Mexico–Gallup Branch (NM)
U of New Mexico–Valencia Cmps (NM)
U of South Carolina at Lancaster (SC)
U of Wisconsin Center–Marathon County (WI)
U of Wisconsin Center–Marinette County (WI)
Vance-Granville Comm Coll (NC)
Ventura Coll (CA)
Vermilion Comm Coll (MN)
Villa Maria Coll of Buffalo (NY)
Vincennes U (IN)
Vincennes University–Jasper Ctr (IN)
Virginia Highlands Comm Coll (VA)
Virginia Western Comm Coll (VA)
Waldorf Coll (IA)
Wallace State Comm Coll (AL)
Walters State Comm Coll (TN)
Washington State Comm Coll (OH)
Waubonsee Comm Coll (IL)
Waycross Coll (GA)
Wayne County Comm Coll (MI)
Wenatchee Valley Coll (WA)
Western Nebraska Comm Coll, Scottsbluff (NE)
Western Oklahoma State Coll (OK)
Western Texas Coll (TX)
Western Wyoming Comm Coll (WY)
West Los Angeles Coll (CA)
West Shore Comm Coll (MI)
West Virginia U at Parkersburg (WV)
Wood Coll (MS)
Wytheville Comm Coll (VA)
Young Harris Coll (GA)
Yuba Coll (CA)

EDUCATIONAL ADMINISTRATION
Brevard Coll (NC)
Comm Coll of the Air Force (AL)

EDUCATIONAL MEDIA
Alamance Comm Coll (NC)
Bellevue Comm Coll (WA)
Bunker Hill Comm Coll (MA)
City Coll of San Francisco (CA)
Comm Coll of the Air Force (AL)
Milwaukee Area Tech Coll (WI)
Polk Comm Coll (FL)
Portland Comm Coll (OR)
Rock Valley Coll (IL)
Tarrant County Jr Coll (TX)

ELECTRICAL AND ELECTRONICS TECHNOLOGIES
Aims Comm Coll (CO)
Alabama Aviation and Tech Coll (AL)
Alabama Southern Comm Coll, Thomasville (AL)
Alamance Comm Coll (NC)
Albuquerque Tech Vocational Inst (NM)
Allen County Comm Coll (KS)
Alpena Comm Coll (MI)
Alvin Comm Coll (TX)
American River Coll (CA)
Angelina Coll (TX)
Anne Arundel Comm Coll (MD)
Anson Comm Coll (NC)
Antelope Valley Coll (CA)
Arapahoe Comm Coll (CO)
Arizona Western Coll (AZ)
Athens Area Tech Inst (GA)
Atlantic Comm Coll (NJ)
Austin Comm Coll (TX)
Bainbridge Coll (GA)
Bakersfield Coll (CA)
Baltimore City Comm Coll (MD)
Barstow Coll (CA)
Barton County Comm Coll (KS)
Bay de Noc Comm Coll (MI)
Belleville Area Coll (IL)
Belmont Tech Coll (OH)
Berean Inst (PA)
Bergen Comm Coll (NJ)
Berkshire Comm Coll (MA)
Bessemer State Tech Coll (AL)
Bishop State Comm Coll (AL)
Bismarck State Coll (ND)
Black Hawk Coll, Moline (IL)
Blackhawk Tech Coll (WI)
Bladen Comm Coll (NC)
Blue Mountain Comm Coll (OR)
Blue Ridge Comm Coll (NC)
Blue Ridge Comm Coll (VA)
Bossier Parish Comm Coll (LA)
Bowling Green State University–Firelands Coll (OH)
Bramson ORT Tech Inst (NY)
Brazosport Coll (TX)
Brevard Comm Coll (FL)
Briarcliffe–The Coll for Business & Tech (NY)
Brookdale Comm Coll (NJ)
Broward Comm Coll (FL)
Brunswick Coll (GA)
Bryant and Stratton Business Inst, Buffalo (NY)
Bryant and Stratton Business Inst, Cicero (NY)
Bryant and Stratton Business Inst, Rochester (NY)

Associate Degree Programs at Two-Year Colleges
Electrical and Electronics Technologies

Bryant and Stratton Business Inst, Rochester (NY)
Bryant and Stratton Business Inst, Syracuse (NY)
Bucks County Comm Coll (PA)
Bunker Hill Comm Coll (MA)
Burlington County Coll (NJ)
Butler County Comm Coll (KS)
Butler County Comm Coll (PA)
Butte Coll (CA)
Cabrillo Coll (CA)
Caldwell Comm Coll and Tech Inst (NC)
Cañada Coll (CA)
Cape Fear Comm Coll (NC)
Capital Comm Tech Coll (CT)
Carl Sandburg Coll (IL)
Casper Coll (WY)
Catawba Valley Comm Coll (NC)
Catonsville Comm Coll (MD)
Cayuga County Comm Coll (NY)
Cecil Comm Coll (MD)
Central Alabama Comm Coll (AL)
Central Carolina Comm Coll (NC)
Central Carolina Tech Coll (SC)
Central Comm College–Grand Island Cmps (NE)
Central Comm College–Hastings Cmps (NE)
Central Comm College–Platte Cmps (NE)
Centralia Coll (WA)
Central Oregon Comm Coll (OR)
Central Piedmont Comm Coll (NC)
Central Texas Coll (TX)
Central Virginia Comm Coll (VA)
Cerritos Coll (CA)
Cerro Coso Comm Coll (CA)
Chabot Coll (CA)
Chaffey Coll (CA)
Charles County Comm Coll (MD)
Charles Stewart Mott Comm Coll (MI)
Chattanooga State Tech Comm Coll (TN)
Chemeketa Comm Coll (OR)
Chesapeake Coll (MD)
Chesterfield-Marlboro Tech Coll (SC)
CHI Inst (PA)
Chippewa Valley Tech Coll (WI)
Cisco Jr Coll (TX)
Citrus Coll (CA)
City Colls of Chicago, Olive-Harvey Coll (IL)
Clarendon Coll (TX)
Clark Coll (WA)
Clovis Comm Coll (NM)
Cochise Coll, Sierra Vista (AZ)
Coll of DuPage (IL)
Coll of Marin (CA)
Coll of San Mateo (CA)
Coll of Southern Idaho (ID)
Coll of the Canyons (CA)
Coll of the Mainland (TX)
Coll of the Sequoias (CA)
Collin County Comm Coll (TX)
Columbia Basin Coll (WA)
Comm Coll of Allegheny County North Cmps (PA)
Comm Coll of Allegheny County South Cmps (PA)
Comm Coll of Beaver County (PA)
Comm Coll of Denver (CO)
Comm Coll of Rhode Island (RI)
Comm Coll of Southern Nevada (NV)
Comm Coll of the Air Force (AL)
Contra Costa Coll (CA)
Copiah-Lincoln Comm Coll (MS)
Corning Comm Coll (NY)
Cosumnes River Coll (CA)
Cowley County Comm Coll and Voc-Tech Sch (KS)
Crowder Coll (MO)
Cuesta Coll (CA)
Cuyahoga Comm Coll, Metropolitan Cmps (OH)
Cuyamaca Coll (CA)
Dabney S Lancaster Comm Coll (VA)
Dalton Coll (GA)
Danville Area Comm Coll (IL)
Davidson County Comm Coll (NC)
Daytona Beach Comm Coll (FL)
De Anza Coll (CA)
Delaware County Comm Coll (PA)
Delaware Tech & Comm Coll, Jack F Owens Cmps (DE)
Delaware Tech & Comm Coll, Stanton/Wilmington Cmps (DE)
Delaware Tech & Comm Coll, Terry Cmps (DE)
Delgado Comm Coll (LA)
Del Mar Coll (TX)
Des Moines Area Comm Coll (IA)
DeVry Tech Inst (NJ)
Dixie Coll (UT)
Dodge City Comm Coll (KS)
Doña Ana Branch Comm Coll (NM)
Don Bosco Tech Inst (CA)
Douglas MacArthur State Tech Coll (AL)
Dundalk Comm Coll (MD)
Durham Tech Comm Coll (NC)
Dyersburg State Comm Coll (TN)
East Central Coll (MO)
East Central Comm Coll (MS)
Eastern Idaho Tech Coll (ID)
Eastern Maine Tech Coll (ME)
Eastern New Mexico University–Roswell (NM)
Eastern Shore Comm Coll (VA)
Eastfield Coll (TX)
East Los Angeles Coll (CA)
East Mississippi Comm Coll (MS)
ECPI Coll of Tech, Hampton (VA)
ECPI Coll of Tech, Virginia Beach (VA)
ECPI Computer Inst, Richmond (VA)
ECPI Computer Inst, Roanoke (VA)
Edgecombe Comm Coll (NC)
Edison Comm Coll (FL)
Edison State Comm Coll (OH)
Edmonds Comm Coll (WA)
El Camino Coll (CA)
Electronic Institutes, Pittsburgh (PA)
El Paso Comm Coll (TX)
Essex County Coll (NJ)
Evergreen Valley Coll (CA)
Florence-Darlington Tech Coll (SC)
Foothill Coll (CA)
Forsyth Tech Comm Coll (NC)
Fort Peck Comm Coll (MT)
Fox Valley Tech Coll (WI)
Franklin Inst of Boston (MA)
Frederick Comm Coll (MD)
Fresno City Coll (CA)
Front Range Comm Coll (CO)
Gainesville Coll (GA)
Garden City Comm Coll (KS)
Garland County Comm Coll (AR)
Genesee Comm Coll (NY)
George Corley Wallace State Comm Coll, Selma (AL)
George C Wallace State Comm Coll, Dothan (AL)
Germanna Comm Coll (VA)
Golden West Coll (CA)
Grand Rapids Comm Coll (MI)
Grayson County Coll (TX)
Great Basin Coll (NV)
Great Lakes Jr Coll of Business (MI)
Green River Comm Coll (WA)
Guilford Tech Comm Coll (NC)
Gwinnett Tech Inst (GA)
Harford Comm Coll (MD)
Harrisburg Area Comm Coll (PA)
Harry M Ayers State Tech Coll (AL)
Hartnell Coll (CA)
Hawkeye Comm Coll (IA)
Heald Business Coll (HI)
Heartland Comm Coll (IL)
Helena Coll of Tech of The U of Montana (MT)
Henry Ford Comm Coll (MI)
Herzing Coll of Business and Tech (AL)
Herzing Coll of Tech (WI)
Highland Comm Coll (IL)
Highland Park Comm Coll (MI)
Hill Coll of the Hill Jr Coll District (TX)
Hocking Coll (OH)
Horry-Georgetown Tech Coll (SC)
Howard Comm Coll (MD)
Hudson Valley Comm Coll (NY)
Hutchinson Comm Coll and Area Vocational Sch (KS)
ICS Ctr for Degree Studies (PA)
Illinois Central Coll (IL)
Illinois Eastern Comm Colls, Wabash Valley Coll (IL)
Illinois Valley Comm Coll (IL)
Indian Hills Comm Coll (IA)
Indian River Comm Coll (FL)
Inst of Electronic Tech (KY)
Iowa Lakes Comm Coll (IA)
Isothermal Comm Coll (NC)
Itawamba Comm Coll (MS)
ITT Tech Inst (ID)
Ivy Tech State Coll–Central Indiana (IN)
Ivy Tech State Coll–Columbus (IN)
Ivy Tech State Coll–Eastcentral (IN)
Ivy Tech State Coll–Kokomo (IN)
Ivy Tech State Coll–Lafayette (IN)
Ivy Tech State Coll–Northcentral (IN)
Ivy Tech State Coll–Northeast (IN)
Ivy Tech State Coll–Northwest (IN)
Ivy Tech State Coll–Southcentral (IN)
Ivy Tech State Coll–Southeast (IN)
Ivy Tech State Coll–Southwest (IN)
Ivy Tech State Coll–Wabash Valley (IN)
Ivy Tech State Coll–Whitewater (IN)
Jefferson Coll (MO)
Jefferson Comm Coll (OH)
J F Drake State Tech Coll (AL)
John A Logan Coll (IL)
John C Calhoun State Comm Coll (AL)
John M Patterson State Tech Coll (AL)
Johnson Tech Inst (PA)
John Wood Comm Coll (IL)
Joliet Jr Coll (IL)
Jones County Jr Coll (MS)
J Sargeant Reynolds Comm Coll (VA)
Kalamazoo Valley Comm Coll (MI)
Kankakee Comm Coll (IL)
Kansas City Kansas Comm Coll (KS)
Kaskaskia Coll (IL)
Kellogg Comm Coll (MI)
Kennebec Valley Tech Coll (ME)
Kent State U, Ashtabula Cmps (OH)
Kent State U, Trumbull Cmps (OH)
Kettering Coll of Medical Arts (OH)
Kirkwood Comm Coll (IA)
Kishwaukee Coll (IL)
Lake Land Coll (IL)
Lakeland Comm Coll (OH)
Lake Michigan Coll (MI)
Lakeshore Tech Coll (WI)
Lake Washington Tech Coll (WA)
Lane Comm Coll (OR)
Lansing Comm Coll (MI)
Laredo Comm Coll (TX)
Las Positas Coll (CA)
Lawson State Comm Coll (AL)
Lee Coll (TX)
Lehigh Carbon Comm Coll (PA)
Lenoir Comm Coll (NC)
Lewis and Clark Comm Coll (IL)
Lincoln Land Comm Coll (IL)
Lincoln Tech Inst, Allentown (PA)
Long Beach City Coll (CA)
Longview Comm Coll (MO)
Lorain County Comm Coll (OH)
Lord Fairfax Comm Coll (VA)
Los Angeles City Coll (CA)
Los Angeles Pierce Coll (CA)
Los Angeles Trade-Tech Coll (CA)
Los Angeles Valley Coll (CA)
Los Medanos Coll (CA)
Lower Columbia Coll (WA)
Luzerne County Comm Coll (PA)
Macomb Comm Coll (MI)
Madison Area Tech Coll (WI)
Maple Woods Comm Coll (MO)
Marion Tech Coll (OH)
Marshalltown Comm Coll (IA)
Massachusetts Bay Comm Coll (MA)
Massasoit Comm Coll (MA)
Mayland Comm Coll (NC)
McDowell Tech Comm Coll (NC)
Merced Coll (CA)
Mercer County Comm Coll (NJ)
Meridian Comm Coll (MS)
Mesa Comm Coll (AZ)
Metropolitan Comm Coll (NE)
Miami-Dade Comm Coll (FL)
Miami University–Hamilton Cmps (OH)
Middlesex County Coll (NJ)
Midland Coll (TX)
Midlands Tech Coll (SC)
Mid-Plains Comm Coll (NE)
Mid-State Tech Coll (WI)
Miles Comm Coll (MT)
Milwaukee Area Tech Coll (WI)
Mineral Area Coll (MO)
Mission Coll (CA)
Mississippi County Comm Coll (AR)
Mississippi Delta Comm Coll (MS)
Mississippi Gulf Coast Comm Coll (MS)
Moberly Area Comm Coll (MO)
Modesto Jr Coll (CA)
Mohawk Valley Comm Coll (NY)
Monroe County Comm Coll (MI)
Montcalm Comm Coll (MI)
Montgomery College–Rockville Cmps (MD)
Montgomery Comm Coll (NC)
Montgomery County Comm Coll (PA)
Moorpark Coll (CA)
Moraine Valley Comm Coll (IL)
Morgan Comm Coll (CO)
Motlow State Comm Coll (TN)
Mountain Empire Comm Coll (VA)
Mountain View Coll (TX)
Mt Hood Comm Coll (OR)
Mt San Antonio Coll (CA)
Murray State Coll (OK)
Muskegon Comm Coll (MI)
Muskingum Area Tech Coll (OH)
Napa Valley Coll (CA)
Nassau Comm Coll (NY)
National Ed Ctr–Spartan Sch of Aeronautics Cmps (OK)
Nebraska Indian Comm Coll (NE)
NEI Coll of Tech (MN)
Neosho County Comm Coll (KS)
New England Inst of Tech (RI)
New Hampshire Tech Coll, Claremont (NH)
New Hampshire Tech Coll, Laconia (NH)
New Hampshire Tech Coll, Manchester (NH)
New Hampshire Tech Coll, Nashua (NH)
New Mexico State University–Carlsbad (NM)
New Mexico State University–Grants (NM)
New River Comm Coll (VA)
Nielsen Electronics Inst (SC)
Northampton County Area Comm Coll (PA)
North Central Missouri Coll (MO)
North Central Tech Coll (OH)
Northcentral Tech Coll (WI)
North Central Texas Coll (TX)
North Dakota State Coll of Science (ND)
Northeast Comm Coll (NE)
Northeastern Oklahoma A&M Coll (OK)
Northeast Iowa Comm Coll, Calmar Cmps (IA)
Northeast Iowa Comm Coll, Peosta Cmps (IA)
Northeast Mississippi Comm Coll (MS)
Northeast State Tech Comm Coll (TN)
Northern Essex Comm Coll (MA)
Northern Maine Tech Coll (ME)
Northern Virginia Comm Coll (VA)
North Harris Coll (TX)
North Idaho Coll (ID)
North Iowa Area Comm Coll (IA)
North Lake Coll (TX)
Northland Comm and Tech Coll (MN)
Northland Pioneer Coll (AZ)
North Seattle Comm Coll (WA)
Northwestern Connecticut Comm-Tech Coll (CT)
Northwestern Michigan Coll (MI)
Northwest Iowa Comm Coll (IA)
Oakland Comm Coll (MI)
Oakton Comm Coll (IL)
Odessa Coll (TX)
Ohlone Coll (CA)
Oklahoma City Comm Coll (OK)
Oklahoma State U, Oklahoma City (OK)
Oklahoma State U, Okmulgee (OK)
Olympic Coll (WA)
Onondaga Comm Coll (NY)
Orangeburg-Calhoun Tech Coll (SC)
Orange Coast Coll (CA)
Orange County Comm Coll (NY)
Owens Comm Coll, Toledo (OH)
Oxnard Coll (CA)
Palau Comm Coll (PW)
Palm Beach Comm Coll (FL)
Palomar Coll (CA)
Paris Jr Coll (TX)
Parkland Coll (IL)
Pasadena City Coll (CA)
Patrick Henry Comm Coll (VA)
Pearl River Comm Coll (MS)
Peninsula Coll (WA)
Pennco Tech (PA)
Pennsylvania Coll of Tech (PA)
Pennsylvania Inst of Tech (PA)
Penn Tech Inst (PA)
Penn Valley Comm Coll (MO)
Peoples Coll (FL)
Phillips Jr Coll, Condie Cmps (CA)
Piedmont Tech Coll (SC)
Piedmont Virginia Comm Coll (VA)
Pikes Peak Comm Coll (CO)
Pima Comm Coll (AZ)
Pines Tech Coll (AR)
Pitt Comm Coll (NC)
Pittsburgh Inst of Aeronautics (PA)
Portland Comm Coll (OR)
Potomac State Coll of West Virginia U (WV)
Prairie State Coll (IL)
Pueblo Comm Coll (CO)
Quinsigamond Comm Coll (MA)
Rancho Santiago Coll (CA)
Randolph Comm Coll (NC)
Ranken Tech Coll (MO)
Raritan Valley Comm Coll (NJ)
Reading Area Comm Coll (PA)
Redlands Comm Coll (OK)
Red Rocks Comm Coll (CO)
Reid State Tech Coll (AL)
Renton Tech Coll (WA)
RETS Tech Ctr (OH)
Richland Comm Coll (IL)
Ricks Coll (ID)
Riverside Comm Coll (CA)
Roanoke-Chowan Comm Coll (NC)
Rock Valley Coll (IL)
Rogue Comm Coll (OR)
Rose State Coll (OK)
Rowan-Cabarrus Comm Coll (NC)
Sacramento City Coll (CA)
Saint Charles County Comm Coll (MO)
St Clair County Comm Coll (MI)
St Paul Tech Coll (MN)
St Philip's Coll (TX)
Salem Comm Coll (NJ)
Salt Lake Comm Coll (UT)
San Antonio Coll (TX)
San Bernardino Valley Coll (CA)
Sandhills Comm Coll (NC)
San Diego City Coll (CA)
San Diego Mesa Coll (CA)
San Jacinto College–Central Cmps (TX)
San Jacinto College–North Cmps (TX)
San Jacinto College–South Cmps (TX)
San Joaquin Delta Coll (CA)
San Jose City Coll (CA)
San Juan Coll (NM)
Santa Barbara City Coll (CA)
Santa Fe Comm Coll (NM)
Santa Monica Coll (CA)
Santa Rosa Jr Coll (CA)
Sauk Valley Comm Coll (IL)
Schenectady County Comm Coll (NY)
Schoolcraft Coll (MI)
Scottsdale Comm Coll (AZ)
Shasta Coll (CA)
Shawnee Comm Coll (IL)
Shelton State Comm Coll (AL)
Sierra Coll (CA)
Sinclair Comm Coll (OH)
Sisseton-Wahpeton Comm Coll (SD)
Skagit Valley Coll (WA)
Snow Coll (UT)
Solano Comm Coll (CA)
Southeast Comm Coll, Lincoln Cmps (NE)
Southeast Comm Coll, Milford Cmps (NE)
Southeastern Illinois Coll (IL)
Southern Arkansas U Tech (AR)
Southern Maine Tech Coll (ME)
Southern Ohio Coll, Cincinnati Cmps (OH)
Southern State Comm Coll (OH)
South Plains Coll (TX)
South Puget Sound Comm Coll (WA)
Southside Virginia Comm Coll (VA)
South Suburban Coll (IL)
Southwestern Coll (CA)
Southwestern Comm Coll (NC)
Southwestern Michigan Coll (MI)
Southwestern Oregon Comm Coll (OR)
Southwest Mississippi Comm Coll (MS)

Southwest Virginia Comm Coll (VA)
Southwest Wisconsin Tech Coll (WI)
Spartanburg Tech Coll (SC)
Spokane Comm Coll (WA)
Spoon River Coll (IL)
Stanly Comm Coll (NC)
Stark Tech Coll (OH)
State Fair Comm Coll (MO)
State Tech Inst at Memphis (TN)
State U of NY Coll of A&T at Morrisville (NY)
State U of NY Coll of Tech at Alfred (NY)
State U of NY Coll of Tech at Canton (NY)
State U of NY Coll of Tech at Farmingdale (NY)
Suffolk County Comm College–Ammerman Cmps (NY)
Suffolk County Comm Coll–Western Cmps (NY)
Surry Comm Coll (NC)
Taft Coll (CA)
Tarrant County Jr Coll (TX)
Tech Career Institutes (NY)
Temple Coll (TX)
Tennessee Inst of Electronics (TN)
Terra State Comm Coll (OH)
Texarkana Coll (TX)
Texas Southmost Coll (TX)
Texas State Tech Coll (TX)
Texas State Tech Coll–Harlingen Cmps (TX)
Texas State Tech Coll–Waco/Marshall Cmps (TX)
Thaddeus Stevens State Sch of Tech (PA)
Thomas Nelson Comm Coll (VA)
Thompson Inst (PA)
Tidewater Comm Coll (VA)
Tompkins Cortland Comm Coll (NY)
Trenholm State Tech Coll (AL)
Triangle Tech, Inc–DuBois Sch (PA)
Triangle Tech, Inc–Erie Sch (PA)
Tri-County Comm Coll (NC)
Tri-County Tech Coll (SC)
Trident Tech Coll (SC)
Trinidad State Jr Coll (CO)
Triton Coll (IL)
Truckee Meadows Comm Coll (NV)
Tulsa Jr Coll (OK)
Tyler Jr Coll (TX)
Umpqua Comm Coll (OR)
U of Alaska Anchorage, Kenai Peninsula Coll (AK)
U of Alaska Anchorage, Matanuska-Susitna Coll (AK)
U of Hawaii–Hawaii Comm Coll (HI)
U of Hawaii–Honolulu Comm Coll (HI)
U of Hawaii–Kauai Comm Coll (HI)
U of Kentucky, Hopkinsville Comm Coll (KY)
U of New Mexico–Los Alamos Branch (NM)
U of North Dakota–Lake Region (ND)
Utah Valley State Coll (UT)
Vance-Granville Comm Coll (NC)
Ventura Coll (CA)
Vermont Tech Coll (VT)
Victor Valley Coll (CA)
Vincennes U (IN)
Virginia Coll (VA)
Virginia Coll at Birmingham (AL)
Virginia Highlands Comm Coll (VA)
Virginia Western Comm Coll (VA)
Wake Tech Comm Coll (NC)
Wallace State Comm Coll (AL)
Washington State Comm Coll (OH)
Washtenaw Comm Coll (MI)
Waubonsee Comm Coll (IL)
Waukesha County Tech Coll (WI)
Waycross Coll (GA)
Westark Comm Coll (AR)
Western Dakota Tech Inst (SD)
Western Iowa Tech Comm Coll (IA)
Western Nebraska Comm Coll, Scottsbluff (NE)
Western Nevada Comm Coll (NV)
Western Wisconsin Tech Coll (WI)
Western Wyoming Comm Coll (WY)
West Los Angeles Coll (CA)
Westmoreland County Comm Coll (PA)
West Shore Comm Coll (MI)
West Virginia Northern Comm Coll (WV)
West Virginia U at Parkersburg (WV)
Wharton County Jr Coll (TX)
William Rainey Harper Coll (IL)
The Williamson Free Sch of Mech Trades (PA)
Willmar Comm Coll (MN)
Willmar Tech Coll (MN)
Wilson Tech Comm Coll (NC)
Wisconsin Indianhead Tech Coll, Superior Cmps (WI)
Wytheville Comm Coll (VA)
York Tech Coll (SC)
Yuba Coll (CA)

ELECTRICAL ENGINEERING TECHNOLOGY

Adirondack Comm Coll (NY)
Aiken Tech Coll (SC)
Albuquerque Tech Vocational Inst (NM)
Anne Arundel Comm Coll (MD)
Augusta Tech Inst (GA)
Austin Comm Coll (TX)
Bay de Noc Comm Coll (MI)
Beaufort County Comm Coll (NC)
Berkshire Comm Coll (MA)
Black Hawk Coll, Moline (IL)
Brevard Comm Coll (FL)
Bristol Comm Coll (MA)
Bronx Comm Coll of City U of NY (NY)
Brookdale Comm Coll (NJ)
Broome Comm Coll (NY)
Butler County Comm Coll (KS)
Cabrillo Coll (CA)
Camden County Coll (NJ)
Capital Comm Tech Coll (CT)
Central Oregon Comm Coll (OR)
Central Piedmont Comm Coll (NC)
Chabot Coll (CA)
Charles Stewart Mott Comm Coll (MI)
Chattahoochee Tech Inst (GA)
Chattanooga State Tech Comm Coll (TN)
Cincinnati State Tech and Comm Coll (OH)
City Coll of San Francisco (CA)
Clark State Comm Coll (OH)
Collin County Comm Coll (TX)
Comm Coll of Allegheny County South Cmps (PA)
Comm Coll of Southern Nevada (NV)
Copiah-Lincoln Comm Coll (MS)
Craven Comm Coll (NC)
Delaware Tech & Comm Coll, Stanton/Wilmington Cmps (DE)
Delgado Comm Coll (LA)
Del Mar Coll (TX)
Delta Coll (MI)
Dunwoody Inst (MN)
Dutchess Comm Coll (NY)
Eastern Maine Tech Coll (ME)
Eastern Oklahoma State Coll (OK)
Edison State Comm Coll (OH)
Erie Comm Coll, North Cmps (NY)
Finger Lakes Comm Coll (NY)
Florida Keys Comm Coll (FL)
Franklin Inst of Boston (MA)
Frank Phillips Coll (TX)
Gadsden State Comm Coll (AL)
Garland County Comm Coll (AR)
Gateway Comm-Tech Coll (CT)
Grayson County Coll (TX)
Hagerstown Jr Coll (MD)
Harrisburg Area Comm Coll (PA)
Hartnell Coll (CA)
Herzing Coll of Business and Tech (GA)
Hill Coll of the Hill Jr Coll District (TX)
Hocking Coll (OH)
Hudson Valley Comm Coll (NY)
ICS Ctr for Degree Studies (PA)
Inst of Electronic Tech (KY)
Iowa Central Comm Coll (IA)
Isothermal Comm Coll (NC)
ITT Tech Inst (WI)
Jackson Comm Coll (MI)
Jamestown Comm Coll (NY)
Jefferson Coll (MO)
Jefferson Comm Coll (OH)
Johnson County Comm Coll (KS)
J Sargeant Reynolds Comm Coll (VA)
Kansas City Kansas Comm Coll (KS)
Kent State U, Ashtabula Cmps (OH)
Kent State U, Tuscarawas Cmps (OH)
Kirkwood Comm Coll (IA)
Lakeshore Tech Coll (WI)
Lane Comm Coll (OR)
Lansing Comm Coll (MI)
Lehigh Carbon Comm Coll (PA)
Los Angeles Harbor Coll (CA)
Los Angeles Trade-Tech Coll (CA)
Los Angeles Valley Coll (CA)
Louisville Tech Inst (KY)
Macomb Comm Coll (MI)
Manatee Comm Coll (FL)
Marion Tech Coll (OH)
Massachusetts Bay Comm Coll (MA)
Mendocino Coll (CA)
Mercer County Comm Coll (NJ)
Miami University–Hamilton Cmps (OH)
Miami University–Middletown Cmps (OH)
Middlesex County Coll (NJ)
Midlands Tech Coll (SC)
Milwaukee Area Tech Coll (WI)
Mohawk Valley Comm Coll (NY)
Monroe Comm Coll (NY)
Motlow State Comm Coll (TN)
Mountain View Coll (TX)
Mount Ida Coll (MA)
Mount Wachusett Comm Coll (MA)
Nashville State Tech Inst (TN)
Naugatuck Valley Community–Tech Coll (CT)
New York City Tech Coll of the City U of NY (NY)
North Central Texas Coll (TX)
North Dakota State Coll of Science (ND)
Northeast Mississippi Comm Coll (MS)
Northern Essex Comm Coll (MA)
Northwest Iowa Comm Coll (IA)
Northwest State Comm Coll (OH)
Norwalk Comm-Tech Coll (CT)
Oakland Comm Coll (MI)
Ocean County Coll (NJ)
Oklahoma State U, Okmulgee (OK)
Onondaga Comm Coll (NY)
Orange County Comm Coll (NY)
Owens Comm Coll, Findlay (OH)
Owens Comm Coll, Toledo (OH)
Pamlico Comm Coll (NC)
Parkland Coll (IL)
Pasadena City Coll (CA)
Pellissippi State Tech Comm Coll (TN)
Penn State U Abington-Ogontz Cmps (PA)
Penn State U Altoona Cmps (PA)
Penn State U Beaver Cmps (PA)
Penn State U Berks Cmps (PA)
Penn State U DuBois Cmps (PA)
Penn State U Fayette Cmps (PA)
Penn State U Hazleton Cmps (PA)
Penn State U McKeesport Cmps (PA)
Penn State U New Kensington Cmps (PA)
Penn State U Schuylkill Cmps (PA)
Penn State U Shenango Cmps (PA)
Penn State U Wilkes-Barre Cmps (PA)
Penn State U York Cmps (PA)
Phillips Jr Coll, Condie Cmps (CA)
Polk Comm Coll (FL)
Portland Comm Coll (OR)
Queensborough Comm Coll of City U of NY (NY)
Reading Area Comm Coll (PA)
Ricks Coll (ID)
Riverside Comm Coll (CA)
Rockland Comm Coll (NY)
Rock Valley Coll (IL)
Rowan-Cabarrus Comm Coll (NC)
Saddleback Coll (CA)
St Louis Comm Coll at Florissant Valley (MO)
St Louis Comm Coll at Forest Park (MO)
St Louis Comm Coll at Meramec (MO)
Salt Lake Comm Coll (UT)
San Jacinto College–Central Cmps (TX)
San Jacinto College–North Cmps (TX)
San Joaquin Delta Coll (CA)
San Juan Coll (NM)
Santa Barbara City Coll (CA)
Santa Monica Coll (CA)
Shasta Coll (CA)
Shelton State Comm Coll (AL)
Southeast Comm Coll, Milford Cmps (NE)
Southeastern Comm Coll (NC)
Southern Maine Tech Coll (ME)
South Suburban Coll (IL)
Southwestern Coll (CA)
Southwestern Comm Coll (IA)
Spokane Comm Coll (WA)
Springfield Tech Comm Coll (MA)
Stark Tech Coll (OH)
State Tech Inst at Memphis (TN)
State U of NY Coll of A&T at Morrisville (NY)
State U of NY Coll of Tech at Alfred (NY)
State U of NY Coll of Tech at Canton (NY)
State U of NY Coll of Tech at Farmingdale (NY)
Suffolk County Comm College–Ammerman Cmps (NY)
Tech Career Institutes (NY)
Thaddeus Stevens State Sch of Tech (PA)
Three Rivers Comm-Tech Coll (CT)
Triangle Tech, Inc, Pittsburgh (PA)
Trident Tech Coll (SC)
U of Cincinnati Clermont Coll (OH)
U of Kentucky, Henderson Comm Coll (KY)
U of Kentucky, Jefferson Comm Coll (KY)
U of Kentucky, Lexington Comm Coll (KY)
U of Kentucky, Madisonville Comm Coll (KY)
U of Kentucky, Maysville Comm Coll (KY)
U of Kentucky, Paducah Comm Coll (KY)
Vermont Tech Coll (VT)
Vincennes U (IN)
Washington State Comm Coll (OH)
Washtenaw Comm Coll (MI)
Wayne County Comm Coll (MI)
Westchester Comm Coll (NY)
Western Piedmont Comm Coll (NC)
Western Wyoming Comm Coll (WY)
Wright State U, Lake Cmps (OH)
Yakima Valley Comm Coll (WA)

ELECTROMECHANICAL TECHNOLOGY

Aiken Tech Coll (SC)
Alamance Comm Coll (NC)
Allegany Comm Coll (MD)
American Inst of Design (PA)
Angelina Coll (TX)
Athens Area Tech Inst (GA)
Augusta Tech Inst (GA)
Belmont Tech Coll (OH)
Blackhawk Tech Coll (WI)
Bramson ORT Tech Inst (NY)
Bristol Comm Coll (MA)
Brookhaven Coll (TX)
Central Comm College–Hastings Cmps (NE)
Central Comm College–Platte Cmps (NE)
Central Maine Tech Coll (ME)
Central Ohio Tech Coll (OH)
Central Piedmont Comm Coll (NC)
Chabot Coll (CA)
Chattahoochee Tech Inst (GA)
Chemeketa Comm Coll (OR)
Chippewa Valley Tech Coll (WI)
Cincinnati State Tech and Comm Coll (OH)
Clark Coll (WA)
Coll of DuPage (IL)
Columbus State Comm Coll (OH)
Comm Coll of Allegheny County North Cmps (PA)
Comm Coll of Allegheny County South Cmps (PA)
Dean Inst of Tech (PA)
DeKalb Tech Inst (GA)
Delaware Tech & Comm Coll, Terry Cmps (DE)
Dutchess Comm Coll (NY)
ECPI Coll of Tech, Hampton (VA)
ECPI Coll of Tech, Virginia Beach (VA)
ECPI Computer Inst, Richmond (VA)
ECPI Computer Inst, Roanoke (VA)
Edison State Comm Coll (OH)
Forsyth Tech Comm Coll (NC)
Gateway Comm Coll (AZ)
Houston Comm Coll System (TX)
Irvine Valley Coll (CA)
Johnson Tech Inst (PA)
Kirkwood Comm Coll (IA)
Lake Land Coll (IL)
Lake Michigan Coll (MI)
Lakeshore Tech Coll (WI)
Lansing Comm Coll (MI)
Long Beach City Coll (CA)
Los Angeles Harbor Coll (CA)
Macomb Comm Coll (MI)
Massasoit Comm Coll (MA)
Meridian Comm Coll (MS)
Miami-Dade Comm Coll (FL)
Miami University–Hamilton Cmps (OH)
Miami University–Middletown Cmps (OH)
Milwaukee Area Tech Coll (WI)
Montgomery College–Germantown Cmps (MD)
Moraine Park Tech Coll (WI)
Mountain View Coll (TX)
Muskegon Comm Coll (MI)
NEI Coll of Tech (MN)
New Hampshire Tech Coll, Manchester (NH)
New Hampshire Tech Coll, Nashua (NH)
New York City Tech Coll of the City U of NY (NY)
Normandale Comm Coll (MN)
Northampton County Area Comm Coll (PA)
North Arkansas Comm/Tech Coll (AR)
Northcentral Tech Coll (WI)
North Seattle Comm Coll (WA)
Northwest Iowa Comm Coll (IA)
Oakland Comm Coll (MI)
Owens Comm Coll, Findlay (OH)
Owens Comm Coll, Toledo (OH)
Parkland Coll (IL)
Pulaski Tech Coll (AR)
Raritan Valley Comm Coll (NJ)
Rockingham Comm Coll (NC)
Rockland Comm Coll (NY)
Salem Comm Coll (NJ)
San Juan Coll (NM)
Sinclair Comm Coll (OH)
Southeast Comm Coll, Milford Cmps (NE)
Southern Arkansas U Tech (AR)
Southwestern Comm Coll (IA)
Southwest Wisconsin Tech Coll (WI)
Springfield Tech Comm Coll (MA)
State U of NY Coll of Tech at Alfred (NY)
Tarrant County Jr Coll (TX)
Terra State Comm Coll (OH)
Texas State Tech Coll–Harlingen Cmps (TX)
Tri-County Tech Coll (SC)
Tulsa Jr Coll (OK)
Union County Coll (NJ)
Washtenaw Comm Coll (MI)
Western Wisconsin Tech Coll (WI)
West Virginia U at Parkersburg (WV)
Wilkes Comm Coll (NC)
Wisconsin Indianhead Tech Coll, New Richmond Cmps (WI)
York Tech Coll (SC)

ELECTRONICS ENGINEERING TECHNOLOGY

Aiken Tech Coll (SC)
Alamance Comm Coll (NC)
Albuquerque Tech Vocational Inst (NM)
Allan Hancock Coll (CA)
Allen County Comm Coll (KS)
Arkansas State University–Beebe Branch (AR)
Asheville-Buncombe Tech Comm Coll (NC)
Athens Area Tech Inst (GA)
Atlanta Metropolitan Coll (GA)
Atlantic Comm Coll (NJ)
Beaufort County Comm Coll (NC)
Berkshire Comm Coll (MA)
Blue Ridge Comm Coll (NC)
Bramson ORT Tech Inst (NY)
Bristol Comm Coll (MA)
Brookdale Comm Coll (NJ)
Broward Comm Coll (FL)
Brown Inst (MN)
Brunswick Comm Coll (NC)
Cape Fear Comm Coll (NC)
Capital Comm Tech Coll (CT)
Catawba Valley Comm Coll (NC)

Associate Degree Programs at Two-Year Colleges
Electronics Engineering Technology–Elementary Education

Central Florida Comm Coll (FL)
Central Ohio Tech Coll (OH)
Central Piedmont Comm Coll (NC)
Chabot Coll (CA)
Chattanooga State Tech Comm Coll (TN)
Chemeketa Comm Coll (OR)
CHI Inst, RETS Cmps (PA)
Cincinnati State Tech and Comm Coll (OH)
City Colls of Chicago, Olive-Harvey Coll (IL)
City Colls of Chicago, Richard J Daley Coll (IL)
Clark Coll (WA)
Clark State Comm Coll (OH)
Cleveland Comm Coll (NC)
Cleveland Inst of Electronics (OH)
Clinton Comm Coll (IA)
Coahoma Comm Coll (MS)
Cochise Coll, Sierra Vista (AZ)
Coll of DuPage (IL)
Coll of Lake County (IL)
Coll of Marin (CA)
Coll of San Mateo (CA)
Coll of The Albemarle (NC)
Coll of the Redwoods (CA)
Collin County Comm Coll (TX)
Columbia State Comm Coll (TN)
Columbus State Comm Coll (OH)
Comm Coll of Allegheny County North Cmps (PA)
Comm Coll of Allegheny County South Cmps (PA)
Comm Coll of Philadelphia (PA)
Comm Coll of Rhode Island (RI)
Cosumnes River Coll (CA)
County Coll of Morris (NJ)
Craven Comm Coll (NC)
Davidson County Comm Coll (NC)
Daytona Beach Comm Coll (FL)
Delaware Tech & Comm Coll, Terry Cmps (DE)
Delgado Comm Coll (LA)
Del Mar Coll (TX)
Delta Coll (MI)
DeVry Tech Inst (NJ)
Dunwoody Inst (MN)
Durham Tech Comm Coll (NC)
Eastern Maine Tech Coll (ME)
ECPI Coll of Tech, Hampton (VA)
ECPI Coll of Tech, Virginia Beach (VA)
ECPI Computer Inst, Richmond (VA)
ECPI Computer Inst, Roanoke (VA)
Edison Comm Coll (FL)
Education America–Tampa Tech Inst Cmps (FL)
Elaine P Nunez Comm Coll (LA)
Electronic Inst, Middletown (PA)
Electronic Institutes, Pittsburgh (PA)
Elgin Comm Coll (IL)
Essex County Coll (NJ)
ETI Tech Coll, Niles (OH)
Fayetteville Tech Comm Coll (NC)
Florence-Darlington Tech Coll (SC)
Florida Comm Coll at Jacksonville (FL)
Floyd Coll (GA)
Forsyth Tech Comm Coll (NC)
Fort Scott Comm Coll (KS)
Gadsden State Comm Coll (AL)
Gaston Coll (NC)
Gateway Coll (NE)
George C Wallace State Comm Coll, Dothan (AL)
Glendale Comm Coll (AZ)
Green River Comm Coll (WA)
Greenville Tech Coll (SC)
Guilford Tech Comm Coll (NC)
Gulf Coast Comm Coll (FL)
Harrisburg Area Comm Coll (PA)
Hawkeye Comm Coll (IA)
Haywood Comm Coll (NC)
Heald Inst of Tech, Martinez (CA)
Heald Inst of Tech, Milpitas (CA)
Heald Inst of Tech, San Francisco (CA)
Hillsborough Comm Coll (FL)
Hinds Comm Coll (MS)
Horry-Georgetown Tech Coll (SC)
Houston Comm Coll System (TX)
Howard Comm Coll (MD)
Hudson County Comm Coll (NJ)
Hutchinson Comm Coll and Area Vocational Sch (KS)
Independence Comm Coll (KS)
Indian River Comm Coll (FL)
Inst of Electronic Tech (KY)
Iowa Central Comm Coll (IA)
Iowa Western Comm Coll (IA)
Isothermal Comm Coll (NC)
ITT Tech Inst (AL)
ITT Tech Inst, Phoenix (AZ)
ITT Tech Inst, Tucson (AZ)
ITT Tech Inst (AR)
ITT Tech Inst, Anaheim (CA)
ITT Tech Inst, Carson (CA)
ITT Tech Inst, Oxnard (CA)
ITT Tech Inst, Sacramento (CA)
ITT Tech Inst, San Bernardino (CA)
ITT Tech Inst, San Diego (CA)
ITT Tech Inst, Van Nuys (CA)
ITT Tech Inst, West Covina (CA)
ITT Tech Inst (CO)
ITT Tech Inst, Fort Lauderdale (FL)
ITT Tech Inst, Jacksonville (FL)
ITT Tech Inst, Tampa (FL)
ITT Tech Inst, Hoffman Estates (IL)
ITT Tech Inst, Evansville (IN)
ITT Tech Inst, Fort Wayne (IN)
ITT Tech Inst, Indianapolis (IN)
ITT Tech Inst (MA)
ITT Tech Inst (MO)
ITT Tech Inst (NE)
ITT Tech Inst, Dayton (OH)
ITT Tech Inst, Youngstown (OH)
ITT Tech Inst (OR)
ITT Tech Inst, Knoxville (TN)
ITT Tech Inst, Memphis (TN)
ITT Tech Inst, Nashville (TN)
ITT Tech Inst, Arlington (TX)
ITT Tech Inst, Austin (TX)
ITT Tech Inst, Garland (TX)
ITT Tech Inst, Houston (TX)
ITT Tech Inst, Houston (TX)
ITT Tech Inst, San Antonio (TX)
ITT Tech Inst (UT)
ITT Tech Inst, Seattle (WA)
ITT Tech Inst, Spokane (WA)
Jackson Comm Coll (MI)
Jefferson Comm Coll (OH)
Jefferson State Comm Coll (AL)
John A Logan Coll (IL)
Johnson County Comm Coll (KS)
Johnston Comm Coll (NC)
John Tyler Comm Coll (VA)
Joliet Jr Coll (IL)
Kalamazoo Valley Comm Coll (MI)
Kansas City Kansas Comm Coll (KS)
Kellogg Comm Coll (MI)
Kent State U, Tuscarawas Cmps (OH)
Kirkwood Comm Coll (IA)
Lake Area Vocational-Tech Inst (SD)
Lake City Comm Coll (FL)
Lake Land Coll (IL)
Lakeland Comm Coll (OH)
Lake-Sumter Comm Coll (FL)
Lamar University–Port Arthur (TX)
Lane Comm Coll (OR)
Lansing Comm Coll (MI)
Lehigh Carbon Comm Coll (PA)
Lenoir Comm Coll (NC)
Lima Tech Coll (OH)
Linn-Benton Comm Coll (OR)
Longview Comm Coll (MO)
Lorain County Comm Coll (OH)
Los Angeles Pierce Coll (CA)
Los Angeles Southwest Coll (CA)
Los Angeles Trade-Tech Coll (CA)
Louisville Tech Inst (KY)
Luzerne County Comm Coll (PA)
Macomb Comm Coll (MI)
Maple Woods Comm Coll (MO)
Massachusetts Bay Comm Coll (MA)
Mayland Comm Coll (NC)
McHenry County Coll (IL)
Mercer County Comm Coll (NJ)
Miami-Dade Comm Coll (FL)
Middlesex Comm Coll (MA)
Middlesex County Coll (NJ)
Mid-State Tech Coll (WI)
Mitchell Comm Coll (NC)
Mohawk Valley Comm Coll (NY)
Montgomery College–Rockville Cmps (MD)
Moraine Valley Comm Coll (IL)
Mountain Empire Comm Coll (VA)
Mountain View Coll (TX)
Nash Comm Coll (NC)
Nashville State Tech Inst (TN)
National Ed Ctr–National Inst of Tech Cmps (WV)
NEI Coll of Tech (MN)
New England Inst of Tech & Florida Culinary Inst (FL)
New Hampshire Tech Coll, Manchester (NH)
New Hampshire Tech Coll, Nashua (NH)
New Hampshire Tech Inst (NH)
New Mexico State University–Grants (NM)
Normandale Comm Coll (MN)
North Central Tech Coll (OH)
North Central Texas Coll (TX)
North Dakota State Coll of Science (ND)
Northeast Comm Coll (NE)
Northeast Iowa Comm Coll, Peosta Cmps (IA)
Northeast Mississippi Comm Coll (MS)
Northeast State Tech Comm Coll (TN)
Northern Essex Comm Coll (MA)
North Hennepin Comm Coll (MN)
North Lake Coll (TX)
North Seattle Comm Coll (WA)
Northwest Mississippi Comm Coll (MS)
Ohlone Coll (CA)
Okaloosa-Walton Comm Coll (FL)
Oklahoma State U, Oklahoma City (OK)
Orangeburg-Calhoun Tech Coll (SC)
Oregon Polytechnic Inst (OR)
Owens Comm Coll, Findlay (OH)
Owens Comm Coll, Toledo (OH)
Ozarks Tech Comm Coll (MO)
Parkland Coll (IL)
Pellissippi State Tech Comm Coll (TN)
Pennsylvania Coll of Tech (PA)
Pennsylvania Inst of Tech (PA)
Penn Valley Comm Coll (MO)
Pensacola Jr Coll (FL)
Piedmont Tech Coll (SC)
Pierce Coll (WA)
Portland Comm Coll (OR)
Prince George's Comm Coll (MD)
Reading Area Comm Coll (PA)
Rend Lake Coll (IL)
RETS Electronic Inst (KY)
RETS Tech Ctr (OH)
Richland Coll (TX)
Richmond Comm Coll (NC)
Ricks Coll (ID)
Riverside Comm Coll (CA)
Rochester Comm Coll (MN)
Rock Valley Coll (IL)
Saint Charles County Comm Coll (MO)
St Johns River Comm Coll (FL)
St Louis Comm Coll at Florissant Valley (MO)
St Louis Comm Coll at Forest Park (MO)
St Petersburg Jr Coll (FL)
St Philip's Coll (TX)
Salt Lake Comm Coll (UT)
San Bernardino Valley Coll (CA)
Sandhills Comm Coll (NC)
San Diego City Coll (CA)
San Joaquin Delta Coll (CA)
San Juan Coll (NM)
Santa Barbara City Coll (CA)
Santa Fe Comm Coll (FL)
Santa Fe Comm Coll (NM)
Santa Monica Coll (CA)
Schoolcraft Coll (MI)
Seminole Comm Coll (FL)
Sierra Coll (CA)
Sinclair Comm Coll (OH)
Snead State Comm Coll (AL)
Southeast Comm Coll, Milford Cmps (NE)
Southeastern Comm Coll, North Cmps, West Burlington (IA)
Southern Arkansas U Tech (AR)
Southern Maine Tech Coll (ME)
Southern U at Shreveport–Bossier City Cmps (LA)
South Florida Comm Coll (FL)
South Suburban Coll (IL)
Southwestern Coll (CA)
Southwestern Indian Polytechnic Inst (NM)
Southwestern Tech Coll (MN)
Spartanburg Tech Coll (SC)
Spokane Comm Coll (WA)
Springfield Tech Comm Coll (MA)
Stark Tech Coll (OH)
State Tech Inst at Memphis (TN)
State U of NY Coll of Tech at Farmingdale (NY)
Surry Comm Coll (NC)
Tech Coll of Municipality of San Juan (PR)
Texas State Tech Coll–Harlingen Cmps (TX)
Thaddeus Stevens State Sch of Tech (PA)
Tomball Coll (TX)
Tri-County Tech Coll (SC)
Trident Tech Coll (SC)
Triton Coll (IL)
Tulsa Jr Coll (OK)
Union County Coll (NJ)
U of Hawaii–Hawaii Comm Coll (HI)
U of Hawaii–Kauai Comm Coll (HI)
Valencia Comm Coll (FL)
Vance-Granville Comm Coll (NC)
Vermont Tech Coll (VT)
Victoria Coll (TX)
Wake Tech Comm Coll (NC)
Washtenaw Comm Coll (MI)
Wayne Comm Coll (NC)
Weatherford Coll (TX)
Western Nebraska Comm Coll, Scottsbluff (NE)
Westmoreland County Comm Coll (PA)
West Virginia U at Parkersburg (WV)
Wilkes Comm Coll (NC)
William Rainey Harper Coll (IL)
Willmar Comm Coll (MN)
Willmar Tech Coll (MN)
Wilson Tech Comm Coll (NC)
Wor-Wic Comm Coll (MD)
Wright State U, Lake Cmps (OH)
York Tech Coll (SC)

ELEMENTARY EDUCATION

Abraham Baldwin Ag Coll (GA)
Alabama Southern Comm Coll, Monroeville (AL)
Alabama Southern Comm Coll, Thomasville (AL)
Allen County Comm Coll (KS)
Angelina Coll (TX)
Anne Arundel Comm Coll (MD)
Atlanta Metropolitan Coll (GA)
Bainbridge Coll (GA)
Bay de Noc Comm Coll (MI)
Beaufort County Comm Coll (NC)
Bee County Coll (TX)
Bismarck State Coll (ND)
Black Hawk Coll, Moline (IL)
Bowling Green State University–Firelands Coll (OH)
Brazosport Coll (TX)
Brevard Comm Coll (FL)
Bristol Comm Coll (MA)
Broward Comm Coll (FL)
Brunswick Coll (GA)
Burlington County Coll (NJ)
Butler County Comm Coll (PA)
Carl Albert State Coll (OK)
Casper Coll (WY)
Catonsville Comm Coll (MD)
Cecil Comm Coll (MD)
Central Coll (KS)
Central Wyoming Coll (WY)
Charles County Comm Coll (MD)
Chattahoochee Valley State Comm Coll (AL)
Chesapeake Coll (MD)
City Colls of Chicago, Harold Washington Coll (IL)
City Colls of Chicago, Harry S Truman Coll (IL)
City Colls of Chicago, Richard J Daley Coll (IL)
City Colls of Chicago, Wilbur Wright Coll (IL)
Clackamas Comm Coll (OR)
Cloud County Comm Coll (KS)
Coahoma Comm Coll (MS)
Coastal Carolina Comm Coll (NC)
Coffeyville Comm Coll (KS)
Coll of Southern Idaho (ID)
Coll of The Albemarle (NC)
Columbia State Comm Coll (TN)
Comm Coll of Allegheny County Allegheny Cmps (PA)
Comm Coll of Allegheny County North Cmps (PA)
Comm Coll of Allegheny County South Cmps (PA)
Comm Coll of Rhode Island (RI)
Copiah-Lincoln Comm Coll (MS)
Copiah-Lincoln Comm College–Natchez Cmps (MS)
Cowley County Comm Coll and Voc-Tech Sch (KS)
Dalton Coll (GA)
Danville Area Comm Coll (IL)
Darton Coll (GA)
DeKalb Coll (GA)
Delta Coll (MI)
Dixie Coll (UT)
Dodge City Comm Coll (KS)
Dundalk Comm Coll (MD)
East Central Coll (MO)
East Central Comm Coll (MS)
Eastern Arizona Coll (AZ)
Eastern Oklahoma State Coll (OK)
Eastern Wyoming Coll (WY)
East Georgia Coll (GA)
East Mississippi Comm Coll (MS)
Edison State Comm Coll (OH)
El Paso Comm Coll (TX)
Essex County Coll (NJ)
Everett Comm Coll (WA)
Frank Phillips Coll (TX)
Frederick Comm Coll (MD)
Fulton-Montgomery Comm Coll (NY)
Gainesville Coll (GA)
Garden City Comm Coll (KS)
Garland County Comm Coll (AR)
Garrett Comm Coll (MD)
Genesee Comm Coll (NY)
Grayson County Coll (TX)
Gulf Coast Comm Coll (FL)
Harford Comm Coll (MD)
Harrisburg Area Comm Coll (PA)
Hill Coll of the Hill Jr Coll District (TX)
Hiwassee Coll (TN)
Holmes Comm Coll (MS)
Holyoke Comm Coll (MA)
Howard Comm Coll (MD)
Hutchinson Comm Coll and Area Vocational Sch (KS)
Illinois Valley Comm Coll (IL)
Independence Comm Coll (KS)
Inter American U of PR, Guayama Cmps (PR)
Iowa Lakes Comm Coll (IA)
Isothermal Comm Coll (NC)
Itawamba Comm Coll (MS)
Jackson State Comm Coll (TN)
James Sprunt Comm Coll (NC)
Jefferson Coll (MO)
Jefferson Davis Comm Coll (AL)
John A Logan Coll (IL)
John C Calhoun State Comm Coll (AL)
Kansas City Kansas Comm Coll (KS)
Kellogg Comm Coll (MI)
Kirkwood Comm Coll (IA)
Kishwaukee Coll (IL)
Labette Comm Coll (KS)
Lake Land Coll (IL)
Lake Michigan Coll (MI)
Lake-Sumter Comm Coll (FL)
Lansing Comm Coll (MI)
Lenoir Comm Coll (NC)
Lincoln Land Comm Coll (IL)
Linn-Benton Comm Coll (OR)
Little Big Horn Coll (MT)
Lon Morris Coll (TX)
Lorain County Comm Coll (OH)
Macon Coll (GA)
Manor Jr Coll (PA)
Mary Holmes Coll (MS)
Meridian Comm Coll (MS)
Miami-Dade Comm Coll (FL)
Miami University–Middletown Cmps (OH)
Middle Georgia Coll (GA)
Mid Michigan Comm Coll (MI)
Mid-Plains Comm Coll (NE)
Mineral Area Coll (MO)
Mississippi Delta Comm Coll (MS)
Mississippi Gulf Coast Comm Coll (MS)
Monroe County Comm Coll (MI)
Montgomery College–Germantown Cmps (MD)
Montgomery College–Takoma Park Cmps (MD)
Montgomery County Comm Coll (PA)
Mountain Empire Comm Coll (VA)
Murray State Coll (OK)
Muskegon Comm Coll (MI)
Navajo Comm Coll (AZ)
Navarro Coll (TX)
New Mexico Jr Coll (NM)
Northeast Comm Coll (NE)
Northeastern Jr Coll (CO)
Northeastern Oklahoma A&M Coll (OK)
Northeast Mississippi Comm Coll (MS)
Northern Oklahoma Coll (OK)
North Idaho Coll (ID)
Northwest Coll (WY)
Northwest-Shoals Comm Coll (AL)
Ocean County Coll (NJ)
Ohio Valley Coll (WV)
Okaloosa-Walton Comm Coll (FL)

Associate Degree Programs at Two-Year Colleges
Elementary Education–Engineering (General)

Orange County Comm Coll (NY)
Otero Jr Coll (CO)
Palm Beach Comm Coll (FL)
Paris Jr Coll (TX)
Parkland Coll (IL)
Pensacola Jr Coll (FL)
Pima Comm Coll (AZ)
Pitt Comm Coll (NC)
Polk Comm Coll (FL)
Portland Comm Coll (OR)
Potomac State Coll of West Virginia U (WV)
Pratt Comm Coll and Area Voc Sch (KS)
Prince George's Comm Coll (MD)
Raritan Valley Comm Coll (NJ)
Reading Area Comm Coll (PA)
Redlands Comm Coll (OK)
Ricks Coll (ID)
Roane State Comm Coll (TN)
Rogers State Coll (OK)
Rose State Coll (OK)
Sage Jr Coll of Albany (NY)
St Catharine Coll (KY)
St Louis Comm Coll at Florissant Valley (MO)
St Louis Comm Coll at Meramec (MO)
Salt Lake Comm Coll (UT)
San Juan Coll (NM)
Sauk Valley Comm Coll (IL)
Seminole Jr Coll (OK)
Seward County Comm Coll (KS)
Shelton State Comm Coll (AL)
Sheridan Coll (WY)
Snow Coll (UT)
Southeast Comm Coll, Beatrice Cmps (NE)
Southern Arkansas U Tech (AR)
Southern State Comm Coll (OH)
South Georgia Coll (GA)
South Suburban Coll (IL)
Southwestern Coll (CA)
Southwestern Comm Coll (IA)
Southwest Mississippi Comm Coll (MS)
Sullivan County Comm Coll (NY)
Three Rivers Comm Coll (MO)
Trinity Valley Comm Coll (TX)
Triton Coll (IL)
Tulsa Jr Coll (OK)
Turtle Mountain Comm Coll (ND)
Ulster County Comm Coll (NY)
Umpqua Comm Coll (OR)
U of Cincinnati Clermont Coll (OH)
U of Kentucky, Jefferson Comm Coll (KY)
U of New Mexico–Gallup Branch (NM)
U of Wisconsin Center–Marathon County (WI)
Vance-Granville Comm Coll (NC)
Vermilion Comm Coll (MN)
Vincennes U (IN)
Vincennes University–Jasper Ctr (IN)
Volunteer State Comm Coll (TN)
Wallace State Comm Coll (AL)
Waycross Coll (GA)
Westark Comm Coll (AR)
Western Nebraska Comm Coll, Scottsbluff (NE)
Western Oklahoma State Coll (OK)
West Shore Comm Coll (MI)
Wood Coll (MS)
Wright State U, Lake Cmps (OH)
Yavapai Coll (AZ)
Yuba Coll (CA)

EMERGENCY MEDICAL TECHNOLOGY

Allen County Comm Coll (KS)
Angelina Coll (TX)
Anne Arundel Comm Coll (MD)
Antelope Valley Coll (CA)
Arapahoe Comm Coll (CO)
Asheville-Buncombe Tech Comm Coll (NC)
Augusta Tech Inst (GA)
Austin Comm Coll (TX)
Bakersfield Coll (CA)
Baltimore City Comm Coll (MD)
Barstow Coll (CA)
Barton County Comm Coll (KS)
Belleville Area Coll (IL)
Belmont Tech Coll (OH)
Bishop State Comm Coll (AL)
Borough of Manhattan Comm Coll of City U of NY (NY)
Bossier Parish Comm Coll (LA)
Brevard Comm Coll (FL)
Broome Comm Coll (NY)
Broward Comm Coll (FL)
Capital Comm Tech Coll (CT)
Casper Coll (WY)
Catawba Valley Comm Coll (NC)
Central Florida Comm Coll (FL)
Cerro Coso Comm Coll (CA)
Chabot Coll (CA)
Charles Stewart Mott Comm Coll (MI)
Chattanooga State Tech Comm Coll (TN)
Chemeketa Comm Coll (OR)
City Colls of Chicago, Harold Washington Coll (IL)
City Colls of Chicago, Malcolm X Coll (IL)
Clark State Comm Coll (OH)
Coastal Carolina Comm Coll (NC)
Coffeyville Comm Coll (KS)
Coll of DuPage (IL)
Coll of the Mainland (TX)
Collin County Comm Coll (TX)
Columbia State Comm Coll (TN)
Columbus State Comm Coll (OH)
Comm Coll of Allegheny County Allegheny Cmps (PA)
Comm Coll of Southern Nevada (NV)
Comm Coll of the Air Force (AL)
Comm Hospital Roanoke Valley–Coll of Health Scis (VA)
Contra Costa Coll (CA)
Corning Comm Coll (NY)
Cosumnes River Coll (CA)
Cowley County Comm Coll and Voc-Tech Sch (KS)
Crafton Hills Coll (CA)
Crowder Coll (MO)
Cuyahoga Comm Coll, Metropolitan Cmps (OH)
Darton Coll (GA)
Daytona Beach Comm Coll (FL)
DeKalb Coll (GA)
DeKalb Tech Inst (GA)
Delgado Comm Coll (LA)
Dixie Coll (UT)
Doña Ana Branch Comm Coll (NM)
East Central Coll (MO)
Eastern New Mexico University–Roswell (NM)
East Los Angeles Coll (CA)
Edison Comm Coll (FL)
Edison State Comm Coll (OH)
Elaine P Nunez Comm Coll (LA)
Erie Comm Coll, South Cmps (NY)
Essex Comm Coll (MD)
Essex County Coll (NJ)
Fiorello H LaGuardia Comm Coll of City U of NY (NY)
Florida Comm Coll at Jacksonville (FL)
Floyd Coll (GA)
Foothill Coll (CA)
Fort Scott Comm Coll (KS)
Gadsden State Comm Coll (AL)
Garland County Comm Coll (AR)
Gaston Coll (NC)
George C Wallace State Comm Coll, Dothan (AL)
Glendale Comm Coll (AZ)
Great Lakes Jr Coll of Business (MI)
Greenville Tech Coll (SC)
Guilford Tech Comm Coll (NC)
Gulf Coast Comm Coll (FL)
Gwinnett Tech Inst (GA)
Harrisburg Area Comm Coll (PA)
Hawkeye Comm Coll (IA)
Henry Ford Comm Coll (MI)
Highland Comm Coll (KS)
Hillsborough Comm Coll (FL)
Hinds Comm Coll (MS)
Hocking Coll (OH)
Hudson Valley Comm Coll (NY)
Independence Comm Coll (KS)
Indian River Comm Coll (FL)
Ivy Tech State Coll–Kokomo (IN)
Ivy Tech State Coll–Southwest (IN)
Jackson State Comm Coll (TN)
Jefferson Coll (MO)
Jefferson Comm Coll (OH)
John A Logan Coll (IL)
John C Calhoun State Comm Coll (AL)
Johnson County Comm Coll (KS)
Jones County Jr Coll (MS)
Kalamazoo Valley Comm Coll (MI)
Kankakee Comm Coll (IL)
Kellogg Comm Coll (MI)
Kennebec Valley Tech Coll (ME)
Lake City Comm Coll (FL)
Lakeland Comm Coll (OH)
Lake Michigan Coll (MI)
Lakeshore Tech Coll (WI)
Lake-Sumter Comm Coll (FL)
Lakewood Comm Coll (MN)
Lamar Comm Coll (CO)
Lansing Comm Coll (MI)
Laredo Comm Coll (TX)
Lima Tech Coll (OH)
Lower Columbia Coll (WA)
Lurleen B Wallace State Jr Coll (AL)
Lutheran Coll of Health Professions (IN)
Luzerne County Comm Coll (PA)
Macomb Comm Coll (MI)
Madison Area Tech Coll (WI)
Massachusetts Bay Comm Coll (MA)
McHenry County Coll (IL)
Meridian Comm Coll (MS)
Miami-Dade Comm Coll (FL)
Midland Coll (TX)
Mid-Plains Comm Coll (NE)
Mississippi Gulf Coast Comm Coll (MS)
Modesto Jr Coll (CA)
Montana State U Coll of Tech-Great Falls (MT)
Montcalm Comm Coll (MI)
Montgomery Coll (TX)
Montgomery Comm Coll (NC)
Moraine Park Tech Coll (WI)
Moraine Valley Comm Coll (IL)
Mt San Antonio Coll (CA)
Muskegon Comm Coll (MI)
Napa Valley Coll (CA)
New Hampshire Tech Inst (NH)
New Mexico Jr Coll (NM)
Nicolet Area Tech Coll (WI)
Northampton County Area Comm Coll (PA)
North Arkansas Comm/Tech Coll (AR)
North Central Missouri Coll (MO)
North Central Texas Coll (TX)
Northeast Alabama State Comm Coll (AL)
Northeastern Jr Coll (CO)
Northeast Metro Tech Coll (MN)
Northeast State Tech Comm Coll (TN)
Northern Virginia Comm Coll (VA)
NorthWest Arkansas Comm Coll (AR)
Norwalk Comm-Tech Coll (CT)
Oakland Comm Coll (MI)
Odessa Coll (TX)
Oklahoma City Comm Coll (OK)
Orange Coast Coll (CA)
Our Lady of the Lake Coll (LA)
Palomar Coll (CA)
Pasco-Hernando Comm Coll (FL)
Penn Valley Comm Coll (MO)
Pensacola Jr Coll (FL)
Pines Tech Coll (AR)
Rancho Santiago Coll (CA)
Redlands Comm Coll (OK)
Rend Lake Coll (IL)
Ricks Coll (ID)
Riverside Comm Coll (CA)
Roane State Comm Coll (TN)
Rockland Comm Coll (NY)
Rogers State Coll (OK)
Saddleback Coll (CA)
St Johns River Comm Coll (FL)
St Louis Comm Coll at Florissant Valley (MO)
St Louis Comm Coll at Meramec (MO)
St Petersburg Jr Coll (FL)
San Diego City Coll (CA)
San Diego Miramar Coll (CA)
San Jacinto College–Central Cmps (TX)
San Jacinto College–North Cmps (TX)
San Joaquin Delta Coll (CA)
Santa Fe Comm Coll (FL)
Santa Rosa Jr Coll (CA)
Scottsdale Comm Coll (AZ)
Seminole Comm Coll (FL)
Shelby State Comm Coll (TN)
Shelton State Comm Coll (AL)
Sinclair Comm Coll (OH)
Skyline Coll (CA)
South Arkansas Comm Coll (AR)
South Coll (FL)
Southeastern Comm Coll, North Cmps, West Burlington (IA)
Southeastern Illinois Coll (IL)
South Suburban Coll (IL)
Southwestern Coll (CA)
Southwest Mississippi Comm Coll (MS)
Tacoma Comm Coll (WA)
Tallahassee Comm Coll (FL)
Tarrant County Jr Coll (TX)
Texarkana Coll (TX)
Texas Southmost Coll (TX)
Texas State Tech Coll (TX)
Tomball Coll (TX)
Trinity Valley Comm Coll (TX)
Umpqua Comm Coll (OR)
U of Cincinnati Raymond Walters Coll (OH)
Valencia Comm Coll (FL)
Volunteer State Comm Coll (TN)
Wake Tech Comm Coll (NC)
Wallace State Comm Coll (AL)
Waycross Coll (GA)
Wayne County Comm Coll (MI)
Weatherford Coll (TX)
Westark Comm Coll (AR)
Western Nebraska Comm Coll, Scottsbluff (NE)
Western Wisconsin Tech Coll (WI)
West Shore Comm Coll (MI)
West Virginia Northern Comm Coll (WV)
Willmar Tech Coll (MN)
Wilson Tech Comm Coll (NC)

ENERGY MANAGEMENT TECHNOLOGIES

Bismarck State Coll (ND)
Brevard Comm Coll (FL)
Cabrillo Coll (CA)
Chattanooga State Tech Comm Coll (TN)
Comm Coll of Allegheny County South Cmps (PA)
Delaware County Comm Coll (PA)
Henry Ford Comm Coll (MI)
Hocking Coll (OH)
Iowa Lakes Comm Coll (IA)
Johnson County Comm Coll (KS)
Lane Comm Coll (OR)
Lassen Coll (CA)
Macomb Comm Coll (MI)
Miles Comm Coll (MT)
Moraine Valley Comm Coll (IL)
Northwest Iowa Comm Coll (IA)
Oakland Comm Coll (MI)
Pratt Comm Coll and Area Voc Sch (KS)
Springfield Tech Comm Coll (MA)
Tulsa Jr Coll (OK)
Vista Comm Coll (CA)
The Williamson Free Sch of Mech Trades (PA)
Wisconsin Indianhead Tech Coll, Superior Cmps (WI)

ENGINEERING (GENERAL)

Adirondack Comm Coll (NY)
Alabama Southern Comm Coll, Monroeville (AL)
Allan Hancock Coll (CA)
Allegany Comm Coll (MD)
Allen County Comm Coll (KS)
Angelina Coll (TX)
Antelope Valley Coll (CA)
Bakersfield Coll (CA)
Baltimore City Comm Coll (MD)
Bee County Coll (TX)
Berkshire Comm Coll (MA)
Bismarck State Coll (ND)
Brazosport Coll (TX)
Brevard Coll (NC)
Bristol Comm Coll (MA)
Brookdale Comm Coll (NJ)
Bucks County Comm Coll (PA)
Burlington County Coll (NJ)
Butler County Comm Coll (KS)
Cañada Coll (CA)
Cape Cod Comm Coll (MA)
Casper Coll (WY)
Catonsville Comm Coll (MD)
Central Coll (KS)
Central Oregon Comm Coll (OR)
Central Texas Coll (TX)
Chabot Coll (CA)
Chaffey Coll (CA)
Charles County Comm Coll (MD)
Chattahoochee Valley State Comm Coll (AL)
Chemeketa Comm Coll (OR)
Citrus Coll (CA)
City Colls of Chicago, Harold Washington Coll (IL)
City Colls of Chicago, Kennedy-King Coll (IL)
City Colls of Chicago, Olive-Harvey Coll (IL)
Clark Coll (WA)
Clinton Comm Coll (IA)
Coffeyville Comm Coll (KS)
Colby Comm Coll (KS)
Coll of Lake County (IL)
Coll of Marin (CA)
Coll of San Mateo (CA)
Coll of the Sequoias (CA)
Coll of the Siskiyous (CA)
Comm Coll of Allegheny County Allegheny Cmps (PA)
Comm Coll of Allegheny County Boyce Cmps (PA)
Comm Coll of Allegheny County South Cmps (PA)
Comm Coll of Philadelphia (PA)
Comm Coll of Rhode Island (RI)
Connors State Coll (OK)
Cuesta Coll (CA)
Cypress Coll (CA)
Danville Area Comm Coll (IL)
Darton Coll (GA)
Daytona Beach Comm Coll (FL)
DeKalb Coll (GA)
Delaware Tech & Comm Coll, Jack F Owens Cmps (DE)
Delaware Tech & Comm Coll, Stanton/Wilmington Cmps (DE)
Delgado Comm Coll (LA)
Dixie Coll (UT)
Dodge City Comm Coll (KS)
Donnelly Coll (KS)
East Central Comm Coll (MS)
East Los Angeles Coll (CA)
Edgecombe Comm Coll (NC)
El Camino Coll (CA)
Essex Comm Coll (MD)
Essex County Coll (NJ)
Everett Comm Coll (WA)
Evergreen Valley Coll (CA)
Finger Lakes Comm Coll (NY)
Foothill Coll (CA)
Frank Phillips Coll (TX)
Frederick Comm Coll (MD)
Fresno City Coll (CA)
Gainesville Coll (GA)
Garden City Comm Coll (KS)
Georgia Military Coll (GA)
Glendale Comm Coll (AZ)
Grays Harbor Coll (WA)
Greenville Tech Coll (SC)
Harford Comm Coll (MD)
Harrisburg Area Comm Coll (PA)
Highland Comm Coll (IL)
Highline Comm Coll (WA)
Hiwassee Coll (TN)
Holmes Comm Coll (MS)
Howard Comm Coll (MD)
Hudson County Comm Coll (NJ)
Hutchinson Comm Coll and Area Vocational Sch (KS)
Imperial Valley Coll (CA)
Independence Comm Coll (KS)
Indian River Comm Coll (FL)
Jackson State Comm Coll (TN)
J Sargeant Reynolds Comm Coll (VA)
Kansas City Kansas Comm Coll (KS)
Kent State U, Trumbull Cmps (OH)
Kirkwood Comm Coll (IA)
Lake Land Coll (IL)
Laney Coll (CA)
Lansing Comm Coll (MI)
Lehigh Carbon Comm Coll (PA)
Lincoln Land Comm Coll (IL)
Long Beach City Coll (CA)
Longview Comm Coll (MO)
Lon Morris Coll (TX)
Lorain County Comm Coll (OH)
Los Angeles City Coll (CA)
Los Angeles Southwest Coll (CA)
Los Angeles Trade-Tech Coll (CA)
Marion Military Inst (AL)
Massachusetts Bay Comm Coll (MA)
Mercer County Comm Coll (NJ)
Miami-Dade Comm Coll (FL)
Middle Georgia Coll (GA)
Middlesex County Coll (NJ)
Midland Coll (TX)
Mineral Area Coll (MO)
Mitchell Coll (CT)
Modesto Jr Coll (CA)
Monterey Peninsula Coll (CA)
Montgomery College–Rockville Cmps (MD)
Montgomery College–Takoma Park Cmps (MD)
Montgomery County Comm Coll (PA)
Motlow State Comm Coll (TN)
Mt San Jacinto Coll (CA)
Murray State Coll (OK)
Napa Valley Coll (CA)
Navarro Coll (TX)
New Mexico Jr Coll (NM)
New Mexico Military Inst (NM)
Northampton County Area Comm Coll (PA)
North Dakota State University–Bottineau (ND)
Northeast Mississippi Comm Coll (MS)
Northern Oklahoma Coll (OK)
Northern Virginia Comm Coll (VA)
North Idaho Coll (ID)
North Shore Comm Coll (MA)

Associate Degree Programs at Two-Year Colleges
Engineering (General)–(Pre)Engineering Sequence

Northwest Coll (WY)
Northwestern Connecticut Comm-Tech Coll (CT)
Northwest Indian Coll (WA)
Ocean County Coll (NJ)
Okaloosa-Walton Comm Coll (FL)
Oklahoma City Comm Coll (OK)
Oklahoma State U, Oklahoma City (OK)
Orangeburg-Calhoun Tech Coll (SC)
Orange Coast Coll (CA)
Palomar Coll (CA)
Paris Jr Coll (TX)
Parkland Coll (IL)
Pasadena City Coll (CA)
Penn Valley Comm Coll (MO)
Pensacola Jr Coll (FL)
Piedmont Tech Coll (SC)
Pima Comm Coll (AZ)
Portland Comm Coll (OR)
Potomac State Coll of West Virginia U (WV)
Prince George's Comm Coll (MD)
Rancho Santiago Coll (CA)
Raritan Valley Comm Coll (NJ)
Reading Area Comm Coll (PA)
Ricks Coll (ID)
Riverside Comm Coll (CA)
Roane State Comm Coll (TN)
Rogers State Coll (OK)
Sacramento City Coll (CA)
Saddleback Coll (CA)
St Louis Comm Coll at Florissant Valley (MO)
Salt Lake Comm Coll (UT)
San Diego Mesa Coll (CA)
San Jacinto College–Central Cmps (TX)
San Joaquin Delta Coll (CA)
San Jose City Coll (CA)
San Juan Coll (NM)
Santa Barbara City Coll (CA)
Santa Fe Comm Coll (FL)
Shasta Coll (CA)
Sheridan Coll (WY)
Sierra Coll (CA)
Snow Coll (UT)
South Plains Coll (TX)
South Seattle Comm Coll (WA)
Southwestern Coll (CA)
Southwest Mississippi Comm Coll (MS)
Southwest Virginia Comm Coll (VA)
State U of NY Coll of Tech at Farmingdale (NY)
Suffolk County Comm College–Ammerman Cmps (NY)
Sullivan County Comm Coll (NY)
Tacoma Comm Coll (WA)
Terra State Comm Coll (OH)
Texarkana Coll (TX)
Thomas Nelson Comm Coll (VA)
Three Rivers Comm-Tech Coll (CT)
Tidewater Comm Coll (VA)
Treasure Valley Comm Coll (OR)
Trinidad State Jr Coll (CO)
Triton Coll (IL)
Tulsa Jr Coll (OK)
Tunxis Comm Tech Coll (CT)
UAB Walker Coll (AL)
Ulster County Comm Coll (NY)
Umpqua Comm Coll (OR)
Union County Coll (NJ)
U of New Mexico–Los Alamos Branch (NM)
Valley Forge Military Coll (PA)
Ventura Coll (CA)
Vermilion Comm Coll (MN)
Vincennes U (IN)
Virginia Western Comm Coll (VA)
Wallace State Comm Coll (AL)
Washington State Comm Coll (OH)
Wayne Comm Coll (NC)
Western Oklahoma State Coll (OK)
Western Wyoming Comm Coll (WY)
West Los Angeles Coll (CA)
Westmoreland County Comm Coll (PA)
Willmar Comm Coll (MN)
Wright State U, Lake Cmps (OH)

ENGINEERING AND APPLIED SCIENCES

Angelina Coll (TX)
Berkshire Comm Coll (MA)
Brevard Coll (NC)
Casper Coll (WY)
Cayuga County Comm Coll (NY)
Centralia Coll (WA)
Central Oregon Comm Coll (OR)
City Colls of Chicago, Harold Washington Coll (IL)
Clackamas Comm Coll (OR)
Colby Comm Coll (KS)
Collin County Comm Coll (TX)
Columbia Basin Coll (WA)
Comm Coll of Allegheny County South Cmps (PA)
Comm Coll of the Air Force (AL)
Contra Costa Coll (CA)
Copiah-Lincoln Comm Coll (MS)
Cumberland County Coll (NJ)
Cuyahoga Comm Coll, Metropolitan Cmps (OH)
De Anza Coll (CA)
Edison Comm Coll (FL)
Edison State Comm Coll (OH)
Erie Comm Coll, City Cmps (NY)
Everett Comm Coll (WA)
Floyd Coll (GA)
Garden City Comm Coll (KS)
Georgia Military Coll (GA)
Gogebic Comm Coll (MI)
Greenville Tech Coll (SC)
Highline Comm Coll (WA)
Hill Coll of the Hill Jr Coll District (TX)
Inver Hills Comm Coll (MN)
Lamar Comm Coll (CO)
Laramie County Comm Coll (WY)
Miami University–Middletown Cmps (OH)
Middle Georgia Coll (GA)
Middlesex County Coll (NJ)
Modesto Jr Coll (CA)
Mohawk Valley Comm Coll (NY)
Moorpark Coll (CA)
Northeast Mississippi Comm Coll (MS)
Northwest Mississippi Comm Coll (MS)
Palo Alto Coll (TX)
Paris Jr Coll (TX)
Rancho Santiago Coll (CA)
Reading Area Comm Coll (PA)
Richland Coll (TX)
St Louis Comm Coll at Forest Park (MO)
San Jose City Coll (CA)
Sinclair Comm Coll (OH)
Southwest Texas Jr Coll (TX)
State U of NY Coll of A&T at Morrisville (NY)
Tulsa Jr Coll (OK)
Washington State Comm Coll (OH)
William Rainey Harper Coll (IL)

ENGINEERING DESIGN

Brazosport Coll (TX)
Brevard Coll (NC)
Brevard Comm Coll (FL)
Catonsville Comm Coll (MD)
Central Texas Coll (TX)
Chattanooga State Tech Comm Coll (TN)
Comm Coll of Allegheny County Boyce Cmps (PA)
Comm Coll of Allegheny County South Cmps (PA)
Dunwoody Inst (MN)
Edison State Comm Coll (OH)
Los Angeles Valley Coll (CA)
Macomb Comm Coll (MI)
Miami-Dade Comm Coll (FL)
Morrison Inst of Tech (IL)
Northwest Indian Coll (WA)
Piedmont Tech Coll (SC)
Rancho Santiago Coll (CA)
Salt Lake Comm Coll (UT)
San Joaquin Delta Coll (CA)
Snead State Comm Coll (AL)
Southeastern Comm Coll, North Cmps, West Burlington (IA)
Southern Maine Tech Coll (ME)
Triton Coll (IL)
Western Iowa Tech Comm Coll (IA)
Wright State U, Lake Cmps (OH)

ENGINEERING SCIENCES

Adirondack Comm Coll (NY)
Allen County Comm Coll (KS)
Bergen Comm Coll (NJ)
Borough of Manhattan Comm Coll of City U of NY (NY)
Brevard Coll (NC)
Brevard Comm Coll (FL)
Broome Comm Coll (NY)
Broward Comm Coll (FL)
Camden County Coll (NJ)
Cayuga County Comm Coll (NY)
Central Texas Coll (TX)
Comm Coll of Allegheny County Boyce Cmps (PA)
Comm Coll of Allegheny County South Cmps (PA)
County Coll of Morris (NJ)
Dundalk Comm Coll (MD)
Dutchess Comm Coll (NY)
Erie Comm Coll, North Cmps (NY)
Everett Comm Coll (WA)
Finger Lakes Comm Coll (NY)
Fulton-Montgomery Comm Coll (NY)
Genesee Comm Coll (NY)
Gloucester County Coll (NJ)
Grand Rapids Comm Coll (MI)
Greenfield Comm Coll (MA)
Herkimer County Comm Coll (NY)
Highland Comm Coll (IL)
Hill Coll of the Hill Jr Coll District (TX)
Holyoke Comm Coll (MA)
Hudson County Comm Coll (NJ)
Jamestown Comm Coll (NY)
Jefferson Comm Coll (NY)
Jones County Jr Coll (MS)
Lake City Comm Coll (FL)
Lake Land Coll (IL)
Massachusetts Bay Comm Coll (MA)
Mercer County Comm Coll (NJ)
Miami-Dade Comm Coll (FL)
Middle Georgia Coll (GA)
Middlesex Community– Tech Coll (CT)
Middlesex County Coll (NJ)
Midland Coll (TX)
Mohawk Valley Comm Coll (NY)
Monroe Comm Coll (NY)
Nassau Comm Coll (NY)
Northern Essex Comm Coll (MA)
North Shore Comm Coll (MA)
Norwalk Comm-Tech Coll (CT)
Onondaga Comm Coll (NY)
Orange County Comm Coll (NY)
Parkland Coll (IL)
Queensborough Comm Coll of City U of NY (NY)
Rancho Santiago Coll (CA)
Reading Area Comm Coll (PA)
St Gregory's Coll (OK)
St Louis Comm Coll at Florissant Valley (MO)
St Louis Comm Coll at Forest Park (MO)
St Louis Comm Coll at Meramec (MO)
Springfield Tech Comm Coll (MA)
State U of NY Coll of A&T at Morrisville (NY)
State U of NY Coll of Tech at Alfred (NY)
State U of NY Coll of Tech at Canton (NY)
State U of NY Coll of Tech at Delhi (NY)
State U of NY Coll of Tech at Farmingdale (NY)
Suffolk County Comm College–Ammerman Cmps (NY)
Sullivan County Comm Coll (NY)
Three Rivers Comm-Tech Coll (CT)
Tompkins Cortland Comm Coll (NY)
Westchester Comm Coll (NY)

(PRE)ENGINEERING SEQUENCE

Abraham Baldwin Ag Coll (GA)
Adirondack Comm Coll (NY)
Alabama Southern Comm Coll, Monroeville (AL)
Alabama Southern Comm Coll, Thomasville (AL)
Alpena Comm Coll (MI)
American River Coll (CA)
Andrew Coll (GA)
Anoka-Ramsey Comm Coll (MN)
Antelope Valley Coll (CA)
Arizona Western Coll (AZ)
Austin Comm Coll (TX)
Barton County Comm Coll (KS)
Bay de Noc Comm Coll (MI)
Belleville Area Coll (IL)
Berkshire Comm Coll (MA)
Bevill State Comm Coll (AL)
Big Bend Comm Coll (WA)
Black Hawk Coll, Moline (IL)
Blue Mountain Comm Coll (OR)
Bowling Green State University–Firelands Coll (OH)
Brazosport Coll (TX)
Brevard Coll (NC)
Bronx Comm Coll of City U of NY (NY)
Broward Comm Coll (FL)
Brunswick Coll (GA)
Burlington County Coll (NJ)
Butler County Comm Coll (KS)
Butler County Comm Coll (PA)
Cabrillo Coll (CA)
Caldwell Comm Coll and Tech Inst (NC)
Cape Cod Comm Coll (MA)
Carl Albert State Coll (OK)
Casper Coll (WY)
Catonsville Comm Coll (MD)
Central Comm College–Platte Cmps (NE)
Centralia Coll (WA)
Central Oregon Comm Coll (OR)
Central Texas Coll (TX)
Central Virginia Comm Coll (VA)
Cerritos Coll (CA)
Cerro Coso Comm Coll (CA)
Chabot Coll (CA)
Charles County Comm Coll (MD)
Charles Stewart Mott Comm Coll (MI)
Chipola Jr Coll (FL)
Cincinnati State Tech and Comm Coll (OH)
City Coll of San Francisco (CA)
City Colls of Chicago, Harold Washington Coll (IL)
City Colls of Chicago, Harry S Truman Coll (IL)
City Colls of Chicago, Kennedy-King Coll (IL)
City Colls of Chicago, Richard J Daley Coll (IL)
City Colls of Chicago, Wilbur Wright Coll (IL)
Clark Coll (WA)
Clinton Comm Coll (IA)
Cloud County Comm Coll (KS)
Coastal Carolina Comm Coll (NC)
Cochise Coll, Douglas (AZ)
Cochise Coll, Sierra Vista (AZ)
Coffeyville Comm Coll (KS)
Colby Comm Coll (KS)
Coll of Eastern Utah (UT)
Coll of The Albemarle (NC)
Coll of the Canyons (CA)
Coll of the Desert (CA)
Coll of the Sequoias (CA)
Collin County Comm Coll (TX)
Columbia State Comm Coll (TN)
Comm Coll of Allegheny County Allegheny Cmps (PA)
Comm Coll of Allegheny County Boyce Cmps (PA)
Comm Coll of Allegheny County South Cmps (PA)
Comm Coll of Philadelphia (PA)
Corning Comm Coll (NY)
Cosumnes River Coll (CA)
County Coll of Morris (NJ)
Cowley County Comm Coll and Voc-Tech Sch (KS)
Crafton Hills Coll (CA)
Crowder Coll (MO)
Cuesta Coll (CA)
Cumberland County Coll (NJ)
Dalton Coll (GA)
Danville Area Comm Coll (IL)
Darton Coll (GA)
Davidson County Comm Coll (NC)
Dean Coll (MA)
De Anza Coll (CA)
DeKalb Coll (GA)
Delaware County Comm Coll (PA)
Del Mar Coll (TX)
Delta Coll (MI)
Dixie Coll (UT)
Dodge City Comm Coll (KS)
East Central Coll (MO)
East Central Comm Coll (MS)
Eastern Arizona Coll (AZ)
Eastern Oklahoma State Coll (OK)
East Los Angeles Coll (CA)
East Mississippi Comm Coll (MS)
Edison State Comm Coll (OH)
Elgin Comm Coll (IL)
Ellsworth Comm Coll (IA)
El Paso Comm Coll (TX)
Enterprise State Jr Coll (AL)
Essex County Coll (NJ)
Everett Comm Coll (WA)
Evergreen Valley Coll (CA)
Fergus Falls Comm Coll (MN)
Finger Lakes Comm Coll (NY)
Fiorello H LaGuardia Comm Coll of City U of NY (NY)
Fort Belknap Coll (MT)
Frank Phillips Coll (TX)
Fresno City Coll (CA)
Garden City Comm Coll (KS)
Gaston Coll (NC)
Gavilan Coll (CA)
Georgia Military Coll (GA)
Golden West Coll (CA)
Grand Rapids Comm Coll (MI)
Grays Harbor Coll (WA)
Grayson County Coll (TX)
Greenfield Comm Coll (MA)
Greenville Tech Coll (SC)
Gulf Coast Comm Coll (FL)
Hagerstown Jr Coll (MD)
Henry Ford Comm Coll (MI)
Herkimer County Comm Coll (NY)
Hibbing Comm Coll (MN)
Highland Comm Coll (IL)
Highland Comm Coll (KS)
Highland Park Comm Coll (MI)
Highline Comm Coll (WA)
Hill Coll of the Hill Jr Coll District (TX)
Hinds Comm Coll (MS)
Hiwassee Coll (TN)
Holyoke Comm Coll (MA)
Horry-Georgetown Tech Coll (SC)
Housatonic Comm-Tech Coll (CT)
Howard Coll (TX)
Hudson County Comm Coll (NJ)
Hudson Valley Comm Coll (NY)
Hutchinson Comm Coll and Area Vocational Sch (KS)
Illinois Valley Comm Coll (IL)
Imperial Valley Coll (CA)
Independence Comm Coll (KS)
Indian River Comm Coll (FL)
Iowa Lakes Comm Coll (IA)
Isothermal Comm Coll (NC)
Itasca Comm Coll (MN)
Itawamba Comm Coll (MS)
Jackson State Comm Coll (TN)
Jamestown Comm Coll (NY)
Jefferson Coll (MO)
Jefferson Comm Coll (NY)
Jefferson State Comm Coll (AL)
John A Logan Coll (IL)
Johnson County Comm Coll (KS)
John Wood Comm Coll (IL)
Joliet Jr Coll (IL)
Kalamazoo Valley Comm Coll (MI)
Kankakee Comm Coll (IL)
Kansas City Kansas Comm Coll (KS)
Kaskaskia Coll (IL)
Kellogg Comm Coll (MI)
Kent State U, Geauga Cmps (OH)
Kingsborough Comm Coll of City U of NY (NY)
Kirkwood Comm Coll (IA)
Kishwaukee Coll (IL)
Labette Comm Coll (KS)
Lake Michigan Coll (MI)
Lake-Sumter Comm Coll (FL)
Lamar Comm Coll (CO)
Lansing Comm Coll (MI)
Laramie County Comm Coll (WY)
Lassen Coll (CA)
Lee Coll (TX)
Lehigh Carbon Comm Coll (PA)
Lenoir Comm Coll (NC)
Lewis and Clark Comm Coll (IL)
Lincoln Land Comm Coll (IL)
Linn-Benton Comm Coll (OR)
Long Beach City Coll (CA)
Longview Comm Coll (MO)
Lon Morris Coll (TX)
Lorain County Comm Coll (OH)
Los Angeles Harbor Coll (CA)
Los Angeles Pierce Coll (CA)
Los Angeles Valley Coll (CA)
Louisburg Coll (NC)
Lower Columbia Coll (WA)
Macomb Comm Coll (MI)
Macon Coll (GA)
Maple Woods Comm Coll (MO)
Marshalltown Comm Coll (IA)
Mary Holmes Coll (MS)
Massachusetts Bay Comm Coll (MA)
Merced Coll (CA)
Meridian Comm Coll (MS)
Mesabi Comm Coll (MN)
Mesa Comm Coll (AZ)
Metropolitan Comm Coll (NE)
Miami-Dade Comm Coll (FL)
Miami University–Middletown Cmps (OH)
Middle Georgia Coll (GA)
Middlesex Comm Coll (MA)
Middlesex Community– Tech Coll (CT)
Midland Coll (TX)
Mid Michigan Comm Coll (MI)
Mid-Plains Comm Coll (NE)
Milwaukee Area Tech Coll (WI)
Mineral Area Coll (MO)
Mission Coll (CA)
Mississippi Gulf Coast Comm Coll (MS)
Moberly Area Comm Coll (MO)
Mohawk Valley Comm Coll (NY)
Monroe County Comm Coll (MI)
Montgomery College–Germantown Cmps (MD)

Peterson's Guide to Two-Year Colleges 1997
83

Associate Degree Programs at Two-Year Colleges
(Pre)Engineering Sequence–English

Montgomery College–Rockville Cmps (MD)
Montgomery College–Takoma Park Cmps (MD)
Moraine Valley Comm Coll (IL)
Motlow State Comm Coll (TN)
Mountain Empire Comm Coll (VA)
Mount Ida Coll (MA)
Mt San Antonio Coll (CA)
Murray State Coll (OK)
Naugatuck Valley Community–Tech Coll (CT)
Navajo Comm Coll (AZ)
Navarro Coll (TX)
Neosho County Comm Coll (KS)
New Mexico Military Inst (NM)
Normandale Comm Coll (MN)
North Central Michigan Coll (MI)
North Central Texas Coll (TX)
North Dakota State Coll of Science (ND)
North Dakota State University–Bottineau (ND)
Northeast Alabama State Comm Coll (AL)
Northeastern Jr Coll (CO)
Northeastern Oklahoma A&M Coll (OK)
Northeast Mississippi Comm Coll (MS)
Northern Virginia Comm Coll (VA)
North Harris Coll (TX)
North Hennepin Comm Coll (MN)
North Shore Comm Coll (MA)
Northwest Coll (WY)
Northwestern Connecticut Comm-Tech Coll (CT)
Northwestern Michigan Coll (MI)
Northwest Mississippi Comm Coll (MS)
Northwest-Shoals Comm Coll (AL)
Oakland Comm Coll (MI)
Oakton Comm Coll (IL)
Odessa Coll (TX)
Ohio Valley Coll (WV)
Ohlone Coll (CA)
Oklahoma City Comm Coll (OK)
Olympic Coll (WA)
Otero Jr Coll (CO)
Palm Beach Comm Coll (FL)
Palo Verde Coll (CA)
Passaic County Comm Coll (NJ)
Pennsylvania Coll of Tech (PA)
Piedmont Virginia Comm Coll (VA)
Pikes Peak Comm Coll (CO)
Polk Comm Coll (FL)
Porterville Coll (CA)
Portland Comm Coll (OR)
Potomac State Coll of West Virginia U (WV)
Prairie State Coll (IL)
Pratt Comm Coll and Area Voc Sch (KS)
Quinebaug Valley Comm-Tech Coll (CT)
Quinsigamond Comm Coll (MA)
Rainy River Comm Coll (MN)
Rancho Santiago Coll (CA)
Raritan Valley Comm Coll (NJ)
Reading Area Comm Coll (PA)
Redlands Comm Coll (OK)
Richland Comm Coll (IL)
Ricks Coll (ID)
Roane State Comm Coll (TN)
Rochester Comm Coll (MN)
Rock Valley Coll (IL)
Rose State Coll (OK)
Saddleback Coll (CA)
Saint Charles County Comm Coll (MO)
St Louis Comm Coll at Florissant Valley (MO)
St Louis Comm Coll at Forest Park (MO)
St Philip's Coll (TX)
Salt Lake Comm Coll (UT)
San Bernardino Valley Coll (CA)
Sandhills Comm Coll (NC)
San Diego City Coll (CA)
San Jacinto College–Central Cmps (TX)
San Jacinto College–South Cmps (TX)
Santa Fe Comm Coll (NM)
Santa Monica Coll (CA)
Sauk Valley Comm Coll (IL)
Schoolcraft Coll (MI)
Scott Comm Coll (IA)
Seward County Comm Coll (KS)
Sheridan Coll (WY)
Shoreline Comm Coll (WA)
Skagit Valley Coll (WA)
Snow Coll (UT)
South Georgia Coll (GA)
South Mountain Comm Coll (AZ)
South Plains Coll (TX)
South Suburban Coll (IL)
SouthWest Collegiate Inst for the Deaf (TX)
Southwestern Coll (CA)
Southwestern Michigan Coll (MI)
Spokane Falls Comm Coll (WA)
Spoon River Coll (IL)
Springfield Coll in Illinois (IL)
Springfield Tech Comm Coll (MA)
State U of NY Coll of A&T at Morrisville (NY)
State U of NY Coll of Tech at Alfred (NY)
State U of NY Coll of Tech at Delhi (NY)
Sullivan County Comm Coll (NY)
Tacoma Comm Coll (WA)
Taft Coll (CA)
Three Rivers Comm-Tech Coll (CT)
Trinidad State Jr Coll (CO)
Trinity Valley Comm Coll (TX)
Triton Coll (IL)
Tulsa Jr Coll (OK)
Turtle Mountain Comm Coll (ND)
UAB Walker Coll (AL)
Umpqua Comm Coll (OR)
U of Cincinnati Raymond Walters Coll (OH)
U of New Mexico–Los Alamos Branch (NM)
U of New Mexico–Valencia Cmps (NM)
U of Wisconsin Center–Marathon County (WI)
Utah Valley State Coll (UT)
Vermilion Comm Coll (MN)
Vincennes U (IN)
Virginia Western Comm Coll (VA)
Wake Tech Comm Coll (NC)
Waldorf Coll (IA)
Walters State Comm Coll (TN)
Washtenaw Comm Coll (MI)
Waubonsee Comm Coll (IL)
Wenatchee Valley Coll (WA)
Western Piedmont Comm Coll (NC)
Western Wyoming Comm Coll (WY)
West Hills Comm Coll (CA)
West Shore Comm Coll (MI)
West Virginia U at Parkersburg (WV)
Wharton County Jr Coll (TX)
William Rainey Harper Coll (IL)
Willmar Comm Coll (MN)
Worthington Comm Coll (MN)
Wright State U, Lake Cmps (OH)
Yakima Valley Comm Coll (WA)
Young Harris Coll (GA)
Yuba Coll (CA)

ENGINEERING TECHNOLOGY

Aiken Tech Coll (SC)
Aims Comm Coll (CO)
Alabama Southern Comm Coll, Thomasville (AL)
Allan Hancock Coll (CA)
Allen County Comm Coll (KS)
American River Coll (CA)
Anne Arundel Comm Coll (MD)
Arizona Western Coll (AZ)
Athens Area Tech Inst (GA)
Atlanta Metropolitan Coll (GA)
Belleville Area Coll (IL)
Berkshire Comm Coll (MA)
Bishop State Comm Coll (AL)
Black Hawk Coll, Moline (IL)
Brookhaven Coll (TX)
Catonsville Comm Coll (MD)
Central Oregon Comm Coll (OR)
Central Piedmont Comm Coll (NC)
Central Texas Coll (TX)
Central Virginia Comm Coll (VA)
Cerro Coso Comm Coll (CA)
Chabot Coll (CA)
Citrus Coll (CA)
City Colls of Chicago, Harold Washington Coll (IL)
Clark Coll (WA)
Clovis Comm Coll (NM)
Coll of Marin (CA)
Coll of San Mateo (CA)
Coll of the Desert (CA)
Collin County Comm Coll (TX)
Columbus State Comm Coll (OH)
Comm Coll of Allegheny County Allegheny Cmps (PA)
Comm Coll of Allegheny County Boyce Cmps (PA)
Comm Coll of Allegheny County South Cmps (PA)
Comm Coll of Philadelphia (PA)
Cowley County Comm Coll and Voc-Tech Sch (KS)
Cuyahoga Comm Coll, Eastern Cmps (OH)
Cuyahoga Comm Coll, Metropolitan Cmps (OH)
Cuyahoga Comm Coll, Western Cmps (OH)
Cuyamaca Coll (CA)
Danville Comm Coll (VA)
Darton Coll (GA)
Davidson County Comm Coll (NC)
De Anza Coll (CA)
DeKalb Tech Inst (GA)
Delaware Tech & Comm Coll, Jack F Owens Cmps (DE)
Delaware Tech & Comm Coll, Terry Cmps (DE)
Delgado Comm Coll (LA)
Delta Coll (MI)
Denmark Tech Coll (SC)
Dodge City Comm Coll (KS)
D-Q U (CA)
East Mississippi Comm Coll (MS)
ECPI Coll of Tech, Hampton (VA)
ECPI Coll of Tech, Virginia Beach (VA)
ECPI Computer Inst, Richmond (VA)
ECPI Computer Inst, Roanoke (VA)
Edison Comm Coll (FL)
Edison State Comm Coll (OH)
Essex County Coll (NJ)
Everett Comm Coll (WA)
Florence-Darlington Tech Coll (SC)
Forsyth Tech Comm Coll (NC)
Franklin Inst of Boston (MA)
Frank Phillips Coll (TX)
Gainesville Coll (GA)
Garden City Comm Coll (KS)
Gateway Comm-Tech Coll (CT)
Glendale Comm Coll (AZ)
Golden West Coll (CA)
Harrisburg Area Comm Coll (PA)
Hawkeye Comm Coll (IA)
Highland Comm Coll (IL)
Highline Comm Coll (WA)
Houston Comm Coll System (TX)
Illinois Central Coll (IL)
Independence Comm Coll (KS)
Indian River Comm Coll (FL)
Jackson State Comm Coll (TN)
Johnson County Comm Coll (KS)
J Sargeant Reynolds Comm Coll (VA)
Kansas City Kansas Comm Coll (KS)
Kent State U, Ashtabula Cmps (OH)
Kent State U, Tuscarawas Cmps (OH)
Lakeland Comm Coll (OH)
Laney Coll (CA)
Lansing Comm Coll (MI)
Laramie County Comm Coll (WY)
Lehigh Carbon Comm Coll (PA)
Lima Tech Coll (OH)
Lorain County Comm Coll (OH)
Los Angeles Harbor Coll (CA)
Louisville Tech Inst (KY)
Lower Columbia Coll (WA)
Macon Coll (GA)
Marion Tech Coll (OH)
Massachusetts Bay Comm Coll (MA)
Meadows Coll of Business (GA)
Mesa Comm Coll (AZ)
Miami-Dade Comm Coll (FL)
Miami University–Hamilton Cmps (OH)
Miami University–Middletown Cmps (OH)
Middle Georgia Coll (GA)
Middlesex Community– Tech Coll (CT)
Middlesex County Coll (NJ)
Midlands Tech Coll (SC)
Montgomery County Comm Coll (PA)
Moorpark Coll (CA)
Moraine Valley Comm Coll (IL)
Morrison Inst of Tech (IL)
Motlow State Comm Coll (TN)
Mountain Empire Comm Coll (VA)
Mountain View Coll (TX)
Mt San Antonio Coll (CA)
Murray State Coll (OK)
Muskegon Comm Coll (MI)
Naugatuck Valley Community–Tech Coll (CT)
New Hampshire Tech Coll, Nashua (NH)
New Hampshire Tech Inst (NH)
New Mexico State University–Alamogordo (NM)
New Mexico State University–Carlsbad (NM)
New York City Tech Coll of the City U of NY (NY)
Normandale Comm Coll (MN)
North Central Michigan Coll (MI)
Northeast Mississippi Comm Coll (MS)
Northeast State Tech Comm Coll (TN)
Norwalk Comm-Tech Coll (CT)
Ocean County Coll (NJ)
Oklahoma State U, Oklahoma City (OK)
Olympic Coll (WA)
Owensboro Comm Coll (KY)
Pasadena City Coll (CA)
Piedmont Tech Coll (SC)
Portland Comm Coll (OR)
Pueblo Comm Coll (CO)
Quinebaug Valley Comm-Tech Coll (CT)
Rancho Santiago Coll (CA)
Rappahannock Comm Coll (VA)
Reading Area Comm Coll (PA)
Ricks Coll (ID)
Rogers State Coll (OK)
St Louis Comm Coll at Florissant Valley (MO)
St Louis Comm Coll at Forest Park (MO)
Salt Lake Comm Coll (UT)
San Antonio Coll (TX)
Sandhills Comm Coll (NC)
San Diego City Coll (CA)
San Jacinto College–Central Cmps (TX)
San Joaquin Delta Coll (CA)
San Juan Coll (NM)
Santa Barbara City Coll (CA)
Sheridan Coll (WY)
Shoreline Comm Coll (WA)
Southeast Tech Inst (SD)
South Seattle Comm Coll (WA)
Southwestern Indian Polytechnic Inst (NM)
Southwestern Michigan Coll (MI)
Southwestern Tech Coll (MN)
Spartanburg Tech Coll (SC)
State Tech Inst at Memphis (TN)
State U of NY Coll of A&T at Morrisville (NY)
State U of NY Coll of Tech at Canton (NY)
Three Rivers Comm Coll (MO)
Three Rivers Comm-Tech Coll (CT)
Triton Coll (IL)
Truckee Meadows Comm Coll (NV)
Tunxis Comm Tech Coll (CT)
Ulster County Comm Coll (NY)
U of Hawaii–Honolulu Comm Coll (HI)
U of Kentucky, Ashland Comm Coll (KY)
U of Kentucky, Henderson Comm Coll (KY)
Vincennes U (IN)
Virginia Highlands Comm Coll (VA)
Washington County Tech Coll (ME)
Washtenaw Comm Coll (MI)
Waycross Coll (GA)
Wayne County Comm Coll (MI)
Westchester Comm Coll (NY)
Williamsburg Tech Coll (SC)
Wright State U, Lake Cmps (OH)
York Tech Coll (SC)

ENGLISH

Abraham Baldwin Ag Coll (GA)
Alabama Southern Comm Coll, Monroeville (AL)
Allan Hancock Coll (CA)
Allen County Comm Coll (KS)
Alpena Comm Coll (MI)
Andrew Coll (GA)
Angelina Coll (TX)
Anne Arundel Comm Coll (MD)
Antelope Valley Coll (CA)
Arizona Western Coll (AZ)
Atlanta Metropolitan Coll (GA)
Austin Comm Coll (TX)
Bainbridge Coll (GA)
Bakersfield Coll (CA)
Barstow Coll (CA)
Barton County Comm Coll (KS)
Bay de Noc Comm Coll (MI)
Bee County Coll (TX)
Bismarck State Coll (ND)
Black Hawk Coll, Moline (IL)
Blinn Coll (TX)
Brazosport Coll (TX)
Brevard Coll (NC)
Brevard Comm Coll (FL)
Brookdale Comm Coll (NJ)
Brunswick Coll (GA)
Burlington County Coll (NJ)
Butler County Comm Coll (KS)
Butler County Comm Coll (PA)
Cañada Coll (CA)
Carl Albert State Coll (OK)
Casper Coll (WY)
Central Coll (KS)
Central Comm College–Platte Cmps (NE)
Centralia Coll (WA)
Central Texas Coll (TX)
Central Wyoming Coll (WY)
Cerritos Coll (CA)
Chabot Coll (CA)
Chaffey Coll (CA)
Chemeketa Comm Coll (OR)
Citrus Coll (CA)
City Coll of San Francisco (CA)
City Colls of Chicago, Harold Washington Coll (IL)
City Colls of Chicago, Wilbur Wright Coll (IL)
Clackamas Comm Coll (OR)
Clark Coll (WA)
Clinton Comm Coll (IA)
Coahoma Comm Coll (MS)
Cochise Coll, Douglas (AZ)
Cochise Coll, Sierra Vista (AZ)
Coffeyville Comm Coll (KS)
Colby Comm Coll (KS)
Coll of Alameda (CA)
Coll of DuPage (IL)
Coll of San Mateo (CA)
Coll of Southern Idaho (ID)
Coll of the Canyons (CA)
Coll of the Desert (CA)
Coll of the Sequoias (CA)
Collin County Comm Coll (TX)
Colorado Mountn Coll, Alpine Cmps (CO)
Colorado Mountn Coll, Roaring Fork Cmps-Spring Valley Ctr (CO)
Colorado Mountn Coll, Timberline Cmps (CO)
Columbia Coll (CA)
Columbia State Comm Coll (TN)
Comm Coll of Allegheny County Allegheny Cmps (PA)
Comm Coll of Allegheny County Boyce Cmps (PA)
Comm Coll of Allegheny County North Cmps (PA)
Comm Coll of Allegheny County South Cmps (PA)
Comm Coll of Southern Nevada (NV)
Connors State Coll (OK)
Contra Costa Coll (CA)
Copiah-Lincoln Comm Coll (MS)
Crafton Hills Coll (CA)
Cypress Coll (CA)
Dalton Coll (GA)
Danville Area Comm Coll (IL)
Darton Coll (GA)
Daytona Beach Comm Coll (FL)
De Anza Coll (CA)
DeKalb Coll (GA)
Del Mar Coll (TX)
Delta Coll (MI)
Dixie Coll (UT)
Dodge City Comm Coll (KS)
Donnelly Coll (KS)
East Central Coll (MO)
East Central Comm Coll (MS)
Eastern Arizona Coll (AZ)
Eastern Oklahoma State Coll (OK)
Eastern Wyoming Coll (WY)
East Georgia Coll (GA)
East Los Angeles Coll (CA)
East Mississippi Comm Coll (MS)
Edison State Comm Coll (OH)
El Camino Coll (CA)
El Paso Comm Coll (TX)
Erie Comm Coll, City Cmps (NY)
Erie Comm Coll, South Cmps (NY)
Essex Comm Coll (MD)
Everett Comm Coll (WA)
Foothill Coll (CA)
Frank Phillips Coll (TX)
Frederick Comm Coll (MD)
Fullerton Coll (CA)
Fulton-Montgomery Comm Coll (NY)
Gainesville Coll (GA)
Galveston Coll (TX)
Garden City Comm Coll (KS)
Gavilan Coll (CA)
Glendale Comm Coll (AZ)
Gordon Coll (GA)
Grossmont Coll (CA)
Gulf Coast Comm Coll (FL)
Harford Comm Coll (MD)
Hartnell Coll (CA)
Herkimer County Comm Coll (NY)
Highland Comm Coll (KS)

Associate Degree Programs at Two-Year Colleges
English–Family Services

Highline Comm Coll (WA)
Hill Coll of the Hill Jr Coll District (TX)
Hinds Comm Coll (MS)
Hiwassee Coll (TN)
Howard Coll (TX)
Hutchinson Comm Coll and Area Vocational Sch (KS)
Illinois Valley Comm Coll (IL)
Imperial Valley Coll (CA)
Independence Comm Coll (KS)
Indian River Comm Coll (FL)
Iowa Lakes Comm Coll (IA)
Irvine Valley Coll (CA)
Itawamba Comm Coll (MS)
Jackson State Comm Coll (TN)
Jefferson Coll (MO)
John A Logan Coll (IL)
John C Calhoun State Comm Coll (AL)
John Wood Comm Coll (IL)
Jones County Jr Coll (MS)
Kansas City Kansas Comm Coll (KS)
Kellogg Comm Coll (MI)
Kemper Military Jr Coll (MO)
Kings River Comm Coll (CA)
Kirkwood Comm Coll (IA)
Kishwaukee Coll (IL)
Labette Comm Coll (KS)
Lake City Comm Coll (FL)
Lake Michigan Coll (MI)
Lamar Comm Coll (CO)
Laramie County Comm Coll (WY)
Lawson State Comm Coll (AL)
Lincoln Land Comm Coll (IL)
Little Hoop Comm Coll (ND)
Long Beach City Coll (CA)
Lon Morris Coll (TX)
Los Angeles City Coll (CA)
Los Angeles Mission Coll (CA)
Lower Columbia Coll (WA)
Macon Coll (GA)
Mendocino Coll (CA)
Miami-Dade Comm Coll (FL)
Miami University–Middletown Cmps (OH)
Middle Georgia Coll (GA)
Middlesex County Coll (NJ)
Midland Coll (TX)
Mid-Plains Comm Coll (NE)
MiraCosta Coll (CA)
Mississippi Delta Comm Coll (MS)
Modesto Jr Coll (CA)
Mohave Comm Coll (AZ)
Monroe County Comm Coll (MI)
Monterey Peninsula Coll (CA)
Montgomery County Comm Coll (PA)
Motlow State Comm Coll (TN)
Mountain Empire Comm Coll (VA)
Murray State Coll (OK)
Muscatine Comm Coll (IA)
Navarro Coll (TX)
New Mexico Jr Coll (NM)
New Mexico Military Inst (NM)
Northeast Comm Coll (NE)
Northeastern Jr Coll (CO)
Northeast Mississippi Comm Coll (MS)
North Idaho Coll (ID)
Northwest Coll (WY)
Northwestern Connecticut Comm-Tech Coll (CT)
Odessa Coll (TX)
Oxnard Coll (CA)
Palm Beach Comm Coll (FL)
Palo Alto Coll (TX)
Palomar Coll (CA)
Palo Verde Coll (CA)
Panama Canal Coll (Republic of Panama)
Parks Jr Coll (CO)
Pasadena City Coll (CA)
Phillips County Comm Coll (AR)
Pikes Peak Comm Coll (CO)
Polk Comm Coll (FL)
Porterville Coll (CA)
Potomac State Coll of West Virginia U (WV)
Pratt Comm Coll and Area Voc Sch (KS)
Quincy Coll (MA)
Rancho Santiago Coll (CA)
Redlands Comm Coll (OK)
Red Rocks Comm Coll (CO)
Ricks Coll (ID)
Rogers State Coll (OK)
Rose State Coll (OK)
Roxbury Comm Coll (MA)
St Gregory's Coll (OK)
St Philip's Coll (TX)
Salem Comm Coll (NJ)
Salt Lake Comm Coll (UT)
San Bernardino Valley Coll (CA)
San Diego City Coll (CA)
San Diego Mesa Coll (CA)
San Diego Miramar Coll (CA)
San Jacinto College–Central Cmps (TX)
San Jacinto College–North Cmps (TX)
San Jacinto College–South Cmps (TX)
San Joaquin Delta Coll (CA)
San Juan Coll (NM)
Santa Barbara City Coll (CA)
Santa Monica Coll (CA)
Santa Rosa Jr Coll (CA)
Sauk Valley Comm Coll (IL)
Scott Comm Coll (IA)
Seward County Comm Coll (KS)
Sheridan Coll (WY)
Skagit Valley Coll (WA)
Skyline Coll (CA)
Solano Comm Coll (CA)
Southern U at Shreveport–Bossier City Cmps (LA)
South Georgia Coll (GA)
SouthWest Collegiate Inst for the Deaf (TX)
Southwestern Coll (CA)
Southwestern Comm Coll (IA)
Southwest Mississippi Comm Coll (MS)
Spoon River Coll (IL)
Suffolk County Comm College–Ammerman Cmps (NY)
Sullivan County Comm Coll (NY)
Sussex County Comm Coll (NJ)
Tacoma Comm Coll (WA)
Taft Coll (CA)
Treasure Valley Comm Coll (OR)
Trinidad State Jr Coll (CO)
Trinity Valley Comm Coll (TX)
Triton Coll (IL)
Tulsa Jr Coll (OK)
Turtle Mountain Comm Coll (ND)
Umpqua Comm Coll (OR)
U of Kentucky, Jefferson Comm Coll (KY)
Vincennes U (IN)
Vista Comm Coll (CA)
Waldorf Coll (IA)
Waubonsee Comm Coll (IL)
Waycross Coll (GA)
Western Nebraska Comm Coll, Scottsbluff (NE)
Western Oklahoma State Coll (OK)
Western Wyoming Comm Coll (WY)
West Los Angeles Coll (CA)
West Valley Coll (CA)
Wharton County Jr Coll (TX)
Wright State U, Lake Cmps (OH)
Young Harris Coll (GA)
Yuba Coll (CA)

ENTOMOLOGY
Chemeketa Comm Coll (OR)
Northeast Mississippi Comm Coll (MS)
Snow Coll (UT)

ENVIRONMENTAL DESIGN
Abraham Baldwin Ag Coll (GA)
Art Inst of Pittsburgh (PA)
Brevard Coll (NC)
Cosumnes River Coll (CA)
Inst of Design and Construction (NY)
Iowa Lakes Comm Coll (IA)
Merritt Coll (CA)
Middle Georgia Coll (GA)
Scottsdale Comm Coll (AZ)

ENVIRONMENTAL EDUCATION
Brevard Coll (NC)
Colorado Mountn Coll, Timberline Cmps (CO)
Iowa Lakes Comm Coll (IA)
Modesto Jr Coll (CA)
New Mexico Jr Coll (NM)
Vermilion Comm Coll (MN)

ENVIRONMENTAL ENGINEERING TECHNOLOGY
Albuquerque Tech Vocational Inst (NM)
Allan Hancock Coll (CA)
Arapahoe Comm Coll (CO)
Berkshire Comm Coll (MA)
Central Carolina Tech Coll (SC)
Central Piedmont Comm Coll (NC)
Chaffey Coll (CA)
Chattanooga State Tech Comm Coll (TN)
Cincinnati State Tech and Comm Coll (OH)
Columbia Basin Coll (WA)
Columbus State Comm Coll (OH)
Comm Coll of Allegheny County South Cmps (PA)
Comm Coll of Denver (CO)
Comm Coll of Philadelphia (PA)
Delaware Tech & Comm Coll, Jack F Owens Cmps (DE)
Eastern Idaho Tech Coll (ID)
Elaine P Nunez Comm Coll (LA)
Gloucester County Coll (NJ)
Harford Comm Coll (MD)
Jackson Comm Coll (MI)
James H Faulkner State Comm Coll (AL)
Kansas City Kansas Comm Coll (KS)
Kemper Military Jr Coll (MO)
Kent State U, Trumbull Cmps (OH)
Keystone Coll (PA)
Massachusetts Bay Comm Coll (MA)
Merced Coll (CA)
Midland Coll (TX)
Montgomery County Comm Coll (PA)
New York City Tech Coll of the City U of NY (NY)
Oakland Comm Coll (MI)
Oklahoma State U, Oklahoma City (OK)
Owens Comm Coll, Findlay (OH)
Owens Comm Coll, Toledo (OH)
Pellissippi State Tech Comm Coll (TN)
Pennsylvania Coll of Tech (PA)
Pima Comm Coll (AZ)
San Diego City Coll (CA)
Schoolcraft Coll (MI)
Shoreline Comm Coll (WA)
Southern Maine Tech Coll (ME)
Springfield Tech Comm Coll (MA)
Three Rivers Comm-Tech Coll (CT)
Tyler Jr Coll (TX)
U of Kentucky, Madisonville Comm Coll (KY)
Vermont Tech Coll (VT)
Wake Tech Comm Coll (NC)
Waubonsee Comm Coll (IL)
Wayne County Comm Coll (MI)
Westchester Comm Coll (NY)
Westmoreland County Comm Coll (PA)

ENVIRONMENTAL HEALTH SCIENCES
Brevard Coll (NC)
Brevard Comm Coll (FL)
Coll of DuPage (IL)
Comm Coll of the Air Force (AL)
Crowder Coll (MO)
Everett Comm Coll (WA)
Grand Rapids Comm Coll (MI)
Kingsborough Comm Coll of City U of NY (NY)
Milwaukee Area Tech Coll (WI)
Northampton County Area Comm Coll (PA)
North Idaho Coll (ID)
Queensborough Comm Coll of City U of NY (NY)
Roane State Comm Coll (TN)
Texas State Tech Coll–Harlingen Cmps (TX)
U of North Dakota–Williston (ND)
Vincennes U (IN)

ENVIRONMENTAL SCIENCES
Adirondack Comm Coll (NY)
Anne Arundel Comm Coll (MD)
Arizona Western Coll (AZ)
Berkshire Comm Coll (MA)
Brevard Coll (NC)
Burlington County Coll (NJ)
Camden County Coll (NJ)
Cañada Coll (CA)
Central Florida Comm Coll (FL)
Coll of the Desert (CA)
Colorado Mountn Coll, Timberline Cmps (CO)
Columbia Coll (CA)
Comm Coll of the Air Force (AL)
Cosumnes River Coll (CA)
County Coll of Morris (NJ)
Delta Coll (MI)
Dixie Coll (UT)
East Los Angeles Coll (CA)
Erie Comm Coll, North Cmps (NY)
Erie Comm Coll, South Cmps (NY)
Everett Comm Coll (WA)
Finger Lakes Comm Coll (NY)
Fort Berthold Comm Coll (ND)
Fullerton Coll (CA)
Grays Harbor Coll (WA)
Harrisburg Area Comm Coll (PA)
Holyoke Comm Coll (MA)
Housatonic Comm-Tech Coll (CT)
Hudson Valley Comm Coll (NY)
Iowa Lakes Comm Coll (IA)
J Sargeant Reynolds Comm Coll (VA)
Kent State U, Salem Cmps (OH)
Kent State U, Tuscarawas Cmps (OH)
Lackawanna Jr Coll (PA)
Lake Land Coll (IL)
Lakewood Comm Coll (MN)
Las Positas Coll (CA)
Macon Coll (GA)
Middle Georgia Coll (GA)
Middlesex Community– Tech Coll (CT)
Midland Coll (TX)
Mitchell Coll (CT)
Mohawk Valley Comm Coll (NY)
Monroe Comm Coll (NY)
Mountain Empire Comm Coll (VA)
Muskingum Area Tech Coll (OH)
Naugatuck Valley Community–Tech Coll (CT)
Newbury Coll (MA)
New Mexico Jr Coll (NM)
Normandale Comm Coll (MN)
North Dakota State University–Bottineau (ND)
Northeast Metro Tech Coll (MN)
Northwest Coll (WY)
Oakland Comm Coll (MI)
Ohio State U Ag Tech Inst (OH)
Pamlico Comm Coll (NC)
Paul Smith's Coll (NY)
Pensacola Jr Coll (FL)
Quincy Coll (MA)
Rancho Santiago Coll (CA)
Raritan Valley Comm Coll (NJ)
Rockland Comm Coll (NY)
Rose State Coll (OK)
St Catharine Coll (KY)
Salish Kootenai Coll (MT)
Salt Lake Comm Coll (UT)
San Bernardino Valley Coll (CA)
San Jacinto College–South Cmps (TX)
Santa Barbara City Coll (CA)
Santa Fe Comm Coll (FL)
Scott Comm Coll (IA)
Southeast Comm Coll, Lincoln Cmps (NE)
State Comm Coll of East St Louis (IL)
State U of NY Coll of A&T at Morrisville (NY)
State U of NY Coll of Tech at Alfred (NY)
State U of NY Coll of Tech at Canton (NY)
Sterling Coll (VT)
Sussex County Comm Coll (NJ)
Texas State Tech Coll (TX)
Truckee Meadows Comm Coll (NV)
Turtle Mountain Comm Coll (ND)
U of Cincinnati Raymond Walters Coll (OH)
U of New Mexico–Los Alamos Branch (NM)
Valencia Comm Coll (FL)
Vermilion Comm Coll (MN)
Vincennes U (IN)
Westchester Comm Coll (NY)
Western Nebraska Comm Coll, Scottsbluff (NE)

ENVIRONMENTAL STUDIES
Berkshire Comm Coll (MA)
Brevard Coll (NC)
Coll of San Mateo (CA)
Colorado Mountn Coll, Timberline Cmps (CO)
Comm Coll of Beaver County (PA)
Comm Coll of Southern Nevada (NV)
De Anza Coll (CA)
Harford Comm Coll (MD)
Iowa Lakes Comm Coll (IA)
Kent State U, Ashtabula Cmps (OH)
Keystone Coll (PA)
Napa Valley Coll (CA)
Saddleback Coll (CA)
Santa Barbara City Coll (CA)
Truckee Meadows Comm Coll (NV)
Vermilion Comm Coll (MN)

EQUESTRIAN STUDIES
Allen County Comm Coll (KS)
Black Hawk Coll, Kewanee (IL)
Brevard Coll (NC)
Central Texas Coll (TX)
Central Wyoming Coll (WY)
Coll of Southern Idaho (ID)
Dawson Comm Coll (MT)
Dodge City Comm Coll (KS)
Ellsworth Comm Coll (IA)
Erie Business Ctr, Main (PA)
Kirkwood Comm Coll (IA)
Lamar Comm Coll (CO)
Laramie County Comm Coll (WY)
Los Angeles Pierce Coll (CA)
Martin Comm Coll (NC)
Mount Ida Coll (MA)
Murray State Coll (OK)
North Central Texas Coll (TX)
Northeastern Jr Coll (CO)
Northwest Coll (WY)
Ohio State U Ag Tech Inst (OH)
Parkland Coll (IL)
Redlands Comm Coll (OK)
Rogers State Coll (OK)
Scott Comm Coll (IA)
Scottsdale Comm Coll (AZ)
Sierra Coll (CA)
State U of NY Coll of A&T at Cobleskill (NY)
State U of NY Coll of A&T at Morrisville (NY)
Western Dakota Tech Inst (SD)
West Hills Comm Coll (CA)
Wood Coll (MS)

ETHNIC STUDIES
Barstow Coll (CA)
Bay Mills Comm Coll (MI)
Coll of Marin (CA)
Coll of San Mateo (CA)
Coll of the Sequoias (CA)
Cosumnes River Coll (CA)
De Anza Coll (CA)
Foothill Coll (CA)
Fresno City Coll (CA)
Highline Comm Coll (WA)
Laney Coll (CA)
Mendocino Coll (CA)
Monterey Peninsula Coll (CA)
Palomar Coll (CA)
Pasadena City Coll (CA)
Rancho Santiago Coll (CA)
Sacramento City Coll (CA)
Santa Barbara City Coll (CA)
Santa Monica Coll (CA)
Skagit Valley Coll (WA)
Solano Comm Coll (CA)
Southwestern Coll (CA)
Yuba Coll (CA)

EUROPEAN STUDIES
Anne Arundel Comm Coll (MD)
Brevard Coll (NC)

FAMILY AND CONSUMER STUDIES
Arizona Western Coll (AZ)
Bakersfield Coll (CA)
Butte Coll (CA)
Central Comm College–Platte Cmps (NE)
Cerro Coso Comm Coll (CA)
Cosumnes River Coll (CA)
Cowley County Comm Coll and Voc-Tech Sch (KS)
Cuesta Coll (CA)
Dixie Coll (UT)
Evergreen Valley Coll (CA)
Grossmont Coll (CA)
Hartnell Coll (CA)
Hiwassee Coll (TN)
Long Beach City Coll (CA)
Los Angeles City Coll (CA)
Los Angeles Mission Coll (CA)
Los Angeles Southwest Coll (CA)
Los Angeles Valley Coll (CA)
Middle Georgia Coll (GA)
Palomar Coll (CA)
Penn State U DuBois Cmps (PA)
Penn State U Fayette Cmps (PA)
Penn State U Mont Alto Cmps (PA)
Penn State U Schuylkill Cmps (PA)
Portland Comm Coll (OR)
Rancho Santiago Coll (CA)
Sacramento City Coll (CA)
San Bernardino Valley Coll (CA)
Southwestern Coll (CA)
Vincennes U (IN)
West Los Angeles Coll (CA)
Yakima Valley Comm Coll (WA)

FAMILY SERVICES
Barstow Coll (CA)
Brevard Coll (NC)
Central Coll (KS)
Comm Coll of Allegheny County North Cmps (PA)
Dixie Coll (UT)
Garden City Comm Coll (KS)
Hiwassee Coll (TN)
Lincoln Land Comm Coll (IL)
Oxnard Coll (CA)
Ricks Coll (ID)
Saddleback Coll (CA)
San Jose City Coll (CA)
Skagit Valley Coll (WA)
Snow Coll (UT)
Willmar Comm Coll (MN)

Peterson's Guide to Two-Year Colleges 1997
85

FARM AND RANCH MANAGEMENT
Abraham Baldwin Ag Coll (GA)
Allen County Comm Coll (KS)
Bismarck State Coll (ND)
Blue Mountain Comm Coll (OR)
Butler County Comm Coll (KS)
Central Coll (KS)
Central Comm College–Platte Cmps (NE)
Central Texas Coll (TX)
Clarendon Coll (TX)
Cloud County Comm Coll (KS)
Colby Comm Coll (KS)
Colorado Northwestern Comm Coll (CO)
Cosumnes River Coll (CA)
Cowley County Comm Coll and Voc-Tech Sch (KS)
Crowder Coll (MO)
Dodge City Comm Coll (KS)
Eastern Oklahoma State Coll (OK)
Eastern Wyoming Coll (WY)
Fort Berthold Comm Coll (ND)
Frank Phillips Coll (TX)
Garden City Comm Coll (KS)
Hawkeye Comm Coll (IA)
Highland Comm Coll (KS)
Hill Coll of the Hill Jr Coll District (TX)
Hutchinson Comm Coll and Area Vocational Sch (KS)
Iowa Western Comm Coll (IA)
Kankakee Comm Coll (IL)
Kirkwood Comm Coll (IA)
Kishwaukee Coll (IL)
Lamar Comm Coll (CO)
Lassen Coll (CA)
Mississippi Delta Comm Coll (MS)
Muscatine Comm Coll (IA)
North Central Missouri Coll (MO)
North Central Texas Coll (TX)
North Dakota State University–Bottineau (ND)
Northeast Comm Coll (NE)
Northeastern Jr Coll (CO)
Northeastern Oklahoma A&M Coll (OK)
Northwest Coll (WY)
Parkland Coll (IL)
Pratt Comm Coll and Area Voc Sch (KS)
Redlands Comm Coll (OK)
Ricks Coll (ID)
Rogers State Coll (OK)
St Catharine Coll (KY)
Seward County Comm Coll (KS)
Snow Coll (UT)
Southwest Texas Jr Coll (TX)
State U of NY Coll of A&T at Morrisville (NY)
Texas State Tech Coll–Harlingen Cmps (TX)
Trinidad State Jr Coll (CO)
Trinity Valley Comm Coll (TX)
Tyler Jr Coll (TX)
U of North Dakota–Lake Region (ND)
Vernon Regional Jr Coll (TX)
Wallace State Comm Coll (AL)
Western Dakota Tech Inst (SD)
Western Nebraska Comm Coll, Scottsbluff (NE)
Western Wisconsin Tech Coll (WI)
Wharton County Jr Coll (TX)
Willmar Tech Coll (MN)

FASHION DESIGN AND TECHNOLOGY
Allen County Comm Coll (KS)
American River Coll (CA)
Art Inst of Dallas (TX)
Art Inst of Fort Lauderdale (FL)
The Art Inst of Philadelphia (PA)
Art Inst of Pittsburgh (PA)
Art Inst of Seattle (WA)
Baltimore City Comm Coll (MD)
Bauder Coll (GA)
Black Hawk Coll, Moline (IL)
Brooks Coll (CA)
Butte Coll (CA)
Cañada Coll (CA)
Central Coll (KS)
Central Texas Coll (TX)
Cerritos Coll (CA)
Chabot Coll (CA)
Chaffey Coll (CA)
Cloud County Comm Coll (KS)
Coll of Alameda (CA)
Coll of DuPage (IL)
Coll of the Sequoias (CA)
Colorado Inst of Art (CO)
Daytona Beach Comm Coll (FL)
East Los Angeles Coll (CA)
El Camino Coll (CA)
El Centro Coll (TX)
El Paso Comm Coll (TX)
Fashion Inst of Design & Merchandising, LA Cmps (CA)
Fashion Inst of Design & Merchandising, SD Cmps (CA)
Fashion Inst of Design & Merchandising, SF Cmps (CA)
Florida Comm Coll at Jacksonville (FL)
Fullerton Coll (CA)
Garden City Comm Coll (KS)
Grand Rapids Comm Coll (MI)
Harcum Coll (PA)
Hesser Coll (NH)
Highland Comm Coll (KS)
Hinds Comm Coll (MS)
Hiwassee Coll (TN)
Houston Comm Coll System (TX)
International Fine Arts Coll (FL)
Itawamba Comm Coll (MS)
Kirkwood Comm Coll (IA)
Long Beach City Coll (CA)
Los Angeles Trade-Tech Coll (CA)
Louisville Tech Inst (KY)
Lowthian Coll (MN)
Merced Coll (CA)
Miami-Dade Comm Coll (FL)
Middlesex County Coll (NJ)
Miss Wade's Fashion Merchandising Coll (TX)
Monroe Comm Coll (NY)
Moorpark Coll (CA)
Mount Ida Coll (MA)
Nassau Comm Coll (NY)
Newbury Coll (MA)
Northeastern Oklahoma A&M Coll (OK)
Northeast Mississippi Comm Coll (MS)
Oakland Comm Coll (MI)
Palm Beach Comm Coll (FL)
Palomar Coll (CA)
Penn Valley Comm Coll (MO)
Pima Comm Coll (AZ)
Rancho Santiago Coll (CA)
Ricks Coll (ID)
Saddleback Coll (CA)
St Philip's Coll (TX)
San Diego Mesa Coll (CA)
San Jacinto College–Central Cmps (TX)
San Jacinto College–North Cmps (TX)
San Jacinto College–South Cmps (TX)
Santa Rosa Jr Coll (CA)
Seattle Central Comm Coll (WA)
Shoreline Comm Coll (WA)
Tulsa Jr Coll (OK)
U of Hawaii–Honolulu Comm Coll (HI)
U of Hawaii–Maui Comm Coll (HI)
Ventura Coll (CA)
Vincennes U (IN)
Virginia Marti Coll of Fashion and Art (OH)
Westmoreland County Comm Coll (PA)
West Valley Coll (CA)
William Rainey Harper Coll (IL)
Wood Tobe–Coburn Sch (NY)

FASHION MERCHANDISING
Abraham Baldwin Ag Coll (GA)
Alamance Comm Coll (NC)
Alexandria Tech Coll (MN)
Allen County Comm Coll (KS)
Allentown Business Sch (PA)
Alvin Comm Coll (TX)
American River Coll (CA)
Antonelli Coll (OH)
Art Inst of Atlanta (GA)
Art Inst of Dallas (TX)
Art Inst of Fort Lauderdale (FL)
The Art Inst of Philadelphia (PA)
Art Inst of Pittsburgh (PA)
Art Inst of Seattle (WA)
Austin Comm Coll (TX)
Baltimore City Comm Coll (MD)
Barton County Comm Coll (KS)
Bauder Coll (GA)
Bay State Coll (MA)
Bellevue Comm Coll (WA)
Berkeley Coll (NJ)
Berkeley Coll, New York (NY)
Berkeley Coll, White Plains (NY)
Black Hawk Coll, Moline (IL)
Bradley Acad for the Visual Arts (PA)
Brevard Comm Coll (FL)
Briarwood Coll (CT)
Brookdale Comm Coll (NJ)
Brookhaven Coll (TX)
Brooks Coll (CA)
Bryant and Stratton Business Inst, E Hills Cmps, Williamsville (NY)
Butler County Comm Coll (KS)
Butte Coll (CA)
Carl Sandburg Coll (IL)
Casco Bay Coll (ME)
Cedar Valley Coll (TX)
Central Coll (KS)
Central Comm College–Platte Cmps (NE)
Central Piedmont Comm Coll (NC)
Central Texas Coll (TX)
Chabot Coll (CA)
Champlain Coll (VT)
City Coll of San Francisco (CA)
Clark Coll (WA)
Cleveland Comm Coll (NC)
Coll of Alameda (CA)
Coll of DuPage (IL)
Coll of the Sequoias (CA)
Collin County Comm Coll (TX)
Colorado Inst of Art (CO)
Commonwealth Business Coll, Merrillville (IN)
Comm Coll of Allegheny County South Cmps (PA)
Comm Coll of Philadelphia (PA)
Comm Coll of Rhode Island (RI)
Cuesta Coll (CA)
Davis Coll (OH)
Dean Coll (MA)
DeKalb Coll (GA)
DeKalb Tech Inst (GA)
Delta Coll (MI)
Des Moines Area Comm Coll (IA)
Dixie Coll (UT)
Doña Ana Branch Comm Coll (NM)
Draughons Jr Coll, Nashville (TN)
Duff's Business Inst (PA)
Eastern Oklahoma State Coll (OK)
Edmonds Comm Coll (WA)
Ellsworth Comm Coll (IA)
El Paso Comm Coll (TX)
Erie Comm Coll, City Cmps (NY)
Evergreen Valley Coll (CA)
Fashion Inst of Design & Merchandising, LA Cmps (CA)
Fashion Inst of Design & Merchandising, SD Cmps (CA)
Fashion Inst of Design & Merchandising, SF Cmps (CA)
Fisher Coll (MA)
Florida Comm Coll at Jacksonville (FL)
Fresno City Coll (CA)
Fullerton Coll (CA)
Garden City Comm Coll (KS)
Gateway Comm-Tech Coll (CT)
Genesee Comm Coll (NY)
Grand Rapids Comm Coll (MI)
Grossmont Coll (CA)
Gulf Coast Comm Coll (FL)
Gwinnett Tech Inst (GA)
Harcum Coll (PA)
Herkimer County Comm Coll (NY)
Hesser Coll (NH)
Hiwassee Coll (TN)
Houston Comm Coll System (TX)
Howard Comm Coll (MD)
Huntington Jr Coll of Business (WV)
Hutchinson Comm Coll and Area Vocational Sch (KS)
ICM Sch of Business (PA)
Indiana Business Coll (IN)
Indian River Comm Coll (FL)
International Fine Arts Coll (FL)
Iowa Western Comm Coll (IA)
James H Faulkner State Comm Coll (AL)
Jefferson State Comm Coll (AL)
John A Logan Coll (IL)
Johnson County Comm Coll (KS)
John Wood Comm Coll (IL)
Joliet Jr Coll (IL)
J Sargeant Reynolds Comm Coll (VA)
Kaskaskia Coll (IL)
Kentucky Coll of Business, Lexington (KY)
Kingsborough Comm Coll of City U of NY (NY)
Kings River Comm Coll (CA)
Kirkwood Comm Coll (IA)
Lansdale Sch of Business (PA)
Laredo Comm Coll (TX)
Las Positas Coll (CA)
LDS Business Coll (UT)
Lee Coll (TX)
Lima Tech Coll (OH)
Long Beach City Coll (CA)
Los Angeles Trade-Tech Coll (CA)
Louisville Tech Inst (KY)
Lowthian Coll (MN)
Macomb Comm Coll (MI)
Madison Area Tech Coll (WI)
Merced Coll (CA)
Mesa Comm Coll (AZ)
Metropolitan Comm Coll (NE)
Miami-Dade Comm Coll (FL)
Middle Georgia Coll (GA)
Middlesex Comm Coll (MA)
Middlesex County Coll (NJ)
Midstate Coll (IL)
Milwaukee Area Tech Coll (WI)
Mineral Area Coll (MO)
Mississippi Gulf Coast Comm Coll (MS)
Miss Wade's Fashion Merchandising Coll (TX)
Modesto Jr Coll (CA)
Monroe Comm Coll (NY)
Monterey Peninsula Coll (CA)
Moraine Valley Comm Coll (IL)
Mount Ida Coll (MA)
Mt San Antonio Coll (CA)
Muskingum Area Tech Coll (OH)
Nassau Comm Coll (NY)
National Business Coll, Danville (VA)
National Business Coll, Lynchburg (VA)
National Business Coll, Roanoke (VA)
Nettleton Career Coll (SD)
Newbury Coll (MA)
Newport Business Inst (PA)
New River Comm Coll (VA)
New York City Tech Coll of the City U of NY (NY)
North Central Missouri Coll (MO)
Northeastern Jr Coll (CO)
Northeastern Oklahoma A&M Coll (OK)
Northeast Mississippi Comm Coll (MS)
North Iowa Area Comm Coll (IA)
Northwestern Business Coll (IL)
Northwest Mississippi Comm Coll (MS)
Oakland Comm Coll (MI)
Odessa Coll (TX)
Ohlone Coll (CA)
Okaloosa-Walton Comm Coll (FL)
Olympic Coll (WA)
Orange Coast Coll (CA)
Owens Comm Coll, Findlay (OH)
Owens Comm Coll, Toledo (OH)
Oxnard Coll (CA)
Palm Beach Comm Coll (FL)
Palomar Coll (CA)
Parks Jr Coll (CO)
Pasadena City Coll (CA)
Penn Valley Comm Coll (MO)
Pensacola Jr Coll (FL)
Piedmont Tech Coll (SC)
Pierce Coll (WA)
Rancho Santiago Coll (CA)
Rasmussen Coll Mankato (MN)
Ricks Coll (ID)
Rochester Comm Coll (MN)
Saddleback Coll (CA)
St Louis Comm Coll at Florissant Valley (MO)
St Petersburg Jr Coll (FL)
San Diego City Coll (CA)
San Diego Mesa Coll (CA)
San Jacinto College–Central Cmps (TX)
San Jacinto College–North Cmps (TX)
San Jacinto College–South Cmps (TX)
San Joaquin Delta Coll (CA)
Santa Fe Comm Coll (FL)
Santa Monica Coll (CA)
Scott Comm Coll (IA)
Scottsdale Comm Coll (AZ)
Shasta Coll (CA)
Shelby State Comm Coll (TN)
Sierra Coll (CA)
Skagit Valley Coll (WA)
Skyline Coll (CA)
Solano Comm Coll (CA)
South Plains Coll (TX)
South Suburban Coll (IL)
Southwest Mississippi Comm Coll (MS)
Spencer Sch of Business (NE)
Spokane Falls Comm Coll (WA)
Tarrant County Jr Coll (TX)
Trinity Valley Comm Coll (TX)
Triton Coll (IL)
Tunxis Comm Tech Coll (CT)
Tyler Jr Coll (TX)
U of North Dakota–Lake Region (ND)
Utah Valley State Coll (UT)
Vincennes U (IN)
Virginia Marti Coll of Fashion and Art (OH)
Wallace State Comm Coll (AL)
Waukesha County Tech Coll (WI)
Wayne Comm Coll (NC)
Western Wisconsin Tech Coll (WI)
Westmoreland County Comm Coll (PA)
William Rainey Harper Coll (IL)
Willmar Tech Coll (MN)
Wisconsin Indianhead Tech Coll, Superior Cmps (WI)
Wood Tobe–Coburn Sch (NY)

FILM AND VIDEO PRODUCTION
Anne Arundel Comm Coll (MD)
The Art Inst of Houston (TX)
Art Inst of Pittsburgh (PA)
Art Inst of Seattle (WA)
City Coll of San Francisco (CA)
Coll of DuPage (IL)
Coll of San Mateo (CA)
Coll of the Canyons (CA)
Colorado Inst of Art (CO)
Cumberland County Coll (NJ)
Daytona Beach Comm Coll (FL)
Everett Comm Coll (WA)
Full Sail Ctr for the Recording Arts (FL)
Hesser Coll (NH)
Holyoke Comm Coll (MA)
Keiser Coll of Tech, Daytona Beach (FL)
Lane Comm Coll (OR)
Lansing Comm Coll (MI)
Miami-Dade Comm Coll (FL)
Minneapolis Comm Coll (MN)
Orange Coast Coll (CA)
Saddleback Coll (CA)
St Louis Comm Coll at Florissant Valley (MO)
St Louis Comm Coll at Meramec (MO)
Scott Comm Coll (IA)
Seattle Central Comm Coll (WA)
Shoreline Comm Coll (WA)
Southern Maine Tech Coll (ME)

FILM STUDIES
Allan Hancock Coll (CA)
Art Inst of Fort Lauderdale (FL)
Cochise Coll, Douglas (AZ)
Cochise Coll, Sierra Vista (AZ)
De Anza Coll (CA)
Lansing Comm Coll (MI)
Long Beach City Coll (CA)
Los Angeles Valley Coll (CA)
Miami-Dade Comm Coll (FL)
Milwaukee Area Tech Coll (WI)
Moorpark Coll (CA)
Orange Coast Coll (CA)
Palomar Coll (CA)
Pensacola Jr Coll (FL)
Tallahassee Comm Coll (FL)
Valencia Comm Coll (FL)
Watkins Inst of Interior Design (TN)

FINANCE/BANKING
Adirondack Comm Coll (NY)
Alabama Southern Comm Coll, Monroeville (AL)
Alexandria Tech Coll (MN)
Allen County Comm Coll (KS)
American Inst of Business (IA)
American River Coll (CA)
Arapahoe Comm Coll (CO)
Arizona Western Coll (AZ)
Austin Comm Coll (TX)
Bakersfield Coll (CA)
Bee County Coll (TX)
Bergen Comm Coll (NJ)
Berkshire Comm Coll (MA)
Black Hawk Coll, Moline (IL)
Blue Ridge Comm Coll (VA)
Borough of Manhattan Comm Coll of City U of NY (NY)
Brevard Comm Coll (FL)
Broward Comm Coll (FL)
Bucks County Comm Coll (PA)
Burlington County Coll (NJ)
Butte Coll (CA)
Camden County Coll (NJ)
Catawba Valley Comm Coll (NC)
Central Coll (KS)
Central Pennsylvania Business Sch (PA)
Central Piedmont Comm Coll (NC)
Central Texas Coll (TX)
Central Virginia Comm Coll (VA)
Chabot Coll (CA)
Chattanooga State Tech Comm Coll (TN)
Chemeketa Comm Coll (OR)
Chipola Jr Coll (FL)
Churchman Business Sch (PA)
Cisco Jr Coll (TX)

Associate Degree Programs at Two-Year Colleges
Finance/Banking–Fire Science

City Coll of San Francisco (CA)
City Colls of Chicago, Harold Washington Coll (IL)
Clark State Comm Coll (OH)
Clovis Comm Coll (NM)
Coll of Southern Idaho (ID)
Coll of The Albemarle (NC)
Coll of the Mainland (TX)
Columbus State Comm Coll (OH)
Comm Coll of Allegheny County Boyce Cmps (PA)
Comm Coll of Allegheny County North Cmps (PA)
Comm Coll of Allegheny County South Cmps (PA)
Comm Coll of Aurora (CO)
Comm Coll of Philadelphia (PA)
Comm Coll of Southern Nevada (NV)
Connors State Coll (OK)
Cosumnes River Coll (CA)
County Coll of Morris (NJ)
Cuyahoga Comm Coll, Eastern Cmps (OH)
Cuyahoga Comm Coll, Western Cmps (OH)
Dalton Coll (GA)
Daytona Beach Comm Coll (FL)
Delaware County Comm Coll (PA)
Del Mar Coll (TX)
Delta Coll (MI)
Dodge City Comm Coll (KS)
Doña Ana Branch Comm Coll (NM)
Eastern New Mexico University–Roswell (NM)
East Los Angeles Coll (CA)
East Mississippi Comm Coll (MS)
Edison Comm Coll (FL)
El Camino Coll (CA)
Elgin Comm Coll (IL)
El Paso Comm Coll (TX)
Enterprise State Jr Coll (AL)
Fayetteville Tech Comm Coll (NC)
Fiorello H LaGuardia Comm Coll of City U of NY (NY)
Florida Comm Coll at Jacksonville (FL)
Florida Keys Comm Coll (FL)
Forsyth Tech Comm Coll (NC)
Fox Valley Tech Coll (WI)
Frank Phillips Coll (TX)
Frederick Comm Coll (MD)
Fresno City Coll (CA)
Fulton-Montgomery Comm Coll (NY)
Gadsden State Comm Coll (AL)
Garland County Comm Coll (AR)
Glendale Comm Coll (AZ)
Gloucester County Coll (NJ)
Grayson County Coll (TX)
Great Lakes Jr Coll of Business (MI)
Gulf Coast Comm Coll (FL)
Hill Coll of the Hill Jr Coll District (TX)
Hillsborough Comm Coll (FL)
Hinds Comm Coll (MS)
Hiwassee Coll (TN)
Hocking Coll (OH)
Holmes Comm Coll (MS)
Howard Coll (TX)
Howard Comm Coll (MD)
Hudson Valley Comm Coll (NY)
Hutchinson Comm Coll and Area Vocational Sch (KS)
ICS Ctr for Degree Studies (PA)
Illinois Central Coll (IL)
Illinois Eastern Comm Colls, Lincoln Trail Coll (IL)
Independence Comm Coll (KS)
Indian River Comm Coll (FL)
International Business Coll (IN)
Iowa Lakes Comm Coll (IA)
Jackson Comm Coll (MI)
Jackson State Comm Coll (TN)
James H Faulkner State Comm Coll (AL)
Jefferson Comm Coll (NY)

Jefferson Comm Coll (OH)
Jefferson Davis Comm Coll (AL)
Jefferson State Comm Coll (AL)
John A Logan Coll (IL)
Joliet Jr Coll (IL)
J Sargeant Reynolds Comm Coll (VA)
Kansas City Kansas Comm Coll (KS)
Kellogg Comm Coll (MI)
Kent State U, Ashtabula Cmps (OH)
Kent State U, East Liverpool Cmps (OH)
Kent State U, Trumbull Cmps (OH)
Kirkwood Comm Coll (IA)
Kirtland Comm Coll (MI)
Lake Area Vocational-Tech Inst (SD)
Lake Land Coll (IL)
Lake Michigan Coll (MI)
Lakeshore Tech Coll (WI)
Lake-Sumter Comm Coll (FL)
Lake Tahoe Comm Coll (CA)
Laney Coll (CA)
Lansing Comm Coll (MI)
Lenoir Comm Coll (NC)
Lewis and Clark Comm Coll (IL)
Lima Tech Coll (OH)
Lorain County Comm Coll (OH)
Los Angeles City Coll (CA)
Los Angeles Mission Coll (CA)
Los Angeles Southwest Coll (CA)
Luzerne County Comm Coll (PA)
Macomb Comm Coll (MI)
Madison Area Tech Coll (WI)
Manatee Comm Coll (FL)
Marion Tech Coll (OH)
Massachusetts Bay Comm Coll (MA)
Mayland Comm Coll (NC)
McLennan Comm Coll (TX)
Mendocino Coll (CA)
Merced Coll (CA)
Mercer County Comm Coll (NJ)
Mesa Comm Coll (AZ)
Metropolitan Comm Coll (NE)
Miami-Dade Comm Coll (FL)
Miami University–Hamilton Cmps (OH)
Miami University–Middletown Cmps (OH)
Middlesex County Coll (NJ)
Midlands Tech Coll (SC)
Mid Michigan Comm Coll (MI)
Milwaukee Area Tech Coll (WI)
Mississippi Gulf Coast Comm Coll (MS)
Modesto Jr Coll (CA)
Mohawk Valley Comm Coll (NY)
Monroe County Comm Coll (MI)
Montgomery College–Germantown Cmps (MD)
Montgomery College–Takoma Park Cmps (MD)
Moraine Valley Comm Coll (IL)
Morton Coll (IL)
Mt San Antonio Coll (CA)
Muscatine Comm Coll (IA)
Muskegon Comm Coll (MI)
Nassau Comm Coll (NY)
Naugatuck Valley Community–Tech Coll (CT)
Neosho County Comm Coll (KS)
Newbury Coll (MA)
The New England Banking Inst (MA)
New Mexico Jr Coll (NM)
New Mexico Military Inst (NM)
Northampton County Area Comm Coll (PA)
North Central Michigan Coll (MI)
North Central Tech Coll (OH)
Northeast Alabama State Comm Coll (AL)
Northeast Texas Comm Coll (TX)

Northern Essex Comm Coll (MA)
North Harris Coll (TX)
NorthWest Arkansas Comm Coll (AR)
Northwest Iowa Comm Coll (IA)
Northwest State Comm Coll (OH)
Norwalk Comm-Tech Coll (CT)
Oakton Comm Coll (IL)
Ocean County Coll (NJ)
Okaloosa-Walton Comm Coll (FL)
Oklahoma City Comm Coll (OK)
Onondaga Comm Coll (NY)
Orangeburg-Calhoun Tech Coll (SC)
Orange County Comm Coll (NY)
Owens Comm Coll, Toledo (OH)
Palm Beach Comm Coll (FL)
Palo Alto Coll (TX)
Palomar Coll (CA)
Parkland Coll (IL)
Pasadena City Coll (CA)
Passaic County Comm Coll (NJ)
Pellissippi State Tech Comm Coll (TN)
Pikes Peak Comm Coll (CO)
Pima Comm Coll (AZ)
Polk Comm Coll (FL)
Porterville Coll (CA)
Prairie State Coll (IL)
Rancho Santiago Coll (CA)
Reading Area Comm Coll (PA)
Redlands Comm Coll (OK)
Ricks Coll (ID)
Rio Salado Comm Coll (AZ)
Riverside Comm Coll (CA)
Robeson Comm Coll (NC)
Rockland Comm Coll (NY)
Rock Valley Coll (IL)
Saint Charles County Comm Coll (MO)
St Louis Comm Coll at Florissant Valley (MO)
St Louis Comm Coll at Forest Park (MO)
St Louis Comm Coll at Meramec (MO)
St Petersburg Jr Coll (FL)
Salt Lake Comm Coll (UT)
San Bernardino Valley Coll (CA)
San Diego City Coll (CA)
San Jacinto College–Central Cmps (TX)
San Jacinto College–South Cmps (TX)
San Juan Coll (NM)
Santa Barbara City Coll (CA)
Santa Fe Comm Coll (FL)
Santa Fe Comm Coll (NM)
Scott Comm Coll (IA)
Scottsdale Comm Coll (AZ)
Seminole Comm Coll (FL)
Seward County Comm Coll (KS)
Shasta Coll (CA)
Sinclair Comm Coll (OH)
Skyline Coll (CA)
Solano Comm Coll (CA)
Southeast Comm Coll, Beatrice Cmps (NE)
Southern Union State Comm Coll (AL)
Southern U at Shreveport–Bossier City Cmps (LA)
Southern West Virginia Comm and Tech Coll (WV)
South Florida Comm Coll (FL)
South Georgia Coll (GA)
South Suburban Coll (IL)
Southwestern Coll (CA)
Southwestern Oregon Comm Coll (OR)
Southwest Mississippi Comm Coll (MS)
Southwest Wisconsin Tech Coll (WI)
Spencer Sch of Business (NE)
Spoon River Coll (IL)
Springfield Tech Comm Coll (MA)
State Fair Comm Coll (MO)

State Tech Inst at Memphis (TN)
State U of NY Coll of A&T at Morrisville (NY)
State U of NY Coll of Tech at Alfred (NY)
Suffolk County Comm Coll–Western Cmps (NY)
Terra State Comm Coll (OH)
Texarkana Coll (TX)
Texas Southmost Coll (TX)
Tidewater Comm Coll (VA)
Trinity Valley Comm Coll (TX)
Truckee Meadows Comm Coll (NV)
Tulsa Jr Coll (OK)
Tyler Jr Coll (TX)
Union County Coll (NJ)
U of Hawaii–Windward Comm Coll (HI)
U of Kentucky, Elizabethtown Comm Coll (KY)
U of Kentucky, Hopkinsville Comm Coll (KY)
U of New Mexico–Gallup Branch (NM)
Utah Valley State Coll (UT)
Valencia Comm Coll (FL)
Vermilion Comm Coll (MN)
Vincennes U (IN)
Vincennes University–Jasper Ctr (IN)
Waldorf Coll (IA)
Wallace State Comm Coll (AL)
Waubonsee Comm Coll (IL)
Wayne County Comm Coll (MI)
Westark Comm Coll (AR)
Westchester Comm Coll (NY)
Western Nevada Comm Coll (NV)
Western Piedmont Comm Coll (NC)
Western Wisconsin Tech Coll (WI)
Westmoreland County Comm Coll (PA)
West Virginia Northern Comm Coll (WV)
West Virginia U at Parkersburg (WV)
William Rainey Harper Coll (IL)
Wisconsin Indianhead Tech Coll, Rice Lake Cmps (WI)
Wright State U, Lake Cmps (OH)
Yuba Coll (CA)

FIRE SCIENCE
Aims Comm Coll (CO)
Alabama Southern Comm Coll, Monroeville (AL)
Alamance Comm Coll (NC)
Albuquerque Tech Vocational Inst (NM)
Allan Hancock Coll (CA)
American River Coll (CA)
Antelope Valley Coll (CA)
Arizona Western Coll (AZ)
Austin Comm Coll (TX)
Bakersfield Coll (CA)
Barstow Coll (CA)
Barton County Comm Coll (KS)
Belleville Area Coll (IL)
Bellevue Comm Coll (WA)
Berkshire Comm Coll (MA)
Bishop State Comm Coll (AL)
Blackhawk Tech Coll (WI)
Black River Tech Coll (AR)
Blinn Coll (TX)
Brevard Comm Coll (FL)
Bristol Comm Coll (MA)
Broome Comm Coll (NY)
Broward Comm Coll (FL)
Bunker Hill Comm Coll (MA)
Butler County Comm Coll (KS)
Butte Coll (CA)
Cabrillo Coll (CA)
Camden County Coll (NJ)
Cape Cod Comm Coll (MA)
Casper Coll (WY)
Catonsville Comm Coll (MD)
Central Florida Comm Coll (FL)
Central Oregon Comm Coll (OR)
Central Piedmont Comm Coll (NC)
Cerro Coso Comm Coll (CA)

Chabot Coll (CA)
Chattahoochee Valley State Comm Coll (AL)
Chattanooga State Tech Comm Coll (TN)
Chemeketa Comm Coll (OR)
Chippewa Valley Tech Coll (WI)
Cisco Jr Coll (TX)
City Coll of San Francisco (CA)
City Colls of Chicago, Harold Washington Coll (IL)
City Colls of Chicago, Richard J Daley Coll (IL)
Clatsop Comm Coll (OR)
Coastal Carolina Comm Coll (NC)
Cochise Coll, Douglas (AZ)
Cochise Coll, Sierra Vista (AZ)
Coconino County Comm Coll (AZ)
Coll of DuPage (IL)
Coll of Lake County (IL)
Coll of Marin (CA)
Coll of San Mateo (CA)
Coll of the Desert (CA)
Coll of the Sequoias (CA)
Coll of the Siskiyous (CA)
Collin County Comm Coll (TX)
Columbia Basin Coll (WA)
Columbia Coll (CA)
Comm Coll of Allegheny County Boyce Cmps (PA)
Comm Coll of Philadelphia (PA)
Comm Coll of Rhode Island (RI)
Comm Coll of Southern Nevada (NV)
Comm Coll of the Air Force (AL)
Corning Comm Coll (NY)
Cosumnes River Coll (CA)
Crafton Hills Coll (CA)
Crowder Coll (MO)
Cuyahoga Comm Coll, Western Cmps (OH)
Davidson County Comm Coll (NC)
Daytona Beach Comm Coll (FL)
DeKalb Coll (GA)
Delaware County Comm Coll (PA)
Delaware Tech & Comm Coll, Stanton/Wilmington Cmps (DE)
Delgado Comm Coll (LA)
Del Mar Coll (TX)
Delta Coll (MI)
Des Moines Area Comm Coll (IA)
Dodge City Comm Coll (KS)
Doña Ana Branch Comm Coll (NM)
Durham Tech Comm Coll (NC)
East Central Coll (MO)
Eastern New Mexico University–Roswell (NM)
East Los Angeles Coll (CA)
East Mississippi Comm Coll (MS)
Edison Comm Coll (FL)
Edmonds Comm Coll (WA)
El Camino Coll (CA)
El Centro Coll (TX)
Elgin Comm Coll (IL)
El Paso Comm Coll (TX)
Erie Comm Coll, South Cmps (NY)
Essex County Coll (NJ)
Feather River Comm Coll District (CA)
Florida Comm Coll at Jacksonville (FL)
Fox Valley Tech Coll (WI)
Frank Phillips Coll (TX)
Fresno City Coll (CA)
Gadsden State Comm Coll (AL)
Galveston Coll (TX)
Garland County Comm Coll (AR)
Gaston Coll (NC)
Gateway Comm-Tech Coll (CT)
George Corley Wallace State Comm Coll, Selma (AL)
Georgia Military Coll (GA)
Glendale Comm Coll (AZ)

Grand Rapids Comm Coll (MI)
Greenfield Comm Coll (MA)
Greenville Tech Coll (SC)
Guilford Tech Comm Coll (NC)
Gulf Coast Comm Coll (FL)
Harrisburg Area Comm Coll (PA)
Hartnell Coll (CA)
Henry Ford Comm Coll (MI)
Hillsborough Comm Coll (FL)
Hocking Coll (OH)
Houston Comm Coll System (TX)
Howard Coll (TX)
Hutchinson Comm Coll and Area Vocational Sch (KS)
Illinois Central Coll (IL)
Imperial Valley Coll (CA)
Indian River Comm Coll (FL)
Iowa Western Comm Coll (IA)
Ivy Tech State Coll–Central Indiana (IN)
Ivy Tech State Coll–Northeast (IN)
Ivy Tech State Coll–Northwest (IN)
James H Faulkner State Comm Coll (AL)
Jefferson Coll (MO)
Jefferson State Comm Coll (AL)
John C Calhoun State Comm Coll (AL)
Johnson County Comm Coll (KS)
John Wood Comm Coll (IL)
Joliet Jr Coll (IL)
J Sargeant Reynolds Comm Coll (VA)
Kalamazoo Valley Comm Coll (MI)
Kansas City Kansas Comm Coll (KS)
Kellogg Comm Coll (MI)
Kilian Comm Coll (SD)
Kirkwood Comm Coll (IA)
Kirtland Comm Coll (MI)
Kishwaukee Coll (IL)
Labette Comm Coll (KS)
Lakeland Comm Coll (OH)
Lake-Sumter Comm Coll (FL)
Lake Tahoe Comm Coll (CA)
Lansing Comm Coll (MI)
Laramie County Comm Coll (WY)
Laredo Comm Coll (TX)
Las Positas Coll (CA)
Lawson State Comm Coll (AL)
Lenoir Comm Coll (NC)
Lewis and Clark Comm Coll (IL)
Lincoln Land Comm Coll (IL)
Long Beach City Coll (CA)
Lorain County Comm Coll (OH)
Los Angeles Harbor Coll (CA)
Los Angeles Valley Coll (CA)
Los Medanos Coll (CA)
Louisiana State U at Eunice (LA)
Lower Columbia Coll (WA)
Luzerne County Comm Coll (PA)
Macomb Comm Coll (MI)
Macon Coll (GA)
Madison Area Tech Coll (WI)
Manatee Comm Coll (FL)
Massasoit Comm Coll (MA)
McHenry County Coll (IL)
Merced Coll (CA)
Mercer County Comm Coll (NJ)
Meridian Comm Coll (MS)
Mesa Comm Coll (AZ)
Miami-Dade Comm Coll (FL)
Middlesex Comm Coll (MA)
Middlesex County Coll (NJ)
Midland Coll (TX)
Mid Michigan Comm Coll (MI)
Miles Comm Coll (MT)
Milwaukee Area Tech Coll (WI)
Mission Coll (CA)
Modesto Jr Coll (CA)
Mohave Comm Coll (AZ)
Monroe Comm Coll (NY)
Montana State U Coll of Tech-Great Falls (MT)
Monterey Peninsula Coll (CA)
Montgomery College–Rockville Cmps (MD)

Associate Degree Programs at Two-Year Colleges
Fire Science–Food Services Technology

Montgomery County Comm Coll (PA)
Moraine Valley Comm Coll (IL)
Mt Hood Comm Coll (OR)
Mt San Antonio Coll (CA)
Mt San Jacinto Coll (CA)
Mount Wachusett Comm Coll (MA)
Naugatuck Valley Community–Tech Coll (CT)
Navarro Coll (TX)
New Hampshire Tech Coll, Laconia (NH)
New Mexico Jr Coll (NM)
New Mexico State University–Carlsbad (NM)
Northern Virginia Comm Coll (VA)
North Hennepin Comm Coll (MN)
Northland Pioneer Coll (AZ)
North Shore Comm Coll (MA)
Northwest-Shoals Comm Coll (AL)
Norwalk Comm-Tech Coll (CT)
Oakton Comm Coll (IL)
Ocean County Coll (NJ)
Odessa Coll (TX)
Oklahoma State U, Oklahoma City (OK)
Olympic Coll (WA)
Onondaga Comm Coll (NY)
Owens Comm Coll, Toledo (OH)
Oxnard Coll (CA)
Ozarks Tech Comm Coll (MO)
Palm Beach Comm Coll (FL)
Palomar Coll (CA)
Parkland Coll (IL)
Pasadena City Coll (CA)
Pasco-Hernando Comm Coll (FL)
Passaic County Comm Coll (NJ)
Penn Valley Comm Coll (MO)
Pensacola Jr Coll (FL)
Pierce Coll (WA)
Pima Comm Coll (AZ)
Polk Comm Coll (FL)
Porterville Coll (CA)
Portland Comm Coll (OR)
Prairie State Coll (IL)
Quinsigamond Comm Coll (MA)
Rancho Santiago Coll (CA)
Red Rocks Comm Coll (CO)
Richland Comm Coll (IL)
Riverside Comm Coll (CA)
Rockland Comm Coll (NY)
Rock Valley Coll (IL)
Rogue Comm Coll (OR)
St Clair County Comm Coll (MI)
St Johns River Comm Coll (FL)
St Louis Comm Coll at Florissant Valley (MO)
St Louis Comm Coll at Forest Park (MO)
St Petersburg Jr Coll (FL)
San Antonio Coll (TX)
San Diego Miramar Coll (CA)
San Jacinto College–Central Cmps (TX)
San Joaquin Delta Coll (CA)
Santa Fe Comm Coll (FL)
Santa Monica Coll (CA)
Santa Rosa Jr Coll (CA)
Schenectady County Comm Coll (NY)
Scottsdale Comm Coll (AZ)
Seminole Comm Coll (FL)
Shasta Coll (CA)
Shorter Coll (AR)
Sierra Coll (CA)
Sinclair Comm Coll (OH)
Solano Comm Coll (CA)
Southeast Comm Coll, Lincoln Cmps (NE)
Southeastern Illinois Coll (IL)
Southern Maine Tech Coll (ME)
South Plains Coll (TX)
South Puget Sound Comm Coll (WA)
South Suburban Coll (IL)
Southwestern Michigan Coll (MI)
Southwestern Oregon Comm Coll (OR)
Spokane Comm Coll (WA)
Springfield Tech Comm Coll (MA)
Stark Tech Coll (OH)
State Comm Coll of East St Louis (IL)
Tarrant County Jr Coll (TX)
Texas Southmost Coll (TX)
Thomas Nelson Comm Coll (VA)
Three Rivers Comm-Tech Coll (CT)
Triton Coll (IL)
Truckee Meadows Comm Coll (NV)
Tulsa Jr Coll (OK)
Tyler Jr Coll (TX)
Umpqua Comm Coll (OR)
Union County Coll (NJ)
U of Alaska Anchorage, Matanuska-Susitna Coll (AK)
U of Hawaii–Hawaii Comm Coll (HI)
U of Hawaii–Honolulu Comm Coll (HI)
U of Hawaii–Maui Comm Coll (HI)
U of Kentucky, Jefferson Comm Coll (KY)
Utah Valley State Coll (UT)
Valencia Comm Coll (FL)
Victor Valley Coll (CA)
Wallace State Comm Coll (AL)
Washtenaw Comm Coll (MI)
Wenatchee Valley Coll (WA)
Western Oklahoma State Coll (OK)
Westmoreland County Comm Coll (PA)
William Rainey Harper Coll (IL)
Wilson Tech Comm Coll (NC)
Yakima Valley Comm Coll (WA)
Yavapai Coll (AZ)
Yuba Coll (CA)

FISH AND GAME MANAGEMENT

Abraham Baldwin Ag Coll (GA)
Alexandria Tech Coll (MN)
Central Oregon Comm Coll (OR)
Chattanooga State Tech Comm Coll (TN)
East Central Coll (MO)
Finger Lakes Comm Coll (NY)
Fox Valley Tech Coll (WI)
Fullerton Coll (CA)
Garrett Comm Coll (MD)
Grays Harbor Coll (WA)
Haywood Comm Coll (NC)
Hocking Coll (OH)
Iowa Lakes Comm Coll (IA)
Kirkwood Comm Coll (IA)
Mid Michigan Comm Coll (MI)
Monterey Peninsula Coll (CA)
Mt Hood Comm Coll (OR)
North Dakota State University–Bottineau (ND)
North Idaho Coll (ID)
Northwest Coll (WY)
Peninsula Coll (WA)
Pratt Comm Coll and Area Voc Sch (KS)
Seward County Comm Coll (KS)
State U of NY Coll of A&T at Cobleskill (NY)
State U of NY Coll of A&T at Morrisville (NY)
Vermilion Comm Coll (MN)
Wayne Comm Coll (NC)

FLIGHT TRAINING

Alabama Aviation and Tech Coll (AL)
Arapahoe Comm Coll (CO)
Belleville Area Coll (IL)
Big Bend Comm Coll (WA)
Broward Comm Coll (FL)
Casper Coll (WY)
Catonsville Comm Coll (MD)
Central Coll (KS)
Central Texas Coll (TX)
Chattanooga State Tech Comm Coll (TN)
Cochise Coll, Douglas (AZ)
Coll of San Mateo (CA)
Colorado Northwestern Comm Coll (CO)
Comm Coll of Allegheny County Allegheny Cmps (PA)
Comm Coll of Beaver County (PA)
Cumberland County Coll (NJ)
Dixie Coll (UT)
Florida Comm Coll at Jacksonville (FL)
Fox Valley Tech Coll (WI)
Frank Phillips Coll (TX)
Fulton-Montgomery Comm Coll (NY)
Green River Comm Coll (WA)
Guilford Tech Comm Coll (NC)
Gulf Coast Comm Coll (FL)
Indian Hills Comm Coll (IA)
Inver Hills Comm Coll (MN)
Iowa Central Comm Coll (IA)
Iowa Lakes Comm Coll (IA)
Jackson Comm Coll (MI)
Kansas City Kansas Comm Coll (KS)
Lane Comm Coll (OR)
Lansing Comm Coll (MI)
Lee Coll (TX)
Lenoir Comm Coll (NC)
Long Beach City Coll (CA)
Mercer County Comm Coll (NJ)
Miami-Dade Comm Coll (FL)
Mt San Antonio Coll (CA)
National Ed Ctr–Spartan Sch of Aeronautics Cmps (OK)
Navarro Coll (TX)
Northern Virginia Comm Coll (VA)
North Shore Comm Coll (MA)
Northwestern Michigan Coll (MI)
Oakland Comm Coll (MI)
Orange Coast Coll (CA)
Palm Beach Comm Coll (FL)
Pasadena City Coll (CA)
Prairie State Coll (IL)
St Petersburg Jr Coll (FL)
Salt Lake Comm Coll (UT)
San Diego Mesa Coll (CA)
San Jacinto College–Central Cmps (TX)
Scott Comm Coll (IA)
Springfield Coll in Illinois (IL)
State U of NY Coll of Tech at Farmingdale (NY)
Texas State Tech Coll–Waco/Marshall Cmps (TX)
Vincennes U (IN)
Wallace State Comm Coll (AL)

FOOD MARKETING

American River Coll (CA)
Austin Comm Coll (TX)
Iowa Central Comm Coll (IA)
Iowa Western Comm Coll (IA)
Kirkwood Comm Coll (IA)
Muskegon Comm Coll (MI)
Northeast Mississippi Comm Coll (MS)
Ohio State U Ag Tech Inst (OH)
State U of NY Coll of Tech at Alfred (NY)
Vincennes U (IN)
Waukesha County Tech Coll (WI)

FOOD SCIENCES

Alamance Comm Coll (NC)
Blackhawk Tech Coll (WI)
Bucks County Comm Coll (PA)
Cabrillo Coll (CA)
Central Piedmont Comm Coll (NC)
Coll of Southern Idaho (ID)
Comm Coll of the Air Force (AL)
Dixie Coll (UT)
El Centro Coll (TX)
Elgin Comm Coll (IL)
Greenfield Comm Coll (MA)
Highland Comm Coll (KS)
Hocking Coll (OH)
Lake Michigan Coll (MI)
Los Angeles City Coll (CA)
Macon Coll (GA)
Miami-Dade Comm Coll (FL)
Moraine Park Tech Coll (WI)
Mt Hood Comm Coll (OR)
Northeast Mississippi Comm Coll (MS)
Oakland Comm Coll (MI)
Ohlone Coll (CA)
Saddleback Coll (CA)
St Louis Comm Coll at Florissant Valley (MO)
San Jacinto College–North Cmps (TX)
South Seattle Comm Coll (WA)
SouthWest Collegiate Inst for the Deaf (TX)
Vincennes U (IN)

FOOD SERVICES MANAGEMENT

Alamance Comm Coll (NC)
Allegany Comm Coll (MD)
American River Coll (CA)
The Art Inst of Houston (TX)
Asheville-Buncombe Tech Comm Coll (NC)
Asnuntuck Comm-Tech Coll (CT)
Baltimore International Culinary Coll (MD)
Belleville Area Coll (IL)
Berkshire Comm Coll (MA)
Brevard Comm Coll (FL)
Brookdale Comm Coll (NJ)
Broward Comm Coll (FL)
Bucks County Comm Coll (PA)
Bunker Hill Comm Coll (MA)
Burlington County Coll (NJ)
Butler County Comm Coll (PA)
Cabrillo Coll (CA)
Camden County Coll (NJ)
Central Coll (KS)
Central Comm College–Hastings Cmps (NE)
Central Piedmont Comm Coll (NC)
Central Texas Coll (TX)
Chaffey Coll (CA)
Charles Stewart Mott Comm Coll (MI)
Chippewa Valley Tech Coll (WI)
City Colls of Chicago, Harold Washington Coll (IL)
City Colls of Chicago, Kennedy-King Coll (IL)
City Colls of Chicago, Malcolm X Coll (IL)
Clark Coll (WA)
Coll of DuPage (IL)
Coll of Lake County (IL)
Columbia Coll (CA)
Columbus State Comm Coll (OH)
Comm Coll of Allegheny County Allegheny Cmps (PA)
Comm Coll of Allegheny County Boyce Cmps (PA)
Comm Coll of Philadelphia (PA)
Comm Coll of Southern Nevada (NV)
Copiah-Lincoln Comm Coll (MS)
Copiah-Lincoln Comm College–Natchez Cmps (MS)
Cosumnes River Coll (CA)
Cuyahoga Comm Coll, Metropolitan Cmps (OH)
Cypress Coll (CA)
Daytona Beach Comm Coll (FL)
Del Mar Coll (TX)
Des Moines Area Comm Coll (IA)
Dixie Coll (UT)
Dutchess Comm Coll (NY)
East Central Coll (MO)
Eastern Maine Tech Coll (ME)
Edmonds Comm Coll (WA)
El Camino Coll (CA)
El Centro Coll (TX)
Elgin Comm Coll (IL)
Enterprise State Jr Coll (AL)
Erie Comm Coll, North Cmps (NY)
Fayetteville Tech Comm Coll (NC)
Fiorello H LaGuardia Comm Coll of City U of NY (NY)
Florida Comm Coll at Jacksonville (FL)
Fox Valley Tech Coll (WI)
Fulton-Montgomery Comm Coll (NY)
Gateway Comm-Tech Coll (CT)
Gogebic Comm Coll (MI)
Greenville Tech Coll (SC)
Grossmont Coll (CA)
Guilford Tech Comm Coll (NC)
Harrisburg Area Comm Coll (PA)
Henry Ford Comm Coll (MI)
Highland Comm Coll (IL)
Hinds Comm Coll (MS)
Hiwassee Coll (TN)
Hocking Coll (OH)
Indian River Comm Coll (FL)
Inver Hills Comm Coll (MN)
Iowa Western Comm Coll (IA)
Ivy Tech State Coll–Central Indiana (IN)
Jefferson Comm Coll (OH)
Jefferson State Comm Coll (AL)
John Wood Comm Coll (IL)
Joliet Jr Coll (IL)
Keystone Coll (PA)
Kirkwood Comm Coll (IA)
Lake Michigan Coll (MI)
Lane Comm Coll (OR)
Lansing Comm Coll (MI)
Lewis and Clark Comm Coll (IL)
Lexington Coll (IL)
Lincoln Land Comm Coll (IL)
Long Beach City Coll (CA)
Los Angeles City Coll (CA)
Manchester Comm-Tech Coll (CT)
Merced Coll (CA)
Meridian Comm Coll (MS)
Metropolitan Comm Coll (NE)
Middlesex County Coll (NJ)
Mission Coll (CA)
Mohawk Valley Comm Coll (NY)
Monroe Comm Coll (NY)
Montgomery College–Rockville Cmps (MD)
Moraine Valley Comm Coll (IL)
Mount Wachusett Comm Coll (MA)
Muskegon Comm Coll (MI)
Nassau Comm Coll (NY)
Naugatuck Valley Community–Tech Coll (CT)
Newbury Coll (MA)
New Hampshire Tech Coll, Berlin (NH)
Nicolet Area Tech Coll (WI)
North Central Tech Coll (OH)
Northeast Mississippi Comm Coll (MS)
Northern Virginia Comm Coll (VA)
Northwestern Michigan Coll (MI)
Norwalk Comm-Tech Coll (CT)
Oakland Comm Coll (MI)
Oklahoma State U, Okmulgee (OK)
Onondaga Comm Coll (NY)
Orange Coast Coll (CA)
Palm Beach Comm Coll (FL)
Palomar Coll (CA)
Parkland Coll (IL)
Pennsylvania Coll of Tech (PA)
Penn Valley Comm Coll (MO)
Pierce Coll (WA)
Pikes Peak Comm Coll (CO)
Pima Comm Coll (AZ)
Pueblo Comm Coll (CO)
Quincy Coll (MA)
Rancho Santiago Coll (CA)
Ricks Coll (ID)
Rockland Comm Coll (NY)
Saddleback Coll (CA)
St Louis Comm Coll at Florissant Valley (MO)
St Philip's Coll (TX)
San Diego City Coll (CA)
San Diego Mesa Coll (CA)
San Jacinto College–Central Cmps (TX)
San Joaquin Delta Coll (CA)
Santa Barbara City Coll (CA)
Schoolcraft Coll (MI)
Scottsdale Comm Coll (AZ)
Seminole Comm Coll (FL)
Sinclair Comm Coll (OH)
Skagit Valley Coll (WA)
Southeast Comm Coll, Lincoln Cmps (NE)
Southern Maine Tech Coll (ME)
South Plains Coll (TX)
South Puget Sound Comm Coll (WA)
South Seattle Comm Coll (WA)
Southwestern Comm Coll (NC)
State Fair Comm Coll (MO)
State U of NY Coll of A&T at Cobleskill (NY)
State U of NY Coll of A&T at Morrisville (NY)
State U of NY Coll of Tech at Delhi (NY)
Suffolk County Comm Coll–Eastern Cmps (NY)
Three Rivers Comm-Tech Coll (CT)
Tulsa Jr Coll (OK)
U of Hawaii–Kapiolani Comm Coll (HI)
Vermilion Comm Coll (MN)
Vincennes U (IN)
Wallace State Comm Coll (AL)
Washtenaw Comm Coll (MI)
Westchester Comm Coll (NY)
Western Wisconsin Tech Coll (WI)
Westmoreland County Comm Coll (PA)
West Shore Comm Coll (MI)
Wilkes Comm Coll (NC)
William Rainey Harper Coll (IL)
Wisconsin Indianhead Tech Coll, Ashland Cmps (WI)
Yakima Valley Comm Coll (WA)
Yuba Coll (CA)

FOOD SERVICES TECHNOLOGY

Adirondack Comm Coll (NY)
Alamance Comm Coll (NC)
Anne Arundel Comm Coll (MD)
Anson Comm Coll (NC)
Arapahoe Comm Coll (CO)
Blackhawk Tech Coll (WI)
Burlington County Coll (NJ)
Butler County Comm Coll (PA)
Cabrillo Coll (CA)
Central Comm College–Hastings Cmps (NE)
Central Piedmont Comm Coll (NC)
Central Texas Coll (TX)
Cerritos Coll (CA)
Chattanooga State Tech Comm Coll (TN)
Chippewa Valley Tech Coll (WI)
Clark Coll (WA)
Coll of DuPage (IL)
Columbia Coll (CA)
Columbus State Comm Coll (OH)
Comm Coll of Allegheny County Allegheny Cmps (PA)
Comm Coll of Allegheny County Boyce Cmps (PA)
Comm Coll of Southern Nevada (NV)
Comm Coll of the Air Force (AL)
Cosumnes River Coll (CA)
Delaware Tech & Comm Coll, Stanton/Wilmington Cmps (DE)
Edmonds Comm Coll (WA)
El Centro Coll (TX)
Elgin Comm Coll (IL)
Fresno City Coll (CA)
Grand Rapids Comm Coll (MI)
Henry Ford Comm Coll (MI)
Hiwassee Coll (TN)
Illinois Eastern Comm Colls, Lincoln Trail Coll (IL)
Indian Hills Comm Coll (IA)
Iowa Western Comm Coll (IA)
Kirkwood Comm Coll (IA)
Lake Michigan Coll (MI)

Associate Degree Programs at Two-Year Colleges
Food Services Technology–Geology

Lane Comm Coll (OR)
Lenoir Comm Coll (NC)
Los Angeles City Coll (CA)
Luzerne County Comm Coll (PA)
Miami-Dade Comm Coll (FL)
Milwaukee Area Tech Coll (WI)
Mission Coll (CA)
Modesto Jr Coll (CA)
Mohawk Valley Comm Coll (NY)
Monroe Comm Coll (NY)
Montcalm Comm Coll (MI)
North Dakota State Coll of Science (ND)
Northeast Texas Comm Coll (TX)
North Seattle Comm Coll (WA)
Northwestern Michigan Coll (MI)
Oakland Comm Coll (MI)
Oklahoma State U, Okmulgee (OK)
Olympic Coll (WA)
Orange Coast Coll (CA)
Owens Comm Coll, Findlay (OH)
Owens Comm Coll, Toledo (OH)
Palomar Coll (CA)
Pennsylvania Coll of Tech (PA)
Richland Comm Coll (IL)
Saddleback Coll (CA)
St Louis Comm Coll at Florissant Valley (MO)
San Joaquin Delta Coll (CA)
Shawnee Comm Coll (IL)
Sierra Coll (CA)
Skagit Valley Coll (WA)
Southern Maine Tech Coll (ME)
South Puget Sound Comm Coll (WA)
South Seattle Comm Coll (WA)
Southwest Wisconsin Tech Coll (WI)
Spokane Comm Coll (WA)
Stark Tech Coll (OH)
State U of NY Coll of A&T at Cobleskill (NY)
State U of NY Coll of A&T at Morrisville (NY)
Sullivan County Comm Coll (NY)
Tarrant County Jr Coll (TX)
Texas State Tech Coll–Harlingen Cmps (TX)
Texas State Tech Coll–Waco/Marshall Cmps (TX)
Trenholm State Tech Coll (AL)
Truckee Meadows Comm Coll (NV)
U of Hawaii–Hawaii Comm Coll (HI)
U of Hawaii–Honolulu Comm Coll (HI)
U of Hawaii–Leeward Comm Coll (HI)
U of Hawaii–Maui Comm Coll (HI)
Ventura Coll (CA)
Victor Valley Coll (CA)
Washtenaw Comm Coll (MI)
Westchester Comm Coll (NY)
Wisconsin Indianhead Tech Coll, Ashland Cmps (WI)

FORENSIC SCIENCES
Clark State Comm Coll (OH)
New River Comm Coll (VA)
Tunxis Comm Tech Coll (CT)

FORESTRY
Abraham Baldwin Ag Coll (GA)
Adirondack Comm Coll (NY)
Alabama Southern Comm Coll, Thomasville (AL)
Allegany Comm Coll (MD)
Andrew Coll (GA)
Atlanta Metropolitan Coll (GA)
Bainbridge Coll (GA)
Bakersfield Coll (CA)
Barton County Comm Coll (KS)
Bevill State Comm Coll (AL)
Brevard Coll (NC)
Brunswick Coll (GA)
Camden County Coll (NJ)
Casper Coll (WY)
Cerritos Coll (CA)
Chattahoochee Valley State Comm Coll (AL)
Chattanooga State Tech Comm Coll (TN)
Chemeketa Comm Coll (OR)
City Coll of San Francisco (CA)
Colby Comm Coll (KS)
Coll of Southern Idaho (ID)
Coll of the Redwoods (CA)
Coll of the Siskiyous (CA)
Colorado Northwestern Comm Coll (CO)
Copiah-Lincoln Comm College–Natchez Cmps (MS)
Dalton Coll (GA)
Darton Coll (GA)
Daytona Beach Comm Coll (FL)
Delta Coll (MI)
Dixie Coll (UT)
Dodge City Comm Coll (KS)
East Central Coll (MO)
Eastern Arizona Coll (AZ)
Eastern Oklahoma State Coll (OK)
East Mississippi Comm Coll (MS)
Erie Comm Coll, City Cmps (NY)
Erie Comm Coll, South Cmps (NY)
Fullerton Coll (CA)
Gainesville Coll (GA)
Glendale Comm Coll (AZ)
Grand Rapids Comm Coll (MI)
Gulf Coast Comm Coll (FL)
Highland Comm Coll (KS)
Hiwassee Coll (TN)
Hocking Coll (OH)
Holmes Comm Coll (MS)
Hutchinson Comm Coll and Area Vocational Sch (KS)
Itasca Comm Coll (MN)
Jefferson Coll (MO)
Joliet Jr Coll (IL)
Keystone Coll (PA)
Kirkwood Comm Coll (IA)
Lake City Comm Coll (FL)
Lake Land Coll (IL)
Miami-Dade Comm Coll (FL)
Middle Georgia Coll (GA)
Modesto Jr Coll (CA)
Monroe Comm Coll (NY)
Mountain Empire Comm Coll (VA)
New Hampshire Tech Coll, Berlin (NH)
North Country Comm Coll (NY)
North Dakota State University–Bottineau (ND)
Northeastern Jr Coll (CO)
Northeastern Oklahoma A&M Coll (OK)
Northeast Mississippi Comm Coll (MS)
North Idaho Coll (ID)
Northwest Coll (WY)
Northwest Mississippi Comm Coll (MS)
Northwest-Shoals Comm Coll (AL)
Palo Verde Coll (CA)
Paul Smith's Coll (NY)
Pensacola Jr Coll (FL)
Potomac State Coll of West Virginia U (WV)
Rancho Santiago Coll (CA)
Ricks Coll (ID)
Rockland Comm Coll (NY)
Salish Kootenai Coll (MT)
Sierra Coll (CA)
Snow Coll (UT)
Spokane Comm Coll (WA)
State U of NY Coll of A&T at Morrisville (NY)
State U of NY Coll of Tech at Delhi (NY)
Sterling Coll (VT)
Sullivan County Comm Coll (NY)
Tacoma Comm Coll (WA)
Treasure Valley Comm Coll (OR)
Trinidad State Jr Coll (CO)
Tulsa Jr Coll (OK)
Umpqua Comm Coll (OR)
U of Kentucky, Jefferson Comm Coll (KY)
Vermilion Comm Coll (MN)
Vincennes U (IN)
Waycross Coll (GA)
Western Nebraska Comm Coll, Scottsbluff (NE)

FOREST TECHNOLOGY
Abraham Baldwin Ag Coll (GA)
Adirondack Comm Coll (NY)
Alabama Southern Comm Coll, Monroeville (AL)
Allegany Comm Coll (MD)
American River Coll (CA)
Brevard Coll (NC)
Centralia Coll (WA)
Central Oregon Comm Coll (OR)
Chattanooga State Tech Comm Coll (TN)
Chemeketa Comm Coll (OR)
Columbia Coll (CA)
Dabney S Lancaster Comm Coll (VA)
Eastern Oklahoma State Coll (OK)
East Mississippi Comm Coll (MS)
El Camino Coll (CA)
Erie Comm Coll, City Cmps (NY)
Erie Comm Coll, North Cmps (NY)
Feather River Comm Coll District (CA)
Flathead Valley Comm Coll (MT)
Fox Valley Tech Coll (WI)
Fulton-Montgomery Comm Coll (NY)
Green River Comm Coll (WA)
Hartnell Coll (CA)
Haywood Comm Coll (NC)
Hiwassee Coll (TN)
Hocking Coll (OH)
Horry-Georgetown Tech Coll (SC)
Itasca Comm Coll (MN)
Itawamba Comm Coll (MS)
Jefferson Comm Coll (NY)
Jones County Jr Coll (MS)
Kings River Comm Coll (CA)
Lake City Comm Coll (FL)
Lurleen B Wallace State Jr Coll (AL)
Modesto Jr Coll (CA)
Montgomery Comm Coll (NC)
Mt Hood Comm Coll (OR)
Mt San Antonio Coll (CA)
North Country Comm Coll (NY)
North Dakota State University–Bottineau (ND)
Northeast Mississippi Comm Coll (MS)
Orangeburg-Calhoun Tech Coll (SC)
Pasadena City Coll (CA)
Paul Smith's Coll (NY)
Pennsylvania Coll of Tech (PA)
Penn State U Mont Alto Cmps (PA)
Pensacola Jr Coll (FL)
Potomac State Coll of West Virginia U (WV)
Reid State Tech Coll (AL)
Salish Kootenai Coll (MT)
Santa Rosa Jr Coll (CA)
Sierra Coll (CA)
Southeastern Comm Coll (NC)
Southeastern Illinois Coll (IL)
Southwestern Oregon Comm Coll (OR)
State U of NY Coll of A&T at Cobleskill (NY)
State U of NY Coll of A&T at Morrisville (NY)
State U of NY Coll of Environ Sci & For Ranger Sch (NY)
State U of NY Coll of Tech at Canton (NY)
State U of NY Coll of Tech at Delhi (NY)
Sullivan County Comm Coll (NY)
Treasure Valley Comm Coll (OR)
U of Alaska Anchorage, Kenai Peninsula Coll (AK)
U of Kentucky, Hazard Comm Coll (KY)
Vermilion Comm Coll (MN)
Waycross Coll (GA)
Wayne Comm Coll (NC)

FRENCH
Austin Comm Coll (TX)
Bee County Coll (TX)
Black Hawk Coll, Moline (IL)
Brazosport Coll (TX)
Brevard Coll (NC)
Brevard Comm Coll (FL)
Cañada Coll (CA)
Casper Coll (WY)
Centralia Coll (WA)
Cerritos Coll (CA)
Chaffey Coll (CA)
Cisco Jr Coll (TX)
City Colls of Chicago, Harold Washington Coll (IL)
Clark Coll (WA)
Coll of Marin (CA)
Coll of San Mateo (CA)
Coll of the Canyons (CA)
Coll of the Desert (CA)
Coll of the Sequoias (CA)
Collin County Comm Coll (TX)
Comm Coll of Allegheny County Allegheny Cmps (PA)
Contra Costa Coll (CA)
Copiah-Lincoln Comm Coll (MS)
Crafton Hills Coll (CA)
Dixie Coll (UT)
East Central Coll (MO)
Eastern Arizona Coll (AZ)
East Los Angeles Coll (CA)
Foothill Coll (CA)
Glendale Comm Coll (AZ)
Grossmont Coll (CA)
Imperial Valley Coll (CA)
Independence Comm Coll (KS)
John Wood Comm Coll (IL)
Kansas City Kansas Comm Coll (KS)
Kirkwood Comm Coll (IA)
Lansing Comm Coll (MI)
Lee Coll (TX)
Long Beach City Coll (CA)
Lon Morris Coll (TX)
Los Angeles City Coll (CA)
Los Angeles Mission Coll (CA)
Los Angeles Valley Coll (CA)
Mendocino Coll (CA)
Merritt Coll (CA)
Miami-Dade Comm Coll (FL)
Middlesex County Coll (NJ)
Midland Coll (TX)
MiraCosta Coll (CA)
Modesto Jr Coll (CA)
Monterey Peninsula Coll (CA)
New Mexico Military Inst (NM)
Northeast Comm Coll (NE)
North Idaho Coll (ID)
Pasadena City Coll (CA)
Polk Comm Coll (FL)
Red Rocks Comm Coll (CO)
Ricks Coll (ID)
San Bernardino Valley Coll (CA)
San Diego Mesa Coll (CA)
San Joaquin Delta Coll (CA)
Santa Barbara City Coll (CA)
Santa Monica Coll (CA)
Santa Rosa Jr Coll (CA)
Sauk Valley Comm Coll (IL)
Skyline Coll (CA)
Snow Coll (UT)
Solano Comm Coll (CA)
South Georgia Coll (GA)
Southwestern Coll (CA)
Triton Coll (IL)
Tulsa Jr Coll (OK)
U of Kentucky, Jefferson Comm Coll (KY)
Vincennes U (IN)
Western Nebraska Comm Coll, Scottsbluff (NE)
Western Wyoming Comm Coll (WY)
West Los Angeles Coll (CA)
West Valley Coll (CA)
Young Harris Coll (GA)

FUNERAL SERVICE
American Acad McAllister Inst of Funeral Service (NY)
Bishop State Comm Coll (AL)
Briarwood Coll (CT)
Catonsville Comm Coll (MD)
City Colls of Chicago, Malcolm X Coll (IL)
Commonwealth Inst of Funeral Service (TX)
Cypress Coll (CA)
Dallas Inst of Funeral Service (TX)
Delgado Comm Coll (LA)
Delta Coll (MI)
East Mississippi Comm Coll (MS)
Fayetteville Tech Comm Coll (NC)
Fiorello H LaGuardia Comm Coll of City U of NY (NY)
Florence-Darlington Tech Coll (SC)
Forsyth Tech Comm Coll (NC)
Gupton-Jones Coll of Funeral Service (GA)
Herkimer County Comm Coll (NY)
Highland Comm Coll (KS)
Hudson Valley Comm Coll (NY)
Hutchinson Comm Coll and Area Vocational Sch (KS)
Jefferson State Comm Coll (AL)
John A Gupton Coll (TN)
John Tyler Comm Coll (VA)
Kansas City Kansas Comm Coll (KS)
Mercer County Comm Coll (NJ)
Miami-Dade Comm Coll (FL)
Mid-America Coll of Funeral Service (IN)
Milwaukee Area Tech Coll (WI)
Monroe County Comm Coll (MI)
Mt Hood Comm Coll (OR)
Mount Ida Coll (MA)
Nassau Comm Coll (NY)
Northampton County Area Comm Coll (PA)
Northwest Mississippi Comm Coll (MS)
Pittsburgh Inst of Mortuary Science, Inc (PA)
Red River Tech Coll (AR)
St Louis Comm Coll at Forest Park (MO)
San Antonio Coll (TX)
San Francisco Coll of Mortuary Science (CA)
Simmons Inst of Funeral Service (NY)
State U of NY Coll of Tech at Canton (NY)
Vincennes U (IN)

GEOGRAPHY
Alexandria Tech Coll (MN)
Allen County Comm Coll (KS)
Atlanta Metropolitan Coll (GA)
Bakersfield Coll (CA)
Brunswick Coll (GA)
Cañada Coll (CA)
Cerritos Coll (CA)
Chemeketa Comm Coll (OR)
Clackamas Comm Coll (OR)
Clark Coll (WA)
Coll of Alameda (CA)
Coll of Southern Idaho (ID)
Coll of the Canyons (CA)
Coll of the Desert (CA)
Collin County Comm Coll (TX)
Columbia State Comm Coll (TN)
Contra Costa Coll (CA)
Cypress Coll (CA)
Darton Coll (GA)
Del Mar Coll (TX)
Dixie Coll (UT)
East Central Coll (MO)
East Los Angeles Coll (CA)
El Camino Coll (CA)
Essex Comm Coll (MD)
Everett Comm Coll (WA)
Foothill Coll (CA)
Fresno City Coll (CA)
Grossmont Coll (CA)
Hill Coll of the Hill Jr Coll District (TX)
Jackson State Comm Coll (TN)
Jefferson Coll (MO)
Joliet Jr Coll (IL)
Lake Land Coll (IL)
Lake Michigan Coll (MI)
Lansing Comm Coll (MI)
Lincoln Land Comm Coll (IL)
Little Hoop Comm Coll (ND)
Los Angeles Mission Coll (CA)
Los Angeles Valley Coll (CA)
Miami University–Middletown Cmps (OH)
Mississippi Delta Comm Coll (MS)
Modesto Jr Coll (CA)
Montgomery College–Rockville Cmps (MD)
Motlow State Comm Coll (TN)
Parks Jr Coll (CO)
Pasadena City Coll (CA)
Polk Comm Coll (FL)
Rancho Santiago Coll (CA)
Ricks Coll (ID)
Saddleback Coll (CA)
Salt Lake Comm Coll (UT)
San Bernardino Valley Coll (CA)
San Diego Miramar Coll (CA)
Santa Barbara City Coll (CA)
Santa Monica Coll (CA)
Santa Rosa Jr Coll (CA)
Skagit Valley Coll (WA)
Snow Coll (UT)
Southwestern Coll (CA)
Triton Coll (IL)
Tulsa Jr Coll (OK)
U of Kentucky, Jefferson Comm Coll (KY)
Vermilion Comm Coll (MN)
Vincennes U (IN)
Western Nebraska Comm Coll, Scottsbluff (NE)
West Hills Comm Coll (CA)
West Los Angeles Coll (CA)
Wright State U, Lake Cmps (OH)

GEOLOGY
Arizona Western Coll (AZ)
Atlanta Metropolitan Coll (GA)
Austin Comm Coll (TX)
Bakersfield Coll (CA)
Barton County Comm Coll (KS)
Bee County Coll (TX)
Brevard Coll (NC)
Brunswick Coll (GA)
Cañada Coll (CA)
Casper Coll (WY)
Centralia Coll (WA)
Central Texas Coll (TX)
Cerritos Coll (CA)
Chaffey Coll (CA)
Chemeketa Comm Coll (OR)
City Coll of San Francisco (CA)
Clackamas Comm Coll (OR)
Clark Coll (WA)
Coll of Marin (CA)
Coll of San Mateo (CA)
Coll of the Canyons (CA)
Coll of the Desert (CA)
Collin County Comm Coll (TX)
Colorado Mountn Coll, Alpine Cmps (CO)
Contra Costa Coll (CA)
Cosumnes River Coll (CA)
Crafton Hills Coll (CA)
Cuesta Coll (CA)
Cypress Coll (CA)
Dalton Coll (GA)
Daytona Beach Comm Coll (FL)
Del Mar Coll (TX)
Delta Coll (MI)
Dixie Coll (UT)
East Central Coll (MO)
Eastern Arizona Coll (AZ)
East Georgia Coll (GA)
East Los Angeles Coll (CA)
El Camino Coll (CA)
El Paso Comm Coll (TX)
Everett Comm Coll (WA)
Foothill Coll (CA)
Fullerton Coll (CA)
Gainesville Coll (GA)

Peterson's Guide to Two-Year Colleges 1997

89

Associate Degree Programs at Two-Year Colleges
Geology–Health Science

Glendale Comm Coll (AZ)
Grand Rapids Comm Coll (MI)
Grays Harbor Coll (WA)
Grayson County Coll (TX)
Great Basin Coll (NV)
Grossmont Coll (CA)
Gulf Coast Comm Coll (FL)
Highland Comm Coll (IL)
Highland Comm Coll (KS)
Hill Coll of the Hill Jr Coll District (TX)
Howard Coll (TX)
Hutchinson Comm Coll and Area Vocational Sch (KS)
Iowa Lakes Comm Coll (IA)
Lansing Comm Coll (MI)
Lincoln Land Comm Coll (IL)
Los Angeles Valley Coll (CA)
Miami-Dade Comm Coll (FL)
Miami University–Middletown Cmps (OH)
Middle Georgia Coll (GA)
Midland Coll (TX)
Modesto Jr Coll (CA)
Monterey Peninsula Coll (CA)
Moorpark Coll (CA)
North Idaho Coll (ID)
Odessa Coll (TX)
Palo Alto Coll (TX)
Palomar Coll (CA)
Pasadena City Coll (CA)
Pikes Peak Comm Coll (CO)
Pima Comm Coll (AZ)
Polk Comm Coll (FL)
Potomac State Coll of West Virginia U (WV)
Rancho Santiago Coll (CA)
Red Rocks Comm Coll (CO)
Ricks Coll (ID)
Saddleback Coll (CA)
San Bernardino Valley Coll (CA)
San Jacinto College–Central Cmps (TX)
San Joaquin Delta Coll (CA)
San Juan Coll (NM)
Santa Barbara City Coll (CA)
Santa Monica Coll (CA)
Santa Rosa Jr Coll (CA)
Sierra Coll (CA)
Snow Coll (UT)
Southwestern Coll (CA)
Tacoma Comm Coll (WA)
Tomball Coll (TX)
Triton Coll (IL)
Tulsa Jr Coll (OK)
Vincennes U (IN)
Western Wyoming Comm Coll (WY)
West Hills Comm Coll (CA)
West Los Angeles Coll (CA)
Young Harris Coll (GA)

GERMAN
Austin Comm Coll (TX)
Bakersfield Coll (CA)
Bee County Coll (TX)
Black Hawk Coll, Moline (IL)
Brevard Coll (NC)
Brevard Comm Coll (FL)
Cañada Coll (CA)
Casper Coll (WY)
Cerritos Coll (CA)
Chaffey Coll (CA)
City Colls of Chicago, Harold Washington Coll (IL)
Clark Coll (WA)
Coll of DuPage (IL)
Coll of Marin (CA)
Coll of San Mateo (CA)
Coll of the Canyons (CA)
Collin County Comm Coll (TX)
Comm Coll of Allegheny County Allegheny Cmps (PA)
Contra Costa Coll (CA)
Dixie Coll (UT)
East Central Coll (MO)
El Camino Coll (CA)
Everett Comm Coll (WA)
Foothill Coll (CA)
Glendale Comm Coll (AZ)
Grossmont Coll (CA)
John Wood Comm Coll (IL)
Kansas City Kansas Comm Coll (KS)
Lansing Comm Coll (MI)
Lee Coll (TX)
Long Beach City Coll (CA)
Los Angeles City Coll (CA)
Miami-Dade Comm Coll (FL)
Midland Coll (TX)
Modesto Jr Coll (CA)
Monterey Peninsula Coll (CA)
New Mexico Military Inst (NM)
North Idaho Coll (ID)
Pasadena City Coll (CA)
Polk Comm Coll (FL)
Red Rocks Comm Coll (CO)
Ricks Coll (ID)
San Bernardino Valley Coll (CA)
San Diego Mesa Coll (CA)
San Jacinto College–Central Cmps (TX)
San Joaquin Delta Coll (CA)
Santa Barbara City Coll (CA)
Santa Monica Coll (CA)
Santa Rosa Jr Coll (CA)
Solano Comm Coll (CA)
Triton Coll (IL)
Tulsa Jr Coll (OK)
Vincennes U (IN)
Waldorf Coll (IA)
Western Nebraska Comm Coll, Scottsbluff (NE)
Western Wyoming Comm Coll (WY)
West Valley Coll (CA)

GERONTOLOGY
American River Coll (CA)
Baltimore City Comm Coll (MD)
Camden County Coll (NJ)
Chaffey Coll (CA)
Charles Stewart Mott Comm Coll (MI)
Chemeketa Comm Coll (OR)
Columbus State Comm Coll (OH)
Comm Coll of Allegheny County North Cmps (PA)
Comm Coll of Philadelphia (PA)
Comm Coll of Rhode Island (RI)
Connors State Coll (OK)
Cosumnes River Coll (CA)
Edmonds Comm Coll (WA)
El Camino Coll (CA)
Elgin Comm Coll (IL)
Eugenio María de Hostos Comm Coll of City U of NY (NY)
Fiorello H LaGuardia Comm Coll of City U of NY (NY)
Gateway Comm-Tech Coll (CT)
Genesee Comm Coll (NY)
Grand Rapids Comm Coll (MI)
Hudson County Comm Coll (NJ)
Ivy Tech State Coll–Central Indiana (IN)
Ivy Tech State Coll–Eastcentral (IN)
Kalamazoo Valley Comm Coll (MI)
Kellogg Comm Coll (MI)
Lansing Comm Coll (MI)
Macomb Comm Coll (MI)
Manchester Comm-Tech Coll (CT)
Mitchell Coll (CT)
Montgomery College–Rockville Cmps (MD)
Montgomery County Comm Coll (PA)
Naugatuck Valley Community–Tech Coll (CT)
Nebraska Indian Comm Coll (NE)
New Hampshire Tech Coll, Manchester (NH)
New York City Tech Coll of the City U of NY (NY)
Northern Virginia Comm Coll (VA)
North Shore Comm Coll (MA)
Oakland Comm Coll (MI)
Ocean County Coll (NJ)
Oklahoma City Comm Coll (OK)
Palomar Coll (CA)
Pikes Peak Comm Coll (CO)
Rancho Santiago Coll (CA)
Reading Area Comm Coll (PA)
Saddleback Coll (CA)
Sinclair Comm Coll (OH)
Southwestern Oregon Comm Coll (OR)
Spokane Falls Comm Coll (WA)
Union County Coll (NJ)
Wayne Comm Coll (NC)
Willmar Comm Coll (MN)

GRAPHIC ARTS
Aims Comm Coll (CO)
Allan Hancock Coll (CA)
Alpena Comm Coll (MI)
American Acad of Art (IL)
Antonelli Inst (PA)
Arapahoe Comm Coll (CO)
Art Inst of Fort Lauderdale (FL)
Art Inst of Pittsburgh (PA)
Art Inst of Seattle (WA)
Bradford Sch (OH)
Bradley Acad for the Visual Arts (PA)
Brevard Coll (NC)
Bucks County Comm Coll (PA)
Bunker Hill Comm Coll (MA)
Burlington County Coll (NJ)
Butler County Comm Coll (PA)
Catonsville Comm Coll (MD)
Central Maine Tech Coll (ME)
Central Piedmont Comm Coll (NC)
Chabot Coll (CA)
Chattanooga State Tech Comm Coll (TN)
Chemeketa Comm Coll (OR)
Clark Coll (WA)
Clovis Comm Coll (NM)
Coahoma Comm Coll (MS)
Coll of DuPage (IL)
Coll of San Mateo (CA)
Coll of the Redwoods (CA)
Coll of the Sequoias (CA)
Colorado Mountn Coll, Roaring Fork Cmps-Spring Valley Ctr (CO)
Columbus State Comm Coll (OH)
Comm Coll of Allegheny County Allegheny Cmps (PA)
Comm Coll of Allegheny County South Cmps (PA)
Comm Coll of Aurora (CO)
Comm Coll of Denver (CO)
Comm Coll of Southern Nevada (NV)
County Coll of Morris (NJ)
Cuyahoga Comm Coll, Western Cmps (OH)
Davis Coll (OH)
Daytona Beach Comm Coll (FL)
Delaware County Comm Coll (PA)
Dixie Coll (UT)
Don Bosco Tech Inst (CA)
Eastfield Coll (TX)
Elgin Comm Coll (IL)
Erie Comm Coll, South Cmps (NY)
Everett Comm Coll (WA)
Florida Comm Coll at Jacksonville (FL)
Foothill Coll (CA)
Forsyth Tech Comm Coll (NC)
Fort Scott Comm Coll (KS)
Fox Valley Tech Coll (WI)
Fresno City Coll (CA)
Front Range Comm Coll (CO)
Fulton-Montgomery Comm Coll (NY)
Garden City Comm Coll (KS)
Garland County Comm Coll (AR)
George C Wallace State Comm Coll, Dothan (AL)
Glendale Comm Coll (AZ)
Golden West Coll (CA)
Greenfield Comm Coll (MA)
Harrisburg Area Comm Coll (PA)
Hartnell Coll (CA)
Hawkeye Comm Coll (IA)
Henry Ford Comm Coll (MI)
Highland Comm Coll (IL)
Housatonic Comm-Tech Coll (CT)
Houston Comm Coll System (TX)
Hutchinson Comm Coll and Area Vocational Sch (KS)
Illinois Central Coll (IL)
International Business Coll (IN)
Inver Hills Comm Coll (MN)
Iowa Western Comm Coll (IA)
Isothermal Comm Coll (NC)
Ivy Tech State Coll–Wabash Valley (IN)
J F Drake State Tech Coll (AL)
John C Calhoun State Comm Coll (AL)
Kellogg Comm Coll (MI)
Lakeland Comm Coll (OH)
Lake-Sumter Comm Coll (FL)
Lane Comm Coll (OR)
Lassen Coll (CA)
Lee Coll (TX)
Lenoir Comm Coll (NC)
Lincoln Land Comm Coll (IL)
Linn-Benton Comm Coll (OR)
Macomb Comm Coll (MI)
Maryland Coll of Art and Design (MD)
Mercer County Comm Coll (NJ)
Metropolitan Comm Coll (NE)
Miami-Dade Comm Coll (FL)
Middlesex County Coll (NJ)
Midland Coll (TX)
Midlands Tech Coll (SC)
Mid Michigan Comm Coll (MI)
Miles Comm Coll (MT)
Mission Coll (CA)
Mitchell Coll (CT)
Mohawk Valley Comm Coll (NY)
Monroe Comm Coll (NY)
Monterey Peninsula Coll (CA)
Montgomery County Comm Coll (PA)
Moorpark Coll (CA)
Moraine Park Tech Coll (WI)
Mt Hood Comm Coll (OR)
Mount Ida Coll (MA)
Mt San Antonio Coll (CA)
Muskegon Comm Coll (MI)
Nashville State Tech Inst (TN)
Newbury Coll (MA)
New Hampshire Tech Coll, Laconia (NH)
New Mexico Jr Coll (NM)
New York City Tech Coll of the City U of NY (NY)
North Dakota State Coll of Science (ND)
Northern Oklahoma Coll (OK)
North Hennepin Comm Coll (MN)
Northwest Coll (WY)
Northwestern Connecticut Comm-Tech Coll (CT)
Norwalk Comm-Tech Coll (CT)
Oakland Comm Coll (MI)
Ohlone Coll (CA)
Okaloosa-Walton Comm Coll (FL)
Oklahoma City Comm Coll (OK)
Onondaga Comm Coll (NY)
Palomar Coll (CA)
Parkland Coll (IL)
Pennsylvania Coll of Tech (PA)
Pensacola Jr Coll (FL)
Petit Jean Tech Coll (AR)
Piedmont Tech Coll (SC)
Pikes Peak Comm Coll (CO)
Pima Comm Coll (AZ)
Pittsburgh Tech Inst (PA)
Porterville Coll (CA)
Portland Comm Coll (OR)
Pratt Comm Coll and Area Voc Sch (KS)
Raritan Valley Comm Coll (NJ)
Riverside Comm Coll (CA)
Rockland Comm Coll (NY)
Rogers State Coll (OK)
Sage Jr Coll of Albany (NY)
St Johns River Comm Coll (FL)
St Louis Comm Coll at Meramec (MO)
St Petersburg Jr Coll (FL)
Salt Lake Comm Coll (UT)
San Diego City Coll (CA)
San Joaquin Delta Coll (CA)
Santa Barbara City Coll (CA)
Santa Fe Comm Coll (FL)
Santa Monica Coll (CA)
Santa Rosa Jr Coll (CA)
Seattle Central Comm Coll (WA)
Shasta Coll (CA)
Shoreline Comm Coll (WA)
Sinclair Comm Coll (OH)
Skagit Valley Coll (WA)
Southeast Tech Inst (SD)
Southern Arkansas U Tech (AR)
South Suburban Coll (IL)
Southwestern Coll (CA)
Southwestern Indian Polytechnic Inst (NM)
Southwestern Michigan Coll (MI)
Spokane Falls Comm Coll (WA)
Springfield Tech Comm Coll (MA)
Suffolk County Comm Coll–Eastern Cmps (NY)
Sullivan County Comm Coll (NY)
Sussex County Comm Coll (NJ)
Terra State Comm Coll (OH)
Texas State Tech Coll–Waco/Marshall Cmps (TX)
Thomas Nelson Comm Coll (VA)
Tidewater Comm Coll (VA)
Tompkins Cortland Comm Coll (NY)
Triton Coll (IL)
Truckee Meadows Comm Coll (NV)
Tunxis Comm Tech Coll (CT)
Tyler Jr Coll (TX)
Ulster County Comm Coll (NY)
Union County Coll (NJ)
U of Hawaii–Honolulu Comm Coll (HI)
U of Hawaii–Leeward Comm Coll (HI)
U of Maine at Augusta (ME)
Utah Valley State Coll (UT)
Valencia Comm Coll (FL)
Vernon Regional Jr Coll (TX)
Villa Maria Coll of Buffalo (NY)
Vincennes U (IN)
Washtenaw Comm Coll (MI)
Watkins Inst of Interior Design (TN)
Western Oklahoma State Coll (OK)
Western Wisconsin Tech Coll (WI)
Westmoreland County Comm Coll (PA)

GUIDANCE AND COUNSELING
Brevard Coll (NC)
Central Coll (KS)
Dundalk Comm Coll (MD)
East Los Angeles Coll (CA)
Pratt Comm Coll and Area Voc Sch (KS)
Western Nebraska Comm Coll, Scottsbluff (NE)

HEALTH EDUCATION
Andrew Coll (GA)
Angelina Coll (TX)
Anne Arundel Comm Coll (MD)
Atlanta Metropolitan Coll (GA)
Bainbridge Coll (GA)
Bee County Coll (TX)
Bismarck State Coll (ND)
Blinn Coll (TX)
Brevard Coll (NC)
Bucks County Comm Coll (PA)
Butler County Comm Coll (KS)
Cañada Coll (CA)
Central Coll (KS)
Central Texas Coll (TX)
Chabot Coll (CA)
Chemeketa Comm Coll (OR)
Chesapeake Coll (MD)
Coahoma Comm Coll (MS)
Coll of the Sequoias (CA)
Columbia Coll (CA)
Columbia State Comm Coll (TN)
Comm Coll of Allegheny County Allegheny Cmps (PA)
Copiah-Lincoln Comm Coll (MS)
Dalton Coll (GA)
Darton Coll (GA)
Daytona Beach Comm Coll (FL)
Del Mar Coll (TX)
Donnelly Coll (KS)
East Central Comm Coll (MS)
East Georgia Coll (GA)
East Mississippi Comm Coll (MS)
El Paso Comm Coll (TX)
Florida National Coll (FL)
Fulton-Montgomery Comm Coll (NY)
Gulf Coast Comm Coll (FL)
Harford Comm Coll (MD)
Hartnell Coll (CA)
Hesser Coll (NH)
Highland Comm Coll (KS)
Hill Coll of the Hill Jr Coll District (TX)
Howard Comm Coll (MD)
Lake Land Coll (IL)
Little Hoop Comm Coll (ND)
Los Angeles Mission Coll (CA)
Middle Georgia Coll (GA)
Mississippi Delta Comm Coll (MS)
Modesto Jr Coll (CA)
Motlow State Comm Coll (TN)
Nassau Comm Coll (NY)
Northeast Mississippi Comm Coll (MS)
Northwest Coll (WY)
Palm Beach Comm Coll (FL)
Polk Comm Coll (FL)
Pratt Comm Coll and Area Voc Sch (KS)
Prince George's Comm Coll (MD)
St Catharine Coll (KY)
St Philip's Coll (TX)
Salem Comm Coll (NJ)
Sanford-Brown Coll, Hazelwood (MO)
San Joaquin Delta Coll (CA)
Santa Rosa Jr Coll (CA)
South Georgia Coll (GA)
SouthWest Collegiate Inst for the Deaf (TX)
State Comm Coll of East St Louis (IL)
Umpqua Comm Coll (OR)
U of New Mexico–Gallup Branch (NM)
Vermilion Comm Coll (MN)
Volunteer State Comm Coll (TN)
Waldorf Coll (IA)
Waycross Coll (GA)
Westmoreland County Comm Coll (PA)
William Rainey Harper Coll (IL)
Young Harris Coll (GA)
Yuba Coll (CA)

HEALTH SCIENCE
Arizona Western Coll (AZ)
Barton County Comm Coll (KS)
Bay Mills Comm Coll (MI)
Borough of Manhattan Comm Coll of City U of NY (NY)
Brevard Coll (NC)
Bucks County Comm Coll (PA)
Butte Coll (CA)
Cabrillo Coll (CA)
Cañada Coll (CA)
City Colls of Chicago, Kennedy-King Coll (IL)
City Colls of Chicago, Malcolm X Coll (IL)
Coll of the Canyons (CA)
Collin County Comm Coll (TX)
Comm Coll of the Air Force (AL)
Cuyahoga Comm Coll, Eastern Cmps (OH)
Cuyahoga Comm Coll, Metropolitan Cmps (OH)
Cuyahoga Comm Coll, Western Cmps (OH)
Cypress Coll (CA)

Associate Degree Programs at Two-Year Colleges
Health Science–History

Daytona Beach Comm Coll (FL)
Dixie Coll (UT)
Draughons Jr Coll (AL)
El Paso Comm Coll (TX)
Garland County Comm Coll (AR)
Gateway Comm Coll (AZ)
Glendale Comm Coll (AZ)
Grand Rapids Comm Coll (MI)
Greenville Tech Coll (SC)
Harcum Coll (PA)
Hill Coll of the Hill Jr Coll District (TX)
Hiwassee Coll (TN)
Kalamazoo Valley Comm Coll (MI)
Kansas City Kansas Comm Coll (KS)
Keiser Coll of Tech, Fort Lauderdale (FL)
Long Beach City Coll (CA)
Macon Coll (GA)
Manor Jr Coll (PA)
Merritt Coll (CA)
Mission Coll (CA)
Mitchell Coll (CT)
Mohave Comm Coll (AZ)
Mount Ida Coll (MA)
Murray State Coll (OK)
Navajo Comm Coll (AZ)
New Mexico Jr Coll (NM)
Northeastern Jr Coll (CO)
Northeast Mississippi Comm Coll (MS)
Northwestern Connecticut Comm-Tech Coll (CT)
Ohlone Coll (CA)
Palo Alto Coll (TX)
Palomar Coll (CA)
Palo Verde Coll (CA)
Pikes Peak Comm Coll (CO)
Redlands Comm Coll (OK)
Ricks Coll (ID)
Salt Lake Comm Coll (UT)
San Joaquin Delta Coll (CA)
Santa Fe Comm Coll (NM)
Shorter Coll (AR)
Southeast Tech Inst (SD)
Southwestern Michigan Coll (MI)
Southwest Mississippi Comm Coll (MS)
Spoon River Coll (IL)
Springfield Coll in Illinois (IL)
Tulsa Jr Coll (OK)
Union County Coll (NJ)
U of Wisconsin Center–Marathon County (WI)
West Hills Comm Coll (CA)

HEALTH SERVICES ADMINISTRATION

Berkeley Coll (NJ)
Berkeley Coll, New York (NY)
Berkeley Coll, White Plains (NY)
Brevard Coll (NC)
Central Comm College–Hastings Cmps (NE)
Central Piedmont Comm Coll (NC)
City Colls of Chicago, Malcolm X Coll (IL)
Cleveland State Comm Coll (TN)
Coll of DuPage (IL)
Comm Coll of the Air Force (AL)
Delaware County Comm Coll (PA)
Des Moines Area Comm Coll (IA)
ECPI Coll of Tech, Hampton (VA)
ECPI Coll of Tech, Virginia Beach (VA)
ECPI Computer Inst, Richmond (VA)
ECPI Computer Inst, Roanoke (VA)
Essex Comm Coll (MD)
Essex County Coll (NJ)
Garland County Comm Coll (AR)
Gateway Comm Coll (AZ)
Herkimer County Comm Coll (NY)
Highland Park Comm Coll (MI)
Illinois Central Coll (IL)
Indian Hills Comm Coll (IA)
Inver Hills Comm Coll (MN)
Iowa Lakes Comm Coll (IA)
Keiser Coll of Tech, Daytona Beach (FL)
Luzerne County Comm Coll (PA)
Mendocino Coll (CA)
Mitchell Coll (CT)
North Idaho Coll (ID)
Oakland Comm Coll (MI)
Ozarks Tech Comm Coll (MO)
Pensacola Jr Coll (FL)
St Petersburg Jr Coll (FL)
South Plains Coll (TX)
Tyler Jr Coll (TX)
Virginia Coll at Birmingham (AL)

HEATING/ REFRIGERATION/AIR CONDITIONING

Alabama Southern Comm Coll, Thomasville (AL)
Alamance Comm Coll (NC)
Anson Comm Coll (NC)
Antelope Valley Coll (CA)
Arizona Western Coll (AZ)
Athens Area Tech Inst (GA)
Austin Comm Coll (TX)
Belleville Area Coll (IL)
Belmont Tech Coll (OH)
Bismarck State Coll (ND)
Blue Ridge Comm Coll (NC)
Brazosport Coll (TX)
Brunswick Comm Coll (NC)
Cape Fear Comm Coll (NC)
Central Comm College–Grand Island Cmps (NE)
Central Comm College–Hastings Cmps (NE)
Central Texas Coll (TX)
Cerro Coso Comm Coll (CA)
Chattanooga State Tech Comm Coll (TN)
CHI Inst (PA)
Chippewa Valley Tech Coll (WI)
City Colls of Chicago, Kennedy-King Coll (IL)
Clovis Comm Coll (NM)
Coastal Carolina Comm Coll (NC)
Coll of DuPage (IL)
Coll of Lake County (IL)
Coll of Southern Idaho (ID)
Coll of the Desert (CA)
Coll of the Mainland (TX)
Coll of the Sequoias (CA)
Columbus State Comm Coll (OH)
Comm Coll of Allegheny County Boyce Cmps (PA)
Comm Coll of Allegheny County North Cmps (PA)
Comm Coll of Allegheny County South Cmps (PA)
Comm Coll of Denver (CO)
Comm Coll of Southern Nevada (NV)
Comm Coll of the Air Force (AL)
Craven Comm Coll (NC)
Daytona Beach Comm Coll (FL)
Delaware County Comm Coll (PA)
Del Mar Coll (TX)
Doña Ana Branch Comm Coll (NM)
Dundalk Comm Coll (MD)
Dunwoody Inst (MN)
East Central Coll (MO)
Eastern Maine Tech Coll (ME)
Eastern Wyoming Coll (WY)
Eastfield Coll (TX)
Elaine P Nunez Comm Coll (LA)
El Camino Coll (CA)
Elgin Comm Coll (IL)
El Paso Comm Coll (TX)
Fayetteville Tech Comm Coll (NC)
Florence-Darlington Tech Coll (SC)
Floyd Coll (GA)
Forsyth Tech Comm Coll (NC)
Frank Phillips Coll (TX)
Fresno City Coll (CA)
Gadsden State Comm Coll (AL)
Gateway Comm Coll (AZ)
George C Wallace State Comm Coll, Dothan (AL)
Grand Rapids Comm Coll (MI)
Grayson County Coll (TX)
Greenville Tech Coll (SC)
Harry M Ayers State Tech Coll (AL)
Hawkeye Comm Coll (IA)
Henry Ford Comm Coll (MI)
Horry-Georgetown Tech Coll (SC)
Hudson Valley Comm Coll (NY)
Illinois Eastern Comm Colls, Lincoln Trail Coll (IL)
Indian River Comm Coll (FL)
ITT Tech Inst, Dayton (OH)
Ivy Tech State Coll–Central Indiana (IN)
Ivy Tech State Coll–Columbus (IN)
Ivy Tech State Coll–Eastcentral (IN)
Ivy Tech State Coll–Kokomo (IN)
Ivy Tech State Coll–Lafayette (IN)
Ivy Tech State Coll–Northcentral (IN)
Ivy Tech State Coll–Northeast (IN)
Ivy Tech State Coll–Northwest (IN)
Ivy Tech State Coll–Southcentral (IN)
Ivy Tech State Coll–Southwest (IN)
Ivy Tech State Coll–Wabash Valley (IN)
Ivy Tech State Coll–Whitewater (IN)
Jefferson Coll (MO)
John A Logan Coll (IL)
John C Calhoun State Comm Coll (AL)
John M Patterson State Tech Coll (AL)
Johnson County Comm Coll (KS)
John Wood Comm Coll (IL)
J Sargeant Reynolds Comm Coll (VA)
Kalamazoo Valley Comm Coll (MI)
Kankakee Comm Coll (IL)
Kansas City Kansas Comm Coll (KS)
Kirkwood Comm Coll (IA)
Labette Comm Coll (KS)
Lamar University–Port Arthur (TX)
Lane Comm Coll (OR)
Laney Coll (CA)
Lansing Comm Coll (MI)
Lee Coll (TX)
Lehigh Carbon Comm Coll (PA)
Linn-Benton Comm Coll (OR)
Long Beach City Coll (CA)
Los Angeles Trade-Tech Coll (CA)
Luzerne County Comm Coll (PA)
Macomb Comm Coll (MI)
Maple Woods Comm Coll (MO)
Martin Comm Coll (NC)
Massasoit Comm Coll (MA)
Mercer County Comm Coll (NJ)
Metropolitan Comm Coll (NE)
Miami-Dade Comm Coll (FL)
Middlesex County Coll (NJ)
Midland Coll (TX)
Midlands Tech Coll (SC)
Mid Michigan Comm Coll (MI)
Mid-Plains Comm Coll (NE)
Milwaukee Area Tech Coll (WI)
Mohawk Valley Comm Coll (NY)
Monroe Comm Coll (NY)
Moraine Valley Comm Coll (IL)
Morton Coll (IL)
Mountain Empire Comm Coll (VA)
Mt San Antonio Coll (CA)
New England Inst of Tech (RI)
New England Inst of Tech & Florida Culinary Inst (FL)
New Hampshire Tech Coll, Manchester (NH)
New York City Tech Coll of the City U of NY (NY)
North Central Tech Coll (OH)
North Dakota State Coll of Science (ND)
Northeast Comm Coll (NE)
Northeast Mississippi Comm Coll (MS)
Northern Maine Tech Coll (ME)
Northern Virginia Comm Coll (VA)
North Harris Coll (TX)
North Idaho Coll (ID)
North Iowa Area Comm Coll (IA)
North Lake Coll (TX)
North Seattle Comm Coll (WA)
Oakland Comm Coll (MI)
Oakton Comm Coll (IL)
Odessa Coll (TX)
Okaloosa-Walton Comm Coll (FL)
Oklahoma State U, Oklahoma City (OK)
Oklahoma State U, Okmulgee (OK)
Orange Coast Coll (CA)
Oxnard Coll (CA)
Ozarks Tech Comm Coll (MO)
Paris Jr Coll (TX)
Pennsylvania Coll of Tech (PA)
Penn Valley Comm Coll (MO)
Petit Jean Tech Coll (AR)
Phillips County Comm Coll (AR)
Piedmont Tech Coll (SC)
Pikes Peak Comm Coll (CO)
Pima Comm Coll (AZ)
Pitt Comm Coll (NC)
Ranken Tech Coll (MO)
Raritan Valley Comm Coll (NJ)
Rend Lake Coll (IL)
Renton Tech Coll (WA)
RETS Tech Ctr (OH)
Riverside Comm Coll (CA)
Roanoke-Chowan Comm Coll (NC)
Rockingham Comm Coll (NC)
St Philip's Coll (TX)
Salem Comm Coll (NJ)
Salt Lake Comm Coll (UT)
San Bernardino Valley Coll (CA)
San Jacinto College–South Cmps (TX)
San Joaquin Delta Coll (CA)
San Jose City Coll (CA)
Sauk Valley Comm Coll (IL)
Scott Comm Coll (IA)
Shelton State Comm Coll (AL)
Southeast Comm Coll, Milford Cmps (NE)
Southern Maine Tech Coll (ME)
South Plains Coll (TX)
Spokane Comm Coll (WA)
Springfield Tech Comm Coll (MA)
State U of NY Coll of Tech at Alfred (NY)
State U of NY Coll of Tech at Canton (NY)
State U of NY Coll of Tech at Delhi (NY)
Tarrant County Jr Coll (TX)
Terra State Comm Coll (OH)
Texarkana Coll (TX)
Texas State Tech Coll–Harlingen Cmps (TX)
Texas State Tech Coll–Waco/ Marshall Cmps (TX)
Thaddeus Stevens State Sch of Tech (PA)
Tomball Coll (TX)
Triangle Tech, Inc, Pittsburgh (PA)
Triangle Tech, Inc–Greensburg Ctr (PA)
Tri-County Tech Coll (SC)
Trinity Valley Comm Coll (TX)
Triton Coll (IL)
Truckee Meadows Comm Coll (NV)
Tulsa Jr Coll (OK)
Tyler Jr Coll (TX)
U of Alaska Anchorage, Matanuska-Susitna Coll (AK)
U of Hawaii–Honolulu Comm Coll (HI)
Vance-Granville Comm Coll (NC)
Virginia Highlands Comm Coll (VA)
Wallace State Comm Coll (AL)
Walla Walla Comm Coll (WA)
Washington State Comm Coll (OH)
Washtenaw Comm Coll (MI)
Waubonsee Comm Coll (IL)
Wenatchee Valley Coll (WA)
Western Wisconsin Tech Coll (WI)
Westmoreland County Comm Coll (PA)
West Virginia Northern Comm Coll (WV)
William Rainey Harper Coll (IL)
York Tech Coll (SC)

HEBREW

Los Angeles Valley Coll (CA)

HISPANIC STUDIES

Colorado Mountn Coll, Timberline Cmps (CO)
Contra Costa Coll (CA)
San Diego City Coll (CA)

HISTORIC PRESERVATION

Belmont Tech Coll (OH)

HISTORY

Abraham Baldwin Ag Coll (GA)
Alabama Southern Comm Coll, Monroeville (AL)
Allen County Comm Coll (KS)
Andrew Coll (GA)
Angelina Coll (TX)
Antelope Valley Coll (CA)
Atlanta Metropolitan Coll (GA)
Atlantic Comm Coll (NJ)
Austin Comm Coll (TX)
Bainbridge Coll (GA)
Bakersfield Coll (CA)
Barstow Coll (CA)
Barton County Comm Coll (KS)
Bay de Noc Comm Coll (MI)
Bee County Coll (TX)
Bergen Comm Coll (NJ)
Bismarck State Coll (ND)
Black Hawk Coll, Moline (IL)
Blinn Coll (TX)
Brazosport Coll (TX)
Brevard Coll (NC)
Brevard Comm Coll (FL)
Bronx Comm Coll of City U of NY (NY)
Brunswick Coll (GA)
Burlington County Coll (NJ)
Butler County Comm Coll (KS)
Cañada Coll (CA)
Cape Cod Comm Coll (MA)
Casper Coll (WY)
Central Coll (KS)
Central Comm College–Platte Cmps (NE)
Centralia Coll (WA)
Central Texas Coll (TX)
Cerritos Coll (CA)
Chabot Coll (CA)
Chaffey Coll (CA)
Chemeketa Comm Coll (OR)
Cisco Jr Coll (TX)
Clackamas Comm Coll (OR)
Clarendon Coll (TX)
Clark Coll (WA)
Clinton Comm Coll (IA)
Cloud County Comm Coll (KS)
Cochise Coll, Douglas (AZ)
Cochise Coll, Sierra Vista (AZ)
Coffeyville Comm Coll (KS)
Colby Comm Coll (KS)
Coll of Alameda (CA)
Coll of DuPage (IL)
Coll of Marin (CA)
Coll of Southern Idaho (ID)
Coll of the Canyons (CA)
Coll of the Desert (CA)
Coll of the Sequoias (CA)
Coll of the Siskiyous (CA)
Collin County Comm Coll (TX)
Columbia Coll (CA)
Columbia State Comm Coll (TN)
Comm Coll of Allegheny County Allegheny Cmps (PA)
Comm Coll of Allegheny County South Cmps (PA)
Comm Coll of Southern Nevada (NV)
Connors State Coll (OK)
Contra Costa Coll (CA)
Copiah-Lincoln Comm Coll (MS)
Crafton Hills Coll (CA)
Cypress Coll (CA)
Dalton Coll (GA)
Danville Area Comm Coll (IL)
Darton Coll (GA)
Daytona Beach Comm Coll (FL)
De Anza Coll (CA)
Del Mar Coll (TX)
Dixie Coll (UT)
Dodge City Comm Coll (KS)
Donnelly Coll (KS)
East Central Coll (MO)
East Central Comm Coll (MS)
Eastern Arizona Coll (AZ)
Eastern Oklahoma State Coll (OK)
Eastern Wyoming Coll (WY)
East Georgia Coll (GA)
East Los Angeles Coll (CA)
East Mississippi Comm Coll (MS)
El Camino Coll (CA)
Ellsworth Comm Coll (IA)
El Paso Comm Coll (TX)
Essex Comm Coll (MD)
Everett Comm Coll (WA)
Foothill Coll (CA)
Frank Phillips Coll (TX)
Fresno City Coll (CA)
Fullerton Coll (CA)
Fulton-Montgomery Comm Coll (NY)
Gainesville Coll (GA)
Galveston Coll (TX)
Gavilan Coll (CA)
Glendale Comm Coll (AZ)
Gordon Coll (GA)
Grossmont Coll (CA)
Gulf Coast Comm Coll (FL)
Harford Comm Coll (MD)
Hartnell Coll (CA)
Hibbing Comm Coll (MN)
Highland Comm Coll (IL)
Highland Comm Coll (KS)
Hill Coll of the Hill Jr Coll District (TX)
Hiwassee Coll (TN)
Hutchinson Comm Coll and Area Vocational Sch (KS)
Independence Comm Coll (KS)
Indian River Comm Coll (FL)
Iowa Lakes Comm Coll (IA)
Irvine Valley Coll (CA)
Itawamba Comm Coll (MS)
Jackson State Comm Coll (TN)
Jefferson Coll (MO)
Jefferson Davis Comm Coll (AL)
John A Logan Coll (IL)
John Wood Comm Coll (IL)
Joliet Jr Coll (IL)
Kansas City Kansas Comm Coll (KS)
Kellogg Comm Coll (MI)
Kemper Military Jr Coll (MO)
Kirkwood Comm Coll (IA)
Kishwaukee Coll (IL)
Labette Comm Coll (KS)
Lake Land Coll (IL)
Lake Michigan Coll (MI)
Lamar Comm Coll (CO)
Lansing Comm Coll (MI)
Lassen Coll (CA)
Lincoln Land Comm Coll (IL)
Little Hoop Comm Coll (ND)
Lon Morris Coll (TX)
Lorain County Comm Coll (OH)
Los Angeles City Coll (CA)
Los Angeles Mission Coll (CA)

Los Angeles Valley Coll (CA)
Lower Columbia Coll (WA)
Macon Coll (GA)
Miami-Dade Comm Coll (FL)
Miami University–Middletown Cmps (OH)
Middle Georgia Coll (GA)
Middlesex County Coll (NJ)
Mid Michigan Comm Coll (MI)
Mineral Area Coll (MO)
MiraCosta Coll (CA)
Mississippi Delta Comm Coll (MS)
Moberly Area Comm Coll (MO)
Modesto Jr Coll (CA)
Mohave Comm Coll (AZ)
Monroe Comm Coll (NY)
Monterey Peninsula Coll (CA)
Motlow State Comm Coll (TN)
Murray State Coll (OK)
Naugatuck Valley Community–Tech Coll (CT)
New Mexico Jr Coll (NM)
New Mexico Military Inst (NM)
Northeast Comm Coll (NE)
Northeastern Jr Coll (CO)
Northeast Mississippi Comm Coll (MS)
Northern Essex Comm Coll (MA)
North Idaho Coll (ID)
Northwest Coll (WY)
Odessa Coll (TX)
Oklahoma City Comm Coll (OK)
Otero Jr Coll (CO)
Oxnard Coll (CA)
Palm Beach Comm Coll (FL)
Palo Alto Coll (TX)
Palo Verde Coll (CA)
Pasadena City Coll (CA)
Pensacola Jr Coll (FL)
Pikes Peak Comm Coll (CO)
Polk Comm Coll (FL)
Porterville Coll (CA)
Potomac State Coll of West Virginia U (WV)
Pratt Comm Coll and Area Voc Sch (KS)
Rancho Santiago Coll (CA)
Redlands Comm Coll (OK)
Red Rocks Comm Coll (CO)
Ricks Coll (ID)
Rogers State Coll (OK)
Rose State Coll (OK)
Saddleback Coll (CA)
St Catharine Coll (KY)
St Gregory's Coll (OK)
St Philip's Coll (TX)
Salem Comm Coll (NJ)
San Bernardino Valley Coll (CA)
San Jacinto College–Central Cmps (TX)
San Jacinto College–South Cmps (TX)
San Joaquin Delta Coll (CA)
San Jose City Coll (CA)
San Juan Coll (NM)
Santa Barbara City Coll (CA)
Santa Monica Coll (CA)
Santa Rosa Jr Coll (CA)
Sauk Valley Comm Coll (IL)
Scott Comm Coll (IA)
Seward County Comm Coll (KS)
Sheridan Coll (WY)
Skagit Valley Coll (WA)
Skyline Coll (CA)
Snow Coll (UT)
Solano Comm Coll (CA)
Southern U at Shreveport–Bossier City Cmps (LA)
South Georgia Coll (GA)
South Mountain Comm Coll (AZ)
SouthWest Collegiate Inst for the Deaf (TX)
Southwestern Coll (CA)
Southwestern Comm Coll (IA)
Southwest Mississippi Comm Coll (MS)
Southwest Missouri State University– West Plains (MO)
Spoon River Coll (IL)
State Comm Coll of East St Louis (IL)
Tacoma Comm Coll (WA)
Treasure Valley Comm Coll (OR)
Trinity Valley Comm Coll (TX)
Triton Coll (IL)
Tulsa Jr Coll (OK)
Turtle Mountain Comm Coll (ND)
Umpqua Comm Coll (OR)
U of Kentucky, Jefferson Comm Coll (KY)
Vermilion Comm Coll (MN)
Vincennes U (IN)
Waldorf Coll (IA)
Waubonsee Comm Coll (IL)
Waycross Coll (GA)
Wenatchee Valley Coll (WA)
Western Nebraska Comm Coll, Scottsbluff (NE)
Western Wyoming Comm Coll (WY)
West Los Angeles Coll (CA)
West Shore Comm Coll (MI)
West Valley Coll (CA)
Willmar Comm Coll (MN)
Wright State U, Lake Cmps (OH)
Young Harris Coll (GA)
Yuba Coll (CA)

HISTORY OF PHILOSOPHY

Iowa Lakes Comm Coll (IA)

HISTORY OF SCIENCE

Iowa Lakes Comm Coll (IA)

HOME ECONOMICS

Abraham Baldwin Ag Coll (GA)
Allan Hancock Coll (CA)
Allen County Comm Coll (KS)
Antelope Valley Coll (CA)
Atlanta Metropolitan Coll (GA)
Bacone Coll (OK)
Bainbridge Coll (GA)
Barton County Comm Coll (KS)
Brunswick Coll (GA)
Butte Coll (CA)
Cañada Coll (CA)
Central Coll (KS)
Central Comm College–Platte Cmps (NE)
Cerritos Coll (CA)
Chaffey Coll (CA)
Chemeketa Comm Coll (OR)
City Colls of Chicago, Kennedy-King Coll (IL)
Cloud County Comm Coll (KS)
Coffeyville Comm Coll (KS)
Colby Comm Coll (KS)
Coll of DuPage (IL)
Coll of the Sequoias (CA)
Coll of the Siskiyous (CA)
Connors State Coll (OK)
Contra Costa Coll (CA)
Copiah-Lincoln Comm College–Natchez Cmps (MS)
Dalton Coll (GA)
Delta Coll (MI)
Dixie Coll (UT)
East Central Coll (MO)
East Los Angeles Coll (CA)
El Camino Coll (CA)
Fresno City Coll (CA)
Fullerton Coll (CA)
Glendale Comm Coll (AZ)
Grays Harbor Coll (WA)
Grayson County Coll (TX)
Gulf Coast Comm Coll (FL)
Highland Comm Coll (KS)
Hill Coll of the Hill Jr Coll District (TX)
Hinds Comm Coll (MS)
Hiwassee Coll (TN)
Holyoke Comm Coll (MA)
Houston Comm Coll System (TX)
Hutchinson Comm Coll and Area Vocational Sch (KS)
Indian River Comm Coll (FL)
Itawamba Comm Coll (MS)
Jackson State Comm Coll (TN)
Jones County Jr Coll (MS)
Kings River Comm Coll (CA)
Lake Land Coll (IL)
Lamar University–Port Arthur (TX)
Lansing Comm Coll (MI)
Linn-Benton Comm Coll (OR)
Long Beach City Coll (CA)
Los Angeles City Coll (CA)
Los Angeles Valley Coll (CA)
Merced Coll (CA)
Mesa Comm Coll (AZ)
Middle Georgia Coll (GA)
Mississippi Delta Comm Coll (MS)
Modesto Jr Coll (CA)
Monterey Peninsula Coll (CA)
Moorpark Coll (CA)
Mt San Antonio Coll (CA)
North Dakota State University–Bottineau (ND)
Northeastern Jr Coll (CO)
Northeastern Oklahoma A&M Coll (OK)
Northeast Mississippi Comm Coll (MS)
Northwest Coll (WY)
Ohlone Coll (CA)
Orange Coast Coll (CA)
Oxnard Coll (CA)
Palm Beach Comm Coll (FL)
Palomar Coll (CA)
Penn Valley Comm Coll (MO)
Pensacola Jr Coll (FL)
Pima Comm Coll (AZ)
Polk Comm Coll (FL)
Portland Comm Coll (OR)
Pratt Comm Coll and Area Voc Sch (KS)
Ricks Coll (ID)
Riverside Comm Coll (CA)
Rose State Coll (OK)
Saddleback Coll (CA)
San Jacinto College–Central Cmps (TX)
San Jacinto College–North Cmps (TX)
San Joaquin Delta Coll (CA)
Santa Monica Coll (CA)
Shasta Coll (CA)
Shelton State Comm Coll (AL)
Sierra Coll (CA)
Skagit Valley Coll (WA)
Skyline Coll (CA)
Snow Coll (UT)
Solano Comm Coll (CA)
South Mountain Comm Coll (AZ)
Southwestern Coll (CA)
U of Kentucky, Jefferson Comm Coll (KY)
Ventura Coll (CA)
Vermilion Comm Coll (MN)
Vincennes U (IN)
Waldorf Coll (IA)
Yuba Coll (CA)

HOME ECONOMICS EDUCATION

American River Coll (CA)
Brevard Comm Coll (FL)
Central Coll (KS)
Central Comm College–Platte Cmps (NE)
Cloud County Comm Coll (KS)
Coll of the Sequoias (CA)
Copiah-Lincoln Comm Coll (MS)
East Georgia Coll (GA)
Hiwassee Coll (TN)
Itawamba Comm Coll (MS)
Jones County Jr Coll (MS)
Kansas City Kansas Comm Coll (KS)
Los Angeles Mission Coll (CA)
Middle Georgia Coll (GA)
Northeast Mississippi Comm Coll (MS)
Northwest Coll (WY)
Northwest Mississippi Comm Coll (MS)
Okaloosa-Walton Comm Coll (FL)
Ricks Coll (ID)
U of Kentucky, Jefferson Comm Coll (KY)

HORTICULTURE

Abraham Baldwin Ag Coll (GA)
Alamance Comm Coll (NC)
American River Coll (CA)
Anne Arundel Comm Coll (MD)
Anoka-Ramsey Comm Coll (MN)
Bacone Coll (OK)
Bakersfield Coll (CA)
Belleville Area Coll (IL)
Blue Ridge Comm Coll (NC)
Butte Coll (CA)
Cabrillo Coll (CA)
Cape Cod Comm Coll (MA)
Catawba Valley Comm Coll (NC)
Central Coll (KS)
Central Comm College–Hastings Cmps (NE)
Central Lakes Coll (MN)
Central Piedmont Comm Coll (NC)
Chabot Coll (CA)
Cincinnati State Tech and Comm Coll (OH)
City Coll of San Francisco (CA)
City Colls of Chicago, Richard J Daley Coll (IL)
Clark Coll (WA)
Clark State Comm Coll (OH)
Coll of DuPage (IL)
Coll of Lake County (IL)
Coll of San Mateo (CA)
Coll of the Desert (CA)
Coll of the Sequoias (CA)
Collin County Comm Coll (TX)
Comm Coll of Allegheny County South Cmps (PA)
Comm Coll of Southern Nevada (NV)
Cosumnes River Coll (CA)
Cumberland County Coll (NJ)
Danville Area Comm Coll (IL)
Des Moines Area Comm Coll (IA)
East Central Coll (MO)
Eastern Oklahoma State Coll (OK)
Edison Comm Coll (FL)
Edmonds Comm Coll (WA)
El Camino Coll (CA)
Elgin Comm Coll (IL)
Fayetteville Tech Comm Coll (NC)
Finger Lakes Comm Coll (NY)
Forsyth Tech Comm Coll (NC)
Frank Phillips Coll (TX)
Front Range Comm Coll (CO)
Fullerton Coll (CA)
Gwinnett Tech Inst (GA)
Hartnell Coll (CA)
Hawkeye Comm Coll (IA)
Haywood Comm Coll (NC)
Hill Coll of the Hill Jr Coll District (TX)
Houston Comm Coll System (TX)
Illinois Central Coll (IL)
Indian Hills Comm Coll (IA)
Joliet Jr Coll (IL)
Jones County Jr Coll (MS)
J Sargeant Reynolds Comm Coll (VA)
Kansas City Kansas Comm Coll (KS)
Kent State U, Salem Cmps (OH)
Kirkwood Comm Coll (IA)
Kishwaukee Coll (IL)
Lake Washington Tech Coll (WA)
Lansing Comm Coll (MI)
Las Positas Coll (CA)
Lenoir Comm Coll (NC)
Linn-Benton Comm Coll (OR)
Long Beach City Coll (CA)
Lord Fairfax Comm Coll (VA)
Los Angeles Pierce Coll (CA)
Luzerne County Comm Coll (PA)
Mayland Comm Coll (NC)
McHenry County Coll (IL)
Meridian Comm Coll (MS)
Merritt Coll (CA)
Mesa Comm Coll (AZ)
Metropolitan Comm Coll (NE)
Miami-Dade Comm Coll (FL)
MiraCosta Coll (CA)
Mississippi County Comm Coll (AR)
Mississippi Gulf Coast Comm Coll (MS)
Moorpark Coll (CA)
Mt Hood Comm Coll (OR)
Mt San Antonio Coll (CA)
Naugatuck Valley Community–Tech Coll (CT)
Nebraska Coll of Tech Agriculture (NE)
North Dakota State University–Bottineau (ND)
Northeastern Jr Coll (CO)
Northeastern Oklahoma A&M Coll (OK)
Northeast Mississippi Comm Coll (MS)
Northern Virginia Comm Coll (VA)
Northwest Coll (WY)
Ohio State U Ag Tech Inst (OH)
Oklahoma State U, Oklahoma City (OK)
Orange Coast Coll (CA)
Palo Alto Coll (TX)
Pensacola Jr Coll (FL)
Petit Jean Tech Coll (AR)
Polk Comm Coll (FL)
Potomac State Coll of West Virginia U (WV)
Randolph Comm Coll (NC)
Richland Coll (TX)
Ricks Coll (ID)
Rockingham Comm Coll (NC)
Saddleback Coll (CA)
St Catharine Coll (KY)
St Clair County Comm Coll (MI)
St Louis Comm Coll at Meramec (MO)
Sampson Comm Coll (NC)
San Jacinto College–Central Cmps (TX)
Santa Barbara City Coll (CA)
Santa Rosa Jr Coll (CA)
Shasta Coll (CA)
Shawnee Comm Coll (IL)
Sierra Coll (CA)
Southern Maine Tech Coll (ME)
South Puget Sound Comm Coll (WA)
South Seattle Comm Coll (WA)
Spartanburg Tech Coll (SC)
Spokane Comm Coll (WA)
State U of NY Coll of A&T at Cobleskill (NY)
State U of NY Coll of A&T at Morrisville (NY)
State U of NY Coll of Tech at Alfred (NY)
State U of NY Coll of Tech at Delhi (NY)
State U of NY Coll of Tech at Farmingdale (NY)
Suffolk County Comm Coll–Eastern Cmps (NY)
Surry Comm Coll (NC)
Tarrant County Jr Coll (TX)
Trident Tech Coll (SC)
Trinity Valley Comm Coll (TX)
Triton Coll (IL)
Tulsa Jr Coll (OK)
Tyler Jr Coll (TX)
U of Hawaii–Maui Comm Coll (HI)
U of Kentucky, Jefferson Comm Coll (KY)
Vermont Tech Coll (VT)
Victor Valley Coll (CA)
Vincennes U (IN)
Wallace State Comm Coll (AL)
Western Piedmont Comm Coll (NC)
Westmoreland County Comm Coll (PA)
West Virginia Northern Comm Coll (WV)
William Rainey Harper Coll (IL)
The Williamson Free Sch of Mech Trades (PA)

HOSPITALITY SERVICES

Adirondack Comm Coll (NY)
American Inst of Business (IA)
Atlantic Comm Coll (NJ)
Bay State Coll (MA)
Beal Coll (ME)
Berkeley Coll, White Plains (NY)
Bucks County Comm Coll (PA)
Butler County Comm Coll (PA)
Central Oregon Comm Coll (OR)
Central Piedmont Comm Coll (NC)
Central Texas Coll (TX)
Chaparral Career Coll (AZ)
Chemeketa Comm Coll (OR)
Chippewa Valley Tech Coll (WI)
City Colls of Chicago, Harold Washington Coll (IL)
Coll of DuPage (IL)
Colorado Mountn Coll, Alpine Cmps (CO)
Columbus State Comm Coll (OH)
Comm Coll of Southern Nevada (NV)
Cuyahoga Comm Coll, Metropolitan Cmps (OH)
Daytona Beach Comm Coll (FL)
Delaware Tech & Comm Coll, Jack F Owens Cmps (DE)
Doña Ana Branch Comm Coll (NM)
East Central Coll (MO)
Edison Comm Coll (FL)
El Centro Coll (TX)
Erie Comm Coll, City Cmps (NY)
Florida National Coll (FL)
Fox Valley Tech Coll (WI)
Greenville Tech Coll (SC)
Gulf Coast Comm Coll (FL)
Harcum Coll (PA)
Harford Comm Coll (MD)
Henry Ford Comm Coll (MI)
Highland Comm Coll (IL)
Hillsborough Comm Coll (FL)
Hocking Coll (OH)
Holyoke Comm Coll (MA)
ICS Ctr for Degree Studies (PA)
Indiana Business Coll (IN)
ITT Tech Inst, Indianapolis (IN)
Ivy Tech State Coll–Central Indiana (IN)
Ivy Tech State Coll–Northeast (IN)
Ivy Tech State Coll–Northwest (IN)
Jackson Comm Coll (MI)
James H Faulkner State Comm Coll (AL)
Jefferson Comm Coll (NY)
Jefferson State Comm Coll (AL)
Johnson County Comm Coll (KS)
Katharine Gibbs Sch (MA)
Keystone Coll (PA)
Lakeland Comm Coll (OH)
Lake Michigan Coll (MI)
Lane Comm Coll (OR)
Lansdale Sch of Business (PA)
Lansing Comm Coll (MI)
Lexington Coll (IL)
Linn-Benton Comm Coll (OR)
Madison Area Tech Coll (WI)
Marian Court Coll (MA)
Massachusetts Bay Comm Coll (MA)
Massasoit Comm Coll (MA)
Middlesex County Coll (NJ)
Mid Michigan Comm Coll (MI)
Midstate Coll (IL)
Mohawk Valley Comm Coll (NY)
Monroe Coll, Bronx (NY)
Monroe Coll, New Rochelle (NY)
Monterey Peninsula Coll (CA)
Mt Hood Comm Coll (OR)
Muskegon Comm Coll (MI)
National Business Coll, Roanoke (VA)
Naugatuck Valley Community–Tech Coll (CT)
New Hampshire Tech Coll, Laconia (NH)
Normandale Comm Coll (MN)
Northwestern Business Coll (IL)
Northwestern Michigan Coll (MI)
Oakland Comm Coll (MI)
Oklahoma State U, Okmulgee (OK)
Ozarks Tech Comm Coll (MO)
Parkland Coll (IL)
Parks Jr Coll (CO)

92
Peterson's Guide to Two-Year Colleges 1997

Associate Degree Programs at Two-Year Colleges
Hospitality Services–Humanities

Pasco-Hernando Comm Coll (FL)
Paul Smith's Coll (NY)
Phillips Jr Coll of Springfield (MO)
Pima Comm Coll (AZ)
Rainy River Comm Coll (MN)
Rio Salado Comm Coll (AZ)
Rock Valley Coll (IL)
San Diego City Coll (CA)
Scottsdale Comm Coll (AZ)
Seattle Central Comm Coll (WA)
Sheridan Coll (WY)
Sisseton-Wahpeton Comm Coll (SD)
Southern Maine Tech Coll (ME)
South Seattle Comm Coll (WA)
State U of NY Coll of A&T at Morrisville (NY)
Sullivan County Comm Coll (NY)
Three Rivers Comm-Tech Coll (CT)
Triton Coll (IL)
Truckee Meadows Comm Coll (NV)
U of Cincinnati Clermont Coll (OH)
U of Hawaii–Kauai Comm Coll (HI)
Utah Valley State Coll (UT)
Valencia Comm Coll (FL)
Vermilion Comm Coll (MN)
Westmoreland County Comm Coll (PA)
William Rainey Harper Coll (IL)
Wisconsin Indianhead Tech Coll, Ashland Cmps (WI)

HOTEL AND RESTAURANT MANAGEMENT

Alexandria Tech Coll (MN)
Allegany Comm Coll (MD)
American Inst of Commerce (IA)
American River Coll (CA)
Anne Arundel Comm Coll (MD)
Asheville-Buncombe Tech Comm Coll (NC)
Austin Comm Coll (TX)
Bakersfield Coll (CA)
Baltimore International Culinary Coll (MD)
Bay State Coll (MA)
Beal Coll (ME)
Bergen Comm Coll (NJ)
Berkeley Coll, White Plains (NY)
Berkshire Comm Coll (MA)
Bismarck State Coll (ND)
Black Hawk Coll, Moline (IL)
Brevard Comm Coll (FL)
Briarwood Coll (CT)
Broome Comm Coll (NY)
Broward Comm Coll (FL)
Bryant and Stratton Business Inst, Albany (NY)
Bryant and Stratton Business Inst, Lackawanna (NY)
Bryant and Stratton Business Inst, Rochester (NY)
Bryant and Stratton Business Inst, Syracuse (NY)
Bryant and Stratton Coll, Parma (OH)
Bucks County Comm Coll (PA)
Bunker Hill Comm Coll (MA)
Burlington County Coll (NJ)
Butler County Comm Coll (KS)
Cape Cod Comm Coll (MA)
Cape Fear Comm Coll (NC)
Carl Albert State Coll (OK)
Central Comm College–Hastings Cmps (NE)
Central Oregon Comm Coll (OR)
Central Pennsylvania Business Sch (PA)
Central Piedmont Comm Coll (NC)
Central Texas Coll (TX)
Chaffey Coll (CA)
Champlain Coll (VT)
Chattanooga State Tech Comm Coll (TN)
Chemeketa Comm Coll (OR)
Cincinnati State Tech and Comm Coll (OH)
City Coll of San Francisco (CA)
City Colls of Chicago, Harold Washington Coll (IL)
Cochise Coll, Sierra Vista (AZ)
Coll of DuPage (IL)
Coll of Southern Idaho (ID)
Coll of the Canyons (CA)
Colorado Mountn Coll, Alpine Cmps (CO)
Columbia Coll (CA)
Columbus State Comm Coll (OH)
Comm Coll of Allegheny County Boyce Cmps (PA)
Comm Coll of Allegheny County North Cmps (PA)
Comm Coll of Denver (CO)
Comm Coll of Philadelphia (PA)
Comm Coll of Southern Nevada (NV)
Comm Coll of the Air Force (AL)
Copiah-Lincoln Comm College–Natchez Cmps (MS)
County Coll of Morris (NJ)
Cowley County Comm Coll and Voc-Tech Sch (KS)
Cuyahoga Comm Coll, Metropolitan Cmps (OH)
Cypress Coll (CA)
Daytona Beach Comm Coll (FL)
DeKalb Coll (GA)
Delaware County Comm Coll (PA)
Delaware Tech & Comm Coll, Jack F Owens Cmps (DE)
Del Mar Coll (TX)
Des Moines Area Comm Coll (IA)
Dixie Coll (UT)
East Central Coll (MO)
El Centro Coll (TX)
Elgin Comm Coll (IL)
Erie Comm Coll, City Cmps (NY)
Essex County Coll (NJ)
Finger Lakes Comm Coll (NY)
Fisher Coll (MA)
Flathead Valley Comm Coll (MT)
Florida Comm Coll at Jacksonville (FL)
Florida National Coll (FL)
Floyd Coll (GA)
Gainesville Coll (GA)
Galveston Coll (TX)
Garrett Comm Coll (MD)
Gateway Comm-Tech Coll (CT)
Genesee Comm Coll (NY)
Gogebic Comm Coll (MI)
Grand Rapids Comm Coll (MI)
Gwinnett Tech Inst (GA)
Harrisburg Area Comm Coll (PA)
Heald Business Coll (HI)
Henry Ford Comm Coll (MI)
Hesser Coll (NH)
Highland Park Comm Coll (MI)
Hillsborough Comm Coll (FL)
Hinds Comm Coll (MS)
Hocking Coll (OH)
Holyoke Comm Coll (MA)
Horry-Georgetown Tech Coll (SC)
Houston Comm Coll System (TX)
Hutchinson Comm Coll and Area Vocational Sch (KS)
ICM Sch of Business (PA)
Indiana Business Coll (IN)
Indian River Comm Coll (FL)
Iowa Western Comm Coll (IA)
ITT Tech Inst, San Diego (CA)
ITT Tech Inst (OR)
Ivy Tech State Coll–Central Indiana (IN)
James H Faulkner State Comm Coll (AL)
Jefferson Coll (MO)
Jefferson Comm Coll (NY)
Johnson County Comm Coll (KS)
Joliet Jr Coll (IL)
J Sargeant Reynolds Comm Coll (VA)
Katharine Gibbs Sch, Melville (NY)
Keystone Coll (PA)
Kirkwood Comm Coll (IA)
Knoxville Business Coll (TN)
Lackawanna Jr Coll (PA)
Lake-Sumter Comm Coll (FL)
Lake Tahoe Comm Coll (CA)
Lake Washington Tech Coll (WA)
Lane Comm Coll (OR)
Lansing Comm Coll (MI)
Laramie County Comm Coll (WY)
Laredo Comm Coll (TX)
Lehigh Carbon Comm Coll (PA)
Lewis and Clark Comm Coll (IL)
Lexington Coll (IL)
Long Beach City Coll (CA)
Los Angeles Valley Coll (CA)
Luzerne County Comm Coll (PA)
MacCormac Jr Coll (IL)
Macon Coll (GA)
Manatee Comm Coll (FL)
Manchester Comm-Tech Coll (CT)
Massasoit Comm Coll (MA)
Mercer County Comm Coll (NJ)
Meridian Comm Coll (MS)
Metropolitan Comm Coll (NE)
Miami-Dade Comm Coll (FL)
Middlesex Comm Coll (MA)
Middlesex County Coll (NJ)
Mid-State Tech Coll (WI)
Milwaukee Area Tech Coll (WI)
MiraCosta Coll (CA)
Mississippi Gulf Coast Comm Coll (MS)
Mohawk Valley Comm Coll (NY)
Monroe Comm Coll (NY)
Monterey Peninsula Coll (CA)
Montgomery College–Rockville Cmps (MD)
Montgomery County Comm Coll (PA)
Moraine Park Tech Coll (WI)
Moraine Valley Comm Coll (IL)
Mount Ida Coll (MA)
Mt San Antonio Coll (CA)
Muskegon Comm Coll (MI)
Nassau Comm Coll (NY)
National Business Coll, Roanoke (VA)
Naugatuck Valley Community–Tech Coll (CT)
Newbury Coll (MA)
New Hampshire Tech Inst (NH)
New York City Tech Coll of the City U of NY (NY)
Nicolet Area Tech Coll (WI)
Normandale Comm Coll (MN)
Northampton County Area Comm Coll (PA)
North Arkansas Comm/Tech Coll (AR)
North Central Tech Coll (OH)
Northeastern Oklahoma A&M Coll (OK)
Northeast Mississippi Comm Coll (MS)
Northern Essex Comm Coll (MA)
Northern Virginia Comm Coll (VA)
Northwestern Michigan Coll (MI)
Northwest Indian Coll (WA)
Northwest Mississippi Comm Coll (MS)
Norwalk Comm-Tech Coll (CT)
Oakland Comm Coll (MI)
Oakton Comm Coll (IL)
Okaloosa-Walton Comm Coll (FL)
Onondaga Comm Coll (NY)
Orange Coast Coll (CA)
Owens Comm Coll, Toledo (OH)
Oxnard Coll (CA)
Palm Beach Comm Coll (FL)
Parkland Coll (IL)
Parks Jr Coll (CO)
Paul Smith's Coll (NY)
Peirce Coll (PA)
Pennsylvania Coll of Tech (PA)
Penn State U Beaver Cmps (PA)
Penn State U Berks Cmps (PA)
Penn Valley Comm Coll (MO)
Pensacola Jr Coll (FL)
Pima Comm Coll (AZ)
Quincy Coll (MA)
Quinsigamond Comm Coll (MA)
Rainy River Comm Coll (MN)
Raritan Valley Comm Coll (NJ)
Rasmussen Coll Eagan (MN)
Rock Valley Coll (IL)
St Louis Comm Coll at Forest Park (MO)
St Philip's Coll (TX)
San Bernardino Valley Coll (CA)
Sandhills Comm Coll (NC)
San Diego Mesa Coll (CA)
San Jacinto College–Central Cmps (TX)
Santa Barbara City Coll (CA)
Santa Fe Comm Coll (NM)
Schenectady County Comm Coll (NY)
Schiller International U (Switzerland)
Scottsdale Comm Coll (AZ)
Seattle Central Comm Coll (WA)
Sinclair Comm Coll (OH)
Skagit Valley Coll (WA)
Skyline Coll (CA)
South Coll (FL)
South Coll (GA)
Southern Arkansas U Tech (AR)
Southern Maine Tech Coll (ME)
Southern U at Shreveport–Bossier City Cmps (LA)
South Florida Comm Coll (FL)
Spokane Comm Coll (WA)
State Tech Inst at Memphis (TN)
State U of NY Coll of A&T at Cobleskill (NY)
State U of NY Coll of A&T at Morrisville (NY)
State U of NY Coll of Tech at Delhi (NY)
Stratton Coll (WI)
Suffolk County Comm Coll–Eastern Cmps (NY)
Sullivan County Comm Coll (NY)
Swiss Hospitality Inst "Cesar Ritz" (CT)
Texas Southmost Coll (TX)
Three Rivers Comm-Tech Coll (CT)
Tompkins Cortland Comm Coll (NY)
Trident Tech Coll (SC)
Triton Coll (IL)
Trocaire Coll (NY)
Tulsa Jr Coll (OK)
U of Hawaii–Hawaii Comm Coll (HI)
U of Hawaii–Kapiolani Comm Coll (HI)
U of Hawaii–Maui Comm Coll (HI)
Utah Valley State Coll (UT)
Vermilion Comm Coll (MN)
Vincennes U (IN)
Wake Tech Comm Coll (NC)
Washtenaw Comm Coll (MI)
Westchester Comm Coll (NY)
Westmoreland County Comm Coll (PA)
Wilkes Comm Coll (NC)
Wor-Wic Comm Coll (MD)
Yakima Valley Comm Coll (WA)
Yavapai Coll (AZ)

HUMAN DEVELOPMENT

Central Wyoming Coll (WY)
Coll of Alameda (CA)
Comm Coll of Allegheny County Allegheny Cmps (PA)
Comm Coll of Allegheny County South Cmps (PA)
Cuesta Coll (CA)
Gloucester County Coll (NJ)
Harford Comm Coll (MD)
Imperial Valley Coll (CA)
Orange Coast Coll (CA)
Rancho Santiago Coll (CA)
Saddleback Coll (CA)
Shoreline Comm Coll (WA)
SouthWest Collegiate Inst for the Deaf (TX)
Western Nebraska Comm Coll, Scottsbluff (NE)

HUMAN ECOLOGY

Brevard Coll (NC)
Greenfield Comm Coll (MA)
Monroe Comm Coll (NY)
Sterling Coll (VT)
Vermilion Comm Coll (MN)

HUMANITIES

Abraham Baldwin Ag Coll (GA)
Adirondack Comm Coll (NY)
Andrew Coll (GA)
Angelina Coll (TX)
Anne Arundel Comm Coll (MD)
Antelope Valley Coll (CA)
Atlantic Comm Coll (NJ)
Barstow Coll (CA)
Barton County Comm Coll (KS)
Bay de Noc Comm Coll (MI)
Bevill State Comm Coll (AL)
Bowling Green State University–Firelands Coll (OH)
Brevard Coll (NC)
Brookdale Comm Coll (NJ)
Bucks County Comm Coll (PA)
Butler County Comm Coll (PA)
Cañada Coll (CA)
Casper Coll (WY)
Cayuga County Comm Coll (NY)
Central Coll (KS)
Centralia Coll (WA)
Central Oregon Comm Coll (OR)
Central Texas Coll (TX)
Cerro Coso Comm Coll (CA)
Chabot Coll (CA)
Chaffey Coll (CA)
Chemeketa Comm Coll (OR)
Chesapeake Coll (MD)
City Colls of Chicago, Harold Washington Coll (IL)
City Colls of Chicago, Richard J Daley Coll (IL)
Clark Coll (WA)
Clinton Comm Coll (NY)
Cloud County Comm Coll (KS)
Coffeyville Comm Coll (KS)
Colby Comm Coll (KS)
Coll of Alameda (CA)
Coll of DuPage (IL)
Coll of Marin (CA)
Coll of San Mateo (CA)
Coll of the Canyons (CA)
Coll of the Sequoias (CA)
Colorado Mountn Coll, Alpine Cmps (CO)
Colorado Mountn Coll, Roaring Fork Cmps-Spring Valley Ctr (CO)
Colorado Mountn Coll, Timberline Cmps (CO)
Columbia Coll (CA)
Columbia-Greene Comm Coll (NY)
Comm Coll of Allegheny County Allegheny Cmps (PA)
Comm Coll of Allegheny County Boyce Cmps (PA)
Comm Coll of Allegheny County North Cmps (PA)
Comm Coll of Allegheny County South Cmps (PA)
Contra Costa Coll (CA)
Corning Comm Coll (NY)
Cosumnes River Coll (CA)
County Coll of Morris (NJ)
Crafton Hills Coll (CA)
Danville Area Comm Coll (IL)
Daytona Beach Comm Coll (FL)
Dean Coll (MA)
De Anza Coll (CA)
Dixie Coll (UT)
Dodge City Comm Coll (KS)
Dutchess Comm Coll (NY)
East Central Coll (MO)
Eastern Wyoming Coll (WY)
Erie Comm Coll, City Cmps (NY)
Erie Comm Coll, North Cmps (NY)
Erie Comm Coll, South Cmps (NY)
Finger Lakes Comm Coll (NY)
Foothill Coll (CA)
Fresno City Coll (CA)
Fulton-Montgomery Comm Coll (NY)
Galveston Coll (TX)
Garden City Comm Coll (KS)
Gogebic Comm Coll (MI)
Golden West Coll (CA)
Grays Harbor Coll (WA)
Greenfield Comm Coll (MA)
Harford Comm Coll (MD)
Herkimer County Comm Coll (NY)
Highline Comm Coll (WA)
Hill Coll of the Hill Jr Coll District (TX)
Hiwassee Coll (TN)
Housatonic Comm-Tech Coll (CT)
Imperial Valley Coll (CA)
Independence Comm Coll (KS)
Iowa Lakes Comm Coll (IA)
Irvine Valley Coll (CA)
Jamestown Comm Coll (NY)
Jefferson Comm Coll (NY)
John A Logan Coll (IL)
John Wood Comm Coll (IL)
Kansas City Kansas Comm Coll (KS)
Kirkwood Comm Coll (IA)
Lake Tahoe Comm Coll (CA)
Lamar Comm Coll (CO)
Laney Coll (CA)
Lassen Coll (CA)
Lehigh Carbon Comm Coll (PA)
Lincoln Coll, Normal (IL)
Lincoln Land Comm Coll (IL)
Lon Morris Coll (TX)
Los Angeles Mission Coll (CA)
Los Angeles Southwest Coll (CA)
Luzerne County Comm Coll (PA)
Mendocino Coll (CA)
Merced Coll (CA)
Mercer County Comm Coll (NJ)
Merritt Coll (CA)
Miami-Dade Comm Coll (FL)
Middle Georgia Coll (GA)
Modesto Jr Coll (CA)
Mohawk Valley Comm Coll (NY)
Montgomery County Comm Coll (PA)
Mt San Jacinto Coll (CA)
Napa Valley Coll (CA)
Nassau Comm Coll (NY)
Newbury Coll (MA)
New Mexico Military Inst (NM)
Northeastern Jr Coll (CO)
North Seattle Comm Coll (WA)
Northwest Coll (WY)
Norwalk Comm-Tech Coll (CT)
Okaloosa-Walton Comm Coll (FL)
Oklahoma City Comm Coll (OK)
Onondaga Comm Coll (NY)
Orange County Comm Coll (NY)
Otero Jr Coll (CO)
Passaic County Comm Coll (NJ)
Pikes Peak Comm Coll (CO)
Polk Comm Coll (FL)
Pratt Comm Coll and Area Voc Sch (KS)
Quincy Coll (MA)
Reading Area Comm Coll (PA)
Redlands Comm Coll (OK)
Red Rocks Comm Coll (CO)
Ricks Coll (ID)

Peterson's Guide to Two-Year Colleges 1997
93

Associate Degree Programs at Two-Year Colleges
Humanities–Industrial and Heavy Equipment Maintenance

Rogue Comm Coll (OR)
Roxbury Comm Coll (MA)
Sacramento City Coll (CA)
Saddleback Coll (CA)
Sage Jr Coll of Albany (NY)
St Catharine Coll (KY)
St Gregory's Coll (OK)
Salem Comm Coll (NJ)
Salt Lake Comm Coll (UT)
San Diego Miramar Coll (CA)
San Joaquin Delta Coll (CA)
Santa Rosa Jr Coll (CA)
Schenectady County Comm Coll (NY)
Sheridan Coll (WY)
Skagit Valley Coll (WA)
Snow Coll (UT)
Southwestern Comm Coll (IA)
Southwest Mississippi Comm Coll (MS)
Springfield Tech Comm Coll (MA)
State U of NY Coll of A&T at Cobleskill (NY)
State U of NY Coll of A&T at Morrisville (NY)
State U of NY Coll of Tech at Alfred (NY)
State U of NY Coll of Tech at Canton (NY)
Suffolk County Comm College–Ammerman Cmps (NY)
Sullivan County Comm Coll (NY)
Tacoma Comm Coll (WA)
Tompkins Cortland Comm Coll (NY)
Treasure Valley Comm Coll (OR)
Tulsa Jr Coll (OK)
Ulster County Comm Coll (NY)
Umpqua Comm Coll (OR)
U of Cincinnati Raymond Walters Coll (OH)
Victor Valley Coll (CA)
Westchester Comm Coll (NY)
Western Oklahoma State Coll (OK)
Western Wyoming Comm Coll (WY)
West Hills Comm Coll (CA)
William Rainey Harper Coll (IL)
Willmar Comm Coll (MN)

HUMAN RESOURCES
Brevard Comm Coll (FL)
Chemeketa Comm Coll (OR)
Comm Coll of Allegheny County South Cmps (PA)
Comm Coll of the Air Force (AL)
Cumberland County Coll (NJ)
Essex Comm Coll (MD)
Houston Comm Coll System (TX)
Inver Hills Comm Coll (MN)
Jackson State Comm Coll (TN)
Marian Court Coll (MA)
Moraine Valley Comm Coll (IL)
New Hampshire Tech Inst (NH)
Okaloosa-Walton Comm Coll (FL)
Reading Area Comm Coll (PA)
Rockingham Comm Coll (NC)
St Paul Tech Coll (MN)
Tyler Jr Coll (TX)
Umpqua Comm Coll (OR)

HUMAN SERVICES
Aiken Tech Coll (SC)
Allan Hancock Coll (CA)
American River Coll (CA)
Angelina Coll (TX)
Anne Arundel Comm Coll (MD)
Arizona Western Coll (AZ)
Asnuntuck Comm-Tech Coll (CT)
Atlanta Metropolitan Coll (GA)
Austin Comm Coll (MN)
Austin Comm Coll (TX)
Baltimore City Comm Coll (MD)
Bay de Noc Comm Coll (MI)

Bay Mills Comm Coll (MI)
Berkshire Comm Coll (MA)
Blackfeet Comm Coll (MT)
Blue Mountain Comm Coll (OR)
Borough of Manhattan Comm Coll of City U of NY (NY)
Bowling Green State University–Firelands Coll (OH)
Bristol Comm Coll (MA)
Bronx Comm Coll of City U of NY (NY)
Brookdale Comm Coll (NJ)
Bucks County Comm Coll (PA)
Bunker Hill Comm Coll (MA)
Camden County Coll (NJ)
Cañada Coll (CA)
Castle Coll (NH)
Central Comm College–Hastings Cmps (NE)
Central Ohio Tech Coll (OH)
Central Piedmont Comm Coll (NC)
Central Wyoming Coll (WY)
Chabot Coll (CA)
Champlain Coll (VT)
Charles County Comm Coll (MD)
Chatfield Coll (OH)
Chemeketa Comm Coll (OR)
Chesapeake Coll (MD)
Cisco Jr Coll (TX)
Clackamas Comm Coll (OR)
Clark State Comm Coll (OH)
Cleveland State Comm Coll (TN)
Clovis Comm Coll (NM)
Coll of DuPage (IL)
Coll of Lake County (IL)
Columbia-Greene Comm Coll (NY)
Comm Coll of Allegheny County Allegheny Cmps (PA)
Comm Coll of Allegheny County North Cmps (PA)
Comm Coll of Allegheny County South Cmps (PA)
Comm Coll of Denver (CO)
Comm Coll of Rhode Island (RI)
Comm Coll of Vermont (VT)
Corning Comm Coll (NY)
Cosumnes River Coll (CA)
County Coll of Morris (NJ)
Crafton Hills Coll (CA)
Cuesta Coll (CA)
Cypress Coll (CA)
Danville Area Comm Coll (IL)
Dawson Comm Coll (MT)
Daytona Beach Comm Coll (FL)
Dean Coll (MA)
Delaware Tech & Comm Coll, Jack F Owens Cmps (DE)
Delaware Tech & Comm Coll, Stanton/Wilmington Cmps (DE)
Delaware Tech & Comm Coll, Terry Cmps (DE)
Denmark Tech Coll (SC)
Des Moines Area Comm Coll (IA)
Edison Comm Coll (FL)
Edison State Comm Coll (OH)
Edmonds Comm Coll (WA)
Elgin Comm Coll (IL)
Ellsworth Comm Coll (IA)
El Paso Comm Coll (TX)
Essex County Coll (NJ)
Everett Comm Coll (WA)
Finger Lakes Comm Coll (NY)
Fiorello H LaGuardia Comm Coll of City U of NY (NY)
Flathead Valley Comm Coll (MT)
Florence-Darlington Tech Coll (SC)
Florida Comm Coll at Jacksonville (FL)
Floyd Coll (GA)
Fond du Lac Tribal and Comm Coll (MN)
Fort Belknap Coll (MT)
Fort Berthold Comm Coll (ND)
Fort Peck Comm Coll (MT)
Frederick Comm Coll (MD)
Fresno City Coll (CA)

Fulton-Montgomery Comm Coll (NY)
Gadsden State Comm Coll (AL)
Gateway Comm-Tech Coll (CT)
Genesee Comm Coll (NY)
Glendale Comm Coll (AZ)
Grays Harbor Coll (WA)
Greenfield Comm Coll (MA)
Gulf Coast Comm Coll (FL)
Hagerstown Jr Coll (MD)
Harrisburg Area Comm Coll (PA)
Hartnell Coll (CA)
Herkimer County Comm Coll (NY)
Hesser Coll (NH)
Highland Comm Coll (IL)
Hillsborough Comm Coll (FL)
Hiwassee Coll (TN)
Holyoke Comm Coll (MA)
Housatonic Comm-Tech Coll (CT)
Hudson County Comm Coll (NJ)
Hudson Valley Comm Coll (NY)
Indian River Comm Coll (FL)
Inver Hills Comm Coll (MN)
Iowa Western Comm Coll (IA)
Itasca Comm Coll (MN)
Itawamba Comm Coll (MS)
Ivy Tech State Coll–Central Indiana (IN)
Ivy Tech State Coll–Eastcentral (IN)
Jamestown Comm Coll (NY)
Jefferson Comm Coll (NY)
John Tyler Comm Coll (VA)
Kellogg Comm Coll (MI)
Kent State U, Ashtabula Cmps (OH)
Kent State U, Salem Cmps (OH)
Keystone Coll (PA)
Kilian Comm Coll (SD)
Kirkwood Comm Coll (IA)
Lackawanna Jr Coll (PA)
Lake Area Vocational-Tech Inst (SD)
Lake Land Coll (IL)
Lakeland Comm Coll (OH)
Lakewood Comm Coll (MN)
Lansing Comm Coll (MI)
Lima Tech Coll (OH)
Long Beach City Coll (CA)
Longview Comm Coll (MO)
Los Angeles City Coll (CA)
Luzerne County Comm Coll (PA)
Madison Area Tech Coll (WI)
Manchester Comm-Tech Coll (CT)
Manor Jr Coll (PA)
Marion Tech Coll (OH)
Massachusetts Bay Comm Coll (MA)
Massasoit Comm Coll (MA)
Mendocino Coll (CA)
Merced Coll (CA)
Mesabi Comm Coll (MN)
Metropolitan Comm Coll (NE)
Middlesex Community–Tech Coll (CT)
Midlands Tech Coll (SC)
Milwaukee Area Tech Coll (WI)
Minneapolis Comm Coll (MN)
Mississippi Gulf Coast Comm Coll (MS)
Mitchell Coll (CT)
Mitchell Comm Coll (NC)
Modesto Jr Coll (CA)
Mohawk Valley Comm Coll (NY)
Monroe Comm Coll (NY)
Montgomery Coll (TX)
Montgomery County Comm Coll (PA)
Mount Ida Coll (MA)
Mount Wachusett Comm Coll (MA)
Naugatuck Valley Community–Tech Coll (CT)
Nebraska Indian Comm Coll (NE)
New Hampshire Tech Coll, Berlin (NH)
New Hampshire Tech Coll, Laconia (NH)
New Hampshire Tech Coll, Nashua (NH)

New Hampshire Tech Inst (NH)
New York City Tech Coll of the City U of NY (NY)
Niagara County Comm Coll (NY)
North Central Tech Coll (OH)
Northeast Iowa Comm Coll, Peosta Cmps (IA)
Northern Virginia Comm Coll (VA)
North Harris Coll (TX)
North Idaho Coll (ID)
Northland Comm and Tech Coll (MN)
Northwestern Connecticut Comm-Tech Coll (CT)
Northwest Indian Coll (WA)
Northwest State Comm Coll (OH)
Norwalk Comm-Tech Coll (CT)
Odessa Coll (TX)
Onondaga Comm Coll (NY)
Owensboro Comm Coll (KY)
Pasadena City Coll (CA)
Pasco-Hernando Comm Coll (FL)
Pennsylvania Coll of Tech (PA)
Piedmont Tech Coll (SC)
Pitt Comm Coll (NC)
Porterville Coll (CA)
Pratt Comm Coll and Area Voc Sch (KS)
Quinebaug Valley Comm-Tech Coll (CT)
Quinsigamond Comm Coll (MA)
Raritan Valley Comm Coll (NJ)
Reading Area Comm Coll (PA)
Redlands Comm Coll (OK)
Richmond Comm Coll (NC)
Rochester Comm Coll (MN)
Rock Valley Coll (IL)
Rogue Comm Coll (OR)
Sacramento City Coll (CA)
Saddleback Coll (CA)
Saint Charles County Comm Coll (MO)
St Louis Comm Coll at Florissant Valley (MO)
St Louis Comm Coll at Forest Park (MO)
St Louis Comm Coll at Meramec (MO)
St Petersburg Jr Coll (FL)
Salish Kootenai Coll (MT)
Salt Lake Comm Coll (UT)
San Bernardino Valley Coll (CA)
Sandhills Comm Coll (NC)
San Jose City Coll (CA)
Sauk Valley Comm Coll (IL)
Schenectady County Comm Coll (NY)
Seattle Central Comm Coll (WA)
Shawnee Comm Coll (IL)
Sinclair Comm Coll (OH)
Skagit Valley Coll (WA)
Southeast Comm Coll, Lincoln Cmps (NE)
Southeastern Illinois Coll (IL)
Southside Virginia Comm Coll (VA)
South Suburban Coll (IL)
Southwestern Oregon Comm Coll (OR)
Southwest Virginia Comm Coll (VA)
Springfield Tech Comm Coll (MA)
Standing Rock Coll (ND)
Stark Tech Coll (OH)
State U of NY Coll of Tech at Alfred (NY)
State U of NY Coll of Tech at Canton (NY)
Sullivan County Comm Coll (NY)
Sussex County Comm Coll (NJ)
Tacoma Comm Coll (WA)
Three Rivers Comm-Tech Coll (CT)
Tomball Coll (TX)
Tompkins Cortland Comm Coll (NY)
Tunxis Comm Tech Coll (CT)
Turtle Mountain Comm Coll (ND)

Ulster County Comm Coll (NY)
U of Alaska Anchorage, Matanuska-Susitna Coll (AK)
U of Hawaii–Honolulu Comm Coll (HI)
U of Hawaii–Leeward Comm Coll (HI)
U of Hawaii–Maui Comm Coll (HI)
U of Kentucky, Henderson Comm Coll (KY)
U of Kentucky, Hopkinsville Comm Coll (KY)
U of Maine at Augusta (ME)
U of New Mexico–Gallup Branch (NM)
U of New Mexico–Valencia Cmps (NM)
Utah Valley State Coll (UT)
Ventura Coll (CA)
Virginia Highlands Comm Coll (VA)
Waldorf Coll (IA)
Waubonsee Comm Coll (IL)
Wayne Comm Coll (NC)
Westchester Comm Coll (NY)
Western Nebraska Comm Coll, Scottsbluff (NE)
Western Wisconsin Tech Coll (WI)
Westmoreland County Comm Coll (PA)
West Virginia Northern Comm Coll (WV)
Willmar Comm Coll (MN)
Willmar Tech Coll (MN)
Worthington Comm Coll (MN)
Yuba Coll (CA)

ILLUSTRATION
American Acad of Art (IL)
Art Inst of Fort Lauderdale (FL)
The Art Inst of Philadelphia (PA)
Art Inst of Pittsburgh (PA)
Baltimore City Comm Coll (MD)
Bunker Hill Comm Coll (MA)
Colorado Inst of Art (CO)
Cuyamaca Coll (CA)
Davis Coll (OH)
Harcum Coll (PA)
Houston Comm Coll System (TX)
Hussian Sch of Art (PA)
Lansing Comm Coll (MI)
Los Angeles Pierce Coll (CA)
Macomb Comm Coll (MI)
Maryland Coll of Art and Design (MD)
Mohawk Valley Comm Coll (NY)
Montgomery College–Rockville Cmps (MD)
Mount Ida Coll (MA)
Oakland Comm Coll (MI)
Oklahoma State U, Okmulgee (OK)
Palomar Coll (CA)
Ricks Coll (ID)
Salt Lake Comm Coll (UT)
San Bernardino Valley Coll (CA)
Union County Coll (NJ)
Washtenaw Comm Coll (MI)
Willmar Tech Coll (MN)

INDUSTRIAL ADMINISTRATION
Alamance Comm Coll (NC)
Asnuntuck Comm-Tech Coll (CT)
Black Hawk Coll, Kewanee (IL)
Bowling Green State University–Firelands Coll (OH)
Butler County Comm Coll (PA)
Catawba Valley Comm Coll (NC)
Central Carolina Comm Coll (NC)
City Colls of Chicago, Harold Washington Coll (IL)
City Colls of Chicago, Harry S Truman Coll (IL)
City Colls of Chicago, Richard J Daley Coll (IL)

Cleveland Comm Coll (NC)
Coll of Lake County (IL)
Comm Coll of the Air Force (AL)
Cumberland County Coll (NJ)
Daytona Beach Comm Coll (FL)
Durham Tech Comm Coll (NC)
Elaine P Nunez Comm Coll (LA)
Elgin Comm Coll (IL)
Florida Comm Coll at Jacksonville (FL)
Forsyth Tech Comm Coll (NC)
Fox Valley Tech Coll (WI)
Gaston Coll (NC)
Guilford Tech Comm Coll (NC)
International Business Coll (IN)
Iowa Western Comm Coll (IA)
Ivy Tech State Coll–Eastcentral (IN)
Johnston Comm Coll (NC)
Lake Michigan Coll (MI)
Lehigh Carbon Comm Coll (PA)
Lenoir Comm Coll (NC)
Lima Tech Coll (OH)
Lord Fairfax Comm Coll (VA)
Los Angeles Mission Coll (CA)
Los Medanos Coll (CA)
McDowell Tech Comm Coll (NC)
McHenry County Coll (IL)
Monroe County Comm Coll (MI)
Mt San Antonio Coll (CA)
Okaloosa-Walton Comm Coll (FL)
Oxnard Coll (CA)
Pasadena City Coll (CA)
Prairie State Coll (IL)
Reading Area Comm Coll (PA)
Rowan-Cabarrus Comm Coll (NC)
Salt Lake Comm Coll (UT)
Solano Comm Coll (CA)
Southwestern Coll (CA)
State Tech Inst at Memphis (TN)
Tallahassee Comm Coll (FL)
Terra State Comm Coll (OH)
Three Rivers Comm-Tech Coll (CT)
Tidewater Comm Coll (VA)
Trident Tech Coll (SC)
Triton Coll (IL)
Tulsa Jr Coll (OK)
U of Cincinnati Raymond Walters Coll (OH)
Vance-Granville Comm Coll (NC)
Wallace State Comm Coll (AL)
West Los Angeles Coll (CA)
Wilson Tech Comm Coll (NC)
York Tech Coll (SC)

INDUSTRIAL AND HEAVY EQUIPMENT MAINTENANCE
Alabama Southern Comm Coll, Thomasville (AL)
Allan Hancock Coll (CA)
Anson Comm Coll (NC)
Big Bend Comm Coll (WA)
Brazosport Coll (TX)
Centralia Coll (WA)
Clark Coll (WA)
Coll of Lake County (IL)
Comm Coll of Southern Nevada (NV)
Delaware Tech & Comm Coll, Jack F Owens Cmps (DE)
Del Mar Coll (TX)
Des Moines Area Comm Coll (IA)
Dundalk Comm Coll (MD)
Eastern Maine Tech Coll (ME)
Elgin Comm Coll (IL)
Grays Harbor Coll (WA)
Grayson County Coll (TX)
Guilford Tech Comm Coll (NC)
Hawkeye Comm Coll (IA)
Illinois Eastern Comm Colls, Olney Central Coll (IL)

Associate Degree Programs at Two-Year Colleges
Industrial and Heavy Equipment Maintenance–Insurance

Indian Hills Comm Coll (IA)
Ivy Tech State Coll–Central Indiana (IN)
Ivy Tech State Coll–Columbus (IN)
Ivy Tech State Coll–Eastcentral (IN)
Ivy Tech State Coll–Lafayette (IN)
Ivy Tech State Coll–Northcentral (IN)
Ivy Tech State Coll–Northeast (IN)
Ivy Tech State Coll–Northwest (IN)
Ivy Tech State Coll–Southcentral (IN)
Ivy Tech State Coll–Southeast (IN)
Ivy Tech State Coll–Southwest (IN)
Ivy Tech State Coll–Wabash Valley (IN)
Ivy Tech State Coll–Whitewater (IN)
John M Patterson State Tech Coll (AL)
Kaskaskia Coll (IL)
Lane Comm Coll (OR)
Lansing Comm Coll (MI)
Lawson State Comm Coll (AL)
Lenoir Comm Coll (NC)
Longview Comm Coll (MO)
Los Angeles Trade-Tech Coll (CA)
Lower Columbia Coll (WA)
Marshalltown Comm Coll (IA)
McDowell Tech Comm Coll (NC)
Mesa Comm Coll (AZ)
Metropolitan Comm Coll (NE)
Nebraska Coll of Tech Agriculture (NE)
Northeast State Tech Comm Coll (TN)
North Idaho Coll (ID)
Northwest Iowa Comm Coll (IA)
Oklahoma State U, Okmulgee (OK)
Owens Comm Coll, Toledo (OH)
Pennsylvania Coll of Tech (PA)
Red Rocks Comm Coll (CO)
Rich Mountain Comm Coll (AR)
Robeson Comm Coll (NC)
Rogue Comm Coll (OR)
Salt Lake Comm Coll (UT)
San Jacinto College–Central Cmps (TX)
Shasta Coll (CA)
Sheridan Coll (WY)
South Seattle Comm Coll (WA)
Spokane Comm Coll (WA)
State U of NY Coll of Tech at Alfred (NY)
Texas State Tech Coll–Waco/Marshall Cmps (TX)
Trinidad State Jr Coll (CO)
Vincennes U (IN)
Wake Tech Comm Coll (NC)
Walla Walla Comm Coll (WA)
Waycross Coll (GA)
Western Wisconsin Tech Coll (WI)
Yakima Valley Comm Coll (WA)
York Tech Coll (SC)

INDUSTRIAL ARTS

Allen County Comm Coll (KS)
American River Coll (CA)
Anson Comm Coll (NC)
Art Inst of Pittsburgh (PA)
Bakersfield Coll (CA)
Bucks County Comm Coll (PA)
Butler County Comm Coll (KS)
Cañada Coll (CA)
Carl Albert State Coll (OK)
Casper Coll (WY)
Central Coll (KS)
Cerritos Coll (CA)
Chabot Coll (CA)
Coll of the Sequoias (CA)
Comm Coll of Allegheny County South Cmps (PA)
Comm Coll of Beaver County (PA)
Contra Costa Coll (CA)
Cowley County Comm Coll and Voc-Tech Sch (KS)
Delgado Comm Coll (LA)
Delta Coll (MI)
Dodge City Comm Coll (KS)
Eastern Oklahoma State Coll (OK)
El Camino Coll (CA)
El Paso Comm Coll (TX)
Everett Comm Coll (WA)
Fort Scott Comm Coll (KS)
Fresno City Coll (CA)
Fullerton Coll (CA)
Garden City Comm Coll (KS)
Highland Comm Coll (KS)
Hinds Comm Coll (MS)
Howard Coll (TX)
Hutchinson Comm Coll and Area Vocational Sch (KS)
Itawamba Comm Coll (MS)
Kishwaukee Coll (IL)
Lake Land Coll (IL)
Lake Michigan Coll (MI)
Long Beach City Coll (CA)
Los Angeles Pierce Coll (CA)
Merced Coll (CA)
Modesto Jr Coll (CA)
Mt San Antonio Coll (CA)
Muskegon Comm Coll (MI)
New Mexico Jr Coll (NM)
Northeastern Oklahoma A&M Coll (OK)
Phillips County Comm Coll (AR)
Porterville Coll (CA)
Pratt Comm Coll and Area Voc Sch (KS)
Ricks Coll (ID)
Rockingham Comm Coll (NC)
Rogers State Coll (OK)
Saddleback Coll (CA)
San Diego City Coll (CA)
San Juan Coll (NM)
Santa Monica Coll (CA)
Santa Rosa Jr Coll (CA)
Shoreline Comm Coll (WA)
Sierra Coll (CA)
Skagit Valley Coll (WA)
Southeast Comm Coll, Milford Cmps (NE)
Taft Coll (CA)
Thaddeus Stevens State Sch of Tech (PA)
U of Hawaii–Honolulu Comm Coll (HI)
Vermilion Comm Coll (MN)
Washtenaw Comm Coll (MI)
Waubonsee Comm Coll (IL)
Western Piedmont Comm Coll (NC)
Western Wyoming Comm Coll (WY)

INDUSTRIAL DESIGN

Art Inst of Fort Lauderdale (FL)
The Art Inst of Philadelphia (PA)
Art Inst of Pittsburgh (PA)
Art Inst of Seattle (WA)
Cabrillo Coll (CA)
Chaffey Coll (CA)
Colorado Inst of Art (CO)
Comm Coll of Allegheny County Allegheny Cmps (PA)
Comm Coll of Allegheny County South Cmps (PA)
Delgado Comm Coll (LA)
Iowa Western Comm Coll (IA)
Ivy Tech State Coll–Northeast (IN)
Kishwaukee Coll (IL)
Las Positas Coll (CA)
Milwaukee Area Tech Coll (WI)
Mt San Antonio Coll (CA)
Navarro Coll (TX)
Northwest Iowa Comm Coll (IA)
Oklahoma State U, Oklahoma City (OK)
Orange Coast Coll (CA)
Pima Comm Coll (AZ)
Portland Comm Coll (OR)
Ricks Coll (ID)
Rock Valley Coll (IL)
Southeast Comm Coll, Milford Cmps (NE)
Washtenaw Comm Coll (MI)

INDUSTRIAL ENGINEERING TECHNOLOGY

Allen County Comm Coll (KS)
American Inst of Commerce (IA)
Arizona Western Coll (AZ)
Bakersfield Coll (CA)
Blackhawk Tech Coll (WI)
Blue Ridge Comm Coll (NC)
Brazosport Coll (TX)
Brevard Comm Coll (FL)
Butler County Comm Coll (KS)
Caldwell Comm Coll and Tech Inst (NC)
Catawba Valley Comm Coll (NC)
Catonsville Comm Coll (MD)
Central Ohio Tech Coll (OH)
Chabot Coll (CA)
Charles Stewart Mott Comm Coll (MI)
Chemeketa Comm Coll (OR)
City Coll of San Francisco (CA)
City Colls of Chicago, Harold Washington Coll (IL)
Clackamas Comm Coll (OR)
Clark Coll (WA)
Clark State Comm Coll (OH)
Cleveland State Comm Coll (TN)
Coffeyville Comm Coll (KS)
Coll of the Mainland (TX)
Comm Coll of Allegheny County South Cmps (PA)
Comm Coll of Vermont (VT)
Corning Comm Coll (NY)
Craven Comm Coll (NC)
Crowder Coll (MO)
Cuesta Coll (CA)
Cumberland County Coll (NJ)
Cuyahoga Comm Coll, Metropolitan Cmps (OH)
Danville Area Comm Coll (IL)
De Anza Coll (CA)
Delaware Tech & Comm Coll, Stanton/Wilmington Cmps (DE)
Delaware Tech & Comm Coll, Terry Cmps (DE)
Edison State Comm Coll (OH)
Erie Comm Coll, North Cmps (NY)
Erie Comm Coll, South Cmps (NY)
Fox Valley Tech Coll (WI)
Garden City Comm Coll (KS)
Gaston Coll (NC)
Greenfield Comm Coll (MA)
Greenville Tech Coll (SC)
Halifax Comm Coll (NC)
Harrisburg Area Comm Coll (PA)
Henry Ford Comm Coll (MI)
Hocking Coll (OH)
Hudson Valley Comm Coll (NY)
ICS Ctr for Degree Studies (PA)
Illinois Eastern Comm Colls, Lincoln Trail Coll (IL)
Illinois Valley Comm Coll (IL)
Inst of Electronic Tech (KY)
Ivy Tech State Coll–Kokomo (IN)
Ivy Tech State Coll–Northwest (IN)
Jackson Comm Coll (MI)
Jackson State Comm Coll (TN)
Jefferson Comm Coll (OH)
John C Calhoun State Comm Coll (AL)
Kellogg Comm Coll (MI)
Kent State U, Ashtabula Cmps (OH)
Kent State U, Geauga Cmps (OH)
Kent State U, Trumbull Cmps (OH)
Kent State U, Tuscarawas Cmps (OH)
Kings River Comm Coll (CA)
Lake Land Coll (IL)
Lakeland Comm Coll (OH)
Lake Michigan Coll (MI)
Lansing Comm Coll (MI)
Lenoir Comm Coll (NC)
Lima Tech Coll (OH)
Long Beach City Coll (CA)
Los Angeles Harbor Coll (CA)
Los Angeles Pierce Coll (CA)
Lower Columbia Coll (WA)
Manchester Comm-Tech Coll (CT)
Marion Tech Coll (OH)
McHenry County Coll (IL)
Meridian Comm Coll (MS)
Miami-Dade Comm Coll (FL)
Miami University–Middletown Cmps (OH)
Middlesex County Coll (NJ)
Milwaukee Area Tech Coll (WI)
Mississippi County Comm Coll (AR)
Montcalm Comm Coll (MI)
Moraine Park Tech Coll (WI)
Moraine Valley Comm Coll (IL)
Mt Hood Comm Coll (OR)
Muscatine Comm Coll (IA)
Muskegon Comm Coll (MI)
Nashville State Tech Inst (TN)
Naugatuck Valley Community–Tech Coll (CT)
Navarro Coll (TX)
NEI Coll of Tech (MN)
New Hampshire Tech Inst (NH)
Northcentral Tech Coll (WI)
North Dakota State Coll of Science (ND)
Northeast Mississippi Comm Coll (MS)
Northwest Iowa Comm Coll (IA)
Northwest State Comm Coll (OH)
Oakland Comm Coll (MI)
Oklahoma State U, Oklahoma City (OK)
Owens Comm Coll, Findlay (OH)
Owens Comm Coll, Toledo (OH)
Patrick Henry Comm Coll (VA)
Pennsylvania Coll of Tech (PA)
Piedmont Tech Coll (SC)
Pitt Comm Coll (NC)
Rancho Santiago Coll (CA)
Reading Area Comm Coll (PA)
Rend Lake Coll (IL)
Richland Comm Coll (IL)
Ricks Coll (ID)
Rock Valley Coll (IL)
St Clair County Comm Coll (MI)
St Louis Comm Coll at Forest Park (MO)
Salem Comm Coll (NJ)
Sampson Comm Coll (NC)
San Antonio Coll (TX)
Schenectady County Comm Coll (NY)
Shoreline Comm Coll (WA)
Sinclair Comm Coll (OH)
Southern Arkansas U Tech (AR)
Southern State Comm Coll (OH)
South Suburban Coll (IL)
Southwestern Coll (CA)
Southwestern Oregon Comm Coll (OR)
Springfield Tech Comm Coll (MA)
Stark Tech Coll (OH)
State Tech Inst at Memphis (TN)
State U of NY Coll of A&T at Morrisville (NY)
State U of NY Coll of Tech at Canton (NY)
Tennessee Inst of Electronics (TN)
Terra State Comm Coll (OH)
Three Rivers Comm Coll (MO)
Trident Tech Coll (SC)
Ulster County Comm Coll (NY)
U of Kentucky, Hopkinsville Comm Coll (KY)
Vance-Granville Comm Coll (NC)
Vermilion Comm Coll (MN)
Vincennes University–Jasper Ctr (IN)
Wake Tech Comm Coll (NC)
Washtenaw Comm Coll (MI)
Waukesha County Tech Coll (WI)
Wayne County Comm Coll (MI)
Western Piedmont Comm Coll (NC)
Wright State U, Lake Cmps (OH)
York Tech Coll (SC)

INFORMATION SCIENCE

Alexandria Tech Coll (MN)
Broome Comm Coll (NY)
Bucks County Comm Coll (PA)
Cayuga County Comm Coll (NY)
Chippewa Valley Tech Coll (WI)
City Colls of Chicago, Wilbur Wright Coll (IL)
Coffeyville Comm Coll (KS)
Coll of the Redwoods (CA)
Comm Coll of Allegheny County Allegheny Cmps (PA)
Comm Coll of Allegheny County Boyce Cmps (PA)
Comm Coll of Allegheny County South Cmps (PA)
Comm Coll of Beaver County (PA)
Comm Coll of the Air Force (AL)
Darton Coll (GA)
ECPI Coll of Tech, Hampton (VA)
ECPI Coll of Tech, Virginia Beach (VA)
ECPI Computer Inst, Richmond (VA)
ECPI Computer Inst, Roanoke (VA)
Edmonds Comm Coll (WA)
El Paso Comm Coll (TX)
Florida Comm Coll at Jacksonville (FL)
Harford Comm Coll (MD)
Harrisburg Area Comm Coll (PA)
Henry Ford Comm Coll (MI)
Illinois Eastern Comm Colls, Frontier Comm Coll (IL)
Illinois Eastern Comm Colls, Lincoln Trail Coll (IL)
Illinois Eastern Comm Colls, Olney Central Coll (IL)
Illinois Eastern Comm Colls, Wabash Valley Coll (IL)
Jamestown Business Coll (NY)
Jefferson Coll (MO)
Johnson County Comm Coll (KS)
John Wood Comm Coll (IL)
Luzerne County Comm Coll (PA)
MacCormac Jr Coll (IL)
Massachusetts Bay Comm Coll (MA)
Miami University–Middletown Cmps (OH)
Montgomery Coll (TX)
Montgomery College–Germantown Cmps (MD)
Montgomery College–Rockville Cmps (MD)
Montgomery College–Takoma Park Cmps (MD)
Motlow State Comm Coll (TN)
NEI Coll of Tech (MN)
Nicolet Area Tech Coll (WI)
Northern Essex Comm Coll (MA)
North Harris Coll (TX)
Orange County Comm Coll (NY)
Pellissippi State Tech Comm Coll (TN)
Saddleback Coll (CA)
Shoreline Comm Coll (WA)
South Georgia Coll (GA)
South Puget Sound Comm Coll (WA)
Sussex County Comm Coll (NJ)
Texas State Tech Coll–Harlingen Cmps (TX)
Texas State Tech Coll–Waco/Marshall Cmps (TX)
Tulsa Jr Coll (OK)
U of Cincinnati Clermont Coll (OH)
Waycross Coll (GA)
Westchester Comm Coll (NY)
Westmoreland County Comm Coll (PA)
William Rainey Harper Coll (IL)

INSTRUMENTATION TECHNOLOGY

Albuquerque Tech Vocational Inst (NM)
Belleville Area Coll (IL)
Brazosport Coll (TX)
Butler County Comm Coll (PA)
Cape Fear Comm Coll (NC)
Central Carolina Comm Coll (NC)
Chabot Coll (CA)
Chattanooga State Tech Comm Coll (TN)
Colorado Northwestern Comm Coll (CO)
Comm Coll of Allegheny County South Cmps (PA)
Comm Coll of Rhode Island (RI)
Comm Coll of the Air Force (AL)
Copiah-Lincoln Comm College–Natchez Cmps (MS)
Delaware Tech & Comm Coll, Stanton/Wilmington Cmps (DE)
East Mississippi Comm Coll (MS)
Henry Ford Comm Coll (MI)
John M Patterson State Tech Coll (AL)
John Tyler Comm Coll (VA)
Lenoir Comm Coll (NC)
Lower Columbia Coll (WA)
Miami-Dade Comm Coll (FL)
Mid-State Tech Coll (WI)
Monroe Comm Coll (NY)
National Ed Ctr–Spartan Sch of Aeronautics Cmps (OK)
New River Comm Coll (VA)
North Dakota State Coll of Science (ND)
Northeast State Tech Comm Coll (TN)
Northwest Iowa Comm Coll (IA)
Oklahoma State U, Oklahoma City (OK)
Orangeburg-Calhoun Tech Coll (SC)
Phillips County Comm Coll (AR)
Ranken Tech Coll (MO)
St Cloud Tech Coll (MN)
St Johns River Comm Coll (FL)
Salem Comm Coll (NJ)
San Juan Coll (NM)
Texas State Tech Coll–Harlingen Cmps (TX)
Texas State Tech Coll–Waco/Marshall Cmps (TX)
U of Alaska Anchorage, Kenai Peninsula Coll (AK)
Western Wyoming Comm Coll (WY)
Yakima Valley Comm Coll (WA)

INSURANCE

Alabama Southern Comm Coll, Monroeville (AL)
Austin Comm Coll (TX)
Brookdale Comm Coll (NJ)
Broward Comm Coll (FL)
Central Piedmont Comm Coll (NC)
City Coll of San Francisco (CA)
Columbia-Greene Comm Coll (NY)
County Coll of Morris (NJ)
Daytona Beach Comm Coll (FL)
Delaware County Comm Coll (PA)
Durham Tech Comm Coll (NC)
Enterprise State Jr Coll (AL)
Fayetteville Tech Comm Coll (NC)

Associate Degree Programs at Two-Year Colleges
Insurance–Journalism

Florida Comm Coll at Jacksonville (FL)
Fox Valley Tech Coll (WI)
Fresno City Coll (CA)
Hudson Valley Comm Coll (NY)
Hutchinson Comm Coll and Area Vocational Sch (KS)
Isothermal Comm Coll (NC)
John C Calhoun State Comm Coll (AL)
Lansing Comm Coll (MI)
Lenoir Comm Coll (NC)
Long Beach City Coll (CA)
Macon Coll (GA)
Madison Area Tech Coll (WI)
Merced Coll (CA)
Mesa Comm Coll (AZ)
Metropolitan Comm Coll (NE)
Miami University–Hamilton Cmps (OH)
Mohawk Valley Comm Coll (NY)
Motlow State Comm Coll (TN)
North Dakota State Coll of Science (ND)
Northeast Mississippi Comm Coll (MS)
Northwest Iowa Comm Coll (IA)
Oklahoma City Comm Coll (OK)
Onondaga Comm Coll (NY)
Rancho Santiago Coll (CA)
Richland Comm Coll (IL)
Rockland Comm Coll (NY)
St Catharine Coll (KY)
San Diego City Coll (CA)
Southwestern Tech Coll (MN)
Suffolk County Comm College–Ammerman Cmps (NY)
Sullivan County Comm Coll (NY)
Trinity Valley Comm Coll (TX)
Tulsa Jr Coll (OK)
Vincennes U (IN)
Waukesha County Tech Coll (WI)
Westchester Comm Coll (NY)
William Rainey Harper Coll (IL)

INTERDISCIPLINARY STUDIES
Aiken Tech Coll (SC)
Bowling Green State University–Firelands Coll (OH)
Brevard Coll (NC)
Central Texas Coll (TX)
Central Wyoming Coll (WY)
Chabot Coll (CA)
Columbia-Greene Comm Coll (NY)
Comm Coll of Allegheny County Allegheny Cmps (PA)
Comm Coll of Allegheny County South Cmps (PA)
Del Mar Coll (TX)
Harcum Coll (PA)
Hawkeye Comm Coll (IA)
Hudson Valley Comm Coll (NY)
Jefferson Coll (MO)
Kilian Comm Coll (SD)
Moraine Valley Comm Coll (IL)
Mt San Jacinto Coll (CA)
North Shore Comm Coll (MA)
Pasadena City Coll (CA)
Stark Tech Coll (OH)
State U of NY Coll of Tech at Canton (NY)
State U of NY Coll of Tech at Delhi (NY)
Triton Coll (IL)
The U of Akron–Wayne Coll (OH)
Vermilion Comm Coll (MN)
Volunteer State Comm Coll (TN)
Walters State Comm Coll (TN)
Willmar Comm Coll (MN)

INTERIOR DESIGN
Alexandria Tech Coll (MN)
Allan Hancock Coll (CA)
American Inst of Design (PA)
American River Coll (CA)
Antonelli Coll (OH)
Antonelli Inst (PA)
Arapahoe Comm Coll (CO)
Art Inst of Atlanta (GA)
Art Inst of Dallas (TX)
Art Inst of Fort Lauderdale (FL)
The Art Inst of Houston (TX)
The Art Inst of Philadelphia (PA)
Art Inst of Pittsburgh (PA)
Art Inst of Seattle (WA)
Bakersfield Coll (CA)
Barton County Comm Coll (KS)
Bauder Coll (GA)
Bellevue Comm Coll (WA)
Berkeley Coll (NJ)
Black Hawk Coll, Moline (IL)
Bradley Acad for the Visual Arts (PA)
Brevard Coll (NC)
Brooks Coll (CA)
Broward Comm Coll (FL)
Bryant and Stratton Business Inst, E Hills Cmps, Williamsville (NY)
Cañada Coll (CA)
Carteret Comm Coll (NC)
Catonsville Comm Coll (MD)
Central Coll (KS)
Central Comm College–Platte Cmps (NE)
Central Piedmont Comm Coll (NC)
Chaffey Coll (CA)
City Coll of San Francisco (CA)
Coll of DuPage (IL)
Coll of Marin (CA)
Coll of the Canyons (CA)
Coll of the Desert (CA)
Coll of the Sequoias (CA)
Colorado Inst of Art (CO)
Cosumnes River Coll (CA)
Cuesta Coll (CA)
Cuyahoga Comm Coll, Eastern Cmps (OH)
Cuyahoga Comm Coll, Metropolitan Cmps (OH)
Davis Coll (OH)
Daytona Beach Comm Coll (FL)
Delgado Comm Coll (LA)
Delta Coll (MI)
Dixie Coll (UT)
East Central Coll (MO)
El Camino Coll (CA)
El Centro Coll (TX)
Ellsworth Comm Coll (IA)
El Paso Comm Coll (TX)
Fashion Inst of Design & Merchandising, LA Cmps (CA)
Fashion Inst of Design & Merchandising, SD Cmps (CA)
Fashion Inst of Design & Merchandising, SF Cmps (CA)
Florida Comm Coll at Jacksonville (FL)
Fox Valley Tech Coll (WI)
Fullerton Coll (CA)
Garden City Comm Coll (KS)
Grand Rapids Comm Coll (MI)
Grossmont Coll (CA)
Gwinnett Tech Inst (GA)
Halifax Comm Coll (NC)
Harcum Coll (PA)
Harford Comm Coll (MD)
Hawkeye Comm Coll (IA)
Henry Ford Comm Coll (MI)
Hesser Coll (NH)
Highline Comm Coll (WA)
Hillsborough Comm Coll (FL)
Hiwassee Coll (TN)
Houston Comm Coll System (TX)
Hutchinson Comm Coll and Area Vocational Sch (KS)
Illinois Central Coll (IL)
Indian River Comm Coll (FL)
International Fine Arts Coll (FL)
Inver Hills Comm Coll (MN)
Ivy Tech State Coll–Kokomo (IN)
Ivy Tech State Coll–Northcentral (IN)
Ivy Tech State Coll–Southwest (IN)
Jefferson State Comm Coll (AL)
Johnson County Comm Coll (KS)
Joliet Jr Coll (IL)
Kirkwood Comm Coll (IA)
Las Positas Coll (CA)
LDS Business Coll (UT)
Long Beach City Coll (CA)
Los Angeles Harbor Coll (CA)
Los Angeles Valley Coll (CA)
Louisville Tech Inst (KY)
Lowthian Coll (MN)
Madison Area Tech Coll (WI)
Massachusetts Bay Comm Coll (MA)
Mesa Comm Coll (AZ)
Metropolitan Comm Coll (NE)
Miami-Dade Comm Coll (FL)
Miss Wade's Fashion Merchandising Coll (TX)
Modesto Jr Coll (CA)
Monroe Comm Coll (NY)
Monterey Peninsula Coll (CA)
Montgomery College–Rockville Cmps (MD)
Mount Ida Coll (MA)
Mt San Antonio Coll (CA)
Nassau Comm Coll (NY)
Newbury Coll (MA)
New England Inst of Tech (RI)
Northampton County Area Comm Coll (PA)
Northeastern Oklahoma A&M Coll (OK)
Northeast Mississippi Comm Coll (MS)
Northern Virginia Comm Coll (VA)
North Harris Coll (TX)
Northwest Coll (WY)
Ohlone Coll (CA)
Okaloosa-Walton Comm Coll (FL)
Onondaga Comm Coll (NY)
Orange Coast Coll (CA)
Palm Beach Comm Coll (FL)
Palomar Coll (CA)
Pasadena City Coll (CA)
Pellissippi State Tech Comm Coll (TN)
Pima Comm Coll (AZ)
Prairie State Coll (IL)
Rancho Santiago Coll (CA)
Randolph Comm Coll (NC)
Ricks Coll (ID)
Saddleback Coll (CA)
Sage Jr Coll of Albany (NY)
St Louis Comm Coll at Meramec (MO)
St Petersburg Jr Coll (FL)
St Philip's Coll (TX)
San Bernardino Valley Coll (CA)
San Diego City Coll (CA)
San Diego Mesa Coll (CA)
San Jacinto College–Central Cmps (TX)
San Jacinto College–North Cmps (TX)
San Joaquin Delta Coll (CA)
Santa Monica Coll (CA)
Scott Comm Coll (IA)
Scottsdale Comm Coll (AZ)
Seminole Comm Coll (FL)
Sierra Coll (CA)
Sinclair Comm Coll (OH)
Southern Coll (FL)
Southwestern Coll (CA)
Spokane Falls Comm Coll (WA)
Suffolk County Comm Coll–Eastern Cmps (NY)
Triton Coll (IL)
Tulsa Jr Coll (OK)
Villa Maria Coll of Buffalo (NY)
Vincennes U (IN)
Virginia Coll at Birmingham (AL)
Virginia Marti Coll of Fashion and Art (OH)
Wallace State Comm Coll (AL)
Watkins Inst of Interior Design (TN)
Western Piedmont Comm Coll (NC)
Western Wisconsin Tech Coll (WI)
West Valley Coll (CA)
William Rainey Harper Coll (IL)

INTERNATIONAL BUSINESS
Arapahoe Comm Coll (CO)
Berkeley Coll (NJ)
Berkeley Coll, New York (NY)
Berkeley Coll, White Plains (NY)
Brevard Coll (NC)
Broome Comm Coll (NY)
Catonsville Comm Coll (MD)
Cincinnati State Tech and Comm Coll (OH)
City Colls of Chicago, Harold Washington Coll (IL)
Comm Coll of Philadelphia (PA)
Edmonds Comm Coll (WA)
El Paso Comm Coll (TX)
Erie Comm Coll, City Cmps (NY)
Fisher Coll (MA)
Frederick Comm Coll (MD)
Fullerton Coll (CA)
Gainesville Coll (GA)
Gateway Comm Coll (AZ)
Glendale Comm Coll (AZ)
Grossmont Coll (CA)
Hudson Valley Comm Coll (NY)
Iowa Western Comm Coll (IA)
Keystone Coll (PA)
Kirkwood Comm Coll (IA)
Lansing Comm Coll (MI)
Laredo Comm Coll (TX)
Long Beach City Coll (CA)
Luzerne County Comm Coll (PA)
MacCormac Jr Coll (IL)
Metropolitan Comm Coll (NE)
Mohawk Valley Comm Coll (NY)
Monroe Comm Coll (NY)
Monterey Peninsula Coll (CA)
Montgomery College–Germantown Cmps (MD)
Northern Virginia Comm Coll (VA)
Northland Comm and Tech Coll (MN)
Oakton Comm Coll (IL)
Oklahoma State U, Oklahoma City (OK)
Palomar Coll (CA)
Paradise Valley Comm Coll (AZ)
Pima Comm Coll (AZ)
Raritan Valley Comm Coll (NJ)
Richland Coll (TX)
Rio Salado Comm Coll (AZ)
Rock Valley Coll (IL)
St Louis Comm Coll at Forest Park (MO)
St Paul Tech Coll (MN)
Schiller International U (Switzerland)
Shoreline Comm Coll (WA)
Spokane Falls Comm Coll (WA)
Tacoma Comm Coll (WA)
Tompkins Cortland Comm Coll (NY)
Triton Coll (IL)
Tulsa Jr Coll (OK)
Utah Valley State Coll (UT)
Westchester Comm Coll (NY)
William Rainey Harper Coll (IL)

INTERNATIONAL ECONOMICS
Tulsa Jr Coll (OK)

INTERNATIONAL STUDIES
Allan Hancock Coll (CA)
Brevard Coll (NC)
Bronx Comm Coll of City U of NY (NY)
Clackamas Comm Coll (OR)
Cochise Coll, Douglas (AZ)
Cochise Coll, Sierra Vista (AZ)
County Coll of Morris (NJ)
De Anza Coll (CA)
Edmonds Comm Coll (WA)
Foothill Coll (CA)
Glendale Comm Coll (AZ)
Kalamazoo Valley Comm Coll (MI)
Kellogg Comm Coll (MI)
Macomb Comm Coll (MI)
Massachusetts Bay Comm Coll (MA)
Miami-Dade Comm Coll (FL)
Mohawk Valley Comm Coll (NY)
Naugatuck Valley Community–Tech Coll (CT)
Northern Essex Comm Coll (MA)
Sage Jr Coll of Albany (NY)
Salt Lake Comm Coll (UT)
Santa Barbara City Coll (CA)
Tulsa Jr Coll (OK)
Union County Coll (NJ)

ITALIAN
Casper Coll (WY)
Chabot Coll (CA)
City Colls of Chicago, Harold Washington Coll (IL)
Coll of the Desert (CA)
Comm Coll of Allegheny County Allegheny Cmps (PA)
Contra Costa Coll (CA)
El Camino Coll (CA)
Glendale Comm Coll (AZ)
Los Angeles Mission Coll (CA)
Los Angeles Valley Coll (CA)
Miami-Dade Comm Coll (FL)
Modesto Jr Coll (CA)
San Diego Mesa Coll (CA)
San Joaquin Delta Coll (CA)
Triton Coll (IL)
Tulsa Jr Coll (OK)
West Valley Coll (CA)

JAPANESE
Austin Comm Coll (TX)
City Colls of Chicago, Harold Washington Coll (IL)
Clark Coll (WA)
East Los Angeles Coll (CA)
El Camino Coll (CA)
Everett Comm Coll (WA)
Foothill Coll (CA)
Glendale Comm Coll (AZ)
John Wood Comm Coll (IL)
MiraCosta Coll (CA)
St Catharine Coll (KY)
San Joaquin Delta Coll (CA)
Snow Coll (UT)
Tacoma Comm Coll (WA)
Tulsa Jr Coll (OK)

JAZZ
Brevard Coll (NC)
Comm Coll of Rhode Island (RI)
Iowa Lakes Comm Coll (IA)
Kirkwood Comm Coll (IA)
Miami-Dade Comm Coll (FL)
Northwest Coll (WY)
U of Maine at Augusta (ME)

JEWELRY AND METALSMITHING
Art Inst of Pittsburgh (PA)
Garden City Comm Coll (KS)
Gem City Coll (IL)
Haywood Comm Coll (NC)
Highline Comm Coll (WA)
Inst of American Indian Arts (NM)
John Wood Comm Coll (IL)
Mohave Comm Coll (AZ)
Monterey Peninsula Coll (CA)
Oklahoma State U, Okmulgee (OK)
Palomar Coll (CA)
Paris Jr Coll (TX)
Pasadena City Coll (CA)
Pueblo Comm Coll (CO)
San Antonio Coll (TX)
Virginia Marti Coll of Fashion and Art (OH)

JOURNALISM
Abraham Baldwin Ag Coll (GA)
Allen County Comm Coll (KS)
American River Coll (CA)
Andrew Coll (GA)
Angelina Coll (TX)
Atlanta Metropolitan Coll (GA)
Austin Comm Coll (TX)
Bacone Coll (OK)
Bainbridge Coll (GA)
Bakersfield Coll (CA)
Barton County Comm Coll (KS)
Bay de Noc Comm Coll (MI)
Bee County Coll (TX)
Bismarck State Coll (ND)
Black Hawk Coll, Moline (IL)
Brevard Coll (NC)
Brevard Comm Coll (FL)
Bucks County Comm Coll (PA)
Burlington County Coll (NJ)
Butler County Comm Coll (KS)
Cañada Coll (CA)
Carl Albert State Coll (OK)
Casper Coll (WY)
Central Coll (KS)
Central Texas Coll (TX)
Cerritos Coll (CA)
Chabot Coll (CA)
Chaffey Coll (CA)
Chemeketa Comm Coll (OR)
Citrus Coll (CA)
City Coll of San Francisco (CA)
City Colls of Chicago, Harold Washington Coll (IL)
City Colls of Chicago, Harry S Truman Coll (IL)
City Colls of Chicago, Richard J Daley Coll (IL)
City Colls of Chicago, Wilbur Wright Coll (IL)
Clackamas Comm Coll (OR)
Clark Coll (WA)
Clinton Comm Coll (IA)
Cloud County Comm Coll (KS)
Cochise Coll, Douglas (AZ)
Cochise Coll, Sierra Vista (AZ)
Coffeyville Comm Coll (KS)
Colby Comm Coll (KS)
Coll of Marin (CA)
Coll of San Mateo (CA)
Coll of the Canyons (CA)
Coll of the Desert (CA)
Coll of the Sequoias (CA)
Collin County Comm Coll (TX)
Comm Coll of Allegheny County Allegheny Cmps (PA)
Comm Coll of Allegheny County Boyce Cmps (PA)
Comm Coll of Allegheny County South Cmps (PA)
Connors State Coll (OK)
Contra Costa Coll (CA)
Copiah-Lincoln Comm Coll (MS)
Cosumnes River Coll (CA)
County Coll of Morris (NJ)
Cowley County Comm Coll and Voc-Tech Sch (KS)
Cuesta Coll (CA)
Dalton Coll (GA)
Danville Area Comm Coll (IL)
Darton Coll (GA)
Daytona Beach Comm Coll (FL)
Dean Coll (MA)
De Anza Coll (CA)
Delaware Tech & Comm Coll, Jack F Owens Cmps (DE)
Del Mar Coll (TX)
Delta Coll (MI)
Dodge City Comm Coll (KS)
East Central Coll (MO)
East Central Comm Coll (MS)
Eastern Oklahoma State Coll (OK)
Eastern Wyoming Coll (WY)
East Los Angeles Coll (CA)
El Camino Coll (CA)
Enterprise State Jr Coll (AL)
Everett Comm Coll (WA)
Fiorello H LaGuardia Comm Coll of City U of NY (NY)
Fresno City Coll (CA)
Fullerton Coll (CA)
Gainesville Coll (GA)
Garden City Comm Coll (KS)
Gavilan Coll (CA)
Glendale Comm Coll (AZ)
Golden West Coll (CA)
Gordon Coll (GA)
Grays Harbor Coll (WA)
Grayson County Coll (TX)
Gulf Coast Comm Coll (FL)
Herkimer County Comm Coll (NY)

Associate Degree Programs at Two-Year Colleges
Journalism–Law Enforcement/Police Sciences

Highland Comm Coll (KS)
Highline Comm Coll (WA)
Hill Coll of the Hill Jr Coll District (TX)
Hinds Comm Coll (MS)
Housatonic Comm-Tech Coll (CT)
Howard Coll (TX)
Hutchinson Comm Coll and Area Vocational Sch (KS)
Illinois Valley Comm Coll (IL)
Imperial Valley Coll (CA)
Indian River Comm Coll (FL)
Iowa Central Comm Coll (IA)
Iowa Lakes Comm Coll (IA)
Iowa Western Comm Coll (IA)
Itawamba Comm Coll (MS)
Jefferson Coll (MO)
John A Logan Coll (IL)
Kansas City Kansas Comm Coll (KS)
Kellogg Comm Coll (MI)
Kingsborough Comm Coll of City U of NY (NY)
Kirkwood Comm Coll (IA)
Lake Land Coll (IL)
Lake-Sumter Comm Coll (FL)
Laney Coll (CA)
Lansing Comm Coll (MI)
Laramie County Comm Coll (WY)
Lassen Coll (CA)
Lincoln Land Comm Coll (IL)
Linn-Benton Comm Coll (OR)
Long Beach City Coll (CA)
Lorain County Comm Coll (OH)
Los Angeles City Coll (CA)
Los Angeles Mission Coll (CA)
Los Angeles Pierce Coll (CA)
Los Angeles Trade-Tech Coll (CA)
Los Angeles Valley Coll (CA)
Los Medanos Coll (CA)
Luzerne County Comm Coll (PA)
Macon Coll (GA)
McLennan Comm Coll (TX)
Miami-Dade Comm Coll (FL)
Middle Georgia Coll (GA)
Middlesex County Coll (NJ)
Midland Coll (TX)
MiraCosta Coll (CA)
Modesto Jr Coll (CA)
Monroe County Comm Coll (MI)
Moorpark Coll (CA)
Mt Hood Comm Coll (OR)
Mt San Antonio Coll (CA)
Muscatine Comm Coll (IA)
Navarro Coll (TX)
Northeast Comm Coll (NE)
Northeastern Jr Coll (CO)
Northeastern Oklahoma A&M Coll (OK)
Northeast Mississippi Comm Coll (MS)
Northern Essex Comm Coll (MA)
North Harris Coll (TX)
North Idaho Coll (ID)
Northwest Coll (WY)
Northwest Mississippi Comm Coll (MS)
Ocean County Coll (NJ)
Ohlone Coll (CA)
Oxnard Coll (CA)
Palm Beach Comm Coll (FL)
Palo Alto Coll (TX)
Palomar Coll (CA)
Parkland Coll (IL)
Pasadena City Coll (CA)
Pensacola Jr Coll (FL)
Pikes Peak Comm Coll (CO)
Polk Comm Coll (FL)
Potomac State Coll of West Virginia U (WV)
Rancho Santiago Coll (CA)
Raritan Valley Comm Coll (NJ)
Redlands Comm Coll (OK)
Ricks Coll (ID)
Rose State Coll (OK)
Saddleback Coll (CA)
St Catharine Coll (KY)
St Clair County Comm Coll (MI)
St Louis Comm Coll at Florissant Valley (MO)
St Louis Comm Coll at Meramec (MO)
Salem Comm Coll (NJ)
San Bernardino Valley Coll (CA)
San Diego City Coll (CA)
San Diego Miramar Coll (CA)
San Jacinto College–Central Cmps (TX)
San Joaquin Delta Coll (CA)
San Juan Coll (NM)
Santa Monica Coll (CA)
Seward County Comm Coll (KS)
Sierra Coll (CA)
Skyline Coll (CA)
Solano Comm Coll (CA)
Southeast Comm Coll, Beatrice Cmps (NE)
South Georgia Coll (GA)
South Plains Coll (TX)
SouthWest Collegiate Inst for the Deaf (TX)
Southwestern Coll (CA)
Southwestern Comm Coll (IA)
Southwestern Michigan Coll (MI)
State U of NY Coll of A&T at Morrisville (NY)
Suffolk County Comm College–Ammerman Cmps (NY)
Sussex County Comm Coll (NJ)
Tacoma Comm Coll (WA)
Taft Coll (CA)
Texarkana Coll (TX)
Trinidad State Jr Coll (CO)
Trinity Valley Comm Coll (TX)
Triton Coll (IL)
Tulsa Jr Coll (OK)
Turtle Mountain Comm Coll (ND)
Ulster County Comm Coll (NY)
Umpqua Comm Coll (OR)
Ventura Coll (CA)
Vincennes U (IN)
Waldorf Coll (IA)
Waubonsee Comm Coll (IL)
Western Nebraska Comm Coll, Scottsbluff (NE)
Western Oklahoma State Coll (OK)
Western Texas Coll (TX)
Western Wyoming Comm Coll (WY)
West Los Angeles Coll (CA)
White Pines Coll (NH)
William Rainey Harper Coll (IL)
Willmar Comm Coll (MN)
Young Harris Coll (GA)

LABOR AND INDUSTRIAL RELATIONS

Comm Coll of Allegheny County Allegheny Cmps (PA)
Cumberland County Coll (NJ)
Kingsborough Comm Coll of City U of NY (NY)
Long Beach City Coll (CA)
Los Angeles Trade-Tech Coll (CA)
Macomb Comm Coll (MI)
Mid-State Tech Coll (WI)
Rockingham Comm Coll (NC)
San Jose City Coll (CA)
Sinclair Comm Coll (OH)
Thomas Nelson Comm Coll (VA)
Tulsa Jr Coll (OK)
Vance-Granville Comm Coll (NC)
Wallace State Comm Coll (AL)

LABORATORY ANIMAL MEDICINE

Colby Comm Coll (KS)
Los Angeles Pierce Coll (CA)
Manor Jr Coll (PA)
Mount Ida Coll (MA)
Redlands Comm Coll (OK)
State U of NY Coll of Tech at Delhi (NY)

LABORATORY TECHNOLOGIES

Athens Area Tech Inst (GA)
Augusta Tech Inst (GA)
Bucks County Comm Coll (PA)
Burlington County Coll (NJ)
Camden County Coll (NJ)
Cecil Comm Coll (MD)
Central Maine Tech Coll (ME)
Charles Stewart Mott Comm Coll (MI)
Chippewa Valley Tech Coll (WI)
Comm Coll of Allegheny County South Cmps (PA)
Comm Coll of the Air Force (AL)
County Coll of Morris (NJ)
Darton Coll (GA)
Delaware Tech & Comm Coll, Jack F Owens Cmps (DE)
Eastern Idaho Tech Coll (ID)
Ellsworth Comm Coll (IA)
Fergus Falls Comm Coll (MN)
Florida Comm Coll at Jacksonville (FL)
Frederick Comm Coll (MD)
Harcum Coll (PA)
Harford Comm Coll (MD)
Herkimer County Comm Coll (NY)
Howard Comm Coll (MD)
Hutchinson Comm Coll and Area Vocational Sch (KS)
Iowa Lakes Comm Coll (IA)
Ivy Tech State Coll–Central Indiana (IN)
Jefferson Comm Coll (NY)
Lake Michigan Coll (MI)
Madison Area Tech Coll (WI)
Martin Comm Coll (NC)
Medical Inst of Minnesota (MN)
Mercer County Comm Coll (NJ)
Meridian Comm Coll (MS)
Mohawk Valley Comm Coll (NY)
Northwest-Shoals Comm Coll (AL)
Ohio State U Ag Tech Inst (OH)
Portland Comm Coll (OR)
Reading Area Comm Coll (PA)
Shoreline Comm Coll (WA)
U of Cincinnati Raymond Walters Coll (OH)
Vincennes U (IN)
Western Wyoming Comm Coll (WY)

LABOR STUDIES

Black Hawk Coll, Moline (IL)
Bucks County Comm Coll (PA)
Bunker Hill Comm Coll (MA)
City Coll of San Francisco (CA)
Coll of the Mainland (TX)
Comm Coll of Allegheny County Allegheny Cmps (PA)
Comm Coll of Rhode Island (RI)
Dundalk Comm Coll (MD)
El Camino Coll (CA)
Laney Coll (CA)
Los Angeles Trade-Tech Coll (CA)
Onondaga Comm Coll (NY)
San Diego City Coll (CA)
San Jose City Coll (CA)
Sinclair Comm Coll (OH)
Southwestern Coll of Business, Cincinnati (OH)
Tompkins Cortland Comm Coll (NY)
Tulsa Jr Coll (OK)
Wayne County Comm Coll (MI)

LANDSCAPE ARCHITECTURE/DESIGN

American River Coll (CA)
Anne Arundel Comm Coll (MD)
Antelope Valley Coll (CA)
Art Inst of Pittsburgh (PA)
Butte Coll (CA)
Catonsville Comm Coll (MD)
City Coll of San Francisco (CA)
Coll of Lake County (IL)
Coll of Marin (CA)
Coll of San Mateo (CA)
Columbus State Comm Coll (OH)
Comm Coll of Allegheny County South Cmps (PA)
Edmonds Comm Coll (WA)
Finger Lakes Comm Coll (NY)
Foothill Coll (CA)
Front Range Comm Coll (CO)
Grayson County Coll (TX)
Keystone Coll (PA)
Kirkwood Comm Coll (IA)
Kishwaukee Coll (IL)
Lake City Comm Coll (FL)
Lansing Comm Coll (MI)
Lenoir Comm Coll (NC)
Los Angeles Pierce Coll (CA)
Merced Coll (CA)
Mercer County Comm Coll (NJ)
Merritt Coll (CA)
Miami-Dade Comm Coll (FL)
Monroe Comm Coll (NY)
Mt San Antonio Coll (CA)
North Dakota State University–Bottineau (ND)
Northeast Mississippi Comm Coll (MS)
Oakland Comm Coll (MI)
Oklahoma State U, Oklahoma City (OK)
Onondaga Comm Coll (NY)
Pasadena City Coll (CA)
Pima Comm Coll (AZ)
Portland Comm Coll (OR)
Ricks Coll (ID)
Saddleback Coll (CA)
St Catharine Coll (KY)
San Diego Mesa Coll (CA)
Santa Rosa Jr Coll (CA)
South Seattle Comm Coll (WA)
Southwestern Coll (CA)
Springfield Tech Comm Coll (MA)
State U of NY Coll of A&T at Morrisville (NY)
State U of NY Coll of Tech at Canton (NY)
State U of NY Coll of Tech at Delhi (NY)
State U of NY Coll of Tech at Farmingdale (NY)
Trinidad State Jr Coll (CO)
Triton Coll (IL)
Truckee Meadows Comm Coll (NV)
Tulsa Jr Coll (OK)
Vermont Tech Coll (VT)
Vincennes U (IN)
Wake Tech Comm Coll (NC)
Western Texas Coll (TX)
West Valley Coll (CA)
William Rainey Harper Coll (IL)

LANDSCAPING/GROUNDS MAINTENANCE

Abraham Baldwin Ag Coll (GA)
Anoka-Ramsey Comm Coll (MN)
Brunswick Comm Coll (NC)
Chabot Coll (CA)
Clark Coll (WA)
Clark State Comm Coll (OH)
Coll of DuPage (IL)
Coll of Lake County (IL)
Coll of Marin (CA)
Coll of San Mateo (CA)
Collin County Comm Coll (TX)
Comm Coll of Allegheny County South Cmps (PA)
Comm Coll of Southern Nevada (NV)
Cosumnes River Coll (CA)
County Coll of Morris (NJ)
Cuyahoga Comm Coll, Eastern Cmps (OH)
Cuyamaca Coll (CA)
Danville Area Comm Coll (IL)
DeKalb Coll (GA)
Edmonds Comm Coll (WA)
Grayson County Coll (TX)
Hinds Comm Coll (MS)
Horry-Georgetown Tech Coll (SC)
Inver Hills Comm Coll (MN)
James H Faulkner State Comm Coll (AL)
Joliet Jr Coll (IL)
Kishwaukee Coll (IL)
Los Angeles Pierce Coll (CA)
Merritt Coll (CA)
Milwaukee Area Tech Coll (WI)
MiraCosta Coll (CA)
Northeastern Jr Coll (CO)
Ohio State U Ag Tech Inst (OH)
Owens Comm Coll, Toledo (OH)
Pennsylvania Coll of Tech (PA)
St Catharine Coll (KY)
Sandhills Comm Coll (NC)
Southern Maine Tech Coll (ME)
South Puget Sound Comm Coll (WA)
South Seattle Comm Coll (WA)
Southwestern Coll (CA)
Spokane Comm Coll (WA)
State U of NY Coll of A&T at Cobleskill (NY)
State U of NY Coll of A&T at Morrisville (NY)
State U of NY Coll of Tech at Alfred (NY)
State U of NY Coll of Tech at Delhi (NY)
Triton Coll (IL)
Vermont Tech Coll (VT)
Walla Walla Comm Coll (WA)
William Rainey Harper Coll (IL)

LAND USE MANAGEMENT AND RECLAMATION

Colorado Mountn Coll, Timberline Cmps (CO)
Fullerton Coll (CA)
Merritt Coll (CA)
Mountain Empire Comm Coll (VA)
St Catharine Coll (KY)
Southwest Virginia Comm Coll (VA)
Vermilion Comm Coll (MN)

LASER TECHNOLOGIES

Central Carolina Comm Coll (NC)
Cincinnati State Tech and Comm Coll (OH)
Indian Hills Comm Coll (IA)
Ivy Tech State Coll–Wabash Valley (IN)
Northcentral Tech Coll (WI)
Queensborough Comm Coll of City U of NY (NY)
Springfield Tech Comm Coll (MA)
Vincennes U (IN)

LATIN

Tulsa Jr Coll (OK)

LATIN AMERICAN STUDIES

City Coll of San Francisco (CA)
Cypress Coll (CA)
Fullerton Coll (CA)
Miami-Dade Comm Coll (FL)
Pasadena City Coll (CA)
San Diego City Coll (CA)

LAW ENFORCEMENT/ POLICE SCIENCES

Abraham Baldwin Ag Coll (GA)
Adirondack Comm Coll (NY)
Aims Comm Coll (CO)
Alamance Comm Coll (NC)
Alexandria Tech Coll (MN)
Allan Hancock Coll (CA)
Allen County Comm Coll (KS)
Alpena Comm Coll (MI)
Alvin Comm Coll (TX)
Anne Arundel Comm Coll (MD)
Antelope Valley Coll (CA)
Arapahoe Comm Coll (CO)
Arizona Western Coll (AZ)
Asheville-Buncombe Tech Comm Coll (NC)
Atlantic Comm Coll (NJ)
Austin Comm Coll (MN)
Austin Comm Coll (TX)
Bakersfield Coll (CA)
Baltimore City Comm Coll (MD)
Barstow Coll (CA)
Barton County Comm Coll (KS)
Bay de Noc Comm Coll (MI)
Beaufort County Comm Coll (NC)
Bee County Coll (TX)
Belleville Area Coll (IL)
Bellevue Comm Coll (WA)
Berkshire Comm Coll (MA)
Black Hawk Coll, Moline (IL)
Blackhawk Tech Coll (WI)
Bladen Comm Coll (NC)
Blue Mountain Comm Coll (OR)
Bossier Parish Comm Coll (LA)
Brazosport Coll (TX)
Brevard Comm Coll (FL)
Broward Comm Coll (FL)
Bucks County Comm Coll (PA)
Bunker Hill Comm Coll (MA)
Burlington County Coll (NJ)
Butler County Comm Coll (KS)
Butte Coll (CA)
Carl Sandburg Coll (IL)
Casper Coll (WY)
Catonsville Comm Coll (MD)
Cayuga County Comm Coll (NY)
Cecil Comm Coll (MD)
Central Carolina Comm Coll (NC)
Central Florida Comm Coll (FL)
Central Ohio Tech Coll (OH)
Central Piedmont Comm Coll (NC)
Central Texas Coll (TX)
Central Virginia Comm Coll (VA)
Cerritos Coll (CA)
Chabot Coll (CA)
Champlain Coll (VT)
Charles Stewart Mott Comm Coll (MI)
Chattahoochee Tech Inst (GA)
Chemeketa Comm Coll (OR)
Chippewa Valley Tech Coll (WI)
Cisco Jr Coll (TX)
Citrus Coll (CA)
City Coll of San Francisco (CA)
City Colls of Chicago, Harold Washington Coll (IL)
City Colls of Chicago, Harry S Truman Coll (IL)
City Colls of Chicago, Richard J Daley Coll (IL)
City Colls of Chicago, Wilbur Wright Coll (IL)
Clackamas Comm Coll (OR)
Clark Coll (WA)
Clark State Comm Coll (OH)
Cleveland State Comm Coll (TN)
Clinton Comm Coll (IA)
Clinton Comm Coll (NY)
Cochise Coll, Douglas (AZ)
Cochise Coll, Sierra Vista (AZ)
Coll of DuPage (IL)
Coll of Marin (CA)
Coll of San Mateo (CA)
Coll of Southern Idaho (ID)
Coll of the Canyons (CA)
Coll of the Desert (CA)
Coll of the Sequoias (CA)
Coll of the Siskiyous (CA)
Colorado Northwestern Comm Coll (CO)
Columbia Basin Coll (WA)
Columbus State Comm Coll (OH)
Comm Coll of Allegheny County Boyce Cmps (PA)
Comm Coll of Allegheny County South Cmps (PA)
Comm Coll of Beaver County (PA)
Comm Coll of Rhode Island (RI)
Comm Coll of the Air Force (AL)
Connors State Coll (OK)
Contra Costa Coll (CA)
Copiah-Lincoln Comm Coll (MS)

Peterson's Guide to Two-Year Colleges 1997
97

Associate Degree Programs at Two-Year Colleges
Law Enforcement/Police Sciences–Legal Secretarial Studies

Cowley County Comm Coll and Voc-Tech Sch (KS)
Cumberland County Coll (NJ)
Cuyahoga Comm Coll, Metropolitan Cmps (OH)
Cuyahoga Comm Coll, Western Cmps (OH)
Danville Area Comm Coll (IL)
Davidson County Comm Coll (NC)
Dawson Comm Coll (MT)
Daytona Beach Comm Coll (FL)
Dean Coll (MA)
De Anza Coll (CA)
Delaware Tech & Comm Coll, Stanton/Wilmington Cmps (DE)
Del Mar Coll (TX)
Delta Coll (MI)
Des Moines Area Comm Coll (IA)
Durham Tech Comm Coll (NC)
Dyersburg State Comm Coll (TN)
East Arkansas Comm Coll (AR)
East Central Coll (MO)
Eastern Arizona Coll (AZ)
Eastern Wyoming Coll (WY)
East Los Angeles Coll (CA)
East Mississippi Comm Coll (MS)
Edison State Comm Coll (OH)
El Camino Coll (CA)
El Centro Coll (TX)
Elgin Comm Coll (IL)
El Paso Comm Coll (TX)
Enterprise State Jr Coll (AL)
Erie Comm Coll, North Cmps (NY)
Essex County Coll (NJ)
Everett Comm Coll (WA)
Feather River Comm Coll District (CA)
Fergus Falls Comm Coll (MN)
Finger Lakes Comm Coll (NY)
Floyd Coll (GA)
Fond du Lac Tribal and Comm Coll (MN)
Forsyth Tech Comm Coll (NC)
Fox Valley Tech Coll (WI)
Frank Phillips Coll (TX)
Fullerton Coll (CA)
Galveston Coll (TX)
Garden City Comm Coll (KS)
Gavilan Coll (CA)
George Corley Wallace State Comm Coll, Selma (AL)
George C Wallace State Comm Coll, Dothan (AL)
Germanna Comm Coll (VA)
Glendale Comm Coll (AZ)
Gloucester County Coll (NJ)
Golden West Coll (CA)
Grand Rapids Comm Coll (MI)
Grays Harbor Coll (WA)
Grayson County Coll (TX)
Green River Comm Coll (WA)
Greenville Tech Coll (SC)
Grossmont Coll (CA)
Guilford Tech Comm Coll (NC)
Hagerstown Jr Coll (MD)
Halifax Comm Coll (NC)
Harrisburg Area Comm Coll (PA)
Hawkeye Comm Coll (IA)
Henry Ford Comm Coll (MI)
Herkimer County Comm Coll (NY)
Hesser Coll (NH)
Hibbing Comm Coll (MN)
Highland Comm Coll (KS)
Highline Comm Coll (WA)
Hill Coll of the Hill Jr Coll District (TX)
Hillsborough Comm Coll (FL)
Hinds Comm Coll (MS)
Hocking Coll (OH)
Holyoke Comm Coll (MA)
Houston Comm Coll System (TX)
Howard Coll (TX)
Hutchinson Comm Coll and Area Vocational Sch (KS)
Illinois Central Coll (IL)
Illinois Eastern Comm Colls, Olney Central Coll (IL)
Illinois Valley Comm Coll (IL)
Imperial Valley Coll (CA)
Indian River Comm Coll (FL)
Inter American U of PR, Guayama Cmps (PR)
Inver Hills Comm Coll (MN)
Iowa Central Comm Coll (IA)
Iowa Lakes Comm Coll (IA)
Iowa Western Comm Coll (IA)
Isothermal Comm Coll (NC)
Itawamba Comm Coll (MS)
Jackson Comm Coll (MI)
Jamestown Comm Coll (NY)
Jefferson Comm Coll (OH)
Jefferson Davis Comm Coll (AL)
Jefferson State Comm Coll (AL)
John C Calhoun State Comm Coll (AL)
Johnson County Comm Coll (KS)
Johnston Comm Coll (NC)
John Tyler Comm Coll (VA)
John Wood Comm Coll (IL)
Joliet Jr Coll (IL)
Jones County Jr Coll (MS)
J Sargeant Reynolds Comm Coll (VA)
Kalamazoo Valley Comm Coll (MI)
Kankakee Comm Coll (IL)
Kansas City Kansas Comm Coll (KS)
Kaskaskia Coll (IL)
Kellogg Comm Coll (MI)
Kent State U, Ashtabula Cmps (OH)
Kent State U, Tuscarawas Cmps (OH)
Kings River Comm Coll (CA)
Kirkwood Comm Coll (IA)
Kishwaukee Coll (IL)
Labette Comm Coll (KS)
Lake City Comm Coll (FL)
Lake Land Coll (IL)
Lakeland Comm Coll (OH)
Lake Michigan Coll (MI)
Lake Tahoe Comm Coll (CA)
Lansing Comm Coll (MI)
Laramie County Comm Coll (WY)
Laredo Comm Coll (TX)
Las Positas Coll (CA)
Lassen Coll (CA)
Lawson State Comm Coll (AL)
Lee Coll (TX)
Lehigh Carbon Comm Coll (PA)
Lenoir Comm Coll (NC)
Lewis and Clark Comm Coll (IL)
Lima Tech Coll (OH)
Lincoln Land Comm Coll (IL)
Longview Comm Coll (MO)
Lorain County Comm Coll (OH)
Los Angeles City Coll (CA)
Los Angeles Harbor Coll (CA)
Los Angeles Mission Coll (CA)
Los Angeles Southwest Coll (CA)
Los Angeles Valley Coll (CA)
Louisiana State U at Eunice (LA)
Lower Columbia Coll (WA)
Macomb Comm Coll (MI)
Macon Coll (GA)
Madison Area Tech Coll (WI)
Manchester Comm-Tech Coll (CT)
Maple Woods Comm Coll (MO)
Massachusetts Bay Comm Coll (MA)
Massasoit Comm Coll (MA)
Mayland Comm Coll (NC)
McLennan Comm Coll (TX)
Mendocino Coll (CA)
Merced Coll (CA)
Mercer County Comm Coll (NJ)
Meridian Comm Coll (MS)
Mesabi Comm Coll (MN)
Metropolitan Comm Coll (NE)
Miami-Dade Comm Coll (FL)
Middlesex County Coll (NJ)
Midland Coll (TX)
Mid-State Tech Coll (WI)
Milwaukee Area Tech Coll (WI)
Mineral Area Coll (MO)
Minneapolis Comm Coll (MN)
MiraCosta Coll (CA)
Mississippi Gulf Coast Comm Coll (MS)
Moberly Area Comm Coll (MO)
Modesto Jr Coll (CA)
Mohave Comm Coll (AZ)
Monroe Comm Coll (NY)
Monroe County Comm Coll (MI)
Monterey Peninsula Coll (CA)
Montgomery College–Rockville Cmps (MD)
Montgomery Comm Coll (NC)
Montgomery County Comm Coll (PA)
Moorpark Coll (CA)
Morton Coll (IL)
Mountain Empire Comm Coll (VA)
Mt San Antonio Coll (CA)
Mt San Jacinto Coll (CA)
Napa Valley Coll (CA)
Nash Comm Coll (NC)
Navarro Coll (TX)
Neosho County Comm Coll (KS)
New Mexico Jr Coll (NM)
New Mexico Military Inst (NM)
New Mexico State University–Alamogordo (NM)
New River Comm Coll (VA)
Nicolet Area Tech Coll (WI)
Normandale Comm Coll (MN)
North Central Michigan Coll (MI)
Northcentral Tech Coll (WI)
North Central Texas Coll (TX)
North Dakota State Coll of Science (ND)
Northeast Comm Coll (NE)
Northeastern Jr Coll (CO)
Northeast Mississippi Comm Coll (MS)
Northern Virginia Comm Coll (VA)
North Harris Coll (TX)
North Hennepin Comm Coll (MN)
North Idaho Coll (ID)
North Iowa Area Comm Coll (IA)
Northland Comm and Tech Coll (MN)
Northwestern Connecticut Comm-Tech Coll (CT)
Northwestern Michigan Coll (MI)
Northwest Mississippi Comm Coll (MS)
Northwest-Shoals Comm Coll (AL)
Oakland Comm Coll (MI)
Oakton Comm Coll (IL)
Odessa Coll (TX)
Ohlone Coll (CA)
Okaloosa-Walton Comm Coll (FL)
Oklahoma State U, Oklahoma City (OK)
Orangeburg-Calhoun Tech Coll (SC)
Orange County Comm Coll (NY)
Owens Comm Coll, Findlay (OH)
Owens Comm Coll, Toledo (OH)
Palau Comm Coll (PW)
Palm Beach Comm Coll (FL)
Palomar Coll (CA)
Palo Verde Coll (CA)
Parkland Coll (IL)
Penn Valley Comm Coll (MO)
Pensacola Jr Coll (FL)
Piedmont Virginia Comm Coll (VA)
Pitt Comm Coll (NC)
Polk Comm Coll (FL)
Porterville Coll (CA)
Prairie State Coll (IL)
Pueblo Comm Coll (CO)
Quincy Coll (MA)
Rancho Santiago Coll (CA)
Rappahannock Comm Coll (VA)
Raritan Valley Comm Coll (NJ)
Redlands Comm Coll (OK)
Richland Comm Coll (IL)
Ricks Coll (ID)
Rio Salado Comm Coll (AZ)
Riverside Comm Coll (CA)
Roane State Comm Coll (TN)
Robeson Comm Coll (NC)
Rochester Comm Coll (MN)
Rockingham Comm Coll (NC)
Rogers State Coll (OK)
Saint Charles County Comm Coll (MO)
St Louis Comm Coll at Florissant Valley (MO)
St Louis Comm Coll at Meramec (MO)
St Petersburg Jr Coll (FL)
Salt Lake Comm Coll (UT)
San Antonio Coll (TX)
San Bernardino Valley Coll (CA)
Sandhills Comm Coll (NC)
San Diego Miramar Coll (CA)
San Jacinto College–Central Cmps (TX)
San Jacinto College–North Cmps (TX)
San Joaquin Delta Coll (CA)
San Juan Coll (NM)
Santa Barbara City Coll (CA)
Santa Fe Comm Coll (FL)
Santa Monica Coll (CA)
Santa Rosa Jr Coll (CA)
Sauk Valley Comm Coll (IL)
Scott Comm Coll (IA)
Seminole Jr Coll (OK)
Seward County Comm Coll (KS)
Shawnee Comm Coll (IL)
Sheridan Coll (WY)
Shoreline Comm Coll (WA)
Sierra Coll (CA)
Sinclair Comm Coll (OH)
Skagit Valley Coll (WA)
Skyline Coll (CA)
Southeastern Illinois Coll (IL)
Southern Maine Tech Coll (ME)
South Plains Coll (TX)
South Suburban Coll (IL)
Southwestern Coll (CA)
Southwestern Comm Coll (NC)
Southwest Virginia Comm Coll (VA)
Spartanburg Methodist Coll (SC)
Spokane Comm Coll (WA)
Spoon River Coll (IL)
Springfield Tech Comm Coll (MA)
State Fair Comm Coll (MO)
State U of NY Coll of Tech at Canton (NY)
State U of NY Coll of Tech at Farmingdale (NY)
Suffolk County Comm College–Ammerman Cmps (NY)
Suffolk County Comm Coll–Eastern Cmps (NY)
Sullivan County Comm Coll (NY)
Tacoma Comm Coll (WA)
Temple Coll (TX)
Terra State Comm Coll (OH)
Texarkana Coll (TX)
Texas Southmost Coll (TX)
Thomas Nelson Comm Coll (VA)
Three Rivers Comm Coll (MO)
Treasure Valley Comm Coll (OR)
Trinidad State Jr Coll (CO)
Trinity Valley Comm Coll (TX)
Triton Coll (IL)
Truckee Meadows Comm Coll (NV)
Tulsa Jr Coll (OK)
Tyler Jr Coll (TX)
U of Alaska Southeast, Sitka Cmps (AK)
U of Hawaii–Honolulu Comm Coll (HI)
U of Kentucky, Hopkinsville Comm Coll (KY)
U of New Mexico–Gallup Branch (NM)
U of North Dakota–Lake Region (ND)
Vance-Granville Comm Coll (NC)
Vermilion Comm Coll (MN)
Victoria Coll (TX)
Victor Valley Coll (CA)
Vincennes U (IN)
Vincennes University–Jasper Ctr (IN)
Virginia Highlands Comm Coll (VA)
Wake Tech Comm Coll (NC)
Waldorf Coll (IA)
Wallace State Comm Coll (AL)
Washtenaw Comm Coll (MI)
Waukesha County Tech Coll (WI)
Wayne Comm Coll (NC)
Wayne County Comm Coll (MI)
Westchester Comm Coll (NY)
Western Dakota Tech Inst (SD)
Western Iowa Tech Comm Coll (IA)
Western Nevada Comm Coll (NV)
Western Oklahoma State Coll (OK)
Western Piedmont Comm Coll (NC)
Western Texas Coll (TX)
Western Wisconsin Tech Coll (WI)
Western Wyoming Comm Coll (WY)
West Los Angeles Coll (CA)
Westmoreland County Comm Coll (PA)
West Shore Comm Coll (MI)
West Valley Coll (CA)
Whatcom Comm Coll (WA)
William Rainey Harper Coll (IL)
Willmar Comm Coll (MN)
Wisconsin Indianhead Tech Coll, Rice Lake Cmps (WI)
Wor-Wic Comm Coll (MD)
Wytheville Comm Coll (VA)
Yakima Valley Comm Coll (WA)
Yavapai Coll (AZ)
Yuba Coll (CA)

LEGAL SECRETARIAL STUDIES

Acad of Business Coll (AZ)
Alexandria Tech Coll (MN)
Allan Hancock Coll (CA)
Allegany Comm Coll (MD)
Allen County Comm Coll (KS)
Allentown Business Sch (PA)
Alvin Comm Coll (TX)
American Inst of Business (IA)
American Inst of Commerce (IA)
American River Coll (CA)
Andover Coll (ME)
Anoka-Ramsey Comm Coll (MN)
Anson Comm Coll (NC)
Aquinas Coll at Milton (MA)
Aquinas Coll at Newton (MA)
Arapahoe Comm Coll (CO)
Austin Comm Coll (TX)
Baker Coll of Jackson (MI)
Bakersfield Coll (CA)
Baltimore City Comm Coll (MD)
Bay State Coll (MA)
Beal Coll (ME)
Bee County Coll (TX)
Belleville Area Coll (IL)
Berean Inst (PA)
Bergen Comm Coll (NJ)
Big Bend Comm Coll (WA)
Bismarck State Coll (ND)
Black Hawk Coll, Kewanee (IL)
Black Hawk Coll, Moline (IL)
Blackhawk Tech Coll (WI)
Blinn Coll (TX)
Bradford Sch (OH)
Bramson ORT Tech Inst (NY)
Brazosport Coll (TX)
Briarwood Coll (CT)
Bristol Comm Coll (MA)
Broward Comm Coll (FL)
Bryant and Stratton Business Inst, Albany (NY)
Bryant and Stratton Business Inst, Buffalo (NY)
Bryant and Stratton Business Inst, Cicero (NY)
Bryant and Stratton Business Inst, Rochester (NY)
Bryant and Stratton Business Inst, Syracuse (NY)
Bryant and Stratton Business Inst, E Hills Cmps, Williamsville (NY)
Bryant and Stratton Coll, Parma (OH)
Bucks County Comm Coll (PA)
Bunker Hill Comm Coll (MA)
Burlington County Coll (NJ)
Butler County Comm Coll (KS)
Butler County Comm Coll (PA)
Butte Coll (CA)
Cambria-Rowe Business Coll (PA)
Cape Cod Comm Coll (MA)
Carl Albert State Coll (OK)
Carteret Comm Coll (NC)
Casco Bay Coll (ME)
Casper Coll (WY)
Castle Coll (NH)
Catonsville Comm Coll (MD)
Cedar Valley Coll (TX)
Central Carolina Comm Coll (NC)
Central City Business Inst (NY)
Central Coll (KS)
Central Comm College–Grand Island Cmps (NE)
Central Comm College–Hastings Cmps (NE)
Central Comm College–Platte Cmps (NE)
Central Florida Comm Coll (FL)
Centralia Coll (WA)
Central Lakes Coll (MN)
Central Oregon Comm Coll (OR)
Central Pennsylvania Business Sch (PA)
Central Piedmont Comm Coll (NC)
Central Texas Coll (TX)
Cerritos Coll (CA)
Chabot Coll (CA)
Chaffey Coll (CA)
Champlain Coll (VT)
Chaparral Career Coll (AZ)
Charles Stewart Mott Comm Coll (MI)
Chattahoochee Valley State Comm Coll (AL)
Chattanooga State Tech Comm Coll (TN)
Chemeketa Comm Coll (OR)
Chesapeake Coll (MD)
Chicago Coll of Commerce (IL)
Chippewa Valley Tech Coll (WI)
Churchman Business Sch (PA)
City Coll of San Francisco (CA)
Clark Coll (WA)
Clatsop Comm Coll (OR)
Coastal Carolina Comm Coll (NC)
Cochise Coll, Douglas (AZ)
Cochise Coll, Sierra Vista (AZ)
Coffeyville Comm Coll (KS)
Colby Comm Coll (KS)
Coll of DuPage (IL)
Coll of The Albemarle (NC)
Coll of the Redwoods (CA)
Collin County Comm Coll (TX)
Columbus State Comm Coll (OH)
Commonwealth Business Coll, LaPorte (IN)
Commonwealth Business Coll, Merrillville (IN)
Comm Coll of Allegheny County Allegheny Cmps (PA)
Comm Coll of Allegheny County North Cmps (PA)
Comm Coll of Allegheny County South Cmps (PA)
Comm Coll of Denver (CO)
Comm Coll of Philadelphia (PA)
Comm Coll of Rhode Island (RI)
Comm Coll of Southern Nevada (NV)
Craven Comm Coll (NC)
Crowder Coll (MO)
Cumberland County Coll (NJ)

Associate Degree Programs at Two-Year Colleges
Legal Secretarial Studies–Liberal Arts/General Studies

Dabney S Lancaster Comm Coll (VA)
Danville Area Comm Coll (IL)
Darton Coll (GA)
Davis Coll (OH)
Daytona Beach Comm Coll (FL)
DeKalb Tech Inst (GA)
Delaware Tech & Comm Coll, Jack F Owens Cmps (DE)
Del Mar Coll (TX)
Delta Coll (MI)
Des Moines Area Comm Coll (IA)
Dodge City Comm Coll (KS)
Draughons Jr Coll (AL)
Draughons Jr Coll (KY)
DuBois Business Coll (PA)
Duff's Business Inst (PA)
Dundalk Comm Coll (MD)
East Central Coll (MO)
Eastern Idaho Tech Coll (ID)
Eastern Oklahoma State Coll (OK)
Eastern Wyoming Coll (WY)
Eastfield Coll (TX)
East Los Angeles Coll (CA)
Edmonds Comm Coll (WA)
Ellsworth Comm Coll (IA)
Enterprise State Jr Coll (AL)
Erie Business Ctr, Main (PA)
Erie Business Ctr South (PA)
Fergus Falls Comm Coll (MN)
Finger Lakes Comm Coll (NY)
Fiorello H LaGuardia Comm Coll of City U of NY (NY)
Fisher Coll (MA)
Florida Keys Comm Coll (FL)
Florida National Coll (FL)
Fort Scott Comm Coll (KS)
Fox Valley Tech Coll (WI)
Frank Phillips Coll (TX)
Frederick Comm Coll (MD)
Fresno City Coll (CA)
Front Range Comm Coll (CO)
Fullerton Coll (CA)
Fulton-Montgomery Comm Coll (NY)
Gadsden State Comm Coll (AL)
Garden City Comm Coll (KS)
Gaston Coll (NC)
Gateway Comm-Tech Coll (CT)
Gavilan Coll (CA)
Gem City Coll (IL)
Gloucester County Coll (NJ)
Gogebic Comm Coll (MI)
Golden West Coll (CA)
Grand Rapids Comm Coll (MI)
Grays Harbor Coll (WA)
Grayson County Coll (TX)
Green River Comm Coll (WA)
Grossmont Coll (CA)
Hagerstown Business Coll (MD)
Hamilton Business Coll (IA)
Harrisburg Area Comm Coll (PA)
Heald Business Coll, Concord (CA)
Heald Business Coll, Fresno (CA)
Heald Business Coll, Hayward (CA)
Heald Business Coll, Rancho Cordova (CA)
Heald Business Coll, San Francisco (CA)
Heald Business Coll (HI)
Helena Coll of Tech of The U of Montana (MT)
Henry Ford Comm Coll (MI)
Herkimer County Comm Coll (NY)
Herzing Coll of Business and Tech (AL)
Hesser Coll (NH)
Hibbing Comm Coll (MN)
Highland Comm Coll (KS)
Highland Park Comm Coll (MI)
Highline Comm Coll (WA)
Hillsborough Comm Coll (FL)
Hocking Coll (OH)
Holyoke Comm Coll (MA)
Howard Comm Coll (MD)
Huntington Jr Coll of Business (WV)
Hutchinson Comm Coll and Area Vocational Sch (KS)
ICM Sch of Business (PA)
Indiana Business Coll (IN)
Interboro Inst (NY)
Inver Hills Comm Coll (MN)
Iowa Lakes Comm Coll (IA)
Iowa Western Comm Coll (IA)
Itasca Comm Coll (MN)
Jackson Comm Coll (MI)
James H Faulkner State Comm Coll (AL)
Jamestown Business Coll (NY)
Jefferson Coll (MO)
Jefferson Comm Coll (OH)
John A Logan Coll (IL)
Johnson County Comm Coll (KS)
John Wood Comm Coll (IL)
J Sargeant Reynolds Comm Coll (VA)
Kalamazoo Valley Comm Coll (MI)
Kankakee Comm Coll (IL)
Kansas City Kansas Comm Coll (KS)
Kaskaskia Coll (IL)
Katharine Gibbs Sch (CT)
Katharine Gibbs Sch (MA)
Kellogg Comm Coll (MI)
Kelsey Jenney Coll (CA)
Kent State U, Ashtabula Cmps (OH)
Kent State U, East Liverpool Cmps (OH)
Kentucky Coll of Business, Lexington (KY)
Kilian Comm Coll (SD)
Kirkwood Comm Coll (IA)
Kirtland Comm Coll (MI)
Kishwaukee Coll (IL)
Knoxville Business Coll (TN)
Labette Comm Coll (KS)
Lackawanna Jr Coll (PA)
Lake Land Coll (IL)
Lake Michigan Coll (MI)
Lamar Comm Coll (CO)
Lamar University–Port Arthur (TX)
Lamson Jr Coll, Mesa (AZ)
Lane Comm Coll (OR)
Lansing Comm Coll (MI)
Laramie County Comm Coll (WY)
Lassen Coll (CA)
Lawson State Comm Coll (AL)
LDS Business Coll (UT)
Lee Coll (TX)
Lehigh Carbon Comm Coll (PA)
Lenoir Comm Coll (NC)
Lewis and Clark Comm Coll (IL)
Lewis Coll of Business (MI)
Lima Tech Coll (OH)
Lincoln Coll, Normal (IL)
Lincoln Sch of Commerce (NE)
Linn-Benton Comm Coll (OR)
Long Beach City Coll (CA)
Longview Comm Coll (MO)
Los Angeles City Coll (CA)
Los Angeles Harbor Coll (CA)
Los Angeles Pierce Coll (CA)
Lower Columbia Coll (WA)
MacCormac Jr Coll (IL)
Macomb Comm Coll (MI)
Madison Jr Coll of Business (WI)
Manchester Comm-Tech Coll (CT)
Manor Jr Coll (PA)
Maple Woods Comm Coll (MO)
Marian Court Coll (MA)
Massasoit Comm Coll (MA)
Mater Dei Coll (NY)
McCook Comm Coll (NE)
McIntosh Coll (NH)
McLennan Comm Coll (TX)
Merced Coll (CA)
Mercer County Comm Coll (NJ)
Metropolitan Comm Coll (NE)
Miami-Dade Comm Coll (FL)
Miami-Jacobs Coll (OH)
Miami University–Middletown Cmps (OH)
Michiana Coll (IN)
Middlesex Community–Tech Coll (CT)
Middlesex County Coll (NJ)
Midland Coll (TX)
Mid Michigan Comm Coll (MI)
Mid-Plains Comm Coll (NE)
Midstate Coll (IL)
Mid-State Coll (ME)
Milwaukee Area Tech Coll (WI)
Mohawk Valley Comm Coll (NY)
Monroe Comm Coll (NY)
Monroe County Comm Coll (MI)
Montana State U Coll of Tech-Great Falls (MT)
Montcalm Comm Coll (MI)
Monterey Peninsula Coll (CA)
Montgomery College–Rockville Cmps (MD)
Montgomery College–Takoma Park Cmps (MD)
Moraine Valley Comm Coll (IL)
Morton Coll (IL)
Mountain Empire Comm Coll (VA)
Mountain View Coll (TX)
Mt Hood Comm Coll (OR)
Mt San Antonio Coll (CA)
Muskegon Comm Coll (MI)
Napa Valley Coll (CA)
Nash Comm Coll (NC)
Nassau Comm Coll (NY)
National Business Coll, Bluefield (VA)
National Business Coll, Charlottesville (VA)
National Business Coll, Danville (VA)
National Business Coll, Harrisonburg (VA)
National Business Coll, Lynchburg (VA)
National Business Coll, Martinsville (VA)
National Business Coll, Roanoke (VA)
Naugatuck Valley Community–Tech Coll (CT)
Navarro Coll (TX)
Nebraska Coll of Business (NE)
New Mexico Jr Coll (NM)
Newport Business Inst (PA)
New York City Tech Coll of the City U of NY (NY)
Nicolet Area Tech Coll (WI)
Normandale Comm Coll (MN)
Northampton County Area Comm Coll (PA)
North Central Michigan Coll (MI)
Northcentral Tech Coll (WI)
North Central Texas Coll (TX)
North Dakota State Coll of Science (ND)
North Dakota State University–Bottineau (ND)
Northeast Alabama State Comm Coll (AL)
Northeast Comm Coll (NE)
Northeastern Jr Coll (CO)
Northeastern Oklahoma A&M Coll (OK)
Northeast Mississippi Comm Coll (MS)
Northeast Texas Comm Coll (TX)
Northern Maine Tech Coll (ME)
North Idaho Coll (ID)
North Iowa Area Comm Coll (IA)
North Lake Coll (TX)
Northland Comm and Tech Coll (MN)
North Shore Comm Coll (MA)
Northwestern Business Coll (IL)
Northwestern Coll (OH)
Northwestern Michigan Coll (MI)
Northwest Mississippi Comm Coll (MS)
Northwest State Comm Coll (OH)
Oakland Comm Coll (MI)
Odessa Coll (TX)
Oklahoma State U, Okmulgee (OK)
Olean Business Inst (NY)
Olympic Coll (WA)
Orangeburg-Calhoun Tech Coll (SC)
Orange Coast Coll (CA)
Otero Jr Coll (CO)
Palm Beach Comm Coll (FL)
Palomar Coll (CA)
Parkland Coll (IL)
Pasadena City Coll (CA)
Pellissippi State Tech Comm Coll (TN)
Penn Commercial, Inc (PA)
Penn Valley Comm Coll (MO)
Pensacola Jr Coll (FL)
Phillips Jr Coll, Condie Cmps (CA)
Piedmont Comm Coll (NC)
Pierce Coll (WA)
Pima Comm Coll (AZ)
Portland Comm Coll (OR)
Prairie State Coll (IL)
Prince George's Comm Coll (MD)
Prospect Hall (FL)
Pueblo Comm Coll (CO)
Quincy Coll (MA)
Rasmussen Coll Mankato (MN)
Rasmussen Coll Minnetonka (MN)
Rasmussen Coll St Cloud (MN)
Reading Area Comm Coll (PA)
Renton Tech Coll (WA)
Richland Comm Coll (IL)
Roane State Comm Coll (TN)
Rochester Business Inst (NY)
Rockingham Comm Coll (NC)
Rogers State Coll (OK)
Rose State Coll (OK)
Roxbury Comm Coll (MA)
Sacramento City Coll (CA)
Saddleback Coll (CA)
St Catharine Coll (KY)
St Clair County Comm Coll (MI)
St Louis Comm Coll at Meramec (MO)
St Philip's Coll (TX)
Salem Comm Coll (NJ)
San Antonio Coll (TX)
San Diego City Coll (CA)
San Diego Mesa Coll (CA)
San Jacinto College–Central Cmps (TX)
San Jacinto College–North Cmps (TX)
San Jacinto College–South Cmps (TX)
Santa Fe Comm Coll (FL)
Scott Comm Coll (IA)
Shasta Coll (CA)
Shawnee Comm Coll (IL)
Sierra Coll (CA)
Sinclair Comm Coll (OH)
Skyline Coll (CA)
Solano Comm Coll (CA)
Southeast Comm Coll, Beatrice Cmps (NE)
Southern Ohio Coll, Northern Kentucky Cmps (KY)
South Florida Comm Coll (FL)
South Plains Coll (TX)
South Puget Sound Comm Coll (WA)
Southwestern Coll (CA)
Southwestern Michigan Coll (MI)
Southwestern Tech Coll (MN)
Southwest Mississippi Comm Coll (MS)
Southwest Wisconsin Tech Coll (WI)
Spencer Sch of Business (NE)
Spokane Comm Coll (WA)
Spoon River Coll (IL)
Springfield Tech Comm Coll (MA)
Stanly Comm Coll (NC)
Stark Tech Coll (OH)
State Fair Comm Coll (MO)
State Tech Inst at Memphis (TN)
State U of NY Coll of A&T at Cobleskill (NY)
State U of NY Coll of A&T at Morrisville (NY)
State U of NY Coll of Tech at Delhi (NY)
Stevens Henager Coll (UT)
Stratton Coll (WI)
Suffolk County Comm College–Ammerman Cmps (NY)
Suffolk County Comm Coll–Eastern Cmps (NY)
Suffolk County Comm Coll–Western Cmps (NY)
Surry Comm Coll (NC)
Tallahassee Comm Coll (FL)
Terra State Comm Coll (OH)
Texas Southmost Coll (TX)
Texas State Tech Coll–Harlingen Cmps (TX)
Thaddeus Stevens State Sch of Tech (PA)
Thomas Nelson Comm Coll (VA)
Three Rivers Comm-Tech Coll (CT)
Tomball Coll (TX)
Treasure Valley Comm Coll (OR)
Trenholm State Tech Coll (AL)
Trinity Valley Comm Coll (TX)
Triton Coll (IL)
Trocaire Coll (NY)
Truckee Meadows Comm Coll (NV)
Tulsa Jr Coll (OK)
Tunxis Comm Tech Coll (CT)
Tyler Jr Coll (TX)
Umpqua Comm Coll (OR)
U of Cincinnati Clermont Coll (OH)
U of Cincinnati Raymond Walters Coll (OH)
U of Hawaii–Kapiolani Comm Coll (HI)
U of New Mexico–Gallup Branch (NM)
U of North Dakota–Lake Region (ND)
Utah Valley State Coll (UT)
Valencia Comm Coll (FL)
Vance-Granville Comm Coll (NC)
Vincennes U (IN)
Vincennes University–Jasper Ctr (IN)
Wake Tech Comm Coll (NC)
Wallace State Comm Coll (AL)
Walla Walla Comm Coll (WA)
Waubonsee Comm Coll (IL)
Wayne Comm Coll (NC)
Wayne County Comm Coll (MI)
Webster Coll, Ocala (FL)
Wenatchee Valley Coll (WA)
Westark Comm Coll (AR)
Westchester Comm Coll (NY)
Western Piedmont Comm Coll (NC)
Western Wisconsin Tech Coll (WI)
Western Wyoming Comm Coll (WY)
West Los Angeles Coll (CA)
Westmoreland County Comm Coll (PA)
West Shore Comm Coll (MI)
West Valley Coll (CA)
West Virginia Career Coll, Morgantown (WV)
West Virginia Northern Comm Coll (WV)
William Rainey Harper Coll (IL)
Williamsport Sch of Commerce (PA)
Willmar Comm Coll (MN)
Willmar Tech Coll (MN)
Wright State U, Lake Cmps (OH)
Yakima Valley Comm Coll (WA)
Yavapai Coll (AZ)

LEGAL STUDIES

Atlantic Comm Coll (NJ)
Catonsville Comm Coll (MD)
Central City Business Inst (NY)
Central Texas Coll (TX)
City Colls of Chicago, Harold Washington Coll (IL)
City Colls of Chicago, Harry S Truman Coll (IL)
City Colls of Chicago, Kennedy-King Coll (IL)
City Colls of Chicago, Richard J Daley Coll (IL)
Clovis Comm Coll (NM)
Coll of the Siskiyous (CA)
Del Mar Coll (TX)
Delta Coll (MI)
Draughons Jr Coll, Nashville (TN)
Edison Comm Coll (FL)
Edison State Comm Coll (OH)
Edmonds Comm Coll (WA)
El Centro Coll (TX)
Florida National Coll (FL)
Greenville Tech Coll (SC)
Gulf Coast Comm Coll (FL)
Hillsborough Comm Coll (FL)
Iowa Lakes Comm Coll (IA)
John C Calhoun State Comm Coll (AL)
Kellogg Comm Coll (MI)
Kelsey Jenney Coll (CA)
Kilian Comm Coll (SD)
Kirkwood Comm Coll (IA)
MacCormac Jr Coll (IL)
Macomb Comm Coll (MI)
Manatee Comm Coll (FL)
Maria Coll (NY)
McIntosh Coll (NH)
Metropolitan Comm Coll (NE)
Miami-Dade Comm Coll (FL)
Midlands Tech Coll (SC)
Mount Ida Coll (MA)
Navarro Coll (TX)
Nebraska Coll of Business (NE)
Northeast Metro Tech Coll (MN)
North Harris Coll (TX)
Northland Comm and Tech Coll (MN)
Norwalk Comm-Tech Coll (CT)
Okaloosa-Walton Comm Coll (FL)
Oxnard Coll (CA)
Palo Alto Coll (TX)
Pasadena City Coll (CA)
Pasco-Hernando Comm Coll (FL)
Pennsylvania Coll of Tech (PA)
Rancho Santiago Coll (CA)
Rasmussen Coll Mankato (MN)
Reading Area Comm Coll (PA)
Saddleback Coll (CA)
Sage Jr Coll of Albany (NY)
St Louis Comm Coll at Florissant Valley (MO)
St Philip's Coll (TX)
San Juan Coll (NM)
Santa Fe Comm Coll (FL)
Sussex County Comm Coll (NJ)
Trident Tech Coll (SC)
Utah Valley State Coll (UT)
Vernon Regional Jr Coll (TX)
West Virginia Career Coll, Charleston (WV)

LIBERAL ARTS/GENERAL STUDIES

Abraham Baldwin Ag Coll (GA)
Adirondack Comm Coll (NY)
Aiken Tech Coll (SC)
Aims Comm Coll (CO)
Alabama Southern Comm Coll, Monroeville (AL)
Alabama Southern Comm Coll, Thomasville (AL)
Alamance Comm Coll (NC)
Albuquerque Tech Vocational Inst (NM)
Allan Hancock Coll (CA)
Allegany Comm Coll (MD)
Allen County Comm Coll (KS)
Alpena Comm Coll (MI)
Alvin Comm Coll (TX)
American River Coll (CA)
Ancilla Coll (IN)
Angelina Coll (TX)
Anne Arundel Comm Coll (MD)
Anoka-Ramsey Comm Coll (MN)
Anson Comm Coll (NC)
Antelope Valley Coll (CA)
Aquinas Coll (TN)
Aquinas Coll at Milton (MA)
Aquinas Coll at Newton (MA)
Arapahoe Comm Coll (CO)
Arizona Western Coll (AZ)
Arkansas State University–Beebe Branch (AR)
Asheville-Buncombe Tech Comm Coll (NC)
Asnuntuck Comm-Tech Coll (CT)

Peterson's Guide to Two-Year Colleges 1997

99

Associate Degree Programs at Two-Year Colleges
Liberal Arts/General Studies

Assumption Coll for Sisters (NJ)
Atlantic Comm Coll (NJ)
Austin Comm Coll (MN)
Austin Comm Coll (TX)
Bacone Coll (OK)
Bainbridge Coll (GA)
Bakersfield Coll (CA)
Baltimore City Comm Coll (MD)
Barstow Coll (CA)
Barton County Comm Coll (KS)
Bay de Noc Comm Coll (MI)
Bay Mills Comm Coll (MI)
Beaufort County Comm Coll (NC)
Bee County Coll (TX)
Belleville Area Coll (IL)
Bellevue Comm Coll (WA)
Bergen Comm Coll (NJ)
Berkshire Comm Coll (MA)
Bethany Lutheran Coll (MN)
Bevill State Comm Coll (AL)
Big Bend Comm Coll (WA)
Bishop State Comm Coll (AL)
Bismarck State Coll (ND)
Blackfeet Comm Coll (MT)
Black Hawk Coll, Kewanee (IL)
Black Hawk Coll, Moline (IL)
Bladen Comm Coll (NC)
Blue Mountain Comm Coll (OR)
Blue Ridge Comm Coll (NC)
Blue Ridge Comm Coll (VA)
Borough of Manhattan Comm Coll of City U of NY (NY)
Bossier Parish Comm Coll (LA)
Bowling Green State University–Firelands Coll (OH)
Brazosport Coll (TX)
Brevard Coll (NC)
Brevard Comm Coll (FL)
Briarwood Coll (CT)
Bristol Comm Coll (MA)
Bronx Comm Coll of City U of NY (NY)
Brookdale Comm Coll (NJ)
Brookhaven Coll (TX)
Broome Comm Coll (NY)
Broward Comm Coll (FL)
Brunswick Coll (GA)
Brunswick Comm Coll (NC)
Bucks County Comm Coll (PA)
Bunker Hill Comm Coll (MA)
Burlington County Coll (NJ)
Butler County Comm Coll (KS)
Butler County Comm Coll (PA)
Butte Coll (CA)
Cabrillo Coll (CA)
Caldwell Comm Coll and Tech Inst (NC)
Camden County Coll (NJ)
Cañada Coll (CA)
Cape Cod Comm Coll (MA)
Cape Fear Comm Coll (NC)
Capital Comm Tech Coll (CT)
Carl Sandburg Coll (IL)
Carteret Comm Coll (NC)
Casper Coll (WY)
Catawba Valley Comm Coll (NC)
Catonsville Comm Coll (MD)
Cayuga County Comm Coll (NY)
Cecil Comm Coll (MD)
Cedar Valley Coll (TX)
Central Alabama Comm Coll (AL)
Central Carolina Comm Coll (NC)
Central Coll (KS)
Central Comm College–Platte Cmps (NE)
Central Florida Comm Coll (FL)
Centralia Coll (WA)
Central Lakes Coll (MN)
Central Oregon Comm Coll (OR)
Central Piedmont Comm Coll (NC)
Central Texas Coll (TX)
Central Virginia Comm Coll (VA)
Central Wyoming Coll (WY)
Cerritos Coll (CA)
Cerro Coso Comm Coll (CA)

Chabot Coll (CA)
Chaffey Coll (CA)
Champlain Coll (VT)
Chandler-Gilbert Comm Coll (AZ)
Charles County Comm Coll (MD)
Charles Stewart Mott Comm Coll (MI)
Chatfield Coll (OH)
Chattahoochee Valley State Comm Coll (AL)
Chattanooga State Tech Comm Coll (TN)
Chemeketa Comm Coll (OR)
Chesapeake Coll (MD)
Chesterfield-Marlboro Tech Coll (SC)
Chipola Jr Coll (FL)
City Colls of Chicago, Harry S Truman Coll (IL)
City Colls of Chicago, Kennedy-King Coll (IL)
City Colls of Chicago, Malcolm X Coll (IL)
City Colls of Chicago, Olive-Harvey Coll (IL)
City Colls of Chicago, Richard J Daley Coll (IL)
City Colls of Chicago, Wilbur Wright Coll (IL)
Clackamas Comm Coll (OR)
Clarendon Coll (TX)
Clark Coll (WA)
Clark State Comm Coll (OH)
Clatsop Comm Coll (OR)
Cleveland Comm Coll (NC)
Cleveland State Comm Coll (TN)
Clinton Comm Coll (IA)
Clinton Comm Coll (NY)
Cloud County Comm Coll (KS)
Clovis Comm Coll (NM)
Coahoma Comm Coll (MS)
Coastal Carolina Comm Coll (NC)
Coastline Comm Coll (CA)
Cochise Coll, Douglas (AZ)
Cochise Coll, Sierra Vista (AZ)
Coconino County Comm Coll (AZ)
Coffeyville Comm Coll (KS)
Colby Comm Coll (KS)
Coll of Alameda (CA)
Coll of DuPage (IL)
Coll of Eastern Utah (UT)
Coll of Lake County (IL)
Coll of Marin (CA)
Coll of Micronesia–FSM (FM)
Coll of St Catherine–Minneapolis (MN)
Coll of San Mateo (CA)
Coll of Southern Idaho (ID)
Coll of The Albemarle (NC)
Coll of the Canyons (CA)
Coll of the Desert (CA)
Coll of the Sequoias (CA)
Collin County Comm Coll (TX)
Colorado Mountn Coll, Alpine Cmps (CO)
Colorado Mountn Coll, Roaring Fork Cmps-Spring Valley Ctr (CO)
Colorado Mountn Coll, Timberline Cmps (CO)
Colorado Northwestern Comm Coll (CO)
Columbia Basin Coll (WA)
Columbia Coll (CA)
Columbia-Greene Comm Coll (NY)
Columbia State Comm Coll (TN)
Columbus State Comm Coll (OH)
Comm Coll of Allegheny County Allegheny Cmps (PA)
Comm Coll of Allegheny County Boyce Cmps (PA)
Comm Coll of Allegheny County North Cmps (PA)
Comm Coll of Allegheny County South Cmps (PA)
Comm Coll of Aurora (CO)
Comm Coll of Beaver County (PA)
Comm Coll of Denver (CO)
Comm Coll of Philadelphia (PA)

Comm Coll of Rhode Island (RI)
Comm Coll of Southern Nevada (NV)
Comm Coll of Vermont (VT)
Connors State Coll (OK)
Contra Costa Coll (CA)
Copiah-Lincoln Comm Coll (MS)
Copiah-Lincoln Comm College–Natchez Cmps (MS)
Corning Comm Coll (NY)
Cossatot Tech Coll (AR)
Cosumnes River Coll (CA)
Cottey Coll (MO)
County Coll of Morris (NJ)
Cowley County Comm Coll and Voc-Tech Sch (KS)
Crafton Hills Coll (CA)
Craven Comm Coll (NC)
Crowder Coll (MO)
Cuesta Coll (CA)
Cumberland County Coll (NJ)
Cuyahoga Comm Coll, Eastern Cmps (OH)
Cuyahoga Comm Coll, Metropolitan Cmps (OH)
Cuyahoga Comm Coll, Western Cmps (OH)
Cuyamaca Coll (CA)
Cypress Coll (CA)
Dabney S Lancaster Comm Coll (VA)
Dalton Coll (GA)
Danville Area Comm Coll (IL)
Danville Comm Coll (VA)
Darton Coll (GA)
Davidson County Comm Coll (NC)
Dawson Comm Coll (MT)
Daytona Beach Comm Coll (FL)
Dean Coll (MA)
De Anza Coll (CA)
Deep Springs Coll (CA)
Delaware County Comm Coll (PA)
Delgado Comm Coll (LA)
Del Mar Coll (TX)
Delta Coll (MI)
Des Moines Area Comm Coll (IA)
Diablo Valley Coll (CA)
Dixie Coll (UT)
Dodge City Comm Coll (KS)
Donnelly Coll (KS)
D-Q U (CA)
Dull Knife Memorial Coll (MT)
Dundalk Comm Coll (MD)
Durham Tech Comm Coll (NC)
Dutchess Comm Coll (NY)
Dyersburg State Comm Coll (TN)
East Arkansas Comm Coll (AR)
East Central Coll (MO)
East Central Comm Coll (MS)
Eastern Arizona Coll (AZ)
Eastern New Mexico University–Roswell (NM)
Eastern Shore Comm Coll (VA)
Eastern Wyoming Coll (WY)
Eastfield Coll (TX)
East Georgia Coll (GA)
East Los Angeles Coll (CA)
East Mississippi Comm Coll (MS)
Edgecombe Comm Coll (NC)
Edison Comm Coll (FL)
Edison State Comm Coll (OH)
Edmonds Comm Coll (WA)
Elaine P Nunez Comm Coll (LA)
El Camino Coll (CA)
El Centro Coll (TX)
Elgin Comm Coll (IL)
Ellsworth Comm Coll (IA)
El Paso Comm Coll (TX)
Emory U, Oxford Coll (GA)
Enterprise State Jr Coll (AL)
Erie Comm Coll, City Cmps (NY)
Erie Comm Coll, North Cmps (NY)
Erie Comm Coll, South Cmps (NY)
Essex Comm Coll (MD)
Essex County Coll (NJ)

Eugenio María de Hostos Comm Coll of City U of NY (NY)
Everett Comm Coll (WA)
Evergreen Valley Coll (CA)
Fairleigh Dickinson U, Edward Williams Coll (NJ)
Fayetteville Tech Comm Coll (NC)
Feather River Comm Coll District (CA)
Fergus Falls Comm Coll (MN)
Finger Lakes Comm Coll (NY)
Fiorello H LaGuardia Comm Coll of City U of NY (NY)
Fisher Coll (MA)
Flathead Valley Comm Coll (MT)
Florida Coll (FL)
Florida Comm Coll at Jacksonville (FL)
Florida Keys Comm Coll (FL)
Florida National Coll (FL)
Floyd Coll (GA)
Fond du Lac Tribal and Comm Coll (MN)
Foothill Coll (CA)
Fort Belknap Coll (MT)
Fort Berthold Comm Coll (ND)
Fort Peck Comm Coll (MT)
Fort Scott Comm Coll (KS)
Frank Phillips Coll (TX)
Frederick Comm Coll (MD)
Fresno City Coll (CA)
Front Range Comm Coll (CO)
Fullerton Coll (CA)
Fulton-Montgomery Comm Coll (NY)
Gadsden State Comm Coll (AL)
Gainesville Coll (GA)
Galveston Coll (TX)
Garden City Comm Coll (KS)
Garland County Comm Coll (AR)
Garrett Comm Coll (MD)
Gaston Coll (NC)
Gateway Comm Coll (AZ)
Gateway Comm-Tech Coll (CT)
Gavilan Coll (CA)
Genesee Comm Coll (NY)
George C Wallace State Comm Coll, Dothan (AL)
Georgia Military Coll (GA)
Germanna Comm Coll (VA)
Glendale Comm Coll (AZ)
Glen Oaks Comm Coll (MI)
Gloucester County Coll (NJ)
Gogebic Comm Coll (MI)
Golden West Coll (CA)
Gordon Coll (GA)
Grand Rapids Comm Coll (MI)
Grays Harbor Coll (WA)
Grayson County Coll (TX)
Great Basin Coll (NV)
Greenfield Comm Coll (MA)
Green River Comm Coll (WA)
Greenville Tech Coll (SC)
Grossmont Coll (CA)
Guilford Tech Comm Coll (NC)
Gulf Coast Comm Coll (FL)
Hagerstown Jr Coll (MD)
Halifax Comm Coll (NC)
Harcum Coll (PA)
Harford Comm Coll (MD)
Harrisburg Area Comm Coll (PA)
Hartnell Coll (CA)
Haskell Indian Nations U (KS)
Hawaii Tokai International Coll (HI)
Hawkeye Comm Coll (IA)
Haywood Comm Coll (NC)
Henry Ford Comm Coll (MI)
Herkimer County Comm Coll (NY)
Hesser Coll (NH)
Hesston Coll (KS)
Hibbing Comm Coll (MN)
Highland Comm Coll (IL)
Highland Comm Coll (KS)
Highland Park Comm Coll (MI)
Hill Coll of the Hill Jr Coll District (TX)
Hillsborough Comm Coll (FL)
Hinds Comm Coll (MS)
Hiwassee Coll (TN)
Holmes Comm Coll (MS)

Holy Cross Coll (IN)
Holyoke Comm Coll (MA)
Housatonic Comm-Tech Coll (CT)
Houston Comm Coll System (TX)
Howard Comm Coll (MD)
Hudson County Comm Coll (NJ)
Hudson Valley Comm Coll (NY)
Hutchinson Comm Coll and Area Vocational Sch (KS)
Illinois Central Coll (IL)
Illinois Eastern Comm Colls, Frontier Comm Coll (IL)
Illinois Eastern Comm Colls, Lincoln Trail Coll (IL)
Illinois Eastern Comm Colls, Olney Central Coll (IL)
Illinois Eastern Comm Colls, Wabash Valley Coll (IL)
Illinois Valley Comm Coll (IL)
Imperial Valley Coll (CA)
Independence Comm Coll (KS)
Indian Hills Comm Coll (IA)
Indian River Comm Coll (FL)
Inver Hills Comm Coll (MN)
Iowa Central Comm Coll (IA)
Iowa Lakes Comm Coll (IA)
Iowa Western Comm Coll (IA)
Irvine Valley Coll (CA)
Isothermal Comm Coll (NC)
Itasca Comm Coll (MN)
Itawamba Comm Coll (MS)
Jackson Comm Coll (MI)
Jackson State Comm Coll (TN)
Jacksonville Coll (TX)
James H Faulkner State Comm Coll (AL)
James Sprunt Comm Coll (NC)
Jamestown Comm Coll (NY)
Jefferson Coll (MO)
Jefferson Comm Coll (NY)
Jefferson Davis Comm Coll (AL)
Jefferson State Comm Coll (AL)
John A Logan Coll (IL)
John C Calhoun State Comm Coll (AL)
Johnson County Comm Coll (KS)
Johnston Comm Coll (NC)
John Tyler Comm Coll (VA)
John Wood Comm Coll (IL)
Joliet Jr Coll (IL)
J Sargeant Reynolds Comm Coll (VA)
Kalamazoo Valley Comm Coll (MI)
Kankakee Comm Coll (IL)
Kansas City Kansas Comm Coll (KS)
Kaskaskia Coll (IL)
Kellogg Comm Coll (MI)
Kemper Military Jr Coll (MO)
Kent State U, Ashtabula Cmps (OH)
Kent State U, East Liverpool Cmps (OH)
Kent State U, Geauga Cmps (OH)
Kent State U, Salem Cmps (OH)
Kent State U, Stark Cmps (OH)
Kent State U, Trumbull Cmps (OH)
Kent State U, Tuscarawas Cmps (OH)
Kettering Coll of Medical Arts (OH)
Keystone Coll (PA)
Kingsborough Comm Coll of City U of NY (NY)
Kings River Comm Coll (CA)
Kirkwood Comm Coll (IA)
Kirtland Comm Coll (MI)
Kishwaukee Coll (IL)
Labette Comm Coll (KS)
Lackawanna Jr Coll (PA)
Lake City Comm Coll (FL)
Lake Land Coll (IL)
Lakeland Comm Coll (OH)
Lake Michigan Coll (MI)
Lake-Sumter Comm Coll (FL)
Lake Tahoe Comm Coll (CA)
Lakewood Comm Coll (MN)
Lamar Comm Coll (CO)

Lamar University–Orange (TX)
Lamar University–Port Arthur (TX)
Landmark Coll (VT)
Lane Comm Coll (OR)
Laney Coll (CA)
Lansing Comm Coll (MI)
Laramie County Comm Coll (WY)
Laredo Comm Coll (TX)
Las Positas Coll (CA)
Lassen Coll (CA)
Lawson State Comm Coll (AL)
LDS Business Coll (UT)
Lee Coll (TX)
Lehigh Carbon Comm Coll (PA)
Lenoir Comm Coll (NC)
Lewis and Clark Comm Coll (IL)
Lewis Coll of Business (MI)
Lincoln Coll, Lincoln (IL)
Lincoln Land Comm Coll (IL)
Linn-Benton Comm Coll (OR)
Little Big Horn Coll (MT)
Little Hoop Comm Coll (ND)
Long Beach City Coll (CA)
Longview Comm Coll (MO)
Lon Morris Coll (TX)
Lorain County Comm Coll (OH)
Lord Fairfax Comm Coll (VA)
Los Angeles City Coll (CA)
Los Angeles Harbor Coll (CA)
Los Angeles Mission Coll (CA)
Los Angeles Pierce Coll (CA)
Los Angeles Trade-Tech Coll (CA)
Los Angeles Valley Coll (CA)
Los Medanos Coll (CA)
Louisburg Coll (NC)
Louisiana State U at Alexandria (LA)
Louisiana State U at Eunice (LA)
Lower Columbia Coll (WA)
Lurleen B Wallace State Jr Coll (AL)
Luzerne County Comm Coll (PA)
Macomb Comm Coll (MI)
Macon Coll (GA)
Madison Area Tech Coll (WI)
Manatee Comm Coll (FL)
Manchester Comm-Tech Coll (CT)
Manor Jr Coll (PA)
Maple Woods Comm Coll (MO)
Maria Coll (NY)
Marian Court Coll (MA)
Marion Military Inst (AL)
Marshalltown Comm Coll (IA)
Martin Comm Coll (NC)
Mary Holmes Coll (MS)
Marymount Coll, Palos Verdes, California (CA)
Massachusetts Bay Comm Coll (MA)
Massasoit Comm Coll (MA)
Mater Dei Coll (NY)
Mayland Comm Coll (NC)
McCook Comm Coll (NE)
McDowell Tech Comm Coll (NC)
McHenry County Coll (IL)
McLennan Comm Coll (TX)
Mendocino Coll (CA)
Merced Coll (CA)
Mercer County Comm Coll (NJ)
Meridian Comm Coll (MS)
Merritt Coll (CA)
Mesabi Comm Coll (MN)
Mesa Comm Coll (AZ)
Metropolitan Comm Coll (NE)
Miami-Dade Comm Coll (FL)
Miami University–Hamilton Cmps (OH)
Miami University–Middletown Cmps (OH)
Middle Georgia Coll (GA)
Middlesex Comm Coll (MA)
Middlesex Community–Tech Coll (CT)
Middlesex County Coll (NJ)
Midland Coll (TX)
Midlands Tech Coll (SC)
Mid Michigan Comm Coll (MI)
Mid-Plains Comm Coll (NE)
Miles Comm Coll (MT)

Associate Degree Programs at Two-Year Colleges
Liberal Arts/General Studies

Milwaukee Area Tech Coll (WI)
Mineral Area Coll (MO)
Minneapolis Comm Coll (MN)
MiraCosta Coll (CA)
Mission Coll (CA)
Mississippi County Comm Coll (AR)
Mississippi Delta Comm Coll (MS)
Mississippi Gulf Coast Comm Coll (MS)
Mitchell Coll (CT)
Mitchell Comm Coll (NC)
Moberly Area Comm Coll (MO)
Modesto Jr Coll (CA)
Mohave Comm Coll (AZ)
Mohawk Valley Comm Coll (NY)
Monroe Comm Coll (NY)
Monroe County Comm Coll (MI)
Montcalm Comm Coll (MI)
Monterey Peninsula Coll (CA)
Montgomery College–Germantown Cmps (MD)
Montgomery College–Rockville Cmps (MD)
Montgomery College–Takoma Park Cmps (MD)
Montgomery Comm Coll (NC)
Montgomery County Comm Coll (PA)
Moorpark Coll (CA)
Moraine Valley Comm Coll (IL)
Morgan Comm Coll (CO)
Morton Coll (IL)
Motlow State Comm Coll (TN)
Mountain Empire Comm Coll (VA)
Mountain View Coll (TX)
Mt Hood Comm Coll (OR)
Mount Ida Coll (MA)
Mt San Antonio Coll (CA)
Mount Wachusett Comm Coll (MA)
Murray State Coll (OK)
Muscatine Comm Coll (IA)
Muskegon Comm Coll (MI)
Nash Comm Coll (NC)
Nassau Comm Coll (NY)
Naugatuck Valley Community–Tech Coll (CT)
Navajo Comm Coll (AZ)
Nebraska Indian Comm Coll (NE)
NEI Coll of Tech (MN)
Neosho County Comm Coll (KS)
New Mexico Jr Coll (NM)
New Mexico Military Inst (NM)
New Mexico State University–Alamogordo (NM)
New Mexico State University–Carlsbad (NM)
New Mexico State University–Grants (NM)
New River Comm Coll (VA)
New York City Tech Coll of the City U of NY (NY)
Niagara County Comm Coll (NY)
Nicolet Area Tech Coll (WI)
Normandale Comm Coll (MN)
Northampton County Area Comm Coll (PA)
North Arkansas Comm/Tech Coll (AR)
North Central Michigan Coll (MI)
North Central Missouri Coll (MO)
North Central Texas Coll (TX)
North Country Comm Coll (NY)
North Dakota State Coll of Science (ND)
North Dakota State University–Bottineau (ND)
Northeast Alabama State Comm Coll (AL)
Northeast Comm Coll (NE)
Northeastern Jr Coll (CO)
Northeast Iowa Comm Coll, Calmar Cmps (IA)
Northeast Mississippi Comm Coll (MS)
Northeast State Tech Comm Coll (TN)
Northern Essex Comm Coll (MA)
Northern Marianas Coll (MP)
Northern Oklahoma Coll (OK)
Northern Virginia Comm Coll (VA)
North Florida Comm Coll (FL)
North Harris Coll (TX)
North Hennepin Comm Coll (MN)
North Idaho Coll (ID)
North Iowa Area Comm Coll (IA)
North Lake Coll (TX)
Northland Comm and Tech Coll (MN)
Northland Pioneer Coll (AZ)
North Seattle Comm Coll (WA)
North Shore Comm Coll (MA)
NorthWest Arkansas Comm Coll (AR)
Northwest Coll (WY)
Northwestern Connecticut Comm-Tech Coll (CT)
Northwestern Michigan Coll (MI)
Northwest Iowa Comm Coll (IA)
Northwest Mississippi Comm Coll (MS)
Northwest-Shoals Comm Coll (AL)
Norwalk Comm-Tech Coll (CT)
Oakland Comm Coll (MI)
Oakton Comm Coll (IL)
Ocean County Coll (NJ)
Odessa Coll (TX)
Ohio University–Southern Cmps (OH)
Ohio Valley Coll (WV)
Ohlone Coll (CA)
Okaloosa-Walton Comm Coll (FL)
Olympic Coll (WA)
Onondaga Comm Coll (NY)
Orangeburg-Calhoun Tech Coll (SC)
Orange Coast Coll (CA)
Orange County Comm Coll (NY)
Otero Jr Coll (CO)
Owensboro Comm Coll (KY)
Owens Comm Coll, Findlay (OH)
Owens Comm Coll, Toledo (OH)
Oxnard Coll (CA)
Ozarka Tech Coll (AR)
Palau Comm Coll (PW)
Palm Beach Comm Coll (FL)
Palo Alto Coll (TX)
Palomar Coll (CA)
Palo Verde Coll (CA)
Pamlico Comm Coll (NC)
Panama Canal Coll (Republic of Panama)
Paradise Valley Comm Coll (AZ)
Paris Jr Coll (TX)
Parkland Coll (IL)
Pasadena City Coll (CA)
Pasco-Hernando Comm Coll (FL)
Patrick Henry Comm Coll (VA)
Paul D Camp Comm Coll (VA)
Paul Smith's Coll (NY)
Peace Coll (NC)
Pearl River Comm Coll (MS)
Peirce Coll (PA)
Pellissippi State Tech Comm Coll (TN)
Peninsula Coll (WA)
Pennsylvania Coll of Tech (PA)
Penn State U Abington-Ogontz Cmps (PA)
Penn State U Allentown Cmps (PA)
Penn State U Altoona Cmps (PA)
Penn State U Beaver Cmps (PA)
Penn State U Berks Cmps (PA)
Penn State U Delaware County Cmps (PA)
Penn State U DuBois Cmps (PA)
Penn State U Fayette Cmps (PA)
Penn State U Hazleton Cmps (PA)
Penn State U McKeesport Cmps (PA)
Penn State U Mont Alto Cmps (PA)
Penn State U New Kensington Cmps (PA)
Penn State U Schuylkill Cmps (PA)
Penn State U Shenango Cmps (PA)
Penn State U Wilkes-Barre Cmps (PA)
Penn State U Worthington Scranton Cmps (PA)
Penn State U York Cmps (PA)
Penn Valley Comm Coll (MO)
Pensacola Jr Coll (FL)
Petit Jean Tech Coll (AR)
Phillips County Comm Coll (AR)
Piedmont Comm Coll (NC)
Piedmont Virginia Comm Coll (VA)
Pierce Coll (WA)
Pikes Peak Comm Coll (CO)
Pima Comm Coll (AZ)
Pitt Comm Coll (NC)
Polk Comm Coll (FL)
Porterville Coll (CA)
Portland Comm Coll (OR)
Potomac State Coll of West Virginia U (WV)
Prairie State Coll (IL)
Pratt Comm Coll and Area Voc Sch (KS)
Prince George's Comm Coll (MD)
Pueblo Comm Coll (CO)
Queensborough Comm Coll of City U of NY (NY)
Quincy Coll (MA)
Quinebaug Valley Comm-Tech Coll (CT)
Quinsigamond Comm Coll (MA)
Rainy River Comm Coll (MN)
Rancho Santiago Coll (CA)
Randolph Comm Coll (NC)
Ranger Coll (TX)
Rappahannock Comm Coll (VA)
Raritan Valley Comm Coll (NJ)
Reading Area Comm Coll (PA)
Redlands Comm Coll (OK)
Red River Tech Coll (AR)
Red Rocks Comm Coll (CO)
Rend Lake Coll (IL)
Richard Bland Coll of the Coll of William and Mary (VA)
Richland Coll (TX)
Richland Comm Coll (IL)
Richmond Comm Coll (NC)
Rich Mountain Comm Coll (AR)
Ricks Coll (ID)
Rio Hondo Coll (CA)
Riverside Comm Coll (CA)
Roane State Comm Coll (TN)
Roanoke-Chowan Comm Coll (NC)
Rochester Comm Coll (MN)
Rockingham Comm Coll (NC)
Rockland Comm Coll (NY)
Rock Valley Coll (IL)
Rogers State Coll (OK)
Rogue Comm Coll (OR)
Rose State Coll (OK)
Rowan-Cabarrus Comm Coll (NC)
Roxbury Comm Coll (MA)
Sacramento City Coll (CA)
Saddleback Coll (CA)
Sage Jr Coll of Albany (NY)
Saint Augustine Coll (IL)
St Catharine Coll (KY)
Saint Charles County Comm Coll (MO)
St Clair County Comm Coll (MI)
St Gregory's Coll (OK)
St Johns River Comm Coll (FL)
St Louis Comm Coll at Florissant Valley (MO)
St Louis Comm Coll at Forest Park (MO)
St Louis Comm Coll at Meramec (MO)
Saint Mary's Coll (NC)
St Petersburg Jr Coll (FL)
St Philip's Coll (TX)
Salem Comm Coll (NJ)
Salish Kootenai Coll (MT)
Salt Lake Comm Coll (UT)
Sampson Comm Coll (NC)
San Antonio Coll (TX)
San Bernardino Valley Coll (CA)
Sandhills Comm Coll (NC)
San Diego City Coll (CA)
San Diego Mesa Coll (CA)
San Diego Miramar Coll (CA)
San Jacinto College–Central Cmps (TX)
San Joaquin Delta Coll (CA)
San Jose City Coll (CA)
San Juan Coll (NM)
Santa Barbara City Coll (CA)
Santa Fe Comm Coll (FL)
Santa Fe Comm Coll (NM)
Santa Monica Coll (CA)
Santa Rosa Jr Coll (CA)
Sauk Valley Comm Coll (IL)
Schenectady County Comm Coll (NY)
Schoolcraft Coll (MI)
Scott Comm Coll (IA)
Seattle Central Comm Coll (WA)
Seminole Comm Coll (FL)
Seminole Jr Coll (OK)
Seward County Comm Coll (KS)
Shawnee Comm Coll (IL)
Shelby State Comm Coll (TN)
Shelton State Comm Coll (AL)
Sheridan Coll (WY)
Shoreline Comm Coll (WA)
Shorter Coll (AR)
Sierra Coll (CA)
Sinclair Comm Coll (OH)
Sisseton-Wahpeton Comm Coll (SD)
Skagit Valley Coll (WA)
Skyline Coll (CA)
Snead State Comm Coll (AL)
Snow Coll (UT)
Solano Comm Coll (CA)
South Arkansas Comm Coll (AR)
Southeast Comm Coll, Beatrice Cmps (NE)
Southeast Comm Coll, Lincoln Cmps (NE)
Southeastern Comm Coll (NC)
Southeastern Comm Coll, North Cmps, West Burlington (IA)
Southeastern Comm Coll, South Cmps, Keokuk (IA)
Southern Arkansas U Tech (AR)
Southern State Comm Coll (OH)
Southern Union State Comm Coll (AL)
Southern West Virginia Comm and Tech Coll (WV)
South Florida Comm Coll (FL)
South Georgia Coll (GA)
South Mountain Comm Coll (AZ)
South Plains Coll (TX)
South Puget Sound Comm Coll (WA)
South Seattle Comm Coll (WA)
Southside Virginia Comm Coll (VA)
South Suburban Coll (IL)
Southwestern Coll (CA)
Southwestern Comm Coll (IA)
Southwestern Comm Coll (NC)
Southwestern Indian Polytechnic Inst (NM)
Southwestern Michigan Coll (MI)
Southwestern Oklahoma State U at Sayre (OK)
Southwestern Oregon Comm Coll (OR)
Southwest Mississippi Comm Coll (MS)
Southwest Texas Jr Coll (TX)
Southwest Virginia Comm Coll (VA)
Spartanburg Methodist Coll (SC)
Spokane Comm Coll (WA)
Spokane Falls Comm Coll (WA)
Spoon River Coll (IL)
Springfield Coll in Illinois (IL)
Springfield Tech Comm Coll (MA)
Standing Rock Coll (ND)
State Comm Coll of East St Louis (IL)
State Fair Comm Coll (MO)
State U of NY Coll of A&T at Cobleskill (NY)
State U of NY Coll of A&T at Morrisville (NY)
State U of NY Coll of Tech at Alfred (NY)
State U of NY Coll of Tech at Canton (NY)
State U of NY Coll of Tech at Delhi (NY)
State U of NY Coll of Tech at Farmingdale (NY)
Stone Child Coll (MT)
Suffolk County Comm College–Ammerman Cmps (NY)
Suffolk County Comm Coll–Eastern Cmps (NY)
Suffolk County Comm Coll–Western Cmps (NY)
Sullivan County Comm Coll (NY)
Surry Comm Coll (NC)
Sussex County Comm Coll (NJ)
Tacoma Comm Coll (WA)
Taft Coll (CA)
Tallahassee Comm Coll (FL)
Tarrant County Jr Coll (TX)
Tech Coll of Municipality of San Juan (PR)
Temple Coll (TX)
Texarkana Coll (TX)
Texas Southmost Coll (TX)
Thomas Nelson Comm Coll (VA)
Three Rivers Comm Coll (MO)
Three Rivers Comm-Tech Coll (CT)
Tidewater Comm Coll (VA)
Tomball Coll (TX)
Tompkins Cortland Comm Coll (NY)
Treasure Valley Comm Coll (OR)
Tri-County Comm Coll (NC)
Tri-County Tech Coll (SC)
Trinidad State Jr Coll (CO)
Trinity Valley Comm Coll (TX)
Triton Coll (IL)
Trocaire Coll (NY)
Truckee Meadows Comm Coll (NV)
Truett-McConnell Coll (GA)
Tulsa Jr Coll (OK)
Tunxis Comm Tech Coll (CT)
Turtle Mountain Comm Coll (ND)
Tyler Jr Coll (TX)
UAB Walker Coll (AL)
Ulster County Comm Coll (NY)
Umpqua Comm Coll (OR)
Union County Coll (NJ)
The U of Akron–Wayne Coll (OH)
U of Alaska Anchorage, Kenai Peninsula Coll (AK)
U of Alaska Anchorage, Kodiak Coll (AK)
U of Alaska Anchorage, Matanuska-Susitna Coll (AK)
U of Alaska, Prince William Sound Comm Coll (AK)
U of Alaska Southeast, Ketchikan Cmps (AK)
U of Alaska Southeast, Sitka Cmps (AK)
U of Cincinnati Clermont Coll (OH)
U of Cincinnati Raymond Walters Coll (OH)
U of Hawaii–Hawaii Comm Coll (HI)
U of Hawaii–Honolulu Comm Coll (HI)
U of Hawaii–Kapiolani Comm Coll (HI)
U of Hawaii–Kauai Comm Coll (HI)
U of Hawaii–Leeward Comm Coll (HI)
U of Hawaii–Maui Comm Coll (HI)
U of Hawaii–Windward Comm Coll (HI)
U of Kentucky, Ashland Comm Coll (KY)
U of Kentucky, Elizabethtown Comm Coll (KY)
U of Kentucky, Hazard Comm Coll (KY)
U of Kentucky, Hopkinsville Comm Coll (KY)
U of Kentucky, Jefferson Comm Coll (KY)
U of Kentucky, Lexington Comm Coll (KY)
U of Kentucky, Maysville Comm Coll (KY)
U of Kentucky, Prestonsburg Comm Coll (KY)
U of Kentucky, Southeast Comm Coll (KY)
U of Maine at Augusta (ME)
U of New Mexico–Gallup Branch (NM)
U of New Mexico–Los Alamos Branch (NM)
U of New Mexico–Valencia Cmps (NM)
U of North Dakota–Lake Region (ND)
U of North Dakota–Williston (ND)
U of Pittsburgh–Titusville (PA)
U of South Carolina at Beaufort (SC)
U of South Carolina at Lancaster (SC)
U of South Carolina at Sumter (SC)
U of South Carolina at Union (SC)
U of South Carolina Salkehatchie Regional Cmps (SC)
U of Wisconsin Center–Baraboo/Sauk County (WI)
U of Wisconsin Center–Barron County (WI)
U of Wisconsin Center–Fond du Lac (WI)
U of Wisconsin Center–Fox Valley (WI)
U of Wisconsin Center–Manitowoc County (WI)
U of Wisconsin Center–Marathon County (WI)
U of Wisconsin Center–Marinette County (WI)
U of Wisconsin Center–Marshfield/Wood County (WI)
U of Wisconsin Center–Richland (WI)
U of Wisconsin Center–Rock County (WI)
U of Wisconsin Center–Sheboygan County (WI)
U of Wisconsin Center–Washington County (WI)
U of Wisconsin Center–Waukesha County (WI)
Utah Valley State Coll (UT)
Valencia Comm Coll (FL)
Valley Forge Military Coll (PA)
Vance-Granville Comm Coll (NC)
Ventura Coll (CA)
Vermilion Comm Coll (MN)
Vernon Regional Jr Coll (TX)
Victoria Coll (TX)
Victor Valley Coll (CA)
Villa Maria Coll of Buffalo (NY)
Vincennes U (IN)
Vincennes University–Jasper Ctr (IN)
Virginia Highlands Comm Coll (VA)
Virginia Western Comm Coll (VA)
Vista Comm Coll (CA)
Volunteer State Comm Coll (TN)
Wake Tech Comm Coll (NC)
Waldorf Coll (IA)
Wallace State Comm Coll (AL)
Walla Walla Comm Coll (WA)
Walters State Comm Coll (TN)

Peterson's Guide to Two-Year Colleges 1997
101

Associate Degree Programs at Two-Year Colleges
Liberal Arts/General Studies–Manufacturing Technology

Warren County Comm Coll (NJ)
Washington State Comm Coll (OH)
Washtenaw Comm Coll (MI)
Waubonsee Comm Coll (IL)
Waycross Coll (GA)
Wayne Comm Coll (NC)
Wayne County Comm Coll (MI)
Weatherford Coll (TX)
Wenatchee Valley Coll (WA)
Wentworth Military Acad and Jr Coll (MO)
Westark Comm Coll (AR)
Westchester Comm Coll (NY)
Western Nebraska Comm Coll, Scottsbluff (NE)
Western Nevada Comm Coll (NV)
Western Oklahoma State Coll (OK)
Western Piedmont Comm Coll (NC)
Western Texas Coll (TX)
Western Wyoming Comm Coll (WY)
West Hills Comm Coll (CA)
West Los Angeles Coll (CA)
Westmoreland County Comm Coll (PA)
West Shore Comm Coll (MI)
West Valley Coll (CA)
West Virginia Northern Comm Coll (WV)
West Virginia U at Parkersburg (WV)
Whatcom Comm Coll (WA)
White Pines Coll (NH)
Wilkes Comm Coll (NC)
William Rainey Harper Coll (IL)
Williamsburg Tech Coll (SC)
Willmar Comm Coll (MN)
Wilson Tech Comm Coll (NC)
Wood Coll (MS)
Worthington Comm Coll (MN)
Wor-Wic Comm Coll (MD)
Wright State U, Lake Cmps (OH)
Wytheville Comm Coll (VA)
Yakima Valley Comm Coll (WA)
Yavapai Coll (AZ)
York Tech Coll (SC)
Young Harris Coll (GA)
Yuba Coll (CA)

LIBRARY SCIENCE
Allen County Comm Coll (KS)
Alpena Comm Coll (MI)
Brookdale Comm Coll (NJ)
Central Coll (KS)
City Coll of San Francisco (CA)
City Colls of Chicago, Wilbur Wright Coll (IL)
Clovis Comm Coll (NM)
Colby Comm Coll (KS)
Coll of DuPage (IL)
Coll of Lake County (IL)
Coll of Southern Idaho (ID)
Comm Coll of Philadelphia (PA)
Copiah-Lincoln Comm Coll (MS)
Cuesta Coll (CA)
Dixie Coll (UT)
Doña Ana Branch Comm Coll (NM)
East Central Coll (MO)
East Central Comm Coll (MS)
Foothill Coll (CA)
Fresno City Coll (CA)
Fullerton Coll (CA)
Gulf Coast Comm Coll (FL)
Hartnell Coll (CA)
Highland Comm Coll (KS)
Highline Comm Coll (WA)
Hutchinson Comm Coll and Area Vocational Sch (KS)
Illinois Central Coll (IL)
Indian River Comm Coll (FL)
Itawamba Comm Coll (MS)
Joliet Jr Coll (IL)
Lawson State Comm Coll (AL)
Lenoir Comm Coll (NC)
Lewis and Clark Comm Coll (IL)
Los Angeles Valley Coll (CA)
Merced Coll (CA)
Mesa Comm Coll (AZ)
Middle Georgia Coll (GA)
Northeast Mississippi Comm Coll (MS)
Northland Pioneer Coll (AZ)
Northwest Mississippi Comm Coll (MS)
Oakland Comm Coll (MI)
Oxnard Coll (CA)
Palo Alto Coll (TX)
Palomar Coll (CA)
Pasadena City Coll (CA)
Portland Comm Coll (OR)
Rancho Santiago Coll (CA)
Rock Valley Coll (IL)
Rose State Coll (OK)
Sacramento City Coll (CA)
Southwestern Comm Coll (IA)
Spokane Falls Comm Coll (WA)
U of Cincinnati Raymond Walters Coll (OH)
U of Maine at Augusta (ME)
Wallace State Comm Coll (AL)
Western Oklahoma State Coll (OK)

LINGUISTICS
Foothill Coll (CA)

LITERATURE
Allen County Comm Coll (KS)
Andrew Coll (GA)
Atlantic Comm Coll (NJ)
Austin Comm Coll (MN)
Bergen Comm Coll (NJ)
Blinn Coll (TX)
Brevard Coll (NC)
Chabot Coll (CA)
The Coll of Saint Thomas More (TX)
Comm Coll of Allegheny County South Cmps (PA)
Comm Coll of Southern Nevada (NV)
East Central Comm Coll (MS)
Eastern Wyoming Coll (WY)
Foothill Coll (CA)
Hutchinson Comm Coll and Area Vocational Sch (KS)
Iowa Lakes Comm Coll (IA)
Irvine Valley Coll (CA)
Jackson State Comm Coll (TN)
Kansas City Kansas Comm Coll (KS)
Lamar Comm Coll (CO)
Lamar University–Orange (TX)
Lincoln Land Comm Coll (IL)
Lon Morris Coll (TX)
Miami-Dade Comm Coll (FL)
Middle Georgia Coll (GA)
Midland Coll (TX)
Oklahoma City Comm Coll (OK)
Otero Jr Coll (CO)
Palm Beach Comm Coll (FL)
Polk Comm Coll (FL)
Pratt Comm Coll and Area Voc Sch (KS)
Redlands Comm Coll (OK)
Sacramento City Coll (CA)
Saddleback Coll (CA)
St Louis Comm Coll at Meramec (MO)
San Jacinto College–Central Cmps (TX)
San Joaquin Delta Coll (CA)
San Juan Coll (NM)
Seward County Comm Coll (KS)
Skagit Valley Coll (WA)
Skyline Coll (CA)
Southwestern Comm Coll (IA)

MACHINE AND TOOL TECHNOLOGIES
Aiken Tech Coll (SC)
Alamance Comm Coll (NC)
Alexandria Tech Coll (MN)
Allan Hancock Coll (CA)
Allen County Comm Coll (KS)
Alpena Comm Coll (MI)
Anson Comm Coll (NC)
Asheville-Buncombe Tech Comm Coll (NC)
Athens Area Tech Inst (GA)
Bakersfield Coll (CA)
Bay de Noc Comm Coll (MI)
Bessemer State Tech Coll (AL)
Black Hawk Coll, Moline (IL)
Blue Ridge Comm Coll (NC)
Brunswick Coll (GA)
Cape Fear Comm Coll (NC)
Casper Coll (WY)
Catonsville Comm Coll (MD)
Central Carolina Tech Coll (SC)
Central Comm College–Hastings Cmps (NE)
Central Comm College–Platte Cmps (NE)
Central Maine Tech Coll (ME)
Central Oregon Comm Coll (OR)
Central Piedmont Comm Coll (NC)
Cerritos Coll (CA)
Cerro Coso Comm Coll (CA)
Chattanooga State Tech Comm Coll (TN)
Chemeketa Comm Coll (OR)
Chesterfield-Marlboro Tech Coll (SC)
Chippewa Valley Tech Coll (WI)
City Colls of Chicago, Richard J Daley Coll (IL)
City Colls of Chicago, Wilbur Wright Coll (IL)
Clark Coll (WA)
Coffeyville Comm Coll (KS)
Coll of DuPage (IL)
Coll of Eastern Utah (UT)
Coll of Lake County (IL)
Coll of Marin (CA)
Coll of San Mateo (CA)
Coll of the Redwoods (CA)
Columbia Basin Coll (WA)
Comm Coll of Allegheny County North Cmps (PA)
Comm Coll of Rhode Island (RI)
Corning Comm Coll (NY)
Cowley County Comm Coll and Voc-Tech Sch (KS)
De Anza Coll (CA)
Delgado Comm Coll (LA)
Del Mar Coll (TX)
Delta Coll (MI)
Des Moines Area Comm Coll (IA)
Dunwoody Inst (MN)
Durham Tech Comm Coll (NC)
Eastern Maine Tech Coll (ME)
Elgin Comm Coll (IL)
Fayetteville Tech Comm Coll (NC)
Florence-Darlington Tech Coll (SC)
Forsyth Tech Comm Coll (NC)
Fresno City Coll (CA)
Front Range Comm Coll (CO)
Gadsden State Comm Coll (AL)
Gateway Comm Coll (AZ)
George Corley Wallace State Comm Coll, Selma (AL)
George C Wallace State Comm Coll, Dothan (AL)
Grays Harbor Coll (WA)
Grayson County Coll (TX)
Green River Comm Coll (WA)
Greenville Tech Coll (SC)
Gwinnett Tech Inst (GA)
Harry M Ayers State Tech Coll (AL)
Hartnell Coll (CA)
Hawkeye Comm Coll (IA)
Haywood Comm Coll (NC)
Helena Coll of Tech of The U of Montana (MT)
Hill Coll of the Hill Jr Coll District (TX)
Hinds Comm Coll (MS)
Horry-Georgetown Tech Coll (SC)
Hudson Valley Comm Coll (NY)
Illinois Eastern Comm Colls, Wabash Valley Coll (IL)
Indian Hills Comm Coll (IA)
Inver Hills Comm Coll (MN)
Iowa Central Comm Coll (IA)
Iowa Western Comm Coll (IA)
Isothermal Comm Coll (NC)
ITT Tech Inst, Evansville (IN)
ITT Tech Inst, Fort Wayne (IN)
ITT Tech Inst, Dayton (OH)
Ivy Tech State Coll–Eastcentral (IN)
Ivy Tech State Coll–Kokomo (IN)
Ivy Tech State Coll–Lafayette (IN)
Ivy Tech State Coll–Northcentral (IN)
Ivy Tech State Coll–Northeast (IN)
Ivy Tech State Coll–Northwest (IN)
Ivy Tech State Coll–Wabash Valley (IN)
Jackson Comm Coll (MI)
Jefferson Coll (MO)
J F Drake State Tech Coll (AL)
John A Logan Coll (IL)
John C Calhoun State Comm Coll (AL)
John M Patterson State Tech Coll (AL)
Johnson Tech Inst (PA)
John Wood Comm Coll (IL)
Kalamazoo Valley Comm Coll (MI)
Kankakee Comm Coll (IL)
Kellogg Comm Coll (MI)
Kishwaukee Coll (IL)
Lake Area Vocational-Tech Inst (SD)
Lakeland Comm Coll (OH)
Lake Michigan Coll (MI)
Lake Washington Tech Coll (WA)
Laney Coll (CA)
Lansing Comm Coll (MI)
Lee Coll (TX)
Lewis and Clark Comm Coll (IL)
Long Beach City Coll (CA)
Lorain County Comm Coll (OH)
Los Angeles Pierce Coll (CA)
Los Angeles Valley Coll (CA)
Lower Columbia Coll (WA)
Macomb Comm Coll (MI)
Maple Woods Comm Coll (MO)
Marshalltown Comm Coll (IA)
McDowell Tech Comm Coll (NC)
Meridian Comm Coll (MS)
Midlands Tech Coll (SC)
Mid Michigan Comm Coll (MI)
Mid-Plains Comm Coll (NE)
MiraCosta Coll (CA)
Moberly Area Comm Coll (MO)
Mohawk Valley Comm Coll (NY)
Montcalm Comm Coll (MI)
Moraine Park Tech Coll (WI)
Moraine Valley Comm Coll (IL)
Mt San Antonio Coll (CA)
Muskegon Comm Coll (MI)
Napa Valley Coll (CA)
New Hampshire Tech Coll, Berlin (NH)
New Hampshire Tech Coll, Nashua (NH)
New Mexico Jr Coll (NM)
New River Comm Coll (VA)
New York City Tech Coll of the City U of NY (NY)
Nicolet Area Tech Coll (WI)
North Arkansas Comm/Tech Coll (AR)
North Central Tech Coll (OH)
Northcentral Tech Coll (WI)
North Central Texas Coll (TX)
North Dakota State Coll of Science (ND)
Northeast State Tech Comm Coll (TN)
Northern Essex Comm Coll (MA)
North Idaho Coll (ID)
Oakland Comm Coll (MI)
Oakton Comm Coll (IL)
Odessa Coll (TX)
Oklahoma City Comm Coll (OK)
Oklahoma State U, Okmulgee (OK)
Onondaga Comm Coll (NY)
Orangeburg-Calhoun Tech Coll (SC)
Orange Coast Coll (CA)
Owens Comm Coll, Toledo (OH)
Oxnard Coll (CA)
Pasadena City Coll (CA)
Pellissippi State Tech Comm Coll (TN)
Petit Jean Tech Coll (AR)
Piedmont Tech Coll (SC)
Pikes Peak Comm Coll (CO)
Pima Comm Coll (AZ)
Portland Comm Coll (OR)
Pueblo Comm Coll (CO)
Randolph Comm Coll (NC)
Ranken Tech Coll (MO)
Reading Area Comm Coll (PA)
Renton Tech Coll (WA)
Richmond Comm Coll (NC)
Rich Mountain Comm Coll (AR)
Ricks Coll (ID)
St Clair County Comm Coll (MI)
St Cloud Tech Coll (MN)
St Philip's Coll (TX)
Salt Lake Comm Coll (UT)
San Bernardino Valley Coll (CA)
San Diego City Coll (CA)
San Joaquin Delta Coll (CA)
San Jose City Coll (CA)
San Juan Coll (NM)
Santa Rosa Jr Coll (CA)
Scott Comm Coll (IA)
Shawnee Comm Coll (IL)
Sheridan Coll (WY)
Shoreline Comm Coll (WA)
Sinclair Comm Coll (OH)
Solano Comm Coll (CA)
South Arkansas Comm Coll (AR)
Southeast Comm Coll, Lincoln Cmps (NE)
Southeast Comm Coll, Milford Cmps (NE)
Southeastern Comm Coll, North Cmps, West Burlington (IA)
Southern Maine Tech Coll (ME)
South Plains Coll (TX)
South Suburban Coll (IL)
Southwestern Michigan Coll (MI)
Southwestern Oregon Comm Coll (OR)
Southwestern Tech Coll (MN)
Southwest Mississippi Comm Coll (MS)
Southwest Wisconsin Tech Coll (WI)
Spartanburg Tech Coll (SC)
Spokane Comm Coll (WA)
State Fair Comm Coll (MO)
Tarrant County Jr Coll (TX)
Texas State Tech Coll–Waco/Marshall Cmps (TX)
Thaddeus Stevens State Sch of Tech (PA)
Tri-County Tech Coll (SC)
Trident Tech Coll (SC)
Triton Coll (IL)
U of Alaska Anchorage, Kenai Peninsula Coll (AK)
Utah Valley State Coll (UT)
Ventura Coll (CA)
Vincennes U (IN)
Virginia Highlands Comm Coll (VA)
Wake Tech Comm Coll (NC)
Wallace State Comm Coll (AL)
Walla Walla Comm Coll (WA)
Washtenaw Comm Coll (MI)
Waubonsee Comm Coll (IL)
Waukesha County Tech Coll (WI)
Waycross Coll (GA)
Westark Comm Coll (AR)
Westchester Comm Coll (NY)
Western Nevada Comm Coll (NV)
Western Wisconsin Tech Coll (WI)
Western Wyoming Comm Coll (WY)
West Shore Comm Coll (MI)
West Virginia U at Parkersburg (WV)
William Rainey Harper Coll (IL)
The Williamson Free Sch of Mech Trades (PA)
Willmar Tech Coll (MN)
Wytheville Comm Coll (VA)
Yavapai Coll (AZ)
York Tech Coll (SC)
Yuba Coll (CA)

MANAGEMENT INFORMATION SYSTEMS
Alexandria Tech Coll (MN)
Allen County Comm Coll (KS)
Arapahoe Comm Coll (CO)
Central Virginia Comm Coll (VA)
Central Wyoming Coll (WY)
Chandler-Gilbert Comm Coll (AZ)
Cincinnati State Tech and Comm Coll (OH)
Coconino County Comm Coll (AZ)
Coll of San Mateo (CA)
Comm Coll of Allegheny County South Cmps (PA)
Cosumnes River Coll (CA)
Delaware County Comm Coll (PA)
Dunwoody Inst (MN)
East Central Coll (MO)
Evergreen Valley Coll (CA)
Fugazzi Coll (KY)
Grayson County Coll (TX)
Gwinnett Tech Inst (GA)
Harrisburg Area Comm Coll (PA)
Herzing Coll of Business and Tech (GA)
Hesser Coll (NH)
John Wood Comm Coll (IL)
Keiser Coll of Tech, Daytona Beach (FL)
Kentucky Coll of Business, Lexington (KY)
Kirkwood Comm Coll (IA)
Lake Washington Tech Coll (WA)
Lamar Comm Coll (CO)
Laney Coll (CA)
Lansing Comm Coll (MI)
Merced Coll (CA)
Miami-Dade Comm Coll (FL)
Napa Valley Coll (CA)
NEI Coll of Tech (MN)
The New England Banking Inst (MA)
New Hampshire Tech Coll, Manchester (NH)
North Hennepin Comm Coll (MN)
Ouachita Tech Coll (AR)
Ozarka Tech Coll (AR)
Parkland Coll (IL)
Raritan Valley Comm Coll (NJ)
Saint Augustine Coll (IL)
Shasta Coll (CA)
Southern Maine Tech Coll (ME)
South Suburban Coll (IL)
Stark Tech Coll (OH)
State U of NY Coll of Tech at Farmingdale (NY)
Texas State Tech Coll (TX)
Triton Coll (IL)
Tulsa Jr Coll (OK)
U of Cincinnati Raymond Walters Coll (OH)
U of Kentucky, Ashland Comm Coll (KY)
U of Kentucky, Hopkinsville Comm Coll (KY)
U of Kentucky, Southeast Comm Coll (KY)
Vincennes U (IN)
Vincennes University–Jasper Ctr (IN)
Westchester Business Inst (NY)
William Rainey Harper Coll (IL)
Wright State U, Lake Cmps (OH)
Yakima Valley Comm Coll (WA)
Yavapai Coll (AZ)

MANUFACTURING TECHNOLOGY
Aiken Tech Coll (SC)
Alexandria Tech Coll (MN)
Allen County Comm Coll (KS)
Anne Arundel Comm Coll (MD)
Austin Comm Coll (TX)
Bergen Comm Coll (NJ)
Black Hawk Coll, Moline (IL)

Associate Degree Programs at Two-Year Colleges
Manufacturing Technology–Marketing/Retailing/Merchandising

Blue Ridge Comm Coll (NC)
Bowling Green State University–Firelands Coll (OH)
Brookhaven Coll (TX)
Cape Fear Comm Coll (NC)
Capital Comm Tech Coll (CT)
Catonsville Comm Coll (MD)
Central Comm College–Grand Island Cmps (NE)
Central Comm College–Hastings Cmps (NE)
Central Florida Comm Coll (FL)
Central Ohio Tech Coll (OH)
Central Oregon Comm Coll (OR)
Central Piedmont Comm Coll (NC)
Cerritos Coll (CA)
Chemeketa Comm Coll (OR)
Cincinnati State Tech and Comm Coll (OH)
Clackamas Comm Coll (OR)
Clark State Comm Coll (OH)
Coll of DuPage (IL)
Comm Coll of Allegheny County North Cmps (PA)
Comm Coll of Allegheny County South Cmps (PA)
Comm Coll of Beaver County (PA)
Comm Coll of Vermont (VT)
County Coll of Morris (NJ)
Danville Area Comm Coll (IL)
De Anza Coll (CA)
Dodge City Comm Coll (KS)
Don Bosco Tech Inst (CA)
Erie Comm Coll, City Cmps (NY)
Everett Comm Coll (WA)
Evergreen Valley Coll (CA)
Fashion Inst of Design & Merchandising, LA Cmps (CA)
Fashion Inst of Design & Merchandising, SD Cmps (CA)
Forsyth Tech Comm Coll (NC)
Fullerton Coll (CA)
Gateway Comm Coll (AZ)
Gateway Comm-Tech Coll (CT)
Gloucester County Coll (NJ)
Grand Rapids Comm Coll (MI)
Greenville Tech Coll (SC)
Harrisburg Area Comm Coll (PA)
Hartnell Coll (CA)
Haywood Comm Coll (NC)
Heartland Comm Coll (IL)
Henry Ford Comm Coll (MI)
Houston Comm Coll System (TX)
Illinois Central Coll (IL)
Ivy Tech State Coll–Columbus (IN)
Ivy Tech State Coll–Kokomo (IN)
Ivy Tech State Coll–Lafayette (IN)
Ivy Tech State Coll–Northcentral (IN)
Ivy Tech State Coll–Northeast (IN)
Ivy Tech State Coll–Northwest (IN)
Ivy Tech State Coll–Southcentral (IN)
Ivy Tech State Coll–Southeast (IN)
Ivy Tech State Coll–Wabash Valley (IN)
Ivy Tech State Coll–Whitewater (IN)
Jackson Comm Coll (MI)
Jefferson Comm Coll (OH)
Johnson County Comm Coll (KS)
Joliet Jr Coll (IL)
Kellogg Comm Coll (MI)
Kent State U, Ashtabula Cmps (OH)
Kent State U, Salem Cmps (OH)
Kings River Comm Coll (CA)
Kirkwood Comm Coll (IA)
Kirtland Comm Coll (MI)
Kishwaukee Coll (IL)
Labette Comm Coll (KS)
Lake Land Coll (IL)
Lakeland Comm Coll (OH)
Lake Michigan Coll (MI)
Lane Comm Coll (OR)
Lansing Comm Coll (MI)
Lima Tech Coll (OH)
Linn-Benton Comm Coll (OR)
Lorain County Comm Coll (OH)
Los Angeles Pierce Coll (CA)
Los Angeles Trade-Tech Coll (CA)
Meridian Comm Coll (MS)
Mesa Comm Coll (AZ)
Miami University–Hamilton Cmps (OH)
Miami University–Middletown Cmps (OH)
Middlesex County Coll (NJ)
Mid-State Tech Coll (WI)
Mineral Area Coll (MO)
MiraCosta Coll (CA)
Mohawk Valley Comm Coll (NY)
Monroe Comm Coll (NY)
Monroe County Comm Coll (MI)
Mt Hood Comm Coll (OR)
Muskingum Area Tech Coll (OH)
Naugatuck Valley Community–Tech Coll (CT)
New Hampshire Tech Coll, Claremont (NH)
New Hampshire Tech Coll, Laconia (NH)
New Hampshire Tech Coll, Nashua (NH)
Northampton County Area Comm Coll (PA)
North Central Tech Coll (OH)
North Dakota State Coll of Science (ND)
Northeast State Tech Comm Coll (TN)
North Hennepin Comm Coll (MN)
North Shore Comm Coll (MA)
Northwestern Michigan Coll (MI)
Oakland Comm Coll (MI)
Ocean County Coll (NJ)
Ohio State U Ag Tech Inst (OH)
Oklahoma State U, Okmulgee (OK)
Ouachita Tech Coll (AR)
Owens Comm Coll, Toledo (OH)
Ozarks Tech Comm Coll (MO)
Passaic County Comm Coll (NJ)
Pellissippi State Tech Comm Coll (TN)
Pennsylvania Coll of Tech (PA)
Pennsylvania Inst of Tech (PA)
Penn State U Abington-Ogontz Cmps (PA)
Penn State U Altoona Cmps (PA)
Penn State U Beaver Cmps (PA)
Penn State U Berks Cmps (PA)
Penn State U DuBois Cmps (PA)
Penn State U Fayette Cmps (PA)
Penn State U Hazleton Cmps (PA)
Penn State U McKeesport Cmps (PA)
Penn State U New Kensington Cmps (PA)
Penn State U Schuylkill Cmps (PA)
Penn State U Shenango Cmps (PA)
Penn State U Wilkes-Barre Cmps (PA)
Penn State U Worthington Scranton Cmps (PA)
Penn State U York Cmps (PA)
Pensacola Jr Coll (FL)
Piedmont Tech Coll (SC)
Pierce Coll (WA)
Pima Comm Coll (AZ)
Pitt Comm Coll (NC)
Prairie State Coll (IL)
Pulaski Tech Coll (AR)
Raritan Valley Comm Coll (NJ)
Richland Coll (TX)
Ricks Coll (ID)
Rock Valley Coll (IL)
Rogue Comm Coll (OR)
Rowan-Cabarrus Comm Coll (NC)
St Clair County Comm Coll (MI)
St Louis Comm Coll at Forest Park (MO)
St Paul Tech Coll (MN)
Salt Lake Comm Coll (UT)
San Antonio Coll (TX)
Sandhills Comm Coll (NC)
San Diego City Coll (CA)
Schoolcraft Coll (MI)
Scott Comm Coll (IA)
Seminole Comm Coll (FL)
Shoreline Comm Coll (WA)
Sierra Coll (CA)
Sinclair Comm Coll (OH)
Southeast Comm Coll, Milford Cmps (NE)
Southwestern Coll (CA)
Southwestern Michigan Coll (MI)
Southwestern Tech Coll (MN)
Southwest Missouri State University– West Plains (MO)
Spokane Comm Coll (WA)
Spoon River Coll (IL)
Springfield Tech Comm Coll (MA)
State U of NY Coll of A&T at Morrisville (NY)
State U of NY Coll of Tech at Canton (NY)
Suffolk County Comm College–Ammerman Cmps (NY)
Temple Coll (TX)
Terra State Comm Coll (OH)
Texas State Tech Coll–Harlingen Cmps (TX)
Texas State Tech Coll–Waco/Marshall Cmps (TX)
Three Rivers Comm-Tech Coll (CT)
Trident Tech Coll (SC)
Triton Coll (IL)
U of Cincinnati Raymond Walters Coll (OH)
Wake Tech Comm Coll (NC)
Washington State Comm Coll (OH)
Washtenaw Comm Coll (MI)
Waubonsee Comm Coll (IL)
West Shore Comm Coll (MI)
William Rainey Harper Coll (IL)
Wilson Tech Comm Coll (NC)
Wright State U, Lake Cmps (OH)
Yakima Valley Comm Coll (WA)
Yavapai Coll (AZ)
Yuba Coll (CA)

MARINE BIOLOGY

Brevard Coll (NC)
Daytona Beach Comm Coll (FL)
Florida Keys Comm Coll (FL)
Grays Harbor Coll (WA)
Gulf Coast Comm Coll (FL)
Mitchell Coll (CT)
Polk Comm Coll (FL)
Ricks Coll (ID)
Shoreline Comm Coll (WA)
Southern Maine Tech Coll (ME)
State U of NY Coll of A&T at Morrisville (NY)

MARINE SCIENCES

Anne Arundel Comm Coll (MD)
Atlantic Comm Coll (NJ)
Coll of Micronesia–FSM (FM)
Coll of the Redwoods (CA)
Indian River Comm Coll (FL)
Mitchell Coll (CT)
Saddleback Coll (CA)
State U of NY Coll of A&T at Morrisville (NY)

MARINE TECHNOLOGY

Cape Fear Comm Coll (NC)
Coll of Marin (CA)
Coll of Oceaneering (CA)
Florida Keys Comm Coll (FL)
Gulf Coast Comm Coll (FL)
Highline Comm Coll (WA)
Kingsborough Comm Coll of City U of NY (NY)
Louisville Tech Inst (KY)
New England Inst of Tech (RI)
New Hampshire Tech Coll, Laconia (NH)
Northeastern Jr Coll (CO)
Northern Marianas Coll (MP)
North Idaho Coll (ID)
Northwest Indian Coll (WA)
Orange Coast Coll (CA)
Rancho Santiago Coll (CA)
Saddleback Coll (CA)
Santa Barbara City Coll (CA)
Seattle Central Comm Coll (WA)
Shoreline Comm Coll (WA)
Skagit Valley Coll (WA)
Suffolk County Comm College–Ammerman Cmps (NY)
Suffolk County Comm Coll–Eastern Cmps (NY)
U of Hawaii–Honolulu Comm Coll (HI)
Washington County Tech Coll (ME)

MARITIME SCIENCES

Northwestern Michigan Coll (MI)

MARKETING/RETAILING/MERCHANDISING

Abraham Baldwin Ag Coll (GA)
Adirondack Comm Coll (NY)
Aiken Tech Coll (SC)
Aims Comm Coll (CO)
Alexandria Tech Coll (MN)
Allen County Comm Coll (KS)
Allentown Business Sch (PA)
American Inst of Business (IA)
American River Coll (CA)
Anne Arundel Comm Coll (MD)
Anoka-Ramsey Comm Coll (MN)
Anson Comm Coll (NC)
Arapahoe Comm Coll (CO)
Arizona Western Coll (AZ)
Art Inst of Fort Lauderdale (FL)
Art Inst of Pittsburgh (PA)
Asheville-Buncombe Tech Comm Coll (NC)
Athens Area Tech Inst (GA)
Atlantic Comm Coll (NJ)
Austin Comm Coll (TX)
Bainbridge Coll (GA)
Baker Coll of Jackson (MI)
Baltimore City Comm Coll (MD)
Barstow Coll (CA)
Bay de Noc Comm Coll (MI)
Belleville Area Coll (IL)
Bellevue Comm Coll (WA)
Berkeley Coll, New York (NY)
Berkeley Coll, White Plains (NY)
Berkshire Comm Coll (MA)
Big Bend Comm Coll (WA)
Bismarck State Coll (ND)
Black Hawk Coll, Moline (IL)
Blackhawk Tech Coll (WI)
Blue Mountain Comm Coll (OR)
Blue Ridge Comm Coll (NC)
Borough of Manhattan Comm Coll of City U of NY (NY)
Bowling Green State University–Firelands Coll (OH)
Bramson ORT Tech Inst (NY)
Brazosport Coll (TX)
Brevard Coll (NC)
Brevard Comm Coll (FL)
Bristol Comm Coll (MA)
Bronx Comm Coll of City U of NY (NY)
Brookdale Comm Coll (NJ)
Brookhaven Coll (TX)
Broome Comm Coll (NY)
Broward Comm Coll (FL)
The Brown Mackie Coll (KS)
Brunswick Coll (GA)
Bryant and Stratton Business Inst, Albany (NY)
Bryant and Stratton Business Inst, Buffalo (NY)
Bryant and Stratton Business Inst, Rochester (NY)
Bryant and Stratton Business Inst, Rochester (NY)
Bryant and Stratton Business Inst, E Hills Cmps, Williamsville (NY)
Bryant and Stratton Coll, Parma (OH)
Bucks County Comm Coll (PA)
Bunker Hill Comm Coll (MA)
Butler County Comm Coll (KS)
Butler County Comm Coll (PA)
Butte Coll (CA)
Camden County Coll (NJ)
Carl Sandburg Coll (IL)
Casper Coll (WY)
Catonsville Comm Coll (MD)
Cayuga County Comm Coll (NY)
Cecil Comm Coll (MD)
Cedar Valley Coll (TX)
Central Carolina Comm Coll (NC)
Central Carolina Tech Coll (SC)
Central City Business Inst (NY)
Central Comm College–Platte Cmps (NE)
Centralia Coll (WA)
Central Lakes Coll (MN)
Central Oregon Comm Coll (OR)
Central Pennsylvania Business Sch (PA)
Central Piedmont Comm Coll (NC)
Central Texas Coll (TX)
Central Virginia Comm Coll (VA)
Cerritos Coll (CA)
Chaffey Coll (CA)
Champlain Coll (VT)
Charles Stewart Mott Comm Coll (MI)
Chattahoochee Tech Inst (GA)
Chesterfield-Marlboro Tech Coll (SC)
Chippewa Valley Tech Coll (WI)
Cincinnati State Tech and Comm Coll (OH)
Cisco Jr Coll (TX)
City Coll of San Francisco (CA)
City Colls of Chicago, Harold Washington Coll (IL)
City Colls of Chicago, Harry S Truman Coll (IL)
City Colls of Chicago, Kennedy-King Coll (IL)
City Colls of Chicago, Malcolm X Coll (IL)
City Colls of Chicago, Olive-Harvey Coll (IL)
City Colls of Chicago, Richard J Daley Coll (IL)
City Colls of Chicago, Wilbur Wright Coll (IL)
Clackamas Comm Coll (OR)
Clark Coll (WA)
Clinton Comm Coll (IA)
Clovis Comm Coll (NM)
Coffeyville Comm Coll (KS)
Coll of Alameda (CA)
Coll of DuPage (IL)
Coll of Lake County (IL)
Coll of Marin (CA)
Coll of San Mateo (CA)
Coll of Southern Idaho (ID)
Coll of the Desert (CA)
Coll of the Sequoias (CA)
Collin County Comm Coll (TX)
Colorado Mountn Coll, Alpine Cmps (CO)
Columbia Basin Coll (WA)
Columbia Jr Coll of Business (SC)
Columbia State Comm Coll (TN)
Columbus State Comm Coll (OH)
Comm Coll of Allegheny County Allegheny Cmps (PA)
Comm Coll of Allegheny County Boyce Cmps (PA)
Comm Coll of Allegheny County North Cmps (PA)
Comm Coll of Allegheny County South Cmps (PA)
Comm Coll of Aurora (CO)
Comm Coll of Beaver County (PA)
Comm Coll of Denver (CO)
Comm Coll of Philadelphia (PA)
Comm Coll of Rhode Island (RI)
Comm Coll of Southern Nevada (NV)
Copiah-Lincoln Comm College–Natchez Cmps (MS)
Cosumnes River Coll (CA)
County Coll of Morris (NJ)
Cowley County Comm Coll and Voc-Tech Sch (KS)
Crafton Hills Coll (CA)
Craven Comm Coll (NC)
Crowder Coll (MO)
Cuesta Coll (CA)
Cumberland County Coll (NJ)
Cuyahoga Comm Coll, Eastern Cmps (OH)
Cuyahoga Comm Coll, Metropolitan Cmps (OH)
Cuyahoga Comm Coll, Western Cmps (OH)
Cypress Coll (CA)
Dalton Coll (GA)
Danville Area Comm Coll (IL)
Danville Comm Coll (VA)
Darton Coll (GA)
Daytona Beach Comm Coll (FL)
Dean Coll (MA)
De Anza Coll (CA)
DeKalb Coll (GA)
DeKalb Tech Inst (GA)
Delaware Tech & Comm Coll, Jack F Owens Cmps (DE)
Delta Coll (MI)
Des Moines Area Comm Coll (IA)
Dixie Coll (UT)
Dodge City Comm Coll (KS)
East Central Coll (MO)
Eastern Arizona Coll (AZ)
Eastern Idaho Tech Coll (ID)
Eastern Oklahoma State Coll (OK)
East Los Angeles Coll (CA)
Edison State Comm Coll (OH)
Edmonds Comm Coll (WA)
El Camino Coll (CA)
Elgin Comm Coll (IL)
Ellsworth Comm Coll (IA)
Enterprise State Jr Coll (AL)
Erie Business Ctr, Main (PA)
Erie Business Ctr South (PA)
Erie Comm Coll, City Cmps (NY)
Essex Comm Coll (MD)
Everett Comm Coll (WA)
Fashion Inst of Design & Merchandising, LA Cmps (CA)
Fashion Inst of Design & Merchandising, SD Cmps (CA)
Fashion Inst of Design & Merchandising, SF Cmps (CA)
Fayetteville Tech Comm Coll (NC)
Fergus Falls Comm Coll (MN)
Finger Lakes Comm Coll (NY)
Florence-Darlington Tech Coll (SC)
Florida Comm Coll at Jacksonville (FL)
Forsyth Tech Comm Coll (NC)
Fort Berthold Comm Coll (ND)
Fox Valley Tech Coll (WI)
Frederick Comm Coll (MD)
Fresno City Coll (CA)
Front Range Comm Coll (CO)
Fullerton Coll (CA)
Gadsden State Comm Coll (AL)
Gainesville Coll (GA)
Garden City Comm Coll (KS)
Gaston Coll (NC)
Genesee Comm Coll (NY)

Peterson's Guide to Two-Year Colleges 1997
103

Associate Degree Programs at Two-Year Colleges
Marketing/Retailing/Merchandising–Mathematics

Glendale Comm Coll (AZ)
Gloucester County Coll (NJ)
Golden West Coll (CA)
Grand Rapids Comm Coll (MI)
Greenfield Comm Coll (MA)
Green River Comm Coll (WA)
Greenville Tech Coll (SC)
Grossmont Coll (CA)
Guilford Tech Comm Coll (NC)
Gulf Coast Comm Coll (FL)
Gwinnett Tech Inst (GA)
Hagerstown Business Coll (MD)
Hagerstown Jr Coll (MD)
Halifax Comm Coll (NC)
Harcum Coll (PA)
Harford Comm Coll (MD)
Harrisburg Area Comm Coll (PA)
Hartnell Coll (CA)
Hawkeye Comm Coll (IA)
Henry Ford Comm Coll (MI)
Herkimer County Comm Coll (NY)
Hesser Coll (NH)
Highland Comm Coll (IL)
Hillsborough Comm Coll (FL)
Hinds Comm Coll (MS)
Hocking Coll (OH)
Houston Comm Coll System (TX)
Hudson Valley Comm Coll (NY)
Hutchinson Comm Coll and Area Vocational Sch (KS)
ICS Ctr for Degree Studies (PA)
Illinois Central Coll (IL)
Illinois Valley Comm Coll (IL)
Imperial Valley Coll (CA)
Indian River Comm Coll (FL)
Inter American U of PR, Guayama Cmps (PR)
Inver Hills Comm Coll (MN)
Iowa Western Comm Coll (IA)
Isothermal Comm Coll (NC)
Itawamba Comm Coll (MS)
Ivy Tech State Coll–Central Indiana (IN)
Ivy Tech State Coll–Columbus (IN)
Ivy Tech State Coll–Eastcentral (IN)
Ivy Tech State Coll–Kokomo (IN)
Ivy Tech State Coll–Lafayette (IN)
Ivy Tech State Coll–Northcentral (IN)
Ivy Tech State Coll–Northeast (IN)
Ivy Tech State Coll–Northwest (IN)
Ivy Tech State Coll–Southwest (IN)
Ivy Tech State Coll–Wabash Valley (IN)
Ivy Tech State Coll–Whitewater (IN)
Jackson Comm Coll (MI)
Jackson State Comm Coll (TN)
James H Faulkner State Comm Coll (AL)
Jamestown Business Coll (NY)
Jefferson Coll (MO)
Jefferson Comm Coll (NY)
Jefferson Davis Comm Coll (AL)
Jefferson State Comm Coll (AL)
John A Logan Coll (IL)
John C Calhoun State Comm Coll (AL)
Johnson County Comm Coll (KS)
John Wood Comm Coll (IL)
Joliet Jr Coll (IL)
Kalamazoo Valley Comm Coll (MI)
Kankakee Comm Coll (IL)
Kansas City Kansas Comm Coll (KS)
Kent State U, Ashtabula Cmps (OH)
Kent State U, Trumbull Cmps (OH)
Kingsborough Comm Coll of City U of NY (NY)
Kirkwood Comm Coll (IA)
Kirtland Comm Coll (MI)
Kishwaukee Coll (IL)
Lackawanna Jr Coll (PA)
Lake Area Vocational-Tech Inst (SD)
Lake City Comm Coll (FL)
Lake Land Coll (IL)
Lake Michigan Coll (MI)
Lakeshore Tech Coll (WI)
Lake Tahoe Comm Coll (CA)
Lakewood Comm Coll (MN)
Lamar Comm Coll (CO)
Laney Coll (CA)
Lansing Comm Coll (MI)
Laredo Comm Coll (TX)
Las Positas Coll (CA)
LDS Business Coll (UT)
Lenoir Comm Coll (NC)
Lewis and Clark Comm Coll (IL)
Lima Tech Coll (OH)
Lincoln Coll, Normal (IL)
Lincoln Land Comm Coll (IL)
Little Hoop Comm Coll (ND)
Long Beach City Coll (CA)
Longview Comm Coll (MO)
Lorain County Comm Coll (OH)
Los Angeles City Coll (CA)
Los Angeles Pierce Coll (CA)
Los Angeles Southwest Coll (CA)
Los Angeles Valley Coll (CA)
Lower Columbia Coll (WA)
MacCormac Jr Coll (IL)
Macomb Comm Coll (MI)
Macon Coll (GA)
Madison Area Tech Coll (WI)
Madison Jr Coll of Business (WI)
Manatee Comm Coll (FL)
Manchester Comm-Tech Coll (CT)
Maple Woods Comm Coll (MO)
Marion Tech Coll (OH)
Marshalltown Comm Coll (IA)
Massachusetts Bay Comm Coll (MA)
Massasoit Comm Coll (MA)
McCann Sch of Business (PA)
McDowell Tech Comm Coll (NC)
McHenry County Coll (IL)
Merced Coll (CA)
Meridian Comm Coll (MS)
Mesabi Comm Coll (MN)
Mesa Comm Coll (AZ)
Metropolitan Comm Coll (NE)
Miami-Dade Comm Coll (FL)
Miami-Jacobs Coll (OH)
Miami University–Middletown Cmps (OH)
Middle Georgia Coll (GA)
Middlesex Comm Coll (MA)
Middlesex Community-Tech Coll (CT)
Middlesex County Coll (NJ)
Midlands Tech Coll (SC)
Mid Michigan Comm Coll (MI)
Midstate Coll (IL)
Mid-State Tech Coll (WI)
Miles Comm Coll (MT)
Milwaukee Area Tech Coll (WI)
Mineral Area Coll (MO)
MiraCosta Coll (CA)
Mission Coll (CA)
Mississippi Gulf Coast Comm Coll (MS)
Miss Wade's Fashion Merchandising Coll (TX)
Moberly Area Comm Coll (MO)
Modesto Jr Coll (CA)
Mohave Comm Coll (AZ)
Mohawk Valley Comm Coll (NY)
Monroe Comm Coll (NY)
Monroe County Comm Coll (MI)
Monterey Peninsula Coll (CA)
Montgomery College–Germantown Cmps (MD)
Montgomery College–Rockville Cmps (MD)
Montgomery College–Takoma Park Cmps (MD)
Montgomery County Comm Coll (PA)
Moorpark Coll (CA)
Moraine Valley Comm Coll (IL)
Morton Coll (IL)
Mountain Empire Comm Coll (VA)
Mt Hood Comm Coll (OR)
Mount Ida Coll (MA)
Mt San Antonio Coll (CA)
Mount Wachusett Comm Coll (MA)
Muskegon Comm Coll (MI)
Muskingum Area Tech Coll (OH)
Napa Valley Coll (CA)
Nash Comm Coll (NC)
Nassau Comm Coll (NY)
National Business Coll, Bluefield (VA)
National Business Coll, Danville (VA)
National Business Coll, Harrisonburg (VA)
National Business Coll, Lynchburg (VA)
National Business Coll, Martinsville (VA)
National Business Coll, Roanoke (VA)
Naugatuck Valley Community–Tech Coll (CT)
Navarro Coll (TX)
Neosho County Comm Coll (KS)
Newbury Coll (MA)
The New England Banking Inst (MA)
New Hampshire Tech Coll, Manchester (NH)
New Hampshire Tech Coll, Nashua (NH)
New Hampshire Tech Inst (NH)
New Mexico Jr Coll (NM)
New River Comm Coll (VA)
New York City Tech Coll of the City U of NY (NY)
Nicolet Area Tech Coll (WI)
Normandale Comm Coll (MN)
North Central Michigan Coll (MI)
North Central Missouri Coll (MO)
Northcentral Tech Coll (WI)
North Dakota State University–Bottineau (ND)
Northeast Comm Coll (NE)
Northeastern Jr Coll (CO)
Northeastern Oklahoma A&M Coll (OK)
Northeast Iowa Comm Coll, Calmar Cmps (IA)
Northeast Iowa Comm Coll, Peosta Cmps (IA)
Northern Essex Comm Coll (MA)
Northern Marianas Coll (MP)
Northern Virginia Comm Coll (VA)
North Harris Coll (TX)
North Hennepin Comm Coll (MN)
North Iowa Area Comm Coll (IA)
Northland Comm and Tech Coll (MN)
North Shore Comm Coll (MA)
Northwest Coll (WY)
Northwestern Business Coll (IL)
Northwestern Coll (OH)
Northwestern Connecticut Comm-Tech Coll (CT)
Northwestern Michigan Coll (MI)
Northwest Iowa Comm Coll (IA)
Northwest State Comm Coll (OH)
Norwalk Comm-Tech Coll (CT)
Oakland Comm Coll (MI)
Oakton Comm Coll (IL)
Ocean County Coll (NJ)
Ohlone Coll (CA)
Oklahoma State U, Okmulgee (OK)
Orange Coast Coll (CA)
Orange County Comm Coll (NY)
Otero Jr Coll (CO)
Owens Comm Coll, Findlay (OH)
Owens Comm Coll, Toledo (OH)
Oxnard Coll (CA)
Palm Beach Comm Coll (FL)
Palomar Coll (CA)
Palo Verde Coll (CA)
Parkland Coll (IL)
Pasadena City Coll (CA)
Pasco-Hernando Comm Coll (FL)
Passaic County Comm Coll (NJ)
Pearl River Comm Coll (MS)
Pellissippi State Tech Comm Coll (TN)
Penn Valley Comm Coll (MO)
Petit Jean Tech Coll (AR)
Piedmont Tech Coll (SC)
Piedmont Virginia Comm Coll (VA)
Pierce Coll (WA)
Pikes Peak Comm Coll (CO)
Pitt Comm Coll (NC)
Polk Comm Coll (FL)
Portland Comm Coll (OR)
Prairie State Coll (IL)
Pratt Comm Coll and Area Voc Sch (KS)
Prince George's Comm Coll (MD)
Quincy Coll (MA)
Rancho Santiago Coll (CA)
Raritan Valley Comm Coll (NJ)
Rasmussen Coll Mankato (MN)
Rasmussen Coll Minnetonka (MN)
Rasmussen Coll St Cloud (MN)
Reading Area Comm Coll (PA)
Red Rocks Comm Coll (CO)
Rend Lake Coll (IL)
Ricks Coll (ID)
Riverside Comm Coll (CA)
Rochester Business Inst (NY)
Rochester Comm Coll (MN)
Rockland Comm Coll (NY)
Rock Valley Coll (IL)
Sage Jr Coll of Albany (NY)
Saint Charles County Comm Coll (MO)
St Clair County Comm Coll (MI)
St Cloud Tech Coll (MN)
St Johns River Comm Coll (FL)
St Petersburg Jr Coll (FL)
Salem Comm Coll (NJ)
Salt Lake Comm Coll (UT)
San Bernardino Valley Coll (CA)
San Diego City Coll (CA)
San Diego Mesa Coll (CA)
San Jacinto College–Central Cmps (TX)
San Joaquin Delta Coll (CA)
San Jose City Coll (CA)
Santa Barbara City Coll (CA)
Santa Fe Comm Coll (FL)
Sauk Valley Comm Coll (IL)
Schoolcraft Coll (MI)
Seminole Comm Coll (FL)
Seward County Comm Coll (KS)
Shasta Coll (CA)
Shelby State Comm Coll (TN)
Shoreline Comm Coll (WA)
Sierra Coll (CA)
Sinclair Comm Coll (OH)
Skagit Valley Coll (WA)
Solano Comm Coll (CA)
Southern U at Shreveport–Bossier City Cmps (LA)
South Florida Comm Coll (FL)
South Plains Coll (TX)
South Suburban Coll (IL)
Southwestern Coll (CA)
Southwestern Comm Coll (IA)
Southwestern Indian Polytechnic Inst (NM)
Southwestern Michigan Coll (MI)
Southwestern Oregon Comm Coll (OR)
Southwest Mississippi Comm Coll (MS)
Southwest Wisconsin Tech Coll (WI)
Spartanburg Tech Coll (SC)
Spokane Comm Coll (WA)
Springfield Tech Comm Coll (MA)
Standing Rock Coll (ND)
Stark Tech Coll (OH)
State Fair Comm Coll (MO)
State U of NY Coll of A&T at Morrisville (NY)
State U of NY Coll of Tech at Alfred (NY)
State U of NY Coll of Tech at Canton (NY)
State U of NY Coll of Tech at Delhi (NY)
Stratton Coll (WI)
Suffolk County Comm College–Ammerman Cmps (NY)
Suffolk County Comm Coll–Eastern Cmps (NY)
Suffolk County Comm Coll–Western Cmps (NY)
Sullivan County Comm Coll (NY)
Tarrant County Jr Coll (TX)
Terra State Comm Coll (OH)
Thomas Nelson Comm Coll (VA)
Three Rivers Comm Coll (MO)
Three Rivers Comm-Tech Coll (CT)
Tidewater Comm Coll (VA)
Tompkins Cortland Comm Coll (NY)
Trident Tech Coll (SC)
Trinity Valley Comm Coll (TX)
Triton Coll (IL)
Trocaire Coll (NY)
Truckee Meadows Comm Coll (NV)
Tulsa Jr Coll (OK)
Tunxis Comm Tech Coll (CT)
Tyler Jr Coll (TX)
Ulster County Comm Coll (NY)
Umpqua Comm Coll (OR)
Union County Coll (NJ)
U of Cincinnati Raymond Walters Coll (OH)
U of Hawaii–Kapiolani Comm Coll (HI)
U of Hawaii–Maui Comm Coll (HI)
U of North Dakota–Lake Region (ND)
U of North Dakota–Williston (ND)
Utah Valley State Coll (UT)
Vincennes U (IN)
Wallace State Comm Coll (AL)
Walla Walla Comm Coll (WA)
Washington State Comm Coll (OH)
Washtenaw Comm Coll (MI)
Waubonsee Comm Coll (IL)
Waukesha County Tech Coll (WI)
Wayne Comm Coll (NC)
Wayne County Comm Coll (MI)
Westchester Business Inst (NY)
Westchester Comm Coll (NY)
Western Iowa Tech Comm Coll (IA)
Western Nebraska Comm Coll, Scottsbluff (NE)
Western Nevada Comm Coll (NV)
Western Piedmont Comm Coll (NC)
Western Texas Coll (TX)
Western Wisconsin Tech Coll (WI)
Western Wyoming Comm Coll (WY)
West Los Angeles Coll (CA)
Westmoreland County Comm Coll (PA)
West Shore Comm Coll (MI)
West Valley Coll (CA)
West Virginia U at Parkersburg (WV)
William Rainey Harper Coll (IL)
Willmar Tech Coll (MN)
Wisconsin Indianhead Tech Coll, New Richmond Cmps (WI)
Wisconsin Indianhead Tech Coll, Rice Lake Cmps (WI)
Wisconsin Indianhead Tech Coll, Superior Cmps (WI)
Wright State U, Lake Cmps (OH)
Yakima Valley Comm Coll (WA)
Yuba Coll (CA)

MARRIAGE AND FAMILY COUNSELING

Central Coll (KS)
Colby Comm Coll (KS)
Hiwassee Coll (TN)
Tallahassee Comm Coll (FL)

MATERIALS SCIENCES

Clark Coll (WA)
Contra Costa Coll (CA)
Elgin Comm Coll (IL)
Erie Comm Coll, North Cmps (NY)
Greenville Tech Coll (SC)
Henry Ford Comm Coll (MI)
Kalamazoo Valley Comm Coll (MI)
Kent State U, Ashtabula Cmps (OH)
Macomb Comm Coll (MI)
Mt San Antonio Coll (CA)
Neosho County Comm Coll (KS)
New Mexico State University–Alamogordo (NM)
Northern Essex Comm Coll (MA)
North Hennepin Comm Coll (MN)
Rock Valley Coll (IL)
St Louis Comm Coll at Meramec (MO)
Schenectady County Comm Coll (NY)
Tulsa Jr Coll (OK)
William Rainey Harper Coll (IL)

MATHEMATICS

Abraham Baldwin Ag Coll (GA)
Adirondack Comm Coll (NY)
Alabama Southern Comm Coll, Monroeville (AL)
Alabama Southern Comm Coll, Thomasville (AL)
Allen County Comm Coll (KS)
Alpena Comm Coll (MI)
Alvin Comm Coll (TX)
American River Coll (CA)
Andrew Coll (GA)
Angelina Coll (TX)
Anne Arundel Comm Coll (MD)
Antelope Valley Coll (CA)
Arizona Western Coll (AZ)
Arkansas State University–Beebe Branch (AR)
Atlanta Metropolitan Coll (GA)
Atlantic Comm Coll (NJ)
Austin Comm Coll (TX)
Bainbridge Coll (GA)
Bakersfield Coll (CA)
Barstow Coll (CA)
Barton County Comm Coll (KS)
Bay de Noc Comm Coll (MI)
Bee County Coll (TX)
Bergen Comm Coll (NJ)
Bismarck State Coll (ND)
Black Hawk Coll, Moline (IL)
Blinn Coll (TX)
Borough of Manhattan Comm Coll of City U of NY (NY)
Brazosport Coll (TX)
Brevard Coll (NC)
Brevard Comm Coll (FL)
Bristol Comm Coll (MA)
Bronx Comm Coll of City U of NY (NY)
Brookdale Comm Coll (NJ)
Brunswick Coll (GA)
Bucks County Comm Coll (PA)
Butler County Comm Coll (KS)
Butler County Comm Coll (PA)
Butte Coll (CA)
Cañada Coll (CA)
Cape Cod Comm Coll (MA)
Carl Albert State Coll (OK)
Casper Coll (WY)
Cayuga County Comm Coll (NY)
Central Comm College–Grand Island Cmps (NE)
Central Comm College–Hastings Cmps (NE)

Associate Degree Programs at Two-Year Colleges
Mathematics–Mechanical Engineering Technology

Central Comm College–Platte Cmps (NE)
Central Oregon Comm Coll (OR)
Central Texas Coll (TX)
Central Wyoming Coll (WY)
Cerritos Coll (CA)
Chabot Coll (CA)
Chaffey Coll (CA)
Chattahoochee Valley State Comm Coll (AL)
Chemeketa Comm Coll (OR)
Chesapeake Coll (MD)
Cisco Jr Coll (TX)
City Coll of San Francisco (CA)
City Colls of Chicago, Harold Washington Coll (IL)
City Colls of Chicago, Kennedy-King Coll (IL)
City Colls of Chicago, Olive-Harvey Coll (IL)
Clackamas Comm Coll (OR)
Clark Coll (WA)
Clinton Comm Coll (IA)
Coffeyville Comm Coll (KS)
Colby Comm Coll (KS)
Coll of Alameda (CA)
Coll of DuPage (IL)
Coll of Lake County (IL)
Coll of Marin (CA)
Coll of San Mateo (CA)
Coll of Southern Idaho (ID)
Coll of the Canyons (CA)
Coll of the Desert (CA)
Coll of the Sequoias (CA)
Coll of the Siskiyous (CA)
Collin County Comm Coll (TX)
Colorado Mountn Coll, Alpine Cmps (CO)
Colorado Mountn Coll, Roaring Fork Cmps-Spring Valley Ctr (CO)
Colorado Mountn Coll, Timberline Cmps (CO)
Columbia Coll (CA)
Columbia-Greene Comm Coll (NY)
Columbia State Comm Coll (TN)
Comm Coll of Allegheny County Allegheny Cmps (PA)
Comm Coll of Allegheny County Boyce Cmps (PA)
Comm Coll of Allegheny County North Cmps (PA)
Comm Coll of Allegheny County South Cmps (PA)
Comm Coll of Southern Nevada (NV)
Connors State Coll (OK)
Contra Costa Coll (CA)
Corning Comm Coll (NY)
Cosumnes River Coll (CA)
County Coll of Morris (NJ)
Crafton Hills Coll (CA)
Crowder Coll (MO)
Cuesta Coll (CA)
Cumberland County Coll (NJ)
Cypress Coll (CA)
Dalton Coll (GA)
Danville Area Comm Coll (IL)
Darton Coll (GA)
Daytona Beach Comm Coll (FL)
De Anza Coll (CA)
Del Mar Coll (TX)
Dixie Coll (UT)
Dodge City Comm Coll (KS)
Donnelly Coll (KS)
Dutchess Comm Coll (NY)
East Central Coll (MO)
East Central Comm Coll (MS)
Eastern Arizona Coll (AZ)
Eastern Oklahoma State Coll (OK)
Eastern Wyoming Coll (WY)
East Georgia Coll (GA)
East Los Angeles Coll (CA)
East Mississippi Comm Coll (MS)
Edison State Comm Coll (OH)
El Camino Coll (CA)
Ellsworth Comm Coll (IA)
El Paso Comm Coll (TX)
Erie Comm Coll, North Cmps (NY)
Essex Comm Coll (MD)
Essex County Coll (NJ)
Everett Comm Coll (WA)
Finger Lakes Comm Coll (NY)
Foothill Coll (CA)
Fort Berthold Comm Coll (ND)
Frank Phillips Coll (TX)
Frederick Comm Coll (MD)
Fresno City Coll (CA)
Front Range Comm Coll (CO)
Fullerton Coll (CA)
Fulton-Montgomery Comm Coll (NY)
Gainesville Coll (GA)
Galveston Coll (TX)
Garden City Comm Coll (KS)
Garrett Comm Coll (MD)
Gavilan Coll (CA)
Genesee Comm Coll (NY)
Gogebic Comm Coll (MI)
Golden West Coll (CA)
Gordon Coll (GA)
Grayson County Coll (TX)
Greenfield Comm Coll (MA)
Grossmont Coll (CA)
Gulf Coast Comm Coll (FL)
Hagerstown Jr Coll (MD)
Harford Comm Coll (MD)
Harrisburg Area Comm Coll (PA)
Hartnell Coll (CA)
Herkimer County Comm Coll (NY)
Highland Comm Coll (IL)
Highland Comm Coll (KS)
Highline Comm Coll (WA)
Hill Coll of the Hill Jr Coll District (TX)
Hinds Comm Coll (MS)
Hiwassee Coll (TN)
Housatonic Comm-Tech Coll (CT)
Howard Coll (TX)
Hudson Valley Comm Coll (NY)
Hutchinson Comm Coll and Area Vocational Sch (KS)
Imperial Valley Coll (CA)
Independence Comm Coll (KS)
Indian River Comm Coll (FL)
Iowa Lakes Comm Coll (IA)
Irvine Valley Coll (CA)
Itawamba Comm Coll (MS)
Jackson State Comm Coll (TN)
Jamestown Comm Coll (NY)
Jefferson Coll (MO)
Jefferson Comm Coll (NY)
John A Logan Coll (IL)
John C Calhoun State Comm Coll (AL)
John Wood Comm Coll (IL)
Joliet Jr Coll (IL)
Jones County Jr Coll (MS)
Kansas City Kansas Comm Coll (KS)
Kellogg Comm Coll (MI)
Kemper Military Jr Coll (MO)
Kings River Comm Coll (CA)
Kirkwood Comm Coll (IA)
Kishwaukee Coll (IL)
Labette Comm Coll (KS)
Lake City Comm Coll (FL)
Lake Land Coll (IL)
Lake Michigan Coll (MI)
Lake Tahoe Comm Coll (CA)
Lamar Comm Coll (CO)
Lamar University–Orange (TX)
Laney Coll (CA)
Laramie County Comm Coll (WY)
Lassen Coll (CA)
Lawson State Comm Coll (AL)
Lee Coll (TX)
Lehigh Carbon Comm Coll (PA)
Lincoln Land Comm Coll (IL)
Linn-Benton Comm Coll (OR)
Little Big Horn Coll (MT)
Little Hoop Comm Coll (ND)
Long Beach City Coll (CA)
Lon Morris Coll (TX)
Lorain County Comm Coll (OH)
Los Angeles City Coll (CA)
Los Angeles Mission Coll (CA)
Los Angeles Valley Coll (CA)
Los Medanos Coll (CA)
Lower Columbia Coll (WA)
Luzerne County Comm Coll (PA)
Macon Coll (GA)
Mary Holmes Coll (MS)
Mendocino Coll (CA)
Merced Coll (CA)
Mercer County Comm Coll (NJ)
Merritt Coll (CA)
Mesa Comm Coll (AZ)
Miami-Dade Comm Coll (FL)
Miami University–Middletown Cmps (OH)
Middle Georgia Coll (GA)
Middlesex County Coll (NJ)
Midland Coll (TX)
Mid Michigan Comm Coll (MI)
Mid-Plains Comm Coll (NE)
Mineral Area Coll (MO)
MiraCosta Coll (CA)
Mission Coll (CA)
Mississippi Delta Comm Coll (MS)
Moberly Area Comm Coll (MO)
Modesto Jr Coll (CA)
Mohave Comm Coll (AZ)
Mohawk Valley Comm Coll (NY)
Monroe Comm Coll (NY)
Monroe County Comm Coll (MI)
Monterey Peninsula Coll (CA)
Montgomery College–Rockville Cmps (MD)
Montgomery College–Takoma Park Cmps (MD)
Montgomery County Comm Coll (PA)
Moorpark Coll (CA)
Motlow State Comm Coll (TN)
Mountain Empire Comm Coll (VA)
Mt San Jacinto Coll (CA)
Murray State Coll (OK)
Muscatine Comm Coll (IA)
Nassau Comm Coll (NY)
Naugatuck Valley Community–Tech Coll (CT)
Navarro Coll (TX)
New Mexico Jr Coll (NM)
New Mexico Military Inst (NM)
Niagara County Comm Coll (NY)
Northampton County Area Comm Coll (PA)
North Country Comm Coll (NY)
North Dakota State University–Bottineau (ND)
Northeast Comm Coll (NE)
Northeastern Jr Coll (CO)
Northeastern Oklahoma A&M Coll (OK)
Northeast Mississippi Comm Coll (MS)
Northern Virginia Comm Coll (VA)
North Harris Coll (TX)
North Idaho Coll (ID)
North Seattle Comm Coll (WA)
Northwest Coll (WY)
Northwestern Connecticut Comm-Tech Coll (CT)
Northwest Mississippi Comm Coll (MS)
Odessa Coll (TX)
Okaloosa-Walton Comm Coll (FL)
Oklahoma City Comm Coll (OK)
Onondaga Comm Coll (NY)
Orange Coast Coll (CA)
Otero Jr Coll (CO)
Owens Comm Coll, Findlay (OH)
Owens Comm Coll, Toledo (OH)
Oxnard Coll (CA)
Palm Beach Comm Coll (FL)
Palo Alto Coll (TX)
Panama Canal Coll (Republic of Panama)
Paris Jr Coll (TX)
Parkland Coll (IL)
Pasadena City Coll (CA)
Passaic County Comm Coll (NJ)
Paul Smith's Coll (NY)
Phillips County Comm Coll (AR)
Pikes Peak Comm Coll (CO)
Pima Comm Coll (AZ)
Polk Comm Coll (FL)
Porterville Coll (CA)
Potomac State Coll of West Virginia U (WV)
Pratt Comm Coll and Area Voc Sch (KS)
Quincy Coll (MA)
Rancho Santiago Coll (CA)
Raritan Valley Comm Coll (NJ)
Redlands Comm Coll (OK)
Red Rocks Comm Coll (CO)
Ricks Coll (ID)
Roane State Comm Coll (TN)
Rockland Comm Coll (NY)
Rogers State Coll (OK)
Rogue Comm Coll (OR)
Rose State Coll (OK)
Roxbury Comm Coll (MA)
Sacramento City Coll (CA)
Saddleback Coll (CA)
St Catharine Coll (KY)
St Gregory's Coll (OK)
St Louis Comm Coll at Florissant Valley (MO)
St Louis Comm Coll at Forest Park (MO)
St Louis Comm Coll at Meramec (MO)
St Philip's Coll (TX)
Salem Comm Coll (NJ)
San Bernardino Valley Coll (CA)
Sandhills Comm Coll (NC)
San Diego City Coll (CA)
San Diego Mesa Coll (CA)
San Diego Miramar Coll (CA)
San Jacinto College–Central Cmps (TX)
San Jacinto College–South Cmps (TX)
San Joaquin Delta Coll (CA)
San Juan Coll (NM)
Santa Barbara City Coll (CA)
Santa Monica Coll (CA)
Santa Rosa Jr Coll (CA)
Sauk Valley Comm Coll (IL)
Schenectady County Comm Coll (NY)
Scott Comm Coll (IA)
Scottsdale Comm Coll (AZ)
Seward County Comm Coll (KS)
Skagit Valley Coll (WA)
Skyline Coll (CA)
Snow Coll (UT)
Solano Comm Coll (CA)
Southern U at Shreveport–Bossier City Cmps (LA)
South Georgia Coll (GA)
South Mountain Comm Coll (AZ)
South Suburban Coll (IL)
SouthWest Collegiate Inst for the Deaf (TX)
Southwestern Coll (CA)
Southwestern Comm Coll (IA)
Spoon River Coll (IL)
State Comm Coll of East St Louis (IL)
State U of NY Coll of A&T at Cobleskill (NY)
State U of NY Coll of A&T at Morrisville (NY)
State U of NY Coll of Tech at Alfred (NY)
Suffolk County Comm College–Ammerman Cmps (NY)
Sussex County Comm Coll (NJ)
Tacoma Comm Coll (WA)
Taft Coll (CA)
Terra State Comm Coll (OH)
Texarkana Coll (TX)
Tompkins Cortland Comm Coll (NY)
Treasure Valley Comm Coll (OR)
Trinity Valley Comm Coll (TX)
Triton Coll (IL)
Tulsa Jr Coll (OK)
Turtle Mountain Comm Coll (ND)
Ulster County Comm Coll (NY)
Umpqua Comm Coll (OR)
U of Kentucky, Jefferson Comm Coll (KY)
U of South Carolina Salkehatchie Regional Cmps (SC)
U of Wisconsin Center–Marathon County (WI)
Vermilion Comm Coll (MN)
Vincennes U (IN)
Waldorf Coll (IA)
Washington State Comm Coll (OH)
Waubonsee Comm Coll (IL)
Waycross Coll (GA)
Wenatchee Valley Coll (WA)
Western Nebraska Comm Coll, Scottsbluff (NE)
Western Nevada Comm Coll (NV)
Western Oklahoma State Coll (OK)
Western Wyoming Comm Coll (WY)
West Hills Comm Coll (CA)
West Los Angeles Coll (CA)
West Shore Comm Coll (MI)
West Valley Coll (CA)
Wharton County Jr Coll (TX)
Wilkes Comm Coll (NC)
William Rainey Harper Coll (IL)
Willmar Comm Coll (MN)
Young Harris Coll (GA)
Yuba Coll (CA)

MECHANICAL DESIGN TECHNOLOGY

Adirondack Comm Coll (NY)
Alamance Comm Coll (NC)
Allen County Comm Coll (KS)
American Inst of Design (PA)
Anoka-Ramsey Comm Coll (MN)
Anson Comm Coll (NC)
Arapahoe Comm Coll (CO)
Black Hawk Coll, Moline (IL)
Blackhawk Tech Coll (WI)
Blue Ridge Comm Coll (VA)
Bowling Green State University–Firelands Coll (OH)
Butler County Comm Coll (KS)
Butler County Comm Coll (PA)
Cape Fear Comm Coll (NC)
Cayuga County Comm Coll (NY)
Central Maine Tech Coll (ME)
Chattanooga State Tech Comm Coll (TN)
Chemeketa Comm Coll (OR)
Chesterfield-Marlboro Tech Coll (SC)
Chippewa Valley Tech Coll (WI)
Clark Coll (WA)
Coll of DuPage (IL)
Coll of The Albemarle (NC)
Columbus State Comm Coll (OH)
Comm Coll of Allegheny County Boyce Cmps (PA)
Comm Coll of Allegheny County South Cmps (PA)
Comm Coll of Rhode Island (RI)
Comm Coll of Southern Nevada (NV)
Dabney S Lancaster Comm Coll (VA)
De Anza Coll (CA)
Delta Coll (MI)
Edgecombe Comm Coll (NC)
Forsyth Tech Comm Coll (NC)
Fox Valley Tech Coll (WI)
Garden City Comm Coll (KS)
Hartnell Coll (CA)
Hawkeye Comm Coll (IA)
Heartland Comm Coll (IL)
Illinois Central Coll (IL)
Illinois Valley Comm Coll (IL)
Iowa Western Comm Coll (IA)
Isothermal Comm Coll (NC)
Ivy Tech State Coll–Central Indiana (IN)
Ivy Tech State Coll–Columbus (IN)
Ivy Tech State Coll–Kokomo (IN)
Ivy Tech State Coll–Lafayette (IN)
Ivy Tech State Coll–Northcentral (IN)
Ivy Tech State Coll–Northeast (IN)
Ivy Tech State Coll–Northwest (IN)
Ivy Tech State Coll–Southcentral (IN)
Ivy Tech State Coll–Wabash Valley (IN)
Jefferson Coll (MO)
Johnson Tech Inst (PA)
Joliet Jr Coll (IL)
Kirkwood Comm Coll (IA)
Lake Michigan Coll (MI)
Lakeshore Tech Coll (WI)
Lansing Comm Coll (MI)
Lenoir Comm Coll (NC)
Lima Tech Coll (OH)
Lorain County Comm Coll (OH)
Los Angeles Valley Coll (CA)
Louisville Tech Inst (KY)
Luzerne County Comm Coll (PA)
Macomb Comm Coll (MI)
Madison Area Tech Coll (WI)
McHenry County Coll (IL)
Mid-State Tech Coll (WI)
Mohawk Valley Comm Coll (NY)
Montgomery College–Rockville Cmps (MD)
Moraine Park Tech Coll (WI)
Moraine Valley Comm Coll (IL)
Morrison Inst of Tech (IL)
Mountain Empire Comm Coll (VA)
Mt San Antonio Coll (CA)
New Hampshire Tech Coll, Berlin (NH)
New Hampshire Tech Coll, Manchester (NH)
Normandale Comm Coll (MN)
Northcentral Tech Coll (WI)
North Dakota State Coll of Science (ND)
Northeast Iowa Comm Coll, Calmar Cmps (IA)
North Iowa Area Comm Coll (IA)
Northwest Iowa Comm Coll (IA)
Northwest Mississippi Comm Coll (MS)
Oakland Comm Coll (MI)
Oakton Comm Coll (IL)
Oklahoma City Comm Coll (OK)
Owens Comm Coll, Toledo (OH)
Pennsylvania Inst of Tech (PA)
Piedmont Tech Coll (SC)
Pikes Peak Comm Coll (CO)
Prairie State Coll (IL)
Raritan Valley Comm Coll (NJ)
Richland Coll (TX)
Ricks Coll (ID)
Rock Valley Coll (IL)
St Cloud Tech Coll (MN)
Sauk Valley Comm Coll (IL)
Schoolcraft Coll (MI)
Southeast Comm Coll, Milford Cmps (NE)
South Suburban Coll (IL)
Southwestern Michigan Coll (MI)
Southwest Wisconsin Tech Coll (WI)
Spokane Comm Coll (WA)
Springfield Tech Comm Coll (MA)
State U of NY Coll of Tech at Alfred (NY)
Thaddeus Stevens State Sch of Tech (PA)
Triangle Tech, Inc, Pittsburgh (PA)
Triangle Tech, Inc–Erie Sch (PA)
Triangle Tech, Inc–Greensburg Ctr (PA)
Waubonsee Comm Coll (IL)
Western Wisconsin Tech Coll (WI)
Westmoreland County Comm Coll (PA)
William Rainey Harper Coll (IL)

MECHANICAL ENGINEERING TECHNOLOGY

Alexandria Tech Coll (MN)
Anne Arundel Comm Coll (MD)

Associate Degree Programs at Two-Year Colleges
Mechanical Engineering Technology–Medical Assistant Technologies

Asheville-Buncombe Tech Comm Coll (NC)
Augusta Tech Inst (GA)
Belmont Tech Coll (OH)
Black Hawk Coll, Moline (IL)
Blue Ridge Comm Coll (NC)
Brevard Comm Coll (FL)
Bristol Comm Coll (MA)
Broome Comm Coll (NY)
Broward Comm Coll (FL)
Brunswick Coll (GA)
Butler County Comm Coll (KS)
Camden County Coll (NJ)
Capital Comm Tech Coll (CT)
Catawba Valley Comm Coll (NC)
Central Ohio Tech Coll (OH)
Central Oregon Comm Coll (OR)
Central Piedmont Comm Coll (NC)
Central Virginia Comm Coll (VA)
Charles Stewart Mott Comm Coll (MI)
Chattanooga State Tech Comm Coll (TN)
Chippewa Valley Tech Coll (WI)
Cincinnati State Tech and Comm Coll (OH)
Citrus Coll (CA)
City Coll of San Francisco (CA)
City Colls of Chicago, Wilbur Wright Coll (IL)
Clackamas Comm Coll (OR)
Clark Coll (WA)
Clark State Comm Coll (OH)
Coffeyville Comm Coll (KS)
Coll of Lake County (IL)
Columbus State Comm Coll (OH)
Columbus Tech Inst (GA)
Comm Coll of Allegheny County Boyce Cmps (PA)
Comm Coll of Allegheny County South Cmps (PA)
Comm Coll of Rhode Island (RI)
Comm Coll of Southern Nevada (NV)
Corning Comm Coll (NY)
County Coll of Morris (NJ)
Cuyahoga Comm Coll, Metropolitan Cmps (OH)
Danville Area Comm Coll (IL)
DeKalb Coll (GA)
Delaware County Comm Coll (PA)
Delaware Tech & Comm Coll, Stanton/Wilmington Cmps (DE)
Delta Coll (MI)
Dixie Coll (UT)
ECPI Coll of Tech, Hampton (VA)
ECPI Coll of Tech, Virginia Beach (VA)
ECPI Computer Inst, Richmond (VA)
ECPI Computer Inst, Roanoke (VA)
Edgecombe Comm Coll (NC)
Erie Comm Coll, North Cmps (NY)
Finger Lakes Comm Coll (NY)
Fox Valley Tech Coll (WI)
Franklin Inst of Boston (MA)
Gadsden State Comm Coll (AL)
Garden City Comm Coll (KS)
Gaston Coll (NC)
Gateway Comm-Tech Coll (CT)
Grayson County Coll (TX)
Greenville Tech Coll (SC)
Hagerstown Jr Coll (MD)
Harrisburg Area Comm Coll (PA)
Hawkeye Comm Coll (IA)
Highland Comm Coll (IL)
Hudson Valley Comm Coll (NY)
Hutchinson Comm Coll and Area Vocational Sch (KS)
ICS Ctr for Degree Studies (PA)
Illinois Valley Comm Coll (IL)
Iowa Western Comm Coll (IA)
Isothermal Comm Coll (NC)
Jamestown Comm Coll (NY)
Jefferson Comm Coll (OH)
Jefferson State Comm Coll (AL)
John C Calhoun State Comm Coll (AL)
John Tyler Comm Coll (VA)
Kalamazoo Valley Comm Coll (MI)
Kent State U, Ashtabula Cmps (OH)
Kent State U, Trumbull Cmps (OH)
Kent State U, Tuscarawas Cmps (OH)
Kirkwood Comm Coll (IA)
Lakeland Comm Coll (OH)
Lake Michigan Coll (MI)
Lansing Comm Coll (MI)
Lehigh Carbon Comm Coll (PA)
Lima Tech Coll (OH)
Lord Fairfax Comm Coll (VA)
Los Angeles Trade-Tech Coll (CA)
Los Angeles Valley Coll (CA)
Louisville Tech Inst (KY)
Lower Columbia Coll (WA)
Marion Tech Coll (OH)
Massachusetts Bay Comm Coll (MA)
Meridian Comm Coll (MS)
Miami University–Middletown Cmps (OH)
Middle Georgia Coll (GA)
Middlesex County Coll (NJ)
Midlands Tech Coll (SC)
Mid Michigan Comm Coll (MI)
Milwaukee Area Tech Coll (WI)
Mohawk Valley Comm Coll (NY)
Monroe Comm Coll (NY)
Montgomery College–Rockville Cmps (MD)
Morrison Inst of Tech (IL)
Mt Hood Comm Coll (OR)
Nashville State Tech Inst (TN)
Naugatuck Valley Community–Tech Coll (CT)
New Hampshire Tech Inst (NH)
New York City Tech Coll of the City U of NY (NY)
Normandale Comm Coll (MN)
North Central Tech Coll (OH)
Northeastern Oklahoma A&M Coll (OK)
Northeast Iowa Comm Coll, Peosta Cmps (IA)
Northern Virginia Comm Coll (VA)
Northwest Iowa Comm Coll (IA)
Northwest State Comm Coll (OH)
Norwalk Comm-Tech Coll (CT)
Onondaga Comm Coll (NY)
Orangeburg-Calhoun Tech Coll (SC)
Owens Comm Coll, Findlay (OH)
Owens Comm Coll, Toledo (OH)
Pasadena City Coll (CA)
Pellissippi State Tech Comm Coll (TN)
Pennsylvania Inst of Tech (PA)
Penn State U Abington-Ogontz Cmps (PA)
Penn State U Altoona Cmps (PA)
Penn State U Beaver Cmps (PA)
Penn State U Berks Cmps (PA)
Penn State U DuBois Cmps (PA)
Penn State U Fayette Cmps (PA)
Penn State U Hazleton Cmps (PA)
Penn State U McKeesport Cmps (PA)
Penn State U New Kensington Cmps (PA)
Penn State U Schuylkill Cmps (PA)
Penn State U Shenango Cmps (PA)
Penn State U Wilkes-Barre Cmps (PA)
Penn State U York Cmps (PA)
Piedmont Tech Coll (SC)
Portland Comm Coll (OR)
Potomac State Coll of West Virginia U (WV)
Prairie State Coll (IL)
Queensborough Comm Coll of City U of NY (NY)
Reading Area Comm Coll (PA)
Red Rocks Comm Coll (CO)
Richland Coll (TX)
Richmond Comm Coll (NC)
Ricks Coll (ID)
Rochester Comm Coll (MN)
Rockland Comm Coll (NY)
St Louis Comm Coll at Florissant Valley (MO)
St Louis Comm Coll at Forest Park (MO)
Salt Lake Comm Coll (UT)
San Antonio Coll (TX)
San Jacinto College–South Cmps (TX)
San Joaquin Delta Coll (CA)
San Juan Coll (NM)
Shasta Coll (CA)
Shoreline Comm Coll (WA)
Sinclair Comm Coll (OH)
Southeast Comm Coll, Milford Cmps (NE)
Southeastern Comm Coll, North Cmps, West Burlington (IA)
Southern Arkansas U Tech (AR)
Southern U at Shreveport–Bossier City Cmps (LA)
Southwestern Tech Coll (MN)
Spartanburg Tech Coll (SC)
Spokane Comm Coll (WA)
Springfield Tech Comm Coll (MA)
Stark Tech Coll (OH)
State Tech Inst at Memphis (TN)
State U of NY Coll of A&T at Morrisville (NY)
State U of NY Coll of Tech at Alfred (NY)
State U of NY Coll of Tech at Canton (NY)
State U of NY Coll of Tech at Farmingdale (NY)
Suffolk County Comm College–Ammerman Cmps (NY)
Tarrant County Jr Coll (TX)
Terra State Comm Coll (OH)
Texas State Tech Coll–Waco/Marshall Cmps (TX)
Thomas Nelson Comm Coll (VA)
Three Rivers Comm-Tech Coll (CT)
Trident Tech Coll (SC)
Tulsa Jr Coll (OK)
Union County Coll (NJ)
U of Hawaii–Hawaii Comm Coll (HI)
U of Kentucky, Jefferson Comm Coll (KY)
U of Kentucky, Lexington Comm Coll (KY)
U of Kentucky, Madisonville Comm Coll (KY)
Vermont Tech Coll (VT)
Vincennes U (IN)
Virginia Western Comm Coll (VA)
Wake Tech Comm Coll (NC)
Washington State Comm Coll (OH)
Washtenaw Comm Coll (MI)
Westchester Comm Coll (NY)
Western Iowa Tech Comm Coll (IA)
Westmoreland County Comm Coll (PA)
West Virginia U at Parkersburg (WV)
William Rainey Harper Coll (IL)
Wisconsin Indianhead Tech Coll, Rice Lake Cmps (WI)
Wright State U, Lake Cmps (OH)
Wytheville Comm Coll (VA)
York Tech Coll (SC)

MEDICAL ASSISTANT TECHNOLOGIES

Allan Hancock Coll (CA)
Allen County Comm Coll (KS)
American Inst of Commerce (IA)
Andover Coll (ME)
Anne Arundel Comm Coll (MD)
Anson Comm Coll (NC)
Antelope Valley Coll (CA)
Aquinas Coll at Milton (MA)
Aquinas Coll at Newton (MA)
Arapahoe Comm Coll (CO)
Athens Area Tech Inst (GA)
ATI Health Education Ctr (FL)
Atlanta Metropolitan Coll (GA)
Austin Comm Coll (TX)
Baker Coll of Jackson (MI)
Bay State Coll (MA)
Beal Coll (ME)
Belleville Area Coll (IL)
Belmont Tech Coll (OH)
Bergen Comm Coll (NJ)
Blair Jr Coll (CO)
Bossier Parish Comm Coll (LA)
Bradford Sch (OH)
Brevard Comm Coll (FL)
Briarwood Coll (CT)
Broome Comm Coll (NY)
Broward Comm Coll (FL)
Brown Inst (MN)
Bryant and Stratton Business Inst, Albany (NY)
Bryant and Stratton Business Inst, Buffalo (NY)
Bryant and Stratton Business Inst, Rochester (NY)
Bryant and Stratton Business Inst, Rochester (NY)
Bryant and Stratton Business Inst, Syracuse (NY)
Bryant and Stratton Business Inst, E Hills Cmps, Williamsville (NY)
Bryant and Stratton Coll, Parma (OH)
Bryant and Stratton Coll, Richmond Heights (OH)
Bucks County Comm Coll (PA)
Burlington County Coll (NJ)
Butler County Comm Coll (PA)
Carteret Comm Coll (NC)
Cecils Jr Coll of Business (NC)
Central Carolina Comm Coll (NC)
Central City Business Inst (NY)
Central Comm College–Hastings Cmps (NE)
Central Pennsylvania Business Sch (PA)
Central Piedmont Comm Coll (NC)
Cerritos Coll (CA)
Chabot Coll (CA)
Charter Coll (AK)
Chemeketa Comm Coll (OR)
Cincinnati State Tech and Comm Coll (OH)
Colby Comm Coll (KS)
Coll of Marin (CA)
Coll of San Mateo (CA)
Coll of Southern Idaho (ID)
Coll of the Desert (CA)
Colorado Northwestern Comm Coll (CO)
Commonwealth Business Coll, LaPorte (IN)
Commonwealth Business Coll, Merrillville (IN)
Comm Coll of Allegheny County Allegheny Cmps (PA)
Comm Coll of Allegheny County South Cmps (PA)
Comm Coll of Aurora (CO)
Comm Coll of Philadelphia (PA)
Comm Coll of the Air Force (AL)
Cosumnes River Coll (CA)
Cuesta Coll (CA)
Cuyahoga Comm Coll, Metropolitan Cmps (OH)
Davidson County Comm Coll (NC)
Davis Coll (OH)
De Anza Coll (CA)
Delaware County Comm Coll (PA)
Delaware Tech & Comm Coll, Jack F Owens Cmps (DE)
Delta Coll (MI)
Des Moines Area Comm Coll (IA)
Draughons Jr Coll (AL)
Draughons Jr Coll (KY)
Draughons Jr Coll, Nashville (TN)
Duff's Business Inst (PA)
Dutchess Comm Coll (NY)
Eastern Idaho Tech Coll (ID)
Eastern Oklahoma State Coll (OK)
East Los Angeles Coll (CA)
Edgecombe Comm Coll (NC)
Edmonds Comm Coll (WA)
El Camino Coll (CA)
El Centro Coll (TX)
El Paso Comm Coll (TX)
Erie Business Ctr, Main (PA)
Erie Comm Coll, North Cmps (NY)
ETI Tech Coll, Niles (OH)
Everett Comm Coll (WA)
Fisher Coll (MA)
Florida National Coll (FL)
Forsyth Tech Comm Coll (NC)
Fresno City Coll (CA)
Fugazzi Coll (KY)
Gadsden State Comm Coll (AL)
Gaston Coll (NC)
Gateway Coll (NE)
Gem City Coll (IL)
George Corley Wallace State Comm Coll, Selma (AL)
Great Lakes Jr Coll of Business (MI)
Grossmont Coll (CA)
Guilford Tech Comm Coll (NC)
Gwinnett Tech Inst (GA)
Hagerstown Business Coll (MD)
Harcum Coll (PA)
Harford Comm Coll (MD)
Haywood Comm Coll (NC)
Henry Ford Comm Coll (MI)
Hesser Coll (NH)
Highland Park Comm Coll (MI)
Highline Comm Coll (WA)
Hiwassee Coll (TN)
Hocking Coll (OH)
Hudson County Comm Coll (NJ)
Huntington Jr Coll of Business (WV)
Hutchinson Comm Coll and Area Vocational Sch (KS)
ICM Sch of Business (PA)
Imperial Valley Coll (CA)
Indiana Business Coll (IN)
Inst of Career Education (FL)
Iowa Central Comm Coll (IA)
Iowa Western Comm Coll (IA)
Ivy Tech State Coll–Central Indiana (IN)
Ivy Tech State Coll–Columbus (IN)
Ivy Tech State Coll–Eastcentral (IN)
Ivy Tech State Coll–Kokomo (IN)
Ivy Tech State Coll–Lafayette (IN)
Ivy Tech State Coll–Northcentral (IN)
Ivy Tech State Coll–Northeast (IN)
Ivy Tech State Coll–Northwest (IN)
Ivy Tech State Coll–Southcentral (IN)
Ivy Tech State Coll–Southwest (IN)
Ivy Tech State Coll–Wabash Valley (IN)
Ivy Tech State Coll–Whitewater (IN)
Jackson Comm Coll (MI)
James Sprunt Comm Coll (NC)
Jefferson Comm Coll (OH)
Jefferson Davis Comm Coll (AL)
John C Calhoun State Comm Coll (AL)
J Sargeant Reynolds Comm Coll (VA)
Kalamazoo Valley Comm Coll (MI)
Keiser Coll of Tech, Daytona Beach (FL)
Keiser Coll of Tech, Sarasota (FL)
Kelsey Jenney Coll (CA)
Kirkwood Comm Coll (IA)
Knoxville Business Coll (TN)
Lake Area Vocational-Tech Inst (SD)
Lakeshore Tech Coll (WI)
Lake Tahoe Comm Coll (CA)
Lake Washington Tech Coll (WA)
Lansdale Sch of Business (PA)
Lansing Comm Coll (MI)
Laredo Comm Coll (TX)
LDS Business Coll (UT)
Lehigh Carbon Comm Coll (PA)
Lenoir Comm Coll (NC)
Long Beach City Coll (CA)
Lower Columbia Coll (WA)
Massasoit Comm Coll (MA)
McCarrie Schools of Health Sci and Tech (PA)
McIntosh Coll (NH)
Meadows Coll of Business (GA)
Median Sch of Allied Health Careers (PA)
Medical Inst of Minnesota (MN)
Merced Coll (CA)
Miami-Dade Comm Coll (FL)
Miami-Jacobs Coll (OH)
Michiana Coll (IN)
Middlesex Comm Coll (MA)
Midstate Coll (IL)
Mid-State Coll (ME)
Modesto Jr Coll (CA)
Montana State U Coll of Tech-Great Falls (MT)
Monterey Peninsula Coll (CA)
Montgomery College–Takoma Park Cmps (MD)
Montgomery Comm Coll (NC)
Mt Hood Comm Coll (OR)
Muskingum Area Tech Coll (OH)
National Business Coll, Bluefield (VA)
National Business Coll, Charlottesville (VA)
National Business Coll, Danville (VA)
National Business Coll, Harrisonburg (VA)
National Business Coll, Lynchburg (VA)
National Business Coll, Roanoke (VA)
National Ed Ctr–National Inst of Tech Cmps (WV)
Nettleton Career Coll (SD)
Newbury Coll (MA)
New England Inst of Tech (RI)
New England Inst of Tech & Florida Culinary Inst (FL)
New Hampshire Tech Coll, Claremont (NH)
New Mexico Jr Coll (NM)
Newport Business Inst (PA)
Niagara County Comm Coll (NY)
North Dakota State University–Bottineau (ND)
Northeast Mississippi Comm Coll (MS)
North Iowa Area Comm Coll (IA)
North Seattle Comm Coll (WA)
Northwestern Business Coll (IL)
Northwestern Coll (OH)
Northwestern Connecticut Comm-Tech Coll (CT)
Northwestern Michigan Coll (MI)
Oakland Comm Coll (MI)
Ohio Inst of Photography and Tech (OH)
Ohlone Coll (CA)
Olympic Coll (WA)
Omaha Coll of Health Careers (NE)
Orangeburg-Calhoun Tech Coll (SC)
Orange Coast Coll (CA)
Our Lady of the Lake Coll (LA)
Owensboro Jr Coll of Business (KY)
Palomar Coll (CA)
Pamlico Comm Coll (NC)

Associate Degree Programs at Two-Year Colleges
Medical Assistant Technologies–Medical Records Services

Parks Jr Coll (CO)
Pasadena City Coll (CA)
Penn Commercial, Inc (PA)
Phillips Jr Coll (UT)
Phillips Jr Coll of Springfield (MO)
Piedmont Tech Coll (SC)
Pima Medical Inst (NM)
Pitt Comm Coll (NC)
Portland Comm Coll (OR)
PPI Health Careers Sch (CO)
Pueblo Coll of Business and Tech (CO)
Quinebaug Valley Comm-Tech Coll (CT)
Rasmussen Coll Mankato (MN)
Renton Tech Coll (WA)
RETS Tech Ctr (OH)
Riverside Comm Coll (CA)
Rochester Comm Coll (MN)
Rockingham Comm Coll (NC)
Saddleback Coll (CA)
Salem Comm Coll (NJ)
Salt Lake Comm Coll (UT)
San Antonio Coll (TX)
San Diego Mesa Coll (CA)
Sanford-Brown Coll, North Kansas City (MO)
Sanford-Brown Coll, St Charles (MO)
Santa Rosa Jr Coll (CA)
Sawyer Coll of Business, Cleveland (OH)
Sawyer Coll of Business, Cleveland Heights (OH)
Scott Comm Coll (IA)
Shasta Coll (CA)
Shelby State Comm Coll (TN)
Shelton State Comm Coll (AL)
Sinclair Comm Coll (OH)
South Coll (FL)
South Coll (GA)
Southeastern Comm Coll, North Cmps, West Burlington (IA)
Southern Maine Tech Coll (ME)
Southern Ohio Coll, Cincinnati Cmps (OH)
Southern Ohio Coll, Northern Kentucky Cmps (KY)
Southern State Comm Coll (OH)
South Puget Sound Comm Coll (WA)
South Suburban Coll (IL)
Southwestern Coll of Business, Cincinnati (OH)
Southwestern Coll of Business, Cincinnati (OH)
Southwestern Coll of Business, Dayton (OH)
Southwest Florida Coll of Business (FL)
Spencer Sch of Business (NE)
Spokane Falls Comm Coll (WA)
Springfield Tech Comm Coll (MA)
Stanly Comm Coll (NC)
Stark Tech Coll (OH)
State U of NY Coll of Tech at Alfred (NY)
Stratton Coll (WI)
Thompson Inst (PA)
Tri-County Comm Coll (NC)
Trocaire Coll (NY)
Tulsa Jr Coll (OK)
U of Alaska Southeast, Sitka Cmps (AK)
U of Hawaii–Kapiolani Comm Coll (HI)
Vincennes U (IN)
Virginia Coll at Birmingham (AL)
Wake Tech Comm Coll (NC)
Waldorf Coll (IA)
Wallace State Comm Coll (AL)
Ward Stone Coll (FL)
Wayne Comm Coll (NC)
Webster Coll, Ocala (FL)
Wenatchee Valley Coll (WA)
Western Piedmont Comm Coll (NC)
Western Wisconsin Tech Coll (WI)
Western Wyoming Comm Coll (WY)
West Valley Coll (CA)
West Virginia Career Coll, Charleston (WV)
Whatcom Comm Coll (WA)
Wilkes Comm Coll (NC)
William Rainey Harper Coll (IL)
Willmar Tech Coll (MN)

MEDICAL ILLUSTRATION

Atlanta Metropolitan Coll (GA)

MEDICAL LABORATORY TECHNOLOGY

Alabama Southern Comm Coll, Monroeville (AL)
Alamance Comm Coll (NC)
Albuquerque Tech Vocational Inst (NM)
Alexandria Tech Coll (MN)
Allegany Comm Coll (MD)
Alvin Comm Coll (TX)
Angelina Coll (TX)
Apollo College–Phoenix, Inc (AZ)
Arapahoe Comm Coll (CO)
Arkansas State University–Beebe Branch (AR)
Asheville-Buncombe Tech Comm Coll (NC)
Atlanta Metropolitan Coll (GA)
Augusta Tech Inst (GA)
Austin Comm Coll (TX)
Barton County Comm Coll (KS)
Beaufort County Comm Coll (NC)
Belleville Area Coll (IL)
Bergen Comm Coll (NJ)
Bismarck State Coll (ND)
Brevard Comm Coll (FL)
Bristol Comm Coll (MA)
Bronx Comm Coll of City U of NY (NY)
Brookdale Comm Coll (NJ)
Broome Comm Coll (NY)
Broward Comm Coll (FL)
Brunswick Coll (GA)
Camden County Coll (NJ)
Catonsville Comm Coll (MD)
Central Maine Tech Coll (ME)
Central Piedmont Comm Coll (NC)
Central Texas Coll (TX)
Central Virginia Comm Coll (VA)
Chippewa Valley Tech Coll (WI)
Cincinnati State Tech and Comm Coll (OH)
City Colls of Chicago, Malcolm X Coll (IL)
Clark State Comm Coll (OH)
Cleveland State Comm Coll (TN)
Clinton Comm Coll (IA)
Clinton Comm Coll (NY)
Coastal Carolina Comm Coll (NC)
Coll of Lake County (IL)
Columbia State Comm Coll (TN)
Columbus State Comm Coll (OH)
Comm Coll of Allegheny County Allegheny Cmps (PA)
Comm Coll of Allegheny County South Cmps (PA)
Comm Coll of Beaver County (PA)
Comm Coll of Philadelphia (PA)
Comm Coll of Rhode Island (RI)
Comm Coll of Southern Nevada (NV)
Comm Coll of the Air Force (AL)
Copiah-Lincoln Comm Coll (MS)
County Coll of Morris (NJ)
Cumberland Sch of Tech (LA)
Cumberland Sch of Tech (TN)
Cuyahoga Comm Coll, Metropolitan Cmps (OH)
Dalton Coll (GA)
Darton Coll (GA)
Davidson County Comm Coll (NC)
DeKalb Tech Inst (GA)
Delaware Tech & Comm Coll, Jack F Owens Cmps (DE)
Del Mar Coll (TX)
Des Moines Area Comm Coll (IA)
Dutchess Comm Coll (NY)
Eastern Maine Tech Coll (ME)
Eastern Oklahoma State Coll (OK)
El Centro Coll (TX)
Elgin Comm Coll (IL)
El Paso Comm Coll (TX)
Erie Comm Coll, North Cmps (NY)
Essex Comm Coll (MD)
Eugenio María de Hostos Comm Coll of City U of NY (NY)
Fergus Falls Comm Coll (MN)
Florence-Darlington Tech Coll (SC)
Florida Comm Coll at Jacksonville (FL)
Gadsden State Comm Coll (AL)
Gainesville Coll (GA)
Garland County Comm Coll (AR)
Genesee Comm Coll (NY)
George Corley Wallace State Comm Coll, Selma (AL)
George C Wallace State Comm Coll, Dothan (AL)
Grayson County Coll (TX)
Greenville Tech Coll (SC)
Halifax Comm Coll (NC)
Harcum Coll (PA)
Harford Comm Coll (MD)
Harrisburg Area Comm Coll (PA)
Hawkeye Comm Coll (IA)
Herkimer County Comm Coll (NY)
Hibbing Comm Coll (MN)
Highland Park Comm Coll (MI)
Hinds Comm Coll (MS)
Housatonic Comm-Tech Coll (CT)
Houston Comm Coll System (TX)
Hudson Valley Comm Coll (NY)
Hutchinson Comm Coll and Area Vocational Sch (KS)
Illinois Central Coll (IL)
Indian River Comm Coll (FL)
Iowa Central Comm Coll (IA)
Ivy Tech State Coll–Northcentral (IN)
Ivy Tech State Coll–Wabash Valley (IN)
Jefferson Comm Coll (NY)
Jefferson Comm Coll (OH)
Jefferson State Comm Coll (AL)
John A Logan Coll (IL)
John C Calhoun State Comm Coll (AL)
Johnson County Comm Coll (KS)
John Wood Comm Coll (IL)
J Sargeant Reynolds Comm Coll (VA)
Kankakee Comm Coll (IL)
Kellogg Comm Coll (MI)
Lake Area Vocational-Tech Inst (SD)
Lake City Comm Coll (FL)
Lakeland Comm Coll (OH)
Lamar University–Orange (TX)
Laredo Comm Coll (TX)
Lewis and Clark Comm Coll (IL)
Lorain County Comm Coll (OH)
Macon Coll (GA)
Madison Area Tech Coll (WI)
Manchester Comm-Tech Coll (CT)
Manor Jr Coll (PA)
Marion Tech Coll (OH)
Massachusetts Bay Comm Coll (MA)
Massasoit Comm Coll (MA)
McCarrie Schools of Health Sci and Tech (PA)
McLennan Comm Coll (TX)
Medical Inst of Minnesota (MN)
Mercer County Comm Coll (NJ)
Meridian Comm Coll (MS)
Miami-Dade Comm Coll (FL)
Middle Georgia Coll (GA)
Middlesex Comm Coll (MA)
Middlesex County Coll (NJ)
Midlands Tech Coll (SC)
Mid-Plains Comm Coll (NE)
Milwaukee Area Tech Coll (WI)
Mineral Area Coll (MO)
Mississippi Delta Comm Coll (MS)
Mississippi Gulf Coast Comm Coll (MS)
Montgomery College–Takoma Park Cmps (MD)
Montgomery County Comm Coll (PA)
Moraine Valley Comm Coll (IL)
Mount Wachusett Comm Coll (MA)
Nassau Comm Coll (NY)
Navarro Coll (TX)
New Hampshire Tech Coll, Claremont (NH)
New Mexico Jr Coll (NM)
New Mexico State University–Alamogordo (NM)
New York City Tech Coll of the City U of NY (NY)
North Arkansas Comm/Tech Coll (AR)
North Dakota State University–Bottineau (ND)
Northeast Iowa Comm Coll, Calmar Cmps (IA)
Northeast Iowa Comm Coll, Peosta Cmps (IA)
Northeast Mississippi Comm Coll (MS)
Northern Virginia Comm Coll (VA)
Oakland Comm Coll (MI)
Oakton Comm Coll (IL)
Ocean County Coll (NJ)
Odessa Coll (TX)
Orangeburg-Calhoun Tech Coll (SC)
Orange County Comm Coll (NY)
Pamlico Comm Coll (NC)
Penn State U DuBois Cmps (PA)
Penn State U Hazleton Cmps (PA)
Penn State U New Kensington Cmps (PA)
Penn State U Shenango Cmps (PA)
Phillips County Comm Coll (AR)
Portland Comm Coll (OR)
PPI Health Careers Sch (CO)
Queensborough Comm Coll of City U of NY (NY)
Reading Area Comm Coll (PA)
Redlands Comm Coll (OK)
Rend Lake Coll (IL)
Ricks Coll (ID)
Roane State Comm Coll (TN)
Rochester Comm Coll (MN)
Rockland Comm Coll (NY)
Rose State Coll (OK)
St Louis Comm Coll at Forest Park (MO)
St Paul Tech Coll (MN)
St Petersburg Jr Coll (FL)
St Philip's Coll (TX)
Salt Lake Comm Coll (UT)
San Bernardino Valley Coll (CA)
Sandhills Comm Coll (NC)
San Diego Mesa Coll (CA)
San Jacinto College–Central Cmps (TX)
Sauk Valley Comm Coll (IL)
Scott Comm Coll (IA)
Seminole Jr Coll (OK)
Seward County Comm Coll (KS)
Shelby State Comm Coll (TN)
Shelton State Comm Coll (AL)
Shoreline Comm Coll (WA)
Shorter Coll (AR)
South Arkansas Comm Coll (AR)
Southeast Comm Coll, Lincoln Cmps (NE)
Southeastern Comm Coll (NC)
Southeastern Comm Coll, North Cmps, West Burlington (IA)
Southeastern Illinois Coll (IL)
Southern U at Shreveport–Bossier City Cmps (LA)
Southern West Virginia Comm and Tech Coll (WV)
SouthWest Collegiate Inst for the Deaf (TX)
Southwestern Coll of Business, Cincinnati (OH)
Southwestern Comm Coll (IA)
Southwestern Comm Coll (NC)
Southwestern Oklahoma State U at Sayre (OK)
Spartanburg Tech Coll (SC)
Springfield Tech Comm Coll (MA)
Stark Tech Coll (OH)
State U of NY Coll of A&T at Cobleskill (NY)
State U of NY Coll of A&T at Morrisville (NY)
State U of NY Coll of Tech at Alfred (NY)
State U of NY Coll of Tech at Canton (NY)
State U of NY Coll of Tech at Farmingdale (NY)
Tarrant County Jr Coll (TX)
Temple Coll (TX)
Texas Southmost Coll (TX)
Thomas Nelson Comm Coll (VA)
Three Rivers Comm Coll (MO)
Tompkins Cortland Comm Coll (NY)
Tri-County Tech Coll (SC)
Trident Tech Coll (SC)
Trocaire Coll (NY)
Tulsa Jr Coll (OK)
Tyler Jr Coll (TX)
U of Hawaii–Kapiolani Comm Coll (HI)
U of Kentucky, Hazard Comm Coll (KY)
U of Kentucky, Madisonville Comm Coll (KY)
U of Kentucky, Somerset Comm Coll (KY)
U of Maine at Augusta (ME)
U of New Mexico–Gallup Branch (NM)
Victoria Coll (TX)
Vincennes U (IN)
Wake Tech Comm Coll (NC)
Wallace State Comm Coll (AL)
Walters State Comm Coll (TN)
Washington State Comm Coll (OH)
Waycross Coll (GA)
Wayne County Comm Coll (MI)
Wenatchee Valley Coll (WA)
Westark Comm Coll (AR)
Westchester Comm Coll (NY)
Western Iowa Tech Comm Coll (IA)
Western Piedmont Comm Coll (NC)
Western Wisconsin Tech Coll (WI)
West Virginia Northern Comm Coll (WV)
Wharton County Jr Coll (TX)
Wytheville Comm Coll (VA)
York Tech Coll (SC)

MEDICAL RECORDS SERVICES

Adirondack Comm Coll (NY)
Alabama Southern Comm Coll, Monroeville (AL)
Anoka-Ramsey Comm Coll (MN)
Arapahoe Comm Coll (CO)
Baltimore City Comm Coll (MD)
Barton County Comm Coll (KS)
Belleville Area Coll (IL)
Berkeley Coll, White Plains (NY)
Bishop State Comm Coll (AL)
Black Hawk Coll, Moline (IL)
Bowling Green State University–Firelands Coll (OH)
Briarwood Coll (CT)
Bristol Comm Coll (MA)
Broome Comm Coll (NY)
Brunswick Coll (GA)
Brunswick Comm Coll (NC)
Bryant and Stratton Business Inst, Rochester (NY)
Butler County Comm Coll (KS)
Cabrillo Coll (CA)
Cape Fear Comm Coll (NC)
Central Comm College–Platte Cmps (NE)
Central Oregon Comm Coll (OR)
Central Piedmont Comm Coll (NC)
Central Texas Coll (TX)
Chabot Coll (CA)
Chattanooga State Tech Comm Coll (TN)
Chemeketa Comm Coll (OR)
Chippewa Valley Tech Coll (WI)
Cincinnati State Tech and Comm Coll (OH)
City Coll of San Francisco (CA)
City Colls of Chicago, Harry S Truman Coll (IL)
Clark Coll (WA)
Coll of DuPage (IL)
Coll of Lake County (IL)
Coll of St Catherine–Minneapolis (MN)
Columbia Jr Coll of Business (SC)
Columbus State Comm Coll (OH)
Comm Coll of Allegheny County Allegheny Cmps (PA)
Comm Coll of Philadelphia (PA)
Comm Coll of Southern Nevada (NV)
Comm Hospital Roanoke Valley–Coll of Health Scis (VA)
Cosumnes River Coll (CA)
Cuyahoga Comm Coll, Metropolitan Cmps (OH)
Cypress Coll (CA)
Dalton Coll (GA)
Darton Coll (GA)
Davidson County Comm Coll (NC)
Daytona Beach Comm Coll (FL)
Delgado Comm Coll (LA)
Dodge City Comm Coll (KS)
Draughons Jr Coll, Nashville (TN)
Durham Tech Comm Coll (NC)
East Central Comm Coll (MS)
East Los Angeles Coll (CA)
ECPI Coll of Tech, Hampton (VA)
ECPI Coll of Tech, Virginia Beach (VA)
ECPI Computer Inst, Richmond (VA)
ECPI Computer Inst, Roanoke (VA)
Edgecombe Comm Coll (NC)
Elaine P Nunez Comm Coll (LA)
El Centro Coll (TX)
Elgin Comm Coll (IL)
El Paso Comm Coll (TX)
Enterprise State Jr Coll (AL)
Erie Business Ctr South (PA)
Erie Comm Coll, North Cmps (NY)
Florence-Darlington Tech Coll (SC)
Florida Comm Coll at Jacksonville (FL)
Fort Berthold Comm Coll (ND)
Fresno City Coll (CA)
Gadsden State Comm Coll (AL)
Garland County Comm Coll (AR)
George Corley Wallace State Comm Coll, Selma (AL)
Gogebic Comm Coll (MI)
Gulf Coast Comm Coll (FL)
Hagerstown Business Coll (MD)
Heald Business Coll, Rancho Cordova (CA)

Peterson's Guide to Two-Year Colleges 1997
107

Associate Degree Programs at Two-Year Colleges
Medical Records Services–Medical Secretarial Studies

Henry Ford Comm Coll (MI)
Hesser Coll (NH)
Highland Comm Coll (KS)
Highland Park Comm Coll (MI)
Hinds Comm Coll (MS)
Hiwassee Coll (TN)
Hocking Coll (OH)
Holmes Comm Coll (MS)
Holyoke Comm Coll (MA)
Houston Comm Coll System (TX)
Howard Coll (TX)
Hudson County Comm Coll (NJ)
Hutchinson Comm Coll and Area Vocational Sch (KS)
Illinois Central Coll (IL)
Imperial Valley Coll (CA)
Indiana Business Coll (IN)
Indian Hills Comm Coll (IA)
Indian River Comm Coll (FL)
Itawamba Comm Coll (MS)
James Sprunt Comm Coll (NC)
Jefferson State Comm Coll (AL)
John A Logan Coll (IL)
Johnson County Comm Coll (KS)
John Wood Comm Coll (IL)
Kennebec Valley Tech Coll (ME)
Kingsborough Comm Coll of City U of NY (NY)
Kirkwood Comm Coll (IA)
Labouré Coll (MA)
LDS Business Coll (UT)
Lee Coll (TX)
Lehigh Carbon Comm Coll (PA)
Lincoln Sch of Commerce (NE)
Massachusetts Bay Comm Coll (MA)
McCook Comm Coll (NE)
McLennan Comm Coll (TX)
Medical Inst of Minnesota (MN)
Meridian Comm Coll (MS)
Miami-Dade Comm Coll (FL)
Michiana Coll (IN)
Middle Georgia Coll (GA)
Midlands Tech Coll (SC)
Mississippi Delta Comm Coll (MS)
Mohawk Valley Comm Coll (NY)
Monroe Comm Coll (NY)
Montana State U Coll of Tech-Great Falls (MT)
Montgomery Coll (TX)
Montgomery College– Takoma Park Cmps (MD)
Moraine Park Tech Coll (WI)
Moraine Valley Comm Coll (IL)
Motlow State Comm Coll (TN)
Newport Business Inst (PA)
North Central Texas Coll (TX)
North Dakota State Coll of Science (ND)
Northeast Iowa Comm Coll, Calmar Cmps (IA)
Northern Essex Comm Coll (MA)
Northern Virginia Comm Coll (VA)
North Hennepin Comm Coll (MN)
Northland Comm and Tech Coll (MN)
North Shore Comm Coll (MA)
Northwest Iowa Comm Coll (IA)
Northwest Mississippi Comm Coll (MS)
Northwest State Comm Coll (OH)
Oakton Comm Coll (IL)
Oklahoma City Comm Coll (OK)
Onondaga Comm Coll (NY)
Ozarka Tech Coll (AR)
Pennsylvania Inst of Tech (PA)
Penn Valley Comm Coll (MO)
Pensacola Jr Coll (FL)
Pima Comm Coll (AZ)
Pima Medical Inst (NM)
Pitt Comm Coll (NC)
Portland Comm Coll (OR)

Prince George's Comm Coll (MD)
Pueblo Comm Coll (CO)
Rasmussen Coll Eagan (MN)
Rasmussen Coll Mankato (MN)
Rasmussen Coll St Cloud (MN)
Reading Area Comm Coll (PA)
Roane State Comm Coll (TN)
Rockland Comm Coll (NY)
Rose State Coll (OK)
Saint Charles County Comm Coll (MO)
St Petersburg Jr Coll (FL)
St Philip's Coll (TX)
San Diego Mesa Coll (CA)
Schoolcraft Coll (MI)
Shelton State Comm Coll (AL)
Shoreline Comm Coll (WA)
Sinclair Comm Coll (OH)
South Arkansas Comm Coll (AR)
Southeastern Illinois Coll (IL)
Southern U at Shreveport– Bossier City Cmps (LA)
South Plains Coll (TX)
Spokane Comm Coll (WA)
Stark Tech Coll (OH)
State Fair Comm Coll (MO)
State U of NY Coll of Tech at Alfred (NY)
Tacoma Comm Coll (WA)
Tarrant County Jr Coll (TX)
Tech Coll of Municipality of San Juan (PR)
Texas State Tech Coll– Harlingen Cmps (TX)
Trenholm State Tech Coll (AL)
Trocaire Coll (NY)
Tulsa Jr Coll (OK)
Turtle Mountain Comm Coll (ND)
United Tribes Tech Coll (ND)
Vermilion Comm Coll (MN)
Vincennes U (IN)
Volunteer State Comm Coll (TN)
Wallace State Comm Coll (AL)
Ward Stone Coll (FL)
Western Dakota Tech Inst (SD)
Western Wisconsin Tech Coll (WI)
Westmoreland County Comm Coll (PA)
West Valley Coll (CA)
Wharton County Jr Coll (TX)
Willmar Comm Coll (MN)
Willmar Tech Coll (MN)

MEDICAL SECRETARIAL STUDIES

Adirondack Comm Coll (NY)
Alamance Comm Coll (NC)
Alexandria Tech Coll (MN)
Allegany Comm Coll (MD)
Allen County Comm Coll (KS)
Allentown Business Sch (PA)
Alvin Comm Coll (TX)
American Inst of Business (IA)
American Inst of Commerce (IA)
American River Coll (CA)
Andover Coll (ME)
Anoka-Ramsey Comm Coll (MN)
Anson Comm Coll (NC)
Aquinas Coll at Milton (MA)
Aquinas Coll at Newton (MA)
Athens Area Tech Inst (GA)
Baker Coll of Jackson (MI)
Baltimore City Comm Coll (MD)
Barton County Comm Coll (KS)
Bay State Coll (MA)
Beal Coll (ME)
Beaufort County Comm Coll (NC)
Belleville Area Coll (IL)
Berean Inst (PA)
Bergen Comm Coll (NJ)
Big Bend Comm Coll (WA)
Bismarck State Coll (ND)
Black Hawk Coll, Kewanee (IL)
Black Hawk Coll, Moline (IL)

Blair Jr Coll (CO)
Blue Mountain Comm Coll (OR)
Brazosport Coll (TX)
Briarwood Coll (CT)
Bristol Comm Coll (MA)
Bronx Comm Coll of City U of NY (NY)
Broward Comm Coll (FL)
Brunswick Coll (GA)
Bryant and Stratton Business Inst, Albany (NY)
Bryant and Stratton Business Inst, Buffalo (NY)
Bryant and Stratton Business Inst, Lackawanna (NY)
Bryant and Stratton Business Inst, Rochester (NY)
Bryant and Stratton Business Inst, Rochester (NY)
Bryant and Stratton Business Inst, Syracuse (NY)
Bryant and Stratton Business Inst, E Hills Cmps, Williamsville (NY)
Bryant and Stratton Coll, Parma (OH)
Bucks County Comm Coll (PA)
Bunker Hill Comm Coll (MA)
Butler County Comm Coll (KS)
Butler County Comm Coll (PA)
Butte Coll (CA)
Cabrillo Coll (CA)
Caldwell Comm Coll and Tech Inst (NC)
Cambria-Rowe Business Coll (PA)
Cape Cod Comm Coll (MA)
Carl Albert State Coll (OK)
Casco Bay Coll (ME)
Castle Coll (NH)
Catonsville Comm Coll (MD)
Central Carolina Comm Coll (NC)
Central City Business Inst (NY)
Central Coll (KS)
Central Comm College– Grand Island Cmps (NE)
Central Comm College– Hastings Cmps (NE)
Central Comm College– Platte Cmps (NE)
Central Florida Comm Coll (FL)
Centralia Coll (WA)
Central Lakes Coll (MN)
Central Maine Tech Coll (ME)
Central Oregon Comm Coll (OR)
Central Pennsylvania Business Sch (PA)
Central Piedmont Comm Coll (NC)
Central Texas Coll (TX)
Cerritos Coll (CA)
Chaffey Coll (CA)
Champlain Coll (VT)
Chaparral Career Coll (AZ)
Chattanooga State Tech Comm Coll (TN)
Chemeketa Comm Coll (OR)
Chesapeake Coll (MD)
Chicago Coll of Commerce (IL)
Churchman Business Sch (PA)
City Colls of Chicago, Harold Washington Coll (IL)
City Colls of Chicago, Harry S Truman Coll (IL)
City Colls of Chicago, Richard J Daley Coll (IL)
Clark Coll (WA)
Clark State Comm Coll (OH)
Clatsop Comm Coll (OR)
Cleveland Comm Coll (NC)
Coastal Carolina Comm Coll (NC)
Cochise Coll, Douglas (AZ)
Cochise Coll, Sierra Vista (AZ)
Coffeyville Comm Coll (KS)
Colby Comm Coll (KS)
Coll of Marin (CA)
Coll of San Mateo (CA)
Coll of The Albemarle (NC)
Collin County Comm Coll (TX)
Colorado Northwestern Comm Coll (CO)

Columbia Jr Coll of Business (SC)
Columbus State Comm Coll (OH)
Commonwealth Business Coll, LaPorte (IN)
Commonwealth Business Coll, Merrillville (IN)
Comm Coll of Allegheny County Boyce Cmps (PA)
Comm Coll of Allegheny County North Cmps (PA)
Comm Coll of Allegheny County South Cmps (PA)
Comm Coll of Aurora (CO)
Comm Coll of Beaver County (PA)
Comm Coll of Denver (CO)
Comm Coll of Philadelphia (PA)
Comm Coll of Rhode Island (RI)
Cosumnes River Coll (CA)
Crafton Hills Coll (CA)
Craven Comm Coll (NC)
Crowder Coll (MO)
Cypress Coll (CA)
Dabney S Lancaster Comm Coll (VA)
Danville Area Comm Coll (IL)
Darton Coll (GA)
Davis Coll (OH)
Daytona Beach Comm Coll (FL)
Delaware Tech & Comm Coll, Jack F Owens Cmps (DE)
Delaware Tech & Comm Coll, Stanton/Wilmington Cmps (DE)
Delta Coll (MI)
Des Moines Area Comm Coll (IA)
Dodge City Comm Coll (KS)
DuBois Business Coll (PA)
Duff's Business Inst (PA)
Dundalk Comm Coll (MD)
Durham Tech Comm Coll (NC)
East Central Coll (MO)
Eastern Wyoming Coll (WY)
East Los Angeles Coll (CA)
ECPI Coll of Tech, Hampton (VA)
ECPI Coll of Tech, Virginia Beach (VA)
ECPI Computer Inst, Richmond (VA)
ECPI Computer Inst, Roanoke (VA)
Edgecombe Comm Coll (NC)
Edmonds Comm Coll (WA)
Elgin Comm Coll (IL)
Ellsworth Comm Coll (IA)
Enterprise State Jr Coll (AL)
Erie Business Ctr, Main (PA)
Erie Business Ctr South (PA)
Essex County Coll (NJ)
Eugenio María de Hostos Comm Coll of City U of NY (NY)
Everett Comm Coll (WA)
Fergus Falls Comm Coll (MN)
Finger Lakes Comm Coll (NY)
Flathead Valley Comm Coll (MT)
Florida Keys Comm Coll (FL)
Florida National Coll (FL)
Fort Scott Comm Coll (KS)
Frederick Comm Coll (MD)
Fresno City Coll (CA)
Fulton-Montgomery Comm Coll (NY)
Gadsden State Comm Coll (AL)
Garland County Comm Coll (AR)
Gateway Comm-Tech Coll (CT)
Gem City Coll (IL)
George C Wallace State Comm Coll, Dothan (AL)
Gloucester County Coll (NJ)
Gogebic Comm Coll (MI)
Grand Rapids Comm Coll (MI)
Grays Harbor Coll (WA)
Great Lakes Jr Coll of Business (MI)
Green River Comm Coll (WA)
Grossmont Coll (CA)
Guilford Tech Comm Coll (NC)

Hagerstown Business Coll (MD)
Halifax Comm Coll (NC)
Hamilton Business Coll (IA)
Harcum Coll (PA)
Hawkeye Comm Coll (IA)
Heald Business Coll, Concord (CA)
Heald Business Coll, Fresno (CA)
Heald Business Coll, Hayward (CA)
Heald Business Coll, San Francisco (CA)
Heald Business Coll (HI)
Helena Coll of Tech of The U of Montana (MT)
Henry Ford Comm Coll (MI)
Herkimer County Comm Coll (NY)
Hesser Coll (NH)
Hibbing Comm Coll (MN)
Highland Comm Coll (KS)
Highland Park Comm Coll (MI)
Hillsborough Comm Coll (FL)
Hiwassee Coll (TN)
Hocking Coll (OH)
Howard Coll (TX)
Howard Comm Coll (MD)
Hudson Valley Comm Coll (NY)
Huntington Jr Coll of Business (WV)
Hutchinson Comm Coll and Area Vocational Sch (KS)
ICM Sch of Business (PA)
Illinois Eastern Comm Colls, Olney Central Coll (IL)
Indiana Business Coll (IN)
Indian River Comm Coll (FL)
Inst of Career Education (FL)
Interboro Inst (NY)
Inver Hills Comm Coll (MN)
Iowa Western Comm Coll (IA)
Itasca Comm Coll (MN)
Jackson Comm Coll (MI)
Jamestown Business Coll (NY)
Jefferson Coll (MO)
Jefferson Comm Coll (NY)
Jefferson Comm Coll (OH)
Johnson County Comm Coll (KS)
Johnston Comm Coll (NC)
John Wood Comm Coll (IL)
Kalamazoo Valley Comm Coll (MI)
Kankakee Comm Coll (IL)
Katharine Gibbs Sch (CT)
Katharine Gibbs Sch (MA)
Kellogg Comm Coll (MI)
Kelsey Jenney Coll (CA)
Kilian Comm Coll (SD)
Kirkwood Comm Coll (IA)
Kirtland Comm Coll (MI)
Knoxville Business Coll (TN)
Labette Comm Coll (KS)
Lackawanna Jr Coll (PA)
Lake Land Coll (IL)
Lake Michigan Coll (MI)
Lakeshore Tech Coll (WI)
Lake Tahoe Comm Coll (CA)
Lamar Comm Coll (CO)
Lamar University–Port Arthur (TX)
Lansdale Sch of Business (PA)
Lansing Comm Coll (MI)
Lassen Coll (CA)
LDS Business Coll (UT)
Lenoir Comm Coll (NC)
Lewis and Clark Comm Coll (IL)
Lewis Coll of Business (MI)
Lima Tech Coll (OH)
Lincoln Coll, Normal (IL)
Lincoln Sch of Commerce (NE)
Linn-Benton Comm Coll (OR)
Long Beach City Coll (CA)
Longview Comm Coll (MO)
Los Angeles City Coll (CA)
Los Angeles Harbor Coll (CA)
Lower Columbia Coll (WA)
Luzerne County Comm Coll (PA)
MacCormac Jr Coll (IL)
Macomb Comm Coll (MI)
Madison Area Tech Coll (WI)
Madison Jr Coll of Business (WI)
Manchester Comm-Tech Coll (CT)

Manor Jr Coll (PA)
Maple Woods Comm Coll (MO)
Marian Court Coll (MA)
Marion Tech Coll (OH)
Mater Dei Coll (NY)
Mayland Comm Coll (NC)
McIntosh Coll (NH)
McLennan Comm Coll (TX)
Merced Coll (CA)
Mesa Comm Coll (AZ)
Metropolitan Comm Coll (NE)
Miami-Dade Comm Coll (FL)
Miami-Jacobs Coll (OH)
Miami University–Middletown Cmps (OH)
Michiana Coll (IN)
Middlesex Community– Tech Coll (CT)
Midlands Tech Coll (SC)
Mid-Plains Comm Coll (NE)
Midstate Coll (IL)
Mid-State Coll (ME)
Miles Comm Coll (MT)
Milwaukee Area Tech Coll (WI)
Mohawk Valley Comm Coll (NY)
Monroe County Comm Coll (MI)
Montana State U Coll of Tech-Great Falls (MT)
Montcalm Comm Coll (MI)
Monterey Peninsula Coll (CA)
Montgomery College– Germantown Cmps (MD)
Montgomery College– Takoma Park Cmps (MD)
Moraine Park Tech Coll (WI)
Morton Coll (IL)
Mt Hood Comm Coll (OR)
Mt San Antonio Coll (CA)
Muscatine Comm Coll (IA)
Muskegon Comm Coll (MI)
Nash Comm Coll (NC)
Nassau Comm Coll (NY)
National Business Coll, Bluefield (VA)
National Business Coll, Charlottesville (VA)
National Business Coll, Danville (VA)
National Business Coll, Harrisonburg (VA)
National Business Coll, Lynchburg (VA)
National Business Coll, Martinsville (VA)
National Business Coll, Roanoke (VA)
Naugatuck Valley Community–Tech Coll (CT)
Nebraska Coll of Business (NE)
New Hampshire Tech Coll, Manchester (NH)
New Mexico Jr Coll (NM)
Newport Business Inst (PA)
New River Comm Coll (VA)
Niagara County Comm Coll (NY)
Nicolet Area Tech Coll (WI)
Normandale Comm Coll (MN)
Northampton County Area Comm Coll (PA)
Northcentral Tech Coll (WI)
North Dakota State Coll of Science (ND)
North Dakota State University–Bottineau (ND)
Northeast Alabama State Comm Coll (AL)
Northeast Comm Coll (NE)
Northeastern Jr Coll (CO)
Northeastern Oklahoma A&M Coll (OK)
Northeast Mississippi Comm Coll (MS)
Northeast Texas Comm Coll (TX)
Northern Essex Comm Coll (MA)
Northern Maine Tech Coll (ME)
North Idaho Coll (ID)
North Iowa Area Comm Coll (IA)
Northland Comm and Tech Coll (MN)
North Seattle Comm Coll (WA)
North Shore Comm Coll (MA)
Northwestern Business Coll (IL)

Associate Degree Programs at Two-Year Colleges
Medical Secretarial Studies–Modern Languages

Northwestern Coll (OH)
Northwest Mississippi Comm Coll (MS)
Northwest State Comm Coll (OH)
Oakland Comm Coll (MI)
Ohlone Coll (CA)
Oklahoma State U, Okmulgee (OK)
Olean Business Inst (NY)
Omaha Coll of Health Careers (NE)
Orangeburg-Calhoun Tech Coll (SC)
Orange Coast Coll (CA)
Otero Jr Coll (CO)
Palomar Coll (CA)
Parkland Coll (IL)
Pearl River Comm Coll (MS)
Peirce Coll (PA)
Penn Commercial, Inc (PA)
Pennsylvania Inst of Tech (PA)
Penn Valley Comm Coll (MO)
Pensacola Jr Coll (FL)
Phillips County Comm Coll (AR)
Piedmont Comm Coll (NC)
Pima Comm Coll (AZ)
Pima Medical Inst (NM)
Pitt Comm Coll (NC)
Polk Comm Coll (FL)
Portland Comm Coll (OR)
Potomac State Coll of West Virginia U (WV)
Prince George's Comm Coll (MD)
Prospect Hall (FL)
Pueblo Comm Coll (CO)
Quincy Coll (MA)
Rasmussen Coll Eagan (MN)
Rasmussen Coll Mankato (MN)
Rasmussen Coll Minnetonka (MN)
Rasmussen Coll St Cloud (MN)
Reading Area Comm Coll (PA)
Renton Tech Coll (WA)
Richland Comm Coll (IL)
Riverside Comm Coll (CA)
Roane State Comm Coll (TN)
Rochester Business Inst (NY)
Rochester Comm Coll (MN)
Rockingham Comm Coll (NC)
Rock Valley Coll (IL)
Rowan-Cabarrus Comm Coll (NC)
Roxbury Comm Coll (MA)
Sacramento City Coll (CA)
St Catharine Coll (KY)
St Clair County Comm Coll (MI)
St Philip's Coll (TX)
Salem Comm Coll (NJ)
Salt Lake Comm Coll (UT)
Sandhills Comm Coll (NC)
San Jacinto College–Central Cmps (TX)
Santa Fe Comm Coll (FL)
Santa Rosa Jr Coll (CA)
Scott Comm Coll (IA)
Scottsdale Comm Coll (AZ)
Shawnee Comm Coll (IL)
Shelby State Comm Coll (TN)
Shelton State Comm Coll (AL)
Shoreline Comm Coll (WA)
Sierra Coll (CA)
Sinclair Comm Coll (OH)
Skagit Valley Coll (WA)
Southeast Comm Coll, Beatrice Cmps (NE)
Southeast Comm Coll, Lincoln Cmps (NE)
Southern Ohio Coll, Cincinnati Cmps (OH)
Southern U at Shreveport–Bossier City Cmps (LA)
South Plains Coll (TX)
South Puget Sound Comm Coll (WA)
South Suburban Coll (IL)
Southwestern Coll of Business, Cincinnati (OH)
Southwestern Coll of Business, Middletown (OH)
Southwestern Michigan Coll (MI)
Southwestern Oklahoma State U at Sayre (OK)
Southwestern Oregon Comm Coll (OR)
Southwestern Tech Coll (MN)
Spartanburg Tech Coll (SC)
Spencer Sch of Business (NE)
Spokane Comm Coll (WA)
Spoon River Coll (IL)
Springfield Tech Comm Coll (MA)
Stanly Comm Coll (NC)
State Fair Comm Coll (MO)
State U of NY Coll of A&T at Morrisville (NY)
Stevens Henager Coll (UT)
Stratton Coll (WI)
Suffolk County Comm Coll–Western Cmps (NY)
Surry Comm Coll (NC)
Tacoma Comm Coll (WA)
Temple Coll (TX)
Terra State Comm Coll (OH)
Three Rivers Comm-Tech Coll (CT)
Tomball Coll (TX)
Trenholm State Tech Coll (AL)
Trident Tech Coll (SC)
Trocaire Coll (NY)
Truckee Meadows Comm Coll (NV)
Tulsa Jr Coll (OK)
Tunxis Comm Tech Coll (CT)
Tyler Jr Coll (TX)
Umpqua Comm Coll (OR)
U of Cincinnati Clermont Coll (OH)
U of Cincinnati Raymond Walters Coll (OH)
U of North Dakota–Lake Region (ND)
Utah Valley State Coll (UT)
Valencia Comm Coll (FL)
Vance-Granville Comm Coll (NC)
Ventura Coll (CA)
Vermilion Comm Coll (MN)
Vincennes U (IN)
Vincennes University–Jasper Ctr (IN)
Wake Tech Comm Coll (NC)
Wallace State Comm Coll (AL)
Walla Walla Comm Coll (WA)
Walters State Comm Coll (TN)
Washington State Comm Coll (OH)
Washtenaw Comm Coll (MI)
Wayne Comm Coll (NC)
Wayne County Comm Coll (MI)
Webster Coll, Ocala (FL)
Wenatchee Valley Coll (WA)
Westchester Business Inst (NY)
Western Piedmont Comm Coll (NC)
Western Wisconsin Tech Coll (WI)
Western Wyoming Comm Coll (WY)
West Los Angeles Coll (CA)
Westmoreland County Comm Coll (PA)
West Shore Comm Coll (MI)
West Valley Coll (CA)
West Virginia Career Coll, Charleston (WV)
West Virginia Northern Comm Coll (WV)
Whatcom Comm Coll (WA)
William Rainey Harper Coll (IL)
Williamsport Sch of Commerce (PA)
Willmar Comm Coll (MN)
Willmar Tech Coll (MN)
Wright State U, Lake Cmps (OH)
Wytheville Comm Coll (VA)
Yakima Valley Comm Coll (WA)

MEDICAL TECHNOLOGY

Alabama Southern Comm Coll, Thomasville (AL)
Andrew Coll (GA)
Angelina Coll (TX)
Anne Arundel Comm Coll (MD)
Antelope Valley Coll (CA)
Arapahoe Comm Coll (CO)
Athens Area Tech Inst (GA)
Atlanta Metropolitan Coll (GA)
Bevill State Comm Coll (AL)
Bismarck State Coll (ND)
Brevard Coll (NC)
Broward Comm Coll (FL)
Brunswick Coll (GA)
Butte Coll (CA)
Casper Coll (WY)
Catawba Valley Comm Coll (NC)
Central Piedmont Comm Coll (NC)
Central Texas Coll (TX)
Charles Stewart Mott Comm Coll (MI)
Chattahoochee Valley State Comm Coll (AL)
Chipola Jr Coll (FL)
Chippewa Valley Tech Coll (WI)
Cisco Jr Coll (TX)
City Colls of Chicago, Harry S Truman Coll (IL)
City Colls of Chicago, Kennedy-King Coll (IL)
City Colls of Chicago, Malcolm X Coll (IL)
City Colls of Chicago, Richard J Daley Coll (IL)
City Colls of Chicago, Wilbur Wright Coll (IL)
Clark Coll (WA)
Coahoma Comm Coll (MS)
Coll of St Catherine–Minneapolis (MN)
Columbus State Comm Coll (OH)
Comm Coll of Allegheny County Allegheny Cmps (PA)
Comm Coll of Allegheny County South Cmps (PA)
Comm Coll of Southern Nevada (NV)
Cuyahoga Comm Coll, Western Cmps (OH)
Dalton Coll (GA)
Del Mar Coll (TX)
Delta Coll (MI)
Dixie Coll (UT)
Dodge City Comm Coll (KS)
Eastern Oklahoma State Coll (OK)
El Centro Coll (TX)
Ellsworth Comm Coll (IA)
Florida Comm Coll at Jacksonville (FL)
Fort Scott Comm Coll (KS)
Garland County Comm Coll (AR)
Glendale Comm Coll (AZ)
Grayson County Coll (TX)
Grossmont Coll (CA)
Gulf Coast Comm Coll (FL)
Highland Comm Coll (KS)
Highland Park Comm Coll (MI)
Holmes Comm Coll (MS)
Holyoke Comm Coll (MA)
Howard Comm Coll (MD)
Hutchinson Comm Coll and Area Vocational Sch (KS)
Jackson Comm Coll (MI)
Jackson State Comm Coll (TN)
Joliet Jr Coll (IL)
Keystone Coll (PA)
Labouré Coll (MA)
Lawson State Comm Coll (AL)
Lower Columbia Coll (WA)
Massachusetts Bay Comm Coll (MA)
Medical Inst of Minnesota (MN)
Miami-Dade Comm Coll (FL)
Monroe County Comm Coll (MI)
National Sch of Tech, Inc (FL)
North Dakota State Coll of Science (ND)
Northeastern Jr Coll (CO)
Northeast Mississippi Comm Coll (MS)
North Idaho Coll (ID)
Northwest Mississippi Comm Coll (MS)
Northwest-Shoals Comm Coll (AL)
Oakland Comm Coll (MI)
Okaloosa-Walton Comm Coll (FL)
Orange Coast Coll (CA)
Pensacola Jr Coll (FL)
Reading Area Comm Coll (PA)
Renton Tech Coll (WA)
St Philip's Coll (TX)
South Suburban Coll (IL)
Southwestern Oklahoma State U at Sayre (OK)
Springfield Coll in Illinois (IL)
Springfield Tech Comm Coll (MA)
Suffolk County Comm Coll–Western Cmps (NY)
Tarrant County Jr Coll (TX)
Temple Coll (TX)
Turtle Mountain Comm Coll (ND)
U of Cincinnati Raymond Walters Coll (OH)
U of Kentucky, Henderson Comm Coll (KY)
U of Wisconsin Center–Marathon County (WI)
Vincennes U (IN)
Ward Stone Coll (FL)
Waycross Coll (GA)
Westchester Comm Coll (NY)
Western Wisconsin Tech Coll (WI)
Young Harris Coll (GA)

MENTAL HEALTH/ REHABILITATION COUNSELING

Alvin Comm Coll (TX)
Anne Arundel Comm Coll (MD)
Atlanta Metropolitan Coll (GA)
Belmont Tech Coll (OH)
Blue Ridge Comm Coll (VA)
Catonsville Comm Coll (MD)
Chemeketa Comm Coll (OR)
Chippewa Valley Tech Coll (WI)
City Colls of Chicago, Harold Washington Coll (IL)
City Colls of Chicago, Kennedy-King Coll (IL)
Colby Comm Coll (KS)
Coll of Lake County (IL)
Columbus State Comm Coll (OH)
Comm Coll of Allegheny County North Cmps (PA)
Comm Coll of Philadelphia (PA)
Comm Coll of Rhode Island (RI)
Cuyahoga Comm Coll, Metropolitan Cmps (OH)
Del Mar Coll (TX)
Dull Knife Memorial Coll (MT)
Dundalk Comm Coll (MD)
Dutchess Comm Coll (NY)
Edmonds Comm Coll (WA)
Elgin Comm Coll (IL)
El Paso Comm Coll (TX)
Erie Comm Coll, City Cmps (NY)
Essex Comm Coll (MD)
Evergreen Valley Coll (CA)
Fiorello H LaGuardia Comm Coll of City U of NY (NY)
Fort Peck Comm Coll (MT)
Fresno City Coll (CA)
Gadsden State Comm Coll (AL)
Gateway Comm-Tech Coll (CT)
Housatonic Comm-Tech Coll (CT)
Houston Comm Coll System (TX)
Ivy Tech State Coll–Central Indiana (IN)
Ivy Tech State Coll–Eastcentral (IN)
John Wood Comm Coll (IL)
Kingsborough Comm Coll of City U of NY (NY)
Lac Courte Oreilles Ojibwa Comm Coll (WI)
Lenoir Comm Coll (NC)
Los Angeles City Coll (CA)
Macomb Comm Coll (MI)
Marshalltown Comm Coll (IA)
McLennan Comm Coll (TX)
Metropolitan Comm Coll (NE)
Middlesex Comm Coll (MA)
Middlesex Community–Tech Coll (CT)
Midland Coll (TX)
Minneapolis Comm Coll (MN)
Montgomery College–Takoma Park Cmps (MD)
Mt Hood Comm Coll (OR)
Mt San Antonio Coll (CA)
Muskingum Area Tech Coll (OH)
Naugatuck Valley Community–Tech Coll (CT)
New Hampshire Tech Coll, Berlin (NH)
New Hampshire Tech Inst (NH)
North Country Comm Coll (NY)
Northern Essex Comm Coll (MA)
Northern Virginia Comm Coll (VA)
North Shore Comm Coll (MA)
Oakland Comm Coll (MI)
Orange County Comm Coll (NY)
Oxnard Coll (CA)
Pierce Coll (WA)
Porterville Coll (CA)
Pueblo Coll of Business and Tech (CO)
Reading Area Comm Coll (PA)
Rio Salado Comm Coll (AZ)
Saint Augustine Coll (IL)
St Clair County Comm Coll (MI)
San Bernardino Valley Coll (CA)
Sandhills Comm Coll (NC)
Sauk Valley Comm Coll (IL)
Sinclair Comm Coll (OH)
Southern U at Shreveport–Bossier City Cmps (LA)
South Plains Coll (TX)
South Suburban Coll (IL)
Southwestern Comm Coll (NC)
State Comm Coll of East St Louis (IL)
Sullivan County Comm Coll (NY)
Tarrant County Jr Coll (TX)
Tunxis Comm Tech Coll (CT)
U of Alaska, Prince William Sound Comm Coll (AK)
U of Kentucky, Hopkinsville Comm Coll (KY)
U of Kentucky, Jefferson Comm Coll (KY)
Virginia Western Comm Coll (VA)
Wallace State Comm Coll (AL)
Wayne Comm Coll (NC)
Willmar Comm Coll (MN)
Wor-Wic Comm Coll (MD)
Yuba Coll (CA)

METALLURGICAL TECHNOLOGY

Albuquerque Tech Vocational Inst (NM)
Comm Coll of the Air Force (AL)
Don Bosco Tech Inst (CA)
Erie Comm Coll, North Cmps (NY)
Great Basin Coll (NV)
Linn-Benton Comm Coll (OR)
Macomb Comm Coll (MI)
Moberly Area Comm Coll (MO)
Mohawk Valley Comm Coll (NY)
Murray State Coll (OK)
Ricks Coll (ID)
Sierra Coll (CA)
Southeast Comm Coll, Milford Cmps (NE)
Southern Maine Tech Coll (ME)

METALLURGY

Cerritos Coll (CA)
Mt San Antonio Coll (CA)
Schoolcraft Coll (MI)
Southeast Comm Coll, Milford Cmps (NE)

METEOROLOGY

City Coll of San Francisco (CA)
Comm Coll of the Air Force (AL)
Daytona Beach Comm Coll (FL)
Gulf Coast Comm Coll (FL)
Modesto Jr Coll (CA)
Okaloosa-Walton Comm Coll (FL)

MEXICAN-AMERICAN/ CHICANO STUDIES

Cerritos Coll (CA)
Coll of Alameda (CA)
East Los Angeles Coll (CA)
Fresno City Coll (CA)
Laney Coll (CA)
Los Angeles City Coll (CA)
Pasadena City Coll (CA)
Rancho Santiago Coll (CA)
San Diego City Coll (CA)
San Diego Mesa Coll (CA)
San Joaquin Delta Coll (CA)
Santa Barbara City Coll (CA)
Solano Comm Coll (CA)
Southwestern Coll (CA)
Yuba Coll (CA)

MIDDLE SCHOOL EDUCATION

Gainesville Coll (GA)
Lincoln Land Comm Coll (IL)
Miami-Dade Comm Coll (FL)
Middle Georgia Coll (GA)
South Georgia Coll (GA)
Vincennes U (IN)

MILITARY SCIENCE

Brevard Comm Coll (FL)
Comm Coll of the Air Force (AL)
Dodge City Comm Coll (KS)
Georgia Military Coll (GA)
Kemper Military Jr Coll (MO)
Lansing Comm Coll (MI)
Middle Georgia Coll (GA)
New Mexico Military Inst (NM)
Polk Comm Coll (FL)
Ricks Coll (ID)
Sacramento City Coll (CA)

MINING TECHNOLOGY

Belleville Area Coll (IL)
Casper Coll (WY)
Coll of Eastern Utah (UT)
Eastern Arizona Coll (AZ)
Great Basin Coll (NV)
Hutchinson Comm Coll and Area Vocational Sch (KS)
Illinois Eastern Comm Colls, Wabash Valley Coll (IL)
Ivy Tech State Coll–Wabash Valley (IN)
Mountain Empire Comm Coll (VA)
Rend Lake Coll (IL)
Sierra Coll (CA)
Southeastern Illinois Coll (IL)
Southwest Virginia Comm Coll (VA)
Trinidad State Jr Coll (CO)
U of Kentucky, Madisonville Comm Coll (KY)
U of Kentucky, Southeast Comm Coll (KY)

MINISTRIES

Andrew Coll (GA)
Brevard Coll (NC)
Central Coll (KS)
Hiwassee Coll (TN)
Lon Morris Coll (TX)
Okaloosa-Walton Comm Coll (FL)
Southeastern Baptist Theological Sem (NC)
Waldorf Coll (IA)
Wood Coll (MS)

MODERN LANGUAGES

Antelope Valley Coll (CA)
Bay Mills Comm Coll (MI)
Brevard Comm Coll (FL)
Cape Cod Comm Coll (MA)
Central Texas Coll (TX)
Citrus Coll (CA)
City Colls of Chicago, Harry S Truman Coll (IL)

Associate Degree Programs at Two-Year Colleges
Modern Languages–Music Therapy

City Colls of Chicago, Richard J Daley Coll (IL)
City Colls of Chicago, Wilbur Wright Coll (IL)
Coll of the Sequoias (CA)
Comm Coll of Allegheny County Allegheny Cmps (PA)
Comm Coll of the Air Force (AL)
East Central Coll (MO)
Eastern Arizona Coll (AZ)
Everett Comm Coll (WA)
Galveston Coll (TX)
Hutchinson Comm Coll and Area Vocational Sch (KS)
Imperial Valley Coll (CA)
Independence Comm Coll (KS)
Itawamba Comm Coll (MS)
Kishwaukee Coll (IL)
Lon Morris Coll (TX)
Macon Coll (GA)
Middlesex County Coll (NJ)
Midland Coll (TX)
Northwest Coll (WY)
Odessa Coll (TX)
Okaloosa-Walton Comm Coll (FL)
Oklahoma City Comm Coll (OK)
Otero Jr Coll (CO)
Palo Alto Coll (TX)
Pasadena City Coll (CA)
Polk Comm Coll (FL)
Rancho Santiago Coll (CA)
Rose State Coll (OK)
St Louis Comm Coll at Meramec (MO)
St Philip's Coll (TX)
San Diego City Coll (CA)
San Jacinto College–Central Cmps (TX)
San Juan Coll (NM)
Tyler Jr Coll (TX)
Vincennes U (IN)

MUSEUM STUDIES

Central Coll (KS)
Inst of American Indian Arts (NM)

MUSIC

Abraham Baldwin Ag Coll (GA)
Alabama Southern Comm Coll, Thomasville (AL)
Allan Hancock Coll (CA)
Allen County Comm Coll (KS)
Alvin Comm Coll (TX)
American River Coll (CA)
Andrew Coll (GA)
Angelina Coll (TX)
Anne Arundel Comm Coll (MD)
Antelope Valley Coll (CA)
Arizona Western Coll (AZ)
Atlanta Metropolitan Coll (GA)
Austin Comm Coll (TX)
Bakersfield Coll (CA)
Barton County Comm Coll (KS)
Bee County Coll (TX)
Bergen Comm Coll (NJ)
Bismarck State Coll (ND)
Black Hawk Coll, Moline (IL)
Blinn Coll (TX)
Borough of Manhattan Comm Coll of City U of NY (NY)
Brazosport Coll (TX)
Brevard Coll (NC)
Brevard Comm Coll (FL)
Bronx Comm Coll of City U of NY (NY)
Brookdale Comm Coll (NJ)
Bucks County Comm Coll (PA)
Burlington County Coll (NJ)
Butler County Comm Coll (KS)
Butte Coll (CA)
Caldwell Comm Coll and Tech Inst (NC)
Cañada Coll (CA)
Cape Cod Comm Coll (MA)
Carl Albert State Coll (OK)
Casper Coll (WY)
Catonsville Comm Coll (MD)
Cedar Valley Coll (TX)
Central Coll (KS)
Central Comm College–Platte Cmps (NE)
Centralia Coll (WA)
Central Piedmont Comm Coll (NC)
Central Texas Coll (TX)
Central Wyoming Coll (WY)
Cerritos Coll (CA)
Chabot Coll (CA)
Chaffey Coll (CA)
Charles Stewart Mott Comm Coll (MI)
Chattahoochee Valley State Comm Coll (AL)
Chesapeake Coll (MD)
Citrus Coll (CA)
City Coll of San Francisco (CA)
City Colls of Chicago, Harold Washington Coll (IL)
City Colls of Chicago, Olive-Harvey Coll (IL)
City Colls of Chicago, Richard J Daley Coll (IL)
City Colls of Chicago, Wilbur Wright Coll (IL)
Clackamas Comm Coll (OR)
Clark Coll (WA)
Cloud County Comm Coll (KS)
Coastal Carolina Comm Coll (NC)
Coffeyville Comm Coll (KS)
Colby Comm Coll (KS)
Coll of DuPage (IL)
Coll of Marin (CA)
Coll of San Mateo (CA)
Coll of Southern Idaho (ID)
Coll of The Albemarle (NC)
Coll of the Desert (CA)
Coll of the Sequoias (CA)
Coll of the Siskiyous (CA)
Collin County Comm Coll (TX)
Columbia Coll (CA)
Columbia State Comm Coll (TN)
Comm Coll of Allegheny County Allegheny Cmps (PA)
Comm Coll of Allegheny County Boyce Cmps (PA)
Comm Coll of Allegheny County South Cmps (PA)
Comm Coll of Philadelphia (PA)
Comm Coll of Rhode Island (RI)
Comm Coll of Southern Nevada (NV)
Comm Coll of the Air Force (AL)
Connors State Coll (OK)
Contra Costa Coll (CA)
Cosumnes River Coll (CA)
County Coll of Morris (NJ)
Cowley County Comm Coll and Voc-Tech Sch (KS)
Crafton Hills Coll (CA)
Crowder Coll (MO)
Cypress Coll (CA)
Darton Coll (GA)
Daytona Beach Comm Coll (FL)
Dean Coll (MA)
De Anza Coll (CA)
DeKalb Coll (GA)
Delgado Comm Coll (LA)
Del Mar Coll (TX)
Delta Coll (MI)
Dixie Coll (UT)
Dodge City Comm Coll (KS)
East Central Coll (MO)
East Central Comm Coll (MS)
Eastern Arizona Coll (AZ)
Eastern Oklahoma State Coll (OK)
Eastern Wyoming Coll (WY)
East Los Angeles Coll (CA)
East Mississippi Comm Coll (MS)
Edison Comm Coll (FL)
El Camino Coll (CA)
El Paso Comm Coll (TX)
Essex Comm Coll (MD)
Essex County Coll (NJ)
Everett Comm Coll (WA)
Finger Lakes Comm Coll (NY)
Foothill Coll (CA)
Fort Scott Comm Coll (KS)
Frank Phillips Coll (TX)
Fresno City Coll (CA)
Fullerton Coll (CA)
Gainesville Coll (GA)
Galveston Coll (TX)
Garden City Comm Coll (KS)
Garrett Comm Coll (MD)
Gavilan Coll (CA)
Glendale Comm Coll (AZ)
Golden West Coll (CA)
Grand Rapids Comm Coll (MI)
Grays Harbor Coll (WA)
Grayson County Coll (TX)
Green River Comm Coll (WA)
Grossmont Coll (CA)
Gulf Coast Comm Coll (FL)
Harford Comm Coll (MD)
Harrisburg Area Comm Coll (PA)
Highland Comm Coll (KS)
Highline Comm Coll (WA)
Hill Coll of the Hill Jr Coll District (TX)
Hinds Comm Coll (MS)
Hiwassee Coll (TN)
Holyoke Comm Coll (MA)
Houston Comm Coll System (TX)
Howard Comm Coll (MD)
Imperial Valley Coll (CA)
Independence Comm Coll (KS)
Indian River Comm Coll (FL)
Iowa Lakes Comm Coll (IA)
Isothermal Comm Coll (NC)
Itawamba Comm Coll (MS)
Jackson State Comm Coll (TN)
Jefferson Coll (MO)
Jefferson Davis Comm Coll (AL)
John Wood Comm Coll (IL)
Joliet Jr Coll (IL)
Jones County Jr Coll (MS)
Kansas City Kansas Comm Coll (KS)
Kellogg Comm Coll (MI)
Kingsborough Comm Coll of City U of NY (NY)
Kings River Comm Coll (CA)
Kirkwood Comm Coll (IA)
Kishwaukee Coll (IL)
Labette Comm Coll (KS)
Lake City Comm Coll (FL)
Lake Michigan Coll (MI)
Lake-Sumter Comm Coll (FL)
Lake Tahoe Comm Coll (CA)
Laney Coll (CA)
Laramie County Comm Coll (WY)
Lee Coll (TX)
Lewis and Clark Comm Coll (IL)
Lincoln Land Comm Coll (IL)
Long Beach City Coll (CA)
Lon Morris Coll (TX)
Lorain County Comm Coll (OH)
Los Angeles City Coll (CA)
Los Angeles Mission Coll (CA)
Los Angeles Pierce Coll (CA)
Los Angeles Southwest Coll (CA)
Los Angeles Valley Coll (CA)
Los Medanos Coll (CA)
Lower Columbia Coll (WA)
Macon Coll (GA)
Manchester Comm-Tech Coll (CT)
McLennan Comm Coll (TX)
Mendocino Coll (CA)
Merced Coll (CA)
Mercer County Comm Coll (NJ)
Mesa Comm Coll (AZ)
Miami-Dade Comm Coll (FL)
Middle Georgia Coll (GA)
Middlesex County Coll (NJ)
Midland Coll (TX)
Mid-Plains Comm Coll (NE)
Milwaukee Area Tech Coll (WI)
Mineral Area Coll (MO)
MiraCosta Coll (CA)
Mississippi Delta Comm Coll (MS)
Moberly Area Comm Coll (MO)
Modesto Jr Coll (CA)
Mohave Comm Coll (AZ)
Monroe Comm Coll (NY)
Monterey Peninsula Coll (CA)
Montgomery College–Rockville Cmps (MD)
Moorpark Coll (CA)
Morton Coll (IL)
Motlow State Comm Coll (TN)
Mt San Jacinto Coll (CA)
Muscatine Comm Coll (IA)
Napa Valley Coll (CA)
Nassau Comm Coll (NY)
Naugatuck Valley Community–Tech Coll (CT)
Navarro Coll (TX)
New Mexico Jr Coll (NM)
Niagara County Comm Coll (NY)
Northeast Comm Coll (NE)
Northeastern Jr Coll (CO)
Northeastern Oklahoma A&M Coll (OK)
Northeast Mississippi Comm Coll (MS)
Northern Essex Comm Coll (MA)
Northern Virginia Comm Coll (VA)
North Harris Coll (TX)
North Idaho Coll (ID)
North Seattle Comm Coll (WA)
Northwest Coll (WY)
Northwest-Shoals Comm Coll (AL)
Odessa Coll (TX)
Okaloosa-Walton Comm Coll (FL)
Oklahoma City Comm Coll (OK)
Onondaga Comm Coll (NY)
Orange Coast Coll (CA)
Palm Beach Comm Coll (FL)
Palo Alto Coll (TX)
Palomar Coll (CA)
Parkland Coll (IL)
Pasadena City Coll (CA)
Peace Coll (NC)
Pensacola Jr Coll (FL)
Phillips County Comm Coll (AR)
Pima Comm Coll (AZ)
Polk Comm Coll (FL)
Porterville Coll (CA)
Potomac State Coll of West Virginia U (WV)
Pratt Comm Coll and Area Voc Sch (KS)
Prince George's Comm Coll (MD)
Rancho Santiago Coll (CA)
Raritan Valley Comm Coll (NJ)
Redlands Comm Coll (OK)
Ricks Coll (ID)
Riverside Comm Coll (CA)
Rose State Coll (OK)
Sacramento City Coll (CA)
Saddleback Coll (CA)
St Catharine Coll (KY)
St Louis Comm Coll at Florissant Valley (MO)
St Louis Comm Coll at Forest Park (MO)
St Louis Comm Coll at Meramec (MO)
St Philip's Coll (TX)
San Bernardino Valley Coll (CA)
Sandhills Comm Coll (NC)
San Diego City Coll (CA)
San Diego Mesa Coll (CA)
San Jacinto College–Central Cmps (TX)
San Jacinto College–North Cmps (TX)
San Jacinto College–South Cmps (TX)
San Joaquin Delta Coll (CA)
San Juan Coll (NM)
Santa Barbara City Coll (CA)
Santa Monica Coll (CA)
Santa Rosa Jr Coll (CA)
Sauk Valley Comm Coll (IL)
Schenectady County Comm Coll (NY)
Seward County Comm Coll (KS)
Shasta Coll (CA)
Shelton State Comm Coll (AL)
Sheridan Coll (WY)
Shoreline Comm Coll (WA)
Sinclair Comm Coll (OH)
Skagit Valley Coll (WA)
Skyline Coll (CA)
Snow Coll (UT)
Solano Comm Coll (CA)
Southeastern Comm Coll (NC)
South Mountain Comm Coll (AZ)
South Plains Coll (TX)
South Suburban Coll (IL)
Southwestern Coll (CA)
Southwestern Comm Coll (IA)
Southwest Mississippi Comm Coll (MS)
Southwest Virginia Comm Coll (VA)
Spokane Falls Comm Coll (WA)
Springfield Coll in Illinois (IL)
Suffolk County Comm College–Ammerman Cmps (NY)
Tacoma Comm Coll (WA)
Texarkana Coll (TX)
Texas Southmost Coll (TX)
Three Rivers Comm Coll (MO)
Tidewater Comm Coll (VA)
Treasure Valley Comm Coll (OR)
Trinidad State Jr Coll (CO)
Trinity Valley Comm Coll (TX)
Triton Coll (IL)
Truett-McConnell Coll (GA)
Tulsa Jr Coll (OK)
Tyler Jr Coll (TX)
Umpqua Comm Coll (OR)
Union County Coll (NJ)
U of Wisconsin Center–Marathon County (WI)
Ventura Coll (CA)
Vermilion Comm Coll (MN)
Victor Valley Coll (CA)
Villa Maria Coll of Buffalo (NY)
Vincennes U (IN)
Waldorf Coll (IA)
Wallace State Comm Coll (AL)
Waubonsee Comm Coll (IL)
Wenatchee Valley Coll (WA)
Westchester Comm Coll (NY)
Western Nebraska Comm Coll, Scottsbluff (NE)
Western Wyoming Comm Coll (WY)
West Los Angeles Coll (CA)
West Valley Coll (CA)
Wharton County Jr Coll (TX)
Wilkes Comm Coll (NC)
William Rainey Harper Coll (IL)
Willmar Comm Coll (MN)
Yavapai Coll (AZ)
Young Harris Coll (GA)
Yuba Coll (CA)

MUSICAL INSTRUMENT TECHNOLOGY

Brevard Coll (NC)
Hartnell Coll (CA)
Houston Comm Coll System (TX)
Orange Coast Coll (CA)
Queensborough Comm Coll of City U of NY (NY)
Renton Tech Coll (WA)

MUSIC BUSINESS

American River Coll (CA)
Art Inst of Atlanta (GA)
Art Inst of Dallas (TX)
Art Inst of Fort Lauderdale (FL)
The Art Inst of Philadelphia (PA)
Art Inst of Pittsburgh (PA)
Art Inst of Seattle (WA)
Brevard Coll (NC)
Houston Comm Coll System (TX)
Independence Comm Coll (KS)
Los Medanos Coll (CA)
Orange Coast Coll (CA)
San Jacinto College–Central Cmps (TX)
San Jacinto College–North Cmps (TX)
Schenectady County Comm Coll (NY)
Villa Maria Coll of Buffalo (NY)

MUSIC EDUCATION

Angelina Coll (TX)
Bee County Coll (TX)
Brevard Coll (NC)
Casper Coll (WY)
Central Coll (KS)
Central Comm College–Platte Cmps (NE)
Chattahoochee Valley State Comm Coll (AL)
Coffeyville Comm Coll (KS)
Colby Comm Coll (KS)
Coll of Southern Idaho (ID)
Comm Coll of Allegheny County Allegheny Cmps (PA)
Copiah-Lincoln Comm Coll (MS)
Del Mar Coll (TX)
Delta Coll (MI)
Dodge City Comm Coll (KS)
East Central Comm Coll (MS)
Eastern Arizona Coll (AZ)
Eastern Wyoming Coll (WY)
Essex Comm Coll (MD)
Essex County Coll (NJ)
Frank Phillips Coll (TX)
Frederick Comm Coll (MD)
Gainesville Coll (GA)
Highland Comm Coll (IL)
Hill Coll of the Hill Jr Coll District (TX)
Hiwassee Coll (TN)
Holmes Comm Coll (MS)
Howard Coll (TX)
Hutchinson Comm Coll and Area Vocational Sch (KS)
Independence Comm Coll (KS)
Iowa Lakes Comm Coll (IA)
Itawamba Comm Coll (MS)
John C Calhoun State Comm Coll (AL)
John Wood Comm Coll (IL)
Jones County Jr Coll (MS)
Kansas City Kansas Comm Coll (KS)
Lon Morris Coll (TX)
Miami-Dade Comm Coll (FL)
Middle Georgia Coll (GA)
Midland Coll (TX)
Mid-Plains Comm Coll (NE)
Mississippi Delta Comm Coll (MS)
Northeastern Jr Coll (CO)
Northeast Mississippi Comm Coll (MS)
North Idaho Coll (ID)
Northwest Coll (WY)
Northwest Mississippi Comm Coll (MS)
Ohio Valley Coll (WV)
Parkland Coll (IL)
Polk Comm Coll (FL)
Potomac State Coll of West Virginia U (WV)
Ricks Coll (ID)
Roane State Comm Coll (TN)
Sandhills Comm Coll (NC)
Shelton State Comm Coll (AL)
Snow Coll (UT)
Southwestern Comm Coll (IA)
Southwest Mississippi Comm Coll (MS)
Treasure Valley Comm Coll (OR)
Tulsa Jr Coll (OK)
Umpqua Comm Coll (OR)
U of Kentucky, Jefferson Comm Coll (KY)
Vincennes U (IN)
Waldorf Coll (IA)
Walters State Comm Coll (TN)
Wenatchee Valley Coll (WA)
Western Oklahoma State Coll (OK)
Young Harris Coll (GA)

MUSIC HISTORY

Brevard Coll (NC)
Cañada Coll (CA)
Del Mar Coll (TX)
Hill Coll of the Hill Jr Coll District (TX)
Polk Comm Coll (FL)
Snow Coll (UT)

MUSIC THERAPY

Brevard Coll (NC)

Associate Degree Programs at Two-Year Colleges
Music Therapy–Nursing

Hill Coll of the Hill Jr Coll District (TX)
Pasadena City Coll (CA)

NATIVE AMERICAN STUDIES
Bacone Coll (OK)
Blackfeet Comm Coll (MT)
Brevard Coll (NC)
Central Wyoming Coll (WY)
D-Q U (CA)
Fort Belknap Coll (MT)
Fort Peck Comm Coll (MT)
Fresno City Coll (CA)
Itasca Comm Coll (MN)
Lac Courte Oreilles Ojibwa Comm Coll (WI)
Navajo Comm Coll (AZ)
Nebraska Indian Comm Coll (NE)
Northeastern Oklahoma A&M Coll (OK)
Palomar Coll (CA)
Pima Comm Coll (AZ)
Rogers State Coll (OK)
Salish Kootenai Coll (MT)
Santa Barbara City Coll (CA)
Sisseton-Wahpeton Comm Coll (SD)
Standing Rock Coll (ND)

NATURAL RESOURCE MANAGEMENT
American River Coll (CA)
Antelope Valley Coll (CA)
Bacone Coll (OK)
Butte Coll (CA)
Central Carolina Tech Coll (SC)
Central Wyoming Coll (WY)
Coll of the Desert (CA)
Coll of the Siskiyous (CA)
Colorado Northwestern Comm Coll (CO)
Columbia Coll (CA)
Delta Coll (MI)
Dull Knife Memorial Coll (MT)
Finger Lakes Comm Coll (NY)
Fort Belknap Coll (MT)
Fort Peck Comm Coll (MT)
Frank Phillips Coll (TX)
Fulton-Montgomery Comm Coll (NY)
Garrett Comm Coll (MD)
Greenfield Comm Coll (MA)
Haskell Indian Nations U (KS)
Hocking Coll (OH)
Lord Fairfax Comm Coll (VA)
Los Angeles Pierce Coll (CA)
Modesto Jr Coll (CA)
Nebraska Coll of Tech Agriculture (NE)
Nebraska Indian Comm Coll (NE)
New Hampshire Tech Coll, Berlin (NH)
North Dakota State University–Bottineau (ND)
Northwest Coll (WY)
Ohio State U Ag Tech Inst (OH)
Pennsylvania Coll of Tech (PA)
Sacramento City Coll (CA)
Salish Kootenai Coll (MT)
San Joaquin Delta Coll (CA)
Shasta Coll (CA)
Snow Coll (UT)
Southwestern Indian Polytechnic Inst (NM)
Spokane Comm Coll (WA)
State U of NY Coll of A&T at Morrisville (NY)
Sterling Coll (VT)
Treasure Valley Comm Coll (OR)
Trinidad State Jr Coll (CO)
Turtle Mountain Comm Coll (ND)
Ventura Coll (CA)
Vermilion Comm Coll (MN)
Vincennes U (IN)
Wayne County Comm Coll (MI)

NATURAL SCIENCES
Andrew Coll (GA)
Black Hawk Coll, Moline (IL)
Brevard Coll (NC)
Cabrillo Coll (CA)

Cañada Coll (CA)
Casper Coll (WY)
Central Comm College–Platte Cmps (NE)
Centralia Coll (WA)
Central Texas Coll (TX)
Chabot Coll (CA)
Citrus Coll (CA)
Clark Coll (WA)
Coll of Marin (CA)
Coll of the Canyons (CA)
Colorado Mountn Coll, Roaring Fork Cmps-Spring Valley Ctr (CO)
Comm Coll of Allegheny County Boyce Cmps (PA)
Cypress Coll (CA)
Dalton Coll (GA)
Delaware County Comm Coll (PA)
Dixie Coll (UT)
Feather River Comm Coll District (CA)
Fiorello H LaGuardia Comm Coll of City U of NY (NY)
Fresno City Coll (CA)
Galveston Coll (TX)
Gavilan Coll (CA)
Golden West Coll (CA)
Highline Comm Coll (WA)
Independence Comm Coll (KS)
Iowa Lakes Comm Coll (IA)
Jackson State Comm Coll (TN)
Jefferson Comm Coll (NY)
Kellogg Comm Coll (MI)
Lake Tahoe Comm Coll (CA)
Lassen Coll (CA)
Lehigh Carbon Comm Coll (PA)
Mary Holmes Coll (MS)
Merced Coll (CA)
Miami-Dade Comm Coll (FL)
Middle Georgia Coll (GA)
Mid-Plains Comm Coll (NE)
Moorpark Coll (CA)
Naugatuck Valley Community–Tech Coll (CT)
North Dakota State University–Bottineau (ND)
Northeastern Jr Coll (CO)
Northern Virginia Comm Coll (VA)
North Seattle Comm Coll (WA)
Northwest Coll (WY)
Ohlone Coll (CA)
Passaic County Comm Coll (NJ)
Polk Comm Coll (FL)
Porterville Coll (CA)
Redlands Comm Coll (OK)
Riverside Comm Coll (CA)
Sacramento City Coll (CA)
Saddleback Coll (CA)
St Gregory's Coll (OK)
St Philip's Coll (TX)
Salish Kootenai Coll (MT)
San Jacinto College–South Cmps (TX)
San Joaquin Delta Coll (CA)
Santa Barbara City Coll (CA)
Seward County Comm Coll (KS)
Sisseton-Wahpeton Comm Coll (SD)
Skagit Valley Coll (WA)
Snow Coll (UT)
Southern U at Shreveport-Bossier City Cmps (LA)
Southwestern Comm Coll (IA)
Sullivan County Comm Coll (NY)
Umpqua Comm Coll (OR)
U of Pittsburgh–Titusville (PA)
Victor Valley Coll (CA)
Western Wyoming Comm Coll (WY)
Young Harris Coll (GA)

NEAR AND MIDDLE EASTERN STUDIES
Wayne County Comm Coll (MI)

NUCLEAR MEDICAL TECHNOLOGY
Bronx Comm Coll of City U of NY (NY)
Broward Comm Coll (FL)
Bunker Hill Comm Coll (MA)

Caldwell Comm Coll and Tech Inst (NC)
Chattanooga State Tech Comm Coll (TN)
Coll of DuPage (IL)
Comm Coll of Allegheny County Allegheny Cmps (PA)
Comm Coll of Denver (CO)
Comm Coll of the Air Force (AL)
Delaware Tech & Comm Coll, Stanton/Wilmington Cmps (DE)
Delgado Comm Coll (LA)
Forsyth Tech Comm Coll (NC)
Galveston Coll (TX)
Gateway Comm Coll (AZ)
Gateway Comm-Tech Coll (CT)
Gloucester County Coll (NJ)
Harrisburg Area Comm Coll (PA)
Hillsborough Comm Coll (FL)
Houston Comm Coll System (TX)
Kettering Coll of Medical Arts (OH)
Lorain County Comm Coll (OH)
Los Angeles City Coll (CA)
Oakland Comm Coll (MI)
Owens Comm Coll, Findlay (OH)
Owens Comm Coll, Toledo (OH)
Prince George's Comm Coll (MD)
Santa Fe Comm Coll (FL)
Springfield Tech Comm Coll (MA)
Triton Coll (IL)
U of Cincinnati Raymond Walters Coll (OH)
U of Kentucky, Lexington Comm Coll (KY)
Valencia Comm Coll (FL)
Vincennes U (IN)

NUCLEAR TECHNOLOGY
Aiken Tech Coll (SC)
Chattanooga State Tech Comm Coll (TN)
Columbia Basin Coll (WA)
Eastern Idaho Tech Coll (ID)
Front Range Comm Coll (CO)
Georgia Military Coll (GA)
Joliet Jr Coll (IL)
Luzerne County Comm Coll (PA)
Monroe County Comm Coll (MI)
Muscatine Comm Coll (IA)
New Mexico State University–Carlsbad (NM)
Salem Comm Coll (NJ)
Santa Fe Comm Coll (NM)
Terra State Comm Coll (OH)
Texas State Tech Coll–Waco/Marshall Cmps (TX)
Three Rivers Comm-Tech Coll (CT)
Westmoreland County Comm Coll (PA)

NURSING
Abraham Baldwin Ag Coll (GA)
Adirondack Comm Coll (NY)
Alabama Southern Comm Coll, Monroeville (AL)
Alabama Southern Comm Coll, Thomasville (AL)
Alamance Comm Coll (NC)
Albuquerque Tech Vocational Inst (NM)
Allan Hancock Coll (CA)
Allegany Comm Coll (MD)
Alpena Comm Coll (MI)
Alvin Comm Coll (TX)
American River Coll (CA)
Ancilla Coll (IN)
Andrew Coll (GA)
Angelina Coll (TX)
Anne Arundel Comm Coll (MD)
Anoka-Ramsey Comm Coll (MN)
Antelope Valley Coll (CA)
Aquinas Coll (TN)
Arapahoe Comm Coll (CO)

Arizona Western Coll (AZ)
Arkansas State University–Beebe Branch (AR)
Asheville-Buncombe Tech Comm Coll (NC)
Athens Area Tech Inst (GA)
Atlanta Metropolitan Coll (GA)
Atlantic Comm Coll (NJ)
Austin Comm Coll (MN)
Austin Comm Coll (TX)
Bacone Coll (OK)
Bainbridge Coll (GA)
Bakersfield Coll (CA)
Baltimore City Comm Coll (MD)
Barton County Comm Coll (KS)
Bay de Noc Comm Coll (MI)
Beaufort County Comm Coll (NC)
Bee County Coll (TX)
Belleville Area Coll (IL)
Bellevue Comm Coll (WA)
Belmont Tech Coll (OH)
Bergen Comm Coll (NJ)
Berkshire Comm Coll (MA)
Bevill State Comm Coll (AL)
Big Bend Comm Coll (WA)
Bishop State Comm Coll (AL)
Bismarck State Coll (ND)
Black Hawk Coll, Kewanee (IL)
Black Hawk Coll, Moline (IL)
Blackhawk Tech Coll (WI)
Blinn Coll (TX)
Blue Mountain Comm Coll (OR)
Blue Ridge Comm Coll (NC)
Blue Ridge Comm Coll (VA)
Borough of Manhattan Comm Coll of City U of NY (NY)
Bowling Green State University–Firelands Coll (OH)
Brazosport Coll (TX)
Brevard Coll (NC)
Brevard Comm Coll (FL)
Bristol Comm Coll (MA)
Bronx Comm Coll of City U of NY (NY)
Brookdale Comm Coll (NJ)
Brookhaven Coll (TX)
Broome Comm Coll (NY)
Broward Comm Coll (FL)
Brunswick Coll (GA)
Brunswick Comm Coll (NC)
Bucks County Comm Coll (PA)
Bunker Hill Comm Coll (MA)
Burlington County Coll (NJ)
Butler County Comm Coll (KS)
Butler County Comm Coll (PA)
Butte Coll (CA)
Cabrillo Coll (CA)
Caldwell Comm Coll and Tech Inst (NC)
Camden County Coll (NJ)
Cape Cod Comm Coll (MA)
Cape Fear Comm Coll (NC)
Capital Comm Tech Coll (CT)
Carl Albert State Coll (OK)
Carl Sandburg Coll (IL)
Casper Coll (WY)
Catawba Valley Comm Coll (NC)
Cath Med Ctr of Brooklyn & Queens Sch of Nursing (NY)
Catonsville Comm Coll (MD)
Cayuga County Comm Coll (NY)
Cecil Comm Coll (MD)
Central Alabama Comm Coll (AL)
Central Carolina Comm Coll (NC)
Central Carolina Tech Coll (SC)
Central Comm College–Grand Island Cmps (NE)
Central Comm College–Platte Cmps (NE)
Central Florida Comm Coll (FL)
Centralia Coll (WA)
Central Lakes Coll (MN)
Central Maine Medical Ctr Sch of Nursing (ME)
Central Maine Tech Coll (ME)
Central Ohio Tech Coll (OH)

Central Oregon Comm Coll (OR)
Central Piedmont Comm Coll (NC)
Central Texas Coll (TX)
Central Wyoming Coll (WY)
Cerritos Coll (CA)
Cerro Coso Comm Coll (CA)
Chabot Coll (CA)
Chaffey Coll (CA)
Charles County Comm Coll (MD)
Charles Stewart Mott Comm Coll (MI)
Chattahoochee Valley State Comm Coll (AL)
Chattanooga State Tech Comm Coll (TN)
Chemeketa Comm Coll (OR)
Chesterfield-Marlboro Tech Coll (SC)
Chipola Jr Coll (FL)
Chippewa Valley Tech Coll (WI)
Cincinnati State Tech and Comm Coll (OH)
Cisco Jr Coll (TX)
City Coll of San Francisco (CA)
City Colls of Chicago, Harry S Truman Coll (IL)
City Colls of Chicago, Kennedy-King Coll (IL)
City Colls of Chicago, Malcolm X Coll (IL)
City Colls of Chicago, Olive-Harvey Coll (IL)
City Colls of Chicago, Richard J Daley Coll (IL)
Clackamas Comm Coll (OR)
Clark Coll (WA)
Clark State Comm Coll (OH)
Clatsop Comm Coll (OR)
Cleveland State Comm Coll (TN)
Clinton Comm Coll (IA)
Clinton Comm Coll (NY)
Cloud County Comm Coll (KS)
Clovis Comm Coll (NM)
Coastal Carolina Comm Coll (NC)
Cochise Coll, Douglas (AZ)
Cochise Coll, Sierra Vista (AZ)
Cochran Sch of Nursing (NY)
Coffeyville Comm Coll (KS)
Colby Comm Coll (KS)
Coll of DuPage (IL)
Coll of Eastern Utah (UT)
Coll of Lake County (IL)
Coll of Marin (CA)
Coll of Micronesia–FSM (FM)
Coll of St Catherine–Minneapolis (MN)
Coll of San Mateo (CA)
Coll of Southern Idaho (ID)
Coll of The Albemarle (NC)
Coll of the Canyons (CA)
Coll of the Desert (CA)
Coll of the Mainland (TX)
Coll of the Redwoods (CA)
Coll of the Sequoias (CA)
Collin County Comm Coll (TX)
Colorado Mountn Coll, Roaring Fork Cmps-Spring Valley Ctr (CO)
Columbia Basin Coll (WA)
Columbia-Greene Comm Coll (NY)
Columbia State Comm Coll (TN)
Columbus State Comm Coll (OH)
Comm Coll of Allegheny County Allegheny Cmps (PA)
Comm Coll of Allegheny County Boyce Cmps (PA)
Comm Coll of Allegheny County North Cmps (PA)
Comm Coll of Allegheny County South Cmps (PA)
Comm Coll of Beaver County (PA)
Comm Coll of Denver (CO)
Comm Coll of Philadelphia (PA)
Comm Coll of Rhode Island (RI)
Comm Coll of Southern Nevada (NV)

Comm Hospital Roanoke Valley–Coll of Health Scis (VA)
Connors State Coll (OK)
Contra Costa Coll (CA)
Copiah-Lincoln Comm Coll (MS)
Corning Comm Coll (NY)
County Coll of Morris (NJ)
Craven Comm Coll (NC)
Crowder Coll (MO)
Cuesta Coll (CA)
Cumberland County Coll (NJ)
Cuyahoga Comm Coll, Eastern Cmps (OH)
Cuyahoga Comm Coll, Metropolitan Cmps (OH)
Cuyahoga Comm Coll, Western Cmps (OH)
Cypress Coll (CA)
Dabney S Lancaster Comm Coll (VA)
Dalton Coll (GA)
Danville Area Comm Coll (IL)
Darton Coll (GA)
Davidson County Comm Coll (NC)
Daytona Beach Comm Coll (FL)
De Anza Coll (CA)
DeKalb Coll (GA)
Delaware County Comm Coll (PA)
Delaware Tech & Comm Coll, Jack F Owens Cmps (DE)
Delaware Tech & Comm Coll, Stanton/Wilmington Cmps (DE)
Delaware Tech & Comm Coll, Terry Cmps (DE)
Delgado Comm Coll (LA)
Del Mar Coll (TX)
Delta Coll (MI)
Des Moines Area Comm Coll (IA)
Dixie Coll (UT)
Dodge City Comm Coll (KS)
Doña Ana Branch Comm Coll (NM)
Donnelly Coll (KS)
Durham Tech Comm Coll (NC)
Dutchess Comm Coll (NY)
Dyersburg State Comm Coll (TN)
East Central Coll (MO)
East Central Comm Coll (MS)
Eastern Arizona Coll (AZ)
Eastern Maine Tech Coll (ME)
Eastern New Mexico University–Roswell (NM)
Eastern Oklahoma State Coll (OK)
Eastern Shore Comm Coll (VA)
East Georgia Coll (GA)
East Los Angeles Coll (CA)
East Mississippi Comm Coll (MS)
Edgecombe Comm Coll (NC)
Edison Comm Coll (FL)
Edison State Comm Coll (OH)
El Camino Coll (CA)
El Centro Coll (TX)
Elgin Comm Coll (IL)
Ellsworth Comm Coll (IA)
El Paso Comm Coll (TX)
Erie Comm Coll, City Cmps (NY)
Erie Comm Coll, North Cmps (NY)
Essex Comm Coll (MD)
Essex County Coll (NJ)
Eugenio María de Hostos Comm Coll of City U of NY (NY)
Everett Comm Coll (WA)
Evergreen Valley Coll (CA)
Fayetteville Tech Comm Coll (NC)
Fergus Falls Comm Coll (MN)
Finger Lakes Comm Coll (NY)
Fiorello H LaGuardia Comm Coll of City U of NY (NY)
Florence-Darlington Tech Coll (SC)
Florida Comm Coll at Jacksonville (FL)
Florida Keys Comm Coll (FL)
Floyd Coll (GA)

Peterson's Guide to Two-Year Colleges 1997   111

Associate Degree Programs at Two-Year Colleges
Nursing

Forsyth Tech Comm Coll (NC)
Fort Berthold Comm Coll (ND)
Fort Scott Comm Coll (KS)
Fox Valley Tech Coll (WI)
Frank Phillips Coll (TX)
Frederick Comm Coll (MD)
Fresno City Coll (CA)
Front Range Comm Coll (CO)
Fullerton Coll (CA)
Fulton-Montgomery Comm Coll (NY)
Gadsden State Comm Coll (AL)
Galveston Coll (TX)
Garden City Comm Coll (KS)
Garland County Comm Coll (AR)
Gaston Coll (NC)
Gateway Comm Coll (AZ)
Gavilan Coll (CA)
Genesee Comm Coll (NY)
George Corley Wallace State Comm Coll, Selma (AL)
George C Wallace State Comm Coll, Dothan (AL)
Germanna Comm Coll (VA)
Glendale Comm Coll (AZ)
Glen Oaks Comm Coll (MI)
Gloucester County Coll (NJ)
Gogebic Comm Coll (MI)
Golden West Coll (CA)
Gordon Coll (GA)
Grand Rapids Comm Coll (MI)
Grays Harbor Coll (WA)
Grayson County Coll (TX)
Great Basin Coll (NV)
Great Lakes Jr Coll of Business (MI)
Greenfield Comm Coll (MA)
Greenville Tech Coll (SC)
Grossmont Coll (CA)
Guilford Tech Comm Coll (NC)
Gulf Coast Comm Coll (FL)
Hagerstown Jr Coll (MD)
Halifax Comm Coll (NC)
Harford Comm Coll (MD)
Harrisburg Area Comm Coll (PA)
Hartnell Coll (CA)
Hawkeye Comm Coll (IA)
Haywood Comm Coll (NC)
Heartland Comm Coll (IL)
Helene Fuld Coll of Nursing of North General Hosp (NY)
Henry Ford Comm Coll (MI)
Hesston Coll (KS)
Hibbing Comm Coll (MN)
Highland Comm Coll (IL)
Highland Comm Coll (KS)
Highland Park Comm Coll (MI)
Highline Comm Coll (WA)
Hill Coll of the Hill Jr Coll District (TX)
Hillsborough Comm Coll (FL)
Hinds Comm Coll (MS)
Hiwassee Coll (TN)
Hocking Coll (OH)
Holmes Comm Coll (MS)
Holyoke Comm Coll (MA)
Horry-Georgetown Tech Coll (SC)
Housatonic Comm-Tech Coll (CT)
Houston Comm Coll System (TX)
Howard Coll (TX)
Howard Comm Coll (MD)
Hudson Valley Comm Coll (NY)
Hutchinson Comm Coll and Area Vocational Sch (KS)
Illinois Central Coll (IL)
Illinois Eastern Comm Colls, Olney Central Coll (IL)
Illinois Valley Comm Coll (IL)
Imperial Valley Coll (CA)
Independence Comm Coll (KS)
Indian Hills Comm Coll (IA)
Indian River Comm Coll (FL)
Inter American U of PR, Guayama Cmps (PR)
Inver Hills Comm Coll (MN)
Iowa Central Comm Coll (IA)
Iowa Western Comm Coll (IA)
Itawamba Comm Coll (MS)
Ivy Tech State Coll–Central Indiana (IN)
Ivy Tech State Coll–Columbus (IN)
Ivy Tech State Coll–Lafayette (IN)
Ivy Tech State Coll–Northcentral (IN)
Ivy Tech State Coll–Northwest (IN)
Ivy Tech State Coll–Southcentral (IN)
Ivy Tech State Coll–Southeast (IN)
Ivy Tech State Coll–Southwest (IN)
Ivy Tech State Coll–Whitewater (IN)
Jackson Comm Coll (MI)
Jackson State Comm Coll (TN)
James Sprunt Comm Coll (NC)
Jamestown Comm Coll (NY)
Jefferson Coll (MO)
Jefferson Comm Coll (NY)
Jefferson Davis Comm Coll (AL)
Jefferson State Comm Coll (AL)
Jewish Hospital Coll of Nursing and Allied Health (MO)
John A Logan Coll (IL)
John C Calhoun State Comm Coll (AL)
Johnson County Comm Coll (KS)
Johnston Comm Coll (NC)
John Tyler Comm Coll (VA)
John Wood Comm Coll (IL)
Joliet Jr Coll (IL)
Jones County Jr Coll (MS)
J Sargeant Reynolds Comm Coll (VA)
Kalamazoo Valley Comm Coll (MI)
Kankakee Comm Coll (IL)
Kansas City Kansas Comm Coll (KS)
Kaskaskia Coll (IL)
Kellogg Comm Coll (MI)
Kemper Military Jr Coll (MO)
Kennebec Valley Tech Coll (ME)
Kent State U, Ashtabula Cmps (OH)
Kent State U, East Liverpool Cmps (OH)
Kent State U, Tuscarawas Cmps (OH)
Kettering Coll of Medical Arts (OH)
Keystone Coll (PA)
Kingsborough Comm Coll of City U of NY (NY)
Kirkwood Comm Coll (IA)
Kirtland Comm Coll (MI)
Kishwaukee Coll (IL)
Labette Comm Coll (KS)
Labouré Coll (MA)
Lake City Comm Coll (FL)
Lake Land Coll (IL)
Lakeland Comm Coll (OH)
Lake Michigan Coll (MI)
Lakeshore Tech Coll (WI)
Lake-Sumter Comm Coll (FL)
Lakewood Comm Coll (MN)
Lamar Comm Coll (CO)
Lamar University–Orange (TX)
Lamar University–Port Arthur (TX)
Lane Comm Coll (OR)
Lansing Comm Coll (MI)
Laramie County Comm Coll (WY)
Laredo Comm Coll (TX)
Lassen Coll (CA)
Lawson State Comm Coll (AL)
Lee Coll (TX)
Lehigh Carbon Comm Coll (PA)
Lenoir Comm Coll (NC)
Lewis and Clark Comm Coll (IL)
Lima Tech Coll (OH)
Lincoln Coll, Normal (IL)
Lincoln Land Comm Coll (IL)
Linn-Benton Comm Coll (OR)
Long Beach City Coll (CA)
Long Island Coll Hospital Sch of Nursing (NY)
Lorain County Comm Coll (OH)
Los Angeles Harbor Coll (CA)
Los Angeles Pierce Coll (CA)
Los Angeles Southwest Coll (CA)
Los Angeles Trade-Tech Coll (CA)
Los Angeles Valley Coll (CA)
Los Medanos Coll (CA)
Louise Harkey Sch of Nurs–Cabarrus Memorial Hosp (NC)
Louisiana State U at Alexandria (LA)
Louisiana State U at Eunice (LA)
Lower Columbia Coll (WA)
Lutheran Coll of Health Professions (IN)
Luzerne County Comm Coll (PA)
Macomb Comm Coll (MI)
Macon Coll (GA)
Madison Area Tech Coll (WI)
Manatee Comm Coll (FL)
Manor Jr Coll (PA)
Maria Coll (NY)
Maric Coll of Medical Careers (CA)
Marion Tech Coll (OH)
Marshalltown Comm Coll (IA)
Mary Holmes Coll (MS)
Massachusetts Bay Comm Coll (MA)
Massasoit Comm Coll (MA)
Mayland Comm Coll (NC)
McCarrie Schools of Health Sci and Tech (PA)
McDowell Tech Comm Coll (NC)
McLennan Comm Coll (TX)
Meadows Coll of Business (GA)
Merced Coll (CA)
Mercer County Comm Coll (NJ)
Mercy Coll of Northwest Ohio (OH)
Meridian Comm Coll (MS)
Merritt Coll (CA)
Mesa Comm Coll (AZ)
Metropolitan Comm Coll (NE)
Miami-Dade Comm Coll (FL)
Miami University–Hamilton Cmps (OH)
Miami University–Middletown Cmps (OH)
Middle Georgia Coll (GA)
Middlesex Comm Coll (MA)
Middlesex County Coll (NJ)
Midland Coll (TX)
Midlands Tech Coll (SC)
Mid Michigan Comm Coll (MI)
Mid-Plains Comm Coll (NE)
Mid-State Tech Coll (WI)
Miles Comm Coll (MT)
Milwaukee Area Tech Coll (WI)
Mineral Area Coll (MO)
Minneapolis Comm Coll (MN)
MiraCosta Coll (CA)
Mississippi County Comm Coll (AR)
Mississippi Delta Comm Coll (MS)
Mississippi Gulf Coast Comm Coll (MS)
Mitchell Comm Coll (NC)
Moberly Area Comm Coll (MO)
Modesto Jr Coll (CA)
Mohave Comm Coll (AZ)
Mohawk Valley Comm Coll (NY)
Monroe Comm Coll (NY)
Monroe County Comm Coll (MI)
Montana State U Coll of Tech-Great Falls (MT)
Montcalm Comm Coll (MI)
Monterey Peninsula Coll (CA)
Montgomery Coll (TX)
Montgomery College–Takoma Park Cmps (MD)
Montgomery County Comm Coll (PA)
Moorpark Coll (CA)
Moraine Park Tech Coll (WI)
Moraine Valley Comm Coll (IL)
Morton Coll (IL)
Motlow State Comm Coll (TN)
Mountain Empire Comm Coll (VA)
Mt Hood Comm Coll (OR)
Mt San Antonio Coll (CA)
Mt San Jacinto Coll (CA)
Mount Wachusett Comm Coll (MA)
Murray State Coll (OK)
Muskegon Comm Coll (MI)
Napa Valley Coll (CA)
Nash Comm Coll (NC)
Nassau Comm Coll (NY)
Naugatuck Valley Community–Tech Coll (CT)
Navarro Coll (TX)
Neosho County Comm Coll (KS)
New Hampshire Tech Coll, Berlin (NH)
New Hampshire Tech Coll, Claremont (NH)
New Hampshire Tech Coll, Manchester (NH)
New Hampshire Tech Inst (NH)
New Mexico Jr Coll (NM)
New Mexico State University–Alamogordo (NM)
New Mexico State University–Carlsbad (NM)
New York City Tech Coll of the City U of NY (NY)
Niagara County Comm Coll (NY)
Nicolet Area Tech Coll (WI)
Normandale Comm Coll (MN)
Northampton County Area Comm Coll (PA)
North Arkansas Comm/Tech Coll (AR)
North Central Michigan Coll (MI)
North Central Missouri Coll (MO)
North Central Tech Coll (OH)
Northcentral Tech Coll (WI)
North Central Texas Coll (TX)
North Country Comm Coll (NY)
North Dakota State Coll of Science (ND)
Northeast Alabama State Comm Coll (AL)
Northeast Comm Coll (NE)
Northeastern Jr Coll (CO)
Northeastern Oklahoma A&M Coll (OK)
Northeast Iowa Comm Coll, Calmar Cmps (IA)
Northeast Iowa Comm Coll, Peosta Cmps (IA)
Northeast Mississippi Comm Coll (MS)
Northeast Texas Comm Coll (TX)
Northern Essex Comm Coll (MA)
Northern Maine Tech Coll (ME)
Northern Marianas Coll (MP)
Northern Oklahoma Coll (OK)
Northern Virginia Comm Coll (VA)
North Harris Coll (TX)
North Hennepin Comm Coll (MN)
North Idaho Coll (ID)
North Iowa Area Comm Coll (IA)
Northland Comm and Tech Coll (MN)
Northland Pioneer Coll (AZ)
North Shore Comm Coll (MA)
NorthWest Arkansas Comm Coll (AR)
Northwest Coll (WY)
Northwestern Michigan Coll (MI)
Northwest Iowa Comm Coll (IA)
Northwest Mississippi Comm Coll (MS)
Northwest-Shoals Comm Coll (AL)
Northwest State Comm Coll (OH)
Norwalk Comm-Tech Coll (CT)
Oakland Comm Coll (MI)
Oakton Comm Coll (IL)
Ocean County Coll (NJ)
Odessa Coll (TX)
Ohio Valley Coll (WV)
Ohlone Coll (CA)
Okaloosa-Walton Comm Coll (FL)
Oklahoma City Comm Coll (OK)
Oklahoma State U, Oklahoma City (OK)
Olympic Coll (WA)
Onondaga Comm Coll (NY)
Orangeburg-Calhoun Tech Coll (SC)
Orange County Comm Coll (NY)
Otero Jr Coll (CO)
Our Lady of the Lake Coll (LA)
Owensboro Comm Coll (KY)
Owens Comm Coll, Findlay (OH)
Owens Comm Coll, Toledo (OH)
Ozarka Tech Coll (AR)
Palm Beach Comm Coll (FL)
Palo Alto Coll (TX)
Palomar Coll (CA)
Paris Jr Coll (TX)
Parkland Coll (IL)
Pasadena City Coll (CA)
Pasco-Hernando Comm Coll (FL)
Passaic County Comm Coll (NJ)
Patrick Henry Comm Coll (VA)
Pearl River Comm Coll (MS)
Peninsula Coll (WA)
Pennsylvania Coll of Tech (PA)
Penn State U Altoona Cmps (PA)
Penn State U Fayette Cmps (PA)
Penn State U Mont Alto Cmps (PA)
Penn State U Worthington Scranton Cmps (PA)
Penn Valley Comm Coll (MO)
Pensacola Jr Coll (FL)
Phillips Beth Israel Sch of Nursing (NY)
Phillips County Comm Coll (AR)
Piedmont Comm Coll (NC)
Piedmont Tech Coll (SC)
Piedmont Virginia Comm Coll (VA)
Pikes Peak Comm Coll (CO)
Pima Comm Coll (AZ)
Pitt Comm Coll (NC)
Polk Comm Coll (FL)
Portland Comm Coll (OR)
Prairie State Coll (IL)
Pratt Comm Coll and Area Voc Sch (KS)
Prince George's Comm Coll (MD)
Pueblo Comm Coll (CO)
Queensborough Comm Coll of City U of NY (NY)
Quincy Coll (MA)
Quinsigamond Comm Coll (MA)
Rancho Santiago Coll (CA)
Randolph Comm Coll (NC)
Rappahannock Comm Coll (VA)
Raritan Valley Comm Coll (NJ)
Reading Area Comm Coll (PA)
Redlands Comm Coll (OK)
Rend Lake Coll (IL)
Richland Comm Coll (IL)
Richmond Comm Coll (NC)
Rich Mountain Comm Coll (AR)
Ricks Coll (ID)
Rio Hondo Coll (CA)
Riverside Comm Coll (CA)
Roane State Comm Coll (TN)
Roanoke-Chowan Comm Coll (NC)
Robeson Comm Coll (NC)
Rochester Comm Coll (MN)
Rockingham Comm Coll (NC)
Rockland Comm Coll (NY)
Rock Valley Coll (IL)
Rogers State Coll (OK)
Rogue Comm Coll (OR)
Rose State Coll (OK)
Rowan-Cabarrus Comm Coll (NC)
Roxbury Comm Coll (MA)
Sacramento City Coll (CA)
Saddleback Coll (CA)
St Catharine Coll (KY)
Saint Charles County Comm Coll (MO)
St Clair County Comm Coll (MI)
St Cloud Tech Coll (MN)
St Louis Comm Coll at Florissant Valley (MO)
St Louis Comm Coll at Forest Park (MO)
St Louis Comm Coll at Meramec (MO)
St Petersburg Jr Coll (FL)
St Philip's Coll (TX)
St Vincent's Coll (CT)
Salem Comm Coll (NJ)
Salish Kootenai Coll (MT)
Salt Lake Comm Coll (UT)
Sampson Comm Coll (NC)
San Antonio Coll (TX)
San Bernardino Valley Coll (CA)
Sandhills Comm Coll (NC)
San Diego City Coll (CA)
Sanford-Brown Coll, Des Peres (MO)
Sanford-Brown Coll, St Charles (MO)
San Jacinto College–Central Cmps (TX)
San Jacinto College–North Cmps (TX)
San Jacinto College–South Cmps (TX)
San Joaquin Delta Coll (CA)
San Juan Coll (NM)
Santa Barbara City Coll (CA)
Santa Fe Comm Coll (FL)
Santa Fe Comm Coll (NM)
Santa Monica Coll (CA)
Santa Rosa Jr Coll (CA)
Sauk Valley Comm Coll (IL)
Schoolcraft Coll (MI)
Scott Comm Coll (IA)
Scottsdale Comm Coll (AZ)
Seattle Central Comm Coll (WA)
Seminole Comm Coll (FL)
Seminole Jr Coll (OK)
Seward County Comm Coll (KS)
Shasta Coll (CA)
Shawnee Comm Coll (IL)
Shelby State Comm Coll (TN)
Shelton State Comm Coll (AL)
Sheridan Coll (WY)
Shoreline Comm Coll (WA)
Shorter Coll (AR)
Sierra Coll (CA)
Sinclair Comm Coll (OH)
Sisseton-Wahpeton Comm Coll (SD)
Skagit Valley Coll (WA)
Solano Comm Coll (CA)
Southeast Comm Coll, Lincoln Cmps (NE)
Southeastern Comm Coll (NC)
Southeastern Comm Coll, North Cmps, West Burlington (IA)
Southeastern Comm Coll, South Cmps, Keokuk (IA)
Southeastern Illinois Coll (IL)
Southern Arkansas U Tech (AR)
Southern Maine Tech Coll (ME)
Southern State Comm Coll (OH)
Southern Union State Comm Coll (AL)
Southern West Virginia Comm and Tech Coll (WV)
South Florida Comm Coll (FL)
South Georgia Coll (GA)
South Plains Coll (TX)
South Puget Sound Comm Coll (WA)
Southside Virginia Comm Coll (VA)
South Suburban Coll (IL)
Southwestern Coll (CA)
Southwestern Comm Coll (NC)
Southwestern Michigan Coll (MI)
Southwestern Oklahoma State U at Sayre (OK)
Southwestern Oregon Comm Coll (OR)

Associate Degree Programs at Two-Year Colleges
Nursing–Optical Technologies

Southwest Mississippi Comm Coll (MS)
Southwest Missouri State University– West Plains (MO)
Southwest Virginia Comm Coll (VA)
Southwest Wisconsin Tech Coll (WI)
Spokane Comm Coll (WA)
Springfield Coll in Illinois (IL)
Springfield Tech Comm Coll (MA)
Stanly Comm Coll (NC)
Stark Tech Coll (OH)
State Comm Coll of East St Louis (IL)
State Fair Comm Coll (MO)
State U of NY Coll of A&T at Morrisville (NY)
State U of NY Coll of Tech at Alfred (NY)
State U of NY Coll of Tech at Canton (NY)
State U of NY Coll of Tech at Delhi (NY)
State U of NY Coll of Tech at Farmingdale (NY)
Suffolk County Comm College–Ammerman Cmps (NY)
Suffolk County Comm Coll–Western Cmps (NY)
Sullivan County Comm Coll (NY)
Surry Comm Coll (NC)
Tacoma Comm Coll (WA)
Tallahassee Comm Coll (FL)
Tarrant County Jr Coll (TX)
Tech Coll of Municipality of San Juan (PR)
Temple Coll (TX)
Texarkana Coll (TX)
Texas Southmost Coll (TX)
Texas State Tech Coll (TX)
Thomas Nelson Comm Coll (VA)
Three Rivers Comm Coll (MO)
Three Rivers Comm-Tech Coll (CT)
Tidewater Comm Coll (VA)
Tomball Coll (TX)
Tompkins Cortland Comm Coll (NY)
Treasure Valley Comm Coll (OR)
Tri-County Comm Coll (NC)
Tri-County Tech Coll (SC)
Trident Tech Coll (SC)
Trinidad State Jr Coll (CO)
Trinity Valley Comm Coll (TX)
Triton Coll (IL)
Trocaire Coll (NY)
Truckee Meadows Comm Coll (NV)
Tulsa Jr Coll (OK)
Turtle Mountain Comm Coll (ND)
Tyler Jr Coll (TX)
UAB Walker Coll (AL)
Ulster County Comm Coll (NY)
Umpqua Comm Coll (OR)
Union County Coll (NJ)
United Tribes Tech Coll (ND)
U of Cincinnati Raymond Walters Coll (OH)
U of Hawaii–Hawaii Comm Coll (HI)
U of Hawaii–Kapiolani Comm Coll (HI)
U of Hawaii–Kauai Comm Coll (HI)
U of Hawaii–Maui Comm Coll (HI)
U of Kentucky, Ashland Comm Coll (KY)
U of Kentucky, Elizabethtown Comm Coll (KY)
U of Kentucky, Hazard Comm Coll (KY)
U of Kentucky, Henderson Comm Coll (KY)
U of Kentucky, Hopkinsville Comm Coll (KY)
U of Kentucky, Jefferson Comm Coll (KY)
U of Kentucky, Lexington Comm Coll (KY)
U of Kentucky, Madisonville Comm Coll (KY)
U of Kentucky, Maysville Comm Coll (KY)
U of Kentucky, Paducah Comm Coll (KY)
U of Kentucky, Prestonsburg Comm Coll (KY)
U of Kentucky, Somerset Comm Coll (KY)
U of Kentucky, Southeast Comm Coll (KY)
U of Maine at Augusta (ME)
U of New Mexico–Gallup Branch (NM)
U of South Carolina at Lancaster (SC)
U of Wisconsin Center–Marathon County (WI)
U of Wisconsin Center–Marinette County (WI)
Valencia Comm Coll (FL)
Vance-Granville Comm Coll (NC)
Ventura Coll (CA)
Vernon Regional Jr Coll (TX)
Victoria Coll (TX)
Victor Valley Coll (CA)
Vincennes U (IN)
Virginia Highlands Comm Coll (VA)
Virginia Western Comm Coll (VA)
Wake Tech Comm Coll (NC)
Waldorf Coll (IA)
Wallace State Comm Coll (AL)
Walla Walla Comm Coll (WA)
Walters State Comm Coll (TN)
Washington State Comm Coll (OH)
Washtenaw Comm Coll (MI)
Waubonsee Comm Coll (IL)
Waukesha County Tech Coll (WI)
Waycross Coll (GA)
Wayne Comm Coll (NC)
Wayne County Comm Coll (MI)
Wenatchee Valley Coll (WA)
Westark Comm Coll (AR)
Westchester Comm Coll (NY)
Western Iowa Tech Comm Coll (IA)
Western Nebraska Comm Coll, Scottsbluff (NE)
Western Nevada Comm Coll (NV)
Western Oklahoma State Coll (OK)
Western Piedmont Comm Coll (NC)
Western Wisconsin Tech Coll (WI)
Western Wyoming Comm Coll (WY)
Westmoreland County Comm Coll (PA)
West Shore Comm Coll (MI)
West Virginia Northern Comm Coll (WV)
West Virginia U at Parkersburg (WV)
Wharton County Jr Coll (TX)
Whatcom Comm Coll (WA)
Wilkes Comm Coll (NC)
William Rainey Harper Coll (IL)
Willmar Comm Coll (MN)
Wilson Tech Comm Coll (NC)
Wisconsin Indianhead Tech Coll, Ashland Cmps (WI)
Wisconsin Indianhead Tech Coll, New Richmond Cmps (WI)
Wisconsin Indianhead Tech Coll, Rice Lake Cmps (WI)
Wisconsin Indianhead Tech Coll, Superior Cmps (WI)
Worthington Comm Coll (MN)
Wor-Wic Comm Coll (MD)
Wytheville Comm Coll (VA)
Yakima Valley Comm Coll (WA)
Yavapai Coll (AZ)
York Tech Coll (SC)
Young Harris Coll (GA)
Yuba Coll (CA)

NUTRITION

American Acad of Nutrition (TN)
Camden County Coll (NJ)
Central Coll (KS)
City Coll of San Francisco (CA)
City Colls of Chicago, Malcolm X Coll (IL)
Clackamas Comm Coll (OR)
Colby Comm Coll (KS)
Comm Coll of Allegheny County Allegheny Cmps (PA)
Comm Coll of Philadelphia (PA)
Cuesta Coll (CA)
Daytona Beach Comm Coll (FL)
Dixie Coll (UT)
Dutchess Comm Coll (NY)
Holyoke Comm Coll (MA)
Kansas City Kansas Comm Coll (KS)
Mohawk Valley Comm Coll (NY)
Normandale Comm Coll (MN)
Ohlone Coll (CA)
Okaloosa-Walton Comm Coll (FL)
Orange Coast Coll (CA)
Owens Comm Coll, Toledo (OH)
Palm Beach Comm Coll (FL)
Rancho Santiago Coll (CA)
Ricks Coll (ID)
Saddleback Coll (CA)
San Diego Mesa Coll (CA)
San Jacinto College–Central Cmps (TX)
Santa Rosa Jr Coll (CA)
Sinclair Comm Coll (OH)
Snow Coll (UT)
State U of NY Coll of Tech at Farmingdale (NY)
Vincennes U (IN)

OCCUPATIONAL SAFETY AND HEALTH

Broome Comm Coll (NY)
Camden County Coll (NJ)
Catonsville Comm Coll (MD)
Central Maine Tech Coll (ME)
Delaware Tech & Comm Coll, Stanton/Wilmington Cmps (DE)
Las Positas Coll (CA)
Mt San Antonio Coll (CA)
Northampton County Area Comm Coll (PA)
NorthWest Arkansas Comm Coll (AR)
Salem Comm Coll (NJ)
San Diego City Coll (CA)
San Diego Miramar Coll (CA)
San Jacinto College–Central Cmps (TX)
Texas State Tech Coll–Waco/Marshall Cmps (TX)
Trinidad State Jr Coll (CO)
Truckee Meadows Comm Coll (NV)
U of Hawaii–Honolulu Comm Coll (HI)
Wallace State Comm Coll (AL)

OCCUPATIONAL THERAPY

Alabama Southern Comm Coll, Monroeville (AL)
Allegany Comm Coll (MD)
Andrew Coll (GA)
Anoka-Ramsey Comm Coll (MN)
Apollo College–Phoenix, Inc (AZ)
Arapahoe Comm Coll (CO)
Atlanta Metropolitan Coll (GA)
Atlantic Comm Coll (NJ)
Austin Comm Coll (MN)
Austin Comm Coll (TX)
Barton County Comm Coll (KS)
Bay State Coll (MA)
Brevard Coll (NC)
Briarwood Coll (CT)
Bristol Comm Coll (MA)
Brunswick Coll (GA)
Brunswick Comm Coll (NC)
Caldwell Comm Coll and Tech Inst (NC)
Casper Coll (WY)
Catonsville Comm Coll (MD)
Central Florida Comm Coll (FL)
Champlain Coll (VT)
Charles Stewart Mott Comm Coll (MI)
Chattanooga State Tech Comm Coll (TN)
Cincinnati State Tech and Comm Coll (OH)
City Colls of Chicago, Harold Washington Coll (IL)
City Colls of Chicago, Wilbur Wright Coll (IL)
Coll of DuPage (IL)
Coll of St Catherine–Minneapolis (MN)
Comm Coll of Allegheny County Boyce Cmps (PA)
Comm Coll of Southern Nevada (NV)
Comm Coll of the Air Force (AL)
Comm Hospital Roanoke Valley–Coll of Health Scis (VA)
Cuyahoga Comm Coll, Metropolitan Cmps (OH)
Dalton Coll (GA)
Danville Area Comm Coll (IL)
Daytona Beach Comm Coll (FL)
Delgado Comm Coll (LA)
Durham Tech Comm Coll (NC)
East Central Comm Coll (MS)
Eastern New Mexico University–Roswell (NM)
Erie Comm Coll, North Cmps (NY)
Everett Comm Coll (WA)
Fiorello H LaGuardia Comm Coll of City U of NY (NY)
Fox Valley Tech Coll (WI)
Gadsden State Comm Coll (AL)
Genesee Comm Coll (NY)
George Corley Wallace State Comm Coll, Selma (AL)
Grand Rapids Comm Coll (MI)
Green River Comm Coll (WA)
Gulf Coast Comm Coll (FL)
Harcum Coll (PA)
Herkimer County Comm Coll (NY)
Hesser Coll (NH)
Highland Comm Coll (KS)
Hillsborough Comm Coll (FL)
Houston Comm Coll System (TX)
Hutchinson Comm Coll and Area Vocational Sch (KS)
Illinois Central Coll (IL)
Iowa Central Comm Coll (IA)
Ivy Tech State Coll–Central Indiana (IN)
Jefferson State Comm Coll (AL)
John A Logan Coll (IL)
Johnson County Comm Coll (KS)
Kansas City Kansas Comm Coll (KS)
Kennebec Valley Tech Coll (ME)
Kent State U, East Liverpool Cmps (OH)
Keystone Coll (PA)
Kirkwood Comm Coll (IA)
Lake Area Vocational-Tech Inst (SD)
Lake-Sumter Comm Coll (FL)
Lehigh Carbon Comm Coll (PA)
Madison Area Tech Coll (WI)
Manchester Comm-Tech Coll (CT)
Manor Jr Coll (PA)
Maria Coll (NY)
Maric Coll of Medical Careers (CA)
Massachusetts Bay Comm Coll (MA)
Middle Georgia Coll (GA)
Milwaukee Area Tech Coll (WI)
Modesto Jr Coll (CA)
Montana State U Coll of Tech-Great Falls (MT)
Monterey Peninsula Coll (CA)
Moraine Valley Comm Coll (IL)
Mt Hood Comm Coll (OR)
Mount Ida Coll (MA)
Muskingum Area Tech Coll (OH)
Nashville State Tech Inst (TN)
Navarro Coll (TX)
New Hampshire Tech Coll, Claremont (NH)
North Central Texas Coll (TX)
North Dakota State Coll of Science (ND)
Northeast Mississippi Comm Coll (MS)
North Shore Comm Coll (MA)
Oklahoma City Comm Coll (OK)
Orange County Comm Coll (NY)
Palm Beach Comm Coll (FL)
Parkland Coll (IL)
Pasadena City Coll (CA)
Pennsylvania Coll of Tech (PA)
Penn State U Berks Cmps (PA)
Penn State U Mont Alto Cmps (PA)
Penn Valley Comm Coll (MO)
Pitt Comm Coll (NC)
Pueblo Comm Coll (CO)
Quinsigamond Comm Coll (MA)
Ricks Coll (ID)
Roane State Comm Coll (TN)
Rockland Comm Coll (NY)
Sacramento City Coll (CA)
Saint Charles County Comm Coll (MO)
St Louis Comm Coll at Meramec (MO)
St Philip's Coll (TX)
Salt Lake Comm Coll (UT)
Sanford-Brown Coll, Des Peres (MO)
San Jacinto College–South Cmps (TX)
Schoolcraft Coll (MI)
Sinclair Comm Coll (OH)
Southeastern Illinois Coll (IL)
South Suburban Coll (IL)
Southwestern Comm Coll (NC)
Springfield Tech Comm Coll (MA)
Stanly Comm Coll (NC)
Stark Tech Coll (OH)
Tacoma Comm Coll (WA)
Trident Tech Coll (SC)
Tulsa Jr Coll (OK)
Union County Coll (NJ)
U of Hawaii–Kapiolani Comm Coll (HI)
U of Pittsburgh–Titusville (PA)
U of Wisconsin Center–Marathon County (WI)
Vincennes U (IN)
Wallace State Comm Coll (AL)
Wayne County Comm Coll (MI)
Western Iowa Tech Comm Coll (IA)
Western Wisconsin Tech Coll (WI)
Yakima Valley Comm Coll (WA)

OCEANOGRAPHY

Arizona Western Coll (AZ)
Everett Comm Coll (WA)
Fullerton Coll (CA)
Grays Harbor Coll (WA)
Gulf Coast Comm Coll (FL)
Miami-Dade Comm Coll (FL)
Mitchell Coll (CT)
Northeast Mississippi Comm Coll (MS)
Shoreline Comm Coll (WA)
Southern Maine Tech Coll (ME)
Southwestern Coll (CA)
Tacoma Comm Coll (WA)

OPERATING ROOM TECHNOLOGY

Austin Comm Coll (TX)
Baltimore City Comm Coll (MD)
Catawba Valley Comm Coll (NC)
Central Wyoming Coll (WY)
Cincinnati State Tech and Comm Coll (OH)
Coastal Carolina Comm Coll (NC)
Coll of DuPage (IL)
Columbus State Comm Coll (OH)
Comm Coll of Allegheny County Boyce Cmps (PA)
Comm Coll of Denver (CO)
Comm Coll of the Air Force (AL)
Cuyahoga Comm Coll, Western Cmps (OH)
Delaware County Comm Coll (PA)
Delta Coll (MI)
Edgecombe Comm Coll (NC)
El Centro Coll (TX)
Gateway Comm Coll (AZ)
Highland Park Comm Coll (MI)
Hinds Comm Coll (MS)
Ivy Tech State Coll–Central Indiana (IN)
Ivy Tech State Coll–Lafayette (IN)
Ivy Tech State Coll–Northwest (IN)
Lake City Comm Coll (FL)
Lansing Comm Coll (MI)
Lorain County Comm Coll (OH)
Lutheran Coll of Health Professions (IN)
Luzerne County Comm Coll (PA)
Manchester Comm-Tech Coll (CT)
Marshalltown Comm Coll (IA)
Massachusetts Bay Comm Coll (MA)
McCarrie Schools of Health Sci and Tech (PA)
Mt Hood Comm Coll (OR)
Nassau Comm Coll (NY)
New England Inst of Tech (RI)
Niagara County Comm Coll (NY)
Northcentral Tech Coll (WI)
Odessa Coll (TX)
Our Lady of the Lake Coll (LA)
Owens Comm Coll, Toledo (OH)
Ozarks Tech Comm Coll (MO)
Pines Tech Coll (AR)
Quincy Coll (MA)
Renton Tech Coll (WA)
St Cloud Tech Coll (MN)
St Louis Comm Coll at Forest Park (MO)
St Philip's Coll (TX)
Salt Lake Comm Coll (UT)
Sandhills Comm Coll (NC)
San Jacinto College–Central Cmps (TX)
Southeastern Illinois Coll (IL)
Southern Maine Tech Coll (ME)
Southern U at Shreveport–Bossier City Cmps (LA)
South Plains Coll (TX)
Spokane Comm Coll (WA)
Springfield Tech Comm Coll (MA)
Tarrant County Jr Coll (TX)
Trinity Valley Comm Coll (TX)
Trocaire Coll (NY)
Ward Stone Coll (FL)
Waycross Coll (GA)
Westark Comm Coll (AR)
Western Wisconsin Tech Coll (WI)
West Virginia Northern Comm Coll (WV)
York Tech Coll (SC)

OPTICAL TECHNOLOGIES

Albuquerque Tech Vocational Inst (NM)
Bunker Hill Comm Coll (MA)
Camden County Coll (NJ)
Durham Tech Comm Coll (NC)
Elaine P Nunez Comm Coll (LA)
Essex County Coll (NJ)
George C Wallace State Comm Coll, Dothan (AL)
Lakeshore Tech Coll (WI)
McCarrie Schools of Health Sci and Tech (PA)
Mesabi Comm Coll (MN)
Miami-Dade Comm Coll (FL)
Mid-Plains Comm Coll (NE)
Monroe Comm Coll (NY)
Moorpark Coll (CA)

Associate Degree Programs at Two-Year Colleges
Optical Technologies–Paralegal Studies

Pennsylvania Coll of Tech (PA)
Pikes Peak Comm Coll (CO)
Pima Comm Coll (AZ)
Portland Comm Coll (OR)
Roane State Comm Coll (TN)
Schoolcraft Coll (MI)
Southern Ohio Coll, Cincinnati Cmps (OH)
Southwestern Indian Polytechnic Inst (NM)
U of Kentucky, Madisonville Comm Coll (KY)
Vincennes U (IN)

OPTOMETRIC/ OPHTHALMIC TECHNOLOGIES
Anoka-Ramsey Comm Coll (MN)
Comm Coll of Allegheny County South Cmps (PA)
Comm Coll of Aurora (CO)
Comm Coll of the Air Force (AL)
Cuyahoga Comm Coll, Metropolitan Cmps (OH)
DeKalb Coll (GA)
DeKalb Tech Inst (GA)
East Mississippi Comm Coll (MS)
El Paso Comm Coll (TX)
Erie Comm Coll, North Cmps (NY)
Hillsborough Comm Coll (FL)
Interboro Inst (NY)
J Sargeant Reynolds Comm Coll (VA)
Lakeland Comm Coll (OH)
Los Angeles City Coll (CA)
Massachusetts Bay Comm Coll (MA)
Mater Dei Coll (NY)
Metropolitan Comm Coll (NE)
Miami-Dade Comm Coll (FL)
Middlesex Community– Tech Coll (CT)
New Hampshire Tech Coll, Nashua (NH)
New York City Tech Coll of the City U of NY (NY)
Owens Comm Coll, Findlay (OH)
Owens Comm Coll, Toledo (OH)
Portland Comm Coll (OR)
Pueblo Comm Coll (CO)
Raritan Valley Comm Coll (NJ)
St Cloud Tech Coll (MN)
St Petersburg Jr Coll (FL)
Seattle Central Comm Coll (WA)
Southwestern Tech Coll (MN)
Spokane Comm Coll (WA)
Thomas Nelson Comm Coll (VA)
Triton Coll (IL)
Tyler Jr Coll (TX)
Westmoreland County Comm Coll (PA)

ORNAMENTAL HORTICULTURE
Abraham Baldwin Ag Coll (GA)
Bakersfield Coll (CA)
Bergen Comm Coll (NJ)
Bessemer State Tech Coll (AL)
Bronx Comm Coll of City U of NY (NY)
Butte Coll (CA)
Central Florida Comm Coll (FL)
Cerritos Coll (CA)
Chabot Coll (CA)
Cincinnati State Tech and Comm Coll (OH)
City Coll of San Francisco (CA)
Clackamas Comm Coll (OR)
Clark Coll (WA)
Coll of DuPage (IL)
Coll of San Mateo (CA)
Coll of the Desert (CA)
Coll of the Sequoias (CA)
Collin County Comm Coll (TX)
Comm Coll of Allegheny County South Cmps (PA)

Comm Coll of Southern Nevada (NV)
Cumberland County Coll (NJ)
Cuyamaca Coll (CA)
Danville Area Comm Coll (IL)
Dundalk Comm Coll (MD)
Edmonds Comm Coll (WA)
El Camino Coll (CA)
Finger Lakes Comm Coll (NY)
Foothill Coll (CA)
Forsyth Tech Comm Coll (NC)
Fullerton Coll (CA)
Glendale Comm Coll (AZ)
Golden West Coll (CA)
Gwinnett Tech Inst (GA)
Hartnell Coll (CA)
Hawkeye Comm Coll (IA)
Hillsborough Comm Coll (FL)
Howard Coll (TX)
Kings River Comm Coll (CA)
Kirkwood Comm Coll (IA)
Kishwaukee Coll (IL)
Lenoir Comm Coll (NC)
Los Angeles Pierce Coll (CA)
Mendocino Coll (CA)
Merced Coll (CA)
Mercer County Comm Coll (NJ)
Mesa Comm Coll (AZ)
Metropolitan Comm Coll (NE)
Miami-Dade Comm Coll (FL)
Mississippi Gulf Coast Comm Coll (MS)
Modesto Jr Coll (CA)
Monterey Peninsula Coll (CA)
Mt Hood Comm Coll (OR)
Mt San Antonio Coll (CA)
Niagara County Comm Coll (NY)
Northwestern Michigan Coll (MI)
Ohio State U Ag Tech Inst (OH)
Orange Coast Coll (CA)
Pennsylvania Coll of Tech (PA)
Pensacola Jr Coll (FL)
Petit Jean Tech Coll (AR)
Polk Comm Coll (FL)
Richland Coll (TX)
Ricks Coll (ID)
Saddleback Coll (CA)
San Joaquin Delta Coll (CA)
Santa Barbara City Coll (CA)
Santa Fe Comm Coll (FL)
Shasta Coll (CA)
Sierra Coll (CA)
Solano Comm Coll (CA)
South Florida Comm Coll (FL)
Southwestern Coll (CA)
Spokane Comm Coll (WA)
State U of NY Coll of A&T at Cobleskill (NY)
State U of NY Coll of Tech at Alfred (NY)
State U of NY Coll of Tech at Farmingdale (NY)
Texas State Tech Coll–Waco/ Marshall Cmps (TX)
Triton Coll (IL)
Tyler Jr Coll (TX)
Valencia Comm Coll (FL)
Ventura Coll (CA)
Vincennes U (IN)
Wharton County Jr Coll (TX)
The Williamson Free Sch of Mech Trades (PA)
Yuba Coll (CA)

PAINTING/DRAWING
Allen County Comm Coll (KS)
American Acad of Art (IL)
Art Inst of Fort Lauderdale (FL)
Austin Comm Coll (MN)
Berkshire Comm Coll (MA)
Brevard Coll (NC)
Cañada Coll (CA)
Central Texas Coll (TX)
Chabot Coll (CA)
City Colls of Chicago, Harold Washington Coll (IL)
Coffeyville Comm Coll (KS)
Colby Comm Coll (KS)
Coll of San Mateo (CA)
Comm Coll of Allegheny County South Cmps (PA)
Delgado Comm Coll (LA)
East Central Comm Coll (MS)
Everett Comm Coll (WA)

Gavilan Coll (CA)
Grossmont Coll (CA)
Henry Ford Comm Coll (MI)
Inst of American Indian Arts (NM)
Iowa Lakes Comm Coll (IA)
John Wood Comm Coll (IL)
Lassen Coll (CA)
Lincoln Coll, Normal (IL)
Lon Morris Coll (TX)
Luzerne County Comm Coll (PA)
Midland Coll (TX)
Moberly Area Comm Coll (MO)
Monterey Peninsula Coll (CA)
Northeastern Jr Coll (CO)
Northeast Mississippi Comm Coll (MS)
Northwest Coll (WY)
Palomar Coll (CA)
Pasadena City Coll (CA)
Polk Comm Coll (FL)
Sandhills Comm Coll (NC)
San Jacinto College–Central Cmps (TX)
San Jacinto College–North Cmps (TX)
San Joaquin Delta Coll (CA)
Seward County Comm Coll (KS)
Springfield Tech Comm Coll (MA)
Vermilion Comm Coll (MN)

PAPER AND PULP SCIENCES
Alabama Southern Comm Coll, Thomasville (AL)
Bay de Noc Comm Coll (MI)
Dabney S Lancaster Comm Coll (VA)
Fox Valley Tech Coll (WI)
Lower Columbia Coll (WA)
State U of NY Coll of Tech at Canton (NY)
Tacoma Comm Coll (WA)
Texarkana Coll (TX)

PARALEGAL STUDIES
Acad of Business Coll (AZ)
Albuquerque Tech Vocational Inst (NM)
Alvin Comm Coll (TX)
American River Coll (CA)
Andover Coll (ME)
Anne Arundel Comm Coll (MD)
Arapahoe Comm Coll (CO)
Athens Area Tech Inst (GA)
Atlantic Comm Coll (NJ)
Austin Comm Coll (TX)
Baltimore City Comm Coll (MD)
Beal Coll (ME)
Belleville Area Coll (IL)
Bergen Comm Coll (NJ)
Berkeley Coll (NJ)
Berkeley Coll, New York (NY)
Berkeley Coll, White Plains (NY)
Blair Jr Coll (CO)
Bradford Sch (OH)
Briarcliffe–The Coll for Business & Tech (NY)
Briarwood Coll (CT)
Bronx Comm Coll of City U of NY (NY)
Brookdale Comm Coll (NJ)
Broome Comm Coll (NY)
Broward Comm Coll (FL)
The Brown Mackie Coll (KS)
The Brown Mackie Coll–Olathe Cmps (KS)
Bryant and Stratton Business Inst, Cicero (NY)
Bryant and Stratton Business Inst, Rochester (NY)
Bryant and Stratton Business Inst, E Hills Cmps, Williamsville (NY)
Bucks County Comm Coll (PA)
Caldwell Comm Coll and Tech Inst (NC)
Cañada Coll (CA)
Cape Cod Comm Coll (MA)
Cape Fear Comm Coll (NC)
Carteret Comm Coll (NC)
Casco Bay Coll (ME)
Casper Coll (WY)
Castle Coll (NH)

Cecils Jr Coll of Business (NC)
Central Carolina Comm Coll (NC)
Central Carolina Tech Coll (SC)
Central Comm College– Grand Island Cmps (NE)
Central Florida Comm Coll (FL)
Central Pennsylvania Business Sch (PA)
Central Piedmont Comm Coll (NC)
Central Texas Coll (TX)
Champlain Coll (VT)
Charles County Comm Coll (MD)
Charles Stewart Mott Comm Coll (MI)
Charter Coll (AK)
Chippewa Valley Tech Coll (WI)
Clark Coll (WA)
Clark State Comm Coll (OH)
Cleveland State Comm Coll (TN)
Coastal Carolina Comm Coll (NC)
Coll of The Albemarle (NC)
Coll of the Sequoias (CA)
Columbia Basin Coll (WA)
Columbia Jr Coll of Business (SC)
Columbus State Comm Coll (OH)
Commonwealth Business Coll, Merrillville (IN)
Comm Coll of Allegheny County Allegheny Cmps (PA)
Comm Coll of Allegheny County Boyce Cmps (PA)
Comm Coll of Aurora (CO)
Comm Coll of Denver (CO)
Comm Coll of Philadelphia (PA)
Comm Coll of Rhode Island (RI)
Comm Coll of Southern Nevada (NV)
Comm Coll of the Air Force (AL)
Corning Comm Coll (NY)
Cuyahoga Comm Coll, Western Cmps (OH)
Davidson County Comm Coll (NC)
Daytona Beach Comm Coll (FL)
Dean Coll (MA)
De Anza Coll (CA)
Delta Coll (MI)
Des Moines Area Comm Coll (IA)
Doña Ana Branch Comm Coll (NM)
Draughons Jr Coll (AL)
Duff's Business Inst (PA)
Dundalk Comm Coll (MD)
Durham Tech Comm Coll (NC)
Eastern New Mexico University–Roswell (NM)
Edgecombe Comm Coll (NC)
Edison State Comm Coll (OH)
Edmonds Comm Coll (WA)
El Camino Coll (CA)
El Centro Coll (TX)
Elgin Comm Coll (IL)
Erie Business Ctr, Main (PA)
Erie Comm Coll, City Cmps (NY)
ETI Tech Coll, Niles (OH)
Eugenio María de Hostos Comm Coll of City U of NY (NY)
Evergreen Valley Coll (CA)
Fayetteville Tech Comm Coll (NC)
Fiorello H LaGuardia Comm Coll of City U of NY (NY)
Fisher Coll (MA)
Florence-Darlington Tech Coll (SC)
Florida Comm Coll at Jacksonville (FL)
Florida National Coll (FL)
Floyd Coll (GA)
Forsyth Tech Comm Coll (NC)
Frederick Comm Coll (MD)
Fresno City Coll (CA)

Fullerton Coll (CA)
Gadsden State Comm Coll (AL)
Gainesville Coll (GA)
Gem City Coll (IL)
Genesee Comm Coll (NY)
Gogebic Comm Coll (MI)
Great Lakes Jr Coll of Business (MI)
Greenville Tech Coll (SC)
Guilford Tech Comm Coll (NC)
Gulf Coast Comm Coll (FL)
Hagerstown Business Coll (MD)
Hagerstown Jr Coll (MD)
Harford Comm Coll (MD)
Harrisburg Area Comm Coll (PA)
Henry Ford Comm Coll (MI)
Herkimer County Comm Coll (NY)
Hesser Coll (NH)
Highline Comm Coll (WA)
Hinds Comm Coll (MS)
Horry-Georgetown Tech Coll (SC)
Houston Comm Coll System (TX)
Hudson County Comm Coll (NJ)
Hutchinson Comm Coll and Area Vocational Sch (KS)
Illinois Central Coll (IL)
Indian River Comm Coll (FL)
Interboro Inst (NY)
International Business Coll (IN)
Inver Hills Comm Coll (MN)
Iowa Lakes Comm Coll (IA)
Iowa Western Comm Coll (IA)
Itasca Comm Coll (MN)
Ivy Tech State Coll–Central Indiana (IN)
Ivy Tech State Coll–Northeast (IN)
Jefferson Comm Coll (NY)
John C Calhoun State Comm Coll (AL)
Johnson County Comm Coll (KS)
Johnston Comm Coll (NC)
Kansas City Kansas Comm Coll (KS)
Keiser Coll of Tech, Daytona Beach (FL)
Keiser Coll of Tech, Sarasota (FL)
Kellogg Comm Coll (MI)
Kelsey Jenney Coll (CA)
Kirkwood Comm Coll (IA)
Knoxville Business Coll (TN)
Lakeland Comm Coll (OH)
Lakeshore Tech Coll (WI)
Lamar University–Port Arthur (TX)
Lamson Jr Coll, Mesa (AZ)
Lansdale Sch of Business (PA)
Lansing Comm Coll (MI)
Laramie County Comm Coll (WY)
Lee Coll (TX)
Lehigh Carbon Comm Coll (PA)
Lima Tech Coll (OH)
Lincoln Coll, Normal (IL)
Lincoln Sch of Commerce (NE)
Luzerne County Comm Coll (PA)
MacCormac Jr Coll (IL)
Macomb Comm Coll (MI)
Manchester Comm-Tech Coll (CT)
Manor Jr Coll (PA)
Marion Tech Coll (OH)
Massachusetts Bay Comm Coll (MA)
McCann Sch of Business (PA)
McCook Comm Coll (NE)
McIntosh Coll (NH)
McLennan Comm Coll (TX)
Mercer County Comm Coll (NJ)
Merritt Coll (CA)
Mesabi Comm Coll (MN)
Metropolitan Comm Coll (NE)
Miami-Dade Comm Coll (FL)
Middle Georgia Coll (GA)
Middlesex County Coll (NJ)
Midland Coll (TX)
Midstate Coll (IL)

Milwaukee Area Tech Coll (WI)
Mississippi Gulf Coast Comm Coll (MS)
Montcalm Comm Coll (MI)
Montgomery College– Takoma Park Cmps (MD)
Mount Ida Coll (MA)
Mt San Antonio Coll (CA)
Muskingum Area Tech Coll (OH)
Napa Valley Coll (CA)
Nassau Comm Coll (NY)
National Inst for Paralegal Arts and Sciences (FL)
Naugatuck Valley Community–Tech Coll (CT)
Navarro Coll (TX)
Nettleton Career Coll (SD)
Newbury Coll (MA)
New Hampshire Tech Coll, Laconia (NH)
New Hampshire Tech Coll, Nashua (NH)
New Mexico State University–Grants (NM)
New River Comm Coll (VA)
New York City Tech Coll of the City U of NY (NY)
North Central Tech Coll (OH)
North Central Texas Coll (TX)
Northeast Alabama State Comm Coll (AL)
Northeast Mississippi Comm Coll (MS)
Northern Essex Comm Coll (MA)
Northern Virginia Comm Coll (VA)
North Hennepin Comm Coll (MN)
Northland Comm and Tech Coll (MN)
North Shore Comm Coll (MA)
Northwestern Business Coll (IL)
Northwestern Connecticut Comm-Tech Coll (CT)
Northwestern Michigan Coll (MI)
Northwest Mississippi Comm Coll (MS)
Northwest State Comm Coll (OH)
Norwalk Comm-Tech Coll (CT)
Ocean County Coll (NJ)
Okaloosa-Walton Comm Coll (FL)
Olean Business Inst (NY)
Orangeburg-Calhoun Tech Coll (SC)
Ouachita Tech Coll (AR)
Owensboro Jr Coll of Business (KY)
Palomar Coll (CA)
Paralegal Inst, Inc (AZ)
Peirce Coll (PA)
Pellissippi State Tech Comm Coll (TN)
Pennsylvania Coll of Tech (PA)
Penn Valley Comm Coll (MO)
Pensacola Jr Coll (FL)
Phillips Jr Coll (UT)
Phillips Jr Coll, Condie Cmps (CA)
Phillips Jr Coll of Springfield (MO)
Pierce Coll (WA)
Pima Comm Coll (AZ)
Pitt Comm Coll (NC)
Portland Comm Coll (OR)
Prince George's Comm Coll (MD)
Prospect Hall (FL)
Pueblo Coll of Business and Tech (CO)
Pueblo Comm Coll (CO)
Quincy Coll (MA)
Raritan Valley Comm Coll (NJ)
Rasmussen Coll Mankato (MN)
RETS Tech Ctr (OH)
Rockingham Comm Coll (NC)
Rogers State Coll (OK)
Rowan-Cabarrus Comm Coll (NC)
Saddleback Coll (CA)
St Louis Comm Coll at Meramec (MO)
St Petersburg Jr Coll (FL)
St Philip's Coll (TX)

Associate Degree Programs at Two-Year Colleges
Paralegal Studies–Photography

Salt Lake Comm Coll (UT)
Sandhills Comm Coll (NC)
San Diego City Coll (CA)
San Diego Miramar Coll (CA)
Sanford-Brown Coll, Des Peres (MO)
Sanford-Brown Coll, Hazelwood (MO)
Sanford-Brown Coll, St Charles (MO)
San Jacinto College–Central Cmps (TX)
San Juan Coll (NM)
Santa Fe Comm Coll (NM)
Sawyer Coll of Business, Cleveland Heights (OH)
Schenectady County Comm Coll (NY)
Seminole Comm Coll (FL)
Shasta Coll (CA)
Shorter Coll (AR)
Sinclair Comm Coll (OH)
Skagit Valley Coll (WA)
Skyline Coll (CA)
South Coll (FL)
South Coll (GA)
Southern Coll (FL)
Southern U at Shreveport–Bossier City Cmps (LA)
South Puget Sound Comm Coll (WA)
South Suburban Coll (IL)
Southwestern Comm Coll (NC)
Southwestern Michigan Coll (MI)
Southwest Florida Coll of Business (FL)
Southwest Missouri State University– West Plains (MO)
Spokane Comm Coll (WA)
Stenotype Acad (NY)
Suffolk County Comm College–Ammerman Cmps (NY)
Sullivan County Comm Coll (NY)
Surry Comm Coll (NC)
Tallahassee Comm Coll (FL)
Tarrant County Jr Coll (TX)
Tompkins Cortland Comm Coll (NY)
Tulsa Jr Coll (OK)
U of Cincinnati Clermont Coll (OH)
U of Hawaii–Kapiolani Comm Coll (HI)
U of North Dakota–Lake Region (ND)
Valencia Comm Coll (FL)
Vincennes U (IN)
Virginia Coll at Birmingham (AL)
Volunteer State Comm Coll (TN)
Wallace State Comm Coll (AL)
Ward Stone Coll (FL)
Warren County Comm Coll (NJ)
Westchester Comm Coll (NY)
Western Dakota Tech Inst (SD)
Western Piedmont Comm Coll (NC)
Western Wisconsin Tech Coll (WI)
West Los Angeles Coll (CA)
Westmoreland County Comm Coll (PA)
Whatcom Comm Coll (WA)
William Rainey Harper Coll (IL)
Wilson Tech Comm Coll (NC)
Woodbury Coll (VT)
Yavapai Coll (AZ)

PARKS MANAGEMENT

Antelope Valley Coll (CA)
Brevard Coll (NC)
Butler County Comm Coll (PA)
Butte Coll (CA)
Finger Lakes Comm Coll (NY)
Frederick Comm Coll (MD)
Garland County Comm Coll (AR)
Garrett Comm Coll (MD)
Hawkeye Comm Coll (IA)
Hiwassee Coll (TN)
Hocking Coll (OH)
Horry-Georgetown Tech Coll (SC)
Hutchinson Comm Coll and Area Vocational Sch (KS)
Kirkwood Comm Coll (IA)
Monterey Peninsula Coll (CA)
Mt San Antonio Coll (CA)
Muskingum Area Tech Coll (OH)
North Dakota State University–Bottineau (ND)
Northwest Coll (WY)
Northwestern Connecticut Comm-Tech Coll (CT)
Palomar Coll (CA)
Paul Smith's Coll (NY)
Potomac State Coll of West Virginia U (WV)
Santa Fe Comm Coll (FL)
Santa Rosa Jr Coll (CA)
Skagit Valley Coll (WA)
Spokane Comm Coll (WA)
State U of NY Coll of A&T at Cobleskill (NY)
State U of NY Coll of A&T at Morrisville (NY)
State U of NY Coll of Tech at Delhi (NY)
Vermilion Comm Coll (MN)
Western Texas Coll (TX)
West Valley Coll (CA)
William Rainey Harper Coll (IL)

PASTORAL STUDIES

Brevard Coll (NC)
Central Coll (KS)
Hesston Coll (KS)
Hiwassee Coll (TN)
Southeastern Baptist Theological Sem (NC)

PEACE STUDIES

Berkshire Comm Coll (MA)

PEST CONTROL TECHNOLOGY

Los Angeles Pierce Coll (CA)

PETROLEUM TECHNOLOGY

Bakersfield Coll (CA)
Barton County Comm Coll (KS)
Bee County Coll (TX)
Comm Coll of the Air Force (AL)
Eastern New Mexico University–Roswell (NM)
Frank Phillips Coll (TX)
Hocking Coll (OH)
Midland Coll (TX)
New Mexico Jr Coll (NM)
Odessa Coll (TX)
Oklahoma State U, Oklahoma City (OK)
South Plains Coll (TX)
Tulsa Jr Coll (OK)
Tyler Jr Coll (TX)
U of Alaska Anchorage, Kenai Peninsula Coll (AK)
Ventura Coll (CA)

PHARMACY/ PHARMACEUTICAL SCIENCES

Abraham Baldwin Ag Coll (GA)
Allen County Comm Coll (KS)
Andrew Coll (GA)
Angelina Coll (TX)
Bainbridge Coll (GA)
Barton County Comm Coll (KS)
Bee County Coll (TX)
Bismarck State Coll (ND)
Casper Coll (WY)
Cerritos Coll (CA)
City Coll of San Francisco (CA)
City Colls of Chicago, Kennedy-King Coll (IL)
City Colls of Chicago, Malcolm X Coll (IL)
City Colls of Chicago, Olive-Harvey Coll (IL)
City Colls of Chicago, Richard J Daley Coll (IL)
Colby Comm Coll (KS)
Columbia State Comm Coll (TN)
Comm Coll of Allegheny County South Cmps (PA)
Comm Coll of Southern Nevada (NV)
Comm Coll of the Air Force (AL)
Cuyahoga Comm Coll, Eastern Cmps (OH)
Cuyahoga Comm Coll, Western Cmps (OH)
Darton Coll (GA)
Del Mar Coll (TX)
Dixie Coll (UT)
Dodge City Comm Coll (KS)
Donnelly Coll (KS)
Durham Tech Comm Coll (NC)
East Central Coll (MO)
East Central Comm Coll (MS)
El Paso Comm Coll (TX)
Fayetteville Tech Comm Coll (NC)
Foothill Coll (CA)
Frank Phillips Coll (TX)
Gateway Comm-Tech Coll (CT)
Glendale Comm Coll (AZ)
Highland Comm Coll (KS)
Hiwassee Coll (TN)
Holmes Comm Coll (MS)
Howard Coll (TX)
Howard Comm Coll (MD)
Huertas Jr Coll (PR)
Hutchinson Comm Coll and Area Vocational Sch (KS)
Indian River Comm Coll (FL)
Iowa Lakes Comm Coll (IA)
Isothermal Comm Coll (NC)
Kansas City Kansas Comm Coll (KS)
Kellogg Comm Coll (MI)
Lakeshore Tech Coll (WI)
Lake-Sumter Comm Coll (FL)
Lorain County Comm Coll (OH)
Luzerne County Comm Coll (PA)
Macon Coll (GA)
Massachusetts Bay Comm Coll (MA)
Mercy Coll of Northwest Ohio (OH)
Miami-Dade Comm Coll (FL)
Mid Michigan Comm Coll (MI)
Monroe Comm Coll (NY)
Monroe County Comm Coll (MI)
Mount Ida Coll (MA)
Muscatine Comm Coll (IA)
Navarro Coll (TX)
North Central Tech Coll (OH)
Northeastern Jr Coll (CO)
Northeast Mississippi Comm Coll (MS)
North Idaho Coll (ID)
North Seattle Comm Coll (WA)
Northwest-Shoals Comm Coll (AL)
Oakland Comm Coll (MI)
Pasadena City Coll (CA)
Pima Comm Coll (AZ)
Reading Area Comm Coll (PA)
Rock Valley Coll (IL)
Rogers State Coll (OK)
St Clair County Comm Coll (MI)
St Philip's Coll (TX)
Scott Comm Coll (IA)
Shelton State Comm Coll (AL)
South Suburban Coll (IL)
Southwestern Michigan Coll (MI)
Tacoma Comm Coll (WA)
Turtle Mountain Comm Coll (ND)
U of Cincinnati Clermont Coll (OH)
Vincennes U (IN)
Wake Tech Comm Coll (NC)
Washtenaw Comm Coll (MI)
Westchester Comm Coll (NY)
William Rainey Harper Coll (IL)

PHILOSOPHY

Andrew Coll (GA)
Atlanta Metropolitan Coll (GA)
Bakersfield Coll (CA)
Barton County Comm Coll (KS)
Bergen Comm Coll (NJ)
Brevard Coll (NC)
Burlington County Coll (NJ)
Cañada Coll (CA)
Cape Cod Comm Coll (MA)
Cerritos Coll (CA)
Chaffey Coll (CA)
Chemeketa Comm Coll (OR)
City Colls of Chicago, Harold Washington Coll (IL)
City Colls of Chicago, Olive-Harvey Coll (IL)
Clackamas Comm Coll (OR)
Clark Coll (WA)
Coll of Alameda (CA)
Coll of DuPage (IL)
Coll of Marin (CA)
The Coll of Saint Thomas More (TX)
Coll of the Desert (CA)
Collin County Comm Coll (TX)
Comm Coll of Allegheny County South Cmps (PA)
Contra Costa Coll (CA)
Crafton Hills Coll (CA)
Cypress Coll (CA)
Danville Area Comm Coll (IL)
Darton Coll (GA)
Daytona Beach Comm Coll (FL)
De Anza Coll (CA)
Dixie Coll (UT)
Donnelly Coll (KS)
East Central Coll (MO)
East Los Angeles Coll (CA)
El Camino Coll (CA)
Essex Comm Coll (MD)
Everett Comm Coll (WA)
Foothill Coll (CA)
Fullerton Coll (CA)
Glendale Comm Coll (AZ)
Grossmont Coll (CA)
Gulf Coast Comm Coll (FL)
Harford Comm Coll (MD)
Indian River Comm Coll (FL)
Iowa Lakes Comm Coll (IA)
John Wood Comm Coll (IL)
Kansas City Kansas Comm Coll (KS)
Kellogg Comm Coll (MI)
Lake Michigan Coll (MI)
Lincoln Coll, Normal (IL)
Lincoln Land Comm Coll (IL)
Lon Morris Coll (TX)
Los Angeles Mission Coll (CA)
Lower Columbia Coll (WA)
McLennan Comm Coll (TX)
Miami-Dade Comm Coll (FL)
Miami University–Middletown Cmps (OH)
MiraCosta Coll (CA)
Modesto Jr Coll (CA)
Monterey Peninsula Coll (CA)
Muscatine Comm Coll (IA)
Northeastern Oklahoma A&M Coll (OK)
Oxnard Coll (CA)
Palm Beach Comm Coll (FL)
Palo Alto Coll (TX)
Pasadena City Coll (CA)
Pensacola Jr Coll (FL)
Polk Comm Coll (FL)
Rancho Santiago Coll (CA)
Saddleback Coll (CA)
St Gregory's Coll (OK)
San Bernardino Valley Coll (CA)
San Diego Miramar Coll (CA)
San Jacinto College–Central Cmps (TX)
San Joaquin Delta Coll (CA)
San Juan Coll (NM)
Santa Barbara City Coll (CA)
Santa Monica Coll (CA)
Sauk Valley Comm Coll (IL)
Skagit Valley Coll (WA)
Skyline Coll (CA)
Snow Coll (UT)
South Georgia Coll (GA)
SouthWest Collegiate Inst for the Deaf (TX)
Southwestern Coll (CA)
State Comm Coll of East St Louis (IL)
Tacoma Comm Coll (WA)
Triton Coll (IL)
Tulsa Jr Coll (OK)
U of Kentucky, Jefferson Comm Coll (KY)
West Los Angeles Coll (CA)
Yuba Coll (CA)

PHOTOGRAPHY

Adirondack Comm Coll (NY)
Allan Hancock Coll (CA)
Andrew Coll (GA)
Anne Arundel Comm Coll (MD)
Antelope Valley Coll (CA)
Antonelli Coll (OH)
Antonelli Inst (PA)
Art Inst of Atlanta (GA)
Art Inst of Dallas (TX)
Art Inst of Fort Lauderdale (FL)
The Art Inst of Houston (TX)
The Art Inst of Philadelphia (PA)
Art Inst of Pittsburgh (PA)
Art Inst of Seattle (WA)
Austin Comm Coll (TX)
Bakersfield Coll (CA)
Bergen Comm Coll (NJ)
Brevard Coll (NC)
Butte Coll (CA)
Carteret Comm Coll (NC)
Casper Coll (WY)
Catonsville Comm Coll (MD)
Cecil Comm Coll (MD)
Cerritos Coll (CA)
Chabot Coll (CA)
Chaffey Coll (CA)
Charles Stewart Mott Comm Coll (MI)
Citrus Coll (CA)
City Coll of San Francisco (CA)
City Colls of Chicago, Olive-Harvey Coll (IL)
City Colls of Chicago, Richard J Daley Coll (IL)
Clark State Comm Coll (OH)
Cochise Coll, Douglas (AZ)
Cochise Coll, Sierra Vista (AZ)
Coll of DuPage (IL)
Coll of San Mateo (CA)
Coll of Southern Idaho (ID)
Collin County Comm Coll (TX)
Colorado Inst of Art (CO)
Colorado Mountn Coll, Roaring Fork Cmps-Spring Valley Ctr (CO)
Columbia Coll (CA)
Comm Coll of Allegheny County South Cmps (PA)
Comm Coll of Denver (CO)
Comm Coll of Philadelphia (PA)
Comm Coll of Southern Nevada (NV)
Comm Coll of the Air Force (AL)
Cosumnes River Coll (CA)
County Coll of Morris (NJ)
Cuyahoga Comm Coll, Western Cmps (OH)
Cypress Coll (CA)
Daytona Beach Comm Coll (FL)
De Anza Coll (CA)
Dundalk Comm Coll (MD)
East Los Angeles Coll (CA)
El Camino Coll (CA)
El Paso Comm Coll (TX)
Everett Comm Coll (WA)
Fiorello H LaGuardia Comm Coll of City U of NY (NY)
Foothill Coll (CA)
Fort Scott Comm Coll (KS)
Fresno City Coll (CA)
Greenfield Comm Coll (MA)
Grossmont Coll (CA)
Gwinnett Tech Inst (GA)
Harford Comm Coll (MD)
Harrisburg Area Comm Coll (PA)
Hawkeye Comm Coll (IA)
Herkimer County Comm Coll (NY)
Hill Coll of the Hill Jr Coll District (TX)
Holyoke Comm Coll (MA)
Houston Comm Coll System (TX)
Howard Comm Coll (MD)
Hutchinson Comm Coll and Area Vocational Sch (KS)
Inst of American Indian Arts (NM)
Iowa Lakes Comm Coll (IA)
Ivy Tech State Coll–Columbus (IN)
Ivy Tech State Coll–Northcentral (IN)
Ivy Tech State Coll–Southcentral (IN)
Ivy Tech State Coll–Southwest (IN)
John C Calhoun State Comm Coll (AL)
Laney Coll (CA)
Lansing Comm Coll (MI)
Lassen Coll (CA)
Long Beach City Coll (CA)
Los Angeles City Coll (CA)
Los Angeles Pierce Coll (CA)
Los Angeles Trade-Tech Coll (CA)
Los Angeles Valley Coll (CA)
Luzerne County Comm Coll (PA)
Macomb Comm Coll (MI)
Madison Area Tech Coll (WI)
McDowell Tech Comm Coll (NC)
Mercer County Comm Coll (NJ)
Metropolitan Comm Coll (NE)
Miami-Dade Comm Coll (FL)
Middlesex County Coll (NJ)
Milwaukee Area Tech Coll (WI)
Modesto Jr Coll (CA)
Monterey Peninsula Coll (CA)
Montgomery College–Rockville Cmps (MD)
Moorpark Coll (CA)
Mt San Antonio Coll (CA)
Mt San Jacinto Coll (CA)
Napa Valley Coll (CA)
Nashville State Tech Inst (TN)
Northeastern Oklahoma A&M Coll (OK)
Northeast Mississippi Comm Coll (MS)
Northern Virginia Comm Coll (VA)
North Harris Coll (TX)
Northland Pioneer Coll (AZ)
Northwest Coll (WY)
Oakland Comm Coll (MI)
Odessa Coll (TX)
Ohio Inst of Photography and Tech (OH)
Oklahoma State U, Okmulgee (OK)
Onondaga Comm Coll (NY)
Orange Coast Coll (CA)
Palm Beach Comm Coll (FL)
Palomar Coll (CA)
Pasadena City Coll (CA)
Porterville Coll (CA)
Prairie State Coll (IL)
Rancho Santiago Coll (CA)
Randolph Comm Coll (NC)
Ricks Coll (ID)
Riverside Comm Coll (CA)
Saddleback Coll (CA)
Sage Jr Coll of Albany (NY)
St Gregory's Coll (OK)
St Louis Comm Coll at Florissant Valley (MO)
St Louis Comm Coll at Forest Park (MO)
St Louis Comm Coll at Meramec (MO)
San Bernardino Valley Coll (CA)
San Diego City Coll (CA)
San Joaquin Delta Coll (CA)
Santa Monica Coll (CA)
Scottsdale Comm Coll (AZ)
Seattle Central Comm Coll (WA)
Shoreline Comm Coll (WA)
Sierra Coll (CA)
Solano Comm Coll (CA)
SouthWest Collegiate Inst for the Deaf (TX)
Southwestern Coll (CA)
Sullivan County Comm Coll (NY)
Thomas Nelson Comm Coll (VA)
Tyler Jr Coll (TX)
Union County Coll (NJ)
U of Maine at Augusta (ME)
Ventura Coll (CA)
Villa Maria Coll of Buffalo (NY)
Washtenaw Comm Coll (MI)
Watkins Inst of Interior Design (TN)

Associate Degree Programs at Two-Year Colleges
Photography–Physical Sciences

Western Wyoming Comm Coll (WY)
Westmoreland County Comm Coll (PA)
White Pines Coll (NH)
Willmar Comm Coll (MN)
Willmar Tech Coll (MN)
Yuba Coll (CA)

PHYSICAL EDUCATION

Abraham Baldwin Ag Coll (GA)
Alabama Southern Comm Coll, Monroeville (AL)
Alabama Southern Comm Coll, Thomasville (AL)
Allen County Comm Coll (KS)
Alvin Comm Coll (TX)
Andrew Coll (GA)
Angelina Coll (TX)
Anne Arundel Comm Coll (MD)
Antelope Valley Coll (CA)
Arizona Western Coll (AZ)
Barstow Coll (CA)
Barton County Comm Coll (KS)
Bay de Noc Comm Coll (MI)
Bee County Coll (TX)
Berkshire Comm Coll (MA)
Bishop State Comm Coll (AL)
Bismarck State Coll (ND)
Black Hawk Coll, Moline (IL)
Blinn Coll (TX)
Borough of Manhattan Comm Coll of City U of NY (NY)
Brevard Coll (NC)
Brevard Comm Coll (FL)
Brunswick Coll (GA)
Bucks County Comm Coll (PA)
Burlington County Coll (NJ)
Butler County Comm Coll (KS)
Butler County Comm Coll (PA)
Butte Coll (CA)
Cabrillo Coll (CA)
Cañada Coll (CA)
Cape Cod Comm Coll (MA)
Carl Albert State Coll (OK)
Casper Coll (WY)
Central Coll (KS)
Central Comm College–Platte Cmps (NE)
Centralia Coll (WA)
Central Oregon Comm Coll (OR)
Central Texas Coll (TX)
Central Wyoming Coll (WY)
Cerritos Coll (CA)
Chabot Coll (CA)
Chaffey Coll (CA)
Chattahoochee Valley State Comm Coll (AL)
Chemeketa Comm Coll (OR)
Chesapeake Coll (MD)
Cisco Jr Coll (TX)
Citrus Coll (CA)
City Colls of Chicago, Harry S Truman Coll (IL)
City Colls of Chicago, Wilbur Wright Coll (IL)
Clackamas Comm Coll (OR)
Clark Coll (WA)
Clinton Comm Coll (IA)
Clinton Comm Coll (NY)
Cloud County Comm Coll (KS)
Clovis Comm Coll (NM)
Cochise Coll, Douglas (AZ)
Cochise Coll, Sierra Vista (AZ)
Coffeyville Comm Coll (KS)
Colby Comm Coll (KS)
Coll of DuPage (IL)
Coll of Marin (CA)
Coll of Southern Idaho (ID)
Coll of the Canyons (CA)
Coll of the Desert (CA)
Coll of the Sequoias (CA)
Coll of the Siskiyous (CA)
Columbia Coll (CA)
Columbia State Comm Coll (TN)
Comm Coll of Allegheny County Allegheny Cmps (PA)
Connors State Coll (OK)
Copiah-Lincoln Comm Coll (MS)
Cowley County Comm Coll and Voc-Tech Sch (KS)
Crafton Hills Coll (CA)
Crowder Coll (MO)
Cuesta Coll (CA)
Cypress Coll (CA)
Dalton Coll (GA)
Danville Area Comm Coll (IL)
Darton Coll (GA)
Daytona Beach Comm Coll (FL)
Dean Coll (MA)
De Anza Coll (CA)
DeKalb Coll (GA)
Del Mar Coll (TX)
Dixie Coll (UT)
Dodge City Comm Coll (KS)
East Central Coll (MO)
Eastern Arizona Coll (AZ)
Eastern Oklahoma State Coll (OK)
Eastern Wyoming Coll (WY)
East Georgia Coll (GA)
East Los Angeles Coll (CA)
El Camino Coll (CA)
Ellsworth Comm Coll (IA)
Essex Comm Coll (MD)
Essex County Coll (NJ)
Everett Comm Coll (WA)
Finger Lakes Comm Coll (NY)
Foothill Coll (CA)
Frank Phillips Coll (TX)
Frederick Comm Coll (MD)
Fullerton Coll (CA)
Fulton-Montgomery Comm Coll (NY)
Gadsden State Comm Coll (AL)
Gainesville Coll (GA)
Galveston Coll (TX)
Garden City Comm Coll (KS)
Garrett Comm Coll (MD)
Gavilan Coll (CA)
Genesee Comm Coll (NY)
Glendale Comm Coll (AZ)
Gloucester County Coll (NJ)
Grayson County Coll (TX)
Gulf Coast Comm Coll (FL)
Hagerstown Jr Coll (MD)
Harrisburg Area Comm Coll (PA)
Haskell Indian Nations U (KS)
Herkimer County Comm Coll (NY)
Highland Comm Coll (KS)
Hill Coll of the Hill Jr Coll District (TX)
Hiwassee Coll (TN)
Howard Coll (TX)
Hudson Valley Comm Coll (NY)
Hutchinson Comm Coll and Area Vocational Sch (KS)
Imperial Valley Coll (CA)
Independence Comm Coll (KS)
Indian River Comm Coll (FL)
Iowa Lakes Comm Coll (IA)
Itawamba Comm Coll (MS)
Jackson State Comm Coll (TN)
Jefferson Coll (MO)
Jefferson Davis Comm Coll (AL)
John A Logan Coll (IL)
John C Calhoun State Comm Coll (AL)
John Wood Comm Coll (IL)
Joliet Jr Coll (IL)
Jones County Jr Coll (MS)
Kansas City Kansas Comm Coll (KS)
Kellogg Comm Coll (MI)
Kemper Military Jr Coll (MO)
Kings River Comm Coll (CA)
Kirkwood Comm Coll (IA)
Kishwaukee Coll (IL)
Labette Comm Coll (KS)
Lake Land Coll (IL)
Lake Michigan Coll (MI)
Lake Tahoe Comm Coll (CA)
Lansing Comm Coll (MI)
Laramie County Comm Coll (WY)
Lassen Coll (CA)
Lee Coll (TX)
Lincoln Coll, Normal (IL)
Lincoln Land Comm Coll (IL)
Linn-Benton Comm Coll (OR)
Long Beach City Coll (CA)
Lon Morris Coll (TX)
Lorain County Comm Coll (OH)
Los Angeles Mission Coll (CA)
Los Angeles Valley Coll (CA)
Lower Columbia Coll (WA)
Luzerne County Comm Coll (PA)
Macon Coll (GA)
Manchester Comm-Tech Coll (CT)
Mary Holmes Coll (MS)
McLennan Comm Coll (TX)
Mendocino Coll (CA)
Merced Coll (CA)
Miami-Dade Comm Coll (FL)
Middle Georgia Coll (GA)
Middlesex County Coll (NJ)
Midland Coll (TX)
Mid-Plains Comm Coll (NE)
Mineral Area Coll (MO)
Mississippi Delta Comm Coll (MS)
Mitchell Coll (CT)
Modesto Jr Coll (CA)
Mohawk Valley Comm Coll (NY)
Monroe Comm Coll (NY)
Monterey Peninsula Coll (CA)
Montgomery College–Rockville Cmps (MD)
Montgomery County Comm Coll (PA)
Motlow State Comm Coll (TN)
Mt San Jacinto Coll (CA)
Murray State Coll (OK)
Muscatine Comm Coll (IA)
Nassau Comm Coll (NY)
Navarro Coll (TX)
New Mexico Jr Coll (NM)
New Mexico Military Inst (NM)
North Dakota State Coll of Science (ND)
North Dakota State University–Bottineau (ND)
Northeast Comm Coll (NE)
Northeastern Jr Coll (CO)
Northeastern Oklahoma A&M Coll (OK)
Northeast Mississippi Comm Coll (MS)
Northern Essex Comm Coll (MA)
North Harris Coll (TX)
Northwest Coll (WY)
Northwest Mississippi Comm Coll (MS)
Odessa Coll (TX)
Ohio Valley Coll (WV)
Okaloosa-Walton Comm Coll (FL)
Orange Coast Coll (CA)
Oxnard Coll (CA)
Palm Beach Comm Coll (FL)
Palo Alto Coll (TX)
Palomar Coll (CA)
Parkland Coll (IL)
Pasadena City Coll (CA)
Pensacola Jr Coll (FL)
Polk Comm Coll (FL)
Porterville Coll (CA)
Potomac State Coll of West Virginia U (WV)
Pratt Comm Coll and Area Voc Sch (KS)
Prince George's Comm Coll (MD)
Rancho Santiago Coll (CA)
Redlands Comm Coll (OK)
Ricks Coll (ID)
Roane State Comm Coll (TN)
Rose State Coll (OK)
Sacramento City Coll (CA)
Saddleback Coll (CA)
St Catharine Coll (KY)
St Philip's Coll (TX)
Salem Comm Coll (NJ)
San Bernardino Valley Coll (CA)
San Diego City Coll (CA)
San Diego Mesa Coll (CA)
San Diego Miramar Coll (CA)
San Jacinto College–North Cmps (TX)
San Jacinto College–South Cmps (TX)
San Joaquin Delta Coll (CA)
San Juan Coll (NM)
Santa Barbara City Coll (CA)
Santa Monica Coll (CA)
Santa Rosa Jr Coll (CA)
Sauk Valley Comm Coll (IL)
Seminole Jr Coll (OK)
Seward County Comm Coll (KS)
Shelton State Comm Coll (AL)
Sheridan Coll (WY)
Sinclair Comm Coll (OH)
Skagit Valley Coll (WA)
Skyline Coll (CA)
Snow Coll (UT)
Solano Comm Coll (CA)
South Georgia Coll (GA)
South Mountain Comm Coll (AZ)
South Plains Coll (TX)
SouthWest Collegiate Inst for the Deaf (TX)
Southwestern Comm Coll (IA)
Southwest Mississippi Comm Coll (MS)
Spoon River Coll (IL)
State U of NY Coll of Tech at Delhi (NY)
Taft Coll (CA)
Treasure Valley Comm Coll (OR)
Trinidad State Jr Coll (CO)
Trinity Valley Comm Coll (TX)
Triton Coll (IL)
Tulsa Jr Coll (OK)
Umpqua Comm Coll (OR)
U of New Mexico–Gallup Branch (NM)
Vermilion Comm Coll (MN)
Vincennes U (IN)
Waldorf Coll (IA)
Walters State Comm Coll (TN)
Waubonsee Comm Coll (IL)
Waycross Coll (GA)
Wenatchee Valley Coll (WA)
Western Oklahoma State Coll (OK)
Western Wyoming Comm Coll (WY)
West Hills Comm Coll (CA)
West Los Angeles Coll (CA)
West Valley Coll (CA)
Wharton County Jr Coll (TX)
William Rainey Harper Coll (IL)
Willmar Comm Coll (MN)
Wood Coll (MS)
Yavapai Coll (AZ)
Yuba Coll (CA)

PHYSICAL FITNESS/ EXERCISE SCIENCE

Bergen Comm Coll (NJ)
Brevard Coll (NC)
Butler County Comm Coll (PA)
Camden County Coll (NJ)
Cañada Coll (CA)
Colorado Mountn Coll, Alpine Cmps (CO)
Columbia-Greene Comm Coll (NY)
Comm Coll of Allegheny County South Cmps (PA)
Dean Coll (MA)
Dundalk Comm Coll (MD)
Essex Comm Coll (MD)
Henry Ford Comm Coll (MI)
Hocking Coll (OH)
Houston Comm Coll System (TX)
Kansas City Kansas Comm Coll (KS)
Monterey Peninsula Coll (CA)
Mount Ida Coll (MA)
Naugatuck Valley Community–Tech Coll (CT)
New Hampshire Tech Coll, Manchester (NH)
Northeast Mississippi Comm Coll (MS)
North Lake Coll (TX)
Oakland Comm Coll (MI)
Orange Coast Coll (CA)
Orange County Comm Coll (NY)
Pima Comm Coll (AZ)
Spokane Falls Comm Coll (WA)
U of New Mexico–Gallup Branch (NM)
Vincennes U (IN)
William Rainey Harper Coll (IL)

PHYSICAL SCIENCES

Abraham Baldwin Ag Coll (GA)
Allen County Comm Coll (KS)
Alvin Comm Coll (TX)
American River Coll (CA)
Angelina Coll (TX)
Arkansas State University–Beebe Branch (AR)
Austin Comm Coll (TX)
Barton County Comm Coll (KS)
Bevill State Comm Coll (AL)
Black Hawk Coll, Moline (IL)
Blinn Coll (TX)
Bowling Green State University–Firelands Coll (OH)
Brevard Coll (NC)
Butler County Comm Coll (PA)
Butte Coll (CA)
Carl Albert State Coll (OK)
Casper Coll (WY)
Central Coll (KS)
Central Comm College–Grand Island Cmps (NE)
Central Comm College–Hastings Cmps (NE)
Central Comm College–Platte Cmps (NE)
Centralia Coll (WA)
Central Oregon Comm Coll (OR)
Central Texas Coll (TX)
Central Wyoming Coll (WY)
Cerro Coso Comm Coll (CA)
Chaffey Coll (CA)
Chesapeake Coll (MD)
Cincinnati State Tech and Comm Coll (OH)
Citrus Coll (CA)
City Colls of Chicago, Harold Washington Coll (IL)
City Colls of Chicago, Wilbur Wright Coll (IL)
Clark Coll (WA)
Clinton Comm Coll (IA)
Cloud County Comm Coll (KS)
Coll of DuPage (IL)
Coll of Lake County (IL)
Coll of San Mateo (CA)
Coll of the Canyons (CA)
Colorado Mountn Coll, Alpine Cmps (CO)
Columbia Coll (CA)
Crowder Coll (MO)
Dixie Coll (UT)
Dodge City Comm Coll (KS)
East Central Comm Coll (MS)
Eastern Arizona Coll (AZ)
Eastern Oklahoma State Coll (OK)
El Camino Coll (CA)
Ellsworth Comm Coll (IA)
Fort Scott Comm Coll (KS)
Frank Phillips Coll (TX)
Frederick Comm Coll (MD)
Fresno City Coll (CA)
Front Range Comm Coll (CO)
Galveston Coll (TX)
Garland County Comm Coll (AR)
Gloucester County Coll (NJ)
Golden West Coll (CA)
Gordon Coll (GA)
Harrisburg Area Comm Coll (PA)
Highland Comm Coll (IL)
Highland Comm Coll (KS)
Hill Coll of the Hill Jr Coll District (TX)
Howard Comm Coll (MD)
Hutchinson Comm Coll and Area Vocational Sch (KS)
Illinois Eastern Comm Colls, Lincoln Trail Coll (IL)
Imperial Valley Coll (CA)
Independence Comm Coll (KS)
Iowa Lakes Comm Coll (IA)
Jackson State Comm Coll (TN)
Jefferson Coll (MO)
John Wood Comm Coll (IL)
Jones County Jr Coll (MS)
Kemper Military Jr Coll (MO)
Kings River Comm Coll (CA)
Kishwaukee Coll (IL)
Lake Land Coll (IL)
Lake Michigan Coll (MI)
Lamar Comm Coll (CO)
Long Beach City Coll (CA)
Los Angeles Mission Coll (CA)
McLennan Comm Coll (TX)
Mendocino Coll (CA)
Merced Coll (CA)
Miami-Dade Comm Coll (FL)
Middle Georgia Coll (GA)
Middlesex County Coll (NJ)
Midland Coll (TX)
Mid-Plains Comm Coll (NE)
MiraCosta Coll (CA)
Mitchell Coll (CT)
Moberly Area Comm Coll (MO)
Modesto Jr Coll (CA)
Montgomery County Comm Coll (PA)
Motlow State Comm Coll (TN)
Naugatuck Valley Community–Tech Coll (CT)
Navarro Coll (TX)
Neosho County Comm Coll (KS)
North Dakota State Coll of Science (ND)
Northeastern Jr Coll (CO)
North Idaho Coll (ID)
Northwest Coll (WY)
Northwestern Connecticut Comm-Tech Coll (CT)
Ohio Valley Coll (WV)
Ohlone Coll (CA)
Orange County Comm Coll (NY)
Otero Jr Coll (CO)
Ozarks Tech Comm Coll (MO)
Palm Beach Comm Coll (FL)
Parkland Coll (IL)
Pasadena City Coll (CA)
Pennsylvania Coll of Tech (PA)
Penn State U Beaver Cmps (PA)
Penn State U McKeesport Cmps (PA)
Penn State U New Kensington Cmps (PA)
Penn State U Schuylkill Cmps (PA)
Penn State U Shenango Cmps (PA)
Polk Comm Coll (FL)
Portland Comm Coll (OR)
Pratt Comm Coll and Area Voc Sch (KS)
Quincy Coll (MA)
Redlands Comm Coll (OK)
Ricks Coll (ID)
Riverside Comm Coll (CA)
Roane State Comm Coll (TN)
Rogers State Coll (OK)
Roxbury Comm Coll (MA)
Sacramento City Coll (CA)
Saddleback Coll (CA)
Sage Jr Coll of Albany (NY)
Salt Lake Comm Coll (UT)
San Bernardino Valley Coll (CA)
San Diego City Coll (CA)
San Diego Mesa Coll (CA)
San Diego Miramar Coll (CA)
San Jacinto College–Central Cmps (TX)
San Joaquin Delta Coll (CA)
Santa Rosa Jr Coll (CA)
Scott Comm Coll (IA)
Seward County Comm Coll (KS)
Skyline Coll (CA)
Snow Coll (UT)
Southeast Comm Coll, Beatrice Cmps (NE)
Southwestern Coll (CA)
Southwestern Comm Coll (IA)
Southwest Mississippi Comm Coll (MS)
Spoon River Coll (IL)
State U of NY Coll of Tech at Canton (NY)
Sullivan County Comm Coll (NY)
Tacoma Comm Coll (WA)
Taft Coll (CA)
Treasure Valley Comm Coll (OR)
Trinity Valley Comm Coll (TX)
Ulster County Comm Coll (NY)
Umpqua Comm Coll (OR)
Union County Coll (NJ)
U of Wisconsin Center–Marathon County (WI)
Vermilion Comm Coll (MN)
Waldorf Coll (IA)
Washington State Comm Coll (OH)

Associate Degree Programs at Two-Year Colleges
Physical Sciences–Plumbing

Waubonsee Comm Coll (IL)
Western Oklahoma State Coll (OK)
Western Wyoming Comm Coll (WY)
William Rainey Harper Coll (IL)
Willmar Comm Coll (MN)

PHYSICAL THERAPY
Alabama Southern Comm Coll, Monroeville (AL)
Andrew Coll (GA)
Angelina Coll (TX)
Anoka-Ramsey Comm Coll (MN)
Arapahoe Comm Coll (CO)
Atlanta Metropolitan Coll (GA)
Atlantic Comm Coll (NJ)
Austin Comm Coll (MN)
Baltimore City Comm Coll (MD)
Barton County Comm Coll (KS)
Bay State Coll (MA)
Belleville Area Coll (IL)
Berkshire Comm Coll (MA)
Bevill State Comm Coll (AL)
Blackhawk Tech Coll (WI)
Bossier Parish Comm Coll (LA)
Brevard Coll (NC)
Brevard Comm Coll (FL)
Broome Comm Coll (NY)
Broward Comm Coll (FL)
Brunswick Coll (GA)
Butler County Comm Coll (KS)
Butler County Comm Coll (PA)
Caldwell Comm Coll and Tech Inst (NC)
Cañada Coll (CA)
Cape Cod Comm Coll (MA)
Casper Coll (WY)
Central Coll (KS)
Central Florida Comm Coll (FL)
Central Ohio Tech Coll (OH)
Central Pennsylvania Business Sch (PA)
Central Piedmont Comm Coll (NC)
Central Wyoming Coll (WY)
Cerritos Coll (CA)
Chattanooga State Tech Comm Coll (TN)
City Coll of San Francisco (CA)
Colby Comm Coll (KS)
Coll of St Catherine–Minneapolis (MN)
Collin County Comm Coll (TX)
Columbia State Comm Coll (TN)
Comm Coll of Allegheny County Boyce Cmps (PA)
Comm Coll of Rhode Island (RI)
Comm Coll of the Air Force (AL)
Comm Hospital Roanoke Valley–Coll of Health Scis (VA)
Cowley County Comm Coll and Voc-Tech Sch (KS)
Cuyahoga Comm Coll, Metropolitan Cmps (OH)
Dalton Coll (GA)
Danville Area Comm Coll (IL)
Daytona Beach Comm Coll (FL)
De Anza Coll (CA)
Delgado Comm Coll (LA)
Delta Coll (MI)
Dixie Coll (UT)
Dodge City Comm Coll (KS)
Donnelly Coll (KS)
East Central Comm Coll (MS)
El Paso Comm Coll (TX)
Essex County Coll (NJ)
Fayetteville Tech Comm Coll (NC)
Fiorello H LaGuardia Comm Coll of City U of NY (NY)
Fisher Coll (MA)
Florence-Darlington Tech Coll (SC)
Gateway Comm Coll (AZ)
Genesee Comm Coll (NY)
George Corley Wallace State Comm Coll, Selma (AL)
Glendale Comm Coll (AZ)
Green River Comm Coll (WA)
Greenville Tech Coll (SC)
Gulf Coast Comm Coll (FL)
Gwinnett Tech Inst (GA)
Harcum Coll (PA)
Herkimer County Comm Coll (NY)
Hesser Coll (NH)
Highland Comm Coll (KS)
Hiwassee Coll (TN)
Holmes Comm Coll (MS)
Housatonic Comm-Tech Coll (CT)
Houston Comm Coll System (TX)
Howard Coll (TX)
Hutchinson Comm Coll and Area Vocational Sch (KS)
Illinois Central Coll (IL)
Indian Hills Comm Coll (IA)
Indian River Comm Coll (FL)
Iowa Central Comm Coll (IA)
Ivy Tech State Coll–Eastcentral (IN)
Ivy Tech State Coll–Kokomo (IN)
Ivy Tech State Coll–Northeast (IN)
Ivy Tech State Coll–Northwest (IN)
Jackson State Comm Coll (TN)
Jefferson State Comm Coll (AL)
Johnson County Comm Coll (KS)
John Tyler Comm Coll (VA)
Kansas City Kansas Comm Coll (KS)
Kaskaskia Coll (IL)
Kellogg Comm Coll (MI)
Kennebec Valley Tech Coll (ME)
Kent State U, Ashtabula Cmps (OH)
Kent State U, East Liverpool Cmps (OH)
Keystone Coll (PA)
Lake Area Vocational-Tech Inst (SD)
Lake City Comm Coll (FL)
Lake-Sumter Comm Coll (FL)
Laredo Comm Coll (TX)
Lawson State Comm Coll (AL)
Lehigh Carbon Comm Coll (PA)
Lima Tech Coll (OH)
Lutheran Coll of Health Professions (IN)
Macomb Comm Coll (MI)
Macon Coll (GA)
Manor Jr Coll (PA)
Maria Coll (NY)
Martin Comm Coll (NC)
Massachusetts Bay Comm Coll (MA)
McLennan Comm Coll (TX)
Meridian Comm Coll (MS)
Miami-Dade Comm Coll (FL)
Michiana Coll (IN)
Mid Michigan Comm Coll (MI)
Mid-Plains Comm Coll (NE)
Milwaukee Area Tech Coll (WI)
Monroe County Comm Coll (MI)
Montana State U Coll of Tech-Great Falls (MT)
Monterey Peninsula Coll (CA)
Morgan Comm Coll (CO)
Morton Coll (IL)
Motlow State Comm Coll (TN)
Mt Hood Comm Coll (OR)
Mount Wachusett Comm Coll (MA)
Nash Comm Coll (NC)
Newbury Coll (MA)
New Hampshire Tech Coll, Claremont (NH)
New Hampshire Tech Coll, Manchester (NH)
Niagara County Comm Coll (NY)
North Central Tech Coll (OH)
Northeast Comm Coll (NE)
Northeastern Oklahoma A&M Coll (OK)
Northeast Mississippi Comm Coll (MS)
Northern Virginia Comm Coll (VA)
North Shore Comm Coll (MA)
NorthWest Arkansas Comm Coll (AR)
Northwest Coll (WY)
Oakton Comm Coll (IL)
Odessa Coll (TX)
Oklahoma City Comm Coll (OK)
Onondaga Comm Coll (NY)
Orange County Comm Coll (NY)
Owens Comm Coll, Findlay (OH)
Owens Comm Coll, Toledo (OH)
Palm Beach Comm Coll (FL)
Penn State U DuBois Cmps (PA)
Penn State U Hazleton Cmps (PA)
Penn State U Mont Alto Cmps (PA)
Penn State U Shenango Cmps (PA)
Penn Valley Comm Coll (MO)
Pensacola Jr Coll (FL)
Polk Comm Coll (FL)
Professional Skills Inst (OH)
Pueblo Comm Coll (CO)
Quincy Coll (MA)
Ricks Coll (ID)
Roane State Comm Coll (TN)
Rogers State Coll (OK)
St Louis Comm Coll at Meramec (MO)
St Petersburg Jr Coll (FL)
St Philip's Coll (TX)
San Diego Mesa Coll (CA)
Sanford-Brown Coll, Des Peres (MO)
Sanford-Brown Coll, Hazelwood (MO)
Sanford-Brown Coll, North Kansas City (MO)
San Jacinto College–South Cmps (TX)
San Juan Coll (NM)
Scott Comm Coll (IA)
Seminole Comm Coll (FL)
Shelby State Comm Coll (TN)
Sinclair Comm Coll (OH)
South Plains Coll (TX)
Southwestern Comm Coll (NC)
Spokane Falls Comm Coll (WA)
Springfield Coll in Illinois (IL)
Springfield Tech Comm Coll (MA)
Stanly Comm Coll (NC)
Stark Tech Coll (OH)
Suffolk County Comm College–Ammerman Cmps (NY)
Tacoma Comm Coll (WA)
Tarrant County Jr Coll (TX)
Trident Tech Coll (SC)
Triton Coll (IL)
Tulsa Jr Coll (OK)
Turtle Mountain Comm Coll (ND)
Union County Coll (NJ)
U of Hawaii–Kapiolani Comm Coll (HI)
U of Kentucky, Jefferson Comm Coll (KY)
U of Kentucky, Paducah Comm Coll (KY)
U of North Dakota–Williston (ND)
U of Pittsburgh–Titusville (PA)
Vincennes U (IN)
Virginia Highlands Comm Coll (VA)
Volunteer State Comm Coll (TN)
Wallace State Comm Coll (AL)
Waycross Coll (GA)
Western Wisconsin Tech Coll (WI)
Wharton County Jr Coll (TX)
Whatcom Comm Coll (WA)
Wytheville Comm Coll (VA)
Young Harris Coll (GA)

PHYSICIAN'S ASSISTANT STUDIES
Barton County Comm Coll (KS)
Brunswick Coll (GA)
Cuyahoga Comm Coll, Western Cmps (OH)
Dalton Coll (GA)
Darton Coll (GA)
Essex Comm Coll (MD)
Floyd Coll (GA)
Foothill Coll (CA)
Gulf Coast Comm Coll (FL)
Hartnell Coll (CA)
Hudson Valley Comm Coll (NY)
Kettering Coll of Medical Arts (OH)
Metropolitan Comm Coll (NE)
Modesto Jr Coll (CA)
Tulsa Jr Coll (OK)
Western Iowa Tech Comm Coll (IA)

PHYSICS
Allan Hancock Coll (CA)
Allen County Comm Coll (KS)
Andrew Coll (GA)
Arizona Western Coll (AZ)
Atlanta Metropolitan Coll (GA)
Austin Comm Coll (TX)
Bakersfield Coll (CA)
Barton County Comm Coll (KS)
Bee County Coll (TX)
Bergen Comm Coll (NJ)
Blinn Coll (TX)
Brazosport Coll (TX)
Brevard Coll (NC)
Brunswick Coll (GA)
Burlington County Coll (NJ)
Butler County Comm Coll (KS)
Casper Coll (WY)
Central Texas Coll (TX)
Cerritos Coll (CA)
Chabot Coll (CA)
Chaffey Coll (CA)
Chattahoochee Valley State Comm Coll (AL)
Chemeketa Comm Coll (OR)
City Colls of Chicago, Harold Washington Coll (IL)
City Colls of Chicago, Kennedy-King Coll (IL)
City Colls of Chicago, Olive-Harvey Coll (IL)
Clackamas Comm Coll (OR)
Clark Coll (WA)
Clinton Comm Coll (IA)
Coll of DuPage (IL)
Coll of Marin (CA)
Coll of San Mateo (CA)
Coll of Southern Idaho (ID)
Coll of the Desert (CA)
Coll of the Siskiyous (CA)
Collin County Comm Coll (TX)
Columbia Coll (CA)
Columbia State Comm Coll (TN)
Comm Coll of Allegheny County Allegheny Cmps (PA)
Comm Coll of Allegheny County Boyce Cmps (PA)
Comm Coll of Allegheny County South Cmps (PA)
Contra Costa Coll (CA)
Crafton Hills Coll (CA)
Cuesta Coll (CA)
Cypress Coll (CA)
Dalton Coll (GA)
Darton Coll (GA)
Daytona Beach Comm Coll (FL)
De Anza Coll (CA)
Del Mar Coll (TX)
Dixie Coll (UT)
Dodge City Comm Coll (KS)
East Central Coll (MO)
Eastern Arizona Coll (AZ)
El Camino Coll (CA)
El Paso Comm Coll (TX)
Essex Comm Coll (MD)
Everett Comm Coll (WA)
Finger Lakes Comm Coll (NY)
Foothill Coll (CA)
Fullerton Coll (CA)
Gainesville Coll (GA)
Glendale Comm Coll (AZ)
Grayson County Coll (TX)
Grossmont Coll (CA)
Gulf Coast Comm Coll (FL)
Hagerstown Jr Coll (MD)
Harford Comm Coll (MD)
Highland Comm Coll (IL)
Hill Coll of the Hill Jr Coll District (TX)
Holyoke Comm Coll (MA)
Hutchinson Comm Coll and Area Vocational Sch (KS)
Indian River Comm Coll (FL)
John A Logan Coll (IL)
John Wood Comm Coll (IL)
Joliet Jr Coll (IL)
Kellogg Comm Coll (MI)
Lamar Comm Coll (CO)
Lincoln Land Comm Coll (IL)
Lon Morris Coll (TX)
Lorain County Comm Coll (OH)
Los Angeles City Coll (CA)
Los Angeles Harbor Coll (CA)
Lower Columbia Coll (WA)
Macon Coll (GA)
Mercer County Comm Coll (NJ)
Miami-Dade Comm Coll (FL)
Miami University–Middletown Cmps (OH)
Middle Georgia Coll (GA)
Middlesex County Coll (NJ)
MiraCosta Coll (CA)
Modesto Jr Coll (CA)
Mohawk Valley Comm Coll (NY)
Monroe Comm Coll (NY)
Monterey Peninsula Coll (CA)
Motlow State Comm Coll (TN)
Navarro Coll (TX)
New Mexico Military Inst (NM)
Northampton County Area Comm Coll (PA)
Northeast Comm Coll (NE)
North Idaho Coll (ID)
Northwest Coll (WY)
Odessa Coll (TX)
Okaloosa-Walton Comm Coll (FL)
Oklahoma City Comm Coll (OK)
Palo Alto Coll (TX)
Pasadena City Coll (CA)
Phillips County Comm Coll (AR)
Pikes Peak Comm Coll (CO)
Pima Comm Coll (AZ)
Rancho Santiago Coll (CA)
Redlands Comm Coll (OK)
Red Rocks Comm Coll (CO)
Ricks Coll (ID)
Rose State Coll (OK)
Saddleback Coll (CA)
San Bernardino Valley Coll (CA)
San Diego Mesa Coll (CA)
San Diego Miramar Coll (CA)
San Juan Coll (NM)
Santa Barbara City Coll (CA)
Santa Monica Coll (CA)
Sauk Valley Comm Coll (IL)
Skyline Coll (CA)
Snow Coll (UT)
Solano Comm Coll (CA)
Southern U at Shreveport–Bossier City Cmps (LA)
South Georgia Coll (GA)
South Mountain Comm Coll (AZ)
SouthWest Collegiate Inst for the Deaf (TX)
Southwestern Coll (CA)
Spoon River Coll (IL)
State Comm Coll of East St Louis (IL)
State U of NY Coll of A&T at Morrisville (NY)
State U of NY Coll of Tech at Canton (NY)
Tacoma Comm Coll (WA)
Terra State Comm Coll (OH)
Texarkana Coll (TX)
Triton Coll (IL)
Vermilion Comm Coll (MN)
Vincennes U (IN)
Waubonsee Comm Coll (IL)
Western Nebraska Comm Coll, Scottsbluff (NE)
West Hills Comm Coll (CA)
West Los Angeles Coll (CA)
West Valley Coll (CA)
Young Harris Coll (GA)

PHYSIOLOGY
Atlantic Comm Coll (NJ)
Chabot Coll (CA)
Comm Coll of the Air Force (AL)
Joliet Jr Coll (IL)
Modesto Jr Coll (CA)
Snow Coll (UT)

PIANO/ORGAN
Angelina Coll (TX)
Brevard Coll (NC)
Colby Comm Coll (KS)
Frank Phillips Coll (TX)
Hill Coll of the Hill Jr Coll District (TX)
Iowa Lakes Comm Coll (IA)
Itawamba Comm Coll (MS)
Jackson State Comm Coll (TN)
Lon Morris Coll (TX)
Miami-Dade Comm Coll (FL)
Northeastern Oklahoma A&M Coll (OK)
Ricks Coll (ID)
St Catharine Coll (KY)
San Jacinto College–North Cmps (TX)
Waldorf Coll (IA)

PLASTICS TECHNOLOGY
Cerritos Coll (CA)
Clark Coll (WA)
Coll of DuPage (IL)
Cumberland County Coll (NJ)
Davidson County Comm Coll (NC)
Delaware County Comm Coll (PA)
Elaine P Nunez Comm Coll (LA)
Grand Rapids Comm Coll (MI)
Ivy Tech State Coll–Northcentral (IN)
Ivy Tech State Coll–Southwest (IN)
Ivy Tech State Coll–Wabash Valley (IN)
Kalamazoo Valley Comm Coll (MI)
Lorain County Comm Coll (OH)
Macomb Comm Coll (MI)
Massachusetts Bay Comm Coll (MA)
Mount Wachusett Comm Coll (MA)
Northampton County Area Comm Coll (PA)
Northeastern Oklahoma A&M Coll (OK)
Northeast Iowa Comm Coll, Peosta Cmps (IA)
Northwestern Michigan Coll (MI)
Oakland Comm Coll (MI)
Pennsylvania Coll of Tech (PA)
Quinebaug Valley Comm-Tech Coll (CT)
Ricks Coll (ID)
St Clair County Comm Coll (MI)
Schenectady County Comm Coll (NY)
Southeast Comm Coll, Milford Cmps (NE)
Terra State Comm Coll (OH)
Tyler Jr Coll (TX)
Willmar Tech Coll (MN)

PLUMBING
Bakersfield Coll (CA)
Cecil Comm Coll (MD)
Coll of San Mateo (CA)
Comm Coll of Allegheny County North Cmps (PA)
Dixie Coll (UT)
Fayetteville Tech Comm Coll (NC)
Forsyth Tech Comm Coll (NC)
Fresno City Coll (CA)
Gateway Comm Coll (AZ)
Haywood Comm Coll (NC)
John M Patterson State Tech Coll (AL)
Lansing Comm Coll (MI)
Los Angeles Trade-Tech Coll (CA)
Luzerne County Comm Coll (PA)
Macomb Comm Coll (MI)

Peterson's Guide to Two-Year Colleges 1997
117

Associate Degree Programs at Two-Year Colleges
Plumbing–Practical Nursing

Nebraska Indian Comm Coll (NE)
New England Inst of Tech (RI)
Northern Maine Tech Coll (ME)
Oklahoma State U, Okmulgee (OK)
Palomar Coll (CA)
Ranken Tech Coll (MO)
St Cloud Tech Coll (MN)
St Louis Comm Coll at Forest Park (MO)
St Philip's Coll (TX)
Salt Lake Comm Coll (UT)
Sisseton-Wahpeton Comm Coll (SD)
Southeast Comm Coll, Milford Cmps (NE)
Southern Maine Tech Coll (ME)
State U of NY Coll of Tech at Alfred (NY)
State U of NY Coll of Tech at Canton (NY)
State U of NY Coll of Tech at Delhi (NY)
Thaddeus Stevens State Sch of Tech (PA)
Truckee Meadows Comm Coll (NV)
Wake Tech Comm Coll (NC)

POLITICAL SCIENCE/ GOVERNMENT
Abraham Baldwin Ag Coll (GA)
Allen County Comm Coll (KS)
Antelope Valley Coll (CA)
Atlanta Metropolitan Coll (GA)
Austin Comm Coll (TX)
Bainbridge Coll (GA)
Bakersfield Coll (CA)
Barton County Comm Coll (KS)
Bay de Noc Comm Coll (MI)
Bee County Coll (TX)
Bergen Comm Coll (NJ)
Bismarck State Coll (ND)
Black Hawk Coll, Moline (IL)
Brazosport Coll (TX)
Brevard Comm Coll (NC)
Brunswick Coll (GA)
Burlington County Coll (NJ)
Butler County Comm Coll (KS)
Butte Coll (CA)
Cañada Coll (CA)
Casper Coll (WY)
Centralia Coll (WA)
Central Texas Coll (TX)
Cerritos Coll (CA)
Chabot Coll (CA)
Chaffey Coll (CA)
Chemeketa Comm Coll (OR)
Clackamas Comm Coll (OR)
Clark Coll (WA)
Clinton Comm Coll (IA)
Cochise Coll, Douglas (AZ)
Cochise Coll, Sierra Vista (AZ)
Coffeyville Comm Coll (KS)
Colby Comm Coll (KS)
Coll of Alameda (CA)
Coll of DuPage (IL)
Coll of Marin (CA)
Coll of Southern Idaho (ID)
Coll of the Canyons (CA)
Coll of the Desert (CA)
Coll of the Siskiyous (CA)
Collin County Comm Coll (TX)
Columbia State Comm Coll (TN)
Comm Coll of Allegheny County Boyce Cmps (PA)
Comm Coll of Allegheny County South Cmps (PA)
Contra Costa Coll (CA)
Copiah-Lincoln Comm College–Natchez Cmps (MS)
Crafton Hills Coll (CA)
Cypress Coll (CA)
Dalton Coll (GA)
Darton Coll (GA)
De Anza Coll (CA)
Del Mar Coll (TX)
Dixie Coll (UT)
Dodge City Comm Coll (KS)
Donnelly Coll (KS)
East Central Coll (MO)
East Central Comm Coll (MS)
Eastern Arizona Coll (AZ)
Eastern Oklahoma State Coll (OK)
Eastern Wyoming Coll (WY)
East Georgia Coll (GA)
East Los Angeles Coll (CA)
El Camino Coll (CA)
Ellsworth Comm Coll (IA)
El Paso Comm Coll (TX)
Essex Comm Coll (MD)
Everett Comm Coll (WA)
Finger Lakes Comm Coll (NY)
Foothill Coll (CA)
Frank Phillips Coll (TX)
Fresno City Coll (CA)
Fullerton Coll (CA)
Gainesville Coll (GA)
Gavilan Coll (CA)
Gordon Coll (GA)
Grossmont Coll (CA)
Gulf Coast Comm Coll (FL)
Harford Comm Coll (MD)
Highland Comm Coll (IL)
Highland Comm Coll (KS)
Hill Coll of the Hill Jr Coll District (TX)
Hinds Comm Coll (MS)
Hiwassee Coll (TN)
Hutchinson Comm Coll and Area Vocational Sch (KS)
Independence Comm Coll (KS)
Iowa Lakes Comm Coll (IA)
Itawamba Comm Coll (MS)
Jackson State Comm Coll (TN)
Jefferson Coll (MO)
Jefferson Davis Comm Coll (AL)
John A Logan Coll (IL)
John Wood Comm Coll (IL)
Joliet Jr Coll (IL)
Kansas City Kansas Comm Coll (KS)
Kellogg Comm Coll (MI)
Kirkwood Comm Coll (IA)
Lake Land Coll (IL)
Lake Michigan Coll (MI)
Laramie County Comm Coll (WY)
Lawson State Comm Coll (AL)
Lincoln Land Comm Coll (IL)
Lon Morris Coll (TX)
Lorain County Comm Coll (OH)
Lower Columbia Coll (WA)
Macon Coll (GA)
Marshalltown Comm Coll (IA)
Merced Coll (CA)
Miami-Dade Comm Coll (FL)
Miami University–Middletown Cmps (OH)
Middle Georgia Coll (GA)
Middlesex County Coll (NJ)
Mid-Plains Comm Coll (NE)
Mississippi Delta Comm Coll (MS)
Mitchell Coll (CT)
Modesto Jr Coll (CA)
Monroe Comm Coll (NY)
Monterey Peninsula Coll (CA)
Northeastern Oklahoma A&M Coll (OK)
Northeast Mississippi Comm Coll (MS)
Northern Essex Comm Coll (MA)
North Harris Coll (TX)
North Idaho Coll (ID)
Northwest Coll (WY)
Odessa Coll (TX)
Oklahoma City Comm Coll (OK)
Otero Jr Coll (CO)
Palm Beach Comm Coll (FL)
Palo Verde Coll (CA)
Pasadena City Coll (CA)
Pikes Peak Comm Coll (CO)
Pima Comm Coll (AZ)
Potomac State Coll of West Virginia U (WV)
Rancho Santiago Coll (CA)
Reading Area Comm Coll (PA)
Redlands Comm Coll (OK)
Red Rocks Comm Coll (CO)
Ricks Coll (ID)
Rogers State Coll (OK)
Rose State Coll (OK)
Saddleback Coll (CA)
St Philip's Coll (TX)
Salem Comm Coll (NJ)
San Bernardino Valley Coll (CA)
San Diego City Coll (CA)
San Jacinto College–Central Cmps (TX)
San Joaquin Delta Coll (CA)
San Juan Coll (NM)
Santa Barbara City Coll (CA)
Santa Monica Coll (CA)
Santa Rosa Jr Coll (CA)
Sauk Valley Comm Coll (IL)
Scott Comm Coll (IA)
Skagit Valley Coll (WA)
Skyline Coll (CA)
Snow Coll (UT)
Solano Comm Coll (CA)
South Georgia Coll (GA)
South Mountain Comm Coll (AZ)
SouthWest Collegiate Inst for the Deaf (TX)
Southwestern Coll (CA)
Southwestern Comm Coll (IA)
Spoon River Coll (IL)
State Comm Coll of East St Louis (IL)
Tacoma Comm Coll (WA)
Treasure Valley Comm Coll (OR)
Trinity Valley Comm Coll (TX)
Triton Coll (IL)
Tulsa Jr Coll (OK)
Umpqua Comm Coll (OR)
U of Kentucky, Jefferson Comm Coll (KY)
Vermilion Comm Coll (MN)
Vincennes U (IN)
Waubonsee Comm Coll (IL)
Waycross Coll (GA)
Western Wyoming Comm Coll (WY)
West Los Angeles Coll (CA)
West Shore Comm Coll (MI)
Young Harris Coll (GA)

POLLUTION CONTROL TECHNOLOGIES
Bay de Noc Comm Coll (MI)
Broward Comm Coll (FL)
Central Alabama Comm Coll (AL)
Cosumnes River Coll (CA)
Ellsworth Comm Coll (IA)
Foothill Coll (CA)
Green River Comm Coll (WA)
Iowa Lakes Comm Coll (IA)
Ivy Tech State Coll–Central Indiana (IN)
Ivy Tech State Coll–Northwest (IN)
Milwaukee Area Tech Coll (WI)
Napa Valley Coll (CA)
Southern Maine Tech Coll (ME)
Ulster County Comm Coll (NY)
Vermilion Comm Coll (MN)
Westchester Comm Coll (NY)

PORTUGUESE
Miami-Dade Comm Coll (FL)
Modesto Jr Coll (CA)

POSTAL MANAGEMENT
Angelina Coll (TX)
Bevill State Comm Coll (AL)
Central Piedmont Comm Coll (NC)
Connors State Coll (OK)
Cuyahoga Comm Coll, Metropolitan Cmps (OH)
Daytona Beach Comm Coll (FL)
Fayetteville Tech Comm Coll (NC)
Frank Phillips Coll (TX)
Gateway Comm-Tech Coll (CT)
Gulf Coast Comm Coll (FL)
Hillsborough Comm Coll (FL)
Hinds Comm Coll (MS)
Jefferson State Comm Coll (AL)
Lenoir Comm Coll (NC)
Longview Comm Coll (MO)
Macon Coll (GA)
Mayland Comm Coll (NC)
Miami-Dade Comm Coll (FL)
Minneapolis Comm Coll (MN)
Mississippi Gulf Coast Comm Coll (MS)
Northwest Coll (WY)
San Antonio Coll (TX)
San Diego City Coll (CA)
South Plains Coll (TX)
Tarrant County Jr Coll (TX)
Tyler Jr Coll (TX)
Wallace State Comm Coll (AL)

POULTRY SCIENCES
Crowder Coll (MO)
Gainesville Coll (GA)
Modesto Jr Coll (CA)
Northeast Texas Comm Coll (TX)
Wallace State Comm Coll (AL)
Wayne Comm Coll (NC)

PRACTICAL NURSING
Alexandria Tech Coll (MN)
Allan Hancock Coll (CA)
Alpena Comm Coll (MI)
Angelina Coll (TX)
Antelope Valley Coll (CA)
Arizona Western Coll (AZ)
Athens Area Tech Inst (GA)
Bainbridge Coll (GA)
Bay de Noc Comm Coll (MI)
Bee County Coll (TX)
Belmont Tech Coll (OH)
Berkshire Comm Coll (MA)
Bessemer State Tech Coll (AL)
Bevill State Comm Coll (AL)
Big Bend Comm Coll (WA)
Black Hawk Coll, Moline (IL)
Blinn Coll (TX)
Blue Mountain Comm Coll (OR)
Brazosport Coll (TX)
Brevard Comm Coll (FL)
Butte Coll (CA)
Carl Sandburg Coll (IL)
Carteret Comm Coll (NC)
Casper Coll (WY)
Central Comm College–Grand Island Cmps (NE)
Central Comm College–Platte Cmps (NE)
Centralia Coll (WA)
Central Oregon Comm Coll (OR)
Central Piedmont Comm Coll (NC)
Central Texas Coll (TX)
Cerro Coso Comm Coll (CA)
Charles County Comm Coll (MD)
Charles Stewart Mott Comm Coll (MI)
Chattahoochee Valley State Comm Coll (AL)
Chemeketa Comm Coll (OR)
Citrus Coll (CA)
City Coll of San Francisco (CA)
Clark Coll (WA)
Clark State Comm Coll (OH)
Clinton Comm Coll (IA)
Coastal Carolina Comm Coll (NC)
Coffeyville Comm Coll (KS)
Colby Comm Coll (KS)
Coll of Southern Idaho (ID)
Coll of the Canyons (CA)
Colorado Mountn Coll, Roaring Fork Cmps-Spring Valley Ctr (CO)
Comm Coll of Beaver County (PA)
Comm Coll of Southern Nevada (NV)
Contra Costa Coll (CA)
Danville Area Comm Coll (IL)
Daytona Beach Comm Coll (FL)
Delaware Tech & Comm Coll, Jack F Owens Cmps (DE)
Delaware Tech & Comm Coll, Terry Cmps (DE)
Dodge City Comm Coll (KS)
Douglas MacArthur State Tech Coll (AL)
Durham Tech Comm Coll (NC)
East Arkansas Comm Coll (AR)
Eastern Maine Tech Coll (ME)
Elaine P Nunez Comm Coll (LA)
El Camino Coll (CA)
El Centro Coll (TX)
Elgin Comm Coll (IL)
Everett Comm Coll (WA)
Fayetteville Tech Comm Coll (NC)
Fergus Falls Comm Coll (MN)
Fresno City Coll (CA)
Galveston Coll (TX)
Gateway Comm Coll (AZ)
Gavilan Coll (CA)
George Corley Wallace State Comm Coll, Selma (AL)
Gogebic Comm Coll (MI)
Grand Rapids Comm Coll (MI)
Green River Comm Coll (WA)
Harrisburg Area Comm Coll (PA)
Hawkeye Comm Coll (IA)
Heartland Comm Coll (IL)
Helena Coll of Tech of The U of Montana (MT)
Highland Park Comm Coll (MI)
Hill Coll of the Hill Jr Coll District (TX)
Hinds Comm Coll (MS)
Horry-Georgetown Tech Coll (SC)
Howard Coll (TX)
Howard Comm Coll (MD)
Illinois Eastern Comm Colls, Olney Central Coll (IL)
Imperial Valley Coll (CA)
Indian Hills Comm Coll (IA)
Indian River Comm Coll (FL)
Iowa Central Comm Coll (IA)
Iowa Western Comm Coll (IA)
Isothermal Comm Coll (NC)
Itasca Comm Coll (MN)
Jackson Comm Coll (MI)
Jefferson Coll (MO)
Jefferson Comm Coll (OH)
John A Logan Coll (IL)
John C Calhoun State Comm Coll (AL)
John Wood Comm Coll (IL)
Jones County Jr Coll (MS)
Kellogg Comm Coll (MI)
Kingwood Coll (TX)
Kirkwood Comm Coll (IA)
Kirtland Comm Coll (MI)
Lake Area Vocational-Tech Inst (SD)
Lake City Comm Coll (FL)
Lake Michigan Coll (MI)
Lamar Comm Coll (CO)
Lansing Comm Coll (MI)
Lassen Coll (CA)
Lehigh Carbon Comm Coll (PA)
Lincoln Coll, Normal (IL)
Los Angeles Valley Coll (CA)
Lower Columbia Coll (WA)
Marshalltown Comm Coll (IA)
Massachusetts Bay Comm Coll (MA)
Merced Coll (CA)
Meridian Comm Coll (MS)
Merritt Coll (CA)
Metropolitan Comm Coll (NE)
Midland Coll (TX)
Mid Michigan Comm Coll (MI)
Mid-Plains Comm Coll (NE)
MiraCosta Coll (CA)
Mission Coll (CA)
Moberly Area Comm Coll (MO)
Modesto Jr Coll (CA)
Montana State U Coll of Tech-Great Falls (MT)
Montcalm Comm Coll (MI)
Montgomery Coll (TX)
Muscatine Comm Coll (IA)
Navarro Coll (TX)
Neosho County Comm Coll (KS)
New Mexico Jr Coll (NM)
New River Comm Coll (VA)
Niagara County Comm Coll (NY)
North Dakota State Coll of Science (ND)
Northeast Comm Coll (NE)
Northeastern Jr Coll (CO)
Northeast Iowa Comm Coll, Peosta Cmps (IA)
Northern Maine Tech Coll (ME)
North Idaho Coll (ID)
Northland Comm and Tech Coll (MN)
North Seattle Comm Coll (WA)
Northwest Coll (WY)
Northwestern Michigan Coll (MI)
Northwest Iowa Comm Coll (IA)
Northwest Mississippi Comm Coll (MS)
Northwest-Shoals Comm Coll (AL)
Oakland Comm Coll (MI)
Olympic Coll (WA)
Ozarks Tech Comm Coll (MO)
Pasadena City Coll (CA)
Pennsylvania Coll of Tech (PA)
Petit Jean Tech Coll (AR)
Phillips County Comm Coll (AR)
Porterville Coll (CA)
Quincy Coll (MA)
Rainy River Comm Coll (MN)
Reading Area Comm Coll (PA)
Reid State Tech Coll (AL)
Richmond Comm Coll (NC)
Riverside Comm Coll (CA)
Robeson Comm Coll (NC)
Rockingham Comm Coll (NC)
St Cloud Tech Coll (MN)
St Philip's Coll (TX)
Salt Lake Comm Coll (UT)
Sampson Comm Coll (NC)
Sandhills Comm Coll (NC)
San Diego City Coll (CA)
San Jacinto College–South Cmps (TX)
San Joaquin Delta Coll (CA)
Santa Barbara City Coll (CA)
Scott Comm Coll (IA)
Seward County Comm Coll (KS)
Shelton State Comm Coll (AL)
Sheridan Coll (WY)
Sierra Coll (CA)
Skagit Valley Coll (WA)
Southeast Comm Coll, Beatrice Cmps (NE)
Southeastern Comm Coll, North Cmps, West Burlington (IA)
Southeastern Comm Coll, South Cmps, Keokuk (IA)
Southeastern Illinois Coll (IL)
Southern Maine Tech Coll (ME)
Southern State Comm Coll (OH)
South Plains Coll (TX)
South Puget Sound Comm Coll (WA)
South Suburban Coll (IL)
Southwestern Michigan Coll (MI)
Southwest Wisconsin Tech Coll (WI)
Spokane Comm Coll (WA)
State Fair Comm Coll (MO)
Surry Comm Coll (NC)
Temple Coll (TX)
Texarkana Coll (TX)
Trinidad State Jr Coll (CO)
Trinity Valley Comm Coll (TX)
Triton Coll (IL)
Tyler Jr Coll (TX)
Union County Coll (NJ)
U of Hawaii–Hawaii Comm Coll (HI)
U of North Dakota–Williston (ND)
Utah Valley State Coll (UT)
Vance-Granville Comm Coll (NC)
Vermont Tech Coll (VT)
Vernon Regional Jr Coll (TX)
Vincennes U (IN)
Wallace State Comm Coll (AL)
Walla Walla Comm Coll (WA)
Washington State Comm Coll (OH)
Wenatchee Valley Coll (WA)
Western Nebraska Comm Coll, Scottsbluff (NE)
Western Nevada Comm Coll (NV)
Western Texas Coll (TX)
Western Wyoming Comm Coll (WY)

Associate Degree Programs at Two-Year Colleges
Practical Nursing–Purchasing/Inventory Management

Westmoreland County Comm Coll (PA)
West Shore Comm Coll (MI)
William Rainey Harper Coll (IL)
Willmar Tech Coll (MN)
Wilson Tech Comm Coll (NC)
Yuba Coll (CA)

PRINTING TECHNOLOGIES
Allen County Comm Coll (KS)
Austin Comm Coll (TX)
Catonsville Comm Coll (MD)
Central Comm College–Hastings Cmps (NE)
Central Piedmont Comm Coll (NC)
Central Texas Coll (TX)
Chattanooga State Tech Comm Coll (TN)
Chemeketa Comm Coll (OR)
Cincinnati State Tech and Comm Coll (OH)
City Coll of San Francisco (CA)
City Colls of Chicago, Kennedy-King Coll (IL)
Clark Coll (WA)
Clinton Comm Coll (IA)
Colby Comm Coll (KS)
Coll of DuPage (IL)
Columbus State Comm Coll (OH)
Comm Coll of Allegheny County South Cmps (PA)
Comm Coll of Southern Nevada (NV)
Comm Coll of the Air Force (AL)
Delta Coll (MI)
Des Moines Area Comm Coll (IA)
Don Bosco Tech Inst (CA)
Dunwoody Inst (MN)
Erie Comm Coll, South Cmps (NY)
Forsyth Tech Comm Coll (NC)
Fox Valley Tech Coll (WI)
Fresno City Coll (CA)
Fullerton Coll (CA)
Fulton-Montgomery Comm Coll (NY)
Gogebic Comm Coll (MI)
Golden West Coll (CA)
Highline Comm Coll (WA)
Hinds Comm Coll (MS)
Hutchinson Comm Coll and Area Vocational Sch (KS)
Iowa Lakes Comm Coll (IA)
Ivy Tech State Coll–Wabash Valley (IN)
John M Patterson State Tech Coll (AL)
Kirkwood Comm Coll (IA)
Lakeshore Tech Coll (WI)
Laney Coll (CA)
Lenoir Comm Coll (NC)
Los Angeles Trade-Tech Coll (CA)
Luzerne County Comm Coll (PA)
Macomb Comm Coll (MI)
Madison Area Tech Coll (WI)
Metropolitan Comm Coll (NE)
Milwaukee Area Tech Coll (WI)
Mission Coll (CA)
Modesto Jr Coll (CA)
Monroe Comm Coll (NY)
Montgomery College–Rockville Cmps (MD)
Moorpark Coll (CA)
New York City Tech Coll of the City U of NY (NY)
Northcentral Tech Coll (WI)
Northeastern Oklahoma A&M Coll (OK)
Northern Oklahoma Coll (OK)
Northwest Coll (WY)
Oakland Comm Coll (MI)
Oklahoma State U, Okmulgee (OK)
Ozarks Tech Comm Coll (MO)
Palomar Coll (CA)
Petit Jean Tech Coll (AR)
Phillips County Comm Coll (AR)
Sacramento City Coll (CA)
San Diego City Coll (CA)
San Jacinto College–Central Cmps (TX)
San Joaquin Delta Coll (CA)
Santa Monica Coll (CA)
Seattle Central Comm Coll (WA)
Shoreline Comm Coll (WA)
Sinclair Comm Coll (OH)
South Suburban Coll (IL)
Springfield Tech Comm Coll (MA)
Tarrant County Jr Coll (TX)
Terra State Comm Coll (OH)
Texas State Tech Coll–Waco/Marshall Cmps (TX)
Thaddeus Stevens State Sch of Tech (PA)
Triton Coll (IL)
Tyler Jr Coll (TX)
Vincennes U (IN)
Washtenaw Comm Coll (MI)
Western Wisconsin Tech Coll (WI)
Westmoreland County Comm Coll (PA)

PRINTMAKING
Brevard Coll (NC)
Coll of San Mateo (CA)
Inst of American Indian Arts (NM)
Northwest Mississippi Comm Coll (MS)

PSYCHOLOGY
Abraham Baldwin Ag Coll (GA)
Alabama Southern Comm Coll, Monroeville (AL)
Allegany Comm Coll (MD)
Allen County Comm Coll (KS)
Andrew Coll (GA)
Antelope Valley Coll (CA)
Atlanta Metropolitan Coll (GA)
Austin Comm Coll (TX)
Bainbridge Coll (GA)
Bakersfield Coll (CA)
Barton County Comm Coll (KS)
Bay de Noc Comm Coll (MI)
Bee County Coll (TX)
Bergen Comm Coll (NJ)
Bishop State Comm Coll (AL)
Bismarck State Coll (ND)
Black Hawk Coll, Moline (IL)
Brazosport Coll (TX)
Brevard Coll (NC)
Bronx Comm Coll of City U of NY (NY)
Brookdale Comm Coll (NJ)
Brunswick Coll (GA)
Bucks County Comm Coll (PA)
Burlington County Coll (NJ)
Butler County Comm Coll (KS)
Butte Coll (CA)
Cañada Coll (CA)
Cape Cod Comm Coll (MA)
Carl Albert State Coll (OK)
Casper Coll (WY)
Central Coll (KS)
Central Comm College–Grand Island Cmps (NE)
Central Comm College–Hastings Cmps (NE)
Central Comm College–Platte Cmps (NE)
Centralia Coll (WA)
Central Texas Coll (TX)
Central Wyoming Coll (WY)
Cerritos Coll (CA)
Chabot Coll (CA)
Chaffey Coll (CA)
Chemeketa Comm Coll (OR)
Cisco Jr Coll (TX)
City Coll of San Francisco (CA)
Clackamas Comm Coll (OR)
Clark Coll (WA)
Clinton Comm Coll (IA)
Clovis Comm Coll (NM)
Cochise Coll, Douglas (AZ)
Cochise Coll, Sierra Vista (AZ)
Coffeyville Comm Coll (KS)
Colby Comm Coll (KS)
Coll of Alameda (CA)
Coll of DuPage (IL)
Coll of Marin (CA)
Coll of Southern Idaho (ID)
Coll of the Canyons (CA)
Coll of the Desert (CA)
Coll of the Siskiyous (CA)
Collin County Comm Coll (TX)
Colorado Mountn Coll, Roaring Fork Cmps-Spring Valley Ctr (CO)
Colorado Mountn Coll, Timberline Cmps (CO)
Columbia Coll (CA)
Columbia State Comm Coll (TN)
Comm Coll of Allegheny County Allegheny Cmps (PA)
Comm Coll of Allegheny County North Cmps (PA)
Comm Coll of Allegheny County South Cmps (PA)
Connors State Coll (OK)
Crafton Hills Coll (CA)
Cuesta Coll (CA)
Cypress Coll (CA)
Dalton Coll (GA)
Danville Area Comm Coll (IL)
Darton Coll (GA)
Daytona Beach Comm Coll (FL)
De Anza Coll (CA)
Del Mar Coll (TX)
Delta Coll (MI)
Dixie Coll (UT)
Dodge City Comm Coll (KS)
Donnelly Coll (KS)
East Central Coll (MO)
East Central Comm Coll (MS)
Eastern Arizona Coll (AZ)
Eastern Oklahoma State Coll (OK)
Eastern Wyoming Coll (WY)
East Georgia Coll (GA)
East Los Angeles Coll (CA)
East Mississippi Comm Coll (MS)
El Camino Coll (CA)
Ellsworth Comm Coll (IA)
El Paso Comm Coll (TX)
Essex Comm Coll (MD)
Everett Comm Coll (WA)
Finger Lakes Comm Coll (NY)
Foothill Coll (CA)
Frank Phillips Coll (TX)
Frederick Comm Coll (MD)
Fresno City Coll (CA)
Fullerton Coll (CA)
Fulton-Montgomery Comm Coll (NY)
Gainesville Coll (GA)
Garrett Comm Coll (MD)
Gavilan Coll (CA)
Genesee Comm Coll (NY)
Glendale Comm Coll (AZ)
Gordon Coll (GA)
Grays Harbor Coll (WA)
Grayson County Coll (TX)
Gulf Coast Comm Coll (FL)
Harford Comm Coll (MD)
Harrisburg Area Comm Coll (PA)
Hesser Coll (NH)
Highland Comm Coll (IL)
Highland Comm Coll (KS)
Highline Comm Coll (WA)
Hill Coll of the Hill Jr Coll District (TX)
Hinds Comm Coll (MS)
Hiwassee Coll (TN)
Howard Comm Coll (MD)
Hutchinson Comm Coll and Area Vocational Sch (KS)
Imperial Valley Coll (CA)
Independence Comm Coll (KS)
Indian River Comm Coll (FL)
Iowa Lakes Comm Coll (IA)
Itawamba Comm Coll (MS)
Jackson State Comm Coll (TN)
Jefferson Coll (MO)
John A Logan Coll (IL)
John Wood Comm Coll (IL)
Joliet Jr Coll (IL)
Kansas City Kansas Comm Coll (KS)
Kellogg Comm Coll (MI)
Kemper Military Jr Coll (MO)
Kirkwood Comm Coll (IA)
Lake Michigan Coll (MI)
Laramie County Comm Coll (WY)
Lassen Coll (CA)
Lawson State Comm Coll (AL)
Lincoln Coll, Normal (IL)
Lincoln Land Comm Coll (IL)
Lon Morris Coll (TX)
Lorain County Comm Coll (OH)
Los Angeles City Coll (CA)
Los Angeles Mission Coll (CA)
Los Angeles Valley Coll (CA)
Los Medanos Coll (CA)
Lower Columbia Coll (WA)
Macon Coll (GA)
Manor Jr Coll (PA)
Miami-Dade Comm Coll (FL)
Miami University–Middletown Cmps (OH)
Middle Georgia Coll (GA)
Middlesex County Coll (NJ)
Midland Coll (TX)
Mid Michigan Comm Coll (MI)
Mineral Area Coll (MO)
MiraCosta Coll (CA)
Mitchell Coll (CT)
Moberly Area Comm Coll (MO)
Modesto Jr Coll (CA)
Mohave Comm Coll (AZ)
Monroe County Comm Coll (MI)
Monterey Peninsula Coll (CA)
Montgomery County Comm Coll (PA)
Motlow State Comm Coll (TN)
Muscatine Comm Coll (IA)
Navajo Comm Coll (AZ)
Navarro Coll (TX)
Newbury Coll (MA)
Northeastern Jr Coll (CO)
Northeastern Oklahoma A&M Coll (OK)
Northeast Mississippi Comm Coll (MS)
North Idaho Coll (ID)
Northwest Coll (WY)
Odessa Coll (TX)
Ohio Valley Coll (WV)
Oklahoma City Comm Coll (OK)
Otero Jr Coll (CO)
Owens Comm Coll, Findlay (OH)
Owens Comm Coll, Toledo (OH)
Palm Beach Comm Coll (FL)
Palo Alto Coll (TX)
Palo Verde Coll (CA)
Parks Jr Coll (CO)
Pasadena City Coll (CA)
Pikes Peak Comm Coll (CO)
Polk Comm Coll (FL)
Potomac State Coll of West Virginia U (WV)
Pratt Comm Coll and Area Voc Sch (KS)
Quincy Coll (MA)
Rancho Santiago Coll (CA)
Raritan Valley Comm Coll (NJ)
Reading Area Comm Coll (PA)
Redlands Comm Coll (OK)
Red Rocks Comm Coll (CO)
Ricks Coll (ID)
Rose State Coll (OK)
Sacramento City Coll (CA)
Saddleback Coll (CA)
St Philip's Coll (TX)
San Antonio Coll (TX)
San Bernardino Valley Coll (CA)
San Diego City Coll (CA)
San Diego Mesa Coll (CA)
San Diego Miramar Coll (CA)
San Jacinto College–Central Cmps (TX)
San Jacinto College–South Cmps (TX)
San Joaquin Delta Coll (CA)
San Juan Coll (NM)
Santa Barbara City Coll (CA)
Santa Monica Coll (CA)
Santa Rosa Jr Coll (CA)
Sauk Valley Comm Coll (IL)
Scott Comm Coll (IA)
Seward County Comm Coll (KS)
Skagit Valley Coll (WA)
Skyline Coll (CA)
Solano Comm Coll (CA)
South Georgia Coll (GA)
South Mountain Comm Coll (AZ)
SouthWest Collegiate Inst for the Deaf (TX)
Southwestern Coll (CA)
Southwestern Comm Coll (IA)
Spoon River Coll (IL)
State Comm Coll of East St Louis (IL)
Sullivan County Comm Coll (NY)
Sussex County Comm Coll (NJ)
Tacoma Comm Coll (WA)
Trinidad State Jr Coll (CO)
Trinity Valley Comm Coll (TX)
Triton Coll (IL)
Tulsa Jr Coll (OK)
Tyler Jr Coll (TX)
Umpqua Comm Coll (OR)
Vermilion Comm Coll (MN)
Vincennes U (IN)
Vincennes University–Jasper Ctr (IN)
Waldorf Coll (IA)
Waubonsee Comm Coll (IL)
Waycross Coll (GA)
Western Nebraska Comm Coll, Scottsbluff (NE)
Western Wyoming Comm Coll (WY)
West Hills Comm Coll (CA)
West Los Angeles Coll (CA)
West Shore Comm Coll (MI)
West Valley Coll (CA)
Willmar Comm Coll (MN)
Wright State U, Lake Cmps (OH)
Young Harris Coll (GA)
Yuba Coll (CA)

PUBLIC ADMINISTRATION
Anne Arundel Comm Coll (MD)
Barton County Comm Coll (KS)
Bay Mills Comm Coll (MI)
Bismarck State Coll (ND)
Borough of Manhattan Comm Coll of City U of NY (NY)
Brevard Coll (NC)
Cañada Coll (CA)
City Coll of San Francisco (CA)
Comm Coll of Allegheny County Allegheny Cmps (PA)
Comm Coll of Allegheny County South Cmps (PA)
County Coll of Morris (NJ)
Darton Coll (GA)
Del Mar Coll (TX)
East Central Coll (MO)
East Los Angeles Coll (CA)
Eugenio María de Hostos Comm Coll of City U of NY (NY)
Everett Comm Coll (WA)
Fayetteville Tech Comm Coll (NC)
Fort Berthold Comm Coll (ND)
Fresno City Coll (CA)
Hinds Comm Coll (MS)
Housatonic Comm-Tech Coll (CT)
Hudson County Comm Coll (NJ)
Hutchinson Comm Coll and Area Vocational Sch (KS)
Itawamba Comm Coll (MS)
Jefferson Coll (MO)
Kemper Military Jr Coll (MO)
Laramie County Comm Coll (WY)
Lehigh Carbon Comm Coll (PA)
Los Angeles City Coll (CA)
Macon Coll (GA)
Miami-Dade Comm Coll (FL)
Middle Georgia Coll (GA)
Mitchell Coll (CT)
Modesto Jr Coll (CA)
Mountain Empire Comm Coll (VA)
Mount Ida Coll (MA)
Nebraska Indian Comm Coll (NE)
Northeast Comm Coll (NE)
Northeast Mississippi Comm Coll (MS)
Northern Marianas Coll (MP)
Northwest Coll (WY)
Palomar Coll (CA)
Passaic County Comm Coll (NJ)
Pima Comm Coll (AZ)
Reading Area Comm Coll (PA)
Red Rocks Comm Coll (CO)
Rio Salado Comm Coll (AZ)
Salem Comm Coll (NJ)
San Antonio Coll (TX)
San Joaquin Delta Coll (CA)
San Jose City Coll (CA)
San Juan Coll (NM)
Santa Rosa Jr Coll (CA)
Scottsdale Comm Coll (AZ)
Sinclair Comm Coll (OH)
Solano Comm Coll (CA)
Southwestern Coll (CA)
Thomas Nelson Comm Coll (VA)
Three Rivers Comm-Tech Coll (CT)
Union County Coll (NJ)
U of New Mexico–Gallup Branch (NM)
Vincennes U (IN)
Westchester Comm Coll (NY)
Westmoreland County Comm Coll (PA)

PUBLIC AFFAIRS AND POLICY STUDIES
Anne Arundel Comm Coll (MD)
Comm Coll of the Air Force (AL)
Del Mar Coll (TX)
Fort Scott Comm Coll (KS)
Hill Coll of the Hill Jr Coll District (TX)
Macon Coll (GA)
Mount Ida Coll (MA)
Northwest Coll (WY)
Tallahassee Comm Coll (FL)

PUBLIC HEALTH
City Coll of San Francisco (CA)
Hill Coll of the Hill Jr Coll District (TX)
Kingsborough Comm Coll of City U of NY (NY)

PUBLIC RELATIONS
American Inst of Business (IA)
Bee County Coll (TX)
Black Hawk Coll, Moline (IL)
Brevard Coll (NC)
Champlain Coll (VT)
Colby Comm Coll (KS)
Comm Coll of Beaver County (PA)
Cosumnes River Coll (CA)
Edmonds Comm Coll (WA)
Glendale Comm Coll (AZ)
Golden West Coll (CA)
Gulf Coast Comm Coll (FL)
Harford Comm Coll (MD)
Kellogg Comm Coll (MI)
Kirkwood Comm Coll (IA)
Long Beach City Coll (CA)
Los Angeles City Coll (CA)
Middle Georgia Coll (GA)
Modesto Jr Coll (CA)
Northeast Mississippi Comm Coll (MS)
Northwestern Business Coll (IL)
Parkland Coll (IL)
St Louis Comm Coll at Meramec (MO)
Vincennes U (IN)

PUBLISHING
Front Range Comm Coll (CO)
Milwaukee Area Tech Coll (WI)
Parkland Coll (IL)
Western Wisconsin Tech Coll (WI)
Westmoreland County Comm Coll (PA)

PURCHASING/INVENTORY MANAGEMENT
Cincinnati State Tech and Comm Coll (OH)
Columbus State Comm Coll (OH)
Comm Coll of Allegheny County Allegheny Cmps (PA)

Associate Degree Programs at Two-Year Colleges
Purchasing/Inventory Management–Radiological Technology

De Anza Coll (CA)
Fresno City Coll (CA)
Fullerton Coll (CA)
Metropolitan Comm Coll (NE)
Northern Virginia Comm Coll (VA)
Shoreline Comm Coll (WA)
Tulsa Jr Coll (OK)
William Rainey Harper Coll (IL)

QUALITY CONTROL TECHNOLOGY
Arkansas State University–Beebe Branch (AR)
Austin Comm Coll (TX)
Bowling Green State University–Firelands Coll (OH)
Butler County Comm Coll (PA)
Catonsville Comm Coll (MD)
Central Carolina Comm Coll (NC)
Chaffey Coll (CA)
Charles Stewart Mott Comm Coll (MI)
Chippewa Valley Tech Coll (WI)
Coll of Lake County (IL)
Coll of the Canyons (CA)
Columbia Basin Coll (WA)
Columbus State Comm Coll (OH)
Comm Coll of Allegheny County North Cmps (PA)
Contra Costa Coll (CA)
Cumberland County Coll (NJ)
Fort Scott Comm Coll (KS)
Grand Rapids Comm Coll (MI)
Heartland Comm Coll (IL)
Henry Ford Comm Coll (MI)
Illinois Eastern Comm Colls, Frontier Comm Coll (IL)
Illinois Eastern Comm Colls, Lincoln Trail Coll (IL)
Ivy Tech State Coll–Central Indiana (IN)
Ivy Tech State Coll–Columbus (IN)
Ivy Tech State Coll–Kokomo (IN)
Ivy Tech State Coll–Lafayette (IN)
Ivy Tech State Coll–Northcentral (IN)
Ivy Tech State Coll–Northeast (IN)
Ivy Tech State Coll–Wabash Valley (IN)
John C Calhoun State Comm Coll (AL)
Kishwaukee Coll (IL)
Lamar Comm Coll (CO)
Lansing Comm Coll (MI)
Lima Tech Coll (OH)
Long Beach City Coll (CA)
Longview Comm Coll (MO)
Lorain County Comm Coll (OH)
Los Angeles Pierce Coll (CA)
Los Angeles Southwest Coll (CA)
Macomb Comm Coll (MI)
Mesa Comm Coll (AZ)
Mid-State Tech Coll (WI)
Monroe Comm Coll (NY)
Moraine Valley Comm Coll (IL)
Mountain View Coll (TX)
Mt San Antonio Coll (CA)
National Ed Ctr–Spartan Sch of Aeronautics Cmps (OK)
Naugatuck Valley Community–Tech Coll (CT)
New Hampshire Tech Coll, Nashua (NH)
North Central Tech Coll (OH)
Northeast Metro Tech Coll (MN)
Northwest State Comm Coll (OH)
Oakland Comm Coll (MI)
Oklahoma State U, Oklahoma City (OK)
Onondaga Comm Coll (NY)
Owens Comm Coll, Findlay (OH)
Owens Comm Coll, Toledo (OH)
Pennsylvania Coll of Tech (PA)

Prince George's Comm Coll (MD)
Rock Valley Coll (IL)
St Clair County Comm Coll (MI)
Schenectady County Comm Coll (NY)
Schoolcraft Coll (MI)
Sinclair Comm Coll (OH)
Southeast Comm Coll, Milford Cmps (NE)
South Seattle Comm Coll (WA)
Tarrant County Jr Coll (TX)
Terra State Comm Coll (OH)
Tri-County Tech Coll (SC)
U of Kentucky, Elizabethtown Comm Coll (KY)
Ventura Coll (CA)
Washtenaw Comm Coll (MI)
Waubonsee Comm Coll (IL)
Westark Comm Coll (AR)
Wisconsin Indianhead Tech Coll, Rice Lake Cmps (WI)

RADIO AND TELEVISION STUDIES
Adirondack Comm Coll (NY)
Allegany Comm Coll (MD)
Alvin Comm Coll (TX)
Art Inst of Pittsburgh (PA)
Austin Comm Coll (TX)
Black Hawk Coll, Moline (IL)
Brevard Comm Coll (FL)
Bucks County Comm Coll (PA)
Catonsville Comm Coll (MD)
Cayuga County Comm Coll (NY)
Central Carolina Comm Coll (NC)
Centralia Coll (WA)
Central Texas Coll (TX)
Central Wyoming Coll (WY)
Chabot Coll (CA)
Chattahoochee Valley State Comm Coll (AL)
Chattanooga State Tech Comm Coll (TN)
City Colls of Chicago, Kennedy-King Coll (IL)
Clarendon Coll (TX)
Coahoma Comm Coll (MS)
Coffeyville Comm Coll (KS)
Colby Comm Coll (KS)
Coll of DuPage (IL)
Coll of San Mateo (CA)
Comm Coll of Southern Nevada (NV)
Cosumnes River Coll (CA)
Cuesta Coll (CA)
Daytona Beach Comm Coll (FL)
De Anza Coll (CA)
Del Mar Coll (TX)
Delta Coll (MI)
Dodge City Comm Coll (KS)
Douglas MacArthur State Tech Coll (AL)
Draughons Jr Coll, Nashville (TN)
Florida Comm Coll at Jacksonville (FL)
Foothill Coll (CA)
Fugazzi Coll (KY)
Fullerton Coll (CA)
Gaston Coll (NC)
George C Wallace State Comm Coll, Dothan (AL)
Golden West Coll (CA)
Green River Comm Coll (WA)
Grossmont Coll (CA)
Gulf Coast Comm Coll (FL)
Herkimer County Comm Coll (NY)
Holmes Comm Coll (MS)
Hutchinson Comm Coll and Area Vocational Sch (KS)
Illinois Eastern Comm Colls, Wabash Valley Coll (IL)
Iowa Central Comm Coll (IA)
Isothermal Comm Coll (NC)
Kellogg Comm Coll (MI)
Kirkwood Comm Coll (IA)
Lane Comm Coll (OR)
Laney Coll (CA)
Lansing Comm Coll (MI)
Lassen Coll (CA)
Lawson State Comm Coll (AL)
Lewis and Clark Comm Coll (IL)
Los Angeles City Coll (CA)

Los Angeles Southwest Coll (CA)
Los Angeles Valley Coll (CA)
Mercer County Comm Coll (NJ)
Miami-Dade Comm Coll (FL)
Middlesex Community–Tech Coll (CT)
Milwaukee Area Tech Coll (WI)
Modesto Jr Coll (CA)
Montgomery College–Rockville Cmps (MD)
Mt Hood Comm Coll (OR)
Mt San Antonio Coll (CA)
Napa Valley Coll (CA)
Navarro Coll (TX)
NEI Coll of Tech (MN)
Newbury Coll (MA)
New England Inst of Tech (RI)
Northampton County Area Comm Coll (PA)
Northeast Comm Coll (NE)
Northeastern Jr Coll (CO)
Northeast Mississippi Comm Coll (MS)
Northland Comm and Tech Coll (MN)
Northwest Mississippi Comm Coll (MS)
Odessa Coll (TX)
Ohlone Coll (CA)
Onondaga Comm Coll (NY)
Oxnard Coll (CA)
Palomar Coll (CA)
Parkland Coll (IL)
Pasadena City Coll (CA)
Ricks Coll (ID)
Rogers State Coll (OK)
Saddleback Coll (CA)
St Louis Comm Coll at Florissant Valley (MO)
San Antonio Coll (TX)
San Bernardino Valley Coll (CA)
San Diego City Coll (CA)
Santa Monica Coll (CA)
Southwestern Comm Coll (NC)
Sullivan County Comm Coll (NY)
Tompkins Cortland Comm Coll (NY)
Tri-County Tech Coll (SC)
Vincennes U (IN)
Virginia Western Comm Coll (VA)
Washington State Comm Coll (OH)
Western Wisconsin Tech Coll (WI)
Wilkes Comm Coll (NC)
Willmar Tech Coll (MN)

RADIOLOGICAL SCIENCES
Brookdale Comm Coll (NJ)
Comm Coll of Southern Nevada (NV)
Darton Coll (GA)
Edison Comm Coll (FL)
El Centro Coll (TX)
Foothill Coll (CA)
Garland County Comm Coll (AR)
Gateway Comm Coll (AZ)
Hillsborough Comm Coll (FL)
Hudson Valley Comm Coll (NY)
Kettering Coll of Medical Arts (OH)
Laredo Comm Coll (TX)
Los Angeles City Coll (CA)
Medical Inst of Minnesota (MN)
Miami-Dade Comm Coll (FL)
Monroe County Comm Coll (NY)
New Mexico State University–Carlsbad (NM)
Pitt Comm Coll (NC)
Ricks Coll (ID)
Western Wyoming Comm Coll (WY)

RADIOLOGICAL TECHNOLOGY
Aims Comm Coll (CO)
Alabama Southern Comm Coll, Monroeville (AL)
Allegany Comm Coll (MD)
Angelina Coll (TX)

Anne Arundel Comm Coll (MD)
Asheville-Buncombe Tech Comm Coll (NC)
Athens Area Tech Inst (GA)
Atlanta Metropolitan Coll (GA)
Austin Comm Coll (TX)
Bacone Coll (OK)
Bakersfield Coll (CA)
Belleville Area Coll (IL)
Bellevue Comm Coll (WA)
Bergen Comm Coll (NJ)
Bevill State Comm Coll (AL)
Blinn Coll (TX)
Brevard Comm Coll (FL)
Broome Comm Coll (NY)
Broward Comm Coll (FL)
Brunswick Coll (GA)
Bunker Hill Comm Coll (MA)
Burlington County Coll (NJ)
Caldwell Comm Coll and Tech Inst (NC)
Camden County Coll (NJ)
Cañada Coll (CA)
Capital Comm Tech Coll (CT)
Carl Sandburg Coll (IL)
Carteret Comm Coll (NC)
Casper Coll (WY)
Central Florida Comm Coll (FL)
Central Maine Tech Coll (ME)
Central Ohio Tech Coll (OH)
Central Virginia Comm Coll (VA)
Chaffey Coll (CA)
Champlain Coll (VT)
Charles Stewart Mott Comm Coll (MI)
Chattahoochee Valley State Comm Coll (AL)
Chattanooga State Tech Comm Coll (TN)
Chesapeake Coll (MD)
Chippewa Valley Tech Coll (WI)
City Coll of San Francisco (CA)
City Colls of Chicago, Malcolm X Coll (IL)
City Colls of Chicago, Wilbur Wright Coll (IL)
Cleveland Comm Coll (NC)
Clovis Comm Coll (NM)
Coll of DuPage (IL)
Coll of Lake County (IL)
Coll of St Catherine–Minneapolis (MN)
Columbia State Comm Coll (TN)
Columbus State Comm Coll (OH)
Comm Coll of Allegheny County Allegheny Cmps (PA)
Comm Coll of Allegheny County Boyce Cmps (PA)
Comm Coll of Denver (CO)
Comm Coll of Philadelphia (PA)
Comm Coll of Rhode Island (RI)
Comm Coll of Southern Nevada (NV)
Comm Coll of the Air Force (AL)
Copiah-Lincoln Comm Coll (MS)
Crafton Hills Coll (CA)
Cumberland County Coll (NJ)
Cuyahoga Comm Coll, Western Cmps (OH)
Cypress Coll (CA)
Danville Area Comm Coll (IL)
Darton Coll (GA)
Daytona Beach Comm Coll (FL)
Delaware Tech & Comm Coll, Stanton/Wilmington Cmps (DE)
Delgado Comm Coll (LA)
Del Mar Coll (TX)
Delta Coll (MI)
Doña Ana Branch Comm Coll (NM)
Eastern Idaho Tech Coll (ID)
Eastern Maine Tech Coll (ME)
Edgecombe Comm Coll (NC)
El Centro Coll (TX)
El Paso Comm Coll (TX)
Erie Comm Coll, City Cmps (NY)
Essex Comm Coll (MD)

Essex County Coll (NJ)
Eugenio María de Hostos Comm Coll of City U of NY (NY)
Fayetteville Tech Comm Coll (NC)
Florence-Darlington Tech Coll (SC)
Florida Comm Coll at Jacksonville (FL)
Floyd Coll (GA)
Foothill Coll (CA)
Forsyth Tech Comm Coll (NC)
Fresno City Coll (CA)
Gadsden State Comm Coll (AL)
Galveston Coll (TX)
Garland County Comm Coll (AR)
Gateway Comm Coll (AZ)
Gateway Comm-Tech Coll (CT)
George Corley Wallace State Comm Coll, Selma (AL)
Grand Rapids Comm Coll (MI)
Greenville Tech Coll (SC)
Gulf Coast Comm Coll (FL)
Gwinnett Tech Inst (GA)
Hagerstown Jr Coll (MD)
Harrisburg Area Comm Coll (PA)
Highland Comm Coll (KS)
Hillsborough Comm Coll (FL)
Hinds Comm Coll (MS)
Holyoke Comm Coll (MA)
Horry-Georgetown Tech Coll (SC)
Houston Comm Coll System (TX)
Hudson Valley Comm Coll (NY)
Hutchinson Comm Coll and Area Vocational Sch (KS)
Illinois Central Coll (IL)
Illinois Eastern Comm Colls, Olney Central Coll (IL)
Indian Hills Comm Coll (IA)
Indian River Comm Coll (FL)
Iowa Central Comm Coll (IA)
Itawamba Comm Coll (MS)
Ivy Tech State Coll–Central Indiana (IN)
Ivy Tech State Coll–Wabash Valley (IN)
Jackson Comm Coll (MI)
Jackson State Comm Coll (TN)
Jefferson Comm Coll (OH)
Jefferson State Comm Coll (AL)
John C Calhoun State Comm Coll (AL)
Johnson County Comm Coll (KS)
Johnston Comm Coll (NC)
Kankakee Comm Coll (IL)
Kansas City Kansas Comm Coll (KS)
Kaskaskia Coll (IL)
Kellogg Comm Coll (MI)
Kent State U, Salem Cmps (OH)
Kettering Coll of Medical Arts (OH)
Keystone Coll (PA)
Kishwaukee Coll (IL)
Labette Comm Coll (KS)
Labouré Coll (MA)
Lakeland Comm Coll (OH)
Lake Michigan Coll (MI)
Lakeshore Tech Coll (WI)
Lakewood Comm Coll (MN)
Lansing Comm Coll (MI)
Laramie County Comm Coll (WY)
Laredo Comm Coll (TX)
Las Positas Coll (CA)
Lima Tech Coll (OH)
Lincoln Land Comm Coll (IL)
Long Beach City Coll (CA)
Lorain County Comm Coll (OH)
Los Angeles City Coll (CA)
Louisiana State U at Eunice (LA)
Lutheran Coll of Health Professions (IN)
Madison Area Tech Coll (WI)
Manatee Comm Coll (FL)
Marion Tech Coll (OH)
Marshalltown Comm Coll (IA)

Massachusetts Bay Comm Coll (MA)
Massasoit Comm Coll (MA)
McLennan Comm Coll (TX)
Medical Inst of Minnesota (MN)
Merced Coll (CA)
Mercer County Comm Coll (NJ)
Meridian Comm Coll (MS)
Merritt Coll (CA)
Metropolitan Comm Coll (NE)
Miami-Dade Comm Coll (FL)
Miami University–Middletown Cmps (OH)
Middlesex Comm Coll (MA)
Middlesex Community–Tech Coll (CT)
Middlesex County Coll (NJ)
Midland Coll (TX)
Midlands Tech Coll (SC)
Mid Michigan Comm Coll (MI)
Mid-Plains Comm Coll (NE)
Milwaukee Area Tech Coll (WI)
Mineral Area Coll (MO)
Mississippi Delta Comm Coll (MS)
Mississippi Gulf Coast Comm Coll (MS)
Modesto Jr Coll (CA)
Mohawk Valley Comm Coll (NY)
Monroe Comm Coll (NY)
Montcalm Comm Coll (MI)
Montgomery College–Takoma Park Cmps (MD)
Moraine Valley Comm Coll (IL)
Mt San Antonio Coll (CA)
Muskingum Area Tech Coll (OH)
Nassau Comm Coll (NY)
Naugatuck Valley Community–Tech Coll (CT)
New Hampshire Tech Inst (NH)
New Mexico State University–Carlsbad (NM)
New York City Tech Coll of the City U of NY (NY)
Niagara County Comm Coll (NY)
Normandale Comm Coll (MN)
Northampton County Area Comm Coll (PA)
North Arkansas Comm/Tech Coll (AR)
North Central Tech Coll (OH)
Northcentral Tech Coll (WI)
North Country Comm Coll (NY)
Northeast Iowa Comm Coll, Peosta Cmps (IA)
Northeast Mississippi Comm Coll (MS)
Northern Essex Comm Coll (MA)
Northern Virginia Comm Coll (VA)
North Shore Comm Coll (MA)
NorthWest Arkansas Comm Coll (AR)
Northwest Coll (WY)
Oakland Comm Coll (MI)
Odessa Coll (TX)
Orangeburg-Calhoun Tech Coll (SC)
Orange Coast Coll (CA)
Orange County Comm Coll (NY)
Our Lady of the Lake Coll (LA)
Owensboro Comm Coll (KY)
Owens Comm Coll, Findlay (OH)
Owens Comm Coll, Toledo (OH)
Palm Beach Comm Coll (FL)
Parkland Coll (IL)
Pasadena City Coll (CA)
Passaic County Comm Coll (NJ)
Pennsylvania Coll of Tech (PA)
Penn Valley Comm Coll (MO)
Pensacola Jr Coll (FL)
Phillips County Comm Coll (AR)
Piedmont Tech Coll (SC)
Pima Comm Coll (AZ)
Pima Medical Inst (CO)
Pima Medical Inst (NM)
Pitt Comm Coll (NC)

Associate Degree Programs at Two-Year Colleges
Radiological Technology–Recreation and Leisure Services

Polk Comm Coll (FL)
Portland Comm Coll (OR)
Prince George's Comm Coll (MD)
Pueblo Comm Coll (CO)
Quinsigamond Comm Coll (MA)
Reading Area Comm Coll (PA)
Roane State Comm Coll (TN)
Rochester Comm Coll (MN)
Rose State Coll (OK)
Rowan-Cabarrus Comm Coll (NC)
St Louis Comm Coll at Forest Park (MO)
St Petersburg Jr Coll (FL)
St Philip's Coll (TX)
St Vincent's Coll (CT)
Salt Lake Comm Coll (UT)
Sandhills Comm Coll (NC)
San Diego Mesa Coll (CA)
San Jacinto College–Central Cmps (TX)
San Joaquin Delta Coll (CA)
Santa Barbara City Coll (CA)
Santa Fe Comm Coll (FL)
Santa Rosa Jr Coll (CA)
Sauk Valley Comm Coll (IL)
Scott Comm Coll (IA)
Shelby State Comm Coll (TN)
Sinclair Comm Coll (OH)
South Arkansas Comm Coll (AR)
Southeast Comm Coll, Lincoln Cmps (NE)
Southeastern Comm Coll, North Cmps, West Burlington (IA)
Southern Maine Tech Coll (ME)
Southern U at Shreveport–Bossier City Cmps (LA)
Southern West Virginia Comm and Tech Coll (WV)
South Plains Coll (TX)
South Suburban Coll (IL)
Southwestern Comm Coll (NC)
Southwestern Oklahoma State U at Sayre (OK)
Southwest Virginia Comm Coll (VA)
Spartanburg Tech Coll (SC)
Springfield Tech Comm Coll (MA)
Tacoma Comm Coll (WA)
Tarrant County Jr Coll (TX)
Texas Southmost Coll (TX)
Trident Tech Coll (SC)
Triton Coll (IL)
Trocaire Coll (NY)
Truckee Meadows Comm Coll (NV)
Tulsa Jr Coll (OK)
Tyler Jr Coll (TX)
Union County Coll (NJ)
U of Cincinnati Raymond Walters Coll (OH)
U of Hawaii–Kapiolani Comm Coll (HI)
U of Kentucky, Hazard Comm Coll (KY)
U of Kentucky, Lexington Comm Coll (KY)
U of Kentucky, Madisonville Comm Coll (KY)
U of Kentucky, Paducah Comm Coll (KY)
Utah Valley State Coll (UT)
Valencia Comm Coll (FL)
Vance-Granville Comm Coll (NC)
Virginia Highlands Comm Coll (VA)
Virginia Western Comm Coll (VA)
Volunteer State Comm Coll (TN)
Wake Tech Comm Coll (NC)
Wallace State Comm Coll (AL)
Walters State Comm Coll (TN)
Washtenaw Comm Coll (MI)
Waycross Coll (GA)
Wenatchee Valley Coll (WA)
Westark Comm Coll (AR)
Westchester Comm Coll (NY)
Western Nebraska Comm Coll, Scottsbluff (NE)
Western Wisconsin Tech Coll (WI)
Western Wyoming Comm Coll (WY)
West Virginia Northern Comm Coll (WV)
Wharton County Jr Coll (TX)
Willmar Comm Coll (MN)
Wor-Wic Comm Coll (MD)
Yakima Valley Comm Coll (WA)
York Tech Coll (SC)
Yuba Coll (CA)

RANGE MANAGEMENT
Central Texas Coll (TX)
Colby Comm Coll (KS)
Dixie Coll (UT)
Eastern Oklahoma State Coll (OK)
Lamar Comm Coll (CO)
Modesto Jr Coll (CA)
North Dakota State University–Bottineau (ND)
Northeastern Oklahoma A&M Coll (OK)
Northeast Texas Comm Coll (TX)
Northwest Coll (WY)
Ricks Coll (ID)
St Catharine Coll (KY)
Snow Coll (UT)
Treasure Valley Comm Coll (OR)
Trinity Valley Comm Coll (TX)
Vermilion Comm Coll (MN)

READING EDUCATION
Allen County Comm Coll (KS)
Bay Mills Comm Coll (MI)
East Mississippi Comm Coll (MS)
Laney Coll (CA)
Merritt Coll (CA)

REAL ESTATE
Alamance Comm Coll (NC)
Allan Hancock Coll (CA)
American River Coll (CA)
Angelina Coll (TX)
Anne Arundel Comm Coll (MD)
Antelope Valley Coll (CA)
Austin Comm Coll (TX)
Bakersfield Coll (CA)
Barstow Coll (CA)
Belleville Area Coll (IL)
Bellevue Comm Coll (WA)
Bergen Comm Coll (NJ)
Black Hawk Coll, Moline (IL)
Blinn Coll (TX)
Borough of Manhattan Comm Coll of City U of NY (NY)
Brazosport Coll (TX)
Brevard Comm Coll (FL)
Brunswick Comm Coll (NC)
Bucks County Comm Coll (PA)
Butler County Comm Coll (KS)
Butte Coll (CA)
Cabrillo Coll (CA)
Camden County Coll (NJ)
Carl Sandburg Coll (IL)
Casco Bay Coll (ME)
Catawba Valley Comm Coll (NC)
Catonsville Comm Coll (MD)
Central Piedmont Comm Coll (NC)
Central Texas Coll (TX)
Cerritos Coll (CA)
Chabot Coll (CA)
Chaffey Coll (CA)
Chattahoochee Valley State Comm Coll (AL)
Chemeketa Comm Coll (OR)
Chippewa Valley Tech Coll (WI)
Cincinnati State Tech and Comm Coll (OH)
Cisco Jr Coll (TX)
Citrus Coll (CA)
City Coll of San Francisco (CA)
Clark Coll (WA)
Clovis Comm Coll (NM)
Coll of DuPage (IL)
Coll of Marin (CA)
Coll of San Mateo (CA)
Coll of Southern Idaho (ID)
Coll of the Canyons (CA)
Coll of the Desert (CA)
Coll of the Mainland (TX)
Coll of the Redwoods (CA)
Coll of the Sequoias (CA)
Coll of the Siskiyous (CA)
Collin County Comm Coll (TX)
Columbia Basin Coll (WA)
Columbia-Greene Comm Coll (NY)
Columbus State Comm Coll (OH)
Comm Coll of Allegheny County Allegheny Cmps (PA)
Comm Coll of Allegheny County Boyce Cmps (PA)
Comm Coll of Allegheny County North Cmps (PA)
Comm Coll of Allegheny County South Cmps (PA)
Comm Coll of Philadelphia (PA)
Comm Coll of Rhode Island (RI)
Comm Coll of Southern Nevada (NV)
Contra Costa Coll (CA)
Cosumnes River Coll (CA)
Cuesta Coll (CA)
Cuyahoga Comm Coll, Eastern Cmps (OH)
Cuyahoga Comm Coll, Metropolitan Cmps (OH)
Cuyahoga Comm Coll, Western Cmps (OH)
Cuyamaca Coll (CA)
Danville Area Comm Coll (IL)
De Anza Coll (CA)
Del Mar Coll (TX)
Delta Coll (MI)
Dodge City Comm Coll (KS)
Dundalk Comm Coll (MD)
Durham Tech Comm Coll (NC)
East Los Angeles Coll (CA)
East Mississippi Comm Coll (MS)
Edgecombe Comm Coll (NC)
Edison State Comm Coll (OH)
El Camino Coll (CA)
Elgin Comm Coll (IL)
El Paso Comm Coll (TX)
Enterprise State Jr Coll (AL)
Evergreen Valley Coll (CA)
Fayetteville Tech Comm Coll (NC)
Florida Comm Coll at Jacksonville (FL)
Foothill Coll (CA)
Forsyth Tech Comm Coll (NC)
Fresno City Coll (CA)
Fullerton Coll (CA)
Glendale Comm Coll (AZ)
Golden West Coll (CA)
Grayson County Coll (TX)
Green River Comm Coll (WA)
Gulf Coast Comm Coll (FL)
Harrisburg Area Comm Coll (PA)
Hartnell Coll (CA)
Haywood Comm Coll (NC)
Henry Ford Comm Coll (MI)
Hill Coll of the Hill Jr Coll District (TX)
Hinds Comm Coll (MS)
Houston Comm Coll System (TX)
Hudson Valley Comm Coll (NY)
Illinois Central Coll (IL)
Independence Comm Coll (KS)
Iowa Lakes Comm Coll (IA)
Isothermal Comm Coll (NC)
Itasca Comm Coll (MN)
Jackson State Comm Coll (TN)
Jefferson Comm Coll (OH)
Jefferson State Comm Coll (AL)
John C Calhoun State Comm Coll (AL)
Joliet Jr Coll (IL)
J Sargeant Reynolds Comm Coll (VA)
Kankakee Comm Coll (IL)
Kent State U, Ashtabula Cmps (OH)
Kent State U, Trumbull Cmps (OH)
Kingwood Coll (TX)
Kishwaukee Coll (IL)
Lake Tahoe Comm Coll (CA)
Lamar University–Orange (TX)
Lane Comm Coll (OR)
Lansing Comm Coll (MI)
Laredo Comm Coll (TX)
Las Positas Coll (CA)
Lehigh Carbon Comm Coll (PA)
Lincoln Land Comm Coll (IL)
Long Beach City Coll (CA)
Lorain County Comm Coll (OH)
Los Angeles City Coll (CA)
Los Angeles Harbor Coll (CA)
Los Angeles Mission Coll (CA)
Los Angeles Pierce Coll (CA)
Los Angeles Southwest Coll (CA)
Los Angeles Trade-Tech Coll (CA)
Los Angeles Valley Coll (CA)
Los Medanos Coll (CA)
Lower Columbia Coll (WA)
Luzerne County Comm Coll (PA)
Madison Area Tech Coll (WI)
Manchester Comm-Tech Coll (CT)
Massachusetts Bay Comm Coll (MA)
Mayland Comm Coll (NC)
McHenry County Coll (IL)
McLennan Comm Coll (TX)
Mendocino Coll (CA)
Merced Coll (CA)
Merritt Coll (CA)
Mesa Comm Coll (AZ)
Metropolitan Comm Coll (NE)
Miami University–Hamilton Cmps (OH)
Miami University–Middletown Cmps (OH)
Mid-Plains Comm Coll (NE)
Milwaukee Area Tech Coll (WI)
MiraCosta Coll (CA)
Mission Coll (CA)
Modesto Jr Coll (CA)
Monterey Peninsula Coll (CA)
Montgomery Coll (TX)
Montgomery College–Takoma Park Cmps (MD)
Montgomery County Comm Coll (PA)
Moorpark Coll (CA)
Moraine Valley Comm Coll (IL)
Morton Coll (IL)
Motlow State Comm Coll (TN)
Mt San Antonio Coll (CA)
Mt San Jacinto Coll (CA)
Napa Valley Coll (CA)
Navarro Coll (TX)
New Hampshire Tech Coll, Laconia (NH)
New Mexico Jr Coll (NM)
New Mexico State University–Alamogordo (NM)
Nicolet Area Tech Coll (WI)
North Central Texas Coll (TX)
North Dakota State Coll of Science (ND)
Northeast Alabama State Comm Coll (AL)
Northeast Comm Coll (NE)
Northeastern Oklahoma A&M Coll (OK)
Northeast Texas Comm Coll (TX)
Northern Essex Comm Coll (MA)
Northern Virginia Comm Coll (VA)
North Harris Coll (TX)
North Lake Coll (TX)
North Seattle Comm Coll (WA)
Northwest Mississippi Comm Coll (MS)
Northwest State Comm Coll (OH)
Oakton Comm Coll (IL)
Ocean County Coll (NJ)
Ohlone Coll (CA)
Okaloosa-Walton Comm Coll (FL)
Oklahoma City Comm Coll (OK)
Olympic Coll (WA)
Orangeburg-Calhoun Tech Coll (SC)
Orange County Comm Coll (NY)
Oxnard Coll (CA)
Palomar Coll (CA)
Paris Jr Coll (TX)
Parkland Coll (IL)
Pasadena City Coll (CA)
Peninsula Coll (WA)
Pima Comm Coll (AZ)
Polk Comm Coll (FL)
Porterville Coll (CA)
Portland Comm Coll (OR)
Prairie State Coll (IL)
Rainy River Comm Coll (MN)
Rancho Santiago Coll (CA)
Raritan Valley Comm Coll (NJ)
Red Rocks Comm Coll (CO)
Richland Coll (TX)
Riverside Comm Coll (CA)
Rockland Comm Coll (NY)
Sacramento City Coll (CA)
Saddleback Coll (CA)
St Cloud Tech Coll (MN)
St Louis Comm Coll at Florissant Valley (MO)
St Louis Comm Coll at Meramec (MO)
St Petersburg Jr Coll (FL)
San Antonio Coll (TX)
San Bernardino Valley Coll (CA)
San Diego City Coll (CA)
San Diego Mesa Coll (CA)
San Diego Miramar Coll (CA)
San Jacinto College–Central Cmps (TX)
San Jacinto College–North Cmps (TX)
San Jacinto College–South Cmps (TX)
San Jose City Coll (CA)
San Juan Coll (NM)
Santa Barbara City Coll (CA)
Santa Fe Comm Coll (NM)
Santa Monica Coll (CA)
Scottsdale Comm Coll (AZ)
Shasta Coll (CA)
Sierra Coll (CA)
Sinclair Comm Coll (OH)
Southeastern Illinois Coll (IL)
Southern Ohio Coll, Cincinnati Cmps (OH)
Southern State Comm Coll (OH)
South Plains Coll (TX)
South Suburban Coll (IL)
Southwestern Coll (CA)
Southwestern Coll of Business, Cincinnati (OH)
Spokane Falls Comm Coll (WA)
State U of NY Coll of Tech at Canton (NY)
Suffolk County Comm College–Ammerman Cmps (NY)
Suffolk County Comm Coll–Eastern Cmps (NY)
Suffolk County Comm Coll–Western Cmps (NY)
Surry Comm Coll (NC)
Terra State Comm Coll (OH)
Texarkana Coll (TX)
Tidewater Comm Coll (VA)
Trinity Valley Comm Coll (TX)
Triton Coll (IL)
Truckee Meadows Comm Coll (NV)
Tulsa Jr Coll (OK)
Tyler Jr Coll (TX)
U of Cincinnati Raymond Walters Coll (OH)
U of Kentucky, Ashland Comm Coll (KY)
U of Kentucky, Elizabethtown Comm Coll (KY)
U of Kentucky, Jefferson Comm Coll (KY)
U of Kentucky, Lexington Comm Coll (KY)
U of Kentucky, Madisonville Comm Coll (KY)
U of Kentucky, Paducah Comm Coll (KY)
U of Kentucky, Prestonsburg Comm Coll (KY)
U of New Mexico–Valencia Cmps (NM)
Utica Sch of Commerce (NY)
Valencia Comm Coll (FL)
Ventura Coll (CA)
Victoria Coll (TX)
Victor Valley Coll (CA)
Vincennes U (IN)
Wake Tech Comm Coll (NC)
Wallace State Comm Coll (AL)
Waubonsee Comm Coll (IL)
Waukesha County Tech Coll (WI)
Westchester Comm Coll (NY)
Western Nebraska Comm Coll, Scottsbluff (NE)
Western Nevada Comm Coll (NV)
West Los Angeles Coll (CA)
Westmoreland County Comm Coll (PA)
Whatcom Comm Coll (WA)
William Rainey Harper Coll (IL)
Willmar Comm Coll (MN)
Wytheville Comm Coll (VA)
Yuba Coll (CA)

RECREATIONAL FACILITIES MANAGEMENT
Abraham Baldwin Ag Coll (GA)
Brevard Coll (NC)
Brunswick Comm Coll (NC)
Catawba Valley Comm Coll (NC)
Coll of the Desert (CA)
Colorado Mountn Coll, Alpine Cmps (CO)
Colorado Mountn Coll, Timberline Cmps (CO)
Cuesta Coll (CA)
Dean Coll (MA)
Mohawk Valley Comm Coll (NY)
North Country Comm Coll (NY)
Potomac State Coll of West Virginia U (WV)
State U of NY Coll of A&T at Cobleskill (NY)
State U of NY Coll of A&T at Morrisville (NY)
State U of NY Coll of Tech at Delhi (NY)
Sullivan County Comm Coll (NY)

RECREATION AND LEISURE SERVICES
Allan Hancock Coll (CA)
Allegany Comm Coll (MD)
American River Coll (CA)
Atlanta Metropolitan Coll (GA)
Bee County Coll (TX)
Bellevue Comm Coll (WA)
Bergen Comm Coll (NJ)
Borough of Manhattan Comm Coll of City U of NY (NY)
Brevard Coll (NC)
Brookdale Comm Coll (NJ)
Brunswick Coll (GA)
Cabrillo Coll (CA)
Camden County Coll (NJ)
Cape Cod Comm Coll (MA)
Catonsville Comm Coll (MD)
Central Coll (KS)
Central Comm College–Platte Cmps (NE)
Centralia Coll (WA)
Cerritos Coll (CA)
Chabot Coll (CA)
Charles Stewart Mott Comm Coll (MI)
Chesapeake Coll (MD)
City Coll of San Francisco (CA)
City Colls of Chicago, Harold Washington Coll (IL)
City Colls of Chicago, Kennedy-King Coll (IL)
Coll of the Desert (CA)
Colorado Mountn Coll, Timberline Cmps (CO)
Comm Coll of Southern Nevada (NV)
Comm Coll of the Air Force (AL)
Cowley County Comm Coll and Voc-Tech Sch (KS)
Crowder Coll (MO)
Cypress Coll (CA)
Dean Coll (MA)
De Anza Coll (CA)
Del Mar Coll (TX)

Associate Degree Programs at Two-Year Colleges
Recreation and Leisure Services–Retail Management

Des Moines Area Comm Coll (IA)
Dutchess Comm Coll (NY)
East Central Coll (MO)
East Georgia Coll (GA)
Enterprise State Jr Coll (AL)
Erie Comm Coll, City Cmps (NY)
Erie Comm Coll, South Cmps (NY)
Fayetteville Tech Comm Coll (NC)
Feather River Comm Coll District (CA)
Florida Keys Comm Coll (FL)
Frederick Comm Coll (MD)
Fresno City Coll (CA)
Fullerton Coll (CA)
Garrett Comm Coll (MD)
Glendale Comm Coll (AZ)
Gordon Coll (GA)
Greenfield Comm Coll (MA)
Hartnell Coll (CA)
Hudson Valley Comm Coll (NY)
Hutchinson Comm Coll and Area Vocational Sch (KS)
Iowa Lakes Comm Coll (IA)
Jefferson Davis Comm Coll (AL)
Jefferson State Comm Coll (AL)
John C Calhoun State Comm Coll (AL)
J Sargeant Reynolds Comm Coll (VA)
Kansas City Kansas Comm Coll (KS)
Kingsborough Comm Coll of City U of NY (NY)
Kirkwood Comm Coll (IA)
Lake Land Coll (IL)
Lawson State Comm Coll (AL)
Little Hoop Comm Coll (ND)
Los Medanos Coll (CA)
Luzerne County Comm Coll (PA)
Madison Area Tech Coll (WI)
Merritt Coll (CA)
Miami-Dade Comm Coll (FL)
Middlesex County Coll (NJ)
Mitchell Coll (CT)
Modesto Jr Coll (CA)
Mohawk Valley Comm Coll (NY)
Monroe Comm Coll (NY)
Montgomery College–Rockville Cmps (MD)
Moorpark Coll (CA)
Moraine Valley Comm Coll (IL)
Mount Ida Coll (MA)
Mt San Antonio Coll (CA)
Muskegon Comm Coll (MI)
Muskingum Area Tech Coll (OH)
New Mexico Jr Coll (NM)
North Country Comm Coll (NY)
Northeast Mississippi Comm Coll (MS)
Northern Essex Comm Coll (MA)
Northern Virginia Comm Coll (VA)
Northwest Coll (WY)
Northwestern Connecticut Comm-Tech Coll (CT)
Norwalk Comm-Tech Coll (CT)
Onondaga Comm Coll (NY)
Orange County Comm Coll (NY)
Palomar Coll (CA)
Pasadena City Coll (CA)
Polk Comm Coll (FL)
Rancho Santiago Coll (CA)
Ricks Coll (ID)
San Bernardino Valley Coll (CA)
San Diego City Coll (CA)
San Diego Mesa Coll (CA)
Santa Barbara City Coll (CA)
Santa Monica Coll (CA)
Skagit Valley Coll (WA)
Skyline Coll (CA)
Southeastern Comm Coll (NC)
South Georgia Coll (GA)
Southwestern Comm Coll (NC)
State U of NY Coll of Tech at Delhi (NY)
Suffolk County Comm College–Ammerman Cmps (NY)
Sussex County Comm Coll (NJ)
Taft Coll (CA)
Tompkins Cortland Comm Coll (NY)
Tyler Jr Coll (TX)
Ulster County Comm Coll (NY)
U of Hawaii–Leeward Comm Coll (HI)
Vance-Granville Comm Coll (NC)
Ventura Coll (CA)
Vermilion Comm Coll (MN)
Vincennes U (IN)
Walla Walla Comm Coll (WA)
Wenatchee Valley Coll (WA)
Young Harris Coll (GA)
Waldorf Coll (IA)
Wallace State Comm Coll (AL)
Young Harris Coll (GA)

RESPIRATORY THERAPY
Alabama Southern Comm Coll, Monroeville (AL)
Albuquerque Tech Vocational Inst (NM)
Allegany Comm Coll (MD)
Alvin Comm Coll (TX)
American River Coll (CA)
Andrew Coll (GA)
Angelina Coll (TX)
Apollo College–Phoenix, Inc (AZ)
Athens Area Tech Inst (GA)
ATI Health Education Ctr (FL)
Atlantic Comm Coll (NJ)
Augusta Tech Inst (GA)
Baltimore City Comm Coll (MD)
Barton County Comm Coll (KS)
Belleville Area Coll (IL)
Bergen Comm Coll (NJ)
Berkshire Comm Coll (MA)
Bevill State Comm Coll (AL)
Bishop State Comm Coll (AL)
Black Hawk Coll, Moline (IL)
Borough of Manhattan Comm Coll of City U of NY (NY)
Bossier Parish Comm Coll (LA)
Bowling Green State University–Firelands Coll (OH)
Brookdale Comm Coll (NJ)
Broward Comm Coll (FL)
Brunswick Coll (GA)
Butte Coll (CA)
Camden County Coll (NJ)
Carteret Comm Coll (NC)
Central Florida Comm Coll (FL)
Central Piedmont Comm Coll (NC)
Champlain Coll (VT)
Charles Stewart Mott Comm Coll (MI)
Chattanooga State Tech Comm Coll (TN)
Cincinnati State Tech and Comm Coll (OH)
City Coll of San Francisco (CA)
City Colls of Chicago, Malcolm X Coll (IL)
Coll of DuPage (IL)
Coll of St Catherine–Minneapolis (MN)
Coll of the Desert (CA)
Collin County Comm Coll (TX)
Columbia State Comm Coll (TN)
Columbus State Comm Coll (OH)
Comm Coll of Allegheny County Allegheny Cmps (PA)
Comm Coll of Philadelphia (PA)
Comm Coll of Rhode Island (RI)
Comm Coll of Southern Nevada (NV)
Comm Hospital Roanoke Valley–Coll of Health Scis (VA)
Copiah-Lincoln Comm College–Natchez Cmps (MS)
County Coll of Morris (NJ)
Crafton Hills Coll (CA)
Cuyahoga Comm Coll, Western Cmps (OH)
Dalton Coll (GA)
Danville Area Comm Coll (IL)
Darton Coll (GA)
Daytona Beach Comm Coll (FL)
Delaware County Comm Coll (PA)
Delaware Tech & Comm Coll, Stanton/Wilmington Cmps (DE)
Delgado Comm Coll (LA)
Del Mar Coll (TX)
Delta Coll (MI)
Des Moines Area Comm Coll (IA)
Dixie Coll (UT)
Dodge City Comm Coll (KS)
Doña Ana Branch Comm Coll (NM)
Durham Tech Comm Coll (NC)
East Central Coll (MO)
East Los Angeles Coll (CA)
Edgecombe Comm Coll (NC)
Edison Comm Coll (FL)
El Camino Coll (CA)
El Centro Coll (TX)
El Paso Comm Coll (TX)
Erie Comm Coll, North Cmps (NY)
Essex Comm Coll (MD)
Fayetteville Tech Comm Coll (NC)
Flagler Career Inst (FL)
Florence-Darlington Tech Coll (SC)
Florida Comm Coll at Jacksonville (FL)
Floyd Coll (GA)
Foothill Coll (CA)
Forsyth Tech Comm Coll (NC)
Frederick Comm Coll (MD)
Fresno City Coll (CA)
Front Range Comm Coll (CO)
Gadsden State Comm Coll (AL)
Gateway Comm Coll (AZ)
Genesee Comm Coll (NY)
George Corley Wallace State Comm Coll, Selma (AL)
George C Wallace State Comm Coll, Dothan (AL)
Gloucester County Coll (NJ)
Greenville Tech Coll (SC)
Grossmont Coll (CA)
Gulf Coast Comm Coll (FL)
Gwinnett Tech Inst (GA)
Harrisburg Area Comm Coll (PA)
Hawkeye Comm Coll (IA)
Henry Ford Comm Coll (MI)
Hibbing Comm Coll (MN)
Highland Comm Coll (KS)
Highline Comm Coll (WA)
Hinds Comm Coll (MS)
Holmes Comm Coll (MS)
Houston Comm Coll System (TX)
Howard Coll (TX)
Hudson Valley Comm Coll (NY)
Illinois Central Coll (IL)
Indian River Comm Coll (FL)
Itawamba Comm Coll (MS)
Ivy Tech State Coll–Central Indiana (IN)
Ivy Tech State Coll–Lafayette (IN)
Ivy Tech State Coll–Northeast (IN)
Ivy Tech State Coll–Northwest (IN)
Jackson State Comm Coll (TN)
Jefferson Comm Coll (OH)
John C Calhoun State Comm Coll (AL)
Johnson County Comm Coll (KS)
J Sargeant Reynolds Comm Coll (VA)
Kalamazoo Valley Comm Coll (MI)
Kansas City Kansas Comm Coll (KS)
Kaskaskia Coll (IL)
Kennebec Valley Tech Coll (ME)
Kettering Coll of Medical Arts (OH)
Kirkwood Comm Coll (IA)
Labette Comm Coll (KS)
Lakeland Comm Coll (OH)
Lane Comm Coll (OR)
Lansing Comm Coll (MI)
Lehigh Carbon Comm Coll (PA)
Lima Tech Coll (OH)
Lincoln Land Comm Coll (IL)
Long Beach City Coll (CA)
Los Angeles Valley Coll (CA)
Louisiana State U at Eunice (LA)
Luzerne County Comm Coll (PA)
Macomb Comm Coll (MI)
Macon Coll (GA)
Madison Area Tech Coll (WI)
Manatee Comm Coll (FL)
Manchester Comm-Tech Coll (CT)
Massachusetts Bay Comm Coll (MA)
Massasoit Comm Coll (MA)
McLennan Comm Coll (TX)
Mercer County Comm Coll (NJ)
Meridian Comm Coll (MS)
Metropolitan Comm Coll (NE)
Miami-Dade Comm Coll (FL)
Middle Georgia Coll (GA)
Midland Coll (TX)
Midlands Tech Coll (SC)
Mid-Plains Comm Coll (NE)
Mid-State Tech Coll (WI)
Milwaukee Area Tech Coll (WI)
MiraCosta Coll (CA)
Mississippi Gulf Coast Comm Coll (MS)
Modesto Jr Coll (CA)
Mohawk Valley Comm Coll (NY)
Monroe County Comm Coll (MI)
Montana State U Coll of Tech-Great Falls (MT)
Moraine Valley Comm Coll (IL)
Mountain Empire Comm Coll (VA)
Mt Hood Comm Coll (OR)
Mt San Antonio Coll (CA)
Napa Valley Coll (CA)
Nassau Comm Coll (NY)
Newbury Coll (MA)
New Hampshire Tech Coll, Claremont (NH)
North Central Tech Coll (OH)
Northeast Iowa Comm Coll, Peosta Cmps (IA)
Northeast Mississippi Comm Coll (MS)
Northern Essex Comm Coll (MA)
Northern Virginia Comm Coll (VA)
North Harris Coll (TX)
North Shore Comm Coll (MA)
NorthWest Arkansas Comm Coll (AR)
Northwest Mississippi Comm Coll (MS)
Norwalk Comm-Tech Coll (CT)
Oakland Comm Coll (MI)
Odessa Coll (TX)
Ohlone Coll (CA)
Onondaga Comm Coll (NY)
Orangeburg-Calhoun Tech Coll (SC)
Orange Coast Coll (CA)
Ozarks Tech Comm Coll (MO)
Parkland Coll (IL)
Passaic County Comm Coll (NJ)
Pearl River Comm Coll (MS)
Penn Valley Comm Coll (MO)
Pensacola Jr Coll (FL)
Piedmont Tech Coll (SC)
Pima Comm Coll (AZ)
Pima Medical Inst (CO)
Pitt Comm Coll (NC)
Prince George's Comm Coll (MD)
Pueblo Comm Coll (CO)
Quinsigamond Comm Coll (MA)
Raritan Valley Comm Coll (NJ)
Reading Area Comm Coll (PA)
Red River Tech Coll (AR)
Roane State Comm Coll (TN)
Rochester Comm Coll (MN)
Rockland Comm Coll (NY)
Rock Valley Coll (IL)
Rogue Comm Coll (OR)
Rose State Coll (OK)
Saint Augustine Coll (IL)
St Cloud Tech Coll (MN)
St Louis Comm Coll at Forest Park (MO)
St Paul Tech Coll (MN)
St Petersburg Jr Coll (FL)
St Philip's Coll (TX)
Sandhills Comm Coll (NC)
San Jacinto College–Central Cmps (TX)
Santa Fe Comm Coll (FL)
Santa Monica Coll (CA)
Scott Comm Coll (IA)
Seattle Central Comm Coll (WA)
Seminole Comm Coll (FL)
Seward County Comm Coll (KS)
Shelton State Comm Coll (AL)
Sheridan Coll (WY)
Sinclair Comm Coll (OH)
Southeast Comm Coll, Lincoln Cmps (NE)
Southern Maine Tech Coll (ME)
Southern U at Shreveport-Bossier City Cmps (LA)
South Plains Coll (TX)
Southside Virginia Comm Coll (VA)
Southwestern Comm Coll (NC)
Southwest Virginia Comm Coll (VA)
Spartanburg Tech Coll (SC)
Spokane Comm Coll (WA)
Springfield Tech Comm Coll (MA)
Stanly Comm Coll (NC)
Stark Tech Coll (OH)
Sussex County Comm Coll (NJ)
Tacoma Comm Coll (WA)
Tallahassee Comm Coll (FL)
Tarrant County Jr Coll (TX)
Temple Coll (TX)
Texas Southmost Coll (TX)
Trident Tech Coll (SC)
Triton Coll (IL)
Tulsa Jr Coll (OK)
Tyler Jr Coll (TX)
Union County Coll (NJ)
U of Hawaii–Kapiolani Comm Coll (HI)
U of Kentucky, Jefferson Comm Coll (KY)
U of Kentucky, Lexington Comm Coll (KY)
U of Kentucky, Madisonville Comm Coll (KY)
Valencia Comm Coll (FL)
Ventura Coll (CA)
Victoria Coll (TX)
Victor Valley Coll (CA)
Vincennes U (IN)
Volunteer State Comm Coll (TN)
Wallace State Comm Coll (AL)
Walla Walla Comm Coll (WA)
Warren County Comm Coll (NJ)
Washtenaw Comm Coll (MI)
Waycross Coll (GA)
Westark Comm Coll (AR)
Westchester Comm Coll (NY)
Western Wisconsin Tech Coll (WI)
Western Wyoming Comm Coll (WY)
West Virginia Northern Comm Coll (WV)

RETAIL MANAGEMENT
Alexandria Tech Coll (MN)
Allen County Comm Coll (KS)
American Inst of Business (IA)
American Inst of Commerce (IA)
American River Coll (CA)
Anne Arundel Comm Coll (MD)
Arapahoe Comm Coll (CO)
Art Inst of Pittsburgh (PA)
Atlantic Comm Coll (NJ)
Austin Comm Coll (TX)
Bay State Coll (MA)
Bergen Comm Coll (NJ)
Berkeley Coll (NJ)
Berkeley Coll, New York (NY)
Berkeley Coll, White Plains (NY)
Bessemer State Tech Coll (AL)
Bismarck State Coll (ND)
Black Hawk Coll, Moline (IL)
Borough of Manhattan Comm Coll of City U of NY (NY)
Bowling Green State University–Firelands Coll (OH)
Briarwood Coll (CT)
Bristol Comm Coll (MA)

REHABILITATION THERAPY
Edmonds Comm Coll (WA)
Iowa Lakes Comm Coll (IA)
Middlesex County Coll (NJ)
Vermont Tech Coll (VT)
William Rainey Harper Coll (IL)

RELIGIOUS EDUCATION
Brevard Comm Coll (NC)
Lon Morris Coll (TX)
Northeast Mississippi Comm Coll (MS)
Waldorf Coll (IA)

RELIGIOUS STUDIES
Andrew Coll (GA)
Brevard Coll (NC)
Central Coll (KS)
Chaffey Coll (CA)
Clackamas Comm Coll (OR)
Cowley County Comm Coll and Voc-Tech Sch (KS)
Crafton Hills Coll (CA)
East Central Coll (MO)
Fullerton Coll (CA)
Lon Morris Coll (TX)
Mater Dei Coll (NY)
Northern Virginia Comm Coll (VA)
Ohio Valley Coll (WV)
Orange Coast Coll (CA)
Palm Beach Comm Coll (FL)
Pasadena City Coll (CA)
Pensacola Jr Coll (FL)
Queen of the Holy Rosary Coll (CA)
St Hyacinth Coll and Sem (MA)
San Bernardino Valley Coll (CA)
San Joaquin Delta Coll (CA)
State Comm Coll of East St Louis (IL)
Trinity Valley Comm Coll (TX)

122   Peterson's Guide to Two-Year Colleges 1997

Associate Degree Programs at Two-Year Colleges
Retail Management–Science

Brookhaven Coll (TX)
Bucks County Comm Coll (PA)
Bunker Hill Comm Coll (MA)
Butler County Comm Coll (KS)
Butler County Comm Coll (PA)
Cabrillo Coll (CA)
Cañada Coll (CA)
Cape Cod Comm Coll (MA)
Casper Coll (WY)
Cayuga County Comm Coll (NY)
Central City Business Inst (NY)
Centralia Coll (WA)
Central Pennsylvania Business Sch (PA)
Central Piedmont Comm Coll (NC)
Central Texas Coll (TX)
Central Virginia Comm Coll (VA)
Central Wyoming Coll (WY)
Chabot Coll (CA)
Champlain Coll (VT)
Chattanooga State Tech Comm Coll (TN)
Cisco Jr Coll (TX)
City Colls of Chicago, Harold Washington Coll (IL)
Clark Coll (WA)
Clinton Comm Coll (NY)
Coffeyville Comm Coll (KS)
Coll of Lake County (IL)
Coll of Marin (CA)
Coll of San Mateo (CA)
Coll of Southern Idaho (ID)
Colorado Mountn Coll, Alpine Cmps (CO)
Columbus State Comm Coll (OH)
Comm Coll of Allegheny County Allegheny Cmps (PA)
Comm Coll of Allegheny County Boyce Cmps (PA)
Comm Coll of Allegheny County North Cmps (PA)
Comm Coll of Allegheny County South Cmps (PA)
Comm Coll of Philadelphia (PA)
Comm Coll of Rhode Island (RI)
Comm Coll of Southern Nevada (NV)
County Coll of Morris (NJ)
Cowley County Comm Coll and Voc-Tech Sch (KS)
Dean Coll (MA)
DeKalb Coll (GA)
Delaware County Comm Coll (PA)
Delaware Tech & Comm Coll, Jack F Owens Cmps (DE)
Del Mar Coll (TX)
Delta Coll (MI)
Des Moines Area Comm Coll (IA)
Doña Ana Branch Comm Coll (NM)
Dutchess Comm Coll (NY)
Eastern Arizona Coll (AZ)
Edison State Comm Coll (OH)
Edmonds Comm Coll (WA)
Elgin Comm Coll (IL)
Ellsworth Comm Coll (IA)
Enterprise State Jr Coll (AL)
Erie Comm Coll, City Cmps (NY)
Everett Comm Coll (WA)
Fashion Inst of Design & Merchandising, LA Cmps (CA)
Fashion Inst of Design & Merchandising, SD Cmps (CA)
Fashion Inst of Design & Merchandising, SF Cmps (CA)
Finger Lakes Comm Coll (NY)
Florida Comm Coll at Jacksonville (FL)
Fort Scott Comm Coll (KS)
Fox Valley Tech Coll (WI)
Garden City Comm Coll (KS)
Gateway Comm-Tech Coll (CT)
Genesee Comm Coll (NY)
Glendale Comm Coll (AZ)
Gloucester County Coll (NJ)
Golden West Coll (CA)
Green River Comm Coll (WA)
Grossmont Coll (CA)
Harcum Coll (PA)
Harford Comm Coll (MD)
Harrisburg Area Comm Coll (PA)
Heald Business Coll (HI)
Hesser Coll (NH)
Hocking Coll (OH)
Holyoke Comm Coll (MA)
Howard Comm Coll (MD)
Hutchinson Comm Coll and Area Vocational Sch (KS)
Indian River Comm Coll (FL)
Iowa Lakes Comm Coll (IA)
Iowa Western Comm Coll (IA)
Jefferson Coll (MO)
Jefferson Comm Coll (NY)
Jefferson Comm Coll (OH)
Jefferson State Comm Coll (AL)
John A Logan Coll (IL)
John C Calhoun State Comm Coll (AL)
Kankakee Comm Coll (IL)
Kingsborough Comm Coll of City U of NY (NY)
Kirkwood Comm Coll (IA)
Lake Land Coll (IL)
Lansing Comm Coll (MI)
Laramie County Comm Coll (WY)
LDS Business Coll (UT)
Lenoir Comm Coll (NC)
Lima Tech Coll (OH)
Lincoln Land Comm Coll (IL)
Long Beach City Coll (CA)
Lorain County Comm Coll (OH)
Los Angeles City Coll (CA)
Los Angeles Valley Coll (CA)
MacCormac Jr Coll (IL)
Massachusetts Bay Comm Coll (MA)
Merced Coll (CA)
Middlesex Comm Coll (MA)
Middlesex County Coll (NJ)
Midland Coll (TX)
Mid-State Tech Coll (WI)
Miles Comm Coll (MT)
Milwaukee Area Tech Coll (WI)
Modesto Jr Coll (CA)
Mohawk Valley Comm Coll (NY)
Monroe Comm Coll (NY)
Montgomery College–Germantown Cmps (MD)
Moraine Valley Comm Coll (IL)
Mount Ida Coll (MA)
Nassau Comm Coll (NY)
Navarro Coll (TX)
Newbury Coll (MA)
Newport Business Inst (PA)
Niagara County Comm Coll (NY)
North Country Comm Coll (NY)
North Dakota State University–Bottineau (ND)
North Hennepin Comm Coll (MN)
North Iowa Area Comm Coll (IA)
Northland Comm and Tech Coll (MN)
Northwest Coll (WY)
Northwest Iowa Comm Coll (IA)
Oakland Comm Coll (MI)
Ocean County Coll (NJ)
Orange County Comm Coll (NY)
Parkland Coll (IL)
Parks Jr Coll (CO)
Passaic County Comm Coll (NJ)
Pennsylvania Coll of Tech (PA)
Quincy Coll (MA)
Quinsigamond Comm Coll (MA)
Rancho Santiago Coll (CA)
Raritan Valley Comm Coll (NJ)
Reading Area Comm Coll (PA)
Rock Valley Coll (IL)
Roxbury Comm Coll (MA)
Saddleback Coll (CA)
St Cloud Tech Coll (MN)
Salem Comm Coll (NJ)
Salt Lake Comm Coll (UT)
Shasta Coll (CA)
Shoreline Comm Coll (WA)
Sinclair Comm Coll (OH)
Skagit Valley Coll (WA)
Southeast Comm Coll, Lincoln Cmps (NE)
South Plains Coll (TX)
South Suburban Coll (IL)
Southwestern Comm Coll (IA)
Spartanburg Methodist Coll (SC)
Spencer Sch of Business (NE)
Spokane Falls Comm Coll (WA)
State Fair Comm Coll (MO)
State U of NY Coll of Tech at Alfred (NY)
State U of NY Coll of Tech at Canton (NY)
Suffolk County Comm College–Ammerman Cmps (NY)
Suffolk County Comm Coll–Eastern Cmps (NY)
Suffolk County Comm Coll–Western Cmps (NY)
Sullivan County Comm Coll (NY)
Surry Comm Coll (NC)
Sussex County Comm Coll (NJ)
Tarrant County Jr Coll (TX)
Texarkana Coll (TX)
Texas Southmost Coll (TX)
Three Rivers Comm-Tech Coll (CT)
Triton Coll (IL)
Tulsa Jr Coll (OK)
Ulster County Comm Coll (NY)
U of Hawaii–Leeward Comm Coll (HI)
U of Kentucky, Madisonville Comm Coll (KY)
U of Kentucky, Maysville Comm Coll (KY)
U of Kentucky, Paducah Comm Coll (KY)
Utah Valley State Coll (UT)
Walla Walla Comm Coll (WA)
Westchester Comm Coll (NY)
Western Oklahoma State Coll (OK)
Western Wisconsin Tech Coll (WI)
West Los Angeles Coll (CA)
Westmoreland County Comm Coll (PA)
West Shore Comm Coll (MI)
Willmar Comm Coll (MN)
Wright State U, Lake Cmps (OH)

ROBOTICS
Alexandria Tech Coll (MN)
Allen County Comm Coll (KS)
Black Hawk Coll, Moline (IL)
Brookdale Comm Coll (NJ)
Camden County Coll (NJ)
Catawba Valley Comm Coll (NC)
Cecil Comm Coll (MD)
Central Oregon Comm Coll (OR)
Central Texas Coll (TX)
Charles Stewart Mott Comm Coll (MI)
Chattanooga State Tech Comm Coll (TN)
Comm Coll of Allegheny County South Cmps (PA)
Comm Coll of Beaver County (PA)
Cumberland County Coll (NJ)
Delaware County Comm Coll (PA)
Des Moines Area Comm Coll (IA)
Dutchess Comm Coll (NY)
Erie Comm Coll, City Cmps (NY)
Henry Ford Comm Coll (MI)
Hill Coll of the Hill Jr Coll District (TX)
Hutchinson Comm Coll and Area Vocational Sch (KS)
Illinois Central Coll (IL)
Indian Hills Comm Coll (IA)
Ivy Tech State Coll–Central Indiana (IN)
Ivy Tech State Coll–Columbus (IN)
Ivy Tech State Coll–Eastcentral (IN)
Ivy Tech State Coll–Kokomo (IN)
Ivy Tech State Coll–Lafayette (IN)
Ivy Tech State Coll–Northcentral (IN)
Ivy Tech State Coll–Northeast (IN)
Ivy Tech State Coll–Northwest (IN)
Ivy Tech State Coll–Southcentral (IN)
Ivy Tech State Coll–Southeast (IN)
Ivy Tech State Coll–Southwest (IN)
Ivy Tech State Coll–Wabash Valley (IN)
Ivy Tech State Coll–Whitewater (IN)
Jackson Comm Coll (MI)
Jefferson Coll (MO)
Kansas City Kansas Comm Coll (KS)
Kellogg Comm Coll (MI)
Kirkwood Comm Coll (IA)
Lansing Comm Coll (MI)
Lima Tech Coll (OH)
Lorain County Comm Coll (OH)
Louisville Tech Inst (KY)
Luzerne County Comm Coll (PA)
Macomb Comm Coll (MI)
Middlesex County Coll (NJ)
Mountain View Coll (TX)
Nashville State Tech Inst (TN)
New Hampshire Tech Coll, Nashua (NH)
Northeast Mississippi Comm Coll (MS)
North Iowa Area Comm Coll (IA)
Northwest Iowa Comm Coll (IA)
Oakland Comm Coll (MI)
Oklahoma State U, Okmulgee (OK)
Owens Comm Coll, Findlay (OH)
Owens Comm Coll, Toledo (OH)
Pennsylvania Coll of Tech (PA)
Phillips Jr Coll, Condie Cmps (CA)
Piedmont Tech Coll (SC)
Raritan Valley Comm Coll (NJ)
Richland Coll (TX)
Saint Charles County Comm Coll (MO)
St Clair County Comm Coll (MI)
St Louis Comm Coll at Forest Park (MO)
San Diego City Coll (CA)
Schoolcraft Coll (MI)
Scott Comm Coll (IA)
Sinclair Comm Coll (OH)
Skagit Valley Coll (WA)
Southeastern Comm Coll, North Cmps, West Burlington (IA)
Southern Arkansas U Tech (AR)
Southern State Comm Coll (OH)
South Seattle Comm Coll (WA)
South Suburban Coll (IL)
Southwestern Tech Coll (MN)
Spokane Comm Coll (WA)
Springfield Tech Comm Coll (MA)
Texas State Tech Coll (TX)
Tulsa Jr Coll (OK)
Union County Coll (NJ)
Vincennes U (IN)
Wake Tech Comm Coll (NC)
Washtenaw Comm Coll (MI)
Waubonsee Comm Coll (IL)
Western Nevada Comm Coll (NV)
Westmoreland County Comm Coll (PA)

ROMANCE LANGUAGES
Coll of the Desert (CA)
Highline Comm Coll (WA)
Lon Morris Coll (TX)
Middlesex County Coll (NJ)
Tacoma Comm Coll (WA)

RUSSIAN
Austin Comm Coll (TX)
Comm Coll of Allegheny County Allegheny Cmps (PA)
Dixie Coll (UT)
El Camino Coll (CA)
Everett Comm Coll (WA)
Glendale Comm Coll (AZ)
Modesto Jr Coll (CA)
Ricks Coll (ID)
San Diego Mesa Coll (CA)
Tacoma Comm Coll (WA)
Tulsa Jr Coll (OK)

SACRED MUSIC
Brevard Coll (NC)
Northern Virginia Comm Coll (VA)

SAFETY AND SECURITY TECHNOLOGIES
Columbus State Comm Coll (OH)
Comm Coll of the Air Force (AL)
Cuyahoga Comm Coll, Western Cmps (OH)
Hudson County Comm Coll (NJ)
Hudson Valley Comm Coll (NY)
Interboro Inst (NY)
Ivy Tech State Coll–Northwest (IN)
Lakeland Comm Coll (OH)
Macomb Comm Coll (MI)
Moraine Valley Comm Coll (IL)
Mt Hood Comm Coll (OR)
Oakland Comm Coll (MI)
San Jacinto College–Central Cmps (TX)
Schoolcraft Coll (MI)
Truckee Meadows Comm Coll (NV)

SANITATION TECHNOLOGY
Bay de Noc Comm Coll (MI)
Bevill State Comm Coll (AL)
Kirkwood Comm Coll (IA)
Palomar Coll (CA)
Red Rocks Comm Coll (CO)

SCIENCE
Abraham Baldwin Ag Coll (GA)
Adirondack Comm Coll (NY)
Aiken Tech Coll (SC)
Alabama Southern Comm Coll, Monroeville (AL)
Allen County Comm Coll (KS)
American River Coll (CA)
Andrew Coll (GA)
Angelina Coll (TX)
Anne Arundel Comm Coll (MD)
Antelope Valley Coll (CA)
Arapahoe Comm Coll (CO)
Arizona Western Coll (AZ)
Atlantic Comm Coll (NJ)
Baltimore City Comm Coll (MD)
Barstow Coll (CA)
Bee County Coll (TX)
Bevill State Comm Coll (AL)
Blinn Coll (TX)
Borough of Manhattan Comm Coll of City U of NY (NY)
Bowling Green State University–Firelands Coll (OH)
Brazosport Coll (TX)
Brevard Coll (NC)
Brevard Comm Coll (FL)
Brookdale Comm Coll (NJ)
Brunswick Coll (GA)
Burlington County Coll (NJ)
Cabrillo Coll (CA)
Caldwell Comm Coll and Tech Inst (NC)
Cañada Coll (CA)
Cape Cod Comm Coll (MA)
Casper Coll (WY)
Catonsville Comm Coll (MD)
Central Coll (KS)
Centralia Coll (WA)
Central Oregon Comm Coll (OR)
Central Texas Coll (TX)
Central Virginia Comm Coll (VA)
Cerro Coso Comm Coll (CA)
Chabot Coll (CA)
Chemeketa Comm Coll (OR)
Chesapeake Coll (MD)
Chipola Jr Coll (FL)
Cincinnati State Tech and Comm Coll (OH)
City Colls of Chicago, Wilbur Wright Coll (IL)
Clackamas Comm Coll (OR)
Clark Coll (WA)
Cleveland Comm Coll (NC)
Clinton Comm Coll (IA)
Clinton Comm Coll (NY)
Cloud County Comm Coll (KS)
Coastal Carolina Comm Coll (NC)
Coconino County Comm Coll (AZ)
Coffeyville Comm Coll (KS)
Colby Comm Coll (KS)
Coll of Alameda (CA)
Coll of DuPage (IL)
Coll of Lake County (IL)
Coll of The Albemarle (NC)
Coll of the Canyons (CA)
Coll of the Mainland (TX)
Coll of the Sequoias (CA)
Collin County Comm Coll (TX)
Colorado Mountn Coll, Alpine Cmps (CO)
Colorado Mountn Coll, Roaring Fork Cmps-Spring Valley Ctr (CO)
Colorado Mountn Coll, Timberline Cmps (CO)
Colorado Northwestern Comm Coll (CO)
Columbia-Greene Comm Coll (NY)
Comm Coll of Allegheny County Allegheny Cmps (PA)
Comm Coll of Allegheny County South Cmps (PA)
Comm Coll of Aurora (CO)
Comm Coll of Philadelphia (PA)
Comm Coll of Rhode Island (RI)
Comm Coll of Southern Nevada (NV)
Comm Hospital Roanoke Valley–Coll of Health Scis (VA)
Copiah-Lincoln Comm Coll (MS)
Corning Comm Coll (NY)
Cosumnes River Coll (CA)
Cottey Coll (MO)
County Coll of Morris (NJ)
Crafton Hills Coll (CA)
Craven Comm Coll (NC)
Cumberland County Coll (NJ)
Cypress Coll (CA)
Dabney S Lancaster Comm Coll (VA)
Dalton Coll (GA)
Danville Area Comm Coll (IL)
Danville Comm Coll (VA)
Davidson County Comm Coll (NC)
Daytona Beach Comm Coll (FL)
Dean Coll (MA)
DeKalb Coll (GA)
Delgado Comm Coll (LA)
Dixie Coll (UT)
Dodge City Comm Coll (KS)
Donnelly Coll (KS)
Dutchess Comm Coll (NY)
East Central Comm Coll (MS)
Eastern Shore Comm Coll (VA)
Eastern Wyoming Coll (WY)
East Mississippi Comm Coll (MS)
Edgecombe Comm Coll (NC)
Elaine P Nunez Comm Coll (LA)
Elgin Comm Coll (IL)
Ellsworth Comm Coll (IA)
Enterprise State Jr Coll (AL)

Peterson's Guide to Two-Year Colleges 1997
123

Erie Comm Coll, City Cmps (NY)
Erie Comm Coll, North Cmps (NY)
Erie Comm Coll, South Cmps (NY)
Fergus Falls Comm Coll (MN)
Finger Lakes Comm Coll (NY)
Fiorello H LaGuardia Comm Coll of City U of NY (NY)
Floyd Coll (GA)
Foothill Coll (CA)
Fort Berthold Comm Coll (ND)
Frank Phillips Coll (TX)
Fresno City Coll (CA)
Front Range Comm Coll (CO)
Fulton-Montgomery Comm Coll (NY)
Gadsden State Comm Coll (AL)
Gainesville Coll (GA)
Galveston Coll (TX)
Garden City Comm Coll (KS)
Gavilan Coll (CA)
Georgia Military Coll (GA)
Germanna Comm Coll (VA)
Glen Oaks Comm Coll (MI)
Golden West Coll (CA)
Gordon Coll (GA)
Grand Rapids Comm Coll (MI)
Grays Harbor Coll (WA)
Great Basin Coll (NV)
Greenfield Comm Coll (MA)
Greenville Tech Coll (SC)
Guilford Tech Comm Coll (NC)
Harford Comm Coll (MD)
Herkimer County Comm Coll (NY)
Highland Comm Coll (IL)
Highline Comm Coll (WA)
Hill Coll of the Hill Jr Coll District (TX)
Houston Comm Coll System (TX)
Howard Comm Coll (MD)
Illinois Central Coll (IL)
Illinois Eastern Comm Colls, Frontier Comm Coll (IL)
Illinois Eastern Comm Colls, Lincoln Trail Coll (IL)
Imperial Valley Coll (CA)
Independence Comm Coll (KS)
Iowa Central Comm Coll (IA)
Iowa Lakes Comm Coll (IA)
Irvine Valley Coll (CA)
Isothermal Comm Coll (NC)
Itawamba Comm Coll (MS)
Jackson State Comm Coll (TN)
Jacksonville Coll (TX)
James Sprunt Comm Coll (NC)
Jamestown Comm Coll (NY)
Jefferson Coll (MO)
Jefferson Comm Coll (NY)
Jefferson Davis Comm Coll (AL)
John Wood Comm Coll (IL)
Jones County Jr Coll (MS)
J Sargeant Reynolds Comm Coll (VA)
Kalamazoo Valley Comm Coll (MI)
Kellogg Comm Coll (MI)
Kent State U, Stark Cmps (OH)
Kirkwood Comm Coll (IA)
Kirtland Comm Coll (MI)
Lakeland Comm Coll (OH)
Lake Tahoe Comm Coll (CA)
Lamar Comm Coll (CO)
Lamar University–Port Arthur (TX)
Laney Coll (CA)
Lansing Comm Coll (MI)
Lassen Coll (CA)
Lee Coll (TX)
Lehigh Carbon Comm Coll (PA)
Lewis and Clark Comm Coll (IL)
Lincoln Land Comm Coll (IL)
Little Big Horn Coll (MT)
Long Beach City Coll (CA)
Longview Comm Coll (MO)
Lorain County Comm Coll (OH)
Lord Fairfax Comm Coll (VA)
Los Angeles City Coll (CA)
Louisburg Coll (NC)
Louisiana State U at Alexandria (LA)
Luzerne County Comm Coll (PA)
Manor Jr Coll (PA)
Maple Woods Comm Coll (MO)
Marion Military Inst (AL)
Marshalltown Comm Coll (IA)
Massasoit Comm Coll (MA)
McHenry County Coll (IL)
Merced Coll (CA)
Merritt Coll (CA)
Miami University–Middletown Cmps (OH)
Middle Georgia Coll (GA)
Middlesex Community– Tech Coll (CT)
Middlesex County Coll (NJ)
Midland Coll (TX)
Mid Michigan Comm Coll (MI)
Mid-Plains Comm Coll (NE)
Mineral Area Coll (MO)
Mississippi Gulf Coast Comm Coll (MS)
Mitchell Coll (CT)
Mitchell Comm Coll (NC)
Moberly Area Comm Coll (MO)
Mohawk Valley Comm Coll (NY)
Monroe Comm Coll (NY)
Montgomery Comm Coll (NC)
Moraine Valley Comm Coll (IL)
Morgan Comm Coll (CO)
Morton Coll (IL)
Mountain Empire Comm Coll (VA)
Mount Ida Coll (MA)
Mt San Jacinto Coll (CA)
Murray State Coll (OK)
Napa Valley Coll (CA)
Nassau Comm Coll (NY)
Naugatuck Valley Community–Tech Coll (CT)
Navarro Coll (TX)
Neosho County Comm Coll (KS)
New Mexico Jr Coll (NM)
New Mexico Military Inst (NM)
New River Comm Coll (VA)
Niagara County Comm Coll (NY)
North Central Texas Coll (TX)
North Country Comm Coll (NY)
North Dakota State Coll of Science (ND)
North Dakota State University–Bottineau (ND)
Northeast Alabama State Comm Coll (AL)
Northeastern Jr Coll (CO)
Northeast Mississippi Comm Coll (MS)
Northern Essex Comm Coll (MA)
Northern Oklahoma Coll (OK)
Northern Virginia Comm Coll (VA)
North Harris Coll (TX)
North Idaho Coll (ID)
North Seattle Comm Coll (WA)
Northwest Coll (WY)
Northwest Mississippi Comm Coll (MS)
Oakland Comm Coll (MI)
Oakton Comm Coll (IL)
Ohio University–Southern Cmps (OH)
Okaloosa-Walton Comm Coll (FL)
Oklahoma City Comm Coll (OK)
Olympic Coll (WA)
Onondaga Comm Coll (NY)
Orangeburg-Calhoun Tech Coll (SC)
Orange County Comm Coll (NY)
Otero Jr Coll (CO)
Paris Jr Coll (TX)
Pasadena City Coll (CA)
Passaic County Comm Coll (NJ)
Patrick Henry Comm Coll (VA)
Paul Smith's Coll (NY)
Penn Valley Comm Coll (MO)
Pensacola Jr Coll (FL)
Phillips County Comm Coll (AR)
Piedmont Tech Coll (SC)
Piedmont Virginia Comm Coll (VA)
Pikes Peak Comm Coll (CO)
Porterville Coll (CA)
Portland Comm Coll (OR)
Potomac State Coll of West Virginia U (WV)
Pratt Comm Coll and Area Voc Sch (KS)
Pueblo Comm Coll (CO)
Quincy Coll (MA)
Rainy River Comm Coll (MN)
Rancho Santiago Coll (CA)
Rappahannock Comm Coll (VA)
Raritan Valley Comm Coll (NJ)
Redlands Comm Coll (OK)
Red Rocks Comm Coll (CO)
Richard Bland Coll of the Coll of William and Mary (VA)
Richland Comm Coll (IL)
Riverside Comm Coll (CA)
Rockingham Comm Coll (NC)
Rockland Comm Coll (NY)
Rogue Comm Coll (OR)
Rowan-Cabarrus Comm Coll (NC)
Sacramento City Coll (CA)
Sage Jr Coll of Albany (NY)
St Catharine Coll (KY)
St Clair County Comm Coll (MI)
St Louis Comm Coll at Meramec (MO)
Salem Comm Coll (NJ)
San Antonio Coll (TX)
Sandhills Comm Coll (NC)
San Jacinto College–Central Cmps (TX)
San Jacinto College–South Cmps (TX)
Santa Fe Comm Coll (NM)
Santa Rosa Jr Coll (CA)
Schenectady County Comm Coll (NY)
Schoolcraft Coll (MI)
Scott Comm Coll (IA)
Seattle Central Comm Coll (WA)
Seward County Comm Coll (KS)
Shawnee Comm Coll (IL)
Sheridan Coll (WY)
Shoreline Comm Coll (WA)
Shorter Coll (AR)
Skagit Valley Coll (WA)
Skyline Coll (CA)
Solano Comm Coll (CA)
Southeast Comm Coll, Beatrice Cmps (NE)
Southeast Comm Coll, Lincoln Cmps (NE)
Southeastern Comm Coll (NC)
South Georgia Coll (GA)
South Plains Coll (TX)
South Seattle Comm Coll (WA)
Southside Virginia Comm Coll (VA)
Southwestern Coll (CA)
Southwestern Comm Coll (IA)
Southwestern Michigan Coll (MI)
Southwest Mississippi Comm Coll (MS)
Southwest Texas Jr Coll (TX)
Southwest Virginia Comm Coll (VA)
Spartanburg Methodist Coll (SC)
Spoon River Coll (IL)
Springfield Coll in Illinois (IL)
State Comm Coll of East St Louis (IL)
State U of NY Coll of A&T at Cobleskill (NY)
State U of NY Coll of Tech at Alfred (NY)
State U of NY Coll of Tech at Canton (NY)
Suffolk County Comm College–Ammerman Cmps (NY)
Sullivan County Comm Coll (NY)
Tacoma Comm Coll (WA)
Thomas Nelson Comm Coll (VA)
Tidewater Comm Coll (VA)
Tompkins Cortland Comm Coll (NY)
Treasure Valley Comm Coll (OR)
Trident Tech Coll (SC)
Trinidad State Jr Coll (CO)
Triton Coll (IL)
Turtle Mountain Comm Coll (ND)
UAB Walker Coll (AL)
Ulster County Comm Coll (NY)
Umpqua Comm Coll (OR)
The U of Akron–Wayne Coll (OH)
U of Kentucky, Elizabethtown Comm Coll (KY)
U of Kentucky, Hazard Comm Coll (KY)
U of Kentucky, Hopkinsville Comm Coll (KY)
U of New Mexico–Gallup Branch (NM)
U of New Mexico–Los Alamos Branch (NM)
U of South Carolina at Beaufort (SC)
U of South Carolina at Lancaster (SC)
U of South Carolina at Sumter (SC)
U of South Carolina at Union (SC)
U of South Carolina Salkehatchie Regional Cmps (SC)
U of Wisconsin Center–Barron County (WI)
U of Wisconsin Center–Marathon County (WI)
U of Wisconsin Center–Richland (WI)
Valley Forge Military Coll (PA)
Vermilion Comm Coll (MN)
Vernon Regional Jr Coll (TX)
Victor Valley Coll (CA)
Virginia Highlands Comm Coll (VA)
Virginia Western Comm Coll (VA)
Wake Tech Comm Coll (NC)
Waldorf Coll (IA)
Washington State Comm Coll (OH)
Waubonsee Comm Coll (IL)
Wayne Comm Coll (NC)
Weatherford Coll (TX)
Westchester Comm Coll (NY)
Western Wyoming Comm Coll (WY)
West Shore Comm Coll (MI)
Wilkes Comm Coll (NC)
William Rainey Harper Coll (IL)
Williamsburg Tech Coll (SC)
Willmar Comm Coll (MN)
Wytheville Comm Coll (VA)
York Tech Coll (SC)
Young Harris Coll (GA)
Yuba Coll (CA)

SCIENCE EDUCATION

Angelina Coll (TX)
Brevard Coll (NC)
Brevard Comm Coll (FL)
Central Coll (KS)
Central Comm College–Platte Cmps (NE)
Colby Comm Coll (KS)
Comm Coll of Allegheny County South Cmps (PA)
Comm Coll of Southern Nevada (NV)
Dutchess Comm Coll (NY)
East Central Comm Coll (MS)
Eastern Arizona Coll (AZ)
Eastern Oklahoma State Coll (OK)
Fayetteville Tech Comm Coll (NC)
Gulf Coast Comm Coll (FL)
Harrisburg Area Comm Coll (PA)
Holmes Comm Coll (MS)
Hutchinson Comm Coll and Area Vocational Sch (KS)
Independence Comm Coll (KS)
Iowa Central Comm Coll (IA)
Iowa Lakes Comm Coll (IA)
Itawamba Comm Coll (MS)
Jones County Jr Coll (MS)
Miami-Dade Comm Coll (FL)
Middle Georgia Coll (GA)
Mississippi Delta Comm Coll (MS)
Northeast Mississippi Comm Coll (MS)
Northwest Coll (WY)
Ranger Coll (TX)
Sandhills Comm Coll (NC)
Snow Coll (UT)
South Georgia Coll (GA)
Vermilion Comm Coll (MN)
Vincennes U (IN)

SCULPTURE

Brevard Coll (NC)
Grossmont Coll (CA)
Inst of American Indian Arts (NM)
Mercer County Comm Coll (NJ)
Monterey Peninsula Coll (CA)
Polk Comm Coll (FL)
St Gregory's Coll (OK)

SECRETARIAL STUDIES/ OFFICE MANAGEMENT

Abraham Baldwin Ag Coll (GA)
Acad of Business Coll (AZ)
Adirondack Comm Coll (NY)
Aiken Tech Coll (SC)
Aims Comm Coll (CO)
Alabama Southern Comm Coll, Monroeville (AL)
Alabama Southern Comm Coll, Thomasville (AL)
Albuquerque Tech Vocational Inst (NM)
Alexandria Tech Coll (MN)
Allan Hancock Coll (CA)
Allegany Comm Coll (MD)
Allen County Comm Coll (KS)
Allentown Business Sch (PA)
Alpena Comm Coll (MI)
Alvin Comm Coll (TX)
American Inst of Business (IA)
American Inst of Commerce (IA)
American River Coll (CA)
Ancilla Coll (IN)
Andover Coll (ME)
Angelina Coll (TX)
Anne Arundel Comm Coll (MD)
Anoka-Ramsey Comm Coll (MN)
Anson Comm Coll (NC)
Antelope Valley Coll (CA)
Aquinas Coll at Milton (MA)
Aquinas Coll at Newton (MA)
Arapahoe Comm Coll (CO)
Arizona Western Coll (AZ)
Asheville-Buncombe Tech Comm Coll (NC)
Asnuntuck Comm-Tech Coll (CT)
Athens Area Tech Inst (GA)
Atlanta Metropolitan Coll (GA)
Atlantic Comm Coll (NJ)
Augusta Tech Inst (GA)
Austin Comm Coll (TX)
Bacone Coll (OK)
Bainbridge Coll (GA)
Baker Coll of Jackson (MI)
Bakersfield Coll (CA)
Baltimore City Comm Coll (MD)
Barstow Coll (CA)
Barton County Comm Coll (KS)
Bay Mills Comm Coll (MI)
Bay State Coll (MA)
Beal Coll (ME)
Beaufort County Comm Coll (NC)
Bee County Coll (TX)
Belleville Area Coll (IL)
Bellevue Comm Coll (WA)
Belmont Tech Coll (OH)
Berean Inst (PA)
Bergen Comm Coll (NJ)
Berkeley Coll (NJ)
Berkeley Coll, New York (NY)
Berkeley Coll, White Plains (NY)
Berkshire Comm Coll (MA)
Bessemer State Tech Coll (AL)
Bevill State Comm Coll (AL)
Big Bend Comm Coll (WA)
Bishop State Comm Coll (AL)
Bismarck State Coll (ND)
Blackfeet Comm Coll (MT)
Black Hawk Coll, Kewanee (IL)
Black Hawk Coll, Moline (IL)
Blackhawk Tech Coll (WI)
Bladen Comm Coll (NC)
Blair Jr Coll (CO)
Blinn Coll (TX)
Blue Mountain Comm Coll (OR)
Blue Ridge Comm Coll (NC)
Blue Ridge Comm Coll (VA)
Borough of Manhattan Comm Coll of City U of NY (NY)
Bossier Parish Comm Coll (LA)
Bowling Green State University–Firelands Coll (OH)
Bradford Sch (OH)
Bramson ORT Tech Inst (NY)
Brazosport Coll (TX)
Brevard Comm Coll (FL)
Briarcliffe–The Coll for Business & Tech (NY)
Briarwood Coll (CT)
Bristol Comm Coll (MA)
Bronx Comm Coll of City U of NY (NY)
Brookdale Comm Coll (NJ)
Brookhaven Coll (TX)
Broome Comm Coll (NY)
Broward Comm Coll (FL)
The Brown Mackie Coll (KS)
Brunswick Coll (GA)
Brunswick Comm Coll (NC)
Bryant and Stratton Business Inst, Albany (NY)
Bryant and Stratton Business Inst, Buffalo (NY)
Bryant and Stratton Business Inst, Cicero (NY)
Bryant and Stratton Business Inst, Lackawanna (NY)
Bryant and Stratton Business Inst, Rochester (NY)
Bryant and Stratton Business Inst, Rochester (NY)
Bryant and Stratton Business Inst, Syracuse (NY)
Bryant and Stratton Business Inst, E Hills Cmps, Williamsville (NY)
Bryant and Stratton Coll, Parma (OH)
Bryant and Stratton Coll, Richmond Heights (OH)
Bucks County Comm Coll (PA)
Bunker Hill Comm Coll (MA)
Burlington County Coll (NJ)
Butler County Comm Coll (KS)
Butler County Comm Coll (PA)
Butte Coll (CA)
Caldwell Comm Coll and Tech Inst (NC)
Cambria-Rowe Business Coll (PA)
Camden County Coll (NJ)
Cañada Coll (CA)
Cape Cod Comm Coll (MA)
Cape Fear Comm Coll (NC)
Capital Comm Tech Coll (CT)
Carl Albert State Coll (OK)
Carl Sandburg Coll (IL)
Carteret Comm Coll (NC)
Casco Bay Coll (ME)
Casper Coll (WY)
Castle Coll (NH)
Catawba Valley Comm Coll (NC)
Catonsville Comm Coll (MD)
Cayuga County Comm Coll (NY)
Cecil Comm Coll (MD)
Cecils Jr Coll of Business (NC)
Central Alabama Comm Coll (AL)
Central Carolina Comm Coll (NC)
Central Carolina Tech Coll (SC)
Central City Business Inst (NY)
Central Coll (KS)
Central Comm College–Grand Island Cmps (NE)
Central Comm College–Hastings Cmps (NE)

Associate Degree Programs at Two-Year Colleges
Secretarial Studies/Office Management

Central Comm College–Platte Cmps (NE)
Central Florida Comm Coll (FL)
Central Lakes Coll (MN)
Central Maine Tech Coll (ME)
Central Ohio Tech Coll (OH)
Central Oregon Comm Coll (OR)
Central Pennsylvania Business Sch (PA)
Central Piedmont Comm Coll (NC)
Central Texas Coll (TX)
Central Virginia Comm Coll (VA)
Central Wyoming Coll (WY)
Cerritos Coll (CA)
Chabot Coll (CA)
Chaffey Coll (CA)
Champlain Coll (VT)
Chaparral Career Coll (AZ)
Charles Stewart Mott Comm Coll (MI)
Chattahoochee Valley State Comm Coll (AL)
Chattanooga State Tech Comm Coll (TN)
Chemeketa Comm Coll (OR)
Chesapeake Coll (MD)
Chesterfield-Marlboro Tech Coll (SC)
Chippewa Valley Tech Coll (WI)
Churchman Business Sch (PA)
Cincinnati State Tech and Comm Coll (OH)
Citrus Coll (CA)
City Colls of Chicago, Kennedy-King Coll (IL)
City Colls of Chicago, Malcolm X Coll (IL)
City Colls of Chicago, Olive-Harvey Coll (IL)
City Colls of Chicago, Richard J Daley Coll (IL)
City Colls of Chicago, Wilbur Wright Coll (IL)
Clackamas Comm Coll (OR)
Clark Coll (WA)
Clark State Comm Coll (OH)
Clatsop Comm Coll (OR)
Cleveland Comm Coll (NC)
Cleveland State Comm Coll (TN)
Clinton Comm Coll (IA)
Clinton Comm Coll (NY)
Cloud County Comm Coll (KS)
Clovis Comm Coll (NM)
Coahoma Comm Coll (MS)
Coastal Carolina Comm Coll (NC)
Cochise Coll, Douglas (AZ)
Cochise Coll, Sierra Vista (AZ)
Coffeyville Comm Coll (KS)
Colby Comm Coll (KS)
Coll of Alameda (CA)
Coll of DuPage (IL)
Coll of Eastern Utah (UT)
Coll of Lake County (IL)
Coll of Marin (CA)
Coll of San Mateo (CA)
Coll of Southern Idaho (ID)
Coll of The Albemarle (NC)
Coll of the Canyons (CA)
Coll of the Desert (CA)
Coll of the Redwoods (CA)
Coll of the Sequoias (CA)
Coll of the Siskiyous (CA)
Collin County Comm Coll (TX)
Colorado Northwestern Comm Coll (CO)
Columbia Basin Coll (WA)
Columbia Coll (CA)
Columbia-Greene Comm Coll (NY)
Columbia Jr Coll of Business (SC)
Columbia State Comm Coll (TN)
Columbus State Comm Coll (OH)
Columbus Tech Inst (GA)
Commonwealth Business Coll, LaPorte (IN)
Commonwealth Business Coll, Merrillville (IN)
Comm Coll of Allegheny County Allegheny Cmps (PA)
Comm Coll of Allegheny County Boyce Cmps (PA)
Comm Coll of Allegheny County North Cmps (PA)
Comm Coll of Allegheny County South Cmps (PA)
Comm Coll of Aurora (CO)
Comm Coll of Beaver County (PA)
Comm Coll of Denver (CO)
Comm Coll of Philadelphia (PA)
Comm Coll of Rhode Island (RI)
Comm Coll of Southern Nevada (NV)
Comm Coll of the Air Force (AL)
Comm Coll of Vermont (VT)
Connors State Coll (OK)
Contra Costa Coll (CA)
Copiah-Lincoln Comm College–Natchez Cmps (MS)
Corning Comm Coll (NY)
County Coll of Morris (NJ)
Cowley County Comm Coll and Voc-Tech Sch (KS)
Crafton Hills Coll (CA)
Craven Comm Coll (NC)
Crowder Coll (MO)
Cuesta Coll (CA)
Cumberland County Coll (NJ)
Cumberland Sch of Tech (LA)
Cumberland Sch of Tech (TN)
Cuyahoga Comm Coll, Eastern Cmps (OH)
Cuyahoga Comm Coll, Metropolitan Cmps (OH)
Cuyahoga Comm Coll, Western Cmps (OH)
Cypress Coll (CA)
Dabney S Lancaster Comm Coll (VA)
Dalton Coll (GA)
Danville Comm Coll (VA)
Darton Coll (GA)
Davidson County Comm Coll (NC)
Davis Coll (OH)
Dawson Comm Coll (MT)
Daytona Beach Comm Coll (FL)
De Anza Coll (CA)
Delaware County Comm Coll (PA)
Delaware Tech & Comm Coll, Jack F Owens Cmps (DE)
Delaware Tech & Comm Coll, Stanton/Wilmington Cmps (DE)
Delaware Tech & Comm Coll, Terry Cmps (DE)
Delgado Comm Coll (LA)
Del Mar Coll (TX)
Delta Coll (MI)
Denmark Tech Coll (SC)
Des Moines Area Comm Coll (IA)
Dixie Coll (UT)
Dodge City Comm Coll (KS)
Doña Ana Branch Comm Coll (NM)
Douglas MacArthur State Tech Coll (AL)
Draughons Jr Coll, Nashville (TN)
DuBois Business Coll (PA)
Duff's Business Inst (PA)
Dull Knife Memorial Coll (MT)
Dundalk Comm Coll (MD)
Durham Tech Comm Coll (NC)
Dutchess Comm Coll (NY)
East Central Coll (MO)
Eastern Arizona Coll (AZ)
Eastern Idaho Tech Coll (ID)
Eastern Maine Tech Coll (ME)
Eastern New Mexico University–Roswell (NM)
Eastern Oklahoma State Coll (OK)
Eastern Shore Comm Coll (VA)
Eastern Wyoming Coll (WY)
Eastfield Coll (TX)
East Los Angeles Coll (CA)
East Mississippi Comm Coll (MS)
Edgecombe Comm Coll (NC)
Edison State Comm Coll (OH)
Edmonds Comm Coll (WA)
Elaine P Nunez Comm Coll (LA)
El Camino Coll (CA)
Elgin Comm Coll (IL)
Ellsworth Comm Coll (IA)
El Paso Comm Coll (TX)
Enterprise State Jr Coll (AL)
Erie Business Ctr, Main (PA)
Erie Business Ctr South (PA)
Erie Comm Coll, City Cmps (NY)
Erie Comm Coll, North Cmps (NY)
Erie Comm Coll, South Cmps (NY)
Essex County Coll (NJ)
Eugenio María de Hostos Comm Coll of City U of NY (NY)
Everett Comm Coll (WA)
Evergreen Valley Coll (CA)
Fayetteville Tech Comm Coll (NC)
Feather River Comm Coll District (CA)
Fergus Falls Comm Coll (MN)
Finger Lakes Comm Coll (NY)
Fiorello H LaGuardia Comm Coll of City U of NY (NY)
Fisher Coll (MA)
Flathead Valley Comm Coll (MT)
Florence-Darlington Tech Coll (SC)
Florida Comm Coll at Jacksonville (FL)
Florida Keys Comm Coll (FL)
Florida National Coll (FL)
Floyd Coll (GA)
Foothill Coll (CA)
Forsyth Tech Comm Coll (NC)
Fort Belknap Coll (MT)
Fort Berthold Comm Coll (ND)
Fort Peck Comm Coll (MT)
Fort Scott Comm Coll (KS)
Fox Valley Tech Coll (WI)
Frank Phillips Coll (TX)
Frederick Comm Coll (MD)
Fresno City Coll (CA)
Front Range Comm Coll (CO)
Fulton-Montgomery Comm Coll (NY)
Gadsden State Comm Coll (AL)
Galveston Coll (TX)
Garland County Comm Coll (AR)
Garrett Comm Coll (MD)
Gaston Coll (NC)
Gateway Comm Coll (AZ)
Gavilan Coll (CA)
Gem City Coll (IL)
Genesee Comm Coll (NY)
George C Wallace State Comm Coll, Dothan (AL)
Germanna Comm Coll (VA)
Glendale Comm Coll (AZ)
Gloucester County Coll (NJ)
Gogebic Comm Coll (MI)
Golden West Coll (CA)
Gordon Coll (GA)
Grand Rapids Comm Coll (MI)
Grays Harbor Coll (WA)
Grayson County Coll (TX)
Great Basin Coll (NV)
Great Lakes Jr Coll of Business (MI)
Greenfield Comm Coll (MA)
Green River Comm Coll (WA)
Greenville Tech Coll (SC)
Grossmont Coll (CA)
Guilford Tech Comm Coll (NC)
Gulf Coast Comm Coll (FL)
Gwinnett Tech Inst (GA)
Hagerstown Business Coll (MD)
Hagerstown Jr Coll (MD)
Halifax Comm Coll (NC)
Harford Comm Coll (MD)
Harrisburg Area Comm Coll (PA)
Hartnell Coll (CA)
Haskell Indian Nations U (KS)
Hawkeye Comm Coll (IA)
Haywood Comm Coll (NC)
Heald Business Coll, Concord (CA)
Heald Business Coll, Fresno (CA)
Heald Business Coll, Hayward (CA)
Heald Business Coll, Rancho Cordova (CA)
Heald Business Coll, San Francisco (CA)
Heald Business Coll (HI)
Heartland Comm Coll (IL)
Helena Coll of Tech of The U of Montana (MT)
Henry Ford Comm Coll (MI)
Herkimer County Comm Coll (NY)
Herzing Coll of Business and Tech (AL)
Herzing Coll of Business and Tech (GA)
Hesser Coll (NH)
Hesston Coll (KS)
Hibbing Comm Coll (MN)
Highland Comm Coll (IL)
Highland Comm Coll (KS)
Highland Park Comm Coll (MI)
Highline Comm Coll (WA)
Hill Coll of the Hill Jr Coll District (TX)
Hillsborough Comm Coll (FL)
Hinds Comm Coll (MS)
Hiwassee Coll (TN)
Hocking Coll (OH)
Holmes Comm Coll (MS)
Holyoke Comm Coll (MA)
Horry-Georgetown Tech Coll (SC)
Housatonic Comm-Tech Coll (CT)
Houston Comm Coll System (TX)
Howard Comm Coll (MD)
Hudson County Comm Coll (NJ)
Hudson Valley Comm Coll (NY)
Huertas Jr Coll (PR)
Huntington Jr Coll of Business (WV)
Hutchinson Comm Coll and Area Vocational Sch (KS)
ICM Sch of Business (PA)
Illinois Central Coll (IL)
Illinois Eastern Comm Colls, Frontier Comm Coll (IL)
Illinois Eastern Comm Colls, Lincoln Trail Coll (IL)
Illinois Eastern Comm Colls, Olney Central Coll (IL)
Illinois Eastern Comm Colls, Wabash Valley Coll (IL)
Illinois Valley Comm Coll (IL)
Imperial Valley Coll (CA)
Independence Comm Coll (KS)
Indiana Business Coll (IN)
Indian River Comm Coll (FL)
Inst of Career Education (FL)
Inter American U of PR, Guayama Cmps (PR)
Interboro Inst (NY)
International Business Coll (IN)
Inver Hills Comm Coll (MN)
Iowa Central Comm Coll (IA)
Iowa Lakes Comm Coll (IA)
Iowa Western Comm Coll (IA)
Irvine Valley Coll (CA)
Isothermal Comm Coll (NC)
Itasca Comm Coll (MN)
Itawamba Comm Coll (MS)
Ivy Tech State Coll–Central Indiana (IN)
Ivy Tech State Coll–Columbus (IN)
Ivy Tech State Coll–Eastcentral (IN)
Ivy Tech State Coll–Kokomo (IN)
Ivy Tech State Coll–Lafayette (IN)
Ivy Tech State Coll–Northcentral (IN)
Ivy Tech State Coll–Northeast (IN)
Ivy Tech State Coll–Northwest (IN)
Ivy Tech State Coll–Southcentral (IN)
Ivy Tech State Coll–Southeast (IN)
Ivy Tech State Coll–Southwest (IN)
Ivy Tech State Coll–Wabash Valley (IN)
Ivy Tech State Coll–Whitewater (IN)
Jackson Comm Coll (MI)
Jackson State Comm Coll (TN)
James Sprunt Comm Coll (NC)
Jamestown Business Coll (NY)
Jefferson Coll (MO)
Jefferson Comm Coll (NY)
Jefferson Comm Coll (OH)
Jefferson Davis Comm Coll (AL)
Jefferson State Comm Coll (AL)
J F Drake State Tech Coll (AL)
John C Calhoun State Comm Coll (AL)
Johnson County Comm Coll (KS)
Johnston Comm Coll (NC)
John Tyler Comm Coll (VA)
John Wood Comm Coll (IL)
Joliet Jr Coll (IL)
J Sargeant Reynolds Comm Coll (VA)
Kalamazoo Valley Comm Coll (MI)
Kankakee Comm Coll (IL)
Kansas City Kansas Comm Coll (KS)
Kaskaskia Coll (IL)
Katharine Gibbs Sch (CT)
Katharine Gibbs Sch (MA)
Katharine Gibbs Sch (NJ)
Katharine Gibbs Sch, Melville (NY)
Kellogg Comm Coll (MI)
Kelsey Jenney Coll (CA)
Kennebec Valley Tech Coll (ME)
Kent State U, Ashtabula Cmps (OH)
Kent State U, Salem Cmps (OH)
Kent State U, Trumbull Cmps (OH)
Kent State U, Tuscarawas Cmps (OH)
Kentucky Coll of Business, Lexington (KY)
Kilian Comm Coll (SD)
Kingsborough Comm Coll of City U of NY (NY)
Kings River Comm Coll (CA)
Kirkwood Comm Coll (IA)
Kirtland Comm Coll (MI)
Kishwaukee Coll (IL)
Knoxville Business Coll (TN)
Labette Comm Coll (KS)
Lac Courte Oreilles Ojibwa Comm Coll (WI)
Lackawanna Jr Coll (PA)
Lake Area Vocational-Tech Inst (SD)
Lake City Comm Coll (FL)
Lake Land Coll (IL)
Lakeland Comm Coll (OH)
Lakeshore Tech Coll (WI)
Lake Tahoe Comm Coll (CA)
Lakewood Comm Coll (MN)
Lamar Comm Coll (CO)
Lamar University–Orange (TX)
Lamar University–Port Arthur (TX)
Lamson Jr Coll, Mesa (AZ)
Lane Comm Coll (OR)
Laney Coll (CA)
Lansdale Sch of Business (PA)
Lansing Comm Coll (MI)
Laramie County Comm Coll (WY)
Laredo Comm Coll (TX)
Las Positas Coll (CA)
Lassen Coll (CA)
Lawson State Comm Coll (AL)
LDS Business Coll (UT)
Lee Coll (TX)
Lehigh Carbon Comm Coll (PA)
Lenoir Comm Coll (NC)
Lewis and Clark Comm Coll (IL)
Lewis Coll of Business (MI)
Lima Tech Coll (OH)
Lincoln Land Comm Coll (IL)
Lincoln Sch of Commerce (NE)
Linn-Benton Comm Coll (OR)
Little Hoop Comm Coll (ND)
Long Beach City Coll (CA)
Longview Comm Coll (MO)
Lorain County Comm Coll (OH)
Lord Fairfax Comm Coll (VA)
Los Angeles City Coll (CA)
Los Angeles Harbor Coll (CA)
Los Angeles Mission Coll (CA)
Los Angeles Pierce Coll (CA)
Los Angeles Southwest Coll (CA)
Los Angeles Valley Coll (CA)
Los Medanos Coll (CA)
Louisburg Coll (NC)
Louisiana State U at Alexandria (LA)
Louisiana State U at Eunice (LA)
Lower Columbia Coll (WA)
Luzerne County Comm Coll (PA)
MacCormac Jr Coll (IL)
Macomb Comm Coll (MI)
Macon Coll (GA)
Madison Area Tech Coll (WI)
Madison Jr Coll of Business (WI)
Manatee Comm Coll (FL)
Manchester Comm-Tech Coll (CT)
Manor Jr Coll (PA)
Maple Woods Comm Coll (MO)
Marian Court Coll (MA)
Marion Tech Coll (OH)
Marshalltown Comm Coll (IA)
Martin Comm Coll (NC)
Mary Holmes Coll (MS)
Massachusetts Bay Comm Coll (MA)
Massasoit Comm Coll (MA)
Mater Dei Coll (NY)
Mayland Comm Coll (NC)
McCann Sch of Business (PA)
McCook Comm Coll (NE)
McDowell Tech Comm Coll (NC)
McHenry County Coll (IL)
McIntosh Coll (NH)
McLennan Comm Coll (TX)
Meadows Coll of Business (GA)
Mendocino Coll (CA)
Merced Coll (CA)
Mercer County Comm Coll (NJ)
Meridian Comm Coll (MS)
Merritt Coll (CA)
Mesabi Comm Coll (MN)
Mesa Comm Coll (AZ)
Metropolitan Comm Coll (NE)
Miami-Dade Comm Coll (FL)
Miami-Jacobs Coll (OH)
Miami University–Hamilton Cmps (OH)
Miami University–Middletown Cmps (OH)
Michiana Coll (IN)
Middle Georgia Coll (GA)
Middlesex Comm Coll (MA)
Middlesex Community- Tech Coll (CT)
Middlesex County Coll (NJ)
Midland Coll (TX)
Midlands Tech Coll (SC)
Mid Michigan Comm Coll (MI)
Mid-Plains Comm Coll (NE)
Midstate Coll (IL)
Mid-State Coll (ME)
Mid-State Tech Coll (WI)
Miles Comm Coll (MT)
Milwaukee Area Tech Coll (WI)
Mineral Area Coll (MO)
MiraCosta Coll (CA)
Mission Coll (CA)
Mississippi County Comm Coll (AR)
Mississippi Gulf Coast Comm Coll (MS)
Mitchell Coll (CT)
Mitchell Comm Coll (NC)
Moberly Area Comm Coll (MO)
Modesto Jr Coll (CA)
Mohawk Valley Comm Coll (NY)
Monroe Coll, Bronx (NY)
Monroe Coll, New Rochelle (NY)
Monroe Comm Coll (NY)

Peterson's Guide to Two-Year Colleges 1997
125

Associate Degree Programs at Two-Year Colleges

Secretarial Studies/Office Management

Monroe County Comm Coll (MI)
Montana State U Coll of Tech-Great Falls (MT)
Montcalm Comm Coll (MI)
Monterey Peninsula Coll (CA)
Montgomery Coll (TX)
Montgomery College–Germantown Cmps (MD)
Montgomery College–Rockville Cmps (MD)
Montgomery College–Takoma Park Cmps (MD)
Montgomery Comm Coll (NC)
Montgomery County Comm Coll (PA)
Moorpark Coll (CA)
Moraine Park Tech Coll (WI)
Moraine Valley Comm Coll (IL)
Morgan Comm Coll (CO)
Morton Coll (IL)
Motlow State Comm Coll (TN)
Mountain Empire Comm Coll (VA)
Mount Ida Coll (MA)
Mt San Antonio Coll (CA)
Mt San Jacinto Coll (CA)
Mount Wachusett Comm Coll (MA)
Murray State Coll (OK)
Muscatine Comm Coll (IA)
Muskegon Comm Coll (MI)
Muskingum Area Tech Coll (OH)
Napa Valley Coll (CA)
Nash Comm Coll (NC)
Nashville State Tech Inst (TN)
Nassau Comm Coll (NY)
National Business Coll, Bluefield (VA)
National Business Coll, Bristol (VA)
National Business Coll, Charlottesville (VA)
National Business Coll, Danville (VA)
National Business Coll, Harrisonburg (VA)
National Business Coll, Lynchburg (VA)
National Business Coll, Martinsville (VA)
National Business Coll, Roanoke (VA)
Naugatuck Valley Community–Tech Coll (CT)
Navajo Comm Coll (AZ)
Navarro Coll (TX)
Nebraska Coll of Business (NE)
Nebraska Indian Comm Coll (NE)
Neosho County Comm Coll (KS)
Nettleton Career Coll (SD)
New England Inst of Tech (RI)
New England Inst of Tech & Florida Culinary Inst (FL)
New Hampshire Tech Coll, Berlin (NH)
New Hampshire Tech Coll, Laconia (NH)
New Hampshire Tech Coll, Manchester (NH)
New Mexico Jr Coll (NM)
New Mexico State University–Alamogordo (NM)
New Mexico State University–Carlsbad (NM)
New Mexico State University–Grants (NM)
Newport Business Inst (PA)
New River Comm Coll (VA)
New York City Tech Coll of the City U of NY (NY)
Niagara County Comm Coll (NY)
Nicolet Area Tech Coll (WI)
Normandale Comm Coll (MN)
Northampton County Area Comm Coll (PA)
North Central Michigan Coll (MI)
North Central Missouri Coll (MO)
North Central Tech Coll (OH)
Northcentral Tech Coll (WI)
North Central Texas Coll (TX)
North Country Comm Coll (NY)
North Dakota State Coll of Science (ND)
North Dakota State University–Bottineau (ND)
Northeast Alabama State Comm Coll (AL)
Northeast Comm Coll (NE)
Northeastern Jr Coll (CO)
Northeastern Oklahoma A&M Coll (OK)
Northeast Iowa Comm Coll, Peosta Cmps (IA)
Northeast Mississippi Comm Coll (MS)
Northeast State Tech Comm Coll (TN)
Northeast Texas Comm Coll (TX)
Northern Essex Comm Coll (MA)
Northern Maine Tech Coll (ME)
Northern Marianas Coll (MP)
Northern Oklahoma Coll (OK)
Northern Virginia Comm Coll (VA)
North Harris Coll (TX)
North Hennepin Comm Coll (MN)
North Idaho Coll (ID)
North Iowa Area Comm Coll (IA)
North Lake Coll (TX)
Northland Comm and Tech Coll (MN)
Northland Pioneer Coll (AZ)
North Seattle Comm Coll (WA)
North Shore Comm Coll (MA)
NorthWest Arkansas Comm Coll (AR)
Northwest Coll (WY)
Northwestern Business Coll (IL)
Northwestern Coll (OH)
Northwestern Connecticut Comm-Tech Coll (CT)
Northwestern Michigan Coll (MI)
Northwest Indian Coll (WA)
Northwest Iowa Comm Coll (IA)
Northwest Mississippi Comm Coll (MS)
Northwest-Shoals Comm Coll (AL)
Northwest State Comm Coll (OH)
Norwalk Comm-Tech Coll (CT)
Oakland Comm Coll (MI)
Oakton Comm Coll (IL)
Ocean County Coll (NJ)
Odessa Coll (TX)
Ohio Valley Coll (WV)
Ohlone Coll (CA)
Okaloosa-Walton Comm Coll (FL)
Oklahoma State U, Okmulgee (OK)
Olean Business Inst (NY)
Olympic Coll (WA)
Onondaga Comm Coll (NY)
Orangeburg-Calhoun Tech Coll (SC)
Orange Coast Coll (CA)
Orange County Comm Coll (NY)
Otero Jr Coll (CO)
Ouachita Tech Coll (AR)
Owensboro Comm Coll (KY)
Owensboro Jr Coll of Business (KY)
Owens Comm Coll, Findlay (OH)
Owens Comm Coll, Toledo (OH)
Oxnard Coll (CA)
Ozarka Tech Coll (AR)
Palau Comm Coll (PW)
Palm Beach Comm Coll (FL)
Palomar Coll (CA)
Palo Verde Coll (CA)
Pamlico Comm Coll (NC)
Paradise Valley Comm Coll (AZ)
Parkland Coll (IL)
Parks Coll (NM)
Parks Jr Coll (CO)
Pasadena City Coll (CA)
Pasco-Hernando Comm Coll (FL)
Passaic County Comm Coll (NJ)
Patrick Henry Comm Coll (VA)
Paul D Camp Comm Coll (VA)
Pearl River Comm Coll (MS)
Peirce Coll (PA)
Pellissippi State Tech Comm Coll (TN)
Peninsula Coll (WA)
Penn Commercial, Inc (PA)
Pennsylvania Coll of Tech (PA)
Pennsylvania Inst of Tech (PA)
Penn Valley Comm Coll (MO)
Pensacola Jr Coll (FL)
Petit Jean Tech Coll (AR)
Phillips County Comm Coll (AR)
Phillips Jr Coll (UT)
Phillips Jr Coll, Condie Cmps (CA)
Phillips Jr Coll of Springfield (MO)
Piedmont Comm Coll (NC)
Piedmont Tech Coll (SC)
Piedmont Virginia Comm Coll (VA)
Pierce Coll (WA)
Pikes Peak Comm Coll (CO)
Pima Comm Coll (AZ)
Pine Tech Coll (MN)
Pitt Comm Coll (NC)
Porterville Coll (CA)
Portland Comm Coll (OR)
Potomac State Coll of West Virginia U (WV)
Prairie State Coll (IL)
Pratt Comm Coll and Area Voc Sch (KS)
Prince George's Comm Coll (MD)
Prospect Hall (FL)
Pueblo Coll of Business and Tech (CO)
Pueblo Comm Coll (CO)
Queensborough Comm Coll of City U of NY (NY)
Quincy Coll (MA)
Quinebaug Valley Comm-Tech Coll (CT)
Quinsigamond Comm Coll (MA)
Rainy River Comm Coll (MN)
Ramírez Coll of Business and Tech (PR)
Randolph Comm Coll (NC)
Ranger Coll (TX)
Rappahannock Comm Coll (VA)
Raritan Valley Comm Coll (NJ)
Rasmussen Coll Mankato (MN)
Rasmussen Coll Minnetonka (MN)
Rasmussen Coll St Cloud (MN)
Reading Area Comm Coll (PA)
Redlands Comm Coll (OK)
Red Rocks Comm Coll (CO)
Reid State Tech Coll (AL)
Rend Lake Coll (IL)
Renton Tech Coll (WA)
RETS Tech Ctr (OH)
Richland Coll (TX)
Richland Comm Coll (IL)
Richmond Comm Coll (NC)
Rich Mountain Comm Coll (AR)
Ricks Coll (ID)
Riverside Comm Coll (CA)
Roane State Comm Coll (TN)
Roanoke-Chowan Comm Coll (NC)
Robeson Comm Coll (NC)
Rochester Business Inst (NY)
Rochester Comm Coll (MN)
Rockingham Comm Coll (NC)
Rockland Comm Coll (NY)
Rock Valley Coll (IL)
Rogers State Coll (OK)
Rogue Comm Coll (OR)
Rose State Coll (OK)
Roxbury Comm Coll (MA)
Sacramento City Coll (CA)
Saddleback Coll (CA)
Sage Jr Coll of Albany (NY)
Saint Augustine Coll (IL)
St Catharine Coll (KY)
Saint Charles County Comm Coll (MO)
St Clair County Comm Coll (MI)
St Cloud Tech Coll (MN)
St Johns River Comm Coll (FL)
St Louis Comm Coll at Florissant Valley (MO)
St Louis Comm Coll at Forest Park (MO)
St Louis Comm Coll at Meramec (MO)
St Paul Tech Coll (MN)
St Petersburg Jr Coll (FL)
St Philip's Coll (TX)
Salem Comm Coll (NJ)
Salish Kootenai Coll (MT)
Salt Lake Comm Coll (UT)
Sampson Comm Coll (NC)
San Bernardino Valley Coll (CA)
Sandhills Comm Coll (NC)
San Diego City Coll (CA)
San Diego Mesa Coll (CA)
San Diego Miramar Coll (CA)
Sanford-Brown Coll, Des Peres (MO)
Sanford-Brown Coll, Hazelwood (MO)
Sanford-Brown Coll, St Charles (MO)
San Jacinto College–Central Cmps (TX)
San Jacinto College–South Cmps (TX)
San Jose City Coll (CA)
San Juan Coll (NM)
Santa Barbara City Coll (CA)
Santa Fe Comm Coll (NM)
Santa Monica Coll (CA)
Sauk Valley Comm Coll (IL)
Sawyer Coll of Business, Cleveland (OH)
Schenectady County Comm Coll (NY)
Schoolcraft Coll (MI)
Scott Comm Coll (IA)
Scottsdale Comm Coll (AZ)
Seattle Central Comm Coll (WA)
Seminole Comm Coll (FL)
Seminole Jr Coll (OK)
Seward County Comm Coll (KS)
Shasta Coll (CA)
Shawnee Comm Coll (IL)
Shelby State Comm Coll (TN)
Shelton State Comm Coll (AL)
Sheridan Coll (WY)
Shoreline Comm Coll (WA)
Shorter Coll (AR)
Sierra Coll (CA)
Sinclair Comm Coll (OH)
Skyline Coll (CA)
Snow Coll (UT)
South Arkansas Comm Coll (AR)
South Coll (FL)
South Coll (GA)
Southeast Comm Coll, Beatrice Cmps (NE)
Southeast Comm Coll, Lincoln Cmps (NE)
Southeastern Comm Coll (NC)
Southeastern Comm Coll, North Cmps, West Burlington (IA)
Southeastern Comm Coll, South Cmps, Keokuk (IA)
Southeastern Illinois Coll (IL)
Southern Arkansas U Tech (AR)
Southern Coll (FL)
Southern Ohio Coll, Cincinnati Cmps (OH)
Southern Ohio Coll, Northeast Cmps (OH)
Southern Ohio Coll, Northern Kentucky Cmps (KY)
Southern State Comm Coll (OH)
Southern Union State Comm Coll (AL)
Southern West Virginia Comm and Tech Coll (WV)
South Florida Comm Coll (FL)
South Georgia Coll (GA)
South Mountain Comm Coll (AZ)
South Plains Coll (TX)
South Puget Sound Comm Coll (WA)
South Seattle Comm Coll (WA)
Southside Virginia Comm Coll (VA)
South Suburban Coll (IL)
Southwestern Coll (CA)
Southwestern Coll of Business, Cincinnati (OH)
Southwestern Coll of Business, Cincinnati (OH)
Southwestern Coll of Business, Dayton (OH)
Southwestern Coll of Business, Middletown (OH)
Southwestern Comm Coll (IA)
Southwestern Comm Coll (NC)
Southwestern Indian Polytechnic Inst (NM)
Southwestern Michigan Coll (MI)
Southwestern Oregon Comm Coll (OR)
Southwest Florida Coll of Business (FL)
Southwest Mississippi Comm Coll (MS)
Southwest Virginia Comm Coll (VA)
Southwest Wisconsin Tech Coll (WI)
Spartanburg Methodist Coll (SC)
Spencer Sch of Business (NE)
Spokane Comm Coll (WA)
Spokane Falls Comm Coll (WA)
Spoon River Coll (IL)
Springfield Tech Comm Coll (MA)
Standing Rock Coll (ND)
Stanly Comm Coll (NC)
Stark Tech Coll (OH)
State Comm Coll of East St Louis (IL)
State Fair Comm Coll (MO)
State Tech Inst at Memphis (TN)
State U of NY Coll of A&T at Cobleskill (NY)
State U of NY Coll of A&T at Morrisville (NY)
State U of NY Coll of Tech at Alfred (NY)
State U of NY Coll of Tech at Canton (NY)
State U of NY Coll of Tech at Delhi (NY)
Stevens Henager Coll (UT)
Stone Child Coll (MT)
Stratton Coll (WI)
Suffolk County Comm College–Ammerman Cmps (NY)
Suffolk County Comm Coll–Eastern Cmps (NY)
Suffolk County Comm Coll–Western Cmps (NY)
Sullivan County Comm Coll (NY)
Surry Comm Coll (NC)
Sussex County Comm Coll (NJ)
Tacoma Comm Coll (WA)
Taft Coll (CA)
Tallahassee Comm Coll (FL)
Tarrant County Jr Coll (TX)
Taylor Business Inst (NY)
Tech Career Institutes (NY)
Tech Coll of Municipality of San Juan (PR)
Temple Coll (TX)
Terra State Comm Coll (OH)
Texarkana Coll (TX)
Texas Southmost Coll (TX)
Texas State Tech Coll (TX)
Texas State Tech Coll–Harlingen Cmps (TX)
Thomas Nelson Comm Coll (VA)
Three Rivers Comm Coll (MO)
Three Rivers Comm-Tech Coll (CT)
Tidewater Comm Coll (VA)
Tompkins Cortland Comm Coll (NY)
Treasure Valley Comm Coll (OR)
Trenholm State Tech Coll (AL)
Tri-County Comm Coll (NC)
Tri-County Tech Coll (SC)
Trident Tech Coll (SC)
Trinidad State Jr Coll (CO)
Triton Coll (IL)
Trocaire Coll (NY)
Truckee Meadows Comm Coll (NV)
Tulsa Jr Coll (OK)
Tunxis Comm Tech Coll (CT)
Turtle Mountain Comm Coll (ND)
Tyler Jr Coll (TX)
Ulster County Comm Coll (NY)
Umpqua Comm Coll (OR)
Union County Coll (NJ)
The U of Akron–Wayne Coll (OH)
U of Alaska Anchorage, Kenai Peninsula Coll (AK)
U of Alaska Anchorage, Kodiak Coll (AK)
U of Alaska Anchorage, Matanuska-Susitna Coll (AK)
U of Alaska, Prince William Sound Comm Coll (AK)
U of Alaska Southeast, Ketchikan Cmps (AK)
U of Cincinnati Clermont Coll (OH)
U of Cincinnati Raymond Walters Coll (OH)
U of Hawaii–Hawaii Comm Coll (HI)
U of Hawaii–Kapiolani Comm Coll (HI)
U of Hawaii–Kauai Comm Coll (HI)
U of Hawaii–Leeward Comm Coll (HI)
U of Hawaii–Maui Comm Coll (HI)
U of Hawaii–Windward Comm Coll (HI)
U of Kentucky, Ashland Comm Coll (KY)
U of Kentucky, Elizabethtown Comm Coll (KY)
U of Kentucky, Hazard Comm Coll (KY)
U of Kentucky, Henderson Comm Coll (KY)
U of Kentucky, Hopkinsville Comm Coll (KY)
U of Kentucky, Lexington Comm Coll (KY)
U of Kentucky, Madisonville Comm Coll (KY)
U of Kentucky, Maysville Comm Coll (KY)
U of Kentucky, Paducah Comm Coll (KY)
U of Kentucky, Somerset Comm Coll (KY)
U of Kentucky, Southeast Comm Coll (KY)
U of New Mexico–Gallup Branch (NM)
U of New Mexico–Los Alamos Branch (NM)
U of New Mexico–Valencia Cmps (NM)
U of North Dakota–Lake Region (ND)
U of North Dakota–Williston (ND)
U of South Carolina at Lancaster (SC)
Utah Valley State Coll (UT)
Utica Sch of Commerce (NY)
Valencia Comm Coll (FL)
Vance-Granville Comm Coll (NC)
Ventura Coll (CA)
Vermont Tech Coll (VT)
Vernon Regional Jr Coll (TX)
Victoria Coll (TX)
Victor Valley Coll (CA)
Villa Maria Coll of Buffalo (NY)
Vincennes U (IN)
Vincennes University–Jasper Ctr (IN)
Virginia Coll (VA)
Virginia Coll at Birmingham (AL)
Virginia Highlands Comm Coll (VA)
Virginia Western Comm Coll (VA)
Vista Comm Coll (CA)
Volunteer State Comm Coll (TN)
Wake Tech Comm Coll (NC)

Associate Degree Programs at Two-Year Colleges
Secretarial Studies/Office Management–Social Work

Wallace State Comm Coll (AL)
Walla Walla Comm Coll (WA)
Walters State Comm Coll (TN)
Warren County Comm Coll (NJ)
Washington State Comm Coll (OH)
Washtenaw Comm Coll (MI)
Waubonsee Comm Coll (IL)
Waukesha County Tech Coll (WI)
Waycross Coll (GA)
Wayne Comm Coll (NC)
Wayne County Comm Coll (MI)
Weatherford Coll (TX)
Webster Coll, Ocala (FL)
Wenatchee Valley Coll (WA)
Westark Comm Coll (AR)
Westchester Business Inst (NY)
Westchester Comm Coll (NY)
Western Dakota Tech Inst (SD)
Western Iowa Tech Comm Coll (IA)
Western Nebraska Comm Coll, Scottsbluff (NE)
Western Nevada Comm Coll (NV)
Western Piedmont Comm Coll (NC)
Western Texas Coll (TX)
Western Wisconsin Tech Coll (WI)
Western Wyoming Comm Coll (WY)
West Hills Comm Coll (CA)
West Los Angeles Coll (CA)
Westmoreland County Comm Coll (PA)
West Shore Comm Coll (MI)
West Valley Coll (CA)
West Virginia Career Coll, Charleston (WV)
West Virginia Northern Comm Coll (WV)
West Virginia U at Parkersburg (WV)
Wharton County Jr Coll (TX)
Whatcom Comm Coll (WA)
Wilkes Comm Coll (NC)
William Rainey Harper Coll (IL)
Williamsburg Tech Coll (SC)
Williamsport Sch of Commerce (PA)
Willmar Comm Coll (MN)
Willmar Tech Coll (MN)
Wilson Tech Comm Coll (NC)
Wisconsin Indianhead Tech Coll, Ashland Cmps (WI)
Wisconsin Indianhead Tech Coll, New Richmond Cmps (WI)
Wisconsin Indianhead Tech Coll, Rice Lake Cmps (WI)
Wisconsin Indianhead Tech Coll, Superior Cmps (WI)
Wood Coll (MS)
Wood Tobe–Coburn Sch (NY)
Wor-Wic Comm Coll (MD)
Wright State U, Lake Cmps (OH)
Wytheville Comm Coll (VA)
Yakima Valley Comm Coll (WA)
Yavapai Coll (AZ)
York Tech Coll (SC)
Yuba Coll (CA)

SOCIAL SCIENCE
Abraham Baldwin Ag Coll (GA)
Adirondack Comm Coll (NY)
Alabama Southern Comm Coll, Monroeville (AL)
Alabama Southern Comm Coll, Thomasville (AL)
Allan Hancock Coll (CA)
Allegany Comm Coll (MD)
Allen County Comm Coll (KS)
American River Coll (CA)
Andrew Coll (GA)
Angelina Coll (TX)
Anne Arundel Comm Coll (MD)
Antelope Valley Coll (CA)
Arizona Western Coll (AZ)
Arkansas State University–Beebe Branch (AR)

Atlantic Comm Coll (NJ)
Barstow Coll (CA)
Bay Mills Comm Coll (MI)
Bevill State Comm Coll (AL)
Bismarck State Coll (ND)
Bowling Green State University–Firelands Coll (OH)
Brazosport Coll (TX)
Brevard Coll (NC)
Brookdale Comm Coll (NJ)
Bucks County Comm Coll (PA)
Butler County Comm Coll (KS)
Butte Coll (CA)
Cañada Coll (CA)
Carl Albert State Coll (OK)
Casper Coll (WY)
Catonsville Comm Coll (MD)
Central Coll (KS)
Centralia Coll (WA)
Central Oregon Comm Coll (OR)
Central Texas Coll (TX)
Central Wyoming Coll (WY)
Cerro Coso Comm Coll (CA)
Chabot Coll (CA)
Chaffey Coll (CA)
Chemeketa Comm Coll (OR)
Chesapeake Coll (MD)
Citrus Coll (CA)
City Coll of San Francisco (CA)
City Colls of Chicago, Harold Washington Coll (IL)
City Colls of Chicago, Olive-Harvey Coll (IL)
Clackamas Comm Coll (OR)
Clark Coll (WA)
Clinton Comm Coll (IA)
Clinton Comm Coll (NY)
Cloud County Comm Coll (KS)
Cochise Coll, Douglas (AZ)
Cochise Coll, Sierra Vista (AZ)
Coffeyville Comm Coll (KS)
Coll of Alameda (CA)
Coll of San Mateo (CA)
Coll of the Canyons (CA)
Coll of the Desert (CA)
Coll of the Sequoias (CA)
Coll of the Siskiyous (CA)
Colorado Mountn Coll, Alpine Cmps (CO)
Colorado Mountn Coll, Roaring Fork Cmps-Spring Valley Ctr (CO)
Colorado Mountn Coll, Timberline Cmps (CO)
Columbia-Greene Comm Coll (NY)
Comm Coll of Allegheny County Allegheny Cmps (PA)
Comm Coll of Allegheny County North Cmps (PA)
Comm Coll of Allegheny County South Cmps (PA)
Comm Coll of Southern Nevada (NV)
Comm Coll of Vermont (VT)
Corning Comm Coll (NY)
Cosumnes River Coll (CA)
County Coll of Morris (NJ)
Cypress Coll (CA)
Danville Area Comm Coll (IL)
Daytona Beach Comm Coll (FL)
Dean Coll (MA)
De Anza Coll (CA)
Dixie Coll (UT)
Dodge City Comm Coll (KS)
D-Q U (CA)
Dutchess Comm Coll (NY)
East Central Comm Coll (MS)
Eastern Wyoming Coll (WY)
East Mississippi Comm Coll (MS)
Edison Comm Coll (FL)
El Paso Comm Coll (TX)
Enterprise State Jr Coll (AL)
Erie Comm Coll, City Cmps (NY)
Erie Comm Coll, North Cmps (NY)
Essex County Coll (NJ)
Feather River Comm Coll District (CA)
Finger Lakes Comm Coll (NY)
Foothill Coll (CA)
Fresno City Coll (CA)

Front Range Comm Coll (CO)
Fulton-Montgomery Comm Coll (NY)
Galveston Coll (TX)
Garden City Comm Coll (KS)
Garrett Comm Coll (MD)
Gavilan Coll (CA)
Gogebic Comm Coll (MI)
Harford Comm Coll (MD)
Harrisburg Area Comm Coll (PA)
Herkimer County Comm Coll (NY)
Highline Comm Coll (WA)
Hill Coll of the Hill Jr Coll District (TX)
Hinds Comm Coll (MS)
Housatonic Comm-Tech Coll (CT)
Houston Comm Coll System (TX)
Howard Coll (TX)
Howard Comm Coll (MD)
Hutchinson Comm Coll and Area Vocational Sch (KS)
Imperial Valley Coll (CA)
Indian River Comm Coll (FL)
Iowa Lakes Comm Coll (IA)
Irvine Valley Coll (CA)
Itawamba Comm Coll (MS)
Jackson State Comm Coll (TN)
Jamestown Comm Coll (NY)
John Wood Comm Coll (IL)
Kings River Comm Coll (CA)
Kirkwood Comm Coll (IA)
Kishwaukee Coll (IL)
Labette Comm Coll (KS)
Lake Land Coll (IL)
Lake-Sumter Comm Coll (FL)
Lake Tahoe Comm Coll (CA)
Lamar Comm Coll (CO)
Lamar University–Orange (TX)
Lamar University–Port Arthur (TX)
Laney Coll (CA)
Laredo Comm Coll (TX)
Lassen Coll (CA)
Lawson State Comm Coll (AL)
Lehigh Carbon Comm Coll (PA)
Lincoln Coll, Normal (IL)
Long Beach City Coll (CA)
Lon Morris Coll (TX)
Lorain County Comm Coll (OH)
Los Angeles Mission Coll (CA)
Los Angeles Southwest Coll (CA)
Lower Columbia Coll (WA)
Luzerne County Comm Coll (PA)
Mary Holmes Coll (MS)
Mendocino Coll (CA)
Merced Coll (CA)
Merritt Coll (CA)
Miami-Dade Comm Coll (FL)
Middle Georgia Coll (GA)
Middlesex County Coll (NJ)
Midland Coll (TX)
Mid-Plains Comm Coll (NE)
Mineral Area Coll (MO)
MiraCosta Coll (CA)
Mission Coll (CA)
Moberly Area Comm Coll (MO)
Modesto Jr Coll (CA)
Mohawk Valley Comm Coll (NY)
Monroe Comm Coll (NY)
Montgomery College–Rockville Cmps (MD)
Montgomery College–Takoma Park Cmps (MD)
Montgomery County Comm Coll (PA)
Motlow State Comm Coll (TN)
Mt San Jacinto Coll (CA)
Nassau Comm Coll (NY)
Navajo Comm Coll (AZ)
Navarro Coll (TX)
New Mexico Military Inst (NM)
Niagara County Comm Coll (NY)
Northeastern Jr Coll (CO)
Northeastern Oklahoma A&M Coll (OK)
Northeast Mississippi Comm Coll (MS)

North Idaho Coll (ID)
North Seattle Comm Coll (WA)
Northwest Coll (WY)
Northwestern Connecticut Comm-Tech Coll (CT)
Odessa Coll (TX)
Ohlone Coll (CA)
Okaloosa-Walton Comm Coll (FL)
Otero Jr Coll (CO)
Owens Comm Coll, Findlay (OH)
Owens Comm Coll, Toledo (OH)
Palm Beach Comm Coll (FL)
Panama Canal Coll (Republic of Panama)
Pasadena City Coll (CA)
Phillips County Comm Coll (AR)
Piedmont Comm Coll (NC)
Polk Comm Coll (FL)
Porterville Coll (CA)
Pratt Comm Coll and Area Voc Sch (KS)
Quincy Coll (MA)
Raritan Valley Comm Coll (NJ)
Reading Area Comm Coll (PA)
Redlands Comm Coll (OK)
Riverside Comm Coll (CA)
Roane State Comm Coll (TN)
Rogue Comm Coll (OR)
Roxbury Comm Coll (MA)
Sacramento City Coll (CA)
Saddleback Coll (CA)
Sage Jr Coll of Albany (NY)
St Catharine Coll (KY)
St Gregory's Coll (OK)
Salem Comm Coll (NJ)
Salt Lake Comm Coll (UT)
San Diego City Coll (CA)
San Diego Mesa Coll (CA)
San Diego Miramar Coll (CA)
San Jacinto College–South Cmps (TX)
San Joaquin Delta Coll (CA)
Santa Rosa Jr Coll (CA)
Schenectady County Comm Coll (NY)
Scott Comm Coll (IA)
Sheridan Coll (WY)
Shorter Coll (AR)
Skagit Valley Coll (WA)
Skyline Coll (CA)
Solano Comm Coll (CA)
SouthWest Collegiate Inst for the Deaf (TX)
Southwestern Comm Coll (IA)
Southwest Mississippi Comm Coll (MS)
Spoon River Coll (IL)
Springfield Tech Comm Coll (MA)
State U of NY Coll of A&T at Cobleskill (NY)
State U of NY Coll of A&T at Morrisville (NY)
State U of NY Coll of Tech at Alfred (NY)
State U of NY Coll of Tech at Canton (NY)
Suffolk County Comm College–Ammerman Cmps (NY)
Sullivan County Comm Coll (NY)
Sussex County Comm Coll (NJ)
Tacoma Comm Coll (WA)
Taft Coll (CA)
Tompkins Cortland Comm Coll (NY)
Treasure Valley Comm Coll (OR)
Triton Coll (IL)
Tulsa Jr Coll (OK)
Turtle Mountain Comm Coll (ND)
Tyler Jr Coll (TX)
UAB Walker Coll (AL)
Ulster County Comm Coll (NY)
Umpqua Comm Coll (OR)
U of Wisconsin Center–Marathon County (WI)
Victor Valley Coll (CA)
Vincennes U (IN)
Vincennes University–Jasper Ctr (IN)
Waldorf Coll (IA)

Warren County Comm Coll (NJ)
Waubonsee Comm Coll (IL)
Westchester Comm Coll (NY)
Western Oklahoma State Coll (OK)
Western Wyoming Comm Coll (WY)
West Hills Comm Coll (CA)
West Valley Coll (CA)
William Rainey Harper Coll (IL)
Yuba Coll (CA)

SOCIAL WORK
Abraham Baldwin Ag Coll (GA)
Aiken Tech Coll (SC)
Allegany Comm Coll (MD)
Allen County Comm Coll (KS)
Andrew Coll (GA)
Angelina Coll (TX)
Anson Comm Coll (NC)
Asheville-Buncombe Tech Comm Coll (NC)
Atlanta Metropolitan Coll (GA)
Atlantic Comm Coll (NJ)
Austin Comm Coll (TX)
Barton County Comm Coll (KS)
Bay de Noc Comm Coll (MI)
Beaufort County Comm Coll (NC)
Bowling Green State University–Firelands Coll (OH)
Brevard Coll (NC)
Butler County Comm Coll (KS)
Casper Coll (WY)
Central Carolina Comm Coll (NC)
Central Comm College–Platte Cmps (NE)
Central Piedmont Comm Coll (NC)
Champlain Coll (VT)
Charles Stewart Mott Comm Coll (MI)
Chemeketa Comm Coll (OR)
Chipola Jr Coll (FL)
City Coll of San Francisco (CA)
City Colls of Chicago, Harold Washington Coll (IL)
City Colls of Chicago, Kennedy-King Coll (IL)
City Colls of Chicago, Richard J Daley Coll (IL)
Clark State Comm Coll (OH)
Clinton Comm Coll (IA)
Coahoma Comm Coll (MS)
Cochise Coll, Douglas (AZ)
Cochise Coll, Sierra Vista (AZ)
Coffeyville Comm Coll (KS)
Colby Comm Coll (KS)
Columbus State Comm Coll (OH)
Comm Coll of Allegheny County Allegheny Cmps (PA)
Comm Coll of Allegheny County North Cmps (PA)
Comm Coll of Allegheny County South Cmps (PA)
Comm Coll of Rhode Island (RI)
Comm Coll of the Air Force (AL)
Connors State Coll (OK)
Cowley County Comm Coll and Voc-Tech Sch (KS)
Cumberland County Coll (NJ)
Dalton Coll (GA)
Danville Area Comm Coll (IL)
Dean Coll (MA)
Del Mar Coll (TX)
Delta Coll (MI)
Dodge City Comm Coll (KS)
East Central Coll (MO)
Eastfield Coll (TX)
East Los Angeles Coll (CA)
Edgecombe Comm Coll (NC)
Edmonds Comm Coll (WA)
El Camino Coll (CA)
Ellsworth Comm Coll (IA)
Finger Lakes Comm Coll (NY)
Gainesville Coll (GA)
Galveston Coll (TX)
Gaston Coll (NC)

Glendale Comm Coll (AZ)
Gogebic Comm Coll (MI)
Gulf Coast Comm Coll (FL)
Halifax Comm Coll (NC)
Harrisburg Area Comm Coll (PA)
Hawkeye Comm Coll (IA)
Herkimer County Comm Coll (NY)
Hesser Coll (NH)
Highland Comm Coll (KS)
Hill Coll of the Hill Jr Coll District (TX)
Hiwassee Coll (TN)
Holmes Comm Coll (MS)
Illinois Eastern Comm Colls, Wabash Valley Coll (IL)
Indian River Comm Coll (FL)
Iowa Central Comm Coll (IA)
Iowa Lakes Comm Coll (IA)
Itawamba Comm Coll (MS)
Jackson State Comm Coll (TN)
Jefferson Coll (MO)
John A Logan Coll (IL)
Kansas City Kansas Comm Coll (KS)
Kellogg Comm Coll (MI)
Kirkwood Comm Coll (IA)
Lamar Comm Coll (CO)
Lawson State Comm Coll (AL)
Lincoln Land Comm Coll (IL)
Lorain County Comm Coll (OH)
Manchester Comm-Tech Coll (CT)
Massachusetts Bay Comm Coll (MA)
Mater Dei Coll (NY)
Miami-Dade Comm Coll (FL)
Middle Georgia Coll (GA)
Mineral Area Coll (MO)
Mississippi Delta Comm Coll (MS)
Mitchell Coll (CT)
Modesto Jr Coll (CA)
Monroe County Comm Coll (MI)
Motlow State Comm Coll (TN)
Mount Ida Coll (MA)
Muskingum Area Tech Coll (OH)
Naugatuck Valley Community–Tech Coll (CT)
Navajo Comm Coll (AZ)
Northampton County Area Comm Coll (PA)
Northeastern Jr Coll (CO)
Northeastern Oklahoma A&M Coll (OK)
Northeast Mississippi Comm Coll (MS)
Northland Comm and Tech Coll (MN)
Northwest Coll (WY)
Northwest Mississippi Comm Coll (MS)
Oakland Comm Coll (MI)
Ohio Valley Coll (WV)
Okaloosa-Walton Comm Coll (FL)
Palm Beach Comm Coll (FL)
Pikes Peak Comm Coll (CO)
Pima Comm Coll (AZ)
Potomac State Coll of West Virginia U (WV)
Pratt Comm Coll and Area Voc Sch (KS)
Reading Area Comm Coll (PA)
Ricks Coll (ID)
Rio Salado Comm Coll (AZ)
Rock Valley Coll (IL)
Sacramento City Coll (CA)
St Catharine Coll (KY)
San Diego City Coll (CA)
Seward County Comm Coll (KS)
Shawnee Comm Coll (IL)
Shorter Coll (AR)
Southern U at Shreveport–Bossier City Cmps (LA)
South Plains Coll (TX)
South Suburban Coll (IL)
Southwestern Coll (CA)
Spokane Falls Comm Coll (WA)
State Comm Coll of East St Louis (IL)
Sullivan County Comm Coll (NY)
Texas Southmost Coll (TX)

Associate Degree Programs at Two-Year Colleges
Social Work–Sports Administration

Tulsa Jr Coll (OK)
Turtle Mountain Comm Coll (ND)
Umpqua Comm Coll (OR)
The U of Akron–Wayne Coll (OH)
U of Cincinnati Clermont Coll (OH)
U of Cincinnati Raymond Walters Coll (OH)
U of Kentucky, Jefferson Comm Coll (KY)
Vincennes U (IN)
Vincennes University–Jasper Ctr (IN)
Waldorf Coll (IA)
Washington State Comm Coll (OH)
Waubonsee Comm Coll (IL)
Western Nebraska Comm Coll, Scottsbluff (NE)
West Shore Comm Coll (MI)
West Virginia Northern Comm Coll (WV)
West Virginia U at Parkersburg (WV)
White Pines Coll (NH)
Wilkes Comm Coll (NC)
Willmar Comm Coll (MN)
Wright State U, Lake Cmps (OH)

SOCIOLOGY
Abraham Baldwin Ag Coll (GA)
Allegany Comm Coll (MD)
Allen County Comm Coll (KS)
Andrew Coll (GA)
Antelope Valley Coll (CA)
Atlanta Metropolitan Coll (GA)
Atlantic Comm Coll (NJ)
Austin Comm Coll (TX)
Bainbridge Coll (GA)
Bakersfield Coll (CA)
Barton County Comm Coll (KS)
Bay de Noc Comm Coll (MI)
Bee County Coll (TX)
Bergen Comm Coll (NJ)
Black Hawk Coll, Moline (IL)
Brazosport Coll (TX)
Brevard Coll (NC)
Brookdale Comm Coll (NJ)
Brunswick Coll (GA)
Burlington County Coll (NJ)
Butler County Comm Coll (KS)
Cañada Coll (CA)
Casper Coll (WY)
Central Comm College–Platte Cmps (NE)
Centralia Coll (WA)
Central Texas Coll (TX)
Cerritos Coll (CA)
Chabot Coll (CA)
Chaffey Coll (CA)
Chemeketa Comm Coll (OR)
Chesapeake Coll (MD)
Clackamas Comm Coll (OR)
Clark Coll (WA)
Coffeyville Comm Coll (KS)
Colby Comm Coll (KS)
Coll of Alameda (CA)
Coll of DuPage (IL)
Coll of Marin (CA)
Coll of Southern Idaho (ID)
Coll of the Desert (CA)
Coll of the Sequoias (CA)
Coll of the Siskiyous (CA)
Collin County Comm Coll (TX)
Columbia Coll (CA)
Columbia State Comm Coll (TN)
Comm Coll of Allegheny County Allegheny Cmps (PA)
Comm Coll of Allegheny County South Cmps (PA)
Comm Coll of Southern Nevada (NV)
Connors State Coll (OK)
Contra Costa Coll (CA)
Crafton Hills Coll (CA)
Cypress Coll (CA)
Dalton Coll (GA)
Darton Coll (GA)
Daytona Beach Comm Coll (FL)
De Anza Coll (CA)
Del Mar Coll (TX)
Dixie Coll (UT)
East Central Coll (MO)
Eastern Arizona Coll (AZ)
Eastern Oklahoma State Coll (OK)
Eastern Wyoming Coll (WY)
East Georgia Coll (GA)
East Los Angeles Coll (CA)
East Mississippi Comm Coll (MS)
El Camino Coll (CA)
Ellsworth Comm Coll (IA)
El Paso Comm Coll (TX)
Essex Comm Coll (MD)
Everett Comm Coll (WA)
Finger Lakes Comm Coll (NY)
Foothill Coll (CA)
Frank Phillips Coll (TX)
Fresno City Coll (CA)
Fullerton Coll (CA)
Gainesville Coll (GA)
Garden City Comm Coll (KS)
Garrett Comm Coll (MD)
Gavilan Coll (CA)
Glendale Comm Coll (AZ)
Gordon Coll (GA)
Grays Harbor Coll (WA)
Grayson County Coll (TX)
Gulf Coast Comm Coll (FL)
Harford Comm Coll (MD)
Highland Comm Coll (IL)
Highland Comm Coll (KS)
Hill Coll of the Hill Jr Coll District (TX)
Hinds Comm Coll (MS)
Hiwassee Coll (TN)
Hutchinson Comm Coll and Area Vocational Sch (KS)
Independence Comm Coll (KS)
Indian River Comm Coll (FL)
Iowa Central Comm Coll (IA)
Iowa Lakes Comm Coll (IA)
Itawamba Comm Coll (MS)
Jackson State Comm Coll (TN)
Jefferson Coll (MO)
John Wood Comm Coll (IL)
Joliet Jr Coll (IL)
Kansas City Kansas Comm Coll (KS)
Kellogg Comm Coll (MI)
Kemper Military Jr Coll (MO)
Kirkwood Comm Coll (IA)
Lake City Comm Coll (FL)
Lake Michigan Coll (MI)
Laramie County Comm Coll (WY)
Lincoln Land Comm Coll (IL)
Lon Morris Coll (TX)
Lorain County Comm Coll (OH)
Los Angeles City Coll (CA)
Los Angeles Mission Coll (CA)
Los Angeles Valley Coll (CA)
Los Medanos Coll (CA)
Lower Columbia Coll (WA)
Macon Coll (GA)
Miami-Dade Comm Coll (FL)
Miami University–Middletown Cmps (OH)
Middle Georgia Coll (GA)
Middlesex County Coll (NJ)
Mid Michigan Comm Coll (MI)
Mid-Plains Comm Coll (NE)
Mineral Area Coll (MO)
MiraCosta Coll (CA)
Modesto Jr Coll (CA)
Mohave Comm Coll (AZ)
Monterey Peninsula Coll (CA)
Motlow State Comm Coll (TN)
Muscatine Comm Coll (IA)
Navarro Coll (TX)
Newbury Coll (MA)
Northeastern Oklahoma A&M Coll (OK)
North Harris Coll (TX)
North Idaho Coll (ID)
Northwest Coll (WY)
Northwest Mississippi Comm Coll (MS)
Odessa Coll (TX)
Oklahoma City Comm Coll (OK)
Oxnard Coll (CA)
Palo Alto Coll (TX)
Palo Verde Coll (CA)
Pasadena City Coll (CA)
Penn State U Hazleton Cmps (PA)
Pikes Peak Comm Coll (CO)
Pima Comm Coll (AZ)
Polk Comm Coll (FL)
Potomac State Coll of West Virginia U (WV)
Pratt Comm Coll and Area Voc Sch (KS)
Quincy Coll (MA)
Rancho Santiago Coll (CA)
Raritan Valley Comm Coll (NJ)
Redlands Comm Coll (OK)
Red Rocks Comm Coll (CO)
Ricks Coll (ID)
Rose State Coll (OK)
Saddleback Coll (CA)
Sage Jr Coll of Albany (NY)
St Catharine Coll (KY)
St Philip's Coll (TX)
Salem Comm Coll (NJ)
San Bernardino Valley Coll (CA)
San Diego City Coll (CA)
San Diego Mesa Coll (CA)
San Diego Miramar Coll (CA)
San Jacinto College–Central Cmps (TX)
San Jacinto College–North Cmps (TX)
San Jacinto College–South Cmps (TX)
San Joaquin Delta Coll (CA)
San Juan Coll (NM)
Santa Barbara City Coll (CA)
Santa Monica Coll (CA)
Santa Rosa Jr Coll (CA)
Sauk Valley Comm Coll (IL)
Scott Comm Coll (IA)
Seward County Comm Coll (KS)
Skagit Valley Coll (WA)
Skyline Coll (CA)
Snow Coll (UT)
Southern U at Shreveport–Bossier City Cmps (LA)
South Georgia Coll (GA)
South Mountain Comm Coll (AZ)
Southwestern Coll (CA)
Southwestern Comm Coll (IA)
Spoon River Coll (IL)
State Comm Coll of East St Louis (IL)
State U of NY Coll of A&T at Cobleskill (NY)
Tacoma Comm Coll (WA)
Treasure Valley Comm Coll (OR)
Trinity Valley Comm Coll (TX)
Tulsa Jr Coll (OK)
Umpqua Comm Coll (OR)
U of Kentucky, Jefferson Comm Coll (KY)
Vermilion Comm Coll (MN)
Vincennes U (IN)
Vincennes University–Jasper Ctr (IN)
Waldorf Coll (IA)
Waycross Coll (GA)
Wenatchee Valley Coll (WA)
Western Nebraska Comm Coll, Scottsbluff (NE)
Western Oklahoma State Coll (OK)
Western Wyoming Comm Coll (WY)
West Los Angeles Coll (CA)
West Shore Comm Coll (MI)
West Valley Coll (CA)
Willmar Comm Coll (MN)
Wright State U, Lake Cmps (OH)
Young Harris Coll (GA)

SOIL CONSERVATION
Nebraska Coll of Tech Agriculture (NE)
Northwest Coll (WY)
Ohio State U Ag Tech Inst (OH)
Snow Coll (UT)
Southeast Comm Coll, Beatrice Cmps (NE)
Trinidad State Jr Coll (CO)
Vermilion Comm Coll (MN)

SOLAR TECHNOLOGIES
Cabrillo Coll (CA)
Cerro Coso Comm Coll (CA)
Chabot Coll (CA)
Comm Coll of Allegheny County South Cmps (PA)
Dixie Coll (UT)
Fresno City Coll (CA)
Oakland Comm Coll (MI)
Red Rocks Comm Coll (CO)
San Jose City Coll (CA)
Southeast Comm Coll, Milford Cmps (NE)
Truckee Meadows Comm Coll (NV)
Western Iowa Tech Comm Coll (IA)

SPANISH
Allan Hancock Coll (CA)
Allen County Comm Coll (KS)
Arizona Western Coll (AZ)
Austin Comm Coll (TX)
Bakersfield Coll (CA)
Barstow Comm Coll (CA)
Black Hawk Coll, Moline (IL)
Blinn Coll (TX)
Brazosport Coll (TX)
Brevard Coll (NC)
Brevard Comm Coll (FL)
Cabrillo Coll (CA)
Cañada Coll (CA)
Casper Coll (WY)
Central Texas Coll (TX)
Cerritos Coll (CA)
Chabot Coll (CA)
Chaffey Coll (CA)
City Colls of Chicago, Harold Washington Coll (IL)
Clark Coll (WA)
Cochise Coll, Douglas (AZ)
Coll of Alameda (CA)
Coll of DuPage (IL)
Coll of Marin (CA)
Coll of San Mateo (CA)
Coll of the Canyons (CA)
Coll of the Sequoias (CA)
Collin County Comm Coll (TX)
Comm Coll of Allegheny County Allegheny Cmps (PA)
Contra Costa Coll (CA)
Crafton Hills Coll (CA)
De Anza Coll (CA)
Dixie Coll (UT)
East Central Coll (MO)
Eastern Arizona Coll (AZ)
East Los Angeles Coll (CA)
El Camino Coll (CA)
Everett Comm Coll (WA)
Florida National Coll (FL)
Foothill Coll (CA)
Fresno City Coll (CA)
Gavilan Coll (CA)
Glendale Comm Coll (AZ)
Gordon Coll (GA)
Grossmont Coll (CA)
Hill Coll of the Hill Jr Coll District (TX)
Hutchinson Comm Coll and Area Vocational Sch (KS)
Imperial Valley Coll (CA)
Independence Comm Coll (KS)
Jefferson Coll (MO)
John Wood Comm Coll (IL)
Kansas City Kansas Comm Coll (KS)
Kings River Comm Coll (CA)
Kirkwood Comm Coll (IA)
Lake Tahoe Comm Coll (CA)
Lee Coll (TX)
Long Beach City Coll (CA)
Lon Morris Coll (TX)
Los Angeles City Coll (CA)
Los Angeles Mission Coll (CA)
Los Angeles Southwest Coll (CA)
Los Angeles Valley Coll (CA)
Mendocino Coll (CA)
Merritt Coll (CA)
Miami-Dade Comm Coll (FL)
Middle Georgia Coll (GA)
Middlesex County Coll (NJ)
Midland Coll (TX)
MiraCosta Coll (CA)
Modesto Jr Coll (CA)
Monterey Peninsula Coll (CA)
New Mexico Military Inst (NM)
North Idaho Coll (ID)
Ohio Valley Coll (WV)
Oxnard Coll (CA)
Panama Canal Coll (Republic of Panama)
Pasadena City Coll (CA)
Polk Comm Coll (FL)
Red Rocks Comm Coll (CO)
Ricks Coll (ID)
St Catharine Coll (KY)
St Philip's Coll (TX)
San Bernardino Valley Coll (CA)
San Diego Mesa Coll (CA)
San Diego Miramar Coll (CA)
San Jacinto College–Central Cmps (TX)
San Jacinto College–North Cmps (TX)
San Joaquin Delta Coll (CA)
Santa Barbara City Coll (CA)
Santa Rosa Jr Coll (CA)
Sauk Valley Comm Coll (IL)
Sheridan Coll (WY)
Skagit Valley Coll (WA)
Skyline Coll (CA)
Snow Coll (UT)
Solano Comm Coll (CA)
South Georgia Coll (GA)
Southwestern Coll (CA)
Tacoma Comm Coll (WA)
Trinity Valley Comm Coll (TX)
Triton Coll (IL)
Tulsa Jr Coll (OK)
U of Kentucky, Jefferson Comm Coll (KY)
Vincennes U (IN)
Vista Comm Coll (CA)
Waldorf Coll (IA)
Western Nebraska Comm Coll, Scottsbluff (NE)
Western Oklahoma State Coll (OK)
Western Wyoming Comm Coll (WY)
West Los Angeles Coll (CA)
West Valley Coll (CA)
Wharton County Jr Coll (TX)
Young Harris Coll (GA)

SPEECH/RHETORIC/PUBLIC ADDRESS/DEBATE
Abraham Baldwin Ag Coll (GA)
Alabama Southern Comm Coll, Thomasville (AL)
Andrew Coll (GA)
Arkansas State University–Beebe Branch (AR)
Austin Comm Coll (TX)
Bainbridge Coll (GA)
Bakersfield Coll (CA)
Bee County Coll (TX)
Bismarck State Coll (ND)
Black Hawk Coll, Moline (IL)
Blinn Coll (TX)
Brazosport Coll (TX)
Brevard Comm Coll (FL)
Brookdale Comm Coll (NJ)
Cañada Coll (CA)
Casper Coll (WY)
Cerritos Coll (CA)
Chaffey Coll (CA)
Chemeketa Comm Coll (OR)
City Colls of Chicago, Harold Washington Coll (IL)
City Colls of Chicago, Harry S Truman Coll (IL)
City Colls of Chicago, Richard J Daley Coll (IL)
City Colls of Chicago, Wilbur Wright Coll (IL)
Clark Coll (WA)
Colby Comm Coll (KS)
Coll of Marin (CA)
Coll of San Mateo (CA)
Coll of the Desert (CA)
Coll of the Sequoias (CA)
Collin County Comm Coll (TX)
Columbia State Comm Coll (TN)
Connors State Coll (OK)
Crafton Hills Coll (CA)
Cypress Coll (CA)
Dalton Coll (GA)
Darton Coll (GA)
Del Mar Coll (TX)
Dixie Coll (UT)
Dodge City Comm Coll (KS)
East Central Coll (MO)
Eastern Oklahoma State Coll (OK)
East Los Angeles Coll (CA)
El Camino Coll (CA)
El Paso Comm Coll (TX)
Everett Comm Coll (WA)
Foothill Coll (CA)
Fullerton Coll (CA)
Gainesville Coll (GA)
Garden City Comm Coll (KS)
Grayson County Coll (TX)
Grossmont Coll (CA)
Hill Coll of the Hill Jr Coll District (TX)
Howard Coll (TX)
Hutchinson Comm Coll and Area Vocational Sch (KS)
Indian River Comm Coll (FL)
Iowa Lakes Comm Coll (IA)
Irvine Valley Coll (CA)
Itawamba Comm Coll (MS)
Jefferson Coll (MO)
John Wood Comm Coll (IL)
Kellogg Comm Coll (MI)
Kings River Comm Coll (CA)
Kishwaukee Coll (IL)
Lake Land Coll (IL)
Lansing Comm Coll (MI)
Laramie County Comm Coll (WY)
Long Beach City Coll (CA)
Lon Morris Coll (TX)
Los Angeles City Coll (CA)
Los Angeles Mission Coll (CA)
Los Angeles Valley Coll (CA)
Macon Coll (GA)
Mendocino Coll (CA)
Miami-Dade Comm Coll (FL)
Middle Georgia Coll (GA)
Midland Coll (TX)
MiraCosta Coll (CA)
Modesto Jr Coll (CA)
Monroe County Comm Coll (MI)
Navarro Coll (TX)
Northeast Comm Coll (NE)
Northern Virginia Comm Coll (VA)
North Harris Coll (TX)
Northwest Coll (WY)
Odessa Coll (TX)
Ohio Valley Coll (WV)
Palo Alto Coll (TX)
Palomar Coll (CA)
Pasadena City Coll (CA)
Pima Comm Coll (AZ)
Pratt Comm Coll and Area Voc Sch (KS)
Redlands Comm Coll (OK)
Rose State Coll (OK)
Sacramento City Coll (CA)
Saddleback Coll (CA)
St Louis Comm Coll at Meramec (MO)
St Philip's Coll (TX)
San Diego City Coll (CA)
San Diego Mesa Coll (CA)
San Joaquin Delta Coll (CA)
San Juan Coll (NM)
Santa Barbara City Coll (CA)
Santa Rosa Jr Coll (CA)
Sauk Valley Comm Coll (IL)
Seward County Comm Coll (KS)
Skagit Valley Coll (WA)
Skyline Coll (CA)
South Georgia Coll (GA)
Southwestern Coll (CA)
Spoon River Coll (IL)
Tacoma Comm Coll (WA)
Trinity Valley Comm Coll (TX)
Triton Coll (IL)
Tyler Jr Coll (TX)
Vermilion Comm Coll (MN)
Waldorf Coll (IA)
Waubonsee Comm Coll (IL)
Western Oklahoma State Coll (OK)
West Los Angeles Coll (CA)
West Valley Coll (CA)
Wharton County Jr Coll (TX)
Willmar Comm Coll (MN)

SPEECH THERAPY
Modesto Jr Coll (CA)
Northeast Mississippi Comm Coll (MS)
Ricks Coll (ID)

SPORTS ADMINISTRATION
Barton County Comm Coll (KS)
Brevard Coll (NC)
Butler County Comm Coll (PA)
Champlain Coll (VT)
Columbus State Comm Coll (OH)
Comm Coll of Allegheny County North Cmps (PA)
Dean Coll (MA)

Associate Degree Programs at Two-Year Colleges
Sports Administration–Theater Arts/Drama

Herkimer County Comm Coll (NY)
Holyoke Comm Coll (MA)
Mitchell Coll (CT)
New Mexico Military Inst (NM)
Northampton County Area Comm Coll (PA)
Sullivan County Comm Coll (NY)
Vincennes U (IN)

SPORTS MEDICINE
Barton County Comm Coll (KS)
Brevard Coll (NC)
Coffeyville Comm Coll (KS)
Coll of the Sequoias (CA)
Colorado Mountn Coll, Alpine Cmps (CO)
Dean Coll (MA)
Dodge City Comm Coll (KS)
Essex Comm Coll (MD)
Fort Scott Comm Coll (KS)
Highland Comm Coll (KS)
Hutchinson Comm Coll and Area Vocational Sch (KS)
Independence Comm Coll (KS)
Lorain County Comm Coll (OH)
Mitchell Coll (CT)
Mount Ida Coll (MA)
Neosho County Comm Coll (KS)
New Hampshire Tech Coll, Manchester (NH)
New Mexico Jr Coll (NM)
Northland Comm and Tech Coll (MN)
Pratt Comm Coll and Area Voc Sch (KS)
Ricks Coll (ID)
Seward County Comm Coll (KS)
Wenatchee Valley Coll (WA)

STATISTICS
Brevard Coll (NC)
Chabot Coll (CA)
Daytona Beach Comm Coll (FL)
Pasadena City Coll (CA)
U of Kentucky, Jefferson Comm Coll (KY)

STRINGED INSTRUMENTS
Kansas City Kansas Comm Coll (KS)
Miami-Dade Comm Coll (FL)

STUDIO ART
American Acad of Art (IL)
Atlantic Comm Coll (NJ)
Bee County Coll (TX)
Berkshire Comm Coll (MA)
Brevard Coll (NC)
Catonsville Comm Coll (MD)
Chabot Coll (CA)
City Colls of Chicago, Harold Washington Coll (IL)
Coll of the Siskiyous (CA)
Del Mar Coll (TX)
Finger Lakes Comm Coll (NY)
Foothill Coll (CA)
Garden City Comm Coll (KS)
Holyoke Comm Coll (MA)
Inst of American Indian Arts (NM)
Iowa Lakes Comm Coll (IA)
Kansas City Kansas Comm Coll (KS)
Kellogg Comm Coll (MI)
Lansing Comm Coll (MI)
Lon Morris Coll (TX)
Los Medanos Coll (CA)
Maryland Coll of Art and Design (MD)
Middlesex Community–Tech Coll (CT)
Middlesex County Coll (NJ)
Midland Coll (TX)
Mohawk Valley Comm Coll (NY)
Monterey Peninsula Coll (CA)
Montgomery College–Rockville Cmps (MD)
Mount Ida Coll (MA)

Mount Wachusett Comm Coll (MA)
Nassau Comm Coll (NY)
Northeastern Jr Coll (CO)
Oakland Comm Coll (MI)
Polk Comm Coll (FL)
Raritan Valley Comm Coll (NJ)
Sandhills Comm Coll (NC)
San Diego Miramar Coll (CA)
San Jacinto College–Central Cmps (TX)
Sinclair Comm Coll (OH)
Skyline Coll (CA)
U of New Mexico–Gallup Branch (NM)
U of New Mexico–Los Alamos Branch (NM)
West Shore Comm Coll (MI)

SURVEYING TECHNOLOGY
Asheville-Buncombe Tech Comm Coll (NC)
Austin Comm Coll (TX)
Bakersfield Coll (CA)
Catonsville Comm Coll (MD)
Central Piedmont Comm Coll (NC)
Chabot Coll (CA)
Chattanooga State Tech Comm Coll (TN)
Chemeketa Comm Coll (OR)
Chippewa Valley Tech Coll (WI)
Cincinnati State Tech and Comm Coll (OH)
Comm Coll of Allegheny County Boyce Cmps (PA)
Comm Coll of Allegheny County South Cmps (PA)
Comm Coll of Beaver County (PA)
Comm Coll of Southern Nevada (NV)
Comm Coll of the Air Force (AL)
Cuyamaca Coll (CA)
Delaware Tech & Comm Coll, Terry Cmps (DE)
Eastern Oklahoma State Coll (OK)
Flathead Valley Comm Coll (MT)
Frank Phillips Coll (TX)
Guilford Tech Comm Coll (NC)
Hawkeye Comm Coll (IA)
Indian River Comm Coll (FL)
Lansing Comm Coll (MI)
Lincoln Land Comm Coll (IL)
Macomb Comm Coll (MI)
Mercer County Comm Coll (NJ)
Miami-Dade Comm Coll (FL)
Middle Georgia Coll (GA)
Middlesex County Coll (NJ)
Mid-State Tech Coll (WI)
Milwaukee Area Tech Coll (WI)
Mohawk Valley Comm Coll (NY)
Morrison Inst of Tech (IL)
Mt San Antonio Coll (CA)
New Hampshire Tech Coll, Berlin (NH)
Nicolet Area Tech Coll (WI)
Ocean County Coll (NJ)
Oklahoma State U, Oklahoma City (OK)
Palm Beach Comm Coll (FL)
Palomar Coll (CA)
Paul Smith's Coll (NY)
Pennsylvania Coll of Tech (PA)
Penn State U Wilkes-Barre Cmps (PA)
Petit Jean Tech Coll (AR)
Rancho Santiago Coll (CA)
Red Rocks Comm Coll (CO)
Renton Tech Coll (WA)
Sacramento City Coll (CA)
Salt Lake Comm Coll (UT)
Sandhills Comm Coll (NC)
San Jacinto College–Central Cmps (TX)
San Joaquin Delta Coll (CA)
Santa Fe Comm Coll (NM)
Sierra Coll (CA)
Sinclair Comm Coll (OH)
Southeast Comm Coll, Milford Cmps (NE)
State U of NY Coll of Tech at Alfred (NY)

Sullivan County Comm Coll (NY)
Terra State Comm Coll (OH)
Treasure Valley Comm Coll (OR)
Tulsa Jr Coll (OK)
Tyler Jr Coll (TX)
Valencia Comm Coll (FL)
Vincennes U (IN)
Wake Tech Comm Coll (NC)

SYSTEMS SCIENCE
Dunwoody Inst (MN)
Luzerne County Comm Coll (PA)
Miami University–Middletown Cmps (OH)
Pensacola Jr Coll (FL)

TEACHER AIDE STUDIES
Alamance Comm Coll (NC)
Angelina Coll (TX)
Antelope Valley Coll (CA)
Athens Area Tech Inst (GA)
Atlanta Metropolitan Coll (GA)
Barstow Coll (CA)
Big Bend Comm Coll (WA)
Blackfeet Comm Coll (MT)
Brevard Comm Coll (FL)
Bucks County Comm Coll (PA)
Carteret Comm Coll (NC)
Catawba Valley Comm Coll (NC)
Central Comm College–Platte Cmps (NE)
Chabot Coll (CA)
Charles Stewart Mott Comm Coll (MI)
Chemeketa Comm Coll (OR)
City Colls of Chicago, Harold Washington Coll (IL)
City Colls of Chicago, Harry S Truman Coll (IL)
City Colls of Chicago, Kennedy-King Coll (IL)
City Colls of Chicago, Malcolm X Coll (IL)
City Colls of Chicago, Richard J Daley Coll (IL)
Clark Coll (WA)
Cochise Coll, Douglas (AZ)
Cochise Coll, Sierra Vista (AZ)
Colby Comm Coll (KS)
Coll of Micronesia–FSM (FM)
Coll of the Desert (CA)
Comm Coll of Allegheny County South Cmps (PA)
Comm Coll of Southern Nevada (NV)
Comm Coll of Vermont (VT)
Craven Comm Coll (NC)
Danville Area Comm Coll (IL)
Des Moines Area Comm Coll (IA)
East Central Coll (MO)
Eastern Wyoming Coll (WY)
Ellsworth Comm Coll (IA)
Essex Comm Coll (MD)
Florida Comm Coll at Jacksonville (FL)
Fort Scott Comm Coll (KS)
Fresno City Coll (CA)
Fulton-Montgomery Comm Coll (NY)
Garden City Comm Coll (KS)
Indian River Comm Coll (FL)
Iowa Central Comm Coll (IA)
Isothermal Comm Coll (NC)
John A Logan Coll (IL)
Joliet Jr Coll (IL)
Kirkwood Comm Coll (IA)
Kishwaukee Coll (IL)
Lac Courte Oreilles Ojibwa Comm Coll (WI)
Lake Michigan Coll (MI)
Lakeshore Tech Coll (WI)
Lamar Comm Coll (CO)
Lansing Comm Coll (MI)
Lewis and Clark Comm Coll (IL)
Lincoln Land Comm Coll (IL)
Los Angeles City Coll (CA)
Los Angeles Mission Coll (CA)
Los Angeles Southwest Coll (CA)
Manchester Comm-Tech Coll (CT)

McDowell Tech Comm Coll (NC)
Merced Coll (CA)
Mercer County Comm Coll (NJ)
Mesa Comm Coll (AZ)
Miami-Dade Comm Coll (FL)
Middlesex County Coll (NJ)
MiraCosta Coll (CA)
Montgomery County Comm Coll (PA)
Moorpark Coll (CA)
Moraine Valley Comm Coll (IL)
Mount Ida Coll (MA)
Nash Comm Coll (NC)
Neosho County Comm Coll (KS)
Northeast Mississippi Comm Coll (MS)
Northland Pioneer Coll (AZ)
North Shore Comm Coll (MA)
Odessa Coll (TX)
Palomar Coll (CA)
Pasadena City Coll (CA)
Pima Comm Coll (AZ)
Prairie State Coll (IL)
Renton Tech Coll (WA)
Robeson Comm Coll (NC)
Rockingham Comm Coll (NC)
Saddleback Coll (CA)
St Cloud Tech Coll (MN)
St Philip's Coll (TX)
Sandhills Comm Coll (NC)
San Diego City Coll (CA)
San Jose City Coll (CA)
Shasta Coll (CA)
Shoreline Comm Coll (WA)
Sierra Coll (CA)
Southeastern Comm Coll (NC)
Southern U at Shreveport–Bossier City Cmps (LA)
South Suburban Coll (IL)
Southwest Texas Jr Coll (TX)
Spokane Falls Comm Coll (WA)
Thomas Nelson Comm Coll (VA)
Vance-Granville Comm Coll (NC)
West Shore Comm Coll (MI)

TECHNICAL WRITING
Austin Comm Coll (TX)
Black Hawk Coll, Moline (IL)
Brevard Comm Coll (FL)
Cincinnati State Tech and Comm Coll (OH)
Clark Coll (WA)
Coll of Lake County (IL)
Columbus State Comm Coll (OH)
Comm Coll of Allegheny County South Cmps (PA)
De Anza Coll (CA)
El Camino Coll (CA)
Florida National Coll (FL)
Front Range Comm Coll (CO)
Golden West Coll (CA)
Houston Comm Coll System (TX)
Kellogg Comm Coll (MI)
North Shore Comm Coll (MA)
Oklahoma State U, Oklahoma City (OK)
Paul Smith's Coll (NY)
Rock Valley Coll (IL)
San Diego Mesa Coll (CA)
Terra State Comm Coll (OH)
Three Rivers Comm-Tech Coll (CT)
Washtenaw Comm Coll (MI)

TECHNOLOGY AND PUBLIC AFFAIRS
Montgomery County Comm Coll (PA)
Ohio State U Ag Tech Inst (OH)
Pines Tech Coll (AR)

TELECOMMUNICATIONS
Anne Arundel Comm Coll (MD)
Bossier Parish Comm Coll (LA)
Briarcliffe–The Coll for Business & Tech (NY)
Brookdale Comm Coll (NJ)

Bucks County Comm Coll (PA)
Butte Coll (CA)
Cayuga County Comm Coll (NY)
Central Carolina Comm Coll (NC)
Central Texas Coll (TX)
Central Wyoming Coll (WY)
Chaffey Coll (CA)
CHI Inst (PA)
City Colls of Chicago, Richard J Daley Coll (IL)
Clark Coll (WA)
Coffeyville Comm Coll (KS)
Colby Comm Coll (KS)
Comm Coll of Beaver County (PA)
Comm Coll of the Air Force (AL)
County Coll of Morris (NJ)
Cuesta Coll (CA)
Cuyahoga Comm Coll, Metropolitan Cmps (OH)
Daytona Beach Comm Coll (FL)
Dean Coll (MA)
Delaware County Comm Coll (PA)
Des Moines Area Comm Coll (IA)
DeVry Tech Inst (NJ)
ECPI Coll of Tech, Hampton (VA)
ECPI Coll of Tech, Virginia Beach (VA)
ECPI Computer Inst, Richmond (VA)
ECPI Computer Inst, Roanoke (VA)
Erie Comm Coll, South Cmps (NY)
Fiorello H LaGuardia Comm Coll of City U of NY (NY)
Gadsden State Comm Coll (AL)
Golden West Coll (CA)
Grossmont Coll (CA)
Gwinnett Tech Inst (GA)
Heald Inst of Tech, Milpitas (CA)
Herkimer County Comm Coll (NY)
Highland Comm Coll (KS)
Hocking Coll (OH)
Howard Comm Coll (MD)
Hudson Valley Comm Coll (NY)
Illinois Eastern Comm Colls, Lincoln Trail Coll (IL)
Inver Hills Comm Coll (MN)
Iowa Central Comm Coll (IA)
Jefferson Coll (MO)
Kansas City Kansas Comm Coll (KS)
Kirkwood Comm Coll (IA)
Lake Land Coll (IL)
Lansing Comm Coll (MI)
Lee Coll (TX)
Long Beach City Coll (CA)
Los Angeles City Coll (CA)
Mercer County Comm Coll (NJ)
Midlands Tech Coll (SC)
Montgomery College–Germantown Cmps (MD)
Montgomery County Comm Coll (PA)
Moorpark Coll (CA)
Moraine Valley Comm Coll (IL)
Mount Wachusett Comm Coll (MA)
Napa Valley Coll (CA)
NEI Coll of Tech (MN)
New England Inst of Tech (RI)
New Hampshire Tech Coll, Nashua (NH)
New York City Tech Coll of the City U of NY (NY)
Niagara County Comm Coll (NY)
Northwest Mississippi Comm Coll (MS)
Onondaga Comm Coll (NY)
Owens Comm Coll, Findlay (OH)
Owens Comm Coll, Toledo (OH)
Oxnard Coll (CA)
Palomar Coll (CA)
Pasadena City Coll (CA)
Pima Comm Coll (AZ)
Rancho Santiago Coll (CA)

Raritan Valley Comm Coll (NJ)
Reading Area Comm Coll (PA)
St Louis Comm Coll at Florissant Valley (MO)
San Bernardino Valley Coll (CA)
San Diego City Coll (CA)
Schenectady County Comm Coll (NY)
Seminole Comm Coll (FL)
Skyline Coll (CA)
Solano Comm Coll (CA)
South Plains Coll (TX)
South Puget Sound Comm Coll (WA)
Southwestern Coll (CA)
Springfield Tech Comm Coll (MA)
State Tech Inst at Memphis (TN)
Suffolk County Comm College–Ammerman Cmps (NY)
Tech Coll of Municipality of San Juan (PR)
Tulsa Jr Coll (OK)
U of North Dakota–Lake Region (ND)
Wake Tech Comm Coll (NC)
Waldorf Coll (IA)

TEXTILE ARTS
Fashion Inst of Design & Merchandising, LA Cmps (CA)
Fulton-Montgomery Comm Coll (NY)
Haywood Comm Coll (NC)
Highland Comm Coll (KS)
Hiwassee Coll (TN)
Inst of American Indian Arts (NM)
Monterey Peninsula Coll (CA)
Pasadena City Coll (CA)

TEXTILES AND CLOTHING
Art Inst of Fort Lauderdale (FL)
Bradley Acad for the Visual Arts (PA)
Brooks Coll (CA)
Central Alabama Comm Coll (AL)
El Centro Coll (TX)
Fashion Inst of Design & Merchandising, LA Cmps (CA)
Fashion Inst of Design & Merchandising, SF Cmps (CA)
Hawkeye Comm Coll (IA)
Hinds Comm Coll (MS)
Hiwassee Coll (TN)
Indian River Comm Coll (FL)
John M Patterson State Tech Coll (AL)
Lawson State Comm Coll (AL)
Long Beach City Coll (CA)
Los Angeles City Coll (CA)
Middle Georgia Coll (GA)
Modesto Jr Coll (CA)
Monterey Peninsula Coll (CA)
Mount Ida Coll (MA)
Northeastern Oklahoma A&M Coll (OK)
Palm Beach Comm Coll (FL)
Ricks Coll (ID)
St Philip's Coll (TX)
Tri-County Tech Coll (SC)

THEATER ARTS/DRAMA
Allen County Comm Coll (KS)
Alvin Comm Coll (TX)
American Acad of Dramatic Arts (NY)
American Acad of Dramatic Arts/West (CA)
American River Coll (CA)
Andrew Coll (GA)
Antelope Valley Coll (CA)
Arizona Western Coll (AZ)
Bainbridge Coll (GA)
Bakersfield Coll (CA)
Barstow Coll (CA)
Barton County Comm Coll (KS)
Bee County Coll (TX)
Bergen Comm Coll (NJ)

Associate Degree Programs at Two-Year Colleges
Theater Arts/Drama–Urban Studies

Berkshire Comm Coll (MA)
Bismarck State Coll (ND)
Black Hawk Coll, Moline (IL)
Blinn Coll (TX)
Brevard Coll (NC)
Brevard Comm Coll (FL)
Bristol Comm Coll (MA)
Brookdale Comm Coll (NJ)
Bucks County Comm Coll (PA)
Burlington County Coll (NJ)
Butler County Comm Coll (KS)
Camden County Coll (NJ)
Cañada Coll (CA)
Cape Cod Comm Coll (MA)
Casper Coll (WY)
Catonsville Comm Coll (MD)
Central Comm College–Platte Cmps (NE)
Centralia Coll (WA)
Central Wyoming Coll (WY)
Cerritos Coll (CA)
Chaffey Coll (CA)
Chattahoochee Valley State Comm Coll (AL)
Citrus Coll (CA)
City Colls of Chicago, Harold Washington Coll (IL)
City Colls of Chicago, Richard J Daley Coll (IL)
Clackamas Comm Coll (OR)
Clark Coll (WA)
Clark State Comm Coll (OH)
Coffeyville Comm Coll (KS)
Colby Comm Coll (KS)
Coll of DuPage (IL)
Coll of Marin (CA)
Coll of Southern Idaho (ID)
Coll of The Albemarle (NC)
Coll of the Desert (CA)
Coll of the Sequoias (CA)
Collin County Comm Coll (TX)
Colorado Mountn Coll, Roaring Fork Cmps-Spring Valley Ctr (CO)
Columbia Coll (CA)
Comm Coll of Allegheny County Allegheny Cmps (PA)
Comm Coll of Allegheny County Boyce Cmps (PA)
Comm Coll of Allegheny County South Cmps (PA)
Comm Coll of Rhode Island (RI)
Comm Coll of Southern Nevada (NV)
Cosumnes River Coll (CA)
County Coll of Morris (NJ)
Cowley County Comm Coll and Voc-Tech Sch (KS)
Crafton Hills Coll (CA)
Cumberland County Coll (NJ)
Cypress Coll (CA)
Darton Coll (GA)
Daytona Beach Comm Coll (FL)
Dean Coll (MA)
De Anza Coll (CA)
DeKalb Coll (GA)
Delgado Comm Coll (LA)
Del Mar Coll (TX)
Delta Coll (MI)
Dixie Coll (UT)
Dodge City Comm Coll (KS)
East Central Coll (MO)
Eastern Arizona Coll (AZ)
Eastern Oklahoma State Coll (OK)
Eastern Wyoming Coll (WY)
East Los Angeles Coll (CA)
El Camino Coll (CA)
El Paso Comm Coll (TX)
Essex Comm Coll (MD)
Everett Comm Coll (WA)
Fashion Inst of Design & Merchandising, LA Cmps (CA)
Finger Lakes Comm Coll (NY)
Foothill Coll (CA)
Fresno City Coll (CA)
Fullerton Coll (CA)
Fulton-Montgomery Comm Coll (NY)
Gainesville Coll (GA)
Galveston Coll (TX)
Garden City Comm Coll (KS)
Genesee Comm Coll (NY)
Glendale Comm Coll (AZ)
Gordon Coll (GA)
Grays Harbor Coll (WA)
Grayson County Coll (TX)
Grossmont Coll (CA)
Guilford Tech Comm Coll (NC)
Gulf Coast Comm Coll (FL)
Harrisburg Area Comm Coll (PA)
Henry Ford Comm Coll (MI)
Highland Comm Coll (IL)
Highland Comm Coll (KS)
Hill Coll of the Hill Jr Coll District (TX)
Hinds Comm Coll (MS)
Holyoke Comm Coll (MA)
Houston Comm Coll System (TX)
Howard Coll (TX)
Howard Comm Coll (MD)
Jefferson Coll (MO)
Jefferson Davis Comm Coll (AL)
John C Calhoun State Comm Coll (AL)
John Wood Comm Coll (IL)
Joliet Jr Coll (IL)
Kansas City Kansas Comm Coll (KS)
KD Studio (TX)
Kellogg Comm Coll (MI)
Kingsborough Comm Coll of City U of NY (NY)
Kings River Comm Coll (CA)
Kirkwood Comm Coll (IA)
Lake City Comm Coll (FL)
Lake Land Coll (IL)
Lake Michigan Coll (MI)
Lake Tahoe Comm Coll (CA)
Laney Coll (CA)
Laramie County Comm Coll (WY)
Lee Coll (TX)
Lincoln Land Comm Coll (IL)
Linn-Benton Comm Coll (OR)
Long Beach City Coll (CA)
Lon Morris Coll (TX)
Lorain County Comm Coll (OH)
Los Angeles City Coll (CA)
Los Angeles Mission Coll (CA)
Los Angeles Pierce Coll (CA)
Los Angeles Southwest Coll (CA)
Los Angeles Valley Coll (CA)
Lower Columbia Coll (WA)
Macon Coll (GA)
Manchester Comm-Tech Coll (CT)
Massachusetts Bay Comm Coll (MA)
Massasoit Comm Coll (MA)
Mendocino Coll (CA)
Merced Coll (CA)
Mercer County Comm Coll (NJ)
Miami-Dade Comm Coll (FL)
Middle Georgia Coll (GA)
Middlesex Comm Coll (MA)
Middlesex County Coll (NJ)
Mid Michigan Comm Coll (MI)
Mid-Plains Comm Coll (NE)
MiraCosta Coll (CA)
Mississippi Delta Comm Coll (MS)
Modesto Jr Coll (CA)
Monterey Peninsula Coll (CA)
Montgomery College–Rockville Cmps (MD)
Moorpark Coll (CA)
Navarro Coll (TX)
New Mexico Jr Coll (NM)
Niagara County Comm Coll (NY)
Northeast Comm Coll (NE)
Northeastern Jr Coll (CO)
Northeastern Oklahoma A&M Coll (OK)
Northeast Mississippi Comm Coll (MS)
Northern Essex Comm Coll (MA)
North Harris Coll (TX)
North Idaho Coll (ID)
Northwest Coll (WY)
Oklahoma City Comm Coll (OK)
Otero Jr Coll (CO)
Oxnard Coll (CA)
Palm Beach Comm Coll (FL)
Palomar Coll (CA)
Pasadena City Coll (CA)
Pensacola Jr Coll (FL)
Phillips County Comm Coll (AR)
Piedmont Virginia Comm Coll (VA)
Pikes Peak Comm Coll (CO)
Pima Comm Coll (AZ)
Prairie State Coll (IL)
Queensborough Comm Coll of City U of NY (NY)
Rancho Santiago Coll (CA)
Raritan Valley Comm Coll (NJ)
Ricks Coll (ID)
Riverside Comm Coll (CA)
Rockland Comm Coll (NY)
Rose State Coll (OK)
Sacramento City Coll (CA)
Saddleback Coll (CA)
St Johns River Comm Coll (FL)
St Louis Comm Coll at Florissant Valley (MO)
St Louis Comm Coll at Meramec (MO)
St Philip's Coll (TX)
San Diego City Coll (CA)
San Jacinto College–Central Cmps (TX)
San Jacinto College–North Cmps (TX)
San Joaquin Delta Coll (CA)
San Juan Coll (NM)
Santa Barbara City Coll (CA)
Santa Monica Coll (CA)
Santa Rosa Jr Coll (CA)
Sauk Valley Comm Coll (IL)
Schenectady County Comm Coll (NY)
Schoolcraft Coll (MI)
Scottsdale Comm Coll (AZ)
Seward County Comm Coll (KS)
Shasta Coll (CA)
Sinclair Comm Coll (OH)
Snow Coll (UT)
Southwestern Coll (CA)
Spoon River Coll (IL)
Suffolk County Comm College–Ammerman Cmps (NY)
Texarkana Coll (TX)
Three Rivers Comm-Tech Coll (CT)
Treasure Valley Comm Coll (OR)
Trinidad State Jr Coll (CO)
Trinity Valley Comm Coll (TX)
Triton Coll (IL)
Tulsa Jr Coll (OK)
Umpqua Comm Coll (OR)
Union County Coll (NJ)
Valencia Comm Coll (FL)
Ventura Coll (CA)
Vermilion Comm Coll (MN)
Vernon Regional Jr Coll (TX)
Victor Valley Coll (CA)
Vincennes U (IN)
Virginia Highlands Comm Coll (VA)
Waldorf Coll (IA)
Waubonsee Comm Coll (IL)
Western Nebraska Comm Coll, Scottsbluff (NE)
Western Wyoming Comm Coll (WY)
West Valley Coll (CA)
Wharton County Jr Coll (TX)
Wilkes Comm Coll (NC)
Willmar Comm Coll (MN)
Young Harris Coll (GA)
Yuba Coll (CA)

THEOLOGY

Assumption Coll for Sisters (NJ)
Brevard Coll (NC)
Central Coll (KS)
The Coll of Saint Thomas More (TX)
Highland Comm Coll (KS)
Lon Morris Coll (TX)
Northeast Mississippi Comm Coll (MS)
St Gregory's Coll (OK)
Southeastern Baptist Theological Sem (NC)
Waldorf Coll (IA)

TOURISM AND TRAVEL

Adirondack Comm Coll (NY)
Allentown Business Sch (PA)
American Inst of Business (IA)
American Inst of Commerce (IA)
Arapahoe Comm Coll (CO)
Art Inst of Fort Lauderdale (FL)
Art Inst of Seattle (WA)
Atlantic Comm Coll (NJ)
Bay State Coll (MA)
Beal Coll (ME)
Berkeley Coll (NJ)
Berkeley Coll, New York (NY)
Berkeley Coll, White Plains (NY)
Blair Jr Coll (CO)
Blue Ridge Comm Coll (NC)
Borough of Manhattan Comm Coll of City U of NY (NY)
Bradford Sch (OH)
Briarwood Coll (CT)
Broome Comm Coll (NY)
Broward Comm Coll (FL)
Bryant and Stratton Business Inst, Albany (NY)
Bryant and Stratton Business Inst, Cicero (NY)
Bryant and Stratton Business Inst, Lackawanna (NY)
Bryant and Stratton Business Inst, Rochester (NY)
Bryant and Stratton Business Inst, Syracuse (NY)
Bryant and Stratton Business Inst, E Hills Cmps, Williamsville (NY)
Butte Coll (CA)
Cañada Coll (CA)
Casco Bay Coll (ME)
Central Pennsylvania Business Sch (PA)
Central Piedmont Comm Coll (NC)
Chabot Coll (CA)
Champlain Coll (VT)
City Colls of Chicago, Harold Washington Coll (IL)
Cloud County Comm Coll (KS)
Coll of DuPage (IL)
Columbus State Comm Coll (OH)
Cypress Coll (CA)
Danville Area Comm Coll (IL)
Davis Coll (OH)
Daytona Beach Comm Coll (FL)
Dixie Coll (UT)
East Central Coll (MO)
Edmonds Comm Coll (WA)
Elgin Comm Coll (IL)
El Paso Comm Coll (TX)
Erie Business Ctr, Main (PA)
Erie Business Ctr South (PA)
Finger Lakes Comm Coll (NY)
Fiorello H LaGuardia Comm Coll of City U of NY (NY)
Fisher Coll (MA)
Florida National Coll (FL)
Foothill Coll (CA)
Fugazzi Coll (KY)
Fullerton Coll (CA)
Genesee Comm Coll (NY)
Grays Harbor Coll (WA)
Gwinnett Tech Inst (GA)
Hamilton Business Coll (IA)
Harcum Coll (PA)
Harrisburg Area Comm Coll (PA)
Heald Business Coll (HI)
Herkimer County Comm Coll (NY)
Hesser Coll (NH)
Highline Comm Coll (WA)
Hocking Coll (OH)
Holyoke Comm Coll (MA)
Houston Comm Coll System (TX)
Hutchinson Comm Coll and Area Vocational Sch (KS)
ICM Sch of Business (PA)
Indiana Business Coll (IN)
Inst of Career Education (FL)
Jefferson Comm Coll (NY)
John A Logan Coll (IL)
Kansas City Kansas Comm Coll (KS)
Kent State U, Trumbull Cmps (OH)
Keystone Coll (PA)
Kingsborough Comm Coll of City U of NY (NY)
Lakeland Comm Coll (OH)
Lansing Comm Coll (MI)
Lehigh Carbon Comm Coll (PA)
Lincoln Coll, Normal (IL)
Lincoln Land Comm Coll (IL)
Lincoln Sch of Commerce (NE)
Long Beach City Coll (CA)
Lorain County Comm Coll (OH)
Los Angeles City Coll (CA)
Los Medanos Coll (CA)
Luzerne County Comm Coll (PA)
MacCormac Jr Coll (IL)
Madison Area Tech Coll (WI)
Maple Woods Comm Coll (MO)
Marian Court Coll (MA)
Massachusetts Bay Comm Coll (MA)
Massasoit Comm Coll (MA)
Mayland Comm Coll (NC)
McIntosh Coll (NH)
Miami-Dade Comm Coll (FL)
Midstate Coll (IL)
Mid-State Coll (ME)
MiraCosta Coll (CA)
Monroe Comm Coll (NY)
Moraine Valley Comm Coll (IL)
Mt Hood Comm Coll (OR)
Mount Ida Coll (MA)
Muskingum Area Tech Coll (OH)
National Business Coll, Charlottesville (VA)
National Business Coll, Roanoke (VA)
Nettleton Career Coll (SD)
Newbury Coll (MA)
New Hampshire Tech Inst (NH)
Newport Business Inst (PA)
Northampton County Area Comm Coll (PA)
Northeastern Jr Coll (CO)
Northern Essex Comm Coll (MA)
Northern Virginia Comm Coll (VA)
North Harris Coll (TX)
North Shore Comm Coll (MA)
Northwest Coll (WY)
Northwestern Business Coll (IL)
Northwestern Michigan Coll (MI)
Oklahoma City Comm Coll (OK)
Palomar Coll (CA)
Parks Jr Coll (CO)
Pasadena City Coll (CA)
Paul Smith's Coll (NY)
Peoples Coll (FL)
Phillips Jr Coll (UT)
Phillips Jr Coll, Condie Cmps (CA)
Pima Comm Coll (AZ)
Pueblo Comm Coll (CO)
Quincy Coll (MA)
Quinsigamond Comm Coll (MA)
Rancho Santiago Coll (CA)
Raritan Valley Comm Coll (NJ)
Rasmussen Coll Eagan (MN)
Rasmussen Coll Mankato (MN)
Rasmussen Coll St Cloud (MN)
Reading Area Comm Coll (PA)
RETS Tech Ctr (OH)
Rockingham Comm Coll (NC)
Rockland Comm Coll (NY)
Saddleback Coll (CA)
St Louis Comm Coll at Forest Park (MO)
San Diego City Coll (CA)
San Diego Mesa Coll (CA)
Sanford-Brown Coll, Des Peres (MO)
Schenectady County Comm Coll (NY)
Sinclair Comm Coll (OH)
Southern Ohio Coll, Cincinnati Cmps (OH)
Southern U at Shreveport–Bossier City Cmps (LA)
Southwestern Coll (CA)
Spencer Sch of Business (NE)
State U of NY Coll of A&T at Cobleskill (NY)
State U of NY Coll of A&T at Morrisville (NY)
State U of NY Coll of Tech at Delhi (NY)
Stratton Coll (WI)
Suffolk County Comm Coll–Eastern Cmps (NY)
Sullivan County Comm Coll (NY)
Taylor Business Inst (NY)
Three Rivers Comm-Tech Coll (CT)
Tompkins Cortland Comm Coll (NY)
Tulsa Jr Coll (OK)
U of Alaska Southeast, Ketchikan Cmps (AK)
Waubonsee Comm Coll (IL)
Westchester Comm Coll (NY)
West Los Angeles Coll (CA)
Westmoreland County Comm Coll (PA)
Willmar Comm Coll (MN)
Yakima Valley Comm Coll (WA)

TRANSPORTATION TECHNOLOGIES

Catawba Valley Comm Coll (NC)
Catonsville Comm Coll (MD)
Central Piedmont Comm Coll (NC)
Chattanooga State Tech Comm Coll (TN)
City Coll of San Francisco (CA)
City Colls of Chicago, Harold Washington Coll (IL)
City Colls of Chicago, Richard J Daley Coll (IL)
Coll of DuPage (IL)
Comm Coll of Denver (CO)
Comm Coll of the Air Force (AL)
Delaware Tech & Comm Coll, Stanton/Wilmington Cmps (DE)
Elgin Comm Coll (IL)
Florida Comm Coll at Jacksonville (FL)
Fort Scott Comm Coll (KS)
Fresno City Coll (CA)
Front Range Comm Coll (CO)
Green River Comm Coll (WA)
Henry Ford Comm Coll (MI)
Illinois Eastern Comm Colls, Wabash Valley Coll (IL)
Jackson State Comm Coll (TN)
John C Calhoun State Comm Coll (AL)
Johnson County Comm Coll (KS)
Johnson Tech Inst (PA)
Los Angeles Trade-Tech Coll (CA)
Middlesex County Coll (NJ)
Milwaukee Area Tech Coll (WI)
Mt San Antonio Coll (CA)
Muskegon Comm Coll (MI)
Nassau Comm Coll (NY)
Northeast Iowa Comm Coll, Peosta Cmps (IA)
North Hennepin Comm Coll (MN)
Oklahoma State U, Oklahoma City (OK)
Oxnard Coll (CA)
Sacramento City Coll (CA)
Salt Lake Comm Coll (UT)
San Diego City Coll (CA)
San Diego Miramar Coll (CA)
Sinclair Comm Coll (OH)
Southeast Comm Coll, Milford Cmps (NE)
Triton Coll (IL)
Tulsa Jr Coll (OK)
Utah Valley State Coll (UT)
West Hills Comm Coll (CA)

URBAN STUDIES

Brunswick Coll (GA)
Comm Coll of Rhode Island (RI)
Lorain County Comm Coll (OH)
Union County Coll (NJ)
U of Cincinnati Raymond Walters Coll (OH)

Associate Degree Programs at Two-Year Colleges
Veterinary Sciences–Welding Technology

VETERINARY SCIENCES

Bel-Rea Inst of Animal Tech (CO)
Black Hawk Coll, Moline (IL)
Brevard Coll (NC)
Brevard Comm Coll (FL)
Casper Coll (WY)
City Coll of San Francisco (CA)
Colby Comm Coll (KS)
Del Mar Coll (TX)
Dixie Coll (UT)
Eastern Oklahoma State Coll (OK)
Eastern Wyoming Coll (WY)
Grayson County Coll (TX)
Highland Comm Coll (KS)
Hinds Comm Coll (MS)
Hiwassee Coll (TN)
Holmes Comm Coll (MS)
Holyoke Comm Coll (MA)
Howard Comm Coll (MD)
Hutchinson Comm Coll and Area Vocational Sch (KS)
Isothermal Comm Coll (NC)
Itawamba Comm Coll (MS)
Kansas City Kansas Comm Coll (KS)
Kellogg Comm Coll (MI)
Kirkwood Comm Coll (IA)
Lake Land Coll (IL)
Lake-Sumter Comm Coll (FL)
Lorain County Comm Coll (OH)
Macomb Comm Coll (MI)
Manor Jr Coll (PA)
Miami-Dade Comm Coll (FL)
Middle Georgia Coll (GA)
Mid-Plains Comm Coll (NE)
Monroe County Comm Coll (MI)
Murray State Coll (OK)
Navarro Coll (TX)
Northeastern Jr Coll (CO)
Northeastern Oklahoma A&M Coll (OK)
North Harris Coll (TX)
Northwest-Shoals Comm Coll (AL)
Palo Alto Coll (TX)
Pasadena City Coll (CA)
Reading Area Comm Coll (PA)
St Petersburg Jr Coll (FL)
Snow Coll (UT)
Suffolk County Comm Coll–Western Cmps (NY)
Tacoma Comm Coll (WA)
Vincennes U (IN)
Waldorf Coll (IA)
Yuba Coll (CA)

VETERINARY TECHNOLOGY

Bel-Rea Inst of Animal Tech (CO)
Blue Ridge Comm Coll (VA)
Cedar Valley Coll (TX)
Central Carolina Comm Coll (NC)
Colby Comm Coll (KS)
Colorado Mountn Coll, Roaring Fork Cmps-Spring Valley Ctr (CO)
Columbia State Comm Coll (TN)
Columbus State Comm Coll (OH)
Cosumnes River Coll (CA)
Cuyahoga Comm Coll, Western Cmps (OH)
Eastern Wyoming Coll (WY)
Essex Comm Coll (MD)
Fiorello H LaGuardia Comm Coll of City U of NY (NY)
Foothill Coll (CA)
Harcum Coll (PA)
Hartnell Coll (CA)
Holyoke Comm Coll (MA)
Jefferson Coll (MO)
Johnson County Comm Coll (KS)
Johnson Tech Inst (PA)
Kirkwood Comm Coll (IA)
Los Angeles Pierce Coll (CA)
Madison Area Tech Coll (WI)
Maple Woods Comm Coll (MO)
Medical Inst of Minnesota (MN)
Midland Coll (TX)
Mount Ida Coll (MA)
Murray State Coll (OK)
Nebraska Coll of Tech Agriculture (NE)
Northeast Comm Coll (NE)
Northern Virginia Comm Coll (VA)
Northwestern Connecticut Comm-Tech Coll (CT)
Omaha Coll of Health Careers (NE)
Parkland Coll (IL)
Pierce Coll (WA)
San Diego Mesa Coll (CA)
Snead State Comm Coll (AL)
State U of NY Coll of Tech at Canton (NY)
State U of NY Coll of Tech at Delhi (NY)
Tomball Coll (TX)
Tri-County Tech Coll (SC)
Turtle Mountain Comm Coll (ND)
U of Cincinnati Raymond Walters Coll (OH)
Vermont Tech Coll (VT)
Wayne County Comm Coll (MI)
Willmar Comm Coll (MN)
Willmar Tech Coll (MN)
Yuba Coll (CA)

VOCATIONAL EDUCATION

Atlanta Metropolitan Coll (GA)
Barstow Coll (CA)
Blue Ridge Comm Coll (NC)
Butler County Comm Coll (KS)
Comm Coll of Allegheny County North Cmps (PA)
Comm Coll of Allegheny County South Cmps (PA)
Comm Coll of the Air Force (AL)
Copiah-Lincoln Comm Coll (MS)
Cypress Coll (CA)
Dalton Coll (GA)
Del Mar Coll (TX)
East Los Angeles Coll (CA)
ECPI Coll of Tech, Hampton (VA)
ECPI Coll of Tech, Virginia Beach (VA)
ECPI Computer Inst, Richmond (VA)
ECPI Computer Inst, Roanoke (VA)
Ellsworth Comm Coll (IA)
Florence-Darlington Tech Coll (SC)
Florida National Coll (FL)
Gainesville Coll (GA)
Garden City Comm Coll (KS)
Garland County Comm Coll (AR)
Guilford Tech Comm Coll (NC)
Isothermal Comm Coll (NC)
Itawamba Comm Coll (MS)
Lenoir Comm Coll (NC)
Little Hoop Comm Coll (ND)
Mid-Plains Comm Coll (NE)
Montgomery Coll (TX)
Moraine Valley Comm Coll (IL)
Neosho County Comm Coll (KS)
New Mexico Jr Coll (NM)
Northeastern Jr Coll (CO)
Northeastern Oklahoma A&M Coll (OK)
Northeast Iowa Comm Coll, Calmar Cmps (IA)
Northeast Mississippi Comm Coll (MS)
Northwest Coll (WY)
Northwest Mississippi Comm Coll (MS)
Palo Alto Coll (TX)
Pennsylvania Coll of Tech (PA)
Piedmont Comm Coll (NC)
Portland Comm Coll (OR)
Red River Tech Coll (AR)
Ricks Coll (ID)
Snead State Comm Coll (AL)
Snow Coll (UT)
Southeastern Comm Coll, North Cmps, West Burlington (IA)
South Seattle Comm Coll (WA)
Spartanburg Tech Coll (SC)
Tulsa Jr Coll (OK)
Turtle Mountain Comm Coll (ND)
Victor Valley Coll (CA)
Wenatchee Valley Coll (WA)

VOICE

Alvin Comm Coll (TX)
Angelina Coll (TX)
Bee County Coll (TX)
Brevard Coll (NC)
Butler County Comm Coll (KS)
Coffeyville Comm Coll (KS)
Colby Comm Coll (KS)
Del Mar Coll (TX)
Hill Coll of the Hill Jr Coll District (TX)
Iowa Lakes Comm Coll (IA)
Jackson State Comm Coll (TN)
Jones County Jr Coll (MS)
Kirkwood Comm Coll (IA)
Lansing Comm Coll (MI)
Lon Morris Coll (TX)
Navarro Coll (TX)
Polk Comm Coll (FL)
San Jacinto College–North Cmps (TX)
Snow Coll (UT)
Southwestern Comm Coll (IA)
Waldorf Coll (IA)

WATER RESOURCES

Bay de Noc Comm Coll (MI)
Brevard Comm Coll (FL)
Cecil Comm Coll (MD)
Citrus Coll (CA)
Clackamas Comm Coll (OR)
Coll of the Canyons (CA)
Colorado Mountn Coll, Timberline Cmps (CO)
Delta Coll (MI)
Dodge City Comm Coll (KS)
Doña Ana Branch Comm Coll (NM)
Fort Scott Comm Coll (KS)
Fresno City Coll (CA)
Gadsden State Comm Coll (AL)
Gateway Comm Coll (AZ)
Grays Harbor Coll (WA)
Green River Comm Coll (WA)
Imperial Valley Coll (CA)
Indian River Comm Coll (FL)
Iowa Lakes Comm Coll (IA)
Kirkwood Comm Coll (IA)
Kishwaukee Coll (IL)
Lawson State Comm Coll (AL)
Linn-Benton Comm Coll (OR)
Los Angeles Trade-Tech Coll (CA)
Milwaukee Area Tech Coll (WI)
Moraine Park Tech Coll (WI)
Mountain Empire Comm Coll (VA)
New Hampshire Tech Coll, Berlin (NH)
Northeast Alabama State Comm Coll (AL)
Palomar Coll (CA)
Rancho Santiago Coll (CA)
Red Rocks Comm Coll (CO)
Rio Salado Comm Coll (AZ)
St Petersburg Jr Coll (FL)
San Diego Mesa Coll (CA)
San Joaquin Delta Coll (CA)
Santa Barbara City Coll (CA)
Southeastern Illinois Coll (IL)
Spokane Comm Coll (WA)
Ventura Coll (CA)
Vermilion Comm Coll (MN)

WELDING TECHNOLOGY

Aims Comm Coll (CO)
Alamance Comm Coll (NC)
Alexandria Tech Coll (MN)
Allan Hancock Coll (CA)
American River Coll (CA)
Angelina Coll (TX)
Anson Comm Coll (NC)
Antelope Valley Coll (CA)
Arizona Western Coll (AZ)
Austin Comm Coll (TX)
Bainbridge Coll (GA)
Bakersfield Coll (CA)
Barton County Comm Coll (KS)
Bee County Coll (TX)
Belleville Area Coll (IL)
Belmont Tech Coll (OH)
Big Bend Comm Coll (WA)
Bismarck State Coll (ND)
Blue Ridge Comm Coll (NC)
Brazosport Coll (TX)
Brunswick Coll (GA)
Butler County Comm Coll (KS)
Butte Coll (CA)
Cabrillo Coll (CA)
Casper Coll (WY)
Cecil Comm Coll (MD)
Central Comm College–Grand Island Cmps (NE)
Central Comm College–Hastings Cmps (NE)
Central Comm College–Platte Cmps (NE)
Centralia Coll (WA)
Central Maine Tech Coll (ME)
Central Oregon Comm Coll (OR)
Central Piedmont Comm Coll (NC)
Central Texas Coll (TX)
Central Wyoming Coll (WY)
Cerritos Coll (CA)
Cerro Coso Comm Coll (CA)
Chabot Coll (CA)
Chattanooga State Tech Comm Coll (TN)
Chemeketa Comm Coll (OR)
Chippewa Valley Tech Coll (WI)
Cisco Jr Coll (TX)
Clark Coll (WA)
Clatsop Comm Coll (OR)
Coastal Carolina Comm Coll (NC)
Cochise Coll, Sierra Vista (AZ)
Coffeyville Comm Coll (KS)
Coll of DuPage (IL)
Coll of Eastern Utah (UT)
Coll of San Mateo (CA)
Coll of Southern Idaho (ID)
Coll of the Canyons (CA)
Coll of the Desert (CA)
Coll of the Redwoods (CA)
Coll of the Sequoias (CA)
Coll of the Siskiyous (CA)
Columbia Basin Coll (WA)
Comm Coll of Allegheny County North Cmps (PA)
Comm Coll of Allegheny County South Cmps (PA)
Comm Coll of Denver (CO)
Comm Coll of Southern Nevada (NV)
Contra Costa Coll (CA)
Cowley County Comm Coll and Voc-Tech Sch (KS)
Cuesta Coll (CA)
Danville Area Comm Coll (IL)
Delaware Tech & Comm Coll, Jack F Owens Cmps (DE)
Delgado Comm Coll (LA)
Del Mar Coll (TX)
Delta Coll (MI)
Dodge City Comm Coll (KS)
Doña Ana Branch Comm Coll (NM)
Douglas MacArthur State Tech Coll (AL)
East Central Coll (MO)
Eastern Arizona Coll (AZ)
Eastern Maine Tech Coll (ME)
Eastern New Mexico University–Roswell (NM)
Eastern Wyoming Coll (WY)
El Camino Coll (CA)
Elgin Comm Coll (IL)
El Paso Comm Coll (TX)
Everett Comm Coll (WA)
Fayetteville Tech Comm Coll (NC)
Forsyth Tech Comm Coll (NC)
Fort Scott Comm Coll (KS)
Fox Valley Tech Coll (WI)
Frank Phillips Coll (TX)
Fresno City Coll (CA)
Front Range Comm Coll (CO)
Garden City Comm Coll (KS)
Gaston Coll (NC)
George Corley Wallace State Comm Coll, Selma (AL)
George C Wallace State Comm Coll, Dothan (AL)
Grand Rapids Comm Coll (MI)
Grays Harbor Coll (WA)
Grayson County Coll (TX)
Great Basin Coll (NV)
Green River Comm Coll (WA)
Hartnell Coll (CA)
Hawkeye Comm Coll (IA)
Haywood Comm Coll (NC)
Heartland Comm Coll (IL)
Helena Coll of Tech of The U of Montana (MT)
Highland Park Comm Coll (MI)
Hill Coll of the Hill Jr Coll District (TX)
Hinds Comm Coll (MS)
Illinois Central Coll (IL)
Illinois Eastern Comm Colls, Olney Central Coll (IL)
Imperial Valley Coll (CA)
Iowa Central Comm Coll (IA)
Iowa Western Comm Coll (IA)
Isothermal Comm Coll (NC)
Ivy Tech State Coll–Southcentral (IN)
Jefferson Coll (MO)
Jefferson Comm Coll (OH)
John A Logan Coll (IL)
John C Calhoun State Comm Coll (AL)
John M Patterson State Tech Coll (AL)
Johnson Tech Inst (PA)
John Wood Comm Coll (IL)
Kalamazoo Valley Comm Coll (MI)
Kankakee Comm Coll (IL)
Kansas City Kansas Comm Coll (KS)
Kaskaskia Coll (IL)
Kellogg Comm Coll (MI)
Kings River Comm Coll (CA)
Kirkwood Comm Coll (IA)
Kirtland Comm Coll (MI)
Kishwaukee Coll (IL)
Lake Area Vocational-Tech Inst (SD)
Lakeshore Tech Coll (WI)
Lane Comm Coll (OR)
Laney Coll (CA)
Lansing Comm Coll (MI)
Las Positas Coll (CA)
Lassen Coll (CA)
Lee Coll (TX)
Lenoir Comm Coll (NC)
Lincoln Land Comm Coll (IL)
Linn-Benton Comm Coll (OR)
Long Beach City Coll (CA)
Los Angeles Pierce Coll (CA)
Los Angeles Trade-Tech Coll (CA)
Los Medanos Coll (CA)
Lower Columbia Coll (WA)
Macomb Comm Coll (MI)
Madison Area Tech Coll (WI)
McDowell Tech Comm Coll (NC)
Mendocino Coll (CA)
Metropolitan Comm Coll (NE)
Midland Coll (TX)
Mid Michigan Comm Coll (MI)
Mid-Plains Comm Coll (NE)
Milwaukee Area Tech Coll (WI)
Mississippi Gulf Coast Comm Coll (MS)
Moberly Area Comm Coll (MO)
Modesto Jr Coll (CA)
Mohawk Valley Comm Coll (NY)
Monroe County Comm Coll (MI)
Montcalm Comm Coll (MI)
Moraine Valley Comm Coll (IL)
Mountain Empire Comm Coll (VA)
Mountain View Coll (TX)
Mt San Antonio Coll (CA)
Muskegon Comm Coll (MI)
Napa Valley Coll (CA)
Neosho County Comm Coll (KS)
New Hampshire Tech Coll, Manchester (NH)
New Mexico Jr Coll (NM)
New Mexico State University–Carlsbad (NM)
New River Comm Coll (VA)
Northcentral Tech Coll (WI)
North Central Texas Coll (TX)
North Dakota State Coll of Science (ND)
Northeast Comm Coll (NE)
Northeastern Oklahoma A&M Coll (OK)
Northeast Iowa Comm Coll, Peosta Cmps (IA)
Northeast State Tech Comm Coll (TN)
North Harris Coll (TX)
North Idaho Coll (ID)
North Iowa Area Comm Coll (IA)
Northland Comm and Tech Coll (MN)
Northland Pioneer Coll (AZ)
Northwest Coll (WY)
Northwest Iowa Comm Coll (IA)
Oakland Comm Coll (MI)
Odessa Coll (TX)
Okaloosa-Walton Comm Coll (FL)
Olympic Coll (WA)
Orange Coast Coll (CA)
Owens Comm Coll, Findlay (OH)
Owens Comm Coll, Toledo (OH)
Oxnard Coll (CA)
Ozarks Tech Comm Coll (MO)
Palomar Coll (CA)
Paris Jr Coll (TX)
Pasadena City Coll (CA)
Pennsylvania Coll of Tech (PA)
Petit Jean Tech Coll (AR)
Phillips County Comm Coll (AR)
Piedmont Comm Coll (NC)
Pikes Peak Comm Coll (CO)
Pima Comm Coll (AZ)
Porterville Coll (CA)
Portland Comm Coll (OR)
Prairie State Coll (IL)
Pueblo Comm Coll (CO)
Rancho Santiago Coll (CA)
Randolph Comm Coll (NC)
Ranger Coll (TX)
Red Rocks Comm Coll (CO)
Reid State Tech Coll (AL)
Rend Lake Coll (IL)
Ricks Coll (ID)
Riverside Comm Coll (CA)
Roanoke-Chowan Comm Coll (NC)
Rock Valley Coll (IL)
St Clair County Comm Coll (MI)
St Cloud Tech Coll (MN)
St Philip's Coll (TX)
Salt Lake Comm Coll (UT)
San Bernardino Valley Coll (CA)
San Diego City Coll (CA)
San Jacinto College–Central Cmps (TX)
San Jacinto College–North Cmps (TX)
San Juan Coll (NM)
Santa Monica Coll (CA)
Schoolcraft Coll (MI)
Shasta Coll (CA)
Shawnee Comm Coll (IL)
Shelton State Comm Coll (AL)
Sheridan Coll (WY)
Sierra Coll (CA)
Solano Comm Coll (CA)
South Arkansas Comm Coll (AR)
Southeast Comm Coll, Lincoln Cmps (NE)
Southeast Comm Coll, Milford Cmps (NE)
Southeastern Comm Coll (NC)
Southeastern Comm Coll, North Cmps, West Burlington (IA)
Southeastern Illinois Coll (IL)
Southern West Virginia Comm and Tech Coll (WV)
South Plains Coll (TX)
South Puget Sound Comm Coll (WA)
South Seattle Comm Coll (WA)
SouthWest Collegiate Inst for the Deaf (TX)
Southwestern Comm Coll (IA)
Southwestern Michigan Coll (MI)
Southwestern Oregon Comm Coll (OR)

Peterson's Guide to Two-Year Colleges 1997
131

Associate Degree Programs at Two-Year Colleges
Welding Technology–Zoology

Southwest Mississippi Comm Coll (MS)
Southwest Missouri State University– West Plains (MO)
Southwest Wisconsin Tech Coll (WI)
Spokane Comm Coll (WA)
Spokane Falls Comm Coll (WA)
State Fair Comm Coll (MO)
State U of NY Coll of Tech at Delhi (NY)
Surry Comm Coll (NC)
Tarrant County Jr Coll (TX)
Terra State Comm Coll (OH)
Texarkana Coll (TX)
Texas State Tech Coll– Harlingen Cmps (TX)
Texas State Tech Coll–Waco/ Marshall Cmps (TX)
Treasure Valley Comm Coll (OR)
Triangle Tech, Inc–DuBois Sch (PA)
Tri-County Tech Coll (SC)
Trinity Valley Comm Coll (TX)
Triton Coll (IL)
Truckee Meadows Comm Coll (NV)
Tyler Jr Coll (TX)
U of Alaska Southeast, Sitka Cmps (AK)
U of Hawaii–Hawaii Comm Coll (HI)
U of Hawaii–Honolulu Comm Coll (HI)
U of Hawaii–Maui Comm Coll (HI)
U of New Mexico–Gallup Branch (NM)
Utah Valley State Coll (UT)
Vance-Granville Comm Coll (NC)
Ventura Coll (CA)
Victor Valley Coll (CA)
Vincennes U (IN)
Wallace State Comm Coll (AL)
Walla Walla Comm Coll (WA)
Washtenaw Comm Coll (MI)
Waycross Coll (GA)
Wayne County Comm Coll (MI)
Welder Training and Testing Inst (PA)
Westark Comm Coll (AR)
Western Nebraska Comm Coll, Scottsbluff (NE)
Western Nevada Comm Coll (NV)
Western Oklahoma State Coll (OK)
Western Texas Coll (TX)
Western Wisconsin Tech Coll (WI)
Western Wyoming Comm Coll (WY)
West Hills Comm Coll (CA)
Westmoreland County Comm Coll (PA)
West Shore Comm Coll (MI)
West Virginia U at Parkersburg (WV)
Willmar Tech Coll (MN)
Wisconsin Indianhead Tech Coll, Rice Lake Cmps (WI)
Yavapai Coll (AZ)
York Tech Coll (SC)
Yuba Coll (CA)

WESTERN CIVILIZATION AND CULTURE
Brevard Coll (NC)
Comm Coll of Allegheny County South Cmps (PA)
Lamar Comm Coll (CO)
Lansing Comm Coll (MI)
Lon Morris Coll (TX)

WILDLIFE BIOLOGY
Brevard Coll (NC)
Colby Comm Coll (KS)

Dodge City Comm Coll (KS)
Eastern Arizona Coll (AZ)
Ellsworth Comm Coll (IA)
Everett Comm Coll (WA)
Feather River Comm Coll District (CA)
Garrett Comm Coll (MD)
Grays Harbor Coll (WA)
Holmes Comm Coll (MS)
Kirkwood Comm Coll (IA)
North Dakota State University–Bottineau (ND)
Northeastern Oklahoma A&M Coll (OK)
Northeast Mississippi Comm Coll (MS)
North Idaho Coll (ID)
Northwest Coll (WY)
Pratt Comm Coll and Area Voc Sch (KS)
Southwestern Comm Coll (IA)
State U of NY Coll of A&T at Cobleskill (NY)
Tacoma Comm Coll (WA)
Vermilion Comm Coll (MN)
Waldorf Coll (IA)

WILDLIFE MANAGEMENT
Abraham Baldwin Ag Coll (GA)
Brevard Coll (NC)
Butler County Comm Coll (KS)
Cabrillo Coll (CA)
Casper Coll (WY)
Central Texas Coll (TX)
Cerritos Coll (CA)
Chattahoochee Valley State Comm Coll (AL)
Chattanooga State Tech Comm Coll (TN)
City Coll of San Francisco (CA)
Coll of DuPage (IL)
Coll of the Siskiyous (CA)
Dixie Coll (UT)
East Central Coll (MO)
Eastern Oklahoma State Coll (OK)
Finger Lakes Comm Coll (NY)
Flathead Valley Comm Coll (MT)
Frederick Comm Coll (MD)
Fullerton Coll (CA)
Garrett Comm Coll (MD)
Grays Harbor Coll (WA)
Haywood Comm Coll (NC)
Hiwassee Coll (TN)
Hocking Coll (OH)
Hutchinson Comm Coll and Area Vocational Sch (KS)
Iowa Lakes Comm Coll (IA)
Itasca Comm Coll (MN)
Kirkwood Comm Coll (IA)
Lake Land Coll (IL)
Laramie County Comm Coll (WY)
Monterey Peninsula Coll (CA)
Moorpark Coll (CA)
Mt San Antonio Coll (CA)
Murray State Coll (OK)
North Dakota State University–Bottineau (ND)
Northeastern Oklahoma A&M Coll (OK)
Northeast Mississippi Comm Coll (MS)
North Idaho Coll (ID)
Northwest Coll (WY)
Penn State U DuBois Cmps (PA)
Potomac State Coll of West Virginia U (WV)
Pratt Comm Coll and Area Voc Sch (KS)
Ricks Coll (ID)
Seward County Comm Coll (KS)
Shawnee Comm Coll (IL)
Snow Coll (UT)
Southeastern Illinois Coll (IL)
Spokane Comm Coll (WA)

State U of NY Coll of A&T at Cobleskill (NY)
State U of NY Coll of A&T at Morrisville (NY)
Sterling Coll (VT)
Tacoma Comm Coll (WA)
Treasure Valley Comm Coll (OR)
Turtle Mountain Comm Coll (ND)
Vermilion Comm Coll (MN)
Waldorf Coll (IA)
Wayne Comm Coll (NC)
Western Nebraska Comm Coll, Scottsbluff (NE)

WIND AND PERCUSSION INSTRUMENTS
Brevard Coll (NC)
Coffeyville Comm Coll (KS)
Iowa Lakes Comm Coll (IA)
Itawamba Comm Coll (MS)
Jackson State Comm Coll (TN)
Kirkwood Comm Coll (IA)
Miami-Dade Comm Coll (FL)

WOMEN'S STUDIES
Bergen Comm Coll (NJ)
Cabrillo Coll (CA)
Chabot Coll (CA)
City Coll of San Francisco (CA)
Cosumnes River Coll (CA)
Fresno City Coll (CA)
Monterey Peninsula Coll (CA)
Northern Essex Comm Coll (MA)
Rancho Santiago Coll (CA)
Sacramento City Coll (CA)
Saddleback Coll (CA)
Suffolk County Comm College–Ammerman Cmps (NY)
Tompkins Cortland Comm Coll (NY)
West Valley Coll (CA)
Yuba Coll (CA)

WOOD SCIENCES
Bakersfield Coll (CA)
Fresno City Coll (CA)
Haywood Comm Coll (NC)
Hiwassee Coll (TN)
Illinois Eastern Comm Colls, Olney Central Coll (IL)
Keystone Coll (PA)
Laney Coll (CA)
Pennsylvania Coll of Tech (PA)
Potomac State Coll of West Virginia U (WV)
State U of NY Coll of A&T at Morrisville (NY)
Western Wisconsin Tech Coll (WI)

WORD PROCESSING
Abraham Baldwin Ag Coll (GA)
Alexandria Tech Coll (MN)
Allen County Comm Coll (KS)
Anoka-Ramsey Comm Coll (MN)
Baker Coll of Jackson (MI)
Bay de Noc Comm Coll (MI)
Bergen Comm Coll (NJ)
Berkeley Coll (NJ)
Berkeley Coll, New York (NY)
Berkeley Coll, White Plains (NY)
Brazosport Coll (TX)
Briarwood Coll (CT)
Bristol Comm Coll (MA)
Bryant and Stratton Business Inst, Buffalo (NY)
Bryant and Stratton Business Inst, Rochester (NY)
Bryant and Stratton Business Inst, Rochester (NY)

Bucks County Comm Coll (PA)
Butler County Comm Coll (PA)
Camden County Coll (NJ)
Castle Coll (NH)
Central Coll (KS)
Central Texas Coll (TX)
Chabot Coll (CA)
Chaffey Coll (CA)
Chattahoochee Tech Inst (GA)
CHI Inst (PA)
Cincinnati State Tech and Comm Coll (OH)
Clovis Comm Coll (NM)
Colby Comm Coll (KS)
Coll of DuPage (IL)
Coll of the Desert (CA)
Coll of Lake County (IL)
Coll of the Redwoods (CA)
Coll of the Sequoias (CA)
Collin County Comm Coll (TX)
Colorado Northwestern Comm Coll (CO)
Commonwealth Business Coll, LaPorte (IN)
Comm Coll of Beaver County (PA)
Comm Coll of Southern Nevada (NV)
Corning Comm Coll (NY)
County Coll of Morris (NJ)
Cowley County Comm Coll and Voc-Tech Sch (KS)
Cumberland County Coll (NJ)
Cuyahoga Comm Coll, Eastern Cmps (OH)
Cuyahoga Comm Coll, Metropolitan Cmps (OH)
Davis Coll (OH)
Daytona Beach Comm Coll (FL)
Del Mar Coll (TX)
Doña Ana Branch Comm Coll (NM)
Durham Tech Comm Coll (NC)
Eastern Wyoming Coll (WY)
ECPI Coll of Tech, Hampton (VA)
ECPI Coll of Tech, Virginia Beach (VA)
ECPI Computer Inst, Richmond (VA)
ECPI Computer Inst, Roanoke (VA)
Elgin Comm Coll (IL)
Erie Comm Coll, City Cmps (NY)
Erie Comm Coll, North Cmps (NY)
Erie Comm Coll, South Cmps (NY)
Eugenio María de Hostos Comm Coll of City U of NY (NY)
Everett Comm Coll (WA)
Flathead Valley Comm Coll (MT)
Fox Valley Tech Coll (WI)
Fresno City Coll (CA)
Fulton-Montgomery Comm Coll (NY)
Garland County Comm Coll (AR)
Gateway Comm Coll (AZ)
Gateway Comm-Tech Coll (CT)
Gogebic Comm Coll (MI)
Great Lakes Jr Coll of Business (MI)
Hamilton Business Coll (IA)
Hesser Coll (NH)
Hill Coll of the Hill Jr Coll District (TX)
Holyoke Comm Coll (MA)
Housatonic Comm-Tech Coll (CT)
Houston Comm Coll System (TX)
Indian River Comm Coll (FL)
Jefferson Comm Coll (NY)

Kansas City Kansas Comm Coll (KS)
Kaskaskia Coll (IL)
Kilian Comm Coll (SD)
Kingwood Coll (TX)
Kirtland Comm Coll (MI)
Kishwaukee Coll (IL)
Lamar Comm Coll (CO)
Lamar University–Port Arthur (TX)
Laney Coll (CA)
Lansdale Sch of Business (PA)
Lansing Comm Coll (MI)
Lehigh Carbon Comm Coll (PA)
Lincoln Coll, Normal (IL)
Longview Comm Coll (MO)
Luzerne County Comm Coll (PA)
MacCormac Jr Coll (IL)
Macomb Comm Coll (MI)
Madison Area Tech Coll (WI)
Massachusetts Bay Comm Coll (MA)
Merritt Coll (CA)
Middlesex Comm Coll (MA)
Mid Michigan Comm Coll (MI)
Modesto Jr Coll (CA)
Mohawk Valley Comm Coll (NY)
Monroe Coll, Bronx (NY)
Monroe Coll, New Rochelle (NY)
Montcalm Comm Coll (MI)
Monterey Peninsula Coll (CA)
Moraine Valley Comm Coll (IL)
Mt Hood Comm Coll (OR)
Nassau Comm Coll (NY)
New Mexico Jr Coll (NM)
New Mexico State University–Carlsbad (NM)
New River Comm Coll (VA)
Niagara County Comm Coll (NY)
North Arkansas Comm/Tech Coll (AR)
Northeast Alabama State Comm Coll (AL)
Northeast Iowa Comm Coll, Peosta Cmps (IA)
Northern Essex Comm Coll (MA)
Northwest State Comm Coll (OH)
Ohlone Coll (CA)
Olympic Coll (WA)
Onondaga Comm Coll (NY)
Orange Coast Coll (CA)
Paradise Valley Comm Coll (AZ)
Parkland Coll (IL)
Pasadena City Coll (CA)
Petit Jean Tech Coll (AR)
Phillips Jr Coll, Condie Cmps (CA)
Pierce Coll (WA)
Prince George's Comm Coll (MD)
Prospect Hall (FL)
Rasmussen Coll Eagan (MN)
Rasmussen Coll Mankato (MN)
Rock Valley Coll (IL)
Roxbury Comm Coll (MA)
Saddleback Coll (CA)
Saint Charles County Comm Coll (MO)
St Clair County Comm Coll (MI)
St Cloud Tech Coll (MN)
St Johns River Comm Coll (FL)
Schoolcraft Coll (MI)
Scott Comm Coll (IA)
Seattle Central Comm Coll (WA)
South Mountain Comm Coll (AZ)
South Suburban Coll (IL)
Southwest Wisconsin Tech Coll (WI)
Spokane Comm Coll (WA)

Spokane Falls Comm Coll (WA)
Springfield Tech Comm Coll (MA)
State U of NY Coll of A&T at Morrisville (NY)
State U of NY Coll of Tech at Alfred (NY)
State U of NY Coll of Tech at Delhi (NY)
Stratton Coll (WI)
Sullivan County Comm Coll (NY)
Tacoma Comm Coll (WA)
Texas Southmost Coll (TX)
Three Rivers Comm-Tech Coll (CT)
Triton Coll (IL)
U of Kentucky, Hazard Comm Coll (KY)
U of New Mexico–Valencia Cmps (NM)
Utica Sch of Commerce (NY)
Valencia Comm Coll (FL)
Washtenaw Comm Coll (MI)
Westark Comm Coll (AR)
Westchester Business Inst (NY)
Western Nevada Comm Coll (NV)
Western Wyoming Comm Coll (WY)
West Shore Comm Coll (MI)
West Virginia Career Coll, Charleston (WV)
William Rainey Harper Coll (IL)
Willmar Tech Coll (MN)
Wright State U, Lake Cmps (OH)

ZOOLOGY
Carl Albert State Coll (OK)
Casper Coll (WY)
Catonsville Comm Coll (MD)
Central Coll (KS)
Cerritos Coll (CA)
Chabot Coll (CA)
Chemeketa Comm Coll (OR)
Clark Coll (WA)
Colby Comm Coll (KS)
Coll of the Siskiyous (CA)
Connors State Coll (OK)
Daytona Beach Comm Coll (FL)
Dixie Coll (UT)
East Central Coll (MO)
El Camino Coll (CA)
Everett Comm Coll (WA)
Foothill Coll (CA)
Frank Phillips Coll (TX)
Fullerton Coll (CA)
Grays Harbor Coll (WA)
Hill Coll of the Hill Jr Coll District (TX)
Jackson State Comm Coll (TN)
Joliet Jr Coll (IL)
Miami University–Middletown Cmps (OH)
Middle Georgia Coll (GA)
Modesto Jr Coll (CA)
Northeastern Jr Coll (CO)
Northeast Mississippi Comm Coll (MS)
North Idaho Coll (ID)
Palm Beach Comm Coll (FL)
Palomar Coll (CA)
Polk Comm Coll (FL)
Rancho Santiago Coll (CA)
Redlands Comm Coll (OK)
Ricks Coll (ID)
San Bernardino Valley Coll (CA)
San Jacinto College–Central Cmps (TX)
Snow Coll (UT)
Southwestern Coll (CA)
Spoon River Coll (IL)
Tacoma Comm Coll (WA)
Tulsa Jr Coll (OK)
U of Kentucky, Jefferson Comm Coll (KY)
Vincennes U (IN)

Associate Degree Programs at Four-Year Colleges

ACCOUNTING
Adrian Coll (MI)
Alaska Pacific U (AK)
Alvernia Coll (PA)
Andrews U (MI)
Armstrong U (CA)
Baker Coll of Auburn Hills (MI)
Baker Coll of Cadillac (MI)
Baker Coll of Flint (MI)
Baker Coll of Mount Clemens (MI)
Baker Coll of Muskegon (MI)
Baker Coll of Owosso (MI)
Baker Coll of Port Huron (MI)
Bartlesville Wesleyan Coll (OK)
Bayamón Tech U Coll (PR)
Becker College–Leicester Cmps (MA)
Becker College–Worcester Cmps (MA)
Benedictine Coll (KS)
Bethel Coll (IN)
Brewton-Parker Coll (GA)
Brigham Young University–Hawaii Cmps (HI)
California U of Pennsylvania (PA)
Calumet Coll of Saint Joseph (IN)
Cazenovia Coll (NY)
Chestnut Hill Coll (PA)
Clayton State Coll (GA)
Cleary Coll (MI)
Coll of Mount St Joseph (OH)
Coll of St Joseph (VT)
Coll of Saint Mary (NE)
Columbia Union Coll (MD)
Dakota Wesleyan U (SD)
Daniel Webster Coll (NH)
Davenport Coll of Business, Grand Rapids (MI)
Davenport Coll of Business, Kalamazoo Cmps (MI)
Davenport Coll of Business, Lansing Cmps (MI)
David N Myers Coll (OH)
Davis & Elkins Coll (WV)
Denver Tech Coll (CO)
Detroit Coll of Business, Dearborn (MI)
Detroit Coll of Business, Warren Cmps (MI)
Eastern New Mexico U (NM)
Evangel Coll (MO)
Fairmont State Coll (WV)
Faulkner U (AL)
Five Towns Coll (NY)
Fort Lauderdale Coll (FL)
Franciscan U of Steubenville (OH)
Franklin U (OH)
Friends U (KS)
Gannon U (PA)
Goldey-Beacom Coll (DE)
Grambling State U (LA)
Gwynedd-Mercy Coll (PA)
Hannibal-LaGrange Coll (MO)
Hilbert Coll (NY)
Humphreys Coll (CA)
Huntington Coll (IN)
Husson Coll (ME)
Immaculata Coll (PA)
Indiana Inst of Tech (IN)
Indiana U East (IN)
Indiana U of Pennsylvania (PA)
Indiana U–Purdue U Fort Wayne (IN)
Indiana Wesleyan U (IN)
Inter American U of PR, Arecibo Cmps (PR)
Inter American U of PR, Fajardo Cmps (PR)
Inter American U of PR, Ponce Cmps (PR)
Inter American U of PR, San Germán Cmps (PR)
International Coll (FL)
International Coll of the Cayman Islands (Cayman Islands)
Johnson & Wales U (RI)
Johnson State Coll (VT)
Jones Coll (FL)
Kansas State U (KS)
King's Coll (PA)
Lake Superior State U (MI)
Lasell Coll (MA)
Lewis-Clark State Coll (ID)
Manchester Coll (IN)
Marian Coll (IN)
Marygrove Coll (MI)
Mayville State U (ND)
Merrimack Coll (MA)
Methodist Coll (NC)
Midland Lutheran Coll (NE)
Missouri Southern State Coll (MO)
Montana State University–Billings (MT)
Morrison Coll (NV)
Mount Aloysius Coll (PA)
Mount Marty Coll (SD)
Mount Olive Coll (NC)
Mount St Clare Coll (IA)
National Coll, Colorado Springs (CO)
National Coll, Denver (CO)
National Coll (NM)
National Coll (SD)
National College–St Paul Cmps (MN)
National College–Sioux Falls Branch (SD)
New Hampshire Coll (NH)
New York Inst of Tech (NY)
Northeastern U (MA)
Northern State U (SD)
Northwestern Coll (MN)
Northwestern State U of Louisiana (LA)
Northwood U (MI)
Northwood U, Florida Cmps (FL)
Oakland City U (IN)
Oakwood Coll (AL)
Oglala Lakota Coll (SD)
Ohio U (OH)
Ohio University–Lancaster (OH)
Orlando Coll (FL)
Pace U (NY)
Philadelphia Coll of Bible (PA)
Pikeville Coll (KY)
Point Park Coll (PA)
Presentation Coll (SD)
Purdue U North Central (IN)
Rivier Coll (NH)
Robert Morris Coll (IL)
Sacred Heart U (CT)
Saint Francis Coll (IN)
Saint Francis Coll (PA)
St John's U (NY)
Saint Joseph's U (PA)
Shawnee State U (OH)
Shepherd Coll (WV)
Siena Heights Coll (MI)
Sinte Gleska U (SD)
Southeastern U (DC)
Southern Coll of Seventh-day Adventists (TN)
Southern Vermont Coll (VT)
Southwestern Christian Coll (TX)
Southwest State U (MN)
Strayer Coll (DC)
Sullivan Coll (KY)
Tampa Coll (FL)
Tampa College–Lakeland (FL)
Tampa Coll, Pinellas Ctr (FL)
Teikyo Post U (CT)
Thiel Coll (PA)
Thomas Coll (ME)
Thomas Edison State Coll (NJ)
Thomas More Coll (KY)
Tiffin U (OH)
Trinity Coll of Vermont (VT)
Tri-State U (IN)
Union Coll (KY)
U Coll of Cape Breton (NS, Canada)
U of Akron (OH)
U of Alaska Anchorage (AK)
U of Alaska Fairbanks (AK)
The U of Charleston (WV)
U of Cincinnati (OH)
U of Dubuque (IA)
The U of Findlay (OH)
U of Great Falls (MT)
U of Maine at Machias (ME)
U of Mary (ND)
U of Massachusetts Lowell (MA)
U of Minnesota, Crookston (MN)
U of Puerto Rico at Arecibo (PR)
U of Puerto Rico at Ponce (PR)
U of Puerto Rico, Humacao U Coll (PR)
U of Rio Grande (OH)
U of Southern Maine (ME)
U of the District of Columbia (DC)
U of the Virgin Islands (VI)
U of Toledo (OH)
U of West Alabama (AL)
Urbana U (OH)
Villa Julie Coll (MD)
Walsh U (OH)
Webber Coll (FL)
West Coast U (CA)
West Virginia State Coll (WV)
West Virginia U Inst of Tech (WV)
Wright State U (OH)
Xavier U (OH)
Youngstown State U (OH)

ADVERTISING
Endicott Coll (MA)
Fashion Inst of Tech (NY)
International Acad of Merchandising & Design, Ltd (IL)
Johnson & Wales U (RI)
Martin Methodist Coll (TN)
Northwood U (MI)
Northwood U, Florida Cmps (FL)
Northwood U, Texas Cmps (TX)
Pacific Union Coll (CA)
U of the District of Columbia (DC)
West Virginia State Coll (WV)

AEROSPACE ENGINEERING
Daniel Webster Coll (NH)

AEROSPACE SCIENCES
Coll of Aeronautics (NY)
Daniel Webster Coll (NH)
Embry-Riddle Aeronautical U, Extended Cmps (FL)
Indiana State U (IN)
Weber State U (UT)

AFRICAN STUDIES
Grambling State U (LA)

AGRICULTURAL BUSINESS
Andrews U (MI)
Brewton-Parker Coll (GA)
Clayton State Coll (GA)
Dickinson State U (ND)
Dordt Coll (IA)
Lindsey Wilson Coll (KY)
Martin Methodist Coll (TN)
MidAmerica Nazarene Coll (KS)
Montana State University–Northern (MT)
Morehead State U (KY)
Northwestern Coll (MN)
The Ohio State U (OH)
Penn State U at Erie, The Behrend Coll (PA)
Penn State U Univ Park Cmps (PA)
Southwest State U (MN)
U of Minnesota, Crookston (MN)

AGRICULTURAL ECONOMICS
Purdue U, West Lafayette (IN)

AGRICULTURAL EDUCATION
Andrews U (MI)
U of New Hampshire, Durham (NH)

AGRICULTURAL SCIENCES
Andrews U (MI)
Becker College–Leicester Cmps (MA)
Becker College–Worcester Cmps (MA)
Clayton State Coll (GA)
Fort Lewis Coll (CO)
Lincoln U (MO)
North Carolina State U (NC)
Oglala Lakota Coll (SD)
Northwood U, Florida Cmps (FL)
Northwood U, Texas Cmps (TX)
Pacific Union Coll (CA)
U of the District of Columbia (DC)
West Virginia State Coll (WV)

AGRICULTURAL TECHNOLOGIES
Andrews U (MI)
Clayton State Coll (GA)
Eastern Kentucky U (KY)
Montana State University–Northern (MT)
Morehead State U (KY)
North Carolina State U (NC)
The Ohio State U (OH)
Purdue U, West Lafayette (IN)
Thomas Edison State Coll (NJ)
U of Alaska Anchorage (AK)
U of Minnesota, Crookston (MN)
Utah State U (UT)
Virginia Polytechnic Inst and State U (VA)
Western Kentucky U (KY)

AGRONOMY/SOIL AND CROP SCIENCES
Andrews U (MI)
Becker College–Leicester Cmps (MA)
The Ohio State U (OH)
Purdue U, West Lafayette (IN)
U of Minnesota, Crookston (MN)

AIRCRAFT AND MISSILE MAINTENANCE
Central Missouri State U (MO)
Clayton State Coll (GA)
Coll of Aeronautics (NY)
Embry-Riddle Aeronautical U (FL)
Embry-Riddle Aeronautical U, Extended Cmps (FL)
Idaho State U (ID)
Kansas State U (KS)
LeTourneau U (TX)
Lewis U (IL)
Purdue U, West Lafayette (IN)
Southern Illinois U at Carbondale (IL)
U of Alaska Fairbanks (AK)
Wentworth Inst of Tech (MA)

AIR TRAFFIC CONTROL
Averett Coll (VA)
Purdue U, West Lafayette (IN)
Thomas Edison State Coll (NJ)
U of Alaska Anchorage (AK)

South Dakota State U (SD)
Southern Arkansas University–Magnolia (AR)
Southern Utah U (UT)
U of Delaware (DE)
U of Maine at Presque Isle (ME)
U of Minnesota, Crookston (MN)
U of the Virgin Islands (VI)

AMERICAN STUDIES
Indiana U South Bend (IN)
Martin Methodist Coll (TN)

ANIMAL SCIENCES
Andrews U (MI)
Becker College–Leicester Cmps (MA)
Becker College–Worcester Cmps (MA)
North Carolina State U (NC)
The Ohio State U (OH)
Purdue U, West Lafayette (IN)
Sul Ross State U (TX)
U of Connecticut, Storrs (CT)
U of Minnesota, Crookston (MN)
U of New Hampshire, Durham (NH)
U of Puerto Rico at Arecibo (PR)

ANTHROPOLOGY
Crown Coll (MN)
West Chester U of Pennsylvania (PA)

APPLIED ART
Brewton-Parker Coll (GA)
Friends U (KS)
National Coll (NM)
Newschool of Architecture (CA)
Northern Michigan U (MI)
Reinhardt Coll (GA)
Rochester Inst of Tech (NY)
Schiller International U, American Coll of Switzerland (Switzerland)
Shepherd Coll (WV)
Suomi Coll (MI)
U of Bridgeport (CT)
U of Maine at Presque Isle (ME)
U of Wisconsin–Green Bay (WI)
Valdosta State U (GA)
Villa Julie Coll (MD)
Western Montana Coll of The U of Montana (MT)

APPLIED MATHEMATICS
Central Methodist Coll (MO)
Southwestern Christian Coll (TX)
U of Massachusetts Lowell (MA)

ARCHAEOLOGY
Baltimore Hebrew U (MD)
Weber State U (UT)

ARCHITECTURAL TECHNOLOGIES
Andrews U (MI)
Baker Coll of Flint (MI)
Baker Coll of Muskegon (MI)
Baker Coll of Owosso (MI)
Baker Coll of Port Huron (MI)
Central Missouri State U (MO)

Peterson's Guide to Two-Year Colleges 1997

Associate Degree Programs at Four-Year Colleges
Architectural Technologies–Business Administration/Commerce/Management

Clayton State Coll (GA)
Coll of Staten Island of the City U of New York (NY)
Denver Tech Coll (CO)
Ferris State U (MI)
Indiana State U (IN)
Indiana U–Purdue U Fort Wayne (IN)
Indiana U–Purdue U Indianapolis (IN)
Morehead State U (KY)
Newschool of Architecture (CA)
New York Inst of Tech (NY)
Purdue U Calumet (IN)
Purdue U North Central (IN)
Rochester Inst of Tech (NY)
Southern Illinois U at Carbondale (IL)
Thomas Edison State Coll (NJ)
U of Alaska Anchorage (AK)
U of Cincinnati (OH)
U of the District of Columbia (DC)
U of Toledo (OH)
Weber State U (UT)
Wentworth Inst of Tech (MA)
Western Kentucky U (KY)
West Virginia State Coll (WV)

ART EDUCATION
Clayton State Coll (GA)
Immaculata Coll (PA)
Martin Methodist Coll (TN)

ART/FINE ARTS
Adrian Coll (MI)
Armstrong State Coll (GA)
Ashland U (OH)
Bethel Coll (IN)
Black Hills State U (SD)
Brewton-Parker Coll (GA)
CAD Inst (AZ)
Carroll Coll (MT)
Clarke Coll (IA)
Clayton State Coll (GA)
Coll of Mount St Joseph (OH)
Concordia Coll (OR)
The Defiance Coll (OH)
Eastern New Mexico U (NM)
Endicott Coll (MA)
Fashion Inst of Tech (NY)
Felician Coll (NJ)
Friends U (KS)
Grace Coll (IN)
Grand View Coll (IA)
Immaculata Coll (PA)
Indiana U East (IN)
Indiana Wesleyan U (IN)
John Brown U (AR)
Kendall Coll (IL)
Lasell Coll (MA)
Lourdes Coll (OH)
Madonna U (MI)
Maharishi U of Management (IA)
Manchester Coll (IN)
Marian Coll (IN)
Martin Methodist Coll (TN)
Mesa State Coll (CO)
Methodist Coll (NC)
Montreat Coll (NC)
Mount Olive Coll (NC)
Mount St Clare Coll (IA)
Newschool of Architecture (CA)
Northern Michigan U (MI)
Northern State U (SD)
Ohio University–Lancaster (OH)
Pace U (NY)
Parsons Sch of Design, New Sch for Social Research (NY)
Pine Manor Coll (MA)
Pontifical Catholic U of Puerto Rico (PR)
Reinhardt Coll (GA)
Richmond Coll, The American International U in London (United Kingdom)
Rivier Coll (NH)
Rochester Inst of Tech (NY)
Sacred Heart U (CT)
Shawnee State U (OH)
Siena Heights Coll (MI)
Sinte Gleska U (SD)
Southern Coll of Seventh-day Adventists (TN)
State U of NY Empire State Coll (NY)
Suomi Coll (MI)
Thomas Coll (GA)
Thomas More Coll (KY)
Union Coll (NE)
Unity Coll (ME)
U of Akron (OH)
U of Rio Grande (OH)
U of Wisconsin–Green Bay (WI)
Villa Julie Coll (MD)
West Virginia State Coll (WV)
York Coll of Pennsylvania (PA)

ART HISTORY
Chestnut Hill Coll (PA)
Kendall Coll (IL)
Lourdes Coll (OH)
Pine Manor Coll (MA)
West Chester U of Pennsylvania (PA)

ARTS ADMINISTRATION
Endicott Coll (MA)
Glenville State Coll (WV)

ASIAN/ORIENTAL STUDIES
Grambling State U (LA)

ASTRONOMY
West Chester U of Pennsylvania (PA)

ATHLETIC TRAINING
Endicott Coll (MA)

AUDIO ENGINEERING
Five Towns Coll (NY)

AUTOMOTIVE TECHNOLOGIES
Andrews U (MI)
Austin Peay State U (TN)
Boise State U (ID)
Central Missouri State U (MO)
Denver Inst of Tech (CO)
Ferris State U (MI)
Georgia Southwestern Coll (GA)
Grambling State U (LA)
Idaho State U (ID)
Lamar University–Beaumont (TX)
LeTourneau U (TX)
Marshall U (WV)
McPherson Coll (KS)
Mesa State Coll (CO)
Montana State University–Billings (MT)
Montana State University–Northern (MT)
Northern Michigan U (MI)
Oakland City U (IN)
Pittsburg State U (KS)
Southern Illinois U at Carbondale (IL)
Southern Utah U (UT)
U of Akron (OH)
U of Alaska Anchorage (AK)
U of Alaska Southeast (AK)
Walla Walla Coll (WA)
Weber State U (UT)
Western New Mexico U (NM)
West Virginia U Inst of Tech (WV)

AVIATION ADMINISTRATION
Clayton State Coll (GA)
Daniel Webster Coll (NH)
Embry-Riddle Aeronautical U (FL)
Embry-Riddle Aeronautical U, Extended Cmps (FL)
Northern Kentucky U (KY)
Purdue U, West Lafayette (IN)
Saint Louis U (MO)
U of Alaska Anchorage (AK)
U of Dubuque (IA)
U of Minnesota, Crookston (MN)
U of the District of Columbia (DC)

AVIATION TECHNOLOGY
Andrews U (MI)
Baker Coll of Flint (MI)
Baker Coll of Muskegon (MI)
Central Missouri State U (MO)
Clayton State Coll (GA)
The Coll of West Virginia (WV)
Embry-Riddle Aeronautical U (FL)
Embry-Riddle Aeronautical U, Extended Cmps (FL)
Fairmont State Coll (WV)
Georgia Southwestern Coll (GA)
Indiana State U (IN)
Kansas State U (KS)
LeTourneau U (TX)
Lewis U (IL)
Marshall U (WV)
Northern Michigan U (MI)
Ohio U (OH)
Purdue U, West Lafayette (IN)
Rocky Mountain Coll (MT)
Saint Louis U (MO)
Southern Illinois U at Carbondale (IL)
Thomas Edison State Coll (NJ)
U of Alaska Anchorage (AK)
U of Alaska Fairbanks (AK)
U of Minnesota, Crookston (MN)
U of New Haven (CT)
U of the District of Columbia (DC)
Walla Walla Coll (WA)
Wentworth Inst of Tech (MA)

BEHAVIORAL SCIENCES
Bartlesville Wesleyan Coll (OK)
Circleville Bible Coll (OH)
Coll for Lifelong Learning of the U System of NH (NH)
Edinboro U of Pennsylvania (PA)
Felician Coll (NJ)
Lewis-Clark State Coll (ID)
Martin Methodist Coll (TN)
Methodist Coll (NC)
Mount Aloysius Coll (PA)
North Central Bible Coll (MN)

BIBLICAL LANGUAGES
Baltimore Hebrew U (MD)
Bethel Coll (IN)
North Central Bible Coll (MN)

BIBLICAL STUDIES
Alaska Bible Coll (AK)
Arizona Coll of the Bible (AZ)
Baltimore Hebrew U (MD)
Berean U of the Assemblies of God (MO)
Bethel Coll (IN)
Boise Bible Coll (ID)
Brewton-Parker Coll (GA)
Briercrest Bible Coll (SK, Canada)
Calvary Bible Coll and Theological Sem (MO)
Central Bible Coll (MO)
Central Christian Coll of the Bible (MO)
Cincinnati Bible Coll and Sem (OH)
Circleville Bible Coll (OH)
Clear Creek Baptist Bible Coll (KY)
Covenant Coll (GA)
The Criswell Coll (TX)
Crown Coll (MN)
Dallas Baptist U (TX)
Dallas Christian Coll (TX)
East Coast Bible Coll (NC)
Eastern Mennonite U (VA)
Eastern Nazarene Coll (MA)
Faith Baptist Bible Coll and Theological Sem (IA)
Faulkner U (AL)
Florida Bible Coll (FL)
Florida Christian Coll (FL)
Fresno Pacific Coll (CA)
Grace U (NE)
Hobe Sound Bible Coll (FL)
Houghton Coll (NY)
Indiana Wesleyan U (IN)
International Bible Coll (AL)
John Brown U (AR)
Johnson Bible Coll (TN)
Kentucky Christian Coll (KY)
Lancaster Bible Coll (PA)
Lexington Baptist Coll (KY)
L I F E Bible Coll (CA)
Lincoln Christian Coll (IL)
Lutheran Bible Inst of Seattle (WA)
Manhattan Christian Coll (KS)
Montreat Coll (NC)
Nazarene Bible Coll (CO)
North Central Bible Coll (MN)
Northwest Christian Coll (OR)
Northwestern Coll (MN)
Oak Hills Bible Coll (MN)
Oakwood Coll (AL)
Pacific Christian Coll (CA)
Pacific Union Coll (CA)
Patten Coll (CA)
Practical Bible Coll (NY)
Reformed Bible Coll (MI)
Roanoke Bible Coll (NC)
Simpson Coll (CA)
Southeastern Baptist Coll (MS)
Southeastern Bible Coll (AL)
Southwestern Assemblies of God U (TX)
Southwestern Christian Coll (TX)
Southwestern Coll (AZ)
Tabor Coll (KS)
Taylor U, Fort Wayne Cmps (IN)
Trinity Bible Coll (ND)
Trinity Coll of Florida (FL)
Universidad Adventista de las Antillas (PR)
Warner Pacific Coll (OR)
Washington Bible Coll (MD)
Western Baptist Coll (OR)
William Tyndale Coll (MI)

BIOCHEMICAL TECHNOLOGY
Weber State U (UT)

BIOLOGY/BIOLOGICAL SCIENCES
Adrian Coll (MI)
Bartlesville Wesleyan Coll (OK)
Bethel Coll (IN)
Brewton-Parker Coll (GA)
Clayton State Coll (GA)
Crown Coll (MN)
Cumberland U (TN)
Felician Coll (NJ)
Fresno Pacific Coll (CA)
Grand View Coll (IA)
Indiana U East (IN)
Indiana U South Bend (IN)
Indiana Wesleyan U (IN)
Lindsey Wilson Coll (KY)
Lourdes Coll (OH)
Madonna U (MI)
Maharishi U of Management (IA)
Martin Methodist Coll (TN)
Mesa State Coll (CO)
Methodist Coll (NC)
Montana Tech of The U of Montana (MT)
Mount Olive Coll (NC)
Mount St Clare Coll (IA)
Northern Michigan U (MI)
Pine Manor Coll (MA)
Presentation Coll (SD)
Reinhardt Coll (GA)
Rochester Inst of Tech (NY)
Sacred Heart U (CT)
Shawnee State U (OH)
Thomas Edison State Coll (NJ)
Thomas More Coll (KY)
U of Dubuque (IA)
U of Hartford (CT)
U of Minnesota, Crookston (MN)
U of New Hampshire at Manchester (NH)
U of New Haven (CT)
U of Rio Grande (OH)
The U of Tampa (FL)
U of Wisconsin–Green Bay (WI)
Villa Julie Coll (MD)
Wright State U (OH)
York Coll of Pennsylvania (PA)

BIOMEDICAL TECHNOLOGIES
Andrews U (MI)
Baker Coll of Flint (MI)
Baker Coll of Muskegon (MI)
Baker Coll of Owosso (MI)
Edinboro U of Pennsylvania (PA)
Faulkner U (AL)
Penn State U at Erie, The Behrend Coll (PA)
Southern Illinois U at Carbondale (IL)
U of Arkansas for Medical Sciences (AR)

BIOTECHNOLOGY
Northeastern U (MA)
U of the District of Columbia (DC)
Villa Julie Coll (MD)
Weber State U (UT)

BOTANY/PLANT SCIENCES
Northern Michigan U (MI)

BROADCASTING
Becker College–Leicester Cmps (MA)
Becker College–Worcester Cmps (MA)
Black Hills State U (SD)
Calvary Bible Coll and Theological Sem (MO)
The Coll of West Virginia (WV)
Cornerstone Coll (MI)
Endicott Coll (MA)
Evangel Coll (MO)
Five Towns Coll (NY)
International Coll of the Cayman Islands (Cayman Islands)
John Brown U (AR)
Manchester Coll (IN)
Martin Methodist Coll (TN)
Morehead State U (KY)
North Central Bible Coll (MN)
Northern Michigan U (MI)
Northwestern Coll (MN)
Ohio University–Zanesville (OH)
Salem-Teikyo U (WV)
Trevecca Nazarene U (TN)

BUSINESS ADMINISTRATION/ COMMERCE/ MANAGEMENT
Adrian Coll (MI)
Alabama State U (AL)
Alaska Pacific U (AK)
Alderson-Broaddus Coll (WV)
Alvernia Coll (PA)
The American Coll (CA)
The American Coll (GA)
The American Coll (United Kingdom)
American Coll of Higher Studies of Anatolia Coll (Greece)
American Indian Coll of the Assemblies of God, Inc (AZ)
American International Coll (MA)
Anderson U (IN)
Andrews U (MI)
Anna Maria Coll (MA)
Armstrong U (CA)
Ashland U (OH)
Baker Coll of Auburn Hills (MI)
Baker Coll of Cadillac (MI)
Baker Coll of Flint (MI)
Baker Coll of Mount Clemens (MI)
Baker Coll of Muskegon (MI)
Baker Coll of Owosso (MI)
Baker Coll of Port Huron (MI)
Ball State U (IN)
Bartlesville Wesleyan Coll (OK)
Bayamón Central U (PR)
Bayamón Tech U Coll (PR)
Becker College–Leicester Cmps (MA)
Becker College–Worcester Cmps (MA)
Benedictine Coll (KS)
Bentley Coll (MA)
Bethany Coll of the Assemblies of God (CA)
Bethel Coll (IN)
Brescia Coll (KY)
Brewton-Parker Coll (GA)
Bryan Coll (TN)
California U of Pennsylvania (PA)
Calumet Coll of Saint Joseph (IN)
Campbellsville U (KY)
Cardinal Stritch Coll (WI)
Carroll Coll (MT)
Central Baptist Coll (AR)
Chaminade U of Honolulu (HI)
Charleston Southern U (SC)
Chestnut Hill Coll (PA)
City U (WA)
Clarion U of Pennsylvania (PA)
Clayton State Coll (GA)
Cleary Coll (MI)
Coll for Lifelong Learning of the U System of NH (NH)
Coll of Insurance (NY)
Coll of Mount St Joseph (OH)
Coll of Mount Saint Vincent (NY)
Coll of St Joseph (VT)
Coll of Saint Mary (NE)
Coll of Santa Fe (NM)
Coll of Staten Island of the City U of New York (NY)
The Coll of West Virginia (WV)
Columbia Coll (MO)
Concordia Coll (AL)
Concordia Coll (NY)
Concordia Coll (OR)
Covenant Coll (GA)
Crown Coll (MN)
Cumberland Coll (TN)
Dakota State U (SD)
Dakota Wesleyan U (SD)
Dallas Baptist U (TX)
Daniel Webster Coll (NH)
Davenport Coll of Business, Grand Rapids (MI)
Davenport Coll of Business, Kalamazoo Cmps (MI)
Davenport Coll of Business, Lansing Cmps (MI)
David N Myers Coll (OH)
Davis & Elkins Coll (WV)
The Defiance Coll (OH)
Denver Tech Coll (CO)
Detroit Coll of Business, Dearborn (MI)
Detroit Coll of Business–Flint (MI)
Detroit Coll of Business, Warren Cmps (MI)
Dickinson State U (ND)
Eastern New Mexico U (NM)
East Texas Baptist U (TX)
East-West U (IL)
Edinboro U of Pennsylvania (PA)
Endicott Coll (MA)
Fairmont State Coll (WV)
Faulkner U (AL)
Felician Coll (NJ)
Five Towns Coll (NY)
Fort Lauderdale Coll (FL)
Franciscan U of Steubenville (OH)
Franklin U (OH)
Free Will Baptist Bible Coll (TN)
Fresno Pacific Coll (CA)
Friends U (KS)
Gannon U (PA)
Geneva Coll (PA)
Golden Gate U (CA)
Goldey-Beacom Coll (DE)
Grace Bible Coll (MI)
Grand View Coll (IA)
Gwynedd-Mercy Coll (PA)
Heritage Coll (WA)
Hilbert Coll (NY)
Humphreys Coll (CA)
Huntington Coll (IN)
Huron U (SD)
Husson Coll (ME)
Idaho State U (ID)
Immaculata Coll (PA)
Indiana Inst of Tech (IN)
Indiana State U (IN)
Indiana U East (IN)

Indiana U Northwest (IN)
Indiana U of Pennsylvania (PA)
Indiana U–Purdue U Fort Wayne (IN)
Indiana U South Bend (IN)
Indiana Wesleyan U (IN)
Inter American U of PR, Arecibo Cmps (PR)
Inter American U of PR, Fajardo Cmps (PR)
Inter American U of PR, Ponce Cmps (PR)
Inter American U of PR, San Germán Cmps (PR)
International Coll (FL)
International Coll of the Cayman Islands (Cayman Islands)
Johnson & Wales U (RI)
Johnson State Coll (VT)
Jones Coll (FL)
Kansas Wesleyan U (KS)
King's Coll (PA)
LaGrange Coll (GA)
Lake Superior State U (MI)
La Salle U (PA)
Lasell Coll (MA)
Lincoln Memorial U (TN)
Lindsey Wilson Coll (KY)
Long Island U, Brooklyn Cmps (NY)
Louisiana Tech U (LA)
Lourdes Coll (OH)
Lyndon State Coll (VT)
MacMurray Coll (IL)
Madonna U (MI)
Maharishi U of Management (IA)
Maine Maritime Acad (ME)
Manchester Coll (IN)
Marian Coll (IN)
Marietta Coll (OH)
Marshall U (WV)
Martin Methodist Coll (TN)
Marygrove Coll (MI)
Mayville State U (ND)
Medgar Evers Coll of the City U of New York (NY)
Mercyhurst Coll (PA)
Merrimack Coll (MA)
Mesa State Coll (CO)
Methodist Coll (NC)
MidAmerica Nazarene Coll (KS)
Midway Coll (KY)
Missouri Baptist Coll (MO)
Missouri Valley Coll (MO)
Montana State University–Northern (MT)
Montreat Coll (NC)
Morehead State U (KY)
Morrison Coll (NV)
Mount Aloysius Coll (PA)
Mount Marty Coll (SD)
Mount Olive Coll (NC)
Mount St Clare Coll (IA)
Mount St Mary's Coll (CA)
Mount Senario Coll (WI)
Mount Vernon Nazarene Coll (OH)
Murray State U (KY)
National Coll, Colorado Springs (CO)
National Coll, Denver (CO)
National Coll (MO)
National Coll (NM)
National Coll (SD)
National College–St Paul Cmps (MN)
National College–Sioux Falls Branch (SD)
New Hampshire Coll (NH)
New York Inst of Tech (NY)
Niagara U (NY)
Nicholls State U (LA)
North Central Bible Coll (MN)
Northeastern U (MA)
Northern Kentucky U (KY)
Northern Michigan U (MI)
Northern State U (SD)
Northwest Coll of the Assemblies of God (WA)
Northwestern Coll (MN)
Northwestern State U of Louisiana (LA)
Northwood U (MI)
Northwood U, Florida Cmps (FL)
Northwood U, Texas Cmps (TX)
Notre Dame Coll of Ohio (OH)
Nyack Coll (NY)
Oakland City U (IN)
Oglala Lakota Coll (SD)
Ohio U (OH)
Ohio University–Chillicothe (OH)
Ohio University–Lancaster (OH)
Oklahoma Panhandle State U (OK)
Orlando Coll (FL)
Pace U (NY)
Penn State U at Erie, The Behrend Coll (PA)
Penn State U at Harrisburg—The Capital Coll (PA)
Penn State U Univ Park Cmps (PA)
Philadelphia Coll of Bible (PA)
Phillips U (OK)
Pikeville Coll (KY)
Pine Manor Coll (MA)
Point Park Coll (PA)
Pontifical Catholic U of Puerto Rico (PR)
Presentation Coll (SD)
Purdue U North Central (IN)
Reinhardt Coll (GA)
Richmond Coll, The American International U in London (United Kingdom)
Rivier Coll (NH)
Robert Morris Coll (IL)
Robert Morris Coll (PA)
Rochester Inst of Tech (NY)
Roger Williams U (RI)
Rust Coll (MS)
Sacred Heart U (CT)
Saint Francis Coll (IN)
St Francis Coll (NY)
Saint Francis Coll (PA)
St John's U (NY)
Saint Joseph's Coll (IN)
Saint Joseph's U (PA)
Saint Mary-of-the-Woods Coll (IN)
Saint Peter's Coll, Jersey City (NJ)
Salve Regina U (RI)
Schiller International U, Paris (France)
Schiller International U, Strasbourg (France)
Schiller International U, Heidelberg (Germany)
Schiller International U (Spain)
Schiller International U, London (United Kingdom)
Shawnee State U (OH)
Shaw U (NC)
Sheldon Jackson Coll (AK)
Shepherd Coll (WV)
Siena Heights Coll (MI)
Sinte Gleska U (SD)
Southeastern Baptist Coll (MS)
Southeastern U (DC)
Southern Nazarene U (OK)
Southern Vermont Coll (VT)
Southern Wesleyan U (SC)
Southwest Baptist U (MO)
Southwestern Assemblies of God U (TX)
Southwestern Christian Coll (TX)
Southwest State U (MN)
Spalding U (KY)
State U of NY Empire State Coll (NY)
Strayer Coll (DC)
Sue Bennett Coll (KY)
Sullivan Coll (KY)
Suomi Coll (MI)
Tampa Coll (FL)
Tampa College–Lakeland (FL)
Tampa Coll, Pinellas Ctr (FL)
Taylor U (IN)
Taylor U, Fort Wayne Cmps (IN)
Teikyo Post U (CT)
Thomas Coll (GA)
Thomas Coll (ME)
Thomas Edison State Coll (NJ)
Thomas More Coll (KY)
Tiffin U (OH)
Trinity Bible Coll (ND)
Trinity Coll of Vermont (VT)
Tri-State U (IN)
Troy State U, Troy (AL)
Troy State U at Dothan (AL)
Troy State U Montgomery (AL)
Tulane U (LA)
Union Coll (NE)
Universidad Adventista de las Antillas (PR)
U Coll of Cape Breton (NS, Canada)
U of Akron (OH)
U of Alaska Anchorage (AK)
U of Alaska Fairbanks (AK)
U of Bridgeport (CT)
The U of Charleston (WV)
U of Cincinnati (OH)
U of Dubuque (IA)
The U of Findlay (OH)
U of Great Falls (MT)
U of Indianapolis (IN)
U of La Verne (CA)
U of Maine at Fort Kent (ME)
U of Maine at Machias (ME)
U of Mary (ND)
U of Massachusetts Lowell (MA)
U of Minnesota, Crookston (MN)
U of New Hampshire, Durham (NH)
U of New Hampshire at Manchester (NH)
U of New Haven (CT)
U of Phoenix (AZ)
U of Puerto Rico, Aguadilla Regional Coll (PR)
U of Puerto Rico at Arecibo (PR)
U of Puerto Rico at Ponce (PR)
U of Puerto Rico, Humacao U Coll (PR)
U of Rio Grande (OH)
U of Sioux Falls (SD)
U of Southern Indiana (IN)
U of Southern Maine (ME)
U of the State of NY, Regents Coll (NY)
U of the Virgin Islands (VI)
U of Toledo (OH)
U of Wisconsin–Green Bay (WI)
Upper Iowa U (IA)
Urbana U (OH)
Villa Julie Coll (MD)
Walla Walla Coll (WA)
Walsh U (OH)
Waynesburg Coll (PA)
Webber Coll (FL)
Wesley Coll (DE)
West Coast U (CA)
Western Baptist Coll (OR)
Western Kentucky U (KY)
Western Montana Coll of The U of Montana (MT)
West Virginia State Coll (WV)
West Virginia U Inst of Tech (WV)
Williams Baptist Coll (AR)
William Tyndale Coll (MI)
Wright State U (OH)
Xavier U (OH)
York Coll (NE)
York Coll of Pennsylvania (PA)
Youngstown State U (OH)

BUSINESS ECONOMICS
Urbana U (OH)
York Coll of Pennsylvania (PA)

BUSINESS EDUCATION
Atlanta Christian Coll (GA)
Clayton State Coll (GA)
Concordia Coll (AL)
Faulkner U (AL)
Inter American U of PR, Fajardo Cmps (PR)
Lindsey Wilson Coll (KY)
Martin Methodist Coll (TN)
Selma U (AL)
Sinte Gleska U (SD)
U of the District of Columbia (DC)

BUSINESS MACHINE TECHNOLOGIES
Boise State U (ID)
Faulkner U (AL)
Ferris State U (MI)
Gallaudet U (DC)
Idaho State U (ID)
Johnson & Wales U (RI)
Lamar University–Beaumont (TX)
U of Akron (OH)
U of New Mexico (NM)

CARPENTRY
Andrews U (MI)
Austin Peay State U (TN)
Boise State U (ID)
Oglala Lakota Coll (SD)
Southern Utah U (UT)
Western New Mexico U (NM)

CARTOGRAPHY
Ferris State U (MI)
Western Kentucky U (KY)

CERAMIC ART AND DESIGN
Endicott Coll (MA)
Friends U (KS)
Northern Michigan U (MI)
Parsons Sch of Design, New Sch for Social Research (NY)
Rochester Inst of Tech (NY)
U of Bridgeport (CT)

CHEMICAL ENGINEERING TECHNOLOGY
Ball State U (IN)
Ferris State U (MI)
Kansas State U (KS)
Lawrence Tech U (MI)
U Coll of Cape Breton (NS, Canada)
U of Akron (OH)
U of Cincinnati (OH)
U of Puerto Rico at Arecibo (PR)
U of the District of Columbia (DC)
U of the State of NY, Regents Coll (NY)
U of Toledo (OH)
Weber State U (UT)
West Virginia State Coll (WV)

CHEMISTRY
Adrian Coll (MI)
Bartlesville Wesleyan Coll (OK)
Bethel Coll (IN)
Calumet Coll of Saint Joseph (IN)
Central Methodist Coll (MO)
Chestnut Hill Coll (PA)
Clayton State Coll (GA)
Grand View Coll (IA)
Indiana U East (IN)
Indiana U South Bend (IN)
Indiana Wesleyan U (IN)
Inter American U of PR, Arecibo Cmps (PR)
Keene State Coll (NH)
Lake Superior State U (MI)
Lindsey Wilson Coll (KY)
Lourdes Coll (OH)
Madonna U (MI)
Maharishi U of Management (IA)
Martin Methodist Coll (TN)
Methodist Coll (NC)
Millersville U of Pennsylvania (PA)
Mount St Clare Coll (IA)
Northern Michigan U (MI)
Ohio Dominican Coll (OH)
Reinhardt Coll (GA)
Rochester Inst of Tech (NY)
Sacred Heart U (CT)
Saint Joseph's U (PA)
Siena Heights Coll (MI)
Thomas Edison State Coll (NJ)
Thomas More Coll (KY)
U of Indianapolis (IN)
U of Massachusetts Lowell (MA)
U of New Haven (CT)
U of Puerto Rico, Humacao U Coll (PR)
U of Rio Grande (OH)
The U of Tampa (FL)
U of Wisconsin–Green Bay (WI)
Villa Julie Coll (MD)
Wright State U (OH)
York Coll of Pennsylvania (PA)

CHILD CARE/CHILD AND FAMILY STUDIES
Alabama A&M U (AL)
Alabama State U (AL)
Andrews U (MI)
Becker College–Leicester Cmps (MA)
Becker College–Worcester Cmps (MA)
Boise State U (ID)
California U of Pennsylvania (PA)
Cazenovia Coll (NY)
Centenary Coll (NJ)
Coll for Lifelong Learning of the U System of NH (NH)
Coll of Staten Island of the City U of New York (NY)
Crown Coll (MN)
Eastern Kentucky U (KY)
Endicott Coll (MA)
Evangel Coll (MO)
Fairmont State Coll (WV)
Ferris State U (MI)
Friends U (KS)
Grambling State U (LA)
Hannibal-LaGrange Coll (MO)
Henderson State U (AR)
Lamar University–Beaumont (TX)
Lasell Coll (MA)
La Sierra U (CA)
Madonna U (MI)
Maranatha Baptist Bible Coll (WI)
Marygrove Coll (MI)
Midway Coll (KY)
Mount St Clare Coll (IA)
Murray State U (KY)
Northern Michigan U (MI)
Ohio University–Lancaster (OH)
Oklahoma Panhandle State U (OK)
Plymouth State Coll of the U System of NH (NH)
Purdue U Calumet (IN)
Reformed Bible Coll (MI)
Silver Lake Coll (WI)
Southeast Missouri State U (MO)
Southern Nazarene U (OK)
Southern Utah U (UT)
Trevecca Nazarene U (TN)
U of Akron (OH)
U of Alaska Fairbanks (AK)
U of Cincinnati (OH)
U of Maine at Machias (ME)
U of Minnesota, Crookston (MN)
U of Rio Grande (OH)
U of the District of Columbia (DC)
U of Toledo (OH)
Villa Julie Coll (MD)
Washburn U of Topeka (KS)
Weber State U (UT)
Youngstown State U (OH)

CHILD PSYCHOLOGY/ CHILD DEVELOPMENT
Abilene Christian U (TX)
Central Missouri State U (MO)
Franciscan U of Steubenville (OH)
Fresno Pacific Coll (CA)
Lewis-Clark State Coll (ID)
Madonna U (MI)
Morehead State U (KY)
Olivet Nazarene U (IL)
Pine Manor Coll (MA)
Plymouth State Coll of the U System of NH (NH)
Siena Heights Coll (MI)
Southern Vermont Coll (VT)
Southwest Baptist U (MO)
Southwestern Christian Coll (TX)
U of Akron (OH)
U of Alaska Fairbanks (AK)
U of Sioux Falls (SD)
U of Wisconsin–Green Bay (WI)
Villa Julie Coll (MD)
Western Montana Coll of The U of Montana (MT)

CITY/COMMUNITY/ REGIONAL PLANNING
U of the District of Columbia (DC)
U of Wisconsin–Green Bay (WI)
West Chester U of Pennsylvania (PA)

CIVIL ENGINEERING TECHNOLOGY
Alabama A&M U (AL)
Bayamón Tech U Coll (PR)
Coll of Staten Island of the City U of New York (NY)
Eastern New Mexico U (NM)
Fairmont State Coll (WV)
Ferris State U (MI)
Idaho State U (ID)
Indiana U–Purdue U Fort Wayne (IN)
Indiana U–Purdue U Indianapolis (IN)
Kansas State U (KS)
Lewis-Clark State Coll (ID)
Michigan Tech U (MI)
Montana State University–Northern (MT)
Murray State U (KY)
New Mexico State U (NM)
Northeastern U (MA)
Point Park Coll (PA)
Purdue U Calumet (IN)
Purdue U North Central (IN)
Roger Williams U (RI)
Southern U and A&M Coll (LA)
Thomas Edison State Coll (NJ)
U Coll of Cape Breton (NS, Canada)
U of Cincinnati (OH)
U of Massachusetts Lowell (MA)
U of New Hampshire, Durham (NH)
U of New Haven (CT)
U of Puerto Rico at Ponce (PR)
U of Southern Indiana (IN)
U of the District of Columbia (DC)
U of Toledo (OH)
Wentworth Inst of Tech (MA)
Western Kentucky U (KY)
West Virginia U Inst of Tech (WV)
Youngstown State U (OH)

COMMERCIAL ART
The American Coll (CA)
The American Coll (GA)
The American Coll (United Kingdom)
Bethel Coll (IN)
Black Hills State U (SD)
Brigham Young University–Hawaii Cmps (HI)
Cardinal Stritch Coll (WI)
Endicott Coll (MA)
Fairmont State Coll (WV)
Fashion Inst of Tech (NY)
Ferris State U (MI)
Friends U (KS)
Indiana U–Purdue U Fort Wayne (IN)
Madonna U (MI)
Northern Michigan U (MI)
Northern State U (SD)
Oakwood Coll (AL)
Orlando Coll (FL)
Parsons Sch of Design, New Sch for Social Research (NY)
Pratt Inst (NY)
Rochester Inst of Tech (NY)
Saint Francis Coll (IN)
Schiller International U, London (United Kingdom)
Shepherd Coll (WV)
Silver Lake Coll (WI)
Southern Illinois U at Carbondale (IL)
Southern Nazarene U (OK)
Tampa Coll (FL)
U of Akron (OH)
U of Bridgeport (CT)
Waynesburg Coll (PA)
Western Montana Coll of The U of Montana (MT)

Peterson's Guide to Two-Year Colleges 1997 135

COMMUNICATION
Becker College–Leicester Cmps (MA)
Becker College–Worcester Cmps (MA)
Bethel Coll (IN)
Black Hills State U (SD)
Brigham Young University–Hawaii Cmps (HI)
Calumet Coll of Saint Joseph (IN)
Carroll Coll (MT)
Castleton State Coll (VT)
Clarke Coll (IA)
Clayton State Coll (GA)
Coll of Mount St Joseph (OH)
Coll of Saint Mary (NE)
Cornerstone Coll (MI)
Creighton U (NE)
Endicott Coll (MA)
Evangel Coll (MO)
Fashion Inst of Tech (NY)
Franklin Coll Switzerland (Switzerland)
Fresno Pacific Coll (CA)
Grand View Coll (IA)
Huron U (SD)
Indiana Wesleyan U (IN)
Kentucky Wesleyan Coll (KY)
Lewis-Clark State Coll (ID)
Lyndon State Coll (VT)
Madonna U (MI)
Martin Methodist Coll (TN)
Methodist Coll (NC)
Montana State University–Northern (MT)
Montreat Coll (NC)
New York Inst of Tech (NY)
North Central Bible Coll (MN)
Northern Michigan U (MI)
Oglala Lakota Coll (SD)
Pace U (NY)
Point Park Coll (PA)
Reinhardt Coll (GA)
Sacred Heart U (CT)
Salem-Teikyo U (WV)
Southwestern Assemblies of God U (TX)
Thomas More Coll (KY)
Tri-State U (IN)
U of Dubuque (IA)
U of Hartford (CT)
U of Puerto Rico, Humacao U Coll (PR)
U of Rio Grande (OH)
U of Southern Indiana (IN)
U of Wisconsin–Green Bay (WI)
Villa Julie Coll (MD)
West Chester U of Pennsylvania (PA)
West Virginia State Coll (WV)
Wright State U (OH)
Xavier U (OH)

COMMUNICATION EQUIPMENT TECHNOLOGY
Central Missouri State U (MO)
East Stroudsburg U of Pennsylvania (PA)
Ferris State U (MI)
Idaho State U (ID)
West Chester U of Pennsylvania (PA)

COMMUNITY SERVICES
Alabama State U (AL)
California U of Pennsylvania (PA)
Cazenovia Coll (NY)
Fairmont State Coll (WV)
Martin Methodist Coll (TN)
Midland Lutheran Coll (NE)
Montana State University–Northern (MT)
State U of NY Empire State Coll (NY)
Thomas Edison State Coll (NJ)
U of Akron (OH)
The U of Findlay (OH)
Wright State U (OH)

COMPUTER GRAPHICS
The Art Inst of Illinois (IL)
Baker Coll of Cadillac (MI)
Cogswell Polytechnical Coll (CA)
International Acad of Merchandising & Design (FL)
International Acad of Merchandising & Design, Ltd (IL)
Newschool of Architecture (CA)
Robert Morris Coll (IL)
Villa Julie Coll (MD)

COMPUTER INFORMATION SYSTEMS
Andrews U (MI)
Arkansas State U (AR)
Baker Coll of Cadillac (MI)
Baker Coll of Mount Clemens (MI)
Baker Coll of Muskegon (MI)
Baker Coll of Owosso (MI)
Ball State U (IN)
Bartlesville Wesleyan Coll (OK)
Bayamón Central U (PR)
Becker College–Worcester Cmps (MA)
Benedictine Coll (KS)
Calumet Coll of Saint Joseph (IN)
Campbellsville U (KY)
Clayton State Coll (GA)
Coll of Mount St Joseph (OH)
Coll of St Joseph (VT)
Coll of Saint Mary (NE)
The Coll of West Virginia (WV)
Colorado Christian U (CO)
Columbia Coll (MO)
Dakota State U (SD)
Daniel Webster Coll (NH)
Davenport Coll of Business, Grand Rapids (MI)
Davenport Coll of Business, Kalamazoo Cmps (MI)
Davenport Coll of Business, Lansing Cmps (MI)
Denver Tech Coll (CO)
Detroit Coll of Business, Dearborn (MI)
Detroit Coll of Business–Flint (MI)
Detroit Coll of Business, Warren Cmps (MI)
Faulkner U (AL)
Friends U (KS)
Goldey-Beacom Coll (DE)
Humphreys Coll (CA)
Huron U (SD)
Husson Coll (ME)
Indiana Inst of Tech (IN)
Indiana Wesleyan U (IN)
Jones Coll (FL)
Kansas Newman Coll (KS)
Kansas State U (KS)
King's Coll (PA)
Michigan Christian Coll (MI)
Midway Coll (KY)
Montana State University–Northern (MT)
Morehead State U (KY)
Morrison Coll (NV)
Mount Olive Coll (NC)
Mount St Clare Coll (IA)
National Coll, Colorado Springs (CO)
National Coll, Denver (CO)
National Coll (MO)
National Coll (NM)
National Coll (SD)
National College–St Paul Cmps (MN)
National College–Sioux Falls Branch (SD)
New Hampshire Coll (NH)
Northwestern Coll (MN)
Northwestern State U of Louisiana (LA)
Oakwood Coll (AL)
Oklahoma Panhandle State U (OK)
Pace U (NY)
Pacific Union Coll (CA)
Purdue U North Central (IN)
Robert Morris Coll (IL)
Roger Williams U (RI)
St Francis Coll (NY)
Shepherd Coll (WV)
Siena Heights Coll (MI)
Southeastern U (DC)
Southern Utah U (UT)
Southwestern Adventist Coll (TX)
Strayer Coll (DC)
Sue Bennett Coll (KY)
Thomas Coll (ME)
Thomas More Coll (KY)
Trevecca Nazarene U (TN)
Tulane U (LA)
Union Coll (KY)
Union Coll (NE)
U Coll of Cape Breton (NS, Canada)
U of Alaska Anchorage (AK)
The U of Charleston (WV)
U of Cincinnati (OH)
U of Maine at Machias (ME)
U of Massachusetts Lowell (MA)
U of Minnesota, Crookston (MN)
U of Scranton (PA)
U of Southern Indiana (IN)
The U of Tampa (FL)
U of Toledo (OH)
U of Wisconsin–Green Bay (WI)
Villa Julie Coll (MD)
Washburn U of Topeka (KS)
Weber State U (UT)
West Coast U (CA)
Western Kentucky U (KY)
Western Montana Coll of The U of Montana (MT)
Xavier U (OH)
Youngstown State U (OH)

COMPUTER MANAGEMENT
Coll for Lifelong Learning of the U System of NH (NH)
Daniel Webster Coll (NH)
Davenport Coll of Business, Lansing Cmps (MI)
Faulkner U (AL)
Five Towns Coll (NY)
International Coll of the Cayman Islands (Cayman Islands)
Northwood U (MI)
Northwood U, Florida Cmps (FL)
U of Great Falls (MT)

COMPUTER PROGRAMMING
Andrews U (MI)
Atlantic Union Coll (MA)
Baker Coll of Flint (MI)
Baker Coll of Muskegon (MI)
Baker Coll of Owosso (MI)
California U of Pennsylvania (PA)
Castleton State Coll (VT)
Cleary Coll (MI)
Columbus Coll (GA)
Dakota State U (SD)
Daniel Webster Coll (NH)
Davenport Coll of Business, Grand Rapids (MI)
Davenport Coll of Business, Kalamazoo Cmps (MI)
Denver Tech Coll (CO)
Eastern Mennonite U (VA)
Endicott Coll (MA)
Fort Lauderdale Coll (FL)
Friends U (KS)
Gwynedd-Mercy Coll (PA)
Humphreys Coll (CA)
Idaho State U (ID)
Johnson & Wales U (RI)
Jones Coll (FL)
Kansas State U (KS)
Lindsey Wilson Coll (KY)
Martin Methodist Coll (TN)
Midland Lutheran Coll (NE)
Missouri Southern State Coll (MO)
National Coll (SD)
National College–Sioux Falls Branch (SD)
New York U (NY)
Oakland City U (IN)
Oregon Inst of Tech (OR)
Orlando Coll (FL)
Pontifical Catholic U of Puerto Rico (PR)
Purdue U, West Lafayette (IN)
Purdue U Calumet (IN)
Purdue U North Central (IN)
Robert Morris Coll (IL)
Saint Francis Coll (PA)
Saint Joseph's U (PA)
Selma U (AL)
Shawnee State U (OH)
Shepherd Coll (WV)
Tampa Coll (FL)
Tampa College–Lakeland (FL)
Tiffin U (OH)
Trinity Coll of Vermont (VT)
U of Akron (OH)
U of Arkansas at Little Rock (AR)
U of Cincinnati (OH)
U of Pittsburgh at Bradford (PA)
U of Puerto Rico, Aguadilla Regional Coll (PR)
U of Rio Grande (OH)
U of Southern Maine (ME)
U of Toledo (OH)
Villa Julie Coll (MD)
Walla Walla Coll (WA)
West Virginia State Coll (WV)
York Coll of Pennsylvania (PA)

COMPUTER SCIENCE
Alabama A&M U (AL)
Baker Coll of Owosso (MI)
Bayamón Tech U Coll (PR)
Bethel Coll (IN)
Brigham Young University–Hawaii Cmps (HI)
California U of Pennsylvania (PA)
Cardinal Stritch Coll (WI)
Carroll Coll (MT)
Central Methodist Coll (MO)
Clayton State Coll (GA)
Columbia Union Coll (MD)
Columbus Coll (GA)
Creighton U (NE)
Davis & Elkins Coll (WV)
The Defiance Coll (OH)
Denver Tech Coll (CO)
East Texas Baptist U (TX)
East-West U (IL)
Edinboro U of Pennsylvania (PA)
Felician Coll (NJ)
Franklin U (OH)
Friends U (KS)
Glenville State Coll (WV)
Grand View Coll (IA)
Grantham Coll of Engineering (LA)
Heritage Coll (WA)
Humphreys Coll (CA)
Indiana U East (IN)
Indiana U South Bend (IN)
Inter American U of PR, Arecibo Cmps (PR)
Inter American U of PR, Fajardo Cmps (PR)
Inter American U of PR, Ponce Cmps (PR)
International Coll (FL)
Johnson & Wales U (RI)
Kansas Wesleyan U (KS)
Keene State Coll (NH)
Kendall Coll (IL)
Kentucky State U (KY)
Lincoln U (MO)
Lyndon State Coll (VT)
Madonna U (MI)
Maharishi U of Management (IA)
Manchester Coll (IN)
Martin Methodist Coll (TN)
Marygrove Coll (MI)
McNeese State U (LA)
Medgar Evers Coll of the City U of New York (NY)
Merrimack Coll (MA)
Mesa State Coll (CO)
Methodist Coll (NC)
Michigan Christian Coll (MI)
Millersville U of Pennsylvania (PA)
Montana Tech of The U of Montana (MT)
Morrison Coll (NV)
Mount Aloysius Coll (PA)
New Mexico Highlands U (NM)
Northwood U (MI)
Oakland City U (IN)
Oglala Lakota Coll (SD)
Ohio University–Lancaster (OH)
Penn State U Univ Park Cmps (PA)
Philadelphia Coll of Bible (PA)
Phillips U (OK)
Point Park Coll (PA)
Purdue U, West Lafayette (IN)
Rivier Coll (NH)
Robert Morris Coll (IL)
Rochester Inst of Tech (NY)
Sacred Heart U (CT)
St Francis Coll (NY)
Saint Joseph's Coll (IN)
Saint Joseph's U (PA)
Selma U (AL)
Southeastern U (DC)
Southern Coll of Seventh-day Adventists (TN)
Southern Nazarene U (OK)
Southern U at New Orleans (LA)
Southwestern Christian Coll (TX)
Sullivan Coll (KY)
Tabor Coll (KS)
Tampa Coll (FL)
Tampa College–Lakeland (FL)
Tampa Coll, Pinellas Ctr (FL)
Thiel Coll (PA)
Thomas Edison State Coll (NJ)
Trevecca Nazarene U (TN)
Troy State U, Troy (AL)
Troy State U Montgomery (AL)
Universidad Adventista de las Antillas (PR)
U of Dubuque (IA)
The U of Findlay (OH)
U of Great Falls (MT)
U of Maine at Fort Kent (ME)
U of New Haven (CT)
U of Puerto Rico at Arecibo (PR)
U of Puerto Rico at Ponce (PR)
U of Rio Grande (OH)
U of the State of NY, Regents Coll (NY)
U of the Virgin Islands (VI)
U of West Alabama (AL)
Weber State U (UT)
Wentworth Inst of Tech (MA)
West Coast U (CA)
West Georgia Coll (GA)
West Virginia State Coll (WV)
Wiley Coll (TX)
William Tyndale Coll (MI)

COMPUTER TECHNOLOGIES
Andrews U (MI)
Baker Coll of Flint (MI)
Baker Coll of Owosso (MI)
CAD Inst (AZ)
Capitol Coll (MD)
Clayton State Coll (GA)
Coleman Coll (CA)
Coll of Staten Island of the City U of New York (NY)
Eastern Kentucky U (KY)
Edinboro U of Pennsylvania (PA)
Gallaudet U (DC)
Glenville State Coll (WV)
Grantham Coll of Engineering (LA)
Idaho State U (ID)
Indiana U–Purdue U Fort Wayne (IN)
Indiana U–Purdue U Indianapolis (IN)
Kansas State U (KS)
Lake Superior State U (MI)
Lewis-Clark State Coll (ID)
Madonna U (MI)
Marshall U (WV)
Marygrove Coll (MI)
Missouri Southern State Coll (MO)
Montana State University–Billings (MT)
Mount Vernon Nazarene Coll (OH)
National Coll (SD)
Northeastern U (MA)
Northwestern State U of Louisiana (LA)
Oakland City U (IN)
Ohio U (OH)
Ohio University–Lancaster (OH)
Oregon Inst of Tech (OR)
Pace U (NY)
Purdue U, West Lafayette (IN)
Purdue U Calumet (IN)
Purdue U North Central (IN)
Rochester Inst of Tech (NY)
Rocky Mountain Coll (MT)
St John's U (NY)
Southeast Missouri State U (MO)
Thomas Edison State Coll (NJ)
Tri-State U (IN)
U of Cincinnati (OH)
U of Hartford (CT)
U of Indianapolis (IN)
U of Minnesota, Crookston (MN)
U of the District of Columbia (DC)
U of the State of NY, Regents Coll (NY)
U of Toledo (OH)
Weber State U (UT)
Wentworth Inst of Tech (MA)
William Tyndale Coll (MI)

CONSERVATION
The Ohio State U (OH)
U of Minnesota, Crookston (MN)

CONSTRUCTION MANAGEMENT
Andrews U (MI)
Baker Coll of Flint (MI)
John Brown U (AR)
Pratt Inst (NY)
Purdue U, West Lafayette (IN)
U of New Hampshire, Durham (NH)

CONSTRUCTION TECHNOLOGIES
Abilene Christian U (TX)
Andrews U (MI)
Austin Peay State U (TN)
Baker Coll of Owosso (MI)
Bayamón Tech U Coll (PR)
Central Missouri State U (MO)
East Tennessee State U (TN)
Fairmont State Coll (WV)
Ferris State U (MI)
Grambling State U (LA)
Lawrence Tech U (MI)
Missouri Western State Coll (MO)
Morehead State U (KY)
Northern Michigan U (MI)
The Ohio State U (OH)
Purdue U, West Lafayette (IN)
Purdue U Calumet (IN)
Purdue U North Central (IN)
Southern Illinois U at Carbondale (IL)
Thomas Edison State Coll (NJ)
U Coll of Cape Breton (NS, Canada)
U of Akron (OH)
U of Alaska Southeast (AK)
U of Arkansas at Little Rock (AR)
U of Cincinnati (OH)
U of Nebraska at Omaha (NE)
U of Nebraska–Lincoln (NE)
U of New Hampshire, Durham (NH)
U of Toledo (OH)
Wentworth Inst of Tech (MA)
Western New Mexico U (NM)

CORRECTIONS
Armstrong State Coll (GA)
Eastern Kentucky U (KY)
John Jay Coll of Criminal Justice of City U of NY (NY)
Lake Superior State U (MI)
Lamar University–Beaumont (TX)
Marygrove Coll (MI)
Morehead State U (KY)
Murray State U (KY)
Northeastern U (MA)
Sue Bennett Coll (KY)
U of Indianapolis (IN)
U of New Haven (CT)
U of the District of Columbia (DC)
U of Toledo (OH)

Associate Degree Programs at Four-Year Colleges
Corrections–Economics

Washburn U of Topeka (KS)
Weber State U (UT)
York Coll of Pennsylvania (PA)

COSMETOLOGY
Idaho State U (ID)
Lamar University–Beaumont (TX)

COURT REPORTING
Davenport Coll of Business, Grand Rapids (MI)
Humphreys Coll (CA)
Johnson & Wales U (RI)
Orlando Coll (FL)
Southern Illinois U at Carbondale (IL)
U of Cincinnati (OH)
Villa Julie Coll (MD)
Washburn U of Topeka (KS)

CREATIVE WRITING
Manchester Coll (IN)
U of Maine at Presque Isle (ME)
The U of Tampa (FL)
West Chester U of Pennsylvania (PA)

CRIMINAL JUSTICE
Adrian Coll (MI)
Anderson U (IN)
Armstrong State Coll (GA)
Ashland U (OH)
Augusta Coll (GA)
Austin Peay State U (TN)
Ball State U (IN)
Becker College–Leicester Cmps (MA)
Becker College–Worcester Cmps (MA)
Bemidji State U (MN)
Boise State U (ID)
Calumet Coll of Saint Joseph (IN)
Cameron U (OK)
Campbellsville U (KY)
Castleton State Coll (VT)
Chaminade U of Honolulu (HI)
Clayton State Coll (GA)
The Coll of West Virginia (WV)
Columbia Coll (MO)
Columbus Coll (GA)
The Defiance Coll (OH)
Eastern Kentucky U (KY)
Edinboro U of Pennsylvania (PA)
Endicott Coll (MA)
Fairmont State Coll (WV)
Fort Valley State Coll (GA)
Georgia Southern U (GA)
Glenville State Coll (WV)
Grambling State U (LA)
Hannibal-LaGrange Coll (MO)
Hilbert Coll (NY)
Idaho State U (ID)
Indiana U East (IN)
Indiana U Kokomo (IN)
Indiana U Northwest (IN)
Indiana U of Pennsylvania (PA)
Indiana U–Purdue U Fort Wayne (IN)
Indiana U–Purdue U Indianapolis (IN)
Indiana U South Bend (IN)
Indiana Wesleyan U (IN)
Johnson & Wales U (RI)
Kansas Wesleyan U (KS)
King's Coll (PA)
LaGrange Coll (GA)
Lake Superior State U (MI)
Lewis-Clark State Coll (ID)
Lincoln U (MO)
Louisiana Coll (LA)
Lourdes Coll (OH)
MacMurray Coll (IL)
Madonna U (MI)
Manchester Coll (IN)
Martin Methodist Coll (TN)
McNeese State U (LA)
Mercyhurst Coll (PA)
Methodist Coll (NC)
Michigan Christian Coll (MI)
Missouri Western State Coll (MO)

Morningside Coll (IA)
Mount Senario Coll (WI)
Murray State U (KY)
New Mexico State U (NM)
New York Inst of Tech (NY)
Nicholls State U (LA)
Northeast Louisiana U (LA)
Northern Michigan U (MI)
Northern State U (SD)
Oglala Lakota Coll (SD)
Reinhardt Coll (GA)
St Francis Coll (NY)
St John's U (NY)
Saint Joseph's U (PA)
Salve Regina U (RI)
Siena Heights Coll (MI)
Southeastern Louisiana U (LA)
Southern U and A&M Coll (LA)
Southern Utah U (UT)
Southern Vermont Coll (VT)
Suffolk U (MA)
Suomi Coll (MI)
Tampa Coll (FL)
Tampa College–Lakeland (FL)
Tampa Coll, Pinellas Ctr (FL)
Taylor U, Fort Wayne Cmps (IN)
Tennessee Tech U (TN)
Thomas Edison State Coll (NJ)
Thomas More Coll (KY)
Tri-State U (IN)
Troy State U, Troy (AL)
Union Coll (KY)
U of Akron (OH)
U of Cincinnati (OH)
U of Great Falls (MT)
U of Indianapolis (IN)
U of Maine at Fort Kent (ME)
U of Maine at Presque Isle (ME)
U of Massachusetts Lowell (MA)
U of New Haven (CT)
U of Scranton (PA)
U of South Carolina–Aiken (SC)
U of South Dakota (SD)
U of Southwestern Louisiana (LA)
U of the District of Columbia (DC)
Washburn U of Topeka (KS)
Weber State U (UT)
West Chester U of Pennsylvania (PA)
Western New Mexico U (NM)
West Georgia Coll (GA)
West Virginia State Coll (WV)
Xavier U (OH)
York Coll of Pennsylvania (PA)
Youngstown State U (OH)

CRIMINOLOGY
Endicott Coll (MA)
Faulkner U (AL)
Indiana State U (IN)
Marquette U (WI)
Mount Aloysius Coll (PA)
U of the District of Columbia (DC)

CULINARY ARTS
Boise State U (ID)
Endicott Coll (MA)
Idaho State U (ID)
Johnson & Wales U (FL)
Johnson & Wales U (RI)
Johnson & Wales U (SC)
Kendall Coll (IL)
Mercyhurst Coll (PA)
Montana State University–Billings (MT)
New Hampshire Coll (NH)
New York Inst of Tech (NY)
Nicholls State U (LA)
Purdue U Calumet (IN)
Saint Francis Coll (PA)
Shepherd Coll (WV)
Sullivan Coll (KY)
U of Akron (OH)
U of Alaska Fairbanks (AK)
U of New Hampshire, Durham (NH)

CYTOTECHNOLOGY
Lebanon Valley Coll (PA)
Mount St Clare Coll (IA)

DAIRY SCIENCES
Eastern Kentucky U (KY)
U of Minnesota, Crookston (MN)
U of New Hampshire, Durham (NH)

DATA PROCESSING
Baker Coll of Auburn Hills (MI)
Baker Coll of Cadillac (MI)
Baker Coll of Flint (MI)
Baker Coll of Mount Clemens (MI)
Baker Coll of Muskegon (MI)
Baker Coll of Owosso (MI)
Baker Coll of Port Huron (MI)
Cameron U (OK)
Campbellsville U (KY)
Clayton State Coll (GA)
Columbus Coll (GA)
Davenport Coll of Business, Kalamazoo Cmps (MI)
Dordt Coll (IA)
Eastern Mennonite U (VA)
Felician Coll (NJ)
Georgia Southwestern Coll (GA)
Hawaii Pacific U (HI)
Humphreys Coll (CA)
Huron U (SD)
Idaho State U (ID)
Johnson State Coll (VT)
Jones Coll (FL)
Lake Superior State U (MI)
Lamar University–Beaumont (TX)
Lincoln U (MO)
Midland Lutheran Coll (NE)
Minot State U (ND)
Missouri Southern State Coll (MO)
Montana State University–Billings (MT)
Mount Vernon Nazarene Coll (OH)
Murray State U (KY)
New York Inst of Tech (NY)
New York U (NY)
Northern Michigan U (MI)
Northern State U (SD)
Northwood U (MI)
Orlando Coll (FL)
Quincy U (IL)
Sacred Heart U (CT)
Saint Francis Coll (PA)
St John's U (NY)
Saint Peter's Coll, Jersey City (NJ)
Shawnee State U (OH)
Shepherd Coll (WV)
Sinte Gleska U (SD)
Tampa Coll (FL)
Tampa College–Lakeland (FL)
Thomas Edison State Coll (NJ)
U of Akron (OH)
U of Cincinnati (OH)
U of Indianapolis (IN)
U of Rio Grande (OH)
U of the Virgin Islands (VI)
U of Toledo (OH)
Valdosta State U (GA)
Weber State U (UT)
Western Montana Coll of The U of Montana (MT)
West Virginia U Inst of Tech (WV)
Wright State U (OH)

DEAF INTERPRETER TRAINING
Bethel Coll (IN)
Cincinnati Bible Coll and Sem (OH)
Eastern Kentucky U (KY)
Gardner-Webb U (NC)
Madonna U (MI)
Mount Aloysius Coll (PA)
Nebraska Christian Coll (NE)
North Central Bible Coll (MN)
Roanoke Bible Coll (NC)
Rochester Inst of Tech (NY)
U of Akron (OH)
U of Arkansas at Little Rock (AR)
William Woods U (MO)

DENTAL SERVICES
Armstrong State Coll (GA)
Baker Coll of Port Huron (MI)

Brewton-Parker Coll (GA)
Clayton State Coll (GA)
Columbus Coll (GA)
East Tennessee State U (TN)
Ferris State U (MI)
Indiana U Bloomington (IN)
Indiana U Northwest (IN)
Indiana U–Purdue U Fort Wayne (IN)
Indiana U–Purdue U Indianapolis (IN)
Indiana U South Bend (IN)
Lamar University–Beaumont (TX)
Louisiana State U Medical Ctr (LA)
Mankato State U (MN)
Medical Coll of Georgia (GA)
Missouri Southern State Coll (MO)
Mount St Clare Coll (IA)
New York U (NY)
Northeastern U (MA)
Northeast Louisiana U (LA)
Northwestern State U of Louisiana (LA)
Oregon Inst of Tech (OR)
Shawnee State U (OH)
Southern Arkansas University–Magnolia (AR)
Southern Illinois U at Carbondale (IL)
Tennessee State U (TN)
U of Alaska Anchorage (AK)
U of Arkansas for Medical Sciences (AR)
U of Bridgeport (CT)
U of Central Arkansas (AR)
U of Louisville (KY)
U of New Haven (CT)
U of New Mexico (NM)
U of Puerto Rico Medical Sciences Cmps (PR)
U of South Dakota (SD)
U of Southern Indiana (IN)
U of Vermont (VT)
Villa Julie Coll (MD)
Weber State U (UT)
Westbrook Coll (ME)
Western Kentucky U (KY)
West Liberty State Coll (WV)
West Virginia U Inst of Tech (WV)
Wichita State U (KS)
Youngstown State U (OH)

DIETETICS
Ball State U (IN)
Faulkner U (AL)
Marian Coll (IN)
Oakwood Coll (AL)
Olivet Nazarene U (IL)
Pacific Union Coll (CA)
Purdue U Calumet (IN)
Rochester Inst of Tech (NY)
U of Minnesota, Crookston (MN)
U of New Hampshire, Durham (NH)
U of West Alabama (AL)
Youngstown State U (OH)

DRAFTING AND DESIGN
Abilene Christian U (TX)
Andrews U (MI)
Baker Coll of Auburn Hills (MI)
Baker Coll of Flint (MI)
Baker Coll of Mount Clemens (MI)
Baker Coll of Muskegon (MI)
Baker Coll of Owosso (MI)
Black Hills State U (SD)
Boise State U (ID)
Bryant and Stratton Coll, Cleveland (OH)
California U of Pennsylvania (PA)
Cameron U (OK)
Central Missouri State U (MO)
Clayton State Coll (GA)
Denver Inst of Tech (CO)
Denver Tech Coll (CO)
Eastern Kentucky U (KY)
Eastern New Mexico U (NM)
Fairmont State Coll (WV)
Ferris State U (MI)
Grambling State U (LA)
Hamilton Tech Coll (IA)
Idaho State U (ID)
Indiana State U (IN)

Indiana U–Purdue U Fort Wayne (IN)
Indiana U–Purdue U Indianapolis (IN)
Indiana U South Bend (IN)
Johnson & Wales U (RI)
Keene State Coll (NH)
Kentucky State U (KY)
Lake Superior State U (MI)
Lamar University–Beaumont (TX)
LeTourneau U (TX)
Lewis-Clark State Coll (ID)
Lincoln U (MO)
McNeese State U (LA)
Missouri Southern State Coll (MO)
Montana State University–Billings (MT)
Montana State University–Northern (MT)
Morehead State U (KY)
Murray State U (KY)
Northern Michigan U (MI)
Northern State U (SD)
Northwestern State U of Louisiana (LA)
Ohio University–Lancaster (OH)
Pace U (NY)
Rochester Inst of Tech (NY)
Saint Francis Coll (PA)
Southeastern Louisiana U (LA)
Southern Utah U (UT)
Thomas Edison State Coll (NJ)
Tri-State U (IN)
U of Akron (OH)
U of Alaska Fairbanks (AK)
U of Cincinnati (OH)
U of Nebraska–Lincoln (NE)
U of Puerto Rico at Ponce (PR)
U of Rio Grande (OH)
U of Toledo (OH)
Utah State U (UT)
Weber State U (UT)
Western Kentucky U (KY)
Western New Mexico U (NM)
West Virginia State Coll (WV)
West Virginia U Inst of Tech (WV)
Wright State U (OH)
Youngstown State U (OH)

DRUG AND ALCOHOL/SUBSTANCE ABUSE COUNSELING
Calumet Coll of Saint Joseph (IN)
Indiana Wesleyan U (IN)
Kansas Newman Coll (KS)
Keene State Coll (NH)
U of Alaska Fairbanks (AK)
U of Great Falls (MT)
U of Toledo (OH)

EARLY CHILDHOOD EDUCATION
Arkansas Tech U (AR)
Atlantic Union Coll (MA)
Becker College–Leicester Cmps (MA)
Becker College–Worcester Cmps (MA)
Bethany Coll of the Assemblies of God (CA)
Bethel Coll (IN)
Brewton-Parker Coll (GA)
California Coll for Health Sciences (CA)
California U of Pennsylvania (PA)
Cazenovia Coll (NY)
Chaminade U of Honolulu (HI)
Clayton State Coll (GA)
Coll for Lifelong Learning of the U System of NH (NH)
Coll of Mount St Joseph (OH)
Coll of Saint Mary (NE)
Columbia Union Coll (MD)
Eastern Nazarene Coll (MA)
Edinboro U of Pennsylvania (PA)
Endicott Coll (MA)
Franciscan U of Steubenville (OH)
Friends U (KS)
Gannon U (PA)
Indiana State U (IN)

Indiana U–Purdue U Fort Wayne (IN)
Indiana U–Purdue U Indianapolis (IN)
Indiana U South Bend (IN)
Kansas Wesleyan U (KS)
Keene State Coll (NH)
Kendall Coll (IL)
Lake Superior State U (MI)
Lasell Coll (MA)
Lourdes Coll (OH)
Lynn U (FL)
Malone Coll (OH)
Manchester Coll (IN)
Maranatha Baptist Bible Coll (WI)
Marian Coll (IN)
Martin Methodist Coll (TN)
Mayville State U (ND)
Mercyhurst Coll (PA)
Mesa State Coll (CO)
Michigan Christian Coll (MI)
Midland Lutheran Coll (NE)
Midway Coll (KY)
Montana State University–Billings (MT)
Morehead State U (KY)
Mount Aloysius Coll (PA)
Mount St Clare Coll (IA)
Mount St Mary's Coll (CA)
Mount Vernon Nazarene Coll (OH)
New York U (NY)
Notre Dame Coll (NH)
Oglala Lakota Coll (SD)
Ohio Dominican Coll (OH)
Pace U (NY)
Pacific Christian Coll (CA)
Pacific Union Coll (CA)
Point Park Coll (PA)
Purdue U Calumet (IN)
Rivier Coll (NH)
Rust Coll (MS)
Taylor U (IN)
Taylor U, Fort Wayne Cmps (IN)
Teikyo Post U (CT)
Tennessee State U (TN)
Thomas Edison State Coll (NJ)
Tougaloo Coll (MS)
U of Alaska Anchorage (AK)
U of Alaska Fairbanks (AK)
U of Alaska Southeast (AK)
U of Arkansas at Pine Bluff (AR)
U of Great Falls (MT)
U of Minnesota, Crookston (MN)
U of Sioux Falls (SD)
U of Southern Indiana (IN)
U of Wisconsin–Green Bay (WI)
Villa Julie Coll (MD)
Washburn U of Topeka (KS)
Western Montana Coll of The U of Montana (MT)
William Tyndale Coll (MI)
Wilmington Coll (DE)
Xavier U (OH)

EARTH SCIENCE
Adrian Coll (MI)
Indiana U East (IN)
U of Wisconsin–Green Bay (WI)
West Chester U of Pennsylvania (PA)

EAST EUROPEAN AND SOVIET STUDIES
Baltimore Hebrew U (MD)

ECOLOGY
Southeastern U (DC)
Southern Vermont Coll (VT)
U of Wisconsin–Green Bay (WI)

ECONOMICS
Adrian Coll (MI)
Bethel Coll (IN)
Brewton-Parker Coll (GA)
Clayton State Coll (GA)
Franklin Coll Switzerland (Switzerland)
Grand View Coll (IA)
Indiana U South Bend (IN)
Martin Methodist Coll (TN)
Methodist Coll (NC)

Associate Degree Programs at Four-Year Colleges
Economics–English

Montana State University–Northern (MT)
Northern Michigan U (MI)
Reinhardt Coll (GA)
Sacred Heart U (CT)
State U of NY Empire State Coll (NY)
Strayer Coll (DC)
Thomas More Coll (KY)
U of Sioux Falls (SD)
The U of Tampa (FL)
U of Wisconsin–Green Bay (WI)
Wright State U (OH)

EDUCATION
Alabama State U (AL)
Andrews U (MI)
Baltimore Hebrew U (MD)
Bayamón Tech U Coll (PR)
Brewton-Parker Coll (GA)
Calvary Bible Coll and Theological Sem (MO)
Cazenovia Coll (NY)
Central Baptist Coll (AR)
Cincinnati Bible Coll and Sem (OH)
Circleville Bible Coll (OH)
Clayton State Coll (GA)
The Coll of West Virginia (WV)
Eastern Mennonite U (VA)
Eastern New Mexico U (NM)
Edinboro U of Pennsylvania (PA)
Endicott Coll (MA)
Evangel Coll (MO)
Florida Bible Coll (FL)
Friends U (KS)
Georgia Southern U (GA)
Lamar University–Beaumont (TX)
Louisiana Coll (LA)
Maharishi U of Management (IA)
Manhattan Christian Coll (KS)
Martin Methodist Coll (TN)
Medgar Evers Coll of the City U of New York (NY)
Milligan Coll (TN)
Mount St Clare Coll (IA)
New Mexico State U (NM)
North American Baptist Coll & Edmonton Baptist Sem (AB, Canada)
Pontifical Catholic U of Puerto Rico (PR)
Reinhardt Coll (GA)
Selma U (AL)
Shawnee State U (OH)
Sinte Gleska U (SD)
Southwestern Assemblies of God U (TX)
State U of NY Empire State Coll (NY)
Sue Bennett Coll (KY)
Suomi Coll (MI)
U of Akron (OH)
U of Puerto Rico at Arecibo (PR)
U of Wisconsin–Green Bay (WI)
Villa Julie Coll (MD)
Wright State U (OH)
York Coll (NE)

EDUCATIONAL MEDIA
Bayamón Central U (PR)
Ferris State U (MI)
Indiana U Bloomington (IN)
West Chester U of Pennsylvania (PA)

ELECTRICAL AND ELECTRONICS TECHNOLOGIES
Alabama A&M U (AL)
Austin Peay State U (TN)
Baker Coll of Muskegon (MI)
Bayamón Tech U Coll (PR)
Boise State U (ID)
Bryant and Stratton Coll, Cleveland (OH)
Central Missouri State U (MO)
Clayton State Coll (GA)
Cogswell Polytechnical Coll (CA)
Denver Inst of Tech (CO)
Denver Tech Coll (CO)
DeVry Inst of Tech (AZ)

DeVry Inst of Tech, Pomona (CA)
DeVry Inst of Tech (GA)
DeVry Inst of Tech, Addison (IL)
DeVry Inst of Tech, Chicago (IL)
DeVry Inst of Tech (MO)
DeVry Inst of Tech (OH)
DeVry Inst of Tech (TX)
Eastern New Mexico U (NM)
Edinboro U of Pennsylvania (PA)
Embry-Riddle Aeronautical U (FL)
Fairmont State Coll (WV)
Ferris State U (MI)
Fort Valley State Coll (GA)
Georgia Southwestern Coll (GA)
Idaho State U (ID)
Indiana State U (IN)
Johnson & Wales U (RI)
Keene State Coll (NH)
Kentucky State U (KY)
Lake Superior State U (MI)
Lamar University–Beaumont (TX)
Lewis-Clark State Coll (ID)
Lincoln U (MO)
Marshall U (WV)
McNeese State U (LA)
Mesa State Coll (CO)
Michigan Tech U (MI)
Morehead State U (KY)
New Mexico State U (NM)
Northern Michigan U (MI)
Northern State U (SD)
Northwestern State U of Louisiana (LA)
Oglala Lakota Coll (SD)
Ohio U (OH)
Ohio University–Lancaster (OH)
Pittsburg State U (KS)
Shepherd Coll (WV)
Southern Illinois U at Carbondale (IL)
Southern U and A&M Coll (LA)
Southern Utah U (UT)
Thomas Edison State Coll (NJ)
U Coll of Cape Breton (NS, Canada)
U of Akron (OH)
U of Alaska Anchorage (AK)
U of Cincinnati (OH)
U of Puerto Rico, Aguadilla Regional Coll (PR)
U of Puerto Rico, Humacao U Coll (PR)
U of Rio Grande (OH)
U of the District of Columbia (DC)
U of the State of NY, Regents Coll (NY)
U of Toledo (OH)
Washburn U of Topeka (KS)
Weber State U (UT)
West Virginia U Inst of Tech (WV)
Wright State U (OH)

ELECTRICAL ENGINEERING TECHNOLOGY
Andrews U (MI)
Central Missouri State U (MO)
Coll of Staten Island of the City U of New York (NY)
Eastern Kentucky U (KY)
Eastern New Mexico U (NM)
Gallaudet U (DC)
Gannon U (PA)
Grambling State U (LA)
Idaho State U (ID)
Indiana U–Purdue U Fort Wayne (IN)
Indiana U–Purdue U Indianapolis (IN)
Indiana U South Bend (IN)
Kansas State U (KS)
Lake Superior State U (MI)
Lawrence Tech U (MI)
Merrimack Coll (MA)
Michigan Tech U (MI)
Milwaukee Sch of Engineering (WI)
Murray State U (KY)
New Mexico State U (NM)
New York Inst of Tech (NY)

Northeastern U (MA)
Penn State U at Erie, The Behrend Coll (PA)
Penn State U Univ Park Cmps (PA)
Point Park Coll (PA)
Purdue U, West Lafayette (IN)
Purdue U Calumet (IN)
Purdue U North Central (IN)
Roger Williams U (RI)
U of Cincinnati (OH)
U of New Haven (CT)
U of Southern Indiana (IN)
U of the District of Columbia (DC)
U of Toledo (OH)
Western Kentucky U (KY)
West Virginia U Inst of Tech (WV)
Wichita State U (KS)
Youngstown State U (OH)

ELECTROMECHANICAL TECHNOLOGY
Clayton State Coll (GA)
Coll of Staten Island of the City U of New York (NY)
Denver Tech Coll (CO)
Idaho State U (ID)
Michigan Tech U (MI)
Morehead State U (KY)
New Mexico State U (NM)
Rochester Inst of Tech (NY)
Shawnee State U (OH)
U of the District of Columbia (DC)
U of the State of NY, Regents Coll (NY)
Walla Walla Coll (WA)
Wentworth Inst of Tech (MA)

ELECTRONICS ENGINEERING TECHNOLOGY
Baker Coll of Flint (MI)
Baker Coll of Muskegon (MI)
Baker Coll of Owosso (MI)
Boise State U (ID)
Bryant and Stratton Coll, Cleveland (OH)
Capitol Coll (MD)
Central Missouri State U (MO)
Clayton State Coll (GA)
The Coll of West Virginia (WV)
Colorado Tech U (CO)
Columbus Coll (GA)
Denver Tech Coll (CO)
Eastern Kentucky U (KY)
Fairmont State Coll (WV)
Ferris State U (MI)
Franklin U (OH)
Grantham Coll of Engineering (LA)
Hamilton Tech Coll (IA)
Marshall U (WV)
Mesa State Coll (CO)
Missouri Tech Sch (MO)
Missouri Western State Coll (MO)
Montana State University–Northern (MT)
New Mexico State U (NM)
Northwestern State U of Louisiana (LA)
Ohio University–Lancaster (OH)
Oregon Inst of Tech (OR)
Shepherd Coll (WV)
Thomas Edison State Coll (NJ)
U of Akron (OH)
U of Arkansas at Little Rock (AR)
U of Hartford (CT)
U of Massachusetts Lowell (MA)
U of Nebraska–Lincoln (NE)
U of the District of Columbia (DC)
U of Toledo (OH)
Weber State U (UT)
Wentworth Inst of Tech (MA)
West Virginia State Coll (WV)

ELEMENTARY EDUCATION
Clayton State Coll (GA)
The Coll of West Virginia (WV)

Concordia Coll (AL)
Endicott Coll (MA)
Florida Bible Coll (FL)
Grace U (NE)
Inter American U of PR, Arecibo Cmps (PR)
Inter American U of PR, Fajardo Cmps (PR)
Inter American U of PR, Ponce Cmps (PR)
Mount St Clare Coll (IA)
New Mexico Highlands U (NM)
Oglala Lakota Coll (SD)
Ozark Christian Coll (MO)
Shawnee State U (OH)
Union Coll (KY)
U of Akron (OH)
U of Puerto Rico at Arecibo (PR)
Villa Julie Coll (MD)
Wright State U (OH)
York Coll (NE)

EMERGENCY MEDICAL TECHNOLOGY
American Coll of Prehospital Medicine (LA)
Arkansas State U (AR)
Baker Coll of Mount Clemens (MI)
Ball State U (IN)
California U of Pennsylvania (PA)
Clayton State Coll (GA)
Davenport Coll of Business, Grand Rapids (MI)
Eastern Kentucky U (KY)
Faulkner U (AL)
Hannibal-LaGrange Coll (MO)
Indiana U–Purdue U Indianapolis (IN)
Marshall U (WV)
Nicholls State U (LA)
Saint Francis Coll (PA)
Shawnee State U (OH)
Shepherd Coll (WV)
Southwest Baptist U (MO)
U of Alaska Anchorage (AK)
U of Arkansas for Medical Sciences (AR)
U of New Mexico (NM)
U of Puerto Rico Medical Sciences Cmps (PR)
U of Southwestern Louisiana (LA)
U of the District of Columbia (DC)
U of Toledo (OH)
U of West Alabama (AL)
Valdosta State U (GA)
Weber State U (UT)
Youngstown State U (OH)

ENERGY MANAGEMENT TECHNOLOGIES
U of Cincinnati (OH)

ENGINEERING (GENERAL)
Brescia Coll (KY)
Clayton State Coll (GA)
Cogswell Polytechnical Coll (CA)
Columbia Union Coll (MD)
Daniel Webster Coll (NH)
Faulkner U (AL)
Geneva Coll (PA)
Mesa State Coll (CO)
Montana Tech of The U of Montana (MT)
Shepherd Coll (WV)
Southern Arkansas University–Magnolia (AR)
Union Coll (NE)
U Coll of Cape Breton (NS, Canada)

ENGINEERING AND APPLIED SCIENCES
DeVry Inst of Tech, Long Beach (CA)
U of Arkansas at Little Rock (AR)
West Coast U (CA)

ENGINEERING DESIGN
East Tennessee State U (TN)
LeTourneau U (TX)

Thomas Edison State Coll (NJ)

ENGINEERING SCIENCES
Coll of Staten Island of the City U of New York (NY)
Daniel Webster Coll (NH)
Merrimack Coll (MA)
Morehead State U (KY)
U of Cincinnati (OH)

(PRE)ENGINEERING SEQUENCE
Adams State Coll (CO)
Anderson U (IN)
Andrews U (MI)
Aquinas Coll (MI)
Atlantic Union Coll (MA)
Ball State U (IN)
Bayamón Tech U Coll (PR)
Bethel Coll (MN)
Bluefield Coll (VA)
Boise State U (ID)
Brescia Coll (KY)
Brewton-Parker Coll (GA)
Briar Cliff Coll (IA)
Campbell U (NC)
Charleston Southern U (SC)
Clayton State Coll (GA)
Coll of Santa Fe (NM)
Columbia Coll (MO)
Columbus Coll (GA)
Covenant Coll (GA)
Deree Coll (Greece)
Dickinson State U (ND)
Eastern Kentucky U (KY)
Eastern Mennonite U (VA)
Eastern New Mexico U (NM)
Edgewood Coll (WI)
Edinboro U of Pennsylvania (PA)
Faulkner U (AL)
Ferris State U (MI)
Fort Lewis Coll (CO)
Fort Valley State Coll (GA)
Friends U (KS)
Georgia Southwestern Coll (GA)
Hannibal-LaGrange Coll (MO)
Houghton Coll (NY)
Huntingdon Coll (AL)
Huntington Coll (IN)
Indiana State U (IN)
Indiana U–Purdue U Fort Wayne (IN)
Kansas Newman Coll (KS)
Keene State Coll (NH)
Kentucky Wesleyan Coll (KY)
King's Coll (PA)
LaGrange Coll (GA)
La Sierra U (CA)
Lewis-Clark State Coll (ID)
Lindsey Wilson Coll (KY)
Loras Coll (IA)
MacMurray Coll (IL)
Malone Coll (OH)
Mankato State U (MN)
Marian Coll (IN)
Marshall U (WV)
McPherson Coll (KS)
Medgar Evers Coll of the City U of New York (NY)
Mesa State Coll (CO)
Methodist Coll (NC)
Midland Lutheran Coll (NE)
Minot State U (ND)
Missouri Southern State Coll (MO)
Montana State University–Billings (MT)
Montana Tech of The U of Montana (MT)
Montreat Coll (NC)
Moorhead State U (MN)
Morehead State U (KY)
Morningside Coll (IA)
Morris Brown Coll (GA)
Mount Vernon Nazarene Coll (OH)
Niagara U (NY)
Northern Kentucky U (KY)
Northern State U (SD)
Northwestern Coll (MN)
Northwestern State U of Louisiana (LA)
Pacific Union Coll (CA)
Phillips U (OK)
Purdue U North Central (IN)
Quincy U (IL)
Reinhardt Coll (GA)

Richmond Coll, The American International U in London (United Kingdom)
Samford U (AL)
Schiller International U, London (United Kingdom)
Schreiner Coll (TX)
Shawnee State U (OH)
Shepherd Coll (WV)
Siena Heights Coll (MI)
Southern Coll of Seventh-day Adventists (TN)
Southern U and A&M Coll (LA)
Southwestern Christian Coll (TX)
Sue Bennett Coll (KY)
Suomi Coll (MI)
Tabor Coll (KS)
Thiel Coll (PA)
Thomas More Coll (KY)
Trevecca Nazarene U (TN)
Troy State U, Troy (AL)
Union Coll (KY)
Union Coll (NE)
U of Central Arkansas (AR)
The U of Findlay (OH)
U of New Hampshire, Durham (NH)
U of New Mexico (NM)
U of Pittsburgh at Bradford (PA)
U of Scranton (PA)
U of Sioux Falls (SD)
U of South Carolina–Aiken (SC)
U of South Dakota (SD)
U of Southern Indiana (IN)
U of the Ozarks (AR)
U of Wisconsin–Green Bay (WI)
U of Wisconsin–La Crosse (WI)
U of Wisconsin–Superior (WI)
Valdosta State U (GA)
Washburn U of Topeka (KS)
Weber State U (UT)
West Georgia Coll (GA)
West Virginia State Coll (WV)
Winona State U (MN)
Xavier U (OH)
York Coll (NE)

ENGINEERING TECHNOLOGY
Andrews U (MI)
California U of Pennsylvania (PA)
Clayton State Coll (GA)
Cogswell Polytechnical Coll (CA)
Coll of Aeronautics (NY)
Edinboro U of Pennsylvania (PA)
Embry-Riddle Aeronautical U (FL)
Fairmont State Coll (WV)
Gallaudet U (DC)
Gannon U (PA)
Grantham Coll of Engineering (LA)
Indiana Inst of Tech (IN)
Indiana U–Purdue U Fort Wayne (IN)
John Brown U (AR)
Lake Superior State U (MI)
Marshall U (WV)
Michigan Tech U (MI)
New Mexico State U (NM)
Nicholls State U (LA)
Northwestern State U of Louisiana (LA)
Pacific Union Coll (CA)
Point Park Coll (PA)
Purdue U, West Lafayette (IN)
Purdue U North Central (IN)
Southern Coll of Tech (GA)
U of Alaska Anchorage (AK)
U of Arkansas at Little Rock (AR)
U of Southern Indiana (IN)
U of the District of Columbia (DC)
U of Toledo (OH)
Wentworth Inst of Tech (MA)

ENGLISH
Acad of the New Church Coll (PA)
Adrian Coll (MI)
Bethel Coll (IN)

Associate Degree Programs at Four-Year Colleges
English–Guidance and Counseling

Brewton-Parker Coll (GA)
Calumet Coll of Saint Joseph (IN)
Carroll Coll (MT)
Central Methodist Coll (MO)
Clayton State Coll (GA)
Coll of Mount Saint Vincent (NY)
Coll of Santa Fe (NM)
Crown Coll (MN)
Felician Coll (NJ)
Fresno Pacific Coll (CA)
Hannibal-LaGrange Coll (MO)
Indiana U South Bend (IN)
Indiana Wesleyan U (IN)
Lindsey Wilson Coll (KY)
Lourdes Coll (OH)
Madonna U (MI)
Manchester Coll (IN)
Martin Methodist Coll (TN)
Mesa State Coll (CO)
Methodist Coll (NC)
Montreat Coll (NC)
Mount St Clare Coll (IA)
Northern Michigan U (MI)
Pine Manor Coll (MA)
Presentation Coll (SD)
Reinhardt Coll (GA)
Richmond Coll, The American International U in London (United Kingdom)
Sacred Heart U (CT)
Salem-Teikyo U (WV)
Selma U (AL)
Siena Heights Coll (MI)
Suomi Coll (MI)
Teikyo Post U (CT)
Thomas More Coll (KY)
Tri-State U (IN)
Troy State U Montgomery (AL)
U of Dubuque (IA)
U of Rio Grande (OH)
The U of Tampa (FL)
U of the District of Columbia (DC)
U of Wisconsin–Green Bay (WI)
Urbana U (OH)
Wright State U (OH)
Xavier U (OH)

ENVIRONMENTAL DESIGN
U of Wisconsin–Green Bay (WI)

ENVIRONMENTAL ENGINEERING TECHNOLOGY
Baker Coll of Flint (MI)
Baker Coll of Owosso (MI)
Baker Coll of Port Huron (MI)
Glenville State Coll (WV)
Mesa State Coll (CO)
U Coll of Cape Breton (NS, Canada)
Wentworth Inst of Tech (MA)

ENVIRONMENTAL HEALTH SCIENCES
Missouri Southern State Coll (MO)
Montana State University–Northern (MT)

ENVIRONMENTAL SCIENCES
Adrian Coll (MI)
Alaska Pacific U (AK)
The Defiance Coll (OH)
Dickinson State U (ND)
Ohio University–Chillicothe (OH)
Saint Francis Coll (IN)
Thomas Edison State Coll (NJ)
U of Cincinnati (OH)
U of Dubuque (IA)
The U of Findlay (OH)
U of Puerto Rico, Aguadilla Regional Coll (PR)
U of Toledo (OH)
U of Wisconsin–Green Bay (WI)

ENVIRONMENTAL STUDIES
Adrian Coll (MI)
Becker College–Leicester Cmps (MA)
Becker College–Worcester Cmps (MA)
The Coll of West Virginia (WV)
Montreat Coll (NC)
Rocky Mountain Coll (MT)
Southern Vermont Coll (VT)
U of Dubuque (IA)

EQUESTRIAN STUDIES
Cazenovia Coll (NY)
Centenary Coll (NJ)
Delaware Valley Coll (PA)
Johnson & Wales U (RI)
Midway Coll (KY)
Murray State U (KY)
The Ohio State U (OH)
Rocky Mountain Coll (MT)
Saint Mary-of-the-Woods Coll (IN)
Teikyo Post U (CT)
The U of Findlay (OH)
U of Massachusetts Amherst (MA)
U of Minnesota, Crookston (MN)
U of New Hampshire, Durham (NH)

ETHNIC STUDIES
Baltimore Hebrew U (MD)
West Chester U of Pennsylvania (PA)

EUROPEAN STUDIES
Franklin Coll Switzerland (Switzerland)

FARM AND RANCH MANAGEMENT
Dickinson State U (ND)
Johnson & Wales U (RI)
Midway Coll (KY)
Oklahoma Panhandle State U (OK)

FASHION DESIGN AND TECHNOLOGY
The American Coll (CA)
The American Coll (GA)
The American Coll (United Kingdom)
The Art Inst of Illinois (IL)
Bassist Coll (OR)
Cazenovia Coll (NY)
Fashion Inst of Tech (NY)
Indiana U Bloomington (IN)
International Acad of Merchandising & Design (FL)
International Acad of Merchandising & Design, Ltd (IL)
Louise Salinger Acad of Fashion (CA)
O'More Coll of Design (TN)
Parsons Sch of Design, New Sch for Social Research (NY)

FASHION MERCHANDISING
The American Coll (CA)
The American Coll (GA)
The American Coll (United Kingdom)
The Art Inst of Illinois (IL)
Baker Coll of Flint (MI)
Baker Coll of Muskegon (MI)
Baker Coll of Owosso (MI)
Baker Coll of Port Huron (MI)
Bay Path Coll (MA)
Centenary Coll (NJ)
Central Missouri State U (MO)
Davis & Elkins Coll (WV)
Endicott Coll (MA)
Fairmont State Coll (WV)
Fashion Inst of Tech (NY)
Ferris State U (MI)
Idaho State U (ID)
International Acad of Merchandising & Design (FL)
International Acad of Merchandising & Design, Ltd (IL)
Johnson & Wales U (RI)
Laboratory Inst of Merchandising (NY)
Lasell Coll (MA)
Louise Salinger Acad of Fashion (CA)
Lynn U (FL)
Madonna U (MI)
Marygrove Coll (MI)
Methodist Coll (NC)
Morehead State U (KY)
Northwood U (MI)
Northwood U, Florida Cmps (FL)
Northwood U, Texas Cmps (TX)
O'More Coll of Design (TN)
Parsons Sch of Design, New Sch for Social Research (NY)
Shepherd Coll (WV)
Southern Arkansas University–Magnolia (AR)
Teikyo Post U (CT)
U of Akron (OH)
U of Bridgeport (CT)
U of the District of Columbia (DC)
Webber Coll (FL)
Weber State U (UT)
West Virginia State Coll (WV)

FILM AND VIDEO PRODUCTION
The American Coll (CA)
The American Coll (GA)
The American Coll (United Kingdom)
Five Towns Coll (NY)
Orlando Coll (FL)
Rochester Inst of Tech (NY)

FILM STUDIES
Fort Lauderdale Coll (FL)
Indiana U South Bend (IN)
West Chester U of Pennsylvania (PA)

FINANCE/BANKING
Armstrong U (CA)
Bayamón Tech U Coll (PR)
Clayton State Coll (GA)
Coll of Staten Island of the City U of New York (NY)
The Coll of West Virginia (WV)
Detroit Coll of Business, Dearborn (MI)
Detroit Coll of Business, Warren Cmps (MI)
Fairmont State Coll (WV)
Hilbert Coll (NY)
Indiana U Kokomo (IN)
Indiana U South Bend (IN)
Indiana Wesleyan U (IN)
International Coll of the Cayman Islands (Cayman Islands)
Johnson & Wales U (RI)
Marian Coll (IN)
Marshall U (WV)
Methodist Coll (NC)
Northeastern U (MA)
Northern State U (SD)
Northwood U (MI)
Northwood U, Florida Cmps (FL)
Pace U (NY)
Point Park Coll (PA)
Sacred Heart U (CT)
Saint Joseph's U (PA)
Saint Peter's Coll, Jersey City (NJ)
Schiller International U, London (United Kingdom)
Shawnee State U (OH)
Shepherd Coll (WV)
Southeastern U (DC)
Thomas Coll (ME)
Thomas Edison State Coll (NJ)
Troy State U Montgomery (AL)
U of Akron (OH)
U of Alaska Fairbanks (AK)
U of Cincinnati (OH)
U of Indianapolis (IN)
U of Massachusetts Lowell (MA)
U of Puerto Rico at Arecibo (PR)
Walsh U (OH)
Washburn U of Topeka (KS)
Waynesburg Coll (PA)
Webber Coll (FL)
Western Kentucky U (KY)
West Virginia State Coll (WV)
Youngstown State U (OH)

FIRE SCIENCE
Eastern Kentucky U (KY)
Lake Superior State U (MI)
Lamar University–Beaumont (TX)
Madonna U (MI)
Providence Coll (RI)
Shepherd Coll (WV)
Thomas Edison State Coll (NJ)
U of Akron (OH)
U of Alaska Anchorage (AK)
U of Alaska Fairbanks (AK)
U of Cincinnati (OH)
U of Nebraska at Omaha (NE)
U of Nebraska–Lincoln (NE)
U of New Haven (CT)
U of the District of Columbia (DC)

FISH AND GAME MANAGEMENT
Sheldon Jackson Coll (AK)
Winona State U (MN)

FLIGHT TRAINING
Andrews U (MI)
Central Missouri State U (MO)
Daniel Webster Coll (NH)
Embry-Riddle Aeronautical U (FL)
Indiana State U (IN)
Kansas State U (KS)
Purdue U, West Lafayette (IN)
Saint Louis U (MO)
Southern Illinois U at Carbondale (IL)
U of Alaska Anchorage (AK)
U of Alaska Fairbanks (AK)
U of Dubuque (IA)
U of Minnesota, Crookston (MN)
U of New Haven (CT)
Winona State U (MN)

FOOD MARKETING
The Ohio State U (OH)
Saint Joseph's U (PA)

FOOD SCIENCES
Austin Peay State U (TN)
Lamar University–Beaumont (TX)
Louisiana Tech U (LA)
Thomas Edison State Coll (NJ)

FOOD SERVICES MANAGEMENT
Andrews U (MI)
Austin Peay State U (TN)
Ball State U (IN)
Black Hills State U (SD)
Endicott Coll (MA)
Fairmont State Coll (WV)
Ferris State U (MI)
Glenville State Coll (WV)
Indiana U–Purdue U Fort Wayne (IN)
Indiana U–Purdue U Indianapolis (IN)
Lamar University–Beaumont (TX)
Nicholls State U (LA)
Northern Michigan U (MI)
Northwood U (MI)
Northwood U, Florida Cmps (FL)
Purdue U Calumet (IN)
Rochester Inst of Tech (NY)
Shepherd Coll (WV)
U of Akron (OH)
U of Alaska Southeast (AK)
U of Minnesota, Crookston (MN)
U of New Hampshire, Durham (NH)
Washburn U of Topeka (KS)

FOOD SERVICES TECHNOLOGY
Austin Peay State U (TN)
Endicott Coll (MA)
Idaho State U (ID)
Johnson & Wales U (SC)
Morehead State U (KY)
Murray State U (KY)
Purdue U, West Lafayette (IN)
Purdue U Calumet (IN)
U of Akron (OH)
U of Alaska Anchorage (AK)
U of the District of Columbia (DC)

FORENSIC SCIENCES
Austin Peay State U (TN)

FORESTRY
Clayton State Coll (GA)
Columbus Coll (GA)
Sheldon Jackson Coll (AK)
Thomas Edison State Coll (NJ)
U of Alaska Anchorage (AK)
U of Maine at Fort Kent (ME)
Winona State U (MN)

FOREST TECHNOLOGY
Glenville State Coll (WV)
Michigan Tech U (MI)
Penn State U Univ Park Cmps (PA)
Sheldon Jackson Coll (AK)
Unity Coll (ME)
U of New Hampshire, Durham (NH)

FRENCH
Adrian Coll (MI)
Bethel Coll (IN)
Brewton-Parker Coll (GA)
Chestnut Hill Coll (PA)
Clayton State Coll (GA)
Franklin Coll Switzerland (Switzerland)
Indiana U South Bend (IN)
Lourdes Coll (OH)
Methodist Coll (NC)
Montana State University–Northern (MT)
Mount St Clare Coll (IA)
Northern Michigan U (MI)
Reinhardt Coll (GA)
U of Wisconsin–Green Bay (WI)
Xavier U (OH)

FUNERAL SERVICE
Cincinnati Coll of Mortuary Science (OH)
Lynn U (FL)
Point Park Coll (PA)
Southern Illinois U at Carbondale (IL)

GEOGRAPHY
Northern Michigan U (MI)
The U of Tampa (FL)
Wright State U (OH)

GEOLOGY
Castleton State Coll (VT)
Clayton State Coll (GA)
Mesa State Coll (CO)
West Chester U of Pennsylvania (PA)
Wright State U (OH)

GERMAN
Adrian Coll (MI)
Indiana U South Bend (IN)
Methodist Coll (NC)
Northern Michigan U (MI)
U of Wisconsin–Green Bay (WI)

GERONTOLOGY
Aquinas Coll (MI)
Bethel Coll (IN)
California U of Pennsylvania (PA)
Coll of Mount St Joseph (OH)
King's Coll (PA)
Loras Coll (IA)
Lourdes Coll (OH)
Madonna U (MI)
Manchester Coll (IN)
Mankato State U (MN)
Millersville U of Pennsylvania (PA)
Ohio Dominican Coll (OH)
Pontifical Catholic U of Puerto Rico (PR)
Siena Heights Coll (MI)
Southern Vermont Coll (VT)
Sue Bennett Coll (KY)
Thomas More Coll (KY)
U of Pittsburgh at Bradford (PA)
U of Toledo (OH)
West Virginia State Coll (WV)
Winona State U (MN)

GRAPHIC ARTS
Andrews U (MI)
Art Acad of Cincinnati (OH)
The Art Inst of Illinois (IL)
Baker Coll of Auburn Hills (MI)
Baker Coll of Flint (MI)
Baker Coll of Mount Clemens (MI)
Baker Coll of Muskegon (MI)
Baker Coll of Owosso (MI)
Baker Coll of Port Huron (MI)
Becker College–Leicester Cmps (MA)
Becker College–Worcester Cmps (MA)
Black Hills State U (SD)
Cardinal Stritch Coll (WI)
Central Missouri State U (MO)
Cogswell Polytechnical Coll (CA)
Coll of Mount St Joseph (OH)
Denver Inst of Tech (CO)
Endicott Coll (MA)
Felician Coll (NJ)
Idaho State U (ID)
Indiana U South Bend (IN)
Lewis-Clark State Coll (ID)
Mesa State Coll (CO)
Montana State University–Northern (MT)
Morehead State U (KY)
Murray State U (KY)
Newschool of Architecture (CA)
Northern Michigan U (MI)
Northwestern Coll (MN)
Parsons Sch of Design, New Sch for Social Research (NY)
Pratt Inst (NY)
Purdue U, West Lafayette (IN)
Rivier Coll (NH)
Robert Morris Coll (IL)
Rochester Inst of Tech (NY)
Sacred Heart U (CT)
Shepherd Coll (WV)
Southern Illinois U at Carbondale (IL)
Tampa Coll (FL)
U of Bridgeport (CT)
U of New Haven (CT)
Villa Julie Coll (MD)
Virginia Intermont Coll (VA)
Walla Walla Coll (WA)
Western Kentucky U (KY)

GREEK
North Central Bible Coll (MN)

GUIDANCE AND COUNSELING
Crown Coll (MN)
Martin Methodist Coll (TN)
Oglala Lakota Coll (SD)
Our Lady of Holy Cross Coll (LA)
Thomas Edison State Coll (NJ)

Associate Degree Programs at Four-Year Colleges
Health Education–International Business

HEALTH EDUCATION
Bethel Coll (IN)
Clayton State Coll (GA)
Martin Methodist Coll (TN)

HEALTH SCIENCE
Becker College–Leicester Cmps (MA)
Becker College–Worcester Cmps (MA)
Bloomsburg U of Pennsylvania (PA)
California Coll for Health Sciences (CA)
Covenant Coll (GA)
Indiana U–Purdue U Fort Wayne (IN)
Kansas Newman Coll (KS)
Kendall Coll (IL)
Lasell Coll (MA)
Martin Methodist Coll (TN)
Mount Vernon Nazarene Coll (OH)
Northwest Coll of the Assemblies of God (WA)
Park Coll (MO)
Pine Manor Coll (MA)
Shawnee State U (OH)
Southern Nazarene U (OK)
Suomi Coll (MI)
Union Coll (NE)
U of Great Falls (MT)
U of Rio Grande (OH)

HEALTH SERVICES ADMINISTRATION
Baker Coll of Auburn Hills (MI)
Baker Coll of Flint (MI)
Baker Coll of Muskegon (MI)
Bay Path Coll (MA)
Benedictine Coll (KS)
Davenport Coll of Business, Kalamazoo Cmps (MI)
Davis & Elkins Coll (WV)
Denver Inst of Tech (CO)
International Coll (FL)
Martin Methodist Coll (TN)
Methodist Coll (NC)
Providence Coll (RI)
Purdue U North Central (IN)
Saint Joseph's U (PA)
Southeastern U (DC)
U of Scranton (PA)
West Virginia U Inst of Tech (WV)

HEATING/ REFRIGERATION/AIR CONDITIONING
Boise State U (ID)
Central Missouri State U (MO)
Denver Inst of Tech (CO)
Ferris State U (MI)
Lamar University–Beaumont (TX)
Lewis-Clark State Coll (ID)
Montana State University–Billings (MT)
Northern Michigan U (MI)
Oakland City U (IN)
U of Alaska Anchorage (AK)
U of Cincinnati (OH)

HEBREW
Baltimore Hebrew U (MD)
North Central Bible Coll (MN)

HISTORY
Acad of the New Church Coll (PA)
Adrian Coll (MI)
Bethel Coll (IN)
Brewton-Parker Coll (GA)
Chaminade U of Honolulu (HI)
Chestnut Hill Coll (PA)
Clayton State Coll (GA)
Coll of Mount Saint Vincent (NY)
Crown Coll (MN)
Felician Coll (NJ)
Franklin Coll Switzerland (Switzerland)
Fresno Pacific Coll (CA)
Grand View Coll (IA)
Indiana U East (IN)
Indiana U South Bend (IN)
Indiana Wesleyan U (IN)
Lindsey Wilson Coll (KY)
Lourdes Coll (OH)
Marian Coll (IN)
Martin Methodist Coll (TN)
Methodist Coll (NC)
Millersville U of Pennsylvania (PA)
Mount St Clare Coll (IA)
North Central Bible Coll (MN)
Northern Michigan U (MI)
Pine Manor Coll (MA)
Reinhardt Coll (GA)
Richmond Coll, The American International U in London (United Kingdom)
Sacred Heart U (CT)
State U of NY Empire State Coll (NY)
Suomi Coll (MI)
Teikyo Post U (CT)
Thomas More Coll (KY)
Troy State U Montgomery (AL)
U of Dubuque (IA)
U of Rio Grande (OH)
The U of Tampa (FL)
U of the District of Columbia (DC)
U of Wisconsin–Green Bay (WI)
Villa Julie Coll (MD)
West Chester U of Pennsylvania (PA)
Wright State U (OH)
Xavier U (OH)

HISTORY OF PHILOSOPHY
Martin Methodist Coll (TN)

HOME ECONOMICS
Adrian Coll (MI)
Andrews U (MI)
Brewton-Parker Coll (GA)
Clayton State Coll (GA)
Mount Vernon Nazarene Coll (OH)
Oglala Lakota Coll (SD)
Olivet Nazarene U (IL)
U of Alaska Anchorage (AK)

HORTICULTURE
Andrews U (MI)
Boise State U (ID)
Eastern Kentucky U (KY)
Ferris State U (MI)
Murray State U (KY)
North Carolina State U (NC)
The Ohio State U (OH)
Purdue U, West Lafayette (IN)
Thomas Edison State Coll (NJ)
U of Connecticut, Storrs (CT)
U of Guelph (ON, Canada)
U of Massachusetts Amherst (MA)
U of Minnesota, Crookston (MN)
U of New Hampshire, Durham (NH)
Utah State U (UT)

HOSPITALITY SERVICES
Alaska Pacific U (AK)
Baker Coll of Owosso (MI)
Bay Path Coll (MA)
Black Hills State U (SD)
Davenport Coll of Business, Grand Rapids (MI)
Endicott Coll (MA)
Johnson & Wales U (FL)
Kendall Coll (IL)
Lewis-Clark State Coll (ID)
National Coll (NM)
Robert Morris Coll (IL)
Tiffin U (OH)
U Coll of Cape Breton (NS, Canada)
U of Akron (OH)
U of Alaska Southeast (AK)
U of Minnesota, Crookston (MN)
Washburn U of Topeka (KS)
Youngstown State U (OH)

HOTEL AND RESTAURANT MANAGEMENT
Baker Coll of Flint (MI)
Baker Coll of Muskegon (MI)
Baker Coll of Owosso (MI)
Baker Coll of Port Huron (MI)
Becker College–Leicester Cmps (MA)
Becker College–Worcester Cmps (MA)
Black Hills State U (SD)
Davenport Coll of Business, Grand Rapids (MI)
Denver Inst of Tech (CO)
Endicott Coll (MA)
Fort Lauderdale Coll (FL)
Glenville State Coll (WV)
Indiana U–Purdue U Indianapolis (IN)
International Coll of the Cayman Islands (Cayman Islands)
Johnson & Wales U (RI)
Johnson & Wales U (SC)
Kendall Coll (IL)
Lasell Coll (MA)
Mercyhurst Coll (PA)
Mesa State Coll (CO)
National Coll, Colorado Springs (CO)
National Coll (NM)
National College–Sioux Falls Branch (SD)
Northeastern U (MA)
Northwood U (MI)
Northwood U, Florida Cmps (FL)
Northwood U, Texas Cmps (TX)
Penn State U Univ Park Cmps (PA)
Presentation Coll (SD)
Purdue U, West Lafayette (IN)
Purdue U Calumet (IN)
Purdue U North Central (IN)
Rochester Inst of Tech (NY)
Schiller International U, Strasbourg (France)
Shepherd Coll (WV)
Siena Heights Coll (MI)
Southeastern U (DC)
Sullivan Coll (KY)
Thomas Edison State Coll (NJ)
Tiffin U (OH)
U of Akron (OH)
U of Indianapolis (IN)
U of Minnesota, Crookston (MN)
U of New Haven (CT)
U of Southern Maine (ME)
U of the Virgin Islands (VI)
Webber Coll (FL)
West Virginia State Coll (WV)

HUMAN DEVELOPMENT
Brescia Coll (KY)
Plymouth State Coll of the U System of NH (NH)
State U of NY Empire State Coll (NY)
U of Wisconsin–Green Bay (WI)

HUMANITIES
Acad of the New Church Coll (PA)
Bayamón Tech U Coll (PR)
Canisius Coll (NY)
Crown Coll (MN)
Faulkner U (AL)
Felician Coll (NJ)
Immaculata Coll (PA)
Johnson State Coll (VT)
Martin Methodist Coll (TN)
Mesa State Coll (CO)
Michigan Tech U (MI)
Montana State University–Northern (MT)
Mount St Clare Coll (IA)
New Coll of California (CA)
Ohio U (OH)
Saint Joseph's Coll (IN)
Saint Peter's Coll, Jersey City (NJ)
Shawnee State U (OH)
Sheldon Jackson Coll (AK)
Southwestern Christian Coll (TX)
State U of NY Empire State Coll (NY)
Thomas Coll (GA)
Thomas Edison State Coll (NJ)
U of Cincinnati (OH)
U of Hartford (CT)
U of Maine at Presque Isle (ME)
U of Puerto Rico at Arecibo (PR)
U of Sioux Falls (SD)
U of Wisconsin–Green Bay (WI)
Urbana U (OH)
Villa Julie Coll (MD)
Washburn U of Topeka (KS)

HUMAN RESOURCES
Indiana Inst of Tech (IN)
Mount St Clare Coll (IA)
New Hampshire Coll (NH)
Purdue U, West Lafayette (IN)
Thomas Edison State Coll (NJ)
U of Richmond (VA)
Western Montana Coll of The U of Montana (MT)

HUMAN SERVICES
Bay Path Coll (MA)
Becker College–Leicester Cmps (MA)
Becker College–Worcester Cmps (MA)
Cazenovia Coll (NY)
Coll of Mount St Joseph (OH)
Edinboro U of Pennsylvania (PA)
Endicott Coll (MA)
Grace Bible Coll (MI)
Hilbert Coll (NY)
Indiana Inst of Tech (IN)
Indiana U East (IN)
Kendall Coll (IL)
Lasell Coll (MA)
La Sierra U (CA)
Martin Methodist Coll (TN)
Merrimack Coll (MA)
Montreat Coll (NC)
Mount Vernon Nazarene Coll (OH)
Northern Kentucky U (KY)
Oglala Lakota Coll (SD)
Ohio U (OH)
Ohio University–Chillicothe (OH)
Plymouth State Coll of the U System of NH (NH)
Saint Joseph's U (PA)
Sinte Gleska U (SD)
Southern Vermont Coll (VT)
State U of NY Empire State Coll (NY)
Sue Bennett Coll (KY)
Suomi Coll (MI)
Thomas Edison State Coll (NJ)
Trinity Coll of Vermont (VT)
U of Akron (OH)
U of Alaska Anchorage (AK)
U of Alaska Fairbanks (AK)
U of Cincinnati (OH)
U of Great Falls (MT)
U of Maine at Fort Kent (ME)
U of New Mexico (NM)
Walsh U (OH)

ILLUSTRATION
Fashion Inst of Tech (NY)
Northern Michigan U (MI)
Parsons Sch of Design, New Sch for Social Research (NY)
Pratt Inst (NY)
Purdue U, West Lafayette (IN)
Rochester Inst of Tech (NY)
Sacred Heart U (CT)
U of Bridgeport (CT)
Western Kentucky U (KY)

INDUSTRIAL ADMINISTRATION
Andrews U (MI)
Baker Coll of Flint (MI)
Ball State U (IN)
Coll of Staten Island of the City U of New York (NY)
Morehead State U (KY)
Northern Kentucky U (KY)
Purdue U North Central (IN)

INDUSTRIAL AND HEAVY EQUIPMENT MAINTENANCE
Ferris State U (MI)
Lewis-Clark State Coll (ID)
Mesa State Coll (CO)
U of Alaska Fairbanks (AK)

INDUSTRIAL ARTS
Andrews U (MI)
Eastern Kentucky U (KY)
U of Cincinnati (OH)

INDUSTRIAL DESIGN
Bassist Coll (OR)
Central Missouri State U (MO)
Ferris State U (MI)
Indiana U–Purdue U Fort Wayne (IN)
Ohio U (OH)
Ohio University–Lancaster (OH)
Parsons Sch of Design, New Sch for Social Research (NY)
Wentworth Inst of Tech (MA)

INDUSTRIAL ENGINEERING TECHNOLOGY
Bayamón Tech U Coll (PR)
Coll of Staten Island of the City U of New York (NY)
Indiana U East (IN)
Indiana U–Purdue U Fort Wayne (IN)
Kansas State U (KS)
Lawrence Tech U (MI)
Murray State U (KY)
New Mexico State U (NM)
Ohio U (OH)
Purdue U Calumet (IN)
Purdue U North Central (IN)
Roger Williams U (RI)
Southern Arkansas University–Magnolia (AR)
Thomas Edison State Coll (NJ)
U of Arkansas at Pine Bluff (AR)
U of Cincinnati (OH)
U of Massachusetts Lowell (MA)
U of New Haven (CT)
U of Puerto Rico at Ponce (PR)
U of Southwestern Louisiana (LA)

INFORMATION SCIENCE
Andrews U (MI)
Coleman Coll (CA)
Detroit Coll of Business, Dearborn (MI)
Detroit Coll of Business, Warren Cmps (MI)
Johnson State Coll (VT)
King's Coll (PA)
Pacific Union Coll (CA)
Rivier Coll (NH)
Sacred Heart U (CT)
U of Cincinnati (OH)
Western Montana Coll of The U of Montana (MT)
Wiley Coll (TX)

INSTRUMENTATION TECHNOLOGY
Bayamón Tech U Coll (PR)
Clayton State Coll (GA)
Idaho State U (ID)
McNeese State U (LA)
Shawnee State U (OH)

INSURANCE
Coll of Insurance (NY)
International Coll of the Cayman Islands (Cayman Islands)
Mercyhurst Coll (PA)

INTERDISCIPLINARY STUDIES
Acad of the New Church Coll (PA)
Austin Peay State U (TN)
Briar Cliff Coll (IA)
Cameron U (OK)
Central Methodist Coll (MO)
Coll of Mount Saint Vincent (NY)
Friends U (KS)
Heritage Coll (WA)
Kansas State U (KS)
Montana State University–Northern (MT)
Morehead State U (KY)
North Central Bible Coll (MN)
Northwest Coll of the Assemblies of God (WA)
Ohio Dominican Coll (OH)
Sheldon Jackson Coll (AK)
Southwestern Coll of Christian Ministries (OK)
State U of NY Empire State Coll (NY)
Toccoa Falls Coll (GA)
Troy State U Montgomery (AL)
U of Akron (OH)
U of Alaska Fairbanks (AK)
U of Sioux Falls (SD)
U of Wisconsin–Green Bay (WI)
Villa Julie Coll (MD)
West Chester U of Pennsylvania (PA)

INTERIOR DESIGN
The American Coll (CA)
The American Coll (GA)
The American Coll (United Kingdom)
Andrews U (MI)
The Art Inst of Illinois (IL)
Baker Coll of Auburn Hills (MI)
Baker Coll of Flint (MI)
Baker Coll of Mount Clemens (MI)
Baker Coll of Muskegon (MI)
Baker Coll of Owosso (MI)
Bassist Coll (OR)
Bay Path Coll (MA)
Becker College–Leicester Cmps (MA)
Becker College–Worcester Cmps (MA)
Centenary Coll (NJ)
Coll of Mount St Joseph (OH)
Eastern Kentucky U (KY)
Endicott Coll (MA)
Fairmont State Coll (WV)
Fashion Inst of Tech (NY)
Harrington Inst of Interior Design (IL)
Indiana U–Purdue U Fort Wayne (IN)
International Acad of Merchandising & Design (FL)
International Acad of Merchandising & Design, Ltd (IL)
Lasell Coll (MA)
Marian Coll (IN)
Martin Methodist Coll (TN)
Morehead State U (KY)
New York Sch of Interior Design (NY)
Pacific Union Coll (CA)
Parsons Sch of Design, New Sch for Social Research (NY)
Robert Morris Coll (IL)
Rochester Inst of Tech (NY)
Southern Utah U (UT)
Teikyo Post U (CT)
The U of Charleston (WV)
U of New Haven (CT)
Weber State U (UT)
Wentworth Inst of Tech (MA)

INTERNATIONAL BUSINESS
Armstrong U (CA)
Fort Lauderdale Coll (FL)

Franklin Coll Switzerland (Switzerland)
New Hampshire Coll (NH)
Saint Peter's Coll, Jersey City (NJ)
Schiller International U (FL)
Schiller International U, Paris (France)
Schiller International U, Strasbourg (France)
Schiller International U, Heidelberg (Germany)
Schiller International U (Spain)
Schiller International U, London (United Kingdom)
Thomas Edison State Coll (NJ)

INTERNATIONAL RELATIONS
Franklin Coll Switzerland (Switzerland)
Insto Tecno Estudios Sups Monterrey (Mexico)

INTERNATIONAL STUDIES
Adrian Coll (MI)
Franklin Coll Switzerland (Switzerland)
Thomas More Coll (KY)

ITALIAN
Franklin Coll Switzerland (Switzerland)
Immaculata Coll (PA)
U of La Verne (CA)

JAPANESE
Winona State U (MN)

JAZZ
American Conservatory of Music (IL)
Five Towns Coll (NY)
Indiana U South Bend (IN)

JEWELRY AND METALSMITHING
Endicott Coll (MA)
Fashion Inst of Tech (NY)
Northern Michigan U (MI)
Parsons Sch of Design, New Sch for Social Research (NY)
Rochester Inst of Tech (NY)

JOURNALISM
Ball State U (IN)
Bethel Coll (IN)
Calumet Coll of Saint Joseph (IN)
Clayton State Coll (GA)
Creighton U (NE)
Davis & Elkins Coll (WV)
Endicott Coll (MA)
Evangel Coll (MO)
John Brown U (AR)
Madonna U (MI)
Manchester Coll (IN)
Morehead State U (KY)
North Central Bible Coll (MN)
Point Park Coll (PA)
Reinhardt Coll (GA)
U of New Haven (CT)

JUDAIC STUDIES
Baltimore Hebrew U (MD)

LABOR AND INDUSTRIAL RELATIONS
Providence Coll (RI)
Youngstown State U (OH)

LABORATORY TECHNOLOGIES
Evangel Coll (MO)
Lewis-Clark State Coll (ID)
Marshall U (WV)
The Ohio State U (OH)
Purdue U North Central (IN)
Southern Nazarene U (OK)
Thomas Edison State Coll (NJ)
Villa Julie Coll (MD)

LABOR STUDIES
Indiana U Bloomington (IN)
Indiana U Kokomo (IN)
Indiana U Northwest (IN)
Indiana U–Purdue U Fort Wayne (IN)
Indiana U–Purdue U Indianapolis (IN)
Indiana U South Bend (IN)
State U of NY Empire State Coll (NY)
Youngstown State U (OH)

LANDSCAPE ARCHITECTURE/DESIGN
Eastern Kentucky U (KY)
Temple U, Philadelphia (PA)
U of New Hampshire, Durham (NH)

LANDSCAPING/GROUNDS MAINTENANCE
Eastern Kentucky U (KY)
North Carolina State U (NC)
The Ohio State U (OH)
U of Massachusetts Amherst (MA)
U of New Hampshire, Durham (NH)

LASER TECHNOLOGIES
Pacific Union Coll (CA)

LAW ENFORCEMENT/ POLICE SCIENCES
Arkansas State U (AR)
Armstrong State Coll (GA)
Austin Peay State U (TN)
Becker College–Leicester Cmps (MA)
Becker College–Worcester Cmps (MA)
Castleton State Coll (VT)
Columbia Coll (MO)
The Defiance Coll (OH)
Eastern Kentucky U (KY)
Idaho State U (ID)
Indiana State U (IN)
Inter American U of PR, Fajardo Cmps (PR)
Inter American U of PR, Ponce Cmps (PR)
John Jay Coll of Criminal Justice of City U of NY (NY)
Lake Superior State U (MI)
Lewis-Clark State Coll (ID)
MacMurray Coll (IL)
Madonna U (MI)
Marshall U (WV)
Martin Methodist Coll (TN)
Mercyhurst Coll (PA)
Middle Tennessee State U (TN)
Missouri Southern State Coll (MO)
Murray State U (KY)
Northeastern U (MA)
Northern Kentucky U (KY)
Northern Michigan U (MI)
Northern State U (SD)
Ohio U (OH)
Ohio University–Chillicothe (OH)
Ohio University–Lancaster (OH)
Oklahoma Panhandle State U (OK)
Salve Regina U (RI)
Southern U and A&M Coll (LA)
Thomas Edison State Coll (NJ)
Tiffin U (OH)
U of Akron (OH)
U of Arkansas at Little Rock (AR)
U of Arkansas at Pine Bluff (AR)
U of Cincinnati (OH)
U of Indianapolis (IN)
U of New Haven (CT)
U of Southwestern Louisiana (LA)
U of the District of Columbia (DC)
U of the Virgin Islands (VI)
U of Toledo (OH)
U of Wisconsin–Superior (WI)
Washburn U of Topeka (KS)
Weber State U (UT)
Western Connecticut State U (CT)
Western New Mexico U (NM)
Wright State U (OH)
York Coll of Pennsylvania (PA)
Youngstown State U (OH)

LEGAL SECRETARIAL STUDIES
Baker Coll of Auburn Hills (MI)
Baker Coll of Flint (MI)
Baker Coll of Mount Clemens (MI)
Baker Coll of Muskegon (MI)
Baker Coll of Owosso (MI)
Baker Coll of Port Huron (MI)
Ball State U (IN)
Becker College–Leicester Cmps (MA)
Becker College–Worcester Cmps (MA)
Central Missouri State U (MO)
Clayton State Coll (GA)
The Coll of West Virginia (WV)
Concordia Coll (NY)
Davenport Coll of Business, Grand Rapids (MI)
Davenport Coll of Business, Kalamazoo Cmps (MI)
David N Myers Coll (OH)
Detroit Coll of Business, Dearborn (MI)
Detroit Coll of Business–Flint (MI)
Detroit Coll of Business, Warren Cmps (MI)
Ferris State U (MI)
Georgia Southwestern Coll (GA)
Hannibal-LaGrange Coll (MO)
Humphreys Coll (CA)
Husson Coll (ME)
Johnson & Wales U (RI)
Lamar University–Beaumont (TX)
La Sierra U (CA)
Lewis-Clark State Coll (ID)
Marshall U (WV)
Martin Methodist Coll (TN)
Mayville State U (ND)
Mesa State Coll (CO)
Midland Lutheran Coll (NE)
Minot State U (ND)
Montana State University–Billings (MT)
Morrison Coll (NV)
New Mexico State U (NM)
Northern Michigan U (MI)
Northwestern Coll (MN)
Ohio University–Lancaster (OH)
Oregon Inst of Tech (OR)
Pacific Union Coll (CA)
Presentation Coll (SD)
Robert Morris Coll (IL)
Sacred Heart U (CT)
Southern Illinois U at Carbondale (IL)
Sullivan Coll (KY)
Thomas Coll (ME)
U Coll of Cape Breton (NS, Canada)
U of Akron (OH)
U of Cincinnati (OH)
U of Richmond (VA)
U of Rio Grande (OH)
U of Toledo (OH)
Villa Julie Coll (MD)
Washburn U of Topeka (KS)
Waynesburg Coll (PA)
Western Montana Coll of The U of Montana (MT)
Western New Mexico U (NM)
West Virginia U Inst of Tech (WV)
Wright State U (OH)
York Coll of Pennsylvania (PA)

LEGAL STUDIES
Bay Path Coll (MA)
Clayton State Coll (GA)
East Texas Baptist U (TX)
Hartford Coll for Women (CT)
Hilbert Coll (NY)
Jones Coll (FL)
Lake Superior State U (MI)
Marshall U (WV)
Marywood Coll (PA)
Ohio Dominican Coll (OH)
Roger Williams U (RI)
Southeastern U (DC)
Sue Bennett Coll (KY)
Teikyo Post U (CT)
U of Alaska Southeast (AK)
U of Bridgeport (CT)
U of Detroit Mercy (MI)
U of Hartford (CT)
U of Toledo (OH)
William Woods U (MO)

LIBERAL ARTS/GENERAL STUDIES
Acad of the New Church Coll (PA)
Adams State Coll (CO)
Alabama State U (AL)
Albertus Magnus Coll (CT)
Alderson-Broaddus Coll (WV)
Alverno Coll (WI)
Ambassador U (TX)
American Coll of Higher Studies of Anatolia Coll (Greece)
American International Coll (MA)
American U (DC)
Anderson Coll (SC)
Anderson U (IN)
Andrews U (MI)
Aquinas Coll (MI)
Arkansas State U (AR)
Arkansas Tech U (AR)
Armstrong State Coll (GA)
Ashland U (OH)
Augusta Coll (GA)
Ball State U (IN)
Baptist Bible Coll of Pennsylvania (PA)
Bartlesville Wesleyan Coll (OK)
Bay Path Coll (MA)
Becker College–Leicester Cmps (MA)
Becker College–Worcester Cmps (MA)
Bemidji State U (MN)
Bethany Coll of the Assemblies of God (CA)
Bethel Coll (IN)
Bethel Coll (MN)
Boricua Coll (NY)
Brewton-Parker Coll (GA)
Briar Cliff Coll (IA)
Bryan Coll (TN)
Bryant Coll (RI)
Burlington Coll (VT)
Calumet Coll of Saint Joseph (IN)
Campbell U (NC)
Cardinal Stritch Coll (WI)
Castleton State Coll (VT)
Cazenovia Coll (NY)
Centenary Coll (NJ)
Charleston Southern U (SC)
Charter Oak State Coll (CT)
City U (WA)
Clarion U of Pennsylvania (PA)
Clarke Coll (IA)
Clearwater Christian Coll (FL)
Colby-Sawyer Coll (NH)
Coll for Lifelong Learning of the U System of NH (NH)
Coll of Mount St Joseph (OH)
Coll of Mount Saint Vincent (NY)
Coll of St Joseph (VT)
Coll of Saint Mary (NE)
Coll of Staten Island of the City U of New York (NY)
The Coll of West Virginia (WV)
Colorado Christian U (CO)
Columbia Coll (MO)
Columbia Union Coll (MD)
Columbus Coll (GA)
Concordia Coll (AL)
Concordia Coll (MI)
Concordia Coll, St Paul (MN)
Concordia Coll (NY)
Concordia U (OR)
Concordia U at Austin (TX)
Crown Coll (MN)
Cumberland U (TN)
Dakota State U (SD)
Dakota Wesleyan U (SD)
Dallas Baptist U (TX)
Daniel Webster Coll (NH)
Dickinson State U (ND)
Dominican Coll of Blauvelt (NY)
Dominion Coll (WA)
Eastern Coll (PA)
Eastern Connecticut State U (CT)
Eastern Mennonite U (VA)
Eastern Nazarene Coll (MA)
Eastern New Mexico U (NM)
East Texas Baptist U (TX)
East-West U (IL)
Edgewood Coll (WI)
Edinboro U of Pennsylvania (PA)
Emmanuel Coll (GA)
Emmanuel Coll (MA)
Endicott Coll (MA)
Faulkner U (AL)
Felician Coll (NJ)
Ferris State U (MI)
Five Towns Coll (NY)
Florida A&M U (FL)
Florida Atlantic U (FL)
Florida State U (FL)
Franciscan U of Steubenville (OH)
Franklin Coll Switzerland (Switzerland)
Fresno Pacific Coll (CA)
Grace Bible Coll (MI)
Grace U (NE)
Grand View Coll (IA)
Gwynedd-Mercy Coll (PA)
Hannibal-LaGrange Coll (MO)
Hartford Coll for Women (CT)
Heritage Coll (WA)
Hilbert Coll (NY)
Humphreys Coll (CA)
Huron U (SD)
Idaho State U (ID)
Immaculata Coll (PA)
Indiana State U (IN)
Indiana U Bloomington (IN)
Indiana U East (IN)
Indiana U Kokomo (IN)
Indiana U Northwest (IN)
Indiana U of Pennsylvania (PA)
Indiana U–Purdue U Fort Wayne (IN)
Indiana U–Purdue U Indianapolis (IN)
Indiana U South Bend (IN)
Indiana Wesleyan U (IN)
International Coll of the Cayman Islands (Cayman Islands)
John Brown U (AR)
Johnson State Coll (VT)
John Wesley Coll (NC)
Kansas Newman Coll (KS)
Kansas State U (KS)
Keene State Coll (NH)
Kendall Coll (IL)
Kentucky State U (KY)
LaGrange Coll (GA)
Lake Superior State U (MI)
La Salle U (PA)
Lasell Coll (MA)
Lebanon Valley Coll (PA)
Lewis-Clark State Coll (ID)
Long Island U, C W Post Cmps (NY)
Loras Coll (IA)
Louisiana Tech U (LA)
Lourdes Coll (OH)
Lyndon State Coll (VT)
Mankato State U (MN)
Marian Coll (IN)
Marietta Coll (OH)
Martin Methodist Coll (TN)
Marycrest International U (IA)
Marygrove Coll (MI)
McNeese State U (LA)
Medaille Coll (NY)
Medgar Evers Coll of the City U of New York (NY)
Mercy Coll (NY)
Merrimack Coll (MA)
Mesa State Coll (CO)
Methodist Coll (NC)
Michigan Christian Coll (MI)
Mid-America Bible Coll (OK)
MidAmerica Nazarene Coll (KS)
Millersville U of Pennsylvania (PA)
Minnesota Bible Coll (MN)
Missouri Baptist Coll (MO)
Molloy Coll (NY)
Monmouth U (NJ)
Montana State University–Northern (MT)
Montana Tech of The U of Montana (MT)
Montreat Coll (NC)
Moorhead State U (MN)
Morehead State U (KY)
Mount Aloysius Coll (PA)
Mount Olive Coll (NC)
Mount St Clare Coll (IA)
Mount St Mary's Coll (CA)
Mount Senario Coll (WI)
Mount Vernon Coll (DC)
Mount Vernon Nazarene Coll (OH)
Murray State U (KY)
National Coll (SD)
National U (CA)
Neumann Coll (PA)
New Hampshire Coll (NH)
New Mexico Inst of Mining and Tech (NM)
New Mexico State U (NM)
New York U (NY)
Niagara U (NY)
North American Baptist Coll & Edmonton Baptist Sem (AB, Canada)
North Central Bible Coll (MN)
Northeast Louisiana U (LA)
Northern Michigan U (MI)
Northern State U (SD)
Northwest Christian Coll (OR)
Northwest Coll of the Assemblies of God (WA)
Northwestern Coll (MN)
Northwestern State U of Louisiana (LA)
Notre Dame Coll (NH)
Nyack Coll (NY)
Oakland City U (IN)
Oglala Lakota Coll (SD)
Ohio State U at Marion (OH)
Ohio State University–Lima Cmps (OH)
Ohio State University–Mansfield Cmps (OH)
Ohio State University–Newark Cmps (OH)
Ohio University–Chillicothe (OH)
Ohio University–Lancaster (OH)
Ohio University–Zanesville (OH)
Oregon Inst of Tech (OR)
Pace U (NY)
Pacific Christian Coll (CA)
Pacific Union Coll (CA)
Patten Coll (CA)
Penn State U at Erie, The Behrend Coll (PA)
Penn State U at Harrisburg—The Capital Coll (PA)
Pine Manor Coll (MA)
Point Park Coll (PA)
Presentation Coll (SD)
Reformed Bible Coll (MI)
Reinhardt Coll (GA)
Richmond Coll, The American International U in London (United Kingdom)
Rivier Coll (NH)
Robert Morris Coll (PA)
Rochester Inst of Tech (NY)
Sacred Heart Major Sem (MI)
Sacred Heart U (CT)
St Cloud State U (MN)
St John's U (NY)
Saint Joseph's U (PA)
Saint Leo Coll (FL)
St Louis Christian Coll (MO)
Saint Martin's Coll (WA)
Saint Mary-of-the-Woods Coll (IN)
Salem-Teikyo U (WV)
Salve Regina U (RI)
Samford U (AL)
Schiller International U (FL)
Schiller International U, Paris (France)
Schiller International U, Heidelberg (Germany)
Schiller International U (Spain)
Schiller International U, London (United Kingdom)
Schiller International U, American Coll of Switzerland (Switzerland)
Schreiner Coll (TX)
Selma U (AL)
Shawnee State U (OH)

Associate Degree Programs at Four-Year Colleges
Liberal Arts/General Studies–Medical Laboratory Technology

Sheldon Jackson Coll (AK)
Shepherd Coll (WV)
Siena Heights Coll (MI)
Silver Lake Coll (WI)
Simon's Rock Coll of Bard (MA)
Simpson Coll (CA)
Sinte Gleska U (SD)
Southeastern Bible Coll (AL)
Southern Arkansas University–Magnolia (AR)
Southern Coll of Seventh-day Adventists (TN)
Southern Coll of Tech (GA)
Southern Connecticut State U (CT)
Southern Vermont Coll (VT)
Southwestern Christian Coll (TX)
Spring Arbor Coll (MI)
Stephens Coll (MO)
Strayer Coll (DC)
Sue Bennett Coll (KY)
Suomi Coll (MI)
Taylor U, Fort Wayne Cmps (IN)
Teikyo Post U (CT)
Thiel Coll (PA)
Thomas Coll (GA)
Thomas Coll (ME)
Thomas Edison State Coll (NJ)
Thomas More Coll (KY)
Toccoa Falls Coll (GA)
Touro Coll (NY)
Trevecca Nazarene U (TN)
Trinity Bible Coll (ND)
Trinity Coll of Vermont (VT)
Tri-State U (IN)
Troy State U, Troy (AL)
Troy State U at Dothan (AL)
Troy State U Montgomery (AL)
United States International U (CA)
United States International U-Africa (Kenya)
United States International U-Mexico (Mexico)
U of Akron (OH)
U of Alaska Fairbanks (AK)
U of Alaska Southeast (AK)
U of Arkansas at Little Rock (AR)
U of Arkansas at Monticello (AR)
U of Bridgeport (CT)
U of Central Florida (FL)
The U of Charleston (WV)
U of Cincinnati (OH)
U of Delaware (DE)
U of Dubuque (IA)
U of Hartford (CT)
U of Indianapolis (IN)
U of La Verne (CA)
U of Maine at Fort Kent (ME)
U of Maine at Machias (ME)
U of Maine at Presque Isle (ME)
U of Minnesota, Crookston (MN)
U of Mobile (AL)
The U of Montana–Missoula (MT)
U of New Hampshire, Durham (NH)
U of New Hampshire at Manchester (NH)
U of New Haven (CT)
U of Pennsylvania (PA)
U of Puerto Rico, Aguadilla Regional Coll (PR)
U of Puerto Rico at Ponce (PR)
U of Southern Maine (ME)
U of South Florida (FL)
U of Southwestern Louisiana (LA)
U of the State of NY, Regents Coll (NY)
U of Toledo (OH)
U of Wisconsin–Eau Claire (WI)
U of Wisconsin–Green Bay (WI)
U of Wisconsin–La Crosse (WI)
U of Wisconsin–Oshkosh (WI)
U of Wisconsin–Platteville (WI)
U of Wisconsin–Stevens Point (WI)
U of Wisconsin–Superior (WI)

U of Wisconsin–Whitewater (WI)
Upper Iowa U (IA)
Villa Julie Coll (MD)
Villanova U (PA)
Virginia Intermont Coll (VA)
Walsh U (OH)
Warner Southern Coll (FL)
Washburn U of Topeka (KS)
Waynesburg Coll (PA)
Wesley Coll (DE)
West Chester U of Pennsylvania (PA)
Western Connecticut State U (CT)
Western International U (AZ)
Western Kentucky U (KY)
Western New England Coll (MA)
Western Oregon State Coll (OR)
West Virginia State Coll (WV)
West Virginia U Inst of Tech (WV)
Williams Baptist Coll (AR)
William Tyndale Coll (MI)
Wilmington Coll (DE)
Wilson Coll (PA)
Winona State U (MN)
York Coll (NE)
York Coll of Pennsylvania (PA)

LIBRARY SCIENCE
Missouri Baptist Coll (MO)
Ohio Dominican Coll (OH)
U of the District of Columbia (DC)

LINGUISTICS
Bartlesville Wesleyan Coll (OK)

LITERATURE
Central Methodist Coll (MO)
Crown Coll (MN)
Franklin Coll Switzerland (Switzerland)
Friends U (KS)
Maharishi U of Management (IA)
Manchester Coll (IN)
Montreat Coll (NC)
North Central Bible Coll (MN)
Pace U (NY)
Richmond Coll, The American International U in London (United Kingdom)
Sacred Heart U (CT)
U of Wisconsin–Green Bay (WI)
West Chester U of Pennsylvania (PA)

MACHINE AND TOOL TECHNOLOGIES
Boise State U (ID)
Coll of Aeronautics (NY)
Edinboro U of Pennsylvania (PA)
Ferris State U (MI)
Idaho State U (ID)
Lamar University–Beaumont (TX)
Mesa State Coll (CO)
Morehead State U (KY)
Southern Illinois U at Carbondale (IL)
Weber State U (UT)
Western New Mexico U (NM)

MANAGEMENT INFORMATION SYSTEMS
Adrian Coll (MI)
Armstrong U (CA)
Daniel Webster Coll (NH)
Fort Lauderdale Coll (FL)
Husson Coll (ME)
King's Coll (PA)
Lindsey Wilson Coll (KY)
National Coll (NM)
National College–Sioux Falls Branch (SD)
Northeastern U (MA)
Northern Michigan U (MI)
Selma U (AL)
Southeastern U (DC)
Taylor U (IN)

MANUFACTURING TECHNOLOGY
Andrews U (MI)
Baker Coll of Muskegon (MI)
Bayamón Tech U Coll (PR)
Central Missouri State U (MO)
Coleman Coll (CA)
Eastern Kentucky U (KY)
Edinboro U of Pennsylvania (PA)
Fairmont State Coll (WV)
Fashion Inst of Tech (NY)
Ferris State U (MI)
Georgia Southwestern Coll (GA)
Indiana U–Purdue U Indianapolis (IN)
Keene State Coll (NH)
Mesa State Coll (CO)
Milwaukee Sch of Engineering (WI)
Montana State University–Northern (MT)
Morehead State U (KY)
Northern Kentucky U (KY)
Ohio U (OH)
Ohio University–Lancaster (OH)
Oklahoma Panhandle State U (OK)
Purdue U, West Lafayette (IN)
Purdue U Calumet (IN)
Southwest State U (MN)
Tri-State U (IN)
U of Akron (OH)
U of Arkansas at Little Rock (AR)
U of Cincinnati (OH)
U of Nebraska at Omaha (NE)
U of Nebraska–Lincoln (NE)
U of Rio Grande (OH)
Weber State U (UT)
Wentworth Inst of Tech (MA)
Western Kentucky U (KY)
Wright State U (OH)

MARINE SCIENCES
State U of NY Maritime Coll (NY)
U of the District of Columbia (DC)

MARINE TECHNOLOGY
Thomas Edison State Coll (NJ)
U of Alaska Southeast (AK)

MARITIME SCIENCES
Maine Maritime Acad (ME)
Martin Methodist Coll (TN)

MARKETING/RETAILING/MERCHANDISING
Armstrong U (CA)
Baker Coll of Auburn Hills (MI)
Baker Coll of Cadillac (MI)
Baker Coll of Flint (MI)
Baker Coll of Mount Clemens (MI)
Baker Coll of Muskegon (MI)
Baker Coll of Owosso (MI)
Baker Coll of Port Huron (MI)
Ball State U (IN)
Bayamón Tech U Coll (PR)
Bay Path Coll (MA)
Becker College–Leicester Cmps (MA)
Boise State U (ID)
Clayton State Coll (GA)
Cleary Coll (MI)
Daniel Webster Coll (NH)
Davenport Coll of Business, Grand Rapids (MI)
Davenport Coll of Business, Kalamazoo Cmps (MI)
Davenport Coll of Business, Lansing Cmps (MI)
David N Myers Coll (OH)
Detroit Coll of Business, Dearborn (MI)
Detroit Coll of Business–Flint (MI)
Detroit Coll of Business, Warren Cmps (MI)
Endicott Coll (MA)
Fairmont State Coll (WV)

Fashion Inst of Tech (NY)
Ferris State U (MI)
Five Towns Coll (NY)
Fort Lauderdale Coll (FL)
Idaho State U (ID)
Indiana U–Purdue U Fort Wayne (IN)
Inter American U of PR, Fajardo Cmps (PR)
International Acad of Merchandising & Design, Ltd (IL)
Johnson & Wales U (RI)
Jones Coll (FL)
King's Coll (PA)
Lasell Coll (MA)
Lewis-Clark State Coll (ID)
Louise Salinger Acad of Fashion (CA)
Martin Methodist Coll (TN)
New Hampshire Coll (NH)
Northeastern U (MA)
Northern Michigan U (MI)
Northern State U (SD)
Northwestern State U of Louisiana (LA)
Northwood U (MI)
Northwood U, Florida Cmps (FL)
Northwood U, Texas Cmps (TX)
Orlando Coll (FL)
Purdue U North Central (IN)
Rochester Inst of Tech (NY)
Saint Joseph's U (PA)
Saint Peter's Coll, Jersey City (NJ)
Schiller International U, London (United Kingdom)
Shawnee State U (OH)
Shepherd Coll (WV)
Southern Nazarene U (OK)
Southwest State U (MN)
Strayer Coll (DC)
Sullivan Coll (KY)
Tampa Coll (FL)
Tampa College–Lakeland (FL)
Teikyo Post U (CT)
Thomas Coll (ME)
Thomas Edison State Coll (NJ)
Touro Coll (NY)
Union Coll (KY)
U Coll of Cape Breton (NS, Canada)
U of Akron (OH)
U of Bridgeport (CT)
U of Cincinnati (OH)
U of Dubuque (IA)
U of Minnesota, Crookston (MN)
U of New Hampshire, Durham (NH)
U of Puerto Rico at Arecibo (PR)
U of Sioux Falls (SD)
U of Southern Maine (ME)
U of the District of Columbia (DC)
U of Toledo (OH)
Walsh U (OH)
Webber Coll (FL)
Weber State U (UT)
West Virginia State Coll (WV)
Wright State U (OH)
Youngstown State U (OH)

MARRIAGE AND FAMILY COUNSELING
Martin Methodist Coll (TN)

MATERIALS SCIENCES
Penn State U at Erie, The Behrend Coll (PA)
Thomas Edison State Coll (NJ)
U of New Hampshire, Durham (NH)

MATHEMATICS
Acad of the New Church Coll (PA)
Adrian Coll (MI)
Andrews U (MI)
Bethel Coll (IN)
Brewton-Parker Coll (GA)
Central Baptist Coll (AR)
Clayton State Coll (GA)
Creighton U (NE)

Felician Coll (NJ)
Fresno Pacific Coll (CA)
Grand View Coll (IA)
Heritage Coll (WA)
Indiana U East (IN)
Indiana Wesleyan U (IN)
Lindsey Wilson Coll (KY)
Madonna U (MI)
Maharishi U of Management (IA)
Martin Methodist Coll (TN)
Mesa State Coll (CO)
Methodist Coll (NC)
Mount St Clare Coll (IA)
Northern Michigan U (MI)
Reinhardt Coll (GA)
Rochester Inst of Tech (NY)
Sacred Heart U (CT)
State U of NY Empire State Coll (NY)
Thomas Coll (GA)
Thomas Edison State Coll (NJ)
Thomas More Coll (KY)
Tri-State U (IN)
Troy State U Montgomery (AL)
U of Dubuque (IA)
U of Great Falls (MT)
U of Massachusetts Lowell (MA)
U of Rio Grande (OH)
The U of Tampa (FL)
U of Wisconsin–Green Bay (WI)
Wright State U (OH)
York Coll of Pennsylvania (PA)

MECHANICAL DESIGN TECHNOLOGY
Alabama A&M U (AL)
Clayton State Coll (GA)
Denver Tech Coll (CO)
Ferris State U (MI)
Indiana U–Purdue U Fort Wayne (IN)
Indiana U–Purdue U Indianapolis (IN)
LeTourneau U (TX)
Lincoln U (MO)
Michigan Tech U (MI)
U of Akron (OH)
Wright State U (OH)

MECHANICAL ENGINEERING TECHNOLOGY
Alabama A&M U (AL)
Andrews U (MI)
Ball State U (IN)
Bayamón Tech U Coll (PR)
Cogswell Polytechnical Coll (CA)
Coll of Staten Island of the City U of New York (NY)
Fairmont State Coll (WV)
Ferris State U (MI)
Franklin U (OH)
Gannon U (PA)
Indiana U East (IN)
Indiana U–Purdue U Fort Wayne (IN)
Indiana U–Purdue U Indianapolis (IN)
Indiana U South Bend (IN)
Kansas State U (KS)
Lake Superior State U (MI)
Lawrence Tech U (MI)
Michigan Tech U (MI)
Milwaukee Sch of Engineering (WI)
Murray State U (KY)
New Mexico State U (NM)
New York Inst of Tech (NY)
Northeastern U (MA)
The Ohio State U (OH)
Penn State U at Erie, The Behrend Coll (PA)
Penn State U Univ Park Cmps (PA)
Point Park Coll (PA)
Purdue U, West Lafayette (IN)
Purdue U Calumet (IN)
Purdue U North Central (IN)
Roger Williams U (RI)
Shawnee State U (OH)
Thomas Edison State Coll (NJ)
U Coll of Cape Breton (NS, Canada)

U of Akron (OH)
U of Arkansas at Little Rock (AR)
U of Cincinnati (OH)
U of Massachusetts Lowell (MA)
U of New Haven (CT)
U of Southern Indiana (IN)
U of the District of Columbia (DC)
U of the State of NY, Regents Coll (NY)
U of Toledo (OH)
Weber State U (UT)
Wentworth Inst of Tech (MA)
West Virginia U Inst of Tech (WV)
Youngstown State U (OH)

MEDICAL ASSISTANT TECHNOLOGIES
Arkansas Tech U (AR)
Baker Coll of Auburn Hills (MI)
Baker Coll of Cadillac (MI)
Baker Coll of Flint (MI)
Baker Coll of Mount Clemens (MI)
Baker Coll of Muskegon (MI)
Baker Coll of Owosso (MI)
Baker Coll of Port Huron (MI)
Brewton-Parker Coll (GA)
California Coll for Health Sciences (CA)
Clayton State Coll (GA)
The Coll of West Virginia (WV)
Concordia U Wisconsin (WI)
Davenport Coll of Business, Grand Rapids (MI)
Davenport Coll of Business, Kalamazoo Cmps (MI)
Denver Inst of Tech (CO)
Denver Tech Coll (CO)
Eastern Kentucky U (KY)
East Tennessee State U (TN)
East Texas Baptist U (TX)
Faulkner U (AL)
Husson Coll (ME)
International Coll (FL)
Johnson & Wales U (RI)
Jones Coll (FL)
Mount Aloysius Coll (PA)
Mount St Clare Coll (IA)
National Coll (SD)
Orlando Coll (FL)
Palmer Coll of Chiropractic (IA)
Robert Morris Coll (IL)
Tampa Coll (FL)
Tampa Coll, Pinellas Ctr (FL)
Trevecca Nazarene U (TN)
U of Akron (OH)
U of Alaska Anchorage (AK)
U of Toledo (OH)
U of West Alabama (AL)
West Virginia State Coll (WV)
Youngstown State U (OH)

MEDICAL ILLUSTRATION
Clayton State Coll (GA)

MEDICAL LABORATORY TECHNOLOGY
Arkansas State U (AR)
Baker Coll of Owosso (MI)
Bluefield Coll (VA)
Clayton State Coll (GA)
Coll of Staten Island of the City U of New York (NY)
The Coll of West Virginia (WV)
Columbia Union Coll (MD)
Dakota State U (SD)
Eastern Kentucky U (KY)
East Tennessee State U (TN)
Edinboro U of Pennsylvania (PA)
Fairmont State Coll (WV)
Faulkner U (AL)
Felician Coll (NJ)
Ferris State U (MI)
Friends U (KS)
The George Washington U (DC)
Indiana State U (IN)
Indiana U Northwest (IN)
Indiana Wesleyan U (IN)
Madonna U (MI)
Mansfield U of Pennsylvania (PA)

Associate Degree Programs at Four-Year Colleges
Medical Laboratory Technology–Nursing

Marshall U (WV)
Martin Methodist Coll (TN)
Mount Aloysius Coll (PA)
Northeastern U (MA)
Northern Michigan U (MI)
Penn State U Univ Park Cmps (PA)
Presentation Coll (SD)
Rochester Inst of Tech (NY)
Shawnee State U (OH)
Southern Nazarene U (OK)
U of Alaska Anchorage (AK)
U of Cincinnati (OH)
U of Maine at Presque Isle (ME)
U of Puerto Rico at Arecibo (PR)
U of Rio Grande (OH)
U of the District of Columbia (DC)
Villa Julie Coll (MD)
Weber State U (UT)
Youngstown State U (OH)

MEDICAL RECORDS SERVICES
Baker Coll of Auburn Hills (MI)
Baker Coll of Cadillac (MI)
Baker Coll of Flint (MI)
Baker Coll of Mount Clemens (MI)
Baker Coll of Muskegon (MI)
Baker Coll of Owosso (MI)
Baker Coll of Port Huron (MI)
Boise State U (ID)
California Coll for Health Sciences (CA)
Clayton State Coll (GA)
Coll of Saint Mary (NE)
Columbus Coll (GA)
Dakota State U (SD)
Davenport Coll of Business, Kalamazoo Cmps (MI)
Denver Inst of Tech (CO)
Eastern Kentucky U (KY)
Fairmont State Coll (WV)
Faulkner U (AL)
Ferris State U (MI)
Gwynedd-Mercy Coll (PA)
Indiana U Northwest (IN)
Inter American U of PR, San Germán Cmps (PR)
International Coll (FL)
Louisiana Tech U (LA)
Marshall U (WV)
Medical Coll of Georgia (GA)
Missouri Western State Coll (MO)
Montana State University–Billings (MT)
Moorhead State U (MN)
National Coll (SD)
Presentation Coll (SD)
Rochester Inst of Tech (NY)
Universidad Adventista de las Antillas (PR)
U of Toledo (OH)
U of West Alabama (AL)
Washburn U of Topeka (KS)
Weber State U (UT)
Western Kentucky U (KY)

MEDICAL SECRETARIAL STUDIES
Baker Coll of Auburn Hills (MI)
Baker Coll of Cadillac (MI)
Baker Coll of Flint (MI)
Baker Coll of Mount Clemens (MI)
Baker Coll of Muskegon (MI)
Baker Coll of Owosso (MI)
Baker Coll of Port Huron (MI)
Becker College–Leicester Cmps (MA)
Becker College–Worcester Cmps (MA)
Boise State U (ID)
The Coll of West Virginia (WV)
Concordia Coll (NY)
Concordia U Wisconsin (WI)
Davenport Coll of Business, Grand Rapids (MI)
Davenport Coll of Business, Kalamazoo Cmps (MI)
Davenport Coll of Business, Lansing Cmps (MI)
Denver Inst of Tech (CO)
Denver Tech Coll (CO)

Detroit Coll of Business, Dearborn (MI)
Detroit Coll of Business–Flint (MI)
Dickinson State U (ND)
Hannibal-LaGrange Coll (MO)
Humphreys Coll (CA)
Husson Coll (ME)
Johnson & Wales U (RI)
Lamar University–Beaumont (TX)
La Sierra U (CA)
Lewis-Clark State Coll (ID)
Marshall U (WV)
Martin Methodist Coll (TN)
Mayville State U (ND)
Mesa State Coll (CO)
Midland Lutheran Coll (NE)
Minot State U (ND)
Montana State University–Billings (MT)
Morrison Coll (NV)
Mount St Clare Coll (IA)
Northern Michigan U (MI)
Ohio University–Lancaster (OH)
Oregon Inst of Tech (OR)
Pacific Union Coll (CA)
Presentation Coll (SD)
Robert Morris Coll (IL)
Southern Illinois U at Carbondale (IL)
Sullivan Coll (KY)
Thomas Coll (ME)
Trevecca Nazarene U (TN)
Universidad Adventista de las Antillas (PR)
U of Akron (OH)
U of Cincinnati (OH)
U of Rio Grande (OH)
U of Toledo (OH)
Villa Julie Coll (MD)
Walla Walla Coll (WA)
Washburn U of Topeka (KS)
Waynesburg Coll (PA)
Western Montana Coll of The U of Montana (MT)
Western New Mexico U (NM)
West Virginia U Inst of Tech (WV)
Wright State U (OH)
York Coll of Pennsylvania (PA)

MEDICAL TECHNOLOGY
Clayton State Coll (GA)
The Coll of West Virginia (WV)
Columbia Union Coll (MD)
Eastern Coll (PA)
Faulkner U (AL)
Gwynedd-Mercy Coll (PA)
Indiana State U (IN)
Kansas Newman Coll (KS)
Marygrove Coll (MI)
Mount St Clare Coll (IA)
Northern Michigan U (MI)
Purdue U North Central (IN)
Rochester Inst of Tech (NY)
Valdosta State U (GA)
Weber State U (UT)

MENTAL HEALTH/REHABILITATION COUNSELING
Evangel Coll (MO)
Indiana U–Purdue U Fort Wayne (IN)
Lake Superior State U (MI)
U of Toledo (OH)
Washburn U of Topeka (KS)

METALLURGICAL TECHNOLOGY
Purdue U Calumet (IN)

METEOROLOGY
Western Kentucky U (KY)

MILITARY SCIENCE
Indiana State U (IN)
Methodist Coll (NC)
Weber State U (UT)

MINING TECHNOLOGY
Arkansas Tech U (AR)

MINISTRIES
Atlantic Union Coll (MA)
Berean U of the Assemblies of God (MO)
Bethany Coll of the Assemblies of God (CA)
Boise Bible Coll (ID)
Brescia Coll (KY)
Calvary Bible Coll and Theological Sem (MO)
Carson-Newman Coll (TN)
Circleville Bible Coll (OH)
Clear Creek Baptist Bible Coll (KY)
Creighton U (NE)
Eastern Nazarene Coll (MA)
Faith Baptist Bible Coll and Theological Sem (IA)
Faulkner U (AL)
Florida Bible Coll (FL)
Florida Christian Coll (FL)
Free Will Baptist Bible Coll (TN)
Griggs U (MD)
Hobe Sound Bible Coll (FL)
Indiana Wesleyan U (IN)
Manchester Coll (IN)
Manhattan Christian Coll (KS)
MidAmerica Nazarene Coll (KS)
Montreat Coll (NC)
Mount Olive Coll (NC)
Nazarene Bible Coll (CO)
Nebraska Christian Coll (NE)
North Central Bible Coll (MN)
Nyack Coll (NY)
Pacific Union Coll (CA)
Sacred Heart Major Sem (MI)
St Louis Christian Coll (MO)
Taylor U, Fort Wayne Cmps (IN)
Trevecca Nazarene U (TN)
Warner Pacific Coll (OR)

MODERN LANGUAGES
North Central Bible Coll (MN)
The U of Tampa (FL)
Wesley Coll (DE)
Xavier U (OH)
York Coll of Pennsylvania (PA)

MUSIC
Adrian Coll (MI)
Bethel Coll (IN)
Brewton-Parker Coll (GA)
Brigham Young University–Hawaii Cmps (HI)
Calvary Bible Coll and Theological Sem (MO)
Central Baptist Coll (AR)
Chestnut Hill Coll (PA)
Clayton State Coll (GA)
Crown Coll (MN)
East Coast Bible Coll (NC)
Emmanuel Coll (GA)
Five Towns Coll (NY)
Fresno Pacific Coll (CA)
Grand View Coll (IA)
Indiana U South Bend (IN)
Indiana Wesleyan U (IN)
John Brown U (AR)
Kentucky Wesleyan Coll (KY)
Lourdes Coll (OH)
Maharishi U of Management (IA)
Marian Coll (IN)
Martin Methodist Coll (TN)
Mesa State Coll (CO)
Methodist Coll (NC)
Montreat Coll (NC)
Mount Olive Coll (NC)
Mount St Clare Coll (IA)
North American Baptist Coll & Edmonton Baptist Sem (AB, Canada)
North Central Bible Coll (MN)
Northern Michigan U (MI)
Northwestern Coll (MN)
Reinhardt Coll (GA)
Saint Joseph's Coll (IN)
Silver Lake Coll (WI)
Southern Coll of Seventh-day Adventists (TN)
Suomi Coll (MI)
Thomas Coll (GA)
Thomas More Coll (KY)
U of Rio Grande (OH)
The U of Tampa (FL)
U of the District of Columbia (DC)

West Chester U of Pennsylvania (PA)
Williams Baptist Coll (AR)
York Coll of Pennsylvania (PA)

MUSICAL INSTRUMENT TECHNOLOGY
Cogswell Polytechnical Coll (CA)
Five Towns Coll (NY)
Indiana U Bloomington (IN)
Shenandoah U (VA)

MUSIC BUSINESS
Five Towns Coll (NY)
Friends U (KS)
Glenville State Coll (WV)

MUSIC EDUCATION
Bethel Coll (IN)
Calvary Bible Coll and Theological Sem (MO)
Martin Methodist Coll (TN)
Montreat Coll (NC)
Union Coll (NE)

NATIVE AMERICAN STUDIES
Montana State University–Northern (MT)
Mount Senario Coll (WI)
Oglala Lakota Coll (SD)
Sinte Gleska U (SD)
The U of Montana–Missoula (MT)
U of Wisconsin–Superior (WI)

NATURAL RESOURCE MANAGEMENT
Heritage Coll (WA)
Lake Superior State U (MI)
Mount Vernon Nazarene Coll (OH)
Oglala Lakota Coll (SD)
Purdue U, West Lafayette (IN)
Sinte Gleska U (SD)
U of Minnesota, Crookston (MN)

NATURAL SCIENCES
Bayamón Tech U Coll (PR)
Charleston Southern U (SC)
Felician Coll (NJ)
Fresno Pacific Coll (CA)
Gwynedd-Mercy Coll (PA)
Lourdes Coll (OH)
Madonna U (MI)
Medgar Evers Coll of the City U of New York (NY)
Michigan Christian Coll (MI)
Roberts Wesleyan Coll (NY)
Thomas Coll (GA)
Thomas Edison State Coll (NJ)
Universidad Metropolitana (PR)
U of Cincinnati (OH)
U of Puerto Rico at Arecibo (PR)
U of Puerto Rico at Ponce (PR)
U of Toledo (OH)
U of Wisconsin–Green Bay (WI)
Villanova U (PA)
York Coll (NE)

NAVAL SCIENCES
Southern U and A&M Coll (LA)
Thomas Edison State Coll (NJ)
Weber State U (UT)

NEAR AND MIDDLE EASTERN STUDIES
Baltimore Hebrew U (MD)

NUCLEAR MEDICAL TECHNOLOGY
Ball State U (IN)
Ferris State U (MI)

The George Washington U (DC)
Mass Coll of Pharmacy and Allied Health Sciences (MA)
Medical Coll of Georgia (GA)
The U of Findlay (OH)
U of New Mexico (NM)
U of Vermont (VT)
West Virginia State Coll (WV)

NUCLEAR TECHNOLOGY
American Tech Inst (TN)
Arkansas Tech U (AR)
Thomas Edison State Coll (NJ)
U of the State of NY, Regents Coll (NY)

NURSING
Abilene Christian U (TX)
Alcorn State U (MS)
Alvernia Coll (PA)
Angelo State U (TX)
Arkansas State U (AR)
Armstrong State Coll (GA)
Atlantic Union Coll (MA)
Augusta Coll (GA)
Ball State U (IN)
Bartlesville Wesleyan Coll (OK)
Becker College–Leicester Cmps (MA)
Becker College–Worcester Cmps (MA)
Bethel Coll (IN)
Boise State U (ID)
Cameron U (OK)
Cardinal Stritch Coll (WI)
Castleton State Coll (VT)
Central Methodist Coll (MO)
Clarion U of Pennsylvania (PA)
Clayton State Coll (GA)
Coll of Saint Mary (NE)
Coll of Staten Island of the City U of New York (NY)
Columbia Coll (MO)
Columbus Coll (GA)
Covenant Coll (GA)
Dakota Wesleyan U (SD)
Davis & Elkins Coll (WV)
Deaconess Coll of Nursing (MO)
Dickinson State U (ND)
Eastern Kentucky U (KY)
East Tennessee State U (TN)
Endicott Coll (MA)
Fairmont State Coll (WV)
Felician Coll (NJ)
Ferris State U (MI)
Gannon U (PA)
Gardner-Webb U (NC)
Georgia Southwestern Coll (GA)
Gwynedd-Mercy Coll (PA)
Hannibal-LaGrange Coll (MO)
Hardin-Simmons U (TX)
Heritage Coll (WA)
Houston Baptist U (TX)
Huron U (SD)
Indiana State U (IN)
Indiana U East (IN)
Indiana U Kokomo (IN)
Indiana U Northwest (IN)
Indiana U–Purdue U Fort Wayne (IN)
Indiana U–Purdue U Indianapolis (IN)
Indiana U South Bend (IN)
Inter American U of PR, Arecibo Cmps (PR)
Inter American U of PR, Fajardo Cmps (PR)
Inter American U of PR, Ponce Cmps (PR)
Kansas Newman Coll (KS)
Kansas Wesleyan U (KS)
Kentucky State U (KY)
Kentucky Wesleyan Coll (KY)
Lamar University–Beaumont (TX)
Lasell Coll (MA)
Lebanon Valley Coll (PA)
Lincoln Memorial U (TN)
Lincoln U (MO)
Lock Haven U of Pennsylvania (PA)
Louisiana State U Medical Ctr (LA)
Louisiana Tech U (LA)
Marshall U (WV)

Marymount U (VA)
McMurry U (TX)
Mesa State Coll (CO)
Midway Coll (KY)
Mississippi U for Women (MS)
Montana State University–Northern (MT)
Morehead State U (KY)
Mount Aloysius Coll (PA)
Mount St Mary's Coll (CA)
Nebraska Methodist Coll of Nursing & Allied Health (NE)
Nicholls State U (LA)
North Central Bible Coll (MN)
Northern Kentucky U (KY)
North Georgia Coll (GA)
Northwestern State U of Louisiana (LA)
Norwich U (VT)
Nyack Coll (NY)
Oakwood Coll (AL)
Oglala Lakota Coll (SD)
Ohio U (OH)
Ohio University–Chillicothe (OH)
Ohio University–Zanesville (OH)
Pace U (NY)
Pacific Union Coll (CA)
Park Coll (MO)
Penn State U Univ Park Cmps (PA)
Pikeville Coll (KY)
Presentation Coll (SD)
Purdue U Calumet (IN)
Purdue U North Central (IN)
Reinhardt Coll (GA)
Rivier Coll (NH)
Saint Joseph's Coll (IN)
Salve Regina U (RI)
Samford U (AL)
Shawnee State U (OH)
Shenandoah U (VA)
Shepherd Coll (WV)
Southeast Missouri State U (MO)
Southern Arkansas University–Magnolia (AR)
Southern Coll of Seventh-day Adventists (TN)
Southern Vermont Coll (VT)
Southwestern Adventist Coll (TX)
Sue Bennett Coll (KY)
Sul Ross State U (TX)
Suomi Coll (MI)
Tarleton State U (TX)
Tennessee State U (TN)
Thomas Coll (GA)
Troy State U, Troy (AL)
Universidad Adventista de las Antillas (PR)
Universidad Metropolitana (PR)
U of Alaska Anchorage (AK)
U of Arkansas at Little Rock (AR)
The U of Charleston (WV)
U of Cincinnati (OH)
U of Indianapolis (IN)
U of Maine at Presque Isle (ME)
U of Mobile (AL)
U of New England (ME)
U of Pittsburgh at Bradford (PA)
U of Puerto Rico at Arecibo (PR)
U of Puerto Rico, Humacao U Coll (PR)
U of Rio Grande (OH)
U of South Carolina–Aiken (SC)
U of South Carolina–Spartanburg (SC)
U of South Dakota (SD)
U of Southern Indiana (IN)
The U of Texas–Pan American (TX)
U of the District of Columbia (DC)
U of the State of NY, Regents Coll (NY)
U of the Virgin Islands (VI)
U of Toledo (OH)
U of West Alabama (AL)
Walsh U (OH)
Weber State U (UT)
Wesley Coll (DE)
Western Kentucky U (KY)
Western New Mexico U (NM)
West Georgia Coll (GA)

Peterson's Guide to Two-Year Colleges 1997

Associate Degree Programs at Four-Year Colleges
Nursing–Public Administration

West Virginia U Inst of Tech (WV)

NUTRITION
Eastern Kentucky U (KY)
Madonna U (MI)
Pacific Union Coll (CA)
Rochester Inst of Tech (NY)
Youngstown State U (OH)

OCCUPATIONAL SAFETY AND HEALTH
Ferris State U (MI)
Lamar University–Beaumont (TX)
Montana Tech of The U of Montana (MT)
Murray State U (KY)
Shepherd Coll (WV)
U of Cincinnati (OH)
U of New Haven (CT)
Washburn U of Topeka (KS)

OCCUPATIONAL THERAPY
Baker Coll of Flint (MI)
Baker Coll of Muskegon (MI)
Bay Path Coll (MA)
Becker College–Leicester Cmps (MA)
Becker College–Worcester Cmps (MA)
Clayton State Coll (GA)
Denver Inst of Tech (CO)
Faulkner U (AL)
Lasell Coll (MA)
Lebanon Valley Coll (PA)
Lourdes Coll (OH)
Medical Coll of Georgia (GA)
Mount Aloysius Coll (PA)
Mount St Mary's Coll (CA)
Northeast Louisiana U (LA)
Oakwood Coll (AL)
Penn State U Univ Park Cmps (PA)
Shawnee State U (OH)
Southern Nazarene U (OK)
Southwest Baptist U (MO)
U of Puerto Rico at Arecibo (PR)
U of Puerto Rico at Ponce (PR)
U of Puerto Rico, Humacao U Coll (PR)
U of West Alabama (AL)
Walla Walla Coll (WA)
Wichita State U (KS)

OPERATING ROOM TECHNOLOGY
Baker Coll of Flint (MI)
Baker Coll of Mount Clemens (MI)
Baker Coll of Muskegon (MI)
Mount Aloysius Coll (PA)
Presentation Coll (SD)
U of Akron (OH)
U of Arkansas for Medical Sciences (AR)

OPERATIONS RESEARCH
Thomas Edison State Coll (NJ)
U of Louisville (KY)

OPTICAL TECHNOLOGIES
Capitol Coll (MD)
Ferris State U (MI)
Indiana U Bloomington (IN)
Pacific Union Coll (CA)
Rochester Inst of Tech (NY)
U of the State of NY, Regents Coll (NY)

OPTOMETRIC/OPHTHALMIC TECHNOLOGIES
Ferris State U (MI)
Indiana U Bloomington (IN)
U of Puerto Rico Medical Sciences Cmps (PR)

ORNAMENTAL HORTICULTURE
Eastern Kentucky U (KY)
Ferris State U (MI)

Morehead State U (KY)
North Carolina State U (NC)
The Ohio State U (OH)
U of Massachusetts Amherst (MA)
U of New Hampshire, Durham (NH)
Utah State U (UT)

PAINTING/DRAWING
Endicott Coll (MA)
Northern Michigan U (MI)
Parsons Sch of Design, New Sch for Social Research (NY)
Rochester Inst of Tech (NY)
Sacred Heart U (CT)

PAPER AND PULP SCIENCES
Northeast Louisiana U (LA)

PARALEGAL STUDIES
Anna Maria Coll (MA)
Atlantic Union Coll (MA)
Bay Path Coll (MA)
Becker College–Leicester Cmps (MA)
Becker College–Worcester Cmps (MA)
Bentley Coll (MA)
Boise State U (ID)
Bryant and Stratton Coll, Cleveland (OH)
Clarion U of Pennsylvania (PA)
Clayton State Coll (GA)
Coll of Mount St Joseph (OH)
Coll of Saint Mary (NE)
The Coll of West Virginia (WV)
Davenport Coll of Business, Grand Rapids (MI)
Davenport Coll of Business, Kalamazoo Cmps (MI)
David N Myers Coll (OH)
Eastern Kentucky U (KY)
East Texas Baptist U (TX)
Elms Coll (MA)
Endicott Coll (MA)
Faulkner U (AL)
Ferris State U (MI)
Fort Lauderdale Coll (FL)
Gannon U (PA)
Hartford Coll for Women (CT)
Hilbert Coll (NY)
Huntingdon Coll (AL)
Husson Coll (ME)
Indiana U South Bend (IN)
Indiana Wesleyan U (IN)
International Coll (FL)
Johnson & Wales U (RI)
Jones Coll (FL)
King's Coll (PA)
Lewis-Clark State Coll (ID)
Long Island U, Brooklyn Cmps (NY)
Madonna U (MI)
Marshall U (WV)
McNeese State U (LA)
Merrimack Coll (MA)
Midway Coll (KY)
Missouri Western State Coll (MO)
Morrison Coll (NV)
Mount Aloysius Coll (PA)
National Coll (SD)
National College–Sioux Falls Branch (SD)
Nicholls State U (LA)
Notre Dame Coll of Ohio (OH)
Oglala Lakota Coll (SD)
Orlando Coll (FL)
Rocky Mountain Coll (MT)
Sacred Heart U (CT)
St John's U (NY)
Saint Mary-of-the-Woods Coll (IN)
Samford U (AL)
Shawnee State U (OH)
Suffolk U (MA)
Sullivan Coll (KY)
Tampa Coll (FL)
Tampa College–Lakeland (FL)
Tampa Coll, Pinellas Ctr (FL)
Teikyo Post U (CT)
Thomas Coll (ME)
Thomas Edison State Coll (NJ)

Union Coll (NE)
U Coll of Cape Breton (NS, Canada)
U of Alaska Anchorage (AK)
U of Alaska Fairbanks (AK)
U of Alaska Southeast (AK)
U of Bridgeport (CT)
U of Cincinnati (OH)
The U of Findlay (OH)
U of Great Falls (MT)
U of Hartford (CT)
U of Indianapolis (IN)
U of La Verne (CA)
U of Louisville (KY)
U of Toledo (OH)
U of Wisconsin–Superior (WI)
Villa Julie Coll (MD)
Washburn U of Topeka (KS)
Wesley Coll (DE)
Western Kentucky U (KY)
Wichita State U (KS)
Widener U (PA)

PARKS MANAGEMENT
Becker College–Leicester Cmps (MA)
Eastern Kentucky U (KY)
Martin Methodist Coll (TN)
U of Maine at Machias (ME)
U of Massachusetts Amherst (MA)

PASTORAL STUDIES
Berean U of the Assemblies of God (MO)
Boise Bible Coll (ID)
Calvary Bible Coll and Theological Sem (MO)
East Coast Bible Coll (NC)
Florida Bible Coll (FL)
Indiana Wesleyan U (IN)
Mercyhurst Coll (PA)
Nebraska Christian Coll (NE)
North Central Bible Coll (MN)
Notre Dame Coll of Ohio (OH)
Oakwood Coll (AL)
Spalding U (KY)

PEACE STUDIES
West Chester U of Pennsylvania (PA)

PEST CONTROL TECHNOLOGY
Alaska Pacific U (AK)

PETROLEUM TECHNOLOGY
Glenville State Coll (WV)
McNeese State U (LA)
Nicholls State U (LA)
U of Alaska Anchorage (AK)

PHARMACY/PHARMACEUTICAL SCIENCES
Baker Coll of Muskegon (MI)
Clayton State Coll (GA)
Columbus Coll (GA)
Emmanuel Coll (GA)
Martin Methodist Coll (TN)
Mount Aloysius Coll (PA)
Mount St Clare Coll (IA)
Notre Dame Coll (NH)
Southern Nazarene U (OK)
U of Central Arkansas (AR)
U of Puerto Rico at Arecibo (PR)
Walla Walla Coll (WA)

PHILOSOPHY
Adrian Coll (MI)
Baltimore Hebrew U (MD)
Bethel Coll (IN)
Clayton State Coll (GA)
Grand View Coll (IA)
Indiana U South Bend (IN)
Lourdes Coll (OH)
Martin Methodist Coll (TN)
Marycrest International U (IA)
Methodist Coll (NC)
Mount St Clare Coll (IA)
North Central Bible Coll (MN)
Northern Michigan U (MI)
Sacred Heart U (CT)

Saint John's Sem Coll of Liberal Arts (MA)
Suomi Coll (MI)
Thomas More Coll (KY)
The U of Tampa (FL)
U of the District of Columbia (DC)
U of Wisconsin–Green Bay (WI)
West Chester U of Pennsylvania (PA)
York Coll of Pennsylvania (PA)

PHOTOGRAPHY
Andrews U (MI)
Brescia Coll (KY)
Endicott Coll (MA)
Fashion Inst of Tech (NY)
Northern Michigan U (MI)
Pacific Union Coll (CA)
Paier Coll of Art, Inc (CT)
Parsons Sch of Design, New Sch for Social Research (NY)
Rochester Inst of Tech (NY)
St John's U (NY)
Shepherd Coll (WV)
U of Bridgeport (CT)
Villa Julie Coll (MD)

PHYSICAL EDUCATION
Adrian Coll (MI)
Bayamón Tech U Coll (PR)
Becker College–Leicester Cmps (MA)
Becker College–Worcester Cmps (MA)
Bethel Coll (IN)
Brewton-Parker Coll (GA)
Clayton State Coll (GA)
Endicott Coll (MA)
Fresno Pacific Coll (CA)
Martin Methodist Coll (TN)
Methodist Coll (NC)
Montreat Coll (NC)
Shawnee State U (OH)
U Coll of Cape Breton (NS, Canada)
U of Rio Grande (OH)

PHYSICAL FITNESS/EXERCISE SCIENCE
Atlantic Union Coll (MA)
Becker College–Leicester Cmps (MA)
Becker College–Worcester Cmps (MA)
Brewton-Parker Coll (GA)
Denver Tech Coll (CO)
Manchester Coll (IN)
Thomas Coll (GA)
Thomas More Coll (KY)

PHYSICAL SCIENCES
Faulkner U (AL)
Martin Methodist Coll (TN)
Olivet Nazarene U (IL)
Roberts Wesleyan Coll (NY)
U of Hartford (CT)
U of the District of Columbia (DC)
Villa Julie Coll (MD)
Western Montana Coll of The U of Montana (MT)

PHYSICAL THERAPY
Alvernia Coll (PA)
Baker Coll of Cadillac (MI)
Baker Coll of Flint (MI)
Baker Coll of Muskegon (MI)
Becker College–Leicester Cmps (MA)
Becker College–Worcester Cmps (MA)
Clayton State Coll (GA)
The Coll of West Virginia (WV)
Davenport Coll of Business, Lansing Cmps (MI)
Denver Tech Coll (CO)
Endicott Coll (MA)
Fairleigh Dickinson U, Teaneck-Hackensack Cmps (NJ)
Faulkner U (AL)
Knoxville Coll (TN)
Lasell Coll (MA)
Lebanon Valley Coll (PA)

Lynn U (FL)
Martin Methodist Coll (TN)
Midway Coll (KY)
Missouri Western State Coll (MO)
Mount Aloysius Coll (PA)
Mount St Clare Coll (IA)
Mount St Mary's Coll (CA)
New York U (NY)
Oakwood Coll (AL)
Shawnee State U (OH)
Southern Illinois U at Carbondale (IL)
Suomi Coll (MI)
U of Central Arkansas (AR)
U of Cincinnati (OH)
U of Evansville (IN)
U of Puerto Rico at Arecibo (PR)
U of Puerto Rico at Ponce (PR)
U of Puerto Rico, Humacao U Coll (PR)
U of West Alabama (AL)
Walla Walla Coll (WA)
Washburn U of Topeka (KS)
Wichita State U (KS)

PHYSICIAN'S ASSISTANT STUDIES
Mount St Clare Coll (IA)
U of Alaska Southeast (AK)

PHYSICS
Adrian Coll (MI)
Clayton State Coll (GA)
Grand View Coll (IA)
Maharishi U of Management (IA)
Mesa State Coll (CO)
Thomas Edison State Coll (NJ)
Thomas More Coll (KY)
U of the Virgin Islands (VI)
U of Wisconsin–Green Bay (WI)
York Coll of Pennsylvania (PA)

PHYSIOLOGY
Martin Methodist Coll (TN)

PIANO/ORGAN
Alverno Coll (WI)
Andrews U (MI)
Bethel Coll (IN)
Brewton-Parker Coll (GA)
Five Towns Coll (NY)
John Brown U (AR)
Pacific Union Coll (CA)

PLASTICS TECHNOLOGY
Ferris State U (MI)
Shawnee State U (OH)
U of Toledo (OH)

POLITICAL SCIENCE/GOVERNMENT
Adrian Coll (MI)
Brewton-Parker Coll (GA)
Clayton State Coll (GA)
Fresno Pacific Coll (CA)
Grand View Coll (IA)
Indiana U East (IN)
Indiana U South Bend (IN)
Indiana Wesleyan U (IN)
Medaille Coll (NY)
Methodist Coll (NC)
Northern Michigan U (MI)
Pine Manor Coll (MA)
Richmond Coll, The American International U in London (United Kingdom)
Rocky Mountain Coll (MT)
Sacred Heart U (CT)
Thomas More Coll (KY)
Troy State U Montgomery (AL)
U of Scranton (PA)
The U of Tampa (FL)
U of Wisconsin–Green Bay (WI)
Villa Julie Coll (MD)
West Chester U of Pennsylvania (PA)
Xavier U (OH)
York Coll of Pennsylvania (PA)

POLLUTION CONTROL TECHNOLOGIES
U of Cincinnati (OH)
U of the District of Columbia (DC)
U of Toledo (OH)

POSTAL MANAGEMENT
Washburn U of Topeka (KS)

PRACTICAL NURSING
Brewton-Parker Coll (GA)
Clayton State Coll (GA)
Dickinson State U (ND)
Grace U (NE)
Lamar University–Beaumont (TX)
Montana State University–Billings (MT)
Weber State U (UT)

PRINTING TECHNOLOGIES
Alabama A&M U (AL)
Andrews U (MI)
Ball State U (IN)
California U of Pennsylvania (PA)
Fairmont State Coll (WV)
Ferris State U (MI)
Idaho State U (ID)
Lewis-Clark State Coll (ID)
Murray State U (KY)
Pacific Union Coll (CA)
Pittsburg State U (KS)
Rochester Inst of Tech (NY)
U of the District of Columbia (DC)
West Virginia U Inst of Tech (WV)

PSYCHOLOGY
Adrian Coll (MI)
Bay Path Coll (MA)
Bethel Coll (IN)
Brewton-Parker Coll (GA)
Central Methodist Coll (MO)
Clayton State Coll (GA)
Crown Coll (MN)
Davis & Elkins Coll (WV)
Eastern New Mexico U (NM)
Endicott Coll (MA)
Felician Coll (NJ)
Fresno Pacific Coll (CA)
Heritage Coll (WA)
Indiana U East (IN)
Indiana U South Bend (IN)
Lourdes Coll (OH)
Maharishi U of Management (IA)
Marian Coll (IN)
Martin Methodist Coll (TN)
Methodist Coll (NC)
Montana State University–Billings (MT)
Mount Olive Coll (NC)
Mount St Clare Coll (IA)
Pine Manor Coll (MA)
Rocky Mountain Coll (MT)
Sacred Heart U (CT)
Siena Heights Coll (MI)
Simpson Coll (CA)
Southwestern Assemblies of God U (TX)
Southwestern Christian Coll (TX)
Teikyo Post U (CT)
Thomas Edison State Coll (NJ)
Thomas More Coll (KY)
Troy State U Montgomery (AL)
U of Rio Grande (OH)
The U of Tampa (FL)
U of Wisconsin–Green Bay (WI)
Villa Julie Coll (MD)
West Chester U of Pennsylvania (PA)
Wright State U (OH)
Xavier U (OH)

PUBLIC ADMINISTRATION
David N Myers Coll (OH)
Indiana U–Purdue U Fort Wayne (IN)
Madonna U (MI)
Medgar Evers Coll of the City U of New York (NY)
Mount Aloysius Coll (PA)

Associate Degree Programs at Four-Year Colleges
Public Administration–Secretarial Studies/Office Management

Plymouth State Coll of the U System of NH (NH)
Point Park Coll (PA)
Siena Heights Coll (MI)
Southeastern U (DC)
Thomas Edison State Coll (NJ)
U of Richmond (VA)
U of Scranton (PA)
U of the District of Columbia (DC)
U of Wisconsin–Green Bay (WI)
West Chester U of Pennsylvania (PA)

PUBLIC AFFAIRS AND POLICY STUDIES
Indiana U Bloomington (IN)
Indiana U Northwest (IN)
Indiana U–Purdue U Fort Wayne (IN)
Indiana U–Purdue U Indianapolis (IN)
Indiana U South Bend (IN)

PUBLIC HEALTH
Martin Methodist Coll (TN)
Thomas Edison State Coll (NJ)
U of Alaska Fairbanks (AK)

PUBLIC RELATIONS
Black Hills State U (SD)
Huron U (SD)
John Brown U (AR)
Johnson & Wales U (RI)
Madonna U (MI)
U of Central Arkansas (AR)
U of Richmond (VA)
Xavier U (OH)

PURCHASING/INVENTORY MANAGEMENT
Marshall U (WV)
Mercyhurst Coll (PA)
Northeastern U (MA)
Saint Joseph's U (PA)
Thomas Edison State Coll (NJ)

QUALITY CONTROL TECHNOLOGY
Baker Coll of Cadillac (MI)
Baker Coll of Flint (MI)
Baker Coll of Muskegon (MI)
Baker Coll of Owosso (MI)
Eastern Kentucky U (KY)
U of Cincinnati (OH)
U of Puerto Rico, Aguadilla Regional Coll (PR)
U of Toledo (OH)

RABBINICAL/TALMUDIC STUDIES
Baltimore Hebrew U (MD)

RADIO AND TELEVISION STUDIES
Ashland U (OH)
Black Hills State U (SD)
Endicott Coll (MA)
Lewis-Clark State Coll (ID)
Morehead State U (KY)
Ohio U (OH)
Ohio University–Zanesville (OH)
Rust Coll (MS)
Salem-Teikyo U (WV)
Trevecca Nazarene U (TN)
U of Puerto Rico at Arecibo (PR)
West Chester U of Pennsylvania (PA)
Xavier U (OH)
York Coll of Pennsylvania (PA)

RADIOLOGICAL SCIENCES
Clayton State Coll (GA)
Indiana U–Purdue U Indianapolis (IN)
Mesa State Coll (CO)

Nebraska Methodist Coll of Nursing & Allied Health (NE)
Thomas Edison State Coll (NJ)
Washburn U of Topeka (KS)
Weber State U (UT)

RADIOLOGICAL TECHNOLOGY
Andrews U (MI)
Arkansas State U (AR)
Armstrong State Coll (GA)
Baker Coll of Muskegon (MI)
Baker Coll of Owosso (MI)
Ball State U (IN)
Boise State U (ID)
Clarkson Coll (NE)
East Tennessee State U (TN)
Fairleigh Dickinson U, Teaneck-Hackensack Cmps (NJ)
Faulkner U (AL)
Ferris State U (MI)
Fort Hays State U (KS)
Gannon U (PA)
The George Washington U (DC)
Gwynedd-Mercy Coll (PA)
Holy Family Coll (PA)
Idaho State U (ID)
Indiana U Northwest (IN)
Indiana U–Purdue U Fort Wayne (IN)
Indiana U South Bend (IN)
Inter American U of PR, San Germán Cmps (PR)
Kansas Newman Coll (KS)
LaGrange Coll (GA)
Lamar University–Beaumont (TX)
Lebanon Valley Coll (PA)
Mansfield U of Pennsylvania (PA)
Marian Coll (IN)
Marshall U (WV)
Marygrove Coll (MI)
Mass Coll of Pharmacy and Allied Health Sciences (MA)
Medical Coll of Georgia (GA)
Mesa State Coll (CO)
Midwestern State U (TX)
Missouri Southern State Coll (MO)
Morehead State U (KY)
Northeastern U (MA)
Northern Kentucky U (KY)
Presentation Coll (SD)
Robert Morris Coll (PA)
Saint Francis Coll (IN)
Saint Joseph's Coll (ME)
Shawnee State U (OH)
Southern Illinois U at Carbondale (IL)
State U of NY Health Science Ctr at Syracuse (NY)
Thomas Edison State Coll (NJ)
U of Akron (OH)
U of Arkansas for Medical Sciences (AR)
The U of Charleston (WV)
U of Cincinnati (OH)
U of Louisville (KY)
U of New Mexico (NM)
U of Puerto Rico Medical Sciences Cmps (PR)
U of Southern Indiana (IN)
U of the District of Columbia (DC)
U of Vermont (VT)
U of West Alabama (AL)
Virginia Commonwealth U (VA)
Washburn U of Topeka (KS)
Weber State U (UT)
Xavier U (OH)

RANGE MANAGEMENT
Abilene Christian U (TX)
Weber State U (UT)

READING EDUCATION
Pacific Christian Coll (CA)

REAL ESTATE
Davis & Elkins Coll (WV)
Eastern New Mexico U (NM)
Fairmont State Coll (WV)
Ferris State U (MI)

Five Towns Coll (NY)
Franklin U (OH)
Lamar University–Beaumont (TX)
Marshall U (WV)
Morehead State U (KY)
Northeastern U (MA)
Robert Morris Coll (IL)
Saint Francis Coll (PA)
Shawnee State U (OH)
Southern U and A&M Coll (LA)
Southern U at New Orleans (LA)
Thomas Coll (ME)
Thomas Edison State Coll (NJ)
U of Akron (OH)
U of Cincinnati (OH)
U of Maine at Machias (ME)
U of Richmond (VA)
U of Southern Maine (ME)
U of Toledo (OH)
Western Kentucky U (KY)
Xavier U (OH)

RECREATIONAL FACILITIES MANAGEMENT
Indiana Inst of Tech (IN)
U of Maine at Machias (ME)
Webber Coll (FL)

RECREATION AND LEISURE SERVICES
Becker College–Leicester Cmps (MA)
Becker College–Worcester Cmps (MA)
Bethel Coll (IN)
Brewton-Parker Coll (GA)
Clayton State Coll (GA)
Columbus Coll (GA)
Eastern Kentucky U (KY)
Indiana Inst of Tech (IN)
Johnson & Wales U (RI)
Mount Olive Coll (NC)
Northern Michigan U (MI)
Oklahoma Panhandle State U (OK)
Southwest Baptist U (MO)
Thomas Edison State Coll (NJ)
U of Great Falls (MT)
U of Maine at Machias (ME)
U of Maine at Presque Isle (ME)
U of the District of Columbia (DC)

RECREATION THERAPY
Gannon U (PA)
Indiana Inst of Tech (IN)
Johnson & Wales U (RI)
Lourdes Coll (OH)
U of Southern Maine (ME)

REHABILITATION THERAPY
Clarion U of Pennsylvania (PA)
Thomas Edison State Coll (NJ)

RELIGIOUS EDUCATION
Boise Bible Coll (ID)
Calvary Bible Coll and Theological Sem (MO)
Central Baptist Coll (AR)
Central Bible Coll (MO)
Cincinnati Bible Coll and Sem (OH)
Circleville Bible Coll (OH)
Cornerstone Coll (MI)
East Coast Bible Coll (NC)
Eastern Nazarene Coll (MA)
Florida Baptist Theological Coll (FL)
Florida Bible Coll (FL)
Great Lakes Christian Coll (MI)
Houghton Coll (NY)
Indiana Wesleyan U (IN)
Manhattan Christian Coll (KS)
Mercyhurst Coll (PA)
Methodist Coll (NC)
MidAmerica Nazarene Coll (KS)
Missouri Baptist Coll (MO)
Nazarene Bible Coll (CO)

Nebraska Christian Coll (NE)
North Central Bible Coll (MN)
Reformed Bible Coll (MI)
Southern Coll of Seventh-day Adventists (TN)
Warner Pacific Coll (OR)
Washington Bible Coll (MD)

RELIGIOUS STUDIES
Adrian Coll (MI)
Atlantic Union Coll (MA)
Baltimore Hebrew U (MD)
Boise Bible Coll (ID)
Brewton-Parker Coll (GA)
Calumet Coll of Saint Joseph (IN)
Cardinal Stritch U (WI)
Circleville Bible Coll (OH)
The Criswell Coll (TX)
East Coast Bible Coll (NC)
Felician Coll (NJ)
Grace Bible Coll (MI)
Grand View Coll (IA)
Griggs U (MD)
Holy Apostles Coll and Sem (CT)
ICI U (TX)
Indiana U South Bend (IN)
Liberty U (VA)
L I F E Bible Coll (CA)
Lourdes Coll (OH)
Madonna U (MI)
Manchester Coll (IN)
Maranatha Baptist Bible Coll (WI)
Martin Methodist Coll (TN)
MidAmerica Nazarene Coll (KS)
Missouri Baptist Coll (MO)
Montreat Coll (NC)
Mount Marty Coll (SD)
Mount Olive Coll (NC)
New Orleans Baptist Theological Sem (LA)
Northwest Christian Coll (OR)
Oakwood Coll (AL)
Presentation Coll (SD)
Sacred Heart U (CT)
Southwestern Christian Coll (TX)
Southwestern Coll (AZ)
Suomi Coll (MI)
Tabor Coll (KS)
Thomas More Coll (KY)
Trevecca Nazarene U (TN)
U of Great Falls (MT)
U of Sioux Falls (SD)
Washington Bible Coll (MD)
West Chester U of Pennsylvania (PA)

RESPIRATORY THERAPY
Armstrong State Coll (GA)
Ball State U (IN)
Boise State U (ID)
California Coll for Health Sciences (CA)
The Coll of West Virginia (WV)
Columbia Union Coll (MD)
Columbus Coll (GA)
Dakota State U (SD)
East Tennessee State U (TN)
Fairleigh Dickinson U, Teaneck-Hackensack Cmps (NJ)
Faulkner U (AL)
Ferris State U (MI)
Gannon U (PA)
Gwynedd-Mercy Coll (PA)
Indiana U Northwest (IN)
Indiana U–Purdue U Indianapolis (IN)
Lamar University–Beaumont (TX)
Mansfield U of Pennsylvania (PA)
Marygrove Coll (MI)
Midland Lutheran Coll (NE)
Nebraska Methodist Coll of Nursing & Allied Health (NE)
Nicholls State U (LA)
Northern Kentucky U (KY)
Our Lady of Holy Cross Coll (LA)
Point Park Coll (PA)
Sacred Heart U (CT)
Shawnee State U (OH)
Shenandoah U (VA)
Southern Illinois U at Carbondale (IL)

State U of NY Health Science Ctr at Syracuse (NY)
Thomas Edison State Coll (NJ)
Universidad Adventista de las Antillas (PR)
U of Akron (OH)
U of Arkansas for Medical Sciences (AR)
The U of Charleston (WV)
U of Great Falls (MT)
U of Louisville (KY)
U of Pittsburgh at Johnstown (PA)
U of Southern Indiana (IN)
U of the District of Columbia (DC)
U of Toledo (OH)
U of West Alabama (AL)
Walla Walla Coll (WA)
Weber State U (UT)
West Chester U of Pennsylvania (PA)
Wichita State U (KS)
York Coll of Pennsylvania (PA)
Youngstown State U (OH)

RETAIL MANAGEMENT
Baker Coll of Flint (MI)
Baker Coll of Muskegon (MI)
Baker Coll of Owosso (MI)
Bassist Coll (OR)
Endicott Coll (MA)
Fairmont State Coll (WV)
Fashion Inst of Tech (NY)
Idaho State U (ID)
Johnson & Wales U (RI)
Lasell Coll (MA)
Lewis-Clark State Coll (ID)
Marshall U (WV)
Northwood U (MI)
Shepherd Coll (WV)
Sullivan Coll (KY)
Thomas Coll (ME)
Thomas Edison State Coll (NJ)
U of Bridgeport (CT)
U of Minnesota, Crookston (MN)
U of Toledo (OH)
Weber State U (UT)
Western Kentucky U (KY)
York Coll of Pennsylvania (PA)

ROBOTICS
California U of Pennsylvania (PA)
Clayton State Coll (GA)
Georgia Southwestern Coll (GA)
Indiana U–Purdue U Fort Wayne (IN)
Lamar University–Beaumont (TX)
Pacific Union Coll (CA)
Shawnee State U (OH)
U of Cincinnati (OH)
Western Kentucky U (KY)

SACRED MUSIC
Aquinas Coll (MI)
Bethel Coll (IN)
Boise Bible Coll (ID)
Calvary Bible Coll and Theological Sem (MO)
Central Bible Coll (MO)
Cincinnati Bible Coll and Sem (OH)
Circleville Bible Coll (OH)
Florida Baptist Theological Coll (FL)
Gwynedd-Mercy Coll (PA)
Immaculata Coll (PA)
Manhattan Christian Coll (KS)
MidAmerica Nazarene Coll (KS)
Mount Vernon Nazarene Coll (OH)
Nazarene Bible Coll (CO)
Nebraska Christian Coll (NE)
North Central Bible Coll (MN)
Southeastern Baptist Coll (MS)

SAFETY AND SECURITY TECHNOLOGIES
Eastern Kentucky U (KY)

John Jay Coll of Criminal Justice of City of NY (NY)
Keene State Coll (NH)
Lamar University–Beaumont (TX)
Madonna U (MI)
Ohio U (OH)
Ohio University–Chillicothe (OH)
U of Cincinnati (OH)
U of New Haven (CT)

SCANDINAVIAN LANGUAGES/STUDIES
Suomi Coll (MI)

SCIENCE
Acad of the New Church Coll (PA)
Aquinas Coll (MI)
Bayamón Tech U Coll (PR)
Bethel Coll (IN)
Cameron U (OK)
Clayton State Coll (GA)
Crown Coll (MN)
Cumberland U (TN)
Davenport Coll of Business, Lansing Cmps (MI)
Heritage Coll (WA)
Idaho State U (ID)
Indiana U East (IN)
Indiana Wesleyan U (IN)
Loras Coll (IA)
Madonna U (MI)
Martin Methodist Coll (TN)
Medgar Evers Coll of the City U of New York (NY)
Michigan Christian Coll (MI)
Montana Tech of The U of Montana (MT)
Mount Olive Coll (NC)
Mount St Clare Coll (IA)
Northwestern Coll (MN)
Ohio University–Chillicothe (OH)
Ohio University–Lancaster (OH)
Ohio University–Zanesville (OH)
Pace U (NY)
Penn State U Univ Park Cmps (PA)
Reinhardt Coll (GA)
Sacred Heart U (CT)
Selma U (AL)
Shawnee State U (OH)
Southern Arkansas University–Magnolia (AR)
State U of NY Empire State Coll (NY)
Sue Bennett Coll (KY)
Tri-State U (IN)
U of Cincinnati (OH)
U of Puerto Rico, Aguadilla Regional Coll (PR)
Valparaiso U (IN)
Villa Julie Coll (MD)
Washburn U of Topeka (KS)
Western Montana Coll of The U of Montana (MT)

SCIENCE EDUCATION
Bethel Coll (IN)
Martin Methodist Coll (TN)
U of Cincinnati (OH)

SECONDARY EDUCATION
Southern Coll of Seventh-day Adventists (TN)

SECRETARIAL STUDIES/ OFFICE MANAGEMENT
Adams State Coll (CO)
Alabama State U (AL)
Anderson U (IN)
Arkansas State U (AR)
Arkansas Tech U (AR)
Atlanta Christian Coll (GA)
Atlantic Union Coll (MA)
Austin Peay State U (TN)
Baker Coll of Auburn Hills (MI)
Baker Coll of Cadillac (MI)
Baker Coll of Flint (MI)
Baker Coll of Mount Clemens (MI)
Baker Coll of Muskegon (MI)
Baker Coll of Owosso (MI)
Baker Coll of Port Huron (MI)

Peterson's Guide to Two-Year Colleges 1997

Associate Degree Programs at Four-Year Colleges
Secretarial Studies/Office Management–Tourism and Travel

Baptist Bible Coll of Pennsylvania (PA)
Bartlesville Wesleyan Coll (OK)
Bayamón Central U (PR)
Bayamón Tech U Coll (PR)
Becker College–Leicester Cmps (MA)
Becker College–Worcester Cmps (MA)
Bethel Coll (IN)
Black Hills State U (SD)
Brewton-Parker Coll (GA)
Campbellsville U (KY)
Cedarville Coll (OH)
Central Missouri State U (MO)
Cincinnati Bible Coll and Sem (OH)
Clayton State Coll (GA)
Clearwater Christian Coll (FL)
Cleary Coll (MI)
Coleman Coll (CA)
Coll of Staten Island of the City U of New York (NY)
The Coll of West Virginia (WV)
Concordia Coll (NY)
Concordia U Wisconsin (WI)
Crown Coll (MN)
Dakota State U (SD)
Dallas Christian Coll (TX)
Davenport Coll of Business, Grand Rapids (MI)
Davenport Coll of Business, Kalamazoo Cmps (MI)
Davenport Coll of Business, Lansing Cmps (MI)
David N Myers Coll (OH)
Davis & Elkins Coll (WV)
Detroit Coll of Business, Dearborn (MI)
Detroit Coll of Business–Flint (MI)
Detroit Coll of Business, Warren Cmps (MI)
Dickinson State U (ND)
Dordt Coll (IA)
Eastern Kentucky U (KY)
Eastern New Mexico U (NM)
Eastern Oregon State Coll (OR)
East Texas Baptist U (TX)
Emmanuel Coll (GA)
Evangel Coll (MO)
Fairmont State Coll (WV)
Faith Baptist Bible Coll and Theological Sem (IA)
Faulkner U (AL)
Ferris State U (MI)
Five Towns Coll (NY)
Fort Hays State U (KS)
Fort Valley State Coll (GA)
Free Will Baptist Bible Coll (TN)
Gallaudet U (DC)
Georgia Southwestern Coll (GA)
Glenville State Coll (WV)
Goldey-Beacom Coll (DE)
Grace Coll (IN)
Hannibal-LaGrange Coll (MO)
Henderson State U (AR)
Hobe Sound Bible Coll (FL)
Humphreys Coll (CA)
Huntington Coll (IN)
Husson Coll (ME)
Idaho State U (ID)
Indiana State U (IN)
Indiana U of Pennsylvania (PA)
Indiana U–Purdue U Fort Wayne (IN)
Inter American U of PR, Arecibo Cmps (PR)
Inter American U of PR, Fajardo Cmps (PR)
Inter American U of PR, Ponce Cmps (PR)
Inter American U of PR, San Germán Cmps (PR)
International Coll of the Cayman Islands (Cayman Islands)
John Brown U (AR)
Johnson & Wales U (RI)
Jones Coll (FL)
Kentucky Christian Coll (KY)
Kentucky State U (KY)
Lake Superior State U (MI)
Lamar University–Beaumont (TX)
Lancaster Bible Coll (PA)
La Sierra U (CA)
Lewis-Clark State Coll (ID)
Lincoln Christian Coll (IL)
Lincoln U (MO)
Louisiana Coll (LA)
Louisiana Tech U (LA)
Maranatha Baptist Bible Coll (WI)
Marshall U (WV)
Martin Methodist Coll (TN)
Mayville State U (ND)
McNeese State U (LA)
Medgar Evers Coll of the City U of New York (NY)
Mercyhurst Coll (PA)
Mesa State Coll (CO)
Middle Tennessee State U (TN)
Montana State University–Billings (MT)
Morehead State U (KY)
Morrison Coll (NV)
Mount Vernon Nazarene Coll (OH)
Murray State U (KY)
Nebraska Christian Coll (NE)
Nicholls State U (LA)
North Central Bible Coll (MN)
Northeast Louisiana U (LA)
Northern Michigan U (MI)
Northern State U (SD)
Northwestern Coll (IA)
Northwestern Coll (MN)
Northwestern State U of Louisiana (LA)
Northwest Nazarene Coll (ID)
Oakland City U (IN)
Oakwood Coll (AL)
Oglala Lakota Coll (SD)
Ohio U (OH)
Ohio University–Chillicothe (OH)
Ohio University–Lancaster (OH)
Oklahoma Panhandle State U (OK)
Olivet Nazarene U (IL)
Oregon Inst of Tech (OR)
Pace U (NY)
Pacific Union Coll (CA)
Pillsbury Baptist Bible Coll (MN)
Pontifical Catholic U of Puerto Rico (PR)
Presentation Coll (SD)
Reformed Bible Coll (MI)
Robert Morris Coll (IL)
Robert Morris Coll (PA)
St Louis Christian Coll (MO)
Selma U (AL)
Shawnee State U (OH)
Shepherd Coll (WV)
Southeastern Baptist Coll (MS)
Southeastern Louisiana U (LA)
Southern Arkansas University–Magnolia (AR)
Southern Coll of Seventh-day Adventists (TN)
Southern Illinois U at Carbondale (IL)
Southern Nazarene U (OK)
Southern U at New Orleans (LA)
Southwest Baptist U (MO)
Southwestern Adventist Coll (TX)
Southwest Missouri State U (MO)
Southwest State U (MN)
Sullivan Coll (KY)
Sul Ross State U (TX)
Tabor Coll (KS)
Tampa College–Lakeland (FL)
Tennessee State U (TN)
Thomas Coll (ME)
Trevecca Nazarene U (TN)
Trinity Bible Coll (ND)
Union Coll (KY)
Union Coll (NE)
Universidad Adventista de las Antillas (PR)
U Coll of Cape Breton (NS, Canada)
U of Akron (OH)
U of Alaska Anchorage (AK)
U of Alaska Fairbanks (AK)
U of Alaska Southeast (AK)
U of Arkansas, Fayetteville (AR)
U of Central Arkansas (AR)
U of Cincinnati (OH)
The U of Findlay (OH)
U of Georgia (GA)
U of Maine at Machias (ME)
U of Minnesota, Crookston (MN)
U of Puerto Rico, Aguadilla Regional Coll (PR)
U of Puerto Rico at Arecibo (PR)
U of Puerto Rico at Ponce (PR)
U of Puerto Rico, Cayey U Coll (PR)
U of Puerto Rico, Humacao U Coll (PR)
U of Rio Grande (OH)
U of Sioux Falls (SD)
U of Southern Indiana (IN)
U of the District of Columbia (DC)
U of the Ozarks (AR)
U of the Virgin Islands (VI)
U of Toledo (OH)
Utah State U (UT)
Villa Julie Coll (MD)
Washburn U of Topeka (KS)
Wayland Baptist U (TX)
Waynesburg Coll (PA)
Weber State U (UT)
Western Kentucky U (KY)
Western Montana Coll of The U of Montana (MT)
Western New Mexico U (NM)
West Georgia Coll (GA)
West Virginia State Coll (WV)
West Virginia U Inst of Tech (WV)
Wiley Coll (TX)
Williams Baptist Coll (AR)
Winona State U (MN)
Wright State U (OH)
York Coll (NE)
York Coll of Pennsylvania (PA)
Youngstown State U (OH)

SOCIAL SCIENCE
Acad of the New Church Coll (PA)
Adrian Coll (MI)
Bayamón Tech U Coll (PR)
Bethel Coll (IN)
Brewton-Parker Coll (GA)
Campbellsville U (KY)
Canisius Coll (NY)
Chaminade U of Honolulu (HI)
Clayton State Coll (GA)
Coll of Mount Saint Vincent (NY)
Cumberland U (TN)
Divine Word Coll (IA)
Endicott Coll (MA)
Evangel Coll (MO)
Faulkner U (AL)
Felician Coll (NJ)
Heritage Coll (WA)
Indiana Wesleyan U (IN)
Lindsey Wilson Coll (KY)
Lourdes Coll (OH)
Madonna U (MI)
Mesa State Coll (CO)
Montana State University–Northern (MT)
Montreat Coll (NC)
Ohio University–Zanesville (OH)
Richmond Coll, The American International U in London (United Kingdom)
Saint Peter's Coll, Jersey City (NJ)
Selma U (AL)
Shawnee State U (OH)
Southwestern Assemblies of God U (TX)
State U of NY Empire State Coll (NY)
Suomi Coll (MI)
Touro Coll (NY)
Tri-State U (IN)
Troy State U Montgomery (AL)
U of Cincinnati (OH)
The U of Findlay (OH)
U of Hartford (CT)
U of Puerto Rico at Arecibo (PR)
U of Scranton (PA)
U of Sioux Falls (SD)
U of Southern Indiana (IN)
U of Toledo (OH)
U of Wisconsin–Green Bay (WI)
Villa Julie Coll (MD)
Warner Pacific Coll (OR)

SOCIAL WORK
Calumet Coll of Saint Joseph (IN)
The Coll of West Virginia (WV)
Endicott Coll (MA)
Indiana U East (IN)
Lourdes Coll (OH)
Martin Methodist Coll (TN)
Marycrest International U (IA)
Methodist Coll (NC)
Morehead State U (KY)
New York U (NY)
Northern State U (SD)
Northwest Nazarene Coll (ID)
Oglala Lakota Coll (SD)
Siena Heights Coll (MI)
Southern U at New Orleans (LA)
Suffolk U (MA)
U of Cincinnati (OH)
U of Rio Grande (OH)
U of Wisconsin–Green Bay (WI)
Wright State U (OH)
Youngstown State U (OH)

SOCIOLOGY
Adrian Coll (MI)
Bethel Coll (IN)
Brewton-Parker Coll (GA)
Cardinal Stritch Coll (WI)
Chestnut Hill Coll (PA)
Clayton State Coll (GA)
Crown Coll (MN)
Felician Coll (NJ)
Fresno Pacific Coll (CA)
Friends U (KS)
Grand View Coll (IA)
Indiana U East (IN)
Indiana U South Bend (IN)
Lourdes Coll (OH)
Martin Methodist Coll (TN)
Methodist Coll (NC)
Montana State University–Billings (MT)
Mount St Clare Coll (IA)
Northern Michigan U (MI)
Sacred Heart U (CT)
Selma U (AL)
Teikyo Post U (CT)
Thomas More Coll (KY)
U of Dubuque (IA)
U of Rio Grande (OH)
The U of Tampa (FL)
U of Wisconsin–Green Bay (WI)
Villa Julie Coll (MD)
West Chester U of Pennsylvania (PA)
Wright State U (OH)
Xavier U (OH)

SOIL CONSERVATION
U of Minnesota, Crookston (MN)

SPANISH
Adrian Coll (MI)
Bethel Coll (IN)
Chestnut Hill Coll (PA)
Clayton State Coll (GA)
Friends U (KS)
Methodist Coll (NC)
Montreat Coll (NC)
Mount St Clare Coll (IA)
Northern Michigan U (MI)
Sacred Heart U (CT)
Southwestern Assemblies of God U (TX)
The U of Tampa (FL)
U of Wisconsin–Green Bay (WI)
Xavier U (OH)

SPEECH/RHETORIC/PUBLIC ADDRESS/DEBATE
Brigham Young University–Hawaii Cmps (HI)
Clayton State Coll (GA)
Indiana U South Bend (IN)
Northern Michigan U (MI)
West Chester U of Pennsylvania (PA)

SPEECH THERAPY
Mount St Clare Coll (IA)

SPORTS ADMINISTRATION
Becker College–Leicester Cmps (MA)
Becker College–Worcester Cmps (MA)
Endicott Coll (MA)
Webber Coll (FL)

SPORTS MEDICINE
Denver Tech Coll (CO)
Endicott Coll (MA)

STRINGED INSTRUMENTS
American Conservatory of Music (IL)
Brigham Young University–Hawaii Cmps (HI)
Five Towns Coll (NY)
Indiana U Bloomington (IN)

STUDIO ART
Cazenovia Coll (NY)
Chestnut Hill Coll (PA)
Endicott Coll (MA)
Manchester Coll (IN)
Pine Manor Coll (MA)
Rochester Inst of Tech (NY)
Shepherd Coll (WV)
Suomi Coll (MI)
U of New Hampshire at Manchester (NH)
U of Wisconsin–Green Bay (WI)
West Chester U of Pennsylvania (PA)

SURVEYING TECHNOLOGY
Bayamón Tech U Coll (PR)
Denver Inst of Tech (CO)
East Tennessee State U (TN)
Ferris State U (MI)
Glenville State Coll (WV)
Kansas State U (KS)
Northeastern U (MA)
Penn State U Univ Park Cmps (PA)
Thomas Edison State Coll (NJ)
U of Akron (OH)
U of Alaska Anchorage (AK)
U of New Hampshire, Durham (NH)
West Virginia U Inst of Tech (WV)

TEACHER AIDE STUDIES
Alabama State U (AL)
Alverno Coll (WI)
Boise State U (ID)
Brewton-Parker Coll (GA)
California U of Pennsylvania (PA)
Centenary Coll (NJ)
Concordia Coll, St Paul (MN)
Dordt Coll (IA)
Eastern Mennonite U (VA)
Georgia Southern U (GA)
Johnson State Coll (VT)
Lamar University–Beaumont (TX)
Louisiana Coll (LA)
Martin Methodist Coll (TN)
Missouri Valley Coll (MO)
New Mexico Highlands U (NM)
New Mexico State U (NM)
Olivet Nazarene U (IL)
Our Lady of Holy Cross Coll (LA)
St John's U (NY)
Union Coll (KY)
U of Akron (OH)
U of Maine at Fort Kent (ME)

TECHNICAL WRITING
Ferris State U (MI)

TECHNOLOGY AND PUBLIC AFFAIRS
U of New Hampshire, Durham (NH)

TELECOMMUNICATIONS
Cameron U (OK)
Capitol Coll (MD)
Clayton State Coll (GA)
Coll of Saint Mary (NE)
Columbia College–Hollywood, Hollywood (CA)
Ferris State U (MI)
Idaho State U (ID)
Penn State U at Erie, The Behrend Coll (PA)
Salem-Teikyo U (WV)

TEXTILE ARTS
Fashion Inst of Tech (NY)
Parsons Sch of Design, New Sch for Social Research (NY)
Rochester Inst of Tech (NY)

TEXTILES AND CLOTHING
Andrews U (MI)
Fashion Inst of Tech (NY)
Indiana U Bloomington (IN)
Louise Salinger Acad of Fashion (CA)
Thomas Coll (ME)

THEATER ARTS/DRAMA
Adrian Coll (MI)
Bethel Coll (IN)
Brigham Young University–Hawaii Cmps (HI)
Clayton State Coll (GA)
Indiana U Bloomington (IN)
Indiana U South Bend (IN)
Marian Coll (IN)
Martin Methodist Coll (TN)
Mesa State Coll (CO)
Methodist Coll (NC)
Montana State University–Northern (MT)
Northern Michigan U (MI)
Pace U (NY)
Pine Manor Coll (MA)
Rocky Mountain Coll (MT)
Southern Oregon State Coll (OR)
Suomi Coll (MI)
Thomas More Coll (KY)
U of Rio Grande (OH)
U of Sioux Falls (SD)
U of Wisconsin–Green Bay (WI)
Villa Julie Coll (MD)
West Chester U of Pennsylvania (PA)

THEOLOGY
Appalachian Bible Coll (WV)
Baptist Missionary Assoc Theol Sem (TX)
Berean U of the Assemblies of God (MO)
Briar Cliff Coll (IA)
Calvary Bible Coll and Theological Sem (MO)
Circleville Bible Coll (OH)
Creighton U (NE)
The Criswell Coll (TX)
Florida Baptist Theological Coll (FL)
Florida Bible Coll (FL)
Franciscan U of Steubenville (OH)
Griggs Coll (MD)
Marian Coll (IN)
Martin Methodist Coll (TN)
Mount St Clare Coll (IA)
Ohio Dominican Coll (OH)
Ozark Christian Coll (MO)
San Jose Christian Coll (CA)
Southwestern Coll (AZ)
Washington Bible Coll (MD)
Williams Baptist Coll (AR)
Xavier U (OH)

TOURISM AND TRAVEL
Alaska Pacific U (AK)
Baker Coll of Flint (MI)
Baker Coll of Muskegon (MI)
Baker Coll of Owosso (MI)
Baker Coll of Port Huron (MI)

Associate Degree Programs at Four-Year Colleges
Tourism and Travel–Zoology

Bay Path Coll (MA)
Becker College–Leicester Cmps (MA)
Becker College–Worcester Cmps (MA)
Black Hills State U (SD)
Brigham Young University–Hawaii Cmps (HI)
The Coll of West Virginia (WV)
Columbia Coll (MO)
Davenport Coll of Business, Kalamazoo Cmps (MI)
Detroit Coll of Business, Dearborn (MI)
Huron U (SD)
International Coll of the Cayman Islands (Cayman Islands)
Johnson & Wales U (RI)
Johnson & Wales U (SC)
Lasell Coll (MA)
Mesa State Coll (CO)
Midland Lutheran Coll (NE)
Morrison Coll (NV)
Mount St Mary's Coll (CA)
National Coll, Colorado Springs (CO)
National Coll (MO)
National Coll (SD)
National College–St Paul Cmps (MN)
National College–Sioux Falls Branch (SD)
Robert Morris Coll (IL)
Rochester Inst of Tech (NY)
Schiller International U (FL)
Schiller International U, London (United Kingdom)

Sullivan Coll (KY)
Suomi Coll (MI)
U of Akron (OH)
U of Alaska Southeast (AK)
U of Indianapolis (IN)
U of New Haven (CT)
Villa Julie Coll (MD)
Webber Coll (FL)
Western Montana Coll of The U of Montana (MT)

TRANSPORTATION TECHNOLOGIES
Central Missouri State U (MO)
Maine Maritime Acad (ME)
Montana State University–Northern (MT)
Northeastern U (MA)
Thomas Edison State Coll (NJ)
U of Akron (OH)
U of Cincinnati (OH)
U of Toledo (OH)
Weber State U (UT)

URBAN STUDIES
Clayton State Coll (GA)
Taylor U, Fort Wayne Cmps (IN)
U of the District of Columbia (DC)
U of Wisconsin–Green Bay (WI)

VETERINARY SCIENCES
Becker College–Leicester Cmps (MA)

Becker College–Worcester Cmps (MA)
Clayton State Coll (GA)
Fort Valley State Coll (GA)
Martin Methodist Coll (TN)
McNeese State U (LA)
Medaille Coll (NY)
Mount St Clare Coll (IA)

VETERINARY TECHNOLOGY
Becker College–Leicester Cmps (MA)
Becker College–Worcester Cmps (MA)
Fairmont State Coll (WV)
Fort Valley State Coll (GA)
Lincoln Memorial U (TN)
Medaille Coll (NY)
Morehead State U (KY)
National Coll (SD)
Northwestern State U of Louisiana (LA)
Purdue U, West Lafayette (IN)
Sul Ross State U (TX)

VOCATIONAL EDUCATION
Arkansas State U (AR)
Cincinnati Bible Coll and Sem (OH)

Eastern Kentucky U (KY)
Murray State U (KY)
Sinte Gleska U (SD)
U of Alaska Anchorage (AK)
U of Central Arkansas (AR)
Valdosta State U (GA)
Western Kentucky U (KY)

VOICE
Bethel Coll (IN)
Brewton-Parker Coll (GA)
Calvary Bible Coll and Theological Sem (MO)
Five Towns Coll (NY)

WATER RESOURCES
Lake Superior State U (MI)
Montana State University–Northern (MT)
Thomas Edison State Coll (NJ)
U of the District of Columbia (DC)
U of Toledo (OH)

WELDING TECHNOLOGY
Boise State U (ID)
Ferris State U (MI)
Lamar University–Beaumont (TX)
Lewis-Clark State Coll (ID)

Mesa State Coll (CO)
Montana State University–Billings (MT)
Montana State University–Northern (MT)
Morehead State U (KY)
Oakland City U (IN)
U of Alaska Anchorage (AK)
U of Alaska Fairbanks (AK)
U of Alaska Southeast (AK)
U of the State of NY, Regents Coll (NY)
Western New Mexico U (NM)

WESTERN CIVILIZATION AND CULTURE
Bayamón Tech U Coll (PR)

WILDLIFE BIOLOGY
Martin Methodist Coll (TN)

WILDLIFE MANAGEMENT
Becker College–Leicester Cmps (MA)
Martin Methodist Coll (TN)
U of Minnesota, Crookston (MN)
Winona State U (MN)

WIND AND PERCUSSION INSTRUMENTS
Five Towns Coll (NY)

WOMEN'S STUDIES
Indiana U South Bend (IN)

U of Wisconsin–Green Bay (WI)
West Chester U of Pennsylvania (PA)

WORD PROCESSING
Baker Coll of Auburn Hills (MI)
Baker Coll of Cadillac (MI)
Baker Coll of Flint (MI)
Baker Coll of Mount Clemens (MI)
Baker Coll of Muskegon (MI)
Baker Coll of Owosso (MI)
Baker Coll of Port Huron (MI)
Baltimore Hebrew U (MD)
Calumet Coll of Saint Joseph (IN)
Davis & Elkins Coll (WV)
Faulkner U (AL)
Grambling State U (LA)
McNeese State U (LA)
Montana State University–Billings (MT)
National Coll (SD)
Northern Michigan U (MI)
Philadelphia Coll of Bible (PA)
Shepherd Coll (WV)
U of Akron (OH)
U of Toledo (OH)
Villa Julie Coll (MD)

ZOOLOGY
Martin Methodist Coll (TN)

Recent Institutional Changes

Following is an alphabetical listing of institutions that have recently closed, merged with other institutions, or changed their name or status. In the case of a name change, the former name appears first, followed by the new name.

Antonelli Institute of Art and Photography (Cincinnati, Ohio); name changed to Antonelli College.

Berkeley College of Business (West Paterson, New Jersey); name changed to Berkeley College.

Brainerd Community College (Brainerd, Minnesota); name changed to Central Lakes College.

The Brown Mackie College-Overland Park Campus (Olathe, Kansas); name changed to The Brown Mackie College-Olathe Campus.

Bryant and Stratton Business Institute (Parma, Ohio); name changed to Bryant and Stratton College.

Bryant and Stratton Business Institute (Richmond Heights, Ohio); name changed to Bryant and Stratton College.

The Career Center (West Palm Beach, Florida); name changed to Institute of Career Education.

Delaware Technical & Community College, Southern Campus (Georgetown, Delaware); name changed to Delaware Technical & Community College, Jack F. Owens Campus.

Gateway Electronics Institute (Omaha, Nebraska); name changed to Gateway College.

Heart of the Ozarks Technical Community College (Springfield, Missouri); name changed to Ozarks Technical Community College.

Helene Fuld School of Nursing of North General Hospital (New York, New York); name changed to Helene Fuld College of Nursing of North General Hospital.

Hocking Technical College (Nelsonville, Ohio); name changed to Hocking College.

Hutchinson Community College (Hutchinson, Kansas); name changed to Hutchinson Community College and Area Vocational School.

Indiana Vocational Technical College System (Columbus, Evansville, Fort Wayne, Gary, Indianapolis, Kokomo, Lafayette, Madison, Muncie, Richmond, Sellersburg, South Bend, and Terre Haute, Indiana); name changed to Ivy Tech State College.

Jordan College (Cedar Springs, Michigan); closed.

Latter-Day Saints Business College (Salt Lake City, Utah); name changed to LDS Business College.

Lees College (Jackson, Kentucky); merged with Hazard Community College.

Lexington Institute of Hospitality Careers (Chicago, Illinois); name changed to Lexington College.

Massey College of Business and Technology (Atlanta, Georgia); name changed to Herzing College of Business and Technology.

Meadows Junior College (Columbus, Georgia); name changed to Meadows College of Business.

National Education Center-Tampa Technical Institute Campus (Tampa, Florida); name changed to Education America-Tampa Technical Institute Campus.

National Education Center-Vale Technical Institute Campus (Blairsville, Pennsylvania); name changed to Remington Education Center-Vale Campus.

Nettleton Junior College (Sioux Falls, South Dakota); name changed to Nettleton Career College.

New Kensington Commercial School (Lower Burrell, Pennsylvania); name changed to Newport Business Institute.

Northern Nevada Community College (Elko, Nevada); name changed to Great Basin College.

North Florida Junior College (Madison, Florida); name changed to North Florida Community College.

North Harris Montgomery Community College District (Houston, Texas); name changed to North Harris College.

Northland Community College (Thief River Falls, Minnesota); name changed to Northland Community and Technical College.

Oklahoma Junior College (Oklahoma City, Oklahoma); closed.

Penn Commercial College (Washington, Pennsylvania); name changed to Penn Commercial, Inc..

Pennsylvania State University Ogontz Campus (Abington, Pennsylvania); name changed to Pennsylvania State University Abington-Ogontz Campus.

Peoples College of Independent Studies (Kissimmee, Florida); name changed to Peoples College.

Pratt Community College (Pratt, Kansas); name changed to Pratt Community College and Area Vocational School.

RETS Education Center (Broomall, Pennsylvania); name changed to CHI Institute, RETS Campus.

St. Vincent's College of Nursing (Bridgeport, Connecticut); name changed to St. Vincent's College.

Southern Ohio College, Fairfield Campus (Fairfield, Ohio); merged with Southern Ohio College, Cincinnati Campus.

Southern Virginia College (Buena Vista, Virginia); closed.

Southern West Virginia Community College (Mount Gay, West Virginia); name changed to Southern West Virginia Community and Technical College.

Temple Junior College (Temple, Texas); name changed to Temple College.

Texas State Technical College at Amarillo (Amarillo, Texas); name changed to Amarillo Technical Center, a Division of Amarillo College and merged with Amarillo College.

Tokai International College (Honolulu, Hawaii); name changed to Hawaii Tokai International College.

Tunxis Community College (Farmington, Connecticut); name changed to Tunxis Community Technical College.

Western Nebraska Community College-Scottsbluff Campus (Scottsbluff, Nebraska) ; information included in Western Nebraska Community College.

Wisconsin School of Electronics (Madison, Wisconsin); name changed to Herzing College of Technology.

College Profiles and Special Announcements

This section contains detailed factual profiles of colleges, covering such items as background facts, enrollment figures, faculty size, admission and graduation requirements, expenses, financial aid, special programs, career services, sports (including athletic scholarships), majors, and whom to contact for more information. In addition, there are Special Announcements from college administrators about new programs or special events.

The data in each of these profiles, collected from fall 1995 to spring 1996, come solely from Peterson's Annual Survey of Undergraduate Institutions, which was sent to deans or admission officers at each institution.

ALABAMA

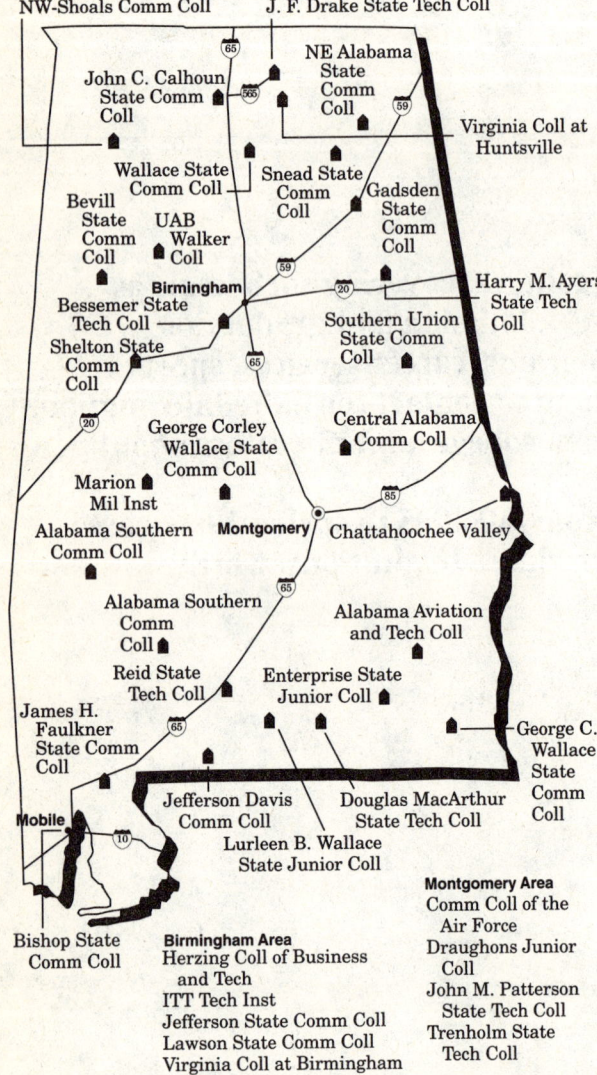

Birmingham Area
Herzing Coll of Business and Tech
ITT Tech Inst
Jefferson State Comm Coll
Lawson State Comm Coll
Virginia Coll at Birmingham

Montgomery Area
Comm Coll of the Air Force
Draughons Junior Coll
John M. Patterson State Tech Coll
Trenholm State Tech Coll

ALABAMA AVIATION AND TECHNICAL COLLEGE
Ozark, Alabama

UG Enrollment: 293	Tuition & Fees (AL Res): $1476
Application Deadline: rolling	Room Only: $1140

GENERAL State-supported, 2-year, primarily men. Part of Alabama College System. Awards certificates, diplomas, transfer associate, terminal associate degrees. Founded 1960. *Setting:* 19-acre small-town campus. *Total enrollment:* 293. *Faculty:* 38 (15 full-time, 7% with terminal degrees, 23 part-time); student-faculty ratio is 10:1.
ENROLLMENT PROFILE 293 students from 22 states and territories, 7 other countries. 11% women, 16% part-time, 78% state residents, 42% transferred in, 5% international, 55% 25 or older, 2% Native American, 4% Hispanic, 21% African American, 2% Asian American. *Areas of study chosen:* 100% engineering and applied sciences.
FIRST-YEAR CLASS 60 total; 103 applied, 98% were accepted, 58% of whom enrolled.
ACADEMIC PROGRAM Core, honor code. Calendar: quarters. 200 courses offered in 1995-96. Academic remediation for entering students, services for LD students, advanced placement, summer session for credit, part-time degree program (daytime, evenings, summer).
GENERAL DEGREE REQUIREMENTS 105 quarter hours; 15 quarter hours of math/science.
MAJORS Aircraft and missile maintenance, aviation technology, electrical and electronics technologies, flight training.
LIBRARY Learning Resources Center with 6,042 books, 3,500 microform titles, 175 periodicals, 1,699 records, tapes, and CDs. Acquisition spending 1994-95: $43,215.
COMPUTERS ON CAMPUS 30 computers for student use in computer center, learning resource center, library. Staffed computer lab on campus provides training in use of computers, software.
COLLEGE LIFE *Social organizations:* 3 open to all. *Most popular organizations:* Professional Aviation Maintenance Association, Precision Flight Team, Student Government. *Major annual events:* Blood Drive, Substance Abuse Prevention Program. *Student services:* personal-psychological counseling. *Campus security:* local police patrol.
HOUSING 70 college housing spaces available; all were occupied 1995-96. No special consideration for freshman housing applicants. Off-campus living permitted. *Option:* coed (1 building) housing available. Resident assistants live in dorms.
CAREER PLANNING *Placement office:* 1 full-time, 1 part-time staff. *Director:* Dr. Eva Sasser, Career Development Director, 334-774-5113. *Services:* job fairs, resume referral, career counseling, careers library, job interviews. Students must register sophomore year. 120 organizations recruited on campus 1994-95.
EXPENSES FOR 1995-96 State resident tuition: $1296 full-time, $24 per quarter hour part-time. Nonresident tuition: $2592 full-time, $48 per quarter hour part-time. Part-time mandatory fees: $2 per quarter hour. Full-time mandatory fees: $180. College room only: $1140.
FINANCIAL AID *College-administered undergrad aid 1995-96:* need-based scholarships, non-need scholarships, low-interest long-term loans from external sources ($3063), Federal Work-Study, 4 part-time jobs. *Required forms:* institutional; accepted: FAFSA. *Priority deadline:* 8/1. *Waivers:* full or partial for employees or children of employees and senior citizens.
APPLYING Open admission. *Option:* midyear entrance. *Required:* TOEFL for international students, ACT ASSET. Test scores used for counseling/placement. *Application deadline:* rolling.
APPLYING/TRANSFER *Required:* standardized test scores. *Application deadline:* rolling. *Contact:* Dr. Eva Sasser, Counselor, 334-774-5113.
CONTACT Mr. Robert J. Miller Jr., Student Development Coordinator, Alabama Aviation and Technical College, Ozark, AL 36361-1209, 334-774-5113 Ext. 220 or toll-free 800-624-3468. *Fax:* 334-774-5113 Ext. 258. College video available.

ALABAMA SOUTHERN COMMUNITY COLLEGE
Monroeville, Alabama

UG Enrollment: 1,800	Tuition & Fees (AL Res): $1293
Application Deadline: 9/10	Room & Board: N/Avail

GENERAL State-supported, 2-year, coed. Part of Alabama College System. Awards certificates, transfer associate, terminal associate degrees. Founded 1965. *Setting:* 80-acre rural campus. *Educational spending 1994-95:* $1705 per undergrad. *Total enrollment:* 1,800. *Faculty:* 107 (41 full-time, 10% with terminal degrees, 66 part-time).
ENROLLMENT PROFILE 1,800 students from 5 states and territories. 66% women, 36% part-time, 98% state residents, 10% transferred in, 36% 25 or older, 0% Native American, 0% Hispanic, 33% African American, 0% Asian American. *Areas of study chosen:* 52% interdisciplinary studies, 8% education, 6% social sciences, 4% agriculture, 4% engineering and applied sciences, 3% performing arts, 2% premed.
FIRST-YEAR CLASS 825 total; 900 applied, 100% were accepted, 92% of whom enrolled.
ACADEMIC PROGRAM Core. Calendar: quarters. Academic remediation for entering students, advanced placement, honors program, summer session for credit, part-time degree program (daytime, evenings, summer), adult/continuing education programs.
GENERAL DEGREE REQUIREMENTS 96 quarter hours; math/science requirements vary according to program.
MAJORS Accounting, art/fine arts, biology/biological sciences, biomedical technologies, business administration/commerce/management, business education, chemistry, computer programming, computer science, computer technologies, early childhood education, economics, education, elementary education, engineering (general), (pre)engineering sequence, English, finance/banking, fire science, forest technology, history, insurance, liberal arts/general studies, mathematics, medical laboratory technology, medical records services, nursing, occupational therapy, physical education, physical therapy, psychology, radiological technology, respiratory therapy, science, secretarial studies/office management, social science.
LIBRARY Dennis Stone Forte Library plus 1 other, with 43,000 books, 2,816 microform titles, 670 periodicals, 357 records, tapes, and CDs. Acquisition spending 1994-95: $21,601.
COMPUTERS ON CAMPUS 51 computers for student use in computer labs, learning resource center, business department, classrooms. Academic computing expenditure 1994-95: $156,906.
COLLEGE LIFE Drama-theater group, choral group. *Most popular organizations:* Student Government Association, Students In Free Enterprise, Circle K, Phi Theta Kappa, Ethnic Student Society. *Major annual events:* Homecoming, Blue/White Day, Spring Theater Production. *Student services:* personal-psychological counseling.
HOUSING College housing not available.
ATHLETICS Member NJCAA. *Intercollegiate:* baseball M(s), basketball M(s)/W(s). *Contact:* Mr. Rob Jenkins, Basketball Coach, 334-575-3156.
CAREER PLANNING *Placement office:* 2 full-time, 1 part-time staff; $32,000 operating expenditure 1994-95. *Director:* Ms. Angelis Smith, ABE Director, 334-575-3156. *Services:* career counseling, careers library.
EXPENSES FOR 1996-97 State resident tuition: $1056 full-time, $24 per quarter hour part-time. Nonresident tuition: $2112 full-time, $48 per quarter hour part-time. Part-time mandatory fees per quarter range from $5.50 to $59. Full-time mandatory fees: $237.
FINANCIAL AID *College-administered undergrad aid 1995-96:* 36 need-based scholarships (average $1017), 50 non-need scholarships (average $1017), Federal Work-Study, 36 part-time jobs. *Required forms:* institutional, FAFSA; accepted: CSS Financial Aid PROFILE. *Priority deadline:* 9/1. *Waivers:* full or partial for minority students, employees or children of employees, and senior citizens.
APPLYING Open admission. *Options:* early entrance, midyear entrance. *Required:* school transcript, ACT ASSET. *Recommended:* ACT. Test scores used for counseling/placement. *Application deadline:* 9/10. Preference given to district residents.
APPLYING/TRANSFER *Required:* standardized test scores, high school transcript, college transcript. *Application deadline:* 9/10.
CONTACT Ms. Jana Horton, Admissions Coordinator, Alabama Southern Community College, Monroeville, AL 36460, 334-575-3156 Ext. 222.

ALABAMA SOUTHERN COMMUNITY COLLEGE
Thomasville, Alabama

UG Enrollment: 1,225 **Tuition & Fees (AL Res): $1245**
Application Deadline: rolling **Room & Board: N/Avail**

GENERAL State-supported, 2-year, coed. Part of Alabama College System. Awards certificates, transfer associate, terminal associate degrees. Founded 1965. ***Setting:*** 40-acre rural campus. ***Total enrollment:*** 1,225. ***Faculty:*** 119 (96 full-time, 23 part-time).
ENROLLMENT PROFILE 1,225 students: 60% women, 18% part-time, 100% state residents, 15% transferred in, 45% African American. ***Most popular recent major:*** nursing.
FIRST-YEAR CLASS 775 total. Of the students who applied, 95% were accepted, 75% of whom enrolled.
ACADEMIC PROGRAM Core. Calendar: quarters. Academic remediation for entering students, services for LD students, summer session for credit, adult/continuing education programs.
GENERAL DEGREE REQUIREMENTS 96 quarter hours; computer course.
MAJORS Agricultural business, agricultural sciences, art/fine arts, biology/biological sciences, business administration/commerce/management, chemistry, computer information systems, computer science, criminal justice, education, electrical and electronics technologies, elementary education, (pre)engineering sequence, engineering technology, forestry, heating/refrigeration/air conditioning, industrial and heavy equipment maintenance, liberal arts/general studies, mathematics, medical technology, music, nursing, paper and pulp sciences, physical education, secretarial studies/office management, social science, speech/rhetoric/public address/debate.
COMPUTERS ON CAMPUS 130 computers for student use in computer center, various buildings provide access to main academic computer. Staffed computer lab on campus provides training in use of computers, software.
COLLEGE LIFE ***Student services:*** personal-psychological counseling.
HOUSING College housing not available.
ATHLETICS Member NJCAA. ***Intercollegiate:*** baseball M, basketball M. ***Intramural:*** basketball, table tennis (Ping-Pong). ***Contact:*** Mr. Terry Sellers, Athletic Director, 334-575-3156.
CAREER PLANNING ***Service:*** career counseling.
EXPENSES FOR 1996–97 State resident tuition: $1245 full-time. Nonresident tuition: $2179 full-time. Part-time tuition per quarter ranges from $25.50 to $279 for state residents, $44.60 to $488 for nonresidents.
FINANCIAL AID ***College-administered undergrad aid 1995–96:*** non-need scholarships. ***Required forms:*** institutional, FAFSA. ***Application deadline:*** continuous. ***Waivers:*** full or partial for senior citizens.
APPLYING Open admission. ***Required:*** school transcript, ACT ASSET. Test scores used for counseling/placement. ***Application deadline:*** rolling. ***Notification:*** continuous.
APPLYING/TRANSFER ***Required:*** standardized test scores, college transcript. ***Recommended:*** minimum 2.0 college GPA. ***Application deadline:*** rolling. ***Notification:*** continuous.
CONTACT Mr. David Phillips, Dean of Students, Alabama Southern Community College, Thomasville, AL 36784-0489, 334-636-9642 Ext. 639. ***Fax:*** 334-636-8123.

BESSEMER STATE TECHNICAL COLLEGE
Bessemer, Alabama

UG Enrollment: 1,840 **Tuition & Fees (AL Res): $1680**
Application Deadline: 9/1 **Room & Board: N/Avail**

GENERAL State-supported, 2-year, coed. Part of Alabama College System. Awards certificates, diplomas, terminal associate degrees. Founded 1966. ***Setting:*** 60-acre small-town campus with easy access to Birmingham. ***Endowment:*** $51,542. ***Educational spending 1994–95:*** $3177 per undergrad. ***Total enrollment:*** 1,840. ***Faculty:*** 119 (51 full-time, 68 part-time); student-faculty ratio is 15:1.
ENROLLMENT PROFILE 1,840 students: 38% women, 56% part-time, 99% state residents, 38% transferred in, 8% have need-based financial aid, 63% 25 or older, 34% African American. ***Areas of study chosen:*** 18% health professions and related sciences, 12% computer and information sciences, 12% engineering and applied sciences, 9% business management and administrative services, 4% agriculture. ***Most popular recent majors:*** practical nursing, electrical and electronics technologies, computer science.
FIRST-YEAR CLASS 712 total; 1,434 applied, 68% were accepted, 73% of whom enrolled.
ACADEMIC PROGRAM Calendar: quarters. Academic remediation for entering students, services for LD students, advanced placement, part-time degree program (daytime, evenings), internships.
GENERAL DEGREE REQUIREMENTS 120 quarter hours; 10 quarter hours of math; computer course for accounting, retail management, electrical and electronics technology, nursing majors.
MAJORS Accounting, automotive technologies, computer graphics, computer science, construction technologies, drafting and design, electrical and electronics technologies, machine and tool technologies, ornamental horticulture, practical nursing, retail management, secretarial studies/office management.
COMPUTERS ON CAMPUS 180 computers for student use in computer labs, learning resource center. Academic computing expenditure 1994–95: $97,740.
COLLEGE LIFE ***Campus security:*** 24-hour patrols, student patrols.
HOUSING College housing not available.
CAREER PLANNING ***Placement office:*** 1 full-time staff; $134,206 operating expenditure 1994–95. ***Director:*** Ms. Sundra Smith, Job Placement Director, 205-428-6391. ***Services:*** resume referral, career counseling, careers library. 49 organizations recruited on campus 1994–95.
AFTER GRADUATION 73% of class of 1994 had job offers within 6 months.
EXPENSES FOR 1996–97 State resident tuition: $1440 full-time, $24 per quarter hour part-time. Nonresident tuition: $2880 full-time, $48 per quarter hour part-time. Part-time mandatory fees: $60 per quarter. Full-time mandatory fees: $240.
FINANCIAL AID ***College-administered undergrad aid 1995–96:*** 150 need-based scholarships (average $650), 100 non-need scholarships (average $1110), short-term loans (average $200), 75 Federal Work-Study (averaging $800). ***Required forms:*** institutional, FAFSA; accepted: CSS Financial Aid PROFILE. ***Priority deadline:*** 9/1. ***Waivers:*** full or partial for employees or children of employees and senior citizens.
APPLYING ***Required:*** school transcript, ACT ASSET. Test scores used for admission and counseling/placement. ***Application deadline:*** 9/1. ***Notification:*** continuous until 9/1.
APPLYING/TRANSFER ***Entrance:*** minimally difficult. ***Application deadline:*** 9/1. ***Notification:*** continuous until 9/1.
CONTACT Mr. Jim Natale, Director of Admissions, Bessemer State Technical College, Bessemer, AL 35021-0308, 205-428-6391 Ext. 359 or toll-free 800-235-5368 (in-state). ***Fax:*** 205-424-5119. College video available.

BEVILL STATE COMMUNITY COLLEGE
Sumiton, Alabama

UG Enrollment: 4,597 **Tuition & Fees (AL Res): $883**
Application Deadline: rolling **Room & Board: N/Avail**

GENERAL State-supported, 2-year, coed. Part of Alabama College System. Awards transfer associate, terminal associate degrees. Founded 1969. ***Setting:*** 23-acre rural campus with easy access to Birmingham. ***Total enrollment:*** 4,597. ***Faculty:*** 63 (16 full-time, 25% with terminal degrees, 47 part-time); student-faculty ratio is 18:1.
ENROLLMENT PROFILE 4,597 students from 4 states and territories. 67% women, 46% part-time, 99% state residents, 13% transferred in, 43% 25 or older, 12% African American. ***Areas of study chosen:*** 77% interdisciplinary studies.
FIRST-YEAR CLASS 2,357 total. Of the students who applied, 100% were accepted, 96% of whom enrolled.
ACADEMIC PROGRAM Core. Calendar: quarters. Academic remediation for entering students, services for LD students, advanced placement, honors program, summer session for credit, part-time degree program (daytime, evenings, summer), adult/continuing education programs, co-op programs. Off-campus study at University of Alabama at Birmingham, Wallace State Community College, Shelton State Community College, Northwest Alabama State Technical College.
GENERAL DEGREE REQUIREMENTS 96 quarter hours; computer course for all associate of science degree students and transfer students.
MAJORS Accounting, business administration/commerce/management, computer technologies, data processing, education, (pre)engineering sequence, forestry, humanities, liberal arts/general studies, medical technology, nursing, physical sciences, physical therapy, postal management, practical nursing, radiological technology, respiratory therapy, sanitation technology, science, secretarial studies/office management, social science.
LIBRARY 31,690 books, 90,766 microform titles, 192 periodicals, 1,913 records, tapes, and CDs. Acquisition spending 1994–95: $97,111.
COMPUTERS ON CAMPUS 65 computers for student use in computer center, library. Academic computing expenditure 1994–95: $93,250.
COLLEGE LIFE Choral group. ***Most popular organizations:*** Student LPN Club, Phi Beta Lambda, Campus Ministries. ***Major annual events:*** Homecoming, Field Day, Christmas Concert. ***Student services:*** personal-psychological counseling.
HOUSING College housing not available.
ATHLETICS Member NJCAA. ***Intercollegiate:*** baseball M(s), basketball M(s)/W(s), softball W(s), volleyball W(s). ***Intramural:*** basketball, football, softball, swimming and diving, table tennis (Ping-Pong), tennis, volleyball. ***Contact:*** Mr. Don Bell, Athletic Director, 205-932-3221.
CAREER PLANNING ***Placement office:*** 3 full-time staff; $130,200 operating expenditure 1994–95. ***Director:*** Ms. Patsy Hubbert, Counselor, 205-932-3221. ***Services:*** resume preparation, career counseling, careers library.
EXPENSES FOR 1995–96 State resident tuition: $858 full-time, $22 per quarter hour part-time. Nonresident tuition: $1501 full-time, $38.50 per quarter hour part-time. Part-time mandatory fees: $11 per quarter. Full-time mandatory fees: $25.
FINANCIAL AID ***College-administered undergrad aid 1995–96:*** need-based scholarships, 240 non-need scholarships (averaging $1000), Federal Work-Study, part-time jobs. ***Required forms:*** FAFSA; accepted: CSS Financial Aid PROFILE. ***Priority deadline:*** 6/1. ***Payment plan:*** deferred payment. ***Waivers:*** full or partial for employees or children of employees and senior citizens.
APPLYING Open admission. ***Options:*** early entrance, deferred entrance, midyear entrance. ***Required:*** school transcript, TOEFL for international students, ACT ASSET. ***Required for some:*** ACT. Test scores used for counseling/placement. ***Application deadline:*** rolling.
APPLYING/TRANSFER ***Required:*** standardized test scores, high school transcript, college transcript. ***Entrance:*** noncompetitive. ***Application deadline:*** rolling.
CONTACT Mrs. Nelda S. Oswalt, Director of Admissions and Records, Bevill State Community College, Sumiton, AL 35148, 205-932-3221 Ext. 5101.

BISHOP STATE COMMUNITY COLLEGE
Mobile, Alabama

UG Enrollment: 4,127 **Tuition & Fees (AL Res): $1341**
Application Deadline: rolling **Room & Board: N/Avail**

GENERAL State-supported, 2-year, coed. Part of Alabama College System. Awards certificates, diplomas, transfer associate, terminal associate degrees. Founded 1965. ***Setting:*** 9-acre urban campus. ***Endowment:*** $275,124. ***Educational spending 1994–95:*** $2290 per undergrad. ***Total enrollment:*** 4,127. ***Faculty:*** 257 (131 full-time, 1% with terminal degrees, 126 part-time); student-faculty ratio is 16:1. ***Notable Alumni:*** Dr. Yvonne Kennedy.
ENROLLMENT PROFILE 4,127 students: 63% women, 45% part-time, 97% state residents, 3% transferred in, 46% have need-based financial aid, 2% have non-need-based financial aid, 1% international, 57% 25 or older, 1% Native American, 1% Hispanic, 58% African American, 1% Asian American. ***Areas of study chosen:*** 41% health professions and related sciences, 34% education, 22% vocational and home economics, 3% computer and information sciences. ***Most popular recent major:*** nursing.
FIRST-YEAR CLASS 729 total; 1,150 applied, 91% were accepted, 70% of whom enrolled.

Peterson's Guide to Two-Year Colleges 1997

151

Bishop State Community College (continued)

ACADEMIC PROGRAM Core, honor code. Calendar: quarters. Academic remediation for entering students, services for LD students, tutorials, summer session for credit, part-time degree program (daytime, evenings), adult/continuing education programs, co-op programs and internships. ROTC: Army.

GENERAL DEGREE REQUIREMENTS 96 quarter hours; math/science requirements vary according to program; internship (some majors).

MAJORS Accounting, business administration/commerce/management, carpentry, chemical engineering technology, child care/child and family studies, computer information systems, computer technologies, cosmetology, criminal justice, culinary arts, data processing, deaf interpreter training, early childhood education, electrical and electronics technologies, emergency medical technology, engineering technology, fire science, funeral service, liberal arts/general studies, medical records services, nursing, physical education, psychology, respiratory therapy, secretarial studies/office management.

LIBRARY Minnie Slade Bishop Library with 48,970 books, 2,928 microform titles, 243 periodicals, 2,000 records, tapes, and CDs. Acquisition spending 1994–95: $54,333.

COMPUTERS ON CAMPUS 96 computers for student use in computer center, computer labs, learning resource center, library. Staffed computer lab on campus provides training in use of computers, software.

COLLEGE LIFE Choral group, student-run newspaper. 20% vote in student government elections. ***Major annual event:*** Homecoming. ***Campus security:*** 24-hour emergency response devices and patrols.

HOUSING College housing not available.

ATHLETICS Member NJCAA. ***Intercollegiate:*** baseball M, basketball M(s)/W(s), softball W. ***Contact:*** Mr. Johnny Shelwood, Athletic Director, 334-690-6436.

CAREER PLANNING ***Placement office:*** 1 full-time staff; $75,000 operating expenditure 1994–95. ***Director:*** Mr. Marcine Chatman, Director of Career and Placement, 334-690-6447. ***Services:*** career counseling, careers library, job interviews. 21 organizations recruited on campus 1994–95.

EXPENSES FOR 1995–96 State resident tuition: $1200 full-time, $25 per credit hour part-time. Nonresident tuition: $2400 full-time, $50 per credit hour part-time. Part-time mandatory fees per quarter range from $14 to $54. Full-time mandatory fees: $141.

FINANCIAL AID ***College-administered undergrad aid 1995–96:*** need-based scholarships, non-need scholarships, low-interest long-term loans from external sources, Federal Work-Study, part-time jobs. ***Required forms:*** institutional, FAFSA; accepted: CSS Financial Aid PROFILE. ***Priority deadline:*** 8/20. ***Waivers:*** full or partial for senior citizens.

APPLYING Open admission. ***Options:*** early entrance, deferred entrance. ***Required:*** school transcript, TOEFL for international students. Test scores used for counseling/placement. ***Application deadline:*** rolling. ***Notification:*** continuous until 9/17.

APPLYING/TRANSFER ***Required:*** high school transcript, college transcript. ***Application deadline:*** rolling. ***Notification:*** continuous until 9/17. ***Contact:*** Ms. Lisa Dewberry, Academic Counselor, 334-690-6423.

CONTACT Mr. Terry Hazzard, Dean of Students, Bishop State Community College, 351 North Broad Street, Mobile, AL 36603-5898, 334-690-6419.

CENTRAL ALABAMA COMMUNITY COLLEGE
Alexander City, Alabama

UG Enrollment: 1,917	**Tuition & Fees (AL Res): $1312**
Application Deadline: 9/9	**Room & Board: N/Avail**

GENERAL State-supported, 2-year, coed. Part of Alabama College System. Awards certificates, transfer associate, terminal associate degrees. Founded 1965. ***Setting:*** 100-acre small-town campus. ***Research spending 1994–95:*** $60,657. ***Total enrollment:*** 1,917. ***Faculty:*** 140 (55 full-time, 99% with terminal degrees, 85 part-time); student-faculty ratio is 15:1.

ENROLLMENT PROFILE 1,917 students from 4 states and territories, 3 other countries. 55% women, 65% part-time, 98% state residents, 33% transferred in, 1% international, 43% 25 or older, 0% Native American, 0% Hispanic, 15% African American, 0% Asian American.

FIRST-YEAR CLASS 600 total; 850 applied, 100% were accepted, 71% of whom enrolled.

ACADEMIC PROGRAM Core, interdisciplinary curriculum. Calendar: quarters. Average class size 23 in required courses. Academic remediation for entering students, services for LD students, advanced placement, tutorials, summer session for credit, part-time degree program (daytime, evenings, summer), adult/continuing education programs, co-op programs and internships.

GENERAL DEGREE REQUIREMENTS 96 quarter hours; 15 quarter hours of math/science; computer course for secretarial studies, textiles, business, drafting and design majors.

MAJORS Business administration/commerce/management, computer information systems, computer programming, computer science, drafting and design, electrical and electronics technologies, liberal arts/general studies, nursing, pollution control technologies, secretarial studies/office management, textiles and clothing.

LIBRARY Thomas D. Russell Library with 35,000 books, 455 periodicals, 1,155 records, tapes, and CDs.

COMPUTERS ON CAMPUS 70 computers for student use in computer center provide access to main academic computer. Staffed computer lab on campus provides training in use of computers, software. Academic computing expenditure 1994–95: $9.7 million.

COLLEGE LIFE Orientation program (4 days, $91). Drama-theater group, choral group, student-run radio station. ***Social organizations:*** 6 open to all. ***Most popular organizations:*** Cultural Unity, Baptist Campus Ministry, Student Government Association. ***Major annual events:*** Fall Fest, Spring Fest. ***Student services:*** personal-psychological counseling. ***Campus security:*** evening security.

HOUSING College housing not available.

ATHLETICS Member NJCAA. ***Intercollegiate:*** baseball M(s), golf M(s), softball W(s), tennis M(s)/W(s), volleyball W(s). ***Contact:*** Mr. Larry Ginanggrosso, Athletic Director, 205-234-6346 Ext. 6269.

CAREER PLANNING ***Director:*** Ms. Amelia Pearson, Dean of Student Affairs, 205-234-6346. ***Service:*** career counseling.

AFTER GRADUATION 33% of students completing a degree program in 1994–95 went directly on to further study.

EXPENSES FOR 1995–96 State resident tuition: $1312 full-time, $30.50 per quarter hour part-time. Nonresident tuition: $2100 full-time, $49.25 per quarter hour part-time.

FINANCIAL AID ***College-administered undergrad aid 1995–96:*** need-based scholarships, non-need scholarships. ***Required forms:*** FAFSA. ***Application deadline:*** continuous. ***Waivers:*** full or partial for senior citizens.

APPLYING Open admission. ***Options:*** Common Application, early entrance. ***Required:*** school transcript, ACT ASSET. ***Required for some:*** interview. Test scores used for counseling/placement. ***Application deadline:*** 9/9.

APPLYING/TRANSFER ***Required:*** college transcript. ***Required for some:*** standardized test scores, high school transcript, interview. ***Entrance:*** noncompetitive. ***Application deadline:*** 9/9. ***Contact:*** Ms. Bettie McMillan, Admissions Assistant, 205-234-6346 Ext. 6238.

CONTACT Ms. Amelia Pearson, Dean of Student Affairs, Central Alabama Community College, Alexander City, AL 35011-0699, 205-234-6346 Ext. 210.

CHATTAHOOCHEE VALLEY STATE COMMUNITY COLLEGE
Phenix City, Alabama

UG Enrollment: 2,101	**Tuition & Fees (AL Res): $1327**
Application Deadline: rolling	**Room & Board: N/Avail**

GENERAL State-supported, 2-year, coed. Awards transfer associate, terminal associate degrees. Founded 1974. ***Setting:*** 103-acre small-town campus. ***Endowment:*** $35,758. ***Total enrollment:*** 2,101. ***Faculty:*** 107 (39 full-time, 7% with terminal degrees, 68 part-time).

ENROLLMENT PROFILE 2,101 students from 10 states and territories, 8 other countries. 61% women, 39% men, 43% part-time, 97% state residents, 27% transferred in, 1% international, 51% 25 or older, 0% Native American, 1% Hispanic, 41% African American, 1% Asian American. ***Most popular recent majors:*** computer information systems, business administration/commerce/management, liberal arts/general studies.

FIRST-YEAR CLASS 773 total; 920 applied, 100% were accepted, 84% of whom enrolled.

ACADEMIC PROGRAM Core, honor code. Calendar: quarters. Academic remediation for entering students, advanced placement, self-designed majors, honors program, summer session for credit, part-time degree program (daytime, evenings, weekends, summer), adult/continuing education programs. Off-campus study at Troy State University.

GENERAL DEGREE REQUIREMENTS 96 hours; 5 hours of math and science; computer course.

MAJORS Accounting, agricultural business, agricultural economics, agricultural sciences, art education, biology/biological sciences, business administration/commerce/management, business education, chemistry, child care/child and family studies, computer information systems, criminal justice, data processing, elementary education, engineering (general), fire science, forestry, legal secretarial studies, liberal arts/general studies, mathematics, medical technology, music, music education, nursing, physical education, physics, practical nursing, radio and television studies, radiological technology, real estate, secretarial studies/office management, theater arts/drama, wildlife management.

LIBRARY Estelle Bain Owens Learning Resource Center and Library with 53,723 books, 116 microform titles, 115 periodicals, 1 on-line bibliographic service, 4 CD-ROMs, 1,326 records, tapes, and CDs. Acquisition spending 1994–95: $11,069.

COMPUTERS ON CAMPUS 60 computers for student use in computer center, computer labs, physics lab, library provide access to Internet. Staffed computer lab on campus.

COLLEGE LIFE Drama-theater group, choral group, student-run newspaper. ***Student services:*** personal-psychological counseling. ***Campus security:*** 24-hour emergency response devices and patrols, student patrols.

HOUSING College housing not available.

ATHLETICS Member NJCAA. ***Intercollegiate:*** baseball M(s), basketball M(s)/W(s), cross-country running M(s)/W(s), softball W(s), tennis M(s)/W(s). ***Contact:*** Mr. Doug Key, Athletic Director, 334-291-4908.

CAREER PLANNING ***Placement office:*** $29,289 operating expenditure 1994–95. ***Service:*** career counseling.

AFTER GRADUATION 18% of students completing a degree program in 1994–95 went directly on to further study.

EXPENSES FOR 1995–96 State resident tuition: $1327 full-time, $29.50 per quarter hour part-time. Nonresident tuition: $2323 full-time, $51.62 per quarter hour part-time. Georgia residents of Stewart, Harris, Muscogee, and Chattahoochee counties pay state resident tuition rates.

FINANCIAL AID ***College-administered undergrad aid 1995–96:*** 562 need-based scholarships (average $1305), 20 Federal Work-Study (averaging $2500). ***Required forms:*** FAFSA. ***Application deadline:*** continuous. ***Waivers:*** full or partial for senior citizens.

APPLYING Open admission. ***Options:*** Common Application, early entrance. ***Required for some:*** ACT, TOEFL for international students. Test scores used for counseling/placement. ***Application deadline:*** rolling. ***Notification:*** continuous. Preference given to state residents.

APPLYING/TRANSFER ***Required for some:*** college transcript. ***Entrance:*** noncompetitive. ***Application deadline:*** rolling. ***Notification:*** continuous.

CONTACT Mrs. Patricia W. Weeks, Director of Admissions, Chattahoochee Valley State Community College, Phenix City, AL 36869-7928, 334-291-4928 or toll-free 800-842-2822 (in-state). ***Fax:*** 334-291-4980.

COMMUNITY COLLEGE OF THE AIR FORCE
Maxwell Air Force Base, Alabama

UG Enrollment: 410,100	**Comprehensive Fee: $0**
Application Deadline: rolling	**Room & Board: N/App**

GENERAL Federally supported, 2-year, coed. Awards certificates, terminal associate degrees (courses conducted at 140 branch locations worldwide). Founded 1972. ***Setting:*** suburban campus. ***Total enrollment:*** 410,100. ***Faculty:*** 6,028 (all full-time, 1% with terminal degrees); student-faculty ratio is 20:1.

ENROLLMENT PROFILE 410,100 students from 58 states and territories. 16% women, 0% part-time, 0% transferred in, 0% have need-based financial aid, 0% have non-need-based financial aid, 0% international, 82% 25 or older, 15% African American. ***Areas of study chosen:*** 35% engineering and applied sciences, 34% business management and administrative services, 7% health professions and related sciences, 5% computer and

information sciences, 2% biological and life sciences, 2% communications and journalism, 2% interdisciplinary studies, 2% physical sciences, 2% psychology, 2% social sciences, 1% area and ethnic studies, 1% education, 1% fine arts, 1% foreign language and literature, 1% liberal arts/general studies, 1% library and information studies, 1% natural resource sciences. *Most popular recent majors:* aircraft and missile maintenance, electrical and electronics technologies, criminal justice.
FIRST-YEAR CLASS Of the students who applied, 100% were accepted, 100% of whom enrolled.
ACADEMIC PROGRAM Core. Calendar: continuous. 3,669 courses offered in 1995–96. Academic remediation for entering students, advanced placement, adult/continuing education programs, internships.
GENERAL DEGREE REQUIREMENTS 64 semester hours; 3 semester hours of intermediate algebra; computer course for most majors; internship (some majors).
MAJORS Accounting, aerospace sciences, aircraft and missile maintenance, air traffic control, automotive technologies, aviation administration, aviation technology, biomedical technologies, business administration/commerce/management, civil engineering technology, communication, communication equipment technology, computer technologies, construction management, criminal justice, dental services, ecology, educational administration, educational media, electrical and electronics technologies, emergency medical technology, engineering and applied sciences, environmental health sciences, environmental sciences, fire science, food sciences, food services technology, health science, health services administration, heating/refrigeration/air conditioning, hotel and restaurant management, human resources, industrial administration, information science, instrumentation technology, laboratory technologies, law enforcement/police sciences, medical assistant technologies, medical laboratory technology, metallurgical technology, meteorology, military science, modern languages, music, nuclear medical technology, occupational therapy, operating room technology, optometric/ophthalmic technologies, paralegal studies, petroleum technology, pharmacy/pharmaceutical sciences, photography, physical therapy, physiology, printing technologies, public affairs and policy studies, radiological technology, recreation and leisure services, safety and security technologies, secretarial studies/office management, social work, surveying technology, telecommunications, transportation technologies, vocational education.
LIBRARY Air Force Library Service with 5 million books, 5.4 million microform titles, 56,654 periodicals, 425,849 records, tapes, and CDs.
COMPUTERS ON CAMPUS Computers for student use in computer labs, classrooms. Staffed computer lab on campus.
COLLEGE LIFE *Student services:* legal services, health clinic, personal-psychological counseling. *Campus security:* 24-hour emergency response devices and patrols.
HOUSING 121,495 college housing spaces available; all were occupied 1995–96. Freshmen guaranteed college housing. Off-campus living permitted. *Option:* coed housing available.
ATHLETICS *Intramural:* badminton, baseball, basketball, bowling, cross-country running, football, golf, racquetball, softball, squash, table tennis (Ping-Pong), tennis, track and field, volleyball, weight lifting.
CAREER PLANNING *Service:* career counseling.
EXPENSES FOR 1996–97 Comprehensive fee: $0. Tuition, room and board, medical and dental care are provided by the U.S. government. Each student receives a salary from which to pay for uniforms, supplies, and personal expenses.
FINANCIAL AID *Acceptable forms:* United States Air Force Tuition Assistance Form. *Application deadline:* continuous. *Waivers:* full or partial for minority students and adult students.
APPLYING Open admission. *Required:* Armed Services Vocational Aptitude Battery. Test scores used for admission. *Application deadline:* rolling. *Notification:* continuous.
APPLYING/TRANSFER *Application deadline:* rolling. *Notification:* continuous.
CONTACT C.M.Sgt. Lloyd L. Wilson, Director of Admissions/Registrar, Community College of the Air Force, Maxwell Air Force Base, AL 36112-6613, 334-953-6436. *Fax:* 334-953-5231. *E-mail:* wilson@ccaf.au.af.mil. College video available.

DOUGLAS MACARTHUR STATE TECHNICAL COLLEGE
Opp, Alabama

UG Enrollment: 630	Tuition & Fees (AL Res): $936
Application Deadline: rolling	Room & Board: N/Avail

GENERAL State-supported, 2-year, coed. Awards certificates, diplomas, terminal associate degrees. Founded 1965. *Setting:* 96-acre small-town campus. *Total enrollment:* 630. *Faculty:* 26 (24 full-time, 2 part-time).
ENROLLMENT PROFILE 630 students from 2 states and territories. 52% women, 19% part-time, 94% state residents, 15% transferred in, 66% have need-based financial aid, 30% have non-need-based financial aid, 58% 25 or older, 0% Native American, 0% Hispanic, 18% African American, 0% Asian American. *Most popular recent majors:* practical nursing, secretarial studies/office management, electrical and electronics technologies.
FIRST-YEAR CLASS 175 total. Of the students who applied, 100% were accepted, 95% of whom enrolled.
ACADEMIC PROGRAM Honor code. Calendar: quarters. Academic remediation for entering students, summer session for credit, part-time degree program (daytime), co-op programs.
GENERAL DEGREE REQUIREMENTS 112 quarter hours; math requirement varies according to program.
MAJORS Accounting, automotive technologies, carpentry, computer programming, computer science, cosmetology, drafting and design, electrical and electronics technologies, practical nursing, radio and television studies, secretarial studies/office management, welding technology.
LIBRARY 3,000 books, 15 periodicals, 250 records, tapes, and CDs.
COMPUTERS ON CAMPUS 78 computers for student use in computer center, computer labs, drafting department.
HOUSING College housing not available.
CAREER PLANNING *Service:* career counseling.
EXPENSES FOR 1996–97 State resident tuition: $936 full-time, $22 per quarter hour part-time. Nonresident tuition: $1566 full-time, $37 per quarter hour part-time.
FINANCIAL AID *College-administered undergrad aid 1995–96:* need-based scholarships, 150 non-need scholarships (average $936). *Required forms:* FAFSA. *Application deadline:* continuous. *Waivers:* full or partial for senior citizens.
APPLYING Open admission. *Option:* early entrance. *Required:* school transcript, ACT ASSET. Test scores used for admission and counseling/placement. *Application deadline:* rolling. *Notification:* continuous.
APPLYING/TRANSFER *Required:* standardized test scores, high school transcript, college transcript. *Entrance:* noncompetitive. *Application deadline:* rolling. *Notification:* continuous.
CONTACT Ms. Susan Dee, Admissions Officer, Douglas MacArthur State Technical College, Opp, AL 36467-1419, 334-493-3573 Ext. 260. College video available.

DRAUGHONS JUNIOR COLLEGE
Montgomery, Alabama

UG Enrollment: 209	Tuition & Fees: $5085
Application Deadline: rolling	Room & Board: N/Avail

GENERAL Proprietary, 2-year, coed. Awards certificates, terminal associate degrees. Founded 1887. *Setting:* urban campus. *Total enrollment:* 209. *Faculty:* 30 (6 full-time, 37% with terminal degrees, 24 part-time); student-faculty ratio is 7:1.
ENROLLMENT PROFILE 209 students: 84% women, 16% men, 21% part-time, 25% transferred in, 90% have need-based financial aid, 10% have non-need-based financial aid, 70% 25 or older, 58% African American. *Areas of study chosen:* 25% liberal arts/general studies, 23% business management and administrative services, 19% health professions and related sciences, 11% computer and information sciences.
FIRST-YEAR CLASS 68 total; 170 applied, 82% were accepted, 80% of whom enrolled. 5% from top 10% of their high school class, 10% from top quarter, 25% from top half.
ACADEMIC PROGRAM Core, business curriculum. Calendar: quarters. Academic remediation for entering students, tutorials, summer session for credit, part-time degree program (evenings), co-op programs and internships.
GENERAL DEGREE REQUIREMENTS 102 quarter credits; 1 math course; computer course; internship (some majors).
MAJORS Accounting, business administration/commerce/management, computer information systems, health science, legal secretarial studies, medical assistant technologies, paralegal studies.
LIBRARY Draughons Junior College Library with 3,750 books, 22 periodicals, 2 on-line bibliographic services. Acquisition spending 1994–95: $15,000.
COMPUTERS ON CAMPUS 37 computers for student use in computer labs, library. Staffed computer lab on campus provides training in use of computers, software. Academic computing expenditure 1994–95: $50,000.
COLLEGE LIFE *Campus security:* evening security guard.
HOUSING College housing not available.
CAREER PLANNING *Placement office:* 1 full-time staff; $23,000 operating expenditure 1994–95. *Director:* Mr. Basil Manly, Director of Placement, 334-263-1013. *Services:* resume preparation, resume referral, career counseling, job interviews. Students must register sophomore year.
AFTER GRADUATION 77% of class of 1994 had job offers within 6 months.
EXPENSES FOR 1996–97 *Application fee:* $25. Tuition: $5085 full-time, $1295 per quarter part-time.
FINANCIAL AID *College-administered undergrad aid 1995–96:* need-based scholarships, non-need scholarships, low-interest long-term loans from external sources, 17 Federal Work-Study (averaging $1300). *Required forms:* FAFSA. *Application deadline:* continuous. *Payment plans:* installment, deferred payment. *Waivers:* full or partial for employees or children of employees.
APPLYING *Option:* midyear entrance. *Required:* school transcript, SAT I or ACT. Test scores used for admission and counseling/placement. *Application deadline:* rolling.
APPLYING/TRANSFER *Required:* standardized test scores, high school transcript.
CONTACT Mr. Richard Singer, Director of Admissions, Draughons Junior College, 122 Commerce Street, Montgomery, AL 36104-2538, 334-263-1013. *Fax:* 334-262-7326.

ENTERPRISE STATE JUNIOR COLLEGE
Enterprise, Alabama

UG Enrollment: 1,822	Tuition & Fees (AL Res): $1422
Application Deadline: rolling	Room & Board: N/Avail

GENERAL State-supported, 2-year, coed. Part of Alabama College System. Awards transfer associate, terminal associate degrees. Founded 1965. *Setting:* 100-acre small-town campus. *Total enrollment:* 1,822. *Faculty:* 125 (54 full-time, 71 part-time); student-faculty ratio is 20:1.
ENROLLMENT PROFILE 1,822 students: 59% women, 41% men, 41% part-time, 99% state residents, 32% transferred in, 21% 25 or older, 1% Native American, 1% Hispanic, 15% African American, 1% Asian American.
FIRST-YEAR CLASS 1,200 total. Of the students who applied, 100% were accepted, 98% of whom enrolled.
ACADEMIC PROGRAM Core. Calendar: quarters. Academic remediation for entering students, advanced placement, tutorials, honors program, summer session for credit, part-time degree program (daytime, evenings), adult/continuing education programs, internships. Off-campus study at Alabama Aviation and Technical College, Wallace State Community College.
GENERAL DEGREE REQUIREMENTS 96 quarter hours; 3 math/science courses including at least 1 course each in math and science.
MAJORS Agricultural business, aircraft and missile maintenance, automotive technologies, aviation technology, business administration/commerce/management, child care/child and family studies, communication, computer science, criminal justice, early childhood education, education, (pre)engineering sequence, finance/banking, food services management, insurance, journalism, law enforcement/police sciences, legal secretarial studies, liberal arts/general studies, marketing/retailing/merchandising, medical records services, medical secretarial studies, real estate, recreation and leisure services, retail management, science, secretarial studies/office management, social science.
LIBRARY Snuggs Hall with 45,076 books, 349 periodicals, 626 records, tapes, and CDs.
COMPUTERS ON CAMPUS 100 computers for student use in computer center, classroom labs.
COLLEGE LIFE Choral group, student-run newspaper. *Student services:* personal-psychological counseling, women's center. *Campus security:* security personnel.
HOUSING College housing not available.

Enterprise State Junior College (continued)

ATHLETICS Member NJCAA. ***Intercollegiate:*** baseball M, basketball M(s), golf M, softball W, tennis M/W, volleyball W. ***Intramural:*** basketball, football, volleyball. ***Contact:*** Dr. David Chalker, Athletic Director, 334-347-2623 Ext. 235.
CAREER PLANNING ***Placement office:*** 2 full-time staff. ***Director:*** Mr. Freddie Alford, Director of Career Development Center, 334-347-2623 Ext. 297. ***Services:*** job fairs, career counseling, careers library, job bank, job interviews.
EXPENSES FOR 1995–96 State resident tuition: $1200 full-time, $25 per quarter hour part-time. Nonresident tuition: $2400 full-time, $50 per quarter hour part-time. Part-time mandatory fees per quarter range from $5.50 to $59. Full-time mandatory fees: $222.
FINANCIAL AID ***College-administered undergrad aid 1995–96:*** need-based scholarships, non-need scholarships, low-interest long-term loans from external sources, Federal Work-Study. ***Required forms:*** institutional, FAFSA; accepted: CSS Financial Aid PROFILE. ***Application deadline:*** continuous. ***Waivers:*** full or partial for employees or children of employees and senior citizens.
APPLYING Open admission. ***Options:*** early entrance, deferred entrance, midyear entrance. ***Required:*** school transcript, TOEFL for international students. Test scores used for counseling/placement. ***Application deadline:*** rolling. ***Notification:*** continuous.
APPLYING/TRANSFER ***Required:*** college transcript. ***Entrance:*** noncompetitive. ***Application deadline:*** rolling. ***Notification:*** continuous. ***Contact:*** Mr. Freddie Alford, Senior College Liaison, 334-347-2623 Ext. 297.
CONTACT Ms. Robin Wyatt, Director of Admissions, Enterprise State Junior College, Enterprise, AL 36331-1300, 334-347-2623 Ext. 234.

GADSDEN STATE COMMUNITY COLLEGE
Gadsden, Alabama

UG Enrollment: 6,243	**Tuition & Fees (AL Res): $1437**
Application Deadline: rolling	**Room & Board: $2250**

GENERAL State-supported, 2-year, coed. Part of Alabama College System. Awards certificates, transfer associate, terminal associate degrees. Founded 1985. ***Setting:*** 275-acre small-town campus with easy access to Birmingham. ***Endowment:*** $1.3 million. ***Total enrollment:*** 6,243. ***Faculty:*** 323 (149 full-time, 7% with terminal degrees, 174 part-time); student-faculty ratio is 20:1. ***Notable Alumni:*** Dr. Garry Magouirk, physician; Jeff Cook, musician with group "Alabama"; Randy Jones, leading producer for Nationwide Insurance; James L. Brown, owner and CEO of Economy Rental Car; Dr. Lynn Wright, former chief scientist for Strategic Defense Initiative.
ENROLLMENT PROFILE 6,243 students from 10 states and territories, 38 other countries. 52% women, 48% men, 50% part-time, 96% state residents, 18% transferred in, 22% have need-based financial aid, 8% have non-need-based financial aid, 3% international, 47% 25 or older, 1% Native American, 1% Hispanic, 18% African American, 3% Asian American. ***Most popular recent majors:*** business administration/commerce/management, nursing, liberal arts/general studies.
FIRST-YEAR CLASS 4,831 applied, 100% were accepted, 80% of whom enrolled.
ACADEMIC PROGRAM Core, interdisciplinary curriculum. Calendar: quarters. 1,074 courses offered in 1995–96. Academic remediation for entering students, English as a second language program offered during academic year and summer, services for LD students, advanced placement, summer session for credit, part-time degree program (daytime, evenings, summer), external degree programs, adult/continuing education programs, co-op programs.
GENERAL DEGREE REQUIREMENTS 96 quarter hours; internship (some majors).
MAJORS Broadcasting, business administration/commerce/management, carpentry, civil engineering technology, computer graphics, computer science, court reporting, criminal justice, drafting and design, drug and alcohol/substance abuse counseling, early childhood education, electrical engineering technology, electronics engineering technology, emergency medical technology, finance/banking, fire science, heating/refrigeration/air conditioning, human services, legal secretarial studies, liberal arts/general studies, machine and tool technologies, marketing/retailing/merchandising, mechanical engineering technology, medical assistant technologies, medical laboratory technology, medical records services, medical secretarial studies, mental health/rehabilitation counseling, nursing, occupational therapy, paralegal studies, physical education, radiological technology, respiratory therapy, science, secretarial studies/office management, telecommunications, water resources.
LIBRARY Meadows Library with 72,915 books, 356 microform titles, 303 periodicals, 1,372 records, tapes, and CDs. Acquisition spending 1994–95: $72,293.
COMPUTERS ON CAMPUS 200 computers for student use in computer center, computer labs, learning resource center, classrooms, library. Staffed computer lab on campus provides training in use of computers, software.
COLLEGE LIFE Drama-theater group, choral group, student-run newspaper, radio station. ***Social organizations:*** 18 open to all. ***Most popular organizations:*** Science, Math & Engineering, Student Government Association, Circle K, Phi Beta Lambda, VICA. ***Major annual events:*** Get on Board Days, G-Day, College Fest. ***Student services:*** women's center. ***Campus security:*** 24-hour patrols.
HOUSING 110 college housing spaces available; all were occupied 1995–96. No special consideration for freshman housing applicants. Off-campus living permitted. ***Option:*** coed housing available. Resident assistants live in dorms.
ATHLETICS Member NJCAA. ***Intercollegiate:*** baseball M(s), basketball M(s)/W(s), cross-country running M(s)/W(s), golf M(s), softball W(s), tennis M(s), volleyball W(s). ***Intramural:*** basketball, volleyball. ***Contact:*** Dr. Riley Whitaker, Athletic Director, 205-549-8311.
CAREER PLANNING ***Placement office:*** $74,334 operating expenditure 1994–95. ***Director:*** Ms. Deborah Beverly, Director, Counseling Services, 205-549-8376. ***Services:*** job fairs, resume preparation, resume referral, career counseling, careers library, job bank, job interviews. 87 organizations recruited on campus 1994–95.
AFTER GRADUATION 74% of class of 1994 had job offers within 6 months.
EXPENSES FOR 1996–97 State resident tuition: $1392 full-time, $29 per quarter hour part-time. Nonresident tuition: $2592 full-time, $54 per quarter hour part-time. Part-time mandatory fees per quarter range from $5 to $15. Full-time mandatory fees: $45. College room and board: $2250.
FINANCIAL AID ***College-administered undergrad aid 1995–96:*** 250 need-based scholarships (average $650), non-need scholarships (average $1200), Federal Work-Study, part-time jobs. ***Required forms:*** institutional, FAFSA. ***Priority deadline:*** 4/15. ***Waivers:*** full or partial for employees or children of employees and senior citizens.
APPLYING Open admission. ***Options:*** early entrance, deferred entrance, midyear entrance. ***Required:*** school transcript. ***Required for some:*** ACT, TOEFL for international students. ***Application deadline:*** rolling.
APPLYING/TRANSFER ***Required:*** college transcript. ***Entrance:*** noncompetitive. ***Application deadline:*** rolling.
CONTACT Ms. Cynthia Whisenhunt, Director of Admissions and Success Center, Gadsden State Community College, Gadsden, AL 35902-0227, 205-549-8229 or toll-free 800-226-5563. ***Fax:*** 205-549-8444.

GEORGE CORLEY WALLACE STATE COMMUNITY COLLEGE
Selma, Alabama

UG Enrollment: 1,847	**Tuition & Fees (AL Res): $1176**
Application Deadline: rolling	**Room & Board: N/Avail**

GENERAL State-supported, 2-year, coed. Part of Alabama College System. Awards certificates, diplomas, transfer associate, terminal associate degrees. Founded 1966. ***Setting:*** small-town campus. ***Total enrollment:*** 1,847. ***Faculty:*** 78 (55 full-time, 23 part-time); student-faculty ratio is 18:1.
ENROLLMENT PROFILE 1,847 students from 2 states and territories, 4 other countries. 61% women, 35% part-time, 99% state residents, 5% transferred in, 31% 25 or older, 0% Native American, 0% Hispanic, 34% African American, 0% Asian American. ***Most popular recent majors:*** nursing, business education, drafting and design.
FIRST-YEAR CLASS 450 total; 581 applied, 100% were accepted, 77% of whom enrolled. 5% from top 10% of their high school class, 15% from top quarter, 45% from top half.
ACADEMIC PROGRAM Core, honor code. Calendar: quarters. Academic remediation for entering students, services for LD students, advanced placement, tutorials, summer session for credit, part-time degree program (daytime, evenings, weekends, summer), adult/continuing education programs.
GENERAL DEGREE REQUIREMENTS 98 quarter hours; 15 quarter hours of math/science; computer course.
MAJORS Accounting, biomedical technologies, business administration/commerce/management, business education, computer programming, computer science, criminal justice, drafting and design, electrical and electronics technologies, fire science, law enforcement/police sciences, machine and tool technologies, medical assistant technologies, medical laboratory technology, medical records services, nursing, occupational therapy, physical therapy, practical nursing, radiological technology, respiratory therapy, welding technology.
LIBRARY George Corley Wallace Library with 29,500 books, 200 microform titles, 50 periodicals, 800 records, tapes, and CDs.
COMPUTERS ON CAMPUS 100 computers for student use in computer center. Staffed computer lab on campus provides training in use of computers, software.
COLLEGE LIFE Choral group. 20% vote in student government elections.
HOUSING College housing not available.
ATHLETICS Member NJCAA. ***Intercollegiate:*** baseball M(s), basketball M(s), softball W(s), tennis M(s)/W(s). ***Intramural:*** badminton, basketball, softball, tennis, volleyball. ***Contact:*** Mr. Lothian Smallwood, Athletic Director, 334-875-2634 Ext. 126.
CAREER PLANNING ***Placement office:*** 3 full-time staff. ***Director:*** Mr. Steve Hickman, Career Counselor, 334-875-2634 Ext. 139. ***Services:*** career counseling, job interviews.
AFTER GRADUATION 25% of students completing a degree program in 1994–95 went directly on to further study.
EXPENSES FOR 1996–97 State resident tuition: $1176 full-time, $24 per quarter hour part-time. Nonresident tuition: $2058 full-time, $42 per quarter hour part-time.
FINANCIAL AID ***College-administered undergrad aid 1995–96:*** 12 need-based scholarships (average $1000), 100 non-need scholarships (average $1000), Federal Work-Study. ***Required forms:*** FAFSA. ***Application deadline:*** continuous to 9/1. ***Waivers:*** full or partial for minority students and senior citizens.
APPLYING Open admission. ***Options:*** Common Application, early entrance, deferred entrance. ***Required:*** ACT ASSET. Test scores used for counseling/placement. ***Application deadline:*** rolling.
APPLYING/TRANSFER ***Required:*** standardized test scores. ***Entrance:*** noncompetitive. ***Application deadline:*** rolling. ***Contact:*** Mr. Steve Hickman, Academic Counselor, 334-875-2634.
CONTACT Mr. Effell Williams, Dean of Students, George Corley Wallace State Community College, 3000 Earl Goodwin Parkway, Selma, AL 36702-1049, 334-875-2634 Ext. 135. ***Fax:*** 334-874-7116. College video available.

GEORGE C. WALLACE STATE COMMUNITY COLLEGE
Dothan, Alabama

UG Enrollment: 4,000	**Tuition & Fees (AL Res): $1320**
Application Deadline: rolling	**Room & Board: N/Avail**

GENERAL State-supported, 2-year, coed. Awards certificates, transfer associate, terminal associate degrees. Founded 1949. ***Setting:*** 200-acre rural campus. ***Total enrollment:*** 4,000. ***Faculty:*** 180.
ENROLLMENT PROFILE 4,000 students from 31 states and territories, 4 other countries. 58% women, 52% part-time, 92% state residents, 12% transferred in, 43% 25 or older, 0% Native American, 1% Hispanic, 13% African American, 1% Asian American.
FIRST-YEAR CLASS Of the students who applied, 99% were accepted.
ACADEMIC PROGRAM Core. Calendar: quarters. Academic remediation for entering students, advanced placement, summer session for credit, part-time degree program (daytime, evenings), adult/continuing education programs, co-op programs and internships. Off-campus study at University of Alabama at Birmingham, Alabama Aviation and Technical College.
GENERAL DEGREE REQUIREMENTS 96 quarter hours; 1 math course; computer course; internship (some majors).
MAJORS Accounting, agricultural technologies, automotive technologies, business administration/commerce/management, carpentry, computer science, criminal justice, data processing, drafting and design, electrical and electronics technologies, electronics engineering technology, emergency medical technology, graphic arts, heating/refrigeration/air

154

Peterson's Guide to Two-Year Colleges 1997

conditioning, law enforcement/police sciences, liberal arts/general studies, machine and tool technologies, medical laboratory technology, medical secretarial studies, nursing, optical technologies, radio and television studies, respiratory therapy, secretarial studies/office management, welding technology.
LIBRARY 45,353 books, 1,372 microform titles, 399 periodicals, 2,964 records, tapes, and CDs.
COMPUTERS ON CAMPUS 75 computers for student use in computer center. Staffed computer lab on campus.
COLLEGE LIFE Drama-theater group, student-run newspaper. *Student services:* personal-psychological counseling, women's center.
HOUSING College housing not available.
ATHLETICS Member NJCAA. *Intercollegiate:* basketball M(s)/W(s), golf M, tennis M(s)/W(s). *Intramural:* basketball, tennis, volleyball. *Contact:* Mr. Gene Dews, Athletic Director, 334-983-3521 Ext. 216.
CAREER PLANNING *Director:* Dr. Jane McMurty, Director of Counseling, 334-983-3521 Ext. 283. *Service:* career counseling.
EXPENSES FOR 1996–97 State resident tuition: $1125 full-time, $25 per quarter hour part-time. Nonresident tuition: $2250 full-time, $50 per quarter hour part-time. Part-time mandatory fees: $6.50 per quarter hour. Full-time mandatory fees: $195.
FINANCIAL AID *College-administered undergrad aid 1995–96:* need-based scholarships, 100 non-need scholarships (average $600), Federal Work-Study. *Required forms:* institutional, FAFSA; accepted: CSS Financial Aid PROFILE. *Application deadline:* continuous.
APPLYING Open admission. *Option:* early entrance. *Required for some:* TOEFL for international students, CAT (for LPN). Test scores used for counseling/placement. *Application deadline:* rolling.
APPLYING/TRANSFER *Required for some:* standardized test scores. *Entrance:* noncompetitive. *Application deadline:* rolling.
CONTACT Mrs. Brenda Barnes, Director of Admissions and Records, George C. Wallace State Community College, Dothan, AL 36303, 334-983-3521 Ext. 302 or toll-free 800-821-1542 (in-state).

HARRY M. AYERS STATE TECHNICAL COLLEGE
Anniston, Alabama

UG Enrollment: 800	Tuition & Fees (AL Res): $966
Application Deadline: rolling	Room & Board: N/Avail

GENERAL State-supported, 2-year, coed. Awards certificates, diplomas, transfer associate, terminal associate degrees. Founded 1966. *Setting:* 25-acre small-town campus with easy access to Birmingham. *Total enrollment:* 800. *Faculty:* 39 (25 full-time, 14 part-time); student-faculty ratio is 16:1.
ENROLLMENT PROFILE 800 students from 2 states and territories. 44% women, 32% part-time, 99% state residents, 7% transferred in, 51% 25 or older, 0% Native American, 1% Hispanic, 10% African American. *Areas of study chosen:* 68% engineering and applied sciences.
FIRST-YEAR CLASS 310 applied, 91% were accepted, 83% of whom enrolled. 15% from top 10% of their high school class, 25% from top quarter, 50% from top half.
ACADEMIC PROGRAM Calendar: quarters. Services for LD students, advanced placement, part-time degree program (daytime, evenings).
GENERAL DEGREE REQUIREMENTS 103 quarter hours; math requirement varies according to program.
MAJORS Drafting and design, electrical and electronics technologies, heating/refrigeration/air conditioning, machine and tool technologies.
LIBRARY Cain Learning Resource Center with 4,645 books, 120 periodicals, 1 CD-ROM.
COMPUTERS ON CAMPUS Computers for student use in computer labs, business education, computer science buildings, library. Staffed computer lab on campus provides training in use of computers, software.
COLLEGE LIFE *Student services:* personal-psychological counseling.
HOUSING College housing not available.
CAREER PLANNING *Placement office:* 1 full-time, 2 part-time staff. *Director:* Mr. T. David Cunningham, Coordinator, Student Services, 205-835-5400. *Services:* resume preparation, resume referral, career counseling, careers library, job bank.
EXPENSES FOR 1995–96 State resident tuition: $966 full-time, $23 per quarter hour part-time. Nonresident tuition: $1691 full-time, $40.25 per quarter hour part-time. Georgia residents pay state resident tuition rates.
FINANCIAL AID *College-administered undergrad aid 1995–96:* need-based scholarships, non-need scholarships. *Required forms:* FAFSA. *Priority deadline:* 8/31.
APPLYING Open admission. *Option:* deferred entrance. *Required:* school transcript, ACT ASSET. Test scores used for counseling/placement. *Application deadline:* rolling. *Notification:* continuous.
APPLYING/TRANSFER *Required:* standardized test scores, high school transcript, college transcript. *Entrance:* noncompetitive. *Application deadline:* rolling. *Notification:* continuous.
CONTACT Mr. Charles Chandler, Acting Director of Student Services, Harry M. Ayers State Technical College, Anniston, AL 36202-1647, 205-835-5410.

HERZING COLLEGE OF BUSINESS AND TECHNOLOGY
Birmingham, Alabama

UG Enrollment: 425	Tuition & Fees: $5625
Application Deadline: rolling	Room & Board: N/Avail

GENERAL Proprietary, 2-year, coed. Part of Herzing Institutes, Inc. Awards terminal associate degrees. Founded 1965. *Setting:* urban campus. *Total enrollment:* 425. *Faculty:* 18 (12 full-time, 100% with terminal degrees, 6 part-time); student-faculty ratio is 21:1.
ENROLLMENT PROFILE 425 students from 3 states and territories, 4 other countries. 60% women, 15% part-time, 92% state residents, 20% transferred in, 1% international, 70% 25 or older, 0% Native American, 0% Hispanic, 40% African American, 0% Asian American. *Areas of study chosen:* 50% business management and administrative services, 25% computer and information sciences, 25% engineering and applied sciences.
FIRST-YEAR CLASS 145 total; 180 applied, 81% were accepted, 100% of whom enrolled.
ACADEMIC PROGRAM Core, job training curriculum, honor code. Calendar: quarters. Advanced placement, self-designed majors, tutorials, summer session for credit, external degree programs, adult/continuing education programs, co-op programs and internships.
GENERAL DEGREE REQUIREMENTS 106 credits; computer course.
MAJORS Business machine technologies, computer information systems, computer programming, computer science, data processing, electrical and electronics technologies, legal secretarial studies, secretarial studies/office management.
COMPUTERS ON CAMPUS 80 computers for student use in computer center, computer labs, classrooms.
COLLEGE LIFE *Student services:* personal-psychological counseling, women's center. *Campus security:* late-night transport-escort service, security guard.
HOUSING College housing not available.
CAREER PLANNING *Placement office:* 1 full-time, 1 part-time staff. *Director:* Ms. Cindy Johnson, Student Services Director, 205-933-8536. *Services:* job fairs, resume preparation, resume referral, career counseling, careers library, job bank, job interviews.
EXPENSES FOR 1996–97 *Application fee:* $20. Tuition: $5625 full-time. Part-time tuition per quarter ranges from $495 to $950.
FINANCIAL AID *College-administered undergrad aid 1995–96:* need-based scholarships, low-interest long-term loans from external sources, Federal Work-Study. *Required forms:* institutional; accepted: CSS Financial Aid PROFILE, FAFSA. *Application deadline:* continuous. *Payment plan:* installment. *Waivers:* full or partial for employees or children of employees.
APPLYING *Options:* early entrance, deferred entrance, midyear entrance. *Recommended:* TOEFL for international students. Test scores used for admission. *Application deadline:* rolling. *Notification:* continuous.
APPLYING/TRANSFER *Entrance:* minimally difficult. *Application deadline:* rolling. *Notification:* continuous. *Contact:* Mr. Michael A. Cates, Director of Admissions, 205-933-8536.
CONTACT Mr. Michael A. Cates, Director of Admissions, Herzing College of Business and Technology, 280 West Valley Avenue, Birmingham, AL 35209, 205-916-2800. College video available.

ITT TECHNICAL INSTITUTE
Birmingham, Alabama

UG Enrollment: 133	Tuition: $15,599/deg prog
Application Deadline: N/R	Room & Board: N/Avail

GENERAL Proprietary, 2-year, coed. Part of ITT Educational Services, Inc. Awards transfer associate, terminal associate degrees. Founded 1994. *Setting:* suburban campus. *Total enrollment:* 133. *Faculty:* 8 (5 full-time, 12% with terminal degrees, 3 part-time); student-faculty ratio is 16:1.
ENROLLMENT PROFILE 133 students: 13% women, 87% men, 0% part-time, 100% state residents, 1% transferred in, 0% international, 0% Native American, 0% Hispanic, 55% African American, 1% Asian American. *Areas of study chosen:* 100% engineering and applied sciences.
FIRST-YEAR CLASS 112 total; 314 applied, 36% were accepted, 100% of whom enrolled. 5% from top 10% of their high school class, 10% from top quarter, 55% from top half.
ACADEMIC PROGRAM Core, technical-based curriculum, honor code. Calendar: quarters. 2 courses offered in 1995–96; average class size 15 in required courses. Academic remediation for entering students, tutorials.
GENERAL DEGREE REQUIREMENT 90 credit hours.
MAJORS Drafting and design, electronics engineering technology.
LIBRARY Learning Resource Center with 200 books, 15 periodicals.
COMPUTERS ON CAMPUS 25 computers for student use in learning resource center, classrooms.
COLLEGE LIFE Student-run newspaper. 100% vote in student government elections. *Most popular organizations:* National Vocational-Technical Honor Society, ISCET. *Major annual events:* Spring Fling, Winter Festival, Blood Drives. *Campus security:* 24-hour emergency response devices.
HOUSING College housing not available.
CAREER PLANNING *Placement office:* 1 full-time staff. *Director:* Ms. Susan Gann, Director of Placement, 205-991-5410. *Services:* job fairs, resume preparation, resume referral, career counseling, careers library, job bank, job interviews.
EXPENSES FOR 1996–97 *Application fee:* $100. Tuition per degree program ranges from $15,599 to $17,690. Full-time mandatory fees range from $540 to $720. Tuition guaranteed not to increase for student's term of enrollment.
FINANCIAL AID *College-administered undergrad aid 1995–96:* need-based scholarships, non-need scholarships, part-time jobs. *Required forms:* FAFSA. *Priority deadline:* 9/1. *Payment plan:* installment.
APPLYING *Option:* deferred entrance. *Required:* school transcript, interview, CPAt. *Recommended:* recommendations. Test scores used for admission. *Notification:* continuous.
APPLYING/TRANSFER *Required:* standardized test scores, high school transcript, interview, college transcript. *Recommended:* recommendations. *Contact:* Mr. George Price, Director of Education, 205-991-5410.
CONTACT Mr. Darrell Gonzales, Director of Recruitment, ITT Technical Institute, Birmingham, AL 35242, 205-991-5410 or toll-free 800-488-7033 (in-state). *Fax:* 205-991-5025. College video available.

JAMES H. FAULKNER STATE COMMUNITY COLLEGE
Bay Minette, Alabama

UG Enrollment: 3,042	Tuition & Fees (AL Res): $1200
Application Deadline: rolling	Room & Board: $2175

GENERAL State-supported, 2-year, coed. Awards certificates, transfer associate, terminal associate degrees. Founded 1965. *Setting:* 105-acre small-town campus. *Educational*

Peterson's Guide to Two-Year Colleges 1997

James H. Faulkner State Community College (continued)

spending 1994–95: $1404 per undergrad. ***Total enrollment:*** 3,042. ***Faculty:*** 157 (52 full-time, 100% with terminal degrees, 105 part-time); student-faculty ratio is 22:1.
ENROLLMENT PROFILE 3,042 students from 12 states and territories, 4 other countries. 61% women, 40% part-time, 98% state residents, 12% transferred in, 32% have need-based financial aid, 5% have non-need-based financial aid, 1% international, 39% 25 or older, 1% Native American, 1% Hispanic, 11% African American, 1% Asian American.
FIRST-YEAR CLASS 1,695 total; 2,000 applied, 90% were accepted, 85% of whom enrolled.
ACADEMIC PROGRAM Calendar: quarters. Academic remediation for entering students, services for LD students, advanced placement, honors program, summer session for credit, part-time degree program (daytime, evenings, summer), adult/continuing education programs, co-op programs and internships.
GENERAL DEGREE REQUIREMENTS 96 quarter hours; computer course; internship (some majors).
MAJORS Commercial art, computer management, computer science, court reporting, culinary arts, dental services, environmental engineering technology, fashion merchandising, finance/banking, fire science, hospitality services, hotel and restaurant management, landscaping/grounds maintenance, legal secretarial studies, liberal arts/general studies, marketing/retailing/merchandising.
LIBRARY Austin Meadows Library with 52,311 books, 212 microform titles, 232 periodicals, 1,234 records, tapes, and CDs. Acquisition spending 1994–95: $108,481.
COMPUTERS ON CAMPUS 175 computers for student use in computer center, computer labs, learning resource center, counseling center, business education department, library. Staffed computer lab on campus provides training in use of computers, software. Academic computing expenditure 1994–95: $165,431.
COLLEGE LIFE Orientation program (2 days, no cost, parents included). Drama-theater group, choral group, student-run newspaper. 10% vote in student government elections. ***Student services:*** personal-psychological counseling. ***Campus security:*** 24-hour patrols, controlled dormitory access.
HOUSING 277 college housing spaces available; all were occupied 1995–96. No special consideration for freshman housing applicants. Off-campus living permitted. ***Option:*** single-sex housing available. Resident assistants live in dorms.
ATHLETICS Member NJCAA. ***Intercollegiate:*** baseball M, basketball M(s)/W(s), golf M(s), softball W, tennis M(s)/W(s), volleyball W(s). ***Intramural:*** basketball, football, racquetball, tennis, volleyball. ***Contact:*** Mr. Jack Robertson, Division Chair/Athletic Director, 334-580-2135.
CAREER PLANNING ***Placement office:*** 2 full-time staff; $703,192 operating expenditure 1994–95. ***Director:*** Dr. Brenda Kennedy, Dean of Student Development, 334-580-2180. ***Services:*** job fairs, resume preparation, career counseling, careers library.
AFTER GRADUATION 72% of students completing a degree program in 1994–95 went directly on to further study.
EXPENSES FOR 1996–97 State resident tuition: $1200 full-time, $25 per quarter hour part-time. Nonresident tuition: $2400 full-time, $50 per quarter hour part-time. College room and board: $2175.
FINANCIAL AID ***College-administered undergrad aid 1995–96:*** need-based scholarships, non-need scholarships, 150 Federal Work-Study (averaging $1500). ***Required forms:*** institutional, FAFSA. ***Priority deadline:*** 7/1. ***Waivers:*** full or partial for employees or children of employees and senior citizens. ***Notification:*** continuous.
APPLYING Open admission. ***Options:*** early entrance, deferred entrance, midyear entrance. ***Required:*** school transcript, TOEFL for international students. ***Recommended:*** ACT ASSET. Test scores used for counseling/placement. ***Application deadline:*** rolling. ***Notification:*** continuous until 9/16.
APPLYING/TRANSFER ***Required:*** high school transcript, college transcript. ***Application deadline:*** rolling. ***Notification:*** continuous until 9/16. ***Contact:*** Ms. Linda Brown, Director of Admissions, 334-580-2134.
CONTACT Ms. Linda Brown, Director of Admissions, James H. Faulkner State Community College, Bay Minette, AL 36507-2619, 334-937-9581 Ext. 2134 or toll-free 800-231-3752 (in-state). ***Fax:*** 334-937-3404.

JEFFERSON DAVIS COMMUNITY COLLEGE
Brewton, Alabama

UG Enrollment: 1,600	**Tuition & Fees (AL Res): $1125**
Application Deadline: rolling	**Room & Board: N/Avail**

GENERAL State-supported, 2-year, coed. Awards transfer associate, terminal associate degrees. Founded 1965. ***Setting:*** 100-acre small-town campus. ***Total enrollment:*** 1,600. ***Faculty:*** 66 (41 full-time, 25 part-time); student-faculty ratio is 25:1.
ENROLLMENT PROFILE 1,600 students from 2 states and territories. 65% women, 30% part-time, 85% state residents, 5% transferred in, 30% 25 or older, 1% Native American, 25% African American. ***Most popular recent majors:*** nursing, liberal arts/general studies, business administration/commerce/management.
FIRST-YEAR CLASS 530 total. Of the students who applied, 100% were accepted, 80% of whom enrolled. 20% from top 10% of their high school class, 70% from top half.
ACADEMIC PROGRAM Calendar: quarters. Academic remediation for entering students, services for LD students, summer session for credit, part-time degree program (daytime, evenings, summer), adult/continuing education programs.
GENERAL DEGREE REQUIREMENTS 96 credit hours; 3 math/science courses; computer course.
MAJORS Applied art, biology/biological sciences, business administration/commerce/management, education, elementary education, finance/banking, history, law enforcement/police sciences, liberal arts/general studies, marketing/retailing/merchandising, medical assistant technologies, music, nursing, physical education, political science/government, recreation and leisure services, science, secretarial studies/office management, theater arts/drama.
LIBRARY 926 books, 330 periodicals, 1,204 records, tapes, and CDs.
COMPUTERS ON CAMPUS 40 computers for student use in business department.
COLLEGE LIFE ***Student services:*** personal-psychological counseling.
HOUSING College housing not available.
ATHLETICS Member NJCAA. ***Intercollegiate:*** basketball M(s)/W(s), golf M(s), tennis M(s)/W(s). ***Intramural:*** basketball, golf, gymnastics, swimming and diving, tennis, track and field, volleyball. ***Contact:*** Mr. Michael Cannon, Athletic Director, 334-368-8118.
CAREER PLANNING ***Director:*** Ms. Sherry Martin, Director of Success Center, 334-867-4832 Ext. 72. ***Service:*** career counseling.
EXPENSES FOR 1995–96 State resident tuition: $990 full-time, $22 per credit hour part-time. Nonresident tuition: $1980 full-time, $44 per credit hour part-time. Part-time mandatory fees: $6 per credit hour. Full-time mandatory fees: $135.
FINANCIAL AID ***College-administered undergrad aid 1995–96:*** need-based scholarships, non-need scholarships, low-interest long-term loans from external sources, Federal Work-Study. ***Application deadline:*** continuous. ***Waivers:*** full or partial for employees or children of employees and senior citizens.
APPLYING Open admission. ***Option:*** early entrance. ***Required:*** school transcript, ACT ASSET. Test scores used for counseling/placement. ***Application deadline:*** rolling.
APPLYING/TRANSFER ***Required:*** college transcript. ***Application deadline:*** rolling.
CONTACT Ms. Cynthia M. Moore, Assistant Dean for Admissions and Records, Jefferson Davis Community College, Brewton, AL 36426, 334-867-4832 Ext. 45.

JEFFERSON STATE COMMUNITY COLLEGE
Birmingham, Alabama

UG Enrollment: 6,749	**Tuition & Fees (AL Res): $1425**
Application Deadline: rolling	**Room & Board: N/Avail**

GENERAL State-supported, 2-year, coed. Part of Alabama College System. Awards transfer associate, terminal associate degrees. Founded 1965. ***Setting:*** 234-acre suburban campus. ***Endowment:*** $850,000. ***Total enrollment:*** 6,749. ***Faculty:*** 268 (108 full-time, 23% with terminal degrees, 160 part-time); student-faculty ratio is 25:1.
ENROLLMENT PROFILE 6,749 students: 62% women, 38% men, 59% part-time, 99% state residents, 18% have need-based financial aid, 18% have non-need-based financial aid, 1% international, 46% 25 or older, 1% Native American, 1% Hispanic, 12% African American, 1% Asian American. ***Areas of study chosen:*** 59% liberal arts/general studies, 16% health professions and related sciences, 10% business management and administrative services, 5% computer and information sciences, 3% vocational and home economics, 2% engineering and applied sciences, 1% agriculture. ***Most popular recent majors:*** nursing, radiological technology, funeral service.
FIRST-YEAR CLASS 1,602 total; 2,910 applied, 100% were accepted, 55% of whom enrolled.
ACADEMIC PROGRAM Core, university parallel and career program curricula, honor code. Calendar: quarters. 501 courses offered in 1995–96. Academic remediation for entering students, services for LD students, advanced placement, honors program, summer session for credit, part-time degree program (daytime, evenings, summer), adult/continuing education programs, internships. ROTC: Army (c), Air Force (c).
GENERAL DEGREE REQUIREMENTS 96 quarter hours; 5 quarter hours of math/science; computer course for most majors; internship (some majors).
MAJORS Accounting, agricultural technologies, architectural technologies, biomedical technologies, business administration/commerce/management, child psychology/child development, civil engineering technology, computer programming, computer science, construction management, criminal justice, culinary arts, electronics engineering technology, (pre)engineering sequence, fashion merchandising, finance/banking, fire science, food services management, funeral service, hospitality services, interior design, law enforcement/police sciences, liberal arts/general studies, marketing/retailing/merchandising, mechanical engineering technology, medical laboratory technology, medical records services, nursing, occupational therapy, physical therapy, postal management, radiological technology, real estate, recreation and leisure services, retail management, secretarial studies/office management.
LIBRARY James B. Allen Library with 73,652 books, 8,269 microform titles, 274 periodicals, 3,698 records, tapes, and CDs. Acquisition spending 1994–95: $21,652.
COMPUTERS ON CAMPUS 475 computers for student use in computer labs, learning resource center, classrooms, library. Staffed computer lab on campus provides training in use of computers, software. Academic computing expenditure 1994–95: $175,000.
COLLEGE LIFE Drama-theater group, choral group, student-run newspaper, radio station. ***Social organizations:*** 20 open to all. ***Most popular organizations:*** Student Government Association, African-American Society, Baptist Campus Ministries, Jefferson State Ambassadors, Jefferson State Singers. ***Major annual events:*** Martin Luther King/Black History Celebration, Jeff/Club Fest, Haunted Trail. ***Student services:*** women's center. ***Campus security:*** 24-hour patrols.
HOUSING College housing not available.
ATHLETICS Member NJCAA. ***Intercollegiate:*** baseball M(s), tennis M(s)/W(s). ***Intramural:*** badminton, basketball, bowling, soccer, softball, tennis, volleyball. ***Contact:*** Mr. Don Green, Athletic Director, 205-853-1200 Ext. 8523.
CAREER PLANNING ***Placement office:*** 1 full-time staff; $68,500 operating expenditure 1994–95. ***Director:*** Ms. Paula Gray, Career Counseling and Placement, 205-853-1200. ***Services:*** resume preparation, careers library, job bank, job interviews. 13 organizations recruited on campus 1994–95.
EXPENSES FOR 1996–97 State resident tuition: $1200 full-time, $25 per quarter hour part-time. Nonresident tuition: $2400 full-time, $50 per quarter hour part-time. Part-time mandatory fees per quarter range from $9 to $49. Full-time mandatory fees: $225.
FINANCIAL AID ***College-administered undergrad aid 1995–96:*** need-based scholarships, 190 non-need scholarships (average $1350), short-term loans (average $300), low-interest long-term loans from external sources (average $2625), Federal Work-Study. ***Required forms:*** institutional, FAFSA. ***Priority deadline:*** 5/1. ***Waivers:*** full or partial for employees or children of employees and senior citizens.
APPLYING Open admission. ***Options:*** early entrance, deferred entrance, midyear entrance. ***Required:*** TOEFL for international students. ***Recommended:*** ACT. ***Required for some:*** school transcript. Test scores used for counseling/placement. ***Application deadline:*** rolling. ***Notification:*** continuous.
APPLYING/TRANSFER ***Recommended:*** standardized test scores. ***Required for some:*** high school transcript. ***Entrance:*** noncompetitive. ***Contact:*** Dr. Rosann Dulce, Registrar, 205-853-1200 Ext. 6069.
CONTACT Dr. Linda Hooten, Associate Dean, Academic Services, Jefferson State Community College, Birmingham, AL 35215-3098, 205-853-1200 Ext. 7948 or toll-free 800-239-5900 (in-state). ***Fax:*** 205-853-0340.

J. F. DRAKE STATE TECHNICAL COLLEGE
Huntsville, Alabama

UG Enrollment: 688 **Tuition & Fees (AL Res): $1248**
Application Deadline: rolling **Room & Board: N/Avail**

GENERAL State-supported, 2-year, coed. Part of State of Alabama Department of Postsecondary Education. Awards certificates, diplomas, transfer associate degrees. Founded 1961. ***Setting:*** 6-acre urban campus. ***Total enrollment:*** 688. ***Faculty:*** 46 (25 full-time, 21 part-time).

ENROLLMENT PROFILE 688 students: 25% women, 30% part-time, 98% state residents, 10% transferred in, 40% African American. ***Most popular recent majors:*** drafting and design, electrical and electronics technologies, computer information systems.

FIRST-YEAR CLASS 230 total; 250 applied, 95% were accepted, 97% of whom enrolled.

ACADEMIC PROGRAM Calendar: quarters. Academic remediation for entering students, services for LD students, co-op programs.

GENERAL DEGREE REQUIREMENTS 96 credit hours; math requirement varies according to program; computer course for business-related majors.

MAJORS Accounting, computer information systems, drafting and design, electrical and electronics technologies, graphic arts, machine and tool technologies, secretarial studies/office management.

COMPUTERS ON CAMPUS 50 computers for student use in business department provide access to main academic computer. Staffed computer lab on campus provides training in use of computers, software.

COLLEGE LIFE Student-run newspaper. 80% vote in student government elections. ***Most popular organizations:*** Phi Beta Lambda, Vocational Industrial Clubs of America. ***Campus security:*** 24-hour patrols.

HOUSING College housing not available.

CAREER PLANNING ***Director:*** Dr. Drexell Boothe, Director of Student Services, 205-539-8161 Ext. 120. ***Service:*** career counseling.

EXPENSES FOR 1996–97 State resident tuition: $1152 (minimum) full-time, $24 per credit hour part-time. Nonresident tuition: $2304 (minimum) full-time, $48 per credit hour part-time. Part-time mandatory fees: $2 per credit hour. Full-time mandatory fees: $96.

FINANCIAL AID ***College-administered undergrad aid 1995–96:*** low-interest long-term loans from external sources. ***Required forms:*** institutional, FAFSA. ***Application deadline:*** continuous. ***Payment plan:*** tuition prepayment.

APPLYING Open admission. ***Option:*** deferred entrance. ***Required:*** school transcript, ACT ASSET. Test scores used for counseling/placement. ***Application deadline:*** rolling.

APPLYING/TRANSFER ***Required:*** college transcript.

CONTACT Mrs. Mary Malone, Admissions Officer, J. F. Drake State Technical College, 3421 Meridian Street North, Huntsville, AL 35811-1584, 205-539-8161 Ext. 110.

JOHN C. CALHOUN STATE COMMUNITY COLLEGE
Decatur, Alabama

UG Enrollment: 7,514 **Tuition & Fees (AL Res): $1449**
Application Deadline: rolling **Room & Board: N/Avail**

GENERAL State-supported, 2-year, coed. Part of Alabama College System. Awards certificates, transfer associate, terminal associate degrees. Founded 1965. ***Setting:*** 98-acre rural campus. ***Total enrollment:*** 7,514. ***Faculty:*** 379 (147 full-time, 18% with terminal degrees, 232 part-time); student-faculty ratio is 20:1.

ENROLLMENT PROFILE 7,514 students: 54% women, 57% part-time, 99% state residents, 23% transferred in, 24% have need-based financial aid, 6% have non-need-based financial aid, 1% international, 46% 25 or older, 1% Native American, 1% Hispanic, 11% African American, 1% Asian American. ***Areas of study chosen:*** 14% interdisciplinary studies, 7% business management and administrative services, 6% health professions and related sciences, 3% computer and information sciences, 3% engineering and applied sciences, 2% education, 2% mathematics, 1% agriculture, 1% biological and life sciences, 1% communications and journalism, 1% fine arts, 1% performing arts, 1% premed, 1% prevet. ***Most popular recent majors:*** nursing, business administration/commerce/management, education.

FIRST-YEAR CLASS 1,565 total; 2,162 applied, 100% were accepted, 72% of whom enrolled.

ACADEMIC PROGRAM Core, interdisciplinary curriculum. Calendar: quarters. 709 courses offered in 1995–96. Academic remediation for entering students, services for LD students, advanced placement, tutorials, honors program, summer session for credit, part-time degree program (daytime, evenings, summer), adult/continuing education programs, co-op programs. ROTC: Army (c).

GENERAL DEGREE REQUIREMENTS 96 quarter hours; internship (some majors).

MAJORS Accounting, agricultural sciences, art education, automotive technologies, biology/biological sciences, biomedical technologies, business administration/commerce/management, business education, carpentry, chemistry, commercial art, computer information systems, corrections, cosmetology, criminal justice, dental services, drafting and design, education, electrical and electronics technologies, elementary education, emergency medical technology, English, fire science, graphic arts, heating/refrigeration/air conditioning, industrial engineering technology, insurance, law enforcement/police sciences, legal studies, liberal arts/general studies, machine and tool technologies, marketing/retailing/merchandising, mathematics, mechanical engineering technology, medical assistant technologies, medical laboratory technology, music education, nursing, paralegal studies, photography, physical education, practical nursing, quality control technology, radiological technology, real estate, recreation and leisure services, respiratory therapy, retail management, secretarial studies/office management, theater arts/drama, transportation technologies, welding technology.

LIBRARY Brewer Library plus 1 other, with 48,605 books, 216 microform titles, 222 periodicals, 10 CD-ROMs, 3,233 records, tapes, and CDs. Acquisition spending 1994–95: $42,165.

COMPUTERS ON CAMPUS 160 computers for student use in computer center, business, English buildings, library.

COLLEGE LIFE Drama-theater group, choral group, student-run newspaper. ***Social organizations:*** 31 open to all. ***Most popular organizations:*** Student Government Association, Black Students Alliance, College Host and Hostess, Students Against Drunk Drivers (SADD), Campus Ministries. ***Major annual events:*** Homecoming, Spring Fest, Comedy Club. ***Student services:*** health clinic, personal-psychological counseling. ***Campus security:*** 24-hour patrols.

HOUSING College housing not available.

ATHLETICS Member NJCAA. ***Intercollegiate:*** baseball M(s), basketball M(s)/W(s), softball W(s). ***Intramural:*** basketball. ***Contact:*** Dr. Jo O'Neal, Dean of Students, 205-306-2500.

CAREER PLANNING ***Placement office:*** 2 full-time staff. ***Director:*** Ms. Pat Swinford, Counselor, Career Services, 205-306-2636. ***Services:*** job fairs, resume preparation, resume referral, career counseling, careers library, job bank, job interviews. 40 organizations recruited on campus 1994–95.

EXPENSES FOR 1995–96 State resident tuition: $1269 full-time, $27 per quarter hour part-time. Nonresident tuition: $2303 full-time, $49 per quarter hour part-time. Part-time mandatory fees: $60 per quarter. Full-time mandatory fees: $180.

FINANCIAL AID ***College-administered undergrad aid 1995–96:*** need-based scholarships, 500 non-need scholarships, short-term loans (average $100), low-interest long-term loans from external sources (average $2000), 50 Federal Work-Study (averaging $1500), 13 part-time jobs. ***Required forms:*** institutional, FAFSA; required for some: state; accepted: CSS Financial Aid PROFILE. ***Priority deadline:*** 4/1. ***Waivers:*** full or partial for employees or children of employees and senior citizens.

APPLYING Open admission except for practical nursing, dental services programs. ***Options:*** early entrance, deferred entrance, midyear entrance. ***Required:*** TOEFL for international students. Test scores used for counseling/placement. ***Application deadline:*** rolling. ***Notification:*** continuous.

APPLYING/TRANSFER ***Application deadline:*** rolling. ***Notification:*** continuous. ***Contact:*** Mr. Wayne Tosh, Director of Admissions and Registrar, 205-306-2500.

CONTACT Mr. Wayne Tosh, Director of Admissions and Registrar, John C. Calhoun State Community College, Decatur, AL 35609-2216, 205-306-2500 or toll-free 800-626-3628 (in-state). ***Fax:*** 205-306-2885.

JOHN M. PATTERSON STATE TECHNICAL COLLEGE
Montgomery, Alabama

UG Enrollment: 1,066 **Tuition & Fees (AL Res): $1260**
Application Deadline: rolling **Room & Board: N/Avail**

GENERAL State-supported, 2-year, coed. Part of Alabama College System. Awards certificates, diplomas, terminal associate degrees. Founded 1962. ***Setting:*** 40-acre urban campus. ***Total enrollment:*** 1,066. ***Faculty:*** 63 (42 full-time, 21 part-time); student-faculty ratio is 20:1.

ENROLLMENT PROFILE 1,066 students: 41% women, 59% men, 46% part-time, 99% state residents, 27% transferred in, 11% have non-need-based financial aid, 1% international, 52% 25 or older, 1% Native American, 1% Hispanic, 49% African American, 1% Asian American. ***Most popular recent majors:*** cosmetology, computer information systems.

FIRST-YEAR CLASS 373 total; 846 applied, 44% of whom enrolled.

ACADEMIC PROGRAM Core, honor code. Calendar: quarters. 421 courses offered in 1995–96; average class size 25 in required courses. Academic remediation for entering students, services for LD students, advanced placement, summer session for credit, part-time degree program (daytime, evenings, summer), adult/continuing education programs, co-op programs and internships.

GENERAL DEGREE REQUIREMENTS 114 credit hours; math/science requirements vary according to program; computer course (varies by major).

MAJORS Automotive technologies, carpentry, computer information systems, construction technologies, cosmetology, drafting and design, electrical and electronics technologies, heating/refrigeration/air conditioning, industrial and heavy equipment maintenance, instrumentation technology, machine and tool technologies, plumbing, printing technologies, textiles and clothing, welding technology.

COMPUTERS ON CAMPUS 116 computers for student use in computer center, computer labs, reading lab, classrooms provide access to main academic computer. Staffed computer lab on campus provides training in use of computers, software.

COLLEGE LIFE ***Major annual event:*** Student Appreciation Day. ***Campus security:*** 24-hour emergency response devices and patrols.

HOUSING College housing not available.

CAREER PLANNING ***Placement office:*** 2 full-time staff. ***Director:*** Mr. Jim Randolph, Coordinator, Co-Op and Placement, 334-288-1080 Ext. 224. ***Services:*** resume preparation, careers library, job bank, job interviews.

AFTER GRADUATION 81% of class of 1994 had job offers within 6 months.

EXPENSES FOR 1996–97 State resident tuition: $1260 full-time. Nonresident tuition: $2520 full-time. Part-time tuition per quarter ranges from $57 to $312 for state residents, $114 to $624 for nonresidents.

FINANCIAL AID ***College-administered undergrad aid 1995–96:*** 119 non-need scholarships, short-term loans. ***Required forms:*** institutional, FAFSA. ***Priority deadline:*** 9/1. ***Waivers:*** full or partial for employees or children of employees and senior citizens.

APPLYING Open admission. ***Options:*** early entrance, midyear entrance. ***Required:*** TOEFL for international students, ACT ASSET. ***Recommended:*** ACT. ***Required for some:*** school transcript. Test scores used for counseling/placement. ***Application deadline:*** rolling.

APPLYING/TRANSFER ***Required:*** college transcript. ***Required for some:*** standardized test scores, high school transcript. ***Entrance:*** noncompetitive. ***Application deadline:*** rolling. ***Contact:*** Dr. Sherryl Byrd, Coordinator of Student Services, 334-288-1080 Ext. 223.

CONTACT Dr. Sherryl Byrd, Coordinator of Student Services, John M. Patterson State Technical College, 3920 Troy Highway, Montgomery, AL 36116-2699, 334-288-1080 Ext. 223.

LAWSON STATE COMMUNITY COLLEGE
Birmingham, Alabama

UG Enrollment: 1,892	Tuition & Fees (AL Res): $1245
Application Deadline: rolling	Room & Board: N/Avail

GENERAL State-supported, 2-year, coed. Part of Alabama College System. Awards certificates, diplomas, transfer associate, terminal associate degrees. Founded 1965. ***Setting:*** 30-acre urban campus. ***Total enrollment:*** 1,892. ***Faculty:*** 112 (58 full-time, 7% with terminal degrees, 54 part-time); student-faculty ratio is 17:1. ***Notable Alumni:*** Larry Langford, mayor of Fairfield, Alabama.
ENROLLMENT PROFILE 1,892 students from 2 states and territories, 3 other countries. 59% women, 41% men, 23% part-time, 98% state residents, 3% transferred in, 80% have need-based financial aid, 1% international, 45% 25 or older, 0% Native American, 0% Hispanic, 96% African American, 1% Asian American. ***Areas of study chosen:*** 38% vocational and home economics, 28% health professions and related sciences, 15% liberal arts/general studies, 8% business management and administrative services, 5% computer and information sciences, 4% social sciences, 3% education, 2% psychology, 1% biological and life sciences, 1% communications and journalism, 1% engineering and applied sciences, 1% mathematics, 1% performing arts, 1% physical sciences, 1% prelaw. ***Most popular recent majors:*** nursing, computer information systems, accounting.
FIRST-YEAR CLASS 433 total; 520 applied, 100% were accepted, 83% of whom enrolled.
ACADEMIC PROGRAM Core, interdisciplinary curriculum, honor code. Calendar: quarters. 326 courses offered in 1995–96. Academic remediation for entering students, Freshman Honors College, honors program, summer session for credit, part-time degree program (daytime, evenings, weekends, summer), adult/continuing education programs, co-op programs and internships.
GENERAL DEGREE REQUIREMENT 96 credits.
MAJORS Accounting, business administration/commerce/management, business education, carpentry, computer information systems, cosmetology, criminal justice, dietetics, drafting and design, education, electrical and electronics technologies, English, fire science, industrial and heavy equipment maintenance, law enforcement/police sciences, legal secretarial studies, liberal arts/general studies, library science, mathematics, medical technology, nursing, physical therapy, political science/government, psychology, radio and television studies, recreation and leisure services, secretarial studies/office management, social science, social work, textiles and clothing, water resources.
LIBRARY Lawson State Library with 31,624 books, 105 microform titles, 152 periodicals, 8 on-line bibliographic services, 8 CD-ROMs, 364 records, tapes, and CDs.
COMPUTERS ON CAMPUS 115 computers for student use in learning resource center, classrooms, library, student center provide access to main academic computer, on-line services. Staffed computer lab on campus provides training in use of computers, software.
COLLEGE LIFE Choral group. 87% vote in student government elections. ***Student services:*** health clinic. ***Campus security:*** 24-hour emergency response devices and patrols, student patrols.
HOUSING College housing not available.
ATHLETICS Member NJCAA. ***Intercollegiate:*** basketball M/W, volleyball W. ***Intramural:*** swimming and diving, tennis, track and field, volleyball, weight lifting. ***Contact:*** Dr. Eric Green, Athletic Director, 205-925-2515 Ext. 365.
CAREER PLANNING ***Placement office:*** 4 full-time staff. ***Director:*** Ms. Charlsie Cook, Director of Student Services, 205-925-2515 Ext. 368. ***Services:*** job fairs, career counseling, careers library, job interviews. Students must register freshman year. 5 organizations recruited on campus 1994–95.
AFTER GRADUATION 2% of students completing a degree program in 1994–95 went directly on to further study.
EXPENSES FOR 1995–96 State resident tuition: $999 full-time. Nonresident tuition: $1617 full-time. Part-time tuition per quarter ranges from $22 to $242 for state residents, $38 to $423 for nonresidents. Full-time mandatory fees per year: $255 for residents, $246 for nonresidents. Part-time mandatory fees per semester range from $15 to $65 for residents, $12 to $62 for nonresidents.
FINANCIAL AID ***College-administered undergrad aid 1995–96:*** need-based scholarships, non-need scholarships, low-interest long-term loans from external sources, Federal Work-Study, part-time jobs. ***Required forms:*** CSS Financial Aid PROFILE, FAFSA. ***Application deadline:*** continuous to 4/15. ***Waivers:*** full or partial for employees or children of employees and senior citizens.
APPLYING Open admission except for nursing, medical technology programs. ***Options:*** Common Application, early entrance, deferred entrance. ***Required:*** school transcript, TOEFL for international students. Test scores used for counseling/placement. ***Application deadline:*** rolling. ***Notification:*** continuous.
APPLYING/TRANSFER ***Entrance:*** noncompetitive. ***Application deadline:*** rolling. ***Notification:*** continuous. ***Contact:*** Dr. Bettye Berry, Director of Transfer Programs, 205-925-2515 Ext. 289.
CONTACT Mrs. Myra P. Davis, Coordinator of Admissions and Records, Lawson State Community College, 3060 Wilson Road, SW, Birmingham, AL 35221-1798, 205-925-2515 Ext. 309. ***Fax:*** 205-929-6316.

LURLEEN B. WALLACE STATE JUNIOR COLLEGE
Andalusia, Alabama

UG Enrollment: 1,147	Tuition & Fees (AL Res): $1170
Application Deadline: rolling	Room & Board: N/Avail

GENERAL State-supported, 2-year, coed. Part of Alabama College System. Awards certificates, transfer associate, terminal associate degrees. Founded 1969. ***Setting:*** 200-acre small-town campus. ***Total enrollment:*** 1,147. ***Faculty:*** 71 (26 full-time, 23% with terminal degrees, 45 part-time); student-faculty ratio is 20:1.
ENROLLMENT PROFILE 1,147 students: 56% women, 44% men, 34% part-time, 99% state residents, 7% transferred in, 0% international, 39% 25 or older, 0% Native American, 0% Hispanic, 13% African American, 0% Asian American. ***Areas of study chosen:*** 82% liberal arts/general studies, 8% health professions and related sciences, 4% natural resource sciences, 3% business management and administrative services, 3% computer and information sciences.
FIRST-YEAR CLASS 349 total; 500 applied, 99% were accepted, 71% of whom enrolled.
ACADEMIC PROGRAM Core. Calendar: quarters. Academic remediation for entering students, advanced placement, Freshman Honors College, tutorials, summer session for credit, part-time degree program (daytime, evenings, summer), adult/continuing education programs, co-op programs.
GENERAL DEGREE REQUIREMENTS 96 quarter hours; 5 quarter hours of math.
MAJORS Business administration/commerce/management, computer programming, computer science, emergency medical technology, forest technology, liberal arts/general studies.
LIBRARY Lurleen B. Wallace Library with 35,278 books, 133 periodicals, 7,735 records, tapes, and CDs. Acquisition spending 1994–95: $6206.
COMPUTERS ON CAMPUS 45 computers for student use in computer center, computer labs, library provide access to main academic computer, Internet. Staffed computer lab on campus provides training in use of computers, software. Academic computing expenditure 1994–95: $105,304.
COLLEGE LIFE Orientation program (3 days, no cost). Drama-theater group, student-run newspaper. ***Most popular organizations:*** Student Government Association, College Ambassadors, Phi Theta Kappa, Mu Alpha Theta, Christian Student Union. ***Major annual events:*** Blue and White Day, Ms. LBW Pageant, Saints' Day. ***Student services:*** personal-psychological counseling.
HOUSING College housing not available.
ATHLETICS Member NJCAA. ***Intercollegiate:*** baseball M(s), basketball M(s)/W(s), cross-country running M(s)/W(s), softball W(s), tennis M(s). ***Intramural:*** tennis. ***Contact:*** Mr. Steve Helms, Athletic Director, 334-222-6591 Ext. 2203.
CAREER PLANNING ***Placement office:*** 1 part-time staff. ***Director:*** Mr. Curtis Thomasson, Director of Counseling, 334-222-6591 Ext. 2272. ***Services:*** resume preparation, career counseling, careers library. Students must register freshman year.
EXPENSES FOR 1995–96 State resident tuition: $990 full-time, $22 per quarter hour part-time. Nonresident tuition: $1980 full-time, $44 per quarter hour part-time. Part-time mandatory fees: $4.50 per quarter hour. Full-time mandatory fees: $180.
FINANCIAL AID ***College-administered undergrad aid 1995–96:*** need-based scholarships (average $300), Federal Work-Study. ***Required forms:*** FAFSA. ***Priority deadline:*** 6/15.
APPLYING Open admission. ***Options:*** early entrance, deferred entrance, midyear entrance. ***Required:*** school transcript, TOEFL for international students. ***Required for some:*** ACT. Test scores used for admission. ***Application deadline:*** rolling. ***Notification:*** continuous until 9/15.
APPLYING/TRANSFER ***Required:*** college transcript, minimum 2.0 college GPA. ***Required for some:*** standardized test scores, high school transcript. ***Application deadline:*** rolling. ***Notification:*** continuous until 9/15. ***Contact:*** Ms. Mackie Stephens, Registrar, 334-222-6591.
CONTACT Ms. Judy Hall, Director of Admission and Financial Aid, Lurleen B. Wallace State Junior College, Andalusia, AL 36420-1418, 334-222-6591 Ext. 271.

MARION MILITARY INSTITUTE
Marion, Alabama

UG Enrollment: 220	Tuition & Fees: $7740
Application Deadline: 8/30	Room & Board: $2800

GENERAL Independent, 2-year, coed. Awards diplomas, transfer associate, terminal associate degrees. Founded 1842. ***Setting:*** 130-acre small-town campus. ***Endowment:*** $1.2 million. ***Educational spending 1994–95:*** $2500 per undergrad. ***Total enrollment:*** 220. ***Faculty:*** 26 (100% of full-time faculty have terminal degrees). ***Notable Alumni:*** Bruce Holloway, Alva Cain, Joseph Cunnigham, Dwight Stone, R. M. Montgomery.
ENROLLMENT PROFILE 220 students from 41 states and territories, 3 other countries. 13% women, 87% men, 0% part-time, 41% state residents, 99% live on campus, 0% transferred in, 96% have need-based financial aid, 50% have non-need-based financial aid, 1% international, 0% 25 or older, 0% Native American, 5% Hispanic, 10% African American, 1% Asian American.
FIRST-YEAR CLASS 120 total; 220 applied, 91% were accepted, 60% of whom enrolled. 20% from top 10% of their high school class, 50% from top quarter, 98% from top half.
ACADEMIC PROGRAM Core, self-designed curriculum, honor code. Calendar: semesters. 75 courses offered in 1995–96. Academic remediation for entering students, English as a second language program, tutorials, part-time degree program (daytime). Off-campus study at Judson College. ROTC: Army.
GENERAL DEGREE REQUIREMENTS 64 credit hours; 6 credit hours of math; 8 credit hours of science.
MAJORS Engineering (general), liberal arts/general studies, science.
LIBRARY Baer Memorial Library with 36,000 books, 140 periodicals, 25 CD-ROMs, 1,954 records, tapes, and CDs. Acquisition spending 1994–95: $12,000.
COMPUTERS ON CAMPUS 21 computers for student use in computer center, library. Staffed computer lab on campus provides training in use of computers, software. Academic computing expenditure 1994–95: $32,000.
COLLEGE LIFE Orientation program (5 days, no cost). Drama-theater group, choral group, marching band, student-run newspaper. 98% vote in student government elections. ***Social organizations:*** 12 open to all. ***Most popular organizations:*** Swamp Foxes, White Knights, Marching Band, Drama Club, Scabbard and Blade. ***Major annual events:*** Military Ball, Gymkhana, Red Carpet Day. ***Student services:*** health clinic, personal-psychological counseling. ***Campus security:*** nighttime security patrol.
HOUSING 550 college housing spaces available; 218 were occupied 1995–96. Freshmen guaranteed college housing. Off-campus living permitted. ***Option:*** single-sex (6 buildings) housing available. Resident assistants live in dorms.
ATHLETICS Member NJCAA. ***Intercollegiate:*** golf M/W, soccer M/W, tennis M/W. ***Intramural:*** baseball, basketball, football, golf, lacrosse, racquetball, soccer, softball, swimming and diving, table tennis (Ping-Pong), tennis, volleyball, water polo, weight lifting. ***Contact:*** Col. J. T. Murfee III, Athletic Director, 334-683-2359.
CAREER PLANNING ***Placement office:*** 1 full-time staff. ***Director:*** Major Suzanne Adams, Director of Counseling, 334-683-2354. ***Services:*** resume preparation, career counseling, careers library.
AFTER GRADUATION 100% of students completing a degree program in 1994–95 went directly on to further study.
ESTIMATED EXPENSES FOR 1996–97 ***Application fee:*** $35. Comprehensive fee of $10,540 includes full-time tuition ($7740) and college room and board ($2800).

FINANCIAL AID ***College-administered undergrad aid 1995–96:*** 53 need-based scholarships (average $450), 100 non-need scholarships (average $3000), low-interest long-term loans from external sources (average $3000), 25 Federal Work-Study (averaging $500), 10 part-time jobs. ***Required forms:*** institutional, FAFSA; accepted: CSS Financial Aid PROFILE, state. ***Application deadline:*** continuous. ***Payment plan:*** installment. ***Waivers:*** full or partial for employees or children of employees. ***Notification:*** continuous.
APPLYING ***Options:*** Common Application, deferred entrance, midyear entrance. ***Required:*** school transcript, minimum 2.0 GPA, recommendations, SAT I or ACT. ***Recommended:*** interview. Test scores used for admission. ***Application deadline:*** 8/30.
APPLYING/TRANSFER ***Required:*** standardized test scores, high school transcript, recommendations, minimum 2.0 high school GPA. ***Recommended:*** interview. ***Entrance:*** moderately difficult. ***Application deadline:*** 8/30. ***Contact:*** Mrs. Evelyn Vetzel, Registrar, 334-683-2304.
CONTACT Col. James L. Waters Jr., Dean of Admissions, Marion Military Institute, Marion, AL 36756, 334-683-2305 or toll-free 800-664-1842 (in-state). ***Fax:*** 334-683-2380. College video available.

NORTHEAST ALABAMA STATE COMMUNITY COLLEGE
Rainsville, Alabama

UG Enrollment: 1,589	Tuition & Fees (AL Res): $1197
Application Deadline: rolling	Room & Board: N/Avail

GENERAL State-supported, 2-year, coed. Part of Alabama College System. Awards certificates, transfer associate, terminal associate degrees. Founded 1963. ***Setting:*** 100-acre rural campus. ***Total enrollment:*** 1,589. ***Faculty:*** 51 (36 full-time, 10% with terminal degrees, 15 part-time); student-faculty ratio is 25:1. ***Notable Alumni:*** Randy Owen, musician.
ENROLLMENT PROFILE 1,589 students: 62% women, 38% men, 37% part-time, 99% state residents, 15% transferred in, 40% have need-based financial aid, 6% have non-need-based financial aid, 1% international, 40% 25 or older, 2% Native American, 1% Hispanic, 1% African American, 1% Asian American. ***Most popular recent majors:*** nursing, liberal arts/general studies, computer science.
FIRST-YEAR CLASS 282 total; 314 applied, 100% were accepted, 90% of whom enrolled.
ACADEMIC PROGRAM Core, pre-liberal arts curriculum, honor code. Calendar: quarters. 500 courses offered in 1995–96. Academic remediation for entering students, services for LD students, advanced placement, tutorials, honors program, summer session for credit, part-time degree program (daytime, evenings, summer), adult/continuing education programs.
GENERAL DEGREE REQUIREMENTS 96 quarter hours; 20 quarter hours of math/science for associate of arts degree; 15 quarter hours of math/science for associate of science degree; computer course for most majors.
MAJORS Business administration/commerce/management, computer information systems, computer science, emergency medical technology, (pre)engineering sequence, finance/banking, legal secretarial studies, liberal arts/general studies, medical secretarial studies, nursing, paralegal studies, real estate, science, secretarial studies/office management, water resources, word processing.
LIBRARY 45,000 books, 142 periodicals, 1 on-line bibliographic service, 500 records, tapes, and CDs.
COMPUTERS ON CAMPUS 40 computers for student use in computer center, computer labs, library provide access to main academic computer. Staffed computer lab on campus provides training in use of computers, software.
COLLEGE LIFE Drama-theater group, choral group. 30% vote in student government elections. ***Social organizations:*** 7 open to all. ***Most popular organizations:*** Baptist Campus Ministry, Theater, SGA, Spectrum Art Club, Choral Group. ***Major annual events:*** Spring Fling, Fall Dance, Graduation. ***Student services:*** personal-psychological counseling. ***Campus security:*** 24-hour emergency response devices and patrols, late-night transport-escort service.
HOUSING College housing not available.
CAREER PLANNING ***Director:*** Dr. Joe Burke, Director of Admissions, 205-638-4418 Ext. 325. ***Services:*** resume preparation, resume referral, career counseling, careers library, job bank.
AFTER GRADUATION 30% of students completing a degree program in 1994–95 went directly on to further study.
EXPENSES FOR 1996–97 State resident tuition: $1197 full-time, $25 per quarter hour part-time. Nonresident tuition: $2157 full-time, $45 per quarter hour part-time.
FINANCIAL AID ***College-administered undergrad aid 1995–96:*** 100 non-need scholarships (averaging $1200), 28 Federal Work-Study (averaging $1500). ***Acceptable forms:*** FAFSA. ***Application deadline:*** continuous. ***Waivers:*** full or partial for employees or children of employees and senior citizens.
APPLYING Open admission. ***Options:*** early entrance, deferred entrance, midyear entrance. ***Required:*** 3 years of high school math and science, TOEFL for international students, ACT ASSET. Test scores used for counseling/placement. ***Application deadline:*** rolling. ***Notification:*** continuous.
APPLYING/TRANSFER ***Required:*** standardized test scores. ***Entrance:*** noncompetitive. ***Application deadline:*** rolling. ***Notification:*** continuous. ***Contact:*** Dr. Joe Burke, Director of Admissions, 205-638-4418 Ext. 325.
CONTACT Dr. Joe Burke, Director of Admissions, Northeast Alabama State Community College, Rainsville, AL 35986-0159, 205-638-4418 Ext. 25.

NORTHWEST-SHOALS COMMUNITY COLLEGE
Muscle Shoals, Alabama

UG Enrollment: 4,545	Tuition & Fees (AL Res): $1437
Application Deadline: rolling	Room & Board: $1170

GENERAL State-supported, 2-year, coed. Part of State of Alabama Department of Postsecondary Education. Awards certificates, diplomas, transfer associate, terminal associate degrees. Founded 1961. ***Setting:*** 205-acre small-town campus. ***Endowment:*** $10,762. ***Research spending 1994–95:*** $203,866. ***Total enrollment:*** 4,545. ***Faculty:*** 176 (73 full-time, 100% with terminal degrees, 103 part-time); student-faculty ratio is 25:1.
ENROLLMENT PROFILE 4,545 students: 54% women, 43% part-time, 95% state residents, 10% transferred in, 0% international, 43% 25 or older, 1% Native American, 1% Hispanic, 9% African American. ***Most popular recent majors:*** nursing, business administration/commerce/management, education.
FIRST-YEAR CLASS 784 total. Of the students who applied, 100% were accepted.
ACADEMIC PROGRAM Core, interdisciplinary curriculum, honor code. Calendar: quarters. 800 courses offered in 1995–96; average class size 25 in required courses. Academic remediation for entering students, self-designed majors, summer session for credit, part-time degree program (daytime, evenings, summer), adult/continuing education programs.
GENERAL DEGREE REQUIREMENTS 96 quarter hours; 1 course in college algebra; 10 quarter hours of science; computer course for most majors.
MAJORS Accounting, agricultural education, business administration/commerce/management, child care/child and family studies, computer information systems, computer science, criminal justice, drafting and design, education, elementary education, (pre)engineering sequence, fire science, forestry, laboratory technologies, law enforcement/police sciences, liberal arts/general studies, medical technology, music, nursing, pharmacy/pharmaceutical sciences, practical nursing, secretarial studies/office management, veterinary sciences.
LIBRARY Larry W. McCoy Learning Resource Center and James Glasgow Library with 60,000 books, 350 microform titles, 250 periodicals, 4 on-line bibliographic services, 30 CD-ROMs, 200 records, tapes, and CDs. Acquisition spending 1994–95: $337,430.
COMPUTERS ON CAMPUS 180 computers for student use in computer center, computer labs, library provide access to main academic computer. Staffed computer lab on campus provides training in use of computers, software.
COLLEGE LIFE Drama-theater group, choral group, student-run newspaper. ***Social organizations:*** 20 open to all. ***Most popular organizations:*** Student Government Association, Science Club, Phi Theta Kappa, Baptist Campus Ministry, Northwest-Shoals Singers. ***Major annual events:*** Homecoming and Dance, Spring Fling, Blood Drive. ***Student services:*** personal-psychological counseling. ***Campus security:*** 24-hour emergency response devices and patrols.
HOUSING 76 college housing spaces available; all were occupied 1995–96. No special consideration for freshman housing applicants. Off-campus living permitted. ***Option:*** coed (1 building) housing available. Resident assistants live in dorms.
ATHLETICS Member NJCAA. ***Intercollegiate:*** baseball M(s), basketball M(s)/W(s), cross-country running M(s)/W(s), softball W(s), tennis M(s)/W(s), volleyball W(s). ***Intramural:*** basketball. ***Contact:*** Mr. Bill Moss, Athletic Director, 205-331-5200.
CAREER PLANNING ***Placement office:*** 2 full-time, 4 part-time staff. ***Director:*** Ms. Charlene Freeman, Coordinator, 205-331-6277. ***Services:*** career counseling, careers library, job bank. Students must register freshman year.
EXPENSES FOR 1996–97 State resident tuition: $1437 full-time, $25 per quarter hour part-time. Nonresident tuition: $2637 full-time, $43.75 per quarter hour part-time. College room and board: $1170. Tuition guaranteed not to increase for student's term of enrollment.
FINANCIAL AID ***College-administered undergrad aid 1995–96:*** 200 non-need scholarships (averaging $400), low-interest long-term loans from external sources (averaging $2281), 45 Federal Work-Study. ***Required forms:*** FAFSA. ***Priority deadline:*** 6/15. ***Payment plan:*** deferred payment. ***Waivers:*** full or partial for employees or children of employees and senior citizens.
APPLYING Open admission except for nursing program. ***Options:*** Common Application, early entrance, midyear entrance. ***Required:*** school transcript, ACT ASSET. ***Recommended:*** TOEFL for international students. ***Required for some:*** ACT. Test scores used for counseling/placement. ***Application deadline:*** rolling.
APPLYING/TRANSFER ***Required:*** high school transcript, college transcript. ***Entrance:*** noncompetitive. ***Application deadline:*** rolling. ***Contact:*** Mr. Charles T. Taylor Sr., Director of Admissions, 205-331-6218.
CONTACT Mr. Charles T. Taylor Sr., Director of Admissions, Northwest-Shoals Community College, P. O. Box 2545, Muscle Shoals, AL 35662, 205-331-6218 or toll-free 800-645-8967 (in-state). ***Fax:*** 205-331-5341.

REID STATE TECHNICAL COLLEGE
Evergreen, Alabama

UG Enrollment: 833	Tuition & Fees (AL Res): $990
Application Deadline: rolling	Room & Board: N/Avail

GENERAL State-supported, 2-year, coed. Part of Alabama College System. Awards terminal associate degrees. Founded 1966. ***Setting:*** 26-acre rural campus. ***Total enrollment:*** 833. ***Faculty:*** 47 (32 full-time, 100% with terminal degrees, 15 part-time); student-faculty ratio is 14:1.
ENROLLMENT PROFILE 833 students from 2 states and territories. 70% women, 42% part-time, 97% state residents, 25% transferred in, 46% have need-based financial aid, 0% international, 55% 25 or older, 1% Native American, 0% Hispanic, 43% African American, 0% Asian American. ***Areas of study chosen:*** 35% health professions and related sciences. ***Most popular recent majors:*** practical nursing, secretarial studies/office management, cosmetology.
FIRST-YEAR CLASS 222 total; 658 applied, 65% of whom enrolled.
ACADEMIC PROGRAM Technical specialties curriculum. Calendar: quarters. Academic remediation for entering students, services for LD students, summer session for credit, part-time degree program (daytime, evenings, summer), adult/continuing education programs.
GENERAL DEGREE REQUIREMENTS 114 credit hours; 5 credit hours of math; computer course for electrical and electronics technology majors.
MAJORS Carpentry, child care/child and family studies, construction technologies, cosmetology, electrical and electronics technologies, forest technology, practical nursing, secretarial studies/office management, welding technology.
COMPUTERS ON CAMPUS 56 computers for student use in computer center, computer labs, learning resource center, library.
COLLEGE LIFE Orientation program (2 days, parents included). Student-run newspaper. ***Social organizations:*** 1 open to all. ***Most popular organization:*** Student Government Association. ***Major annual events:*** Challenge Cup Ambassadors, Talent Show. ***Student services:*** personal-psychological counseling. ***Campus security:*** 24-hour emergency response devices, day and evening security guard.
HOUSING College housing not available.

Peterson's Guide to Two-Year Colleges 1997 159

Reid State Technical College (continued)
CAREER PLANNING ***Placement office:*** 1 full-time staff. ***Director:*** Ms. Diannah Rowger, Director of Job Placement, 334-578-1313 Ext. 141. ***Services:*** job fairs, resume preparation, career counseling, careers library, job bank, job interviews.
EXPENSES FOR 1996–97 State resident tuition: $900 full-time, $20 per credit hour part-time. Nonresident tuition: $1575 full-time, $35 per credit hour part-time. Part-time mandatory fees: $2 per credit hour. Full-time mandatory fees: $90.
FINANCIAL AID ***College-administered undergrad aid 1995–96:*** need-based scholarships, non-need scholarships, part-time jobs. ***Required forms:*** FAFSA. ***Priority deadline:*** 8/31. ***Waivers:*** full or partial for employees or children of employees and senior citizens.
APPLYING Open admission. ***Option:*** early entrance. ***Required:*** school transcript, ACT ASSET, Ability-To-Benefit Admissions Test. Test scores used for counseling/placement. ***Application deadline:*** rolling.
APPLYING/TRANSFER ***Required:*** high school transcript, college transcript, minimum 2.0 college GPA. ***Entrance:*** noncompetitive. ***Application deadline:*** rolling. ***Contact:*** Ms. Vicki P. Hawsey, Registrar, 334-578-1313.
CONTACT Ms. Alesia Stuart, Public Relations/Marketing, Reid State Technical College, PO Box 588, Evergreen, AL 36401-0588, 334-578-1313 Ext. 108. ***Fax:*** 334-578-5355.

SHELTON STATE COMMUNITY COLLEGE
Tuscaloosa, Alabama

UG Enrollment: 6,000	**Tuition & Fees (AL Res): $1389**
Application Deadline: rolling	**Room & Board: N/Avail**

GENERAL State-supported, 2-year, coed. Awards certificates, transfer associate, terminal associate degrees. Founded 1979. ***Setting:*** 40-acre small-town campus with easy access to Birmingham. ***Total enrollment:*** 6,000. ***Faculty:*** 268 (104 full-time, 164 part-time).
ENROLLMENT PROFILE 6,000 students from 2 states and territories, 4 other countries. 55% women, 56% part-time, 97% state residents, 20% transferred in, 2% international, 37% 25 or older, 0% Native American, 0% Hispanic, 23% African American, 0% Asian American.
FIRST-YEAR CLASS 908 total. Of the students who applied, 100% were accepted, 95% of whom enrolled.
ACADEMIC PROGRAM Calendar: semesters. Academic remediation for entering students, services for LD students, advanced placement, summer session for credit, part-time degree program (daytime), adult/continuing education programs. ROTC: Army, Air Force.
GENERAL DEGREE REQUIREMENTS 64 semester hours; 9 semester hours math/science.
MAJORS Art education, automotive technologies, biology/biological sciences, business administration/commerce/management, business education, chemistry, computer science, cosmetology, data processing, drafting and design, early childhood education, education, electrical and electronics technologies, electrical engineering technology, elementary education, emergency medical technology, heating/refrigeration/air conditioning, home economics, liberal arts/general studies, medical assistant technologies, medical laboratory technology, medical records services, medical secretarial studies, music, music education, nursing, pharmacy/pharmaceutical sciences, physical education, practical nursing, respiratory therapy, secretarial studies/office management, welding technology.
LIBRARY 17,031 books, 1,030 microform titles, 1,170 records, tapes, and CDs. Acquisition spending 1994–95: $575,780.
COMPUTERS ON CAMPUS Computers for student use in computer center, computer labs. Staffed computer lab on campus provides training in use of computers, software.
COLLEGE LIFE Choral group. ***Campus security:*** 24-hour emergency response devices and patrols.
HOUSING College housing not available.
ATHLETICS Member NJCAA. ***Intercollegiate:*** baseball M(s), basketball M(s)/W(s), golf M(s), softball M(s), volleyball W(s).
CAREER PLANNING ***Service:*** career counseling.
EXPENSES FOR 1996–97 State resident tuition: $1152 full-time, $36 per semester hour part-time. Nonresident tuition: $2304 full-time, $72 per semester hour part-time. Part-time mandatory fees: $7.50 per semester hour. Full-time mandatory fees: $237.
FINANCIAL AID ***College-administered undergrad aid 1995–96:*** need-based scholarships, non-need scholarships, Federal Work-Study. ***Required forms:*** FAFSA; required for some: institutional. ***Application deadline:*** continuous to 5/1. ***Waivers:*** full or partial for employees or children of employees and senior citizens.
APPLYING Open admission except for practical nursing program. ***Options:*** Common Application, early entrance. ***Required:*** ACT ASSET. ***Required for some:*** TOEFL for international students. Test scores used for counseling/placement. ***Application deadline:*** rolling.
APPLYING/TRANSFER ***Required:*** standardized test scores. ***Application deadline:*** rolling.
CONTACT Ms. Loretta Jones, Assistant to the Dean of Students, Shelton State Community College, Tuscaloosa, AL 35405-4093, 205-759-1541 Ext. 2236. ***Fax:*** 205-759-2495.

SNEAD STATE COMMUNITY COLLEGE
Boaz, Alabama

UG Enrollment: 1,708	**Tuition & Fees (AL Res): $837**
Application Deadline: rolling	**Room & Board: $1643**

GENERAL State-supported, 2-year, coed. Awards certificates, transfer associate, terminal associate degrees. Founded 1935. ***Setting:*** 42-acre small-town campus with easy access to Birmingham. ***Endowment:*** $589,758. ***Research spending 1994–95:*** $70,622. ***Total enrollment:*** 1,708. ***Faculty:*** 81 (28 full-time, 29% with terminal degrees, 53 part-time). ***Notable Alumni:*** Harold O. Chitwood, CEO of Goldkist Inc; Lowell Barron, Alabama state senator.
ENROLLMENT PROFILE 1,708 students from 5 states and territories. 57% women, 43% men, 28% part-time, 99% state residents, 4% live on campus, 0% international, 28% 25 or older, 1% Native American, 1% Hispanic, 2% African American, 1% Asian American. ***Areas of study chosen:*** 72% liberal arts/general studies, 11% engineering and applied sciences, 8% business management and administrative services, 3% agriculture, 3% computer and information sciences, 3% health professions and related sciences. ***Most popular recent majors:*** liberal arts/general studies, business administration/commerce/management.
FIRST-YEAR CLASS 645 total; 936 applied, 100% were accepted, 69% of whom enrolled.
ACADEMIC PROGRAM Core, interdisciplinary curriculum. Calendar: quarters. 494 courses offered in 1995–96. Academic remediation for entering students, advanced placement, summer session for credit, part-time degree program (daytime, evenings), adult/continuing education programs, internships.
GENERAL DEGREE REQUIREMENTS 96 quarter hours; math/science requirements vary according to program; computer course for fire science, criminal justice technology, electronics technology; drafting, management and supervision, air conditioning, child development majors; internship (some majors).
MAJORS Business administration/commerce/management, computer technologies, criminal justice, electronics engineering technology, engineering design, liberal arts/general studies, veterinary technology, vocational education.
LIBRARY McCain Learning Resource Center with 30,681 books, 43 microform titles, 213 periodicals, 20 CD-ROMs, 944 records, tapes, and CDs. Acquisition spending 1994–95: $239,222.
COMPUTERS ON CAMPUS 141 computers for student use in computer labs, learning resource center, classrooms, library provide access to main academic computer. Staffed computer lab on campus provides training in use of computers, software.
COLLEGE LIFE Drama-theater group, choral group, student-run newspaper. 25% vote in student government elections. ***Social organizations:*** 15 open to all. ***Most popular organizations:*** Phi Theta Kappa, Snead Agricultural Organization, Veterinary Technician Association, Student Government Association. ***Student services:*** personal-psychological counseling. ***Campus security:*** late-night transport-escort service, trained security personnel.
HOUSING 70 college housing spaces available; 59 were occupied 1995–96. No special consideration for freshman housing applicants. Off-campus living permitted. ***Option:*** coed (1 building) housing available. Resident assistants live in dorms.
ATHLETICS Member NJCAA. ***Intercollegiate:*** baseball M(s), basketball M(s)/W(s), golf M(s), softball W(s), tennis W(s). ***Contact:*** Dr. David Wilson, Athletic Director, 205-593-5120.
CAREER PLANNING ***Placement office:*** 1 full-time, 1 part-time staff. ***Director:*** Ms. Phyllis Kirk, Director, Counseling Services, 205-593-5120 Ext. 251. ***Services:*** job fairs, resume preparation, career counseling, careers library.
EXPENSES FOR 1995–96 State resident tuition: $720 full-time, $20 per quarter hour part-time. Nonresident tuition: $1440 full-time, $40 per quarter hour part-time. Part-time mandatory fees per quarter range from $7 to $32. Full-time mandatory fees: $117. College room and board: $1643. College room only: $600.
FINANCIAL AID ***College-administered undergrad aid 1995–96:*** need-based scholarships, non-need scholarships, short-term loans, Federal Work-Study, part-time jobs. ***Required forms:*** FAFSA; accepted: CSS Financial Aid PROFILE. ***Priority deadline:*** 4/15. ***Waivers:*** full or partial for employees or children of employees and senior citizens.
APPLYING Open admission. ***Options:*** early entrance, deferred entrance, midyear entrance. ***Required:*** school transcript, ACT ASSET. ***Required for some:*** interview. Test scores used for counseling/placement. ***Application deadline:*** rolling.
APPLYING/TRANSFER ***Required:*** college transcript. ***Application deadline:*** rolling. ***Contact:*** Ms. Joan Osborn, Director of Admissions and Records, 205-593-5120 Ext. 207.
CONTACT Ms. Joan Osborn, Director of Admissions and Records, Snead State Community College, Boaz, AL 35957, 205-593-5120 Ext. 207.

SOUTHERN UNION STATE COMMUNITY COLLEGE
Wadley, Alabama

UG Enrollment: 6,499	**Tuition & Fees (AL Res): $1350**
Application Deadline: rolling	**Room & Board: $1950**

GENERAL State-supported, 2-year, coed. Part of Alabama College System. Awards certificates, diplomas, transfer associate, terminal associate degrees. Founded 1922. ***Setting:*** rural campus. ***Research spending 1994–95:*** $21,765. ***Educational spending 1994–95:*** $757 per undergrad. ***Total enrollment:*** 6,499. ***Faculty:*** 217 (81 full-time, 6% with terminal degrees, 136 part-time); student-faculty ratio is 20:1. ***Notable Alumni:*** Nofflet Williams, retired associate dean for distance learning at University of Kentucky; V. Warren "Rhubarb" Jones, radio personality.
ENROLLMENT PROFILE 6,499 students: 53% women, 47% men, 54% part-time, 95% state residents, 6% live on campus, 1% transferred in, 50% have need-based financial aid, 0% international, 33% 25 or older, 0% Native American, 0% Hispanic, 25% African American, 1% Asian American. ***Most popular recent majors:*** liberal arts/general studies, nursing.
FIRST-YEAR CLASS Of the students who applied, 99% were accepted.
ACADEMIC PROGRAM Core, general education curriculum, honor code. Calendar: quarters. 564 courses offered in 1995–96; average class size 20 in required courses. Academic remediation for entering students, services for LD students, advanced placement, summer session for credit, part-time degree program (daytime, evenings, weekends, summer), adult/continuing education programs, co-op programs and internships. ROTC: Air Force (c).
GENERAL DEGREE REQUIREMENTS 96 quarter hours; 20 quarter hours of math/science; computer course for students without computer competency.
MAJORS Business administration/commerce/management, computer information systems, finance/banking, liberal arts/general studies, nursing, secretarial studies/office management.
LIBRARY McClintock-Ensminger Library plus 2 others, with 90,791 books, 4,923 microform titles, 877 periodicals, 8,992 records, tapes, and CDs. Acquisition spending 1994–95: $72,326.
COMPUTERS ON CAMPUS 225 computers for student use in computer center, computer labs, learning resource center, classrooms, library provide access to main academic computer. Staffed computer lab on campus provides training in use of computers, software.
COLLEGE LIFE Drama-theater group, choral group, student-run newspaper. 10% vote in student government elections. ***Social organizations:*** 12 open to all. ***Most popular organizations:*** Student Government Association, Phi Theta Kappa, Music Club, National Student Nurses Association, Global Environmental Organization of Students. ***Major***

annual events: Homecoming, Spring Fling, Miss Southern Union. ***Student services:*** personal-psychological counseling. ***Campus security:*** 24-hour patrols, controlled dormitory access.
HOUSING 288 college housing spaces available; all were occupied 1995–96. No special consideration for freshman housing applicants. Off-campus living permitted. ***Options:*** coed (1 building), single-sex (2 buildings) housing available. Resident assistants live in dorms.
ATHLETICS Member NSCAA, NJCAA. ***Intercollegiate:*** baseball M(s), basketball M(s)/W(s), cross-country running M(s)/W(s), softball W(s), volleyball W(s). ***Intramural:*** basketball, bowling. ***Contact:*** Mr. Ron Radford, Athletic Director, 205-395-2211.
CAREER PLANNING ***Placement office:*** 1 full-time staff. ***Director:*** Mr. Gary Branch, Director of Career Development and Placement Services, 205-745-6437. ***Services:*** resume preparation, resume referral, career counseling, careers library, job bank, job interviews.
EXPENSES FOR 1995–96 State resident tuition: $1350 full-time, $30.50 per quarter hour part-time. Nonresident tuition: $2475 full-time, $55.50 per quarter hour part-time. College room and board: $1950.
FINANCIAL AID ***College-administered undergrad aid 1995–96:*** need-based scholarships, 207 non-need scholarships (average $1240), short-term loans (average $372), Federal Work-Study, 45 part-time jobs. ***Acceptable forms:*** FAFSA. ***Priority deadline:*** 6/1. ***Waivers:*** full or partial for employees or children of employees and senior citizens.
APPLYING Open admission. ***Options:*** Common Application, early entrance, deferred entrance, midyear entrance. ***Required:*** school transcript, TOEFL for international students. Test scores used for counseling/placement. ***Application deadline:*** rolling. ***Notification:*** continuous.
APPLYING/TRANSFER ***Required:*** high school transcript, college transcript. ***Application deadline:*** rolling. ***Notification:*** continuous. ***Contact:*** Mrs. Susan Salatto, Director of Student Development, 205-395-2211.
CONTACT Mrs. Susan Salatto, Director of Student Development, Southern Union State Community College, Wadley, AL 36276, 205-395-2211. ***Fax:*** 205-395-2215.

TRENHOLM STATE TECHNICAL COLLEGE
Montgomery, Alabama

UG Enrollment: 767	**Tuition & Fees (AL Res): $1267**
Application Deadline: rolling	**Room & Board: N/Avail**

GENERAL State-supported, 2-year, coed. Part of Alabama College System. Awards certificates, diplomas, terminal associate degrees. Founded 1965. ***Setting:*** 85-acre suburban campus. ***Total enrollment:*** 767. ***Faculty:*** 61 (70% of full-time faculty have terminal degrees); student-faculty ratio is 12:1. ***Notable Alumni:*** Greg Calhoun.
ENROLLMENT PROFILE 767 students: 68% women, 32% men, 39% part-time, 99% state residents, 2% transferred in, 71% have need-based financial aid, 1% international, 86% 25 or older, 76% African American. ***Most popular recent majors:*** legal secretarial studies, accounting, dental services.
FIRST-YEAR CLASS 387 total; 836 applied, 74% of whom enrolled.
ACADEMIC PROGRAM Core, honor code. Calendar: quarters. Academic remediation for entering students, services for LD students, tutorials, part-time degree program (daytime, evenings), external degree programs, adult/continuing education programs, co-op programs and internships. Off-campus study.
GENERAL DEGREE REQUIREMENTS 98 quarter hours; math requirement varies according to program; internship (some majors).
MAJORS Accounting, computer information systems, construction technologies, dental services, electrical and electronics technologies, food services technology, legal secretarial studies, medical records services, medical secretarial studies, secretarial studies/office management.
LIBRARY 477 books, 30 periodicals, 250 records, tapes, and CDs.
COMPUTERS ON CAMPUS 186 computers for student use in computer center, classrooms, library. Staffed computer lab on campus.
COLLEGE LIFE Orientation program (3 days, $24). Choral group. 30% vote in student government elections. ***Most popular organizations:*** VICA, Phi Beta Lambda. ***Major annual events:*** Coronation of Miss TSTC, Back to School Festival, Honors Day. ***Campus security:*** 24-hour patrols.
HOUSING College housing not available.
ATHLETICS ***Intramural:*** basketball, softball.
CAREER PLANNING ***Placement office:*** 1 full-time, 1 part-time staff. ***Director:*** Ms. Janet Lewis, Planning and Career Specialist, 334-832-9000. ***Services:*** job fairs, resume preparation, resume referral, career counseling, careers library, job bank, job interviews. Students must register freshman year.
AFTER GRADUATION 19% of students completing a degree program in 1994–95 went directly on to further study.
EXPENSES FOR 1995–96 State resident tuition: $1078 full-time, $22 per credit hour part-time. Nonresident tuition: $2156 full-time, $44 per credit hour part-time. Part-time mandatory fees per quarter range from $19 to $59. Full-time mandatory fees: $189.
FINANCIAL AID ***College-administered undergrad aid 1995–96:*** need-based scholarships, Federal Work-Study, part-time jobs. ***Required forms:*** state, institutional, FAFSA. ***Priority deadline:*** 6/1. ***Payment plan:*** deferred payment. ***Waivers:*** full or partial for senior citizens.
APPLYING Open admission. ***Required:*** school transcript. ***Application deadline:*** rolling.
APPLYING/TRANSFER ***Required:*** college transcript. ***Entrance:*** noncompetitive. ***Application deadline:*** rolling. ***Contact:*** Ms. Mary Carter, Registrar, 334-832-9000.
CONTACT Ms. Carolyn Silverman, Director of Admissions, Trenholm State Technical College, Montgomery, AL 36108-3105, 334-832-9000 Ext. 735. ***Fax:*** 334-832-9777. College video available.

UAB WALKER COLLEGE
Jasper, Alabama

UG Enrollment: 957	**Tuition & Fees (AL Res): $1572**
Application Deadline: rolling	**Room & Board: $1680**

GENERAL State-supported, 2-year, coed. Part of University of Alabama at Birmingham. Awards certificates, transfer associate, terminal associate degrees. Founded 1938. ***Setting:*** 40-acre small-town campus with easy access to Birmingham. ***Total enrollment:*** 957. ***Faculty:*** 52 (19 full-time, 33 part-time); student-faculty ratio is 17:1. ***Notable Alumni:*** Allen Dale Sherer, Gary N. Drummond, Mike Melody, A.J. McDanal, Timothy Sumner Robinson.
ENROLLMENT PROFILE 957 students from 5 states and territories. 67% women, 33% men, 45% part-time, 99% state residents, 5% transferred in, 0% international, 38% 25 or older, 0% Native American, 0% Hispanic, 8% African American, 0% Asian American. ***Most popular recent majors:*** nursing, business administration/commerce/management, liberal arts/general studies.
FIRST-YEAR CLASS 301 total; 394 applied, 100% were accepted, 76% of whom enrolled.
ACADEMIC PROGRAM Core, interdisciplinary curriculum, honor code. Calendar: quarters. 217 courses offered in 1995–96. Academic remediation for entering students, advanced placement, honors program, summer session for credit, part-time degree program (daytime, evenings, weekends, summer), adult/continuing education programs.
GENERAL DEGREE REQUIREMENTS 64 quarter hours; math/science requirements vary according to program; computer course.
MAJORS Business administration/commerce/management, cytotechnology, engineering (general), (pre)engineering sequence, liberal arts/general studies, nursing, science, social science.
LIBRARY Irma Dilg Nicholson Library with 20,637 books, 70 microform titles, 157 periodicals, 615 records, tapes, and CDs.
COMPUTERS ON CAMPUS 28 computers for student use in computer center, nursing, English labs. Staffed computer lab on campus (open 24 hours a day). Academic computing expenditure 1994–95: $100,000.
COLLEGE LIFE Orientation program (2 days, no cost). Drama-theater group, choral group. ***Social organizations:*** 5 open to all. ***Most popular organizations:*** Circle K, Student Government, Rotaract, Phi Theta Kappa, Campus Ministry. ***Major annual events:*** Fall Festival, Homecoming. ***Campus security:*** late-night transport-escort service, security personnel.
HOUSING 152 college housing spaces available; all were occupied 1995–96. No special consideration for freshman housing applicants. Off-campus living permitted.
ATHLETICS Member NJCAA. ***Intercollegiate:*** basketball M(s), golf M, softball W(s). ***Intramural:*** baseball, basketball, football, softball, tennis, volleyball. ***Contact:*** Mr. Glenn R. Clem, Athletic Director, 205-387-5140.
CAREER PLANNING ***Placement office:*** 1 part-time staff; $35,000 operating expenditure 1994–95. ***Director:*** Mr. Randell Pickering, Director of Student Activities and Career Counseling, 205-387-5142. ***Services:*** resume preparation, career counseling, careers library, job interviews.
AFTER GRADUATION 85% of students completing a degree program in 1994–95 went directly on to further study.
EXPENSES FOR 1995–96 ***Application fee:*** $25. State resident tuition: $1416 full-time, $59 per quarter hour part-time. Nonresident tuition: $2832 full-time, $118 per quarter hour part-time. Part-time mandatory fees per quarter range from $21 to $41. Full-time mandatory fees: $156. College room and board: $1680. College room only: $780.
FINANCIAL AID ***College-administered undergrad aid 1995–96:*** need-based scholarships, 115 non-need scholarships (average $600), short-term loans, low-interest long-term loans from external sources (average $2500), Federal Work-Study, 4 part-time jobs. ***Required forms:*** institutional, FAFSA; accepted: CSS Financial Aid PROFILE. ***Priority deadline:*** 7/1. ***Payment plan:*** installment.
APPLYING Open admission except for nursing program. ***Options:*** Common Application, early entrance, deferred entrance. ***Required:*** school transcript, minimum 2.0 GPA, TOEFL for international students. ***Recommended:*** ACT. ***Required for some:*** ACT. Test scores used for counseling/placement. ***Application deadline:*** rolling. ***Notification:*** continuous.
APPLYING/TRANSFER ***Required:*** college transcript. ***Entrance:*** noncompetitive. ***Application deadline:*** rolling. ***Notification:*** continuous. ***Contact:*** Mr. James E. West, Dean of Academic Affairs and Admissions, 205-387-5120.
CONTACT Mr. James E. West, Dean of Academic Affairs and Admissions, UAB Walker College, 1411 Indiana Avenue, Jasper, AL 35501-4967, 205-387-5120 or toll-free 800-777-0372. ***Fax:*** 205-387-5175. College video available.

VIRGINIA COLLEGE AT BIRMINGHAM
Birmingham, Alabama

UG Enrollment: 500	**Tuition & Fees: $4160**
Application Deadline: rolling	**Room & Board: N/Avail**

GENERAL Proprietary, 2-year, coed. Awards diplomas, terminal associate degrees. Founded 1989. ***Total enrollment:*** 500. ***Faculty:*** 36 (10 full-time, 26 part-time).
ENROLLMENT PROFILE 500 students.
FIRST-YEAR CLASS 275 total; 575 applied, 87% were accepted, 55% of whom enrolled.
ACADEMIC PROGRAM Core. Calendar: quarters.
GENERAL DEGREE REQUIREMENTS 96 quarter hours; 1 math course; computer course.
MAJORS Drafting and design, electrical and electronics technologies, health services administration, interior design, medical assistant technologies, paralegal studies, secretarial studies/office management.
HOUSING College housing not available.
EXPENSES FOR 1996–97 Tuition: $4160 (minimum) full-time. Part-time tuition per quarter hour ranges from $130 to $150. One-time mandatory fee: $100.
FINANCIAL AID ***College-administered undergrad aid 1995–96:*** need-based scholarships, low-interest long-term loans from external sources. ***Required forms:*** FAFSA. ***Payment plan:*** installment.
APPLYING ***Required:*** school transcript, CPAt. Test scores used for admission. ***Application deadline:*** rolling. ***Notification:*** continuous.
APPLYING/TRANSFER ***Required:*** standardized test scores, high school transcript, college transcript.
CONTACT Ms. Bibbie McLaughlin, Director of Admissions, Virginia College at Birmingham, Birmingham, AL 35209, 205-802-1200.

Peterson's Guide to Two-Year Colleges 1997 161

Alabama–Alaska

VIRGINIA COLLEGE AT HUNTSVILLE
Huntsville, Alabama

UG Enrollment: 250	Tuition & Fees: $3900
Application Deadline: rolling	Room & Board: N/Avail

GENERAL Proprietary, 2-year, coed. Awards diplomas, terminal associate degrees. *Total enrollment:* 250. *Faculty:* 21 (5 full-time, 16 part-time).
ENROLLMENT PROFILE 250 students.
FIRST-YEAR CLASS Of the students who applied, 95% were accepted, 90% of whom enrolled.
ACADEMIC PROGRAM Calendar: quarters.
GENERAL DEGREE REQUIREMENTS 90 quarter hours; computer course.
HOUSING College housing not available.
EXPENSES FOR 1996–97 Tuition: $3900 (minimum) full-time. Part-time tuition per quarter hour ranges from $130 to $160. One-time mandatory fee: $100.
FINANCIAL AID *College-administered undergrad aid 1995–96:* need-based scholarships, low-interest long-term loans from external sources, Federal Work-Study, part-time jobs. *Required forms:* FAFSA.
APPLYING *Required:* school transcript, CPAt. *Application deadline:* rolling. *Notification:* continuous.
APPLYING/TRANSFER *Required:* standardized test scores, high school transcript. *Recommended:* college transcript. *Entrance:* minimally difficult.
CONTACT Ms. Pat Thomas, Director of Admissions, Virginia College at Huntsville, Huntsville, AL 35805, 205-533-7387.

WALLACE STATE COMMUNITY COLLEGE
Hanceville, Alabama

UG Enrollment: 5,824	Tuition & Fees (AL Res): $999
Application Deadline: rolling	Room Only: $1050

GENERAL State-supported, 2-year, coed. Awards diplomas, transfer associate, terminal associate degrees. Founded 1966. *Setting:* 223-acre rural campus with easy access to Birmingham. *Educational spending 1994–95:* $1462 per undergrad. *Total enrollment:* 5,824. *Faculty:* 301 (121 full-time, 14% with terminal degrees, 180 part-time).
ENROLLMENT PROFILE 5,824 students from 16 states and territories, 6 other countries. 63% women, 37% men, 42% part-time, 99% state residents, 2% live on campus, 20% transferred in, 41% 25 or older, 0% Native American, 0% Hispanic, 2% African American. *Areas of study chosen:* 31% health professions and related sciences, 28% liberal arts/general studies, 22% vocational and home economics, 8% business management and administrative services, 4% education, 2% computer and information sciences, 2% engineering and applied sciences, 1% agriculture, 1% interdisciplinary studies, 1% performing arts. *Most popular recent majors:* liberal arts/general studies, nursing, business administration/commerce/management.
FIRST-YEAR CLASS 1,550 total; 1,650 applied, 98% were accepted, 96% of whom enrolled. 10% from top 10% of their high school class, 20% from top quarter, 40% from top half.
ACADEMIC PROGRAM Interdisciplinary curriculum, honor code. Calendar: quarters. 2,000 courses offered in 1995–96. Academic remediation for entering students, advanced placement, summer session for credit, part-time degree program (daytime, evenings, summer), co-op programs.
GENERAL DEGREE REQUIREMENTS 96 quarter hours; math/science requirements vary according to program; computer course for paralegal, secretarial majors.
MAJORS Accounting, agricultural sciences, art education, automotive technologies, aviation technology, business administration/commerce/management, business education, carpentry, child care/child and family studies, computer programming, computer science, construction technologies, cosmetology, criminal justice, dental services, drafting and design, early childhood education, education, electrical and electronics technologies, elementary education, emergency medical technology, engineering (general), farm and ranch management, fashion merchandising, finance/banking, fire science, flight training, food services management, heating/refrigeration/air conditioning, horticulture, industrial administration, interior design, labor and industrial relations, law enforcement/police sciences, legal secretarial studies, liberal arts/general studies, library science, machine and tool technologies, marketing/retailing/merchandising, medical assistant technologies, medical laboratory technology, medical records services, medical secretarial studies, mental health/rehabilitation counseling, music, nursing, occupational safety and health, occupational therapy, paralegal studies, physical therapy, postal management, poultry sciences, practical nursing, radiological technology, real estate, religious studies, respiratory therapy, secretarial studies/office management, welding technology.
LIBRARY Wallace State College Library with 41,500 books, 30,000 microform titles, 425 periodicals, 200 CD-ROMs, 105 records, tapes, and CDs. Acquisition spending 1994–95: $149,848.
COMPUTERS ON CAMPUS 75 computers for student use in computer center, classrooms, library. Staffed computer lab on campus provides training in use of computers, software. Academic computing expenditure 1994–95: $50,081.
COLLEGE LIFE Choral group. 20% vote in student government elections. *Social organizations:* 7 open to all. *Most popular organizations:* Student Government Association, Vocational Industrial Clubs of America, Student Nurses Association. *Major annual events:* Homecoming, Women's Health Day, Summer Music Workshop. *Student services:* personal-psychological counseling.
HOUSING 94 college housing spaces available; all were occupied 1995–96. No special consideration for freshman housing applicants. Off-campus living permitted. *Option:* single-sex (4 buildings) housing available. Resident assistants live in dorms.
ATHLETICS Member NJCAA. *Intercollegiate:* baseball M(s), basketball M(s)/W(s), cross-country running M(s)/W(s), golf M(s)/W(s), soccer M(s), softball W(s), track and field M(s)/W(s), volleyball W(s). *Intramural:* basketball, softball, tennis, volleyball. *Contact:* Dr. James C. Bailey, President, 205-352-8130.
CAREER PLANNING *Services:* job fairs, resume preparation, career counseling, job interviews. 40 organizations recruited on campus 1994–95.
AFTER GRADUATION 79% of students completing a degree program in 1994–95 went directly on to further study.

EXPENSES FOR 1995–96 State resident tuition: $900 full-time, $20 per quarter hour part-time. Nonresident tuition: $1800 full-time, $40 per quarter hour part-time. Part-time mandatory fees: $2 per quarter hour. Full-time mandatory fees: $99. College room only: $1050.
FINANCIAL AID *College-administered undergrad aid 1995–96:* 125 need-based scholarships (average $900), 133 non-need scholarships (average $1600), 35 Federal Work-Study (averaging $3000), 6 part-time jobs. *Required forms:* institutional, FAFSA. *Priority deadline:* 9/15. *Waivers:* full or partial for employees or children of employees and senior citizens. *Notification:* continuous.
APPLYING Open admission for technical, liberal arts programs. *Options:* early entrance, deferred entrance, midyear entrance. *Required:* school transcript, TOEFL for international students. *Recommended:* ACT. *Required for some:* ACT, nursing exam. Test scores used for counseling/placement. *Application deadline:* rolling. *Notification:* continuous.
APPLYING/TRANSFER *Required:* college transcript. *Recommended:* standardized test scores. *Required for some:* standardized test scores. *Application deadline:* rolling. *Notification:* continuous. *Contact:* Ms. Diane M. Harris, Director of Admissions, 205-352-8129.
CONTACT Ms. Diane M. Harris, Director of Admissions, Wallace State Community College, Hanceville, AL 35077-2000, 205-352-8129.

ALASKA

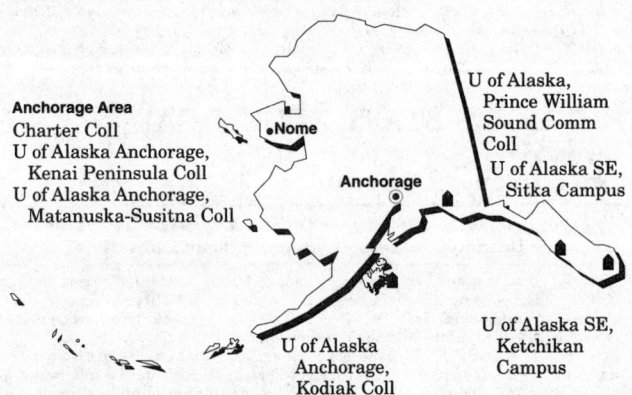

Anchorage Area
Charter Coll
U of Alaska Anchorage, Kenai Peninsula Coll
U of Alaska Anchorage, Matanuska-Susitna Coll

U of Alaska, Prince William Sound Comm Coll
U of Alaska SE, Sitka Campus
U of Alaska Anchorage, Kodiak Coll
U of Alaska SE, Ketchikan Campus

CHARTER COLLEGE
Anchorage, Alaska

Enrollment: N/R	Tuition & Fees: $8700
Application Deadline: rolling	Room & Board: N/Avail

GENERAL Proprietary, 2-year, coed. Awards certificates, transfer associate, terminal associate degrees. Founded 1985. *Setting:* urban campus. *Faculty:* 28 (7 full-time, 21 part-time).
ACADEMIC PROGRAM Calendar: quarters. Part-time degree program (daytime, evenings, summer).
GENERAL DEGREE REQUIREMENTS 90 credit hours; math/science requirements vary according to program; computer course.
MAJORS Accounting, computer science, computer technologies, medical assistant technologies, paralegal studies.
HOUSING College housing not available.
EXPENSES FOR 1995–96 *Application fee:* $20. Tuition: $8700 full-time, $149 per credit hour part-time.
FINANCIAL AID *College-administered undergrad aid 1995–96:* low-interest long-term loans from external sources.
APPLYING *Required:* school transcript, interview. *Application deadline:* rolling. *Notification:* continuous.
APPLYING/TRANSFER *Required:* high school transcript, interview, college transcript. *Application deadline:* rolling. *Notification:* continuous.
CONTACT Ms. Lily Sirianni, Vice-President, Charter College, 2221 East Northern Lights Boulevard, Anchorage, AK 99508, 907-277-1000 or toll-free 800-279-1008 (in-state). *Fax:* 907-274-3342.

UNIVERSITY OF ALASKA ANCHORAGE, KENAI PENINSULA COLLEGE
Soldotna, Alaska

UG Enrollment: 1,658	Tuition & Fees (AK Res): $2145
Application Deadline: rolling	Room & Board: N/Avail

GENERAL State-supported, 2-year, coed. Part of University of Alaska System. Awards certificates, transfer associate, terminal associate degrees. Founded 1964. *Setting:* 360-acre rural campus. *Endowment:* $950,000. *Total enrollment:* 1,658. *Faculty:* 107 (27 full-time, 25% with terminal degrees, 80 part-time).
ENROLLMENT PROFILE 1,658 students: 67% women, 78% part-time, 99% state residents, 76% 25 or older, 4% Native American, 2% Hispanic, 1% African American, 1% Asian American.
FIRST-YEAR CLASS 282 total; 282 applied, 100% were accepted, 100% of whom enrolled.
ACADEMIC PROGRAM Core, honor code. Calendar: semesters. 450 courses offered in 1995–96. Academic remediation for entering students, English as a second language

program offered during academic year, advanced placement, part-time degree program (daytime, evenings), adult/continuing education programs, internships.
GENERAL DEGREE REQUIREMENT 60 credits.
MAJORS Business administration/commerce/management, electrical and electronics technologies, forest technology, instrumentation technology, liberal arts/general studies, machine and tool technologies, petroleum technology, secretarial studies/office management.
LIBRARY Kenai Peninsula College Library with 25,000 books, 95 periodicals, 1 on-line bibliographic service, 2 CD-ROMs, 517 records, tapes, and CDs. Acquisition spending 1994–95: $32,130.
COMPUTERS ON CAMPUS 45 computers for student use in computer labs, classrooms. Staffed computer lab on campus provides training in use of computers, software.
COLLEGE LIFE Drama-theater group, student-run newspaper. 4% vote in student government elections. *Student services:* personal-psychological counseling. *Campus security:* 24-hour emergency response devices.
HOUSING College housing not available.
CAREER PLANNING *Placement office:* 1 part-time staff. *Director:* Ms. Sara Moore, Career Center Coordinator, 907-262-0337. *Services:* resume preparation, career counseling, careers library.
EXPENSES FOR 1996–97 State resident tuition: $2100 (minimum) full-time. Nonresident tuition: $6300 (minimum) full-time. Part-time tuition per credit ranges from $70 to $77 for state residents, $210 to $231 for nonresidents. Part-time mandatory fees: $1.50 per credit. Full-time mandatory fees: $45.
FINANCIAL AID *College-administered undergrad aid 1995–96:* 55 need-based scholarships (average $300), 3 non-need scholarships (average $220), short-term loans (average $100), low-interest long-term loans from external sources (average $2625), 14 Federal Work-Study (averaging $3000), 36 part-time jobs. *Required forms for some financial aid applicants:* state, institutional, FAFSA; accepted: CSS Financial Aid PROFILE. *Priority deadline:* 4/1. *Payment plan:* deferred payment. *Waivers:* full or partial for employees or children of employees and senior citizens. *Average indebtedness of graduates:* $11,000.
APPLYING Open admission. *Options:* Common Application, midyear entrance. *Required:* TOEFL for international students. *Recommended:* school transcript. Test scores used for counseling/placement. *Application deadline:* rolling.
APPLYING/TRANSFER *Required:* high school transcript, interview. *Application deadline:* rolling. *Contact:* Ms. Karen Dorcas, Administrative Assistant, 907-262-0317.
CONTACT Ms. Shelly Love, Data Management Clerk, University of Alaska Anchorage, Kenai Peninsula College, Soldotna, AK 99669-9798, 907-262-0311.

UNIVERSITY OF ALASKA ANCHORAGE, KODIAK COLLEGE
Kodiak, Alaska

UG Enrollment: 948	Tuition & Fees (AK Res): $1466
Application Deadline: rolling	Room & Board: N/Avail

GENERAL State-supported, 2-year, coed. Part of University of Alaska System. Awards certificates, transfer associate, terminal associate degrees. Founded 1968. *Setting:* 68-acre rural campus. *Total enrollment:* 948. *Faculty:* 69 (9 full-time, 40% with terminal degrees, 60 part-time); student-faculty ratio is 12:1.
ENROLLMENT PROFILE 948 students: 70% women, 90% part-time, 100% state residents, 0% transferred in, 5% have need-based financial aid, 5% have non-need-based financial aid, 0% international, 83% 25 or older, 6% Native American, 2% Hispanic, 1% African American, 6% Asian American. *Areas of study chosen:* 60% liberal arts/general studies, 30% business management and administrative services, 10% computer and information sciences.
FIRST-YEAR CLASS 100 total. Of the students who applied, 100% were accepted.
ACADEMIC PROGRAM Core. Calendar: semesters. Advanced placement, part-time degree program (daytime, evenings), adult/continuing education programs.
GENERAL DEGREE REQUIREMENTS 60 credits; 9 credits of math/natural science.
MAJORS Business administration/commerce/management, liberal arts/general studies, secretarial studies/office management.
LIBRARY Carolyn Floyd Library with 20,000 books, 153 microform titles, 100 periodicals, 500 records, tapes, and CDs.
COMPUTERS ON CAMPUS 40 computers for student use in computer center, office occupations lab provide access to main academic computer, e-mail, on-line services. Staffed computer lab on campus provides training in use of computers, software.
HOUSING College housing not available.
CAREER PLANNING *Placement office:* 1 full-time staff. *Director:* Ms. Christine Jamin, Counselor, Career Planning, 907-486-4161. *Services:* career counseling, careers library.
EXPENSES FOR 1995–96 State resident tuition: $1456 (minimum) full-time. Nonresident tuition: $5736 full-time. Part-time tuition per credit ranges from $56 to $75 for state residents, $56 to $225 for nonresidents. Part-time mandatory fees: $10 per year. State resident tuition ranges up to $1950 full-time according to class level. Full-time mandatory fees: $10.
FINANCIAL AID *College-administered undergrad aid 1995–96:* 9 need-based scholarships (averaging $200), 2 non-need scholarships (averaging $200), 1 part-time job. *Required forms:* institutional, FAFSA; required for some: state. *Priority deadline:* 4/1. *Payment plan:* deferred payment. *Waivers:* full or partial for employees or children of employees and senior citizens.
APPLYING Open admission. *Option:* midyear entrance. *Recommended:* ACT ASSET. Test scores used for counseling/placement. *Application deadline:* rolling.
APPLYING/TRANSFER *Recommended:* standardized test scores. *Contact:* Ms. Christine Jamin, Counselor, 907-486-4161.
CONTACT Ms. Fae Gaines, Registrar, University of Alaska Anchorage, Kodiak College, Kodiak, AK 99615-6643, 907-486-4161.

UNIVERSITY OF ALASKA ANCHORAGE, MATANUSKA-SUSITNA COLLEGE
Palmer, Alaska

UG Enrollment: 1,654	Tuition & Fees (AK Res): $2120
Application Deadline: rolling	Room & Board: N/Avail

GENERAL State-supported, 2-year, coed. Part of University of Alaska System. Awards certificates, transfer associate, terminal associate degrees. Founded 1958. *Setting:* 950-acre small-town campus. *Total enrollment:* 1,654. *Faculty:* 113 (13 full-time, 3% with terminal degrees, 100 part-time); student-faculty ratio is 15:1.
ENROLLMENT PROFILE 1,654 students: 70% women, 30% men, 82% part-time, 95% state residents, 20% transferred in, 60% have need-based financial aid, 40% have non-need-based financial aid, 82% 25 or older, 4% Native American, 1% Hispanic, 1% African American, 0% Asian American. *Areas of study chosen:* 60% liberal arts/general studies, 29% vocational and home economics, 10% business management and administrative services. *Most popular recent majors:* liberal arts/general studies, heating/refrigeration/air conditioning, accounting.
FIRST-YEAR CLASS 256 total. Of the students who applied, 100% were accepted, 79% of whom enrolled.
ACADEMIC PROGRAM Core, liberal arts curriculum, honor code. Calendar: semesters. 450 courses offered in 1995–96. Academic remediation for entering students, advanced placement, summer session for credit, part-time degree program (daytime, evenings, weekends, summer), adult/continuing education programs, co-op programs. Off-campus study at Alaska Pacific University, University of Alaska Anchorage.
GENERAL DEGREE REQUIREMENTS 60 credits; computer course for business, accounting majors; internship (some majors).
MAJORS Accounting, business administration/commerce/management, electrical and electronics technologies, fire science, heating/refrigeration/air conditioning, human services, liberal arts/general studies, secretarial studies/office management.
LIBRARY Al Okeson Library with 40,000 books, 200 periodicals, 400 records, tapes, and CDs.
COMPUTERS ON CAMPUS Computer purchase plan available. 60 computers for student use in computer labs, learning resource center, classrooms, library provide access to e-mail. Staffed computer lab on campus provides training in use of software.
COLLEGE LIFE Orientation program (3 days, $69). Choral group, student-run newspaper. 15% vote in student government elections. *Most popular organizations:* Student Government, Math Club. *Major annual events:* Christmas Ball, Spring BBQ. *Student services:* personal-psychological counseling. *Campus security:* 24-hour patrols.
HOUSING College housing not available.
CAREER PLANNING *Service:* career counseling.
AFTER GRADUATION 25% of students completing a degree program in 1994–95 went directly on to further study.
EXPENSES FOR 1996–97 *Application fee:* $35. State resident tuition: $2100 (minimum) full-time. Nonresident tuition: $6300 (minimum) full-time. Part-time tuition per credit ranges from $70 to $77 for state residents, $210 to $231 for nonresidents. Part-time mandatory fees per semester range from $5 to $10. Full-time mandatory fees: $20.
FINANCIAL AID *College-administered undergrad aid 1995–96:* need-based scholarships, 6 non-need scholarships (average $375), low-interest long-term loans from external sources (average $2400), Federal Work-Study, part-time jobs. *Required forms:* CSS Financial Aid PROFILE, institutional, FAFSA. *Priority deadline:* 5/31. *Payment plan:* deferred payment. *Waivers:* full or partial for employees or children of employees and senior citizens.
APPLYING Open admission. *Options:* Common Application, early entrance. *Recommended:* school transcript, minimum 2.0 GPA, 3 years of high school math and science, SAT I or ACT, TOEFL for international students. Test scores used for counseling/placement. *Application deadline:* rolling.
APPLYING/TRANSFER *Recommended:* high school transcript, 3 years of high school math and science, minimum 2.0 high school GPA. *Application deadline:* rolling. *Contact:* Ms. Toni Kahklen-Jones, Counselor, 907-745-9774.
CONTACT Dr. Joseph Emmons, College Director, University of Alaska Anchorage, Matanuska-Susitna College, Palmer, AK 99645-2889, 907-745-9726. *Fax:* 907-745-9711.

UNIVERSITY OF ALASKA, PRINCE WILLIAM SOUND COMMUNITY COLLEGE
Valdez, Alaska

UG Enrollment: 1,508	Tuition & Fees (AK Res): $1850
Application Deadline: rolling	Room & Board: $3050

GENERAL State-supported, 2-year, coed. Part of University of Alaska System. Awards transfer associate, terminal associate degrees. Founded 1978. *Setting:* small-town campus. *Total enrollment:* 1,508. *Faculty:* 63 (10 full-time, 100% with terminal degrees, 53 part-time).
ENROLLMENT PROFILE 1,508 students from 2 states and territories, 2 other countries. 65% women, 86% part-time, 20% transferred in, 76% 25 or older, 6% Native American, 2% Hispanic, 1% African American, 1% Asian American. *Most popular recent majors:* liberal arts/general studies, secretarial studies/office management, mental health/rehabilitation counseling.
FIRST-YEAR CLASS Of the students who applied, 100% were accepted, 100% of whom enrolled.
ACADEMIC PROGRAM Core, honor code. Calendar: semesters. 290 courses offered in 1995–96. Academic remediation for entering students, English as a second language program offered during academic year, summer session for credit, adult/continuing education programs, internships.
GENERAL DEGREE REQUIREMENTS 60 credits; 9 credits of math/science including at least 1 lab science course; computer course for broadcasting, office management technology majors; internship (some majors).
MAJORS Broadcasting, liberal arts/general studies, mental health/rehabilitation counseling, secretarial studies/office management.

Alaska

University of Alaska, Prince William Sound Community College *(continued)*
LIBRARY Valdez Consortium Library with 37,703 books, 34 microform titles, 172 periodicals, 2 on-line bibliographic services, 6 CD-ROMs, 2,459 records, tapes, and CDs. Acquisition spending 1994–95: $37,000.
COMPUTERS ON CAMPUS 25 computers for student use in computer center, library.
COLLEGE LIFE *Student services:* personal-psychological counseling. *Campus security:* student patrols.
HOUSING 70 college housing spaces available; 25 were occupied 1995–96. No special consideration for freshman housing applicants. Off-campus living permitted. Resident assistants live in dorms.
CAREER PLANNING *Service:* career counseling.
EXPENSES FOR 1996–97 *Application fee:* $10. State resident tuition: $1800 full-time, $60 per credit part-time. Nonresident tuition: $5400 full-time, $180 per credit part-time. Part-time mandatory fees per semester range from $2.50 to $25. Full-time mandatory fees: $50. College room and board: $3050. College room only: $1600.
FINANCIAL AID *College-administered undergrad aid 1995–96:* 4 need-based scholarships (average $800), 20 non-need scholarships (average $350), low-interest long-term loans from external sources (average $2000), Federal Work-Study, 4 part-time jobs. *Required forms:* CSS Financial Aid PROFILE, state, institutional, FAFSA. *Priority deadline:* 8/15. *Payment plan:* deferred payment. *Waivers:* full or partial for senior citizens.
APPLYING Open admission. *Option:* early entrance. *Required:* TOEFL for international students, ACT ASSET. Test scores used for counseling/placement. *Application deadline:* rolling.
APPLYING/TRANSFER *Required:* standardized test scores. *Entrance:* noncompetitive. *Application deadline:* rolling.
CONTACT Mr. Doug Desorcie, Student Services Coordinator, University of Alaska, Prince William Sound Community College, PO Box 97, Valdez, AK 99686-0097, 907-835-2678 or toll-free 800-478-8800 (in-state), 800-526-2586 (out-of-state). College video available.

UNIVERSITY OF ALASKA SOUTHEAST, KETCHIKAN CAMPUS
Ketchikan, Alaska

UG Enrollment: 95	Tuition & Fees (AK Res): $2115
Application Deadline: rolling	Room & Board: N/Avail

GENERAL State and locally supported, 2-year, coed. Part of University of Alaska System. Awards transfer associate, terminal associate degrees. Founded 1954. *Setting:* 51-acre small-town campus. *Endowment:* $2.6 million. *Research spending 1994–95:* $92,750. *Total enrollment:* 95. *Faculty:* 27 (7 full-time, 30% with terminal degrees, 20 part-time); student-faculty ratio is 9:1.
ENROLLMENT PROFILE 95 students from 5 states and territories, 1 other country. 72% women, 28% men, 35% part-time, 96% state residents, 1% transferred in, 2% international, 46% 25 or older, 17% Native American, 1% Hispanic, 1% African American, 1% Asian American. *Areas of study chosen:* 68% liberal arts/general studies, 27% business management and administrative services, 4% vocational and home economics. *Most popular recent majors:* liberal arts/general studies, tourism and travel, business administration/commerce/management.
FIRST-YEAR CLASS 47 total; 52 applied, 100% were accepted, 90% of whom enrolled.
ACADEMIC PROGRAM Core, interdisciplinary curriculum. Calendar: semesters. 130 courses offered in 1995–96; average class size 12 in required courses. Academic remediation for entering students, services for LD students, self-designed majors, part-time degree program (daytime, evenings, weekends), adult/continuing education programs, internships. Off-campus study at University of Alaska Southeast, Sheldon Jackson College.
GENERAL DEGREE REQUIREMENTS 60 credits; 1 course each in math and science; computer course for business administration majors; internship (some majors).
MAJORS Business administration/commerce/management, liberal arts/general studies, secretarial studies/office management, tourism and travel.
LIBRARY Ketchikan Campus Library with 54,000 books, 25 microform titles, 175 periodicals, 620 records, tapes, and CDs. Acquisition spending 1994–95: $16,015.
COMPUTERS ON CAMPUS 40 computers for student use in computer center, library, student center provide access to off-campus computing facilities, e-mail, on-line services, Internet. Staffed computer lab on campus (open 24 hours a day) provides training in use of computers, software. Academic computing expenditure 1994–95: $28,054.
COLLEGE LIFE Choral group. 10% vote in student government elections. *Social organizations:* 1 open to all. *Most popular organizations:* Student Council, Phi Theta Kappa, Alpha Beta Gamma. *Student services:* personal-psychological counseling. *Campus security:* 24-hour emergency response devices.
HOUSING College housing not available.
CAREER PLANNING *Services:* resume preparation, career counseling, careers library.
AFTER GRADUATION 90% of students completing a degree program in 1994–95 went directly on to further study.
EXPENSES FOR 1996–97 *Application fee:* $30. State resident tuition: $2100 (minimum) full-time. Nonresident tuition: $5460 (minimum) full-time. Part-time tuition per credit ranges from $70 to $77 for state residents. Part-time tuition per semester ranges from $70 to $2030 for nonresidents. Part-time mandatory fees: $5 per semester (minimum). Full-time tuition ranges up to $2310 for state residents, $5892 for nonresidents, according to class level. Full-time mandatory fees: $15.
FINANCIAL AID *College-administered undergrad aid 1995–96:* 6 need-based scholarships (average $1400), 7 non-need scholarships (average $300), low-interest long-term loans from external sources (average $4000), Federal Work-Study, 4 part-time jobs. *Required forms:* CSS Financial Aid PROFILE, institutional, FAFSA; required for some: state. *Application deadline:* continuous to 5/15.
APPLYING Open admission. *Option:* early entrance. *Required:* school transcript, TOEFL for international students. *Recommended:* SAT I or ACT, ACT ASSET. *Required for some:* essay. Test scores used for counseling/placement. *Application deadline:* rolling.
APPLYING/TRANSFER *Required:* high school transcript, college transcript. *Contact:* Ms. Brenda Jepson, Admissions and Records, 907-225-6177.
CONTACT Mr. William G. Trudeau, Assistant Director of Student Services and Public Relations, University of Alaska Southeast, Ketchikan Campus, Ketchikan, AK 99901-5798, 907-225-6177 Ext. 14. *Fax:* 907-225-3624. *E-mail:* knblj@acad1.alaska.edu. Electronic viewbook available.

UNIVERSITY OF ALASKA SOUTHEAST, SITKA CAMPUS
Sitka, Alaska

UG Enrollment: 1,470	Tuition & Fees (AK Res): $1715
Application Deadline: rolling	Room Only: $2400

GENERAL State-supported, 2-year, coed. Part of University of Alaska System. Awards certificates, transfer associate, terminal associate degrees. Founded 1962. *Setting:* small-town campus. *Educational spending 1994–95:* $1022 per undergrad. *Total enrollment:* 1,470. *Faculty:* 104 (11 full-time, 50% with terminal degrees, 93 part-time); student-faculty ratio is 14:1.
ENROLLMENT PROFILE 1,470 students from 10 states and territories, 2 other countries. 67% women, 33% men, 51% part-time, 97% state residents, 2% live on campus, 5% transferred in, 65% 25 or older, 24% Native American, 1% Hispanic, 1% African American, 2% Asian American. *Most popular recent majors:* liberal arts/general studies, business administration/commerce/management.
FIRST-YEAR CLASS 40 total.
ACADEMIC PROGRAM Core, general studies curriculum, honor code. Calendar: semesters. 500 courses offered in 1995–96. Academic remediation for entering students, English as a second language program offered during academic year, tutorials, summer session for credit, part-time degree program (daytime, evenings), adult/continuing education programs, co-op programs and internships. Off-campus study at Sheldon Jackson College, University of Alaska Southeast.
GENERAL DEGREE REQUIREMENTS 60 credits; computer course for health information management, business information systems majors; internship (some majors).
MAJORS Business administration/commerce/management, computer technologies, law enforcement/police sciences, liberal arts/general studies, medical assistant technologies, welding technology.
LIBRARY Stratton Library with 78,000 books, 380 periodicals, 1 on-line bibliographic service, 4 CD-ROMs, 2,500 records, tapes, and CDs. Acquisition spending 1994–95: $9000.
COMPUTERS ON CAMPUS 40 computers for student use in computer center, computer labs, learning resource center, library, student center, dorms provide access to e-mail, on-line services. Staffed computer lab on campus provides training in use of computers, software. Academic computing expenditure 1994–95: $286,142.
COLLEGE LIFE *Major annual events:* Campus-Wide Picnic, Christmas Tree Lighting. *Student services:* personal-psychological counseling. *Campus security:* 24-hour emergency response devices, controlled dormitory access.
HOUSING 54 college housing spaces available; 21 were occupied 1995–96. No special consideration for freshman housing applicants. Off-campus living permitted. *Option:* coed (1 building) housing available. Resident assistants live in dorms.
CAREER PLANNING *Placement office:* 1 full-time staff; $85,969 operating expenditure 1994–95. *Director:* Mr. Phil Slattery, Counselor, 907-747-6653. *Services:* resume preparation, career counseling, careers library, job bank.
AFTER GRADUATION 40% of students completing a degree program in 1994–95 went directly on to further study.
EXPENSES FOR 1996–97 *Application fee:* $35. State resident tuition: $1680 (minimum) full-time. Nonresident tuition: $4992 (minimum) full-time. Part-time tuition per credit ranges from $70 to $77 for state residents, $70 to $231 for nonresidents. Part-time mandatory fees: $1 per credit. Full-time mandatory fees: $35. College room only: $2400.
FINANCIAL AID *College-administered undergrad aid 1995–96:* 20 need-based scholarships (average $1550), 20 non-need scholarships (average $200), low-interest long-term loans from external sources (average $4000), 10 part-time jobs. *Required forms:* institutional, FAFSA. *Priority deadline:* 5/1. *Payment plan:* deferred payment. *Waivers:* full or partial for employees or children of employees and senior citizens. *Notification:* continuous.
APPLYING Open admission. *Options:* Common Application, early entrance, midyear entrance. *Required:* school transcript, minimum 2.0 GPA. *Recommended:* TOEFL for international students. *Required for some:* essay. Test scores used for counseling/placement. *Application deadline:* continuous.
APPLYING/TRANSFER *Required:* high school transcript, college transcript, minimum 2.0 college GPA, minimum 2.0 high school GPA. *Recommended:* standardized test scores. *Required for some:* essay. *Application deadline:* rolling. *Notification:* continuous. *Contact:* Mr. Phil Slattery, Counselor, 907-747-6653.
CONTACT Mrs. Kathleen Niles, Admissions and Records Clerk, University of Alaska Southeast, Sitka Campus, Sitka, AK 99835-9418, 907-747-6653 Ext. 707. *Fax:* 907-747-7747.

Arizona

ARIZONA

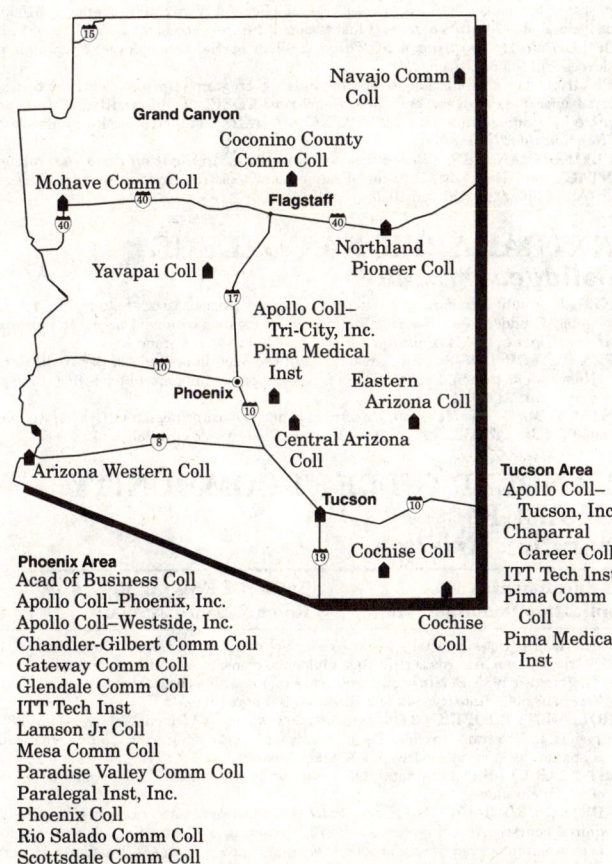

Navajo Comm Coll
Grand Canyon
Coconino County Comm Coll
Mohave Comm Coll
Flagstaff
Northland Pioneer Coll
Yavapai Coll
Apollo Coll–Tri-City, Inc.
Pima Medical Inst
Phoenix
Eastern Arizona Coll
Central Arizona Coll
Arizona Western Coll
Tucson
Cochise Coll

Tucson Area
Apollo Coll–Tucson, Inc.
Chaparral Career Coll
ITT Tech Inst
Pima Comm Coll
Pima Medical Inst

Phoenix Area
Acad of Business Coll
Apollo Coll–Phoenix, Inc.
Apollo Coll–Westside, Inc.
Chandler-Gilbert Comm Coll
Gateway Comm Coll
Glendale Comm Coll
ITT Tech Inst
Lamson Jr Coll
Mesa Comm Coll
Paradise Valley Comm Coll
Paralegal Inst, Inc.
Phoenix Coll
Rio Salado Comm Coll
Scottsdale Comm Coll
South Mountain Comm Coll

ACADEMY OF BUSINESS COLLEGE
Phoenix, Arizona

UG Enrollment: 240	Tuition: $8745/deg prog
Application Deadline: rolling	Room & Board: N/Avail

GENERAL Proprietary, 2-year, coed. Awards certificates, diplomas, terminal associate degrees. Founded 1982. *Setting:* urban campus. *Total enrollment:* 240. *Faculty:* 19 (4 full-time, 15 part-time).
ENROLLMENT PROFILE 240 students: 87% women, 0% part-time, 100% state residents, 30% transferred in. *Most popular recent majors:* paralegal studies, accounting, legal secretarial studies.
ACADEMIC PROGRAM Career-oriented curriculum. Calendar: six-week terms. 11 courses offered in 1995–96. Summer session for credit, internships.
GENERAL DEGREE REQUIREMENT 60 credits.
MAJORS Accounting, computer technologies, legal secretarial studies, paralegal studies, secretarial studies/office management.
COMPUTERS ON CAMPUS 50 computers for student use in computer labs provide access to main academic computer, on-line services, Internet. Staffed computer lab on campus.
COLLEGE LIFE *Social organizations:* 2 open to all. *Most popular organizations:* Collegiate Secretaries International, Toastmasters. *Student services:* personal-psychological counseling.
HOUSING College housing not available.
EXPENSES FOR 1996–97 *Application fee:* $50. Tuition: $8745 per degree program (minimum). Full-time tuition for computer technologies program: $11,770. Full-time mandatory fees: $50 (minimum).
FINANCIAL AID *Required forms:* institutional, FAFSA; required for some: state. *Payment plan:* installment. *Waivers:* full or partial for employees or children of employees.
APPLYING *Required:* school transcript, minimum 2.0 GPA, interview. *Required for some:* essay, 2 recommendations. *Application deadline:* rolling.
CONTACT Mr. Dennis O'Neil, Director of Admissions, Academy of Business College, 3320 West Cheryl Drive, #115, Phoenix, AZ 85051, 602-942-4141. *Fax:* 602-942-9082.

APOLLO COLLEGE–PHOENIX, INC.
Phoenix, Arizona

UG Enrollment: 85	Tuition: $10,832/deg prog
Application Deadline: N/R	Room & Board: N/Avail

GENERAL Proprietary, 2-year. Awards certificates, diplomas, transfer associate, terminal associate degrees. Founded 1976. *Total enrollment:* 85. *Faculty:* 17 (11 full-time, 6 part-time).
ENROLLMENT PROFILE 85 students.
FIRST-YEAR CLASS 30 total; 30 applied, 100% were accepted, 100% of whom enrolled.
ACADEMIC PROGRAM 7 courses offered in 1995–96.
GENERAL DEGREE REQUIREMENTS 66 credit hours; computer course.
MAJORS Medical laboratory technology, occupational therapy, respiratory therapy.
EXPENSES FOR 1996–97 *Application fee:* $75. Tuition per degree program ranges from $10,832 to $14,648.
APPLYING Open admission. *Required:* school transcript. *Required for some:* essay, interview, Wonderlic aptitude test. Test scores used for admission.
APPLYING/TRANSFER *Required:* high school transcript, college transcript. *Required for some:* essay, standardized test scores, interview. *Entrance:* noncompetitive.
CONTACT Ms. Julie Citron, Director of Admissions, Apollo College–Phoenix, Inc., 2701 West Bethany Home Road, Phoenix, AZ 85017, 602-433-1333.

APOLLO COLLEGE–TRI-CITY, INC.
Mesa, Arizona

Enrollment: N/R	Tuition: $10,500/deg prog
Application Deadline: rolling	Room & Board: N/Avail

GENERAL Proprietary, 2-year, coed. Part of Apollo Colleges, Inc. Awards transfer associate, terminal associate degrees. Founded 1977. *Setting:* suburban campus. *Faculty:* 17 (12 full-time, 5 part-time).
ENROLLMENT PROFILE 80% women, 20% men, 0% part-time, 100% state residents, 5% transferred in, 40% have need-based financial aid, 60% have non-need-based financial aid, 0% international, 50% 25 or older, 1% Native American, 1% Hispanic, 0% African American, 0% Asian American.
FIRST-YEAR CLASS 168 total. Of the students who applied, 100% were accepted, 95% of whom enrolled.
ACADEMIC PROGRAM Calendar: semesters.
GENERAL DEGREE REQUIREMENTS 66 credit hours; computer course.
COMPUTERS ON CAMPUS 25 computers for student use in computer labs. Staffed computer lab on campus provides training in use of computers, software.
COLLEGE LIFE *Campus security:* 24-hour emergency response devices, late-night transport-escort service.
CAREER PLANNING *Director:* Ms. Paula Pagano, Placement Director, 602-831-6585.
EXPENSES FOR 1995–96 *Application fee:* $75. Tuition per degree program ranges from $10,500 to $16,500.
FINANCIAL AID *College-administered undergrad aid 1995–96:* need-based scholarships, non-need scholarships.
APPLYING Open admission. *Required:* essay, school transcript, Wonderlic aptitude test. *Required for some:* recommendations, interview. Test scores used for admission. *Application deadline:* rolling. *Notification:* continuous.
APPLYING/TRANSFER *Required:* essay, standardized test scores, high school transcript, college transcript. *Required for some:* recommendations, interview. *Application deadline:* rolling. *Notification:* continuous. *Contact:* Mr. Tim Kulesha, Campus Director, 602-831-6585.
CONTACT Mr. Tim Kulesha, Campus Director, Apollo College–Tri-City, Inc., Mesa, AZ 85210-5004, 602-831-6585 or toll-free 800-36-TRAIN. College video available.

APOLLO COLLEGE–TUCSON, INC.
Tucson, Arizona

UG Enrollment: 320	Tuition & Fees: $5718
Application Deadline: N/R	Room & Board: N/Avail

GENERAL Proprietary, 2-year, coed. Awards diplomas, transfer associate, terminal associate degrees. Founded 1984. *Setting:* suburban campus. *Total enrollment:* 320.
ENROLLMENT PROFILE 320 students: 84% women, 16% men, 90% have need-based financial aid, 10% have non-need-based financial aid, 3% Native American, 35% Hispanic, 5% African American, 1% Asian American.
FIRST-YEAR CLASS 230 applied.
ACADEMIC PROGRAM Calendar: semesters modular courses are offered.
GENERAL DEGREE REQUIREMENTS 67 credits; computer course.
COMPUTERS ON CAMPUS 25 computers for student use in computer labs.
EXPENSES FOR 1996–97 *Application fee:* $75. Tuition: $5718 (minimum) full-time. Full-time tuition ranges up to $13,855 according to program.
FINANCIAL AID *College-administered undergrad aid 1995–96:* need-based scholarships, non-need scholarships.
APPLYING *Required for some:* essay, school transcript, recommendations, campus interview.
CONTACT Ms. Elaine Cue, Campus Director, Apollo College–Tucson, Inc., Tucson, AZ 85705-3227, 520-888-5885 or toll-free 800-36-TRAIN.

APOLLO COLLEGE–WESTSIDE, INC.
Phoenix, Arizona

UG Enrollment: 68	Tuition: $10,500/deg prog
Application Deadline: rolling	Room & Board: N/Avail

Apollo College–Westside, Inc. (continued)
GENERAL Proprietary, 2-year, coed. Part of Apollo Colleges, Inc. Awards transfer associate, terminal associate degrees. ***Setting:*** urban campus. ***Total enrollment:*** 68. ***Faculty:*** 13 (11 full-time, 2 part-time).
ENROLLMENT PROFILE 68 students: 70% women, 30% men, 0% part-time, 100% state residents, 5% transferred in, 40% have need-based financial aid, 60% have non-need-based financial aid, 0% international, 65% 25 or older, 3% Native American, 3% Hispanic, 2% African American, 0% Asian American.
FIRST-YEAR CLASS Of the students who applied, 100% were accepted, 95% of whom enrolled.
ACADEMIC PROGRAM Calendar: semesters.
GENERAL DEGREE REQUIREMENTS 66 credit hours; computer course.
COMPUTERS ON CAMPUS 10 computers for student use in computer labs. Staffed computer lab on campus provides training in use of computers, software.
COLLEGE LIFE ***Campus security:*** 24-hour emergency response devices, late-night transport-escort service.
CAREER PLANNING ***Director:*** Ms. Brenda Kells, Placement Director, 602-433-1333.
EXPENSES FOR 1995–96 ***Application fee:*** $75. Tuition per degree program ranges from $10,500 to $16,500.
FINANCIAL AID ***College-administered undergrad aid 1995–96:*** need-based scholarships, non-need scholarships.
APPLYING Open admission. ***Required:*** essay, school transcript, Wonderlic aptitude test. ***Required for some:*** recommendations, interview. Test scores used for admission. ***Application deadline:*** rolling. ***Notification:*** continuous.
APPLYING/TRANSFER ***Required:*** essay, standardized test scores, high school transcript, college transcript. ***Required for some:*** recommendations, interview. ***Application deadline:*** rolling. ***Notification:*** continuous. ***Contact:*** Ms. Julie Citron, Director of Admissions, 602-433-1333.
CONTACT Ms. Julie Citron, Director of Admissions, Apollo College–Westside, Inc., 2701 West Bethany Home Road, Phoenix, AZ 85017, 602-433-1333 or toll-free 800-36-TRAIN. College video available.

ARIZONA WESTERN COLLEGE
Yuma, Arizona

UG Enrollment: 5,837	**Tuition & Fees (AZ Res): $810**
Application Deadline: rolling	**Room & Board: $3000**

GENERAL State and locally supported, 2-year, coed. Part of Arizona State Community College System. Awards transfer associate, terminal associate degrees. Founded 1962. ***Setting:*** 640-acre rural campus. ***Research spending 1994–95:*** $57,924. ***Educational spending 1994–95:*** $1757 per undergrad. ***Total enrollment:*** 5,837. ***Faculty:*** 236 (96 full-time, 12% with terminal degrees, 140 part-time); student-faculty ratio is 16:1.
ENROLLMENT PROFILE 5,837 students from 45 states and territories, 8 other countries. 59% women, 72% part-time, 90% state residents, 7% live on campus, 8% transferred in, 75% have need-based financial aid, 5% have non-need-based financial aid, 1% international, 53% 25 or older, 2% Native American, 43% Hispanic, 3% African American, 2% Asian American. ***Areas of study chosen:*** 24% health professions and related sciences, 17% liberal arts/general studies, 17% social sciences, 16% business management and administrative services, 15% vocational and home economics, 4% computer and information sciences, 3% agriculture, 2% fine arts, 1% education, 1% engineering and applied sciences, 1% natural resource sciences. ***Most popular recent majors:*** liberal arts/general studies, business administration/commerce/management, nursing.
FIRST-YEAR CLASS 1,042 total. Of the students who applied, 99% were accepted.
ACADEMIC PROGRAM Core, interdisciplinary curriculum, honor code. Calendar: semesters. Academic remediation for entering students, English as a second language program offered during academic year, advanced placement, honors program, summer session for credit, part-time degree program (daytime, evenings, weekends, summer), adult/continuing education programs, co-op programs.
GENERAL DEGREE REQUIREMENT 64 credit hours.
MAJORS Agricultural business, agricultural technologies, art/fine arts, automotive technologies, biology/biological sciences, botany/plant sciences, broadcasting, business administration/commerce/management, chemical engineering technology, chemistry, child psychology/child development, computer information systems, computer science, criminal justice, drafting and design, education, electrical and electronics technologies, (pre)engineering sequence, engineering technology, English, environmental sciences, family and consumer studies, finance/banking, fire science, geology, health science, heating/refrigeration/air conditioning, human services, industrial engineering technology, law enforcement/police sciences, liberal arts/general studies, marketing/retailing/merchandising, mathematics, music, nursing, oceanography, physical education, physics, practical nursing, science, secretarial studies/office management, social science, Spanish, theater arts/drama, welding technology.
LIBRARY Arizona Western College Library with 57,000 books, 120,000 microform titles, 790 periodicals, 2 on-line bibliographic services, 8 CD-ROMs, 1,500 records, tapes, and CDs. Acquisition spending 1994–95: $174,546.
COMPUTERS ON CAMPUS 30 computers for student use in computer center, classrooms. Academic computing expenditure 1994–95: $357,698.
COLLEGE LIFE Drama-theater group, choral group, student-run newspaper, radio station. ***Social organizations:*** 15 open to all. ***Most popular organizations:*** Associated Students Governing Board, MECHA, Umoja, Honors Club, UVU. ***Major annual events:*** Winter Festival, Spring Fling, Christmas Formal. ***Student services:*** health clinic, personal-psychological counseling. ***Campus security:*** 24-hour emergency response devices and patrols, late-night transport-escort service.
HOUSING 390 college housing spaces available; all were occupied 1995–96. No special consideration for freshman housing applicants. Off-campus living permitted. ***Options:*** coed (1 building), single-sex (2 buildings) housing available. Resident assistants live in dorms.
ATHLETICS Member NJCAA. ***Intercollegiate:*** baseball M(s), basketball M(s), football M(s), soccer M(s), softball W(s), volleyball W(s). ***Intramural:*** badminton, basketball, bowling, football, soccer, softball, swimming and diving, table tennis (Ping-Pong), volleyball. ***Contact:*** Mr. Ray Butcher, Athletic Director, 520-344-7536.
CAREER PLANNING ***Placement office:*** 3 full-time, 2 part-time staff; $134,789 operating expenditure 1994–95. ***Director:*** Ms. Carmen Faucon-Woodward, Director of Career Development, 520-344-7604. ***Services:*** job fairs, resume preparation, resume referral, career counseling, careers library, job bank, job interviews. 8 organizations recruited on campus 1994–95.
AFTER GRADUATION 32% of students completing a degree program in 1994–95 went directly on to further study.
EXPENSES FOR 1996–97 State resident tuition: $810 full-time, $27 per credit hour part-time. Nonresident tuition: $5130 full-time. College room and board: $3000. College room only: $1200.
FINANCIAL AID ***College-administered undergrad aid 1995–96:*** need-based scholarships, 190 non-need scholarships (average $400), short-term loans (average $350), low-interest long-term loans from external sources, 400 Federal Work-Study (averaging $1000), 45 part-time jobs. ***Required forms:*** institutional, FAFSA; accepted: CSS Financial Aid PROFILE. ***Priority deadline:*** 4/20. ***Waivers:*** full or partial for employees or children of employees and senior citizens.
APPLYING Open admission except for nursing program. ***Options:*** early entrance, deferred entrance, midyear entrance. ***Required:*** TOEFL for international students. ***Required for some:*** minimum 3.0 GPA, SAT I or ACT. Test scores used for admission. ***Application deadline:*** rolling.
APPLYING/TRANSFER ***Entrance:*** noncompetitive. ***Application deadline:*** rolling.
CONTACT Mr. Dick Lott, Director of Admissions/Registrar, Arizona Western College, Yuma, AZ 85366-0929, 520-726-1050.

CENTRAL ARIZONA COLLEGE
Coolidge, Arizona

GENERAL County-supported, 2-year, coed. Awards transfer associate, terminal associate degrees. Founded 1961. ***Setting:*** 709-acre rural campus with easy access to Phoenix. ***Total enrollment:*** 14,724. ***Faculty:*** 440 (92 full-time, 348 part-time).
EXPENSES FOR 1995–96 State resident tuition: $700 full-time, $25 per credit part-time. Nonresident tuition: $4984 full-time, $37 per credit (minimum) part-time. College room and board: $2920.
CONTACT Ms. Cherie McGlynn, Director of Student Records/Registrar, Central Arizona College, Coolidge, AZ 85228-9779, 602-426-4260. College video available.

CHANDLER-GILBERT COMMUNITY COLLEGE
Chandler, Arizona

UG Enrollment: 3,500	**Tuition & Fees (AZ Res): $1030**
Application Deadline: N/R	**Room & Board: N/Avail**

GENERAL District-supported, 2-year, coed. Part of Maricopa County Community College District System. Awards certificates, diplomas, transfer associate, terminal associate degrees. Founded 1985. ***Setting:*** 80-acre rural campus with easy access to Phoenix. ***Total enrollment:*** 3,500. ***Faculty:*** 140 (40 full-time, 100 part-time).
ENROLLMENT PROFILE 3,500 students: 60% women, 40% men, 75% part-time, 98% state residents, 52% transferred in, 1% international, 42% 25 or older, 1% Native American, 15% Hispanic, 1% African American, 1% Asian American.
FIRST-YEAR CLASS 1,700 total. Of the students who applied, 100% were accepted, 95% of whom enrolled.
ACADEMIC PROGRAM Core, honor code. Calendar: semesters. Average class size 35 in required courses. Academic remediation for entering students, English as a second language program offered during academic year, advanced placement, Freshman Honors College, honors program, summer session for credit, part-time degree program (daytime, evenings, weekends, summer).
GENERAL DEGREE REQUIREMENTS 64 credits; 4 credits of math; 8 credits of science; computer course.
MAJORS Accounting, aircraft and missile maintenance, aviation technology, computer technologies, liberal arts/general studies, management information systems.
COMPUTERS ON CAMPUS Computers for student use in computer labs provide access to main academic computer, e-mail, on-line services, Internet. Staffed computer lab on campus provides training in use of computers, software.
COLLEGE LIFE Choral group, student-run newspaper. ***Student services:*** personal-psychological counseling. ***Campus security:*** 24-hour emergency response devices and patrols, late-night transport-escort service.
HOUSING College housing not available.
CAREER PLANNING ***Service:*** career counseling. 25 organizations recruited on campus 1994–95.
AFTER GRADUATION 95% of students completing a degree program in 1994–95 went directly on to further study.
EXPENSES FOR 1995–96 State resident tuition: $1020 full-time, $34 per credit part-time. Nonresident tuition: $3570 full-time. Nonresident part-time tuition per semester ranges from $59 to $1149. Part-time mandatory fees: $5 per semester. Full-time mandatory fees: $10.
FINANCIAL AID ***Payment plan:*** deferred payment. ***Waivers:*** full or partial for employees or children of employees.
APPLYING Open admission. ***Options:*** Common Application, electronic application, early entrance, midyear entrance. ***Required:*** TOEFL for international students.
APPLYING/TRANSFER ***Required:*** minimum 2.0 college GPA. ***Required for some:*** high school transcript, college transcript. ***Entrance:*** noncompetitive.
CONTACT Ms. Ruth Romano, Supervisor, Admissions and Records, Chandler-Gilbert Community College, Chandler, AZ 85225-2479, 602-732-7319.

CHAPARRAL CAREER COLLEGE
Tucson, Arizona

UG Enrollment: 363	**Tuition & Fees: $5490**
Application Deadline: rolling	**Room & Board: N/Avail**

GENERAL Proprietary, 2-year, coed. Awards transfer associate, terminal associate degrees. Founded 1972. ***Setting:*** suburban campus with easy access to Phoenix. ***Total enrollment:*** 363. ***Faculty:*** 30 (10 full-time, 2% with terminal degrees, 20 part-time).

ENROLLMENT PROFILE 363 students: 70% women, 0% part-time, 100% state residents, 30% transferred in, 0% international, 50% 25 or older.
FIRST-YEAR CLASS 145 total.
ACADEMIC PROGRAM Core. Calendar: 5 five-week modules. Internships.
GENERAL DEGREE REQUIREMENTS 106 credit hours; computer course; internship (some majors).
MAJORS Accounting, business administration/commerce/management, computer programming, hospitality services, legal secretarial studies, medical secretarial studies, secretarial studies/office management.
COMPUTERS ON CAMPUS 65 computers for student use in computer center provide access to e-mail, on-line services. Staffed computer lab on campus provides training in use of computers, software.
COLLEGE LIFE Student-run newspaper. ***Student services:*** personal-psychological counseling. ***Campus security:*** 24-hour emergency response devices.
HOUSING College housing not available.
CAREER PLANNING ***Placement office:*** 1 full-time, 1 part-time staff. ***Director:*** Mr. Frank Maish, Placement Director, 520-327-6866. ***Services:*** job fairs, resume preparation, resume referral, career counseling, job bank, job interviews.
EXPENSES FOR 1996–97 ***Application fee:*** $25. Tuition: $5490 full-time. One-time enrollment fee: $25. Tuition guaranteed not to increase for student's term of enrollment.
FINANCIAL AID ***College-administered undergrad aid 1995–96:*** 46 need-based scholarships (average $250), low-interest long-term loans from external sources (average $3900), 10 part-time jobs. ***Required forms:*** FAFSA. ***Priority deadline:*** 9/20. ***Payment plan:*** installment. ***Waivers:*** full or partial for employees or children of employees.
APPLYING Open admission. ***Option:*** Common Application. ***Required:*** school transcript, CPAt. Test scores used for admission and counseling/placement. ***Application deadline:*** rolling.
APPLYING/TRANSFER ***Required:*** standardized test scores, high school transcript, minimum 2.0 college GPA. ***Required for some:*** college transcript. ***Application deadline:*** rolling.
CONTACT Ms. Rosemary Elkins-DeCook, Admissions Director, Chaparral Career College, Tucson, AZ 85712, 520-327-6866. ***Fax:*** 520-325-0108.

COCHISE COLLEGE
Douglas, Arizona

UG Enrollment: 1,204	**Tuition & Fees (AZ Res): $862**
Application Deadline: rolling	**Room & Board: $3006**

Cochise College is a public community college with campuses in Sierra Vista and Douglas. Unique programs include aviation (pilot training, avionics, and maintenance technology), computer science, nursing, and other vocational and transfer programs. Graduates routinely transfer to Arizona State University, Northern Arizona University, University of Arizona, and Western New Mexico University.

GENERAL State and locally supported, 2-year, coed. Part of Cochise College. Awards certificates, transfer associate, terminal associate degrees. Founded 1962. ***Setting:*** 500-acre rural campus. ***Total enrollment:*** 1,204. ***Faculty:*** 88 (59 full-time, 10% with terminal degrees, 29 part-time); student-faculty ratio is 16:1.
ENROLLMENT PROFILE 1,204 students from 16 states and territories, 7 other countries. 58% women, 42% men, 49% part-time, 83% state residents, 17% live on campus, 6% transferred in, 3% international, 42% 25 or older, 1% Native American, 59% Hispanic, 1% African American, 3% Asian American. ***Areas of study chosen:*** 22% liberal arts/general studies, 11% English language/literature/letters, 8% health professions and related sciences, 7% education, 6% business management and administrative services, 4% psychology, 2% computer and information sciences. ***Most popular recent majors:*** liberal arts/general studies, business administration/commerce/management, nursing.
FIRST-YEAR CLASS 410 total. Of the students who applied, 100% were accepted, 85% of whom enrolled.
ACADEMIC PROGRAM Core, honor code. Calendar: semesters. Academic remediation for entering students, English as a second language program offered during academic year and summer, services for LD students, summer session for credit, part-time degree program (daytime, evenings), adult/continuing education programs, co-op programs and internships.
GENERAL DEGREE REQUIREMENTS 64 credit hours; 1 course each in college algebra and lab science.
MAJORS Agricultural sciences, aircraft and missile maintenance, anthropology, art/fine arts, aviation technology, behavioral sciences, biology/biological sciences, business administration/commerce/management, chemistry, communication, computer information systems, computer programming, computer science, criminal justice, drafting and design, education, (pre)engineering sequence, English, film studies, fire science, flight training, history, international studies, journalism, law enforcement/police sciences, legal secretarial studies, liberal arts/general studies, medical secretarial studies, nursing, photography, physical education, political science/government, psychology, secretarial studies/office management, social science, social work, Spanish, teacher aide studies.
LIBRARY Charles DiPeso Library with 44,925 books, 3,922 microform titles, 402 periodicals, 1 CD-ROM, 2,337 records, tapes, and CDs.
COMPUTERS ON CAMPUS 84 computers for student use in computer labs, tutoring labs, library provide access to e-mail, Internet. Staffed computer lab on campus provides training in use of computers, software.
COLLEGE LIFE Drama-theater group, choral group, student-run newspaper. 38% vote in student government elections. ***Social organizations:*** 6 open to all; 2 national fraternities. ***Most popular organizations:*** Student Government, Phi Theta Kappa. ***Major annual events:*** Red and White Ball, Valentine Dance. ***Student services:*** health clinic, personal-psychological counseling. ***Campus security:*** 24-hour emergency response devices and patrols, controlled dormitory access.
HOUSING 233 college housing spaces available; 198 were occupied 1995–96. No special consideration for freshman housing applicants. Off-campus living permitted. ***Option:*** single-sex (2 buildings) housing available. Resident assistants live in dorms.
ATHLETICS Member NJCAA. ***Intercollegiate:*** baseball M(s), basketball M(s)/W(s), equestrian sports M(s)/W(s). ***Intramural:*** basketball, football, golf, soccer, softball, swimming and diving, tennis, volleyball. ***Contact:*** Dr. James Hall, Director of Athletics, 520-364-0295.
CAREER PLANNING ***Placement office:*** 2 full-time staff. ***Director:*** Mr. Bill Lent, Career Action Center Coordinator, 520-364-0253. ***Services:*** resume preparation, resume referral, career counseling, careers library.
EXPENSES FOR 1996–97 State resident tuition: $832 full-time, $26 per unit part-time. Nonresident tuition: $4896 full-time. Part-time mandatory fees per year range from $30 to $50. Nonresident part-time tuition per credit hour: $39 for the first 6 credit hours, $153 for the next 5 credit hours. Full-time mandatory fees range from $30 to $50. College room and board: $3006.
FINANCIAL AID ***College-administered undergrad aid 1995–96:*** need-based scholarships (average $1850), non-need scholarships (average $300), low-interest long-term loans from external sources (average $3000), Federal Work-Study, part-time jobs. ***Required forms:*** institutional, FAFSA; accepted: CSS Financial Aid PROFILE. ***Priority deadline:*** 4/15. ***Waivers:*** full or partial for employees or children of employees and senior citizens.
APPLYING Open admission except for nursing, professional pilot, aviation maintenance technology programs. ***Options:*** early entrance, deferred entrance, midyear entrance. ***Recommended:*** TOEFL for international students. Test scores used for counseling/placement. ***Application deadline:*** rolling. ***Notification:*** continuous.
APPLYING/TRANSFER ***Entrance:*** noncompetitive. ***Application deadline:*** rolling. ***Notification:*** continuous. ***Contact:*** Mr. Jay Pence, Admissions Counselor, 520-364-0238.
CONTACT Mr. Jay Pence, Admissions Counselor, Cochise College, Douglas, AZ 85607-9724, 520-364-0336 or toll-free 800-966-7946. ***Fax:*** 520-364-0236.

❖ ***See page 722 for a narrative description.*** ❖

COCHISE COLLEGE
Sierra Vista, Arizona

UG Enrollment: 2,614	**Tuition & Fees (AZ Res): $862**
Application Deadline: rolling	**Room & Board: N/Avail**

GENERAL State and locally supported, 2-year, coed. Part of Cochise College. Awards certificates, transfer associate, terminal associate degrees. Founded 1977. ***Setting:*** 200-acre small-town campus with easy access to Tucson. ***Total enrollment:*** 2,614. ***Faculty:*** 253 (50 full-time, 10% with terminal degrees, 203 part-time).
ENROLLMENT PROFILE 2,614 students from 4 states and territories, 3 other countries. 61% women, 39% men, 74% part-time, 98% state residents, 19% transferred in, 67% 25 or older, 1% Native American, 12% Hispanic, 8% African American, 5% Asian American. ***Areas of study chosen:*** 17% liberal arts/general studies, 13% business management and administrative services, 13% computer and information sciences, 12% health professions and related sciences, 7% education, 6% engineering and applied sciences, 3% psychology. ***Most popular recent majors:*** liberal arts/general studies, business administration/commerce/management, computer information systems.
FIRST-YEAR CLASS 463 total. Of the students who applied, 100% were accepted, 83% of whom enrolled.
ACADEMIC PROGRAM Core, honor code. Calendar: semesters. Academic remediation for entering students, English as a second language program offered during academic year and summer, services for LD students, summer session for credit, part-time degree program (daytime, evenings, summer), adult/continuing education programs, co-op programs and internships.
GENERAL DEGREE REQUIREMENTS 64 credit hours; 1 course each in college algebra and lab science.
MAJORS Anthropology, art/fine arts, behavioral sciences, biology/biological sciences, business administration/commerce/management, chemistry, communication, computer information systems, computer programming, computer science, criminal justice, drafting and design, education, electrical and electronics technologies, electronics engineering technology, (pre)engineering sequence, English, film studies, fire science, history, hotel and restaurant management, international studies, journalism, law enforcement/police sciences, legal secretarial studies, liberal arts/general studies, medical secretarial studies, nursing, photography, physical education, political science/government, psychology, secretarial studies/office management, social science, social work, teacher aide studies, welding technology.
LIBRARY 17,440 books, 525 microform titles, 169 periodicals, 2 CD-ROMs, 2,203 records, tapes, and CDs.
COMPUTERS ON CAMPUS 162 computers for student use in computer labs, tutoring lab provide access to e-mail, Internet. Staffed computer lab on campus provides training in use of computers, software.
COLLEGE LIFE Drama-theater group, choral group, student-run newspaper. 42% vote in student government elections. ***Social organizations:*** 6 open to all; 1 national fraternity. ***Most popular organizations:*** Student Government, Phi Theta Kappa. ***Major annual events:*** Red and White Ball, Halloween Dance. ***Student services:*** personal-psychological counseling. ***Campus security:*** 24-hour emergency response devices and patrols.
HOUSING College housing not available.
CAREER PLANNING ***Placement office:*** 1 full-time, 1 part-time staff. ***Director:*** Mr. Ron Olson, Placement Coordinator, 520-515-5457. ***Services:*** resume preparation, resume referral, career counseling, careers library, job interviews.
EXPENSES FOR 1996–97 State resident tuition: $832 full-time, $26 per unit part-time. Nonresident tuition: $4896 full-time. Part-time mandatory fees per year range from $30 to $50. Nonresident part-time tuition per credit hour: $39 for the first 6 credit hours, $153 for the next 5 credit hours. Full-time mandatory fees range from $30 to $50.
FINANCIAL AID ***College-administered undergrad aid 1995–96:*** need-based scholarships, non-need scholarships (average $300), low-interest long-term loans from external sources, Federal Work-Study, part-time jobs. ***Required forms:*** institutional, FAFSA; accepted: CSS Financial Aid PROFILE. ***Priority deadline:*** 4/15. ***Waivers:*** full or partial for employees or children of employees and senior citizens.
APPLYING Open admission except for nursing program. ***Options:*** early entrance, deferred entrance, midyear entrance. ***Recommended:*** TOEFL for international students. Test scores used for counseling/placement. ***Application deadline:*** rolling. ***Notification:*** continuous.
APPLYING/TRANSFER ***Entrance:*** noncompetitive. ***Application deadline:*** rolling. ***Notification:*** continuous. ***Contact:*** Mr. Steven Lane, Admissions Counselor, 520-515-5412.
CONTACT Mr. Steven Lane, Admissions Counselor, Cochise College, Sierra Vista, AZ 85635-2317, 520-515-5412 or toll-free 800-966-7943. ***Fax:*** 520-515-5452.

COCONINO COUNTY COMMUNITY COLLEGE
Flagstaff, Arizona

UG Enrollment: 1,991	Tuition & Fees (AZ Res): $810
Application Deadline: rolling	Room & Board: N/Avail

GENERAL State-supported, 2-year, coed. Awards certificates, transfer associate, terminal associate degrees. Founded 1991. ***Setting:*** 5-acre small-town campus. ***Endowment:*** $11,275. ***Total enrollment:*** 1,991. ***Faculty:*** 201 (25 full-time, 12% with terminal degrees, 176 part-time).

ENROLLMENT PROFILE 1,991 students: 60% women, 40% men, 88% part-time, 1% international, 36% 25 or older, 14% Native American, 9% Hispanic, 1% African American, 1% Asian American. ***Areas of study chosen:*** 50% liberal arts/general studies, 22% vocational and home economics, 10% business management and administrative services, 10% education, 5% health professions and related sciences, 3% engineering and applied sciences. ***Most popular recent majors:*** liberal arts/general studies, accounting.

ACADEMIC PROGRAM Core, interdisciplinary curriculum. Calendar: semesters. 246 courses offered in 1995–96; average class size 20 in required courses. Academic remediation for entering students, services for LD students, advanced placement, summer session for credit, part-time degree program (daytime, evenings), adult/continuing education programs.

GENERAL DEGREE REQUIREMENTS 60 credit hours; 3 credit hours each of math and science; computer course for computer information systems, accounting, business management, office information systems majors.

MAJORS Accounting, business administration/commerce/management, computer information systems, criminal justice, fire science, liberal arts/general studies, management information systems, science.

COMPUTERS ON CAMPUS 100 computers for student use in computer labs, learning resource center provide access to off-campus computing facilities, on-line services, Internet. Staffed computer lab on campus provides training in use of computers, software. Academic computing expenditure 1994–95: $117,140.

COLLEGE LIFE Choral group. ***Social organizations:*** 1 open to all. ***Most popular organization:*** Student Leadership. ***Campus security:*** 24-hour patrols.

HOUSING College housing not available.

EXPENSES FOR 1996–97 ***Application fee:*** $10. State resident tuition: $810 full-time, $27 per credit hour part-time. Nonresident tuition: $3390 full-time, $35 per credit hour part-time.

FINANCIAL AID ***College-administered undergrad aid 1995–96:*** 875 need-based scholarships (average $1000), 26 Federal Work-Study (averaging $3000), 20 part-time jobs. ***Required forms:*** institutional, FAFSA; accepted: CSS Financial Aid PROFILE, state. ***Priority deadline:*** 4/15. ***Payment plan:*** installment. ***Waivers:*** full or partial for employees or children of employees and senior citizens. ***Notification:*** 7/15.

APPLYING Open admission. ***Option:*** midyear entrance. ***Required for some:*** school transcript. Test scores used for counseling/placement. ***Application deadline:*** rolling.

APPLYING/TRANSFER ***Required for some:*** high school transcript, college transcript. ***Application deadline:*** rolling. ***Contact:*** Ms. Linda Newell, Director of Admissions and Registrar, 520-527-1222 Ext. 302.

CONTACT Ms. Maggie Myers, Credentials Evaluator, Coconino County Community College, 3000 North Fourth Street, Flagstaff, AZ 86003, 520-522-1222 Ext. 201 or toll-free 800-350-7122 (out-of-state). ***Fax:*** 520-526-1821. ***E-mail:*** lnewell@coco.cc.az.us.

EASTERN ARIZONA COLLEGE
Thatcher, Arizona

UG Enrollment: 2,269	Tuition & Fees (AZ Res): $628
Application Deadline: rolling	Room & Board: $2902

GENERAL State and locally supported, 2-year, coed. Part of Arizona State Community College System. Awards certificates, transfer associate, terminal associate degrees. Founded 1888. ***Setting:*** 40-acre rural campus. ***Research spending 1994–95:*** $64,225. ***Educational spending 1994–95:*** $1129 per undergrad. ***Total enrollment:*** 2,269. ***Faculty:*** 232 (58 full-time, 100% with terminal degrees, 174 part-time). ***Notable Alumni:*** Tony Sanchez, research officer at Center for Disease Control; Spencer Kimball, retired law professor at University of Chicago; Nolan Richardson, head basketball coach at University of Arkansas; Dr. Wayne McGrath, former president of Eastern Arizona College.

ENROLLMENT PROFILE 2,269 students from 23 states and territories, 4 other countries. 59% women, 41% men, 39% part-time, 94% state residents, 10% transferred in, 10% have need-based financial aid, 8% have non-need-based financial aid, 1% international, 35% 25 or older, 8% Native American, 18% Hispanic, 3% African American, 1% Asian American. ***Areas of study chosen:*** 19% liberal arts/general studies, 18% business management and administrative services, 18% vocational and home economics, 16% education, 10% health professions and related sciences, 4% fine arts, 3% computer and information sciences, 3% premed, 2% engineering and applied sciences, 2% social sciences, 1% agriculture, 1% biological and life sciences, 1% communications and journalism, 1% performing arts, 1% prelaw, 1% psychology. ***Most popular recent major:*** liberal arts/general studies.

FIRST-YEAR CLASS 754 total. Of the students who applied, 100% were accepted.

ACADEMIC PROGRAM Honor code. Calendar: semesters. Academic remediation for entering students, English as a second language program offered during academic year, advanced placement, summer session for credit, part-time degree program (daytime, evenings), adult/continuing education programs, co-op programs.

GENERAL DEGREE REQUIREMENTS 64 semester hours; computer course for agricultural business, agricultural sciences, automotive technologies, bookkeeping, business education, office management majors.

MAJORS Advertising, agricultural business, agricultural sciences, anthropology, art education, art/fine arts, automotive technologies, biology/biological sciences, business administration/commerce/management, business education, chemistry, child care/child and family studies, commercial art, computer information systems, computer science, cosmetology, criminal justice, drafting and design, education, elementary education, (pre)engineering sequence, English, forestry, French, geology, history, law enforcement/police sciences, liberal arts/general studies, marketing/retailing/merchandising, mathematics, mining technology, modern languages, music, music education, nursing, physical education, physical sciences, physics, political science/government, psychology, retail management, science education, secretarial studies/office management, sociology, Spanish, theater arts/drama, welding technology, wildlife biology.

LIBRARY Alumni Library with 53,436 books, 448 microform titles, 256 periodicals, 50 CD-ROMs, 3,988 records, tapes, and CDs. Acquisition spending 1994–95: $274,365.

COMPUTERS ON CAMPUS Computer purchase plan available. Student rooms linked to a campus network. 320 computers for student use in computer center, computer labs, business classrooms, library provide access to e-mail, Internet. Staffed computer lab on campus provides training in use of computers, software. Academic computing expenditure 1994–95: $537,428.

COLLEGE LIFE Drama-theater group, choral group, marching band. 30% vote in student government elections. ***Social organizations:*** 20 open to all. ***Most popular organizations:*** Latter-Day Saints Student Association, Criminal Justice Student Association, Intertribal Club, Sigma Gamma Chi, Mark Allen Dorm Club. ***Major annual events:*** Fall Homecoming, Fall Campus Picnic, Yearbook Party. ***Student services:*** personal-psychological counseling. ***Campus security:*** 24-hour emergency response devices, student patrols, late-night transport-escort service, controlled dormitory access.

HOUSING 280 college housing spaces available; 245 were occupied 1995–96. No special consideration for freshman housing applicants. Off-campus living permitted. ***Option:*** single-sex (3 buildings) housing available. Resident assistants live in dorms.

ATHLETICS Member NJCAA. ***Intercollegiate:*** basketball M(s)/W(s), football M(s), softball W(s), volleyball W(s). ***Intramural:*** basketball, racquetball, softball, swimming and diving, table tennis (Ping-Pong), tennis, volleyball, water polo, weight lifting. ***Contact:*** Mr. Chuck LaVetter, Athletic Director, 520-428-8414.

CAREER PLANNING ***Placement office:*** 3 full-time staff; $127,485 operating expenditure 1994–95. ***Director:*** Mr. Richard D. Spining, Assistant Dean of Counseling, 520-428-8253. ***Services:*** resume preparation, resume referral, career counseling, careers library. 2 organizations recruited on campus 1994–95.

EXPENSES FOR 1995–96 State resident tuition: $628 full-time. Nonresident tuition: $4040 full-time. Part-time tuition per semester ranges from $22 to $269 for state residents, $35 to $1695 for nonresidents. College room and board: $2902 (minimum). College room only: $972.

FINANCIAL AID ***College-administered undergrad aid 1995–96:*** 229 need-based scholarships (averaging $987), 400 non-need scholarships (averaging $1504), short-term loans (averaging $88), low-interest long-term loans from college funds (averaging $739), 243 Federal Work-Study (averaging $1445), 69 part-time jobs. ***Required forms:*** institutional; accepted: CSS Financial Aid PROFILE, FAFSA. ***Priority deadline:*** 4/15. ***Waivers:*** full or partial for employees or children of employees.

APPLYING Open admission. ***Options:*** early entrance, midyear entrance. ***Required:*** TOEFL for international students. ***Recommended:*** ACT. Test scores used for counseling/placement. ***Application deadline:*** rolling.

APPLYING/TRANSFER ***Entrance:*** noncompetitive. ***Application deadline:*** rolling. ***Contact:*** Mrs. Pat Morris, Admissions Clerk, 520-428-8270.

CONTACT Ms. Verlene Anderson, Supervisor of Records, Eastern Arizona College, Thatcher, AZ 85552-0769, 520-428-8251 or toll-free 800-678-3808 (in-state). ***Fax:*** 520-428-8462. ***E-mail:*** admissions@eac.cc.az.us.

GATEWAY COMMUNITY COLLEGE
Phoenix, Arizona

UG Enrollment: 6,804	Tuition & Fees (Area Res): $1098
Application Deadline: rolling	Room & Board: N/Avail

GENERAL State and locally supported, 2-year, coed. Part of Maricopa County Community College District System. Awards certificates, transfer associate, terminal associate degrees. Founded 1968. ***Setting:*** 20-acre urban campus. ***Endowment:*** $3278. ***Total enrollment:*** 6,804. ***Faculty:*** 300 (67 full-time, 15% with terminal degrees, 233 part-time); student-faculty ratio is 25:1.

ENROLLMENT PROFILE 6,804 students from 54 states and territories, 26 other countries. 53% women, 47% men, 91% part-time, 94% state residents, 48% transferred in, 1% international, 75% 25 or older, 4% Native American, 14% Hispanic, 5% African American, 3% Asian American. ***Most popular recent majors:*** nursing, radiological technology.

FIRST-YEAR CLASS 2,497 total; 7,491 applied, 100% were accepted, 33% of whom enrolled.

ACADEMIC PROGRAM Core, liberal arts curriculum, honor code. Calendar: semesters. Academic remediation for entering students, English as a second language program offered during academic year, services for LD students, advanced placement, tutorials, honors program, summer session for credit, part-time degree program (daytime, evenings, summer), adult/continuing education programs, co-op programs and internships.

GENERAL DEGREE REQUIREMENTS 64 credit hours; 1 math course; computer course for most majors; internship (some majors).

MAJORS Accounting, automotive technologies, business administration/commerce/management, carpentry, construction technologies, court reporting, electromechanical technology, health science, health services administration, heating/refrigeration/air conditioning, international business, liberal arts/general studies, machine and tool technologies, manufacturing technology, nuclear medical technology, nursing, operating room technology, physical therapy, plumbing, practical nursing, radiological sciences, radiological technology, respiratory therapy, secretarial studies/office management, water resources, word processing.

LIBRARY Gateway Library with 50,000 books, 300 periodicals. Acquisition spending 1994–95: $7862.

COMPUTERS ON CAMPUS Computer purchase plan available. 300 computers for student use in computer center, computer labs, learning resource center, learning assistance center, classrooms, library, student center, student rooms provide access to main academic computer, on-line services, Internet. Staffed computer lab on campus provides training in use of computers, software. Academic computing expenditure 1994–95: $483,708.

COLLEGE LIFE Student-run newspaper. ***Most popular organizations:*** Native American Indian Organization, Single Parents Association, Black Student Union. ***Major annual events:*** Christmas Buffet, Annual Campus Celebration. ***Student services:*** personal-psychological counseling, women's center. ***Campus security:*** 24-hour emergency response devices and patrols, student patrols, late-night transport-escort service.

HOUSING College housing not available.

CAREER PLANNING *Placement office:* 2 full-time, 1 part-time staff; $16,153 operating expenditure 1994–95. *Director:* Mr. Larry Matje, Coordinator, Career Planning and Placement, 602-392-5040. *Services:* job fairs, resume preparation, resume referral, career counseling, careers library, job bank, job interviews.
AFTER GRADUATION 3% of students completing a degree program in 1994–95 went directly on to further study.
EXPENSES FOR 1996–97 Area resident tuition: $1088 full-time, $34 per credit hour part-time. Nonresident tuition: $5088 full-time, $159 per credit hour part-time. Part-time mandatory fees: $5 per semester. Full-time mandatory fees: $10.
FINANCIAL AID *College-administered undergrad aid 1995–96:* 229 need-based scholarships (averaging $1013), 217 non-need scholarships (averaging $250), short-term loans (averaging $416), low-interest long-term loans from external sources (averaging $1737), 74 Federal Work-Study (averaging $979), part-time jobs. *Required forms:* institutional, FAFSA; required for some: state. *Priority deadline:* 4/15. *Waivers:* full or partial for employees or children of employees.
APPLYING Open admission except for health science, nursing programs. *Options:* early entrance, deferred entrance, midyear entrance. *Required:* TOEFL for international students. *Required for some:* school transcript, 3 years of high school math. Test scores used for counseling/placement. *Application deadline:* rolling. *Notification:* continuous.
APPLYING/TRANSFER *Entrance:* noncompetitive. *Application deadline:* rolling. *Notification:* continuous. *Contact:* Ms. Cathy Meschke, Director, Records and Registration, 602-392-5194.
CONTACT Mrs. Cathy Meschke, Director, Records and Registration, Gateway Community College, 108 North 40th Street, Phoenix, AZ 85034-1795, 602-392-5194. *Fax:* 602-392-5329. *E-mail:* meschke@gwc.maricopa.edu. College video available.

GLENDALE COMMUNITY COLLEGE
Glendale, Arizona

UG Enrollment: 16,235 — **Tuition & Fees (Area Res): $1098**
Application Deadline: 8/19 — **Room & Board: N/Avail**

GENERAL State and locally supported, 2-year, coed. Part of Maricopa County Community College District System. Awards certificates, transfer associate, terminal associate degrees. Founded 1965. *Setting:* 160-acre suburban campus with easy access to Phoenix. *Total enrollment:* 16,235. *Faculty:* 687 (220 full-time, 100% with terminal degrees, 467 part-time); student-faculty ratio is 21:1.
ENROLLMENT PROFILE 16,235 students from 48 states and territories, 36 other countries. 55% women, 74% part-time, 98% state residents, 35% transferred in, 1% international, 53% 25 or older, 2% Native American, 12% Hispanic, 4% African American, 4% Asian American. *Most popular recent majors:* nursing, liberal arts/general studies.
FIRST-YEAR CLASS 4,932 total. Of the students who applied, 100% were accepted.
ACADEMIC PROGRAM Core, honor code. Calendar: semesters. 750 courses offered in 1995–96. Academic remediation for entering students, English as a second language program offered during academic year and summer, services for LD students, advanced placement, self-designed majors, honors program, summer session for credit, part-time degree program (daytime, evenings, weekends, summer), adult/continuing education programs, co-op programs and internships. ROTC: Army (c), Air Force (c).
GENERAL DEGREE REQUIREMENTS 64 credit hours; math/science requirements vary according to program; internship (some majors).
MAJORS Accounting, advertising, agricultural business, art/fine arts, automotive technologies, biology/biological sciences, business administration/commerce/management, chemistry, Chinese, communication, computer graphics, computer information systems, computer technologies, criminal justice, data processing, drafting and design, early childhood education, earth science, economics, education, electronics engineering technology, emergency medical technology, engineering (general), engineering technology, English, finance/banking, fire science, forestry, French, geology, German, graphic arts, health science, history, home economics, human services, international business, international studies, Italian, Japanese, journalism, law enforcement/police sciences, liberal arts/general studies, marketing/retailing/merchandising, medical technology, music, nursing, ornamental horticulture, pharmacy/pharmaceutical sciences, philosophy, physical education, physical therapy, physics, psychology, public relations, real estate, recreation and leisure services, retail management, Russian, secretarial studies/office management, social work, sociology, Spanish, theater arts/drama.
LIBRARY Library-Media Center plus 1 other, with 77,491 books, 148 microform titles, 426 periodicals, 2 on-line bibliographic services, 7 CD-ROMs, 3,176 records, tapes, and CDs. Acquisition spending 1994–95: $686,138.
COMPUTERS ON CAMPUS Computer purchase plan available. 1,200 computers for student use in computer center, computer labs, learning resource center, labs, learning assistance center, classrooms, library, student center. Staffed computer lab on campus provides training in use of computers, software.
COLLEGE LIFE Drama-theater group, choral group, marching band, student-run newspaper. 5% vote in student government elections. *Social organizations:* 40 open to all. *Most popular organizations:* LDS Student Association, Glendale Association of Students, Band, Phi Theta Kappa. *Major annual events:* Student Art Show, Multicultural Week. *Student services:* legal services, personal-psychological counseling. *Campus security:* student patrols, late-night transport-escort service.
HOUSING College housing not available.
ATHLETICS Member NJCAA. *Intercollegiate:* archery W(s), baseball M(s), basketball M(s)/W(s), cross-country running M(s)/W(s), football M(s), golf M(s), soccer M(s), softball W(s), tennis M(s)/W(s), track and field M(s)/W(s), volleyball W(s). *Intramural:* golf, racquetball, softball, table tennis (Ping-Pong), tennis, volleyball. *Contact:* Mr. Pete Pisciotta, Athletic Director, 602-435-3046.
CAREER PLANNING *Placement office:* 1 full-time, 1 part-time staff. *Director:* Ms. Rene Rodgers Barstack, Director of Career Educational Services, 602-435-3281. *Services:* job fairs, resume preparation, career counseling, careers library, job bank, job interviews.
EXPENSES FOR 1995–96 Area resident tuition: $1088 full-time, $34 per credit hour part-time. State resident tuition: $4448 full-time. Nonresident tuition: $5024 full-time. Part-time tuition per credit hour ranges from $59 to $154 for state residents, $59 to $154 for nonresidents. Part-time mandatory fees: $5 per semester. Residents of participating Arizona counties pay area resident tuition rates. Full-time mandatory fees: $10.
FINANCIAL AID *College-administered undergrad aid 1995–96:* need-based scholarships (averaging $445), 1,200 non-need scholarships (averaging $400), short-term loans (averaging $100), low-interest long-term loans from external sources (averaging $2000), Federal Work-Study, 281 part-time jobs. *Required forms:* institutional, FAFSA. *Priority deadline:* 5/15. *Waivers:* full or partial for employees or children of employees.
APPLYING Open admission. *Options:* early entrance, midyear entrance. *Required:* TOEFL for international students. *Recommended:* 3 years of high school math and science, some high school foreign language. *Required for some:* ACT ASSET. Test scores used for counseling/placement. *Application deadline:* 8/19. *Notification:* continuous until 8/19.
APPLYING/TRANSFER *Recommended:* 3 years of high school math and science, some high school foreign language. *Entrance:* noncompetitive. *Application deadline:* 8/19. *Notification:* continuous until 8/19. *Contact:* Ms. Mary Lou Bayless, Associate Dean of Student Services, 602-435-3305.
CONTACT Ms. Mary Lou Bayless, Associate Dean of Student Services, Glendale Community College, Glendale, AZ 85302-3090, 602-435-3305. *Fax:* 602-435-3329.

ITT TECHNICAL INSTITUTE
Phoenix, Arizona

UG Enrollment: 264 — **Tuition: $15,599/deg prog**
Application Deadline: rolling — **Room & Board: N/Avail**

GENERAL Proprietary, primarily 2-year, coed. Part of ITT Educational Services, Inc. Awards terminal associate, bachelor's degrees. Founded 1972. *Setting:* 2-acre urban campus. *Total enrollment:* 264. *Faculty:* 18 (17 full-time, 1 part-time); student-faculty ratio is 18:1.
ENROLLMENT PROFILE 264 students from 14 states and territories. 18% women, 0% part-time, 0% state residents, 0% transferred in, 0% international, 39% 25 or older, 5% Native American, 20% Hispanic, 5% African American, 3% Asian American. *Most popular recent majors:* electronics engineering technology, drafting and design.
FIRST-YEAR CLASS 416 applied, 90% were accepted, 93% of whom enrolled.
ACADEMIC PROGRAM Core. Calendar: quarters. Academic remediation for entering students.
GENERAL DEGREE REQUIREMENTS 90 quarter hours for associate, 180 quarter hours for bachelor's; 1 course each in math and physics; computer course.
MAJORS Computer science, drafting and design, electrical engineering technology (B), electronics engineering technology (B).
LIBRARY 450 books, 6 periodicals, 12 records, tapes, and CDs.
COMPUTERS ON CAMPUS 100 computers for student use in computer center, labs, classrooms.
COLLEGE LIFE *Most popular organization:* Student Activities Council. *Major annual events:* Very Special Arts Fair, APSA Sports Tournaments. *Student services:* personal-psychological counseling.
HOUSING College housing not available.
ATHLETICS *Intramural:* soccer, softball, volleyball.
CAREER PLANNING *Placement office:* 2 full-time, 1 part-time staff. *Director:* Mr. Jon Price, Director of Placement, 602-231-0871. *Services:* resume preparation, resume referral, career counseling, careers library, job bank, job interviews. Students must register sophomore year.
EXPENSES FOR 1996–97 Tuition per degree program ranges from $15,599 to $17,690. Full-time mandatory fees range from $540 to $720. Tuition guaranteed not to increase for student's term of enrollment.
FINANCIAL AID *College-administered undergrad aid 1995–96:* need-based scholarships, low-interest long-term loans from external sources (average $2625), Federal Work-Study. *Required forms:* institutional, FAFSA; accepted: CSS Financial Aid PROFILE, state. *Application deadline:* continuous. *Waivers:* full or partial for employees or children of employees.
APPLYING *Option:* deferred entrance. *Required:* CPAt. Test scores used for admission. *Application deadline:* rolling.
CONTACT Mr. Charles Wilson, Education Supervisor, ITT Technical Institute, 4837 East McDowell Road, Phoenix, AZ 85008-4292, 602-231-0871 or toll-free 800-879-4881 (out-of-state). *Fax:* 602-267-8727.

ITT TECHNICAL INSTITUTE
Tucson, Arizona

UG Enrollment: 212 — **Tuition: $15,599/deg prog**
Application Deadline: rolling — **Room & Board: N/Avail**

GENERAL Proprietary, 2-year, coed. Part of ITT Educational Services, Inc. Awards transfer associate, terminal associate degrees. Founded 1984. *Setting:* 3-acre urban campus. *Total enrollment:* 212. *Faculty:* 12 (8 full-time, 100% with terminal degrees, 4 part-time); student-faculty ratio is 17:1.
ENROLLMENT PROFILE 212 students from 9 states and territories, 3 other countries. 15% women, 0% part-time, 95% state residents, 3% transferred in, 1% international, 50% 25 or older, 5% Native American, 50% Hispanic, 5% African American, 5% Asian American. *Areas of study chosen:* 100% engineering and applied sciences.
FIRST-YEAR CLASS 92 total; 185 applied, 50% were accepted, 100% of whom enrolled. 5% from top 10% of their high school class, 45% from top quarter, 50% from top half.
ACADEMIC PROGRAM Core, engineering curriculum. Calendar: quarters. 65 courses offered in 1995–96. Academic remediation for entering students, English as a second language program, services for LD students, summer session for credit.
GENERAL DEGREE REQUIREMENTS 108 credits; computer course.
MAJORS Drafting and design, electronics engineering technology.
LIBRARY 350 books, 35 periodicals, 4 CD-ROMs, 60 records, tapes, and CDs.
COMPUTERS ON CAMPUS 115 computers for student use in computer center, computer labs, learning resource center, classrooms, library. Staffed computer lab on campus provides training in use of computers, software.
COLLEGE LIFE *Campus security:* monitored surveillance cameras.
HOUSING College housing not available.
CAREER PLANNING *Placement office:* 1 full-time staff. *Director:* Ms. Valerie Muzzuco, Director of Placement, 520-294-2944. *Services:* job fairs, resume preparation, resume referral, career counseling, careers library, job bank, job interviews. Students must register freshman year. 7 organizations recruited on campus 1994–95.
AFTER GRADUATION 85% of class of 1994 had job offers within 6 months.

ITT Technical Institute (continued)
EXPENSES FOR 1996–97 ***Application fee:*** $100. Tuition per degree program ranges from $15,599 to $17,690. Full-time mandatory fees range from $540 to $720.
FINANCIAL AID ***College-administered undergrad aid 1995–96:*** need-based scholarships, Federal Work-Study. ***Required forms:*** CSS Financial Aid PROFILE, institutional, FAFSA; accepted: state. ***Application deadline:*** continuous. ***Payment plan:*** installment. ***Waivers:*** full or partial for employees or children of employees.
APPLYING ***Option:*** deferred entrance. ***Required:*** minimum 2.0 GPA, TOEFL for international students, CPAt (DAT also required for drafting program). ***Recommended:*** 3 years of high school math and science, SAT I, SAT II Subject Tests. Test scores used for admission. ***Application deadline:*** rolling.
APPLYING/TRANSFER ***Entrance:*** moderately difficult. ***Contact:*** Mr. James Grinosky, Director of Education, 520-294-2944.
CONTACT Mr. William Fennelly, Director, ITT Technical Institute, 1840 East Benson Highway, Tucson, AZ 85714-1409, 520-294-2944. College video available.

LAMSON JUNIOR COLLEGE
Mesa, Arizona

UG Enrollment: 73 | **Tuition: $5297/deg prog**
Application Deadline: rolling | **Room & Board: N/Avail**

GENERAL Proprietary, 2-year, coed. Part of National Career Education, Inc. Awards transfer associate, terminal associate degrees. Founded 1889. ***Setting:*** urban campus with easy access to Phoenix. ***Total enrollment:*** 73. ***Faculty:*** 8 (4 full-time, 4 part-time).
ENROLLMENT PROFILE 73 students from 4 states and territories, 5 other countries. 88% women, 0% part-time, 97% state residents, 3% transferred in, 40% 25 or older, 10% Native American, 20% Hispanic, 1% African American, 3% Asian American. ***Most popular recent majors:*** paralegal studies, computer information systems, business administration/commerce/management.
FIRST-YEAR CLASS Of the students who applied, 80% were accepted, 78% of whom enrolled. 1% from top 10% of their high school class, 5% from top quarter, 20% from top half.
ACADEMIC PROGRAM Calendar: quarters. Academic remediation for entering students, English as a second language program offered during academic year, tutorials, summer session for credit, adult/continuing education programs, internships.
GENERAL DEGREE REQUIREMENTS 92 quarter credits; computer course; internship (some majors).
MAJORS Accounting, business administration/commerce/management, computer information systems, legal secretarial studies, paralegal studies, secretarial studies/office management.
COMPUTERS ON CAMPUS 45 computers for student use in computer center, learning center, library. Staffed computer lab on campus provides training in use of computers, software.
COLLEGE LIFE ***Campus security:*** 24-hour patrols.
HOUSING College housing not available.
CAREER PLANNING ***Placement office:*** 1 full-time staff. ***Director:*** Ms. Mary Brinkley, Placement Director, 602-898-7000. ***Services:*** job fairs, resume preparation, resume referral, career counseling, careers library, job bank, job interviews.
AFTER GRADUATION 76% of class of 1994 had job offers within 6 months.
EXPENSES FOR 1995–96 ***Application fee:*** $25. Tuition per degree program ranges from $5297 to $11,408. Full-time mandatory fees: $25. Tuition guaranteed not to increase for student's term of enrollment.
FINANCIAL AID ***College-administered undergrad aid 1995–96:*** non-need scholarships, low-interest long-term loans from external sources, Federal Work-Study. ***Required forms:*** institutional, FAFSA; accepted: CSS Financial Aid PROFILE, state. ***Application deadline:*** continuous. ***Payment plans:*** installment, deferred payment.
APPLYING ***Option:*** midyear entrance. ***Required:*** school transcript, campus interview, CPAt. Test scores used for admission. ***Application deadline:*** rolling. ***Notification:*** continuous.
APPLYING/TRANSFER ***Entrance:*** minimally difficult.
CONTACT Ms. Gail Ballew, Director of Admissions, Lamson Junior College, 1980 West Main, Mesa, AZ 85201-6933, 602-898-7000 Ext. 11. ***Fax:*** 602-833-0814.

MESA COMMUNITY COLLEGE
Mesa, Arizona

UG Enrollment: 22,302 | **Tuition & Fees (Area Res): $1234**
Application Deadline: 8/25 | **Room & Board: N/Avail**

GENERAL State and locally supported, 2-year, coed. Part of Maricopa County Community College District System. Awards certificates, transfer associate, terminal associate degrees. Founded 1965. ***Setting:*** 160-acre urban campus with easy access to Phoenix. ***Total enrollment:*** 22,302. ***Faculty:*** 852 (240 full-time, 25% with terminal degrees, 612 part-time); student-faculty ratio is 29:1. ***Notable Alumni:*** Toby Wright, professional football player with St. Louis Rams.
ENROLLMENT PROFILE 22,302 students from 18 states and territories, 75 other countries. 55% women, 72% part-time, 95% state residents, 37% transferred in, 1% international, 44% 25 or older, 2% Native American, 8% Hispanic, 3% African American, 2% Asian American. ***Most popular recent majors:*** liberal arts/general studies, business administration/commerce/management, nursing.
FIRST-YEAR CLASS 14,496 total; 26,000 applied, 100% were accepted, 56% of whom enrolled.
ACADEMIC PROGRAM Core, comprehensive curriculum, honor code. Calendar: semesters. 519 courses offered in 1995–96. Academic remediation for entering students, English as a second language program offered during academic year and summer, services for LD students, advanced placement, self-designed majors, Freshman Honors College, tutorials, honors program, summer session for credit, part-time degree program (daytime, evenings, weekends, summer), adult/continuing education programs, co-op programs. Off-campus study at Servicemembers Opportunity Colleges. Study abroad in Spain, England, Mexico, Jamaica. ROTC: Army (c), Air Force (c).
GENERAL DEGREE REQUIREMENTS 64 credit hours; 1 course in college algebra; 2 courses in lab science; computer course.
MAJORS Accounting, agricultural business, agricultural technologies, agronomy/soil and crop sciences, art/fine arts, automotive technologies, biology/biological sciences, business administration/commerce/management, child care/child and family studies, criminal justice, data processing, drafting and design, electrical and electronics technologies, (pre)engineering sequence, engineering technology, fashion merchandising, finance/banking, fire science, home economics, horticulture, industrial and heavy equipment maintenance, insurance, interior design, liberal arts/general studies, library science, manufacturing technology, marketing/retailing/merchandising, mathematics, medical secretarial studies, music, nursing, ornamental horticulture, quality control technology, real estate, secretarial studies/office management, teacher aide studies.
LIBRARY Information Commons with 56,224 books, 794 periodicals, 1,257 records, tapes, and CDs. Acquisition spending 1994–95: $175,000.
COMPUTERS ON CAMPUS Computer purchase plan available. 600 computers for student use in computer center, library provide access to Internet. Staffed computer lab on campus provides training in use of computers, software. Academic computing expenditure 1994–95: $1 million.
COLLEGE LIFE Drama-theater group, choral group, student-run newspaper, radio station. ***Social organizations:*** 25 open to all. ***Most popular organizations:*** Mecha, International Student Association, American Indian Association, Asian/Pacific Islander Club. ***Major annual events:*** Bash, Homecoming. ***Student services:*** legal services, personal-psychological counseling. ***Campus security:*** 24-hour emergency response devices and patrols, student patrols.
HOUSING College housing not available.
ATHLETICS Member NJCAA. ***Intercollegiate:*** baseball M, basketball M/W, cross-country running M, football M, golf M/W, soccer M/W, softball W, tennis M/W, track and field M/W, volleyball W, wrestling M. ***Intramural:*** basketball, cross-country running, football, tennis, track and field, volleyball, wrestling. ***Contact:*** Mr. Alan Benedict, Athletic Director, 602-461-7000.
CAREER PLANNING ***Placement office:*** 3 full-time, 3 part-time staff; $200,000 operating expenditure 1994–95. ***Director:*** Ms. Carolyn O'Connor, Director, Career and Educational Planning, 602-461-7429. ***Services:*** job fairs, resume preparation, resume referral, career counseling, careers library, job bank, job interviews. 35 organizations recruited on campus 1994–95.
EXPENSES FOR 1996–97 Area resident tuition: $1224 full-time, $34 per credit hour part-time. Nonresident tuition: $5724 full-time. Nonresident part-time tuition per credit hour ranges from $59 to $159. Part-time mandatory fees: $5 per semester. Residents of participating Arizona counties pay area resident tuition rates. Full-time mandatory fees: $10.
FINANCIAL AID ***College-administered undergrad aid 1995–96:*** 400 need-based scholarships (average $500), short-term loans (average $50), low-interest long-term loans from external sources, Federal Work-Study, 300 part-time jobs. ***Required forms:*** institutional, FAFSA; accepted: CSS Financial Aid PROFILE, state. ***Priority deadline:*** 5/15. ***Waivers:*** full or partial for employees or children of employees. ***Average indebtedness of graduates:*** $2500.
APPLYING Open admission. ***Options:*** early entrance, deferred entrance, midyear entrance. ***Required:*** TOEFL for international students, ACT ASSET. Test scores used for counseling/placement. ***Application deadline:*** 8/25. ***Notification:*** continuous.
APPLYING/TRANSFER ***Contact:*** Ms. Judy Taussig, Director of Educational Support Services, 602-461-7200.
CONTACT Mr. Gordon Benson, Associate Dean of Students, Mesa Community College, 1833 West Southern Avenue, Mesa, AZ 85202-4866, 602-461-7478. ***Fax:*** 602-461-7805.

MOHAVE COMMUNITY COLLEGE
Kingman, Arizona

UG Enrollment: 5,681 | **Tuition & Fees (AZ Res): $670**
Application Deadline: rolling | **Room & Board: N/Avail**

GENERAL State-supported, 2-year, coed. Awards transfer associate, terminal associate degrees. Founded 1971. ***Setting:*** 160-acre small-town campus. ***Total enrollment:*** 5,681. ***Faculty:*** 349 (49 full-time, 300 part-time); student-faculty ratio is 14:1.
ENROLLMENT PROFILE 5,681 students from 11 states and territories, 1 other country. 62% women, 88% part-time, 93% state residents, 10% transferred in, 22% have need-based financial aid, 9% have non-need-based financial aid, 1% international, 72% 25 or older, 3% Native American, 9% Hispanic, 1% African American, 1% Asian American. ***Areas of study chosen:*** 28% liberal arts/general studies, 22% health professions and related sciences, 17% business management and administrative services, 16% vocational and home economics, 7% computer and information sciences, 3% fine arts, 3% social sciences, 2% psychology, 1% biological and life sciences, 1% English language/literature/letters. ***Most popular recent majors:*** liberal arts/general studies, nursing.
FIRST-YEAR CLASS 2,827 total; 5,534 applied, 100% were accepted, 51% of whom enrolled.
ACADEMIC PROGRAM Core, general studies curriculum, honor code. Calendar: semesters. Academic remediation for entering students, English as a second language program offered during academic year and summer, summer session for credit, part-time degree program (daytime, evenings, weekends), adult/continuing education programs.
GENERAL DEGREE REQUIREMENTS 64 semester credits; 1 course in college algebra; 1 course in a foreign language, speech, or computer science.
MAJORS Accounting, art/fine arts, automotive technologies, business administration/commerce/management, ceramic art and design, computer science, English, fire science, health science, history, jewelry and metalsmithing, law enforcement/police sciences, liberal arts/general studies, marketing/retailing/merchandising, mathematics, music, nursing, psychology, sociology.
LIBRARY Mohave Community College Library with 45,849 books, 249 microform titles, 476 periodicals, 1,946 records, tapes, and CDs. Acquisition spending 1994–95: $56,302.
COMPUTERS ON CAMPUS 120 computers for student use in computer center, library. Staffed computer lab on campus provides training in use of computers, software.
COLLEGE LIFE 100% vote in student government elections. ***Campus security:*** 24-hour emergency response devices, late-night transport-escort service.
HOUSING College housing not available.
ATHLETICS ***Intramural:*** basketball, bowling, golf, swimming and diving, tennis, volleyball.
CAREER PLANNING ***Service:*** career counseling.

EXPENSES FOR 1996–97 ***Application fee:*** $5. State resident tuition: $660 full-time. Nonresident tuition: $3776 full-time. Part-time tuition per semester ranges from $90 to $270 for state residents, $100 to $1558 for nonresidents. Part-time mandatory fees: $10 per semester. Full-time mandatory fees: $20.
FINANCIAL AID ***College-administered undergrad aid 1995–96:*** 200 need-based scholarships (average $440), 90 non-need scholarships (average $500), low-interest long-term loans from college funds (average $800), loans from external sources (average $2000), 159 part-time jobs. ***Required forms:*** institutional, FAFSA. ***Priority deadline:*** 4/15. ***Waivers:*** full or partial for employees or children of employees and senior citizens. ***Notification:*** 6/15.
APPLYING Open admission except for nursing, paramedic programs. ***Options:*** early entrance, deferred entrance. ***Required:*** TOEFL for international students. ***Recommended:*** minimum 2.0 GPA, 3 years of high school math and science, some high school foreign language, SAT I or ACT, SAT II Subject Tests. ***Required for some:*** school transcript, campus interview. Test scores used for counseling/placement. ***Application deadline:*** rolling. ***Notification:*** continuous.
APPLYING/TRANSFER ***Recommended:*** minimum 2.0 high school GPA. ***Required for some:*** campus interview, college transcript. ***Entrance:*** noncompetitive. ***Application deadline:*** rolling. ***Notification:*** continuous. ***Contact:*** Dr. Roger L. Johnson, Director of Admissions and Records, 520-757-0847.
CONTACT Dr. Roger L. Johnson, Director of Admissions and Records, Mohave Community College, Kingman, AZ 86401-1299, 520-757-0847. ***Fax:*** 520-757-0836. ***E-mail:*** rogjoh@pops.mohave.cc.az.us.

NAVAJO COMMUNITY COLLEGE
Tsaile, Arizona

UG Enrollment: 1,767 **Tuition & Fees: $620**
Application Deadline: rolling **Room & Board: $2940**

GENERAL Federally supported, 2-year, coed. Awards certificates, transfer associate, terminal associate degrees. Founded 1968. ***Setting:*** 1,200-acre rural campus. ***Endowment:*** $3.5 million. ***Research spending 1994–95:*** $383,607. ***Educational spending 1994–95:*** $1797 per undergrad. ***Total enrollment:*** 1,767. ***Faculty:*** 164 (54 full-time, 110 part-time); student-faculty ratio is 15:1.
ENROLLMENT PROFILE 1,767 students: 75% women, 25% men, 54% part-time, 8% live on campus, 16% transferred in, 1% international, 63% 25 or older, 95% Native American, 0% Hispanic, 0% African American. ***Most popular recent majors:*** elementary education, liberal arts/general studies, social science.
FIRST-YEAR CLASS 450 total. Of the students who applied, 100% were accepted, 100% of whom enrolled.
ACADEMIC PROGRAM Core, honor code. Calendar: semesters. Academic remediation for entering students, services for LD students, summer session for credit, part-time degree program (daytime, evenings, summer), adult/continuing education programs, co-op programs. Off-campus study at members of the American Indian Higher Education Consortium.
GENERAL DEGREE REQUIREMENTS 64 credits; 1 college algebra course; 1 course in Navajo; computer course for business majors.
MAJORS Art/fine arts, business administration/commerce/management, computer information systems, computer science, earth science, elementary education, (pre)engineering sequence, health science, liberal arts/general studies, Native American studies, psychology, secretarial studies/office management, social science, social work.
LIBRARY Tsaile-NCC Library plus 1 other, with 50,000 books, 329 periodicals, 2,750 records, tapes, and CDs. Acquisition spending 1994–95: $93,323.
COMPUTERS ON CAMPUS 262 computers for student use in computer center, computer labs, research center, learning resource center, library provide access to main academic computer, e-mail. Staffed computer lab on campus provides training in use of computers, software. Academic computing expenditure 1994–95: $202,722.
NOTEWORTHY RESEARCH FACILITIES Minority Bio-Medical Research Support Program, Navajo Dryland Environments Laboratory, SIHASINS Science Honor Program.
COLLEGE LIFE Orientation program (2 days, no cost). 75% vote in student government elections. ***Social organizations:*** 7 open to all; 7 social clubs; 20% of eligible men and 20% of eligible women are members. ***Most popular organizations:*** Associate Students of Navajo Community College, Bar-N-Rodeo Club, Red Dawn Indian Club, Native American Church. ***Major annual events:*** Fall Bash, Spring Fling, Farewell Dance. ***Student services:*** health clinic, personal-psychological counseling. ***Campus security:*** 24-hour emergency response devices and patrols, student patrols, late-night transport-escort service.
HOUSING 285 college housing spaces available; 191 were occupied 1995–96. No special consideration for freshman housing applicants. Off-campus living permitted. ***Options:*** coed (1 building), single-sex (9 buildings) housing available. Resident assistants live in dorms.
ATHLETICS Member NSCAA, NJCAA. ***Intercollegiate:*** archery M/W, cross-country running M(s)/W(s). ***Contact:*** Mr. Mark Retasket, Dean of Students, 520-724-6730.
CAREER PLANNING ***Placement office:*** 1 full-time staff. ***Director:*** Mr. Edison Curtis, Student Development Specialist, 520-724-6727. ***Services:*** job fairs, resume preparation, career counseling, careers library.
ESTIMATED EXPENSES FOR 1996–97 Comprehensive fee of $3560 includes full-time tuition ($600), mandatory fees ($20), and college room and board ($2940). College room only: $1120. Part-time tuition: $25 per credit hour. Part-time mandatory fees: $10 per semester.
FINANCIAL AID ***College-administered undergrad aid 1995–96:*** 521 need-based scholarships (average $1470), 21 non-need scholarships (average $1300), 65 Federal Work-Study (averaging $500). ***Required forms:*** institutional, FAFSA; accepted: state. ***Priority deadline:*** 4/15. ***Payment plans:*** installment, deferred payment.
APPLYING Open admission. ***Options:*** Common Application, early entrance. ***Required:*** school transcript, TOEFL for international students. ***Recommended:*** 3 years of high school math and science, SAT I or ACT, SAT II Subject Tests, SAT II: Writing Test. Test scores used for counseling/placement. ***Application deadline:*** rolling. ***Notification:*** continuous. Preference given to Native Americans.
APPLYING/TRANSFER ***Required:*** high school transcript, college transcript. ***Recommended:*** 3 years of high school math and science. ***Entrance:*** noncompetitive. ***Application deadline:*** rolling. ***Notification:*** continuous. ***Contact:*** Ms. Louise Litzin, Registrar, 520-724-6633.
CONTACT Ms. Louise Litzin, Registrar, Navajo Community College, Tsaile, AZ 86556, 520-724-6633. ***Fax:*** 520-724-3349.

❖ ***See page 778 for a narrative description.*** ❖

NORTHLAND PIONEER COLLEGE
Holbrook, Arizona

UG Enrollment: 4,779 **Tuition & Fees (AZ Res): $660**
Application Deadline: rolling **Room Only: $1400**

GENERAL State and locally supported, 2-year, coed. Awards certificates, transfer associate, terminal associate degrees. Founded 1974. ***Setting:*** 40-acre rural campus. ***Total enrollment:*** 4,779. ***Faculty:*** 400 (50 full-time, 15% with terminal degrees, 350 part-time); student-faculty ratio is 16:1.
ENROLLMENT PROFILE 4,779 students from 15 states and territories. 67% women, 33% men, 85% part-time, 99% state residents, 5% transferred in, 15% have need-based financial aid, 2% have non-need-based financial aid, 0% international, 77% 25 or older, 26% Native American, 8% Hispanic, 1% African American, 1% Asian American. ***Most popular recent majors:*** early childhood education, business administration/commerce/management, liberal arts/general studies.
FIRST-YEAR CLASS 1,800 total. Of the students who applied, 100% were accepted.
ACADEMIC PROGRAM Core, liberal studies curriculum, honor code. Calendar: semesters. 962 courses offered in 1995–96. Academic remediation for entering students, English as a second language program offered during academic year, services for LD students, advanced placement, Freshman Honors College, tutorials, honors program, summer session for credit, part-time degree program (daytime, evenings), co-op programs and internships.
GENERAL DEGREE REQUIREMENTS 64 semester hours; math/science requirements vary according to program; computer course for office administration support, business majors.
MAJORS Accounting, business administration/commerce/management, business education, child care/child and family studies, computer science, construction technologies, cosmetology, criminal justice, data processing, early childhood education, electrical and electronics technologies, fire science, liberal arts/general studies, library science, nursing, photography, secretarial studies/office management, teacher aide studies, welding technology.
LIBRARY 60,000 books, 200 microform titles, 240 periodicals, 5,500 records, tapes, and CDs. Acquisition spending 1994–95: $57,000.
COMPUTERS ON CAMPUS 200 computers for student use in computer labs, classrooms, library. Staffed computer lab on campus provides training in use of computers, software. Academic computing expenditure 1994–95: $110,000.
COLLEGE LIFE Drama-theater group, choral group, student-run newspaper. ***Social organizations:*** 5 open to all. ***Student services:*** personal-psychological counseling.
HOUSING 71 college housing spaces available. No special consideration for freshman housing applicants. Off-campus living permitted. ***Option:*** coed (3 buildings) housing available.
ATHLETICS Member NJCAA. ***Intercollegiate:*** basketball M(s)/W(s). ***Contact:*** Mr. Richard Zelenski, Athletic Director, 520-524-6111.
CAREER PLANNING ***Placement office:*** 1 part-time staff; $60,000 operating expenditure 1994–95. ***Director:*** Mr. Chuck Kermes, Placement Director, 520-524-6111. ***Services:*** job fairs, resume preparation, career counseling, careers library, job bank, job interviews. 30 organizations recruited on campus 1994–95.
EXPENSES FOR 1996–97 State resident tuition: $660 full-time, $22 per semester hour part-time. Nonresident tuition: $2760 full-time. Nonresident part-time tuition per semester hour ranges from $42 to $92. College room only: $1400.
FINANCIAL AID ***College-administered undergrad aid 1995–96:*** need-based scholarships, short-term loans (averaging $60), Federal Work-Study. ***Required forms:*** institutional, FAFSA. ***Priority deadline:*** 8/25. ***Waivers:*** full or partial for employees or children of employees and senior citizens.
APPLYING Open admission. ***Option:*** early entrance. ***Application deadline:*** rolling.
APPLYING/TRANSFER ***Entrance:*** noncompetitive.
CONTACT Mr. A. Daniel Simper, Dean of Admissions and Records, Northland Pioneer College, Holbrook, AZ 86025-0610, 520-524-1993. ***Fax:*** 520-524-1997.

PARADISE VALLEY COMMUNITY COLLEGE
Phoenix, Arizona

UG Enrollment: 5,574 **Tuition & Fees (Area Res): $1098**
Application Deadline: rolling **Room & Board: N/Avail**

GENERAL State and locally supported, 2-year, coed. Part of Maricopa County Community College District System. Awards certificates, transfer associate, terminal associate degrees. Founded 1985. ***Setting:*** urban campus. ***Total enrollment:*** 5,574. ***Faculty:*** 260 (59 full-time, 31% with terminal degrees, 201 part-time); student-faculty ratio is 27:1.
ENROLLMENT PROFILE 5,574 students: 63% women, 37% men, 80% part-time, 98% state residents, 45% transferred in, 56% 25 or older, 1% Native American, 5% Hispanic, 1% African American, 2% Asian American.
FIRST-YEAR CLASS Of the students who applied, 100% were accepted.
ACADEMIC PROGRAM Core. Calendar: semesters. Academic remediation for entering students, services for LD students, advanced placement, tutorials, honors program, summer session for credit, adult/continuing education programs, co-op programs.
GENERAL DEGREE REQUIREMENT 60 credit hours.
MAJORS Accounting, business administration/commerce/management, international business, liberal arts/general studies, secretarial studies/office management, word processing.
COMPUTERS ON CAMPUS 350 computers for student use in computer center, computer labs, learning resource center, classrooms. Staffed computer lab on campus provides training in use of computers, software.
COLLEGE LIFE Student-run newspaper. ***Social organizations:*** 16 open to all. ***Most popular organizations:*** Phi Theta Kappa, ECO Watch, Recreational Outing Club, AWARE, Student Christian Association. ***Student services:*** personal-psychological counseling. ***Campus security:*** 24-hour emergency response devices, late-night transport-escort service.

Peterson's Guide to Two-Year Colleges 1997 171

Arizona

Paradise Valley Community College (continued)
HOUSING College housing not available.
ATHLETICS Member NJCAA. *Intercollegiate:* cross-country running M/W. *Intramural:* golf, tennis. *Contact:* Dr. Fred Stahl, Dean of Instruction, 602-493-2713.
CAREER PLANNING *Director:* Ms. Queta Chavez, Chairperson, Counseling And Consultation Division, 602-493-2920. *Services:* job fairs, resume preparation, career counseling, careers library, job bank, job interviews.
EXPENSES FOR 1995–96 Area resident tuition: $1088 full-time, $34 per credit hour part-time. State resident tuition: $3792 full-time. Nonresident tuition: $3888 full-time. Part-time tuition per semester ranges from $56 to $1116 for state residents, $59 to $1149 for nonresidents. Part-time mandatory fees: $5 per semester. Full-time mandatory fees: $10.
FINANCIAL AID *College-administered undergrad aid 1995–96:* 45 need-based scholarships (average $350), 45 non-need scholarships (average $350), short-term loans (average $200), low-interest long-term loans from external sources (average $1200). *Acceptable forms:* CSS Financial Aid PROFILE, state, institutional, FAFSA. *Priority deadline:* 4/15. *Waivers:* full or partial for employees or children of employees.
APPLYING Open admission. *Options:* early entrance, midyear entrance. *Required:* TOEFL for international students. Test scores used for counseling/placement. *Application deadline:* rolling.
APPLYING/TRANSFER *Application deadline:* rolling.
CONTACT Dr. Shirley Green, Associate Dean of Student Services, Paradise Valley Community College, 18401 North 32nd Street, Phoenix, AZ 85032-1200, 602-493-2610. College video available.

PARALEGAL INSTITUTE, INC.
Phoenix, Arizona

UG Enrollment: 600	Tuition: $1500/deg prog
Application Deadline: N/R	Room & Board: N/Avail

GENERAL Proprietary, 2-year. Awards diplomas, terminal associate degrees. Founded 1974. *Total enrollment:* 600.
ENROLLMENT PROFILE 600 students.
FIRST-YEAR CLASS Of the students who applied, 95% were accepted, 100% of whom enrolled.
GENERAL DEGREE REQUIREMENT 60 credits.
MAJOR Paralegal studies.
EXPENSES FOR 1996–97 Tuition per degree program ranges from $1500 to $3200.
CONTACT Mr. John W. Morrison, President, Paralegal Institute, Inc., Phoenix, AZ 85061-1408, 602-272-1855 or toll-free 800-354-1254.

PHOENIX COLLEGE
Phoenix, Arizona

GENERAL State and locally supported, 2-year, coed. Part of Maricopa County Community College District System. Awards transfer associate, terminal associate degrees. Founded 1920. *Setting:* 52-acre urban campus. *Total enrollment:* 11,266. *Faculty:* 540 (150 full-time, 390 part-time); student-faculty ratio is 25:1.
EXPENSES FOR 1995–96 Area resident tuition: $1088 full-time, $34 per credit hour part-time. Nonresident tuition: $5088 full-time. Nonresident part-time tuition per credit hour ranges from $59 to $159. Part-time mandatory fees: $5 per semester. Full-time mandatory fees: $10.
CONTACT Ms. Donna Fischer, Supervisor of Admissions and Records, Phoenix College, 1202 West Thomas Road, Phoenix, AZ 85013-4234, 602-285-7500. *Fax:* 602-285-7813.

PIMA COMMUNITY COLLEGE
Tucson, Arizona

UG Enrollment: 27,960	Tuition & Fees (AZ Res): $940
Application Deadline: rolling	Room & Board: N/Avail

GENERAL State-supported, 2-year, coed. Part of Arizona State Community College System. Awards certificates, transfer associate, terminal associate degrees. Founded 1966. *Setting:* 350-acre urban campus. *Endowment:* $460,000. *Educational spending 1994–95:* $1902 per undergrad. *Total enrollment:* 27,960. *Faculty:* 1,567 (319 full-time, 85% with terminal degrees, 1,248 part-time); student-faculty ratio is 20:1.
ENROLLMENT PROFILE 27,960 students from 48 states and territories, 80 other countries. 55% women, 74% part-time, 94% state residents, 11% transferred in, 2% international, 50% 25 or older, 3% Native American, 26% Hispanic, 4% African American, 4% Asian American. *Most popular recent majors:* liberal arts/general studies, business administration/commerce/management, education.
FIRST-YEAR CLASS 4,924 total; 4,924 applied, 100% were accepted, 100% of whom enrolled. 6% from top 10% of their high school class, 36% from top quarter, 70% from top half.
ACADEMIC PROGRAM Core, general education curriculum, honor code. Calendar: semesters. 1,117 courses offered in 1995–96. Academic remediation for entering students, English as a second language program offered during academic year, services for LD students, self-designed majors, honors program, summer session for credit, part-time degree program (daytime, evenings, summer), adult/continuing education programs, co-op programs and internships. ROTC: Army (c), Naval (c), Air Force (c).
GENERAL DEGREE REQUIREMENTS 60 credit hours; math/science requirements vary according to program.
MAJORS Accounting, aircraft and missile maintenance, anthropology, applied art, archaeology, art/fine arts, Asian/Oriental studies, automotive technologies, biology/biological sciences, business administration/commerce/management, chemistry, child care/child and family studies, commercial art, communication, communication equipment technology, computer graphics, computer programming, computer science, construction technologies, corrections, criminal justice, culinary arts, deaf interpreter training, dental services, drafting and design, drug and alcohol/substance abuse counseling, early childhood education, education, electrical and electronics technologies, elementary education, engineering (general), environmental engineering technology, fashion design and technology, finance/banking, fire science, food services management, geology, graphic arts, heating/refrigeration/air conditioning, home economics, hospitality services, hotel and restaurant management, industrial design, interior design, international business, landscape architecture/design, legal secretarial studies, liberal arts/general studies, machine and tool technologies, manufacturing technology, mathematics, medical records services, medical secretarial studies, music, Native American studies, nursing, optical technologies, paralegal studies, pharmacy/pharmaceutical sciences, physical fitness/exercise science, physics, political science/government, public administration, radiological technology, real estate, respiratory therapy, secretarial studies/office management, social work, sociology, speech/rhetoric/public address/debate, teacher aide studies, telecommunications, theater arts/drama, tourism and travel, welding technology.
LIBRARY Pima College Library with 175,034 books, 1,101 microform titles, 1,471 periodicals, 1 on-line bibliographic service, 5 CD-ROMs, 8,100 records, tapes, and CDs. Acquisition spending 1994–95: $358,327.
COMPUTERS ON CAMPUS Computer purchase plan available. 1,500 computers for student use in computer labs, labs, classrooms. Staffed computer lab on campus provides training in use of computers, software. Academic computing expenditure 1994–95: $88,285.
COLLEGE LIFE Drama-theater group, choral group, student-run newspaper. *Student services:* personal-psychological counseling, women's center. *Campus security:* 24-hour emergency response devices, late-night transport-escort service.
HOUSING College housing not available.
ATHLETICS Member NJCAA. *Intercollegiate:* baseball M(s), basketball M(s)/W(s), cross-country running M(s)/W(s), equestrian sports M(s)/W(s), golf M, soccer M, softball W(s), tennis M(s)/W(s), track and field M(s)/W(s), volleyball W(s). *Intramural:* badminton, basketball, cross-country running, equestrian sports, football, golf, ice hockey, racquetball, soccer, tennis, track and field, volleyball, wrestling. *Contact:* Mr. Larry Toledo, Director, 520-884-6005; Ms. Maureen Murphy, Assistant Athletic Director, 520-884-6009.
CAREER PLANNING *Placement office:* $196,158 operating expenditure 1994–95. *Director:* Dr. John Merren, Director of Occupational Curriculum, 520-748-4901. *Services:* job fairs, resume preparation, career counseling, job bank.
AFTER GRADUATION 16% of students completing a degree program in 1994–95 went directly on to further study.
EXPENSES FOR 1996–97 State resident tuition: $930 full-time, $31 per credit hour part-time. Nonresident tuition: $4500 full-time. Nonresident part-time tuition per semester ranges from $51 to $150. Part-time mandatory fees: $5 per semester. Full-time mandatory fees: $10.
FINANCIAL AID *College-administered undergrad aid 1995–96:* need-based scholarships (average $150), Federal Work-Study, 200 part-time jobs. *Required forms:* FAFSA; accepted: CSS Financial Aid PROFILE. *Priority deadline:* 4/1. *Payment plan:* deferred payment. *Waivers:* full or partial for employees or children of employees.
APPLYING Open admission. *Option:* early entrance. *Required:* TOEFL for international students. *Recommended:* SAT I or ACT. Test scores used for counseling/placement. *Application deadline:* rolling.
APPLYING/TRANSFER *Recommended:* standardized test scores. *Entrance:* noncompetitive. *Application deadline:* rolling.
CONTACT Ms. Nancee Sorenson, Acting Director of Admissions and Records, Pima Community College, 4905 East Broadway, Tucson, AZ 85709-1010, 520-748-4640. *Fax:* 520-884-6728.

❖ *See page 794 for a narrative description.* ❖

PIMA MEDICAL INSTITUTE
Mesa, Arizona

PIMA MEDICAL INSTITUTE
Tucson, Arizona

RIO SALADO COMMUNITY COLLEGE
Phoenix, Arizona

UG Enrollment: 8,754	Tuition & Fees (Area Res): $1098
Application Deadline: rolling	Room & Board: N/Avail

GENERAL State and locally supported, 2-year, coed. Part of Maricopa County Community College District System. Awards certificates, transfer associate, terminal associate degrees. Founded 1978. *Setting:* urban campus. *Total enrollment:* 8,754. *Faculty:* 446 (11 full-time, 100% with terminal degrees, 435 part-time); student-faculty ratio is 18:1.
ENROLLMENT PROFILE 8,754 students from 37 states and territories, 18 other countries. 56% women, 96% part-time, 94% state residents, 43% transferred in, 1% international, 59% 25 or older, 1% Native American, 8% Hispanic, 4% African American, 2% Asian American. *Most popular recent majors:* law enforcement/police sciences, drug and alcohol/substance abuse counseling, social work.
FIRST-YEAR CLASS 4,371 total; 4,371 applied, 100% were accepted, 100% of whom enrolled.
ACADEMIC PROGRAM Core, interdisciplinary curriculum, honor code. Calendar: semesters. 828 courses offered in 1995–96. Academic remediation for entering students, English as a second language program offered during academic year and summer, services for LD students, advanced placement, honors program, summer session for credit, part-time degree program (daytime, evenings, weekends, summer), external degree programs, adult/continuing education programs, co-op programs and internships.
GENERAL DEGREE REQUIREMENTS 64 credit hours; 1 college algebra course; internship (some majors).
MAJORS Accounting, aviation administration, business administration/commerce/management, consumer services, corrections, drug and alcohol/substance abuse counseling, finance/banking, hospitality services, international business, law enforcement/police sciences, mental health/rehabilitation counseling, public administration, social work, water resources.
LIBRARY Rio Salado Professional Library with 10,000 books, 150 periodicals, 2 on-line bibliographic services, 5,100 records, tapes, and CDs. Acquisition spending 1994–95: $38,904.

COMPUTERS ON CAMPUS Computer purchase plan available. 750 computers for student use in computer center, computer labs, learning resource center, library provide access to main academic computer, off-campus computing facilities, on-line services, Internet.
COLLEGE LIFE ***Student services:*** personal-psychological counseling. ***Campus security:*** 24-hour emergency response devices, late-night transport-escort service.
HOUSING College housing not available.
CAREER PLANNING ***Placement office:*** 1 full-time, 2 part-time staff. ***Director:*** Ms. Betty Elliott, Director, Career Education Planning Services, 602-252-3289. ***Services:*** career counseling, careers library.
EXPENSES FOR 1996–97 Area resident tuition: $1088 full-time, $34 per credit hour part-time. Nonresident tuition: $5088 full-time. Nonresident part-time tuition per credit hour ranges from $59 to $159. Part-time mandatory fees: $9 per semester. Residents of participating Arizona counties pay area resident tuition rates. Full-time mandatory fees: $10.
FINANCIAL AID ***College-administered undergrad aid 1995–96:*** 204 need-based scholarships (average $382), 48 non-need scholarships (average $265), low-interest long-term loans, 2 Federal Work-Study (averaging $2500). ***Required forms:*** institutional, FAFSA; accepted: state. ***Priority deadline:*** 3/1. ***Payment plan:*** deferred payment. ***Waivers:*** full or partial for employees or children of employees. ***Notification:*** 7/1.
APPLYING Open admission. ***Options:*** early entrance, deferred entrance, midyear entrance. ***Required:*** TOEFL for international students. ***Required for some:*** ACT ASSET. Test scores used for counseling/placement. ***Application deadline:*** rolling.
APPLYING/TRANSFER ***Entrance:*** noncompetitive.
CONTACT Ms. Deborah Lain, Supervisor of Admissions and Records, Rio Salado Community College, 640 North 1st Avenue, Phoenix, AZ 85003-1558, 602-223-4013. ***Fax:*** 602-223-4331.

SCOTTSDALE COMMUNITY COLLEGE
Scottsdale, Arizona

UG Enrollment: 9,765	**Tuition & Fees (Area Res): $1088**
Application Deadline: rolling	**Room & Board: N/Avail**

GENERAL State and locally supported, 2-year, coed. Part of Maricopa County Community College District System. Awards certificates, diplomas, transfer associate, terminal associate degrees. Founded 1969. ***Setting:*** 160-acre suburban campus with easy access to Phoenix. ***Total enrollment:*** 9,765. ***Faculty:*** 447 (135 full-time, 312 part-time).
ENROLLMENT PROFILE 9,765 students: 57% women, 75% part-time, 93% state residents, 45% transferred in.
FIRST-YEAR CLASS 3,695 total; 3,695 applied, 100% were accepted, 100% of whom enrolled.
ACADEMIC PROGRAM Core. Calendar: semesters. Academic remediation for entering students, English as a second language program offered during academic year, services for LD students, advanced placement, self-designed majors, honors program, summer session for credit, part-time degree program (daytime, evenings), adult/continuing education programs, co-op programs. Off-campus study at Servicemembers Opportunity Colleges.
GENERAL DEGREE REQUIREMENTS 64 credit hours; 1 math course; 2 lab science courses.
MAJORS Accounting, business administration/commerce/management, computer information systems, criminal justice, culinary arts, early childhood education, electrical and electronics technologies, emergency medical technology, environmental design, equestrian studies, fashion merchandising, finance/banking, fire science, food services management, hospitality services, hotel and restaurant management, interior design, mathematics, medical secretarial studies, nursing, photography, public administration, real estate, secretarial studies/office management, theater arts/drama.
COMPUTERS ON CAMPUS 75 computers for student use in computer center, various locations.
COLLEGE LIFE Drama-theater group, choral group, student-run newspaper. ***Student services:*** legal services, personal-psychological counseling, women's center. ***Campus security:*** 24-hour emergency response devices and patrols, student patrols, late-night transport-escort service, 24-hour automatic surveillance cameras.
HOUSING College housing not available.
ATHLETICS Member NJCAA. ***Intercollegiate:*** basketball M/W, cross-country running M/W, football M, golf M/W, tennis M/W, track and field M/W, volleyball W. ***Intramural:*** archery, badminton, basketball, bowling, racquetball, track and field, volleyball.
CAREER PLANNING ***Service:*** career counseling.
EXPENSES FOR 1995–96 Area resident tuition: $1088 full-time, $34 per credit hour part-time. State resident tuition: $4672 full-time. Nonresident tuition: $5088 full-time. Part-time tuition per credit hour ranges from $59 to $146 for state residents, $59 to $159 for nonresidents.
FINANCIAL AID ***College-administered undergrad aid 1995–96:*** need-based scholarships, short-term loans, low-interest long-term loans from external sources, Federal Work-Study, part-time jobs. ***Required forms:*** FAFSA. ***Priority deadline:*** 4/15. ***Payment plan:*** installment. ***Waivers:*** full or partial for employees or children of employees.
APPLYING Open admission. ***Option:*** early entrance. ***Recommended:*** 3 years of high school math, 2 years of high school foreign language. ***Required for some:*** ACT ASSET. Test scores used for counseling/placement. ***Application deadline:*** rolling. ***Notification:*** continuous.
APPLYING/TRANSFER ***Recommended:*** minimum 2.0 college GPA.
CONTACT Mr. John M. Silvester, Associate Dean of Student Personnel Services, Scottsdale Community College, 9000 East Chaparral Road, Scottsdale, AZ 85250-2699, 602-423-6139.

SOUTH MOUNTAIN COMMUNITY COLLEGE
Phoenix, Arizona

UG Enrollment: 2,423	**Tuition & Fees (Area Res): $1002**
Application Deadline: 8/22	**Room & Board: N/Avail**

GENERAL State and locally supported, 2-year, coed. Part of Maricopa County Community College District System. Awards certificates, transfer associate, terminal associate degrees. Founded 1979. ***Setting:*** 108-acre suburban campus. ***Total enrollment:*** 2,423. ***Faculty:*** 184 (42 full-time, 32% with terminal degrees, 142 part-time); student-faculty ratio is 20:1.
ENROLLMENT PROFILE 2,423 students: 58% women, 72% part-time, 96% state residents, 23% transferred in, 40% have need-based financial aid, 4% international, 40% 25 or older, 4% Native American, 43% Hispanic, 16% African American, 3% Asian American. ***Most popular recent major:*** liberal arts/general studies.
FIRST-YEAR CLASS 2,317 total. Of the students who applied, 100% were accepted, 85% of whom enrolled.
ACADEMIC PROGRAM Core. Calendar: semesters. 263 courses offered in 1995–96. Academic remediation for entering students, English as a second language program offered during academic year, services for LD students, advanced placement, honors program, summer session for credit, part-time degree program (daytime, evenings), adult/continuing education programs, co-op programs. ROTC: Air Force (c).
GENERAL DEGREE REQUIREMENTS 62 credit hours; 1 math course; computer course.
MAJORS Art/fine arts, biology/biological sciences, business administration/commerce/management, chemistry, communication, computer information systems, (pre)engineering sequence, history, home economics, liberal arts/general studies, mathematics, music, physical education, physics, political science/government, psychology, secretarial studies/office management, sociology, word processing.
LIBRARY Learning Resource Center with 35,591 books, 450 microform titles, 475 periodicals, 4,450 records, tapes, and CDs.
COMPUTERS ON CAMPUS 150 computers for student use in computer center, computer labs, business building classrooms, library provide access to e-mail, Internet, electronic forum career guidance. Staffed computer lab on campus (open 24 hours a day) provides training in use of computers, software.
COLLEGE LIFE ***Social organizations:*** 9 open to all. ***Major annual events:*** Festive Fall, Multicultural Week, Spring Fling. ***Student services:*** legal services. ***Campus security:*** late-night transport-escort service, 18-hour patrols and campus lockdown.
HOUSING College housing not available.
ATHLETICS Member NJCAA. ***Intercollegiate:*** baseball M, basketball M/W, cross-country running M/W, soccer M, softball W, tennis M/W, track and field M/W, volleyball W. ***Contact:*** Mr. Doug Ferguson, Director of Athletics, 602-243-8238; Ms. Christine Haines, Director of Athletics, 602-243-8244.
CAREER PLANNING ***Director:*** Ms. Ofelia Marin, Coordinator, Job Placement and Career Development, 602-243-8153. ***Services:*** job fairs, career counseling, job bank, job interviews.
AFTER GRADUATION 17% of students completing a degree program in 1994–95 went directly on to further study.
EXPENSES FOR 1996–97 Area resident tuition: $992 full-time, $32 per credit hour part-time. State resident tuition: $4309 full-time. Nonresident tuition: $4867 full-time. Part-time tuition per credit hour ranges from $57 to $139 for state residents, $57 to $157 for nonresidents. Part-time mandatory fees: $5 per semester. Residents of participating Arizona counties pay area resident tuition rates. Full-time mandatory fees: $10.
FINANCIAL AID ***College-administered undergrad aid 1995–96:*** 120 need-based scholarships (average $1000), 75 non-need scholarships (average $150), short-term loans (average $250), low-interest long-term loans from external sources (average $1130), Federal Work-Study, 175 part-time jobs. ***Acceptable forms:*** CSS Financial Aid PROFILE, FAFSA, USAF FAIR. ***Priority deadline:*** 7/1. ***Payment plan:*** deferred payment. ***Waivers:*** full or partial for employees or children of employees.
APPLYING Open admission. ***Application deadline:*** 8/22. ***Notification:*** continuous until 8/22.
APPLYING/TRANSFER ***Entrance:*** noncompetitive. ***Application deadline:*** 8/22. ***Notification:*** continuous until 8/22.
CONTACT Mr. Tony Bracamonte, Associate Dean of Admissions and Records, South Mountain Community College, Phoenix, AZ 85040, 602-243-8120. ***Fax:*** 602-243-8329.

YAVAPAI COLLEGE
Prescott, Arizona

UG Enrollment: 6,297	**Tuition & Fees (AZ Res): $666**
Application Deadline: rolling	**Room & Board: $2950**

GENERAL State and locally supported, 2-year, coed. Part of Arizona State Community College System. Awards certificates, transfer associate, terminal associate degrees. Founded 1966. ***Setting:*** 100-acre small-town campus. ***Endowment:*** $1.2 million. ***Total enrollment:*** 6,297. ***Faculty:*** 487 (87 full-time, 24% with terminal degrees, 400 part-time); student-faculty ratio is 15:1.
ENROLLMENT PROFILE 6,297 students: 63% women, 80% part-time, 94% state residents, 5% transferred in, 20% have need-based financial aid, 8% have non-need-based financial aid, 1% international, 67% 25 or older, 8% Native American, 4% Hispanic, 1% African American, 1% Asian American. ***Most popular recent majors:*** nursing, liberal arts/general studies, business administration/commerce/management.
FIRST-YEAR CLASS 2,055 total. Of the students who applied, 100% were accepted.
ACADEMIC PROGRAM Core, interdisciplinary curriculum, honor code. Calendar: semesters. 1,200 courses offered in 1995–96. Academic remediation for entering students, English as a second language program offered during academic year, services for LD students, advanced placement, tutorials, honors program, summer session for credit, part-time degree program (daytime, evenings, weekends, summer), adult/continuing education programs, co-op programs and internships. Off-campus study at Northern Arizona University. ROTC: Army (c), Air Force (c).
GENERAL DEGREE REQUIREMENTS 64 credits; computer course.
MAJORS Accounting, architectural technologies, art/fine arts, automotive technologies, business administration/commerce/management, carpentry, commercial art, computer information systems, drafting and design, elementary education, fire science, hotel and restaurant management, law enforcement/police sciences, legal secretarial studies, liberal arts/general studies, machine and tool technologies, management information systems, manufacturing technology, music, nursing, paralegal studies, physical education, secretarial studies/office management, welding technology.
LIBRARY Yavapai College Library with 60,000 books, 250 microform titles, 767 periodicals, 2 on-line bibliographic services, 17 CD-ROMs, 13,120 records, tapes, and CDs. Acquisition spending 1994–95: $799,139.

Arizona–Arkansas

Yavapai College (continued)
COMPUTERS ON CAMPUS 150 computers for student use in computer labs, learning center, classrooms, library provide access to main academic computer, off-campus computing facilities, e-mail, on-line services, Internet. Staffed computer lab on campus provides training in use of computers.
COLLEGE LIFE Orientation program (2 days, $30, parents included). Drama-theater group, choral group, student-run newspaper. *Most popular organizations:* Re-Entry Club, Student Nurses Association, Native American Club, International Club, VICA. *Major annual events:* Welcome Week, Homecoming/Parents' Weekend, Earth Day. *Student services:* personal-psychological counseling, women's center. *Campus security:* 24-hour emergency response devices and patrols, late-night transport-escort service, controlled dormitory access.
HOUSING 400 college housing spaces available; all were occupied 1995–96. No special consideration for freshman housing applicants. Off-campus living permitted. *Option:* coed housing available. Resident assistants live in dorms.
ATHLETICS Member NJCAA. *Intercollegiate:* baseball M(s), basketball M(s)/W(s), cross-country running M(s)/W(s), soccer M(s), volleyball W(s). *Contact:* Mr. Vernon Mumment, Director of Athletics, 520-776-2238.
CAREER PLANNING *Placement office:* 2 full-time, 2 part-time staff. *Director:* Ms. Kay Krecker, Career Counselor, 520-776-2116. *Services:* job fairs, resume preparation, career counseling, careers library.
AFTER GRADUATION 80% of students completing a degree program in 1994–95 went directly on to further study.
EXPENSES FOR 1996–97 State resident tuition: $666 full-time. Nonresident tuition: $5666 full-time. Part-time tuition per semester ranges from $47 to $293 for state residents, $53 to $2288 for nonresidents. Part-time mandatory fees: $3 per credit hour. College room and board: $2950 (minimum).
FINANCIAL AID *College-administered undergrad aid 1995–96:* 180 need-based scholarships (average $800), 400 non-need scholarships (average $666), short-term loans (average $200), low-interest long-term loans from external sources (average $2200), 63 Federal Work-Study (averaging $2500), 150 part-time jobs. *Required forms:* FAFSA; required for some: institutional; accepted: CSS Financial Aid PROFILE. *Priority deadline:* 4/15. *Payment plan:* deferred payment. *Waivers:* full or partial for employees or children of employees and senior citizens. *Notification:* 6/15.
APPLYING Open admission except for nursing, gunsmithing programs. *Options:* early entrance, deferred entrance, midyear entrance. *Required:* school transcript, TOEFL for international students. *Recommended:* SAT I or ACT. *Required for some:* essay, recommendations. Test scores used for counseling/placement. *Application deadline:* rolling.
APPLYING/TRANSFER *Required:* high school transcript. *Recommended:* standardized test scores. *Required for some:* essay, recommendations. *Entrance:* noncompetitive. *Application deadline:* rolling. *Contact:* Ms. Dianne Albrecht, Director, Counseling Department, 520-776-2124.
CONTACT Dr. Richard M. Boone, Director of Admissions/Registrar, Yavapai College, Prescott, AZ 86301-3297, 520-776-2147 or toll-free 800-922-6787 (in-state). *Fax:* 520-776-2193. *E-mail:* preg_bob@sizzle.yavapai.cc.az.us. College video available.

ARKANSAS

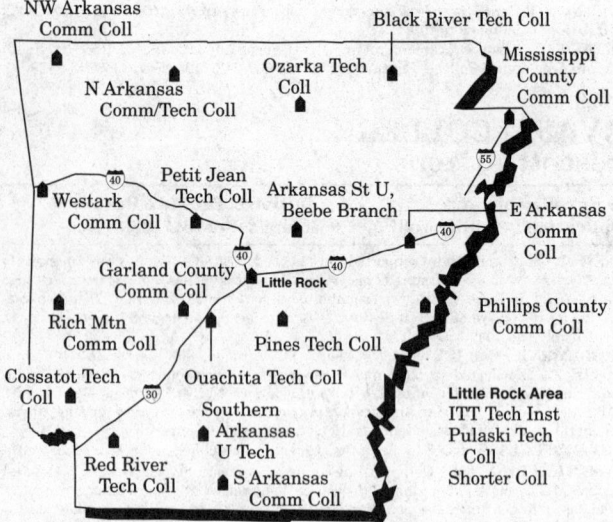

ARKANSAS STATE UNIVERSITY–BEEBE BRANCH
Beebe, Arkansas

UG Enrollment: 1,999	Tuition & Fees (AR Res): $1128
Application Deadline: rolling	Room & Board: $1980

GENERAL State-supported, 2-year, coed. Part of Arkansas State University System. Awards certificates, transfer associate degrees. Founded 1927. *Setting:* 320-acre rural campus with easy access to Memphis. *Total enrollment:* 1,999. *Faculty:* 71 (51 full-time, 20% with terminal degrees, 20 part-time); student-faculty ratio is 24:1.
ENROLLMENT PROFILE 1,999 students: 56% women, 44% men, 33% part-time, 99% state residents, 3% live on campus, 10% transferred in, 38% 25 or older, 2% Native American, 1% Hispanic, 4% African American. *Most popular recent majors:* liberal arts/general studies, business administration/commerce/management.
FIRST-YEAR CLASS 564 total; 700 applied, 100% were accepted, 81% of whom enrolled.
ACADEMIC PROGRAM Core. Calendar: semesters. Academic remediation for entering students, advanced placement, honors program, summer session for credit, part-time degree program (daytime, evenings, weekends, summer), adult/continuing education programs.
GENERAL DEGREE REQUIREMENTS 60 credit hours; computer course for business majors.
MAJORS Agricultural sciences, animal sciences, biology/biological sciences, business administration/commerce/management, computer information systems, computer technologies, drafting and design, electronics engineering technology, liberal arts/general studies, mathematics, medical laboratory technology, nursing, physical sciences, quality control technology, social science, speech/rhetoric/public address/debate.
LIBRARY 53,000 books, 3,400 microform titles, 265 periodicals, 1,600 records, tapes, and CDs.
COMPUTERS ON CAMPUS 69 computers for student use in computer center, computer labs, learning resource center, classrooms. Staffed computer lab on campus (open 24 hours a day) provides training in use of computers, software.
COLLEGE LIFE Drama-theater group, marching band. *Student services:* personal-psychological counseling. *Campus security:* 24-hour emergency response devices and patrols.
HOUSING 156 college housing spaces available; 75 were occupied 1995–96. Freshmen guaranteed college housing. Off-campus living permitted. *Option:* single-sex (2 buildings) housing available. Resident assistants live in dorms.
ATHLETICS *Intramural:* badminton, basketball, bowling, football, racquetball, squash, tennis, track and field, volleyball.
CAREER PLANNING *Service:* career counseling.
EXPENSES FOR 1995–96 State resident tuition: $1080 full-time, $45 per credit hour part-time. Nonresident tuition: $1824 full-time, $76 per credit hour part-time. Part-time mandatory fees: $2 per credit hour. Full-time mandatory fees: $48. College room and board: $1980.
FINANCIAL AID *College-administered undergrad aid 1995–96:* need-based scholarships, 40 non-need scholarships (averaging $1080), low-interest long-term loans from external sources (averaging $2625), Federal Work-Study, 20 part-time jobs. *Required forms:* FAFSA. *Priority deadline:* 6/1. *Payment plan:* installment. *Waivers:* full or partial for senior citizens.
APPLYING Open admission. *Options:* Common Application, early entrance, deferred entrance. *Required:* school transcript, ACT, TOEFL for international students. Test scores used for counseling/placement. *Application deadline:* rolling.
APPLYING/TRANSFER *Required:* standardized test scores, high school transcript, college transcript.
CONTACT Mr. James Washburn, Registrar/Director of Admissions, Arkansas State University–Beebe Branch, Beebe, AR 72012-1008, 501-882-8280 or toll-free 800-632-9985 (in-state). *Fax:* 501-882-6452 Ext. 370.

BLACK RIVER TECHNICAL COLLEGE
Pocahontas, Arkansas

UG Enrollment: 1,189	Tuition & Fees (Area Res): $1178
Application Deadline: rolling	Room & Board: N/Avail

GENERAL State-supported, 2-year, coed. Awards transfer associate, terminal associate degrees. Founded 1972. *Setting:* 55-acre small-town campus. *Total enrollment:* 1,189. *Faculty:* 70 (30 full-time, 40 part-time).
ENROLLMENT PROFILE 1,189 students.
FIRST-YEAR CLASS 738 total. Of the students who applied, 100% were accepted, 80% of whom enrolled.
ACADEMIC PROGRAM Calendar: semesters.
GENERAL DEGREE REQUIREMENTS 62 credit hours; 6 credit hours of math/science; computer course.
MAJORS Data processing, fire science.
COMPUTERS ON CAMPUS 100 computers for student use in computer labs, classrooms provide access to on-line services, Internet. Staffed computer lab on campus provides training in use of computers, software.
HOUSING College housing not available.
EXPENSES FOR 1996–97 Area resident tuition: $1178 full-time, $38 per credit hour part-time. State resident tuition: $1457 full-time, $47 per credit hour part-time. Nonresident tuition: $4309 full-time, $139 per credit hour part-time.
FINANCIAL AID *College-administered undergrad aid 1995–96:* need-based scholarships, non-need scholarships, low-interest long-term loans from external sources. *Required forms:* FAFSA.
APPLYING Open admission. *Required:* school transcript, ACT, ACT ASSET, or SAT I. *Application deadline:* rolling.
APPLYING/TRANSFER *Required:* standardized test scores, high school transcript, college transcript. *Entrance:* noncompetitive. *Application deadline:* rolling.
CONTACT Mr. Jim Ulmer, Director of Admissions, Black River Technical College, Pocahontas, AR 72455, 501-892-4565 or toll-free 800-919-3086. *Fax:* 501-892-3546.

COSSATOT TECHNICAL COLLEGE
DeQueen, Arkansas

UG Enrollment: 800	Tuition & Fees: $912
Application Deadline: N/R	Room & Board: N/Avail

GENERAL State-supported, 2-year, specialized, coed. Awards certificates, diplomas, transfer associate degrees. *Setting:* rural campus. *Total enrollment:* 800. *Faculty:* 31.
ENROLLMENT PROFILE 800 students.
FIRST-YEAR CLASS 231 total. Of the students who applied, 100% were accepted, 70% of whom enrolled.
ACADEMIC PROGRAM Calendar: semesters. Co-op programs.
GENERAL DEGREE REQUIREMENTS 62 credit hours; 1 course in college algebra.

MAJORS Business administration/commerce/management, computer management, liberal arts/general studies.
COMPUTERS ON CAMPUS Computers for student use in learning resource center.
EXPENSES FOR 1996–97 Tuition: $912 full-time, $38 per credit hour part-time.
APPLYING Open admission. ***Required:*** SAT I or ACT, ACT ASSET. ***Recommended:*** school transcript.
APPLYING/TRANSFER ***Recommended:*** high school transcript.
CONTACT Mr. Don Park, Academic Dean, Cossatot Technical College, DeQueen, AR 71832, 501-584-4471.

EAST ARKANSAS COMMUNITY COLLEGE
Forrest City, Arkansas

UG Enrollment: 1,333	**Tuition & Fees (Area Res): $792**
Application Deadline: rolling	**Room & Board: N/Avail**

GENERAL State-supported, 2-year, coed. Awards certificates, transfer associate, terminal associate degrees. Founded 1974. ***Setting:*** 40-acre small-town campus with easy access to Memphis. ***Endowment:*** $28,661. ***Total enrollment:*** 1,333. ***Faculty:*** 101 (42 full-time, 9% with terminal degrees, 59 part-time); student-faculty ratio is 13:1.
ENROLLMENT PROFILE 1,333 students from 4 states and territories. 72% women, 28% men, 44% part-time, 99% state residents, 20% transferred in, 0% international, 47% 25 or older, 0% Native American, 1% Hispanic, 38% African American, 1% Asian American. ***Areas of study chosen:*** 50% liberal arts/general studies, 25% health professions and related sciences, 15% computer and information sciences, 10% business management and administrative services. ***Most popular recent majors:*** liberal arts/general studies, practical nursing, criminal justice.
FIRST-YEAR CLASS 303 total; 481 applied, 100% were accepted, 63% of whom enrolled.
ACADEMIC PROGRAM Core, interdisciplinary curriculum, honor code. Calendar: semesters. 538 courses offered in 1995–96. Academic remediation for entering students, English as a second language program, services for LD students, advanced placement, tutorials, honors program, summer session for credit, part-time degree program (daytime, evenings, weekends, summer), adult/continuing education programs.
GENERAL DEGREE REQUIREMENTS 64 credits; college algebra for associate of arts degree, intermediate algebra for associate of applied science; computer course for associate of applied science degree students.
MAJORS Business administration/commerce/management, computer technologies, criminal justice, drafting and design, law enforcement/police sciences, liberal arts/general studies, practical nursing, secondary education.
LIBRARY Learning Resource Center plus 1 other, with 21,908 books, 109 periodicals, 1 on-line bibliographic service, 1 CD-ROM, 889 records, tapes, and CDs. Acquisition spending 1994–95: $19,385.
COMPUTERS ON CAMPUS 26 computers for student use in computer center. Staffed computer lab on campus provides training in use of computers, software. Academic computing expenditure 1994–95: $128,755.
COLLEGE LIFE Drama-theater group, choral group. ***Social organizations:*** 4 open to all. ***Most popular organizations:*** Gamma Beta Phi, Baptist Student Union, Student Activities Committee, Lambda Alpha Epsilon. ***Major annual events:*** Spring Barbecue, Homecoming. ***Student services:*** personal-psychological counseling. ***Campus security:*** 24-hour emergency response devices, 16-hour patrols by trained security personnel.
HOUSING College housing not available.
CAREER PLANNING ***Placement office:*** 4 full-time staff; $35,000 operating expenditure 1994–95. ***Director:*** Ms. Darcy Clifton, Coordinator of Career Center, 501-633-4480 Ext. 306. ***Services:*** job fairs, resume preparation, resume referral, career counseling, careers library, job bank, job interviews. 45 organizations recruited on campus 1994–95.
AFTER GRADUATION 54% of students completing a degree program in 1994–95 went directly on to further study.
EXPENSES FOR 1996–97 Area resident tuition: $792 full-time, $33 per credit part-time. State resident tuition: $960 full-time, $40 per credit part-time. Nonresident tuition: $1164 full-time, $48.50 per credit part-time.
FINANCIAL AID ***College-administered undergrad aid 1995–96:*** low-interest long-term loans, part-time jobs. ***Required forms:*** FAFSA. ***Priority deadline:*** 5/1. ***Waivers:*** full or partial for senior citizens.
APPLYING Open admission. ***Options:*** early entrance, deferred entrance. ***Required:*** school transcript, TOEFL for international students. ***Recommended:*** ACT, ACT ASSET. ***Required for some:*** ACT, ACT ASSET. Test scores used for counseling/placement. ***Application deadline:*** rolling. ***Notification:*** continuous.
APPLYING/TRANSFER ***Required:*** college transcript. ***Required for some:*** standardized test scores. ***Entrance:*** noncompetitive. ***Application deadline:*** rolling. ***Notification:*** continuous. ***Contact:*** Ms. Leslie Anderson, Assistant Registrar, 501-633-4480 Ext. 206.
CONTACT Ms. Debra Vandiver, Registrar/Director of Admissions, East Arkansas Community College, Forrest City, AR 72335-9598, 501-633-4480 Ext. 219. ***Fax:*** 501-633-7222.

GARLAND COUNTY COMMUNITY COLLEGE
Hot Springs, Arkansas

UG Enrollment: 1,988	**Tuition & Fees (Area Res): $908**
Application Deadline: rolling	**Room & Board: N/Avail**

GENERAL State and locally supported, 2-year, coed. Awards certificates, diplomas, transfer associate, terminal associate degrees. Founded 1973. ***Setting:*** 50-acre suburban campus with easy access to Little Rock. ***Total enrollment:*** 1,988. ***Faculty:*** 109 (56 full-time, 19% with terminal degrees, 53 part-time); student-faculty ratio is 16:1.
ENROLLMENT PROFILE 1,988 students from 30 states and territories, 2 other countries. 66% women, 34% men, 58% part-time, 96% state residents, 30% transferred in, 48% have need-based financial aid, 22% have non-need-based financial aid, 1% international, 55% 25 or older, 2% Native American, 1% Hispanic, 6% African American, 1% Asian American. ***Most popular recent majors:*** nursing, business administration/commerce/management, education.
FIRST-YEAR CLASS 635 total. Of the students who applied, 100% were accepted.
ACADEMIC PROGRAM Core, interdisciplinary curriculum, honor code. Calendar: semesters. 562 courses offered in 1995–96. Academic remediation for entering students, English as a second language program, services for LD students, advanced placement, self-designed majors, tutorials, honors program, summer session for credit, part-time degree program (daytime, evenings, weekends, summer), adult/continuing education programs, co-op programs and internships. Study-abroad program. (5% of students participate)
GENERAL DEGREE REQUIREMENTS 64 semester hours; math/science requirements vary according to program; computer course; internship (some majors).
MAJORS Accounting, art/fine arts, business administration/commerce/management, ceramic art and design, child care/child and family studies, commercial art, computer graphics, computer information systems, computer technologies, criminal justice, data processing, education, electrical and electronics technologies, electrical engineering technology, elementary education, emergency medical technology, finance/banking, fire science, graphic arts, health science, health services administration, liberal arts/general studies, medical laboratory technology, medical records services, medical secretarial studies, medical technology, nursing, parks management, physical sciences, radiological sciences, radiological technology, secretarial studies/office management, vocational education, word processing.
LIBRARY Garland County Community College Library with 15,600 books, 2,700 microform titles, 290 periodicals, 450 records, tapes, and CDs. Acquisition spending 1994–95: $217,351.
COMPUTERS ON CAMPUS 270 computers for student use in computer labs, learning resource center, classrooms, library provide access to main academic computer, off-campus computing facilities, e-mail, on-line services, Internet. Staffed computer lab on campus provides training in use of computers, software. Academic computing expenditure 1994–95: $183,378.
COLLEGE LIFE Orientation program ($35, parents included). Choral group, student-run newspaper. ***Most popular organizations:*** Student Newspaper, Choral Group. ***Student services:*** health clinic, personal-psychological counseling, women's center. ***Campus security:*** 24-hour patrols.
HOUSING College housing not available.
ATHLETICS Member NJCAA. ***Intramural:*** archery, baseball, basketball, soccer, swimming and diving, tennis, volleyball. ***Contact:*** Mr. Ron Garner, Dean of Students, 501-767-9371.
CAREER PLANNING ***Placement office:*** 1 full-time staff. ***Director:*** Ms. Cathy Wells, Counselor, 501-767-9371. ***Services:*** job fairs, resume preparation, resume referral, career counseling, careers library, job bank, job interviews.
EXPENSES FOR 1996–97 Area resident tuition: $888 full-time, $37 per semester hour part-time. State resident tuition: $1104 full-time, $46 per semester hour part-time. Nonresident tuition: $2760 full-time, $115 per semester hour part-time. Part-time mandatory fees: $10 per semester. Full-time mandatory fees: $20.
FINANCIAL AID ***College-administered undergrad aid 1995–96:*** need-based scholarships, non-need scholarships, short-term loans, low-interest long-term loans from external sources, Federal Work-Study, part-time jobs. ***Required forms:*** institutional, FAFSA; required for some: state; accepted: CSS Financial Aid PROFILE. ***Application deadline:*** continuous. ***Waivers:*** full or partial for employees or children of employees and senior citizens.
APPLYING Open admission. ***Options:*** early entrance, deferred entrance, midyear entrance. ***Required:*** school transcript, SAT I or ACT, TOEFL for international students. ***Recommended:*** ACT ASSET. Test scores used for counseling/placement. ***Application deadline:*** rolling.
APPLYING/TRANSFER ***Required:*** standardized test scores, high school transcript. ***Entrance:*** noncompetitive. ***Application deadline:*** rolling. ***Contact:*** Mr. Allen B. Moody, Registrar, 501-767-9371.
CONTACT Mr. Ron Garner, Dean of Students, Garland County Community College, Hot Springs, AR 71913, 501-767-9371. ***Fax:*** 501-767-6896. ***E-mail:*** rphillips@jill.accc.cc.ar.us.

ITT TECHNICAL INSTITUTE
Little Rock, Arkansas

UG Enrollment: 138	**Tuition: $15,599/deg prog**
Application Deadline: rolling	**Room & Board: N/Avail**

GENERAL Proprietary, 2-year, coed. Part of ITT Educational Services, Inc. Awards terminal associate degrees. Founded 1993. ***Setting:*** urban campus. ***Total enrollment:*** 138. ***Faculty:*** 11 (7 full-time, 100% with terminal degrees, 4 part-time).
ENROLLMENT PROFILE 138 students: 16% women, 84% men, 0% part-time, 100% state residents, 36% 25 or older, 33% African American, 1% Asian American. ***Areas of study chosen:*** 100% engineering and applied sciences.
FIRST-YEAR CLASS 65 total.
ACADEMIC PROGRAM Calendar: quarters. Tutorials.
GENERAL DEGREE REQUIREMENT 108 units.
MAJORS Drafting and design, electronics engineering technology.
COLLEGE LIFE ***Campus security:*** 24-hour emergency response devices.
HOUSING College housing not available.
CAREER PLANNING ***Placement office:*** 1 full-time staff. ***Director:*** Ms. Carol Wallace, Director of Placement, 501-565-5550. ***Services:*** job fairs, resume preparation, resume referral, career counseling, careers library, job bank, job interviews. Students must register freshman year. 10 organizations recruited on campus 1994–95.
EXPENSES FOR 1996–97 ***Application fee:*** $100. Tuition per degree program ranges from $15,599 to $17,690. Full-time mandatory fees range from $540 to $720.
FINANCIAL AID ***College-administered undergrad aid 1995–96:*** need-based scholarships, low-interest long-term loans from external sources. ***Required forms:*** institutional, FAFSA. ***Application deadline:*** continuous.
APPLYING ***Option:*** deferred entrance. ***Required:*** school transcript, interview, CPAt. ***Recommended:*** recommendations. Test scores used for admission. ***Application deadline:*** rolling.
APPLYING/TRANSFER ***Required:*** standardized test scores, high school transcript, interview, college transcript. ***Recommended:*** recommendations. ***Application deadline:*** rolling. ***Contact:*** Dr. Pat Hunnicutt, Director of Education, 501-565-5550.
CONTACT Mr. Ken Sullivan, Director, ITT Technical Institute, 4520 South University, Little Rock, AR 72204, 501-565-5550. College video available.

Peterson's Guide to Two-Year Colleges 1997 175

MISSISSIPPI COUNTY COMMUNITY COLLEGE
Blytheville, Arkansas

UG Enrollment: 2,114 **Tuition & Fees (Area Res): $816**
Application Deadline: rolling **Room & Board: N/Avail**

GENERAL State-supported, 2-year, coed. Awards certificates, transfer associate, terminal associate degrees. Founded 1975. ***Setting:*** 80-acre rural campus with easy access to Memphis. ***Research spending 1994–95:*** $82,929. ***Educational spending 1994–95:*** $1054 per undergrad. ***Total enrollment:*** 2,114. ***Faculty:*** 88 (42 full-time, 8% with terminal degrees, 46 part-time).
ENROLLMENT PROFILE 2,114 students from 5 states and territories, 4 other countries. 64% women, 58% part-time, 78% state residents, 7% transferred in, 1% international, 45% 25 or older, 28% African American. ***Areas of study chosen:*** 48% liberal arts/general studies, 30% health professions and related sciences, 15% business management and administrative services, 4% computer and information sciences, 3% engineering and applied sciences, 1% agriculture. ***Most popular recent majors:*** liberal arts/general studies, nursing, business administration/commerce/management.
FIRST-YEAR CLASS 404 total; 439 applied, 100% were accepted, 92% of whom enrolled.
ACADEMIC PROGRAM Core. Calendar: semesters. Average class size 20 in required courses. Academic remediation for entering students, English as a second language program offered during academic year and summer, advanced placement, summer session for credit, part-time degree program (daytime, evenings, weekends, summer), adult/continuing education programs, co-op programs and internships.
GENERAL DEGREE REQUIREMENTS 62 semester hours; 1 math course; computer course for all associate of applied science degree students; internship (some majors).
MAJORS Agricultural technologies, business administration/commerce/management, computer technologies, criminal justice, data processing, electrical and electronics technologies, horticulture, industrial engineering technology, liberal arts/general studies, nursing, secretarial studies/office management.
LIBRARY Mississippi County Library plus 1 other, with 12,478 books, 190 microform titles, 179 periodicals, 1 on-line bibliographic service, 5 CD-ROMs, 340 records, tapes, and CDs. Acquisition spending 1994–95: $55,334.
COMPUTERS ON CAMPUS Computer purchase plan available. 120 computers for student use in computer labs, classrooms provide access to main academic computer, Internet. Staffed computer lab on campus (open 24 hours a day) provides training in use of computers, software. Academic computing expenditure 1994–95: $210,000.
COLLEGE LIFE Choral group. ***Social organizations:*** 12 open to all. ***Most popular organizations:*** Gamma Beta Phi, Drama Club, Nursing Club, Powerlifting Club. ***Major annual events:*** Fall Funfest, Spring Funfest, Evening Student Appreciation Night. ***Campus security:*** security guard during certain evening and weekend hours.
HOUSING College housing not available.
CAREER PLANNING ***Placement office:*** 1 full-time staff; $38,000 operating expenditure 1994–95. ***Director:*** Ms. Shellie Besharse, Coordinator, Career Center, 501-762-1020. ***Services:*** resume preparation, resume referral, career counseling, job interviews.
EXPENSES FOR 1995–96 Area resident tuition: $816 full-time, $34 per semester hour part-time. State resident tuition: $1056 full-time, $44 per semester hour part-time. Nonresident tuition: $1920 full-time, $80 per semester hour part-time. Missouri residents of Pemiscott, Dunklin, and New Madrid counties, and Tennessee residents of Obion, Dyer, Lauderdale, Tipton, and Shelby counties pay state resident tuition rates.
FINANCIAL AID ***College-administered undergrad aid 1995–96:*** 61 need-based scholarships (average $200), 196 non-need scholarships (average $556), low-interest long-term loans from external sources (average $3351), 23 Federal Work-Study (averaging $762), 35 part-time jobs. ***Required forms:*** FAFSA; required for some: institutional; accepted: CSS Financial Aid PROFILE, state. ***Priority deadline:*** 4/15. ***Payment plans:*** installment, deferred payment. ***Waivers:*** full or partial for employees or children of employees and senior citizens. ***Notification:*** continuous. ***Average indebtedness of graduates:*** $2538.
APPLYING Open admission except for nursing programs. ***Options:*** early entrance, deferred entrance. ***Required:*** TOEFL for international students, ACT ASSET. ***Recommended:*** school transcript, ACT. ***Required for some:*** ACT. Test scores used for counseling/placement. ***Application deadline:*** rolling. ***Notification:*** continuous.
APPLYING/TRANSFER ***Required:*** college transcript. ***Entrance:*** noncompetitive. ***Application deadline:*** rolling. ***Notification:*** continuous. ***Contact:*** Ms. June Walters, Assistant Dean of Student Services and Registrar, 501-762-1020 Ext. 106.
CONTACT Mrs. June Walters, Assistant Dean of Student Services and Registrar, Mississippi County Community College, Blytheville, AR 72316-1109, 501-762-1020 Ext. 103. ***Fax:*** 501-763-3704.

NORTH ARKANSAS COMMUNITY/TECHNICAL COLLEGE
Harrison, Arkansas

UG Enrollment: 1,482 **Tuition & Fees (Area Res): $912**
Application Deadline: rolling **Room & Board: N/Avail**

GENERAL State and locally supported, 2-year, coed. Awards certificates, transfer associate, terminal associate degrees. Founded 1974. ***Setting:*** 40-acre small-town campus. ***Total enrollment:*** 1,482. ***Faculty:*** 116 (56 full-time, 80% with terminal degrees, 60 part-time).
ENROLLMENT PROFILE 1,482 students from 13 states and territories. 58% women, 42% men, 39% part-time, 94% state residents, 11% transferred in, 45% 25 or older, 1% Native American, 1% Hispanic, 1% African American, 1% Asian American. ***Areas of study chosen:*** 38% liberal arts/general studies, 15% health professions and related sciences, 7% business management and administrative services, 5% engineering and applied sciences. ***Most popular recent majors:*** liberal arts/general studies, nursing.
FIRST-YEAR CLASS 374 total; 560 applied, 90% were accepted, 74% of whom enrolled.
ACADEMIC PROGRAM Core, transfer/technical curriculum. Calendar: semesters. Academic remediation for entering students, services for LD students, advanced placement, Freshman Honors College, honors program, summer session for credit, part-time degree program (daytime, evenings, weekends), adult/continuing education programs.
GENERAL DEGREE REQUIREMENT 62 credit hours.
MAJORS Automotive technologies, business administration/commerce/management, data processing, electromechanical technology, emergency medical technology, hotel and restaurant management, liberal arts/general studies, machine and tool technologies, medical laboratory technology, nursing, radiological technology, word processing.
LIBRARY NACTC Library plus 1 other, with 23,994 books, 327 microform titles, 374 periodicals, 11 CD-ROMs, 169 records, tapes, and CDs.
COMPUTERS ON CAMPUS Computer purchase plan available. 145 computers for student use in computer center, computer labs, learning resource center, classrooms, library provide access to main academic computer, off-campus computing facilities, e-mail, Internet. Staffed computer lab on campus provides training in use of computers, software.
COLLEGE LIFE Drama-theater group. ***Most popular organization:*** Phi Beta Lambda. ***Student services:*** personal-psychological counseling. ***Campus security:*** 24-hour patrols.
HOUSING College housing not available.
ATHLETICS Member NJCAA. ***Intercollegiate:*** baseball M, basketball M(s)/W(s). ***Intramural:*** archery, badminton, baseball, basketball, football, racquetball, softball, table tennis (Ping-Pong), volleyball. ***Contact:*** Mr. Dorm Saylors, Athletic Director, 501-743-3000 Ext. 279.
CAREER PLANNING ***Placement office:*** 4 full-time staff. ***Director:*** Dr. Jerry Cash, Vice President for Student Services, 501-743-3000 Ext. 239. ***Services:*** job fairs, resume preparation, career counseling, careers library.
EXPENSES FOR 1995–96 Area resident tuition: $912 full-time, $38 per credit hour part-time. State resident tuition: $1128 full-time, $47 per credit hour part-time. Nonresident tuition: $2184 full-time, $91 per credit hour part-time.
FINANCIAL AID ***College-administered undergrad aid 1995–96:*** 274 need-based scholarships (averaging $185), 169 non-need scholarships (averaging $563), short-term loans (averaging $50), low-interest long-term loans from external sources (averaging $1791), Federal Work-Study, part-time jobs. ***Required forms:*** institutional, FAFSA; accepted: CSS Financial Aid PROFILE. ***Priority deadline:*** 5/1. ***Payment plan:*** installment. ***Waivers:*** full or partial for employees or children of employees and senior citizens.
APPLYING Open admission. ***Options:*** deferred entrance, midyear entrance. ***Required:*** ACT, TOEFL for international students, ACT ASSET. ***Recommended:*** school transcript. Test scores used for counseling/placement. ***Application deadline:*** rolling. ***Notification:*** continuous.
APPLYING/TRANSFER ***Recommended:*** high school transcript, college transcript. ***Entrance:*** noncompetitive. ***Contact:*** Ms. Lesli Young, Counselor, 501-743-3000 Ext. 338.
CONTACT Ms. Charla McDonald, Research Assistant, North Arkansas Community/Technical College, Harrison, AR 72601, 501-743-3000 Ext. 221. ***Fax:*** 501-743-6418.

NORTHWEST ARKANSAS COMMUNITY COLLEGE
Bentonville, Arkansas

UG Enrollment: 2,245 **Tuition & Fees (Area Res): $888**
Application Deadline: rolling **Room & Board: N/Avail**

GENERAL State and locally supported, 2-year, coed. Awards transfer associate, terminal associate degrees. Founded 1989. ***Setting:*** 77-acre urban campus. ***Educational spending 1994–95:*** $855 per undergrad. ***Total enrollment:*** 2,245. ***Faculty:*** 151 (40 full-time, 38% with terminal degrees, 111 part-time); student-faculty ratio is 15:1.
ENROLLMENT PROFILE 2,245 students from 4 states and territories, 4 other countries. 60% women, 40% men, 71% part-time, 97% state residents, 32% transferred in, 16% have need-based financial aid, 10% have non-need-based financial aid, 1% international, 42% 25 or older, 1% Native American, 1% Hispanic, 1% African American, 1% Asian American. ***Areas of study chosen:*** 31% liberal arts/general studies, 15% health professions and related sciences, 8% business management and administrative services, 1% social sciences. ***Most popular recent majors:*** business administration/commerce/management, liberal arts/general studies.
FIRST-YEAR CLASS 649 total; 649 applied, 100% were accepted, 100% of whom enrolled.
ACADEMIC PROGRAM Core, interdisciplinary curriculum, honor code. Calendar: semesters. 296 courses offered in 1995–96; average class size 17 in required courses. Academic remediation for entering students, English as a second language program, services for LD students, tutorials, honors program, summer session for credit, part-time degree program (daytime, evenings, summer), adult/continuing education programs, co-op programs and internships.
GENERAL DEGREE REQUIREMENTS 62 credits; 1 college algebra course; computer course; internship (some majors).
MAJORS Accounting, business administration/commerce/management, computer programming, criminal justice, data processing, education, emergency medical technology, finance/banking, liberal arts/general studies, nursing, occupational safety and health, physical therapy, radiological technology, respiratory therapy, secretarial studies/office management.
LIBRARY Library Resource Center plus 1 other, with 15,500 books, 175 microform titles, 159 periodicals, 9 CD-ROMs, 204 records, tapes, and CDs. Acquisition spending 1994–95: $97,485.
COMPUTERS ON CAMPUS 97 computers for student use in computer labs, learning resource center, library. Staffed computer lab on campus.
COLLEGE LIFE Orientation program (2 days, no cost). Drama-theater group, choral group, student-run newspaper. ***Social organizations:*** 2 open to all. ***Most popular organizations:*** Student Advisory Activity Council, Gamma Beta Phi, Phi Beta Lambda. ***Major annual events:*** Red Ribbon Week, Student Organization Fair. ***Campus security:*** 24-hour emergency response devices, student patrols.
HOUSING College housing not available.
CAREER PLANNING ***Placement office:*** 1 full-time staff. ***Director:*** Ms. Debra Davis, Career Center Director, 501-619-4233. ***Services:*** job fairs, resume preparation, career counseling, careers library, job bank, job interviews.
EXPENSES FOR 1996–97 Area resident tuition: $888 full-time, $37 per credit part-time. State resident tuition: $1776 full-time, $74 per credit part-time. Nonresident tuition: $2280 full-time, $95 per credit part-time.
FINANCIAL AID ***College-administered undergrad aid 1995–96:*** 325 need-based scholarships (average $1350), 80 non-need scholarships (average $800), short-term loans (average $25), low-interest long-term loans from external sources (average $2625), part-time jobs. ***Required forms:*** state, institutional, FAFSA. ***Priority deadline:*** 7/1. ***Waivers:*** full or partial for employees or children of employees and senior citizens.

APPLYING Open admission. *Option:* early entrance. *Required:* ACT ASSET. *Recommended:* school transcript, SAT I or ACT. *Required for some:* TOEFL for international students. Test scores used for counseling/placement. *Application deadline:* rolling. *Notification:* continuous.
APPLYING/TRANSFER *Recommended:* college transcript. *Required for some:* standardized test scores, high school transcript. *Contact:* Dr. Bill Path, Registrar/Director of Admissions, 501-636-9222.
CONTACT Ms. Carol Jines, Registrar, NorthWest Arkansas Community College, PO Box 1408, Bentonville, AR 72712-1408, 501-636-9222 Ext. 4136.

OUACHITA TECHNICAL COLLEGE
Malvern, Arkansas

UG Enrollment: 568	Tuition & Fees (AR Res): $1290
Application Deadline: rolling	Room & Board: N/Avail

GENERAL State-supported, 2-year, coed. Awards terminal associate degrees. *Total enrollment:* 568. *Faculty:* 26.
ENROLLMENT PROFILE 568 students.
FIRST-YEAR CLASS 297 total. Of the students who applied, 100% were accepted, 80% of whom enrolled.
ACADEMIC PROGRAM Calendar: semesters.
GENERAL DEGREE REQUIREMENTS 60 credit hours; math/science requirements vary according to program; computer course.
MAJORS Accounting, automotive technologies, computer information systems, management information systems, manufacturing technology, paralegal studies, secretarial studies/office management.
COMPUTERS ON CAMPUS 70 computers for student use.
HOUSING College housing not available.
EXPENSES FOR 1996–97 State resident tuition: $1140 full-time, $38 per credit hour part-time. Nonresident tuition: $1980 full-time, $66 per credit hour part-time. Part-time mandatory fees: $5 per credit hour. Full-time mandatory fees: $150.
APPLYING Open admission. *Required:* school transcript. *Required for some:* SAT I or ACT, ACT ASSET. *Application deadline:* rolling.
APPLYING/TRANSFER *Required:* high school transcript, college transcript. *Entrance:* noncompetitive. *Application deadline:* rolling.
CONTACT Mr. Vaughn Kesterson, Counselor, Ouachita Technical College, Malvern, AR 72104, 501-332-3658.

OZARKA TECHNICAL COLLEGE
Melbourne, Arkansas

UG Enrollment: 453	Tuition & Fees: $845
Application Deadline: 8/28	Room & Board: N/Avail

GENERAL State-supported, 2-year, coed. Awards certificates, transfer associate, terminal associate degrees. Founded 1973. *Setting:* 40-acre rural campus. *Educational spending 1994–95:* $2320 per undergrad. *Total enrollment:* 453. *Faculty:* 42 (14 full-time, 86% with terminal degrees, 28 part-time); student-faculty ratio is 15:1.
ENROLLMENT PROFILE 453 students: 70% women, 60% part-time, 100% state residents, 10% transferred in, 33% have need-based financial aid, 1% have non-need-based financial aid, 0% international, 45% 25 or older, 1% Native American, 1% Hispanic, 0% African American, 1% Asian American. *Areas of study chosen:* 75% liberal arts/general studies, 15% business management and administrative services, 10% health professions and related sciences, 2% vocational and home economics. *Most popular recent majors:* management information systems, automotive technologies, liberal arts/general studies.
FIRST-YEAR CLASS 303 total; 328 applied, 100% were accepted, 92% of whom enrolled. 7% from top 10% of their high school class, 30% from top quarter, 61% from top half.
ACADEMIC PROGRAM Core, general education and technical curriculum, honor code. Calendar: semesters. 82 courses offered in 1995–96. Academic remediation for entering students, services for LD students, tutorials, summer session for credit, part-time degree program (daytime), co-op programs and internships.
GENERAL DEGREE REQUIREMENTS 60 credits; 1 algebra course; computer course for automatic service technology, business information technology, medical transcription, general technology majors; internship (some majors).
MAJORS Automotive technologies, culinary arts, liberal arts/general studies, management information systems, medical records services, nursing, secretarial studies/office management.
LIBRARY Ozarka Technical College Library with 5,500 books, 68 microform titles, 400 periodicals, 5 on-line bibliographic services, 2 CD-ROMs, 650 records, tapes, and CDs. Acquisition spending 1994–95: $35,000.
COMPUTERS ON CAMPUS 40 computers for student use in computer labs, learning resource center, library provide access to on-line services, Internet. Staffed computer lab on campus provides training in use of computers, software.
COLLEGE LIFE 70% vote in student government elections. *Most popular organizations:* VICA, Phi Beta Lambda, Student Council, HOSA, Phi Theta Kappa. *Major annual events:* Activity Day, Career Day. *Student services:* personal-psychological counseling.
HOUSING College housing not available.
CAREER PLANNING *Placement office:* 1 full-time staff. *Director:* Ms. Jean Hall, Counselor, 501-368-7371. *Services:* resume preparation, career counseling, careers library.
AFTER GRADUATION 90% of class of 1994 had job offers within 6 months. 40% of students completing a degree program went directly on to further study.
EXPENSES FOR 1995–96 Tuition: $840 full-time, $35 per credit hour part-time. Part-time mandatory fees: $5 per year. Full-time mandatory fees: $5.
FINANCIAL AID *College-administered undergrad aid 1995–96:* 169 need-based scholarships (average $1285), 19 non-need scholarships (average $420), low-interest long-term loans from external sources, 4 part-time jobs. *Required forms:* FAFSA; accepted: state, institutional. *Priority deadline:* 9/12.
APPLYING Open admission. *Options:* early entrance, midyear entrance. *Required:* school transcript, ACT, ACT ASSET. *Recommended:* minimum 2.0 GPA, 3 years of high school math and science. *Required for some:* essay, recommendations, campus interview. Test scores used for admission and counseling/placement. *Application deadline:* 8/28.

APPLYING/TRANSFER *Required:* standardized test scores, college transcript. *Recommended:* 3 years of high school math and science, minimum 2.0 college GPA, minimum 2.0 high school GPA. *Required for some:* essay, high school transcript, recommendations, campus interview. *Entrance:* noncompetitive. *Application deadline:* 8/28. *Contact:* Mr. Ron C. Helm, Registrar, 501-368-7371.
CONTACT Ms. Jean Hall, Counselor, Ozarka Technical College, Melbourne, AR 72556, 501-368-7371.

PETIT JEAN TECHNICAL COLLEGE
Morrilton, Arkansas

UG Enrollment: 651	Tuition & Fees: $990
Application Deadline: rolling	Room & Board: N/Avail

GENERAL State-supported, 2-year, coed. Awards certificates, diplomas, transfer associate, terminal associate degrees. Founded 1961. *Setting:* 63-acre rural campus. *Total enrollment:* 651. *Faculty:* 54 (29 full-time, 95% with terminal degrees, 25 part-time); student-faculty ratio is 18:1.
ENROLLMENT PROFILE 651 students: 66% women, 34% men, 40% part-time, 100% state residents, 10% transferred in, 44% have need-based financial aid, 6% have non-need-based financial aid, 0% international, 1% Native American, 1% Hispanic, 8% African American, 1% Asian American. *Areas of study chosen:* 32% liberal arts/general studies, 24% engineering and applied sciences, 15% computer and information sciences, 13% business management and administrative services, 9% health professions and related sciences, 5% vocational and home economics, 2% agriculture. *Most popular recent majors:* practical nursing, secretarial studies/office management, child care/child and family studies.
FIRST-YEAR CLASS 311 total; 451 applied, 95% were accepted, 72% of whom enrolled. 5% from top 10% of their high school class, 20% from top quarter, 50% from top half.
ACADEMIC PROGRAM Core, honor code. Calendar: semesters. 160 courses offered in 1995–96. Academic remediation for entering students, services for LD students, advanced placement, self-designed majors, summer session for credit, part-time degree program (daytime, evenings), internships.
GENERAL DEGREE REQUIREMENTS 60 credits; computer course for business, drafting, child care majors.
MAJORS Automotive technologies, child care/child and family studies, computer information systems, drafting and design, graphic arts, heating/refrigeration/air conditioning, horticulture, liberal arts/general studies, machine and tool technologies, marketing/retailing/merchandising, ornamental horticulture, practical nursing, printing technologies, secretarial studies/office management, surveying technology, welding technology, word processing.
LIBRARY Gordon Library with 6,400 books, 76 periodicals, 1 on-line bibliographic service, 50 CD-ROMs, 50 records, tapes, and CDs.
COMPUTERS ON CAMPUS 100 computers for student use in computer labs, learning resource center, classrooms. Staffed computer lab on campus.
COLLEGE LIFE 20% vote in student government elections. *Major annual events:* Fall Fest, Spring Fling. *Student services:* personal-psychological counseling. *Campus security:* 24-hour emergency response devices.
HOUSING College housing not available.
CAREER PLANNING *Placement office:* 2 full-time staff. *Director:* Ms. Skipper Rentfro, Job Placement Assistance/Retention, 501-354-2465. *Services:* job fairs, resume preparation, resume referral, career counseling. Students must register sophomore year.
AFTER GRADUATION 75% of class of 1994 had job offers within 6 months.
EXPENSES FOR 1996–97 Tuition: $960 full-time, $40 per credit hour part-time. Part-time mandatory fees: $10 per semester. Full-time mandatory fees: $30.
FINANCIAL AID *College-administered undergrad aid 1995–96:* 350 need-based scholarships (average $1300), 20 non-need scholarships (average $900), low-interest long-term loans from external sources (average $2000), 20 Federal Work-Study (averaging $800). *Required forms:* institutional, FAFSA. *Priority deadline:* 7/1. *Payment plan:* tuition prepayment. *Waivers:* full or partial for employees or children of employees and senior citizens.
APPLYING Open admission. *Options:* Common Application, early entrance, deferred entrance, midyear entrance. *Required:* school transcript, ACT, TOEFL for international students, ACT ASSET. Test scores used for counseling/placement. *Application deadline:* rolling. *Notification:* continuous.
APPLYING/TRANSFER *Required:* college transcript. *Required for some:* standardized test scores, high school transcript. *Entrance:* noncompetitive. *Application deadline:* rolling. *Notification:* continuous. *Contact:* Mr. Thomas Flowers, Vice President for Student Services, 501-354-2465.
CONTACT Mr. Thomas Flowers, Vice President for Student Services, Petit Jean Technical College, PO Box 586, Morrilton, AR 72110, 501-354-2465 or toll-free 800-264-1094 (in-state). *Fax:* 501-354-9948. College video available.

PHILLIPS COUNTY COMMUNITY COLLEGE
Helena, Arkansas

UG Enrollment: 1,520	Tuition & Fees (Area Res): $840
Application Deadline: 8/25	Room & Board: N/Avail

GENERAL State and locally supported, 2-year, coed. Awards transfer associate, terminal associate degrees. Founded 1965. *Setting:* 80-acre small-town campus with easy access to Memphis. *Total enrollment:* 1,520. *Faculty:* 107 (61 full-time, 46 part-time); student-faculty ratio is 14:1.
ENROLLMENT PROFILE 1,520 students: 74% women, 47% part-time, 100% state residents, 2% transferred in, 0% international, 45% 25 or older, 1% Native American, 1% Hispanic, 54% African American, 1% Asian American. *Most popular recent majors:* nursing, business education, liberal arts/general studies.
FIRST-YEAR CLASS 505 total; 505 applied, 100% were accepted, 100% of whom enrolled.
ACADEMIC PROGRAM Core, honor code. Calendar: semesters. Academic remediation for entering students, services for LD students, advanced placement, summer session for credit, part-time degree program (daytime, evenings), adult/continuing education programs.

Arkansas

Phillips County Community College *(continued)*
GENERAL DEGREE REQUIREMENT 64 semester hours.
MAJORS Agricultural business, art/fine arts, automotive technologies, biology/biological sciences, business administration/commerce/management, business education, chemistry, computer programming, cosmetology, data processing, drafting and design, education, English, heating/refrigeration/air conditioning, industrial arts, instrumentation technology, liberal arts/general studies, mathematics, medical laboratory technology, medical secretarial studies, music, nursing, physics, practical nursing, printing technologies, radiological technology, science, secretarial studies/office management, social science, theater arts/drama, welding technology.
LIBRARY 39,000 books, 7,336 microform titles, 352 periodicals, 4,182 records, tapes, and CDs.
COMPUTERS ON CAMPUS 200 computers for student use in computer center, computer labs, library.
COLLEGE LIFE Drama-theater group, choral group, student-run newspaper. *Student services:* personal-psychological counseling. *Campus security:* 24-hour patrols.
HOUSING College housing not available.
ATHLETICS *Intramural:* basketball, bowling, golf, tennis, volleyball.
CAREER PLANNING *Placement office:* 3 full-time staff. *Director:* Ms. Carolyn Quarrells, Director of Advising, 501-338-6474. *Service:* career counseling.
AFTER GRADUATION 80% of students completing a degree program in 1994–95 went directly on to further study.
EXPENSES FOR 1995–96 Area resident tuition: $840 full-time, $35 per semester hour part-time. State resident tuition: $1056 full-time, $42 per semester hour part-time. Nonresident tuition: $1968 full-time, $82 per semester hour part-time.
FINANCIAL AID *College-administered undergrad aid 1995–96:* 500 need-based scholarships (averaging $1650), 60 non-need scholarships (averaging $850), low-interest long-term loans from external sources, Federal Work-Study. *Required forms:* FAFSA; accepted: CSS Financial Aid PROFILE. *Priority deadline:* 8/1. *Payment plan:* installment. *Waivers:* full or partial for employees or children of employees and senior citizens.
APPLYING Open admission except for nursing program. *Option:* early entrance. *Required:* ACT, TOEFL for international students, ACT ASSET. Test scores used for counseling/placement. *Application deadline:* 8/25. *Notification:* continuous until 8/25.
APPLYING/TRANSFER *Application deadline:* 8/25. *Notification:* continuous until 8/25. *Contact:* Mr. James R. Brasel, Dean of Admissions, 501-338-6474.
CONTACT Mr. James R. Brasel, Dean of Admissions, Phillips County College, Helena, AR 72342-0785, 501-338-6474. *Fax:* 501-338-7452.

PINES TECHNICAL COLLEGE
Pine Bluff, Arkansas

UG Enrollment: 1,231	Tuition & Fees: $900
Application Deadline: 8/21	Room & Board: N/Avail

GENERAL State-supported, 2-year, specialized, coed. Awards certificates, transfer associate, terminal associate degrees. Founded 1991. *Total enrollment:* 1,231. *Faculty:* 100 (60 full-time, 40 part-time).
ENROLLMENT PROFILE 1,231 students.
FIRST-YEAR CLASS 360 total. Of the students who applied, 100% were accepted, 60% of whom enrolled.
ACADEMIC PROGRAM Calendar: semesters. Part-time degree program (daytime, evenings, summer).
GENERAL DEGREE REQUIREMENTS 62 credits; 1 course each in math and science; computer course.
MAJORS Automotive technologies, business administration/commerce/management, drafting and design, electrical and electronics technologies, emergency medical technology, operating room technology, technology and public affairs.
HOUSING College housing not available.
EXPENSES FOR 1996–97 Tuition: $900 full-time, $30 per credit part-time.
APPLYING *Required:* school transcript, SAT I or ACT, ACT ASSET. *Application deadline:* 8/21. *Notification:* continuous.
APPLYING/TRANSFER *Required:* high school transcript, college transcript. *Application deadline:* 8/21. *Notification:* continuous.
CONTACT Dr. Charlotte Cone, Admissions/Enrollment Management Coordinator, Pines Technical College, Pine Bluff, AR 71603, 501-543-5900.

PULASKI TECHNICAL COLLEGE
North Little Rock, Arkansas

UG Enrollment: 1,412	Tuition & Fees (AR Res): $984
Application Deadline: rolling	Room & Board: N/Avail

GENERAL State-supported, 2-year, coed. Awards certificates, transfer associate degrees. Founded 1945. *Setting:* 40-acre urban campus with easy access to Little Rock. *Total enrollment:* 1,412. *Faculty:* 88 (40 full-time, 2% with terminal degrees, 48 part-time).
ENROLLMENT PROFILE 1,412 students.
FIRST-YEAR CLASS 206 total.
ACADEMIC PROGRAM Calendar: semesters. Academic remediation for entering students, services for LD students, summer session for credit, part-time degree program (daytime).
GENERAL DEGREE REQUIREMENTS 63 semester credit hours; computer course for all associate of applied science degree students.
MAJORS Computer information systems, drafting and design, electromechanical technology, manufacturing technology.
COMPUTERS ON CAMPUS 75 computers for student use in computer labs. Staffed computer lab on campus provides training in use of computers, software.
COLLEGE LIFE *Campus security:* security personnel from 7 a.m.– 11:00 p.m.
HOUSING College housing not available.
EXPENSES FOR 1995–96 State resident tuition: $984 full-time, $41 per semester part-time. Nonresident tuition: $1920 full-time, $80 per semester part-time.
FINANCIAL AID *College-administered undergrad aid 1995–96:* 500 need-based scholarships, 300 non-need scholarships, 6 part-time jobs. *Required forms:* state, FAFSA. *Application deadline:* continuous. *Payment plan:* deferred payment. *Waivers:* full or partial for employees or children of employees.
APPLYING Open admission. *Option:* Common Application. *Required:* school transcript, ACT ASSET. *Recommended:* ACT. Test scores used for counseling/placement. *Application deadline:* rolling.
APPLYING/TRANSFER *Required for some:* standardized test scores, high school transcript. *Entrance:* noncompetitive. *Contact:* Ms. Cindy Harkey, Counselor, 501-771-1000.
CONTACT Ms. Cindy Harkey, Counselor, Pulaski Technical College, 3000 West Scenic Drive, North Little Rock, AR 72118, 501-771-1000 Ext. 68. *Fax:* 501-771-2844.

RED RIVER TECHNICAL COLLEGE
Hope, Arkansas

UG Enrollment: 920	Tuition & Fees: $912
Application Deadline: rolling	Room & Board: N/Avail

GENERAL State-supported, 2-year, specialized, coed. Awards certificates, diplomas, transfer associate degrees. Founded 1966. *Setting:* 60-acre rural campus. *Total enrollment:* 920. *Faculty:* 47 (22 full-time, 41% with terminal degrees, 25 part-time); student-faculty ratio is 20:1.
ENROLLMENT PROFILE 920 students from 4 states and territories. 65% women, 35% men, 53% part-time, 99% state residents, 50% have need-based financial aid, 0% international, 46% 25 or older, 1% Native American, 1% Hispanic, 27% African American, 1% Asian American. *Areas of study chosen:* 17% business management and administrative services, 13% health professions and related sciences, 12% vocational and home economics, 6% liberal arts/general studies, 5% education, 2% social sciences, 1% biological and life sciences, 1% engineering and applied sciences, 1% mathematics, 1% prelaw, 1% premed. *Most popular recent major:* respiratory therapy.
FIRST-YEAR CLASS 475 total; 500 applied, 100% were accepted, 95% of whom enrolled.
ACADEMIC PROGRAM Core, honor code. Calendar: semesters. 267 courses offered in 1995–96; average class size 25 in required courses. Academic remediation for entering students, summer session for credit, part-time degree program (daytime, evenings, summer), internships.
GENERAL DEGREE REQUIREMENTS 62 credits; math/science requirements vary according to program; computer course; internship (some majors).
MAJORS Business administration/commerce/management, funeral service, liberal arts/general studies, respiratory therapy, vocational education.
LIBRARY 3,000 books, 1,283 microform titles, 105 periodicals, 1 on-line bibliographic service, 12 CD-ROMs, 195 records, tapes, and CDs. Acquisition spending 1994–95: $40,617.
COMPUTERS ON CAMPUS 30 computers for student use in computer labs, library. Academic computing expenditure 1994–95: $34,973.
COLLEGE LIFE Orientation program (2 days, no cost). *Social organizations:* 4 open to all. *Most popular organizations:* Student Government Association, Phi Theta Kappa, Phi Beta Lambda, Circle K. *Major annual events:* Thanksgiving Cookout, Fish Fry, Halloween Festival. *Campus security:* on-site security during day and evening class hours.
HOUSING College housing not available.
CAREER PLANNING *Services:* resume preparation, career counseling, job bank. Students must register freshman year.
EXPENSES FOR 1996–97 Tuition: $912 full-time.
FINANCIAL AID *College-administered undergrad aid 1995–96:* 10 need-based scholarships (average $456), 25 non-need scholarships (average $456), 1 Federal Work-Study, 8 part-time jobs. *Required forms:* institutional, FAFSA. *Priority deadline:* 7/31. *Payment plan:* installment. *Waivers:* full or partial for employees or children of employees and senior citizens.
APPLYING Open admission. *Required:* school transcript. *Recommended:* ACT, ACT ASSET. Test scores used for counseling/placement. *Application deadline:* rolling.
APPLYING/TRANSFER *Required:* high school transcript, college transcript. *Entrance:* noncompetitive.
CONTACT Ms. Danita Ormand, Director of Admission Services, Red River Technical College, Hope, AR 71801, 501-777-5722 Ext. 27 or toll-free 800-467-1722. *Fax:* 501-777-5951.

RICH MOUNTAIN COMMUNITY COLLEGE
Mena, Arkansas

UG Enrollment: 758	Tuition & Fees (Area Res): $792
Application Deadline: 8/25	Room & Board: N/Avail

GENERAL State and locally supported, 2-year, coed. Awards certificates, transfer associate, terminal associate degrees. Founded 1983. *Setting:* 40-acre small-town campus. *Total enrollment:* 758. *Faculty:* 48 (18 full-time, 30 part-time); student-faculty ratio is 12:1.
ENROLLMENT PROFILE 758 students from 2 states and territories. 65% women, 60% part-time, 96% state residents, 13% transferred in, 50% 25 or older, 4% Native American, 1% Hispanic, 1% Asian American. *Most popular recent majors:* liberal arts/general studies, business administration/commerce/management.
FIRST-YEAR CLASS 225 total. Of the students who applied, 100% were accepted, 95% of whom enrolled.
ACADEMIC PROGRAM Core. Calendar: semesters. Academic remediation for entering students, English as a second language program, services for LD students, summer session for credit, part-time degree program (daytime, evenings), adult/continuing education programs.
GENERAL DEGREE REQUIREMENTS 60 credits; math/science requirements vary according to program; computer course.
MAJORS Automotive technologies, business administration/commerce/management, carpentry, data processing, industrial and heavy equipment maintenance, liberal arts/general studies, machine and tool technologies, nursing, secretarial studies/office management.

LIBRARY St. John Library with 10,000 books, 115 periodicals, 100 records, tapes, and CDs.
COMPUTERS ON CAMPUS 60 computers for student use in computer labs, library.
COLLEGE LIFE Student-run newspaper. *Student services:* personal-psychological counseling.
HOUSING College housing not available.
CAREER PLANNING *Service:* career counseling.
AFTER GRADUATION 75% of students completing a degree program in 1994–95 went directly on to further study.
EXPENSES FOR 1995-96 Area resident tuition: $792 full-time, $33 per credit part-time. State resident tuition: $960 full-time, $40 per credit part-time. Nonresident tuition: $2040 full-time, $85 per credit part-time.
FINANCIAL AID *College-administered undergrad aid 1995–96:* 20 need-based scholarships (average $600), low-interest long-term loans from external sources (average $2500), Federal Work-Study. *Required forms:* state, AFSSA-CSX. *Priority deadline:* 9/1.
APPLYING Open admission. *Option:* early entrance. *Required:* school transcript. *Recommended:* ACT. Test scores used for counseling/placement. *Application deadline:* 8/25. *Notification:* continuous until 8/25.
APPLYING/TRANSFER *Required:* high school transcript. *Recommended:* standardized test scores. *Application deadline:* 8/25. *Notification:* continuous until 8/25.
CONTACT Dr. Richard Black, Dean of Students, Rich Mountain Community College, Mena, AR 71953, 501-394-5012 Ext. 47.

SHORTER COLLEGE
North Little Rock, Arkansas

UG Enrollment: 264	Tuition & Fees: $2200
Application Deadline: rolling	Room & Board: $2400

GENERAL Independent African Methodist Episcopal, 2-year, coed. Awards transfer associate, terminal associate degrees. Founded 1886. *Setting:* urban campus. *Total enrollment:* 264. *Faculty:* 24 (9 full-time, 15 part-time); student-faculty ratio is 8:1.
ENROLLMENT PROFILE 264 students from 5 states and territories. 49% women, 35% part-time, 43% state residents, 23% transferred in, 50% 25 or older, 0% Native American, 0% Hispanic, 90% African American, 0% Asian American. *Most popular recent majors:* business administration/commerce/management, nursing, social science.
FIRST-YEAR CLASS 85 total; 264 applied, 100% were accepted, 32% of whom enrolled. 0% from top 10% of their high school class, 0% from top quarter, 2% from top half.
ACADEMIC PROGRAM Core. Calendar: semesters. Academic remediation for entering students, summer session for credit, part-time degree program (daytime, evenings, weekends, summer), external degree programs, adult/continuing education programs, co-op programs.
GENERAL DEGREE REQUIREMENTS 64 credits; 3 credits of math; 4 credits of science; computer course.
MAJORS Behavioral sciences, business administration/commerce/management, business education, computer programming, computer science, early childhood education, education, fire science, health science, liberal arts/general studies, medical laboratory technology, nursing, paralegal studies, science, secretarial studies/office management, social science, social work.
COMPUTERS ON CAMPUS 10 computers for student use in computer center, library provide access to main academic computer. Staffed computer lab on campus provides training in use of computers.
COLLEGE LIFE Orientation program (2 days, $25). 70% vote in student government elections. *Student services:* legal services, health clinic, personal-psychological counseling.
HOUSING 50 college housing spaces available; 33 were occupied 1995–96. No special consideration for freshman housing applicants. Off-campus living permitted. *Option:* coed housing available.
ATHLETICS Member NJCAA. *Intercollegiate:* basketball M(s)/W. *Intramural:* table tennis (Ping-Pong). *Contact:* Mr. Charles Baker, Basketball Coach, 501-372-3354.
CAREER PLANNING *Service:* career counseling.
AFTER GRADUATION 50% of students completing a degree program in 1994–95 went directly on to further study.
EXPENSES FOR 1995-96 Comprehensive fee of $4600 includes full-time tuition ($2100), mandatory fees ($100), and college room and board ($2400). Part-time tuition per semester ranges from $89 to $775. Tuition guaranteed not to increase for student's term of enrollment.
FINANCIAL AID *College-administered undergrad aid 1995–96:* need-based scholarships, non-need scholarships, Federal Work-Study. *Required forms:* FAFSA; required for some: state. *Application deadline:* continuous. *Payment plan:* installment. *Waivers:* full or partial for employees or children of employees.
APPLYING Open admission. *Options:* Common Application, early entrance, deferred entrance. *Required:* school transcript, TOEFL for international students. Test scores used for admission. *Application deadline:* rolling.
APPLYING/TRANSFER *Required:* high school transcript, college transcript. *Entrance:* noncompetitive. *Application deadline:* rolling.
CONTACT Mrs. Delores Voliber, Registrar, Shorter College, 604 Locust Street, North Little Rock, AR 72114-4885, 501-374-6305.

SOUTH ARKANSAS COMMUNITY COLLEGE
El Dorado, Arkansas

UG Enrollment: 1,000	Tuition & Fees (Area Res): $840
Application Deadline: rolling	Room & Board: N/Avail

GENERAL State-supported, 2-year, coed. Awards certificates, transfer associate, terminal associate degrees. Founded 1975. *Setting:* 4-acre small-town campus. *Total enrollment:* 1,000. *Faculty:* 81 (51 full-time, 30 part-time).
ENROLLMENT PROFILE 1,000 students from 12 states and territories, 1 other country. 70% women, 55% part-time, 94% state residents, 20% transferred in, 46% 25 or older, 0% Native American, 0% Hispanic, 13% African American, 0% Asian American.
FIRST-YEAR CLASS 231 total; 331 applied, 100% were accepted, 70% of whom enrolled.
ACADEMIC PROGRAM Core, honor code. Calendar: semesters. Academic remediation for entering students, services for LD students, advanced placement, summer session for credit, part-time degree program (daytime, evenings), adult/continuing education programs, internships.
GENERAL DEGREE REQUIREMENTS 60 credits; 1 course each in intermediate algebra, natural science and social science; computer course for business majors.
MAJORS Accounting, automotive technologies, computer information systems, emergency medical technology, liberal arts/general studies, machine and tool technologies, medical laboratory technology, medical records services, radiological technology, secretarial studies/office management, welding technology.
LIBRARY 22,652 books, 122 microform titles, 223 periodicals, 1,240 records, tapes, and CDs.
COMPUTERS ON CAMPUS 75 computers for student use in computer center, library.
COLLEGE LIFE Choral group. *Student services:* personal-psychological counseling. *Campus security:* security guard.
HOUSING College housing not available.
ATHLETICS *Intramural:* badminton, basketball, tennis, volleyball.
CAREER PLANNING *Service:* career counseling.
EXPENSES FOR 1995-96 Area resident tuition: $840 full-time, $35 per semester hour part-time. State resident tuition: $1056 full-time, $44 per semester hour part-time. Nonresident tuition: $2040 full-time, $85 per semester hour part-time.
FINANCIAL AID *College-administered undergrad aid 1995–96:* 84 need-based scholarships (average $300), 93 non-need scholarships (average $600), low-interest long-term loans from external sources (average $2000), Federal Work-Study, 6 part-time jobs. *Acceptable forms:* CSS Financial Aid PROFILE, state, institutional, FAFSA. *Priority deadline:* 7/15. *Payment plan:* installment. *Waivers:* full or partial for senior citizens.
APPLYING Open admission. *Options:* early entrance, deferred entrance. *Required:* ACT ASSET. *Recommended:* SAT I or ACT. Test scores used for counseling/placement. *Application deadline:* rolling.
APPLYING/TRANSFER *Required:* standardized test scores. *Entrance:* noncompetitive. *Application deadline:* rolling.
CONTACT Mrs. Elizabeth Dugal, Admissions Counselor, South Arkansas Community College, El Dorado, AR 71731-7010, 501-862-4926 Ext. 243.

SOUTHERN ARKANSAS UNIVERSITY TECH
Camden, Arkansas

UG Enrollment: 1,197	Tuition & Fees (AR Res): $1350
Application Deadline: rolling	Room Only: $1950

GENERAL State-supported, 2-year, coed. Part of Southern Arkansas University System. Awards certificates, transfer associate, terminal associate degrees. Founded 1968. *Setting:* 96-acre rural campus. *Educational spending 1994–95:* $1812 per undergrad. *Total enrollment:* 1,197. *Faculty:* 114 (41 full-time, 73 part-time). *Notable Alumni:* Don Johnson, actor.
ENROLLMENT PROFILE 1,197 students from 4 states and territories. 51% women, 54% part-time, 99% state residents, 8% transferred in, 0% international, 55% 25 or older, 1% Native American, 1% Hispanic, 21% African American, 1% Asian American.
FIRST-YEAR CLASS 141 total; 231 applied, 100% were accepted, 61% of whom enrolled. 10% from top 10% of their high school class, 20% from top quarter, 70% from top half.
ACADEMIC PROGRAM Core, honor code. Calendar: semesters. Academic remediation for entering students, advanced placement, self-designed majors, summer session for credit, part-time degree program (daytime, evenings), adult/continuing education programs, internships.
GENERAL DEGREE REQUIREMENTS 60 credits; internship (some majors).
MAJORS Aviation technology, business administration/commerce/management, computer graphics, computer programming, electrical and electronics technologies, electromechanical technology, electronics engineering technology, elementary education, graphic arts, hotel and restaurant management, industrial engineering technology, liberal arts/general studies, mechanical engineering technology, nursing, robotics, secretarial studies/office management.
LIBRARY Southern Arkansas University Tech Learning Resource Center with 18,045 books, 122 periodicals, 10 CD-ROMs, 611 records, tapes, and CDs. Acquisition spending 1994–95: $76,232.
COMPUTERS ON CAMPUS 49 computers for student use in computer center, learning center, library. Academic computing expenditure 1994–95: $34,081.
COLLEGE LIFE Choral group. *Most popular organizations:* Phi Beta Lambda, Electronics Club, African-American Club. *Major annual events:* Fall Convocation, Spring Fling, High Tech Week. *Student services:* personal-psychological counseling. *Campus security:* 24-hour emergency response devices, patrols by trained security personnel.
HOUSING 72 college housing spaces available; 60 were occupied 1995–96. No special consideration for freshman housing applicants. Off-campus living permitted. *Option:* coed housing available.
ATHLETICS *Intramural:* archery, basketball, football, table tennis (Ping-Pong), tennis, volleyball.
CAREER PLANNING *Service:* career counseling.
EXPENSES FOR 1996-97 State resident tuition: $1350 full-time, $45 per semester hour part-time. Nonresident tuition: $2025 full-time, $67.50 per semester hour part-time. College room only: $1950.
FINANCIAL AID *College-administered undergrad aid 1995–96:* 75 non-need scholarships (average $840), low-interest long-term loans from external sources (average $2000), Federal Work-Study, 15 part-time jobs. *Required forms:* institutional; accepted: CSS Financial Aid PROFILE, FAFSA. *Priority deadline:* 6/30. *Payment plan:* installment. *Waivers:* full or partial for employees or children of employees.
APPLYING Open admission. *Required:* SAT I or ACT, TOEFL for international students, ACT ASSET. Test scores used for counseling/placement. *Application deadline:* rolling.
APPLYING/TRANSFER *Required:* standardized test scores. *Entrance:* noncompetitive. *Application deadline:* rolling.
CONTACT Associate Dean for Enrollment Management, Southern Arkansas University Tech, Camden, AR 71701, 501-574-4529.

Arkansas

WESTARK COMMUNITY COLLEGE
Fort Smith, Arkansas

UG Enrollment: 5,323	Tuition & Fees (Area Res): $884
Application Deadline: rolling	Room & Board: N/Avail

GENERAL State and locally supported, 2-year, coed. Awards transfer associate, terminal associate degrees. Founded 1928. *Setting:* 75-acre suburban campus. *Total enrollment:* 5,323. *Faculty:* 236 (114 full-time, 12% with terminal degrees, 122 part-time); student-faculty ratio is 24:1.

ENROLLMENT PROFILE 5,323 students from 28 states and territories, 14 other countries. 59% women, 55% part-time, 89% state residents, 11% transferred in, 29% have need-based financial aid, 38% have non-need-based financial aid, 1% international, 43% 25 or older, 1% Native American, 1% Hispanic, 3% African American, 2% Asian American. *Most popular recent majors:* elementary education, nursing, business administration/commerce/management.

FIRST-YEAR CLASS 1,079 total; 1,440 applied, 100% were accepted, 75% of whom enrolled. 3% from top 10% of their high school class, 67% from top quarter, 70% from top half.

ACADEMIC PROGRAM Core, honor code. Calendar: semesters. 328 courses offered in 1995–96. Academic remediation for entering students, English as a second language program offered during academic year and summer, services for LD students, advanced placement, self-designed majors, Freshman Honors College, tutorials, honors program, summer session for credit, part-time degree program (daytime, evenings, summer), adult/continuing education programs, co-op programs.

GENERAL DEGREE REQUIREMENTS 60 credit hours; 1 college algebra course; 8 credit hours of science; computer course for associate of applied science degree students; internship (some majors).

MAJORS Accounting, art/fine arts, automotive technologies, business administration/commerce/management, computer information systems, computer programming, computer science, drafting and design, electrical and electronics technologies, elementary education, emergency medical technology, finance/banking, legal secretarial studies, liberal arts/general studies, machine and tool technologies, medical laboratory technology, nursing, operating room technology, quality control technology, radiological technology, respiratory therapy, secretarial studies/office management, welding technology, word processing.

LIBRARY Boreham Library with 50,295 books, 41,343 microform titles, 595 periodicals, 5 CD-ROMs, 2,645 records, tapes, and CDs. Acquisition spending 1994–95: $707,680.

COMPUTERS ON CAMPUS 200 computers for student use in computer center, computer labs, classrooms, library. Academic computing expenditure 1994–95: $545,501.

COLLEGE LIFE Choral group, student-run newspaper. *Social organizations:* 25 open to all. *Most popular organizations:* Student Activities Council, Phi Beta Lambda, Phi Beta Kappa, Spanish Club, Student Publications. *Major annual events:* Miss Westark Pageant, Season of Entertainment, Student/Staff Picnic. *Student services:* personal-psychological counseling, women's center. *Campus security:* 24-hour emergency response devices and patrols.

HOUSING College housing not available.

ATHLETICS Member NJCAA. *Intercollegiate:* baseball M(s), basketball M(s)/W(s). *Intramural:* basketball, bowling, football, soccer, tennis, volleyball. *Contact:* Mr. Jim Wyatt, Athletic Director, 501-788-7590.

CAREER PLANNING *Placement office:* 1 full-time, 1 part-time staff; $26,000 operating expenditure 1994–95. *Director:* Mrs. Leanna Garrett, Career Counselor, 501-788-7405. *Services:* resume preparation, resume referral, career counseling, careers library, job bank, job interviews.

AFTER GRADUATION 47% of students completing a degree program in 1994–95 went directly on to further study.

EXPENSES FOR 1995-96 Area resident tuition: $864 full-time, $36 per credit hour part-time. State resident tuition: $1080 full-time, $45 per credit hour part-time. Nonresident tuition: $2088 full-time, $87 per credit hour part-time. Part-time mandatory fees: $10 per semester. Full-time mandatory fees: $20.

FINANCIAL AID *College-administered undergrad aid 1995–96:* 175 need-based scholarships (average $1400), 325 non-need scholarships (average $600), short-term loans (average $550), low-interest long-term loans from external sources (average $2000), 54 Federal Work-Study (averaging $1500), part-time jobs. *Required forms for some financial aid applicants:* institutional; accepted: CSS Financial Aid PROFILE, state, FAFSA. *Priority deadline:* 6/1. *Payment plan:* installment. *Waivers:* full or partial for employees or children of employees and senior citizens. *Notification:* 7/1.

APPLYING Open admission except for nursing program. *Options:* early entrance, deferred entrance, midyear entrance. *Required:* TOEFL for international students. *Recommended:* ACT, ACT ASSET. Test scores used for counseling/placement. *Application deadline:* rolling.

APPLYING/TRANSFER *Recommended:* standardized test scores. *Entrance:* noncompetitive. *Application deadline:* rolling. *Contact:* Ms. Peggy Forsberg, Director of Advisement, Admissions, and Records, 501-788-7234.

CONTACT Ms. Penny Pendleton, Director of Recruitment and Placement, Westark Community College, Fort Smith, AR 72913-3649, 501-788-7120. College video available.

CALIFORNIA

ALLAN HANCOCK COLLEGE
Santa Maria, California

UG Enrollment: 7,403 **Tuition & Fees (CA Res): $416**
Application Deadline: rolling **Room & Board: N/Avail**

GENERAL State and locally supported, 2-year, coed. Part of California Community Colleges System. Awards certificates, transfer associate, terminal associate degrees. Founded 1920. ***Setting:*** 10-acre small-town campus. ***Endowment:*** $128,575. ***Research spending 1994–95:*** $53,396. ***Educational spending 1994–95:*** $1860 per undergrad. ***Total enrollment:*** 7,403. ***Faculty:*** 404 (124 full-time, 10% with terminal degrees, 280 part-time); student-faculty ratio is 19:1. ***Notable Alumni:*** Robin Williams, actor; Kelly McGillis, actress.
ENROLLMENT PROFILE 7,403 students from 24 states and territories, 6 other countries. 57% women, 43% men, 71% part-time, 96% state residents, 5% transferred in, 2% international, 51% 25 or older, 1% Native American, 25% Hispanic, 5% African American, 3% Asian American. ***Most popular recent majors:*** liberal arts/general studies, nursing, accounting.
FIRST-YEAR CLASS 532 total. Of the students who applied, 100% were accepted.
ACADEMIC PROGRAM Core, honor code. Calendar: semesters. Academic remediation for entering students, English as a second language program offered during academic year and summer, services for LD students, advanced placement, summer session for credit, part-time degree program (daytime, evenings, weekends, summer), adult/continuing education programs, co-op programs. Study abroad in England, Italy (1% of students participate).
GENERAL DEGREE REQUIREMENT 60 units.
MAJORS Accounting, applied art, architectural technologies, art/fine arts, automotive technologies, biology/biological sciences, business administration/commerce/management, chemistry, civil engineering technology, computer information systems, computer science, computer technologies, cosmetology, dance, dental services, early childhood education, electronics engineering technology, engineering (general), engineering technology, English, environmental engineering technology, film studies, fire science, graphic arts, home economics, human services, industrial and heavy equipment maintenance, interior design, international studies, law enforcement/police sciences, legal secretarial studies, liberal arts/general studies, machine and tool technologies, medical assistant technologies, music, nursing, photography, physics, practical nursing, real estate, recreation and leisure services, secretarial studies/office management, social science, Spanish, welding technology.
LIBRARY Learning Resources Center with 47,000 books, 120 microform titles, 421 periodicals, 3 on-line bibliographic services, 9 CD-ROMs, 8,000 records, tapes, and CDs. Acquisition spending 1994–95: $58,990.
COMPUTERS ON CAMPUS 130 computers for student use in computer center, learning resource center, business, English, math, journalism labs, library provide access to Internet. Staffed computer lab on campus provides training in use of computers, software. Academic computing expenditure 1994–95: $504,711.
COLLEGE LIFE Drama-theater group, choral group, student-run newspaper. 5% vote in student government elections. ***Social organizations:*** 10 open to all. ***Most popular organizations:*** MECHA, AHC Student Club, Club Med (medical), Hancock Christian Fellowship, Vocational Industrial Clubs of America. ***Major annual events:*** Chili Cook Off, Blood Drive, Spring Fest. ***Student services:*** legal services, health clinic, personal-psychological counseling. ***Campus security:*** student patrols, late-night transport-escort service.
HOUSING College housing not available.
ATHLETICS ***Intercollegiate:*** baseball M, basketball M/W, cross-country running M/W, football M, golf M, soccer M, softball W, tennis M/W, track and field M/W, volleyball W. ***Contact:*** Mr. John Osborne, Director of Athletics, 805-922-6966 Ext. 3227.
CAREER PLANNING ***Placement office:*** 1 full-time staff; $39,368 operating expenditure 1994–95. ***Director:*** Mr. Jim West, Dean of Matriculation and Counseling Services, 805-922-6966 Ext. 3459. ***Services:*** resume preparation, career counseling, careers library.
ESTIMATED EXPENSES FOR 1996–97 State resident tuition: $0 full-time. Nonresident tuition: $3420 full-time, $114 per unit part-time. Part-time mandatory fees: $13 per unit. Full-time mandatory fees: $416.
FINANCIAL AID ***College-administered undergrad aid 1995–96:*** 164 need-based scholarships (averaging $500), 20 non-need scholarships (averaging $1000), low-interest long-term loans from external sources (averaging $1200), 240 Federal Work-Study (averaging $1000), 100 part-time jobs. ***Required forms:*** institutional, FAFSA. ***Priority deadline:*** 7/1. ***Payment plans:*** installment, deferred payment.
APPLYING Open admission except for nursing, drama, fire technology programs. ***Options:*** early entrance, midyear entrance. ***Required:*** TOEFL for international students. ***Required for some:*** Assessment and Placement Services for Community Colleges. Test scores used for counseling/placement. ***Application deadline:*** rolling. ***Notification:*** continuous.
APPLYING/TRANSFER ***Entrance:*** noncompetitive. ***Application deadline:*** rolling. ***Notification:*** continuous.
CONTACT Ms. Norma Razo, Registrar, Allan Hancock College, Santa Maria, CA 93454-6399, 805-922-6966 Ext. 3272. ***Fax:*** 805-928-7905.

AMERICAN ACADEMY OF DRAMATIC ARTS/WEST
Pasadena, California

UG Enrollment: 208 **Tuition & Fees: $9200**
Application Deadline: rolling **Room & Board: N/Avail**

GENERAL Independent, 2-year, specialized, coed. Awards transfer associate, terminal associate degrees. Founded 1974. ***Setting:*** 4-acre suburban campus with easy access to Los Angeles. ***Educational spending 1994–95:*** $2418 per undergrad. ***Total enrollment:*** 208. ***Faculty:*** 47 (all part-time); student-faculty ratio is 9:1. ***Notable Alumni:*** Robert Redford, Danny DeVito, Anne Bancroft, Gena Rowlands, Jason Robards.
ENROLLMENT PROFILE 208 students from 25 states and territories, 9 other countries. 59% women, 0% part-time, 16% state residents, 71% transferred in, 39% have need-based financial aid, 15% international, 21% 25 or older, 0% Native American, 7% Hispanic, 7% African American, 4% Asian American. ***Areas of study chosen:*** 100% performing arts.
FIRST-YEAR CLASS 60 total; 396 applied, 63% were accepted, 24% of whom enrolled.
ACADEMIC PROGRAM Core, professional actor training curriculum, honor code. Calendar: year-round. 21 courses offered in 1995–96; average class size 16 in required courses.
GENERAL DEGREE REQUIREMENT 70 units.
MAJOR Theater arts/drama.
LIBRARY Bryn Morgan Library with 7,700 books, 24 periodicals, 1,000 records, tapes, and CDs. Acquisition spending 1994–95: $8752.
COLLEGE LIFE 40% vote in student government elections. ***Campus security:*** 24-hour emergency response devices, 8-hour patrols by trained security personnel.
HOUSING College housing not available.
CAREER PLANNING ***Placement office:*** $5040 operating expenditure 1994–95. ***Director:*** Ms. Jackie Margey, Careers Consultant, 818-798-0777. ***Service:*** career counseling.
EXPENSES FOR 1996–97 ***Application fee:*** $35. Tuition: $9000 full-time. Full-time mandatory fees: $200.
FINANCIAL AID ***College-administered undergrad aid 1995–96:*** 26 need-based scholarships (averaging $700), 17 non-need scholarships (averaging $718), short-term loans (averaging $100), low-interest long-term loans from external sources, 4 Federal Work-Study (averaging $2500), 5 part-time jobs. ***Required forms:*** institutional, FAFSA, financial aid transcript; required for some: state; accepted: CSS Financial Aid PROFILE. ***Priority deadline:*** 8/1. ***Payment plan:*** installment.
APPLYING ***Options:*** deferred entrance, midyear entrance. ***Required:*** essay, school transcript, minimum 2.0 GPA, 2 recommendations, interview, audition, TOEFL for international students. ***Recommended:*** minimum 3.0 GPA, SAT I or ACT. Test scores used for counseling/placement. ***Application deadline:*** rolling. ***Notification:*** continuous.
APPLYING/TRANSFER ***Recommended:*** minimum 2.0 college GPA. ***Required for some:*** college transcript. ***Entrance:*** moderately difficult. ***Application deadline:*** rolling. ***Notification:*** continuous. ***Contact:*** Mr. James Wickline, Director of Admissions, 818-798-0777.
CONTACT Mr. James Wickline, Director of Admissions, American Academy of Dramatic Arts/West, Pasadena, CA 91107-2697, 818-798-0777.

❖ *See page 688 for a narrative description.* ❖

AMERICAN RIVER COLLEGE
Sacramento, California

UG Enrollment: 19,695 **Tuition & Fees (CA Res): $390**
Application Deadline: rolling **Room & Board: N/Avail**

GENERAL District-supported, 2-year, coed. Part of Los Rios Community College District System. Awards transfer associate, terminal associate degrees. Founded 1955. ***Setting:*** 153-acre suburban campus. ***Total enrollment:*** 19,695. ***Faculty:*** 700 (350 full-time, 350 part-time).
ENROLLMENT PROFILE 19,695 students: 56% women, 77% part-time, 99% state residents, 22% transferred in, 1% international, 50% 25 or older, 2% Native American, 8% Hispanic, 7% African American, 6% Asian American.
FIRST-YEAR CLASS 3,391 total. Of the students who applied, 100% were accepted.
ACADEMIC PROGRAM Core, honor code. Calendar: semesters. Academic remediation for entering students, English as a second language program offered during academic year and summer, services for LD students, advanced placement, summer session for credit, part-time degree program (daytime, evenings), adult/continuing education programs, co-op programs. Off-campus study.
GENERAL DEGREE REQUIREMENTS 60 units; math proficiency; internship (some majors).
MAJORS Accounting, advertising, art/fine arts, automotive technologies, business administration/commerce/management, carpentry, child care/child and family studies, computer programming, computer technologies, construction technologies, culinary arts, data processing, deaf interpreter training, drafting and design, early childhood education, electrical and electronics technologies, (pre)engineering sequence, engineering technology, fashion design and technology, fashion merchandising, finance/banking, fire science, food marketing, food services management, forest technology, gerontology, home economics education, horticulture, hotel and restaurant management, human services, industrial arts, interior design, journalism, landscape architecture/design, legal secretarial studies, liberal arts/general studies, marketing/retailing/merchandising, mathematics, medical secretarial studies, music, music business, natural resource management, nursing, paralegal studies, physical sciences, real estate, recreation and leisure services, respiratory therapy, retail management, science, secretarial studies/office management, social science, theater arts/drama, welding technology.
LIBRARY 78,400 books, 450 microform titles, 75 periodicals, 6,350 records, tapes, and CDs.
COMPUTERS ON CAMPUS Computers for student use in resource centers, library.
COLLEGE LIFE Drama-theater group, student-run newspaper. ***Student services:*** health clinic, personal-psychological counseling, women's center. ***Campus security:*** 24-hour emergency response devices and patrols, student patrols, late-night transport-escort service.
HOUSING College housing not available.
ATHLETICS ***Intercollegiate:*** basketball M/W, cross-country running M/W, football M, golf M/W, soccer M/W, swimming and diving M/W, tennis M/W, track and field M/W, volleyball M/W. ***Intramural:*** basketball. ***Contact:*** Dr. Bruce Werner, Dean of Physical Education, Athletics, and Recreation, 916-484-8201.
CAREER PLANNING ***Service:*** career counseling.
EXPENSES FOR 1995–96 State resident tuition: $0 full-time. Nonresident tuition: $4140 full-time, $138 per unit part-time. Part-time mandatory fees: $13 per unit. Full-time mandatory fees: $390.
FINANCIAL AID ***College-administered undergrad aid 1995–96:*** need-based scholarships, 63 non-need scholarships (averaging $250), low-interest long-term loans from external sources (averaging $2250), Federal Work-Study, 350 part-time jobs. ***Required forms:*** CSS Financial Aid PROFILE, FAFSA; accepted: state. ***Priority deadline:*** 8/1.
APPLYING Open admission except for nursing, respiratory therapy programs. ***Options:*** Common Application, early entrance, deferred entrance. ***Required:*** TOEFL for international students. ***Recommended:*** SAT I or ACT. ***Required for some:*** nursing exam. Test scores used for counseling/placement. ***Application deadline:*** rolling.
APPLYING/TRANSFER ***Entrance:*** noncompetitive. ***Application deadline:*** rolling.
CONTACT Ms. Jimmy Mraule, Dean of Admissions and Administrative Services, American River College, 4700 College Oak Drive, Sacramento, CA 95841-4286, 916-484-8171.

ANTELOPE VALLEY COLLEGE
Lancaster, California

UG Enrollment: 9,027 | **Tuition & Fees (CA Res): $390**
Application Deadline: rolling | **Room & Board: N/Avail**

GENERAL State and locally supported, 2-year, coed. Part of California Community Colleges System. Awards transfer associate, terminal associate degrees. Founded 1929. ***Setting:*** 160-acre suburban campus with easy access to Los Angeles. ***Total enrollment:*** 9,027. ***Faculty:*** 400 (115 full-time, 285 part-time).
ENROLLMENT PROFILE 9,027 students: 60% women, 75% part-time, 98% state residents, 12% transferred in, 1% international, 53% 25 or older, 2% Native American, 14% Hispanic, 8% African American, 7% Asian American.
FIRST-YEAR CLASS Of the students who applied, 100% were accepted, 100% of whom enrolled.
ACADEMIC PROGRAM Core. Calendar: semesters. Academic remediation for entering students, English as a second language program offered during academic year and summer, services for LD students, advanced placement, honors program, summer session for credit, part-time degree program (daytime, evenings, summer), adult/continuing education programs, co-op programs. Study abroad in France, England, Mexico. ROTC: Air Force (c).
GENERAL DEGREE REQUIREMENTS 60 units; 1 intermediate algebra course.
MAJORS Agricultural sciences, animal sciences, art/fine arts, automotive technologies, biology/biological sciences, business administration/commerce/management, chemistry, child psychology/child development, civil engineering technology, computer programming, computer science, computer technologies, construction technologies, criminal justice, data processing, early childhood education, economics, electrical and electronics technologies, emergency medical technology, engineering (general), (pre)engineering sequence, English, fire science, heating/refrigeration/air conditioning, history, home economics, humanities, landscape architecture/design, law enforcement/police sciences, liberal arts/general studies, mathematics, medical assistant technologies, medical technology, modern languages, music, natural resource management, nursing, parks management, photography, physical education, political science/government, practical nursing, psychology, real estate, science, secretarial studies/office management, social science, sociology, teacher aide studies, theater arts/drama, welding technology.
LIBRARY Antelope Valley College Library with 43,000 books, 6,174 microform titles, 175 periodicals, 5,967 records, tapes, and CDs.
COMPUTERS ON CAMPUS Computers for student use in computer center, 5 labs.
COLLEGE LIFE Drama-theater group, student-run newspaper. ***Student services:*** health clinic, personal-psychological counseling.
HOUSING College housing not available.
ATHLETICS ***Intercollegiate:*** baseball M, basketball M/W, cross-country running M/W, football M, golf M/W, softball W, tennis M/W, track and field M/W, volleyball W. ***Intramural:*** bowling, racquetball, swimming and diving, table tennis (Ping-Pong), volleyball, weight lifting. ***Contact:*** Mr. Brent Carder, Dean of Physical Education, 805-943-3241 Ext. 205.
CAREER PLANNING ***Placement office:*** 2 full-time staff. ***Director:*** Ms. Linda Noteboom, Career Center Coordinator, 805-943-3241 Ext. 237. ***Service:*** career counseling.
EXPENSES FOR 1996–97 State resident tuition: $0 full-time. Nonresident tuition: $3510 full-time, $117 per unit part-time. Part-time mandatory fees: $13 per unit. Full-time mandatory fees: $390.
FINANCIAL AID ***College-administered undergrad aid 1995–96:*** 316 need-based scholarships (average $1736), 20 non-need scholarships (average $375), short-term loans (average $50), low-interest long-term loans from external sources (average $2000), Federal Work-Study, 55 part-time jobs. ***Required forms:*** CSS Financial Aid PROFILE, state, institutional, FAFSA. ***Priority deadline:*** 8/1.
APPLYING Open admission. ***Option:*** early entrance. ***Required:*** school transcript, TOEFL for international students. Test scores used for counseling/placement. ***Application deadline:*** rolling. ***Notification:*** continuous.
APPLYING/TRANSFER ***Required:*** high school transcript, college transcript, minimum 2.0 college GPA. ***Application deadline:*** rolling. ***Notification:*** continuous.
CONTACT Ms. Patricia Hsieh, Dean of Admissions, Antelope Valley College, 3041 West Avenue K, Lancaster, CA 93536-5426, 805-943-3241 Ext. 430.

BAKERSFIELD COLLEGE
Bakersfield, California

UG Enrollment: 12,000 | **Tuition & Fees (CA Res): $405**
Application Deadline: rolling | **Room & Board: N/R**

GENERAL State and locally supported, 2-year, coed. Part of California Community Colleges System. Awards transfer associate, terminal associate degrees. Founded 1913. ***Setting:*** 175-acre urban campus. ***Total enrollment:*** 12,000. ***Faculty:*** 496 (237 full-time, 87% with terminal degrees, 259 part-time).
ENROLLMENT PROFILE 12,000 students: 56% women, 74% part-time, 99% state residents. ***Most popular recent major:*** liberal arts/general studies.
FIRST-YEAR CLASS 7,000 total. Of the students who applied, 100% were accepted, 60% of whom enrolled.
ACADEMIC PROGRAM Core, honor code. Calendar: semesters. Academic remediation for entering students, English as a second language program offered during academic year, services for LD students, summer session for credit, part-time degree program (daytime, evenings, summer), adult/continuing education programs, co-op programs.
GENERAL DEGREE REQUIREMENTS 60 credits; math/science requirements vary according to program.
MAJORS Accounting, agricultural business, animal sciences, anthropology, art education, automotive technologies, biology/biological sciences, broadcasting, business administration/commerce/management, carpentry, chemistry, child care/child and family studies, computer information systems, computer science, corrections, cosmetology, criminal justice, data processing, dental services, dietetics, economics, electrical and electronics technologies, emergency medical technology, engineering (general), English, family and consumer studies, finance/banking, fire science, forestry, geography, geology, German, history, horticulture, hotel and restaurant management, industrial arts, industrial engineering technology, interior design, journalism, law enforcement/police sciences, legal secretarial studies, liberal arts/general studies, machine and tool technologies, mathematics, music, nursing, ornamental horticulture, petroleum technology, philosophy, photography, physics, plumbing, political science/government, psychology, radiological technology, real estate, secretarial studies/office management, sociology, Spanish, speech/rhetoric/public address/debate, surveying technology, theater arts/drama, welding technology, wood sciences.
LIBRARY Grace Van Dyke Bird Library with 64,862 books, 309 microform titles, 298 periodicals, 4 CD-ROMs.
COMPUTERS ON CAMPUS Computers for student use in computer center, library, student center.
COLLEGE LIFE Drama-theater group, choral group, marching band, student-run newspaper, radio station. ***Student services:*** health clinic, women's center. ***Campus security:*** 24-hour patrols, late-night transport-escort service.
HOUSING 122 college housing spaces available; all were occupied 1995–96. No special consideration for freshman housing applicants. Off-campus living permitted. ***Option:*** coed housing available.
ATHLETICS ***Intercollegiate:*** baseball M, basketball M/W, cross-country running M/W, football M, golf M, soccer M, softball W, swimming and diving M/W, tennis M/W, track and field M/W, volleyball W, wrestling M.
CAREER PLANNING ***Service:*** career counseling.
EXPENSES FOR 1996–97 State resident tuition: $0 full-time. Nonresident tuition: $3120 full-time, $104 per unit part-time. Part-time mandatory fees per semester hour range from $28 to $158. Full-time mandatory fees: $405.
FINANCIAL AID ***College-administered undergrad aid 1995–96:*** 200 need-based scholarships (average $250), 115 non-need scholarships (average $400), short-term loans (average $100), low-interest long-term loans from external sources (average $2000), Federal Work-Study, 328 part-time jobs. ***Required forms:*** institutional, FAFSA; required for some: CSS Financial Aid PROFILE, state. ***Priority deadline:*** 5/1.
APPLYING Open admission except for registered nursing, radiological technology programs. ***Required:*** TOEFL for international students. Test scores used for counseling/placement. ***Application deadline:*** rolling. Preference given to district residents for nursing, radiological technology programs.
CONTACT Ms. Nancy Haines, Registrar, Bakersfield College, 1801 Panorama Drive, Bakersfield, CA 93305-1299, 805-395-4301. College video available.

BARSTOW COLLEGE
Barstow, California

UG Enrollment: 2,632 | **Tuition & Fees (CA Res): $390**
Application Deadline: rolling | **Room & Board: N/Avail**

GENERAL State and locally supported, 2-year, coed. Part of California Community Colleges System. Awards transfer associate, terminal associate degrees. Founded 1959. ***Setting:*** 50-acre small-town campus. ***Total enrollment:*** 2,632. ***Faculty:*** 128 (26 full-time, 1% with terminal degrees, 102 part-time).
ENROLLMENT PROFILE 2,632 students from 43 states and territories, 8 other countries. 50% women, 50% men, 76% part-time, 95% state residents, 13% transferred in, 1% international, 66% 25 or older, 2% Native American, 18% Hispanic, 11% African American, 3% Asian American. ***Most popular recent majors:*** humanities, social science.
FIRST-YEAR CLASS 433 total; 881 applied, 100% were accepted, 33% of whom enrolled.
ACADEMIC PROGRAM Core, honor code. Calendar: semesters. Academic remediation for entering students, English as a second language program offered during academic year and summer, services for LD students, self-designed majors, summer session for credit, part-time degree program (daytime, evenings, weekends, summer), external degree programs, adult/continuing education programs, co-op programs.
GENERAL DEGREE REQUIREMENTS 60 units; math/science requirements vary according to program; computer course for business-related majors.
MAJORS Accounting, art/fine arts, automotive technologies, business administration/commerce/management, business machine technologies, child care/child and family studies, computer science, creative writing, drafting and design, early childhood education, economics, education, electrical and electronics technologies, emergency medical technology, English, ethnic studies, family services, fire science, history, humanities, law enforcement/police sciences, liberal arts/general studies, marketing/retailing/merchandising, mathematics, physical education, real estate, science, secretarial studies/office management, social science, Spanish, teacher aide studies, theater arts/drama, vocational education.
LIBRARY 38,000 books, 110 periodicals, 3,000 records, tapes, and CDs.
COMPUTERS ON CAMPUS 20 computers for student use in classrooms.
COLLEGE LIFE Drama-theater group, student-run newspaper. ***Student services:*** personal-psychological counseling. ***Campus security:*** evening security personnel.
HOUSING College housing not available.
ATHLETICS ***Intercollegiate:*** baseball M, basketball M, volleyball W. ***Intramural:*** basketball, bowling.
CAREER PLANNING ***Service:*** career counseling.
EXPENSES FOR 1995–96 State resident tuition: $0 full-time. Nonresident tuition: $3420 full-time, $114 per unit part-time. Part-time mandatory fees: $13 per unit. Full-time mandatory fees: $390.
FINANCIAL AID ***College-administered undergrad aid 1995–96:*** need-based scholarships, short-term loans (average $50), low-interest long-term loans from external sources (average $1000), 30 Federal Work-Study (averaging $2000), 25 part-time jobs. ***Required forms:*** CSS Financial Aid PROFILE, state, institutional, FAFSA. ***Priority deadline:*** 3/15. ***Payment plans:*** installment, deferred payment.
APPLYING Open admission except for allied health programs. ***Options:*** early entrance, deferred entrance. ***Required:*** TOEFL for international students. Test scores used for counseling/placement. ***Application deadline:*** rolling.
APPLYING/TRANSFER ***Entrance:*** noncompetitive. ***Application deadline:*** rolling.
CONTACT Mr. Ray Perea, Dean of Student Services, Barstow College, Barstow, CA 92311-6699, 619-252-2411 Ext. 211. ***Fax:*** 619-252-1875. College video available.

BROOKS COLLEGE
Long Beach, California

UG Enrollment: 720 | **Tuition & Fees: $8310**
Application Deadline: rolling | **Room & Board: $4980**

GENERAL Proprietary, 2-year, coed. Awards terminal associate degrees. Founded 1971. ***Setting:*** 7-acre suburban campus with easy access to Los Angeles. ***Total enrollment:***

Brooks College (continued)
720. ***Faculty:*** 57 (34 full-time, 23 part-time). ***Notable Alumni:*** Julianne Phillips, actress; Byron Lahrs, designer; Kunal Shah, designer for Nicole of California; Candy Barnes Clinton, vice president of merchandising.
ENROLLMENT PROFILE 720 students from 50 states and territories, 17 other countries. 93% women, 0% part-time, 31% state residents, 79% live on campus, 6% transferred in, 5% international, 3% 25 or older, 2% Native American, 10% Hispanic, 8% African American, 3% Asian American. ***Most popular recent majors:*** fashion merchandising, interior design, fashion design and technology.
FIRST-YEAR CLASS 650 total; 1,500 applied, 47% were accepted, 93% of whom enrolled. 10% from top 10% of their high school class, 30% from top quarter, 80% from top half.
ACADEMIC PROGRAM Business and technical curriculum, honor code. Calendar: quarters. Academic remediation for entering students, services for LD students, summer session for credit, co-op programs and internships.
GENERAL DEGREE REQUIREMENTS 88 credit hours; computer course; internship.
MAJORS Fashion design and technology, fashion merchandising, interior design, textiles and clothing.
LIBRARY 15,000 books, 80 periodicals.
COMPUTERS ON CAMPUS 50 computers for student use in computer center, computer labs, library. Staffed computer lab on campus provides training in use of computers, software.
COLLEGE LIFE Student-run newspaper. ***Student services:*** personal-psychological counseling. ***Campus security:*** 24-hour emergency response devices and patrols, controlled dormitory access.
HOUSING 650 college housing spaces available. No special consideration for freshman housing applicants. Off-campus living permitted. ***Option:*** single-sex (3 buildings) housing available. Resident assistants live in dorms.
CAREER PLANNING ***Placement office:*** 2 full-time, 1 part-time staff. ***Director:*** Ms. Cheryl Williams, Director of Career Development, 800-421-3775. ***Services:*** job fairs, resume preparation, resume referral, career counseling, careers library, job bank, job interviews. Students must register freshman year. 80 organizations recruited on campus 1994–95.
AFTER GRADUATION 94% of class of 1994 had job offers within 6 months.
EXPENSES FOR 1996–97 Comprehensive fee of $13,290 includes full-time tuition ($8310) and college room and board ($4980).
FINANCIAL AID ***College-administered undergrad aid 1995–96:*** need-based scholarships, 10 non-need scholarships (averaging $750), low-interest long-term loans from external sources (averaging $2625), part-time jobs. ***Required forms:*** CSS Financial Aid PROFILE, institutional, FAFSA. ***Application deadline:*** continuous to 6/1. ***Payment plan:*** installment.
APPLYING ***Option:*** deferred entrance. ***Required:*** essay, school transcript, minimum 2.0 GPA, recommendations, interview, TOEFL for international students. Test scores used for admission. ***Application deadline:*** rolling. ***Notification:*** continuous.
APPLYING/TRANSFER ***Required:*** essay, high school transcript, recommendations, interview, college transcript, minimum 2.0 high school GPA. ***Entrance:*** moderately difficult. ***Application deadline:*** rolling. ***Notification:*** continuous.
CONTACT Ms. Chelena Adkins, Director of Admissions, Brooks College, Long Beach, CA 90804-3291, 310-498-2441 or toll-free 800-421-3775.

BUTTE COLLEGE
Oroville, California

UG Enrollment: 11,900	**Tuition & Fees (CA Res): $460**
Application Deadline: rolling	**Room & Board: N/Avail**

GENERAL District-supported, 2-year, coed. Part of California Community Colleges System. Awards certificates, transfer associate, terminal associate degrees. Founded 1966. ***Setting:*** 900-acre rural campus. ***Total enrollment:*** 11,900. ***Faculty:*** 561 (123 full-time, 438 part-time).
ENROLLMENT PROFILE 11,900 students from 19 states and territories, 25 other countries. 55% women, 60% part-time, 86% state residents, 15% transferred in, 1% international, 53% 25 or older, 3% Native American, 5% Hispanic, 1% African American, 3% Asian American.
FIRST-YEAR CLASS 4,500 total. Of the students who applied, 100% were accepted. 5% from top 10% of their high school class, 60% from top half.
ACADEMIC PROGRAM Core. Calendar: semesters. Academic remediation for entering students, English as a second language program offered during academic year and summer, services for LD students, advanced placement, honors program, summer session for credit, part-time degree program (daytime, evenings, summer), adult/continuing education programs, internships. Off-campus study at members of the Northeastern California Higher Education Council. Study abroad in England.
GENERAL DEGREE REQUIREMENTS 60 semester units; 1 course each in math and lab science.
MAJORS Accounting, agricultural business, agricultural economics, agricultural sciences, agronomy/soil and crop sciences, animal sciences, applied art, art/fine arts, automotive technologies, biology/biological sciences, business education, civil engineering technology, commercial art, construction technologies, cosmetology, court reporting, criminal justice, data processing, drafting and design, early childhood education, electrical and electronics technologies, family and consumer studies, fashion design and technology, fashion merchandising, finance/banking, fire science, health science, home economics, horticulture, landscape architecture/design, law enforcement/police sciences, legal secretarial studies, liberal arts/general studies, marketing/retailing/merchandising, mathematics, medical secretarial studies, medical technology, music, natural resource management, nursing, ornamental horticulture, parks management, photography, physical education, physical sciences, political science/government, practical nursing, psychology, real estate, respiratory therapy, secretarial studies/office management, social science, telecommunications, tourism and travel, welding technology.
LIBRARY 50,000 books, 220 microform titles, 300 periodicals, 5,050 records, tapes, and CDs.
COMPUTERS ON CAMPUS 65 computers for student use in computer labs, library.
COLLEGE LIFE ***Student services:*** health clinic, personal-psychological counseling.
HOUSING College housing not available.
ATHLETICS ***Intercollegiate:*** basketball M/W, cross-country running M/W, football M, golf M, tennis M/W, track and field M/W, volleyball W, wrestling M. ***Intramural:*** equestrian sports.
CAREER PLANNING ***Service:*** career counseling.
EXPENSES FOR 1995–96 State resident tuition: $0 full-time. Nonresident tuition: $3750 full-time, $125 per unit part-time. Part-time mandatory fees per semester range from $72.50 to $220. Full-time mandatory fees: $460.
FINANCIAL AID ***College-administered undergrad aid 1995–96:*** need-based scholarships (average $50), short-term loans (average $90), Federal Work-Study, part-time jobs. ***Required forms:*** CSS Financial Aid PROFILE, state, institutional, FAFSA. ***Priority deadline:*** 5/15.
APPLYING Open admission except for allied health, criminal justice, fire science programs. ***Option:*** early entrance. ***Required:*** TOEFL for international students. ***Required for some:*** school transcript. Test scores used for counseling/placement. ***Application deadline:*** rolling.
APPLYING/TRANSFER ***Required:*** college transcript. ***Application deadline:*** rolling.
CONTACT Ms. Carly Epting, Registrar, Butte College, Oroville, CA 95965-8399, 916-895-2511.

CABRILLO COLLEGE
Aptos, California

UG Enrollment: 11,805	**Tuition & Fees (CA Res): $498**
Application Deadline: rolling	**Room & Board: N/Avail**

GENERAL District-supported, 2-year, coed. Part of California Community Colleges System. Awards certificates, transfer associate, terminal associate degrees. Founded 1959. ***Setting:*** 120-acre small-town campus with easy access to San Jose. ***Total enrollment:*** 11,805. ***Faculty:*** 552 (207 full-time, 345 part-time).
ENROLLMENT PROFILE 11,805 students: 58% women, 72% part-time, 98% state residents, 16% transferred in, 1% international, 50% 25 or older, 1% Native American, 14% Hispanic, 1% African American, 3% Asian American.
FIRST-YEAR CLASS 2,040 total. Of the students who applied, 100% were accepted, 70% of whom enrolled.
ACADEMIC PROGRAM Core. Calendar: semesters. Academic remediation for entering students, English as a second language program offered during academic year, services for LD students, summer session for credit, part-time degree program (daytime, evenings, summer), adult/continuing education programs.
GENERAL DEGREE REQUIREMENTS 60 semester units; math competence; 1 science course; computer course for physical science majors.
MAJORS Accounting, business administration/commerce/management, business machine technologies, cartography, ceramic art and design, child care/child and family studies, computer programming, computer science, construction management, data processing, dental services, drafting and design, early childhood education, electrical and electronics technologies, electrical engineering technology, energy management technologies, (pre)engineering sequence, fire science, food sciences, food services management, food services technology, health science, horticulture, industrial design, liberal arts/general studies, medical records services, medical secretarial studies, natural sciences, nursing, physical education, real estate, recreation and leisure services, retail management, science, solar technologies, Spanish, welding technology, wildlife management, women's studies.
LIBRARY 60,000 books, 300 periodicals, 1,000 records, tapes, and CDs.
COMPUTERS ON CAMPUS Computers for student use in labs.
COLLEGE LIFE Drama-theater group, student-run newspaper. ***Student services:*** health clinic, personal-psychological counseling, women's center.
HOUSING College housing not available.
ATHLETICS ***Intercollegiate:*** basketball M/W, cross-country running M/W, fencing M/W, football M, golf M/W, swimming and diving M/W, tennis M/W, track and field M/W, wrestling M. ***Intramural:*** basketball, cross-country running, fencing, field hockey, football, golf, gymnastics, sailing, skiing (cross-country), skiing (downhill), soccer, swimming and diving, tennis, track and field, volleyball, wrestling.
CAREER PLANNING ***Service:*** career counseling.
EXPENSES FOR 1996–97 State resident tuition: $0 full-time. Nonresident tuition: $3270 full-time, $109 per unit part-time. Part-time mandatory fees per semester range from $28 to $157. Full-time mandatory fees: $498.
FINANCIAL AID ***College-administered undergrad aid 1995–96:*** 300 need-based scholarships (average $1000), non-need scholarships (average $500), short-term loans (average $50), low-interest long-term loans from college funds (average $1000), loans from external sources (average $2500), Federal Work-Study, 500 part-time jobs. ***Required forms:*** state, FAFSA. ***Priority deadline:*** 4/15.
APPLYING Open admission. ***Option:*** early entrance. ***Required for some:*** school transcript, TOEFL for international students. Test scores used for admission. ***Application deadline:*** rolling.
APPLYING/TRANSFER ***Required:*** college transcript. ***Required for some:*** high school transcript. ***Entrance:*** noncompetitive. ***Application deadline:*** rolling.
CONTACT Ms. Gloria Garing, Registrar, Cabrillo College, Aptos, CA 95003-3194, 408-479-6201.

CAÑADA COLLEGE
Redwood City, California

UG Enrollment: 5,261	**Tuition & Fees (CA Res): $412**
Application Deadline: rolling	**Room & Board: N/Avail**

GENERAL District-supported, 2-year, coed. Part of San Mateo County Community College District System. Awards transfer associate, terminal associate degrees. Founded 1968. ***Setting:*** 131-acre suburban campus with easy access to San Francisco and San Jose. ***Total enrollment:*** 5,261. ***Faculty:*** 263 (109 full-time, 154 part-time). ***Notable Alumni:*** Anna Eshao, congresswoman.
ENROLLMENT PROFILE 5,261 students: 64% women, 36% men, 75% part-time, 97% state residents, 23% transferred in, 7% have need-based financial aid, 0% have non-need-based financial aid, 2% international, 61% 25 or older, 1% Native American, 22% Hispanic, 5% African American, 7% Asian American.

FIRST-YEAR CLASS 974 total. Of the students who applied, 100% were accepted, 100% of whom enrolled.
ACADEMIC PROGRAM Core, honor code. Calendar: semesters. Academic remediation for entering students, English as a second language program offered during academic year and summer, services for LD students, advanced placement, summer session for credit, part-time degree program (daytime, evenings, weekends, summer), adult/continuing education programs, co-op programs. Study abroad in England, France, Italy, Costa Rica.
GENERAL DEGREE REQUIREMENTS 60 credits; computer course.
MAJORS Accounting, anatomy, anthropology, architectural technologies, art education, art/fine arts, art history, biology/biological sciences, business administration/commerce/management, business machine technologies, chemistry, computer information systems, computer programming, computer science, computer technologies, dance, data processing, early childhood education, economics, education, electrical and electronics technologies, engineering (general), English, environmental sciences, fashion design and technology, French, geography, geology, German, health education, health science, history, home economics, humanities, human services, industrial arts, interior design, journalism, liberal arts/general studies, mathematics, music, music history, natural sciences, painting/drawing, paralegal studies, philosophy, physical education, physical fitness/exercise science, physical therapy, political science/government, psychology, public administration, radiological technology, retail management, science, secretarial studies/office management, social science, sociology, Spanish, speech/rhetoric/public address/debate, theater arts/drama, tourism and travel.
LIBRARY 45,902 books, 202 microform titles, 305 periodicals, 2 CD-ROMs, 296 records, tapes, and CDs.
COMPUTERS ON CAMPUS Computer purchase plan available. 55 computers for student use in computer center, labs, classrooms. Staffed computer lab on campus provides training in use of computers, software.
COLLEGE LIFE Drama-theater group, choral group. 10% vote in student government elections. *Social organizations:* 15 open to all. *Most popular organizations:* Latin-American Club, Student Government, Environmental Club, Athletics, Interior Design Club. *Major annual event:* Spring Faire. *Student services:* health clinic, personal-psychological counseling. *Campus security:* 12-hour patrols by trained security personnel.
HOUSING College housing not available.
ATHLETICS *Intercollegiate:* baseball M, basketball M, golf M, soccer M/W, tennis M. *Intramural:* basketball, soccer, tennis, volleyball. *Contact:* Mr. Bruce Edmond, Athletic Director, 415-306-3341.
CAREER PLANNING *Placement office:* 2 full-time, 1 part-time staff. *Director:* Ms. Olivia Martinez, Vice President of Student Services, 415-306-3234. *Services:* job fairs, resume preparation, career counseling, careers library, job bank.
EXPENSES FOR 1996-97 State resident tuition: $0 full-time. Nonresident tuition: $3600 full-time, $120 per unit part-time. Part-time mandatory fees per semester range from $24 to $154. Full-time mandatory fees: $412.
FINANCIAL AID *College-administered undergrad aid 1995-96:* 25 need-based scholarships (average $300), short-term loans (average $50), low-interest long-term loans, 40 Federal Work-Study (averaging $3000), part-time jobs. *Required forms:* CSS Financial Aid PROFILE, institutional, FAFSA. *Priority deadline:* 3/2.
APPLYING Open admission except for radiological technology programs. *Option:* early entrance. *Required:* TOEFL for international students. Test scores used for counseling/placement. *Application deadline:* rolling.
APPLYING/TRANSFER *Entrance:* noncompetitive. *Application deadline:* rolling.
CONTACT Mr. Jose Romero, Lead Records Clerk, Cañada College, Redwood City, CA 94061-1099, 415-306-3395. *Fax:* 415-306-3457.

CERRITOS COLLEGE
Norwalk, California

UG Enrollment: 22,068	Tuition & Fees (CA Res): $425
Application Deadline: rolling	Room & Board: N/Avail

GENERAL State and locally supported, 2-year, coed. Part of California Community Colleges System. Awards transfer associate, terminal associate degrees. Founded 1956. *Setting:* 140-acre suburban campus with easy access to Los Angeles. *Total enrollment:* 22,068. *Faculty:* 642 (217 full-time, 425 part-time).
ENROLLMENT PROFILE 22,068 students: 56% women, 77% part-time, 95% state residents, 7% transferred in, 1% international, 46% 25 or older, 2% Native American, 31% Hispanic, 6% African American, 14% Asian American. *Most popular recent majors:* liberal arts/general studies, business administration/commerce/management, nursing.
FIRST-YEAR CLASS 3,951 total. Of the students who applied, 100% were accepted.
ACADEMIC PROGRAM Core. Calendar: semesters. Academic remediation for entering students, English as a second language program offered during academic year and summer, services for LD students, advanced placement, summer session for credit, part-time degree program (daytime, evenings, summer), adult/continuing education programs. Study-abroad program.
GENERAL DEGREE REQUIREMENTS 64 units; math competence; 2 science courses; computer course for engineering, business-related majors.
MAJORS Accounting, agricultural sciences, anthropology, architectural technologies, art/fine arts, automotive technologies, biology/biological sciences, biomedical technologies, botany/plant sciences, business administration/commerce/management, chemistry, computer programming, computer science, cosmetology, court reporting, data processing, dental services, drafting and design, early childhood education, economics, electrical and electronics technologies, (pre)engineering sequence, English, fashion design and technology, food services technology, forestry, French, geography, geology, German, history, home economics, industrial arts, journalism, law enforcement/police sciences, legal secretarial studies, liberal arts/general studies, machine and tool technologies, manufacturing technology, marketing/retailing/merchandising, mathematics, medical assistant technologies, medical secretarial studies, metallurgy, Mexican-American/Chicano studies, music, nursing, ornamental horticulture, pharmacy/pharmaceutical sciences, philosophy, photography, physical education, physical therapy, physics, plastics technology, political science/government, psychology, real estate, recreation and leisure services, secretarial studies/office management, sociology, Spanish, speech/rhetoric/public address/debate, theater arts/drama, welding technology, wildlife management, zoology.
LIBRARY Wilford Michael Library with 74,502 books, 115 microform titles, 396 periodicals, 11,660 records, tapes, and CDs.
COMPUTERS ON CAMPUS 400 computers for student use in computer center, labs, classrooms, library.

COLLEGE LIFE Drama-theater group, student-run newspaper, radio station. *Social organizations:* 5 local fraternities, 5 local sororities, 40 social clubs; 1% of eligible men and 2% of eligible women are members. *Student services:* legal services, health clinic, personal-psychological counseling, women's center.
HOUSING College housing not available.
ATHLETICS Member NJCAA. *Intercollegiate:* baseball M, basketball M/W, cross-country running M/W, football M, golf M, soccer M, softball W, swimming and diving M/W, tennis M/W, track and field M/W, volleyball W, water polo M, wrestling M. *Contact:* Mr. Frank Mazzota, Interim Dean of Athletics, 310-860-2451 Ext. 575.
CAREER PLANNING *Director:* Dr. David Young, Counselor, 310-860-2451 Ext. 476. *Service:* career counseling.
EXPENSES FOR 1995-96 State resident tuition: $0 full-time. Nonresident tuition: $3420 full-time, $114 per unit part-time. Part-time mandatory fees per semester range from $20.50 to $150.50. Full-time mandatory fees: $425.
FINANCIAL AID *College-administered undergrad aid 1995-96:* need-based scholarships, short-term loans, low-interest long-term loans from external sources. *Required forms:* institutional; accepted: CSS Financial Aid PROFILE, state, FAFSA. *Application deadline:* continuous to 5/1.
APPLYING Open admission. *Options:* early entrance, deferred entrance, midyear entrance. *Required:* TOEFL for international students. *Recommended:* CEPT, Nelson Denny Reading Test. Test scores used for counseling/placement. *Application deadline:* rolling.
APPLYING/TRANSFER *Entrance:* noncompetitive. *Application deadline:* rolling.
CONTACT Dr. Robert Bell, Interim Director of Admissions, Cerritos College, Norwalk, CA 90650-6298, 310-860-2451.

CERRO COSO COMMUNITY COLLEGE
Ridgecrest, California

UG Enrollment: 5,564	Tuition & Fees (CA Res): $312
Application Deadline: rolling	Room & Board: N/Avail

GENERAL State-supported, 2-year, coed. Part of Kern Community College District System. Awards transfer associate, terminal associate degrees. Founded 1973. *Setting:* 320-acre small-town campus. *Total enrollment:* 5,564. *Faculty:* 262 (37 full-time, 225 part-time).
ENROLLMENT PROFILE 5,564 students: 55% women, 45% men, 88% part-time, 96% state residents, 12% transferred in, 70% 25 or older, 3% Native American, 8% Hispanic, 5% African American, 9% Asian American.
FIRST-YEAR CLASS 615 total; 615 applied, 100% were accepted, 100% of whom enrolled.
ACADEMIC PROGRAM Core, honor code. Calendar: semesters. Academic remediation for entering students, English as a second language program offered during academic year and summer, services for LD students, summer session for credit, part-time degree program (daytime, evenings), adult/continuing education programs, co-op programs. Study abroad in England.
GENERAL DEGREE REQUIREMENTS 60 semester units; algebra proficiency; 1 course each in natural and physical science.
MAJORS Art/fine arts, automotive technologies, business administration/commerce/management, business machine technologies, child psychology/child development, computer science, computer technologies, criminal justice, data processing, drafting and design, early childhood education, electrical and electronics technologies, emergency medical technology, (pre)engineering sequence, engineering technology, family and consumer studies, fire science, heating/refrigeration/air conditioning, humanities, liberal arts/general studies, machine and tool technologies, nursing, physical sciences, practical nursing, science, social science, solar technologies, welding technology.
LIBRARY Walter Stiern Memorial Library with 24,000 books, 19 microform titles, 105 periodicals, 1 on-line bibliographic service, 2 CD-ROMs, 1,630 records, tapes, and CDs.
COMPUTERS ON CAMPUS 80 computers for student use in computer center, learning center, business skills lab, library.
COLLEGE LIFE *Most popular organizations:* Special Services Club, Art Club, LVN Club, Athletic Club, Drama Club. *Student services:* personal-psychological counseling. *Campus security:* periodic security patrols by security.
HOUSING College housing not available.
ATHLETICS *Intercollegiate:* baseball M, basketball M, cross-country running M/W, golf M, tennis W, volleyball W. *Contact:* Mr. Bob Weisenthal, Director of Athletics, 619-375-5001 Ext. 219.
CAREER PLANNING *Director:* Ms. June Wasserman, Director of Counseling Services, 619-375-5001 Ext. 219. *Services:* resume preparation, career counseling, careers library.
EXPENSES FOR 1996-97 State resident tuition: $0 full-time. Nonresident tuition: $3600 full-time, $120 per unit part-time. Part-time mandatory fees: $13 per unit. Full-time mandatory fees: $312.
FINANCIAL AID *College-administered undergrad aid 1995-96:* 10 need-based scholarships (average $200), 25 non-need scholarships (average $150), short-term loans (average $50), Federal Work-Study, 50 part-time jobs. *Required forms:* CSS Financial Aid PROFILE, institutional, FAFSA. *Priority deadline:* 5/15. *Payment plan:* installment.
APPLYING Open admission except for nursing program. *Option:* early entrance. *Recommended:* school transcript. *Required for some:* TOEFL for international students. Test scores used for counseling/placement. *Application deadline:* rolling.
APPLYING/TRANSFER *Recommended:* college transcript. *Entrance:* noncompetitive. *Application deadline:* rolling.
CONTACT Dr. Don Mourton, Vice President, Cerro Coso Community College, Ridgecrest, CA 93555-9571, 619-375-5001 Ext. 201. *Fax:* 619-375-5001 Ext. 252.

CHABOT COLLEGE
Hayward, California

UG Enrollment: 13,285	Tuition & Fees (CA Res): $390
Application Deadline: 10/15	Room & Board: N/Avail

GENERAL State-supported, 2-year, coed. Part of California Community Colleges System. Awards certificates, transfer associate, terminal associate degrees. Founded 1961. *Setting:* 245-acre suburban campus with easy access to San Francisco. *Educational spending 1994-95:* $3500 per undergrad. *Total enrollment:* 13,285. *Faculty:* 933 (281 full-

Chabot College (continued)
time, 35% with terminal degrees, 652 part-time); student-faculty ratio is 15:1. ***Notable Alumni:*** Tom Hanks, Honorable Peggy Hora, Jeff Barnes, Lester Conner, Glen DeBoise.
ENROLLMENT PROFILE 13,285 students: 53% women, 79% part-time, 99% state residents, 13% transferred in, 20% have need-based financial aid, 1% international, 47% 25 or older, 1% Native American, 16% Hispanic, 12% African American, 17% Asian American. ***Areas of study chosen:*** 10% liberal arts/general studies, 10% social sciences, 5% communications and journalism, 5% computer and information sciences, 5% engineering and applied sciences, 5% health professions and related sciences, 3% business management and administrative services, 3% fine arts, 2% premed, 1% agriculture, 1% architecture, 1% biological and life sciences, 1% education, 1% English language/literature/letters, 1% foreign language and literature, 1% interdisciplinary studies, 1% library and information studies, 1% mathematics, 1% military science, 1% natural resource sciences, 1% performing arts, 1% philosophy, 1% physical sciences, 1% predentistry, 1% prelaw, 1% prevet, 1% psychology. ***Most popular recent majors:*** business administration/commerce/management, nursing, computer science.
FIRST-YEAR CLASS 5,516 total. Of the students who applied, 100% were accepted, 42% of whom enrolled.
ACADEMIC PROGRAM Core, general education curriculum, honor code. Calendar: semesters. 1,300 courses offered in 1995–96. Academic remediation for entering students, English as a second language program offered during academic year and summer, services for LD students, advanced placement, self-designed majors, summer session for credit, part-time degree program (daytime, evenings, weekends, summer), adult/continuing education programs, internships. Off-campus study at Mills College, California State University, Hayward. Study abroad in Italy, Mexico, England. ROTC: Army (c), Air Force (c).
GENERAL DEGREE REQUIREMENTS 60 semester units; math/science requirements vary according to program.
MAJORS Accounting, advertising, applied mathematics, architectural technologies, art/fine arts, automotive technologies, behavioral sciences, biology/biological sciences, broadcasting, business administration/commerce/management, business economics, business education, business machine technologies, chemistry, civil engineering technology, commercial art, communication, computer information systems, computer science, computer technologies, corrections, criminal justice, data processing, dental services, early childhood education, ecology, economics, education, electrical and electronics technologies, electrical engineering technology, electromechanical technology, electronics engineering technology, emergency medical technology, engineering (general), (pre)engineering sequence, engineering technology, English, fashion design and technology, fashion merchandising, finance/banking, fire science, graphic arts, health education, history, horticulture, humanities, human services, industrial arts, industrial engineering technology, instrumentation technology, interdisciplinary studies, Italian, journalism, landscaping/grounds maintenance, law enforcement/police sciences, legal secretarial studies, liberal arts/general studies, literature, mathematics, medical assistant technologies, medical records services, music, natural sciences, nursing, ornamental horticulture, painting/drawing, photography, physical education, physics, physiology, political science/government, psychology, radio and television studies, real estate, recreation and leisure services, retail management, science, secretarial studies/office management, social science, sociology, solar technologies, Spanish, statistics, studio art, surveying technology, teacher aide studies, tourism and travel, welding technology, women's studies, word processing, zoology.
LIBRARY Chabot Library with 100,000 books, 450 microform titles, 160 periodicals, 6,500 records, tapes, and CDs.
COMPUTERS ON CAMPUS Computer purchase plan available. 1,000 computers for student use in computer center, computer labs, learning resource center, library, student center. Staffed computer lab on campus provides training in use of computers, software. Academic computing expenditure 1994–95: $450,000.
COLLEGE LIFE Orientation program (2 days, no cost). Drama-theater group, choral group, student-run newspaper, radio station. ***Most popular organizations:*** Ski Club, International Club, MECCHA, Muslim Student Union, CARP. ***Major annual events:*** Homecoming, Orientation, International Day. ***Student services:*** legal services, personal-psychological counseling. ***Campus security:*** late-night transport-escort service.
HOUSING College housing not available.
ATHLETICS ***Intercollegiate:*** baseball M, basketball M/W, cross-country running M/W, football M, golf M, soccer M/W, softball W, swimming and diving M/W, tennis M/W, track and field M/W, wrestling M. ***Intramural:*** archery, badminton, basketball, bowling, football, golf, gymnastics, racquetball, skiing (cross-country), skiing (downhill), soccer, softball, swimming and diving, table tennis (Ping-Pong), tennis, track and field, volleyball, weight lifting.
CAREER PLANNING ***Placement office:*** 2 full-time staff; $60,000 operating expenditure 1994–95. ***Director:*** Mrs. Priscilla Leadon, Counselor, 510-786-6720. ***Services:*** job fairs, career counseling, careers library.
AFTER GRADUATION 85% of students completing a degree program in 1994–95 went directly on to further study.
EXPENSES FOR 1996–97 State resident tuition: $0 full-time. Nonresident tuition: $3660 full-time, $122 per unit part-time. Part-time mandatory fees: $13 per unit. Full-time mandatory fees: $390.
FINANCIAL AID ***College-administered undergrad aid 1995–96:*** 100 need-based scholarships (average $400), 35 non-need scholarships (average $300), short-term loans, low-interest long-term loans from external sources, Federal Work-Study, part-time jobs. ***Required forms:*** CSS Financial Aid PROFILE, institutional, FAFSA. ***Priority deadline:*** 6/1.
APPLYING Open admission except for dental hygiene, nursing, emergency medical technician programs. ***Options:*** early entrance, midyear entrance. ***Required:*** TOEFL for international students. Test scores used for counseling/placement. ***Application deadline:*** 10/15. Preference given to state residents.
APPLYING/TRANSFER ***Entrance:*** noncompetitive. ***Application deadline:*** 10/15. ***Contact:*** Mrs. Norma Ambriz, Area Dean of Counseling, 510-786-6718.
CONTACT Mr. Carlo E. Vecchiarelli, District Dean of Admissions and Records, Chabot College, Hayward, CA 94545-5001, 510-786-6714.

CHAFFEY COLLEGE
Rancho Cucamonga, California

UG Enrollment: 12,651	**Tuition & Fees (CA Res): $410**
Application Deadline: rolling	**Room & Board: N/Avail**

GENERAL District-supported, 2-year, coed. Part of California Community Colleges System. Awards certificates, transfer associate, terminal associate degrees. Founded 1883. ***Setting:*** 200-acre suburban campus with easy access to Los Angeles. ***Total enrollment:*** 12,651. ***Faculty:*** 540 (190 full-time, 350 part-time); student-faculty ratio is 27:1.
ENROLLMENT PROFILE 12,651 students: 60% women, 72% part-time, 97% state residents, 10% transferred in, 2% international, 42% 25 or older, 1% Native American, 29% Hispanic, 11% African American, 7% Asian American. ***Most popular recent majors:*** business administration/commerce/management, nursing, liberal arts/general studies.
FIRST-YEAR CLASS 8,000 total; 8,000 applied, 100% were accepted, 100% of whom enrolled.
ACADEMIC PROGRAM Core. Calendar: semesters. Academic remediation for entering students, English as a second language program offered during academic year and summer, services for LD students, advanced placement, honors program, summer session for credit, part-time degree program (daytime, evenings, summer), adult/continuing education programs, co-op programs and internships. Study abroad in Germany, France. ROTC: Army (c).
GENERAL DEGREE REQUIREMENTS 60 units; computer course (varies by major).
MAJORS Accounting, anthropology, art/fine arts, automotive technologies, biology/biological sciences, broadcasting, business administration/commerce/management, business education, ceramic art and design, chemistry, child care/child and family studies, child psychology/child development, computer information systems, corrections, court reporting, dance, dietetics, drafting and design, early childhood education, economics, electrical and electronics technologies, engineering (general), English, environmental engineering technology, fashion design and technology, food services management, French, geology, German, gerontology, history, home economics, hotel and restaurant management, humanities, industrial design, interior design, journalism, legal secretarial studies, liberal arts/general studies, marketing/retailing/merchandising, mathematics, medical secretarial studies, music, nursing, philosophy, photography, physical education, physical sciences, physics, political science/government, psychology, quality control technology, radiological technology, real estate, religious studies, secretarial studies/office management, social science, sociology, Spanish, speech/rhetoric/public address/debate, telecommunications, theater arts/drama, word processing.
LIBRARY Chaffey College Library with 72,000 books, 232 periodicals, 5 CD-ROMs.
COMPUTERS ON CAMPUS Computer purchase plan available. 150 computers for student use in computer center, computer labs, learning resource center, classrooms, library provide access to on-line services.
COLLEGE LIFE Drama-theater group, choral group, student-run newspaper, radio station. 10% vote in student government elections. ***Social organizations:*** 30 open to all. ***Most popular organizations:*** The Associated Students of Chaffey College, Multicultural Club, Style Club. ***Major annual events:*** Club Rush, Toy and Food Drive, ICC Sponsored Events. ***Student services:*** health clinic, personal-psychological counseling. ***Campus security:*** 24-hour emergency response devices, late-night transport-escort service.
HOUSING College housing not available.
ATHLETICS Member NJCAA. ***Intercollegiate:*** baseball M, basketball M/W, cross-country running M/W, football M, golf M/W, swimming and diving M/W, tennis M/W, track and field M/W, volleyball W, water polo M. ***Contact:*** Mr. Bob Olivera, Athletic Director, 909-941-2467.
CAREER PLANNING ***Placement office:*** 16 full-time, 10 part-time staff. ***Director:*** Mr. Victor Oliva, Counselor, 909-941-2814. ***Services:*** job fairs, resume preparation, resume referral, career counseling, careers library, job bank, job interviews.
EXPENSES FOR 1995–96 State resident tuition: $0 full-time. Nonresident tuition: $3480 full-time, $116 per unit part-time. Part-time mandatory fees per semester range from $23 to $153. Full-time mandatory fees: $410.
FINANCIAL AID ***College-administered undergrad aid 1995–96:*** need-based scholarships, non-need scholarships, short-term loans, low-interest long-term loans from external sources, part-time jobs. ***Required forms:*** institutional. ***Application deadline:*** continuous. ***Waivers:*** full or partial for employees or children of employees.
APPLYING Open admission. ***Options:*** early entrance, midyear entrance. ***Recommended:*** TOEFL for international students. Test scores used for counseling/placement. ***Application deadline:*** rolling. ***Notification:*** continuous.
APPLYING/TRANSFER ***Entrance:*** noncompetitive. ***Application deadline:*** rolling. ***Notification:*** continuous. ***Contact:*** Mr. Victor Oliva, Counselor, 909-941-2813.
CONTACT Ms. JoAnne Edmison, Director of Admissions, Registration, and Records, Chaffey College, Rancho Cucamonga, CA 91737-3002, 909-941-2631. ***Fax:*** 909-941-2783.

CITRUS COLLEGE
Glendora, California

UG Enrollment: 10,448	**Tuition & Fees (CA Res): $410**
Application Deadline: 9/1	**Room & Board: N/Avail**

GENERAL State and locally supported, 2-year, coed. Part of California Community Colleges System. Awards transfer associate, terminal associate degrees. Founded 1915. ***Setting:*** 104-acre small-town campus with easy access to Los Angeles. ***Total enrollment:*** 10,448. ***Faculty:*** 392 (132 full-time, 10% with terminal degrees, 260 part-time); student-faculty ratio is 22:1.
ENROLLMENT PROFILE 10,448 students: 56% women, 44% men, 71% part-time, 95% state residents, 2% international, 45% 25 or older, 1% Native American, 32% Hispanic, 7% African American, 10% Asian American. ***Areas of study chosen:*** 10% business management and administrative services, 5% health professions and related sciences, 4% engineering and applied sciences, 3% psychology, 2% fine arts, 1% agriculture, 1% architecture, 1% biological and life sciences, 1% communications and journalism, 1% computer and information sciences, 1% English language/literature/letters, 1% foreign language and literature, 1% library and information studies, 1% mathematics, 1% philosophy, 1% physical sciences, 1% social sciences. ***Most popular recent major:*** business administration/commerce/management.
FIRST-YEAR CLASS 1,900 total. Of the students who applied, 100% were accepted.
ACADEMIC PROGRAM Core, honor code. Calendar: semesters. Academic remediation for entering students, English as a second language program offered during academic year and summer, services for LD students, advanced placement, summer session for credit, part-time degree program (daytime, evenings, weekends, summer), adult/continuing education programs, co-op programs. Study abroad in England, France, Spain, Italy.
GENERAL DEGREE REQUIREMENTS 60 units; math proficiency; computer course (varies by major).
MAJORS Art/fine arts, automotive technologies, behavioral sciences, biology/biological sciences, business administration/commerce/management, computer science, cosmetology, criminal justice, data processing, dental services, drafting and design, electrical and

electronics technologies, engineering (general), engineering technology, English, journalism, law enforcement/police sciences, mechanical engineering technology, modern languages, music, natural sciences, photography, physical education, physical sciences, practical nursing, real estate, secretarial studies/office management, social science, theater arts/drama, water resources.
LIBRARY 57,036 books, 73 microform titles, 393 periodicals, 2,037 records, tapes, and CDs.
COMPUTERS ON CAMPUS 250 computers for student use in various locations throughout campus.
COLLEGE LIFE Drama-theater group, student-run newspaper. 20% vote in student government elections. ***Social organizations:*** 40 open to all. ***Most popular organizations:*** Student Government, Student Activities Club, International Students Association, Latino Students Association. ***Student services:*** legal services, health clinic, personal-psychological counseling. ***Campus security:*** 24-hour patrols, student patrols, late-night transport-escort service.
HOUSING College housing not available.
ATHLETICS ***Intercollegiate:*** baseball M, basketball M/W, cross-country running M/W, football M, golf M, softball W, swimming and diving M/W, tennis M/W, track and field M/W, volleyball W, water polo M. ***Contact:*** Mr. Robert Claprood, Athletic Director, 818-914-8656; Ms. Marianne Kerr, Assistant Athletic Director, 818-914-8656.
CAREER PLANNING ***Director:*** Ms. Penny York, 818-914-8639. ***Services:*** job fairs, resume preparation, career counseling, careers library, job bank, job interviews.
EXPENSES FOR 1995–96 State resident tuition: $0 full-time. Nonresident tuition: $4050 full-time, $135 per unit part-time. Part-time mandatory fees per semester range from $23 to $153. Full-time mandatory fees: $410.
FINANCIAL AID ***College-administered undergrad aid 1995–96:*** need-based scholarships, non-need scholarships, short-term loans, low-interest long-term loans from external sources, Federal Work-Study, part-time jobs. ***Required forms:*** state, institutional, FAFSA; accepted: CSS Financial Aid PROFILE. ***Application deadline:*** continuous to 4/1. ***Waivers:*** full or partial for senior citizens.
APPLYING Open admission. ***Option:*** early entrance. ***Required:*** TOEFL for international students. ***Required for some:*** SAT I or ACT, ACT ASSET. Test scores used for counseling/placement. ***Application deadline:*** 9/1.
APPLYING/TRANSFER ***Required for some:*** standardized test scores. ***Application deadline:*** 9/1. ***Contact:*** Mr. Patrick Cain, 818-914-8531.
CONTACT Mrs. Melanie Cox, Dean of Admissions and Financial Aid, Citrus College, Glendora, CA 91741-1899, 818-914-8517.

CITY COLLEGE OF SAN FRANCISCO
San Francisco, California

Enrollment: N/R	**Tuition & Fees (CA Res): $410**
Application Deadline: rolling	**Room & Board: N/Avail**

GENERAL State and locally supported, 2-year, coed. Part of California Community Colleges System. Awards transfer associate, terminal associate degrees. Founded 1935. ***Setting:*** 56-acre urban campus. ***Faculty:*** 1,117 (479 full-time, 638 part-time).
ENROLLMENT PROFILE 57% women, 76% part-time, 94% state residents, 16% transferred in, 4% international, 56% 25 or older, 1% Native American, 14% Hispanic, 7% African American, 49% Asian American.
FIRST-YEAR CLASS Of the students who applied, 100% were accepted.
ACADEMIC PROGRAM Core. Calendar: semesters. Academic remediation for entering students, English as a second language program offered during academic year and summer, services for LD students, advanced placement, summer session for credit, part-time degree program (daytime, evenings, summer), adult/continuing education programs, internships. Off-campus study at members of The San Francisco Consortium. Study abroad in Mexico, France, Japan, China, Spain. ROTC: Army (c).
GENERAL DEGREE REQUIREMENTS 60 units; math competence; computer course for science majors.
MAJORS Accounting, agricultural business, aircraft and missile maintenance, art/fine arts, Asian/Oriental studies, automotive technologies, aviation technology, black/African-American studies, botany/plant sciences, broadcasting, business administration/commerce/management, chemical engineering technology, chemistry, child psychology/child development, civil engineering technology, computer programming, computer science, construction management, consumer services, court reporting, criminal justice, dental services, dietetics, educational media, electrical engineering technology, (pre)engineering sequence, English, fashion merchandising, film and video production, finance/banking, fire science, forestry, geology, horticulture, hotel and restaurant management, industrial engineering technology, insurance, interior design, journalism, labor studies, landscape architecture/design, Latin American studies, law enforcement/police sciences, legal secretarial studies, library science, marketing/retailing/merchandising, mathematics, mechanical engineering technology, medical records services, meteorology, music, nursing, nutrition, ornamental horticulture, pharmacy/pharmaceutical sciences, photography, physical therapy, practical nursing, printing technologies, psychology, public administration, public health, radiological technology, real estate, recreation and leisure services, respiratory therapy, social science, social work, transportation technologies, veterinary sciences, wildlife management, women's studies.
LIBRARY City College of San Francisco Library with 93,518 books, 236 microform titles, 774 periodicals, 4 CD-ROMs, 21,010 records, tapes, and CDs.
COMPUTERS ON CAMPUS Computers for student use in computer labs, various departments provide access to main academic computer, on-line services. Staffed computer lab on campus.
COLLEGE LIFE Orientation program (2 days). Drama-theater group, student-run newspaper. ***Student services:*** health clinic, personal-psychological counseling, women's center. ***Campus security:*** 24-hour patrols.
HOUSING College housing not available.
ATHLETICS ***Intercollegiate:*** archery W, basketball M(s), cross-country running M(s)/W, fencing W, football M(s), golf M(s), gymnastics W, soccer M(s), swimming and diving M(s), tennis M(s)/W, track and field M(s)/W(s), volleyball M(s)/W, water polo M(s). ***Intramural:*** archery, badminton, basketball, bowling, fencing, football, golf, gymnastics, soccer, swimming and diving, tennis, track and field, volleyball, wrestling.
CAREER PLANNING ***Placement office:*** 6 part-time staff. ***Director:*** Ms. Alliene M. Lawson, Department Head, 415-239-3117. ***Service:*** career counseling.
EXPENSES FOR 1995–96 State resident tuition: $0 full-time. Nonresident tuition: $3630 full-time, $121 per unit part-time. Part-time mandatory fees per semester range from $23 to $153. Full-time mandatory fees: $410.
FINANCIAL AID ***College-administered undergrad aid 1995–96:*** need-based scholarships, low-interest long-term loans from external sources, Federal Work-Study. ***Required forms:*** state, FAFSA. ***Application deadline:*** continuous.
APPLYING Open admission. ***Option:*** early entrance. ***Required:*** TOEFL for international students. Test scores used for counseling/placement. ***Application deadline:*** rolling. ***Notification:*** continuous.
APPLYING/TRANSFER ***Application deadline:*** rolling. ***Notification:*** continuous.
CONTACT Mr. Robert Balesteri, Dean of Admissions and Records, City College of San Francisco, 50 Phelan Avenue, San Francisco, CA 94112-1821, 415-239-3291.

COASTLINE COMMUNITY COLLEGE
Fountain Valley, California

UG Enrollment: 11,950	**Tuition & Fees (CA Res): $390**
Application Deadline: rolling	**Room & Board: N/Avail**

GENERAL State and locally supported, 2-year, coed. Part of Coast Community College District System. Awards transfer associate degrees. Founded 1976. ***Setting:*** urban campus with easy access to Los Angeles. ***Total enrollment:*** 11,950. ***Faculty:*** 340 (50 full-time, 10% with terminal degrees, 290 part-time); student-faculty ratio is 30:1.
ENROLLMENT PROFILE 11,950 students: 63% women, 37% men, 92% part-time, 89% state residents, 0% international, 82% 25 or older, 1% Native American, 8% Hispanic, 2% African American, 19% Asian American. ***Areas of study chosen:*** 23% liberal arts/general studies.
FIRST-YEAR CLASS 4,118 total; 4,118 applied, 100% were accepted, 100% of whom enrolled.
ACADEMIC PROGRAM Core. Calendar: semesters. 720 courses offered in 1995–96. Academic remediation for entering students, English as a second language program offered during academic year and summer, advanced placement, summer session for credit, part-time degree program (daytime, evenings, weekends, summer), external degree programs, adult/continuing education programs, co-op programs.
GENERAL DEGREE REQUIREMENT 60 units.
MAJOR Liberal arts/general studies.
COLLEGE LIFE ***Student services:*** health clinic.
HOUSING College housing not available.
CAREER PLANNING ***Placement office:*** 1 full-time, 1 part-time staff. ***Director:*** Mr. Ron Klien, Instructional Associate, 714-241-6171. ***Services:*** job fairs, resume preparation, career counseling, careers library.
EXPENSES FOR 1995–96 State resident tuition: $0 full-time. Nonresident tuition: $3420 full-time, $114 per unit part-time. Part-time mandatory fees: $13 per unit. Part-time tuition for international students per unit: $114 plus $12 per unit capital outlay fee. Full-time mandatory fees: $390.
FINANCIAL AID ***College-administered undergrad aid 1995–96:*** 120 need-based scholarships (average $500), 90 non-need scholarships (average $250), short-term loans (average $50), low-interest long-term loans from college funds (average $1500), loans from external sources (average $3000), 9 Federal Work-Study (averaging $3000). ***Required forms:*** FAFSA. ***Application deadline:*** continuous. ***Waivers:*** full or partial for minority students, adult students, and senior citizens.
APPLYING Open admission. ***Options:*** Common Application, early entrance, midyear entrance. ***Required for some:*** TOEFL for international students. ***Application deadline:*** rolling.
APPLYING/TRANSFER ***Application deadline:*** rolling. ***Contact:*** Mr. Rendell Drew, Dean of Student Services, 714-241-6162.
CONTACT Mr. Ronald Berggren, Vice President of Student Services, Coastline Community College, 11460 Warner Avenue, Fountain Valley, CA 92708-2597, 714-241-6160.

COLLEGE OF ALAMEDA
Alameda, California

UG Enrollment: 4,858	**Tuition & Fees (CA Res): $394**
Application Deadline: rolling	**Room & Board: N/Avail**

GENERAL State and locally supported, 2-year, coed. Part of Peralta Community College District System. Awards certificates, transfer associate, terminal associate degrees. Founded 1970. ***Setting:*** 62-acre urban campus with easy access to San Francisco. ***Research spending 1994–95:*** $37,247. ***Educational spending 1994–95:*** $953 per undergrad. ***Total enrollment:*** 4,858. ***Faculty:*** 166 (80 full-time, 14% with terminal degrees, 86 part-time); student-faculty ratio is 24:1. ***Notable Alumni:*** Herbert W. Smith, dentist; Denise Lor Alexander, dentist; Tom Robertson, transportation executive; Michael Corrales, executive at United Parcel Services; Lisa Price, executive at Wells Fargo Bank.
ENROLLMENT PROFILE 4,858 students from 18 states and territories, 9 other countries. 56% women, 73% part-time, 97% state residents, 11% transferred in, 1% international, 44% 25 or older, 1% Native American, 9% Hispanic, 30% African American, 32% Asian American. ***Areas of study chosen:*** 10% business management and administrative services, 9% engineering and applied sciences, 6% health professions and related sciences, 4% interdisciplinary studies, 3% computer and information sciences, 3% psychology, 3% social sciences, 3% vocational and home economics, 2% biological and life sciences, 2% fine arts, 2% liberal arts/general studies, 1% architecture, 1% communications and journalism, 1% education, 1% mathematics.
FIRST-YEAR CLASS 1,077 total. Of the students who applied, 100% were accepted, 90% of whom enrolled. 5% from top quarter of their high school class, 60% from top half.
ACADEMIC PROGRAM Honor code. Calendar: semesters. 337 courses offered in 1995–96. Academic remediation for entering students, English as a second language program offered during academic year and summer, services for LD students, summer session for credit, part-time degree program (daytime), adult/continuing education programs, co-op programs. Off-campus study at other units of the Peralta Community College District System.
GENERAL DEGREE REQUIREMENTS 60 semester hours; 3 semester hours of math; computer course.
MAJORS Accounting, anthropology, art/fine arts, automotive technologies, aviation technology, biology/biological sciences, black/African-American studies, business administration/

Peterson's Guide to Two-Year Colleges 1997

187

College of Alameda (continued)
commerce/management, business education, computer information systems, dental services, English, fashion design and technology, fashion merchandising, geography, history, human development, humanities, liberal arts/general studies, marketing/retailing/merchandising, mathematics, Mexican-American/Chicano studies, philosophy, political science/government, psychology, science, secretarial studies/office management, social science, sociology, Spanish.

LIBRARY Learning Resources Center with 40,000 books, 200 periodicals, 3,000 records, tapes, and CDs. Acquisition spending 1994–95: $35,265.

COMPUTERS ON CAMPUS 20 computers for student use in lab.

COLLEGE LIFE Student-run newspaper. 8% vote in student government elections. ***Student services:*** women's center.

HOUSING College housing not available.

ATHLETICS ***Intercollegiate:*** basketball M/W, bowling M/W. ***Intramural:*** golf, soccer, tennis, track and field, volleyball.

CAREER PLANNING ***Placement office:*** $39,325 operating expenditure 1994–95. ***Director:*** Ms. Ruth Phillips, Counselor- Single Parents, 510-748-2208. ***Services:*** resume preparation, career counseling, careers library.

EXPENSES FOR 1996–97 State resident tuition: $0 full-time. Nonresident tuition: $3660 full-time, $122 per semester hour part-time. Part-time mandatory fees: $13 per semester hour. Full-time mandatory fees: $394.

FINANCIAL AID ***College-administered undergrad aid 1995–96:*** need-based scholarships, non-need scholarships, low-interest long-term loans from external sources, Federal Work-Study. ***Required forms:*** state, FAFSA; accepted: CSS Financial Aid PROFILE. ***Application deadline:*** continuous.

APPLYING Open admission. ***Recommended:*** SAT I or ACT. Test scores used for counseling/placement. ***Application deadline:*** rolling.

APPLYING/TRANSFER ***Entrance:*** noncompetitive. ***Application deadline:*** rolling.

CONTACT Mrs. Mary DeCoite, District Admissions Officer, College of Alameda, 555 Atlantic Avenue, Alameda, CA 94501-2109, 510-466-7369.

COLLEGE OF MARIN
Kentfield, California

UG Enrollment: 8,845 | **Tuition & Fees (CA Res): $412**
Application Deadline: rolling | **Room & Board: N/Avail**

GENERAL State and locally supported, 2-year, coed. Part of California Community Colleges System. Awards transfer associate, terminal associate degrees. Founded 1926. ***Setting:*** 410-acre small-town campus with easy access to San Francisco. ***Total enrollment:*** 8,845. ***Faculty:*** 464 (161 full-time, 303 part-time).

ENROLLMENT PROFILE 8,845 students: 62% women, 77% part-time, 92% state residents, 15% transferred in, 1% international, 50% 25 or older, 1% Native American, 7% Hispanic, 3% African American, 8% Asian American.

FIRST-YEAR CLASS 1,923 total. Of the students who applied, 99% were accepted, 99% of whom enrolled.

ACADEMIC PROGRAM Core. Calendar: semesters. Academic remediation for entering students, English as a second language program offered during academic year, services for LD students, summer session for credit, part-time degree program, adult/continuing education programs, co-op programs.

GENERAL DEGREE REQUIREMENTS 60 units; 4 units of intermediate college algebra or demonstrated proficiency; 3 units of natural science.

MAJORS Accounting, applied art, architectural technologies, art/fine arts, automotive technologies, behavioral sciences, biology/biological sciences, business administration/commerce/management, chemistry, communication, computer information systems, computer science, corrections, court reporting, dance, data processing, dental services, early childhood education, ecology, electrical and electronics technologies, electronics engineering technology, engineering (general), engineering technology, ethnic studies, fire science, French, geology, German, history, humanities, interior design, journalism, landscape architecture/design, landscaping/grounds maintenance, law enforcement/police sciences, liberal arts/general studies, machine and tool technologies, marine technology, marketing/retailing/merchandising, mathematics, medical assistant technologies, medical secretarial studies, music, natural sciences, nursing, philosophy, physical education, physics, political science/government, psychology, real estate, retail management, secretarial studies/office management, sociology, Spanish, speech/rhetoric/public address/debate, theater arts/drama.

LIBRARY 85,000 books, 500 periodicals.

COMPUTERS ON CAMPUS 25 computers for student use in computer center, computer labs, learning resource center, classrooms. Staffed computer lab on campus provides training in use of computers, software.

COLLEGE LIFE Drama-theater group, student-run newspaper. ***Student services:*** health clinic, personal-psychological counseling. ***Campus security:*** 24-hour patrols.

HOUSING College housing not available.

ATHLETICS ***Intercollegiate:*** basketball M/W, cross-country running M/W, football M/W, golf M/W, soccer M/W, swimming and diving M/W, tennis M/W, track and field M/W, volleyball M/W, water polo M/W.

CAREER PLANNING ***Service:*** career counseling.

EXPENSES FOR 1995–96 State resident tuition: $0 full-time. Nonresident tuition: $4020 full-time, $134 per unit part-time. Part-time mandatory fees per semester range from $24 to $154. Full-time mandatory fees: $412.

FINANCIAL AID ***College-administered undergrad aid 1995–96:*** need-based scholarships, non-need scholarships, short-term loans, low-interest long-term loans from external sources, Federal Work-Study. ***Required forms:*** CSS Financial Aid PROFILE, state, institutional; required for some: FAFSA. ***Priority deadline:*** 4/30.

APPLYING Open admission. ***Option:*** early entrance. ***Required:*** TOEFL for international students. Test scores used for admission. ***Application deadline:*** rolling. ***Notification:*** continuous.

CONTACT Ms. Pamela J. Mize, Director of Admissions and Records, College of Marin, 1800 Ignaci Boulevard, Kentfield, CA 94904, 415-485-9412.

COLLEGE OF OCEANEERING
Wilmington, California

UG Enrollment: 230 | **Tuition & Fees: $14,050**
Application Deadline: rolling | **Room & Board: N/Avail**

GENERAL Proprietary, 2-year, specialized, primarily men. Awards transfer associate degrees. Founded 1969. ***Setting:*** 5-acre suburban campus with easy access to Los Angeles. ***Total enrollment:*** 230. ***Faculty:*** 11 (all full-time).

ENROLLMENT PROFILE 230 students from 47 states and territories, 2 other countries. 0% part-time, 30% state residents, 0% transferred in, 95% have need-based financial aid, 40% 25 or older, 1% Native American, 3% Hispanic, 1% African American, 2% Asian American.

FIRST-YEAR CLASS Of the students who applied, 100% were accepted, 100% of whom enrolled.

ACADEMIC PROGRAM Core, marine technology curriculum, honor code. Calendar: year-round. Academic remediation for entering students, tutorials. Off-campus study at San Pedro/Wilmington Skills Center.

GENERAL DEGREE REQUIREMENT 90 quarter credits.

MAJOR Marine technology.

COLLEGE LIFE Orientation program (2 weeks, no cost). ***Major annual events:*** Graduation, Cook Outs, Thanksgiving Dinner. ***Student services:*** personal-psychological counseling. ***Campus security:*** 24-hour emergency response devices.

HOUSING College housing not available.

CAREER PLANNING ***Placement office:*** 3 full-time staff. ***Director:*** Ms. Tania Lee, Job Placement Coordinator, 310-834-2501. ***Services:*** resume preparation, resume referral, career counseling, job bank, job interviews. Students must register sophomore year.

EXPENSES FOR 1996–97 ***Application fee:*** $100. Tuition: $13,950 full-time. Full-time mandatory fees: $100.

FINANCIAL AID ***College-administered undergrad aid 1995–96:*** 3 need-based scholarships (average $2750), 2 non-need scholarships (average $13,950), 15 part-time jobs. ***Required forms:*** institutional, FAFSA; required for some: state; accepted: CSS Financial Aid PROFILE. ***Application deadline:*** continuous.

APPLYING Open admission. ***Options:*** Common Application, deferred entrance, midyear entrance. ***Recommended:*** TOEFL for international students. Test scores used for admission. ***Application deadline:*** rolling. ***Notification:*** continuous.

APPLYING/TRANSFER ***Entrance:*** noncompetitive. ***Application deadline:*** rolling. ***Notification:*** continuous.

CONTACT Mrs. Tamera Mendoza, Manager of Admittance, College of Oceaneering, Wilmington, CA 90744-6399, 310-834-2501 or toll-free 800-432-DIVE (in-state), 800-824-9027 (out-of-state). ***Fax:*** 310-834-7132.

COLLEGE OF SAN MATEO
San Mateo, California

UG Enrollment: 11,506 | **Tuition & Fees (CA Res): $410**
Application Deadline: rolling | **Room & Board: N/Avail**

GENERAL State and locally supported, 2-year, coed. Part of California Community Colleges System. Awards certificates, transfer associate, terminal associate degrees. Founded 1922. ***Setting:*** 150-acre suburban campus. ***Total enrollment:*** 11,506. ***Faculty:*** 476 (184 full-time, 292 part-time).

ENROLLMENT PROFILE 11,506 students: 50% women, 71% part-time, 98% state residents, 21% transferred in, 1% international, 51% 25 or older, 1% Native American, 15% Hispanic, 4% African American, 15% Asian American.

FIRST-YEAR CLASS 3,408 total. Of the students who applied, 100% were accepted.

ACADEMIC PROGRAM Core. Calendar: semesters. Academic remediation for entering students, English as a second language program offered during academic year, services for LD students, advanced placement, honors program, summer session for credit, part-time degree program (daytime, evenings, summer), adult/continuing education programs, co-op programs. Study abroad in England, France, Italy, Costa Rica. ROTC: Army (c), Naval (c), Air Force (c).

GENERAL DEGREE REQUIREMENTS 60 semester units; math competence; computer course for business, math, science majors.

MAJORS Accounting, aircraft and missile maintenance, architectural technologies, art/fine arts, aviation technology, biology/biological sciences, biotechnology, broadcasting, business administration/commerce/management, chemistry, commercial art, computer information systems, computer science, construction technologies, cosmetology, dental services, drafting and design, drug and alcohol/substance abuse counseling, electrical and electronics technologies, electronics engineering technology, engineering (general), engineering technology, English, environmental studies, ethnic studies, film and video production, fire science, flight training, French, geology, German, graphic arts, horticulture, humanities, journalism, landscape architecture/design, landscaping/grounds maintenance, law enforcement/police sciences, liberal arts/general studies, machine and tool technologies, management information systems, marketing/retailing/merchandising, mathematics, medical assistant technologies, medical secretarial studies, music, nursing, ornamental horticulture, painting/drawing, photography, physical sciences, physics, plumbing, printmaking, radio and television studies, real estate, retail management, secretarial studies/office management, social science, Spanish, speech/rhetoric/public address/debate, welding technology.

LIBRARY 98,000 books, 395 periodicals.

COMPUTERS ON CAMPUS Students must have own computer. 150 computers for student use in computer center, computer labs provide access to main academic computer. Staffed computer lab on campus provides training in use of computers, software.

COLLEGE LIFE Student-run newspaper. ***Student services:*** health clinic, personal-psychological counseling. ***Campus security:*** 24-hour emergency response devices and patrols.

HOUSING College housing not available.

ATHLETICS ***Intercollegiate:*** basketball M/W, cross-country running M/W, football M, soccer W, tennis W, track and field M/W. ***Contact:*** Mr. Gary Dilley, Athletic Director, 415-574-6462.

CAREER PLANNING ***Director:*** Ms. Elaine Burns, Coordinator of Career Development Center, 415-574-6571. ***Services:*** job fairs, resume preparation, career counseling, careers library.

EXPENSES FOR 1996–97 State resident tuition: $0 full-time. Nonresident tuition: $3990 full-time, $133 per unit part-time. Part-time mandatory fees per semester range from $33 to $163. Full-time mandatory fees: $410.
FINANCIAL AID *College-administered undergrad aid 1995–96:* 300 need-based scholarships (average $1000), non-need scholarships (average $500), short-term loans (average $50), low-interest long-term loans from college funds (average $1000), loans from external sources (average $1000), Federal Work-Study, part-time jobs. *Required forms:* CSS Financial Aid PROFILE, state, institutional, FAFSA. *Priority deadline:* 3/2.
APPLYING Open admission except for nursing program. *Option:* early entrance. *Required:* TOEFL for international students. Test scores used for counseling/placement. *Application deadline:* rolling.
APPLYING/TRANSFER *Required:* college transcript. *Contact:* Ms. Aisha Upshaw, Coordinator of Transfer Center, 415-574-6159.
CONTACT Mr. John Mullen, Dean of Admissions and Records, College of San Mateo, San Mateo, CA 94402-3784, 415-574-6594.

COLLEGE OF THE CANYONS
Santa Clarita, California

UG Enrollment: 6,123	Tuition & Fees (CA Res): $390
Application Deadline: 8/22	Room & Board: N/Avail

GENERAL State and locally supported, 2-year, coed. Part of California Community Colleges System. Awards certificates, transfer associate, terminal associate degrees. Founded 1969. *Setting:* 158-acre suburban campus with easy access to Los Angeles. *Total enrollment:* 6,123. *Faculty:* 260 (70 full-time, 23% with terminal degrees, 190 part-time).
ENROLLMENT PROFILE 6,123 students from 15 states and territories, 14 other countries. 58% women, 70% part-time, 98% state residents, 23% transferred in, 1% international, 43% 25 or older, 1% Native American, 10% Hispanic, 2% African American, 3% Asian American. *Most popular recent majors:* social science, business administration/commerce/management, science.
FIRST-YEAR CLASS 2,186 total. Of the students who applied, 100% were accepted, 95% of whom enrolled.
ACADEMIC PROGRAM Core. Calendar: semesters. 581 courses offered in 1995–96. Academic remediation for entering students, English as a second language program offered during academic year, services for LD students, advanced placement, honors program, summer session for credit, part-time degree program (daytime, evenings, summer), adult/continuing education programs, co-op programs and internships.
GENERAL DEGREE REQUIREMENTS 60 units; 1 math course.
MAJORS Accounting, art/fine arts, biology/biological sciences, business administration/commerce/management, chemistry, child care/child and family studies, child psychology/child development, computer information systems, computer science, criminal justice, drafting and design, early childhood education, electrical and electronics technologies, (pre)engineering sequence, English, film and video production, French, geography, geology, German, health science, history, hotel and restaurant management, humanities, interior design, journalism, law enforcement/police sciences, liberal arts/general studies, mathematics, natural sciences, nursing, physical education, physical sciences, political science/government, practical nursing, psychology, quality control technology, real estate, science, secretarial studies/office management, social science, Spanish, water resources, welding technology.
LIBRARY 41,206 books, 232 periodicals, 4,617 records, tapes, and CDs. Acquisition spending 1994–95: $219,335.
COMPUTERS ON CAMPUS 123 computers for student use in computer center, classrooms, library.
COLLEGE LIFE Drama-theater group, choral group, student-run newspaper. *Student services:* health clinic, personal-psychological counseling. *Campus security:* student patrols, late-night transport-escort service.
HOUSING College housing not available.
ATHLETICS *Intercollegiate:* baseball M, basketball M/W, cross-country running M/W, golf M, softball W, swimming and diving M/W, track and field M/W, volleyball W, water polo M. *Intramural:* football, volleyball. *Contact:* Ms. Beth A. Asmus, Athletic Director, 805-259-7800 Ext. 200.
CAREER PLANNING *Placement office:* 1 full-time, 3 part-time staff. *Director:* Ms. Marge Dieguez, Career Center Specialist, 805-259-7800 Ext. 253. *Services:* job fairs, career counseling, careers library, job bank, job interviews.
AFTER GRADUATION 65% of students completing a degree program in 1994–95 went directly on to further study.
EXPENSES FOR 1996–97 State resident tuition: $0 full-time. Nonresident tuition: $3300 full-time, $110 per unit part-time. Part-time mandatory fees: $13 per unit. Full-time mandatory fees: $390.
FINANCIAL AID *College-administered undergrad aid 1995–96:* need-based scholarships, low-interest long-term loans from external sources, Federal Work-Study, part-time jobs. *Required forms:* CSS Financial Aid PROFILE, institutional, FAFSA. *Priority deadline:* 6/15.
APPLYING Open admission. *Options:* early entrance, midyear entrance. *Required:* TOEFL for international students. *Recommended:* school transcript, SAT I or ACT. Test scores used for counseling/placement. *Application deadline:* 8/22. *Notification:* continuous until 8/22.
APPLYING/TRANSFER *Required:* college transcript. *Recommended:* high school transcript. *Application deadline:* 8/22. *Notification:* continuous until 8/22. *Contact:* Ms. Yvette Cruzalequi, Transfer Center Specialist, 805-259-7800 Ext. 455.
CONTACT Dr. Glenn Hisayasu, Dean of Student Services, College of the Canyons, Santa Clarita, CA 91355-1899, 805-259-7800 Ext. 291.

COLLEGE OF THE DESERT
Palm Desert, California

UG Enrollment: 9,638	Tuition & Fees (CA Res): $410
Application Deadline: rolling	Room & Board: N/Avail

GENERAL State and locally supported, 2-year, coed. Part of California Community Colleges System. Awards transfer associate, terminal associate degrees. Founded 1959. *Setting:* 160-acre small-town campus. *Total enrollment:* 9,638. *Faculty:* 320 (100 full-time, 220 part-time); student-faculty ratio is 30:1.
ENROLLMENT PROFILE 9,638 students from 23 states and territories. 58% women, 80% part-time, 96% state residents, 11% transferred in, 60% 25 or older, 1% Native American, 37% Hispanic, 3% African American, 2% Asian American. *Areas of study chosen:* 4% education, 4% fine arts, 2% architecture, 2% communications and journalism, 2% performing arts, 2% premed, 1% agriculture, 1% engineering and applied sciences, 1% natural resource sciences, 1% prevet, 1% social sciences. *Most popular recent majors:* nursing, business administration/commerce/management, education.
FIRST-YEAR CLASS 1,450 total; 2,250 applied, 100% were accepted.
ACADEMIC PROGRAM Core, comprehensive curriculum. Calendar: semesters. 118 courses offered in 1995–96. Academic remediation for entering students, English as a second language program offered during academic year, services for LD students, honors program, summer session for credit, part-time degree program (daytime, evenings), adult/continuing education programs.
GENERAL DEGREE REQUIREMENTS 60 units; math proficiency; computer course for business, pre-engineering majors.
MAJORS Agricultural business, anthropology, architectural technologies, art/fine arts, automotive technologies, biology/biological sciences, business administration/commerce/management, business economics, chemistry, communication, computer science, construction management, criminal justice, culinary arts, drafting and design, early childhood education, economics, education, (pre)engineering sequence, engineering technology, English, environmental sciences, fire science, French, geography, geology, heating/refrigeration/air conditioning, history, horticulture, interior design, Italian, journalism, law enforcement/police sciences, liberal arts/general studies, marketing/retailing/merchandising, mathematics, medical assistant technologies, music, natural resource management, nursing, ornamental horticulture, philosophy, physical education, physics, political science/government, psychology, real estate, recreational facilities management, recreation and leisure services, respiratory therapy, Romance languages, secretarial studies/office management, social science, sociology, speech/rhetoric/public address/debate, teacher aide studies, theater arts/drama, welding technology, word processing.
LIBRARY College of the Desert Library with 42,000 books, 100 microform titles, 260 periodicals, 4 CD-ROMs, 600 records, tapes, and CDs. Acquisition spending 1994–95: $60,000.
COMPUTERS ON CAMPUS 13 computers for student use in library.
COLLEGE LIFE Drama-theater group, choral group, student-run newspaper. 10% vote in student government elections. *Most popular organizations:* Student Association, International Club, African-Americans for College Education. *Major annual events:* Homecoming, Mayor's Forum, Rotary Awards. *Student services:* health clinic, personal-psychological counseling. *Campus security:* 24-hour emergency response devices, late-night transport-escort service.
HOUSING College housing not available.
ATHLETICS *Intercollegiate:* baseball M, basketball M/W, cross-country running M/W, football M, golf M/W, soccer M, softball W, tennis M/W, track and field M/W, volleyball W. *Intramural:* badminton, basketball, fencing, golf, soccer, softball, swimming and diving, table tennis (Ping-Pong), tennis, volleyball. *Contact:* Mr. John Marman, Athletic Director, 619-773-2581.
CAREER PLANNING *Placement office:* 1 full-time, 1 part-time staff. *Director:* Ms. Jayne Curenta, Counselor, 619-773-2524. *Services:* job fairs, resume preparation, career counseling, careers library.
EXPENSES FOR 1995–96 State resident tuition: $0 full-time. Nonresident tuition: $3390 full-time, $113 per unit part-time. Part-time mandatory fees per semester range from $23 to $153. Full-time mandatory fees: $410.
FINANCIAL AID *College-administered undergrad aid 1995–96:* 50 need-based scholarships (average $250), 40 non-need scholarships (average $250), short-term loans (average $100), low-interest long-term loans from external sources (average $1500), Federal Work-Study, 15 part-time jobs. *Required forms:* CSS Financial Aid PROFILE, state, institutional, FAFSA. *Priority deadline:* 12/17. *Payment plan:* installment.
APPLYING Open admission except for foreign applicants, nursing program. *Option:* early entrance. *Application deadline:* rolling. *Notification:* continuous. Preference given to district residents.
APPLYING/TRANSFER *Entrance:* noncompetitive. *Application deadline:* rolling. *Notification:* continuous.
CONTACT Ms. Kathi Westerfield, Registrar, College of the Desert, Palm Desert, CA 92260-9305, 619-773-2519.

COLLEGE OF THE REDWOODS
Eureka, California

UG Enrollment: 6,968	Tuition & Fees (CA Res): $405
Application Deadline: rolling	Room & Board: $4768

GENERAL State and locally supported, 2-year, coed. Part of California Community Colleges System. Awards certificates, transfer associate, terminal associate degrees. Founded 1964. *Setting:* 322-acre small-town campus. *Endowment:* $629,806. *Total enrollment:* 6,968. *Faculty:* 376 (116 full-time, 260 part-time).
ENROLLMENT PROFILE 6,968 students from 52 states and territories, 32 other countries. 57% women, 67% part-time, 96% state residents, 2% live on campus, 12% transferred in, 1% international, 52% 25 or older, 6% Native American, 6% Hispanic, 1% African American, 3% Asian American. *Most popular recent majors:* business administration/commerce/management, nursing.
FIRST-YEAR CLASS 1,384 total. Of the students who applied, 100% were accepted.
ACADEMIC PROGRAM Core, interdisciplinary curriculum, honor code. Calendar: semesters. Academic remediation for entering students, English as a second language program offered during academic year, services for LD students, advanced placement, honors program, summer session for credit, part-time degree program (daytime, evenings, summer), adult/continuing education programs, co-op programs.
GENERAL DEGREE REQUIREMENTS 60 units; 3 units each of math and biological/physical science; computer course (varies by major).
MAJORS Agricultural business, agronomy/soil and crop sciences, architectural technologies, automotive technologies, business administration/commerce/management, construction technologies, criminal justice, drafting and design, early childhood education, electron-

College of the Redwoods (continued)
ics engineering technology, forestry, graphic arts, information science, legal secretarial studies, machine and tool technologies, marine sciences, nursing, real estate, secretarial studies/office management, welding technology, word processing.
LIBRARY College of the Redwoods Library with 65,195 books, 315 microform titles, 260 periodicals, 419 records, tapes, and CDs.
COMPUTERS ON CAMPUS 387 computers for student use in computer labs, learning resource center, classrooms, dorms. Staffed computer lab on campus.
COLLEGE LIFE Student-run newspaper. ***Most popular organizations:*** Associated Students College of the Redwoods, Veterans Club, Computer Information Systems Club, Math/Science Club, International Students Club. ***Major annual events:*** Wood Fair, Homecoming, Graduation. ***Student services:*** health clinic, personal-psychological counseling. ***Campus security:*** 24-hour emergency response devices and patrols, late-night transport-escort service.
HOUSING 160 college housing spaces available; all were occupied 1995–96. No special consideration for freshman housing applicants. Off-campus living permitted. ***Option:*** coed housing available. Resident assistants live in dorms.
ATHLETICS ***Intercollegiate:*** baseball M, basketball M/W, cross-country running M/W, football M, golf M/W, track and field M/W, volleyball W. ***Contact:*** Mr. Tom Giacomini, Director of Health/Physical Education, 707-445-6922.
CAREER PLANNING ***Placement office:*** 1 full-time staff. ***Director:*** Ms. Rita Zito, Career Guidance Specialist, 707-445-6773. ***Services:*** resume preparation, career counseling, careers library, job bank, job interviews.
EXPENSES FOR 1995–96 State resident tuition: $0 full-time. Nonresident tuition: $3690 full-time, $123 per unit part-time. Part-time mandatory fees per semester range from $20.50 to $150.50. Full-time mandatory fees: $405. College room and board: $4768.
FINANCIAL AID ***College-administered undergrad aid 1995–96:*** 30 need-based scholarships (average $500), 10 non-need scholarships (average $200), short-term loans (average $75), low-interest long-term loans from external sources (average $2000), Federal Work-Study, 150 part-time jobs. ***Required forms:*** state, institutional; accepted: CSS Financial Aid PROFILE, FAFSA. ***Priority deadline:*** 3/1.
APPLYING Open admission except for nursing program, international students. ***Options:*** early entrance, midyear entrance. ***Required:*** TOEFL for international students. Test scores used for counseling/placement. ***Application deadline:*** rolling.
APPLYING/TRANSFER ***Required for some:*** college transcript. ***Entrance:*** noncompetitive. ***Application deadline:*** rolling. ***Contact:*** Mr. Allen Keppner, Director of Transfer Center, 707-445-6744.
CONTACT Vice President of Student Services, College of the Redwoods, Eureka, CA 95501-9300, 707-445-6722 or toll-free 800-641-0400 (in-state).

COLLEGE OF THE SEQUOIAS
Visalia, California

UG Enrollment: 8,721	**Tuition & Fees (CA Res): $410**
Application Deadline: 8/15	**Room & Board: N/Avail**

GENERAL State and locally supported, 2-year, coed. Part of California Community Colleges System. Awards transfer associate, terminal associate degrees. Founded 1925. ***Setting:*** 215-acre suburban campus. ***Educational spending 1994–95:*** $1805 per undergrad. ***Total enrollment:*** 8,721. ***Faculty:*** 445 (145 full-time, 10% with terminal degrees, 300 part-time). ***Notable Alumni:*** Dr. Gerry Hayward, former chancellor of California Community College System; Bob Ojeda, major league baseball player; Jim Wolhford, vice president of Investments and Branch Co-Manager at AG Edwards and Sons; Robert Line, retired superintendent of Visalia Unified School District; Jim Vidak, superintendent of schools for Tulare County.
ENROLLMENT PROFILE 8,721 students: 59% women, 41% men, 53% part-time, 87% state residents, 8% transferred in, 22% have need-based financial aid, 6% have non-need-based financial aid, 1% international, 40% 25 or older, 2% Native American, 34% Hispanic, 3% African American, 4% Asian American. ***Most popular recent majors:*** liberal arts/general studies, business administration/commerce/management, social science.
FIRST-YEAR CLASS 2,038 total; 3,470 applied, 100% were accepted, 100% of whom enrolled. 12% from top 10% of their high school class, 75% from top half.
ACADEMIC PROGRAM Core, honor code. Calendar: semesters. Average class size 35 in required courses. Academic remediation for entering students, English as a second language program offered during academic year, services for LD students, advanced placement, Freshman Honors College, tutorials, honors program, summer session for credit, part-time degree program (daytime, evenings, weekends, summer), adult/continuing education programs, co-op programs and internships. Study abroad in England, France, Italy, Costa Rica (1% of students participate). ROTC: Air Force (c).
GENERAL DEGREE REQUIREMENTS 60 units; 3 units of intermediate algebra.
MAJORS Accounting, agricultural business, agricultural education, agricultural sciences, agricultural technologies, animal sciences, architectural technologies, art/fine arts, automotive technologies, biology/biological sciences, business administration/commerce/management, carpentry, chemistry, child psychology/child development, commercial art, communication, community services, computer graphics, computer information systems, computer programming, computer science, computer technologies, construction technologies, corrections, cosmetology, criminal justice, culinary arts, dairy sciences, deaf interpreter training, drafting and design, early childhood education, electrical and electronics technologies, engineering (general), (pre)engineering sequence, English, ethnic studies, fashion design and technology, fashion merchandising, fire science, French, graphic arts, health education, heating/refrigeration/air conditioning, history, home economics, home economics education, horticulture, humanities, industrial arts, interior design, journalism, law enforcement/police sciences, liberal arts/general studies, marketing/retailing/merchandising, mathematics, modern languages, music, nursing, ornamental horticulture, paralegal studies, physical education, real estate, science, secretarial studies/office management, social science, sociology, Spanish, speech/rhetoric/public address/debate, sports medicine, theater arts/drama, welding technology, word processing.
LIBRARY College of the Sequoias Library with 72,262 books, 3,542 microform titles, 430 periodicals, 3 on-line bibliographic services, 10 CD-ROMs, 2,486 records, tapes, and CDs. Acquisition spending 1994–95: $472,746.
COMPUTERS ON CAMPUS 44 computers for student use in computer labs, tutorial center, classrooms, library provide access to e-mail, on-line services, Internet. Staffed computer lab on campus provides training in use of computers, software. Academic computing expenditure 1994–95: $323,612.
COLLEGE LIFE Drama-theater group, choral group, student-run newspaper. 20% vote in student government elections. ***Social organizations:*** 35 open to all. ***Most popular organizations:*** MECHA Club, Ag Club, Alpha Gamma Sigma, Paralegal Association, Sports Medicine. ***Major annual events:*** Homecoming, Multi-Cultural Fair, Tech Prep Expo. ***Student services:*** health clinic, personal-psychological counseling, women's center. ***Campus security:*** 24-hour emergency response devices and patrols, student patrols, late-night transport-escort service, 18 hour patrols by trained security personnel.
HOUSING College housing not available.
ATHLETICS ***Intercollegiate:*** baseball M, basketball M/W, cross-country running M/W, equestrian sports M/W, football M, golf M/W, softball W, swimming and diving M/W, tennis M/W, track and field M/W, volleyball W, water polo M, wrestling M. ***Intramural:*** basketball. ***Contact:*** Mr. Al Branco, Athletic Director, 209-730-3911.
CAREER PLANNING ***Placement office:*** 1 full-time, 2 part-time staff; $56,679 operating expenditure 1994–95. ***Director:*** Mr. Floyd Hord, Career Center Coordinator, 209-730-3730. ***Services:*** job fairs, resume preparation, career counseling, careers library, job bank.
EXPENSES FOR 1996–97 State resident tuition: $0 full-time. Nonresident tuition: $3562 full-time, $118 per unit part-time. Part-time mandatory fees per semester range from $23 to $153. Full-time mandatory fees: $410.
FINANCIAL AID ***College-administered undergrad aid 1995–96:*** 2,124 need-based scholarships (average $1062), 600 non-need scholarships (average $310), short-term loans (average $150), low-interest long-term loans from external sources, Federal Work-Study, 275 part-time jobs. ***Required forms:*** institutional, FAFSA. ***Priority deadline:*** 3/2.
APPLYING Open admission except for nursing, engineering, chemistry, math, English programs. ***Option:*** early entrance. ***Required:*** school transcript, TOEFL for international students. Test scores used for counseling/placement. ***Application deadline:*** 8/15. ***Notification:*** continuous.
APPLYING/TRANSFER ***Required for some:*** high school transcript, college transcript. ***Application deadline:*** 8/15. ***Notification:*** continuous. ***Contact:*** Mr. Howard Wren, Transfer Counselor, 209-730-3964.
CONTACT Mr. Robert G. Heath, Dean of Admissions/Registrar, College of the Sequoias, Visalia, CA 93277-2234, 209-730-3792.

COLLEGE OF THE SISKIYOUS
Weed, California

UG Enrollment: 2,888	**Tuition & Fees (CA Res): $410**
Application Deadline: rolling	**Room & Board: $3910**

COS is unusual—a small public community college with dorms and a friendly atmosphere. Located in a beautiful alpine, rural setting in northern California, the College has excellent transfer and vocational programs, free support services, and athletic opportunities. Small classes provide personal attention to students.

GENERAL State and locally supported, 2-year, coed. Part of California Community Colleges System. Awards certificates, transfer associate, terminal associate degrees. Founded 1957. ***Setting:*** 260-acre rural campus. ***Total enrollment:*** 2,888. ***Faculty:*** 146 (54 full-time, 5% with terminal degrees, 92 part-time); student-faculty ratio is 16:1.
ENROLLMENT PROFILE 2,888 students from 11 states and territories, 13 other countries. 64% women, 36% men, 68% part-time, 93% state residents, 4% live on campus, 6% transferred in, 45% have need-based financial aid, 2% international, 63% 25 or older, 4% Native American, 6% Hispanic, 2% African American, 4% Asian American. ***Areas of study chosen:*** 8% business management and administrative services, 3% biological and life sciences, 2% engineering and applied sciences, 1% agriculture, 1% physical sciences. ***Most popular recent majors:*** business administration/commerce/management, engineering (general), social science.
FIRST-YEAR CLASS 454 total; 454 applied, 100% were accepted, 100% of whom enrolled.
ACADEMIC PROGRAM Core, honor code. Calendar: semesters. Academic remediation for entering students, English as a second language program offered during academic year, services for LD students, advanced placement, self-designed majors, honors program, summer session for credit, part-time degree program (daytime, evenings), adult/continuing education programs, co-op programs.
GENERAL DEGREE REQUIREMENTS 60 units; math/science requirements vary according to program.
MAJORS Accounting, art education, automotive technologies, biology/biological sciences, botany/plant sciences, business administration/commerce/management, ceramic art and design, civil engineering technology, computer programming, computer science, cosmetology, criminal justice, data processing, engineering (general), fire science, forestry, history, home economics, law enforcement/police sciences, legal studies, mathematics, music, natural resource management, physical education, physics, political science/government, psychology, real estate, secretarial studies/office management, social science, sociology, studio art, welding technology, wildlife management, zoology.
LIBRARY College of the Siskiyous Library with 41,000 books, 29 microform titles, 196 periodicals, 1 on-line bibliographic service, 5,700 records, tapes, and CDs.
COMPUTERS ON CAMPUS 120 computers for student use in computer labs, classrooms provide access to e-mail, Internet. Staffed computer lab on campus provides training in use of computers, software.
COLLEGE LIFE Drama-theater group, choral group. ***Student services:*** legal services, personal-psychological counseling, women's center. ***Campus security:*** controlled dormitory access.
HOUSING 150 college housing spaces available; all were occupied 1995–96. No special consideration for freshman housing applicants. Off-campus living permitted. ***Option:*** coed housing available. Resident assistants live in dorms.
ATHLETICS ***Intercollegiate:*** baseball M, basketball M/W, cross-country running M/W, football M, softball W, track and field M/W, volleyball W. ***Intramural:*** basketball, bowling, skiing (cross-country), skiing (downhill), tennis, volleyball. ***Contact:*** Ms. Sue Gatlin, Director of Athletics, 916-938-5288.
CAREER PLANNING ***Placement office:*** 1 part-time staff. ***Director:*** Mr. Jim Pratt, Career Center Technician, 916-938-4461. ***Services:*** career counseling, careers library.
AFTER GRADUATION 15% of students completing a degree program in 1994–95 went directly on to further study.
EXPENSES FOR 1995–96 State resident tuition: $0 full-time. Nonresident tuition: $3600 full-time, $120 per unit part-time. Part-time mandatory fees per semester range from $23 to $153. Full-time mandatory fees: $410. College room and board: $3910.

FINANCIAL AID *College-administered undergrad aid 1995–96:* need-based scholarships, short-term loans (average $50), low-interest long-term loans from external sources (average $2200), Federal Work-Study. *Required forms:* institutional, FAFSA. *Priority deadline:* 4/29.
APPLYING Open admission. *Options:* Common Application, early entrance, deferred entrance, midyear entrance. *Required:* TOEFL for international students. Test scores used for counseling/placement. *Application deadline:* rolling. *Notification:* continuous.
APPLYING/TRANSFER *Entrance:* noncompetitive. *Application deadline:* rolling. *Notification:* continuous.
CONTACT Dr. James Arack, Vice President of Student Personnel Services, College of the Siskiyous, Weed, CA 96094-2899, 916-938-5215. *Fax:* 916-938-5227.

COLUMBIA COLLEGE
Sonora, California

UG Enrollment: 2,644	Tuition & Fees (CA Res): $390
Application Deadline: rolling	Room & Board: N/Avail

GENERAL State and locally supported, 2-year, coed. Part of Yosemite Community College District System. Awards certificates, transfer associate, terminal associate degrees. Founded 1968. *Setting:* 200-acre rural campus. *Total enrollment:* 2,644. *Faculty:* 121 (46 full-time, 6% with terminal degrees, 75 part-time); student-faculty ratio is 25:1.
ENROLLMENT PROFILE 2,644 students: 62% women, 52% part-time, 23% transferred in, 7% international, 68% 25 or older, 1% Native American, 3% Hispanic, 7% African American, 8% Asian American. *Areas of study chosen:* 30% interdisciplinary studies, 9% social sciences, 6% performing arts, 3% engineering and applied sciences. *Most popular recent majors:* liberal arts/general studies, business administration/commerce/management.
FIRST-YEAR CLASS Of the students who applied, 100% were accepted, 85% of whom enrolled.
ACADEMIC PROGRAM Core, interdisciplinary curriculum, honor code. Calendar: semesters. Average class size 30 in required courses. Academic remediation for entering students, English as a second language program offered during academic year and summer, services for LD students, advanced placement, tutorials, summer session for credit, part-time degree program (daytime, evenings), adult/continuing education programs, internships.
GENERAL DEGREE REQUIREMENTS 60 units; 1 course in college algebra or higher level math course; computer course for business administration majors.
MAJORS Anthropology, art/fine arts, automotive technologies, biology/biological sciences, business administration/commerce/management, chemistry, child psychology/child development, computer science, culinary arts, earth science, English, environmental sciences, fire science, food services management, food services technology, forest technology, health education, history, hotel and restaurant management, humanities, liberal arts/general studies, mathematics, music, natural resource management, photography, physical education, physical sciences, physics, psychology, secretarial studies/office management, sociology, theater arts/drama.
LIBRARY 34,892 books, 205 microform titles, 320 periodicals, 3,148 records, tapes, and CDs.
COMPUTERS ON CAMPUS 85 computers for student use in computer center, computer labs, high tech center, classrooms, library provide access to Internet. Staffed computer lab on campus provides training in use of computers, software.
COLLEGE LIFE Drama-theater group, choral group. 5% vote in student government elections. *Social organizations:* 7 open to all. *Most popular organizations:* International Club, Jazz Club, Ecology Action Club, Christian Club. *Student services:* health clinic. *Campus security:* 24-hour emergency response devices and patrols, late-night transport-escort service.
HOUSING College housing not available.
ATHLETICS *Intercollegiate:* basketball M, tennis M/W, volleyball W. *Contact:* Ms. Morgan McBride, Athletic Director, 209-533-5184.
CAREER PLANNING *Placement office:* 1 part-time staff. *Director:* Ms. Wendy Archer, Career Center Specialist, 209-533-5271. *Services:* job fairs, resume preparation, resume referral, career counseling, careers library. 10 organizations recruited on campus 1994–95.
AFTER GRADUATION 91% of students completing a degree program in 1994–95 went directly on to further study.
EXPENSES FOR 1996–97 State resident tuition: $0 full-time. Nonresident tuition: $3420 full-time, $114 per unit part-time. Part-time mandatory fees: $13 per unit. Full-time mandatory fees: $390.
FINANCIAL AID *College-administered undergrad aid 1995–96:* 330 need-based scholarships (average $450), 80 non-need scholarships (average $375), short-term loans (average $100), low-interest long-term loans from college funds, loans from external sources (average $700), Federal Work-Study, 75 part-time jobs. *Required forms:* institutional, FAFSA; required for some: state. *Application deadline:* continuous.
APPLYING Open admission. *Options:* Common Application, early entrance, deferred entrance, midyear entrance. *Required:* TOEFL for international students, ACT ASSET, CPT. *Required for some:* school transcript. Test scores used for counseling/placement. *Application deadline:* rolling. *Notification:* continuous.
APPLYING/TRANSFER *Required for some:* standardized test scores, high school transcript, some high school foreign language, college transcript. *Entrance:* noncompetitive. *Application deadline:* rolling. *Notification:* continuous.
CONTACT Ms. Kathy Smith, Coordinator, Admissions and Records, Columbia College, Sonora, CA 95370, 209-533-5231.

COMPTON COMMUNITY COLLEGE
Compton, California

GENERAL State and locally supported, 2-year, coed. Part of California Community Colleges System. Awards transfer associate, terminal associate degrees. Founded 1927. *Setting:* 83-acre urban campus with easy access to Los Angeles. *Total enrollment:* 5,700. *Faculty:* 347 (100 full-time, 247 part-time); student-faculty ratio is 15:1.
EXPENSES FOR 1995–96 State resident tuition: $0 full-time. Nonresident tuition: $3210 full-time, $107 per unit part-time. Part-time mandatory fees per semester range from $20 to $150. Full-time mandatory fees: $428.

CONTACT Mr. John Moling, Dean of Student Affairs, Compton Community College, 1111 East Artesia Boulevard, Compton, CA 90221-5393, 310-637-2660 Ext. 2020. College video available.

CONTRA COSTA COLLEGE
San Pablo, California

UG Enrollment: 9,000	Tuition & Fees (CA Res): $390
Application Deadline: rolling	Room & Board: N/Avail

GENERAL State and locally supported, 2-year, coed. Part of Contra Costa Community College District System. Awards certificates, transfer associate degrees. Founded 1948. *Setting:* 83-acre small-town campus with easy access to San Francisco. *Total enrollment:* 9,000. *Faculty:* 222 (117 full-time, 105 part-time).
ENROLLMENT PROFILE 9,000 students from 5 states and territories, 16 other countries. 62% women, 79% part-time, 98% state residents, 11% transferred in, 54% 25 or older, 1% Native American, 16% Hispanic, 28% African American, 14% Asian American. *Most popular recent majors:* nursing, liberal arts/general studies, business administration/commerce/management.
FIRST-YEAR CLASS 1,650 total. Of the students who applied, 100% were accepted, 90% of whom enrolled.
ACADEMIC PROGRAM Core, honor code. Calendar: semesters. Academic remediation for entering students, English as a second language program offered during academic year and summer, services for LD students, honors program, summer session for credit, part-time degree program (daytime, evenings, weekends, summer), adult/continuing education programs, co-op programs. Off-campus study at University of California, Berkeley, members of the Regional Association of East Bay Colleges and Universities. ROTC: Army (c), Naval (c), Air Force (c).
GENERAL DEGREE REQUIREMENTS 60 units; 3 units of math; 6 units of science; computer course.
MAJORS Anthropology, art/fine arts, automotive technologies, biology/biological sciences, biotechnology, black/African-American studies, business administration/commerce/management, chemistry, computer programming, computer science, criminal justice, culinary arts, dental services, drafting and design, early childhood education, electrical and electronics technologies, emergency medical technology, engineering and applied sciences, English, French, geography, geology, German, Hispanic studies, history, home economics, humanities, industrial arts, Italian, journalism, law enforcement/police sciences, liberal arts/general studies, materials sciences, mathematics, music, nursing, philosophy, physics, political science/government, practical nursing, quality control technology, real estate, secretarial studies/office management, sociology, Spanish, welding technology.
LIBRARY 57,017 books, 9,200 microform titles, 333 periodicals, 4,959 records, tapes, and CDs.
COMPUTERS ON CAMPUS 180 computers for student use in labs provide access to main academic computer. Staffed computer lab on campus.
COLLEGE LIFE Drama-theater group, student-run newspaper. *Student services:* personal-psychological counseling, women's center. *Campus security:* 24-hour patrols.
HOUSING College housing not available.
ATHLETICS *Intercollegiate:* baseball M, basketball M/W, cross-country running M/W, football M, softball W, tennis M/W, track and field M/W, volleyball W. *Contact:* Mr. Vince Maiorana, Director of Athletics, 510-235-7800 Ext. 310.
CAREER PLANNING *Director:* Ms. Phyllis Goldman, Director of Counseling, 510-235-7800 Ext. 233. *Service:* career counseling.
EXPENSES FOR 1996–97 State resident tuition: $0 full-time. Nonresident tuition: $3660 full-time, $122 per unit part-time. Part-time mandatory fees: $13 per unit. Full-time mandatory fees: $390.
FINANCIAL AID *College-administered undergrad aid 1995–96:* need-based scholarships, short-term loans (average $50), Federal Work-Study, part-time jobs. *Required forms:* CSS Financial Aid PROFILE, state, FAFSA; required for some: Stafford Student Loan form. *Priority deadline:* 3/2.
APPLYING Open admission. *Options:* Common Application, early entrance. *Recommended:* SAT I or ACT. Test scores used for counseling/placement. *Application deadline:* rolling.
APPLYING/TRANSFER *Entrance:* noncompetitive.
CONTACT Mrs. Jeanette Moore, Office Manager, Contra Costa College, San Pablo, CA 94806-3195, 510-235-7800 Ext. 211.

COSUMNES RIVER COLLEGE
Sacramento, California

UG Enrollment: 11,245	Tuition & Fees (CA Res): $390
Application Deadline: 8/1	Room & Board: N/Avail

GENERAL District-supported, 2-year, coed. Part of Los Rios Community College District System. Awards certificates, transfer associate, terminal associate degrees. Founded 1970. *Setting:* 180-acre rural campus. *Total enrollment:* 11,245. *Faculty:* 425 (125 full-time, 30% with terminal degrees, 300 part-time).
ENROLLMENT PROFILE 11,245 students from 15 states and territories, 26 other countries. 59% women, 77% part-time, 98% state residents, 22% transferred in, 11% have need-based financial aid, 1% international, 52% 25 or older, 2% Native American, 10% Hispanic, 10% African American, 17% Asian American. *Most popular recent majors:* business administration/commerce/management, automotive technologies, communication.
FIRST-YEAR CLASS 2,381 total. Of the students who applied, 100% were accepted.
ACADEMIC PROGRAM Calendar: semesters. Academic remediation for entering students, English as a second language program offered during academic year and summer, services for LD students, advanced placement, tutorials, honors program, summer session for credit, part-time degree program (daytime, evenings, summer), adult/continuing education programs, co-op programs. Study abroad in England, Malaysia, France.
GENERAL DEGREE REQUIREMENTS 60 units; math competence; 3 units of science.
MAJORS Accounting, advertising, agricultural business, agricultural technologies, agronomy/soil and crop sciences, American studies, animal sciences, applied art, architectural technologies, art/fine arts, automotive technologies, biology/biological sciences, broadcasting, business administration/commerce/management, child care/child and family studies, communication, computer information systems, computer management,

Cosumnes River College (continued)
computer programming, construction management, construction technologies, criminal justice, drafting and design, early childhood education, electrical and electronics technologies, electronics engineering technology, emergency medical technology, (pre)engineering sequence, environmental design, environmental sciences, ethnic studies, family and consumer studies, farm and ranch management, finance/banking, fire science, food services management, food services technology, geology, gerontology, horticulture, humanities, human services, interior design, journalism, landscaping/grounds maintenance, liberal arts/general studies, management information systems, marketing/retailing/merchandising, mathematics, medical assistant technologies, medical records services, medical secretarial studies, music, photography, pollution control technologies, public relations, radio and television studies, real estate, science, social science, theater arts/drama, veterinary technology, women's studies.
LIBRARY Cosumnes River College Library with 55,447 books, 21,563 microform titles, 375 periodicals, 2 CD-ROMs, 2,834 records, tapes, and CDs.
COMPUTERS ON CAMPUS Computer purchase plan available. 190 computers for student use in computer center, learning center. Staffed computer lab on campus provides training in use of computers, software.
COLLEGE LIFE Drama-theater group, choral group, student-run newspaper, radio station. ***Social organizations:*** 16 open to all. ***Most popular organizations:*** Latino/Hispanic Scholars Club, Animal Health Technology Club, Christian Club, Club Mesa, Writers' Workshop. ***Student services:*** health clinic, personal-psychological counseling, women's center. ***Campus security:*** 24-hour emergency response devices and patrols, student patrols, late-night transport-escort service.
HOUSING College housing not available.
ATHLETICS ***Intercollegiate:*** baseball M/W, basketball M/W, soccer M/W, softball W, tennis M/W, track and field M/W, volleyball W. ***Intramural:*** badminton, basketball, bowling, golf, soccer, table tennis (Ping-Pong), tennis, track and field, volleyball. ***Contact:*** Mr. Travis L. Parker, Athletic Director, 916-688-7261; Ms. Barbara Peters, Dean of Physical Education, Health, and Athletics, 916-688-7261.
CAREER PLANNING ***Placement office:*** 2 full-time staff. ***Director:*** Mrs. Claudia Hansson, Dean of Counseling, 916-688-7316. ***Services:*** job fairs, resume preparation, career counseling, job interviews.
EXPENSES FOR 1995–96 State resident tuition: $0 full-time. Nonresident tuition: $3750 full-time, $125 per unit part-time. Part-time mandatory fees: $13 per unit. Full-time mandatory fees: $390.
FINANCIAL AID ***College-administered undergrad aid 1995–96:*** need-based scholarships, low-interest long-term loans from external sources, Federal Work-Study, part-time jobs. ***Required forms:*** CSS Financial Aid PROFILE, institutional, FAFSA. ***Priority deadline:*** 8/1. ***Payment plan:*** installment.
APPLYING Open admission except for foreign applicants. ***Options:*** early entrance, midyear entrance. ***Required:*** TOEFL for international students. ***Recommended:*** SAT I or ACT. Test scores used for counseling/placement. ***Application deadline:*** 8/1. ***Notification:*** continuous until 8/15.
APPLYING/TRANSFER ***Application deadline:*** 8/15. ***Notification:*** continuous until 8/15. ***Contact:*** Mr. Hoyt Fong, Transfer Center Coordinator, 916-688-7479.
CONTACT Mr. Barry W. Tucker, Vice President of Student Services, Cosumnes River College, 8401 Center Parkway, Sacramento, CA 95823-5799, 916-688-7410. College video available.

CRAFTON HILLS COLLEGE
Yucaipa, California

UG Enrollment: 5,041 | **Tuition & Fees (CA Res): $432**
Application Deadline: rolling | **Room & Board: N/Avail**

GENERAL State and locally supported, 2-year, coed. Part of California Community Colleges System. Awards transfer associate, terminal associate degrees. Founded 1972. ***Setting:*** 526-acre small-town campus with easy access to Los Angeles. ***Total enrollment:*** 5,041. ***Faculty:*** 184 (64 full-time, 14% with terminal degrees, 120 part-time); student-faculty ratio is 35:1.
ENROLLMENT PROFILE 5,041 students from 12 states and territories, 12 other countries. 56% women, 72% part-time, 95% state residents, 15% transferred in, 11% have need-based financial aid, 6% have non-need-based financial aid, 1% international, 47% 25 or older, 1% Native American, 17% Hispanic, 4% African American, 4% Asian American. ***Most popular recent major:*** liberal arts/general studies.
FIRST-YEAR CLASS 2,066 total; 2,809 applied, 100% were accepted, 74% of whom enrolled.
ACADEMIC PROGRAM Core, honor code. Calendar: semesters. Academic remediation for entering students, services for LD students, advanced placement, self-designed majors, summer session for credit, part-time degree program (daytime, evenings, summer), adult/continuing education programs, co-op programs.
GENERAL DEGREE REQUIREMENTS 60 credits; 1 course each in math and science.
MAJORS Accounting, anthropology, art/fine arts, astronomy, biology/biological sciences, business administration/commerce/management, chemistry, community services, computer science, criminal justice, economics, emergency medical technology, (pre)engineering sequence, English, fire science, French, geology, history, humanities, human services, liberal arts/general studies, marketing/retailing/merchandising, mathematics, medical secretarial studies, music, philosophy, physical education, physics, political science/government, psychology, radiological technology, religious studies, respiratory therapy, science, secretarial studies/office management, sociology, Spanish, speech/rhetoric/public address/debate, theater arts/drama.
LIBRARY 65,731 books, 33 microform titles, 425 periodicals, 2 on-line bibliographic services, 4 CD-ROMs, 1,903 records, tapes, and CDs.
COMPUTERS ON CAMPUS 52 computers for student use in computer center, learning resource center, classrooms. Staffed computer lab on campus.
COLLEGE LIFE Drama-theater group. 3% vote in student government elections. ***Social organizations:*** 9 open to all. ***Major annual events:*** College Night, Career Fair, Native American Gathering (Pow Wow). ***Student services:*** health clinic, personal-psychological counseling. ***Campus security:*** 24-hour patrols.
HOUSING College housing not available.
CAREER PLANNING ***Placement office:*** 1 full-time staff. ***Director:*** Ms. Linda Cook, Job Placement/Career Guidance Specialist, 909-389-3361. ***Services:*** job fairs, resume preparation, career counseling, careers library, job bank.
EXPENSES FOR 1995–96 State resident tuition: $0 full-time. Nonresident tuition: $3420 full-time, $114 per unit part-time. Part-time mandatory fees per semester range from $25 to $164. Full-time mandatory fees: $432.
FINANCIAL AID ***College-administered undergrad aid 1995–96:*** 564 need-based scholarships (average $570), 308 non-need scholarships (average $500), short-term loans (average $100), low-interest long-term loans from external sources (average $2625), Federal Work-Study, 45 part-time jobs. ***Required forms:*** institutional, FAFSA; required for some: state; accepted: CSS Financial Aid PROFILE. ***Priority deadline:*** 6/1.
APPLYING Open admission. ***Options:*** Common Application, early entrance, deferred entrance, midyear entrance. ***Required:*** TOEFL for international students. Test scores used for counseling/placement. ***Application deadline:*** rolling. ***Notification:*** continuous. Preference given to district residents.
APPLYING/TRANSFER ***Entrance:*** noncompetitive. ***Notification:*** continuous. ***Contact:*** Ms. Violet H. Neuman, Coordinator of Counseling, 909-389-3366.
CONTACT Mrs. Ellen Edgar, Registrar, Crafton Hills College, Yucaipa, CA 92399-1799, 909-389-3372. ***Fax:*** 909-794-0423.

CUESTA COLLEGE
San Luis Obispo, California

UG Enrollment: 7,800 | **Tuition & Fees (CA Res): $390**
Application Deadline: rolling | **Room & Board: N/Avail**

GENERAL District-supported, 2-year, coed. Part of California Community Colleges System. Awards transfer associate, terminal associate degrees. Founded 1964. ***Setting:*** 129-acre rural campus. ***Research spending 1994–95:*** $40,102. ***Educational spending 1994–95:*** $1303 per undergrad. ***Total enrollment:*** 7,800. ***Faculty:*** 292 (107 full-time, 185 part-time).
ENROLLMENT PROFILE 7,800 students: 53% women, 56% part-time, 98% state residents, 15% transferred in, 18% have need-based financial aid, 1% international, 33% 25 or older, 1% Native American, 12% Hispanic, 2% African American, 4% Asian American. ***Most popular recent majors:*** liberal arts/general studies, nursing, business administration/commerce/management.
FIRST-YEAR CLASS 1,638 total. Of the students who applied, 100% were accepted, 40% of whom enrolled.
ACADEMIC PROGRAM Core. Calendar: semesters. Academic remediation for entering students, English as a second language program offered during academic year, services for LD students, advanced placement, tutorials, honors program, summer session for credit, part-time degree program (daytime, evenings, summer), adult/continuing education programs. ROTC: Army (c).
GENERAL DEGREE REQUIREMENTS 60 units; math competence; 1 course of biological/physical science.
MAJORS Agricultural technologies, applied art, art/fine arts, arts administration, automotive technologies, biology/biological sciences, business administration/commerce/management, chemistry, child care/child and family studies, communication, computer science, computer technologies, construction technologies, data processing, early childhood education, electrical and electronics technologies, engineering (general), (pre)engineering sequence, family and consumer studies, fashion merchandising, geology, human development, human services, industrial engineering technology, interior design, journalism, liberal arts/general studies, library science, marketing/retailing/merchandising, mathematics, medical assistant technologies, nursing, nutrition, physical education, physics, psychology, radio and television studies, real estate, recreational facilities management, recreation therapy, secretarial studies/office management, telecommunications, welding technology.
LIBRARY Cuesta College Library with 51,202 books, 118 microform titles, 415 periodicals, 1 on-line bibliographic service, 1,382 records, tapes, and CDs. Acquisition spending 1994–95: $848,084.
COMPUTERS ON CAMPUS Computer purchase plan available. 400 computers for student use in computer center, computer labs, learning resource center, labs, classrooms, library. Staffed computer lab on campus. Academic computing expenditure 1994–95: $217,887.
COLLEGE LIFE Orientation program (2 days, $30, parents included). Drama-theater group, choral group, student-run newspaper, radio station. 15% vote in student government elections. ***Social organizations:*** 10 open to all. ***Most popular organizations:*** Associated Students of Cuesta College, Alpha Gamma Sigma, Student Nurses Association. ***Major annual events:*** Student Life Orientation Days, Jazz Festival, Fall Barbecue. ***Student services:*** health clinic, personal-psychological counseling. ***Campus security:*** 24-hour emergency response devices, student patrols, late-night transport-escort service.
HOUSING College housing not available.
ATHLETICS ***Intercollegiate:*** baseball M, basketball M/W, cross-country running M/W, softball W, swimming and diving M/W, tennis W, track and field M/W, volleyball W, water polo M, wrestling M. ***Contact:*** Mr. Warren Hansen, Athletic Director, 805-546-3210.
CAREER PLANNING ***Placement office:*** 1 full-time, 1 part-time staff; $115,518 operating expenditure 1994–95. ***Services:*** resume preparation, career counseling, careers library, job bank, job interviews.
EXPENSES FOR 1996–97 State resident tuition: $0 full-time. Nonresident tuition: $3420 full-time, $114 per unit part-time. Part-time mandatory fees: $13 per unit. Full-time mandatory fees: $390.
FINANCIAL AID ***College-administered undergrad aid 1995–96:*** 520 need-based scholarships (average $340), short-term loans (average $135), low-interest long-term loans from external sources (average $1964), Federal Work-Study. ***Acceptable forms:*** CSS Financial Aid PROFILE, FAFSA. ***Priority deadline:*** 5/1.
APPLYING Open admission. ***Options:*** early entrance, deferred entrance. ***Required:*** school transcript, TOEFL for international students. Test scores used for counseling/placement. ***Application deadline:*** rolling. ***Notification:*** continuous. Preference given to district residents.
APPLYING/TRANSFER ***Entrance:*** noncompetitive. ***Application deadline:*** rolling. ***Notification:*** continuous.
CONTACT Ms. Sandra McLaughlin, Dean of Student Services, Cuesta College, San Luis Obispo, CA 93403-8106, 805-546-3130.

CUYAMACA COLLEGE
El Cajon, California

UG Enrollment: 4,469 **Tuition & Fees (CA Res): $440**
Application Deadline: rolling **Room & Board: N/Avail**

GENERAL State-supported, 2-year, coed. Part of Grossmont-Cuyamaca Community College District System. Awards transfer associate, terminal associate degrees. Founded 1978. ***Setting:*** 165-acre suburban campus with easy access to San Diego. ***Total enrollment:*** 4,469.
ENROLLMENT PROFILE 4,469 students: 49% women, 86% part-time, 98% state residents, 32% transferred in, 1% international, 63% 25 or older, 2% Native American, 10% Hispanic, 2% African American, 5% Asian American.
FIRST-YEAR CLASS 1,825 total. Of the students who applied, 100% were accepted.
ACADEMIC PROGRAM Core. Calendar: semesters. Academic remediation for entering students, English as a second language program offered during academic year, services for LD students, advanced placement, self-designed majors, summer session for credit, part-time degree program (daytime, evenings, weekends, summer), adult/continuing education programs, co-op programs. Study abroad in Mexico. ROTC: Army (c), Air Force (c).
GENERAL DEGREE REQUIREMENTS 60 units; math/science requirements vary according to program.
MAJORS Accounting, air traffic control, architectural technologies, automotive technologies, aviation administration, business administration/commerce/management, child psychology/child development, computer technologies, construction technologies, drafting and design, electrical and electronics technologies, engineering technology, illustration, landscaping/grounds maintenance, liberal arts/general studies, ornamental horticulture, real estate, surveying technology.
LIBRARY 25,000 books, 3,465 microform titles, 300 periodicals, 892 records, tapes, and CDs.
COMPUTERS ON CAMPUS 125 computers for student use in computer center. Staffed computer lab on campus.
COLLEGE LIFE Student-run newspaper. ***Student services:*** health clinic, personal-psychological counseling.
HOUSING College housing not available.
ATHLETICS ***Intercollegiate:*** soccer M.
CAREER PLANNING ***Director:*** Ms. Nancy Davis, Job Development Specialist, 619-670-1980 Ext. 437. ***Service:*** career counseling.
EXPENSES FOR 1996–97 State resident tuition: $0 full-time. Nonresident tuition: $3390 full-time, $113 per unit part-time. Part-time mandatory fees: $13 per unit. Full-time mandatory fees: $440.
FINANCIAL AID ***College-administered undergrad aid 1995–96:*** 62 need-based scholarships, low-interest long-term loans from external sources (average $2600), Federal Work-Study, part-time jobs. ***Required forms:*** institutional, FAFSA; accepted: CSS Financial Aid PROFILE, state. ***Priority deadline:*** 12/18.
APPLYING Open admission. ***Option:*** early entrance. ***Required:*** TOEFL for international students, ACT ASSET. Test scores used for counseling/placement. ***Application deadline:*** rolling.
APPLYING/TRANSFER ***Entrance:*** noncompetitive. ***Application deadline:*** rolling.
CONTACT Mrs. Jeanne Hyde, Associate Dean of Admissions, Cuyamaca College, El Cajon, CA 92019-4304, 619-670-1980 Ext. 302.

CYPRESS COLLEGE
Cypress, California

UG Enrollment: 14,350 **Tuition & Fees (CA Res): $390**
Application Deadline: 8/25 **Room & Board: N/Avail**

GENERAL State and locally supported, 2-year, coed. Part of California Community Colleges System. Awards certificates, transfer associate, terminal associate degrees. Founded 1966. ***Setting:*** 108-acre suburban campus with easy access to Los Angeles. ***Total enrollment:*** 14,350. ***Faculty:*** 434 (209 full-time, 225 part-time); student-faculty ratio is 34:1.
ENROLLMENT PROFILE 14,350 students from 15 states and territories, 18 other countries. 58% women, 66% part-time, 98% state residents, 13% transferred in, 1% international, 45% 25 or older, 1% Native American, 16% Hispanic, 4% African American, 22% Asian American.
FIRST-YEAR CLASS 9,231 total. Of the students who applied, 100% were accepted.
ACADEMIC PROGRAM Core, general education curriculum, honor code. Calendar: semesters. Academic remediation for entering students, English as a second language program offered during academic year, services for LD students, advanced placement, summer session for credit, part-time degree program (daytime, evenings, summer), adult/continuing education programs. Study abroad in England, France, Austria, Italy. ROTC: Army (c), Naval (c), Air Force (c).
GENERAL DEGREE REQUIREMENTS 60 units; math/science requirements vary according to program; computer course.
MAJORS Accounting, advertising, anthropology, applied art, art/fine arts, Asian/Oriental studies, automotive technologies, aviation administration, biology/biological sciences, business administration/commerce/management, chemistry, computer science, court reporting, culinary arts, dance, data processing, dental services, economics, engineering (general), English, food services management, funeral service, geography, geology, health science, history, hotel and restaurant management, human services, Latin American studies, liberal arts/general studies, marketing/retailing/merchandising, mathematics, medical records services, medical secretarial studies, music, natural sciences, nursing, philosophy, photography, physical education, physics, political science/government, psychology, radiological technology, recreation and leisure services, science, secretarial studies/office management, social science, sociology, speech/rhetoric/public address/debate, theater arts/drama, tourism and travel, vocational education.
LIBRARY Cypress College Library with 58,000 books, 257 microform titles, 436 periodicals, 691 records, tapes, and CDs.
COMPUTERS ON CAMPUS 500 computers for student use in computer center, library, student center.
COLLEGE LIFE Drama-theater group, choral group, student-run newspaper, radio station. 12% vote in student government elections. ***Student services:*** legal services, health clinic, personal-psychological counseling, women's center. ***Campus security:*** 24-hour emergency response devices.
HOUSING College housing not available.
ATHLETICS ***Intercollegiate:*** baseball M, basketball M/W, golf M, soccer M/W, softball W, swimming and diving M/W, tennis M/W, volleyball W, water polo M, wrestling M. ***Contact:*** Ms. Diane Henry, Athletic Director, 714-826-2220.
CAREER PLANNING ***Placement office:*** 2 full-time, 5 part-time staff. ***Director:*** Mr. Art Wood, Director of Career Planning Center, 714-826-2220. ***Services:*** job fairs, career counseling, careers library, job bank.
EXPENSES FOR 1996–97 State resident tuition: $0 full-time. Nonresident tuition: $3510 full-time, $117 per unit part-time. Part-time mandatory fees: $13 per unit. Full-time mandatory fees: $390.
FINANCIAL AID ***College-administered undergrad aid 1995–96:*** need-based scholarships, non-need scholarships, Federal Work-Study, part-time jobs. ***Required forms:*** CSS Financial Aid PROFILE, institutional; required for some: state, FAFSA. ***Application deadline:*** continuous.
APPLYING Open admission. ***Options:*** early entrance, midyear entrance. ***Required:*** TOEFL for international students. ***Recommended:*** school transcript. Test scores used for counseling/placement. ***Application deadline:*** 8/25.
APPLYING/TRANSFER ***Required:*** college transcript. ***Entrance:*** noncompetitive. ***Application deadline:*** 8/25.
CONTACT Ms. Carlene A. Gibson, Dean of Admissions and Records, Cypress College, Cypress, CA 90630-5897, 714-826-2220 Ext. 345.

DE ANZA COLLEGE
Cupertino, California

UG Enrollment: 23,497 **Tuition & Fees (CA Res): $471**
Application Deadline: rolling **Room & Board: N/Avail**

GENERAL State and locally supported, 2-year, coed. Part of California Community Colleges System. Awards certificates, diplomas, transfer associate, terminal associate degrees. Founded 1967. ***Setting:*** 112-acre small-town campus with easy access to San Jose and San Francisco. ***Total enrollment:*** 23,497. ***Faculty:*** 890 (345 full-time, 545 part-time).
ENROLLMENT PROFILE 23,497 students from 50 states and territories, 71 other countries. 54% women, 46% men, 67% part-time, 93% state residents, 33% transferred in, 1% international, 52% 25 or older, 1% Native American, 12% Hispanic, 4% African American, 30% Asian American.
FIRST-YEAR CLASS 6,907 total; 8,023 applied, 87% were accepted, 99% of whom enrolled.
ACADEMIC PROGRAM Core, honor code. Calendar: quarters. Academic remediation for entering students, English as a second language program offered during academic year and summer, services for LD students, advanced placement, honors program, summer session for credit, part-time degree program (daytime, evenings, summer), external degree programs, adult/continuing education programs, co-op programs. Study abroad in England, France (1% of students participate). ROTC: Army (c), Air Force (c).
GENERAL DEGREE REQUIREMENTS 90 units; 1 course each in elementary algebra and science; computer course.
MAJORS Accounting, art/fine arts, automotive technologies, behavioral sciences, biochemical technology, biology/biological sciences, biotechnology, business administration/commerce/management, child care/child and family studies, child psychology/child development, communication, computer information systems, computer science, corrections, criminal justice, dance, economics, electrical and electronics technologies, engineering and applied sciences, (pre)engineering sequence, engineering technology, English, environmental studies, ethnic studies, film studies, history, humanities, industrial engineering technology, international studies, journalism, law enforcement/police sciences, liberal arts/general studies, machine and tool technologies, manufacturing technology, marketing/retailing/merchandising, mathematics, mechanical design technology, medical assistant technologies, music, nursing, paralegal studies, philosophy, photography, physical education, physical therapy, physics, political science/government, psychology, purchasing/inventory management, radio and television studies, real estate, recreation and leisure services, secretarial studies/office management, social science, sociology, Spanish, technical writing, theater arts/drama.
LIBRARY A. Robert DeHart Learning Center with 80,000 books, 7,000 microform titles, 927 periodicals, 27,500 records, tapes, and CDs.
COMPUTERS ON CAMPUS 800 computers for student use in computer center, computer labs, library.
COLLEGE LIFE Orientation program (1 week, $4). Drama-theater group, choral group, student-run newspaper. 3% vote in student government elections. ***Social organizations:*** 45 open to all. ***Most popular organizations:*** Disabled Student Union, PTK, Ski Club, Vietnamese Student Club, Photo Club. ***Major annual events:*** Graduation, Orientation, Club Day. ***Student services:*** legal services, health clinic, personal-psychological counseling, women's center. ***Campus security:*** 24-hour emergency response devices, student patrols, late-night transport-escort service.
HOUSING College housing not available.
ATHLETICS ***Intercollegiate:*** baseball M, basketball M/W, cross-country running M/W, football M, golf M/W, soccer M/W, softball W, swimming and diving M/W, tennis M/W, track and field M/W, volleyball M/W, water polo M/W. ***Intramural:*** badminton, basketball, bowling, fencing, golf, gymnastics, racquetball, soccer, swimming and diving, tennis, volleyball, weight lifting. ***Contact:*** Mr. Glen Hanley, Dean of Physical Education/Athletics, 408-864-8402.
CAREER PLANNING ***Placement office:*** 1 full-time staff. ***Director:*** Ms. Shirley Kawazoe, Coordinator, Transfer and Career Planning Center, 408-864-8552. ***Services:*** resume preparation, career counseling, careers library, job interviews. 10 organizations recruited on campus 1994–95.
AFTER GRADUATION 13% of students completing a degree program in 1994–95 went directly on to further study.
EXPENSES FOR 1996–97 State resident tuition: $0 full-time. Nonresident tuition: $3510 full-time, $78 per unit part-time. Part-time mandatory fees per quarter range from $31 to $121. Part-time tuition for international students per unit: $83. Full-time mandatory fees: $471.

California

De Anza College (continued)
FINANCIAL AID *College-administered undergrad aid 1995–96:* 275 need-based scholarships (average $1200), 75 non-need scholarships (average $200), short-term loans (average $100), low-interest long-term loans from external sources (average $2500), 221 Federal Work-Study (averaging $1200), 500 part-time jobs. *Required forms:* institutional, FAFSA; required for some: state; accepted: CSS Financial Aid PROFILE. *Priority deadline:* 3/2.
APPLYING Open admission except for nursing program. *Options:* Common Application, early entrance. *Required:* TOEFL for international students. *Recommended:* 3 years of high school math and science, some high school foreign language. Test scores used for counseling/placement. *Application deadline:* rolling. *Notification:* continuous.
APPLYING/TRANSFER *Entrance:* noncompetitive. *Application deadline:* rolling. *Notification:* continuous.
CONTACT Mrs. Beverly Reeder, Admissions and Records, De Anza College, Cupertino, CA 95014-5793, 408-864-8419.

DEEP SPRINGS COLLEGE
Deep Springs, California

UG Enrollment: 25	Comprehensive Fee: $0
Application Deadline: 11/15	Room & Board: N/App

GENERAL Independent, 2-year, men only. Awards transfer associate degrees. Founded 1917. *Setting:* 3,000-acre rural campus. *Research spending 1994–95:* $65,000. *Educational spending 1994–95:* $34,800 per undergrad. *Total enrollment:* 25. *Faculty:* 20 (4 full-time, 100% with terminal degrees, 16 part-time); student-faculty ratio is 4:1.
ENROLLMENT PROFILE 25 students from 17 states and territories. 0% women, 0% part-time, 3% state residents, 14% transferred in, 0% international, 0% 25 or older, 0% Native American, 0% Hispanic, 0% African American, 0% Asian American. *Areas of study chosen:* 100% liberal arts/general studies.
FIRST-YEAR CLASS 13 total; 220 applied, 8% were accepted, 76% of whom enrolled. 100% from top 10% of their high school class.
ACADEMIC PROGRAM Liberal arts and sciences curriculum, honor code. Calendar: 6 seven-week terms. 40 courses offered in 1995–96. Tutorials, honors program, summer session for credit.
MAJOR Liberal arts/general studies.
LIBRARY 25,000 books, 60 periodicals, 500 records, tapes, and CDs. Acquisition spending 1994–95: $3200.
COMPUTERS ON CAMPUS 6 computers for student use in library. Academic computing expenditure 1994–95: $20,000.
NOTEWORTHY RESEARCH FACILITIES Lab for Desert Ecology.
COLLEGE LIFE Orientation program. Drama-theater group, choral group, student-run radio station. *Most popular organizations:* Student Self-Government, Labor Program. *Major annual events:* Potato Harvest, Cattle Round-up, Thanksgiving Football Game. *Student services:* personal-psychological counseling.
HOUSING 28 college housing spaces available; 25 were occupied 1995–96. Freshmen guaranteed college housing. On-campus residence required through sophomore year. *Option:* single-sex (1 building) housing available.
AFTER GRADUATION 92% of students completing a degree program in 1994–95 went directly on to further study.
EXPENSES FOR 1995–96 Comprehensive fee: $0. All students are on full scholarship.
APPLYING *Option:* early entrance. *Required:* essay, school transcript, 2 years of high school foreign language, campus interview, SAT I, 2 SAT II Subject Tests. Test scores used for admission. *Application deadline:* 11/15. *Notification:* 4/15.
APPLYING/TRANSFER *Required:* essay, standardized test scores, high school transcript, 2 years of high school foreign language, campus interview, college transcript. *Application deadline:* 11/15. *Notification:* 4/15.
CONTACT Dr. L. Jackson Newell, President, Deep Springs College, HC 72, Box 45001, Dyer, NV 89010-9803, 619-872-2000.

DIABLO VALLEY COLLEGE
Pleasant Hill, California

UG Enrollment: 21,000	Tuition & Fees (CA Res): $390
Application Deadline: rolling	Room & Board: N/Avail

GENERAL State and locally supported, 2-year, coed. Part of Contra Costa Community College District System. Awards certificates, transfer associate degrees. Founded 1949. *Setting:* 100-acre small-town campus with easy access to San Francisco. *Total enrollment:* 21,000. *Faculty:* 800 (300 full-time, 500 part-time).
ENROLLMENT PROFILE 21,000 students: 55% women, 70% part-time, 98% state residents, 0% international, 1% Native American, 4% Hispanic, 2% African American, 4% Asian American.
FIRST-YEAR CLASS Of the students who applied, 100% were accepted.
ACADEMIC PROGRAM Core. Calendar: semesters. Academic remediation for entering students, services for LD students, advanced placement, self-designed majors, summer session for credit, part-time degree program (daytime, evenings, weekends, summer), adult/continuing education programs, co-op programs. Study abroad in England. ROTC: Air Force (c).
GENERAL DEGREE REQUIREMENTS 60 units; math proficiency or 1 math course.
MAJOR Liberal arts/general studies.
LIBRARY 73,821 books, 179 microform titles, 428 periodicals, 10,539 records, tapes, and CDs.
COMPUTERS ON CAMPUS 450 computers for student use in computer center, classrooms, library.
COLLEGE LIFE Drama-theater group, student-run newspaper. *Student services:* women's center.
HOUSING College housing not available.
ATHLETICS *Intercollegiate:* basketball M/W, cross-country running M/W, football M, gymnastics W, soccer M, swimming and diving M/W, tennis M/W, track and field M/W, volleyball W, wrestling M.
CAREER PLANNING *Director:* Mr. Paul Nilsen, Manager of Career Information Services, 510-685-1230. *Service:* career counseling.

EXPENSES FOR 1996–97 State resident tuition: $0 full-time. Nonresident tuition: $4050 full-time, $135 per unit part-time. Part-time mandatory fees: $13 per unit. Full-time mandatory fees: $390.
FINANCIAL AID *College-administered undergrad aid 1995–96:* need-based scholarships, 125 non-need scholarships (average $250), low-interest long-term loans from external sources (average $1000), Federal Work-Study, part-time jobs. *Required forms:* FAFSA; required for some: CSS Financial Aid PROFILE. *Priority deadline:* 5/1.
APPLYING Open admission. *Option:* early entrance. *Required:* TOEFL for international students. *Recommended:* school transcript. Test scores used for admission. *Application deadline:* rolling.
APPLYING/TRANSFER *Recommended:* high school transcript. *Application deadline:* rolling.
CONTACT Ms. Jeanette Moore, Director of Admissions and Records, Diablo Valley College, Pleasant Hill, CA 94523-1544, 510-685-1230 Ext. 330.

DON BOSCO TECHNICAL INSTITUTE
Rosemead, California

UG Enrollment: 950	Tuition & Fees: $5000
Application Deadline: 8/1	Room & Board: N/Avail

GENERAL Independent, 2-year, men only, affiliated with Roman Catholic Church. Awards transfer associate, terminal associate degrees (only Don Bosco Technical High School graduates are eligible for admission). Founded 1955. *Setting:* 30-acre suburban campus with easy access to Los Angeles. *Total enrollment:* 950. *Faculty:* 32 (all full-time).
ENROLLMENT PROFILE 950 students: 0% women, 0% part-time, 100% state residents, 0% transferred in, 0% international, 0% 25 or older, 0% Native American, 66% Hispanic, 1% African American, 10% Asian American. *Most popular recent majors:* graphic arts, construction technologies, drafting and design.
FIRST-YEAR CLASS 42 total. Of the students who applied, 95% were accepted, 80% of whom enrolled. 2% from top 10% of their high school class, 13% from top quarter, 36% from top half.
ACADEMIC PROGRAM Core. Calendar: semesters. Advanced placement, co-op programs.
GENERAL DEGREE REQUIREMENTS 64 units; 1 course each in math and science.
MAJORS Automotive technologies, construction technologies, drafting and design, electrical and electronics technologies, graphic arts, manufacturing technology, metallurgical technology, printing technologies.
LIBRARY 16,400 books, 70 periodicals, 800 records, tapes, and CDs.
COMPUTERS ON CAMPUS 75 computers for student use in computer center, computer labs. Staffed computer lab on campus provides training in use of computers, software.
COLLEGE LIFE *Student services:* personal-psychological counseling.
HOUSING College housing not available.
ATHLETICS *Intramural:* baseball, basketball, cross-country running, football, soccer, volleyball, weight lifting.
CAREER PLANNING *Service:* career counseling.
AFTER GRADUATION 85% of students completing a degree program in 1994–95 went directly on to further study.
EXPENSES FOR 1996–97 Tuition: $4800 full-time. Full-time mandatory fees: $200.
FINANCIAL AID *College-administered undergrad aid 1995–96:* 5 need-based scholarships (average $500), low-interest long-term loans from external sources (average $2500), Federal Work-Study, 4 part-time jobs. *Acceptable forms:* CSS Financial Aid PROFILE, state, FAFSA. *Priority deadline:* 3/2. *Payment plan:* installment. *Waivers:* full or partial for employees or children of employees.
APPLYING Open admission. *Required:* minimum 2.0 GPA, 3 years of high school math, 2 years of high school foreign language, recommendations, TOEFL for international students. *Required for some:* SAT I or ACT. Test scores used for admission. *Application deadline:* 8/1.
APPLYING/TRANSFER *Required:* 3 years of high school math, 2 years of high school foreign language, minimum 2.0 high school GPA. *Application deadline:* 8/1.
CONTACT Ms. Margie McTeer, Director of Admissions/College Class Dean, Don Bosco Technical Institute, Rosemead, CA 91770-4299, 818-307-6553. College video available.

D-Q UNIVERSITY
Davis, California

UG Enrollment: 466	Tuition & Fees: $2900
Application Deadline: rolling	Room & Board: $4352

GENERAL Independent, 2-year, coed. Awards certificates, transfer associate, terminal associate degrees. Founded 1971. *Setting:* 640-acre rural campus with easy access to Sacramento. *Total enrollment:* 466. *Faculty:* 31 (17 full-time, 100% with terminal degrees, 14 part-time); student-faculty ratio is 10:1.
ENROLLMENT PROFILE 466 students from 20 states and territories, 1 other country. 70% women, 45% part-time, 85% state residents, 34% transferred in, 50% 25 or older, 71% Native American, 13% Hispanic, 0% African American. *Areas of study chosen:* 60% liberal arts/general studies, 10% computer and information sciences, 10% natural resource sciences, 5% area and ethnic studies, 5% biological and life sciences, 5% business management and administrative services, 5% engineering and applied sciences.
FIRST-YEAR CLASS 73 total. Of the students who applied, 100% were accepted, 85% of whom enrolled. 10% from top half of their high school class.
ACADEMIC PROGRAM Core, honor code. Calendar: semesters. 75 courses offered in 1995–96. Academic remediation for entering students, English as a second language program offered during academic year, self-designed majors, tutorials, summer session for credit, part-time degree program (daytime, evenings), adult/continuing education programs, internships. Off-campus study at members of the American Indian Higher Education Consortium.
GENERAL DEGREE REQUIREMENTS 60 units; math/science requirements vary according to program; internship (some majors).
MAJORS Agricultural sciences, art/fine arts, business administration/commerce/ management, city/community/regional planning, computer science, engineering technology, liberal arts/general studies, Native American studies, social science.
LIBRARY 26,400 books, 10 periodicals.

Peterson's Guide to Two-Year Colleges 1997

COMPUTERS ON CAMPUS 30 computers for student use in computer labs, learning resource center, dorms. Staffed computer lab on campus provides training in use of computers, software.
COLLEGE LIFE Orientation program (1 week, no cost). Student-run newspaper. ***Student services:*** personal-psychological counseling. ***Campus security:*** 24-hour emergency response devices, student patrols, late-night transport-escort service.
HOUSING 40 college housing spaces available; all were occupied 1995–96. Freshmen guaranteed college housing. Off-campus living permitted. ***Option:*** coed (2 buildings) housing available. Resident assistants live in dorms.
ATHLETICS ***Intramural:*** archery, basketball, cross-country running, gymnastics, softball, tennis, track and field, volleyball, wrestling.
CAREER PLANNING ***Service:*** career counseling.
EXPENSES FOR 1996–97 Comprehensive fee of $7252 includes full-time tuition ($2800), mandatory fees ($100), and college room and board ($4352). College room only: $2612. Part-time tuition: $24.50 per unit.
FINANCIAL AID ***College-administered undergrad aid 1995–96:*** 45 need-based scholarships (average $500), Federal Work-Study. ***Acceptable forms:*** CSS Financial Aid PROFILE, state. ***Application deadline:*** continuous to 3/30. ***Payment plan:*** installment. ***Waivers:*** full or partial for minority students and employees or children of employees.
APPLYING Open admission. ***Options:*** early entrance, deferred entrance. ***Required:*** school transcript, TABE. Test scores used for counseling/placement. ***Application deadline:*** rolling.
APPLYING/TRANSFER ***Required:*** high school transcript, college transcript. ***Entrance:*** noncompetitive. ***Application deadline:*** rolling.
CONTACT Ms. Wynona Batcho, Registrar, D-Q University, Davis, CA 95617-0409, 916-758-0470. ***Fax:*** 916-758-4891.

EAST LOS ANGELES COLLEGE
Monterey Park, California

UG Enrollment: 15,100	**Tuition & Fees (CA Res): $390**
Application Deadline: 8/19	**Room & Board: N/Avail**

GENERAL State and locally supported, 2-year, coed. Part of Los Angeles Community College District System. Awards transfer associate, terminal associate degrees. Founded 1945. ***Setting:*** 84-acre urban campus with easy access to Los Angeles. ***Total enrollment:*** 15,100. ***Faculty:*** 450 (250 full-time, 200 part-time).
ENROLLMENT PROFILE 15,100 students: 65% women, 68% part-time, 95% state residents, 10% transferred in, 1% international, 60% 25 or older, 1% Native American, 67% Hispanic, 5% African American, 15% Asian American. ***Most popular recent majors:*** business administration/commerce/management, (pre)engineering sequence.
FIRST-YEAR CLASS 5,000 total. Of the students who applied, 100% were accepted, 80% of whom enrolled.
ACADEMIC PROGRAM Core, honor code. Calendar: semesters. Academic remediation for entering students, English as a second language program offered during academic year, services for LD students, advanced placement, honors program, part-time degree program (daytime, evenings, summer), adult/continuing education programs, co-op programs.
GENERAL DEGREE REQUIREMENTS 60 units; 1 course each in math and science.
MAJORS Accounting, anthropology, architectural technologies, art/fine arts, Asian/Oriental studies, automotive technologies, biology/biological sciences, business administration/commerce/management, chemistry, child care/child and family studies, child psychology/child development, civil engineering technology, computer programming, computer technologies, criminal justice, data processing, drafting and design, electrical and electronics technologies, emergency medical technology, engineering (general), (pre)engineering sequence, English, environmental sciences, fashion design and technology, finance/banking, fire science, French, geography, geology, guidance and counseling, history, home economics, Japanese, journalism, law enforcement/police sciences, legal secretarial studies, liberal arts/general studies, marketing/retailing/merchandising, mathematics, medical assistant technologies, medical records services, medical secretarial studies, Mexican-American/Chicano studies, music, nursing, philosophy, photography, physical education, political science/government, psychology, public administration, real estate, respiratory therapy, secretarial studies/office management, social work, sociology, Spanish, speech/rhetoric/public address/debate, theater arts/drama, vocational education.
LIBRARY 80,000 books, 400 periodicals, 1,227 records, tapes, and CDs.
COMPUTERS ON CAMPUS Computers for student use in learning resource center.
COLLEGE LIFE Drama-theater group, choral group, student-run newspaper, radio station. 10% vote in student government elections. ***Most popular organizations:*** Asian Club, Spanish Club, Chicanos for Creative Medicine. ***Major annual events:*** Cinco de Mayo, Black Week, Asian Week. ***Student services:*** health clinic, personal-psychological counseling. ***Campus security:*** 24-hour emergency response devices and patrols, late-night transport-escort service.
HOUSING College housing not available.
ATHLETICS ***Intercollegiate:*** basketball M, football M, soccer M, softball W, wrestling M. ***Contact:*** Mr. Gilbert Rozavilla, Athletic Director, 213-265-8713.
CAREER PLANNING ***Service:*** career counseling.
AFTER GRADUATION 15% of students completing a degree program in 1994–95 went directly on to further study.
EXPENSES FOR 1996–97 State resident tuition: $0 full-time. Nonresident tuition: $4110 full-time, $137 per unit part-time. Part-time mandatory fees: $13 per unit. Full-time mandatory fees: $390.
FINANCIAL AID ***College-administered undergrad aid 1995–96:*** 60 need-based scholarships (average $100), short-term loans (average $75), low-interest long-term loans, Federal Work-Study, 150 part-time jobs. ***Required forms:*** CSS Financial Aid PROFILE, institutional, FAFSA. ***Priority deadline:*** 4/30.
APPLYING Open admission. ***Option:*** early entrance. ***Application deadline:*** 8/19. ***Notification:*** continuous until 8/19.
APPLYING/TRANSFER ***Application deadline:*** 8/19. ***Notification:*** continuous until 8/19.
CONTACT Mr. Daniel Orneles, Associate Dean of Admissions, East Los Angeles College, 1301 Avenida Cesar Chavez, Monterey Park, CA 91754-6001, 213-265-8650.

EL CAMINO COLLEGE
Torrance, California

UG Enrollment: 21,860	**Tuition & Fees (CA Res): $410**
Application Deadline: rolling	**Room & Board: N/Avail**

GENERAL District-supported, 2-year, coed. Part of California Community Colleges System. Awards certificates, diplomas, transfer associate degrees. Founded 1947. ***Setting:*** 115-acre urban campus with easy access to Los Angeles. ***Total enrollment:*** 21,860. ***Faculty:*** 533 (330 full-time, 203 part-time).
ENROLLMENT PROFILE 21,860 students: 54% women, 77% part-time, 98% state residents, 18% transferred in, 2% international, 45% 25 or older, 1% Native American, 14% Hispanic, 19% African American, 13% Asian American.
FIRST-YEAR CLASS 4,200 total. Of the students who applied, 100% were accepted, 75% of whom enrolled.
ACADEMIC PROGRAM Core. Calendar: semesters. Academic remediation for entering students, English as a second language program offered during academic year, services for LD students, advanced placement, self-designed majors, honors program, summer session for credit, part-time degree program (daytime, evenings, summer), co-op programs.
GENERAL DEGREE REQUIREMENTS 60 units; 1 college math course.
MAJORS Accounting, advertising, American studies, anthropology, architectural technologies, art/fine arts, art history, Asian/Oriental studies, astronomy, automotive technologies, biology/biological sciences, black/African-American studies, botany/plant sciences, business administration/commerce/management, chemistry, construction technologies, cosmetology, culinary arts, data processing, drafting and design, early childhood education, economics, electrical and electronics technologies, engineering (general), English, fashion design and technology, finance/banking, fire science, food services management, forest technology, geography, geology, German, gerontology, heating/refrigeration/air conditioning, history, home economics, horticulture, industrial arts, interior design, Italian, Japanese, journalism, labor studies, law enforcement/police sciences, liberal arts/general studies, marketing/retailing/merchandising, mathematics, medical assistant technologies, music, nursing, ornamental horticulture, paralegal studies, philosophy, photography, physical education, physical sciences, physics, political science/government, practical nursing, psychology, real estate, respiratory therapy, Russian, secretarial studies/office management, social work, sociology, Spanish, speech/rhetoric/public address/debate, technical writing, theater arts/drama, welding technology, zoology.
LIBRARY 116,051 books, 864 periodicals, 3,305 records, tapes, and CDs.
COMPUTERS ON CAMPUS 151 computers for student use in computer center, various locations throughout campus, library.
COLLEGE LIFE Orientation program (2 days, no cost). Drama-theater group, student-run newspaper. ***Student services:*** health clinic, personal-psychological counseling, women's center.
HOUSING College housing not available.
ATHLETICS ***Intercollegiate:*** basketball M/W, cross-country running M/W, football M, golf M, gymnastics W, soccer M, swimming and diving M/W, tennis M/W, track and field M/W, volleyball M/W, wrestling M. ***Intramural:*** archery, badminton, bowling.
CAREER PLANNING ***Service:*** career counseling.
EXPENSES FOR 1996–97 State resident tuition: $0 full-time. Nonresident tuition: $3510 full-time, $117 per unit part-time. Part-time mandatory fees per semester range from $23 to $153. Full-time mandatory fees: $410.
FINANCIAL AID ***College-administered undergrad aid 1995–96:*** 124 need-based scholarships (average $278), short-term loans (average $100), Federal Work-Study, 141 part-time jobs. ***Required forms:*** institutional, FAFSA. ***Application deadline:*** continuous.
APPLYING Open admission. ***Option:*** early entrance. ***Required:*** school transcript, TOEFL for international students. Test scores used for admission. ***Application deadline:*** rolling. ***Notification:*** continuous.
APPLYING/TRANSFER ***Required:*** high school transcript, college transcript. ***Application deadline:*** rolling. ***Notification:*** continuous.
CONTACT Mr. William Robinson, Director of Admissions, El Camino College, 16007 Crenshaw Boulevard, Torrance, CA 90506-0001, 310-660-3418.

EVERGREEN VALLEY COLLEGE
San Jose, California

UG Enrollment: 9,002	**Tuition & Fees (CA Res): $440**
Application Deadline: rolling	**Room & Board: N/Avail**

GENERAL State and locally supported, 2-year, coed. Part of California Community Colleges System. Awards transfer associate, terminal associate degrees. Founded 1975. ***Setting:*** 175-acre urban campus. ***Total enrollment:*** 9,002. ***Faculty:*** 300 (103 full-time, 197 part-time).
ENROLLMENT PROFILE 9,002 students from 23 states and territories, 11 other countries. 54% women, 46% men, 80% part-time, 94% state residents, 2% transferred in, 1% international, 52% 25 or older, 1% Native American, 23% Hispanic, 5% African American, 33% Asian American. ***Most popular recent majors:*** liberal arts/general studies, business administration/commerce/management, drafting and design.
FIRST-YEAR CLASS 2,660 total; 3,409 applied, 100% were accepted, 78% of whom enrolled.
ACADEMIC PROGRAM Core. Calendar: semesters. Academic remediation for entering students, English as a second language program offered during academic year, services for LD students, advanced placement, honors program, summer session for credit, part-time degree program (daytime, evenings, weekends, summer), adult/continuing education programs, co-op programs. Off-campus study at other community colleges in the area. ROTC: Army (c).
GENERAL DEGREE REQUIREMENTS 60 units; computer course.
MAJORS Applied art, automotive technologies, business administration/commerce/management, computer graphics, computer information systems, criminal justice, data processing, drafting and design, electrical and electronics technologies, engineering (general), (pre)engineering sequence, family and consumer studies, fashion merchandising, liberal arts/general studies, management information systems, manufacturing technology, mental health/rehabilitation counseling, nursing, paralegal studies, real estate, secretarial studies/office management.
LIBRARY Evergreen Valley College Library with 42,782 books, 115 microform titles, 368 periodicals, 5,652 records, tapes, and CDs.

Peterson's Guide to Two-Year Colleges 1997

195

Evergreen Valley College (continued)

COMPUTERS ON CAMPUS Computer purchase plan available. 250 computers for student use in computer center, learning resource center. Staffed computer lab on campus provides training in use of computers, software.

COLLEGE LIFE Drama-theater group, choral group, student-run newspaper. ***Student services:*** health clinic, personal-psychological counseling. ***Campus security:*** 24-hour emergency response devices, late-night transport-escort service, patrols by trained security personnel.

HOUSING College housing not available.

ATHLETICS ***Intramural:*** basketball, golf, racquetball, soccer, tennis, volleyball.

CAREER PLANNING ***Placement office:*** 1 full-time staff. ***Director:*** Ms. Vicki Apherton, Library Coordinator, 408-270-6503. ***Services:*** job fairs, career counseling. 22 organizations recruited on campus 1994–95.

EXPENSES FOR 1995–96 State resident tuition: $0 full-time. Nonresident tuition: $3750 full-time, $125 per unit part-time. Part-time mandatory fees per semester range from $24 to $164. Full-time mandatory fees: $440.

FINANCIAL AID ***College-administered undergrad aid 1995–96:*** need-based scholarships (average $250), non-need scholarships (average $250), short-term loans (average $40), 135 Federal Work-Study (averaging $1200), part-time jobs. ***Required forms:*** institutional, FAFSA; accepted: CSS Financial Aid PROFILE. ***Priority deadline:*** 6/16. ***Payment plans:*** installment, deferred payment.

APPLYING Open admission except for nursing program. ***Options:*** early entrance, midyear entrance. ***Required:*** TOEFL for international students. Test scores used for counseling/placement. ***Application deadline:*** rolling. ***Notification:*** continuous.

APPLYING/TRANSFER ***Entrance:*** noncompetitive. ***Application deadline:*** rolling. ***Notification:*** continuous. ***Contact:*** Ms. Josie Gutierrez, Director of Transfer/Career, 408-270-6711.

CONTACT Ms. Linda Harris, Director of Admissions and Records, Evergreen Valley College, 3095 Yerba Buena Road, San Jose, CA 95135-1598, 408-270-6441. ***Fax:*** 408-223-9351.

FASHION INSTITUTE OF DESIGN AND MERCHANDISING, LOS ANGELES CAMPUS
Los Angeles, California

UG Enrollment: 3,038	Tuition & Fees: $12,440
Application Deadline: rolling	Room & Board: N/Avail

The Fashion Institute of Design and Merchandising (FIDM) is an accredited California college offering AA, professional designation, and advanced studies degrees in the fashion, retail, and interior design fields. A culturally diverse student body creates a unique college experience. Campuses are located in Los Angeles, San Francisco, Costa Mesa, and San Diego.

GENERAL Proprietary, 2-year, coed. Part of Fashion Institute of Design and Merchandising. Awards transfer associate degrees. Founded 1969. ***Setting:*** urban campus. ***Total enrollment:*** 3,038. ***Faculty:*** 106 (24 full-time, 82 part-time); student-faculty ratio is 16:1. ***Notable Alumni:*** Karen Kane, owner and designer of Karen Kane; Randolph Duke, fashion designer at Henri Bendel's; Raymond Gallego, president of Architectural Design Concepts; Basha Cohen, vice president of design and buying at Laura Ashley, London; June Durr, director of marketing at Harris Department Stores.

ENROLLMENT PROFILE 3,038 students from 40 states and territories, 29 other countries. 18% part-time, 70% state residents, 34% transferred in, 19% international, 27% 25 or older, 1% Native American, 19% Hispanic, 5% African American, 34% Asian American. ***Most popular recent majors:*** fashion design and technology, marketing/retailing/merchandising, commercial art.

FIRST-YEAR CLASS 690 total. Of the students who applied, 80% were accepted, 70% of whom enrolled.

ACADEMIC PROGRAM Core. Calendar: quarters. Average class size 30 in required courses. Academic remediation for entering students, English as a second language program offered during academic year, advanced placement, summer session for credit, part-time degree program (evenings), adult/continuing education programs, co-op programs and internships. Study abroad in France, Italy, Germany, England, Korea, Mexico, Hong Kong.

GENERAL DEGREE REQUIREMENTS 90 quarter units; completion of a math proficiency test; computer course.

MAJORS Commercial art, fashion design and technology, fashion merchandising, interior design, manufacturing technology, marketing/retailing/merchandising, retail management, textile arts, textiles and clothing, theater arts/drama.

LIBRARY Resource and Research Center with 11,239 books, 217 periodicals, 6,205 records, tapes, and CDs.

COMPUTERS ON CAMPUS Computer purchase plan available. 74 computers for student use in computer center, idea centers provide access to main academic computer. Staffed computer lab on campus provides training in use of software.

NOTEWORTHY RESEARCH FACILITIES Predictive Services, International Fashion Video Library, Costume Museum, Interior Design Workroom, California Historical First Family Collection.

COLLEGE LIFE ***Most popular organizations:*** ASID Student Chapter, International Club, DECA, Association of Manufacturing Students, Honor Society. ***Major annual events:*** Debut Fashion Show, International Food Fair, Career Connection. ***Student services:*** personal-psychological counseling. ***Campus security:*** 24-hour emergency response devices and patrols.

HOUSING College housing not available.

CAREER PLANNING ***Placement office:*** 6 full-time, 2 part-time staff. ***Director:*** Ms. Sharon Calhoun, Director of Career Planning and Placement, 213-624-1200 Ext. 3500. ***Services:*** job fairs, resume preparation, resume referral, career counseling, careers library, job interviews. Students must register freshman year. 22 organizations recruited on campus 1994–95.

AFTER GRADUATION 90% of class of 1994 had job offers within 6 months.

EXPENSES FOR 1996–97 ***Application fee:*** $25. Tuition: $12,115 (minimum) full-time. Full-time tuition ranges up to $13,820 according to program. Full-time mandatory fees range from $325 to $525.

FINANCIAL AID ***College-administered undergrad aid 1995–96:*** 500 need-based scholarships (averaging $750), 150 non-need scholarships (averaging $1000), low-interest long-term loans from external sources (averaging $3000), 20 Federal Work-Study (averaging $3900). ***Required forms:*** institutional, FAFSA. ***Application deadline:*** continuous.

APPLYING ***Options:*** Common Application, deferred entrance. ***Required:*** essay, school transcript, 3 recommendations. ***Recommended:*** minimum 2.0 GPA, SAT I or ACT, SAT II Subject Tests. ***Required for some:*** campus interview, TOEFL for international students. Test scores used for admission and counseling/placement. ***Application deadline:*** rolling.

APPLYING/TRANSFER ***Required:*** essay, high school transcript, 3 recommendations, college transcript, minimum 2.0 college GPA. ***Recommended:*** minimum 2.0 high school GPA. ***Required for some:*** campus interview. ***Entrance:*** moderately difficult. ***Application deadline:*** rolling. ***Contact:*** Ms. Nancy Sims-Redlich, Director of Counseling, 213-624-1200 Ext. 3415.

CONTACT Ms. Susan Aronson, Director of Admissions, Fashion Institute of Design and Merchandising, Los Angeles Campus, 919 South Grand Avenue, Los Angeles, CA 90015-1421, 213-624-1200 Ext. 5400. ***E-mail:*** info@fidm.com. College video available.

❖ ***See page 736 for a narrative description.*** ❖

FASHION INSTITUTE OF DESIGN AND MERCHANDISING, SAN DIEGO CAMPUS
San Diego, California

UG Enrollment: 300	Tuition & Fees: $12,415
Application Deadline: rolling	Room & Board: N/Avail

GENERAL Proprietary, 2-year, coed. Part of Fashion Institute of Design and Merchandising. Awards transfer associate degrees. Founded 1985. ***Setting:*** urban campus. ***Total enrollment:*** 300. ***Faculty:*** 18 (all part-time); student-faculty ratio is 16:1. ***Notable Alumni:*** Alicia Goodman, buyer for Road Runner Sports; Kelly Doan, buyer for Brady's.

ENROLLMENT PROFILE 300 students from 12 states and territories, 4 other countries. 10% part-time, 5% international, 27% 25 or older, 5% Native American, 9% Hispanic, 8% African American. ***Most popular recent majors:*** marketing/retailing/merchandising, interior design.

FIRST-YEAR CLASS 136 total. Of the students who applied, 80% were accepted, 70% of whom enrolled.

ACADEMIC PROGRAM Core. Calendar: quarters. Average class size 25 in required courses. Academic remediation for entering students, English as a second language program, advanced placement, tutorials, summer session for credit, part-time degree program (daytime), co-op programs and internships. Study abroad in France, Italy, Germany, England, Korea, Mexico.

GENERAL DEGREE REQUIREMENTS 90 units; completion of math competency test; computer course.

MAJORS Commercial art, fashion design and technology, fashion merchandising, interior design, manufacturing technology, marketing/retailing/merchandising, retail management.

LIBRARY Resource and Research Center with 1,703 books, 61 periodicals, 301 records, tapes, and CDs.

COMPUTERS ON CAMPUS Computer purchase plan available. 9 computers for student use in computer center, computer labs, idea center, classrooms.

COLLEGE LIFE ***Most popular organizations:*** ASID Student Chapter, DECA, Honor Society. ***Major annual events:*** Debut Fashion Show, International Food Fair, Career Connection. ***Student services:*** personal-psychological counseling. ***Campus security:*** 24-hour emergency response devices and patrols.

HOUSING College housing not available.

CAREER PLANNING ***Placement office:*** 1 full-time, 1 part-time staff. ***Director:*** Ms. Karen Neilson, Placement and Student Activities Coordinator, 619-235-4515. ***Services:*** job fairs, resume preparation, resume referral, career counseling, careers library, job interviews. Students must register freshman year.

AFTER GRADUATION 93% of class of 1994 had job offers within 6 months. 18% of students completing a degree program went directly on to further study.

EXPENSES FOR 1996–97 ***Application fee:*** $25. Tuition: $12,115 full-time. Full-time mandatory fees: $300.

FINANCIAL AID ***Required forms:*** institutional, FAFSA. ***Application deadline:*** continuous.

APPLYING ***Options:*** Common Application, deferred entrance. ***Required:*** essay, school transcript, 3 recommendations. ***Recommended:*** minimum 2.0 GPA, portfolio. ***Required for some:*** campus interview. ***Application deadline:*** rolling.

APPLYING/TRANSFER ***Required:*** essay, 3 recommendations, college transcript, minimum 2.0 college GPA. ***Recommended:*** minimum 2.0 high school GPA. ***Required for some:*** campus interview, portfolio. ***Entrance:*** moderately difficult. ***Application deadline:*** rolling. ***Contact:*** Ms. Nancy Sims-Redlich, Director of Counseling, 619-624-1200 Ext. 3415.

CONTACT Mr. Allen Gueco, Director of Admissions, Fashion Institute of Design and Merchandising, San Diego Campus, 1010 Second Avenue, Suite 200, San Diego, CA 92101, 619-235-4515. ***E-mail:*** info@fidm.com. College video available.

FASHION INSTITUTE OF DESIGN AND MERCHANDISING, SAN FRANCISCO CAMPUS
San Francisco, California

UG Enrollment: 1,690	Tuition & Fees: $12,440
Application Deadline: rolling	Room & Board: N/Avail

GENERAL Proprietary, 2-year, coed. Part of Fashion Institute of Design and Merchandising. Awards transfer associate degrees. Founded 1973. ***Setting:*** urban campus. ***Total enrollment:*** 1,690. ***Faculty:*** 41 (3 full-time, 38 part-time). ***Notable Alumni:*** La T. Naylor, fashion designer at Think Tank; Joyce Johnson, fashion designer at Levi-Strauss; Kevin Flowers, owner and designer at William Flowers; Tuby Flax, owner and retailer at Flax.

ENROLLMENT PROFILE 1,690 students: 18% part-time, 85% state residents, 15% transferred in, 8% international, 13% 25 or older, 2% Native American, 4% Hispanic, 7% African American, 31% Asian American. ***Most popular recent majors:*** fashion design and technology, fashion merchandising, commercial art.

FIRST-YEAR CLASS 760 total. Of the students who applied, 80% were accepted, 70% of whom enrolled.
ACADEMIC PROGRAM Core. Calendar: quarters. Academic remediation for entering students, honors program, summer session for credit, internships. Off-campus study at Fashion Institute of Design and Merchandising, Los Angeles Campus. Study abroad in France, Italy, Japan, England, Korea, Mexico.
GENERAL DEGREE REQUIREMENTS 90 quarter units; completion of a math proficiency test; computer course.
MAJORS Commercial art, fashion design and technology, fashion merchandising, interior design, marketing/retailing/merchandising, retail management, textiles and clothing.
LIBRARY 4,200 books, 156 periodicals, 1,011 records, tapes, and CDs.
COMPUTERS ON CAMPUS 26 computers for student use in computer center, idea center, classrooms.
NOTEWORTHY RESEARCH FACILITIES Predictive Services, Interior Design Workroom, Costume Museum.
COLLEGE LIFE ***Most popular organizations:*** ASID Student Chapter, DECA, Visual Design Form, Honor Society. ***Major annual events:*** Career Connection, Industry Lunch Connections. ***Student services:*** personal-psychological counseling. ***Campus security:*** 24-hour emergency response devices and patrols.
HOUSING College housing not available.
CAREER PLANNING ***Placement office:*** 2 full-time, 1 part-time staff. ***Director:*** Ms. Amy Bollinger, Director of Placement, 415-433-6691. ***Services:*** job fairs, resume preparation, resume referral, career counseling, careers library, job interviews. Students must register freshman year.
AFTER GRADUATION 93% of class of 1994 had job offers within 6 months.
EXPENSES FOR 1996–97 ***Application fee:*** $25. Tuition: $12,115 (minimum) full-time. Full-time tuition ranges up to $13,820 according to program. Full-time mandatory fees range from $325 to $525.
FINANCIAL AID ***College-administered undergrad aid 1995–96:*** 200 need-based scholarships (average $750), 46 non-need scholarships (average $1000), low-interest long-term loans from external sources (average $3000), Federal Work-Study. ***Required forms:*** institutional, FAFSA. ***Application deadline:*** continuous.
APPLYING ***Options:*** Common Application, deferred entrance. ***Recommended:*** SAT I or ACT, SAT II Subject Tests. ***Required for some:*** TOEFL for international students. Test scores used for admission and counseling/placement. ***Application deadline:*** rolling.
APPLYING/TRANSFER ***Required:*** college transcript, minimum 2.0 college GPA. ***Entrance:*** moderately difficult. ***Application deadline:*** rolling. ***Contact:*** Ms. Maria De Palma, Academic Counselor, 415-433-6691.
CONTACT Ms. Jane DeMordant, Director of Admissions, Fashion Institute of Design and Merchandising, San Francisco Campus, 55 Stockton Street, San Francisco, CA 94108-5829, 415-433-6691 Ext. 200. ***E-mail:*** info@fidm.com. College video available.

FEATHER RIVER COMMUNITY COLLEGE DISTRICT
Quincy, California

UG Enrollment: 1,200	**Tuition & Fees (CA Res): $390**
Application Deadline: rolling	**Room & Board: N/Avail**

GENERAL State and locally supported, 2-year, coed. Awards certificates, transfer associate, terminal associate degrees. Founded 1968. ***Setting:*** 150-acre rural campus. ***Total enrollment:*** 1,200. ***Faculty:*** 92 (17 full-time, 75 part-time).
ENROLLMENT PROFILE 1,200 students from 4 states and territories, 1 other country. 60% women, 86% part-time, 96% state residents, 24% transferred in, 68% 25 or older, 3% Native American, 3% Hispanic, 1% African American, 1% Asian American. ***Most popular recent majors:*** forest technology, wildlife biology, recreation and leisure services.
FIRST-YEAR CLASS Of the students who applied, 100% were accepted, 100% of whom enrolled.
ACADEMIC PROGRAM Core. Calendar: semesters. Academic remediation for entering students, English as a second language program offered during academic year, services for LD students, summer session for credit, part-time degree program (daytime, evenings), adult/continuing education programs.
GENERAL DEGREE REQUIREMENTS 60 units; 1 course each in math and science; computer course.
MAJORS Accounting, biology/biological sciences, business administration/commerce/management, criminal justice, fire science, forest technology, law enforcement/police sciences, liberal arts/general studies, natural sciences, recreation and leisure services, secretarial studies/office management, social science, wildlife biology.
LIBRARY 12,516 books, 14 microform titles, 46 periodicals, 312 records, tapes, and CDs.
COMPUTERS ON CAMPUS 25 computers for student use in computer center, learning center. Staffed computer lab on campus.
COLLEGE LIFE Drama-theater group.
HOUSING College housing not available.
ATHLETICS ***Intramural:*** basketball, volleyball.
CAREER PLANNING ***Placement office:*** 1 full-time staff. ***Director:*** Mrs. Jodi Beynon, Program Staff Specialist/Career Center, 916-283-0202 Ext. 288. ***Service:*** career counseling.
EXPENSES FOR 1996–97 State resident tuition: $0 full-time. Nonresident tuition: $3750 full-time, $125 per unit part-time. Part-time mandatory fees: $13 per semester. Tuition for Nevada residents who are eligible for the Good Neighbor Program: $1260 full-time, $42 per unit part-time. Full-time mandatory fees: $390.
FINANCIAL AID ***College-administered undergrad aid 1995–96:*** need-based scholarships, 3 non-need scholarships (average $600), short-term loans (average $50), low-interest long-term loans from external sources (average $1000), Federal Work-Study, 15 part-time jobs. ***Required forms:*** state, FAFSA. ***Priority deadline:*** 4/15.
APPLYING Open admission. ***Option:*** early entrance. ***Required:*** school transcript, TOEFL for international students. ***Recommended:*** SAT I or ACT. Test scores used for counseling/placement. ***Application deadline:*** rolling.
APPLYING/TRANSFER ***Required:*** high school transcript, college transcript. ***Recommended:*** standardized test scores. ***Entrance:*** noncompetitive. ***Application deadline:*** rolling.
CONTACT Ms. Connie West, Registrar, Feather River Community College District, Quincy, CA 95971-6023, 916-283-0202 Ext. 285.

FOOTHILL COLLEGE
Los Altos Hills, California

UG Enrollment: 15,500	**Tuition & Fees (CA Res): $480**
Application Deadline: 9/15	**Room & Board: N/Avail**

GENERAL State and locally supported, 2-year, coed. Part of Foothill/DeAnza Community College District System. Awards certificates, transfer associate, terminal associate degrees. Founded 1958. ***Setting:*** 122-acre suburban campus with easy access to San Jose. ***Total enrollment:*** 15,500. ***Faculty:*** 578 (238 full-time, 340 part-time). ***Notable Alumni:*** Rosalind Creasy, author and horticulturalist; Debbie Fields, owner of Mrs. Fields Cookies; Peter Socrates Manoukian, superior court judge; Rebecca Morgan, California state senator.
ENROLLMENT PROFILE 15,500 students from 51 states and territories, 45 other countries. 49% women, 78% part-time, 98% state residents, 22% transferred in, 1% international, 67% 25 or older, 1% Native American, 6% Hispanic, 3% African American, 9% Asian American. ***Most popular recent majors:*** liberal arts/general studies, radiological technology, business administration/commerce/management.
FIRST-YEAR CLASS 3,000 total; 9,000 applied, 100% were accepted, 33% of whom enrolled. 10% from top 10% of their high school class, 35% from top quarter, 50% from top half.
ACADEMIC PROGRAM Core. Calendar: quarters. Academic remediation for entering students, English as a second language program offered during academic year and summer, services for LD students, advanced placement, self-designed majors, honors program, summer session for credit, part-time degree program (daytime, evenings, weekends, summer), adult/continuing education programs, co-op programs and internships. Study abroad in England, France, Austria, Japan. ROTC: Army (c), Naval (c), Air Force (c).
GENERAL DEGREE REQUIREMENTS 90 quarter units; 1 math course; computer course.
MAJORS Accounting, aerospace sciences, American studies, anthropology, art/fine arts, art history, aviation technology, biology/biological sciences, botany/plant sciences, business administration/commerce/management, chemistry, child psychology/child development, classics, communication, computer science, computer technologies, creative writing, dental services, economics, electrical and electronics technologies, emergency medical technology, engineering (general), English, ethnic studies, French, geography, geology, German, graphic arts, history, humanities, international studies, Japanese, landscape architecture/design, liberal arts/general studies, library science, linguistics, literature, mathematics, music, ornamental horticulture, pharmacy/pharmaceutical sciences, philosophy, photography, physical education, physician's assistant studies, physics, political science/government, pollution control technologies, psychology, radio and television studies, radiological sciences, radiological technology, real estate, respiratory therapy, science, secretarial studies/office management, social science, sociology, Spanish, speech/rhetoric/public address/debate, studio art, theater arts/drama, tourism and travel, veterinary technology, zoology.
LIBRARY Hubert H. Seamens Library with 75,000 books, 200 periodicals.
COMPUTERS ON CAMPUS 200 computers for student use in computer center.
COLLEGE LIFE Drama-theater group, choral group, student-run newspaper, radio station. 35% vote in student government elections. ***Student services:*** legal services, health clinic, personal-psychological counseling, women's center. ***Campus security:*** 24-hour emergency response devices and patrols, late-night transport-escort service.
HOUSING College housing not available.
ATHLETICS ***Intercollegiate:*** baseball M, basketball M/W, cross-country running M/W, football M, golf M/W, soccer M/W, softball W, swimming and diving M/W, tennis M/W, track and field M/W, volleyball W, water polo M. ***Intramural:*** basketball, cross-country running, football, golf, skiing (downhill), swimming and diving, tennis, track and field, volleyball. ***Contact:*** Mr. Tom Chivington, Athletic Director, 415-949-7285.
CAREER PLANNING ***Placement office:*** 1 part-time staff. ***Director:*** Ms. Marky Olsen, Interim Dean of Counseling, 415-949-7136. ***Services:*** job fairs, resume preparation, career counseling, careers library.
EXPENSES FOR 1995–96 ***Application fee:*** $22. State resident tuition: $0 full-time. Nonresident tuition: $3420 full-time, $76 per unit part-time. Part-time mandatory fees per quarter range from $34 to $124. Full-time mandatory fees: $480.
FINANCIAL AID ***College-administered undergrad aid 1995–96:*** need-based scholarships, non-need scholarships, short-term loans (average $75), low-interest long-term loans from external sources, Federal Work-Study, part-time jobs. ***Required forms:*** institutional, FAFSA. ***Application deadline:*** continuous to 3/2. ***Waivers:*** full or partial for employees or children of employees and senior citizens.
APPLYING Open admission except for dental hygiene, allied health programs. ***Required:*** TOEFL for international students. ***Recommended:*** school transcript. Test scores used for counseling/placement. ***Application deadline:*** 9/15. ***Notification:*** continuous.
APPLYING/TRANSFER ***Recommended:*** college transcript. ***Application deadline:*** rolling. ***Notification:*** continuous. ***Contact:*** Ms. Marky Olsen, Interim Dean of Counseling, 415-949-7136.
CONTACT Mr. Steve Barber, Admissions Representative, Foothill College, Los Altos Hills, CA 94022-4599, 415-949-7517.

FRESNO CITY COLLEGE
Fresno, California

UG Enrollment: 17,099	**Tuition & Fees (CA Res): $410**
Application Deadline: rolling	**Room & Board: N/Avail**

GENERAL District-supported, 2-year, coed. Part of California Community Colleges System. Awards transfer associate, terminal associate degrees. Founded 1910. ***Setting:*** 103-acre urban campus. ***Total enrollment:*** 17,099. ***Faculty:*** 832 (271 full-time, 561 part-time); student-faculty ratio is 22:1.
ENROLLMENT PROFILE 17,099 students: 53% women, 47% men, 69% part-time, 97% state residents, 8% transferred in, 80% have need-based financial aid, 1% international, 46% 25 or older, 1% Native American, 30% Hispanic, 8% African American, 13% Asian American. ***Most popular recent majors:*** liberal arts/general studies, business administration/commerce/management.
FIRST-YEAR CLASS 5,469 total; 7,449 applied, 99% were accepted, 74% of whom enrolled.

Fresno City College (continued)
ACADEMIC PROGRAM Core. Calendar: semesters. Academic remediation for entering students, English as a second language program offered during academic year, services for LD students, advanced placement, Freshman Honors College, honors program, summer session for credit, part-time degree program (daytime, evenings, summer), co-op programs. Off-campus study at King's River Community College, California State University, Fresno. Study abroad in England, France, Mexico, Costa Rica (1% of students participate). ROTC: Army (c), Air Force (c).
GENERAL DEGREE REQUIREMENTS 60 units; 1 algebra course; computer course for business administration majors.
MAJORS Accounting, agricultural business, anthropology, archaeology, architectural technologies, art/fine arts, automotive technologies, aviation technology, biology/biological sciences, black/African-American studies, business administration/commerce/management, carpentry, child psychology/child development, civil engineering technology, construction management, construction technologies, corrections, cosmetology, criminal justice, dance, data processing, dental services, dietetics, drafting and design, drug and alcohol/substance abuse counseling, electrical and electronics technologies, engineering (general), (pre)engineering sequence, ethnic studies, fashion merchandising, finance/banking, fire science, food services technology, geography, graphic arts, heating/refrigeration/air conditioning, history, home economics, humanities, human services, industrial arts, insurance, journalism, legal secretarial studies, liberal arts/general studies, library science, machine and tool technologies, marketing/retailing/merchandising, mathematics, medical assistant technologies, medical records services, medical secretarial studies, mental health/rehabilitation counseling, Mexican-American/Chicano studies, music, Native American studies, natural sciences, nursing, paralegal studies, photography, physical sciences, plumbing, political science/government, practical nursing, printing technologies, psychology, public administration, purchasing/inventory management, radiological technology, real estate, recreation and leisure services, respiratory therapy, science, secretarial studies/office management, social science, sociology, solar technologies, Spanish, teacher aide studies, theater arts/drama, transportation technologies, water resources, welding technology, women's studies, wood sciences, word processing.
LIBRARY Fresno City College Library with 67,500 books, 360 microform titles, 13 CD-ROMs, 2,700 records, tapes, and CDs.
COMPUTERS ON CAMPUS 600 computers for student use in various locations throughout campus. Staffed computer lab on campus provides training in use of computers, software.
COLLEGE LIFE Drama-theater group, choral group, marching band, student-run newspaper. ***Most popular organizations:*** MECHA, HMONG Club, ROTORACT, Students in Free Enterprise, Latter Day Saints Student Association. ***Major annual events:*** Showcase, Club Awareness Day, Homecoming. ***Student services:*** health clinic, personal-psychological counseling. ***Campus security:*** 24-hour emergency response devices and patrols, late-night transport-escort service.
HOUSING College housing not available.
ATHLETICS ***Intercollegiate:*** baseball M, basketball M/W, cross-country running M/W, football M, golf M/W, soccer M/W, softball W, tennis M/W, track and field M/W, volleyball W, wrestling M. ***Intramural:*** badminton, basketball, cross-country running, football, golf, gymnastics, soccer, swimming and diving, table tennis (Ping-Pong), tennis, track and field, volleyball, weight lifting, wrestling. ***Contact:*** Mr. Ron Scott, Athletic Director, 209-442-4600 Ext. 8440.
CAREER PLANNING ***Placement office:*** 3 full-time, 2 part-time staff. ***Director:*** Mr. Ryan Cox, Coordinator, Job Placement, 209-442-8294. ***Services:*** job fairs, resume preparation, resume referral, career counseling, careers library, job bank, job interviews. Students must register freshman year. 150 organizations recruited on campus 1994–95.
AFTER GRADUATION 85% of students completing a degree program in 1994–95 went directly on to further study.
EXPENSES FOR 1996–97 State resident tuition: $0 full-time. Nonresident tuition: $3660 full-time, $122 per unit part-time. Part-time mandatory fees per semester range from $23 to $153. Full-time mandatory fees: $410.
FINANCIAL AID ***College-administered undergrad aid 1995–96:*** 411 need-based scholarships, 110 non-need scholarships (average $200), short-term loans (average $50), low-interest long-term loans from external sources, 373 Federal Work-Study, 390 part-time jobs. ***Required forms:*** institutional, FAFSA. ***Priority deadline:*** 4/15. ***Payment plan:*** installment.
APPLYING Open admission. ***Options:*** early entrance, deferred entrance, midyear entrance. ***Required:*** school transcript, TOEFL for international students. ***Recommended:*** 3 years of high school math and science, some high school foreign language, SAT I or ACT, SAT II Subject Tests. Test scores used for counseling/placement. ***Application deadline:*** rolling. ***Notification:*** continuous.
APPLYING/TRANSFER ***Required:*** college transcript. ***Entrance:*** noncompetitive. ***Application deadline:*** rolling. ***Notification:*** continuous. ***Contact:*** Ms. Delfina Flores, Student Services Specialist, 209-442-4600 Ext. 8615.
CONTACT Mr. Joaquin Jimenez, Associate Dean of Students, Admissions, Records and Aid, Fresno City College, 1101 East University Avenue, Fresno, CA 93741-0002, 209-442-8240.

FULLERTON COLLEGE
Fullerton, California

UG Enrollment: 18,007	**Tuition & Fees (CA Res): $415**
Application Deadline: rolling	**Room & Board: N/Avail**

GENERAL State and locally supported, 2-year, coed. Part of North Orange County Community College District System. Awards certificates, transfer associate, terminal associate degrees. Founded 1913. ***Setting:*** 79-acre suburban campus with easy access to Los Angeles. ***Total enrollment:*** 18,007. ***Faculty:*** 678 (276 full-time, 402 part-time).
ENROLLMENT PROFILE 18,007 students: 52% women, 48% men, 49% part-time, 99% state residents, 10% transferred in, 1% international, 40% 25 or older, 2% Native American, 18% Hispanic, 2% African American, 10% Asian American. ***Most popular recent majors:*** liberal arts/general studies, business administration/commerce/management, law enforcement/police sciences.
FIRST-YEAR CLASS 3,459 applied, 100% were accepted, 100% of whom enrolled.
ACADEMIC PROGRAM Core. Calendar: semesters. Academic remediation for entering students, English as a second language program offered during academic year, services for LD students, advanced placement, summer session for credit, part-time degree program (daytime, evenings, weekends, summer), adult/continuing education programs, co-op programs. Study abroad in England, France, Austria. ROTC: Army (c), Naval (c), Air Force (c).
GENERAL DEGREE REQUIREMENTS 60 semester units; 3 semester units each of math and biological/physical science.
MAJORS Accounting, agricultural sciences, anthropology, architectural technologies, art/fine arts, astronomy, automotive technologies, biology/biological sciences, business administration/commerce/management, carpentry, chemistry, child psychology/child development, civil engineering technology, communication, computer information systems, computer science, construction technologies, cosmetology, dance, drafting and design, early childhood education, economics, English, environmental sciences, fashion design and technology, fashion merchandising, fish and game management, forestry, geology, history, home economics, horticulture, industrial arts, interior design, international business, journalism, land use management and reclamation, Latin American studies, law enforcement/police sciences, legal secretarial studies, liberal arts/general studies, library science, manufacturing technology, marketing/retailing/merchandising, mathematics, music, nursing, oceanography, ornamental horticulture, paralegal studies, philosophy, physical education, physics, political science/government, printing technologies, psychology, purchasing/inventory management, radio and television studies, real estate, recreation and leisure services, religious studies, sociology, speech/rhetoric/public address/debate, theater arts/drama, tourism and travel, wildlife management, zoology.
LIBRARY William T. Boyce Library with 113,236 books, 581 microform titles, 600 periodicals, 13 CD-ROMs, 2,281 records, tapes, and CDs.
COMPUTERS ON CAMPUS 600 computers for student use in computer labs, academic departments, library. Staffed computer lab on campus provides training in use of computers, software.
COLLEGE LIFE Drama-theater group, student-run newspaper, radio station. ***Social organizations:*** 24 social clubs. ***Student services:*** legal services, health clinic, personal-psychological counseling, women's center.
HOUSING College housing not available.
ATHLETICS ***Intercollegiate:*** basketball M/W, cross-country running M/W, football M, golf M/W, soccer M, swimming and diving M/W, tennis M/W, track and field M/W, volleyball W, water polo M. ***Contact:*** Ms. Susan Beers, Division Dean, 714-992-7126.
CAREER PLANNING ***Service:*** career counseling.
EXPENSES FOR 1995–96 State resident tuition: $0 full-time. Nonresident tuition: $3420 full-time, $114 per unit part-time. Part-time mandatory fees: $13 per unit. Full-time mandatory fees: $415.
FINANCIAL AID ***College-administered undergrad aid 1995–96:*** 3,000 need-based scholarships (average $1500), 200 non-need scholarships (average $500), short-term loans (average $100), low-interest long-term loans from external sources (average $1300), Federal Work-Study, 1,000 part-time jobs. ***Required forms:*** CSS Financial Aid PROFILE, institutional, FAFSA. ***Priority deadline:*** 7/15.
APPLYING Open admission. ***Option:*** early entrance. ***Required:*** TOEFL for international students. Test scores used for counseling/placement. ***Application deadline:*** rolling.
APPLYING/TRANSFER ***Entrance:*** noncompetitive. ***Application deadline:*** rolling.
CONTACT Ms. Carlene Gibson, Dean of Admissions, Fullerton College, Fullerton, CA 92632-2095, 714-992-7582. ***E-mail:*** gibsonc@nocccd.cc.ca.us.

GAVILAN COLLEGE
Gilroy, California

UG Enrollment: 4,029	**Tuition & Fees (CA Res): $422**
Application Deadline: rolling	**Room & Board: N/Avail**

GENERAL State and locally supported, 2-year, coed. Part of California Community Colleges System. Awards certificates, diplomas, transfer associate, terminal associate degrees. Founded 1919. ***Setting:*** 150-acre rural campus with easy access to San Jose. ***Total enrollment:*** 4,029. ***Faculty:*** 164 (74 full-time, 90 part-time); student-faculty ratio is 30:1.
ENROLLMENT PROFILE 4,029 students from 7 states and territories, 16 other countries. 52% women, 63% part-time, 96% state residents, 17% transferred in, 1% international, 40% 25 or older, 1% Native American, 35% Hispanic, 2% African American, 4% Asian American. ***Areas of study chosen:*** 70% liberal arts/general studies, 8% fine arts, 6% business management and administrative services, 5% health professions and related sciences, 4% vocational and home economics, 3% education, 1% biological and life sciences, 1% computer and information sciences, 1% English language/literature/letters, 1% social sciences.
FIRST-YEAR CLASS 921 total; 1,200 applied, 100% were accepted, 77% of whom enrolled.
ACADEMIC PROGRAM Core, liberal arts curriculum. Calendar: semesters. Academic remediation for entering students, English as a second language program offered during academic year, services for LD students, advanced placement, self-designed majors, tutorials, summer session for credit, part-time degree program (daytime, evenings, summer), adult/continuing education programs, co-op programs and internships.
GENERAL DEGREE REQUIREMENTS 60 units; 9 units of math/science; computer course.
MAJORS Accounting, art/fine arts, automotive technologies, aviation technology, biology/biological sciences, business administration/commerce/management, ceramic art and design, chemistry, child care/child and family studies, child psychology/child development, computer information systems, computer programming, computer science, corrections, cosmetology, criminal justice, drafting and design, early childhood education, (pre)engineering sequence, English, history, journalism, law enforcement/police sciences, legal secretarial studies, liberal arts/general studies, mathematics, music, natural sciences, nursing, painting/drawing, physical education, political science/government, practical nursing, psychology, science, secretarial studies/office management, social science, sociology, Spanish.
LIBRARY 55,440 books, 250 microform titles, 205 periodicals.
COMPUTERS ON CAMPUS 31 computers for student use in learning resource center.
COLLEGE LIFE Drama-theater group, student-run newspaper. 5% vote in student government elections. ***Student services:*** health clinic, personal-psychological counseling. ***Campus security:*** 24-hour emergency response devices and patrols, late-night transport-escort service.
HOUSING College housing not available.
ATHLETICS ***Intercollegiate:*** baseball W, basketball M/W, football M, golf M, soccer M, softball W, tennis M, volleyball W, wrestling M. ***Contact:*** Mr. Bill Perkins, Athletic Director, 408-848-4875.

CAREER PLANNING ***Placement office:*** 1 full-time, 1 part-time staff. ***Director:*** Ms. Aieleen Parker, Director of Transfer Center, 408-848-4818. ***Services:*** resume preparation, career counseling, careers library.
ESTIMATED EXPENSES FOR 1996–97 State resident tuition: $0 full-time. Nonresident tuition: $3840 full-time, $128 per unit part-time. Part-time mandatory fees per semester range from $29 to $159. Part-time tuition for international students per unit: $136. Full-time mandatory fees: $422.
FINANCIAL AID ***College-administered undergrad aid 1995–96:*** need-based scholarships, non-need scholarships, part-time jobs. ***Required forms:*** CSS Financial Aid PROFILE, institutional, FAFSA. ***Priority deadline:*** 8/1.
APPLYING Open admission. ***Option:*** midyear entrance. ***Required:*** TOEFL for international students. ***Required for some:*** school transcript. Test scores used for counseling/placement. ***Application deadline:*** rolling. ***Notification:*** continuous.
APPLYING/TRANSFER ***Required for some:*** college transcript. ***Entrance:*** noncompetitive. ***Application deadline:*** rolling. ***Notification:*** continuous. ***Contact:*** Mr. Lud Oliviera, Counselor, 408-848-4708.
CONTACT Ms. Joy Parker, Director of Admissions, Gavilan College, Gilroy, CA 95020-9599, 408-848-4735.

GLENDALE COMMUNITY COLLEGE
Glendale, California

GENERAL State and locally supported, 2-year, coed. Part of California Community Colleges System. Awards certificates, transfer associate, terminal associate degrees. Founded 1927. ***Setting:*** 119-acre urban campus with easy access to Los Angeles. ***Total enrollment:*** 15,337. ***Faculty:*** 345.
EXPENSES FOR 1995–96 State resident tuition: $0 full-time. Nonresident tuition: $3510 full-time, $117 per unit part-time. Part-time mandatory fees per semester range from $41 to $171. Full-time mandatory fees: $446.
CONTACT Dr. Gary Parker, Dean of Admissions, Glendale Community College, 1500 North Verdugo Road, Glendale, CA 91208-2894, 818-240-1000 Ext. 5116. ***Fax:*** 818-549-9436.

GOLDEN WEST COLLEGE
Huntington Beach, California

UG Enrollment: 12,415	**Tuition & Fees (CA Res): $506**
Application Deadline: rolling	**Room & Board: N/Avail**

GENERAL State and locally supported, 2-year, coed. Part of Coast Community College District System. Awards certificates, transfer associate, terminal associate degrees. Founded 1966. ***Setting:*** 122-acre suburban campus with easy access to Los Angeles. ***Total enrollment:*** 12,415. ***Faculty:*** 421 (200 full-time, 100% with terminal degrees, 221 part-time); student-faculty ratio is 30:1. ***Notable Alumni:*** Martin Yan, Douglas Fabian, Sam Duran, Brenda Premo, Mark Nancina.
ENROLLMENT PROFILE 12,415 students: 52% women, 68% part-time, 97% state residents, 11% transferred in, 1% international, 44% 25 or older, 2% Native American, 11% Hispanic, 2% African American, 32% Asian American. ***Areas of study chosen:*** 16% vocational and home economics, 15% liberal arts/general studies, 10% business management and administrative services, 10% health professions and related sciences, 8% social sciences, 5% engineering and applied sciences, 4% biological and life sciences, 4% physical sciences, 3% computer and information sciences, 3% psychology, 2% communications and journalism, 2% education, 2% English language/literature/letters, 2% fine arts, 2% foreign language and literature, 2% performing arts, 1% agriculture, 1% architecture, 1% interdisciplinary studies, 1% mathematics, 1% natural resource sciences, 1% philosophy, 1% predentistry, 1% prelaw, 1% premed, 1% prevet. ***Most popular recent majors:*** business administration/commerce/management, nursing.
FIRST-YEAR CLASS 3,893 total; 5,500 applied, 100% were accepted, 71% of whom enrolled.
ACADEMIC PROGRAM Core, transfer/vocational curriculum, honor code. Calendar: semesters (summer session). 740 courses offered in 1995–96. Academic remediation for entering students, English as a second language program offered during academic year and summer, advanced placement, self-designed majors, tutorials, summer session for credit, part-time degree program (daytime, evenings, summer), external degree programs, adult/continuing education programs, co-op programs and internships. Study abroad in Mexico, Spain, England, France, Italy, Costa Rica (1% of students participate). ROTC: Air Force (c).
GENERAL DEGREE REQUIREMENTS 60 units; 1 course each in math and biological/physical science; computer course for business administration majors; internship (some majors).
MAJORS Accounting, architectural technologies, art/fine arts, automotive technologies, biology/biological sciences, business administration/commerce/management, cosmetology, criminal justice, deaf interpreter training, drafting and design, electrical and electronics technologies, (pre)engineering sequence, engineering technology, graphic arts, humanities, journalism, law enforcement/police sciences, legal secretarial studies, liberal arts/general studies, marketing/retailing/merchandising, mathematics, music, natural sciences, nursing, ornamental horticulture, physical sciences, printing technologies, public relations, radio and television studies, real estate, retail management, science, secretarial studies/office management, technical writing, telecommunications.
LIBRARY Golden West College Library plus 1 other, with 98,151 books, 50 microform titles, 410 periodicals, 8 CD-ROMs, 5,022 records, tapes, and CDs.
COMPUTERS ON CAMPUS Computer purchase plan available. 600 computers for student use in computer center, computer labs, classrooms, library. Staffed computer lab on campus provides training in use of computers, software.
COLLEGE LIFE Drama-theater group, choral group, student-run newspaper, radio station. 5% vote in student government elections. ***Major annual events:*** College Transfer Day, Gold Rush Days. ***Student services:*** legal services, health clinic, personal-psychological counseling. ***Campus security:*** 24-hour emergency response devices and patrols, late-night transport-escort service.
HOUSING College housing not available.
ATHLETICS Member NJCAA. ***Intercollegiate:*** baseball M, basketball M/W, cross-country running M/W, football M, golf M/W, soccer M/W, softball W, swimming and diving M/W, tennis M/W, track and field M/W, volleyball M/W, water polo M, wrestling M. ***Contact:*** Mr. Thomas Hermstad, Division Dean of Physical Education and Athletics, 714-895-8333.
CAREER PLANNING ***Placement office:*** 1 full-time, 2 part-time staff. ***Director:*** Ms. Belen Genet, Instructional Associate, Career Center, 714-895-8217. ***Services:*** job fairs, resume preparation, resume referral, career counseling, careers library, job bank, job interviews.
AFTER GRADUATION 80% of students completing a degree program in 1994–95 went directly on to further study.
EXPENSES FOR 1996–97 State resident tuition: $0 full-time. Nonresident tuition: $3420 full-time, $114 per unit part-time. Part-time mandatory fees per semester range from $33.50 to $163.50. Full-time mandatory fees: $506.
FINANCIAL AID ***College-administered undergrad aid 1995–96:*** 1,700 need-based scholarships (average $210), 60 non-need scholarships (average $400), short-term loans (average $100), low-interest long-term loans from external sources (average $2053), Federal Work-Study, part-time jobs. ***Required forms:*** state, FAFSA; accepted: CSS Financial Aid PROFILE. ***Priority deadline:*** 6/1. ***Payment plan:*** deferred payment.
APPLYING Open admission except for nursing program. ***Options:*** early entrance, midyear entrance. ***Recommended:*** school transcript, TOEFL for international students, Assessment and Placement Services for Community Colleges. ***Required for some:*** essay, TOEFL for international students, Assessment and Placement Services for Community Colleges. Test scores used for counseling/placement. ***Application deadline:*** rolling. ***Notification:*** continuous.
APPLYING/TRANSFER ***Recommended:*** high school transcript, college transcript. ***Required for some:*** essay, standardized test scores, college transcript. ***Entrance:*** noncompetitive. ***Application deadline:*** rolling. ***Notification:*** continuous. ***Contact:*** Dr. Tom Kosuth, Articulation Counselor, 714-895-8794.
CONTACT Mr. John M. Breihan, Administrative Dean of Admissions and Records, Golden West College, Huntington Beach, CA 92647-2748, 714-895-8121.

GROSSMONT COLLEGE
El Cajon, California

UG Enrollment: 14,500	**Tuition & Fees (CA Res): $410**
Application Deadline: 8/12	**Room & Board: N/Avail**

GENERAL State and locally supported, 2-year, coed. Part of California Community Colleges System. Awards certificates, transfer associate, terminal associate degrees. Founded 1961. ***Setting:*** 135-acre suburban campus with easy access to San Diego. ***Total enrollment:*** 14,500. ***Faculty:*** 600 (201 full-time, 399 part-time); student-faculty ratio is 25:1.
ENROLLMENT PROFILE 14,500 students: 57% women, 64% part-time, 97% state residents, 21% transferred in, 1% international, 38% 25 or older, 1% Native American, 10% Hispanic, 3% African American, 5% Asian American. ***Most popular recent majors:*** liberal arts/general studies, business administration/commerce/management, nursing.
FIRST-YEAR CLASS 2,400 total. Of the students who applied, 100% were accepted.
ACADEMIC PROGRAM Core, honor code. Calendar: semesters. Academic remediation for entering students, English as a second language program offered during academic year and summer, services for LD students, advanced placement, self-designed majors, tutorials, summer session for credit, part-time degree program (daytime, evenings, summer), adult/continuing education programs, co-op programs and internships.
GENERAL DEGREE REQUIREMENTS 60 units; 1 course each in math and lab science; computer course for business majors.
MAJORS Accounting, advertising, art history, biology/biological sciences, business administration/commerce/management, ceramic art and design, chemistry, child care/child and family studies, child psychology/child development, communication, computer information systems, computer management, computer programming, computer science, corrections, creative writing, criminal justice, dance, dietetics, economics, English, family and consumer studies, fashion merchandising, food services management, French, geography, geology, German, history, interior design, international business, law enforcement/police sciences, legal secretarial studies, liberal arts/general studies, marketing/retailing/merchandising, mathematics, medical assistant technologies, medical secretarial studies, medical technology, music, nursing, painting/drawing, philosophy, photography, physics, political science/government, radio and television studies, respiratory therapy, retail management, sculpture, secretarial studies/office management, Spanish, speech/rhetoric/public address/debate, telecommunications, theater arts/drama.
LIBRARY Lewis F. Smith Learning Resource Center with 93,484 books, 326 microform titles, 541 periodicals, 1 CD-ROM, 4,762 records, tapes, and CDs.
COMPUTERS ON CAMPUS Computer purchase plan available. 300 computers for student use in computer center, computer labs, learning resource center, library. Staffed computer lab on campus provides training in use of computers, software.
COLLEGE LIFE Drama-theater group, choral group, student-run newspaper, radio station. 10% vote in student government elections. ***Social organizations:*** 33 open to all. ***Student services:*** legal services, health clinic, personal-psychological counseling. ***Campus security:*** 24-hour emergency response devices, student patrols, late-night transport-escort service.
HOUSING College housing not available.
ATHLETICS ***Intercollegiate:*** baseball M, basketball M/W, cross-country running M, football M, soccer W, softball W, swimming and diving M/W, tennis M/W, track and field M, volleyball W, water polo M/W. ***Contact:*** Mr. Felix Rogers, Athletics Director, 619-465-1700 Ext. 412.
CAREER PLANNING ***Placement office:*** 1 full-time, 2 part-time staff. ***Director:*** Ms. Virginia Steinbach, Dean, Counseling and Guidance, 619-465-1700 Ext. 627. ***Services:*** job fairs, resume preparation, resume referral, career counseling, careers library, job interviews. 50 organizations recruited on campus 1994–95.
EXPENSES FOR 1995–96 State resident tuition: $0 full-time. Nonresident tuition: $3330 full-time, $111 per unit part-time. Part-time mandatory fees per semester range from $23 to $153. Full-time mandatory fees: $410.
FINANCIAL AID ***College-administered undergrad aid 1995–96:*** 513 need-based scholarships (average $564), 61 non-need scholarships (average $567), short-term loans (average $200), low-interest long-term loans from external sources (average $2190), 230 Federal Work-Study (averaging $1845). ***Required forms:*** FAFSA. ***Priority deadline:*** 11/1. ***Waivers:*** full or partial for employees or children of employees.
APPLYING Open admission. ***Options:*** Common Application, early entrance, midyear entrance. ***Required:*** TOEFL for international students. ***Recommended:*** Assessment and Placement Services for Community Colleges. Test scores used for counseling/placement. ***Application deadline:*** 8/12. ***Notification:*** continuous until 8/12.

Peterson's Guide to Two-Year Colleges 1997

199

Grossmont College (continued)

APPLYING/TRANSFER ***Entrance:*** noncompetitive. ***Application deadline:*** 8/12. ***Notification:*** continuous until 8/12. ***Contact:*** Ms. Diane Sandoval, Student Services Specialist, 619-465-1700 Ext. 215.
CONTACT Ms. Sharon Clark, Registrar, Grossmont College, 8800 Grossmont College Drive, El Cajon, CA 92020-1799, 619-465-1700 Ext. 170.

HARTNELL COLLEGE
Salinas, California

UG Enrollment: 7,500	**Tuition & Fees (CA Res): $390**
Application Deadline: rolling	**Room & Board: N/Avail**

GENERAL District-supported, 2-year, coed. Part of California Community Colleges System. Awards certificates, transfer associate, terminal associate degrees. Founded 1920. ***Setting:*** 50-acre small-town campus with easy access to San Jose. ***Total enrollment:*** 7,500. ***Faculty:*** 363 (95 full-time, 268 part-time).
ENROLLMENT PROFILE 7,500 students from 4 states and territories, 14 other countries. 54% women, 70% part-time, 96% state residents, 5% transferred in, 1% international, 1% Native American, 39% Hispanic, 4% African American, 5% Asian American. ***Areas of study chosen:*** 20% liberal arts/general studies, 10% health professions and related sciences, 5% English language/literature/letters, 4% engineering and applied sciences, 4% fine arts, 3% foreign language and literature, 3% mathematics, 3% social sciences, 1% education, 1% library and information studies, 1% natural resource sciences, 1% performing arts. ***Most popular recent majors:*** liberal arts/general studies, business administration/commerce/management, nursing.
FIRST-YEAR CLASS 1,500 total. Of the students who applied, 97% were accepted, 75% of whom enrolled. 1% from top 10% of their high school class, 50% from top half.
ACADEMIC PROGRAM Core, honor code. Calendar: semesters. Academic remediation for entering students, English as a second language program offered during academic year, services for LD students, self-designed majors, tutorials, honors program, summer session for credit, part-time degree program (daytime, evenings, summer), adult/continuing education programs, co-op programs. Study abroad in England, Spain, China, France.
GENERAL DEGREE REQUIREMENTS 60 semester units; math competence; 1 science course.
MAJORS Agricultural business, agronomy/soil and crop sciences, animal sciences, anthropology, art/fine arts, automotive technologies, business administration/commerce/management, business machine technologies, carpentry, child care/child and family studies, child psychology/child development, computer science, construction technologies, criminal justice, data processing, drafting and design, early childhood education, economics, electrical and electronics technologies, electrical engineering technology, English, family and consumer studies, fire science, forest technology, graphic arts, health education, history, horticulture, human services, liberal arts/general studies, library science, machine and tool technologies, manufacturing technology, marketing/retailing/merchandising, mathematics, mechanical design technology, musical instrument technology, nursing, ornamental horticulture, physician's assistant studies, real estate, recreation and leisure services, secretarial studies/office management, veterinary technology, welding technology.
LIBRARY Hartnell College Library plus 1 other, with 70,000 books, 8,200 microform titles, 480 periodicals, 4,700 records, tapes, and CDs.
COMPUTERS ON CAMPUS 75 computers for student use in computer labs.
COLLEGE LIFE Drama-theater group. ***Social organizations:*** 20 open to all. ***Most popular organizations:*** Chicano Students Club, Alpha Gamma Sigma. ***Major annual events:*** College Night, Western Stage, Spring Conference Day. ***Student services:*** women's center. ***Campus security:*** 24-hour emergency response devices, student patrols, late-night transport-escort service.
HOUSING College housing not available.
ATHLETICS ***Intercollegiate:*** basketball M/W, cross-country running M/W, football M, golf M, soccer M, swimming and diving M/W, tennis M/W, track and field M/W, water polo M. ***Contact:*** Mr. Marv Grim, Dean of Physical Education, Health Education, and Recreation, 408-755-6837.
CAREER PLANNING ***Director:*** Ms. Sheri Gray, Director of Admissions, 408-755-6711. ***Services:*** job fairs, resume preparation, career counseling, job bank.
EXPENSES FOR 1996–97 State resident tuition: $0 full-time. Nonresident tuition: $3600 full-time, $120 per unit part-time. Part-time mandatory fees: $13 per unit. Full-time mandatory fees: $390.
FINANCIAL AID ***College-administered undergrad aid 1995–96:*** 100 need-based scholarships (averaging $300), 70 non-need scholarships (averaging $300), short-term loans (averaging $100), low-interest long-term loans from external sources (averaging $800), Federal Work-Study, 300 part-time jobs. ***Required forms:*** CSS Financial Aid PROFILE, state, institutional, FAFSA. ***Priority deadline:*** 5/30.
APPLYING Open admission except for allied health programs. ***Options:*** early entrance, deferred entrance, midyear entrance. ***Required:*** TOEFL for international students. ***Recommended:*** SAT I or ACT. ***Required for some:*** school transcript. Test scores used for counseling/placement. ***Application deadline:*** rolling. ***Notification:*** continuous.
APPLYING/TRANSFER ***Recommended:*** standardized test scores. ***Required for some:*** high school transcript. ***Application deadline:*** rolling. ***Notification:*** continuous. ***Contact:*** Ms. Maria Castillo, Counselor, 408-755-6007.
CONTACT Ms. Sheri Gray, Director of Admissions, Hartnell College, Salinas, CA 93901-1697, 408-755-6711.

HEALD BUSINESS COLLEGE
Concord, California

UG Enrollment: 472	**Tuition & Fees: $8000**
Application Deadline: rolling	**Room & Board: N/Avail**

GENERAL Independent, 2-year, specialized, coed. Part of Heald Colleges of California. Awards terminal associate degrees. Founded 1863. ***Setting:*** urban campus with easy access to San Francisco. ***Total enrollment:*** 472. ***Faculty:*** 15 (9 full-time, 6 part-time); student-faculty ratio is 22:1.
ENROLLMENT PROFILE 472 students: 70% women, 0% part-time, 97% state residents, 10% transferred in, 2% international, 30% 25 or older, 1% Native American, 10% Hispanic, 5% African American, 10% Asian American. ***Most popular recent majors:*** secretarial studies/office management, accounting.
FIRST-YEAR CLASS 112 total; 150 applied, 90% were accepted, 70% of whom enrolled.
ACADEMIC PROGRAM Core. Calendar: quarters. English as a second language program offered during academic year, tutorials, co-op programs.
GENERAL DEGREE REQUIREMENTS 104 quarter credits; 2 math courses; 1 science course; computer course.
MAJORS Accounting, computer information systems, data processing, legal secretarial studies, medical secretarial studies, secretarial studies/office management.
COMPUTERS ON CAMPUS Students must have own computer. 180 computers for student use in classrooms provide access to main academic computer. Staffed computer lab on campus provides training in use of computers, software.
COLLEGE LIFE ***Major annual events:*** Orientation, Graduation.
HOUSING College housing not available.
CAREER PLANNING ***Placement office:*** 1 full-time staff. ***Director:*** Ms. Leslie Baldwin, Placement Director, 510-827-1300. ***Services:*** job fairs, resume preparation, resume referral, career counseling, job interviews.
EXPENSES FOR 1996–97 ***Application fee:*** $25. Tuition: $8000 full-time.
FINANCIAL AID ***College-administered undergrad aid 1995–96:*** need-based scholarships, non-need scholarships, low-interest long-term loans from external sources, Federal Work-Study, part-time jobs. ***Acceptable forms:*** CSS Financial Aid PROFILE, state, FAFSA. ***Application deadline:*** continuous. ***Payment plans:*** tuition prepayment, installment. ***Waivers:*** full or partial for employees or children of employees.
APPLYING ***Option:*** deferred entrance. ***Required:*** TOEFL for international students, CPT. Test scores used for counseling/placement. ***Application deadline:*** rolling.
APPLYING/TRANSFER ***Required:*** standardized test scores. ***Entrance:*** minimally difficult. ***Contact:*** Ms. Linda Avila, Dean of Instruction, 510-827-1300.
CONTACT Ms. Kate Pereira, Director of Admissions, Heald Business College, 2150 John Glenn Drive, Concord, CA 94520-5618, 510-827-1300.

HEALD BUSINESS COLLEGE
Fresno, California

UG Enrollment: 500	**Tuition & Fees: $5785**
Application Deadline: rolling	**Room & Board: N/Avail**

GENERAL Independent, 2-year, specialized, coed. Part of Heald Colleges of California. Awards diplomas, transfer associate, terminal associate degrees. Founded 1891. ***Setting:*** 3-acre suburban campus. ***Total enrollment:*** 500. ***Faculty:*** 21 (16 full-time, 98% with terminal degrees, 5 part-time); student-faculty ratio is 20:1.
ENROLLMENT PROFILE 500 students from 6 states and territories, 3 other countries. 65% women, 1% part-time, 90% state residents, 10% transferred in, 5% international, 20% 25 or older, 5% Native American, 30% Hispanic, 10% African American, 10% Asian American.
FIRST-YEAR CLASS 320 total. Of the students who applied, 88% were accepted, 81% of whom enrolled.
ACADEMIC PROGRAM Core, business-oriented curriculum. Calendar: quarters. Academic remediation for entering students, tutorials, summer session for credit, part-time degree program (evenings), adult/continuing education programs.
GENERAL DEGREE REQUIREMENTS 103 quarter units; math/science requirements vary according to program; computer course.
MAJORS Accounting, computer information systems, legal secretarial studies, medical secretarial studies, secretarial studies/office management.
COMPUTERS ON CAMPUS 135 computers for student use in classrooms.
HOUSING College housing not available.
CAREER PLANNING ***Placement office:*** 1 full-time staff. ***Director:*** Mr. Dennis Yee, Director of Placement, 209-438-4222. ***Services:*** resume preparation, resume referral, career counseling, job interviews. Students must register freshman year.
EXPENSES FOR 1996–97 ***Application fee:*** $25. Tuition: $5760 (minimum) full-time. Full-time tuition ranges up to $6300 according to program. Full-time mandatory fees: $25. Tuition guaranteed not to increase for student's term of enrollment.
FINANCIAL AID ***Payment plans:*** installment, deferred payment.
APPLYING ***Required:*** school transcript, CPAt. ***Application deadline:*** rolling.
APPLYING/TRANSFER ***Required:*** college transcript. ***Entrance:*** minimally difficult.
CONTACT Ms. Ruth Johnson, Director of Admissions, Heald Business College, 255 West Bullard Avenue, Fresno, CA 93704-1706, 209-438-4222.

HEALD BUSINESS COLLEGE
Hayward, California

UG Enrollment: 500	**Tuition & Fees: $6000**
Application Deadline: rolling	**Room & Board: N/Avail**

GENERAL Independent, 2-year, coed. Part of Heald Colleges of California. Awards transfer associate, terminal associate degrees. Founded 1863. ***Setting:*** urban campus with easy access to San Francisco. ***Total enrollment:*** 500. ***Faculty:*** 16 (8 full-time, 8 part-time); student-faculty ratio is 20:1.
ENROLLMENT PROFILE 500 students: 50% women, 5% part-time, 100% state residents, 30% 25 or older, 15% Hispanic, 20% Asian American.
FIRST-YEAR CLASS 70 total. Of the students who applied, 90% were accepted.
ACADEMIC PROGRAM Calendar: quarters. Academic remediation for entering students, part-time degree program (evenings).
GENERAL DEGREE REQUIREMENTS 103 quarter units; 1 math course; computer course.
MAJORS Accounting, computer science, legal secretarial studies, medical secretarial studies, secretarial studies/office management.
COMPUTERS ON CAMPUS 230 computers for student use in computer center provide access to main academic computer.
COLLEGE LIFE ***Student services:*** personal-psychological counseling.
HOUSING College housing not available.
CAREER PLANNING ***Service:*** career counseling.
EXPENSES FOR 1996–97 ***Application fee:*** $50. Tuition: $6000 full-time, $50 per unit part-time. Tuition guaranteed not to increase for student's term of enrollment.
FINANCIAL AID ***College-administered undergrad aid 1995–96:*** need-based scholarships, 3 non-need scholarships (average $4900), short-term loans, low-interest long-term

loans from external sources (average $2625), Federal Work-Study, part-time jobs. *Required forms:* FAFSA; accepted: CSS Financial Aid PROFILE. *Application deadline:* continuous.
APPLYING Open admission. *Required:* CPAt. *Recommended:* TOEFL for international students. *Application deadline:* rolling.
APPLYING/TRANSFER *Required:* standardized test scores.
CONTACT Mr. Todd Wheeler, Director of Admissions, Heald Business College, 777 Southland Drive, Suite 210, Hayward, CA 94545-1557, 510-784-7000.

HEALD BUSINESS COLLEGE
Oakland, California

GENERAL Independent, 2-year, coed. Part of Heald Colleges of California. Awards transfer associate, terminal associate degrees. Founded 1863. *Setting:* urban campus with easy access to San Francisco. *Educational spending 1994–95:* $6300 per undergrad. *Total enrollment:* 300. *Faculty:* 20 (15 full-time, 5 part-time); student-faculty ratio is 20:1. *Notable Alumni:* Rose Bird, former chief justice of California.
EXPENSES FOR 1995–96 *Application fee:* $25. Tuition: $5850 full-time, $500 per course part-time. Tuition guaranteed not to increase for student's term of enrollment.
CONTACT Mr. Klint Schahrer, Director of Admissions, Heald Business College, 1000 Broadway, Suite 290, Oakland, CA 94607-4040, 510-444-0201. *Fax:* 510-839-2084. College video available.

HEALD BUSINESS COLLEGE
Rancho Cordova, California

UG Enrollment: 600	Tuition: $11,700/deg prog
Application Deadline: 10/15	Room & Board: N/Avail

GENERAL Independent, 2-year, coed. Part of Heald Colleges of California. Awards terminal associate degrees. Founded 1863. *Setting:* 1-acre small-town campus with easy access to Sacramento. *Total enrollment:* 600. *Faculty:* 20 (15 full-time, 5 part-time).
ENROLLMENT PROFILE 600 students: 70% women, 5% part-time, 95% state residents, 20% transferred in, 20% 25 or older, 1% Native American, 13% Hispanic, 8% African American, 3% Asian American.
FIRST-YEAR CLASS 150 total. Of the students who applied, 85% were accepted. 12% from top 10% of their high school class, 40% from top quarter, 74% from top half.
ACADEMIC PROGRAM Core. Calendar: quarters. Academic remediation for entering students, summer session for credit, adult/continuing education programs, internships.
GENERAL DEGREE REQUIREMENTS 116 quarter units; 1 course each in math and science; computer course.
MAJORS Accounting, computer science, data processing, legal secretarial studies, medical records services, secretarial studies/office management.
LIBRARY 8,800 books, 87 periodicals, 331 records, tapes, and CDs.
COMPUTERS ON CAMPUS 225 computers for student use in classrooms.
COLLEGE LIFE *Campus security:* late-night transport-escort service.
HOUSING College housing not available.
CAREER PLANNING *Service:* career counseling.
EXPENSES FOR 1995–96 *Application fee:* $50. Full-time tuition per degree program: $13,200 for evening program, $11,700 for day program.
FINANCIAL AID *College-administered undergrad aid 1995–96:* need-based scholarships, 4 non-need scholarships (average $4500), low-interest long-term loans from college funds (average $2500), loans from external sources (average $2500), Federal Work-Study, 12 part-time jobs. *Required forms:* CSS Financial Aid PROFILE, state, FAFSA. *Priority deadline:* 10/1.
APPLYING *Required:* school transcript, campus interview, TOEFL for international students. Test scores used for admission and counseling/placement. *Application deadline:* 10/15.
APPLYING/TRANSFER *Required:* high school transcript, campus interview, college transcript. *Entrance:* minimally difficult. *Application deadline:* 10/15. *Contact:* Ms. Gabriel Meehan, Dean, 916-638-1616.
CONTACT Mr. Steve Do, Director of Admissions, Heald Business College, 2910 Prospect Park Drive, Rancho Cordova, CA 95670-6005, 916-638-1616 Ext. 304 or toll-free 800-499-4333 (out-of-state).

HEALD BUSINESS COLLEGE
Salinas, California

HEALD BUSINESS COLLEGE
San Francisco, California

UG Enrollment: 600	Tuition & Fees: $8400
Application Deadline: rolling	Room & Board: N/Avail

GENERAL Independent, 2-year, coed. Part of Heald Colleges of California. Awards transfer associate, terminal associate degrees. Founded 1863. *Setting:* 1-acre urban campus. *Total enrollment:* 600. *Faculty:* 25 (16 full-time, 9 part-time); student-faculty ratio is 20:1.
ENROLLMENT PROFILE 600 students: 75% women, 21% part-time, 83% state residents, 10% transferred in, 17% international, 34% 25 or older, 0% Native American, 18% Hispanic, 14% African American, 18% Asian American.
FIRST-YEAR CLASS 200 total. Of the students who applied, 90% were accepted, 95% of whom enrolled.
ACADEMIC PROGRAM Core. Calendar: quarters. Academic remediation for entering students, English as a second language program, advanced placement, summer session for credit, internships.
GENERAL DEGREE REQUIREMENTS 110 credit hours; 1 course each in math and science; computer course.
MAJORS Accounting, business education, computer information systems, data processing, legal secretarial studies, medical secretarial studies, secretarial studies/office management.
LIBRARY 600 books, 50 periodicals, 100 records, tapes, and CDs.
COMPUTERS ON CAMPUS 185 computers for student use in computer labs, classrooms. Staffed computer lab on campus provides training in use of computers, software.
HOUSING College housing not available.
CAREER PLANNING *Service:* career counseling.
EXPENSES FOR 1996–97 Tuition: $8400 full-time, $650 per course part-time.
FINANCIAL AID *College-administered undergrad aid 1995–96:* 2 need-based scholarships (average $5000), 1 non-need scholarship ($5000), low-interest long-term loans from external sources, Federal Work-Study, part-time jobs. *Required forms:* CSS Financial Aid PROFILE, state, FAFSA. *Application deadline:* continuous.
APPLYING *Option:* deferred entrance. *Required:* school transcript, TOEFL for international students, CPAt. *Application deadline:* rolling.
APPLYING/TRANSFER *Required:* standardized test scores, high school transcript. *Entrance:* minimally difficult. *Application deadline:* rolling.
CONTACT Dr. Linda Sempliner, Director, Heald Business College, 1453 Mission Street, San Francisco, CA 94103-2552, 415-673-5500. *Fax:* 415-626-1404.

HEALD BUSINESS COLLEGE
San Jose, California

UG Enrollment: 304	Tuition: $13,275/deg prog
Application Deadline: N/R	Room & Board: N/Avail

GENERAL Independent, 2-year. Awards terminal associate degrees. *Total enrollment:* 304.
ENROLLMENT PROFILE 304 students.
FIRST-YEAR CLASS 75 total.
ACADEMIC PROGRAM Calendar: quarters.
GENERAL DEGREE REQUIREMENTS 102 units; computer course.
EXPENSES FOR 1996–97 Tuition: $13,275 per degree program. Part-time tuition per unit: $130.
APPLYING *Required:* school transcript.
APPLYING/TRANSFER *Required:* high school transcript, college transcript.
CONTACT Mr. Charles Reese, Director of Admissions, Heald Business College, San Jose, CA 95134, 408-955-9555.

HEALD BUSINESS COLLEGE
Santa Rosa, California

GENERAL Independent, 2-year, coed. Part of Heald Colleges of California. Awards terminal associate degrees. Founded 1984. *Setting:* small-town campus with easy access to San Francisco. *Total enrollment:* 210. *Faculty:* 14 (8 full-time, 6 part-time); student-faculty ratio is 21:1.
EXPENSES FOR 1995–96 *Application fee:* $25. Tuition: $7800 full-time. Tuition guaranteed not to increase for student's term of enrollment.
CONTACT Mr. Gordon Kent, Admissions Counselor, Heald Business College, 100 Professional Center Drive, Santa Rosa, CA 95403-3116, 707-525-1300.

HEALD BUSINESS COLLEGE
Stockton, California

HEALD INSTITUTE OF TECHNOLOGY
Hayward, California

UG Enrollment: 349	Tuition & Fees: $6300
Application Deadline: N/R	Room & Board: N/Avail

GENERAL Independent, 2-year. Awards terminal associate degrees. *Total enrollment:* 349.
ENROLLMENT PROFILE 349 students.
FIRST-YEAR CLASS Of the students who applied, 100% were accepted.
GENERAL DEGREE REQUIREMENTS 102 units; 1 math course; computer course.
EXPENSES FOR 1996–97 *Application fee:* $50. Tuition: $6300 full-time.
CONTACT Mr. Brent Javaine, Director of Admissions, Heald Institute of Technology, Hayward, CA 94545, 510-783-2100.

HEALD INSTITUTE OF TECHNOLOGY
Martinez, California

UG Enrollment: 430	Tuition & Fees: $7200
Application Deadline: 10/1	Room & Board: N/Avail

GENERAL Independent, 2-year, coed. Part of Heald Colleges of California. Awards certificates, terminal associate degrees. Founded 1863. *Setting:* 5-acre small-town campus with easy access to San Francisco. *Educational spending 1994–95:* $6700 per undergrad. *Total enrollment:* 430. *Faculty:* 15 (all full-time); student-faculty ratio is 29:1.
ENROLLMENT PROFILE 430 students: 15% women, 0% part-time, 100% state residents, 20% transferred in, 70% 25 or older, 1% Native American, 15% Hispanic, 10% African American, 15% Asian American. *Areas of study chosen:* 100% engineering and applied sciences.
FIRST-YEAR CLASS 95 total. Of the students who applied, 83% were accepted, 100% of whom enrolled.
ACADEMIC PROGRAM Electronic technology curriculum, honor code. Calendar: quarters. 18 courses offered in 1995–96. Academic remediation for entering students, advanced placement, summer session for credit, adult/continuing education programs.
GENERAL DEGREE REQUIREMENTS 102 units; 1 quarter of math; 3 quarters of science; computer course.
MAJORS Computer technologies, electronics engineering technology.
LIBRARY Learning Resource Center plus 1 other, with 500 books, 50 periodicals. Acquisition spending 1994–95: $10,000.

Peterson's Guide to Two-Year Colleges 1997

California

Heald Institute of Technology (continued)
COMPUTERS ON CAMPUS Computer purchase plan available. 60 computers for student use in lab provide access to main academic computer. Staffed computer lab on campus (open 24 hours a day) provides training in use of computers, software.
COLLEGE LIFE Orientation program (3 days, no cost). *Campus security:* 24-hour emergency response devices.
HOUSING College housing not available.
CAREER PLANNING *Placement office:* 1 full-time staff; $10,000 operating expenditure 1994–95. *Director:* Ms. Melissa Johnson, Director of Graduate Services, 510-228-9000. *Services:* job fairs, resume preparation, resume referral, career counseling, job bank, job interviews.
EXPENSES FOR 1996–97 *Application fee:* $50. Tuition: $7200 full-time.
FINANCIAL AID *College-administered undergrad aid 1995–96:* need-based scholarships, short-term loans, low-interest long-term loans from external sources (average $2600), Federal Work-Study, part-time jobs. *Required forms:* CSS Financial Aid PROFILE, FAFSA. *Application deadline:* continuous.
APPLYING *Options:* electronic application, early entrance, deferred entrance. *Required:* school transcript. *Application deadline:* 10/1. *Notification:* continuous.
APPLYING/TRANSFER *Required:* high school transcript. *Entrance:* minimally difficult.
CONTACT Mr. Joseph Cañas, Admissions Counselor, Heald Institute of Technology, 2860 Howe Road, Martinez, CA 94553-4000, 510-228-9000. College video and electronic viewbook available.

HEALD INSTITUTE OF TECHNOLOGY
Milpitas, California

UG Enrollment: 470	Tuition & Fees: $8400
Application Deadline: rolling	Room & Board: N/Avail

GENERAL Independent, 2-year, coed. Part of Heald Colleges of California. Awards certificates, terminal associate degrees. Founded 1863. *Setting:* small-town campus. *Total enrollment:* 470. *Faculty:* 30 (24 full-time, 6 part-time); student-faculty ratio is 20:1.
ENROLLMENT PROFILE 470 students: 15% women, 5% part-time, 95% state residents, 15% transferred in, 80% have need-based financial aid, 13% have non-need-based financial aid, 1% international, 50% 25 or older, 1% Native American, 30% Hispanic, 5% African American, 25% Asian American. *Areas of study chosen:* 100% engineering and applied sciences.
FIRST-YEAR CLASS 300 total; 475 applied, 76% were accepted, 83% of whom enrolled.
ACADEMIC PROGRAM Core. Calendar: quarters.
GENERAL DEGREE REQUIREMENTS 102 credit hours; 1 math course; computer course.
MAJORS Computer technologies, electronics engineering technology, telecommunications.
LIBRARY 1,500 books, 45 periodicals, 39 records, tapes, and CDs.
COMPUTERS ON CAMPUS Computer purchase plan available. 125 computers for student use in computer labs provide access to on-line services, Internet. Staffed computer lab on campus provides training in use of computers, software.
COLLEGE LIFE *Student services:* personal-psychological counseling.
HOUSING College housing not available.
CAREER PLANNING *Service:* career counseling. 20 organizations recruited on campus 1994–95.
AFTER GRADUATION 93% of class of 1994 had job offers within 6 months.
EXPENSES FOR 1996–97 *Application fee:* $50. Tuition: $8400 full-time. Tuition guaranteed not to increase for student's term of enrollment.
FINANCIAL AID *College-administered undergrad aid 1995–96:* need-based scholarships, 60 non-need scholarships (average $500), low-interest long-term loans from external sources (average $4000), Federal Work-Study, 20 part-time jobs. *Required forms:* institutional, FAFSA; accepted: CSS Financial Aid PROFILE, state. *Priority deadline:* 10/14. *Payment plan:* installment. *Waivers:* full or partial for employees or children of employees.
APPLYING *Required:* school transcript, minimum 2.0 GPA, interview. Test scores used for counseling/placement. *Application deadline:* rolling.
APPLYING/TRANSFER *Entrance:* moderately difficult.
CONTACT Mr. Douglas Remington, Director of Admissions, Heald Institute of Technology, Milpitas, CA 95035, 408-295-8000 Ext. 17. *Fax:* 408-374-5645. *E-mail:* sjtadm@heald.edu.

HEALD INSTITUTE OF TECHNOLOGY
Sacramento, California

HEALD INSTITUTE OF TECHNOLOGY
San Francisco, California

UG Enrollment: 400	Tuition & Fees: $8400
Application Deadline: rolling	Room & Board: N/Avail

GENERAL Independent, 2-year, specialized, primarily men. Part of Heald Colleges of California. Awards terminal associate degrees. Founded 1863. *Setting:* 3-acre urban campus. *Total enrollment:* 400. *Faculty:* 18 (15 full-time, 3 part-time).
ENROLLMENT PROFILE 400 students: 20% women, 0% part-time, 97% state residents, 5% transferred in, 33% have need-based financial aid, 40% have non-need-based financial aid, 3% international, 70% 25 or older, 5% Native American, 15% Hispanic, 10% African American, 25% Asian American.
FIRST-YEAR CLASS 90 total. Of the students who applied, 47% were accepted, 87% of whom enrolled.
ACADEMIC PROGRAM Core. Calendar: quarters. Academic remediation for entering students, honors program.
GENERAL DEGREE REQUIREMENTS 102 credits; math/science requirements vary according to program; computer course.
MAJOR Electronics engineering technology.

COMPUTERS ON CAMPUS Computer purchase plan available. 60 computers for student use in labs provide access to e-mail, on-line services, Internet. Staffed computer lab on campus provides training in use of computers, software.
COLLEGE LIFE *Student services:* personal-psychological counseling.
HOUSING College housing not available.
CAREER PLANNING *Service:* career counseling.
EXPENSES FOR 1996–97 *Application fee:* $25. Tuition: $8400 full-time.
FINANCIAL AID *College-administered undergrad aid 1995–96:* need-based scholarships, non-need scholarships, short-term loans, low-interest long-term loans from external sources, Federal Work-Study, part-time jobs. *Required forms:* state, institutional, FAFSA. *Application deadline:* continuous.
APPLYING *Required:* school transcript, minimum 2.0 GPA, 3 years of high school math and science, campus interview, TOEFL for international students. *Recommended:* SAT I. Test scores used for admission. *Application deadline:* rolling. *Notification:* continuous.
APPLYING/TRANSFER *Entrance:* minimally difficult. *Application deadline:* rolling. *Notification:* continuous.
CONTACT Mr. Rod Maulis, Director of Admissions, Heald Institute of Technology, 250 Executive Park Boulevard, #1000, San Francisco, CA 94134-3306, 415-822-2900. College video available.

IMPERIAL VALLEY COLLEGE
Imperial, California

UG Enrollment: 5,696	Tuition & Fees (CA Res): $390
Application Deadline: N/R	Room & Board: N/Avail

GENERAL State and locally supported, 2-year, coed. Part of California Community Colleges System. Awards certificates, transfer associate, terminal associate degrees. Founded 1922. *Setting:* 160-acre rural campus. *Total enrollment:* 5,696. *Faculty:* 288 (98 full-time, 190 part-time); student-faculty ratio is 22:1.
ENROLLMENT PROFILE 5,696 students: 62% women, 54% part-time, 98% state residents, 3% transferred in, 1% international, 0% Native American, 74% Hispanic, 1% African American, 1% Asian American. *Most popular recent majors:* liberal arts/general studies, social science, business administration/commerce/management.
FIRST-YEAR CLASS 1,372 total. Of the students who applied, 100% were accepted, 90% of whom enrolled.
ACADEMIC PROGRAM Core, honor code. Calendar: semesters. 1,450 courses offered in 1995–96. Academic remediation for entering students, English as a second language program offered during academic year, services for LD students, self-designed majors, summer session for credit, part-time degree program (daytime, evenings, summer), adult/continuing education programs. Off-campus study.
GENERAL DEGREE REQUIREMENTS 60 units; 1 algebra course; 3 units of natural science; computer course for business majors; internship (some majors).
MAJORS Accounting, agricultural business, agricultural sciences, agricultural technologies, anthropology, art/fine arts, automotive technologies, behavioral sciences, business administration/commerce/management, computer information systems, criminal justice, data processing, early childhood education, engineering (general), (pre)engineering sequence, English, fire science, French, human development, humanities, journalism, law enforcement/police sciences, liberal arts/general studies, marketing/retailing/merchandising, mathematics, medical assistant technologies, medical records services, modern languages, music, nursing, physical education, physical sciences, practical nursing, psychology, science, secretarial studies/office management, social science, Spanish, water resources, welding technology.
LIBRARY Spencer Library with 51,726 books, 478 microform titles, 456 periodicals, 2,362 records, tapes, and CDs.
COMPUTERS ON CAMPUS 120 computers for student use in computer center, business department. Staffed computer lab on campus.
COLLEGE LIFE Choral group. 10% vote in student government elections. *Student services:* personal-psychological counseling, women's center. *Campus security:* student patrols.
HOUSING College housing not available.
ATHLETICS *Intercollegiate:* baseball M, basketball M, soccer M, softball W, tennis M/W, volleyball W. *Intramural:* basketball, tennis, volleyball. *Contact:* Dr. James Walker, Vice President of Academic Services, 619-352-8320.
CAREER PLANNING *Director:* Mr. Jim Grevatt, Counselor, 619-352-8320 Ext. 253. *Service:* career counseling.
EXPENSES FOR 1996–97 State resident tuition: $0 full-time. Nonresident tuition: $3420 full-time, $114 per unit part-time. Part-time mandatory fees: $13 per unit. Full-time mandatory fees: $390.
FINANCIAL AID *College-administered undergrad aid 1995–96:* 6,000 need-based scholarships (average $300), 147 non-need scholarships (average $250), short-term loans (average $50), Federal Work-Study, 200 part-time jobs. *Required forms:* CSS Financial Aid PROFILE, institutional, FAFSA. *Priority deadline:* 5/1.
APPLYING Open admission. *Recommended:* school transcript. *Required for some:* school transcript. Test scores used for counseling/placement. *Notification:* continuous.
APPLYING/TRANSFER *Recommended:* college transcript. *Application deadline:* rolling. *Notification:* continuous.
CONTACT Mrs. Sandra Standiford, Dean of Admissions and Student Activities, Imperial Valley College, Imperial, CA 92251-0158, 619-352-8320 Ext. 200.

IRVINE VALLEY COLLEGE
Irvine, California

UG Enrollment: 10,300	Tuition & Fees (CA Res): $410
Application Deadline: rolling	Room & Board: N/Avail

GENERAL State and locally supported, 2-year, coed. Part of Saddleback Community College District. Awards certificates, transfer associate degrees. Founded 1979. *Setting:* 20-acre suburban campus with easy access to Los Angeles. *Total enrollment:* 10,300. *Faculty:* 344 (94 full-time, 250 part-time).
ENROLLMENT PROFILE 10,300 students: 60% women, 80% part-time, 90% state residents, 1% transferred in, 4% international, 55% 25 or older, 1% Native American, 5%

California

Hispanic, 1% African American, 2% Asian American. *Most popular recent majors:* business administration/commerce/management, liberal arts/general studies.
FIRST-YEAR CLASS Of the students who applied, 100% were accepted, 95% of whom enrolled.
ACADEMIC PROGRAM Core, honor code. Calendar: semesters. Academic remediation for entering students, English as a second language program offered during academic year and summer, services for LD students, advanced placement, summer session for credit, part-time degree program (daytime, evenings, weekends, summer), adult/continuing education programs, co-op programs.
GENERAL DEGREE REQUIREMENTS 60 units; 1 math/analytic reasoning course.
MAJORS Accounting, art/fine arts, behavioral sciences, biology/biological sciences, business administration/commerce/management, business machine technologies, computer technologies, creative writing, criminal justice, data processing, electromechanical technology, English, history, humanities, liberal arts/general studies, literature, mathematics, science, secretarial studies/office management, social science, speech/rhetoric/public address/debate.
LIBRARY Irvine Valley College Library with 24,000 books, 100 microform titles, 250 periodicals, 800 records, tapes, and CDs.
COMPUTERS ON CAMPUS Computer purchase plan available. 125 computers for student use in computer center provide access to e-mail, on-line services. Staffed computer lab on campus provides training in use of computers, software.
COLLEGE LIFE Drama-theater group, student-run newspaper. 1% vote in student government elections. *Student services:* health clinic, personal-psychological counseling, women's center. *Campus security:* late-night transport-escort service.
HOUSING College housing not available.
ATHLETICS *Intercollegiate:* basketball M/W, cross-country running M/W, soccer M/W, tennis M/W, volleyball M.
CAREER PLANNING *Service:* career counseling.
EXPENSES FOR 1996-97 State resident tuition: $0 full-time. Nonresident tuition: $4500 full-time, $150 per unit part-time. Part-time mandatory fees per semester range from $23 to $153. Full-time mandatory fees: $410.
FINANCIAL AID *College-administered undergrad aid 1995–96:* need-based scholarships, non-need scholarships, short-term loans, low-interest long-term loans from external sources, Federal Work-Study, part-time jobs. *Required forms:* state, institutional, FAFSA; accepted: CSS Financial Aid PROFILE. *Priority deadline:* 3/15. *Payment plan:* deferred payment.
APPLYING Open admission. *Options:* Common Application, early entrance. *Required:* TOEFL for international students. Test scores used for counseling/placement. *Application deadline:* rolling. *Notification:* continuous.
APPLYING/TRANSFER *Entrance:* noncompetitive. *Notification:* continuous.
CONTACT Mr. Jess Craig, Dean of Students, Irvine Valley College, Irvine, CA 92720-4399, 714-559-3410. *Fax:* 714-559-3443. *E-mail:* c_bennet@ivc.cc.ca.edu.

ITT TECHNICAL INSTITUTE
Anaheim, California

UG Enrollment: 702	Tuition: $15,429/deg prog
Application Deadline: rolling	Room & Board: N/Avail

GENERAL Proprietary, primarily 2-year, coed. Part of ITT Educational Services, Inc. Awards transfer associate, terminal associate, bachelor's degrees. Founded 1982. *Setting:* 5-acre suburban campus with easy access to Los Angeles. *Total enrollment:* 702. *Faculty:* 25 (20 full-time, 8% with terminal degrees, 5 part-time); student-faculty ratio is 28:1.
ENROLLMENT PROFILE 702 students: 13% women, 0% part-time, 99% state residents, 3% transferred in, 1% international, 24% 25 or older, 1% Native American, 27% Hispanic, 5% African American, 16% Asian American. *Areas of study chosen:* 100% engineering and applied sciences. *Most popular recent major:* electronics engineering technology.
FIRST-YEAR CLASS 342 total; 593 applied, 89% were accepted, 65% of whom enrolled. 5% from top 10% of their high school class, 20% from top quarter, 55% from top half.
ACADEMIC PROGRAM Core. Calendar: quarters. Academic remediation for entering students.
GENERAL DEGREE REQUIREMENT 180 credits for bachelor's.
MAJORS Drafting and design, electronics engineering technology (B).
LIBRARY 300 books, 3 periodicals.
COMPUTERS ON CAMPUS 85 computers for student use in computer center, classrooms, library.
COLLEGE LIFE Student-run newspaper. *Campus security:* 24-hour emergency response devices and patrols.
HOUSING College housing not available.
CAREER PLANNING *Placement office:* 3 full-time, 1 part-time staff. *Director:* Ms. Cindy Ball, Placement Director, 714-535-3700 Ext. 20. *Services:* job fairs, resume preparation, resume referral, career counseling, careers library, job bank, job interviews. Students must register freshman year.
EXPENSES FOR 1995-96 *Application fee:* $100. Tuition for associate degree program ranges from $15,429 to $17,690. Tuition for bachelor's degree program: $25,800. Tuition guaranteed not to increase for student's term of enrollment.
FINANCIAL AID *College-administered undergrad aid 1995–96:* need-based scholarships, non-need scholarships, low-interest long-term loans from external sources, Federal Work-Study. *Required forms:* institutional, FAFSA; accepted: CSS Financial Aid PROFILE, state. *Application deadline:* continuous.
APPLYING *Options:* Common Application, deferred entrance. *Required:* CPAt verbal and arithmetic tests. Test scores used for admission. *Application deadline:* rolling. *Notification:* continuous.
APPLYING/TRANSFER *Entrance:* moderately difficult. *Application deadline:* rolling. *Notification:* continuous. *Contact:* Mr. Timothy Mayo, Director of Education, 714-535-3700.
CONTACT Mr. Louis E. Osborn, Director of Recruitment, ITT Technical Institute, Anaheim, CA 92801-9938, 714-535-3700. College video available.

ITT TECHNICAL INSTITUTE
Carson, California

UG Enrollment: 467	Tuition: $15,599/deg prog
Application Deadline: rolling	Room & Board: N/Avail

GENERAL Proprietary, 2-year, coed. Part of ITT Educational Services, Inc. Awards terminal associate degrees. Founded 1987. *Setting:* urban campus with easy access to Los Angeles. *Total enrollment:* 467. *Faculty:* 21 (16 full-time, 99% with terminal degrees, 5 part-time).
ENROLLMENT PROFILE 467 students: 18% women, 0% part-time, 100% state residents, 25% transferred in, 30% 25 or older, 1% Native American, 43% Hispanic, 21% African American, 18% Asian American. *Areas of study chosen:* 100% engineering and applied sciences.
FIRST-YEAR CLASS 189 total; 374 applied, 80% were accepted, 60% of whom enrolled.
ACADEMIC PROGRAM Core, technical curriculum, honor code. Calendar: quarters. Academic remediation for entering students, tutorials, co-op programs.
GENERAL DEGREE REQUIREMENT 91 credits.
MAJORS Drafting and design, electronics engineering technology.
LIBRARY 1,200 books, 10 periodicals, 12 records, tapes, and CDs.
COMPUTERS ON CAMPUS 44 computers for student use in computer labs, learning resource center, drafting labs.
COLLEGE LIFE *Campus security:* 24-hour emergency response devices, late-night transport-escort service.
HOUSING College housing not available.
CAREER PLANNING *Placement office:* 2 full-time staff. *Director:* Ms. Fay Wease, Director of Placement, 310-835-5595. *Services:* job fairs, resume preparation, resume referral, career counseling, careers library, job bank, job interviews.
EXPENSES FOR 1996-97 Tuition per degree program ranges from $15,599 to $17,690. Full-time mandatory fees range from $540 to $720. Tuition guaranteed not to increase for student's term of enrollment.
FINANCIAL AID *College-administered undergrad aid 1995–96:* need-based scholarships, low-interest long-term loans from external sources, Federal Work-Study, part-time jobs. *Required forms:* FAFSA. *Application deadline:* continuous. *Payment plan:* installment.
APPLYING *Option:* deferred entrance. *Required:* CPAt. *Required for some:* minimum 2.0 GPA. *Application deadline:* rolling.
APPLYING/TRANSFER *Required for some:* minimum 2.0 high school GPA. *Entrance:* moderately difficult. *Application deadline:* rolling. *Contact:* Mr. Gary Wilson, Director of Education, 310-835-5595.
CONTACT Mr. James Sorchilla, Director of Recruitment, ITT Technical Institute, 2035 East 223rd Street, Carson, CA 90810-1610, 310-835-5595 Ext. 17. College video available.

ITT TECHNICAL INSTITUTE
Oxnard, California

UG Enrollment: 294	Tuition: $15,599/deg prog
Application Deadline: rolling	Room & Board: N/Avail

GENERAL Proprietary, 2-year, coed. Part of ITT Educational Services, Inc. Awards transfer associate, terminal associate degrees. Founded 1993. *Setting:* urban campus with easy access to Los Angeles. *Total enrollment:* 294. *Faculty:* 13 (10 full-time, 1% with terminal degrees, 3 part-time).
ENROLLMENT PROFILE 294 students.
FIRST-YEAR CLASS 145 total; 213 applied.
ACADEMIC PROGRAM Core. Calendar: quarters.
GENERAL DEGREE REQUIREMENTS 90 credit hours; computer course.
MAJORS Drafting and design, electronics engineering technology.
COMPUTERS ON CAMPUS 4 computers for student use in learning resource center. Staffed computer lab on campus.
COLLEGE LIFE *Campus security:* 24-hour emergency response devices and patrols.
HOUSING College housing not available.
CAREER PLANNING *Placement office:* 1 full-time staff. *Director:* Mr. Anthony Michaelides, Director of Placement, 805-988-0143. *Services:* job fairs, resume preparation, resume referral, career counseling, careers library, job bank, job interviews. Students must register freshman year.
EXPENSES FOR 1996-97 *Application fee:* $100. Tuition per degree program ranges from $15,599 to $17,690. Full-time mandatory fees range from $540 to $720.
FINANCIAL AID *College-administered undergrad aid 1995–96:* need-based scholarships, non-need scholarships, Federal Work-Study. *Required forms:* institutional, FAFSA. *Application deadline:* continuous. *Payment plans:* tuition prepayment, installment. *Waivers:* full or partial for employees or children of employees.
APPLYING *Option:* deferred entrance. *Required:* school transcript, recommendations, interview, CPAt. *Recommended:* minimum 2.0 GPA. Test scores used for admission. *Application deadline:* rolling.
APPLYING/TRANSFER *Required:* minimum 2.0 college GPA. *Required for some:* college transcript. *Application deadline:* rolling. *Contact:* Mr. Arnulfo Runas, Director of Education, 805-988-0143.
CONTACT Mr. Ted Morgan, Director of Recruitment, ITT Technical Institute, 2051 Solar Drive, Suite 150, Oxnard, CA 93030, 805-988-0143. College video available.

ITT TECHNICAL INSTITUTE
Sacramento, California

UG Enrollment: 419	Tuition: $15,599/deg prog
Application Deadline: rolling	Room & Board: N/Avail

GENERAL Proprietary, primarily 2-year, coed. Part of ITT Educational Services, Inc. Awards terminal associate, bachelor's degrees. Founded 1954. *Setting:* 5-acre urban campus. *Total enrollment:* 419. *Faculty:* 15 (13 full-time, 2 part-time); student-faculty ratio is 23:1. *Notable Alumni:* Adrian Aguianaga, drafter at Price Technical; Kayleen

Peterson's Guide to Two-Year Colleges 1997

California

ITT Technical Institute (continued)

Smart, CAD drafter at Grinnel Fire Protection; Shane Cheatham, technician at Chuck E. Cheese; Richard Lawson, telecom technician at Franchise Tax Board; Caroline Larrabee, technician at Indy Electronics.

ENROLLMENT PROFILE 419 students: 10% women, 40% 25 or older, 1% Native American, 15% Hispanic, 7% African American, 12% Asian American. *Areas of study chosen:* 100% engineering and applied sciences. *Most popular recent major:* electronics engineering technology.

FIRST-YEAR CLASS 162 total; 311 applied.

ACADEMIC PROGRAM Core, career-specific curriculum, honor code. Calendar: quarters. Tutorials, summer session for credit.

MAJORS Drafting and design, electronics engineering technology.

LIBRARY 1,732 books, 20 periodicals, 37 records, tapes, and CDs.

COMPUTERS ON CAMPUS 32 computers for student use in computer labs, learning resource center.

COLLEGE LIFE *Major annual events:* Christmas Party, Halloween Costume Contest, All School Picnic. *Campus security:* 24-hour emergency response devices, late-night transport-escort service.

HOUSING College housing not available.

ATHLETICS *Intramural:* softball, volleyball.

CAREER PLANNING *Placement office:* 2 full-time, 1 part-time staff. *Director:* Ms. Gloria Rivas, Director of Placement, 916-366-3900. *Services:* resume preparation, resume referral, career counseling, job bank, job interviews. Students must register freshman year.

EXPENSES FOR 1996–97 *Application fee:* $100. Tuition per degree program ranges from $15,599 to $17,690. Tuition guaranteed not to increase for student's term of enrollment.

FINANCIAL AID *College-administered undergrad aid 1995–96:* need-based scholarships, low-interest long-term loans from external sources, Federal Work-Study, 1 part-time job. *Required forms:* institutional, FAFSA; accepted: CSS Financial Aid PROFILE, state. *Application deadline:* continuous to 8/23. *Payment plan:* installment. *Waivers:* full or partial for employees or children of employees.

APPLYING *Option:* deferred entrance. *Required:* ACT, CPAt. Test scores used for admission. *Application deadline:* rolling.

APPLYING/TRANSFER *Application deadline:* rolling. *Contact:* Mr. Jay Johanneson, Director of Education, 916-366-3900.

CONTACT Mr. Carlos Llarena, Director of Recruitment, ITT Technical Institute, 9700 Goethe Road, Sacramento, CA 95827-3500, 916-366-3900 or toll-free 800-488-8466. *Fax:* 916-366-9225. College video available.

ITT TECHNICAL INSTITUTE
San Bernardino, California

UG Enrollment: 511	Tuition & Fees: $6786
Application Deadline: rolling	Room & Board: N/Avail

GENERAL Proprietary, primarily 2-year, coed. Part of ITT Educational Services, Inc. Awards terminal associate, bachelor's degrees. Founded 1987. *Setting:* urban campus with easy access to Los Angeles. *Total enrollment:* 511. *Faculty:* 24 (18 full-time, 5% with terminal degrees, 6 part-time); student-faculty ratio is 30:1.

ENROLLMENT PROFILE 511 students: 12% women, 0% part-time, 98% state residents, 1% transferred in, 0% international, 20% 25 or older, 2% Native American, 20% Hispanic, 10% African American, 3% Asian American. *Areas of study chosen:* 100% engineering and applied sciences.

FIRST-YEAR CLASS 322 total; 650 applied, 91% were accepted, 55% of whom enrolled. 5% from top 10% of their high school class, 15% from top quarter, 40% from top half.

ACADEMIC PROGRAM Core. Calendar: quarters. Academic remediation for entering students, services for LD students, tutorials, honors program, summer session for credit.

MAJORS Drafting and design, electronics engineering technology, industrial design (B).

LIBRARY 500 books, 6 periodicals.

COMPUTERS ON CAMPUS 89 computers for student use in computer center, computer labs, library, student center provide access to on-line services, Internet.

COLLEGE LIFE Choral group. *Most popular organizations:* International Society of Certified Electronic Technicians, American Drafting and Design Association, Student Activity Council. *Campus security:* late-night transport-escort service, off-duty police patrols.

HOUSING College housing not available.

CAREER PLANNING *Placement office:* 2 full-time, 1 part-time staff. *Director:* Ms. Teri Kittredge, Director of Placement, 909-889-3800. *Services:* job fairs, resume preparation, resume referral, career counseling, careers library, job bank, job interviews.

EXPENSES FOR 1996–97 *Application fee:* $100. Tuition: $6786 (minimum) full-time. Tuition per quarter ranges from $2262 to $2763.

FINANCIAL AID *College-administered undergrad aid 1995–96:* need-based scholarships, non-need scholarships, low-interest long-term loans from external sources, Federal Work-Study. *Required forms:* institutional, FAFSA; accepted: CSS Financial Aid PROFILE, state. *Application deadline:* continuous. *Payment plan:* installment. *Waivers:* full or partial for employees or children of employees.

APPLYING *Option:* deferred entrance. *Required:* CPAt. Test scores used for admission. *Application deadline:* rolling.

APPLYING/TRANSFER *Application deadline:* rolling. *Contact:* Ms. Luka Mbewe, Director of Education, 909-889-3800.

CONTACT Mr. Cliff Kline, Director of Recruitment, ITT Technical Institute, 630 East Brier Drive, Suite 150, San Bernardino, CA 92408-2800, 909-889-3800 Ext. 20 or toll-free 800-942-0088 (out-of-state). *Fax:* 909-888-6970. College video available.

ITT TECHNICAL INSTITUTE
San Diego, California

UG Enrollment: 663	Tuition: $15,429/deg prog
Application Deadline: rolling	Room & Board: N/Avail

GENERAL Proprietary, primarily 2-year, coed. Part of ITT Educational Services, Inc. Awards terminal associate, bachelor's degrees. Founded 1981. *Setting:* suburban campus. *Total enrollment:* 663. *Faculty:* 34 (22 full-time, 91% with terminal degrees, 12 part-time); student-faculty ratio is 26:1.

ENROLLMENT PROFILE 663 students from 4 states and territories, 8 other countries. 17% women, 0% part-time, 90% state residents, 1% transferred in, 1% international, 37% 25 or older, 1% Native American, 28% Hispanic, 8% African American, 10% Asian American. *Areas of study chosen:* 100% engineering and applied sciences. *Most popular recent majors:* electronics engineering technology, drafting and design.

FIRST-YEAR CLASS 335 total; 544 applied, 96% were accepted, 64% of whom enrolled.

ACADEMIC PROGRAM Core. Calendar: quarters. Academic remediation for entering students, tutorials, summer session for credit.

GENERAL DEGREE REQUIREMENTS 91 credit hours for associate; internship (some majors).

MAJORS Drafting and design, electronics engineering technology (B), hotel and restaurant management.

LIBRARY Learning Resource Center with 480 books, 8 periodicals.

COMPUTERS ON CAMPUS 4 computers for student use in computer labs, learning resource center, classrooms provide access to Internet. Staffed computer lab on campus (open 24 hours a day) provides training in use of computers, software.

COLLEGE LIFE *Social organizations:* 1 open to all. *Most popular organization:* The Users Group. *Major annual events:* Blood Drive, Halloween Costume Day, Student/Staff Picnic. *Campus security:* 24-hour emergency response devices.

HOUSING College housing not available.

CAREER PLANNING *Placement office:* 3 full-time staff. *Director:* Ms. Leslie Boucher, Director of Placement, 619-571-8500. *Services:* job fairs, resume preparation, resume referral, career counseling, careers library, job bank, job interviews. Students must register freshman year. 37 organizations recruited on campus 1994–95.

AFTER GRADUATION 81% of class of 1994 had job offers within 6 months.

EXPENSES FOR 1995–96 *Application fee:* $100. Tuition per degree program ranges from $15,429 to $17,690 for associate, $25,117 to $28,060 for bachelor's. Tuition guaranteed not to increase for student's term of enrollment.

FINANCIAL AID *College-administered undergrad aid 1995–96:* need-based scholarships, short-term loans, low-interest long-term loans from external sources, Federal Work-Study, part-time jobs. *Required forms:* state, institutional, FAFSA; accepted: CSS Financial Aid PROFILE. *Priority deadline:* 9/20. *Payment plan:* installment. *Waivers:* full or partial for employees or children of employees.

APPLYING *Option:* deferred entrance. *Required:* interview, CPAt. Test scores used for admission. *Application deadline:* rolling.

APPLYING/TRANSFER *Entrance:* noncompetitive. *Application deadline:* rolling. *Contact:* Mr. Granerson Hester, Director of Education, 619-571-8500.

CONTACT Ms. Sheryl Schulgen, Director of Recruitment, ITT Technical Institute, San Diego, CA 92123, 619-571-8500. *Fax:* 619-462-9418. College video available.

ITT TECHNICAL INSTITUTE
Van Nuys, California

UG Enrollment: 410	Tuition: $15,429/deg prog
Application Deadline: rolling	Room & Board: N/Avail

GENERAL Proprietary, 2-year, coed. Part of ITT Educational Services, Inc. Awards terminal associate degrees. Founded 1982. *Setting:* urban campus. *Total enrollment:* 410. *Faculty:* 15 (13 full-time, 2 part-time).

ENROLLMENT PROFILE 410 students: 2% women, 0% part-time, 100% state residents, 0% transferred in, 0% international, 80% 25 or older, 0% Native American, 30% Hispanic, 10% African American, 15% Asian American.

FIRST-YEAR CLASS 100 total; 250 applied, 60% were accepted, 67% of whom enrolled. 20% from top 10% of their high school class, 40% from top half.

ACADEMIC PROGRAM Core, honor code. Calendar: quarters. Academic remediation for entering students.

GENERAL DEGREE REQUIREMENTS 121 credit hours; computer course.

MAJORS Drafting and design, electronics engineering technology.

LIBRARY 300 books.

COMPUTERS ON CAMPUS 50 computers for student use in computer center. Staffed computer lab on campus (open 24 hours a day) provides training in use of computers.

COLLEGE LIFE *Campus security:* 24-hour emergency response devices and patrols.

HOUSING College housing not available.

CAREER PLANNING *Placement office:* 2 full-time, 1 part-time staff. *Director:* Mrs. Sylvia Weocher, Director of Placement, 818-989-1177. *Services:* resume preparation, resume referral, career counseling, job interviews.

EXPENSES FOR 1995–96 *Application fee:* $100. Tuition per degree program ranges from $15,429 to $17,690. Tuition guaranteed not to increase for student's term of enrollment.

FINANCIAL AID *College-administered undergrad aid 1995–96:* need-based scholarships, low-interest long-term loans from external sources. *Required forms:* institutional, FAFSA; accepted: CSS Financial Aid PROFILE, state. *Priority deadline:* 9/1. *Payment plan:* installment. *Waivers:* full or partial for employees or children of employees.

APPLYING *Option:* Common Application. *Required:* school transcript, SRA verbal and arithmetic tests, SRA achievement series, reading and math. Test scores used for admission. *Application deadline:* rolling. *Notification:* continuous.

APPLYING/TRANSFER *Required:* college transcript. *Application deadline:* rolling. *Notification:* continuous.

CONTACT Mr. Robert Quintero, Director of Recruitment, ITT Technical Institute, 6723 Van Nuys Boulevard, Van Nuys, CA 91405-4620, 818-989-1177 Ext. 22. College video available.

ITT TECHNICAL INSTITUTE
West Covina, California

UG Enrollment: 681	Tuition: $16,379/deg prog
Application Deadline: rolling	Room & Board: N/Avail

GENERAL Proprietary, primarily 2-year, coed. Part of ITT Educational Services, Inc. Awards terminal associate, bachelor's degrees. Founded 1982. *Setting:* 4-acre suburban campus with easy access to Los Angeles. *Total enrollment:* 681. *Faculty:* 28 (15 full-time, 13 part-time).
ENROLLMENT PROFILE 681 students: 8% women, 0% part-time, 1% international, 30% 25 or older, 1% Native American, 50% Hispanic, 10% African American, 16% Asian American. *Areas of study chosen:* 100% engineering and applied sciences. *Most popular recent majors:* electronics engineering technology, drafting and design.
FIRST-YEAR CLASS 250 total; 430 applied, 58% of whom enrolled.
ACADEMIC PROGRAM Core, technical curriculum. Calendar: quarters. 76 courses offered in 1995-96. Academic remediation for entering students.
GENERAL DEGREE REQUIREMENTS 108 credits for associate, 180 credits for bachelor's; 5 credits each of math and physics; computer course.
MAJORS Drafting and design, electronics engineering technology, manufacturing technology (B), robotics (B).
LIBRARY 1,550 books, 10 periodicals, 5 records, tapes, and CDs.
COMPUTERS ON CAMPUS 75 computers for student use in classrooms, library provide access to Internet. Staffed computer lab on campus provides training in use of computers, software.
COLLEGE LIFE *Most popular organizations:* Society of Manufacturing Engineers, Drafting Association. *Major annual events:* High-Tech Day, Career Fair. *Campus security:* 24-hour emergency response devices.
HOUSING College housing not available.
CAREER PLANNING *Placement office:* 3 full-time, 1 part-time staff. *Director:* Mr. Barrett Van Buren, Director of Placement, 818-960-8681. *Services:* job fairs, resume preparation, resume referral, career counseling, careers library, job bank, job interviews. Students must register freshman year.
AFTER GRADUATION 85% of class of 1994 had job offers within 6 months.
EXPENSES FOR 1996-97 *Application fee:* $100. Full-time tuition per degree program: $16,379 to $18,575 for associate, $26,551 for bachelor's. Tuition guaranteed not to increase for student's term of enrollment.
FINANCIAL AID *College-administered undergrad aid 1995-96:* need-based scholarships, low-interest long-term loans from external sources, Federal Work-Study, part-time jobs. Average total aid for freshmen: $4902, meeting 60% of need. *Required forms:* institutional, FAFSA; accepted: CSS Financial Aid PROFILE, state. *Priority deadline:* 9/1. *Payment plan:* installment. *Waivers:* full or partial for employees or children of employees.
APPLYING *Option:* deferred entrance. *Required:* school transcript, 2 recommendations, interview, CPAt. Test scores used for admission. *Application deadline:* rolling.
APPLYING/TRANSFER *Required:* high school transcript, 2 recommendations, interview. *Recommended:* college transcript. *Entrance:* minimally difficult. *Application deadline:* rolling. *Contact:* Mr. Douglas Bolton, Director of Education, 818-960-8681.
CONTACT Mr. Lou Osburn, Director of Recruitment, ITT Technical Institute, 1530 West Cameron Avenue, West Covina, CA 91790-2711, 818-960-8681. *Fax:* 818-960-4299. College video available.

KELSEY JENNEY COLLEGE
San Diego, California

UG Enrollment: 900	Tuition & Fees: $8388
Application Deadline: rolling	Room & Board: N/Avail

GENERAL Independent, 2-year, coed. Awards terminal associate degrees. Founded 1863. *Setting:* urban campus. *Total enrollment:* 900. *Faculty:* 50 (23 full-time, 27 part-time); student-faculty ratio is 20:1.
ENROLLMENT PROFILE 900 students: 75% women, 10% part-time, 98% state residents, 1% transferred in, 2% international, 20% 25 or older, 2% Native American, 60% Hispanic, 20% African American, 10% Asian American. *Most popular recent majors:* paralegal studies, court reporting, accounting.
FIRST-YEAR CLASS Of the students who applied, 95% were accepted. 0% from top 10% of their high school class, 5% from top quarter, 20% from top half.
ACADEMIC PROGRAM Core, honor code. Calendar: quarters. 80 courses offered in 1995-96. Summer session for credit, part-time degree program (daytime, evenings), adult/continuing education programs.
GENERAL DEGREE REQUIREMENTS 96 quarter units; 1 course each in math and science; computer course; internship (some majors).
MAJORS Accounting, business administration/commerce/management, computer information systems, computer science, court reporting, legal secretarial studies, legal studies, medical assistant technologies, medical secretarial studies, paralegal studies, secretarial studies/office management.
COMPUTERS ON CAMPUS Students must have own computer. 120 computers for student use in computer center provide access to main academic computer, on-line services, Internet. Staffed computer lab on campus provides training in use of computers, software.
COLLEGE LIFE *Student services:* personal-psychological counseling. *Campus security:* 24-hour emergency response devices, late-night transport-escort service.
HOUSING College housing not available.
CAREER PLANNING *Placement office:* 1 full-time staff. *Director:* Mrs. Peggy Webb, Director of Placement, 619-549-5070. *Services:* resume preparation, resume referral, career counseling, job interviews.
EXPENSES FOR 1996-97 *Application fee:* $75. Tuition: $8388 (minimum) full-time, $150 per quarter hour part-time. Full-time tuition ranges up to $16,776 according to program.
FINANCIAL AID *College-administered undergrad aid 1995-96:* 50 need-based scholarships (average $400), low-interest long-term loans from external sources (average $2625), Federal Work-Study, 2 part-time jobs. *Required forms:* institutional, FAFSA; accepted: CSS Financial Aid PROFILE, state. *Application deadline:* continuous. *Payment plans:* tuition prepayment, installment.
APPLYING Open admission. *Option:* deferred entrance. *Required:* school transcript. *Recommended:* TOEFL for international students. Test scores used for admission. *Application deadline:* rolling.
APPLYING/TRANSFER *Entrance:* noncompetitive. *Application deadline:* rolling. *Contact:* Ms. Charlene Dackerman, Director, 619-549-5070.
CONTACT Ms. Debbie Glenn, Director of Admissions, Kelsey Jenney College, 7310 Miramar Road, Suite 300, San Diego, CA 92126, 619-233-7418. College video available.

KINGS RIVER COMMUNITY COLLEGE
Reedley, California

UG Enrollment: 6,278	Tuition & Fees (CA Res): $390
Application Deadline: rolling	Room Only: $1500

GENERAL State and locally supported, 2-year, coed. Part of State Center Community College District System. Awards certificates, diplomas, transfer associate, terminal associate degrees. Founded 1926. *Setting:* 350-acre rural campus. *Total enrollment:* 6,278. *Faculty:* 221 (76 full-time, 145 part-time).
ENROLLMENT PROFILE 6,278 students from 15 states and territories, 7 other countries. 63% women, 56% part-time, 98% state residents, 16% transferred in, 1% international, 53% 25 or older, 2% Native American, 31% Hispanic, 2% African American, 4% Asian American. *Most popular recent majors:* liberal arts/general studies, aviation technology, agricultural sciences.
FIRST-YEAR CLASS 2,206 total. Of the students who applied, 100% were accepted, 89% of whom enrolled.
ACADEMIC PROGRAM Core. Calendar: semesters. Academic remediation for entering students, English as a second language program offered during academic year, services for LD students, advanced placement, honors program, summer session for credit, part-time degree program (daytime, evenings), adult/continuing education programs, co-op programs. ROTC: Air Force (c).
GENERAL DEGREE REQUIREMENTS 60 units; 1 course in college algebra; computer course.
MAJORS Accounting, agricultural business, agricultural sciences, agronomy/soil and crop sciences, animal sciences, art/fine arts, automotive technologies, aviation technology, biology/biological sciences, business administration/commerce/management, child psychology/child development, computer information systems, computer science, dental services, English, fashion merchandising, forest technology, home economics, industrial engineering technology, law enforcement/police sciences, liberal arts/general studies, manufacturing technology, mathematics, music, ornamental horticulture, physical education, physical sciences, secretarial studies/office management, social science, Spanish, speech/rhetoric/public address/debate, theater arts/drama, welding technology.
LIBRARY 30,000 books, 125 periodicals, 2,155 records, tapes, and CDs.
COMPUTERS ON CAMPUS Computers for student use in computer center, agriculture, business departments, library. Staffed computer lab on campus.
COLLEGE LIFE Drama-theater group, student-run newspaper. *Student services:* personal-psychological counseling.
HOUSING 204 college housing spaces available; 180 were occupied 1995-96. No special consideration for freshman housing applicants. Off-campus living permitted. *Option:* coed housing available. Resident assistants live in dorms.
ATHLETICS *Intercollegiate:* basketball M/W, cross-country running M/W, football M, golf M, tennis M/W, track and field M/W, volleyball W. *Intramural:* basketball, football, swimming and diving, tennis, track and field, volleyball. *Contact:* Mr. John Perkins, Director of Athletics, 209-638-3641 Ext. 360.
CAREER PLANNING *Director:* Mr. Joe Russo, 209-638-3641 Ext. 364. *Service:* career counseling.
EXPENSES FOR 1996-97 State resident tuition: $0 full-time. Nonresident tuition: $4050 full-time, $135 per unit part-time. Part-time mandatory fees: $13 per unit. Full-time mandatory fees: $390. College room only: $1500.
FINANCIAL AID *College-administered undergrad aid 1995-96:* need-based scholarships, non-need scholarships (average $100), Federal Work-Study, part-time jobs. *Required forms:* CSS Financial Aid PROFILE, FAFSA. *Priority deadline:* 5/1.
APPLYING Open admission. *Required:* school transcript, TOEFL for international students. *Recommended:* SAT I or ACT. *Required for some:* CGP. Test scores used for counseling/placement. *Application deadline:* rolling.
APPLYING/TRANSFER *Required:* college transcript. *Recommended:* standardized test scores.
CONTACT Mr. Moire C. Charters, Associate Dean of Admissions, Kings River Community College, Reedley, CA 93654-2099, 209-638-3641 Ext. 221.

LAKE TAHOE COMMUNITY COLLEGE
South Lake Tahoe, California

UG Enrollment: 2,700	Tuition & Fees (CA Res): $417
Application Deadline: rolling	Room & Board: N/Avail

GENERAL State and locally supported, 2-year, coed. Part of California Community Colleges System. Awards certificates, transfer associate, terminal associate degrees. Founded 1975. *Setting:* 164-acre small-town campus. *Total enrollment:* 2,700. *Faculty:* 164 (24 full-time, 140 part-time).
ENROLLMENT PROFILE 2,700 students: 58% women, 42% men, 89% part-time, 95% state residents, 16% transferred in, 71% 25 or older, 2% Native American, 15% Hispanic, 2% African American, 3% Asian American.
FIRST-YEAR CLASS Of the students who applied, 100% were accepted.
ACADEMIC PROGRAM Core, honor code. Calendar: quarters. Academic remediation for entering students, English as a second language program offered during academic year and summer, services for LD students, summer session for credit, part-time degree program (daytime), internships.
GENERAL DEGREE REQUIREMENTS 90 units; math/science requirements vary according to program; 2 courses in science including 1 lab science course; computer course.
MAJORS Accounting, art/fine arts, business administration/commerce/management, computer science, criminal justice, dance, early childhood education, finance/banking, fire science, hotel and restaurant management, humanities, law enforcement/police sciences, liberal arts/general studies, marketing/retailing/merchandising, mathematics, medical assistant technologies, medical secretarial studies, music, natural sciences, physical education, real estate, science, secretarial studies/office management, social science, Spanish, theater arts/drama.
LIBRARY Lake Tahoe Community College Library with 38,124 books, 347 microform titles, 367 periodicals, 1 CD-ROM, 2,717 records, tapes, and CDs.
COMPUTERS ON CAMPUS 105 computers for student use in computer center, computer labs, learning resource center, classrooms. Staffed computer lab on campus provides training in use of computers, software.

Lake Tahoe Community College (continued)

COLLEGE LIFE Drama-theater group. ***Social organizations:*** 4 open to all. ***Most popular organizations:*** Associated Student Council, Alpha Gamma Sigma, Foreign Language Club, Art Club. ***Major annual events:*** AIDS Awareness Day, Day of the Young Child, Annual Student/Staff Picnic. ***Student services:*** personal-psychological counseling.

HOUSING College housing not available.

ATHLETICS ***Intramural:*** cross-country running, volleyball. ***Contact:*** Mr. Mark Meka, Athletic Director/Physical Education Instructor, 916-541-4660 Ext. 246.

CAREER PLANNING ***Placement office:*** 1 part-time staff. ***Director:*** Mr. Robert Sanfilippo, Counselor, 916-541-4660 Ext. 231. ***Services:*** job fairs, resume preparation, career counseling, careers library, job interviews.

EXPENSES FOR 1995–96 State resident tuition: $0 full-time. Nonresident tuition: $3735 full-time. Part-time mandatory fees per quarter range from $13 to $103. Nonresident part-time tuition per unit: $28 for the first 6 units, $83 for the next 5 units. Part-time tuition per unit for Nevada residents who are eligible for the Good Neighbor Program: $37. Full-time mandatory fees: $417.

FINANCIAL AID ***College-administered undergrad aid 1995–96:*** 4 need-based scholarships (average $200), 2 non-need scholarships (average $200), short-term loans (average $50), low-interest long-term loans from external sources (average $2500), Federal Work-Study. ***Required forms:*** institutional, FAFSA; required for some: state. ***Priority deadline:*** 7/1.

APPLYING Open admission. ***Options:*** early entrance, midyear entrance. ***Required:*** TOEFL for international students. Test scores used for counseling/placement. ***Application deadline:*** rolling. ***Notification:*** continuous.

APPLYING/TRANSFER ***Entrance:*** noncompetitive. ***Application deadline:*** rolling. ***Notification:*** continuous.

CONTACT Ms. Linda Stevenson, Director of Admissions and Records, Lake Tahoe Community College, South Lake Tahoe, CA 96150-4524, 916-541-4660 Ext. 273. ***Fax:*** 916-541-7852.

LANEY COLLEGE
Oakland, California

UG Enrollment: 10,454	**Tuition & Fees (CA Res): $394**
Application Deadline: rolling	**Room & Board: N/Avail**

GENERAL State and locally supported, 2-year, coed. Part of Peralta Community College District System. Awards certificates, transfer associate, terminal associate degrees. Founded 1953. ***Setting:*** urban campus with easy access to San Francisco. ***Research spending 1994–95:*** $68,724. ***Educational spending 1994–95:*** $824 per undergrad. ***Total enrollment:*** 10,454. ***Faculty:*** 315 (130 full-time, 185 part-time); student-faculty ratio is 33:1.

ENROLLMENT PROFILE 10,454 students: 57% women, 71% part-time, 98% state residents, 10% transferred in, 1% international, 57% 25 or older, 1% Native American, 10% Hispanic, 39% African American, 30% Asian American. ***Areas of study chosen:*** 9% business management and administrative services, 9% engineering and applied sciences, 5% fine arts, 5% health professions and related sciences, 4% computer and information sciences, 4% interdisciplinary studies, 3% liberal arts/general studies, 3% social sciences, 2% biological and life sciences, 2% psychology, 1% architecture, 1% communications and journalism, 1% education, 1% mathematics.

FIRST-YEAR CLASS 2,313 total. Of the students who applied, 98% were accepted.

ACADEMIC PROGRAM Core. Calendar: semesters. 597 courses offered in 1995–96. Academic remediation for entering students, services for LD students, summer session for credit, part-time degree program (daytime, evenings), adult/continuing education programs.

GENERAL DEGREE REQUIREMENTS 60 semester hours; 3 semester hours of math; computer course.

MAJORS Accounting, architectural technologies, art/fine arts, Asian/Oriental studies, black/African-American studies, broadcasting, business administration/commerce/management, carpentry, ceramic art and design, commercial art, computer information systems, computer programming, construction management, cosmetology, culinary arts, dance, engineering (general), engineering technology, ethnic studies, finance/banking, heating/refrigeration/air conditioning, humanities, journalism, labor studies, liberal arts/general studies, machine and tool technologies, management information systems, marketing/retailing/merchandising, mathematics, Mexican-American/Chicano studies, music, photography, printing technologies, radio and television studies, reading education, science, secretarial studies/office management, social science, theater arts/drama, welding technology, wood sciences, word processing.

LIBRARY Laney Library with 78,054 books, 6,611 microform titles, 209 periodicals, 811 records, tapes, and CDs. Acquisition spending 1994–95: $20,000.

COMPUTERS ON CAMPUS 30 computers for student use in computer labs.

COLLEGE LIFE Drama-theater group, student-run newspaper. ***Most popular organizations:*** La Raza Club, African Student Union, Vision Christian Society, Asian/Pacific Islander Club, Vietnamese Student Club. ***Major annual events:*** Cinco de Mayo, Black History Month, Multi-Cultural Day.

HOUSING College housing not available.

ATHLETICS ***Intercollegiate:*** baseball M, football M, softball W, volleyball W. ***Contact:*** Mr. Stan Peters, Athletic Director, 510-464-3478.

CAREER PLANNING ***Service:*** career counseling.

EXPENSES FOR 1996–97 State resident tuition: $0 full-time. Nonresident tuition: $3660 full-time, $122 per semester hour part-time. Part-time mandatory fees: $13 per semester hour. Full-time mandatory fees: $394.

FINANCIAL AID ***College-administered undergrad aid 1995–96:*** need-based scholarships, Federal Work-Study. ***Required forms:*** FAFSA. ***Priority deadline:*** 4/10.

APPLYING Open admission. ***Option:*** early entrance. ***Required:*** TOEFL for international students. Test scores used for counseling/placement. ***Application deadline:*** rolling.

APPLYING/TRANSFER ***Entrance:*** noncompetitive.

CONTACT Mrs. Mary DeCoite, District Admissions Officer, Laney College, 900 Fallon Street, Oakland, CA 94607-4893, 510-466-7369.

LAS POSITAS COLLEGE
Livermore, California

UG Enrollment: 5,600	**Tuition & Fees (CA Res): $390**
Application Deadline: N/R	**Room & Board: N/Avail**

GENERAL State-supported, 2-year, coed. Part of California Community Colleges System. Awards certificates, diplomas, transfer associate, terminal associate degrees. Founded 1988. ***Setting:*** 150-acre suburban campus with easy access to Oakland and San Francisco. ***Total enrollment:*** 5,600. ***Faculty:*** 165 full-time.

ENROLLMENT PROFILE 5,600 students: 58% women, 83% part-time, 4% transferred in, 1% international, 52% 25 or older, 2% Native American, 9% Hispanic, 2% African American, 4% Asian American. ***Most popular recent majors:*** liberal arts/general studies, business administration/commerce/management, computer science.

FIRST-YEAR CLASS 1,400 total. Of the students who applied, 100% were accepted.

ACADEMIC PROGRAM Core, honor code. Calendar: semesters. Academic remediation for entering students, English as a second language program offered during academic year and summer, services for LD students, advanced placement, self-designed majors, tutorials, summer session for credit, part-time degree program (daytime, evenings, weekends, summer), internships.

GENERAL DEGREE REQUIREMENTS 60 units; 1 course each in math and science.

MAJORS Accounting, automotive technologies, business administration/commerce/management, computer information systems, computer science, drafting and design, early childhood education, education, electrical and electronics technologies, environmental sciences, fashion merchandising, fire science, horticulture, industrial design, interior design, law enforcement/police sciences, liberal arts/general studies, marketing/retailing/merchandising, occupational safety and health, radiological technology, real estate, secretarial studies/office management, welding technology.

COMPUTERS ON CAMPUS Computers for student use in computer center, computer labs, learning resource center, classrooms, library provide access to Internet. Staffed computer lab on campus provides training in use of computers, software.

COLLEGE LIFE 10% vote in student government elections. ***Social organizations:*** 23 open to all. ***Campus security:*** 24-hour emergency response devices, late-night transport-escort service.

HOUSING College housing not available.

ATHLETICS ***Intercollegiate:*** cross-country running M/W, soccer M/W. ***Intramural:*** basketball, fencing, racquetball, soccer, softball, volleyball. ***Contact:*** Ms. Sophie Rheinheimer, Athletic Director, 510-373-5800 Ext. 5862.

CAREER PLANNING ***Placement office:*** 1 full-time staff. ***Director:*** Ms. Lettie Camp, Counselor Assistant, 510-373-5823. ***Services:*** job fairs, resume preparation, career counseling, careers library, job bank, job interviews.

EXPENSES FOR 1995–96 State resident tuition: $0 full-time. Nonresident tuition: $3660 full-time, $122 per unit part-time. Part-time mandatory fees: $13 per unit. Full-time mandatory fees: $390.

FINANCIAL AID ***College-administered undergrad aid 1995–96:*** 9 Federal Work-Study (averaging $1225). ***Required forms:*** FAFSA, income verification. ***Priority deadline:*** 7/1.

APPLYING Open admission. ***Required:*** TOEFL for international students. ***Recommended:*** school transcript. Test scores used for counseling/placement.

APPLYING/TRANSFER ***Required:*** college transcript.

CONTACT Ms. Sylvia Rodriquez, Registrar, Las Positas College, Livermore, CA 94550-7650, 510-373-4942.

LASSEN COLLEGE
Susanville, California

UG Enrollment: 2,951	**Tuition & Fees (CA Res): $405**
Application Deadline: rolling	**Room & Board: $4006**

GENERAL State and locally supported, 2-year, coed. Part of California Community Colleges System. Awards certificates, transfer associate, terminal associate degrees. Founded 1925. ***Setting:*** 100-acre rural campus. ***Total enrollment:*** 2,951. ***Faculty:*** 204 (44 full-time, 160 part-time); student-faculty ratio is 15:1.

ENROLLMENT PROFILE 2,951 students from 12 states and territories, 3 other countries. 57% women, 67% part-time, 94% state residents, 10% transferred in, 5% international, 58% 25 or older, 6% Native American, 5% Hispanic, 2% African American, 2% Asian American.

FIRST-YEAR CLASS 1,178 total.

ACADEMIC PROGRAM Core. Calendar: semesters. Academic remediation for entering students, English as a second language program offered during academic year, services for LD students, advanced placement, summer session for credit, part-time degree program (daytime, evenings, summer), adult/continuing education programs, co-op programs and internships. Off-campus study at members of the Northeastern California Higher Education Council.

GENERAL DEGREE REQUIREMENTS 60 units; 1 math course; computer course for journalism, math, business-related majors.

MAJORS Accounting, agricultural business, agricultural economics, agricultural sciences, agricultural technologies, agronomy/soil and crop sciences, applied art, art/fine arts, automotive technologies, biology/biological sciences, botany/plant sciences, business administration/commerce/management, business machine technologies, carpentry, ceramic art and design, chemistry, commercial art, communication, communication equipment technology, computer science, construction technologies, cosmetology, drafting and design, early childhood education, energy management technologies, (pre)engineering sequence, farm and ranch management, graphic arts, history, humanities, journalism, law enforcement/police sciences, legal secretarial studies, liberal arts/general studies, mathematics, medical secretarial studies, natural sciences, nursing, painting/drawing, photography, physical education, practical nursing, psychology, radio and television studies, science, secretarial studies/office management, social science, welding technology.

LIBRARY Lassen College Library with 15,000 books, 100 periodicals, 150 records, tapes, and CDs.

COMPUTERS ON CAMPUS Computer purchase plan available. 30 computers for student use in computer center. Staffed computer lab on campus provides training in use of computers, software.

COLLEGE LIFE Drama-theater group, student-run newspaper. *Most popular organization:* Lassen Student Union. *Major annual events:* Career Day, Vocational Olympics, Skunk Days. *Student services:* legal services, health clinic.
HOUSING 100 college housing spaces available; 60 were occupied 1995–96. Off-campus living permitted. *Option:* coed housing available. Resident assistants live in dorms.
ATHLETICS Member NJCAA. *Intercollegiate:* basketball M/W, cross-country running M/W, golf M/W, riflery M/W, softball W, track and field M/W, volleyball W, wrestling M. *Intramural:* basketball, cross-country running, equestrian sports, football, golf, gymnastics, racquetball, riflery, sailing, skiing (cross-country), skiing (downhill), softball, swimming and diving, tennis, track and field, volleyball, weight lifting, wrestling. *Contact:* Ms. Donna Pritchard, Athletic Director, 916-257-6181 Ext. 117.
CAREER PLANNING *Director:* Ms. Ann Wyngate, Director of Career Center, 916-257-6181 Ext. 124. *Services:* resume preparation, career counseling, careers library.
EXPENSES FOR 1996–97 State resident tuition: $0 full-time. Nonresident tuition: $3810 full-time, $127 per unit part-time. Part-time mandatory fees per semester range from $20.50 to $150.50. Full-time mandatory fees: $405. College room and board: $4006.
FINANCIAL AID *College-administered undergrad aid 1995–96:* need-based scholarships, short-term loans (averaging $60), low-interest long-term loans, Federal Work-Study, part-time jobs. *Required forms:* CSS Financial Aid PROFILE, FAFSA; required for some: state. *Priority deadline:* 6/30.
APPLYING Open admission. *Option:* early entrance. *Required:* TOEFL for international students. *Recommended:* school transcript, ACT. Test scores used for counseling/placement. *Application deadline:* rolling. *Notification:* continuous.
APPLYING/TRANSFER *Recommended:* standardized test scores, high school transcript, college transcript. *Entrance:* noncompetitive. *Application deadline:* rolling. *Notification:* continuous.
CONTACT Mr. Jim Goubert, Counselor, Lassen College, Susanville, CA 96130, 916-257-6181 Ext. 106.

LONG BEACH CITY COLLEGE
Long Beach, California

UG Enrollment: 24,000	Tuition & Fees (CA Res): $410
Application Deadline: rolling	Room & Board: N/Avail

GENERAL State-supported, 2-year, coed. Part of California Community Colleges System. Awards transfer associate, terminal associate degrees. Founded 1927. *Setting:* 40-acre urban campus with easy access to Los Angeles. *Research spending 1994–95:* $30,000. *Total enrollment:* 24,000. *Faculty:* 763 (247 full-time, 516 part-time); student-faculty ratio is 32:1.
ENROLLMENT PROFILE 24,000 students: 54% women, 89% part-time, 92% state residents, 12% transferred in, 1% international, 61% 25 or older, 1% Native American, 21% Hispanic, 11% African American, 15% Asian American. *Areas of study chosen:* 36% liberal arts/general studies, 17% health professions and related sciences, 11% business management and administrative services, 8% engineering and applied sciences, 5% computer and information sciences, 5% social sciences, 4% education, 4% vocational and home economics, 1% biological and life sciences, 1% physical sciences. *Most popular recent majors:* liberal arts/general studies, nursing, electrical and electronics technologies.
FIRST-YEAR CLASS 6,300 total. Of the students who applied, 100% were accepted.
ACADEMIC PROGRAM Core, honor code. Calendar: semesters. Academic remediation for entering students, English as a second language program offered during academic year and summer, services for LD students, advanced placement, honors program, summer session for credit, part-time degree program (daytime, evenings, summer); adult/continuing education programs.
GENERAL DEGREE REQUIREMENTS 60 units; 1 life science course; 1 year of a foreign language; computer course.
MAJORS Accounting, advertising, architectural technologies, art/fine arts, automotive technologies, aviation technology, biology/biological sciences, business administration/commerce/management, carpentry, child psychology/child development, computer programming, criminal justice, dance, data processing, dental services, dietetics, drafting and design, early childhood education, electrical and electronics technologies, electromechanical technology, engineering (general), (pre)engineering sequence, English, family and consumer studies, fashion design and technology, fashion merchandising, film studies, fire science, flight training, food services management, French, German, health science, heating/refrigeration/air conditioning, home economics, horticulture, hotel and restaurant management, human services, industrial arts, industrial engineering technology, insurance, interior design, international business, journalism, labor and industrial relations, legal secretarial studies, liberal arts/general studies, machine and tool technologies, marketing/retailing/merchandising, mathematics, medical assistant technologies, medical secretarial studies, music, nursing, photography, physical education, physical sciences, public relations, quality control technology, radiological technology, real estate, respiratory therapy, retail management, science, secretarial studies/office management, social science, Spanish, speech/rhetoric/public address/debate, telecommunications, textiles and clothing, theater arts/drama, tourism and travel, welding technology.
LIBRARY Long Beach City College Library with 250,000 books. Acquisition spending 1994–95: $115,000.
COMPUTERS ON CAMPUS Computer purchase plan available. 200 computers for student use in computer center, computer labs, library. Academic computing expenditure 1994–95: $1 million.
COLLEGE LIFE Drama-theater group, choral group, marching band, student-run newspaper. *Social organizations:* 55 open to all; 5 local fraternities, 6 local sororities. *Most popular organizations:* American Criminal Justice Association, AGS Scholarship Organization, Lesbian, Gay, Bisexual Student Union, Vietnamese Club, Network Christian Fellowship. *Major annual events:* Homecoming, Spring Sing, Mini-Grand Prix. *Student services:* personal-psychological counseling, women's center. *Campus security:* 24-hour emergency response devices and patrols, student patrols, late-night transport-escort service.
HOUSING College housing not available.
ATHLETICS Member NJCAA. *Intercollegiate:* baseball M, basketball M/W, cross-country running M/W, football M, golf M, soccer M/W, softball W, swimming and diving M/W, tennis M/W, track and field M/W, volleyball M/W, water polo M. *Intramural:* archery, basketball, bowling, football, golf, racquetball, soccer, softball, swimming and diving, tennis, track and field, volleyball, weight lifting, wrestling. *Contact:* Mr. Chuck McFerrin, Director, Men's Athletics, 310-420-4239; Ms. Mickie Davis, Director, Women's Athletics, 310-420-4053.

CAREER PLANNING *Placement office:* $120,000 operating expenditure 1994–95. *Director:* Ms. Dorothy Mitchell, Director, Career Planning, 310-420-4292. *Services:* resume preparation, career counseling, careers library, job bank, job interviews.
AFTER GRADUATION 20% of students completing a degree program in 1994–95 went directly on to further study.
EXPENSES FOR 1996–97 State resident tuition: $0 full-time. Nonresident tuition: $3810 full-time, $127 per unit part-time. Part-time mandatory fees per semester range from $23 to $153. Full-time mandatory fees: $410.
FINANCIAL AID *College-administered undergrad aid 1995–96:* need-based scholarships, non-need scholarships, short-term loans, Federal Work-Study, part-time jobs. *Required forms:* institutional, FAFSA. *Application deadline:* continuous to 8/1.
APPLYING Open admission except for nursing program. *Option:* early entrance. *Required:* TOEFL for international students. *Recommended:* school transcript. Test scores used for counseling/placement. *Application deadline:* rolling.
APPLYING/TRANSFER *Recommended:* high school transcript, college transcript. *Entrance:* noncompetitive. *Contact:* Ms. Mary B. Williams, Transfer Center Director, 310-420-4557.
CONTACT Mr. Gopal Raman, Dean of Admissions and Records, Long Beach City College, 4901 East Carson Street, Long Beach, CA 90808-1780, 310-420-4130. College video available.

LOS ANGELES CITY COLLEGE
Los Angeles, California

UG Enrollment: 15,217	Tuition & Fees (CA Res): $390
Application Deadline: 9/5	Room & Board: N/Avail

GENERAL District-supported, 2-year, coed. Part of Los Angeles Community College District System. Awards certificates, transfer associate, terminal associate degrees. Founded 1929. *Setting:* 42-acre urban campus. *Total enrollment:* 15,217. *Faculty:* 625 (200 full-time, 5% with terminal degrees, 425 part-time). *Notable Alumni:* William Wilson, Paul Winfield, Mark Hamill, Cindy Williams, Robert Vaughn.
ENROLLMENT PROFILE 15,217 students from 52 states and territories, 36 other countries. 54% women, 66% part-time, 94% state residents, 62% 25 or older, 1% Native American, 38% Hispanic, 14% African American, 22% Asian American.
FIRST-YEAR CLASS 3,807 total. Of the students who applied, 100% were accepted, 85% of whom enrolled.
ACADEMIC PROGRAM Core, honor code. Calendar: semesters. Academic remediation for entering students, English as a second language program offered during academic year and summer, services for LD students, advanced placement, honors program, summer session for credit, part-time degree program (daytime), adult/continuing education programs. Study abroad in Mexico, France, England, Germany, Spain, Japan, Italy, Portugal, Australia. ROTC: Army (c), Naval (c), Air Force (c).
GENERAL DEGREE REQUIREMENTS 60 units; 1 course each in math and natural science.
MAJORS Accounting, advertising, American studies, applied art, architectural technologies, art/fine arts, biology/biological sciences, black/African-American studies, broadcasting, business administration/commerce/management, ceramic art and design, chemistry, child care/child and family studies, child psychology/child development, communication, computer programming, computer technologies, corrections, criminal justice, data processing, dental services, dietetics, drafting and design, electrical and electronics technologies, engineering (general), English, family and consumer studies, finance/banking, food sciences, food services management, food services technology, French, German, history, home economics, human services, journalism, law enforcement/police sciences, legal secretarial studies, liberal arts/general studies, marketing/retailing/merchandising, mathematics, medical secretarial studies, mental health/rehabilitation counseling, Mexican-American/Chicano studies, music, nuclear medical technology, optometric/ophthalmic technologies, photography, physics, psychology, public administration, public relations, radio and television studies, radiological sciences, radiological technology, real estate, retail management, science, secretarial studies/office management, sociology, Spanish, speech/rhetoric/public address/debate, teacher aide studies, telecommunications, textiles and clothing, theater arts/drama, tourism and travel.
LIBRARY 150,000 books, 150 periodicals.
COMPUTERS ON CAMPUS 200 computers for student use in computer center, library. Staffed computer lab on campus provides training in use of computers, software.
COLLEGE LIFE Drama-theater group, choral group, marching band, student-run newspaper. 10% vote in student government elections. *Student services:* health clinic, personal-psychological counseling. *Campus security:* 24-hour emergency response devices and patrols, student patrols, late-night transport-escort service.
HOUSING College housing not available.
ATHLETICS *Intercollegiate:* basketball M, cross-country running M, football M, gymnastics M, track and field M/W, volleyball M/W. *Intramural:* archery, badminton, basketball, bowling, golf, gymnastics, soccer, swimming and diving, table tennis (Ping-Pong), tennis, weight lifting, wrestling. *Contact:* Mr. Jack Boyer, Department Chairperson, Physical Education, 213-953-4835.
CAREER PLANNING *Director:* Ms. Betty McKiver, Director, 213-953-4290. *Service:* career counseling.
EXPENSES FOR 1995–96 State resident tuition: $0 full-time. Nonresident tuition: $3750 full-time, $125 per unit part-time. Part-time mandatory fees: $13 per unit. Full-time mandatory fees: $390.
FINANCIAL AID *College-administered undergrad aid 1995–96:* 426 need-based scholarships (average $320), non-need scholarships, short-term loans (average $100), low-interest long-term loans from external sources (average $2500), Federal Work-Study, 1,000 part-time jobs. *Required forms:* CSS Financial Aid PROFILE, state, institutional, FAFSA. *Priority deadline:* 5/1.
APPLYING Open admission except for foreign applicants, optics, radiological technology programs. *Required:* TOEFL for international students. Test scores used for admission. *Application deadline:* 9/5. *Notification:* continuous until 9/5.
APPLYING/TRANSFER *Entrance:* noncompetitive. *Application deadline:* 9/5. *Notification:* continuous until 9/5. *Contact:* Dr. Martha Sklar, Director, 213-953-4281.
CONTACT Mr. Leonard Walton, Chief Admissions Officer, Los Angeles City College, 855 North Vermont Avenue, Los Angeles, CA 90029-3590, 213-953-4381. College video available.

LOS ANGELES HARBOR COLLEGE
Wilmington, California

UG Enrollment: 7,603 **Tuition & Fees (CA Res): $405**
Application Deadline: 8/15 **Room & Board: N/Avail**

GENERAL State and locally supported, 2-year, coed. Part of Los Angeles Community College District System. Awards certificates, transfer associate, terminal associate degrees. Founded 1949. ***Setting:*** 80-acre suburban campus. ***Total enrollment:*** 7,603. ***Faculty:*** 313 (98 full-time, 215 part-time); student-faculty ratio is 25:1.
ENROLLMENT PROFILE 7,603 students from 14 states and territories, 16 other countries. 59% women, 73% part-time, 98% state residents, 14% transferred in, 1% international, 49% 25 or older, 2% Native American, 36% Hispanic, 17% African American, 18% Asian American.
FIRST-YEAR CLASS 2,272 total. Of the students who applied, 100% were accepted.
ACADEMIC PROGRAM Core. Calendar: semesters. Academic remediation for entering students, English as a second language program offered during academic year, services for LD students, advanced placement, Freshman Honors College, honors program, summer session for credit, part-time degree program (daytime, evenings, weekends, summer), external degree programs, adult/continuing education programs, co-op programs. Off-campus study at California State University, Dominguez Hills. Study abroad in England.
GENERAL DEGREE REQUIREMENTS 60 units; math/science requirements vary according to program; computer course for most majors.
MAJORS Accounting, architectural technologies, automotive technologies, biology/biological sciences, black/African-American studies, business administration/commerce/management, child psychology/child development, computer information systems, computer technologies, data processing, drafting and design, electrical engineering technology, electromechanical technology, (pre)engineering sequence, engineering technology, fire science, industrial engineering technology, interior design, law enforcement/police sciences, legal secretarial studies, liberal arts/general studies, medical secretarial studies, nursing, physics, real estate, secretarial studies/office management.
LIBRARY 82,790 books, 302 periodicals.
COMPUTERS ON CAMPUS 50 computers for student use in computer center, library, student center.
COLLEGE LIFE Drama-theater group, choral group, student-run radio station. 5% vote in student government elections. ***Student services:*** legal services, health clinic, personal-psychological counseling. ***Campus security:*** 24-hour emergency response devices and patrols.
HOUSING College housing not available.
ATHLETICS ***Intercollegiate:*** baseball M, basketball M/W, football M, soccer M, tennis W. ***Contact:*** Mr. James O'Brien, Athletic Director, 310-522-8345.
CAREER PLANNING ***Placement office:*** 3 full-time staff. ***Director:*** Ms. Joy Fisher, Counselor, 310-522-8386. ***Services:*** career counseling, careers library.
EXPENSES FOR 1996–97 State resident tuition: $0 full-time. Nonresident tuition: $3570 full-time, $119 per unit part-time. Part-time mandatory fees per semester range from $20.50 to $150.50. Full-time mandatory fees: $405.
FINANCIAL AID ***College-administered undergrad aid 1995–96:*** low-interest long-term loans, part-time jobs. ***Acceptable forms:*** CSS Financial Aid PROFILE, institutional, FAFSA. ***Application deadline:*** 3/15.
APPLYING Open admission except for nursing program. ***Options:*** early entrance, deferred entrance, midyear entrance. ***Required:*** TOEFL for international students. Test scores used for counseling/placement. ***Application deadline:*** 8/15.
APPLYING/TRANSFER ***Entrance:*** noncompetitive. ***Application deadline:*** 8/15.
CONTACT Assistant Dean of Admissions and Records, Los Angeles Harbor College, Wilmington, CA 90744-2311, 310-522-8318. College video available.

LOS ANGELES MISSION COLLEGE
Sylmar, California

UG Enrollment: 6,027 **Tuition & Fees (CA Res): $390**
Application Deadline: N/R **Room & Board: N/Avail**

GENERAL State and locally supported, 2-year, coed. Part of Los Angeles Community College District System. Awards transfer associate, terminal associate degrees. Founded 1974. ***Setting:*** 22-acre small-town campus with easy access to Los Angeles. ***Total enrollment:*** 6,027. ***Faculty:*** 115 (42 full-time, 73 part-time).
ENROLLMENT PROFILE 6,027 students: 65% women, 73% part-time, 98% state residents, 1% transferred in, 1% international, 55% 25 or older, 2% Native American, 64% Hispanic, 6% African American, 5% Asian American. ***Most popular recent majors:*** computer programming, liberal arts/general studies, English.
FIRST-YEAR CLASS 1,726 total. Of the students who applied, 100% were accepted.
ACADEMIC PROGRAM Core, honor code. Calendar: semesters. Academic remediation for entering students, English as a second language program offered during academic year and summer, services for LD students, advanced placement, summer session for credit, part-time degree program (daytime, evenings), external degree programs, adult/continuing education programs, co-op programs.
GENERAL DEGREE REQUIREMENTS 60 credits; 1 course each in math and lab science.
MAJORS Accounting, art education, aviation technology, biology/biological sciences, business administration/commerce/management, chemistry, child psychology/child development, computer programming, consumer services, culinary arts, economics, English, family and consumer studies, finance/banking, French, geography, health education, history, home economics education, humanities, industrial administration, Italian, journalism, law enforcement/police sciences, liberal arts/general studies, mathematics, music, philosophy, physical education, physical sciences, psychology, real estate, secretarial studies/office management, social science, sociology, Spanish, speech/rhetoric/public address/debate, teacher aide studies, theater arts/drama.
LIBRARY 40,000 books, 62 microform titles, 450 periodicals, 1,850 records, tapes, and CDs.
COMPUTERS ON CAMPUS 103 computers for student use in computer center, library provide access to main academic computer, on-line services.
COLLEGE LIFE Drama-theater group, student-run newspaper. 2% vote in student government elections. ***Student services:*** personal-psychological counseling, women's center. ***Campus security:*** 24-hour emergency response devices and patrols, student patrols.
HOUSING College housing not available.
ATHLETICS ***Intercollegiate:*** baseball M, cross-country running M/W, golf M, soccer M. ***Contact:*** Mr. John Klitsner, Athletic Director, 818-837-1201.
CAREER PLANNING ***Placement office:*** 1 full-time, 4 part-time staff. ***Director:*** Ms. Joanne Flink, Counselor, 818-364-7652. ***Services:*** job fairs, career counseling, careers library.
EXPENSES FOR 1995–96 State resident tuition: $0 full-time. Nonresident tuition: $3570 full-time, $119 per unit part-time. Part-time mandatory fees per semester range from $20.50 to $150.50. Full-time mandatory fees: $390.
FINANCIAL AID ***College-administered undergrad aid 1995–96:*** need-based scholarships, non-need scholarships, short-term loans (average $100), low-interest long-term loans from external sources (average $2500), Federal Work-Study, 55 part-time jobs. ***Required forms:*** CSS Financial Aid PROFILE, state, institutional, FAFSA. ***Priority deadline:*** 8/1.
APPLYING Open admission. ***Option:*** early entrance. ***Required:*** TOEFL for international students. Test scores used for counseling/placement. ***Notification:*** continuous until 9/25.
CONTACT Ms. Angela Merrill, Admissions Supervisor, Los Angeles Mission College, Sylmar, CA 91342-3200, 818-364-7658.

LOS ANGELES PIERCE COLLEGE
Woodland Hills, California

UG Enrollment: 18,212 **Tuition & Fees (CA Res): $419**
Application Deadline: 8/20 **Room & Board: N/Avail**

GENERAL State and locally supported, 2-year, coed. Part of Los Angeles Community College District System. Awards certificates, transfer associate, terminal associate degrees. Founded 1947. ***Setting:*** 425-acre suburban campus with easy access to Los Angeles. ***Total enrollment:*** 18,212. ***Faculty:*** 519 (288 full-time, 40% with terminal degrees, 231 part-time).
ENROLLMENT PROFILE 18,212 students from 2 states and territories, 48 other countries. 54% women, 70% part-time, 98% state residents, 48% 25 or older, 1% Native American, 13% Hispanic, 4% African American, 17% Asian American. ***Areas of study chosen:*** 71% liberal arts/general studies, 9% health professions and related sciences, 5% vocational and home economics, 4% agriculture, 3% business management and administrative services, 2% computer and information sciences, 2% engineering and applied sciences, 2% performing arts, 1% architecture, 1% foreign language and literature. ***Most popular recent majors:*** liberal arts/general studies, nursing, (pre)engineering sequence.
FIRST-YEAR CLASS 2,425 total. Of the students who applied, 100% were accepted.
ACADEMIC PROGRAM Core, liberal arts curriculum, honor code. Calendar: semesters. Academic remediation for entering students, English as a second language program offered during academic year, services for LD students, advanced placement, honors program, summer session for credit, part-time degree program (daytime, evenings, summer), adult/continuing education programs, co-op programs and internships. Study abroad in Mexico, England, Spain, France, Italy, Australia (1% of students participate).
GENERAL DEGREE REQUIREMENTS 60 credits; 1 math course; internship (some majors).
MAJORS Accounting, agricultural business, agricultural sciences, agronomy/soil and crop sciences, animal sciences, architectural technologies, art/fine arts, automotive technologies, business administration/commerce/management, commercial art, computer programming, computer science, computer technologies, construction technologies, data processing, deaf interpreter training, drafting and design, electrical and electronics technologies, electronics engineering technology, (pre)engineering sequence, equestrian studies, horticulture, illustration, industrial arts, industrial engineering technology, journalism, laboratory animal medicine, landscape architecture/design, landscaping/grounds maintenance, legal secretarial studies, liberal arts/general studies, machine and tool technologies, manufacturing technology, marketing/retailing/merchandising, music, natural resource management, nursing, ornamental horticulture, pest control technology, photography, quality control technology, real estate, secretarial studies/office management, theater arts/drama, veterinary technology, welding technology.
LIBRARY Pierce College Library plus 1 other, with 106,122 books, 6,022 microform titles, 395 periodicals, 5,223 records, tapes, and CDs. Acquisition spending 1994–95: $40,412.
COMPUTERS ON CAMPUS 60 computers for student use in computer center, learning resource center. Staffed computer lab on campus provides training in use of computers, software. Academic computing expenditure 1994–95: $169,525.
COLLEGE LIFE Drama-theater group, choral group, student-run newspaper. 5% vote in student government elections. ***Social organizations:*** 28 open to all. ***Most popular organizations:*** Alpha Gamma Sigma, Club Latino United for Education, United African-American Student Association, Hillel Club, Filipino Club. ***Major annual events:*** Club Day, Job Fair, University Day. ***Student services:*** health clinic, personal-psychological counseling, women's center. ***Campus security:*** 24-hour patrols.
HOUSING College housing not available.
ATHLETICS Member NJCAA. ***Intercollegiate:*** baseball M, basketball W, football M, softball W, swimming and diving M/W, tennis M/W, volleyball M/W, water polo M. ***Intramural:*** archery, badminton, basketball, bowling, cross-country running, equestrian sports, fencing, golf, racquetball, skiing (downhill), soccer, swimming and diving, tennis, volleyball, weight lifting. ***Contact:*** Ms. Marian McWilliams, Athletic Director, 818-719-6421.
CAREER PLANNING ***Placement office:*** 5 part-time staff; $109,420 operating expenditure 1994–95. ***Director:*** Mr. Rudy Dompe, Counselor, 818-719-6440. ***Services:*** job fairs, career counseling, careers library.
EXPENSES FOR 1995–96 State resident tuition: $0 full-time. Nonresident tuition: $3750 full-time, $125 per unit part-time. Part-time mandatory fees per semester range from $27.50 to $157.50. Full-time mandatory fees: $419.
FINANCIAL AID ***College-administered undergrad aid 1995–96:*** 2 need-based scholarships (average $1000), 15 non-need scholarships (average $100), short-term loans (average $50), low-interest long-term loans from external sources (average $1625), Federal Work-Study, 120 part-time jobs. ***Required forms:*** CSS Financial Aid PROFILE; required for some: state, FAFSA. ***Priority deadline:*** 5/24.

APPLYING Open admission except for nursing, honors programs. ***Options:*** early entrance, midyear entrance. ***Required for some:*** TOEFL for international students. Test scores used for counseling/placement. ***Application deadline:*** 8/20.
APPLYING/TRANSFER ***Entrance:*** noncompetitive. ***Contact:*** Mr. Rudy Dompe, Counselor, 818-719-6440.
CONTACT Ms. Shelley L. Gerstl, Associate Dean of Admissions and Records, Los Angeles Pierce College, Woodland Hills, CA 91371-0001, 818-719-6448.

LOS ANGELES SOUTHWEST COLLEGE
Los Angeles, California

UG Enrollment: 5,802 **Tuition & Fees (CA Res): $390**
Application Deadline: 9/9 **Room & Board: N/Avail**

GENERAL State and locally supported, 2-year, coed. Part of Los Angeles Community College District System. Awards certificates, diplomas, transfer associate, terminal associate degrees. Founded 1967. ***Setting:*** 69-acre urban campus. ***Total enrollment:*** 5,802. ***Faculty:*** 223 (75 full-time, 148 part-time); student-faculty ratio is 37:1. ***Notable Alumni:*** Chris Mims.
ENROLLMENT PROFILE 5,802 students from 20 states and territories, 4 other countries. 72% women, 77% part-time, 98% state residents, 16% transferred in, 63% 25 or older, 0% Native American, 24% Hispanic, 74% African American, 1% Asian American. ***Areas of study chosen:*** 6% health professions and related sciences, 2% computer and information sciences, 1% biological and life sciences, 1% business management and administrative services, 1% communications and journalism, 1% education, 1% engineering and applied sciences, 1% English language/literature/letters, 1% interdisciplinary studies, 1% liberal arts/general studies, 1% mathematics, 1% performing arts, 1% psychology, 1% social sciences.
FIRST-YEAR CLASS 485 total. Of the students who applied, 100% were accepted, 40% of whom enrolled.
ACADEMIC PROGRAM Core, honor code. Calendar: semesters. 550 courses offered in 1995–96. Academic remediation for entering students, English as a second language program offered during academic year, services for LD students, Freshman Honors College, tutorials, honors program, summer session for credit, part-time degree program (daytime, evenings), adult/continuing education programs, co-op programs and internships.
GENERAL DEGREE REQUIREMENTS 60 units; 1 course each in math and science.
MAJORS Accounting, African studies, behavioral sciences, child care/child and family studies, child psychology/child development, computer science, criminal justice, data processing, deaf interpreter training, drafting and design, early childhood education, economics, education, electronics engineering technology, engineering (general), family and consumer studies, finance/banking, humanities, law enforcement/police sciences, marketing/retailing/merchandising, music, nursing, quality control technology, radio and television studies, real estate, secretarial studies/office management, social science, Spanish, teacher aide studies, theater arts/drama.
LIBRARY Main library plus 1 other, with 60,000 books, 120 microform titles, 600 periodicals.
COMPUTERS ON CAMPUS Students must have own computer. 40 computers for student use in computer center, library provide access to Internet. Staffed computer lab on campus provides training in use of computers, software.
COLLEGE LIFE Choral group, student-run newspaper. 20% vote in student government elections. ***Social organizations:*** 8 open to all. ***Campus security:*** 24-hour emergency response devices and patrols, student patrols, late-night transport-escort service.
HOUSING College housing not available.
ATHLETICS ***Intercollegiate:*** cross-country running M/W, football M, track and field M/W. ***Intramural:*** archery, badminton, basketball, bowling, cross-country running, golf, volleyball. ***Contact:*** Mr. Henry Washington, Director of Athletics, 213-241-5432.
CAREER PLANNING ***Placement office:*** 2 part-time staff. ***Director:*** Dr. Manque Winters, Chairperson of Counseling, 213-241-5200. ***Services:*** job fairs, career counseling, careers library. 3 organizations recruited on campus 1994–95.
EXPENSES FOR 1996–97 State resident tuition: $0 full-time. Nonresident tuition: $4290 full-time, $143 per unit part-time. Part-time mandatory fees: $13 per unit. Full-time mandatory fees: $390.
FINANCIAL AID ***College-administered undergrad aid 1995–96:*** need-based scholarships, short-term loans (average $50), low-interest long-term loans from external sources (average $2500), Federal Work-Study, part-time jobs. ***Required forms:*** CSS Financial Aid PROFILE, institutional, FAFSA. ***Priority deadline:*** 7/15. ***Payment plan:*** deferred payment. ***Waivers:*** full or partial for minority students.
APPLYING Open admission except for nursing program. ***Option:*** early entrance. ***Recommended:*** 3 years of high school math and science, some high school foreign language. ***Application deadline:*** 9/9. ***Notification:*** continuous until 9/9.
APPLYING/TRANSFER ***Entrance:*** noncompetitive. ***Contact:*** Ms. Brenda A. Scranton, Dean, Student Services, 213-241-5280.
CONTACT Ms. Marilyn May, Associate Dean of Student Services, Los Angeles Southwest College, 1600 West Imperial Highway, Los Angeles, CA 90047-4810, 213-241-5320.

LOS ANGELES TRADE-TECHNICAL COLLEGE
Los Angeles, California

UG Enrollment: 13,373 **Tuition & Fees (CA Res): $390**
Application Deadline: 8/28 **Room & Board: N/Avail**

GENERAL State and locally supported, 2-year, coed. Part of Los Angeles Community College District System. Awards certificates, diplomas, transfer associate, terminal associate degrees. Founded 1925. ***Setting:*** 25-acre urban campus. ***Total enrollment:*** 13,373. ***Faculty:*** 600 (200 full-time, 95% with terminal degrees, 400 part-time); student-faculty ratio is 21:1.
ENROLLMENT PROFILE 13,373 students from 25 states and territories, 20 other countries. 49% women, 64% part-time, 98% state residents, 17% transferred in, 1% international, 57% 25 or older, 2% Native American, 38% Hispanic, 32% African American, 15% Asian American.
FIRST-YEAR CLASS 2,675 total. Of the students who applied, 100% were accepted, 96% of whom enrolled.
ACADEMIC PROGRAM Core. Calendar: semesters. Academic remediation for entering students, English as a second language program offered during academic year and summer, services for LD students, advanced placement, summer session for credit, part-time degree program (daytime, evenings, summer), adult/continuing education programs, co-op programs.
GENERAL DEGREE REQUIREMENTS 60 units; 1 course each in math and science.
MAJORS Accounting, architectural technologies, automotive technologies, business administration/commerce/management, carpentry, chemical engineering technology, commercial art, computer information systems, computer programming, computer technologies, construction technologies, cosmetology, culinary arts, data processing, drafting and design, electrical and electronics technologies, electrical engineering technology, electronics engineering technology, engineering (general), fashion design and technology, fashion merchandising, heating/refrigeration/air conditioning, industrial and heavy equipment maintenance, journalism, labor and industrial relations, labor studies, liberal arts/general studies, manufacturing technology, mechanical engineering technology, nursing, photography, plumbing, printing technologies, real estate, transportation technologies, water resources, welding technology.
LIBRARY 98,000 books, 367 periodicals, 12,000 records, tapes, and CDs.
COMPUTERS ON CAMPUS 150 computers for student use in computer center, library. Staffed computer lab on campus.
COLLEGE LIFE Choral group, student-run newspaper. ***Student services:*** health clinic, personal-psychological counseling, women's center. ***Campus security:*** 24-hour patrols, student patrols, late-night transport-escort service.
HOUSING College housing not available.
ATHLETICS ***Intercollegiate:*** basketball M/W, cross-country running M/W, tennis M, track and field M/W. ***Contact:*** Mr. James Brown, Athletics Director, 213-744-9443.
CAREER PLANNING ***Placement office:*** 3 full-time, 20 part-time staff. ***Director:*** Ms. Eve Madigan, Director, 213-744-9492. ***Services:*** resume preparation, career counseling, careers library. Students must register freshman year.
EXPENSES FOR 1996–97 State resident tuition: $0 full-time. Nonresident tuition: $4140 full-time, $138 per unit part-time. Part-time mandatory fees: $13 per unit. Full-time mandatory fees: $390.
FINANCIAL AID ***College-administered undergrad aid 1995–96:*** need-based scholarships, low-interest long-term loans from external sources, Federal Work-Study, part-time jobs. ***Required forms:*** FAFSA. ***Priority deadline:*** 5/1.
APPLYING Open admission. ***Options:*** early entrance, deferred entrance. ***Required:*** TOEFL for international students. ***Recommended:*** school transcript, 3 years of high school math and science. Test scores used for counseling/placement. ***Application deadline:*** 8/28.
APPLYING/TRANSFER ***Entrance:*** noncompetitive. ***Contact:*** Ms. Billie Ambers, Counselor, 213-744-9449.
CONTACT Mr. Robert Richards, Associate Dean of Admissions and Records, Los Angeles Trade-Technical College, 400 West Washington Boulevard, Los Angeles, CA 90015-4108, 213-744-9420. ***Fax:*** 213-748-7334. College video available.

LOS ANGELES VALLEY COLLEGE
Van Nuys, California

UG Enrollment: 17,768 **Tuition & Fees (CA Res): $407**
Application Deadline: 9/8 **Room & Board: N/Avail**

GENERAL State and locally supported, 2-year, coed. Part of Los Angeles Community College District System. Awards transfer associate, terminal associate degrees. Founded 1949. ***Setting:*** 105-acre suburban campus. ***Total enrollment:*** 17,768. ***Faculty:*** 482.
ENROLLMENT PROFILE 17,768 students: 57% women, 77% part-time, 99% state residents, 16% transferred in, 1% international, 48% 25 or older, 1% Native American, 22% Hispanic, 7% African American, 12% Asian American.
FIRST-YEAR CLASS 10,577 total; 13,941 applied, 100% were accepted, 76% of whom enrolled.
ACADEMIC PROGRAM Core, general education curriculum. Calendar: semesters. 1,700 courses offered in 1995–96. Academic remediation for entering students, English as a second language program offered during academic year and summer, services for LD students, self-designed majors, honors program, summer session for credit, part-time degree program (daytime, evenings, summer), adult/continuing education programs, co-op programs and internships.
GENERAL DEGREE REQUIREMENTS 60 units; 1 math course; internship (some majors).
MAJORS Accounting, advertising, art/fine arts, biology/biological sciences, black/African-American studies, broadcasting, business administration/commerce/management, business machine technologies, ceramic art and design, child care/child and family studies, child psychology/child development, civil engineering technology, commercial art, communication, computer information systems, computer programming, criminal justice, data processing, drafting and design, early childhood education, economics, electrical and electronics technologies, electrical engineering technology, engineering design, (pre)engineering sequence, family and consumer studies, film studies, fire science, French, geography, geology, Hebrew, history, home economics, hotel and restaurant management, interior design, Italian, journalism, law enforcement/police sciences, liberal arts/general studies, library science, machine and tool technologies, marketing/retailing/merchandising, mathematics, mechanical design technology, mechanical engineering technology, music, nursing, photography, physical education, practical nursing, psychology, radio and television studies, real estate, respiratory therapy, retail management, secretarial studies/office management, sociology, Spanish, speech/rhetoric/public address/debate, theater arts/drama.
LIBRARY Los Angeles Valley Library with 115,000 books, 760 microform titles, 400 periodicals, 6 CD-ROMs.
COMPUTERS ON CAMPUS 40 computers for student use in computer center.
COLLEGE LIFE Drama-theater group, student-run newspaper, radio station. ***Major annual events:*** Graduation, Dean's Tea. ***Student services:*** legal services, personal-psychological counseling, women's center. ***Campus security:*** 24-hour emergency response devices and patrols, student patrols, late-night transport-escort service.
HOUSING College housing not available.
ATHLETICS ***Intercollegiate:*** basketball M/W, cross-country running M/W, fencing M/W, football M, gymnastics M/W, swimming and diving M/W, tennis M/W, track and field M/W, volleyball M/W, water polo M, wrestling M. ***Intramural:*** badminton, basketball, cross-country running, fencing, football, golf, gymnastics, skiing (cross-country), skiing (downhill), soccer, swimming and diving, tennis, track and field, volleyball, water polo, wrestling. ***Contact:*** Mr. Gary Honjio, Physical Education Chairperson, 818-781-1200 Ext. 212.

Los Angeles Valley College (continued)

CAREER PLANNING ***Placement office:*** 2 full-time, 2 part-time staff. ***Director:*** Ms. Barbara Goldberg, Director, 818-781-1200 Ext. 246. ***Services:*** job fairs, resume preparation, career counseling, careers library.
EXPENSES FOR 1996–97 State resident tuition: $0 full-time. Nonresident tuition: $4140 full-time, $138 per unit part-time. Part-time mandatory fees per semester range from $21.50 to $151.50. Full-time mandatory fees: $407.
FINANCIAL AID ***College-administered undergrad aid 1995–96:*** 90 need-based scholarships (average $300), 20 non-need scholarships (average $150), short-term loans (average $100), low-interest long-term loans from external sources (average $700), Federal Work-Study, part-time jobs. ***Required forms:*** state, institutional; accepted: CSS Financial Aid PROFILE, FAFSA. ***Priority deadline:*** 6/30.
APPLYING Open admission except for allied health programs. ***Option:*** early entrance. ***Required:*** ACT, TOEFL for international students. ***Recommended:*** school transcript. Test scores used for counseling/placement. ***Application deadline:*** 9/8.
APPLYING/TRANSFER ***Recommended:*** college transcript. ***Entrance:*** noncompetitive. ***Application deadline:*** 9/8.
CONTACT Mr. Billy Reed, Associate Dean of Admissions and Records, Los Angeles Valley College, Van Nuys, CA 91401-4096, 818-781-1200 Ext. 257. ***Fax:*** 818-785-4672.

LOS MEDANOS COLLEGE
Pittsburg, California

UG Enrollment: 7,311 | **Tuition & Fees (CA Res): $390**
Application Deadline: 9/1 | **Room & Board: N/Avail**

GENERAL District-supported, 2-year, coed. Part of California Community Colleges System. Awards transfer associate, terminal associate degrees. Founded 1974. ***Setting:*** 120-acre suburban campus with easy access to San Francisco. ***Total enrollment:*** 7,311. ***Faculty:*** 236 (94 full-time, 142 part-time); student-faculty ratio is 30:1.
ENROLLMENT PROFILE 7,311 students: 61% women, 39% men, 76% part-time, 99% state residents, 15% transferred in, 1% international, 53% 25 or older, 1% Native American, 18% Hispanic, 10% African American, 5% Asian American. ***Most popular recent majors:*** liberal arts/general studies, nursing, accounting.
FIRST-YEAR CLASS 1,768 total; 1,768 applied, 100% were accepted, 100% of whom enrolled.
ACADEMIC PROGRAM Core, honor code. Calendar: semesters. 343 courses offered in 1995–96. Academic remediation for entering students, English as a second language program offered during academic year, services for LD students, summer session for credit, part-time degree program (daytime, evenings), co-op programs.
GENERAL DEGREE REQUIREMENTS 57 units; math proficiency; 1 course each in biological science and physical science; computer course.
MAJORS Accounting, anthropology, art/fine arts, behavioral sciences, biology/biological sciences, business administration/commerce/management, business economics, chemistry, child psychology/child development, drafting and design, electrical and electronics technologies, fire science, industrial administration, journalism, liberal arts/general studies, mathematics, music, music business, nursing, psychology, real estate, recreation and leisure services, secretarial studies/office management, sociology, studio art, tourism and travel, welding technology.
LIBRARY Learning Resource Center with 14,246 books, 21 microform titles, 229 periodicals, 4 CD-ROMs, 5,449 records, tapes, and CDs.
COMPUTERS ON CAMPUS 200 computers for student use in computer center, computer labs, learning resource center, classrooms. Staffed computer lab on campus.
COLLEGE LIFE Choral group, student-run newspaper. ***Social organizations:*** 16 open to all. ***Most popular organizations:*** Alpha Gamma Sigma, Christian Fellowship Club, Student Nurses Association, La Raza Club. ***Student services:*** personal-psychological counseling, women's center. ***Campus security:*** 24-hour patrols, student patrols, late-night transport-escort service.
HOUSING College housing not available.
ATHLETICS ***Intercollegiate:*** baseball M, basketball M/W, football M, soccer M, softball W, volleyball W. ***Contact:*** Mrs. Shirley Baskin, Athletic Director, 510-439-2181 Ext. 217.
CAREER PLANNING ***Placement office:*** 1 part-time staff. ***Director:*** Ms. Ofelia Marino, Career Counselor, 510-439-2181. ***Services:*** resume preparation, career counseling, careers library.
EXPENSES FOR 1995–96 State resident tuition: $0 full-time. Nonresident tuition: $3810 full-time, $127 per unit part-time. Part-time mandatory fees: $13 per unit. Full-time mandatory fees: $390.
FINANCIAL AID ***College-administered undergrad aid 1995–96:*** need-based scholarships, low-interest long-term loans from external sources, Federal Work-Study, part-time jobs. ***Required forms:*** institutional. ***Application deadline:*** continuous to 5/1.
APPLYING Open admission. ***Option:*** Common Application. ***Required:*** TOEFL for international students. ***Required for some:*** Assessment and Placement Services for Community Colleges. Test scores used for counseling/placement. ***Application deadline:*** 9/1. ***Notification:*** continuous until 9/1.
APPLYING/TRANSFER ***Entrance:*** noncompetitive. ***Application deadline:*** 9/1. ***Notification:*** continuous until 9/1. ***Contact:*** Ms. Shirley Baskin, Dean of Behavioral Sciences, 510-439-2181 Ext. 217.
CONTACT Ms. Gail Newman, Director of Admissions and Records, Los Medanos College, Pittsburg, CA 94565-5197, 510-439-2181 Ext. 250.

MARIC COLLEGE OF MEDICAL CAREERS
San Diego, California

UG Enrollment: 1,100 | **Tuition & Fees: $4155**
Application Deadline: N/R | **Room & Board: N/Avail**

GENERAL Proprietary, 2-year, coed. Awards certificates, transfer associate degrees. Founded 1976. ***Setting:*** 4-acre urban campus. ***Total enrollment:*** 1,100. ***Faculty:*** 65 (45 full-time, 20 part-time).
ENROLLMENT PROFILE 1,100 students: 60% women, 40% men, 80% have need-based financial aid, 20% have non-need-based financial aid, 60% 25 or older, 20% Hispanic, 20% African American, 20% Asian American. ***Areas of study chosen:*** 85% health professions and related sciences, 15% business management and administrative services.
ACADEMIC PROGRAM Core. Calendar: modular. Average class size 40 in required courses. Academic remediation for entering students.
GENERAL DEGREE REQUIREMENTS 42 credits; computer course for most majors.
MAJORS Nursing, occupational therapy.
COMPUTERS ON CAMPUS 100 computers for student use in computer center, computer labs, research center, classrooms, library. Staffed computer lab on campus provides training in use of computers, software.
COLLEGE LIFE ***Campus security:*** 24-hour patrols.
HOUSING College housing not available.
CAREER PLANNING ***Director:*** Ms. Melva Duran, Director of Placement, 619-654-3620. ***Services:*** job fairs, resume preparation, resume referral, career counseling, careers library, job bank, job interviews. Students must register freshman year. 50 organizations recruited on campus 1994–95.
AFTER GRADUATION 80% of class of 1994 had job offers within 6 months.
EXPENSES FOR 1995–96 Tuition: $4155 (minimum) full-time. Full-time tuition and fees range up to $15,373 according to program.
FINANCIAL AID ***College-administered undergrad aid 1995–96:*** need-based scholarships, non-need scholarships. ***Acceptable forms:*** state, FAFSA.
APPLYING ***Option:*** Common Application. ***Required:*** essay, school transcript, interview, CPAt. ***Notification:*** continuous.
CONTACT Mr. Peter Marquez, Admissions Representative, Maric College of Medical Careers, 3666 Kearny Villa Road, San Diego, CA 92123-1995, 619-654-3623.

MARYMOUNT COLLEGE, PALOS VERDES, CALIFORNIA
Rancho Palos Verdes, California

UG Enrollment: 852 | **Tuition & Fees: $13,080**
Application Deadline: 8/15 | **Room & Board: $6400**

GENERAL Independent Roman Catholic, 2-year, coed. Awards transfer associate degrees. Founded 1932. ***Setting:*** 26-acre suburban campus with easy access to Los Angeles. ***Educational spending 1994–95:*** $4211 per undergrad. ***Total enrollment:*** 852. ***Faculty:*** 66 (52 full-time, 40% with terminal degrees, 14 part-time); student-faculty ratio is 16:1.
ENROLLMENT PROFILE 852 students from 27 states and territories, 27 other countries. 56% women, 44% men, 30% part-time, 70% state residents, 13% transferred in, 40% have need-based financial aid, 2% have non-need-based financial aid, 18% international, 20% 25 or older, 1% Native American, 18% Hispanic, 4% African American, 10% Asian American. ***Areas of study chosen:*** 100% liberal arts/general studies.
FIRST-YEAR CLASS 371 total; 864 applied, 98% were accepted, 44% of whom enrolled.
ACADEMIC PROGRAM Core, liberal arts curriculum, honor code. Calendar: semesters. 311 courses offered in 1995–96. Academic remediation for entering students, English as a second language program offered during academic year and summer, services for LD students, advanced placement, tutorials, honors program, summer session for credit, part-time degree program (daytime, weekends), adult/continuing education programs, internships. Study abroad in England (3% of students participate). ROTC: Air Force (c).
GENERAL DEGREE REQUIREMENT 60 units.
MAJOR Liberal arts/general studies.
LIBRARY College Library plus 1 other, with 40,000 books, 225 periodicals, 1 on-line bibliographic service, 2 CD-ROMs, 4,100 records, tapes, and CDs. Acquisition spending 1994–95: $84,208.
COMPUTERS ON CAMPUS Computer purchase plan available. 30 computers for student use in computer center, learning resource center, library provide access to main academic computer, e-mail. Staffed computer lab on campus provides training in use of computers, software. Academic computing expenditure 1994–95: $103,030.
COLLEGE LIFE Orientation program (4 days, $45, parents included). Drama-theater group, choral group, student-run newspaper. ***Social organizations:*** 15 open to all. ***Most popular organizations:*** Alianza Latina, Volunteer Club, Ski Club, African-American Student Union, Cross-Cultural Club. ***Major annual events:*** International Week, Major and Career Week, Black History Month. ***Student services:*** health clinic, personal-psychological counseling. ***Campus security:*** 24-hour patrols, late-night transport-escort service, controlled dormitory access.
HOUSING 230 college housing spaces available; all were occupied 1995–96. Freshmen given priority for college housing. Off-campus living permitted. ***Option:*** coed (3 buildings) housing available. Resident assistants live in dorms.
ATHLETICS Member NJCAA. ***Intercollegiate:*** tennis M(s)/W(s). ***Intramural:*** basketball, football, golf, soccer, softball, swimming and diving, tennis, volleyball, water polo. ***Contact:*** Ms. Adrienne-Ann Mullen, Director of Student Life, 310-377-5501.
CAREER PLANNING ***Placement office:*** 1 full-time, 2 part-time staff; $42,251 operating expenditure 1994–95. ***Director:*** Mr. Ed Ogle, Director of Advisement and Transfer, 310-377-5501. ***Services:*** job fairs, resume preparation, career counseling, job bank.
AFTER GRADUATION 92% of students completing a degree program in 1994–95 went directly on to further study.
EXPENSES FOR 1996–97 ***Application fee:*** $25. Comprehensive fee of $19,480 includes full-time tuition ($12,950 minimum), mandatory fees ($130), and college room and board ($6400). Part-time tuition: $595 per unit. Part-time mandatory fees: $60 per year. Full-time tuition for international students: $13,950.
FINANCIAL AID ***College-administered undergrad aid 1995–96:*** 272 need-based scholarships (average $6253), 34 non-need scholarships (average $4192), short-term loans (average $75), low-interest long-term loans from external sources (average $2800), 80 Federal Work-Study (averaging $1100), 38 part-time jobs. ***Required forms:*** institutional, FAFSA; required for some: state. ***Priority deadline:*** 3/2. ***Payment plan:*** installment. ***Waivers:*** full or partial for employees or children of employees. ***Notification:*** 4/25.
APPLYING ***Options:*** Common Application, early entrance, deferred entrance, midyear entrance. ***Required:*** school transcript. ***Recommended:*** minimum 2.0 GPA, SAT I or ACT, TOEFL for international students. ***Required for some:*** recommendations. Test scores used for counseling/placement. ***Application deadline:*** 8/15. ***Notification:*** continuous until 9/1.
APPLYING/TRANSFER ***Required:*** high school transcript, college transcript. ***Recommended:*** standardized test scores, minimum 2.0 college GPA. ***Required for some:*** recommendations. ***Entrance:*** minimally difficult. ***Application deadline:*** 8/15. ***Notification:*** continuous until 9/1. ***Contact:*** Ms. Nina Lococo, Director of Admissions and School Relations, 310-377-5501.

CONTACT Ms. Nina Lococo, Director of Admissions and School Relations, Marymount College, Palos Verdes, California, Rancho Palos Verdes, CA 90275-6299, 310-377-5501. ***Fax:*** 310-377-6223.

MENDOCINO COLLEGE
Ukiah, California

UG Enrollment: 3,400	Tuition & Fees (CA Res): $410
Application Deadline: rolling	Room & Board: N/Avail

GENERAL State and locally supported, 2-year, coed. Part of California Community Colleges System. Awards transfer associate, terminal associate degrees. Founded 1973. ***Setting:*** 127-acre rural campus. ***Total enrollment:*** 3,400. ***Faculty:*** 169 (42 full-time, 127 part-time).
ENROLLMENT PROFILE 3,400 students from 16 states and territories, 3 other countries. 59% women, 76% part-time, 97% state residents, 15% transferred in, 60% 25 or older, 3% Native American, 4% Hispanic, 1% African American, 1% Asian American. ***Most popular recent majors:*** computer information systems, secretarial studies/office management, liberal arts/general studies.
FIRST-YEAR CLASS 784 total. Of the students who applied, 100% were accepted, 98% of whom enrolled.
ACADEMIC PROGRAM Core, honor code. Calendar: semesters. Academic remediation for entering students, English as a second language program offered during academic year, services for LD students, advanced placement, honors program, summer session for credit, part-time degree program (daytime, evenings), adult/continuing education programs, co-op programs and internships.
GENERAL DEGREE REQUIREMENTS 60 units; 3 units of math; computer course for business administration majors.
MAJORS Accounting, animal sciences, art/fine arts, automotive technologies, biology/biological sciences, business administration/commerce/management, child care/child and family studies, child psychology/child development, computer information systems, criminal justice, data processing, electrical engineering technology, English, ethnic studies, finance/banking, French, health services administration, humanities, human services, law enforcement/police sciences, liberal arts/general studies, mathematics, music, ornamental horticulture, physical education, physical sciences, real estate, secretarial studies/office management, social science, Spanish, speech/rhetoric/public address/debate, theater arts/drama, welding technology.
LIBRARY Lowery Library with 27,441 books, 42 microform titles, 275 periodicals, 562 records, tapes, and CDs.
COMPUTERS ON CAMPUS 72 computers for student use in computer labs.
COLLEGE LIFE Drama-theater group, student-run newspaper. ***Social organizations:*** 14 open to all. ***Student services:*** personal-psychological counseling. ***Campus security:*** student patrols.
HOUSING College housing not available.
ATHLETICS ***Intercollegiate:*** baseball M, basketball M/W, football M, volleyball W. ***Contact:*** Mr. Dan Drew, Athletic Director, 707-468-3036.
CAREER PLANNING ***Placement office:*** 2 full-time, 2 part-time staff. ***Director:*** Mrs. Marie Myers, Career Center Specialist, 707-468-3045. ***Services:*** job fairs, resume preparation, resume referral, career counseling, careers library, job bank, job interviews.
AFTER GRADUATION 10% of students completing a degree program in 1994–95 went directly on to further study.
EXPENSES FOR 1995–96 State resident tuition: $0 full-time. Nonresident tuition: $4290 full-time, $143 per unit part-time. Part-time mandatory fees per semester range from $23 to $153. Full-time mandatory fees: $410.
FINANCIAL AID ***College-administered undergrad aid 1995–96:*** need-based scholarships, low-interest long-term loans from external sources, Federal Work-Study, part-time jobs. ***Required forms:*** CSS Financial Aid PROFILE, institutional; accepted: FAFSA. ***Priority deadline:*** 5/1.
APPLYING Open admission. ***Options:*** early entrance, deferred entrance. ***Required:*** TOEFL for international students. ***Recommended:*** SAT I or ACT. Test scores used for counseling/placement. ***Application deadline:*** rolling. ***Notification:*** continuous. Preference given to state residents.
APPLYING/TRANSFER ***Application deadline:*** rolling. ***Notification:*** continuous. ***Contact:*** Mr. Jerry Harrison, Transfer Center Coordinator, 707-468-3118.
CONTACT Mr. Joe Madrigal, Dean of Student Services, Mendocino College, Ukiah, CA 95482-0300, 707-468-3105.

MERCED COLLEGE
Merced, California

UG Enrollment: 6,327	Tuition & Fees (CA Res): $422
Application Deadline: rolling	Room & Board: N/Avail

GENERAL State and locally supported, 2-year, coed. Part of California Community Colleges System. Awards transfer associate, terminal associate degrees. Founded 1962. ***Setting:*** 168-acre small-town campus. ***Total enrollment:*** 6,327. ***Faculty:*** 421 (145 full-time, 276 part-time); student-faculty ratio is 20:1.
ENROLLMENT PROFILE 6,327 students from 30 states and territories, 10 other countries. 60% women, 40% men, 47% part-time, 95% state residents, 8% transferred in, 1% international, 42% 25 or older, 2% Native American, 29% Hispanic, 5% African American, 11% Asian American. ***Areas of study chosen:*** 17% vocational and home economics, 14% social sciences, 9% business management and administrative services, 9% physical sciences, 7% health professions and related sciences, 7% liberal arts/general studies, 5% biological and life sciences, 5% English language/literature/letters, 5% foreign language and literature, 5% mathematics, 3% computer and information sciences, 3% fine arts, 2% agriculture, 2% engineering and applied sciences, 2% performing arts, 1% communications and journalism, 1% natural resource sciences, 1% philosophy.
FIRST-YEAR CLASS 1,504 total; 2,616 applied, 100% were accepted.
ACADEMIC PROGRAM Core, honor code. Calendar: semesters. Academic remediation for entering students, English as a second language program offered during academic year, services for LD students, advanced placement, honors program, summer session for credit, part-time degree program (daytime, evenings, summer), adult/continuing education programs, co-op programs. Off-campus study at several local community colleges. Study abroad in England, Spain. ROTC: Army (c).
GENERAL DEGREE REQUIREMENTS 60 units; proficiency in elementary algebra; computer course for business-related majors.
MAJORS Accounting, agricultural business, agricultural sciences, agronomy/soil and crop sciences, aircraft and missile maintenance, animal sciences, applied art, art/fine arts, automotive technologies, business administration/commerce/management, carpentry, child psychology/child development, computer science, computer technologies, construction technologies, data processing, dental services, dietetics, early childhood education, electrical and electronics technologies, (pre)engineering sequence, environmental engineering technology, fashion design and technology, fashion merchandising, finance/banking, fire science, food services management, home economics, humanities, human services, industrial arts, insurance, landscape architecture/design, law enforcement/police sciences, legal secretarial studies, liberal arts/general studies, library science, management information systems, marketing/retailing/merchandising, mathematics, medical assistant technologies, medical secretarial studies, music, natural sciences, nursing, ornamental horticulture, physical education, physical sciences, political science/government, practical nursing, radiological technology, real estate, retail management, science, secretarial studies/office management, social science, teacher aide studies, theater arts/drama.
LIBRARY Lesher Library with 35,000 books, 400 periodicals, 500 records, tapes, and CDs.
COMPUTERS ON CAMPUS 400 computers for student use in computer center, learning resource center.
COLLEGE LIFE Drama-theater group, choral group, student-run newspaper. ***Social organizations:*** 30 open to all. ***Student services:*** legal services, health clinic, personal-psychological counseling, women's center. ***Campus security:*** 24-hour patrols, late-night transport-escort service.
HOUSING College housing not available.
ATHLETICS ***Intercollegiate:*** baseball M, basketball M/W, bowling M/W, cross-country running M, equestrian sports M/W, football M, golf M/W, soccer M, softball W, swimming and diving M/W, tennis M/W, track and field M/W, volleyball W, water polo M. ***Contact:*** Mr. Steve Cassidy, Athletic Director, 209-384-6026.
CAREER PLANNING ***Director:*** Ms. Karol Protzmann, Director of Job Placement, Careers, Transfer Center, 209-384-6244. ***Services:*** job fairs, resume preparation, career counseling, careers library, job bank, job interviews.
AFTER GRADUATION 80% of students completing a degree program in 1994–95 went directly on to further study.
EXPENSES FOR 1995–96 State resident tuition: $0 full-time. Nonresident tuition: $3420 full-time, $114 per unit part-time. Part-time mandatory fees per semester range from $29 to $159. Full-time mandatory fees: $422.
FINANCIAL AID ***College-administered undergrad aid 1995–96:*** 1,303 need-based scholarships (average $800), 418 non-need scholarships (average $400), short-term loans (average $300), Federal Work-Study, 100 part-time jobs. ***Required forms:*** state, FAFSA; accepted: CSS Financial Aid PROFILE. ***Priority deadline:*** 6/1. ***Payment plan:*** deferred payment.
APPLYING Open admission except for allied health programs, foreign students. ***Option:*** early entrance. ***Required:*** TOEFL for international students. ***Recommended:*** 3 years of high school math and science, some high school foreign language, SAT I or ACT. Test scores used for counseling/placement. ***Application deadline:*** rolling. ***Notification:*** continuous.
APPLYING/TRANSFER ***Recommended:*** 3 years of high school math and science, some high school foreign language. ***Entrance:*** noncompetitive. ***Application deadline:*** rolling. ***Notification:*** continuous.
CONTACT Ms. Helen Torres, Admissions Clerk, Merced College, Merced, CA 95348-2898, 209-384-6187. ***Fax:*** 209-384-6339.

MERRITT COLLEGE
Oakland, California

UG Enrollment: 5,123	Tuition & Fees (CA Res): $394
Application Deadline: 8/28	Room & Board: N/Avail

GENERAL State and locally supported, 2-year, coed. Part of Peralta Community College District System. Awards certificates, transfer associate, terminal associate degrees. Founded 1953. ***Setting:*** 130-acre urban campus with easy access to San Francisco. ***Research spending 1994–95:*** $34,939. ***Educational spending 1994–95:*** $1076 per undergrad. ***Total enrollment:*** 5,123. ***Faculty:*** 201 (94 full-time, 100% with terminal degrees, 107 part-time).
ENROLLMENT PROFILE 5,123 students: 66% women, 34% men, 74% part-time, 99% state residents, 14% transferred in, 1% international, 55% 25 or older, 1% Native American, 11% Hispanic, 47% African American, 13% Asian American. ***Areas of study chosen:*** 14% health professions and related sciences, 6% business management and administrative services, 4% computer and information sciences, 3% agriculture, 3% engineering and applied sciences, 3% interdisciplinary studies, 3% social sciences, 2% fine arts, 2% psychology, 1% biological and life sciences, 1% liberal arts/general studies.
FIRST-YEAR CLASS 1,084 total. Of the students who applied, 100% were accepted. 40% from top half of their high school class.
ACADEMIC PROGRAM Core. Calendar: semesters. 358 courses offered in 1995–96. Academic remediation for entering students, English as a second language program offered during academic year, services for LD students, summer session for credit, part-time degree program (daytime, evenings, weekends, summer), adult/continuing education programs, co-op programs. Off-campus study at Holy Names College, Mills College, University of California, Berkeley.
GENERAL DEGREE REQUIREMENTS 60 semester hours; 3 semester hours of math; computer course.
MAJORS Accounting, architectural technologies, black/African-American studies, business administration/commerce/management, business education, child care/child and family studies, community services, computer information systems, computer programming, computer technologies, early childhood education, economics, environmental design, French, health science, horticulture, humanities, landscape architecture/design, landscaping/grounds maintenance, land use management and reclamation, liberal arts/general studies, mathematics, nursing, paralegal studies, practical nursing, radiological technology, reading education, real estate, recreation and leisure services, science, secretarial studies/office management, social science, Spanish, word processing.
LIBRARY Merritt College Library with 80,000 books, 100 microform titles, 200 periodicals, 4 CD-ROMs. Acquisition spending 1994–95: $19,454.

Merritt College (continued)
COMPUTERS ON CAMPUS 20 computers for student use in lab. Staffed computer lab on campus (open 24 hours a day).
COLLEGE LIFE Student-run newspaper. 2% vote in student government elections. ***Student services:*** women's center.
HOUSING College housing not available.
ATHLETICS ***Intercollegiate:*** basketball M, cross-country running M, fencing M, gymnastics M/W, soccer M, tennis M/W, track and field M.
CAREER PLANNING ***Placement office:*** 1 full-time, 1 part-time staff; $31,000 operating expenditure 1994–95. ***Director:*** Ms. Debra Jacks, Coordinator of Career Center, 510-436-2444. ***Services:*** job fairs, resume preparation, careers library. 6 organizations recruited on campus 1994–95.
EXPENSES FOR 1996–97 State resident tuition: $0 full-time. Nonresident tuition: $3660 full-time, $122 per semester hour part-time. Part-time mandatory fees: $13 per semester hour. Full-time mandatory fees: $394.
FINANCIAL AID ***College-administered undergrad aid 1995–96:*** need-based scholarships, Federal Work-Study, part-time jobs. ***Required forms:*** CSS Financial Aid PROFILE, FAFSA. ***Application deadline:*** continuous.
APPLYING Open admission. ***Options:*** early entrance, deferred entrance. ***Recommended:*** SAT I or ACT. Test scores used for counseling/placement. ***Application deadline:*** 8/28. ***Notification:*** continuous.
APPLYING/TRANSFER ***Entrance:*** noncompetitive. ***Notification:*** continuous.
CONTACT Ms. Mary DeColte, District Admissions Officer, Merritt College, 12500 Campus Drive, Oakland, CA 94619-3196, 510-466-7369. ***E-mail:*** hperdue@peralta.cc.ca.us.

MIRACOSTA COLLEGE
Oceanside, California

UG Enrollment: 8,038	**Tuition & Fees (CA Res): $420**
Application Deadline: rolling	**Room & Board: N/Avail**

GENERAL State-supported, 2-year, coed. Part of California Community Colleges System. Awards certificates, transfer associate degrees. Founded 1934. ***Setting:*** 131-acre small-town campus with easy access to San Diego. ***Research spending 1994–95:*** $102,545. ***Total enrollment:*** 8,038. ***Faculty:*** 388 (93 full-time, 295 part-time); student-faculty ratio is 22:1.
ENROLLMENT PROFILE 8,038 students from 37 states and territories, 13 other countries. 59% women, 72% part-time, 90% state residents, 20% transferred in, 1% international, 46% 25 or older, 3% Native American, 15% Hispanic, 5% African American, 5% Asian American. ***Most popular recent majors:*** business administration/commerce/management, liberal arts/general studies.
FIRST-YEAR CLASS 1,273 total; 7,187 applied, 100% were accepted, 18% of whom enrolled.
ACADEMIC PROGRAM Core. Calendar: semesters. Academic remediation for entering students, English as a second language program offered during academic year and summer, services for LD students, advanced placement, tutorials, honors program, summer session for credit, part-time degree program (daytime, evenings, summer), adult/continuing education programs. Study abroad in England, Spain, France, Mexico, Costa Rica.
GENERAL DEGREE REQUIREMENTS 60 units; computer course for business majors; internship (some majors).
MAJORS Accounting, art/fine arts, automotive technologies, behavioral sciences, biology/biological sciences, business administration/commerce/management, chemistry, child psychology/child development, computer information systems, computer technologies, cosmetology, criminal justice, dance, drafting and design, early childhood education, English, French, history, horticulture, hotel and restaurant management, Japanese, journalism, landscaping/grounds maintenance, law enforcement/police sciences, liberal arts/general studies, machine and tool technologies, manufacturing technology, marketing/retailing/merchandising, mathematics, music, nursing, philosophy, physical sciences, physics, practical nursing, psychology, real estate, respiratory therapy, secretarial studies/office management, social science, sociology, Spanish, speech/rhetoric/public address/debate, teacher aide studies, theater arts/drama, tourism and travel.
LIBRARY MiraCosta College Library plus 2 others, with 53,227 books, 509 periodicals, 11 CD-ROMs, 5,784 records, tapes, and CDs. Acquisition spending 1994–95: $149,000.
COMPUTERS ON CAMPUS Computer purchase plan available. 275 computers for student use in computer center, computer labs, learning resource center, business, English departments, classrooms, library provide access to main academic computer, e-mail, Internet. Staffed computer lab on campus provides training in use of computers, software.
COLLEGE LIFE Drama-theater group, choral group, student-run newspaper. ***Social organizations:*** 29 open to all. ***Most popular organizations:*** African-American Student Alliance, Spanish Club, Cultural Exchange Program, Phi Theta Kappa, Friends of EOPS. ***Major annual events:*** Career Day Fair, Christmas Angel Exchange, Cinco de Mayo. ***Student services:*** health clinic, personal-psychological counseling, women's center. ***Campus security:*** late-night transport-escort service, security during class hours.
HOUSING College housing not available.
ATHLETICS Member NJCAA. ***Intercollegiate:*** basketball M, cross-country running W, track and field W. ***Intramural:*** basketball, cross-country running, golf, tennis, track and field. ***Contact:*** Mr. Clete Adelman, Chairperson of Athletics, 619-757-2121 Ext. 420.
CAREER PLANNING ***Placement office:*** 1 full-time, 2 part-time staff; $117,344 operating expenditure 1994–95. ***Director:*** Ms. Diane Baum, Career Placement Manager, 619-757-2121. ***Services:*** job fairs, resume preparation, resume referral, career counseling, job interviews.
ESTIMATED EXPENSES FOR 1996–97 State resident tuition: $0 full-time. Nonresident tuition: $3420 full-time, $114 per unit part-time. Part-time mandatory fees per semester range from $24 to $163. Full-time mandatory fees: $420.
FINANCIAL AID ***College-administered undergrad aid 1995–96:*** need-based scholarships (average $420), 150 non-need scholarships (average $250), low-interest long-term loans from external sources (average $2000), 143 Federal Work-Study (averaging $1200), 167 part-time jobs. ***Required forms for some financial aid applicants:*** state; accepted: CSS Financial Aid PROFILE, FAFSA. ***Priority deadline:*** 4/26. ***Payment plan:*** deferred payment. ***Waivers:*** full or partial for employees or children of employees.
APPLYING Open admission except for nursing program. ***Options:*** Common Application, early entrance, deferred entrance, midyear entrance. ***Required:*** TOEFL for international students. Test scores used for counseling/placement. ***Application deadline:*** rolling.
APPLYING/TRANSFER ***Entrance:*** noncompetitive. ***Application deadline:*** rolling.
CONTACT Ms. Norma Cooper, Registrar, MiraCosta College, Oceanside, CA 92056-3899, 619-757-2121 Ext. 287.

MISSION COLLEGE
Santa Clara, California

UG Enrollment: 8,750	**Tuition & Fees (CA Res): $431**
Application Deadline: rolling	**Room & Board: N/Avail**

GENERAL State and locally supported, 2-year, coed. Part of California Community Colleges System. Awards transfer associate, terminal associate degrees. Founded 1977. ***Setting:*** 167-acre urban campus with easy access to San Jose and San Francisco. ***Total enrollment:*** 8,750. ***Faculty:*** 376 (108 full-time, 268 part-time); student-faculty ratio is 25:1.
ENROLLMENT PROFILE 8,750 students: 50% women, 79% part-time, 98% state residents, 16% transferred in, 1% international, 64% 25 or older, 1% Native American, 14% Hispanic, 5% African American, 51% Asian American. ***Most popular recent major:*** business administration/commerce/management.
FIRST-YEAR CLASS 2,705 total. Of the students who applied, 100% were accepted.
ACADEMIC PROGRAM Core. Calendar: semesters. Academic remediation for entering students, English as a second language program offered during academic year, services for LD students, summer session for credit, part-time degree program (daytime, evenings, weekends, summer), adult/continuing education programs, co-op programs. ROTC: Army (c), Air Force (c).
GENERAL DEGREE REQUIREMENTS 60 units; math/science requirements vary according to program; computer course (varies by major).
MAJORS Accounting, art/fine arts, business administration/commerce/management, commercial art, computer information systems, computer technologies, drafting and design, electrical and electronics technologies, (pre)engineering sequence, fire science, food services management, food services technology, graphic arts, health science, liberal arts/general studies, marketing/retailing/merchandising, mathematics, practical nursing, printing technologies, real estate, secretarial studies/office management, social science.
LIBRARY 43,456 books, 68 microform titles, 323 periodicals, 2,914 records, tapes, and CDs.
COMPUTERS ON CAMPUS Computer purchase plan available. 60 computers for student use in computer labs. Staffed computer lab on campus.
COLLEGE LIFE ***Student services:*** personal-psychological counseling. ***Campus security:*** 24-hour emergency response devices, late-night transport-escort service.
HOUSING College housing not available.
ATHLETICS ***Intercollegiate:*** baseball M, soccer M, tennis M. ***Contact:*** Mr. R. J. Smith, Athletic Director, 408-988-2200.
CAREER PLANNING ***Placement office:*** 1 full-time staff. ***Director:*** Ms. Susan Monahan, Director, 408-748-2729. ***Services:*** job fairs, resume preparation, career counseling, careers library, job interviews.
EXPENSES FOR 1995–96 State resident tuition: $0 full-time. Nonresident tuition: $3600 full-time, $120 per unit part-time. Part-time mandatory fees per semester range from $25 to $165. Full-time mandatory fees: $431.
FINANCIAL AID ***College-administered undergrad aid 1995–96:*** need-based scholarships (averaging $100), Federal Work-Study, part-time jobs. ***Required forms:*** FAFSA. ***Priority deadline:*** 5/1.
APPLYING Open admission except for nursing program. ***Option:*** early entrance. ***Required:*** TOEFL for international students. Test scores used for counseling/placement. ***Application deadline:*** rolling. ***Notification:*** continuous. Preference given to district residents.
APPLYING/TRANSFER ***Entrance:*** noncompetitive. ***Notification:*** continuous.
CONTACT Mr. R. Dan Mataragas, Dean of Student Services, Mission College, 3000 Mission College Boulevard, Santa Clara, CA 95054-1897, 408-748-2772.

MODESTO JUNIOR COLLEGE
Modesto, California

UG Enrollment: 14,774	**Tuition & Fees (CA Res): $403**
Application Deadline: rolling	**Room & Board: N/Avail**

GENERAL State and locally supported, 2-year, coed. Part of Yosemite Community College District System. Awards transfer associate degrees. Founded 1921. ***Setting:*** urban campus. ***Total enrollment:*** 14,774. ***Faculty:*** 494 (210 full-time, 284 part-time).
ENROLLMENT PROFILE 14,774 students: 56% women, 44% men, 76% part-time, 93% state residents, 5% transferred in, 1% international, 58% 25 or older, 1% Native American, 22% Hispanic, 2% African American, 7% Asian American.
FIRST-YEAR CLASS 4,194 total; 4,194 applied, 100% were accepted, 100% of whom enrolled.
ACADEMIC PROGRAM Core, honor code. Calendar: semesters. Academic remediation for entering students, English as a second language program offered during academic year and summer, services for LD students, advanced placement, Freshman Honors College, honors program, summer session for credit, part-time degree program (daytime, evenings, weekends, summer), adult/continuing education programs, co-op programs.
GENERAL DEGREE REQUIREMENTS 62.5 units; math competence.
MAJORS Accounting, agricultural business, agricultural economics, agricultural sciences, agronomy/soil and crop sciences, anatomy, animal sciences, anthropology, art education, art/fine arts, art history, astronomy, automotive technologies, biology/biological sciences, botany/plant sciences, business administration/commerce/management, chemistry, child care/child and family studies, computer science, construction technologies, corrections, criminal justice, dairy sciences, dental services, earth science, economics, electrical and electronics technologies, emergency medical technology, engineering (general), engineering and applied sciences, English, environmental education, fashion merchandising, finance/banking, fire science, food services technology, forestry, forest technology, French, geography, geology, German, health education, history, home economics, humanities, human services, industrial arts, interior design, Italian, journalism, law enforcement/police sci-

ences, liberal arts/general studies, marketing/retailing/merchandising, mathematics, medical assistant technologies, meteorology, music, natural resource management, nursing, occupational therapy, ornamental horticulture, philosophy, photography, physical education, physical sciences, physician's assistant studies, physics, physiology, political science/government, Portuguese, poultry sciences, practical nursing, printing technologies, psychology, public administration, public relations, radio and television studies, radiological technology, range management, real estate, recreation and leisure services, respiratory therapy, retail management, Russian, secretarial studies/office management, social science, social work, sociology, Spanish, speech/rhetoric/public address/debate, speech therapy, textiles and clothing, theater arts/drama, welding technology, word processing, zoology.
LIBRARY 65,000 books, 40 periodicals, 6,000 records, tapes, and CDs.
COMPUTERS ON CAMPUS 95 computers for student use in computer center, West Campus Study Center, library provide access to Internet. Staffed computer lab on campus provides training in use of computers, software.
COLLEGE LIFE Drama-theater group, choral group, student-run newspaper. *Campus security:* 24-hour emergency response devices and patrols, late-night transport-escort service.
HOUSING College housing not available.
ATHLETICS *Intercollegiate:* baseball M, basketball M/W, cross-country running M/W, football M, golf M, gymnastics W, soccer M, softball W, swimming and diving M/W, tennis M/W, track and field M/W, volleyball W, water polo M, wrestling·M. *Intramural:* basketball, tennis. *Contact:* Mr. Douglas Hodge, Dean of Physical Education, Recreation, Health Education, 209-575-6399.
CAREER PLANNING *Placement office:* 1 full-time, 1 part-time staff. *Director:* Ms. Leticia Cavazos, Coordinator, Career Information, 209-575-6239. *Services:* career counseling, careers library. 48 organizations recruited on campus 1994–95.
ESTIMATED EXPENSES FOR 1996–97 State resident tuition: $0 full-time. Nonresident tuition: $3534 full-time, $114 per unit part-time. Part-time mandatory fees: $13 per unit. Full-time mandatory fees: $403.
FINANCIAL AID *College-administered undergrad aid 1995–96:* need-based scholarships, 357 Federal Work-Study, part-time jobs. *Required forms:* CSS Financial Aid PROFILE, institutional, FAFSA. *Priority deadline:* 2/1.
APPLYING Open admission. *Options:* early entrance, deferred entrance. *Required:* TOEFL for international students. *Recommended:* school transcript. Test scores used for counseling/placement. *Application deadline:* rolling. *Notification:* continuous.
APPLYING/TRANSFER *Recommended:* high school transcript, college transcript. *Entrance:* noncompetitive. *Application deadline:* rolling. *Notification:* continuous. *Contact:* Ms. Linda Wong, Counselor, Transfer Center, 209-575-6039.
CONTACT Dr. Julius Manrique, Associate Dean of Student Services, Modesto Junior College, 435 College Avenue, Modesto, CA 95350-5800, 209-575-6040.

MONTEREY PENINSULA COLLEGE
Monterey, California

UG Enrollment: 8,300	Tuition & Fees (CA Res): $430
Application Deadline: rolling	Room & Board: N/Avail

GENERAL State-supported, 2-year, coed. Part of California Community Colleges System. Awards transfer associate, terminal associate degrees. Founded 1947. *Setting:* 87-acre small-town campus. *Total enrollment:* 8,300. *Faculty:* 388 (138 full-time, 250 part-time).
ENROLLMENT PROFILE 8,300 students from 29 states and territories, 47 other countries. 60% women, 40% men, 82% part-time, 97% state residents, 13% transferred in, 2% international, 1% Native American, 8% Hispanic, 6% African American, 10% Asian American. *Most popular recent majors:* liberal arts/general studies, business administration/commerce/management.
FIRST-YEAR CLASS 3,200 total; 3,200 applied, 100% were accepted, 100% of whom enrolled.
ACADEMIC PROGRAM Core. Calendar: semesters. Academic remediation for entering students, English as a second language program offered during academic year and summer, services for LD students, advanced placement, summer session for credit, part-time degree program (daytime, evenings, weekends, summer), adult/continuing education programs, co-op programs.
GENERAL DEGREE REQUIREMENT 60 credits.
MAJORS Accounting, anthropology, art/fine arts, art history, automotive technologies, biology/biological sciences, business administration/commerce/management, ceramic art and design, chemistry, child care/child and family studies, communication, computer information systems, computer science, computer technologies, corrections, criminal justice, dance, data processing, dental services, drafting and design, early childhood education, economics, engineering (general), English, ethnic studies, fashion merchandising, fire science, fish and game management, French, geology, German, graphic arts, history, home economics, hospitality services, hotel and restaurant management, interior design, international business, jewelry and metalsmithing, law enforcement/police sciences, legal secretarial studies, liberal arts/general studies, marketing/retailing/merchandising, mathematics, medical assistant technologies, medical secretarial studies, music, nursing, occupational therapy, ornamental horticulture, painting/drawing, parks management, philosophy, photography, physical education, physical fitness/exercise science, physical therapy, physics, political science/government, psychology, real estate, sculpture, secretarial studies/office management, sociology, Spanish, studio art, textile arts, textiles and clothing, theater arts/drama, wildlife management, women's studies, word processing.
LIBRARY Monterey Peninsula College Library with 50,000 books, 214 microform titles, 320 periodicals, 8 CD-ROMs, 2,500 records, tapes, and CDs.
COMPUTERS ON CAMPUS 120 computers for student use in various departments, labs, library.
COLLEGE LIFE Drama-theater group, student-run newspaper. *Student services:* legal services, health clinic, personal-psychological counseling.
HOUSING College housing not available.
ATHLETICS *Intercollegiate:* baseball M, basketball M, cross-country running M/W, football M, golf M/W, softball W, swimming and diving M/W, tennis M/W, track and field M/W, volleyball W.
CAREER PLANNING *Service:* career counseling.
EXPENSES FOR 1996–97 State resident tuition: $0 full-time. Nonresident tuition: $3270 full-time, $109 per unit part-time. Part-time mandatory fees range from $33 to $163 per semester. Full-time mandatory fees: $430.
FINANCIAL AID *College-administered undergrad aid 1995–96:* 215 need-based scholarships (average $500), 30 non-need scholarships (average $500), short-term loans (average $100), 82 Federal Work-Study (averaging $2000), 161 part-time jobs. *Required forms:* institutional. *Priority deadline:* 3/2.
APPLYING Open admission except for nonresident aliens. *Options:* early entrance, midyear entrance. *Required:* TOEFL for international students. Test scores used for counseling/placement. *Application deadline:* rolling. *Notification:* continuous.
APPLYING/TRANSFER *Entrance:* noncompetitive. *Application deadline:* rolling. *Notification:* continuous.
CONTACT Dr. Sharon Congiglio, Dean of Student Success and Enrollment Services, Monterey Peninsula College, Monterey, CA 93940-4799, 408-646-4006.

MOORPARK COLLEGE
Moorpark, California

UG Enrollment: 10,226	Tuition & Fees (CA Res): $410
Application Deadline: rolling	Room & Board: N/Avail

GENERAL County-supported, 2-year, coed. Part of Ventura County Community College District System. Awards transfer associate, terminal associate degrees. Founded 1967. *Setting:* 121-acre small-town campus with easy access to Los Angeles. *Total enrollment:* 10,226. *Faculty:* 450 (150 full-time, 300 part-time); student-faculty ratio is 26:1.
ENROLLMENT PROFILE 10,226 students: 55% women, 60% part-time, 99% state residents, 15% transferred in, 1% international, 42% 25 or older, 2% Native American, 11% Hispanic, 2% African American, 8% Asian American. *Areas of study chosen:* 85% liberal arts/general studies, 5% business management and administrative services, 5% health professions and related sciences, 2% biological and life sciences, 1% computer and information sciences. *Most popular recent majors:* liberal arts/general studies, business administration/commerce/management, wildlife management.
FIRST-YEAR CLASS 3,218 total; 3,600 applied, 100% were accepted, 89% of whom enrolled.
ACADEMIC PROGRAM Core, honor code. Calendar: semesters. Academic remediation for entering students, English as a second language program offered during academic year, services for LD students, advanced placement, summer session for credit, part-time degree program (daytime, evenings, summer), adult/continuing education programs, co-op programs.
GENERAL DEGREE REQUIREMENTS 60 units; 1 course each in college algebra and natural science.
MAJORS Accounting, agricultural sciences, agronomy/soil and crop sciences, animal sciences, art/fine arts, automotive technologies, behavioral sciences, biology/biological sciences, broadcasting, business administration/commerce/management, business machine technologies, chemistry, commercial art, computer information systems, computer science, data processing, early childhood education, electrical and electronics technologies, engineering and applied sciences, engineering technology, fashion design and technology, film studies, geology, graphic arts, home economics, horticulture, journalism, law enforcement/police sciences, liberal arts/general studies, marketing/retailing/merchandising, mathematics, music, natural sciences, nursing, optical technologies, photography, printing technologies, real estate, recreation and leisure services, secretarial studies/office management, teacher aide studies, telecommunications, theater arts/drama, wildlife management.
LIBRARY 50,000 books, 100 periodicals.
COMPUTERS ON CAMPUS 80 computers for student use in learning resource center, 3 labs, library, student center. Staffed computer lab on campus provides training in use of computers, software.
COLLEGE LIFE Student-run newspaper. *Student services:* health clinic, personal-psychological counseling, women's center. *Campus security:* 24-hour patrols.
HOUSING College housing not available.
ATHLETICS *Intercollegiate:* basketball M/W, cross-country running M/W, football M, golf M, soccer M/W, tennis M/W, track and field M/W, volleyball W, wrestling M. *Intramural:* skiing (downhill). *Contact:* Mr. John Keever, Athletic Director, 805-378-1457.
CAREER PLANNING *Service:* career counseling.
EXPENSES FOR 1996–97 State resident tuition: $0 full-time. Nonresident tuition: $3420 full-time, $114 per unit part-time. Part-time mandatory fees per semester range from $23 to $153. Full-time mandatory fees: $410.
FINANCIAL AID *College-administered undergrad aid 1995–96:* need-based scholarships, Federal Work-Study, part-time jobs. *Required forms:* institutional, FAFSA; accepted: CSS Financial Aid PROFILE, state. *Application deadline:* continuous.
APPLYING Open admission except for nursing, exotic animal training programs. *Options:* early entrance, deferred entrance. *Required:* TOEFL for international students. Test scores used for counseling/placement. *Application deadline:* rolling. *Notification:* continuous.
APPLYING/TRANSFER *Entrance:* noncompetitive. *Application deadline:* rolling. *Notification:* continuous. *Contact:* Ms. Debra Goertzen, Counselor Assistant, 805-378-1551.
CONTACT Ms. Kathy Colborn, Registrar, Moorpark College, Moorpark, CA 93021-2899, 805-378-1410. College video available.

❖ *See page 822 for a narrative description.* ❖

MT. SAN ANTONIO COLLEGE
Walnut, California

UG Enrollment: 32,000	Tuition & Fees (CA Res): $460
Application Deadline: rolling	Room & Board: N/Avail

GENERAL District-supported, 2-year, coed. Part of California Community Colleges System. Awards transfer associate, terminal associate degrees. Founded 1946. *Setting:* 433-acre small-town campus with easy access to Los Angeles. *Total enrollment:* 32,000. *Faculty:* 799 (278 full-time, 521 part-time).
ENROLLMENT PROFILE 32,000 students from 51 states and territories. 54% women, 67% part-time, 94% state residents, 9% transferred in, 2% international, 38% 25 or older, 1% Native American, 35% Hispanic, 7% African American, 17% Asian American. *Most popular recent majors:* liberal arts/general studies, nursing, business administration/commerce/management.

Mt. San Antonio College (continued)

FIRST-YEAR CLASS Of the students who applied, 100% were accepted.

ACADEMIC PROGRAM Core, honor code. Calendar: semesters. Academic remediation for entering students, English as a second language program offered during academic year, services for LD students, honors program, summer session for credit, part-time degree program (daytime), adult/continuing education programs, co-op programs. Study abroad in England, Mexico, France.

GENERAL DEGREE REQUIREMENTS 60 units; math/science requirements vary according to program; computer course (varies by major).

MAJORS Accounting, advertising, agricultural business, agricultural sciences, agricultural technologies, agronomy/soil and crop sciences, aircraft and missile maintenance, air traffic control, animal sciences, architectural technologies, aviation technology, business administration/commerce/management, business education, child care/child and family studies, civil engineering technology, commercial art, computer science, computer technologies, construction management, corrections, dairy sciences, data processing, deaf interpreter training, drafting and design, early childhood education, electrical and electronics technologies, emergency medical technology, (pre)engineering sequence, engineering technology, fashion merchandising, finance/banking, fire science, flight training, forest technology, graphic arts, heating/refrigeration/air conditioning, home economics, horticulture, hotel and restaurant management, industrial administration, industrial arts, industrial design, interior design, journalism, landscape architecture/design, law enforcement/police sciences, legal secretarial studies, liberal arts/general studies, machine and tool technologies, marketing/retailing/merchandising, materials sciences, mechanical design technology, medical secretarial studies, mental health/rehabilitation counseling, metallurgy, nursing, occupational safety and health, ornamental horticulture, paralegal studies, parks management, photography, quality control technology, radio and television studies, radiological technology, real estate, recreation and leisure services, respiratory therapy, secretarial studies/office management, surveying technology, transportation technologies, welding technology, wildlife management.

LIBRARY 76,181 books, 900 microform titles, 1,295 periodicals, 2 CD-ROMs, 15,000 records, tapes, and CDs. Acquisition spending 1994–95: $1.2 million.

COMPUTERS ON CAMPUS 162 computers for student use in computer center, library.

COLLEGE LIFE Drama-theater group, choral group, student-run newspaper, radio station. ***Most popular organizations:*** Alpha Gamma Sigma, Mexican-Chicano Association, Student Government. ***Major annual events:*** Student of Distinction Brunch, Student Blood Drive, Student Awards Presentation. ***Student services:*** legal services, health clinic, personal-psychological counseling, women's center. ***Campus security:*** late-night transport-escort service.

HOUSING College housing not available.

ATHLETICS ***Intercollegiate:*** baseball M, basketball M/W, cross-country running M/W, football M, golf M, soccer M/W, softball W, swimming and diving M/W, tennis M/W, track and field M/W, volleyball M/W, water polo M, wrestling M. ***Contact:*** Ms. Linda Garrison, Dean, Physical Education, Athletics and Dance Division, 909-594-5611 Ext. 4630.

CAREER PLANNING ***Placement office:*** 3 full-time, 1 part-time staff. ***Director:*** Ms. Yolanda Villegas, Director, Job Placement, 909-594-5611 Ext. 4510. ***Services:*** job fairs, resume preparation, career counseling, careers library, job interviews.

EXPENSES FOR 1995–96 State resident tuition: $0 full-time. Nonresident tuition: $3450 full-time, $115 per unit part-time. Part-time mandatory fees per semester range from $34 to $174. Full-time mandatory fees range from $460 to $520.

FINANCIAL AID ***College-administered undergrad aid 1995–96:*** 704 need-based scholarships (average $300), 100 non-need scholarships (average $50), short-term loans (average $100), low-interest long-term loans from external sources (average $2000), Federal Work-Study, 300 part-time jobs. ***Required forms:*** state, FAFSA. ***Priority deadline:*** 4/15. ***Payment plan:*** deferred payment.

APPLYING Open admission. ***Options:*** early entrance, deferred entrance. ***Required:*** TOEFL for international students, ACT ASSET. ***Recommended:*** school transcript, SAT I or ACT. Test scores used for counseling/placement. ***Application deadline:*** rolling. ***Notification:*** continuous.

APPLYING/TRANSFER ***Required:*** standardized test scores. ***Recommended:*** high school transcript, college transcript. ***Entrance:*** noncompetitive. ***Application deadline:*** rolling. ***Notification:*** continuous.

CONTACT Ms. Lynn Hanks, Director of Admissions and Records, Mt. San Antonio College, Walnut, CA 91789-1399, 909-594-5611 Ext. 4415.

MT. SAN JACINTO COLLEGE
San Jacinto, California

UG Enrollment: 5,627	**Tuition & Fees (CA Res): $390**
Application Deadline: rolling	**Room & Board: N/Avail**

GENERAL State and locally supported, 2-year, coed. Part of California Community Colleges System. Awards transfer associate, terminal associate degrees. Founded 1963. ***Setting:*** 180-acre suburban campus with easy access to San Diego. ***Total enrollment:*** 5,627. ***Faculty:*** 215 (70 full-time, 1% with terminal degrees, 145 part-time).

ENROLLMENT PROFILE 5,627 students from 14 states and territories, 10 other countries. 61% women, 39% men, 72% part-time, 0% transferred in, 1% international, 46% 25 or older, 3% Native American, 18% Hispanic, 4% African American, 2% Asian American. ***Most popular recent majors:*** humanities, social science, interdisciplinary studies.

FIRST-YEAR CLASS 4,134 total; 4,134 applied, 100% were accepted, 100% of whom enrolled.

ACADEMIC PROGRAM Core, honor code. Calendar: semesters. Academic remediation for entering students, English as a second language program offered during academic year, services for LD students, advanced placement, summer session for credit, part-time degree program (daytime, evenings, summer), co-op programs.

GENERAL DEGREE REQUIREMENTS 60 units; 1 course in math; 6 units of natural/physical science.

MAJORS Art/fine arts, automotive technologies, behavioral sciences, business administration/commerce/management, computer science, dance, early childhood education, engineering (general), fire science, humanities, interdisciplinary studies, law enforcement/police sciences, mathematics, music, nursing, photography, physical education, real estate, science, secretarial studies/office management, social science.

LIBRARY Milo P. Johnson Library with 28,000 books, 330 periodicals, 2 CD-ROMs. Acquisition spending 1994–95: $60,000.

COMPUTERS ON CAMPUS 35 computers for student use in classrooms, library.

COLLEGE LIFE Drama-theater group. 4% vote in student government elections. ***Student services:*** personal-psychological counseling. ***Campus security:*** part-time security personnel.

HOUSING College housing not available.

ATHLETICS ***Intercollegiate:*** baseball M, basketball M/W, football M, golf M, tennis M/W, volleyball W. ***Contact:*** Mr. John Chambers, Athletic Director, 909-487-6752 Ext. 1561.

CAREER PLANNING ***Placement office:*** 2 full-time staff. ***Director:*** Ms. Linda Schlotthauer, Career Center Technician, 909-487-6752 Ext. 1442. ***Services:*** resume preparation, career counseling, careers library. 9 organizations recruited on campus 1994–95.

EXPENSES FOR 1995–96 State resident tuition: $0 full-time. Nonresident tuition: $3420 full-time, $114 per unit part-time. Part-time mandatory fees: $13 per unit. Full-time mandatory fees: $390.

FINANCIAL AID ***College-administered undergrad aid 1995–96:*** need-based scholarships, Federal Work-Study, 20 part-time jobs. ***Required forms:*** CSS Financial Aid PROFILE, institutional, FAFSA. ***Priority deadline:*** 8/1. ***Payment plan:*** installment.

APPLYING Open admission except for nursing program. ***Option:*** early entrance. ***Required:*** TOEFL for international students, Assessment and Placement Services for Community Colleges. Test scores used for counseling/placement. ***Application deadline:*** rolling.

APPLYING/TRANSFER ***Required:*** college transcript. ***Application deadline:*** rolling. ***Contact:*** Ms. Rosa Ramos, Transfer Specialist, 909-487-6752.

CONTACT Ms. Elida Gonzales, Director of Admissions and Records, Mt. San Jacinto College, San Jacinto, CA 92583-2399, 909-487-6752 Ext. 1414 or toll-free 800-624-5561 (in-state). ***Fax:*** 909-487-9240. ***E-mail:*** e_gonzales@msjc.cc.ca.us. College video available.

NAPA VALLEY COLLEGE
Napa, California

UG Enrollment: 7,000	**Tuition & Fees (CA Res): $392**
Application Deadline: rolling	**Room & Board: N/Avail**

GENERAL State and locally supported, 2-year, coed. Part of California Community Colleges System. Awards certificates, transfer associate, terminal associate degrees. Founded 1942. ***Setting:*** 188-acre suburban campus with easy access to San Francisco. ***Total enrollment:*** 7,000. ***Faculty:*** 304 (104 full-time, 200 part-time); student-faculty ratio is 23:1. ***Notable Alumni:*** Dick Vermeil, Major General Frank Humpert, Senator Mike Thompson, Delores Fisher.

ENROLLMENT PROFILE 7,000 students from 12 states and territories, 21 other countries. 58% women, 72% part-time, 92% state residents, 67% transferred in, 2% international, 44% 25 or older, 2% Native American, 16% Hispanic, 5% African American, 9% Asian American.

FIRST-YEAR CLASS 1,217 total; 1,350 applied, 100% were accepted, 90% of whom enrolled.

ACADEMIC PROGRAM Core, honor code. Calendar: semesters. 456 courses offered in 1995–96; average class size 22 in required courses. Academic remediation for entering students, English as a second language program offered during academic year and summer, services for LD students, advanced placement, tutorials, summer session for credit, part-time degree program (daytime, evenings), co-op programs. Study abroad in Mexico, France.

GENERAL DEGREE REQUIREMENTS 60 units; 1 math course; internship (some majors).

MAJORS Accounting, agricultural sciences, art/fine arts, behavioral sciences, biomedical technologies, business administration/commerce/management, child care/child and family studies, communication equipment technology, computer science, corrections, cosmetology, criminal justice, data processing, drafting and design, early childhood education, electrical and electronics technologies, emergency medical technology, engineering (general), environmental studies, humanities, law enforcement/police sciences, legal secretarial studies, machine and tool technologies, management information systems, marketing/retailing/merchandising, music, nursing, paralegal studies, photography, pollution control technologies, radio and television studies, real estate, respiratory therapy, science, secretarial studies/office management, telecommunications, welding technology.

LIBRARY Napa Valley College Library plus 1 other, with 42,000 books, 2,500 microform titles, 250 periodicals, 2 on-line bibliographic services, 1 CD-ROM, 10,800 records, tapes, and CDs. Acquisition spending 1994–95: $324,149.

COMPUTERS ON CAMPUS 30 computers for student use in computer center, library. Staffed computer lab on campus provides training in use of computers.

COLLEGE LIFE Drama-theater group, choral group, student-run newspaper. 30% vote in student government elections. ***Most popular organizations:*** Hispano-Americano Club, African-American Club, Environmental Action Coalition, International Student Club, Phi Theta Kappa. ***Major annual events:*** Black History Month, Cinco de Mayo Festival, Native American Pow Wow. ***Student services:*** personal-psychological counseling, women's center. ***Campus security:*** late-night transport-escort service.

HOUSING College housing not available.

ATHLETICS Member NJCAA. ***Intercollegiate:*** baseball M, basketball M/W, cross-country running M/W, golf M/W, soccer M, softball W, swimming and diving M/W, tennis M/W, volleyball W, wrestling M. ***Intramural:*** archery, badminton, basketball, bowling, fencing, golf, gymnastics, racquetball, rugby, skiing (cross-country), skiing (downhill), soccer, swimming and diving, tennis, volleyball, water polo, weight lifting, wrestling. ***Contact:*** Ms. Nadine Wade-Gravett, Dean, Athletics/Physical Education, 707-253-3220.

CAREER PLANNING ***Placement office:*** 3 full-time, 4 part-time staff; $217,052 operating expenditure 1994–95. ***Director:*** Ms. Lauralyn Bauer, Director, Career/Re-Entry Center, 707-253-3050. ***Services:*** job fairs, resume preparation, career counseling, careers library, job bank.

EXPENSES FOR 1996–97 State resident tuition: $0 full-time. Nonresident tuition: $3960 full-time, $132 per unit part-time. Part-time mandatory fees per semester range from $14 to $145. Full-time mandatory fees: $392.

FINANCIAL AID ***College-administered undergrad aid 1995–96:*** 90 need-based scholarships (average $400), 2 non-need scholarships (average $250), short-term loans (average $50), low-interest long-term loans from external sources, Federal Work-Study, 115 part-time jobs. ***Required forms:*** CSS Financial Aid PROFILE, institutional, FAFSA; required for some: state. ***Priority deadline:*** 5/1. ***Payment plan:*** installment.

APPLYING Open admission except for allied health programs. ***Options:*** early entrance, deferred entrance, midyear entrance. ***Required:*** TOEFL for international students.

Required for some: school transcript, SAT I or ACT. Test scores used for counseling/placement. ***Application deadline:*** rolling. ***Notification:*** continuous.
APPLYING/TRANSFER ***Required for some:*** standardized test scores, high school transcript, minimum 3.0 high school GPA. ***Entrance:*** noncompetitive. ***Application deadline:*** rolling. ***Notification:*** continuous.
CONTACT Ms. Delores Smith, Assistant Dean of Admissions and Records, Napa Valley College, Napa, CA 94558-6236, 707-253-3000. ***Fax:*** 707-253-3015. ***E-mail:*** yvongrab@admin.nvc.cc.ca.us.

OHLONE COLLEGE
Fremont, California

UG Enrollment: 8,400	Tuition & Fees: $390
Application Deadline: rolling	Room & Board: N/Avail

GENERAL State and locally supported, 2-year, coed. Part of California Community Colleges System. Awards transfer associate, terminal associate degrees. Founded 1967. ***Setting:*** 530-acre suburban campus with easy access to San Francisco. ***Total enrollment:*** 8,400. ***Faculty:*** 434 (134 full-time, 300 part-time); student-faculty ratio is 20:1.
ENROLLMENT PROFILE 8,400 students from 54 states and territories. 57% women, 71% part-time, 98% state residents, 15% transferred in, 1% international, 49% 25 or older, 1% Native American, 12% Hispanic, 4% African American, 17% Asian American. ***Most popular recent major:*** business administration/commerce/management.
FIRST-YEAR CLASS 1,879 total. Of the students who applied, 99% were accepted, 70% of whom enrolled.
ACADEMIC PROGRAM Core. Calendar: semesters. Academic remediation for entering students, English as a second language program offered during academic year, services for LD students, self-designed majors, honors program, summer session for credit, part-time degree program (daytime, evenings, weekends, summer), adult/continuing education programs, co-op programs. Off-campus study at Contra Costa Community College District, Chabot College, members of the California State University System. Study-abroad program. ROTC: Army (c), Air Force (c).
GENERAL DEGREE REQUIREMENTS 60 units; math proficiency.
MAJORS Accounting, art/fine arts, biology/biological sciences, broadcasting, business administration/commerce/management, child care/child and family studies, communication, computer programming, computer science, consumer services, criminal justice, deaf interpreter training, drafting and design, early childhood education, electrical and electronics technologies, electronics engineering technology, (pre)engineering sequence, fashion merchandising, food sciences, graphic arts, health science, home economics, interior design, journalism, law enforcement/police sciences, liberal arts/general studies, marketing/retailing/merchandising, medical assistant technologies, medical secretarial studies, natural sciences, nursing, nutrition, physical sciences, radio and television studies, real estate, respiratory therapy, secretarial studies/office management, social science, word processing.
LIBRARY Ohlone College Library with 65,000 books, 121 microform titles, 410 periodicals, 10,000 records, tapes, and CDs.
COMPUTERS ON CAMPUS 250 computers for student use in computer center, business labs, library. Staffed computer lab on campus.
COLLEGE LIFE Orientation program (2 days, no cost). Drama-theater group, choral group, student-run newspaper. ***Campus security:*** 24-hour emergency response devices and patrols, late-night transport-escort service.
HOUSING College housing not available.
ATHLETICS Member NJCAA. ***Intercollegiate:*** baseball M, basketball M/W, soccer M/W, softball W, swimming and diving M/W, track and field M/W, volleyball M/W, water polo M. ***Contact:*** Mr. Paul Moore, Athletic Director, 510-659-6042.
CAREER PLANNING ***Placement office:*** 1 full-time, 2 part-time staff. ***Director:*** Ms. Gail Marx, Director of Career Center, 510-659-6115. ***Services:*** job fairs, resume preparation, career counseling, careers library, job bank, job interviews.
EXPENSES FOR 1996–97 State resident tuition: $0 full-time. Nonresident tuition: $3485 full-time, $116.15 per unit part-time. Part-time mandatory fees: $13 per unit. Full-time mandatory fees: $390.
FINANCIAL AID ***College-administered undergrad aid 1995–96:*** 250 need-based scholarships (average $300), 6 non-need scholarships (average $685), short-term loans (average $200), low-interest long-term loans from external sources (average $2625), Federal Work-Study. ***Required forms:*** CSS Financial Aid PROFILE, state, FAFSA. ***Priority deadline:*** 7/1.
APPLYING Open admission except for nursing, respiratory therapy, interpreter preparation programs. ***Options:*** early entrance, midyear entrance. ***Required:*** school transcript, TOEFL for international students. ***Required for some:*** ACT ASSET. Test scores used for counseling/placement. ***Application deadline:*** rolling. ***Notification:*** continuous.
APPLYING/TRANSFER ***Required:*** college transcript. ***Required for some:*** standardized test scores. ***Application deadline:*** rolling. ***Notification:*** continuous.
CONTACT Ms. Kathy Prazak, Admissions and Records Coordinator, Ohlone College, Fremont, CA 94539-5884, 510-659-6108.

ORANGE COAST COLLEGE
Costa Mesa, California

UG Enrollment: 22,009	Tuition & Fees (CA Res): $435
Application Deadline: rolling	Room & Board: N/Avail

GENERAL State and locally supported, 2-year, coed. Part of Coast Community College District System. Awards transfer associate, terminal associate degrees. Founded 1947. ***Setting:*** 200-acre suburban campus with easy access to Los Angeles. ***Total enrollment:*** 22,009. ***Faculty:*** 823 (303 full-time, 25% with terminal degrees, 520 part-time); student-faculty ratio is 30:1.
ENROLLMENT PROFILE 22,009 students from 52 states and territories, 53 other countries. 51% women, 49% men, 66% part-time, 97% state residents, 4% transferred in, 1% international, 42% 25 or older, 1% Native American, 13% Hispanic, 2% African American, 24% Asian American. ***Areas of study chosen:*** 7% business management and administrative services, 5% engineering and applied sciences, 5% health professions and related sciences, 5% liberal arts/general studies, 4% psychology, 3% biological and life sciences, 3% education, 2% architecture, 2% fine arts, 1% area and ethnic studies, 1% computer and information sciences, 1% English language/literature/letters, 1% foreign language and literature, 1% mathematics, 1% performing arts, 1% philosophy, 1% physical sciences, 1% predentistry, 1% social sciences, 1% theology/religion.
FIRST-YEAR CLASS 7,252 total; 10,786 applied, 100% were accepted, 67% of whom enrolled.
ACADEMIC PROGRAM Core, transfer/vocational curriculum, honor code. Calendar: semesters plus summer session. 1,691 courses offered in 1995–96. Academic remediation for entering students, English as a second language program offered during academic year and summer, services for LD students, advanced placement, Freshman Honors College, honors program, summer session for credit, part-time degree program (daytime, evenings, weekends, summer), external degree programs, adult/continuing education programs, co-op programs. Off-campus study at Golden West College, Coastline Community College. Study abroad in Mexico, Spain, Costa Rica, England, France, Italy, Japan. ROTC: Army (c), Air Force (c).
GENERAL DEGREE REQUIREMENTS 60 units; 1 math course; internship (some majors).
MAJORS Accounting, aerospace sciences, animal sciences, architectural technologies, athletic training, aviation technology, behavioral sciences, business administration/commerce/management, business machine technologies, commercial art, communication equipment technology, computer graphics, computer information systems, computer programming, computer technologies, construction technologies, culinary arts, dance, data processing, dental services, dietetics, drafting and design, early childhood education, electrical and electronics technologies, emergency medical technology, engineering (general), fashion merchandising, film and video production, film studies, flight training, food services management, food services technology, heating/refrigeration/air conditioning, home economics, horticulture, hotel and restaurant management, human development, industrial design, interior design, legal secretarial studies, liberal arts/general studies, machine and tool technologies, marine technology, marketing/retailing/merchandising, mathematics, medical assistant technologies, medical secretarial studies, medical technology, music, musical instrument technology, music business, nutrition, ornamental horticulture, photography, physical education, physical fitness/exercise science, radiological technology, religious studies, respiratory therapy, secretarial studies/office management, welding technology, word processing.
LIBRARY Norman E. Watson Library with 91,000 books, 460 periodicals, 1 on-line bibliographic service, 20 CD-ROMs, 1,200 records, tapes, and CDs. Acquisition spending 1994–95: $102,216.
COMPUTERS ON CAMPUS Computer purchase plan available. 400 computers for student use in computer center, computer labs, classrooms, library provide access to main academic computer, on-line services, Internet. Staffed computer lab on campus provides training in use of computers, software. Academic computing expenditure 1994–95: $229,317.
COLLEGE LIFE Drama-theater group, choral group, student-run newspaper. 12% vote in student government elections. ***Student services:*** legal services, health clinic, personal-psychological counseling. ***Campus security:*** 24-hour emergency response devices and patrols, student patrols, late-night transport-escort service.
HOUSING College housing not available.
ATHLETICS ***Intercollegiate:*** baseball M, basketball M/W, crew M/W, cross-country running M/W, football M, golf M/W, sailing M/W, soccer M/W, swimming and diving M/W, tennis M/W, track and field M/W, volleyball M/W, water polo M. ***Contact:*** Mr. Barry Wallace, Athletic Director, 714-432-5766.
CAREER PLANNING ***Placement office:*** 1 full-time, 2 part-time staff; $92,256 operating expenditure 1994–95. ***Director:*** Mr. Steve Woodyard, Director, Placement Center, 714-432-5576. ***Services:*** job fairs, resume preparation, career counseling, job bank, job interviews.
AFTER GRADUATION 10% of students completing a degree program in 1994–95 went directly on to further study.
EXPENSES FOR 1995–96 State resident tuition: $0 full-time. Nonresident tuition: $3360 full-time, $112 per unit part-time. Part-time mandatory fees per semester range from $35.50 to $165.50. Full-time mandatory fees: $435.
FINANCIAL AID ***College-administered undergrad aid 1995–96:*** 256 need-based scholarships (average $300), short-term loans (average $150), low-interest long-term loans from external sources (average $2500), Federal Work-Study, 900 part-time jobs. ***Required forms:*** institutional; required for some: FAFSA. ***Priority deadline:*** 6/1.
APPLYING Open admission except for allied health programs. ***Options:*** early entrance, deferred entrance, midyear entrance. ***Required:*** TOEFL for international students. ***Recommended:*** SAT I or ACT. Test scores used for counseling/placement. ***Application deadline:*** rolling. ***Notification:*** continuous. Preference given to Educational Opportunity Program and Services Students, disabled students.
APPLYING/TRANSFER ***Recommended:*** standardized test scores. ***Entrance:*** noncompetitive. ***Application deadline:*** rolling. ***Notification:*** continuous. ***Contact:*** Mr. Bruce Cary, Counselor of Transfer Center, 714-432-5788.
CONTACT Ms. Nancy Kidder, Administrative Dean, Admissions and Records, Orange Coast College, Costa Mesa, CA 92628-5005, 714-432-5773. ***Fax:*** 714-432-5790.

OXNARD COLLEGE
Oxnard, California

UG Enrollment: 5,073	Tuition & Fees (CA Res): $390
Application Deadline: rolling	Room & Board: N/Avail

GENERAL County-supported, 2-year, coed. Part of Ventura County Community College District System. Awards certificates, transfer associate degrees. Founded 1975. ***Setting:*** 119-acre urban campus. ***Total enrollment:*** 5,073. ***Faculty:*** 288 (79 full-time, 209 part-time).
ENROLLMENT PROFILE 5,073 students from 10 states and territories, 11 other countries. 53% women, 79% part-time, 98% state residents, 18% transferred in, 1% international, 62% 25 or older, 1% Native American, 37% Hispanic, 5% African American, 12% Asian American.
FIRST-YEAR CLASS Of the students who applied, 100% were accepted, 65% of whom enrolled.
ACADEMIC PROGRAM Core. Calendar: semesters. Academic remediation for entering students, English as a second language program offered during academic year and summer, services for LD students, advanced placement, honors program, summer session for credit, part-time degree program (daytime, evenings), adult/continuing education programs.
GENERAL DEGREE REQUIREMENTS 60 units; math/science requirements vary according to program; computer course for most majors.

Peterson's Guide to Two-Year Colleges 1997

215

Oxnard College (continued)
MAJORS Accounting, agricultural business, agricultural technologies, anthropology, art education, automotive technologies, behavioral sciences, biology/biological sciences, business administration/commerce/management, child care/child and family studies, computer information systems, culinary arts, early childhood education, economics, electrical and electronics technologies, English, family services, fashion merchandising, fire science, heating/refrigeration/air conditioning, history, home economics, hotel and restaurant management, industrial administration, journalism, legal studies, liberal arts/general studies, library science, machine and tool technologies, marketing/retailing/merchandising, mathematics, mental health/rehabilitation counseling, philosophy, physical education, radio and television studies, real estate, secretarial studies/office management, sociology, Spanish, telecommunications, theater arts/drama, transportation technologies, welding technology.
LIBRARY 25,223 books, 10 microform titles, 107 periodicals, 1,000 records, tapes, and CDs.
COMPUTERS ON CAMPUS 116 computers for student use in computer center, classrooms.
COLLEGE LIFE Drama-theater group, choral group, student-run newspaper. ***Student services:*** health clinic, personal-psychological counseling, women's center.
HOUSING College housing not available.
ATHLETICS ***Intercollegiate:*** baseball M, basketball M/W, soccer M/W. ***Contact:*** Mr. Ronald Jackson, Acting Athletic Director, 805-985-5847.
CAREER PLANNING ***Director:*** Mrs. Mariel Miller, Job Placement Specialist, 805-986-5838. ***Services:*** job fairs, resume preparation, career counseling, careers library.
EXPENSES FOR 1995–96 ***Application fee:*** $10. State resident tuition: $0 full-time. Nonresident tuition: $3300 full-time, $110 per unit part-time. Part-time mandatory fees: $13 per unit. Full-time mandatory fees: $390.
FINANCIAL AID ***College-administered undergrad aid 1995–96:*** 51 need-based scholarships (average $390), short-term loans (average $50), low-interest long-term loans from external sources (average $2000), Federal Work-Study. ***Required forms:*** CSS Financial Aid PROFILE, institutional, FAFSA. ***Priority deadline:*** 5/10. ***Payment plan:*** deferred payment.
APPLYING Open admission. ***Option:*** early entrance. ***Required:*** TOEFL for international students. Test scores used for counseling/placement. ***Application deadline:*** rolling. ***Notification:*** continuous. Preference given to county residents.
APPLYING/TRANSFER ***Entrance:*** noncompetitive. ***Application deadline:*** rolling. ***Notification:*** continuous.
CONTACT Ms. Delores Tabor-King, Registrar, Oxnard College, 4000 South Rose Avenue, Oxnard, CA 93033-6699, 805-986-5843.

❖ *See page 822 for a narrative description.* ❖

PALOMAR COLLEGE
San Marcos, California

UG Enrollment: 22,945 **Tuition & Fees (CA Res): $410**
Application Deadline: rolling **Room & Board: N/Avail**

GENERAL State and locally supported, 2-year, coed. Part of California Community Colleges System. Awards certificates, transfer associate degrees. Founded 1946. ***Setting:*** 156-acre suburban campus with easy access to San Diego. ***Total enrollment:*** 22,945. ***Faculty:*** 1,097 (307 full-time, 790 part-time); student-faculty ratio is 25:1.
ENROLLMENT PROFILE 22,945 students: 54% women, 46% men, 62% part-time, 89% state residents, 10% transferred in, 6% international, 3% 25 or older, 1% Native American, 19% Hispanic, 3% African American, 4% Asian American. ***Most popular recent majors:*** liberal arts/general studies, accounting.
FIRST-YEAR CLASS 4,978 total; 10,000 applied, 100% were accepted, 47% of whom enrolled.
ACADEMIC PROGRAM Core, honor code. Calendar: semesters. Academic remediation for entering students, English as a second language program offered during academic year, services for LD students, advanced placement, summer session for credit, part-time degree program (daytime, evenings, summer), co-op programs and internships. Study abroad in England, Mexico, France, Costa Rica, Italy.
GENERAL DEGREE REQUIREMENTS 60 units; internship (some majors).
MAJORS Accounting, advertising, American studies, anthropology, applied art, archaeology, art education, art/fine arts, arts administration, astronomy, automotive technologies, aviation administration, aviation technology, biology/biological sciences, business administration/commerce/management, business economics, business education, business machine technologies, carpentry, ceramic art and design, chemistry, child care/child and family studies, child psychology/child development, commercial art, communication, computer information systems, construction technologies, criminal justice, dance, deaf interpreter training, dental services, drafting and design, early childhood education, economics, electrical and electronics technologies, emergency medical technology, engineering (general), English, ethnic studies, family and consumer studies, fashion design and technology, fashion merchandising, film studies, finance/banking, fire science, food services management, food services technology, geology, gerontology, graphic arts, health science, home economics, illustration, interior design, international business, jewelry and metalsmithing, journalism, law enforcement/police sciences, legal secretarial studies, liberal arts/general studies, library science, marketing/retailing/merchandising, medical assistant technologies, medical secretarial studies, music, Native American studies, nursing, painting/drawing, paralegal studies, parks management, photography, physical education, plumbing, printing technologies, public administration, radio and television studies, real estate, recreation and leisure services, sanitation technology, secretarial studies/office management, speech/rhetoric/public address/debate, surveying technology, teacher aide studies, telecommunications, theater arts/drama, tourism and travel, water resources, welding technology, zoology.
LIBRARY Palomar Library with 108,000 books, 2 on-line bibliographic services, 14 CD-ROMs, 777 records, tapes, and CDs.
COMPUTERS ON CAMPUS Computer purchase plan available. 922 computers for student use in computer center, computer labs, labs, library provide access to on-line services, Internet. Staffed computer lab on campus provides training in use of computers, software.
COLLEGE LIFE Drama-theater group, choral group, student-run newspaper, radio station. ***Student services:*** health clinic, personal-psychological counseling. ***Campus security:*** 24-hour patrols, student patrols, late-night transport-escort service.
HOUSING College housing not available.
ATHLETICS Member NAIA. ***Intercollegiate:*** basketball M/W, football M, soccer M, swimming and diving M/W, tennis M/W, volleyball W, water polo M, wrestling M. ***Intramural:*** basketball, bowling, golf, skiing (downhill), soccer, softball, tennis, volleyball, water polo, wrestling. ***Contact:*** Mr. John Woods, Director, 619-744-1150 Ext. 2464.
CAREER PLANNING ***Placement office:*** 2 full-time staff. ***Director:*** Ms. Judith Eberhart, Dean of Counseling, 619-744-1150 Ext. 2194. ***Services:*** job fairs, resume preparation, resume referral, career counseling, job bank, job interviews. 30 organizations recruited on campus 1994–95.
EXPENSES FOR 1996–97 State resident tuition: $0 full-time. Nonresident tuition: $3510 full-time, $117 per unit part-time. Part-time mandatory fees per semester range from $23 to $153. Full-time mandatory fees: $410.
FINANCIAL AID ***College-administered undergrad aid 1995–96:*** need-based scholarships, short-term loans (average $100), Federal Work-Study, part-time jobs. ***Required forms:*** CSS Financial Aid PROFILE, institutional, FAFSA. ***Priority deadline:*** 1/1. ***Payment plan:*** deferred payment. ***Waivers:*** full or partial for employees or children of employees.
APPLYING Open admission. ***Options:*** Common Application, early entrance, midyear entrance. ***Required:*** TOEFL for international students. ***Required for some:*** ACT ASSET. Test scores used for counseling/placement. ***Application deadline:*** rolling. ***Notification:*** continuous.
APPLYING/TRANSFER ***Entrance:*** noncompetitive. ***Application deadline:*** rolling. ***Notification:*** continuous. ***Contact:*** Mr. Bob Larson, Director, 619-744-1150 Ext. 2552.
CONTACT Mr. Herman Lee, Director of Enrollment Services, Palomar College, San Marcos, CA 92069-1487, 619-744-1150 Ext. 2171. ***E-mail:*** herman_lee@palomar.edu. College video and electronic viewbook available.

PALO VERDE COLLEGE
Blythe, California

UG Enrollment: 1,200 **Tuition & Fees (CA Res): $390**
Application Deadline: rolling **Room & Board: N/Avail**

GENERAL State and locally supported, 2-year, coed. Part of California Community Colleges System. Awards transfer associate, terminal associate degrees. Founded 1947. ***Setting:*** 10-acre small-town campus. ***Total enrollment:*** 1,200. ***Faculty:*** 69 (21 full-time, 48 part-time); student-faculty ratio is 17:1.
ENROLLMENT PROFILE 1,200 students from 4 states and territories, 3 other countries. 28% women, 44% part-time, 94% state residents, 8% transferred in, 1% international, 88% 25 or older, 1% Native American, 53% Hispanic, 7% African American, 2% Asian American. ***Most popular recent majors:*** liberal arts/general studies, business administration/commerce/management.
FIRST-YEAR CLASS 250 total; 300 applied, 100% were accepted, 83% of whom enrolled.
ACADEMIC PROGRAM Core, interdisciplinary curriculum. Calendar: semesters. 215 courses offered in 1995–96. Academic remediation for entering students, English as a second language program offered during academic year and summer, services for LD students, advanced placement, summer session for credit, part-time degree program (daytime, evenings), adult/continuing education programs, internships.
GENERAL DEGREE REQUIREMENTS 60 units; 1 math course; computer course.
MAJORS Accounting, agricultural sciences, automotive technologies, behavioral sciences, biology/biological sciences, business administration/commerce/management, child psychology/child development, criminal justice, early childhood education, economics, education, (pre)engineering sequence, English, forestry, health science, history, law enforcement/police sciences, liberal arts/general studies, marketing/retailing/merchandising, political science/government, psychology, secretarial studies/office management, sociology.
LIBRARY Palo Verde College Library with 21,457 books, 135 microform titles, 165 periodicals, 2 CD-ROMs, 2,501 records, tapes, and CDs.
COMPUTERS ON CAMPUS 25 computers for student use in computer center, learning resource center, library. Staffed computer lab on campus provides training in use of computers, software.
COLLEGE LIFE Drama-theater group, student-run newspaper. ***Most popular organizations:*** Extended Opportunity Program and Services Club, Associated Student Body. ***Major annual events:*** 5th of May Celebration, Thanksgiving Lunch, Graduation. ***Student services:*** personal-psychological counseling. ***Campus security:*** student patrols, security personnel during open hours.
HOUSING College housing not available.
CAREER PLANNING ***Director:*** Ms. Susan Black, Counselor, 619-922-6168 Ext. 207. ***Service:*** career counseling.
EXPENSES FOR 1995–96 State resident tuition: $0 full-time. Nonresident tuition: $3210 full-time. Nonresident part-time tuition per unit: $107. Part-time mandatory fees: $13 per unit. Full-time mandatory fees: $390.
FINANCIAL AID ***College-administered undergrad aid 1995–96:*** 190 need-based scholarships (average $1000), 20 non-need scholarships (average $500), low-interest long-term loans from external sources (average $2625), 30 Federal Work-Study (averaging $800), 75 part-time jobs. ***Required forms:*** state, institutional, FAFSA. ***Application deadline:*** continuous to 5/31. ***Payment plan:*** installment.
APPLYING Open admission. ***Options:*** early entrance, midyear entrance. ***Recommended:*** school transcript. ***Required for some:*** TOEFL for international students. Test scores used for counseling/placement. ***Application deadline:*** rolling. ***Notification:*** continuous.
APPLYING/TRANSFER ***Required:*** college transcript. ***Entrance:*** noncompetitive. ***Application deadline:*** rolling. ***Notification:*** continuous. ***Contact:*** Ms. Susan Black, Counselor, 619-922-6168.
CONTACT Dr. Howard B. Markle, Counselor, Palo Verde College, Blythe, CA 92225-1118, 619-922-6168 Ext. 220. ***Fax:*** 619-922-0230.

PASADENA CITY COLLEGE
Pasadena, California

UG Enrollment: 21,756 **Tuition & Fees (CA Res): $410**
Application Deadline: rolling **Room & Board: N/Avail**

GENERAL State and locally supported, 2-year, coed. Part of California Community Colleges System. Awards certificates, transfer associate, terminal associate degrees.

California

Founded 1924. *Setting:* 55-acre urban campus with easy access to Los Angeles. *Total enrollment:* 21,756. *Faculty:* 824 (308 full-time, 100% with terminal degrees, 516 part-time); student-faculty ratio is 27:1.
ENROLLMENT PROFILE 21,756 students from 15 states and territories, 50 other countries. 55% women, 70% part-time, 96% state residents, 11% transferred in, 19% have need-based financial aid, 3% international, 37% 25 or older, 1% Native American, 34% Hispanic, 8% African American, 34% Asian American. *Most popular recent major:* business administration/commerce/management.
FIRST-YEAR CLASS 6,369 total; 17,600 applied, 98% were accepted, 37% of whom enrolled.
ACADEMIC PROGRAM Core, honor code. Calendar: semesters. 980 courses offered in 1995–96. Academic remediation for entering students, English as a second language program offered during academic year and summer, services for LD students, advanced placement, self-designed majors, honors program, summer session for credit, part-time degree program (daytime, evenings, summer), adult/continuing education programs. Study abroad in England.
GENERAL DEGREE REQUIREMENTS 60 units; internship (some majors).
MAJORS Accounting, advertising, African studies, anthropology, architectural technologies, art/fine arts, art history, astronomy, automotive technologies, aviation administration, aviation technology, biology/biological sciences, black/African-American studies, broadcasting, business administration/commerce/management, business education, carpentry, ceramic art and design, ceramic sciences, chemistry, child psychology/child development, civil engineering technology, communication, communication equipment technology, computer information systems, computer programming, computer science, computer technologies, construction technologies, cosmetology, criminal justice, data processing, deaf interpreter training, dental services, drafting and design, early childhood education, economics, electrical and electronics technologies, electrical engineering technology, engineering (general), engineering technology, English, ethnic studies, fashion merchandising, finance/banking, fire science, flight training, forest technology, French, geography, geology, German, history, human services, industrial administration, interdisciplinary studies, interior design, jewelry and metalsmithing, journalism, landscape architecture/design, Latin American studies, legal secretarial studies, legal studies, liberal arts/general studies, library science, machine and tool technologies, marketing/retailing/merchandising, mathematics, mechanical engineering technology, medical assistant technologies, Mexican-American/Chicano studies, modern languages, music, music therapy, nursing, occupational therapy, painting/drawing, pharmacy/pharmaceutical sciences, philosophy, photography, physical education, physical sciences, physics, political science/government, practical nursing, psychology, radio and television studies, radiological technology, real estate, recreation and leisure services, religious studies, science, secretarial studies/office management, social science, sociology, Spanish, speech/rhetoric/public address/debate, statistics, teacher aide studies, telecommunications, textile arts, theater arts/drama, tourism and travel, veterinary sciences, welding technology, word processing.
LIBRARY Pasedena City College Library with 110,000 books, 400 microform titles, 360 periodicals, 3,257 records, tapes, and CDs.
COMPUTERS ON CAMPUS 274 computers for student use in computer center, computer labs, learning resource center, classrooms. Staffed computer lab on campus provides training in use of computers, software.
COLLEGE LIFE Drama-theater group, choral group, marching band, student-run newspaper, radio station. 2% vote in student government elections. *Student services:* health clinic, personal-psychological counseling, women's center. *Campus security:* 24-hour emergency response devices and patrols, late-night transport-escort service.
HOUSING College housing not available.
ATHLETICS *Intercollegiate:* baseball M, basketball M/W, cross-country running M/W, football M, golf M, softball W, swimming and diving M/W, tennis M/W, track and field M/W, volleyball W, water polo M. *Contact:* Mr. Skip Robinson, Department of Athletics Chairperson, 818-585-7218.
CAREER PLANNING *Placement office:* 2 full-time staff. *Director:* Mrs. Dina Chase, Career Center Technician, 818-585-5090. *Service:* career counseling.
EXPENSES FOR 1995–96 State resident tuition: $0 full-time. Nonresident tuition: $3510 full-time, $117 per unit part-time. Part-time mandatory fees per semester range from $23 to $153. Full-time mandatory fees: $410.
FINANCIAL AID *College-administered undergrad aid 1995–96:* 6,469 need-based scholarships (averaging $161), 50 non-need scholarships (averaging $245), short-term loans (averaging $150), low-interest long-term loans from college funds (averaging $500), loans from external sources (averaging $2625), Federal Work-Study, 50 part-time jobs. *Required forms:* institutional; required for some: CSS Financial Aid PROFILE, state, nontaxable income verification; accepted: FAFSA. *Priority deadline:* 5/21.
APPLYING Open admission except for some nonresident aliens. *Options:* early entrance, deferred entrance. *Required:* TOEFL for international students. Test scores used for counseling/placement. *Application deadline:* rolling. *Notification:* continuous.
APPLYING/TRANSFER *Application deadline:* rolling. *Notification:* continuous.
CONTACT Ms. Carol Kaser, Supervisor of Admissions and Records, Pasadena City College, 1570 East Colorado Boulevard, Pasadena, CA 91106-2041, 818-578-7397. *Fax:* 818-585-7915. College video available.

PHILLIPS JUNIOR COLLEGE
Van Nuys, California

GENERAL Proprietary, 2-year, coed. Part of Phillips Colleges, Inc. Awards transfer associate, terminal associate degrees. Founded 1945. *Setting:* urban campus with easy access to Los Angeles. *Total enrollment:* 600. *Faculty:* 19 (5 full-time, 100% with terminal degrees, 14 part-time); student-faculty ratio is 20:1.
EXPENSES FOR 1995–96 *Application fee:* $25. Tuition: $11,700 per degree program.
CONTACT Ms. Sandy Pallet, Director of Admissions, Phillips Junior College, 15350 Sherman Way, Van Nuys, CA 91406-4203, 818-895-2220. *Fax:* 818-895-5282.

PHILLIPS JUNIOR COLLEGE, CONDIE CAMPUS
Campbell, California

Enrollment: N/R	Tuition: $12,225/deg prog
Application Deadline: rolling	Room & Board: N/Avail

GENERAL Proprietary, 2-year, coed. Part of Phillips Colleges, Inc. Awards transfer associate, terminal associate degrees. Founded 1968. *Setting:* 5-acre small-town campus with easy access to San Jose. *Faculty:* 45 (15 full-time, 30 part-time).
ENROLLMENT PROFILE 40% women, 0% part-time, 95% state residents, 20% transferred in, 4% international, 80% 25 or older, 0% Native American, 20% Hispanic, 12% African American, 10% Asian American. *Most popular recent majors:* paralegal studies, electrical and electronics technologies, business administration/commerce/management.
FIRST-YEAR CLASS Of the students who applied, 80% were accepted, 75% of whom enrolled.
ACADEMIC PROGRAM Core. Calendar: quarters. Academic remediation for entering students, summer session for credit.
GENERAL DEGREE REQUIREMENTS 90 credits; 2 math courses; computer course; internship (some majors).
MAJORS Accounting, business administration/commerce/management, computer management, computer programming, computer science, computer technologies, data processing, electrical and electronics technologies, electrical engineering technology, legal secretarial studies, paralegal studies, robotics, secretarial studies/office management, tourism and travel, word processing.
LIBRARY 6,500 books, 60 periodicals, 20 records, tapes, and CDs.
COMPUTERS ON CAMPUS 55 computers for student use in computer center, library.
COLLEGE LIFE *Campus security:* 24-hour emergency response devices.
HOUSING College housing not available.
CAREER PLANNING *Director:* Mr. Frank Sandoval, Placement Director, 408-866-6666 Ext. 41. *Services:* job fairs, resume preparation, resume referral, career counseling, careers library, job bank, job interviews. Students must register freshman year.
EXPENSES FOR 1996–97 *Application fee:* $25. Tuition: $12,225 per degree program. Tuition guaranteed not to increase for student's term of enrollment.
FINANCIAL AID *College-administered undergrad aid 1995–96:* need-based scholarships, short-term loans, low-interest long-term loans from external sources (average $2500), Federal Work-Study, part-time jobs. *Required forms:* institutional; required for some: FAFSA. *Application deadline:* continuous. *Payment plans:* installment, deferred payment. *Waivers:* full or partial for employees or children of employees.
APPLYING *Required:* TOEFL for international students, CPAt. Test scores used for admission and counseling/placement. *Application deadline:* rolling.
APPLYING/TRANSFER *Required for some:* standardized test scores, college transcript. *Entrance:* moderately difficult. *Application deadline:* rolling.
CONTACT Mr. Clarence Hardiman, Director of Admissions, Phillips Junior College, Condie Campus, Campbell, CA 95008-1004, 408-866-6666 Ext. 19. *Fax:* 408-866-5542.

PORTERVILLE COLLEGE
Porterville, California

UG Enrollment: 2,651	Tuition & Fees (CA Res): $420
Application Deadline: rolling	Room & Board: N/Avail

GENERAL State-supported, 2-year, coed. Part of Kern Community College District System. Awards certificates, transfer associate, terminal associate degrees. Founded 1927. *Setting:* 60-acre rural campus. *Total enrollment:* 2,651. *Faculty:* 128 (58 full-time, 5% with terminal degrees, 70 part-time); student-faculty ratio is 14:1.
ENROLLMENT PROFILE 2,651 students: 61% women, 39% men, 59% part-time, 99% state residents, 6% transferred in, 52% have need-based financial aid, 37% have non-need-based financial aid, 1% international, 3% Asian American. *Most popular recent majors:* education, business administration/commerce/management, science.
FIRST-YEAR CLASS 472 total; 472 applied, 100% were accepted, 100% of whom enrolled.
ACADEMIC PROGRAM Core, interdisciplinary curriculum. Calendar: semesters. 301 courses offered in 1995–96. Academic remediation for entering students, English as a second language program offered during academic year, services for LD students, advanced placement, summer session for credit, part-time degree program (daytime, evenings, summer), adult/continuing education programs.
GENERAL DEGREE REQUIREMENTS 60 units; computer course for business, information science majors.
MAJORS Applied art, art/fine arts, automotive technologies, biology/biological sciences, business administration/commerce/management, business education, carpentry, child care/child and family studies, commercial art, computer science, criminal justice, drafting and design, education, (pre)engineering sequence, English, finance/banking, fire science, graphic arts, history, human services, industrial arts, law enforcement/police sciences, liberal arts/general studies, mathematics, mental health/rehabilitation counseling, music, natural sciences, photography, physical education, practical nursing, real estate, science, secretarial studies/office management, social science, welding technology.
LIBRARY Porterville College Library Media Center with 31,557 books, 54 microform titles, 297 periodicals, 48 CD-ROMs, 20 records, tapes, and CDs.
COMPUTERS ON CAMPUS 158 computers for student use in computer center, learning resource center, library. Staffed computer lab on campus provides training in use of computers, software.
COLLEGE LIFE Drama-theater group, choral group. 10% vote in student government elections. *Student services:* personal-psychological counseling. *Campus security:* 24-hour emergency response devices, student patrols.
HOUSING College housing not available.
ATHLETICS *Intercollegiate:* baseball M, basketball M/W, softball W, tennis M/W, volleyball W. *Contact:* Mr. George Nessman, Athletic Director, 209-791-2247.
CAREER PLANNING *Placement office:* 1 part-time staff. *Director:* Mr. Miles Vega, Career Counselor, 209-791-2327. *Services:* job fairs, resume preparation, career counseling.
EXPENSES FOR 1996–97 State resident tuition: $0 full-time. Nonresident tuition: $3120 full-time, $104 per unit part-time. Part-time mandatory fees per semester range from $28 to $158. Full-time mandatory fees: $420.
FINANCIAL AID *College-administered undergrad aid 1995–96:* 450 need-based scholarships (average $575), 20 non-need scholarships (average $250), low-interest long-term loans from external sources, 110 Federal Work-Study, 50 part-time jobs. *Required forms:* institutional, FAFSA, nontaxable income verification; accepted: CSS Financial Aid PROFILE. *Priority deadline:* 3/31.
APPLYING Open admission. *Option:* early entrance. *Required:* TOEFL for international students. Test scores used for counseling/placement. *Application deadline:* rolling.

Peterson's Guide to Two-Year Colleges 1997

Porterville College (continued)
APPLYING/TRANSFER ***Entrance:*** noncompetitive. ***Application deadline:*** rolling. ***Contact:*** Mr. Miles Vega, Counselor, 209-791-2327.
CONTACT Mrs. Norma Hodge, Director of Admissions and Records/Registrar, Porterville College, 100 East College Avenue, Porterville, CA 93257-6058, 209-791-2222.

QUEEN OF THE HOLY ROSARY COLLEGE
Mission San Jose, California

UG Enrollment: 224 | **Tuition & Fees: $2500**
Application Deadline: 7/1 | **Room & Board: N/Avail**

GENERAL Independent Roman Catholic, 2-year, specialized, primarily women. Awards transfer associate, terminal associate degrees. Founded 1930. ***Setting:*** 37-acre suburban campus with easy access to San Francisco. ***Total enrollment:*** 224. ***Faculty:*** 15 (4 full-time, 11 part-time).
ENROLLMENT PROFILE 224 students: 96% women, 4% men, 95% part-time, 0% transferred in, 0% Native American, 0% Hispanic, 0% African American. ***Areas of study chosen:*** 100% theology/religion.
ACADEMIC PROGRAM Core, honor code. Calendar: semesters. Academic remediation for entering students, English as a second language program offered during academic year, summer session for credit, part-time degree program (daytime, summer), external degree programs, adult/continuing education programs.
GENERAL DEGREE REQUIREMENTS 70 credits; math competence.
MAJOR Religious studies.
LIBRARY Karcher Library with 16,000 books, 100 periodicals.
COMPUTERS ON CAMPUS 5 computers for student use in library, student rooms provide access to Internet. Staffed computer lab on campus.
COLLEGE LIFE ***Student services:*** health clinic, personal-psychological counseling. ***Campus security:*** 24-hour emergency response devices.
HOUSING College housing not available.
CAREER PLANNING ***Service:*** career counseling.
AFTER GRADUATION 100% of students completing a degree program in 1994–95 went directly on to further study.
EXPENSES FOR 1995–96 Tuition: $2500 full-time, $100 per unit part-time.
APPLYING Open admission. ***Recommended:*** SAT I or ACT. Test scores used for counseling/placement. ***Application deadline:*** 7/1.
APPLYING/TRANSFER ***Application deadline:*** 7/1. ***Contact:*** Sr. Mary Paul Mehegan, Dean of the College, 510-657-2468 Ext. 322.
CONTACT Sr. Mary Paul Mehegan, Dean of the College, Queen of the Holy Rosary College, Mission San Jose, CA 94539-0391, 510-657-2468 Ext. 322. ***Fax:*** 510-657-1734.

RANCHO SANTIAGO COLLEGE
Santa Ana, California

UG Enrollment: 20,714 | **Tuition & Fees (CA Res): $425**
Application Deadline: 8/21 | **Room & Board: N/Avail**

GENERAL State-supported, 2-year, coed. Part of California Community Colleges System. Awards certificates, transfer associate, terminal associate degrees. Founded 1915. ***Setting:*** 58-acre urban campus with easy access to Los Angeles. ***Total enrollment:*** 20,714. ***Faculty:*** 1,799 (299 full-time, 1,500 part-time); student-faculty ratio is 15:1.
ENROLLMENT PROFILE 20,714 students from 50 states and territories, 50 other countries. 48% women, 81% part-time, 97% state residents, 17% transferred in, 2% international, 63% 25 or older, 2% Native American, 24% Hispanic, 3% African American, 17% Asian American. ***Most popular recent majors:*** liberal arts/general studies, business administration/commerce/management, nursing.
FIRST-YEAR CLASS 14,025 total. Of the students who applied, 100% were accepted.
ACADEMIC PROGRAM Core. Calendar: semesters. Academic remediation for entering students, English as a second language program offered during academic year, services for LD students, advanced placement, honors program, summer session for credit, part-time degree program (daytime, evenings, weekends, summer), external degree programs, adult/continuing education programs, co-op programs. Study abroad in England. ROTC: Air Force (c).
GENERAL DEGREE REQUIREMENTS 60 credits; math requirement varies according to program.
MAJORS Accounting, agricultural sciences, anthropology, architectural technologies, art/fine arts, automotive technologies, biology/biological sciences, black/African-American studies, botany/plant sciences, business administration/commerce/management, carpentry, chemistry, child care/child and family studies, commercial art, computer information systems, computer science, corrections, cosmetology, court reporting, criminal justice, dance, dental services, drafting and design, early childhood education, economics, electrical and electronics technologies, emergency medical technology, engineering (general), engineering and applied sciences, engineering design, engineering sciences, (pre)engineering sequence, engineering technology, English, environmental sciences, ethnic studies, family and consumer studies, fashion design and technology, fashion merchandising, finance/banking, fire science, food services management, forestry, geography, geology, gerontology, history, human development, industrial engineering technology, insurance, interior design, journalism, law enforcement/police sciences, legal studies, liberal arts/general studies, library science, marine technology, marketing/retailing/merchandising, mathematics, Mexican-American/Chicano studies, modern languages, music, nursing, nutrition, philosophy, photography, physical education, physics, political science/government, psychology, real estate, recreation and leisure services, retail management, science, sociology, surveying technology, telecommunications, theater arts/drama, tourism and travel, water resources, welding technology, women's studies, zoology.
LIBRARY 94,500 books, 19 microform titles, 1,250 periodicals, 2,700 records, tapes, and CDs.
COMPUTERS ON CAMPUS 100 computers for student use in computer labs.
COLLEGE LIFE Drama-theater group, choral group, student-run newspaper. ***Student services:*** legal services, health clinic, personal-psychological counseling, women's center. ***Campus security:*** late-night transport-escort service.
HOUSING College housing not available.
ATHLETICS ***Intercollegiate:*** baseball M, basketball M/W, cross-country running M/W, football M, golf M, soccer M, softball W, swimming and diving M, tennis M/W, track and field M/W, volleyball W, water polo M, wrestling M.
CAREER PLANNING ***Service:*** career counseling.
EXPENSES FOR 1996–97 State resident tuition: $0 full-time. Nonresident tuition: $3600 full-time, $120 per unit part-time. Part-time mandatory fees per semester range from $30.50 to $160.50. Full-time mandatory fees: $425.
FINANCIAL AID ***College-administered undergrad aid 1995–96:*** need-based scholarships, non-need scholarships, short-term loans (average $50), low-interest long-term loans from external sources, Federal Work-Study. ***Required forms:*** institutional; accepted: CSS Financial Aid PROFILE, state, FAFSA. ***Priority deadline:*** 5/1. ***Payment plan:*** deferred payment.
APPLYING Open admission. ***Option:*** early entrance. ***Required:*** TOEFL for international students. Test scores used for counseling/placement. ***Application deadline:*** 8/21.
APPLYING/TRANSFER ***Application deadline:*** 8/21.
CONTACT Mrs. Chris Steward, Admissions Clerk, Rancho Santiago College, 1530 West 17th Street, Santa Ana, CA 92706-3398, 714-564-6053.

RIO HONDO COLLEGE
Whittier, California

UG Enrollment: 14,500 | **Tuition & Fees (CA Res): $431**
Application Deadline: 7/10 | **Room & Board: N/Avail**

GENERAL State and locally supported, 2-year, coed. Part of California Community Colleges System. Awards transfer associate, terminal associate degrees. Founded 1960. ***Setting:*** 128-acre suburban campus with easy access to Los Angeles. ***Total enrollment:*** 14,500. ***Faculty:*** 710 (210 full-time, 500 part-time).
ENROLLMENT PROFILE 14,500 students from 5 states and territories, 40 other countries. 52% women, 48% men, 78% part-time, 96% state residents, 11% transferred in, 1% international, 40% 25 or older, 2% Native American, 58% Hispanic, 6% African American, 11% Asian American.
FIRST-YEAR CLASS 3,500 total; 3,500 applied, 100% were accepted, 100% of whom enrolled.
ACADEMIC PROGRAM Core, honor code. Calendar: semesters. Academic remediation for entering students, English as a second language program offered during academic year, services for LD students, advanced placement, tutorials, honors program, summer session for credit, part-time degree program (daytime, evenings, weekends, summer), adult/continuing education programs. Off-campus study. Study abroad in England, Mexico. ROTC: Army (c), Naval (c), Air Force (c).
GENERAL DEGREE REQUIREMENTS 62 units; math competence; computer course for business education majors.
MAJORS Business education, criminal justice, dental services, liberal arts/general studies, nursing.
LIBRARY Main library plus 1 other, with 94,143 books, 479 periodicals, 5,748 records, tapes, and CDs.
COMPUTERS ON CAMPUS Computer purchase plan available. 150 computers for student use in various academic buildings, labs provide access to Internet.
COLLEGE LIFE Drama-theater group, choral group, student-run newspaper, radio station. ***Social organizations:*** 15 open to all. ***Student services:*** legal services, health clinic, personal-psychological counseling, women's center. ***Campus security:*** 24-hour patrols, late-night transport-escort service.
HOUSING College housing not available.
ATHLETICS ***Intercollegiate:*** baseball M, basketball M/W, cross-country running M/W, football M, golf M/W, softball W, swimming and diving M/W, tennis M/W, track and field M, volleyball W, water polo M/W, wrestling M. ***Intramural:*** field hockey, volleyball. ***Contact:*** Ms. Ellie Bewley, Dean of Physical Education, 310-692-0421.
CAREER PLANNING ***Director:*** Ms. Barbara Booth, Director, 310-692-0821. ***Service:*** career counseling.
EXPENSES FOR 1995–96 State resident tuition: $0 full-time. Nonresident tuition: $3270 full-time, $109 per unit part-time. Part-time mandatory fees per semester range from $36 to $166. Full-time mandatory fees: $431.
FINANCIAL AID ***College-administered undergrad aid 1995–96:*** need-based scholarships (average $300). ***Required forms:*** CSS Financial Aid PROFILE, FAFSA. ***Application deadline:*** continuous to 7/15. ***Payment plan:*** installment.
APPLYING Open admission. ***Options:*** early entrance, midyear entrance. ***Required:*** TOEFL for international students. ***Recommended:*** SCAT, ACT ASSET. Test scores used for counseling/placement. ***Application deadline:*** 7/10. ***Notification:*** continuous.
APPLYING/TRANSFER ***Entrance:*** noncompetitive. ***Application deadline:*** 7/10. ***Notification:*** continuous.
CONTACT Dr. Harold T. Huffman, Dean of Admissions and Records, Rio Hondo College, Whittier, CA 90601-1699, 310-692-0921 Ext. 301. ***Fax:*** 310-692-9318.

RIVERSIDE COMMUNITY COLLEGE
Riverside, California

UG Enrollment: 20,000 | **Tuition & Fees (CA Res): $430**
Application Deadline: rolling | **Room & Board: N/Avail**

GENERAL State and locally supported, 2-year, coed. Part of California Community Colleges System. Awards certificates, terminal associate degrees. Founded 1916. ***Setting:*** 109-acre suburban campus with easy access to Los Angeles. ***Total enrollment:*** 20,000. ***Faculty:*** 550 (250 full-time, 300 part-time).
ENROLLMENT PROFILE 20,000 students from 40 states and territories, 31 other countries. 58% women, 77% part-time, 98% state residents, 15% transferred in, 1% international, 50% 25 or older, 2% Native American, 15% Hispanic, 9% African American, 4% Asian American.
FIRST-YEAR CLASS 5,000 total. Of the students who applied, 100% were accepted.
ACADEMIC PROGRAM Core, honor code. Calendar: semesters. Academic remediation for entering students, English as a second language program offered during academic year, services for LD students, advanced placement, summer session for credit, part-time degree program (daytime, evenings, weekends, summer), adult/continuing education programs. Study abroad in England, Mexico, Italy. ROTC: Army (c).

GENERAL DEGREE REQUIREMENTS 60 units; math competence; 3 units of natural science; computer course (varies by major).
MAJORS Accounting, art/fine arts, automotive technologies, behavioral sciences, business administration/commerce/management, commercial art, computer information systems, computer programming, construction technologies, cosmetology, criminal justice, data processing, deaf interpreter training, dental services, drafting and design, early childhood education, electrical and electronics technologies, electrical engineering technology, electronics engineering technology, emergency medical technology, engineering (general), finance/banking, fire science, graphic arts, heating/refrigeration/air conditioning, home economics, law enforcement/police sciences, liberal arts/general studies, marketing/retailing/merchandising, medical assistant technologies, medical secretarial studies, music, natural sciences, nursing, photography, physical sciences, practical nursing, real estate, science, secretarial studies/office management, social science, theater arts/drama, welding technology.
LIBRARY Riverside Community College Library with 75,000 books, 425 periodicals.
COMPUTERS ON CAMPUS 200 computers for student use in computer center, writing lab, library.
COLLEGE LIFE Choral group. ***Social organizations:*** 30 open to all. ***Student services:*** health clinic, personal-psychological counseling. ***Campus security:*** 24-hour patrols, late-night transport-escort service.
HOUSING College housing not available.
ATHLETICS ***Intercollegiate:*** baseball M, basketball M/W, cross-country running M/W, football M, golf M, soccer M, softball W, swimming and diving M/W, tennis M/W, track and field M/W, volleyball W. ***Intramural:*** badminton, basketball, bowling, football, golf, racquetball, soccer, tennis, volleyball, weight lifting. ***Contact:*** Mr. Jim Kross, Athletic Director, 909-684-3240 Ext. 2610.
CAREER PLANNING ***Director:*** Mrs. Jeanie Briesacker, Dean of Counseling and Student Support Services, 909-684-3240. ***Service:*** career counseling.
EXPENSES FOR 1995–96 State resident tuition: $0 full-time. Nonresident tuition: $3420 full-time, $114 per unit part-time. Part-time mandatory fees per semester range from $33 to $163. Full-time mandatory fees: $430.
FINANCIAL AID ***College-administered undergrad aid 1995–96:*** 200 need-based scholarships (average $250), 350 non-need scholarships (average $500), low-interest long-term loans from external sources (average $1750), Federal Work-Study, 300 part-time jobs. ***Required forms:*** state, institutional, FAFSA; accepted: CSS Financial Aid PROFILE. ***Priority deadline:*** 5/31.
APPLYING Open admission. ***Options:*** early entrance, midyear entrance. ***Required:*** ACT, TOEFL for international students, Assessment and Placement Services for Community Colleges. Test scores used for counseling/placement. ***Application deadline:*** rolling. ***Notification:*** continuous.
APPLYING/TRANSFER ***Entrance:*** noncompetitive. ***Application deadline:*** rolling. ***Notification:*** continuous. ***Contact:*** Ms. Jeanie Briesacker, Dean of Counseling and Student Support Services, 909-341-8010.
CONTACT Dr. Margaret Ramey, Director of Admissions and Records, Riverside Community College, Riverside, CA 92506-1293, 909-222-8026.

SACRAMENTO CITY COLLEGE
Sacramento, California

UG Enrollment: 16,039	**Tuition & Fees (CA Res): $390**
Application Deadline: rolling	**Room & Board: N/Avail**

GENERAL State and locally supported, 2-year, coed. Part of California Community Colleges System. Awards certificates, transfer associate, terminal associate degrees. Founded 1916. ***Setting:*** 60-acre urban campus. ***Total enrollment:*** 16,039. ***Faculty:*** 375 (250 full-time, 11% with terminal degrees, 125 part-time).
ENROLLMENT PROFILE 16,039 students from 37 states and territories, 58 other countries. 57% women, 69% part-time, 96% state residents, 20% transferred in, 21% have need-based financial aid, 3% international, 50% 25 or older, 2% Native American, 14% Hispanic, 13% African American, 23% Asian American. ***Most popular recent major:*** business administration/commerce/management.
FIRST-YEAR CLASS 2,584 total; 3,200 applied, 100% were accepted, 81% of whom enrolled. 5% from top 10% of their high school class, 10% from top quarter, 25% from top half.
ACADEMIC PROGRAM Core, liberal arts curriculum, honor code. Calendar: semesters. 500 courses offered in 1995–96; average class size 30 in required courses. Academic remediation for entering students, English as a second language program offered during academic year and summer, services for LD students, advanced placement, self-designed majors, tutorials, honors program, summer session for credit, part-time degree program (daytime, evenings, weekends, summer), adult/continuing education programs, co-op programs. Off-campus study at University of California, Davis, California State University, Sacramento. Study abroad in England, France, Spain.
GENERAL DEGREE REQUIREMENTS 60 units; completion of math competency test or 1 math course; 1 science course.
MAJORS Accounting, advertising, aircraft and missile maintenance, art/fine arts, aviation technology, business administration/commerce/management, communication, computer science, cosmetology, criminal justice, data processing, dental services, drafting and design, early childhood education, electrical and electronics technologies, engineering (general), ethnic studies, family and consumer studies, humanities, human services, legal secretarial studies, liberal arts/general studies, library science, literature, mathematics, medical secretarial studies, military science, music, natural resource management, natural sciences, nursing, occupational therapy, physical education, physical sciences, printing technologies, psychology, real estate, science, secretarial studies/office management, social science, social work, speech/rhetoric/public address/debate, surveying technology, theater arts/drama, transportation technologies, women's studies.
LIBRARY Sacramento City College Library with 80,000 books, 400 periodicals, 1,000 records, tapes, and CDs.
COMPUTERS ON CAMPUS Computer purchase plan available. 450 computers for student use in computer center, computer labs, learning resource center, labs, classrooms, library provide access to Internet. Staffed computer lab on campus provides training in use of computers, software.
COLLEGE LIFE Drama-theater group, choral group, student-run newspaper. 3% vote in student government elections. ***Student services:*** personal-psychological counseling, women's center. ***Campus security:*** 24-hour emergency response devices and patrols, student patrols, late-night transport-escort service.
HOUSING College housing not available.
ATHLETICS ***Intercollegiate:*** basketball M/W, cross-country running M/W, football M, golf M/W, gymnastics M/W, soccer M, softball W, swimming and diving M/W, tennis M/W, track and field M/W, volleyball W, wrestling M. ***Intramural:*** archery, badminton, basketball, bowling, fencing, football, golf, gymnastics, skiing (downhill), soccer, softball, swimming and diving, table tennis (Ping-Pong), tennis, volleyball, weight lifting. ***Contact:*** Mr. Paul Carmazzi, Men's Athletic Director, 916-558-2425; Ms. Debbie Blair, Women's Athletic Director, 916-558-2425.
CAREER PLANNING ***Placement office:*** 1 full-time, 2 part-time staff. ***Director:*** Ms. Susan Leone, SPA, Counseling Services, 916-558-2384. ***Services:*** job fairs, career counseling, careers library, job bank, job interviews. 79 organizations recruited on campus 1994–95.
EXPENSES FOR 1996–97 State resident tuition: $0 full-time. Nonresident tuition: $3750 full-time, $125 per unit part-time. Part-time mandatory fees: $13 per unit. Full-time mandatory fees: $390.
FINANCIAL AID ***College-administered undergrad aid 1995–96:*** 63 need-based scholarships (average $161), 38 non-need scholarships (average $148), low-interest long-term loans from external sources, Federal Work-Study, 295 part-time jobs. ***Required forms:*** CSS Financial Aid PROFILE, FAFSA; required for some: state. ***Priority deadline:*** 3/2. ***Payment plan:*** installment.
APPLYING Open admission. ***Option:*** midyear entrance. ***Required:*** TOEFL for international students. Test scores used for counseling/placement. ***Application deadline:*** rolling. ***Notification:*** continuous.
APPLYING/TRANSFER ***Entrance:*** noncompetitive. ***Application deadline:*** rolling. ***Notification:*** continuous.
CONTACT Mr. Sam T. Sandusky, Dean of Admissions and Financial Aid, Sacramento City College, 3835 Freeport Boulevard, Sacramento, CA 95822-1386, 916-558-2438.

SADDLEBACK COLLEGE
Mission Viejo, California

UG Enrollment: 16,917	**Tuition & Fees (CA Res): $436**
Application Deadline: rolling	**Room & Board: N/Avail**

GENERAL State and locally supported, 2-year, coed. Part of Saddleback Community College District. Awards certificates, transfer associate degrees. Founded 1967. ***Setting:*** 100-acre suburban campus with easy access to Los Angeles and San Diego. ***Total enrollment:*** 16,917. ***Faculty:*** 635 (205 full-time, 40% with terminal degrees, 430 part-time).
ENROLLMENT PROFILE 16,917 students from 37 states and territories, 23 other countries. 62% women, 60% part-time, 95% state residents, 10% transferred in, 10% have need-based financial aid, 1% international, 52% 25 or older, 1% Native American, 10% Hispanic, 1% African American, 9% Asian American. ***Most popular recent majors:*** liberal arts/general studies, nursing.
FIRST-YEAR CLASS 5,508 total; 11,070 applied, 100% were accepted, 50% of whom enrolled. 5% from top 10% of their high school class.
ACADEMIC PROGRAM Core, general education curriculum, honor code. Calendar: semesters. 1,150 courses offered in 1995–96. Academic remediation for entering students, English as a second language program offered during academic year and summer, services for LD students, advanced placement, honors program, summer session for credit, part-time degree program (daytime), adult/continuing education programs, co-op programs. Off-campus study at Irvine Valley College. Study abroad in England, Mexico (1% of students participate).
GENERAL DEGREE REQUIREMENTS 64 units; completion of a math competency test or 1 algebra course; computer course for accounting, science, business majors.
MAJORS Accounting, American studies, anthropology, architectural technologies, art/fine arts, astronomy, automotive technologies, biology/biological sciences, business administration/commerce/management, carpentry, chemical engineering technology, chemistry, child care/child and family studies, child psychology/child development, commercial art, computer information systems, computer programming, computer science, construction technologies, consumer services, cosmetology, drafting and design, drug and alcohol/substance abuse counseling, early childhood education, economics, electrical engineering technology, emergency medical technology, engineering (general), (pre)engineering sequence, environmental studies, family services, fashion design and technology, fashion merchandising, film and video production, food sciences, food services management, food services technology, geography, geology, gerontology, history, home economics, horticulture, human development, humanities, human services, industrial arts, information science, interior design, journalism, landscape architecture/design, legal secretarial studies, legal studies, liberal arts/general studies, literature, marine sciences, marine technology, mathematics, medical assistant technologies, music, natural sciences, nursing, nutrition, ornamental horticulture, paralegal studies, philosophy, photography, physical education, physical sciences, physics, political science/government, psychology, radio and television studies, real estate, retail management, secretarial studies/office management, social science, sociology, speech/rhetoric/public address/debate, teacher aide studies, theater arts/drama, tourism and travel, women's studies, word processing.
LIBRARY James B. Utt Memorial Library with 109,000 books, 132 periodicals, 1 on-line bibliographic service, 1 CD-ROM, 7,400 records, tapes, and CDs.
COMPUTERS ON CAMPUS Computer purchase plan available. 200 computers for student use in computer center, computer labs, learning resource center, library provide access to main academic computer, off-campus computing facilities, Internet. Staffed computer lab on campus provides training in use of computers, software.
COLLEGE LIFE Drama-theater group, choral group, student-run newspaper, radio station. ***Social organizations:*** 19 open to all. ***Student services:*** legal services, health clinic, personal-psychological counseling, women's center. ***Campus security:*** 24-hour emergency response devices and patrols, late-night transport-escort service.
HOUSING College housing not available.
ATHLETICS ***Intercollegiate:*** baseball M, basketball M/W, cross-country running M/W, football M, golf M/W, softball W, swimming and diving M/W, tennis M/W, track and field M/W, volleyball W, water polo M/W. ***Contact:*** Dr. Keith Calkins, Athletic Director, 714-582-4547.
CAREER PLANNING ***Placement office:*** 1 full-time, 2 part-time staff. ***Director:*** Ms. Jerilyn Chuman, Dean, Counseling Services and Special Programs, 714-582-4573. ***Services:*** job fairs, resume preparation, career counseling, careers library, job bank, job interviews. 70 organizations recruited on campus 1994–95.
AFTER GRADUATION 60% of students completing a degree program in 1994–95 went directly on to further study.

Peterson's Guide to Two-Year Colleges 1997

219

Saddleback College (continued)
EXPENSES FOR 1996–97 State resident tuition: $0 full-time. Nonresident tuition: $4800 full-time, $150 per unit part-time. Part-time mandatory fees per semester range from $23 to $153. Full-time mandatory fees: $436.
FINANCIAL AID ***College-administered undergrad aid 1995–96:*** need-based scholarships, non-need scholarships, short-term loans (average $75), low-interest long-term loans, Federal Work-Study, part-time jobs. ***Required forms:*** state, FAFSA. ***Priority deadline:*** 3/15. ***Payment plan:*** deferred payment.
APPLYING Open admission. ***Option:*** early entrance. ***Required:*** TOEFL for international students. Test scores used for counseling/placement. ***Application deadline:*** rolling.
APPLYING/TRANSFER ***Application deadline:*** rolling. ***Contact:*** Ms. Miki Mikolajczak, Transfer Center Director, 714-582-4627.
CONTACT Admissions Office, Saddleback College, Mission Viejo, CA 92692-3697, 714-582-4555. College video and electronic viewbook available.

SALVATION ARMY COLLEGE FOR OFFICER TRAINING
Rancho Palos Verdes, California

Enrollment: N/R	**Comprehensive Fee: $19,960**
Application Deadline: N/R	**Room & Board: N/App**

GENERAL Independent-religious, 2-year, specialized, coed. Awards transfer associate, terminal associate degrees. Founded 1878.
ACADEMIC PROGRAM Calendar: quarters. Academic remediation for entering students, English as a second language program offered during academic year.
COMPUTERS ON CAMPUS Computers for student use in learning resource center, library. Staffed computer lab on campus provides training in use of computers.
EXPENSES FOR 1996–97 ***Application fee:*** $15. Comprehensive fee: $19,960.
CONTACT Admissions Office, Salvation Army College for Officer Training, 30840 Hawthorne Boulevard, Rancho Palos Verdes, CA 90274, 310-377-0481.

SAN BERNARDINO VALLEY COLLEGE
San Bernardino, California

UG Enrollment: 10,673	**Tuition & Fees (CA Res): $180**
Application Deadline: 8/29	**Room & Board: N/Avail**

GENERAL State and locally supported, 2-year, coed. Part of San Bernardino Community College District System. Awards certificates, diplomas, transfer associate, terminal associate degrees. Founded 1926. ***Setting:*** 82-acre campus with easy access to Los Angeles. ***Total enrollment:*** 10,673. ***Faculty:*** 375 (175 full-time, 200 part-time).
ENROLLMENT PROFILE 10,673 students from 2 states and territories. 52% women, 70% part-time, 90% state residents, 22% transferred in, 55% 25 or older, 2% Native American, 17% Hispanic, 11% African American, 4% Asian American.
FIRST-YEAR CLASS 3,000 total. Of the students who applied, 100% were accepted.
ACADEMIC PROGRAM Core. Calendar: semesters. Academic remediation for entering students, services for LD students, summer session for credit, part-time degree program (daytime, evenings, summer), co-op programs.
GENERAL DEGREE REQUIREMENTS 60 semester units; 1 math course or completion of proficiency test; 6 semester units of science.
MAJORS Accounting, aerospace sciences, anthropology, architectural technologies, art/fine arts, astronomy, automotive technologies, biology/biological sciences, botany/plant sciences, business administration/commerce/management, chemical engineering technology, chemistry, child psychology/child development, civil engineering technology, commercial art, computer science, computer technologies, corrections, data processing, dental services, drafting and design, economics, electrical and electronics technologies, electronics engineering technology, (pre)engineering sequence, English, environmental sciences, family and consumer studies, finance/banking, French, geography, geology, German, heating/refrigeration/air conditioning, history, hotel and restaurant management, human services, illustration, interior design, journalism, law enforcement/police sciences, liberal arts/general studies, machine and tool technologies, marketing/retailing/merchandising, mathematics, medical laboratory technology, mental health/rehabilitation counseling, music, nursing, philosophy, photography, physical education, physical sciences, physics, political science/government, psychology, radio and television studies, real estate, recreation and leisure services, religious studies, secretarial studies/office management, sociology, Spanish, telecommunications, welding technology, zoology.
LIBRARY 122,802 books, 5,453 microform titles, 657 periodicals, 605 records, tapes, and CDs.
COMPUTERS ON CAMPUS 80 computers for student use in computer center, learning resource center, library. Staffed computer lab on campus.
COLLEGE LIFE Drama-theater group, student-run newspaper, radio station. ***Student services:*** health clinic, personal-psychological counseling, women's center.
HOUSING College housing not available.
ATHLETICS ***Intercollegiate:*** basketball M/W, cross-country running M/W, football M, golf M, tennis M/W, track and field M/W, volleyball W, wrestling M. ***Intramural:*** basketball, soccer.
CAREER PLANNING ***Service:*** career counseling.
EXPENSES FOR 1996–97 State resident tuition: $0 full-time. Nonresident tuition: $3420 full-time, $114 per unit part-time. Part-time mandatory fees per semester range from $7.50 to $75. Full-time mandatory fees: $180.
FINANCIAL AID ***College-administered undergrad aid 1995–96:*** need-based scholarships, low-interest long-term loans from external sources (average $800), Federal Work-Study, 200 part-time jobs. ***Acceptable forms:*** state. ***Priority deadline:*** 4/30.
APPLYING Open admission. ***Required:*** TOEFL for international students, CGP. Test scores used for counseling/placement. ***Application deadline:*** 8/29.
APPLYING/TRANSFER ***Required:*** standardized test scores.
CONTACT Mr. Daniel T. Angelo, Director of Admissions and Records, San Bernardino Valley College, San Bernardino, CA 92410-2748, 909-888-6511 Ext. 1656.

SAN DIEGO CITY COLLEGE
San Diego, California

UG Enrollment: 12,616	**Tuition & Fees (CA Res): $390**
Application Deadline: 8/15	**Room & Board: N/Avail**

GENERAL State and locally supported, 2-year, coed. Part of San Diego Community College District System. Awards transfer associate, terminal associate degrees. Founded 1914. ***Setting:*** 56-acre urban campus. ***Total enrollment:*** 12,616. ***Faculty:*** 250 (180 full-time, 70 part-time).
ENROLLMENT PROFILE 12,616 students: 48% part-time, 97% state residents, 22% transferred in, 63% 25 or older, 1% Native American, 18% Hispanic, 17% African American, 10% Asian American.
FIRST-YEAR CLASS Of the students who applied, 100% were accepted, 49% of whom enrolled.
ACADEMIC PROGRAM Core. Calendar: semesters. Academic remediation for entering students, services for LD students, self-designed majors, summer session for credit, part-time degree program (daytime, evenings, weekends, summer), external degree programs, adult/continuing education programs, co-op programs. Off-campus study at San Diego State University. ROTC: Air Force (c).
GENERAL DEGREE REQUIREMENTS 60 semester units; math/science requirements vary according to program.
MAJORS Accounting, anthropology, art/fine arts, automotive technologies, behavioral sciences, biology/biological sciences, black/African-American studies, business administration/commerce/management, carpentry, child psychology/child development, commercial art, computer technologies, consumer services, cosmetology, court reporting, data processing, drafting and design, electrical and electronics technologies, electronics engineering technology, emergency medical technology, (pre)engineering sequence, engineering technology, English, environmental engineering technology, fashion merchandising, finance/banking, food services management, graphic arts, Hispanic studies, hospitality services, industrial arts, insurance, interior design, journalism, labor studies, Latin American studies, legal secretarial studies, liberal arts/general studies, machine and tool technologies, manufacturing technology, marketing/retailing/merchandising, mathematics, Mexican-American/Chicano studies, modern languages, music, nursing, occupational safety and health, paralegal studies, photography, physical education, physical sciences, political science/government, postal management, practical nursing, printing technologies, psychology, radio and television studies, real estate, recreation and leisure services, robotics, secretarial studies/office management, social science, social work, sociology, speech/rhetoric/public address/debate, teacher aide studies, telecommunications, theater arts/drama, tourism and travel, transportation technologies, welding technology.
LIBRARY San Diego City College Library with 96,000 books, 350 periodicals, 2,500 records, tapes, and CDs.
COMPUTERS ON CAMPUS 140 computers for student use in computer center, learning resource center, graphics room, library.
COLLEGE LIFE Drama-theater group, student-run newspaper, radio station. ***Student services:*** legal services, health clinic, personal-psychological counseling, women's center. ***Campus security:*** late-night transport-escort service.
HOUSING College housing not available.
ATHLETICS ***Intercollegiate:*** baseball M, basketball M/W, cross-country running M/W, football M, golf M/W, soccer M, softball W, tennis M/W, track and field M/W, volleyball M/W. ***Intramural:*** archery, badminton, baseball, basketball, bowling, racquetball, soccer, softball, swimming and diving, tennis, track and field, volleyball, weight lifting.
CAREER PLANNING ***Placement office:*** 3 full-time, 2 part-time staff. ***Director:*** Ms. Laurel Corona, Dean, Student Development, 619-230-2709. ***Services:*** job fairs, resume preparation, resume referral, career counseling, careers library, job bank, job interviews.
EXPENSES FOR 1996–97 State resident tuition: $0 full-time. Nonresident tuition: $3690 full-time, $123 per unit part-time. Part-time mandatory fees: $13 per unit. Full-time mandatory fees: $390.
FINANCIAL AID ***College-administered undergrad aid 1995–96:*** need-based scholarships (average $1075), non-need scholarships (average $100), short-term loans (average $50), low-interest long-term loans from college funds (average $2500), Federal Work-Study, 350 part-time jobs. ***Required forms:*** CSS Financial Aid PROFILE, institutional; required for some: nontaxable income verification; accepted: FAFSA. ***Priority deadline:*** 5/1.
APPLYING Open admission. ***Required:*** TOEFL for international students. ***Required for some:*** school transcript. Test scores used for counseling/placement. ***Application deadline:*** 8/15.
APPLYING/TRANSFER ***Required:*** college transcript. ***Entrance:*** noncompetitive. ***Application deadline:*** 8/15.
CONTACT Ms. Mari Porter, Admissions Officer, San Diego City College, 1313 Twelfth Avenue, San Diego, CA 92101-4787, 619-230-2400. ***Fax:*** 619-230-2135.

SAN DIEGO MESA COLLEGE
San Diego, California

UG Enrollment: 22,677	**Tuition & Fees (CA Res): $410**
Application Deadline: N/R	**Room & Board: N/Avail**

GENERAL District-supported, 2-year, coed. Part of San Diego Community College District System. Awards certificates, diplomas, transfer associate, terminal associate degrees. Founded 1964. ***Setting:*** 104-acre suburban campus. ***Total enrollment:*** 22,677. ***Faculty:*** 676 (228 full-time, 448 part-time).
ENROLLMENT PROFILE 22,677 students: 54% women, 83% part-time, 97% state residents, 14% transferred in, 1% international, 48% 25 or older, 2% Native American, 12% Hispanic, 6% African American, 13% Asian American. ***Areas of study chosen:*** 7% business management and administrative services, 5% liberal arts/general studies, 5% vocational and home economics, 4% biological and life sciences, 4% health professions and related sciences, 3% computer and information sciences, 3% psychology, 2% engineering and applied sciences, 1% architecture, 1% English language/literature/letters, 1% library and information studies, 1% social sciences.
FIRST-YEAR CLASS Of the students who applied, 100% were accepted.
ACADEMIC PROGRAM Core. Calendar: semesters. 1,800 courses offered in 1995–96. Academic remediation for entering students, services for LD students, honors program,

summer session for credit, part-time degree program (daytime, evenings, weekends, summer), external degree programs, adult/continuing education programs.
GENERAL DEGREE REQUIREMENTS 60 semester hours; math/science requirements vary according to program; 2 courses in a foreign language.
MAJORS Accounting, anthropology, applied art, architectural technologies, art/fine arts, aviation administration, biology/biological sciences, black/African-American studies, business administration/commerce/management, chemistry, child psychology/child development, computer science, construction technologies, consumer services, data processing, dental services, electrical and electronics technologies, engineering (general), English, fashion design and technology, fashion merchandising, flight training, food services management, French, German, hotel and restaurant management, interior design, Italian, landscape architecture/design, legal secretarial studies, liberal arts/general studies, marketing/retailing/merchandising, mathematics, medical assistant technologies, medical laboratory technology, medical records services, Mexican-American/Chicano studies, music, nutrition, physical education, physical sciences, physical therapy, physics, psychology, radiological technology, real estate, recreation and leisure services, Russian, secretarial studies/office management, social science, sociology, Spanish, speech/rhetoric/public address/debate, technical writing, tourism and travel, veterinary technology, water resources.
LIBRARY 84,353 books, 657 periodicals, 2,388 records, tapes, and CDs.
COMPUTERS ON CAMPUS 350 computers for student use in computer center, computer labs, learning resource center, library. Staffed computer lab on campus provides training in use of computers, software.
COLLEGE LIFE Choral group, marching band, student-run newspaper. *Social organizations:* 39 open to all. *Most popular organizations:* Alpha Gamma Sigma, Black Students Association, MECHA, Gay and Lesbian Student Group, Vietnamese Student Organization. *Major annual events:* Festival of Colors, Annual Pow-Wow, Club Rush/Back to School Reception. *Student services:* health clinic. *Campus security:* 24-hour emergency response devices and patrols.
HOUSING College housing not available.
ATHLETICS *Intercollegiate:* baseball M, basketball M/W, cross-country running M/W, football M, golf M, soccer M/W, softball W, swimming and diving M/W, tennis M/W, track and field M/W, volleyball M/W, water polo M, wrestling M. *Intramural:* basketball, skiing (cross-country), skiing (downhill), wrestling. *Contact:* Ms. Judy Stamm, Athletic Director, 619-627-2737.
CAREER PLANNING *Service:* career counseling.
EXPENSES FOR 1996–97 State resident tuition: $0 full-time. Nonresident tuition: $3300 full-time, $110 per unit part-time. Part-time mandatory fees per semester range from $23 to $153. Full-time mandatory fees: $410.
FINANCIAL AID *College-administered undergrad aid 1995–96:* need-based scholarships, low-interest long-term loans from external sources, Federal Work-Study. *Required forms:* FAFSA. *Priority deadline:* 7/1.
APPLYING Open admission. *Option:* early entrance. *Recommended:* ACT. *Required for some:* TOEFL for international students. Test scores used for counseling/placement. *Notification:* continuous.
APPLYING/TRANSFER *Required:* college transcript. *Contact:* Ms. Adrienne Frodente, Articulation Officer, 619-627-2537.
CONTACT Ms. Ivonne Alvorez, Admissions and Records Officer, San Diego Mesa College, San Diego, CA 92111-4998, 619-627-2682. *Fax:* 619-627-2960.

SAN DIEGO MIRAMAR COLLEGE
San Diego, California

UG Enrollment: 8,935	Tuition & Fees (CA Res): $395
Application Deadline: 8/20	Room & Board: N/Avail

GENERAL State and locally supported, 2-year, coed. Part of San Diego Community College District System. Awards transfer associate degrees. Founded 1969. *Setting:* 120-acre suburban campus. *Total enrollment:* 8,935. *Faculty:* 188 (67 full-time, 20% with terminal degrees, 121 part-time). *Notable Alumni:* Jerry Sanders, San Diego chief of police; Monica Higgins, deputy chief of San Diego fire department; Janko Yamamoto, international artist.
ENROLLMENT PROFILE 8,935 students: 48% women, 88% part-time, 98% state residents, 12% transferred in, 6% have need-based financial aid, 1% have non-need-based financial aid, 1% international, 57% 25 or older, 2% Native American, 10% Hispanic, 5% African American, 26% Asian American. *Most popular recent majors:* liberal arts/general studies, fire science, law enforcement/police sciences.
FIRST-YEAR CLASS Of the students who applied, 100% were accepted, 99% of whom enrolled.
ACADEMIC PROGRAM Core. Calendar: semesters. Academic remediation for entering students, English as a second language program offered during academic year and summer, services for LD students, advanced placement, self-designed majors, honors program, summer session for credit, part-time degree program (daytime, evenings, weekends, summer), adult/continuing education programs.
GENERAL DEGREE REQUIREMENTS 60 credits; math competence; computer course for fire technology majors.
MAJORS Accounting, aircraft and missile maintenance, anthropology, applied mathematics, art/fine arts, automotive technologies, aviation technology, biology/biological sciences, biotechnology, business administration/commerce/management, chemistry, child psychology/child development, communication, computer information systems, corrections, criminal justice, emergency medical technology, English, fire science, geography, humanities, journalism, law enforcement/police sciences, liberal arts/general studies, mathematics, occupational safety and health, paralegal studies, philosophy, physical education, physical sciences, physics, psychology, real estate, secretarial studies/office management, social science, sociology, Spanish, studio art, transportation technologies.
LIBRARY Miramar College Library with 18,916 books, 124 microform titles, 135 periodicals, 1 on-line bibliographic service, 3 CD-ROMs, 1,245 records, tapes, and CDs. Acquisition spending 1994–95: $35,492.
COMPUTERS ON CAMPUS 170 computers for student use in computer center, computer labs, learning resource center, classrooms, library provide access to main academic computer, e-mail, on-line services. Staffed computer lab on campus provides training in use of computers, software. Academic computing expenditure 1994–95: $270,672.
COLLEGE LIFE Student-run newspaper. 1% vote in student government elections. *Social organizations:* 9 open to all. *Most popular organizations:* Science Club, International Club, Parent Student Advisory Board, Filipino-American Student Union, Miramar-U. S. Tennis Association. *Major annual event:* Majors Fair. *Student services:* personal-psychological counseling. *Campus security:* 24-hour emergency response devices and patrols.
HOUSING College housing not available.
ATHLETICS *Intramural:* tennis.
CAREER PLANNING *Placement office:* 5 part-time staff; $9849 operating expenditure 1994–95. *Director:* Dr. Palisa Williams Rushin, Transfer Center Director, 619-536-7840. *Services:* resume preparation, career counseling, careers library.
EXPENSES FOR 1996–97 State resident tuition: $0 full-time. Nonresident tuition: $3300 full-time, $110 per unit part-time. Part-time mandatory fees per semester range from $15.50 to $145.50. Full-time mandatory fees: $395.
FINANCIAL AID *College-administered undergrad aid 1995–96:* 89 need-based scholarships (average $300), short-term loans (average $50), low-interest long-term loans from external sources (average $2000), 27 Federal Work-Study (averaging $1000), 5 part-time jobs. *Required forms:* CSS Financial Aid PROFILE, institutional, FAFSA; accepted: state. *Application deadline:* continuous to 5/1.
APPLYING Open admission. *Option:* early entrance. *Required:* TOEFL for international students. Test scores used for counseling/placement. *Application deadline:* 8/20.
APPLYING/TRANSFER *Entrance:* noncompetitive. *Contact:* Ms. Joan Thompson, Counseling Department Chair, 619-536-7840.
CONTACT Mrs. Dana Maxwell, Admissions Office Supervisor, San Diego Miramar College, San Diego, CA 92126-2999, 619-536-7854. *E-mail:* dmaxwell@sdccd.cc.ca.us.

SAN FRANCISCO COLLEGE OF MORTUARY SCIENCE
San Francisco, California

UG Enrollment: 65	Tuition & Fees: $9200
Application Deadline: rolling	Room & Board: N/Avail

GENERAL Independent, 2-year, specialized, coed. Awards terminal associate degrees. Founded 1930. *Setting:* 1-acre urban campus. *Total enrollment:* 65. *Faculty:* 6 (3 full-time, 3 part-time); student-faculty ratio is 11:1.
ENROLLMENT PROFILE 65 students from 10 states and territories. 32% women, 68% men, 0% part-time, 72% state residents, 10% transferred in, 0% international, 50% 25 or older, 0% Native American, 2% Hispanic, 5% African American, 0% Asian American.
FIRST-YEAR CLASS 30 total; 40 applied, 100% were accepted, 75% of whom enrolled. 5% from top 10% of their high school class, 20% from top half.
ACADEMIC PROGRAM Core, honor code. Calendar: trimesters. Summer session for credit.
GENERAL DEGREE REQUIREMENT 69 credits.
MAJOR Funeral service.
LIBRARY 1,000 books, 12 periodicals, 24 records, tapes, and CDs.
COMPUTERS ON CAMPUS 2 computers for student use in classrooms.
COLLEGE LIFE Student-run newspaper. 100% vote in student government elections.
HOUSING College housing not available.
CAREER PLANNING *Service:* career counseling.
EXPENSES FOR 1995–96 *Application fee:* $25. Tuition: $8400 full-time. Full-time mandatory fees: $800. Tuition guaranteed not to increase for student's term of enrollment.
FINANCIAL AID *College-administered undergrad aid 1995–96:* low-interest long-term loans from external sources (averaging $2625), part-time jobs. *Application deadline:* continuous to 9/1.
APPLYING Open admission. *Option:* deferred entrance. *Application deadline:* rolling. *Notification:* continuous.
APPLYING/TRANSFER *Application deadline:* rolling. *Notification:* continuous.
CONTACT Ms. Jacquelyn S. Taylor, President, San Francisco College of Mortuary Science, 1598 Dolores Street, San Francisco, CA 94110-4927, 415-567-0674 Ext. 14. *E-mail:* sfcms@ix.netcom.com.

SAN JOAQUIN DELTA COLLEGE
Stockton, California

UG Enrollment: 17,860	Tuition & Fees (CA Res): $390
Application Deadline: rolling	Room & Board: N/Avail

GENERAL District-supported, 2-year, coed. Part of California Community Colleges System. Awards transfer associate degrees. Founded 1935. *Setting:* 165-acre urban campus with easy access to Sacramento. *Total enrollment:* 17,860. *Faculty:* 579 (229 full-time, 1% with terminal degrees, 350 part-time); student-faculty ratio is 31:1.
ENROLLMENT PROFILE 17,860 students: 55% women, 45% men, 67% part-time, 97% state residents, 3% transferred in, 1% international, 49% 25 or older, 2% Native American, 19% Hispanic, 6% African American, 17% Asian American. *Most popular recent majors:* liberal arts/general studies, nursing, business administration/commerce/management.
FIRST-YEAR CLASS 2,857 total; 2,857 applied, 100% were accepted, 100% of whom enrolled.
ACADEMIC PROGRAM Core, honor code. Calendar: semesters. Academic remediation for entering students, English as a second language program offered during academic year and summer, services for LD students, advanced placement, self-designed majors, honors program, summer session for credit, part-time degree program (daytime, evenings, summer), adult/continuing education programs, co-op programs.
GENERAL DEGREE REQUIREMENTS 60 units; math proficiency.
MAJORS Accounting, agricultural business, agricultural sciences, agricultural technologies, animal sciences, anthropology, art/fine arts, automotive technologies, behavioral sciences, biology/biological sciences, botany/plant sciences, broadcasting, business administration/commerce/management, business economics, carpentry, chemistry, child care/child and family studies, child psychology/child development, civil engineering technology, computer programming, computer science, computer technologies, construction technologies, corrections, culinary arts, dance, drafting and design, early childhood education, economics, electrical and electronics technologies, electrical engineering technology, electronics engineering technology, emergency medical technology, engineering (general), engineering design, engineering technology, English, fashion merchandising, fire science, food services management, food services technology, French, geology, German, graphic arts, health education,

San Joaquin Delta College (continued)
health science, heating/refrigeration/air conditioning, history, home economics, humanities, interior design, Italian, Japanese, journalism, law enforcement/police sciences, liberal arts/general studies, literature, machine and tool technologies, marketing/retailing/merchandising, mathematics, mechanical engineering technology, Mexican-American/Chicano studies, music, natural resource management, natural sciences, nursing, ornamental horticulture, painting/drawing, philosophy, photography, physical education, physical sciences, political science/government, practical nursing, printing technologies, psychology, public administration, radiological technology, religious studies, social science, sociology, Spanish, speech/rhetoric/public address/debate, surveying technology, theater arts/drama, water resources.
LIBRARY Goleman Library with 86,226 books, 614 periodicals, 5,500 records, tapes, and CDs.
COMPUTERS ON CAMPUS 200 computers for student use in labs. Staffed computer lab on campus provides training in use of computers, software.
COLLEGE LIFE Drama-theater group, choral group, student-run newspaper, radio station. ***Social organizations:*** 30 open to all. ***Most popular organizations:*** Alpha Gamma Sigma, MECHA, Vietnamese Club, American Society of Mechanical Engineers. ***Major annual events:*** Job Fair, Club Rush, Cinco de Mayo. ***Student services:*** legal services, personal-psychological counseling. ***Campus security:*** 24-hour emergency response devices and patrols, late-night transport-escort service.
HOUSING College housing not available.
ATHLETICS ***Intercollegiate:*** baseball M, basketball M/W, cross-country running M/W, football M, golf M, skiing (cross-country) M/W, soccer M/W, softball W, swimming and diving M/W, tennis M/W, track and field M/W, volleyball W, water polo M/W, wrestling M. ***Contact:*** Mr. Ernest Marcopulos, Director of Athletics, 209-474-5176.
CAREER PLANNING ***Placement office:*** 5 full-time, 6 part-time staff. ***Director:*** Ms. Marcella Rodgers-Vieiria, Counselor, 209-474-5674. ***Services:*** job fairs, resume preparation, resume referral, career counseling, careers library, job bank, job interviews. 70 organizations recruited on campus 1994–95.
EXPENSES FOR 1996–97 State resident tuition: $0 full-time. Nonresident tuition: $3420 full-time, $114 per unit part-time. Part-time mandatory fees: $13 per unit. Full-time mandatory fees: $390.
FINANCIAL AID ***College-administered undergrad aid 1995–96:*** need-based scholarships, low-interest long-term loans from external sources, Federal Work-Study, part-time jobs. ***Required forms:*** CSS Financial Aid PROFILE, institutional; required for some: FAFSA. ***Priority deadline:*** 5/31.
APPLYING Open admission. ***Options:*** Common Application, early entrance. ***Recommended:*** TOEFL for international students, Michigan Test of English Language Proficiency. Test scores used for counseling/placement. ***Application deadline:*** rolling. ***Notification:*** continuous.
APPLYING/TRANSFER ***Entrance:*** noncompetitive. ***Application deadline:*** rolling. ***Notification:*** continuous. ***Contact:*** Mr. Michael Kerns, Director of the College Center, 209-474-5100.
CONTACT Ms. Cheryl L. Clark, Registrar, San Joaquin Delta College, 5151 Pacific Avenue, Stockton, CA 95207-6370, 209-474-5635. ***Fax:*** 209-474-5649.

SAN JOAQUIN VALLEY COLLEGE
Visalia, California

UG Enrollment: 425 | **Tuition & Fees: $6600**
Application Deadline: N/R | **Room & Board: N/Avail**

GENERAL Independent, 2-year. Awards transfer associate degrees. Founded 1977. ***Setting:*** small-town campus. ***Total enrollment:*** 425.
ENROLLMENT PROFILE 425 students.
FIRST-YEAR CLASS Of the students who applied, 70% were accepted, 90% of whom enrolled.
ACADEMIC PROGRAM Calendar: semesters.
GENERAL DEGREE REQUIREMENTS 60 credits; 3 credits of math/science; computer course.
HOUSING College housing not available.
EXPENSES FOR 1996–97 Tuition: $6500 full-time. Full-time mandatory fees: $100.
APPLYING ***Required:*** school transcript, CPAt. ***Required for some:*** interview.
APPLYING/TRANSFER ***Required:*** standardized test scores, high school transcript, college transcript. ***Required for some:*** interview.
CONTACT Ms. Raelene Vanek, Director of Admissions, San Joaquin Valley College, Visalia, CA 93291, 209-651-2500.

SAN JOSE CITY COLLEGE
San Jose, California

UG Enrollment: 10,044 | **Tuition & Fees (CA Res): $410**
Application Deadline: rolling | **Room & Board: N/Avail**

GENERAL District-supported, 2-year, coed. Part of San Jose/Evergreen Community College District System. Awards transfer associate, terminal associate degrees. Founded 1921. ***Setting:*** 58-acre urban campus. ***Total enrollment:*** 10,044. ***Faculty:*** 390 (165 full-time, 225 part-time).
ENROLLMENT PROFILE 10,044 students: 52% women, 48% men, 83% part-time, 98% state residents, 4% transferred in, 1% international, 56% 25 or older, 1% Native American, 23% Hispanic, 6% African American, 30% Asian American. ***Most popular recent majors:*** history, electrical and electronics technologies, liberal arts/general studies.
FIRST-YEAR CLASS 3,649 total. Of the students who applied, 100% were accepted, 52% of whom enrolled.
ACADEMIC PROGRAM Core. Calendar: semesters. Academic remediation for entering students, English as a second language program offered during academic year, services for LD students, advanced placement, self-designed majors, summer session for credit, part-time degree program (daytime, evenings, weekends, summer), adult/continuing education programs, co-op programs. ROTC: Army (c), Air Force (c).
GENERAL DEGREE REQUIREMENTS 60 units; algebra competence; 1 lab science course; computer course.
MAJORS Accounting, business administration/commerce/management, child care/child and family studies, computer science, computer technologies, construction technologies, cosmetology, criminal justice, data processing, dental services, drafting and design, early childhood education, electrical and electronics technologies, engineering (general), engineering and applied sciences, family services, heating/refrigeration/air conditioning, history, human services, labor and industrial relations, labor studies, liberal arts/general studies, machine and tool technologies, marketing/retailing/merchandising, public administration, real estate, secretarial studies/office management, solar technologies, teacher aide studies.
LIBRARY San Jose City College Library with 54,075 books, 3,049 microform titles, 345 periodicals, 1,829 records, tapes, and CDs.
COMPUTERS ON CAMPUS 48 computers for student use in computer center. Staffed computer lab on campus provides training in use of computers, software.
COLLEGE LIFE Drama-theater group, student-run newspaper, radio station. ***Student services:*** health clinic.
HOUSING College housing not available.
ATHLETICS ***Intercollegiate:*** baseball M, basketball M/W, cross-country running M/W, football M, golf M, softball W, track and field M/W, volleyball W, wrestling M. ***Contact:*** Mr. Burt Bonanno, Athletic Director, 408-298-3730.
CAREER PLANNING ***Director:*** Dr. Alex Reyes, Director of Transfer Center, 408-298-2181 Ext. 3643. ***Service:*** career counseling.
AFTER GRADUATION 12% of students completing a degree program in 1994–95 went directly on to further study.
EXPENSES FOR 1996–97 State resident tuition: $0 full-time. Nonresident tuition: $3360 full-time, $112 per unit part-time. Part-time mandatory fees per semester range from $23 to $153. Full-time mandatory fees: $410.
FINANCIAL AID ***College-administered undergrad aid 1995–96:*** need-based scholarships, non-need scholarships, short-term loans (average $500), low-interest long-term loans from external sources, Federal Work-Study, part-time jobs. ***Required forms:*** institutional. ***Priority deadline:*** 6/15.
APPLYING Open admission. ***Options:*** early entrance, deferred entrance. ***Required:*** TOEFL for international students. Test scores used for counseling/placement. ***Application deadline:*** rolling. Preference given to district residents.
APPLYING/TRANSFER ***Recommended:*** college transcript. ***Entrance:*** noncompetitive. ***Application deadline:*** rolling.
CONTACT Ms. Rosalie Eskew, Director of Admissions/Registrar, San Jose City College, 2100 Moorpark Avenue, San Jose, CA 95128-2797, 408-288-3707.

SANTA BARBARA CITY COLLEGE
Santa Barbara, California

UG Enrollment: 11,288 | **Tuition & Fees (CA Res): $422**
Application Deadline: 8/17 | **Room & Board: N/Avail**

GENERAL District-supported, 2-year, coed. Part of California Community Colleges System. Awards certificates, terminal associate degrees. Founded 1908. ***Setting:*** 65-acre small-town campus. ***Total enrollment:*** 11,288. ***Faculty:*** 468 (202 full-time, 18% with terminal degrees, 266 part-time). ***Notable Alumni:*** Mark Munch, photographer and author; Bill Villa, director of admissions at University of California, Santa Barbara; Jill Rivera, national promotional director of KMGQ-KIST radio; Gary Picaret, assistant superintendent of Santa Barbara County Education Office.
ENROLLMENT PROFILE 11,288 students from 20 states and territories, 60 other countries. 50% women, 58% part-time, 94% state residents, 13% transferred in, 4% international, 34% 25 or older, 1% Native American, 25% Hispanic, 2% African American, 7% Asian American. ***Most popular recent majors:*** liberal arts/general studies, criminal justice, business administration/commerce/management.
FIRST-YEAR CLASS 2,260 total. Of the students who applied, 100% were accepted.
ACADEMIC PROGRAM Core, honor code. Calendar: semesters. Academic remediation for entering students, English as a second language program offered during academic year and summer, services for LD students, advanced placement, honors program, summer session for credit, part-time degree program (daytime, evenings, summer), adult/continuing education programs, co-op programs and internships. Study abroad in England, Mexico, France, China, Spain, Costa Rica, Commonwealth of Independent States, Germany, Italy. ROTC: Army (c).
GENERAL DEGREE REQUIREMENTS 60 units; 1 course each in intermediate algebra and lab science; internship (some majors).
MAJORS Anthropology, art/fine arts, automotive technologies, biology/biological sciences, biomedical technologies, black/African-American studies, business administration/commerce/management, chemistry, communication, computer information systems, computer science, criminal justice, dental services, drafting and design, early childhood education, earth science, economics, electrical and electronics technologies, electrical engineering technology, electronics engineering technology, engineering (general), engineering technology, English, environmental sciences, environmental studies, ethnic studies, finance/banking, food services management, French, geography, geology, German, graphic arts, history, horticulture, hotel and restaurant management, international studies, law enforcement/police sciences, liberal arts/general studies, marine technology, marketing/retailing/merchandising, mathematics, Mexican-American/Chicano studies, music, Native American studies, natural sciences, nursing, ornamental horticulture, philosophy, physical education, physics, political science/government, practical nursing, psychology, radiological technology, real estate, recreation and leisure services, secretarial studies/office management, sociology, Spanish, speech/rhetoric/public address/debate, theater arts/drama, water resources.
LIBRARY Eli Luria Library with 88,000 books, 225 microform titles, 425 periodicals, 2 on-line bibliographic services, 2 CD-ROMs, 14,523 records, tapes, and CDs.
COMPUTERS ON CAMPUS Computer purchase plan available. 225 computers for student use in computer center, computer labs, learning resource center, labs. Staffed computer lab on campus provides training in use of computers, software.
COLLEGE LIFE Drama-theater group, choral group, student-run newspaper. 10% vote in student government elections. ***Social organizations:*** 25 open to all. ***Most popular organizations:*** MECHA, International-Cultural Exchange Club, Ski Club, Computer Club, Astronomy Club. ***Major annual events:*** Cinco de Mayo, Karate Tournament. ***Student services:*** personal-psychological counseling. ***Campus security:*** 24-hour emergency response devices and patrols, late-night transport-escort service.
HOUSING College housing not available.
ATHLETICS ***Intercollegiate:*** baseball M, basketball M/W, cross-country running M/W, football M, golf M, soccer M/W, tennis M/W, track and field M/W, volleyball M/W.

Intramural: softball. ***Contact:*** Mr. Bob Dinaberg, Athletic Director, 805-965-0581 Ext. 2277; Ms. Ellen O'Connor, Assistant Athletic Director, 805-965-0581 Ext. 2270.

CAREER PLANNING ***Placement office:*** 3 full-time, 5 part-time staff. ***Director:*** Mr. Bob Ehrman, Director of Career Advancement Center, 805-965-0581 Ext. 2334. ***Services:*** job fairs, resume preparation, career counseling, careers library, job bank, job interviews.

EXPENSES FOR 1995–96 State resident tuition: $0 full-time. Nonresident tuition: $3420 full-time, $114 per unit part-time. Part-time mandatory fees per semester range from $35 to $165. Full-time mandatory fees: $422.

FINANCIAL AID ***College-administered undergrad aid 1995–96:*** 3,665 need-based scholarships (average $572), 287 non-need scholarships (average $476), short-term loans (average $150), low-interest long-term loans from college funds (average $459), loans from external sources (average $2686), 145 Federal Work-Study (averaging $2400), 60 part-time jobs. ***Required forms:*** institutional; accepted: CSS Financial Aid PROFILE, FAFSA. ***Priority deadline:*** 5/1.

APPLYING Open admission. ***Options:*** early entrance, midyear entrance. ***Required:*** TOEFL for international students. ***Recommended:*** school transcript, SCAT. Test scores used for counseling/placement. ***Application deadline:*** 8/17. ***Notification:*** continuous.

APPLYING/TRANSFER ***Recommended:*** high school transcript, college transcript. ***Entrance:*** noncompetitive. ***Application deadline:*** 8/17. ***Notification:*** continuous. ***Contact:*** Mr. Armando Segura, Director of Transfer Center, 805-965-0581 Ext. 2547.

CONTACT Ms. Jane Craven, Assistant Dean of Admissions and Records, Santa Barbara City College, Santa Barbara, CA 93109-2394, 805-965-0581. ***Fax:*** 805-963-SBCC. ***E-mail:*** info@gate1.sbcc.cc.ca.us.

SANTA MONICA COLLEGE
Santa Monica, California

UG Enrollment: 22,127	**Tuition & Fees (CA Res): $430**
Application Deadline: 8/30	**Room & Board: N/Avail**

GENERAL State and locally supported, 2-year, coed. Part of California Community Colleges System. Awards transfer associate, terminal associate degrees. Founded 1929. ***Setting:*** 40-acre urban campus with easy access to Los Angeles. ***Total enrollment:*** 22,127. ***Faculty:*** 664 (277 full-time, 387 part-time).

ENROLLMENT PROFILE 22,127 students from 20 states and territories, 103 other countries. 56% women, 44% men, 70% part-time, 89% state residents, 16% transferred in, 9% international, 41% 25 or older, 1% Native American, 18% Hispanic, 11% African American, 20% Asian American. ***Areas of study chosen:*** 26% liberal arts/general studies, 15% business management and administrative services, 6% fine arts, 5% engineering and applied sciences, 5% psychology, 3% communications and journalism, 3% health professions and related sciences, 2% architecture, 2% biological and life sciences, 2% education, 2% performing arts. ***Most popular recent majors:*** business administration/commerce/management, liberal arts/general studies, nursing.

FIRST-YEAR CLASS 3,103 total; 5,000 applied, 100% were accepted, 62% of whom enrolled.

ACADEMIC PROGRAM Core, honor code. Calendar: semesters. Academic remediation for entering students, English as a second language program offered during academic year and summer, services for LD students, advanced placement, Freshman Honors College, honors program, summer session for credit, part-time degree program (daytime, evenings, summer), adult/continuing education programs, co-op programs and internships. Study abroad in England, Austria, Spain, France (1% of students participate). ROTC: Army (c).

GENERAL DEGREE REQUIREMENTS 60 units; 1 course in college algebra.

MAJORS Accounting, anthropology, architectural technologies, art/fine arts, astronomy, athletic training, automotive technologies, biology/biological sciences, broadcasting, business administration/commerce/management, chemistry, child psychology/child development, communication, computer information systems, computer programming, construction technologies, cosmetology, criminal justice, dance, data processing, dental services, drafting and design, early childhood education, economics, electrical and electronics technologies, electrical engineering technology, electronics engineering technology, (pre)engineering sequence, English, ethnic studies, fashion merchandising, fire science, French, geography, geology, German, graphic arts, history, home economics, industrial arts, interior design, journalism, law enforcement/police sciences, liberal arts/general studies, mathematics, music, nursing, philosophy, photography, physical education, physics, political science/government, printing technologies, psychology, radio and television studies, real estate, recreation and leisure services, respiratory therapy, secretarial studies/office management, sociology, theater arts/drama, welding technology.

LIBRARY Santa Monica College Library with 105,075 books, 85 microform titles, 447 periodicals, 1 on-line bibliographic service, 15 CD-ROMs. Acquisition spending 1994–95: $81,537.

COMPUTERS ON CAMPUS Computer purchase plan available. 360 computers for student use in computer labs, learning resource center, various locations throughout campus, classrooms, library. Staffed computer lab on campus. Academic computing expenditure 1994–95: $705,864.

COLLEGE LIFE Drama-theater group, choral group, marching band, student-run newspaper. 10% vote in student government elections. ***Social organizations:*** 50 open to all. ***Most popular organizations:*** Club Latino United for Education, African Student Union, Gay and Lesbian Union, Alpha Gamma Sigma, International Speakers Club. ***Major annual events:*** Transfer College Fair, Club Row, International Festival. ***Student services:*** health clinic, personal-psychological counseling, women's center. ***Campus security:*** 24-hour emergency response devices and patrols, late-night transport-escort service.

HOUSING College housing not available.

ATHLETICS Member NJCAA. ***Intercollegiate:*** basketball M/W, cross-country running M/W, football M, soccer W, softball W, swimming and diving M/W, tennis M/W, track and field M/W, volleyball M/W, water polo M/W. ***Contact:*** Ms. Avie Bridges, Athletics Director, 310-450-5150.

CAREER PLANNING ***Placement office:*** 1 full-time, 4 part-time staff; $273,061 operating expenditure 1994–95. ***Director:*** Ms. Brenda Johnson, Assistant Dean, 310-450-5150. ***Services:*** job fairs, resume preparation, career counseling, careers library, job interviews. 140 organizations recruited on campus 1994–95.

AFTER GRADUATION 20% of students completing a degree program in 1994–95 went directly on to further study.

EXPENSES FOR 1995–96 State resident tuition: $0 full-time. Nonresident tuition: $3750 full-time, $125 per unit part-time. Part-time mandatory fees per semester range from $33 to $163. Tuition for international students: $140 per unit. Full-time mandatory fees: $430.

FINANCIAL AID ***College-administered undergrad aid 1995–96:*** need-based scholarships, 250 non-need scholarships (averaging $500), short-term loans (averaging $50), low-interest long-term loans from college funds (averaging $40), loans from external sources (averaging $2625), 250 Federal Work-Study, 200 part-time jobs. ***Required forms:*** FAFSA; accepted: institutional. ***Priority deadline:*** 12/21.

APPLYING Open admission. ***Options:*** early entrance, midyear entrance. ***Required:*** TOEFL for international students. Test scores used for counseling/placement. ***Application deadline:*** 8/30. ***Notification:*** continuous until 8/30.

APPLYING/TRANSFER ***Application deadline:*** 8/30. ***Notification:*** continuous until 8/30. ***Contact:*** Ms. Brenda Johnson, Assistant Dean, 310-450-5150.

CONTACT Mr. Gordon A. Newman, Dean of Admissions and Records, Santa Monica College, 1900 Pico Boulevard, Santa Monica, CA 90405-1644, 310-452-9220.

❖ *See page 802 for a narrative description.* ❖

SANTA ROSA JUNIOR COLLEGE
Santa Rosa, California

UG Enrollment: 21,651	**Tuition & Fees (CA Res): $412**
Application Deadline: rolling	**Room Only: $1750**

GENERAL State and locally supported, 2-year, coed. Part of California Community Colleges System. Awards transfer associate, terminal associate degrees. Founded 1918. ***Setting:*** 93-acre urban campus with easy access to San Francisco. ***Endowment:*** $10.7 million. ***Total enrollment:*** 21,651. ***Faculty:*** 1,130 (271 full-time, 11% with terminal degrees, 859 part-time).

ENROLLMENT PROFILE 21,651 students from 39 states and territories, 43 other countries. 59% women, 41% men, 69% part-time, 98% state residents, 9% transferred in, 1% international, 60% 25 or older, 1% Native American, 11% Hispanic, 2% African American, 3% Asian American. ***Most popular recent majors:*** liberal arts/general studies, science.

FIRST-YEAR CLASS 2,680 total; 2,680 applied, 100% were accepted, 100% of whom enrolled.

ACADEMIC PROGRAM Core. Calendar: semesters. Academic remediation for entering students, English as a second language program offered during academic year and summer, services for LD students, advanced placement, tutorials, summer session for credit, part-time degree program (daytime, evenings, summer), adult/continuing education programs, co-op programs and internships. Off-campus study at California State University, University of California. Study abroad in England, France, Italy (1% of students participate). ROTC: Army (c), Air Force (c).

GENERAL DEGREE REQUIREMENT 60 units.

MAJORS Agricultural business, agricultural sciences, animal sciences, anthropology, applied art, art/fine arts, astronomy, automotive technologies, aviation technology, biology/biological sciences, botany/plant sciences, business administration/commerce/management, chemistry, child psychology/child development, civil engineering technology, communication, construction management, construction technologies, criminal justice, culinary arts, dental services, economics, electrical and electronics technologies, emergency medical technology, English, fashion design and technology, fire science, forest technology, French, geography, geology, German, graphic arts, health education, history, horticulture, humanities, industrial arts, landscape architecture/design, law enforcement/police sciences, liberal arts/general studies, machine and tool technologies, mathematics, medical assistant technologies, medical secretarial studies, music, nursing, nutrition, parks management, physical education, physical sciences, political science/government, psychology, public administration, radiological technology, science, social science, sociology, Spanish, speech/rhetoric/public address/debate, theater arts/drama.

LIBRARY Plover Library with 119,700 books, 493 microform titles, 772 periodicals, 2 CD-ROMs, 2,336 records, tapes, and CDs. Acquisition spending 1994–95: $90,517.

COMPUTERS ON CAMPUS 900 computers for student use in computer center, computer labs, learning resource center, lab, tutorial center, various locations throughout campus, classrooms, library provide access to Internet. Staffed computer lab on campus provides training in use of computers, software.

COLLEGE LIFE Drama-theater group, choral group, student-run newspaper. ***Social organizations:*** 30 open to all. ***Most popular organizations:*** Hemp Club, MECHA, Alpha Gamma Sigma, Ski and Snowboard Club, Phi Theta Kappa. ***Major annual events:*** Day Under the Oaks, Earth Day, Club Days. ***Student services:*** health clinic, personal-psychological counseling, women's center. ***Campus security:*** 24-hour emergency response devices and patrols.

HOUSING 72 college housing spaces available; all were occupied 1995–96. No special consideration for freshman housing applicants. Off-campus living permitted. Sonoma County applicants given priority for college housing. ***Option:*** coed (1 building) housing available. Resident assistants live in dorms.

ATHLETICS ***Intercollegiate:*** baseball M, basketball M/W, cross-country running M/W, football M, golf M, soccer M/W, softball W, swimming and diving M/W, tennis M/W, track and field M/W, volleyball W, water polo M, wrestling M. ***Contact:*** Mr. Ben Partee, Athletic Director, 707-527-4237.

CAREER PLANNING ***Placement office:*** 3 full-time, 3 part-time staff; $96,389 operating expenditure 1994–95. ***Director:*** Ms. Carol Tice, Career Center Director, 707-527-4448. ***Services:*** resume preparation, resume referral, career counseling, careers library, job interviews.

EXPENSES FOR 1995–96 State resident tuition: $0 full-time. Nonresident tuition: $3600 full-time, $120 per unit part-time. Part-time mandatory fees per semester range from $24 to $154. Tuition for international students: $154 per unit. Full-time mandatory fees: $412. College room only: $1750.

FINANCIAL AID ***College-administered undergrad aid 1995–96:*** need-based scholarships (average $350), 3,660 non-need scholarships (average $950), low-interest long-term loans from external sources (average $3000), 392 Federal Work-Study (averaging $3136), 400 part-time jobs. ***Required forms:*** FAFSA; accepted: CSS Financial Aid PROFILE. ***Priority deadline:*** 3/2.

APPLYING Open admission except for allied health programs. ***Options:*** Common Application, early entrance. ***Required:*** TOEFL for international students. Test scores used for counseling/placement. ***Application deadline:*** rolling. ***Notification:*** continuous.

Santa Rosa Junior College (continued)
APPLYING/TRANSFER ***Required for some:*** college transcript. ***Entrance:*** noncompetitive. ***Application deadline:*** rolling. ***Notification:*** continuous. ***Contact:*** Ms. Jan Tracy, Counselor/Director of Transfer Center, 707-527-4874.
CONTACT Mr. Ricardo Navarrette, Dean of Admissions, Santa Rosa Junior College, 1501 Mendocino Avenue, Santa Rosa, CA 95401-4395, 707-527-4510. ***E-mail:*** kim-nikolic@garfield.santarosa.edu.

SHASTA COLLEGE
Redding, California

UG Enrollment: 11,152 **Tuition & Fees (CA Res): $416**
Application Deadline: rolling **Room Only: $1794**

GENERAL State and locally supported, 2-year, coed. Part of California Community Colleges System. Awards transfer associate, terminal associate degrees. Founded 1948. ***Setting:*** 336-acre suburban campus. ***Total enrollment:*** 11,152. ***Faculty:*** 424 (159 full-time, 265 part-time).
ENROLLMENT PROFILE 11,152 students: 63% women, 77% part-time, 99% state residents, 19% transferred in, 1% international, 60% 25 or older, 4% Native American, 3% Hispanic, 1% African American, 2% Asian American.
FIRST-YEAR CLASS 2,130 total. Of the students who applied, 100% were accepted, 95% of whom enrolled.
ACADEMIC PROGRAM Core. Calendar: semesters. Academic remediation for entering students, English as a second language program offered during academic year and summer, services for LD students, advanced placement, tutorials, honors program, summer session for credit, part-time degree program (daytime, evenings), adult/continuing education programs, co-op programs.
GENERAL DEGREE REQUIREMENT 60 semester units.
MAJORS Accounting, agricultural business, agricultural technologies, animal sciences, art/fine arts, automotive technologies, aviation technology, business administration/commerce/management, carpentry, civil engineering technology, commercial art, computer management, computer science, construction technologies, criminal justice, culinary arts, drafting and design, early childhood education, electrical and electronics technologies, electrical engineering technology, engineering (general), fashion merchandising, finance/banking, fire science, graphic arts, home economics, horticulture, industrial and heavy equipment maintenance, legal secretarial studies, management information systems, marketing/retailing/merchandising, mechanical engineering technology, medical assistant technologies, music, natural resource management, nursing, ornamental horticulture, paralegal studies, real estate, retail management, secretarial studies/office management, teacher aide studies, theater arts/drama, welding technology.
LIBRARY Shasta College Learning Resource Center with 66,070 books, 60 microform titles, 377 periodicals, 5 CD-ROMs, 1,955 records, tapes, and CDs.
COMPUTERS ON CAMPUS 250 computers for student use in computer center, computer labs, learning resource center, classrooms.
COLLEGE LIFE Drama-theater group, choral group, student-run newspaper, radio station. ***Student services:*** health clinic, personal-psychological counseling. ***Campus security:*** 18-hour patrols by trained security personnel.
HOUSING 120 college housing spaces available; all were occupied 1995–96. No special consideration for freshman housing applicants. Off-campus living permitted. ***Option:*** coed housing available. Resident assistants live in dorms.
ATHLETICS ***Intercollegiate:*** baseball M, basketball M/W, cross-country running M/W, football M, golf M/W, softball W, tennis M/W, track and field M/W, volleyball W. ***Intramural:*** cross-country running. ***Contact:*** Mr. Joe Golenor, Athletic Director, 916-225-4797.
CAREER PLANNING ***Placement office:*** 2 full-time, 1 part-time staff. ***Director:*** Ms. Irene Helzer, Career Center Coordinator, 916-225-4925. ***Services:*** resume preparation, career counseling, careers library.
EXPENSES FOR 1995–96 State resident tuition: $0 full-time. Nonresident tuition: $3750 full-time, $125 per unit part-time. Part-time mandatory fees per semester range from $26 to $156. Full-time mandatory fees: $416. College room only: $1794.
FINANCIAL AID ***College-administered undergrad aid 1995–96:*** need-based scholarships, non-need scholarships, low-interest long-term loans from external sources, part-time jobs. ***Required forms:*** state, institutional; accepted: CSS Financial Aid PROFILE. ***Priority deadline:*** 8/15.
APPLYING Open admission. ***Options:*** early entrance, midyear entrance. ***Required:*** school transcript, TOEFL for international students. Test scores used for counseling/placement. ***Application deadline:*** rolling. ***Notification:*** continuous.
APPLYING/TRANSFER ***Required:*** high school transcript, college transcript. ***Required for some:*** standardized test scores.
CONTACT Admissions Office, Shasta College, Redding, CA 96049-6006, 916-225-4841.

SIERRA COLLEGE
Rocklin, California

UG Enrollment: 13,567 **Tuition & Fees (CA Res): $405**
Application Deadline: rolling **Room & Board: $3990**

GENERAL State-supported, 2-year, coed. Part of California Community Colleges System. Awards transfer associate, terminal associate degrees. Founded 1936. ***Setting:*** 327-acre rural campus with easy access to Sacramento. ***Research spending 1994–95:*** $192,586. ***Total enrollment:*** 13,567. ***Faculty:*** 518 (143 full-time, 100% with terminal degrees, 375 part-time); student-faculty ratio is 27:1.
ENROLLMENT PROFILE 13,567 students: 55% women, 71% part-time, 99% state residents, 1% live on campus, 12% transferred in, 15% have need-based financial aid, 1% international, 46% 25 or older, 3% Native American, 6% Hispanic, 1% African American, 2% Asian American. ***Most popular recent majors:*** liberal arts/general studies, business administration/commerce/management.
FIRST-YEAR CLASS 2,888 total; 7,181 applied, 100% were accepted, 40% of whom enrolled.
ACADEMIC PROGRAM Core, honor code. Calendar: semesters. Academic remediation for entering students, English as a second language program offered during academic year, services for LD students, advanced placement, summer session for credit, part-time degree program (daytime, evenings), internships. Off-campus study at Hartnell College. Study abroad in Spain, England.
GENERAL DEGREE REQUIREMENTS 60 units; math proficiency; computer course for accounting, business, communication majors.
MAJORS Accounting, agricultural technologies, agronomy/soil and crop sciences, animal sciences, art/fine arts, automotive technologies, biology/biological sciences, business administration/commerce/management, carpentry, chemistry, communication, computer information systems, computer science, computer technologies, construction management, construction technologies, corrections, criminal justice, drafting and design, early childhood education, electrical and electronics technologies, electronics engineering technology, engineering (general), equestrian studies, fashion merchandising, fire science, food services technology, forestry, forest technology, geology, home economics, horticulture, industrial arts, interior design, journalism, law enforcement/police sciences, legal secretarial studies, liberal arts/general studies, manufacturing technology, marketing/retailing/merchandising, medical secretarial studies, metallurgical technology, mining technology, nursing, ornamental horticulture, photography, practical nursing, real estate, secretarial studies/office management, surveying technology, teacher aide studies, welding technology.
LIBRARY Winstead Library plus 1 other, with 69,879 books, 226 microform titles, 189 periodicals, 5 CD-ROMs, 5,590 records, tapes, and CDs. Acquisition spending 1994–95: $1.5 million.
COMPUTERS ON CAMPUS Computer purchase plan available. 430 computers for student use in computer labs, learning resource center, library, student center. Academic computing expenditure 1994–95: $719,802.
COLLEGE LIFE Drama-theater group, student-run newspaper. ***Social organizations:*** 32 open to all. ***Major annual events:*** Scholarship Awards Banquet, Kids Day, Sierra Daze. ***Student services:*** health clinic, personal-psychological counseling. ***Campus security:*** 24-hour emergency response devices and patrols, late-night transport-escort service.
HOUSING 150 college housing spaces available; 143 were occupied 1995–96. No special consideration for freshman housing applicants. Off-campus living permitted. ***Option:*** coed (2 buildings) housing available. Resident assistants live in dorms.
ATHLETICS ***Intercollegiate:*** baseball M, basketball M/W, cross-country running M/W, football M, golf M/W, skiing (cross-country) M/W, skiing (downhill) M/W, softball W, swimming and diving M/W, tennis M/W, track and field M/W, volleyball W, water polo M/W, wrestling M. ***Intramural:*** archery, badminton, basketball, tennis, volleyball. ***Contact:*** Mr. Lew Fellows, Dean of Physical Education, 916-781-0583.
CAREER PLANNING ***Placement office:*** 1 full-time, 2 part-time staff; $18,020 operating expenditure 1994–95. ***Director:*** Dr. James Hirschinger, Dean of Student Services, 916-781-0598. ***Services:*** career counseling, careers library.
EXPENSES FOR 1995–96 ***Application fee:*** $50. State resident tuition: $0 full-time. Nonresident tuition: $3600 full-time, $120 per unit part-time. Part-time mandatory fees per semester range from $20.50 to $150.50. Full-time mandatory fees: $405. College room and board: $3990.
FINANCIAL AID ***College-administered undergrad aid 1995–96:*** 20 need-based scholarships (average $195), 70 non-need scholarships (average $150), short-term loans (average $100), low-interest long-term loans from external sources (average $2625), Federal Work-Study, 150 part-time jobs. ***Required forms:*** institutional, FAFSA; required for some: state; accepted: CSS Financial Aid PROFILE. ***Priority deadline:*** 6/15.
APPLYING Open admission except for early entrance program. ***Options:*** Common Application, early entrance, midyear entrance. ***Required:*** TOEFL for international students, Nelson Denny Reading Test. ***Recommended:*** ACT. Test scores used for counseling/placement. ***Application deadline:*** rolling. ***Notification:*** continuous.
APPLYING/TRANSFER ***Notification:*** continuous. ***Contact:*** Ms. Karen Englefield, Articulation and Transfer Coordinator, 916-624-3333 Ext. 2331.
CONTACT Ms. Mandy Davies, Dean of Student Support Services, Sierra College, Rocklin, CA 95677-3397, 916-624-3333 Ext. 2525.

SKYLINE COLLEGE
San Bruno, California

UG Enrollment: 8,104 **Tuition & Fees (CA Res): $390**
Application Deadline: 8/1 **Room & Board: N/Avail**

GENERAL County-supported, 2-year, coed. Part of San Mateo County Community College District System. Awards transfer associate, terminal associate degrees. Founded 1969. ***Setting:*** 125-acre suburban campus with easy access to San Francisco. ***Total enrollment:*** 8,104. ***Faculty:*** 268 (121 full-time, 147 part-time).
ENROLLMENT PROFILE 8,104 students: 55% women, 45% men, 74% part-time, 99% state residents, 23% transferred in, 1% international, 46% 25 or older, 1% Native American, 21% Hispanic, 5% African American, 36% Asian American. ***Most popular recent majors:*** business administration/commerce/management, computer science, art/fine arts.
FIRST-YEAR CLASS 1,664 total; 2,316 applied, 100% were accepted, 72% of whom enrolled.
ACADEMIC PROGRAM Core, honor code. Calendar: semesters. 625 courses offered in 1995–96. Academic remediation for entering students, English as a second language program offered during academic year and summer, services for LD students, advanced placement, summer session for credit, part-time degree program (daytime, evenings), adult/continuing education programs, co-op programs. Study abroad in England, France, Italy, Mexico.
GENERAL DEGREE REQUIREMENT 60 credits.
MAJORS Accounting, anthropology, applied art, art/fine arts, art history, automotive technologies, biology/biological sciences, business administration/commerce/management, chemistry, computer programming, computer science, cosmetology, criminal justice, data processing, economics, emergency medical technology, English, fashion merchandising, finance/banking, French, history, home economics, hotel and restaurant management, journalism, law enforcement/police sciences, legal secretarial studies, liberal arts/general studies, literature, mathematics, music, paralegal studies, philosophy, physical education, physical sciences, physics, political science/government, psychology, recreation and leisure services, science, secretarial studies/office management, social science, sociology, Spanish, speech/rhetoric/public address/debate, studio art, telecommunications.
LIBRARY 50,000 books, 4,500 microform titles, 244 periodicals, 4,200 records, tapes, and CDs.
COMPUTERS ON CAMPUS 220 computers for student use in computer labs, learning resource center, classrooms, library, student center provide access to Internet. Staffed computer lab on campus.
COLLEGE LIFE Choral group. ***Student services:*** health clinic, personal-psychological counseling. ***Campus security:*** security guards during open hours.

HOUSING College housing not available.
ATHLETICS Member NJCAA. *Intercollegiate:* baseball M, basketball M, cross-country running M/W, soccer M, softball W, track and field M/W, volleyball W, wrestling M. *Contact:* Mr. Ed Johnson, Interim Dean of Physical Education Department, 415-738-4271.
CAREER PLANNING *Placement office:* 1 part-time staff. *Director:* Mr. Eric Larson, Career Center Director, 415-738-4292. *Services:* job fairs, resume preparation, career counseling, careers library, job interviews.
ESTIMATED EXPENSES FOR 1996–97 State resident tuition: $0 full-time. Nonresident tuition: $3990 full-time, $133 per unit part-time. Part-time mandatory fees: $13 per unit. Full-time mandatory fees: $390 (minimum).
FINANCIAL AID *College-administered undergrad aid 1995–96:* 15 need-based scholarships (average $200), 7 non-need scholarships (average $200), low-interest long-term loans from external sources (average $2406), 99 Federal Work-Study (averaging $2558), 100 part-time jobs. *Required forms:* CSS Financial Aid PROFILE, institutional, FAFSA; accepted: state. *Priority deadline:* 3/2. *Payment plan:* deferred payment.
APPLYING Open admission. *Option:* early entrance. *Required:* TOEFL for international students. *Recommended:* SAT I or ACT, SAT II Subject Tests. Test scores used for counseling/placement. *Application deadline:* 8/1. *Notification:* continuous until 8/1.
APPLYING/TRANSFER *Recommended:* standardized test scores. *Entrance:* noncompetitive. *Application deadline:* 8/1. *Notification:* continuous until 8/1. *Contact:* Ms. Linda Miller, Transfer Center Director, 415-738-4423.
CONTACT Mr. Dennis Arreola, Dean of Admissions and Records, Skyline College, San Bruno, CA 94066-1698, 415-738-4251.

SOLANO COMMUNITY COLLEGE
Suisun City, California

UG Enrollment: 9,909	Tuition & Fees (CA Res): $402
Application Deadline: rolling	Room & Board: N/Avail

GENERAL State and locally supported, 2-year, coed. Part of California Community Colleges System. Awards certificates, diplomas, transfer associate degrees. Founded 1945. *Setting:* 192-acre small-town campus with easy access to San Francisco and Sacramento. *Total enrollment:* 9,909. *Faculty:* 374 (147 full-time, 227 part-time); student-faculty ratio is 30:1.
ENROLLMENT PROFILE 9,909 students from 43 states and territories, 6 other countries. 58% women, 72% part-time, 98% state residents, 9% transferred in, 1% international, 51% 25 or older, 1% Native American, 10% Hispanic, 15% African American, 6% Asian American.
FIRST-YEAR CLASS 2,000 total. Of the students who applied, 100% were accepted.
ACADEMIC PROGRAM Core, honor code. Calendar: semesters. Academic remediation for entering students, English as a second language program offered during academic year and summer, services for LD students, advanced placement, honors program, summer session for credit, part-time degree program (daytime, evenings, summer), adult/continuing education programs, co-op programs. Off-campus study at California State University, Hayward, University of California, Davis, University of California, Berkeley. Study abroad in England, Spain.
GENERAL DEGREE REQUIREMENTS 60 credits; 1 math course; 1 course each in physical science and natural science including at least 1 lab science course.
MAJORS Accounting, African studies, aircraft and missile maintenance, art/fine arts, automotive technologies, aviation technology, biology/biological sciences, black/African-American studies, business administration/commerce/management, business machine technologies, chemistry, commercial art, computer programming, cosmetology, criminal justice, drafting and design, early childhood education, electrical and electronics technologies, English, ethnic studies, fashion merchandising, finance/banking, fire science, French, German, history, home economics, industrial administration, journalism, legal secretarial studies, liberal arts/general studies, machine and tool technologies, marketing/retailing/merchandising, mathematics, Mexican-American/Chicano studies, music, nursing, ornamental horticulture, photography, physical education, physics, political science/government, psychology, public administration, science, social science, Spanish, telecommunications, welding technology.
LIBRARY Solano Community College Library with 32,000 books.
COMPUTERS ON CAMPUS 150 computers for student use in learning resource center, labs.
COLLEGE LIFE Drama-theater group, choral group, student-run newspaper. *Social organizations:* 1 national fraternity. *Student services:* personal-psychological counseling. *Campus security:* 24-hour patrols.
HOUSING College housing not available.
ATHLETICS *Intercollegiate:* baseball M, basketball M/W, cross-country running M/W, football M, swimming and diving M/W, track and field M/W, water polo M/W. *Intramural:* swimming and diving, track and field, water polo. *Contact:* Mr. Robert Meyers, Division Dean, Health and Physical Education, 707-864-7126.
CAREER PLANNING *Placement office:* 1 full-time, 1 part-time staff. *Director:* Ms. Jill Hopkins, Career Center Specialist, 707-864-7000 Ext. 480. *Services:* job fairs, career counseling, careers library, job bank, job interviews.
EXPENSES FOR 1996–97 State resident tuition: $0 full-time. Nonresident tuition: $3660 full-time, $122 per unit part-time. Part-time mandatory fees per semester range from $19 to $149. Full-time mandatory fees: $402.
FINANCIAL AID *College-administered undergrad aid 1995–96:* need-based scholarships, low-interest long-term loans from external sources. *Required forms:* CSS Financial Aid PROFILE, state, institutional, FAFSA. *Priority deadline:* 6/1.
APPLYING Open admission. *Options:* early entrance, midyear entrance. *Required:* TOEFL for international students. *Recommended:* SAT I or ACT, SAT II Subject Tests. Test scores used for counseling/placement. *Application deadline:* rolling.
APPLYING/TRANSFER *Application deadline:* rolling. *Contact:* Mr. Jim Bracy, Dean of Student Services, 707-864-7101.
CONTACT Mr. Gerald Fisher, Assistant Dean of Admissions and Records, Solano Community College, Suisun City, CA 94585-3197, 707-864-7171 or toll-free 800-728-6529 (in-state). College video available.

SOUTHWESTERN COLLEGE
Chula Vista, California

UG Enrollment: 15,498	Tuition & Fees (CA Res): $431
Application Deadline: 8/27	Room & Board: N/Avail

GENERAL State and locally supported, 2-year, coed. Part of California Community Colleges System. Awards certificates, transfer associate, terminal associate degrees. Founded 1961. *Setting:* 158-acre suburban campus with easy access to San Diego. *Endowment:* $40.9 million. *Research spending 1994–95:* $351,675. *Total enrollment:* 15,498. *Faculty:* 633 (233 full-time, 14% with terminal degrees, 400 part-time).
ENROLLMENT PROFILE 15,498 students: 54% women, 46% men, 66% part-time, 99% state residents, 8% have need-based financial aid, 1% international, 50% 25 or older, 1% Native American, 54% Hispanic, 6% African American, 16% Asian American. *Most popular recent majors:* business administration/commerce/management, liberal arts/general studies, engineering (general).
FIRST-YEAR CLASS 4,048 applied, 100% were accepted, 100% of whom enrolled.
ACADEMIC PROGRAM Core. Calendar: semesters. Academic remediation for entering students, English as a second language program offered during academic year and summer, services for LD students, Freshman Honors College, tutorials, honors program, summer session for credit, part-time degree program (daytime, evenings, summer), external degree programs, adult/continuing education programs, co-op programs and internships.
GENERAL DEGREE REQUIREMENTS 60 units; 1 course in elementary algebra; computer course.
MAJORS Accounting, African studies, air traffic control, anthropology, architectural technologies, art/fine arts, astronomy, automotive technologies, aviation administration, aviation technology, biology/biological sciences, black/African-American studies, botany/plant sciences, business administration/commerce/management, chemistry, child psychology/child development, communication equipment technology, computer information systems, computer programming, computer science, computer technologies, construction technologies, corrections, criminal justice, dance, drafting and design, early childhood education, earth science, ecology, economics, electrical and electronics technologies, electrical engineering technology, electronics engineering technology, elementary education, emergency medical technology, engineering (general), (pre)engineering sequence, English, ethnic studies, family and consumer studies, finance/banking, French, geography, geology, graphic arts, history, home economics, industrial administration, industrial engineering technology, interior design, journalism, landscape architecture/design, landscaping/grounds maintenance, law enforcement/police sciences, legal secretarial studies, liberal arts/general studies, manufacturing technology, marketing/retailing/merchandising, mathematics, Mexican-American/Chicano studies, music, nursing, oceanography, ornamental horticulture, philosophy, photography, physical sciences, physics, political science/government, psychology, public administration, real estate, recreation and leisure services, science, secretarial studies/office management, social work, sociology, Spanish, speech/rhetoric/public address/debate, telecommunications, theater arts/drama, tourism and travel, zoology.
LIBRARY Southwestern College Library with 71,148 books, 115 microform titles, 741 periodicals, 5 on-line bibliographic services, 40 CD-ROMs, 5,104 records, tapes, and CDs. Acquisition spending 1994–95: $662,806.
COMPUTERS ON CAMPUS Computer purchase plan available. 700 computers for student use in computer center, learning resource center, labs, classrooms, library. Academic computing expenditure 1994–95: $1.1 million.
COLLEGE LIFE Drama-theater group, choral group, student-run newspaper. *Social organizations:* 20 open to all; 1 national fraternity. *Most popular organizations:* MECHA, Business Club, Alpha Phi Epsilon, ABLE (disabled club), Society of Hispanic Engineers. *Major annual events:* Earth Day, Heritage Awareness Day, Human Services Day. *Student services:* health clinic, personal-psychological counseling, women's center. *Campus security:* 24-hour emergency response devices, student patrols, late-night transport-escort service.
HOUSING College housing not available.
ATHLETICS *Intercollegiate:* baseball M, basketball M/W, cross-country running M/W, football M, soccer M, softball W, swimming and diving M/W, tennis M/W, track and field M/W, volleyball M/W. *Intramural:* volleyball. *Contact:* Mr. John Cosentino, Director of Athletics, 619-482-6420.
CAREER PLANNING *Placement office:* 1 full-time, 1 part-time staff; $155,493 operating expenditure 1994–95. *Director:* Ms. Mary Ellene Deason, Counselor of Career Center Coordinator, 619-421-6700 Ext. 5397. *Services:* job fairs, career counseling, careers library.
EXPENSES FOR 1995–96 State resident tuition: $0 full-time. Nonresident tuition: $3270 full-time, $109 per unit part-time. Part-time mandatory fees per semester range from $24.50 to $164.50. Full-time mandatory fees: $431.
FINANCIAL AID *College-administered undergrad aid 1995–96:* need-based scholarships, short-term loans (average $50), Federal Work-Study, part-time jobs. *Required forms for some financial aid applicants:* CSS Financial Aid PROFILE. *Priority deadline:* 3/2. *Payment plan:* deferred payment.
APPLYING Open admission. *Option:* early entrance. *Required:* TOEFL for international students. Test scores used for admission and counseling/placement. *Application deadline:* 8/27. *Notification:* continuous.
APPLYING/TRANSFER *Application deadline:* 8/27. *Notification:* continuous.
CONTACT Ms. Georgia Copeland, Director of Admissions and Records, Southwestern College, Chula Vista, CA 91910-7299, 619-482-6306.

TAFT COLLEGE
Taft, California

UG Enrollment: 532	Tuition & Fees (CA Res): $475
Application Deadline: rolling	Room & Board: $2300

GENERAL State and locally supported, 2-year, coed. Part of California Community Colleges System. Awards transfer associate, terminal associate degrees. Founded 1922. *Setting:* 15-acre small-town campus. *Research spending 1994–95:* $5000. *Total enrollment:* 532. *Faculty:* 64 (24 full-time, 100% with terminal degrees, 40 part-time).
ENROLLMENT PROFILE 532 students from 9 states and territories, 4 other countries. 69% women, 40% part-time, 98% state residents, 6% live on campus, 12% transferred in, 47% 25 or older, 3% Native American, 9% Hispanic, 11% African American, 2% Asian American. *Areas of study chosen:* 16% liberal arts/general studies, 6% business management and administrative services, 5% health professions and related sciences, 5%

Taft College (continued)
vocational and home economics, 4% interdisciplinary studies, 3% biological and life sciences, 1% communications and journalism, 1% computer and information sciences, 1% education, 1% engineering and applied sciences, 1% fine arts, 1% physical sciences, 1% social sciences.
FIRST-YEAR CLASS 99 total. Of the students who applied, 100% were accepted, 85% of whom enrolled.
ACADEMIC PROGRAM Core, transfer/occupational curriculum, honor code. Calendar: semesters. 978 courses offered in 1995–96. Academic remediation for entering students, English as a second language program offered during academic year, services for LD students, advanced placement, summer session for credit, part-time degree program (daytime, evenings, summer), adult/continuing education programs.
GENERAL DEGREE REQUIREMENT 60 units.
MAJORS Accounting, art/fine arts, automotive technologies, biology/biological sciences, business administration/commerce/management, computer science, criminal justice, data processing, dental services, drafting and design, early childhood education, electrical and electronics technologies, (pre)engineering sequence, English, industrial arts, journalism, liberal arts/general studies, mathematics, physical education, physical sciences, recreation and leisure services, secretarial studies/office management, social science.
LIBRARY Taft College Library with 28,000 books, 18 microform titles, 143 periodicals, 3 on-line bibliographic services, 28 CD-ROMs, 1,426 records, tapes, and CDs. Acquisition spending 1994–95: $139,460.
COMPUTERS ON CAMPUS 91 computers for student use in computer center, learning resource center, career center, classrooms provide access to main academic computer. Staffed computer lab on campus. Academic computing expenditure 1994–95: $214,000.
COLLEGE LIFE Student-run newspaper. ***Most popular organizations:*** International Club, Alpha Gamma Sigma. ***Student services:*** personal-psychological counseling. ***Campus security:*** controlled dormitory access, parking lot security.
HOUSING 80 college housing spaces available; 36 were occupied 1995–96. No special consideration for freshman housing applicants. Off-campus living permitted. ***Option:*** coed housing available. Resident assistants live in dorms.
ATHLETICS ***Intercollegiate:*** baseball M, golf M, softball W, volleyball W. ***Contact:*** Mr. Donald Zumbro, Dean of Student Services, 805-763-4282 Ext. 215.
CAREER PLANNING ***Placement office:*** 1 part-time staff; $20,000 operating expenditure 1994–95. ***Director:*** Ms. Karen Kuckreja, Director of Counseling, 805-763-4282. ***Service:*** career counseling.
EXPENSES FOR 1995–96 State resident tuition: $0 full-time. Nonresident tuition: $3420 full-time, $114 per unit part-time. Part-time mandatory fees per semester range from $33 to $163. Full-time mandatory fees: $475. College room and board: $2300 (minimum).
FINANCIAL AID ***College-administered undergrad aid 1995–96:*** need-based scholarships, non-need scholarships, short-term loans, Federal Work-Study, part-time jobs. ***Acceptable forms:*** CSS Financial Aid PROFILE, state, FAFSA. ***Priority deadline:*** 7/30. ***Payment plans:*** installment, deferred payment.
APPLYING Open admission. ***Options:*** early entrance, midyear entrance. ***Required:*** TOEFL for international students. Test scores used for counseling/placement. ***Application deadline:*** rolling.
APPLYING/TRANSFER ***Entrance:*** noncompetitive. ***Application deadline:*** 8/1. ***Contact:*** Ms. Linda West, Director of Financial Aid and Admissions, 805-763-4282 Ext. 263.
CONTACT Ms. Linda West, Director of Financial Aid and Admissions, Taft College, Taft, CA 93268-2317, 805-763-4282 Ext. 263. ***Fax:*** 805-763-1038. College video available.

VENTURA COLLEGE
Ventura, California

UG Enrollment: 10,083	**Tuition & Fees (CA Res): $390**
Application Deadline: 9/1	**Room & Board: N/Avail**

GENERAL State and locally supported, 2-year, coed. Part of California Community Colleges System. Awards certificates, transfer associate, terminal associate degrees. Founded 1925. ***Setting:*** 112-acre suburban campus with easy access to Los Angeles. ***Total enrollment:*** 10,083. ***Faculty:*** 541 (165 full-time, 376 part-time); student-faculty ratio is 22:1. ***Notable Alumni:*** Cedric Ceballos, professional basketball player.
ENROLLMENT PROFILE 10,083 students from 3 states and territories, 15 other countries. 56% women, 72% part-time, 97% state residents, 25% transferred in, 1% international, 47% 25 or older, 2% Native American, 18% Hispanic, 2% African American, 3% Asian American.
FIRST-YEAR CLASS 1,961 total; 2,488 applied, 100% were accepted, 79% of whom enrolled.
ACADEMIC PROGRAM Core. Calendar: semesters. Academic remediation for entering students, English as a second language program offered during academic year, services for LD students, self-designed majors, tutorials, honors program, summer session for credit, part-time degree program (daytime, evenings, summer), adult/continuing education programs. ROTC: Army (c), Air Force (c).
GENERAL DEGREE REQUIREMENTS 60 semester units; 6 semester units of science.
MAJORS Accounting, agricultural business, agronomy/soil and crop sciences, animal sciences, architectural technologies, automotive technologies, business administration/commerce/management, business machine technologies, ceramic art and design, civil engineering technology, commercial art, computer information systems, construction technologies, criminal justice, drafting and design, early childhood education, education, electrical and electronics technologies, engineering (general), fashion design and technology, food services technology, home economics, human services, journalism, liberal arts/general studies, machine and tool technologies, medical secretarial studies, music, natural resource management, nursing, ornamental horticulture, petroleum technology, photography, quality control technology, real estate, recreation and leisure services, respiratory therapy, secretarial studies/office management, theater arts/drama, water resources, welding technology.
LIBRARY Ventura College Library with 70,000 books, 100 microform titles, 300 periodicals, 3,000 records, tapes, and CDs.
COMPUTERS ON CAMPUS 40 computers for student use in computer center, library.
COLLEGE LIFE Drama-theater group, choral group, student-run newspaper. ***Student services:*** health clinic, personal-psychological counseling, women's center. ***Campus security:*** 24-hour patrols, student patrols.
HOUSING College housing not available.
ATHLETICS ***Intercollegiate:*** basketball M/W, cross-country running M/W, football M, golf M, swimming and diving M/W, tennis M/W, track and field M/W, volleyball W, water polo M, wrestling M. ***Contact:*** Mr. Phillip Mathews, Athletic Coordinator, 805-654-6347.
CAREER PLANNING ***Placement office:*** 8 full-time, 1 part-time staff. ***Director:*** Mr. Jeff Ferguson, Dean of Student Services, 805-654-6447. ***Services:*** job fairs, resume preparation, resume referral, career counseling, careers library, job bank, job interviews.
EXPENSES FOR 1996–97 State resident tuition: $0 full-time. Nonresident tuition: $3420 full-time, $114 per unit part-time. Part-time mandatory fees: $13 per semester. Full-time mandatory fees: $390.
FINANCIAL AID ***College-administered undergrad aid 1995–96:*** need-based scholarships, 30 non-need scholarships (average $250), short-term loans (average $100), low-interest long-term loans from external sources (average $1850), Federal Work-Study, part-time jobs. ***Required forms:*** state, institutional; accepted: CSS Financial Aid PROFILE, FAFSA. ***Priority deadline:*** 7/1. ***Waivers:*** full or partial for minority students. ***Notification:*** continuous.
APPLYING Open admission. ***Options:*** early entrance, midyear entrance. ***Required:*** school transcript. ***Required for some:*** TOEFL for international students, Assessment and Placement Services for Community Colleges. Test scores used for counseling/placement. ***Application deadline:*** 9/1. ***Notification:*** continuous until 9/1.
APPLYING/TRANSFER ***Required:*** college transcript. ***Required for some:*** standardized test scores, high school transcript. ***Entrance:*** noncompetitive. ***Notification:*** continuous until 9/1.
CONTACT Ms. Joan Halk, Registrar, Ventura College, Ventura, CA 93003-3899, 805-654-6455. ***Fax:*** 805-654-6466.

❖ *See page 822 for a narrative description.* ❖

VICTOR VALLEY COLLEGE
Victorville, California

UG Enrollment: 8,000	**Tuition & Fees (CA Res): $420**
Application Deadline: rolling	**Room & Board: N/Avail**

GENERAL State-supported, 2-year, coed. Part of California Community Colleges System. Awards certificates, transfer associate, terminal associate degrees. Founded 1961. ***Setting:*** 280-acre small-town campus with easy access to Los Angeles. ***Total enrollment:*** 8,000. ***Faculty:*** 325 (90 full-time, 235 part-time).
ENROLLMENT PROFILE 8,000 students from 10 states and territories, 5 other countries. 65% women, 80% part-time, 86% state residents, 12% transferred in, 60% 25 or older, 1% Native American, 15% Hispanic, 9% African American, 3% Asian American. ***Most popular recent majors:*** nursing, business administration/commerce/management.
FIRST-YEAR CLASS 5,000 total; 5,000 applied, 100% were accepted, 100% of whom enrolled.
ACADEMIC PROGRAM Core, transfer and vocational curriculum, honor code. Calendar: semesters. 1,087 courses offered in 1995–96. Academic remediation for entering students, English as a second language program offered during academic year, services for LD students, self-designed majors, tutorials, honors program, summer session for credit, part-time degree program (daytime, evenings), adult/continuing education programs, co-op programs. ROTC: Naval (c).
GENERAL DEGREE REQUIREMENTS 60 units; 1 course in math; 2 courses in science.
MAJORS Agricultural education, art/fine arts, automotive technologies, biology/biological sciences, business administration/commerce/management, child care/child and family studies, computer information systems, computer science, construction technologies, early childhood education, electrical and electronics technologies, fire science, food services technology, horticulture, humanities, law enforcement/police sciences, liberal arts/general studies, music, natural sciences, nursing, real estate, respiratory therapy, science, secretarial studies/office management, social science, theater arts/drama, vocational education, welding technology.
LIBRARY Victor Valley College Library with 3,582 books, 165 microform titles, 692 periodicals, 2,000 records, tapes, and CDs.
COMPUTERS ON CAMPUS 260 computers for student use in computer center, labs, classrooms, library. Staffed computer lab on campus provides training in use of computers, software.
COLLEGE LIFE Drama-theater group, choral group, student-run newspaper. 2% vote in student government elections. ***Most popular organizations:*** Pep Club, Drama Club, Solar Car Club, Phi Theta Kappa. ***Major annual events:*** Homecoming, Diversity, Red Ribbon Week. ***Student services:*** personal-psychological counseling, women's center. ***Campus security:*** part-time trained security personnel.
HOUSING College housing not available.
ATHLETICS Member NJCAA. ***Intercollegiate:*** baseball M, basketball M/W, football M, golf M/W, soccer W, softball W, tennis M/W, volleyball W, wrestling M. ***Contact:*** Mr. Willie Pringle, Director of Student Activity Athletics, 619-245-4271 Ext. 336.
CAREER PLANNING ***Placement office:*** 3 full-time staff. ***Director:*** Ms. Ruth Green, Director of Student Development Center, 619-245-4271. ***Services:*** career counseling, careers library.
EXPENSES FOR 1995–96 State resident tuition: $0 full-time. Nonresident tuition: $3420 full-time, $114 per unit part-time. Part-time mandatory fees per semester range from $14 to $154. Full-time mandatory fees: $420.
FINANCIAL AID ***College-administered undergrad aid 1995–96:*** need-based scholarships, short-term loans (average $100), Federal Work-Study, part-time jobs. ***Required forms:*** CSS Financial Aid PROFILE, institutional, FAFSA; required for some: state. ***Priority deadline:*** 5/1. ***Payment plan:*** installment.
APPLYING Open admission except for allied health programs. ***Options:*** early entrance, midyear entrance. ***Required:*** TOEFL for international students. Test scores used for counseling/placement. ***Application deadline:*** rolling. ***Notification:*** continuous.
APPLYING/TRANSFER ***Entrance:*** noncompetitive. ***Notification:*** continuous. ***Contact:*** Ms. Ruth Green, Transfer Center Technician, 619-245-4271 Ext. 447.
CONTACT Mrs. Laura White, Dean of Institutional Effectiveness, Victor Valley College, Victorville, CA 92392-5849, 619-245-4271 Ext. 270. ***Fax:*** 619-245-9745.

VISTA COMMUNITY COLLEGE
Berkeley, California

UG Enrollment: 3,171	Tuition & Fees (CA Res): $394
Application Deadline: 9/9	Room & Board: N/Avail

GENERAL State and locally supported, 2-year, coed. Part of Peralta Community College District System. Awards certificates, transfer associate, terminal associate degrees. Founded 1974. *Setting:* urban campus with easy access to San Francisco. *Research spending 1994–95:* $23,897. *Educational spending 1994–95:* $485 per undergrad. *Total enrollment:* 3,171. *Faculty:* 125 (18 full-time, 107 part-time).
ENROLLMENT PROFILE 3,171 students: 66% women, 34% men, 81% part-time, 99% state residents, 17% transferred in, 0% international, 63% 25 or older, 1% Native American, 12% Hispanic, 35% African American, 9% Asian American. *Areas of study chosen:* 15% interdisciplinary studies, 8% business management and administrative services, 8% education, 7% computer and information sciences, 4% fine arts, 4% liberal arts/general studies, 4% social sciences, 2% biological and life sciences, 2% engineering and applied sciences, 2% health professions and related sciences, 2% psychology, 1% architecture, 1% communications and journalism, 1% foreign language and literature.
FIRST-YEAR CLASS 717 total. Of the students who applied, 100% were accepted.
ACADEMIC PROGRAM Core. Calendar: semesters. Academic remediation for entering students, services for LD students, self-designed majors, summer session for credit, part-time degree program (daytime, evenings), adult/continuing education programs. Off-campus study at members of the Downtown Oakland Business Education Consortium. Study-abroad program.
GENERAL DEGREE REQUIREMENTS 60 semester hours; 3 semster hours of math; computer course.
MAJORS Accounting, art/fine arts, biotechnology, business administration/commerce/management, computer information systems, deaf interpreter training, energy management technologies, English, liberal arts/general studies, secretarial studies/office management, Spanish.
COMPUTERS ON CAMPUS 10 computers for student use in computer labs.
HOUSING College housing not available.
CAREER PLANNING *Service:* career counseling.
EXPENSES FOR 1996–97 State resident tuition: $0 full-time. Nonresident tuition: $3660 full-time, $122 per semester hour part-time. Part-time mandatory fees: $13 per semester hour. Full-time mandatory fees: $394.
FINANCIAL AID *College-administered undergrad aid 1995–96:* need-based scholarships, Federal Work-Study, part-time jobs. *Required forms:* CSS Financial Aid PROFILE, FAFSA. *Application deadline:* continuous.
APPLYING Open admission. *Options:* early entrance, deferred entrance. *Application deadline:* 9/9. Preference given to state residents.
APPLYING/TRANSFER *Entrance:* noncompetitive.
CONTACT Mrs. Mary DeCoite, District Admissions Officer, Vista Community College, 2020 Milvia Street, 3rd Floor, Berkeley, CA 94704-5102, 510-466-7369.

WEST HILLS COMMUNITY COLLEGE
Coalinga, California

UG Enrollment: 2,810	Tuition & Fees (CA Res): $390
Application Deadline: rolling	Room & Board: $3084

GENERAL State-supported, 2-year, coed. Part of California Community Colleges System. Awards certificates, diplomas, transfer associate, terminal associate degrees. Founded 1932. *Setting:* 193-acre small-town campus. *Total enrollment:* 2,810. *Faculty:* 107 (47 full-time, 60 part-time).
ENROLLMENT PROFILE 2,810 students from 25 states and territories, 5 other countries. 52% women, 24% part-time, 93% state residents, 4% transferred in, 1% international, 48% 25 or older, 3% Native American, 21% Hispanic, 5% African American, 2% Asian American. *Areas of study chosen:* 51% liberal arts/general studies, 16% social sciences, 11% business management and administrative services, 7% agriculture, 5% health professions and related sciences, 4% psychology, 2% computer and information sciences, 2% engineering and applied sciences, 1% fine arts, 1% mathematics. *Most popular recent majors:* liberal arts/general studies, business administration/commerce/management.
FIRST-YEAR CLASS 2,487 total; 2,850 applied, 100% were accepted, 87% of whom enrolled.
ACADEMIC PROGRAM Core, interdisciplinary curriculum. Calendar: semesters. 441 courses offered in 1995–96. Academic remediation for entering students, English as a second language program offered during academic year and summer, services for LD students, summer session for credit, part-time degree program (daytime, evenings, summer), adult/continuing education programs, co-op programs. Study abroad in England, Italy, Costa Rica, France. ROTC: Naval (c).
GENERAL DEGREE REQUIREMENTS 60 units; 3 units each of math and natural science; computer course (varies by major).
MAJORS Accounting, agricultural business, agricultural technologies, agronomy/soil and crop sciences, animal sciences, art/fine arts, automotive technologies, biology/biological sciences, business administration/commerce/management, chemistry, child care/child and family studies, computer information systems, criminal justice, early childhood education, (pre)engineering sequence, equestrian studies, geography, geology, health science, humanities, liberal arts/general studies, mathematics, physical education, physics, psychology, secretarial studies/office management, social science, transportation technologies, welding technology.
LIBRARY West Hills Community College Library with 32,000 books, 7,000 microform titles, 210 periodicals, 4 CD-ROMs, 1,843 records, tapes, and CDs. Acquisition spending 1994–95: $123,922.
COMPUTERS ON CAMPUS Student rooms linked to a campus network. 82 computers for student use in computer center, computer labs, academic buildings, labs, library. Staffed computer lab on campus. Academic computing expenditure 1994–95: $484,172.
COLLEGE LIFE Orientation program (no cost). Drama-theater group, student-run newspaper. *Student services:* personal-psychological counseling.
HOUSING No special consideration for freshman housing applicants. *Option:* single-sex (2 buildings) housing available. Resident assistants live in dorms.
ATHLETICS *Intercollegiate:* basketball M, football M, softball W, volleyball W. *Contact:* Mr. Jim Grant, Athletic Director, 209-935-0801 Ext. 3251.
CAREER PLANNING *Placement office:* 1 part-time staff; $10,895 operating expenditure 1994–95. *Director:* Ms. Susan Walter, Career Counselor, 209-935-0801 Ext. 3244. *Service:* career counseling.
AFTER GRADUATION 14% of students completing a degree program in 1994–95 went directly on to further study.
EXPENSES FOR 1995–96 State resident tuition: $0 full-time. Nonresident tuition: $3000 full-time, $100 per unit part-time. Part-time mandatory fees: $13 per unit. Full-time mandatory fees: $390. College room and board: $3084.
FINANCIAL AID *College-administered undergrad aid 1995–96:* 560 need-based scholarships (average $200), 27 non-need scholarships (average $1800), short-term loans (average $20), low-interest long-term loans from external sources (average $2625), Federal Work-Study, 100 part-time jobs. *Required forms:* institutional; required for some: state; accepted: CSS Financial Aid PROFILE, FAFSA. *Priority deadline:* 3/2.
APPLYING Open admission. *Options:* early entrance, midyear entrance. *Required:* TOEFL for international students. *Recommended:* SAT I or ACT. Test scores used for counseling/placement. *Application deadline:* rolling. *Notification:* continuous. Preference given to district residents.
APPLYING/TRANSFER *Recommended:* standardized test scores. *Application deadline:* rolling. *Notification:* continuous.
CONTACT Mrs. Darlene Georgatos, Registrar, West Hills Community College, Coalinga, CA 93210-1399, 209-935-0801 Ext. 3217 or toll-free 800-266-1114. *Fax:* 209-935-5655.

WEST LOS ANGELES COLLEGE
Culver City, California

UG Enrollment: 7,400	Tuition & Fees (CA Res): $390
Application Deadline: 8/16	Room & Board: N/Avail

GENERAL State and locally supported, 2-year, coed. Part of Los Angeles Community College District System. Awards transfer associate, terminal associate degrees. Founded 1969. *Setting:* 69-acre urban campus with easy access to Los Angeles. *Total enrollment:* 7,400. *Faculty:* 320 (120 full-time, 200 part-time).
ENROLLMENT PROFILE 7,400 students from 20 states and territories. 64% women, 78% part-time, 99% state residents, 17% transferred in, 76% 25 or older, 1% Native American, 11% Hispanic, 48% African American, 9% Asian American.
FIRST-YEAR CLASS 3,500 total; 8,000 applied, 100% were accepted, 44% of whom enrolled.
ACADEMIC PROGRAM Core. Calendar: semesters. Academic remediation for entering students, English as a second language program offered during academic year and summer, services for LD students, advanced placement, honors program, summer session for credit, part-time degree program (daytime, evenings), adult/continuing education programs, co-op programs. ROTC: Army (c), Air Force (c).
GENERAL DEGREE REQUIREMENTS 60 units; 1 course in college algebra.
MAJORS Accounting, aircraft and missile maintenance, anthropology, art/fine arts, aviation technology, biology/biological sciences, business administration/commerce/management, chemistry, child psychology/child development, computer programming, criminal justice, data processing, dental services, drafting and design, economics, education, electrical and electronics technologies, engineering (general), English, family and consumer studies, French, geography, geology, history, industrial administration, journalism, law enforcement/police sciences, legal secretarial studies, liberal arts/general studies, marketing/retailing/merchandising, mathematics, medical secretarial studies, music, paralegal studies, philosophy, physical education, physics, political science/government, psychology, real estate, retail management, secretarial studies/office management, sociology, Spanish, speech/rhetoric/public address/debate, tourism and travel.
LIBRARY 51,000 books, 400 periodicals, 1,200 records, tapes, and CDs.
COMPUTERS ON CAMPUS Computers for student use in learning resource center, classrooms.
COLLEGE LIFE Choral group. *Student services:* health clinic, personal-psychological counseling. *Campus security:* 24-hour patrols.
HOUSING College housing not available.
ATHLETICS *Intercollegiate:* basketball M, football M, track and field M/W, volleyball W. *Contact:* Mr. James Raack, Athletic Director, 310-287-4590.
CAREER PLANNING *Services:* job fairs, resume preparation, career counseling, careers library.
EXPENSES FOR 1996–97 State resident tuition: $0 full-time. Nonresident tuition: $3750 full-time, $125 per unit part-time. Part-time mandatory fees per semester range from $20.50 to $150.50. Full-time mandatory fees: $390.
FINANCIAL AID *College-administered undergrad aid 1995–96:* need-based scholarships, non-need scholarships, short-term loans (average $50), low-interest long-term loans from external sources, Federal Work-Study, part-time jobs. *Required forms:* CSS Financial Aid PROFILE, FAFSA. *Priority deadline:* 5/31. *Payment plan:* installment.
APPLYING Open admission. *Option:* early entrance. *Recommended:* school transcript. Test scores used for counseling/placement. *Application deadline:* 8/16.
APPLYING/TRANSFER *Required:* college transcript. *Recommended:* high school transcript. *Application deadline:* 8/16.
CONTACT Ms. Adrian Foster, Associate Dean of Student Services, West Los Angeles College, 4800 Freshman Drive, Culver City, CA 90230-3500, 310-287-4246. *Fax:* 310-841-0396. College video available.

WEST VALLEY COLLEGE
Saratoga, California

UG Enrollment: 14,224	Tuition & Fees (CA Res): $436
Application Deadline: rolling	Room & Board: N/Avail

GENERAL State and locally supported, 2-year, coed. Part of California Community Colleges System. Awards certificates, transfer associate, terminal associate degrees. Founded 1963. *Setting:* 143-acre small-town campus with easy access to San Francisco and San Jose. *Total enrollment:* 14,224. *Faculty:* 560 (210 full-time, 350 part-time); student-faculty ratio is 26:1.
ENROLLMENT PROFILE 14,224 students from 2 states and territories, 20 other countries. 60% women, 69% part-time, 89% state residents, 19% transferred in, 3% international, 58% 25 or older, 1% Native American, 9% Hispanic, 3% African American, 10% Asian American.

California–Colorado

West Valley College (continued)
FIRST-YEAR CLASS 2,434 total. Of the students who applied, 100% were accepted.
ACADEMIC PROGRAM Core. Calendar: semesters. Academic remediation for entering students, English as a second language program offered during academic year and summer, services for LD students, tutorials, honors program, summer session for credit, part-time degree program (daytime, evenings), adult/continuing education programs, co-op programs and internships. ROTC: Army (c), Air Force (c).
GENERAL DEGREE REQUIREMENTS 60 units; proficiency in algebra or geometry; computer course for business, engineering, management, marketing majors.
MAJORS Accounting, art/fine arts, biology/biological sciences, business administration/commerce/management, chemistry, computer information systems, court reporting, criminal justice, data processing, drafting and design, early childhood education, economics, English, fashion design and technology, French, German, history, interior design, Italian, landscape architecture/design, law enforcement/police sciences, legal secretarial studies, liberal arts/general studies, marketing/retailing/merchandising, mathematics, medical assistant technologies, medical records services, medical secretarial studies, music, parks management, physical education, physics, psychology, secretarial studies/office management, social science, sociology, Spanish, speech/rhetoric/public address/debate, theater arts/drama, women's studies.
LIBRARY West Valley College Library with 82,959 books, 300 microform titles, 491 periodicals, 2,663 records, tapes, and CDs.
COMPUTERS ON CAMPUS 200 computers for student use in various departments, library.
COLLEGE LIFE Orientation program (3 days, no cost). Drama-theater group, student-run newspaper. *Student services:* health clinic, personal-psychological counseling.
HOUSING College housing not available.
ATHLETICS *Intercollegiate:* basketball M/W, cross-country running M/W, football M, soccer M, swimming and diving M/W, tennis M/W, track and field M/W, volleyball M/W, water polo M, wrestling M. *Intramural:* badminton, basketball, bowling, swimming and diving, tennis, track and field, volleyball. *Contact:* Ms. Diane Tsutsumi, Division Chairperson, Physical Education, 408-867-2200.
CAREER PLANNING *Service:* career counseling.
EXPENSES FOR 1995-96 State resident tuition: $0 full-time. Nonresident tuition: $3600 full-time, $120 per unit part-time. Part-time mandatory fees per semester range from $30 to $165. Full-time mandatory fees: $436.
FINANCIAL AID *College-administered undergrad aid 1995-96:* need-based scholarships, non-need scholarships (average $100), short-term loans (average $75), low-interest long-term loans from external sources (average $2625), Federal Work-Study, 250 part-time jobs. *Required forms:* state; accepted: CSS Financial Aid PROFILE, FAFSA. *Priority deadline:* 5/31.
APPLYING Open admission. *Options:* Common Application, early entrance, midyear entrance. *Required:* TOEFL for international students. Test scores used for counseling/placement. *Application deadline:* rolling. *Notification:* continuous. Preference given to district residents.
APPLYING/TRANSFER *Entrance:* noncompetitive. *Application deadline:* rolling. *Notification:* continuous.
CONTACT Mr. Albert Moore, Admissions and Records Supervisor, West Valley College, 14000 Fruitvale Avenue, Saratoga, CA 95070-5697, 408-741-2533.

YUBA COLLEGE
Marysville, California

UG Enrollment: 9,860	Tuition & Fees (CA Res): $412
Application Deadline: 8/22	Room & Board: $3400

Yuba College is a California community college. On-campus dormitories, athletic facilities, a theater, a library/learning skills center, and laboratory and shop classrooms are available to serve students and the community. Students enjoy small classes. Individual instructor attention. Many opportunities for activities and involvement in collegiate life.

GENERAL State and locally supported, 2-year, coed. Part of California Community Colleges System. Awards transfer associate, terminal associate degrees. Founded 1927. *Setting:* 160-acre rural campus with easy access to Sacramento. *Total enrollment:* 9,860. *Faculty:* 500 (124 full-time, 376 part-time).
ENROLLMENT PROFILE 9,860 students from 38 states and territories, 8 other countries. 58% women, 42% men, 70% part-time, 97% state residents, 9% transferred in, 1% international, 54% 25 or older, 1% Native American, 11% Hispanic, 4% African American, 4% Asian American.
FIRST-YEAR CLASS 3,000 total; 3,000 applied, 100% were accepted, 100% of whom enrolled.
ACADEMIC PROGRAM Core, honor code. Calendar: semesters. Academic remediation for entering students, English as a second language program offered during academic year, services for LD students, advanced placement, honors program, summer session for credit, part-time degree program (daytime, evenings, summer), adult/continuing education programs. Study abroad in Mexico, France, Greece.
GENERAL DEGREE REQUIREMENT 62 units.
MAJORS Accounting, advertising, agricultural business, agricultural sciences, agricultural technologies, agronomy/soil crop sciences, animal sciences, art/fine arts, automotive technologies, biology/biological sciences, black/African-American studies, business administration/commerce/management, chemistry, child care/child and family studies, communication, computer science, corrections, cosmetology, criminal justice, early childhood education, education, electrical and electronics technologies, elementary education, (pre)engineering sequence, English, ethnic studies, finance/banking, fire science, food services management, health education, history, home economics, human services, law enforcement/police sciences, liberal arts/general studies, machine and tool technologies, manufacturing technology, marketing/retailing/merchandising, mathematics, mental health/rehabilitation counseling, Mexican-American/Chicano studies, music, nursing, ornamental horticulture, philosophy, photography, physical education, practical nursing, psychology, radiological technology, real estate, science, secretarial studies/office management, social science, theater arts/drama, veterinary sciences, veterinary technology, welding technology, women's studies.
LIBRARY Yuba College Library with 62,000 books, 530 periodicals.

COLLEGE LIFE Drama-theater group, choral group. *Social organizations:* 18 open to all. *Student services:* health clinic, personal-psychological counseling, women's center. *Campus security:* 24-hour patrols, student patrols.
HOUSING 197 college housing spaces available; all were occupied 1995-96. No special consideration for freshman housing applicants. Off-campus living permitted. *Option:* coed (3 buildings) housing available. Resident assistants live in dorms.
ATHLETICS *Intercollegiate:* baseball M, basketball M/W, cross-country running M/W, football M, tennis M/W, track and field M/W, volleyball W. *Intramural:* basketball, football, golf, skiing (cross-country), skiing (downhill), swimming and diving, tennis, volleyball, weight lifting. *Contact:* Mr. Joe McCarron, Athletic Director, 916-741-6838.
CAREER PLANNING *Placement office:* 1 full-time staff. *Director:* Ms. Alice Epler, Career Center Technician, 916-741-6804. *Service:* career counseling.
EXPENSES FOR 1996-97 State resident tuition: $0 full-time. Nonresident tuition: $3750 full-time, $125 per unit part-time. Part-time mandatory fees per semester range from $24 to $154. Full-time mandatory fees: $412. College room and board: $3400.
FINANCIAL AID *College-administered undergrad aid 1995-96:* 29 need-based scholarships (average $750), 30 non-need scholarships (average $500), short-term loans (average $75), low-interest long-term loans from external sources (average $2500), Federal Work-Study, 25 part-time jobs. *Required forms:* CSS Financial Aid PROFILE, state, institutional, FAFSA. *Priority deadline:* 5/31.
APPLYING Open admission. *Options:* early entrance, deferred entrance, midyear entrance. *Required:* school transcript, TOEFL for international students. *Recommended:* SAT I or ACT. Test scores used for counseling/placement. *Application deadline:* 8/22. *Notification:* continuous.
APPLYING/TRANSFER *Entrance:* noncompetitive. *Application deadline:* 8/22. *Notification:* continuous. *Contact:* Ms. Sheila Daniels, Director of Matriculation and Transfer Center, 916-741-6797.
CONTACT Ms. Susan Singhas, Dean for Admissions, Counseling, and Records, Yuba College, Marysville, CA 95901-7699, 916-741-6705. *Fax:* 916-741-3541.

COLORADO

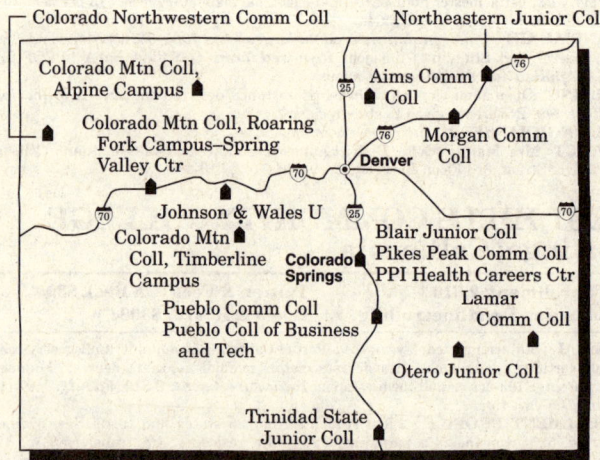

Denver Area
Arapahoe Comm Coll
Bel-Rea Institute of Animal Technology
Colorado Institute of Art
Comm Coll of Aurora
Comm Coll of Denver
Denver Automotive and Diesel Coll
Front Range Comm Coll
ITT Technical Institute
Parks Junior Coll
Pima Medical Inst
Red Rocks Comm Coll

AIMS COMMUNITY COLLEGE
Greeley, Colorado

UG Enrollment: 6,958	Tuition & Fees (Area Res): $1290
Application Deadline: rolling	Room & Board: N/Avail

GENERAL District-supported, 2-year, coed. Awards certificates, diplomas, transfer associate, terminal associate degrees. Founded 1967. *Setting:* 185-acre urban campus with easy access to Denver. *Endowment:* $70,512. *Total enrollment:* 6,958. *Faculty:* 370 (118 full-time, 91% with terminal degrees, 252 part-time); student-faculty ratio is 16:1.
ENROLLMENT PROFILE 6,958 students from 8 states and territories. 62% women, 38% men, 70% part-time, 98% state residents, 1% transferred in, 0% international, 59% 25 or older, 1% Native American, 17% Hispanic, 1% African American, 1% Asian American. *Areas of study chosen:* 57% liberal arts/general studies, 12% business management and administrative services, 11% vocational and home economics, 4% engineering and applied sciences, 4% health professions and related sciences, 3% social sciences, 2% computer

and information sciences. *Most popular recent majors:* liberal arts/general studies, secretarial studies/office management, marketing/retailing/merchandising.
FIRST-YEAR CLASS 1,404 total; 1,799 applied, 100% were accepted, 78% of whom enrolled.
ACADEMIC PROGRAM Core, interdisciplinary curriculum. Calendar: quarters. Academic remediation for entering students, English as a second language program offered during academic year and summer, advanced placement, self-designed majors, Freshman Honors College, tutorials, honors program, summer session for credit, part-time degree program (daytime, evenings, summer), external degree programs, adult/continuing education programs, co-op programs. ROTC: Air Force (c).
GENERAL DEGREE REQUIREMENT 96 quarter hours.
MAJORS Accounting, agricultural technologies, automotive technologies, aviation technology, child care/child and family studies, computer information systems, criminal justice, early childhood education, electrical and electronics technologies, engineering technology, fire science, graphic arts, law enforcement/police sciences, liberal arts/general studies, marketing/retailing/merchandising, radiological technology, secretarial studies/office management, welding technology.
LIBRARY Aims Community College Library with 38,462 books, 413 microform titles, 360 periodicals, 5 on-line bibliographic services, 2 CD-ROMs, 22 records, tapes, and CDs. Acquisition spending 1994–95: $54,046.
COMPUTERS ON CAMPUS Computer purchase plan available. 600 computers for student use in computer labs, learning resource center, classrooms, library provide access to main academic computer, e-mail, on-line services, Internet. Staffed computer lab on campus provides training in use of computers, software. Academic computing expenditure 1994–95: $366,614.
COLLEGE LIFE Drama-theater group, choral group, student-run newspaper, radio station. *Social organizations:* 3 open to all. *Major annual events:* Fall-In Activity, Winter Fest, Spring-Fest/Blowout Activity. *Student services:* personal-psychological counseling, women's center. *Campus security:* 24-hour emergency response devices, daytime and evening patrols by trained security personnel.
HOUSING College housing not available.
ATHLETICS *Intramural:* basketball, volleyball.
CAREER PLANNING *Placement office:* 1 full-time, 1 part-time staff. *Director:* Ms. Sue Davisson, Director, Advising, Assessment and Career Services, 970-330-8008 Ext. 251. *Services:* resume preparation, career counseling, careers library, job interviews.
AFTER GRADUATION 88% of class of 1994 had job offers within 6 months.
EXPENSES FOR 1995–96 Area resident tuition: $1200 full-time, $25 per quarter hour part-time. State resident tuition: $2016 full-time, $42 per quarter hour part-time. Nonresident tuition: $6096 full-time, $127 per quarter hour part-time. Part-time mandatory fees: $2 per quarter hour. Full-time mandatory fees: $90.
FINANCIAL AID *College-administered undergrad aid 1995–96:* 582 need-based scholarships (average $1043), 305 non-need scholarships (average $750), short-term loans (average $50), low-interest long-term loans from college funds, loans from external sources (average $1992), 61 Federal Work-Study (averaging $1075), part-time jobs. *Required forms:* institutional, FAFSA; required for some: state; accepted: CSS Financial Aid PROFILE. *Priority deadline:* 4/15. *Waivers:* full or partial for employees or children of employees and senior citizens. *Notification:* 8/1.
APPLYING Open admission. *Options:* early entrance, deferred entrance. *Required:* TOEFL for international students, CPT. Test scores used for counseling/placement. *Application deadline:* rolling.
APPLYING/TRANSFER *Entrance:* noncompetitive. *Application deadline:* rolling.
CONTACT Ms. Susie Gallardo, Admissions Technician, Aims Community College, Box 69, Greeley, CO 80632-0069, 970-330-8008 Ext. 624. *E-mail:* wgreen@chiron.aims.edu.

ARAPAHOE COMMUNITY COLLEGE
Littleton, Colorado

UG Enrollment: 7,346	Tuition & Fees (CO Res): $1671
Application Deadline: rolling	Room & Board: N/Avail

GENERAL State-supported, 2-year, coed. Part of Colorado Community College and Occupational Education System. Awards certificates, transfer associate, terminal associate degrees. Founded 1965. *Setting:* 52-acre suburban campus with easy access to Denver. *Total enrollment:* 7,346. *Faculty:* 298 (98 full-time, 21% with terminal degrees, 200 part-time); student-faculty ratio is 19:1.
ENROLLMENT PROFILE 7,346 students from 42 states and territories, 29 other countries. 61% women, 39% men, 75% part-time, 95% state residents, 35% transferred in, 3% international, 61% 25 or older, 1% Native American, 6% Hispanic, 1% African American, 2% Asian American. *Most popular recent majors:* nursing, business administration/commerce/management, computer information systems.
FIRST-YEAR CLASS 3,634 total. Of the students who applied, 98% were accepted, 59% of whom enrolled.
ACADEMIC PROGRAM Core. Calendar: semesters. Academic remediation for entering students, English as a second language program offered during academic year and summer, services for LD students, advanced placement, self-designed majors, honors program, summer session for credit, part-time degree program (daytime, evenings, summer), adult/continuing education programs, co-op programs. Off-campus study at Metropolitan State College. Study abroad in United Kingdom. ROTC: Army (c), Air Force (c).
GENERAL DEGREE REQUIREMENTS 61 credit hours; computer course for most majors.
MAJORS Accounting, architectural technologies, automotive technologies, business administration/commerce/management, commercial art, computer information systems, computer programming, computer science, construction management, criminal justice, drafting and design, electrical and electronics technologies, emergency medical technology, environmental engineering technology, finance/banking, flight training, food services technology, graphic arts, interior design, international business, law enforcement/police sciences, legal secretarial studies, liberal arts/general studies, management information systems, marketing/retailing/merchandising, mechanical design technology, medical assistant technologies, medical laboratory technology, medical records services, medical technology, nursing, occupational therapy, paralegal studies, physical therapy, retail management, science, secretarial studies/office management, tourism and travel.
LIBRARY 45,000 books, 10,246 microform titles, 441 periodicals, 3 on-line bibliographic services, 6 CD-ROMs, 2,470 records, tapes, and CDs.

COMPUTERS ON CAMPUS 200 computers for student use in computer center, computer labs, instructional areas, library, student center provide access to main academic computer. Staffed computer lab on campus.
COLLEGE LIFE Drama-theater group, student-run newspaper. *Student services:* personal-psychological counseling, women's center. *Campus security:* 24-hour patrols, late-night transport-escort service.
HOUSING College housing not available.
ATHLETICS *Intercollegiate:* baseball M(c), basketball M(c), soccer M(c), volleyball M(c)/W(c). *Intramural:* basketball, cross-country running, skiing (cross-country), skiing (downhill), soccer, swimming and diving, tennis, volleyball. *Contact:* Mr. Larry Knierim, Coordinator of Recreational Services and Student Clubs, 303-797-5851.
CAREER PLANNING *Director:* Ms. Sharon Wink, Coordinator of Career Services, 303-797-5697. *Service:* career counseling.
AFTER GRADUATION 16% of students completing a degree program in 1994–95 went directly on to further study.
EXPENSES FOR 1996–97 State resident tuition: $1605 full-time, $53.50 per credit hour part-time. Nonresident tuition: $7313 full-time, $243.75 per credit hour part-time. Full-time mandatory fees: $66.
FINANCIAL AID *College-administered undergrad aid 1995–96:* 413 need-based scholarships (averaging $811), 189 non-need scholarships (averaging $451), short-term loans (averaging $100), low-interest long-term loans from college funds (averaging $984), loans from external sources (averaging $2367), Federal Work-Study, 187 part-time jobs. *Required forms:* institutional, FAFSA; accepted: CSS Financial Aid PROFILE. *Priority deadline:* 5/1. *Waivers:* full or partial for senior citizens.
APPLYING Open admission. *Options:* early entrance, deferred entrance. *Required:* TOEFL for international students, ACT, ACT ASSET, or SAT. *Recommended:* school transcript. Test scores used for counseling/placement. *Application deadline:* rolling.
APPLYING/TRANSFER *Required:* standardized test scores. *Recommended:* high school transcript. *Required for some:* college transcript. *Entrance:* noncompetitive. *Application deadline:* rolling.
CONTACT Ms. Linora Newell, Director of Admissions and Enrollment Management, Arapahoe Community College, Littleton, CO 80160-9002, 303-797-5620. *Fax:* 303-797-5970.

BEL-REA INSTITUTE OF ANIMAL TECHNOLOGY
Denver, Colorado

UG Enrollment: 325	Tuition & Fees: $5750
Application Deadline: rolling	Room & Board: N/Avail

GENERAL Proprietary, 2-year, specialized, coed. Awards terminal associate degrees. Founded 1971. *Setting:* 4-acre suburban campus. *Total enrollment:* 325. *Faculty:* 16 (8 full-time, 30% with terminal degrees, 8 part-time); student-faculty ratio is 14:1.
ENROLLMENT PROFILE 325 students from 20 states and territories, 3 other countries. 85% women, 4% part-time, 56% state residents, 18% transferred in, 1% international, 25% 25 or older, 2% Native American, 3% Hispanic, 1% African American, 0% Asian American.
FIRST-YEAR CLASS 122 total; 250 applied, 72% were accepted, 68% of whom enrolled. 16% from top 10% of their high school class, 33% from top quarter, 62% from top half.
ACADEMIC PROGRAM Core, honor code. Calendar: quarters. Academic remediation for entering students, tutorials, internships.
GENERAL DEGREE REQUIREMENTS 114 credits; 1 course each in math and science; internship.
MAJORS Veterinary sciences, veterinary technology.
LIBRARY 1,800 books, 57 periodicals, 200 records, tapes, and CDs.
COMPUTERS ON CAMPUS 4 computers for student use provide access to off-campus computing facilities. Staffed computer lab on campus.
COLLEGE LIFE *Most popular organization:* National Association of Veterinary Technicians. *Student services:* personal-psychological counseling.
HOUSING College housing not available.
CAREER PLANNING *Placement office:* 1 full-time, 1 part-time staff. *Director:* Ms. LeeAnn Henbest, 303-751-8700. *Services:* resume preparation, resume referral, career counseling, job interviews.
EXPENSES FOR 1996–97 *Application fee:* $150. Tuition: $5750 full-time.
FINANCIAL AID *College-administered undergrad aid 1995–96:* need-based scholarships, low-interest long-term loans from external sources (average $2625), Federal Work-Study, 10 part-time jobs. *Required forms:* institutional; accepted: CSS Financial Aid PROFILE, FAFSA. *Priority deadline:* 9/15. *Payment plans:* tuition prepayment, installment.
APPLYING *Option:* Common Application. *Recommended:* minimum 2.0 GPA, interview, SAT I or ACT. *Required for some:* TOEFL for international students. Test scores used for counseling/placement. *Application deadline:* rolling.
APPLYING/TRANSFER *Required:* high school transcript, college transcript, minimum 2.0 high school GPA. *Recommended:* standardized test scores, interview. *Application deadline:* rolling.
CONTACT Ms. Paulette Bottoms, Director, Bel-Rea Institute of Animal Technology, Denver, CO 80231-3048, 303-751-8700 or toll-free 800-950-8001. *Fax:* 303-751-9969.

❖ *See page 704 for a narrative description.* ❖

BLAIR JUNIOR COLLEGE
Colorado Springs, Colorado

UG Enrollment: 290	Tuition: $11,400/deg prog
Application Deadline: rolling	Room & Board: N/Avail

GENERAL Proprietary, 2-year, coed. Part of Phillips Colleges, Inc. Awards diplomas, transfer associate, terminal associate degrees. Founded 1897. *Setting:* 5-acre suburban campus with easy access to Denver. *Total enrollment:* 290. *Faculty:* 28 (12 full-time, 16 part-time); student-faculty ratio is 18:1.
ENROLLMENT PROFILE 290 students from 6 states and territories, 3 other countries. 83% women, 90% state residents, 10% transferred in, 1% international, 69% 25 or older, 1% Native American, 6% Hispanic, 14% African American, 1% Asian American.

Blair Junior College (continued)

FIRST-YEAR CLASS 145 total. Of the students who applied, 96% were accepted.

ACADEMIC PROGRAM Core, honor code. Calendar: quarters. Academic remediation for entering students, English as a second language program offered during academic year, services for LD students, co-op programs and internships.

GENERAL DEGREE REQUIREMENTS 96 credit hours; 1 math course; computer course.

MAJORS Accounting, business administration/commerce/management, computer programming, computer science, medical assistant technologies, medical secretarial studies, paralegal studies, secretarial studies/office management, tourism and travel.

LIBRARY Blair Junior College Library with 6,500 books, 45 periodicals, 365 records, tapes, and CDs.

COMPUTERS ON CAMPUS 72 computers for student use in computer center provide access to main academic computer.

COLLEGE LIFE ***Student services:*** personal-psychological counseling. ***Campus security:*** 24-hour emergency response devices.

HOUSING College housing not available.

ATHLETICS ***Intramural:*** bowling.

CAREER PLANNING ***Placement office:*** 1 full-time staff. ***Director:*** Mr. Bill Utecht, Placement Director, 719-574-1082. ***Services:*** job fairs, resume preparation, resume referral, career counseling, job interviews.

EXPENSES FOR 1996–97 ***Application fee:*** $25. Tuition: $11,400 per degree program. Tuition guaranteed not to increase for student's term of enrollment.

FINANCIAL AID ***College-administered undergrad aid 1995–96:*** need-based scholarships, non-need scholarships, low-interest long-term loans from external sources (average $2500), Federal Work-Study, 6 part-time jobs. ***Required forms:*** institutional, FAFSA; accepted: CSS Financial Aid PROFILE, state. ***Application deadline:*** continuous. ***Payment plan:*** installment. ***Waivers:*** full or partial for employees or children of employees.

APPLYING ***Options:*** early entrance, deferred entrance. ***Required:*** school transcript, CPAt. Test scores used for admission. ***Application deadline:*** rolling. ***Notification:*** continuous.

APPLYING/TRANSFER ***Required:*** college transcript. ***Entrance:*** minimally difficult. ***Application deadline:*** rolling. ***Notification:*** continuous.

CONTACT Ms. Debbie McAtee, Director of Admissions, Blair Junior College, Colorado Springs, CO 80915, 719-574-1082.

COLORADO INSTITUTE OF ART
Denver, Colorado

UG Enrollment: 1,478	**Tuition: $18,540/deg prog**
Application Deadline: rolling	**Room & Board: $4920**

GENERAL Proprietary, 2-year, coed. Part of Education Management Corporation. Awards diplomas, terminal associate degrees. Founded 1952. ***Setting:*** urban campus. ***Total enrollment:*** 1,478. ***Faculty:*** 123 (52 full-time, 71 part-time); student-faculty ratio is 20:1. ***Notable Alumni:*** Dan Price, design director of Denver Nuggets; Quang Ho, artist; Ramon Kelley, artist; Kevin Van Fleet, producer and director; Lynn Gertenbach, artist.

ENROLLMENT PROFILE 1,478 students from 49 states and territories, 14 other countries. 42% women, 58% men, 0% part-time, 50% state residents, 80% have need-based financial aid, 4% international, 28% 25 or older, 3% Native American, 9% Hispanic, 5% African American, 2% Asian American.

FIRST-YEAR CLASS 465 total; 761 applied, 100% were accepted, 61% of whom enrolled.

ACADEMIC PROGRAM Core, competency-based curriculum, honor code. Calendar: quarters. 100 courses offered in 1995–96. Academic remediation for entering students, services for LD students, advanced placement, adult/continuing education programs.

GENERAL DEGREE REQUIREMENTS 90 credits; computer course.

MAJORS Art/fine arts, commercial art, computer graphics, culinary arts, fashion design and technology, fashion merchandising, film and video production, illustration, industrial design, interior design, photography.

LIBRARY 9,220 books, 210 periodicals, 50 CD-ROMs, 605 records, tapes, and CDs.

COMPUTERS ON CAMPUS Computer purchase plan available. 350 computers for student use in computer center, computer labs, learning resource center, classrooms, library. Staffed computer lab on campus provides training in use of computers, software.

COLLEGE LIFE Orientation program (3 days, no cost, parents included). ***Social organizations:*** 1 local fraternity. ***Student services:*** personal-psychological counseling. ***Campus security:*** 24-hour emergency response devices.

HOUSING 150 college housing spaces available; 125 were occupied 1995–96. Freshmen given priority for college housing. Off-campus living permitted. ***Options:*** coed, single-sex housing available. Resident assistants live in dorms.

CAREER PLANNING ***Placement office:*** 9 full-time staff. ***Director:*** Mr. Bruce Walthers, Director of Student Services, 303-837-0825. ***Services:*** job fairs, resume preparation, resume referral, career counseling, job bank, job interviews.

AFTER GRADUATION 85% of class of 1994 had job offers within 6 months.

EXPENSES FOR 1995–96 ***Application fee:*** $50. Tuition per degree program ranges from $18,540 to $27,810. College room and board: $4920.

FINANCIAL AID ***College-administered undergrad aid 1995–96:*** need-based scholarships, non-need scholarships, low-interest long-term loans from external sources, Federal Work-Study, part-time jobs. ***Required forms:*** CSS Financial Aid PROFILE, institutional, FAFSA; required for some: state. ***Application deadline:*** continuous. ***Payment plan:*** installment.

APPLYING ***Option:*** deferred entrance. ***Required:*** essay, school transcript, interview, TOEFL for international students. Test scores used for admission. ***Application deadline:*** rolling.

APPLYING/TRANSFER ***Required:*** essay, high school transcript, interview, college transcript. ***Entrance:*** minimally difficult. ***Application deadline:*** rolling. ***Contact:*** Ms. Barbara Browning, Vice President and Director of Admissions, 303-837-0825 Ext. 520.

CONTACT Ms. Barbara Browning, Vice President and Director of Admissions, Colorado Institute of Art, 200 East Ninth Avenue, Denver, CO 80203-2903, 303-837-0825 Ext. 520 or toll-free 800-275-2420. ***Fax:*** 303-837-0825 Ext. 549. College video available.

COLORADO MOUNTAIN COLLEGE, ALPINE CAMPUS
Steamboat Springs, Colorado

UG Enrollment: 1,262	**Tuition & Fees (Area Res): $1150**
Application Deadline: rolling	**Room & Board: $3700**

GENERAL District-supported, 2-year, coed. Part of Colorado Mountain College District System. Awards certificates, transfer associate, terminal associate degrees. Founded 1965. ***Setting:*** 10-acre rural campus. ***Total enrollment:*** 1,262. ***Faculty:*** 132 (32 full-time, 25% with terminal degrees, 100 part-time).

ENROLLMENT PROFILE 1,262 students from 49 states and territories, 6 other countries. 50% women, 64% part-time, 78% state residents, 12% live on campus, 25% transferred in, 2% international, 50% 25 or older, 1% Native American, 2% Hispanic, 1% African American, 1% Asian American. ***Most popular recent major:*** liberal arts/general studies.

FIRST-YEAR CLASS 198 total; 450 applied, 100% were accepted, 44% of whom enrolled.

ACADEMIC PROGRAM Core. Calendar: semesters. Academic remediation for entering students, services for LD students, advanced placement, tutorials, summer session for credit, part-time degree program (daytime, evenings), adult/continuing education programs, co-op programs and internships.

GENERAL DEGREE REQUIREMENTS 62 credits; 3 credits of math; 4 credits of lab science; internship (some majors).

MAJORS Accounting, behavioral sciences, biology/biological sciences, business administration/commerce/management, computer technologies, English, geology, hospitality services, hotel and restaurant management, humanities, liberal arts/general studies, marketing/retailing/merchandising, mathematics, physical fitness/exercise science, physical sciences, recreational facilities management, retail management, science, social science, sports medicine.

LIBRARY 17,000 books, 32,000 microform titles, 192 periodicals, 2,000 records, tapes, and CDs.

COMPUTERS ON CAMPUS 60 computers for student use in computer center, computer labs, library.

COLLEGE LIFE Orientation program (3 days, parents included). Student-run newspaper. ***Social organizations:*** 8 open to all. ***Most popular organizations:*** Student Government, Environmental Club, Ski Club, International Club, Phi Theta Kappa. ***Major annual events:*** Spring Fling, Winter Carnival. ***Student services:*** personal-psychological counseling. ***Campus security:*** controlled dormitory access.

HOUSING 150 college housing spaces available; all were occupied 1995–96. No special consideration for freshman housing applicants. Off-campus living permitted. ***Option:*** coed (2 buildings) housing available. Resident assistants live in dorms.

ATHLETICS Member NAIA. ***Intercollegiate:*** skiing (cross-country) M(s)/W(s), skiing (downhill) M(s)/W(s). ***Intramural:*** basketball, skiing (cross-country), skiing (downhill), soccer, volleyball. ***Contact:*** Ms. Ames Chandler, Ski Team Coach, 970-879-3288.

CAREER PLANNING ***Placement office:*** 1 full-time staff. ***Director:*** Mr. Dan Schafrick, Counselor, 970-870-4444. ***Services:*** resume preparation, career counseling, job bank.

AFTER GRADUATION 57% of students completing a degree program in 1994–95 went directly on to further study.

EXPENSES FOR 1996–97 Area resident tuition: $1020 full-time, $34 per credit part-time. State resident tuition: $1890 full-time, $63 per credit part-time. Nonresident tuition: $6000 full-time, $200 per credit part-time. Part-time mandatory fees per semester (9 to 11 credits): $50. Full-time mandatory fees: $130. College room and board: $3700.

FINANCIAL AID ***College-administered undergrad aid 1995–96:*** 42 need-based scholarships (average $900), 33 non-need scholarships (average $900), low-interest long-term loans from college funds (average $750), loans from external sources (average $2000), Federal Work-Study, 20 part-time jobs. ***Acceptable forms:*** institutional, FAFSA. ***Priority deadline:*** 3/31. ***Waivers:*** full or partial for employees or children of employees and senior citizens. ***Notification:*** 5/15.

APPLYING Open admission for state residents. ***Options:*** early entrance, deferred entrance, midyear entrance. ***Required:*** TOEFL for international students. ***Recommended:*** SAT I or ACT. ***Required for some:*** school transcript. Test scores used for counseling/placement. ***Application deadline:*** rolling. Preference given to district residents.

APPLYING/TRANSFER ***Recommended:*** college transcript. ***Entrance:*** noncompetitive. ***Application deadline:*** rolling.

CONTACT Ms. Janice Bell, Admissions Assistant, Colorado Mountain College, Alpine Campus, PO Box 10001, Department PG, Glenwood Springs, CO 81602, 970-870-4417 or toll-free 800-621-8559. ***E-mail:*** joinus@coloradomtn.edu.

❖ ***See page 726 for a narrative description.*** ❖

COLORADO MOUNTAIN COLLEGE, ROARING FORK CAMPUS-SPRING VALLEY CENTER
Glenwood Springs, Colorado

UG Enrollment: 868	**Tuition & Fees (Area Res): $1150**
Application Deadline: rolling	**Room & Board: $3700**

The outdoors become a classroom for programs such as the Outdoor Semester in the Rockies and outdoor recreational leadership. Students can train for the ski industry with programs in ski area operations, ski business, resort management, or culinary arts. They can explore unique programs in photography, graphic design, criminal justice, and veterinary technology. Associate degrees are available with transfer agreements.

GENERAL District-supported, 2-year, coed. Part of Colorado Mountain College District System. Awards certificates, transfer associate, terminal associate degrees. Founded 1965. ***Setting:*** 680-acre rural campus. ***Total enrollment:*** 868. ***Faculty:*** 64 (28 full-time, 25% with terminal degrees, 36 part-time).

ENROLLMENT PROFILE 868 students from 48 states and territories, 6 other countries. 59% women, 56% part-time, 84% state residents, 26% live on campus, 1%

230

Peterson's Guide to Two-Year Colleges 1997

international, 51% 25 or older, 1% Native American, 4% Hispanic, 1% African American, 1% Asian American. ***Most popular recent majors:*** liberal arts/general studies, photography, veterinary technology.
FIRST-YEAR CLASS 222 total; 461 applied, 100% were accepted, 48% of whom enrolled.
ACADEMIC PROGRAM Core. Calendar: semesters. Academic remediation for entering students, services for LD students, advanced placement, tutorials, part-time degree program (daytime, evenings, summer), adult/continuing education programs, co-op programs and internships.
GENERAL DEGREE REQUIREMENTS 62 credits; 3 credits of math; 4 credits of lab science; computer course; internship (some majors).
MAJORS Accounting, art/fine arts, behavioral sciences, biology/biological sciences, business administration/commerce/management, commercial art, computer technologies, criminal justice, culinary arts, English, graphic arts, humanities, liberal arts/general studies, mathematics, natural sciences, nursing, photography, practical nursing, psychology, recreation therapy, science, social science, theater arts/drama, veterinary technology.
LIBRARY 36,000 books, 32,000 microform titles, 186 periodicals, 3,400 records, tapes, and CDs.
COMPUTERS ON CAMPUS 45 computers for student use in computer labs, veterinary technology classroom, library. Staffed computer lab on campus.
COLLEGE LIFE Orientation program (3 days, $40, parents included). Drama-theater group. ***Most popular organizations:*** Student Government, Visual Communication Club, World Awareness Society, Peer Mentors, Student Activities Board. ***Major annual event:*** Spring Fest. ***Student services:*** personal-psychological counseling. ***Campus security:*** controlled dormitory access.
HOUSING 160 college housing spaces available; all were occupied 1995–96. No special consideration for freshman housing applicants. Off-campus living permitted. ***Option:*** coed housing available. Resident assistants live in dorms.
ATHLETICS Member NAIA. ***Intercollegiate:*** skiing (cross-country) M/W, skiing (downhill) M/W. ***Intramural:*** basketball, football, skiing (cross-country), skiing (downhill), soccer, volleyball. ***Contact:*** Ms. Ames Chandler, Ski Team Coach, 970-870-4444.
CAREER PLANNING ***Placement office:*** 1 full-time staff. ***Director:*** Ms. Lisa Doak, Assistant Campus Dean of Student Services, 970-945-7481. ***Services:*** resume preparation, career counseling, job bank.
AFTER GRADUATION 57% of students completing a degree program in 1994–95 went directly on to further study.
EXPENSES FOR 1996–97 Area resident tuition: $1020 full-time, $34 per credit part-time. State resident tuition: $1890 full-time, $63 per credit part-time. Nonresident tuition: $6000 full-time, $200 per credit part-time. Part-time mandatory fees per semester (7 to 11 credits): $50. Full-time mandatory fees: $130. College room and board: $3700.
FINANCIAL AID ***College-administered undergrad aid 1995–96:*** 40 need-based scholarships (average $850), 35 non-need scholarships (average $900), low-interest long-term loans from college funds (average $1000), loans from external sources (average $2000), Federal Work-Study, 15 part-time jobs. ***Acceptable forms:*** institutional, FAFSA. ***Priority deadline:*** 3/31. ***Waivers:*** full or partial for employees or children of employees and senior citizens. ***Notification:*** 5/15.
APPLYING Open admission for state residents. ***Options:*** early entrance, deferred entrance, midyear entrance. ***Required:*** TOEFL for international students. ***Recommended:*** SAT I or ACT. ***Required for some:*** school transcript. Test scores used for counseling/placement. ***Application deadline:*** rolling. Preference given to district residents.
APPLYING/TRANSFER ***Recommended:*** college transcript. ***Entrance:*** noncompetitive. ***Application deadline:*** rolling.
CONTACT Ms. Deborah Cutter, Admissions Assistant, Colorado Mountain College, Roaring Fork Campus-Spring Valley Center, PO Box 10001, Department PG, Glenwood Springs, CO 81601, 970-945-7481 or toll-free 800-621-8559. ***E-mail:*** joinus@coloradomtn.edu.

❖ ***See page 726 for a narrative description.*** ❖

COLORADO MOUNTAIN COLLEGE, TIMBERLINE CAMPUS
Leadville, Colorado

UG Enrollment: 576	**Tuition & Fees (Area Res): $1150**
Application Deadline: rolling	**Room & Board: $3700**

GENERAL District-supported, 2-year, coed. Part of Colorado Mountain College District System. Awards certificates, transfer associate, terminal associate degrees. Founded 1965. ***Setting:*** 200-acre rural campus. ***Total enrollment:*** 576. ***Faculty:*** 45 (15 full-time, 20% with terminal degrees, 30 part-time).
ENROLLMENT PROFILE 576 students from 48 states and territories, 6 other countries. 45% women, 76% part-time, 83% state residents, 16% live on campus, 1% international, 62% 25 or older, 1% Native American, 12% Hispanic, 1% African American, 1% Asian American. ***Most popular recent majors:*** environmental sciences, recreational facilities management, liberal arts/general studies.
FIRST-YEAR CLASS 114 total; 271 applied, 100% were accepted, 42% of whom enrolled.
ACADEMIC PROGRAM Core. Calendar: semesters. Average class size 15 in required courses. Academic remediation for entering students, services for LD students, advanced placement, tutorials, part-time degree program (daytime, evenings), adult/continuing education programs, co-op programs and internships.
GENERAL DEGREE REQUIREMENTS 62 credits; 3 credits of math; 4 credits of lab science; internship (some majors).
MAJORS Accounting, art/fine arts, behavioral sciences, biology/biological sciences, business administration/commerce/management, child care/child and family studies, computer technologies, early childhood education, ecology, English, environmental education, environmental sciences, environmental studies, Hispanic studies, humanities, land use management and reclamation, liberal arts/general studies, mathematics, psychology, recreational facilities management, recreation and leisure services, science, social science, water resources.
LIBRARY 25,000 books, 10,000 microform titles, 185 periodicals, 1,100 records, tapes, and CDs.
COMPUTERS ON CAMPUS 30 computers for student use in library.
COLLEGE LIFE Orientation program (3 days, no cost, parents included). ***Most popular organizations:*** Environmental Club, Snow Boarders Club, Outdoors Club, Student Activities Board, Soccer Club. ***Student services:*** personal-psychological counseling. ***Campus security:*** controlled dormitory access.
HOUSING 92 college housing spaces available; all were occupied 1995–96. No special consideration for freshman housing applicants. Off-campus living permitted. ***Option:*** coed housing available. Resident assistants live in dorms.
ATHLETICS Member NAIA. ***Intercollegiate:*** skiing (cross-country) M/W, skiing (downhill) M/W. ***Intramural:*** basketball, skiing (cross-country), skiing (downhill), soccer, volleyball. ***Contact:*** Ms. Ames Chandler, Ski Team Coach, 970-870-4444.
CAREER PLANNING ***Placement office:*** 1 full-time staff. ***Director:*** Ms. Connie Lugeanbeal, Counselor, 719-486-2015. ***Services:*** resume preparation, career counseling, job bank.
AFTER GRADUATION 57% of students completing a degree program in 1994–95 went directly on to further study.
EXPENSES FOR 1996–97 Area resident tuition: $1020 full-time, $34 per credit part-time. State resident tuition: $1890 full-time, $63 per credit part-time. Nonresident tuition: $6000 full-time, $200 per credit part-time. Part-time mandatory fees per semester (9 to 11 credits): $50. Full-time mandatory fees: $130. College room and board: $3700.
FINANCIAL AID ***College-administered undergrad aid 1995–96:*** 45 need-based scholarships (average $600), 31 non-need scholarships (average $900), low-interest long-term loans from college funds (average $700), loans from external sources (average $2000), Federal Work-Study, 20 part-time jobs. ***Acceptable forms:*** institutional, FAFSA. ***Priority deadline:*** 3/31. ***Waivers:*** full or partial for employees or children of employees and senior citizens. ***Notification:*** 5/15.
APPLYING Open admission for state residents. ***Options:*** early entrance, deferred entrance, midyear entrance. ***Required:*** TOEFL for international students. ***Recommended:*** SAT I or ACT. ***Required for some:*** school transcript. Test scores used for counseling/placement. ***Application deadline:*** rolling. Preference given to district residents.
APPLYING/TRANSFER ***Recommended:*** college transcript. ***Entrance:*** noncompetitive. ***Application deadline:*** rolling.
CONTACT Ms. Virginia Espinoza, Admissions Assistant, Colorado Mountain College, Timberline Campus, PO Box 10001, Department PG, Glenwood Springs, CO 81602, 719-486-4291 or toll-free 800-621-8559. ***E-mail:*** joinus@coloradomtn.edu.

❖ ***See page 726 for a narrative description.*** ❖

COLORADO NORTHWESTERN COMMUNITY COLLEGE
Rangely, Colorado

UG Enrollment: 555	**Tuition & Fees (Area Res): $470**
Application Deadline: rolling	**Room & Board: $3736**

GENERAL District-supported, 2-year, coed. Awards transfer associate, terminal associate degrees. Founded 1962. ***Setting:*** 150-acre rural campus. ***Research spending 1994–95:*** $160,346. ***Educational spending 1994–95:*** $4022 per undergrad. ***Total enrollment:*** 555. ***Faculty:*** 209 (44 full-time, 5% with terminal degrees, 165 part-time); student-faculty ratio is 13:1.
ENROLLMENT PROFILE 555 students from 17 states and territories, 6 other countries. 54% women, 46% men, 21% part-time, 83% state residents, 48% live on campus, 16% transferred in, 53% have need-based financial aid, 27% have non-need-based financial aid, 2% international, 41% 25 or older, 1% Native American, 4% Hispanic, 2% African American, 0% Asian American. ***Areas of study chosen:*** 50% liberal arts/general studies, 23% engineering and applied sciences, 9% business management and administrative services, 8% health professions and related sciences, 5% computer and information sciences, 4% agriculture, 1% natural resource sciences. ***Most popular recent majors:*** liberal arts/general studies, dental services, aviation technology.
FIRST-YEAR CLASS 152 total; 281 applied, 81% were accepted, 66% of whom enrolled. 7% from top 10% of their high school class, 26% from top quarter, 48% from top half. 3 valedictorians.
ACADEMIC PROGRAM Core, honor code. Calendar: semesters. Academic remediation for entering students, services for LD students, advanced placement, summer session for credit, part-time degree program (daytime), adult/continuing education programs, internships.
GENERAL DEGREE REQUIREMENTS 62 credits; computer course for most majors.
MAJORS Aircraft and missile maintenance, aviation technology, business administration/commerce/management, computer information systems, computer technologies, corrections, criminal justice, dental services, farm and ranch management, flight training, forestry, instrumentation technology, law enforcement/police sciences, liberal arts/general studies, medical assistant technologies, medical secretarial studies, natural resource management, science, secretarial studies/office management, word processing.
LIBRARY Colorado Northwestern Community College Library plus 1 other, with 19,170 books, 350 microform titles, 291 periodicals, 2,500 records, tapes, and CDs. Acquisition spending 1994–95: $39,445.
COMPUTERS ON CAMPUS 55 computers for student use in computer center, computer labs, learning resource center, business lab, library, dorms provide access to Internet. Staffed computer lab on campus provides training in use of computers, software. Academic computing expenditure 1994–95: $217,047.
COLLEGE LIFE 80% vote in student government elections. ***Most popular organizations:*** Campus Activities Board, SADHA (Student American Dental Hygiene Association, Aero Club, Criminal Justice Club. ***Major annual events:*** All-Nighter Weekend, Crazy Daze. ***Student services:*** personal-psychological counseling. ***Campus security:*** student patrols, late-night transport-escort service.
HOUSING 288 college housing spaces available; 250 were occupied 1995–96. Freshmen guaranteed college housing. On-campus residence required in freshman year. ***Options:*** coed (2 buildings), single-sex (1 building) housing available. Resident assistants live in dorms.
ATHLETICS Member NJCAA. ***Intercollegiate:*** baseball M(s), basketball M(s)/W(s), softball W(s), volleyball W(s), wrestling M(s). ***Intramural:*** basketball, football, golf, racquetball, soccer, softball, table tennis (Ping-Pong), tennis, volleyball. ***Contact:*** Mr. Paul Conrad, Athletic Director, 970-675-3286.
CAREER PLANNING ***Placement office:*** 3 full-time, 1 part-time staff; $145,347 operating expenditure 1994–95. ***Director:*** Ms. Celeste Donovan, Director of Counseling and Career Services, 970-675-3233. ***Services:*** resume preparation, resume referral, career counseling, careers library.
AFTER GRADUATION 61% of students completing a degree program in 1994–95 went directly on to further study.

Peterson's Guide to Two-Year Colleges 1997

231

Colorado Northwestern Community College (continued)
EXPENSES FOR 1996–97 ***Application fee:*** $10. Area resident tuition: $0 full-time. State resident tuition: $1141 full-time, $46 per semester hour part-time. Nonresident tuition: $4190 full-time, $175 per semester hour part-time. Part-time mandatory fees: $11 per semester hour. Full-time mandatory fees: $470. College room and board: $3736.
FINANCIAL AID ***College-administered undergrad aid 1995–96:*** 188 need-based scholarships (average $730), 312 non-need scholarships (average $1084), short-term loans (average $30), low-interest long-term loans from external sources (average $2639), 29 Federal Work-Study (averaging $1800), 107 part-time jobs. ***Required forms:*** institutional, FAFSA. ***Priority deadline:*** 5/1. ***Payment plan:*** installment. ***Waivers:*** full or partial for senior citizens. ***Average indebtedness of graduates:*** $3240.
APPLYING Open admission except for dental hygiene programs. ***Options:*** early entrance, deferred entrance, midyear entrance. ***Required:*** TOEFL for international students. ***Recommended:*** school transcript, ACT. Test scores used for counseling/placement. ***Application deadline:*** rolling.
APPLYING/TRANSFER ***Recommended:*** college transcript. ***Entrance:*** noncompetitive. ***Application deadline:*** rolling.
CONTACT Ms. Susan N. Shafer, Director of Admissions and Records, Colorado Northwestern Community College, Rangely, CO 81648-3598, 970-675-3217 or toll-free 800-562-1105. ***Fax:*** 970-675-3305. College video available.

COMMUNITY COLLEGE OF AURORA
Aurora, Colorado

UG Enrollment: 4,670 — **Tuition & Fees (CO Res): $1532**
Application Deadline: rolling — **Room & Board: N/Avail**

GENERAL State-supported, 2-year, coed. Awards certificates, transfer associate, terminal associate degrees. Founded 1983. ***Setting:*** suburban campus with easy access to Denver. ***Total enrollment:*** 4,670. ***Faculty:*** 197 (18 full-time, 179 part-time); student-faculty ratio is 18:1.
ENROLLMENT PROFILE 4,670 students: 64% women, 84% part-time, 96% state residents, 13% transferred in, 1% international, 68% 25 or older, 1% Native American, 6% Hispanic, 14% African American, 3% Asian American.
FIRST-YEAR CLASS 3,731 total; 3,731 applied, 100% were accepted, 100% of whom enrolled.
ACADEMIC PROGRAM Core. Calendar: semesters. Academic remediation for entering students, English as a second language program offered during academic year, services for LD students, summer session for credit, part-time degree program (daytime, evenings), external degree programs, adult/continuing education programs. Off-campus study at T. H. Pickens Technical Vocational Center.
GENERAL DEGREE REQUIREMENTS 60 semester hours; computer course for accounting, banking and financial services, insurance, flight attendant, management, marketing, metrology, criminal justice majors.
MAJORS Accounting, automotive technologies, business administration/commerce/management, carpentry, computer information systems, criminal justice, early childhood education, finance/banking, graphic arts, liberal arts/general studies, marketing/retailing/merchandising, medical assistant technologies, medical secretarial studies, optometric/ophthalmic technologies, paralegal studies, science, secretarial studies/office management.
LIBRARY 7,440 books, 126 periodicals, 475 records, tapes, and CDs.
COMPUTERS ON CAMPUS 160 computers for student use in computer center, computer labs, research center, learning resource center, classrooms, library, student center provide access to main academic computer, e-mail. Staffed computer lab on campus provides training in use of computers, software.
COLLEGE LIFE Drama-theater group, student-run newspaper. ***Student services:*** women's center. ***Campus security:*** late-night transport-escort service.
HOUSING College housing not available.
CAREER PLANNING ***Service:*** career counseling.
AFTER GRADUATION 20% of students completing a degree program in 1994–95 went directly on to further study.
EXPENSES FOR 1995–96 State resident tuition: $1440 full-time, $48 per semester hour part-time. Nonresident tuition: $4320 full-time, $144 per semester hour part-time. Part-time mandatory fees per semester range from $19 to $38. Full-time mandatory fees: $92.
FINANCIAL AID ***College-administered undergrad aid 1995–96:*** need-based scholarships, non-need scholarships, short-term loans (averaging $75), low-interest long-term loans from external sources, Federal Work-Study. ***Required forms:*** institutional. ***Priority deadline:*** 6/1. ***Payment plan:*** deferred payment. ***Waivers:*** full or partial for employees or children of employees and senior citizens.
APPLYING Open admission. ***Option:*** early entrance. ***Required:*** TOEFL for international students. ***Recommended:*** SAT I or ACT. Test scores used for counseling/placement. ***Application deadline:*** rolling. ***Notification:*** continuous.
APPLYING/TRANSFER ***Recommended:*** standardized test scores. ***Application deadline:*** rolling. ***Notification:*** continuous.
CONTACT Mr. Bryan Doak, Director of Registrations, Records, and Admission, Community College of Aurora, Aurora, CO 80011-9036, 303-360-4700.

COMMUNITY COLLEGE OF DENVER
Denver, Colorado

UG Enrollment: 11,897 — **Tuition & Fees (CO Res): $1822**
Application Deadline: rolling — **Room & Board: N/Avail**

GENERAL State-supported, 2-year, coed. Awards certificates, transfer associate, terminal associate degrees. Founded 1970. ***Setting:*** urban campus. ***Total enrollment:*** 11,897. ***Faculty:*** 596 (96 full-time, 500 part-time); student-faculty ratio is 25:1.
ENROLLMENT PROFILE 11,897 students from 3 states and territories, 38 other countries. 58% women, 68% part-time, 95% state residents, 8% transferred in, 3% international, 51% 25 or older, 2% Native American, 24% Hispanic, 12% African American, 5% Asian American. ***Most popular recent majors:*** liberal arts/general studies, business administration/commerce/management, nursing.
FIRST-YEAR CLASS 5,405 total. Of the students who applied, 100% were accepted.
ACADEMIC PROGRAM Core. Calendar: semesters. Academic remediation for entering students, English as a second language program offered during academic year and summer, services for LD students, advanced placement, summer session for credit, part-time degree program (daytime, evenings, weekends, summer), adult/continuing education programs, co-op programs. Off-campus study at Metropolitan State College, University of Colorado at Denver. Study abroad in England. ROTC: Army (c).
GENERAL DEGREE REQUIREMENTS 60 credit hours; math/science requirements vary according to program.
MAJORS Accounting, aircraft and missile maintenance, automotive technologies, business administration/commerce/management, child care/child and family studies, commercial art, computer programming, computer science, drafting and design, early childhood education, electrical and electronics technologies, environmental engineering technology, graphic arts, heating/refrigeration/air conditioning, hotel and restaurant management, human services, legal secretarial studies, liberal arts/general studies, marketing/retailing/merchandising, medical secretarial studies, nuclear medical technology, nursing, operating room technology, paralegal studies, photography, radiological technology, secretarial studies/office management, transportation technologies, welding technology.
COMPUTERS ON CAMPUS 250 computers for student use in computer labs, media lab provide access to off-campus computing facilities, e-mail, on-line services. Staffed computer lab on campus provides training in use of computers, software.
COLLEGE LIFE Student-run newspaper. ***Social organizations:*** 1 national fraternity, 1 national sorority, 1 local fraternity, 1 local sorority; 1% of eligible men and 1% of eligible women are members. ***Student services:*** legal services, health clinic, women's center.
HOUSING College housing not available.
ATHLETICS ***Intramural:*** archery, badminton, basketball, bowling, cross-country running, equestrian sports, fencing, field hockey, football, golf, gymnastics, racquetball, riflery, rugby, skiing (cross-country), skiing (downhill), soccer, swimming and diving, table tennis (Ping-Pong), tennis, track and field, volleyball, weight lifting.
CAREER PLANNING ***Service:*** career counseling.
EXPENSES FOR 1995–96 State resident tuition: $1567 full-time, $52.25 per credit hour part-time. Nonresident tuition: $7012 full-time, $233.75 per credit hour part-time. Part-time mandatory fees: $8.50 per credit hour. Full-time mandatory fees: $255.
FINANCIAL AID ***College-administered undergrad aid 1995–96:*** need-based scholarships, low-interest long-term loans from external sources, Federal Work-Study. ***Required forms:*** institutional, FAFSA. ***Priority deadline:*** 6/1.
APPLYING Open admission. ***Options:*** early entrance, deferred entrance. ***Required:*** TOEFL for international students. ***Recommended:*** school transcript, ACT. Test scores used for counseling/placement. ***Application deadline:*** rolling.
APPLYING/TRANSFER ***Entrance:*** noncompetitive. ***Application deadline:*** rolling.
CONTACT Ms. Lillian Hunsaker, Director of Education, Planning, and Advising, Community College of Denver, PO Box 173363, Denver, CO 80217-3363, 303-556-2600.

DENVER AUTOMOTIVE AND DIESEL COLLEGE
Denver, Colorado

UG Enrollment: 388 — **Tuition: $4830/deg prog**
Application Deadline: rolling — **Room & Board: N/Avail**

GENERAL Proprietary, 2-year, coed. Awards diplomas, terminal associate degrees. Founded 1963. ***Setting:*** urban campus. ***Total enrollment:*** 388. ***Faculty:*** 25 (all full-time).
ENROLLMENT PROFILE 388 students: 3% women, 2% transferred in, 90% have need-based financial aid, 1% international, 20% 25 or older, 2% Native American, 10% Hispanic, 3% African American, 1% Asian American.
FIRST-YEAR CLASS 90 total. Of the students who applied, 97% were accepted, 80% of whom enrolled. 50% from top half of their high school class.
ACADEMIC PROGRAM Core, honor code. Calendar: 8 six-week terms. 24 courses offered in 1995–96. Services for LD students, summer session for credit.
GENERAL DEGREE REQUIREMENT 108 credit hours.
MAJOR Automotive technologies.
LIBRARY Denver Automotive and Diesel College Library with 1,050 books, 8 periodicals.
COMPUTERS ON CAMPUS 4 computers for student use in classrooms, library.
COLLEGE LIFE Orientation program (2 days, no cost). ***Most popular organization:*** Student Council. ***Student services:*** personal-psychological counseling. ***Campus security:*** 24-hour emergency response devices and patrols.
HOUSING College housing not available.
CAREER PLANNING ***Placement office:*** 2 full-time staff; $30,000 operating expenditure 1994–95. ***Director:*** Mr. Harvey Spychalla, Manager, Career Development, 303-722-5724. ***Services:*** resume preparation, resume referral, career counseling, job bank, job interviews. Students must register freshman year.
EXPENSES FOR 1996–97 ***Application fee:*** $150. Tuition per degree program ranges from $4830 to $15,740.
FINANCIAL AID ***College-administered undergrad aid 1995–96:*** need-based scholarships, low-interest long-term loans from external sources, Federal Work-Study, part-time jobs. ***Required forms:*** FAFSA. ***Application deadline:*** continuous. ***Payment plans:*** installment, deferred payment.
APPLYING ***Application deadline:*** rolling.
CONTACT Mr. John Chalupa, Director of Admissions, Denver Automotive and Diesel College, 405 S. Platte River Dr., Denver, CO 80223-2025, 303-722-5724 or toll-free 800-347-3232. ***Fax:*** 303-778-8264. College video available.

FRONT RANGE COMMUNITY COLLEGE
Westminster, Colorado

UG Enrollment: 11,471 — **Tuition & Fees (CO Res): $1655**
Application Deadline: rolling — **Room & Board: N/Avail**

GENERAL State-supported, 2-year, coed. Awards certificates, transfer associate, terminal associate degrees. Founded 1968. ***Setting:*** 90-acre suburban campus with easy access to Denver. ***Research spending 1994–95:*** $6275. ***Educational spending 1994–95:*** $1622 per undergrad. ***Total enrollment:*** 11,471. ***Faculty:*** 517 (167 full-time, 350 part-time); student-faculty ratio is 15:1.

ENROLLMENT PROFILE 11,471 students from 8 states and territories, 15 other countries. 57% women, 72% part-time, 95% state residents, 15% transferred in, 1% international, 60% 25 or older, 1% Native American, 9% Hispanic, 1% African American, 3% Asian American.
FIRST-YEAR CLASS 3,327 total. Of the students who applied, 100% were accepted, 55% of whom enrolled.
ACADEMIC PROGRAM Core, honor code. Calendar: semesters. 1,800 courses offered in 1995–96. Academic remediation for entering students, English as a second language program offered during academic year and summer, services for LD students, advanced placement, self-designed majors, honors program, summer session for credit, part-time degree program (daytime, evenings, summer), external degree programs, adult/continuing education programs, co-op programs and internships. Off-campus study at Metropolitan State College, University of Colorado at Denver, Colorado State University. Study abroad in England. ROTC: Army (c), Air Force (c).
GENERAL DEGREE REQUIREMENTS 60 credit hours; 1 math course; computer course for most majors; internship (some majors).
MAJORS Accounting, architectural technologies, automotive technologies, biology/biological sciences, business administration/commerce/management, child care/child and family studies, computer information systems, deaf interpreter training, dietetics, drafting and design, early childhood education, electrical and electronics technologies, graphic arts, horticulture, landscape architecture/design, legal secretarial studies, liberal arts/general studies, machine and tool technologies, marketing/retailing/merchandising, mathematics, nuclear technology, nursing, physical sciences, publishing, respiratory therapy, science, secretarial studies/office management, social science, technical writing, transportation technologies, welding technology.
LIBRARY Learning Materials Center with 43,000 books, 509 microform titles, 360 periodicals, 22,000 records, tapes, and CDs. Acquisition spending 1994–95: $158,533.
COMPUTERS ON CAMPUS 500 computers for student use in computer labs, learning resource center, classrooms.
COLLEGE LIFE Student-run newspaper. ***Social organizations:*** 15 open to all. ***Most popular organizations:*** Interfaith Fellowship, Los Estudiantes, Alpha Mu Psi. ***Major annual event:*** Spring Fling BBQ. ***Student services:*** personal-psychological counseling, women's center. ***Campus security:*** 24-hour patrols, late-night transport-escort service.
HOUSING College housing not available.
ATHLETICS ***Intramural:*** basketball, volleyball.
CAREER PLANNING ***Director:*** Ms. Maggie Manuele, Counselor, 303-446-8811 Ext. 5480. ***Services:*** job fairs, career counseling, careers library, job bank, job interviews.
EXPENSES FOR 1995–96 State resident tuition: $1548 full-time, $51 per credit hour part-time. Nonresident tuition: $6738 full-time, $224 per credit hour part-time. Part-time mandatory fees per semester range from $11.95 to $41.45. Full-time mandatory fees: $107.
FINANCIAL AID ***College-administered undergrad aid 1995–96:*** 849 need-based scholarships (average $945), 671 non-need scholarships (average $715), low-interest long-term loans from external sources (average $2418), Federal Work-Study, 278 part-time jobs. ***Required forms for some financial aid applicants:*** institutional; accepted: CSS Financial Aid PROFILE, FAFSA. ***Priority deadline:*** 5/15. ***Waivers:*** full or partial for employees or children of employees.
APPLYING Open admission. ***Options:*** early entrance, deferred entrance. ***Required:*** TOEFL for international students, ACT ASSET. ***Recommended:*** SAT I or ACT. Test scores used for counseling/placement. ***Application deadline:*** rolling.
APPLYING/TRANSFER ***Required:*** standardized test scores. ***Entrance:*** noncompetitive. ***Application deadline:*** rolling.
CONTACT Dr. Patricia Lammers, Director of Admissions and Counseling, Front Range Community College, Westminster, CO 80030-2105, 303-466-8811 Ext. 5471.

ITT TECHNICAL INSTITUTE
Aurora, Colorado

UG Enrollment: 287	**Tuition: $16,379/deg prog**
Application Deadline: rolling	**Room & Board: N/Avail**

GENERAL Proprietary, primarily 2-year, coed. Part of ITT Educational Services, Inc. Awards terminal associate, bachelor's degrees. Founded 1984. ***Setting:*** 2-acre suburban campus with easy access to Denver. ***Total enrollment:*** 287. ***Faculty:*** 16 (14 full-time, 2 part-time); student-faculty ratio is 19:1.
ENROLLMENT PROFILE 287 students from 5 states and territories. 12% women, 88% men, 0% part-time, 96% state residents, 18% transferred in, 0% international, 31% 25 or older, 1% Native American, 19% Hispanic, 6% African American, 6% Asian American. ***Areas of study chosen:*** 100% engineering and applied sciences. ***Most popular recent major:*** electronics engineering technology.
FIRST-YEAR CLASS 86 total; 183 applied, 85% were accepted, 55% of whom enrolled.
ACADEMIC PROGRAM Core, engineering technology curriculum. Calendar: quarters. 56 courses offered in 1995–96. Academic remediation for entering students, summer session for credit.
GENERAL DEGREE REQUIREMENTS 90 credits for associate, 180 credits for bachelor's; computer course.
MAJORS Drafting and design, electronics engineering technology (B).
LIBRARY 1,200 books, 25 periodicals, 15 CD-ROMs, 50 records, tapes, and CDs.
COMPUTERS ON CAMPUS 81 computers for student use in computer center, learning resource center, classrooms provide access to Internet. Staffed computer lab on campus provides training in use of computers, software.
COLLEGE LIFE Student-run newspaper. ***Major annual events:*** Annual School Picnic, Halloween Costume Contest, Thanksgiving Food Drive. ***Campus security:*** 24-hour emergency response devices, late-night transport-escort service.
HOUSING College housing not available.
CAREER PLANNING ***Placement office:*** 1 full-time, 1 part-time staff. ***Director:*** Mr. Stephen Brown, Director of Placement, 303-695-1913. ***Services:*** job fairs, resume preparation, resume referral, career counseling, careers library, job bank, job interviews. Students must register freshman year. 26 organizations recruited on campus 1994–95.
AFTER GRADUATION 93% of class of 1994 had job offers within 6 months. 68% of students completing transfer associate program went directly to 4-year colleges.
EXPENSES FOR 1996–97 ***Application fee:*** $100. Tuition for associate degree program ranges from $16,379 to $18,575. Tuition for bachelor's degree program: $28,747. Full-time mandatory fees: $270. Tuition guaranteed not to increase for student's term of enrollment.
FINANCIAL AID ***College-administered undergrad aid 1995–96:*** need-based scholarships, low-interest long-term loans from external sources, Federal Work-Study, part-time jobs. ***Required forms:*** institutional, FAFSA; accepted: CSS Financial Aid PROFILE. ***Priority deadline:*** 9/1. ***Payment plan:*** installment. ***Waivers:*** full or partial for employees or children of employees.
APPLYING ***Option:*** deferred entrance. ***Required:*** school transcript, campus interview, TOEFL for international students, CPAt. Test scores used for admission and counseling/placement. ***Application deadline:*** rolling.
APPLYING/TRANSFER ***Required:*** standardized test scores, high school transcript, campus interview, college transcript. ***Entrance:*** moderately difficult. ***Application deadline:*** rolling. ***Contact:*** Mr. John Clark, Director of Education, 303-695-1913.
CONTACT Mr. Richard F. Hansen, Director of Recruitment, ITT Technical Institute, Aurora, CO 80014-1476, 303-695-1913 or toll-free 800-395-4488. ***Fax:*** 303-337-0683. College video available.

JOHNSON & WALES UNIVERSITY
Vail, Colorado

UG Enrollment: 39	**Tuition & Fees: $16,507**
Application Deadline: N/R	**Room & Board: N/Avail**

GENERAL Independent, 2-year, coed. Part of Johnson & Wales University. Awards terminal associate degrees (only candidates with bachelor's degree eligible for admission). Founded 1993. ***Setting:*** small-town campus. ***Total enrollment:*** 39. ***Faculty:*** 8 (all part-time). ***Notable Alumni:*** Emeril Lagasse, owner and executive chef of Emeril's; Edmond Abraim, president and CEO of H&B Powerbilt; Lee Geravitz, partner at Clever Cleaver Productions; Steve Cassarino, partner at Clever Cleaver Productions; Joel Scanlon, president of Eastern Butcher Block.
ENROLLMENT PROFILE 39 students from 22 states and territories. 36% women, 64% men, 15% state residents, 50% 25 or older, 3% African American.
FIRST-YEAR CLASS 39 total; 47 applied, 83% were accepted, 100% of whom enrolled.
ACADEMIC PROGRAM Core, professional culinary curriculum, honor code. Calendar: modular. 19 courses offered in 1995–96; average class size 22 in required courses. Services for LD students, adult/continuing education programs, internships.
GENERAL DEGREE REQUIREMENTS 99 credits; internship.
MAJOR Culinary arts.
LIBRARY Johnson & Wales at Vail Resource Center with 380 books, 20 periodicals, 3 CD-ROMs, 18 records, tapes, and CDs.
COMPUTERS ON CAMPUS 4 computers for student use in learning resource center. Staffed computer lab on campus provides training in use of computers, software.
COLLEGE LIFE ***Social organizations:*** 1 open to all. ***Most popular organization:*** Brewing Club. ***Major annual events:*** Graduation, Job Fair, Registration.
HOUSING College housing not available.
CAREER PLANNING ***Placement office:*** 1 full-time staff. ***Director:*** Mr. Todd Rymer, Director, 970-476-2993. ***Services:*** resume preparation, career counseling, careers library.
AFTER GRADUATION 98% of class of 1994 had job offers within 6 months.
EXPENSES FOR 1995–96 Tuition: $13,152 full-time. Full-time mandatory fees: $3355.
FINANCIAL AID ***College-administered undergrad aid 1995–96:*** 26 need-based scholarships (average $2300), non-need scholarships, low-interest long-term loans from college funds (average $1000), loans from external sources (average $4151), 5 Federal Work-Study (averaging $1500). ***Required forms:*** FAFSA. ***Priority deadline:*** 5/1. ***Payment plans:*** tuition prepayment, installment. ***Waivers:*** full or partial for employees or children of employees. ***Notification:*** continuous.
APPLYING ***Option:*** Common Application. ***Required:*** school transcript, TOEFL for international students. ***Recommended:*** SAT I or ACT, SAT II Subject Tests, SAT II: Writing Test. Test scores used for counseling/placement.
APPLYING/TRANSFER ***Required:*** high school transcript, college transcript. ***Recommended:*** standardized test scores.
CONTACT Mr. William Priante, Director of Culinary Admissions, Johnson & Wales University, 8 Abbot Park Place, Providence, RI 02903, 401-598-1000 or toll-free 800-342-5598 (out-of-state). ***E-mail:*** admissions@jwu.edu. College video available.

LAMAR COMMUNITY COLLEGE
Lamar, Colorado

UG Enrollment: 701	**Tuition & Fees (CO Res): $1960**
Application Deadline: 9/16	**Room & Board: $3864**

GENERAL State-supported, 2-year, coed. Part of Colorado Community College and Occupational Education System. Awards certificates, diplomas, transfer associate, terminal associate degrees. Founded 1937. ***Setting:*** 125-acre small-town campus. ***Endowment:*** $200,000. ***Total enrollment:*** 701. ***Faculty:*** 58 (20 full-time, 15% with terminal degrees, 38 part-time); student-faculty ratio is 12:1. ***Notable Alumni:*** Dwayne Nuzum, Elsie Lacy, Pat Robinette.
ENROLLMENT PROFILE 701 students from 26 states and territories, 7 other countries. 58% women, 44% part-time, 91% state residents, 8% transferred in, 79% have need-based financial aid, 21% have non-need-based financial aid, 2% international, 43% 25 or older, 2% Native American, 12% Hispanic, 3% African American, 1% Asian American. ***Areas of study chosen:*** 21% liberal arts/general studies, 12% agriculture, 12% biological and life sciences, 12% computer and information sciences, 6% vocational and home economics, 3% English language/literature/letters, 3% fine arts, 3% health professions and related sciences, 3% mathematics, 3% physical sciences, 3% psychology, 3% social sciences, 2% business management and administrative services, 2% education, 2% engineering and applied sciences, 2% predentistry, 2% prelaw, 2% premed, 2% prevet, 1% communications and journalism, 1% foreign language and literature, 1% natural resource sciences.
FIRST-YEAR CLASS 359 total; 427 applied, 100% were accepted, 84% of whom enrolled.
ACADEMIC PROGRAM Core, interdisciplinary curriculum, honor code. Calendar: semesters. 325 courses offered in 1995–96. Academic remediation for entering students, services for LD students, advanced placement, self-designed majors, summer session for credit, part-time degree program (evenings), adult/continuing education programs, co-op programs and internships.
GENERAL DEGREE REQUIREMENTS 64 semester hours; 1 math course; computer course for most majors; internship (some majors).

Peterson's Guide to Two-Year Colleges 1997

233

Lamar Community College (continued)

MAJORS Accounting, agricultural business, agricultural education, agricultural sciences, agronomy/soil and crop sciences, animal sciences, art/fine arts, behavioral sciences, biology/biological sciences, business administration/commerce/management, business education, communication, community services, computer information systems, computer management, computer programming, computer science, computer technologies, cosmetology, data processing, emergency medical technology, engineering and applied sciences, (pre)engineering sequence, English, equestrian studies, farm and ranch management, history, humanities, legal secretarial studies, liberal arts/general studies, literature, management information systems, marketing/retailing/merchandising, mathematics, medical secretarial studies, nursing, physical sciences, physics, practical nursing, quality control technology, range management, science, secretarial studies/office management, social science, social work, teacher aide studies, Western civilization and culture, word processing.
LIBRARY Learning Resources Center with 26,852 books, 170 microform titles, 134 periodicals, 3 CD-ROMs, 1,005 records, tapes, and CDs. Acquisition spending 1994–95: $28,788.
COMPUTERS ON CAMPUS Computer purchase plan available. 60 computers for student use in computer center, computer labs, research center, learning resource center, classrooms, library, dorms provide access to main academic computer. Staffed computer lab on campus provides training in use of computers, software. Academic computing expenditure 1994–95: $21,820.
COLLEGE LIFE Orientation program (2 days). Drama-theater group, choral group, student-run newspaper. 75% vote in student government elections. ***Major annual events:*** Homecoming, Earth Day, Antelope Night. ***Student services:*** personal-psychological counseling. ***Campus security:*** 24-hour emergency response devices and patrols, student patrols, controlled dormitory access.
HOUSING 170 college housing spaces available; 160 were occupied 1995–96. Freshmen guaranteed college housing. On-campus residence required in freshman year except if 21 or over, married, or living with relatives. ***Option:*** coed housing available. Resident assistants live in dorms.
ATHLETICS Member NJCAA. ***Intercollegiate:*** baseball M(s), basketball M(s), equestrian sports M/W, volleyball W(s). ***Intramural:*** golf. ***Contact:*** Mr. David Shellberg, Associate Dean for Student Services, 719-336-2248 Ext. 241.
CAREER PLANNING ***Services:*** resume preparation, career counseling, careers library.
AFTER GRADUATION 64% of students completing a degree program in 1994–95 went directly on to further study.
ESTIMATED EXPENSES FOR 1996–97 State resident tuition: $1712 full-time, $53.50 per semester hour part-time. Nonresident tuition: $5856 full-time, $183 per semester hour part-time. Part-time mandatory fees: $16.50 per semester hour. Full-time mandatory fees: $248. College room and board: $3864. College room only: $1300.
FINANCIAL AID ***College-administered undergrad aid 1995–96:*** 240 need-based scholarships (averaging $500), 85 non-need scholarships (averaging $500), low-interest long-term loans from external sources (averaging $3065), Federal Work-Study (averaging $1500). ***Required forms:*** institutional, FAFSA. ***Priority deadline:*** 6/1. ***Payment plan:*** installment. ***Waivers:*** full or partial for employees or children of employees and senior citizens. ***Notification:*** 6/30.
APPLYING Open admission. ***Options:*** early entrance, midyear entrance. ***Recommended:*** SAT I or ACT, TOEFL for international students. Test scores used for counseling/placement. ***Application deadline:*** 9/16. Preference given to state residents.
APPLYING/TRANSFER ***Entrance:*** noncompetitive. ***Application deadline:*** 9/16. ***Notification:*** continuous until 9/10. ***Contact:*** Mrs. Dottie Matthew, Registrar, 719-336-2248 Ext. 125.
CONTACT Mrs. Dottie Matthew, Registrar, Lamar Community College, Lamar, CO 81052-3999, 719-336-2248 Ext. 125. ***Fax:*** 719-336-2448. ***E-mail:*** b_carkhuff@mash,colorado.edu. College video available.

MORGAN COMMUNITY COLLEGE
Fort Morgan, Colorado

UG Enrollment: 997	**Tuition & Fees (CO Res): $1698**
Application Deadline: rolling	**Room & Board: N/Avail**

GENERAL State-supported, 2-year, coed. Part of Colorado Community College and Occupational Education System. Awards transfer associate, terminal associate degrees. Founded 1967. ***Setting:*** 20-acre rural campus with easy access to Denver. ***Total enrollment:*** 997. ***Faculty:*** 220 (33 full-time, 187 part-time); student-faculty ratio is 9:1.
ENROLLMENT PROFILE 997 students: 62% women, 38% men, 67% part-time, 98% state residents, 9% transferred in, 0% international, 56% 25 or older, 2% Native American, 10% Hispanic.
FIRST-YEAR CLASS 385 total; 436 applied, 100% were accepted, 88% of whom enrolled.
ACADEMIC PROGRAM Core, honor code. Calendar: semesters. 80 courses offered in 1995–96. Academic remediation for entering students, English as a second language program offered during academic year and summer, services for LD students, advanced placement, tutorials, summer session for credit, part-time degree program (daytime, evenings), adult/continuing education programs, internships.
GENERAL DEGREE REQUIREMENTS 62 credit hours; math/science requirements vary according to major; computer course.
MAJORS Accounting, automotive technologies, business administration/commerce/management, business economics, business education, electrical and electronics technologies, liberal arts/general studies, physical therapy, science, secretarial studies/office management.
LIBRARY Learning Resource Center with 123 books, 70 periodicals, 1 on-line bibliographic service, 4 CD-ROMs, 299 records, tapes, and CDs.
COMPUTERS ON CAMPUS 60 computers for student use in computer center, library provide access to off-campus computing facilities. Staffed computer lab on campus provides training in use of computers, software.
HOUSING College housing not available.
CAREER PLANNING ***Placement office:*** 2 full-time staff. ***Director:*** Ms. Connie Long, Director of Admissions and Retention, 970-867-3081. ***Service:*** career counseling.
EXPENSES FOR 1995–96 State resident tuition: $1620 full-time, $52.25 per credit hour part-time. Nonresident tuition: $7246 full-time, $233.75 per credit hour part-time. Part-time mandatory fees: $2.50 per credit hour. Full-time mandatory fees: $78.
FINANCIAL AID ***College-administered undergrad aid 1995–96:*** 180 need-based scholarships (averaging $1100), 190 non-need scholarships (averaging $725), short-term loans (averaging $50), low-interest long-term loans from external sources (averaging $1870), Federal Work-Study (averaging $800), 30 part-time jobs. ***Required forms:*** institutional; accepted: CSS Financial Aid PROFILE, FAFSA. ***Priority deadline:*** 4/1. ***Waivers:*** full or partial for employees or children of employees and senior citizens.
APPLYING Open admission. ***Options:*** early entrance, deferred entrance. ***Required:*** school transcript. ***Required for some:*** TOEFL for international students. Test scores used for counseling/placement. ***Application deadline:*** rolling.
APPLYING/TRANSFER ***Required:*** high school transcript. ***Application deadline:*** rolling.
CONTACT Student Services, Morgan Community College, Fort Morgan, CO 80701-4399, 970-867-3081 Ext. 109.

NORTHEASTERN JUNIOR COLLEGE
Sterling, Colorado

UG Enrollment: 2,734	**Tuition & Fees (Area Res): $805**
Application Deadline: 8/1	**Room & Board: $3600**

GENERAL State and locally supported, 2-year, coed. Awards certificates, transfer associate, terminal associate degrees. Founded 1941. ***Setting:*** 65-acre small-town campus. ***Endowment:*** $483,000. ***Total enrollment:*** 2,734. ***Faculty:*** 79 (65 full-time, 14 part-time); student-faculty ratio is 20:1. ***Notable Alumni:*** Ms. Marianne Banister, anchor and reporter for KABC-TV; Mr. Wellington Webb, mayor of Denver, Colorado; Mr. Cliff Meely, former NBA player.
ENROLLMENT PROFILE 2,734 students from 13 states and territories, 4 other countries. 54% women, 46% men, 25% part-time, 96% state residents, 3% transferred in, 60% have need-based financial aid, 50% have non-need-based financial aid, 2% international, 16% 25 or older, 1% Native American, 3% Hispanic, 2% African American. ***Areas of study chosen:*** 30% liberal arts/general studies, 15% agriculture, 15% business management and administrative services, 10% health professions and related sciences, 5% biological and life sciences, 5% computer and information sciences, 5% engineering and applied sciences, 3% education, 3% psychology, 2% premed, 2% prevet, 2% social sciences, 1% communications and journalism, 1% mathematics, 1% performing arts. ***Most popular recent majors:*** business administration/commerce/management, psychology, agricultural business.
FIRST-YEAR CLASS 450 total; 790 applied, 99% were accepted. 6% from top 10% of their high school class, 47% from top half.
ACADEMIC PROGRAM Core. Calendar: semesters. Academic remediation for entering students, services for LD students, advanced placement, summer session for credit, part-time degree program (daytime, evenings, summer), adult/continuing education programs, co-op programs. Study-abroad program.
GENERAL DEGREE REQUIREMENTS 62 credit hours; internship (some majors).
MAJORS Accounting, agricultural business, agricultural economics, agricultural education, agricultural sciences, agricultural technologies, agronomy/soil and crop sciences, anatomy, animal sciences, applied mathematics, art education, art/fine arts, automotive technologies, biology/biological sciences, business administration/commerce/management, business education, child care/child and family studies, computer science, computer technologies, corrections, cosmetology, data processing, early childhood education, economics, education, elementary education, emergency medical technology, (pre)engineering sequence, English, equestrian studies, farm and ranch management, fashion merchandising, forestry, health science, history, home economics, horticulture, humanities, journalism, landscaping/grounds maintenance, law enforcement/police sciences, legal secretarial studies, liberal arts/general studies, marine technology, marketing/retailing/merchandising, mathematics, medical secretarial studies, medical technology, music, music education, natural sciences, nursing, painting/drawing, pharmacy/pharmaceutical sciences, physical education, physical sciences, practical nursing, psychology, radio and television studies, science, secretarial studies/office management, social science, social work, studio art, theater arts/drama, tourism and travel, veterinary sciences, vocational education, zoology.
LIBRARY 45,260 books, 414 periodicals, 2,770 records, tapes, and CDs. Acquisition spending 1994–95: $30,000.
COMPUTERS ON CAMPUS 50 computers for student use in computer labs, library provide access to e-mail, Internet. Staffed computer lab on campus provides training in use of computers, software. Academic computing expenditure 1994–95: $50,000.
COLLEGE LIFE Orientation program (2 days, no cost, parents included). Drama-theater group, choral group, student-run newspaper, radio station. ***Social organizations:*** 31 open to all. ***Most popular organizations:*** Associated Student Government, Aggie Club, Rodeo Team and Club, Math/Science Club, Campus Christian Fellowship. ***Major annual events:*** Winter Formal, Spring Formal, Associated Student Government Elections. ***Student services:*** health clinic, personal-psychological counseling, women's center. ***Campus security:*** 24-hour emergency response devices, controlled dormitory access, night patrols by trained security personnel.
HOUSING 410 college housing spaces available; 395 were occupied 1995–96. Freshmen guaranteed college housing. On-campus residence required in freshman year except by special permission. ***Options:*** coed, single-sex (4 buildings) housing available. Resident assistants live in dorms.
ATHLETICS Member NJCAA. ***Intercollegiate:*** basketball M(s)/W(s), equestrian sports M(s)/W(s), golf W, tennis M/W, volleyball W(s). ***Intramural:*** basketball, cross-country running, football, racquetball, soccer, softball, track and field, volleyball. ***Contact:*** Mr. Lowell Roumph, Athletic Director, 970-522-6600 Ext. 624.
CAREER PLANNING ***Placement office:*** 2 full-time, 1 part-time staff; $2000 operating expenditure 1994–95. ***Director:*** Mrs. Judy Giacomini, Director of Counseling, 970-522-6600 Ext. 657. ***Services:*** career counseling, careers library.
AFTER GRADUATION 75% of students completing a degree program in 1994–95 went directly on to further study.
EXPENSES FOR 1995–96 ***Application fee:*** $15. Area resident tuition: $0 full-time, $39 per credit hour part-time. State resident tuition: $940 full-time, $84.50 per credit hour part-time. Nonresident tuition: $3760 full-time, $209 per credit hour part-time. Full-time mandatory fees: $805. College room and board: $3600 (minimum).
FINANCIAL AID ***College-administered undergrad aid 1995–96:*** need-based scholarships, 250 non-need scholarships (averaging $300), low-interest long-term loans from external sources (averaging $600), Federal Work-Study, 30 part-time jobs. ***Required forms:*** state, FAFSA; accepted: CSS Financial Aid PROFILE. ***Priority deadline:*** 4/1. ***Payment plans:*** installment, deferred payment. ***Waivers:*** full or partial for minority students and employees or children of employees.
APPLYING Open admission. ***Options:*** Common Application, early entrance, deferred entrance. ***Required:*** school transcript, TOEFL for international students. ***Required for***

some: SAT I or ACT. Test scores used for counseling/placement. ***Application deadline:*** 8/1. ***Notification:*** continuous until 8/1. Preference given to state residents.
APPLYING/TRANSFER ***Required:*** high school transcript, college transcript. ***Required for some:*** standardized test scores. ***Application deadline:*** 8/1. ***Notification:*** continuous until 8/1.
CONTACT Mr. Tim Adams, Director of Enrollment Management, Northeastern Junior College, Sterling, CO 80751-2344, 970-522-6600 Ext. 652 or toll-free 800-626-4637 (in-state). ***Fax:*** 970-522-4945. ***E-mail:*** tadams@csn.org.

OTERO JUNIOR COLLEGE
La Junta, Colorado

UG Enrollment: 1,000 | **Tuition & Fees (CO Res): $1548**
Application Deadline: 8/30 | **Room & Board: $3780**

GENERAL State-supported, 2-year, coed. Part of Colorado Community College and Occupational Education System. Awards transfer associate, terminal associate degrees. Founded 1941. ***Setting:*** 50-acre rural campus. ***Total enrollment:*** 1,000. ***Faculty:*** 53 (28 full-time, 100% with terminal degrees, 25 part-time); student-faculty ratio is 18:1.
ENROLLMENT PROFILE 1,000 students from 11 states and territories, 2 other countries. 54% women, 35% part-time, 92% state residents, 13% live on campus, 2% transferred in, 70% have need-based financial aid, 10% have non-need-based financial aid, 3% international, 52% 25 or older, 1% Native American, 36% Hispanic, 5% African American, 1% Asian American. ***Areas of study chosen:*** 67% liberal arts/general studies, 12% computer and information sciences, 7% health professions and related sciences, 4% biological and life sciences, 4% business management and administrative services, 3% education, 2% psychology, 1% engineering and applied sciences. ***Most popular recent majors:*** nursing, liberal arts/general studies, computer management.
FIRST-YEAR CLASS 425 total; 621 applied, 100% were accepted, 68% of whom enrolled. 6% from top 10% of their high school class, 28% from top quarter, 65% from top half.
ACADEMIC PROGRAM Core, honor code. Calendar: semesters. 200 courses offered in 1995–96. Academic remediation for entering students, advanced placement, tutorials, summer session for credit, part-time degree program (daytime, evenings), adult/continuing education programs, internships.
GENERAL DEGREE REQUIREMENTS 60 semester hours; computer course for all associate of applied science degree students; internship (some majors).
MAJORS Agricultural business, architectural technologies, automotive technologies, biology/biological sciences, business administration/commerce/management, child care/child and family studies, computer management, computer programming, data processing, early childhood education, education, elementary education, (pre)engineering sequence, history, humanities, legal secretarial studies, liberal arts/general studies, literature, marketing/retailing/merchandising, mathematics, medical secretarial studies, modern languages, nursing, physical sciences, political science/government, psychology, science, secretarial studies/office management, social science, theater arts/drama.
LIBRARY Wheeler Library with 33,000 books, 350 periodicals.
COMPUTERS ON CAMPUS 65 computers for student use in computer center, computer labs, library, dorms provide access to e-mail, Internet. Staffed computer lab on campus.
COLLEGE LIFE Drama-theater group, student-run newspaper. ***Student services:*** personal-psychological counseling. ***Campus security:*** 24-hour patrols, late-night transport-escort service.
HOUSING 166 college housing spaces available; 130 were occupied 1995–96. On-campus residence required in freshman year except if 21 or over, married, or living with relatives. ***Option:*** coed housing available. Resident assistants live in dorms.
ATHLETICS Member NJCAA. ***Intercollegiate:*** baseball M(s), basketball M(s)/W(s), golf M/W, volleyball W(s). ***Intramural:*** basketball, volleyball. ***Contact:*** Mr. Brad Franz, Director of Athletics, 719-384-6829.
CAREER PLANNING ***Placement office:*** 1 full-time staff. ***Director:*** Ms. Janice LaSalle, Director, Counseling Services, 719-384-6869. ***Services:*** job fairs, resume preparation, career counseling, careers library.
AFTER GRADUATION 36% of students completing a degree program in 1994–95 went directly on to further study.
EXPENSES FOR 1996–97 ***Application fee:*** $10. State resident tuition: $1224 full-time, $51 per semester hour part-time. Nonresident tuition: $4026 full-time, $167.75 per semester hour part-time. Part-time mandatory fees: $13.50 per semester hour. Full-time mandatory fees: $324. College room and board: $3780.
FINANCIAL AID ***College-administered undergrad aid 1995–96:*** need-based scholarships (average $1200), non-need scholarships (average $553), Federal Work-Study, part-time jobs. ***Required forms:*** FAFSA. ***Priority deadline:*** 4/15. ***Waivers:*** full or partial for senior citizens.
APPLYING Open admission. ***Options:*** early entrance, midyear entrance. ***Required:*** TOEFL for international students. ***Recommended:*** school transcript, ACT. Test scores used for counseling/placement. ***Application deadline:*** 8/30. ***Notification:*** continuous.
APPLYING/TRANSFER ***Recommended:*** college transcript. ***Required for some:*** college transcript. ***Application deadline:*** 8/30. ***Notification:*** continuous. ***Contact:*** Ms. Janice LaSalle, Director of Counseling Services, 719-384-6869.
CONTACT Dr. James W. Tisdale, Dean of Student Services, Otero Junior College, La Junta, CO 81050-3415, 719-384-6831. ***Fax:*** 719-384-6880. ***E-mail:*** j_schiro@ojc.axp.cccoes.edu.

PARKS JUNIOR COLLEGE
Denver, Colorado

UG Enrollment: 400 | **Tuition: $12,000/deg prog**
Application Deadline: rolling | **Room & Board: N/Avail**

GENERAL Proprietary, 2-year, coed. Awards terminal associate degrees. Founded 1895. ***Setting:*** 11-acre campus. ***Total enrollment:*** 400. ***Faculty:*** 73 (29 full-time, 44 part-time).
ENROLLMENT PROFILE 400 students from 3 states and territories. 75% women, 2% part-time, 98% state residents, 28% transferred in, 30% 25 or older, 2% Native American, 13% Hispanic, 10% African American, 1% Asian American.
FIRST-YEAR CLASS 75 total. Of the students who applied, 90% were accepted, 80% of whom enrolled. 1% from top 10% of their high school class, 9% from top quarter, 56% from top half.
ACADEMIC PROGRAM Core. Calendar: quarters. Summer session for credit, part-time degree program (daytime, evenings), internships.
GENERAL DEGREE REQUIREMENTS 96 credits; math requirement varies according to major; computer course for most majors.
MAJORS Accounting, business administration/commerce/management, computer programming, computer science, data processing, economics, English, fashion merchandising, geography, hospitality services, hotel and restaurant management, medical assistant technologies, psychology, retail management, secretarial studies/office management, tourism and travel.
LIBRARY 2,000 books, 58 periodicals, 24 records, tapes, and CDs.
COMPUTERS ON CAMPUS 66 computers for student use in computer center, computer labs. Staffed computer lab on campus provides training in use of computers, software.
COLLEGE LIFE Student-run newspaper. ***Student services:*** health clinic, personal-psychological counseling.
HOUSING College housing not available.
CAREER PLANNING ***Services:*** job fairs, resume preparation, resume referral, career counseling, careers library, job bank, job interviews.
AFTER GRADUATION 94% of class of 1994 had job offers within 6 months.
EXPENSES FOR 1996–97 ***Application fee:*** $25. Tuition: $12,000 per degree program. Tuition guaranteed not to increase for student's term of enrollment.
FINANCIAL AID ***College-administered undergrad aid 1995–96:*** need-based scholarships, 1 non-need scholarship ($4770), low-interest long-term loans from college funds (average $2500), loans from external sources (average $2500), Federal Work-Study. ***Required forms:*** state, institutional, FAFSA; accepted: CSS Financial Aid PROFILE. ***Priority deadline:*** 9/15.
APPLYING ***Option:*** deferred entrance. ***Required:*** TOEFL for international students, CPAt. Test scores used for admission. ***Application deadline:*** rolling.
APPLYING/TRANSFER ***Required:*** standardized test scores. ***Entrance:*** moderately difficult. ***Application deadline:*** rolling.
CONTACT Mr. Tony Wallace, Director of Admissions, Parks Junior College, Denver, CO 80229-4339, 303-457-2757.

PIKES PEAK COMMUNITY COLLEGE
Colorado Springs, Colorado

UG Enrollment: 6,615 | **Tuition & Fees (CO Res): $1353**
Application Deadline: rolling | **Room & Board: N/Avail**

GENERAL State-supported, 2-year, coed. Awards transfer associate, terminal associate degrees. Founded 1968. ***Setting:*** 212-acre urban campus. ***Total enrollment:*** 6,615. ***Faculty:*** 479 (117 full-time, 362 part-time).
ENROLLMENT PROFILE 6,615 students from 51 states and territories, 10 other countries. 59% women, 41% men, 64% part-time, 97% state residents, 14% transferred in, 1% international, 58% 25 or older, 2% Native American, 9% Hispanic, 8% African American, 4% Asian American.
FIRST-YEAR CLASS 2,891 total; 5,165 applied, 100% were accepted, 56% of whom enrolled.
ACADEMIC PROGRAM Core. Calendar: semesters. Academic remediation for entering students, English as a second language program offered during academic year, services for LD students, advanced placement, summer session for credit, part-time degree program (daytime, evenings, weekends, summer), adult/continuing education programs, co-op programs and internships. ROTC: Army.
GENERAL DEGREE REQUIREMENTS 60 credits; 1 course each in math and science; computer course.
MAJORS Accounting, anthropology, architectural technologies, art/fine arts, automotive technologies, aviation technology, biology/biological sciences, broadcasting, business administration/commerce/management, chemistry, commercial art, communication, computer information systems, computer science, computer technologies, criminal justice, dance, dental services, early childhood education, education, electrical and electronics technologies, (pre)engineering sequence, English, finance/banking, food services management, geology, gerontology, graphic arts, health science, heating/refrigeration/air conditioning, history, humanities, journalism, liberal arts/general studies, machine and tool technologies, marketing/retailing/merchandising, mathematics, mechanical design technology, nursing, optical technologies, physics, political science/government, psychology, science, secretarial studies/office management, social work, sociology, theater arts/drama, welding technology.
LIBRARY 35,120 books, 185 microform titles, 320 periodicals, 3,480 records, tapes, and CDs. Acquisition spending 1994–95: $69,312.
COMPUTERS ON CAMPUS 120 computers for student use in labs, library.
COLLEGE LIFE Drama-theater group, student-run newspaper, radio station. ***Student services:*** women's center. ***Campus security:*** 24-hour emergency response devices.
HOUSING College housing not available.
ATHLETICS ***Intramural:*** basketball, golf, soccer, volleyball.
CAREER PLANNING ***Services:*** job fairs, resume preparation, career counseling, careers library.
EXPENSES FOR 1995–96 State resident tuition: $1254 full-time, $52.50 per credit hour part-time. Nonresident tuition: $5610 full-time, $233.75 per credit hour part-time. Part-time mandatory fees per semester range from $29 to $49.50. Full-time mandatory fees: $99.
FINANCIAL AID ***College-administered undergrad aid 1995–96:*** 3,037 need-based scholarships, non-need scholarships (average $505), low-interest long-term loans from external sources (average $2042), Federal Work-Study. ***Required forms:*** institutional, FAFSA; accepted: CSS Financial Aid PROFILE. ***Priority deadline:*** 7/1. ***Payment plan:*** deferred payment. ***Waivers:*** full or partial for employees or children of employees and senior citizens.
APPLYING Open admission. ***Options:*** early entrance, deferred entrance. ***Recommended:*** SAT I or ACT. ***Required for some:*** TOEFL for international students. Test scores used for counseling/placement. ***Application deadline:*** rolling.
APPLYING/TRANSFER ***Application deadline:*** rolling.
CONTACT Ms. Roberta Erickson, Director of Admissions and Counseling, Pikes Peak Community College, 5675 South Academy Boulevard, Colorado Springs, CO 80906-5498, 719-540-7147. ***E-mail:*** harris@ppcc.colorado.edu.

Peterson's Guide to Two-Year Colleges 1997 235

Colorado

PIMA MEDICAL INSTITUTE
Denver, Colorado

UG Enrollment: 450	Tuition & Fees: $2000
Application Deadline: N/R	Room & Board: N/Avail

GENERAL Proprietary, 2-year, specialized. Awards terminal associate degrees. Founded 1972. *Setting:* urban campus. *Total enrollment:* 450. *Faculty:* 30.
ENROLLMENT PROFILE 450 students.
FIRST-YEAR CLASS 45 total. Of the students who applied, 90% were accepted, 100% of whom enrolled.
ACADEMIC PROGRAM Calendar: modular.
GENERAL DEGREE REQUIREMENTS 76 credits; math/science requirements vary according to program; computer course for most majors.
MAJORS Radiological technology, respiratory therapy.
HOUSING College housing not available.
EXPENSES FOR 1996–97 Application fee: $150. Tuition: $2000 (minimum) full-time. Full-time tuition ranges up to $17,000 according to program.
FINANCIAL AID College-administered undergrad aid 1995–96: need-based scholarships, low-interest long-term loans from external sources. *Required forms:* institutional; accepted: CSS Financial Aid PROFILE, FAFSA. *Application deadline:* continuous.
APPLYING *Required:* school transcript.
APPLYING/TRANSFER *Required:* high school transcript, college transcript.
CONTACT Ms. Susan Wallisa, Admissions Representative, Pima Medical Institute, 1701 West 72nd Avenue, #130, Denver, CO 80221, 303-426-1800.

PPI HEALTH CAREERS SCHOOL
Colorado Springs, Colorado

Enrollment: N/R	Tuition & Fees: $8680
Application Deadline: rolling	Room & Board: N/Avail

GENERAL Proprietary, 2-year, primarily women. Awards terminal associate degrees. Founded 1966. *Setting:* suburban campus. *Faculty:* 22 (4 full-time, 18 part-time); student-faculty ratio is 10:1.
ENROLLMENT PROFILE 90% women, 10% men.
ACADEMIC PROGRAM Calendar: clock hours.
GENERAL DEGREE REQUIREMENTS 99 credit hours; computer course.
MAJORS Medical assistant technologies, medical laboratory technology.
COMPUTERS ON CAMPUS 40 computers for student use.
HOUSING College housing not available.
EXPENSES FOR 1996–97 Tuition: $7680 full-time. Full-time mandatory fees: $1000.
FINANCIAL AID College-administered undergrad aid 1995–96: need-based scholarships, low-interest long-term loans from external sources, Federal Work-Study. *Required forms:* state, institutional, FAFSA; required for some: CSS Financial Aid PROFILE. *Application deadline:* continuous.
APPLYING Open admission. *Option:* Common Application. *Required:* campus interview. *Application deadline:* rolling.
APPLYING/TRANSFER *Required:* campus interview, college transcript, minimum 2.0 college GPA.
CONTACT Mrs. Audrey DeRubis, Director of Admissions, PPI Health Careers School, Colorado Springs, CO 80909, 719-596-7400.

PUEBLO COLLEGE OF BUSINESS AND TECHNOLOGY
Pueblo, Colorado

UG Enrollment: 200	Tuition & Fees: $7680
Application Deadline: rolling	Room & Board: N/Avail

GENERAL Proprietary, 2-year, coed. Awards terminal associate degrees. Founded 1925. *Total enrollment:* 200. *Faculty:* 12.
ENROLLMENT PROFILE 200 students.
FIRST-YEAR CLASS 65 total. Of the students who applied, 80% were accepted, 75% of whom enrolled.
ACADEMIC PROGRAM Calendar: modular.
GENERAL DEGREE REQUIREMENT 96 contact hours.
MAJORS Computer science, medical assistant technologies, mental health/rehabilitation counseling, paralegal studies, secretarial studies/office management.
EXPENSES FOR 1996–97 Tuition: $7680 full-time.
APPLYING *Required:* school transcript. *Application deadline:* rolling.
APPLYING/TRANSFER *Required:* college transcript.
CONTACT Mr. Lorenzo Montoya, Admissions Representative, Pueblo College of Business and Technology, Pueblo, CO 81004, 719-545-3100.

PUEBLO COMMUNITY COLLEGE
Pueblo, Colorado

UG Enrollment: 4,127	Tuition & Fees (CO Res): $2044
Application Deadline: rolling	Room & Board: N/Avail

GENERAL State-supported, 2-year, coed. Part of Colorado Community College and Occupational Education System. Awards certificates, transfer associate, terminal associate degrees. Founded 1979. *Setting:* 35-acre urban campus. *Endowment:* $1.6 million. *Total enrollment:* 4,127. *Faculty:* 288 (100% of full-time faculty have terminal degrees); student-faculty ratio is 16:1.
ENROLLMENT PROFILE 4,127 students: 60% women, 58% part-time, 99% state residents, 5% transferred in, 57% have need-based financial aid, 10% have non-need-based financial aid, 1% international, 62% 25 or older, 2% Native American, 30% Hispanic, 3% African American, 1% Asian American. *Areas of study chosen:* 39% library and information studies, 7% health professions and related sciences. *Most popular recent majors:* nursing, criminal justice.
FIRST-YEAR CLASS 1,472 total; 2,388 applied, 100% were accepted, 62% of whom enrolled.
ACADEMIC PROGRAM Core, general transfer technical curriculum, honor code. Calendar: semesters. 800 courses offered in 1995–96. Academic remediation for entering students, services for LD students, advanced placement, self-designed majors, tutorials, summer session for credit, part-time degree program (daytime, evenings), external degree programs, adult/continuing education programs, co-op programs and internships. Study abroad in England.
GENERAL DEGREE REQUIREMENTS 60 credits; math/science requirements vary according to program; computer course for students without computer competency; internship (some majors).
MAJORS Accounting, automotive technologies, behavioral sciences, broadcasting, business administration/commerce/management, civil engineering technology, computer graphics, computer information systems, corrections, criminal justice, culinary arts, dental services, early childhood education, electrical and electronics technologies, engineering technology, food services management, jewelry and metalsmithing, law enforcement/police sciences, legal secretarial studies, liberal arts/general studies, machine and tool technologies, medical records services, medical secretarial studies, nursing, occupational therapy, optometric/ophthalmic technologies, paralegal studies, physical therapy, radiological technology, respiratory therapy, science, secretarial studies/office management, tourism and travel, welding technology.
LIBRARY Pueblo Community College Learning Resources Center with 21,532 books, 2,563 microform titles, 221 periodicals, 2 on-line bibliographic services, 23 CD-ROMs, 7,452 records, tapes, and CDs. Acquisition spending 1994–95: $110,888.
COMPUTERS ON CAMPUS 212 computers for student use in computer labs, learning resource center, learning center, classrooms, library provide access to main academic computer. Staffed computer lab on campus provides training in use of computers, software. Academic computing expenditure 1994–95: $138,240.
COLLEGE LIFE Choral group. *Social organizations:* 20 open to all. *Most popular organizations:* Criminal Justice Club, Phi Beta Lambda, Automotive Society, Nursing Club, Creating Health Attitudes Together (CHAT). *Major annual events:* Spring Fling, Fall Ball, Christmas Party. *Student services:* personal-psychological counseling, women's center. *Campus security:* 24-hour emergency response devices, student patrols, late-night transport-escort service.
HOUSING College housing not available.
CAREER PLANNING *Placement office:* 1 full-time staff; $295,399 operating expenditure 1994–95. *Director:* Ms. Ruth White, Counselor for Career Services, 719-549-3464. *Services:* resume preparation, career counseling, job bank.
EXPENSES FOR 1996–97 State resident tuition: $1813 full-time. Nonresident tuition: $7522 full-time. Part-time tuition per semester ranges from $72.80 to $684.80 for state residents, $263.10 to $2778 for nonresidents. Part-time mandatory fees: $7.70 per credit. Full-time mandatory fees: $231.
FINANCIAL AID College-administered undergrad aid 1995–96: 1,503 need-based scholarships (average $1100), 292 non-need scholarships (average $580), short-term loans (average $50), low-interest long-term loans from external sources (average $2400), Federal Work-Study. *Required forms:* institutional, FAFSA; required for some: state; accepted: CSS Financial Aid PROFILE. *Priority deadline:* 4/1. *Waivers:* full or partial for minority students, employees or children of employees, and senior citizens.
APPLYING Open admission except for allied health programs. *Options:* early entrance, deferred entrance, midyear entrance. *Required:* TOEFL for international students. *Required for some:* ACT. Test scores used for counseling/placement. *Application deadline:* rolling. *Notification:* continuous until 8/15.
APPLYING/TRANSFER *Required for some:* standardized test scores. *Entrance:* noncompetitive. *Application deadline:* rolling. *Notification:* continuous until 8/15. *Contact:* Ms. Deidre Frazier, Counselor, 719-549-3375.
CONTACT Mr. Dan Cordova, Admissions Counselor, Pueblo Community College, 900 West Orman Avenue, Pueblo, CO 81004-1499, 719-549-3013. *E-mail:* pcc.admit@pcc.cccoes.edu. College video available.

RED ROCKS COMMUNITY COLLEGE
Lakewood, Colorado

UG Enrollment: 6,939	Tuition & Fees (CO Res): $1983
Application Deadline: rolling	Room & Board: N/Avail

GENERAL State-supported, 2-year, coed. Part of Colorado Community College and Occupational Education System. Awards transfer associate, terminal associate degrees. Founded 1969. *Setting:* 120-acre urban campus with easy access to Denver. *Total enrollment:* 6,939. *Faculty:* 276 (63 full-time, 213 part-time).
ENROLLMENT PROFILE 6,939 students from 27 states and territories, 53 other countries. 56% women, 76% part-time, 97% state residents, 14% transferred in, 2% international, 69% 25 or older, 1% Native American, 6% Hispanic, 1% African American, 1% Asian American. *Most popular recent majors:* liberal arts/general studies, criminal justice, computer science.
FIRST-YEAR CLASS 1,704 total. Of the students who applied, 100% were accepted, 90% of whom enrolled.
ACADEMIC PROGRAM Core. Calendar: semesters. Academic remediation for entering students, English as a second language program offered during academic year and summer, summer session for credit, part-time degree program (daytime, evenings, weekends, summer), adult/continuing education programs, co-op programs. Off-campus study at Metropolitan State College, University of Colorado at Denver, Colorado School of Mines. Study abroad in England, Mexico. ROTC: Army (c).
GENERAL DEGREE REQUIREMENTS 60 credits; math/science requirements vary according to program.
MAJORS Accounting, art/fine arts, automotive technologies, biology/biological sciences, business administration/commerce/management, carpentry, chemistry, communication, computer programming, computer science, computer technologies, criminal justice, drafting and design, economics, electrical and electronics technologies, English, fire science, French, geology, German, history, humanities, industrial and heavy equipment maintenance, liberal arts/general studies, marketing/retailing/merchandising, mathematics, mechanical engineering technology, physics, political science/government, psychology, public

administration, real estate, sanitation technology, science, secretarial studies/office management, sociology, solar technologies, Spanish, surveying technology, water resources, welding technology.
LIBRARY 45,511 books, 94,167 microform titles, 304 periodicals, 3,604 records, tapes, and CDs.
COMPUTERS ON CAMPUS 200 computers for student use in computer center, computer labs, library provide access to off-campus computing facilities, e-mail, on-line services. Staffed computer lab on campus provides training in use of computers, software.
COLLEGE LIFE Drama-theater group, student-run newspaper. *Student services:* personal-psychological counseling, women's center. *Campus security:* 24-hour emergency response devices and patrols.
HOUSING College housing not available.
ATHLETICS *Intramural:* volleyball. *Contact:* Mr. Jim Jones, Director of Student Activities, 303-988-6160 Ext. 372.
CAREER PLANNING *Director:* Ms. Nancy Carlson, Director of Job Placement, 303-988-6160 Ext. 389. *Service:* career counseling.
EXPENSES FOR 1996–97 State resident tuition: $1755 full-time, $58.50 per credit hour part-time. Nonresident tuition: $7313 full-time, $243.75 per credit hour part-time. Part-time mandatory fees per semester range from $16.30 to $89.30. Full-time mandatory fees: $228.
FINANCIAL AID *College-administered undergrad aid 1995–96:* need-based scholarships, non-need scholarships, low-interest long-term loans from external sources, Federal Work-Study, part-time jobs. *Required forms:* institutional. *Priority deadline:* 4/1. *Payment plan:* deferred payment. *Waivers:* full or partial for senior citizens.
APPLYING Open admission. *Option:* early entrance. *Required:* TOEFL for international students. Test scores used for counseling/placement. *Application deadline:* rolling. *Notification:* continuous.
APPLYING/TRANSFER *Application deadline:* rolling. *Notification:* continuous.
CONTACT Mr. Bob Schantz, Registrar/Director of Admissions and Records, Red Rocks Community College, 13300 West 6th Avenue, Lakewood, CO 80401, 303-988-6160 Ext. 357. *Fax:* 303-969-8039. College video available.

TRINIDAD STATE JUNIOR COLLEGE
Trinidad, Colorado

UG Enrollment: 2,142	Tuition & Fees (CO Res): $1397
Application Deadline: rolling	Room & Board: $3130

GENERAL State-supported, 2-year, coed. Part of Colorado Community College and Occupational Education System. Awards certificates, transfer associate, terminal associate degrees. Founded 1925. *Setting:* 17-acre small-town campus. *Educational spending 1994–95:* $1542 per undergrad. *Total enrollment:* 2,142. *Faculty:* 111 (50 full-time, 61 part-time); student-faculty ratio is 17:1.
ENROLLMENT PROFILE 2,142 students from 33 states and territories, 11 other countries. 46% women, 28% part-time, 80% state residents, 23% transferred in, 1% international, 26% 25 or older, 1% Native American, 42% Hispanic, 2% African American, 1% Asian American.
FIRST-YEAR CLASS 303 total. Of the students who applied, 100% were accepted.
ACADEMIC PROGRAM Core. Calendar: semesters. Academic remediation for entering students, English as a second language program offered during academic year and summer, services for LD students, advanced placement, tutorials, summer session for credit, part-time degree program (daytime, evenings, weekends, summer), adult/continuing education programs, co-op programs and internships.
GENERAL DEGREE REQUIREMENTS 64 credits; math/science requirements vary according to program; computer course for most majors.
MAJORS Accounting, art education, automotive technologies, biology/biological sciences, business administration/commerce/management, carpentry, chemistry, civil engineering technology, commercial art, computer information systems, computer science, construction technologies, corrections, cosmetology, data processing, drafting and design, early childhood education, education, electrical and electronics technologies, engineering (general), (pre)engineering sequence, English, farm and ranch management, forestry, industrial and heavy equipment maintenance, journalism, landscape architecture/design, law enforcement/police sciences, liberal arts/general studies, mining technology, music, natural resource management, nursing, occupational safety and health, physical education, practical nursing, psychology, science, secretarial studies/office management, soil conservation, theater arts/drama.
LIBRARY Frendenthal Library with 56,000 books, 30 microform titles, 260 periodicals, 1 CD-ROM, 1,788 records, tapes, and CDs. Acquisition spending 1994–95: $127,251.
COMPUTERS ON CAMPUS 125 computers for student use in computer center, computer labs, learning resource center, classrooms, library. Staffed computer lab on campus provides training in use of computers, software. Academic computing expenditure 1994–95: $263,888.
COLLEGE LIFE Drama-theater group, choral group, student-run newspaper. 70% vote in student government elections. *Social organizations:* 10 open to all. *Most popular organizations:* Student Association, International Club, Gunsmithing Club. *Major annual events:* Winter Formal, Trinidad State Junior College Basketball Tourney, Job Fair.
HOUSING 325 college housing spaces available; 182 were occupied 1995–96. No special consideration for freshman housing applicants. Off-campus living permitted. *Option:* single-sex housing available. Resident assistants live in dorms.
ATHLETICS Member NJCAA. *Intercollegiate:* baseball M(s), basketball M(s), golf M(s)/W, volleyball W(s). *Intramural:* badminton, basketball, bowling, football, riflery, skiing (cross-country), skiing (downhill), softball, table tennis (Ping-Pong), tennis, volleyball. *Contact:* Mr. James Toupal, Director of Athletics, 719-846-5510.
CAREER PLANNING *Placement office:* 2 full-time, 1 part-time staff; $78,762 operating expenditure 1994–95. *Director:* Mr. Roger Brunelli, Job Placement, 719-846-5556. *Services:* job fairs, resume preparation, resume referral, career counseling, job interviews.
EXPENSES FOR 1995–96 *Application fee:* $10. State resident tuition: $1254 full-time, $52.25 per semester hour part-time. Nonresident tuition: $4206 full-time, $175.25 per semester hour part-time. Part-time mandatory fees per semester range from $10 to $19. Full-time mandatory fees: $143. College room and board: $3130 (minimum).
FINANCIAL AID *College-administered undergrad aid 1995–96:* 743 need-based scholarships (average $676), 249 non-need scholarships (average $388), short-term loans (average $50), low-interest long-term loans from external sources (average $1727), Federal Work-Study. *Required forms:* institutional, FAFSA. *Priority deadline:* 5/1. *Payment plan:* installment. *Waivers:* full or partial for employees or children of employees and senior citizens. *Notification:* 7/1.
APPLYING Open admission. *Options:* early entrance, deferred entrance, midyear entrance. *Recommended:* SAT I or ACT, SAT II Subject Tests, TOEFL for international students. *Required for some:* ACT, ACT ASSET. Test scores used for counseling/placement. *Application deadline:* rolling. *Notification:* continuous.
APPLYING/TRANSFER *Recommended:* standardized test scores. *Required for some:* standardized test scores. *Entrance:* minimally difficult. *Application deadline:* rolling. *Notification:* continuous. *Contact:* Mr. Roger Brunelli, Counselor, 719-846-5556.
CONTACT Mr. John Giron, Dean of Students, Trinidad State Junior College, Trinidad, CO 81082-2396, 719-846-5621 or toll-free 800-621-8752. *Fax:* 719-846-5667.

CONNECTICUT

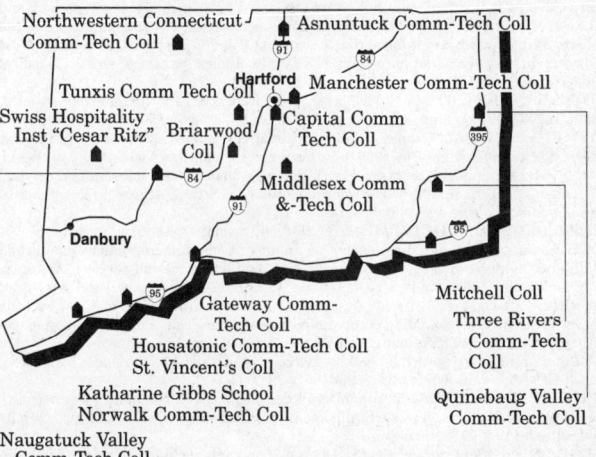

ASNUNTUCK COMMUNITY-TECHNICAL COLLEGE
Enfield, Connecticut

UG Enrollment: 2,051	Tuition & Fees (CT Res): $1722
Application Deadline: rolling	Room & Board: N/Avail

GENERAL State-supported, 2-year, coed. Part of Connecticut Community–Technical College System. Awards transfer associate, terminal associate degrees. Founded 1972. *Setting:* 4-acre small-town campus. *Total enrollment:* 2,051. *Faculty:* 112 (26 full-time, 86 part-time).
ENROLLMENT PROFILE 2,051 students from 2 states and territories, 4 other countries. 70% women, 85% part-time, 97% state residents, 12% transferred in, 1% international, 87% 25 or older, 0% Native American, 0% Hispanic, 1% African American, 0% Asian American. *Most popular recent majors:* business administration/commerce/management, liberal arts/general studies, computer science.
FIRST-YEAR CLASS 654 total; 690 applied, 100% were accepted, 95% of whom enrolled. 20% from top 10% of their high school class, 70% from top half.
ACADEMIC PROGRAM Core, honor code. Calendar: semesters. Academic remediation for entering students, English as a second language program offered during academic year, advanced placement, self-designed majors, summer session for credit, part-time degree program (daytime, evenings, summer), adult/continuing education programs.
GENERAL DEGREE REQUIREMENTS 60 credits; 1 math/science course.
MAJORS Accounting, art/fine arts, business administration/commerce/management, communication, computer programming, computer science, drug and alcohol/substance abuse counseling, food services management, human services, industrial administration, liberal arts/general studies, secretarial studies/office management.
LIBRARY 27,655 books, 298 periodicals, 1,017 records, tapes, and CDs.
COMPUTERS ON CAMPUS 90 computers for student use in computer center, learning resource center, library. Staffed computer lab on campus.
COLLEGE LIFE Drama-theater group. *Social organizations:* 9 open to all. *Student services:* women's center.
HOUSING College housing not available.
CAREER PLANNING *Director:* Ms. Gloria Hill, Counselor, 860-253-3025. *Services:* resume preparation, career counseling.
AFTER GRADUATION 75% of students completing a degree program in 1994–95 went directly on to further study.
EXPENSES FOR 1996–97 *Application fee:* $10. State resident tuition: $1722 full-time, $65 per credit part-time. Nonresident tuition: $4842 full-time, $195 per credit part-time. Tuition for nonresidents who are eligible for the New England Regional Student Program: $2502 full-time, $97.50 per credit part-time.
FINANCIAL AID *College-administered undergrad aid 1995–96:* need-based scholarships, low-interest long-term loans, Federal Work-Study, part-time jobs. *Required forms:* CSS Financial Aid PROFILE, institutional, FAFSA. *Application deadline:* continuous. *Waivers:* full or partial for employees or children of employees and senior citizens.
APPLYING Open admission. *Options:* early entrance, deferred entrance. *Application deadline:* rolling. *Notification:* continuous.
APPLYING/TRANSFER *Application deadline:* rolling. *Notification:* continuous. *Contact:* Ms. Donna Shaw, Assistant Director of Student Services, 860-253-3018.

Asnuntuck Community-Technical College (continued)

CONTACT Mr. Vincent S. Fulginiti, Director of Admissions, Asnuntuck Community-Technical College, Enfield, CT 06082-3800, 860-253-3011. ***Fax:*** 860-253-9310.

BRIARWOOD COLLEGE
Southington, Connecticut

UG Enrollment: 541	**Tuition & Fees: $10,010**
Application Deadline: rolling	**Room Only: $2296**

GENERAL Proprietary, 2-year, coed. Awards certificates, diplomas, transfer associate, terminal associate degrees. Founded 1966. ***Setting:*** 32-acre small-town campus with easy access to Hartford and Boston. ***Endowment:*** $12,700. ***Total enrollment:*** 541. ***Faculty:*** 63 (23 full-time, 40 part-time); student-faculty ratio is 12:1.
ENROLLMENT PROFILE 541 students from 5 states and territories, 6 other countries. 80% women, 20% men, 45% part-time, 95% state residents, 17% live on campus, 30% transferred in, 83% have need-based financial aid, 1% international, 37% 25 or older, 1% Native American, 8% Hispanic, 8% African American, 1% Asian American. ***Areas of study chosen:*** 52% health professions and related sciences, 9% business management and administrative services, 5% vocational and home economics, 3% communications and journalism, 3% computer and information sciences, 3% liberal arts/general studies. ***Most popular recent majors:*** child care/child and family studies, paralegal studies, medical records services.
FIRST-YEAR CLASS 160 total; 392 applied, 100% were accepted, 41% of whom enrolled. 2% from top 10% of their high school class, 17% from top quarter, 50% from top half.
ACADEMIC PROGRAM Transfer and vocational curriculum, honor code. Calendar: semesters. 252 courses offered in 1995–96. Academic remediation for entering students, English as a second language program offered during academic year and summer, services for LD students, tutorials, summer session for credit, part-time degree program, adult/continuing education programs, internships.
GENERAL DEGREE REQUIREMENTS 65 credits; computer course; internship.
MAJORS Accounting, broadcasting, business administration/commerce/management, child care/child and family studies, communication, criminal justice, dental services, dietetics, fashion merchandising, funeral service, hotel and restaurant management, legal secretarial studies, liberal arts/general studies, medical assistant technologies, medical records services, medical secretarial studies, occupational therapy, paralegal studies, retail management, secretarial studies/office management, tourism and travel, word processing.
LIBRARY Pupillo Library with 10,589 books, 150 periodicals, 10 CD-ROMs, 35 records, tapes, and CDs. Acquisition spending 1994–95: $19,000.
COMPUTERS ON CAMPUS 52 computers for student use in computer labs, learning resource center, classrooms, library. Staffed computer lab on campus. Academic computing expenditure 1994–95: $100,000.
COLLEGE LIFE Orientation program (2 days, $25, parents included). Student-run radio station. ***Social organizations:*** 3 open to all. ***Most popular organizations:*** Phi Beta Lambda, Student Government, Yearbook Committee, Psi Beta, Allied Health Club. ***Major annual events:*** Family Day, Spring Prom, Class Night. ***Student services:*** personal-psychological counseling. ***Campus security:*** late-night transport-escort service, 16-hour patrols by trained security personnel.
HOUSING 144 college housing spaces available; 90 were occupied 1995–96. No special consideration for freshman housing applicants. Off-campus living permitted. ***Option:*** single-sex housing available. Resident assistants live in dorms.
ATHLETICS ***Intercollegiate:*** tennis W. ***Intramural:*** basketball, soccer, softball, tennis, volleyball. ***Contact:*** Mr. Jack Bordieri, Activities Director, 860-628-4751.
CAREER PLANNING ***Placement office:*** 1 part-time staff; $32,000 operating expenditure 1994–95. ***Director:*** Ms. Kristine Gradowski, Director of Placement, 860-628-4751. ***Services:*** resume preparation, resume referral, career counseling, job interviews. Students must register sophomore year. 100 organizations recruited on campus 1994–95.
AFTER GRADUATION 82% of class of 1994 had job offers within 6 months. 11% of students completing a degree program went directly on to further study.
EXPENSES FOR 1996–97 ***Application fee:*** $25. Tuition: $9795 full-time, $150 per credit hour part-time. Full-time mandatory fees: $215. College room only: $2296. Tuition guaranteed not to increase for student's term of enrollment.
FINANCIAL AID ***College-administered undergrad aid 1995–96:*** 308 need-based scholarships (average $1107), 6 non-need scholarships (average $750), low-interest long-term loans from external sources (average $2625), 38 part-time jobs. ***Required forms:*** institutional, FAFSA. ***Priority deadline:*** 5/1. ***Payment plan:*** installment. ***Waivers:*** full or partial for employees or children of employees. ***Notification:*** continuous.
APPLYING ***Option:*** midyear entrance. ***Required:*** school transcript. ***Required for some:*** recommendations, campus interview, TOEFL for international students. Test scores used for counseling/placement. ***Application deadline:*** rolling.
APPLYING/TRANSFER ***Required:*** high school transcript, college transcript. ***Entrance:*** minimally difficult. ***Application deadline:*** rolling. ***Contact:*** Ms. Barbara R. MacKay, Registrar/Dean of Enrollment Management, 860-628-4751 Ext. 22.
CONTACT Mrs. Debra LaRoche, Director of Admissions, Briarwood College, Southington, CT 06489-1057, 860-628-4751 Ext. 25 or toll-free 800-952-2444 (in-state). ***Fax:*** 860-628-6444. College video available.

❖ ***See page 714 for a narrative description.*** ❖

CAPITAL COMMUNITY TECHNICAL COLLEGE
Hartford, Connecticut

UG Enrollment: 2,900	**Tuition & Fees (CT Res): $2112**
Application Deadline: rolling	**Room & Board: N/Avail**

GENERAL State-supported, 2-year, coed. Part of Connecticut Community–Technical College System. Awards transfer associate, terminal associate degrees. Founded 1946. ***Setting:*** 10-acre urban campus. ***Total enrollment:*** 2,900. ***Faculty:*** 174 (70 full-time, 104 part-time); student-faculty ratio is 17:1.
ENROLLMENT PROFILE 2,900 students from 4 states and territories, 15 other countries. 62% women, 79% part-time, 97% state residents, 2% international, 67% 25 or older, 0% Native American, 17% Hispanic, 34% African American, 6% Asian American. ***Areas of study chosen:*** 29% liberal arts/general studies, 10% engineering and applied sciences, 8% health professions and related sciences, 4% business management and administrative services, 3% computer and information sciences, 3% education. ***Most popular recent majors:*** nursing, liberal arts/general studies.
FIRST-YEAR CLASS Of the students who applied, 100% were accepted, 50% of whom enrolled.
ACADEMIC PROGRAM Career-preparation curriculum. Calendar: semesters. Academic remediation for entering students, English as a second language program offered during academic year and summer, services for LD students, summer session for credit, part-time degree program (daytime, evenings), adult/continuing education programs.
GENERAL DEGREE REQUIREMENTS 60 credit hours; 1 math course.
MAJORS Accounting, architectural technologies, business administration/commerce/management, chemical engineering technology, civil engineering technology, computer technologies, data processing, drug and alcohol/substance abuse counseling, early childhood education, electrical and electronics technologies, electrical engineering technology, electronics engineering technology, emergency medical technology, liberal arts/general studies, manufacturing technology, mechanical engineering technology, nursing, radiological technology, secretarial studies/office management.
LIBRARY Arthur C. Banks, Jr. Library with 54,188 books, 217 microform titles, 432 periodicals, 6 CD-ROMs, 1,525 records, tapes, and CDs.
COMPUTERS ON CAMPUS 50 computers for student use in computer labs, learning resource center, library. Staffed computer lab on campus.
COLLEGE LIFE ***Student services:*** personal-psychological counseling.
HOUSING College housing not available.
CAREER PLANNING ***Director:*** Ms. Linda Domenitz, Director of Career Development and Placement, 860-520-7832. ***Services:*** job fairs, resume preparation, career counseling, careers library, job bank, job interviews.
EXPENSES FOR 1996–97 State resident tuition: $1560 full-time, $65 per credit hour part-time. Nonresident tuition: $4680 full-time, $195 per credit hour part-time. Part-time mandatory fees: $36 per semester. Full-time mandatory fees: $162.
FINANCIAL AID ***College-administered undergrad aid 1995–96:*** 1,267 need-based scholarships (average $800), 20 non-need scholarships (average $700), short-term loans (average $50), low-interest long-term loans from college funds (average $1000), loans from external sources (average $2625), Federal Work-Study, 80 part-time jobs. ***Required forms:*** institutional, FAFSA. ***Priority deadline:*** 7/15.
APPLYING Open admission except for nursing, emergency medical technology, radiologic technology programs. ***Options:*** early entrance, deferred entrance, midyear entrance. ***Required:*** TOEFL for international students. ***Required for some:*** SAT I. Test scores used for counseling/placement. ***Application deadline:*** rolling. ***Notification:*** continuous until 9/1.
APPLYING/TRANSFER ***Required for some:*** standardized test scores. ***Entrance:*** noncompetitive. ***Application deadline:*** rolling. ***Notification:*** continuous until 9/1.
CONTACT Ms. Judith Pierson, Director of Enrollment Services, Capital Community Technical College, 61 Woodland Street, Hartford, CT 06105-2354, 860-520-7830. College video available.

GATEWAY COMMUNITY-TECHNICAL COLLEGE
New Haven, Connecticut

UG Enrollment: 4,843	**Tuition & Fees (CT Res): $1722**
Application Deadline: 9/9	**Room & Board: N/Avail**

GENERAL State-supported, 2-year, coed. Part of Connecticut Community–Technical College System. Awards certificates, transfer associate, terminal associate degrees. Founded 1968. ***Setting:*** 5-acre urban campus with easy access to New York City. ***Educational spending 1994–95:*** $3341 per undergrad. ***Total enrollment:*** 4,843. ***Faculty:*** 248 (85 full-time, 16% with terminal degrees, 163 part-time); student-faculty ratio is 22:1.
ENROLLMENT PROFILE 4,843 students from 6 states and territories, 29 other countries. 61% women, 39% men, 75% part-time, 98% state residents, 8% transferred in, 22% have need-based financial aid, 1% international, 60% 25 or older, 1% Native American, 7% Hispanic, 18% African American, 3% Asian American. ***Areas of study chosen:*** 32% liberal arts/general studies, 24% business management and administrative services, 17% health professions and related sciences, 8% engineering and applied sciences, 7% computer and information sciences, 6% social sciences, 5% education. ***Most popular recent majors:*** liberal arts/general studies, business administration/commerce/management.
FIRST-YEAR CLASS 1,526 total; 2,624 applied, 100% were accepted, 58% of whom enrolled.
ACADEMIC PROGRAM Calendar: semesters. 600 courses offered in 1995–96. Academic remediation for entering students, English as a second language program offered during academic year and summer, services for LD students, advanced placement, summer session for credit, part-time degree program (daytime, evenings), external degree programs, adult/continuing education programs, internships. Off-campus study at Southern Connecticut State University.
GENERAL DEGREE REQUIREMENTS 60 credit hours; 6 semester hours each of math and science; computer course; internship (some majors).
MAJORS Accounting, automotive technologies, aviation technology, biomedical technologies, business administration/commerce/management, computer graphics, computer technologies, data processing, dietetics, drug and alcohol/substance abuse counseling, early childhood education, electrical engineering technology, engineering technology, fashion merchandising, fire science, food services management, gerontology, hotel and restaurant management, human services, legal secretarial studies, liberal arts/general studies, manufacturing technology, mechanical engineering technology, medical secretarial studies, mental health/rehabilitation counseling, nuclear medical technology, pharmacy/pharmaceutical sciences, postal management, radiological technology, retail management, word processing.
LIBRARY 45,858 books, 95,088 microform titles, 567 periodicals, 3 on-line bibliographic services, 164 CD-ROMs, 1,252 records, tapes, and CDs. Acquisition spending 1994–95: $591,397.
COMPUTERS ON CAMPUS 125 computers for student use in computer center, computer labs, learning resource center, classrooms, library provide access to main academic computer, off-campus computing facilities, on-line services. Staffed computer lab on campus provides training in use of computers, software.
COLLEGE LIFE Drama-theater group. ***Student services:*** health clinic, personal-psychological counseling, women's center. ***Campus security:*** late-night transport-escort service.

HOUSING College housing not available.
ATHLETICS Member NJCAA. *Intercollegiate:* baseball M, basketball M/W, golf M/W, softball W, tennis M/W. *Contact:* Dr. Paul Swann, Director of Athletics, 203-789-7034.
CAREER PLANNING *Placement office:* 2 full-time, 1 part-time staff. *Director:* Mr. Robert A. Miles, Director of Career Development and Job Placement, 203-789-7033. *Services:* job fairs, resume preparation, career counseling, job bank, job interviews.
AFTER GRADUATION 40% of students completing a degree program in 1994–95 went directly on to further study.
EXPENSES FOR 1996–97 *Application fee:* $10. State resident tuition: $1560 full-time, $65 per credit hour part-time. Nonresident tuition: $4680 full-time, $195 per credit hour part-time. Part-time mandatory fees per semester range from $36 to $81. Tuition for nonresidents who are eligible for the New England Regional Student Program: $2340 full-time, $97.50 per credit hour part-time. Full-time mandatory fees: $162.
FINANCIAL AID *College-administered undergrad aid 1995–96:* need-based scholarships, non-need scholarships, low-interest long-term loans from external sources, Federal Work-Study, part-time jobs. *Required forms:* state, institutional, FAFSA; accepted: CSS Financial Aid PROFILE. *Priority deadline:* 4/15. *Waivers:* full or partial for employees or children of employees and senior citizens.
APPLYING Open admission except for radiological technology, postal services management, pharmacy technology, engineering technologies programs. *Options:* early entrance, deferred entrance. *Required:* essay, school transcript, interview, TOEFL for international students. *Recommended:* 3 years of high school math and science. *Required for some:* 3 years of high school math and science. Test scores used for counseling/placement. *Application deadline:* 9/9. *Notification:* continuous until 9/9.
APPLYING/TRANSFER *Required:* high school transcript, college transcript. *Entrance:* noncompetitive. *Application deadline:* 9/9. *Notification:* continuous until 9/9. *Contact:* Mr. Michael Murphy, Director of Counseling, 203-789-7011.
CONTACT Ms. Myrna Garcia-Bowen, Director of Admissions, Gateway Community-Technical College, 60 Sargent Drive, New Haven, CT 06511-5918, 203-789-7043. College video available.

HOUSATONIC COMMUNITY-TECHNICAL COLLEGE
Bridgeport, Connecticut

UG Enrollment: 2,654	Tuition & Fees (CT Res): $1722
Application Deadline: rolling	Room & Board: N/Avail

GENERAL State-supported, 2-year, coed. Part of Connecticut Community–Technical College System. Awards transfer associate, terminal associate degrees. Founded 1966. *Setting:* 4-acre urban campus with easy access to New York City. *Total enrollment:* 2,654. *Faculty:* 137 (45 full-time, 12% with terminal degrees, 92 part-time); student-faculty ratio is 18:1.
ENROLLMENT PROFILE 2,654 students: 70% women, 84% part-time, 99% state residents, 5% transferred in, 1% international, 54% 25 or older, 0% Native American, 20% Hispanic, 28% African American, 3% Asian American. *Areas of study chosen:* 15% business management and administrative services, 6% health professions and related sciences, 2% liberal arts/general studies, 1% fine arts.
FIRST-YEAR CLASS 663 total; 2,182 applied, 99% were accepted.
ACADEMIC PROGRAM Core, liberal arts curriculum. Calendar: semesters. Academic remediation for entering students, English as a second language program offered during academic year, services for LD students, advanced placement, honors program, summer session for credit, part-time degree program (daytime, evenings, summer), adult/continuing education programs, co-op programs and internships. Off-campus study. ROTC: Army (c).
GENERAL DEGREE REQUIREMENTS 60 credits; 3 credits of math; 3 credits of science.
MAJORS Accounting, art/fine arts, aviation technology, business administration/commerce/management, child care/child and family studies, criminal justice, data processing, drug and alcohol/substance abuse counseling, (pre)engineering sequence, environmental sciences, graphic arts, humanities, human services, journalism, liberal arts/general studies, mathematics, medical laboratory technology, mental health/rehabilitation counseling, nursing, physical therapy, public administration, secretarial studies/office management, social science, word processing.
LIBRARY 29,000 books, 300 periodicals, 2 CD-ROMs, 2,100 records, tapes, and CDs. Acquisition spending 1994–95: $77,130.
COMPUTERS ON CAMPUS 100 computers for student use in computer labs, library provide access to main academic computer, off-campus computing facilities. Staffed computer lab on campus.
COLLEGE LIFE Student-run newspaper. 15% vote in student government elections. *Most popular organizations:* Student Senate, Association of Latin American Students, African-American Cultural Society, Art Club. *Student services:* personal-psychological counseling. *Campus security:* 24-hour emergency response devices, late-night transport-escort service.
HOUSING College housing not available.
ATHLETICS *Intramural:* baseball. *Contact:* Mr. Edward Sylvia, Director of Athletics, 203-579-6479.
CAREER PLANNING *Services:* career counseling, careers library.
EXPENSES FOR 1996–97 *Application fee:* $20. State resident tuition: $1560 full-time, $65 per credit part-time. Nonresident tuition: $4680 full-time, $195 per credit part-time. Part-time mandatory fees per semester range from $36 to $81. Tuition for nonresidents who are eligible for the New England Regional Student Program: $2340 full-time, $97.50 per credit part-time. Full-time mandatory fees: $162.
FINANCIAL AID *College-administered undergrad aid 1995–96:* need-based scholarships, Federal Work-Study, part-time jobs. *Required forms:* state, FAFSA. *Priority deadline:* 7/1. *Waivers:* full or partial for senior citizens.
APPLYING Open admission except for drug and alcohol rehabilitation counseling, medical laboratory technology, allied health, phlebotomy programs. *Options:* deferred entrance, midyear entrance. *Required:* school transcript, TOEFL for international students. *Required for some:* recommendations, interview, New Jersey Basic Skills Exam. Test scores used for counseling/placement. *Application deadline:* rolling.
APPLYING/TRANSFER *Required:* college transcript. *Required for some:* recommendations, interview. *Application deadline:* rolling.
CONTACT Ms. Deloris Y. Curtis, Director of Admissions, Housatonic Community-Technical College, 510 Barnum Avenue, Bridgeport, CT 06608-2453, 203-579-6475. College video available.

KATHARINE GIBBS SCHOOL
Norwalk, Connecticut

UG Enrollment: 350	Tuition & Fees: $8105
Application Deadline: rolling	Room & Board: N/Avail

GENERAL Proprietary, 2-year, primarily women. Part of K-III Communications Corporation. Awards certificates, terminal associate degrees. Founded 1975. *Setting:* 2-acre suburban campus with easy access to New York City. *Total enrollment:* 350. *Faculty:* 30 (15 full-time, 15 part-time); student-faculty ratio is 15:1.
ENROLLMENT PROFILE 350 students from 10 states and territories, 2 other countries. 90% women, 0% part-time, 94% state residents, 5% transferred in, 10% 25 or older, 0% Native American, 5% Hispanic, 15% African American, 0% Asian American. *Most popular recent majors:* secretarial studies/office management, legal secretarial studies, medical secretarial studies.
FIRST-YEAR CLASS 200 total. Of the students who applied, 66% were accepted, 93% of whom enrolled. 5% from top 10% of their high school class, 15% from top quarter, 40% from top half.
ACADEMIC PROGRAM Core, honor code. Calendar: quarters. Academic remediation for entering students, adult/continuing education programs, internships.
GENERAL DEGREE REQUIREMENTS 105 credits; computer course; internship (some majors).
MAJORS Legal secretarial studies, medical secretarial studies, secretarial studies/office management.
LIBRARY Sister Barbara Dewey Library with 2,300 books, 500 microform titles, 200 periodicals, 200 records, tapes, and CDs.
COMPUTERS ON CAMPUS 90 computers for student use in computer labs. Staffed computer lab on campus provides training in use of computers, software.
COLLEGE LIFE Student-run newspaper. *Student services:* personal-psychological counseling.
HOUSING College housing not available.
CAREER PLANNING *Services:* resume preparation, resume referral, career counseling, job interviews. Students must register freshman year.
EXPENSES FOR 1996–97 *Application fee:* $25. Tuition: $8105 full-time.
FINANCIAL AID *College-administered undergrad aid 1995–96:* 10 need-based scholarships (average $1000), low-interest long-term loans from external sources (average $2625), Federal Work-Study, 5 part-time jobs. *Required forms:* institutional; required for some: state, FAFSA, nontaxable income verification; accepted: CSS Financial Aid PROFILE. *Application deadline:* continuous. *Payment plan:* installment.
APPLYING *Options:* Common Application, deferred entrance. *Required:* school transcript, CPAt. *Recommended:* SAT I, TOEFL for international students. Test scores used for admission. *Application deadline:* rolling. *Notification:* continuous.
APPLYING/TRANSFER *Required:* college transcript. *Application deadline:* rolling. *Notification:* continuous.
CONTACT Mr. Robert Biangiola, High School Coordinator, Katharine Gibbs School, Norwalk, CT 06851-5754, 203-838-4173 or toll-free 800-845-5333. *Fax:* 203-853-6402. College video available.

MANCHESTER COMMUNITY-TECHNICAL COLLEGE
Manchester, Connecticut

UG Enrollment: 5,400	Tuition & Fees (CT Res): $1722
Application Deadline: rolling	Room & Board: N/Avail

GENERAL State-supported, 2-year, coed. Part of Connecticut Community–Technical College System. Awards transfer associate, terminal associate degrees. Founded 1963. *Setting:* 160-acre small-town campus with easy access to Hartford. *Total enrollment:* 5,400. *Faculty:* 205 (100 full-time, 105 part-time).
ENROLLMENT PROFILE 5,400 students: 61% women, 72% part-time, 98% state residents, 15% transferred in, 1% Hispanic, 4% African American.
FIRST-YEAR CLASS Of the students who applied, 100% were accepted, 75% of whom enrolled.
ACADEMIC PROGRAM Core. Calendar: semesters. Academic remediation for entering students, summer session for credit, part-time degree program (daytime, evenings, weekends), internships. Off-campus study at other institutions in the Connecticut Public Higher Education System. ROTC: Army (c).
GENERAL DEGREE REQUIREMENTS 60 credit hours; math/science requirements vary according to program; computer course for business-related majors.
MAJORS Accounting, art/fine arts, business administration/commerce/management, communication, criminal justice, culinary arts, data processing, early childhood education, food services management, gerontology, hotel and restaurant management, human services, industrial engineering technology, law enforcement/police sciences, legal secretarial studies, liberal arts/general studies, marketing/retailing/merchandising, medical laboratory technology, medical secretarial studies, music, occupational therapy, operating room technology, paralegal studies, physical education, real estate, respiratory therapy, secretarial studies/office management, social work, teacher aide studies, theater arts/drama.
LIBRARY 39,534 books, 62,513 microform titles, 295 periodicals, 1,339 records, tapes, and CDs.
COMPUTERS ON CAMPUS Computers for student use in computer center, various buildings on campus, library.
COLLEGE LIFE Drama-theater group, student-run newspaper. *Student services:* women's center.
HOUSING College housing not available.
ATHLETICS Member NJCAA. *Intercollegiate:* basketball M/W, soccer M, volleyball W. *Contact:* Mr. Patrick Mistretta, Director of Athletics, 860-647-6058.
CAREER PLANNING *Director:* Mr. Carl Ochnio, Director of Career Services and Placement, 860-647-6067. *Service:* career counseling.
EXPENSES FOR 1996–97 State resident tuition: $1560 full-time, $65 per credit hour part-time. Nonresident tuition: $4680 full-time, $195 per credit hour part-time. Full-time mandatory fees: $162.
FINANCIAL AID *College-administered undergrad aid 1995–96:* need-based scholarships, low-interest long-term loans from external sources, Federal Work-Study. *Required forms:* institutional, FAFSA. *Priority deadline:* 6/1.

Manchester Community-Technical College (continued)

APPLYING Open admission except for allied health programs. ***Option:*** early entrance. ***Required:*** school transcript, TOEFL for international students. ***Recommended:*** 3 years of high school math and science. Test scores used for admission. ***Application deadline:*** rolling. ***Notification:*** continuous until 8/30.

APPLYING/TRANSFER ***Required:*** high school transcript, college transcript. ***Recommended:*** 3 years of high school math and science.

CONTACT Mr. Joseph Mesquita, Director of Admissions, Manchester Community-Technical College, Manchester, CT 06045-1046, 860-647-6050.

MIDDLESEX COMMUNITY- TECHNICAL COLLEGE
Middletown, Connecticut

UG Enrollment: 2,785	**Tuition & Fees (CT Res): $1722**
Application Deadline: 8/1	**Room & Board: N/Avail**

GENERAL State-supported, 2-year, coed. Part of Connecticut Community–Technical College System. Awards certificates, transfer associate, terminal associate degrees. Founded 1966. ***Setting:*** 38-acre small-town campus. ***Total enrollment:*** 2,785. ***Faculty:*** 130 (50 full-time, 6% with terminal degrees, 80 part-time); student-faculty ratio is 25:1.

ENROLLMENT PROFILE 2,785 students from 6 states and territories, 11 other countries. 65% women, 35% men, 75% part-time, 98% state residents, 25% transferred in, 68% have non-need-based financial aid, 1% international, 60% 25 or older, 1% Native American, 5% Hispanic, 6% African American, 2% Asian American. ***Areas of study chosen:*** 20% liberal arts/general studies, 15% business management and administrative services, 9% health professions and related sciences, 4% social sciences, 3% communications and journalism, 2% biological and life sciences, 2% computer and information sciences, 2% fine arts, 1% engineering and applied sciences, 1% English language/literature/letters. ***Most popular recent majors:*** liberal arts/general studies, business administration/commerce/management, optometric/ophthalmic technologies.

FIRST-YEAR CLASS 1,319 total; 1,734 applied, 98% were accepted, 77% of whom enrolled.

ACADEMIC PROGRAM Core, honor code. Calendar: semesters. 465 courses offered in 1995–96. Academic remediation for entering students, English as a second language program offered during academic year, services for LD students, advanced placement, self-designed majors, Freshman Honors College, tutorials, honors program, summer session for credit, part-time degree program (daytime, evenings), external degree programs, adult/continuing education programs, internships. Off-campus study at other units of the Connecticut Community College System.

GENERAL DEGREE REQUIREMENTS 60 credits; 1 college algebra course; computer course for accounting, business, marketing, radiological technology, office management majors; internship (some majors).

MAJORS Accounting, applied art, art/fine arts, biotechnology, broadcasting, business administration/commerce/management, commercial art, communication, computer programming, drug and alcohol/substance abuse counseling, engineering sciences, (pre)engineering sequence, engineering technology, environmental sciences, human services, legal secretarial studies, liberal arts/general studies, marketing/retailing/merchandising, medical secretarial studies, mental health/rehabilitation counseling, optometric/ophthalmic technologies, radio and television studies, radiological technology, science, secretarial studies/office management, studio art.

LIBRARY Jean Burr Smith Library plus 1 other, with 45,000 books, 180 periodicals, 2 on-line bibliographic services, 1,900 records, tapes, and CDs.

COMPUTERS ON CAMPUS 50 computers for student use in computer center, various classroom buildings, library provide access to main academic computer, Internet. Staffed computer lab on campus provides training in use of computers, software.

COLLEGE LIFE Choral group, marching band, student-run radio station. ***Social organizations:*** 8 open to all. ***Most popular organizations:*** Art, Human Services, Collegiate Secretaries International, Minority Opportunities in Education, Radio Club. ***Major annual events:*** International Day, Bus Trips, Senior Art Exhibit. ***Student services:*** personal-psychological counseling, women's center. ***Campus security:*** 24-hour patrols.

HOUSING College housing not available.

CAREER PLANNING ***Placement office:*** 3 full-time, 1 part-time staff. ***Services:*** resume preparation, resume referral, career counseling, job bank. 30 organizations recruited on campus 1994–95.

EXPENSES FOR 1996–97 State resident tuition: $1560 full-time, $65 per credit hour part-time. Nonresident tuition: $4680 full-time, $195 per credit hour part-time. Part-time mandatory fees per semester range from $36 to $81. Tuition for nonresidents who are eligible for the New England Regional Student Program: $2340 full-time, $97.50 per credit hour part-time. Full-time mandatory fees: $162.

FINANCIAL AID ***College-administered undergrad aid 1995–96:*** 458 need-based scholarships (average $1135), short-term loans (average $150), low-interest long-term loans from college funds (average $550), loans from external sources (average $2625), 110 Federal Work-Study (averaging $1400). ***Required forms:*** institutional; accepted: CSS Financial Aid PROFILE, FAFSA. ***Priority deadline:*** 7/1. ***Waivers:*** full or partial for employees or children of employees and senior citizens.

APPLYING Open admission except for radiological technology, human services, drug and alcohol counseling, information systems, ophthalmic design and dispensing programs. ***Options:*** early entrance, deferred entrance, midyear entrance. ***Required:*** TOEFL for international students. Test scores used for counseling/placement. ***Application deadline:*** 8/1. ***Notification:*** continuous until 8/1.

APPLYING/TRANSFER ***Entrance:*** noncompetitive. ***Application deadline:*** 8/1. ***Notification:*** continuous until 8/1. ***Contact:*** Ms. Merrily Lyon, Counselor, 860-343-5822.

CONTACT Mr. Richard Muniz, Director of Enrollment Management, Middlesex Community- Technical College, Middletown, CT 06457-4889, 860-343-5719. ***Fax:*** 860-344-7488. College video available.

MITCHELL COLLEGE
New London, Connecticut

UG Enrollment: 509	**Tuition & Fees: $12,715**
Application Deadline: rolling	**Room & Board: $5720**

GENERAL Independent, 2-year, coed. Awards transfer associate, terminal associate degrees. Founded 1938. ***Setting:*** 67-acre suburban campus with easy access to Hartford and Providence. ***Total enrollment:*** 509. ***Faculty:*** 75 (25 full-time, 50 part-time); student-faculty ratio is 10:1.

ENROLLMENT PROFILE 509 students from 26 states and territories, 16 other countries. 46% women, 54% men, 20% part-time, 50% state residents, 90% live on campus, 11% transferred in, 60% have need-based financial aid, 20% have non-need-based financial aid, 9% international, 7% 25 or older, 1% Native American, 6% Hispanic, 10% African American, 1% Asian American. ***Areas of study chosen:*** 50% liberal arts/general studies, 10% biological and life sciences, 10% business management and administrative services, 10% computer and information sciences, 10% education, 5% engineering and applied sciences, 5% health professions and related sciences. ***Most popular recent majors:*** liberal arts/general studies, business administration/commerce/management.

FIRST-YEAR CLASS 268 total; 856 applied, 83% were accepted, 38% of whom enrolled. 1% from top 10% of their high school class, 14% from top quarter, 33% from top half.

ACADEMIC PROGRAM Core, competency-based career-oriented curriculum, honor code. Calendar: semesters. Academic remediation for entering students, English as a second language program offered during academic year and summer, services for LD students, advanced placement, tutorials, summer session for credit, part-time degree program (daytime, evenings, summer), adult/continuing education programs, internships.

GENERAL DEGREE REQUIREMENTS 60 credit hours; 1 course each in math and science; computer course; internship (some majors).

MAJORS Accounting, athletic training, biology/biological sciences, business administration/commerce/management, child care/child and family studies, child psychology/child development, computer information systems, criminal justice, early childhood education, ecology, engineering (general), environmental sciences, gerontology, graphic arts, health science, health services administration, human services, liberal arts/general studies, marine biology, marine sciences, oceanography, physical education, physical sciences, political science/government, psychology, public administration, recreation and leisure services, recreation therapy, science, secretarial studies/office management, social work, sports administration, sports medicine.

LIBRARY Mitchell College Library plus 1 other, with 50,000 books, 85 periodicals, 4 CD-ROMs, 350 records, tapes, and CDs.

COMPUTERS ON CAMPUS Computer purchase plan available. 120 computers for student use in computer center, graphic design classroom, library. Staffed computer lab on campus provides training in use of computers, software.

COLLEGE LIFE Orientation program (3 days, no cost, parents included). Student-run newspaper. ***Most popular organizations:*** International Club, Business Club, Student Government, Student Newspaper. ***Student services:*** health clinic, personal-psychological counseling. ***Campus security:*** 24-hour emergency response devices and patrols, student patrols, late-night transport-escort service, controlled dormitory access.

HOUSING 450 college housing spaces available; all were occupied 1995–96. Freshmen guaranteed college housing. On-campus residence required through sophomore year except if living with relatives. ***Options:*** coed (2 buildings), single-sex (5 buildings) housing available. Resident assistants live in dorms.

ATHLETICS Member NJCAA. ***Intercollegiate:*** baseball M(s), basketball M(s)/W(s), field hockey W(s), golf M(s)/W, sailing M(s)/W(s), soccer M(s)/W(s), softball W(s), tennis M(s), volleyball W(s). ***Intramural:*** badminton, baseball, basketball, field hockey, football, golf, sailing, soccer, softball, tennis, volleyball. ***Contact:*** Mr. Douglas Yarnall, Athletic Director, 860-443-2811 Ext. 261.

CAREER PLANNING ***Placement office:*** 1 full-time staff. ***Director:*** Ms. Cindi Doherty, Student Advisor, 860-701-5080. ***Services:*** resume preparation, career counseling.

AFTER GRADUATION 90% of students completing a degree program in 1994–95 went directly on to further study.

EXPENSES FOR 1996–97 ***Application fee:*** $30. Comprehensive fee of $18,435 includes full-time tuition ($11,935), mandatory fees ($780), and college room and board ($5720). Part-time tuition: $135 per credit hour. Part-time mandatory fees: $15 per semester.

FINANCIAL AID ***College-administered undergrad aid 1995–96:*** 300 need-based scholarships (averaging $3500), non-need scholarships, low-interest long-term loans from external sources (averaging $2625), Federal Work-Study, 25 part-time jobs. ***Required forms:*** FAFSA. ***Priority deadline:*** 3/1. ***Payment plan:*** installment. ***Waivers:*** full or partial for employees or children of employees.

APPLYING ***Options:*** early entrance, deferred entrance, midyear entrance. ***Required:*** essay, school transcript, recommendations, TOEFL for international students. ***Recommended:*** interview, SAT I or ACT, SAT II Subject Tests. ***Required for some:*** minimum 2.0 GPA. Test scores used for counseling/placement. ***Application deadline:*** rolling. ***Notification:*** continuous until 8/30.

APPLYING/TRANSFER ***Required:*** essay, high school transcript, college transcript. ***Recommended:*** interview. ***Required for some:*** standardized test scores. ***Application deadline:*** rolling. ***Notification:*** continuous.

CONTACT Dr. Arthur Forst Jr., Dean of Enrollment Management, Mitchell College, New London, CT 06320-4498, 860-443-2811 or toll-free 800-443-2811 (in-state), 800-223-2769 (out-of-state). ***Fax:*** 860-444-1209. College video available.

❖ *See page 774 for a narrative description.* ❖

NAUGATUCK VALLEY COMMUNITY-TECHNICAL COLLEGE
Waterbury, Connecticut

UG Enrollment: 5,533	**Tuition & Fees (CT Res): $1722**
Application Deadline: rolling	**Room & Board: N/Avail**

GENERAL State-supported, 2-year, coed. Part of Connecticut Community–Technical College System. Awards certificates, transfer associate, terminal associate degrees. Founded 1967. ***Setting:*** 138-acre urban campus. ***Educational spending 1994–95:*** $1400 per undergrad. ***Total enrollment:*** 5,533. ***Faculty:*** 165 (115 full-time, 30% with terminal degrees, 50 part-time); student-faculty ratio is 25:1.

ENROLLMENT PROFILE 5,533 students from 4 states and territories, 15 other countries. 56% women, 44% men, 69% part-time, 98% state residents, 25% transferred in, 38% have need-based financial aid, 1% have non-need-based financial aid, 1% international, 54% 25 or older, 1% Native American, 7% Hispanic, 6% African American, 2% Asian American. ***Areas of study chosen:*** 36% liberal arts/general studies, 16% business management and administrative services, 14% engineering and applied sciences, 12% social sciences, 8% vocational and home economics, 5% education, 5% health professions and related sciences, 4% computer and information sciences. ***Most popular recent majors:*** liberal arts/general studies, business administration/commerce/management, early childhood education.
FIRST-YEAR CLASS 1,250 total; 2,139 applied, 100% were accepted, 58% of whom enrolled.
ACADEMIC PROGRAM Core, honor code. Calendar: semesters. 550 courses offered in 1995–96. Academic remediation for entering students, English as a second language program offered during academic year and summer, services for LD students, advanced placement, self-designed majors, summer session for credit, part-time degree program (daytime, evenings), external degree programs, adult/continuing education programs, co-op programs and internships. Off-campus study at other institutions in the Connecticut Public Higher Education System. Study abroad in England, France, Israel, Italy, Mexico, Spain, China, Germany, Colombia, Cyprus, Ecuador, Greece, Ireland, Scotland, Sweden, Switzerland (1% of students participate).
GENERAL DEGREE REQUIREMENTS 60 credits; math/science requirements vary according to program; computer course for business, engineering technology, hospitality management, automotive technician, legal assistant, nursing, radiologic technology majors; internship (some majors).
MAJORS Accounting, American studies, automotive technologies, business administration/commerce/management, chemical engineering technology, computer information systems, computer programming, criminal justice, drafting and design, drug and alcohol/substance abuse counseling, early childhood education, electrical engineering technology, (pre)engineering sequence, engineering technology, environmental sciences, finance/banking, fire science, food services management, gerontology, history, horticulture, hospitality services, hotel and restaurant management, human services, industrial engineering technology, international studies, legal secretarial studies, liberal arts/general studies, manufacturing technology, marketing/retailing/merchandising, mathematics, mechanical engineering technology, medical secretarial studies, mental health/rehabilitation counseling, music, natural sciences, nursing, paralegal studies, physical fitness/exercise science, physical sciences, quality control technology, radiological technology, science, secretarial studies/office management, social work.
LIBRARY Max R. Traurig Learning Resource Center plus 2 others, with 35,000 books, 222 microform titles, 430 periodicals, 3 on-line bibliographic services, 13 CD-ROMs, 600 records, tapes, and CDs. Acquisition spending 1994–95: $132,282.
COMPUTERS ON CAMPUS 400 computers for student use in computer labs, learning resource center, classrooms. Staffed computer lab on campus. Academic computing expenditure 1994–95: $158,303.
COLLEGE LIFE Drama-theater group, choral group, student-run newspaper. 8% vote in student government elections. ***Social organizations:*** 35 open to all. ***Most popular organizations:*** Student Government, Hispanic Student Union, Black Student Union, Student Action for Mothers in School, Choral Society. ***Major annual events:*** Awards Ceremony, Spring Banquet, Holiday Banquet. ***Student services:*** health clinic, personal-psychological counseling, women's center. ***Campus security:*** 24-hour emergency response devices and patrols, late-night transport-escort service.
HOUSING College housing not available.
ATHLETICS Member NJCAA. ***Intercollegiate:*** baseball M, basketball M/W, softball W. ***Contact:*** Mr. John Salerno, Director of Athletics, 203-575-8072.
CAREER PLANNING ***Placement office:*** 2 full-time, 1 part-time staff. ***Director:*** Dr. Joan W. Donald, Director of Special Programs and Alumni Affairs, 203-575-8121. ***Services:*** resume preparation, resume referral, career counseling, job bank, job interviews. Students must register sophomore year. 12 organizations recruited on campus 1994–95.
AFTER GRADUATION 60% of class of 1994 had job offers within 6 months. 30% of students completing a degree program went directly on to further study.
EXPENSES FOR 1996–97 ***Application fee:*** $10. State resident tuition: $1560 full-time, $65 per credit part-time. Nonresident tuition: $4680 full-time, $195 per credit part-time. Part-time mandatory fees per semester range from $36 to $73.50. Tuition for nonresidents who are eligible for the New England Regional Student Program: $2340 full-time, $97.50 per credit part-time. Full-time mandatory fees: $162.
FINANCIAL AID ***College-administered undergrad aid 1995–96:*** need-based scholarships, 25 non-need scholarships (average $600), low-interest long-term loans from college funds (average $1777), loans from external sources (average $2044), Federal Work-Study, part-time jobs. ***Required forms:*** institutional, FAFSA. ***Priority deadline:*** 7/1. ***Waivers:*** full or partial for employees or children of employees and senior citizens.
APPLYING Open admission except for nursing, radiology, engineering technology, automotive technology, paramedic, respiratory care technician programs. ***Options:*** early entrance, deferred entrance, midyear entrance. ***Required:*** school transcript, TOEFL for international students. ***Required for some:*** campus interview, SAT I. Test scores used for counseling/placement. ***Application deadline:*** rolling. ***Notification:*** continuous.
APPLYING/TRANSFER ***Required:*** high school transcript, college transcript. ***Required for some:*** campus interview. ***Entrance:*** noncompetitive. ***Application deadline:*** rolling. ***Notification:*** continuous. ***Contact:*** Mr. Robert Kaminski, Coordinator of Learning Resources, 203-575-8025.
CONTACT Ms. Nancy M. Merritt, Director of Admissions and Marketing, Naugatuck Valley Community–Technical College, 750 Chase Parkway, Waterbury, CT 06708-3000, 203-575-8078. ***Fax:*** 203-596-8766. College video available.

NORTHWESTERN CONNECTICUT COMMUNITY-TECHNICAL COLLEGE
Winsted, Connecticut

UG Enrollment: 2,116	**Tuition & Fees (CT Res): $1722**
Application Deadline: rolling	**Room & Board: N/Avail**

GENERAL State-supported, 2-year, coed. Part of Connecticut Community–Technical College System. Awards certificates, transfer associate, terminal associate degrees. Founded 1965. ***Setting:*** 5-acre small-town campus with easy access to Hartford. ***Total enrollment:*** 2,116. ***Faculty:*** 92 (37 full-time, 20% with terminal degrees, 55 part-time).
ENROLLMENT PROFILE 2,116 students from 6 states and territories, 10 other countries. 70% women, 78% part-time, 90% state residents, 10% transferred in, 13% have need-based financial aid, 1% international, 62% 25 or older, 1% Native American, 1% Hispanic, 1% African American, 1% Asian American. ***Areas of study chosen:*** 30% liberal arts/general studies, 18% computer and information sciences, 8% biological and life sciences, 8% English language/literature/letters, 5% business management and administrative services, 5% fine arts, 4% foreign language and literature, 4% health professions and related sciences, 3% education, 3% mathematics, 2% physical sciences, 1% engineering and applied sciences, 1% psychology, 1% social sciences. ***Most popular recent majors:*** business administration/commerce/management, criminal justice, deaf interpreter training.
FIRST-YEAR CLASS 439 total; 582 applied, 95% were accepted, 80% of whom enrolled. 5% from top 10% of their high school class, 40% from top half.
ACADEMIC PROGRAM Core. Calendar: semesters. Academic remediation for entering students, English as a second language program offered during academic year, advanced placement, summer session for credit, part-time degree program (daytime, evenings, summer), external degree programs, adult/continuing education programs, internships.
GENERAL DEGREE REQUIREMENTS 62 credits; math requirement varies according to program; computer course for most majors; internship (some majors).
MAJORS Accounting, art/fine arts, behavioral sciences, biology/biological sciences, business administration/commerce/management, child care/child and family studies, commercial art, communication equipment technology, computer graphics, computer information systems, computer programming, computer science, computer technologies, criminal justice, deaf interpreter training, drug and alcohol/substance abuse counseling, early childhood education, electrical and electronics technologies, engineering (general), (pre)engineering sequence, English, graphic arts, health science, human services, law enforcement/police sciences, liberal arts/general studies, marketing/retailing/merchandising, mathematics, medical assistant technologies, paralegal studies, parks management, physical sciences, recreation and leisure services, recreation therapy, secretarial studies/office management, social science, veterinary technology.
LIBRARY Northwestern Connecticut Community–Technical College Learning Center with 43,000 books, 95 microform titles, 250 periodicals, 5 CD-ROMs, 2,000 records, tapes, and CDs.
COMPUTERS ON CAMPUS 90 computers for student use in computer center, computer labs, academic skills center, classrooms, library provide access to main academic computer, Internet. Staffed computer lab on campus provides training in use of computers, software.
COLLEGE LIFE ***Social organizations:*** 10 open to all. ***Most popular organizations:*** Ski Club, Fine Arts Society, Deaf Club, Recreation Club, Early Childhood Educational Club. ***Campus security:*** evening security patrols.
HOUSING College housing not available.
CAREER PLANNING ***Placement office:*** 1 full-time staff. ***Director:*** Mr. Jeff Crothers, Counselor, 860-738-6306. ***Services:*** job fairs, resume preparation, career counseling, careers library, job bank.
AFTER GRADUATION 30% of students completing a degree program in 1994–95 went directly on to further study.
EXPENSES FOR 1996–97 ***Application fee:*** $10. State resident tuition: $1560 full-time, $65 per credit part-time. Nonresident tuition: $4680 full-time, $195 per credit part-time. Part-time mandatory fees: $36 per semester. Tuition for nonresidents who are eligible for the New England Regional Student Program: $2340 full-time, $97.50 per credit part-time. Full-time mandatory fees: $162.
FINANCIAL AID ***College-administered undergrad aid 1995–96:*** 50 need-based scholarships (average $800), 5 non-need scholarships (average $300), low-interest long-term loans from external sources (average $2000), Federal Work-Study, 40 part-time jobs. ***Required forms:*** institutional, FAFSA. ***Priority deadline:*** 6/1. ***Waivers:*** full or partial for employees or children of employees and senior citizens.
APPLYING Open admission. ***Options:*** deferred entrance, midyear entrance. ***Recommended:*** TOEFL for international students. Test scores used for counseling/placement. ***Application deadline:*** rolling. ***Notification:*** continuous until 9/1.
APPLYING/TRANSFER ***Required:*** college transcript. ***Entrance:*** noncompetitive. ***Application deadline:*** rolling. ***Notification:*** continuous until 9/1. ***Contact:*** Ms. Beverly Chrzan, Interim Director of Admissions, 860-738-6329.
CONTACT Ms. Beverly Chrzan, Interim Director of Admissions, Northwestern Connecticut Community–Technical College, Winsted, CT 06098, 860-738-6329. ***Fax:*** 860-379-4465.

NORWALK COMMUNITY-TECHNICAL COLLEGE
Norwalk, Connecticut

UG Enrollment: 5,352	**Tuition & Fees (CT Res): $1722**
Application Deadline: rolling	**Room & Board: N/Avail**

GENERAL State-supported, 2-year, coed. Part of Connecticut Community–Technical College System. Awards transfer associate, terminal associate degrees. Founded 1961. ***Setting:*** 14-acre urban campus with easy access to New York City. ***Endowment:*** $600,000. ***Educational spending 1994–95:*** $1501 per undergrad. ***Total enrollment:*** 5,352. ***Faculty:*** 241 (86 full-time, 10% with terminal degrees, 155 part-time); student-faculty ratio is 24:1.
ENROLLMENT PROFILE 5,352 students from 5 states and territories, 28 other countries. 59% women, 78% part-time, 99% state residents, 16% transferred in, 55% 25 or older, 1% Native American, 11% Hispanic, 17% African American, 4% Asian American. ***Areas of study chosen:*** 24% liberal arts/general studies, 16% engineering and applied sciences, 12% business management and administrative services, 5% computer and information sciences, 4% education, 2% architecture, 2% English language/literature/letters, 2% health professions and related sciences, 1% communications and journalism, 1% mathematics.
FIRST-YEAR CLASS 1,602 total; 2,484 applied, 100% were accepted, 64% of whom enrolled.
ACADEMIC PROGRAM Core, interdisciplinary curriculum, honor code. Calendar: semesters. 450 courses offered in 1995–96. Academic remediation for entering students, English as a second language program offered during academic year and summer, services for LD students, advanced placement, Freshman Honors College, honors program, summer session for credit, part-time degree program (daytime, evenings), adult/continuing education programs, co-op programs and internships. ROTC: Army (c), Air Force (c).

Norwalk Community-Technical College (continued)

GENERAL DEGREE REQUIREMENTS 60 credits; computer course for engineering technology, graphic design, criminal justice, hotel/restaurant management, office administration majors; internship (some majors).
MAJORS Accounting, architectural technologies, art/fine arts, business administration/ commerce/management, civil engineering technology, communication, computer information systems, computer technologies, construction technologies, criminal justice, data processing, drug and alcohol/substance abuse counseling, early childhood education, electrical engineering technology, emergency medical technology, engineering sciences, engineering technology, finance/banking, fire science, food services management, graphic arts, hotel and restaurant management, humanities, human services, legal studies, liberal arts/ general studies, marketing/retailing/merchandising, mechanical engineering technology, nursing, paralegal studies, recreation and leisure services, recreation therapy, respiratory therapy, secretarial studies/office management.
LIBRARY Learning Resource Center with 56,416 books, 74 microform titles, 249 periodicals, 9 CD-ROMs, 1,589 records, tapes, and CDs. Acquisition spending 1994–95: $45,330.
COMPUTERS ON CAMPUS 225 computers for student use in computer center, computer labs, learning resource center, ESL, nursing labs, library provide access to Internet. Staffed computer lab on campus provides training in use of computers, software. Academic computing expenditure 1994–95: $575,720.
COLLEGE LIFE Drama-theater group, choral group, student-run newspaper. 20% vote in student government elections. ***Social organizations:*** 30 open to all. ***Most popular organizations:*** African Culture Club, Archaeology Club, Phi Theta Kappa, Student Advisory Board, Hay Motivo (Hispanic Culture Club). ***Major annual events:*** Student Activities Day, Spring Picnic. ***Student services:*** women's center. ***Campus security:*** security patrols.
HOUSING College housing not available.
ATHLETICS Member NJCAA. ***Intercollegiate:*** baseball M, basketball M, crew M/W, golf M/W, softball W. ***Contact:*** Mr. Curtis Antrum, Director of Athletics, 203-857-7250.
CAREER PLANNING ***Placement office:*** 1 full-time, 1 part-time staff; $114,595 operating expenditure 1994–95. ***Services:*** job fairs, resume preparation, resume referral, career counseling, careers library, job bank, job interviews.
AFTER GRADUATION 40% of students completing a degree program in 1994–95 went directly on to further study.
EXPENSES FOR 1996–97 ***Application fee:*** $10. State resident tuition: $1560 full-time, $65 per credit part-time. Nonresident tuition: $4680 full-time, $195 per credit part-time. Part-time mandatory fees: $36 per semester. Tuition for nonresidents who are eligible for the New England Regional Student Program: $2340 full-time, $97.50 per credit part-time. Full-time mandatory fees: $162.
FINANCIAL AID ***College-administered undergrad aid 1995–96:*** need-based scholarships, non-need scholarships, short-term loans (average $200), low-interest long-term loans from external sources (average $2500), 70 Federal Work-Study (averaging $2000). ***Required forms:*** institutional, FAFSA; accepted: CSS Financial Aid PROFILE. ***Priority deadline:*** 4/15. ***Waivers:*** full or partial for employees or children of employees and senior citizens.
APPLYING Open admission except for allied health programs. ***Options:*** early entrance, midyear entrance. ***Recommended:*** TOEFL for international students. ***Required for some:*** 3 years of high school math. Test scores used for counseling/placement. ***Application deadline:*** rolling. ***Notification:*** continuous.
APPLYING/TRANSFER ***Required for some:*** 3 years of high school math. ***Entrance:*** noncompetitive. ***Application deadline:*** rolling. ***Notification:*** continuous. ***Contact:*** Ms. Carolyn Thomas, Transfer Counselor, 203-857-7033.
CONTACT Ms. Barbara E. Drotman, Director of Enrollment Management, Norwalk Community-Technical College, 188 Richards Avenue, Norwalk, CT 06854-1655, 203-857-7060. ***Fax:*** 203-857-3335. College video available.

QUINEBAUG VALLEY COMMUNITY-TECHNICAL COLLEGE
Danielson, Connecticut

UG Enrollment: 1,120	**Tuition & Fees (CT Res): $1722**
Application Deadline: 9/1	**Room & Board: N/Avail**

GENERAL State-supported, 2-year, coed. Part of Connecticut Community–Technical College System. Awards certificates, transfer associate, terminal associate degrees. Founded 1971. ***Setting:*** 60-acre rural campus. ***Total enrollment:*** 1,120. ***Faculty:*** 55 (19 full-time, 36 part-time); student-faculty ratio is 22:1.
ENROLLMENT PROFILE 1,120 students: 74% women, 26% men, 73% part-time, 95% state residents, 27% transferred in, 1% international, 62% 25 or older, 1% Native American, 7% Hispanic, 2% African American, 1% Asian American.
FIRST-YEAR CLASS 357 total; 523 applied, 100% were accepted, 68% of whom enrolled.
ACADEMIC PROGRAM Core, honor code. Calendar: semesters. Academic remediation for entering students, English as a second language program offered during academic year, services for LD students, advanced placement, tutorials, summer session for credit, part-time degree program (daytime, evenings), external degree programs, adult/continuing education programs.
GENERAL DEGREE REQUIREMENTS 60 credit hours; math proficiency; 1 math course; computer course for business administration majors; internship (some majors).
MAJORS Accounting, art/fine arts, aviation technology, business administration/commerce/ management, drug and alcohol/substance abuse counseling, (pre)engineering sequence, engineering technology, human services, liberal arts/general studies, medical assistant technologies, plastics technology, secretarial studies/office management.
LIBRARY Audrey Beck Library with 26,000 books, 300 periodicals, 1 on-line bibliographic service, 600 records, tapes, and CDs.
COMPUTERS ON CAMPUS 80 computers for student use in computer center, computer labs, learning resource center, library provide access to main academic computer, on-line services, Internet. Staffed computer lab on campus provides training in use of computers, software.
COLLEGE LIFE Student-run newspaper. 30% vote in student government elections. ***Campus security:*** evening security guard.
HOUSING College housing not available.
ATHLETICS ***Intramural:*** basketball, volleyball.
CAREER PLANNING ***Placement office:*** 1 full-time staff. ***Director:*** Ms. Joan MacNeil, Director, Career Services, 860-774-1130. ***Services:*** job fairs, resume preparation, career counseling, careers library.
EXPENSES FOR 1996–97 ***Application fee:*** $10. State resident tuition: $1560 full-time, $65 per credit hour part-time. Nonresident tuition: $4680 full-time, $195 per credit hour part-time. Part-time mandatory fees: $81 per semester. Tuition for nonresidents who are eligible for the New England Regional Student Program: $2340 full-time, $97.50 per credit hour part-time. Full-time mandatory fees: $162.
FINANCIAL AID ***College-administered undergrad aid 1995–96:*** 417 need-based scholarships (averaging $481), 54 non-need scholarships (averaging $381), short-term loans, Federal Work-Study, 20 part-time jobs. ***Required forms:*** institutional, FAFSA. ***Priority deadline:*** 9/1. ***Payment plan:*** deferred payment. ***Waivers:*** full or partial for employees or children of employees and senior citizens.
APPLYING Open admission. ***Options:*** early entrance, deferred entrance, midyear entrance. ***Required for some:*** TOEFL for international students. Test scores used for counseling/placement. ***Application deadline:*** 9/1. ***Notification:*** continuous until 9/1.
APPLYING/TRANSFER ***Entrance:*** noncompetitive. ***Application deadline:*** 9/1. ***Notification:*** continuous until 9/1. ***Contact:*** Mr. Antonio L. Veloso, Director of Admission, 860-774-1130 Ext. 320.
CONTACT Mr. Antonio L. Veloso, Director of Admissions, Quinebaug Valley Community-Technical College, Danielson, CT 06239-1440, 860-774-1130 Ext. 320. ***Fax:*** 860-774-7768.

ST. VINCENT'S COLLEGE
Bridgeport, Connecticut

UG Enrollment: 212	**Tuition & Fees: $7440**
Application Deadline: rolling	**Room Only: $3276**

GENERAL Independent, 2-year, coed. Awards transfer associate degrees. ***Setting:*** urban campus with easy access to New York City. ***Total enrollment:*** 212. ***Faculty:*** 15 (9 full-time, 100% with terminal degrees, 6 part-time).
ENROLLMENT PROFILE 212 students from 2 states and territories. 88% women, 60% part-time, 98% state residents, 5% live on campus, 76% transferred in, 61% have need-based financial aid, 0% have non-need-based financial aid, 0% international, 58% 25 or older, 1% Native American, 4% Hispanic, 9% African American, 3% Asian American. ***Areas of study chosen:*** 100% health professions and related sciences.
FIRST-YEAR CLASS 110 total; 494 applied, 35% were accepted, 64% of whom enrolled. 5% from top 10% of their high school class, 20% from top quarter, 38% from top half.
ACADEMIC PROGRAM Core, health care professional curriculum, honor code. Calendar: semesters. 30 courses offered in 1995–96. Academic remediation for entering students, advanced placement, summer session for credit, part-time degree program (daytime, evenings).
GENERAL DEGREE REQUIREMENTS 72 credits; 1 chemistry course; computer course for radiography majors.
MAJORS Nursing, radiological technology.
LIBRARY Daniel T. Banks Health Science Library with 9,428 books, 332 periodicals, 3 on-line bibliographic services, 3 CD-ROMs, 1,067 records, tapes, and CDs.
COMPUTERS ON CAMPUS 14 computers for student use in computer center, computer labs, library provide access to on-line services, computer-aided instruction. Staffed computer lab on campus provides training in use of computers, software.
COLLEGE LIFE Orientation program (2 days, no cost). Choral group, student-run newspaper. 65% vote in student government elections. ***Social organizations:*** 6 open to all. ***Most popular organizations:*** Community Service, Student Congress, Mentors, Yearbook, Heartbeat. ***Major annual events:*** Beginning of the Year Liturgy, Day of Reflection, Awards Banquet. ***Student services:*** health clinic, personal-psychological counseling. ***Campus security:*** 24-hour patrols, late-night transport-escort service.
HOUSING No special consideration for freshman housing applicants. Off-campus living permitted. ***Option:*** single-sex (1 building) housing available.
CAREER PLANNING ***Services:*** job fairs, resume preparation, career counseling.
EXPENSES FOR 1995–96 ***Application fee:*** $30. Tuition: $7440 full-time, $248 per credit part-time. Part-time mandatory fees: $270 per year. College room only: $3276.
FINANCIAL AID ***College-administered undergrad aid 1995–96:*** 133 need-based scholarships (average $1312), short-term loans (average $500), Federal Work-Study. ***Required forms:*** institutional, FAFSA; required for some: state. ***Priority deadline:*** 4/1. ***Payment plan:*** deferred payment. ***Waivers:*** full or partial for employees or children of employees. ***Notification:*** 6/1.
APPLYING ***Option:*** deferred entrance. ***Required:*** essay, school transcript, recommendations, TOEFL for international students. ***Recommended:*** minimum 3.0 GPA, 3 years of high school math and science, some high school foreign language. ***Required for some:*** interview, SAT I or ACT. Test scores used for counseling/placement. ***Application deadline:*** rolling.
APPLYING/TRANSFER ***Required:*** essay, high school transcript, recommendations, college transcript. ***Recommended:*** 3 years of high school math and science, some high school foreign language, minimum 3.0 college GPA, minimum 3.0 high school GPA. ***Required for some:*** standardized test scores, interview. ***Entrance:*** moderately difficult. ***Application deadline:*** rolling.
CONTACT Ms. Barbara Davis, Dean of Academics, St. Vincent's College, 2800 Main Street, Bridgeport, CT 06606, 203-576-5578.

SWISS HOSPITALITY INSTITUTE "CESAR RITZ"
Washington, Connecticut

UG Enrollment: 100	**Tuition & Fees: $14,500**
Application Deadline: rolling	**Room & Board: $4250**

The Swiss Hospitality Institute César Ritz is the only Swiss college of hospitality management in the United States. Students earn an Associate of Science degree and undertake paid internships in 4- and 5-star American hotels, resorts, and restaurants in preparation for managerial positions in the fastest-growing industry in the world.

GENERAL Proprietary, 2-year, specialized, coed. Awards certificates, transfer associate, terminal associate degrees. Founded 1992. ***Setting:*** 27-acre small-town campus. ***Educational spending 1994–95:*** $2715 per undergrad. ***Total enrollment:*** 100. ***Faculty:*** 32 (10 full-time, 100% with terminal degrees, 22 part-time); student-faculty ratio is 7:1.

242

Peterson's Guide to Two-Year Colleges 1997

ENROLLMENT PROFILE 100 students from 5 states and territories, 23 other countries. 42% women, 58% men, 1% part-time, 33% state residents, 75% live on campus, 15% transferred in, 67% have need-based financial aid, 30% have non-need-based financial aid, 48% international, 31% 25 or older, 0% Native American, 3% Hispanic, 6% African American, 3% Asian American. ***Areas of study chosen:*** 100% business management and administrative services.
FIRST-YEAR CLASS 36 total; 94 applied, 82% were accepted, 47% of whom enrolled. 4% from top 10% of their high school class, 8% from top quarter, 21% from top half.
ACADEMIC PROGRAM Core, hospitality management curriculum, honor code. Calendar: semesters. 33 courses offered in 1995–96. Academic remediation for entering students, English as a second language program offered during academic year, services for LD students, advanced placement, tutorials, part-time degree program (daytime), adult/continuing education programs, co-op programs and internships. Study abroad in Switzerland.
GENERAL DEGREE REQUIREMENTS 62 credits; 3 credits of math; 6 credits of a foreign language; computer course; internship.
MAJOR Hotel and restaurant management.
LIBRARY Swiss Hospitality Institute Library with 77,500 books, 135 periodicals, 4 CD-ROMs, 162 records, tapes, and CDs. Acquisition spending 1994–95: $79,700.
COMPUTERS ON CAMPUS 25 computers for student use in computer labs, library provide access to main academic computer. Staffed computer lab on campus provides training in use of computers, software. Academic computing expenditure 1994–95: $75,171.
COLLEGE LIFE Orientation program (2 days, $25). Student-run newspaper. ***Social organizations:*** 5 open to all. ***Most popular organizations:*** Student Association, Student Newsletter, Yearbook, Community Service. ***Major annual events:*** International Dinner Series, College Open House, Formal Banquets. ***Student services:*** health clinic, personal-psychological counseling. ***Campus security:*** 24-hour emergency response devices, student patrols, controlled dormitory access.
HOUSING 120 college housing spaces available; 75 were occupied 1995–96. Freshmen guaranteed college housing. Off-campus living permitted. ***Option:*** single-sex (4 buildings) housing available. Resident assistants live in dorms.
CAREER PLANNING ***Placement office:*** 1 full-time staff; $50,000 operating expenditure 1994–95. ***Director:*** Ms. Nell Nicholas, Director of Internships and Placement, 860-868-9555 Ext. 132. ***Services:*** job fairs, resume preparation, resume referral, career counseling, careers library, job bank, job interviews. Students must register freshman year.
AFTER GRADUATION 80% of class of 1994 had job offers within 6 months. 40% of students completing a degree program went directly on to further study.
EXPENSES FOR 1996–97 ***Application fee:*** $25. Comprehensive fee of $18,750 includes full-time tuition ($13,000), mandatory fees ($1500), and college room and board ($4250). Part-time tuition: $450 per credit.
FINANCIAL AID ***College-administered undergrad aid 1995–96:*** 82 need-based scholarships (average $4000), 12 non-need scholarships (average $2000), low-interest long-term loans from college funds (average $7000), 28 part-time jobs. ***Required forms:*** institutional; required for some: FAFSA. ***Application deadline:*** continuous. ***Payment plans:*** installment, deferred payment.
APPLYING ***Options:*** Common Application, deferred entrance, midyear entrance. ***Required:*** school transcript, recommendations. ***Recommended:*** SAT I, TOEFL for international students. ***Required for some:*** interview. Test scores used for admission. ***Application deadline:*** rolling.
APPLYING/TRANSFER ***Required:*** high school transcript, recommendations, college transcript. ***Recommended:*** standardized test scores. ***Required for some:*** interview. ***Entrance:*** minimally difficult. ***Application deadline:*** rolling. ***Contact:*** Ms. Karen Lambert, Director of Admission, 860-868-9555 Ext. 126.
CONTACT Ms. Karen Lambert, Director of Admission, Swiss Hospitality Institute "Cesar Ritz", 101 Wykeham Road, Washington, CT 06793-1300, 860-868-9555 or toll-free 800-955-0809. ***Fax:*** 860-868-2114. College video available.

❖ ***See page 816 for a narrative description.*** ❖

THREE RIVERS COMMUNITY-TECHNICAL COLLEGE
Norwich, Connecticut

UG Enrollment: 3,977	**Tuition & Fees (CT Res): $1722**
Application Deadline: rolling	**Room & Board: N/Avail**

GENERAL State-supported, 2-year, coed. Part of Technical/Community College System of Connecticut. Awards certificates, transfer associate, terminal associate degrees (engineering technology programs are offered on the Thames Valley Campus; liberal arts, transfer and career programs are offered on the Mohegan Campus). Founded 1963. ***Setting:*** 40-acre small-town campus with easy access to Hartford. ***Educational spending 1994–95:*** $1019 per undergrad. ***Total enrollment:*** 3,977. ***Faculty:*** 180 (80 full-time, 10% with terminal degrees, 100 part-time).
ENROLLMENT PROFILE 3,977 students: 60% women, 40% men, 76% part-time, 99% state residents, 41% transferred in, 24% have need-based financial aid, 0% international, 61% 25 or older, 1% Native American, 4% Hispanic, 6% African American, 2% Asian American. ***Areas of study chosen:*** 32% liberal arts/general studies, 14% business management and administrative services, 12% engineering and applied sciences, 3% health professions and related sciences, 2% computer and information sciences, 2% natural resource sciences, 1% architecture, 1% education, 1% library and information studies. ***Most popular recent majors:*** liberal arts/general studies, manufacturing technology, nursing.
FIRST-YEAR CLASS 1,043 total; 1,473 applied, 100% were accepted, 71% of whom enrolled.
ACADEMIC PROGRAM Core, career-oriented/technical curriculum, honor code. Calendar: semesters. 1,243 courses offered in 1995–96. Academic remediation for entering students, English as a second language program offered during academic year, services for LD students, advanced placement, self-designed majors, tutorials, summer session for credit, part-time degree program (daytime, evenings, summer), external degree programs, adult/continuing education programs, co-op programs and internships. Study abroad in Ireland, England, Spain, Italy, Costa Rica (2% of students participate).
GENERAL DEGREE REQUIREMENTS 60 credits; computer course; internship (some majors).
MAJORS Accounting, advertising, architectural technologies, art/fine arts, aviation technology, business administration/commerce/management, civil engineering technology, computer programming, computer technologies, corrections, criminal justice, data processing, drafting and design, drug and alcohol/substance abuse counseling, early childhood education, electrical engineering technology, engineering (general), engineering sciences, (pre)engineering sequence, engineering technology, environmental engineering technology, fire science, food services management, hospitality services, hotel and restaurant management, human services, industrial administration, legal secretarial studies, liberal arts/general studies, manufacturing technology, marketing/retailing/merchandising, mechanical engineering technology, medical secretarial studies, nuclear technology, nursing, public administration, retail management, secretarial studies/office management, technical writing, theater arts/drama, tourism and travel, word processing.
LIBRARY Three Rivers Community-Technical College plus 2 others, with 52,517 books, 112 microform titles, 537 periodicals, 1 on-line bibliographic service, 16 CD-ROMs, 1,782 records, tapes, and CDs. Acquisition spending 1994–95: $160,901.
COMPUTERS ON CAMPUS 287 computers for student use in computer labs, learning resource center, labs, library provide access to main academic computer, off-campus computing facilities, Internet. Academic computing expenditure 1994–95: $663,355.
COLLEGE LIFE Drama-theater group, student-run newspaper. 10% vote in student government elections. ***Social organizations:*** 20 open to all; 2 national fraternities. ***Most popular organizations:*** Student Senate/Student Government Association, Theater Guild, Senior Student Ambassadors, Student Nurses Association, African-American Organization. ***Major annual events:*** Student Picnic, Awards Ceremony, Commencement. ***Student services:*** personal-psychological counseling. ***Campus security:*** late-night transport-escort service.
HOUSING College housing not available.
ATHLETICS ***Intercollegiate:*** basketball M, golf M/W. ***Intramural:*** basketball, ice hockey, skiing (downhill). ***Contact:*** Mr. Richard Marien, Director of Athletics, 860-885-2352.
CAREER PLANNING ***Placement office:*** 2 full-time, 3 part-time staff; $146,112 operating expenditure 1994–95. ***Director:*** Ms. Gail Mozzicato, Career Counselor, 860-823-2832. ***Services:*** job fairs, resume preparation, career counseling, careers library, job bank, job interviews. 20 organizations recruited on campus 1994–95.
AFTER GRADUATION 51% of class of 1994 had job offers within 6 months. 45% of students completing a degree program went directly on to further study.
EXPENSES FOR 1996–97 ***Application fee:*** $20. State resident tuition: $1560 full-time, $65 per credit part-time. Nonresident tuition: $4680 full-time, $195 per credit part-time. Part-time mandatory fees per semester range from $36 to $81. Tuition for nonresidents who are eligible for the New England Regional Student Program: $2340 full-time, $97.50 per credit part-time. Full-time mandatory fees: $162.
FINANCIAL AID ***College-administered undergrad aid 1995–96:*** 950 need-based scholarships (average $900), 25 non-need scholarships (average $100), short-term loans (average $300), low-interest long-term loans from external sources (average $2625), Federal Work-Study, 1,500 part-time jobs. ***Required forms:*** institutional, FAFSA. ***Priority deadline:*** 7/15. ***Payment plan:*** deferred payment. ***Waivers:*** full or partial for employees or children of employees and senior citizens.
APPLYING Open admission except for nursing, drug and alcohol rehabilitation counseling, paramedic programs. ***Options:*** early entrance, deferred entrance, midyear entrance. ***Required:*** Accuplacer. ***Recommended:*** school transcript. ***Required for some:*** minimum 3.0 GPA. Test scores used for counseling/placement. ***Application deadline:*** rolling. ***Notification:*** continuous.
APPLYING/TRANSFER ***Required:*** standardized test scores. ***Recommended:*** high school transcript. ***Entrance:*** noncompetitive. ***Application deadline:*** rolling. ***Notification:*** continuous. ***Contact:*** Ms. Barbara Segal, Director of Marketing and Recruitment, 860-823-2845.
CONTACT Ms. Aida Garcia, Admissions and Recruitment Counselor, Mohegan Campus, Three Rivers Community-Technical College, Mahan Drive, Norwich, CT 06360. ***Fax:*** 860-886-0691. College video available.

TUNXIS COMMUNITY TECHNICAL COLLEGE
Farmington, Connecticut

UG Enrollment: 3,675	**Tuition & Fees (CT Res): $1722**
Application Deadline: rolling	**Room & Board: N/Avail**

GENERAL State-supported, 2-year, coed. Part of Connecticut Community–Technical College System. Awards certificates, transfer associate, terminal associate degrees. Founded 1969. ***Setting:*** 12-acre suburban campus with easy access to Hartford. ***Total enrollment:*** 3,675. ***Faculty:*** 175 (45 full-time, 30% with terminal degrees, 130 part-time); student-faculty ratio is 20:1.
ENROLLMENT PROFILE 3,675 students from 2 states and territories, 15 other countries. 67% women, 33% men, 77% part-time, 98% state residents, 13% transferred in, 40% have need-based financial aid, 1% international, 65% 25 or older, 1% Native American, 3% Hispanic, 3% African American, 2% Asian American. ***Areas of study chosen:*** 51% liberal arts/general studies, 25% business management and administrative services, 15% social sciences, 5% health professions and related sciences, 3% computer and information sciences, 1% engineering and applied sciences. ***Most popular recent majors:*** business administration/commerce/management, dental services, liberal arts/general studies.
FIRST-YEAR CLASS 755 total; 1,450 applied.
ACADEMIC PROGRAM Core. Calendar: semesters. Academic remediation for entering students, English as a second language program offered during academic year, summer session for credit, part-time degree program (daytime, evenings), adult/continuing education programs.
GENERAL DEGREE REQUIREMENTS 60 credits; 3 credits of math/science; computer course for accounting, graphic arts majors; internship (some majors).
MAJORS Accounting, applied art, art/fine arts, business administration/commerce/management, commercial art, computer information systems, corrections, criminal justice, data processing, dental services, drug and alcohol/substance abuse counseling, engineering (general), engineering technology, fashion merchandising, forensic sciences, graphic arts, human services, legal secretarial studies, liberal arts/general studies, marketing/retailing/merchandising, medical secretarial studies, mental health/rehabilitation counseling, secretarial studies/office management.
LIBRARY Tunxis Community Technical College Library with 31,901 books, 161 microform titles, 280 periodicals, 6 CD-ROMs, 500 records, tapes, and CDs. Acquisition spending 1994–95: $338,734.

Connecticut–Delaware

Tunxis Community Technical College (continued)
COMPUTERS ON CAMPUS 175 computers for student use in computer center, Academic Support Center, classrooms, library provide access to Internet. Staffed computer lab on campus provides training in use of computers, software.
COLLEGE LIFE 60% vote in student government elections. *Social organizations:* 35 open to all. *Most popular organizations:* Phi Theta Kappa, SADHA, Human Services Club, Minority Student Alliance, Connecticut Secretaries International. *Major annual events:* Art Show, Campus Barbecue, International Students' Day. *Student services:* personal-psychological counseling. *Campus security:* 24-hour patrols.
HOUSING College housing not available.
CAREER PLANNING *Placement office:* 1 part-time staff; $16,000 operating expenditure 1994–95. *Director:* Dr. David Smith, Director of Student Development, 860-679-9541. *Services:* resume preparation, career counseling, careers library, job bank.
EXPENSES FOR 1996–97 *Application fee:* $10. State resident tuition: $1560 full-time, $65 per credit part-time. Nonresident tuition: $4680 full-time, $195 per credit part-time. Part-time mandatory fees per semester range from $36 to $81. Tuition for nonresidents who are eligible for the New England Regional Student Program: $2340 full-time, $97.50 per credit part-time. Full-time mandatory fees: $162.
FINANCIAL AID *College-administered undergrad aid 1995–96:* 404 need-based scholarships (average $742), 25 non-need scholarships (average $300), short-term loans (average $300), low-interest long-term loans from external sources (average $1500), Federal Work-Study, 57 part-time jobs. *Required forms:* institutional, FAFSA; accepted: CSS Financial Aid PROFILE. *Priority deadline:* 6/1. *Waivers:* full or partial for employees or children of employees and senior citizens.
APPLYING Open admission except for dental hygiene, drug and alcohol rehabilitation counseling programs. *Options:* Common Application, deferred entrance. *Required:* school transcript, TOEFL for international students. *Required for some:* Dental Hygiene Candidate Admission Test. Test scores used for admission and counseling/placement. *Application deadline:* rolling. Preference given to state residents.
APPLYING/TRANSFER *Required:* high school transcript. *Required for some:* standardized test scores. *Entrance:* noncompetitive. *Application deadline:* rolling.
CONTACT Ms. Donna Brandeis LaGanga, Director of Admissions, Tunxis Community Technical College, Farmington, CT 06032-3026, 860-679-9512.

DELAWARE

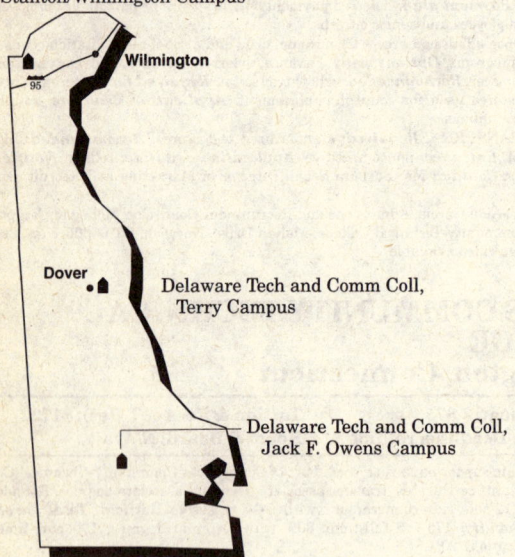

Delaware Tech and Comm Coll, Stanton/Wilmington Campus
Wilmington
Dover
Delaware Tech and Comm Coll, Terry Campus
Delaware Tech and Comm Coll, Jack F. Owens Campus

DELAWARE TECHNICAL & COMMUNITY COLLEGE, JACK F. OWENS CAMPUS
Georgetown, Delaware

UG Enrollment: 3,251	Tuition & Fees (DE Res): $1225
Application Deadline: rolling	Room & Board: N/Avail

GENERAL State-supported, 2-year, coed. Part of Delaware Technical and Community College System. Awards certificates, diplomas, terminal associate degrees. Founded 1967. *Setting:* 120-acre small-town campus. *Total enrollment:* 3,251. *Faculty:* 164 (78 full-time, 86 part-time); student-faculty ratio is 16:1. *Notable Alumni:* Neal Hitchens, author; Allan Ellingsworth, superintendent of Delaware State Police; June Turnasky, professor; J. Everette Moore, attorney; Ruth Miner, lieutenant governor.
ENROLLMENT PROFILE 3,251 students from 4 states and territories, 9 other countries. 64% women, 36% men, 56% part-time, 93% state residents, 5% transferred in, 40% have need-based financial aid, 54% 25 or older, 1% Native American, 1% Hispanic, 14% African American, 1% Asian American. *Areas of study chosen:* 32% health professions and related sciences, 13% business management and administrative services, 6% engineering and applied sciences, 4% computer and information sciences, 2% agriculture, 2% architecture, 1% communications and journalism.
FIRST-YEAR CLASS 775 total. Of the students who applied, 100% were accepted.
ACADEMIC PROGRAM Core. Calendar: semesters. Academic remediation for entering students, English as a second language program offered during academic year and summer, services for LD students, self-designed majors, summer session for credit, part-time degree program (daytime, evenings, summer), external degree programs, adult/continuing education programs, internships.
GENERAL DEGREE REQUIREMENTS 70 credits; internship (some majors).
MAJORS Accounting, agricultural business, architectural technologies, automotive technologies, business administration/commerce/management, carpentry, chemical engineering technology, civil engineering technology, computer programming, construction management, criminal justice, data processing, drafting and design, electrical and electronics technologies, engineering (general), engineering technology, environmental engineering technology, hospitality services, hotel and restaurant management, human services, industrial and heavy equipment maintenance, journalism, laboratory technologies, legal secretarial studies, marketing/retailing/merchandising, medical assistant technologies, medical laboratory technology, medical secretarial studies, nursing, practical nursing, retail management, secretarial studies/office management, welding technology.
LIBRARY Stephen J. Betze Library plus 1 other, with 68,282 books, 150 microform titles, 433 periodicals, 19 CD-ROMs, 1,635 records, tapes, and CDs. Acquisition spending 1994–95: $353,068.
COMPUTERS ON CAMPUS 400 computers for student use in computer center, computer labs, classrooms, library provide access to off-campus computing facilities, on-line services. Staffed computer lab on campus.
COLLEGE LIFE Student-run radio station. *Social organizations:* 7 open to all. *Most popular organizations:* Student Government Association, Student Nursing Association, Phi Beta Kappa, Occupational Therapy Assistant Club, Physical Therapy Assistant Club. *Campus security:* 24-hour patrols, late-night transport-escort service.
HOUSING College housing not available.
ATHLETICS Member NJCAA. *Intercollegiate:* baseball M(s), softball W. *Intramural:* golf. *Contact:* Mr. Terry Johnson, Assistant Dean of Students, 302-856-5400.
CAREER PLANNING *Placement office:* 2 full-time staff. *Director:* Mr. Terry Johnson, Assistant Dean of Students, 302-856-5400. *Services:* job fairs, resume preparation, career counseling, careers library, job bank, job interviews.
EXPENSES FOR 1995–96 State resident tuition: $1200 full-time, $50 per credit part-time. Nonresident tuition: $3000 full-time, $125 per credit part-time. Full-time mandatory fees: $25.
FINANCIAL AID *College-administered undergrad aid 1995–96:* need-based scholarships, low-interest long-term loans from external sources, Federal Work-Study. *Required forms:* institutional, FAFSA; required for some: state. *Priority deadline:* 6/15. *Payment plans:* installment, deferred payment. *Waivers:* full or partial for employees or children of employees and senior citizens.
APPLYING Open admission except for nursing, engineering technology programs. *Option:* early entrance. *Required:* CGP. Test scores used for counseling/placement. *Application deadline:* rolling. *Notification:* continuous. Preference given to state residents.
APPLYING/TRANSFER *Entrance:* noncompetitive. *Application deadline:* rolling. *Notification:* continuous. *Contact:* Ms. Clare A. MacDonald, Counselor, 302-856-5400.
CONTACT Mr. Walton Johnson, Registrar, Delaware Technical & Community College, Jack F. Owens Campus, Box 610, Georgetown, DE 19947, 302-856-5400. *Fax:* 302-856-9461.

DELAWARE TECHNICAL & COMMUNITY COLLEGE, STANTON/WILMINGTON CAMPUS
Newark, Delaware

UG Enrollment: 6,552	Tuition & Fees (DE Res): $1225
Application Deadline: rolling	Room & Board: N/Avail

GENERAL State-supported, 2-year, coed. Part of Delaware Technical and Community College System. Awards certificates, diplomas, terminal associate degrees. Founded 1968. *Setting:* small-town campus with easy access to Philadelphia. *Total enrollment:* 6,552. *Faculty:* 460 (142 full-time, 318 part-time).
ENROLLMENT PROFILE 6,552 students from 4 states and territories, 25 other countries. 57% women, 43% men, 66% part-time, 92% state residents, 8% transferred in, 1% international, 50% 25 or older, 1% Native American, 3% Hispanic, 17% African American, 3% Asian American. *Areas of study chosen:* 23% health professions and related sciences, 12% business management and administrative services, 12% engineering and applied sciences, 4% computer and information sciences, 2% architecture. *Most popular recent majors:* nursing, engineering (general), criminal justice.
FIRST-YEAR CLASS 1,755 total. Of the students who applied, 100% were accepted.
ACADEMIC PROGRAM Core, honor code. Calendar: semesters. Academic remediation for entering students, English as a second language program offered during academic year, services for LD students, summer session for credit, part-time degree program (daytime, evenings, weekends, summer), external degree programs, adult/continuing education programs, co-op programs.
GENERAL DEGREE REQUIREMENTS 70 credits; internship (some majors).
MAJORS Accounting, architectural technologies, biomedical technologies, business administration/commerce/management, chemical engineering technology, civil engineering technology, corrections, criminal justice, data processing, dental services, drafting and design, electrical and electronics technologies, electrical engineering technology, engineering (general), fire science, food services technology, human services, industrial engineering technology, instrumentation technology, law enforcement/police sciences, mechanical engineering technology, medical secretarial studies, nuclear medical technology, nursing, occupational safety and health, radiological technology, respiratory therapy, secretarial studies/office management, transportation technologies.
LIBRARY 47,059 books, 2,924 microform titles, 583 periodicals, 924 records, tapes, and CDs. Acquisition spending 1994–95: $211,150.
COMPUTERS ON CAMPUS 200 computers for student use in computer center.
COLLEGE LIFE *Student services:* health clinic, personal-psychological counseling. *Campus security:* late-night transport-escort service.
HOUSING College housing not available.
ATHLETICS Member NJCAA. *Intercollegiate:* basketball M, soccer M, softball W, tennis M/W, volleyball M/W. *Intramural:* basketball, tennis.

Delaware

CAREER PLANNING *Director:* Ms. Joan Yaskcoe, Counselor, 302-573-5464. *Services:* resume preparation, career counseling, careers library, job bank.
EXPENSES FOR 1995–96 State resident tuition: $1200 full-time, $50 per credit part-time. Nonresident tuition: $3000 full-time, $125 per credit part-time. Full-time mandatory fees: $25.
FINANCIAL AID *College-administered undergrad aid 1995–96:* need-based scholarships, non-need scholarships, low-interest long-term loans from external sources, Federal Work-Study. *Required forms:* CSS Financial Aid PROFILE, institutional; accepted: FAFSA. *Priority deadline:* 7/11. *Waivers:* full or partial for employees or children of employees and senior citizens.
APPLYING Open admission. *Option:* early entrance. *Required:* CGP. *Recommended:* SAT I. Test scores used for counseling/placement. *Application deadline:* rolling. *Notification:* continuous. Preference given to state residents.
APPLYING/TRANSFER *Application deadline:* rolling. *Notification:* continuous.
CONTACT Ms. Rebecca Bailey, Admissions Coordinator, Wilmington, Delaware Technical & Community College, Stanton/Wilmington Campus, Newark, DE 19702, 302-571-5366. *Fax:* 302-577-2548.

DELAWARE TECHNICAL & COMMUNITY COLLEGE, TERRY CAMPUS
Dover, Delaware

UG Enrollment: 1,861	Tuition & Fees (DE Res): $1225
Application Deadline: rolling	Room & Board: N/Avail

GENERAL State-supported, 2-year, coed. Part of Delaware Technical and Community College System. Awards certificates, diplomas, terminal associate degrees. Founded 1972. *Setting:* 70-acre small-town campus. *Total enrollment:* 1,861. *Faculty:* 119 (45 full-time, 74 part-time); student-faculty ratio is 16:1.
ENROLLMENT PROFILE 1,861 students from 4 states and territories, 5 other countries. 62% women, 38% men, 71% part-time, 97% state residents, 7% transferred in, 40% have need-based financial aid, 56% 25 or older, 1% Native American, 2% Hispanic, 17% African American, 2% Asian American. *Areas of study chosen:* 21% health professions and related sciences, 17% business management and administrative services, 9% engineering and applied sciences, 6% computer and information sciences, 5% architecture.
FIRST-YEAR CLASS 482 total. Of the students who applied, 100% were accepted.
ACADEMIC PROGRAM Core. Calendar: semesters. Academic remediation for entering students, services for LD students, summer session for credit, part-time degree program (daytime, evenings, summer), adult/continuing education programs, co-op programs and internships.

GENERAL DEGREE REQUIREMENTS 70 credits; internship (some majors).
MAJORS Accounting, aerospace sciences, architectural technologies, aviation administration, aviation technology, business administration/commerce/management, civil engineering technology, computer programming, computer technologies, construction management, construction technologies, corrections, criminal justice, data processing, drafting and design, early childhood education, electrical and electronics technologies, electromechanical technology, electronics engineering technology, engineering technology, human services, industrial engineering technology, nursing, practical nursing, secretarial studies/office management, surveying technology.
LIBRARY 15,969 books, 53 microform titles, 334 periodicals, 292 on-line bibliographic services, 13 CD-ROMs, 1,486 records, tapes, and CDs. Acquisition spending 1994–95: $265,715.
COMPUTERS ON CAMPUS 125 computers for student use in computer labs, classrooms. Staffed computer lab on campus provides training in use of computers, software.
COLLEGE LIFE 30% vote in student government elections. *Social organizations:* 15 open to all. *Most popular organizations:* Students of Kolor, Human Services Organization, Phi Theta Kappa, Alpha Beta Gamma. *Student services:* personal-psychological counseling.
HOUSING College housing not available.
ATHLETICS *Intercollegiate:* golf M/W.
CAREER PLANNING *Placement office:* 2 full-time staff. *Director:* Ms. Mary Lynn Houghtaling, Coordinator of Assessment Center, 302-739-6186. *Services:* resume preparation, resume referral, career counseling, careers library, job bank, job interviews. Students must register freshman year.
EXPENSES FOR 1995–96 State resident tuition: $1200 full-time, $50 per credit part-time. Nonresident tuition: $3000 full-time, $125 per credit part-time. Full-time mandatory fees: $25.
FINANCIAL AID *College-administered undergrad aid 1995–96:* need-based scholarships, short-term loans, low-interest long-term loans from external sources, Federal Work-Study, part-time jobs. *Required forms:* FAFSA. *Application deadline:* continuous. *Payment plans:* tuition prepayment, installment, deferred pay. *Waivers:* full or partial for employees or children of employees and senior citizens.
APPLYING Open admission except for nursing, engineering technology programs. *Option:* early entrance. *Required:* TOEFL for international students, CGP. Test scores used for counseling/placement. *Application deadline:* rolling. Preference given to state residents.
APPLYING/TRANSFER *Entrance:* noncompetitive. *Application deadline:* rolling.
CONTACT Mr. Kenneth Hogan, Registrar/Admissions Officer, Delaware Technical & Community College, Terry Campus, 1832 North duPont Parkway, Dover, DE 19904, 302-739-5451. *Fax:* 302-739-6169. *E-mail:* khogan@outland.dtcc.edu.

Peterson's Guide to Two-Year Colleges 1997

Florida

FLORIDA

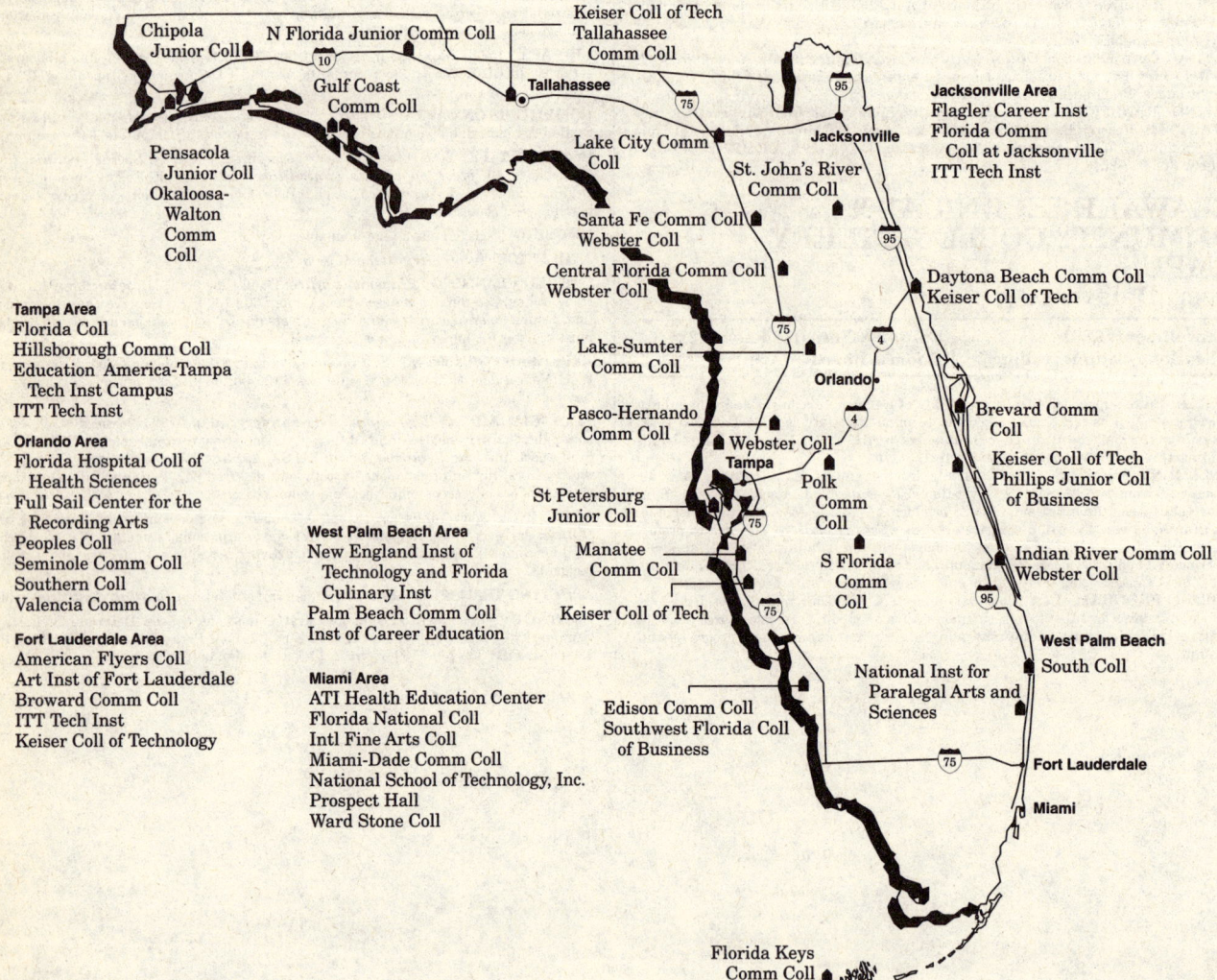

AMERICAN FLYERS COLLEGE
Fort Lauderdale, Florida

UG Enrollment: 50	Tuition & Fees: $9777
Application Deadline: rolling	Room Only: $1700

GENERAL Proprietary, 2-year, coed. Awards transfer associate degrees. Founded 1990. *Setting:* urban campus with easy access to Miami. *Total enrollment:* 50. *Faculty:* 8.
ENROLLMENT PROFILE 50 students.
ACADEMIC PROGRAM Core, aviation-oriented curriculum, honor code. Calendar: semesters.
GENERAL DEGREE REQUIREMENTS 69 credit hours; 3 credit hours of college algebra; computer course.
MAJOR Aviation technology.
LIBRARY Montgomery Library with 1,400 books, 35 periodicals.
COMPUTERS ON CAMPUS 6 computers for student use in computer center, computer labs, library. Staffed computer lab on campus.
COLLEGE LIFE *Campus security:* 24-hour emergency response devices and patrols, student patrols.
HOUSING 63 college housing spaces available; 26 were occupied 1995–96.
CAREER PLANNING *Services:* job fairs, resume preparation, career counseling, careers library, job bank.
EXPENSES FOR 1996-97 *Application fee:* $25. Tuition: $9177 full-time, $266 per credit hour part-time. Part-time mandatory fees: $300 per semester. Full-time mandatory fees: $600. College room only: $1700.
FINANCIAL AID *College-administered undergrad aid 1995–96:* need-based scholarships, non-need scholarships.
APPLYING Open admission. *Required:* TOEFL for international students. *Recommended:* SAT I. Test scores used for counseling/placement. *Application deadline:* rolling.
APPLYING/TRANSFER *Entrance:* noncompetitive. *Application deadline:* rolling. *Contact:* Ms. Sherry Magno, Registrar, 305-772-7500.

CONTACT Ms. Sherry Magno, Registrar, American Flyers College, 5400 NW 21st Terrace, Fort Lauderdale, FL 33309, 305-772-7500 or toll-free 800-327-0808. College video available.

ART INSTITUTE OF FORT LAUDERDALE
Fort Lauderdale, Florida

UG Enrollment: 1,950	Tuition & Fees: $12,600
Application Deadline: rolling	Room Only: $5250

The Art Institute of Fort Lauderdale has been showing students how to turn a passion for the visual and practical arts into a profession since 1968. The Institute offers Associate of Science degree programs in broadcasting, culinary arts, computer animation, fashion design, fashion marketing, industrial design, interior design, multimedia, photography, travel and hospitality, video production, and visual communications. The Bachelor of Science degree in interior design and industrial design is also offered. Faculty members are working professionals with impressive achievements in their respective fields.

GENERAL Proprietary, primarily 2-year, coed. Awards transfer associate, terminal associate, bachelor's degrees. Founded 1968. *Setting:* urban campus with easy access to Miami. *Total enrollment:* 1,950. *Faculty:* 150 (100 full-time, 50 part-time).
ENROLLMENT PROFILE 1,950 students: 50% women, 0% part-time, 50% state residents, 42% transferred in, 12% 25 or older, 1% Native American, 8% Hispanic, 8% African American, 2% Asian American. *Most popular recent majors:* commercial art, music business, interior design.
FIRST-YEAR CLASS 668 total; 1,000 applied, 100% were accepted, 67% of whom enrolled. 15% from top 10% of their high school class, 25% from top quarter, 50% from top half.

ACADEMIC PROGRAM Core. Calendar: quarters. Academic remediation for entering students, advanced placement, summer session for credit, adult/continuing education programs, co-op programs and internships. Off-campus study at 9 members of The Art Institutes. Study-abroad program.
GENERAL DEGREE REQUIREMENTS 96 credits for associate, 180 credits for bachelor's; 1 course each in math and science; computer course for interior design, commercial art, fashion, music and video business majors.
MAJORS Applied art, broadcasting (B), business administration/commerce/management (B), commercial art, culinary arts, fashion design and technology, fashion merchandising (B), film studies, graphic arts, illustration, industrial design, interior design, marketing/retailing/merchandising, music business, painting/drawing, photography, textiles and clothing, tourism and travel.
LIBRARY 14,000 books, 240 periodicals, 6 CD-ROMs.
COMPUTERS ON CAMPUS 125 computers for student use in computer center, computer labs, library. Staffed computer lab on campus provides training in use of computers, software.
COLLEGE LIFE ***Student services:*** personal-psychological counseling.
HOUSING 280 college housing spaces available. No special consideration for freshman housing applicants. Off-campus living permitted. ***Option:*** coed housing available.
CAREER PLANNING ***Service:*** career counseling.
EXPENSES FOR 1995–96 ***Application fee:*** $50. Tuition: $12,600 full-time. One-time mandatory fee: $250. College room only: $5250.
FINANCIAL AID ***College-administered undergrad aid 1995–96:*** need-based scholarships, 12 non-need scholarships (average $3000), low-interest long-term loans from college funds (average $1500), loans from external sources (average $1400), Federal Work-Study, 15 part-time jobs. ***Required forms:*** CSS Financial Aid PROFILE, institutional; required for some: state; accepted: FAFSA. ***Application deadline:*** continuous. ***Payment plan:*** tuition prepayment.
APPLYING ***Option:*** Common Application. ***Recommended:*** SAT I or ACT. ***Required for some:*** TOEFL for international students. Test scores used for counseling/placement. ***Application deadline:*** rolling.
APPLYING/TRANSFER ***Recommended:*** standardized test scores. ***Application deadline:*** rolling. ***Contact:*** Ms. Eileen Northrop, Vice President/Director Admissions, 305-527-1799.
CONTACT Ms. Eileen Northrop, Vice President/Director of Admissions, Art Institute of Fort Lauderdale, 1799 Southeast 17th Street Causeway, Fort Lauderdale, FL 33316-3000, 305-527-1799 Ext. 420 or toll-free 800-275-7603. ***Fax:*** 305-527-1799 Ext. 509. College video available.

❖ ***See page 694 for a narrative description.*** ❖

ATI HEALTH EDUCATION CENTER
Miami, Florida

UG Enrollment: 300	**Tuition: $7995/deg prog**
Application Deadline: rolling	**Room & Board: N/Avail**

GENERAL Proprietary, 2-year, coed. Part of ATI Enterprises Inc., of Florida. Awards transfer associate, terminal associate degrees. Founded 1976. ***Setting:*** 1-acre urban campus. ***Total enrollment:*** 300. ***Faculty:*** 19 (7 full-time, 12 part-time).
ENROLLMENT PROFILE 300 students from 2 states and territories, 5 other countries. 60% women, 0% part-time, 94% state residents, 10% transferred in, 5% international, 50% 25 or older, 1% Native American, 35% Hispanic, 40% African American, 2% Asian American.
FIRST-YEAR CLASS 100 total. Of the students who applied, 70% were accepted, 80% of whom enrolled.
ACADEMIC PROGRAM Calendar: semesters. Academic remediation for entering students, part-time degree program (evenings, summer).
GENERAL DEGREE REQUIREMENT 86 semester hours.
MAJORS Medical assistant technologies, respiratory therapy.
COLLEGE LIFE ***Student services:*** health clinic, personal-psychological counseling.
HOUSING College housing not available.
CAREER PLANNING ***Service:*** career counseling.
EXPENSES FOR 1996–97 ***Application fee:*** $100. Tuition per degree program ranges from $7995 to $13,995. One-time mandatory fee: $100. Tuition guaranteed not to increase for student's term of enrollment.
FINANCIAL AID ***College-administered undergrad aid 1995–96:*** need-based scholarships, low-interest long-term loans from external sources. ***Required forms:*** institutional, FAFSA. ***Application deadline:*** continuous.
APPLYING ***Required:*** school transcript, interview, Wonderlic aptitude test. Test scores used for counseling/placement. ***Application deadline:*** rolling. ***Notification:*** continuous.
APPLYING/TRANSFER ***Required:*** standardized test scores, high school transcript, interview, college transcript. ***Entrance:*** minimally difficult. ***Application deadline:*** rolling. ***Notification:*** continuous.
CONTACT Mr. Chris Cavone, Director of Admissions, ATI Health Education Center, 1395 NW 167th Street, Suite 200, Miami, FL 33169-5742, 305-628-1000.

BREVARD COMMUNITY COLLEGE
Cocoa, Florida

UG Enrollment: 14,341	**Tuition & Fees (FL Res): $1184**
Application Deadline: rolling	**Room & Board: N/Avail**

GENERAL State-supported, 2-year, coed. Part of Florida Community Colleges System. Awards certificates, diplomas, transfer associate, terminal associate degrees. Founded 1960. ***Setting:*** 100-acre suburban campus. ***Total enrollment:*** 14,341. ***Faculty:*** 1,119 (235 full-time, 884 part-time); student-faculty ratio is 15:1. ***Notable Alumni:*** Paul Azinger, professional golfer; Mike Smith, professional golfer; Don Wilson, actor and world-champion kickboxer; Lieutenant Colonel Danny McKnight, decorated military officer.
ENROLLMENT PROFILE 14,341 students from 50 states and territories, 43 other countries. 58% women, 42% men, 69% part-time, 97% state residents, 34% transferred in, 1% international, 57% 25 or older, 0% Native American, 5% Hispanic, 7% African American, 3% Asian American. ***Most popular recent major:*** liberal arts/general studies.
FIRST-YEAR CLASS 2,508 total; 3,350 applied, 100% were accepted, 75% of whom enrolled.
ACADEMIC PROGRAM Core. Calendar: semesters. 1,100 courses offered in 1995–96. Academic remediation for entering students, English as a second language program offered during academic year, services for LD students, self-designed majors, honors program, summer session for credit, part-time degree program (daytime, evenings, summer), external degree programs, adult/continuing education programs, co-op programs. Off-campus study at Malaspina College. Study abroad in Germany. ROTC: Army, Air Force.
GENERAL DEGREE REQUIREMENTS 60 credit hours; math/science requirements vary according to major; computer course for business-related majors; internship (some majors).
MAJORS Accounting, art/fine arts, biology/biological sciences, biomedical technologies, business administration/commerce/management, chemistry, child care/child and family studies, civil engineering technology, commercial art, computer programming, computer science, computer technologies, construction technologies, corrections, cosmetology, criminal justice, data processing, dental services, drafting and design, early childhood education, economics, education, electrical and electronics technologies, electrical engineering technology, elementary education, emergency medical technology, energy management technologies, engineering design, engineering sciences, English, environmental health sciences, fashion merchandising, finance/banking, fire science, food services management, French, German, history, home economics education, hotel and restaurant management, human resources, industrial engineering technology, journalism, law enforcement/police sciences, liberal arts/general studies, marketing/retailing/merchandising, mathematics, mechanical engineering technology, medical assistant technologies, medical laboratory technology, military science, modern languages, music, nursing, physical education, physical therapy, practical nursing, radio and television studies, radiological technology, real estate, science, science education, secretarial studies/office management, Spanish, speech/rhetoric/public address/debate, teacher aide studies, technical writing, theater arts/drama, veterinary sciences, water resources.
LIBRARY Roger Dobson Library plus 3 others, with 147,213 books, 876 microform titles, 1,375 periodicals, 30 on-line bibliographic services, 5,567 records, tapes, and CDs.
COMPUTERS ON CAMPUS 290 computers for student use in computer labs, learning resource center, Disabled Student Center, library provide access to on-line services, Internet. Staffed computer lab on campus provides training in use of computers, software.
NOTEWORTHY RESEARCH FACILITIES Florida Solar Energy Center.
COLLEGE LIFE Orientation program. Drama-theater group, choral group, student-run newspaper. 5% vote in student government elections. ***Most popular organizations:*** Black Student Union, Terraphile Society, Joy Explosion. ***Major annual events:*** Spring Festival, Black Heritage Week. ***Student services:*** personal-psychological counseling, women's center. ***Campus security:*** 24-hour emergency response devices and patrols, late-night transport-escort service.
HOUSING College housing not available.
ATHLETICS Member NJCAA. ***Intercollegiate:*** baseball M, basketball M(s)/W(s), golf M(s), softball W, volleyball W(s). ***Intramural:*** cross-country running, fencing, sailing, soccer, swimming and diving, track and field. ***Contact:*** Dr. Robert A. Anderson, Associate Vice President of Student Services, 407-632-1111.
CAREER PLANNING ***Placement office:*** 10 full-time, 4 part-time staff. ***Director:*** Dr. Anita Moore, Director of the Center for Career Development, 407-632-1111. ***Services:*** job fairs, resume preparation, resume referral, career counseling, careers library, job bank, job interviews.
AFTER GRADUATION 70% of students completing a degree program in 1994–95 went directly on to further study.
EXPENSES FOR 1996–97 ***Application fee:*** $25. State resident tuition: $1184 full-time, $37 per credit hour part-time. Nonresident tuition: $4320 full-time, $135 per credit hour part-time.
FINANCIAL AID ***College-administered undergrad aid 1995–96:*** 560 need-based scholarships (average $500), 1,000 non-need scholarships (average $800), short-term loans (average $200), low-interest long-term loans from external sources (average $2625), 140 Federal Work-Study (averaging $1632), part-time jobs. ***Required forms:*** CSS Financial Aid PROFILE, state; required for some: institutional, FAFSA. ***Priority deadline:*** 5/16. ***Payment plan:*** deferred payment. ***Waivers:*** full or partial for minority students and senior citizens. ***Notification:*** continuous.
APPLYING Open admission. ***Options:*** early entrance, deferred entrance. ***Required:*** school transcript, 3 years of high school math and science. ***Required for some:*** SAT I or ACT, TOEFL for international students, ACT ASSET. Test scores used for counseling/placement. ***Application deadline:*** rolling. ***Notification:*** continuous.
APPLYING/TRANSFER ***Required:*** high school transcript, 3 years of high school math and science, college transcript. ***Required for some:*** standardized test scores. ***Application deadline:*** rolling. ***Notification:*** continuous. ***Contact:*** Ms. Irene Bacca, Dean of Enrollment Services, 407-632-1111.
CONTACT Ms. Margaret Thurman, Supervisor of Admissions, Brevard Community College, 1519 Clearlake Road, Cocoa, FL 32922-6597, 407-632-1111. ***Fax:*** 407-633-4565. College video available.

BROWARD COMMUNITY COLLEGE
Fort Lauderdale, Florida

UG Enrollment: 24,600	**Tuition & Fees (FL Res): $1176**
Application Deadline: N/R	**Room & Board: N/Avail**

GENERAL State-supported, 2-year, coed. Part of Florida Community Colleges System. Awards transfer associate, terminal associate degrees. Founded 1960. ***Setting:*** urban campus with easy access to Miami. ***Total enrollment:*** 24,600. ***Faculty:*** 775 (300 full-time, 475 part-time); student-faculty ratio is 30:1.
ENROLLMENT PROFILE 24,600 students: 61% women, 78% part-time, 56% state residents, 16% transferred in, 4% international, 29% 25 or older, 1% Native American, 15% Hispanic, 19% African American, 3% Asian American. ***Most popular recent majors:*** nursing, business administration/commerce/management, liberal arts/general studies.
FIRST-YEAR CLASS 5,589 total. Of the students who applied, 100% were accepted, 99% of whom enrolled.
ACADEMIC PROGRAM Core. Calendar: trimesters. Academic remediation for entering students, English as a second language program offered during academic year, services for LD students, advanced placement, self-designed majors, honors program, summer session for credit, part-time degree program (daytime, evenings, summer), adult/continuing education programs, co-op programs. Off-campus study. Study abroad in 12 countries, including Spain, England, Israel. ROTC: Army.

Peterson's Guide to Two-Year Colleges 1997 247

Broward Community College (continued)

GENERAL DEGREE REQUIREMENTS 60 semester hours; 6 semester hours of math; 7 semester hours of science; computer course (varies by major).

MAJORS Accounting, architectural technologies, automotive technologies, aviation administration, aviation technology, business administration/commerce/management, child care/child and family studies, civil engineering technology, computer information systems, computer programming, computer science, computer technologies, construction management, corrections, criminal justice, data processing, dental services, early childhood education, electrical and electronics technologies, electronics engineering technology, elementary education, emergency medical technology, engineering sciences, (pre)engineering sequence, finance/banking, fire science, flight training, food services management, hotel and restaurant management, insurance, interior design, law enforcement/police sciences, legal secretarial studies, liberal arts/general studies, marketing/retailing/merchandising, mechanical engineering technology, medical assistant technologies, medical laboratory technology, medical secretarial studies, medical technology, nuclear medical technology, nursing, paralegal studies, physical therapy, pollution control technologies, radiological technology, respiratory therapy, secretarial studies/office management, tourism and travel.

LIBRARY 200,000 books, 600 periodicals.

COMPUTERS ON CAMPUS Computers for student use in computer center, computer labs, learning resource center.

COLLEGE LIFE Drama-theater group, choral group, student-run newspaper. ***Social organizations:*** 5 local fraternities, 5 local sororities. ***Student services:*** personal-psychological counseling, women's center. ***Campus security:*** 24-hour emergency response devices and patrols, late-night transport-escort service.

HOUSING College housing not available.

ATHLETICS Member NJCAA. ***Intercollegiate:*** baseball M(s), basketball M(s)/W(s), golf M(s)/W(s), soccer M(s)/W, tennis M(s)/W(s), wrestling M(s). ***Intramural:*** baseball, basketball, golf, tennis. ***Contact:*** Dr. Thomas Ryan, Athletic Director, 305-475-6755.

CAREER PLANNING ***Placement office:*** 2 full-time, 1 part-time staff. ***Services:*** job fairs, career counseling, careers library, job bank.

AFTER GRADUATION 39% of students completing a degree program in 1994–95 went directly on to further study.

EXPENSES FOR 1995–96 ***Application fee:*** $25. State resident tuition: $1176 full-time, $36.75 per semester hour part-time. Nonresident tuition: $4288 full-time, $134 per semester hour part-time.

FINANCIAL AID ***College-administered undergrad aid 1995–96:*** need-based scholarships, non-need scholarships, low-interest long-term loans from external sources, Federal Work-Study, part-time jobs. ***Required forms:*** CSS Financial Aid PROFILE, institutional, FAFSA. ***Application deadline:*** continuous. ***Payment plans:*** tuition prepayment, deferred payment. ***Waivers:*** full or partial for employees or children of employees and senior citizens.

APPLYING Open admission. ***Options:*** early entrance, deferred entrance. ***Required:*** TOEFL for international students. ***Recommended:*** SAT I or ACT. Test scores used for counseling/placement. Preference given to state residents.

APPLYING/TRANSFER ***Entrance:*** noncompetitive.

CONTACT Mrs. Barbara Bryan, Director of Enrollment Management/Registrar, Broward Community College, 225 East Las Olas Boulevard, Fort Lauderdale, FL 33301-2298, 305-761-7464.

THE CAREER CENTER
Florida—See Institute of Career Education

CENTRAL FLORIDA COMMUNITY COLLEGE
Ocala, Florida

UG Enrollment: 6,068	**Tuition & Fees (FL Res): $1230**
Application Deadline: 8/10	**Room & Board: N/Avail**

GENERAL State and locally supported, 2-year, coed. Part of Florida Community Colleges System. Awards certificates, diplomas, transfer associate, terminal associate degrees. Founded 1957. ***Setting:*** 120-acre small-town campus. ***Endowment:*** $3.4 million. ***Total enrollment:*** 6,068. ***Faculty:*** 219 (104 full-time, 17% with terminal degrees, 115 part-time).

ENROLLMENT PROFILE 6,068 students: 64% women, 59% part-time, 97% state residents, 3% transferred in, 1% international, 1% Native American, 4% Hispanic, 10% African American, 1% Asian American. ***Areas of study chosen:*** 20% vocational and home economics, 19% business management and administrative services, 15% education, 12% liberal arts/general studies, 10% health professions and related sciences, 2% engineering and applied sciences, 2% physical sciences, 1% interdisciplinary studies. ***Most popular recent majors:*** business administration/commerce/management, education, liberal arts/general studies.

FIRST-YEAR CLASS 880 total; 1,900 applied, 100% were accepted, 46% of whom enrolled.

ACADEMIC PROGRAM Core, honor code. Calendar: semesters. Academic remediation for entering students, English as a second language program offered during academic year, services for LD students, advanced placement, Freshman Honors College, honors program, summer session for credit, part-time degree program (daytime, evenings, weekends, summer), adult/continuing education programs, co-op programs. Study abroad in Spain, England.

GENERAL DEGREE REQUIREMENTS 60 credit hours; internship (some majors).

MAJORS Accounting, business administration/commerce/management, child care/child and family studies, computer programming, criminal justice, dental services, drafting and design, education, electronics engineering technology, emergency medical technology, environmental sciences, fire science, law enforcement/police sciences, legal secretarial studies, liberal arts/general studies, manufacturing technology, medical secretarial studies, nursing, occupational therapy, ornamental horticulture, paralegal studies, physical therapy, radiological technology, respiratory therapy, secretarial studies/office management.

LIBRARY Main library plus 1 other, with 63,391 books, 5,409 microform titles, 425 periodicals, 4 on-line bibliographic services, 5 CD-ROMs, 5,235 records, tapes, and CDs. Acquisition spending 1994–95: $145,162.

COMPUTERS ON CAMPUS 175 computers for student use in computer labs, skills lab, classrooms provide access to e-mail, Internet. Staffed computer lab on campus provides training in use of computers, software. Academic computing expenditure 1994–95: $490,281.

COLLEGE LIFE Orientation program (2 days, $38). Drama-theater group, choral group, student-run newspaper. 30% vote in student government elections. ***Social organizations:*** 45 open to all. ***Most popular organizations:*** Student Government, Campus Diplomats. ***Major annual events:*** Homecoming, Student Activities Week, Alcohol Awareness Week. ***Student services:*** personal-psychological counseling, women's center. ***Campus security:*** 24-hour patrols, student patrols, late-night transport-escort service.

HOUSING College housing not available.

ATHLETICS Member NJCAA. ***Intercollegiate:*** baseball M, basketball M(s)/W(s), softball W. ***Intramural:*** basketball, swimming and diving, volleyball. ***Contact:*** Mr. Mike McGinnis, Athletic Director, 904-237-2111 Ext. 325.

CAREER PLANNING ***Placement office:*** 2 full-time staff. ***Director:*** Ms. Amy Mangan, Director of Cooperative Education and Job Placement, 904-237-2111 Ext. 397. ***Services:*** job fairs, resume preparation, resume referral, career counseling, careers library, job bank, job interviews. 60 organizations recruited on campus 1994–95.

AFTER GRADUATION 5% of class of 1994 had job offers within 6 months.

ESTIMATED EXPENSES FOR 1996–97 ***Application fee:*** $20. State resident tuition: $1230 full-time, $38.44 per credit hour part-time. Nonresident tuition: $4405 full-time, $137.68 per credit hour part-time.

FINANCIAL AID ***College-administered undergrad aid 1995–96:*** 187 need-based scholarships (average $800), 310 non-need scholarships (average $800), short-term loans (average $268), low-interest long-term loans from college funds, loans from external sources (average $2625), 23 Federal Work-Study (averaging $1800), 26 part-time jobs. ***Required forms:*** institutional; accepted: CSS Financial Aid PROFILE, FAFSA. ***Priority deadline:*** 5/1. ***Waivers:*** full or partial for employees or children of employees. ***Average indebtedness of graduates:*** $5000.

APPLYING Open admission. ***Option:*** early entrance. ***Required:*** school transcript. ***Recommended:*** SAT I or ACT. Test scores used for counseling/placement. ***Application deadline:*** 8/10. ***Notification:*** continuous.

APPLYING/TRANSFER ***Required:*** college transcript. ***Entrance:*** noncompetitive. ***Application deadline:*** 8/10. ***Notification:*** continuous.

CONTACT Mrs. Captoria Rawls, Director of Admissions and Records, Central Florida Community College, Ocala, FL 34478-1388, 904-237-2111 Ext. 319. ***E-mail:*** rawlsc@cfcc.cc.fl.us.

CHIPOLA JUNIOR COLLEGE
Marianna, Florida

UG Enrollment: 2,273	**Tuition & Fees (FL Res): $1123**
Application Deadline: rolling	**Room & Board: $2464**

GENERAL State-supported, 2-year, coed. Awards certificates, transfer associate, terminal associate degrees. Founded 1947. ***Setting:*** 105-acre small-town campus. ***Total enrollment:*** 2,273. ***Faculty:*** 142 (79 full-time, 63 part-time); student-faculty ratio is 22:1.

ENROLLMENT PROFILE 2,273 students from 8 states and territories, 5 other countries. 52% women, 58% part-time, 95% state residents, 4% transferred in, 1% international, 1% Hispanic, 16% African American, 1% Asian American. ***Most popular recent majors:*** business administration/commerce/management, nursing, education.

FIRST-YEAR CLASS 700 total; 775 applied, 100% were accepted, 90% of whom enrolled.

ACADEMIC PROGRAM Core. Calendar: semesters. Academic remediation for entering students, services for LD students, advanced placement, honors program, summer session for credit, part-time degree program (daytime, evenings, summer), adult/continuing education programs.

GENERAL DEGREE REQUIREMENTS 60 semester hours; 6 semester hours each of math and science.

MAJORS Accounting, agricultural sciences, agronomy/soil and crop sciences, art/fine arts, business administration/commerce/management, communication, computer science, education, (pre)engineering sequence, finance/banking, liberal arts/general studies, medical technology, nursing, science, social work.

LIBRARY Chipola Library with 37,740 books, 285 microform titles, 226 periodicals, 4 CD-ROMs, 1,867 records, tapes, and CDs.

COMPUTERS ON CAMPUS 80 computers for student use in labs, library.

COLLEGE LIFE Drama-theater group, choral group, student-run newspaper. 25% vote in student government elections. ***Most popular organization:*** Drama/Theater Group. ***Major annual events:*** Fall Festival, Homecoming, Spring Frolics. ***Campus security:*** night security personnel.

HOUSING No special consideration for freshman housing applicants. Off-campus living permitted. ***Option:*** single-sex housing available. Resident assistants live in dorms.

ATHLETICS Member NJCAA. ***Intercollegiate:*** baseball M(s), basketball M(s), softball W(s). ***Contact:*** Mr. Monte Towe, Athletic Director, 904-526-2761 Ext. 237.

CAREER PLANNING ***Service:*** career counseling.

AFTER GRADUATION 35% of students completing a degree program in 1994–95 went directly on to further study.

EXPENSES FOR 1995–96 State resident tuition: $1123 full-time, $35.10 per semester hour part-time. Nonresident tuition: $4301 full-time, $134.40 per semester hour part-time. College room and board: $2464. College room only: $1100.

FINANCIAL AID ***College-administered undergrad aid 1995–96:*** 250 need-based scholarships (averaging $500), 214 non-need scholarships (averaging $830), short-term loans (averaging $150), low-interest long-term loans from external sources (averaging $2600), Federal Work-Study, 16 part-time jobs. ***Required forms:*** institutional, FAFSA; accepted: CSS Financial Aid PROFILE, state. ***Priority deadline:*** 7/15.

APPLYING Open admission. ***Option:*** early entrance. ***Required:*** 3 years of high school math and science, SAT I or ACT, TOEFL for international students. Test scores used for counseling/placement. ***Application deadline:*** rolling. ***Notification:*** continuous.

APPLYING/TRANSFER ***Application deadline:*** rolling. ***Notification:*** continuous.

CONTACT Mrs. Annette Widner, Registrar and Admissions Manager, Chipola Junior College, Marianna, FL 32446-3065, 904-526-2761 Ext. 292. ***Fax:*** 904-526-4153.

DAYTONA BEACH COMMUNITY COLLEGE
Daytona Beach, Florida

UG Enrollment: 12,001	Tuition & Fees (FL Res): $1074
Application Deadline: rolling	Room & Board: N/Avail

GENERAL State-supported, 2-year, coed. Part of Florida Community Colleges System. Awards certificates, transfer associate, terminal associate degrees. Founded 1958. ***Setting:*** 93-acre suburban campus with easy access to Orlando. ***Endowment:*** $3.9 million. ***Educational spending 1994–95:*** $1991 per undergrad. ***Total enrollment:*** 12,001. ***Faculty:*** 817 (217 full-time, 18% with terminal degrees, 600 part-time).
ENROLLMENT PROFILE 12,001 students from 41 states and territories, 70 other countries. 64% women, 63% part-time, 93% state residents, 6% transferred in, 30% have need-based financial aid, 5% have non-need-based financial aid, 2% international, 52% 25 or older, 0% Native American, 4% Hispanic, 8% African American, 3% Asian American. ***Most popular recent majors:*** business administration/commerce/management, education, engineering (general).
FIRST-YEAR CLASS 1,464 total; 3,119 applied, 100% were accepted, 47% of whom enrolled.
ACADEMIC PROGRAM Core, honor code. Calendar: semesters. Average class size 22 in required courses. Academic remediation for entering students, English as a second language program offered during academic year and summer, services for LD students, advanced placement, honors program, summer session for credit, part-time degree program (daytime, evenings, summer), adult/continuing education programs, co-op programs and internships. Study abroad in Canada, Mexico, England, China, Japan, Hong Kong. ROTC: Army (c), Air Force (c).
GENERAL DEGREE REQUIREMENTS 60 semester hours; internship (some majors).
MAJORS Accounting, advertising, agricultural sciences, anthropology, architectural technologies, art/fine arts, astronomy, automotive technologies, behavioral sciences, biology/biological sciences, business administration/commerce/management, chemistry, child care/child and family studies, civil engineering technology, communication, computer information systems, computer programming, computer science, construction technologies, corrections, cosmetology, court reporting, criminal justice, criminology, culinary arts, dance, drafting and design, early childhood education, economics, education, electrical and electronics technologies, electronics engineering technology, emergency medical technology, engineering (general), English, fashion design and technology, film and video production, finance/banking, fire science, food services management, forestry, geology, graphic arts, health education, health science, heating/refrigeration/air conditioning, history, hospitality services, hotel and restaurant management, humanities, human services, industrial administration, insurance, interior design, journalism, law enforcement/police sciences, legal secretarial studies, liberal arts/general studies, marine biology, marketing/retailing/merchandising, mathematics, medical records services, medical secretarial studies, meteorology, music, nursing, nutrition, occupational therapy, paralegal studies, philosophy, photography, physical education, physical therapy, physics, postal management, practical nursing, psychology, radio and television studies, radiological technology, respiratory therapy, science, secretarial studies/office management, social science, sociology, statistics, telecommunications, theater arts/drama, tourism and travel, word processing, zoology.
LIBRARY Mary Karl Memorial Library with 77,692 books, 212 microform titles, 421 periodicals, 1 on-line bibliographic service, 9 CD-ROMs, 1,821 records, tapes, and CDs. Acquisition spending 1994–95: $82,939.
COMPUTERS ON CAMPUS 565 computers for student use in computer labs, library. Staffed computer lab on campus. Academic computing expenditure 1994–95: $426,292.
COLLEGE LIFE Drama-theater group, choral group, student-run newspaper. ***Social organizations:*** 20 open to all. ***Most popular organizations:*** Florida Student Nursing Association, International Club. ***Major annual events:*** Cultural Festival, Earth Day, Handicap Awareness Day. ***Student services:*** personal-psychological counseling, women's center. ***Campus security:*** 24-hour patrols, late-night transport-escort service.
HOUSING College housing not available.
ATHLETICS Member NJCAA. ***Intercollegiate:*** basketball M(s), softball W(s). ***Intramural:*** basketball, bowling, fencing, football, racquetball, soccer, table tennis (Ping-Pong), tennis, volleyball. ***Contact:*** Mr. Will Dunne, Athletic Director, 904-255-8131 Ext. 4486.
CAREER PLANNING ***Placement office:*** 3 full-time, 2 part-time staff; $239,514 operating expenditure 1994–95. ***Director:*** Ms. Lucy Bell, Dean, Student Services, 904-255-8131 Ext. 3328. ***Services:*** job fairs, resume preparation, resume referral, career counseling, careers library, job bank, job interviews.
EXPENSES FOR 1995–96 ***Application fee:*** $25. State resident tuition: $1074 full-time, $35.80 per semester hour part-time. Nonresident tuition: $4027 full-time, $134.23 per semester hour part-time.
FINANCIAL AID ***College-administered undergrad aid 1995–96:*** 620 need-based scholarships (average $200), 590 non-need scholarships (average $398), low-interest long-term loans from external sources (average $2600), Federal Work-Study, 65 part-time jobs. ***Required forms:*** institutional, FAFSA. ***Priority deadline:*** 5/1. ***Waivers:*** full or partial for employees or children of employees and senior citizens.
APPLYING Open admission except for nursing, allied health, public services programs. ***Options:*** Common Application, early entrance, deferred entrance, midyear entrance. ***Required:*** school transcript, 3 years of high school math and science, TOEFL for international students, ACT ASSET, CPT. ***Recommended:*** SAT I or ACT, SAT II Subject Tests. Test scores used for counseling/placement. ***Application deadline:*** rolling.
APPLYING/TRANSFER ***Required:*** high school transcript, 3 years of high school math and science, college transcript. ***Required for some:*** standardized test scores. ***Application deadline:*** rolling. ***Contact:*** Mrs. Jackie Alvarez, Assistant Director, Admissions Services, 904-255-8131 Ext. 3322.
CONTACT Mrs. Jackie Alvarez, Assistant Director, Admissions Services, Daytona Beach Community College, Daytona Beach, FL 32120, 904-255-8131 Ext. 3322. ***Fax:*** 904-254-4458.

EDISON COMMUNITY COLLEGE
Fort Myers, Florida

UG Enrollment: 9,836	Tuition & Fees (FL Res): $1073
Application Deadline: 8/15	Room & Board: N/Avail

GENERAL State and locally supported, 2-year, coed. Part of Florida Community Colleges System. Awards certificates, transfer associate, terminal associate degrees. Founded 1962. ***Setting:*** 80-acre urban campus. ***Endowment:*** $7 million. ***Total enrollment:*** 9,836. ***Faculty:*** 724 (124 full-time, 30% with terminal degrees, 600 part-time). ***Notable Alumni:*** Fuzzy Zoeller, professional golfer; Keith Arnold, Florida government official.
ENROLLMENT PROFILE 9,836 students from 25 states and territories, 45 other countries. 60% women, 68% part-time, 85% state residents, 1% international, 43% 25 or older, 0% Native American, 5% African American, 2% Asian American. ***Most popular recent majors:*** liberal arts/general studies, business administration/commerce/management.
FIRST-YEAR CLASS 1,738 total; 3,700 applied, 100% were accepted, 47% of whom enrolled.
ACADEMIC PROGRAM Core, interdisciplinary curriculum, honor code. Calendar: semesters. Academic remediation for entering students, English as a second language program offered during academic year and summer, services for LD students, advanced placement, honors program, summer session for credit, part-time degree program (daytime, evenings, summer), adult/continuing education programs, co-op programs. Study-abroad program.
GENERAL DEGREE REQUIREMENTS 60 credits; math/science requirements vary according to program; computer course (varies by major).
MAJORS Accounting, applied art, art/fine arts, business administration/commerce/management, computer science, criminal justice, dental services, drafting and design, electrical and electronics technologies, electronics engineering technology, emergency medical technology, engineering and applied sciences, engineering technology, finance/banking, fire science, horticulture, hospitality services, human services, legal studies, liberal arts/general studies, music, nursing, radiological sciences, respiratory therapy, social science.
LIBRARY Learning Resources Center with 147,513 books, 460 microform titles, 1,681 periodicals, 6 CD-ROMs, 5,609 records, tapes, and CDs. Acquisition spending 1994–95: $36,271.
COMPUTERS ON CAMPUS Computer purchase plan available. 60 computers for student use in computer labs, classrooms. Academic computing expenditure 1994–95: $682,336.
COLLEGE LIFE Drama-theater group, choral group, student-run newspaper. 5% vote in student government elections. ***Social organizations:*** 20 open to all; 1 national fraternity, 1 national sorority; 5% of eligible men and 5% of eligible women are members. ***Most popular organizations:*** Student Government Association, Phi Sigma Omega, Phi Theta Kappa, African-American Student Association, International Club. ***Major annual events:*** Buc Week, Spring Fling, Taste of the South. ***Student services:*** health clinic, personal-psychological counseling. ***Campus security:*** 24-hour emergency response devices and patrols.
HOUSING College housing not available.
ATHLETICS Member NJCAA. ***Intercollegiate:*** baseball M(s), softball W(s). ***Contact:*** Dr. Harold Nolte, Vice President, Student Services, 941-489-9221.
CAREER PLANNING ***Placement office:*** 1 full-time staff; $528,756 operating expenditure 1994–95. ***Director:*** Ms. Michele Yovonovich, Director, Student Development, 941-489-9497. ***Services:*** career counseling, careers library, job bank.
AFTER GRADUATION 70% of students completing a degree program in 1994–95 went directly on to further study.
EXPENSES FOR 1995–96 State resident tuition: $1073 full-time, $35.75 per credit part-time. Nonresident tuition: $3990 full-time, $133 per credit part-time.
FINANCIAL AID ***College-administered undergrad aid 1995–96:*** 200 need-based scholarships (average $600), 150 non-need scholarships (average $1000), short-term loans (average $300), low-interest long-term loans from external sources (average $2000), Federal Work-Study, 50 part-time jobs. ***Required forms:*** institutional, FAFSA. ***Priority deadline:*** 5/1. ***Waivers:*** full or partial for employees or children of employees and senior citizens.
APPLYING Open admission. ***Options:*** early entrance, deferred entrance, midyear entrance. ***Required:*** SAT I or ACT, TOEFL for international students, CPT, ACT ASSET. ***Required for some:*** 3 years of high school math and science. Test scores used for counseling/placement. ***Application deadline:*** 8/15. ***Notification:*** continuous.
APPLYING/TRANSFER ***Required:*** standardized test scores. ***Application deadline:*** 8/15. ***Notification:*** continuous.
CONTACT Ms. Pat Armstrong, Admissions Specialist, Edison Community College, PO Box 60210, Fort Myers, FL 33906-6210, 941-489-9361. ***Fax:*** 941-489-9127. Electronic view-book available.

EDUCATION AMERICA–TAMPA TECHNICAL INSTITUTE CAMPUS
Tampa, Florida

UG Enrollment: 1,150	Tuition: $14,700/deg prog
Application Deadline: rolling	Room & Board: N/Avail

GENERAL Proprietary, primarily 2-year, coed. Part of Education America, Inc. Awards transfer associate, bachelor's degrees. Founded 1948. ***Setting:*** 10-acre urban campus. ***Total enrollment:*** 1,150. ***Faculty:*** 40 (35 full-time, 5 part-time); student-faculty ratio is 30:1.
ENROLLMENT PROFILE 1,150 students: 0% part-time, 83% state residents, 1% transferred in, 32% 25 or older, 1% Native American, 1% Hispanic, 63% African American, 2% Asian American.
FIRST-YEAR CLASS 287 total; 448 applied, 65% of whom enrolled.
ACADEMIC PROGRAM Core, technical curriculum. Calendar: quarters. 182 courses offered in 1995–96; average class size 45 in required courses. Academic remediation for entering students, tutorials, internships.
GENERAL DEGREE REQUIREMENTS 134 quarter hours for associate, 180 quarter hours for bachelor's; computer course.
MAJORS Business administration/commerce/management, commercial art, computer technologies, electronics engineering technology (B).
LIBRARY Tampa Technical Institute Library with 13,640 books, 121 periodicals, 9 on-line bibliographic services, 5 CD-ROMs, 16 records, tapes, and CDs.
COMPUTERS ON CAMPUS 200 computers for student use in computer center, career center, classrooms, library provide access to Bulletin Board Service. Staffed computer lab on campus provides training in use of software.
COLLEGE LIFE 98% vote in student government elections. ***Social organizations:*** 1 national fraternity, 1 coed fraternity; 30% of eligible men and 10% of eligible women are members. ***Campus security:*** late-night transport-escort service.

Peterson's Guide to Two-Year Colleges 1997

249

Education America–Tampa Technical Institute Campus (continued)
HOUSING College housing not available.
CAREER PLANNING ***Placement office:*** 4 full-time, 1 part-time staff. ***Director:*** Mr. Ray Nunziata, Employer Relations Director, 813-935-5700. ***Services:*** job fairs, resume preparation, resume referral, career counseling, careers library, job bank, job interviews. Students must register freshman year. 226 organizations recruited on campus 1994–95.
AFTER GRADUATION 91% of class of 1994 had job offers within 6 months.
EXPENSES FOR 1995–96 ***Application fee:*** $50. Tuition per degree program ranges from $14,700 to $19,980.
FINANCIAL AID ***College-administered undergrad aid 1995–96:*** need-based scholarships, low-interest long-term loans from external sources (average $1000). ***Required forms:*** institutional; required for some: state, FAFSA; accepted: CSS Financial Aid PROFILE. ***Priority deadline:*** 8/15.
APPLYING Open admission. ***Options:*** Common Application, early entrance, deferred entrance. ***Required:*** school transcript, interview. ***Recommended:*** TOEFL for international students. Test scores used for admission. ***Application deadline:*** rolling.
APPLYING/TRANSFER ***Required:*** high school transcript, interview. ***Required for some:*** college transcript. ***Application deadline:*** rolling.
CONTACT Ms. Kathy Miller, Director of Admissions, Education America–Tampa Technical Institute Campus, 2410 East Busch Boulevard, Tampa, FL 33612-8410, 813-935-5700 or toll-free 800-992-4850 (in-state). College video available.

FLAGLER CAREER INSTITUTE
Jacksonville, Florida

UG Enrollment: 214	**Tuition: $18,000/deg prog**
Application Deadline: N/R	**Room & Board: N/Avail**

GENERAL Proprietary, 2-year, coed. Awards certificates, terminal associate degrees. Founded 1979. ***Setting:*** urban campus. ***Total enrollment:*** 214. ***Faculty:*** 30.
ENROLLMENT PROFILE 214 students: 60% women, 50% part-time, 72% state residents.
FIRST-YEAR CLASS 65 total. Of the students who applied, 25% were accepted, 100% of whom enrolled.
GENERAL DEGREE REQUIREMENTS 66 semester hours; 6 semester hours of math; 1 physical science course; computer course.
MAJOR Respiratory therapy.
COMPUTERS ON CAMPUS 30 computers for student use in computer center, library. Staffed computer lab on campus provides training in use of computers, software.
COLLEGE LIFE Student-run newspaper.
HOUSING College housing not available.
CAREER PLANNING ***Director:*** Mr. Ken Johnson, Placement Director, 904-721-1622.
EXPENSES FOR 1995–96 ***Application fee:*** $25. Tuition: $18,000 per degree program.
APPLYING ***Required:*** essay, school transcript, 3 recommendations, CPAt.
APPLYING/TRANSFER ***Required:*** essay, standardized test scores, high school transcript, 3 recommendations.
CONTACT Ms. Lucretia Williams, Education Representative, Flagler Career Institute, 3225 University Boulevard South, Jacksonville, FL 32216-2757, 904-721-1622.

FLORIDA COLLEGE
Temple Terrace, Florida

UG Enrollment: 378	**Tuition & Fees: $6390**
Application Deadline: 8/15	**Room & Board: $3580**

GENERAL Independent, 2-year, coed. Awards certificates, transfer associate degrees. Founded 1944. ***Setting:*** 195-acre small-town campus with easy access to Tampa. ***Endowment:*** $8 million. ***Educational spending 1994–95:*** $2977 per undergrad. ***Total enrollment:*** 378. ***Faculty:*** 28 (24 full-time, 38% with terminal degrees, 4 part-time); student-faculty ratio is 12:1.
ENROLLMENT PROFILE 378 students from 37 states and territories, 2 other countries. 55% women, 45% men, 2% part-time, 22% state residents, 94% live on campus, 8% transferred in, 21% have need-based financial aid, 32% have non-need-based financial aid, 1% international, 1% 25 or older, 1% Native American, 3% Hispanic, 1% African American, 1% Asian American. ***Areas of study chosen:*** 100% liberal arts/general studies.
FIRST-YEAR CLASS 187 total; 298 applied, 81% were accepted, 78% of whom enrolled. 5 National Merit Scholars, 4 valedictorians.
ACADEMIC PROGRAM Core, honor code. Calendar: semesters. 166 courses offered in 1995–96. Academic remediation for entering students, advanced placement, tutorials. Off-campus study at University of South Florida. ROTC: Army (c).
GENERAL DEGREE REQUIREMENTS 64 semester hours; 6 semester hours each of math and science; computer course.
MAJOR Liberal arts/general studies.
LIBRARY Chatlos Library with 41,622 books, 426 microform titles, 294 periodicals, 30 CD-ROMs, 1,054 records, tapes, and CDs. Acquisition spending 1994–95: $50,555.
COMPUTERS ON CAMPUS 35 computers for student use in computer center, computer labs, library provide access to Internet. Staffed computer lab on campus provides training in use of computers, software. Academic computing expenditure 1994–95: $17,128.
COLLEGE LIFE Orientation program (2 days, no cost, parents included). Drama-theater group, choral group. 99% vote in student government elections. ***Social organizations:*** 15 open to all; societies; 75% of eligible men and 75% of eligible women are members. ***Most popular organizations:*** Drama Workshop, Concert Band, Choral Union, SBGA, YWTO. ***Major annual events:*** Fall Banquet, Spring Banquet, Annual Alumni Basketball Game. ***Student services:*** health clinic, personal-psychological counseling. ***Campus security:*** student patrols.
HOUSING 400 college housing spaces available; 353 were occupied 1995–96. No special consideration for freshman housing applicants. On-campus residence required through sophomore year except if living with relatives or 21 or over. ***Option:*** single-sex housing available. Resident assistants live in dorms.
ATHLETICS Member NJCAA. ***Intercollegiate:*** basketball M(s), golf M/W. ***Intramural:*** basketball, football, soccer, softball, volleyball. ***Contact:*** Dr. Daniel W. Petty, Dean of Student Services, 813-988-5131 Ext. 223.
CAREER PLANNING ***Service:*** career counseling.
EXPENSES FOR 1996–97 ***Application fee:*** $25. Comprehensive fee of $9970 includes full-time tuition ($6270), mandatory fees ($120), and college room and board ($3580). Part-time tuition: $275 per semester hour. Part-time mandatory fees: $30 per semester.
FINANCIAL AID ***College-administered undergrad aid 1995–96:*** 56 need-based scholarships (average $1500), 100 non-need scholarships (average $500), short-term loans (average $25), low-interest long-term loans from college funds (average $1500), loans from external sources (average $2000), 80 part-time jobs. ***Required forms:*** institutional, FAFSA; required for some: state; accepted: CSS Financial Aid PROFILE. ***Priority deadline:*** 4/1. ***Payment plan:*** installment. ***Waivers:*** full or partial for employees or children of employees. ***Average indebtedness of graduates:*** $6000.
APPLYING ***Option:*** midyear entrance. ***Required:*** school transcript, minimum 2.0 GPA, recommendations, ACT, TOEFL for international students. ***Recommended:*** SAT I. Test scores used for counseling/placement. ***Application deadline:*** 8/15. ***Notification:*** continuous.
APPLYING/TRANSFER ***Required:*** high school transcript, recommendations, college transcript, minimum 2.0 college GPA. ***Required for some:*** essay, standardized test scores. ***Application deadline:*** 8/15. ***Contact:*** Ms. Beth Grant, Assistant to Registrar, 813-988-5131 Ext. 6705.
CONTACT Mrs. Mari Smith, Admissions Contact, Florida College, Temple Terrace, FL 33617, 813-988-5131 Ext. 225. College video available.

FLORIDA COMMUNITY COLLEGE AT JACKSONVILLE
Jacksonville, Florida

UG Enrollment: 19,211	**Tuition & Fees (FL Res): $1074**
Application Deadline: rolling	**Room & Board: N/Avail**

GENERAL State-supported, 2-year, coed. Part of Florida Community Colleges System. Awards certificates, transfer associate, terminal associate degrees. Founded 1963. ***Setting:*** urban campus. ***Total enrollment:*** 19,211. ***Faculty:*** 1,533 (391 full-time, 21% with terminal degrees, 1,142 part-time).
ENROLLMENT PROFILE 19,211 students from 46 states and territories, 35 other countries. 61% women, 39% men, 67% part-time, 97% state residents, 5% transferred in, 1% international, 64% 25 or older, 0% Native American, 4% Hispanic, 19% African American, 6% Asian American.
FIRST-YEAR CLASS 3,055 total. Of the students who applied, 100% were accepted, 38% of whom enrolled.
ACADEMIC PROGRAM Honor code. Calendar: semesters. Academic remediation for entering students, English as a second language program offered during academic year, services for LD students, advanced placement, Freshman Honors College, honors program, summer session for credit, part-time degree program (daytime, evenings), adult/continuing education programs. Study-abroad program. ROTC: Naval (c).
GENERAL DEGREE REQUIREMENTS 60 semester hours; math/science requirements vary according to program; computer course (varies by major).
MAJORS Accounting, architectural technologies, automotive technologies, aviation administration, aviation technology, biomedical technologies, business administration/commerce/management, child care/child and family studies, civil engineering technology, computer information systems, computer programming, computer technologies, construction technologies, criminal justice, culinary arts, dental services, dietetics, drafting and design, drug and alcohol/substance abuse counseling, electronics engineering technology, emergency medical technology, fashion design and technology, fashion merchandising, finance/banking, fire science, flight training, food services management, graphic arts, hotel and restaurant management, human services, industrial administration, information science, insurance, interior design, laboratory technologies, liberal arts/general studies, marketing/retailing/merchandising, medical laboratory technology, medical records services, medical technology, nursing, paralegal studies, radio and television studies, radiological technology, real estate, respiratory therapy, retail management, secretarial studies/office management, teacher aide studies, transportation technologies.
LIBRARY Learning Resources Center with 231,378 books, 1,712 microform titles, 1,824 periodicals, 8 on-line bibliographic services.
COMPUTERS ON CAMPUS 2,984 computers for student use in computer labs, classrooms, library provide access to main academic computer, on-line services. Staffed computer lab on campus provides training in use of computers, software.
COLLEGE LIFE Drama-theater group, choral group, student-run newspaper. 10% vote in student government elections. ***Most popular organization:*** Phi Theta Kappa. ***Student services:*** personal-psychological counseling, women's center. ***Campus security:*** 24-hour emergency response devices and patrols, student patrols.
HOUSING College housing not available.
ATHLETICS Member NJCAA. ***Intercollegiate:*** baseball M(s), basketball M(s)/W(s), cross-country running M(s)/W(s), golf M(s), softball W(s), tennis W(s), track and field M(s)/W(s), volleyball W(s). ***Intramural:*** badminton, basketball, bowling, football, golf, soccer, table tennis (Ping-Pong), tennis, volleyball. ***Contact:*** Mr. Ralph Daniel, Athletic Director, 904-646-2202.
CAREER PLANNING ***Director:*** Dr. Elizabeth Cobb, Dean of Student Affairs, 904-381-3443. ***Services:*** job fairs, resume preparation, career counseling, careers library, job bank.
AFTER GRADUATION 81% of students completing a degree program in 1994–95 went directly on to further study.
EXPENSES FOR 1995–96 ***Application fee:*** $25. State resident tuition: $1074 full-time, $35.80 per semester hour part-time. Nonresident tuition: $4026 full-time, $134.80 per semester hour part-time.
FINANCIAL AID ***College-administered undergrad aid 1995–96:*** 1,787 need-based scholarships, 1,244 non-need scholarships (average $778), short-term loans (average $1350), low-interest long-term loans from external sources (average $2501), 798 Federal Work-Study (averaging $817), part-time jobs. ***Required forms:*** institutional, FAFSA; required for some: state; accepted: CSS Financial Aid PROFILE. ***Priority deadline:*** 5/15. ***Payment plan:*** deferred payment. ***Waivers:*** full or partial for employees or children of employees.
APPLYING Open admission. ***Option:*** early entrance. ***Required:*** TOEFL for international students. ***Recommended:*** SAT I or ACT. Test scores used for admission (TOEFL) and counseling/placement (SAT or ACT). ***Application deadline:*** rolling.
APPLYING/TRANSFER ***Recommended:*** standardized test scores.
CONTACT Mrs. Sandra Willis, Registrar, Florida Community College at Jacksonville, 501 West State Street, Jacksonville, FL 32202-4030, 904-632-3110.

Florida

FLORIDA HOSPITAL COLLEGE OF HEALTH SCIENCES
Orlando, Florida

Enrollment: N/R	Tuition & Fees: $3343
Application Deadline: N/R	Room Only: $640

GENERAL Independent, 2-year, specialized. Awards terminal associate degrees.
GENERAL DEGREE REQUIREMENTS 64 semester hours; 1 college algebra course; computer course.
EXPENSES FOR 1996–97 *Application fee:* $20. Tuition: $3168 full-time, $99 per semester hour part-time. Part-time mandatory fees: $35 per term. Full-time mandatory fees: $175. College room only: $640.
APPLYING *Required:* school transcript, ACT. *Required for some:* minimum 2.25 GPA.
APPLYING/TRANSFER *Required:* standardized test scores, high school transcript, college transcript. *Required for some:* minimum 2.25 GPA.
CONTACT Ms. Angela Abraham, Acting Registrar, Florida Hospital College of Health Sciences, Orlando, FL 32803, 407-895-7747.

FLORIDA KEYS COMMUNITY COLLEGE
Key West, Florida

UG Enrollment: 2,200	Tuition & Fees (FL Res): $1128
Application Deadline: rolling	Room & Board: N/Avail

GENERAL State-supported, 2-year, coed. Part of Florida Community Colleges System. Awards certificates, transfer associate, terminal associate degrees. Founded 1965. *Setting:* 20-acre small-town campus. *Total enrollment:* 2,200. *Faculty:* 94 (35 full-time, 20% with terminal degrees, 59 part-time); student-faculty ratio is 23:1.
ENROLLMENT PROFILE 2,200 students from 25 states and territories, 10 other countries. 54% women, 71% part-time, 98% state residents, 2% transferred in, 10% have need-based financial aid, 5% have non-need-based financial aid, 1% international, 57% 25 or older, 0% Native American, 6% Hispanic, 3% African American, 1% Asian American. *Areas of study chosen:* 10% interdisciplinary studies, 10% liberal arts/general studies, 5% biological and life sciences, 5% business management and administrative services, 5% computer and information sciences, 5% engineering and applied sciences, 5% health professions and related sciences. *Most popular recent majors:* liberal arts/general studies, nursing, marine technology.
FIRST-YEAR CLASS 400 total; 400 applied, 100% were accepted, 100% of whom enrolled.
ACADEMIC PROGRAM Core, general education curriculum, honor code. Calendar: trimesters. Academic remediation for entering students, English as a second language program offered during academic year and summer, services for LD students, advanced placement, self-designed majors, summer session for credit, part-time degree program (daytime, evenings, summer), adult/continuing education programs, co-op programs and internships.
GENERAL DEGREE REQUIREMENT 60 credits.
MAJORS Art/fine arts, business administration/commerce/management, business machine technologies, computer programming, computer technologies, electrical engineering technology, finance/banking, legal secretarial studies, liberal arts/general studies, marine biology, marine technology, medical secretarial studies, nursing, recreation and leisure services, secretarial studies/office management.
LIBRARY 23,361 books, 9,050 microform titles, 344 periodicals, 2,878 records, tapes, and CDs.
COMPUTERS ON CAMPUS 109 computers for student use in computer center, labs, library.
COLLEGE LIFE Choral group. *Social organizations:* 7 open to all. *Most popular organizations:* Florida Student Nursing Association, Nurses Pinning Club, Phi Theta Kappa, Scuba Club, Ceramics Club. *Major annual events:* State University System Representatives Visit, Graduation Dance, Fall Ice Cream Social. *Student services:* personal-psychological counseling. *Campus security:* security personnel.
HOUSING College housing not available.
CAREER PLANNING *Placement office:* 1 full-time, 3 part-time staff. *Director:* Mr. Mitchell A. Grabois, Director of Admissions, 305-296-9081 Ext. 284. *Services:* job fairs, resume preparation, resume referral, career counseling, careers library, job bank.
EXPENSES FOR 1995–96 *Application fee:* $15. State resident tuition: $1128 full-time, $35.25 per credit part-time. Nonresident tuition: $4176 full-time, $130.50 per credit part-time.
FINANCIAL AID *College-administered undergrad aid 1995–96:* 6 need-based scholarships (average $294), 40 non-need scholarships (average $500), short-term loans (average $270), low-interest long-term loans from external sources (average $800), Federal Work-Study. *Required forms:* CSS Financial Aid PROFILE, institutional; required for some: state, FAFSA. *Priority deadline:* 5/1. *Payment plan:* tuition prepayment. *Waivers:* full or partial for employees or children of employees.
APPLYING Open admission except for nursing program. *Options:* early entrance, deferred entrance, midyear entrance. *Required:* 3 years of high school math and science, TOEFL for international students. *Required for some:* MAPS. Test scores used for counseling/placement. *Application deadline:* rolling. *Notification:* continuous.
APPLYING/TRANSFER *Required for some:* standardized test scores. *Entrance:* noncompetitive. *Application deadline:* rolling. *Notification:* continuous. *Contact:* Ms. Sharon Toppino, Coordinator of Counseling Services, 305-296-9081 Ext. 250.
CONTACT Mr. Mitchell A. Grabois, Director of Admissions, Florida Keys Community College, Key West, FL 33040-4397, 305-296-9081 Ext. 284.

FLORIDA NATIONAL COLLEGE
Hialeah, Florida

UG Enrollment: 1,100	Tuition & Fees: $4000
Application Deadline: N/R	Room & Board: N/Avail

GENERAL Proprietary, 2-year, coed. Awards certificates, diplomas, transfer associate, terminal associate degrees. Founded 1982. *Setting:* urban campus with easy access to Miami. *Total enrollment:* 1,100. *Faculty:* 70 (50 full-time, 100% with terminal degrees, 20 part-time); student-faculty ratio is 10:1.
ENROLLMENT PROFILE 1,100 students: 60% women, 0% part-time, 5% transferred in, 85% have need-based financial aid, 15% have non-need-based financial aid, 5% international, 0% Native American, 95% Hispanic, 1% African American, 1% Asian American. *Areas of study chosen:* 40% health professions and related sciences, 30% vocational and home economics, 20% computer and information sciences, 10% business management and administrative services.
FIRST-YEAR CLASS Of the students who applied, 90% were accepted.
ACADEMIC PROGRAM Honor code. Calendar: semesters. Academic remediation for entering students, English as a second language program offered during academic year and summer, services for LD students, tutorials, summer session for credit, adult/continuing education programs, co-op programs and internships.
GENERAL DEGREE REQUIREMENTS 60 credits; 2 math courses; computer course; internship (some majors).
MAJORS Accounting, business administration/commerce/management, computer programming, computer science, data processing, dental services, health education, hospitality services, hotel and restaurant management, legal secretarial studies, legal studies, liberal arts/general studies, medical assistant technologies, medical secretarial studies, paralegal studies, secretarial studies/office management, Spanish, technical writing, tourism and travel, vocational education.
LIBRARY 4,000 books, 19 periodicals.
COMPUTERS ON CAMPUS Computers for student use in computer labs. Staffed computer lab on campus provides training in use of computers, software.
COLLEGE LIFE 80% vote in student government elections.
HOUSING College housing not available.
CAREER PLANNING *Services:* job fairs, resume preparation, resume referral, career counseling, careers library, job bank, job interviews.
EXPENSES FOR 1996–97 *Application fee:* $100. Tuition: $4000 full-time. Part-time mandatory fees: $133 per credit.
FINANCIAL AID *College-administered undergrad aid 1995–96:* need-based scholarships, non-need scholarships, Federal Work-Study. *Required forms:* CSS Financial Aid PROFILE, institutional, FAFSA. *Application deadline:* continuous.
APPLYING Open admission. *Option:* early entrance. *Required:* school transcript, TABE.
APPLYING/TRANSFER *Required:* standardized test scores, high school transcript, college transcript.
CONTACT Ms. Maria C. Reguerio, Vice President, Florida National College, 4206 West 12th Avenue, Hialeah, FL 33012, 305-821-3333.

FULL SAIL CENTER FOR THE RECORDING ARTS
Winter Park, Florida

UG Enrollment: 754	Tuition: $20,650/deg prog
Application Deadline: rolling	Room & Board: N/Avail

GENERAL Proprietary, 2-year, coed. Awards terminal associate degrees. Founded 1979. *Setting:* suburban campus with easy access to Orlando. *Research spending 1994–95:* $350,000. *Educational spending 1994–95:* $6429 per undergrad. *Total enrollment:* 754. *Faculty:* 95 (40 full-time, 55 part-time); student-faculty ratio is 8:1. *Notable Alumni:* Felipe Elgueta, assistant engineer; Michelle Salbolchick, live sound engineer; Derrick Perkins, digital audioworkstation programmer; Greg Hancock, live sound systems technician; Ronnie Rivera, assistant audio engineer.
ENROLLMENT PROFILE 754 students from 44 states and territories, 9 other countries. 12% women, 0% part-time, 5% state residents, 0% transferred in, 7% international, 29% 25 or older, 0% Native American, 7% Hispanic, 7% African American, 4% Asian American.
FIRST-YEAR CLASS 754 applied.
ACADEMIC PROGRAM Core, hands-on training curriculum, honor code. Calendar: modular. Academic remediation for entering students, services for LD students, tutorials, summer session for credit, part-time degree program (daytime, evenings, weekends), adult/continuing education programs, internships.
GENERAL DEGREE REQUIREMENTS 81.5 credit hours; computer course.
MAJORS Audio engineering, film and video production.
LIBRARY Full Sail Library with 610 books, 31 periodicals, 1 on-line bibliographic service, 298 records, tapes, and CDs. Acquisition spending 1994–95: $100,000.
COMPUTERS ON CAMPUS Computer purchase plan available. 32 computers for student use in computer labs provide access to Internet. Staffed computer lab on campus. Academic computing expenditure 1994–95: $400,000.
COLLEGE LIFE Orientation program (2 days, no cost). *Most popular organization:* Student Chapter of Audio Engineering Society. *Major annual events:* Annual Speech Tournament, Success Seminar, Entertainment Business. *Campus security:* 24-hour patrols.
HOUSING College housing not available.
CAREER PLANNING *Placement office:* 5 full-time staff; $200,000 operating expenditure 1994–95. *Director:* Ms. Tammy Gilbert, Director of Placement Services, 407-679-0100. *Services:* resume preparation, resume referral, career counseling, careers library, job interviews.
AFTER GRADUATION 10% of students completing a degree program in 1994–95 went directly on to further study.
EXPENSES FOR 1996–97 *Application fee:* $150. Tuition per degree program ranges from $20,650 to $24,600.
FINANCIAL AID *College-administered undergrad aid 1995–96:* low-interest long-term loans from external sources (average $2625). *Required forms:* institutional, FAFSA; accepted: CSS Financial Aid PROFILE. *Application deadline:* continuous. *Payment plan:* installment.
APPLYING Open admission. *Options:* Common Application, early entrance, deferred entrance. *Required:* school transcript. *Required for some:* TOEFL for international students. *Application deadline:* rolling.
APPLYING/TRANSFER *Required:* high school transcript. *Entrance:* noncompetitive. *Application deadline:* rolling.

Full Sail Center for the Recording Arts (continued)

CONTACT Ms. Mary Beth Plank, Admissions Department Manager, Full Sail Center for the Recording Arts, Winter Park, FL 32792-7437, 407-679-6333 Ext. 2141 or toll-free 800-CAN-ROCK. ***Fax:*** 407-678-0070. College video available.

GULF COAST COMMUNITY COLLEGE
Panama City, Florida

UG Enrollment: 5,865	**Tuition & Fees (FL Res): $1083**
Application Deadline: rolling	**Room & Board: N/Avail**

GENERAL State-supported, 2-year, coed. Awards certificates, transfer associate, terminal associate degrees. Founded 1957. ***Setting:*** 80-acre suburban campus. ***Total enrollment:*** 5,865. ***Faculty:*** 348 (104 full-time, 18% with terminal degrees, 244 part-time); student-faculty ratio is 19:1.

ENROLLMENT PROFILE 5,865 students from 10 states and territories, 8 other countries. 57% women, 43% men, 65% part-time, 98% state residents, 8% transferred in, 1% international, 42% 25 or older, 1% Native American, 3% Hispanic, 9% African American, 3% Asian American. ***Most popular recent majors:*** business administration/commerce/ management, nursing.

FIRST-YEAR CLASS 3,081 total; 3,235 applied, 100% were accepted, 95% of whom enrolled.

ACADEMIC PROGRAM Core, honor code. Calendar: semesters. 905 courses offered in 1995–96. Academic remediation for entering students, English as a second language program offered during academic year and summer, services for LD students, advanced placement, self-designed majors, Freshman Honors College, tutorials, honors program, summer session for credit, part-time degree program (daytime, evenings, summer), adult/ continuing education programs, co-op programs.

GENERAL DEGREE REQUIREMENTS 60 credit hours; 6 credit hours of math; 3 credit hours of science; computer course for students without computer competency.

MAJORS Accounting, advertising, anthropology, archaeology, art/fine arts, aviation administration, biology/biological sciences, broadcasting, business administration/commerce/ management, business education, chemistry, child psychology/child development, civil engineering technology, communication, computer programming, computer science, construction technologies, corrections, criminal justice, criminology, culinary arts, dental services, drafting and design, economics, education, electronics engineering technology, elementary education, emergency medical technology, (pre)engineering sequence, English, fashion merchandising, finance/banking, fire science, flight training, forestry, geology, health education, history, home economics, hospitality services, human services, journalism, legal studies, liberal arts/general studies, library science, marine biology, marine technology, marketing/retailing/merchandising, mathematics, medical records services, medical technology, meteorology, music, nursing, occupational therapy, oceanography, paralegal studies, philosophy, physical education, physical therapy, physician's assistant studies, physics, political science/government, postal management, psychology, public relations, radio and television studies, radiological technology, real estate, respiratory therapy, science education, secretarial studies/office management, social work, sociology, theater arts/drama.

LIBRARY Gulf Coast Community College Library with 69,542 books, 304,808 microform titles, 788 periodicals, 6 on-line bibliographic services, 8 CD-ROMs, 3,000 records, tapes, and CDs. Acquisition spending 1994–95: $89,733.

COMPUTERS ON CAMPUS 400 computers for student use in computer center, computer labs, classrooms, library, student center. Staffed computer lab on campus provides training in use of computers, software.

COLLEGE LIFE Orientation program (3 days, $36). Drama-theater group, choral group, student-run newspaper, radio station. ***Social organizations:*** 14 open to all. ***Most popular organizations:*** Student Activities Board, Baptist Campus Ministry, Theater Club, Circle K, International Student Organization. ***Major annual events:*** Homecoming, Spring Luau, Alcohol Awareness Week. ***Student services:*** personal-psychological counseling. ***Campus security:*** patrols by trained security personnel during campus hours.

HOUSING College housing not available.

ATHLETICS Member NJCAA. ***Intercollegiate:*** baseball M(s), basketball M(s)/W, softball W(s). ***Intramural:*** football. ***Contact:*** Mr. John Holdnak, Chairman, Physical Education Division, 904-872-3830.

CAREER PLANNING ***Placement office:*** 1 full-time, 2 part-time staff; $23,862 operating expenditure 1994–95. ***Director:*** Ms. Julie McLeod, Career and Educational Development Specialist, 904-769-1551 Ext. 4856. ***Services:*** job fairs, resume preparation, career counseling, careers library.

AFTER GRADUATION 68% of students completing a degree program in 1994–95 went directly on to further study.

EXPENSES FOR 1995–96 State resident tuition: $1083 full-time, $36.10 per credit hour part-time. Nonresident tuition: $4062 full-time, $135.40 per credit hour part-time.

FINANCIAL AID ***College-administered undergrad aid 1995–96:*** 710 need-based scholarships (average $1120), 589 non-need scholarships (average $1120), short-term loans (average $657), low-interest long-term loans from external sources (average $2200), 55 Federal Work-Study (averaging $1750), 135 part-time jobs. ***Required forms:*** FAFSA; required for some: institutional; accepted: state. ***Priority deadline:*** 4/15.

APPLYING Open admission. ***Options:*** early entrance, deferred entrance, midyear entrance. ***Required:*** school transcript, 3 years of high school math and science, TOEFL for international students, MAPS, TSWE. Test scores used for counseling/placement. ***Application deadline:*** rolling. ***Notification:*** continuous.

APPLYING/TRANSFER ***Required:*** college transcript. ***Required for some:*** standardized test scores, high school transcript. ***Entrance:*** noncompetitive. ***Application deadline:*** rolling. ***Contact:*** Mrs. Kris Bigbie, Transcript Evaluation Specialist, 904-769-1551 Ext. 4888.

CONTACT Mrs. Jackie Kuczenski, Administrative Secretary of Admissions, Gulf Coast Community College, Panama City, FL 32401-1058, 904-769-1551 Ext. 4892.

HILLSBOROUGH COMMUNITY COLLEGE
Tampa, Florida

UG Enrollment: 19,189	**Tuition & Fees (FL Res): $1028**
Application Deadline: rolling	**Room & Board: N/Avail**

GENERAL State-supported, 2-year, coed. Awards transfer associate, terminal associate degrees. Founded 1968. ***Setting:*** urban campus. ***Endowment:*** $1 million. ***Educational spending 1994–95:*** $1916 per undergrad. ***Total enrollment:*** 19,189. ***Faculty:*** 708 (253 full-time, 28% with terminal degrees, 455 part-time); student-faculty ratio is 27:1. ***Notable Alumni:*** Dottie Berger, Hillsborough county commissioner; Mary Ann Stiles, Hillsborough Community College board of trustee member; Melvin Stone, assistant fire marshall; Denise Pomponio, assistant district attorney of Hillsborough County.

ENROLLMENT PROFILE 19,189 students: 58% women, 42% men, 72% part-time, 97% state residents, 8% transferred in, 18% have need-based financial aid, 4% have non-need-based financial aid, 1% international, 44% 25 or older, 1% Native American, 13% Hispanic, 12% African American, 3% Asian American. ***Areas of study chosen:*** 43% liberal arts/general studies, 15% business management and administrative services, 10% health professions and related sciences, 6% computer and information sciences, 5% education, 5% premed, 4% vocational and home economics, 3% engineering and applied sciences, 2% architecture, 2% communications and journalism, 2% prelaw, 1% agriculture, 1% fine arts, 1% performing arts, 1% predentistry, 1% prevet. ***Most popular recent majors:*** liberal arts/general studies, nursing, optometric/ophthalmic technologies.

FIRST-YEAR CLASS 2,428 total; 2,914 applied, 100% were accepted, 83% of whom enrolled.

ACADEMIC PROGRAM Core, career and transfer curriculum, honor code. Calendar: semesters. 571 courses offered in 1995–96; average class size 21 in required courses. Academic remediation for entering students, English as a second language program offered during academic year and summer, services for LD students, advanced placement, summer session for credit, part-time degree program (daytime, evenings, weekends, summer), adult/continuing education programs, co-op programs. Off-campus study at University of South Florida, Linkage Program institutions. Study-abroad program. (1% of students participate) ROTC: Army (c), Air Force (c).

GENERAL DEGREE REQUIREMENTS 60 credits; computer course for accounting, architectural design, business, radiation therapy majors.

MAJORS Accounting, architectural technologies, automotive technologies, biomedical technologies, business administration/commerce/management, child care/child and family studies, computer information systems, computer programming, computer technologies, construction technologies, corrections, criminal justice, data processing, deaf interpreter training, electronics engineering technology, emergency medical technology, finance/ banking, fire science, hospitality services, hotel and restaurant management, human services, interior design, law enforcement/police sciences, legal secretarial studies, legal studies, liberal arts/general studies, marketing/retailing/merchandising, medical secretarial studies, nuclear medical technology, nursing, occupational therapy, optometric/ophthalmic technologies, ornamental horticulture, postal management, radiological sciences, radiological technology, secretarial studies/office management.

LIBRARY Main library plus 4 others, with 94,977 books, 1,302 microform titles, 826 periodicals, 10 CD-ROMs, 4,197 records, tapes, and CDs. Acquisition spending 1994–95: $200,441.

COMPUTERS ON CAMPUS Computer purchase plan available. 560 computers for student use in computer labs, learning resource center, classrooms, library provide access to Internet. Staffed computer lab on campus provides training in use of computers, software. Academic computing expenditure 1994–95: $561,750.

NOTEWORTHY RESEARCH FACILITIES Institute of Florida Studies.

COLLEGE LIFE Drama-theater group, student-run newspaper. 1% vote in student government elections. ***Social organizations:*** 40 open to all; 4 national fraternities; 1% of eligible men and 1% of eligible women are members. ***Most popular organizations:*** Student Government Association, Student Nursing Association, Phi Theta Kappa, Disabled Students Association, Radiography Club. ***Major annual events:*** Halloween Fest, Spring Fling, Valentine's Day Events. ***Student services:*** personal-psychological counseling. ***Campus security:*** 24-hour emergency response devices and patrols.

HOUSING College housing not available.

ATHLETICS Member NJCAA. ***Intercollegiate:*** baseball M(s), basketball M(s)/W(s), softball W(s), tennis W(s), volleyball W(s). ***Contact:*** Mr. Joseph Patton Jr., Athletics Manager, 813-253-7411.

CAREER PLANNING ***Placement office:*** 3 full-time staff; $227,514 operating expenditure 1994–95. ***Director:*** Mr. Howard Sinsley, Associate Vice President for Student Services, 813-253-7054. ***Services:*** job fairs, resume preparation, resume referral, career counseling, careers library, job bank, job interviews. 60 organizations recruited on campus 1994–95.

EXPENSES FOR 1995–96 ***Application fee:*** $20. State resident tuition: $1028 full-time, $34.25 per credit hour part-time. Nonresident tuition: $3945 full-time, $131.50 per credit hour part-time.

FINANCIAL AID ***College-administered undergrad aid 1995–96:*** 1,245 need-based scholarships (averaging $800), 339 non-need scholarships (averaging $800), short-term loans (averaging $350), low-interest long-term loans from college funds (averaging $1000), loans from external sources (averaging $2625), 320 Federal Work-Study (averaging $2000), 300 part-time jobs. ***Required forms:*** institutional, FAFSA, financial aid transcript (for transfers); accepted: CSS Financial Aid PROFILE. ***Priority deadline:*** 4/15. ***Payment plan:*** deferred payment. ***Waivers:*** full or partial for employees or children of employees and senior citizens.

APPLYING Open admission. ***Options:*** Common Application, early entrance, midyear entrance. ***Required:*** school transcript, TOEFL for international students. ***Required for some:*** MAPS. Test scores used for counseling/placement. ***Application deadline:*** rolling.

APPLYING/TRANSFER ***Required:*** college transcript. ***Required for some:*** standardized test scores. ***Application deadline:*** rolling. ***Contact:*** Ms. Peggy Chase, Registrar/ Articulation Officer, 813-253-7004.

CONTACT Ms. Peggy Chase, Registrar/Articulation Officer, Hillsborough Community College, PO Box 31127, Tampa, FL 33631-3127, 813-253-7004. College video available.

INDIAN RIVER COMMUNITY COLLEGE
Fort Pierce, Florida

UG Enrollment: 6,919	**Tuition & Fees (FL Res): $1178**
Application Deadline: rolling	**Room & Board: N/Avail**

GENERAL State-supported, 2-year, coed. Part of Florida Community Colleges System. Awards certificates, transfer associate, terminal associate degrees. Founded 1960. ***Setting:*** 133-acre small-town campus. ***Total enrollment:*** 6,919. ***Faculty:*** 623 (150 full-time, 21% with terminal degrees, 473 part-time); student-faculty ratio is 16:1.

252

Peterson's Guide to Two-Year Colleges 1997

ENROLLMENT PROFILE 6,919 students from 33 states and territories, 12 other countries. 66% women, 68% part-time, 98% state residents, 25% transferred in, 1% international, 51% 25 or older, 1% Native American, 3% Hispanic, 9% African American, 2% Asian American.
FIRST-YEAR CLASS 962 total. Of the students who applied, 100% were accepted.
ACADEMIC PROGRAM Core, honor code. Calendar: semesters. Average class size 35 in required courses. Academic remediation for entering students, English as a second language program offered during academic year, services for LD students, advanced placement, summer session for credit, part-time degree program (daytime, evenings, summer), adult/continuing education programs.
GENERAL DEGREE REQUIREMENTS 60 semester hours; 2 college algebra courses; 1 lab science course.
MAJORS Accounting, agricultural business, anthropology, automotive technologies, biology/biological sciences, business administration/commerce/management, chemistry, child care/child and family studies, civil engineering technology, computer information systems, computer programming, computer science, computer technologies, corrections, cosmetology, criminal justice, dental services, drafting and design, drama therapy, early childhood education, economics, education, electrical and electronics technologies, electronics engineering technology, emergency medical technology, engineering (general), (pre)engineering sequence, engineering technology, English, fashion merchandising, finance/banking, fire science, food services management, heating/refrigeration/air conditioning, history, home economics, hotel and restaurant management, human services, interior design, journalism, law enforcement/police sciences, liberal arts/general studies, library science, marine sciences, marketing/retailing/merchandising, mathematics, medical laboratory technology, medical records services, medical secretarial studies, music, nursing, paralegal studies, pharmacy/pharmaceutical sciences, philosophy, physical education, physical therapy, physics, practical nursing, psychology, radiological technology, respiratory therapy, retail management, secretarial studies/office management, social science, social work, sociology, speech/rhetoric/public address/debate, surveying technology, teacher aide studies, textiles and clothing, water resources, word processing.
LIBRARY Charles S. Miley Learning Resource Center with 50,303 books, 360 microform titles, 494 periodicals, 2 on-line bibliographic services, 83 CD-ROMs, 1,920 records, tapes, and CDs.
COMPUTERS ON CAMPUS 500 computers for student use in computer labs, learning resource center, labs, classrooms, library. Staffed computer lab on campus provides training in use of computers, software.
COLLEGE LIFE Drama-theater group, choral group. ***Social organizations:*** 31 open to all; local fraternities, local sororities; 50% of eligible men and 50% of eligible women are members. ***Most popular organizations:*** Phi Beta Lambda, Distributive Education Club of America, International Club, Cultural Exchange, Human Services Club. ***Major annual events:*** United Way Day, Welcome Back Cookout, Valentine's Day Celebration. ***Student services:*** health clinic, personal-psychological counseling, women's center. ***Campus security:*** 24-hour patrols.
HOUSING College housing not available.
ATHLETICS Member NJCAA. ***Intercollegiate:*** baseball M(s), basketball M(s)/W(s), softball W(s), swimming and diving M(s)/W(s), volleyball W(s). ***Intramural:*** basketball, racquetball, soccer, volleyball. ***Contact:*** Mr. Mike Easom, Athletic Director, 407-462-4700 Ext. 4772; Ms. Christina Hart, Assistant Athletic Director, 407-462-4723.
CAREER PLANNING ***Placement office:*** 2 part-time staff. ***Director:*** Ms. Sharon Mims, Career Planning Advisor, 407-462-4740. ***Services:*** job fairs, resume preparation, resume referral, career counseling, careers library, job bank, job interviews.
EXPENSES FOR 1995–96 State resident tuition: $1178 full-time, $36.80 per semester hour part-time. Nonresident tuition: $4358 full-time, $136.20 per semester hour part-time.
FINANCIAL AID ***College-administered undergrad aid 1995–96:*** 300 need-based scholarships (averaging $1100), 176 non-need scholarships (averaging $803), short-term loans (averaging $450), low-interest long-term loans from external sources (averaging $2349), Federal Work-Study, 6 part-time jobs. ***Acceptable forms:*** state, FAFSA. ***Priority deadline:*** 6/1.
APPLYING Open admission. ***Options:*** early entrance, deferred entrance, midyear entrance. ***Required:*** SAT I or ACT, TOEFL for international students, CPT. Test scores used for counseling/placement. ***Application deadline:*** rolling. ***Notification:*** continuous.
APPLYING/TRANSFER ***Required for some:*** standardized test scores. ***Entrance:*** noncompetitive. ***Application deadline:*** rolling. ***Notification:*** continuous. ***Contact:*** Ms. Ann Tedder, Director of Admissions, 407-462-4740.
CONTACT Mrs. Linda Hays, Associate Dean of Educational Services, Indian River Community College, Fort Pierce, FL 34981-5599, 407-462-4740.

INSTITUTE OF CAREER EDUCATION
West Palm Beach, Florida

UG Enrollment: 180	**Tuition: $1850/deg prog**
Application Deadline: rolling	**Room & Board: N/Avail**

GENERAL Proprietary, 2-year, coed. Awards diplomas, terminal associate degrees. Founded 1975. ***Setting:*** suburban campus. ***Total enrollment:*** 180. ***Faculty:*** 18 (8 full-time, 10 part-time); student-faculty ratio is 10:1.
ENROLLMENT PROFILE 180 students: 97% women, 35% part-time, 98% state residents, 5% transferred in, 2% international, 85% 25 or older, 0% Native American, 10% Hispanic, 24% African American, 1% Asian American.
FIRST-YEAR CLASS 50 total; 71 applied, 86% were accepted, 82% of whom enrolled.
ACADEMIC PROGRAM Core. Calendar: quarters. 71 courses offered in 1995–96. Academic remediation for entering students, part-time degree program (daytime, evenings), co-op programs.
GENERAL DEGREE REQUIREMENTS 1500 hours; computer course; internship (some majors).
MAJORS Accounting, business administration/commerce/management, computer information systems, court reporting, medical assistant technologies, medical secretarial studies, secretarial studies/office management, tourism and travel.
COMPUTERS ON CAMPUS 50 computers for student use in classrooms.
COLLEGE LIFE 50% vote in student government elections. ***Student services:*** personal-psychological counseling.
HOUSING College housing not available.
CAREER PLANNING ***Director:*** Ms. Evelyn Kannawin, Executive Director, 407-881-0220. ***Services:*** resume preparation, resume referral, career counseling, job bank, job interviews.
AFTER GRADUATION 72% of class of 1994 had job offers within 6 months.
EXPENSES FOR 1996–97 ***Application fee:*** $50. Tuition per degree program ranges from $1850 to $14,000.
FINANCIAL AID ***College-administered undergrad aid 1995–96:*** need-based scholarships, low-interest long-term loans from external sources. ***Required forms:*** institutional, FAFSA. ***Application deadline:*** continuous. ***Payment plan:*** installment. ***Waivers:*** full or partial for employees or children of employees.
APPLYING ***Required:*** school transcript, campus interview. ***Required for some:*** TABE. Test scores used for admission. ***Application deadline:*** rolling. ***Notification:*** continuous.
APPLYING/TRANSFER ***Required:*** high school transcript, campus interview, college transcript, minimum 2.0 college GPA. ***Application deadline:*** rolling. ***Notification:*** continuous.
CONTACT Ms. Evelyn Kannawin, Executive Director, Institute of Career Education, West Palm Beach, FL 33407-2192, 407-881-0220.

INTERNATIONAL FINE ARTS COLLEGE
Miami, Florida

UG Enrollment: 790	**Tuition & Fees: $9525**
Application Deadline: rolling	**Room & Board: $2900**

Students learn the most progressive ideas in computer animation, digital audio/video, electronic publishing/commercial art, fashion design, fashion merchandising, film and television, interior design, and visual arts. They use state-of-the-art technology and make invaluable contacts in the fields of their choice, paving the path to success.

GENERAL Proprietary, 2-year, coed. Awards terminal associate degrees. Founded 1965. ***Setting:*** urban campus. ***Total enrollment:*** 790. ***Faculty:*** 48 (8 full-time, 40 part-time); student-faculty ratio is 22:1.
ENROLLMENT PROFILE 790 students from 45 states and territories, 50 other countries. 67% women, 0% part-time, 55% state residents, 26% live on campus, 16% transferred in, 70% have need-based financial aid, 30% have non-need-based financial aid, 25% international, 5% 25 or older, 1% Native American, 45% Hispanic, 12% African American, 4% Asian American. ***Most popular recent majors:*** commercial art, fashion merchandising, fashion design and technology.
FIRST-YEAR CLASS 500 total. Of the students who applied, 70% were accepted, 60% of whom enrolled.
ACADEMIC PROGRAM Core, liberal arts curriculum, honor code. Calendar: semesters. 98 courses offered in 1995–96. Academic remediation for entering students, internships.
GENERAL DEGREE REQUIREMENTS 60 credits; 1 math course; internship (some majors).
MAJORS Commercial art, computer graphics, fashion design and technology, fashion merchandising, interior design.
LIBRARY 10,495 books, 81 periodicals.
COMPUTERS ON CAMPUS Computer purchase plan available. 94 computers for student use in computer center, computer labs, classrooms, library provide access to main academic computer. Staffed computer lab on campus provides training in use of computers, software.
NOTEWORTHY RESEARCH FACILITIES History of Costumes Collection, Fabric Collection.
COLLEGE LIFE ***Most popular organizations:*** Caribbean Students Association, Student Government, DECA. ***Major annual events:*** Halloween Party, Trip to Disney World, Luau Party. ***Student services:*** personal-psychological counseling. ***Campus security:*** student patrols, controlled dormitory access, security service.
HOUSING 196 college housing spaces available; all were occupied 1995–96. Freshmen given priority for college housing. Off-campus living permitted. ***Options:*** coed (1 building), single-sex (1 building) housing available. Resident assistants live in dorms.
CAREER PLANNING ***Placement office:*** 1 full-time staff. ***Director:*** Ms. Dorothy McHale, Director of Placement, 305-373-4684 Ext. 139. ***Services:*** resume preparation, resume referral, career counseling, careers library, job bank.
AFTER GRADUATION 15% of students completing a degree program in 1994–95 went directly on to further study.
EXPENSES FOR 1995–96 ***Application fee:*** $50. Comprehensive fee of $12,425 includes full-time tuition ($9425 minimum), mandatory fees ($100), and college room and board ($2900). Full-time tuition ranges up to $13,500 according to program. Tuition guaranteed not to increase for student's term of enrollment.
FINANCIAL AID ***College-administered undergrad aid 1995–96:*** need-based scholarships, non-need scholarships, low-interest long-term loans from college funds (average $2000), loans from external sources (average $2625), part-time jobs. ***Required forms:*** institutional, FAFSA; accepted: CSS Financial Aid PROFILE. ***Priority deadline:*** 8/30. ***Payment plan:*** installment.
APPLYING ***Options:*** deferred entrance, midyear entrance. ***Required:*** school transcript, two photographs, art portfolio. ***Recommended:*** essay, 2 recommendations, SAT I or ACT. Test scores used for admission. ***Application deadline:*** rolling. ***Notification:*** continuous.
APPLYING/TRANSFER ***Required:*** college transcript. ***Entrance:*** moderately difficult. ***Application deadline:*** rolling. ***Notification:*** continuous. ***Contact:*** Mr. Daniel M. Stack, Dean of the College, 305-373-4684.
CONTACT Ms. Elsia Suarez, Director of Admissions, International Fine Arts College, 1737 North Bayshore Drive, Miami, FL 33132-1121, 305-373-4684 or toll-free 800-225-9023.

❖ *See page 748 for a narrative description.* ❖

ITT TECHNICAL INSTITUTE
Fort Lauderdale, Florida

UG Enrollment: 386	**Tuition: $15,599/deg prog**
Application Deadline: rolling	**Room & Board: N/Avail**

Florida

ITT Technical Institute (continued)
GENERAL Proprietary, 2-year, coed. Part of ITT Educational Services, Inc. Awards terminal associate degrees. Founded 1991. *Setting:* suburban campus with easy access to Miami. *Total enrollment:* 386. *Faculty:* 13 (all full-time); student-faculty ratio is 29:1.
ENROLLMENT PROFILE 386 students: 0% part-time.
FIRST-YEAR CLASS 284 total; 544 applied.
ACADEMIC PROGRAM Core. Calendar: quarters.
GENERAL DEGREE REQUIREMENTS 124 credit hours; computer course.
MAJOR Electronics engineering technology.
LIBRARY Learning Resource Center with 500 books, 15 periodicals.
COMPUTERS ON CAMPUS 25 computers for student use in lab, library.
COLLEGE LIFE *Campus security:* 24-hour emergency response devices.
HOUSING College housing not available.
CAREER PLANNING *Placement office:* 2 full-time staff. *Director:* Ms. Tina Schackne, Director of Placement, 305-476-9300. *Services:* resume preparation, resume referral, career counseling, careers library, job bank, job interviews.
AFTER GRADUATION 87% of class of 1994 had job offers within 6 months.
EXPENSES FOR 1996–97 *Application fee:* $100. Tuition per degree program ranges from $15,599 to $17,690. Full-time mandatory fees range from $540 to $720.
FINANCIAL AID *College-administered undergrad aid 1995–96:* need-based scholarships, low-interest long-term loans from external sources, Federal Work-Study. *Required forms:* institutional, FAFSA; required for some: state; accepted: CSS Financial Aid PROFILE. *Application deadline:* continuous.
APPLYING *Option:* deferred entrance. *Required:* CPAt. Test scores used for admission. *Application deadline:* continuous.
APPLYING/TRANSFER *Application deadline:* rolling. *Contact:* Mr. Leon Nicely, Director of Education, 305-476-9300.
CONTACT Ms. Nan Lough, Director, ITT Technical Institute, Fort Lauderdale, FL 33328-2021, 305-476-9300. College video available.

ITT TECHNICAL INSTITUTE
Jacksonville, Florida

UG Enrollment: 417	Tuition: $15,429/deg prog
Application Deadline: rolling	Room & Board: N/Avail

GENERAL Proprietary, primarily 2-year, coed. Part of ITT Educational Services, Inc. Awards terminal associate, bachelor's degrees. Founded 1991. *Setting:* 1-acre urban campus. *Total enrollment:* 417. *Faculty:* 17 (15 full-time, 94% with terminal degrees, 2 part-time); student-faculty ratio is 30:1.
ENROLLMENT PROFILE 417 students: 14% women, 0% part-time, 98% state residents, 1% transferred in, 97% have need-based financial aid, 0% have non-need-based financial aid, 0% international, 30% 25 or older, 0% Native American, 3% Hispanic, 28% African American, 2% Asian American. *Areas of study chosen:* 100% engineering and applied sciences. *Most popular recent major:* electronics engineering technology.
FIRST-YEAR CLASS 204 total; 491 applied, 59% of whom enrolled.
ACADEMIC PROGRAM Core, honor code. Calendar: quarters. 56 courses offered in 1995–96. Academic remediation for entering students, tutorials.
GENERAL DEGREE REQUIREMENT
MAJORS Drafting and design, electronics engineering technology (B).
LIBRARY Learning Resource Center plus 1 other, with 1,201 books, 20 periodicals, 25 records, tapes, and CDs.
COMPUTERS ON CAMPUS 5 computers for student use in library provide access to Internet.
COLLEGE LIFE *Most popular organizations:* Student Council, Newsletter Staff. *Major annual event:* Annual School Picnic. *Campus security:* 24-hour emergency response devices.
HOUSING College housing not available.
CAREER PLANNING *Placement office:* 2 full-time staff. *Director:* Mr. Brian Quirk, Director of Placement, 904-573-9100. *Services:* job fairs, resume preparation, resume referral, career counseling, careers library, job bank, job interviews.
EXPENSES FOR 1995–96 *Application fee:* $100. Tuition per degree program ranges from $15,429 to $17,690.
FINANCIAL AID *College-administered undergrad aid 1995–96:* need-based scholarships, low-interest long-term loans from college funds, loans from external sources (average $6625), Federal Work-Study, 10 part-time jobs. *Required forms:* institutional, FAFSA; accepted: CSS Financial Aid PROFILE. *Priority deadline:* 8/6. *Payment plan:* installment. *Waivers:* full or partial for employees or children of employees. *Notification:* continuous.
APPLYING *Option:* deferred entrance. *Required:* CPAt, DAT. Test scores used for admission. *Application deadline:* rolling.
APPLYING/TRANSFER *Entrance:* minimally difficult. *Application deadline:* rolling. *Contact:* Mr. Jeff Schillinger, Director of Education, 904-573-9100.
CONTACT Mr. Jeff Schillinger, Director of Education, ITT Technical Institute, 6600 Youngerman Circle, Suite 10, Jacksonville, FL 32244-6630, 904-573-9100. College video available.

ITT TECHNICAL INSTITUTE
Tampa, Florida

UG Enrollment: 582	Tuition: $15,429/deg prog
Application Deadline: rolling	Room & Board: N/Avail

GENERAL Proprietary, primarily 2-year, coed. Part of ITT Educational Services, Inc. Awards transfer associate, terminal associate, bachelor's degrees. Founded 1981. *Setting:* suburban campus with easy access to St. Petersburg. *Total enrollment:* 582. *Faculty:* 24 (19 full-time, 5 part-time); student-faculty ratio is 27:1.
ENROLLMENT PROFILE 582 students from 3 states and territories, 1 other country. 9% women, 0% part-time, 99% state residents, 0% transferred in, 27% 25 or older, 1% Native American, 15% Hispanic, 13% African American, 1% Asian American. *Most popular recent major:* electronics engineering technology.
FIRST-YEAR CLASS 197 total; 325 applied, 82% were accepted, 77% of whom enrolled.

ACADEMIC PROGRAM Core. Calendar: quarters. Academic remediation for entering students.
GENERAL DEGREE REQUIREMENTS 91 credits for associate, 194 credits for bachelor's.
MAJORS Drafting and design, electronics engineering technology (B).
LIBRARY 825 books.
COMPUTERS ON CAMPUS 48 computers for student use in computer labs, library provide access to off-campus computing facilities. Staffed computer lab on campus provides training in use of computers, software.
HOUSING College housing not available.
CAREER PLANNING *Placement office:* 3 full-time, 1 part-time staff. *Director:* Ms. Toni Riggs, Director of Placement, 813-885-2244. *Services:* job fairs, resume preparation, resume referral, career counseling, careers library, job bank, job interviews. 27 organizations recruited on campus 1994–95.
AFTER GRADUATION 88% of class of 1994 had job offers within 6 months. 45% of students completing transfer associate program went directly to 4-year colleges.
EXPENSES FOR 1995–96 *Application fee:* $100. Tuition per degree program ranges from $15,429 to $17,690 for associate, $25,117 to $28,060 for bachelor's. Tuition guaranteed not to increase for student's term of enrollment.
FINANCIAL AID *College-administered undergrad aid 1995–96:* need-based scholarships, low-interest long-term loans from external sources, Federal Work-Study, 2 part-time jobs. *Required forms:* institutional, FAFSA; accepted: CSS Financial Aid PROFILE. *Priority deadline:* 9/11.
APPLYING *Option:* deferred entrance. *Required:* TOEFL for international students. Test scores used for admission. *Application deadline:* rolling. *Notification:* continuous.
APPLYING/TRANSFER *Application deadline:* rolling. *Notification:* continuous.
CONTACT Mr. Joseph Drennen, Director of Recruitment, ITT Technical Institute, Tampa, FL 33634-7350, 813-885-4809. *Fax:* 813-888-6078.

KEISER COLLEGE OF TECHNOLOGY
Daytona Beach, Florida

UG Enrollment: 196	Tuition & Fees: $6658
Application Deadline: N/R	Room & Board: N/Avail

GENERAL Proprietary, 2-year, coed. Awards transfer associate, terminal associate degrees. Founded 1995. *Setting:* 1-acre suburban campus with easy access to Orlando. *Total enrollment:* 196. *Faculty:* 15 (9 full-time, 100% with terminal degrees, 6 part-time); student-faculty ratio is 13:1.
ENROLLMENT PROFILE 196 students. *Most popular recent majors:* medical assistant technologies, business administration/commerce/management, accounting.
FIRST-YEAR CLASS 75 total.
ACADEMIC PROGRAM Calendar: semesters.
GENERAL DEGREE REQUIREMENTS 60 credits; 1 college math course; 2 science courses; computer course.
MAJORS Accounting, business administration/commerce/management, film and video production, health services administration, management information systems, medical assistant technologies, paralegal studies.
LIBRARY Keiser Library with 5,000 books, 30 periodicals, 50 CD-ROMs, 300 records, tapes, and CDs.
COMPUTERS ON CAMPUS 35 computers for student use in computer center, computer labs, library provide access to on-line services, Internet. Staffed computer lab on campus provides training in use of computers, software.
COLLEGE LIFE 3% vote in student government elections. *Social organizations:* national fraternities. *Most popular organization:* Phi Beta Lambda. *Student services:* personal-psychological counseling. *Campus security:* 24-hour emergency response devices.
HOUSING College housing not available.
CAREER PLANNING *Placement office:* 1 full-time staff. *Director:* Ms. Cindy Hodges, Director of Graduate Services, 904-255-1707. *Services:* resume preparation, resume referral, career counseling, job bank, job interviews. Students must register sophomore year.
EXPENSES FOR 1996–97 Tuition: $6560 full-time. Full-time mandatory fees: $98.
FINANCIAL AID *College-administered undergrad aid 1995–96:* need-based scholarships, non-need scholarships, low-interest long-term loans, Federal Work-Study. *Required forms:* institutional, FAFSA. *Application deadline:* continuous.
APPLYING Open admission. *Required:* school transcript, Otis-Lennon School Ability Test.
APPLYING/TRANSFER *Required for some:* college transcript.
CONTACT Ms. Charlene Donnelly, Director of Admissions, Keiser College of Technology, 1491 South Nova Road, Daytona Beach, FL 32114, 904-255-1707.

KEISER COLLEGE OF TECHNOLOGY
Fort Lauderdale, Florida

UG Enrollment: 700	Tuition & Fees: $8698
Application Deadline: rolling	Room & Board: N/Avail

GENERAL Proprietary, 2-year, coed. Awards diplomas, transfer associate, terminal associate degrees. Founded 1977. *Setting:* 4-acre suburban campus with easy access to Miami. *Total enrollment:* 700. *Faculty:* 24 (16 full-time, 60% with terminal degrees, 8 part-time); student-faculty ratio is 18:1.
ENROLLMENT PROFILE 700 students: 60% women, 40% men, 80% state residents, 25% transferred in, 88% have need-based financial aid, 12% have non-need-based financial aid, 18% international, 70% 25 or older, 1% Native American, 12% Hispanic, 25% African American, 6% Asian American. *Areas of study chosen:* 50% health professions and related sciences, 35% computer and information sciences, 15% business management and administrative services.
FIRST-YEAR CLASS 620 total; 890 applied, 78% were accepted, 89% of whom enrolled.
ACADEMIC PROGRAM Core. Calendar: semesters. 154 courses offered in 1995–96; average class size 18 in required courses. Tutorials, adult/continuing education programs, internships.
GENERAL DEGREE REQUIREMENTS 60 credits; 3 credits of math; 6 credits of science; computer course; internship (some majors).
MAJORS Business administration/commerce/management, computer technologies, health science.

COMPUTERS ON CAMPUS Computer purchase plan available. Computers for student use in computer labs, learning resource center, classrooms, library provide access to main academic computer, on-line services. Staffed computer lab on campus provides training in use of computers, software.
COLLEGE LIFE *Campus security:* security guard after 8 p.m.
HOUSING College housing not available.
CAREER PLANNING *Placement office:* 1 full-time staff. *Director:* Ms. Christina Dudash, Director of Student Services, 954-776-4456. *Services:* job fairs, resume preparation, resume referral, career counseling, job interviews.
AFTER GRADUATION 35% of students completing a degree program in 1994–95 went directly on to further study.
ESTIMATED EXPENSES FOR 1996–97 *Application fee:* $50. Tuition: $8600 full-time. Full-time mandatory fees: $98. Tuition guaranteed not to increase for student's term of enrollment.
FINANCIAL AID *College-administered undergrad aid 1995–96:* need-based scholarships, non-need scholarships, low-interest long-term loans from external sources, Federal Work-Study. *Required forms:* institutional, FAFSA. *Priority deadline:* 5/1. *Payment plan:* installment. *Waivers:* full or partial for employees or children of employees. *Notification:* continuous.
APPLYING *Options:* deferred entrance, midyear entrance. *Required:* school transcript, minimum 2.0 GPA, interview. *Recommended:* SAT I or ACT. *Required for some:* TOEFL for international students. Test scores used for admission. *Application deadline:* rolling. *Notification:* continuous.
APPLYING/TRANSFER *Required:* college transcript. *Recommended:* minimum 2.0 college GPA. *Entrance:* minimally difficult. *Application deadline:* rolling. *Notification:* continuous. *Contact:* Ms. Susan Ziegelhofer, Director of Admissions, 954-776-4456.
CONTACT Ms. Susan Ziegelhofer, Director of Admissions, Keiser College of Technology, Fort Lauderdale, FL 33309, 954-776-4456. College video available.

KEISER COLLEGE OF TECHNOLOGY
Melbourne, Florida

UG Enrollment: 428	Tuition & Fees: $6560
Application Deadline: N/R	Room & Board: N/Avail

GENERAL Proprietary, 2-year, specialized. Awards transfer associate, terminal associate degrees. Founded 1989. *Total enrollment:* 428. *Faculty:* 25 (15 full-time, 10 part-time).
ENROLLMENT PROFILE 428 students; 0% part-time.
ACADEMIC PROGRAM Calendar: semesters.
GENERAL DEGREE REQUIREMENTS 60 semester hours; 1 math course; 2 science courses; computer course.
HOUSING College housing not available.
EXPENSES FOR 1995–96 Tuition: $6560 full-time.
APPLYING *Required:* school transcript.
APPLYING/TRANSFER *Required for some:* college transcript.
CONTACT Ms. Shirley Simoni, Director of Admissions, Keiser College of Technology, Melbourne, FL 32901-1461, 407-255-2255.

KEISER COLLEGE OF TECHNOLOGY
Sarasota, Florida

UG Enrollment: 120	Tuition & Fees: $6560
Application Deadline: rolling	Room & Board: N/Avail

GENERAL Proprietary, 2-year, coed. Awards terminal associate degrees. *Setting:* small-town campus with easy access to Tampa. *Total enrollment:* 120. *Faculty:* 4 (all full-time, 25% with terminal degrees).
ENROLLMENT PROFILE 120 students. *Most popular recent majors:* paralegal studies, medical assistant technologies.
ACADEMIC PROGRAM Honor code. Calendar: semesters.
GENERAL DEGREE REQUIREMENTS 60 credits; 1 math course; computer course.
MAJORS Accounting, business administration/commerce/management, computer information systems, medical assistant technologies, paralegal studies.
COMPUTERS ON CAMPUS 20 computers for student use in computer center, computer labs, library.
COLLEGE LIFE *Campus security:* 24-hour patrols, late-night transport-escort service.
HOUSING College housing not available.
EXPENSES FOR 1995–96 *Application fee:* $50. Tuition: $6560 full-time. One-time mandatory fee: $510. Tuition guaranteed not to increase for student's term of enrollment.
FINANCIAL AID *Payment plan:* installment.
APPLYING *Application deadline:* rolling. *Notification:* continuous.
APPLYING/TRANSFER *Application deadline:* rolling. *Notification:* continuous.
CONTACT Mr. Roger Buck, Executive Director, Keiser College of Technology, Sarasota, FL 34236, 941-954-0954. College video available.

KEISER COLLEGE OF TECHNOLOGY
Tallahassee, Florida

LAKE CITY COMMUNITY COLLEGE
Lake City, Florida

UG Enrollment: 2,700	Tuition & Fees (FL Res): $1013
Application Deadline: rolling	Room & Board: $3362

GENERAL State-supported, 2-year, coed. Part of Florida Community Colleges System. Awards certificates, transfer associate, terminal associate degrees. Founded 1962. *Setting:* 132-acre small-town campus with easy access to Jacksonville. *Total enrollment:* 2,700. *Faculty:* 225 (75 full-time, 15% with terminal degrees, 150 part-time).

ENROLLMENT PROFILE 2,700 students from 18 states and territories, 9 other countries. 54% women, 46% men, 47% part-time, 95% state residents, 2% live on campus, 8% transferred in, 1% international, 48% 25 or older, 1% Native American, 2% Hispanic, 11% African American, 1% Asian American. *Areas of study chosen:* 55% liberal arts/general studies, 30% health professions and related sciences, 5% business management and administrative services, 5% computer and information sciences, 5% vocational and home economics. *Most popular recent majors:* liberal arts/general studies, nursing.
FIRST-YEAR CLASS 1,412 applied, 100% were accepted. 8% from top 10% of their high school class.
ACADEMIC PROGRAM Core, interdisciplinary curriculum, honor code. Calendar: semesters. 300 courses offered in 1995–96. Academic remediation for entering students, English as a second language program offered during academic year, services for LD students, advanced placement, summer session for credit, part-time degree program (daytime, evenings, summer), adult/continuing education programs, co-op programs and internships. Study abroad in the Netherlands, Italy, Switzerland, France, England, Scotland.
GENERAL DEGREE REQUIREMENTS 60 semester hours; 6 semester hours of math; 10 semester hours of science.
MAJORS Accounting, business administration/commerce/management, computer programming, corrections, criminal justice, education, electronics engineering technology, emergency medical technology, engineering sciences, English, forestry, forest technology, landscape architecture/design, law enforcement/police sciences, liberal arts/general studies, marketing/retailing/merchandising, mathematics, medical laboratory technology, music, nursing, operating room technology, physical therapy, practical nursing, secretarial studies/office management, sociology, theater arts/drama.
LIBRARY Learning Resources Center with 42,000 books, 10,046 microform titles, 259 periodicals, 152 CD-ROMs, 1,450 records, tapes, and CDs.
COMPUTERS ON CAMPUS 150 computers for student use in computer center, learning resource center provide access to Internet. Staffed computer lab on campus provides training in use of computers, software.
COLLEGE LIFE Drama-theater group, choral group. 30% vote in student government elections. *Social organizations:* 22 open to all. *Most popular organizations:* Student Government, Florida Turf Grass Association, Florida Student Nurses Association, Phi Theta Kappa, Black Student Union. *Major annual events:* Fall Fest, Student Government Awards Banquet, Homecoming. *Campus security:* 24-hour patrols.
HOUSING 92 college housing spaces available; 70 were occupied 1995–96. No special consideration for freshman housing applicants. Off-campus living permitted. *Option:* coed housing available. Resident assistants live in dorms.
ATHLETICS Member NJCAA. *Intercollegiate:* baseball M(s), softball W(s). *Intramural:* volleyball. *Contact:* Mr. Jim Webb, Athletic Director, 904-752-1822 Ext. 1363.
CAREER PLANNING *Placement office:* 5 full-time staff. *Director:* Ms. Juanita Maxwell, Director of Counseling, 904-752-1822 Ext. 1333. *Services:* career counseling, careers library.
AFTER GRADUATION 35% of students completing a degree program in 1994–95 went directly on to further study.
EXPENSES FOR 1995–96 *Application fee:* $15. State resident tuition: $1013 full-time, $33.75 per semester hour part-time. Nonresident tuition: $3915 full-time, $130.50 per semester hour part-time. College room and board: $3362.
FINANCIAL AID *College-administered undergrad aid 1995–96:* need-based scholarships, short-term loans (average $375), low-interest long-term loans from college funds (average $1313), loans from external sources (average $1313), Federal Work-Study. *Required forms:* institutional; accepted: CSS Financial Aid PROFILE, FAFSA. *Priority deadline:* 6/1.
APPLYING Open admission except for nursing, golf course operation, allied health programs. *Options:* early entrance, deferred entrance, midyear entrance. *Required:* 3 years of high school math and science, TOEFL for international students, CPT. *Recommended:* SAT I or ACT. Test scores used for counseling/placement. *Application deadline:* rolling. *Notification:* continuous.
APPLYING/TRANSFER *Required:* standardized test scores, college transcript. *Entrance:* noncompetitive. *Application deadline:* rolling. *Notification:* continuous. *Contact:* Ms. Judy Hammons, Assistant Registrar, 904-752-0822.
CONTACT Mr. Hank Dunn, Director of Admissions and Registrations, Lake City Community College, Lake City, FL 32025, 904-752-1822 Ext. 1288.

LAKE-SUMTER COMMUNITY COLLEGE
Leesburg, Florida

UG Enrollment: 2,700	Tuition & Fees (FL Res): $1160
Application Deadline: rolling	Room & Board: N/Avail

GENERAL State and locally supported, 2-year, coed. Part of Florida Community Colleges System. Awards transfer associate, terminal associate degrees. Founded 1962. *Setting:* 110-acre rural campus with easy access to Orlando. *Total enrollment:* 2,700. *Faculty:* 117 (41 full-time, 76 part-time); student-faculty ratio is 20:1.
ENROLLMENT PROFILE 2,700 students from 4 states and territories, 2 other countries. 65% women, 29% part-time, 98% state residents, 10% transferred in, 1% international, 52% 25 or older, 0% Native American, 1% Hispanic, 6% African American, 0% Asian American. *Most popular recent majors:* liberal arts/general studies, nursing, business administration/commerce/management.
FIRST-YEAR CLASS 699 total; 824 applied, 100% were accepted, 85% of whom enrolled.
ACADEMIC PROGRAM Core. Calendar: semesters. Academic remediation for entering students, services for LD students, advanced placement, summer session for credit, part-time degree program (daytime, evenings, summer), adult/continuing education programs, co-op programs. Off-campus study at University of Central Florida, Valencia Community College, Lake County Area Vocational-Technical Center. ROTC: Air Force (c).
GENERAL DEGREE REQUIREMENTS 60 credits; math/science requirements vary according to program; computer course for business-related majors.
MAJORS Art education, broadcasting, business administration/commerce/management, computer science, computer technologies, criminal justice, electronics engineering technology, elementary education, emergency medical technology, (pre)engineering sequence, finance/banking, fire science, graphic arts, hotel and restaurant management, journalism, liberal arts/general studies, music, nursing, occupational therapy, pharmacy/pharmaceutical sciences, physical therapy, social science, veterinary sciences.
LIBRARY Learning Resources Library with 52,124 books, 397 periodicals, 2,160 records, tapes, and CDs.

Peterson's Guide to Two-Year Colleges 1997

Lake-Sumter Community College (continued)

COMPUTERS ON CAMPUS 250 computers for student use in computer center, media center.

COLLEGE LIFE Drama-theater group, choral group, student-run newspaper. ***Social organizations:*** 19 open to all. ***Student services:*** personal-psychological counseling. ***Campus security:*** student patrols, late-night transport-escort service.

HOUSING College housing not available.

ATHLETICS ***Intramural:*** badminton, basketball, bowling, football, sailing, soccer, table tennis (Ping-Pong), tennis, volleyball, weight lifting.

CAREER PLANNING ***Placement office:*** 1 part-time staff. ***Director:*** Mr. Earl Evans, Director of Student Services, 352-365-3576. ***Services:*** job fairs, resume preparation, career counseling, careers library, job interviews.

EXPENSES FOR 1995–96 ***Application fee:*** $15. State resident tuition: $1160 full-time, $36.25 per semester hour part-time. Nonresident tuition: $4312 full-time, $134.75 per semester hour part-time.

FINANCIAL AID ***College-administered undergrad aid 1995–96:*** 60 need-based scholarships (average $750), 250 non-need scholarships (average $500), short-term loans (average $350), Federal Work-Study. ***Required forms:*** CSS Financial Aid PROFILE, institutional; accepted: FAFSA. ***Priority deadline:*** 4/15. ***Waivers:*** full or partial for senior citizens. ***Notification:*** continuous.

APPLYING Open admission. ***Options:*** early entrance, deferred entrance. ***Required:*** school transcript, TOEFL for international students, MAPS. ***Recommended:*** SAT I or ACT. ***Required for some:*** 3 years of high school math and science. Test scores used for counseling/placement. ***Application deadline:*** rolling. ***Notification:*** continuous.

APPLYING/TRANSFER ***Required:*** standardized test scores, high school transcript, college transcript. ***Entrance:*** noncompetitive. ***Application deadline:*** rolling. ***Notification:*** continuous. ***Contact:*** Ms. Jane Miller, Director of Admissions and Records, 352-365-3568.

CONTACT Ms. Jane Miller, Director of Admissions and Records, Lake-Sumter Community College, Leesburg, FL 34788-8751, 652-365-3568.

MANATEE COMMUNITY COLLEGE
Bradenton, Florida

UG Enrollment: 7,605	**Tuition & Fees (FL Res): $1050**
Application Deadline: 8/20	**Room & Board: N/Avail**

GENERAL State-supported, 2-year, coed. Part of Florida Community Colleges System. Awards certificates, transfer associate, terminal associate degrees. Founded 1957. ***Setting:*** 100-acre suburban campus with easy access to Tampa–St. Petersburg. ***Total enrollment:*** 7,605. ***Faculty:*** 289 (133 full-time, 19% with terminal degrees, 156 part-time).

ENROLLMENT PROFILE 7,605 students from 10 states and territories. 62% women, 38% men, 61% part-time, 93% state residents, 20% transferred in, 4% international, 45% 25 or older, 1% Native American, 3% Hispanic, 6% African American, 1% Asian American. ***Areas of study chosen:*** 59% library and information studies, 4% health professions and related sciences, 3% computer and information sciences, 1% business management and administrative services, 1% engineering and applied sciences. ***Most popular recent majors:*** liberal arts/general studies, nursing, legal studies.

FIRST-YEAR CLASS 1,044 total. Of the students who applied, 100% were accepted, 100% of whom enrolled.

ACADEMIC PROGRAM Core. Calendar: semesters. 580 courses offered in 1995–96. Academic remediation for entering students, English as a second language program offered during academic year, services for LD students, advanced placement, summer session for credit, part-time degree program (daytime, evenings, summer), co-op programs.

GENERAL DEGREE REQUIREMENTS 60 credit hours; math/science requirements vary according to program; computer course.

MAJORS Accounting, automotive technologies, business administration/commerce/management, child psychology/child development, civil engineering technology, computer information systems, computer programming, construction technologies, criminal justice, drafting and design, electrical engineering technology, finance/banking, fire science, hotel and restaurant management, legal studies, liberal arts/general studies, marketing/retailing/merchandising, nursing, radiological technology, respiratory therapy, secretarial studies/office management.

LIBRARY Sara Harlee Library with 61,550 books, 311 microform titles, 418 periodicals, 1 on-line bibliographic service, 10 CD-ROMs, 483 records, tapes, and CDs. Acquisition spending 1994–95: $903,804.

COMPUTERS ON CAMPUS 270 computers for student use in computer labs, technology building, classrooms provide access to Internet. Staffed computer lab on campus provides training in use of computers, software.

COLLEGE LIFE Drama-theater group, student-run newspaper. ***Social organizations:*** 36 open to all. ***Most popular organizations:*** Student Government Association, Phi Theta Kappa, American Chemical Society Student Affiliate, Campus Ministry. ***Major annual events:*** Fall Frolic, Spring Fling, Great Safe Holiday Break Campaign. ***Student services:*** health clinic. ***Campus security:*** 24-hour emergency response devices and patrols, late-night transport-escort service.

HOUSING College housing not available.

ATHLETICS Member NJCAA. ***Intercollegiate:*** baseball M(s), basketball M(s)/W(s), golf M(s), softball W(s), volleyball W(s). ***Intramural:*** basketball, football, softball, volleyball. ***Contact:*** Mr. George Sanders, Athletic Director, 941-755-1511 Ext. 4575.

CAREER PLANNING ***Placement office:*** 2 full-time, 3 part-time staff. ***Director:*** Dr. Jack Dale, Assistant Dean to Educational Services, 941-755-1511 Ext. 4385. ***Services:*** job fairs, resume preparation, resume referral, career counseling, careers library, job bank, job interviews. 29 organizations recruited on campus 1994–95.

AFTER GRADUATION 77% of students completing a degree program in 1994–95 went directly on to further study.

EXPENSES FOR 1995–96 ***Application fee:*** $15. State resident tuition: $1050 full-time, $35 per credit hour part-time. Nonresident tuition: $3810 full-time, $127 per credit hour part-time.

FINANCIAL AID ***College-administered undergrad aid 1995–96:*** need-based scholarships (average $223), non-need scholarships (average $863), short-term loans (average $300), low-interest long-term loans from external sources, Federal Work-Study, 175 part-time jobs. ***Required forms for some financial aid applicants:*** state, institutional; accepted: CSS Financial Aid PROFILE, FAFSA. ***Priority deadline:*** 7/1.

APPLYING Open admission except for allied health programs. ***Option:*** early entrance. ***Required:*** 3 years of high school math and science, TOEFL for international students, MAPS. Test scores used for counseling/placement. ***Application deadline:*** 8/20. ***Notification:*** continuous.

APPLYING/TRANSFER ***Required:*** standardized test scores, 3 years of high school math and science. ***Entrance:*** noncompetitive. ***Application deadline:*** 8/20. ***Notification:*** continuous. ***Contact:*** Mr. James Brown, Associate Dean of Education Services, 941-755-1511 Ext. 4421.

CONTACT Mrs. Yvette Robison, Director of Admissions and Records, Manatee Community College, Bradenton, FL 34206-7046, 941-755-1511 Ext. 4234. ***Fax:*** 941-755-1511 Ext. 4234. College video available.

MIAMI-DADE COMMUNITY COLLEGE
Miami, Florida

UG Enrollment: 51,019	**Tuition & Fees (FL Res): $1177**
Application Deadline: rolling	**Room & Board: N/Avail**

Miami-Dade Community College offers undergraduate study in more than 120 academic areas and professions. The College is internationally recognized as an educational leader in undergraduate programs that are innovative and diverse within a multicultural, multiethnic environment. More than 120,000 credit and noncredit students are enrolled at 5 major campuses and numerous outreach centers.

GENERAL State and locally supported, 2-year, coed. Part of Florida Community Colleges System. Awards transfer associate, terminal associate degrees. Founded 1960. ***Setting:*** urban campus. ***Total enrollment:*** 51,019. ***Faculty:*** 2,070 (886 full-time, 25% with terminal degrees, 1,184 part-time).

ENROLLMENT PROFILE 51,019 students from 31 states and territories, 97 other countries. 58% women, 42% men, 67% part-time, 92% state residents, 4% transferred in, 7% international, 43% 25 or older, 0% Native American, 59% Hispanic, 22% African American, 2% Asian American.

FIRST-YEAR CLASS 26,641 applied, 59% of whom enrolled. 9% from top 10% of their high school class, 23% from top quarter, 52% from top half.

ACADEMIC PROGRAM Core, honor code. Calendar: 16-16-6-6. Academic remediation for entering students, English as a second language program offered during academic year and summer, services for LD students, advanced placement, honors program, summer session for credit, part-time degree program (daytime, evenings, weekends, summer), adult/continuing education programs, co-op programs and internships. Study abroad in France, Italy, England, Mexico, Spain, Costa Rica. ROTC: Army (c), Air Force (c).

GENERAL DEGREE REQUIREMENTS 60 credit hours; 6 credit hours of math/science.

MAJORS Accounting, aerospace sciences, agricultural sciences, American studies, anthropology, architectural technologies, art education, art/fine arts, Asian/Oriental studies, aviation administration, aviation technology, behavioral sciences, biology/biological sciences, broadcasting, business administration/commerce/management, chemistry, child care/child and family studies, civil engineering technology, commercial art, communication, computer graphics, computer information systems, computer programming, computer science, construction technologies, court reporting, criminal justice, dance, data processing, deaf interpreter training, dental services, dietetics, drafting and design, drama therapy, early childhood education, economics, education, electrical and electronics technologies, electromechanical technology, electronics engineering technology, elementary education, emergency medical technology, engineering (general), engineering design, engineering sciences, (pre)engineering sequence, engineering technology, English, fashion design and technology, fashion merchandising, film and video production, film studies, finance/banking, fire science, flight training, food sciences, food services technology, forestry, French, funeral service, geology, German, graphic arts, heating/refrigeration/air conditioning, history, horticulture, hotel and restaurant management, humanities, industrial engineering technology, instrumentation technology, interior design, international studies, Italian, jazz, journalism, landscape architecture/design, Latin American studies, law enforcement/police sciences, legal secretarial studies, legal studies, liberal arts/general studies, literature, management information systems, marketing/retailing/merchandising, mathematics, medical assistant technologies, medical laboratory technology, medical records services, medical secretarial studies, medical technology, middle school education, music, music education, natural sciences, nursing, oceanography, optical technologies, optometric/ophthalmic technologies, ornamental horticulture, paralegal studies, pharmacy/pharmaceutical sciences, philosophy, photography, physical education, physical sciences, physical therapy, physics, piano/organ, political science/government, Portuguese, postal management, psychology, public administration, radio and television studies, radiological sciences, radiological technology, recreation and leisure services, respiratory therapy, science education, secretarial studies/office management, social science, social work, sociology, Spanish, speech/rhetoric/public address/debate, stringed instruments, surveying technology, teacher aide studies, theater arts/drama, tourism and travel, veterinary sciences, wind and percussion instruments.

LIBRARY 331,695 books, 1,921 periodicals, 3 on-line bibliographic services, 41 CD-ROMs.

COMPUTERS ON CAMPUS Computer purchase plan available. 4,423 computers for student use in computer labs, learning resource center, labs, classrooms, library, student center. Staffed computer lab on campus provides training in use of computers, software.

COLLEGE LIFE Drama-theater group, choral group, student-run newspaper, radio station. ***Social organizations:*** national fraternities, national sororities, local fraternities, local sororities; 5% of eligible men and 5% of eligible women are members. ***Student services:*** personal-psychological counseling, women's center. ***Campus security:*** 24-hour patrols.

HOUSING College housing not available.

ATHLETICS Member NJCAA. ***Intercollegiate:*** baseball M(s), basketball M(s)/W(s), golf M(s), swimming and diving M(s)/W(s), tennis M(s)/W(s), track and field M(s), volleyball W(s). ***Intramural:*** badminton, basketball, bowling, fencing, gymnastics, racquetball, squash, swimming and diving, tennis, volleyball, water polo, weight lifting.

CAREER PLANNING ***Services:*** job fairs, career counseling, careers library, job bank.

AFTER GRADUATION 78% of students completing a degree program in 1994–95 went directly on to further study.

EXPENSES FOR 1995–96 ***Application fee:*** $15. State resident tuition: $1177 full-time, $39.25 per credit hour part-time. Nonresident tuition: $4095 full-time, $136.50 per credit hour part-time.

Florida

FINANCIAL AID *College-administered undergrad aid 1995–96:* 8,745 need-based scholarships (average $651), 5,895 non-need scholarships (average $693), short-term loans (average $318), low-interest long-term loans from external sources (average $2291), Federal Work-Study, 118 part-time jobs. *Required forms:* institutional, FAFSA, financial aid transcript (for transfers); required for some: state; accepted: CSS Financial Aid PROFILE. *Priority deadline:* 4/15. *Payment plan:* tuition prepayment.
APPLYING Open admission. *Options:* early entrance, deferred entrance, midyear entrance. *Required:* 3 years of high school math and science, TOEFL for international students, CPT. Test scores used for counseling/placement. *Application deadline:* rolling.
APPLYING/TRANSFER *Required:* standardized test scores, college transcript. *Application deadline:* rolling.
CONTACT Mr. Samuel LaRoue, Director of Admissions and Registration Services, Miami-Dade Community College, 300 Northeast Second Avenue, Miami, FL 33132-2296, 305-237-7478.

❖ *See page 770 for a narrative description.* ❖

NATIONAL EDUCATION CENTER– TAMPA TECHNICAL INSTITUTE CAMPUS
Florida—See Education America–Tampa Technical Institute Campus

NATIONAL INSTITUTE FOR PARALEGAL ARTS AND SCIENCES
Boca Raton, Florida

Enrollment: N/R	Tuition & Fees: $5900
Application Deadline: rolling	Room & Board: N/Avail

GENERAL Proprietary, 2-year, specialized, coed. Awards certificates, diplomas, transfer associate, terminal associate degrees (offers only distance learning degree programs). Founded 1976.
ACADEMIC PROGRAM Core. Calendar: year-round.
GENERAL DEGREE REQUIREMENTS 60 credits; 3 credits of math; computer course.
MAJOR Paralegal studies.
EXPENSES FOR 1996–97 Tuition: $5900 full-time.
APPLYING Open admission. *Required:* campus interview. *Application deadline:* rolling. *Notification:* continuous.
APPLYING/TRANSFER *Required:* campus interview. *Application deadline:* rolling. *Notification:* continuous.
CONTACT Ms. Christina Belanger, Director of Education, National Institute for Paralegal Arts and Sciences, Boca Raton, FL 33432, 407-368-2522 or toll-free 800-669-2555.

NATIONAL SCHOOL OF TECHNOLOGY, INC.
North Miami Beach, Florida

UG Enrollment: 800	Tuition: $5485/deg prog
Application Deadline: rolling	Room & Board: N/Avail

GENERAL Proprietary, 2-year, coed. Awards terminal associate degrees. Founded 1977. *Setting:* urban campus. *Total enrollment:* 800. *Faculty:* 30 (20 full-time, 10 part-time).
ENROLLMENT PROFILE 800 students: 60% women, 60% part-time, 100% state residents, 5% transferred in, 0% international, 90% 25 or older.
ACADEMIC PROGRAM Core. Calendar: continuous. Academic remediation for entering students, English as a second language program offered during academic year, summer session for credit, part-time degree program (daytime, evenings), adult/continuing education programs, co-op programs and internships.
GENERAL DEGREE REQUIREMENTS 1500 clock hours; computer course.
MAJORS Cartography, computer programming, medical technology.
COMPUTERS ON CAMPUS 30 computers for student use in computer center.
HOUSING College housing not available.
CAREER PLANNING *Placement office:* 3 full-time staff. *Director:* Ms. Cheryl Grogan, Director of Career Development, 305-949-9500. *Services:* job fairs, resume preparation, resume referral, career counseling, careers library, job interviews.
EXPENSES FOR 1995–96 *Application fee:* $25. Tuition per degree program ranges from $5485 to $13,200.
FINANCIAL AID *College-administered undergrad aid 1995–96:* non-need scholarships, low-interest long-term loans from external sources, Federal Work-Study. *Required forms:* institutional, FAFSA. *Application deadline:* continuous.
APPLYING Open admission. *Required:* school transcript, interview. *Application deadline:* rolling. *Notification:* continuous.
APPLYING/TRANSFER *Required:* high school transcript, interview, college transcript. *Entrance:* noncompetitive. *Application deadline:* rolling. *Notification:* continuous.
CONTACT Ms. Rosa Iverson, Vice President, National School of Technology, Inc., 1590 NE 162nd Street, #300, North Miami Beach, FL 33162-4744, 305-945-2929.

NEW ENGLAND INSTITUTE OF TECHNOLOGY AND FLORIDA CULINARY INSTITUTE
West Palm Beach, Florida

UG Enrollment: 945	Tuition & Fees: $4950
Application Deadline: rolling	Room & Board: N/Avail

GENERAL Proprietary, 2-year, coed. Awards terminal associate degrees. Founded 1983. *Setting:* 7-acre campus with easy access to Miami. *Total enrollment:* 945. *Faculty:* 68 (all full-time); student-faculty ratio is 20:1.
ENROLLMENT PROFILE 945 students: 41% women, 0% part-time, 95% state residents, 20% transferred in, 3% international, 40% 25 or older, 0% Native American, 12% Hispanic, 34% African American, 4% Asian American.
FIRST-YEAR CLASS 300 total; 1,300 applied, 92% were accepted.
ACADEMIC PROGRAM Calendar: quarters. Academic remediation for entering students, internships.
GENERAL DEGREE REQUIREMENTS 90 quarter credit hours; computer course for medical assistant majors.
MAJORS Automotive technologies, computer programming, culinary arts, drafting and design, electronics engineering technology, heating/refrigeration/air conditioning, medical assistant technologies, secretarial studies/office management.
COMPUTERS ON CAMPUS 58 computers for student use in computer center.
COLLEGE LIFE *Student services:* personal-psychological counseling.
HOUSING College housing not available.
CAREER PLANNING *Placement office:* 2 full-time staff. *Director:* Mr. Noel Shevack, Dean of Instruction, 407-842-8324. *Services:* job fairs, resume preparation, resume referral, career counseling, careers library, job bank, job interviews.
EXPENSES FOR 1996–97 *Application fee:* $150. Tuition: $4800 (minimum) full-time. Tuition for culinary arts program per year: $8550. Full-time mandatory fees: $150. Tuition guaranteed not to increase for student's term of enrollment.
FINANCIAL AID *College-administered undergrad aid 1995–96:* need-based scholarships, low-interest long-term loans from external sources, Federal Work-Study. *Required forms:* CSS Financial Aid PROFILE, institutional, FAFSA. *Priority deadline:* 8/1.
APPLYING Open admission. *Option:* early entrance. *Required:* school transcript. *Application deadline:* rolling. *Notification:* continuous.
APPLYING/TRANSFER *Required:* high school transcript. *Recommended:* college transcript. *Entrance:* noncompetitive. *Application deadline:* rolling. *Notification:* continuous.
CONTACT Mr. Scott Spitolnick, Director of Admissions, New England Institute of Technology and Florida Culinary Institute, West Palm Beach, FL 33407-2384, 407-842-8324. College video available.

NORTH FLORIDA COMMUNITY COLLEGE
Madison, Florida

UG Enrollment: 1,003	Tuition & Fees (FL Res): $992
Application Deadline: rolling	Room & Board: N/Avail

GENERAL State-supported, 2-year, coed. Awards transfer associate degrees. Founded 1958. *Setting:* 109-acre small-town campus. *Total enrollment:* 1,003. *Faculty:* 30 (26 full-time, 100% with terminal degrees, 4 part-time); student-faculty ratio is 26:1. *Notable Alumni:* Allen Boyd, state representative; Jerry M. Blair, state attorney for the third judicial circuit; Malcolm Brady, assistant special agent; Jesse Solomon, former professional football player.
ENROLLMENT PROFILE 1,003 students from 5 states and territories, 3 other countries. 66% women, 34% men, 58% part-time, 99% state residents, 10% transferred in, 55% have need-based financial aid, 45% have non-need-based financial aid, 26% 25 or older, 1% Native American, 2% Hispanic, 17% African American, 1% Asian American.
FIRST-YEAR CLASS 421 total; 451 applied, 93% were accepted, 100% of whom enrolled. 10% from top 10% of their high school class, 30% from top quarter, 80% from top half.
ACADEMIC PROGRAM Core, transfer curriculum, honor code. Calendar: modified semester. 115 courses offered in 1995–96; average class size 22 in required courses. Academic remediation for entering students, services for LD students, advanced placement, summer session for credit, part-time degree program (daytime, evenings, summer), adult/continuing education programs.
GENERAL DEGREE REQUIREMENTS 60 semester hours; 6 semester hours each of math and science.
MAJOR Liberal arts/general studies.
LIBRARY Dr. Marshall Hamilton Library with 34,977 books, 671 microform titles, 116 periodicals, 14 CD-ROMs, 1,887 records, tapes, and CDs. Acquisition spending 1994–95: $40,543.
COMPUTERS ON CAMPUS 34 computers for student use in computer labs, classrooms, library. Staffed computer lab on campus provides training in use of computers, software. Academic computing expenditure 1994–95: $62,000.
COLLEGE LIFE Drama-theater group, choral group, student-run newspaper. 2% vote in student government elections. *Social organizations:* 7 open to all. *Most popular organizations:* Student Government Association, Sentinel Ambassadors, Phi Theta Kappa, African-American Student Union, Fellowship of Christian Athletes. *Student services:* women's center. *Campus security:* 24-hour emergency response devices and patrols.
HOUSING College housing not available.
ATHLETICS Member NJCAA. *Intercollegiate:* baseball M, basketball M(s). *Intramural:* baseball, basketball, racquetball, tennis, volleyball. *Contact:* Mr. Clyde Alexander, Athletic Director, 904-973-2288 Ext. 157.
CAREER PLANNING *Placement office:* 2 full-time, 1 part-time staff. *Director:* Mr. James Catron, Director of Counseling, 904-973-2288 Ext. 127. *Services:* career counseling, careers library.
AFTER GRADUATION 68% of students completing a degree program in 1994–95 went directly on to further study.

Peterson's Guide to Two-Year Colleges 1997

North Florida Community College (continued)
EXPENSES FOR 1995–96 ***Application fee:*** $10. State resident tuition: $992 full-time, $31 per semester hour part-time. Nonresident tuition: $3776 full-time, $118 per semester hour part-time.
FINANCIAL AID ***College-administered undergrad aid 1995–96:*** 280 need-based scholarships (average $1600), 110 non-need scholarships (average $780), short-term loans (average $150), 73 Federal Work-Study (averaging $1011), 46 part-time jobs. ***Required forms:*** FAFSA; accepted: CSS Financial Aid PROFILE. ***Priority deadline:*** 8/20. ***Payment plans:*** tuition prepayment, installment. ***Waivers:*** full or partial for employees or children of employees and senior citizens.
APPLYING Open admission. ***Options:*** Common Application, early entrance. ***Required:*** school transcript, 3 years of high school math and science, SAT I or ACT, TOEFL for international students. ***Recommended:*** 2 years of high school foreign language. Test scores used for counseling/placement. ***Application deadline:*** rolling.
APPLYING/TRANSFER ***Required:*** standardized test scores, high school transcript, college transcript. ***Recommended:*** some high school foreign language. ***Required for some:*** 3 years of high school math and science. ***Entrance:*** noncompetitive. ***Application deadline:*** rolling. ***Contact:*** Mr. James Catron, Director of Counseling, 904-973-2288 Ext. 127.
CONTACT Mrs. Myrtle Hutcherson, Admissions Assistant, North Florida Community College, Madison, FL 32340-1602, 904-973-2288 Ext. 120.

OKALOOSA-WALTON COMMUNITY COLLEGE
Niceville, Florida

UG Enrollment: 5,820	Tuition & Fees (FL Res): $924
Application Deadline: rolling	Room & Board: N/Avail

GENERAL State and locally supported, 2-year, coed. Part of Florida Community Colleges System. Awards transfer associate, terminal associate degrees. Founded 1963. ***Setting:*** 264-acre small-town campus. ***Total enrollment:*** 5,820. ***Faculty:*** 297 (77 full-time, 18% with terminal degrees, 220 part-time); student-faculty ratio is 21:1.
ENROLLMENT PROFILE 5,820 students: 57% women, 88% part-time, 99% state residents, 6% transferred in, 34% have need-based financial aid, 12% have non-need-based financial aid, 55% 25 or older, 1% Native American, 2% Hispanic, 7% African American, 2% Asian American. ***Most popular recent majors:*** liberal arts/general studies, drafting and design, electronics engineering technology.
FIRST-YEAR CLASS 1,569 applied, 100% were accepted, 100% of whom enrolled. 6% from top 10% of their high school class, 16% from top quarter, 31% from top half.
ACADEMIC PROGRAM Core, honor code. Calendar: semesters plus summer sessions. Academic remediation for entering students, English as a second language program offered during academic year, services for LD students, advanced placement, self-designed majors, summer session for credit, part-time degree program (daytime, evenings, summer), adult/continuing education programs.
GENERAL DEGREE REQUIREMENTS 60 semester hours; math/science requirements vary according to program.
MAJORS Accounting, art/fine arts, automotive technologies, aviation technology, biology/biological sciences, business administration/commerce/management, chemistry, child care/child and family studies, computer programming, computer science, construction technologies, criminal justice, dietetics, drafting and design, early childhood education, education, electronics engineering technology, elementary education, engineering (general), fashion merchandising, finance/banking, graphic arts, heating/refrigeration/air conditioning, home economics education, hotel and restaurant management, humanities, human resources, industrial administration, interior design, law enforcement/police sciences, legal studies, liberal arts/general studies, mathematics, medical technology, meteorology, ministries, modern languages, music, nursing, nutrition, paralegal studies, physical education, physics, real estate, science, secretarial studies/office management, social science, social work, welding technology.
LIBRARY 83,981 books, 386 microform titles, 600 periodicals, 20 CD-ROMs, 8,633 records, tapes, and CDs. Acquisition spending 1994–95: $111,888.
COMPUTERS ON CAMPUS Computer purchase plan available. 200 computers for student use in computer labs, learning resource center, teaching labs, classrooms, library. Academic computing expenditure 1994–95: $497,147.
COLLEGE LIFE Drama-theater group, choral group, student-run newspaper. ***Most popular organizations:*** Student Government Association, PTK. ***Major annual events:*** College Night, Drug Prevention Campaign, Student Government Association Picnic. ***Student services:*** health clinic. ***Campus security:*** 24-hour patrols.
HOUSING College housing not available.
ATHLETICS Member NJCAA. ***Intercollegiate:*** baseball M(s), basketball M(s)/W(s), softball W(s). ***Intramural:*** archery, badminton, baseball, basketball, bowling, cross-country running, football, golf, racquetball, soccer, softball, table tennis (Ping-Pong), tennis, volleyball, weight lifting. ***Contact:*** Mr. Mickey Englett, Athletic Director, 904-729-5379.
CAREER PLANNING ***Placement office:*** 1 part-time staff. ***Director:*** Ms. Dianne Avillion, Career Information Counselor, 904-729-5372. ***Services:*** career counseling, careers library.
EXPENSES FOR 1995–96 ***Application fee:*** $15. State resident tuition: $924 full-time, $30.79 per semester hour part-time. Nonresident tuition: $3510 full-time, $117 per semester hour part-time.
FINANCIAL AID ***College-administered undergrad aid 1995–96:*** need-based scholarships, 158 non-need scholarships (averaging $500), short-term loans (averaging $150), low-interest long-term loans from external sources (averaging $2000), Federal Work-Study, 40 part-time jobs. ***Required forms:*** institutional; accepted: CSS Financial Aid PROFILE, FAFSA. ***Priority deadline:*** 4/1. ***Payment plans:*** tuition prepayment, installment, deferred pay. ***Waivers:*** full or partial for employees or children of employees. ***Notification:*** continuous.
APPLYING Open admission. ***Options:*** early entrance, deferred entrance. ***Required:*** TOEFL for international students, ACT, SAT, ACT ASSET, or MAPS. Test scores used for admission and counseling/placement. ***Application deadline:*** rolling. ***Notification:*** continuous. Preference given to state residents.
APPLYING/TRANSFER ***Required:*** standardized test scores. ***Application deadline:*** rolling. ***Notification:*** continuous.
CONTACT Ms. Ann James, Dean of Student Services/Registrar, Okaloosa-Walton Community College, Niceville, FL 32578-1295, 904-729-5223.

PALM BEACH COMMUNITY COLLEGE
Lake Worth, Florida

UG Enrollment: 16,717	Tuition & Fees (FL Res): $1074
Application Deadline: 7/27	Room & Board: N/R

GENERAL State-supported, 2-year, coed. Part of Florida Community Colleges System. Awards certificates, transfer associate, terminal associate degrees. Founded 1933. ***Setting:*** 150-acre urban campus with easy access to West Palm Beach. ***Total enrollment:*** 16,717. ***Faculty:*** 772 (198 full-time, 100% with terminal degrees, 574 part-time); student-faculty ratio is 24:1. ***Notable Alumni:*** Burt Reynolds, actor; Monty Markham, actor; Dante Bichette, baseball player.

ENROLLMENT PROFILE 16,717 students from 40 states and territories, 41 other countries. 60% women, 69% part-time, 95% state residents, 2% live on campus, 17% transferred in, 1% international, 45% 25 or older, 1% Native American, 8% Hispanic, 11% African American, 3% Asian American. ***Areas of study chosen:*** 27% liberal arts/general studies, 13% health professions and related sciences, 12% business management and administrative services, 10% social sciences, 7% vocational and home economics, 4% computer and information sciences, 3% engineering and applied sciences, 2% English language/literature/letters, 2% physical sciences, 1% biological and life sciences, 1% education, 1% fine arts, 1% mathematics, 1% performing arts. ***Most popular recent majors:*** liberal arts/general studies, business administration/commerce/management, nursing.

FIRST-YEAR CLASS 2,376 total. Of the students who applied, 100% were accepted, 100% of whom enrolled. 5% from top 10% of their high school class, 60% from top half.

ACADEMIC PROGRAM Core, honor code. Calendar: semesters. 1,500 courses offered in 1995–96. Academic remediation for entering students, English as a second language program offered during academic year and summer, services for LD students, advanced placement, self-designed majors, honors program, summer session for credit, part-time degree program (daytime, evenings, summer), adult/continuing education programs, co-op programs and internships. Study abroad in England, Mexico, Costa Rica, Spain, Thailand (1% of students participate).

GENERAL DEGREE REQUIREMENTS 60 semester hours; math/science requirements vary according to program.

MAJORS Accounting, art/fine arts, art history, biology/biological sciences, botany/plant sciences, business administration/commerce/management, ceramic art and design, chemistry, commercial art, communication, computer programming, computer science, construction management, criminal justice, data processing, dental services, drafting and design, early childhood education, economics, education, electrical and electronics technologies, elementary education, (pre)engineering sequence, English, fashion design and technology, fashion merchandising, finance/banking, fire science, flight training, food services management, health education, history, home economics, hotel and restaurant management, interior design, journalism, law enforcement/police sciences, legal secretarial studies, liberal arts/general studies, literature, marketing/retailing/merchandising, mathematics, music, nursing, nutrition, occupational therapy, philosophy, photography, physical education, physical sciences, physical therapy, political science/government, psychology, radiological technology, religious studies, secretarial studies/office management, social science, social work, surveying technology, textiles and clothing, theater arts/drama, zoology.

LIBRARY Harold C. Manor Library plus 4 others, with 184,312 books, 1,530 microform titles, 1,656 periodicals, 3,446 records, tapes, and CDs. Acquisition spending 1994–95: $248,223.

COMPUTERS ON CAMPUS Computer purchase plan available. 640 computers for student use in computer center, learning resource center, career center, library. Staffed computer lab on campus provides training in use of computers, software. Academic computing expenditure 1994–95: $5.2 million.

COLLEGE LIFE Drama-theater group, choral group, student-run newspaper. ***Social organizations:*** 27 open to all. ***Most popular organizations:*** Student Government, Phi Theta Kappa, Students for International Understanding, Black Student Union, Drama Club. ***Major annual event:*** Graduation. ***Student services:*** health clinic, women's center. ***Campus security:*** 24-hour emergency response devices and patrols.

HOUSING 600 college housing spaces available; 275 were occupied 1995–96. No special consideration for freshman housing applicants. ***Option:*** single-sex housing available.

ATHLETICS Member NJCAA. ***Intercollegiate:*** baseball M, basketball M(s)/W(s), golf M(s), softball W, tennis M(s)/W(s). ***Intramural:*** basketball, football, racquetball, soccer, tennis, volleyball. ***Contact:*** Mr. Hamid Faquir, Director of Student Athletics, 407-439-8067.

CAREER PLANNING ***Placement office:*** 2 full-time, 1 part-time staff. ***Director:*** Ms. Gail Tomei, Counselor, 407-439-8182. ***Services:*** job fairs, resume preparation, career counseling, careers library, job interviews.

AFTER GRADUATION 90% of students completing a degree program in 1994–95 went directly on to further study.

EXPENSES FOR 1995–96 ***Application fee:*** $20. State resident tuition: $1074 full-time, $35.80 per semester hour part-time. Nonresident tuition: $3996 full-time, $133.20 per semester hour part-time.

FINANCIAL AID ***College-administered undergrad aid 1995–96:*** need-based scholarships (average $450), non-need scholarships (average $300), part-time jobs. ***Required forms:*** FAFSA; accepted: CSS Financial Aid PROFILE. ***Priority deadline:*** 7/27. ***Waivers:*** full or partial for minority students and employees or children of employees.

APPLYING Open admission except for nursing, dental hygiene programs. ***Option:*** early entrance. ***Required:*** TOEFL for international students. ***Recommended:*** SAT I or ACT, CPT, ACT ASSET, MAPS. Test scores used for counseling/placement. ***Application deadline:*** 7/27. ***Notification:*** continuous until 7/27. Preference given to state residents.

APPLYING/TRANSFER ***Entrance:*** minimally difficult. ***Application deadline:*** 7/27. ***Notification:*** continuous until 7/27. ***Contact:*** Ms. Gloria Hill, Records Specialist, 407-439-8205.

CONTACT Mr. Scott MacLachlan, College Registrar and Dean of Student Services, Palm Beach Community College, 4200 Congress Avenue, Lake Worth, FL 33461-4796, 407-439-8106. ***Fax:*** 407-439-8255. College video available.

PASCO-HERNANDO COMMUNITY COLLEGE
Dade City, Florida

UG Enrollment: 5,242	**Tuition & Fees (FL Res): $1092**
Application Deadline: rolling	**Room & Board: N/Avail**

GENERAL State-supported, 2-year, coed. Part of Florida Community Colleges System. Awards certificates, transfer associate, terminal associate degrees. Founded 1972. ***Setting:*** 365-acre small-town campus with easy access to Tampa. ***Total enrollment:*** 5,242. ***Faculty:*** 255 (68 full-time, 26% with terminal degrees, 187 part-time); student-faculty ratio is 25:1. ***Notable Alumni:*** Lucy Morgan, Pulitzer Prize-winning journalist for *St. Peersburg Times*.
ENROLLMENT PROFILE 5,242 students: 66% women, 34% men, 78% part-time, 93% state residents, 4% transferred in, 46% 25 or older, 1% Native American, 2% Hispanic, 3% African American, 2% Asian American. ***Areas of study chosen:*** 63% liberal arts/general studies, 8% health professions and related sciences, 4% business management and administrative services, 3% computer and information sciences. ***Most popular recent majors:*** liberal arts/general studies, business administration/commerce/management, nursing.
FIRST-YEAR CLASS Of the students who applied, 99% were accepted.
ACADEMIC PROGRAM Core, liberal studies/vocational curriculum, honor code. Calendar: semesters. 495 courses offered in 1995–96. Academic remediation for entering students, services for LD students, advanced placement, tutorials, honors program, summer session for credit, part-time degree program (daytime, evenings, summer), adult/continuing education programs, internships. Off-campus study. ROTC: Army (c).
GENERAL DEGREE REQUIREMENTS 60 semester hours; computer course for most majors; internship (some majors).
MAJORS Business administration/commerce/management, computer programming, construction technologies, criminal justice, dental services, emergency medical technology, fire science, hospitality services, human services, legal studies, liberal arts/general studies, marketing/retailing/merchandising, nursing, secretarial studies/office management.
LIBRARY Pottberg Library plus 2 others, with 52,000 books, 2,518 microform titles, 400 periodicals, 1,000 records, tapes, and CDs.
COMPUTERS ON CAMPUS Computer purchase plan available. 300 computers for student use in computer labs, learning resource center, classrooms, library provide access to off-campus computing facilities, on-line services, Internet. Staffed computer lab on campus provides training in use of computers, software.
COLLEGE LIFE Drama-theater group, choral group. ***Social organizations:*** 36 open to all; 1 national fraternity. ***Most popular organizations:*** Student Government, Phi Theta Kappa, Phi Beta Lambda, Human Services, Student Ambassadors. ***Major annual events:*** Fall Club Carnivals, Spring Fling, Welcome Back. ***Campus security:*** 24-hour patrols.
HOUSING College housing not available.
ATHLETICS Member NJCAA. ***Intercollegiate:*** baseball M(s), basketball M(s), softball W, volleyball W(s). ***Intramural:*** basketball, bowling, golf, racquetball, softball, table tennis (Ping-Pong), tennis, volleyball. ***Contact:*** Mr. Bob Bowman, Athletics Director, 352-847-2727.
CAREER PLANNING ***Service:*** career counseling.
EXPENSES FOR 1995–96 ***Application fee:*** $20. State resident tuition: $1092 full-time, $36.40 per semester hour part-time. Nonresident tuition: $4068 full-time, $135.60 per semester hour part-time.
FINANCIAL AID ***College-administered undergrad aid 1995–96:*** 327 need-based scholarships (average $282), 158 non-need scholarships (average $1414), Federal Work-Study. ***Required forms:*** institutional, FAFSA; accepted: CSS Financial Aid PROFILE. ***Priority deadline:*** 5/1.
APPLYING Open admission. ***Options:*** early entrance, deferred entrance, midyear entrance. ***Recommended:*** SAT I or ACT, MAPS. ***Required for some:*** school transcript, 3 years of high school math and science, TOEFL for international students. Test scores used for counseling/placement. ***Application deadline:*** rolling. ***Notification:*** continuous.
APPLYING/TRANSFER ***Required for some:*** college transcript, minimum 2.0 college GPA. ***Application deadline:*** rolling. ***Notification:*** continuous. ***Contact:*** Mr. Michael Malizia, Director of Admissions and Student Records, 352-847-2727.
CONTACT Mr. Michael Malizia, Director of Admissions and Student Records, Pasco-Hernando Community College, Dade City, FL 33525-7599, 352-847-2727.

PENSACOLA JUNIOR COLLEGE
Pensacola, Florida

UG Enrollment: 12,000	**Tuition & Fees (FL Res): $1133**
Application Deadline: 8/30	**Room & Board: N/Avail**

GENERAL State-supported, 2-year, coed. Awards certificates, diplomas, transfer associate, terminal associate degrees. Founded 1948. ***Setting:*** 160-acre suburban campus. ***Endowment:*** $852,309. ***Total enrollment:*** 12,000. ***Faculty:*** 819 (207 full-time, 26% with terminal degrees, 612 part-time).
ENROLLMENT PROFILE 12,000 students from 37 states and territories. 60% women, 71% part-time, 98% state residents, 10% transferred in, 50% 25 or older, 1% Native American, 1% Hispanic, 13% African American, 3% Asian American.
FIRST-YEAR CLASS Of the students who applied, 100% were accepted.
ACADEMIC PROGRAM Core, interdisciplinary curriculum, honor code. Calendar: semesters. Average class size 30 in required courses. Academic remediation for entering students, English as a second language program, services for LD students, advanced placement, honors program, summer session for credit, part-time degree program (daytime, evenings, summer), adult/continuing education programs, co-op programs. Study abroad in Mexico, France, Italy. ROTC: Army.
GENERAL DEGREE REQUIREMENTS 60 semester hours; 6 semester hours of math; 10 semester hours of science.
MAJORS Accounting, agricultural business, agricultural sciences, art education, art/fine arts, automotive technologies, biology/biological sciences, biomedical technologies, business administration/commerce/management, chemistry, child care/child and family studies, civil engineering technology, communication, communication equipment technology, computer information systems, computer science, construction technologies, court reporting, criminal justice, criminology, culinary arts, dental services, dietetics, drafting and design, early childhood education, education, electronics engineering technology, elementary education, emergency medical technology, engineering (general), environmental sciences, fashion merchandising, film studies, fire science, forestry, forest technology, graphic arts, health services administration, history, home economics, horticulture, hotel and restaurant management, journalism, law enforcement/police sciences, legal secretarial studies, liberal arts/general studies, manufacturing technology, medical records services, medical secretarial studies, medical technology, music, nursing, ornamental horticulture, paralegal studies, philosophy, physical education, physical therapy, radiological technology, religious studies, respiratory therapy, science, secretarial studies/office management, systems science, theater arts/drama.
LIBRARY Learning Resource Center plus 2 others, with 18,551 books, 668 microform titles, 1,315 periodicals, 4,084 records, tapes, and CDs. Acquisition spending 1994–95: $277,700.
COMPUTERS ON CAMPUS 175 computers for student use in computer labs, business education department, library provide access to off-campus computing facilities. Staffed computer lab on campus provides training in use of computers, software. Academic computing expenditure 1994–95: $600,000.
COLLEGE LIFE Drama-theater group, choral group, student-run newspaper. ***Social organizations:*** 16 open to all; national fraternities, national sororities. ***Most popular organizations:*** Baptist Student Union, Campus Activities Board, Students for a Multicultural Society, International Council, Engineering Club. ***Major annual events:*** Spring and Fall Cookouts, Fall End of Term Party, Spring End of Term Party. ***Student services:*** health clinic, personal-psychological counseling. ***Campus security:*** 24-hour emergency response devices and patrols, student patrols, late-night transport-escort service.
HOUSING College housing not available.
ATHLETICS Member NJCAA. ***Intercollegiate:*** baseball M(s), basketball M(s)/W(s), softball W(s). ***Intramural:*** archery, badminton, basketball, bowling, cross-country running, golf, gymnastics, racquetball, sailing, swimming and diving, tennis, track and field, volleyball, weight lifting, wrestling. ***Contact:*** Dr. Donn Perry, Director of Athletics, 904-484-1304; Ms. Vicki Carson, Assistant Director of Athletics, 904-484-1000.
CAREER PLANNING ***Services:*** resume preparation, career counseling, job bank.
EXPENSES FOR 1995–96 ***Application fee:*** $20. State resident tuition: $1133 full-time, $37.75 per semester hour part-time. Nonresident tuition: $4050 full-time, $135 per semester hour part-time.
FINANCIAL AID ***College-administered undergrad aid 1995–96:*** 400 need-based scholarships, 540 non-need scholarships, short-term loans (average $300), low-interest long-term loans, 121 Federal Work-Study (averaging $2000), part-time jobs. ***Required forms:*** institutional, FAFSA; accepted: CSS Financial Aid PROFILE, state. ***Priority deadline:*** 4/1. ***Payment plan:*** deferred payment. ***Waivers:*** full or partial for employees or children of employees and senior citizens. ***Notification:*** 7/1. ***Average indebtedness of graduates:*** $2625.
APPLYING Open admission except for health-related programs. ***Option:*** early entrance. ***Required:*** 3 years of high school math and science, TOEFL for international students. Test scores used for counseling/placement. ***Application deadline:*** 8/30. ***Notification:*** continuous until 8/30.
APPLYING/TRANSFER ***Required:*** college transcript. ***Entrance:*** noncompetitive. ***Application deadline:*** 8/30. ***Notification:*** continuous until 8/30.
CONTACT Ms. Martha Flood Caughey, Coordinator of Admissions and Registration, Pensacola Junior College, Pensacola, FL 32504-8998, 904-484-1623. ***Fax:*** 904-484-1829.

PEOPLES COLLEGE
Kissimmee, Florida

UG Enrollment: 380	**Tuition: $1695/deg prog**
Application Deadline: rolling	**Room & Board: N/Avail**

GENERAL Proprietary, 2-year, coed. Awards transfer associate degrees (offers only external degree programs conducted through home study). Founded 1985. ***Setting:*** 31-acre small-town campus with easy access to Orlando. ***Total enrollment:*** 380. ***Faculty:*** 28 (all full-time).
ENROLLMENT PROFILE 380 students from 16 states and territories, 2 other countries. 30% women, 100% part-time, 2% international, 98% 25 or older. ***Most popular recent major:*** computer programming.
FIRST-YEAR CLASS 150 total; 165 applied, 91% were accepted, 100% of whom enrolled.
ACADEMIC PROGRAM Core, honor code. Calendar: quarters. 9 courses offered in 1995–96. Part-time degree program (daytime), external degree programs.
GENERAL DEGREE REQUIREMENT 32 credits.
MAJORS Computer programming, electrical and electronics technologies, tourism and travel.
COMPUTERS ON CAMPUS 5 computers for student use.
COLLEGE LIFE ***Campus security:*** 24-hour emergency response devices and patrols.
HOUSING College housing not available.
CAREER PLANNING ***Placement office:*** 4 full-time staff. ***Director:*** Ms. Donna Montgomery, Manager of Career Employment Services, 407-847-4444. ***Services:*** resume preparation, resume referral, career counseling. Students must register freshman year.
EXPENSES FOR 1995–96 ***Application fee:*** $150. Tuition per degree program ranges from $1695 to $3995.
FINANCIAL AID ***Payment plans:*** tuition prepayment, installment. ***Waivers:*** full or partial for employees or children of employees.
APPLYING Open admission. ***Option:*** midyear entrance. ***Required:*** TOEFL for international students. Test scores used for counseling/placement. ***Application deadline:*** rolling.
APPLYING/TRANSFER ***Entrance:*** noncompetitive.
CONTACT Ms. Leonette Miles, Admissions Supervisor, Peoples College, 233 Academy Drive, PO Box 421768, Kissimmee, FL 34742-1768, 407-847-9677 Ext. 323 or toll-free 800-765-4732. ***E-mail:*** peoples.college@internetmci.com. College video available.

PHILLIPS JUNIOR COLLEGE OF BUSINESS
Melbourne, Florida

GENERAL Proprietary, 2-year, coed. Part of Phillips Colleges, Inc. Awards terminal associate degrees. Founded 1958. ***Setting:*** 2-acre small-town campus with easy access to Orlando. ***Total enrollment:*** 525. ***Faculty:*** 46 (7 full-time, 39 part-time).

Florida

Phillips Junior College of Business (continued)
EXPENSES FOR 1995–96 *Application fee:* $25. Tuition: $11,140 per degree program (minimum). Tuition and fees for film studies program: $12,900.
CONTACT Ms. Cherrie James, Director of Admissions, Phillips Junior College of Business, 2401 North Harbor City Boulevard, Melbourne, FL 32935-6657, 407-254-6459. *Fax:* 407-255-2017.

POLK COMMUNITY COLLEGE
Winter Haven, Florida

UG Enrollment: 6,000	Tuition & Fees (FL Res): $1084
Application Deadline: rolling	Room & Board: N/Avail

GENERAL State-supported, 2-year, coed. Part of Florida Community Colleges System. Awards transfer associate, terminal associate degrees. Founded 1964. *Setting:* 88-acre suburban campus with easy access to Tampa and Orlando. *Total enrollment:* 6,000. *Faculty:* 260 (117 full-time, 143 part-time).
ENROLLMENT PROFILE 6,000 students from 12 states and territories, 20 other countries. 62% women, 65% part-time, 98% state residents, 10% transferred in, 55% 25 or older, 3% Hispanic, 11% African American. *Most popular recent majors:* liberal arts/general studies, business administration/commerce/management, (pre)engineering sequence.
FIRST-YEAR CLASS 800 total. Of the students who applied, 100% were accepted. 13% from top 10% of their high school class, 35% from top quarter, 65% from top half.
ACADEMIC PROGRAM Core. Calendar: 16-16-6-6. Academic remediation for entering students, services for LD students, advanced placement, self-designed majors, summer session for credit, part-time degree program (daytime, evenings, summer), adult/continuing education programs, co-op programs. ROTC: Army.
GENERAL DEGREE REQUIREMENTS 60 credit hours; 2 years of math; computer course (varies by major).
MAJORS Art/fine arts, art history, astronomy, biology/biological sciences, botany/plant sciences, broadcasting, business administration/commerce/management, ceramic art and design, chemistry, civil engineering technology, communication, computer science, corrections, creative writing, criminal justice, data processing, drafting and design, economics, education, educational media, electrical engineering technology, elementary education, (pre)engineering sequence, English, finance/banking, fire science, French, geography, geology, German, health education, history, home economics, horticulture, humanities, journalism, law enforcement/police sciences, liberal arts/general studies, literature, marine biology, marketing/retailing/merchandising, mathematics, medical secretarial studies, military science, modern languages, music, music education, music history, natural sciences, nursing, ornamental horticulture, painting/drawing, philosophy, physical education, physical sciences, physical therapy, psychology, radiological technology, real estate, recreation and leisure services, sculpture, social science, sociology, Spanish, studio art, voice, zoology.
LIBRARY Polk Community College Library with 2,367 books, 225 microform titles, 515 periodicals, 12 CD-ROMs, 642 records, tapes, and CDs.
COMPUTERS ON CAMPUS 340 computers for student use in computer labs, classrooms, library. Staffed computer lab on campus provides training in use of computers, software.
COLLEGE LIFE Drama-theater group. *Student services:* personal-psychological counseling. *Campus security:* 24-hour emergency response devices and patrols.
HOUSING College housing not available.
ATHLETICS Member NJCAA. *Intercollegiate:* baseball M, basketball M(s), softball W(s), volleyball W(s). *Contact:* Dr. Bill Moore, Director of Student Activities and Support, 941-297-1004.
CAREER PLANNING *Services:* career counseling, job interviews.
EXPENSES FOR 1995–96 *Application fee:* $20. State resident tuition: $1084 full-time, $36.13 per credit hour part-time. Nonresident tuition: $4064 full-time, $135.46 per credit hour part-time.
FINANCIAL AID *College-administered undergrad aid 1995–96:* 82 need-based scholarships (average $300), 217 non-need scholarships (average $700), short-term loans (average $300), low-interest long-term loans from external sources (average $2500), Federal Work-Study, 70 part-time jobs. *Required forms for some financial aid applicants:* state, institutional, FAFSA. *Application deadline:* continuous to 6/30.
APPLYING Open admission. *Options:* early entrance, deferred entrance. *Required:* school transcript, 3 years of high school math and science, TOEFL for international students. *Recommended:* 2 years of high school foreign language, SAT I or ACT, MAPS or ACT ASSET. Test scores used for counseling/placement. *Application deadline:* rolling. *Notification:* 8/1.
APPLYING/TRANSFER *Required:* high school transcript, college transcript. *Recommended:* standardized test scores. *Entrance:* noncompetitive. *Application deadline:* rolling. *Notification:* 8/1.
CONTACT Mr. Charles R. Richardson, Assistant to the President/Director of Student Services, Polk Community College, Winter Haven, FL 33881-4299, 941-297-1016.

PROSPECT HALL
Hollywood, Florida

UG Enrollment: 200	Tuition & Fees: $5280
Application Deadline: rolling	Room & Board: N/Avail

GENERAL Proprietary, 2-year, coed. Awards diplomas, terminal associate degrees. Founded 1929. *Setting:* suburban campus with easy access to Miami. *Total enrollment:* 200. *Faculty:* 15 (4 full-time, 100% with terminal degrees, 11 part-time); student-faculty ratio is 20:1.
ENROLLMENT PROFILE 200 students from 5 states and territories, 3 other countries. 75% women, 5% part-time, 80% state residents, 2% transferred in, 4% international, 0% Native American, 14% Hispanic, 48% African American, 0% Asian American. *Most popular recent majors:* business administration/commerce/management, accounting, computer programming.
FIRST-YEAR CLASS 125 total. Of the students who applied, 92% were accepted, 65% of whom enrolled.
ACADEMIC PROGRAM Core, job skills curriculum. Calendar: quarters. Summer session for credit, part-time degree program (daytime, evenings), adult/continuing education programs.
GENERAL DEGREE REQUIREMENTS 96 credits; computer course.
MAJORS Accounting, business administration/commerce/management, computer management, computer programming, legal secretarial studies, medical secretarial studies, paralegal studies, secretarial studies/office management, word processing.
COMPUTERS ON CAMPUS 64 computers for student use in computer labs, learning resource center.
HOUSING College housing not available.
CAREER PLANNING *Services:* job fairs, resume preparation, career counseling, careers library, job bank, job interviews.
AFTER GRADUATION 75% of class of 1994 had job offers within 6 months.
EXPENSES FOR 1995–96 *Application fee:* $20. Tuition: $5280 full-time, $440 per course part-time. Tuition guaranteed not to increase for student's term of enrollment.
FINANCIAL AID *College-administered undergrad aid 1995–96:* need-based scholarships, low-interest long-term loans from external sources. *Required forms:* CSS Financial Aid PROFILE, institutional, FAFSA. *Application deadline:* continuous. *Payment plan:* installment.
APPLYING *Options:* early entrance, deferred entrance. *Required:* school transcript, interview. *Recommended:* SAT I or ACT. *Required for some:* recommendations, TOEFL for international students. Test scores used for counseling/placement. *Application deadline:* rolling.
APPLYING/TRANSFER *Required:* interview, college transcript. *Recommended:* standardized test scores. *Required for some:* recommendations. *Application deadline:* rolling.
CONTACT Dr. Wedad Asch, Admissions Director, Prospect Hall, Hollywood, FL 33020, 305-923-8100 Ext. 20.

ST. JOHNS RIVER COMMUNITY COLLEGE
Palatka, Florida

UG Enrollment: 3,500	Tuition & Fees (FL Res): $1091
Application Deadline: rolling	Room & Board: N/Avail

GENERAL State-supported, 2-year, coed. Awards transfer associate, terminal associate degrees. Founded 1958. *Setting:* 105-acre small-town campus with easy access to Jacksonville. *Total enrollment:* 3,500. *Faculty:* 157 (61 full-time, 13% with terminal degrees, 96 part-time); student-faculty ratio is 22:1.
ENROLLMENT PROFILE 3,500 students: 61% women, 60% part-time, 99% state residents, 13% transferred in, 41% 25 or older, 2% Hispanic, 5% African American, 2% Asian American.
FIRST-YEAR CLASS Of the students who applied, 99% were accepted.
ACADEMIC PROGRAM Core. Calendar: trimesters. Academic remediation for entering students, services for LD students, advanced placement, summer session for credit, part-time degree program (daytime, evenings), adult/continuing education programs.
GENERAL DEGREE REQUIREMENTS 60 credit hours; 1 math course; computer course for technology, business majors.
MAJORS Applied art, art/fine arts, business administration/commerce/management, commercial art, computer programming, criminal justice, dance, electronics engineering technology, emergency medical technology, fire science, graphic arts, instrumentation technology, liberal arts/general studies, marketing/retailing/merchandising, secretarial studies/office management, theater arts/drama, word processing.
LIBRARY 52,721 books, 1,320 microform titles, 508 periodicals, 13 CD-ROMs, 1,828 records, tapes, and CDs.
COMPUTERS ON CAMPUS 170 computers for student use in labs, classrooms. Staffed computer lab on campus.
COLLEGE LIFE Drama-theater group, choral group, student-run newspaper. *Social organizations:* 10 open to all. *Student services:* personal-psychological counseling. *Campus security:* 24-hour patrols.
HOUSING College housing not available.
ATHLETICS Member NJCAA. *Intercollegiate:* baseball M(s), basketball M(s), softball W(s), volleyball W(s). *Contact:* Mr. John C. Tindall, Director of Athletics, 904-312-4162.
CAREER PLANNING *Service:* career counseling.
EXPENSES FOR 1995–96 *Application fee:* $20. State resident tuition: $1091 full-time, $36.35 per credit hour part-time. Nonresident tuition: $4093 full-time, $136.43 per credit hour part-time.
FINANCIAL AID *College-administered undergrad aid 1995–96:* need-based scholarships, Federal Work-Study, part-time jobs. *Acceptable forms:* CSS Financial Aid PROFILE. *Priority deadline:* 5/15. *Waivers:* full or partial for employees or children of employees.
APPLYING Open admission. *Options:* Common Application, early entrance, midyear entrance. *Required:* school transcript, 3 years of high school math and science, TOEFL for international students. Test scores used for counseling/placement. *Application deadline:* rolling. *Notification:* continuous.
APPLYING/TRANSFER *Entrance:* noncompetitive. *Application deadline:* rolling. *Notification:* continuous.
CONTACT Mr. O'Neal W. Williams, Dean of Student Services, St. Johns River Community College, Palatka, FL 32177-3807, 904-328-1571 Ext. 134.

ST. PETERSBURG JUNIOR COLLEGE
St. Petersburg, Florida

UG Enrollment: 19,207	Tuition & Fees (FL Res): $1119
Application Deadline: rolling	Room & Board: N/Avail

GENERAL State and locally supported, 2-year, coed. Awards transfer associate degrees. Founded 1927. *Setting:* suburban campus. *Total enrollment:* 19,207. *Faculty:* 976 (426 full-time, 22% with terminal degrees, 550 part-time).
ENROLLMENT PROFILE 19,207 students from 40 states and territories, 45 other countries. 60% women, 69% part-time, 74% state residents, 6% transferred in, 1% international, 49% 25 or older, 1% Native American, 4% Hispanic, 7% African American, 4% Asian American.
FIRST-YEAR CLASS 2,889 total. Of the students who applied, 100% were accepted, 100% of whom enrolled.
ACADEMIC PROGRAM Core. Calendar: semesters. Academic remediation for entering students, English as a second language program offered during academic year and

summer, services for LD students, advanced placement, Freshman Honors College, tutorials, honors program, summer session for credit, part-time degree program (daytime, evenings, summer), adult/continuing education programs, co-op programs and internships. Off-campus study. Study abroad in China. ROTC: Army.
GENERAL DEGREE REQUIREMENTS 60 semester hours; math/science requirements vary according to program; computer course.
MAJORS Accounting, architectural technologies, aviation administration, business administration/commerce/management, computer information systems, computer programming, construction technologies, corrections, dental services, early childhood education, electronics engineering technology, emergency medical technology, fashion merchandising, finance/banking, fire science, flight training, graphic arts, health services administration, human services, interior design, law enforcement/police sciences, liberal arts/general studies, marketing/retailing/merchandising, medical laboratory technology, medical records services, nursing, optometric/ophthalmic technologies, paralegal studies, physical therapy, radiological technology, real estate, respiratory therapy, secretarial studies/office management, veterinary sciences, water resources.
LIBRARY M. M. Bennett Library with 213,472 books, 347 microform titles, 959 periodicals, 2,713 records, tapes, and CDs.
COMPUTERS ON CAMPUS Computer purchase plan available. 115 computers for student use in computer labs, classrooms provide access to main academic computer, e-mail, Internet.
COLLEGE LIFE Orientation program (2 days, no cost, parents included). Drama-theater group, student-run newspaper, radio station. ***Student services:*** women's center. ***Campus security:*** 24-hour emergency response devices.
HOUSING College housing not available.
ATHLETICS Member NJCAA. ***Intercollegiate:*** basketball M(s)/W(s), golf M(s), swimming and diving M(s)/W(s). ***Intramural:*** basketball, golf, tennis, volleyball. ***Contact:*** Mr. Jeff Davis, Director of Athletics, 813-791-2662.
CAREER PLANNING ***Placement office:*** 5 full-time, 2 part-time staff. ***Director:*** Ms. Bobbie Hinson, Director, 813-791-2492. ***Services:*** job fairs, resume preparation, resume referral, career counseling, careers library, job bank, job interviews.
EXPENSES FOR 1995–96 ***Application fee:*** $22. State resident tuition: $1119 full-time, $37.30 per semester hour part-time. Nonresident tuition: $3996 full-time, $133.21 per semester hour part-time.
FINANCIAL AID ***College-administered undergrad aid 1995–96:*** 921 need-based scholarships (average $870), non-need scholarships, short-term loans, low-interest long-term loans from external sources (average $2361), Federal Work-Study, 221 part-time jobs. ***Required forms:*** institutional; accepted: FAFSA. ***Priority deadline:*** 4/15. ***Payment plan:*** deferred payment. ***Waivers:*** full or partial for employees or children of employees and senior citizens.
APPLYING Open admission. ***Options:*** early entrance, deferred entrance. ***Required:*** school transcript. ***Required for some:*** TOEFL for international students. Test scores used for admission and counseling/placement. ***Application deadline:*** rolling. ***Notification:*** continuous.
APPLYING/TRANSFER ***Required:*** high school transcript, college transcript.
CONTACT Dr. Naomi Williams, Admissions Director/Registrar, St. Petersburg Junior College, St. Petersburg, FL 33781-3489, 813-341-3170. ***Fax:*** 813-341-3150. College video available.

SANTA FE COMMUNITY COLLEGE
Gainesville, Florida

UG Enrollment: 12,286 | **Tuition & Fees (FL Res): $1074**
Application Deadline: rolling | **Room & Board: N/Avail**

GENERAL State and locally supported, 2-year, coed. Part of Florida Community Colleges System. Awards transfer associate, terminal associate degrees (offers bachelor's degree in business administration in conjunction with Saint Leo College). Founded 1966. ***Setting:*** 175-acre suburban campus with easy access to Jacksonville. ***Total enrollment:*** 12,286. ***Faculty:*** 587 (248 full-time, 339 part-time); student-faculty ratio is 18:1.
ENROLLMENT PROFILE 12,286 students: 55% women, 45% men, 51% part-time, 95% state residents, 10% transferred in, 2% international, 35% 25 or older, 1% Native American, 6% Hispanic, 10% African American, 3% Asian American. ***Areas of study chosen:*** 33% liberal arts/general studies, 14% business management and administrative services, 11% health professions and related sciences, 6% education, 6% engineering and applied sciences, 5% social sciences, 3% communications and journalism, 3% fine arts, 3% psychology, 2% agriculture, 2% biological and life sciences, 2% English language/literature/letters, 2% premed, 1% architecture, 1% mathematics, 1% natural resource sciences, 1% performing arts, 1% physical sciences, 1% predentistry, 1% prevet, 1% theology/religion. ***Most popular recent majors:*** nursing, radiological technology, dental services.
FIRST-YEAR CLASS 1,662 total.
ACADEMIC PROGRAM Core, honor code. Calendar: semesters. Academic remediation for entering students, English as a second language program offered during academic year, services for LD students, advanced placement, self-designed majors, honors program, summer session for credit, part-time degree program (daytime, evenings, weekends, summer), adult/continuing education programs, co-op programs. ROTC: Army (c), Naval (c), Air Force (c).
GENERAL DEGREE REQUIREMENTS 60 semester hours; 6 semster hours of math; 7 semester hours of science; computer course (varies by major).
MAJORS Accounting, automotive technologies, biomedical technologies, business administration/commerce/management, child care/child and family studies, communication equipment technology, computer information systems, computer programming, computer technologies, construction technologies, corrections, criminal justice, data processing, dental services, drafting and design, early childhood education, education, electronics engineering technology, emergency medical technology, engineering (general), environmental sciences, fashion merchandising, finance/banking, fire science, graphic arts, law enforcement/police sciences, legal secretarial studies, legal studies, liberal arts/general studies, marketing/retailing/merchandising, medical secretarial studies, nuclear medical technology, nursing, ornamental horticulture, parks management, radiological technology, respiratory therapy.
COMPUTERS ON CAMPUS Computers for student use in computer center provide access to main academic computer, e-mail, on-line services, Internet. Staffed computer lab on campus provides training in use of computers, software.
COLLEGE LIFE Choral group. ***Most popular organizations:*** Black Student Union, Student Government. ***Major annual events:*** Student Orientation, Wild Wednesday, Homecoming. ***Student services:*** legal services, health clinic, personal-psychological counseling, women's center. ***Campus security:*** 24-hour emergency response devices and patrols.
HOUSING College housing not available.
ATHLETICS Member NJCAA. ***Intercollegiate:*** baseball M(s), basketball M(s)/W(s), cross-country running M(s), softball W(s). ***Intramural:*** basketball. ***Contact:*** Mr. Kenny Drost, Director of Health, Exercise and Sports, 352-395-5536.
CAREER PLANNING ***Placement office:*** 1 full-time, 2 part-time staff. ***Director:*** Mr. Jimmy Yawn, Career Resource Coordinator, 352-395-5824. ***Services:*** job fairs, resume preparation, resume referral, career counseling, careers library, job bank, job interviews.
AFTER GRADUATION 89% of students completing a degree program in 1994–95 went directly on to further study.
EXPENSES FOR 1995–96 ***Application fee:*** $30. State resident tuition: $1074 full-time, $35.80 per semester hour part-time. Nonresident tuition: $3999 full-time, $133.30 per semester hour part-time.
FINANCIAL AID ***College-administered undergrad aid 1995–96:*** 976 need-based scholarships (average $525), 378 non-need scholarships (average $1419), short-term loans (average $150), low-interest long-term loans from external sources (average $2510), 282 Federal Work-Study (averaging $1056), 531 part-time jobs. ***Required forms:*** institutional, FAFSA, financial aid transcript (for transfers). ***Priority deadline:*** 3/15. ***Waivers:*** full or partial for employees or children of employees and senior citizens. ***Average indebtedness of graduates:*** $3000.
APPLYING Open admission. ***Option:*** early entrance. ***Required:*** TOEFL for international students, CPT. ***Recommended:*** SAT I or ACT. Test scores used for counseling/placement. ***Application deadline:*** rolling. ***Notification:*** continuous.
APPLYING/TRANSFER ***Required:*** standardized test scores. ***Entrance:*** noncompetitive. ***Application deadline:*** rolling. ***Notification:*** continuous.
CONTACT Mr. Bernard V. Murphy, Coordinator of Admissions, Santa Fe Community College, Gainesville, FL 32606-6200, 352-395-5443. ***Fax:*** 352-395-5581.

SEMINOLE COMMUNITY COLLEGE
Sanford, Florida

UG Enrollment: 6,522 | **Tuition & Fees (FL Res): $1075**
Application Deadline: rolling | **Room & Board: N/Avail**

GENERAL State and locally supported, 2-year, coed. Awards transfer associate, terminal associate degrees. Founded 1966. ***Setting:*** 200-acre small-town campus with easy access to Orlando. ***Total enrollment:*** 6,522. ***Faculty:*** 502 (130 full-time, 17% with terminal degrees, 372 part-time).
ENROLLMENT PROFILE 6,522 students from 25 states and territories, 12 other countries. 56% women, 44% men, 64% part-time, 95% state residents, 5% transferred in, 1% international, 43% 25 or older, 1% Native American, 9% Hispanic, 9% African American, 4% Asian American. ***Most popular recent majors:*** liberal arts/general studies, nursing, paralegal studies.
FIRST-YEAR CLASS 1,851 total. Of the students who applied, 100% were accepted.
ACADEMIC PROGRAM Core, honor code. Calendar: semesters. 519 courses offered in 1995–96. Academic remediation for entering students, English as a second language program offered during academic year and summer, services for LD students, advanced placement, Freshman Honors College, honors program, summer session for credit, part-time degree program (daytime, evenings, summer), adult/continuing education programs, co-op programs and internships. ROTC: Army (c), Air Force (c).
GENERAL DEGREE REQUIREMENTS 64 credit hours; 6 credit hours of math; 9 credit hours of science; 2 years of a foreign language in high school or 6 credit hours in college; internship (some majors).
MAJORS Accounting, architectural technologies, automotive technologies, business administration/commerce/management, child care/child and family studies, civil engineering technology, computer information systems, computer programming, computer technologies, construction management, construction technologies, criminal justice, data processing, drafting and design, electronics engineering technology, emergency medical technology, finance/banking, fire science, food services management, interior design, liberal arts/general studies, manufacturing technology, marketing/retailing/merchandising, nursing, paralegal studies, physical therapy, respiratory therapy, secretarial studies/office management, telecommunications.
LIBRARY Seminole Community College Library with 87,836 books, 817 microform titles, 483 periodicals, 2 on-line bibliographic services, 16 CD-ROMs, 4,151 records, tapes, and CDs.
COMPUTERS ON CAMPUS 175 computers for student use in computer center, various labs.
COLLEGE LIFE Drama-theater group, choral group. ***Social organizations:*** 15 open to all. ***Most popular organizations:*** Phi Beta Lambda, Phi Theta Kappa, Campus Governance Association, International Student Association, Art Club. ***Major annual events:*** Club Week on Green, College Night. ***Student services:*** personal-psychological counseling. ***Campus security:*** 24-hour patrols.
HOUSING College housing not available.
ATHLETICS Member NJCAA. ***Intercollegiate:*** baseball M(s), basketball M(s)/W(s), softball W(s). ***Intramural:*** archery, badminton, basketball, golf, tennis, volleyball, weight lifting. ***Contact:*** Mr. Larry Castle, Coach and Chairperson, 407-328-2090.
CAREER PLANNING ***Placement office:*** 3 full-time, 2 part-time staff. ***Director:*** Mr. William C. Irwin, Counselor/Director of Career Placement, 407-328-2033 Ext. 493. ***Services:*** job fairs, resume preparation, career counseling, careers library, job bank.
EXPENSES FOR 1995–96 ***Application fee:*** $25. State resident tuition: $1075 full-time, $35.82 per credit hour part-time. Nonresident tuition: $3997 full-time, $133.24 per credit hour part-time.
FINANCIAL AID ***College-administered undergrad aid 1995–96:*** 30 need-based scholarships (averaging $800), 100 non-need scholarships (averaging $800), short-term loans (averaging $130), Federal Work-Study. ***Required forms:*** institutional, FAFSA; accepted: CSS Financial Aid PROFILE, state. ***Priority deadline:*** 4/1. ***Payment plan:*** deferred payment. ***Waivers:*** full or partial for employees or children of employees and senior citizens.
APPLYING Open admission except for physical therapy, respiratory therapy, nursing programs. ***Options:*** early entrance, deferred entrance, midyear entrance. ***Required:*** minimum 2.0 GPA, 3 years of high school math and science, 2 years of high school foreign language, SAT I or ACT, TOEFL for international students. Test scores used for counseling/placement. ***Application deadline:*** rolling. ***Notification:*** continuous.

Florida

Seminole Community College (continued)
APPLYING/TRANSFER *Required:* standardized test scores, minimum 2.0 high school GPA. *Entrance:* noncompetitive. *Application deadline:* rolling. *Notification:* continuous. *Contact:* Mr. John Scarpino, Articulation Officer, 407-328-2148.
CONTACT Mr. David Green, Supervisor of Admissions, Seminole Community College, Sanford, FL 32773-6199, 407-328-2041 Ext. 729. College video available.

SOUTH COLLEGE
West Palm Beach, Florida

UG Enrollment: 350	Tuition & Fees: $6780
Application Deadline: N/R	Room & Board: N/Avail

GENERAL Proprietary, 2-year. Awards certificates, transfer associate, terminal associate degrees. Founded 1892. *Total enrollment:* 350.
ENROLLMENT PROFILE 350 students.
FIRST-YEAR CLASS 75 total.
ACADEMIC PROGRAM Calendar: quarters.
GENERAL DEGREE REQUIREMENTS 106 quarter credits; math proficiency; computer course.
MAJORS Accounting, business administration/commerce/management, computer information systems, emergency medical technology, hotel and restaurant management, medical assistant technologies, paralegal studies, secretarial studies/office management.
HOUSING College housing not available.
EXPENSES FOR 1996–97 Tuition: $5085 full-time.
APPLYING Open admission. *Required:* school transcript, SAT I or ACT, CPAt. *Required for some:* interview.
APPLYING/TRANSFER *Required:* standardized test scores, high school transcript, college transcript. *Required for some:* interview.
CONTACT Mrs. Sherri Witt, Director of Admissions, South College, West Palm Beach, FL 33409, 407-697-9200.

SOUTHERN COLLEGE
Orlando, Florida

UG Enrollment: 500	Tuition & Fees: $5085
Application Deadline: rolling	Room & Board: N/Avail

GENERAL Proprietary, 2-year, coed. Awards transfer associate degrees. Founded 1969. *Setting:* 7-acre urban campus. *Total enrollment:* 500. *Faculty:* 53 (13 full-time, 40 part-time).
ENROLLMENT PROFILE 500 students from 15 states and territories, 4 other countries. 81% women, 31% part-time, 93% state residents, 38% transferred in, 1% international, 65% 25 or older, 0% Native American, 16% Hispanic, 11% African American, 2% Asian American. *Areas of study chosen:* 42% prelaw, 21% health professions and related sciences, 14% business management and administrative services, 12% fine arts, 9% computer and information sciences. *Most popular recent majors:* paralegal studies, dental services, business administration/commerce/management.
FIRST-YEAR CLASS 86 total. Of the students who applied, 95% were accepted.
ACADEMIC PROGRAM Core, career-directed curriculum, honor code. Calendar: quarters. 140 courses offered in 1995–96. Academic remediation for entering students, advanced placement, summer session for credit, part-time degree program (daytime, evenings, weekends, summer), co-op programs and internships. Off-campus study at Warner Southern College, Orlando College, Tampa College, Art Institute of Fort Lauderdale, Columbia College.
GENERAL DEGREE REQUIREMENTS 96 quarter hours; computer course (varies by major); internship (some majors).
MAJORS Accounting, business administration/commerce/management, computer programming, data processing, dental services, interior design, paralegal studies, secretarial studies/office management.
LIBRARY Southern College Library with 10,141 books, 141 periodicals.
COMPUTERS ON CAMPUS 48 computers for student use in computer center, computer labs, library.
COLLEGE LIFE Student-run newspaper. *Most popular organizations:* American Society of Interior Designers Student Chapter, Paralegal Studies Group, Dental Assistant Club. *Major annual event:* Annual Student Picnic. *Student services:* personal-psychological counseling. *Campus security:* 24-hour emergency response devices, evening security officer.
HOUSING College housing not available.
CAREER PLANNING *Placement office:* 1 full-time staff. *Director:* Mr. Robert Cummins, Director of Placement, 407-273-1000. *Services:* job fairs, resume preparation, resume referral, career counseling, job interviews.
AFTER GRADUATION 15% of students completing a degree program in 1994–95 went directly on to further study.
EXPENSES FOR 1995–96 *Application fee:* $30. Tuition: $5085 full-time, $113 per quarter hour part-time.
FINANCIAL AID *College-administered undergrad aid 1995–96:* 376 need-based scholarships (average $225), low-interest long-term loans from external sources (average $1800), Federal Work-Study, 5 part-time jobs. *Required forms:* institutional, FAFSA. *Priority deadline:* 9/26. *Payment plan:* installment. *Waivers:* full or partial for employees or children of employees.
APPLYING *Options:* early entrance, deferred entrance, midyear entrance. *Required:* school transcript, interview, TOEFL for international students, TABE. *Recommended:* SAT I or ACT. Test scores used for admission and counseling/placement. *Application deadline:* rolling. *Notification:* continuous.
APPLYING/TRANSFER *Required:* standardized test scores, high school transcript, interview, college transcript. *Entrance:* noncompetitive. *Application deadline:* rolling. *Notification:* continuous.
CONTACT Ms. Sheri Le Tourneau, Director of Admissions, Southern College, 5600 Lake Underhill Road, Orlando, FL 32807-1699, 407-273-1000 Ext. 1207.

SOUTH FLORIDA COMMUNITY COLLEGE
Avon Park, Florida

UG Enrollment: 1,530	Tuition & Fees (FL Res): $1152
Application Deadline: rolling	Room & Board: N/Avail

GENERAL State-supported, 2-year, coed. Part of Florida Community Colleges System. Awards certificates, diplomas, transfer associate, terminal associate degrees. Founded 1965. *Setting:* 80-acre rural campus with easy access to Tampa–St. Petersburg. *Total enrollment:* 1,530. *Faculty:* 202 (42 full-time, 15% with terminal degrees, 160 part-time).
ENROLLMENT PROFILE 1,530 students. *Most popular recent majors:* business administration/commerce/management, education.
FIRST-YEAR CLASS 345 total; 1,200 applied, 90% were accepted, 33% of whom enrolled.
ACADEMIC PROGRAM Core, honor code. Calendar: semesters. Academic remediation for entering students, English as a second language program offered during academic year, advanced placement, summer session for credit, part-time degree program (daytime, evenings), adult/continuing education programs, co-op programs.
GENERAL DEGREE REQUIREMENTS 60 semester hours; math/science requirements vary accor; computer course (varies by major).
MAJORS Accounting, agricultural business, agricultural technologies, business administration/commerce/management, computer programming, construction technologies, criminal justice, culinary arts, drafting and design, education, electronics engineering technology, finance/banking, hotel and restaurant management, legal secretarial studies, liberal arts/general studies, marketing/retailing/merchandising, nursing, ornamental horticulture, secretarial studies/office management.
LIBRARY 42,000 books, 163 microform titles, 237 periodicals, 4 on-line bibliographic services, 558 records, tapes, and CDs. Acquisition spending 1994–95: $25,000.
COMPUTERS ON CAMPUS 312 computers for student use in computer center, classrooms, library provide access to on-line services. Staffed computer lab on campus.
COLLEGE LIFE Drama-theater group, choral group. *Social organizations:* 12 open to all. *Most popular organizations:* Phi Theta Kappa, Student Activities Board, Cheerleaders Club, African-American Association, Adventist Social Club. *Major annual events:* International Jamboree, Back to School Pool Party, Pep Rally. *Student services:* personal-psychological counseling, women's center.
HOUSING College housing not available.
ATHLETICS Member NJCAA. *Intercollegiate:* basketball M(s), volleyball W(s). *Intramural:* archery, bowling, tennis. *Contact:* Dr. Aubrey Gardner, Vice President of Academic Affairs/Athletic Director, 941-453-6661 Ext. 121.
CAREER PLANNING *Placement office:* 1 full-time, 1 part-time staff. *Director:* Mrs. Laura White, Director of Counseling, 941-453-6661 Ext. 410. *Services:* resume preparation, career counseling, careers library.
EXPENSES FOR 1995–96 State resident tuition: $1152 full-time, $36 per semester hour part-time. Nonresident tuition: $4128 full-time, $129 per semester hour part-time.
FINANCIAL AID *College-administered undergrad aid 1995–96:* need-based scholarships (average $350), 95 non-need scholarships, short-term loans (average $200), low-interest long-term loans from external sources (average $1500), 11 Federal Work-Study (averaging $1632), 11 part-time jobs. *Required forms:* institutional, FAFSA. *Priority deadline:* 6/30. *Waivers:* full or partial for employees or children of employees. *Average indebtedness of graduates:* $2500.
APPLYING Open admission. *Options:* early entrance, midyear entrance. *Required:* school transcript, SAT I or ACT, TOEFL for international students, ACT ASSET. Test scores used for counseling/placement. *Application deadline:* rolling. *Notification:* continuous.
APPLYING/TRANSFER *Required:* standardized test scores, college transcript. *Required for some:* high school transcript. *Contact:* Ms. Michelle T. Wampler, Registrar, 941-453-6661 Ext. 139.
CONTACT Mr. William L. Rudy, Dean of Student Services, South Florida Community College, Avon Park, FL 33825-9356, 941-453-6661 Ext. 104.

SOUTHWEST FLORIDA COLLEGE OF BUSINESS
Fort Meyers, Florida

UG Enrollment: 220	Tuition & Fees: $4660
Application Deadline: rolling	Room & Board: N/Avail

GENERAL Independent, 2-year, coed. Awards diplomas, terminal associate degrees. *Setting:* urban campus. *Total enrollment:* 220. *Faculty:* 13 (8 full-time, 5 part-time); student-faculty ratio is 18:1.
ENROLLMENT PROFILE 220 students. *Most popular recent majors:* secretarial studies/office management, paralegal studies, accounting.
ACADEMIC PROGRAM Calendar: quarters. 98 courses offered in 1995–96. Academic remediation for entering students, co-op programs and internships.
GENERAL DEGREE REQUIREMENTS 96 quarter hours; 2 math courses; computer course; internship (some majors).
MAJORS Accounting, business administration/commerce/management, computer information systems, court reporting, medical assistant technologies, paralegal studies, secretarial studies/office management.
COMPUTERS ON CAMPUS 80 computers for student use in classrooms.
HOUSING College housing not available.
CAREER PLANNING *Director:* Ms. Sharron Broadwell, Placement Director, 941-939-4766. *Services:* resume preparation, resume referral, career counseling, job bank, job interviews.
AFTER GRADUATION 86% of class of 1994 had job offers within 6 months.
EXPENSES FOR 1995–96 Tuition: $4560 full-time, $95 per quarter hour part-time. Full-time mandatory fees: $100.
FINANCIAL AID *College-administered undergrad aid 1995–96:* 83 need-based scholarships (averaging $300), 1 non-need scholarship, 10 Federal Work-Study (averaging $2000). *Required forms:* FAFSA. *Application deadline:* continuous. *Waivers:* full or partial for employees or children of employees.

APPLYING Open admission. ***Option:*** Common Application. ***Required:*** TOEFL for international students. ***Recommended:*** school transcript. Test scores used for counseling/placement. ***Application deadline:*** rolling. ***Notification:*** continuous.
APPLYING/TRANSFER ***Application deadline:*** rolling. ***Notification:*** continuous. ***Contact:*** Ms. Mary A. Anderson, Registrar, 941-939-4766.
CONTACT Dr. Connie Cole, Director, Southwest Florida College of Business, Suite 200, 1685 Medical Lane, Fort Meyers, FL 33907, 941-939-4766.

TALLAHASSEE COMMUNITY COLLEGE
Tallahassee, Florida

UG Enrollment: 10,084	**Tuition & Fees (FL Res): $1043**
Application Deadline: 7/24	**Room & Board: N/Avail**

GENERAL State and locally supported, 2-year, coed. Part of Florida Community Colleges System. Awards certificates, transfer associate, terminal associate degrees. Founded 1966. ***Setting:*** 183-acre suburban campus. ***Total enrollment:*** 10,084. ***Faculty:*** 384 (135 full-time, 35% with terminal degrees, 249 part-time); student-faculty ratio is 30:1.
ENROLLMENT PROFILE 10,084 students from 40 states and territories, 39 other countries. 54% women, 46% men, 52% part-time, 96% state residents, 12% transferred in, 1% international, 25% 25 or older, 1% Native American, 4% Hispanic, 23% African American, 1% Asian American. ***Areas of study chosen:*** 92% library and information studies, 6% health professions and related sciences.
FIRST-YEAR CLASS 1,294 total. Of the students who applied, 100% were accepted.
ACADEMIC PROGRAM Core, honor code. Calendar: semesters. 415 courses offered in 1995–96. Academic remediation for entering students, English as a second language program offered during academic year and summer, services for LD students, advanced placement, honors program, summer session for credit, part-time degree program (daytime, evenings, weekends, summer), adult/continuing education programs. Off-campus study at Florida Agricultural and Mechanical University, Florida State University. ROTC: Army, Naval (c), Air Force (c).
GENERAL DEGREE REQUIREMENTS 60 semester hours; 6 semester hours each of math and science.
MAJORS Business administration/commerce/management, civil engineering technology, computer programming, criminal justice, data processing, dental services, emergency medical technology, film studies, industrial administration, legal secretarial studies, liberal arts/general studies, marriage and family counseling, nursing, paralegal studies, public affairs and policy studies, respiratory therapy, secretarial studies/office management.
LIBRARY Tallahassee Community College Library with 78,802 books, 743 microform titles, 697 periodicals, 12 CD-ROMs, 9,504 records, tapes, and CDs. Acquisition spending 1994–95: $120,384.
COMPUTERS ON CAMPUS 100 computers for student use in computer labs, skills, counseling labs, classrooms, library provide access to main academic computer. Staffed computer lab on campus. Academic computing expenditure 1994–95: $1.5 million.
COLLEGE LIFE Drama-theater group, choral group, student-run newspaper. ***Social organizations:*** 13 open to all. ***Most popular organizations:*** Phi Theta Kappa, Student Government, International Student Organization, Black Student Union, Returning Adults Valuing Education. ***Major annual events:*** Student Faculty Day, Turkey Shoot, Campus Concert. ***Student services:*** personal-psychological counseling. ***Campus security:*** late-night transport-escort service.
HOUSING College housing not available.
ATHLETICS Member NJCAA. ***Intercollegiate:*** baseball M(s), basketball M(s)/W(s), softball W(s). ***Intramural:*** badminton, basketball, cross-country running, football, golf, racquetball, softball, table tennis (Ping-Pong), tennis, volleyball, weight lifting. ***Contact:*** Mr. Mike Gillespie, Co-Curricular Specialist, 904-922-8201.
CAREER PLANNING ***Placement office:*** 2 full-time, 1 part-time staff. ***Director:*** Ms. Margaret M. Hardee, Counselor, 904-488-9239. ***Services:*** resume preparation, career counseling, careers library, job bank.
EXPENSES FOR 1995–96 ***Application fee:*** $15. State resident tuition: $1043 full-time, $34.75 per semester hour part-time. Nonresident tuition: $3825 full-time, $127.50 per semester hour part-time.
FINANCIAL AID ***College-administered undergrad aid 1995–96:*** 159 need-based scholarships (averaging $600), non-need scholarships (averaging $500), low-interest long-term loans from external sources (averaging $2300), 231 Federal Work-Study, 38 part-time jobs. ***Required forms:*** institutional, FAFSA. ***Priority deadline:*** 5/15. ***Waivers:*** full or partial for employees or children of employees.
APPLYING Open admission. ***Options:*** early entrance, deferred entrance, midyear entrance. ***Required:*** 3 years of high school math and science, TOEFL for international students, MAPS. Test scores used for counseling/placement. ***Application deadline:*** 7/24.
APPLYING/TRANSFER ***Required:*** standardized test scores. ***Entrance:*** noncompetitive. ***Application deadline:*** 7/24.
CONTACT Mr. Dave Dahlen, Assistant Vice President for Student Services, Tallahassee Community College, Tallahassee, FL 32304-2895, 904-488-9200 Ext. 217. ***E-mail:*** enroll@mail.tallahassee.cc.fl.us.

VALENCIA COMMUNITY COLLEGE
Orlando, Florida

UG Enrollment: 24,121	**Tuition & Fees (FL Res): $1103**
Application Deadline: 8/10	**Room & Board: N/Avail**

GENERAL State-supported, 2-year, coed. Part of Florida Community Colleges System. Awards certificates, transfer associate, terminal associate degrees. Founded 1967. ***Setting:*** 265-acre urban campus. ***Endowment:*** $4.2 million. ***Total enrollment:*** 24,121. ***Faculty:*** 995 (260 full-time, 13% with terminal degrees, 735 part-time); student-faculty ratio is 24:1. ***Notable Alumni:*** Iloma Edwards, Dick Batchelor, Ron Williams, Mary J. Jack, Frederick J. Walsh.
ENROLLMENT PROFILE 24,121 students: 58% women, 42% men, 68% part-time, 99% state residents, 7% transferred in, 41% 25 or older, 1% Native American, 14% Hispanic, 11% African American, 5% Asian American. ***Areas of study chosen:*** 75% liberal arts/general studies, 8% health professions and related sciences, 6% business management and administrative services, 5% engineering and applied sciences, 3% computer and information sciences, 1% agriculture, 1% architecture, 1% performing arts. ***Most popular recent majors:*** liberal arts/general studies, business administration/commerce/management.
FIRST-YEAR CLASS 7,187 total; 10,047 applied, 100% were accepted, 72% of whom enrolled.
ACADEMIC PROGRAM Core. Calendar: semesters. Academic remediation for entering students, English as a second language program offered during academic year, services for LD students, self-designed majors, honors program, summer session for credit, part-time degree program (daytime, evenings, weekends, summer), adult/continuing education programs, co-op programs and internships. Off-campus study. ROTC: Army (c).
GENERAL DEGREE REQUIREMENT 60 semester hours.
MAJORS Accounting, business administration/commerce/management, civil engineering technology, computer programming, construction technologies, criminal justice, dental services, drafting and design, electronics engineering technology, emergency medical technology, environmental sciences, film studies, finance/banking, fire science, graphic arts, hospitality services, legal secretarial studies, liberal arts/general studies, medical secretarial studies, nuclear medical technology, nursing, ornamental horticulture, paralegal studies, radiological technology, real estate, respiratory therapy, secretarial studies/office management, surveying technology, theater arts/drama, word processing.
LIBRARY Learning Resources Center plus 3 others, with 112,578 books, 837 microform titles, 869 periodicals, 4 on-line bibliographic services, 49 CD-ROMs, 4,822 records, tapes, and CDs. Acquisition spending 1994–95: $208,374.
COMPUTERS ON CAMPUS 600 computers for student use in computer labs, learning resource center, classrooms, library. Staffed computer lab on campus provides training in use of computers, software. Academic computing expenditure 1994–95: $685,736.
COLLEGE LIFE Drama-theater group, choral group, student-run newspaper. ***Social organizations:*** 45 open to all. ***Most popular organizations:*** Phi Theta Kappa, Valencia Intercultural Student Association, Student Government Association. ***Major annual events:*** Matador Day, Dickens' Week, Red Ribbon Week. ***Student services:*** personal-psychological counseling, women's center. ***Campus security:*** 24-hour emergency response devices and patrols, student patrols, late-night transport-escort service.
HOUSING College housing not available.
ATHLETICS Member NJCAA. ***Intercollegiate:*** baseball M(s), basketball M(s)/W(s), softball W(s). ***Intramural:*** basketball, table tennis (Ping-Pong), tennis, volleyball. ***Contact:*** Mr. David Jones, Athletic Director, 407-299-5000 Ext. 1408.
CAREER PLANNING ***Placement office:*** 2 full-time, 2 part-time staff; $138,679 operating expenditure 1994–95. ***Services:*** resume preparation, career counseling, careers library.
AFTER GRADUATION 73% of students completing a degree program in 1994–95 went directly on to further study.
EXPENSES FOR 1995–96 ***Application fee:*** $20. State resident tuition: $1103 full-time, $36.75 per semester hour part-time. Nonresident tuition: $3885 full-time, $129.50 per semester hour part-time.
FINANCIAL AID ***College-administered undergrad aid 1995–96:*** need-based scholarships, non-need scholarships, short-term loans (average $200), low-interest long-term loans from external sources, 243 Federal Work-Study (averaging $1521), part-time jobs. ***Required forms:*** institutional, FAFSA; accepted: CSS Financial Aid PROFILE, state. ***Priority deadline:*** 4/1. ***Waivers:*** full or partial for employees or children of employees and senior citizens. ***Notification:*** continuous.
APPLYING Open admission except for health-related programs. ***Options:*** early entrance, deferred entrance, midyear entrance. ***Required:*** school transcript. ***Recommended:*** SAT I or ACT, TOEFL for international students. Test scores used for counseling/placement. ***Application deadline:*** 8/10. Preference given to local residents for health-related programs.
APPLYING/TRANSFER ***Required:*** college transcript. ***Required for some:*** minimum 2.0 college GPA. ***Application deadline:*** 8/10. ***Contact:*** Mr. Charles H. Drosin, Director of Admissions and Records, 407-299-5000 Ext. 1506.
CONTACT Mr. Charles H. Drosin, Director of Admissions and Records, Valencia Community College, PO Box 3028, Orlando, FL 32802-3028, 407-299-5000 Ext. 1506.

WARD STONE COLLEGE
Miami, Florida

UG Enrollment: 500	**Tuition & Fees: $5370**
Application Deadline: rolling	**Room & Board: N/Avail**

GENERAL Proprietary, 2-year, coed. Awards terminal associate degrees. Founded 1975. ***Total enrollment:*** 500. ***Faculty:*** 30.
ENROLLMENT PROFILE 500 students.
FIRST-YEAR CLASS Of the students accepted, 80% enrolled.
ACADEMIC PROGRAM Calendar: semesters. Part-time degree program (daytime, evenings, summer), internships.
GENERAL DEGREE REQUIREMENTS 63 semester hours; internship.
MAJORS Business administration/commerce/management, court reporting, medical assistant technologies, medical records services, medical technology, operating room technology, paralegal studies.
EXPENSES FOR 1995–96 Tuition: $5280 full-time, $165 per credit hour part-time. Part-time mandatory fees: $45 per semester. Full-time mandatory fees: $90.
APPLYING ***Required:*** school transcript, Thurston Mental Alertness Test. ***Application deadline:*** rolling. ***Notification:*** continuous.
APPLYING/TRANSFER ***Required:*** standardized test scores, high school transcript, college transcript. ***Entrance:*** minimally difficult.
CONTACT Ms. Brenda Rahn, Director of Admission, Ward Stone College, Miami, FL 33186, 305-386-9900.

WEBSTER COLLEGE
Fort Pierce, Florida

WEBSTER COLLEGE
Gainesville, Florida

Florida–Georgia

WEBSTER COLLEGE
New Port Richey, Florida

WEBSTER COLLEGE
Ocala, Florida

UG Enrollment: 224	Tuition & Fees: $6825
Application Deadline: rolling	Room & Board: N/Avail

GENERAL Proprietary, 2-year, primarily women. Awards diplomas, terminal associate degrees. Founded 1984. *Setting:* 3-acre suburban campus with easy access to Orlando. *Total enrollment:* 224. *Faculty:* 21 (10 full-time, 75% with terminal degrees, 11 part-time); student-faculty ratio is 14:1.
ENROLLMENT PROFILE 224 students from 5 states and territories. 85% women, 15% men, 0% part-time, 99% state residents, 15% transferred in, 90% have need-based financial aid, 10% have non-need-based financial aid, 0% international, 70% 25 or older, 0% Native American, 3% Hispanic, 9% African American, 1% Asian American. *Areas of study chosen:* 55% health professions and related sciences, 25% business management and administrative services, 20% computer and information sciences. *Most popular recent majors:* medical assistant technologies, accounting, medical secretarial studies.
FIRST-YEAR CLASS 2% from top 10% of their high school class, 28% from top quarter, 70% from top half.
ACADEMIC PROGRAM Core, honor code. Calendar: quarters. Average class size 15 in required courses. Academic remediation for entering students, tutorials, summer session for credit, part-time degree program (daytime, evenings), adult/continuing education programs.
GENERAL DEGREE REQUIREMENTS 90 credits; computer course.
MAJORS Accounting, business administration/commerce/management, data processing, legal secretarial studies, medical assistant technologies, medical secretarial studies, secretarial studies/office management.
LIBRARY Webster College Library with 2,400 books, 32 periodicals, 1 CD-ROM.
COMPUTERS ON CAMPUS 31 computers for student use in computer labs, library provide access to on-line services, Internet. Staffed computer lab on campus provides training in use of computers, software.
COLLEGE LIFE *Student services:* personal-psychological counseling. *Campus security:* 24-hour emergency response devices, late-night transport-escort service.
HOUSING College housing not available.
CAREER PLANNING *Placement office:* 1 full-time staff. *Director:* Ms. Dani Parks, Director of Career Services, 352-629-1941. *Services:* job fairs, resume preparation, resume referral, career counseling, careers library, job bank, job interviews. Students must register freshman year.
AFTER GRADUATION 88% of class of 1994 had job offers within 6 months.
EXPENSES FOR 1996–97 *Application fee:* $250. Tuition: $6825 full-time.
FINANCIAL AID *College-administered undergrad aid 1995–96:* need-based scholarships. *Required forms:* FAFSA. *Priority deadline:* 9/15. *Payment plans:* installment, deferred payment.
APPLYING Open admission. *Options:* deferred entrance, midyear entrance. *Required:* school transcript, minimum 2.0 GPA, campus interview. *Application deadline:* rolling.
APPLYING/TRANSFER *Required:* high school transcript, minimum 2.0 high school GPA. *Recommended:* campus interview, college transcript. *Entrance:* noncompetitive. *Application deadline:* rolling. *Contact:* Mr. Jay Lambeth, Executive Director, 352-629-1941.
CONTACT Mr. Jay Lambeth, Executive Director, Webster College, Ocala, FL 34474, 352-629-1941. College video available.

GEORGIA

ABRAHAM BALDWIN AGRICULTURAL COLLEGE
Tifton, Georgia

UG Enrollment: 2,592	Tuition & Fees (GA Res): $1654
Application Deadline: 9/24	Room & Board: $2430

GENERAL State-supported, 2-year, coed. Part of University System of Georgia. Awards transfer associate, terminal associate degrees. Founded 1933. *Setting:* 390-acre small-town campus. *Total enrollment:* 2,592. *Faculty:* 115 (106 full-time, 32% with terminal degrees, 9 part-time); student-faculty ratio is 25:1.
ENROLLMENT PROFILE 2,592 students from 13 states and territories, 18 other countries. 52% women, 32% part-time, 93% state residents, 28% live on campus, 7% transferred in, 2% international, 31% 25 or older, 0% Native American, 11% African American, 1% Asian American. *Most popular recent majors:* nursing, elementary education, business administration/commerce/management.
FIRST-YEAR CLASS 701 total; 1,477 applied, 59% of whom enrolled.
ACADEMIC PROGRAM Core, interdisciplinary curriculum. Calendar: quarters. Academic remediation for entering students, English as a second language program offered during academic year, services for LD students, advanced placement, tutorials, honors program, summer session for credit, part-time degree program (daytime, evenings), adult/continuing education programs, internships. Off-campus study at Ben Hill Irwin Technical Institute, Moultrie Technical Institute.
GENERAL DEGREE REQUIREMENTS 96 quarter hours; computer course; internship (some majors).
MAJORS Accounting, agricultural business, agricultural economics, agricultural sciences, agricultural technologies, animal sciences, art/fine arts, biology/biological sciences, business administration/commerce/management, chemistry, child care/child and family studies, computer programming, computer science, computer technologies, criminal justice, data processing, early childhood education, ecology, education, elementary education, (pre)engineering sequence, English, environmental design, farm and ranch management, fashion merchandising, fish and game management, forestry, forest technology, history, home economics, horticulture, humanities, journalism, landscaping/grounds maintenance, law enforcement/police sciences, liberal arts/general studies, marketing/retailing/merchandising, mathematics, music, nursing, ornamental horticulture, pharmacy/pharmaceutical sciences, physical education, physical sciences, political science/government,

psychology, recreational facilities management, science, secretarial studies/office management, social science, social work, sociology, speech/rhetoric/public address/debate, wildlife management, word processing.
LIBRARY Baldwin Library with 69,986 books, 570 microform titles, 431 periodicals, 1 on-line bibliographic service, 6 CD-ROMs, 671 records, tapes, and CDs. Acquisition spending 1994–95: $640,974.
COMPUTERS ON CAMPUS 158 computers for student use in computer center, computer labs, library provide access to main academic computer, Internet. Staffed computer lab on campus provides training in use of computers, software.
COLLEGE LIFE Orientation program (2 days, $30, parents included). Drama-theater group, choral group, student-run newspaper, radio station. ***Most popular organizations:*** Rodeo Club, Baptist Student Union, Forestry/Wildlife Club. ***Major annual events:*** Spring Fling, Concerts, Dances. ***Student services:*** health clinic, personal-psychological counseling. ***Campus security:*** 24-hour emergency response devices and patrols, late-night transport-escort service.
HOUSING 1,150 college housing spaces available; 720 were occupied 1995–96. Freshmen guaranteed college housing. On-campus residence required in freshman year. ***Options:*** coed (1 building), single-sex (4 buildings) housing available. Resident assistants live in dorms.
ATHLETICS Member NJCAA. ***Intercollegiate:*** baseball M(s), basketball M(s), softball W(s), tennis M(s)/W(s), volleyball W(s). ***Intramural:*** basketball, bowling, football, soccer, softball, tennis, volleyball. ***Contact:*** Mr. Wayne Cooper, Department Chair for Health, Physical Ed. and Recreation, 912-386-3927.
CAREER PLANNING ***Placement office:*** 1 full-time staff. ***Director:*** Dr. Maggie Martin, Director of Counseling and Testing, 912-386-3231. ***Services:*** job fairs, resume preparation, resume referral, career counseling, careers library, job bank, job interviews.
EXPENSES FOR 1995–96 ***Application fee:*** $5. State resident tuition: $1314 full-time. Nonresident tuition: $3717 full-time. Part-time tuition per quarter ranges from $29 to $290 for state residents, $87 to $870 for nonresidents. Full-time mandatory fees: $340. College room and board: $2430 (minimum). College room only: $1110 (minimum).
FINANCIAL AID ***College-administered undergrad aid 1995–96:*** 1,200 need-based scholarships (average $1400), 100 non-need scholarships (average $1000), short-term loans (average $100), low-interest long-term loans from external sources (average $2500), Federal Work-Study, 200 part-time jobs. ***Required forms:*** institutional, FAFSA; accepted: CSS Financial Aid PROFILE. ***Application deadline:*** continuous. ***Waivers:*** full or partial for senior citizens. ***Notification:*** continuous.
APPLYING Open admission. ***Options:*** Common Application, early entrance, deferred entrance. ***Required:*** school transcript, 3 years of high school math and science, 2 years of high school foreign language, SAT I or ACT, TOEFL for international students. Test scores used for counseling/placement. ***Application deadline:*** 9/24.
APPLYING/TRANSFER ***Required:*** high school transcript, college transcript. ***Required for some:*** standardized test scores.
CONTACT Mr. Garth L. Webb Jr., Director of Admissions, Abraham Baldwin Agricultural College, ABAC 4 2802 Moore Highway, Tifton, GA 31794-2601, 912-386-3230 or toll-free 800-733-3653. ***Fax:*** 912-386-7481. College video available.

ANDREW COLLEGE
Cuthbert, Georgia

UG Enrollment: 305 **Tuition & Fees: $5832**
Application Deadline: 8/15 **Room & Board: $4104**

GENERAL Independent United Methodist, 2-year, coed. Awards certificates, transfer associate degrees. Founded 1854. ***Setting:*** 40-acre small-town campus. ***Endowment:*** $2.7 million. ***Educational spending 1994–95:*** $3926 per undergrad. ***Total enrollment:*** 305. ***Faculty:*** 36 (20 full-time, 35% with terminal degrees, 16 part-time).
ENROLLMENT PROFILE 305 students from 8 states and territories, 10 other countries. 51% women, 49% men, 5% part-time, 74% state residents, 74% live on campus, 3% transferred in, 65% have need-based financial aid, 25% have non-need-based financial aid, 14% international, 3% 25 or older, 0% Native American, 0% Hispanic, 27% African American, 0% Asian American. ***Areas of study chosen:*** 18% health professions and related sciences, 11% business management and administrative services, 9% education, 9% premed, 8% performing arts, 4% engineering and applied sciences, 4% fine arts, 4% prelaw, 2% biological and life sciences, 2% communications and journalism, 2% English language/literature/letters, 1% agriculture, 1% liberal arts/general studies, 1% prevet, 1% theology/religion. ***Most popular recent majors:*** education, music.
FIRST-YEAR CLASS 184 total; 413 applied, 93% were accepted, 48% of whom enrolled.
ACADEMIC PROGRAM Core, interdisciplinary curriculum, honor code. Calendar: quarters. 128 courses offered in 1995–96. Academic remediation for entering students, English as a second language program offered during academic year and summer, services for LD students, advanced placement, tutorials, honors program, summer session for credit, part-time degree program (daytime, evenings, summer), adult/continuing education programs.
GENERAL DEGREE REQUIREMENTS 100 quarter hours; 20 quarter hours of math/science.
MAJORS Agricultural sciences, art/fine arts, biology/biological sciences, business administration/commerce/management, business education, chemistry, communication, dental services, education, (pre)engineering sequence, English, forestry, health education, history, humanities, journalism, literature, mathematics, medical technology, ministries, music, natural sciences, nursing, occupational therapy, pharmacy/pharmaceutical sciences, philosophy, photography, physical education, physical therapy, physics, psychology, religious studies, respiratory therapy, science, social science, social work, sociology, speech/rhetoric/public address/debate, theater arts/drama.
LIBRARY Pitts Library with 40,000 books, 100 periodicals, 700 records, tapes, and CDs. Acquisition spending 1994–95: $28,700.
COMPUTERS ON CAMPUS 30 computers for student use in computer center, learning resource center, library, dorms provide access to main academic computer. Staffed computer lab on campus provides training in use of computers, software.
COLLEGE LIFE Drama-theater group, choral group, student-run newspaper. 40% vote in student government elections. ***Social organizations:*** 10 open to all. ***Most popular organizations:*** Drama Club, Outdoor Club, International Club, BYU. ***Major annual events:*** Homecoming, Valentine Dance, Spring Semi-Formal. ***Student services:*** health clinic, personal-psychological counseling. ***Campus security:*** controlled dormitory access, night patrols by trained security personnel.
HOUSING 300 college housing spaces available; 225 were occupied 1995–96. Freshmen guaranteed college housing. On-campus residence required through sophomore year except if married or living with relatives. ***Options:*** coed (1 building), single-sex (2 buildings) housing available. Resident assistants live in dorms.
ATHLETICS Member NJCAA. ***Intercollegiate:*** baseball M(s), cross-country running M(s)/W(s), soccer M(s)/W(s), softball W(s), tennis M(s)/W(s). ***Intramural:*** archery, badminton, basketball, equestrian sports, fencing, football, racquetball, skiing (downhill), soccer, softball, swimming and diving, table tennis (Ping-Pong), tennis, volleyball, weight lifting, wrestling. ***Contact:*** Mr. James T. Gilbert, Director of Athletics, 912-732-2171 Ext. 153.
CAREER PLANNING ***Placement office:*** 1 part-time staff. ***Director:*** Ms. Mary Beth Lane, Student Development Assistant Director, 912-732-2171. ***Service:*** career counseling.
AFTER GRADUATION 96% of students completing a degree program in 1994–95 went directly on to further study.
EXPENSES FOR 1996–97 ***Application fee:*** $15. Comprehensive fee of $9936 includes full-time tuition ($5832) and college room and board ($4104). College room only: $1941. Part-time tuition: $120 per quarter hour.
FINANCIAL AID ***College-administered undergrad aid 1995–96:*** need-based scholarships, non-need scholarships, low-interest long-term loans from external sources, Federal Work-Study, part-time jobs. ***Required forms:*** institutional, FAFSA; required for some: state; accepted: CSS Financial Aid PROFILE. ***Priority deadline:*** 6/1. ***Payment plan:*** installment. ***Waivers:*** full or partial for employees or children of employees.
APPLYING ***Options:*** early entrance, deferred entrance, midyear entrance. ***Required:*** school transcript, 3 years of high school math and science, SAT I or ACT, TOEFL for international students. ***Recommended:*** minimum 2.0 GPA. ***Required for some:*** essay, 1 recommendation, campus interview. Test scores used for admission and counseling/placement. ***Application deadline:*** 8/15.
APPLYING/TRANSFER ***Required:*** standardized test scores, high school transcript, college transcript. ***Recommended:*** some high school foreign language, minimum 2.0 college GPA, minimum 2.0 high school GPA. ***Required for some:*** essay, 3 years of high school math and science, 1 recommendation. ***Entrance:*** minimally difficult. ***Application deadline:*** 8/15. ***Contact:*** Ms. Claudia Seyle, Director of Admission, 912-732-2171.
CONTACT Ms. Claudia Seyle, Director of Admission, Andrew College, Cuthbert, GA 31740-1395, 912-732-2171 or toll-free 800-664-9250 (out-of-state). ***Fax:*** 912-732-2176. ***E-mail:*** andrewcol@aol.com. College video available.

ART INSTITUTE OF ATLANTA
Atlanta, Georgia

UG Enrollment: 1,408 **Tuition & Fees: $8790**
Application Deadline: rolling **Room Only: $3300**

GENERAL Proprietary, primarily 2-year, coed. Awards diplomas, terminal associate, bachelor's degrees. Founded 1949. ***Setting:*** urban campus. ***Total enrollment:*** 1,408. ***Faculty:*** 91 (43 full-time, 17% with terminal degrees, 48 part-time); student-faculty ratio is 16:1. ***Notable Alumni:*** Gary Clark, photographer for *Southern Living*; Claire Boymer, interior designer for Georgia Institute of Technology; Margaret Sisk, private cook for Anne Cox Chambers.
ENROLLMENT PROFILE 1,408 students from 30 states and territories, 18 other countries. 36% women, 18% part-time, 45% state residents, 44% transferred in, 1% international, 50% 25 or older, 1% Native American, 1% Hispanic, 22% African American, 1% Asian American. ***Most popular recent majors:*** music business, culinary arts, commercial art.
FIRST-YEAR CLASS 1,100 total; 1,723 applied, 99% were accepted, 65% of whom enrolled.
ACADEMIC PROGRAM Professional studies curriculum. Calendar: quarters. 177 courses offered in 1995–96. Academic remediation for entering students, advanced placement, summer session for credit, adult/continuing education programs, co-op programs and internships.
GENERAL DEGREE REQUIREMENTS 96 credits for associate, 192 credits for bachelor's; 1 math course; computer course.
MAJORS Commercial art, culinary arts, fashion merchandising, interior design (B), music business, photography.
LIBRARY 23,559 books, 7 microform titles, 200 periodicals, 2 on-line bibliographic services, 7 CD-ROMs, 710 records, tapes, and CDs. Acquisition spending 1994–95: $104,117.
COMPUTERS ON CAMPUS Computer purchase plan available. 160 computers for student use in computer labs, learning resource center, classrooms, library provide access to main academic computer. Staffed computer lab on campus provides training in use of computers, software.
COLLEGE LIFE Orientation program (3 days, no cost, parents included). ***Most popular organizations:*** Student Council, ASID Student Chapter, Entertainment Management Group. ***Major annual events:*** Institute Day, Annual Alumni Show, Annual Talent Show. ***Student services:*** personal-psychological counseling. ***Campus security:*** 24-hour emergency response devices, security patrols until 11 p.m.
HOUSING 258 college housing spaces available; 253 were occupied 1995–96. No special consideration for freshman housing applicants. Off-campus living permitted. ***Option:*** coed housing available. Resident assistants live in dorms.
CAREER PLANNING ***Placement office:*** 5 full-time staff; $366,325 operating expenditure 1994–95. ***Director:*** Ms. Diana Graves, Director of Employment Assistance, 404-266-1341. ***Services:*** job fairs, career counseling, job bank, job interviews. 188 organizations recruited on campus 1994–95.
AFTER GRADUATION 85% of class of 1994 had job offers within 6 months.
EXPENSES FOR 1995–96 ***Application fee:*** $50. Tuition: $8790 (minimum) full-time. Full-time tuition ranges up to $8940 according to program. One-time enrollment fee: $250. College room only: $3300 (minimum).
FINANCIAL AID ***College-administered undergrad aid 1995–96:*** need-based scholarships, 310 non-need scholarships, low-interest long-term loans from external sources (average $875), Federal Work-Study, part-time jobs. ***Required forms:*** CSS Financial Aid PROFILE, institutional, FAFSA, FARE. ***Priority deadline:*** 7/15. ***Payment plans:*** installment, deferred payment. ***Waivers:*** full or partial for employees or children of employees.
APPLYING ***Options:*** deferred entrance, midyear entrance. ***Required:*** essay, school transcript, interview. ***Required for some:*** minimum 2.0 GPA. ***Application deadline:*** rolling.

Art Institute of Atlanta (continued)
APPLYING/TRANSFER ***Required:*** essay, high school transcript, interview. ***Required for some:*** college transcript, minimum 2.0 college GPA, minimum 2.0 high school GPA. ***Entrance:*** minimally difficult. ***Application deadline:*** rolling. ***Contact:*** Ms. Robyn Rickenback, Director of Admissions, 404-266-1341 Ext. 320.
CONTACT Ms. Robyn Rickenback, Director of Admissions, Art Institute of Atlanta, 3376 Peachtree Road, NE, Atlanta, GA 30326-1018, 404-266-1341 Ext. 320 or toll-free 800-275-4242. College video available.

ATHENS AREA TECHNICAL INSTITUTE
Athens, Georgia

UG Enrollment: 1,653 **Tuition & Fees (GA Res): $771**
Application Deadline: rolling **Room & Board: N/Avail**

GENERAL State-supported, 2-year, coed. Part of Georgia Department of Technical and Adult Education. Awards transfer associate, terminal associate degrees. Founded 1958. ***Setting:*** 41-acre suburban campus with easy access to Atlanta. ***Total enrollment:*** 1,653. ***Faculty:*** 100 (77 full-time, 40% with terminal degrees, 23 part-time); student-faculty ratio is 20:1.
ENROLLMENT PROFILE 1,653 students from 8 states and territories, 6 other countries. 61% women, 48% part-time, 95% state residents, 17% transferred in, 30% have need-based financial aid, 40% have non-need-based financial aid, 1% international, 40% 25 or older, 1% Native American, 1% Hispanic, 21% African American, 2% Asian American. ***Areas of study chosen:*** 25% health professions and related sciences, 24% engineering and applied sciences, 23% business management and administrative services, 8% liberal arts/general studies, 6% computer and information sciences, 5% prelaw, 3% architecture, 3% biological and life sciences, 3% education. ***Most popular recent majors:*** paralegal studies, nursing, respiratory therapy.
FIRST-YEAR CLASS 300 total. Of the students who applied, 89% were accepted, 74% of whom enrolled. 20% from top 10% of their high school class, 80% from top quarter, 100% from top half. 5 class presidents, 6 valedictorians.
ACADEMIC PROGRAM Core, practical applied knowledge curriculum, honor code. Calendar: quarters. 565 courses offered in 1995–96. Academic remediation for entering students, English as a second language program offered during summer, services for LD students, summer session for credit, part-time degree program (daytime, evenings, weekends, summer), adult/continuing education programs, internships.
GENERAL DEGREE REQUIREMENTS 120 credit hours; 1 college algebra course; computer course for paralegal studies, secretarial studies, accounting, engineering technology, electronics engineering technology majors; internship (some majors).
MAJORS Accounting, automotive technologies, biotechnology, business machine technologies, child care/child and family studies, communication equipment technology, computer programming, cosmetology, drafting and design, electrical and electronics technologies, electromechanical technology, electronics engineering technology, engineering technology, heating/refrigeration/air conditioning, laboratory technologies, machine and tool technologies, marketing/retailing/merchandising, medical assistant technologies, medical secretarial studies, medical technology, nursing, paralegal studies, practical nursing, radiological technology, respiratory therapy, secretarial studies/office management, teacher aide studies.
LIBRARY 25,000 books, 350 periodicals.
COMPUTERS ON CAMPUS Computer purchase plan available. 41 computers for student use in computer center, library provide access to e-mail, on-line services, Internet. Staffed computer lab on campus provides training in use of computers, software.
COLLEGE LIFE ***Social organizations:*** local fraternities, local sororities. ***Most popular organizations:*** Athens Technical Student Advisory Council, Phi Theta Kappa, Delta Epsilon Chi, Radiological Technology Society, Organized Black Students Encouraging Unity and Excellence. ***Major annual events:*** Blood Drives, Can-A-Thon, Smoke Out. ***Student services:*** personal-psychological counseling. ***Campus security:*** 24-hour patrols.
HOUSING College housing not available.
CAREER PLANNING ***Director:*** Mr. Jack Newman, Career Planning and Placement Coordinator, 706-355-5133. ***Services:*** resume preparation, resume referral, career counseling, job interviews.
EXPENSES FOR 1995–96 State resident tuition: $756 full-time, $21 per credit hour part-time. Nonresident tuition: $1512 full-time, $42 per credit hour part-time. Full-time mandatory fees: $15.
FINANCIAL AID ***College-administered undergrad aid 1995–96:*** 300 need-based scholarships (average $500), 20 non-need scholarships (average $500), Federal Work-Study, 48 part-time jobs. ***Required forms:*** FAFSA; accepted: CSS Financial Aid PROFILE. ***Priority deadline:*** 9/1. ***Waivers:*** full or partial for senior citizens.
APPLYING Open admission. ***Option:*** early entrance. ***Required:*** school transcript, ACT. ***Required for some:*** SAT I. Test scores used for counseling/placement. ***Application deadline:*** rolling. ***Notification:*** continuous.
APPLYING/TRANSFER ***Required:*** standardized test scores, high school transcript. ***Contact:*** Ms. Faye Mitchum, Registrar, 706-355-5012.
CONTACT Dr. Evelyn Brooks, Director of Admissions, Athens Area Technical Institute, Athens, GA 30601, 706-355-5006. ***Fax:*** 706-369-5753.

ATLANTA METROPOLITAN COLLEGE
Atlanta, Georgia

UG Enrollment: 1,811 **Tuition & Fees (GA Res): $1140**
Application Deadline: 8/12 **Room & Board: N/Avail**

GENERAL State-supported, 2-year, coed. Part of University System of Georgia. Awards transfer associate, terminal associate degrees. Founded 1974. ***Setting:*** 83-acre urban campus. ***Educational spending 1994–95:*** $2087 per undergrad. ***Total enrollment:*** 1,811. ***Faculty:*** 73 (52 full-time, 38% with terminal degrees, 21 part-time); student-faculty ratio is 25:1.
ENROLLMENT PROFILE 1,811 students from 13 states and territories, 20 other countries. 62% women, 38% men, 48% part-time, 95% state residents, 13% transferred in, 38% 25 or older, 0% Native American, 0% Hispanic, 97% African American, 1% Asian American. ***Areas of study chosen:*** 24% business management and administrative services, 20% health professions and related sciences, 13% social sciences, 9% education, 7% communications and journalism, 7% computer and information sciences, 4% biological and life sciences, 4% fine arts, 4% psychology, 3% engineering and applied sciences, 1% mathematics, 1% physical sciences. ***Most popular recent majors:*** business administration/commerce/management, criminal justice.
FIRST-YEAR CLASS 311 total; 723 applied, 59% were accepted, 73% of whom enrolled.
ACADEMIC PROGRAM Core. Calendar: quarters. 840 courses offered in 1995–96. Academic remediation for entering students, summer session for credit, part-time degree program (daytime, evenings, summer), adult/continuing education programs, co-op programs and internships.
GENERAL DEGREE REQUIREMENTS 30 credit hours; 1 math course; computer course for secretarial science, business administration majors.
MAJORS Accounting, agricultural sciences, anthropology, art/fine arts, aviation technology, biology/biological sciences, business administration/commerce/management, business education, chemistry, child psychology/child development, commercial art, computer information systems, computer science, criminal justice, data processing, dental services, early childhood education, economics, electronics engineering technology, elementary education, engineering technology, English, forestry, geography, geology, health education, history, home economics, human services, journalism, mathematics, medical assistant technologies, medical illustration, medical laboratory technology, medical technology, mental health/rehabilitation counseling, music, nursing, occupational therapy, philosophy, physical therapy, physics, political science/government, psychology, radiological technology, recreation and leisure services, secretarial studies/office management, social work, sociology, teacher aide studies, vocational education.
LIBRARY Atlanta Metropolitan College Library with 36,993 books, 132 microform titles, 364 periodicals, 12 CD-ROMs, 1,567 records, tapes, and CDs. Acquisition spending 1994–95: $34,957.
COMPUTERS ON CAMPUS 150 computers for student use in learning resource center, labs, library provide access to Internet. Staffed computer lab on campus provides training in use of computers. Academic computing expenditure 1994–95: $28,111.
COLLEGE LIFE Drama-theater group, choral group. 40% vote in student government elections. ***Social organizations:*** 15 open to all. ***Most popular organizations:*** Communications Club, Art Club, Creative Writing Club, African Culture Club, International Students Club. ***Student services:*** personal-psychological counseling. ***Campus security:*** 24-hour patrols.
HOUSING College housing not available.
ATHLETICS Member NJCAA. ***Intercollegiate:*** basketball M(s), softball W(s). ***Intramural:*** softball, tennis. ***Contact:*** Mr. Bobby Olive, Coordinator, Student Support Services, 404-756-4057.
CAREER PLANNING ***Placement office:*** 3 full-time staff. ***Director:*** Ms. Carolyn Walker, Director Counseling and Testing, 404-756-4055. ***Services:*** job fairs, career counseling, job bank.
EXPENSES FOR 1995–96 ***Application fee:*** $10. State resident tuition: $1140 full-time. Nonresident tuition: $3543 full-time. Part-time tuition per quarter ranges from $69 to $359 for state residents, $136 to $1096 for nonresidents.
FINANCIAL AID ***College-administered undergrad aid 1995–96:*** need-based scholarships, 14 non-need scholarships (average $1000), Federal Work-Study. ***Required forms:*** state, FAFSA; accepted: CSS Financial Aid PROFILE. ***Priority deadline:*** 7/19.
APPLYING ***Options:*** early entrance, deferred entrance. ***Required:*** school transcript, SAT I or ACT, TOEFL for international students. Test scores used for admission. ***Application deadline:*** 8/12. ***Notification:*** continuous until 9/3.
APPLYING/TRANSFER ***Required:*** standardized test scores, college transcript. ***Entrance:*** minimally difficult. ***Application deadline:*** 8/12. ***Notification:*** continuous until 9/3.
CONTACT Mr. John Brown, Acting Director of Admissions, Atlanta Metropolitan College, 1630 Stewart Avenue, SW, Atlanta, GA 30310-4498, 404-756-4004.

AUGUSTA TECHNICAL INSTITUTE
Augusta, Georgia

UG Enrollment: 2,325 **Tuition & Fees: $825**
Application Deadline: rolling **Room & Board: N/Avail**

GENERAL State-supported, 2-year, coed. Part of Department of Technical and Adult Education. Awards certificates, diplomas, terminal associate degrees. Founded 1961. ***Setting:*** 70-acre urban campus. ***Total enrollment:*** 2,325. ***Faculty:*** 189 (89 full-time, 15% with terminal degrees, 100 part-time).
ENROLLMENT PROFILE 2,325 students: 61% women, 39% men, 44% part-time, 98% state residents, 41% have need-based financial aid, 59% have non-need-based financial aid, 1% international, 1% Native American, 1% Hispanic, 41% African American, 1% Asian American.
FIRST-YEAR CLASS Of the students who applied, 90% were accepted, 35% of whom enrolled.
ACADEMIC PROGRAM Core, honor code. Calendar: quarters. 687 courses offered in 1995–96; average class size 35 in required courses. Part-time degree program (daytime, evenings, summer), co-op programs.
GENERAL DEGREE REQUIREMENTS 101 quarter hours; 1 course each in college algebra and science; computer course for accounting, engineering, marketing, medical majors; internship (some majors).
MAJORS Accounting, child care/child and family studies, computer information systems, computer programming, electrical engineering technology, electromechanical technology, laboratory technologies, mechanical engineering technology, medical laboratory technology, sciences, respiratory therapy, secretarial studies/office management.
COMPUTERS ON CAMPUS Computer purchase plan available. 200 computers for student use in computer labs, research center, learning resource center, classrooms, library provide access to on-line services, Internet. Staffed computer lab on campus provides training in use of computers, software.
COLLEGE LIFE ***Most popular organizations:*** VICA, Student Activities, Professional Organizations. ***Major annual events:*** Field Day, Open House. ***Campus security:*** 24-hour emergency response devices, 12-hour patrols by trained security personnel.
HOUSING College housing not available.
ATHLETICS Member NJCAA. ***Contact:*** Mr. Dennis Harville, Vice-President Student Services, 706-771-4028.
CAREER PLANNING ***Placement office:*** 2 full-time staff. ***Director:*** Mr. Homer Solesbee, Director, Career Placement, 706-771-4307. ***Services:*** job fairs, resume preparation, resume referral, career counseling, careers library, job bank, job interviews. 25 organizations recruited on campus 1994–95.

AFTER GRADUATION 92% of class of 1994 had job offers within 6 months.
EXPENSES FOR 1995–96 ***Application fee:*** $15. Tuition: $756 full-time. Part-time tuition per quarter ranges from $21 to $252. Full-time mandatory fees: $69.
FINANCIAL AID ***College-administered undergrad aid 1995–96:*** 1,044 need-based scholarships (average $575), 1,371 non-need scholarships (average $374), 39 Federal Work-Study (averaging $442). ***Required forms:*** institutional; required for some: FAFSA, HOPE alternate application; accepted: CSS Financial Aid PROFILE. ***Priority deadline:*** 8/1.
APPLYING ***Options:*** Common Application, early entrance, midyear entrance. ***Required:*** school transcript, ACT ASSET. ***Required for some:*** SAT I. Test scores used for counseling/placement. ***Application deadline:*** rolling. ***Notification:*** continuous.
APPLYING/TRANSFER ***Required:*** standardized test scores, high school transcript, college transcript. ***Entrance:*** noncompetitive. ***Application deadline:*** rolling. ***Notification:*** continuous. ***Contact:*** Ms. Stephanie Koller, Director of Admissions, 706-771-4027.
CONTACT Ms. Stephanie Koller, Director of Admissions, Augusta Technical Institute, 3116 Deans Bridge Road, Augusta, GA 30906, 706-771-4028. ***Fax:*** 706-771-4034. ***E-mail:*** skoller@augusta.tec.ga.us.

BAINBRIDGE COLLEGE
Bainbridge, Georgia

UG Enrollment: 1,180	**Tuition & Fees (GA Res): $1110**
Application Deadline: 9/18	**Room & Board: N/Avail**

GENERAL State-supported, 2-year, coed. Part of University System of Georgia. Awards certificates, transfer associate, terminal associate degrees. Founded 1972. ***Setting:*** 160-acre small-town campus. ***Total enrollment:*** 1,180. ***Faculty:*** 46 (31 full-time, 15 part-time); student-faculty ratio is 20:1.
ENROLLMENT PROFILE 1,180 students from 3 states and territories. 67% women, 33% men, 54% part-time, 98% state residents, 9% transferred in, 1% international, 40% 25 or older, 0% Native American, 1% Hispanic, 25% African American, 1% Asian American. ***Areas of study chosen:*** 34% vocational and home economics, 20% health professions and related sciences, 14% business management and administrative services, 10% education, 9% liberal arts/general studies, 5% social sciences, 2% English language/literature/letters, 2% mathematics, 2% physical sciences, 1% biological and life sciences, 1% fine arts. ***Most popular recent majors:*** business administration/commerce/management, education, nursing.
FIRST-YEAR CLASS 333 total; 405 applied, 100% were accepted, 82% of whom enrolled. 15% from top 10% of their high school class, 20% from top quarter, 61% from top half. 3 valedictorians.
ACADEMIC PROGRAM Core. Calendar: quarters. Academic remediation for entering students, services for LD students, advanced placement, summer session for credit, part-time degree program (daytime, evenings, summer), adult/continuing education programs. Off-campus study at Darton College.
GENERAL DEGREE REQUIREMENTS 96 quarter hours; computer course for business administration, accounting majors.
MAJORS Accounting, agricultural sciences, art/fine arts, automotive technologies, biology/biological sciences, business administration/commerce/management, business education, chemistry, computer information systems, criminal justice, data processing, drafting and design, early childhood education, education, electrical and electronics technologies, elementary education, English, forestry, health education, history, home economics, journalism, liberal arts/general studies, marketing/retailing/merchandising, mathematics, nursing, pharmacy/pharmaceutical sciences, political science/government, practical nursing, psychology, secretarial studies/office management, sociology, speech/rhetoric/public address/debate, theater arts/drama, welding technology.
LIBRARY Bainbridge College Library with 32,000 books, 330 periodicals, 1,719 records, tapes, and CDs.
COMPUTERS ON CAMPUS 75 computers for student use in computer center, computer labs. Staffed computer lab on campus.
COLLEGE LIFE 15% vote in student government elections. ***Social organizations:*** 5 open to all. ***Campus security:*** 24-hour patrols.
HOUSING College housing not available.
ATHLETICS ***Intramural:*** bowling, table tennis (Ping-Pong), volleyball.
CAREER PLANNING ***Placement office:*** 1 full-time staff. ***Director:*** Mrs. Joan Fryer, Director, 912-248-2579. ***Services:*** resume preparation, career counseling, careers library.
AFTER GRADUATION 30% of students completing a degree program in 1994–95 went directly on to further study.
EXPENSES FOR 1995–96 State resident tuition: $1065 full-time, $29 per quarter hour part-time. Nonresident tuition: $3468 full-time, $96 per quarter hour part-time. Full-time mandatory fees: $45.
FINANCIAL AID ***College-administered undergrad aid 1995–96:*** 972 need-based scholarships, 439 non-need scholarships (averaging $679), short-term loans (averaging $90), low-interest long-term loans from external sources (averaging $1853), Federal Work-Study, 20 part-time jobs. ***Required forms:*** state, institutional, FAFSA; accepted: CSS Financial Aid PROFILE. ***Priority deadline:*** 8/1. ***Waivers:*** full or partial for senior citizens. ***Notification:*** continuous.
APPLYING Open admission. ***Options:*** Common Application, early entrance, deferred entrance, midyear entrance. ***Required:*** TOEFL for international students. ***Required for some:*** 3 years of high school math and science, 2 years of high school foreign language, SAT I or ACT. Test scores used for counseling/placement. ***Application deadline:*** 9/18. ***Notification:*** continuous.
APPLYING/TRANSFER ***Required:*** 3 years of high school math and science, some high school foreign language. ***Application deadline:*** 9/18. ***Notification:*** continuous.
CONTACT Mrs. Connie Boyd, Admissions Counselor, Bainbridge College, Bainbridge, GA 31717, 912-248-2500. ***E-mail:*** cboyd@catfish.bbc.peachnet.edu.

BAUDER COLLEGE
Atlanta, Georgia

UG Enrollment: 500	**Tuition & Fees: $7550**
Application Deadline: rolling	**Room Only: $3200**

GENERAL Proprietary, 2-year, primarily women. Awards transfer associate degrees. Founded 1964. ***Setting:*** suburban campus. ***Total enrollment:*** 500. ***Faculty:*** 40 (100% of full-time faculty have terminal degrees).
ENROLLMENT PROFILE 500 students: 97% women, 0% part-time, 15% state residents, 1% Hispanic, 19% African American.
FIRST-YEAR CLASS 300 total; 600 applied, 50% were accepted, 100% of whom enrolled.
ACADEMIC PROGRAM Core, honor code. Calendar: quarters. Academic remediation for entering students, summer session for credit, internships.
GENERAL DEGREE REQUIREMENTS 90 credit hours; 3 credit hours of math; computer course; internship.
MAJORS Business administration/commerce/management, fashion design and technology, fashion merchandising, interior design.
LIBRARY 4,000 books, 3 microform titles, 65 periodicals, 100 records, tapes, and CDs.
COMPUTERS ON CAMPUS 50 computers for student use in computer center, computer labs, classrooms, library. Staffed computer lab on campus provides training in use of computers, software.
COLLEGE LIFE Drama-theater group, student-run newspaper. ***Student services:*** personal-psychological counseling. ***Campus security:*** 24-hour emergency response devices and patrols.
HOUSING 342 college housing spaces available; 313 were occupied 1995–96. No special consideration for freshman housing applicants. Off-campus living permitted.
CAREER PLANNING ***Placement office:*** 2 full-time staff. ***Director:*** Mrs. Deborah Antonelli, Director of Placement, 404-237-7573. ***Services:*** job fairs, resume preparation, career counseling, careers library, job bank, job interviews.
AFTER GRADUATION 2% of students completing a degree program in 1994–95 went directly on to further study.
EXPENSES FOR 1995–96 Tuition: $7550 full-time. College room only: $3200.
FINANCIAL AID ***College-administered undergrad aid 1995–96:*** need-based scholarships, 7 non-need scholarships (average $1200), low-interest long-term loans from external sources, 15 part-time jobs. ***Required forms:*** institutional, FAFSA. ***Application deadline:*** continuous. ***Payment plans:*** installment, deferred payment.
APPLYING ***Option:*** midyear entrance. ***Recommended:*** SAT I or ACT. ***Application deadline:*** rolling. ***Notification:*** continuous.
APPLYING/TRANSFER ***Entrance:*** minimally difficult. ***Application deadline:*** rolling. ***Notification:*** continuous.
CONTACT Ms. Lillie Lanier, Assistant Director of Admissions, Bauder College, Atlanta, GA 30326, 404-237-7573 or toll-free 800-282-9497 (in-state), 800-241-3797 (out-of-state). ***Fax:*** 404-237-1642. College video available.

BRUNSWICK COLLEGE
Brunswick, Georgia

UG Enrollment: 2,085	**Tuition & Fees (GA Res): $1720**
Application Deadline: 9/20	**Room & Board: N/Avail**

GENERAL State-supported, 2-year, coed. Part of University System of Georgia. Awards transfer associate, terminal associate degrees. Founded 1961. ***Setting:*** 200-acre small-town campus with easy access to Jacksonville. ***Total enrollment:*** 2,085. ***Faculty:*** 79 (60 full-time, 19 part-time); student-faculty ratio is 22:1.
ENROLLMENT PROFILE 2,085 students from 8 states and territories, 5 other countries. 70% women, 30% men, 58% part-time, 94% state residents, 8% transferred in, 1% international, 48% 25 or older, 1% Native American, 1% Hispanic, 23% African American, 1% Asian American. ***Most popular recent majors:*** nursing, science, computer science.
FIRST-YEAR CLASS 910 total; 1,750 applied, 100% were accepted, 52% of whom enrolled. 10% from top 10% of their high school class, 25% from top quarter, 40% from top half.
ACADEMIC PROGRAM Core, honor code. Calendar: quarters. Academic remediation for entering students, advanced placement, summer session for credit, part-time degree program (daytime, evenings, weekends), adult/continuing education programs.
GENERAL DEGREE REQUIREMENTS 96 quarter hours; 10 quarter hours each of math and science.
MAJORS Accounting, agricultural sciences, art/fine arts, biology/biological sciences, business administration/commerce/management, chemistry, computer science, criminal justice, data processing, dental services, drafting and design, economics, education, electrical and electronics technologies, elementary education, (pre)engineering sequence, English, forestry, geography, geology, history, home economics, liberal arts/general studies, machine and tool technologies, marketing/retailing/merchandising, mathematics, mechanical engineering technology, medical laboratory technology, medical records services, medical secretarial studies, medical technology, nursing, occupational therapy, physical education, physical therapy, physician's assistant studies, physics, political science/government, psychology, radiological technology, recreation and leisure services, respiratory therapy, science, secretarial studies/office management, sociology, urban studies, welding technology.
LIBRARY 58,660 books, 503 periodicals, 10 CD-ROMs, 1,015 records, tapes, and CDs. Acquisition spending 1994–95: $139,219.
COMPUTERS ON CAMPUS 111 computers for student use in various labs provide access to e-mail, on-line services. Staffed computer lab on campus provides training in use of computers, software. Academic computing expenditure 1994–95: $40,000.
COLLEGE LIFE Drama-theater group, student-run newspaper. 60% vote in student government elections. ***Social organizations:*** 7 open to all. ***Most popular organizations:*** Association of Nursing Students, Minority Advisement and Social Development Association, Student Government Association. ***Student services:*** personal-psychological counseling. ***Campus security:*** 24-hour patrols, late-night transport-escort service.
HOUSING College housing not available.
ATHLETICS Member NJCAA. ***Intercollegiate:*** basketball M(s), tennis M(s). ***Intramural:*** basketball, tennis, volleyball. ***Contact:*** Mr. Gerald Cox, Athletic Director, 912-262-3299.
CAREER PLANNING ***Placement office:*** 1 full-time staff; $45,267 operating expenditure 1994–95. ***Director:*** Ms. C. A. Lee, Director, Career Development, 912-262-3295. ***Services:*** resume preparation, career counseling.
EXPENSES FOR 1995–96 ***Application fee:*** $5. State resident tuition: $1540 full-time, $29 per quarter hour part-time. Nonresident tuition: $4744 full-time, $96 per quarter hour part-time. Full-time mandatory fees: $180.
FINANCIAL AID ***College-administered undergrad aid 1995–96:*** 50 need-based scholarships (average $500), 100 non-need scholarships (average $800), short-term loans (average $100), low-interest long-term loans from external sources (average $1500), Federal Work-Study, 40 part-time jobs. ***Required forms:*** CSS Financial Aid PROFILE, institutional, FAFSA. ***Priority deadline:*** 9/1.

Peterson's Guide to Two-Year Colleges 1997 267

Georgia

Brunswick College (continued)
APPLYING Open admission except for nursing program. *Option:* deferred entrance. *Required:* school transcript, minimum 2.0 GPA, 3 years of high school math and science, 2 years of high school foreign language, SAT I or ACT, TOEFL for international students. Test scores used for admission and counseling/placement. *Application deadline:* 9/20. *Notification:* continuous. Preference given to state residents.
APPLYING/TRANSFER *Required:* standardized test scores, high school transcript, college transcript, minimum 2.0 college GPA, minimum 2.0 high school GPA. *Required for some:* 3 years of high school math and science, 2 years of high school foreign language. *Entrance:* minimally difficult. *Application deadline:* 9/20. *Notification:* continuous.
CONTACT Dr. Molly DeHart, Director of Admissions/Registrar, Brunswick College, Brunswick, GA 31520-3644, 912-264-7253 or toll-free 800-675-7235. College video available.

CHATTAHOOCHEE TECHNICAL INSTITUTE
Marietta, Georgia

UG Enrollment: 1,930	Tuition & Fees (GA Res): $825
Application Deadline: rolling	Room & Board: N/Avail

GENERAL State-supported, 2-year, coed. Part of Georgia Department of Technical and Adult Education. Awards certificates, diplomas, terminal associate degrees. Founded 1961. *Setting:* suburban campus with easy access to Atlanta. *Total enrollment:* 1,930. *Faculty:* 76 (50 full-time, 2% with terminal degrees, 26 part-time).
ENROLLMENT PROFILE 1,930 students: 65% part-time, 90% state residents, 25% transferred in.
FIRST-YEAR CLASS 1,802 applied, 100% were accepted.
ACADEMIC PROGRAM Core, honor code. Calendar: quarters. 34 courses offered in 1995-96. Services for LD students, self-designed majors, tutorials, part-time degree program (daytime, evenings, summer), internships.
GENERAL DEGREE REQUIREMENTS 90 credit hours; math requirement varies according to program; computer course for most majors; internship (some majors).
MAJORS Accounting, automotive technologies, biomedical technologies, business administration/commerce/management, computer programming, computer technologies, corrections, data processing, electrical engineering technology, electromechanical technology, law enforcement/police sciences, marketing/retailing/merchandising, word processing.
LIBRARY 10,000 books, 194 periodicals.
COMPUTERS ON CAMPUS 200 computers for student use in computer labs, learning resource center, classrooms provide access to main academic computer. Staffed computer lab on campus provides training in use of computers, software.
COLLEGE LIFE 30% vote in student government elections. *Social organizations:* 4 open to all. *Most popular organizations:* Student Government, Vocational Industrial Clubs of America, Institute for Electrical and Electronic Engineers. *Student services:* personal-psychological counseling. *Campus security:* part-time day and full-time evening security.
HOUSING College housing not available.
CAREER PLANNING *Placement office:* 2 full-time staff. *Director:* Ms. Lucylle Shelton, Director of Career Services, 770-528-4515. *Services:* job fairs, resume preparation, resume referral, career counseling, careers library, job bank, job interviews.
EXPENSES FOR 1995-96 *Application fee:* $15. State resident tuition: $756 full-time, $21 per credit hour part-time. Nonresident tuition: $1512 full-time, $42 per credit hour part-time. Part-time mandatory fees: $23 per quarter. Full-time mandatory fees: $69.
FINANCIAL AID *College-administered undergrad aid 1995-96:* 860 need-based scholarships (average $1575), 5 non-need scholarships (average $650), Federal Work-Study. *Required forms:* state, institutional, FAFSA; accepted: CSS Financial Aid PROFILE. *Priority deadline:* 5/1.
APPLYING Open admission. *Options:* early entrance, deferred entrance. *Required:* TOEFL for international students. *Required for some:* school transcript, ACT ASSET. Test scores used for counseling/placement. *Application deadline:* rolling.
APPLYING/TRANSFER *Required:* college transcript. *Entrance:* noncompetitive. *Application deadline:* rolling. *Contact:* Mrs. Anita Martin, Director of Admissions and Registrar, 770-528-4545.
CONTACT Mrs. Anita Martin, Director of Admissions and Registrar, Chattahoochee Technical Institute, Marietta, GA 30060, 770-528-4545.

COLUMBUS TECHNICAL INSTITUTE
Columbus, Georgia

UG Enrollment: 1,964	Tuition & Fees (GA Res): $786
Application Deadline: N/R	Room & Board: N/Avail

GENERAL State-supported, 2-year, specialized. Awards certificates, diplomas, terminal associate degrees. *Total enrollment:* 1,964.
ENROLLMENT PROFILE 1,964 students.
GENERAL DEGREE REQUIREMENTS 100 credit hours; 1 course each in math and science; computer course (varies by major).
MAJORS Accounting, mechanical engineering technology, secretarial studies/office management.
EXPENSES FOR 1995-96 State resident tuition: $756 full-time, $21 per credit part-time. Nonresident tuition: $3024 full-time, $84 per credit part-time. Full-time mandatory fees: $30.
APPLYING *Required:* school transcript, SAT I or ACT. *Required for some:* recommendations, interview. Test scores used for admission.
CONTACT Mr. Alfred West, Director of Admissions, Columbus Technical Institute, Columbus, GA 31904-6572, 706-649-1848.

DALTON COLLEGE
Dalton, Georgia

UG Enrollment: 3,172	Tuition & Fees (GA Res): $1380
Application Deadline: rolling	Room & Board: N/Avail

GENERAL State-supported, 2-year, coed. Part of University System of Georgia. Awards certificates, transfer associate, terminal associate degrees. Founded 1963. *Setting:* 130-acre small-town campus. *Total enrollment:* 3,172. *Faculty:* 109 (93 full-time, 75% with terminal degrees, 16 part-time); student-faculty ratio is 29:1.
ENROLLMENT PROFILE 3,172 students from 3 states and territories. 59% women, 54% part-time, 99% state residents, 3% transferred in, 0% international, 33% 25 or older, 1% Native American, 1% Hispanic, 2% African American, 1% Asian American. *Areas of study chosen:* 25% health professions and related sciences, 22% business management and administrative services, 15% liberal arts/general studies, 14% vocational and home economics, 9% education, 6% social sciences. *Most popular recent majors:* liberal arts/general studies, business administration/commerce/management, nursing.
FIRST-YEAR CLASS 1,200 total. Of the students who applied, 92% were accepted, 88% of whom enrolled.
ACADEMIC PROGRAM Core, honor code. Calendar: quarters. Academic remediation for entering students, services for LD students, advanced placement, summer session for credit, part-time degree program (daytime, evenings, summer), adult/continuing education programs.
GENERAL DEGREE REQUIREMENTS 90 quarter hours; 1 math course; 2 science courses; foreign language requirement varies according to program.
MAJORS Accounting, agricultural sciences, biology/biological sciences, business administration/commerce/management, business education, chemistry, computer programming, computer science, computer technologies, criminal justice, dental services, drafting and design, early childhood education, economics, education, electrical and electronics technologies, elementary education, (pre)engineering sequence, English, finance/banking, forestry, geology, health education, history, home economics, journalism, liberal arts/general studies, marketing/retailing/merchandising, mathematics, medical laboratory technology, medical records services, medical technology, natural sciences, nursing, occupational therapy, physical education, physical therapy, physician's assistant studies, physics, political science/government, psychology, respiratory therapy, science, secretarial studies/office management, social work, sociology, speech/rhetoric/public address/debate, vocational education.
LIBRARY Dalton College Library with 135,890 books, 4,607 microform titles, 707 periodicals, 2 on-line bibliographic services, 41 CD-ROMs, 4,026 records, tapes, and CDs.
COMPUTERS ON CAMPUS Computers for student use in computer center, computer labs, classrooms, library. Staffed computer lab on campus.
COLLEGE LIFE Choral group. 70% vote in student government elections. *Social organizations:* 19 open to all. *Most popular organizations:* Baptist Student Union, Outdoor Adventure Club, College Bowl, Secretarial Science Club. *Major annual events:* Club Registration, Orientation Entertainment, "For the Heck of It" Cookout. *Campus security:* 24-hour patrols.
HOUSING College housing not available.
ATHLETICS *Intercollegiate:* golf M, tennis M. *Intramural:* basketball, football, racquetball, swimming and diving, tennis, volleyball, weight lifting.
CAREER PLANNING *Placement office:* 2 full-time, 1 part-time staff. *Director:* Ms. Sylvia Graves, Director of Financial Aid, 706-272-4545. *Service:* career counseling.
EXPENSES FOR 1996-97 State resident tuition: $1350 full-time, $30 per quarter hour part-time. Nonresident tuition: $4995 full-time, $111 per quarter hour part-time. Part-time mandatory fees per quarter (5 to 11 quarter hours): $10. Full-time mandatory fees: $30.
FINANCIAL AID *College-administered undergrad aid 1995-96:* 30 need-based scholarships (average $200), 214 non-need scholarships (average $500), low-interest long-term loans from external sources (average $2625), Federal Work-Study, part-time jobs. *Required forms:* institutional, FAFSA, financial aid transcript and verification worksheet (for transfers); required for some: state; accepted: CSS Financial Aid PROFILE. *Priority deadline:* 6/1. *Waivers:* full or partial for senior citizens.
APPLYING Open admission. *Option:* early entrance. *Required:* TOEFL for international students. *Required for some:* 3 years of high school math and science, 2 years of high school foreign language, SAT I, SAT II Subject Tests. Test scores used for counseling/placement. *Application deadline:* rolling. *Notification:* continuous.
APPLYING/TRANSFER *Required for some:* standardized test scores. *Entrance:* noncompetitive. *Application deadline:* rolling. *Notification:* continuous. *Contact:* Ms. Angela Wheeler, Assistant Director of Admissions, 706-272-4436.
CONTACT Dr. David F. Hay, Director of Admissions/Registrar, Dalton College, Dalton, GA 30720-3797, 706-272-4436.

DARTON COLLEGE
Albany, Georgia

UG Enrollment: 2,635	Tuition & Fees (GA Res): $1140
Application Deadline: 8/27	Room & Board: N/Avail

GENERAL State-supported, 2-year, coed. Part of University System of Georgia. Awards transfer associate, terminal associate degrees. Founded 1965. *Setting:* 185-acre suburban campus. *Educational spending 1994-95:* $1861 per undergrad. *Total enrollment:* 2,635. *Faculty:* 152 (72 full-time, 31% with terminal degrees, 80 part-time); student-faculty ratio is 24:1.
ENROLLMENT PROFILE 2,635 students: 69% women, 31% men, 52% part-time, 95% state residents, 5% transferred in, 30% have need-based financial aid, 30% have non-need-based financial aid, 41% 25 or older, 1% Hispanic, 27% African American, 1% Asian American. *Areas of study chosen:* 30% health professions and related sciences, 8% social sciences, 7% business management and administrative services, 6% education, 5% communications and journalism, 5% fine arts, 3% engineering and applied sciences, 2% computer and information sciences, 2% physical sciences, 2% premed, 2% psychology, 1% biological and life sciences, 1% performing arts, 1% prevet. *Most popular recent majors:* nursing, business administration/commerce/management, early childhood education.
FIRST-YEAR CLASS 700 total; 1,379 applied, 99% were accepted, 51% of whom enrolled. 5% from top 10% of their high school class, 15% from top quarter, 40% from top half.

ACADEMIC PROGRAM Core, transfer curriculum. Calendar: quarters. Academic remediation for entering students, services for LD students, advanced placement, self-designed majors, honors program, summer session for credit, part-time degree program (daytime, evenings), adult/continuing education programs, co-op programs. ROTC: Army (c).
GENERAL DEGREE REQUIREMENTS 90 quarter hours; computer course for most majors.
MAJORS Accounting, agricultural sciences, anthropology, art/fine arts, biology/biological sciences, business administration/commerce/management, business economics, business education, chemistry, computer programming, computer science, corrections, criminal justice, data processing, dental services, early childhood education, economics, education, elementary education, emergency medical technology, engineering (general), (pre)engineering sequence, engineering technology, English, forestry, geography, health education, history, information science, journalism, laboratory technologies, legal secretarial studies, liberal arts/general studies, marketing/retailing/merchandising, mathematics, medical laboratory technology, medical records services, medical secretarial studies, music, nursing, pharmacy/pharmaceutical sciences, philosophy, physical education, physician's assistant studies, physics, political science/government, psychology, public administration, radiological sciences, radiological technology, respiratory therapy, secretarial studies/office management, sociology, speech/rhetoric/public address/debate, theater arts/drama.
LIBRARY Weatherbee Learning Resources Center with 67,507 books, 7,769 microform titles, 773 periodicals, 2,188 records, tapes, and CDs.
COMPUTERS ON CAMPUS Computer purchase plan available. 350 computers for student use in computer center, computer labs, classroom labs, library provide access to off-campus computing facilities, e-mail, Internet. Staffed computer lab on campus provides training in use of computers, software.
COLLEGE LIFE Drama-theater group, choral group. ***Student services:*** personal-psychological counseling, women's center. ***Campus security:*** student patrols, late-night transport-escort service.
HOUSING College housing not available.
ATHLETICS ***Intercollegiate:*** baseball M, basketball W, golf M/W, softball W, tennis M/W. ***Intramural:*** badminton, basketball, bowling, football, volleyball. ***Contact:*** Ms. Nancy Abraham, Athletic Director, 912-430-6796.
CAREER PLANNING ***Placement office:*** 4 part-time staff. ***Director:*** Ms. Jane Runge, Director, Career Development, 912-430-6865. ***Services:*** job fairs, resume preparation, career counseling, careers library, job bank.
AFTER GRADUATION 80% of students completing a degree program in 1994–95 went directly on to further study.
EXPENSES FOR 1995–96 ***Application fee:*** $5. State resident tuition: $1020 full-time, $29 per quarter hour part-time. Nonresident tuition: $3423 full-time, $67 per quarter hour part-time. Full-time mandatory fees: $120.
FINANCIAL AID ***College-administered undergrad aid 1995–96:*** 20 need-based scholarships (average $300), 175 non-need scholarships (average $240), low-interest long-term loans from external sources (average $750), 90 Federal Work-Study (averaging $1050), 110 part-time jobs. ***Required forms:*** CSS Financial Aid PROFILE, institutional; required for some: state; accepted: FAFSA. ***Priority deadline:*** 9/1.
APPLYING ***Option:*** early entrance. ***Required for some:*** 3 years of high school math and science, 2 years of high school foreign language, SAT I. Test scores used for counseling/placement. ***Application deadline:*** 8/27. ***Notification:*** continuous until 9/15.
APPLYING/TRANSFER ***Required for some:*** 3 years of high school math and science, 2 years of high school foreign language. ***Entrance:*** minimally difficult. ***Application deadline:*** 8/27. ***Notification:*** continuous until 9/15.
CONTACT Mr. Charles T. Edwards, Registrar, Darton College, Albany, GA 31707-3098, 912-430-6742. ***Fax:*** 912-430-2926. ***E-mail:*** darton@cavalier.dartnet.peachnet.edu.

DEKALB COLLEGE
Decatur, Georgia

UG Enrollment: 16,073 | **Tuition & Fees (GA Res): $1273**
Application Deadline: 8/13 | **Room & Board: N/Avail**

GENERAL State-supported, 2-year, coed. Part of University System of Georgia. Awards certificates, transfer associate, terminal associate degrees. Founded 1964. ***Setting:*** 100-acre suburban campus with easy access to Atlanta. ***Educational spending 1994–95:*** $1261 per undergrad. ***Total enrollment:*** 16,073. ***Faculty:*** 1,050 (335 full-time, 23% with terminal degrees, 715 part-time); student-faculty ratio is 20:1.
ENROLLMENT PROFILE 16,073 students from 14 states and territories, 102 other countries. 61% women, 65% part-time, 95% state residents, 6% transferred in, 4% international, 41% 25 or older, 1% Native American, 2% Hispanic, 30% African American, 6% Asian American. ***Areas of study chosen:*** 43% liberal arts/general studies, 18% health professions and related sciences, 15% business management and administrative services, 5% education, 3% computer and information sciences, 3% engineering and applied sciences, 3% psychology, 3% social sciences, 2% biological and life sciences, 1% agriculture, 1% communications and journalism, 1% English language/literature/letters, 1% fine arts, 1% foreign language and literature, 1% mathematics, 1% philosophy, 1% predentistry, 1% premed, 1% vocational and home economics. ***Most popular recent majors:*** business administration/commerce/management, nursing.
FIRST-YEAR CLASS 2,008 total; 2,934 applied, 100% were accepted, 68% of whom enrolled.
ACADEMIC PROGRAM Core, interdisciplinary curriculum, honor code. Calendar: quarters. Academic remediation for entering students, English as a second language program offered during academic year, services for LD students, advanced placement, honors program, summer session for credit, part-time degree program (daytime, evenings, weekends, summer), adult/continuing education programs. ROTC: Army (c).
GENERAL DEGREE REQUIREMENTS 100 credit hours; computer course for business administration majors.
MAJORS Accounting, applied art, art/fine arts, automotive technologies, behavioral sciences, broadcasting, business administration/commerce/management, business economics, business education, business machine technologies, chemistry, child care/child and family studies, computer programming, computer science, computer technologies, data processing, deaf interpreter training, dental services, early childhood education, economics, elementary education, emergency medical technology, engineering (general), (pre)engineering sequence, English, fashion merchandising, fire science, hotel and restaurant management, landscaping/grounds maintenance, marketing/retailing/merchandising, mechanical engineering technology, music, nursing, optometric/ophthalmic technologies, physical education, retail management, science, theater arts/drama.
LIBRARY DeKalb College Library with 185,458 books, 32,156 microform titles, 942 periodicals. Acquisition spending 1994–95: $488,088.
COMPUTERS ON CAMPUS 50 computers for student use in computer labs, classrooms, library provide access to main academic computer, e-mail, on-line services, Internet.
COLLEGE LIFE Orientation program (2 days). Drama-theater group, choral group, student-run newspaper, radio station. 10% vote in student government elections. ***Social organizations:*** 45 open to all. ***Student services:*** personal-psychological counseling. ***Campus security:*** 24-hour emergency response devices and patrols.
HOUSING College housing not available.
ATHLETICS Member NJCAA. ***Intercollegiate:*** baseball M(s), basketball M(s), soccer M(s)/W(s), softball W, tennis M(s)/W(s), volleyball W. ***Intramural:*** basketball. ***Contact:*** Mr. Gregory Ward, Athletic Director, 404-551-3128.
CAREER PLANNING ***Placement office:*** 15 full-time staff. ***Director:*** Ms. Marjorie Cowan, Coordinator, Access Center, 404-244-5017. ***Service:*** career counseling.
EXPENSES FOR 1995–96 State resident tuition: $1150 full-time, $23 per credit hour part-time. Nonresident tuition: $3463 full-time, $69 per credit hour part-time. Part-time mandatory fees: $41 per quarter. Full-time mandatory fees: $123.
FINANCIAL AID ***College-administered undergrad aid 1995–96:*** 2,805 need-based scholarships (averaging $1895), non-need scholarships, Federal Work-Study, 348 part-time jobs. ***Required forms:*** CSS Financial Aid PROFILE, institutional, FAFSA. ***Application deadline:*** 7/1.
APPLYING ***Options:*** early entrance, midyear entrance. ***Required:*** school transcript, 3 years of high school math and science, some high school foreign language, SAT I or ACT, TOEFL for international students. Test scores used for admission. ***Application deadline:*** 8/13. ***Notification:*** continuous.
APPLYING/TRANSFER ***Required:*** college transcript. ***Recommended:*** high school transcript. ***Entrance:*** minimally difficult. ***Application deadline:*** 8/13. ***Notification:*** continuous.
CONTACT Dr. William C. Crews, Vice President, DeKalb College, 555 North Indian Creek Drive, Clarkston, GA 30021-2396, 404-299-4564. ***Fax:*** 404-299-4574.

DEKALB TECHNICAL INSTITUTE
Clarkston, Georgia

UG Enrollment: 4,347 | **Tuition & Fees (GA Res): $336**
Application Deadline: N/R | **Room & Board: N/Avail**

GENERAL State-supported, 2-year. Awards certificates, diplomas, terminal associate degrees. ***Setting:*** suburban campus with easy access to Atlanta. ***Total enrollment:*** 4,347. ***Faculty:*** 492 (92 full-time, 400 part-time).
ENROLLMENT PROFILE 4,347 students.
FIRST-YEAR CLASS 312 total. Of the students who applied, 100% were accepted.
ACADEMIC PROGRAM Calendar: quarters.
GENERAL DEGREE REQUIREMENTS 100 credit hours; 1 math course; computer course.
MAJORS Accounting, automotive technologies, computer programming, computer technologies, drafting and design, electromechanical technology, emergency medical technology, engineering technology, fashion merchandising, legal secretarial studies, marketing/retailing/merchandising, medical laboratory technology, optometric/ophthalmic technologies.
EXPENSES FOR 1996–97 ***Application fee:*** $15. State resident tuition: $756 full-time, $21 per credit hour part-time. Nonresident tuition: $1512 full-time, $42 per credit hour part-time. Part-time mandatory fees: $42 per quarter. Full-time mandatory fees: $126.
FINANCIAL AID ***College-administered undergrad aid 1995–96:*** non-need scholarships. ***Acceptable forms:*** state.
APPLYING Open admission.
CONTACT Mr. Larry Teems, Dean of Student Services, DeKalb Technical Institute, Clarkston, GA 30021, 404-297-9522.

EAST GEORGIA COLLEGE
Swainsboro, Georgia

UG Enrollment: 905 | **Tuition & Fees (GA Res): $1350**
Application Deadline: rolling | **Room & Board: N/Avail**

GENERAL State-supported, 2-year, coed. Part of University System of Georgia. Awards transfer associate, terminal associate degrees. Founded 1973. ***Setting:*** 207-acre rural campus. ***Endowment:*** $32,000. ***Educational spending 1994–95:*** $1211 per undergrad. ***Total enrollment:*** 905. ***Faculty:*** 46 (21 full-time, 65% with terminal degrees, 25 part-time). ***Notable Alumni:*** Edith Pundt, president of Bank of Wadley; Richard McNeely, attorney; Barbara Jordan, principal, Wadley Middle School; Michael Wells, pharmacist; Bill Mitchell, director of research and development at Oxford Industries.
ENROLLMENT PROFILE 905 students from 5 states and territories. 65% women, 35% men, 21% part-time, 98% state residents, 5% transferred in, 44% have need-based financial aid, 5% have non-need-based financial aid, 0% international, 4% 25 or older, 1% Native American, 1% Hispanic, 20% African American, 1% Asian American. ***Most popular recent majors:*** education, business administration/commerce/management.
FIRST-YEAR CLASS 236 total; 416 applied, 81% were accepted, 70% of whom enrolled.
ACADEMIC PROGRAM Core, honor code. Calendar: quarters. Academic remediation for entering students, services for LD students, advanced placement, summer session for credit, part-time degree program (daytime, evenings, summer), adult/continuing education programs.
GENERAL DEGREE REQUIREMENTS 99 quarter hours; 20 quarter hours of math/science.
MAJORS Agricultural sciences, anthropology, art/fine arts, biology/biological sciences, business administration/commerce/management, business education, chemistry, criminal justice, education, elementary education, English, geology, health education, history, home economics education, liberal arts/general studies, mathematics, nursing, physical education, political science/government, psychology, recreation and leisure services, sociology.
LIBRARY East Georgia College Library with 42,000 books, 97 microform titles, 203 periodicals, 50 on-line bibliographic services, 1 CD-ROM, 988 records, tapes, and CDs. Acquisition spending 1994–95: $39,289.

East Georgia College (continued)

COMPUTERS ON CAMPUS 65 computers for student use in computer center, classrooms provide access to Internet. Staffed computer lab on campus. Academic computing expenditure 1994–95: $46,721.

COLLEGE LIFE Drama-theater group, choral group, student-run newspaper. 51% vote in student government elections. ***Social organizations:*** 5 open to all. ***Most popular organizations:*** Hoopee Bird, Student Government, Yearbook, Gamma Beta Phi, Wiregrass. ***Major annual events:*** Free Food Days, Honors Day, Convocation. ***Student services:*** personal-psychological counseling. ***Campus security:*** 24-hour patrols.

HOUSING College housing not available.

ATHLETICS ***Intramural:*** archery, badminton, basketball, football, golf, softball, table tennis (Ping-Pong), tennis, volleyball, weight lifting.

CAREER PLANNING ***Placement office:*** 1 full-time staff. ***Director:*** Mr. Bennie Brinson, Director of Student Services, 912-237-7831 Ext. 1023. ***Service:*** career counseling.

AFTER GRADUATION 85% of students completing a degree program in 1994–95 went directly on to further study.

EXPENSES FOR 1996–97 State resident tuition: $1305 full-time, $29 per quarter hour part-time. Nonresident tuition: $4320 full-time, $96 per quarter hour part-time. Part-time mandatory fees: $15 per quarter. Full-time mandatory fees: $45.

FINANCIAL AID ***College-administered undergrad aid 1995–96:*** 94 need-based scholarships (average $414), 34 non-need scholarships (average $638), short-term loans (average $193), low-interest long-term loans from external sources (average $1749), Federal Work-Study, 34 part-time jobs. ***Required forms:*** FAFSA; required for some: institutional; accepted: CSS Financial Aid PROFILE, AFSSA-CSX. ***Priority deadline:*** 8/1.

APPLYING ***Options:*** early entrance, deferred entrance. ***Required:*** school transcript. ***Recommended:*** 3 years of high school math and science, some high school foreign language. ***Required for some:*** SAT I or ACT, TOEFL for international students. Test scores used for counseling/placement. ***Application deadline:*** rolling. ***Notification:*** continuous.

APPLYING/TRANSFER ***Required:*** high school transcript. ***Recommended:*** 3 years of high school math and science, some high school foreign language. ***Entrance:*** minimally difficult. ***Application deadline:*** rolling. ***Notification:*** continuous. ***Contact:*** Ms. Denise Griffin, Admissions Specialist, 912-237-7831 Ext. 1002.

CONTACT Ms. Denise Griffin, Admissions Specialist, East Georgia College, Swainsboro, GA 30401-2699, 912-237-7831 Ext. 1002. ***E-mail:*** smith@mail.ega.peachnet.edu.

EMORY UNIVERSITY, OXFORD COLLEGE
Oxford, Georgia

UG Enrollment: 600	**Tuition & Fees: $14,150**
Application Deadline: rolling	**Room & Board: $4750**

GENERAL Independent Methodist, 2-year, coed. Part of Emory University. Awards transfer associate degrees. Founded 1836. ***Setting:*** 150-acre small-town campus with easy access to Atlanta. ***Total enrollment:*** 600. ***Faculty:*** 43 (39 full-time, 4 part-time); student-faculty ratio is 10:1.

ENROLLMENT PROFILE 600 students from 32 states and territories, 9 other countries. 62% women, 1% part-time, 61% state residents, 95% live on campus, 2% transferred in, 3% international, 0% 25 or older, 4% Hispanic, 11% African American, 6% Asian American.

FIRST-YEAR CLASS 329 total; 729 applied, 79% were accepted, 57% of whom enrolled. 4 National Merit Scholars.

ACADEMIC PROGRAM Core. Calendar: semesters. Services for LD students, advanced placement, self-designed majors, tutorials, summer session for credit, internships. Study abroad in France, Spain, Mexico, Scotland, England, Israel, Austria, Italy, Cyprus.

GENERAL DEGREE REQUIREMENTS 68 semester hours; 1 math course; 2 lab science courses.

MAJOR Liberal arts/general studies.

LIBRARY Hoke O'Kelly Library with 67,366 books, 446 microform titles, 327 periodicals, 15 CD-ROMs, 877 records, tapes, and CDs.

COMPUTERS ON CAMPUS 86 computers for student use in computer center, computer labs, learning resource center, classroom buildings, classrooms, library provide access to e-mail, Internet. Staffed computer lab on campus provides training in use of computers, software.

NOTEWORTHY RESEARCH FACILITIES Carter Presidential Library, Yerkes Primate Center.

COLLEGE LIFE Orientation program (4 days, $100, parents included). Drama-theater group, choral group, student-run newspaper. ***Most popular organizations:*** Drama Club, Oxford Fellowship. ***Major annual events:*** Fall Retreat, Oxford Day, Leadership at Oxford. ***Student services:*** health clinic, personal-psychological counseling. ***Campus security:*** late-night transport-escort service.

HOUSING 517 college housing spaces available; 505 were occupied 1995–96. Freshmen guaranteed college housing. On-campus residence required through sophomore year. ***Options:*** freshmen-only, coed housing available. Resident assistants live in dorms.

ATHLETICS ***Intramural:*** badminton, basketball, cross-country running, football, golf, soccer, softball, swimming and diving, table tennis (Ping-Pong), tennis, track and field, volleyball, water polo, weight lifting, wrestling. ***Contact:*** Mr. Seth Bussey, Director of Intramurals, 770-784-8355.

AFTER GRADUATION 99% of students completing a degree program in 1994–95 went directly on to further study.

EXPENSES FOR 1996–97 ***Application fee:*** $35. Comprehensive fee of $18,900 includes full-time tuition ($14,000), mandatory fees ($150), and college room and board ($4750). College room only: $3070. Part-time tuition: $583 per semester hour.

FINANCIAL AID ***College-administered undergrad aid 1995–96:*** 165 need-based scholarships (average $5450), 51 non-need scholarships (average $6070), low-interest long-term loans from college funds (average $7100), loans from external sources (average $2215), Federal Work-Study, 80 part-time jobs. ***Required forms:*** CSS Financial Aid PROFILE; required for some: state; accepted: FAFSA. ***Priority deadline:*** 4/1. ***Payment plan:*** tuition prepayment. ***Waivers:*** full or partial for employees or children of employees. ***Notification:*** 4/15.

APPLYING ***Options:*** early entrance, deferred entrance. ***Required:*** school transcript, 3 years of high school math, SAT I or ACT, TOEFL for international students. ***Recommended:*** essay, minimum 3.0 GPA, 3 years of high school science, 2 years of high school foreign language, SAT II Subject Tests. Test scores used for admission. ***Application deadline:*** rolling. ***Notification:*** continuous.

APPLYING/TRANSFER ***Required:*** 3 years of high school math. ***Recommended:*** 3 years of high school science, 2 years of high school foreign language, minimum 3.0 high school GPA. ***Entrance:*** moderately difficult. ***Application deadline:*** rolling. ***Notification:*** continuous.

CONTACT Ms. Jennifer B. Taylor, Director of Admissions and Financial Aid, Emory University, Oxford College, Oxford, GA 30267, 770-784-8328 or toll-free 800-723-8328 (in-state). ***Fax:*** 770-784-8359.

FLOYD COLLEGE
Rome, Georgia

UG Enrollment: 3,048	**Tuition & Fees (GA Res): $1089**
Application Deadline: rolling	**Room & Board: N/Avail**

GENERAL State-supported, 2-year, coed. Part of University System of Georgia. Awards transfer associate, terminal associate degrees. Founded 1970. ***Setting:*** 212-acre rural campus with easy access to Atlanta. ***Educational spending 1994–95:*** $1484 per undergrad. ***Total enrollment:*** 3,048. ***Faculty:*** 66 (51 full-time, 56% with terminal degrees, 15 part-time).

ENROLLMENT PROFILE 3,048 students from 2 states and territories, 2 other countries. 65% women, 47% part-time, 98% state residents, 20% transferred in, 1% international, 1% Native American, 1% Hispanic, 8% African American, 1% Asian American. ***Most popular recent majors:*** nursing, business administration/commerce/management.

FIRST-YEAR CLASS 385 total; 617 applied, 100% were accepted, 55% of whom enrolled. 3 class presidents, 1 valedictorian.

ACADEMIC PROGRAM Core. Calendar: quarters. Academic remediation for entering students, services for LD students, advanced placement, Freshman Honors College, honors program, summer session for credit, part-time degree program (daytime, evenings, summer).

GENERAL DEGREE REQUIREMENTS 102 quarter hours; 1 math course; computer course.

MAJORS Art/fine arts, automotive technologies, business administration/commerce/management, computer information systems, computer programming, deaf interpreter training, dental services, electronics engineering technology, emergency medical technology, engineering and applied sciences, heating/refrigeration/air conditioning, hotel and restaurant management, human services, law enforcement/police sciences, liberal arts/general studies, nursing, paralegal studies, physician's assistant studies, radiological technology, respiratory therapy, science, secretarial studies/office management.

LIBRARY Floyd College Library with 48,000 books, 200 microform titles, 350 periodicals, 500 records, tapes, and CDs. Acquisition spending 1994–95: $820,389.

COMPUTERS ON CAMPUS 75 computers for student use in computer center, library provide access to main academic computer, on-line services. Staffed computer lab on campus provides training in use of computers. Academic computing expenditure 1994–95: $99,006.

COLLEGE LIFE Student-run newspaper. 25% vote in student government elections. ***Most popular organizations:*** Scholars Bowl, Baptist Student Union, Health, Physical Education, and Recreation Club. ***Major annual events:*** Family Day, Health Week, Mister/Miss Floyd College Dance. ***Campus security:*** 24-hour patrols.

HOUSING College housing not available.

ATHLETICS ***Intramural:*** basketball, bowling, football, tennis, volleyball.

CAREER PLANNING ***Placement office:*** 2 full-time staff. ***Director:*** Ms. Phyllis Weatherly, Director of Guidance Services, 706-295-6336. ***Services:*** resume preparation, career counseling, careers library.

AFTER GRADUATION 39% of students completing a degree program in 1994–95 went directly on to further study.

EXPENSES FOR 1995–96 State resident tuition: $1044 full-time, $29 per quarter hour part-time. Nonresident tuition: $3420 full-time, $96 per quarter hour part-time. Part-time mandatory fees: $15 per quarter. Full-time mandatory fees: $45.

FINANCIAL AID ***College-administered undergrad aid 1995–96:*** need-based scholarships, non-need scholarships, low-interest long-term loans from external sources, Federal Work-Study, part-time jobs. ***Required forms:*** CSS Financial Aid PROFILE, state, institutional; required for some: FAFSA. ***Priority deadline:*** 6/30. ***Waivers:*** full or partial for senior citizens.

APPLYING Open admission. ***Required:*** school transcript, 3 years of high school math and science, 2 years of high school foreign language, TOEFL for international students. ***Recommended:*** minimum 2.0 GPA. ***Required for some:*** SAT I or ACT. Test scores used for admission and counseling/placement. ***Application deadline:*** rolling. ***Notification:*** continuous.

APPLYING/TRANSFER ***Required:*** 3 years of high school math and science, 2 years of high school foreign language. ***Application deadline:*** rolling. ***Notification:*** continuous.

CONTACT Mr. William P. Kerr, Chairman of Enrollment Management, Floyd College, Rome, GA 30162-1864, 706-295-6339 or toll-free 800-332-2406 (in-state). ***Fax:*** 706-295-6610. ***E-mail:*** pkern@jason.fc.peachnet.edu. College video available.

GAINESVILLE COLLEGE
Gainesville, Georgia

UG Enrollment: 2,646	**Tuition & Fees (GA Res): $1083**
Application Deadline: rolling	**Room & Board: N/Avail**

GENERAL State-supported, 2-year, coed. Part of University System of Georgia. Awards transfer associate, terminal associate degrees. Founded 1964. ***Setting:*** 150-acre small-town campus with easy access to Atlanta. ***Total enrollment:*** 2,646. ***Faculty:*** 102 (88 full-time, 33% with terminal degrees, 14 part-time); student-faculty ratio is 25:1.

ENROLLMENT PROFILE 2,646 students from 25 states and territories, 12 other countries. 59% women, 41% men, 40% part-time, 97% state residents, 20% transferred in, 1% international, 26% 25 or older, 1% Native American, 2% Hispanic, 4% African American, 1% Asian American. ***Most popular recent majors:*** business administration/commerce/management, education, science.

FIRST-YEAR CLASS 507 total; 686 applied, 87% were accepted, 85% of whom enrolled.

ACADEMIC PROGRAM Core, honor code. Calendar: quarters. Average class size 20 in required courses. Academic remediation for entering students, services for LD students, advanced placement, summer session for credit, part-time degree program (daytime, evenings, summer), adult/continuing education programs, internships.
GENERAL DEGREE REQUIREMENTS 90 quarter hours; 20 quarter hours of math/science; computer course for engineering, health, physical education, forestry, anthropology majors; internship (some majors).
MAJORS Accounting, agricultural sciences, anthropology, art education, art/fine arts, automotive technologies, biology/biological sciences, business administration/commerce/management, business education, chemistry, child care/child and family studies, computer science, criminal justice, dental services, early childhood education, education, electrical and electronics technologies, elementary education, engineering (general), engineering technology, English, forestry, geology, history, hotel and restaurant management, international business, journalism, liberal arts/general studies, marketing/retailing/merchandising, mathematics, medical laboratory technology, middle school education, music, music education, paralegal studies, physical education, physics, political science/government, poultry sciences, psychology, science, social work, sociology, speech/rhetoric/public address/debate, theater arts/drama, vocational education.
LIBRARY John Harrison Hosch Library with 63,194 books, 398 periodicals, 2,799 records, tapes, and CDs. Acquisition spending 1994–95: $51,111.
COMPUTERS ON CAMPUS 250 computers for student use in computer labs, research center, learning resource center, classrooms, library provide access to main academic computer, off-campus computing facilities, e-mail, on-line services, Internet. Staffed computer lab on campus provides training in use of computers, software. Academic computing expenditure 1994–95: $92,129.
COLLEGE LIFE Drama-theater group, choral group, student-run newspaper. 12% vote in student government elections. ***Social organizations:*** 26 open to all. ***Most popular organizations:*** Student Newspaper, Baptist Student Union, Student Government Association, Prelaw/Political Science Club. ***Major annual events:*** Field Day, Jazz on the Green, Honors Day. ***Student services:*** personal-psychological counseling. ***Campus security:*** 24-hour patrols.
HOUSING College housing not available.
ATHLETICS ***Intramural:*** badminton, basketball, bowling, football, golf, soccer, softball, tennis, volleyball, water polo.
CAREER PLANNING ***Placement office:*** 1 full-time, 4 part-time staff; $125,032 operating expenditure 1994–95. ***Director:*** Ms. Diane Carey-Bradley, Career Counselor, 770-718-3669. ***Services:*** job fairs, resume preparation, career counseling, careers library, job bank, job interviews. 50 organizations recruited on campus 1994–95.
AFTER GRADUATION 80% of students completing a degree program in 1994–95 went directly on to further study.
EXPENSES FOR 1995–96 ***Application fee:*** $15. State resident tuition: $1020 full-time, $29 per quarter hour part-time. Nonresident tuition: $3486 full-time, $96 per quarter hour part-time. Full-time mandatory fees: $63.
FINANCIAL AID ***College-administered undergrad aid 1995–96:*** 349 need-based scholarships (average $443), 276 non-need scholarships (average $350), low-interest long-term loans from external sources (average $2005), 53 Federal Work-Study (averaging $1800), 72 part-time jobs. ***Required forms:*** institutional, FAFSA. ***Priority deadline:*** 4/15. ***Waivers:*** full or partial for senior citizens. ***Notification:*** 7/15.
APPLYING Open admission. ***Option:*** early entrance. ***Required:*** 3 years of high school math and science, 2 years of high school foreign language, SAT I or ACT, TOEFL for international students. Test scores used for counseling/placement. ***Application deadline:*** rolling. ***Notification:*** continuous.
APPLYING/TRANSFER ***Required:*** 3 years of high school science, college transcript. ***Required for some:*** 2 years of high school foreign language. ***Entrance:*** noncompetitive. ***Application deadline:*** rolling. ***Notification:*** continuous. ***Contact:*** Ms. Carol Nobles, Director of Admissions, 770-718-3822.
CONTACT Ms. Carol Nobles, Director of Admissions, Gainesville College, Gainesville, GA 30503-1358, 770-718-3822.

GEORGIA MILITARY COLLEGE
Milledgeville, Georgia

UG Enrollment: 3,495	Tuition & Fees: $4153
Application Deadline: rolling	Room & Board: $3915

GENERAL State and locally supported, 2-year, coed. Awards transfer associate, terminal associate degrees. Founded 1879. ***Setting:*** 40-acre small-town campus. ***Total enrollment:*** 3,495. ***Faculty:*** 179 (33 full-time, 10% with terminal degrees, 146 part-time); student-faculty ratio is 14:1.
ENROLLMENT PROFILE 3,495 students from 29 states and territories, 4 other countries. 48% women, 61% part-time, 84% state residents, 13% transferred in, 70% have need-based financial aid, 20% have non-need-based financial aid, 1% international, 27% 25 or older, 1% Native American, 2% Hispanic, 41% African American, 1% Asian American. ***Most popular recent majors:*** liberal arts/general studies, business administration/commerce/management, communication.
FIRST-YEAR CLASS 1,925 total. Of the students who applied, 94% were accepted, 85% of whom enrolled.
ACADEMIC PROGRAM Core, honor code. Calendar: quarters. Academic remediation for entering students, advanced placement, summer session for credit, part-time degree program (evenings), external degree programs. Off-campus study at Georgia College. ROTC: Army.
GENERAL DEGREE REQUIREMENTS 90 quarter hours; 5 quarter hours of math; 10 quarter hours of lab science; computer course.
MAJORS Business administration/commerce/management, communication, criminal justice, engineering (general), engineering and applied sciences, (pre)engineering sequence, fire science, liberal arts/general studies, military science, nuclear technology, science.
LIBRARY Sibley-Cone Library with 20,000 books, 52 microform titles, 150 periodicals.
COMPUTERS ON CAMPUS 40 computers for student use in computer center, computer labs provide access to e-mail, on-line services. Staffed computer lab on campus provides training in use of computers, software.
COLLEGE LIFE Marching band, student-run newspaper. ***Major annual event:*** Parades. ***Student services:*** personal-psychological counseling. ***Campus security:*** 24-hour emergency response devices and patrols.
HOUSING 186 college housing spaces available; 124 were occupied 1995–96. Freshmen guaranteed college housing. On-campus residence required through sophomore year except for local residents or by special permission; ROTC required to live on campus. ***Option:*** coed housing available.
ATHLETICS Member NSCAA. ***Intercollegiate:*** football M(s), riflery M(s)/W(s). ***Intramural:*** basketball, cross-country running, football, golf, soccer, tennis, track and field, volleyball. ***Contact:*** Mr. Robert Nunn, Athletic Director, 912-454-2690.
CAREER PLANNING ***Service:*** career counseling.
EXPENSES FOR 1995–96 ***Application fee:*** $25. Comprehensive fee of $8068 includes full-time tuition ($3753), mandatory fees ($400), and college room and board ($3915). College room only: $1725. Part-time tuition: $69.50 per quarter hour.
FINANCIAL AID ***College-administered undergrad aid 1995–96:*** need-based scholarships (averaging $500), non-need scholarships, Federal Work-Study, 6 part-time jobs. ***Required forms:*** CSS Financial Aid PROFILE, FAFSA. ***Application deadline:*** continuous to 8/1.
APPLYING ***Options:*** early entrance, deferred entrance. ***Required:*** school transcript, TOEFL for international students. ***Recommended:*** SAT I or ACT. ***Required for some:*** SAT I or ACT. Test scores used for admission (for ROTC only) and counseling/placement. ***Application deadline:*** rolling.
APPLYING/TRANSFER ***Required:*** high school transcript. ***Recommended:*** standardized test scores. ***Required for some:*** standardized test scores. ***Entrance:*** minimally difficult. ***Application deadline:*** rolling.
CONTACT Capt. David Bill, Director of Recruiting, Georgia Military College, Milledgeville, GA 31061, 912-454-2707 or toll-free 800-342-0413. ***Fax:*** 912-454-2188. College video available.

GORDON COLLEGE
Barnesville, Georgia

UG Enrollment: 2,204	Tuition & Fees (GA Res): $1140
Application Deadline: 9/5	Room & Board: $2130

GENERAL State-supported, 2-year, coed. Part of University System of Georgia. Awards certificates, transfer associate, terminal associate degrees. Founded 1852. ***Setting:*** 125-acre small-town campus with easy access to Atlanta. ***Endowment:*** $2.1 million. ***Total enrollment:*** 2,204. ***Faculty:*** 115 (68 full-time, 54% with terminal degrees, 47 part-time); student-faculty ratio is 19:1.
ENROLLMENT PROFILE 2,204 students: 63% women, 37% men, 38% part-time, 99% state residents, 15% live on campus, 21% transferred in, 44% have need-based financial aid, 10% have non-need-based financial aid, 1% international, 26% 25 or older, 1% Native American, 1% Hispanic, 16% African American, 1% Asian American. ***Areas of study chosen:*** 32% health professions and related sciences, 12% business management and administrative services, 11% liberal arts/general studies, 7% education, 4% social sciences, 3% biological and life sciences, 3% psychology, 2% mathematics, 2% performing arts, 1% agriculture, 1% communications and journalism, 1% computer and information sciences, 1% English language/literature/letters, 1% fine arts, 1% foreign language and literature, 1% physical sciences. ***Most popular recent majors:*** nursing, business administration/commerce/management, education.
FIRST-YEAR CLASS 683 total; 808 applied, 98% were accepted, 86% of whom enrolled.
ACADEMIC PROGRAM Core. Calendar: quarters. 240 courses offered in 1995–96; average class size 29 in required courses. Academic remediation for entering students, services for LD students, advanced placement, tutorials, summer session for credit, part-time degree program (daytime, evenings, summer), adult/continuing education programs, co-op programs.
GENERAL DEGREE REQUIREMENTS 96 quarter hours; 1 college algebra course.
MAJORS Agricultural sciences, art/fine arts, behavioral sciences, biology/biological sciences, business administration/commerce/management, computer science, education, English, history, journalism, liberal arts/general studies, mathematics, nursing, physical sciences, political science/government, psychology, recreation and leisure services, science, secretarial studies/office management, sociology, Spanish, theater arts/drama.
LIBRARY Hightower Library with 72,619 books, 237 microform titles, 214 periodicals, 8 CD-ROMs, 2,113 records, tapes, and CDs. Acquisition spending 1994–95: $71,702.
COMPUTERS ON CAMPUS Student rooms linked to a campus network. 75 computers for student use in computer center, library. Staffed computer lab on campus provides training in use of computers, software. Academic computing expenditure 1994–95: $176,981.
COLLEGE LIFE Drama-theater group, choral group. ***Social organizations:*** 13 open to all. ***Most popular organizations:*** Explorers, Minority Advisement Program, Georgia Association of Nursing Students, Baptist Student Union, Phi Beta Lambda. ***Major annual events:*** Gordon Days, Homecoming, Spring Fling. ***Student services:*** personal-psychological counseling. ***Campus security:*** 24-hour patrols, late-night transport-escort service.
HOUSING 343 college housing spaces available; 341 were occupied 1995–96. No special consideration for freshman housing applicants. Off-campus living permitted. ***Option:*** single-sex (4 buildings) housing available. Resident assistants live in dorms.
ATHLETICS Member NJCAA. ***Intercollegiate:*** baseball M(s), soccer M(s), softball W(s), tennis W(s). ***Intramural:*** badminton, basketball, football, racquetball, soccer, softball, table tennis (Ping-Pong), tennis, volleyball. ***Contact:*** Dr. Katrina Tobin, Vice President for Student Affairs, 770-358-5056.
CAREER PLANNING ***Placement office:*** 1 part-time staff. ***Director:*** Dr. Katrina Tobin, Vice President for Student Affairs, 770-358-5056. ***Services:*** resume preparation, career counseling, careers library, job bank, job interviews.
AFTER GRADUATION 50% of students completing a degree program in 1994–95 went directly on to further study.
EXPENSES FOR 1995–96 State resident tuition: $1020 full-time, $29 per quarter hour part-time. Nonresident tuition: $3423 full-time, $96 per quarter hour part-time. Part-time mandatory fees: $40 per quarter. Full-time mandatory fees: $120. College room and board: $2130.
FINANCIAL AID ***College-administered undergrad aid 1995–96:*** 780 need-based scholarships (average $1357), 672 non-need scholarships (average $905), low-interest long-term loans from external sources (average $2074), 42 Federal Work-Study (averaging $1275), 47 part-time jobs. ***Required forms:*** institutional, FAFSA. ***Priority deadline:*** 6/1. ***Waivers:*** full or partial for senior citizens.
APPLYING Open admission. ***Options:*** early entrance, deferred entrance, midyear entrance. ***Required:*** SAT I or ACT. ***Required for some:*** 3 years of high school math and science, 2 years of high school foreign language. Test scores used for counseling/placement. ***Application deadline:*** 9/5.

Georgia

Gordon College (continued)
APPLYING/TRANSFER *Entrance:* noncompetitive. *Application deadline:* 9/5. *Contact:* Ms. Janet Adams, Registrar, 770-358-5000.
CONTACT Dr. Mary Jean Simmons, Director of Enrollment Services, Gordon College, Barnesville, GA 30204-1762, 770-358-5021 or toll-free 800-282-6504 (in-state). *E-mail:* steve_e@hawk.gdn.peachnet.edu. College video available.

GUPTON-JONES COLLEGE OF FUNERAL SERVICE
Decatur, Georgia

UG Enrollment: 325	Tuition & Fees: $5625
Application Deadline: rolling	Room & Board: N/Avail

GENERAL Independent, 2-year, specialized, coed. Part of Pierce Mortuary Colleges, Inc. Awards diplomas, terminal associate degrees. Founded 1920. *Setting:* 3-acre suburban campus with easy access to Atlanta. *Total enrollment:* 325. *Faculty:* 10 (8 full-time, 2 part-time); student-faculty ratio is 30:1.
ENROLLMENT PROFILE 325 students from 11 states and territories, 1 other country. 35% women, 40% state residents, 1% transferred in, 20% 25 or older, 0% Native American, 0% Hispanic, 40% African American, 0% Asian American.
FIRST-YEAR CLASS Of the students who applied, 100% were accepted, 71% of whom enrolled. 15% from top 10% of their high school class, 30% from top half.
ACADEMIC PROGRAM Core, honor code. Calendar: quarters. Academic remediation for entering students, summer session for credit.
GENERAL DEGREE REQUIREMENTS 107 quarter hours; 1 course in business math; 6 quarter hours of anatomy, 5 quarter hours each of chemistry and microbiology, 4 quarter hours of pathology; computer course.
MAJOR Funeral service.
LIBRARY Russell Millison Library with 3,500 books, 15 periodicals, 50 records, tapes, and CDs.
COMPUTERS ON CAMPUS 5 computers for student use in computer center.
COLLEGE LIFE 95% vote in student government elections. *Social organizations:* 1 national fraternity; 10% of eligible men are members.
HOUSING College housing not available.
CAREER PLANNING *Service:* career counseling.
EXPENSES FOR 1995–96 Tuition: $5600 full-time. Full-time mandatory fees: $25.
FINANCIAL AID College-administered undergrad aid 1995–96: low-interest long-term loans from external sources (averaging $2625). *Required forms:* FAFSA; accepted: CSS Financial Aid PROFILE, state. *Priority deadline:* 9/12.
APPLYING Open admission. *Application deadline:* rolling.
APPLYING/TRANSFER *Entrance:* noncompetitive.
CONTACT Ms. Beverly Wheaton, Registrar, Gupton-Jones College of Funeral Service, Decatur, GA 30035-4022, 404-593-2257.

GWINNETT TECHNICAL INSTITUTE
Lawrenceville, Georgia

UG Enrollment: 4,000	Tuition & Fees (GA Res): $1200
Application Deadline: N/R	Room & Board: N/Avail

GENERAL State-supported, 2-year, coed. Awards certificates, diplomas, terminal associate degrees. Founded 1984. *Setting:* 92-acre suburban campus with easy access to Atlanta. *Total enrollment:* 4,000. *Faculty:* 84 (all full-time, 15% with terminal degrees).
ENROLLMENT PROFILE 4,000 students: 52% women, 66% part-time, 98% state residents, 61% transferred in, 1% international, 62% 25 or older, 1% Native American, 7% Hispanic, 8% African American, 5% Asian American. *Areas of study chosen:* 25% engineering and applied sciences, 20% computer and information sciences, 16% health professions and related sciences. *Most popular recent majors:* computer science, horticulture.
FIRST-YEAR CLASS Of the students who applied, 60% were accepted, 75% of whom enrolled.
ACADEMIC PROGRAM Calendar: quarters. Academic remediation for entering students, English as a second language program offered during academic year, services for LD students, advanced placement, summer session for credit, part-time degree program (daytime, evenings), adult/continuing education programs.
GENERAL DEGREE REQUIREMENTS 98 quarter hours; math requirement varies according to program; computer course.
MAJORS Accounting, automotive technologies, computer programming, computer science, construction management, dental services, drafting and design, electrical and electronics technologies, emergency medical technology, fashion merchandising, horticulture, hotel and restaurant management, interior design, machine and tool technologies, management information systems, marketing/retailing/merchandising, medical assistant technologies, ornamental horticulture, photography, physical therapy, radiological technology, respiratory therapy, secretarial studies/office management, telecommunications, tourism and travel.
LIBRARY Gwinnett Technical Institute Media Center with 16,800 books, 269 periodicals, 1 on-line bibliographic service, 4 CD-ROMs, 430 records, tapes, and CDs.
COMPUTERS ON CAMPUS 264 computers for student use in computer labs, library provide access to off-campus computing facilities, on-line services. Staffed computer lab on campus provides training in use of computers, software.
COLLEGE LIFE *Major annual events:* Fall Festival, Spring Fling, Awards Day. *Student services:* personal-psychological counseling. *Campus security:* patrols by campus police.
HOUSING College housing not available.
EXPENSES FOR 1996–97 State resident tuition: $1200 full-time, $25 per quarter hour part-time. Nonresident tuition: $2208 full-time, $46 per quarter hour part-time.
FINANCIAL AID *College-administered undergrad aid 1995–96:* 25 need-based scholarships (average $500), 505 non-need scholarships (average $1200), low-interest long-term loans from external sources (average $1968), Federal Work-Study. *Required forms:* FAFSA; accepted: CSS Financial Aid PROFILE. *Priority deadline:* 7/1. *Waivers:* full or partial for senior citizens.

APPLYING *Required:* school transcript, SAT I or ACT, ACT ASSET. Test scores used for counseling/placement.
APPLYING/TRANSFER *Required:* standardized test scores, high school transcript, college transcript.
CONTACT Mr. Peter Atkinson, Director of Admissions, Gwinnett Technical Institute, Lawrenceville, GA 30246-1505, 770-962-7580 Ext. 115.

HERZING COLLEGE OF BUSINESS AND TECHNOLOGY
Atlanta, Georgia

UG Enrollment: 400	Tuition: $11,400/deg prog
Application Deadline: rolling	Room & Board: N/Avail

GENERAL Proprietary, 2-year, coed. Part of Herzing Institutes, Inc. Awards terminal associate degrees. Founded 1949. *Setting:* urban campus. *Total enrollment:* 400. *Faculty:* 40 (all full-time); student-faculty ratio is 13:1.
ENROLLMENT PROFILE 400 students from 5 states and territories, 22 other countries. 60% women, 0% part-time, 90% state residents, 15% transferred in, 30% 25 or older, 0% Native American, 1% Hispanic, 90% African American, 1% Asian American.
FIRST-YEAR CLASS 300 total.
ACADEMIC PROGRAM Hands-on training curriculum. Calendar: quarters. 96 courses offered in 1995–96. Academic remediation for entering students, honors program, internships.
GENERAL DEGREE REQUIREMENTS 100 credit hours; math/science requirements vary according to program; computer course.
MAJORS Accounting, business administration/commerce/management, business education, business machine technologies, computer information systems, computer management, computer technologies, data processing, electrical engineering technology, management information systems, secretarial studies/office management.
LIBRARY Loretta Herzing Library with 6,000 books, 25 periodicals.
COMPUTERS ON CAMPUS 125 computers for student use in computer center.
HOUSING College housing not available.
CAREER PLANNING *Placement office:* 1 full-time, 1 part-time staff. *Director:* Mr. Nick Blunden, Director of Employment Assistance and Corporate Training, 404-816-4533. *Services:* job fairs, resume preparation, resume referral, career counseling, job interviews.
AFTER GRADUATION 20% of students completing a degree program in 1994–95 went directly on to further study.
EXPENSES FOR 1996–97 *Application fee:* $30. Tuition per degree program ranges from $11,400 to $16,200.
FINANCIAL AID *College-administered undergrad aid 1995–96:* 4 need-based scholarships (average $1000), low-interest long-term loans from college funds (average $2500), loans from external sources (average $750), Federal Work-Study. *Required forms:* institutional, FAFSA. *Application deadline:* continuous.
APPLYING *Required:* school transcript, interview, Wonderlic aptitude test. Test scores used for admission and counseling/placement. *Application deadline:* rolling. *Notification:* continuous.
APPLYING/TRANSFER *Required:* standardized test scores, high school transcript, interview, college transcript, minimum 2.0 college GPA. *Entrance:* moderately difficult. *Application deadline:* rolling. *Notification:* continuous. *Contact:* Mr. Hank Lewis, Faculty Director, 404-816-4533.
CONTACT Ms. Cathleen Cortese, Director, Herzing College of Business and Technology, 3355 Lenox Road, Suite 100, Atlanta, GA 30326, 404-816-4533 or toll-free 800-426-2779.

MACON COLLEGE
Macon, Georgia

UG Enrollment: 4,500	Tuition & Fees (GA Res): $1170
Application Deadline: rolling	Room & Board: N/Avail

GENERAL State-supported, 2-year, coed. Part of University System of Georgia. Awards transfer associate degrees. Founded 1968. *Setting:* 167-acre urban campus. *Total enrollment:* 4,500. *Faculty:* 141; student-faculty ratio is 25:1.
ENROLLMENT PROFILE 4,500 students: 67% women, 64% part-time, 93% state residents, 10% transferred in, 1% international, 49% 25 or older, 1% Native American, 1% Hispanic, 22% African American, 1% Asian American.
FIRST-YEAR CLASS 601 total. Of the students who applied, 90% were accepted.
ACADEMIC PROGRAM Core, career and transfer curriculum, honor code. Calendar: quarters. Academic remediation for entering students, English as a second language program offered during academic year, advanced placement, honors program, summer session for credit, part-time degree program (daytime, evenings, summer), adult/continuing education programs, co-op programs and internships. Study-abroad program.
GENERAL DEGREE REQUIREMENTS 96 quarter hours; 1 algebra course; 2 lab science courses.
MAJORS Accounting, agricultural sciences, art/fine arts, biology/biological sciences, business administration/commerce/management, business education, chemistry, communication, computer information systems, computer programming, computer science, computer technologies, corrections, criminal justice, data processing, dental services, economics, education, elementary education, (pre)engineering sequence, engineering technology, English, environmental sciences, fire science, food sciences, health science, history, hotel and restaurant management, insurance, journalism, law enforcement/police sciences, liberal arts/general studies, marketing/retailing/merchandising, mathematics, medical laboratory technology, modern languages, music, nursing, pharmacy/pharmaceutical sciences, physical education, physical therapy, physics, political science/government, postal management, psychology, public administration, public affairs and policy studies, respiratory therapy, secretarial studies/office management, sociology, speech/rhetoric/public address/debate, theater arts/drama.
LIBRARY Macon College Library with 73,520 books, 1,225 microform titles, 390 periodicals, 3,315 records, tapes, and CDs.
COMPUTERS ON CAMPUS 95 computers for student use in computer labs provide access to e-mail, Internet. Staffed computer lab on campus.

COLLEGE LIFE Drama-theater group, choral group, student-run newspaper. 36% vote in student government elections. *Most popular organizations:* Student Government, Macon College Association of Nursing Students, Macon College Association of Premedicine. *Student services:* personal-psychological counseling. *Campus security:* 24-hour patrols, late-night transport-escort service.
HOUSING College housing not available.
ATHLETICS Member NJCAA. *Intercollegiate:* basketball M(s), softball W(s). *Intramural:* basketball, football, golf, softball, tennis, volleyball. *Contact:* Mr. Jimmy Anderson, Director of Athletics, 912-471-2774.
CAREER PLANNING *Placement office:* 4 full-time staff. *Director:* Ms. Ann Lloyd, Director of Counseling and Testing, 912-471-2714. *Services:* job fairs, resume preparation, career counseling, careers library. 15 organizations recruited on campus 1994–95.
EXPENSES FOR 1995–96 State resident tuition: $1170 full-time. Nonresident tuition: $3510 full-time. Part-time tuition per quarter ranges from $29 to $319 for state residents, $96 to $989 for nonresidents.
FINANCIAL AID *College-administered undergrad aid 1995–96:* need-based scholarships, non-need scholarships, low-interest long-term loans from external sources, Federal Work-Study, part-time jobs. *Required forms:* institutional, FAFSA. *Priority deadline:* 4/1. *Waivers:* full or partial for senior citizens. *Notification:* continuous.
APPLYING *Options:* early entrance, midyear entrance. *Required:* school transcript, 3 years of high school science, SAT I or ACT, TOEFL for international students. *Recommended:* 3 years of high school math, some high school foreign language. Test scores used for counseling/placement. *Application deadline:* rolling. *Notification:* continuous.
APPLYING/TRANSFER *Required for some:* 3 years of high school math and science, 2 years of high school foreign language. *Application deadline:* rolling. *Notification:* continuous.
CONTACT Ms. Dee B. Minter, Director of Admissions, Macon College, 100 College Station Drive, Macon, GA 31297, 912-471-2800 or toll-free 800-272-7619.

MACON TECHNICAL INSTITUTE
Macon, Georgia

CONTACT Ms. Cathy Pittman, Director of Admissions, Macon Technical Institute, Macon, GA 31206, 912-757-3400.

MASSEY COLLEGE OF BUSINESS AND TECHNOLOGY
Georgia—See Herzing College of Business and Technology

MEADOWS COLLEGE OF BUSINESS
Columbus, Georgia

UG Enrollment: 260	Tuition & Fees: $3635
Application Deadline: 9/15	Room & Board: N/Avail

GENERAL Proprietary, 2-year, coed. Awards diplomas, terminal associate degrees. Founded 1971. *Setting:* 4-acre urban campus. *Total enrollment:* 260. *Faculty:* 22 (18 full-time, 5% with terminal degrees, 4 part-time); student-faculty ratio is 15:1.
ENROLLMENT PROFILE 260 students from 28 states and territories, 2 other countries. 71% women, 0% part-time, 80% state residents, 36% transferred in, 42% 25 or older, 1% Native American, 3% Hispanic, 68% African American, 2% Asian American. *Areas of study chosen:* 43% health professions and related sciences, 32% computer and information sciences, 25% business management and administrative services. *Most popular recent majors:* computer science, secretarial studies/office management, nursing.
FIRST-YEAR CLASS 150 total; 161 applied.
ACADEMIC PROGRAM Core, honor code. Calendar: quarters. 51 courses offered in 1995–96. Academic remediation for entering students, advanced placement, summer session for credit, part-time degree program (daytime, evenings, weekends, summer), co-op programs and internships.
GENERAL DEGREE REQUIREMENTS 96 quarter hours; 4 quarter hours each of math and physical science; computer course.
MAJORS Accounting, computer science, engineering technology, medical assistant technologies, nursing, secretarial studies/office management.
LIBRARY Meadows College Library with 5,100 books, 40 periodicals.
COMPUTERS ON CAMPUS 70 computers for student use in computer center, computer labs, classrooms, library. Staffed computer lab on campus provides training in use of computers, software.
COLLEGE LIFE Orientation program (4 days, no cost). Student-run newspaper. *Campus security:* 24-hour emergency response devices.
HOUSING College housing not available.
ATHLETICS *Intercollegiate:* basketball M/W. *Intramural:* basketball, volleyball.
CAREER PLANNING *Placement office:* 1 full-time staff. *Director:* Mr. Louis Jasinski, Placement Director, 706-327-7668. *Services:* resume preparation, resume referral, career counseling, careers library, job bank, job interviews. Students must register freshman year.
EXPENSES FOR 1996–97 *Application fee:* $20. Tuition: $3585 full-time. Full-time mandatory fees: $50. Tuition guaranteed not to increase for student's term of enrollment.
FINANCIAL AID *College-administered undergrad aid 1995–96:* 3 need-based scholarships (average $2200), short-term loans (average $1000), low-interest long-term loans from college funds, loans from external sources (average $2000), Federal Work-Study, part-time jobs. *Required forms:* CSS Financial Aid PROFILE, institutional, FAFSA; required for some: state. *Priority deadline:* 9/15. *Payment plan:* installment. *Waivers:* full or partial for employees or children of employees.
APPLYING Open admission. *Required:* school transcript, campus interview. *Required for some:* CPAt. Test scores used for counseling/placement. *Application deadline:* 9/15.
APPLYING/TRANSFER *Required:* high school transcript, campus interview, college transcript. *Required for some:* standardized test scores. *Entrance:* noncompetitive. *Application deadline:* 9/15. *Contact:* Ms. Phelecia Jackson, Registrar, 706-327-7668.
CONTACT Mr. John Mills, Director of the College, Meadows College of Business, 1170 Brown Avenue, Columbus, GA 31906-2405, 706-327-7668.

MIDDLE GEORGIA COLLEGE
Cochran, Georgia

UG Enrollment: 2,049	Tuition & Fees (GA Res): $1260
Application Deadline: rolling	Room & Board: $2775

Middle Georgia College is a 2-year coeducational unit of the University System of Georgia. Of the total enrollment of approximately 2,050, about 650 students live on campus. Transfer programs are offered in nearly all academic disciplines, including engineering, computer science, and architecture. There are also several career programs.

GENERAL State-supported, 2-year, coed. Part of University System of Georgia. Awards certificates, transfer associate, terminal associate degrees. Founded 1884. *Setting:* 165-acre rural campus. *Total enrollment:* 2,049. *Faculty:* 82 (60 full-time, 40% with terminal degrees, 22 part-time); student-faculty ratio is 19:1.
ENROLLMENT PROFILE 2,049 students from 19 states and territories, 12 other countries. 54% women, 42% part-time, 97% state residents, 4% transferred in, 1% international, 23% 25 or older, 1% Native American, 4% Hispanic, 24% African American, 6% Asian American. *Most popular recent majors:* nursing, business administration/commerce/management, engineering (general).
FIRST-YEAR CLASS 892 total; 1,690 applied, 91% were accepted, 58% of whom enrolled.
ACADEMIC PROGRAM Core. Calendar: quarters. 212 courses offered in 1995–96. Academic remediation for entering students, advanced placement, honors program, summer session for credit, part-time degree program (daytime, evenings, summer), adult/continuing education programs, co-op programs.
GENERAL DEGREE REQUIREMENTS 100 quarter hours; 1 college algebra course; computer course for engineering, business administration majors.
MAJORS Accounting, agricultural sciences, applied art, applied mathematics, art education, art/fine arts, aviation administration, behavioral sciences, biology/biological sciences, business administration/commerce/management, business education, chemistry, commercial art, computer science, criminal justice, data processing, drafting and design, education, elementary education, engineering (general), engineering and applied sciences, engineering sciences, (pre)engineering sequence, engineering technology, English, environmental design, environmental sciences, family and consumer studies, fashion merchandising, forestry, geology, health education, history, home economics, home economics education, humanities, journalism, liberal arts/general studies, library science, literature, marketing/retailing/merchandising, mathematics, mechanical engineering technology, medical laboratory technology, medical records services, middle school education, military science, music, music education, natural sciences, nursing, occupational therapy, paralegal studies, physical education, physical sciences, physics, political science/government, psychology, public administration, public relations, respiratory therapy, science, science education, secretarial studies/office management, social science, social work, sociology, Spanish, speech/rhetoric/public address/debate, surveying technology, textiles and clothing, theater arts/drama, veterinary sciences, zoology.
LIBRARY Roberts Memorial Library with 91,120 books, 27,020 microform titles, 398 periodicals, 1 on-line bibliographic service, 70 CD-ROMs, 5,290 records, tapes, and CDs.
COMPUTERS ON CAMPUS 288 computers for student use in computer labs, learning resource center, classrooms, library provide access to e-mail, on-line services, Internet. Staffed computer lab on campus provides training in use of computers, software.
COLLEGE LIFE Orientation program (2 days, $25). Drama-theater group, choral group, student-run newspaper. *Social organizations:* 35 open to all. *Most popular organizations:* Baptist Student Union, Student Government Association, Minority Alliance, Midga Show Choir, Engineering Club. *Major annual events:* Halloween Carnival Dance, Homecoming, Honors Day. *Student services:* health clinic, personal-psychological counseling. *Campus security:* 24-hour emergency response devices, late-night transport-escort service, patrols by police officers.
HOUSING 830 college housing spaces available; 610 were occupied 1995–96. Freshmen guaranteed college housing. On-campus residence required through sophomore year except if married or living with relatives. *Option:* single-sex (5 buildings) housing available. Resident assistants live in dorms.
ATHLETICS Member NJCAA. *Intercollegiate:* baseball M, basketball M, football M, softball W, tennis W, volleyball W. *Intramural:* basketball, football, softball, swimming and diving, tennis. *Contact:* Mr. Robert Sapp, Athletic Director, 912-934-3044.
CAREER PLANNING *Director:* Dr. Randall Ursrey, Vice President of Student Affairs, 912-934-6221. *Service:* career counseling.
EXPENSES FOR 1995–96 *Application fee:* $5. State resident tuition: $1020 full-time, $29 per quarter hour part-time. Nonresident tuition: $3423 full-time, $96 per quarter hour part-time. Full-time mandatory fees: $240. College room and board: $2775. College room only: $1290.
FINANCIAL AID *College-administered undergrad aid 1995–96:* 7 need-based scholarships (average $1078), 61 non-need scholarships (average $956), low-interest long-term loans from external sources (average $2036), Federal Work-Study, 31 part-time jobs. *Required forms:* institutional, FAFSA. *Priority deadline:* 7/1.
APPLYING *Options:* early entrance, deferred entrance, midyear entrance. *Required:* school transcript, SAT I or ACT, TOEFL for international students. *Required for some:* 3 years of high school math and science, 2 years of high school foreign language. Test scores used for counseling/placement. *Application deadline:* rolling. *Notification:* continuous.
APPLYING/TRANSFER *Required for some:* standardized test scores, high school transcript, college transcript. *Entrance:* minimally difficult. *Application deadline:* rolling. *Notification:* continuous. *Contact:* Mr. George K. Hinton, Registrar/Director of Admissions, 912-934-3036.
CONTACT Mr. George K. Hinton, Registrar/Director of Admissions, Middle Georgia College, Cochran, GA 31014-1599, 912-934-3036. *Fax:* 912-934-3199. *E-mail:* ltravis@warrior.mgc.peachnet.edu.

OXFORD COLLEGE
Georgia—See Emory University, Oxford College

SAVANNAH TECHNICAL INSTITUTE
Savannah, Georgia

UG Enrollment: 2,022	**Tuition & Fees (GA Res): $858**
Application Deadline: N/R	**Room & Board: N/Avail**

GENERAL State-supported, 2-year. Awards terminal associate degrees. ***Total enrollment:*** 2,022.
ENROLLMENT PROFILE 2,022 students.
GENERAL DEGREE REQUIREMENTS 115 quarter hours; 1 college algebra course; computer course for most majors.
EXPENSES FOR 1996–97 State resident tuition: $828 full-time, $21 per credit part-time. Nonresident tuition: $1584 full-time, $42 per credit part-time. Part-time mandatory fees: $15 per term. Full-time mandatory fees: $30.
APPLYING ***Required:*** ACT ASSET.
APPLYING/TRANSFER ***Required:*** standardized test scores.
CONTACT Dr. David Whitis, Enrollment Director, Savannah Technical Institute, Savannah, GA 31499, 912-351-6362.

SOUTH COLLEGE
Savannah, Georgia

UG Enrollment: 308	**Tuition & Fees: $5110**
Application Deadline: rolling	**Room & Board: N/Avail**

GENERAL Proprietary, primarily 2-year, coed. Awards certificates, transfer associate, terminal associate, bachelor's degrees. Founded 1899. ***Setting:*** 5-acre suburban campus. ***Total enrollment:*** 308. ***Faculty:*** 54 (19 full-time, 100% with terminal degrees, 35 part-time).
ENROLLMENT PROFILE 308 students: 83% women, 17% men, 33% part-time, 98% state residents, 68% 25 or older, 0% Native American, 4% Hispanic, 38% African American, 1% Asian American. ***Most popular recent majors:*** medical assistant technologies, paralegal studies, business administration/commerce/management.
FIRST-YEAR CLASS 33 total; 86 applied, 84% were accepted, 46% of whom enrolled.
ACADEMIC PROGRAM Core, honor code. Calendar: quarters. 131 courses offered in 1995–96. Academic remediation for entering students, tutorials, summer session for credit, part-time degree program (daytime, evenings, weekends, summer), adult/continuing education programs, internships.
GENERAL DEGREE REQUIREMENTS 120 quarter hours for associate, 180 quarter hours for bachelor's; 1 course in algebra; internship (some majors).
MAJORS Accounting, business administration/commerce/management (B), computer information systems, hotel and restaurant management, medical assistant technologies, paralegal studies, secretarial studies/office management.
LIBRARY South College Library with 13,000 books, 50 periodicals, 1 on-line bibliographic service, 3 CD-ROMs, 148 records, tapes, and CDs.
COMPUTERS ON CAMPUS 50 computers for student use in computer labs, library provide access to on-line services, Internet. Staffed computer lab on campus provides training in use of computers, software.
COLLEGE LIFE 50% vote in student government elections. ***Most popular organizations:*** Medical Assisting Club, Paralegal Club. ***Student services:*** personal-psychological counseling. ***Campus security:*** late-night transport-escort service.
HOUSING College housing not available.
CAREER PLANNING ***Placement office:*** 1 full-time staff. ***Director:*** Ms. Maureen Hamilton, Job Placement Director, 912-925-8111. ***Services:*** resume preparation, resume referral, career counseling, careers library, job interviews. Students must register sophomore year.
EXPENSES FOR 1995–96 ***Application fee:*** $25. Tuition: $5085 full-time. Part-time tuition per quarter ranges from $660 to $1550. Full-time mandatory fees: $25.
FINANCIAL AID ***College-administered undergrad aid 1995–96:*** need-based scholarships, 1 non-need scholarship ($1500), short-term loans (average $300), low-interest long-term loans from college funds (average $750), loans from external sources (average $875), Federal Work-Study. ***Required forms:*** institutional, FAFSA. ***Priority deadline:*** 10/3. ***Waivers:*** full or partial for employees or children of employees.
APPLYING ***Options:*** Common Application, early entrance, deferred entrance, midyear entrance. ***Required:*** recommendations, TOEFL for international students, CPAt. ***Recommended:*** SAT I or ACT. Test scores used for admission and counseling/placement. ***Application deadline:*** rolling. ***Notification:*** continuous.
APPLYING/TRANSFER ***Required:*** recommendations, minimum 2.0 college GPA. ***Recommended:*** standardized test scores. ***Entrance:*** minimally difficult. ***Application deadline:*** rolling. ***Notification:*** continuous. ***Contact:*** Mrs. Connie Simpson, Registrar, 912-651-8134.
CONTACT Mr. Robin Manning, Director of Admissions, South College, Savannah, GA 31406-4881, 912-651-8100 Ext. 14. ***Fax:*** 912-356-1409.

SOUTH GEORGIA COLLEGE
Douglas, Georgia

UG Enrollment: 1,171	**Tuition & Fees (GA Res): $1128**
Application Deadline: 8/26	**Room & Board: $2550**

GENERAL State-supported, 2-year, coed. Part of University System of Georgia. Awards certificates, transfer associate, terminal associate degrees. Founded 1906. ***Setting:*** 250-acre small-town campus. ***Endowment:*** $150,321. ***Total enrollment:*** 1,171. ***Faculty:*** 51 (44 full-time, 29% with terminal degrees, 7 part-time); student-faculty ratio is 25:1.
ENROLLMENT PROFILE 1,171 students from 6 states and territories, 4 other countries. 67% women, 38% part-time, 98% state residents, 13% live on campus, 22% transferred in, 38% have need-based financial aid, 23% have non-need-based financial aid, 1% international, 33% 25 or older, 0% Native American, 1% Hispanic, 19% African American, 1% Asian American. ***Areas of study chosen:*** 36% health professions and related sciences, 16% liberal arts/general studies, 13% education, 11% business management and administrative services, 9% social sciences, 5% computer and information sciences, 3% psychology, 2% agriculture, 2% biological and life sciences, 1% communications and journalism, 1% mathematics, 1% physical sciences. ***Most popular recent majors:*** nursing, education, business administration/commerce/management.
FIRST-YEAR CLASS 290 total; 470 applied, 100% were accepted, 62% of whom enrolled.
ACADEMIC PROGRAM Core, honor code. Calendar: quarters. Academic remediation for entering students, services for LD students, advanced placement, summer session for credit, part-time degree program (daytime, evenings, summer), adult/continuing education programs.
GENERAL DEGREE REQUIREMENT 96 quarter hours.
MAJORS Accounting, agricultural business, agricultural sciences, animal sciences, biology/biological sciences, business administration/commerce/management, business education, chemistry, communication, computer information systems, computer programming, computer science, criminal justice, early childhood education, education, elementary education, (pre)engineering sequence, English, finance/banking, French, health education, history, information science, journalism, liberal arts/general studies, mathematics, middle school education, nursing, philosophy, physical education, physics, political science/government, psychology, recreation and leisure services, science, science education, secretarial studies/office management, sociology, Spanish, speech/rhetoric/public address/debate.
LIBRARY William S. Smith Library with 81,282 books, 38,662 microform titles, 333 periodicals, 3 on-line bibliographic services, 18 CD-ROMs, 3,886 records, tapes, and CDs. Acquisition spending 1994–95: $55,909.
COMPUTERS ON CAMPUS 80 computers for student use in classroom buildings, library, student center provide access to off-campus computing facilities, on-line services. Staffed computer lab on campus provides training in use of computers, software.
COLLEGE LIFE Orientation program (2 days, no cost, parents included). Drama-theater group, student-run newspaper. 25% vote in student government elections. ***Social organizations:*** 12 open to all. ***Most popular organizations:*** Georgia Association of Student Nurses, Baptist Student Union, Agricultural Club, Residents Assistants Club, Student Organization for Black Unity. ***Student services:*** personal-psychological counseling. ***Campus security:*** 24-hour emergency response devices and patrols, controlled dormitory access.
HOUSING 500 college housing spaces available; 167 were occupied 1995–96. Freshmen guaranteed college housing. On-campus residence required in freshman year except for veterans, or if married, 20 or over, or living within commuting distance. ***Option:*** single-sex housing available. Resident assistants live in dorms.
ATHLETICS Member NJCAA. ***Intercollegiate:*** baseball M(s), basketball M(s), softball W(s), tennis W(s). ***Intramural:*** basketball, football, golf, soccer, tennis, volleyball. ***Contact:*** Dr. Grace M. James, Chairperson, Division of Health, Physical Ed. and Recreation, 912-383-4255.
CAREER PLANNING ***Director:*** Dr. Wendell Duncan, Vice President for Student Affairs, 912-383-4244. ***Services:*** career counseling, careers library, job bank.
EXPENSES FOR 1995–96 ***Application fee:*** $5. State resident tuition: $1020 full-time, $29 per quarter hour part-time. Nonresident tuition: $3423 full-time, $96 per quarter hour part-time. Part-time mandatory fees: $30 per quarter. Full-time mandatory fees: $108. College room and board: $2550 (minimum). College room only: $1170 (minimum).
FINANCIAL AID ***College-administered undergrad aid 1995–96:*** 446 need-based scholarships (average $1977), 207 non-need scholarships (average $1368), short-term loans (average $972), low-interest long-term loans from external sources (average $2475), Federal Work-Study, 30 part-time jobs. ***Required forms:*** institutional, FAFSA; required for some: state, verification worksheet. ***Priority deadline:*** 7/10. ***Waivers:*** full or partial for senior citizens.
APPLYING ***Options:*** early entrance, deferred entrance, midyear entrance. ***Required:*** TOEFL for international students. ***Required for some:*** 3 years of high school math and science, 2 years of high school foreign language, SAT I or ACT. Test scores used for counseling/placement. ***Application deadline:*** 8/26. ***Notification:*** continuous.
APPLYING/TRANSFER ***Required for some:*** standardized test scores, 3 years of high school science, some high school foreign language. ***Entrance:*** minimally difficult. ***Application deadline:*** 8/26. ***Notification:*** continuous.
CONTACT Dr. Kenneth Foshee, Director of Admissions, Records, and Research, South Georgia College, Douglas, GA 31533-5098, 912-383-4200 or toll-free 800-342-6364 (in-state). ***Fax:*** 912-383-4392. ***E-mail:*** kfoshee@tiger.sgc.peachnet.edu.

THOMAS TECHNICAL INSTITUTE
Thomasville, Georgia

UG Enrollment: 998	**Tuition & Fees (GA Res): $792**
Application Deadline: N/R	**Room & Board: N/Avail**

GENERAL State-supported, 2-year, coed. Awards certificates, terminal associate degrees. Founded 1963. ***Total enrollment:*** 998. ***Faculty:*** 45.
ENROLLMENT PROFILE 998 students.
ACADEMIC PROGRAM Calendar: quarters.
GENERAL DEGREE REQUIREMENTS 143 quarter hours; math/science requirements vary according to program; computer course for most majors.
EXPENSES FOR 1996–97 State resident tuition: $756 full-time, $21 per quarter hour part-time. Nonresident tuition: $1512 full-time, $42 per quarter hour part-time. Part-time mandatory fees: $12 per quarter hour. Full-time mandatory fees: $36.
APPLYING Open admission. ***Required:*** SAT I, ACT ASSET.
APPLYING/TRANSFER ***Required:*** standardized test scores.
CONTACT Mr. Thomas Ceccacci, Vice President of Student Services, Thomas Technical Institute, Thomasville, GA 31792, 912-225-4096.

TRUETT-MCCONNELL COLLEGE
Cleveland, Georgia

UG Enrollment: 1,957	**Tuition & Fees: $5100**
Application Deadline: 9/1	**Room & Board: $2775**

Truett-McConnell College is a 2-year coeducational institution located in the Blue Ridge Mountains. The College is fully accredited and is sponsored by the Georgia Baptist Convention. The music department is accredited by NASM. Degrees offered are AA, AM, AB, AAS, and AGS. Men and women compete in intercollegiate athletics through the NJCAA.

GENERAL Independent Baptist, 2-year, coed. Awards transfer associate, terminal associate degrees. Founded 1946. ***Setting:*** 310-acre rural campus with easy access to Atlanta. ***Total enrollment:*** 1,957. ***Faculty:*** 39 (30 full-time, 30% with terminal degrees, 9 part-time).

ENROLLMENT PROFILE 1,957 students from 6 states and territories, 11 other countries. 48% women, 12% part-time, 95% state residents, 5% transferred in, 45% have need-based financial aid, 90% have non-need-based financial aid, 3% international, 5% 25 or older, 0% Native American, 0% Hispanic, 8% African American, 1% Asian American.

FIRST-YEAR CLASS 493 total. 12% from top 10% of their high school class, 30% from top quarter, 55% from top half.

ACADEMIC PROGRAM Core, honor code. Calendar: quarters. 190 courses offered in 1995–96. Academic remediation for entering students, English as a second language program offered during academic year, advanced placement, honors program, summer session for credit, part-time degree program (daytime).

GENERAL DEGREE REQUIREMENTS 90 quarter hours; 1 math course; computer course for business majors.

MAJORS Business administration/commerce/management, liberal arts/general studies, music.

LIBRARY Cofer Library with 32,000 books, 2,538 microform titles, 163 periodicals, 1,702 records, tapes, and CDs. Acquisition spending 1994–95: $99,992.

COMPUTERS ON CAMPUS 16 computers for student use in computer center.

COLLEGE LIFE Drama-theater group, choral group. ***Most popular organizations:*** Baptist Student Union, College Choir, Student Government Association. ***Major annual events:*** Homecoming Week, Orientation Week, Alumni Day. ***Student services:*** health clinic. ***Campus security:*** 24-hour weekday patrols, 18-hour weekend patrols by trained security personnel.

HOUSING 400 college housing spaces available; 340 were occupied 1995–96. No special consideration for freshman housing applicants. On-campus residence required through sophomore year except if living with relatives or married. ***Option:*** single-sex housing available. Resident assistants live in dorms.

ATHLETICS Member NJCAA. ***Intercollegiate:*** baseball M(s), basketball M(s)/W(s), soccer M(s), softball W(s), squash W. ***Intramural:*** baseball, basketball, football, golf, tennis, volleyball. ***Contact:*** Mr. Peter Dees, Athletic Director, 706-865-2134.

AFTER GRADUATION 97% of students completing a degree program in 1994–95 went directly on to further study.

EXPENSES FOR 1995–96 ***Application fee:*** $20. Comprehensive fee of $7875 includes full-time tuition ($5100) and college room and board ($2775). College room only: $1425. Tuition for extension (off-campus) courses: $4230 full-time, $94 per quarter hour part-time.

FINANCIAL AID ***College-administered undergrad aid 1995–96:*** need-based scholarships, non-need scholarships, low-interest long-term loans, Federal Work-Study, part-time jobs. ***Required forms:*** FAFSA; required for some: state, institutional; accepted: CSS Financial Aid PROFILE. ***Priority deadline:*** 4/15. ***Payment plan:*** installment. ***Waivers:*** full or partial for employees or children of employees and senior citizens.

APPLYING ***Options:*** early entrance, deferred entrance, midyear entrance. ***Required:*** minimum 2.0 GPA, SAT I or ACT, TOEFL for international students. ***Recommended:*** 3 years of high school math and science, some high school foreign language. Test scores used for counseling/placement. ***Application deadline:*** 9/1. ***Notification:*** continuous.

APPLYING/TRANSFER ***Required:*** standardized test scores, minimum 2.0 high school GPA. ***Recommended:*** 3 years of high school math and science, some high school foreign language. ***Entrance:*** minimally difficult.

CONTACT Ms. Penny Loggins, Director of Admissions, Truett-McConnell College, Cleveland, GA 30528-9799, 706-865-2138 or toll-free 800-342-8857 (in-state). ***Fax:*** 706-865-0975.

WAYCROSS COLLEGE
Waycross, Georgia

UG Enrollment: 885	Tuition & Fees (GA Res): $1073
Application Deadline: rolling	Room & Board: N/Avail

GENERAL State-supported, 2-year, coed. Part of University System of Georgia. Awards transfer associate, terminal associate degrees. Founded 1976. ***Setting:*** 150-acre small-town campus. ***Endowment:*** $85,583. ***Total enrollment:*** 885. ***Faculty:*** 51 (21 full-time, 30 part-time).

ENROLLMENT PROFILE 885 students: 71% women, 35% part-time, 99% state residents, 10% transferred in, 1% international, 43% 25 or older, 1% Hispanic, 13% African American, 1% Asian American. ***Areas of study chosen:*** 33% health professions and related sciences, 12% education, 11% social sciences, 8% biological and life sciences, 7% business management and administrative services, 4% engineering and applied sciences, 3% computer and information sciences, 3% mathematics, 2% liberal arts/general studies. ***Most popular recent majors:*** education, business administration/commerce/management, psychology.

FIRST-YEAR CLASS 166 total. 15% from top 10% of their high school class, 25% from top quarter, 75% from top half.

ACADEMIC PROGRAM Core. Calendar: quarters. Academic remediation for entering students, advanced placement, summer session for credit, part-time degree program (daytime, evenings, summer), adult/continuing education programs. Off-campus study at South Georgia College, Valdosta State University, Albany State College, Okefenokee Technical Institute, Altamaha Technical Institute, Georgia Southern University.

GENERAL DEGREE REQUIREMENTS 93 quarter hours; math/science requirements vary according to program; computer course for business administration, forestry majors.

MAJORS Accounting, agricultural sciences, automotive technologies, biology/biological sciences, business administration/commerce/management, business education, chemistry, child psychology/child development, computer science, cosmetology, criminal justice, dental services, drafting and design, education, electrical and electronics technologies, elementary education, emergency medical technology, engineering technology, English, forestry, forest technology, health education, history, industrial and heavy equipment maintenance, information science, liberal arts/general studies, machine and tool technologies, mathematics, medical laboratory technology, medical technology, nursing, operating room technology, physical education, physical therapy, political science/government, psychology, radiological technology, respiratory therapy, secretarial studies/office management, sociology, welding technology.

LIBRARY Waycross College Library with 32,461 books, 118 microform titles, 251 periodicals, 19 CD-ROMs, 1,760 records, tapes, and CDs. Acquisition spending 1994–95: $64,176.

COMPUTERS ON CAMPUS 56 computers for student use in computer center, writing lab. Staffed computer lab on campus provides training in use of computers, software. Academic computing expenditure 1994–95: $24,931.

COLLEGE LIFE Drama-theater group, choral group, student-run newspaper. ***Social organizations:*** 9 open to all. ***Most popular organizations:*** Black Student Alliance, Georgia Association of Nursing Students, Baptist Student Union, Sigma Club, Student Government Association. ***Major annual events:*** Spring Fest, Breakfast with Santa. ***Student services:*** personal-psychological counseling. ***Campus security:*** late-night transport-escort service, security guards.

HOUSING College housing not available.

ATHLETICS ***Intramural:*** bowling, football, golf, racquetball, softball, table tennis (Ping-Pong), tennis, volleyball.

CAREER PLANNING ***Director:*** Ms. Christine Rogers, Coordinator of Guidance Services and Student Activities, 912-285-6012. ***Services:*** career counseling, careers library, job bank, job interviews. 15 organizations recruited on campus 1994–95.

EXPENSES FOR 1995–96 State resident tuition: $1020 full-time, $29 per quarter hour part-time. Nonresident tuition: $2403 full-time, $67 per quarter hour part-time. Part-time mandatory fees: $17.50 per quarter. Full-time mandatory fees: $53.

FINANCIAL AID ***College-administered undergrad aid 1995–96:*** need-based scholarships, non-need scholarships, short-term loans, low-interest long-term loans from external sources, Federal Work-Study, part-time jobs. ***Required forms:*** institutional; accepted: CSS Financial Aid PROFILE, state, FAFSA. ***Priority deadline:*** 6/1. ***Waivers:*** full or partial for senior citizens.

APPLYING Open admission. ***Options:*** early entrance, deferred entrance. ***Required:*** TOEFL for international students. ***Required for some:*** 3 years of high school math and science, 2 years of high school foreign language, SAT I. Test scores used for admission and counseling/placement. ***Application deadline:*** rolling. ***Notification:*** continuous.

APPLYING/TRANSFER ***Required for some:*** 3 years of high school math and science, 2 years of high school foreign language. ***Application deadline:*** rolling. ***Notification:*** continuous. ***Contact:*** Ms. Jacqueline J. Luke, Director of Admissions, Financial Aid, Student Records, 912-285-6133.

CONTACT Ms. Jacqueline J. Luke, Director of Admissions, Financial Aid, Student Records, Waycross College, Waycross, GA 31503-9248, 912-285-6133. ***Fax:*** 912-287-4909.

YOUNG HARRIS COLLEGE
Young Harris, Georgia

UG Enrollment: 519	Tuition & Fees: $6400
Application Deadline: rolling	Room & Board: $3505

GENERAL Independent United Methodist, 2-year, coed. Awards transfer associate degrees. Founded 1886. ***Setting:*** 700-acre rural campus. ***Endowment:*** $26 million. ***Total enrollment:*** 519. ***Faculty:*** 35 (32 full-time, 47% with terminal degrees, 3 part-time); student-faculty ratio is 14:1. ***Notable Alumni:*** Zell Miller, Trisha Yearwood.

ENROLLMENT PROFILE 519 students from 10 states and territories, 2 other countries. 50% women, 1% part-time, 91% state residents, 90% live on campus, 4% transferred in, 1% international, 1% 25 or older, 1% Hispanic, 1% African American, 1% Asian American. ***Most popular recent majors:*** science, business administration/commerce/management, sociology.

FIRST-YEAR CLASS 304 total; 671 applied, 91% were accepted, 50% of whom enrolled.

ACADEMIC PROGRAM Core, liberal arts curriculum. Calendar: quarters. 150 courses offered in 1995–96; average class size 17 in required courses. Academic remediation for entering students, advanced placement, summer session for credit, part-time degree program (daytime), internships.

GENERAL DEGREE REQUIREMENTS 93 quarter hours; 1 algebra course; 2 science courses; computer course for most majors; internship (some majors).

MAJORS Agricultural sciences, art education, art/fine arts, biology/biological sciences, business administration/commerce/management, chemistry, criminal justice, education, (pre)engineering sequence, English, French, geology, health education, history, journalism, liberal arts/general studies, mathematics, medical technology, music, music education, natural sciences, nursing, physical therapy, physics, political science/government, psychology, recreation and leisure services, religious studies, science, sociology, Spanish, theater arts/drama.

LIBRARY J. Lon Duckworth Library with 44,339 books, 119 microform titles, 285 periodicals, 725 records, tapes, and CDs. Acquisition spending 1994–95: $44,000.

COMPUTERS ON CAMPUS Student rooms linked to a campus network. 60 computers for student use in computer center provide access to e-mail, Internet. Staffed computer lab on campus provides training in use of computers, software.

COLLEGE LIFE Orientation program (2 days, $50, parents included). Drama-theater group, choral group, student-run newspaper. 60% vote in student government elections. ***Social organizations:*** 36 open to all; 4 local fraternities, 3 local sororities; 25% of eligible men and 25% of eligible women are members. ***Student services:*** health clinic, personal-psychological counseling. ***Campus security:*** 24-hour emergency response devices and patrols.

HOUSING 442 college housing spaces available; 440 were occupied 1995–96. Freshmen guaranteed college housing. On-campus residence required through sophomore year except by special permission or if living with parents. ***Option:*** coed housing available. Resident assistants live in dorms.

ATHLETICS Member NJCAA. ***Intercollegiate:*** baseball M(s), soccer M(s), softball W(s), tennis W(s). ***Intramural:*** badminton, basketball, football, soccer, softball, swimming and diving, tennis, track and field, volleyball, water polo, weight lifting. ***Contact:*** Dr. John Kniess, Athletic Director, 800-241-3754.

CAREER PLANNING ***Placement office:*** 1 full-time staff. ***Director:*** Ms. Gayle Nichols, Senior College Transfer Counselor, 706-379-3111 Ext. 5161. ***Service:*** career counseling.

AFTER GRADUATION 93% of students completing a degree program in 1994–95 went directly on to further study.

EXPENSES FOR 1995–96 ***Application fee:*** $25. Comprehensive fee of $9905 includes full-time tuition ($5860), mandatory fees ($540), and college room and board ($3505). College room only: $1470. Part-time tuition: $195 per quarter hour. Part-time mandatory fees: $540 per year. Georgia residents receive a tuition equalization grant of $2500 per year.

Georgia–Hawaii

Young Harris College (continued)
FINANCIAL AID *College-administered undergrad aid 1995–96:* 120 need-based scholarships (average $1500), 200 non-need scholarships (average $1000), low-interest long-term loans from college funds (average $1000), loans from external sources (average $2625), Federal Work-Study, 175 part-time jobs. *Required forms:* CSS Financial Aid PROFILE, state, institutional. *Priority deadline:* 6/1. *Payment plan:* installment. *Waivers:* full or partial for employees or children of employees.
APPLYING *Options:* early entrance, deferred entrance, midyear entrance. *Required:* school transcript, SAT I, TOEFL for international students. *Recommended:* 3 years of high school math and science, some high school foreign language. Test scores used for admission. *Application deadline:* rolling. *Notification:* continuous.
APPLYING/TRANSFER *Required:* standardized test scores, high school transcript, college transcript, minimum 2.0 college GPA. *Recommended:* 3 years of high school math and science, some high school foreign language. *Entrance:* minimally difficult. *Application deadline:* rolling. *Notification:* continuous.
CONTACT Mr. George L. Dyer, Director of Admissions, Young Harris College, Young Harris, GA 30582-0098, 706-379-3111 Ext. 116 or toll-free 800-241-3754 (in-state). *Fax:* 706-379-4306.

HAWAII

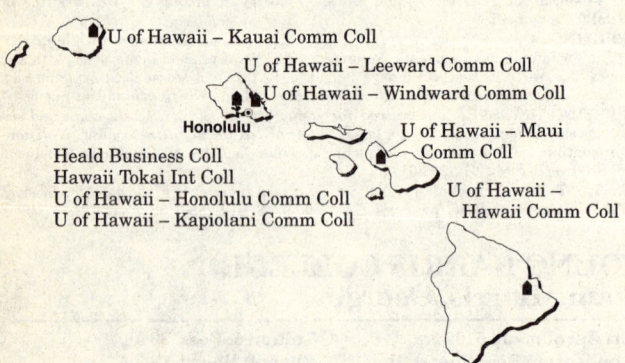

HAWAII TOKAI INTERNATIONAL COLLEGE
Honolulu, Hawaii

UG Enrollment: 84	Tuition & Fees: $6975
Application Deadline: rolling	Room & Board: N/Avail

GENERAL Independent, 2-year, coed. Awards certificates, transfer associate degrees. Founded 1992. *Setting:* urban campus. *Total enrollment:* 84. *Faculty:* 12 full-time; student-faculty ratio is 10:1.
ENROLLMENT PROFILE 84 students: 45% women, 55% men, 0% part-time, 10% state residents, 0% transferred in, 90% international, 15% 25 or older, 10% Native American, 0% Hispanic, 0% African American, 85% Asian American. *Areas of study chosen:* 70% liberal arts/general studies.
FIRST-YEAR CLASS 29 total. Of the students who applied, 100% were accepted, 50% of whom enrolled.
ACADEMIC PROGRAM Core, traditional liberal arts curriculum. Calendar: quarters. 66 courses offered in 1995–96; average class size 12 in required courses. English as a second language program offered during academic year, tutorials, summer session for credit.
GENERAL DEGREE REQUIREMENTS 60 credits; 1 course each in math and science.
MAJOR Liberal arts/general studies.
COMPUTERS ON CAMPUS 22 computers for student use in computer labs, library provide access to off-campus computing facilities, on-line services. Staffed computer lab on campus (open 24 hours a day) provides training in use of computers, software.
COLLEGE LIFE Student-run newspaper. 50% vote in student government elections. *Campus security:* 24-hour patrols.
EXPENSES FOR 1996–97 Tuition: $6900 full-time, $275 per credit part-time. Part-time mandatory fees: $25 per quarter. Full-time mandatory fees: $75.
FINANCIAL AID *Priority deadline:* 4/1.
APPLYING Open admission. *Option:* midyear entrance. *Required:* essay. *Recommended:* school transcript, recommendations, TOEFL for international students. *Application deadline:* rolling. *Notification:* continuous.
APPLYING/TRANSFER *Required:* essay. *Recommended:* high school transcript, recommendations. *Contact:* Ms. Teri Durland, Admissions Officer, 808-973-4150.
CONTACT Ms. Teri Durland, Admissions Officer, Hawaii Tokai International College, 2241 Kapiolani Boulevard, Honolulu, HI 96826-4310, 808-973-4150.

HEALD BUSINESS COLLEGE
Honolulu, Hawaii

UG Enrollment: 650	Tuition: $16,800/deg prog
Application Deadline: rolling	Room & Board: N/Avail

GENERAL Independent, 2-year, coed. Awards diplomas, terminal associate degrees. Founded 1863. *Setting:* urban campus. *Total enrollment:* 650. *Faculty:* 39 (19 full-time, 20 part-time).
ENROLLMENT PROFILE 650 students: 65% women, 2% part-time, 80% state residents, 10% transferred in. *Most popular recent majors:* accounting, tourism and travel.
FIRST-YEAR CLASS 177 total; 500 applied, 100% were accepted, 35% of whom enrolled.
ACADEMIC PROGRAM Core. Calendar: quarters. Academic remediation for entering students, English as a second language program offered during academic year and summer, summer session for credit, part-time degree program (daytime, evenings), internships.
GENERAL DEGREE REQUIREMENTS 102 quarter hours; computer course.
MAJORS Accounting, business administration/commerce/management, computer information systems, electrical and electronics technologies, hotel and restaurant management, legal secretarial studies, medical secretarial studies, retail management, secretarial studies/office management, tourism and travel.
COMPUTERS ON CAMPUS 350 computers for student use in learning resource center, classrooms.
HOUSING College housing not available.
CAREER PLANNING *Placement office:* 2 part-time staff. *Director:* Miss Anita Cottier, Placement Director, 808-955-1500. *Services:* resume preparation, resume referral, career counseling, job bank, job interviews.
EXPENSES FOR 1995–96 Tuition: $16,800 per degree program.
FINANCIAL AID *College-administered undergrad aid 1995–96:* low-interest long-term loans from external sources. *Required forms:* CSS Financial Aid PROFILE, FAFSA. *Priority deadline:* 7/20. *Payment plans:* tuition prepayment, installment. *Waivers:* full or partial for employees or children of employees.
APPLYING Open admission. *Options:* early entrance, deferred entrance. *Required:* school transcript, interview, CPAt. *Recommended:* TOEFL for international students. Test scores used for counseling/placement. *Application deadline:* rolling. *Notification:* continuous.
APPLYING/TRANSFER *Required:* college transcript. *Required for some:* interview. *Application deadline:* rolling.
CONTACT Ms. Evelyn Schemmel, Director, Heald Business College, 1500 Kapiolani Boulevard, Honolulu, HI 96814-3797, 808-955-1500 Ext. 22. *Fax:* 808-955-6964.

TOKAI INTERNATIONAL COLLEGE
Hawaii—See Hawaii Tokai International College

UNIVERSITY OF HAWAII–HAWAII COMMUNITY COLLEGE
Hilo, Hawaii

UG Enrollment: 2,800	Tuition & Fees (HI Res): $1010
Application Deadline: 8/1	Room & Board: $3454

GENERAL State-supported, 2-year, coed. Awards certificates, diplomas, transfer associate degrees. Founded 1954. *Total enrollment:* 2,800. *Faculty:* 98 (92 full-time, 6 part-time).
ENROLLMENT PROFILE 2,800 students from 25 states and territories, 36 other countries. 58% women, 59% part-time, 93% state residents, 19% transferred in, 30% have need-based financial aid, 5% have non-need-based financial aid, 2% international, 64% 25 or older, 6% Native American, 2% Hispanic, 1% African American, 57% Asian American. *Areas of study chosen:* 41% liberal arts/general studies, 22% vocational and home economics, 14% business management and administrative services, 12% health professions and related services, 5% education, 3% computer and information sciences, 2% agriculture.
FIRST-YEAR CLASS Of the students who applied, 100% were accepted.
ACADEMIC PROGRAM Calendar: semesters. Part-time degree program (daytime, evenings).
GENERAL DEGREE REQUIREMENTS 60 credits; 1 math/science course.
MAJORS Accounting, agricultural sciences, automotive technologies, carpentry, criminal justice, data processing, drafting and design, early childhood education, electrical and electronics technologies, electronics engineering technology, fire science, food services technology, hotel and restaurant management, liberal arts/general studies, mechanical engineering technology, nursing, practical nursing, secretarial studies/office management, welding technology.
COMPUTERS ON CAMPUS Computer purchase plan available. 100 computers for student use in computer labs, learning resource center, classrooms provide access to off-campus computing facilities, e-mail. Staffed computer lab on campus provides training in use of computers, software.
EXPENSES FOR 1996–97 State resident tuition: $960 full-time, $32 per credit hour part-time. Nonresident tuition: $6390 full-time, $213 per credit hour part-time. Part-time mandatory fees: $2.41 per credit hour. Full-time mandatory fees: $50. College room and board: $3454. College room only: $1448.
FINANCIAL AID *College-administered undergrad aid 1995–96:* 255 need-based scholarships (average $600), 180 non-need scholarships (average $450), low-interest long-term loans from external sources (average $2300), Federal Work-Study, 80 part-time jobs. *Required forms:* FAFSA. *Priority deadline:* 3/1.
APPLYING Open admission. *Required:* TOEFL for international students. Test scores used for admission. *Application deadline:* 8/1.
APPLYING/TRANSFER *Entrance:* noncompetitive.
CONTACT Mr. David Loeding, Registrar, University of Hawaii–Hawaii Community College, Hilo, HI 96720-4091, 808-933-3661. *E-mail:* loeding@hawada.hawcc.hawaii.edu.

UNIVERSITY OF HAWAII–HONOLULU COMMUNITY COLLEGE
Honolulu, Hawaii

UG Enrollment: 4,717	Tuition & Fees (HI Res): $524
Application Deadline: 7/1	Room & Board: N/Avail

GENERAL State-supported, 2-year, coed. Part of University of Hawaii System. Awards certificates, transfer associate, terminal associate degrees. Founded 1920. *Setting:* 20-acre urban campus. *Total enrollment:* 4,717. *Faculty:* 285 (155 full-time, 130 part-time).

ENROLLMENT PROFILE 4,717 students from 24 states and territories, 45 other countries. 44% women, 56% men, 71% part-time, 92% state residents, 45% transferred in, 13% have need-based financial aid, 1% international, 43% 25 or older, 20% Native American, 2% Hispanic, 1% African American, 55% Asian American. *Areas of study chosen:* 60% vocational and home economics, 40% liberal arts/general studies. *Most popular recent majors:* liberal arts/general studies, cosmetology, human services.
FIRST-YEAR CLASS 909 total; 1,616 applied, 94% were accepted, 60% of whom enrolled.
ACADEMIC PROGRAM Core. Calendar: semesters. 399 courses offered in 1995–96. Academic remediation for entering students, English as a second language program offered during academic year, services for LD students, advanced placement, summer session for credit, part-time degree program (daytime, evenings), co-op programs and internships. Study-abroad program. (1% of students participate) ROTC: Army (c).
GENERAL DEGREE REQUIREMENTS 60 semester hours; math/science requirements vary according to program.
MAJORS Architectural technologies, automotive technologies, aviation technology, carpentry, commercial art, cosmetology, drafting and design, early childhood education, electrical and electronics technologies, engineering technology, fashion design and technology, fire science, food services technology, graphic arts, heating/refrigeration/air conditioning, human services, industrial arts, law enforcement/police sciences, liberal arts/general studies, marine technology, occupational safety and health, welding technology.
LIBRARY 54,300 books, 140 microform titles, 245 periodicals.
COMPUTERS ON CAMPUS 175 computers for student use in computer center, learning center, academic labs, library provide access to e-mail. Staffed computer lab on campus.
COLLEGE LIFE Student-run newspaper. *Student services:* health clinic. *Campus security:* 24-hour emergency response devices.
HOUSING College housing not available.
CAREER PLANNING *Placement office:* 10 full-time staff. *Director:* Ms. Sherrie Rupert, Career Counselor, 808-845-9130. *Services:* job fairs, resume preparation, career counseling, careers library, job bank. 26 organizations recruited on campus 1994–95.
EXPENSES FOR 1995–96 State resident tuition: $504 full-time, $21 per semester hour part-time. Nonresident tuition: $3096 full-time, $129 per semester hour part-time. Full-time mandatory fees: $20.
FINANCIAL AID *College-administered undergrad aid 1995–96:* 741 need-based scholarships (average $601), 289 non-need scholarships (average $147), short-term loans (average $136), low-interest long-term loans from college funds (average $723), loans from external sources (average $1650), 22 Federal Work-Study (averaging $1164), 191 part-time jobs. *Required forms:* institutional, FAFSA. *Priority deadline:* 4/1. *Waivers:* full or partial for employees or children of employees and senior citizens. *Notification:* 5/15.
APPLYING Open admission except for foreign applicants. *Options:* Common Application, early entrance. *Required:* TOEFL for international students. Test scores used for admission. *Application deadline:* 7/1. *Notification:* continuous until 7/1. Preference given to state residents.
APPLYING/TRANSFER *Application deadline:* 7/1. *Notification:* continuous until 7/1.
CONTACT Admissions Office, University of Hawaii–Honolulu Community College, 874 Dillingham Boulevard, Honolulu, HI 96817-4598, 808-845-9129. *E-mail:* ar_miyasaki@hccada.hcc.hawaii.edu.

UNIVERSITY OF HAWAII–KAPIOLANI COMMUNITY COLLEGE
Honolulu, Hawaii

UG Enrollment: 7,283	Tuition & Fees (HI Res): $524
Application Deadline: 7/1	Room & Board: N/Avail

GENERAL State-supported, 2-year, coed. Part of University of Hawaii System. Awards certificates, transfer associate, terminal associate degrees. Founded 1957. *Setting:* 52-acre urban campus. *Total enrollment:* 7,283. *Faculty:* 317 (190 full-time, 127 part-time).
ENROLLMENT PROFILE 7,283 students from 27 states and territories. 59% women, 41% men, 64% part-time, 97% state residents, 13% transferred in, 9% have need-based financial aid, 2% have non-need-based financial aid, 2% international, 40% 25 or older, 1% Native American, 1% Hispanic, 1% African American, 69% Asian American.
FIRST-YEAR CLASS 1,319 total; 10,000 applied, 100% were accepted, 13% of whom enrolled.
ACADEMIC PROGRAM Core, honor code. Calendar: semesters. Academic remediation for entering students, English as a second language program offered during academic year, services for LD students, advanced placement, honors program, summer session for credit, part-time degree program (daytime, evenings, weekends), adult/continuing education programs, co-op programs and internships. Off-campus study at other units of the University of Hawaii System. ROTC: Army (c), Air Force (c).
GENERAL DEGREE REQUIREMENTS 60 credits; math/science requirements vary according to program; proficiency in a foreign language; computer course for accounting, marketing, hotel operations, medical assistant majors; internship (some majors).
MAJORS Accounting, culinary arts, data processing, food services management, hotel and restaurant management, legal secretarial studies, liberal arts/general studies, marketing/retailing/merchandising, medical assistant technologies, medical laboratory technology, nursing, occupational therapy, paralegal studies, physical therapy, radiological technology, respiratory therapy, secretarial studies/office management.
LIBRARY Lama Library with 50,000 books, 600 periodicals, 400 records, tapes, and CDs.
COMPUTERS ON CAMPUS 175 computers for student use in computer center, learning resource center.
COLLEGE LIFE Orientation program. Choral group, student-run newspaper. *Campus security:* 24-hour patrols.
HOUSING College housing not available.
ATHLETICS *Intramural:* bowling, volleyball.
CAREER PLANNING *Placement office:* 14 full-time staff. *Director:* Ms. Rosemae Harrington, Coordinator, 808-734-9500. *Services:* job fairs, resume preparation, resume referral, career counseling, careers library, job bank, job interviews.
EXPENSES FOR 1995–96 State resident tuition: $504 full-time, $21 per credit part-time. Nonresident tuition: $3096 full-time, $129 per credit part-time. Part-time mandatory fees per semester range from $5 to $10. Full-time mandatory fees: $20.
FINANCIAL AID *College-administered undergrad aid 1995–96:* 625 need-based scholarships (averaging $350), 150 non-need scholarships (averaging $175), short-term loans (averaging $100), low-interest long-term loans from college funds (averaging $1200), loans from external sources (averaging $1500), Federal Work-Study, 300 part-time jobs. *Required forms:* FAFSA. *Priority deadline:* 5/1. *Waivers:* full or partial for employees or children of employees and senior citizens.
APPLYING Open admission. *Option:* early entrance. *Required:* TOEFL for international students. Test scores used for admission. *Application deadline:* 7/1. *Notification:* continuous until 8/15. Preference given to state residents.
APPLYING/TRANSFER *Entrance:* noncompetitive. *Application deadline:* 7/1. *Notification:* continuous until 8/15.
CONTACT Ms. Cynthia N. Kimura, Coordinator of Enrollment Services, University of Hawaii–Kapiolani Community College, 4303 Diamond Head Road, Honolulu, HI 96816-4421, 808-734-9559.

UNIVERSITY OF HAWAII–KAUAI COMMUNITY COLLEGE
Lihue, Hawaii

UG Enrollment: 1,143	Tuition & Fees (HI Res): $778
Application Deadline: 8/1	Room & Board: N/Avail

GENERAL State-supported, 2-year, coed. Part of University of Hawaii System. Awards certificates, transfer associate degrees. Founded 1965. *Setting:* 100-acre small-town campus. *Total enrollment:* 1,143. *Faculty:* 78 (56 full-time, 22 part-time).
ENROLLMENT PROFILE 1,143 students: 66% women, 34% men, 49% part-time, 96% state residents, 7% transferred in, 1% international, 37% 25 or older, 21% Native American, 2% Hispanic, 1% African American, 47% Asian American. *Areas of study chosen:* 51% liberal arts/general studies, 49% vocational and home economics. *Most popular recent majors:* liberal arts/general studies, accounting.
FIRST-YEAR CLASS 507 total; 699 applied, 99% were accepted, 73% of whom enrolled.
ACADEMIC PROGRAM Core, liberal arts, trade, and vocational curriculum, honor code. Calendar: semesters. 355 courses offered in 1995–96. Academic remediation for entering students, English as a second language program offered during academic year, services for LD students, tutorials, summer session for credit, part-time degree program (daytime, evenings), co-op programs.
GENERAL DEGREE REQUIREMENTS 60 credits; computer course for electronics technology, accounting, office administration and technology majors; internship (some majors).
MAJORS Accounting, automotive technologies, carpentry, culinary arts, early childhood education, electrical and electronics technologies, electronics engineering technology, hospitality services, liberal arts/general studies, nursing, secretarial studies/office management.
LIBRARY S. W. Wilcox II Learning Resource Center plus 1 other, with 45,342 books, 193 periodicals, 5,278 records, tapes, and CDs.
COMPUTERS ON CAMPUS 173 computers for student use in computer center, business lab, learning center provide access to e-mail, Internet. Staffed computer lab on campus provides training in use of computers, software.
COLLEGE LIFE Drama-theater group, choral group. 14% vote in student government elections. *Social organizations:* 5 open to all. *Most popular organizations:* International Students Club, Pamantasan Club, Hawaiian Club. *Student services:* personal-psychological counseling. *Campus security:* student patrols.
HOUSING College housing not available.
ATHLETICS *Intramural:* basketball, table tennis (Ping-Pong), tennis.
CAREER PLANNING *Placement office:* 4 full-time staff. *Director:* Ms. Sharon Chiba, Counselor, 808-245-8258. *Service:* career counseling.
EXPENSES FOR 1996–97 State resident tuition: $768 full-time, $32 per credit part-time. Nonresident tuition: $5162 full-time, $213 per credit part-time. Full-time mandatory fees: $10.
FINANCIAL AID *College-administered undergrad aid 1995–96:* 80 need-based scholarships (average $250), 100 non-need scholarships (average $480), short-term loans (average $100), low-interest long-term loans from college funds (average $1000), loans from external sources (average $3000), 7 Federal Work-Study (averaging $2000). *Required forms for some financial aid applicants:* state, institutional; accepted: CSS Financial Aid PROFILE, FAFSA. *Priority deadline:* 4/1.
APPLYING Open admission except for nursing, electronics technology, welding, facilities engineering programs. *Options:* Common Application, early entrance, midyear entrance. *Required:* TOEFL for international students. *Recommended:* SCAT, Nelson Denny Reading Test, Lee Clark Arithmetic Test. *Required for some:* 3 years of high school science. Test scores used for counseling/placement. *Application deadline:* 8/1. *Notification:* continuous until 8/1. Preference given to state residents.
APPLYING/TRANSFER *Application deadline:* 8/1. *Notification:* continuous until 8/1.
CONTACT Ms. Alison Shigematsu, Admissions Officer and Registrar, University of Hawaii–Kauai Community College, Lihue, HI 96766-9591, 808-245-8226.

UNIVERSITY OF HAWAII–LEEWARD COMMUNITY COLLEGE
Pearl City, Hawaii

UG Enrollment: 6,330	Tuition & Fees (HI Res): $897
Application Deadline: 8/15	Room & Board: N/Avail

GENERAL State-supported, 2-year, coed. Part of University of Hawaii System. Awards transfer associate, terminal associate degrees. Founded 1968. *Setting:* 49-acre suburban campus with easy access to Honolulu. *Total enrollment:* 6,330. *Faculty:* 264 (156 full-time, 108 part-time).
ENROLLMENT PROFILE 6,330 students from 25 states and territories. 58% women, 42% men, 55% part-time, 88% state residents, 14% transferred in, 36% 25 or older, 1% Native American, 2% Hispanic, 2% African American, 64% Asian American.
FIRST-YEAR CLASS 1,297 total; of those who applied, 100% were accepted, 67% of whom enrolled.
ACADEMIC PROGRAM Calendar: semesters. Academic remediation for entering students, English as a second language program offered during academic year, services for LD students, honors program, summer session for credit, part-time degree program

Hawaii

University of Hawaii–Leeward Community College (continued)
(daytime, evenings, weekends, summer); adult/continuing education programs, co-op programs. Off-campus study at other units of the University of Hawaii System. ROTC: Army, Air Force (c).
GENERAL DEGREE REQUIREMENTS 60 credits; computer course for management majors.
MAJORS Accounting, automotive technologies, business administration/commerce/management, computer science, drafting and design, food services technology, graphic arts, human services, liberal arts/general studies, recreation and leisure services, retail management, secretarial studies/office management.
LIBRARY 58,000 books, 400 microform titles, 315 periodicals, 3,113 records, tapes, and CDs.
COMPUTERS ON CAMPUS 162 computers for student use in computer center, academic departments, student center.
COLLEGE LIFE Orientation program (2 days, no cost). Drama-theater group, student-run newspaper. *Student services:* health clinic. *Campus security:* 24-hour patrols, late-night transport-escort service.
HOUSING College housing not available.
ATHLETICS *Intramural:* basketball, bowling, golf, tennis, volleyball.
CAREER PLANNING *Service:* career counseling.
EXPENSES FOR 1995–96 State resident tuition: $504 full-time, $21 per credit part-time. Nonresident tuition: $3096 full-time, $129 per credit part-time. Part-time mandatory fees per semester range from $3 to $7.50. Full-time mandatory fees: $15.
FINANCIAL AID *College-administered undergrad aid 1995–96:* 300 need-based scholarships (averaging $400), 50 non-need scholarships (averaging $480), short-term loans (averaging $127), low-interest long-term loans from college funds (averaging $1000), loans from external sources (averaging $2400), 43 Federal Work-Study (averaging $1700), 300 part-time jobs. *Required forms:* FAFSA; required for some: institutional. *Priority deadline:* 4/15.
APPLYING Open admission. *Option:* early entrance. *Required:* TOEFL for international students. *Required for some:* school transcript, recommendations. Test scores used for admission. *Application deadline:* 8/15. *Notification:* 4/1. Preference given to state residents.
APPLYING/TRANSFER *Application deadline:* 8/15. *Notification:* 4/1.
CONTACT Ms. Veda Tokashiki, Clerk, University of Hawaii–Leeward Community College, Pearl City, HI 96782-3366, 808-455-0218. *Fax:* 808-455-0471.

UNIVERSITY OF HAWAII–MAUI COMMUNITY COLLEGE
Kahului, Hawaii

UG Enrollment: 2,759	Tuition & Fees (HI Res): $978
Application Deadline: rolling	Room Only: $1532

GENERAL State-supported, 2-year, coed. Part of University of Hawaii System. Awards certificates, transfer associate, terminal associate degrees. Founded 1967. *Setting:* 77-acre rural campus. *Total enrollment:* 2,759. *Faculty:* 148 (80 full-time, 68 part-time); student-faculty ratio is 30:1.
ENROLLMENT PROFILE 2,759 students: 63% women, 66% part-time, 92% state residents, 4% transferred in, 5% international, 45% 25 or older, 17% Native American, 2% Hispanic, 40% Asian American. *Areas of study chosen:* 34% liberal arts/general studies, 30% vocational and home economics, 4% health professions and related sciences, 1% agriculture.
FIRST-YEAR CLASS 794 total; 1,322 applied, 99% were accepted, 61% of whom enrolled.
ACADEMIC PROGRAM Core, honor code. Calendar: semesters. Academic remediation for entering students, services for LD students, summer session for credit, part-time degree program (daytime, evenings, weekends, summer), external degree programs, adult/continuing education programs, co-op programs.
GENERAL DEGREE REQUIREMENTS 60 credits; computer course for accounting, business majors.
MAJORS Accounting, agricultural technologies, automotive technologies, carpentry, construction technologies, criminal justice, fashion design and technology, fire science, food services technology, horticulture, hotel and restaurant management, human services, liberal arts/general studies, marketing/retailing/merchandising, nursing, secretarial studies/office management, welding technology.
LIBRARY Maui Community College Library with 42,523 books, 311 microform titles, 524 periodicals, 1 on-line bibliographic service, 8 CD-ROMs, 896 records, tapes, and CDs.
COMPUTERS ON CAMPUS 218 computers for student use in computer center, learning resource center, classrooms, library, student center provide access to e-mail, on-line services. Staffed computer lab on campus provides training in use of computers, software.
COLLEGE LIFE Student-run newspaper. *Social organizations:* social clubs; 50% of eligible men and 50% of eligible women are members. *Student services:* personal-psychological counseling. *Campus security:* 24-hour emergency response devices and patrols.
HOUSING 55 college housing spaces available; all were occupied 1995–96. Freshmen given priority for college housing. Off-campus living permitted. *Option:* coed housing available.
ATHLETICS *Intramural:* basketball, golf, table tennis (Ping-Pong), tennis, volleyball.
CAREER PLANNING *Services:* job fairs, career counseling, careers library.
EXPENSES FOR 1996–97 State resident tuition: $960 full-time, $32 per credit part-time. Nonresident tuition: $6390 full-time, $213 per credit part-time. Part-time mandatory fees per semester range from $5.50 to $10. Full-time mandatory fees: $18. College room only: $1532 (minimum).
FINANCIAL AID *College-administered undergrad aid 1995–96:* 200 need-based scholarships (averaging $115), 50 non-need scholarships (averaging $300), short-term loans (averaging $200), low-interest long-term loans from college funds (averaging $700), loans from external sources (averaging $2500), Federal Work-Study, 139 part-time jobs. *Required forms:* institutional, FAFSA. *Priority deadline:* 5/1. *Waivers:* full or partial for employees or children of employees and senior citizens. *Notification:* continuous.
APPLYING Open admission. *Option:* early entrance. *Required:* TOEFL for international students, CTBS. *Required for some:* school transcript, 3 years of high school science. Test scores used for counseling/placement. *Application deadline:* rolling.
APPLYING/TRANSFER *Required:* standardized test scores. *Required for some:* 3 years of high school science. *Entrance:* noncompetitive. *Application deadline:* rolling.
Contact: Mr. Stephen Kameda, Director of Admissions and Records, 808-242-1267.
CONTACT Mr. Stephen Kameda, Director of Admissions and Records, University of Hawaii–Maui Community College, Kahului, HI 96732, 808-242-1267. College video available.

UNIVERSITY OF HAWAII–WINDWARD COMMUNITY COLLEGE
Kaneohe, Hawaii

UG Enrollment: 1,666	Tuition & Fees (HI Res): $788
Application Deadline: rolling	Room & Board: N/Avail

GENERAL State-supported, 2-year, coed. Part of University of Hawaii System. Awards certificates, transfer associate, terminal associate degrees. Founded 1972. *Setting:* 78-acre small-town campus with easy access to Honolulu. *Total enrollment:* 1,666. *Faculty:* 80 (41 full-time, 39 part-time); student-faculty ratio is 15:1.
ENROLLMENT PROFILE 1,666 students: 64% part-time, 87% state residents, 19% transferred in, 43% 25 or older, 21% Native American, 1% Hispanic, 1% African American, 25% Asian American.
ACADEMIC PROGRAM Core. Calendar: semesters. Academic remediation for entering students, advanced placement, summer session for credit, part-time degree program (daytime, evenings), adult/continuing education programs, co-op programs. ROTC: Army (c), Air Force (c).
GENERAL DEGREE REQUIREMENTS 60 credits; math/science requirements vary according to program.
MAJORS Accounting, automotive technologies, finance/banking, liberal arts/general studies, secretarial studies/office management.
LIBRARY 34,748 books, 76 microform titles, 323 periodicals, 2,000 records, tapes, and CDs.
COMPUTERS ON CAMPUS Computer purchase plan available. 70 computers for student use in classrooms, library.
COLLEGE LIFE Drama-theater group, student-run newspaper. *Social organizations:* 5 open to all. *Student services:* personal-psychological counseling.
HOUSING College housing not available.
CAREER PLANNING *Placement office:* 1 full-time, 1 part-time staff. *Director:* Ms. Kelly Martino, Career Counselor, 808-235-7414. *Service:* career counseling.
EXPENSES FOR 1996–97 State resident tuition: $768 full-time, $32 per credit part-time. Nonresident tuition: $5112 full-time, $213 per credit part-time. Part-time mandatory fees per semester range from $5.50 to $60.50. Full-time mandatory fees: $20.
FINANCIAL AID *College-administered undergrad aid 1995–96:* need-based scholarships (average $350), non-need scholarships (average $350), short-term loans (average $50), low-interest long-term loans from external sources (average $1000), Federal Work-Study, 100 part-time jobs. *Required forms:* CSS Financial Aid PROFILE, institutional, FAFSA. *Priority deadline:* 4/1.
APPLYING Open admission. *Option:* early entrance. *Required:* TOEFL for international students. Test scores used for admission. *Application deadlines:* rolling, 7/1 for nonresidents. *Notification:* continuous until 8/1. Preference given to state residents.
APPLYING/TRANSFER *Entrance:* noncompetitive. *Application deadline:* rolling. *Notification:* continuous until 8/1.
CONTACT Mr. Charles Heaukulani, Registrar, University of Hawaii–Windward Community College, Kaneohe, HI 96744-3528, 808-235-0077 Ext. 432.

IDAHO

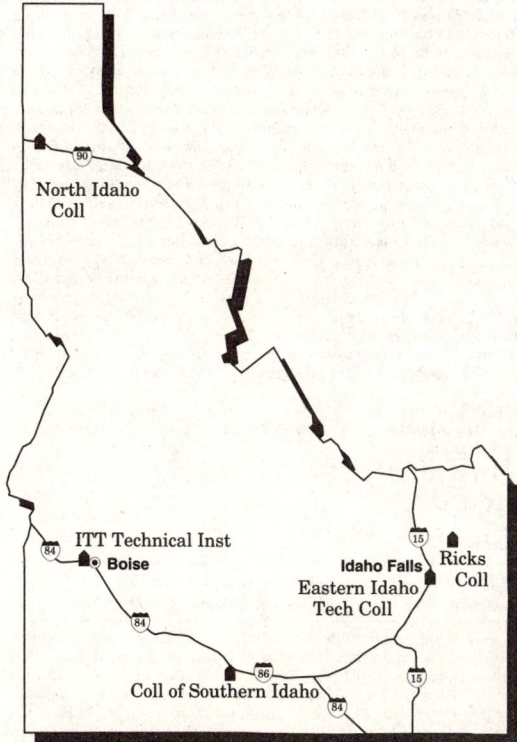

COLLEGE OF SOUTHERN IDAHO
Twin Falls, Idaho

UG Enrollment: 4,342	Tuition & Fees (Area Res): $1000
Application Deadline: rolling	Room & Board: $3130

GENERAL State and locally supported, 2-year, coed. Awards certificates, transfer associate, terminal associate degrees. Founded 1964. *Setting:* 287-acre small-town campus. *Total enrollment:* 4,342. *Faculty:* 248 (118 full-time, 130 part-time); student-faculty ratio is 18:1.
ENROLLMENT PROFILE 4,342 students from 16 states and territories, 24 other countries. 63% women, 50% part-time, 94% state residents, 2% transferred in, 1% international, 52% 25 or older, 1% Native American, 6% Hispanic, 1% African American, 1% Asian American. *Most popular recent majors:* liberal arts/general studies, elementary education, nursing.
FIRST-YEAR CLASS 1,600 total. Of the students accepted, 100% enrolled.
ACADEMIC PROGRAM Core. Calendar: semesters. Academic remediation for entering students, English as a second language program offered during academic year, advanced placement, honors program, summer session for credit, part-time degree program (daytime, evenings), adult/continuing education programs, co-op programs.
GENERAL DEGREE REQUIREMENTS 64 credits; computer course for most majors.
MAJORS Accounting, agricultural business, agricultural sciences, anthropology, art/fine arts, automotive technologies, behavioral sciences, biology/biological sciences, business education, chemistry, child care/child and family studies, commercial art, computer science, criminal justice, culinary arts, drafting and design, education, electrical and electronics technologies, elementary education, English, equestrian studies, finance/banking, food sciences, forestry, geography, heating/refrigeration/air conditioning, history, hotel and restaurant management, law enforcement/police sciences, liberal arts/general studies, library science, marketing/retailing/merchandising, mathematics, medical assistant technologies, music, music education, nursing, photography, physical education, physics, political science/government, practical nursing, psychology, real estate, retail management, secretarial studies/office management, sociology, theater arts/drama, welding technology.
LIBRARY CSD Library with 46,908 books, 274 periodicals.
COMPUTERS ON CAMPUS 250 computers for student use in computer labs, classrooms, dorms provide access to e-mail, Internet. Staffed computer lab on campus.
COLLEGE LIFE Drama-theater group, choral group. *Social organizations:* 42 open to all. *Most popular organization:* Ski Club. *Major annual events:* Homecoming, Environmental Awareness Week, Ski Day. *Student services:* legal services, health clinic, personal-psychological counseling, women's center. *Campus security:* 24-hour emergency response devices and patrols, controlled dormitory access.
HOUSING 250 college housing spaces available; 150 were occupied 1995–96. No special consideration for freshman housing applicants. Off-campus living permitted. *Option:* coed housing available. Resident assistants live in dorms.
ATHLETICS Member NJCAA. *Intercollegiate:* baseball M(s), basketball M(s)/W(s), cross-country running M(s)/W(s), equestrian sports M(s)/W(s), track and field M(s)/W(s), volleyball W(s). *Intramural:* basketball, bowling, racquetball, softball, tennis, volleyball. *Contact:* Mr. Boyd Grant, Athletic Director, 208-733-9554.
CAREER PLANNING *Placement office:* 3 full-time staff. *Director:* Mr. Colin Randolph, Career Development Director, 208-733-9554 Ext. 2286. *Services:* resume preparation, career counseling, careers library, job bank, job interviews. 2 organizations recruited on campus 1994–95.
EXPENSES FOR 1995–96 Area resident tuition: $1000 full-time, $50 per credit part-time. Nonresident tuition: $2400 full-time, $120 per credit part-time. College room and board: $3130.
FINANCIAL AID *College-administered undergrad aid 1995–96:* 500 need-based scholarships (average $450), 500 non-need scholarships (average $1800), short-term loans, low-interest long-term loans from external sources (average $3000), 800 Federal Work-Study (averaging $1600), 100 part-time jobs. *Required forms:* institutional, FAFSA. *Priority deadline:* 3/1. *Waivers:* full or partial for employees or children of employees and senior citizens. *Notification:* 5/1.
APPLYING Open admission except for nursing program. *Options:* Common Application, deferred entrance. *Required:* school transcript, TOEFL for international students. *Required for some:* ACT ASSET. Test scores used for counseling/placement. *Application deadline:* rolling.
APPLYING/TRANSFER *Required:* high school transcript, college transcript. *Entrance:* minimally difficult. *Application deadline:* rolling.
CONTACT Dr. John S. Martin, Director of Admissions, Registration, and Records, College of Southern Idaho, Twin Falls, ID 83303-1238, 208-733-9554 Ext. 2232. *Fax:* 208-736-3014. *E-mail:* ccarlile@taylor.csi.cc.id.us.

EASTERN IDAHO TECHNICAL COLLEGE
Idaho Falls, Idaho

UG Enrollment: 365	Tuition & Fees (ID Res): $1058
Application Deadline: 8/15	Room & Board: N/Avail

GENERAL State-supported, 2-year, coed. Awards certificates, terminal associate degrees. Founded 1970. *Setting:* 40-acre small-town campus. *Total enrollment:* 365. *Faculty:* 71 (38 full-time, 33 part-time); student-faculty ratio is 15:1.
ENROLLMENT PROFILE 365 students from 7 states and territories. 53% women, 47% men, 14% part-time, 98% state residents, 27% transferred in, 81% have need-based financial aid, 10% have non-need-based financial aid, 0% international, 44% 25 or older, 1% Native American, 4% Hispanic, 1% African American, 1% Asian American. *Areas of study chosen:* 20% health professions and related sciences, 19% engineering and applied sciences, 8% computer and information sciences.
FIRST-YEAR CLASS 128 total; 750 applied, 100% of whom enrolled.
ACADEMIC PROGRAM Occupational specific curriculum, honor code. Calendar: semesters. Academic remediation for entering students, English as a second language program offered during academic year, services for LD students, advanced placement, summer session for credit, part-time degree program (daytime), adult/continuing education programs, co-op programs and internships.
GENERAL DEGREE REQUIREMENTS 64 credits; computer course; internship (some majors).
MAJORS Accounting, agricultural technologies, automotive technologies, chemistry, computer technologies, electrical and electronics technologies, environmental engineering technology, laboratory technologies, legal secretarial studies, marketing/retailing/merchandising, medical assistant technologies, nuclear technology, radiological technology, secretarial studies/office management.
LIBRARY 9,700 books, 32 periodicals. Acquisition spending 1994–95: $28,053.
COMPUTERS ON CAMPUS 102 computers for student use in computer labs, learning resource center, classrooms, library provide access to e-mail, Internet.
COLLEGE LIFE *Student services:* personal-psychological counseling. *Campus security:* evening and weekend patrols by trained security personnel.
HOUSING College housing not available.
CAREER PLANNING *Placement office:* 1 full-time staff. *Director:* Mr. Dan Strakal, Placement/High School Relations Officer, 208-524-3000 Ext. 3337. *Services:* resume preparation, resume referral, career counseling, job bank, job interviews.
AFTER GRADUATION 87% of class of 1994 had job offers within 6 months.
EXPENSES FOR 1995–96 *Application fee:* $10. State resident tuition: $1058 full-time, $49 per credit part-time. Nonresident tuition: $3678 full-time, $98 per credit part-time.
FINANCIAL AID *College-administered undergrad aid 1995–96:* 60 need-based scholarships (averaging $660), 33 non-need scholarships (averaging $500), short-term loans (averaging $300), low-interest long-term loans from external sources (averaging $3749), 23 Federal Work-Study (averaging $1000), 10 part-time jobs. *Required forms:* institutional, FAFSA; accepted: CSS Financial Aid PROFILE. *Application deadline:* continuous to 6/1.
APPLYING Open admission. *Option:* deferred entrance. *Required:* school transcript, CPT. Test scores used for counseling/placement. *Application deadline:* 8/15.
APPLYING/TRANSFER *Required:* standardized test scores, high school transcript, college transcript. *Entrance:* noncompetitive. *Contact:* Ms. Beverly Bush, Registrar, 208-524-3000 Ext. 3361.
CONTACT Mr. Steve Albiston, Student Services Manager, Eastern Idaho Technical College, Idaho Falls, ID 83404-5788, 208-524-3000 Ext. 3366 or toll-free 800-662-0261. *Fax:* 208-524-3007. College video available.

ITT TECHNICAL INSTITUTE
Boise, Idaho

UG Enrollment: 339	Tuition: $15,599/deg prog
Application Deadline: rolling	Room & Board: N/Avail

GENERAL Proprietary, 2-year, coed. Part of ITT Educational Services, Inc. Awards terminal associate degrees. Founded 1906. *Setting:* 1-acre urban campus. *Total enrollment:* 339. *Faculty:* 18 (17 full-time, 80% with terminal degrees, 1 part-time); student-faculty ratio is 21:1.
ENROLLMENT PROFILE 339 students from 3 states and territories, 1 other country. *Most popular recent major:* electrical and electronics technologies.
FIRST-YEAR CLASS 168 total; 394 applied, 90% were accepted, 47% of whom enrolled.

Peterson's Guide to Two-Year Colleges 1997

ITT Technical Institute (continued)
ACADEMIC PROGRAM Honor code. Calendar: quarters. 5 courses offered in 1995–96. Academic remediation for entering students, English as a second language program, tutorials, co-op programs.
GENERAL DEGREE REQUIREMENTS 108 credit hours; math/science requirements vary according to program; computer course (varies by major).
MAJORS Drafting and design, electrical and electronics technologies.
COMPUTERS ON CAMPUS 126 computers for student use in computer center, labs, classrooms.
COLLEGE LIFE ***Campus security:*** 24-hour emergency response devices.
HOUSING College housing not available.
CAREER PLANNING ***Placement office:*** 2 full-time staff. ***Director:*** Ms. Joan Cramer, Director of Placement, 208-322-8844. ***Services:*** resume preparation, resume referral, job bank, job interviews. Students must register freshman year.
AFTER GRADUATION 80% of class of 1994 had job offers within 6 months.
EXPENSES FOR 1996–97 ***Application fee:*** $100. Tuition per degree program ranges from $15,599 to $17,690. Full-time mandatory fees range from $540 to $720.
FINANCIAL AID ***College-administered undergrad aid 1995–96:*** need-based scholarships, low-interest long-term loans from external sources, Federal Work-Study. ***Required forms:*** institutional, FAFSA. ***Application deadline:*** continuous. ***Payment plan:*** installment. ***Waivers:*** full or partial for employees or children of employees.
APPLYING ***Option:*** deferred entrance. ***Required:*** minimum 2.0 GPA, CPAt. Test scores used for admission. ***Application deadline:*** rolling.
APPLYING/TRANSFER ***Application deadline:*** rolling. ***Contact:*** Ms. Jennifer Kandler, Director of Education, 208-322-8844.
CONTACT Mr. Bart Vanry, Director of Recruitment, ITT Technical Institute, 12302 West Explorer Drive, Boise, ID 83713, 208-322-8844. ***Fax:*** 208-322-0173. College video available.

NORTH IDAHO COLLEGE
Coeur d'Alene, Idaho

UG Enrollment: 3,312	**Tuition & Fees (ID Res): $1004**
Application Deadline: 8/7	**Room & Board: $3410**

GENERAL State and locally supported, 2-year, coed. Awards certificates, transfer associate, terminal associate degrees. Founded 1933. ***Setting:*** 42-acre small-town campus. ***Endowment:*** $2.6 million. ***Educational spending 1994–95:*** $1993 per undergrad. ***Total enrollment:*** 3,312. ***Faculty:*** 260 (109 full-time, 151 part-time); student-faculty ratio is 16:1.
ENROLLMENT PROFILE 3,312 students from 24 states and territories, 8 other countries. 60% women, 40% men, 41% part-time, 88% state residents, 3% live on campus, 9% transferred in, 1% international, 36% 25 or older, 2% Native American, 2% Hispanic, 1% African American, 1% Asian American.
FIRST-YEAR CLASS 1,175 total; 1,567 applied, 97% were accepted, 77% of whom enrolled. 7% from top 10% of their high school class, 22% from top quarter, 52% from top half.
ACADEMIC PROGRAM Core, honor code. Calendar: semesters. Academic remediation for entering students, English as a second language program offered during academic year and summer, services for LD students, advanced placement, summer session for credit, part-time degree program (daytime), adult/continuing education programs, co-op programs and internships. Off-campus study at Lewis-Clark State College, University of Idaho.
GENERAL DEGREE REQUIREMENTS 64 credits; computer course for most majors; internship (some majors).
MAJORS Agricultural sciences, anthropology, art/fine arts, astronomy, automotive technologies, biology/biological sciences, botany/plant sciences, business administration/commerce/management, business education, carpentry, chemistry, child psychology/child development, commercial art, communication, computer programming, computer science, criminal justice, culinary arts, drafting and design, education, electrical and electronics technologies, elementary education, engineering (general), English, environmental health sciences, fish and game management, forestry, French, geology, German, health services administration, heating/refrigeration/air conditioning, history, human services, industrial and heavy equipment maintenance, journalism, law enforcement/police sciences, legal secretarial studies, liberal arts/general studies, machine and tool technologies, marine technology, mathematics, medical secretarial studies, medical technology, music, music education, nursing, pharmacy/pharmaceutical sciences, physical sciences, physics, political science/government, practical nursing, psychology, science, secretarial studies/office management, social science, sociology, Spanish, theater arts/drama, welding technology, wildlife biology, wildlife management, zoology.
LIBRARY North Idaho College Library with 38,179 books, 236 microform titles, 629 periodicals, 46 CD-ROMs, 469 records, tapes, and CDs. Acquisition spending 1994–95: $708,850.
COMPUTERS ON CAMPUS Computer purchase plan available. 137 computers for student use in computer labs, business department, language, math, commercial art labs, library provide access to on-line services, Internet. Staffed computer lab on campus provides training in use of computers, software. Academic computing expenditure 1994–95: $151,827.
COLLEGE LIFE Drama-theater group, choral group, student-run newspaper. 10% vote in student government elections. ***Social organizations:*** 25 open to all; 1 national fraternity, 1 national sorority; 2% of eligible men and 2% of eligible women are members. ***Most popular organizations:*** Ski Club, Baptist Student Ministries, Foreign Language Club, Residence Hall Association, Journalism Club. ***Major annual event:*** World Game. ***Student services:*** legal services, health clinic, personal-psychological counseling, women's center. ***Campus security:*** 24-hour emergency response devices and patrols, late-night transport-escort service.
HOUSING 96 college housing spaces available; all were occupied 1995–96. No special consideration for freshman housing applicants. Off-campus living permitted. ***Option:*** coed (1 building) housing available. Resident assistants live in dorms.
ATHLETICS Member NJCAA. ***Intercollegiate:*** basketball M(s)/W(s), cross-country running M(s)/W(s), track and field M(s)/W(s), volleyball W(s), wrestling M(s). ***Intramural:*** badminton, basketball, bowling, crew, cross-country running, football, golf, racquetball, riflery, sailing, skiing (cross-country), skiing (downhill), table tennis (Ping-Pong), tennis, volleyball. ***Contact:*** Mr. James Headley, Athletic Director, 208-769-3351.
CAREER PLANNING ***Placement office:*** 1 full-time, 1 part-time staff; $36,344 operating expenditure 1994–95. ***Director:*** Ms. Gail Laferriere, Career Development Specialist, 208-769-7700. ***Services:*** job fairs, resume preparation, career counseling, careers library, job bank.
EXPENSES FOR 1995–96 ***Application fee:*** $10. Area residents tuition: $980 full-time. State resident tuition: $1980 full-time. Nonresident tuition: $3286 full-time. Part-time tuition per semester ranges from $66 to $490 for area residents, $129 to $990 for state residents, $210 to $1643 for nonresidents. Tuition for nonresidents who are eligible for the Western Undergraduate Exchange Program: $2936 full-time. Tuition for Washington residents: $1868 full-time. Full-time mandatory fees: $20. College room and board: $3410.
FINANCIAL AID ***College-administered undergrad aid 1995–96:*** 388 need-based scholarships (average $464), 331 non-need scholarships (average $882), short-term loans (average $142), low-interest long-term loans from college funds (average $864), loans from external sources (average $2750), Federal Work-Study, 63 part-time jobs. ***Required forms:*** institutional, FAFSA; accepted: CSS Financial Aid PROFILE. ***Priority deadline:*** 3/15. ***Waivers:*** full or partial for employees or children of employees and senior citizens.
APPLYING Open admission except for nursing program. ***Options:*** early entrance, deferred entrance, midyear entrance. ***Required:*** TOEFL for international students. ***Recommended:*** 3 years of high school math and science, SAT I or ACT. ***Required for some:*** essay, school transcript, minimum 2.0 GPA, 3 recommendations, county residency certificate, ACT ASSET. Test scores used for counseling/placement. ***Application deadline:*** 8/7.
APPLYING/TRANSFER ***Recommended:*** standardized test scores, 3 years of high school math and science, college transcript. ***Required for some:*** essay, standardized test scores, county residency certificate. ***Entrance:*** noncompetitive. ***Application deadline:*** 8/7. ***Contact:*** Mr. M. Kirk Keonig, Director of Admissions and Financial Aid, 208-769-3311.
CONTACT Mr. M. Kirk Koenig, Director of Admissions and Financial Aid, North Idaho College, Coeur d'Alene, ID 83814-2199, 208-769-3311. ***Fax:*** 208-769-3431. ***E-mail:*** admit@nidc.edu. College video available.

RICKS COLLEGE
Rexburg, Idaho

UG Enrollment: 7,956	**Tuition & Fees: $1870**
Application Deadline: 2/15	**Room & Board: $2300**

GENERAL Independent, 2-year, coed, affiliated with Church of Jesus Christ of Latter-day Saints. Awards transfer associate, terminal associate degrees. Founded 1888. ***Setting:*** 255-acre small-town campus. ***Total enrollment:*** 7,956. ***Faculty:*** 387 (335 full-time, 27% with terminal degrees, 52 part-time); student-faculty ratio is 25:1. ***Notable Alumni:*** Annette Forsgren Winchestor, columnist; Lyndon Ricks, attorney; Nephi Bierwolf, certified public accountant; Drew Kiser, land developer; Steve Flint, university professor.
ENROLLMENT PROFILE 7,956 students from 50 states and territories, 43 other countries. 58% women, 42% men, 3% part-time, 32% state residents, 20% live on campus, 10% transferred in, 60% have need-based financial aid, 25% have non-need-based financial aid, 3% international, 2% 25 or older, 1% Native American, 1% Hispanic, 1% African American, 1% Asian American. ***Areas of study chosen:*** 27% liberal arts/general studies, 17% education, 10% business management and administrative services, 10% health professions and related sciences, 7% biological and life sciences, 7% social sciences, 5% engineering and applied sciences, 4% agriculture, 3% communications and journalism, 3% computer and information sciences, 3% fine arts, 3% performing arts, 3% premed, 3% vocational and home economics, 2% English language/literature/letters, 2% psychology, 1% foreign language and literature, 1% mathematics, 1% prelaw.
FIRST-YEAR CLASS 2,355 total; 5,355 applied, 57% were accepted, 77% of whom enrolled.
ACADEMIC PROGRAM Core, general liberal arts curriculum, honor code. Calendar: semesters. 1,000 courses offered in 1995–96. Academic remediation for entering students, advanced placement, honors program, summer session for credit, part-time degree program (daytime, evenings, summer), adult/continuing education programs, internships.
GENERAL DEGREE REQUIREMENTS 64 semester hours; computer course for agriculture, business, engineering majors; internship (some majors).
MAJORS Accounting, advertising, agricultural business, agricultural economics, agricultural sciences, agronomy/soil and crop sciences, animal sciences, architectural technologies, art/fine arts, automotive technologies, biology/biological sciences, botany/plant sciences, broadcasting, business administration/commerce/management, business education, carpentry, chemical engineering technology, chemistry, child care/child and family studies, civil engineering technology, commercial art, communication, computer information systems, computer programming, computer science, construction technologies, criminal justice, dairy sciences, dance, data processing, dental services, dietetics, drafting and design, early childhood education, ecology, economics, education, electrical and electronics technologies, electrical engineering technology, electronics engineering technology, elementary education, emergency medical technology, engineering (general), (pre)engineering sequence, engineering technology, English, family services, farm and ranch management, fashion design and technology, fashion merchandising, finance/banking, food services management, forestry, French, geography, geology, German, health science, history, home economics, home economics education, horticulture, humanities, illustration, industrial arts, industrial design, industrial engineering technology, interior design, journalism, landscape architecture/design, law enforcement/police sciences, liberal arts/general studies, machine and tool technologies, manufacturing technology, marine biology, marketing/retailing/merchandising, mathematics, mechanical design technology, mechanical engineering technology, medical laboratory technology, metallurgical technology, military science, music, music education, nursing, nutrition, occupational therapy, ornamental horticulture, photography, physical education, physical sciences, physical therapy, physics, piano/organ, plastics technology, political science/government, psychology, radio and television studies, radiological sciences, range management, recreation and leisure services, Russian, secretarial studies/office management, social work, sociology, Spanish, speech therapy, sports medicine, textiles and clothing, theater arts/drama, vocational education, welding technology, wildlife management, zoology.
LIBRARY David O'McKay Library with 143,290 books, 136,349 microform titles, 876 periodicals, 11,817 records, tapes, and CDs.
COMPUTERS ON CAMPUS 380 computers for student use in computer center, library provide access to on-line services, Internet. Staffed computer lab on campus provides training in use of computers, software.

Idaho

COLLEGE LIFE Drama-theater group, choral group, student-run newspaper, radio station. 30% vote in student government elections. *Social organizations:* 60 open to all; 1 national fraternity, 1 national sorority; 5% of eligible men and 10% of eligible women are members. *Most popular organizations:* R Friends, Dance Committee, Student Activities Committee. *Major annual events:* Homecoming, Men's Week, Women's Week. *Student services:* legal services, health clinic, personal-psychological counseling. *Campus security:* 24-hour emergency response devices and patrols, late-night transport-escort service.

HOUSING 1,364 college housing spaces available; all were occupied 1995–96. No special consideration for freshman housing applicants. Off-campus living permitted. *Option:* single-sex (8 buildings) housing available. Resident assistants live in dorms.

ATHLETICS Member NJCAA. *Intercollegiate:* baseball M(s), basketball M(s)/W(s), cross-country running M(s)/W(s), football M(s), track and field M(s)/W(s), volleyball W(s), wrestling M(s). *Intramural:* archery, badminton, basketball, bowling, cross-country running, football, golf, racquetball, skiing (downhill), soccer, softball, swimming and diving, table tennis (Ping-Pong), tennis, volleyball, water polo, wrestling. *Contact:* Dr. Don Rydalch, Athletic Director, 208-356-2103.

CAREER PLANNING *Placement office:* 11 full-time staff. *Director:* Dr. Vance Hendricks, Director of Counseling, 208-356-1100. *Services:* resume preparation, resume referral, career counseling, careers library, job interviews.

AFTER GRADUATION 90% of students completing a degree program in 1994–95 went directly on to further study.

EXPENSES FOR 1996–97 *Application fee:* $15. Comprehensive fee of $4170 includes full-time tuition ($1870 minimum) and college room and board ($2300 minimum). College room only: $1300 (minimum). Part-time tuition: $76 per semester hour (minimum). Tuition for non-church members: $3648 full-time, $114 per semester hour part-time.

FINANCIAL AID *College-administered undergrad aid 1995–96:* 800 need-based scholarships (average $486), 2,300 non-need scholarships (average $850), short-term loans (average $245), 1,300 part-time jobs. *Acceptable forms:* CSS Financial Aid PROFILE, FAFSA. *Priority deadline:* 5/1. *Waivers:* full or partial for employees or children of employees.

APPLYING *Options:* early entrance, midyear entrance. *Required:* essay, school transcript, 2 recommendations, interview, SAT I or ACT, TOEFL for international students. Test scores used for admission and counseling/placement. *Application deadline:* 2/15. *Notification:* continuous until 8/1. Preference given to Latter-day Saints Church members.

APPLYING/TRANSFER *Required:* essay, standardized test scores, high school transcript, 2 recommendations, interview, college transcript, 2.5 minimum college GPA. *Entrance:* moderately difficult. *Application deadline:* 2/15. *Notification:* continuous until 8/1. *Contact:* Mr. P. Scott Ferguson, Director of Academic Advising, 208-356-1030.

CONTACT Mr. Guy Hollingworth, Assistant Director of Admissions, Ricks College, Rexburg, ID 83460-4107, 208-356-1026. *E-mail:* birchm@ricks.edu. Electronic viewbook available.

Illinois

ILLINOIS

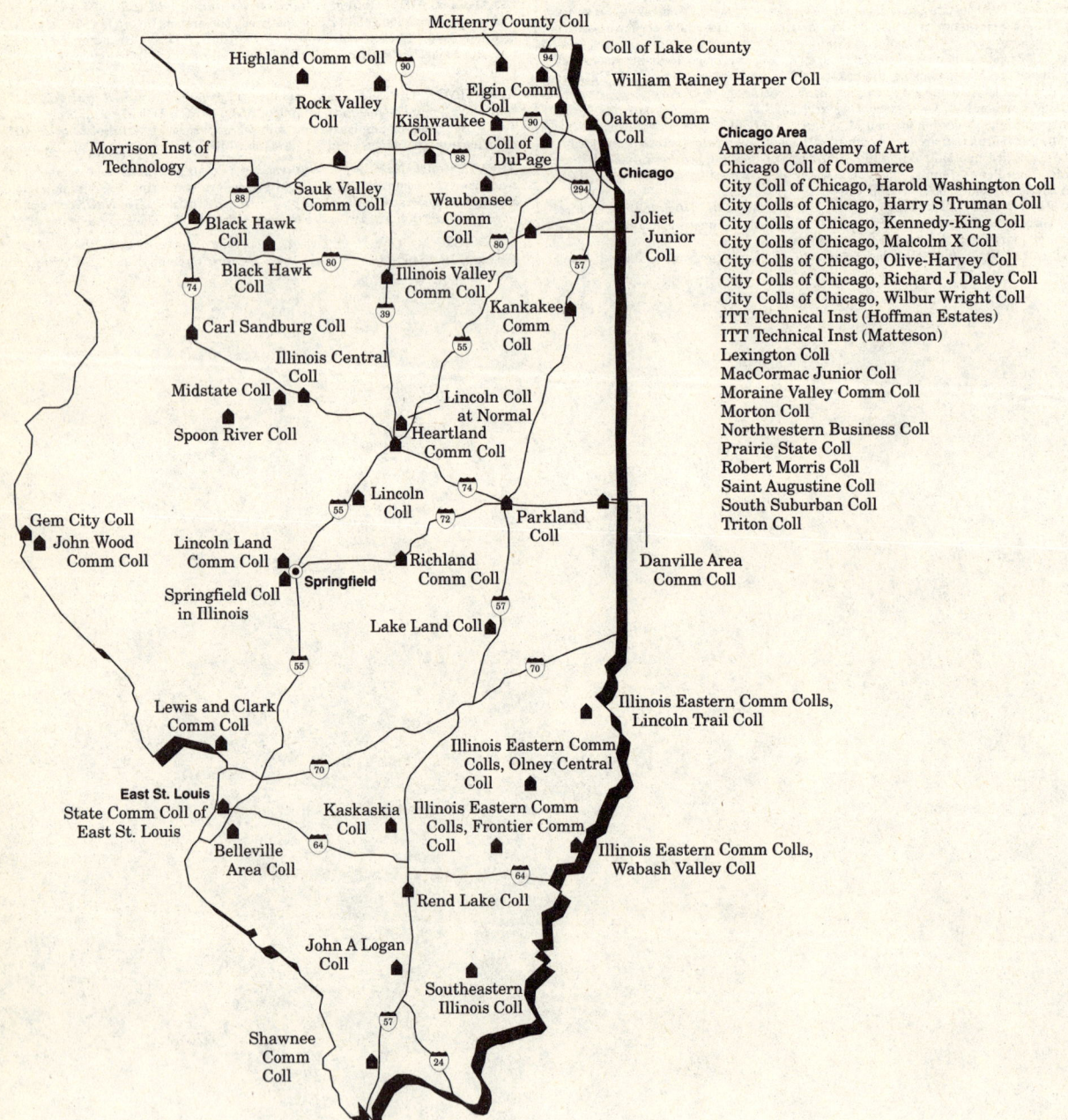

AMERICAN ACADEMY OF ART
Chicago, Illinois

UG Enrollment: 392	**Tuition & Fees:** $11,280
Application Deadline: rolling	**Room & Board:** N/Avail

GENERAL Proprietary, 2-year, specialized, coed. Awards terminal associate degrees. Founded 1923. *Setting:* urban campus. *Educational spending 1994–95:* $1867 per undergrad. *Total enrollment:* 392. *Faculty:* 34 (14 full-time, 36% with terminal degrees, 20 part-time).

ENROLLMENT PROFILE 392 students from 8 states and territories, 1 other country. 33% women, 17% part-time, 78% state residents, 19% transferred in, 68% have need-based financial aid, 0% have non-need-based financial aid, 47% 25 or older, 0% Native American, 16% Hispanic, 7% African American, 5% Asian American. *Areas of study chosen:* 100% fine arts. *Most popular recent majors:* illustration, graphic arts, computer graphics.

FIRST-YEAR CLASS 186 total. Of the students accepted, 69% enrolled.

ACADEMIC PROGRAM Core, art studio with general education curriculum, honor code. Calendar: semesters plus summer session. 88 courses offered in 1995–96. Academic remediation for entering students, tutorials, summer session for credit, part-time degree program (daytime, evenings, summer), adult/continuing education programs, internships.

GENERAL DEGREE REQUIREMENTS 64 semester hours; 1 quantitative reasoning course; 2 science courses; computer course for electronic design majors.

MAJORS Advertising, applied art, art/fine arts, commercial art, computer graphics, graphic arts, illustration, painting/drawing, studio art.

LIBRARY Irving Shapiro Library with 1,471 books, 25 periodicals. Acquisition spending 1994–95: $5188.

COMPUTERS ON CAMPUS Computer purchase plan available. 2 computers for student use in library. Academic computing expenditure 1994–95: $8460.
COLLEGE LIFE 80% vote in student government elections. ***Major annual events:*** Student Art Show, Faculty Art Show, Visiting Artist Program. ***Campus security:*** 24-hour emergency response devices.
HOUSING College housing not available.
CAREER PLANNING ***Placement office:*** 1 full-time staff; $27,000 operating expenditure 1994–95. ***Director:*** Mr. John Brunetti, Career Services Coordinator, 312-461-0600. ***Services:*** resume preparation, resume referral, career counseling, careers library, job bank, job interviews. Students must register sophomore year.
EXPENSES FOR 1995–96 ***Application fee:*** $25. Tuition: $11,280 full-time.
FINANCIAL AID ***College-administered undergrad aid 1995–96:*** need-based scholarships, low-interest long-term loans from external sources (average $2625), 9 part-time jobs. ***Required forms:*** state, institutional, FAFSA. ***Priority deadline:*** 7/31. ***Payment plan:*** installment.
APPLYING ***Required:*** TOEFL for international students. Test scores used for admission. ***Application deadline:*** rolling.
APPLYING/TRANSFER ***Entrance:*** moderately difficult. ***Application deadline:*** rolling. ***Contact:*** Ms. Marcia Thomas, Registrar, 312-461-0600.
CONTACT Ms. Mary Ellen Taylor, Director of Admissions, American Academy of Art, 332 South Michigan Ave, Suite 300, Chicago, IL 60604-4302, 312-461-0600. College video available.

BELLEVILLE AREA COLLEGE
Belleville, Illinois

UG Enrollment: 15,267 | **Tuition & Fees (Area Res): $1360**
Application Deadline: rolling | **Room & Board: N/Avail**

GENERAL District-supported, 2-year, coed. Part of Illinois Community College System. Awards certificates, diplomas, transfer associate, terminal associate degrees. Founded 1946. ***Setting:*** 150-acre suburban campus with easy access to St. Louis. ***Research spending 1994–95:*** $60,507. ***Total enrollment:*** 15,267. ***Faculty:*** 893 (127 full-time, 17% with terminal degrees, 766 part-time); student-faculty ratio is 16:1. ***Notable Alumni:*** Jerry F. Costello, member of House of Representatives; Robert H. Graebe, founder and retired CEO of Rolto Industries; William Badgley, retired CEO and chairman of the board of Magna Bank; Terry Lengfelder, managing partner for central region of Arthur Anderson and Company.
ENROLLMENT PROFILE 15,267 students from 4 states and territories, 16 other countries. 59% women, 41% men, 74% part-time, 98% state residents, 1% transferred in, 60% 25 or older, 1% Native American, 1% Hispanic, 8% African American, 2% Asian American. ***Most popular recent major:*** liberal arts/general studies.
FIRST-YEAR CLASS 3,653 total; 3,653 applied, 100% were accepted, 100% of whom enrolled.
ACADEMIC PROGRAM Core, honor code. Calendar: semesters. 1,055 courses offered in 1995–96. Academic remediation for entering students, English as a second language program offered during academic year, services for LD students, tutorials, summer session for credit, part-time degree program (daytime, evenings, summer), adult/continuing education programs, co-op programs and internships. Off-campus study at other Illinois community colleges. ROTC: Air Force.
GENERAL DEGREE REQUIREMENTS 64 credit hours; 8 credit hours of math/science; computer course for some majors; internship (some majors).
MAJORS Accounting, aircraft and missile maintenance, aviation technology, business administration/commerce/management, business education, carpentry, chemical engineering technology, child care/child and family studies, computer graphics, computer information systems, construction management, criminal justice, data processing, drafting and design, electrical and electronics technologies, emergency medical technology, (pre)engineering sequence, engineering technology, fire science, flight training, food services management, heating/refrigeration/air conditioning, horticulture, instrumentation technology, law enforcement/police sciences, legal secretarial studies, liberal arts/general studies, marketing/retailing/merchandising, medical assistant technologies, medical laboratory technology, medical records services, medical secretarial studies, mining technology, nursing, paralegal studies, physical therapy, radiological technology, real estate, respiratory therapy, secretarial studies/office management, welding technology.
LIBRARY Belleville Area College Library plus 2 others, with 80,721 books, 183 microform titles, 537 periodicals, 12 CD-ROMs, 1,099 records, tapes, and CDs. Acquisition spending 1994–95: $100,301.
COMPUTERS ON CAMPUS Computer purchase plan available. 250 computers for student use in computer center, computer labs, learning resource center, classrooms, library. Staffed computer lab on campus provides training in use of computers, software. Academic computing expenditure 1994–95: $558,898.
COLLEGE LIFE Drama-theater group, choral group, student-run newspaper. 2% vote in student government elections. ***Social organizations:*** 35 open to all. ***Most popular organizations:*** College Activities Board, Phi Beta Kappa, Student Nurses Association, Horticulture Club, Data Processing Management Association. ***Major annual events:*** Spring Blast, Fall Fest, Summer Picnic. ***Student services:*** personal-psychological counseling, women's center. ***Campus security:*** 24-hour emergency response devices and patrols, student patrols, late-night transport-escort service.
HOUSING College housing not available.
ATHLETICS Member NJCAA. ***Intercollegiate:*** baseball M(s), basketball M(s)/W(s), soccer M(s), softball W(s), tennis M(s)/W(s), volleyball W(s). ***Intramural:*** basketball, bowling, golf, softball, tennis, volleyball. ***Contact:*** Mr. Jay Harrington, Athletic Director, 618-235-2700 Ext. 271.
CAREER PLANNING ***Placement office:*** 3 full-time, 5 part-time staff. ***Director:*** Ms. Martha Nelson, Director, 618-235-2700 Ext. 562. ***Services:*** job fairs, resume preparation, resume referral, career counseling, careers library, job bank, job interviews.
EXPENSES FOR 1996–97 ***Application fee:*** $10. Area resident tuition: $1360 full-time, $42.50 per credit hour part-time. State resident tuition: $2912 full-time, $91 per credit hour part-time. Nonresident tuition: $5088 full-time, $159 per credit hour part-time.
FINANCIAL AID ***College-administered undergrad aid 1995–96:*** 451 need-based scholarships (average $447), 255 non-need scholarships (average $1182), short-term loans (average $50), low-interest long-term loans from external sources (average $2625), 153 Federal Work-Study (averaging $1069), 395 part-time jobs. ***Required forms:*** institutional, FAFSA; accepted: CSS Financial Aid PROFILE. ***Priority deadline:*** 5/31. ***Payment plan:*** deferred payment. ***Waivers:*** full or partial for employees or children of employees and senior citizens. ***Average indebtedness of graduates:*** $3600.
APPLYING Open admission. ***Options:*** early entrance, deferred entrance, midyear entrance. ***Required:*** TOEFL for international students. ***Required for some:*** ACT, ACT ASSET. Test scores used for counseling/placement. ***Application deadline:*** rolling.
APPLYING/TRANSFER ***Required for some:*** standardized test scores. ***Application deadline:*** rolling. ***Contact:*** Ms. Jann Haskins, Director of Admissions, 618-235-2700 Ext. 400.
CONTACT Ms. Jann Haskins, Director of Admissions, Belleville Area College, Belleville, IL 62221-5899, 618-235-2700 Ext. 400 or toll-free 800-222-5131 (in-state). ***Fax:*** 618-235-1578.

BLACK HAWK COLLEGE
Kewanee, Illinois

UG Enrollment: 765 | **Tuition & Fees (Area Res): $1590**
Application Deadline: rolling | **Room & Board: N/Avail**

GENERAL State and locally supported, 2-year, coed. Part of Black Hawk College District System. Awards transfer associate, terminal associate degrees. Founded 1967. ***Setting:*** 102-acre rural campus. ***Total enrollment:*** 765. ***Faculty:*** 46 (23 full-time, 23 part-time).
ENROLLMENT PROFILE 765 students: 57% women, 43% men, 45% part-time, 97% state residents, 9% transferred in, 36% 25 or older, 0% Native American, 2% Hispanic, 2% African American. ***Most popular recent majors:*** liberal arts/general studies, agricultural technologies, agricultural business.
FIRST-YEAR CLASS 502 applied, 100% were accepted.
ACADEMIC PROGRAM Core. Calendar: semesters. Academic remediation for entering students, advanced placement, self-designed majors, summer session for credit, part-time degree program (daytime, evenings, summer), adult/continuing education programs, co-op programs. Study abroad in Austria, England.
GENERAL DEGREE REQUIREMENT 64 semester hours.
MAJORS Agricultural business, agricultural sciences, agricultural technologies, automotive technologies, business administration/commerce/management, business education, business machine technologies, equestrian studies, industrial administration, legal secretarial studies, liberal arts/general studies, medical secretarial studies, nursing, secretarial studies/office management.
LIBRARY 15,819 books, 3,531 microform titles, 254 periodicals, 300 records, tapes, and CDs.
COMPUTERS ON CAMPUS 62 computers for student use in computer center. Staffed computer lab on campus.
COLLEGE LIFE 10% vote in student government elections. ***Student services:*** personal-psychological counseling.
HOUSING College housing not available.
ATHLETICS Member NJCAA. ***Intercollegiate:*** basketball M(s)/W(s), track and field M(s)/W(s). ***Intramural:*** basketball. ***Contact:*** Mr. Nelson Lay, Athletic Director, 309-852-5671 Ext. 269.
CAREER PLANNING ***Placement office:*** 1 full-time staff. ***Director:*** Mr. Larry Crawford, Career Placement Counselor, 309-796-1311 Ext. 1358. ***Service:*** career counseling.
EXPENSES FOR 1996–97 Area resident tuition: $1470 full-time, $49 per semester hour part-time. State resident tuition: $3150 full-time, $105 per semester hour part-time. Nonresident tuition: $5670 full-time, $189 per semester hour part-time. Part-time mandatory fees: $4 per semester hour. Full-time mandatory fees: $120.
FINANCIAL AID ***College-administered undergrad aid 1995–96:*** need-based scholarships, non-need scholarships, 50 Federal Work-Study (averaging $1000), part-time jobs. ***Required forms:*** FAFSA; accepted: CSS Financial Aid PROFILE, state. ***Priority deadline:*** 7/15. ***Payment plan:*** deferred payment. ***Waivers:*** full or partial for employees or children of employees and senior citizens.
APPLYING Open admission except for nursing program. ***Options:*** early entrance, deferred entrance, midyear entrance. ***Required:*** school transcript, TOEFL for international students, ACT ASSET. Test scores used for counseling/placement. ***Application deadline:*** rolling. ***Notification:*** continuous.
APPLYING/TRANSFER ***Required:*** high school transcript, college transcript. ***Application deadline:*** rolling. ***Notification:*** continuous. ***Contact:*** Mrs. Patricia Varner, Director of Educational Services, 309-852-5671 Ext. 222.
CONTACT Mrs. Patricia Varner, Director of Educational Services, Black Hawk College, Kewanee, IL 61443, 309-852-5671 Ext. 222.

BLACK HAWK COLLEGE
Moline, Illinois

UG Enrollment: 6,335 | **Tuition & Fees (Area Res): $1696**
Application Deadline: rolling | **Room & Board: N/Avail**

GENERAL State and locally supported, 2-year, coed. Part of Black Hawk College District System. Awards transfer associate, terminal associate degrees. Founded 1946. ***Setting:*** 149-acre suburban campus. ***Total enrollment:*** 6,335. ***Faculty:*** 488 (153 full-time, 335 part-time).
ENROLLMENT PROFILE 6,335 students: 62% women, 57% part-time, 95% state residents, 21% transferred in, 0% international, 63% 25 or older, 0% Native American, 5% Hispanic, 5% African American, 1% Asian American. ***Most popular recent majors:*** liberal arts/general studies, business administration/commerce/management, elementary education.
FIRST-YEAR CLASS Of the students who applied, 100% were accepted.
ACADEMIC PROGRAM Core. Calendar: semesters. Academic remediation for entering students, English as a second language program offered during academic year, advanced placement, summer session for credit, part-time degree program (daytime, evenings, summer), adult/continuing education programs. Off-campus study at Scott Community College. Study abroad in Austria, England.
GENERAL DEGREE REQUIREMENTS 64 semester hours; math/science requirements vary according to program.
MAJORS Accounting, anthropology, archaeology, art/fine arts, automotive technologies, biology/biological sciences, broadcasting, business administration/commerce/management, chemistry, child care/child and family studies, commercial art, computer programming,

Peterson's Guide to Two-Year Colleges 1997

283

Black Hawk College (continued)
computer science, computer technologies, cosmetology, culinary arts, data processing, dental services, drafting and design, earth science, economics, education, electrical and electronics technologies, electrical engineering technology, elementary education, (pre)engineering sequence, engineering technology, English, fashion design and technology, fashion merchandising, finance/banking, French, German, history, hotel and restaurant management, interior design, journalism, labor studies, law enforcement/police sciences, legal secretarial studies, liberal arts/general studies, machine and tool technologies, manufacturing technology, marketing/retailing/merchandising, mathematics, mechanical design technology, mechanical engineering technology, medical records services, medical secretarial studies, music, natural sciences, nursing, physical education, physical sciences, political science/ government, practical nursing, psychology, public relations, radio and television studies, real estate, respiratory therapy, retail management, robotics, secretarial studies/office management, sociology, Spanish, speech/rhetoric/public address/debate, technical writing, theater arts/drama, veterinary sciences.
LIBRARY Quad City Campus Library with 44,758 books, 383 microform titles, 521 periodicals, 725 records, tapes, and CDs.
COMPUTERS ON CAMPUS 130 computers for student use in library.
COLLEGE LIFE Drama-theater group, student-run newspaper, radio station. ***Campus security:*** 24-hour patrols.
HOUSING College housing not available.
ATHLETICS Member NJCAA. ***Intercollegiate:*** basketball M/W, golf M, volleyball W. ***Intramural:*** basketball, golf, skiing (cross-country), skiing (downhill), soccer, swimming and diving, tennis, track and field, volleyball, wrestling.
CAREER PLANNING ***Placement office:*** 2 full-time staff. ***Director:*** Mr. Larry Crawford, Director of Placement, 309-796-1311 Ext. 1358. ***Services:*** resume preparation, career counseling, careers library.
EXPENSES FOR 1996–97 Area resident tuition: $1696 full-time, $53 per semester hour part-time. State resident tuition: $4160 full-time, $130 per semester hour part-time. Nonresident tuition: $7296 full-time, $228 per semester hour part-time.
FINANCIAL AID ***College-administered undergrad aid 1995–96:*** 86 need-based scholarships (averaging $590), 113 non-need scholarships (averaging $270), low-interest long-term loans from external sources (averaging $1538), Federal Work-Study, 158 part-time jobs. ***Required forms for some financial aid applicants:*** institutional; accepted: CSS Financial Aid PROFILE, state, FAFSA. ***Priority deadline:*** 5/15. ***Payment plan:*** deferred payment. ***Waivers:*** full or partial for employees or children of employees and senior citizens.
APPLYING Open admission except for nursing program. ***Option:*** early entrance. ***Required:*** school transcript. ***Required for some:*** ACT, ACT ASSET. Test scores used for counseling/placement. ***Application deadline:*** rolling.
APPLYING/TRANSFER ***Required:*** college transcript. ***Required for some:*** standardized test scores. ***Entrance:*** noncompetitive.
CONTACT Ms. Judy Miller, Coordinator of New Student Services, Black Hawk College, Moline, IL 61265-5899, 309-796-1311 Ext. 1238.

CARL SANDBURG COLLEGE
Galesburg, Illinois

UG Enrollment: 3,000 **Tuition & Fees (Area Res): $1745**
Application Deadline: rolling **Room & Board: N/Avail**

GENERAL State and locally supported, 2-year, coed. Part of Illinois Community College System. Awards transfer associate, terminal associate degrees. Founded 1967. ***Setting:*** 105-acre small-town campus. ***Educational spending 1994–95:*** $1150 per undergrad. ***Total enrollment:*** 3,000. ***Faculty:*** 208 (58 full-time, 5% with terminal degrees, 150 part-time); student-faculty ratio is 12:1.
ENROLLMENT PROFILE 3,000 students from 5 states and territories, 2 other countries. 54% women, 78% part-time, 80% state residents, 14% transferred in, 1% international, 1% Native American, 3% Hispanic, 8% African American, 1% Asian American. ***Most popular recent majors:*** liberal arts/general studies, nursing.
FIRST-YEAR CLASS Of the students who applied, 100% were accepted, 95% of whom enrolled.
ACADEMIC PROGRAM Honor code. Calendar: semesters. Academic remediation for entering students, English as a second language program offered during academic year, services for LD students, advanced placement, self-designed majors, summer session for credit, part-time degree program (daytime, evenings, summer), adult/continuing education programs, co-op programs and internships. ROTC: Army (c).
GENERAL DEGREE REQUIREMENTS 64 semester hours; 8 semester hours of math; 6 semester hours of lab science; computer course for all associate of science degree students; internship (some majors).
MAJORS Accounting, agricultural business, agricultural technologies, automotive technologies, business administration/commerce/management, child psychology/child development, cosmetology, criminal justice, data processing, drafting and design, electrical and electronics technologies, fashion merchandising, law enforcement/police sciences, liberal arts/general studies, marketing/retailing/merchandising, nursing, practical nursing, radiological technology, real estate, secretarial studies/office management.
LIBRARY LRC plus 1 other, with 39,900 books, 290 periodicals, 3 CD-ROMs, 2,638 records, tapes, and CDs. Acquisition spending 1994–95: $34,775.
COMPUTERS ON CAMPUS 110 computers for student use in computer labs. Staffed computer lab on campus provides training in use of computers, software.
COLLEGE LIFE Drama-theater group, choral group. 4% vote in student government elections. ***Student services:*** personal-psychological counseling. ***Campus security:*** 24-hour emergency response devices and patrols.
HOUSING College housing not available.
ATHLETICS Member NJCAA. ***Intercollegiate:*** baseball M(s), basketball M(s)/W(s), volleyball W(s). ***Contact:*** Mr. William Hungate, Athletic Director, 309-344-2518.
CAREER PLANNING ***Placement office:*** 1 full-time staff; $31,000 operating expenditure 1994–95. ***Director:*** Ms. Janis Hipple, Coordinator of Career Planning and Placement, 309-344-2518 Ext. 246. ***Services:*** job fairs, resume preparation, resume referral, career counseling, careers library, job interviews.
AFTER GRADUATION 63% of students completing a degree program in 1994–95 went directly on to further study.
EXPENSES FOR 1996–97 Area resident tuition: $1590 full-time, $53 per semester hour part-time. State resident tuition: $3480 full-time, $116 per semester hour part-time. Nonresident tuition: $6510 full-time, $217 per semester hour part-time. Part-time mandatory fees: $6 per semester hour. Full-time mandatory fees: $155.
FINANCIAL AID ***College-administered undergrad aid 1995–96:*** 140 need-based scholarships (average $400), 31 non-need scholarships (average $500), short-term loans, Federal Work-Study. ***Required forms:*** institutional; accepted: CSS Financial Aid PROFILE, FAFSA. ***Application deadline:*** continuous. ***Payment plan:*** deferred payment. ***Waivers:*** full or partial for employees or children of employees and senior citizens. ***Notification:*** continuous.
APPLYING Open admission for district residents. ***Options:*** early entrance, deferred entrance, midyear entrance. ***Required:*** school transcript, TOEFL for international students. ***Recommended:*** 3 years of high school math and science, some high school foreign language. Test scores used for counseling/placement. ***Application deadline:*** rolling.
APPLYING/TRANSFER ***Required:*** high school transcript, college transcript. ***Recommended:*** 3 years of high school math and science, some high school foreign language. ***Entrance:*** noncompetitive. ***Application deadline:*** rolling.
CONTACT Mr. Phillip J. Mackey, Dean of Student Services, Carl Sandburg College, Galesburg, IL 61401-9576, 309-344-2518 Ext. 227.

CHICAGO COLLEGE OF COMMERCE
Chicago, Illinois

UG Enrollment: 292 **Tuition & Fees: $8170**
Application Deadline: rolling **Room & Board: N/Avail**

GENERAL Proprietary, 2-year, primarily women. Awards certificates, terminal associate degrees. Founded 1950. ***Setting:*** urban campus. ***Total enrollment:*** 292. ***Faculty:*** 18 (6 full-time, 84% with terminal degrees, 12 part-time); student-faculty ratio is 16:1. ***Notable Alumni:*** Jerome E. Miller, former president of NSRA and head of Illinois State Court Official Reporters; G. Allen Sonntag, Illinois speed contest champion; Richard Dadgigian, federal official reporter.
ENROLLMENT PROFILE 292 students from 2 states and territories. 96% women, 4% men, 60% part-time, 98% state residents, 12% transferred in, 0% international, 79% 25 or older, 1% Native American, 9% Hispanic, 32% African American, 1% Asian American. ***Areas of study chosen:*** 100% business management and administrative services.
FIRST-YEAR CLASS 128 total; 156 applied, 96% were accepted, 86% of whom enrolled.
ACADEMIC PROGRAM Core. Calendar: quarters. Advanced placement, summer session for credit, part-time degree program (evenings, weekends).
GENERAL DEGREE REQUIREMENTS 90 credits; internship (some majors).
MAJORS Court reporting, legal secretarial studies, medical secretarial studies.
LIBRARY Main library plus 1 other, with 1,000 books, 5 periodicals, 1,050 records, tapes, and CDs.
COMPUTERS ON CAMPUS 20 computers for student use in computer center, computer labs, classrooms. Staffed computer lab on campus provides training in use of computers, software.
COLLEGE LIFE ***Most popular organization:*** Student Council. ***Major annual event:*** Holiday Party. ***Campus security:*** 24-hour emergency response devices, guard on duty during building hours.
HOUSING College housing not available.
CAREER PLANNING ***Placement office:*** 1 full-time staff. ***Director:*** Ms. Sharon A. Zeman, Registrar, 312-236-3312. ***Services:*** resume preparation, resume referral, career counseling, job interviews.
EXPENSES FOR 1995–96 ***Application fee:*** $40. Tuition: $8000 full-time, $1000 per quarter part-time. Part-time mandatory fees: $170 per year. Full-time mandatory fees: $170.
FINANCIAL AID ***College-administered undergrad aid 1995–96:*** 60 need-based scholarships (average $150), low-interest long-term loans from external sources. ***Required forms:*** CSS Financial Aid PROFILE, institutional, FAFSA. ***Priority deadline:*** 6/11. ***Payment plans:*** tuition prepayment, installment.
APPLYING Open admission. ***Option:*** deferred entrance. ***Recommended:*** ACT. Test scores used for counseling/placement. ***Application deadline:*** rolling.
APPLYING/TRANSFER ***Entrance:*** noncompetitive. ***Application deadline:*** rolling. ***Contact:*** Ms. Sharon Zeman, Registrar, 312-236-3312.
CONTACT Ms. Sharon Zeman, Registrar, Chicago College of Commerce, 11 East Adams Street, Chicago, IL 60603-6301, 312-236-3312.

CITY COLLEGES OF CHICAGO, HAROLD WASHINGTON COLLEGE
Chicago, Illinois

UG Enrollment: 7,745 **Tuition & Fees (Area Res): $1285**
Application Deadline: rolling **Room & Board: N/Avail**

GENERAL State and locally supported, 2-year, coed. Part of City Colleges of Chicago System. Awards certificates, transfer associate, terminal associate degrees. Founded 1962. ***Setting:*** 1-acre urban campus. ***Total enrollment:*** 7,745. ***Faculty:*** 681 (142 full-time, 23% with terminal degrees, 539 part-time).
ENROLLMENT PROFILE 7,745 students: 63% women, 37% men, 77% part-time, 94% state residents, 11% transferred in, 3% international, 61% 25 or older, 1% Native American, 15% Hispanic, 49% African American, 11% Asian American. ***Areas of study chosen:*** 12% liberal arts/general studies, 4% business management and administrative services, 4% engineering and applied sciences, 4% health professions and related sciences, 3% computer and information sciences, 2% education, 1% architecture, 1% biological and life sciences, 1% fine arts, 1% premed, 1% social sciences.
FIRST-YEAR CLASS 2,588 total; 5,521 applied, 100% were accepted, 47% of whom enrolled.
ACADEMIC PROGRAM Core, interdisciplinary curriculum, honor code. Calendar: semesters. 700 courses offered in 1995–96; average class size 25 in required courses. Academic remediation for entering students, English as a second language program offered during academic year and summer, services for LD students, advanced placement, tutorials, summer session for credit, part-time degree program (daytime, evenings, summer), adult/continuing education programs, co-op programs and internships. ROTC: Air Force (c).
GENERAL DEGREE REQUIREMENTS 60 credit hours; internship (some majors).

MAJORS Accounting, architectural technologies, art/fine arts, automotive technologies, biology/biological sciences, business administration/commerce/management, ceramic art and design, chemistry, child care/child and family studies, child psychology/child development, commercial art, computer science, corrections, criminal justice, data processing, drafting and design, early childhood education, elementary education, emergency medical technology, engineering (general), engineering and applied sciences, (pre)engineering sequence, engineering technology, English, finance/banking, fire science, food services management, French, German, hospitality services, hotel and restaurant management, humanities, industrial administration, industrial engineering technology, international business, Italian, Japanese, journalism, law enforcement/police sciences, legal studies, marketing/retailing/merchandising, mathematics, medical secretarial studies, mental health/rehabilitation counseling, music, occupational therapy, painting/drawing, philosophy, physical sciences, physics, recreation and leisure services, retail management, social science, social work, Spanish, speech/rhetoric/public address/debate, studio art, teacher aide studies, theater arts/drama, tourism and travel, transportation technologies.
LIBRARY Main library plus 1 other, with 60,000 books, 145 microform titles, 325 periodicals, 28 CD-ROMs, 3,000 records, tapes, and CDs. Acquisition spending 1994–95: $160,000.
COMPUTERS ON CAMPUS 325 computers for student use in computer center, computer labs, language lab, library provide access to main academic computer, Internet. Staffed computer lab on campus provides training in use of computers, software.
COLLEGE LIFE Orientation program (2 days, no cost). Drama-theater group, choral group, student-run newspaper. ***Social organizations:*** 15 open to all. ***Most popular organizations:*** Phi Theta Kappa, Organization of Latin American Students, Black Student Union, Student Government Association, Global Friendship. ***Major annual events:*** Black History Month Activities, Hispanic-American History Month, Women's History Month. ***Student services:*** personal-psychological counseling, women's center. ***Campus security:*** 24-hour emergency response devices.
HOUSING College housing not available.
CAREER PLANNING ***Placement office:*** 1 full-time, 1 part-time staff; $98,757 operating expenditure 1994–95. ***Director:*** Ms. Carolyn Gabriel, Director of Career Guidance and Job Placement, 312-553-5665. ***Services:*** job fairs, resume preparation, resume referral, career counseling, careers library, job bank, job interviews. 70 organizations recruited on campus 1994–95.
EXPENSES FOR 1995–96 Area resident tuition: $1245 full-time, $41.50 per credit hour part-time. State resident tuition: $3565 full-time, $118.85 per credit hour part-time. Nonresident tuition: $4408 full-time, $146.95 per credit hour part-time. Part-time mandatory fees: $20 per semester. Full-time mandatory fees: $40.
FINANCIAL AID ***College-administered undergrad aid 1995–96:*** 25 non-need scholarships (average $900), low-interest long-term loans from external sources (average $2100), 95 Federal Work-Study, part-time jobs. ***Required forms:*** institutional, FAFSA, proof of citizenship, financial aid transcript from previous institution; accepted: CSS Financial Aid PROFILE. ***Priority deadline:*** 8/15. ***Payment plans:*** installment, deferred payment. ***Waivers:*** full or partial for employees or children of employees and senior citizens. ***Notification:*** continuous.
APPLYING Open admission. ***Options:*** early entrance, deferred entrance, midyear entrance. ***Recommended:*** SAT I or ACT, TOEFL for international students. Test scores used for counseling/placement. ***Application deadline:*** rolling. ***Notification:*** continuous.
APPLYING/TRANSFER ***Recommended:*** college transcript. ***Entrance:*** noncompetitive. ***Application deadline:*** rolling. ***Notification:*** continuous. ***Contact:*** Ms. Tina Hirsch, Director of Transfer Center, 312-553-3000.
CONTACT Ms. Elizabeth Silk, Assistant Dean for Research and Planning, City Colleges of Chicago, Harold Washington College, 30 East Lake Street, Chicago, IL 60601-2420, 312-553-5926. ***Fax:*** 312-553-6077.

CITY COLLEGES OF CHICAGO, HARRY S TRUMAN COLLEGE
Chicago, Illinois

UG Enrollment: 4,620 **Tuition & Fees (Area Res): $1305**
Application Deadline: rolling **Room & Board: N/Avail**

GENERAL State and locally supported, 2-year, coed. Part of City Colleges of Chicago System. Awards transfer associate, terminal associate degrees. Founded 1956. ***Setting:*** 5-acre urban campus. ***Total enrollment:*** 4,620. ***Faculty:*** 160 (70% of full-time faculty have terminal degrees); student-faculty ratio is 25:1.
ENROLLMENT PROFILE 4,620 students: 55% women, 64% part-time, 98% state residents, 4% transferred in, 2% international, 70% 25 or older, 1% Native American, 13% Hispanic, 20% African American, 24% Asian American. ***Most popular recent majors:*** nursing, medical records services, computer information systems.
FIRST-YEAR CLASS 1,092 total; 1,092 applied, 100% were accepted, 100% of whom enrolled.
ACADEMIC PROGRAM Core, honor code. Calendar: semesters. Academic remediation for entering students, English as a second language program offered during academic year, services for LD students, advanced placement, honors program, summer session for credit, part-time degree program (daytime, evenings, weekends, summer), adult/continuing education programs, co-op programs.
GENERAL DEGREE REQUIREMENTS 60 semester hours; 3 semester hours of math/science; internship (some majors).
MAJORS Accounting, art/fine arts, business administration/commerce/management, chemical engineering technology, child psychology/child development, computer information systems, drafting and design, education, elementary education, (pre)engineering sequence, industrial administration, journalism, law enforcement/police sciences, legal studies, liberal arts/general studies, marketing/retailing/merchandising, medical records services, medical secretarial studies, medical technology, modern languages, nursing, physical education, speech/rhetoric/public address/debate, teacher aide studies.
LIBRARY 59,750 books, 395 microform titles, 250 periodicals, 21,900 records, tapes, and CDs.
COMPUTERS ON CAMPUS 150 computers for student use in computer center, computer labs.
COLLEGE LIFE Drama-theater group, student-run newspaper. ***Social organizations:*** 40 open to all. ***Student services:*** personal-psychological counseling. ***Campus security:*** 24-hour patrols, late-night transport-escort service.
HOUSING College housing not available.
ATHLETICS Member NJCAA. ***Intercollegiate:*** baseball M, basketball M/W, tennis M/W, wrestling M. ***Intramural:*** basketball, swimming and diving, tennis, volleyball. ***Contact:*** Mr. Richard Kampwirth, Chairperson of Physical Education Program, 312-907-4660.
CAREER PLANNING ***Placement office:*** 1 full-time, 1 part-time staff. ***Director:*** Mr. Steven Parker, Director, Placement Services, 312-907-4730. ***Services:*** job fairs, career counseling, job bank, job interviews.
EXPENSES FOR 1995–96 Area resident tuition: $1245 full-time, $41.50 per semester hour part-time. State resident tuition: $3565 full-time, $118.85 per semester hour part-time. Nonresident tuition: $4408 full-time, $146.95 per semester hour part-time. Part-time mandatory fees: $20 per semester. Full-time mandatory fees: $60.
FINANCIAL AID ***College-administered undergrad aid 1995–96:*** 969 need-based scholarships (average $781), 377 non-need scholarships (average $170), low-interest long-term loans from external sources (average $3000), Federal Work-Study, 21 part-time jobs. ***Required forms:*** institutional, FAFSA, proof of citizenship, financial aid transcript from previous institution; accepted: CSS Financial Aid PROFILE. ***Application deadline:*** continuous to 7/15. ***Payment plans:*** installment, deferred payment. ***Waivers:*** full or partial for employees or children of employees and senior citizens. ***Notification:*** continuous.
APPLYING Open admission. ***Options:*** early entrance, deferred entrance. ***Required:*** ACT. ***Recommended:*** TOEFL for international students. Test scores used for counseling/placement. ***Application deadline:*** rolling. ***Notification:*** continuous until 9/8.
APPLYING/TRANSFER ***Required:*** standardized test scores. ***Entrance:*** noncompetitive. ***Application deadline:*** rolling. ***Notification:*** continuous until 9/8.
CONTACT Ms. Cathy Battle, Director of Admissions, City Colleges of Chicago, Harry S Truman College, 1145 West Wilson Avenue, Chicago, IL 60640-5616, 312-907-4750. ***Fax:*** 312-989-6135.

CITY COLLEGES OF CHICAGO, KENNEDY-KING COLLEGE
Chicago, Illinois

UG Enrollment: 2,539 **Tuition & Fees (Area Res): $1285**
Application Deadline: rolling **Room & Board: N/Avail**

GENERAL State and locally supported, 2-year, coed. Part of City Colleges of Chicago System. Awards certificates, transfer associate, terminal associate degrees. Founded 1935. ***Setting:*** 18-acre urban campus. ***Total enrollment:*** 2,539. ***Faculty:*** 106 (103 full-time, 28% with terminal degrees, 3 part-time); student-faculty ratio is 28:1. ***Notable Alumni:*** Dempsy Travis, Dr. Carmen Hudson White, Fred Rice, Gwendolyn Brooks, Christine Houston.
ENROLLMENT PROFILE 2,539 students: 71% women, 61% part-time, 99% state residents, 4% transferred in, 1% international, 61% 25 or older, 1% Native American, 1% Hispanic, 96% African American, 1% Asian American. ***Most popular recent majors:*** liberal arts/general studies, nursing, business administration/commerce/management.
FIRST-YEAR CLASS 423 total; 710 applied, 100% were accepted, 62% of whom enrolled. 20% from top 10% of their high school class, 35% from top quarter, 45% from top half.
ACADEMIC PROGRAM Core, honor code. Calendar: semesters. Academic remediation for entering students, English as a second language program offered during academic year, advanced placement, honors program, summer session for credit, part-time degree program (daytime, evenings, weekends, summer), adult/continuing education programs, co-op programs and internships.
GENERAL DEGREE REQUIREMENTS 60 semester hours; math/science requirements vary according to program.
MAJORS Accounting, architectural technologies, automotive technologies, biology/biological sciences, broadcasting, business administration/commerce/management, chemistry, child care/child and family studies, commercial art, data processing, early childhood education, education, engineering (general), (pre)engineering sequence, food services management, health science, heating/refrigeration/air conditioning, home economics, legal studies, liberal arts/general studies, marketing/retailing/merchandising, mathematics, medical technology, mental health/rehabilitation counseling, nursing, pharmacy/pharmaceutical sciences, physics, printing technologies, radio and television studies, recreation and leisure services, secretarial studies/office management, social work, teacher aide studies.
LIBRARY Harold Washington Library with 41,906 books, 164 microform titles, 264 periodicals, 29,422 records, tapes, and CDs.
COMPUTERS ON CAMPUS Computer purchase plan available. 40 computers for student use in computer labs. Staffed computer lab on campus.
COLLEGE LIFE Orientation program (2 days, no cost, parents included). Drama-theater group, choral group, student-run newspaper, radio station. ***Social organizations:*** 12 open to all; national fraternities; 1% of eligible men are members. ***Most popular organizations:*** Phi Theta Kappa, Phi Beta Lambda, Herman Bryant Auto Club, Communication Art Guild, Print Club (POP). ***Major annual events:*** Freshmen Reception, Honors Convocation, Career Week. ***Student services:*** personal-psychological counseling. ***Campus security:*** late-night transport-escort service.
HOUSING College housing not available.
ATHLETICS Member NJCAA. ***Intercollegiate:*** basketball M(s), track and field M/W. ***Intramural:*** basketball, volleyball. ***Contact:*** Ms. Kathleen Welch, Dean of Student Services, 312-602-5081.
CAREER PLANNING ***Placement office:*** 2 part-time staff. ***Director:*** Mr. Darnell Sanford, Coordinator, 312-602-5111. ***Services:*** job fairs, resume preparation, career counseling, careers library, job bank, job interviews.
EXPENSES FOR 1995–96 Area resident tuition: $1245 full-time, $41.50 per semester hour part-time. State resident tuition: $3565 full-time, $118.85 per semester hour part-time. Nonresident tuition: $4408 full-time, $146.95 per semester hour part-time. Part-time mandatory fees: $20 per semester. Full-time mandatory fees: $40.
FINANCIAL AID ***College-administered undergrad aid 1995–96:*** 491 need-based scholarships (average $359), 27 non-need scholarships (average $332), low-interest long-term loans from external sources, Federal Work-Study, 10 part-time jobs. ***Required forms:*** institutional, FAFSA, proof of citizenship, financial aid transcript from previous institution; accepted: CSS Financial Aid PROFILE. ***Priority deadline:*** 8/19. ***Payment plans:*** installment, deferred payment. ***Waivers:*** full or partial for employees or children of employees and senior citizens. ***Notification:*** continuous.
APPLYING Open admission. ***Options:*** early entrance, deferred entrance, midyear entrance. ***Required:*** 3 years of high school math and science, some high school foreign language. ***Recommended:*** SAT I or ACT, TOEFL for international students. Test scores used for counseling/placement. ***Application deadline:*** rolling. Preference given to city residents.

Peterson's Guide to Two-Year Colleges 1997 285

City Colleges of Chicago, Kennedy-King College (continued)

APPLYING/TRANSFER ***Recommended:*** standardized test scores. ***Entrance:*** noncompetitive. ***Application deadline:*** rolling. ***Contact:*** Ms. Kathie House, Director of University Transfer Center, 312-602-5425.

CONTACT Mrs. Iver Watson, Clerical Supervisor for Admissions, City Colleges of Chicago, Kennedy-King College, 6800 South Wentworth Avenue, Chicago, IL 60621-3733, 312-602-5000 Ext. 5055. College video available.

CITY COLLEGES OF CHICAGO, MALCOLM X COLLEGE
Chicago, Illinois

UG Enrollment: 3,480 | **Tuition & Fees (Area Res): $1285**
Application Deadline: rolling | **Room & Board: N/Avail**

GENERAL State and locally supported, 2-year, coed. Part of City Colleges of Chicago System. Awards certificates, transfer associate, terminal associate degrees. Founded 1911. ***Setting:*** 20-acre urban campus. ***Educational spending 1994–95:*** $2561 per undergrad. ***Total enrollment:*** 3,480. ***Faculty:*** 93 (83 full-time, 10 part-time).

ENROLLMENT PROFILE 3,480 students: 73% women, 69% part-time, 99% state residents, 24% transferred in, 1% international, 41% 25 or older, 1% Native American, 9% Hispanic, 74% African American, 6% Asian American. ***Areas of study chosen:*** 45% health professions and related sciences, 44% liberal arts/general studies, 9% business management and administrative services, 1% computer and information sciences, 1% education. ***Most popular recent majors:*** nursing, liberal arts/general studies, radiological technology.

FIRST-YEAR CLASS 1,006 total; 1,500 applied, 100% were accepted, 67% of whom enrolled. 10% from top 10% of their high school class, 25% from top quarter, 35% from top half.

ACADEMIC PROGRAM Core, honor code. Calendar: semesters. Academic remediation for entering students, English as a second language program offered during academic year, services for LD students, advanced placement, self-designed majors, tutorials, honors program, summer session for credit, part-time degree program (daytime, evenings, summer), adult/continuing education programs, co-op programs. ROTC: Air Force (c).

GENERAL DEGREE REQUIREMENTS 60 credit hours; 1 course each in biology and algebra; computer course for respiratory therapy, mortuary science majors.

MAJORS Accounting, art/fine arts, business administration/commerce/management, child psychology/child development, computer management, data processing, dietetics, early childhood education, emergency medical technology, food services management, funeral service, health science, health services administration, liberal arts/general studies, marketing/retailing/merchandising, medical laboratory technology, medical technology, nursing, nutrition, pharmacy/pharmaceutical sciences, radiological technology, respiratory therapy, secretarial studies/office management, teacher aide studies.

LIBRARY 50,000 books, 1,970 microform titles, 490 periodicals, 11,700 records, tapes, and CDs. Acquisition spending 1994–95: $528,144.

COMPUTERS ON CAMPUS 75 computers for student use in computer center, computer labs, learning resource center, library provide access to on-line services. Staffed computer lab on campus provides training in use of computers, software. Academic computing expenditure 1994–95: $304,402.

COLLEGE LIFE Orientation program (3 days, no cost). Student-run newspaper. 50% vote in student government elections. ***Most popular organizations:*** Student Government Association, Phi Beta Lambda, Canal Technology Club. ***Major annual events:*** Homecoming, Black History Month, Cinco de Mayo. ***Student services:*** personal-psychological counseling. ***Campus security:*** 24-hour emergency response devices and patrols.

HOUSING College housing not available.

ATHLETICS Member NJCAA. ***Intercollegiate:*** baseball M, basketball M/W. ***Intramural:*** tennis, volleyball. ***Contact:*** Mr. Dan Davis, Athletic Director, 312-850-7491.

CAREER PLANNING ***Placement office:*** 2 full-time, 1 part-time staff; $338,221 operating expenditure 1994–95. ***Director:*** Mr. Robert Kelly, Coordinator of Career Planning and Placement, 312-850-7087. ***Services:*** job fairs, resume preparation, career counseling, careers library, job bank, job interviews.

EXPENSES FOR 1995–96 Area resident tuition: $1245 full-time, $41.50 per credit hour part-time. State resident tuition: $3565 full-time, $118.85 per credit hour part-time. Nonresident tuition: $4408 full-time, $146.95 per credit hour part-time. Part-time mandatory fees: $20 per semester. Full-time mandatory fees: $40.

FINANCIAL AID ***College-administered undergrad aid 1995–96:*** 2,600 need-based scholarships (average $1271), non-need scholarships, low-interest long-term loans from college funds (average $623), loans from external sources, Federal Work-Study. ***Required forms:*** institutional, FAFSA, proof of citizenship, financial aid transcript from previous institution; accepted: CSS Financial Aid PROFILE, state. ***Application deadline:*** continuous to 8/15. ***Payment plan:*** deferred payment. ***Waivers:*** full or partial for employees or children of employees and senior citizens.

APPLYING Open admission except for allied health programs. ***Options:*** Common Application, early entrance, deferred entrance. ***Required:*** school transcript, minimum 2.0 GPA, 3 years of high school math and science, some high school foreign language. ***Recommended:*** TOEFL for international students. ***Required for some:*** SAT I or ACT, SAT II Subject Tests. Test scores used for counseling/placement. ***Application deadline:*** rolling. Preference given to state residents.

APPLYING/TRANSFER ***Required:*** high school transcript, 3 years of high school math and science, some high school foreign language, minimum 2.0 high school GPA. ***Required for some:*** standardized test scores, campus interview. ***Entrance:*** noncompetitive. ***Application deadline:*** rolling. ***Contact:*** Ms. Kathi Holley, Director of Transfer Center, 312-850-7091.

CONTACT Mr. Ivan R. Lane, Registrar, City Colleges of Chicago, Malcolm X College, 1900 West Van Buren Street, Chicago, IL 60612-3145, 312-850-7125. ***Fax:*** 312-850-7092. College video available.

CITY COLLEGES OF CHICAGO, OLIVE-HARVEY COLLEGE
Chicago, Illinois

UG Enrollment: 3,419 | **Tuition & Fees (Area Res): $1285**
Application Deadline: rolling | **Room & Board: N/Avail**

GENERAL State and locally supported, 2-year, coed. Part of City Colleges of Chicago System. Awards certificates, transfer associate, terminal associate degrees. Founded 1970. ***Setting:*** 67-acre urban campus. ***Total enrollment:*** 3,419. ***Faculty:*** 143 (102 full-time, 76% with terminal degrees, 41 part-time).

ENROLLMENT PROFILE 3,419 students: 71% women, 29% men, 63% part-time, 100% state residents, 4% transferred in, 70% have need-based financial aid, 0% international, 45% 25 or older, 1% Native American, 6% Hispanic, 91% African American, 1% Asian American. ***Areas of study chosen:*** 57% liberal arts/general studies, 6% computer and information sciences, 4% business management and administrative services, 4% health professions and related sciences, 4% social sciences, 1% architecture. ***Most popular recent majors:*** liberal arts/general studies, nursing.

FIRST-YEAR CLASS 664 total. Of the students who applied, 100% were accepted, 95% of whom enrolled.

ACADEMIC PROGRAM Core, honor code. Calendar: semesters. 344 courses offered in 1995–96. Academic remediation for entering students, services for LD students, honors program, summer session for credit, part-time degree program (daytime, evenings, summer), adult/continuing education programs, co-op programs. Study abroad in Denmark, England. ROTC: Air Force (c).

GENERAL DEGREE REQUIREMENTS 60 credit hours; internship (some majors).

MAJORS Accounting, architectural technologies, art/fine arts, biology/biological sciences, black/African-American studies, business administration/commerce/management, chemistry, child psychology/child development, computer technologies, data processing, dental services, early childhood education, earth science, electrical and electronics technologies, electronics engineering technology, engineering (general), liberal arts/general studies, marketing/retailing/merchandising, mathematics, music, nursing, pharmacy/pharmaceutical sciences, philosophy, photography, physics, secretarial studies/office management, social science.

LIBRARY Olga Haley Library with 48,580 books, 157 microform titles, 325 periodicals, 3,003 records, tapes, and CDs. Acquisition spending 1994–95: $77,512.

COMPUTERS ON CAMPUS 290 computers for student use in computer center, computer labs, learning resource center, data processing, typing lab, engineering department, library provide access to Internet. Staffed computer lab on campus provides training in use of computers, software. Academic computing expenditure 1994–95: $243,000.

COLLEGE LIFE Drama-theater group, student-run newspaper. 65% vote in student government elections. ***Student services:*** personal-psychological counseling, women's center, men's center. ***Campus security:*** 24-hour emergency response devices and patrols.

HOUSING College housing not available.

ATHLETICS Member NJCAA. ***Intercollegiate:*** basketball M(s), volleyball W(s). ***Intramural:*** basketball, gymnastics, soccer, swimming and diving, tennis, track and field, volleyball, wrestling. ***Contact:*** Mr. Dan Parker, Dean of Student Services, 312-291-6211.

CAREER PLANNING ***Placement office:*** 1 part-time staff; $54,000 operating expenditure 1994–95. ***Director:*** Mr. Dan Parker, Dean of Student Services, 312-291-6211. ***Services:*** job fairs, resume preparation, resume referral, career counseling, careers library, job bank, job interviews.

EXPENSES FOR 1995–96 Area resident tuition: $1245 full-time, $41.50 per credit hour part-time. State resident tuition: $3565 full-time, $118.85 per credit hour part-time. Nonresident tuition: $4408 full-time, $146.95 per credit hour part-time. Part-time mandatory fees: $20 per semester. Full-time mandatory fees: $40.

FINANCIAL AID ***College-administered undergrad aid 1995–96:*** 1,600 need-based scholarships (average $1150), 100 non-need scholarships (average $494), low-interest long-term loans from external sources (average $2625), 182 Federal Work-Study (averaging $1303), 35 part-time jobs. ***Required forms:*** institutional, FAFSA, proof of citizenship, financial aid transcript from previous institution; accepted: CSS Financial Aid PROFILE, state. ***Priority deadline:*** 6/15. ***Payment plan:*** installment. ***Waivers:*** full or partial for employees or children of employees and senior citizens.

APPLYING Open admission except for nursing, computer electronics programs. ***Options:*** Common Application, early entrance, deferred entrance, midyear entrance. ***Required:*** 3 years of high school math and science, 2 years of high school foreign language, SAT I or ACT, TOEFL for international students. Test scores used for admission and counseling/placement. ***Application deadline:*** rolling. Preference given to city residents.

APPLYING/TRANSFER ***Required:*** standardized test scores, 3 years of high school math and science, some high school foreign language. ***Entrance:*** noncompetitive. ***Application deadline:*** rolling. ***Contact:*** Ms. Paula Causher, Director of Transfer Center, 312-291-6251.

CONTACT Mrs. Ruby M. Howard, Director of Admissions and Registrar, City Colleges of Chicago, Olive-Harvey College, 10001 South Woodlawn Avenue, Chicago, IL 60628-1645, 312-291-6380. ***Fax:*** 312-291-6304.

CITY COLLEGES OF CHICAGO, RICHARD J. DALEY COLLEGE
Chicago, Illinois

UG Enrollment: 4,679 | **Tuition & Fees (Area Res): $1285**
Application Deadline: rolling | **Room & Board: N/Avail**

GENERAL State and locally supported, 2-year, coed. Part of City Colleges of Chicago System. Awards transfer associate, terminal associate degrees. Founded 1960. ***Setting:*** 25-acre urban campus. ***Research spending 1994–95:*** $1 million. ***Total enrollment:*** 4,679. ***Faculty:*** 155 (123 full-time, 23% with terminal degrees, 32 part-time); student-faculty ratio is 31:1.

ENROLLMENT PROFILE 4,679 students: 58% women, 63% part-time, 99% state residents, 7% transferred in, 1% international, 54% 25 or older, 1% Native American, 32% Hispanic, 30% African American, 3% Asian American. ***Areas of study chosen:*** 39% liberal arts/general studies, 26% business management and administrative services, 12% education, 10% health professions and related sciences, 1% architecture, 1% computer

and information sciences, 1% engineering and applied sciences. ***Most popular recent majors:*** liberal arts/general studies, business administration/commerce/management, nursing.
FIRST-YEAR CLASS 988 total; 988 applied, 100% were accepted, 100% of whom enrolled.
ACADEMIC PROGRAM Core, honor code. Calendar: semesters. Academic remediation for entering students, English as a second language program offered during academic year, services for LD students, advanced placement, honors program, summer session for credit, part-time degree program (daytime, evenings, weekends, summer), adult/continuing education programs. ROTC: Air Force (c).
GENERAL DEGREE REQUIREMENTS 60 credit hours; math/science requirements vary according to program.
MAJORS Accounting, architectural technologies, art/fine arts, aviation technology, business administration/commerce/management, child care/child and family studies, child psychology/child development, communication, data processing, dental services, drafting and design, education, electronics engineering technology, elementary education, (pre)engineering sequence, fire science, horticulture, humanities, industrial administration, journalism, law enforcement/police sciences, legal studies, liberal arts/general studies, machine and tool technologies, marketing/retailing/merchandising, medical secretarial studies, medical technology, modern languages, music, nursing, pharmacy/pharmaceutical sciences, photography, secretarial studies/office management, social work, speech/rhetoric/public address/debate, teacher aide studies, telecommunications, theater arts/drama, transportation technologies.
LIBRARY Main library plus 1 other, with 53,201 books, 84 microform titles, 275 periodicals, 2,720 records, tapes, and CDs. Acquisition spending 1994–95: $75,000.
COMPUTERS ON CAMPUS 80 computers for student use in computer center, computer labs, library.
COLLEGE LIFE Drama-theater group, student-run newspaper. ***Most popular organizations:*** Latin Student Organization, Student Government Association, African-American Culture Club. ***Student services:*** personal-psychological counseling, women's center. ***Campus security:*** 24-hour patrols.
HOUSING College housing not available.
CAREER PLANNING ***Placement office:*** 1 full-time staff; $350,000 operating expenditure 1994–95. ***Director:*** Ms. Charlene Appling, Coordinator of Placement Services, 312-838-7500 Ext. 7773. ***Services:*** job fairs, resume preparation, resume referral, career counseling, careers library, job interviews.
EXPENSES FOR 1995–96 Area resident tuition: $1245 full-time, $41.50 per credit hour part-time. State resident tuition: $3565 full-time, $118.85 per credit hour part-time. Nonresident tuition: $4408 full-time, $146.95 per credit hour part-time. Part-time mandatory fees: $20 per semester. Full-time mandatory fees: $40.
FINANCIAL AID ***College-administered undergrad aid 1995–96:*** 1,044 need-based scholarships, non-need scholarships, low-interest long-term loans from external sources (averaging $2625), 140 Federal Work-Study (averaging $1507), 14 part-time jobs. ***Required forms:*** institutional, FAFSA, proof of citizenship, financial aid transcript from previous institution. ***Application deadline:*** continuous to 12/23. ***Waivers:*** full or partial for employees or children of employees and senior citizens. ***Notification:*** continuous.
APPLYING Open admission except for nursing program. ***Options:*** Common Application, early entrance, deferred entrance. ***Recommended:*** ACT. ***Required for some:*** ACT, TOEFL for international students. Test scores used for counseling/placement. ***Application deadline:*** rolling. Preference given to city residents.
APPLYING/TRANSFER ***Recommended:*** standardized test scores. ***Required for some:*** standardized test scores. ***Entrance:*** noncompetitive. ***Application deadline:*** rolling.
CONTACT Ms. Karla Reynolds, Registrar, City Colleges of Chicago, Richard J. Daley College, 7500 South Pulaski Road, Chicago, IL 60652-1242, 312-838-7599.

CITY COLLEGES OF CHICAGO, WILBUR WRIGHT COLLEGE
Chicago, Illinois

UG Enrollment: 6,949	Tuition & Fees (Area Res): $1285
Application Deadline: rolling	Room & Board: N/Avail

GENERAL State and locally supported, 2-year, coed. Part of City Colleges of Chicago System. Awards transfer associate, terminal associate degrees. Founded 1934. ***Setting:*** 9-acre urban campus. ***Total enrollment:*** 6,949. ***Faculty:*** 161 (all full-time). ***Notable Alumni:*** Matt Rodriguez, Chicago police chief; Kim Novak, actress.
ENROLLMENT PROFILE 6,949 students: 59% women, 69% part-time, 99% state residents, 1% transferred in, 1% international, 43% 25 or older, 1% Native American, 23% Hispanic, 12% African American, 11% Asian American. ***Areas of study chosen:*** 13% health professions and related sciences, 12% business management and administrative services, 11% premed, 10% biological and life sciences, 10% education, 10% liberal arts/general studies, 8% communications and journalism, 8% computer and information sciences, 5% engineering and applied sciences, 5% prelaw, 3% architecture, 2% natural resource sciences, 2% psychology, 1% theology/religion. ***Most popular recent majors:*** liberal arts/general studies, radiological technology, business administration/commerce/management.
FIRST-YEAR CLASS 1,192 total; 2,533 applied, 100% were accepted, 47% of whom enrolled. 5% from top 10% of their high school class, 18% from top quarter, 46% from top half.
ACADEMIC PROGRAM Core, honor code. Calendar: semesters. 368 courses offered in 1995–96; average class size 33 in required courses. Academic remediation for entering students, English as a second language program offered during academic year, honors program, summer session for credit, part-time degree program (daytime, evenings, weekends, summer), adult/continuing education programs, internships. ROTC: Air Force (c).
GENERAL DEGREE REQUIREMENTS 60 credit hours; math/science requirements vary according to program.
MAJORS Accounting, architectural technologies, art/fine arts, business administration/commerce/management, commercial art, data processing, elementary education, (pre)engineering sequence, English, information science, journalism, law enforcement/police sciences, liberal arts/general studies, library science, machine and tool technologies, marketing/retailing/merchandising, mechanical engineering technology, medical technology, modern languages, music, occupational therapy, physical education, physical sciences, radiological technology, science, secretarial studies/office management, speech/rhetoric/public address/debate.
LIBRARY Learning Resource Center plus 1 other, with 67,389 books, 12,256 microform titles, 550 periodicals, 15,165 records, tapes, and CDs.
COMPUTERS ON CAMPUS 534 computers for student use in computer center, library. Staffed computer lab on campus provides training in use of computers, software.
COLLEGE LIFE Orientation program (2 days, $125). Drama-theater group, choral group, student-run newspaper, radio station. 10% vote in student government elections. ***Social organizations:*** 23 open to all. ***Most popular organizations:*** Student Government, Circle K, Alumni, Phi Theta Kappa, Black Student Union. ***Major annual events:*** Ethnic Food Fair, Hispanic Month Celebration, Student Graduations. ***Student services:*** health clinic, personal-psychological counseling. ***Campus security:*** 24-hour emergency response devices and patrols, student patrols, late-night transport-escort service.
HOUSING College housing not available.
ATHLETICS Member NJCAA. ***Intercollegiate:*** basketball W, cross-country running M/W, soccer M, swimming and diving M/W, tennis M/W, track and field M/W, volleyball W, wrestling M. ***Intramural:*** basketball, cross-country running, swimming and diving, tennis, volleyball, weight lifting. ***Contact:*** Mr. Dennis Lewis, Coach, 312-481-8437.
CAREER PLANNING ***Placement office:*** 2 full-time, 4 part-time staff. ***Director:*** Ms. Daisy Mitchell, Director of Job Placement Services, 312-481-8528. ***Services:*** job fairs, resume preparation, resume referral, career counseling, careers library, job bank, job interviews. 660 organizations recruited on campus 1994–95.
AFTER GRADUATION 52% of students completing a degree program in 1994–95 went directly on to further study.
EXPENSES FOR 1995–96 Area resident tuition: $1245 full-time, $41.50 per credit hour part-time. State resident tuition: $3565 full-time, $118.85 per credit hour part-time. Nonresident tuition: $4408 full-time, $146.95 per credit hour part-time. Full-time mandatory fees: $40.
FINANCIAL AID ***College-administered undergrad aid 1995–96:*** 1,443 need-based scholarships (averaging $1266), 89 non-need scholarships (averaging $352), low-interest long-term loans from external sources (averaging $2072), Federal Work-Study, 30 part-time jobs. ***Required forms:*** institutional, FAFSA, proof of citizenship, financial aid transcript from previous institution; accepted: CSS Financial Aid PROFILE. ***Priority deadline:*** 8/15. ***Waivers:*** full or partial for employees or children of employees.
APPLYING Open admission. ***Options:*** Common Application, early entrance, deferred entrance. ***Required:*** ACT. ***Recommended:*** school transcript, recommendations, TOEFL for international students. Test scores used for counseling/placement. ***Application deadline:*** rolling. ***Notification:*** continuous. Preference given to city residents.
APPLYING/TRANSFER ***Required:*** college transcript, minimum 2.0 college GPA. ***Entrance:*** noncompetitive. ***Application deadline:*** rolling. ***Notification:*** continuous. ***Contact:*** Mr. Dennis Lewis, 312-481-8550.
CONTACT Ms. Amy Aiello, Assistant Dean of Student Services, City Colleges of Chicago, Wilbur Wright College, 4300 North Narragansett Avenue, Chicago, IL 60634-1591, 312-481-8206. College video available.

COLLEGE OF DUPAGE
Glen Ellyn, Illinois

UG Enrollment: 33,920	Tuition & Fees (Area Res): $1392
Application Deadline: rolling	Room & Board: N/Avail

GENERAL State and locally supported, 2-year, coed. Part of Illinois Community College System. Awards certificates, transfer associate, terminal associate degrees. Founded 1967. ***Setting:*** 273-acre suburban campus with easy access to Chicago. ***Total enrollment:*** 33,920. ***Faculty:*** 1,819 (319 full-time, 22% with terminal degrees, 1,500 part-time); student-faculty ratio is 23:1. ***Notable Alumni:*** James Belushi, actor.
ENROLLMENT PROFILE 33,920 students: 58% women, 42% men, 72% part-time, 99% state residents, 0% international, 48% 25 or older, 0% Native American, 8% Hispanic, 3% African American, 9% Asian American. ***Areas of study chosen:*** 27% business management and administrative services, 15% liberal arts/general studies, 12% health professions and related sciences, 9% education, 5% engineering and applied sciences, 5% social sciences, 4% computer and information sciences, 4% psychology, 3% architecture, 3% fine arts, 3% performing arts, 2% biological and life sciences, 2% communications and journalism, 1% agriculture, 1% English language/literature/letters, 1% foreign language and literature, 1% mathematics, 1% physical sciences, 1% vocational and home economics. ***Most popular recent majors:*** liberal arts/general studies, tourism and travel, nursing.
FIRST-YEAR CLASS 10,220 total. Of the students who applied, 100% were accepted.
ACADEMIC PROGRAM Core, transfer and vocational curriculum, honor code. Calendar: quarters. 1,545 courses offered in 1995–96. Academic remediation for entering students, English as a second language program offered during academic year and summer, services for LD students, advanced placement, self-designed majors, tutorials, honors program, summer session for credit, part-time degree program (daytime, evenings, weekends, summer), external degree programs, adult/continuing education programs, co-op programs and internships. Off-campus study. Study abroad in 17 countries, including China, Costa Rica, Colombia, England, Ecuador, France, Germany, Greece, Israel, Japan, Mexico, Portugal, Russia, Spain, Switzerland. ROTC: Army (c).
GENERAL DEGREE REQUIREMENTS 96 quarter hours; internship (some majors).
MAJORS Accounting, architectural technologies, automotive technologies, biology/biological sciences, business administration/commerce/management, child care/child and family studies, commercial art, communication, communication equipment technology, computer information systems, computer science, computer technologies, corrections, criminal justice, culinary arts, drafting and design, drug and alcohol/substance abuse counseling, early childhood education, education, electrical and electronics technologies, electromechanical technology, electronics engineering technology, emergency medical technology, English, environmental health sciences, fashion design and technology, fashion merchandising, film and video production, fire science, food services management, food services technology, German, graphic arts, health services administration, heating/refrigeration/air conditioning, history, home economics, horticulture, hospitality services, hotel and restaurant management, humanities, human services, interior design, landscaping/grounds maintenance, law enforcement/police sciences, legal secretarial studies, liberal arts/general studies, library science, machine and tool technologies, manufacturing technology, marketing/retailing/merchandising, mathematics, mechanical design technology, medical records services, music, nuclear medical technology, nursing, occupational therapy, operating room technology, ornamental horticulture, philosophy, photography, physical education, physical sciences, physics, plastics technology, political science/government, printing technologies, psychology, radio and television studies, radiological technology, real estate, recreation therapy, respiratory therapy, science, secretarial studies/office

Peterson's Guide to Two-Year Colleges 1997 287

College of DuPage (continued)
management, sociology, Spanish, theater arts/drama, tourism and travel, transportation technologies, welding technology, wildlife management, word processing.
LIBRARY Learning Resource Center with 130,709 books, 1,015 periodicals, 2 on-line bibliographic services, 16 CD-ROMs, 16,906 records, tapes, and CDs. Acquisition spending 1994–95: $591,121.
COMPUTERS ON CAMPUS Computer purchase plan available. 1,100 computers for student use in computer center, computer labs, learning resource center, library. Staffed computer lab on campus.
NOTEWORTHY RESEARCH FACILITIES Center for Asian Studies.
COLLEGE LIFE Drama-theater group, choral group, student-run newspaper. 1% vote in student government elections. ***Social organizations:*** 52 open to all. ***Most popular organizations:*** Student Government Association, Intervarsity-Campus Christian Fellowship, Phi Theta Kappa, International Student Association, Student Activities Board. ***Major annual events:*** Hypnotist Jim Wand Show, Annual Pool Tournament, Street Fair. ***Student services:*** health clinic, personal-psychological counseling. ***Campus security:*** 24-hour emergency response devices and patrols, student patrols, late-night transport-escort service.
HOUSING College housing not available.
ATHLETICS Member NJCAA. ***Intercollegiate:*** baseball M, basketball M/W, football M, golf M, soccer M/W, softball W, swimming and diving M/W, tennis M/W, track and field M/W, volleyball W, wrestling M. ***Intramural:*** basketball, bowling, football, golf, racquetball, soccer, softball, swimming and diving, tennis, volleyball, weight lifting. ***Contact:*** Mr. Ralph Miller, Athletic Director, 708-942-2364.
CAREER PLANNING ***Placement office:*** 2 full-time, 2 part-time staff; $183,475 operating expenditure 1994–95. ***Director:*** Ms. Nancy Wajler, Manager of Career Services, 708-942-2230. ***Services:*** job fairs, resume preparation, resume referral, career counseling, careers library, job bank, job interviews. 50 organizations recruited on campus 1994–95.
AFTER GRADUATION 72% of students completing a degree program in 1994–95 went directly on to further study.
EXPENSES FOR 1996–97 ***Application fee:*** $10. Area resident tuition: $1392 full-time, $29 per quarter hour part-time. State resident tuition: $4368 full-time, $91 per quarter hour part-time. Nonresident tuition: $5616 full-time, $117 per quarter hour part-time.
FINANCIAL AID ***College-administered undergrad aid 1995–96:*** 166 need-based scholarships (average $921), 661 non-need scholarships (average $213), low-interest long-term loans from external sources (average $2229), Federal Work-Study, 810 part-time jobs. ***Required forms:*** institutional, FAFSA; accepted: CSS Financial Aid PROFILE. ***Priority deadline:*** 6/1. ***Waivers:*** full or partial for employees or children of employees and senior citizens.
APPLYING Open admission. ***Options:*** early entrance, deferred entrance, midyear entrance. ***Required:*** TOEFL for international students. ***Recommended:*** 3 years of high school math and science, 4 years of high school English, 3 years of high school social studies, SAT I or ACT. Test scores used for counseling/placement. ***Application deadline:*** rolling. ***Notification:*** continuous.
APPLYING/TRANSFER ***Entrance:*** noncompetitive. ***Application deadline:*** rolling. ***Notification:*** continuous. ***Contact:*** Mr. Leo Torres, Transfer Specialist, 708-942-3314.
CONTACT Mrs. Suzanne M. Blasi, Coordinator of Admission Services, College of DuPage, Glen Ellyn, IL 60137, 708-942-2441.

COLLEGE OF LAKE COUNTY
Grayslake, Illinois

UG Enrollment: 14,865	Tuition & Fees (Area Res): $1581
Application Deadline: rolling	Room & Board: N/Avail

GENERAL District-supported, 2-year, coed. Part of Illinois Community College System. Awards certificates, transfer associate, terminal associate degrees. Founded 1967. ***Setting:*** 232-acre suburban campus with easy access to Chicago and Milwaukee. ***Total enrollment:*** 14,865. ***Faculty:*** 822 (183 full-time, 639 part-time); student-faculty ratio is 20:1.
ENROLLMENT PROFILE 14,865 students from 2 states and territories, 21 other countries. 58% women, 42% men, 81% part-time, 97% state residents, 10% transferred in, 1% international, 60% 25 or older, 0% Native American, 11% Hispanic, 7% African American, 4% Asian American. ***Most popular recent majors:*** liberal arts/general studies, data processing, business administration/commerce/management.
FIRST-YEAR CLASS 2,553 total; 2,860 applied, 100% were accepted, 89% of whom enrolled.
ACADEMIC PROGRAM Core, interdisciplinary curriculum. Calendar: semesters. 700 courses offered in 1995–96. Academic remediation for entering students, English as a second language program offered during academic year and summer, services for LD students, advanced placement, self-designed majors, honors program, summer session for credit, part-time degree program (daytime, evenings, weekends, summer), external degree programs, adult/continuing education programs, co-op programs and internships. Off-campus study at McHenry County College, Gateway Technical College, Oakton Community College, William Rainey Harper College. Study abroad in England, Austria, Costa Rica.
GENERAL DEGREE REQUIREMENTS 63 credit hours; math/science requirements vary according to program; computer course for architecture, business management, health information technology, library media technology, engineering technology, technical communications majors.
MAJORS Accounting, architectural technologies, automotive technologies, business administration/commerce/management, chemical engineering technology, civil engineering technology, computer information systems, computer programming, computer technologies, construction technologies, criminal justice, data processing, drafting and design, drug and alcohol/substance abuse counseling, electronics engineering technology, engineering (general), fire science, food services management, heating/refrigeration/air conditioning, horticulture, human services, industrial administration, industrial and heavy equipment maintenance, landscape architecture/design, landscaping/grounds maintenance, liberal arts/general studies, library science, machine and tool technologies, marketing/retailing/merchandising, mathematics, mechanical engineering technology, medical laboratory technology, medical records services, mental health/rehabilitation counseling, nursing, physical sciences, quality control technology, radiological technology, retail management, science, secretarial studies/office management, technical writing, word processing.
LIBRARY College of Lake County Library with 110,745 books, 201 microform titles, 740 periodicals, 4 on-line bibliographic services, 55 CD-ROMs, 1,634 records, tapes, and CDs. Acquisition spending 1994–95: $1.4 million.
COMPUTERS ON CAMPUS Computer purchase plan available. 600 computers for student use in computer center, computer labs, learning resource center, academic buildings, classrooms, library provide access to main academic computer. Staffed computer lab on campus provides training in use of computers, software. Academic computing expenditure 1994–95: $202,091.
COLLEGE LIFE Drama-theater group, choral group, student-run newspaper, radio station. ***Social organizations:*** 26 open to all. ***Most popular organizations:*** Hispanic Club, Black Student Union, Engineering Club, Phi Theta Kappa, Phi Beta Lambda. ***Major annual events:*** 2nd City, Engineering Club Mousetrap Derby, Hypnotist Jim Wand Show. ***Student services:*** health clinic, personal-psychological counseling. ***Campus security:*** 24-hour emergency response devices and patrols, late-night transport-escort service.
HOUSING College housing not available.
ATHLETICS Member NJCAA. ***Intercollegiate:*** baseball M, basketball M/W, cross-country running M/W, golf M, soccer M/W, softball W, tennis M/W, volleyball W, wrestling M. ***Intramural:*** basketball, fencing, skiing (downhill), swimming and diving, volleyball. ***Contact:*** Mr. Gene Hanson, Associate Dean, 847-223-6601 Ext. 2477.
CAREER PLANNING ***Placement office:*** 19 full-time, 4 part-time staff; $1.4 million operating expenditure 1994–95. ***Director:*** Ms. Terri Berryman, Director of Career Placement Services, 847-223-6601 Ext. 2572. ***Services:*** job fairs, resume preparation, career counseling, careers library, job bank, job interviews.
EXPENSES FOR 1996–97 Area resident tuition: $1581 full-time, $51 per credit hour part-time. State resident tuition: $6138 full-time, $197.99 per credit hour part-time. Nonresident tuition: $7644 full-time, $246.58 per credit hour part-time.
FINANCIAL AID ***College-administered undergrad aid 1995–96:*** need-based scholarships, 136 non-need scholarships (average $730), short-term loans (average $170), low-interest long-term loans from external sources (average $1926), 98 Federal Work-Study (averaging $1102), 108 part-time jobs. ***Required forms:*** institutional, FAFSA; accepted: CSS Financial Aid PROFILE. ***Priority deadline:*** 6/1. ***Payment plan:*** installment. ***Waivers:*** full or partial for employees or children of employees and senior citizens.
APPLYING Open admission except for health programs. ***Options:*** early entrance, deferred entrance, midyear entrance. ***Required:*** TOEFL for international students. ***Recommended:*** school transcript, 3 years of high school math and science, some high school foreign language, SAT I or ACT. Test scores used for counseling/placement. ***Application deadline:*** rolling. ***Notification:*** continuous. Preference given to district residents.
APPLYING/TRANSFER ***Recommended:*** 3 years of high school math and science, college transcript. ***Application deadline:*** rolling. ***Notification:*** continuous. ***Contact:*** Mr. Curtis L. Denny, Director of Admissions, 847-223-6601 Ext. 2384.
CONTACT Mr. Curtis L. Denny, Director of Admissions, College of Lake County, Grayslake, IL 60030-1198, 847-223-6601 Ext. 2384. ***E-mail:*** curtdenny@clc.cc.il.us. College video available.

DALEY COLLEGE
Illinois—See City Colleges of Chicago, Richard J. Daley College

DANVILLE AREA COMMUNITY COLLEGE
Danville, Illinois

Enrollment: N/R	Tuition & Fees (Area Res): $1178
Application Deadline: rolling	Room & Board: N/Avail

GENERAL State and locally supported, 2-year, coed. Part of Illinois Community College System. Awards certificates, transfer associate, terminal associate degrees. Founded 1946. ***Setting:*** 50-acre small-town campus. ***Endowment:*** $978,329. ***Faculty:*** 168 (55 full-time, 113 part-time).
ENROLLMENT PROFILE 65% women, 35% men, 58% part-time, 93% state residents, 0% international, 52% 25 or older, 0% Native American, 1% Hispanic, 8% African American, 1% Asian American. ***Most popular recent majors:*** liberal arts/general studies, business administration/commerce/management.
FIRST-YEAR CLASS Of the students who applied, 100% were accepted. 2% from top 10% of their high school class, 45% from top half.
ACADEMIC PROGRAM Core. Calendar: semesters. Average class size 24 in required courses. Academic remediation for entering students, English as a second language program offered during academic year, services for LD students, advanced placement, self-designed majors, summer session for credit, part-time degree program (daytime, evenings, summer), adult/continuing education programs, co-op programs and internships.
GENERAL DEGREE REQUIREMENTS 62 credits; math/science requirements vary according to program; internship (some majors).
MAJORS Accounting, agricultural business, agricultural sciences, art/fine arts, automotive technologies, biology/biological sciences, business administration/commerce/management, child care/child and family studies, computer information systems, computer programming, criminal justice, data processing, drafting and design, drug and alcohol/substance abuse counseling, early childhood education, education, electrical and electronics technologies, elementary education, engineering (general), (pre)engineering sequence, English, history, horticulture, humanities, human services, industrial engineering technology, journalism, landscaping/grounds maintenance, law enforcement/police sciences, legal secretarial studies, liberal arts/general studies, manufacturing technology, marketing/retailing/merchandising, mathematics, mechanical engineering technology, medical secretarial studies, nursing, occupational therapy, ornamental horticulture, philosophy, physical education, physical therapy, practical nursing, psychology, radiological technology, real estate, respiratory therapy, science, social science, social work, teacher aide studies, tourism and travel, welding technology.
LIBRARY 40,000 books, 8,051 microform titles, 444 periodicals, 3,700 records, tapes, and CDs.
COMPUTERS ON CAMPUS 288 computers for student use in computer labs, math labs, classrooms, library provide access to Internet. Staffed computer lab on campus provides training in use of computers, software.
COLLEGE LIFE ***Student services:*** personal-psychological counseling. ***Campus security:*** 24-hour patrols.
HOUSING College housing not available.

ATHLETICS Member NJCAA. ***Intercollegiate:*** baseball M(s), basketball M(s)/W(s), cross-country running M(s), golf M(s), track and field M(s)/W(s), volleyball W(s). ***Intramural:*** basketball, cross-country running, racquetball. ***Contact:*** Mr. John Spezia, Athletics Director, 217-443-8780.
CAREER PLANNING ***Placement office:*** 2 full-time, 1 part-time staff. ***Director:*** Ms. Viv Dudley, Career Services Coordinator, 217-443-8753. ***Services:*** job fairs, resume preparation, resume referral, career counseling, careers library, job bank, job interviews.
EXPENSES FOR 1995–96 Area resident tuition: $1178 full-time, $38 per semester hour part-time. State resident tuition: $3733 full-time, $120.43 per semester hour part-time. Nonresident tuition: $6112 full-time, $197.17 per semester hour part-time.
FINANCIAL AID ***College-administered undergrad aid 1995–96:*** 600 need-based scholarships (averaging $2500), 190 non-need scholarships (averaging $1000), short-term loans, Federal Work-Study, part-time jobs. ***Required forms:*** institutional, FAFSA. ***Application deadline:*** continuous. ***Payment plans:*** installment, deferred payment. ***Waivers:*** full or partial for minority students, employees or children of employees, and senior citizens. ***Notification:*** 6/1.
APPLYING Open admission. ***Options:*** early entrance, deferred entrance. ***Required:*** school transcript, 3 years of high school math, TOEFL for international students. Test scores used for counseling/placement. ***Application deadline:*** rolling.
APPLYING/TRANSFER ***Application deadline:*** rolling.
CONTACT Ms. Heidi Gnadt, Director of Admissions, Danville Area Community College, Danville, IL 61832-5199, 217-443-8800. ***E-mail:*** register@jaguar.dacc.cc.il.us.

ELGIN COMMUNITY COLLEGE
Elgin, Illinois

UG Enrollment: 8,589	Tuition & Fees (Area Res): $1200
Application Deadline: rolling	Room & Board: N/Avail

GENERAL State and locally supported, 2-year, coed. Part of Illinois Community College System. Awards certificates, diplomas, transfer associate, terminal associate degrees. Founded 1949. ***Setting:*** 100-acre suburban campus with easy access to Chicago. ***Total enrollment:*** 8,589. ***Faculty:*** 459 (109 full-time, 350 part-time); student-faculty ratio is 20:1.
ENROLLMENT PROFILE 8,589 students: 57% women, 43% men, 75% part-time, 99% state residents, 7% transferred in, 1% international, 53% 25 or older, 0% Native American, 17% Hispanic, 4% African American, 4% Asian American.
FIRST-YEAR CLASS 2,203 total. Of the students who applied, 100% were accepted. 20% from top quarter of their high school class, 53% from top half.
ACADEMIC PROGRAM Core. Calendar: semesters. Academic remediation for entering students, English as a second language program offered during academic year and summer, services for LD students, advanced placement, self-designed majors, tutorials, honors program, summer session for credit, part-time degree program (daytime, evenings), adult/continuing education programs, co-op programs and internships. Off-campus study at McHenry County College, Waubonsee Community College, College of DuPage, William Rainey Harper College, Rock Valley College, Illinois Valley Community College, College of Lake County.
GENERAL DEGREE REQUIREMENTS 60 credit hours; internship (some majors).
MAJORS Accounting, art/fine arts, automotive technologies, business administration/commerce/management, child care/child and family studies, computer graphics, computer programming, criminal justice, culinary arts, data processing, dental services, drafting and design, drug and alcohol/substance abuse counseling, electronics engineering technology, (pre)engineering sequence, finance/banking, fire science, food sciences, food services management, food services technology, gerontology, graphic arts, heating/refrigeration/air conditioning, horticulture, hotel and restaurant management, human services, industrial administration, industrial and heavy equipment maintenance, law enforcement/police sciences, liberal arts/general studies, machine and tool technologies, marketing/retailing/merchandising, materials sciences, medical laboratory technology, medical records services, medical secretarial studies, mental health/rehabilitation counseling, nursing, paralegal studies, practical nursing, real estate, retail management, science, secretarial studies/office management, tourism and travel, transportation technologies, welding technology, word processing.
LIBRARY Renner Learning Resource Center with 65,000 books, 67 microform titles, 375 periodicals, 2 on-line bibliographic services, 15 CD-ROMs, 3,000 records, tapes, and CDs.
COMPUTERS ON CAMPUS 400 computers for student use in computer center, computer labs, learning resource center, special labs, classrooms, library, student center. Staffed computer lab on campus provides training in use of computers, software.
COLLEGE LIFE Drama-theater group, choral group, student-run newspaper. ***Social organizations:*** 17 open to all. ***Most popular organizations:*** Phi Theta Kappa, United Students of All Cultures, Organization of Latin American Students, Black Student Association, Office Administration Association. ***Major annual events:*** May Fest, International Week. ***Student services:*** personal-psychological counseling. ***Campus security:*** 24-hour patrols.
HOUSING College housing not available.
ATHLETICS Member NJCAA. ***Intercollegiate:*** baseball M(s), basketball M(s)/W(s), golf M(s)/W, soccer M, softball W, tennis M(s)/W(s), volleyball M(c)/W(s). ***Contact:*** Mr. Steve Murray, Director of Student Life and Intercollegiate Athletics, 847-697-1000 Ext. 7414.
CAREER PLANNING ***Placement office:*** 2 full-time, 2 part-time staff. ***Director:*** Ms. Gayle Saunders, Associate Dean, Counseling, 847-697-1000 Ext. 7422. ***Services:*** job fairs, resume preparation, career counseling, careers library, job bank, job interviews. 50 organizations recruited on campus 1994–95.
EXPENSES FOR 1996–97 ***Application fee:*** $15. Area resident tuition: $1200 full-time, $40 per credit hour part-time. State resident tuition: $5427 full-time, $180.91 per credit hour part-time. Nonresident tuition: $6346 full-time, $211.54 per credit hour part-time.
FINANCIAL AID ***College-administered undergrad aid 1995–96:*** 540 need-based scholarships (average $665), 411 non-need scholarships (average $628), short-term loans (average $480), low-interest long-term loans from external sources (average $1820), 89 Federal Work-Study (averaging $1223), 148 part-time jobs. ***Required forms:*** institutional, FAFSA; accepted: CSS Financial Aid PROFILE. ***Priority deadline:*** 5/1. ***Payment plan:*** deferred payment. ***Waivers:*** full or partial for employees or children of employees. ***Notification:*** 6/1.
APPLYING Open admission except for nursing program. ***Options:*** early entrance, midyear entrance. ***Required:*** TOEFL for international students. ***Recommended:*** ACT. Test scores used for counseling/placement. ***Application deadline:*** rolling. ***Notification:*** continuous.
APPLYING/TRANSFER ***Recommended:*** standardized test scores. ***Entrance:*** noncompetitive. ***Application deadline:*** rolling. ***Notification:*** continuous.
CONTACT Ms. Roberta Haskins, Registrar, Elgin Community College, Elgin, IL 60123-7193, 847-888-7385. College video available.

GEM CITY COLLEGE
Quincy, Illinois

UG Enrollment: 250	Tuition & Fees: $3600
Application Deadline: rolling	Room & Board: N/Avail

GENERAL Proprietary, 2-year, coed. Awards diplomas, terminal associate degrees. Founded 1870. ***Setting:*** small-town campus. ***Total enrollment:*** 250. ***Faculty:*** 18 (16 full-time, 2 part-time); student-faculty ratio is 10:1.
ENROLLMENT PROFILE 250 students from 10 states and territories, 1 other country. 65% women, 10% part-time, 60% state residents, 1% transferred in, 40% 25 or older, 1% African American. ***Areas of study chosen:*** 55% vocational and home economics, 15% business management and administrative services, 15% computer and information sciences, 15% health professions and related sciences.
FIRST-YEAR CLASS 110 total; 120 applied, 100% were accepted, 92% of whom enrolled. 10% from top 10% of their high school class, 20% from top quarter, 40% from top half.
ACADEMIC PROGRAM Skill based curriculum, honor code. Calendar: quarters. 50 courses offered in 1995–96. Academic remediation for entering students, tutorials, summer session for credit, part-time degree program (daytime), adult/continuing education programs, internships.
GENERAL DEGREE REQUIREMENT Internship (some majors).
MAJORS Accounting, business administration/commerce/management, computer information systems, computer science, cosmetology, jewelry and metalsmithing, legal secretarial studies, medical assistant technologies, medical secretarial studies, paralegal studies, secretarial studies/office management.
LIBRARY 2,700 books, 40 periodicals, 15 records, tapes, and CDs.
COMPUTERS ON CAMPUS 40 computers for student use in computer center, computer labs. Staffed computer lab on campus provides training in use of computers, software.
COLLEGE LIFE ***Student services:*** personal-psychological counseling.
HOUSING College housing not available.
CAREER PLANNING ***Placement office:*** 1 part-time staff. ***Services:*** resume preparation, resume referral, career counseling, job interviews.
EXPENSES FOR 1995–96 ***Application fee:*** $25. Tuition: $3600 full-time, $300 per course part-time. Tuition guaranteed not to increase for student's term of enrollment.
FINANCIAL AID ***College-administered undergrad aid 1995–96:*** low-interest long-term loans from external sources (averaging $2500). ***Acceptable forms:*** CSS Financial Aid PROFILE, FAFSA. ***Application deadline:*** continuous. ***Payment plan:*** installment.
APPLYING Open admission. ***Options:*** early entrance, deferred entrance. ***Application deadline:*** rolling.
APPLYING/TRANSFER ***Entrance:*** noncompetitive. ***Application deadline:*** rolling.
CONTACT Admissions Director, Gem City College, PO Box 179, Quincy, IL 62306-0179, 217-222-0391. College video available.

HAROLD WASHINGTON COLLEGE
Illinois—See City Colleges of Chicago, Harold Washington College

HEARTLAND COMMUNITY COLLEGE
Bloomington, Illinois

UG Enrollment: 2,769	Tuition & Fees (Area Res): $1080
Application Deadline: rolling	Room & Board: N/Avail

GENERAL District-supported, 2-year, coed. Part of Illinois Community College System. Awards certificates, transfer associate, terminal associate degrees. Founded 1990. ***Setting:*** urban campus. ***Endowment:*** $125,000. ***Educational spending 1994–95:*** $1300 per undergrad. ***Total enrollment:*** 2,769. ***Faculty:*** 191 (31 full-time, 19% with terminal degrees, 160 part-time); student-faculty ratio is 14:1.
ENROLLMENT PROFILE 2,769 students: 62% women, 74% part-time, 94% state residents, 57% transferred in, 33% 25 or older, 1% Native American, 2% Hispanic, 9% African American, 3% Asian American.
FIRST-YEAR CLASS 976 total; 1,051 applied, 100% were accepted, 93% of whom enrolled.
ACADEMIC PROGRAM Core. Calendar: semesters. Academic remediation for entering students, services for LD students, advanced placement, tutorials, summer session for credit, part-time degree program (daytime, evenings), adult/continuing education programs, co-op programs and internships. Study abroad in England, Germany, Mexico. ROTC: Army (c).
GENERAL DEGREE REQUIREMENTS 60 semester hours; 3 semester hours each of math and science; internship (some majors).
MAJORS Aircraft and missile maintenance, business administration/commerce/management, child care/child and family studies, computer information systems, computer programming, computer science, drafting and design, early childhood education, electrical and electronics technologies, manufacturing technology, mechanical design technology, nursing, practical nursing, quality control technology, secretarial studies/office management, welding technology.
COMPUTERS ON CAMPUS 300 computers for student use in computer center, computer labs, learning resource center, classrooms, library provide access to main academic computer, on-line services. Staffed computer lab on campus provides training in use of computers, software. Academic computing expenditure 1994–95: $225,500.

Peterson's Guide to Two-Year Colleges 1997 289

Heartland Community College (continued)

COLLEGE LIFE 1% vote in student government elections. ***Social organizations:*** 18 open to all. ***Most popular organizations:*** Environmental Club, Early Childhood Club, Student Government, Nursing Club. ***Major annual events:*** Fall Fest, Spring Fest, Chili Cook-off. ***Campus security:*** evening security.

HOUSING College housing not available.

CAREER PLANNING ***Placement office:*** 2 part-time staff; $9300 operating expenditure 1994–95. ***Director:*** Ms. Christine Riley, Director of Advisement and Enrollment Services, 309-827-0500 Ext. 204. ***Services:*** resume preparation, resume referral, career counseling, careers library, job bank, job interviews. 10 organizations recruited on campus 1994–95.

AFTER GRADUATION 94% of students completing a degree program in 1994–95 went directly on to further study.

EXPENSES FOR 1996–97 Area resident tuition: $1080 full-time, $36 per semester hour part-time. State resident tuition: $3646 full-time, $121.54 per semester hour part-time. Nonresident tuition: $5266 full-time, $175.52 per semester hour part-time.

FINANCIAL AID ***College-administered undergrad aid 1995–96:*** 82 need-based scholarships (average $1650), 12 non-need scholarships (average $1000), Federal Work-Study, 20 part-time jobs. ***Required forms:*** institutional, FAFSA; accepted: CSS Financial Aid PROFILE. ***Priority deadline:*** 6/1. ***Waivers:*** full or partial for minority students, employees or children of employees, and senior citizens.

APPLYING Open admission. ***Required:*** TOEFL for international students. ***Recommended:*** school transcript, SAT II: Writing Test. ***Required for some:*** 3 years of high school math, ACT. Test scores used for counseling/placement. ***Application deadline:*** rolling.

APPLYING/TRANSFER ***Recommended:*** standardized test scores. ***Required for some:*** minimum 2.0 college GPA. ***Entrance:*** noncompetitive. ***Application deadline:*** rolling. ***Contact:*** Mr. Fred Peterson, Dean of Student Services, 309-827-0500 Ext. 202.

CONTACT Ms. Christine Riley, Director of Advisement and Enrollment Services, Heartland Community College, 1226 Towanda Avenue, Bloomington, IL 61701, 309-827-0500 Ext. 204.

HIGHLAND COMMUNITY COLLEGE
Freeport, Illinois

UG Enrollment: 2,663	**Tuition & Fees (Area Res): $1240**
Application Deadline: rolling	**Room & Board: N/Avail**

GENERAL State and locally supported, 2-year, coed. Part of Illinois Community College System. Awards transfer associate, terminal associate degrees. Founded 1962. ***Setting:*** 240-acre rural campus. ***Total enrollment:*** 2,663. ***Faculty:*** 169 (46 full-time, 100% with terminal degrees, 123 part-time); student-faculty ratio is 19:1.

ENROLLMENT PROFILE 2,663 students: 68% women, 32% men, 63% part-time, 99% state residents, 3% transferred in, 1% international, 58% 25 or older, 1% Native American, 1% Hispanic, 7% African American, 1% Asian American. ***Most popular recent majors:*** business administration/commerce/management, science, liberal arts/general studies.

FIRST-YEAR CLASS 326 total. Of the students who applied, 100% were accepted. 12% from top 10% of their high school class, 28% from top quarter, 70% from top half.

ACADEMIC PROGRAM Core, honor code. Calendar: semesters. Academic remediation for entering students, English as a second language program offered during academic year and summer, services for LD students, self-designed majors, tutorials, summer session for credit, part-time degree program (daytime, evenings), adult/continuing education programs.

GENERAL DEGREE REQUIREMENTS 62 credit hours; math/science requirements vary according to porgram; computer course for most majors.

MAJORS Accounting, agricultural business, agricultural technologies, art/fine arts, automotive technologies, business administration/commerce/management, chemistry, child care/child and family studies, computer science, criminal justice, data processing, drafting and design, early childhood education, education, electrical and electronics technologies, engineering (general), engineering sciences, (pre)engineering sequence, engineering technology, food services management, geology, graphic arts, history, hospitality services, human services, liberal arts/general studies, marketing/retailing/merchandising, mathematics, mechanical engineering technology, music education, nursing, physical sciences, physics, political science/government, psychology, science, secretarial studies/office management, sociology, theater arts/drama.

LIBRARY Highland Library with 40,392 books, 3,036 microform titles, 227 periodicals, 4 on-line bibliographic services, 18 CD-ROMs, 2,000 records, tapes, and CDs. Acquisition spending 1994–95: $149,391.

COMPUTERS ON CAMPUS 75 computers for student use in computer labs, library provide access to off-campus computing facilities. Staffed computer lab on campus provides training in use of computers.

COLLEGE LIFE Drama-theater group, choral group, student-run newspaper, radio station. 25% vote in student government elections. ***Student services:*** personal-psychological counseling. ***Campus security:*** 24-hour patrols.

HOUSING College housing not available.

ATHLETICS Member NJCAA. ***Intercollegiate:*** baseball M/W, basketball M(s)/W(s), golf M(s)/W(s), softball W, volleyball W(s). ***Intramural:*** basketball, golf, racquetball, volleyball. ***Contact:*** Mr. Pete Norman, Athletic Director, 815-235-6121 Ext. 264.

CAREER PLANNING ***Placement office:*** 1 full-time, 2 part-time staff. ***Director:*** Ms. Kathryn Rossi, Coordinator of Career Services, 815-235-6121 Ext. 286. ***Services:*** job fairs, resume preparation, career counseling, job bank.

AFTER GRADUATION 82% of students completing a degree program in 1994–95 went directly on to further study.

EXPENSES FOR 1996–97 Area resident tuition: $1240 full-time, $40 per credit hour part-time. State resident tuition: $3991 full-time, $128.73 per credit hour part-time. Nonresident tuition: $5047 full-time, $162.81 per credit hour part-time.

FINANCIAL AID ***College-administered undergrad aid 1995–96:*** 80 need-based scholarships (average $500), 40 non-need scholarships (average $400), low-interest long-term loans from external sources (average $2000), Federal Work-Study, 30 part-time jobs. ***Required forms:*** institutional, FAFSA; accepted: CSS Financial Aid PROFILE. ***Priority deadline:*** 6/1. ***Waivers:*** full or partial for employees or children of employees and senior citizens.

APPLYING Open admission except for nursing programs. ***Options:*** early entrance, deferred entrance, midyear entrance. ***Required:*** TOEFL for international students. ***Recommended:*** 3 years of high school math and science, ACT. ***Required for some:*** ACT. Test scores used for counseling/placement. ***Application deadline:*** rolling. Preference given to district residents.

APPLYING/TRANSFER ***Recommended:*** standardized test scores, 3 years of high school math and science. ***Application deadline:*** rolling.

CONTACT Mr. Karl Richards, Director of Admissions and Records, Highland Community College, Freeport, IL 61032-9341, 815-235-6121 Ext. 285. ***Fax:*** 815-235-6130. College video available.

ILLINOIS CENTRAL COLLEGE
East Peoria, Illinois

UG Enrollment: 11,680	**Tuition & Fees (Area Res): $1344**
Application Deadline: rolling	**Room & Board: N/Avail**

GENERAL State and locally supported, 2-year, coed. Part of Illinois Community College System. Awards certificates, transfer associate, terminal associate degrees. Founded 1967. ***Setting:*** 430-acre suburban campus. ***Total enrollment:*** 11,680. ***Faculty:*** 626 (176 full-time, 8% with terminal degrees, 450 part-time); student-faculty ratio is 20:1.

ENROLLMENT PROFILE 11,680 students: 59% women, 69% part-time, 99% state residents, 5% transferred in, 12% have need-based financial aid, 41% have non-need-based financial aid, 1% international, 55% 25 or older, 1% Native American, 1% Hispanic, 6% African American, 1% Asian American. ***Areas of study chosen:*** 10% education, 5% fine arts, 3% agriculture, 3% architecture, 3% engineering and applied sciences, 3% library and information studies, 2% communications and journalism, 2% premed, 1% performing arts, 1% prevet, 1% social sciences. ***Most popular recent majors:*** liberal arts/general studies, science, business administration/commerce/management.

FIRST-YEAR CLASS 2,500 total. Of the students who applied, 100% were accepted.

ACADEMIC PROGRAM Calendar: semesters. 800 courses offered in 1995–96. Academic remediation for entering students, English as a second language program offered during summer, services for LD students, advanced placement, honors program, summer session for credit, part-time degree program (daytime, evenings, weekends), adult/continuing education programs, internships.

GENERAL DEGREE REQUIREMENTS 64 semester hours; math/science requirements vary according to program; internship (some majors).

MAJORS Accounting, agricultural business, agricultural technologies, architectural technologies, automotive technologies, business administration/commerce/management, child psychology/child development, commercial art, court reporting, data processing, dental services, electrical and electronics technologies, engineering technology, finance/banking, fire science, graphic arts, health services administration, horticulture, interior design, law enforcement/police sciences, liberal arts/general studies, library science, manufacturing technology, marketing/retailing/merchandising, mechanical design technology, medical laboratory technology, medical records services, nursing, occupational therapy, paralegal studies, physical therapy, radiological technology, real estate, respiratory therapy, robotics, science, secretarial studies/office management, welding technology.

LIBRARY 82,492 books, 37,992 microform titles, 563 periodicals, 10 CD-ROMs, 1,449 records, tapes, and CDs. Acquisition spending 1994–95: $565,766.

COMPUTERS ON CAMPUS 200 computers for student use in academic labs provide access to off-campus computing facilities, on-line services. Staffed computer lab on campus provides training in use of computers, software. Academic computing expenditure 1994–95: $309,888.

COLLEGE LIFE Drama-theater group, choral group, student-run newspaper. ***Most popular organizations:*** Student Association for the Environment, Horticulture Club. ***Major annual events:*** Fine Arts Festival, Gaming Fair, Train Fair. ***Student services:*** health clinic, personal-psychological counseling.

HOUSING College housing not available.

ATHLETICS Member NJCAA. ***Intercollegiate:*** baseball M(s), basketball M(s)/W(s), golf M, softball W(s), volleyball W(s). ***Intramural:*** basketball, golf, soccer, table tennis (Ping-Pong), tennis, volleyball. ***Contact:*** Mr. Carroll Herman, Athletic Director, 309-694-5119.

CAREER PLANNING ***Placement office:*** 1 full-time, 2 part-time staff; $112,043 operating expenditure 1994–95. ***Director:*** Mr. Lanny C. Spanninger, Director, Student Support Services, 309-694-5321. ***Services:*** job fairs, resume preparation, resume referral, career counseling, careers library, job bank, job interviews.

AFTER GRADUATION 89% of students completing a degree program in 1994–95 went directly on to further study.

EXPENSES FOR 1996–97 Area resident tuition: $1344 full-time, $42 per semester hour part-time. State resident tuition: $4160 full-time, $130 per semester hour part-time. Nonresident tuition: $5760 full-time, $180 per semester hour part-time.

FINANCIAL AID ***College-administered undergrad aid 1995–96:*** 12 need-based scholarships (average $480), 12 non-need scholarships (average $500), short-term loans (average $120), low-interest long-term loans from external sources (average $1000), Federal Work-Study, 164 part-time jobs. ***Required forms:*** state, institutional, FAFSA; accepted: CSS Financial Aid PROFILE. ***Application deadline:*** continuous to 10/1. ***Payment plans:*** installment, deferred payment. ***Waivers:*** full or partial for employees or children of employees and senior citizens.

APPLYING Open admission except for college transfer associate programs, health applied science programs. ***Options:*** early entrance, midyear entrance. ***Required:*** school transcript, TOEFL for international students. ***Required for some:*** ACT. Test scores used for counseling/placement. ***Application deadline:*** rolling. ***Notification:*** continuous.

APPLYING/TRANSFER ***Required for some:*** college transcript. ***Entrance:*** noncompetitive. ***Application deadline:*** rolling. ***Notification:*** continuous.

CONTACT Mrs. Joanne Bannon-Gray, Director of Enrollment Management, Illinois Central College, Admissions Office, 1 College Drive, East Peoria, IL 61635-0001, 309-694-5354 or toll-free 800-422-2293 (in-state). ***Fax:*** 309-694-5450. College video available.

ILLINOIS EASTERN COMMUNITY COLLEGES, FRONTIER COMMUNITY COLLEGE
Fairfield, Illinois

UG Enrollment: 1,904	**Tuition & Fees (Area Res): $944**
Application Deadline: rolling	**Room & Board: N/Avail**

GENERAL State and locally supported, 2-year, coed. Part of Illinois Eastern Community College System. Awards certificates, transfer associate, terminal associate degrees. Founded 1976. ***Setting:*** 8-acre rural campus. ***Total enrollment:*** 1,904. ***Faculty:*** 158 (3 full-time, 155 part-time).
ENROLLMENT PROFILE 1,904 students: 73% women, 27% men, 91% part-time, 100% state residents, 0% transferred in, 24% have need-based financial aid, 0% international, 71% 25 or older, 0% Native American, 0% Hispanic, 0% African American, 0% Asian American. ***Areas of study chosen:*** 54% liberal arts/general studies, 33% vocational and home economics, 10% computer and information sciences, 3% business management and administrative services.
FIRST-YEAR CLASS 1,281 total; 1,281 applied, 100% were accepted, 100% of whom enrolled.
ACADEMIC PROGRAM Core, honor code. Calendar: semesters. 666 courses offered in 1995–96. Academic remediation for entering students, English as a second language program offered during academic year, services for LD students, advanced placement, self-designed majors, tutorials, summer session for credit, part-time degree program (daytime, evenings, weekends, summer), external degree programs, adult/continuing education programs, co-op programs.
GENERAL DEGREE REQUIREMENT 64 credits.
MAJORS Computer information systems, information science, liberal arts/general studies, quality control technology, science, secretarial studies/office management.
LIBRARY 7,986 books, 55 microform titles, 110 periodicals, 544 records, tapes, and CDs. System-wide acquisition spending 1994–95: $55,424.
COMPUTERS ON CAMPUS 42 computers for student use in computer center.
HOUSING College housing not available.
CAREER PLANNING ***Service:*** career counseling.
EXPENSES FOR 1995–96 ***Application fee:*** $10. Area resident tuition: $944 full-time, $29.50 per credit hour part-time. State resident tuition: $3716 full-time, $116.12 per credit hour part-time. Nonresident tuition: $4884 full-time, $152.64 per credit hour part-time. One-time mandatory fee: $10.
FINANCIAL AID ***College-administered undergrad aid 1995–96:*** need-based scholarships, low-interest long-term loans from external sources, 13 Federal Work-Study (averaging $349). ***Required forms:*** institutional, FAFSA. ***Priority deadline:*** 7/1. ***Waivers:*** full or partial for employees or children of employees and senior citizens.
APPLYING Open admission. ***Options:*** early entrance, deferred entrance. ***Required:*** school transcript, SAT I or ACT, TOEFL for international students, ACT ASSET. ***Recommended:*** 3 years of high school math and science, some high school foreign language. Test scores used for counseling/placement. ***Application deadline:*** rolling. ***Notification:*** continuous. Preference given to district residents.
APPLYING/TRANSFER ***Required:*** college transcript. ***Entrance:*** noncompetitive. ***Application deadline:*** rolling. ***Notification:*** continuous.
CONTACT Mrs. Suzanne Brooks, Coordinator of Registration and Records, Illinois Eastern Community Colleges, Frontier Community College, Fairfield, IL 62837-2601, 618-842-3711 Ext. 4406. ***Fax:*** 618-842-6340. College video available.

ILLINOIS EASTERN COMMUNITY COLLEGES, LINCOLN TRAIL COLLEGE
Robinson, Illinois

UG Enrollment: 1,127	**Tuition & Fees (Area Res): $944**
Application Deadline: rolling	**Room & Board: N/Avail**

GENERAL State and locally supported, 2-year, coed. Part of Illinois Eastern Community College System. Awards certificates, transfer associate, terminal associate degrees. Founded 1969. ***Setting:*** 120-acre rural campus. ***Total enrollment:*** 1,127. ***Faculty:*** 77 (23 full-time, 54 part-time).
ENROLLMENT PROFILE 1,127 students: 56% women, 44% men, 54% part-time, 91% state residents, 0% transferred in, 44% have need-based financial aid, 53% 25 or older, 0% Native American, 1% Hispanic, 6% African American, 1% Asian American. ***Areas of study chosen:*** 68% liberal arts/general studies, 14% vocational and home economics, 5% business management and administrative services, 5% computer and information sciences, 3% agriculture, 3% architecture, 1% education, 1% engineering and applied sciences.
FIRST-YEAR CLASS 774 total; 774 applied, 100% were accepted, 100% of whom enrolled.
ACADEMIC PROGRAM Core, honor code. Calendar: semesters. 815 courses offered in 1995–96. Academic remediation for entering students, English as a second language program offered during academic year, services for LD students, advanced placement, self-designed majors, tutorials, summer session for credit, part-time degree program (daytime, evenings, weekends, summer), external degree programs, adult/continuing education programs, co-op programs and internships.
GENERAL DEGREE REQUIREMENTS 64 credits; internship (some majors).
MAJORS Art/fine arts, biology/biological sciences, computer programming, data processing, drafting and design, education, finance/banking, food services technology, heating/refrigeration/air conditioning, industrial engineering technology, information science, liberal arts/general studies, physical sciences, quality control technology, science, secretarial studies/office management, telecommunications.
LIBRARY 25,584 books, 166 periodicals, 954 records, tapes, and CDs. System-wide acquisition spending 1994–95: $55,424.
COMPUTERS ON CAMPUS 96 computers for student use in learning resource center, classrooms, library.
COLLEGE LIFE Drama-theater group. ***Social organizations:*** 1 national fraternity. ***Student services:*** personal-psychological counseling.
HOUSING College housing not available.
ATHLETICS Member NJCAA. ***Intercollegiate:*** basketball M(s)/W(s), golf M/W, volleyball W(s). ***Intramural:*** basketball, volleyball. ***Contact:*** Mr. Terry Collins, Coach, 618-544-8657.
CAREER PLANNING ***Service:*** career counseling.
EXPENSES FOR 1995–96 ***Application fee:*** $10. Area resident tuition: $944 full-time, $29.50 per credit hour part-time. State resident tuition: $3716 full-time, $116.12 per credit hour part-time. Nonresident tuition: $4884 full-time, $152.64 per credit hour part-time. One-time mandatory fee: $10.
FINANCIAL AID ***College-administered undergrad aid 1995–96:*** need-based scholarships, low-interest long-term loans from external sources, 57 Federal Work-Study (averaging $500). ***Required forms:*** institutional, FAFSA. ***Priority deadline:*** 7/1. ***Waivers:*** full or partial for employees or children of employees and senior citizens.
APPLYING Open admission. ***Options:*** early entrance, deferred entrance. ***Required:*** school transcript, SAT I or ACT, TOEFL for international students, ACT ASSET. ***Recommended:*** 3 years of high school math and science, some high school foreign language. Test scores used for counseling/placement. ***Application deadline:*** rolling. ***Notification:*** continuous. Preference given to district residents.
APPLYING/TRANSFER ***Required:*** college transcript. ***Entrance:*** noncompetitive. ***Application deadline:*** rolling. ***Notification:*** continuous.
CONTACT Mrs. Becky Mikeworth, Director of Admissions, Illinois Eastern Community Colleges, Lincoln Trail College, Robinson, IL 62454, 618-544-8657 Ext. 1137. ***Fax:*** 618-544-7423. College video available.

ILLINOIS EASTERN COMMUNITY COLLEGES, OLNEY CENTRAL COLLEGE
Olney, Illinois

UG Enrollment: 1,486	**Tuition & Fees (Area Res): $944**
Application Deadline: rolling	**Room & Board: N/Avail**

GENERAL State and locally supported, 2-year, coed. Part of Illinois Eastern Community College System. Awards certificates, transfer associate, terminal associate degrees. Founded 1962. ***Setting:*** 128-acre rural campus. ***Total enrollment:*** 1,486. ***Faculty:*** 72 (42 full-time, 30 part-time).
ENROLLMENT PROFILE 1,486 students: 63% women, 37% men, 45% part-time, 99% state residents, 0% transferred in, 52% have need-based financial aid, 1% international, 47% 25 or older, 0% Native American, 0% Hispanic, 1% African American, 0% Asian American. ***Areas of study chosen:*** 44% liberal arts/general studies, 31% health professions and related sciences, 11% vocational and home economics, 7% business management and administrative services, 4% prelaw, 3% computer and information sciences.
FIRST-YEAR CLASS 812 total; 812 applied, 100% were accepted, 100% of whom enrolled.
ACADEMIC PROGRAM Core, honor code. Calendar: semesters. 788 courses offered in 1995–96. Academic remediation for entering students, English as a second language program offered during academic year, services for LD students, advanced placement, self-designed majors, tutorials, summer session for credit, part-time degree program (daytime, evenings, weekends, summer), external degree programs, adult/continuing education programs, co-op programs and internships.
GENERAL DEGREE REQUIREMENTS 64 credits; internship (some majors).
MAJORS Accounting, automotive technologies, cosmetology, industrial and heavy equipment maintenance, information science, law enforcement/police sciences, liberal arts/general studies, medical secretarial studies, nursing, practical nursing, radiological technology, secretarial studies/office management, welding technology, wood sciences.
LIBRARY Anderson Learning Resources Center with 27,515 books, 158 periodicals, 473 records, tapes, and CDs. System-wide acquisition spending 1994–95: $55,424.
COMPUTERS ON CAMPUS 125 computers for student use in computer labs, learning resource center, classrooms, library.
COLLEGE LIFE Drama-theater group, student-run newspaper. ***Student services:*** personal-psychological counseling, women's center.
HOUSING College housing not available.
ATHLETICS Member NJCAA. ***Intercollegiate:*** basketball M(s)/W(s), volleyball W(s). ***Intramural:*** basketball. ***Contact:*** Mr. Dennis Conley, Athletic Director, 618-395-4351.
CAREER PLANNING ***Service:*** career counseling.
EXPENSES FOR 1995–96 ***Application fee:*** $10. Area resident tuition: $944 full-time, $29.50 per credit hour part-time. State resident tuition: $3716 full-time, $116.12 per credit hour part-time. Nonresident tuition: $4884 full-time, $152.64 per credit hour part-time. One-time mandatory fee: $10.
FINANCIAL AID ***College-administered undergrad aid 1995–96:*** need-based scholarships, low-interest long-term loans from external sources, 87 Federal Work-Study (averaging $462), part-time jobs. ***Required forms:*** institutional, FAFSA. ***Priority deadline:*** 7/1. ***Waivers:*** full or partial for employees or children of employees and senior citizens.
APPLYING Open admission. ***Options:*** early entrance, deferred entrance. ***Required:*** school transcript, SAT I or ACT, TOEFL for international students, ACT ASSET. ***Recommended:*** 3 years of high school math and science, some high school foreign language. Test scores used for counseling/placement. ***Application deadline:*** rolling. ***Notification:*** continuous. Preference given to district residents.
APPLYING/TRANSFER ***Required:*** college transcript. ***Entrance:*** noncompetitive. ***Application deadline:*** rolling. ***Notification:*** continuous.
CONTACT Mrs. Chris Webber, Assistant Dean for Student Services, Illinois Eastern Community Colleges, Olney Central College, Olney, IL 62450, 618-395-4351 Ext. 2237. ***Fax:*** 618-392-5212. College video available.

ILLINOIS EASTERN COMMUNITY COLLEGES, WABASH VALLEY COLLEGE
Mount Carmel, Illinois

UG Enrollment: 2,023	**Tuition & Fees (Area Res): $944**
Application Deadline: rolling	**Room & Board: N/Avail**

GENERAL State and locally supported, 2-year, coed. Part of Illinois Eastern Community College System. Awards certificates, transfer associate, terminal associate degrees. Founded 1960. ***Setting:*** 40-acre rural campus. ***Total enrollment:*** 2,023. ***Faculty:*** 78 (40 full-time, 38 part-time).
ENROLLMENT PROFILE 2,023 students: 45% women, 67% part-time, 97% state residents, 0% transferred in, 34% have need-based financial aid, 2% international, 67% 25 or older, 0% Native American, 1% African American, 1% Asian American. ***Areas of study chosen:*** 54% liberal arts/general studies, 21% vocational and home economics, 8% agriculture, 8% business management and administrative services, 6% education, 4% communications and journalism, 3% computer and information sciences.
FIRST-YEAR CLASS 1,319 total; 1,319 applied, 100% were accepted, 100% of whom enrolled.
ACADEMIC PROGRAM Core, honor code. Calendar: semesters. 1,083 courses offered in 1995–96. Academic remediation for entering students, English as a second language

Illinois Eastern Community Colleges, Wabash Valley College (continued)
program offered during academic year, services for LD students, advanced placement, self-designed majors, tutorials, summer session for credit, part-time degree program (daytime, evenings, weekends, summer), external degree programs, adult/continuing education programs, co-op programs and internships.
GENERAL DEGREE REQUIREMENTS 64 credits; internship (some majors).
MAJORS Agricultural business, agricultural technologies, art/fine arts, business administration/commerce/management, child care/child and family studies, cosmetology, court reporting, electrical and electronics technologies, information science, liberal arts/general studies, machine and tool technologies, mining technology, radio and television studies, secretarial studies/office management, social work, transportation technologies.
LIBRARY Bauer Media Center with 24,294 books, 27,030 microform titles, 253 periodicals, 2,887 records, tapes, and CDs. System-wide acquisition spending 1994–95: $55,424.
COMPUTERS ON CAMPUS 100 computers for student use in learning resource center, classrooms, library.
COLLEGE LIFE Drama-theater group, student-run newspaper, radio station.
HOUSING College housing not available.
ATHLETICS Member NJCAA. ***Intercollegiate:*** basketball M(s)/W(s), golf M, tennis M, volleyball W(s). ***Intramural:*** basketball, cross-country running, volleyball. ***Contact:*** Mr. Mark Coomes, 618-262-8641.
CAREER PLANNING ***Service:*** career counseling.
EXPENSES FOR 1995–96 ***Application fee:*** $10. Area resident tuition: $944 full-time, $29.50 per credit hour part-time. State resident tuition: $3716 full-time, $116.12 per credit hour part-time. Nonresident tuition: $4884 full-time, $152.64 per credit hour part-time. One-time mandatory fee: $10.
FINANCIAL AID ***College-administered undergrad aid 1995–96:*** need-based scholarships, low-interest long-term loans from external sources (averaging $2000), 80 Federal Work-Study (averaging $504), part-time jobs. ***Required forms:*** institutional, FAFSA. ***Priority deadline:*** 7/1. ***Waivers:*** full or partial for employees or children of employees and senior citizens.
APPLYING Open admission. ***Options:*** early entrance, deferred entrance. ***Required:*** school transcript, SAT I or ACT, TOEFL for international students, ACT ASSET. ***Recommended:*** 3 years of high school math and science, some high school foreign language. Test scores used for counseling/placement. ***Application deadline:*** rolling. ***Notification:*** continuous. Preference given to district residents.
APPLYING/TRANSFER ***Required:*** college transcript. ***Entrance:*** noncompetitive. ***Application deadline:*** rolling. ***Notification:*** continuous.
CONTACT Mrs. Diana Spear, Assistant Dean for Student Services, Illinois Eastern Community Colleges, Wabash Valley College, Mount Carmel, IL 62863-2657, 618-262-8641 Ext. 3246. ***Fax:*** 618-262-5347. College video available.

ILLINOIS VALLEY COMMUNITY COLLEGE
Oglesby, Illinois

UG Enrollment: 4,281	**Tuition & Fees (Area Res): $1214**
Application Deadline: rolling	**Room & Board: N/Avail**

GENERAL District-supported, 2-year, coed. Part of Illinois Community College System. Awards transfer associate, terminal associate degrees. Founded 1924. ***Setting:*** 410-acre rural campus with easy access to Chicago. ***Total enrollment:*** 4,281. ***Faculty:*** 189 (68 full-time, 121 part-time).
ENROLLMENT PROFILE 4,281 students: 61% women, 39% men, 64% part-time, 100% state residents, 11% transferred in, 0% international, 6% 25 or older, 0% Native American, 2% Hispanic, 2% African American.
FIRST-YEAR CLASS 1,241 total. Of the students who applied, 100% were accepted, 73% of whom enrolled.
ACADEMIC PROGRAM Core. Calendar: semesters. Academic remediation for entering students, services for LD students, advanced placement, self-designed majors, Freshman Honors College, summer session for credit, part-time degree program (daytime, evenings, summer), adult/continuing education programs, internships. Off-campus study at Sauk Valley Community College, Kishwaukee College, Kankakee Community College, Joliet Junior College, Rock Valley College, Elgin Community College, Waubonsee Community College.
GENERAL DEGREE REQUIREMENTS 64 semester hours; computer course (varies by major); internship (some majors).
MAJORS Accounting, agricultural business, agricultural sciences, automotive technologies, business administration/commerce/management, carpentry, child care/child and family studies, computer programming, criminal justice, data processing, drafting and design, education, electrical and electronics technologies, elementary education, (pre)engineering sequence, English, industrial engineering technology, journalism, law enforcement/police sciences, liberal arts/general studies, marketing/retailing/merchandising, mechanical design technology, mechanical engineering technology, nursing, secretarial studies/office management.
LIBRARY Jacobs Library with 58,250 books, 504 periodicals, 3,400 records, tapes, and CDs.
COMPUTERS ON CAMPUS 420 computers for student use in labs, library.
COLLEGE LIFE Drama-theater group, choral group, student-run newspaper. ***Social organizations:*** 3 open to all. ***Student services:*** personal-psychological counseling. ***Campus security:*** 24-hour patrols.
HOUSING College housing not available.
ATHLETICS ***Intercollegiate:*** basketball M/W, football M, tennis M/W. ***Intramural:*** basketball, gymnastics, volleyball. ***Contact:*** Mr. Paul Kinley, Athletic Director, 815-224-2720 Ext. 472.
CAREER PLANNING ***Placement office:*** 2 full-time staff. ***Director:*** Mr. John Marzetta, Director of Placement, 815-224-2720 Ext. 214. ***Services:*** job fairs, resume preparation, resume referral, career counseling, careers library, job bank, job interviews.
EXPENSES FOR 1996–97 Area resident tuition: $1152 full-time, $36 per semester hour part-time. State resident tuition: $3504 full-time, $109.49 per semester hour part-time. Nonresident tuition: $4512 full-time, $141 per semester hour part-time. Part-time mandatory fees per semester range from $4.75 to $22.25. Full-time mandatory fees: $62.
FINANCIAL AID ***College-administered undergrad aid 1995–96:*** need-based scholarships, non-need scholarships, short-term loans, Federal Work-Study, part-time jobs. ***Required forms:*** FAFSA; accepted: CSS Financial Aid PROFILE. ***Application deadline:*** continuous.
APPLYING Open admission except for nursing, dental assistant programs. ***Options:*** early entrance, deferred entrance. ***Required:*** school transcript, TOEFL for international students. ***Recommended:*** ACT. Test scores used for counseling/placement. ***Application deadline:*** rolling. ***Notification:*** continuous.
APPLYING/TRANSFER ***Required:*** high school transcript, college transcript. ***Recommended:*** standardized test scores. ***Application deadline:*** rolling. ***Notification:*** continuous.
CONTACT Dr. Robert Marshall, Director of Admissions and Records, Illinois Valley Community College, Oglesby, IL 61348-9691, 815-224-2720 Ext. 437. ***Fax:*** 815-224-3033. College video available.

ITT TECHNICAL INSTITUTE
Hoffman Estates, Illinois

UG Enrollment: 470	**Tuition: $15,429/deg prog**
Application Deadline: rolling	**Room & Board: N/Avail**

GENERAL Proprietary, primarily 2-year, coed. Part of ITT Educational Services, Inc. Awards terminal associate, bachelor's degrees. Founded 1986. ***Setting:*** 1-acre suburban campus with easy access to Chicago. ***Total enrollment:*** 470. ***Faculty:*** 18 (all full-time, 85% with terminal degrees); student-faculty ratio is 26:1.
ENROLLMENT PROFILE 470 students: 5% women, 0% part-time, 100% state residents, 0% transferred in, 0% international, 30% 25 or older, 0% Native American, 14% Hispanic, 15% African American, 2% Asian American. ***Areas of study chosen:*** 100% engineering and applied sciences. ***Most popular recent major:*** electronics engineering technology.
FIRST-YEAR CLASS 202 total; 314 applied, 93% were accepted, 65% of whom enrolled. 5% from top 10% of their high school class, 45% from top quarter, 50% from top half.
ACADEMIC PROGRAM Core, honor code. Calendar: quarters. Academic remediation for entering students.
MAJORS Drafting and design, electronics engineering technology.
COMPUTERS ON CAMPUS 53 computers for student use in computer labs, classrooms, library. Staffed computer lab on campus provides training in use of computers, software.
COLLEGE LIFE ***Social organizations:*** 3 open to all. ***Most popular organizations:*** Student Council, Certified Electronics Technician Association, ISEEE. ***Major annual events:*** Blood Drive, Toys for Tots. ***Campus security:*** 24-hour emergency response devices.
HOUSING College housing not available.
CAREER PLANNING ***Placement office:*** 1 full-time staff. ***Director:*** Ms. Kathy Echelmeyer, Director of Placement, 708-519-9300. ***Services:*** job fairs, resume preparation, resume referral, career counseling, job bank, job interviews. Students must register freshman year.
EXPENSES FOR 1995–96 Tuition per degree program ranges from $15,429 to $17,690. Full-time mandatory fees: $200. Tuition guaranteed not to increase for student's term of enrollment.
FINANCIAL AID ***College-administered undergrad aid 1995–96:*** need-based scholarships, low-interest long-term loans from external sources, Federal Work-Study, part-time jobs. ***Required forms:*** institutional, FAFSA; required for some: Veterans Administration Form. ***Application deadline:*** continuous. ***Payment plan:*** installment.
APPLYING ***Option:*** deferred entrance. ***Required:*** CPAt. Test scores used for admission. ***Application deadline:*** rolling.
APPLYING/TRANSFER ***Contact:*** Mr. Vaughn C. Hardacker, Director of Education, 708-519-9300 Ext. 20.
CONTACT Mr. James M. Burke, Director of Recruitment, ITT Technical Institute, Hoffman Estates, IL 60195-3717, 708-519-9300 Ext. 26. College video available.

ITT TECHNICAL INSTITUTE
Matteson, Illinois

UG Enrollment: 331	**Tuition: $16,379/deg prog**
Application Deadline: rolling	**Room & Board: N/Avail**

GENERAL Proprietary, 2-year, coed. Part of ITT Educational Services, Inc. Awards diplomas, transfer associate, terminal associate degrees. Founded 1993. ***Setting:*** suburban campus with easy access to Chicago. ***Total enrollment:*** 331. ***Faculty:*** 14 (13 full-time, 14% with terminal degrees, 1 part-time).
ENROLLMENT PROFILE 331 students: 16% women, 0% part-time, 100% state residents, 0% international, 10% 25 or older, 0% Native American, 10% Hispanic, 49% African American, 2% Asian American. ***Areas of study chosen:*** 100% engineering and applied sciences.
FIRST-YEAR CLASS 195 total; 340 applied, 97% were accepted.
ACADEMIC PROGRAM Honor code. Calendar: quarters. Academic remediation for entering students.
GENERAL DEGREE REQUIREMENTS 118 units; computer course.
LIBRARY Learning Resources Center with 400 books, 25 periodicals.
COMPUTERS ON CAMPUS 52 computers for student use in computer labs, learning resource center, classrooms provide access to Internet. Staffed computer lab on campus provides training in use of computers, software.
COLLEGE LIFE 85% vote in student government elections. ***Most popular organization:*** Student Advisory Committee. ***Major annual event:*** Picnic. ***Campus security:*** 24-hour patrols, student patrols, escort service.
HOUSING College housing not available.
CAREER PLANNING ***Placement office:*** 1 full-time staff. ***Director:*** Ms. Sandee Rusiniak, Director of Placement, 708-747-2571. ***Services:*** job fairs, resume preparation, resume referral, career counseling, careers library, job bank, job interviews. Students must register freshman year.
EXPENSES FOR 1996–97 ***Application fee:*** $100. Tuition per degree program ranges from $16,379 to $18,575. Tuition guaranteed not to increase for student's term of enrollment.
FINANCIAL AID ***College-administered undergrad aid 1995–96:*** need-based scholarships, non-need scholarships, short-term loans, low-interest long-term loans, Federal Work-Study, part-time jobs. ***Required forms:*** institutional, FAFSA. ***Priority deadline:*** 9/15. ***Payment plan:*** installment.
APPLYING ***Option:*** deferred entrance. ***Required:*** CPAt. Test scores used for admission. ***Application deadline:*** rolling.

APPLYING/TRANSFER ***Entrance:*** moderately difficult. ***Application deadline:*** rolling. ***Contact:*** Ms. Mary Wheeler, Director of Education, 708-747-2571.
CONTACT Mr. Chet Will, Director of Recruitment, ITT Technical Institute, Matteson, IL 60443, 708-747-2571 Ext. 108. College video available.

JOHN A. LOGAN COLLEGE
Carterville, Illinois

UG Enrollment: 4,897 **Tuition & Fees (Area Res): $930**
Application Deadline: 8/25 **Room & Board: N/Avail**

GENERAL State and locally supported, 2-year, coed. Part of Illinois Community College System. Awards certificates, transfer associate, terminal associate degrees. Founded 1967. ***Setting:*** 160-acre rural campus. ***Total enrollment:*** 4,897. ***Faculty:*** 246 (93 full-time, 13% with terminal degrees, 153 part-time); student-faculty ratio is 25:1.
ENROLLMENT PROFILE 4,897 students: 56% women, 42% part-time, 99% state residents, 20% transferred in, 0% international, 37% 25 or older, 0% Native American, 1% Hispanic, 7% African American, 1% Asian American. ***Areas of study chosen:*** 19% vocational and home economics, 9% business management and administrative services, 9% education, 6% health professions and related sciences, 5% computer and information sciences, 4% liberal arts/general studies, 3% engineering and applied sciences, 3% psychology, 2% biological and life sciences, 1% communications and journalism, 1% English language/literature/letters, 1% fine arts, 1% mathematics, 1% physical sciences, 1% premed, 1% prevet, 1% social sciences.
FIRST-YEAR CLASS 1,272 total. 5% from top 10% of their high school class, 65% from top half.
ACADEMIC PROGRAM Core, honor code. Calendar: semesters. Academic remediation for entering students, services for LD students, advanced placement, summer session for credit, part-time degree program (daytime, evenings, summer), adult/continuing education programs, co-op programs and internships. Off-campus study at Belleville Area College, Rend Lake College, Illinois Eastern Community Colleges, Shawnee College, Southern Illinois University at Carbondale, Southeastern Illinois College. Study abroad in England, Mexico. ROTC: Army (c), Air Force (c).
GENERAL DEGREE REQUIREMENTS 62 semester hours; 5 semester hours of math; 12 semester hours of science; computer course for engineering majors.
MAJORS Accounting, agricultural sciences, art education, art/fine arts, automotive technologies, biology/biological sciences, business administration/commerce/management, business education, chemistry, computer information systems, computer science, cosmetology, criminal justice, data processing, deaf interpreter training, dental services, drafting and design, early childhood education, education, electrical and electronics technologies, electronics engineering technology, elementary education, emergency medical technology, (pre)engineering sequence, English, fashion merchandising, finance/banking, heating/refrigeration/air conditioning, history, humanities, journalism, legal secretarial studies, liberal arts/general studies, machine and tool technologies, marketing/retailing/merchandising, mathematics, medical laboratory technology, medical records services, nursing, occupational therapy, physical education, physics, political science/government, practical nursing, psychology, retail management, social work, teacher aide studies, tourism and travel, welding technology.
LIBRARY Learning Resource Center with 33,306 books, 7,370 microform titles, 298 periodicals, 4,347 records, tapes, and CDs.
COMPUTERS ON CAMPUS 150 computers for student use in computer labs, library provide access to Internet. Staffed computer lab on campus provides training in use of computers, software.
COLLEGE LIFE Drama-theater group, choral group, student-run newspaper. ***Campus security:*** 24-hour emergency response devices and patrols.
HOUSING College housing not available.
ATHLETICS Member NJCAA. ***Intercollegiate:*** baseball M, basketball M/W, golf M, softball W, tennis M/W, volleyball W. ***Contact:*** Mr. John Sala, Athletic Director, 618-985-3741 Ext. 439.
CAREER PLANNING ***Director:*** Dr. Julie O'Brien, Director of Career Development Center, 618-985-3741. ***Services:*** career counseling, job bank.
EXPENSES FOR 1995–96 Area resident tuition: $930 full-time, $30 per semester hour part-time. State resident tuition: $2976 full-time, $96.01 per semester hour part-time. Nonresident tuition: $4595 full-time, $148.23 per semester hour part-time.
FINANCIAL AID ***College-administered undergrad aid 1995–96:*** need-based scholarships, non-need scholarships, short-term loans (average $50), low-interest long-term loans from external sources, Federal Work-Study. ***Required forms:*** institutional, FAFSA. ***Priority deadline:*** 4/1. ***Waivers:*** full or partial for employees or children of employees and senior citizens.
APPLYING Open admission except for nursing program. ***Options:*** early entrance, midyear entrance. ***Required:*** school transcript, ACT ASSET. ***Recommended:*** SAT I or ACT. Test scores used for counseling/placement. ***Application deadline:*** 8/25. ***Notification:*** continuous.
APPLYING/TRANSFER ***Entrance:*** noncompetitive. ***Application deadline:*** 8/25. ***Notification:*** continuous. ***Contact:*** Dr. Larry Chapman, Dean for Student Services, 618-985-3741.
CONTACT Dr. Larry Chapman, Dean for Student Services, John A. Logan College, Carterville, IL 62918, 618-985-3741. ***Fax:*** 618-985-2248.

JOHN WOOD COMMUNITY COLLEGE
Quincy, Illinois

UG Enrollment: 2,300 **Tuition & Fees (Area Res): $1568**
Application Deadline: rolling **Room & Board: N/Avail**

GENERAL District-supported, 2-year, coed. Part of Illinois Community College System. Awards transfer associate, terminal associate degrees. Founded 1974. ***Setting:*** small-town campus. ***Total enrollment:*** 2,300. ***Faculty:*** 156 (31 full-time, 125 part-time).
ENROLLMENT PROFILE 2,300 students from 3 states and territories. 65% women, 62% part-time, 98% state residents, 3% transferred in, 1% international, 59% 25 or older, 1% Native American, 1% Hispanic, 2% African American, 1% Asian American.
FIRST-YEAR CLASS 950 total; 1,100 applied, 100% were accepted, 86% of whom enrolled. 5% from top 10% of their high school class, 8% from top quarter, 65% from top half.
ACADEMIC PROGRAM Core. Calendar: semesters. Academic remediation for entering students, English as a second language program offered during academic year and summer, services for LD students, advanced placement, self-designed majors, summer session for credit, part-time degree program (daytime, evenings, summer), external degree programs, adult/continuing education programs, co-op programs and internships. Off-campus study at members of the Quincy Area Education Consortium, Southeastern Community College (IA), Blessing Hospital, Quincy Area Vocational Technical Center. Study abroad in England.
GENERAL DEGREE REQUIREMENTS 64 credit hours; 1 math course; computer course.
MAJORS Accounting, agricultural business, agricultural sciences, agricultural technologies, animal sciences, art/fine arts, automotive technologies, biology/biological sciences, business administration/commerce/management, chemistry, child care/child and family studies, classics, communication, communication equipment technology, computer information systems, computer programming, computer science, cosmetology, dietetics, drafting and design, economics, education, electrical and electronics technologies, (pre)engineering sequence, English, fashion merchandising, fire science, food services management, French, German, heating/refrigeration/air conditioning, history, humanities, information science, Japanese, jewelry and metalsmithing, law enforcement/police sciences, legal secretarial studies, liberal arts/general studies, machine and tool technologies, management information systems, marketing/retailing/merchandising, mathematics, medical laboratory technology, medical records services, medical secretarial studies, mental health/rehabilitation counseling, music, music education, nursing, painting/drawing, philosophy, physical education, physical sciences, physics, political science/government, practical nursing, psychology, science, secretarial studies/office management, social science, sociology, Spanish, speech/rhetoric/public address/debate, theater arts/drama, welding technology.
LIBRARY 369,700 books, 1,002 periodicals, 69,000 records, tapes, and CDs.
COMPUTERS ON CAMPUS Computer purchase plan available. 125 computers for student use in labs. Staffed computer lab on campus provides training in use of computers, software.
COLLEGE LIFE ***Student services:*** personal-psychological counseling.
HOUSING College housing not available.
ATHLETICS ***Intercollegiate:*** basketball M/W, cross-country running M, football M, golf M/W, tennis M/W, volleyball W. ***Intramural:*** basketball, golf, soccer, tennis, volleyball.
CAREER PLANNING ***Service:*** career counseling.
EXPENSES FOR 1995–96 Area resident tuition: $1568 full-time, $49 per semester hour part-time. State resident tuition: $4289 full-time, $134.03 per semester hour part-time. Nonresident tuition: $7057 full-time, $220.52 per semester hour part-time.
FINANCIAL AID ***College-administered undergrad aid 1995–96:*** need-based scholarships, 10 non-need scholarships (average $640), low-interest long-term loans from external sources (average $1800), Federal Work-Study, 10 part-time jobs. ***Required forms:*** FAFSA; required for some: state; accepted: CSS Financial Aid PROFILE, institutional. ***Priority deadline:*** 6/1.
APPLYING Open admission except for broadcast electronics program. ***Option:*** early entrance. ***Required:*** school transcript, TOEFL for international students, ACT ASSET. ***Recommended:*** SAT I or ACT. Test scores used for counseling/placement. ***Application deadline:*** rolling. ***Notification:*** continuous. Preference given to district residents.
APPLYING/TRANSFER ***Required:*** college transcript. ***Entrance:*** noncompetitive. ***Application deadline:*** rolling. ***Notification:*** continuous.
CONTACT Mr. Mark C. McNett, Director of Admissions, John Wood Community College, Quincy, IL 62301-9147, 217-224-6500 Ext. 4339. ***E-mail:*** macnett@speedy.jwcc.cc.il.us.

JOLIET JUNIOR COLLEGE
Joliet, Illinois

UG Enrollment: 10,417 **Tuition & Fees (Area Res): $1325**
Application Deadline: rolling **Room & Board: N/Avail**

GENERAL State and locally supported, 2-year, coed. Part of Illinois Community College System. Awards certificates, diplomas, transfer associate, terminal associate degrees. Founded 1901. ***Setting:*** suburban campus with easy access to Chicago. ***Total enrollment:*** 10,417. ***Faculty:*** 496 (146 full-time, 25% with terminal degrees, 350 part-time); student-faculty ratio is 18:1.
ENROLLMENT PROFILE 10,417 students: 58% women, 70% part-time, 99% state residents, 2% transferred in, 0% international, 51% 25 or older, 1% Native American, 5% Hispanic, 8% African American, 1% Asian American.
FIRST-YEAR CLASS 2,632 total; 4,032 applied, 100% were accepted, 65% of whom enrolled.
ACADEMIC PROGRAM Core. Calendar: semesters. Academic remediation for entering students, English as a second language program offered during academic year, services for LD students, advanced placement, summer session for credit, part-time degree program (daytime, evenings), adult/continuing education programs, internships.
GENERAL DEGREE REQUIREMENTS 64 credits; 3 credits of math; computer course for technology majors.
MAJORS Accounting, agricultural business, agricultural education, art/fine arts, automotive technologies, biology/biological sciences, business administration/commerce/management, business economics, chemistry, child psychology/child development, community services, computer information systems, conservation, construction technologies, corrections, culinary arts, ecology, education, electrical and electronics technologies, electronics engineering technology, (pre)engineering sequence, fashion merchandising, finance/banking, fire science, food services management, forestry, geography, history, horticulture, hotel and restaurant management, interior design, landscaping/grounds maintenance, law enforcement/police sciences, liberal arts/general studies, library science, manufacturing technology, marketing/retailing/merchandising, mathematics, mechanical design technology, medical technology, music, nuclear technology, nursing, physical education, physics, physiology, political science/government, psychology, real estate, secretarial studies/office management, sociology, teacher aide studies, theater arts/drama, zoology.
LIBRARY 74,865 books, 126 microform titles, 482 periodicals, 3,169 records, tapes, and CDs. Acquisition spending 1994–95: $146,400.
COMPUTERS ON CAMPUS 180 computers for student use in computer labs provide access to e-mail. Staffed computer lab on campus provides training in use of computers, software. Academic computing expenditure 1994–95: $89,500.

Peterson's Guide to Two-Year Colleges 1997 293

Joliet Junior College (continued)

COLLEGE LIFE Drama-theater group, student-run newspaper. 1% vote in student government elections. ***Social organizations:*** 20 open to all; 2 national fraternities, 1 eating club; 1% of eligible men and 1% of eligible women are members. ***Student services:*** personal-psychological counseling. ***Campus security:*** 24-hour emergency response devices and patrols, student patrols, late-night transport-escort service.
HOUSING College housing not available.
ATHLETICS Member NJCAA. ***Intercollegiate:*** basketball M/W, football M, tennis M/W, volleyball W.
CAREER PLANNING ***Placement office:*** 1 full-time, 2 part-time staff; $37,600 operating expenditure 1994–95. ***Director:*** Ms. Teri Cullen, Director of Alumni and Placement Services, 815-729-9020 Ext. 2218. ***Services:*** job fairs, resume preparation, resume referral, career counseling, job interviews.
AFTER GRADUATION 85% of students completing a degree program in 1994–95 went directly on to further study.
EXPENSES FOR 1996–97 Area resident tuition: $1248 full-time, $39 per credit part-time. State resident tuition: $4479 full-time, $139.96 per credit part-time. Nonresident tuition: $5482 full-time, $171.30 per credit part-time. Part-time mandatory fees: $8 per credit. Full-time mandatory fees: $77.
FINANCIAL AID ***College-administered undergrad aid 1995–96:*** 100 need-based scholarships (average $90), 100 non-need scholarships (average $370), short-term loans (average $400), low-interest long-term loans from external sources (average $2700), Federal Work-Study, 350 part-time jobs. ***Required forms:*** institutional; accepted: CSS Financial Aid PROFILE, state. ***Priority deadline:*** 8/21.
APPLYING Open admission except for nursing program. ***Options:*** early entrance, deferred entrance. ***Required:*** school transcript, TOEFL for international students. ***Recommended:*** SAT I or ACT. Test scores used for counseling/placement. ***Application deadline:*** rolling. Preference given to district residents.
APPLYING/TRANSFER ***Required:*** college transcript. ***Entrance:*** noncompetitive. ***Application deadline:*** rolling.
CONTACT Mr. George Maniates, Director of Admissions and Enrollment Management, Joliet Junior College, Joliet, IL 60431-9352, 815-729-9020 Ext. 2311. ***E-mail:*** gmaniate@jjc.cc.il.us.

KANKAKEE COMMUNITY COLLEGE
Kankakee, Illinois

UG Enrollment: 3,776 | **Tuition & Fees (Area Res): $1216**
Application Deadline: rolling | **Room & Board: N/Avail**

GENERAL State and locally supported, 2-year, coed. Part of Illinois Community College System. Awards certificates, transfer associate, terminal associate degrees. Founded 1966. ***Setting:*** 178-acre small-town campus with easy access to Chicago. ***Total enrollment:*** 3,776. ***Faculty:*** 222 (47 full-time, 175 part-time); student-faculty ratio is 20:1.
ENROLLMENT PROFILE 3,776 students: 60% women, 67% part-time, 97% state residents, 16% transferred in, 0% international, 25% 25 or older, 0% Native American, 1% Hispanic, 10% African American, 1% Asian American. ***Most popular recent majors:*** nursing, liberal arts/general studies.
FIRST-YEAR CLASS 2,640 total. Of the students who applied, 100% were accepted.
ACADEMIC PROGRAM Core. Calendar: semesters. Academic remediation for entering students, English as a second language program offered during academic year and summer, services for LD students, advanced placement, self-designed majors, honors program, summer session for credit, part-time degree program (daytime, evenings, summer), adult/continuing education programs, co-op programs and internships. Off-campus study at Olivet Nazarene University. Study abroad in England, Austria, Spain.
GENERAL DEGREE REQUIREMENTS 64 semester hours; computer course for most majors.
MAJORS Accounting, agricultural business, agricultural sciences, art/fine arts, automotive technologies, business administration/commerce/management, child care/child and family studies, computer technologies, electrical and electronics technologies, emergency medical technology, (pre)engineering sequence, farm and ranch management, heating/refrigeration/air conditioning, law enforcement/police sciences, legal secretarial studies, liberal arts/general studies, machine and tool technologies, marketing/retailing/merchandising, medical laboratory technology, medical secretarial studies, nursing, radiological technology, real estate, retail management, secretarial studies/office management, welding technology.
LIBRARY 35,150 books, 21,595 microform titles, 265 periodicals, 1,150 records, tapes, and CDs.
COMPUTERS ON CAMPUS 120 computers for student use in computer center, computer labs, learning resource center, library. Staffed computer lab on campus provides training in use of computers, software.
COLLEGE LIFE Orientation program (4 days, $40). Student-run newspaper. ***Student services:*** personal-psychological counseling. ***Campus security:*** 24-hour patrols.
HOUSING College housing not available.
ATHLETICS Member NJCAA. ***Intercollegiate:*** baseball M(s), basketball M(s)/W(s), softball W(s), volleyball W(s). ***Intramural:*** basketball, football, golf, tennis, volleyball. ***Contact:*** Mr. David Holstein, Athletic Director, 815-933-0210.
CAREER PLANNING ***Placement office:*** 2 full-time staff. ***Services:*** resume preparation, resume referral, career counseling, job bank, job interviews.
EXPENSES FOR 1995–96 Area resident tuition: $1136 full-time, $35.50 per semester hour part-time. State resident tuition: $2464 full-time, $77 per semester hour part-time. Nonresident tuition: $6388 full-time, $199.65 per semester hour part-time. Part-time mandatory fees: $2.50 per semester hour. Full-time mandatory fees: $80.
FINANCIAL AID ***College-administered undergrad aid 1995–96:*** need-based scholarships, 150 non-need scholarships (average $400), Federal Work-Study, 50 part-time jobs. ***Required forms:*** institutional, FAFSA; accepted: CSS Financial Aid PROFILE. ***Priority deadline:*** 6/1. ***Payment plan:*** deferred payment. ***Waivers:*** full or partial for employees or children of employees and senior citizens.
APPLYING Open admission except for allied health programs. ***Option:*** early entrance. ***Required:*** school transcript, TOEFL for international students. ***Recommended:*** ACT ASSET. ***Required for some:*** 3 years of high school science, ACT ASSET. Test scores used for counseling/placement. ***Application deadline:*** rolling. ***Notification:*** continuous. Preference given to district residents for allied health programs.
APPLYING/TRANSFER ***Required:*** college transcript. ***Required for some:*** 3 years of high school science. ***Application deadline:*** rolling. ***Notification:*** continuous. ***Contact:*** Mrs. Lisa Hendrickson, Coordinator, Transfer Programs, 815-933-0245.
CONTACT Mr. Thomas D. Dolliger, Assistant Dean of Student Services, Kankakee Community College, Kankakee, IL 60901-0888, 815-933-0242. ***Fax:*** 815-933-0217. College video available.

KASKASKIA COLLEGE
Centralia, Illinois

UG Enrollment: 2,916 | **Tuition & Fees (Area Res): $1082**
Application Deadline: rolling | **Room & Board: N/Avail**

GENERAL State and locally supported, 2-year, coed. Part of Illinois Community College System. Awards transfer associate, terminal associate degrees. Founded 1966. ***Setting:*** 195-acre rural campus with easy access to St. Louis. ***Total enrollment:*** 2,916. ***Faculty:*** 220 (63 full-time, 6% with terminal degrees, 157 part-time); student-faculty ratio is 18:1.
ENROLLMENT PROFILE 2,916 students: 63% women, 37% men, 52% part-time, 99% state residents, 2% transferred in, 1% international, 45% 25 or older, 1% Native American, 1% Hispanic, 4% African American, 1% Asian American. ***Areas of study chosen:*** 33% liberal arts/general studies, 26% vocational and home economics, 11% health professions and related sciences, 5% biological and life sciences, 5% business management and administrative services, 2% computer and information sciences, 1% agriculture, 1% engineering and applied sciences. ***Most popular recent majors:*** liberal arts/general studies, nursing, business administration/commerce/management.
FIRST-YEAR CLASS 906 total.
ACADEMIC PROGRAM Core, honor code. Calendar: semesters. 500 courses offered in 1995–96. Academic remediation for entering students, English as a second language program offered during academic year and summer, services for LD students, self-designed majors, summer session for credit, part-time degree program (daytime, evenings, weekends, summer), adult/continuing education programs, co-op programs and internships. Off-campus study at Belleville Area College, Illinois Eastern Community Colleges, Lake Land College, Rend Lake College, Shawnee Community College. ROTC: Army.
GENERAL DEGREE REQUIREMENTS 64 semester hours; 6 semester hours of math/science; computer course; internship (some majors).
MAJORS Accounting, agricultural business, automotive technologies, business administration/commerce/management, child care/child and family studies, computer information systems, criminal justice, drafting and design, electrical and electronics technologies, (pre)engineering sequence, fashion merchandising, industrial and heavy equipment maintenance, law enforcement/police sciences, legal secretarial studies, liberal arts/general studies, nursing, physical therapy, radiological technology, respiratory therapy, secretarial studies/office management, welding technology, word processing.
LIBRARY Kaskaskia College Library with 26,977 books, 17 microform titles, 116 periodicals, 750 CD-ROMs.
COMPUTERS ON CAMPUS 160 computers for student use in computer center, computer labs, learning resource center, classrooms, library provide access to main academic computer, e-mail, Internet. Staffed computer lab on campus provides training in use of computers, software.
COLLEGE LIFE Orientation program (2 days, $44). Drama-theater group, choral group, student-run newspaper. ***Social organizations:*** 20 open to all. ***Major annual event:*** Student Picnic. ***Student services:*** personal-psychological counseling. ***Campus security:*** 24-hour patrols, late-night transport-escort service.
HOUSING College housing not available.
ATHLETICS Member NJCAA. ***Intercollegiate:*** baseball M(s), basketball M(s)/W(s), softball W(s), volleyball W(s). ***Intramural:*** baseball, basketball, softball, volleyball. ***Contact:*** Mr. George F. Carling, Athletic Director, 618-532-1981 Ext. 346.
CAREER PLANNING ***Placement office:*** 1 part-time staff. ***Director:*** Mr. Rennie Minton, Counselor Specialist, 618-532-1981 Ext. 303. ***Services:*** job fairs, resume preparation, resume referral, career counseling, careers library, job interviews.
EXPENSES FOR 1995–96 ***Application fee:*** $10. Area resident tuition: $1024 full-time, $32 per semester hour part-time. State resident tuition: $2624 full-time, $82 per semester hour part-time. Nonresident tuition: $5088 full-time, $159 per semester hour part-time. Part-time mandatory fees: $1.80 per semester hour. Full-time mandatory fees: $58.
FINANCIAL AID ***College-administered undergrad aid 1995–96:*** 52 need-based scholarships, 84 non-need scholarships (average $1088), short-term loans (average $50), low-interest long-term loans from external sources (average $2625), 43 Federal Work-Study (averaging $1978), 160 part-time jobs. ***Required forms:*** state, FAFSA; accepted: CSS Financial Aid PROFILE. ***Priority deadline:*** 7/1. ***Payment plans:*** installment, deferred payment. ***Waivers:*** full or partial for employees or children of employees and senior citizens.
APPLYING Open admission except for allied health programs. ***Options:*** Common Application, early entrance, deferred entrance, midyear entrance. ***Required:*** school transcript, TOEFL for international students. ***Recommended:*** ACT. ***Required for some:*** interview, ACT. Test scores used for counseling/placement. ***Application deadline:*** rolling. ***Notification:*** continuous. Preference given to district residents.
APPLYING/TRANSFER ***Required:*** high school transcript, college transcript. ***Required for some:*** standardized test scores. ***Application deadline:*** rolling. ***Notification:*** continuous. ***Contact:*** Ms. Bonnie Sanders, Counselor Specialist, 618-532-1981 Ext. 304.
CONTACT Ms. Jan Ripperda, Admissions Officer, Kaskaskia College, Centralia, IL 62801-7878, 618-532-1981 Ext. 240 or toll-free 800-642-0859 (in-state).

KENNEDY-KING COLLEGE
Illinois—See City Colleges of Chicago, Kennedy-King College

KISHWAUKEE COLLEGE
Malta, Illinois

UG Enrollment: 3,690 **Tuition & Fees (Area Res): $1216**
Application Deadline: rolling **Room & Board: N/Avail**

GENERAL State and locally supported, 2-year, coed. Part of Illinois Community College System. Awards certificates, transfer associate, terminal associate degrees. Founded 1967. ***Setting:*** 120-acre rural campus with easy access to Chicago. ***Total enrollment:*** 3,690. ***Faculty:*** 198 (67 full-time, 10% with terminal degrees, 131 part-time); student-faculty ratio is 17:1.

ENROLLMENT PROFILE 3,690 students from 5 states and territories, 4 other countries. 58% women, 42% men, 52% part-time, 98% state residents, 22% transferred in, 1% international, 51% 25 or older, 1% Native American, 9% Hispanic, 7% African American, 3% Asian American. ***Areas of study chosen:*** 24% liberal arts/general studies, 11% health professions and related sciences, 5% education, 4% biological and life sciences, 3% business management and administrative services, 2% architecture, 2% communications and journalism, 2% engineering and applied sciences, 2% psychology, 1% agriculture, 1% computer and information sciences, 1% English language/literature/letters, 1% fine arts, 1% mathematics, 1% performing arts, 1% physical sciences, 1% prelaw, 1% premed, 1% prevet, 1% social sciences.

FIRST-YEAR CLASS 1,020 total. Of the students who applied, 100% were accepted, 90% of whom enrolled.

ACADEMIC PROGRAM Core, multidisciplinary curriculum, honor code. Calendar: semesters. 681 courses offered in 1995–96; average class size 21 in required courses. Academic remediation for entering students, English as a second language program offered during academic year and summer, services for LD students, advanced placement, summer session for credit, part-time degree program (daytime, evenings, summer), external degree programs, adult/continuing education programs, co-op programs and internships. Off-campus study at 6 other Illinois community colleges. ROTC: Army (c).

GENERAL DEGREE REQUIREMENTS 64 semester hours; 3 semester hours of math; 7 semester hours of science; computer course for office management, agriculture, automotive technologies, drafting and design, electrical and electronics technology, horticulture, marketing, radiological technology majors; internship (some majors).

MAJORS Agricultural business, agricultural sciences, agricultural technologies, art/fine arts, automotive technologies, biology/biological sciences, business administration/commerce/management, chemistry, child care/child and family studies, data processing, drafting and design, education, electrical and electronics technologies, elementary education, (pre)engineering sequence, English, farm and ranch management, fire science, history, horticulture, industrial arts, industrial design, landscape architecture/design, landscaping/grounds maintenance, law enforcement/police sciences, legal secretarial studies, liberal arts/general studies, machine and tool technologies, manufacturing technology, marketing/retailing/merchandising, mathematics, modern languages, music, nursing, ornamental horticulture, physical education, physical sciences, quality control technology, radiological technology, real estate, secretarial studies/office management, social science, speech/rhetoric/public address/debate, teacher aide studies, water resources, welding technology, word processing.

LIBRARY Learning Resource Center with 33,000 books, 73 microform titles, 240 periodicals, 400 records, tapes, and CDs.

COMPUTERS ON CAMPUS Computer purchase plan available. 200 computers for student use in computer labs, learning resource center, library provide access to e-mail, Internet. Staffed computer lab on campus provides training in use of computers, software.

COLLEGE LIFE Drama-theater group, choral group, student-run newspaper. ***Social organizations:*** 9 open to all. ***Most popular organizations:*** Student Association, Phi Theta Kappa, Horticulture Club, Student Nursing Association, International Club. ***Major annual events:*** Awards and Recognition Ceremony, Black History Month/Soul Food Buffet, Women's History Month. ***Student services:*** health clinic, personal-psychological counseling. ***Campus security:*** 24-hour patrols.

HOUSING College housing not available.

ATHLETICS Member NJCAA. ***Intercollegiate:*** baseball M(s), basketball M(s)/W(s), golf M(s), soccer M(s), softball W(s), volleyball W(s). ***Intramural:*** basketball, volleyball. ***Contact:*** Ms. Jodi Lord, Athletic Director, 815-825-2086 Ext. 308.

CAREER PLANNING ***Placement office:*** 1 full-time staff. ***Director:*** Ms. Frances Loubere, Coordinator of Career Planning, 815-825-2086 Ext. 338. ***Services:*** resume preparation, career counseling, careers library, job bank. 5 organizations recruited on campus 1994–95.

AFTER GRADUATION 60% of students completing a degree program in 1994–95 went directly on to further study.

EXPENSES FOR 1996–97 Area resident tuition: $1216 full-time, $38 per semester hour part-time. State resident tuition: $4855 full-time, $151.71 per semester hour part-time. Nonresident tuition: $5942 full-time, $185.69 per semester hour part-time. Part-time mandatory fees: $3.75 per semester hour.

FINANCIAL AID ***College-administered undergrad aid 1995–96:*** 10 need-based scholarships (averaging $100), 15 non-need scholarships (averaging $200), short-term loans (averaging $50), low-interest long-term loans from external sources (averaging $2050), 80 Federal Work-Study (averaging $700), 80 part-time jobs. ***Required forms:*** institutional, FAFSA; required for some: state; accepted: CSS Financial Aid PROFILE. ***Priority deadline:*** 6/1.

APPLYING Open admission except for nursing, radiological technology programs. ***Options:*** Common Application, early entrance, deferred entrance, midyear entrance. ***Required:*** TOEFL for international students. ***Required for some:*** school transcript, minimum 2.0 GPA, ACT. Test scores used for counseling/placement. ***Application deadline:*** rolling. ***Notification:*** continuous.

APPLYING/TRANSFER ***Recommended:*** college transcript. ***Required for some:*** high school transcript, college transcript, minimum 2.0 high school GPA. ***Application deadline:*** rolling. ***Notification:*** continuous. ***Contact:*** Ms. Lea Houdek, Director of Admissions, Registration and Records, 815-825-2086 Ext. 218.

CONTACT Ms. Lea Houdek, Director of Admissions, Registration and Records, Kishwaukee College, Malta, IL 60150, 815-825-2086 Ext. 218.

LAKE LAND COLLEGE
Mattoon, Illinois

UG Enrollment: 4,734 **Tuition & Fees (Area Res): $1498**
Application Deadline: rolling **Room & Board: N/Avail**

GENERAL State and locally supported, 2-year, coed. Part of Illinois Community College System. Awards certificates, transfer associate, terminal associate degrees. Founded 1966. ***Setting:*** 304-acre rural campus. ***Total enrollment:*** 4,734. ***Faculty:*** 424 (255 full-time, 80% with terminal degrees, 169 part-time).

ENROLLMENT PROFILE 4,734 students: 54% women, 46% men, 55% part-time, 99% state residents, 10% transferred in, 27% have need-based financial aid, 35% have non-need-based financial aid, 1% international, 48% 25 or older, 1% Native American, 1% Hispanic, 6% African American, 1% Asian American. ***Areas of study chosen:*** 14% health professions and related sciences, 13% social sciences, 9% business management and administrative services, 5% education, 4% engineering and applied sciences, 3% agriculture, 2% communications and journalism, 2% computer and information sciences, 2% psychology, 1% architecture, 1% biological and life sciences, 1% fine arts, 1% liberal arts/general studies, 1% natural resource sciences, 1% prelaw, 1% premed, 1% prevet. ***Most popular recent majors:*** business administration/commerce/management, elementary education, agricultural business.

FIRST-YEAR CLASS 1,428 total; 1,908 applied, 100% were accepted, 75% of whom enrolled.

ACADEMIC PROGRAM Core, honor code. Calendar: semesters. Average class size 22 in required courses. Academic remediation for entering students, English as a second language program offered during academic year and summer, services for LD students, tutorials, honors program, summer session for credit, part-time degree program (daytime, evenings, summer), external degree programs, adult/continuing education programs, co-op programs and internships.

GENERAL DEGREE REQUIREMENTS 64 semester hours; math/science requirements vary according to program; computer course for drafting and design, electronics technology, management majors; internship (some majors).

MAJORS Accounting, agricultural business, agricultural sciences, agricultural technologies, architectural technologies, automotive technologies, biology/biological sciences, broadcasting, business administration/commerce/management, child care/child and family studies, civil engineering technology, computer science, data processing, dental services, drafting and design, economics, electrical and electronics technologies, electromechanical technology, electronics engineering technology, elementary education, engineering (general), engineering sciences, environmental sciences, finance/banking, forestry, geography, health education, history, home economics, human services, industrial arts, industrial engineering technology, journalism, law enforcement/police sciences, legal secretarial studies, liberal arts/general studies, manufacturing technology, marketing/retailing/merchandising, mathematics, medical secretarial studies, nursing, physical education, physical sciences, political science/government, recreation and leisure services, retail management, secretarial studies/office management, social science, speech/rhetoric/public address/debate, telecommunications, theater arts/drama, veterinary sciences, wildlife management.

LIBRARY Virgil H. Judge Learning Resource Center with 32,270 books, 217 periodicals, 1 on-line bibliographic service, 8 CD-ROMs, 1,719 records, tapes, and CDs. Acquisition spending 1994–95: $257,670.

COMPUTERS ON CAMPUS 350 computers for student use in computer center, computer labs, learning resource center, classrooms, library provide access to main academic computer, on-line services, Internet. Staffed computer lab on campus provides training in use of computers, software.

COLLEGE LIFE Student-run newspaper, radio station. 4% vote in student government elections. ***Social organizations:*** 18 open to all. ***Most popular organizations:*** Agriculture Production and Management Club, Cosmetology Club, Agriculture Transfer Club, Phi Theta Kappa, Civil Engineering Technology Club. ***Major annual events:*** Spring Carnival, Alcohol Awareness Week, Blood Drives. ***Student services:*** personal-psychological counseling. ***Campus security:*** 24-hour patrols.

HOUSING College housing not available.

ATHLETICS Member NJCAA. ***Intercollegiate:*** baseball M(s), basketball M(s)/W(s), softball W(s), tennis M(s), volleyball W(s). ***Intramural:*** basketball, bowling, golf, softball, volleyball. ***Contact:*** Mr. Jim Dudley, Athletic Director, 217-234-5294.

CAREER PLANNING ***Placement office:*** 2 full-time staff; $66,009 operating expenditure 1994–95. ***Director:*** Ms. Teresa Grissom, Director of Career Planning and Placement, 217-234-5346. ***Services:*** resume preparation, resume referral, career counseling, careers library, job bank, job interviews. 44 organizations recruited on campus 1994–95.

AFTER GRADUATION 93% of class of 1994 had job offers within 6 months.

EXPENSES FOR 1996–97 ***Application fee:*** $10. Area resident tuition: $1248 full-time, $39 per semester hour part-time. State resident tuition: $3262 full-time, $101.94 per semester hour part-time. Nonresident tuition: $6354 full-time, $198.56 per semester hour part-time. Part-time mandatory fees: $10 per semester hour. Full-time mandatory fees: $250.

FINANCIAL AID ***College-administered undergrad aid 1995–96:*** 285 need-based scholarships (averaging $900), 563 non-need scholarships (averaging $1348), low-interest long-term loans from external sources (averaging $2008), Federal Work-Study, 27 part-time jobs. ***Required forms:*** institutional; accepted: CSS Financial Aid PROFILE, state, FAFSA, SINGLEFILE Form of United Student Aid Funds. ***Priority deadline:*** 4/15. ***Payment plan:*** deferred payment. ***Waivers:*** full or partial for employees or children of employees and senior citizens. ***Notification:*** continuous.

APPLYING Open admission except for dental services, nursing, physical therapist assistant, civil engineering technology, John Deere agricultural technology programs. ***Options:*** early entrance, midyear entrance. ***Required:*** TOEFL for international students. ***Recommended:*** ACT. ***Required for some:*** 3 years of high school math, recommendations, ACT. Test scores used for counseling/placement. ***Application deadline:*** rolling. ***Notification:*** continuous. Preference given to district residents.

APPLYING/TRANSFER ***Required for some:*** 3 years of high school math. ***Entrance:*** noncompetitive. ***Application deadline:*** rolling. ***Notification:*** continuous. ***Contact:*** Mr. David Greeson, Vice President, Academic Services, 217-234-5225.

CONTACT Mrs. Linda Von Behren, Director of Admission Services, Lake Land College, Mattoon, IL 61938-9366, 217-234-5254 or toll-free 800-252-4121 (in-state).

Peterson's Guide to Two-Year Colleges 1997 295

LEWIS AND CLARK COMMUNITY COLLEGE
Godfrey, Illinois

UG Enrollment: 5,303 **Tuition & Fees (Area Res): $1280**
Application Deadline: rolling **Room & Board: N/Avail**

GENERAL District-supported, 2-year, coed. Part of Illinois Community College System. Awards transfer associate, terminal associate degrees. Founded 1970. ***Setting:*** 275-acre small-town campus with easy access to St. Louis. ***Educational spending 1994–95:*** $1044 per undergrad. ***Total enrollment:*** 5,303. ***Faculty:*** 305 (80 full-time, 225 part-time); student-faculty ratio is 20:1.
ENROLLMENT PROFILE 5,303 students from 2 states and territories, 3 other countries. 63% women, 71% part-time, 98% state residents, 49% 25 or older, 1% Hispanic, 6% African American. ***Most popular recent major:*** nursing.
FIRST-YEAR CLASS 1,670 total. Of the students who applied, 100% were accepted, 100% of whom enrolled. 6% from top 10% of their high school class, 25% from top quarter, 43% from top half.
ACADEMIC PROGRAM Core. Calendar: semesters. Academic remediation for entering students, services for LD students, honors program, summer session for credit, part-time degree program (daytime, evenings), adult/continuing education programs. Off-campus study at Blackburn College. Study abroad in England, Austria, Costa Rica.
GENERAL DEGREE REQUIREMENTS 64 credit hours; math/science requirements vary according to major; computer course (varies by major).
MAJORS Accounting, agricultural business, agricultural sciences, art/fine arts, automotive technologies, biology/biological sciences, broadcasting, business administration/commerce/management, child care/child and family studies, computer programming, court reporting, criminal justice, data processing, dental services, drafting and design, early childhood education, electrical and electronics technologies, (pre)engineering sequence, finance/banking, fire science, food services management, hotel and restaurant management, law enforcement/police sciences, legal secretarial studies, liberal arts/general studies, library science, machine and tool technologies, marketing/retailing/merchandising, medical laboratory technology, medical secretarial studies, music, nursing, radio and television studies, science, secretarial studies/office management, teacher aide studies.
LIBRARY 30,000 books, 85 microform titles, 315 periodicals, 1,800 records, tapes, and CDs. Acquisition spending 1994–95: $138,269.
COMPUTERS ON CAMPUS 300 computers for student use in computer center, computer labs, research center, learning resource center, classroom lab, classrooms, library provide access to off-campus computing facilities. Staffed computer lab on campus provides training in use of computers, software. Academic computing expenditure 1994–95: $144,420.
COLLEGE LIFE Drama-theater group, choral group, student-run newspaper, radio station. ***Social organizations:*** 25 open to all. ***Most popular organizations:*** Phi Beta Lambda, Data Processing Club, Nursing Club, Medical Laboratory Technicians Club, Music Club. ***Major annual event:*** Springfest. ***Student services:*** health clinic, personal-psychological counseling, women's center. ***Campus security:*** 24-hour emergency response devices and patrols.
HOUSING College housing not available.
ATHLETICS Member NJCAA. ***Intercollegiate:*** baseball M, basketball W(s), golf M, soccer M(s)/W, tennis M(s)/W(s), volleyball W(s). ***Intramural:*** basketball, bowling, golf, tennis, volleyball. ***Contact:*** Mr. George Terry, Dean of Student Activities and Athletics, 618-466-3411 Ext. 3500.
CAREER PLANNING ***Placement office:*** 2 full-time staff; $48,687 operating expenditure 1994–95. ***Director:*** Mr. Steve Campbell, Assistant Director, Employment Assistance, 618-466-3411. ***Services:*** job fairs, resume preparation, career counseling, careers library, job bank.
EXPENSES FOR 1996–97 Area resident tuition: $1184 full-time, $37 per credit hour part-time. State resident tuition: $3584 full-time, $112 per credit hour part-time. Nonresident tuition: $6400 full-time, $200 per credit hour part-time. Part-time mandatory fees: $3 per credit hour. Full-time mandatory fees: $96.
FINANCIAL AID ***College-administered undergrad aid 1995–96:*** need-based scholarships, non-need scholarships, short-term loans, low-interest long-term loans from external sources, Federal Work-Study, part-time jobs. ***Required forms:*** institutional; required for some: state; accepted: CSS Financial Aid PROFILE, FAFSA. ***Application deadline:*** 12/20. ***Payment plans:*** installment, deferred payment. ***Waivers:*** full or partial for employees or children of employees and senior citizens.
APPLYING Open admission. ***Options:*** early entrance, deferred entrance, midyear entrance. ***Required:*** 4 years of high school math and science, TOEFL for international students. ***Recommended:*** school transcript. Test scores used for counseling/placement. ***Application deadline:*** rolling. ***Notification:*** continuous.
APPLYING/TRANSFER ***Recommended:*** college transcript. ***Application deadline:*** rolling. ***Notification:*** continuous.
CONTACT Ms. Carla Totten, Director of Enrollment Services for Admissions Services, Lewis and Clark Community College, Godfrey, IL 62035-2466, 618-466-3411 Ext. 5100 or toll-free 800-642-1794 (in-state). College video available.

LEXINGTON COLLEGE
Chicago, Illinois

UG Enrollment: 44 **Tuition & Fees: $5470**
Application Deadline: rolling **Room & Board: $3475**

GENERAL Independent, 2-year, women only. Awards transfer associate, terminal associate degrees. Founded 1977. ***Setting:*** urban campus. ***Educational spending 1994–95:*** $2806 per undergrad. ***Total enrollment:*** 44. ***Faculty:*** 12 (2 full-time, 100% with terminal degrees, 10 part-time); student-faculty ratio is 5:1.
ENROLLMENT PROFILE 44 students from 6 states and territories, 5 other countries. 100% women, 9% part-time, 70% state residents, 30% live on campus, 7% transferred in, 73% have need-based financial aid, 17% international, 20% 25 or older, 0% Native American, 27% Hispanic, 16% African American, 7% Asian American. ***Most popular recent majors:*** food services management, hotel and restaurant management, dietetics.
FIRST-YEAR CLASS 21 total; 23 applied, 100% were accepted, 91% of whom enrolled. 11% from top quarter of their high school class, 50% from top half.
ACADEMIC PROGRAM Core, interdisciplinary curriculum, honor code. Calendar: semesters. 29 courses offered in 1995–96. Academic remediation for entering students, English as a second language program offered during academic year, tutorials, part-time degree program (daytime), adult/continuing education programs, co-op programs and internships.
GENERAL DEGREE REQUIREMENTS 64 credits; 1 business math course; computer course; internship.
MAJORS Culinary arts, dietetics, food services management, hospitality services, hotel and restaurant management.
LIBRARY Lexington College Library with 2,000 books, 30 periodicals, 20 records, tapes, and CDs. Acquisition spending 1994–95: $3325.
COMPUTERS ON CAMPUS 5 computers for student use in computer center provide access to software. Staffed computer lab on campus provides training in use of computers, software. Academic computing expenditure 1994–95: $5000.
COLLEGE LIFE Orientation program (2 days, no cost). Student-run newspaper. 100% vote in student government elections. ***Major annual events:*** Cultural Appreciation Week, Taste of Lexington, Family Christmas Party. ***Student services:*** health clinic, personal-psychological counseling, women's center. ***Campus security:*** 24-hour emergency response devices, late-night transport-escort service, patrols by municipal security personnel.
HOUSING 12 college housing spaces available; all were occupied 1995–96. No special consideration for freshman housing applicants. Off-campus living permitted. ***Option:*** single-sex (1 building) housing available. Resident assistants live in dorms.
CAREER PLANNING ***Placement office:*** 1 part-time staff; $7000 operating expenditure 1994–95. ***Director:*** Mrs. Kathy Dornhecker, Job Placement Coordinator, 312-779-3800. ***Services:*** resume preparation, career counseling, job bank, job interviews.
AFTER GRADUATION 100% of class of 1994 had job offers within 6 months. 7% of students completing a degree program went directly on to further study.
EXPENSES FOR 1995–96 ***Application fee:*** $25. Comprehensive fee of $8945 includes full-time tuition ($5400), mandatory fees ($70), and college room and board ($3475). Part-time tuition: $150 per credit. Part-time mandatory fees: $30 per semester. Tuition guaranteed not to increase for student's term of enrollment.
FINANCIAL AID ***College-administered undergrad aid 1995–96:*** 3 need-based scholarships (average $250), 2 part-time jobs. ***Required forms:*** state, FAFSA. ***Application deadline:*** continuous to 10/1. ***Payment plan:*** installment. ***Waivers:*** full or partial for employees or children of employees. ***Notification:*** continuous.
APPLYING Open admission. ***Option:*** midyear entrance. ***Required:*** school transcript, minimum 2.0 GPA. ***Recommended:*** campus interview, ACT. ***Required for some:*** recommendations. Test scores used for counseling/placement. ***Application deadline:*** rolling.
APPLYING/TRANSFER ***Required:*** high school transcript, college transcript. ***Recommended:*** campus interview, minimum 2.0 college GPA, minimum 2.0 high school GPA. ***Entrance:*** minimally difficult. ***Application deadline:*** rolling. ***Contact:*** Ms. Mary Jane Markel, Director of Admissions, 312-779-3800.
CONTACT Ms. Mary Jane Markel, Director of Admissions, Lexington College, 10840 South Western Avenue, Chicago, IL 60643-3294, 312-779-3800. ***Fax:*** 312-779-7450.

LINCOLN COLLEGE
Lincoln, Illinois

UG Enrollment: 570 **Tuition & Fees: $9310**
Application Deadline: rolling **Room & Board: $4150**

GENERAL Independent, 2-year, coed. Awards transfer associate degrees. Founded 1865. ***Setting:*** 38-acre small-town campus. ***Total enrollment:*** 570. ***Faculty:*** 42 (29 full-time, 13 part-time); student-faculty ratio is 13:1.
ENROLLMENT PROFILE 570 students from 15 states and territories, 3 other countries. 46% women, 11% part-time, 92% state residents, 7% transferred in, 2% international, 6% 25 or older, 0% Native American, 8% Hispanic, 12% African American, 1% Asian American.
FIRST-YEAR CLASS 320 total; 560 applied, 62% were accepted, 72% of whom enrolled. 5% from top 10% of their high school class, 17% from top quarter, 43% from top half. 2 valedictorians.
ACADEMIC PROGRAM Core, honor code. Calendar: semesters. Average class size 16 in required courses. Academic remediation for entering students, Freshman Honors College, tutorials, honors program, summer session for credit, part-time degree program (daytime, evenings).
GENERAL DEGREE REQUIREMENTS 61 hours; 3 hours of math; 8 hours of science; computer course (varies by major).
MAJOR Liberal arts/general studies.
LIBRARY McKinstry Library with 37,000 books, 135 microform titles, 361 periodicals, 2,000 records, tapes, and CDs.
COMPUTERS ON CAMPUS 65 computers for student use in computer center, computer labs, learning resource center, classrooms, library provide access to on-line services, Internet. Staffed computer lab on campus provides training in use of computers, software.
COLLEGE LIFE Orientation program (3 days, no cost, parents included). Drama-theater group, choral group, student-run newspaper, radio station. ***Major annual events:*** Parents' Weekend, Spring Formal, Commencement. ***Student services:*** health clinic. ***Campus security:*** 24-hour emergency response devices, controlled dormitory access.
HOUSING 340 college housing spaces available; 335 were occupied 1995–96. Freshmen guaranteed college housing. On-campus residence required through sophomore year. ***Option:*** single-sex housing available. Resident assistants live in dorms.
ATHLETICS Member NJCAA. ***Intercollegiate:*** baseball M(s), basketball M(s)/W(s), golf M(s)/W(s), soccer M(s)/W(s), softball W(s), swimming and diving M(s)/W(s), tennis M/W, volleyball W(s), wrestling M(s). ***Intramural:*** basketball, bowling, equestrian sports, football, golf, racquetball, soccer, softball, swimming and diving, table tennis (Ping-Pong), track and field, volleyball, water polo, weight lifting, wrestling. ***Contact:*** Mr. Allen Pickering, Athletic Director, 217-732-3155 Ext. 302.
CAREER PLANNING ***Placement office:*** 1 full-time, 4 part-time staff. ***Director:*** Ms. Paula Knopp, Transfer Coordinator, 217-732-3155. ***Services:*** resume preparation, career counseling, careers library. 5 organizations recruited on campus 1994–95.
AFTER GRADUATION 83% of students completing a degree program in 1994–95 went directly on to further study.
EXPENSES FOR 1996–97 ***Application fee:*** $25. Comprehensive fee of $13,460 includes full-time tuition ($8950), mandatory fees ($360), and college room and board ($4150). College room only: $1550. Part-time tuition per semester ranges from $137 to $1507. Tuition guaranteed not to increase for student's term of enrollment.

296 Peterson's Guide to Two-Year Colleges 1997

FINANCIAL AID ***College-administered undergrad aid 1995–96:*** 200 need-based scholarships (average $1438), 151 non-need scholarships (average $1100), low-interest long-term loans from external sources (average $1175), 121 Federal Work-Study (averaging $800), 30 part-time jobs. ***Required forms:*** institutional, FAFSA; accepted: CSS Financial Aid PROFILE. ***Priority deadline:*** 8/14. ***Payment plans:*** installment, deferred payment. ***Waivers:*** full or partial for employees or children of employees.
APPLYING ***Options:*** early entrance, deferred entrance, midyear entrance. ***Required:*** school transcript, SAT I or ACT, TOEFL for international students. ***Required for some:*** 1 recommendation, interview. Test scores used for admission and counseling/placement. ***Application deadline:*** rolling.
APPLYING/TRANSFER ***Required:*** interview. ***Recommended:*** college transcript. ***Required for some:*** standardized test scores, high school transcript, 1 recommendation. ***Entrance:*** minimally difficult. ***Application deadline:*** rolling. ***Contact:*** Mr. Roderick Rumler, Dean of Student Enrollment and Management, 217-732-3155 Ext. 250.
CONTACT Mr. Roderick Rumler, Dean of Student Enrollment and Management, Lincoln College, Lincoln, IL 62656-1699, 217-732-3155 Ext. 250 or toll-free 800-569-0556. ***Fax:*** 217-732-8455. College video available.

❖ *See pages 754 for narrative description.* ❖

LINCOLN COLLEGE
Normal, Illinois

UG Enrollment: 600	**Tuition & Fees: $9310**
Application Deadline: rolling	**Room & Board: $4150**

GENERAL Independent, 2-year, coed. Awards certificates, transfer associate, terminal associate degrees. Founded 1865. ***Endowment:*** $12 million. ***Total enrollment:*** 600. ***Faculty:*** 60 (5 full-time, 30% with terminal degrees, 55 part-time); student-faculty ratio is 15:1.
ENROLLMENT PROFILE 600 students from 13 states and territories, 4 other countries. 66% women, 45% part-time, 90% state residents, 20% transferred in, 75% have need-based financial aid, 25% have non-need-based financial aid, 1% international, 25% 25 or older, 1% Native American, 1% Hispanic, 24% African American, 1% Asian American.
FIRST-YEAR CLASS 400 total; 600 applied, 70% were accepted, 80% of whom enrolled. 5% from top 10% of their high school class, 15% from top quarter, 60% from top half.
ACADEMIC PROGRAM Core, liberal arts curriculum, honor code. Calendar: semesters. 227 courses offered in 1995–96. Academic remediation for entering students, tutorials, honors program, summer session for credit, part-time degree program (daytime, evenings, weekends, summer), adult/continuing education programs, co-op programs and internships.
GENERAL DEGREE REQUIREMENTS 61 credit hours; 15 credit hours of math/science including at least 3 credit hours of math and 8 credit hours of science; computer course.
MAJORS Accounting, applied art, art education, behavioral sciences, business economics, business education, computer graphics, computer information systems, computer management, computer programming, computer science, corrections, data processing, economics, education, humanities, legal secretarial studies, marketing/retailing/merchandising, medical secretarial studies, nursing, painting/drawing, paralegal studies, philosophy, physical education, practical nursing, psychology, social science, tourism and travel, word processing.
LIBRARY Milner Library plus 1 other, with 1.2 million books, 1.8 million microform titles.
COMPUTERS ON CAMPUS Computers for student use in computer center, computer labs, learning resource center, classrooms, library, dorms provide access to Internet. Staffed computer lab on campus provides training in use of computers, software.
COLLEGE LIFE Orientation program (1 week, $300). 60% vote in student government elections. ***Social organizations:*** local fraternities, local sororities; 40% of eligible men and 60% of eligible women are members. ***Most popular organization:*** Phi Theta Kappa. ***Major annual events:*** Intramurals, Concerts, Trips. ***Student services:*** health clinic. ***Campus security:*** 24-hour emergency response devices and patrols, student patrols, controlled dormitory access.
HOUSING 150 in college housing during 1995–96. Freshmen guaranteed college housing. On-campus residence required in freshman year. ***Options:*** coed, single-sex, international student housing available. Resident assistants live in dorms.
ATHLETICS ***Intercollegiate:*** baseball M, basketball M/W, golf M/W, soccer M/W, softball W, swimming and diving M/W, volleyball W, wrestling M. ***Intramural:*** ice hockey, lacrosse. ***Contact:*** Mr. Mike Riley, Assistant Director of Admissions, 217-732-3155.
CAREER PLANNING ***Placement office:*** 1 full-time staff. ***Director:*** Mrs. Paula Knopp, Transfer Coordinator, 217-732-3155. ***Services:*** job fairs, resume preparation, career counseling.
AFTER GRADUATION 87% of students completing a degree program in 1994–95 went directly on to further study.
EXPENSES FOR 1996–97 ***Application fee:*** $25. Comprehensive fee of $13,460 includes full-time tuition ($8950), mandatory fees ($360), and college room and board ($4150). College room only: $1550. Part-time tuition per semester ranges from $137 to $1507. Tuition guaranteed not to increase for student's term of enrollment.
FINANCIAL AID ***College-administered undergrad aid 1995–96:*** need-based scholarships, 600 non-need scholarships (averaging $1500), short-term loans, low-interest long-term loans. ***Required forms:*** state, FAFSA; accepted: CSS Financial Aid PROFILE. ***Priority deadline:*** 5/1. ***Payment plan:*** installment. ***Waivers:*** full or partial for employees or children of employees. ***Notification:*** continuous.
APPLYING ***Options:*** deferred entrance, midyear entrance. ***Required:*** school transcript, campus interview, TOEFL for international students. ***Required for some:*** 2 recommendations, SAT I or ACT. Test scores used for counseling/placement. ***Application deadline:*** rolling.
APPLYING/TRANSFER ***Required:*** high school transcript, campus interview, college transcript. ***Required for some:*** standardized test scores, 2 recommendations. ***Entrance:*** moderately difficult. ***Application deadline:*** rolling. ***Contact:*** Mrs. Paula Knopp, Transfer Coordinator, 217-732-3155.
CONTACT Mr. Joe Hendrix, Associate Director of Admissions, Lincoln College, 715 West Raab Road, Normal, IL 61761, 309-452-0500 or toll-free 800-569-0558. ***Fax:*** 309-454-5652. College video available.

❖ *See page 756 for a narrative description.* ❖

LINCOLN LAND COMMUNITY COLLEGE
Springfield, Illinois

UG Enrollment: 11,016	**Tuition & Fees (Area Res): $1175**
Application Deadline: rolling	**Room & Board: N/Avail**

GENERAL District-supported, 2-year, coed. Part of Illinois Community College System. Awards certificates, transfer associate, terminal associate degrees. Founded 1967. ***Setting:*** 241-acre suburban campus. ***Total enrollment:*** 11,016. ***Faculty:*** 245 (115 full-time, 20% with terminal degrees, 130 part-time).
ENROLLMENT PROFILE 11,016 students from 3 states and territories, 3 other countries. 58% women, 42% men, 75% part-time, 96% state residents, 4% transferred in, 1% international, 50% 25 or older, 1% Native American, 1% Hispanic, 4% African American, 1% Asian American.
FIRST-YEAR CLASS Of the students who applied, 100% were accepted, 85% of whom enrolled.
ACADEMIC PROGRAM Core, interdisciplinary curriculum, honor code. Calendar: semesters. 350 courses offered in 1995–96; average class size 30 in required courses. Academic remediation for entering students, English as a second language program offered during academic year, services for LD students, advanced placement, tutorials, honors program, summer session for credit, part-time degree program (daytime, evenings, weekends, summer), external degree programs, adult/continuing education programs, internships. Off-campus study at Foreign Language/International Studies Consortium.
GENERAL DEGREE REQUIREMENTS 60 credit hours; math/science requirements vary according to program; computer course for some majors; internship (some majors).
MAJORS Accounting, agricultural business, agricultural sciences, agricultural technologies, aircraft and missile maintenance, architectural technologies, art education, art/fine arts, art history, automotive technologies, aviation administration, behavioral sciences, biology/biological sciences, business administration/commerce/management, carpentry, chemistry, child care/child and family studies, civil engineering technology, communication, computer programming, computer science, construction technologies, corrections, criminal justice, data processing, drafting and design, economics, education, electrical and electronics technologies, elementary education, engineering (general), (pre)engineering sequence, English, family services, fire science, food services management, geography, geology, graphic arts, history, humanities, journalism, law enforcement/police sciences, liberal arts/general studies, literature, marketing/retailing/merchandising, mathematics, middle school education, music, nursing, philosophy, physical education, physics, political science/government, psychology, radiological technology, real estate, respiratory therapy, retail management, science, secretarial studies/office management, social work, sociology, surveying technology, teacher aide studies, theater arts/drama, tourism and travel, welding technology.
LIBRARY Learning Resource Center plus 1 other, with 72,956 books, 1,365 microform titles, 438 periodicals, 150 CD-ROMs, 10,500 records, tapes, and CDs. Acquisition spending 1994–95: $612,821.
COMPUTERS ON CAMPUS 130 computers for student use in computer center, classrooms, library provide access to on-line services. Staffed computer lab on campus provides training in use of computers, software. Academic computing expenditure 1994–95: $219,306.
COLLEGE LIFE Drama-theater group, choral group, student-run newspaper. 5% vote in student government elections. ***Social organizations:*** 26 open to all. ***Most popular organizations:*** Student Senate, Phi Theta Kappa, Model Illinois Government, Student Newspaper, Madrigals. ***Major annual event:*** Graduation. ***Student services:*** personal-psychological counseling, women's center. ***Campus security:*** 24-hour emergency response devices and patrols.
HOUSING College housing not available.
ATHLETICS Member NJCAA. ***Intercollegiate:*** baseball M(s), basketball M(s)/W(s), soccer M(s), volleyball W(s). ***Intramural:*** basketball, bowling, tennis, volleyball. ***Contact:*** Mr. David Laubersheimer, Athletic Director, 217-786-2240.
CAREER PLANNING ***Placement office:*** 2 full-time, 1 part-time staff; $42,530 operating expenditure 1994–95. ***Director:*** Ms. Sue Ramm, Director of Career Planning and Placement Services, 217-786-2232. ***Services:*** job fairs, resume preparation, career counseling, careers library, job bank.
EXPENSES FOR 1996–97 Area resident tuition: $1170 full-time, $39 per credit hour part-time. State resident tuition: $2434 full-time, $81.13 per credit hour part-time. Nonresident tuition: $3998 full-time, $133.27 per credit hour part-time. Full-time mandatory fees: $5.
FINANCIAL AID ***College-administered undergrad aid 1995–96:*** need-based scholarships, 202 non-need scholarships (average $375), short-term loans (average $100), low-interest long-term loans from college funds (average $775), loans from external sources (average $1591), Federal Work-Study, 201 part-time jobs. ***Required forms:*** state, institutional; accepted: CSS Financial Aid PROFILE, FAFSA. ***Priority deadline:*** 4/1. ***Payment plans:*** tuition prepayment, deferred payment. ***Waivers:*** full or partial for minority students, employees or children of employees, and senior citizens.
APPLYING Open admission except for allied health programs. ***Options:*** early entrance, deferred entrance, midyear entrance. ***Required:*** TOEFL for international students, ACT ASSET. ***Recommended:*** school transcript, 3 years of high school math, ACT. Test scores used for counseling/placement. ***Application deadline:*** rolling. ***Notification:*** continuous.
APPLYING/TRANSFER ***Required:*** college transcript. ***Recommended:*** standardized test scores. ***Entrance:*** noncompetitive. ***Application deadline:*** rolling. ***Notification:*** continuous. ***Contact:*** Mr. Ron Gregoire, Director of Admissions, 217-786-2243.
CONTACT Mr. Ron Gregoire, Director of Admissions, Lincoln Land Community College, Springfield, IL 62794-9256, 217-786-2243 or toll-free 800-727-4161 (in-state). ***Fax:*** 217-786-2492.

MacCORMAC JUNIOR COLLEGE
Chicago, Illinois

UG Enrollment: 569	**Tuition & Fees: $7530**
Application Deadline: rolling	**Room & Board: N/Avail**

GENERAL Independent, 2-year, coed. Awards certificates, diplomas, transfer associate, terminal associate degrees. Founded 1904. ***Setting:*** 8-acre urban campus. ***Total enrollment:*** 569. ***Faculty:*** 41 (30 full-time, 11 part-time); student-faculty ratio is 15:1.

Peterson's Guide to Two-Year Colleges 1997 297

Illinois

MacCormac Junior College (continued)
ENROLLMENT PROFILE 569 students from 7 states and territories, 14 other countries. 70% women, 30% men, 28% part-time, 95% state residents, 24% transferred in, 1% international, 20% 25 or older, 42% Hispanic, 9% African American, 1% Asian American. *Most popular recent majors:* court reporting, paralegal studies, accounting.
FIRST-YEAR CLASS 271 total. 72% from top half of their high school class.
ACADEMIC PROGRAM Core, honor code. Calendar: quarters. 92 courses offered in 1995–96. Academic remediation for entering students, English as a second language program offered during academic year and summer, advanced placement, tutorials, honors program, summer session for credit, part-time degree program (daytime, evenings), adult/continuing education programs, internships.
GENERAL DEGREE REQUIREMENTS 96 quarter hours; computer course; internship (some majors).
MAJORS Accounting, business administration/commerce/management, court reporting, hotel and restaurant management, information science, international business, legal secretarial studies, legal studies, marketing/retailing/merchandising, medical secretarial studies, paralegal studies, retail management, secretarial studies/office management, tourism and travel, word processing.
LIBRARY MacCormac Junior College Library with 11,000 books, 140 periodicals, 3,000 records, tapes, and CDs.
COMPUTERS ON CAMPUS 118 computers for student use in computer center.
COLLEGE LIFE *Social organizations:* 2 open to all. *Most popular organizations:* Student Activities Committee, Phi Theta Kappa. *Major annual events:* Halloween Party, Christmas Dance, All College Picnic. *Campus security:* late-night transport-escort service.
HOUSING College housing not available.
ATHLETICS *Intramural:* badminton, basketball, bowling, volleyball.
CAREER PLANNING *Director:* Mr. Jack Lenberg, Director of Placement, 312-922-1884. *Services:* job fairs, resume preparation, resume referral, career counseling, careers library, job bank, job interviews. Students must register sophomore year.
AFTER GRADUATION 20% of students completing a degree program in 1994–95 went directly on to further study.
EXPENSES FOR 1996–97 *Application fee:* $20. Tuition: $7500 full-time, $208 per quarter hour part-time. Full-time mandatory fees: $30.
FINANCIAL AID *College-administered undergrad aid 1995–96:* need-based scholarships, non-need scholarships (average $3450), low-interest long-term loans from external sources (average $2625), Federal Work-Study, part-time jobs. *Required forms:* FAFSA; accepted: CSS Financial Aid PROFILE. *Application deadline:* continuous. *Payment plan:* installment. *Waivers:* full or partial for employees or children of employees.
APPLYING *Options:* Common Application, deferred entrance, midyear entrance. *Required:* school transcript, ACT, TOEFL for international students. *Recommended:* interview, SAT I. Test scores used for admission. *Application deadline:* rolling. *Notification:* continuous.
APPLYING/TRANSFER *Required:* high school transcript, college transcript. *Recommended:* interview. *Entrance:* moderately difficult. *Application deadline:* rolling. *Notification:* continuous. *Contact:* Mr. Alan B. Solid, Director of Student Services and Admissions, 312-941-1200 Ext. 15.
CONTACT Mr. Alan B. Solid, Director of Student Services and Admissions, MacCormac Junior College, 506 South Wabash Avenue, Chicago, IL 60605-1667, 312-941-1200 Ext. 15. *Fax:* 312-941-0937.

❖ *See page 758 for a narrative description.* ❖

MALCOLM X COLLEGE
Illinois—See City Colleges of Chicago, Malcolm X College

McHENRY COUNTY COLLEGE
Crystal Lake, Illinois

UG Enrollment: 4,933	Tuition & Fees (Area Res): $1184
Application Deadline: rolling	Room & Board: N/Avail

GENERAL State and locally supported, 2-year, coed. Part of Illinois Community College System. Awards certificates, transfer associate, terminal associate degrees. Founded 1967. *Setting:* 108-acre suburban campus with easy access to Chicago. *Total enrollment:* 4,933. *Faculty:* 232 (72 full-time, 7% with terminal degrees, 160 part-time); student-faculty ratio is 18:1.
ENROLLMENT PROFILE 4,933 students: 59% women, 41% men, 74% part-time, 95% state residents, 6% transferred in, 5% have need-based financial aid, 1% international, 53% 25 or older, 1% Native American, 8% Hispanic, 1% African American, 1% Asian American. *Most popular recent majors:* liberal arts/general studies, science.
FIRST-YEAR CLASS 1,903 total; 2,432 applied, 100% were accepted, 78% of whom enrolled.
ACADEMIC PROGRAM Core. Calendar: semesters. Academic remediation for entering students, English as a second language program offered during academic year and summer, services for LD students, advanced placement, honors program, summer session for credit, part-time degree program (daytime, evenings, weekends, summer), adult/continuing education programs, internships.
GENERAL DEGREE REQUIREMENTS 60 semester hours; 1 math course; 2 lab science courses; computer course.
MAJORS Accounting, automotive technologies, child care/child and family studies, computer information systems, criminal justice, electronics engineering technology, emergency medical technology, fire science, horticulture, industrial administration, industrial engineering technology, liberal arts/general studies, marketing/retailing/merchandising, mechanical design technology, real estate, science, secretarial studies/office management.
LIBRARY 39,089 books, 9,469 microform titles, 240 periodicals, 6,975 records, tapes, and CDs.
COMPUTERS ON CAMPUS 100 computers for student use in computer center, computer labs, learning resource center, classrooms, library provide access to main academic computer, Internet. Staffed computer lab on campus provides training in use of computers, software.

COLLEGE LIFE Drama-theater group, choral group, student-run newspaper. *Student services:* legal services, personal-psychological counseling. *Campus security:* 24-hour emergency response devices and patrols, late-night transport-escort service.
HOUSING College housing not available.
ATHLETICS Member NJCAA. *Intercollegiate:* baseball M, basketball M/W, soccer M, softball W, tennis M/W, volleyball W. *Contact:* Mr. Wally Reynolds, Director of Athletics and Student Activities, 815-455-8547.
CAREER PLANNING *Placement office:* 1 full-time, 2 part-time staff. *Director:* Mr. Mike Weimer, Counselor, 815-455-8906. *Services:* job fairs, resume preparation, career counseling, careers library.
EXPENSES FOR 1996–97 Area resident tuition: $1170 full-time, $39 per semester hour part-time. State resident tuition: $5342 full-time, $178.08 per semester hour part-time. Nonresident tuition: $6123 full-time, $204.11 per semester hour part-time. Part-time mandatory fees: $7 per semester hour. Full-time mandatory fees: $14.
FINANCIAL AID *College-administered undergrad aid 1995–96:* need-based scholarships, short-term loans (average $100), low-interest long-term loans, Federal Work-Study, 100 part-time jobs. *Required forms:* state, institutional, FAFSA. *Application deadline:* continuous. *Payment plans:* installment, deferred payment. *Waivers:* full or partial for employees or children of employees and senior citizens.
APPLYING Open admission. *Options:* early entrance, deferred entrance. *Required:* school transcript, TOEFL for international students. *Recommended:* 3 years of high school math and science, ACT. Test scores used for counseling/placement. *Application deadline:* rolling. *Notification:* continuous.
APPLYING/TRANSFER *Recommended:* standardized test scores. *Required for some:* high school transcript, college transcript. *Application deadline:* rolling. *Notification:* continuous. *Contact:* Ms. Wondy Manser, Director of Admissions and Records, 815-455-8716.
CONTACT Ms. Wendy Manser, Director of Admissions and Records, McHenry County College, Crystal Lake, IL 60012-2761, 815-455-8716. College video available.

MIDSTATE COLLEGE
Peoria, Illinois

UG Enrollment: 284	Tuition & Fees: $5730
Application Deadline: rolling	Room & Board: N/Avail

GENERAL Proprietary, 2-year, coed. Awards diplomas, terminal associate degrees. Founded 1888. *Setting:* 1-acre urban campus. *Total enrollment:* 284. *Faculty:* 58 (18 full-time, 40 part-time).
ENROLLMENT PROFILE 284 students from 6 states and territories, 3 other countries. 95% women, 29% part-time, 94% state residents, 34% transferred in, 36% 25 or older, 0% Native American, 1% Hispanic, 10% African American, 2% Asian American. *Most popular recent majors:* court reporting, paralegal studies, medical assistant technologies.
FIRST-YEAR CLASS 112 total; 171 applied, 65% were accepted, 100% of whom enrolled. 11% from top 10% of their high school class, 21% from top quarter, 76% from top half.
ACADEMIC PROGRAM Core. Calendar: quarters. Academic remediation for entering students, Freshman Honors College, tutorials, honors program, summer session for credit, part-time degree program (daytime, evenings, summer), co-op programs and internships.
GENERAL DEGREE REQUIREMENTS 92 quarter hours; computer course; internship (some majors).
MAJORS Accounting, aviation administration, business administration/commerce/management, computer information systems, computer science, court reporting, fashion merchandising, hospitality services, legal secretarial studies, marketing/retailing/merchandising, medical assistant technologies, medical secretarial studies, paralegal studies, secretarial studies/office management, tourism and travel.
LIBRARY Barbara Fields Library with 7,908 books, 90 periodicals, 1,585 records, tapes, and CDs.
COMPUTERS ON CAMPUS 49 computers for student use in computer center, classrooms, library provide access to Internet. Staffed computer lab on campus provides training in use of computers, software.
COLLEGE LIFE *Social organizations:* 2 open to all; 1 national sorority, 1 local fraternity, social clubs; 40% of eligible men and 45% of eligible women are members. *Campus security:* late-night transport-escort service.
HOUSING College housing not available.
CAREER PLANNING *Placement office:* 1 full-time, 1 part-time staff. *Director:* Miss Rhonda Urban, Career Development Coordinator, 309-673-6365. *Services:* resume preparation, resume referral, career counseling, job interviews. Students must register sophomore year.
EXPENSES FOR 1996–97 *Application fee:* $25. Tuition: $5700 full-time, $475 per course part-time. Part-time mandatory fees: $10 per quarter. Full-time mandatory fees: $30.
FINANCIAL AID *College-administered undergrad aid 1995–96:* 200 need-based scholarships (average $200), low-interest long-term loans from external sources (average $2625), Federal Work-Study, 5 part-time jobs. *Required forms:* institutional, FAFSA; required for some: verification worksheet; accepted: CSS Financial Aid PROFILE, state. *Priority deadline:* 9/30. *Payment plan:* installment. *Waivers:* full or partial for employees or children of employees. *Average indebtedness of graduates:* $5250.
APPLYING *Options:* Common Application, early entrance, deferred entrance, midyear entrance. *Required:* school transcript, TOEFL for international students, Wonderlic aptitude test. *Recommended:* SAT I or ACT. Test scores used for admission. *Application deadline:* rolling.
APPLYING/TRANSFER *Required:* high school transcript, college transcript. *Entrance:* minimally difficult. *Application deadline:* rolling. *Contact:* Ms. Margaret J. Padilla, Dean of College, 309-673-6365.
CONTACT Mr. Steve Sergeant, Director of Admissions and Marketing, Midstate College, 244 South West Jefferson Street, Peoria, IL 61602-1489, 309-673-6365. *Fax:* 309-673-5814.

MORAINE VALLEY COMMUNITY COLLEGE
Palos Hills, Illinois

UG Enrollment: 12,813 | **Tuition & Fees (Area Res): $1452**
Application Deadline: rolling | **Room & Board: N/Avail**

GENERAL State and locally supported, 2-year, coed. Part of Illinois Community College System. Awards certificates, transfer associate, terminal associate degrees. Founded 1967. ***Setting:*** 292-acre suburban campus with easy access to Chicago. ***Endowment:*** $9.2 million. ***Educational spending 1994–95:*** $1353 per undergrad. ***Total enrollment:*** 12,813. ***Faculty:*** 592 (162 full-time, 20% with terminal degrees, 430 part-time); student-faculty ratio is 23:1.

ENROLLMENT PROFILE 12,813 students from 2 states and territories, 24 other countries. 58% women, 42% men, 63% part-time, 96% state residents, 9% transferred in, 24% have need-based financial aid, 16% have non-need-based financial aid, 3% international, 40% 25 or older, 1% Native American, 5% Hispanic, 3% African American, 1% Asian American. ***Areas of study chosen:*** 41% liberal arts/general studies, 14% business management and administrative services, 6% engineering and applied sciences, 6% health professions and related sciences, 6% interdisciplinary studies, 3% vocational and home economics, 1% education. ***Most popular recent majors:*** liberal arts/general studies, science, nursing.

FIRST-YEAR CLASS 3,651 total; 4,731 applied, 100% were accepted, 77% of whom enrolled. 7% from top 10% of their high school class, 25% from top quarter, 55% from top half.

ACADEMIC PROGRAM Core, honor code. Calendar: semesters. 2,780 courses offered in 1995–96; average class size 21 in required courses. Academic remediation for entering students, English as a second language program offered during academic year and summer, services for LD students, advanced placement, tutorials, summer session for credit, part-time degree program (daytime, evenings, weekends), adult/continuing education programs, internships. Study abroad in England, Austria, Mexico, Costa Rica (1% of students participate).

GENERAL DEGREE REQUIREMENTS 62 semester hours; 3 semester hours of math; 8 semester hours of science; computer course for medical records services, drafting and design, quality control technology, most business majors; internship (some majors).

MAJORS Automotive technologies, business administration/commerce/management, business machine technologies, child care/child and family studies, communication equipment technology, computer graphics, computer information systems, computer management, computer programming, computer science, computer technologies, criminal justice, culinary arts, data processing, drafting and design, drug and alcohol/substance abuse counseling, education, electrical and electronics technologies, electronics engineering technology, emergency medical technology, energy management technologies, (pre)engineering sequence, engineering technology, fashion merchandising, finance/banking, fire science, food services management, heating/refrigeration/air conditioning, hotel and restaurant management, human resources, industrial engineering technology, interdisciplinary studies, legal secretarial studies, liberal arts/general studies, machine and tool technologies, marketing/retailing/merchandising, mechanical design technology, medical laboratory technology, medical records services, nursing, occupational therapy, quality control technology, radiological technology, real estate, recreation and leisure services, recreation therapy, respiratory therapy, retail management, safety and security technologies, science, secretarial studies/office management, teacher aide studies, telecommunications, tourism and travel, vocational education, welding technology, word processing.

LIBRARY Robert E. Turner Learning Resources Center plus 1 other, with 79,696 books, 543 microform titles, 912 periodicals, 3 on-line bibliographic services, 36 CD-ROMs, 3,977 records, tapes, and CDs. Acquisition spending 1994–95: $204,297.

COMPUTERS ON CAMPUS 435 computers for student use in computer center, computer labs, learning resource center, classrooms, library. Staffed computer lab on campus provides training in use of computers, software. Academic computing expenditure 1994–95: $1.5 million.

COLLEGE LIFE Drama-theater group, choral group, student-run newspaper. 4% vote in student government elections. ***Social organizations:*** 25 open to all. ***Most popular organizations:*** Student Newspaper, Student Volunteerism, Alliance of Latin American Students, Phi Theta Kappa, Inter Club Council. ***Major annual events:*** Spring Fest, Phi Theta Kappa Initiation, Student Activities Benefit. ***Student services:*** personal-psychological counseling, women's center. ***Campus security:*** 24-hour emergency response devices and patrols, late-night transport-escort service, programs in accident prevention, crime prevention, safety and security.

HOUSING College housing not available.

ATHLETICS Member NJCAA. ***Intercollegiate:*** baseball M(s), basketball M(s)/W(s), golf M(s), soccer M(s)/W(s), softball W(s), tennis W(s), volleyball W(s). ***Intramural:*** badminton, basketball, softball, volleyball. ***Contact:*** Mr. William Finn, Director of Athletics, 708-974-5213.

CAREER PLANNING ***Placement office:*** 4 full-time staff; $116,282 operating expenditure 1994–95. ***Director:*** Dr. Sharon Katterman, Director, Job Placement, 708-974-5737. ***Services:*** resume preparation, resume referral, job interviews. 48 organizations recruited on campus 1994–95.

AFTER GRADUATION 78% of students completing a degree program in 1994–95 went directly on to further study.

EXPENSES FOR 1996–97 Area resident tuition: $1302 full-time, $42 per semester hour part-time. State resident tuition: $4991 full-time, $161 per semester hour part-time. Nonresident tuition: $5611 full-time, $181 per semester hour part-time. Part-time mandatory fees: $5 per semester hour. Full-time mandatory fees: $150.

FINANCIAL AID ***College-administered undergrad aid 1995–96:*** 500 need-based scholarships (average $1100), 425 non-need scholarships (average $600), low-interest long-term loans from external sources (average $1800), 100 Federal Work-Study (averaging $1000), 250 part-time jobs. ***Required forms for some financial aid applicants:*** state, institutional, FAFSA. ***Priority deadline:*** 6/1. ***Payment plan:*** installment. ***Waivers:*** full or partial for employees or children of employees and senior citizens. ***Average indebtedness of graduates:*** $3600.

APPLYING Open admission except for allied health, nursing programs. ***Options:*** early entrance, deferred entrance, midyear entrance. ***Required:*** school transcript, ACT ASSET, Nelson Denny Reading Test. ***Recommended:*** 3 years of high school math and science, some high school foreign language, ACT, TOEFL for international students. ***Required for some:*** minimum 2.0 GPA, ACT. Test scores used for counseling/placement. ***Application deadline:*** rolling. ***Notification:*** continuous. Preference given to district residents for allied health, nursing programs.

APPLYING/TRANSFER ***Required:*** high school transcript, college transcript. ***Recommended:*** standardized test scores, 3 years of high school math and science, some high school foreign language, minimum 2.0 college GPA. ***Entrance:*** noncompetitive. ***Application deadline:*** rolling. ***Notification:*** continuous. ***Contact:*** Ms. Patricia Fine, Dean of Student Services and College Activities, 708-974-5345.

CONTACT Ms. Patricia Fine, Dean of Student Services and College Activities, Moraine Valley Community College, 10900 South 88th Avenue, Palos Hills, IL 60465-0937, 708-974-5345. ***Fax:*** 708-974-0681.

MORRISON INSTITUTE OF TECHNOLOGY
Morrison, Illinois

UG Enrollment: 173 | **Tuition & Fees: $7170**
Application Deadline: rolling | **Room Only: $1000**

Morrison Institute of Technology offers the associate degree in engineering technology, with specializations in design and drafting (mechanical CAD—computer-aided drafting) and in building construction (architectural CAD). Classes begin in August and January. Small class size allows students to spend 20–40 hours per week at the computer. Morrison is accredited by TAC/ABET and offers students in-field experience as well as the most up-to-date equipment available in CAD. A very safe campus. The placement rate is more than 90%.

GENERAL Independent, 2-year, specialized, coed. Awards transfer associate, terminal associate degrees. Founded 1973. ***Setting:*** 17-acre small-town campus. ***Total enrollment:*** 173. ***Faculty:*** 15 (13 full-time, 2 part-time).

ENROLLMENT PROFILE 173 students from 5 states and territories. 13% women, 0% part-time, 95% state residents, 0% transferred in, 73% have need-based financial aid, 5% have non-need-based financial aid, 0% international, 20% 25 or older, 0% Native American, 3% Hispanic, 7% African American, 1% Asian American. ***Areas of study chosen:*** 100% engineering and applied sciences. ***Most popular recent majors:*** drafting and design, construction technologies.

FIRST-YEAR CLASS 93 total; 128 applied, 100% were accepted, 73% of whom enrolled. 5% from top 10% of their high school class, 10% from top quarter, 50% from top half.

ACADEMIC PROGRAM Core, technical curriculum. Calendar: semesters. 28 courses offered in 1995–96. Self-designed majors, tutorials, part-time degree program (daytime).

GENERAL DEGREE REQUIREMENTS 68 semester hours; computer course.

MAJORS Architectural technologies, civil engineering technology, computer graphics, computer technologies, construction technologies, drafting and design, engineering design, engineering technology, mechanical design technology, mechanical engineering technology, surveying technology.

LIBRARY 4,800 books, 39 periodicals, 40 records, tapes, and CDs. Acquisition spending 1994–95: $3000.

COMPUTERS ON CAMPUS 72 computers for student use in computer center, computer labs, technical building, classrooms, library. Staffed computer lab on campus provides training in use of computers, software. Academic computing expenditure 1994–95: $50,000.

COLLEGE LIFE Drama-theater group. ***Major annual event:*** Turkey Day. ***Campus security:*** controlled dormitory access.

HOUSING 150 college housing spaces available; 130 were occupied 1995–96. Freshmen given priority for college housing. On-campus residence required in freshman year. ***Option:*** coed (1 building) housing available. Resident assistants live in dorms.

ATHLETICS ***Intramural:*** basketball, bowling, golf, skiing (cross-country), skiing (downhill), softball, table tennis (Ping-Pong), tennis, track and field, volleyball, weight lifting.

CAREER PLANNING ***Placement office:*** 1 full-time staff; $30,000 operating expenditure 1994–95. ***Director:*** Mr. Michael Geerts, Vice President, Academic Affairs, 815-772-7218. ***Services:*** resume preparation, resume referral, career counseling, careers library, job interviews. Students must register sophomore year. 230 organizations recruited on campus 1994–95.

AFTER GRADUATION 100% of class of 1994 had job offers within 6 months. 6% of students completing a degree program went directly on to further study.

EXPENSES FOR 1996–97 ***Application fee:*** $25. Tuition: $7130 full-time, $297 per semester hour part-time. Part-time mandatory fees: $20 per semester. Full-time mandatory fees: $40. College room only: $1000.

FINANCIAL AID ***College-administered undergrad aid 1995–96:*** 50 need-based scholarships (averaging $2000), 12 non-need scholarships (averaging $500), low-interest long-term loans from external sources (averaging $2000), Federal Work-Study, part-time jobs. ***Required forms:*** state, institutional; required for some: FAFSA, AFSSA-CSX; accepted: CSS Financial Aid PROFILE. ***Application deadline:*** continuous. ***Payment plans:*** installment, deferred payment. ***Waivers:*** full or partial for children of alumni.

APPLYING Open admission. ***Options:*** deferred entrance, midyear entrance. ***Required:*** school transcript, TOEFL for international students. ***Recommended:*** 3 years of high school math, campus interview, SAT I or ACT. Test scores used for admission and counseling/placement. ***Application deadline:*** rolling. ***Notification:*** continuous until 8/22.

APPLYING/TRANSFER ***Required:*** high school transcript, college transcript. ***Recommended:*** standardized test scores, 3 years of high school math, campus interview. ***Entrance:*** noncompetitive. ***Contact:*** Dr. Dale W. Trimpe, Director of Admissions, 815-772-7218.

CONTACT Dr. Dale W. Trimpe, Director of Admissions, Morrison Institute of Technology, Morrison, IL 61270-0410, 815-772-7218. ***Fax:*** 815-772-7584. College video available.

MORTON COLLEGE
Cicero, Illinois

UG Enrollment: 4,050 | **Tuition & Fees (Area Res): $1488**
Application Deadline: rolling | **Room & Board: N/Avail**

Peterson's Guide to Two-Year Colleges 1997

299

Morton College (continued)

GENERAL State and locally supported, 2-year, coed. Part of Illinois Community College System. Awards certificates, transfer associate, terminal associate degrees. Founded 1924. ***Setting:*** 25-acre suburban campus with easy access to Chicago. ***Total enrollment:*** 4,050. ***Faculty:*** 214 (53 full-time, 161 part-time); student-faculty ratio is 18:1.
ENROLLMENT PROFILE 4,050 students from 2 states and territories. 59% women, 41% men, 81% part-time, 99% state residents, 3% transferred in, 16% have need-based financial aid, 10% have non-need-based financial aid, 0% international, 53% 25 or older, 1% Native American, 42% Hispanic, 1% African American, 2% Asian American. ***Most popular recent majors:*** nursing, liberal arts/general studies, physical therapy.
FIRST-YEAR CLASS 1,187 total.
ACADEMIC PROGRAM Core. Calendar: semesters. Average class size 18 in required courses. Academic remediation for entering students, English as a second language program offered during academic year and summer, services for LD students, advanced placement, self-designed majors, summer session for credit, part-time degree program (daytime, evenings), adult/continuing education programs, internships.
GENERAL DEGREE REQUIREMENTS 62 semester hours; math/science requirements vary according to program.
MAJORS Accounting, art/fine arts, automotive technologies, business administration/commerce/management, data processing, dental services, drafting and design, finance/banking, heating/refrigeration/air conditioning, law enforcement/police sciences, legal secretarial studies, liberal arts/general studies, marketing/retailing/merchandising, medical secretarial studies, music, nursing, physical therapy, real estate, science, secretarial studies/office management.
LIBRARY Learning Resource Center with 40,972 books, 68,133 microform titles, 327 periodicals, 3 on-line bibliographic services, 8 CD-ROMs, 3,547 records, tapes, and CDs. Acquisition spending 1994–95: $73,494.
COMPUTERS ON CAMPUS Computer purchase plan available. 150 computers for student use in learning resource center, academic departments, classrooms provide access to main academic computer. Staffed computer lab on campus provides training in use of computers, software. Academic computing expenditure 1994–95: $157,218.
COLLEGE LIFE Drama-theater group, choral group, student-run newspaper. 6% vote in student government elections. ***Social organizations:*** 20 open to all. ***Most popular organizations:*** Hispanic Heritage Club, Program Board, Student Senate, Law Enforcement Association, Nursing Club. ***Major annual events:*** Welcome Week, Health Week, Comedy/Variety Series. ***Campus security:*** 24-hour patrols, cameras on campus.
HOUSING College housing not available.
ATHLETICS Member NJCAA. ***Intercollegiate:*** baseball M(s), basketball M(s)/W(s), cross-country running M(s)/W(s), golf M(s)/W(s), soccer M, softball W(s), volleyball W(s). ***Intramural:*** basketball, bowling, cross-country running, racquetball, skiing (downhill), volleyball, weight lifting. ***Contact:*** Mr. George Fejt, Coordinator of Athletics, 708-656-8000 Ext. 370.
CAREER PLANNING ***Placement office:*** $3420 operating expenditure 1994–95. ***Service:*** career counseling. 17 organizations recruited on campus 1994–95.
AFTER GRADUATION 40% of class of 1994 had job offers within 6 months.
EXPENSES FOR 1996–97 ***Application fee:*** $10. Area resident tuition: $1457 full-time, $47 per semester hour part-time. State resident tuition: $4674 full-time, $150.78 per semester hour part-time. Nonresident tuition: $5703 full-time, $183.98 per semester hour part-time. Part-time mandatory fees: $1 per semester hour. Full-time mandatory fees: $31.
FINANCIAL AID ***College-administered undergrad aid 1995–96:*** 15 need-based scholarships (average $500), 45 non-need scholarships (average $750), low-interest long-term loans from external sources (average $2625), 15 Federal Work-Study (averaging $1000), 65 part-time jobs. ***Required forms:*** institutional, FAFSA; accepted: CSS Financial Aid PROFILE. ***Priority deadline:*** 6/1. ***Payment plan:*** deferred payment. ***Waivers:*** full or partial for employees or children of employees. ***Notification:*** continuous.
APPLYING Open admission except for nursing, physical therapy assistant, dental assistant programs. ***Option:*** midyear entrance. ***Required:*** school transcript, 3 years of high school math and science, TOEFL for international students. ***Recommended:*** SAT I or ACT. ***Application deadline:*** rolling. Preference given to district residents for nursing, physical therapy assistant, dental assisting programs.
APPLYING/TRANSFER ***Required:*** high school transcript, college transcript. ***Entrance:*** noncompetitive. ***Application deadline:*** rolling.
CONTACT Ms. Patricia A. Matijevic, Director of Admissions and Records, Morton College, Cicero, IL 60650-4398, 708-656-8000 Ext. 342. ***Fax:*** 708-656-9592.

NORTHWESTERN BUSINESS COLLEGE
Chicago, Illinois

UG Enrollment: 610 | **Tuition: $8840/deg prog**
Application Deadline: rolling | **Room & Board: N/Avail**

GENERAL Proprietary, 2-year, coed. Awards diplomas, transfer associate, terminal associate degrees. Founded 1902. ***Setting:*** 3-acre urban campus. ***Total enrollment:*** 610. ***Faculty:*** 41 (14 full-time, 15% with terminal degrees, 27 part-time); student-faculty ratio is 13:1.
ENROLLMENT PROFILE 610 students: 78% women, 58% part-time, 98% state residents, 7% transferred in, 1% international, 21% 25 or older, 0% Native American, 43% Hispanic, 25% African American, 7% Asian American.
FIRST-YEAR CLASS 209 total; 211 applied, 100% were accepted, 99% of whom enrolled.
ACADEMIC PROGRAM Core, honor code. Calendar: quarters. Academic remediation for entering students, summer session for credit, part-time degree program (daytime, evenings), internships.
GENERAL DEGREE REQUIREMENTS 100 quarter hours; 8 quarter hours of business math; computer course.
MAJORS Accounting, advertising, business administration/commerce/management, computer programming, computer science, data processing, fashion merchandising, hospitality services, legal secretarial studies, marketing/retailing/merchandising, medical assistant technologies, medical secretarial studies, paralegal studies, public relations, secretarial studies/office management, tourism and travel.
LIBRARY Edward G. Schumacher Memorial Library with 2,000 books, 20 periodicals.
COMPUTERS ON CAMPUS 69 computers for student use in computer center, computer labs, classrooms, library provide access to on-line services. Staffed computer lab on campus provides training in use of computers, software.
HOUSING College housing not available.
CAREER PLANNING ***Placement office:*** 1 full-time, 2 part-time staff. ***Director:*** Ms. Nancy Loglisci, Director of Career Development, 312-777-4220. ***Services:*** job fairs, resume preparation, resume referral, career counseling, job bank, job interviews.
EXPENSES FOR 1995–96 ***Application fee:*** $25. Tuition per degree program ranges from $8840 to $24,000. Full-time mandatory fees: $45.
FINANCIAL AID ***College-administered undergrad aid 1995–96:*** need-based scholarships, low-interest long-term loans from college funds (averaging $1200), loans from external sources (averaging $2500). ***Acceptable forms:*** FAFSA. ***Application deadline:*** continuous to 8/25.
APPLYING ***Required:*** school transcript, CPAt, ACT or SAT. ***Application deadline:*** rolling.
APPLYING/TRANSFER ***Required:*** standardized test scores, college transcript.
CONTACT Ms. Nancy Baker, Director of Admissions, Northwestern Business College, 4829 North Lipps Avenue, Chicago, IL 60630-2298, 312-481-3730.

❖ *See page 786 for a narrative description.* ❖

OAKTON COMMUNITY COLLEGE
Des Plaines, Illinois

UG Enrollment: 10,976 | **Tuition & Fees (Area Res): $1098**
Application Deadline: rolling | **Room & Board: N/Avail**

GENERAL District-supported, 2-year, coed. Part of Illinois Community College System. Awards transfer associate, terminal associate degrees. Founded 1969. ***Setting:*** 160-acre suburban campus. ***Research spending 1994–95:*** $311,702. ***Total enrollment:*** 10,976. ***Faculty:*** 625 (151 full-time, 474 part-time).
ENROLLMENT PROFILE 10,976 students: 57% women, 43% men, 73% part-time, 86% state residents, 12% transferred in, 0% international, 46% 25 or older, 0% Native American, 4% Hispanic, 4% African American, 10% Asian American. ***Areas of study chosen:*** 51% liberal arts/general studies, 8% business management and administrative services, 7% health professions and related sciences, 5% computer and information sciences, 3% biological and life sciences, 3% engineering and applied sciences, 1% architecture.
FIRST-YEAR CLASS 2,266 total. Of the students who applied, 99% were accepted, 86% of whom enrolled. 1% from top 10% of their high school class, 10% from top quarter, 45% from top half.
ACADEMIC PROGRAM Core, honor code. Calendar: semesters. 856 courses offered in 1995–96. Academic remediation for entering students, English as a second language program offered during academic year, services for LD students, advanced placement, honors program, summer session for credit, part-time degree program (daytime, evenings, summer), adult/continuing education programs. Off-campus study. Study abroad in England, Austria.
GENERAL DEGREE REQUIREMENTS 60 semester hours; internship (some majors).
MAJORS Accounting, architectural technologies, automotive technologies, biomedical technologies, business administration/commerce/management, computer programming, computer science, data processing, early childhood education, electrical and electronics technologies, (pre)engineering sequence, finance/banking, fire science, heating/refrigeration/air conditioning, hotel and restaurant management, international business, law enforcement/police sciences, liberal arts/general studies, machine and tool technologies, marketing/retailing/merchandising, mechanical design technology, medical laboratory technology, medical records services, nursing, physical therapy, real estate, science, secretarial studies/office management.
LIBRARY 81,668 books, 699 periodicals, 3 on-line bibliographic services, 14 CD-ROMs, 7,000 records, tapes, and CDs. Acquisition spending 1994–95: $164,850.
COMPUTERS ON CAMPUS 750 computers for student use in computer center, computer labs provide access to e-mail, on-line services, Internet. Staffed computer lab on campus (open 24 hours a day) provides training in use of computers, software. Academic computing expenditure 1994–95: $128,320.
COLLEGE LIFE Drama-theater group, choral group, student-run newspaper. ***Student services:*** health clinic, personal-psychological counseling. ***Campus security:*** 24-hour emergency response devices and patrols, student patrols, late-night transport-escort service.
HOUSING College housing not available.
ATHLETICS Member NJCAA. ***Intercollegiate:*** baseball M, basketball M/W, cross-country running M/W, golf M/W, soccer M, softball W, tennis M/W, track and field M/W, volleyball W, wrestling M. ***Intramural:*** badminton, bowling, volleyball. ***Contact:*** Mr. Tom Jorndt, Director of Athletics, 847-635-1754.
CAREER PLANNING ***Placement office:*** 2 full-time, 1 part-time staff. ***Director:*** Ms. Gerry Aiuppa, Manager of Career Placement, 847-635-1736. ***Services:*** resume preparation, career counseling, careers library, job bank. 46 organizations recruited on campus 1994–95.
EXPENSES FOR 1996–97 ***Application fee:*** $25. Area resident tuition: $1050 full-time, $35 per semester hour part-time. State resident tuition: $3840 full-time, $128 per semester hour part-time. Nonresident tuition: $4590 full-time, $153 per semester hour part-time. Tuition and fees per semester hour for district residents over 60 years of age: $16.50. Full-time mandatory fees: $48.
FINANCIAL AID ***College-administered undergrad aid 1995–96:*** 178 need-based scholarships (average $230), 73 non-need scholarships (average $376), short-term loans (average $100), low-interest long-term loans from external sources (average $1180), 15 Federal Work-Study (averaging $1200), part-time jobs. ***Required forms:*** state, institutional, FAFSA, IVF, federal tax forms; accepted: CSS Financial Aid PROFILE. ***Priority deadline:*** 6/1. ***Waivers:*** full or partial for employees or children of employees and senior citizens. ***Notification:*** continuous. ***Average indebtedness of graduates:*** $1975.
APPLYING Open admission. ***Option:*** early entrance. ***Required:*** school transcript. ***Recommended:*** ACT. ***Required for some:*** TOEFL for international students. Test scores used for counseling/placement. ***Application deadline:*** rolling. ***Notification:*** continuous.
APPLYING/TRANSFER ***Required:*** high school transcript. ***Recommended:*** standardized test scores. ***Entrance:*** noncompetitive. ***Application deadline:*** rolling. ***Notification:*** continuous.
CONTACT Mr. Dale Cohen, Admissions Specialist, Oakton Community College, Des Plaines, IL 60016-1268, 847-635-1703. ***Fax:*** 847-635-1706.

OLIVE-HARVEY COLLEGE
Illinois—See City Colleges of Chicago, Olive-Harvey College

PARKLAND COLLEGE
Champaign, Illinois

UG Enrollment: 8,403 **Tuition & Fees (Area Res): $1350**
Application Deadline: rolling **Room & Board: N/Avail**

GENERAL District-supported, 2-year, coed. Part of Illinois Community College System. Awards certificates, transfer associate, terminal associate degrees. Founded 1967. ***Setting:*** 233-acre suburban campus. ***Total enrollment:*** 8,403. ***Faculty:*** 487 (154 full-time, 100% with terminal degrees, 333 part-time); student-faculty ratio is 18:1.

ENROLLMENT PROFILE 8,403 students from 25 states and territories, 56 other countries. 58% women, 57% part-time, 4% transferred in, 60% have need-based financial aid, 3% international, 49% 25 or older, 1% Native American, 2% Hispanic, 11% African American, 3% Asian American. ***Areas of study chosen:*** 21% business management and administrative services, 20% health professions and related sciences, 14% liberal arts/general studies, 10% education, 5% communications and journalism, 4% engineering and applied sciences, 3% computer and information sciences, 2% fine arts, 2% mathematics, 1% agriculture, 1% architecture, 1% area and ethnic studies, 1% biological and life sciences, 1% English language/literature/letters, 1% interdisciplinary studies, 1% performing arts, 1% physical sciences. ***Most popular recent majors:*** nursing, business administration/commerce/management, liberal arts/general studies.

FIRST-YEAR CLASS 2,559 total. Of the students who applied, 100% were accepted.

ACADEMIC PROGRAM Honor code. Calendar: semesters. 997 courses offered in 1995–96. Academic remediation for entering students, English as a second language program offered during academic year and summer, services for LD students, advanced placement, tutorials, summer session for credit, part-time degree program (daytime, evenings), adult/continuing education programs, co-op programs and internships. Off-campus study at University of Illinois at Urbana-Champaign. Study abroad in England, Austria. ROTC: Army (c), Naval (c), Air Force (c).

GENERAL DEGREE REQUIREMENTS 60 semester hours; math/science requirements vary according to program; internship (some majors).

MAJORS Accounting, advertising, agricultural business, agricultural sciences, agricultural technologies, aircraft and missile maintenance, applied art, art/fine arts, automotive technologies, biology/biological sciences, broadcasting, business administration/commerce/management, business education, child psychology/child development, commercial art, communication, communication equipment technology, computer graphics, computer information systems, computer programming, computer science, computer technologies, construction technologies, corrections, criminal justice, data processing, dental services, early childhood education, education, electrical and electronics technologies, electrical engineering technology, electromechanical technology, electronics engineering technology, elementary education, engineering (general), engineering sciences, equestrian studies, farm and ranch management, finance/banking, fire science, food services management, graphic arts, hospitality services, hotel and restaurant management, journalism, law enforcement/police sciences, legal secretarial studies, liberal arts/general studies, management information systems, marketing/retailing/merchandising, mathematics, medical secretarial studies, music, music education, nursing, occupational therapy, physical education, physical sciences, public relations, publishing, radio and television studies, radiological technology, real estate, respiratory therapy, retail management, secretarial studies/office management, veterinary technology, word processing.

LIBRARY Parkland College Library with 104,000 books, 255 microform titles, 560 periodicals, 5 CD-ROMs, 3,700 records, tapes, and CDs. Acquisition spending 1994–95: $170,765.

COMPUTERS ON CAMPUS Computer purchase plan available. 500 computers for student use in computer center, computer labs, learning resource center, labs, classrooms, library. Academic computing expenditure 1994–95: $800,000.

COLLEGE LIFE Drama-theater group, choral group, student-run newspaper, radio station. ***Social organizations:*** 24 open to all; local fraternities, local sororities. ***Most popular organizations:*** Black Student Association, Student Nurses Association, Veterinary Technology Association, International Student Association, Phi Theta Kappa. ***Major annual events:*** Spring Fling, Black History Month, Volunteer Fair. ***Student services:*** personal-psychological counseling, women's center. ***Campus security:*** 24-hour emergency response devices and patrols, late-night transport-escort service.

HOUSING College housing not available.

ATHLETICS Member NJCAA. ***Intercollegiate:*** baseball M(s), basketball M(s)/W(s), cross-country running M(s)/W(s), golf M(s), softball W(s), tennis M(s), track and field M(s)/W(s), volleyball W(s). ***Intramural:*** basketball, bowling, golf, softball, tennis, volleyball. ***Contact:*** Mr. Jim Reed, Director of Athletics, 217-351-2297.

CAREER PLANNING ***Placement office:*** 3 full-time staff; $100,000 operating expenditure 1994–95. ***Director:*** Mr. Gerry Hough, Director, Career Planning and Placement, 217-351-2412. ***Services:*** job fairs, resume preparation, resume referral, career counseling, careers library, job bank, job interviews.

EXPENSES FOR 1996–97 Area resident tuition: $1350 full-time, $45 per semester hour part-time. State resident tuition: $4383 full-time, $146.11 per semester hour part-time. Nonresident tuition: $5947 full-time, $198.24 per semester hour part-time.

FINANCIAL AID ***College-administered undergrad aid 1995–96:*** need-based scholarships, non-need scholarships, short-term loans (averaging $150), low-interest long-term loans from college funds, loans from external sources, Federal Work-Study, part-time jobs. ***Required forms:*** institutional, FAFSA, SINGLEFILE Form of United Student Aid Funds; accepted: CSS Financial Aid PROFILE. ***Application deadline:*** continuous to 3/15. ***Payment plan:*** installment. ***Waivers:*** full or partial for employees or children of employees and senior citizens. ***Notification:*** continuous.

APPLYING Open admission except for allied health and nursing programs. ***Options:*** early entrance, deferred entrance, midyear entrance. ***Recommended:*** school transcript. ***Required for some:*** 3 years of high school math and science, ACT, TOEFL for international students. Test scores used for counseling/placement. ***Application deadline:*** rolling. ***Notification:*** continuous.

APPLYING/TRANSFER ***Recommended:*** high school transcript. ***Required for some:*** standardized test scores, 3 years of high school math and science. ***Entrance:*** noncompetitive. ***Application deadline:*** rolling. ***Notification:*** continuous. ***Contact:*** Ms. Lenita Epinger, Director/Transfer Center, 217-373-3824.

CONTACT Ms. Rosiland Minor, Admissions Representative, Parkland College, Champaign, IL 61821-1899, 217-351-2482 or toll-free 800-346-8089 (in-state). ***Fax:*** 217-351-7640. College video available.

PRAIRIE STATE COLLEGE
Chicago Heights, Illinois

UG Enrollment: 5,000 **Tuition & Fees (Area Res): $1696**
Application Deadline: rolling **Room & Board: N/Avail**

GENERAL State and locally supported, 2-year, coed. Part of Illinois Community College System. Awards certificates, transfer associate, terminal associate degrees. Founded 1958. ***Setting:*** 68-acre suburban campus with easy access to Chicago. ***Total enrollment:*** 5,000. ***Faculty:*** 289 (89 full-time, 200 part-time).

ENROLLMENT PROFILE 5,000 students from 2 states and territories. 60% women, 76% part-time, 92% state residents, 1% transferred in, 0% international, 53% 25 or older, 5% Hispanic, 25% African American, 1% Asian American. ***Most popular recent majors:*** liberal arts/general studies, nursing.

FIRST-YEAR CLASS 1,000 total. Of the students who applied, 100% were accepted, 74% of whom enrolled.

ACADEMIC PROGRAM Core. Calendar: semesters. Academic remediation for entering students, English as a second language program offered during academic year and summer, services for LD students, self-designed majors, summer session for credit, part-time degree program (daytime, evenings, weekends), adult/continuing education programs. Study-abroad program.

GENERAL DEGREE REQUIREMENTS 62 credit hours; 1 math course.

MAJORS Art education, art/fine arts, art history, automotive technologies, business administration/commerce/management, child care/child and family studies, child psychology/child development, computer information systems, computer programming, criminal justice, dental services, drafting and design, early childhood education, electrical and electronics technologies, (pre)engineering sequence, finance/banking, fire science, flight training, industrial administration, interior design, law enforcement/police sciences, legal secretarial studies, liberal arts/general studies, manufacturing technology, marketing/retailing/merchandising, mechanical design technology, mechanical engineering technology, nursing, photography, real estate, secretarial studies/office management, teacher aide studies, theater arts/drama, welding technology.

LIBRARY 46,000 books, 2,363 microform titles, 511 periodicals, 28,019 records, tapes, and CDs.

COMPUTERS ON CAMPUS 72 computers for student use in student labs. Staffed computer lab on campus.

COLLEGE LIFE Drama-theater group, choral group, student-run newspaper. ***Social organizations:*** 25 social clubs; 15% of eligible men and 15% of eligible women are members. ***Student services:*** personal-psychological counseling. ***Campus security:*** 24-hour patrols.

HOUSING College housing not available.

ATHLETICS ***Intramural:*** basketball, volleyball.

CAREER PLANNING ***Service:*** career counseling.

EXPENSES FOR 1996–97 ***Application fee:*** $10. Area resident tuition: $1696 full-time, $53 per credit hour part-time. State resident tuition: $3648 full-time, $125 per credit hour part-time. Nonresident tuition: $4832 full-time, $156 per credit hour part-time.

FINANCIAL AID ***College-administered undergrad aid 1995–96:*** need-based scholarships, 27 non-need scholarships (average $870), low-interest long-term loans from external sources (average $926), Federal Work-Study, part-time jobs. ***Required forms:*** state, FAFSA; required for some: CSS Financial Aid PROFILE, institutional. ***Priority deadline:*** 4/1. ***Payment plan:*** installment. ***Waivers:*** full or partial for employees or children of employees and senior citizens.

APPLYING Open admission. ***Options:*** Common Application, deferred entrance. ***Required:*** school transcript, TOEFL for international students. Test scores used for counseling/placement. ***Application deadline:*** rolling.

APPLYING/TRANSFER ***Required:*** high school transcript, college transcript. ***Application deadline:*** rolling.

CONTACT Mrs. Carol Cleator, Admissions Office Supervisor, Prairie State College, Chicago Heights, IL 60411-1275, 708-709-3516.

REND LAKE COLLEGE
Ina, Illinois

UG Enrollment: 3,759 **Tuition & Fees (Area Res): $1056**
Application Deadline: 8/17 **Room & Board: N/Avail**

GENERAL State-supported, 2-year, coed. Part of Illinois Community College System. Awards certificates, transfer associate, terminal associate degrees. Founded 1967. ***Setting:*** 350-acre rural campus. ***Total enrollment:*** 3,759. ***Faculty:*** 201 (62 full-time, 100% with terminal degrees, 139 part-time); student-faculty ratio is 15:1.

ENROLLMENT PROFILE 3,759 students from 4 states and territories, 3 other countries. 51% women, 77% part-time, 98% state residents, 25% transferred in, 46% have need-based financial aid, 13% have non-need-based financial aid, 55% 25 or older, 0% Native American, 0% Hispanic, 1% African American.

FIRST-YEAR CLASS 1,671 total. Of the students who applied, 100% were accepted, 100% of whom enrolled.

ACADEMIC PROGRAM Core, honor code. Calendar: semesters. 1,300 courses offered in 1995–96. Academic remediation for entering students, English as a second language program offered during academic year, services for LD students, advanced placement, summer session for credit, part-time degree program (daytime, evenings, summer), adult/continuing education programs, co-op programs and internships. ROTC: Air Force (c).

GENERAL DEGREE REQUIREMENTS 64 semester hours; computer course for most majors; internship (some majors).

MAJORS Accounting, agricultural business, agricultural technologies, architectural technologies, automotive technologies, business administration/commerce/management, construction management, construction technologies, criminal justice, culinary arts, electronics engineering technology, emergency medical technology, heating/refrigeration/air conditioning, industrial engineering technology, liberal arts/general studies, marketing/retailing/merchandising, medical laboratory technology, mining technology, nursing, secretarial studies/office management, welding technology.

LIBRARY 36,000 books, 18 microform titles, 348 periodicals, 2,300 records, tapes, and CDs. Acquisition spending 1994–95: $221,746.

Peterson's Guide to Two-Year Colleges 1997

301

Rend Lake College (continued)

COMPUTERS ON CAMPUS 115 computers for student use in computer center, computer labs, classrooms, library. Staffed computer lab on campus provides training in use of computers, software.

COLLEGE LIFE Student-run newspaper. ***Most popular organizations:*** Agriculturist/ Automotive Club, Christian Fellowship Club, Criminal Justice Club, Human Services Club, Phi Theta Kappa. ***Major annual events:*** Career Day, Homecoming. ***Campus security:*** 24-hour emergency response devices and patrols, student patrols, late-night transport-escort service.

HOUSING College housing not available.

ATHLETICS Member NJCAA. ***Intercollegiate:*** baseball M, basketball M(s)/W(s), golf M, softball W, tennis M/W. ***Contact:*** Mr. Tim Wills, Athletic Director, 618-437-5321.

CAREER PLANNING ***Placement office:*** 3 full-time staff. ***Director:*** Mr. Rex Duncan, Director of Cooperative Education and Job Placement, 618-437-5321 Ext. 352. ***Services:*** job fairs, career counseling, job bank, job interviews.

EXPENSES FOR 1996–97 Area resident tuition: $1056 full-time, $33 per semester hour part-time. State resident tuition: $2989 full-time, $93.40 per semester hour part-time. Nonresident tuition: $6043 full-time, $188.83 per semester hour part-time.

FINANCIAL AID ***College-administered undergrad aid 1995–96:*** need-based scholarships, 151 non-need scholarships (average $505), low-interest long-term loans from external sources, Federal Work-Study, part-time jobs. ***Required forms:*** FAFSA. ***Application deadline:*** continuous.

APPLYING Open admission except for nursing program. ***Options:*** early entrance, deferred entrance. ***Required:*** school transcript, TOEFL for international students, ACT ASSET. ***Required for some:*** ACT. Test scores used for counseling/placement. ***Application deadline:*** 8/17.

APPLYING/TRANSFER ***Entrance:*** noncompetitive. ***Application deadline:*** 8/17. ***Contact:*** Mr. Jay Lewis, Director of Counseling, 618-437-5321 Ext. 265.

CONTACT Mr. David Schwartz, Director of Admissions and Records, Rend Lake College, Ina, IL 62846-9801, 618-437-5321 Ext. 230. ***E-mail:*** schwartz@rlc.cc.il.us.

RICHLAND COMMUNITY COLLEGE
Decatur, Illinois

UG Enrollment: 3,384	**Tuition & Fees (Area Res): $1185**
Application Deadline: rolling	**Room & Board: N/Avail**

GENERAL District-supported, 2-year, coed. Part of Illinois Community College System. Awards certificates, transfer associate, terminal associate degrees. Founded 1971. ***Setting:*** 117-acre small-town campus. ***Total enrollment:*** 3,384. ***Faculty:*** 224 (54 full-time, 10% with terminal degrees, 170 part-time); student-faculty ratio is 19:1.

ENROLLMENT PROFILE 3,384 students: 63% women, 37% men, 61% part-time, 100% state residents, 17% transferred in, 33% have need-based financial aid, 0% have non-need-based financial aid, 0% international, 48% 25 or older, 0% Native American, 1% Hispanic, 9% African American, 1% Asian American. ***Most popular recent majors:*** liberal arts/ general studies, computer information systems, secretarial studies/office management.

FIRST-YEAR CLASS 901 total; 901 applied, 100% were accepted, 100% of whom enrolled. 1% from top 10% of their high school class, 8% from top quarter, 62% from top half.

ACADEMIC PROGRAM Core, honor code. Calendar: semesters. 78 courses offered in 1995–96. Academic remediation for entering students, English as a second language program offered during academic year, services for LD students, advanced placement, self-designed majors, honors program, summer session for credit, part-time degree program (daytime, evenings, summer), adult/continuing education programs.

GENERAL DEGREE REQUIREMENTS 60 semester hours; 1 math course; internship (some majors).

MAJORS Accounting, agricultural business, automotive technologies, business administration/commerce/management, child care/child and family studies, computer information systems, construction technologies, drafting and design, electrical and electronics technologies, (pre)engineering sequence, fire science, food services technology, industrial engineering technology, insurance, law enforcement/police sciences, legal secretarial studies, liberal arts/general studies, medical secretarial studies, nursing, science, secretarial studies/office management.

LIBRARY Kitty Lindsay Library with 27,000 books, 135 microform titles, 245 periodicals, 2,110 records, tapes, and CDs.

COMPUTERS ON CAMPUS 150 computers for student use in computer labs, learning resource center, classrooms, library, student center provide access to Internet. Staffed computer lab on campus.

COLLEGE LIFE Student-run newspaper. 5% vote in student government elections. ***Social organizations:*** 35 open to all. ***Most popular organizations:*** Student Senate, Forensics Club, Drama Club, Black Student Association, Student Activities Board. ***Campus security:*** 24-hour emergency response devices and patrols.

HOUSING College housing not available.

CAREER PLANNING ***Placement office:*** 1 full-time, 1 part-time staff. ***Director:*** Ms. Kathy Sorensen, Director of Job Placement, 217-875-7200 Ext. 280. ***Services:*** job fairs, resume preparation, resume referral, career counseling, careers library, job bank, job interviews. 50 organizations recruited on campus 1994–95.

AFTER GRADUATION 60% of students completing a degree program in 1994–95 went directly on to further study.

EXPENSES FOR 1995–96 Area resident tuition: $1110 full-time, $37 per semester hour part-time. State resident tuition: $3814 full-time, $127.13 per semester hour part-time. Nonresident tuition: $4764 full-time, $158.81 per semester hour part-time. Part-time mandatory fees: $2.50 per semester hour. Full-time mandatory fees: $75.

FINANCIAL AID ***College-administered undergrad aid 1995–96:*** need-based scholarships, low-interest long-term loans from external sources (average $2200), Federal Work-Study, part-time jobs. ***Required forms:*** FAFSA; required for some: institutional. ***Application deadline:*** continuous to 5/31. ***Waivers:*** full or partial for senior citizens.

APPLYING Open admission. ***Options:*** Common Application, early entrance, midyear entrance. ***Required:*** school transcript, TOEFL for international students. Test scores used for counseling/placement. ***Application deadline:*** rolling.

APPLYING/TRANSFER ***Required:*** high school transcript, college transcript. ***Entrance:*** noncompetitive. ***Application deadline:*** rolling.

CONTACT Mr. D. Michael Beube, Director of Admissions and Records, Richland Community College, Decatur, IL 62521-8513, 217-875-7200 Ext. 286. ***Fax:*** 217-875-6991. College video available.

ROBERT MORRIS COLLEGE
Chicago, Illinois

UG Enrollment: 3,100	**Tuition & Fees: $9750**
Application Deadline: rolling	**Room & Board: N/Avail**

Robert Morris College recognizes diversity among its student body; this diversity requires options to fit individual needs and circumstances. Three levels of academic achievement are offered: a diploma in 10 months, an associate degree in 15 months, and a Bachelor of Business Administration degree in 3 years or less. The College is recognized as having one of the lowest tuition rates of any baccalaureate degree–granting private college in the state.

GENERAL Independent, primarily 2-year, coed. Awards transfer associate, terminal associate, bachelor's degrees. Founded 1913. ***Setting:*** urban campus. ***Total enrollment:*** 3,100. ***Faculty:*** 210 (60 full-time, 150 part-time); student-faculty ratio is 20:1.

ENROLLMENT PROFILE 3,100 students from 3 states and territories, 3 other countries. 76% women, 5% part-time, 95% state residents, 14% transferred in, 15% 25 or older, 32% Hispanic, 40% African American, 3% Asian American. ***Most popular recent majors:*** accounting, business administration/commerce/management, secretarial studies/ office management.

FIRST-YEAR CLASS 1,880 total; 3,965 applied, 60% were accepted, 79% of whom enrolled. 6% from top 10% of their high school class, 18% from top quarter, 51% from top half.

ACADEMIC PROGRAM Core, honor code. Calendar: 5 ten-week academic sessions per year. Academic remediation for entering students, advanced placement, tutorials, honors program, summer session for credit, part-time degree program (evenings), adult/ continuing education programs, co-op programs and internships. Study abroad in Austria.

GENERAL DEGREE REQUIREMENTS 100 quarter hours for associate, 180 quarter hours for bachelor's; 4 hours each of math and science; computer course; internship (some majors).

MAJORS Accounting (B), business administration/commerce/management (B), computer graphics (B), computer information systems (B), computer programming, computer science (B), graphic arts, hospitality services, interior design, legal secretarial studies, medical assistant technologies, medical secretarial studies, real estate, secretarial studies/ office management (B), tourism and travel.

LIBRARY Thomas Jefferson Library with 65,000 books, 300 periodicals, 3 on-line bibliographic services, 150 CD-ROMs, 1,500 records, tapes, and CDs.

COMPUTERS ON CAMPUS 452 computers for student use in computer center, computer labs, learning resource center, classrooms, library, student center provide access to Internet. Staffed computer lab on campus provides training in use of computers, software.

COLLEGE LIFE Drama-theater group, student-run newspaper. ***Student services:*** personal-psychological counseling. ***Campus security:*** 24-hour emergency response devices and patrols, late-night transport-escort service.

HOUSING College housing not available.

ATHLETICS Member NAIA. ***Intercollegiate:*** baseball M, basketball M/W, soccer M/W, softball W, volleyball W. ***Contact:*** Mr. Eric Dennis, Director of Athletics, 312-836-4627.

CAREER PLANNING ***Placement office:*** 15 full-time staff. ***Director:*** Ms. Leigh Delisi, Director for Placement, 312-836-4772. ***Services:*** job fairs, resume preparation, resume referral, career counseling, careers library, job bank, job interviews.

EXPENSES FOR 1996–97 ***Application fee:*** $20. Tuition: $9750 full-time, $200 per quarter hour part-time.

FINANCIAL AID ***College-administered undergrad aid 1995–96:*** need-based scholarships (average $790), low-interest long-term loans from external sources (average $3559), 325 Federal Work-Study (averaging $764), 35 part-time jobs. ***Required forms:*** FAFSA; required for some: state, institutional. ***Priority deadline:*** 4/1. ***Payment plan:*** installment. ***Waivers:*** full or partial for employees or children of employees.

APPLYING ***Required:*** school transcript, campus interview, TOEFL for international students. ***Recommended:*** minimum 2.0 GPA, SAT I or ACT. Test scores used for counseling/placement. ***Application deadline:*** rolling.

APPLYING/TRANSFER ***Required:*** campus interview, college transcript, minimum 2.0 college GPA. ***Entrance:*** minimally difficult. ***Contact:*** Ms. Wilma Purpura, Transfer Coordinator, 312-836-4792.

CONTACT Ms. Jean Norris, Dean of Admissions, Robert Morris College, 180 North LaSalle Street, Chicago, IL 60601-2501, 312-836-4635 or toll-free 800-225-1520. ***E-mail:*** enroll@rmcil.edu. College video available.

❖ ***See page 798 for a narrative description.*** ❖

ROCK VALLEY COLLEGE
Rockford, Illinois

UG Enrollment: 8,936	**Tuition & Fees (Area Res): $1264**
Application Deadline: 8/22	**Room & Board: N/Avail**

GENERAL District-supported, 2-year, coed. Part of Illinois Community College System. Awards certificates, transfer associate, terminal associate degrees. Founded 1964. ***Setting:*** 217-acre suburban campus with easy access to Chicago. ***Total enrollment:*** 8,936. ***Faculty:*** 222 (139 full-time, 83 part-time).

ENROLLMENT PROFILE 8,936 students from 2 states and territories, 4 other countries. 55% women, 45% men, 76% part-time, 98% state residents, 6% transferred in, 54% 25 or older, 0% Native American, 3% Hispanic, 6% African American, 2% Asian American. ***Most popular recent majors:*** nursing, respiratory therapy.

FIRST-YEAR CLASS 2,243 total. Of the students who applied, 100% were accepted.

ACADEMIC PROGRAM Core, honor code. Calendar: semesters. 2,100 courses offered in 1995–96. Academic remediation for entering students, services for LD students, advanced placement, self-designed majors, summer session for credit, part-time degree program (daytime, evenings, weekends, summer), adult/continuing education programs, co-op programs and internships. Study abroad in England, Austria, Mexico.

GENERAL DEGREE REQUIREMENTS 64 semester hours; computer course for business, electronics technology majors.

MAJORS Accounting, automotive technologies, aviation technology, business administration/ commerce/management, child care/child and family studies, computer science, computer

technologies, construction technologies, criminal justice, data processing, drafting and design, earth science, educational media, electrical and electronics technologies, electrical engineering technology, electronics engineering technology, (pre)engineering sequence, finance/banking, fire science, hospitality services, hotel and restaurant management, human services, industrial design, industrial engineering technology, international business, liberal arts/general studies, library science, manufacturing technology, marketing/retailing/merchandising, materials sciences, mechanical design technology, medical secretarial studies, nursing, pharmacy/pharmaceutical sciences, quality control technology, respiratory therapy, retail management, secretarial studies/office management, social work, technical writing, welding technology, word processing.
LIBRARY Educational Resource Center with 64,000 books, 183 periodicals, 4,870 records, tapes, and CDs. Acquisition spending 1994–95: $37,200.
COMPUTERS ON CAMPUS 130 computers for student use in computer center, computer labs, library provide access to main academic computer. Staffed computer lab on campus provides training in use of software. Academic computing expenditure 1994–95: $173,800.
COLLEGE LIFE Drama-theater group, choral group, student-run newspaper. 5% vote in student government elections. *Social organizations:* 12 open to all. *Most popular organizations:* Black Student Alliance, Phi Theta Kappa, Adults on Campus, Intervarsity Club, Christian Fellowship. *Major annual events:* New Student Week, Homecoming Week, May Fest. *Student services:* personal-psychological counseling. *Campus security:* 24-hour emergency response devices and patrols, late-night transport-escort service.
HOUSING College housing not available.
ATHLETICS Member NJCAA. *Intercollegiate:* baseball M, basketball M/W, football M, golf M, softball W, tennis M/W, volleyball W. *Intramural:* basketball, skiing (downhill). *Contact:* Mr. Ed Gavigan, Athletic Director, 815-654-4400; Ms. Heidi Hutchinson, Coordinator, Women's Athletics, 815-654-4461.
CAREER PLANNING *Placement office:* 1 part-time staff. *Director:* Mr. Mike Sleezer, Coordinator/Career Center, 815-654-4356. *Services:* resume preparation, career counseling, careers library.
EXPENSES FOR 1996-97 Area resident tuition: $1184 full-time, $37 per semester hour part-time. State resident tuition: $4512 full-time, $141 per semester hour part-time. Nonresident tuition: $7200 full-time, $225 per semester hour part-time. Full-time mandatory fees: $80.
FINANCIAL AID *College-administered undergrad aid 1995–96:* 356 need-based scholarships (averaging $300), 121 non-need scholarships (averaging $500), short-term loans (averaging $100), low-interest long-term loans from external sources (averaging $2100), Federal Work-Study, 125 part-time jobs. *Required forms for some financial aid applicants:* institutional; accepted: state, FAFSA. *Priority deadline:* 6/1. *Waivers:* full or partial for employees or children of employees and senior citizens.
APPLYING Open admission. *Option:* early entrance. *Required:* school transcript, TOEFL for international students. *Recommended:* 3 years of high school math and science, ACT. *Required for some:* ACT. Test scores used for counseling/placement. *Application deadline:* 8/22. *Notification:* continuous.
APPLYING/TRANSFER *Entrance:* noncompetitive. *Application deadline:* 8/22. *Notification:* continuous.
CONTACT Mr. Peter Lonsway, Director of Admissions and Records, Rock Valley College, 3301 North Mulford Road, Rockford, IL 61114-5699, 815-654-4286. *Fax:* 815-654-5568. *E-mail:* adad1pl@rvcux1.rvc.cc.il.us. College video available.

SAINT AUGUSTINE COLLEGE
Chicago, Illinois

UG Enrollment: 1,345	Tuition & Fees: $6000
Application Deadline: rolling	Room & Board: N/Avail

GENERAL Independent, 2-year, coed. Awards transfer associate, terminal associate degrees (bilingual Spanish/English degree programs). Founded 1980. *Setting:* 4-acre urban campus. *Endowment:* $340,028. *Educational spending 1994–95:* $1649 per undergrad. *Total enrollment:* 1,345. *Faculty:* 156 (20 full-time, 6% with terminal degrees, 136 part-time).
ENROLLMENT PROFILE 1,345 students: 72% women, 28% men, 6% part-time, 100% state residents, 97% have need-based financial aid, 1% have non-need-based financial aid, 0% international, 67% 25 or older, 0% Native American, 94% Hispanic, 2% African American, 1% Asian American. *Areas of study chosen:* 48% liberal arts/general studies, 23% business management and administrative services, 19% computer and information sciences, 6% health professions and related sciences, 4% education.
FIRST-YEAR CLASS 543 total. Of the students who applied, 100% were accepted.
ACADEMIC PROGRAM Core, bilingual liberal arts curriculum, honor code. Calendar: semesters. 131 courses offered in 1995–96. Academic remediation for entering students, English as a second language program offered during academic year, summer session for credit, part-time degree program (daytime, evenings), co-op programs and internships.
GENERAL DEGREE REQUIREMENTS 60 semester hours; 1 algebra course; computer course for liberal arts, early childhood education, respiratory therapy majors; internship (some majors).
MAJORS Accounting, business administration/commerce/management, early childhood education, liberal arts/general studies, management information systems, mental health/rehabilitation counseling, respiratory therapy, secretarial studies/office management.
LIBRARY 12,789 books, 126 periodicals, 30 CD-ROMs, 600 records, tapes, and CDs. Acquisition spending 1994–95: $9467.
COMPUTERS ON CAMPUS 50 computers for student use in computer labs, learning resource center provide access to main academic computer. Staffed computer lab on campus provides training in use of computers, software.
COLLEGE LIFE Orientation program (2 days, no cost). Choral group, student-run newspaper. *Major annual events:* Student Alliance Week, Hispanic History Week. *Student services:* personal-psychological counseling. *Campus security:* late-night transport-escort service.
HOUSING College housing not available.
ATHLETICS *Intramural:* soccer, volleyball.
CAREER PLANNING *Service:* career counseling.
EXPENSES FOR 1996-97 Tuition: $5850 full-time, $195 per semester hour part-time. Part-time mandatory fees: $75 per semester. Full-time mandatory fees: $150.
FINANCIAL AID *College-administered undergrad aid 1995–96:* 100 need-based scholarships (average $200), 6 non-need scholarships (average $1000), low-interest long-term loans from external sources (average $2200), Federal Work-Study. *Required forms:* CSS Financial Aid PROFILE, institutional, FAFSA; required for some: Stafford Student Loan form. *Priority deadline:* 6/1. *Payment plan:* installment.
APPLYING Open admission. *Options:* deferred entrance, midyear entrance. Test scores used for counseling/placement. *Application deadline:* rolling.
APPLYING/TRANSFER *Entrance:* noncompetitive. *Application deadline:* rolling. *Contact:* Mr. Derick Johnson, Director, Transfer Center, 312-878-8756.
CONTACT Ms. Guadalupe Moreno, Director of Admissions, Saint Augustine College, 1333 West Argyle, Chicago, IL 60640-3501, 312-878-8756 Ext. 232.

SAUK VALLEY COMMUNITY COLLEGE
Dixon, Illinois

UG Enrollment: 2,635	Tuition & Fees (Area Res): $1376
Application Deadline: rolling	Room & Board: N/Avail

GENERAL District-supported, 2-year, coed. Part of Illinois Community College System. Awards certificates, transfer associate, terminal associate degrees. Founded 1965. *Setting:* 165-acre rural campus. *Total enrollment:* 2,635. *Faculty:* 152 (62 full-time, 90 part-time).
ENROLLMENT PROFILE 2,635 students: 59% women, 60% part-time, 99% state residents, 2% transferred in, 50% 25 or older, 1% Native American, 5% Hispanic, 1% African American, 1% Asian American.
FIRST-YEAR CLASS 560 total; 1,250 applied, 100% were accepted, 45% of whom enrolled. 5% from top 10% of their high school class, 21% from top quarter, 53% from top half.
ACADEMIC PROGRAM Core, honor code. Calendar: semesters. 1,200 courses offered in 1995–96. Academic remediation for entering students, English as a second language program offered during academic year, self-designed majors, tutorials, honors program, part-time degree program (daytime, evenings, summer), adult/continuing education programs, co-op programs and internships. Off-campus study at Highland Community College, Illinois Valley Community College, Rock Valley College, Kishwaukee College.
GENERAL DEGREE REQUIREMENT 64 semester hours.
MAJORS Accounting, anthropology, art/fine arts, biology/biological sciences, business administration/commerce/management, chemistry, child care/child and family studies, corrections, criminal justice, data processing, drafting and design, economics, education, electrical and electronics technologies, elementary education, (pre)engineering sequence, English, French, heating/refrigeration/air conditioning, history, human services, law enforcement/police sciences, liberal arts/general studies, marketing/retailing/merchandising, mathematics, mechanical design technology, medical laboratory technology, mental health/rehabilitation counseling, music, nursing, philosophy, physical education, physics, political science/government, psychology, radiological technology, secretarial studies/office management, sociology, Spanish, speech/rhetoric/public address/debate, theater arts/drama.
LIBRARY 55,000 books, 51 microform titles, 268 periodicals, 2 CD-ROMs, 7,810 records, tapes, and CDs. Acquisition spending 1994–95: $61,481.
COMPUTERS ON CAMPUS 100 computers for student use in computer center provide access to main academic computer, e-mail, Internet. Staffed computer lab on campus provides training in use of computers, software. Academic computing expenditure 1994–95: $175,000.
COLLEGE LIFE Orientation program (4 days, $41). Drama-theater group, choral group. *Social organizations:* 10 open to all. *Student services:* personal-psychological counseling. *Campus security:* 24-hour emergency response devices and patrols, late-night transport-escort service.
HOUSING College housing not available.
ATHLETICS Member NJCAA. *Intercollegiate:* baseball M(s), basketball M(s)/W(s), golf M(s), softball W, tennis M(s)/W(s), volleyball W(s). *Intramural:* basketball, tennis, volleyball. *Contact:* Mr. Russ Damhoff, Athletic Director, 815-288-5511 Ext. 234.
CAREER PLANNING *Service:* career counseling.
EXPENSES FOR 1996-97 Area resident tuition: $1376 full-time, $43 per semester hour part-time. State resident tuition: $3764 full-time, $117.63 per semester hour part-time. Nonresident tuition: $4886 full-time, $152.68 per semester hour part-time.
FINANCIAL AID *College-administered undergrad aid 1995–96:* need-based scholarships (average $800), non-need scholarships, short-term loans (average $150), low-interest long-term loans from external sources (average $2625), Federal Work-Study, part-time jobs. *Required forms:* institutional, FAFSA; accepted: CSS Financial Aid PROFILE. *Priority deadline:* 8/1. *Waivers:* full or partial for employees or children of employees and senior citizens.
APPLYING Open admission except for health programs. *Options:* early entrance, deferred entrance. *Required:* ACT ASSET. *Recommended:* school transcript, TOEFL for international students. Test scores used for counseling/placement. *Application deadline:* rolling. *Notification:* continuous.
APPLYING/TRANSFER *Required:* standardized test scores. *Recommended:* high school transcript, college transcript. *Entrance:* moderately difficult. *Application deadline:* rolling. *Notification:* continuous. *Contact:* Ms. Charla Minson, Counselor, 815-288-5511 Ext. 208.
CONTACT Mr. Steve Ullrick, Director of Admissions, Records, and Placement, Sauk Valley Community College, Dixon, IL 61021, 815-288-5511 Ext. 310.

SHAWNEE COMMUNITY COLLEGE
Ullin, Illinois

UG Enrollment: 2,288	Tuition & Fees (Area Res): $936
Application Deadline: rolling	Room & Board: N/Avail

GENERAL State and locally supported, 2-year, coed. Part of Illinois Community College System. Awards transfer associate, terminal associate degrees. Founded 1967. *Setting:* 163-acre rural campus. *Total enrollment:* 2,288. *Faculty:* 176 (43 full-time, 14% with terminal degrees, 133 part-time).
ENROLLMENT PROFILE 2,288 students from 3 states and territories. 62% women, 38% men, 68% part-time, 98% state residents, 1% transferred in, 54% 25 or older, 0% Native American, 1% Hispanic, 13% African American, 1% Asian American. *Most popular recent majors:* liberal arts/general studies, science.

Shawnee Community College (continued)

FIRST-YEAR CLASS 1,464 total. Of the students who applied, 100% were accepted. 5% from top 10% of their high school class, 20% from top quarter, 60% from top half.

ACADEMIC PROGRAM Core. Calendar: semesters. Academic remediation for entering students, services for LD students, summer session for credit, part-time degree program (daytime, evenings, weekends, summer), adult/continuing education programs, internships.

GENERAL DEGREE REQUIREMENTS 64 semester hours; 8 semester hours of math/science; computer course for accounting, business administration majors.

MAJORS Accounting, agricultural business, agricultural sciences, agronomy/soil and crop sciences, animal sciences, automotive technologies, business administration/commerce/management, child care/child and family studies, computer information systems, cosmetology, electrical and electronics technologies, food services technology, horticulture, human services, law enforcement/police sciences, legal secretarial studies, liberal arts/general studies, machine and tool technologies, medical secretarial studies, nursing, science, secretarial studies/office management, social work, welding technology, wildlife management.

LIBRARY Shawnee Community College Library with 37,000 books, 245 periodicals.

COMPUTERS ON CAMPUS 40 computers for student use in computer center, library.

COLLEGE LIFE Drama-theater group, choral group, student-run newspaper. ***Major annual events:*** Homecoming, Fall Fest, Spring Fest.

HOUSING College housing not available.

ATHLETICS Member NJCAA. ***Intercollegiate:*** baseball M(s), basketball M(s)/W(s), golf M, softball W(s), tennis M, volleyball W(s). ***Intramural:*** badminton, baseball, basketball, golf, softball, table tennis (Ping-Pong), tennis, volleyball, weight lifting. ***Contact:*** Mr. Jim Byassee, Athletic Director, 618-634-2242.

CAREER PLANNING ***Placement office:*** 2 full-time staff. ***Director:*** Ms. Jean Ellen Boyd, 618-634-2242. ***Services:*** job fairs, resume preparation, resume referral, career counseling, careers library, job interviews. Students must register sophomore year.

AFTER GRADUATION 60% of students completing a degree program in 1994–95 went directly on to further study.

EXPENSES FOR 1996–97 Area resident tuition: $936 full-time, $29.25 per semester hour part-time. State resident tuition: $3088 full-time, $96.49 per semester hour part-time. Nonresident tuition: $6691 full-time, $209.08 per semester hour part-time. Tuition for residents of participating counties: $1672 full-time, $52.25 per semester hour part-time.

FINANCIAL AID ***College-administered undergrad aid 1995–96:*** 201 need-based scholarships (average $235), 176 non-need scholarships (average $1200), low-interest long-term loans from external sources (average $2206), 38 Federal Work-Study (averaging $855), 50 part-time jobs. ***Required forms:*** institutional; required for some: FAFSA. ***Priority deadline:*** 7/15. ***Payment plan:*** installment. ***Waivers:*** full or partial for employees or children of employees and senior citizens. ***Notification:*** continuous. ***Average indebtedness of graduates:*** $4769.

APPLYING Open admission except for health programs. ***Options:*** early entrance, deferred entrance. ***Required:*** school transcript, ACT ASSET. ***Recommended:*** ACT. ***Required for some:*** 3 years of high school math, ACT. Test scores used for counseling/placement. ***Application deadline:*** rolling. ***Notification:*** continuous. Preference given to district residents.

APPLYING/TRANSFER ***Required:*** standardized test scores. ***Recommended:*** college transcript. ***Required for some:*** 3 years of high school math. ***Entrance:*** noncompetitive. ***Application deadline:*** rolling. ***Notification:*** continuous.

CONTACT Mr. James Dumas, Dean of Student Services, Shawnee Community College, Ullin, IL 62992-9725, 618-634-2242 Ext. 245. ***Fax:*** 618-634-9028.

SOUTHEASTERN ILLINOIS COLLEGE
Harrisburg, Illinois

UG Enrollment: 3,382 — **Tuition & Fees (Area Res): $960**
Application Deadline: 9/1 — **Room & Board: N/Avail**

GENERAL State-supported, 2-year, coed. Part of Illinois Community College System. Awards certificates, transfer associate, terminal associate degrees. Founded 1960. ***Setting:*** 140-acre rural campus. ***Total enrollment:*** 3,382. ***Faculty:*** 184 (47 full-time, 14% with terminal degrees, 137 part-time); student-faculty ratio is 20:1.

ENROLLMENT PROFILE 3,382 students from 5 states and territories, 2 other countries. 48% women, 69% part-time, 95% state residents, 5% transferred in, 2% international, 40% 25 or older, 1% Native American, 1% Hispanic, 13% African American, 1% Asian American. ***Most popular recent majors:*** nursing, business administration/commerce/management.

FIRST-YEAR CLASS 1,169 total. Of the students who applied, 100% were accepted.

ACADEMIC PROGRAM Core. Calendar: semesters. Academic remediation for entering students, services for LD students, advanced placement, tutorials, summer session for credit, part-time degree program (daytime, evenings, summer), adult/continuing education programs, internships.

GENERAL DEGREE REQUIREMENTS 62 semester hours; math/science requirements vary according to program; internship (some majors).

MAJORS Accounting, agricultural technologies, automotive technologies, business administration/commerce/management, child care/child and family studies, computer information systems, corrections, electrical and electronics technologies, emergency medical technology, fire science, forest technology, human services, law enforcement/police sciences, medical laboratory technology, medical records services, mining technology, nursing, occupational therapy, operating room technology, practical nursing, real estate, secretarial studies/office management, water resources, welding technology, wildlife management.

LIBRARY 37,000 books, 32 microform titles, 300 periodicals, 10 CD-ROMs, 1,700 records, tapes, and CDs.

COMPUTERS ON CAMPUS 78 computers for student use in learning electronics labs, classrooms, library. Staffed computer lab on campus.

COLLEGE LIFE Choral group, student-run newspaper. ***Social organizations:*** 13 open to all. ***Most popular organizations:*** Math and Science Club, Phi Theta Kappa, Forestry Club, Phi Beta Lambda. ***Student services:*** personal-psychological counseling. ***Campus security:*** student patrols, evening security guard.

HOUSING College housing not available.

ATHLETICS Member NJCAA. ***Intercollegiate:*** basketball M(s)/W(s). ***Intramural:*** basketball, softball. ***Contact:*** Mr. Virgil Motsinger, Director of Athletics, 618-252-6376 Ext. 395.

CAREER PLANNING ***Placement office:*** 1 full-time staff. ***Director:*** Ms. Phyllis Dover, Career Counselor, 618-252-6376. ***Services:*** job fairs, resume preparation, career counseling, careers library. 73 organizations recruited on campus 1994–95.

EXPENSES FOR 1996–97 Area resident tuition: $960 full-time, $30 per semester hour part-time. State resident tuition: $3777 full-time, $118.03 per semester hour part-time. Nonresident tuition: $4953 full-time, $154.78 per semester hour part-time.

FINANCIAL AID ***College-administered undergrad aid 1995–96:*** 1,881 need-based scholarships (averaging $1266), 75 non-need scholarships (averaging $1000), short-term loans (averaging $100), low-interest long-term loans from external sources, 25 Federal Work-Study (averaging $1750), 15 part-time jobs. ***Required forms:*** institutional, FAFSA; required for some: state. ***Priority deadline:*** 4/1. ***Payment plan:*** installment. ***Waivers:*** full or partial for employees or children of employees and senior citizens. ***Notification:*** 7/1. ***Average indebtedness of graduates:*** $3136.

APPLYING Open admission except for nursing, medical records technology, medical lab technology, operating room technology, game management, occupational therapy programs. ***Options:*** early entrance, deferred entrance, midyear entrance. ***Required:*** school transcript, TOEFL for international students, ACT ASSET. ***Recommended:*** 3 years of high school math and science, some high school foreign language, ACT. Test scores used for counseling/placement. ***Application deadline:*** 9/1. ***Notification:*** continuous. Preference given to district residents.

APPLYING/TRANSFER ***Required:*** standardized test scores, high school transcript, college transcript. ***Recommended:*** 3 years of high school math and science, some high school foreign language. ***Entrance:*** noncompetitive. ***Application deadline:*** 9/1. ***Notification:*** continuous. ***Contact:*** Dr. Dave Nudo, Director of Counseling, 618-252-6376.

CONTACT Ms. Dana Keating, Director of Admissions and Records, Southeastern Illinois College, Harrisburg, IL 62946-9804, 618-252-6376.

SOUTH SUBURBAN COLLEGE
South Holland, Illinois

UG Enrollment: 6,185 — **Tuition & Fees (Area Res): $1449**
Application Deadline: rolling — **Room & Board: N/Avail**

GENERAL State and locally supported, 2-year, coed. Part of Illinois Community College System. Awards certificates, transfer associate, terminal associate degrees. Founded 1927. ***Setting:*** suburban campus with easy access to Chicago. ***Total enrollment:*** 6,185. ***Faculty:*** 382 (111 full-time, 20% with terminal degrees, 271 part-time).

ENROLLMENT PROFILE 6,185 students: 70% women, 30% men, 67% part-time, 98% state residents, 6% transferred in, 27% have need-based financial aid, 0% international, 49% 25 or older, 0% Native American, 5% Hispanic, 37% African American, 1% Asian American.

FIRST-YEAR CLASS 703 total. Of the students who applied, 100% were accepted. 2% from top 10% of their high school class, 5% from top quarter, 18% from top half. 4 National Merit Scholars.

ACADEMIC PROGRAM Core, interdisciplinary curriculum, honor code. Calendar: semesters. 553 courses offered in 1995–96. Academic remediation for entering students, English as a second language program offered during academic year, advanced placement, honors program, summer session for credit, part-time degree program (daytime, evenings, weekends, summer), adult/continuing education programs, co-op programs and internships.

GENERAL DEGREE REQUIREMENTS 62 semester hours; 1 algebra course; computer course; internship (some majors).

MAJORS Accounting, advertising, architectural technologies, art/fine arts, aviation technology, biomedical technologies, business administration/commerce/management, chemical engineering technology, chemistry, child care/child and family studies, computer information systems, construction technologies, cosmetology, court reporting, criminal justice, data processing, drafting and design, early childhood education, electrical and electronics technologies, electrical engineering technology, electronics engineering technology, elementary education, emergency medical technology, (pre)engineering sequence, fashion merchandising, finance/banking, fire science, graphic arts, human services, industrial engineering technology, law enforcement/police sciences, liberal arts/general studies, machine and tool technologies, management information systems, marketing/retailing/merchandising, mathematics, mechanical design technology, medical assistant technologies, medical secretarial studies, medical technology, mental health/rehabilitation counseling, music, nursing, occupational therapy, paralegal studies, pharmacy/pharmaceutical sciences, practical nursing, printing technologies, radiological technology, real estate, retail management, robotics, secretarial studies/office management, social work, teacher aide studies, word processing.

LIBRARY South Suburban College with 38,475 books, 2 microform titles, 401 periodicals, 89 CD-ROMs, 261 records, tapes, and CDs. Acquisition spending 1994–95: $41,680.

COMPUTERS ON CAMPUS 131 computers for student use in computer center, classroom area, library provide access to main academic computer, on-line services, Internet. Staffed computer lab on campus. Academic computing expenditure 1994–95: $584,602.

COLLEGE LIFE Drama-theater group, choral group, student-run newspaper. 25% vote in student government elections. ***Social organizations:*** 20 open to all. ***Most popular organizations:*** Returning Adult Organization, Business Professionals, Gamers Guild, Christian Fellowship, PAC Rats. ***Major annual events:*** Welcome Back Week, Pre-Finals Celebration, Discovering Diversity. ***Student services:*** personal-psychological counseling. ***Campus security:*** 24-hour emergency response devices and patrols.

HOUSING College housing not available.

ATHLETICS Member NJCAA. ***Intercollegiate:*** baseball M, basketball M/W, cross-country running M/W, softball W, tennis M/W, volleyball W. ***Intramural:*** baseball, basketball, bowling, cross-country running, golf, soccer, softball, tennis, volleyball. ***Contact:*** Mr. Robert Marshall, Vice President of Student Services, 708-210-5728.

CAREER PLANNING ***Placement office:*** 1 full-time, 2 part-time staff; $687,065 operating expenditure 1994–95. ***Director:*** Ms. Dale Barz, Counselor, 708-596-2000 Ext. 392. ***Services:*** job fairs, resume preparation, resume referral, career counseling, careers library, job bank, job interviews.

AFTER GRADUATION 61% of students completing a degree program in 1994–95 went directly on to further study.

EXPENSES FOR 1995–96 ***Application fee:*** $20. Area resident tuition: $1410 full-time, $47 per semester hour part-time. State resident tuition: $4523 full-time, $150.75

per semester hour part-time. Nonresident tuition: $6263 full-time, $208.75 per semester hour part-time. Part-time mandatory fees per semester range from $2.75 to $8.50. Full-time mandatory fees: $39.
FINANCIAL AID *College-administered undergrad aid 1995–96:* 432 need-based scholarships, 25 non-need scholarships (averaging $900), Federal Work-Study, 89 part-time jobs. *Acceptable forms:* CSS Financial Aid PROFILE, state, institutional, FAFSA. *Priority deadline:* 8/26. *Payment plan:* deferred payment. *Waivers:* full or partial for employees or children of employees and senior citizens. *Notification:* 9/30.
APPLYING Open admission. *Options:* early entrance, deferred entrance, midyear entrance. *Required:* school transcript, 3 years of high school math, ACT ASSET. *Recommended:* minimum 2.0 GPA, 3 years of high school science, some high school foreign language, TOEFL for international students. *Required for some:* essay, recommendations, interview. Test scores used for counseling/placement. *Application deadline:* rolling. *Notification:* continuous. Preference given to district residents for nursing program.
APPLYING/TRANSFER *Required:* 3 years of high school math, college transcript, minimum 2.0 college GPA. *Recommended:* 3 years of high school science, some high school foreign language, minimum 3.0 college GPA. *Required for some:* interview. *Entrance:* noncompetitive. *Application deadline:* rolling. *Notification:* continuous. *Contact:* Mr. Michael Wilensky, Transfer Admissions Counselor, 708-596-2000 Ext. 516.
CONTACT Mr. Robert Pinkerton, Registrar, South Suburban College, South Holland, IL 60473-1270, 708-596-2000 or toll-free 800-248-4772 (out-of-state). *Fax:* 708-210-5710. College video available.

SPOON RIVER COLLEGE
Canton, Illinois

UG Enrollment: 1,950	Tuition & Fees (Area Res): $1408
Application Deadline: rolling	Room & Board: N/Avail

GENERAL State-supported, 2-year, coed. Part of Illinois Community College System. Awards transfer associate, terminal associate degrees. Founded 1959. *Setting:* 160-acre rural campus. *Educational spending 1994–95:* $1275 per undergrad. *Total enrollment:* 1,950. *Faculty:* 136 (36 full-time, 100 part-time); student-faculty ratio is 18:1.
ENROLLMENT PROFILE 1,950 students from 2 states and territories, 5 other countries. 60% women, 40% men, 49% part-time, 97% state residents, 14% transferred in, 2% international, 50% 25 or older, 0% Native American, 1% Hispanic, 6% African American, 1% Asian American. *Most popular recent majors:* business administration/commerce/management, communication, electrical and electronics technologies.
FIRST-YEAR CLASS 1,166 total. Of the students who applied, 100% were accepted, 90% of whom enrolled.
ACADEMIC PROGRAM Core. Calendar: semesters. Academic remediation for entering students, English as a second language program offered during academic year, services for LD students, advanced placement, honors program, summer session for credit, part-time degree program (daytime), adult/continuing education programs. ROTC: Army.
GENERAL DEGREE REQUIREMENTS 64 semester hours; computer course.
MAJORS Accounting, agricultural education, agricultural technologies, art/fine arts, automotive technologies, biology/biological sciences, botany/plant sciences, business administration/commerce/management, business education, chemistry, child care/child and family studies, communication, criminal justice, data processing, early childhood education, education, electrical and electronics technologies, (pre)engineering sequence, English, finance/banking, health science, history, law enforcement/police sciences, legal secretarial studies, liberal arts/general studies, manufacturing technology, mathematics, medical secretarial studies, physical education, physical sciences, physics, political science/government, psychology, science, secretarial studies/office management, social science, sociology, speech/rhetoric/public address/debate, theater arts/drama, zoology.
LIBRARY Learning Resource Center with 34,269 books, 296 periodicals. Acquisition spending 1994–95: $248,116.
COMPUTERS ON CAMPUS 34 computers for student use in computer labs, library.
COLLEGE LIFE Drama-theater group. *Social organizations:* 9 open to all. *Most popular organizations:* Student Senate, Student and Cultural Affairs Committee, PEACE, Peer Ambassadors. *Major annual events:* Crusaders' Day, Homecoming, May Ball. *Student services:* personal-psychological counseling. *Campus security:* 24-hour emergency response devices.
HOUSING College housing not available.
ATHLETICS Member NJCAA. *Intercollegiate:* baseball M(s), basketball M(s)/W(s), golf M(s), softball W(s), volleyball W(s). *Intramural:* bowling. *Contact:* Mr. Heath Rose, Director of Student Activities and Athletics, 309-647-4645.
CAREER PLANNING *Director:* Mr. Jack Frame, Counselor, 309-647-4645. *Service:* career counseling.
AFTER GRADUATION 75% of students completing a degree program in 1994–95 went directly on to further study.
EXPENSES FOR 1995–96 Area resident tuition: $1408 full-time, $44 per semester hour part-time. State resident tuition: $1824 full-time, $57 per semester hour part-time. Nonresident tuition: $5845 full-time, $182.66 per semester hour part-time.
FINANCIAL AID *College-administered undergrad aid 1995–96:* 10 need-based scholarships (average $260), 60 non-need scholarships (average $864), short-term loans (average $150), low-interest long-term loans from external sources (average $2500), Federal Work-Study, 40 part-time jobs. *Required forms:* FAFSA; accepted: CSS Financial Aid PROFILE, state, institutional. *Application deadline:* continuous. *Payment plan:* installment. *Waivers:* full or partial for employees or children of employees and senior citizens.
APPLYING Open admission. *Option:* early entrance. *Required:* school transcript, 3 years of high school math and science, TOEFL for international students. *Recommended:* some high school foreign language, SAT I or ACT. Test scores used for counseling/placement. *Application deadline:* rolling.
APPLYING/TRANSFER *Entrance:* noncompetitive. *Application deadline:* rolling. *Contact:* Ms. Sharon Wrenn, Associate Dean of Student Development, 309-647-4645.
CONTACT Ms. Sharon Wrenn, Associate Dean of Student Development, Spoon River College, Canton, IL 61520-9801, 309-647-4645. *Fax:* 309-647-6498. College video available.

SPRINGFIELD COLLEGE IN ILLINOIS
Springfield, Illinois

UG Enrollment: 465	Tuition & Fees: $5850
Application Deadline: rolling	Room Only: $1800

GENERAL Independent, 2-year, coed, affiliated with Roman Catholic Church. Awards transfer associate degrees. Founded 1929. *Setting:* 8-acre urban campus. *Total enrollment:* 465. *Faculty:* 45 (17 full-time, 28 part-time); student-faculty ratio is 10:1.
ENROLLMENT PROFILE 465 students: 64% women, 29% part-time, 97% state residents, 27% transferred in, 1% international, 24% 25 or older, 1% Native American, 1% Hispanic, 11% African American, 1% Asian American. *Most popular recent majors:* liberal arts/general studies, nursing, business administration/commerce/management.
FIRST-YEAR CLASS 181 total; 254 applied, 88% were accepted, 81% of whom enrolled.
ACADEMIC PROGRAM Core, honor code. Calendar: semesters. Academic remediation for entering students, advanced placement, self-designed majors, tutorials, summer session for credit, part-time degree program (daytime, evenings), adult/continuing education programs. Off-campus study at Illinois College, MacMurray College, Sangamon State University, Lincoln Land Community College.
GENERAL DEGREE REQUIREMENTS 60 semester hours; 3 semester hours of math; 8 semester hours of science.
MAJORS Art/fine arts, business administration/commerce/management, computer science, education, (pre)engineering sequence, flight training, health science, liberal arts/general studies, medical technology, music, nursing, physical therapy, science.
LIBRARY Charles E. Becker Library plus 1 other, with 24,405 books, 11 microform titles, 329 periodicals, 1,854 records, tapes, and CDs.
COMPUTERS ON CAMPUS 23 computers for student use in computer center, library. Staffed computer lab on campus provides training in use of computers, software.
COLLEGE LIFE Student-run newspaper. 20% vote in student government elections. *Social organizations:* 7 open to all; 1 national fraternity. *Most popular organizations:* Alpha Phi Omega, Student Activity Council, Sculpture Club. *Student services:* personal-psychological counseling.
HOUSING 32 college housing spaces available; 31 were occupied 1995–96. Off-campus living permitted. *Option:* coed (1 building) housing available.
ATHLETICS Member NJCAA. *Intercollegiate:* basketball M(s), soccer M(s), softball W(s), tennis W(s), volleyball W(s). *Intramural:* basketball, tennis, volleyball. *Contact:* Mr. Joe Mackey, Athletic Director, 217-525-1420 Ext. 237.
CAREER PLANNING *Service:* career counseling.
AFTER GRADUATION 86% of students completing a degree program in 1994–95 went directly on to further study.
EXPENSES FOR 1996–97 *Application fee:* $15. Tuition: $5700 full-time, $238 per semester hour part-time. Full-time mandatory fees: $150. College room only: $1800.
FINANCIAL AID *College-administered undergrad aid 1995–96:* 70 need-based scholarships (average $365), 101 non-need scholarships (average $575), low-interest long-term loans from external sources (average $2158), Federal Work-Study, 6 part-time jobs. *Required forms:* institutional; accepted: CSS Financial Aid PROFILE, state, FAFSA. *Priority deadline:* 4/1. *Payment plan:* installment. *Waivers:* full or partial for employees or children of employees.
APPLYING *Options:* early entrance, midyear entrance. *Required:* ACT, TOEFL for international students. *Recommended:* minimum 2.0 GPA, 3 years of high school math and science. *Required for some:* some high school foreign language. Test scores used for counseling/placement. *Application deadline:* rolling.
APPLYING/TRANSFER *Required:* standardized test scores. *Recommended:* 3 years of high school math and science, minimum 2.0 high school GPA. *Required for some:* some high school foreign language. *Entrance:* moderately difficult. *Application deadline:* rolling. *Contact:* Mr. Eldon Brown, Transfer Coordinator, 217-525-1420 Ext. 232.
CONTACT Ms. Deirdre Blankenberger, Director of Enrollment Management, Springfield College in Illinois, 1500 North Fifth Street, Springfield, IL 62702-2643, 217-525-1420 Ext. 252 or toll-free 800-635-7289 (in-state). *Fax:* 217-789-1698.

STATE COMMUNITY COLLEGE OF EAST ST. LOUIS
East St. Louis, Illinois

UG Enrollment: 1,268	Tuition & Fees (IL Res): $1044
Application Deadline: rolling	Room & Board: N/Avail

GENERAL State-supported, 2-year, coed. Part of Illinois Community College System. Awards transfer associate, terminal associate degrees. Founded 1969. *Setting:* urban campus with easy access to St. Louis. *Total enrollment:* 1,268. *Faculty:* 83 (43 full-time, 40 part-time).
ENROLLMENT PROFILE 1,268 students: 65% women, 56% part-time, 100% state residents, 1% transferred in, 59% 25 or older, 98% African American. *Most popular recent majors:* nursing, business administration/commerce/management, science.
FIRST-YEAR CLASS 400 total. Of the students who applied, 100% were accepted, 33% of whom enrolled. 3% from top 10% of their high school class, 12% from top quarter, 60% from top half.
ACADEMIC PROGRAM Calendar: semesters. Academic remediation for entering students, part-time degree program (daytime, evenings, summer), internships.
GENERAL DEGREE REQUIREMENTS 60 semester hours; 3 semester hours each of math and science; computer course for business, law enforcement, nursing, science, math majors; internship (some majors).
MAJORS Accounting, applied mathematics, biology/biological sciences, business administration/commerce/management, chemistry, child care/child and family studies, child psychology/child development, community services, computer programming, computer science, construction management, data processing, economics, education, environmental sciences, fire science, health education, history, liberal arts/general studies, mathematics, mental health/rehabilitation counseling, nursing, philosophy, physics, political science/government, psychology, religious studies, science, secretarial studies/office management, social work, sociology.
COMPUTERS ON CAMPUS 90 computers for student use in labs, classrooms. Staffed computer lab on campus (open 24 hours a day) provides training in use of computers, software.

State Community College of East St. Louis (continued)

COLLEGE LIFE ***Social organizations:*** 1 local fraternity, 1 local sorority; 10% of eligible men and 15% of eligible women are members. ***Student services:*** health clinic, personal-psychological counseling. ***Campus security:*** 24-hour patrols.
HOUSING College housing not available.
ATHLETICS Member NJCAA. ***Intercollegiate:*** baseball M, basketball M. ***Intramural:*** basketball, softball.
CAREER PLANNING ***Services:*** resume preparation, resume referral, career counseling, job interviews.
EXPENSES FOR 1995–96 ***Application fee:*** $2. State resident tuition: $1020 full-time, $34 per semester hour part-time. Nonresident tuition: $4680 full-time, $156 per semester hour part-time. Full-time mandatory fees: $24.
FINANCIAL AID ***College-administered undergrad aid 1995–96:*** need-based scholarships, non-need scholarships, short-term loans, Federal Work-Study. ***Required forms:*** institutional; accepted: CSS Financial Aid PROFILE, state, FAFSA. ***Priority deadline:*** 3/1. ***Payment plans:*** installment, deferred payment. ***Waivers:*** full or partial for senior citizens.
APPLYING Open admission except for nursing program. ***Option:*** Common Application. ***Required for some:*** ACT. Test scores used for admission. ***Application deadline:*** rolling.
APPLYING/TRANSFER ***Required for some:*** standardized test scores. ***Entrance:*** noncompetitive.
CONTACT Mrs. Banks, Admissions and Records Officer, State Community College of East St. Louis, 601 James R Thompson Boulevard, East St. Louis, IL 62201-1100. ***Fax:*** 618-583-2660.

TRITON COLLEGE
River Grove, Illinois

UG Enrollment: 12,050	**Tuition & Fees (Area Res): $1490**
Application Deadline: rolling	**Room & Board: N/Avail**

GENERAL State-supported, 2-year, coed. Part of Illinois Community College System. Awards certificates, transfer associate, terminal associate degrees. Founded 1964. ***Setting:*** 100-acre suburban campus with easy access to Chicago. ***Total enrollment:*** 12,050. ***Faculty:*** 715 (166 full-time, 32% with terminal degrees, 549 part-time).
ENROLLMENT PROFILE 12,050 students: 55% women, 45% men, 68% part-time, 99% state residents, 0% international, 48% 25 or older, 0% Native American, 11% Hispanic, 22% African American, 6% Asian American. ***Most popular recent majors:*** liberal arts/general studies, science.
FIRST-YEAR CLASS 2,749 total; 5,349 applied, 100% were accepted, 51% of whom enrolled.
ACADEMIC PROGRAM Core, general education curriculum, honor code. Calendar: semesters. Academic remediation for entering students, English as a second language program offered during academic year and summer, services for LD students, advanced placement, self-designed majors, Freshman Honors College, honors program, summer session for credit, part-time degree program (daytime, evenings, weekends, summer), adult/continuing education programs, co-op programs and internships.
GENERAL DEGREE REQUIREMENTS 64 credits; computer course for most majors.
MAJORS Accounting, advertising, anthropology, art/fine arts, automotive technologies, biology/biological sciences, business administration/commerce/management, chemistry, communication, computer graphics, computer information systems, computer science, computer technologies, construction management, construction technologies, court reporting, criminal justice, culinary arts, data processing, drafting and design, drug and alcohol/substance abuse counseling, early childhood education, economics, education, electrical and electronics technologies, electronics engineering technology, elementary education, engineering (general), engineering design, (pre)engineering sequence, engineering technology, English, fashion merchandising, fire science, French, geography, geology, German, graphic arts, heating/refrigeration/air conditioning, history, horticulture, hospitality services, hotel and restaurant management, industrial administration, interdisciplinary studies, interior design, international business, Italian, journalism, landscape architecture/design, landscaping/grounds maintenance, law enforcement/police sciences, legal secretarial studies, liberal arts/general studies, machine and tool technologies, management information systems, manufacturing technology, marketing/retailing/merchandising, mathematics, music, nuclear medical technology, nursing, optometric/ophthalmic technologies, ornamental horticulture, philosophy, physical education, physical therapy, physics, political science/government, practical nursing, printing technologies, psychology, radiological technology, real estate, respiratory therapy, retail management, science, secretarial studies/office management, social science, Spanish, speech/rhetoric/public address/debate, theater arts/drama, transportation technologies, welding technology, word processing.
LIBRARY Learning Resource Center with 81,680 books, 708 periodicals, 8 CD-ROMs, 624 records, tapes, and CDs.
COMPUTERS ON CAMPUS 350 computers for student use in computer center provide access to e-mail, Internet. Staffed computer lab on campus provides training in use of computers, software.
COLLEGE LIFE Drama-theater group, choral group, student-run newspaper, radio station. ***Social organizations:*** 34 open to all. ***Most popular organizations:*** Student Government, Program Board. ***Major annual events:*** Triton Spirit Week, World's Largest Sober Party. ***Student services:*** health clinic, personal-psychological counseling. ***Campus security:*** 24-hour emergency response devices and patrols.
HOUSING College housing not available.
ATHLETICS Member NJCAA. ***Intercollegiate:*** baseball M, basketball M/W, soccer M, softball W, swimming and diving M/W, volleyball W, wrestling M. ***Intramural:*** badminton, basketball, swimming and diving, tennis, volleyball, weight lifting. ***Contact:*** Mr. Tom Doyle, Head of Men's and Women's Sports, 708-456-0300 Ext. 3781.
CAREER PLANNING ***Placement office:*** 1 full-time, 12 part-time staff. ***Director:*** Ms. Lois Pye, Director of Career Services Center, 708-456-0300 Ext. 3805. ***Services:*** job fairs, resume preparation, resume referral, career counseling, careers library, job bank, job interviews.
AFTER GRADUATION 68% of students completing a degree program in 1994–95 went directly on to further study.
EXPENSES FOR 1996–97 Area resident tuition: $1376 full-time, $43 per credit hour part-time. State resident tuition: $4012 full-time, $125.37 per credit hour part-time. Nonresident tuition: $6116 full-time, $191.11 per credit hour part-time. Part-time mandatory fees per semester range from $9.50 to $47.50. Full-time mandatory fees: $114.
FINANCIAL AID ***College-administered undergrad aid 1995–96:*** 2,800 need-based scholarships (average $500), 60 non-need scholarships (average $550), short-term loans (average $200), low-interest long-term loans from external sources (average $1800), Federal Work-Study, 63 part-time jobs. ***Required forms:*** state, institutional; accepted: CSS Financial Aid PROFILE, FAFSA. ***Priority deadline:*** 4/15. ***Payment plan:*** installment. ***Waivers:*** full or partial for employees or children of employees and senior citizens.
APPLYING Open admission except for some allied health programs. ***Options:*** early entrance, deferred entrance, midyear entrance. ***Required:*** school transcript, TOEFL for international students. ***Recommended:*** SAT I or ACT. ***Required for some:*** 3 years of high school math and science. Test scores used for counseling/placement. ***Application deadline:*** rolling. Preference given to district residents.
APPLYING/TRANSFER ***Required:*** high school transcript, college transcript. ***Recommended:*** standardized test scores. ***Entrance:*** noncompetitive. ***Application deadline:*** rolling. ***Contact:*** Ms. Mary Jo Hall, Director of Transfer Center, 708-456-0300 Ext. 3731.
CONTACT Ms. Gail Fuller, Director of Admission and Records, Triton College, River Grove, IL 60171-9983, 708-456-0300 Ext. 3397.

TRUMAN COLLEGE
Illinois—See City Colleges of Chicago, Harry S Truman College

WAUBONSEE COMMUNITY COLLEGE
Sugar Grove, Illinois

UG Enrollment: 7,460	**Tuition & Fees (Area Res): $1276**
Application Deadline: rolling	**Room & Board: N/Avail**

GENERAL District-supported, 2-year, coed. Part of Illinois Community College System. Awards certificates, transfer associate, terminal associate degrees. Founded 1966. ***Setting:*** 235-acre rural campus with easy access to Chicago. ***Educational spending 1994–95:*** $807 per undergrad. ***Total enrollment:*** 7,460. ***Faculty:*** 494 (70 full-time, 18% with terminal degrees, 424 part-time); student-faculty ratio is 16:1.
ENROLLMENT PROFILE 7,460 students: 61% women, 79% part-time, 100% state residents, 14% transferred in, 0% international, 54% 25 or older, 1% Native American, 16% Hispanic, 5% African American, 1% Asian American. ***Areas of study chosen:*** 19% business management and administrative services, 17% health professions and related sciences, 14% vocational and home economics, 11% liberal arts/general studies, 9% education, 6% engineering and applied sciences, 6% social sciences, 4% computer and information sciences, 4% psychology, 3% biological and life sciences, 2% fine arts, 2% physical sciences, 1% communications and journalism, 1% English language/literature/letters, 1% performing arts. ***Most popular recent majors:*** business administration/commerce/management, education, nursing.
FIRST-YEAR CLASS 902 total; 1,207 applied, 100% were accepted, 75% of whom enrolled. 10% from top 10% of their high school class, 21% from top half.
ACADEMIC PROGRAM Core, interdisciplinary curriculum. Calendar: semesters. 596 courses offered in 1995–96. Academic remediation for entering students, services for LD students, advanced placement, honors program, summer session for credit, part-time degree program (daytime, evenings, summer), adult/continuing education programs. Study abroad in England, Mexico. ROTC: Army (c).
GENERAL DEGREE REQUIREMENTS 64 semester hours; math/science requirements vary according to program.
MAJORS Accounting, art/fine arts, automotive technologies, biology/biological sciences, business administration/commerce/management, chemistry, communication, computer information systems, criminal justice, deaf interpreter training, drafting and design, early childhood education, earth science, economics, education, electrical and electronics technologies, (pre)engineering sequence, English, environmental engineering technology, finance/banking, heating/refrigeration/air conditioning, history, human services, industrial arts, journalism, legal secretarial studies, liberal arts/general studies, machine and tool technologies, manufacturing technology, marketing/retailing/merchandising, mathematics, mechanical design technology, music, nursing, physical education, physical sciences, physics, political science/government, psychology, quality control technology, real estate, robotics, science, secretarial studies/office management, social science, social work, speech/rhetoric/public address/debate, theater arts/drama, tourism and travel.
LIBRARY Learning Resource Center with 50,336 books, 428 microform titles, 614 periodicals, 2 on-line bibliographic services, 13 CD-ROMs, 2,158 records, tapes, and CDs. Acquisition spending 1994–95: $114,650.
COMPUTERS ON CAMPUS 120 computers for student use in computer center provide access to main academic computer, e-mail. Academic computing expenditure 1994–95: $526,530.
COLLEGE LIFE Drama-theater group, choral group, student-run newspaper. ***Social organizations:*** 18 open to all. ***Most popular organizations:*** Latino Unidos, Phi Theta Kappa, Association of International Studies. ***Major annual events:*** College Night, Careerfest. ***Campus security:*** 24-hour patrols, late-night transport-escort service.
HOUSING College housing not available.
ATHLETICS Member NJCAA. ***Intercollegiate:*** baseball M, basketball M(s)/W(s), cross-country running M(s)/W(s), golf M(s), soccer M(s), softball W(s), tennis M(s)/W(s), volleyball W(s), wrestling M(s). ***Intramural:*** basketball, bowling, table tennis (Ping-Pong), volleyball. ***Contact:*** Mr. David L. Randall, Athletic Manager, 603-466-7900.
CAREER PLANNING ***Placement office:*** 8 full-time, 11 part-time staff; $34,522 operating expenditure 1994–95. ***Director:*** Mr. Robert W. Baker, Dean of Student Development, 603-466-7900 Ext. 2375. ***Services:*** job fairs, resume preparation, resume referral, career counseling, careers library, job bank, job interviews.
AFTER GRADUATION 85% of students completing a degree program in 1994–95 went directly on to further study.
EXPENSES FOR 1996–97 ***Application fee:*** $10. Area resident tuition: $1248 full-time, $39 per semester hour part-time. State resident tuition: $6048 full-time, $189 per semester hour part-time. Nonresident tuition: $7014 full-time, $219.18 per semester hour part-time. Part-time mandatory fees: $2 per semester. Full-time mandatory fees: $28.
FINANCIAL AID ***College-administered undergrad aid 1995–96:*** 700 need-based scholarships (average $600), 120 non-need scholarships (average $250), Federal Work-Study, 110 part-time jobs. ***Required forms:*** state, institutional; accepted: CSS Financial Aid PROFILE, FAFSA. ***Priority deadline:*** 7/1. ***Payment plan:*** deferred payment. ***Waivers:*** full or partial for employees or children of employees and senior citizens.

APPLYING Open admission except for nursing, respiratory therapy, interpreter training, auto body, nurse assistant programs. *Options:* early entrance, deferred entrance, midyear entrance. *Required:* TOEFL for international students. *Recommended:* school transcript, ACT. *Required for some:* essay, 3 years of high school math and science, some high school foreign language. Test scores used for counseling/placement. *Application deadline:* rolling. Preference given to district residents.

APPLYING/TRANSFER *Recommended:* standardized test scores, high school transcript. *Required for some:* essay, college transcript. *Entrance:* noncompetitive. *Application deadline:* rolling. *Contact:* Ms. Carol Alfrey, Manager of Student Development Grants, 603-466-7900.

CONTACT Office of Admissions and Records, Waubonsee Community College, Sugar Grove, IL 60554-9799, 603-466-7900 Ext. 2232. *Fax:* 603-466-4964.

WILLIAM RAINEY HARPER COLLEGE
Palatine, Illinois

UG Enrollment: 13,744	Tuition & Fees (Area Res): $1310
Application Deadline: rolling	Room & Board: N/Avail

GENERAL State and locally supported, 2-year, coed. Part of Illinois Community College System. Awards certificates, transfer associate, terminal associate degrees. Founded 1965. *Setting:* 200-acre suburban campus with easy access to Chicago. *Research spending 1994–95:* $208,565. *Educational spending 1994–95:* $2650 per undergrad. *Total enrollment:* 13,744. *Faculty:* 1,018 (218 full-time, 20% with terminal degrees, 800 part-time). *Notable Alumni:* Rheinhold Weege, television writer and producer; John Loprieno, actor; Rosemary Mulligan, state representative.

ENROLLMENT PROFILE 13,744 students: 58% women, 69% part-time, 99% state residents, 34% transferred in, 1% international, 49% 25 or older, 0% Native American, 6% Hispanic, 3% African American, 9% Asian American. *Areas of study chosen:* 41% liberal arts/general studies, 13% business management and administrative services, 10% health professions and related sciences, 8% education, 7% engineering and applied sciences, 6% computer and information sciences, 3% physical sciences, 3% social sciences, 2% biological and life sciences, 2% vocational and home economics, 1% agriculture, 1% architecture, 1% fine arts, 1% foreign language and literature, 1% performing arts.

FIRST-YEAR CLASS 4,080 total; 4,802 applied, 100% were accepted, 85% of whom enrolled. 34% from top quarter of their high school class, 50% from top half.

ACADEMIC PROGRAM Core, transfer and career training curriculum, honor code. Calendar: semesters. 1,557 courses offered in 1995–96. Academic remediation for entering students, English as a second language program offered during academic year and summer, services for LD students, advanced placement, honors program, summer session for credit, part-time degree program (daytime, evenings, weekends, summer); adult/continuing education programs, co-op programs and internships. Study abroad in England, Austria, Mexico, the Netherlands (1% of students participate).

GENERAL DEGREE REQUIREMENTS 60 semester hours; internship (some majors).

MAJORS Accounting, architectural technologies, art/fine arts, biology/biological sciences, business administration/commerce/management, child care/child and family studies, computer information systems, computer management, computer programming, computer science, computer technologies, criminal justice, culinary arts, data processing, deaf interpreter training, dental services, dietetics, drafting and design, early childhood education, electrical and electronics technologies, electronics engineering technology, engineering and applied sciences, (pre)engineering sequence, fashion design and technology, fashion merchandising, finance/banking, fire science, food services management, health education, heating/refrigeration/air conditioning, horticulture, hospitality services, humanities, information science, insurance, interior design, international business, journalism, landscape architecture/design, landscaping/grounds maintenance, law enforcement/police sciences, legal secretarial studies, liberal arts/general studies, machine and tool technologies, management information systems, manufacturing technology, marketing/retailing/merchandising, materials sciences, mathematics, mechanical design technology, mechanical engineering technology, medical assistant technologies, medical secretarial studies, music, nursing, paralegal studies, parks management, pharmacy/pharmaceutical sciences, physical education, physical fitness/exercise science, physical sciences, practical nursing, purchasing/inventory management, real estate, rehabilitation therapy, science, secretarial studies/office management, social science, word processing.

LIBRARY Harper College Library with 111,109 books, 449 microform titles, 831 periodicals, 4 on-line bibliographic services, 4,512 records, tapes, and CDs. Acquisition spending 1994–95: $290,791.

COMPUTERS ON CAMPUS Computer purchase plan available. 800 computers for student use in computer center, computer labs, learning resource center, classrooms, library provide access to main academic computer. Staffed computer lab on campus provides training in use of computers, software. Academic computing expenditure 1994–95: $2.9 million.

COLLEGE LIFE Orientation program (2 days, no cost, parents included). Drama-theater group, choral group, student-run newspaper, radio station. 5% vote in student government elections. *Social organizations:* 48 open to all. *Most popular organizations:* Student Radio Station, Program Board, Student Senate, Nursing Club, Harper's Bazaar. *Major annual events:* Intercultural Week, Wellness Week, Summer Family Series. *Student services:* legal services, health clinic, personal-psychological counseling, women's center. *Campus security:* 24-hour emergency response devices and patrols, late-night transport-escort service.

HOUSING College housing not available.

ATHLETICS Member NJCAA. *Intercollegiate:* baseball M, basketball M/W, cross-country running M/W, football M, golf M, soccer M, softball W, swimming and diving M/W, tennis M/W, track and field M/W, volleyball W, wrestling M. *Intramural:* badminton, basketball, field hockey, football, racquetball, skiing (cross-country), skiing (downhill), soccer, swimming and diving, table tennis (Ping-Pong), tennis, volleyball. *Contact:* Mr. Roger Bechtold, Athletic Coordinator, 847-925-6000; Ms. Martha Lynn Bolt, Assistant Athletic Coordinator, 847-925-6000.

CAREER PLANNING *Placement office:* 8 full-time, 2 part-time staff; $64,470 operating expenditure 1994–95. *Director:* Mr. Russ Mills, Director of Student Support Services, 847-925-6220. *Services:* job fairs, resume preparation, resume referral, career counseling, careers library, job bank, job interviews.

AFTER GRADUATION 67% of students completing a degree program in 1994–95 went directly on to further study.

EXPENSES FOR 1996-97 *Application fee:* $15. Area resident tuition: $1260 full-time, $42 per semester hour part-time. State resident tuition: $5686 full-time, $189.53 per semester hour part-time. Nonresident tuition: $6547 full-time, $218.24 per semester hour part-time. Part-time mandatory fees: $25 per year. Full-time mandatory fees: $50.

FINANCIAL AID *College-administered undergrad aid 1995–96:* 171 need-based scholarships, 83 non-need scholarships, short-term loans (average $300), low-interest long-term loans from external sources (average $2470), 109 Federal Work-Study (averaging $2202), 500 part-time jobs. *Required forms:* institutional, FAFSA. *Priority deadline:* 5/1. *Waivers:* full or partial for employees or children of employees and senior citizens. *Notification:* 7/1. *Average indebtedness of graduates:* $5300.

APPLYING Open admission. *Options:* early entrance, deferred entrance, midyear entrance. *Required:* school transcript, TOEFL for international students. *Required for some:* minimum 2.0 GPA, SAT I or ACT. Test scores used for counseling/placement. *Application deadline:* rolling. *Notification:* continuous.

APPLYING/TRANSFER *Required for some:* college transcript, minimum 2.0 high school GPA. *Entrance:* noncompetitive. *Application deadline:* rolling. *Notification:* continuous. *Contact:* Ms. Sheryl Otto, Transfer Coordinator, 847-925-6522.

CONTACT Ms. Amy Hauenstein, Admissions Outreach Coordinator, William Rainey Harper College, Palatine, IL 60067-7398, 847-397-3000 Ext. 6247. *E-mail:* info@harper.cc.il.us.

WRIGHT COLLEGE
Illinois—See City Colleges of Chicago, Wilbur Wright College

Indiana

INDIANA

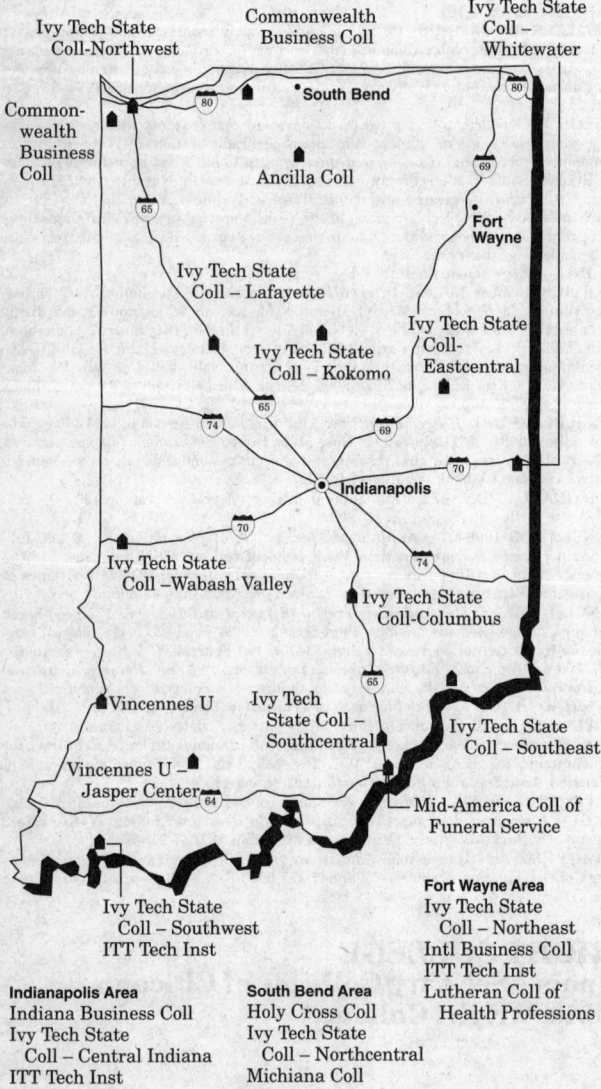

Ivy Tech State Coll-Northwest
Commonwealth Business Coll
Ivy Tech State Coll – Whitewater
South Bend
Commonwealth Business Coll
Ancilla Coll
Fort Wayne
Ivy Tech State Coll – Lafayette
Ivy Tech State Coll – Kokomo
Ivy Tech State Coll-Eastcentral
Indianapolis
Ivy Tech State Coll –Wabash Valley
Ivy Tech State Coll-Columbus
Vincennes U
Ivy Tech State Coll – Southcentral
Ivy Tech State Coll – Southeast
Vincennes U – Jasper Center
Mid-America Coll of Funeral Service

Fort Wayne Area
Ivy Tech State Coll – Northeast
Intl Business Coll
ITT Tech Inst
Lutheran Coll of Health Professions

Ivy Tech State Coll – Southwest
ITT Tech Inst

Indianapolis Area
Indiana Business Coll
Ivy Tech State Coll – Central Indiana
ITT Tech Inst
Lincoln Tech Inst

South Bend Area
Holy Cross Coll
Ivy Tech State Coll – Northcentral
Michiana Coll

ANCILLA COLLEGE
Donaldson, Indiana

UG Enrollment: 709	Tuition & Fees: $3160
Application Deadline: rolling	Room & Board: N/Avail

GENERAL Independent Roman Catholic, 2-year, coed. Awards certificates, transfer associate, terminal associate degrees. Founded 1937. *Setting:* 63-acre rural campus with easy access to Chicago. *Endowment:* $403,501. *Educational spending 1994–95:* $962 per undergrad. *Total enrollment:* 709. *Faculty:* 35 (12 full-time, 16% with terminal degrees, 23 part-time); student-faculty ratio is 20:1. *Notable Alumni:* Holly Shorter-Pifer, attorney; Margo DeMont, director of Leighton Center; Larry Faulstich, banker; Dan Weaver, entrepreneur.
ENROLLMENT PROFILE 709 students from 2 states and territories, 1 other country. 70% women, 30% men, 63% part-time, 98% state residents, 20% transferred in, 1% international, 58% 25 or older, 0% Native American, 1% Hispanic, 1% African American, 1% Asian American. *Areas of study chosen:* 26% business management and administrative services, 17% health professions and related sciences, 9% education, 5% social sciences, 4% computer and information sciences, 3% biological and life sciences, 1% English language/literature/letters, 1% fine arts, 1% liberal arts/general studies. *Most popular recent majors:* business administration/commerce/management, nursing, education.
FIRST-YEAR CLASS 287 total. Of the students who applied, 100% were accepted, 86% of whom enrolled. 10% from top 10% of their high school class, 45% from top quarter, 75% from top half.
ACADEMIC PROGRAM Core, interdisciplinary curriculum, honor code. Calendar: semesters. Academic remediation for entering students, self-designed majors, summer session for credit, part-time degree program (daytime, evenings, weekends, summer), adult/continuing education programs, co-op programs.
GENERAL DEGREE REQUIREMENT 60 semester hours.

MAJORS Business administration/commerce/management, computer science, criminal justice, education, liberal arts/general studies, nursing, secretarial studies/office management.
LIBRARY Ball Library with 27,274 books, 108 microform titles, 218 periodicals, 1 CD-ROM, 3,410 records, tapes, and CDs. Acquisition spending 1994–95: $13,520.
COMPUTERS ON CAMPUS 20 computers for student use in computer center. Staffed computer lab on campus. Academic computing expenditure 1994–95: $66,641.
COLLEGE LIFE Choral group. 40% vote in student government elections. *Social organizations:* 1 open to all. *Most popular organizations:* Student Senate, Scripta Literary Magazine. *Major annual event:* Homecoming. *Campus security:* 24-hour patrols, late-night transport-escort service.
HOUSING College housing not available.
ATHLETICS *Intercollegiate:* basketball M(s)/W(s), cross-country running M(s), golf M(s)/W(s), soccer M(s)/W(s), tennis M(s)/W. *Intramural:* basketball, golf, tennis. *Contact:* Mr. Gene Reese, Athletic Coordinator, 219-936-8898.
CAREER PLANNING *Placement office:* $41,357 operating expenditure 1994–95. *Service:* career counseling.
AFTER GRADUATION 60% of students completing a degree program in 1994–95 went directly on to further study.
EXPENSES FOR 1995–96 *Application fee:* $25. Tuition: $3080 full-time, $99 per semester hour part-time. Part-time mandatory fees: $45 per semester. Full-time mandatory fees: $80.
FINANCIAL AID *College-administered undergrad aid 1995–96:* 30 need-based scholarships (averaging $300), 8 non-need scholarships (averaging $200), short-term loans (averaging $400), low-interest long-term loans from external sources (averaging $1200), Federal Work-Study, 2 part-time jobs. *Required forms:* institutional, FAFSA; required for some: CSS Financial Aid PROFILE. *Priority deadline:* 5/1. *Payment plan:* deferred payment. *Waivers:* full or partial for employees or children of employees.
APPLYING Open admission. *Options:* early entrance, deferred entrance, midyear entrance. *Required for some:* school transcript, SAT I or ACT. Test scores used for counseling/placement. *Application deadline:* rolling.
APPLYING/TRANSFER *Required for some:* college transcript. *Entrance:* noncompetitive. *Application deadline:* rolling. *Contact:* Ms. Sarah Robinson, Director of Student Services, 219-936-8898.
CONTACT Ms. Kathryn Castle, Director of Admissions and Financial Aid, Ancilla College, Donaldson, IN 46513, 219-936-8898. *Fax:* 219-935-1785. College video available.

COMMONWEALTH BUSINESS COLLEGE
LaPorte, Indiana

UG Enrollment: 115	Tuition & Fees: $4680
Application Deadline: rolling	Room & Board: N/Avail

GENERAL Proprietary, 2-year, coed. Part of Commonwealth Business College, Inc. Awards certificates, diplomas, transfer associate, terminal associate degrees. Founded 1890. *Setting:* 2-acre rural campus with easy access to Chicago. *Total enrollment:* 115. *Faculty:* 11 (3 full-time, 8 part-time); student-faculty ratio is 15:1. *Notable Alumni:* Anita Way, Carol Couch, Mari Bailey, Virginia Hartog, Riki Starnes.
ENROLLMENT PROFILE 115 students from 2 states and territories. 96% women, 59% part-time, 96% state residents, 3% transferred in, 0% international, 44% 25 or older, 0% Native American, 2% Hispanic, 10% African American, 0% Asian American.
FIRST-YEAR CLASS 40 total. Of the students who applied, 85% were accepted, 95% of whom enrolled. 3% from top 10% of their high school class, 22% from top quarter, 75% from top half.
ACADEMIC PROGRAM Core, honor code. Calendar: quarters. Advanced placement, self-designed majors, tutorials, summer session for credit, part-time degree program (daytime, evenings), adult/continuing education programs, internships.
GENERAL DEGREE REQUIREMENTS 85 credits; computer course; internship (some majors).
MAJORS Accounting, business administration/commerce/management, legal secretarial studies, medical assistant technologies, medical secretarial studies, secretarial studies/office management, word processing.
COMPUTERS ON CAMPUS 12 computers for student use in computer labs. Staffed computer lab on campus provides training in use of computers, software.
COLLEGE LIFE Student-run newspaper. 75% vote in student government elections. *Social organizations:* 1 local fraternity, 1 local sorority. *Campus security:* 24-hour emergency response devices.
HOUSING College housing not available.
CAREER PLANNING *Service:* career counseling. Students must register sophomore year.
EXPENSES FOR 1996–97 *Application fee:* $25. Tuition: $4680 full-time, $390 per course part-time.
FINANCIAL AID *College-administered undergrad aid 1995–96:* short-term loans, low-interest long-term loans from external sources. *Required forms:* institutional, FAFSA. *Priority deadline:* 9/1. *Payment plan:* installment. *Waivers:* full or partial for employees or children of employees.
APPLYING *Options:* early entrance, deferred entrance. *Required:* school transcript, ABLE, Wonderlic aptitude test. Test scores used for counseling/placement. *Application deadline:* rolling. *Notification:* continuous.
APPLYING/TRANSFER *Required:* high school transcript, college transcript. *Entrance:* minimally difficult. *Application deadline:* rolling. *Notification:* continuous.
CONTACT Mr. Richard Singer, Director of Admissions, Commonwealth Business College, LaPorte, IN 46350, 219-362-3643. *Fax:* 219-324-0112. College video available.

COMMONWEALTH BUSINESS COLLEGE
Merrillville, Indiana

UG Enrollment: 180	Tuition & Fees: $4680
Application Deadline: rolling	Room & Board: N/Avail

GENERAL Proprietary, 2-year, coed. Part of Commonwealth Business College, Inc. Awards certificates, diplomas, terminal associate degrees. Founded 1890. *Setting:* 2-acre small-town campus with easy access to Chicago. *Total enrollment:* 180. *Faculty:* 12 (3 full-time, 9 part-time).

ENROLLMENT PROFILE 180 students: 90% women, 19% part-time, 98% state residents, 15% transferred in, 0% international, 40% 25 or older, 0% Native American, 10% Hispanic, 19% African American, 0% Asian American.
FIRST-YEAR CLASS 50 total. Of the students accepted, 98% enrolled.
ACADEMIC PROGRAM Core. Calendar: quarters. Self-designed majors, summer session for credit, part-time degree program (daytime, evenings), adult/continuing education programs, internships.
GENERAL DEGREE REQUIREMENTS 85 credits; internship (some majors).
MAJORS Accounting, business administration/commerce/management, computer science, fashion merchandising, legal secretarial studies, medical assistant technologies, medical secretarial studies, paralegal studies, secretarial studies/office management.
COMPUTERS ON CAMPUS 15 computers for student use in computer labs provide access to main academic computer. Staffed computer lab on campus provides training in use of computers, software.
COLLEGE LIFE ***Campus security:*** 24-hour emergency response devices.
HOUSING College housing not available.
CAREER PLANNING ***Director:*** Ms. Laura Smith, Placement Director, 219-769-3321. ***Services:*** job fairs, resume preparation, resume referral, career counseling, job bank, job interviews. Students must register freshman year.
EXPENSES FOR 1996–97 ***Application fee:*** $25. Tuition: $4680 full-time, $390 per course part-time.
FINANCIAL AID ***College-administered undergrad aid 1995–96:*** low-interest long-term loans from external sources. ***Required forms:*** FAFSA. ***Priority deadline:*** 9/1. ***Payment plan:*** installment. ***Waivers:*** full or partial for employees or children of employees.
APPLYING ***Options:*** Common Application, early entrance, deferred entrance, midyear entrance. ***Required:*** school transcript, Wonderlic aptitude test, ABLE. Test scores used for admission. ***Application deadline:*** rolling. ***Notification:*** continuous.
APPLYING/TRANSFER ***Required:*** college transcript. ***Entrance:*** minimally difficult. ***Application deadline:*** rolling. ***Notification:*** continuous.
CONTACT Ms. Anne Scharff, Director of Admissions, Commonwealth Business College, Merrillville, IN 46410, 309-762-2100. ***Fax:*** 219-738-1076.

HOLY CROSS COLLEGE
Notre Dame, Indiana

UG Enrollment: 445	**Tuition & Fees: $6450**
Application Deadline: rolling	**Room & Board: N/Avail**

Holy Cross College is a small, private, nonresidential college offering a strong liberal arts / business transfer curriculum. It features small classes, personal attention, and a caring, accessible faculty. Located adjacent to the University of Notre Dame and Saint Mary's College. Credits earned are transferable to these and other 4-year institutions nationwide. Remarkably diverse student body representing up to 27 states and several other countries.

GENERAL Independent Roman Catholic, 2-year, coed. Awards transfer associate degrees. Founded 1966. ***Setting:*** 150-acre urban campus. ***Total enrollment:*** 445. ***Faculty:*** 32 (20 full-time, 12 part-time); student-faculty ratio is 13:1.
ENROLLMENT PROFILE 445 students from 27 states and territories, 3 other countries. 42% women, 58% men, 9% part-time, 70% state residents, 12% transferred in, 50% have need-based financial aid, 3% international, 6% 25 or older, 0% Native American, 1% Hispanic, 5% African American, 1% Asian American.
FIRST-YEAR CLASS 202 total; 400 applied, 96% were accepted, 52% of whom enrolled. 5% from top 10% of their high school class, 10% from top quarter, 50% from top half.
ACADEMIC PROGRAM Core. Calendar: semesters. Academic remediation for entering students, advanced placement, summer session for credit, part-time degree program (daytime, evenings). Off-campus study at members of the Northern Indiana Consortium for Education. ROTC: Army (c), Air Force (c).
GENERAL DEGREE REQUIREMENTS 61 semester hours; 1 course each in math and science.
MAJOR Liberal arts/general studies.
LIBRARY 14,000 books, 150 periodicals.
COMPUTERS ON CAMPUS 32 computers for student use in computer center, computer labs, library. Staffed computer lab on campus provides training in use of computers, software.
COLLEGE LIFE Student-run newspaper. ***Most popular organizations:*** Student Advisory Committee, Campus Ministry, Volunteers in Support of Admissions. ***Major annual events:*** Campus Open House, All College Picnic, Opening Mass. ***Student services:*** personal-psychological counseling.
HOUSING College housing not available.
ATHLETICS ***Intramural:*** basketball, football, volleyball.
CAREER PLANNING ***Service:*** career counseling.
AFTER GRADUATION 85% of students completing a degree program in 1994–95 went directly on to further study.
EXPENSES FOR 1996–97 ***Application fee:*** $30. Tuition: $6400 full-time, $215 per semester hour part-time. Part-time mandatory fees: $50 per year. Full-time mandatory fees: $50.
FINANCIAL AID ***College-administered undergrad aid 1995–96:*** 40 need-based scholarships (average $300), low-interest long-term loans from external sources (average $2300), Federal Work-Study, 2 part-time jobs. ***Required forms:*** institutional, FAFSA; required for some: state; accepted: CSS Financial Aid PROFILE. ***Priority deadline:*** 3/1. ***Payment plan:*** installment. ***Waivers:*** full or partial for employees or children of employees.
APPLYING ***Options:*** deferred entrance, midyear entrance. ***Required:*** essay, school transcript, minimum 2.0 GPA, SAT I or ACT. ***Recommended:*** 3 years of high school math and science, some high school foreign language, campus interview, TOEFL for international students. Test scores used for admission and counseling/placement. ***Application deadline:*** rolling.
APPLYING/TRANSFER ***Required:*** essay, standardized test scores, high school transcript, college transcript, minimum 2.0 college GPA, minimum 2.0 high school GPA. ***Recommended:*** 3 years of high school math and science, some high school foreign language, campus interview. ***Entrance:*** minimally difficult. ***Application deadline:*** rolling.
CONTACT Mr. Vincent M. Duke, Director of Admissions, Holy Cross College, PO Box 308, Notre Dame, IN 46556-0308, 219-233-6813 Ext. 483. ***E-mail:*** hccadmis@gnn.com. College video available.

INDIANA BUSINESS COLLEGE
Indianapolis, Indiana

UG Enrollment: 1,700	**Tuition & Fees: $5685**
Application Deadline: rolling	**Room & Board: N/Avail**

GENERAL Proprietary, 2-year, coed. Awards transfer associate, terminal associate degrees. Founded 1902. ***Setting:*** 1-acre urban campus. ***Total enrollment:*** 1,700. ***Faculty:*** 70; student-faculty ratio is 20:1.
ENROLLMENT PROFILE 1,700 students: 75% women, 25% part-time, 98% state residents, 1% transferred in, 35% 25 or older, 12% African American.
FIRST-YEAR CLASS 800 total. Of the students who applied, 95% were accepted, 80% of whom enrolled. 10% from top 10% of their high school class, 20% from top quarter, 45% from top half.
ACADEMIC PROGRAM Honor code. Calendar: quarters. Summer session for credit, part-time degree program (daytime, evenings), adult/continuing education programs, co-op programs and internships.
GENERAL DEGREE REQUIREMENTS 99 quarter credit hours; computer course.
MAJORS Accounting, business administration/commerce/management, fashion merchandising, hospitality services, hotel and restaurant management, legal secretarial studies, medical assistant technologies, medical records services, medical secretarial studies, secretarial studies/office management, tourism and travel.
COMPUTERS ON CAMPUS Computers for student use in computer labs. Staffed computer lab on campus provides training in use of computers, software.
COLLEGE LIFE ***Student services:*** personal-psychological counseling. ***Campus security:*** 24-hour patrols.
HOUSING College housing not available.
CAREER PLANNING ***Service:*** career counseling. 100 organizations recruited on campus 1994–95.
AFTER GRADUATION 93% of class of 1994 had job offers within 6 months.
EXPENSES FOR 1996–97 ***Application fee:*** $30. Tuition: $5685 full-time, $99 per credit hour part-time.
FINANCIAL AID ***College-administered undergrad aid 1995–96:*** need-based scholarships, non-need scholarships, low-interest long-term loans from external sources, Federal Work-Study, part-time jobs. ***Acceptable forms:*** CSS Financial Aid PROFILE, state, institutional, FAFSA. ***Priority deadline:*** 9/1. ***Payment plan:*** installment.
APPLYING ***Option:*** deferred entrance. ***Required:*** school transcript, minimum 2.0 GPA, interview. ***Application deadline:*** rolling. ***Notification:*** continuous.
APPLYING/TRANSFER ***Required:*** high school transcript, interview, college transcript, minimum 2.0 college GPA, minimum 2.0 high school GPA. ***Entrance:*** minimally difficult. ***Application deadline:*** rolling. ***Notification:*** continuous.
CONTACT Mr. Joseph H. Davis, Vice President of Marketing, Indiana Business College, 802 North Meridian Street, Indianapolis, IN 46204-1108, 317-264-5656 or toll-free 800-999-9229. College video available.

❖ ***See page 746 for a narrative description.*** ❖

INDIANA VOCATIONAL TECHNICAL COLLEGES
Indiana—See Ivy Tech State Colleges

INTERNATIONAL BUSINESS COLLEGE
Fort Wayne, Indiana

UG Enrollment: 512	**Tuition: $13,405/deg prog**
Application Deadline: 8/31	**Room Only: $3040**

GENERAL Proprietary, 2-year, primarily women. Awards diplomas, terminal associate degrees. Founded 1889. ***Setting:*** 2-acre suburban campus. ***Total enrollment:*** 512. ***Faculty:*** 33 (9 full-time, 24 part-time); student-faculty ratio is 27:1.
ENROLLMENT PROFILE 512 students: 80% women, 29% part-time, 70% state residents, 5% transferred in, 1% international, 21% 25 or older, 1% Hispanic, 3% African American. ***Areas of study chosen:*** 71% business management and administrative services, 18% health professions and related sciences, 6% computer and information sciences.
FIRST-YEAR CLASS 400 total. Of the students who applied, 85% were accepted. 10% from top 10% of their high school class, 15% from top quarter, 75% from top half.
ACADEMIC PROGRAM Core. Calendar: modular for day division, semesters for evening division. Part-time degree program (evenings), adult/continuing education programs, co-op programs and internships.
GENERAL DEGREE REQUIREMENTS 1600 hours; computer course.
MAJORS Accounting, business administration/commerce/management, computer programming, computer technologies, finance/banking, graphic arts, industrial administration, paralegal studies, secretarial studies/office management.
LIBRARY 2,000 books, 100 periodicals, 300 records, tapes, and CDs.
COMPUTERS ON CAMPUS 150 computers for student use in computer center. Staffed computer lab on campus provides training in use of computers, software.
COLLEGE LIFE ***Social organizations:*** 3 open to all. ***Most popular organizations:*** Student Senate, Collegiate Secretarial Institute, Accounting Club. ***Campus security:*** controlled dormitory access.
HOUSING 170 college housing spaces available; all were occupied 1995–96. Off-campus living permitted.
CAREER PLANNING ***Services:*** job fairs, resume preparation, resume referral, career counseling, job interviews. Students must register freshman year.
EXPENSES FOR 1996–97 Tuition: $13,405 per degree program. College room only: $3040. Tuition guaranteed not to increase for student's term of enrollment.
FINANCIAL AID ***College-administered undergrad aid 1995–96:*** need-based scholarships, 10 non-need scholarships (average $500), low-interest long-term loans from college funds (average $1000), loans from external sources (average $2000), Federal Work-Study, part-time jobs. ***Required forms:*** institutional; required for some: FAFSA; accepted: CSS Financial Aid PROFILE. ***Priority deadline:*** 8/31.
APPLYING ***Option:*** deferred entrance. ***Required:*** school transcript. ***Application deadline:*** 8/31.
APPLYING/TRANSFER ***Required for some:*** college transcript.

Peterson's Guide to Two-Year Colleges 1997

309

International Business College (continued)
CONTACT Ms. Marianne Likens, Inside Admissions Manager, International Business College, Fort Wayne, IN 46804-1217, 219-432-8702.

ITT TECHNICAL INSTITUTE
Evansville, Indiana

UG Enrollment: 300	**Tuition: $15,429/deg prog**
Application Deadline: rolling	**Room & Board: N/Avail**

GENERAL Proprietary, 2-year, coed. Part of ITT Educational Services, Inc. Awards transfer associate, terminal associate degrees. Founded 1966. ***Setting:*** 5-acre urban campus. ***Total enrollment:*** 300. ***Faculty:*** 13 (12 full-time, 86% with terminal degrees, 1 part-time); student-faculty ratio is 23:1.
ENROLLMENT PROFILE 300 students from 3 states and territories, 1 other country. 10% women, 90% men, 0% part-time, 1% international, 20% 25 or older, 0% Native American, 0% Hispanic, 6% African American, 0% Asian American. ***Areas of study chosen:*** 100% engineering and applied sciences.
FIRST-YEAR CLASS 149 total; 340 applied, 44% were accepted, 100% of whom enrolled.
ACADEMIC PROGRAM Core, direct practical application curriculum, honor code. Calendar: quarters. Academic remediation for entering students, tutorials, summer session for credit.
GENERAL DEGREE REQUIREMENTS 108 credits; math/science requirements vary according to program; computer course.
MAJORS Electronics engineering technology, machine and tool technologies.
LIBRARY 1,400 books, 45 periodicals, 10 CD-ROMs, 90 records, tapes, and CDs.
COMPUTERS ON CAMPUS 81 computers for student use in learning resource center, classrooms.
COLLEGE LIFE ***Campus security:*** 24-hour emergency response devices, late-night transport-escort service.
HOUSING College housing not available.
CAREER PLANNING ***Placement office:*** 1 full-time, 1 part-time staff. ***Director:*** Ms. V. Conner, Director of Placement, 812-479-1441. ***Services:*** job fairs, resume preparation, resume referral, career counseling, careers library, job bank, job interviews. Students must register freshman year. 15 organizations recruited on campus 1994–95.
AFTER GRADUATION 52% of class of 1994 had job offers within 6 months. 10% of students completing a degree program went directly on to further study.
EXPENSES FOR 1995–96 ***Application fee:*** $100. Tuition: $15,429 per degree program. Tuition guaranteed not to increase for student's term of enrollment.
FINANCIAL AID ***College-administered undergrad aid 1995–96:*** need-based scholarships, low-interest long-term loans from external sources, Federal Work-Study, 2 part-time jobs. ***Required forms:*** institutional, FAFSA; accepted: CSS Financial Aid PROFILE, state. ***Priority deadline:*** 9/1. ***Payment plans:*** installment, deferred payment. ***Waivers:*** full or partial for employees or children of employees.
APPLYING ***Option:*** deferred entrance. ***Required:*** school transcript, CPAt. Test scores used for admission. ***Application deadline:*** rolling. ***Notification:*** continuous.
APPLYING/TRANSFER ***Application deadline:*** rolling. ***Notification:*** continuous. ***Contact:*** Mr. Joseph Sweeney, Director of Education, 812-479-1441.
CONTACT Mr. Ken Butler, Director, ITT Technical Institute, 5115 Oak Grove Road, Evansville, IN 47715-2340, 812-479-1441. College video available.

ITT TECHNICAL INSTITUTE
Fort Wayne, Indiana

UG Enrollment: 767	**Tuition: $15,429/deg prog**
Application Deadline: rolling	**Room & Board: N/Avail**

GENERAL Proprietary, primarily 2-year, coed. Part of ITT Educational Services, Inc. Awards terminal associate, bachelor's degrees. Founded 1967. ***Setting:*** 5-acre urban campus. ***Total enrollment:*** 767. ***Faculty:*** 31 (all full-time).
ENROLLMENT PROFILE 767 students. ***Most popular recent majors:*** electronics engineering technology, machine and tool technologies, robotics.
FIRST-YEAR CLASS 512 total; 1,320 applied.
ACADEMIC PROGRAM Core. Calendar: quarters. Tutorials, summer session for credit.
GENERAL DEGREE REQUIREMENTS 110 quarter hour credits for associate, 180 quarter hour credits for bachelor's.
MAJORS Architectural technologies, automotive technologies, electronics engineering technology, industrial design (B), machine and tool technologies, robotics (B).
LIBRARY 4,521 books, 34 periodicals, 10 CD-ROMs, 162 records, tapes, and CDs.
COMPUTERS ON CAMPUS 109 computers for student use in computer labs, learning resource center, classrooms, student rooms.
HOUSING College housing not available.
CAREER PLANNING ***Placement office:*** 3 full-time, 1 part-time staff. ***Director:*** Ms. Phyllis Patton, Director of Placement, 219-484-4107. ***Services:*** job fairs, resume preparation, resume referral, career counseling, careers library, job bank, job interviews. 37 organizations recruited on campus 1994–95.
AFTER GRADUATION 96% of class of 1994 had job offers within 6 months.
EXPENSES FOR 1995–96 Full-time tuition per degree program ranges up to $17,690 for associate, $25,800 to $31,645 for bac helor's. Full-time mandatory fees: $720. Tuition guaranteed not to increase for student's term of enrollment.
FINANCIAL AID ***College-administered undergrad aid 1995–96:*** need-based scholarships, low-interest long-term loans from external sources, Federal Work-Study. ***Required forms:*** institutional, FAFSA; accepted: CSS Financial Aid PROFILE. ***Priority deadline:*** 9/6. ***Payment plan:*** installment. ***Waivers:*** full or partial for employees or children of employees.
APPLYING ***Option:*** deferred entrance. ***Required:*** CPAt. Test scores used for admission. ***Application deadline:*** rolling. ***Notification:*** continuous.
APPLYING/TRANSFER ***Entrance:*** minimally difficult. ***Application deadline:*** rolling. ***Notification:*** continuous. ***Contact:*** Mr. Willie Vaughn, Director of Education, 219-484-4107.
CONTACT Mr. John T. Hayes, Director of Recruitment, ITT Technical Institute, 4919 Coldwater Road, Fort Wayne, IN 46825-5532, 219-484-4107 Ext. 244 or toll-free 800-866-4488. College video available.

ITT TECHNICAL INSTITUTE
Indianapolis, Indiana

UG Enrollment: 860	**Tuition: $15,429/deg prog**
Application Deadline: rolling	**Room & Board: N/Avail**

GENERAL Proprietary, primarily 2-year, coed. Part of ITT Educational Services, Inc. Awards terminal associate, bachelor's degrees. Founded 1966. ***Setting:*** 10-acre suburban campus. ***Total enrollment:*** 860. ***Faculty:*** 42 (40 full-time, 2 part-time); student-faculty ratio is 22:1.
ENROLLMENT PROFILE 860 students: 20% women, 0% part-time, 85% state residents, 3% transferred in, 12% 25 or older, 2% Native American, 1% Hispanic, 15% African American, 3% Asian American. ***Most popular recent majors:*** electronics engineering technology, drafting and design.
FIRST-YEAR CLASS 526 total; 1,006 applied, 97% were accepted.
ACADEMIC PROGRAM Core. Calendar: quarters. 7 courses offered in 1995–96. Adult/continuing education programs, co-op programs and internships.
GENERAL DEGREE REQUIREMENTS 130 quarter hours for associate, 200 quarter hours for bachelor's; computer course for business, electronics engineering technology, automated manufacturing technology majors; internship (some majors).
MAJORS Architectural technologies, chemical engineering technology, computer graphics (B), drafting and design, electronics engineering technology (B), hospitality services (B), manufacturing technology (B), robotics (B).
LIBRARY 2,700 books, 18 periodicals, 35 records, tapes, and CDs.
COMPUTERS ON CAMPUS 110 computers for student use in labs, library.
COLLEGE LIFE ***Most popular organizations:*** Electronics Club, Architectural Club. ***Major annual event:*** Very Special Arts Day. ***Student services:*** personal-psychological counseling. ***Campus security:*** 24-hour emergency response devices.
HOUSING College housing not available.
ATHLETICS ***Intramural:*** basketball, bowling.
CAREER PLANNING ***Placement office:*** 3 full-time, 1 part-time staff. ***Director:*** Mr. Bill Kingery, Director of Placement, 317-875-8640. ***Service:*** career counseling. Students must register senior year.
EXPENSES FOR 1995–96 ***Application fee:*** $100. Tuition per degree program ranges from $15,429 to $17,690 for associate, $25,117 to $28,060 for bachelor's. Tuition guaranteed not to increase for student's term of enrollment.
FINANCIAL AID ***College-administered undergrad aid 1995–96:*** need-based scholarships, 12 non-need scholarships, low-interest long-term loans from external sources (average $2100), Federal Work-Study, 3 part-time jobs. ***Required forms:*** institutional, FAFSA; accepted: CSS Financial Aid PROFILE, state. ***Priority deadline:*** 9/1. ***Payment plan:*** installment. ***Waivers:*** full or partial for employees or children of employees.
APPLYING ***Option:*** deferred entrance. ***Required:*** TOEFL for international students, CPAt. Test scores used for admission. ***Application deadline:*** rolling. ***Notification:*** continuous.
APPLYING/TRANSFER ***Application deadline:*** rolling. ***Notification:*** continuous. ***Contact:*** Dr. David Cline, Director of Education, 317-875-8640.
CONTACT Mrs. Bunty Cantwell, Director of Recruitment, ITT Technical Institute, 9511 Angola Court, Indianapolis, IN 46268-1119, 317-875-8640 Ext. 240. ***Fax:*** 317-875-8641. College video available.

IVY TECH STATE COLLEGE–CENTRAL INDIANA
Indianapolis, Indiana

UG Enrollment: 5,428	**Tuition & Fees (IN Res): $1809**
Application Deadline: rolling	**Room & Board: N/Avail**

GENERAL State-supported, 2-year, coed. Part of Ivy Tech State College System. Awards transfer associate, terminal associate degrees. Founded 1963. ***Setting:*** 10-acre urban campus. ***System endowment:*** $1.2 million. ***Total enrollment:*** 5,428. ***Faculty:*** 326 (117 full-time, 209 part-time); student-faculty ratio is 17:1.
ENROLLMENT PROFILE 5,428 students: 55% women, 45% men, 79% part-time, 100% state residents, 3% transferred in, 64% 25 or older, 1% Native American, 1% Hispanic, 19% African American, 1% Asian American. ***Areas of study chosen:*** 34% engineering and applied sciences, 26% liberal arts/general studies, 16% business management and administrative services, 12% computer and information sciences, 12% health professions and related sciences. ***Most popular recent majors:*** nursing, paralegal studies, respiratory therapy.
FIRST-YEAR CLASS 1,645 total; 2,673 applied, 100% were accepted, 62% of whom enrolled.
ACADEMIC PROGRAM Core. Calendar: semesters. 554 courses offered in 1995–96. Academic remediation for entering students, English as a second language program offered during academic year and summer, services for LD students, advanced placement, summer session for credit, part-time degree program (daytime, evenings, summer), adult/continuing education programs, co-op programs. Off-campus study at Indiana University–Purdue University at Indianapolis, Butler University, Marian College, University of Indianapolis, Martin University, Franklin College.
GENERAL DEGREE REQUIREMENTS 60 credits; computer course (varies by major); internship (some majors).
MAJORS Accounting, architectural technologies, automotive technologies, business administration/commerce/management, child care/child and family studies, computer information systems, computer programming, criminal justice, culinary arts, drafting and design, electrical and electronics technologies, fire science, food services management, gerontology, heating/refrigeration/air conditioning, hospitality services, hotel and restaurant management, human services, industrial and heavy equipment maintenance, laboratory technologies, marketing/retailing/merchandising, mechanical design technology, medical assistant technologies, mental health/rehabilitation counseling, nursing, occupational therapy, operating room technology, paralegal studies, pollution control technologies, quality control technology, radiological technology, respiratory therapy, robotics, secretarial studies/office management.
LIBRARY 13,000 books, 367 periodicals, 8 CD-ROMs, 6,365 records, tapes, and CDs. System-wide acquisition spending 1994–95: $56,036.

COMPUTERS ON CAMPUS 120 computers for student use in computer center, computer labs, library provide access to main academic computer. Staffed computer lab on campus.
COLLEGE LIFE Student-run newspaper. ***Student services:*** personal-psychological counseling. ***Campus security:*** 24-hour patrols, late-night transport-escort service.
HOUSING College housing not available.
CAREER PLANNING ***Placement office:*** 3 full-time, 1 part-time staff. ***Director:*** Ms. Betty Beverly, Placement Manager, 317-921-4994. ***Services:*** resume preparation, resume referral, career counseling, job bank, job interviews.
ESTIMATED EXPENSES FOR 1996–97 State resident tuition: $1809 full-time, $60.30 per credit part-time. Nonresident tuition: $3293 full-time, $109.75 per credit part-time.
FINANCIAL AID ***College-administered undergrad aid 1995–96:*** 803 need-based scholarships (average $642), 30 non-need scholarships (average $493), low-interest long-term loans from external sources (average $2111), Federal Work-Study, part-time jobs. ***Required forms:*** institutional, FAFSA; accepted: CSS Financial Aid PROFILE. ***Application deadline:*** continuous. ***Waivers:*** full or partial for employees or children of employees.
APPLYING Open admission except for allied health programs. ***Options:*** early entrance, deferred entrance. ***Required:*** school transcript, TOEFL for international students, ACT ASSET. ***Application deadline:*** rolling. ***Notification:*** continuous. Preference given to state residents.
APPLYING/TRANSFER ***Required:*** standardized test scores, high school transcript. ***Entrance:*** noncompetitive. ***Application deadline:*** rolling. ***Notification:*** continuous. ***Contact:*** Ms. Sonia Dickerson, Enrollment Manager, 317-921-4612.
CONTACT Ms. Sonia Dickerson, Enrollment Manager, Ivy Tech State College–Central Indiana, 1 West 26th Street, PO Box 1763, Indianapolis, IN 46206-1763, 317-921-4612.

IVY TECH STATE COLLEGE–COLUMBUS
Columbus, Indiana

UG Enrollment: 2,849 | **Tuition & Fees (IN Res): $1809**
Application Deadline: rolling | **Room & Board: N/Avail**

GENERAL State-supported, 2-year, coed. Part of Ivy Tech State College System. Awards transfer associate, terminal associate degrees. Founded 1963. ***Setting:*** small-town campus with easy access to Indianapolis. ***System endowment:*** $1.2 million. ***Total enrollment:*** 2,849. ***Faculty:*** 200 (50 full-time, 150 part-time); student-faculty ratio is 14:1.
ENROLLMENT PROFILE 2,849 students: 60% women, 40% men, 74% part-time, 100% state residents, 12% transferred in, 0% international, 65% 25 or older, 1% Native American, 1% Hispanic, 2% African American, 1% Asian American. ***Areas of study chosen:*** 32% engineering and applied sciences, 23% business management and administrative services, 17% liberal arts/general studies, 15% health professions and related sciences, 13% communications and journalism. ***Most popular recent majors:*** nursing, electrical and electronics technologies, drafting and design.
FIRST-YEAR CLASS 650 total; 941 applied, 100% were accepted, 69% of whom enrolled.
ACADEMIC PROGRAM Core. Calendar: semesters. 462 courses offered in 1995–96. Academic remediation for entering students, English as a second language program offered during academic year and summer, services for LD students, summer session for credit, part-time degree program (daytime, evenings), adult/continuing education programs, internships.
GENERAL DEGREE REQUIREMENTS 60 credits; computer course (varies by major); internship (some majors).
MAJORS Accounting, architectural technologies, automotive technologies, business administration/commerce/management, commercial art, computer information systems, computer programming, drafting and design, electrical and electronics technologies, heating/refrigeration/air conditioning, industrial and heavy equipment maintenance, manufacturing technology, marketing/retailing/merchandising, mechanical design technology, medical assistant technologies, nursing, photography, quality control technology, robotics, secretarial studies/office management.
LIBRARY 5,480 books, 126 periodicals, 30 records, tapes, and CDs. System-wide acquisition spending 1994–95: $23,488.
COMPUTERS ON CAMPUS Computers for student use in computer center. Staffed computer lab on campus.
HOUSING College housing not available.
CAREER PLANNING ***Placement office:*** 1 full-time staff. ***Director:*** Ms. Brenda Hotopp, Placement Coordinator, 812-372-9925. ***Services:*** resume preparation, resume referral, career counseling, job bank, job interviews.
ESTIMATED EXPENSES FOR 1996–97 State resident tuition: $1809 full-time, $60.30 per credit part-time. Nonresident tuition: $3293 full-time, $109.75 per credit part-time.
FINANCIAL AID ***College-administered undergrad aid 1995–96:*** 540 need-based scholarships (average $763), 31 non-need scholarships (average $352), low-interest long-term loans from external sources (average $1882), Federal Work-Study, part-time jobs. ***Required forms:*** institutional, FAFSA; accepted: CSS Financial Aid PROFILE. ***Application deadline:*** continuous. ***Payment plans:*** installment, deferred payment. ***Waivers:*** full or partial for employees or children of employees.
APPLYING Open admission except for allied health programs. ***Options:*** early entrance, deferred entrance. ***Required:*** school transcript, TOEFL for international students, ACT ASSET. ***Application deadline:*** rolling. ***Notification:*** continuous. Preference given to state residents.
APPLYING/TRANSFER ***Required:*** standardized test scores, high school transcript. ***Entrance:*** noncompetitive. ***Application deadline:*** rolling. ***Notification:*** continuous. ***Contact:*** Ms. Lucinda Nord, Admissions Coordinator, 812-372-9925.
CONTACT Ms. Lucinda Nord, Admissions Coordinator, Ivy Tech State College–Columbus, Columbus, IN 47203-1868, 812-372-9925 or toll-free 800-922-4838 (in-state).

IVY TECH STATE COLLEGE–EASTCENTRAL
Muncie, Indiana

UG Enrollment: 2,140 | **Tuition & Fees (IN Res): $1809**
Application Deadline: rolling | **Room & Board: N/Avail**

GENERAL State-supported, 2-year, coed. Part of Ivy Tech State College System. Awards transfer associate, terminal associate degrees. Founded 1968. ***Setting:*** 15-acre suburban campus with easy access to Indianapolis. ***System endowment:*** $1.2 million. ***Total enrollment:*** 2,140. ***Faculty:*** 249 (42 full-time, 207 part-time); student-faculty ratio is 9:1.
ENROLLMENT PROFILE 2,140 students: 65% women, 35% men, 58% part-time, 100% state residents, 4% transferred in, 0% international, 60% 25 or older, 1% Native American, 1% Hispanic, 7% African American, 0% Asian American. ***Areas of study chosen:*** 31% health professions and related sciences, 29% engineering and applied sciences, 19% business management and administrative services, 11% computer and information sciences, 10% liberal arts/general studies. ***Most popular recent majors:*** medical assistant technologies, secretarial studies/office management, child care/child and family studies.
FIRST-YEAR CLASS 667 total; 1,030 applied, 100% were accepted, 65% of whom enrolled.
ACADEMIC PROGRAM Core. Calendar: semesters. 601 courses offered in 1995–96. Academic remediation for entering students, services for LD students, advanced placement, part-time degree program (daytime, evenings, summer), adult/continuing education programs, internships.
GENERAL DEGREE REQUIREMENTS 60 credits; computer course (varies by major); internship (some majors).
MAJORS Accounting, automotive technologies, biomedical technologies, business administration/commerce/management, carpentry, child care/child and family studies, computer information systems, computer programming, construction technologies, drafting and design, electrical and electronics technologies, gerontology, heating/refrigeration/air conditioning, human services, industrial administration, industrial and heavy equipment maintenance, machine and tool technologies, marketing/retailing/merchandising, medical assistant technologies, mental health/rehabilitation counseling, physical therapy, robotics, secretarial studies/office management.
LIBRARY 3,116 books, 62 periodicals. System-wide acquisition spending 1994–95: $46,415.
COMPUTERS ON CAMPUS Computers for student use in computer center. Staffed computer lab on campus.
HOUSING College housing not available.
CAREER PLANNING ***Placement office:*** 1 full-time staff. ***Director:*** Ms. Rudy Murray, Career Counselor, 317-289-2291. ***Services:*** resume preparation, resume referral, career counseling, job bank, job interviews.
ESTIMATED EXPENSES FOR 1996–97 State resident tuition: $1809 full-time, $60.30 per credit part-time. Nonresident tuition: $3293 full-time, $109.75 per credit part-time.
FINANCIAL AID ***College-administered undergrad aid 1995–96:*** 625 need-based scholarships (average $374), 10 non-need scholarships (average $263), short-term loans, low-interest long-term loans from external sources (average $2147), Federal Work-Study. ***Required forms:*** institutional; required for some: CSS Financial Aid PROFILE, state, FAFSA. ***Application deadline:*** continuous. ***Payment plan:*** installment. ***Waivers:*** full or partial for employees or children of employees.
APPLYING Open admission except for allied health programs. ***Options:*** early entrance, deferred entrance. ***Required:*** school transcript, TOEFL for international students, ACT ASSET. Test scores used for counseling/placement. ***Application deadline:*** rolling. Preference given to state residents.
APPLYING/TRANSFER ***Required:*** standardized test scores, high school transcript. ***Entrance:*** noncompetitive. ***Application deadline:*** rolling.
CONTACT Ms. Rudy Murray, Career Counselor, Ivy Tech State College–Eastcentral, Muncie, IN 47302-9448, 317-289-2291 Ext. 408.

IVY TECH STATE COLLEGE–KOKOMO
Kokomo, Indiana

UG Enrollment: 1,570 | **Tuition & Fees (IN Res): $1809**
Application Deadline: rolling | **Room & Board: N/Avail**

GENERAL State-supported, 2-year, coed. Part of Ivy Tech State College System. Awards transfer associate, terminal associate degrees. Founded 1968. ***Setting:*** 20-acre small-town campus with easy access to Indianapolis. ***System endowment:*** $1.2 million. ***Total enrollment:*** 1,570. ***Faculty:*** 141 (34 full-time, 107 part-time); student-faculty ratio is 11:1.
ENROLLMENT PROFILE 1,570 students: 61% women, 39% men, 76% part-time, 100% state residents, 1% transferred in, 66% 25 or older, 1% Native American, 2% Hispanic, 4% African American, 1% Asian American. ***Areas of study chosen:*** 30% engineering and applied sciences, 24% business management and administrative services, 19% computer and information sciences, 14% liberal arts/general studies, 13% health professions and related sciences. ***Most popular recent majors:*** secretarial studies/office management, computer information systems, medical assistant technologies.
FIRST-YEAR CLASS 515 total; 1,091 applied, 100% were accepted, 47% of whom enrolled.
ACADEMIC PROGRAM Core. Calendar: semesters. 358 courses offered in 1995–96. Academic remediation for entering students, services for LD students, advanced placement, summer session for credit, part-time degree program (daytime, evenings), adult/continuing education programs, co-op programs and internships.
GENERAL DEGREE REQUIREMENTS 60 credits; computer course (varies by major); internship (some majors).
MAJORS Accounting, architectural technologies, automotive technologies, business administration/commerce/management, carpentry, computer information systems, computer programming, construction technologies, drafting and design, electrical and electronics technologies, emergency medical technology, heating/refrigeration/air conditioning, industrial engineering technology, interior design, machine and tool technologies, manufacturing technology, marketing/retailing/merchandising, mechanical design technology, medical assistant technologies, physical therapy, quality control technology, robotics, secretarial studies/office management.
LIBRARY 3,473 books, 4 microform titles, 28 CD-ROMs, 597 records, tapes, and CDs. System-wide acquisition spending 1994–95: $24,795.
COMPUTERS ON CAMPUS 220 computers for student use in computer center, library. Staffed computer lab on campus.
COLLEGE LIFE ***Student services:*** personal-psychological counseling.
HOUSING College housing not available.
CAREER PLANNING ***Placement office:*** 1 full-time staff. ***Director:*** Ms. Mary Bennett, Career Services Coordinator, 317-459-0561. ***Services:*** job fairs, resume preparation, resume referral, career counseling, job bank, job interviews.

Ivy Tech State College–Kokomo (continued)
ESTIMATED EXPENSES FOR 1996–97 State resident tuition: $1809 full-time, $60.30 per credit part-time. Nonresident tuition: $3293 full-time, $109.75 per credit part-time.
FINANCIAL AID ***College-administered undergrad aid 1995–96:*** 286 need-based scholarships (average $368), 108 non-need scholarships (average $206), short-term loans (average $552), low-interest long-term loans from external sources (average $1954), 31 Federal Work-Study (averaging $1429), 5 part-time jobs. ***Required forms:*** institutional, FAFSA; accepted: CSS Financial Aid PROFILE. ***Waivers:*** full or partial for employees or children of employees.
APPLYING Open admission except for allied health programs. ***Option:*** early entrance. ***Required:*** school transcript, TOEFL for international students, ACT ASSET. Test scores used for counseling/placement. ***Application deadline:*** rolling. Preference given to state residents.
APPLYING/TRANSFER ***Required:*** standardized test scores, high school transcript. ***Entrance:*** noncompetitive. ***Application deadline:*** rolling. ***Contact:*** Ms. Judy Young, Enrollment Manager, 317-459-0561.
CONTACT Ms. Judy Young, Enrollment Manager, Ivy Tech State College–Kokomo, Kokomo, IN 46903-1373, 317-459-0561.

IVY TECH STATE COLLEGE–LAFAYETTE
Lafayette, Indiana

UG Enrollment: 2,187	**Tuition & Fees (IN Res): $1809**
Application Deadline: rolling	**Room & Board: N/Avail**

GENERAL State-supported, 2-year, coed. Part of Ivy Tech State College System. Awards certificates, transfer associate, terminal associate degrees. Founded 1968. ***Setting:*** suburban campus with easy access to Indianapolis. ***System endowment:*** $1.2 million. ***Total enrollment:*** 2,187. ***Faculty:*** 146 (40 full-time, 106 part-time); student-faculty ratio is 15:1.
ENROLLMENT PROFILE 2,187 students from 3 states and territories. 60% women, 40% men, 68% part-time, 99% state residents, 10% transferred in, 0% international, 51% 25 or older, 1% Native American, 1% Hispanic, 2% African American, 1% Asian American. ***Areas of study chosen:*** 28% engineering and applied sciences, 25% liberal arts/general studies, 21% business management and administrative services, 17% health professions and related sciences, 9% computer and information sciences. ***Most popular recent majors:*** nursing, accounting, secretarial studies/office management.
FIRST-YEAR CLASS 563 total; 908 applied, 100% were accepted, 62% of whom enrolled.
ACADEMIC PROGRAM Core. Calendar: semesters. 346 courses offered in 1995–96. Academic remediation for entering students, services for LD students, advanced placement, summer session for credit, part-time degree program (daytime, evenings, weekends, summer).
GENERAL DEGREE REQUIREMENTS 60 credits; computer course (varies by major); internship (some majors).
MAJORS Accounting, architectural technologies, automotive technologies, business administration/commerce/management, computer information systems, computer programming, drafting and design, electrical and electronics technologies, heating/refrigeration/air conditioning, industrial and heavy equipment maintenance, machine and tool technologies, manufacturing technology, marketing/retailing/merchandising, mechanical design technology, medical assistant technologies, nursing, operating room technology, quality control technology, respiratory therapy, robotics, secretarial studies/office management.
LIBRARY 7,060 books, 132 periodicals, 3 CD-ROMs, 2,066 records, tapes, and CDs. System-wide acquisition spending 1994–95: $30,331.
COMPUTERS ON CAMPUS 125 computers for student use in computer center. Staffed computer lab on campus.
COLLEGE LIFE Student-run newspaper. ***Student services:*** personal-psychological counseling.
HOUSING College housing not available.
CAREER PLANNING ***Placement office:*** 1 full-time staff. ***Director:*** Mr. Greg Bayer, Placement Coordinator, 317-772-9100. ***Services:*** resume preparation, resume referral, career counseling, job bank.
ESTIMATED EXPENSES FOR 1996–97 State resident tuition: $1809 full-time, $60.30 per credit part-time. Nonresident tuition: $3293 full-time, $109.75 per credit part-time.
FINANCIAL AID ***College-administered undergrad aid 1995–96:*** 279 need-based scholarships (averaging $389), 60 non-need scholarships (averaging $375), low-interest long-term loans from external sources (averaging $1958), 52 Federal Work-Study (averaging $1398). ***Required forms:*** institutional, FAFSA; accepted: CSS Financial Aid PROFILE. ***Payment plan:*** deferred payment. ***Waivers:*** full or partial for employees or children of employees, adult students, and senior citizens.
APPLYING Open admission except for allied health programs. ***Required:*** school transcript, TOEFL for international students, ACT ASSET. ***Application deadline:*** rolling. Preference given to state residents.
APPLYING/TRANSFER ***Required:*** standardized test scores, high school transcript. ***Entrance:*** noncompetitive. ***Contact:*** Ms. Judy Dopplefeld, Admissions Manager, 317-772-9116.
CONTACT Ms. Judy Dopplefeld, Admissions Manager, Ivy Tech State College–Lafayette, Lafayette, IN 47903-6299, 317-772-9116 or toll-free 800-699-IVTC (out-of-state).

IVY TECH STATE COLLEGE–NORTHCENTRAL
South Bend, Indiana

UG Enrollment: 2,787	**Tuition & Fees (IN Res): $1809**
Application Deadline: rolling	**Room & Board: N/Avail**

GENERAL State-supported, 2-year, coed. Part of Ivy Tech State College System. Awards certificates, transfer associate, terminal associate degrees. Founded 1968. ***Setting:*** 4-acre suburban campus. ***System endowment:*** $1.2 million. ***Total enrollment:*** 2,787. ***Faculty:*** 226 (57 full-time, 169 part-time); student-faculty ratio is 12:1.
ENROLLMENT PROFILE 2,787 students from 4 states and territories. 59% women, 41% men, 78% part-time, 97% state residents, 5% transferred in, 70% 25 or older, 1% Native American, 2% Hispanic, 10% African American, 1% Asian American. ***Areas of study chosen:*** 33% engineering and applied sciences, 20% business management and administrative services, 17% liberal arts/general studies, 16% computer and information sciences, 14% health professions and related sciences. ***Most popular recent majors:*** nursing, accounting, secretarial studies/office management.
FIRST-YEAR CLASS 885 total; 1,817 applied, 100% were accepted, 49% of whom enrolled.
ACADEMIC PROGRAM Core. Calendar: semesters. 712 courses offered in 1995–96. Academic remediation for entering students, services for LD students, advanced placement, summer session for credit, part-time degree program (daytime, evenings, summer), adult/continuing education programs, co-op programs. Off-campus study at members of the Northern Indiana Consortium for Education.
GENERAL DEGREE REQUIREMENTS 60 credits; computer course (varies by major); internship (some majors).
MAJORS Accounting, architectural technologies, automotive technologies, business administration/commerce/management, commercial art, communication, communication equipment technology, computer information systems, cosmetology, drafting and design, electrical and electronics technologies, heating/refrigeration/air conditioning, industrial and heavy equipment maintenance, interior design, machine and tool technologies, manufacturing technology, marketing/retailing/merchandising, mechanical design technology, medical assistant technologies, medical laboratory technology, nursing, photography, plastics technology, quality control technology, robotics, secretarial studies/office management.
LIBRARY 4,650 books, 215 periodicals, 2 CD-ROMs. Acquisition spending 1994–95: $57,430.
COMPUTERS ON CAMPUS 80 computers for student use in computer center, library. Staffed computer lab on campus.
COLLEGE LIFE ***Student services:*** personal-psychological counseling, women's center.
HOUSING College housing not available.
ATHLETICS ***Intramural:*** basketball, softball, volleyball.
CAREER PLANNING ***Placement office:*** 1 full-time staff. ***Director:*** Ms. Pam Decker, Placement Coordinator, 219-289-7001. ***Services:*** resume preparation, resume referral, career counseling, job bank, job interviews.
ESTIMATED EXPENSES FOR 1996–97 State resident tuition: $1809 full-time, $60.30 per credit part-time. Nonresident tuition: $3293 full-time, $109.75 per credit part-time.
FINANCIAL AID ***College-administered undergrad aid 1995–96:*** 575 need-based scholarships (averaging $236), 175 non-need scholarships (averaging $291), short-term loans (averaging $438), low-interest long-term loans from external sources (averaging $1743), 79 Federal Work-Study (averaging $1301), part-time jobs. ***Required forms:*** institutional, FAFSA; accepted: CSS Financial Aid PROFILE. ***Application deadline:*** continuous. ***Waivers:*** full or partial for employees or children of employees.
APPLYING Open admission except for allied health programs. ***Options:*** early entrance, deferred entrance. ***Required:*** school transcript, TOEFL for international students, CGP, ACT ASSET. Test scores used for counseling/placement. ***Application deadline:*** rolling. Preference given to state residents.
APPLYING/TRANSFER ***Required:*** standardized test scores, high school transcript. ***Entrance:*** noncompetitive. ***Application deadline:*** rolling. ***Contact:*** Mr. Ed Grams, Enrollment Manager, 219-289-7001.
CONTACT Ms. Joan Wagner, Student Services Secretary, Ivy Tech State College–Northcentral, South Bend, IN 46619-3837, 219-289-7001 Ext. 322.

IVY TECH STATE COLLEGE–NORTHEAST
Fort Wayne, Indiana

UG Enrollment: 3,411	**Tuition & Fees (IN Res): $1809**
Application Deadline: rolling	**Room & Board: N/Avail**

GENERAL State-supported, 2-year, coed. Part of Ivy Tech State College System. Awards certificates, transfer associate, terminal associate degrees. Founded 1969. ***Setting:*** 22-acre urban campus. ***System endowment:*** $1.2 million. ***Total enrollment:*** 3,411. ***Faculty:*** 280 (56 full-time, 224 part-time); student-faculty ratio is 12:1.
ENROLLMENT PROFILE 3,411 students from 5 states and territories. 58% women, 42% men, 76% part-time, 97% state residents, 3% transferred in, 63% 25 or older, 1% Native American, 1% Hispanic, 8% African American, 1% Asian American. ***Areas of study chosen:*** 32% engineering and applied sciences, 22% business management and administrative services, 22% health professions and related sciences, 16% liberal arts/general studies, 8% computer and information sciences. ***Most popular recent majors:*** medical assistant technologies, child care/child and family studies, accounting.
FIRST-YEAR CLASS 1,536 total; 2,385 applied, 100% were accepted, 64% of whom enrolled.
ACADEMIC PROGRAM Core. Calendar: semesters. 450 courses offered in 1995–96. Academic remediation for entering students, services for LD students, advanced placement, summer session for credit, part-time degree program (daytime, evenings, summer), adult/continuing education programs, internships.
GENERAL DEGREE REQUIREMENTS 60 credits; computer course (varies by major); internship (some majors).
MAJORS Accounting, architectural technologies, automotive technologies, business administration/commerce/management, carpentry, child care/child and family studies, computer information systems, construction technologies, culinary arts, data processing, drafting and design, electrical and electronics technologies, fire science, heating/refrigeration/air conditioning, hospitality services, industrial and heavy equipment maintenance, industrial design, machine and tool technologies, manufacturing technology, marketing/retailing/merchandising, mechanical design technology, medical assistant technologies, paralegal studies, physical therapy, quality control technology, respiratory therapy, robotics, secretarial studies/office management.
LIBRARY 4,958 books, 125 periodicals. System-wide acquisition spending 1994–95: $44,911.
COMPUTERS ON CAMPUS 158 computers for student use in computer center, computer labs, labs, library. Staffed computer lab on campus.
COLLEGE LIFE ***Campus security:*** late-night transport-escort service.
HOUSING College housing not available.
CAREER PLANNING ***Placement office:*** 1 full-time staff. ***Director:*** Mr. Merland Beyler, Placement Manager, 219-482-9171. ***Services:*** job fairs, resume preparation, resume referral, career counseling, job bank, job interviews.
ESTIMATED EXPENSES FOR 1996–97 State resident tuition: $1809 full-time, $60.30 per credit part-time. Nonresident tuition: $3293 full-time, $109.75 per credit part-time.

FINANCIAL AID *College-administered undergrad aid 1995–96:* 690 need-based scholarships (averaging $279), 103 non-need scholarships (averaging $319), low-interest long-term loans from college funds (averaging $297), loans from external sources (averaging $1882), 51 Federal Work-Study (averaging $1442). *Required forms:* institutional, FAFSA; accepted: CSS Financial Aid PROFILE. *Application deadline:* continuous. *Waivers:* full or partial for employees or children of employees.
APPLYING Open admission except for allied health programs. *Option:* early entrance. *Required:* school transcript, TOEFL for international students, ACT ASSET. Test scores used for counseling/placement. *Application deadline:* rolling. Preference given to state residents.
APPLYING/TRANSFER *Required:* standardized test scores, high school transcript. *Entrance:* noncompetitive. *Application deadline:* rolling. *Contact:* Mr. James Aschliman, Admissions Coordinator, 219-480-4211.
CONTACT Mr. James Aschliman, Admissions Coordinator, Ivy Tech State College–Northeast, 3800 North Anthony Boulevard, Fort Wayne, IN 46805-1430, 219-480-4211. College video available.

IVY TECH STATE COLLEGE–NORTHWEST
Gary, Indiana

UG Enrollment: 2,570	Tuition & Fees (IN Res): $1809
Application Deadline: rolling	Room & Board: N/Avail

GENERAL State-supported, 2-year, coed. Part of Ivy Tech State College System. Awards certificates, transfer associate, terminal associate degrees. Founded 1963. *Setting:* 13-acre urban campus with easy access to Chicago. *System endowment:* $1.2 million. *Total enrollment:* 2,570. *Faculty:* 221 (56 full-time, 165 part-time); student-faculty ratio is 12:1.
ENROLLMENT PROFILE 2,570 students from 4 states and territories. 58% women, 42% men, 65% part-time, 99% state residents, 10% transferred in, 56% 25 or older, 0% Native American, 13% Hispanic, 32% African American, 1% Asian American. *Areas of study chosen:* 30% engineering and applied sciences, 29% liberal arts/general studies, 18% business management and administrative services, 13% health professions and related sciences, 10% computer and information sciences. *Most popular recent majors:* computer information systems, business administration/commerce/management, electrical and electronics technologies.
FIRST-YEAR CLASS 716 total; 1,365 applied, 100% were accepted, 52% of whom enrolled.
ACADEMIC PROGRAM Core. Calendar: semesters. 639 courses offered in 1995–96. Academic remediation for entering students, English as a second language program offered during academic year and summer, services for LD students, advanced placement, summer session for credit, part-time degree program (daytime, evenings, summer), adult/continuing education programs, internships.
GENERAL DEGREE REQUIREMENTS 60 credits; computer course (varies by major); internship (some majors).
MAJORS Accounting, automotive technologies, business administration/commerce/management, computer information systems, computer programming, culinary arts, drafting and design, electrical and electronics technologies, fire science, heating/refrigeration/air conditioning, hospitality services, industrial and heavy equipment maintenance, industrial engineering technology, machine and tool technologies, manufacturing technology, marketing/retailing/merchandising, mechanical design technology, medical assistant technologies, nursing, operating room technology, physical therapy, pollution control technologies, respiratory therapy, robotics, safety and security technologies, secretarial studies/office management.
COMPUTERS ON CAMPUS 150 computers for student use in computer center. Staffed computer lab on campus.
COLLEGE LIFE Orientation program (2 days, no cost).
HOUSING College housing not available.
ATHLETICS *Intramural:* basketball, softball.
CAREER PLANNING *Placement office:* 1 full-time staff. *Director:* Mr. Fred Jackson, Counselor, 219-981-1111. *Services:* resume preparation, resume referral, career counseling, job bank, job interviews.
ESTIMATED EXPENSES FOR 1996–97 State resident tuition: $1809 full-time, $60.30 per credit part-time. Nonresident tuition: $3293 full-time, $109.75 per credit part-time.
FINANCIAL AID *College-administered undergrad aid 1995–96:* 521 need-based scholarships (averaging $243), 46 non-need scholarships (averaging $207), 22 Federal Work-Study (averaging $741). *Required forms:* institutional, FAFSA; accepted: CSS Financial Aid PROFILE. *Application deadline:* continuous. *Waivers:* full or partial for employees or children of employees.
APPLYING Open admission except for allied health programs. *Option:* deferred entrance. *Required:* school transcript, TOEFL for international students, CGP, ACT ASSET. Test scores used for counseling/placement. *Application deadline:* rolling. Preference given to state residents.
APPLYING/TRANSFER *Required:* standardized test scores, high school transcript. *Entrance:* noncompetitive. *Application deadline:* rolling.
CONTACT Ms. Charlotte Malone, Recruitment Counselor, Ivy Tech State College–Northwest, 1440 East 35th Avenue, Gary, IN 46409-1499, 219-981-1111 Ext. 216. College video available.

IVY TECH STATE COLLEGE–SOUTHCENTRAL
Sellersburg, Indiana

UG Enrollment: 1,890	Tuition & Fees (IN Res): $1809
Application Deadline: rolling	Room & Board: N/Avail

GENERAL State-supported, 2-year, coed. Part of Ivy Tech State College System. Awards transfer associate, terminal associate degrees. Founded 1968. *Setting:* 63-acre small-town campus with easy access to Louisville. *System endowment:* $1.2 million. *Total enrollment:* 1,890. *Faculty:* 128 (36 full-time, 92 part-time); student-faculty ratio is 15:1.
ENROLLMENT PROFILE 1,890 students from 4 states and territories. 63% women, 37% men, 73% part-time, 93% state residents, 7% transferred in, 61% 25 or older, 1% Native American, 0% Hispanic, 2% African American, 0% Asian American. *Areas of study chosen:* 32% engineering and applied sciences, 29% health professions and related sciences, 18% business management and administrative services, 13% liberal arts/general studies, 8% computer and information sciences. *Most popular recent majors:* nursing, industrial and heavy equipment maintenance, computer information systems.
FIRST-YEAR CLASS 566 total; 855 applied, 100% were accepted, 66% of whom enrolled.
ACADEMIC PROGRAM Core. Calendar: semesters. 274 courses offered in 1995–96. Academic remediation for entering students, services for LD students, advanced placement, summer session for credit, part-time degree program (daytime, evenings), adult/continuing education programs, co-op programs and internships.
GENERAL DEGREE REQUIREMENTS 60 credits; computer course (varies by major); internship (some majors).
MAJORS Accounting, architectural technologies, automotive technologies, business administration/commerce/management, commercial art, computer information systems, computer programming, construction technologies, drafting and design, electrical and electronics technologies, heating/refrigeration/air conditioning, industrial and heavy equipment maintenance, manufacturing technology, mechanical design technology, medical assistant technologies, nursing, photography, robotics, secretarial studies/office management, welding technology.
COMPUTERS ON CAMPUS 73 computers for student use in computer center, classrooms, library provide access to main academic computer. Staffed computer lab on campus.
HOUSING College housing not available.
CAREER PLANNING *Placement office:* 1 full-time staff. *Director:* Ms. Mary Beth Hackman, Career and Employment Services Coordinator, 812-246-3301. *Services:* job fairs, resume preparation, resume referral, career counseling, job bank, job interviews.
ESTIMATED EXPENSES FOR 1996–97 State resident tuition: $1809 full-time, $60.30 per credit part-time. Nonresident tuition: $3293 full-time, $109.75 per credit part-time.
FINANCIAL AID *College-administered undergrad aid 1995–96:* 289 need-based scholarships (averaging $594), 19 non-need scholarships (averaging $707), low-interest long-term loans from external sources (averaging $2164), Federal Work-Study. *Required forms:* institutional, FAFSA; required for some: CSS Financial Aid PROFILE, state, SINGLEFILE Form of United Student Aid Funds. *Application deadline:* continuous. *Waivers:* full or partial for employees or children of employees.
APPLYING Open admission except for computer programming, drafting, electronics, allied health programs. *Options:* early entrance, deferred entrance. *Required:* school transcript, TOEFL for international students, ACT ASSET. Test scores used for counseling/placement. *Application deadline:* rolling. *Notification:* continuous. Preference given to state residents.
APPLYING/TRANSFER *Required:* standardized test scores, high school transcript. *Entrance:* noncompetitive. *Application deadline:* rolling. *Notification:* continuous. *Contact:* Mr. Randy G. Emily, Admissions Coordinator, 812-246-3301.
CONTACT Mr. Randy G. Emily, Admissions Coordinator, Ivy Tech State College–Southcentral, Sellersburg, IN 47172-1829, 812-246-3301.

IVY TECH STATE COLLEGE–SOUTHEAST
Madison, Indiana

UG Enrollment: 866	Tuition & Fees (IN Res): $1809
Application Deadline: rolling	Room & Board: N/Avail

GENERAL State-supported, 2-year, coed. Part of Ivy Tech State College System. Awards transfer associate, terminal associate degrees. Founded 1963. *Setting:* 5-acre small-town campus with easy access to Louisville. *System endowment:* $1.2 million. *Total enrollment:* 866. *Faculty:* 81 (30 full-time, 51 part-time); student-faculty ratio is 11:1.
ENROLLMENT PROFILE 866 students from 4 states and territories. 77% women, 23% men, 67% part-time, 93% state residents, 3% transferred in, 66% 25 or older, 0% Native American, 0% Hispanic, 1% African American, 1% Asian American. *Areas of study chosen:* 27% business management and administrative services, 22% health professions and related sciences, 20% liberal arts/general studies, 19% computer and information sciences, 12% engineering and applied sciences. *Most popular recent majors:* nursing, computer information systems, accounting.
FIRST-YEAR CLASS 257 total; 404 applied, 100% were accepted, 64% of whom enrolled. 5% from top 10% of their high school class, 25% from top quarter, 50% from top half.
ACADEMIC PROGRAM Core. Calendar: semesters. 237 courses offered in 1995–96. Academic remediation for entering students, services for LD students, advanced placement, summer session for credit, part-time degree program (daytime, evenings), co-op programs and internships.
GENERAL DEGREE REQUIREMENTS 60 credits; computer course (varies by major); internship (some majors).
MAJORS Accounting, automotive technologies, business administration/commerce/management, computer information systems, computer programming, electrical and electronics technologies, industrial and heavy equipment maintenance, manufacturing technology, nursing, robotics, secretarial studies/office management.
COMPUTERS ON CAMPUS Computers for student use in computer center. Staffed computer lab on campus.
HOUSING College housing not available.
ATHLETICS *Intramural:* basketball.
CAREER PLANNING *Placement office:* 1 full-time staff. *Director:* Ms. Jill Woodburn, Career Counselor/Placement Coordinator, 812-265-2580. *Services:* resume preparation, resume referral, career counseling, job bank, job interviews.
ESTIMATED EXPENSES FOR 1996–97 State resident tuition: $1809 full-time, $60.30 per credit part-time. Nonresident tuition: $3293 full-time, $109.75 per credit part-time.
FINANCIAL AID *College-administered undergrad aid 1995–96:* 101 need-based scholarships (average $435), 16 non-need scholarships (average $754), short-term loans (average $50), low-interest long-term loans from external sources (average $2114), Federal Work-Study. *Required forms:* institutional, FAFSA; accepted: CSS Financial Aid PROFILE. *Waivers:* full or partial for employees or children of employees.
APPLYING Open admission except for allied health programs. *Required:* school transcript, TOEFL for international students, ACT ASSET. *Application deadline:* rolling. Preference given to state residents.
APPLYING/TRANSFER *Required:* standardized test scores, high school transcript. *Entrance:* noncompetitive. *Application deadline:* rolling. *Contact:* Ms. Gay Jefferies, Financial Aid/Admissions Counselor, 812-265-2580.

Ivy Tech State College–Southeast (continued)
CONTACT Ms. Gay Jefferies, Financial Aid/Admissions Counselor, Ivy Tech State College–Southeast, Madison, IN 47250-1883, 812-265-2580.

IVY TECH STATE COLLEGE–SOUTHWEST
Evansville, Indiana

UG Enrollment: 2,795	**Tuition & Fees (IN Res): $1809**
Application Deadline: rolling	**Room & Board: N/Avail**

GENERAL State-supported, 2-year, coed. Part of Ivy Tech State College System. Awards transfer associate, terminal associate degrees. Founded 1963. ***Setting:*** 15-acre suburban campus. ***System endowment:*** $1.2 million. ***Total enrollment:*** 2,795. ***Faculty:*** 235 (46 full-time, 189 part-time); student-faculty ratio is 12:1.
ENROLLMENT PROFILE 2,795 students from 4 states and territories. 58% women, 42% men, 75% part-time, 96% state residents, 10% transferred in, 63% 25 or older, 1% Native American, 0% Hispanic, 4% African American, 0% Asian American. ***Areas of study chosen:*** 38% engineering and applied sciences, 22% business management and administrative services, 15% health professions and related sciences, 15% liberal arts/general studies, 10% computer and information sciences. ***Most popular recent majors:*** nursing, secretarial studies/office management, medical assistant technologies.
FIRST-YEAR CLASS 942 total; 1,613 applied, 100% were accepted, 58% of whom enrolled.
ACADEMIC PROGRAM Core. Calendar: semesters. 381 courses offered in 1995–96. Academic remediation for entering students, services for LD students, advanced placement, summer session for credit, part-time degree program (daytime, evenings), internships.
GENERAL DEGREE REQUIREMENTS 60 credits; computer course (varies by major); internship (some majors).
MAJORS Accounting, automotive technologies, business administration/commerce/management, commercial art, computer information systems, computer programming, drafting and design, electrical and electronics technologies, emergency medical technology, heating/refrigeration/air conditioning, industrial and heavy equipment maintenance, interior design, marketing/retailing/merchandising, medical assistant technologies, nursing, photography, plastics technology, robotics, secretarial studies/office management.
LIBRARY 5,000 books, 129 periodicals, 3 CD-ROMs, 150 records, tapes, and CDs. System-wide acquisition spending 1994–95: $24,733.
COMPUTERS ON CAMPUS 50 computers for student use in computer center, computer labs, learning resource center, library. Staffed computer lab on campus.
HOUSING College housing not available.
CAREER PLANNING ***Placement office:*** 1 full-time staff. ***Director:*** Mr. Richard Hettenbach, Placement Services Manager, 812-426-2865. ***Services:*** job fairs, resume preparation, resume referral, career counseling, job bank, job interviews.
AFTER GRADUATION 1% of students completing a degree program in 1994–95 went directly on to further study.
ESTIMATED EXPENSES FOR 1996–97 State resident tuition: $1809 full-time, $60.30 per credit part-time. Nonresident tuition: $3293 full-time, $109.75 per credit part-time.
FINANCIAL AID ***College-administered undergrad aid 1995–96:*** 525 need-based scholarships (average $497), 15 non-need scholarships (average $376), short-term loans (average $100), low-interest long-term loans from external sources (average $1943), Federal Work-Study. ***Required forms:*** institutional, FAFSA; accepted: CSS Financial Aid PROFILE. ***Application deadline:*** continuous. ***Waivers:*** full or partial for employees or children of employees.
APPLYING Open admission except for allied health programs. ***Options:*** early entrance, deferred entrance. ***Required:*** school transcript, TOEFL for international students, ACT ASSET. Test scores used for counseling/placement. ***Application deadline:*** rolling. ***Notification:*** continuous. Preference given to state residents.
APPLYING/TRANSFER ***Required:*** standardized test scores, high school transcript. ***Entrance:*** noncompetitive. ***Application deadline:*** rolling. ***Notification:*** continuous. ***Contact:*** Ms. Mary Hess, Admissions Manager, 812-426-1437.
CONTACT Ms. Mary Hess, Admissions Manager, Ivy Tech State College–Southwest, Evansville, IN 47710-3398, 812-426-1437.

IVY TECH STATE COLLEGE–WABASH VALLEY
Terre Haute, Indiana

UG Enrollment: 2,447	**Tuition & Fees (IN Res): $1809**
Application Deadline: rolling	**Room & Board: N/Avail**

GENERAL State-supported, 2-year, coed. Part of Ivy Tech State College System. Awards transfer associate, terminal associate degrees. Founded 1966. ***Setting:*** 55-acre suburban campus with easy access to Indianapolis. ***System endowment:*** $1.2 million. ***Total enrollment:*** 2,447. ***Faculty:*** 167 (63 full-time, 104 part-time); student-faculty ratio is 15:1.
ENROLLMENT PROFILE 2,447 students from 2 states and territories. 55% women, 45% men, 55% part-time, 96% state residents, 3% transferred in, 50% 25 or older, 1% Native American, 1% Hispanic, 3% African American, 1% Asian American. ***Areas of study chosen:*** 38% engineering and applied sciences, 20% liberal arts/general studies, 17% health professions and related sciences, 16% business management and administrative services, 9% computer and information sciences. ***Most popular recent majors:*** medical laboratory technology, accounting, drafting and design.
FIRST-YEAR CLASS 910 total; 1,289 applied, 100% were accepted, 71% of whom enrolled.
ACADEMIC PROGRAM Core. Calendar: semesters. 473 courses offered in 1995–96. Academic remediation for entering students, services for LD students, advanced placement, summer session for credit, part-time degree program (daytime, evenings), adult/continuing education programs, co-op programs.
GENERAL DEGREE REQUIREMENTS 60 credits; computer course (varies by major); internship (some majors).
MAJORS Accounting, aircraft and missile maintenance, architectural technologies, automotive technologies, business administration/commerce/management, carpentry, computer information systems, computer programming, construction technologies, drafting and design, electrical and electronics technologies, graphic arts, heating/refrigeration/air conditioning, industrial and heavy equipment maintenance, laser technologies, machine and tool technologies, manufacturing technology, marketing/retailing/merchandising, mechanical design technology, medical assistant technologies, medical laboratory technology, mining technology, plastics technology, printing technologies, quality control technology, radiological technology, robotics, secretarial studies/office management.
LIBRARY 1,800 books, 60 periodicals, 5 CD-ROMs. Acquisition spending 1994–95: $13,370.
COMPUTERS ON CAMPUS 100 computers for student use in computer center. Staffed computer lab on campus.
COLLEGE LIFE ***Student services:*** personal-psychological counseling, women's center.
HOUSING College housing not available.
ATHLETICS ***Intramural:*** basketball, bowling, softball.
CAREER PLANNING ***Placement office:*** 1 full-time staff. ***Director:*** Ms. Dot Farr Lindsay, Placement/Transfer Services Coordinator, 812-299-1121. ***Services:*** job fairs, resume preparation, resume referral, career counseling, job bank, job interviews.
ESTIMATED EXPENSES FOR 1996–97 State resident tuition: $1809 full-time, $60.30 per credit part-time. Nonresident tuition: $3293 full-time, $109.75 per credit part-time.
FINANCIAL AID ***College-administered undergrad aid 1995–96:*** 448 need-based scholarships (average $482), 16 non-need scholarships (average $651), short-term loans, low-interest long-term loans from external sources (average $1889), part-time jobs. ***Required forms:*** institutional, FAFSA; accepted: CSS Financial Aid PROFILE. ***Waivers:*** full or partial for employees or children of employees.
APPLYING Open admission except for allied health programs. ***Options:*** early entrance, deferred entrance. ***Required:*** school transcript, TOEFL for international students, ACT ASSET. Test scores used for counseling/placement. ***Application deadline:*** rolling. ***Notification:*** continuous. Preference given to state residents.
APPLYING/TRANSFER ***Required:*** standardized test scores, high school transcript. ***Entrance:*** noncompetitive. ***Application deadline:*** rolling. ***Notification:*** continuous. ***Contact:*** Ms. Charlotte Bukowski, Enrollment/Admissions Manager, 812-299-1121.
CONTACT Ms. Charlotte Bukowski, Enrollment/Admissions Manager, Ivy Tech State College–Wabash Valley, Terre Haute, IN 47802, 812-299-1121.

IVY TECH STATE COLLEGE–WHITEWATER
Richmond, Indiana

UG Enrollment: 1,028	**Tuition & Fees (IN Res): $1809**
Application Deadline: rolling	**Room & Board: N/Avail**

GENERAL State-supported, 2-year, coed. Part of Ivy Tech State College System. Awards transfer associate, terminal associate degrees. Founded 1963. ***Setting:*** 23-acre small-town campus with easy access to Indianapolis. ***System endowment:*** $1.2 million. ***Total enrollment:*** 1,028. ***Faculty:*** 112 (21 full-time, 91 part-time); student-faculty ratio is 9:1.
ENROLLMENT PROFILE 1,028 students from 4 states and territories. 71% women, 29% men, 74% part-time, 97% state residents, 2% transferred in, 63% 25 or older, 1% Native American, 1% Hispanic, 4% African American, 0% Asian American. ***Areas of study chosen:*** 26% engineering and applied sciences, 23% business management and administrative services, 22% health professions and related sciences, 18% computer and information sciences, 11% liberal arts/general studies. ***Most popular recent majors:*** medical assistant technologies, nursing, computer information systems.
FIRST-YEAR CLASS 300 total; 590 applied, 100% were accepted, 51% of whom enrolled.
ACADEMIC PROGRAM Core. Calendar: semesters. 251 courses offered in 1995–96. Academic remediation for entering students, services for LD students, advanced placement, self-designed majors, summer session for credit, part-time degree program (daytime, evenings, weekends, summer), adult/continuing education programs, co-op programs. Off-campus study at Indiana University East.
GENERAL DEGREE REQUIREMENTS 60 credits; computer course (varies by major); internship (some majors).
MAJORS Accounting, automotive technologies, business administration/commerce/management, carpentry, child care/child and family studies, child psychology/child development, computer information systems, computer programming, construction technologies, electrical and electronics technologies, heating/refrigeration/air conditioning, industrial and heavy equipment maintenance, manufacturing technology, marketing/retailing/merchandising, medical assistant technologies, nursing, robotics, secretarial studies/office management.
LIBRARY 56,000 books.
COMPUTERS ON CAMPUS 80 computers for student use in computer center, classrooms. Staffed computer lab on campus.
COLLEGE LIFE ***Student services:*** personal-psychological counseling.
HOUSING College housing not available.
CAREER PLANNING ***Placement office:*** 1 full-time staff. ***Director:*** Mr. Charles Tillman, Admissions/Placement Manager, 317-966-2656 Ext. 36. ***Services:*** job fairs, resume preparation, resume referral, career counseling, job bank, job interviews.
ESTIMATED EXPENSES FOR 1996–97 State resident tuition: $1809 full-time, $60.30 per credit part-time. Nonresident tuition: $3293 full-time, $109.75 per credit part-time.
FINANCIAL AID ***College-administered undergrad aid 1995–96:*** 289 need-based scholarships (average $551), 24 non-need scholarships (average $241), low-interest long-term loans from external sources (average $1947), Federal Work-Study. ***Required forms:*** institutional, FAFSA; accepted: CSS Financial Aid PROFILE. ***Application deadline:*** continuous. ***Payment plans:*** installment, deferred payment. ***Waivers:*** full or partial for employees or children of employees.
APPLYING Open admission except for allied health programs. ***Option:*** early entrance. ***Required:*** school transcript, TOEFL for international students, ACT ASSET. Test scores used for counseling/placement. ***Application deadline:*** rolling. Preference given to state residents.
APPLYING/TRANSFER ***Required:*** standardized test scores, high school transcript. ***Entrance:*** noncompetitive. ***Application deadline:*** rolling. ***Contact:*** Ms. Linda Przybysz, Admissions Coordinator, 317-966-2656.
CONTACT Ms. Linda Przybysz, Admissions Coordinator, Ivy Tech State College–Whitewater, Richmond, IN 47374-1220, 317-966-2656.

LINCOLN TECHNICAL INSTITUTE
Indianapolis, Indiana

UG Enrollment: 400	Tuition: $13,500/deg prog
Application Deadline: rolling	Room & Board: N/Avail

GENERAL Proprietary, 2-year, coed. Part of Lincoln Technical Institute, Inc. Awards certificates, terminal associate degrees. Founded 1946. *Total enrollment:* 400. *Faculty:* 20 (18 full-time, 2 part-time); student-faculty ratio is 25:1.
ENROLLMENT PROFILE 400 students from 2 states and territories, 1 other country. 5% women, 0% part-time, 60% state residents, 5% transferred in, 1% international, 25% 25 or older, 1% Native American, 1% Hispanic, 10% African American, 1% Asian American.
FIRST-YEAR CLASS 100 total.
ACADEMIC PROGRAM Calendar: modular. Summer session for credit.
GENERAL DEGREE REQUIREMENT 59 credits.
MAJORS Automotive technologies, drafting and design.
LIBRARY 800 books, 500 microform titles, 15 periodicals.
COLLEGE LIFE Orientation program (3 days, no cost). *Student services:* personal-psychological counseling.
HOUSING College housing not available.
CAREER PLANNING *Service:* career counseling.
EXPENSES FOR 1996-97 Tuition: $13,500 per degree program. Full-time mandatory fees: $150. Tuition guaranteed not to increase for student's term of enrollment.
FINANCIAL AID *College-administered undergrad aid 1995-96:* need-based scholarships, 15 non-need scholarships (average $5000), short-term loans, low-interest long-term loans from college funds (average $2400), loans from external sources (average $2625), Federal Work-Study. *Required forms:* institutional, FAFSA. *Application deadline:* continuous.
APPLYING *Required:* school transcript, interview. *Application deadline:* rolling.
APPLYING/TRANSFER *Required:* high school transcript, interview, college transcript. *Entrance:* minimally difficult.
CONTACT Ms. Cindy Ryan, Director of High School Admissions, Lincoln Technical Institute, 1201 Stadium Drive, Indianapolis, IN 46202-2194, 317-632-5553 or toll-free 800-382-4857 (in-state), 800-554-4465 (out-of-state).

LUTHERAN COLLEGE OF HEALTH PROFESSIONS
Fort Wayne, Indiana

UG Enrollment: 649	Tuition & Fees: $5550
Application Deadline: 6/1	Room Only: $1888

GENERAL Independent Lutheran, primarily 2-year, primarily women. Awards transfer associate, bachelor's degrees. Founded 1987. *Setting:* urban campus. *Endowment:* $170,000. *Educational spending 1994-95:* $3000 per undergrad. *Total enrollment:* 649. *Faculty:* 55 (31 full-time, 15% with terminal degrees, 24 part-time); student-faculty ratio is 9:1.
ENROLLMENT PROFILE 649 students from 8 states and territories. 88% women, 12% men, 59% part-time, 88% state residents, 6% live on campus, 70% transferred in, 55% have need-based financial aid, 0% have non-need-based financial aid, 0% international, 53% 25 or older, 1% Native American, 2% Hispanic, 2% African American, 0% Asian American. *Areas of study chosen:* 100% health professions and related sciences.
FIRST-YEAR CLASS 68 total; 154 applied, 63% were accepted, 70% of whom enrolled. 19% from top 10% of their high school class, 35% from top quarter, 94% from top half.
ACADEMIC PROGRAM Calendar: semesters. 135 courses offered in 1995-96. Services for LD students, advanced placement, summer session for credit.
GENERAL DEGREE REQUIREMENTS 65 semester hours for associate, 126 semester hours for bachelor's; computer course for emergency medical services, physical therapy assistant, surgical technology majors.
MAJORS Emergency medical technology, nursing (B), operating room technology, physical therapy, physician's assistant studies (B), radiological technology.
LIBRARY Health Sciences Library with 5,736 books, 6,036 microform titles, 307 periodicals, 6 on-line bibliographic services, 1,215 records, tapes, and CDs. Acquisition spending 1994-95: $62,000.
COMPUTERS ON CAMPUS 33 computers for student use in computer labs, learning resource center, library. Staffed computer lab on campus provides training in use of computers, software.
COLLEGE LIFE 90% vote in student government elections. *Social organizations:* 2 open to all. *Most popular organizations:* Student Government, Student Nursing Association, PA Student Organization. *Major annual event:* Casa Luncheons. *Student services:* health clinic, personal-psychological counseling. *Campus security:* 24-hour emergency response devices and patrols, late-night transport-escort service, controlled dormitory access.
HOUSING 45 college housing spaces available; 40 were occupied 1995-96. No special consideration for freshman housing applicants. Off-campus living permitted. *Option:* single-sex (1 building) housing available. Resident assistants live in dorms.
CAREER PLANNING *Placement office:* 1 part-time staff. *Director:* Ms. Linda Jackson, Student Services Coordinator, 219-458-2451. *Services:* resume preparation, career counseling, careers library, job bank.
AFTER GRADUATION 92% of class of 1994 had job offers within 6 months.
EXPENSES FOR 1996-97 *Application fee:* $30. Tuition: $5550 full-time, $185 per semester hour part-time. College room only: $1888.
FINANCIAL AID *College-administered undergrad aid 1995-96:* 100 need-based scholarships (average $230). *Required forms:* institutional, FAFSA. *Priority deadline:* 3/1. *Payment plan:* installment.
APPLYING *Options:* deferred entrance, midyear entrance. *Required:* essay, school transcript, minimum 2.0 GPA, 2 recommendations, SAT I or ACT, TOEFL for international students. *Recommended:* minimum 3.0 GPA, 3 years of high school math and science, some high school foreign language. *Required for some:* interview. Test scores used for admission. *Application deadline:* 6/1. *Notification:* continuous until 7/15.
APPLYING/TRANSFER *Required:* essay, high school transcript, 2 recommendations, college transcript, minimum 2.0 college GPA. *Recommended:* 3 years of high school math and science, some high school foreign language, minimum 3.0 high school GPA. *Required for some:* standardized test scores, interview, minimum 2.0 college GPA.

Entrance: moderately difficult. *Application deadline:* 6/1. *Notification:* continuous until 7/15. *Contact:* Mr. Frank C. Guzik, Director of Admissions, 219-458-2446.
CONTACT Mr. Frank C. Guzik, Director of Admissions, Lutheran College of Health Professions, 3024 Fairfield Avenue, Fort Wayne, IN 46807-1697, 219-458-2446. *Fax:* 219-458-3077.

MICHIANA COLLEGE
South Bend, Indiana

UG Enrollment: 325	Tuition & Fees: $7532
Application Deadline: rolling	Room & Board: N/Avail

GENERAL Proprietary, 2-year, coed. Awards terminal associate degrees. Founded 1882. *Setting:* 5-acre urban campus with easy access to Chicago. *Total enrollment:* 325. *Faculty:* 13 (8 full-time, 5 part-time); student-faculty ratio is 19:1.
ENROLLMENT PROFILE 325 students from 4 states and territories. 34% part-time, 98% state residents, 20% transferred in, 58% 25 or older, 1% Native American, 2% Hispanic, 12% African American, 0% Asian American. *Areas of study chosen:* 68% business management and administrative services, 32% health professions and related sciences. *Most popular recent majors:* accounting, secretarial studies/office management, medical assistant technologies.
FIRST-YEAR CLASS 47 total.
ACADEMIC PROGRAM Core, business-related curriculum, honor code. Calendar: quarters. 120 courses offered in 1995-96. Tutorials, summer session for credit, part-time degree program (evenings), adult/continuing education programs.
GENERAL DEGREE REQUIREMENTS 96 credit hours; 2 business math courses or 1 medical math course.
MAJORS Accounting, business administration/commerce/management, computer management, computer programming, data processing, legal secretarial studies, medical assistant technologies, medical records services, medical secretarial studies, physical therapy, secretarial studies/office management.
LIBRARY Michiana College Resource Center with 4,300 books, 36 periodicals, 200 records, tapes, and CDs.
COMPUTERS ON CAMPUS 34 computers for student use in computer center.
COLLEGE LIFE *Social organizations:* 4 open to all. *Most popular organizations:* Accounting Association, Data Processing Management Association, AAMA, Collegiate Secretaries International. *Student services:* personal-psychological counseling. *Campus security:* 24-hour emergency response devices.
HOUSING College housing not available.
CAREER PLANNING *Placement office:* 1 full-time staff. *Director:* Ms. Phyllis Stegman, Placement Coordinator, 219-237-0774. *Services:* resume preparation, resume referral, career counseling, job bank, job interviews.
AFTER GRADUATION 10% of students completing a degree program in 1994-95 went directly on to further study.
EXPENSES FOR 1996-97 *Application fee:* $50. Tuition: $7282 (minimum) full-time, $280 per course part-time. Part-time mandatory fees: $160 per year. Full-time mandatory fees: $250.
FINANCIAL AID *College-administered undergrad aid 1995-96:* need-based scholarships, 20 non-need scholarships (average $600), low-interest long-term loans from external sources (average $2625), Federal Work-Study. *Required forms:* FAFSA; accepted: CSS Financial Aid PROFILE. *Priority deadline:* 8/30.
APPLYING *Options:* Common Application, deferred entrance. *Required:* Wonderlic aptitude test. Test scores used for admission. *Application deadline:* rolling.
APPLYING/TRANSFER *Required:* minimum 2.0 college GPA. *Entrance:* minimally difficult. *Application deadline:* rolling. *Contact:* Mr. Dave Krueper, President, 219-237-0774.
CONTACT Mr. Dave Krueper, President, Michiana College, 1030 East Jefferson Boulevard, South Bend, IN 46617-3123, 219-237-0774 or toll-free 800-743-2447 (out-of-state). College video available.

MID-AMERICA COLLEGE OF FUNERAL SERVICE
Jeffersonville, Indiana

UG Enrollment: 141	Tuition: $10,500/deg prog
Application Deadline: rolling	Room & Board: N/Avail

GENERAL Independent, 2-year, specialized, primarily men. Awards diplomas, terminal associate degrees. Founded 1905. *Setting:* 3-acre small-town campus with easy access to Louisville. *Total enrollment:* 141. *Faculty:* 5 (all full-time).
ENROLLMENT PROFILE 141 students: 26% women, 0% part-time, 100% state residents, 0% transferred in, 0% international, 13% 25 or older, 0% Native American, 0% Hispanic, 0% African American, 0% Asian American.
FIRST-YEAR CLASS 17 total; 21 applied, 95% were accepted, 85% of whom enrolled.
ACADEMIC PROGRAM Core. Calendar: quarters. Academic remediation for entering students.
GENERAL DEGREE REQUIREMENTS 127 quarter hours; 1 course each in math and science; computer course.
MAJOR Funeral service.
LIBRARY 1,500 books, 20 periodicals.
COLLEGE LIFE Orientation program (2 days, no cost).
HOUSING College housing not available.
CAREER PLANNING *Service:* career counseling.
EXPENSES FOR 1996-97 *Application fee:* $25. Tuition: $10,500 per degree program.
FINANCIAL AID *College-administered undergrad aid 1995-96:* low-interest long-term loans from external sources (average $2625). *Acceptable forms:* CSS Financial Aid PROFILE, state, FAFSA. *Application deadline:* continuous. *Payment plan:* tuition prepayment.
APPLYING Open admission. *Option:* deferred entrance. *Required:* school transcript. *Application deadline:* rolling.
APPLYING/TRANSFER *Required:* high school transcript, college transcript. *Entrance:* noncompetitive.

Mid-America College of Funeral Service (continued)
CONTACT Mr. Richard Nelson, Dean of Students, Mid-America College of Funeral Service, Jeffersonville, IN 47130-9630, 812-288-8878 or toll-free 800-221-6158.

VINCENNES UNIVERSITY
Vincennes, Indiana

UG Enrollment: 6,500 | **Tuition & Fees (IN Res): $2267**
Application Deadline: rolling | **Room & Board: $3712**

GENERAL State-supported, 2-year, coed. Awards transfer associate, terminal associate degrees. Founded 1801. ***Setting:*** 95-acre small-town campus. ***Total enrollment:*** 6,500. ***Faculty:*** 400 (395 full-time, 5 part-time). ***Notable Alumni:*** David Goodnow, anchor for CNN News.
ENROLLMENT PROFILE 6,500 students from 25 states and territories, 30 other countries. 43% women, 57% men, 25% part-time, 91% state residents, 6% transferred in, 5% 25 or older, 1% Native American, 3% Hispanic, 6% African American. ***Most popular recent majors:*** nursing, business administration/commerce/management, law enforcement/ police sciences.
FIRST-YEAR CLASS 2,210 total; 5,140 applied, 98% were accepted. 5% from top 10% of their high school class, 10% from top quarter, 75% from top half.
ACADEMIC PROGRAM Core. Calendar: semesters. Academic remediation for entering students, English as a second language program offered during academic year and summer, services for LD students, advanced placement, self-designed majors, tutorials, summer session for credit, part-time degree program (daytime, evenings, weekends, summer), external degree programs, adult/continuing education programs, co-op programs and internships. Off-campus study at 30 universities in Indiana. ROTC: Army (c).
GENERAL DEGREE REQUIREMENTS 64 credits; math/science requirements vary according to program; computer course.
MAJORS Accounting, actuarial science, advertising, agricultural business, agricultural technologies, aircraft and missile maintenance, anthropology, archaeology, architectural technologies, art education, art/fine arts, athletic training, automotive technologies, aviation technology, behavioral sciences, biology/biological sciences, broadcasting, business administration/commerce/management, business education, chemistry, child care/child and family studies, civil engineering technology, commercial art, communication, communication equipment technology, computer information systems, computer management, computer programming, computer science, computer technologies, conservation, construction management, construction technologies, corrections, cosmetology, criminal justice, culinary arts, deaf interpreter training, dental services, dietetics, drafting and design, early childhood education, earth science, economics, education, electrical and electronics technologies, electrical engineering technology, elementary education, engineering (general), (pre)engineering sequence, engineering technology, English, environmental health sciences, environmental sciences, family and consumer studies, fashion design and technology, fashion merchandising, finance/banking, flight training, food marketing, food sciences, food services management, forestry, French, funeral service, geography, geology, German, graphic arts, history, home economics, horticulture, hotel and restaurant management, industrial and heavy equipment maintenance, insurance, interior design, journalism, laboratory technologies, landscape architecture/design, laser technologies, law enforcement/police sciences, legal secretarial studies, liberal arts/general studies, machine and tool technologies, management information systems, marketing/retailing/merchandising, mathematics, mechanical engineering technology, medical assistant technologies, medical laboratory technology, medical records services, medical secretarial studies, medical technology, middle school education, modern languages, music, music education, natural resource management, nuclear medical technology, nursing, nutrition, occupational therapy, optical technologies, ornamental horticulture, paralegal studies, pharmacy/pharmaceutical sciences, physical education, physical fitness/exercise science, physical therapy, physics, political science/ government, practical nursing, printing technologies, psychology, public administration, public relations, radio and television studies, real estate, recreation and leisure services, recreation therapy, respiratory therapy, robotics, science education, secretarial studies/ office management, social science, social work, sociology, Spanish, sports administration, surveying technology, theater arts/drama, veterinary sciences, welding technology, zoology.
LIBRARY Vincennes University Library with 85,000 books, 600 periodicals, 1,800 records, tapes, and CDs.
COMPUTERS ON CAMPUS 200 computers for student use in computer center, computer labs, learning resource center, classrooms, library, student center, dorms provide access to main academic computer, e-mail, Internet. Staffed computer lab on campus provides training in use of computers, software.
COLLEGE LIFE Drama-theater group, choral group, student-run newspaper, radio station. ***Social organizations:*** 4 national fraternities, 1 national sorority, local fraternities, 1 local sorority; 5% of eligible men and 1% of eligible women are members. ***Student services:*** health clinic, personal-psychological counseling. ***Campus security:*** 24-hour patrols, student patrols, late-night transport-escort service, controlled dormitory access, surveillance cameras.
HOUSING 2,800 college housing spaces available; all were occupied 1995–96. Freshmen given priority for college housing. On-campus residence required in freshman year except if living with relatives or 21 or over. ***Option:*** coed housing available. Resident assistants live in dorms.
ATHLETICS Member NJCAA. ***Intercollegiate:*** baseball M(s), basketball M(s)/W(s), bowling M(s)/W(s), cross-country running M(s)/W, soccer M/W, swimming and diving M(s)/ W(s), tennis M(s), track and field M(s)/W(s), volleyball M/W(s). ***Intramural:*** archery, badminton, basketball, bowling, cross-country running, gymnastics, racquetball, skiing (downhill), soccer, swimming and diving, tennis, track and field, volleyball, weight lifting, wrestling. ***Contact:*** Mr. Dan Sparks, Athletic Director, 812-885-4511.
CAREER PLANNING ***Placement office:*** 2 full-time staff. ***Director:*** Mrs. Alice Bond, Director of Career Center, 812-885-4501. ***Services:*** resume preparation, resume referral, career counseling, careers library, job bank, job interviews. Students must register sophomore year. 30 organizations recruited on campus 1994–95.
AFTER GRADUATION 94% of class of 1994 had job offers within 6 months.
EXPENSES FOR 1995–96 ***Application fee:*** $20. State resident tuition: $2231 full-time, $74.35 per credit part-time. Nonresident tuition: $3233 full-time, $180 per credit part-time. Tuition for Illinois residents of Crawford, Lawrence, Richland, and Wabash counties: $107.50 per credit. Part-time mandatory fees (7 to 11 credits): $18 per semester. Full-time mandatory fees: $36. College room and board: $3712 (minimum).
FINANCIAL AID ***College-administered undergrad aid 1995–96:*** 700 need-based scholarships (average $400), 175 non-need scholarships (average $300), low-interest long-term loans from college funds (average $800), loans from external sources (average $1800), 180 Federal Work-Study. ***Required forms:*** CSS Financial Aid PROFILE, institutional, FAFSA. ***Application deadline:*** 3/1. ***Payment plan:*** installment. ***Waivers:*** full or partial for employees or children of employees.
APPLYING Open admission except for health-related programs. ***Options:*** Common Application, early entrance. ***Required:*** school transcript. ***Recommended:*** SAT I. ***Required for some:*** some high school foreign language, SAT I. Test scores used for counseling/ placement. ***Application deadline:*** rolling. ***Notification:*** continuous until 8/1.
APPLYING/TRANSFER ***Recommended:*** standardized test scores. ***Required for some:*** standardized test scores. ***Entrance:*** minimally difficult. ***Application deadline:*** rolling. ***Notification:*** continuous.
CONTACT Mr. Stephen M. Simonds, Director of Admissions, Vincennes University, Vincennes, IN 47591-5202, 812-888-4313 or toll-free 800-742-9198 (in-state). ***Fax:*** 812-888-5868. ***E-mail:*** simonds@vunet.vinu.edu.

VINCENNES UNIVERSITY–JASPER CENTER
Jasper, Indiana

UG Enrollment: 1,206 | **Tuition & Fees (IN Res): $2256**
Application Deadline: rolling | **Room & Board: N/Avail**

GENERAL State-supported, 2-year, coed. Part of Vincennes University. Awards certificates, transfer associate, terminal associate degrees. Founded 1970. ***Setting:*** 120-acre small-town campus. ***Total enrollment:*** 1,206. ***Faculty:*** 62 (19 full-time, 43 part-time); student-faculty ratio is 17:1.
ENROLLMENT PROFILE 1,206 students: 71% women, 77% part-time, 100% state residents, 30% have need-based financial aid, 5% have non-need-based financial aid, 50% 25 or older, 1% Native American, 1% African American. ***Areas of study chosen:*** 39% liberal arts/general studies, 33% business management and administrative services, 11% social sciences, 5% engineering and applied sciences, 4% computer and information sciences, 4% education, 4% health professions and related sciences.
FIRST-YEAR CLASS 196 total; 241 applied, 100% were accepted, 81% of whom enrolled. 6% from top 10% of their high school class, 24% from top quarter, 54% from top half.
ACADEMIC PROGRAM Honor code. Calendar: semesters. Academic remediation for entering students, advanced placement, summer session for credit, part-time degree program (daytime, evenings, summer), adult/continuing education programs.
GENERAL DEGREE REQUIREMENTS 62 credit hours; 6 credit hours of math/ science; computer course.
MAJORS Accounting, behavioral sciences, business administration/commerce/ management, business education, computer programming, education, elementary education, finance/banking, industrial engineering technology, law enforcement/police sciences, legal secretarial studies, liberal arts/general studies, management information systems, medical secretarial studies, psychology, secretarial studies/office management, social science, social work, sociology.
LIBRARY Ruxer Library with 14,000 books, 25 microform titles, 160 periodicals, 20 CD-ROMs, 200 records, tapes, and CDs.
COMPUTERS ON CAMPUS 48 computers for student use in computer center, study skills lab, library provide access to e-mail, Internet.
COLLEGE LIFE Student-run newspaper. ***Student services:*** personal-psychological counseling.
HOUSING College housing not available.
CAREER PLANNING ***Service:*** career counseling.
EXPENSES FOR 1995–96 ***Application fee:*** $20. State resident tuition: $2231 full-time, $74.35 per credit hour part-time. Nonresident tuition: $5400 full-time, $180 per credit hour part-time. Full-time mandatory fees: $25.
FINANCIAL AID ***College-administered undergrad aid 1995–96:*** 12 need-based scholarships, 10 non-need scholarships (average $760), low-interest long-term loans from external sources (average $2782), 8 Federal Work-Study (averaging $1472). ***Required forms for some financial aid applicants:*** institutional, FAFSA. ***Application deadline:*** continuous. ***Payment plan:*** installment. ***Waivers:*** full or partial for employees or children of employees and senior citizens.
APPLYING Open admission. ***Required:*** school transcript, TOEFL for international students. ***Recommended:*** SAT I or ACT. ***Required for some:*** SAT I or ACT. Test scores used for counseling/placement. ***Application deadline:*** rolling.
APPLYING/TRANSFER ***Required:*** high school transcript, college transcript. ***Required for some:*** standardized test scores. ***Application deadline:*** rolling.
CONTACT Mrs. Virginia Eichmiller, Admissions Counselor, Vincennes University–Jasper Center, Jasper, IN 47546-9393, 812-482-3030 Ext. 23. ***Fax:*** 812-482-3040. ***E-mail:*** veichmil@vunet.vinu.edu. College video available.

IOWA

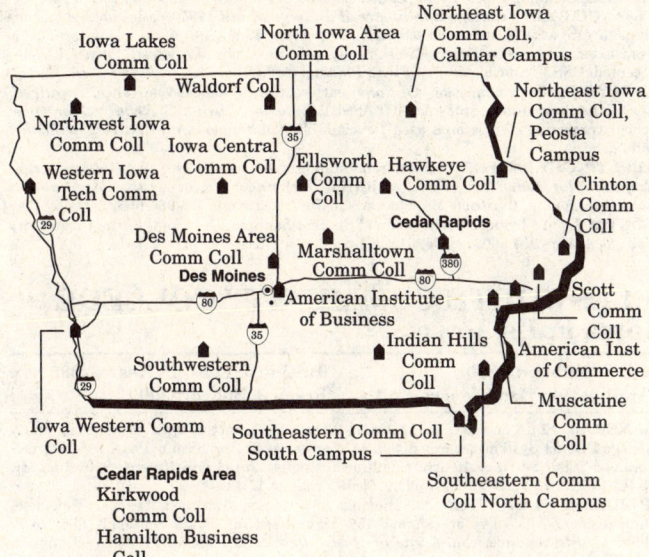

AMERICAN INSTITUTE OF BUSINESS
Des Moines, Iowa

UG Enrollment: 916	Tuition & Fees: $5925
Application Deadline: rolling	Room Only: $1935

GENERAL Independent, 2-year, coed. Awards diplomas, terminal associate degrees. Founded 1921. *Setting:* 20-acre urban campus. *Endowment:* $4.9 million. *Educational spending 1994–95:* $1512 per undergrad. *Total enrollment:* 916. *Faculty:* 47 (25 full-time, 15% with terminal degrees, 22 part-time); student-faculty ratio is 25:1. *Notable Alumni:* Michele Matt-Yanna, president of the Trainers Group, Inc.; Larry Pedersen, president of Devine Office Systems; Donald Lamberti, chairman and CEO of Casey's General Stores, Inc.; Pat Pithan major accounts manager at Imaging Technologies; Melinda Huisinga, human resources vice president at National Travelers Insurance.
ENROLLMENT PROFILE 916 students: 81% women, 22% part-time, 96% state residents, 19% transferred in, 0% international, 11% 25 or older, 0% Native American, 0% Hispanic, 2% African American, 3% Asian American. *Areas of study chosen:* 90% business management and administrative services. *Most popular recent majors:* accounting, finance/banking, court reporting.
FIRST-YEAR CLASS 322 total; 362 applied, 100% were accepted, 89% of whom enrolled. 25% from top quarter of their high school class, 56% from top half.
ACADEMIC PROGRAM Core, specialized business/vocational curriculum, honor code. Calendar: year-round. 132 courses offered in 1995–96. Academic remediation for entering students, summer session for credit, part-time degree program (daytime, evenings, summer), adult/continuing education programs, internships.
GENERAL DEGREE REQUIREMENTS 64 credit hours; 1 college math course; computer course; internship (some majors).
MAJORS Accounting, business administration/commerce/management, computer management, court reporting, finance/banking, hospitality services, legal secretarial studies, marketing/retailing/merchandising, medical secretarial studies, public relations, retail management, secretarial studies/office management, tourism and travel.
LIBRARY 5,400 books, 15 microform titles, 195 periodicals, 1 CD-ROM, 5,000 records, tapes, and CDs. Acquisition spending 1994–95: $10,751.
COMPUTERS ON CAMPUS 138 computers for student use in computer center, library, dorms provide access to Internet. Staffed computer lab on campus provides training in use of computers, software. Academic computing expenditure 1994–95: $194,703.
COLLEGE LIFE *Social organizations:* 12 open to all; 1 national fraternity, 1 national sorority; 10% of eligible men and 10% of eligible women are members. *Most popular organizations:* Business Management Institute, Institute of Management Accountants, Collegiate Secretaries International, Data Processing Management Association, Student Court Reporters Association. *Major annual events:* Family Day, Parents' Weekend, Formal. *Student services:* personal-psychological counseling. *Campus security:* 24-hour emergency response devices, controlled dormitory access.
HOUSING 671 college housing spaces available; 650 were occupied 1995–96. Freshmen guaranteed college housing. On-campus residence required through sophomore year except if 21 or over, married, or living with relatives. *Option:* coed housing available.
ATHLETICS *Intramural:* basketball, bowling, football, golf, volleyball.
CAREER PLANNING *Placement office:* 2 full-time staff; $73,098 operating expenditure 1994–95. *Director:* Mr. Terry Wilson, Director of Student Alumni Employment, 515-244-4221. *Services:* job fairs, resume preparation, resume referral, career counseling, careers library, job bank, job interviews. Students must register sophomore year. 50 organizations recruited on campus 1994–95.
AFTER GRADUATION 96% of class of 1994 had job offers within 6 months.
EXPENSES FOR 1995–96 *Application fee:* $25. Tuition: $5925 full-time, $145 per credit part-time. College room only: $1935. Tuition guaranteed not to increase for student's term of enrollment.

FINANCIAL AID *College-administered undergrad aid 1995–96:* 166 need-based scholarships (averaging $456), 532 non-need scholarships (averaging $911), low-interest long-term loans from external sources (averaging $2725), 105 Federal Work-Study (averaging $812), 127 part-time jobs. *Required forms:* institutional, FAFSA. *Priority deadline:* 4/1. *Payment plan:* installment. *Waivers:* full or partial for employees or children of employees. *Notification:* continuous.
APPLYING Open admission. *Required:* school transcript, campus interview. *Recommended:* ACT. Test scores used for counseling/placement. *Application deadline:* rolling.
APPLYING/TRANSFER *Required:* high school transcript, campus interview, college transcript. *Recommended:* standardized test scores. *Application deadline:* rolling.
Contact: Ms. Judith Charles, Registrar, 515-244-4221.
CONTACT Mr. Tom Shively, Director of Admissions, American Institute of Business, 2500 Fleur Drive, Des Moines, IA 50321-1799, 515-244-4221 or toll-free 800-444-1921. *Fax:* 515-244-6773. *E-mail:* inquiry@aib.edu.

AMERICAN INSTITUTE OF COMMERCE
Davenport, Iowa

UG Enrollment: 482	Tuition & Fees: $6085
Application Deadline: N/R	Room & Board: N/Avail

GENERAL Proprietary, 2-year, coed. Awards diplomas, terminal associate degrees. Founded 1937. *Setting:* suburban campus. *Total enrollment:* 482. *Faculty:* 34 (16 full-time, 18 part-time); student-faculty ratio is 15:1.
ENROLLMENT PROFILE 482 students from 2 states and territories. 83% women, 17% men, 39% part-time, 64% state residents, 42% transferred in, 0% international, 44% 25 or older, 0% Native American, 6% Hispanic, 7% African American, 1% Asian American. *Areas of study chosen:* 9% health professions and related sciences, 7% business management and administrative services, 7% computer and information sciences. *Most popular recent majors:* tourism and travel, medical assistant technologies, secretarial studies/office management.
FIRST-YEAR CLASS 189 total.
ACADEMIC PROGRAM Calendar: quarters. Academic remediation for entering students, part-time degree program (daytime, evenings), adult/continuing education programs, internships.
GENERAL DEGREE REQUIREMENTS 90 credits; 3 credits of math; 6 credits of science; computer course; internship (some majors).
MAJORS Accounting, broadcasting, business administration/commerce/management, computer programming, court reporting, hotel and restaurant management, industrial engineering technology, legal secretarial studies, medical assistant technologies, medical secretarial studies, retail management, secretarial studies/office management, tourism and travel.
LIBRARY AIC Library with 7,000 books, 120 periodicals, 1 on-line bibliographic service, 13 CD-ROMs, 250 records, tapes, and CDs. Acquisition spending 1994–95: $28,000.
COMPUTERS ON CAMPUS 75 computers for student use in computer labs, classrooms, library, student center provide access to Internet. Staffed computer lab on campus provides training in use of computers, software.
COLLEGE LIFE Student-run radio station. *Student services:* personal-psychological counseling.
HOUSING College housing not available.
CAREER PLANNING *Placement office:* 1 full-time, 2 part-time staff. *Director:* Ms. Jane Bollmann, Employment Search Coordinator, 319-355-3500. *Services:* resume preparation, resume referral, career counseling, job bank, job interviews. Students must register freshman year.
AFTER GRADUATION 90% of class of 1994 had job offers within 6 months.
EXPENSES FOR 1996–97 *Application fee:* $25. Tuition: $6075 full-time, $135 per credit hour part-time. Part-time mandatory fees: $5 per quarter. Full-time mandatory fees: $10. Tuition guaranteed not to increase for student's term of enrollment.
FINANCIAL AID *College-administered undergrad aid 1995–96:* 150 need-based scholarships (averaging $500), 40 Federal Work-Study (averaging $1000), 25 part-time jobs. *Required forms:* institutional, FAFSA; required for some: state. *Priority deadline:* 9/12. *Waivers:* full or partial for employees or children of employees. *Notification:* continuous. *Average indebtedness of graduates:* $5500.
APPLYING *Option:* early entrance. *Required:* school transcript, campus interview, CPAt.
APPLYING/TRANSFER *Required:* standardized test scores, high school transcript, campus interview, college transcript. *Entrance:* minimally difficult.
CONTACT Mr. Jim Vernetti, Director of Admissions, American Institute of Commerce, Davenport, IA 52807-2095, 319-355-3500.

CLINTON COMMUNITY COLLEGE
Clinton, Iowa

UG Enrollment: 1,125	Tuition & Fees (IA Res): $1635
Application Deadline: rolling	Room & Board: N/Avail

GENERAL State-supported, 2-year, coed. Part of Eastern Iowa Community College District System. Awards certificates, diplomas, transfer associate, terminal associate degrees. Founded 1946. *Setting:* 20-acre small-town campus. *Total enrollment:* 1,125. *Faculty:* 75 (35 full-time, 40 part-time).
ENROLLMENT PROFILE 1,125 students from 9 states and territories, 1 other country. 65% women, 50% part-time, 89% state residents, 23% transferred in, 1% international, 50% 25 or older, 1% Native American, 1% Hispanic, 2% African American, 1% Asian American.
FIRST-YEAR CLASS 429 total. Of the students who applied, 100% were accepted, 82% of whom enrolled. 12% from top 10% of their high school class, 17% from top quarter, 55% from top half.
ACADEMIC PROGRAM Core. Calendar: semesters. Academic remediation for entering students, English as a second language program offered during academic year, services for LD students, advanced placement, self-designed majors, tutorials, summer session for credit, part-time degree program (daytime, evenings), adult/continuing education programs, co-op programs and internships.

Peterson's Guide to Two-Year Colleges 1997   317

Clinton Community College (continued)
GENERAL DEGREE REQUIREMENTS 64 semester hours; 3 semester hours of math, 8 semester hours of science for associate of arts degree; 6 semester hours of math, 12 semester hours of science for associate of science degree; computer course.
MAJORS Accounting, architectural technologies, art/fine arts, biology/biological sciences, business administration/commerce/management, chemistry, communication, computer programming, computer science, computer technologies, criminal justice, culinary arts, drafting and design, economics, education, electronics engineering technology, engineering (general), (pre)engineering sequence, English, history, journalism, law enforcement/police sciences, liberal arts/general studies, marketing/retailing/merchandising, mathematics, medical laboratory technology, nursing, physical education, physical sciences, physics, political science/government, practical nursing, printing technologies, psychology, science, secretarial studies/office management, social science, social work.
LIBRARY Clinton Community College Library with 18,701 books, 12 microform titles, 155 periodicals, 1 on-line bibliographic service, 2 CD-ROMs, 773 records, tapes, and CDs.
COMPUTERS ON CAMPUS 37 computers for student use in computer labs. Staffed computer lab on campus.
COLLEGE LIFE Drama-theater group, student-run newspaper. ***Student services:*** personal-psychological counseling.
HOUSING College housing not available.
ATHLETICS Member NJCAA. ***Intercollegiate:*** basketball M(s), volleyball W. ***Intramural:*** basketball, bowling, football, golf, racquetball, skiing (downhill), tennis, volleyball, weight lifting.
CAREER PLANNING ***Director:*** Dr. Neil Mandsager, Dean of Student Development, 319-242-6841 Ext. 370. ***Services:*** job fairs, resume preparation, resume referral, career counseling, careers library, job bank, job interviews.
EXPENSES FOR 1995–96 ***Application fee:*** $20. State resident tuition: $1470 full-time, $49 per semester hour part-time. Nonresident tuition: $2205 full-time, $73.50 per semester hour part-time. Part-time mandatory fees: $5.50 per semester hour. Full-time mandatory fees: $165.
FINANCIAL AID ***College-administered undergrad aid 1995–96:*** 60 need-based scholarships (averaging $300), 15 non-need scholarships (averaging $300), short-term loans, low-interest long-term loans from external sources (averaging $2500), Federal Work-Study. ***Required forms:*** institutional, FAFSA; accepted: CSS Financial Aid PROFILE, state, SINGLEFILE Form of United Student Aid Funds. ***Priority deadline:*** 4/20.
APPLYING Open admission except for nursing program. ***Options:*** early entrance, deferred entrance, midyear entrance. ***Required:*** school transcript, TOEFL for international students. ***Recommended:*** ACT. Test scores used for admission and counseling/placement. ***Application deadline:*** rolling. ***Notification:*** continuous.
APPLYING/TRANSFER ***Required:*** high school transcript, college transcript. ***Recommended:*** standardized test scores. ***Entrance:*** noncompetitive. ***Application deadline:*** rolling. ***Notification:*** continuous.
CONTACT Mrs. Sue Carmody, Assistant Dean of Student Development, Clinton Community College, Clinton, IA 52732-6299, 319-242-6841 Ext. 349.

DES MOINES AREA COMMUNITY COLLEGE
Ankeny, Iowa

UG Enrollment: 10,287	**Tuition & Fees (IA Res): $1771**
Application Deadline: rolling	**Room & Board: N/Avail**

GENERAL State and locally supported, 2-year, coed. Part of Iowa Area Community Colleges System. Awards certificates, diplomas, transfer associate, terminal associate degrees. Founded 1966. ***Setting:*** 362-acre small-town campus. ***Educational spending 1994–95:*** $2409 per undergrad. ***Total enrollment:*** 10,287. ***Faculty:*** 240 full-time; student-faculty ratio is 24:1.
ENROLLMENT PROFILE 10,287 students from 21 states and territories, 16 other countries. 61% women, 39% men, 58% part-time, 98% state residents, 5% transferred in, 2% international, 46% 25 or older, 1% Hispanic, 3% African American, 2% Asian American.
FIRST-YEAR CLASS 4,541 total. Of the students who applied, 100% were accepted. 8% from top 10% of their high school class, 35% from top quarter, 74% from top half.
ACADEMIC PROGRAM Core, honor code. Calendar: semesters. 950 courses offered in 1995–96. Academic remediation for entering students, English as a second language program offered during academic year and summer, services for LD students, advanced placement, self-designed majors, honors program, summer session for credit, part-time degree program (daytime, evenings), adult/continuing education programs, co-op programs. Off-campus study at Drake University, Grand View College.
GENERAL DEGREE REQUIREMENTS 64 credit hours; internship (some majors).
MAJORS Accounting, agricultural business, automotive technologies, biomedical technologies, business administration/commerce/management, child care/child and family studies, commercial art, computer programming, computer technologies, corrections, criminal justice, culinary arts, data processing, dental services, drafting and design, education, electrical and electronics technologies, fashion merchandising, fire science, food services management, health services administration, horticulture, hotel and restaurant management, human services, industrial and heavy equipment maintenance, law enforcement/police sciences, legal secretarial studies, liberal arts/general studies, machine and tool technologies, marketing/retailing/merchandising, medical assistant technologies, medical laboratory technology, medical secretarial studies, nursing, paralegal studies, printing technologies, recreation and leisure services, respiratory therapy, retail management, robotics, secretarial studies/office management, teacher aide studies, telecommunications.
LIBRARY 56,857 books, 48 microform titles, 570 periodicals, 1,313 records, tapes, and CDs.
COMPUTERS ON CAMPUS Computer purchase plan available. 700 computers for student use in computer center, computer labs, classrooms, library provide access to main academic computer. Staffed computer lab on campus provides training in use of computers, software.
COLLEGE LIFE Drama-theater group, student-run newspaper. 15% vote in student government elections. ***Student services:*** health clinic, personal-psychological counseling, women's center. ***Campus security:*** 24-hour emergency response devices and patrols, late-night transport-escort service.
HOUSING College housing not available.
ATHLETICS Member NJCAA. ***Intercollegiate:*** basketball M(s)/W(s), golf M/W. ***Intramural:*** basketball, football, golf, soccer, volleyball.
CAREER PLANNING ***Placement office:*** 2 full-time, 1 part-time staff. ***Director:*** Ms. Dorothy Thornton, Placement Officer, 515-964-6243. ***Services:*** resume preparation, career counseling, careers library, job bank, job interviews.
EXPENSES FOR 1996–97 State resident tuition: $1566 full-time, $49 per semester hour part-time. Nonresident tuition: $3132 full-time, $98 per semester hour part-time. Part-time mandatory fees: $6.40 per semester hour. Full-time mandatory fees: $205.
FINANCIAL AID ***College-administered undergrad aid 1995–96:*** need-based scholarships (average $200), non-need scholarships (average $300), low-interest long-term loans from external sources, Federal Work-Study, part-time jobs. ***Required forms:*** FAFSA; accepted: CSS Financial Aid PROFILE. ***Priority deadline:*** 3/1.
APPLYING Open admission. ***Options:*** early entrance, deferred entrance. ***Required:*** TOEFL for international students, ACT ASSET. ***Recommended:*** ACT. ***Required for some:*** school transcript. Test scores used for counseling/placement. ***Application deadline:*** rolling.
APPLYING/TRANSFER ***Required:*** standardized test scores, college transcript. ***Required for some:*** high school transcript. ***Entrance:*** noncompetitive. ***Application deadline:*** rolling. ***Contact:*** Ms. Sharon Van Tuyl, Registrar, 515-964-6562.
CONTACT Mr. Lynn Albrecht, Dean of Student Services, Des Moines Area Community College, Ankeny, IA 50021-8995, 515-964-6210 or toll-free 800-362-2127 (in-state).

ELLSWORTH COMMUNITY COLLEGE
Iowa Falls, Iowa

UG Enrollment: 850	**Tuition & Fees (IA Res): $2088**
Application Deadline: rolling	**Room & Board: $3000**

GENERAL State and locally supported, 2-year, coed. Part of Iowa Valley Community College District System. Awards diplomas, transfer associate, terminal associate degrees. Founded 1890. ***Setting:*** 10-acre small-town campus. ***Total enrollment:*** 850. ***Faculty:*** 50 (41 full-time, 9 part-time); student-faculty ratio is 15:1.
ENROLLMENT PROFILE 850 students: 49% women, 51% men, 21% part-time, 94% state residents, 34% live on campus, 15% transferred in, 1% international, 30% 25 or older, 5% African American. ***Areas of study chosen:*** 20% liberal arts/general studies, 20% vocational and home economics, 16% business management and administrative services, 13% social sciences, 10% biological and life sciences, 10% health professions and related sciences, 9% agriculture, 2% fine arts. ***Most popular recent majors:*** business administration/commerce/management, education, liberal arts/general studies.
FIRST-YEAR CLASS 450 total; 630 applied, 98% were accepted, 73% of whom enrolled. 5% from top 10% of their high school class, 40% from top half.
ACADEMIC PROGRAM Core. Calendar: semesters. Average class size 25 in required courses. Academic remediation for entering students, services for LD students, advanced placement, self-designed majors, honors program, summer session for credit, part-time degree program (daytime, evenings, summer), adult/continuing education programs, co-op programs and internships.
GENERAL DEGREE REQUIREMENTS 64 semester hours; 7 semester hours of math/science for associate of science degree; 8 semester hours of math/science for associate of arts degree; computer course; internship (some majors).
MAJORS Accounting, agricultural business, art education, art/fine arts, biology/biological sciences, biotechnology, business administration/commerce/management, child care/child and family studies, child psychology/child development, commercial art, conservation, corrections, criminal justice, data processing, drug and alcohol/substance abuse counseling, early childhood education, economics, education, (pre)engineering sequence, equestrian studies, fashion merchandising, history, human services, interior design, laboratory technologies, legal secretarial studies, liberal arts/general studies, marketing/retailing/merchandising, mathematics, medical secretarial studies, medical technology, nursing, physical education, physical sciences, political science/government, pollution control technologies, psychology, retail management, science, secretarial studies/office management, social work, sociology, teacher aide studies, vocational education, wildlife biology.
LIBRARY Osgood Learning Resource Center with 25,500 books, 300 periodicals, 2,360 records, tapes, and CDs. Acquisition spending 1994–95: $28,934.
COMPUTERS ON CAMPUS 50 computers for student use in computer center, mathematics building, trades and industry building, classrooms, library. Staffed computer lab on campus provides training in use of computers, software. Academic computing expenditure 1994–95: $64,589.
COLLEGE LIFE Drama-theater group, choral group, student-run newspaper. 40% vote in student government elections. ***Social organizations:*** 10 open to all. ***Most popular organizations:*** Non-Traditional Student Organization, Drama Club, Agriculture-Science Club, Criminal Justice Club. ***Major annual events:*** Family Day, Homecoming, Cabin Fever Weekend. ***Student services:*** personal-psychological counseling. ***Campus security:*** 24-hour emergency response devices, controlled dormitory access, security personnel 10 p.m.- 6 a.m.
HOUSING 380 college housing spaces available; 300 were occupied 1995–96. Freshmen given priority for college housing. On-campus residence required in freshman year. ***Option:*** single-sex (2 buildings) housing available. Resident assistants live in dorms.
ATHLETICS Member NJCAA. ***Intercollegiate:*** baseball M(s), basketball M(s)/W(s), football M(s), golf M, softball W(s), volleyball W(s), wrestling M(s). ***Intramural:*** baseball, basketball, equestrian sports, football, racquetball, rugby, softball, swimming and diving, tennis, volleyball, water polo, weight lifting. ***Contact:*** Mr. Rick Dawson, Director of Athletics/Activities, 515-648-4611 Ext. 270.
CAREER PLANNING ***Placement office:*** 2 full-time staff. ***Director:*** Ms. Nancy Walters, Counselor, 515-648-4611. ***Services:*** resume preparation, career counseling, careers library.
AFTER GRADUATION 90% of students completing a degree program in 1994–95 went directly on to further study.
EXPENSES FOR 1995–96 ***Application fee:*** $25. State resident tuition: $1856 full-time, $58 per semester hour part-time. Nonresident tuition: $3712 full-time, $116 per semester hour part-time. Part-time mandatory fees: $116 per semester. Full-time mandatory fees: $232. College room and board: $3000.
FINANCIAL AID ***College-administered undergrad aid 1995–96:*** need-based scholarships, 120 non-need scholarships (average $880), low-interest long-term loans from external sources (average $2300), Federal Work-Study, 65 part-time jobs. ***Acceptable forms:*** CSS Financial Aid PROFILE, FAFSA. ***Priority deadline:*** 6/1. ***Payment plan:*** installment.
APPLYING Open admission for state residents. ***Options:*** early entrance, deferred entrance, midyear entrance. ***Required:*** school transcript, TOEFL for international students.

Recommended: ACT. *Required for some:* ACT. Test scores used for counseling/placement. *Application deadlines:* rolling, 8/1 for nonresidents. *Notification:* continuous.
APPLYING/TRANSFER *Required:* high school transcript, college transcript. *Required for some:* standardized test scores. *Entrance:* noncompetitive. *Application deadline:* rolling. *Notification:* continuous. *Contact:* Mr. Philip Rusley, Director of Admissions and Registrar, 515-648-4611.
CONTACT Mr. Philip Rusley, Director of Admissions and Registrar, Ellsworth Community College, Iowa Falls, IA 50126-1199, 515-648-4611 Ext. 241. *Fax:* 515-648-3128. College video available.

HAMILTON BUSINESS COLLEGE
Cedar Rapids, Iowa

UG Enrollment: 353	Tuition & Fees: $6185
Application Deadline: rolling	Room & Board: N/Avail

GENERAL Proprietary, 2-year, primarily women. Awards certificates, diplomas, terminal associate degrees. Founded 1900. *Setting:* 4-acre suburban campus. *Total enrollment:* 353. *Faculty:* 19 (10 full-time, 100% with terminal degrees, 9 part-time); student-faculty ratio is 23:1.
ENROLLMENT PROFILE 353 students: 85% women, 30% part-time, 100% state residents, 25% transferred in, 80% have need-based financial aid, 0% international, 83% 25 or older, 0% Native American, 0% Hispanic, 4% African American, 1% Asian American. *Areas of study chosen:* 100% business management and administrative services. *Most popular recent majors:* accounting, business administration/commerce/management, medical secretarial studies.
FIRST-YEAR CLASS 100 total. Of the students who applied, 80% were accepted, 80% of whom enrolled. 5% from top 10% of their high school class, 15% from top quarter.
ACADEMIC PROGRAM Core, interdisciplinary curriculum, honor code. Calendar: quarters. 133 courses offered in 1995–96; average class size 25 in required courses. Academic remediation for entering students, tutorials, part-time degree program (evenings, summer), adult/continuing education programs, co-op programs and internships.
GENERAL DEGREE REQUIREMENTS 92 credit hours; 8 credit hours of math/science; computer course.
MAJORS Accounting, business administration/commerce/management, business machine technologies, computer information systems, data processing, legal secretarial studies, medical secretarial studies, tourism and travel, word processing.
LIBRARY Hamilton Business College Library with 5,500 books, 40 periodicals, 50 CD-ROMs, 200 records, tapes, and CDs. Acquisition spending 1994–95: $50,000.
COMPUTERS ON CAMPUS Computer purchase plan available. 50 computers for student use in computer labs, library provide access to Internet. Staffed computer lab on campus provides training in use of computers, software. Academic computing expenditure 1994–95: $150,000.
COLLEGE LIFE Student-run newspaper. 30% vote in student government elections. *Social organizations:* 4 open to all. *Most popular organizations:* Phi Beta Lambda, Student Activities Board, Collegiate Secretaries International, Travel Club. *Major annual events:* End of Quarter Bash, Awards Program, Alumni Picnic. *Campus security:* 24-hour emergency response devices.
HOUSING College housing not available.
CAREER PLANNING *Placement office:* 1 full-time, 1 part-time staff; $35,000 operating expenditure 1994–95. *Director:* Ms. Denae Zigtema, Employment Search Coordinator, 319-363-0481. *Services:* job fairs, resume preparation, resume referral, career counseling, careers library, job bank, job interviews. 50 organizations recruited on campus 1994–95.
AFTER GRADUATION 98% of class of 1994 had job offers within 6 months.
EXPENSES FOR 1996–97 *Application fee:* $25. Tuition: $5985 full-time, $133 per credit hour part-time. Part-time mandatory fees: $100 per year. Full-time mandatory fees: $200.
FINANCIAL AID *College-administered undergrad aid 1995–96:* 210 need-based scholarships (average $159), 2 Federal Work-Study (averaging $543), 12 part-time jobs. *Required forms:* FAFSA. *Priority deadline:* 3/15. *Payment plans:* tuition prepayment, installment.
APPLYING *Options:* Common Application, early entrance, deferred entrance, midyear entrance. *Required:* school transcript, minimum 2.0 GPA, interview, CPAt. Test scores used for admission and counseling/placement. *Application deadline:* rolling.
APPLYING/TRANSFER *Required:* college transcript. *Required for some:* minimum 2.0 college GPA. *Contact:* Mr. David Omar, Academic Dean, 319-363-0481.
CONTACT Mr. Don Erwin, Director of Admissions, Hamilton Business College, Cedar Rapids, IA 52404, 319-363-0481 or toll-free 800-728-0481. *Fax:* 319-363-3812.

HAWKEYE COMMUNITY COLLEGE
Waterloo, Iowa

UG Enrollment: 3,530	Tuition & Fees (IA Res): $2175
Application Deadline: rolling	Room & Board: N/Avail

GENERAL State and locally supported, 2-year, coed. Part of Iowa Area Community Colleges System. Awards certificates, diplomas, transfer associate, terminal associate degrees. Founded 1967. *Setting:* 320-acre rural campus. *Total enrollment:* 3,530. *Faculty:* 203 (111 full-time, 39% with terminal degrees, 92 part-time); student-faculty ratio is 20:1.
ENROLLMENT PROFILE 3,530 students from 4 states and territories, 8 other countries. 58% women, 42% men, 30% part-time, 99% state residents, 12% transferred in, 81% have need-based financial aid, 11% have non-need-based financial aid, 33% 25 or older, 1% Native American, 1% Hispanic, 6% African American, 1% Asian American. *Areas of study chosen:* 49% liberal arts/general studies, 13% engineering and applied sciences, 11% business management and administrative services, 10% health professions and related sciences, 7% fine arts, 4% agriculture, 3% social sciences, 2% architecture, 1% interdisciplinary studies. *Most popular recent majors:* liberal arts/general studies, criminal justice, practical nursing.
FIRST-YEAR CLASS 1,143 total; 1,989 applied, 78% of whom enrolled. 17% from top quarter of their high school class, 53% from top half.
ACADEMIC PROGRAM Technical and general education curriculum, honor code. Calendar: semesters. 630 courses offered in 1995–96. Academic remediation for entering students, services for LD students, advanced placement, summer session for credit, part-time degree program (daytime, evenings, weekends, summer), external degree programs, adult/continuing education programs, co-op programs and internships. ROTC: Army (c).
GENERAL DEGREE REQUIREMENTS 64 credits; computer course for all associate of science and associate of applied science degree students; internship (some majors).
MAJORS Accounting, agricultural business, agricultural technologies, agronomy/soil and crop sciences, aircraft and missile maintenance, animal sciences, architectural technologies, automotive technologies, aviation technology, biology/biological sciences, business administration/commerce/management, child care/child and family studies, civil engineering technology, commercial art, computer technologies, corrections, criminal justice, dental services, drafting and design, education, electrical and electronics technologies, electronics engineering technology, emergency medical technology, engineering technology, farm and ranch management, graphic arts, heating/refrigeration/air conditioning, horticulture, industrial and heavy equipment maintenance, interdisciplinary studies, interior design, law enforcement/police sciences, liberal arts/general studies, machine and tool technologies, marketing/retailing/merchandising, mechanical design technology, mechanical engineering technology, medical laboratory technology, medical secretarial studies, nursing, ornamental horticulture, parks management, photography, practical nursing, respiratory therapy, secretarial studies/office management, social work, surveying technology, textiles and clothing, welding technology.
LIBRARY 18,200 books, 85 microform titles, 534 periodicals, 12 CD-ROMs, 804 records, tapes, and CDs. Acquisition spending 1994–95: $542,827.
COMPUTERS ON CAMPUS 304 computers for student use in computer labs, learning resource center, classrooms, library provide access to main academic computer.
COLLEGE LIFE *Social organizations:* 10 open to all. *Major annual events:* Fall Fest, Spring Splurge, Hypnotist. *Student services:* personal-psychological counseling, women's center. *Campus security:* 24-hour patrols.
HOUSING College housing not available.
ATHLETICS *Intramural:* basketball, bowling, golf, skiing (cross-country), skiing (downhill), softball, swimming and diving, volleyball, weight lifting, wrestling.
CAREER PLANNING *Placement office:* 6 full-time, 2 part-time staff; $271,822 operating expenditure 1994–95. *Director:* Ms. Dianne Shultz, Director of Student Development, 319-296-4027. *Services:* job fairs, resume preparation, resume referral, career counseling, careers library, job bank, job interviews. Students must register sophomore year.
EXPENSES FOR 1995–96 State resident tuition: $1920 full-time, $64 per credit part-time. Nonresident tuition: $3840 full-time, $128 per credit part-time. Part-time mandatory fees: $8.50 per credit. Full-time mandatory fees: $255.
FINANCIAL AID *College-administered undergrad aid 1995–96:* 498 need-based scholarships (averaging $400), 12 non-need scholarships (averaging $1037), short-term loans (averaging $50), low-interest long-term loans from college funds (averaging $1700), loans from external sources (averaging $2900), 68 Federal Work-Study (averaging $1900), 18 part-time jobs. *Required forms:* FAFSA. *Priority deadline:* 3/31. *Payment plan:* installment.
APPLYING Open admission. *Options:* deferred entrance, midyear entrance. *Required:* school transcript, TOEFL for international students, ACT ASSET. *Required for some:* 3 years of high school math, SAT I or ACT. Test scores used for counseling/placement. *Application deadline:* rolling. *Notification:* continuous.
APPLYING/TRANSFER *Required:* high school transcript, college transcript. *Required for some:* 3 years of high school math. *Entrance:* noncompetitive. *Application deadline:* rolling. *Notification:* continuous. *Contact:* Mr. David Fish, Director of Enrollment Management, 319-296-2320 Ext. 1214.
CONTACT Mr. David Fish, Director of Enrollment Management, Hawkeye Community College, Waterloo, IA 50704-8015, 319-296-2320 Ext. 1214. *Fax:* 319-296-2874. College video available.

INDIAN HILLS COMMUNITY COLLEGE
Ottumwa, Iowa

UG Enrollment: 3,292	Tuition & Fees (IA Res): $1500
Application Deadline: rolling	Room & Board: $2115

GENERAL State and locally supported, 2-year, coed. Part of Iowa Area Community Colleges System. Awards certificates, diplomas, transfer associate, terminal associate degrees. Founded 1966. *Setting:* 400-acre small-town campus. *Total enrollment:* 3,292. *Faculty:* 137 (125 full-time, 4% with terminal degrees, 12 part-time).
ENROLLMENT PROFILE 3,292 students from 20 states and territories. 56% women, 44% men, 28% part-time, 90% state residents, 15% live on campus, 8% transferred in, 32% 25 or older, 1% Native American, 1% Hispanic, 1% African American, 1% Asian American. *Most popular recent majors:* liberal arts/general studies, practical nursing, electrical and electronics technologies.
FIRST-YEAR CLASS 1,231 total; 1,500 applied, 92% were accepted, 89% of whom enrolled. 20% from top 10% of their high school class.
ACADEMIC PROGRAM Calendar: semesters. Academic remediation for entering students, English as a second language program offered during academic year and summer, services for LD students, self-designed majors, honors program, summer session for credit, part-time degree program (daytime, evenings, summer), adult/continuing education programs, co-op programs and internships.
GENERAL DEGREE REQUIREMENTS 61 semester hours; computer course for health science majors; internship (some majors).
MAJORS Agricultural technologies, automotive technologies, aviation technology, biotechnology, business administration/commerce/management, child care/child and family studies, computer programming, computer technologies, criminal justice, drafting and design, electrical and electronics technologies, flight training, food services technology, health services administration, horticulture, industrial and heavy equipment maintenance, laser technologies, liberal arts/general studies, machine and tool technologies, medical records services, nursing, physical therapy, practical nursing, radiological technology, robotics.
LIBRARY 50,982 books, 82 microform titles, 347 periodicals, 7,630 records, tapes, and CDs.
COMPUTERS ON CAMPUS 94 computers for student use in computer center, library.
COLLEGE LIFE Drama-theater group. *Most popular organizations:* Student Senate, Warriors Club. *Major annual events:* Foundation Auction, Art on the Lawn Festival. *Student services:* personal-psychological counseling, women's center. *Campus security:* 24-hour emergency response devices and patrols.

Indian Hills Community College (continued)

HOUSING 496 college housing spaces available; all were occupied 1995–96. No special consideration for freshman housing applicants. Off-campus living permitted. ***Options:*** coed, single-sex housing available. Resident assistants live in dorms.

ATHLETICS Member NJCAA. ***Intercollegiate:*** baseball M, basketball M, golf M, softball W, volleyball W(c). ***Intramural:*** basketball, fencing, football, racquetball, riflery, tennis, volleyball. ***Contact:*** Mr. Kelly Conrad, Athletic Director, 515-683-5136.

CAREER PLANNING ***Service:*** career counseling.

AFTER GRADUATION 45% of students completing a degree program in 1994–95 went directly on to further study.

EXPENSES FOR 1995–96 State resident tuition: $1320 full-time, $44 per semester hour part-time. Nonresident tuition: $1980 full-time, $66 per semester hour part-time. Part-time mandatory fees: $6 per semester hour. Full-time mandatory fees: $180. College room and board: $2115.

FINANCIAL AID ***College-administered undergrad aid 1995–96:*** 127 need-based scholarships (averaging $210), 323 non-need scholarships (averaging $210), short-term loans (averaging $50), low-interest long-term loans from external sources (averaging $1000), Federal Work-Study, 22 part-time jobs. ***Required forms:*** CSS Financial Aid PROFILE; accepted: FAFSA. ***Priority deadline:*** 3/1.

APPLYING Open admission except for nursing, technology programs. ***Option:*** early entrance. ***Required:*** TOEFL for international students, ACT ASSET. ***Required for some:*** school transcript, 3 years of high school math, ACT. Test scores used for counseling/placement. ***Application deadline:*** rolling.

APPLYING/TRANSFER ***Required:*** college transcript. ***Required for some:*** high school transcript, 3 years of high school math. ***Application deadline:*** rolling.

CONTACT Mrs. Jane Sapp, Admissions Officer, Indian Hills Community College, Ottumwa, IA 52501-1398, 515-683-5155 or toll-free 800-726-2585.

IOWA CENTRAL COMMUNITY COLLEGE
Fort Dodge, Iowa

UG Enrollment: 2,627	**Tuition & Fees (IA Res): $1898**
Application Deadline: rolling	**Room & Board: $2860**

GENERAL State and locally supported, 2-year, coed. Part of Iowa Department of Education Division of Community Colleges. Awards certificates, diplomas, transfer associate, terminal associate degrees. Founded 1966. ***Setting:*** 110-acre small-town campus. ***Total enrollment:*** 2,627. ***Faculty:*** 133 (86 full-time, 1% with terminal degrees, 47 part-time); student-faculty ratio is 16:1.

ENROLLMENT PROFILE 2,627 students: 54% women, 46% men, 50% part-time, 98% state residents, 8% transferred in, 60% have need-based financial aid, 10% have non-need-based financial aid, 1% international, 43% 25 or older, 1% Native American, 1% Hispanic, 1% African American, 1% Asian American. ***Most popular recent major:*** business administration/commerce/management.

FIRST-YEAR CLASS 1,847 total; 2,400 applied, 90% of whom enrolled. 10% from top 10% of their high school class, 20% from top quarter, 40% from top half.

ACADEMIC PROGRAM Core. Calendar: semesters. Academic remediation for entering students, English as a second language program offered during academic year, services for LD students, advanced placement, tutorials, summer session for credit, part-time degree program (daytime, evenings, summer), adult/continuing education programs, co-op programs and internships. Study abroad in Spain, Germany, Mexico (1% of students participate).

GENERAL DEGREE REQUIREMENTS 60 semester hours; 4 semester hours each of math and science; computer course for accounting majors; internship (some majors).

MAJORS Accounting, automotive technologies, aviation administration, broadcasting, business administration/commerce/management, business education, carpentry, child care/child and family studies, communication, community services, computer science, data processing, drafting and design, education, electrical engineering technology, electronics engineering technology, flight training, food marketing, journalism, law enforcement/police sciences, liberal arts/general studies, machine and tool technologies, medical assistant technologies, medical laboratory technology, nursing, occupational therapy, physical therapy, practical nursing, radio and television studies, radiological technology, science, science education, secretarial studies/office management, social work, sociology, teacher aide studies, telecommunications, welding technology.

LIBRARY Iowa Central Community College Library plus 1 other, with 55,000 books, 130 microform titles, 350 periodicals, 12 CD-ROMs, 350 records, tapes, and CDs.

COMPUTERS ON CAMPUS Computer purchase plan available. 250 computers for student use in computer center, computer labs, learning resource center, labs, various locations, library, student center, dorms provide access to main academic computer, on-line services.

COLLEGE LIFE Orientation program (4 days, no cost, parents included). Drama-theater group, choral group, student-run newspaper, radio station. ***Student services:*** health clinic, personal-psychological counseling. ***Campus security:*** 24-hour emergency response devices and patrols, student patrols, late-night transport-escort service, controlled dormitory access.

HOUSING 420 college housing spaces available; 175 were occupied 1995–96. No special consideration for freshman housing applicants. Off-campus living permitted. ***Option:*** single-sex housing available. Resident assistants live in dorms.

ATHLETICS Member NJCAA. ***Intercollegiate:*** baseball M, basketball M(s)/W(s), football M(s), golf M/W, softball W, volleyball W, wrestling M(s). ***Intramural:*** basketball, football, golf, softball, table tennis (Ping-Pong), tennis, volleyball, weight lifting, wrestling. ***Contact:*** Mr. Denis Pichler, Athletic Director, 515-576-7201 Ext. 2428.

CAREER PLANNING ***Placement office:*** 1 part-time staff. ***Director:*** Mr. Dave Raedeker, Director of Placement, 515-576-7201 Ext. 2407. ***Services:*** job fairs, resume preparation, resume referral, career counseling, careers library, job interviews.

AFTER GRADUATION 45% of students completing a degree program in 1994–95 went directly on to further study.

EXPENSES FOR 1996–97 State resident tuition: $1650 full-time, $55 per semester hour part-time. Nonresident tuition: $2475 full-time, $83 per semester hour part-time. Part-time mandatory fees: $8.25 per semester hour. Full-time mandatory fees: $248. College room and board: $2860.

FINANCIAL AID ***College-administered undergrad aid 1995–96:*** 130 need-based scholarships (average $200), non-need scholarships, short-term loans (average $200), low-interest long-term loans from external sources (average $1500), 75 Federal Work-Study (averaging $1000). ***Required forms:*** institutional, FAFSA; accepted: CSS Financial Aid PROFILE. ***Priority deadline:*** 4/1. ***Payment plan:*** deferred payment.

APPLYING Open admission. ***Option:*** early entrance. ***Required:*** ACT, TOEFL for international students, ACT ASSET. ***Recommended:*** school transcript. ***Required for some:*** school transcript. Test scores used for counseling/placement. ***Application deadline:*** rolling.

APPLYING/TRANSFER ***Required:*** college transcript. ***Entrance:*** noncompetitive. ***Application deadline:*** rolling. ***Contact:*** Mr. Doug Thompson, Registrar, 515-576-7201.

CONTACT Mr. Arne Ebner, Director of Admissions, Iowa Central Community College, Fort Dodge, IA 50501-5798, 515-576-7201 Ext. 2400. ***E-mail:*** admis@duke.iccc.cc.ia.us. College video available.

IOWA LAKES COMMUNITY COLLEGE
Estherville, Iowa

UG Enrollment: 2,068	**Tuition & Fees (IA Res): $1978**
Application Deadline: rolling	**Room & Board: $2240**

GENERAL State and locally supported, 2-year, coed. Part of Iowa Area Community Colleges System. Awards certificates, diplomas, transfer associate, terminal associate degrees. Founded 1967. ***Setting:*** 20-acre small-town campus. ***Total enrollment:*** 2,068. ***Faculty:*** 40.

ENROLLMENT PROFILE 2,068 students from 10 states and territories, 6 other countries. 50% women, 16% part-time, 98% state residents, 12% transferred in, 12% 25 or older, 1% African American. ***Most popular recent majors:*** criminal justice, environmental studies, business administration/commerce/management.

FIRST-YEAR CLASS 940 total; 1,551 applied, 94% of whom enrolled.

ACADEMIC PROGRAM Core. Calendar: semesters. Academic remediation for entering students, services for LD students, honors program, summer session for credit, part-time degree program (daytime, evenings, weekends, summer), adult/continuing education programs, co-op programs and internships.

GENERAL DEGREE REQUIREMENTS 64 credit hours; math/science requirements vary according to program; computer course; internship (some majors).

MAJORS Accounting, applied art, art education, art/fine arts, art history, astronomy, aviation administration, behavioral sciences, biology/biological sciences, botany/plant sciences, business administration/commerce/management, business machine technologies, ceramic art and design, chemical engineering technology, chemistry, child care/child and family studies, child psychology/child development, commercial art, communication, computer programming, computer science, conservation, criminal justice, data processing, drafting and design, earth science, ecology, economics, education, electrical and electronics technologies, elementary education, energy management technologies, (pre)engineering sequence, English, environmental design, environmental education, environmental sciences, environmental studies, finance/banking, fish and game management, flight training, geology, health services administration, history, history of philosophy, history of science, humanities, jazz, journalism, laboratory technologies, law enforcement/police sciences, legal secretarial studies, legal studies, liberal arts/general studies, literature, mathematics, music, music education, natural sciences, painting/drawing, paralegal studies, pharmacy/pharmaceutical sciences, philosophy, photography, physical education, physical sciences, piano/organ, political science/government, pollution control technologies, printing technologies, psychology, real estate, recreation and leisure services, rehabilitation therapy, retail management, science, science education, secretarial studies/office management, social science, social work, sociology, speech/rhetoric/public address/debate, studio art, voice, water resources, wildlife management, wind and percussion instruments.

LIBRARY 25,861 books, 232 microform titles, 178 periodicals, 2,832 records, tapes, and CDs.

COMPUTERS ON CAMPUS 200 computers for student use in computer center, computer labs, learning resource center, library.

COLLEGE LIFE Choral group, student-run newspaper, radio station. ***Social organizations:*** 35 open to all. ***Major annual events:*** Homecoming, Estherville Winter Sports, Snow Sculptures Festival. ***Student services:*** personal-psychological counseling, women's center.

HOUSING 120 college housing spaces available; all were occupied 1995–96. No special consideration for freshman housing applicants. Off-campus living permitted. ***Option:*** coed housing available.

ATHLETICS Member NJCAA. ***Intercollegiate:*** baseball M(s), basketball M(s)/W(s), football M(s), golf M(s), softball W(s), weight lifting M/W. ***Intramural:*** basketball, football, golf, racquetball, skiing (cross-country), skiing (downhill), softball, table tennis (Ping-Pong), tennis, volleyball, weight lifting. ***Contact:*** Mr. Bob Grems, Athletic Director, 712-362-2604.

CAREER PLANNING ***Service:*** career counseling.

AFTER GRADUATION 60% of students completing a degree program in 1994–95 went directly on to further study.

EXPENSES FOR 1995–96 State resident tuition: $1728 full-time, $54 per semester hour part-time. Nonresident tuition: $2630 full-time, $90 per semester hour part-time. Part-time mandatory fees: $12.25 per semester. Full-time mandatory fees: $250. College room and board: $2240 (minimum). College room only: $1170.

FINANCIAL AID ***College-administered undergrad aid 1995–96:*** 328 need-based scholarships (averaging $1050), 180 non-need scholarships (averaging $150), low-interest long-term loans from external sources (averaging $2500), Federal Work-Study, part-time jobs. ***Required forms:*** institutional, FAFSA; accepted: CSS Financial Aid PROFILE. ***Priority deadline:*** 9/1. ***Payment plan:*** installment.

APPLYING Open admission except for allied health, aviation programs. ***Options:*** early entrance, midyear entrance. ***Required:*** school transcript, TOEFL for international students. ***Recommended:*** ACT. ***Required for some:*** recommendations, interview, ACT. Test scores used for counseling/placement. ***Application deadline:*** rolling.

APPLYING/TRANSFER ***Required:*** high school transcript, college transcript. ***Required for some:*** standardized test scores, recommendations, interview. ***Application deadline:*** rolling. ***Contact:*** Mr. John G. Nelson, Director of Admissions, 712-362-2604 Ext. 146.

CONTACT Mr. John G. Nelson, Director of Admissions, Iowa Lakes Community College, Estherville, IA 51334-2295, 712-362-2604 Ext. 146 or toll-free 800-242-5106. ***Fax:*** 712-362-2260.

IOWA WESTERN COMMUNITY COLLEGE
Council Bluffs, Iowa

UG Enrollment: 3,638 **Tuition & Fees (IA Res): $2100**
Application Deadline: rolling **Room & Board: $3000**

GENERAL District-supported, 2-year, coed. Part of Iowa Department of Education Division of Community Colleges. Awards certificates, diplomas, transfer associate, terminal associate degrees. Founded 1966. ***Setting:*** 282-acre suburban campus with easy access to Omaha. ***Total enrollment:*** 3,638. ***Faculty:*** 218 (112 full-time, 98% with terminal degrees, 106 part-time).
ENROLLMENT PROFILE 3,638 students from 28 states and territories, 10 other countries. 57% women, 51% part-time, 90% state residents, 5% transferred in, 1% international, 36% 25 or older, 1% Native American, 1% Hispanic, 1% African American, 1% Asian American. ***Areas of study chosen:*** 46% liberal arts/general studies, 16% business management and administrative services, 15% health professions and related sciences, 8% vocational and home economics, 7% computer and information sciences, 5% engineering and applied sciences, 3% agriculture. ***Most popular recent majors:*** business administration/commerce/management, nursing, criminal justice.
FIRST-YEAR CLASS 1,434 total; 1,581 applied, 95% were accepted, 96% of whom enrolled.
ACADEMIC PROGRAM Core, honor code. Calendar: semesters. 112 courses offered in 1995–96. Academic remediation for entering students, English as a second language program offered during academic year and summer, services for LD students, tutorials, summer session for credit, part-time degree program (daytime, evenings, weekends, summer), adult/continuing education programs, co-op programs and internships. ROTC: Army (c), Air Force (c).
GENERAL DEGREE REQUIREMENTS 60 semester hours; math/science requirements vary according to program; computer course for all associate of science degree students; internship (some majors).
MAJORS Accounting, agricultural business, architectural technologies, automotive technologies, aviation technology, business administration/commerce/management, child care/child and family studies, civil engineering technology, computer programming, criminal justice, culinary arts, deaf interpreter training, drug and alcohol/substance abuse counseling, electronics engineering technology, farm and ranch management, fashion merchandising, fire science, food marketing, food services management, food services technology, graphic arts, hotel and restaurant management, human services, industrial administration, industrial design, international business, journalism, law enforcement/police sciences, legal secretarial studies, liberal arts/general studies, machine and tool technologies, marketing/retailing/merchandising, mechanical design technology, mechanical engineering technology, medical assistant technologies, medical secretarial studies, nursing, paralegal studies, practical nursing, retail management, secretarial studies/office management, welding technology.
LIBRARY 59,200 books, 207 periodicals, 1 on-line bibliographic service, 15 CD-ROMs, 1,579 records, tapes, and CDs. Acquisition spending 1994–95: $39,822.
COMPUTERS ON CAMPUS 195 computers for student use in computer center, labs, library, dorms. Staffed computer lab on campus provides training in use of computers, software. Academic computing expenditure 1994–95: $1.1 million.
COLLEGE LIFE Drama-theater group, choral group, student-run newspaper. ***Social organizations:*** 21 open to all. ***Most popular organizations:*** Student Senate, Health Occupations Student Association, Volunteer Institute Program, Data Processing Student Association, Phi Theta Kappa. ***Major annual events:*** Career Awareness Fair, Renaissance Faire, Annual Job Expo. ***Student services:*** personal-psychological counseling. ***Campus security:*** 24-hour patrols, late-night transport-escort service.
HOUSING 524 college housing spaces available; 500 were occupied 1995–96. No special consideration for freshman housing applicants. Off-campus living permitted. ***Option:*** coed (2 buildings) housing available. Resident assistants live in dorms.
ATHLETICS Member NJCAA. ***Intercollegiate:*** baseball M(s), basketball M(s), softball W(s), volleyball W(s). ***Intramural:*** baseball, basketball, football, tennis, volleyball. ***Contact:*** Mr. Michael P. Wulbecker, Athletic Director, 712-325-3324; Ms. Brenda Hampton, Associate Athletic Director, 712-325-3402.
CAREER PLANNING ***Placement office:*** 9 full-time, 11 part-time staff; $652,497 operating expenditure 1994–95. ***Director:*** Ms. Bonnie J. Gioiello, Director, Career Center, 712-325-3282. ***Services:*** job fairs, resume preparation, resume referral, career counseling, careers library, job bank, job interviews.
AFTER GRADUATION 72% of students completing a degree program in 1994–95 went directly on to further study.
EXPENSES FOR 1996–97 ***Application fee:*** $15. State resident tuition: $2100 full-time, $70 per credit hour part-time. Nonresident tuition: $2985 full-time, $99.50 per credit hour part-time. College room and board: $3000. College room only: $1500.
FINANCIAL AID ***College-administered undergrad aid 1995–96:*** 25 need-based scholarships (average $300), 200 non-need scholarships (average $250), short-term loans (average $150), low-interest long-term loans from external sources (average $2000), 70 Federal Work-Study (averaging $2000), 120 part-time jobs. ***Required forms:*** institutional, FAFSA; required for some: state; accepted: Stafford Student Loan form. ***Priority deadline:*** 5/1. ***Payment plan:*** installment. ***Waivers:*** full or partial for senior citizens.
APPLYING Open admission except for nursing, technical programs. ***Options:*** early entrance, deferred entrance. ***Required:*** school transcript, TOEFL for international students. ***Recommended:*** ACT. ***Required for some:*** ACT ASSET. Test scores used for counseling/placement. ***Application deadline:*** rolling. ***Notification:*** continuous until 8/25.
APPLYING/TRANSFER ***Required:*** college transcript. ***Entrance:*** noncompetitive. ***Application deadline:*** rolling. ***Notification:*** continuous until 8/25.
CONTACT Mrs. Shirley Davis, Executive Secretary, Iowa Western Community College, Council Bluffs, IA 51502, 712-325-3283 or toll-free 800-432-5852. ***Fax:*** 712-325-3720.

KIRKWOOD COMMUNITY COLLEGE
Cedar Rapids, Iowa

UG Enrollment: 10,025 **Tuition & Fees (IA Res): $1705**
Application Deadline: rolling **Room & Board: N/Avail**

GENERAL State and locally supported, 2-year, coed. Part of Iowa Department of Education Division of Community Colleges. Awards transfer associate, terminal associate degrees. Founded 1966. ***Setting:*** 320-acre suburban campus. ***Total enrollment:*** 10,025. ***Faculty:*** 477 (207 full-time, 100% with terminal degrees, 270 part-time).
ENROLLMENT PROFILE 10,025 students from 17 states and territories, 49 other countries. 58% women, 46% part-time, 97% state residents, 10% transferred in, 2% international, 40% 25 or older, 1% Native American, 1% Hispanic, 2% African American, 1% Asian American. ***Most popular recent major:*** computer programming.
FIRST-YEAR CLASS 5,887 total. Of the students who applied, 98% were accepted. 10% from top 10% of their high school class, 60% from top half.
ACADEMIC PROGRAM Core. Calendar: semesters. Academic remediation for entering students, English as a second language program offered during academic year, services for LD students, advanced placement, self-designed majors, honors program, summer session for credit, part-time degree program (daytime, evenings, weekends, summer), adult/continuing education programs, co-op programs and internships. Off-campus study at Iowa State University, University of Northern Iowa, St. Ambrose University.
GENERAL DEGREE REQUIREMENTS 62 semester hours; 3 semester hours of math; 6 semester hours of science; computer course for business, agriculture, industrial technology, health majors; internship (some majors).
MAJORS Accounting, agricultural business, agricultural education, agricultural sciences, agronomy/soil and crop sciences, animal sciences, applied art, art education, art/fine arts, automotive technologies, biology/biological sciences, biotechnology, broadcasting, business administration/commerce/management, business education, ceramic art and design, child care/child and family studies, child psychology/child development, communication, communication equipment technology, computer programming, computer science, conservation, construction technologies, corrections, criminal justice, culinary arts, data processing, drafting and design, early childhood education, education, electrical and electronics technologies, electrical engineering technology, electromechanical technology, electronics engineering technology, elementary education, engineering (general), (pre)engineering sequence, English, equestrian studies, farm and ranch management, fashion design and technology, fashion merchandising, finance/banking, fire science, fish and game management, food marketing, food services management, food services technology, forestry, French, heating/refrigeration/air conditioning, history, horticulture, hotel and restaurant management, humanities, human services, interior design, international business, jazz, journalism, landscape architecture/design, law enforcement/police sciences, legal secretarial studies, legal studies, liberal arts/general studies, management information systems, manufacturing technology, marketing/retailing/merchandising, mathematics, mechanical design technology, mechanical engineering technology, medical assistant technologies, medical records services, medical secretarial studies, music, nursing, occupational therapy, ornamental horticulture, paralegal studies, parks management, physical education, political science/government, practical nursing, printing technologies, psychology, public relations, radio and television studies, recreation and leisure services, respiratory therapy, retail management, robotics, sanitation technology, science, secretarial studies/office management, social science, social work, sociology, Spanish, teacher aide studies, telecommunications, theater arts/drama, veterinary sciences, veterinary technology, voice, water resources, welding technology, wildlife biology, wildlife management, wind and percussion instruments.
LIBRARY 56,118 books, 540 periodicals, 1,643 records, tapes, and CDs.
COMPUTERS ON CAMPUS 450 computers for student use in computer center, academic departments.
COLLEGE LIFE Orientation program (2 days, $53). Drama-theater group, choral group, student-run newspaper. ***Social organizations:*** 45 open to all. ***Major annual events:*** Homecoming, Fall Orientation, Graduation Ceremonies. ***Student services:*** legal services, health clinic, personal-psychological counseling. ***Campus security:*** 24-hour patrols.
HOUSING College housing not available.
ATHLETICS Member NJCAA. ***Intercollegiate:*** baseball M(s), basketball M(s)/W(s), golf M(s), soccer M/W, softball W(s), volleyball W(s). ***Intramural:*** basketball, football, golf, racquetball, soccer, softball, tennis, volleyball, weight lifting. ***Contact:*** Mr. Ted Oglesby, Athletic Director, 319-398-5462.
CAREER PLANNING ***Placement office:*** 13 full-time, 5 part-time staff. ***Director:*** Mr. Bob Burns, Director, Student Development, 319-398-5471. ***Service:*** career counseling.
ESTIMATED EXPENSES FOR 1996–97 State resident tuition: $1705 full-time, $55 per semester hour part-time. Nonresident tuition: $3162 full-time, $102 per semester hour part-time.
FINANCIAL AID ***College-administered undergrad aid 1995–96:*** 790 need-based scholarships (averaging $559), 40 non-need scholarships (averaging $425), short-term loans (averaging $30), low-interest long-term loans from external sources (averaging $2426), Federal Work-Study, 308 part-time jobs. ***Required forms:*** institutional, FAFSA. ***Priority deadline:*** 3/15. ***Payment plan:*** installment. ***Waivers:*** full or partial for senior citizens. ***Notification:*** continuous.
APPLYING Open admission. ***Option:*** early entrance. ***Required:*** school transcript, ACT, ACT ASSET. Test scores used for counseling/placement. ***Application deadline:*** rolling. ***Notification:*** continuous.
APPLYING/TRANSFER ***Required:*** college transcript. ***Entrance:*** noncompetitive. ***Application deadline:*** rolling. ***Notification:*** continuous. ***Contact:*** Ms. Karen Friest, Records Evaluator, 319-398-5577.
CONTACT Mr. Doug Bannon, Director of Admissions, Kirkwood Community College, Cedar Rapids, IA 52406-2068, 319-398-5517 or toll-free 800-332-2055. ***Fax:*** 319-398-1244.

MARSHALLTOWN COMMUNITY COLLEGE
Marshalltown, Iowa

UG Enrollment: 1,248 **Tuition & Fees (IA Res): $2096**
Application Deadline: rolling **Room & Board: N/Avail**

GENERAL District-supported, 2-year, coed. Part of Iowa Valley Community College District System. Awards diplomas, transfer associate, terminal associate degrees. Founded 1927. ***Setting:*** 200-acre small-town campus. ***Endowment:*** $654,643. ***Total enrollment:*** 1,248. ***Faculty:*** 107 (39 full-time, 100% with terminal degrees, 68 part-time); student-faculty ratio is 15:1. ***Notable Alumni:*** Michael Voght, museum director at Marshall County Historical Society; Chad Harbarts, sports information director at University of Missouri; Craig Wiley, industrial hygienist at Terracon Enviromental Inc.; Dr. Marsha Anderson, veterinarian at Humane Society of Missouri; Mr. Martin Mitchell, mortician.

Marshalltown Community College (continued)

ENROLLMENT PROFILE 1,248 students from 3 states and territories, 6 other countries. 66% women, 39% part-time, 99% state residents, 4% transferred in, 55% have need-based financial aid, 3% have non-need-based financial aid, 34% 25 or older, 2% Native American, 1% Hispanic, 1% African American, 1% Asian American. ***Areas of study chosen:*** 42% liberal arts/general studies, 20% business management and administrative services, 15% health professions and related sciences, 5% education, 4% computer and information sciences, 3% engineering and applied sciences, 2% social sciences, 1% agriculture, 1% biological and life sciences, 1% communications and journalism, 1% fine arts, 1% natural resource sciences, 1% prelaw, 1% prevet, 1% psychology, 1% vocational and home economics. ***Most popular recent majors:*** liberal arts/general studies, nursing, business administration/commerce/management.

FIRST-YEAR CLASS 177 total.

ACADEMIC PROGRAM Core, arts, sciences, and vocational technology curriculum, honor code. Calendar: semesters. 185 courses offered in 1995–96. Academic remediation for entering students, English as a second language program offered during academic year, services for LD students, advanced placement, self-designed majors, summer session for credit, part-time degree program (daytime, evenings, summer), adult/continuing education programs, co-op programs and internships. ROTC: Air Force (c).

GENERAL DEGREE REQUIREMENTS 64 credits; math/science requirements vary according to program; internship (some majors).

MAJORS Accounting, business administration/commerce/management, child care/child and family studies, community services, computer science, dental services, drafting and design, economics, electrical and electronics technologies, (pre)engineering sequence, industrial and heavy equipment maintenance, liberal arts/general studies, machine and tool technologies, marketing/retailing/merchandising, mental health/rehabilitation counseling, nursing, operating room technology, political science/government, practical nursing, radiological technology, science, secretarial studies/office management.

LIBRARY Learning Resource Center with 39,348 books, 127 microform titles, 216 periodicals, 1 on-line bibliographic service, 32 CD-ROMs, 491 records, tapes, and CDs. Acquisition spending 1994–95: $49,763.

COMPUTERS ON CAMPUS 250 computers for student use in computer center, computer labs, learning resource center, Student Senate office, student newspaper office, various labs, library. Staffed computer lab on campus provides training in use of computers, software. Academic computing expenditure 1994–95: $158,190.

COLLEGE LIFE Student-run newspaper. 30% vote in student government elections. ***Most popular organizations:*** Student Activities Council, Student Senate, College Community Connection, SAMS, International Student Association. ***Major annual events:*** Homecoming Events, Popcorn Days, Hypnotist. ***Student services:*** personal-psychological counseling.

HOUSING College housing not available.

ATHLETICS Member NJCAA. ***Intercollegiate:*** baseball M(s), basketball M(s)/W(s), golf M(s)/W(s), softball W(s). ***Intramural:*** racquetball, volleyball. ***Contact:*** Mr. Mike Marquis, Athletic Director, 515-752-7106 Ext. 225.

CAREER PLANNING ***Placement office:*** 3 full-time staff; $84,071 operating expenditure 1994–95. ***Director:*** Ms. Diane Rozell, Employment Specialist, 515-752-7106 Ext. 344. ***Services:*** job fairs, resume preparation, resume referral, career counseling, careers library, job bank, job interviews.

AFTER GRADUATION 80% of students completing a degree program in 1994–95 went directly on to further study.

EXPENSES FOR 1996–97 ***Application fee:*** $25. State resident tuition: $1856 full-time, $58 per credit hour part-time. Nonresident tuition: $3712 full-time, $116 per credit hour part-time. Part-time mandatory fees: $96 per semester. Full-time mandatory fees range from $240 to $315.

FINANCIAL AID ***College-administered undergrad aid 1995–96:*** 100 need-based scholarships (average $200), 20 non-need scholarships (average $200), short-term loans (average $800), Federal Work-Study, 5 part-time jobs. ***Required forms:*** institutional, FAFSA. ***Priority deadline:*** 3/15. ***Payment plans:*** installment, deferred payment. ***Waivers:*** full or partial for senior citizens. ***Notification:*** 6/15.

APPLYING Open admission. ***Options:*** early entrance, midyear entrance. ***Required:*** school transcript, TOEFL for international students. ***Recommended:*** ACT. Test scores used for counseling/placement. ***Application deadline:*** rolling. ***Notification:*** continuous.

APPLYING/TRANSFER ***Required:*** high school transcript, college transcript. ***Recommended:*** standardized test scores. ***Application deadline:*** rolling. ***Notification:*** continuous. ***Contact:*** Ms. Sylvia Grandgeorge, Associate Dean, Student Services, 515-752-7106 Ext. 232.

CONTACT Ms. Sylvia Grandgeorge, Associate Dean, Student Services, Marshalltown Community College, Marshalltown, IA 50158-4760, 515-752-7106 Ext. 232.

MUSCATINE COMMUNITY COLLEGE
Muscatine, Iowa

UG Enrollment: 1,250	**Tuition & Fees (IA Res): $1635**
Application Deadline: rolling	**Room & Board: N/Avail**

GENERAL State-supported, 2-year, coed. Part of Eastern Iowa Community College District System. Awards certificates, diplomas, transfer associate, terminal associate degrees. Founded 1929. ***Setting:*** 25-acre small-town campus. ***Total enrollment:*** 1,250. ***Faculty:*** 95 (36 full-time, 30% with terminal degrees, 59 part-time); student-faculty ratio is 17:1.

ENROLLMENT PROFILE 1,250 students from 6 states and territories, 7 other countries. 58% women, 42% men, 50% part-time, 94% state residents, 2% transferred in, 49% 25 or older, 1% Native American, 6% Hispanic, 1% African American, 1% Asian American.

FIRST-YEAR CLASS 427 total. Of the students who applied, 100% were accepted, 93% of whom enrolled.

ACADEMIC PROGRAM Core. Calendar: semesters. Academic remediation for entering students, English as a second language program offered during academic year, services for LD students, advanced placement, tutorials, honors program, summer session for credit, part-time degree program (daytime, evenings, summer), adult/continuing education programs, co-op programs and internships.

GENERAL DEGREE REQUIREMENTS 64 credits; 3 credits of math; 8 credits of science; computer course; internship (some majors).

MAJORS Accounting, agricultural business, biology/biological sciences, business administration/commerce/management, business machine technologies, chemistry, child care/child and family studies, computer science, conservation, economics, education, English, farm and ranch management, finance/banking, industrial engineering technology, journalism, liberal arts/general studies, mathematics, medical secretarial studies, music, nuclear technology, pharmacy/pharmaceutical sciences, philosophy, physical education, practical nursing, psychology, secretarial studies/office management, sociology.

LIBRARY Muscatine Community College Library with 19,588 books, 176 periodicals, 963 records, tapes, and CDs.

COMPUTERS ON CAMPUS 57 computers for student use in computer center, library.

COLLEGE LIFE Drama-theater group, choral group, student-run newspaper. ***Student services:*** personal-psychological counseling.

HOUSING College housing not available.

ATHLETICS Member NJCAA. ***Intercollegiate:*** baseball M(s), softball W(s). ***Intramural:*** table tennis (Ping-Pong), tennis, water polo.

CAREER PLANNING ***Director:*** Mr. Tom Savage, Counselor/Job Developer, 319-263-8290 Ext. 136. ***Services:*** job fairs, resume preparation, resume referral, career counseling, careers library, job bank, job interviews.

EXPENSES FOR 1995–96 ***Application fee:*** $20. State resident tuition: $1470 full-time, $49 per credit hour part-time. Nonresident tuition: $2205 full-time, $72.50 per credit hour part-time. Part-time mandatory fees: $5.50 per credit hour. Full-time mandatory fees: $165.

FINANCIAL AID ***College-administered undergrad aid 1995–96:*** 136 need-based scholarships (average $675), 60 non-need scholarships (average $400), low-interest long-term loans from external sources (average $2200), Federal Work-Study. ***Required forms:*** FAFSA; accepted: CSS Financial Aid PROFILE, state, SINGLEFILE Form of United Student Aid Funds. ***Priority deadline:*** 6/1. ***Waivers:*** full or partial for employees or children of employees. ***Notification:*** continuous.

APPLYING Open admission. ***Options:*** early entrance, deferred entrance, midyear entrance. ***Required:*** school transcript, TOEFL for international students, ACT ASSET. Test scores used for counseling/placement. ***Application deadline:*** rolling. ***Notification:*** continuous.

APPLYING/TRANSFER ***Required:*** college transcript. ***Entrance:*** noncompetitive. ***Application deadline:*** rolling. ***Notification:*** continuous.

CONTACT Ms. Bev Knoernschild, Admissions Counselor, Muscatine Community College, Muscatine, IA 52761-5396, 319-263-8250 Ext. 165 or toll-free 800-462-3255 (in-state). ***Fax:*** 319-264-8341.

NORTHEAST IOWA COMMUNITY COLLEGE, CALMAR CAMPUS
Calmar, Iowa

UG Enrollment: 900	**Tuition & Fees (IA Res): $2232**
Application Deadline: rolling	**Room & Board: N/Avail**

GENERAL State and locally supported, 2-year, coed. Part of Iowa Area Community Colleges System. Awards transfer associate, terminal associate degrees. Founded 1966. ***Setting:*** 210-acre small-town campus. ***Total enrollment:*** 900. ***Faculty:*** 137 (93 full-time, 44 part-time).

ENROLLMENT PROFILE 900 students: 62% women, 23% part-time, 99% state residents, 12% transferred in, 38% 25 or older, 2% Native American, 2% Hispanic, 0% African American, 2% Asian American.

FIRST-YEAR CLASS 500 total. Of the students who applied, 100% were accepted. 7% from top 10% of their high school class, 25% from top half.

ACADEMIC PROGRAM Core, honor code. Calendar: semesters. Academic remediation for entering students, services for LD students, summer session for credit, part-time degree program (daytime, evenings, weekends, summer), adult/continuing education programs, co-op programs and internships. Off-campus study at Upper Iowa University.

GENERAL DEGREE REQUIREMENTS 64 credit hours; computer course; internship (some majors).

MAJORS Accounting, agricultural business, computer technologies, construction technologies, dairy sciences, electrical and electronics technologies, liberal arts/general studies, marketing/retailing/merchandising, mechanical design technology, medical laboratory technology, medical records services, nursing, vocational education.

LIBRARY 14,195 books, 312 periodicals.

COMPUTERS ON CAMPUS 120 computers for student use in computer center, labs, library.

COLLEGE LIFE 90% vote in student government elections. ***Student services:*** personal-psychological counseling. ***Campus security:*** security personnel on weekday nights.

HOUSING College housing not available.

ATHLETICS ***Intramural:*** basketball, bowling, football, golf, skiing (cross-country), skiing (downhill), swimming and diving, tennis, volleyball.

CAREER PLANNING ***Service:*** career counseling.

EXPENSES FOR 1995–96 State resident tuition: $1984 full-time, $62 per credit part-time. Nonresident tuition: $3968 full-time, $124 per credit part-time. Part-time mandatory fees: $8.25 per credit. Full-time mandatory fees: $248.

FINANCIAL AID ***College-administered undergrad aid 1995–96:*** need-based scholarships, short-term loans, low-interest long-term loans from external sources, Federal Work-Study. ***Required forms:*** CSS Financial Aid PROFILE, institutional, FAFSA. ***Priority deadline:*** 3/1. ***Payment plan:*** deferred payment.

APPLYING Open admission. ***Required:*** school transcript, ACT ASSET. ***Recommended:*** SAT I or ACT, TOEFL for international students. Test scores used for counseling/placement. ***Application deadline:*** rolling. ***Notification:*** continuous.

APPLYING/TRANSFER ***Required:*** standardized test scores, high school transcript, college transcript. ***Application deadline:*** rolling. ***Notification:*** continuous.

CONTACT Ms. Martha Keune, Admissions Representative, Northeast Iowa Community College, Calmar Campus, Calmar, IA 52132-0480, 319-562-3263 Ext. 307 or toll-free 800-728-2256.

NORTHEAST IOWA COMMUNITY COLLEGE, PEOSTA CAMPUS
Peosta, Iowa

UG Enrollment: 1,700 | **Tuition & Fees (IA Res): $2108**
Application Deadline: rolling | **Room & Board: N/Avail**

GENERAL State and locally supported, 2-year, coed. Part of Iowa Area Community Colleges System. Awards transfer associate, terminal associate degrees. Founded 1970. ***Setting:*** 95-acre small-town campus. ***Total enrollment:*** 1,700. ***Faculty:*** 66 (48 full-time, 18 part-time).
ENROLLMENT PROFILE 1,700 students from 5 states and territories, 5 other countries. 69% women, 35% part-time, 96% state residents, 20% transferred in, 27% 25 or older, 1% Native American, 1% Hispanic, 1% African American, 1% Asian American. ***Most popular recent majors:*** nursing, human services, business administration/commerce/management.
FIRST-YEAR CLASS 800 total. Of the students who applied, 100% were accepted.
ACADEMIC PROGRAM Core. Calendar: semesters. Academic remediation for entering students, English as a second language program offered during academic year, services for LD students, self-designed majors, summer session for credit, adult/continuing education programs, co-op programs and internships. Off-campus study at Upper Iowa University, Clarke College, University of Dubuque, Loras College.
GENERAL DEGREE REQUIREMENTS 64 credit hours; 9 credit hours of math/science; computer course.
MAJORS Accounting, agricultural business, agricultural economics, agricultural technologies, architectural technologies, automotive technologies, business administration/commerce/management, carpentry, child care/child and family studies, computer information systems, computer programming, construction management, construction technologies, data processing, drafting and design, electrical and electronics technologies, electronics engineering technology, human services, marketing/retailing/merchandising, mechanical engineering technology, medical laboratory technology, nursing, plastics technology, practical nursing, radiological technology, respiratory therapy, secretarial studies/office management, transportation technologies, welding technology, word processing.
LIBRARY Main library plus 1 other, with 10,163 books, 74 microform titles, 141 periodicals.
COMPUTERS ON CAMPUS 80 computers for student use in computer center, library.
COLLEGE LIFE Choral group, student-run newspaper. ***Most popular organizations:*** Student Senate, Iowa Organization for the Associate Degree in Nursing, Health Occupations Students of America. ***Major annual events:*** Fall Picnic, Halloween Week Activities, Schick Super Hoops Tournament. ***Student services:*** personal-psychological counseling. ***Campus security:*** 24-hour emergency response devices, late-night transport-escort service.
HOUSING College housing not available.
ATHLETICS ***Intramural:*** basketball, bowling, football, golf, skiing (cross-country), skiing (downhill), softball, swimming and diving, table tennis (Ping-Pong), tennis, volleyball.
CAREER PLANNING ***Placement office:*** 1 part-time staff. ***Director:*** Ms. Betty Phillips, Financial Planning/Career Counseling Director, 800-728-7367. ***Services:*** job fairs, resume preparation, career counseling, careers library, job bank, job interviews. Students must register sophomore year.
EXPENSES FOR 1995–96 State resident tuition: $1860 full-time, $62 per credit part-time. Nonresident tuition: $3720 full-time, $124 per credit part-time. Part-time mandatory fees: $8.25 per credit. Full-time mandatory fees: $248.
FINANCIAL AID ***College-administered undergrad aid 1995–96:*** need-based scholarships, non-need scholarships, short-term loans, low-interest long-term loans from external sources, Federal Work-Study. ***Required forms:*** CSS Financial Aid PROFILE, institutional, FAFSA. ***Priority deadline:*** 4/1. ***Waivers:*** full or partial for employees or children of employees.
APPLYING Open admission except for allied health programs. ***Required:*** school transcript, ACT ASSET. ***Recommended:*** TOEFL for international students. ***Required for some:*** ACT. Test scores used for counseling/placement. ***Application deadline:*** rolling. ***Notification:*** continuous.
APPLYING/TRANSFER ***Required:*** standardized test scores, high school transcript, college transcript. ***Entrance:*** noncompetitive. ***Application deadline:*** rolling. ***Notification:*** continuous.
CONTACT Mr. Lee J. Noethe, Admissions Representative, Northeast Iowa Community College, Peosta Campus, Peosta, IA 52068-9776, 319-556-5110 Ext. 211 or toll-free 800-728-PEOSTA. College video available.

NORTH IOWA AREA COMMUNITY COLLEGE
Mason City, Iowa

UG Enrollment: 2,771 | **Tuition & Fees (IA Res): $1840**
Application Deadline: rolling | **Room & Board: $2916**

GENERAL State and locally supported, 2-year, coed. Part of Iowa Area Community Colleges System. Awards diplomas, transfer associate, terminal associate degrees. Founded 1918. ***Setting:*** 320-acre rural campus. ***Total enrollment:*** 2,771. ***Faculty:*** 107 (87 full-time, 20 part-time).
ENROLLMENT PROFILE 2,771 students from 18 states and territories, 2 other countries. 56% women, 44% men, 36% part-time, 98% state residents, 7% transferred in, 1% international, 30% 25 or older, 1% Native American, 1% Hispanic, 1% African American, 1% Asian American. ***Most popular recent majors:*** liberal arts/general studies, nursing, business administration/commerce/management.
FIRST-YEAR CLASS 1,863 total. Of the students who applied, 100% were accepted. 5% from top 10% of their high school class, 14% from top quarter, 31% from top half. 2 National Merit Scholars.
ACADEMIC PROGRAM Core. Calendar: semesters. Academic remediation for entering students, English as a second language program offered during academic year and summer, services for LD students, advanced placement, self-designed majors, honors program, summer session for credit, part-time degree program (daytime, evenings, summer), external degree programs, adult/continuing education programs, co-op programs.
GENERAL DEGREE REQUIREMENTS 60 semester hours; 1 course each in math and science.
MAJORS Accounting, agricultural business, agricultural economics, agricultural technologies, agronomy/soil and crop sciences, animal sciences, automotive technologies, business administration/commerce/management, computer science, electrical and electronics technologies, fashion merchandising, heating/refrigeration/air conditioning, law enforcement/police sciences, legal secretarial studies, liberal arts/general studies, marketing/retailing/merchandising, mechanical design technology, medical assistant technologies, medical secretarial studies, nursing, retail management, robotics, secretarial studies/office management, welding technology.
LIBRARY 33,657 books, 4,151 microform titles, 334 periodicals, 2,371 records, tapes, and CDs.
COMPUTERS ON CAMPUS 300 computers for student use in computer center, department labs, library provide access to main academic computer, e-mail, Internet. Staffed computer lab on campus provides training in use of computers, software.
COLLEGE LIFE Drama-theater group, student-run newspaper. ***Most popular organizations:*** Student Senate, School Newspaper. ***Student services:*** personal-psychological counseling.
HOUSING 460 college housing spaces available; all were occupied 1995–96. No special consideration for freshman housing applicants. On-campus residence required in freshman year. ***Option:*** coed (2 buildings) housing available. Resident assistants live in dorms.
ATHLETICS Member NJCAA. ***Intercollegiate:*** basketball M(s)/W(s), football M(s), golf M(s)/W(s), volleyball W. ***Intramural:*** basketball, football, golf, skiing (cross-country), skiing (downhill), tennis, volleyball, weight lifting. ***Contact:*** Mr. Jerry Dunbar, Athletic Director, 515-421-4281.
CAREER PLANNING ***Director:*** Ms. Kay Field, Director of Employment and Career Services, 515-421-4370. ***Service:*** career counseling.
AFTER GRADUATION 50% of students completing a degree program in 1994–95 went directly on to further study.
EXPENSES FOR 1996–97 State resident tuition: $1840 full-time, $55.40 per semester hour part-time. Nonresident tuition: $2700 full-time, $83.10 per semester hour part-time. Part-time mandatory fees per semester range from $12.65 to $73.15. College room and board: $2916.
FINANCIAL AID ***College-administered undergrad aid 1995–96:*** need-based scholarships, short-term loans, low-interest long-term loans from external sources, Federal Work-Study, part-time jobs. ***Acceptable forms:*** CSS Financial Aid PROFILE, FAFSA. ***Priority deadline:*** 8/1.
APPLYING Open admission except for electronics, nursing, mechanical design technology programs. ***Options:*** early entrance, deferred entrance. ***Required:*** school transcript, TOEFL for international students. ***Recommended:*** ACT. ***Required for some:*** ACT. Test scores used for counseling/placement. ***Application deadline:*** rolling. ***Notification:*** continuous.
APPLYING/TRANSFER ***Required:*** high school transcript, college transcript. ***Application deadline:*** rolling. ***Notification:*** continuous. ***Contact:*** Mr. Jerry Torgerson, Transfer Relations, 515-421-4205.
CONTACT Mr. Tom Dunn, Enrollment Specialist, North Iowa Area Community College, Mason City, IA 50401-7299, 515-421-4246 or toll-free 800-392-5685 (in-state). College video available.

NORTHWEST IOWA COMMUNITY COLLEGE
Sheldon, Iowa

UG Enrollment: 684 | **Tuition & Fees (IA Res): $1830**
Application Deadline: rolling | **Room Only: $1700**

GENERAL State-supported, 2-year, coed. Part of Iowa Department of Education Division of Community Colleges. Awards diplomas, transfer associate, terminal associate degrees. Founded 1966. ***Setting:*** 263-acre small-town campus. ***Educational spending 1994–95:*** $3554 per undergrad. ***Total enrollment:*** 684. ***Faculty:*** 51 (36 full-time, 6% with terminal degrees, 15 part-time); student-faculty ratio is 12:1.
ENROLLMENT PROFILE 684 students from 9 states and territories. 48% women, 52% men, 32% part-time, 96% state residents, 6% live on campus, 13% transferred in, 0% international, 25% 25 or older, 1% Native American, 1% Hispanic, 0% African American, 0% Asian American.
FIRST-YEAR CLASS 397 total; 909 applied, 95% were accepted, 46% of whom enrolled.
ACADEMIC PROGRAM General and vocational curriculum, honor code. Calendar: semesters. 374 courses offered in 1995–96. Academic remediation for entering students, English as a second language program, services for LD students, summer session for credit, part-time degree program, adult/continuing education programs, co-op programs.
GENERAL DEGREE REQUIREMENTS 60 credit hours; math/science requirements vary according to program; internship (some majors).
MAJORS Accounting, agricultural business, agricultural technologies, automotive technologies, carpentry, computer programming, computer science, construction technologies, drafting and design, electrical and electronics technologies, electrical engineering technology, electromechanical technology, energy management technologies, finance/banking, industrial and heavy equipment maintenance, industrial design, industrial engineering technology, instrumentation technology, insurance, liberal arts/general studies, marketing/retailing/merchandising, mechanical design technology, mechanical engineering technology, medical records services, nursing, practical nursing, retail management, robotics, secretarial studies/office management, welding technology.
LIBRARY Northwest Iowa Community College Library plus 1 other, with 10,000 books, 288 periodicals, 7 CD-ROMs. Acquisition spending 1994–95: $125,961.
COMPUTERS ON CAMPUS 86 computers for student use in computer center, learning resource center, classrooms, library provide access to main academic computer, e-mail. Staffed computer lab on campus. Academic computing expenditure 1994–95: $17,718.
COLLEGE LIFE Choral group. 30% vote in student government elections. ***Social organizations:*** 3 open to all. ***Student services:*** personal-psychological counseling. ***Campus security:*** 24-hour emergency response devices.
HOUSING 36 college housing spaces available; 33 were occupied 1995–96. No special consideration for freshman housing applicants. Off-campus living permitted. ***Option:*** coed (1 building) housing available. Resident assistants live in dorms.
ATHLETICS ***Intramural:*** basketball, bowling, football, golf, racquetball, riflery, volleyball, weight lifting, wrestling.

Peterson's Guide to Two-Year Colleges 1997 323

Northwest Iowa Community College (continued)

CAREER PLANNING ***Placement office:*** 1 full-time, 1 part-time staff; $380,081 operating expenditure 1994–95. ***Director:*** Ms. Donna Brinkman, Coordinator of Career Center, 712-324-5061 Ext. 112. ***Services:*** resume preparation, resume referral, career counseling, careers library, job bank, job interviews.

EXPENSES FOR 1996–97 ***Application fee:*** $10. State resident tuition: $1620 full-time, $54 per credit hour part-time. Nonresident tuition: $2430 full-time, $81 per credit hour part-time. Part-time mandatory fees per credit hour range from $7 to $13. Full-time mandatory fees: $210. College room only: $1700.

FINANCIAL AID ***College-administered undergrad aid 1995–96:*** 10 need-based scholarships (average $100), 30 non-need scholarships (average $1100), short-term loans (average $50), 30 Federal Work-Study (averaging $600), 10 part-time jobs. ***Required forms:*** institutional, FAFSA. ***Priority deadline:*** 4/19. ***Payment plan:*** deferred payment.

APPLYING Open admission. ***Option:*** Common Application. ***Required:*** school transcript, TOEFL for international students, ACT ASSET. Test scores used for counseling/placement. ***Application deadline:*** rolling. ***Notification:*** continuous.

APPLYING/TRANSFER ***Required:*** college transcript. ***Required for some:*** standardized test scores, minimum 2.0 high school GPA. ***Entrance:*** noncompetitive. ***Application deadline:*** rolling. ***Notification:*** continuous. ***Contact:*** Mr. Gene McDaniel, Registrar, 712-324-5061 Ext. 141.

CONTACT Ms. Bonnie Brands, Director of Admissions, Northwest Iowa Community College, 603 West Park Street, Sheldon, IA 51201-1046, 712-324-5061 Ext. 124 or toll-free 800-352-4907. ***Fax:*** 712-324-4136. College video available.

SCOTT COMMUNITY COLLEGE
Bettendorf, Iowa

UG Enrollment: 4,000	**Tuition & Fees (IA Res): $1744**
Application Deadline: 8/30	**Room & Board: N/Avail**

GENERAL State and locally supported, 2-year, coed. Part of Eastern Iowa Community College District System. Awards transfer associate, terminal associate degrees. Founded 1966. ***Setting:*** 181-acre urban campus. ***Total enrollment:*** 4,000. ***Faculty:*** 235 (85 full-time, 100% with terminal degrees, 150 part-time); student-faculty ratio is 25:1.

ENROLLMENT PROFILE 4,000 students from 18 states and territories, 19 other countries. 56% women, 50% part-time, 93% state residents, 12% transferred in, 1% international, 1% Native American, 2% Hispanic, 9% African American, 2% Asian American.

FIRST-YEAR CLASS 1,200 total. Of the students who applied, 100% were accepted, 80% of whom enrolled.

ACADEMIC PROGRAM Core. Calendar: semesters. Academic remediation for entering students, English as a second language program offered during academic year and summer, services for LD students, summer session for credit, part-time degree program (daytime, evenings, weekends, summer), adult/continuing education programs, co-op programs and internships. Off-campus study at Black Hawk College.

GENERAL DEGREE REQUIREMENTS 64 credit hours; computer course; internship (some majors).

MAJORS Accounting, art/fine arts, automotive technologies, aviation technology, behavioral sciences, business administration/commerce/management, communication, computer programming, computer science, criminal justice, culinary arts, deaf interpreter training, drafting and design, education, (pre)engineering sequence, English, environmental sciences, equestrian studies, fashion merchandising, film and video production, finance/banking, flight training, heating/refrigeration/air conditioning, history, interior design, law enforcement/police sciences, legal secretarial studies, liberal arts/general studies, machine and tool technologies, manufacturing technology, mathematics, medical assistant technologies, medical laboratory technology, medical secretarial studies, nursing, pharmacy/pharmaceutical sciences, physical sciences, physical therapy, political science/government, practical nursing, psychology, radiological technology, respiratory therapy, robotics, science, secretarial studies/office management, social science, sociology, word processing.

LIBRARY Scott Community College Library with 20,000 books, 702 microform titles, 183 periodicals, 1,500 records, tapes, and CDs.

COMPUTERS ON CAMPUS 40 computers for student use in computer center. Staffed computer lab on campus.

COLLEGE LIFE Drama-theater group. ***Social organizations:*** 3 open to all. ***Most popular organizations:*** Student Government, Campus Activities Board. ***Student services:*** personal-psychological counseling. ***Campus security:*** 24-hour emergency response devices.

HOUSING College housing not available.

CAREER PLANNING ***Placement office:*** 2 full-time staff. ***Director:*** Ms. Kris Barkdoll, Associate Dean for Enrollment Management, 319-359-7531 Ext. 360. ***Services:*** job fairs, resume preparation, resume referral, career counseling, careers library, job bank, job interviews.

EXPENSES FOR 1995–96 ***Application fee:*** $20. State resident tuition: $1568 full-time, $49 per credit part-time. Nonresident tuition: $2352 full-time, $73.50 per credit part-time. Part-time mandatory fees: $5.50 per credit. Full-time mandatory fees: $176.

FINANCIAL AID ***College-administered undergrad aid 1995–96:*** need-based scholarships, short-term loans (averaging $50), low-interest long-term loans from external sources (averaging $2625), Federal Work-Study. ***Required forms:*** institutional, FAFSA; accepted: CSS Financial Aid PROFILE. ***Priority deadline:*** 6/1. ***Waivers:*** full or partial for employees or children of employees and senior citizens. ***Notification:*** continuous.

APPLYING Open admission. ***Options:*** early entrance, deferred entrance. ***Required:*** TOEFL for international students, College Board Diagnostic tests. ***Recommended:*** school transcript, ACT. Test scores used for counseling/placement. ***Application deadline:*** 8/30. ***Notification:*** continuous until 8/30.

APPLYING/TRANSFER ***Required for some:*** standardized test scores, high school transcript, college transcript. ***Application deadline:*** 8/30. ***Notification:*** continuous until 8/30. ***Contact:*** Ms. Kris Barkdoll, Associate Dean of Enrollment Management, 319-359-7531.

CONTACT Ms. Lisa Miller, Admissions Specialist, Scott Community College, 500 Belmont Road, Bettendorf, IA 52722-6804, 319-359-7531 Ext. 202 or toll-free 800-462-3255 (in-state). College video available.

SOUTHEASTERN COMMUNITY COLLEGE, NORTH CAMPUS
West Burlington, Iowa

UG Enrollment: 1,791	**Tuition & Fees (IA Res): $1566**
Application Deadline: rolling	**Room & Board: $2600**

GENERAL State and locally supported, 2-year, coed. Part of Iowa Department of Education Division of Community Colleges. Awards diplomas, transfer associate, terminal associate degrees. Founded 1968. ***Setting:*** 160-acre small-town campus. ***Total enrollment:*** 1,791. ***Faculty:*** 94 (12 full-time, 82 part-time); student-faculty ratio is 19:1.

ENROLLMENT PROFILE 1,791 students from 8 states and territories. 61% women, 34% part-time, 92% state residents, 3% live on campus, 18% transferred in, 0% international, 34% 25 or older, 0% Native American, 1% Hispanic, 2% African American, 1% Asian American.

FIRST-YEAR CLASS 710 total; 1,177 applied, 100% were accepted, 60% of whom enrolled.

ACADEMIC PROGRAM Core, honor code. Calendar: semesters. Average class size 35 in required courses. Academic remediation for entering students, English as a second language program offered during academic year and summer, services for LD students, advanced placement, summer session for credit, part-time degree program (daytime, evenings), adult/continuing education programs, co-op programs and internships.

GENERAL DEGREE REQUIREMENTS 62 credits; computer course for medical assistant technologies majors; internship (some majors).

MAJORS Accounting, agricultural business, agronomy/soil and crop sciences, automotive technologies, business administration/commerce/management, child care/child and family studies, computer information systems, computer programming, construction management, construction technologies, cosmetology, criminal justice, drafting and design, drug and alcohol/substance abuse counseling, electronics engineering technology, emergency medical technology, engineering design, liberal arts/general studies, machine and tool technologies, mechanical engineering technology, medical assistant technologies, medical laboratory technology, nursing, practical nursing, radiological technology, robotics, secretarial studies/office management, vocational education, welding technology.

LIBRARY 39,304 books, 16,779 microform titles, 282 periodicals, 10 CD-ROMs, 1,800 records, tapes, and CDs.

COMPUTERS ON CAMPUS 100 computers for student use in computer center, library. Staffed computer lab on campus provides training in use of computers, software.

COLLEGE LIFE Choral group. 20% vote in student government elections. ***Social organizations:*** 15 open to all. ***Most popular organizations:*** Student Senate, Criminal Justice Club, Art Club. ***Major annual events:*** Welcome to Campus Picnic, Spring Fling. ***Campus security:*** controlled dormitory access, night patrols by trained security personnel.

HOUSING 64 college housing spaces available; all were occupied 1995–96. No special consideration for freshman housing applicants. Off-campus living permitted. ***Option:*** single-sex housing available. Resident assistants live in dorms.

ATHLETICS Member NJCAA. ***Intercollegiate:*** baseball M, basketball M(s), golf M, softball W(s), volleyball W(s). ***Intramural:*** basketball, bowling, softball, volleyball, weight lifting. ***Contact:*** Mr. Steve Swanson, Athletic Director, 319-752-2731 Ext. 163.

CAREER PLANNING ***Placement office:*** 1 full-time staff. ***Director:*** Mr. Tony Takai, Counselor/Evaluator, 319-752-2731. ***Services:*** resume preparation, career counseling, careers library.

EXPENSES FOR 1995–96 State resident tuition: $1395 full-time, $46.50 per credit hour part-time. Nonresident tuition: $2093 full-time, $69.75 per credit hour part-time. Part-time mandatory fees: $5.50 per credit hour. Full-time mandatory fees: $171. College room and board: $2600. College room only: $1500.

FINANCIAL AID ***College-administered undergrad aid 1995–96:*** 980 need-based scholarships (average $2000), 10 non-need scholarships (average $200), low-interest long-term loans from external sources (average $2200), 91 Federal Work-Study, 8 part-time jobs. ***Required forms:*** institutional; required for some: state; accepted: CSS Financial Aid PROFILE, FAFSA. ***Priority deadline:*** 4/15. ***Payment plan:*** deferred payment. ***Waivers:*** full or partial for employees or children of employees.

APPLYING Open admission except for computer programming, nursing, electronics, medical assistant, medical laboratory technology, manufacturing technology, engineering design programs. ***Options:*** early entrance, deferred entrance, midyear entrance. ***Required:*** TOEFL for international students, ACT ASSET. ***Recommended:*** ACT. Test scores used for counseling/placement. ***Application deadline:*** rolling.

APPLYING/TRANSFER ***Entrance:*** noncompetitive. ***Application deadline:*** rolling. ***Contact:*** Mr. Wally Wilson, Counselor, 319-752-2731 Ext. 136.

CONTACT Mr. Steve Rheinschmidt, Admissions Counselor, Southeastern Community College, North Campus, West Burlington, IA 52655-0605, 319-752-2731 Ext. 137 or toll-free 800-828-7322 (in-state).

SOUTHEASTERN COMMUNITY COLLEGE, SOUTH CAMPUS
Keokuk, Iowa

UG Enrollment: 599	**Tuition & Fees (IA Res): $1760**
Application Deadline: rolling	**Room & Board: N/Avail**

GENERAL State and locally supported, 2-year, coed. Part of Iowa Department of Education Division of Community Colleges. Awards certificates, diplomas, transfer associate, terminal associate degrees. Founded 1967. ***Setting:*** 3-acre small-town campus. ***Total enrollment:*** 599. ***Faculty:*** 26 (19 full-time, 7 part-time); student-faculty ratio is 23:1.

ENROLLMENT PROFILE 599 students from 4 states and territories, 1 other country. 71% women, 40% part-time, 66% state residents, 10% transferred in, 1% Hispanic, 1% African American, 1% Asian American. ***Most popular recent majors:*** liberal arts/general studies, nursing, secretarial studies/office management.

FIRST-YEAR CLASS 250 total; 400 applied, 100% were accepted, 63% of whom enrolled.

ACADEMIC PROGRAM Core, general studies/vocational curriculum. Calendar: semesters. Academic remediation for entering students, services for LD students, advanced placement, summer session for credit, part-time degree program (daytime, evenings), adult/continuing education programs. Off-campus study at John Wood Community College, Carl Sandburg College, Iowa Wesleyan College.

GENERAL DEGREE REQUIREMENT 62 credit hours.

MAJORS Business administration/commerce/management, computer information systems, cosmetology, liberal arts/general studies, nursing, practical nursing, secretarial studies/office management.
LIBRARY 10,000 books, 70 periodicals, 1,024 records, tapes, and CDs.
COMPUTERS ON CAMPUS 40 computers for student use in computer center provide access to Internet. Staffed computer lab on campus provides training in use of computers, software.
COLLEGE LIFE Drama-theater group, choral group, student-run newspaper. ***Social organizations:*** 5 open to all. ***Student services:*** personal-psychological counseling.
HOUSING College housing not available.
ATHLETICS ***Intercollegiate:*** golf M/W, soccer M. ***Intramural:*** basketball, bowling, volleyball.
CAREER PLANNING ***Service:*** career counseling.
EXPENSES FOR 1996–97 State resident tuition: $1552 full-time, $48.50 per credit hour part-time. Nonresident tuition: $2328 full-time, $72.75 per credit hour part-time. Part-time mandatory fees: $6.50 per credit hour. Full-time mandatory fees: $208.
FINANCIAL AID ***College-administered undergrad aid 1995–96:*** need-based scholarships, non-need scholarships (average $500), low-interest long-term loans from external sources, Federal Work-Study. ***Acceptable forms:*** CSS Financial Aid PROFILE, FAFSA. ***Priority deadline:*** 7/1. ***Payment plan:*** deferred payment. ***Waivers:*** full or partial for employees or children of employees and senior citizens.
APPLYING Open admission except for nursing programs. ***Options:*** early entrance, deferred entrance. ***Required:*** TOEFL for international students, ACT ASSET. ***Recommended:*** school transcript, ACT. ***Required for some:*** school transcript. Test scores used for counseling/placement. ***Application deadline:*** rolling.
APPLYING/TRANSFER ***Recommended:*** college transcript. ***Required for some:*** college transcript. ***Entrance:*** noncompetitive. ***Application deadline:*** rolling. ***Contact:*** Ms. Louise Orozco, Academic Counselor, 319-524-3221 Ext. 412.
CONTACT Mrs. Tonya Little, Admissions Coordinator, Southeastern Community College, South Campus, Keokuk, IA 52632-6007, 319-524-3221 Ext. 416 or toll-free 800-344-7045 (in-state). ***Fax:*** 319-524-3221 Ext. 409.

SOUTHWESTERN COMMUNITY COLLEGE
Creston, Iowa

UG Enrollment: 1,211	**Tuition & Fees (IA Res): $1922**
Application Deadline: 9/4	**Room & Board: $2760**

GENERAL State-supported, 2-year, coed. Part of Iowa Department of Education Division of Community Colleges. Awards diplomas, transfer associate, terminal associate degrees. Founded 1966. ***Setting:*** 420-acre rural campus. ***Total enrollment:*** 1,211. ***Faculty:*** 86 (43 full-time, 100% with terminal degrees, 43 part-time).
ENROLLMENT PROFILE 1,211 students: 58% women, 44% part-time, 94% state residents, 8% live on campus, 6% transferred in, 82% have need-based financial aid, 18% have non-need-based financial aid, 2% international, 40% 25 or older, 0% Native American, 1% Hispanic, 1% African American, 1% Asian American. ***Areas of study chosen:*** 64% liberal arts/general studies, 36% vocational and home economics. ***Most popular recent majors:*** business administration/commerce/management, education.
FIRST-YEAR CLASS 398 total; 922 applied, 94% were accepted, 46% of whom enrolled.
ACADEMIC PROGRAM Core, interdisciplinary and vocational curriculum. Calendar: semesters. 319 courses offered in 1995–96. Academic remediation for entering students, services for LD students, advanced placement, self-designed majors, summer session for credit, part-time degree program (daytime, evenings, summer), adult/continuing education programs, co-op programs and internships.
GENERAL DEGREE REQUIREMENTS 62 credit hours; computer course for business administration, accounting, secretarial studies majors; internship (some majors).
MAJORS Accounting, agricultural sciences, art education, art/fine arts, business administration/commerce/management, carpentry, computer programming, drafting and design, economics, education, electrical engineering technology, electromechanical technology, elementary education, English, history, humanities, journalism, liberal arts/general studies, library science, literature, marketing/retailing/merchandising, mathematics, medical laboratory technology, music, music education, natural sciences, physical education, physical sciences, political science/government, psychology, retail management, science, secretarial studies/office management, social science, sociology, voice, welding technology, wildlife biology.
LIBRARY Learning Resources Center with 14,750 books, 165 periodicals, 2 on-line bibliographic services, 730 records, tapes, and CDs. Acquisition spending 1994–95: $80,989.
COMPUTERS ON CAMPUS 110 computers for student use in computer center, computer labs, learning resource center, library. Staffed computer lab on campus.
COLLEGE LIFE Choral group, student-run newspaper. ***Major annual events:*** Homecoming, Career Day, Vocational Area Competitions. ***Student services:*** personal-psychological counseling. ***Campus security:*** 24-hour patrols.
HOUSING 73 college housing spaces available; 51 were occupied 1995–96. No special consideration for freshman housing applicants. Off-campus living permitted. ***Option:*** single-sex housing available. Resident assistants live in dorms.
ATHLETICS Member NJCAA. ***Intercollegiate:*** baseball M(s), basketball M(s)/W(s), softball W(s), volleyball W(s). ***Intramural:*** basketball, table tennis (Ping-Pong), volleyball. ***Contact:*** Mr. Ron Clinton, Athletic Director, 515-782-7081 Ext. 257.
CAREER PLANNING ***Placement office:*** 2 full-time, 2 part-time staff; $85,000 operating expenditure 1994–95. ***Director:*** Ms. Pat Butcher, Coordinator of Farm Focus, 515-782-7081 Ext. 250. ***Services:*** resume preparation, resume referral, career counseling, careers library. 10 organizations recruited on campus 1994–95.
AFTER GRADUATION 80% of class of 1994 had job offers within 6 months. 85% of students completing a degree program went directly on to further study.
EXPENSES FOR 1996–97 State resident tuition: $1612 full-time, $52 per credit hour part-time. Nonresident tuition: $2418 full-time, $78 per credit hour part-time. Part-time mandatory fees: $10 per credit hour. Full-time mandatory fees: $310. College room and board: $2760.
FINANCIAL AID ***College-administered undergrad aid 1995–96:*** need-based scholarships, 80 non-need scholarships (average $400), 67 Federal Work-Study (averaging $1326). ***Required forms:*** institutional; accepted: CSS Financial Aid PROFILE, state, FAFSA. ***Application deadline:*** continuous.
APPLYING Open admission except for allied health programs. ***Options:*** early entrance, deferred entrance, midyear entrance. ***Required:*** ACT, TOEFL for international students, ACT ASSET. ***Recommended:*** school transcript. ***Required for some:*** school transcript. Test scores used for counseling/placement. ***Application deadline:*** 9/4. ***Notification:*** continuous.
APPLYING/TRANSFER ***Required:*** college transcript. ***Entrance:*** noncompetitive. ***Application deadline:*** 9/4. ***Notification:*** continuous. ***Contact:*** Mr. Paul B. Somers, Director of Admissions, 515-782-7081.
CONTACT Mr. Bill Hitesman, Acting Director of Student Services, Southwestern Community College, Creston, IA 50801, 515-782-7081 Ext. 231 or toll-free 800-247-4023 (in-state). ***Fax:*** 515-782-3312. ***E-mail:*** somers@swcc.cc.ia.us.

WALDORF COLLEGE
Forest City, Iowa

UG Enrollment: 588	**Tuition & Fees: $10,575**
Application Deadline: rolling	**Room & Board: $3825**

Waldorf College is an innovative 2- and 3-year college of liberal arts and sciences that offers the first 2 years of most bachelor's degree programs and BA degrees in 2 programs. Waldorf's bachelor's degrees are offered in a unique accelerated 3-year format leading to business and communications degrees.

GENERAL Independent Lutheran, primarily 2-year, coed. Awards transfer associate, bachelor's degrees. Founded 1903. ***Setting:*** 29-acre small-town campus. ***Total enrollment:*** 588. ***Faculty:*** 52 (31 full-time, 30% with terminal degrees, 21 part-time); student-faculty ratio is 13:1. ***Notable Alumni:*** John K. Hanson, founder and chairman of Winnebago Industries, Inc.; Herbert D. Ihle, president of Diversified Financial Services; Marguerite L. Johnson, contributing editor at *Time*; Dr. Randy P. Juhl, dean of School of Pharmacy at University of Pittsburgh; Elling B. Halvorson, CEO of Papillon Airways, Inc.
ENROLLMENT PROFILE 588 students from 22 states and territories, 20 other countries. 40% women, 60% men, 10% part-time, 60% state residents, 95% live on campus, 3% transferred in, 96% have need-based financial aid, 4% have non-need-based financial aid, 15% international, 11% 25 or older, 1% Native American, 1% Hispanic, 2% African American, 1% Asian American. ***Most popular recent majors:*** business administration/commerce/management, education, communication.
FIRST-YEAR CLASS 317 total; 723 applied, 87% were accepted, 51% of whom enrolled. 6% from top 10% of their high school class, 12% from top quarter, 40% from top half.
ACADEMIC PROGRAM Core, honor code. Calendar: semesters. 245 courses offered in 1995–96. Academic remediation for entering students, English as a second language program offered during academic year and summer, services for LD students, advanced placement, Freshman Honors College, honors program, summer session for credit, part-time degree program (evenings), adult/continuing education programs, co-op programs and internships.
GENERAL DEGREE REQUIREMENTS 64 semester hours for associate, 124 semester hours for bachelor's; 8 semester hours of science including at least 1 lab science course; internship (some majors).
MAJORS Accounting, art education, art/fine arts, behavioral sciences, biblical studies, biology/biological sciences, business administration/commerce/management (B), chemistry, child care/child and family studies, child psychology/child development, commercial art, communication (B), community services, computer information systems, computer programming, computer science, data processing, early childhood education, education, (pre)engineering sequence, English, finance/banking (B), German, health education, history, home economics, human services, journalism (B), law enforcement/police sciences, liberal arts/general studies, mathematics, medical assistant technologies, ministries, music, music education, nursing, physical education, physical sciences, piano/organ, psychology, religious education, religious studies, science, social science, social work, sociology, Spanish, speech/rhetoric/public address/debate, telecommunications, theater arts/drama, theology, veterinary sciences, voice, wildlife biology, wildlife management.
LIBRARY Voss Memorial Library plus 1 other, with 35,736 books, 41,868 microform titles, 215 periodicals, 2 on-line bibliographic services, 22 CD-ROMs, 273 records, tapes, and CDs.
COMPUTERS ON CAMPUS Computer purchase plan available. Student rooms linked to a campus network. 85 computers for student use in computer center, Academic Achievement Center, library provide access to main academic computer, e-mail, Internet. Staffed computer lab on campus provides training in use of computers, software.
COLLEGE LIFE Orientation program (3 days, no cost, parents included). Drama-theater group, choral group, student-run newspaper, radio station. 70% vote in student government elections. ***Student services:*** health clinic, personal-psychological counseling. ***Campus security:*** late-night transport-escort service, controlled dormitory access, evening and night patrols by trained security personnel.
HOUSING 500 college housing spaces available; all were occupied 1995–96. Freshmen guaranteed college housing. On-campus residence required through sophomore year except if living with relatives or by special permission. ***Options:*** coed (2 buildings), single-sex (2 buildings) housing available. Resident assistants live in dorms.
ATHLETICS Member NJCAA. ***Intercollegiate:*** baseball M(s), basketball M(s)/W(s), football M(s), golf M(s), soccer M(s), softball W(s), volleyball W(s), wrestling M(s). ***Intramural:*** basketball, football, racquetball, soccer, softball, tennis, volleyball. ***Contact:*** Mr. Dennis Jerome, Athletic Director, 515-582-8182.
CAREER PLANNING ***Placement office:*** 2 full-time staff. ***Director:*** Ms. Twylah Kragel, Registrar, 515-582-8139. ***Service:*** career counseling.
AFTER GRADUATION 86% of students completing transfer associate program in 1994–95 went directly to 4-year colleges.
EXPENSES FOR 1996–97 ***Application fee:*** $20. Comprehensive fee of $14,400 includes full-time tuition ($10,425), mandatory fees ($150), and college room and board ($3825). Part-time tuition: $115 per credit. Tuition guaranteed not to increase for student's term of enrollment.
FINANCIAL AID ***College-administered undergrad aid 1995–96:*** need-based scholarships, non-need scholarships, low-interest long-term loans from external sources, Federal Work-Study, part-time jobs. ***Acceptable forms:*** FAFSA. ***Application deadline:*** continuous. ***Payment plans:*** installment, deferred payment. ***Waivers:*** full or partial for employees or children of employees. ***Notification:*** continuous.
APPLYING ***Options:*** early entrance, midyear entrance. ***Required:*** school transcript, SAT I or ACT. ***Recommended:*** minimum 2.0 GPA, 3 years of high school math and sci-

Peterson's Guide to Two-Year Colleges 1997 325

Iowa–Kansas

Waldorf College (continued)
ence, some high school foreign language. **Required for some:** campus interview. Test scores used for counseling/placement. **Application deadline:** rolling. **Notification:** continuous.
APPLYING/TRANSFER Required: standardized test scores, high school transcript, college transcript. **Recommended:** minimum 2.0 high school GPA. **Required for some:** campus interview. **Application deadline:** rolling. **Notification:** continuous. **Contact:** Ms. Twylah Kragel, Registrar, 515-582-8139.
CONTACT Mr. Steven Lovik, Dean of Admission and Financial Aid, Waldorf College, Forest City, IA 50436-1713, 515-582-8112 or toll-free 800-292-1903. **Fax:** 515-582-8111. College video available.

WESTERN IOWA TECH COMMUNITY COLLEGE
Sioux City, Iowa

UG Enrollment: 3,000	Tuition & Fees (IA Res): $1888
Application Deadline: rolling	Room & Board: N/Avail

GENERAL State-supported, 2-year, coed. Part of Iowa Department of Education Division of Community Colleges. Awards transfer associate, terminal associate degrees. Founded 1966. **Setting:** 145-acre urban campus. **Total enrollment:** 3,000. **Faculty:** 157; student-faculty ratio is 15:1.
ENROLLMENT PROFILE 3,000 students: 42% women, 1% part-time, 88% state residents, 12% transferred in, 28% 25 or older, 2% Native American, 1% Hispanic, 1% African American, 1% Asian American. **Most popular recent majors:** nursing, law enforcement/police sciences, architectural technologies.
FIRST-YEAR CLASS 1,700 total. Of the students who applied, 97% were accepted.
ACADEMIC PROGRAM Calendar: semesters. Academic remediation for entering students, services for LD students, summer session for credit, part-time degree program (daytime, evenings), external degree programs, adult/continuing education programs, co-op programs.
GENERAL DEGREE REQUIREMENTS 64 semester credit hours; computer course.
MAJORS Accounting, agricultural business, agricultural technologies, architectural technologies, automotive technologies, business administration/commerce/management, computer programming, construction technologies, drafting and design, early childhood education, electrical and electronics technologies, engineering design, law enforcement/police sciences, marketing/retailing/merchandising, mechanical engineering technology, medical laboratory technology, nursing, occupational therapy, physician's assistant studies, secretarial studies/office management, solar technologies.
COMPUTERS ON CAMPUS 25 computers for student use in learning resource center provide access to main academic computer.
COLLEGE LIFE Student services: health clinic, personal-psychological counseling.
HOUSING College housing not available.
ATHLETICS Intercollegiate: golf M/W. **Intramural:** basketball, bowling, volleyball.
CAREER PLANNING Service: career counseling.
EXPENSES FOR 1995–96 Application fee: $10. State resident tuition: $1760 full-time, $55 per semester hour part-time. Nonresident tuition: $3520 full-time, $110 per semester hour part-time. Part-time mandatory fees: $4 per semester hour. Full-time mandatory fees: $128.
FINANCIAL AID College-administered undergrad aid 1995–96: need-based scholarships, short-term loans, Federal Work-Study, part-time jobs. **Required forms for some financial aid applicants:** FAFSA; accepted: CSS Financial Aid PROFILE. **Application deadline:** continuous.
APPLYING Open admission except for health occupations programs. **Option:** deferred entrance. **Required:** school transcript, TOEFL for international students, CPT. Test scores used for admission. **Application deadline:** rolling. **Notification:** continuous.
APPLYING/TRANSFER Required: standardized test scores, high school transcript, college transcript. **Entrance:** noncompetitive.
CONTACT Mr. Walter Brockamp, Director of Admissions, Western Iowa Tech Community College, 4647 Stone Avenue, PO Box 5199, Sioux City, IA 51102-5199, 712-274-6400 Ext. 1353.

KANSAS

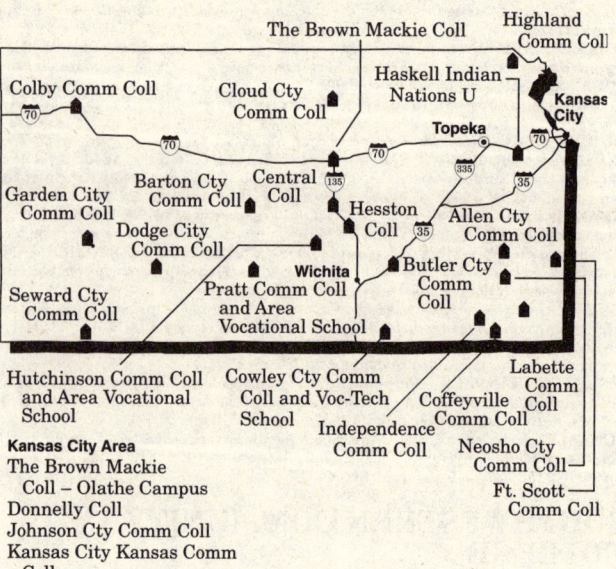

ALLEN COUNTY COMMUNITY COLLEGE
Iola, Kansas

UG Enrollment: 1,689	Tuition & Fees (KS Res): $1176
Application Deadline: 9/10	Room & Board: $2700

GENERAL State and locally supported, 2-year, coed. Part of Kansas State Board of Education. Awards transfer associate, terminal associate degrees. Founded 1923. **Setting:** 88-acre small-town campus. **Educational spending 1994–95:** $1312 per undergrad. **Total enrollment:** 1,689. **Faculty:** 135 (35 full-time, 100 part-time); student-faculty ratio is 12:1.
ENROLLMENT PROFILE 1,689 students from 11 states and territories, 9 other countries. 55% women, 69% part-time, 98% state residents, 10% live on campus, 4% transferred in, 62% 25 or older, 1% Native American, 1% Hispanic, 1% African American.
FIRST-YEAR CLASS 245 total. Of the students who applied, 100% were accepted, 67% of whom enrolled. 13% from top 10% of their high school class, 25% from top quarter, 51% from top half.
ACADEMIC PROGRAM Core, honor code. Calendar: semesters. Academic remediation for entering students, services for LD students, self-designed majors, summer session for credit, part-time degree program (daytime, evenings, summer), adult/continuing education programs, co-op programs.
GENERAL DEGREE REQUIREMENTS 64 credit hours; 1 course each in college algebra and lab science; computer course for business administration, accounting, business education, secretarial, marketing education majors.
MAJORS Accounting, advertising, agricultural business, agricultural education, agricultural sciences, agricultural technologies, agronomy/soil and crop sciences, animal sciences, art education, art/fine arts, behavioral sciences, biology/biological sciences, business administration/commerce/management, business education, ceramic art and design, chemistry, child care/child and family studies, commercial art, communication, computer information systems, computer programming, computer science, computer technologies, construction management, construction technologies, criminal justice, cytotechnology, data processing, deaf interpreter training, drafting and design, early childhood education, economics, education, electrical and electronics technologies, electronics engineering technology, elementary education, emergency medical technology, engineering (general), engineering sciences, engineering technology, English, equestrian studies, farm and ranch management, fashion design and technology, fashion merchandising, finance/banking, geography, history, home economics, industrial arts, industrial engineering technology, journalism, law enforcement/police sciences, legal secretarial studies, liberal arts/general studies, library science, literature, machine and tool technologies, management information systems, manufacturing technology, marketing/retailing/merchandising, mathematics, mechanical design technology, medical assistant technologies, medical secretarial studies, music, painting/drawing, pharmacy/pharmaceutical sciences, physical education, physical sciences, physics, political science/government, printing technologies, psychology, reading education, retail management, robotics, science, secretarial studies/office management, social science, social work, sociology, Spanish, theater arts/drama, word processing.
LIBRARY 48,524 books, 178 microform titles, 256 periodicals, 153 CD-ROMs, 1,531 records, tapes, and CDs. Acquisition spending 1994–95: $96,655.
COMPUTERS ON CAMPUS 65 computers for student use in computer center, learning resource center, classrooms, library, student center provide access to Internet. Staffed computer lab on campus provides training in use of computers, software. Academic computing expenditure 1994–95: $31,100.
COLLEGE LIFE Choral group, student-run newspaper. **Most popular organizations:** Intramurals, ASK Club, Student Senate, Phi Theta Kappa. **Major annual events:** Homecoming, Club Calf Sale, Fall Frolic. **Student services:** personal-psychological counseling. **Campus security:** controlled dormitory access.

HOUSING 156 college housing spaces available; 150 were occupied 1995–96. No special consideration for freshman housing applicants. ***Option:*** coed (2 buildings) housing available. Resident assistants live in dorms.
ATHLETICS Member NJCAA. ***Intercollegiate:*** baseball M(s), basketball M(s)/W(s), cross-country running M(s)/W(s), golf M(s), soccer M(s), softball W(s), track and field M(s)/W(s), volleyball W(s). ***Intramural:*** basketball, football, soccer, softball, table tennis (Ping-Pong), tennis, volleyball. ***Contact:*** Mr. Larry Manes, 316-365-5116.
CAREER PLANNING ***Placement office:*** 3 full-time, 2 part-time staff; $40,000 operating expenditure 1994–95. ***Director:*** Ms. Gladys Groves, Director of Instructional Resource Center, 316-365-5116 Ext. 250. ***Services:*** resume preparation, career counseling, careers library, job bank, job interviews.
EXPENSES FOR 1996–97 State resident tuition: $1176 full-time, $42 per credit hour part-time. Nonresident tuition: $1176 full-time, $42 per credit hour part-time. Tuition for international students: $67 per credit hour. College room and board: $2700.
FINANCIAL AID ***College-administered undergrad aid 1995–96:*** need-based scholarships, 241 non-need scholarships (average $450), Federal Work-Study, 56 part-time jobs. ***Acceptable forms:*** FAFSA. ***Priority deadline:*** 8/1. ***Payment plan:*** installment. ***Waivers:*** full or partial for employees or children of employees and senior citizens.
APPLYING Open admission. ***Options:*** Common Application, early entrance, deferred entrance. ***Required:*** school transcript, TOEFL for international students. ***Recommended:*** ACT. ***Required for some:*** ACT ASSET. Test scores used for counseling/placement. ***Application deadline:*** 9/10. ***Notification:*** continuous.
APPLYING/TRANSFER ***Required:*** high school transcript, college transcript. ***Recommended:*** standardized test scores. ***Entrance:*** noncompetitive. ***Application deadline:*** 9/10. ***Notification:*** continuous.
CONTACT Mr. Mike Schlies, Dean of Student Services, Allen County Community College, Iola, KS 66749-1607, 316-365-5116. ***Fax:*** 316-365-3284. College video available.

BARTON COUNTY COMMUNITY COLLEGE
Great Bend, Kansas

UG Enrollment: 10,000 — **Tuition & Fees (KS Res): $1184**
Application Deadline: rolling — **Room & Board: $2500**

GENERAL State and locally supported, 2-year, coed. Part of Kansas State Board of Education. Awards transfer associate, terminal associate degrees. Founded 1969. ***Setting:*** 140-acre rural campus. ***Total enrollment:*** 10,000. ***Faculty:*** 292 (63 full-time, 12% with terminal degrees, 229 part-time).
ENROLLMENT PROFILE 10,000 students from 23 states and territories, 7 other countries. 56% women, 44% men, 80% part-time, 98% state residents, 30% transferred in, 1% international, 65% 25 or older, 1% Native American, 4% Hispanic, 12% African American, 2% Asian American. ***Most popular recent major:*** business administration/commerce/management.
FIRST-YEAR CLASS 2,600 total; 3,000 applied, 100% were accepted, 87% of whom enrolled. 13% from top 10% of their high school class, 40% from top quarter, 85% from top half.
ACADEMIC PROGRAM Calendar: semesters. Academic remediation for entering students, English as a second language program offered during academic year, services for LD students, advanced placement, self-designed majors, summer session for credit, part-time degree program (daytime, evenings, weekends, summer), external degree programs, adult/continuing education programs, co-op programs and internships.
GENERAL DEGREE REQUIREMENTS 64 credit hours; 3 credit hours of math/science.
MAJORS Agricultural sciences, anthropology, applied art, art/fine arts, automotive technologies, biology/biological sciences, business administration/commerce/management, chemistry, child care/child and family studies, computer information systems, computer science, cosmetology, criminal justice, cytotechnology, drafting and design, economics, education, electrical and electronics technologies, emergency medical technology, (pre)engineering sequence, English, fashion merchandising, fire science, forestry, geology, health science, history, home economics, humanities, interior design, journalism, law enforcement/police sciences, liberal arts/general studies, mathematics, medical laboratory technology, medical records services, medical secretarial studies, music, nursing, occupational therapy, petroleum technology, pharmacy/pharmaceutical sciences, philosophy, physical education, physical sciences, physical therapy, physician's assistant studies, physics, political science/government, psychology, public administration, respiratory therapy, secretarial studies/office management, social work, sociology, sports administration, sports medicine, theater arts/drama, welding technology.
LIBRARY Barton County Community College Library with 28,000 books, 213 periodicals, 283 records, tapes, and CDs.
COMPUTERS ON CAMPUS 100 computers for student use in computer center, computer labs, library provide access to e-mail, on-line services, Internet. Staffed computer lab on campus provides training in use of computers, software.
COLLEGE LIFE Orientation program (3 days, $102, parents included). Drama-theater group, choral group, student-run newspaper. ***Student services:*** health clinic, personal-psychological counseling. ***Campus security:*** 24-hour emergency response devices and patrols.
HOUSING 280 college housing spaces available; all were occupied 1995–96. No special consideration for freshman housing applicants. Off-campus living permitted.
ATHLETICS Member NJCAA. ***Intercollegiate:*** baseball M(s), basketball M(s)/W(s), cross-country running M(s)/W(s), golf M(s), tennis M(s)/W(s), track and field M(s)/W(s), volleyball W(s). ***Intramural:*** basketball, bowling, football, golf, swimming and diving, table tennis (Ping-Pong), tennis, track and field, volleyball. ***Contact:*** Mr. Jerry McCarty, Athletic Director, 316-792-2701 Ext. 178.
CAREER PLANNING ***Placement office:*** 2 full-time staff. ***Director:*** Mr. Louis Pivonka, Career/Placement Counselor, 316-792-2701 Ext. 144. ***Services:*** job fairs, resume preparation, career counseling, careers library, job bank.
ESTIMATED EXPENSES FOR 1996–97 State resident tuition: $800 full-time, $25 per credit hour part-time. Nonresident tuition: $2400 full-time, $75 per credit hour part-time. Part-time mandatory fees: $12 per credit hour. Full-time mandatory fees: $384. College room and board: $2500 (minimum).
FINANCIAL AID ***College-administered undergrad aid 1995–96:*** 150 need-based scholarships (average $300), 400 non-need scholarships (average $500), short-term loans (average $50), low-interest long-term loans from college funds (average $1000), loans from external sources (average $2000), Federal Work-Study, 200 part-time jobs. ***Required forms:*** institutional, FAFSA; accepted: CSS Financial Aid PROFILE. ***Priority deadline:*** 3/1. ***Waivers:*** full or partial for employees or children of employees and senior citizens.
APPLYING Open admission. ***Option:*** early entrance. ***Required:*** TOEFL for international students. ***Recommended:*** ACT. Test scores used for counseling/placement. ***Application deadline:*** rolling.
APPLYING/TRANSFER ***Application deadline:*** rolling.
CONTACT Mr. Matt Gotschall, Director of Student Affairs, Barton County Community College, Great Bend, KS 67530-9283, 316-792-2701 Ext. 226. ***Fax:*** 316-792-3238. ***E-mail:*** crowther/@cougar.barton.cc.ks.us. College video available.

THE BROWN MACKIE COLLEGE
Salina, Kansas

UG Enrollment: 611 — **Tuition & Fees: $7175**
Application Deadline: rolling — **Room & Board: N/Avail**

GENERAL Proprietary, 2-year, coed. Awards diplomas, transfer associate, terminal associate degrees. Founded 1892. ***Setting:*** small-town campus. ***Total enrollment:*** 611. ***Faculty:*** 23 (8 full-time, 4% with terminal degrees, 15 part-time); student-faculty ratio is 25:1.
ENROLLMENT PROFILE 611 students from 8 states and territories. 70% women, 2% part-time, 99% state residents, 37% transferred in, 34% 25 or older, 20% Native American, 6% Hispanic, 20% African American, 1% Asian American.
FIRST-YEAR CLASS 391 total; 583 applied, 99% were accepted, 68% of whom enrolled. 1% from top 10% of their high school class, 2% from top quarter, 50% from top half.
ACADEMIC PROGRAM Core, interdisciplinary curriculum. Calendar: semesters plus 4 six-week terms. 125 courses offered in 1995–96. Academic remediation for entering students, services for LD students, advanced placement, part-time degree program (daytime, evenings), adult/continuing education programs, co-op programs and internships.
GENERAL DEGREE REQUIREMENTS 64 semester hours; 1 math course; computer course; internship (some majors).
MAJORS Accounting, business administration/commerce/management, court reporting, criminal justice, marketing/retailing/merchandising, paralegal studies, secretarial studies/office management.
LIBRARY Irene Carlson Memorial Library with 6,824 books, 41 periodicals, 53 records, tapes, and CDs.
COMPUTERS ON CAMPUS 75 computers for student use in computer center, computer labs, learning resource center, classrooms. Staffed computer lab on campus provides training in use of computers, software.
COLLEGE LIFE Student-run newspaper. 35% vote in student government elections. ***Major annual events:*** Commencement, Summer Picnic, Thanksgiving/Christmas Dinner.
HOUSING College housing not available.
ATHLETICS Member NJCAA. ***Intercollegiate:*** baseball M, basketball M/W, softball W, volleyball W. ***Contact:*** Mr. Francis Flax, Athletic Director, 913-825-5422; Ms. Cheryl Aherns, Assistant Coach, 913-825-5422.
CAREER PLANNING ***Placement office:*** 1 full-time staff. ***Director:*** Mrs. June Day-Lambert, Career Services Director, 913-825-5422. ***Services:*** job fairs, resume preparation, resume referral, career counseling, job interviews.
AFTER GRADUATION 15% of students completing a degree program in 1994–95 went directly on to further study.
EXPENSES FOR 1996–97 Tuition: $6975 full-time, $218 per semester hour part-time. Full-time mandatory fees: $200.
FINANCIAL AID ***College-administered undergrad aid 1995–96:*** need-based scholarships, non-need scholarships (average $750), low-interest long-term loans from college funds, loans from external sources, Federal Work-Study, part-time jobs. ***Required forms for some financial aid applicants:*** state, FAFSA; accepted: CSS Financial Aid PROFILE. ***Application deadline:*** continuous. ***Payment plan:*** installment. ***Waivers:*** full or partial for employees or children of employees and senior citizens.
APPLYING Open admission. ***Option:*** midyear entrance. ***Required:*** school transcript, ACT ASSET, Wonderlic aptitude test. Test scores used for counseling/placement. ***Application deadline:*** rolling. ***Notification:*** continuous.
APPLYING/TRANSFER ***Required:*** college transcript. ***Entrance:*** minimally difficult. ***Contact:*** Dr. Robert S. Fitch, Interim Dean of Academic Affairs, 913-825-5422.
CONTACT Mr. Larry D. Schafer, Vice President of the College and Director of Admissions, The Brown Mackie College, Salina, KS 67401-2810, 913-825-5422 or toll-free 800-365-0433. ***Fax:*** 913-827-7623.

THE BROWN MACKIE COLLEGE-OLATHE CAMPUS
Olathe, Kansas

UG Enrollment: 300 — **Tuition & Fees: $6890**
Application Deadline: 8/15 — **Room & Board: N/Avail**

GENERAL Proprietary, 2-year, coed. Part of The Brown Mackie College. Awards diplomas, terminal associate degrees. Founded 1892. ***Setting:*** suburban campus with easy access to Kansas City. ***Educational spending 1994–95:*** $909 per undergrad. ***Total enrollment:*** 300. ***Faculty:*** 29 (12 full-time, 73% with terminal degrees, 17 part-time); student-faculty ratio is 10:1.
ENROLLMENT PROFILE 300 students from 2 states and territories, 1 other country. 78% women, 2% part-time, 99% state residents, 95% have need-based financial aid, 5% have non-need-based financial aid, 0% Native American, 2% Hispanic, 22% African American, 1% Asian American. ***Areas of study chosen:*** 97% business management and administrative services. ***Most popular recent majors:*** business administration/commerce/management, paralegal studies.
FIRST-YEAR CLASS 200 total; 210 applied, 95% were accepted, 100% of whom enrolled.
ACADEMIC PROGRAM Core, honor code. Calendar: semesters. 150 courses offered in 1995–96. Summer session for credit, part-time degree program (daytime, evenings, summer), internships.
GENERAL DEGREE REQUIREMENTS 64 credit hours; 1 course each in college algebra and human anatomy; computer course; internship (some majors).
MAJORS Accounting, business administration/commerce/management, court reporting, paralegal studies.

The Brown Mackie College-Olathe Campus (continued)

LIBRARY The Brown Mackie College Library with 5,579 books, 25 periodicals, 1 on-line bibliographic service, 15 records, tapes, and CDs. Acquisition spending 1994–95: $55,678.

COMPUTERS ON CAMPUS 60 computers for student use in computer labs, classrooms, library provide access to on-line services, Internet. Staffed computer lab on campus provides training in use of computers, software. Academic computing expenditure 1994–95: $280,000.

COLLEGE LIFE ***Major annual events:*** Summer Picnic, Christmas Party, Thanksgiving Dinner Party. ***Student services:*** personal-psychological counseling. ***Campus security:*** 24-hour emergency response devices, late-night transport-escort service.

HOUSING College housing not available.

CAREER PLANNING ***Placement office:*** 1 full-time staff; $15,000 operating expenditure 1994–95. ***Director:*** Mr. Paul Ostrom, Director, 913-768-1900. ***Services:*** job fairs, resume preparation, resume referral, career counseling, careers library, job bank, job interviews.

EXPENSES FOR 1996–97 ***Application fee:*** $25. Tuition: $6540 full-time, $218 per credit hour part-time. Part-time mandatory fees: $350 per year. Full-time mandatory fees: $350. Tuition guaranteed not to increase for student's term of enrollment.

FINANCIAL AID ***College-administered undergrad aid 1995–96:*** 111 need-based scholarships (average $1070), 75 non-need scholarships (average $2782), 1 part-time job. ***Required forms:*** FAFSA. ***Priority deadline:*** 8/15. ***Payment plan:*** installment. ***Waivers:*** full or partial for employees or children of employees. ***Notification:*** continuous.

APPLYING Open admission. ***Options:*** deferred entrance, midyear entrance. ***Required:*** essay, school transcript, interview, ACT. ***Recommended:*** minimum 2.0 GPA, 3 years of high school math and science. ***Application deadline:*** 8/15. ***Notification:*** continuous until 8/20.

APPLYING/TRANSFER ***Required:*** essay, standardized test scores, high school transcript, interview, college transcript, minimum 2.0 college GPA. ***Recommended:*** 3 years of high school math and science, minimum 2.0 high school GPA. ***Entrance:*** noncompetitive. ***Application deadline:*** 8/15. ***Notification:*** continuous until 8/20. ***Contact:*** Dr. Robert Veach, Dean of Academic Affairs, 913-768-1900.

CONTACT Mr. Paul Ostrom, Director, The Brown Mackie College-Olathe Campus, Olathe, KS 66061, 913-768-1900.

BUTLER COUNTY COMMUNITY COLLEGE
El Dorado, Kansas

UG Enrollment: 7,931	**Tuition & Fees (KS Res): $1271**
Application Deadline: 8/20	**Room & Board: $3100**

GENERAL State and locally supported, 2-year, coed. Part of Kansas State Board of Education. Awards transfer associate, terminal associate degrees. Founded 1927. ***Setting:*** 80-acre small-town campus. ***Total enrollment:*** 7,931. ***Faculty:*** 573.

ENROLLMENT PROFILE 7,931 students from 18 states and territories, 21 other countries. 60% women, 70% part-time, 97% state residents, 20% transferred in, 50% 25 or older, 2% Native American, 2% Hispanic, 6% African American, 3% Asian American.

FIRST-YEAR CLASS 1,730 total. Of the students who applied, 100% were accepted, 83% of whom enrolled.

ACADEMIC PROGRAM Core. Calendar: semesters. Academic remediation for entering students, services for LD students, self-designed majors, honors program, summer session for credit, part-time degree program (daytime, evenings, summer), adult/continuing education programs, co-op programs.

GENERAL DEGREE REQUIREMENTS 62 credit hours; math/science requirements vary according to program; computer course.

MAJORS Accounting, advertising, agricultural business, agricultural sciences, agricultural technologies, art education, art/fine arts, automotive technologies, behavioral sciences, biology/biological sciences, business administration/commerce/management, business education, business machine technologies, carpentry, ceramic art and design, chemistry, child care/child and family studies, civil engineering technology, commercial art, communication, computer programming, computer science, construction technologies, criminal justice, cytotechnology, data processing, drafting and design, early childhood education, electrical and electronics technologies, electrical engineering technology, engineering (general), (pre)engineering sequence, English, farm and ranch management, fashion merchandising, fire science, health education, history, hotel and restaurant management, industrial arts, industrial engineering technology, journalism, law enforcement/police sciences, legal secretarial studies, liberal arts/general studies, marketing/retailing/merchandising, mathematics, mechanical design technology, mechanical engineering technology, medical records services, medical secretarial studies, music, nursing, physical education, physical therapy, physics, political science/government, psychology, real estate, retail management, secretarial studies/office management, social science, social work, sociology, theater arts/drama, vocational education, voice, welding technology, wildlife management.

LIBRARY 38,000 books, 13,100 microform titles, 220 periodicals, 500 records, tapes, and CDs.

COMPUTERS ON CAMPUS 90 computers for student use in computer center, classrooms, library.

COLLEGE LIFE Drama-theater group, student-run newspaper. ***Student services:*** personal-psychological counseling. ***Campus security:*** 24-hour emergency response devices and patrols, controlled dormitory access.

HOUSING 210 college housing spaces available; all were occupied 1995–96. Off-campus living permitted.

ATHLETICS Member NJCAA. ***Intercollegiate:*** baseball M(s), basketball M(s)/W(s), cross-country running M(s)/W(s), football M(s), golf M(s), softball W(s), tennis M(s)/W(s), track and field M(s)/W(s), volleyball W(s). ***Intramural:*** basketball, bowling, football, golf, softball, table tennis (Ping-Pong), tennis, track and field, volleyball.

CAREER PLANNING ***Service:*** career counseling.

EXPENSES FOR 1996–97 State resident tuition: $1271 full-time, $41 per credit hour part-time. Nonresident tuition: $2976 full-time, $96 per credit hour part-time. College room and board: $3100 (minimum).

FINANCIAL AID ***College-administered undergrad aid 1995–96:*** need-based scholarships (average $300), non-need scholarships (average $300), low-interest long-term loans from external sources, part-time jobs. ***Required forms:*** institutional, FAFSA; accepted: CSS Financial Aid PROFILE. ***Priority deadline:*** 5/1.

APPLYING Open admission. ***Options:*** early entrance, deferred entrance. ***Required:*** school transcript, TOEFL for international students. ***Recommended:*** ACT. ***Required for some:*** ACT ASSET. Test scores used for counseling/placement. ***Application deadline:*** 8/20. ***Notification:*** continuous.

APPLYING/TRANSFER ***Required:*** high school transcript, minimum 2.0 college GPA. ***Entrance:*** noncompetitive. ***Application deadline:*** 8/20. ***Notification:*** continuous.

CONTACT Mr. Neal Hoelting, Director of Admissions, Butler County Community College, El Dorado, KS 67042-3280, 316-321-2222 Ext. 245.

CENTRAL COLLEGE
McPherson, Kansas

UG Enrollment: 323	**Tuition & Fees: $8850**
Application Deadline: rolling	**Room & Board: $3300**

GENERAL Independent Free Methodist, primarily 2-year, coed. Awards transfer associate, terminal associate, bachelor's degrees. Founded 1884. ***Setting:*** 16-acre small-town campus. ***Total enrollment:*** 323. ***Faculty:*** 24 (16 full-time, 8 part-time); student-faculty ratio is 16:1.

ENROLLMENT PROFILE 323 students from 30 states and territories, 5 other countries. 42% women, 58% men, 6% part-time, 21% state residents, 2% transferred in, 3% international, 3% 25 or older, 1% Native American, 5% Hispanic, 10% African American, 3% Asian American. ***Most popular recent majors:*** business administration/commerce/management, religious studies, education.

FIRST-YEAR CLASS 158 total; 874 applied, 63% were accepted, 29% of whom enrolled.

ACADEMIC PROGRAM Core. Calendar: 4-1-4. Academic remediation for entering students, advanced placement, self-designed majors, part-time degree program (daytime), adult/continuing education programs, co-op programs and internships. Off-campus study at McPherson College.

GENERAL DEGREE REQUIREMENTS 60 credit hours for associate; 8 credit hours of math/science.

MAJORS Accounting, agricultural business, architectural technologies, art education, art/fine arts, automotive technologies, aviation technology, behavioral sciences, biblical studies, biology/biological sciences, business administration/commerce/management, business economics, business education, carpentry, child care/child and family studies, child psychology/child development, communication, computer programming, computer science, construction technologies, criminal justice, data processing, dietetics, drafting and design, early childhood education, economics, education, elementary education, engineering (general), English, family services, farm and ranch management, fashion design and technology, fashion merchandising, finance/banking, flight training, food services management, guidance and counseling, health education, history, home economics, home economics education, horticulture, humanities, industrial arts, interior design, journalism, legal secretarial studies, liberal arts/general studies, library science, marriage and family counseling, medical secretarial studies, ministries (B), museum studies, music, music education, nutrition, pastoral studies, physical education, physical sciences, physical therapy, psychology, recreation and leisure services, religious studies (B), science, science education, secretarial studies/office management, social science, theology, word processing, zoology.

LIBRARY Briner Library with 25,000 books, 120 periodicals, 50 records, tapes, and CDs.

COMPUTERS ON CAMPUS 30 computers for student use in computer center, library provide access to e-mail, on-line services, Internet. Staffed computer lab on campus provides training in use of computers, software.

COLLEGE LIFE Orientation program (3 days, no cost). Drama-theater group, choral group, student-run newspaper. ***Student services:*** health clinic, personal-psychological counseling.

HOUSING 335 college housing spaces available; 292 were occupied 1995–96. Freshmen guaranteed college housing. On-campus residence required through sophomore year. ***Option:*** single-sex housing available. Resident assistants live in dorms.

ATHLETICS Member NSCAA, NJCAA. ***Intercollegiate:*** baseball M(s), basketball M(s)/W(s), cross-country running M(s)/W(s), golf M, soccer M(s)/W(s), softball W(s), tennis M(s)/W(s), volleyball W(s). ***Intramural:*** basketball, bowling, golf, soccer, volleyball.

CAREER PLANNING ***Director:*** Ms. Karen Mayse, Director of Guidance Center, 316-241-0723. ***Services:*** job fairs, resume preparation, career counseling, careers library.

AFTER GRADUATION 70% of students completing transfer associate program in 1994–95 went directly to 4-year colleges.

EXPENSES FOR 1996–97 ***Application fee:*** $10. Comprehensive fee of $12,150 includes full-time tuition ($8850) and college room and board ($3300). Part-time tuition: $235 per credit hour.

FINANCIAL AID ***College-administered undergrad aid 1995–96:*** need-based scholarships, 250 non-need scholarships (average $917), low-interest long-term loans from college funds (average $1000), loans from external sources (average $2250), Federal Work-Study, 160 part-time jobs. ***Acceptable forms:*** CSS Financial Aid PROFILE, FAFSA. ***Priority deadline:*** 8/15. ***Payment plans:*** installment, deferred payment. ***Waivers:*** full or partial for employees or children of employees.

APPLYING ***Options:*** early entrance, deferred entrance. ***Required:*** school transcript, minimum 2.0 GPA, 1 recommendation, SAT I or ACT. ***Recommended:*** interview. Test scores used for admission and counseling/placement. ***Application deadline:*** rolling.

APPLYING/TRANSFER ***Required:*** standardized test scores, high school transcript, 1 recommendation, college transcript, minimum 2.0 high school GPA. ***Recommended:*** interview. ***Application deadline:*** rolling.

CONTACT Mr. Greg G. Gossell, Director of Enrollment, Central College, McPherson, KS 67460-5799, 316-241-0723 Ext. 334. ***Fax:*** 316-241-6032.

CLOUD COUNTY COMMUNITY COLLEGE
Concordia, Kansas

UG Enrollment: 3,112	**Tuition & Fees (KS Res): $1110**
Application Deadline: 9/11	**Room & Board: $2600**

GENERAL State and locally supported, 2-year, coed. Part of Kansas Community College System. Awards certificates, diplomas, transfer associate, terminal associate degrees.

Founded 1965. ***Setting:*** 35-acre rural campus. ***Total enrollment:*** 3,112. ***Faculty:*** 218 (38 full-time, 8% with terminal degrees, 180 part-time); student-faculty ratio is 15:1.
ENROLLMENT PROFILE 3,112 students from 12 states and territories, 2 other countries. 73% women, 78% part-time, 99% state residents, 35% transferred in, 67% 25 or older, 1% Native American, 2% African American, 1% Asian American.
FIRST-YEAR CLASS 1,250 total. Of the students who applied, 100% were accepted, 91% of whom enrolled. 5% from top 10% of their high school class, 20% from top quarter, 75% from top half.
ACADEMIC PROGRAM Core. Calendar: semesters. Academic remediation for entering students, services for LD students, advanced placement, summer session for credit, part-time degree program (daytime, evenings, summer), adult/continuing education programs, co-op programs and internships.
GENERAL DEGREE REQUIREMENTS 64 credit hours; 6 credit hours of math; 8 credit hours of science; internship (some majors).
MAJORS Agricultural business, art/fine arts, aviation technology, behavioral sciences, biology/biological sciences, broadcasting, business administration/commerce/management, child care/child and family studies, criminal justice, drafting and design, education, elementary education, (pre)engineering sequence, farm and ranch management, fashion design and technology, history, home economics, home economics education, humanities, journalism, liberal arts/general studies, music, nursing, physical education, physical sciences, science, secretarial studies/office management, social science, tourism and travel.
LIBRARY 18,010 books, 70 microform titles, 142 periodicals, 1,620 records, tapes, and CDs.
COMPUTERS ON CAMPUS 57 computers for student use in computer labs, learning resource center, science area. Staffed computer lab on campus provides training in use of computers, software.
COLLEGE LIFE Orientation program (2 days). Drama-theater group, choral group, student-run newspaper, radio station. ***Most popular organizations:*** Fellowship of Christian Athletes, Block and Bridle Club, Student Senate. ***Major annual event:*** Homecoming. ***Student services:*** health clinic. ***Campus security:*** 24-hour emergency response devices.
HOUSING 236 college housing spaces available; 234 were occupied 1995–96. No special consideration for freshman housing applicants. Off-campus living permitted. ***Option:*** single-sex housing available.
ATHLETICS Member NJCAA. ***Intercollegiate:*** basketball M(s)/W(s), cross-country running M(s)/W(s), golf M(s)/W(s), soccer M(s), tennis M(s)/W(s), track and field M(s)/W(s), volleyball W(s). ***Intramural:*** baseball, basketball, softball, volleyball. ***Contact:*** Mr. Dennis Erkenbrack, Athletic Director, 913-243-1435.
CAREER PLANNING ***Director:*** Mr. Jack Kaufman, Director of Career Assistance Center, 913-243-1435. ***Service:*** career counseling.
AFTER GRADUATION 78% of students completing a degree program in 1994–95 went directly on to further study.
EXPENSES FOR 1995–96 State resident tuition: $810 full-time, $27 per credit hour part-time. Nonresident tuition: $2025 full-time, $67.50 per credit hour part-time. Part-time mandatory fees: $10 per credit hour. Full-time mandatory fees: $300. College room and board: $2600. College room only: $1690.
FINANCIAL AID ***College-administered undergrad aid 1995–96:*** need-based scholarships, 550 non-need scholarships (average $475), low-interest long-term loans from external sources (average $1250), Federal Work-Study, part-time jobs. ***Required forms:*** FAFSA; accepted: CSS Financial Aid PROFILE. ***Priority deadline:*** 4/1.
APPLYING Open admission. ***Options:*** early entrance, deferred entrance. ***Required:*** school transcript, ACT ASSET. ***Recommended:*** ACT. Test scores used for counseling/placement. ***Application deadline:*** 9/11. ***Notification:*** continuous.
APPLYING/TRANSFER ***Required:*** standardized test scores, high school transcript, college transcript. ***Application deadline:*** 9/11. ***Notification:*** continuous.
CONTACT Ms. Peggy Rice, Director of Admissions, Cloud County Community College, Concordia, KS 66901-1002, 913-243-1435 Ext. 209 or toll-free 800-729-5101.

COFFEYVILLE COMMUNITY COLLEGE
Coffeyville, Kansas

UG Enrollment: 2,380	**Tuition & Fees (KS Res): $1180**
Application Deadline: rolling	**Room & Board: $2700**

GENERAL State and locally supported, 2-year, coed. Part of Kansas State Board of Education. Awards transfer associate, terminal associate degrees. Founded 1923. ***Setting:*** 8-acre small-town campus with easy access to Tulsa. ***Total enrollment:*** 2,380. ***Faculty:*** 86 (50 full-time, 36 part-time); student-faculty ratio is 25:1.
ENROLLMENT PROFILE 2,380 students from 15 states and territories, 10 other countries. 54% women, 55% part-time, 87% state residents, 12% transferred in, 3% international, 40% 25 or older, 2% Native American, 1% Hispanic, 11% African American, 1% Asian American. ***Most popular recent majors:*** business administration/commerce/management, education, agricultural economics.
FIRST-YEAR CLASS 679 total. Of the students who applied, 100% were accepted. 10% from top 10% of their high school class, 20% from top quarter, 40% from top half.
ACADEMIC PROGRAM Core. Calendar: semesters. Academic remediation for entering students, English as a second language program offered during academic year, self-designed majors, summer session for credit, part-time degree program (daytime, evenings), adult/continuing education programs, co-op programs.
GENERAL DEGREE REQUIREMENTS 64 credit hours; 1 algebra course; 5 credit hours of lab science; computer course.
MAJORS Accounting, agricultural business, agricultural economics, agricultural education, agricultural sciences, agricultural technologies, animal sciences, applied art, art/fine arts, automotive technologies, behavioral sciences, biology/biological sciences, botany/plant sciences, broadcasting, business administration/commerce/management, business education, business machine technologies, carpentry, chemistry, communication, communication equipment technology, computer information systems, computer programming, computer science, construction technologies, drafting and design, economics, education, elementary education, emergency medical technology, engineering (general), (pre)engineering sequence, English, history, home economics, humanities, industrial engineering technology, information science, journalism, legal secretarial studies, liberal arts/general studies, machine and tool technologies, marketing/retailing/merchandising, mathematics, mechanical engineering technology, medical secretarial studies, music, music education, nursing, painting/drawing, physical education, political science/government, practical nursing, psychology, radio and television studies, retail management, science, secretarial studies/office management, social science, social work, sociology, sports medicine, telecommunications, theater arts/drama, voice, welding technology, wind and percussion instruments.
LIBRARY 25,611 books, 246 periodicals, 573 records, tapes, and CDs.
COMPUTERS ON CAMPUS 75 computers for student use in computer labs.
COLLEGE LIFE Drama-theater group, choral group, marching band, student-run newspaper. ***Most popular organizations:*** Student Government Association, Phi Theta Kappa, Sociology Club. ***Major annual events:*** Homecoming, Foundation Dinner and Auction, Super Klutz Competition. ***Student services:*** health clinic, personal-psychological counseling, women's center.
HOUSING 325 college housing spaces available; 320 were occupied 1995–96. No special consideration for freshman housing applicants. Off-campus living permitted. ***Option:*** coed housing available. Resident assistants live in dorms.
ATHLETICS Member NJCAA. ***Intercollegiate:*** baseball M(s), basketball M(s)/W(s), cross-country running M(s)/W(s), football M(s), golf M(s), soccer M(s), softball W(s), track and field M(s)/W(s), volleyball W(s). ***Intramural:*** basketball, bowling, racquetball, soccer, table tennis (Ping-Pong), tennis, weight lifting. ***Contact:*** Mr. Terry Beeson, Athletic Director, 316-251-7700 Ext. 2069.
CAREER PLANNING ***Service:*** career counseling.
EXPENSES FOR 1996–97 State resident tuition: $1180 full-time, $36 per credit hour part-time. Nonresident tuition: $2656 full-time, $82 per credit hour part-time. College room and board: $2700.
FINANCIAL AID ***College-administered undergrad aid 1995–96:*** need-based scholarships, 275 non-need scholarships (average $450), low-interest long-term loans from external sources (average $1000), Federal Work-Study, 20 part-time jobs. ***Required forms:*** state, FAFSA; accepted: CSS Financial Aid PROFILE. ***Priority deadline:*** 8/1. ***Payment plan:*** installment. ***Waivers:*** full or partial for employees or children of employees and senior citizens.
APPLYING Open admission. ***Options:*** early entrance, deferred entrance. ***Required:*** school transcript. ***Recommended:*** ACT, TOEFL for international students. Test scores used for counseling/placement. ***Application deadline:*** rolling. ***Notification:*** continuous.
APPLYING/TRANSFER ***Required:*** college transcript. ***Application deadline:*** rolling. ***Notification:*** continuous.
CONTACT Mrs. Helen Ellerman, Director of Admissions and Financial Aid, Coffeyville Community College, Coffeyville, KS 67337-5063, 316-251-7700 Ext. 2057.

COLBY COMMUNITY COLLEGE
Colby, Kansas

UG Enrollment: 1,150	**Tuition & Fees (KS Res): $1116**
Application Deadline: rolling	**Room & Board: $2816**

Colby Community College offers 2-year career programs in veterinary technology, physical therapist assistant studies, nursing, data processing, executive secretarial studies, and radio/television; transfer curricula in health, physical education, arts and letters, behavioral science, business, mass communications, and math/science; preprofessional options in law and medicine; baccalaureate programs in business and elementary education through area universities; and a College-owned farm operated by agriculture students.

GENERAL State and locally supported, 2-year, coed. Awards certificates, diplomas, transfer associate, terminal associate degrees. Founded 1964. ***Setting:*** 80-acre small-town campus. ***Endowment:*** $1.1 million. ***Educational spending 1994–95:*** $2426 per undergrad. ***Total enrollment:*** 1,150. ***Faculty:*** 63 (59 full-time, 20% with terminal degrees, 4 part-time); student-faculty ratio is 22:1.
ENROLLMENT PROFILE 1,150 students from 11 states and territories, 5 other countries. 51% women, 49% men, 30% part-time, 73% state residents, 5% transferred in, 2% international, 9% 25 or older, 1% Native American, 2% Hispanic, 5% African American, 1% Asian American. ***Areas of study chosen:*** 20% health professions and related sciences, 15% agriculture, 6% education, 5% communications and journalism, 5% computer and information sciences, 5% English language/literature/letters, 5% liberal arts/general studies, 5% physical sciences, 4% business management and administrative services, 4% engineering and applied sciences, 3% biological and life sciences, 3% fine arts, 3% interdisciplinary studies, 3% psychology, 2% mathematics, 2% natural resource sciences, 2% social sciences, 1% library and information studies, 1% performing arts, 1% philosophy, 1% predentistry, 1% prelaw, 1% premed, 1% prevet, 1% vocational and home economics.
FIRST-YEAR CLASS 583 total; 757 applied, 100% were accepted, 77% of whom enrolled. 12% from top 10% of their high school class, 25% from top quarter, 66% from top half. 10 class presidents, 8 valedictorians.
ACADEMIC PROGRAM Core, honor code. Calendar: semesters. 290 courses offered in 1995–96. Academic remediation for entering students, services for LD students, advanced placement, self-designed majors, tutorials, summer session for credit, part-time degree program (daytime, evenings, summer), external degree programs, adult/continuing education programs, co-op programs and internships.
GENERAL DEGREE REQUIREMENTS 62 semester hours; 3 semester hours of math; computer course for business majors; internship (some majors).
MAJORS Accounting, agricultural business, agricultural economics, agricultural education, agricultural sciences, agricultural technologies, agronomy/soil and crop sciences, animal sciences, applied art, art/fine arts, behavioral sciences, biology/biological sciences, broadcasting, business administration/commerce/management, business economics, business education, ceramic art and design, chemistry, child care/child and family studies, commercial art, computer programming, computer science, criminal justice, data processing, early childhood education, earth science, education, engineering (general), engineering and applied sciences, (pre)engineering sequence, English, farm and ranch management, forestry, history, home economics, humanities, journalism, laboratory animal medicine, legal secretarial studies, liberal arts/general studies, library science, marriage and family counseling, mathematics, medical assistant technologies, medical secretarial studies, mental health/rehabilitation counseling, music, music education, nursing, nutrition, painting/drawing, pharmacy/pharmaceutical sciences, physical education, physical therapy, piano/organ, political science/government, practical nursing, printing technologies, psychology, public relations, radio and television studies, range management, science, science education, secretarial studies/office management, social work, sociology, speech/rhetoric/public address/debate, teacher aide studies, telecommunications, theater arts/drama, veterinary sciences, veterinary technology, voice, wildlife biology, word processing, zoology.

Peterson's Guide to Two-Year Colleges 1997 329

Colby Community College (continued)
LIBRARY Davis Library with 32,000 books, 150 microform titles, 350 periodicals, 3,000 records, tapes, and CDs. Acquisition spending 1994–95: $28,648.
COMPUTERS ON CAMPUS Computer purchase plan available. 37 computers for student use in computer center, computer labs, Comprehensive Learning Center, library provide access to main academic computer, on-line services, Internet. Staffed computer lab on campus provides training in use of computers, software. Academic computing expenditure 1994–95: $32,000.
COLLEGE LIFE Drama-theater group, choral group, student-run newspaper, radio station. ***Social organizations:*** 16 open to all. ***Most popular organizations:*** KSNEA, Physical Therapist Assistant Club, Block and Bridle, SVTA, COPNS. ***Major annual events:*** AG Olympics, Spring Formal, Circus of the Stars. ***Student services:*** health clinic, personal-psychological counseling, women's center. ***Campus security:*** 24-hour emergency response devices and patrols, student patrols.
HOUSING 264 college housing spaces available; 253 were occupied 1995–96. No special consideration for freshman housing applicants. Off-campus living permitted. ***Option:*** single-sex (2 buildings) housing available. Resident assistants live in dorms.
ATHLETICS Member NJCAA. ***Intercollegiate:*** baseball M(s), basketball M(s)/W(s), cross-country running M(s)/W(s), equestrian sports M/W, softball W(s), track and field M(s)/W(s), volleyball W(s), wrestling M(s). ***Intramural:*** basketball, bowling, football, golf, racquetball, softball, swimming and diving, tennis, volleyball, weight lifting. ***Contact:*** Mr. Jason Nuss, Athletic Director, 913-462-3984 Ext. 280.
CAREER PLANNING ***Service:*** career counseling.
AFTER GRADUATION 60% of students completing a degree program in 1994–95 went directly on to further study.
EXPENSES FOR 1995–96 ***Application fee:*** $10. State resident tuition: $837 full-time, $27 per semester hour part-time. Nonresident tuition: $2511 full-time, $81 per semester hour part-time. Part-time mandatory fees: $9 per semester hour. Full-time mandatory fees: $279. College room and board: $2816.
FINANCIAL AID ***College-administered undergrad aid 1995–96:*** need-based scholarships, 400 non-need scholarships (average $500), short-term loans (average $175), low-interest long-term loans from external sources (average $1995), Federal Work-Study, 20 part-time jobs. ***Required forms:*** FAFSA. ***Application deadline:*** continuous. ***Payment plan:*** deferred payment. ***Waivers:*** full or partial for employees or children of employees and senior citizens.
APPLYING Open admission except for animal science, health-related programs. ***Options:*** early entrance, deferred entrance, midyear entrance. ***Required:*** TOEFL for international students. ***Recommended:*** SAT I or ACT. Test scores used for counseling/placement. ***Application deadline:*** rolling. ***Notification:*** continuous.
APPLYING/TRANSFER ***Recommended:*** standardized test scores, 3 years of high school math and science. ***Entrance:*** moderately difficult. ***Application deadline:*** rolling. ***Notification:*** continuous. ***Contact:*** Ms. Monica Kane, Transfer and Articulations Specialist, 913-462-3984 Ext. 314.
CONTACT Mr. Gary Schultz, Dean of Students, Colby Community College, 1255 South Range, Colby, KS 67701-4099, 913-462-3984. ***Fax:*** 913-462-4600.

COWLEY COUNTY COMMUNITY COLLEGE AND VOCATIONAL-TECHNICAL SCHOOL
Arkansas City, Kansas

UG Enrollment: 3,054 — **Tuition & Fees (KS Res): $1088**
Application Deadline: 9/1 — **Room & Board: $2440**

GENERAL State and locally supported, 2-year, coed. Part of Kansas State Board of Education. Awards certificates, diplomas, transfer associate, terminal associate degrees. Founded 1922. ***Setting:*** 19-acre small-town campus. ***Total enrollment:*** 3,054. ***Faculty:*** 184 (44 full-time, 95% with terminal degrees, 140 part-time); student-faculty ratio is 18:1.
ENROLLMENT PROFILE 3,054 students: 60% women, 57% part-time, 96% state residents, 7% live on campus, 9% transferred in, 1% international, 46% 25 or older, 2% Native American, 2% Hispanic, 2% African American, 1% Asian American. ***Most popular recent majors:*** business administration/commerce/management, education.
FIRST-YEAR CLASS 1,041 total. Of the students who applied, 100% were accepted, 80% of whom enrolled.
ACADEMIC PROGRAM Core. Calendar: semesters. 295 courses offered in 1995–96. Academic remediation for entering students, English as a second language program offered during academic year, advanced placement, self-designed majors, summer session for credit, part-time degree program (daytime, evenings, summer), external degree programs, adult/continuing education programs, co-op programs.
GENERAL DEGREE REQUIREMENTS 62 credits; computer course.
MAJORS Accounting, agricultural sciences, agricultural technologies, agronomy/soil and crop sciences, aircraft and missile maintenance, art/fine arts, automotive technologies, business administration/commerce/management, chemistry, child care/child and family studies, computer graphics, computer technologies, corrections, cosmetology, criminal justice, drafting and design, education, electrical and electronics technologies, elementary education, emergency medical technology, (pre)engineering sequence, engineering technology, family and consumer studies, farm and ranch management, hotel and restaurant management, industrial arts, journalism, law enforcement/police sciences, liberal arts/general studies, machine and tool technologies, marketing/retailing/merchandising, music, physical education, physical therapy, recreation and leisure services, religious studies, retail management, secretarial studies/office management, social work, theater arts/drama, welding technology, word processing.
LIBRARY Renn Memorial Library with 26,000 books, 85 microform titles, 100 periodicals, 1 on-line bibliographic service, 4 CD-ROMs, 4,500 records, tapes, and CDs.
COMPUTERS ON CAMPUS 53 computers for student use in computer center, business classrooms, library. Staffed computer lab on campus provides training in use of computers, software.
COLLEGE LIFE Orientation program (2 days, no cost, parents included). Drama-theater group, choral group, student-run newspaper. 10% vote in student government elections. ***Social organizations:*** 21 open to all. ***Most popular organizations:*** Volunteer Club, Alcohol and Drug Abuse Awareness, Phi Theta Kappa, Student Government Association, Phi Beta Lambda. ***Major annual events:*** Mr. Cinderfella, Puttin' on the Hits, Homecoming. ***Student services:*** health clinic. ***Campus security:*** student patrols, dormitory entrances are locked at night.
HOUSING 250 college housing spaces available; 192 were occupied 1995–96. No special consideration for freshman housing applicants. Off-campus living permitted. ***Options:*** coed (1 building), single-sex (2 buildings) housing available. Resident assistants live in dorms.
ATHLETICS Member NJCAA. ***Intercollegiate:*** baseball M(s), basketball M(s)/W(s), softball W(s), tennis M(s)/W(s), volleyball W(s). ***Intramural:*** basketball, bowling, table tennis (Ping-Pong), tennis, volleyball.
CAREER PLANNING ***Placement office:*** 1 full-time staff. ***Director:*** Mrs. Susan Rush, Director of Testing and Placement, 316-441-5312. ***Services:*** career counseling, careers library.
AFTER GRADUATION 46% of students completing a degree program in 1994–95 went directly on to further study.
EXPENSES FOR 1995–96 State resident tuition: $800 full-time, $34 per credit hour part-time. Nonresident tuition: $2272 full-time, $80 per credit hour part-time. Full-time mandatory fees: $288. College room and board: $2440.
FINANCIAL AID ***College-administered undergrad aid 1995–96:*** need-based scholarships, non-need scholarships, short-term loans, low-interest long-term loans from external sources, Federal Work-Study, part-time jobs. ***Required forms:*** institutional; required for some: FAFSA; accepted: CSS Financial Aid PROFILE. ***Priority deadline:*** 4/1. ***Payment plan:*** installment. ***Waivers:*** full or partial for employees or children of employees.
APPLYING Open admission. ***Options:*** early entrance, deferred entrance, midyear entrance. ***Required:*** school transcript. ***Recommended:*** 3 years of high school math, ACT, TOEFL for international students. ***Required for some:*** ACT ASSET. Test scores used for counseling/placement. ***Application deadline:*** 9/1. ***Notification:*** continuous until 9/1.
APPLYING/TRANSFER ***Required:*** college transcript. ***Application deadline:*** 9/1. ***Notification:*** continuous until 9/1.
CONTACT Mrs. Susan Rush, Director of Testing and Placement, Cowley County Community College and Vocational-Technical School, Arkansas City, KS 67005-2662, 316-441-5312 or toll-free 800-593-CCCC. ***Fax:*** 316-441-5350. College video available.

DODGE CITY COMMUNITY COLLEGE
Dodge City, Kansas

UG Enrollment: 2,676 — **Tuition & Fees (KS Res): $1302**
Application Deadline: rolling — **Room & Board: $3200**

GENERAL State and locally supported, 2-year, coed. Part of Kansas State Board of Education. Awards certificates, transfer associate, terminal associate degrees. Founded 1935. ***Setting:*** 143-acre small-town campus. ***Total enrollment:*** 2,676. ***Faculty:*** 163 (55 full-time, 108 part-time); student-faculty ratio is 18:1.
ENROLLMENT PROFILE 2,676 students from 20 states and territories, 5 other countries. 62% women, 62% part-time, 98% state residents, 20% live on campus, 3% transferred in, 1% international, 67% 25 or older, 1% Native American, 6% Hispanic, 3% African American, 2% Asian American. ***Most popular recent majors:*** liberal arts/general studies, nursing, agricultural business.
FIRST-YEAR CLASS 1,381 total; 1,614 applied, 100% were accepted, 86% of whom enrolled. 5% from top 10% of their high school class, 50% from top half.
ACADEMIC PROGRAM Core. Calendar: semesters. Academic remediation for entering students, English as a second language program offered during academic year, advanced placement, self-designed majors, tutorials, summer session for credit, part-time degree program (daytime, evenings, summer), external degree programs, adult/continuing education programs, co-op programs and internships.
GENERAL DEGREE REQUIREMENTS 62 credit hours; math/science requirements vary according to program; computer course.
MAJORS Accounting, agricultural business, agricultural economics, agricultural technologies, agronomy/soil and crop sciences, animal sciences, art/fine arts, athletic training, automotive technologies, behavioral sciences, biology/biological sciences, broadcasting, business administration/commerce/management, chemistry, child care/child and family studies, communication, communication equipment technology, computer information systems, computer programming, computer science, construction technologies, cosmetology, criminal justice, data processing, dental services, education, electrical and electronics technologies, elementary education, engineering (general), (pre)engineering sequence, engineering technology, English, equestrian studies, farm and ranch management, finance/banking, fire science, forestry, history, humanities, industrial arts, journalism, legal secretarial studies, liberal arts/general studies, manufacturing technology, marketing/retailing/merchandising, mathematics, medical records services, medical secretarial studies, medical technology, military science, music, music education, nursing, pharmacy/pharmaceutical sciences, physical education, physical sciences, physical therapy, physics, political science/government, practical nursing, psychology, radio and television studies, real estate, respiratory therapy, science, secretarial studies/office management, social science, social work, speech/rhetoric/public address/debate, sports medicine, theater arts/drama, water resources, welding technology, wildlife biology.
LIBRARY 30,000 books, 50 microform titles, 225 periodicals, 25 records, tapes, and CDs.
COMPUTERS ON CAMPUS 125 computers for student use in computer center, English department, library.
COLLEGE LIFE Drama-theater group, choral group, student-run newspaper, radio station. ***Major annual events:*** Homecoming, Spring Fling, Multi-Culture Day. ***Student services:*** health clinic, personal-psychological counseling.
HOUSING 350 college housing spaces available; 302 were occupied 1995–96. No special consideration for freshman housing applicants. Off-campus living permitted. ***Options:*** coed, international student housing available. Resident assistants live in dorms.
ATHLETICS Member NJCAA. ***Intercollegiate:*** baseball M(s), basketball M(s)/W(s), cross-country running M(s)/W(s), equestrian sports M/W, football M(s), golf M(s), softball W(s), volleyball W(s). ***Intramural:*** basketball, bowling, football, golf, racquetball, volleyball, weight lifting. ***Contact:*** Mr. Mike Ryan, Athletic Director, 316-227-9347.
CAREER PLANNING ***Placement office:*** 1 full-time, 1 part-time staff. ***Director:*** Mr. Bill Glennen, Testing and Placement Counselor, 316-227-9268. ***Services:*** job fairs, resume preparation, career counseling, careers library, job bank, job interviews.
AFTER GRADUATION 92% of students completing a degree program in 1994–95 went directly on to further study.
EXPENSES FOR 1996–97 State resident tuition: $930 full-time, $30 per credit hour part-time. Nonresident tuition: $1395 full-time, $45 per credit hour part-time. Part-time mandatory fees: $12 per credit hour. Full-time mandatory fees: $372. College room and board: $3200.

FINANCIAL AID ***College-administered undergrad aid 1995–96:*** need-based scholarships (average $800), 833 non-need scholarships (average $700), low-interest long-term loans from external sources (average $1500), Federal Work-Study, part-time jobs. ***Required forms:*** FAFSA; accepted: CSS Financial Aid PROFILE. ***Priority deadline:*** 4/1. ***Payment plan:*** installment. ***Waivers:*** full or partial for employees or children of employees and senior citizens.
APPLYING Open admission. ***Options:*** early entrance, deferred entrance. ***Required:*** school transcript, TOEFL for international students, ACT ASSET. ***Recommended:*** SAT I or ACT, SAT II Subject Tests. Test scores used for counseling/placement. ***Application deadline:*** rolling. ***Notification:*** continuous.
APPLYING/TRANSFER ***Required:*** standardized test scores, high school transcript, college transcript. ***Entrance:*** noncompetitive. ***Application deadline:*** rolling. ***Notification:*** continuous.
CONTACT Ms. Debbie Lloyd, Director of Admissions, Dodge City Community College, Dodge City, KS 67801-2399, 316-225-1321 Ext. 217 or toll-free 800-742-9519 (in-state), 800-262-4565 (out-of-state). ***Fax:*** 316-225-0918.

DONNELLY COLLEGE
Kansas City, Kansas

UG Enrollment: 409	**Tuition & Fees: $2800**
Application Deadline: rolling	**Room & Board: N/Avail**

GENERAL Independent Roman Catholic, 2-year, coed. Awards certificates, diplomas, transfer associate, terminal associate degrees. Founded 1949. ***Setting:*** 4-acre urban campus. ***Endowment:*** $3 million. ***Educational spending 1994–95:*** $1945 per undergrad. ***Total enrollment:*** 409. ***Faculty:*** 48 (22 full-time, 25% with terminal degrees, 26 part-time); student-faculty ratio is 9:1.
ENROLLMENT PROFILE 409 students from 15 states and territories, 28 other countries. 65% women, 28% part-time, 79% state residents, 11% transferred in, 7% international, 55% 25 or older, 2% Native American, 12% Hispanic, 46% African American, 2% Asian American. ***Areas of study chosen:*** 20% health professions and related sciences, 15% liberal arts/general studies, 10% education, 5% engineering and applied sciences, 2% communications and journalism, 2% prevet, 2% social sciences, 1% architecture.
FIRST-YEAR CLASS 55 total. Of the students who applied, 100% were accepted.
ACADEMIC PROGRAM Core. Calendar: semesters. 450 courses offered in 1995–96. Academic remediation for entering students, English as a second language program offered during academic year and summer, services for LD students, summer session for credit, part-time degree program (daytime, evenings), external degree programs.
GENERAL DEGREE REQUIREMENTS 64 credit hours; 3 credit hours of math; 6 credit hours of science; computer course; internship (some majors).
MAJORS Accounting, business administration/commerce/management, computer science, data processing, drafting and design, early childhood education, education, engineering (general), English, health education, history, liberal arts/general studies, mathematics, nursing, pharmacy/pharmaceutical sciences, philosophy, physical therapy, political science/government, psychology, science.
LIBRARY Trant Memorial Library with 30,000 books, 130 periodicals, 6 CD-ROMs, 1,500 records, tapes, and CDs. Acquisition spending 1994–95: $68,500.
COMPUTERS ON CAMPUS 25 computers for student use in computer center, computer labs, library. Staffed computer lab on campus provides training in use of computers, software. Academic computing expenditure 1994–95: $65,000.
COLLEGE LIFE ***Student services:*** personal-psychological counseling. ***Campus security:*** 24-hour emergency response devices.
HOUSING College housing not available.
CAREER PLANNING ***Placement office:*** 1 full-time, 1 part-time staff; $51,000 operating expenditure 1994–95. ***Director:*** Ms. Latoria Chinn, Director of Career Planning and Placement, 913-621-6070 Ext. 44. ***Services:*** job fairs, resume preparation, resume referral, career counseling, careers library, job bank, job interviews.
AFTER GRADUATION 66% of students completing a degree program in 1994–95 went directly on to further study.
EXPENSES FOR 1996–97 Tuition: $2800 full-time, $110 per credit hour part-time.
FINANCIAL AID ***College-administered undergrad aid 1995–96:*** need-based scholarships, non-need scholarships, short-term loans, low-interest long-term loans from external sources, Federal Work-Study, part-time jobs. ***Priority deadline:*** 6/30. ***Waivers:*** full or partial for senior citizens.
APPLYING Open admission. ***Options:*** early entrance, deferred entrance. ***Recommended:*** school transcript, TOEFL for international students. Test scores used for counseling/placement. ***Application deadline:*** rolling.
APPLYING/TRANSFER ***Application deadline:*** rolling. ***Contact:*** Ms. Laura Loehr, Transfer Counselor, 913-621-6070 Ext. 50.
CONTACT Mr. Paul Gordon, Director of Admissions and Financial Aid, Donnelly College, 608 North 18th Street, Kansas City, KS 66102-4298, 913-621-6070.

FORT SCOTT COMMUNITY COLLEGE
Fort Scott, Kansas

UG Enrollment: 1,651	**Tuition & Fees (KS Res): $1200**
Application Deadline: 8/15	**Room & Board: $2275**

GENERAL State and locally supported, 2-year, coed. Awards transfer associate, terminal associate degrees. Founded 1919. ***Setting:*** 147-acre small-town campus. ***Total enrollment:*** 1,651. ***Faculty:*** 59 (51 full-time, 8 part-time); student-faculty ratio is 19:1.
ENROLLMENT PROFILE 1,651 students from 24 states and territories, 7 other countries. 57% women, 43% men, 48% part-time, 86% state residents, 12% transferred in, 8% have need-based financial aid, 1% international, 40% 25 or older, 1% Native American, 1% Hispanic, 8% African American, 1% Asian American. ***Most popular recent majors:*** education, business administration/commerce/management, agricultural sciences.
FIRST-YEAR CLASS 1,104 total. Of the students who applied, 100% were accepted, 75% of whom enrolled. 30% from top 10% of their high school class, 70% from top half.
ACADEMIC PROGRAM Core. Calendar: semesters. Academic remediation for entering students, English as a second language program offered during academic year, services for LD students, self-designed majors, tutorials, summer session for credit, part-time degree program (daytime, evenings, weekends, summer), external degree programs, adult/continuing education programs, co-op programs and internships.
GENERAL DEGREE REQUIREMENTS 60 semester hours; 1 college algebra course; computer course; internship (some majors).
MAJORS Accounting, agricultural business, agricultural economics, agricultural education, agricultural sciences, agricultural technologies, agronomy/soil and crop sciences, animal sciences, architectural technologies, athletic training, business administration/commerce/management, computer science, cosmetology, criminal justice, drafting and design, education, electronics engineering technology, emergency medical technology, graphic arts, industrial arts, legal secretarial studies, liberal arts/general studies, medical secretarial studies, medical technology, music, nursing, photography, physical sciences, public affairs and policy studies, quality control technology, retail management, secretarial studies/office management, sports medicine, teacher aide studies, transportation technologies, water resources, welding technology.
LIBRARY Learning Resource Center with 23,610 books, 119 periodicals, 3 CD-ROMs, 100 records, tapes, and CDs.
COMPUTERS ON CAMPUS Computer purchase plan available. 95 computers for student use in computer center, computer labs, learning resource center, classrooms, library provide access to off-campus computing facilities, on-line services, Internet. Staffed computer lab on campus provides training in use of computers, software.
COLLEGE LIFE Drama-theater group, choral group, marching band. 45% vote in student government elections. ***Most popular organizations:*** Aggie Club, Student Nurses Association. ***Major annual events:*** Homecoming, Spring Fling, Zook Day. ***Student services:*** personal-psychological counseling. ***Campus security:*** 24-hour patrols, controlled dormitory access.
HOUSING 130 college housing spaces available; all were occupied 1995–96. No special consideration for freshman housing applicants. Off-campus living permitted. ***Option:*** coed housing available.
ATHLETICS Member NJCAA. ***Intercollegiate:*** baseball M(s), basketball M(s)/W(s), football M(s), softball W(s), volleyball W(s). ***Intramural:*** basketball, cross-country running, racquetball, soccer, softball, table tennis (Ping-Pong), tennis, track and field, volleyball, weight lifting. ***Contact:*** Mr. Ron Chismar, Athletic Director, 316-223-2700 Ext. 24.
CAREER PLANNING ***Director:*** Ms. Evelyn Johnson, Career Counselor, 316-223-2700 Ext. 380. ***Services:*** job fairs, resume preparation, career counseling, careers library, job bank, job interviews. 14 organizations recruited on campus 1994–95.
EXPENSES FOR 1996–97 State resident tuition: $1200 full-time, $40 per semester hour part-time. Nonresident tuition: $2700 full-time, $90 per semester hour part-time. College room and board: $2275 (minimum).
FINANCIAL AID ***College-administered undergrad aid 1995–96:*** need-based scholarships, non-need scholarships, short-term loans, low-interest long-term loans from external sources (average $2500), Federal Work-Study, 155 part-time jobs. ***Required forms:*** FAFSA. ***Application deadline:*** continuous. ***Waivers:*** full or partial for employees or children of employees.
APPLYING Open admission. ***Options:*** early entrance, deferred entrance, midyear entrance. ***Required for some:*** ACT. Test scores used for counseling/placement. ***Application deadline:*** 8/15.
APPLYING/TRANSFER ***Application deadline:*** 8/15.
CONTACT Mr. Pat Flynn, Director of Admissions, Fort Scott Community College, Fort Scott, KS 66701, 316-223-2700 Ext. 87 or toll-free 800-874-3722.

GARDEN CITY COMMUNITY COLLEGE
Garden City, Kansas

UG Enrollment: 2,204	**Tuition & Fees (KS Res): $1120**
Application Deadline: rolling	**Room & Board: $2770**

GENERAL District-supported, 2-year, coed. Part of Kansas State Board of Education. Awards certificates, transfer associate, terminal associate degrees. Founded 1919. ***Setting:*** 12-acre rural campus. ***Endowment:*** $2 million. ***Total enrollment:*** 2,204. ***Faculty:*** 148 (67 full-time, 81 part-time); student-faculty ratio is 20:1.
ENROLLMENT PROFILE 2,204 students from 18 states and territories, 5 other countries. 58% women, 66% part-time, 97% state residents, 12% live on campus, 4% transferred in, 31% have need-based financial aid, 56% have non-need-based financial aid, 1% international, 52% 25 or older, 1% Native American, 10% Hispanic, 1% Asian American. ***Areas of study chosen:*** 35% liberal arts/general studies, 13% business management and administrative services, 13% education, 7% health professions and related sciences, 7% vocational and home economics, 5% biological and life sciences, 4% agriculture, 4% premed, 2% performing arts, 2% psychology, 1% architecture, 1% communications and journalism, 1% computer and information sciences, 1% engineering and applied sciences, 1% fine arts, 1% mathematics, 1% prevet, 1% social sciences. ***Most popular recent majors:*** business administration/commerce/management, education, criminal justice.
FIRST-YEAR CLASS 509 total. Of the students who applied, 100% were accepted, 100% of whom enrolled. 17% from top 10% of their high school class, 19% from top quarter, 34% from top half. 7 class presidents, 5 valedictorians.
ACADEMIC PROGRAM Core, interdisciplinary curriculum, honor code. Calendar: semesters. 325 courses offered in 1995–96. Academic remediation for entering students, English as a second language program offered during academic year and summer, services for LD students, advanced placement, self-designed majors, tutorials, summer session for credit, part-time degree program (daytime, evenings, weekends, summer), external degree programs, adult/continuing education programs, co-op programs and internships.
GENERAL DEGREE REQUIREMENTS 64 credit hours; 1 college algebra course; internship (some majors).
MAJORS Accounting, agricultural business, agricultural economics, agricultural sciences, agricultural technologies, athletic training, automotive technologies, business administration/commerce/management, carpentry, ceramic art and design, child care/child and family studies, child psychology/child development, computer graphics, computer information systems, computer programming, computer science, computer technologies, construction technologies, cosmetology, criminal justice, drafting and design, education, electrical and electronics technologies, elementary education, engineering (general), engineering and applied sciences, (pre)engineering sequence, engineering technology, English, family services, farm and ranch management, fashion design and technology, fashion merchandising, graphic arts, humanities, industrial arts, industrial engineering technology, interior design, jewelry and metalsmithing, journalism, law enforcement/police sciences, legal secretarial studies, liberal arts/general studies, marketing/retailing/merchandising, mathematics, mechanical design technology, mechanical engineering

Garden City Community College (continued)
technology, music, nursing, physical education, retail management, science, social science, sociology, speech/rhetoric/public address/debate, studio art, teacher aide studies, theater arts/drama, vocational education, welding technology.
LIBRARY Saffell Library with 43,698 books, 2,709 microform titles, 222 periodicals, 11 CD-ROMs, 1,166 records, tapes, and CDs. Acquisition spending 1994–95: $114,486.
COMPUTERS ON CAMPUS Computer purchase plan available. 122 computers for student use in computer center, computer labs, learning resource center, library, student center, dorms provide access to main academic computer. Staffed computer lab on campus provides training in use of computers, software. Academic computing expenditure 1994–95: $217,256.
COLLEGE LIFE Drama-theater group, choral group. 10% vote in student government elections. ***Social organizations:*** 23 open to all. ***Most popular organizations:*** Student Government, Hispanic American Leadership Organization (HALO), Newman Club, Criminal Justice Organization (TEL), Phi Theta Kappa. ***Major annual events:*** Earth Day, Homecoming, Hispanic Day. ***Student services:*** health clinic, personal-psychological counseling. ***Campus security:*** 24-hour emergency response devices and patrols, late-night transport-escort service, controlled dormitory access.
HOUSING 234 college housing spaces available; all were occupied 1995–96. No special consideration for freshman housing applicants. Off-campus living permitted. ***Option:*** coed (2 buildings) housing available. Resident assistants live in dorms.
ATHLETICS Member NJCAA. ***Intercollegiate:*** baseball M(s), basketball M(s)/W(s), cross-country running M(s)/W(s), football M(s), track and field M(s)/W(s), volleyball W(s). ***Intramural:*** archery, basketball, bowling, football, racquetball, riflery, table tennis (Ping-Pong), tennis, track and field, volleyball. ***Contact:*** Mr. Dennis Perryman, Athletic Director, 316-276-7611.
CAREER PLANNING ***Placement office:*** 2 full-time, 1 part-time staff; $79,227 operating expenditure 1994–95. ***Director:*** Ms. Barb Thoman, Career Counselor, 316-276-7611. ***Services:*** resume preparation, career counseling, careers library, job bank, job interviews.
AFTER GRADUATION 60% of students completing a degree program in 1994–95 went directly on to further study.
EXPENSES FOR 1996–97 State resident tuition: $896 full-time, $28 per credit hour part-time. Nonresident tuition: $2080 full-time, $65 per credit hour part-time. Part-time mandatory fees: $7 per credit hour. Full-time mandatory fees: $224. College room and board: $2770 (minimum).
FINANCIAL AID ***College-administered undergrad aid 1995–96:*** 187 need-based scholarships (average $300), 982 non-need scholarships (average $500), low-interest long-term loans from external sources (average $2200), 44 Federal Work-Study (averaging $1300), 48 part-time jobs. ***Required forms:*** institutional, FAFSA; accepted: CSS Financial Aid PROFILE. ***Priority deadline:*** 7/1. ***Payment plans:*** installment, deferred payment. ***Waivers:*** full or partial for employees or children of employees and senior citizens.
APPLYING Open admission. ***Options:*** early entrance, deferred entrance, midyear entrance. ***Required:*** TOEFL for international students. ***Recommended:*** school transcript, ACT, SAT II Subject Tests. Test scores used for counseling/placement. ***Application deadline:*** rolling.
APPLYING/TRANSFER ***Recommended:*** high school transcript, college transcript. ***Entrance:*** noncompetitive. ***Application deadline:*** rolling. ***Contact:*** Ms. Barb Thoman, Career Counselor, 316-276-7611.
CONTACT Ms. Becky Besack, Director of Admissions, Garden City Community College, Garden City, KS 67846-6399, 316-276-7611.

HASKELL INDIAN NATIONS UNIVERSITY
Lawrence, Kansas

UG Enrollment: 809	**Tuition & Fees: $105**
Application Deadline: 7/15	**Room & Board: N/R**

GENERAL Federally supported, primarily 2-year, coed. Awards transfer associate, terminal associate, bachelor's degrees. Founded 1884. ***Setting:*** 320-acre suburban campus. ***Total enrollment:*** 809. ***Faculty:*** 68 (63 full-time, 100% with terminal degrees, 5 part-time); student-faculty ratio is 15:1.
ENROLLMENT PROFILE 809 students from 37 states and territories. 44% women, 5% part-time, 18% state residents, 10% transferred in, 1% 25 or older, 100% Native American.
FIRST-YEAR CLASS 265 total; 461 applied, 100% were accepted, 57% of whom enrolled. 10% from top 10% of their high school class, 50% from top half.
ACADEMIC PROGRAM Core. Calendar: semesters. Academic remediation for entering students, self-designed majors, summer session for credit, part-time degree program (daytime). Off-campus study at members of the American Indian Higher Education Consortium, Kansas City Regional Council for Higher Education, University of Kansas.
GENERAL DEGREE REQUIREMENTS 61 credit hours for associate, 138 credit hours for bachelor's; math/science requirements vary according to major; computer course for natural science majors.
MAJORS Accounting, business administration/commerce/management, computer information systems, computer technologies, elementary education (B), liberal arts/general studies, natural resource management, physical education, secretarial studies/office management.
LIBRARY 40,000 books, 6,000 microform titles, 525 periodicals, 9,000 records, tapes, and CDs.
COMPUTERS ON CAMPUS 35 computers for student use in learning resource center, library, student center.
COLLEGE LIFE Orientation program (2 days, no cost). Drama-theater group, choral group, student-run newspaper. ***Social organizations:*** social clubs; 30% of eligible men and 35% of eligible women are members. ***Student services:*** health clinic, personal-psychological counseling. ***Campus security:*** 24-hour patrols.
HOUSING 750 college housing spaces available; 740 were occupied 1995–96. No special consideration for freshman housing applicants. Off-campus living permitted. ***Options:*** freshmen-only, coed (1 building), single-sex (6 buildings) housing available. Resident assistants live in dorms.
ATHLETICS Member NJCAA. ***Intercollegiate:*** basketball M/W, cross-country running M/W, football M, track and field M/W, volleyball W. ***Intramural:*** golf, racquetball, weight lifting.
CAREER PLANNING ***Placement office:*** 1 full-time, 1 part-time staff. ***Director:*** Ms. Maggie Necefer, Director, Placement Center, 913-749-8485. ***Service:*** career counseling.
EXPENSES FOR 1996–97 ***Application fee:*** $5. Tuition: $0 full-time. One-time mandatory fee: $70. Full-time mandatory fees: $105.
FINANCIAL AID ***College-administered undergrad aid 1995–96:*** Federal Work-Study, part-time jobs. ***Required forms:*** institutional, FAFSA. ***Priority deadline:*** 5/1.
APPLYING ***Required:*** school transcript, ACT. ***Recommended:*** 1 year of high school foreign language. Test scores used for counseling/placement. ***Application deadline:*** 7/15. ***Notification:*** continuous. Preference given to applicants with at least one-fourth Native American ancestry or tribal membership.
APPLYING/TRANSFER ***Required:*** standardized test scores, high school transcript. ***Recommended:*** 1 year of high school foreign language. ***Application deadline:*** 7/15. ***Notification:*** continuous.
CONTACT Ms. Ellen Allen, Director of Admissions and Records, Haskell Indian Nations University, Lawrence, KS 66046-4800, 913-749-8454. College video available.

HESSTON COLLEGE
Hesston, Kansas

UG Enrollment: 472	**Tuition & Fees: $9750**
Application Deadline: rolling	**Room & Board: $3900**

GENERAL Independent Mennonite, 2-year, coed. Awards transfer associate, terminal associate degrees. Founded 1909. ***Setting:*** 50-acre small-town campus with easy access to Wichita. ***Total enrollment:*** 472. ***Faculty:*** 48 (22 full-time, 26 part-time); student-faculty ratio is 14:1.
ENROLLMENT PROFILE 472 students from 31 states and territories, 29 other countries. 50% women, 15% part-time, 35% state residents, 65% live on campus, 5% transferred in, 65% have need-based financial aid, 28% have non-need-based financial aid, 20% international. ***Most popular recent majors:*** nursing, business administration/commerce/management, aviation technology.
FIRST-YEAR CLASS 175 total. Of the students accepted, 40% enrolled. 14% from top 10% of their high school class, 37% from top quarter, 61% from top half.
ACADEMIC PROGRAM Core, honor code. Calendar: 4-1-4. Academic remediation for entering students, English as a second language program offered during academic year, services for LD students, advanced placement, summer session for credit, part-time degree program (daytime), co-op programs.
GENERAL DEGREE REQUIREMENTS 64 credit hours; math proficiency or 1 math course; computer course for business administration majors.
MAJORS Aviation technology, biblical studies, business administration/commerce/management, business education, computer science, early childhood education, liberal arts/general studies, nursing, pastoral studies, secretarial studies/office management.
LIBRARY Mary Miller Library with 35,000 books, 225 periodicals, 1,200 records, tapes, and CDs.
COMPUTERS ON CAMPUS 45 computers for student use in computer labs, learning resource center, library provide access to e-mail, Internet. Staffed computer lab on campus provides training in use of computers, software.
COLLEGE LIFE Orientation program (2 days, no cost, parents included). Drama-theater group, choral group. ***Student services:*** personal-psychological counseling. ***Campus security:*** 24-hour emergency response devices.
HOUSING 370 college housing spaces available; 325 were occupied 1995–96. Freshmen guaranteed college housing. On-campus residence required through sophomore year except if 23 or over. ***Option:*** single-sex (4 buildings) housing available. Resident assistants live in dorms.
ATHLETICS Member NJCAA. ***Intercollegiate:*** baseball M(s), basketball M(s)/W(s), golf M/W, soccer M(s), softball W, tennis M(s)/W(s), volleyball W(s). ***Intramural:*** baseball, basketball, golf, racquetball, skiing (downhill), soccer, softball, tennis, volleyball. ***Contact:*** Mr. Art Mullet, Athletic Director, 316-327-8274.
CAREER PLANNING ***Placement office:*** 1 full-time, 1 part-time staff. ***Director:*** Ms. Star Gipson, Director of Career Services, 316-327-8186. ***Services:*** job fairs, resume preparation, career counseling, careers library, job bank. 30 organizations recruited on campus 1994–95.
AFTER GRADUATION 65% of students completing a degree program in 1994–95 went directly on to further study.
EXPENSES FOR 1996–97 ***Application fee:*** $15. Comprehensive fee of $13,650 includes full-time tuition ($9750) and college room and board ($3900). Part-time tuition per credit hour: $190 for the first 5 credit hours, $376 for the next 6 credit hours.
FINANCIAL AID ***College-administered undergrad aid 1995–96:*** 70 need-based scholarships (average $1370), 297 non-need scholarships (average $2800), low-interest long-term loans from college funds (average $500), loans from external sources (average $3280), Federal Work-Study, 44 part-time jobs. ***Required forms:*** FAFSA; required for some: state. ***Priority deadline:*** 5/1. ***Payment plan:*** installment. ***Waivers:*** full or partial for employees or children of employees.
APPLYING Open admission except for nursing program. ***Options:*** early entrance, deferred entrance, midyear entrance. ***Required:*** school transcript, TOEFL for international students. ***Recommended:*** SAT I or ACT. Test scores used for counseling/placement. ***Application deadline:*** rolling.
APPLYING/TRANSFER ***Required:*** high school transcript, college transcript. ***Recommended:*** standardized test scores. ***Entrance:*** noncompetitive. ***Application deadline:*** rolling.
CONTACT Mr. Clark Roth, Director of Admissions, Hesston College, Hesston, KS 67062-2093, 316-327-4223 Ext. 212 or toll-free 800-995-2757. ***Fax:*** 316-327-8300. ***E-mail:*** admissions@hesston.edu. College video available.

HIGHLAND COMMUNITY COLLEGE
Highland, Kansas

UG Enrollment: 2,654	**Tuition & Fees (KS Res): $1240**
Application Deadline: 8/20	**Room & Board: $2750**

GENERAL State and locally supported, 2-year, coed. Part of Kansas Community College System. Awards certificates, transfer associate, terminal associate degrees. Founded 1858. ***Setting:*** 20-acre rural campus. ***Total enrollment:*** 2,654. ***Faculty:*** 195 (35 full-time, 160 part-time).
ENROLLMENT PROFILE 2,654 students from 9 states and territories. 52% women, 61% part-time, 92% state residents, 11% transferred in, 31% 25 or older, 5% Native

American, 1% Hispanic, 9% African American. *Most popular recent majors:* business administration/commerce/management, liberal arts/general studies.
FIRST-YEAR CLASS 580 total. Of the students who applied, 95% were accepted. 11% from top 10% of their high school class, 38% from top quarter, 67% from top half. 5 National Merit Scholars.
ACADEMIC PROGRAM Core. Calendar: semesters. Academic remediation for entering students, services for LD students, advanced placement, self-designed majors, summer session for credit, part-time degree program (daytime, evenings, weekends, summer), adult/continuing education programs, co-op programs and internships. Off-campus study at Northeast Kansas Area Vocational Technical School. ROTC: Army (c).
GENERAL DEGREE REQUIREMENTS 62 credit hours; 3 credit hours of math; 8 credit hours of science; computer course for business, art majors; internship (some majors).
MAJORS Accounting, advertising, agricultural business, agricultural economics, agricultural education, agricultural sciences, agronomy/soil and crop sciences, animal sciences, art/fine arts, automotive technologies, biology/biological sciences, business administration/commerce/management, business education, carpentry, chemistry, commercial art, computer information systems, computer science, conservation, construction technologies, criminal justice, cytotechnology, dairy sciences, data processing, dental services, drafting and design, education, emergency medical technology, (pre)engineering sequence, English, farm and ranch management, fashion design and technology, food sciences, forestry, funeral service, geology, health education, history, home economics, industrial arts, journalism, law enforcement/police sciences, legal secretarial studies, liberal arts/general studies, library science, mathematics, medical records services, medical secretarial studies, medical technology, music, nursing, occupational therapy, pharmacy/pharmaceutical sciences, physical education, physical sciences, physical therapy, political science/government, psychology, radiological technology, respiratory therapy, secretarial studies/office management, social work, sociology, sports medicine, telecommunications, textile arts, theater arts/drama, theology, veterinary sciences.
LIBRARY 30,000 books, 18,000 microform titles, 268 periodicals, 2,086 records, tapes, and CDs.
COMPUTERS ON CAMPUS Computer purchase plan available. 94 computers for student use in computer center, learning skills center provide access to on-line services. Staffed computer lab on campus provides training in use of computers, software.
COLLEGE LIFE Drama-theater group, student-run newspaper.
HOUSING 325 college housing spaces available; all were occupied 1995–96. No special consideration for freshman housing applicants. Off-campus living permitted. *Options:* coed, single-sex housing available. Resident assistants live in dorms.
ATHLETICS Member NJCAA. *Intercollegiate:* basketball M(s)/W(s), cross-country running M(s)/W(s), football M(s), track and field M(s)/W(s), volleyball W(s). *Intramural:* basketball, cross-country running, football, tennis, track and field, volleyball. *Contact:* Mr. Tom Smith, Director of Athletics, 913-442-3236 Ext. 275.
CAREER PLANNING *Service:* career counseling.
EXPENSES FOR 1996–97 State resident tuition: $899 full-time, $29 per credit hour part-time. Nonresident tuition: $2697 full-time, $87 per credit hour part-time. Part-time mandatory fees: $11 per credit hour. Full-time mandatory fees: $341. College room and board: $2750. College room only: $1500.
FINANCIAL AID *College-administered undergrad aid 1995–96:* need-based scholarships (average $410), non-need scholarships (average $510), short-term loans (average $50), Federal Work-Study, part-time jobs. *Required forms:* FAFSA; accepted: CSS Financial Aid PROFILE. *Priority deadline:* 4/15.
APPLYING Open admission for state residents. *Option:* early entrance. *Required:* school transcript, TOEFL for international students, ACT ASSET. *Recommended:* ACT. Test scores used for counseling/placement. *Application deadline:* 8/20. *Notification:* continuous. Preference given to state residents.
APPLYING/TRANSFER *Required:* college transcript. *Entrance:* moderately difficult. *Application deadline:* 8/20. *Notification:* continuous.
CONTACT Mr. David Reist, Dean of Student Services, Highland Community College, Highland, KS 66035-0068, 913-442-6020.

HUTCHINSON COMMUNITY COLLEGE AND AREA VOCATIONAL SCHOOL
Hutchinson, Kansas

UG Enrollment: 3,621	Tuition & Fees (KS Res): $1280
Application Deadline: rolling	Room & Board: $2590

GENERAL State and locally supported, 2-year, coed. Part of Kansas Community College System. Awards transfer associate, terminal associate degrees. Founded 1928. *Setting:* 47-acre small-town campus. *Total enrollment:* 3,621. *Faculty:* 264 (100 full-time, 164 part-time); student-faculty ratio is 15:1.
ENROLLMENT PROFILE 3,621 students: 56% women, 63% part-time, 97% state residents, 16% transferred in, 1% international, 54% 25 or older, 1% Native American, 3% Hispanic, 1% African American, 1% Asian American.
FIRST-YEAR CLASS 2,080 total; 5,810 applied, 100% were accepted, 36% of whom enrolled.
ACADEMIC PROGRAM Core. Calendar: semesters. Academic remediation for entering students, English as a second language program offered during academic year, services for LD students, advanced placement, self-designed majors, tutorials, summer session for credit, part-time degree program (daytime, evenings, weekends, summer), adult/continuing education programs, co-op programs and internships. ROTC: Army (c).
GENERAL DEGREE REQUIREMENTS 64 credit hours; 1 course each in algebra and lab science; computer course for secretarial studies majors.
MAJORS Accounting, advertising, agricultural business, agricultural technologies, art/fine arts, automotive technologies, biology/biological sciences, broadcasting, business administration/commerce/management, carpentry, chemistry, child care/child and family studies, commercial art, computer programming, computer science, computer technologies, construction technologies, corrections, cytotechnology, data processing, dental services, drafting and design, early childhood education, economics, education, electrical and electronics technologies, electronics engineering technology, elementary education, engineering (general), (pre)engineering sequence, English, farm and ranch management, fashion merchandising, finance/banking, fire science, forestry, funeral service, geology, graphic arts, history, home economics, hotel and restaurant management, industrial arts, insurance, interior design, journalism, laboratory technologies, law enforcement/police sciences, legal secretarial studies, liberal arts/general studies, library science, literature, marketing/retailing/merchandising, mathematics, mechanical engineering technology, medical assistant technologies, medical laboratory technology, medical records services, medical secretarial studies, medical technology, mining technology, modern languages, music education, nursing, occupational therapy, paralegal studies, parks management, pharmacy/pharmaceutical sciences, photography, physical education, physical sciences, physical therapy, physics, political science/government, printing technologies, psychology, public administration, radio and television studies, radiological technology, recreation and leisure services, retail management, robotics, science education, secretarial studies/office management, social science, sociology, Spanish, speech/rhetoric/public address/debate, sports medicine, tourism and travel, veterinary sciences, wildlife management.
LIBRARY 40,000 books, 212 microform titles, 292 periodicals, 1,007 records, tapes, and CDs.
COMPUTERS ON CAMPUS 140 computers for student use in classrooms, library.
COLLEGE LIFE Drama-theater group, choral group, marching band, student-run newspaper, radio station. *Student services:* health clinic, personal-psychological counseling.
HOUSING 400 college housing spaces available; 389 were occupied 1995–96. No special consideration for freshman housing applicants. Off-campus living permitted. *Option:* single-sex housing available. Resident assistants live in dorms.
ATHLETICS Member NJCAA. *Intercollegiate:* baseball M, basketball M(s)/W(s), bowling M/W, cross-country running M(s)/W(s), football M(s), golf M(s), softball W, tennis M(s)/W(s), track and field M(s)/W(s), volleyball W(s). *Intramural:* badminton, basketball, football, racquetball, soccer, tennis, track and field, volleyball. *Contact:* Mr. Jack Morris, Dean of Students, 316-665-3531.
CAREER PLANNING *Service:* career counseling.
EXPENSES FOR 1996–97 State resident tuition: $960 full-time, $30 per credit hour part-time. Nonresident tuition: $2880 full-time, $90 per credit hour part-time. Part-time mandatory fees: $10 per credit hour. Full-time mandatory fees: $320. College room and board: $2590.
FINANCIAL AID *College-administered undergrad aid 1995–96:* 298 need-based scholarships (average $433), 245 non-need scholarships (average $238), short-term loans (average $200), low-interest long-term loans from external sources (average $1372), Federal Work-Study, part-time jobs. *Required forms:* institutional, FAFSA; accepted: CSS Financial Aid PROFILE. *Priority deadline:* 3/1. *Payment plan:* deferred payment. *Waivers:* full or partial for employees or children of employees and senior citizens.
APPLYING Open admission except for allied health programs. *Options:* early entrance, deferred entrance, midyear entrance. *Required:* TOEFL for international students. *Recommended:* school transcript, ACT. *Required for some:* ACT, ACT ASSET. Test scores used for counseling/placement. *Application deadline:* rolling.
APPLYING/TRANSFER *Required for some:* college transcript. *Application deadline:* rolling.
CONTACT Ms. Laurie Fox, Director of Admissions and Records, Hutchinson Community College and Area Vocational School, Hutchinson, KS 67501-5894, 316-665-3536 or toll-free 800-289-3501. *E-mail:* foxl@hutchcc.edu.

INDEPENDENCE COMMUNITY COLLEGE
Independence, Kansas

UG Enrollment: 1,848	Tuition & Fees (KS Res): $1120
Application Deadline: rolling	Room & Board: $2580

GENERAL State-supported, 2-year, coed. Part of Kansas State Board of Education. Awards transfer associate, terminal associate degrees. Founded 1925. *Setting:* 68-acre small-town campus. *Total enrollment:* 1,848. *Faculty:* 153 (33 full-time, 120 part-time); student-faculty ratio is 17:1. *Notable Alumni:* Bill Kurtis, Jim Halsey.
ENROLLMENT PROFILE 1,848 students from 16 states and territories, 19 other countries. 61% women, 65% part-time, 96% state residents, 10% live on campus, 8% transferred in, 3% international, 54% 25 or older, 1% Native American, 2% Hispanic, 5% African American, 1% Asian American.
FIRST-YEAR CLASS 1,200 total. Of the students who applied, 100% were accepted, 58% of whom enrolled.
ACADEMIC PROGRAM Core, interdisciplinary curriculum, honor code. Calendar: semesters. Academic remediation for entering students, English as a second language program offered during academic year and summer, advanced placement, self-designed majors, tutorials, summer session for credit, part-time degree program (daytime, evenings, weekends, summer), adult/continuing education programs, co-op programs and internships. Off-campus study.
GENERAL DEGREE REQUIREMENTS 64 semester hours; 1 college algebra course; computer course.
MAJORS Accounting, art education, athletic training, biology/biological sciences, business administration/commerce/management, business education, chemistry, child care/child and family studies, civil engineering technology, cosmetology, data processing, drafting and design, early childhood education, electronics engineering technology, elementary education, emergency medical technology, engineering (general), (pre)engineering sequence, engineering technology, English, finance/banking, French, history, humanities, liberal arts/general studies, mathematics, modern languages, music, music business, music education, natural sciences, nursing, physical education, physical sciences, political science/government, psychology, real estate, science, science education, secretarial studies/office management, sociology, Spanish, sports medicine.
LIBRARY Independence Community College Library plus 1 other, with 32,372 books, 116 microform titles, 166 periodicals, 1,099 records, tapes, and CDs.
COMPUTERS ON CAMPUS 75 computers for student use in computer center, computer labs, secretarial science center. Staffed computer lab on campus provides training in use of computers, software.
COLLEGE LIFE Drama-theater group, choral group, student-run newspaper. *Most popular organizations:* Student Senate, Phi Theta Kappa, Student Ambassadors, Campus Christians. *Major annual events:* Homecoming, Winter Formal, Fall/Spring Picnic. *Student services:* personal-psychological counseling. *Campus security:* night patrol.
HOUSING 96 college housing spaces available; 90 were occupied 1995–96. No special consideration for freshman housing applicants. Off-campus living permitted. *Options:* single-sex (4 buildings), international student housing available. Resident assistants live in dorms.

Independence Community College (continued)
ATHLETICS Member NJCAA. ***Intercollegiate:*** baseball M(s), basketball M(s)/W(s), cross-country running M(s)/W(s), football M(s), tennis M(s)/W(s), track and field M(s)/W(s), volleyball W(s). ***Intramural:*** basketball. ***Contact:*** Mr. Darren Brunson, Director of Athletics, 316-331-4100 Ext. 282.
CAREER PLANNING ***Placement office:*** 3 full-time, 1 part-time staff. ***Director:*** Ms. Evelyn Musgrove, Counselor, 316-331-4100 Ext. 237. ***Services:*** job fairs, resume preparation, career counseling, job interviews.
EXPENSES FOR 1996–97 State resident tuition: $800 full-time, $25 per semester hour part-time. Nonresident tuition: $2400 full-time, $75 per semester hour part-time. Part-time mandatory fees: $10 per semester hour. Part-time tuition for international students per semester hour: $93.50. Full-time mandatory fees: $320. College room and board: $2580.
FINANCIAL AID ***College-administered undergrad aid 1995–96:*** 150 need-based scholarships (average $250), 700 non-need scholarships (average $200), low-interest long-term loans from external sources (average $2000), Federal Work-Study, 30 part-time jobs. ***Acceptable forms:*** CSS Financial Aid PROFILE, state, institutional, FAFSA. ***Application deadline:*** continuous. ***Payment plans:*** installment, deferred payment. ***Waivers:*** full or partial for employees or children of employees, adult students, and senior citizens.
APPLYING Open admission. ***Options:*** early entrance, midyear entrance. ***Required:*** school transcript, TOEFL for international students. ***Recommended:*** SAT I or ACT. Test scores used for counseling/placement. ***Application deadline:*** rolling.
APPLYING/TRANSFER ***Required:*** high school transcript, college transcript. ***Recommended:*** standardized test scores. ***Entrance:*** noncompetitive. ***Application deadline:*** rolling. ***Contact:*** Miss Dixie Schierlman, Director, Student Programs, Admissions, Registration, 316-331-4100 Ext. 276.
CONTACT Miss Dixie Schierlman, Director, Student Programs, Admissions, Registration, Independence Community College, Independence, KS 67301-0708, 316-331-4100 Ext. 276 or toll-free 800-842-6063. ***Fax:*** 316-331-5344. College video available.

JOHNSON COUNTY COMMUNITY COLLEGE
Overland Park, Kansas

UG Enrollment: 15,477	**Tuition & Fees (KS Res): $1248**
Application Deadline: rolling	**Room & Board: N/Avail**

GENERAL State and locally supported, 2-year, coed. Part of Kansas State Board of Education. Awards certificates, transfer associate, terminal associate degrees. Founded 1967. ***Setting:*** 220-acre suburban campus with easy access to Kansas City. ***Total enrollment:*** 15,477. ***Faculty:*** 615 (270 full-time, 38% with terminal degrees, 345 part-time); student-faculty ratio is 21:1.
ENROLLMENT PROFILE 15,477 students from 13 states and territories, 20 other countries. 56% women, 44% men, 70% part-time, 94% state residents, 12% transferred in, 1% international, 44% 25 or older, 0% Native American, 2% Hispanic, 3% African American, 3% Asian American.
FIRST-YEAR CLASS 2,274 total. Of the students who applied, 100% were accepted.
ACADEMIC PROGRAM Core, honor code. Calendar: semesters. Academic remediation for entering students, English as a second language program offered during academic year and summer, services for LD students, advanced placement, self-designed majors, honors program, summer session for credit, part-time degree program (daytime, evenings, summer), adult/continuing education programs, co-op programs and internships. Off-campus study at Metropolitan Community College.
GENERAL DEGREE REQUIREMENTS 64 credit hours; computer course for data processing majors.
MAJORS Accounting, automotive technologies, aviation technology, biomedical technologies, business administration/commerce/management, civil engineering technology, commercial art, computer science, computer technologies, criminal justice, culinary arts, data processing, deaf interpreter training, dental services, drafting and design, electrical engineering technology, electronics engineering technology, emergency medical technology, energy management technologies, (pre)engineering sequence, engineering technology, fashion merchandising, fire science, heating/refrigeration/air conditioning, hospitality services, hotel and restaurant management, information science, interior design, law enforcement/police sciences, legal secretarial studies, liberal arts/general studies, manufacturing technology, marketing/retailing/merchandising, medical laboratory technology, medical records services, medical secretarial studies, nursing, occupational therapy, paralegal studies, physical therapy, radiological technology, respiratory therapy, secretarial studies/office management, transportation technologies, veterinary technology.
LIBRARY Johnson County Community College Library with 79,000 books, 400,000 microform titles, 720 periodicals, 4 on-line bibliographic services, 4,000 records, tapes, and CDs. Acquisition spending 1994–95: $212,350.
COMPUTERS ON CAMPUS Computer purchase plan available. 800 computers for student use in computer center, computer labs, learning resource center, classrooms provide access to main academic computer. Staffed computer lab on campus provides training in use of computers, software.
COLLEGE LIFE Drama-theater group, student-run newspaper. ***Campus security:*** 24-hour emergency response devices and patrols, late-night transport-escort service.
HOUSING College housing not available.
ATHLETICS Member NJCAA. ***Intercollegiate:*** basketball M(s)/W(s), equestrian sports M/W, golf M(s), soccer M, tennis M(s)/W(s), track and field M(s)/W(s), volleyball W(s). ***Intramural:*** basketball, cross-country running, soccer, tennis, volleyball. ***Contact:*** Ms. Lori DeGarmo, Director, Physical Education and Athletics, 913-469-8500.
CAREER PLANNING ***Placement office:*** 6 full-time, 8 part-time staff. ***Director:*** Ms. Gloria Campbell, Acting Program Director, 913-469-3870. ***Services:*** resume preparation, career counseling, careers library, job bank, job interviews.
EXPENSES FOR 1995–96 ***Application fee:*** $10. State resident tuition: $1024 full-time, $32 per credit hour part-time. Nonresident tuition: $3136 full-time, $98 per credit hour part-time. Part-time mandatory fees: $7 per credit hour. Full-time mandatory fees: $224.
FINANCIAL AID ***College-administered undergrad aid 1995–96:*** 442 need-based scholarships (average $412), 702 non-need scholarships (average $382), low-interest long-term loans from college funds (average $470), loans from external sources (average $1336), Federal Work-Study, 102 part-time jobs. ***Required forms:*** institutional, FAFSA; required for some: state; accepted: CSS Financial Aid PROFILE. ***Priority deadline:*** 4/5. ***Waivers:*** full or partial for employees or children of employees and senior citizens. ***Notification:*** continuous.
APPLYING Open admission except for nursing, dental hygiene, paralegal, respiratory therapy, interpreter training, emergency medical technology programs. ***Options:*** early entrance, midyear entrance. ***Required:*** TOEFL for international students. ***Required for some:*** school transcript, ACT, ACT ASSET. Test scores used for counseling/placement. ***Application deadline:*** rolling. ***Notification:*** continuous.
APPLYING/TRANSFER ***Required for some:*** standardized test scores, college transcript. ***Entrance:*** noncompetitive. ***Application deadline:*** rolling. ***Notification:*** continuous. ***Contact:*** Dr. Pat Long, Dean of Student Services, 913-469-8500 Ext. 3806.
CONTACT Dr. Pat Long, Dean of Student Services, Johnson County Community College, Overland Park, KS 66210-1299, 913-469-8500 Ext. 3806. College video available.

KANSAS CITY KANSAS COMMUNITY COLLEGE
Kansas City, Kansas

UG Enrollment: 6,000	**Tuition & Fees (KS Res): $1080**
Application Deadline: rolling	**Room & Board: N/Avail**

GENERAL State and locally supported, 2-year, coed. Part of Kansas State Board of Education. Awards certificates, transfer associate, terminal associate degrees. Founded 1923. ***Setting:*** 148-acre suburban campus. ***Endowment:*** $314,498. ***Total enrollment:*** 6,000. ***Faculty:*** 357 (127 full-time, 17% with terminal degrees, 230 part-time); student-faculty ratio is 19:1.
ENROLLMENT PROFILE 6,000 students from 9 states and territories, 6 other countries. 59% women, 70% part-time, 97% state residents, 15% transferred in, 1% international, 53% 25 or older, 1% Native American, 4% Hispanic, 22% African American, 1% Asian American. ***Most popular recent majors:*** business administration/commerce/management, computer programming, liberal arts/general studies.
FIRST-YEAR CLASS 1,567 total. Of the students who applied, 100% were accepted, 76% of whom enrolled. 12% from top 10% of their high school class, 14% from top quarter, 20% from top half.
ACADEMIC PROGRAM Core, honor code. Calendar: semesters. Academic remediation for entering students, English as a second language program offered during academic year, services for LD students, advanced placement, self-designed majors, honors program, summer session for credit, part-time degree program (daytime, evenings, summer), adult/continuing education programs, co-op programs and internships.
GENERAL DEGREE REQUIREMENTS 60 credit hours; 1 math/science course; computer course for most majors; internship (some majors).
MAJORS Accounting, agricultural business, art education, art/fine arts, art history, automotive technologies, biology/biological sciences, biomedical technologies, business administration/commerce/management, carpentry, ceramic art and design, chemistry, child care/child and family studies, commercial art, computer information systems, computer programming, computer science, computer technologies, corrections, cosmetology, criminal justice, data processing, drafting and design, early childhood education, economics, education, electrical and electronics technologies, electrical engineering technology, electronics engineering technology, elementary education, engineering (general), (pre)engineering sequence, engineering technology, English, environmental engineering technology, finance/banking, fire science, flight training, French, funeral service, German, health science, heating/refrigeration/air conditioning, history, home economics education, horticulture, humanities, journalism, law enforcement/police sciences, legal secretarial studies, liberal arts/general studies, literature, marketing/retailing/merchandising, mathematics, music, music education, nursing, nutrition, occupational therapy, paralegal studies, pharmacy/pharmaceutical sciences, philosophy, physical education, physical fitness/exercise science, physical therapy, political science/government, psychology, radiological technology, recreation and leisure services, recreation therapy, respiratory therapy, robotics, secretarial studies/office management, social work, sociology, Spanish, stringed instruments, studio art, telecommunications, theater arts/drama, tourism and travel, veterinary sciences, welding technology, word processing.
LIBRARY 60,000 books, 526 periodicals, 12 CD-ROMs, 2,650 records, tapes, and CDs. Acquisition spending 1994–95: $368,581.
COMPUTERS ON CAMPUS 80 computers for student use in computer center. Academic computing expenditure 1994–95: $462,735.
COLLEGE LIFE Choral group, student-run newspaper. ***Social organizations:*** 21 open to all. ***Most popular organizations:*** Student Senate, Phi Theta Kappa, Sigma Phi Sigma, International Student Organization, Student Nurses Association. ***Major annual events:*** Last Class Bash, Evening Student Appreciation Week, Global Celebrations International Festival. ***Campus security:*** 24-hour emergency response devices and patrols, late-night transport-escort service.
HOUSING College housing not available.
ATHLETICS Member NJCAA. ***Intercollegiate:*** baseball M(s), basketball M(s)/W(s), cross-country running M(s)/W(s), golf M(s), soccer M(s), softball W(s), track and field M(s)/W(s), volleyball W(s). ***Contact:*** Mr. Duane Shaw, Athletic Director, 913-334-1100 Ext. 150.
CAREER PLANNING ***Placement office:*** 1 full-time staff; $34,583 operating expenditure 1994–95. ***Director:*** Ms. Linda Wyatt, Coordinator Career Planning and Placement, 913-334-1100 Ext. 243. ***Services:*** job fairs, resume preparation, resume referral, career counseling, careers library, job bank, job interviews.
AFTER GRADUATION 40% of students completing a degree program in 1994–95 went directly on to further study.
EXPENSES FOR 1996–97 State resident tuition: $1080 full-time, $36 per credit hour part-time. Nonresident tuition: $2880 full-time, $96 per credit hour part-time.
FINANCIAL AID ***College-administered undergrad aid 1995–96:*** need-based scholarships, 53 non-need scholarships (average $500), low-interest long-term loans from external sources (average $1500), Federal Work-Study, 25 part-time jobs. ***Required forms:*** FAFSA. ***Priority deadline:*** 4/15.
APPLYING Open admission. ***Options:*** early entrance, deferred entrance. ***Required:*** school transcript, ACT ASSET. ***Recommended:*** SAT I or ACT, TOEFL for international students. ***Required for some:*** SAT I. Test scores used for counseling/placement. ***Application deadline:*** rolling. ***Notification:*** continuous.
APPLYING/TRANSFER ***Required for some:*** high school transcript, college transcript. ***Entrance:*** moderately difficult. ***Application deadline:*** rolling. ***Notification:*** continuous. ***Contact:*** Mr. Nick Perica, Director of Counseling, 913-334-1100 Ext. 167.
CONTACT Dr. Barbara Bauer, Registrar, Kansas City Kansas Community College, Kansas City, KS 66112-3003, 913-334-1100 Ext. 121.

LABETTE COMMUNITY COLLEGE
Parsons, Kansas

UG Enrollment: 2,598	Tuition & Fees (KS Res): $1320
Application Deadline: rolling	Room & Board: $2200

GENERAL State and locally supported, 2-year, coed. Part of Kansas State Board of Education. Awards transfer associate, terminal associate degrees. Founded 1923. *Setting:* 4-acre small-town campus. *Total enrollment:* 2,598. *Faculty:* 234 (36 full-time, 2% with terminal degrees, 198 part-time); student-faculty ratio is 16:1.
ENROLLMENT PROFILE 2,598 students from 7 states and territories, 4 other countries. 67% women, 68% part-time, 96% state residents, 6% transferred in, 1% international, 40% 25 or older, 2% Native American, 1% Hispanic, 3% African American, 1% Asian American. *Areas of study chosen:* 4% education, 3% fine arts, 1% communications and journalism, 1% engineering and applied sciences, 1% performing arts, 1% social sciences.
FIRST-YEAR CLASS 1,286 total; 1,500 applied, 100% were accepted, 86% of whom enrolled. 13% from top 10% of their high school class, 49% from top half.
ACADEMIC PROGRAM Honor code. Calendar: semesters. Academic remediation for entering students, English as a second language program offered during academic year and summer, services for LD students, advanced placement, summer session for credit, part-time degree program (daytime, evenings, summer); adult/continuing education programs, co-op programs and internships. ROTC: Army (c).
GENERAL DEGREE REQUIREMENTS 62 credit hours; 3 credit hours of college algebra; 5 credit hours of science; internship (some majors).
MAJORS Accounting, art/fine arts, behavioral sciences, biology/biological sciences, business administration/commerce/management, chemistry, child care/child and family studies, commercial art, computer science, criminal justice, data processing, drafting and design, early childhood education, education, elementary education, (pre)engineering sequence, English, fire science, heating/refrigeration/air conditioning, history, law enforcement/police sciences, legal secretarial studies, liberal arts/general studies, manufacturing technology, mathematics, medical secretarial studies, music, nursing, physical education, radiological technology, respiratory therapy, secretarial studies/office management, social science.
LIBRARY Labette Community College Library with 26,000 books, 56 microform titles, 235 periodicals, 540 records, tapes, and CDs.
COMPUTERS ON CAMPUS 66 computers for student use in computer center, classroom labs. Staffed computer lab on campus provides training in use of computers, software.
COLLEGE LIFE Choral group. *Social organizations:* 18 open to all. *Most popular organizations:* Adult Women Who Are Returning to Education (AWARE), Phi Beta Lambda. *Student services:* personal-psychological counseling.
HOUSING 48 college housing spaces available; all were occupied 1995-96. Off-campus living permitted. *Option:* coed housing available.
ATHLETICS Member NJCAA. *Intercollegiate:* baseball M(s), basketball M(s)/W(s), tennis W(s), volleyball W(s), wrestling M(s). *Contact:* Mr. Tom Hilton, Athletic Director, 316-421-0911.
AFTER GRADUATION 30% of students completing a degree program in 1994-95 went directly on to further study.
EXPENSES FOR 1996-97 State resident tuition: $1110 full-time, $37 per credit hour part-time. Nonresident tuition: $2760 full-time, $92 per credit hour part-time. Full-time mandatory fees: $210. College room and board: $2200.
FINANCIAL AID *College-administered undergrad aid 1995-96:* need-based scholarships. *Required forms:* FAFSA. *Application deadline:* continuous. *Payment plans:* installment, deferred payment.
APPLYING Open admission except for nursing program. *Option:* early entrance. *Required:* TOEFL for international students. *Recommended:* school transcript, ACT. Test scores used for counseling/placement. *Application deadline:* rolling. *Notification:* continuous.
APPLYING/TRANSFER *Recommended:* high school transcript, college transcript. *Application deadline:* rolling. *Notification:* continuous.
CONTACT Dr. Jeff Stevenson, Dean of Academic and Student Affairs, Labette Community College, Parsons, KS 67357-4299, 316-421-6700.

NEOSHO COUNTY COMMUNITY COLLEGE
Chanute, Kansas

UG Enrollment: 1,666	Tuition & Fees (KS Res): $1110
Application Deadline: 9/15	Room & Board: $2600

GENERAL State and locally supported, 2-year, coed. Part of Kansas State Board of Education. Awards transfer associate, terminal associate degrees. Founded 1936. *Setting:* 50-acre small-town campus. *Endowment:* $370,000. *Educational spending 1994-95:* $1400 per undergrad. *Total enrollment:* 1,666. *Faculty:* 96 (10% of full-time faculty have terminal degrees); student-faculty ratio is 18:1.
ENROLLMENT PROFILE 1,666 students from 15 states and territories, 3 other countries. 65% women, 60% part-time, 98% state residents, 5% live on campus, 10% transferred in, 58% 25 or older, 1% Native American, 3% Hispanic, 5% African American, 1% Asian American. *Areas of study chosen:* 25% business management and administrative services, 25% education, 15% health professions and related sciences, 5% architecture, 2% engineering and applied sciences, 2% premed, 2% social sciences. *Most popular recent majors:* accounting, business machine technologies, nursing.
FIRST-YEAR CLASS 254 total. Of the students who applied, 100% were accepted, 47% of whom enrolled. 8% from top 10% of their high school class, 20% from top quarter, 60% from top half.
ACADEMIC PROGRAM Core. Calendar: semesters. 200 courses offered in 1995-96. Academic remediation for entering students, services for LD students, advanced placement, self-designed majors, summer session for credit, part-time degree program (daytime, evenings, summer); adult/continuing education programs.
GENERAL DEGREE REQUIREMENTS 62 semester hours; computer course.
MAJORS Accounting, business administration/commerce/management, business machine technologies, carpentry, computer information systems, computer science, construction technologies, criminal justice, electrical and electronics technologies, (pre)engineering sequence, finance/banking, law enforcement/police sciences, liberal arts/general studies, marketing/retailing/merchandising, materials sciences, nursing, physical sciences, practical nursing, science, secretarial studies/office management, sports medicine, teacher aide studies, vocational education, welding technology.
LIBRARY Chapman Library with 33,000 books, 154 microform titles, 200 periodicals, 2 CD-ROMs, 1,500 records, tapes, and CDs. Acquisition spending 1994-95: $134,428.
COMPUTERS ON CAMPUS 100 computers for student use in computer center, English lab, library, dorms provide access to main academic computer. Staffed computer lab on campus provides training in use of computers, software. Academic computing expenditure 1994-95: $74,731.
COLLEGE LIFE Drama-theater group, choral group, student-run newspaper. 50% vote in student government elections. *Social organizations:* 4 open to all. *Most popular organizations:* Business Club, Science Club, Student Nurses Association, Fellowship of Christian Athletes, Non-Traditional Student Organization. *Major annual events:* Homecoming, Fun-in-the-Sun Week, Halloween Dance. *Student services:* personal-psychological counseling. *Campus security:* controlled dormitory access.
HOUSING 100 college housing spaces available; all were occupied 1995-96. No special consideration for freshman housing applicants. On-campus residence required in freshman year except if 21 or over or living with relatives. *Option:* coed housing available. Resident assistants live in dorms.
ATHLETICS Member NJCAA. *Intercollegiate:* baseball M(s), basketball M(s)/W(s), cross-country running M(s)/W(s), softball W(s), track and field M(s), volleyball W(s). *Intramural:* basketball, cross-country running, softball, track and field, volleyball. *Contact:* Dr. Leon Hazen, Acting Dean of Academic and Student Services, 316-431-6222 Ext. 212.
CAREER PLANNING Placement office: 3 full-time, 3 part-time staff; $35,000 operating expenditure 1994-95. *Director:* Mrs. Joyce Shipman, CAVE Director, 316-431-6222 Ext. 279. *Services:* resume preparation, career counseling, careers library.
AFTER GRADUATION 60% of students completing a degree program in 1994-95 went directly on to further study.
EXPENSES FOR 1996-97 State resident tuition: $1110 full-time, $37 per semester hour part-time. Nonresident tuition: $2670 full-time, $89 per semester hour part-time. College room and board: $2600.
FINANCIAL AID *College-administered undergrad aid 1995-96:* need-based scholarships, non-need scholarships, low-interest long-term loans from external sources, Federal Work-Study, part-time jobs. *Acceptable forms:* CSS Financial Aid PROFILE, FAFSA. *Priority deadline:* 8/1. *Payment plan:* installment. *Waivers:* full or partial for employees or children of employees and senior citizens. *Notification:* 10/1.
APPLYING Open admission. *Options:* Common Application, early entrance, midyear entrance. *Required:* school transcript, TOEFL for international students, Accuplacer. *Recommended:* ACT. Test scores used for counseling/placement. *Application deadline:* 9/15. *Notification:* continuous.
APPLYING/TRANSFER *Required:* high school transcript, college transcript. *Recommended:* standardized test scores. *Application deadline:* 9/15. *Notification:* continuous. *Contact:* Ms. Kim Tomlinson, Director of Counseling and Retention, 316-431-2820 Ext. 213.
CONTACT Ms. Deb Scheer, Director of Recruiting, Neosho County Community College, Chanute, KS 66720-2699, 316-431-2820 Ext. 264 or toll-free 800-729-6222. *Fax:* 316-431-6222.

PRATT COMMUNITY COLLEGE AND AREA VOCATIONAL SCHOOL
Pratt, Kansas

UG Enrollment: 1,349	Tuition & Fees (KS Res): $1226
Application Deadline: rolling	Room & Board: $2672

GENERAL District-supported, 2-year, coed. Part of Kansas State Board of Education. Awards certificates, transfer associate, terminal associate degrees. Founded 1938. *Setting:* 80-acre rural campus with easy access to Wichita. *Endowment:* $750,000. *Total enrollment:* 1,349. *Faculty:* 54 (44 full-time, 4% with terminal degrees, 10 part-time); student-faculty ratio is 18:1.
ENROLLMENT PROFILE 1,349 students from 17 states and territories, 3 other countries. 55% women, 60% part-time, 97% state residents, 6% transferred in, 1% international, 36% 25 or older, 1% Native American, 1% Hispanic, 2% African American, 1% Asian American.
FIRST-YEAR CLASS 580 total; 913 applied, 100% were accepted, 23% of whom enrolled. 9% from top 10% of their high school class, 22% from top quarter, 48% from top half.
ACADEMIC PROGRAM Core, honor code. Calendar: semesters. Academic remediation for entering students, advanced placement, tutorials, summer session for credit, part-time degree program (daytime, evenings), adult/continuing education programs, co-op programs.
GENERAL DEGREE REQUIREMENTS 64 credit hours; 3 credit hours of math; 9 credit hours of lab science; computer course.
MAJORS Accounting, agricultural business, agricultural economics, agricultural education, agricultural sciences, agricultural technologies, aircraft and missile maintenance, applied art, art education, art/fine arts, athletic training, automotive technologies, aviation technology, biology/biological sciences, broadcasting, business administration/commerce/management, business education, carpentry, chemistry, child care/child and family studies, commercial art, communication, construction technologies, early childhood education, education, elementary education, energy management technologies, (pre)engineering sequence, English, farm and ranch management, fish and game management, graphic arts, guidance and counseling, health education, history, home economics, humanities, human services, industrial arts, liberal arts/general studies, literature, marketing/retailing/merchandising, mathematics, music, nursing, physical education, physical sciences, psychology, science, secretarial studies/office management, social science, social work, sociology, speech/rhetoric/public address/debate, sports medicine, wildlife biology, wildlife management.
LIBRARY 26,000 books, 250 periodicals.
COMPUTERS ON CAMPUS 100 computers for student use in computer center, computer labs, learning resource center, classrooms, library. Staffed computer lab on campus provides training in use of computers, software.
COLLEGE LIFE Drama-theater group, choral group, student-run newspaper. *Social organizations:* 15 open to all; 1 local sorority. *Most popular organizations:* Phi Theta Kappa, Student Senate, Baptist Student Union, Distributive Education Club of America

Kansas–Kentucky

Pratt Community College and Area Vocational School (continued)
(DECA), Business Professionals Club. *Major annual events:* Spring Formal, Intramurals. *Student services:* personal-psychological counseling. *Campus security:* 24-hour patrols, late-night transport-escort service, controlled dormitory access.
HOUSING 168 college housing spaces available; 164 were occupied 1995–96. No special consideration for freshman housing applicants. On-campus residence required through sophomore year if scholarship recipient. *Options:* coed (1 building), single-sex (2 buildings) housing available. Resident assistants live in dorms.
ATHLETICS Member NJCAA. *Intercollegiate:* baseball M(s), basketball M(s)/W(s), cross-country running M(s)/W(s), softball W(s), tennis M(s)/W(s), track and field M(s)/W(s), volleyball W(s). *Intramural:* basketball, bowling, softball, table tennis (Ping-Pong), volleyball, weight lifting. *Contact:* Mr. Don Schwartz, Athletic Director, 316-672-5641.
EXPENSES FOR 1996–97 State resident tuition: $896 full-time, $28 per credit hour part-time. Nonresident tuition: $2688 full-time, $84 per credit hour part-time. Part-time mandatory fees: $11 per credit hour. Full-time mandatory fees: $330. College room and board: $2672.
FINANCIAL AID *College-administered undergrad aid 1995–96:* 70 need-based scholarships (average $325), 130 non-need scholarships (average $1050), low-interest long-term loans from external sources (average $2490), Federal Work-Study, 20 part-time jobs. *Required forms:* institutional, FAFSA; required for some: state. *Priority deadline:* 4/15. *Waivers:* full or partial for employees or children of employees. *Notification:* 7/1.
APPLYING Open admission. *Options:* Common Application, early entrance. *Required:* school transcript, TOEFL for international students. *Recommended:* ACT. Test scores used for counseling/placement. *Application deadline:* rolling.
APPLYING/TRANSFER *Required:* high school transcript, college transcript. *Recommended:* standardized test scores. *Application deadline:* rolling. *Contact:* Ms. Lisa Kolm, Registrar, 316-672-5641 Ext. 219.
CONTACT Ms. Kirsten Funk, Director of Admissions, Pratt Community College and Area Vocational School, Pratt, KS 67124-8317, 316-672-5641 Ext. 222. *Fax:* 316-672-5288.

SEWARD COUNTY COMMUNITY COLLEGE
Liberal, Kansas

UG Enrollment: 1,899	Tuition & Fees (KS Res): $1504
Application Deadline: 8/15	Room & Board: $2800

GENERAL State and locally supported, 2-year, coed. Part of Kansas State Board of Education. Awards certificates, transfer associate, terminal associate degrees. Founded 1969. *Setting:* 120-acre rural campus. *Endowment:* $8.5 million. *Total enrollment:* 1,899. *Faculty:* 147 (42 full-time, 105 part-time).
ENROLLMENT PROFILE 1,899 students from 10 states and territories, 2 other countries. 58% women, 42% men, 68% part-time, 84% state residents, 27% transferred in, 1% international, 72% 25 or older, 1% Native American, 9% Hispanic, 5% African American, 5% Asian American. *Areas of study chosen:* 9% social sciences, 8% fine arts, 5% agriculture, 4% communications and journalism, 4% premed, 3% education, 2% prevet, 1% architecture, 1% engineering and applied sciences, 1% natural resource sciences, 1% performing arts.
FIRST-YEAR CLASS 501 total; 582 applied, 97% of whom enrolled. 9% from top 10% of their high school class, 34% from top quarter, 72% from top half. 14 National Merit Scholars, 31 class presidents, 24 valedictorians.
ACADEMIC PROGRAM Core, honor code. Calendar: semesters. 394 courses offered in 1995–96. Academic remediation for entering students, English as a second language program offered during academic year, self-designed majors, summer session for credit, part-time degree program (daytime, evenings, summer), external degree programs, adult/continuing education programs, co-op programs and internships.
GENERAL DEGREE REQUIREMENTS 64 credit hours; 3 credit hours of college algebra; computer course for business administration, accounting, mathematics, advertising majors; internship (some majors).
MAJORS Accounting, agricultural sciences, art/fine arts, athletic training, biology/biological sciences, business administration/commerce/management, chemistry, child care/child and family studies, communication, computer programming, computer science, data processing, economics, education, elementary education, (pre)engineering sequence, English, farm and ranch management, finance/banking, fish and game management, history, journalism, law enforcement/police sciences, liberal arts/general studies, literature, marketing/retailing/merchandising, mathematics, medical laboratory technology, music, natural sciences, nursing, painting/drawing, physical education, physical sciences, practical nursing, psychology, respiratory therapy, science, secretarial studies/office management, social work, sociology, speech/rhetoric/public address/debate, sports medicine, theater arts/drama, wildlife management.
LIBRARY Learning Resource Center plus 1 other, with 32,746 books, 647 microform titles, 301 periodicals, 32 CD-ROMs, 146 records, tapes, and CDs. Acquisition spending 1994–95: $22,112.
COMPUTERS ON CAMPUS 102 computers for student use in computer center, labs provide access to main academic computer. Staffed computer lab on campus provides training in use of computers, software. Academic computing expenditure 1994–95: $90,882.
COLLEGE LIFE Orientation program (2 days). Drama-theater group, choral group, student-run newspaper. 36% vote in student government elections. *Social organizations:* 28 open to all. *Most popular organizations:* HALO, ATLAS, Block and Bridle, DECA, Sigma Chi Chi. *Major annual events:* Homecoming/Family Day, Pancake Day, Octoberfest. *Campus security:* late-night transport-escort service.
HOUSING 136 college housing spaces available; 118 were occupied 1995–96. No special consideration for freshman housing applicants. Off-campus living permitted. *Option:* coed housing available.
ATHLETICS Member NJCAA. *Intercollegiate:* baseball M(s), basketball M(s)/W(s), tennis M(s)/W(s), volleyball W(s). *Contact:* Mr. Galen McSpadden, Athletic Director, 316-629-2730.
CAREER PLANNING *Placement office:* 3 full-time, 4 part-time staff; $74,566 operating expenditure 1994–95. *Director:* Ms. Sheila Orth, Career Counseling Coordinator, 316-624-1951. *Services:* job fairs, resume preparation, career counseling, careers library, job bank, job interviews. 62 organizations recruited on campus 1994–95.
AFTER GRADUATION 67% of students completing a degree program in 1994–95 went directly on to further study.

EXPENSES FOR 1996–97 State resident tuition: $1184 full-time, $37 per credit hour part-time. Nonresident tuition: $1600 full-time, $50 per credit hour part-time. Part-time mandatory fees: $10 per credit hour. Full-time mandatory fees: $320. College room and board: $2800.
FINANCIAL AID *College-administered undergrad aid 1995–96:* 369 need-based scholarships (average $1427), 529 non-need scholarships (average $927), short-term loans (average $200), low-interest long-term loans from external sources (average $1803), Federal Work-Study, 167 part-time jobs. *Required forms:* institutional, FAFSA; required for some: state. *Application deadline:* continuous to 8/20.
APPLYING Open admission. *Options:* early entrance, deferred entrance. *Required:* school transcript, TOEFL for international students. *Recommended:* ACT. *Required for some:* minimum 2.0 GPA, recommendations, interview. Test scores used for counseling/placement. *Application deadline:* 8/15. *Notification:* continuous.
APPLYING/TRANSFER *Required:* high school transcript, college transcript. *Recommended:* standardized test scores. *Required for some:* recommendations, interview, minimum 2.0 college GPA, minimum 2.0 high school GPA. *Entrance:* noncompetitive. *Application deadline:* 8/15. *Notification:* continuous. *Contact:* Ms. Gale Buck, Registrar, 316-629-2616.
CONTACT Mr. Jerry Headrick, Director of Guidance, Seward County Community College, Liberal, KS 67905-1137, 316-624-1951 or toll-free 800-373-9951. *Fax:* 316-629-2725.

KENTUCKY

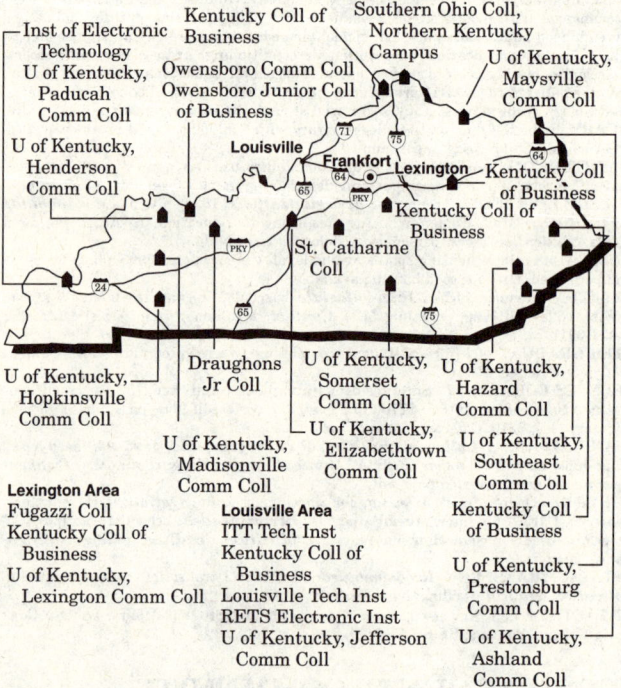

ASHLAND COMMUNITY COLLEGE
Kentucky—See University of Kentucky, Ashland Community College

DRAUGHONS JUNIOR COLLEGE
Bowling Green, Kentucky

UG Enrollment: 160	Tuition & Fees: $4350
Application Deadline: N/R	Room & Board: N/Avail

GENERAL Proprietary, 2-year, primarily women. Awards transfer associate degrees. *Setting:* suburban campus. *Total enrollment:* 160. *Faculty:* 17 (4 full-time, 13 part-time).
ENROLLMENT PROFILE 160 students: 92% women, 8% men.
FIRST-YEAR CLASS 41 total. Of the students who applied, 100% were accepted, 90% of whom enrolled.
ACADEMIC PROGRAM Calendar: semesters.
GENERAL DEGREE REQUIREMENTS 60 credit hours; 1 math course; computer course.
MAJORS Accounting, business administration/commerce/management, computer information systems, legal secretarial studies, medical assistant technologies.
EXPENSES FOR 1996–97 Tuition: $4350 full-time, $145 per credit hour part-time. One-time mandatory fee: $90.
APPLYING Open admission.
CONTACT Mr. William Greene, Director of Admissions, Draughons Junior College, Bowling Green, KY 42103, 615-361-7555.

Kentucky

ELIZABETHTOWN COMMUNITY COLLEGE
Kentucky— See University of Kentucky, Elizabethtown Community College

FUGAZZI COLLEGE
Lexington, Kentucky

UG Enrollment: 202	Tuition & Fees: $5516
Application Deadline: rolling	Room & Board: N/Avail

GENERAL Proprietary, 2-year, coed. Awards terminal associate degrees. Founded 1915. *Setting:* urban campus with easy access to Cincinnati and Louisville. *Total enrollment:* 202. *Faculty:* 30 (2 full-time, 28 part-time); student-faculty ratio is 9:1.
ENROLLMENT PROFILE 202 students from 2 states and territories. 60% women, 3% part-time, 99% state residents, 0% international, 25% 25 or older, 0% Native American, 0% Hispanic, 35% African American, 1% Asian American. *Most popular recent majors:* medical assistant technologies, computer programming, business administration/commerce/management.
FIRST-YEAR CLASS 95 total; 185 applied, 100% were accepted, 51% of whom enrolled.
ACADEMIC PROGRAM Core. Calendar: quarters. Academic remediation for entering students, summer session for credit, part-time degree program (daytime, evenings, summer), co-op programs.
GENERAL DEGREE REQUIREMENTS 96 credit hours; 1 math course; computer course.
MAJORS Broadcasting, business administration/commerce/management, computer programming, computer technologies, management information systems, medical assistant technologies, radio and television studies, tourism and travel.
LIBRARY 3,000 books, 15 periodicals, 200 records, tapes, and CDs.
COMPUTERS ON CAMPUS 19 computers for student use in computer center, computer annex.
COLLEGE LIFE *Student services:* personal-psychological counseling.
HOUSING College housing not available.
CAREER PLANNING *Director:* Ms. Lynn Johnson, Career Counselor, 606-266-0401. *Services:* job fairs, resume preparation, resume referral, career counseling, job interviews.
EXPENSES FOR 1996-97 Tuition: $5496 full-time, $114.50 per credit hour part-time. Part-time mandatory fees: $20 per year. Full-time mandatory fees: $20.
FINANCIAL AID *College-administered undergrad aid 1995-96:* need-based scholarships, 60 non-need scholarships (average $150), low-interest long-term loans from college funds (average $1500), loans from external sources (average $2625), Federal Work-Study. *Required forms:* FAFSA. *Priority deadline:* 9/14. *Payment plan:* installment.
APPLYING Open admission. *Option:* deferred entrance. *Required:* school transcript. Test scores used for counseling/placement. *Application deadline:* rolling.
APPLYING/TRANSFER *Application deadline:* rolling.
CONTACT Mrs. Marianne Kohler, Director of Admissions, Fugazzi College, 406 Lafayette Avenue, Lexington, KY 40502-2140, 606-266-0401.

HAZARD COMMUNITY COLLEGE
Kentucky—See University of Kentucky, Hazard Community College

HENDERSON COMMUNITY COLLEGE
Kentucky—See University of Kentucky, Henderson Community College

HOPKINSVILLE COMMUNITY COLLEGE
Kentucky— See University of Kentucky, Hopkinsville Community College

INSTITUTE OF ELECTRONIC TECHNOLOGY
Paducah, Kentucky

UG Enrollment: 149	Tuition: $12,090/deg prog
Application Deadline: rolling	Room & Board: N/Avail

GENERAL Proprietary, 2-year, specialized, primarily men. Awards terminal associate degrees. Founded 1964. *Setting:* small-town campus. *Total enrollment:* 149. *Faculty:* 5 (all full-time); student-faculty ratio is 25:1.
ENROLLMENT PROFILE 149 students from 4 states and territories. 5% women, 0% part-time, 45% state residents, 0% transferred in, 0% international, 38% 25 or older, 0% Native American, 0% Hispanic, 10% African American, 0% Asian American.
FIRST-YEAR CLASS 79 total; 87 applied, 95% were accepted, 95% of whom enrolled. 9% from top 10% of their high school class, 26% from top quarter, 60% from top half.
ACADEMIC PROGRAM Honor code. Calendar: trimesters. Summer session for credit, co-op programs.
GENERAL DEGREE REQUIREMENTS 72 semester hours; math/science requirements vary according to program; computer course.
MAJORS Communication equipment technology, computer technologies, electrical and electronics technologies, electrical engineering technology, electronics engineering technology, industrial engineering technology.
COMPUTERS ON CAMPUS 17 computers for student use in computer center.
HOUSING College housing not available.
CAREER PLANNING *Service:* career counseling.
EXPENSES FOR 1995-96 Tuition: $12,090 per degree program. Full-time mandatory fees: $75. Tuition guaranteed not to increase for student's term of enrollment.
FINANCIAL AID *College-administered undergrad aid 1995-96:* low-interest long-term loans from external sources (average $2625), 120 part-time jobs. *Required forms:* FAFSA; required for some: CSS Financial Aid PROFILE, state. *Priority deadline:* 6/1. *Payment plans:* installment, deferred payment.
APPLYING Open admission. *Option:* deferred entrance. *Required:* school transcript. *Application deadline:* rolling.
APPLYING/TRANSFER *Entrance:* noncompetitive. *Application deadline:* rolling.
CONTACT Mr. Arnold Harris, Director of Admissions, Institute of Electronic Technology, Paducah, KY 42001, 502-444-9676 Ext. 4 or toll-free 800-995-4438 (in-state). *Fax:* 502-441-7202.

ITT TECHNICAL INSTITUTE
Louisville, Kentucky

CONTACT Mr. Ron Robie, Director of Recruitment, ITT Technical Institute, Louisville, KY 40223-5392, 502-327-7424. College video available.

JEFFERSON COMMUNITY COLLEGE
Kentucky—See University of Kentucky, Jefferson Community College

KENTUCKY COLLEGE OF BUSINESS
Danville, Kentucky

UG Enrollment: 92	Tuition & Fees: $5526
Application Deadline: N/R	Room & Board: N/Avail

GENERAL Proprietary, 2-year. Awards diplomas, terminal associate degrees. Founded 1975. *Total enrollment:* 92. *Faculty:* 39.
ENROLLMENT PROFILE 92 students.
FIRST-YEAR CLASS 16 total. Of the students who applied, 100% were accepted.
ACADEMIC PROGRAM Calendar: quarters.
GENERAL DEGREE REQUIREMENTS 96 credit hours; computer course.
EXPENSES FOR 1996-97 Tuition: $5496 full-time, $114.50 per credit hour part-time. Part-time mandatory fees: $30 per year. Full-time mandatory fees: $30.
APPLYING Open admission. *Required:* school transcript.
APPLYING/TRANSFER *Required:* college transcript.
CONTACT Mr. Larry Weathers, Director of Admissions, Kentucky College of Business, Danville, KY 40422, 606-236-6991.

KENTUCKY COLLEGE OF BUSINESS
Florence, Kentucky

UG Enrollment: 85	Tuition & Fees: $5526
Application Deadline: N/R	Room & Board: N/Avail

GENERAL Proprietary, 2-year. Awards diplomas, terminal associate degrees. Founded 1941. *Total enrollment:* 85. *Faculty:* 21 (3 full-time, 18 part-time).
ENROLLMENT PROFILE 85 students.
FIRST-YEAR CLASS 16 total. Of the students who applied, 100% were accepted.
ACADEMIC PROGRAM Calendar: quarters.
GENERAL DEGREE REQUIREMENTS 96 credit hours; computer course.
EXPENSES FOR 1996-97 Tuition: $5496 full-time, $114.50 per credit hour part-time. Part-time mandatory fees: $30 per year. Full-time mandatory fees: $30.
APPLYING Open admission. *Required:* school transcript.
APPLYING/TRANSFER *Required:* college transcript.
CONTACT Mr. Larry Steele, Director of Admissions, Kentucky College of Business, Florence, KY 41042, 606-525-6510.

KENTUCKY COLLEGE OF BUSINESS
Lexington, Kentucky

UG Enrollment: 119	Tuition & Fees: $5496
Application Deadline: rolling	Room & Board: N/Avail

GENERAL Proprietary, 2-year, coed. Part of Education Systems Incorporated. Awards transfer associate, terminal associate degrees. Founded 1947. *Setting:* urban campus. *Total enrollment:* 119. *Faculty:* 30 (6 full-time, 24 part-time).
ENROLLMENT PROFILE 119 students: 80% women, 30% part-time, 100% state residents, 2% transferred in, 1% Native American, 0% Hispanic, 18% African American, 0% Asian American.
FIRST-YEAR CLASS Of the students who applied, 100% were accepted.
ACADEMIC PROGRAM Core. Calendar: quarters. Part-time degree program (daytime, evenings), internships.
GENERAL DEGREE REQUIREMENT 96 credit hours.
MAJORS Accounting, business administration/commerce/management, fashion merchandising, legal secretarial studies, management information systems, secretarial studies/office management.
COLLEGE LIFE *Student services:* personal-psychological counseling.
HOUSING College housing not available.
CAREER PLANNING *Director:* Ms. Natasha Lacy, Career Placement Center Director, 606-253-0621. *Service:* career counseling.
EXPENSES FOR 1996-97 *Application fee:* $20. Tuition: $5496 full-time, $114.50 per credit hour part-time. One-time mandatory fee: $20.

Kentucky

Kentucky College of Business *(continued)*
FINANCIAL AID *College-administered undergrad aid 1995–96:* need-based scholarships, low-interest long-term loans from external sources, Federal Work-Study. *Required forms:* FAFSA. *Application deadline:* continuous.
APPLYING Open admission. *Required:* school transcript. *Recommended:* TOEFL for international students. Test scores used for counseling/placement. *Application deadline:* rolling.
APPLYING/TRANSFER *Required:* high school transcript. *Entrance:* noncompetitive. *Application deadline:* rolling.
CONTACT Ms. Sandra Connelly, Admissions Representative, Kentucky College of Business, 628 East Main Street, Lexington, KY 40508-2312, 606-253-0621.

KENTUCKY COLLEGE OF BUSINESS
Louisville, Kentucky

UG Enrollment: 155	Tuition & Fees: $5536
Application Deadline: N/R	Room & Board: N/Avail

GENERAL Proprietary, 2-year. Awards diplomas, terminal associate degrees. Founded 1990. *Total enrollment:* 155. *Faculty:* 21 (8 full-time, 13 part-time).
ENROLLMENT PROFILE 155 students.
ACADEMIC PROGRAM Calendar: quarters.
GENERAL DEGREE REQUIREMENTS 96 credit hours; 1 business math course; computer course.
HOUSING College housing not available.
EXPENSES FOR 1996–97 Tuition: $5496 full-time, $114.50 per credit hour part-time. Part-time mandatory fees: $10 per quarter hour. Full-time mandatory fees: $40.
APPLYING Open admission. *Required:* school transcript.
APPLYING/TRANSFER *Required:* college transcript.
CONTACT Ms. Kelly Harris, Director of Admissions, Kentucky College of Business, Louisville, KY 40216, 502-447-7634.

KENTUCKY COLLEGE OF BUSINESS
Pikeville, Kentucky

UG Enrollment: 88	Tuition & Fees: $5496
Application Deadline: N/R	Room & Board: N/Avail

GENERAL Proprietary, 2-year. Awards diplomas, terminal associate degrees. Founded 1976. *Total enrollment:* 88.
ENROLLMENT PROFILE 88 students.
ACADEMIC PROGRAM Calendar: quarters.
GENERAL DEGREE REQUIREMENTS 96 credit hours; 1 math course; computer course.
EXPENSES FOR 1996–97 Tuition: $5496 full-time, $114.50 per credit hour part-time.
APPLYING Open admission. *Required:* school transcript.
APPLYING/TRANSFER *Required:* college transcript.
CONTACT Ms. Lois Atkins, Admissions Representative, Kentucky College of Business, Pikeville, KY 41501, 606-432-5477.

KENTUCKY COLLEGE OF BUSINESS
Richmond, Kentucky

UG Enrollment: 140	Tuition & Fees: $5526
Application Deadline: N/R	Room & Board: N/Avail

GENERAL Proprietary, 2-year. Awards diplomas, terminal associate degrees. Founded 1976. *Total enrollment:* 140. *Faculty:* 20 (3 full-time, 17 part-time).
ENROLLMENT PROFILE 140 students.
FIRST-YEAR CLASS 80 total. Of the students who applied, 100% were accepted, 80% of whom enrolled.
ACADEMIC PROGRAM Calendar: quarters.
GENERAL DEGREE REQUIREMENTS 96 credit hours; 1 business math course; computer course.
EXPENSES FOR 1996–97 Tuition: $5496 full-time, $114.50 per credit hour part-time. Part-time mandatory fees: $30 per year. Full-time mandatory fees: $30.
APPLYING Open admission. *Required:* school transcript.
APPLYING/TRANSFER *Required:* college transcript.
CONTACT Mr. Michael Bullock, Admissions Representative, Kentucky College of Business, Richmond, KY 40475, 606-623-8956.

LEXINGTON COMMUNITY COLLEGE
Kentucky—See University of Kentucky, Lexington Community College

LOUISVILLE TECHNICAL INSTITUTE
Louisville, Kentucky

UG Enrollment: 488	Tuition & Fees: $8805
Application Deadline: 10/5	Room Only: $2610

GENERAL Proprietary, 2-year, coed. Awards terminal associate degrees. Founded 1961. *Setting:* 10-acre suburban campus. *Total enrollment:* 488. *Faculty:* 41 (19 full-time, 22 part-time); student-faculty ratio is 14:1.
ENROLLMENT PROFILE 488 students from 13 states and territories. 11% women, 4% part-time, 95% state residents, 10% transferred in, 0% international, 40% 25 or older, 2% Hispanic, 16% African American, 2% Asian American. *Areas of study chosen:* 20% engineering and applied sciences, 15% architecture. *Most popular recent majors:* drafting and design, engineering technology, interior design.
FIRST-YEAR CLASS 141 total; 210 applied, 80% were accepted, 83% of whom enrolled. 14% from top 10% of their high school class, 76% from top half.
ACADEMIC PROGRAM Core, honor code. Calendar: quarters. Academic remediation for entering students, advanced placement, self-designed majors, summer session for credit, part-time degree program (daytime, evenings, summer), adult/continuing education programs, co-op programs and internships.
GENERAL DEGREE REQUIREMENTS 54 credit hours; math/science requirements vary according to program; computer course; internship (some majors).
MAJORS Architectural technologies, computer technologies, drafting and design, electrical engineering technology, electronics engineering technology, engineering technology, fashion design and technology, fashion merchandising, interior design, marine technology, mechanical design technology, mechanical engineering technology, robotics.
COMPUTERS ON CAMPUS 65 computers for student use in computer center.
COLLEGE LIFE *Campus security:* 24-hour emergency response devices, controlled dormitory access.
HOUSING 50 college housing spaces available; 15 were occupied 1995–96. Freshmen given priority for college housing. Off-campus living permitted. *Option:* coed (1 building) housing available. Resident assistants live in dorms.
ATHLETICS *Intramural:* basketball, bowling, softball.
CAREER PLANNING *Placement office:* 1 full-time, 1 part-time staff. *Director:* Ms. Sandy Zorn, Graduate Employment Services Director, 502-456-6509. *Services:* job fairs, resume preparation, resume referral, career counseling, job interviews. Students must register sophomore year.
EXPENSES FOR 1996–97 *Application fee:* $100. Tuition: $8520 full-time, $185 per credit hour part-time. Full-time mandatory fees: $285. College room only: $2610. Tuition guaranteed not to increase for student's term of enrollment.
FINANCIAL AID *College-administered undergrad aid 1995–96:* need-based scholarships, short-term loans, low-interest long-term loans from college funds, loans from external sources, Federal Work-Study, part-time jobs. *Required forms:* state, institutional, FAFSA; required for some: CSS Financial Aid PROFILE. *Priority deadline:* 10/10. *Payment plan:* installment. *Waivers:* full or partial for employees or children of employees.
APPLYING *Options:* early entrance, deferred entrance. *Required:* school transcript, interview, TOEFL for international students. Test scores used for admission and counseling/placement. *Application deadline:* 10/5. *Notification:* continuous.
APPLYING/TRANSFER *Required:* high school transcript, interview, college transcript. *Required for some:* standardized test scores. *Application deadline:* 10/5. *Notification:* continuous. *Contact:* Mr. Joe Santoro, Director of Admissions, 502-456-6509.
CONTACT Mr. Joe Santoro, Director of Admissions, Louisville Technical Institute, Louisville, KY 40218-4528, 502-456-6509. *Fax:* 502-456-2341.

MADISONVILLE COMMUNITY COLLEGE
Kentucky—See University of Kentucky, Madisonville Community College

MAYSVILLE COMMUNITY COLLEGE
Kentucky—See University of Kentucky, Maysville Community College

OWENSBORO COMMUNITY COLLEGE
Owensboro, Kentucky

UG Enrollment: 2,614	Tuition & Fees (KY Res): $1000
Application Deadline: rolling	Room & Board: N/Avail

GENERAL State-supported, 2-year, coed. Part of University of Kentucky Community College System. Awards transfer associate, terminal associate degrees. Founded 1986. *Setting:* 102-acre suburban campus. *Total enrollment:* 2,614. *Faculty:* 124 (57 full-time, 100% with terminal degrees, 67 part-time); student-faculty ratio is 23:1.
ENROLLMENT PROFILE 2,614 students from 3 states and territories. 63% women, 58% part-time, 99% state residents, 21% transferred in, 0% international, 52% 25 or older, 1% Native American, 0% Hispanic, 2% African American, 0% Asian American.
FIRST-YEAR CLASS 404 total; 762 applied, 100% were accepted, 53% of whom enrolled. 6% from top 10% of their high school class, 16% from top quarter, 43% from top half.
ACADEMIC PROGRAM Core, honor code. Calendar: semesters. Academic remediation for entering students, advanced placement, honors program, summer session for credit, part-time degree program (daytime, evenings), adult/continuing education programs, co-op programs and internships.
GENERAL DEGREE REQUIREMENTS 60 semester hours; 3 semsester hours of math; 6 semester hours of science; computer course; internship (some majors).
MAJORS Accounting, business administration/commerce/management, computer information systems, data processing, engineering technology, human services, liberal arts/general studies, nursing, radiological technology, secretarial studies/office management.
COMPUTERS ON CAMPUS 70 computers for student use in computer center, learning resource center, library provide access to main academic computer, e-mail, on-line services. Staffed computer lab on campus provides training in use of computers, software.
COLLEGE LIFE Drama-theater group, choral group, student-run newspaper, radio station. *Student services:* personal-psychological counseling. *Campus security:* 24-hour emergency response devices.
HOUSING College housing not available.
ATHLETICS *Intramural:* basketball.
CAREER PLANNING *Placement office:* 1 full-time staff. *Director:* Ms. Sylvia Lovett, Director of Cooperative Education and Placement, 502-686-4465. *Services:* job fairs, resume preparation, resume referral, career counseling, job bank, job interviews.
AFTER GRADUATION 49% of students completing a degree program in 1994–95 went directly on to further study.
EXPENSES FOR 1996–97 State resident tuition: $1000 full-time, $42 per semester hour part-time. Nonresident tuition: $3000 full-time, $126 per semester hour part-time.
FINANCIAL AID *College-administered undergrad aid 1995–96:* 975 need-based scholarships (average $640), non-need scholarships (average $500), short-term loans (aver-

Kentucky

age $150), low-interest long-term loans from college funds (average $200), loans from external sources (average $1500), Federal Work-Study, 35 part-time jobs. *Required forms:* CSS Financial Aid PROFILE, state. *Priority deadline:* 4/1. *Payment plan:* deferred payment. *Waivers:* full or partial for senior citizens.
APPLYING Open admission. *Required:* school transcript, 3 years of high school math and science, ACT, TOEFL for international students. Test scores used for counseling/placement. *Application deadline:* rolling. *Notification:* continuous.
APPLYING/TRANSFER *Required:* standardized test scores, high school transcript, 3 years of high school math and science. *Application deadline:* rolling. *Notification:* continuous. *Contact:* Ms. Diane Garrard, Admissions Counselor, 502-686-4400.
CONTACT Ms. Diane Garrard, Admissions Counselor, Owensboro Community College, Owensboro, KY 42303-1899, 502-686-4400.

OWENSBORO JUNIOR COLLEGE OF BUSINESS
Owensboro, Kentucky

UG Enrollment: 175	Tuition & Fees: $4080
Application Deadline: rolling	Room & Board: N/Avail

GENERAL Proprietary, 2-year, coed. Awards transfer associate degrees. Founded 1963. *Setting:* 1-acre small-town campus. *Total enrollment:* 175. *Faculty:* 13 (10 full-time, 3 part-time); student-faculty ratio is 10:1. *Notable Alumni:* Janet Kidd, paralegal; Carol Gray, administrative assistant to the President of Owensboro Junior College of Business; Madoline Dombrosky, assistant registrar of Owensboro Junior College of Business.
ENROLLMENT PROFILE 175 students from 2 states and territories. 95% women, 5% men, 5% part-time, 85% state residents, 15% transferred in, 0% international, 35% 25 or older, 0% Native American, 0% Hispanic, 5% African American, 0% Asian American. *Areas of study chosen:* 40% health professions and related sciences, 25% computer and information sciences, 15% business management and administrative services. *Most popular recent majors:* medical assistant technologies, computer science, paralegal studies.
FIRST-YEAR CLASS 87 total. Of the students who applied, 75% were accepted, 75% of whom enrolled. 5% from top 10% of their high school class, 20% from top quarter, 70% from top half.
ACADEMIC PROGRAM Core, honor code. Calendar: quarters. 59 courses offered in 1995-96. Academic remediation for entering students, advanced placement, summer session for credit, part-time degree program (daytime, evenings), adult/continuing education programs.
GENERAL DEGREE REQUIREMENTS 96 credit hours; computer course.
MAJORS Business administration/commerce/management, computer science, data processing, medical assistant technologies, paralegal studies, secretarial studies/office management.
LIBRARY Owensboro Junior College Library with 3,700 books, 37 periodicals.
COMPUTERS ON CAMPUS 80 computers for student use in computer center. Staffed computer lab on campus provides training in use of computers.
COLLEGE LIFE *Student services:* personal-psychological counseling. *Campus security:* security officer at night.
HOUSING College housing not available.
CAREER PLANNING *Placement office:* 2 part-time staff. *Director:* Ms. Paula Houston, Placement Director, 502-926-4040. *Services:* job fairs, resume preparation, resume referral, career counseling, job bank, job interviews.
EXPENSES FOR 1996-97 *Application fee:* $10. Tuition: $4080 full-time, $85 per quarter hour part-time.
FINANCIAL AID *College-administered undergrad aid 1995-96:* need-based scholarships, non-need scholarships, low-interest long-term loans from external sources (average $1500), Federal Work-Study, 5 part-time jobs. *Required forms:* CSS Financial Aid PROFILE; required for some: state; accepted: FAFSA. *Priority deadline:* 10/1. *Payment plan:* installment.
APPLYING *Options:* deferred entrance, midyear entrance. *Required for some:* SAT I or ACT. Test scores used for admission. *Application deadline:* rolling.
APPLYING/TRANSFER *Required for some:* standardized test scores, minimum 2.0 college GPA. *Entrance:* minimally difficult. *Application deadline:* rolling. *Contact:* Ms. Dorothy Holbrook, Vice President, 502-926-4040.
CONTACT Mr. Mark Gabis, President, Owensboro Junior College of Business, Owensboro, KY 42303, 502-926-4040.

PADUCAH COMMUNITY COLLEGE
Kentucky—See University of Kentucky, Paducah Community College

PRESTONSBURG COMMUNITY COLLEGE
Kentucky— See University of Kentucky, Prestonsburg Community College

RETS ELECTRONIC INSTITUTE
Louisville, Kentucky

UG Enrollment: 300	Tuition & Fees: $7395
Application Deadline: rolling	Room Only: $2250

GENERAL Proprietary, 2-year, specialized, coed. Awards terminal associate degrees. Founded 1935. *Setting:* suburban campus. *Total enrollment:* 300. *Faculty:* 19 (18 full-time, 1 part-time); student-faculty ratio is 29:1.
ENROLLMENT PROFILE 300 students: 8% women, 0% part-time, 75% state residents, 3% transferred in.
FIRST-YEAR CLASS 100 total. Of the students who applied, 90% were accepted.
ACADEMIC PROGRAM Core. Calendar: trimesters. Academic remediation for entering students.
GENERAL DEGREE REQUIREMENTS 90 semester hours; computer course.
MAJOR Electronics engineering technology.
COLLEGE LIFE *Campus security:* 24-hour emergency response devices.
HOUSING 750 college housing spaces available. Freshmen given priority for college housing.
EXPENSES FOR 1995-96 *Application fee:* $75. Tuition: $7395 full-time. College room only: $2250. Tuition guaranteed not to increase for student's term of enrollment.
FINANCIAL AID *College-administered undergrad aid 1995-96:* need-based scholarships, low-interest long-term loans from external sources, Federal Work-Study. *Required forms:* CSS Financial Aid PROFILE, state. *Application deadline:* continuous. *Payment plan:* installment. *Waivers:* full or partial for employees or children of employees.
APPLYING *Required:* campus interview, CPAt. Test scores used for admission and counseling/placement. *Application deadline:* rolling. *Notification:* continuous.
APPLYING/TRANSFER *Application deadline:* rolling. *Notification:* continuous.
CONTACT Mr. Barry McConaghy, Director of Admissions, RETS Electronic Institute, 300 Highrise Drive, Louisville, KY 40213, 502-968-7191 or toll-free 800-999-7387.

RETS MEDICAL AND BUSINESS INSTITUTE
Kentucky—See CHI Institute, RETS Campus, Broomall, PA

ST. CATHARINE COLLEGE
St. Catharine, Kentucky

UG Enrollment: 442	Tuition & Fees: $4800
Application Deadline: rolling	Room & Board: $3100

GENERAL Independent Roman Catholic, 2-year, coed. Awards certificates, transfer associate, terminal associate degrees. Founded 1931. *Setting:* 643-acre rural campus with easy access to Louisville. *Endowment:* $300,000. *Total enrollment:* 442. *Faculty:* 50 (35 full-time, 33% with terminal degrees, 15 part-time); student-faculty ratio is 10:1. *Notable Alumni:* Sandy Welch, educational television personality; Deborah Dawahare, attorney.
ENROLLMENT PROFILE 442 students: 61% women, 37% part-time, 85% state residents, 19% live on campus, 5% transferred in, 87% have need-based financial aid, 13% have non-need-based financial aid, 6% international, 39% 25 or older, 1% Native American, 0% Hispanic, 11% African American, 4% Asian American. *Areas of study chosen:* 28% business management and administrative services, 19% education, 13% computer and information sciences, 9% engineering and applied sciences, 7% agriculture, 4% social sciences, 3% fine arts, 1% mathematics. *Most popular recent majors:* business administration/commerce/management, elementary education, biology/biological sciences.
FIRST-YEAR CLASS 151 total; 220 applied, 92% of whom enrolled. 20% from top 10% of their high school class, 30% from top quarter, 50% from top half. 2 valedictorians.
ACADEMIC PROGRAM Core, interdisciplinary curriculum, honor code. Calendar: semesters. Academic remediation for entering students, English as a second language program offered during academic year, services for LD students, advanced placement, summer session for credit, part-time degree program (daytime, evenings, weekends, summer), co-op programs and internships.
GENERAL DEGREE REQUIREMENTS 66 semester hours; math/science requirements vary according to program; computer course for business majors; internship (some majors).
MAJORS Accounting, agricultural business, agricultural sciences, animal sciences, art education, art/fine arts, art history, aviation administration, aviation technology, biblical studies, biology/biological sciences, business administration/commerce/management, business economics, business education, business machine technologies, ceramic art and design, chemistry, computer information systems, computer technologies, criminal justice, dance, early childhood education, education, elementary education, environmental sciences, farm and ranch management, health education, history, horticulture, humanities, insurance, Japanese, journalism, landscape architecture/design, landscaping/grounds maintenance, land use management and reclamation, legal secretarial studies, liberal arts/general studies, mathematics, medical secretarial studies, music, nursing, physical education, piano/organ, range management, science, secretarial studies/office management, social science, social work, sociology, Spanish.
LIBRARY St. Catharine College Library with 22,000 books, 2,500 microform titles, 37 periodicals, 3 on-line bibliographic services, 1 CD-ROM, 3,600 records, tapes, and CDs.
COMPUTERS ON CAMPUS 60 computers for student use in computer center, computer labs, library provide access to main academic computer. Staffed computer lab on campus provides training in use of computers, software.
COLLEGE LIFE Drama-theater group, choral group, student-run newspaper. 40% vote in student government elections. *Social organizations:* 5 social clubs; 20% of eligible men and 30% of eligible women are members. *Most popular organizations:* African-American Club, International Club, Student Government, Phi Theta Kappa. *Major annual events:* Homecoming Weekend, Christmas Dance, Awards Banquet. *Student services:* personal-psychological counseling. *Campus security:* 24-hour emergency response devices, night security guard.
HOUSING 60 college housing spaces available; 50 were occupied 1995-96. No special consideration for freshman housing applicants. Off-campus living permitted. *Option:* coed housing available. Resident assistants live in dorms.
ATHLETICS Member NJCAA. *Intercollegiate:* baseball M(s)/W(s), basketball M(s)/W(s), softball W(s). *Intramural:* archery, badminton, golf, tennis, volleyball. *Contact:* Mr. Stan Hardin, Athletic Director, 606-336-5082.
CAREER PLANNING *Services:* resume preparation, career counseling, careers library, job interviews.
AFTER GRADUATION 80% of students completing a degree program in 1994-95 went directly on to further study.
EXPENSES FOR 1995-96 *Application fee:* $15. Comprehensive fee of $7900 includes full-time tuition ($4700), mandatory fees ($100), and college room and board ($3100). Part-time tuition: $150 per semester hour. Part-time mandatory fees per semester range from $55 to $65.

Peterson's Guide to Two-Year Colleges 1997

Kentucky

St. Catharine College (continued)
FINANCIAL AID *College-administered undergrad aid 1995–96:* need-based scholarships, non-need scholarships, low-interest long-term loans from external sources, 27 Federal Work-Study. *Required forms:* CSS Financial Aid PROFILE, state, institutional; accepted: FAFSA. *Priority deadline:* 3/15. *Payment plans:* installment, deferred payment. *Waivers:* full or partial for employees or children of employees and senior citizens.
APPLYING Open admission. *Options:* early entrance, midyear entrance. *Required:* TOEFL for international students. *Required for some:* school transcript, SAT I or ACT. Test scores used for counseling/placement. *Application deadline:* rolling.
APPLYING/TRANSFER *Required:* high school transcript, college transcript. *Required for some:* standardized test scores. *Entrance:* noncompetitive. *Application deadline:* rolling. *Contact:* Mr. Jesse Wheat, Director of Admissions, 606-336-5082 Ext. 216.
CONTACT Mr. Jesse Wheat, Director of Admissions, St. Catharine College, St. Catharine, KY 40061-9499, 606-336-5082 Ext. 216. *Fax:* 606-336-5031.

SOMERSET COMMUNITY COLLEGE
Kentucky—See University of Kentucky, Somerset Community College

SOUTHEAST COMMUNITY COLLEGE
Kentucky—See University of Kentucky, Southeast Community College

SOUTHERN OHIO COLLEGE, NORTHERN KENTUCKY CAMPUS
Fort Mitchell, Kentucky

UG Enrollment: 215	Tuition & Fees: $7740
Application Deadline: rolling	Room & Board: N/Avail

GENERAL Proprietary, 2-year, coed. Part of American Education Centers, Inc. Awards transfer associate degrees. Founded 1927. *Setting:* 5-acre suburban campus with easy access to Cincinnati. *Total enrollment:* 215. *Faculty:* 19 (3 full-time, 16 part-time); student-faculty ratio is 10:1.
ENROLLMENT PROFILE 215 students from 3 states and territories, 1 other country. 48% women, 9% part-time, 98% state residents, 20% transferred in, 42% 25 or older, 0% African American. *Most popular recent majors:* computer science, accounting, medical assistant technologies.
FIRST-YEAR CLASS 36 total; 47 applied, 77% were accepted, 100% of whom enrolled. 5% from top 10% of their high school class, 10% from top quarter, 25% from top half.
ACADEMIC PROGRAM Core, interdisciplinary curriculum, honor code. Calendar: quarters. Average class size 10 in required courses. Academic remediation for entering students, summer session for credit, part-time degree program (daytime, evenings, summer), adult/continuing education programs, internships.
GENERAL DEGREE REQUIREMENTS 102 quarter credits; computer course; internship (some majors).
MAJORS Accounting, business administration/commerce/management, computer science, legal secretarial studies, medical assistant technologies, secretarial studies/office management.
LIBRARY 1,500 books, 50 periodicals.
COMPUTERS ON CAMPUS 50 computers for student use in computer center, labs, library. Staffed computer lab on campus provides training in use of computers, software.
COLLEGE LIFE *Major annual events:* Summer Cook-Out, Chili Cook-Off, Halloween. *Student services:* personal-psychological counseling. *Campus security:* 24-hour emergency response devices, late-night transport-escort service.
HOUSING College housing not available.
CAREER PLANNING *Placement office:* 1 full-time staff. *Director:* Mr. Ed Pangburn, Employment Assistance Director, 606-341-5627. *Services:* resume preparation, resume referral, career counseling, job interviews. Students must register sophomore year.
AFTER GRADUATION 10% of students completing a degree program in 1994–95 went directly on to further study.
EXPENSES FOR 1996-97 *Application fee:* $50. Tuition: $7650 full-time, $150 per quarter hour part-time. Part-time mandatory fees: $90 per year. Full-time mandatory fees: $90.
FINANCIAL AID *College-administered undergrad aid 1995–96:* low-interest long-term loans from external sources (average $1240), 1 Federal Work-Study (averaging $946). *Required forms:* FAFSA. *Priority deadline:* 5/1. *Payment plan:* installment.
APPLYING *Options:* Common Application, early entrance, deferred entrance, midyear entrance. *Required:* school transcript, interview, Assessment and Placement Services for Community Colleges. Test scores used for admission. *Application deadline:* rolling.
APPLYING/TRANSFER *Required:* high school transcript, interview. *Recommended:* college transcript. *Application deadline:* rolling. *Contact:* Ms. Annarose Browning, Dean of Admissions, 606-341-5627.
CONTACT Ms. Annarose Browning, Dean of Admissions, Southern Ohio College, Northern Kentucky Campus, Fort Mitchell, KY 41017-2191, 606-341-5627. *Fax:* 606-341-6483.

UNIVERSITY OF KENTUCKY, ASHLAND COMMUNITY COLLEGE
Ashland, Kentucky

UG Enrollment: 2,560	Tuition & Fees (KY Res): $980
Application Deadline: 8/20	Room & Board: N/Avail

GENERAL State-supported, 2-year, coed. Part of University of Kentucky Community College System. Awards transfer associate, terminal associate degrees. Founded 1937. *Setting:* 47-acre small-town campus. *Total enrollment:* 2,560. *Faculty:* 128 (72 full-time, 11% with terminal degrees, 56 part-time); student-faculty ratio is 22:1. *Notable Alumni:* Burl Osborne, editor and CEO of The Dallas Morning News; Duane Gillam, president of Scurlock Oil Company; Phillip Bruce Leslie, attorney and chairman of ACC advisory board.
ENROLLMENT PROFILE 2,560 students from 15 states and territories. 68% women, 32% men, 42% part-time, 78% state residents, 4% transferred in, 40% have need-based financial aid, 0% international, 44% 25 or older, 0% Native American, 1% African American. *Areas of study chosen:* 11% computer and information sciences, 9% health professions and related sciences, 7% education, 5% business management and administrative services, 5% social sciences, 2% engineering and applied sciences, 2% premed, 1% communications and journalism. *Most popular recent majors:* nursing, business administration/commerce/management, accounting.
FIRST-YEAR CLASS 617 total; 1,783 applied, 100% were accepted, 35% of whom enrolled. 10% from top 10% of their high school class, 30% from top quarter, 65% from top half.
ACADEMIC PROGRAM Core, general studies curriculum, honor code. Calendar: semesters. 368 courses offered in 1995–96. Academic remediation for entering students, services for LD students, advanced placement, honors program, summer session for credit, part-time degree program (daytime, evenings, summer), adult/continuing education programs, co-op programs and internships. Off-campus study at University of Kentucky, other area colleges.
GENERAL DEGREE REQUIREMENTS 60 credit hours; math/science requirements vary according to program; computer course.
MAJORS Accounting, business administration/commerce/management, computer information systems, engineering technology, liberal arts/general studies, management information systems, nursing, real estate, secretarial studies/office management.
LIBRARY 37,658 books, 11,507 microform titles, 353 periodicals, 4 CD-ROMs, 1,717 records, tapes, and CDs. Acquisition spending 1994–95: $33,711.
COMPUTERS ON CAMPUS 150 computers for student use in computer center, computer labs, classrooms, library provide access to main academic computer, e-mail. Staffed computer lab on campus.
COLLEGE LIFE Drama-theater group, choral group, student-run newspaper. *Social organizations:* 11 open to all. *Most popular organizations:* Phi Theta Kappa, Phi Beta Lambda, Kentucky Association of Nursing Students, Baptist Student Union/Students for Christ, Circle K. *Major annual events:* Back to School Barbecue/United Way Fund Raiser, Spring Fling, Red Cross Bloodmobiles. *Student services:* personal-psychological counseling. *Campus security:* 24-hour emergency response devices, electronic surveillance of bookstore and business office.
HOUSING College housing not available.
ATHLETICS *Intramural:* archery, badminton, basketball, bowling, fencing, golf, tennis, volleyball.
CAREER PLANNING *Placement office:* 1 full-time staff. *Director:* Mr. John Schornick, Career Counselor, 606-329-2999 Ext. 611. *Services:* job fairs, resume preparation, career counseling, careers library, job interviews.
AFTER GRADUATION 40% of students completing a degree program in 1994–95 went directly on to further study.
EXPENSES FOR 1995-96 State resident tuition: $980 full-time, $41 per credit hour part-time. Nonresident tuition: $2952 full-time, $123 per credit hour part-time.
FINANCIAL AID *College-administered undergrad aid 1995–96:* need-based scholarships, non-need scholarships (averaging $960), low-interest long-term loans from external sources (averaging $2000), Federal Work-Study, 8 part-time jobs. *Required forms:* institutional, FAFSA; accepted: CSS Financial Aid PROFILE, state. *Priority deadline:* 3/15. *Waivers:* full or partial for employees and children of employees and senior citizens. *Notification:* continuous.
APPLYING Open admission except for nursing program. *Options:* early entrance, deferred entrance, midyear entrance. *Required:* school transcript, TOEFL for international students. *Recommended:* ACT. *Required for some:* 3 years of high school math, Career Planning Program. Test scores used for counseling/placement. *Application deadline:* 8/20.
APPLYING/TRANSFER *Required for some:* 3 years of high school math. *Entrance:* noncompetitive. *Application deadline:* 8/20. *Contact:* Mr. Dan Bailey, Coordinator, 606-329-2999 Ext. 231.
CONTACT Mrs. Willie G. McCullough, Dean of Student Affairs, University of Kentucky, Ashland Community College, Ashland, KY 41101-3683, 606-329-2999 Ext. 290. *Fax:* 606-325-8124. *E-mail:* ccsashsa@ukcc.uky.edu.

UNIVERSITY OF KENTUCKY, ELIZABETHTOWN COMMUNITY COLLEGE
Elizabethtown, Kentucky

UG Enrollment: 3,766	Tuition & Fees (KY Res): $1000
Application Deadline: rolling	Room & Board: N/Avail

GENERAL State-supported, 2-year, coed. Part of University of Kentucky Community College System. Awards transfer associate, terminal associate degrees. Founded 1964. *Setting:* 40-acre small-town campus with easy access to Louisville. *Total enrollment:* 3,766. *Faculty:* 170 (88 full-time, 12% with terminal degrees, 82 part-time).
ENROLLMENT PROFILE 3,766 students. 64% women, 61% part-time, 99% state residents, 5% transferred in, 52% 25 or older, 2% Native American, 2% Hispanic, 11% African American, 2% Asian American. *Most popular recent majors:* liberal arts/general studies, nursing, science.
FIRST-YEAR CLASS 835 total. Of the students who applied, 100% were accepted, 60% of whom enrolled.
ACADEMIC PROGRAM Core, honor code. Calendar: semesters. Academic remediation for entering students, services for LD students, advanced placement, summer session for credit, part-time degree program (daytime, evenings, summer), external degree programs, adult/continuing education programs, co-op programs and internships.
GENERAL DEGREE REQUIREMENTS 60 credits; math/science requirements vary according to program; computer course; internship (some majors).
MAJORS Business administration/commerce/management, computer information systems, dental services, finance/banking, liberal arts/general studies, nursing, quality control technology, real estate, science, secretarial studies/office management.
LIBRARY ECC Media Center with 35,175 books, 240 periodicals, 2,250 records, tapes, and CDs.

COMPUTERS ON CAMPUS 70 computers for student use in computer center provide access to main academic computer. Staffed computer lab on campus provides training in use of computers, software.
COLLEGE LIFE Drama-theater group, choral group, student-run newspaper. *Social organizations:* 18 open to all. *Most popular organizations:* Baptist Student Union, Kentucky Association of Nursing Students. *Major annual events:* Fall Festival, Hanging of the Greens, Social Science Seminar. *Student services:* personal-psychological counseling.
HOUSING College housing not available.
ATHLETICS *Intramural:* basketball, football, soccer, table tennis (Ping-Pong), tennis, volleyball.
CAREER PLANNING *Placement office:* 5 full-time, 2 part-time staff. *Director:* Mr. Jim Brown, Director of Career Connections, 502-769-2371. *Services:* resume preparation, career counseling, careers library.
EXPENSES FOR 1996–97 State resident tuition: $1000 full-time, $42 per credit part-time. Nonresident tuition: $3000 full-time, $126 per credit part-time.
FINANCIAL AID *College-administered undergrad aid 1995–96:* need-based scholarships, non-need scholarships, low-interest long-term loans from external sources, Federal Work-Study. *Required forms:* CSS Financial Aid PROFILE, institutional, FAFSA. *Priority deadline:* 4/15. *Payment plan:* deferred payment. *Waivers:* full or partial for senior citizens.
APPLYING Open admission for state residents. *Option:* early entrance. *Required:* essay, school transcript, TOEFL for international students, ACT ASSET. *Required for some:* ACT. Test scores used for admission and counseling/placement. *Application deadline:* rolling. *Notification:* continuous.
APPLYING/TRANSFER *Required:* college transcript. *Entrance:* minimally difficult. *Application deadline:* rolling. *Notification:* continuous.
CONTACT Miss Sharon Spratt, Student Affairs Officer, University of Kentucky, Elizabethtown Community College, Elizabethtown, KY 42701-3081, 502-769-2371 Ext. 309. *Fax:* 502-769-1632.

UNIVERSITY OF KENTUCKY, HAZARD COMMUNITY COLLEGE
Hazard, Kentucky

UG Enrollment: 1,690	Tuition & Fees (KY Res): $1000
Application Deadline: 12/1	Room & Board: N/Avail

GENERAL State-supported, 2-year, coed. Part of University of Kentucky Community College System. Awards transfer associate degrees. Founded 1968. *Setting:* 34-acre rural campus. *Total enrollment:* 1,690. *Faculty:* 119 (64 full-time, 55 part-time); student-faculty ratio is 17:1.
ENROLLMENT PROFILE 1,690 students from 3 states and territories. 72% women, 28% men, 37% part-time, 99% state residents, 26% transferred in, 0% international, 39% 25 or older, 1% Native American, 0% Hispanic, 1% African American, 0% Asian American. *Most popular recent majors:* nursing, radiological technology, business administration/commerce/management.
FIRST-YEAR CLASS 790 total; 1,196 applied, 100% were accepted, 66% of whom enrolled. 15% from top 10% of their high school class, 50% from top half.
ACADEMIC PROGRAM Core, honor code. Calendar: semesters. Academic remediation for entering students, honors program, summer session for credit, part-time degree program (daytime, evenings, weekends, summer), adult/continuing education programs.
GENERAL DEGREE REQUIREMENTS 60 credit hours; 1 course each in math and science; computer course.
MAJORS Business administration/commerce/management, data processing, forest technology, liberal arts/general studies, medical laboratory technology, nursing, radiological technology, science, secretarial studies/office management, word processing.
LIBRARY 36,350 books, 7,150 microform titles, 150 periodicals, 890 records, tapes, and CDs.
COMPUTERS ON CAMPUS 18 computers for student use in learning resource center, library.
COLLEGE LIFE Drama-theater group, choral group. *Student services:* personal-psychological counseling. *Campus security:* late-night transport-escort service.
HOUSING College housing not available.
ATHLETICS *Intramural:* basketball.
CAREER PLANNING *Service:* career counseling.
EXPENSES FOR 1996–97 State resident tuition: $1000 full-time, $42 per credit hour part-time. Nonresident tuition: $3000 full-time, $125 per credit hour part-time.
FINANCIAL AID *College-administered undergrad aid 1995–96:* need-based scholarships, non-need scholarships, low-interest long-term loans from external sources, Federal Work-Study, part-time jobs. *Required forms:* CSS Financial Aid PROFILE, institutional, FAFSA. *Priority deadline:* 4/1.
APPLYING Open admission for state residents. *Option:* early entrance. *Required:* school transcript, ACT, TOEFL for international students. Test scores used for counseling/placement. *Application deadline:* 12/1. *Notification:* continuous.
APPLYING/TRANSFER *Required:* college transcript. *Application deadline:* 12/1. *Notification:* continuous.
CONTACT Mr. Virgil Lykins, Director of Admissions, University of Kentucky, Hazard Community College, 1 Community College Drive, Hazard, KY 41701-2403, 606-436-5721 Ext. 377.

UNIVERSITY OF KENTUCKY, HENDERSON COMMUNITY COLLEGE
Henderson, Kentucky

UG Enrollment: 1,396	Tuition & Fees (KY Res): $980
Application Deadline: 9/1	Room & Board: N/Avail

GENERAL State-supported, 2-year, coed. Part of University of Kentucky Community College System. Awards transfer associate, terminal associate degrees. Founded 1963. *Setting:* 120-acre small-town campus. *Total enrollment:* 1,396. *Faculty:* 96 (44 full-time, 1% with terminal degrees, 52 part-time).

ENROLLMENT PROFILE 1,396 students from 3 states and territories. 69% women, 54% part-time, 94% state residents, 12% transferred in, 0% international, 34% 25 or older, 1% Native American, 5% African American. *Areas of study chosen:* 6% education, 3% engineering and applied sciences, 1% agriculture, 1% architecture, 1% communications and journalism, 1% premed.
FIRST-YEAR CLASS Of the students who applied, 100% were accepted.
ACADEMIC PROGRAM Core. Calendar: semesters. Academic remediation for entering students, summer session for credit, part-time degree program (daytime), adult/continuing education programs, co-op programs and internships.
GENERAL DEGREE REQUIREMENTS 60 credits; math/science requirements vary according to program; computer course; internship (some majors).
MAJORS Business administration/commerce/management, communication, data processing, electrical engineering technology, engineering technology, human services, medical technology, nursing, secretarial studies/office management.
LIBRARY Hartfield Learning Resource Center plus 1 other, with 19,000 books, 300 periodicals, 1,000 records, tapes, and CDs.
COMPUTERS ON CAMPUS 200 computers for student use in computer labs, library.
COLLEGE LIFE Drama-theater group, student-run radio station. *Student services:* personal-psychological counseling. *Campus security:* 24-hour emergency response devices.
HOUSING College housing not available.
ATHLETICS *Intramural:* basketball, football, softball, table tennis (Ping-Pong).
CAREER PLANNING *Placement office:* 1 full-time staff. *Director:* Ms. Teresa Hamilton, Career Planning and Placement Coordinator, 502-827-1867. *Services:* resume preparation, resume referral, career counseling, careers library, job bank, job interviews.
EXPENSES FOR 1995–96 State resident tuition: $980 full-time, $41 per credit hour part-time. Nonresident tuition: $2940 full-time, $123 per credit hour part-time.
FINANCIAL AID *College-administered undergrad aid 1995–96:* 15 need-based scholarships (average $430), 75 non-need scholarships (average $430), short-term loans (average $200), Federal Work-Study, 10 part-time jobs. *Required forms:* CSS Financial Aid PROFILE, institutional. *Application deadline:* 3/15.
APPLYING Open admission. *Required:* 3 years of high school math, ACT, TOEFL for international students, ACT COMPASS. Test scores used for admission and counseling/placement. *Application deadline:* 9/1.
APPLYING/TRANSFER *Required:* standardized test scores. *Required for some:* 3 years of high school math. *Entrance:* noncompetitive. *Application deadline:* 9/1.
CONTACT Ms. Patty Mitchell, Dean of Student Affairs, University of Kentucky, Henderson Community College, Henderson, KY 42420-4623, 502-827-1867 Ext. 256.

UNIVERSITY OF KENTUCKY, HOPKINSVILLE COMMUNITY COLLEGE
Hopkinsville, Kentucky

UG Enrollment: 2,898	Tuition & Fees (KY Res): $1092
Application Deadline: rolling	Room & Board: N/Avail

GENERAL State-supported, 2-year, coed. Part of University of Kentucky Community College System. Awards transfer associate, terminal associate degrees. Founded 1965. *Setting:* 70-acre small-town campus with easy access to Nashville. *Total enrollment:* 2,898. *Faculty:* 158 (48 full-time, 110 part-time); student-faculty ratio is 18:1.
ENROLLMENT PROFILE 2,898 students from 11 states and territories, 3 other countries. 52% women, 48% men, 75% part-time, 96% state residents, 11% transferred in, 60% have need-based financial aid, 4% have non-need-based financial aid, 51% 25 or older, 2% Native American, 4% Hispanic, 20% African American, 2% Asian American. *Areas of study chosen:* 25% health professions and related sciences, 15% business management and administrative services, 12% education, 5% social sciences, 4% biological and life sciences, 4% interdisciplinary studies, 4% psychology, 3% communications and journalism, 3% computer and information sciences, 3% English language/literature/letters, 3% liberal arts/general studies, 2% fine arts, 2% foreign language and literature, 2% predentistry, 2% prelaw, 2% premed, 1% agriculture, 1% architecture, 1% area and ethnic studies, 1% library and information studies, 1% mathematics, 1% natural resource sciences, 1% performing arts, 1% philosophy, 1% physical sciences, 1% prevet. *Most popular recent major:* nursing.
FIRST-YEAR CLASS 647 total. Of the students who applied, 100% were accepted, 75% of whom enrolled. 3% from top 10% of their high school class, 20% from top quarter, 75% from top half. 2 class presidents, 3 valedictorians.
ACADEMIC PROGRAM Core. Calendar: semesters. Academic remediation for entering students, advanced placement, honors program, summer session for credit, part-time degree program (daytime, evenings), adult/continuing education programs.
GENERAL DEGREE REQUIREMENTS 60 credit hours; 3 credit hours each of math and science; computer course (varies by major).
MAJORS Business administration/commerce/management, early childhood education, electrical and electronics technologies, finance/banking, human services, industrial engineering technology, law enforcement/police sciences, liberal arts/general studies, management information systems, mental health/rehabilitation counseling, nursing, science, secretarial studies/office management.
LIBRARY 43,542 books, 2,156 microform titles, 232 periodicals, 5,624 records, tapes, and CDs.
COMPUTERS ON CAMPUS 110 computers for student use in labs, library. Staffed computer lab on campus provides training in use of computers.
COLLEGE LIFE Student-run newspaper. *Social organizations:* 12 open to all; 1 local fraternity; 2% of eligible men are members. *Most popular organizations:* Baptist Student Union, Circle K, Minority Student Union, Donovan Scholars. *Major annual events:* Fun Day, Appreciation Day. *Campus security:* late-night transport-escort service.
HOUSING College housing not available.
ATHLETICS *Intramural:* basketball, football, table tennis (Ping-Pong), volleyball.
CAREER PLANNING *Placement office:* 2 full-time staff. *Director:* Ms. Kay Lancaster, Coordinator for Counseling Services, 502-886-3921. *Services:* job fairs, resume preparation, resume referral, career counseling, careers library, job interviews. 25 organizations recruited on campus 1994–95.
EXPENSES FOR 1996–97 State resident tuition: $1000 full-time, $42 per credit hour part-time. Nonresident tuition: $3000 full-time, $125 per credit hour part-time. Part-time mandatory fees per semester range from $10 to $46. Full-time mandatory fees: $92.

Kentucky

University of Kentucky, Hopkinsville Community College (continued)
FINANCIAL AID *College-administered undergrad aid 1995–96:* need-based scholarships, 50 non-need scholarships (average $150), low-interest long-term loans from external sources, Federal Work-Study. *Required forms:* CSS Financial Aid PROFILE; required for some: institutional, FAFSA. *Priority deadline:* 6/15. *Waivers:* full or partial for employees or children of employees and senior citizens.
APPLYING Open admission except for nursing program. *Options:* Common Application, early entrance, deferred entrance. *Required:* ACT, TOEFL for international students. Test scores used for counseling/placement. *Application deadline:* rolling. *Notification:* continuous.
APPLYING/TRANSFER *Required:* standardized test scores. *Entrance:* noncompetitive. *Application deadline:* rolling. *Notification:* continuous. *Contact:* Ms. Kay Lancaster, Coordinator of Counseling Services, 502-886-3921.
CONTACT Ms. Ruth Ann Rettie, Registrar, University of Kentucky, Hopkinsville Community College, Hopkinsville, KY 42241-2100, 502-886-3921. *E-mail:* ccshopsa@ukcc.uky.edu.

UNIVERSITY OF KENTUCKY, JEFFERSON COMMUNITY COLLEGE
Louisville, Kentucky

UG Enrollment: 9,273	Tuition & Fees (KY Res): $984
Application Deadline: rolling	Room & Board: N/Avail

GENERAL State-supported, 2-year, coed. Part of University of Kentucky Community College System. Awards transfer associate, terminal associate degrees. Founded 1968. *Setting:* 10-acre urban campus. *Total enrollment:* 9,273. *Faculty:* 490 (240 full-time, 25% with terminal degrees, 250 part-time).
ENROLLMENT PROFILE 9,273 students: 64% women, 71% part-time, 99% state residents, 6% transferred in, 54% 25 or older, 1% Native American, 2% Hispanic, 21% African American, 2% Asian American.
FIRST-YEAR CLASS 5,033 total. Of the students who applied, 100% were accepted, 50% of whom enrolled. 5% from top 10% of their high school class, 20% from top quarter, 60% from top half.
ACADEMIC PROGRAM Core, honor code. Calendar: semesters. Academic remediation for entering students, services for LD students, honors program, summer session for credit, part-time degree program (daytime, evenings, summer), adult/continuing education programs, co-op programs. Off-campus study at members of the Kentuckiana Metroversity. ROTC: Army (c).
GENERAL DEGREE REQUIREMENTS 62 credits; 1 course each in math and natural science; computer course.
MAJORS Accounting, applied mathematics, art education, art/fine arts, automotive technologies, biology/biological sciences, business administration/commerce/management, business education, chemical engineering technology, chemistry, child care/child and family studies, civil engineering technology, commercial art, communication, computer programming, computer science, culinary arts, data processing, early childhood education, economics, education, electrical engineering technology, elementary education, English, fire science, forestry, French, geography, history, home economics, home economics education, horticulture, liberal arts/general studies, mathematics, mechanical engineering technology, mental health/rehabilitation counseling, music education, nursing, philosophy, physical therapy, political science/government, real estate, respiratory therapy, social work, sociology, Spanish, statistics, zoology.
LIBRARY 47,889 books, 1,576 microform titles, 495 periodicals, 1,113 records, tapes, and CDs.
COMPUTERS ON CAMPUS 100 computers for student use in labs. Staffed computer lab on campus provides training in use of computers, software.
COLLEGE LIFE Drama-theater group, student-run newspaper. *Student services:* personal-psychological counseling. *Campus security:* 24-hour emergency response devices and patrols, late-night transport-escort service.
HOUSING College housing not available.
CAREER PLANNING *Service:* career counseling.
EXPENSES FOR 1995–96 State resident tuition: $984 full-time, $41 per credit hour part-time. Nonresident tuition: $2952 full-time, $123 per credit hour part-time.
FINANCIAL AID *College-administered undergrad aid 1995–96:* need-based scholarships, 174 non-need scholarships (average $100), low-interest long-term loans from external sources (average $663), Federal Work-Study, 20 part-time jobs. *Required forms:* CSS Financial Aid PROFILE, state, institutional, FAFSA. *Priority deadline:* 6/15.
APPLYING Open admission. *Option:* early entrance. *Required:* ACT, TOEFL for international students. Test scores used for counseling/placement. *Application deadline:* rolling. *Notification:* continuous.
APPLYING/TRANSFER *Required:* standardized test scores. *Entrance:* noncompetitive. *Application deadline:* rolling. *Notification:* continuous.
CONTACT Mr. Ronald Walford, Admissions Officer/Registrar, Downtown Campus, University of Kentucky, Jefferson Community College, 109 East Broadway, Louisville, KY 40202-2005, 502-584-0181 Ext. 2148.

UNIVERSITY OF KENTUCKY, LEXINGTON COMMUNITY COLLEGE
Lexington, Kentucky

UG Enrollment: 5,225	Tuition & Fees (KY Res): $1954
Application Deadline: 8/12	Room & Board: N/Avail

GENERAL State-supported, 2-year, coed. Part of University of Kentucky Community College System. Awards transfer associate, terminal associate degrees. Founded 1965. *Setting:* 10-acre urban campus. *Total enrollment:* 5,225. *Faculty:* 302 (132 full-time, 170 part-time); student-faculty ratio is 19:1.
ENROLLMENT PROFILE 5,225 students from 28 states and territories, 5 other countries. 58% women, 44% part-time, 99% state residents, 39% transferred in, 39% 25 or older, 1% Native American, 1% Hispanic, 6% African American. *Most popular recent majors:* nursing, liberal arts/general studies.
FIRST-YEAR CLASS 1,288 total. Of the students who applied, 100% were accepted.
ACADEMIC PROGRAM Core. Calendar: semesters. Academic remediation for entering students, services for LD students, advanced placement, summer session for credit, part-time degree program (daytime), adult/continuing education programs, co-op programs. ROTC: Army (c), Air Force (c).
GENERAL DEGREE REQUIREMENTS 60 credits hours; math/science requirements vary according to program; computer course.
MAJORS Accounting, architectural technologies, business administration/commerce/management, computer information systems, dental services, electrical engineering technology, liberal arts/general studies, mechanical engineering technology, nuclear medical technology, nursing, radiological technology, real estate, respiratory therapy, secretarial studies/office management.
LIBRARY 20,000 books, 52 microform titles, 180 periodicals, 800 records, tapes, and CDs.
COMPUTERS ON CAMPUS 80 computers for student use in computer center, library. Staffed computer lab on campus provides training in use of computers, software.
COLLEGE LIFE Choral group. *Student services:* health clinic, personal-psychological counseling.
HOUSING College housing not available.
ATHLETICS *Intramural:* basketball, football, golf, racquetball, soccer, swimming and diving, tennis, track and field, volleyball, water polo, wrestling.
CAREER PLANNING *Placement office:* 2 full-time staff. *Director:* Ms. Judy Johnson, Student Employment Services Coordinator, 606-257-4735. *Services:* career counseling, careers library, job interviews.
EXPENSES FOR 1995–96 State resident tuition: $1954 full-time, $74 per credit hour part-time. Nonresident tuition: $5194 full-time, $209 per credit hour part-time.
FINANCIAL AID *College-administered undergrad aid 1995–96:* need-based scholarships, 10 non-need scholarships (average $905), short-term loans (average $100), low-interest long-term loans from external sources (average $1000), Federal Work-Study, 9 part-time jobs. *Required forms:* CSS Financial Aid PROFILE, institutional. *Priority deadline:* 4/15. *Waivers:* full or partial for employees or children of employees and senior citizens.
APPLYING Open admission except for health technology programs. *Option:* early entrance. *Required:* ACT, TOEFL for international students. *Recommended:* 3 years of high school math and science. Test scores used for counseling/placement. *Application deadline:* 8/12. Preference given to state residents.
APPLYING/TRANSFER *Application deadline:* 8/12.
CONTACT Mrs. Shelbie Hugle, Coordinator of Admission Services, University of Kentucky, Lexington Community College, 203 Oswald Building, Cooper Drive, Lexington, KY 40506-0235, 606-257-4872.

UNIVERSITY OF KENTUCKY, MADISONVILLE COMMUNITY COLLEGE
Madisonville, Kentucky

UG Enrollment: 2,533	Tuition & Fees (KY Res): $1000
Application Deadline: rolling	Room & Board: N/Avail

GENERAL State-supported, 2-year, coed. Part of University of Kentucky Community College System. Awards transfer associate, terminal associate degrees. Founded 1968. *Setting:* 150-acre small-town campus. *Total enrollment:* 2,533. *Faculty:* 167 (68 full-time, 99 part-time); student-faculty ratio is 18:1.
ENROLLMENT PROFILE 2,533 students: 70% women, 60% part-time, 100% state residents, 13% transferred in, 0% international, 0% Native American, 5% African American. *Most popular recent majors:* nursing, business administration/commerce/management.
FIRST-YEAR CLASS 1,127 total. Of the students who applied, 100% were accepted.
ACADEMIC PROGRAM Core. Calendar: semesters. Academic remediation for entering students, advanced placement, summer session for credit, part-time degree program (daytime, evenings, summer), adult/continuing education programs, co-op programs.
GENERAL DEGREE REQUIREMENTS 60 credits; math/science requirements vary according to program; computer course.
MAJORS Accounting, biomedical technologies, business administration/commerce/management, computer information systems, electrical engineering technology, environmental engineering technology, mechanical engineering technology, medical laboratory technology, mining technology, nursing, optical technologies, radiological technology, real estate, respiratory therapy, retail management, secretarial studies/office management.
LIBRARY 24,000 books.
COMPUTERS ON CAMPUS 35 computers for student use in computer labs.
COLLEGE LIFE Drama-theater group. 30% vote in student government elections. *Student services:* personal-psychological counseling. *Campus security:* evening patrols.
HOUSING College housing not available.
ATHLETICS *Intramural:* basketball, bowling, golf, tennis, volleyball.
CAREER PLANNING *Director:* Ms. Paula Pendergraff, Counselor, 502-821-2250 Ext. 2181. *Services:* job fairs, resume preparation, career counseling, careers library.
EXPENSES FOR 1996–97 State resident tuition: $1000 full-time, $42 per credit hour part-time. Nonresident tuition: $3000 full-time, $126 per credit hour part-time.
FINANCIAL AID *College-administered undergrad aid 1995–96:* need-based scholarships, short-term loans, low-interest long-term loans, Federal Work-Study, part-time jobs. *Required forms:* CSS Financial Aid PROFILE, institutional, FAFSA. *Priority deadline:* 4/1. *Waivers:* full or partial for employees or children of employees and senior citizens.
APPLYING Open admission. *Options:* early entrance, deferred entrance. *Required:* ACT, TOEFL for international students. *Required for some:* ACT ASSET. Test scores used for counseling/placement. *Application deadline:* rolling. *Notification:* continuous.
APPLYING/TRANSFER *Required:* standardized test scores. *Application deadline:* rolling. *Notification:* continuous.
CONTACT Mr. Bob Renn, Admissions Officer, University of Kentucky, Madisonville Community College, Madisonville, KY 42431-9185, 502-821-2250 Ext. 114.

UNIVERSITY OF KENTUCKY, MAYSVILLE COMMUNITY COLLEGE
Maysville, Kentucky

UG Enrollment: 1,409	Tuition & Fees (KY Res): $1000
Application Deadline: rolling	Room & Board: N/Avail

GENERAL State-supported, 2-year, coed. Part of University of Kentucky Community College System. Awards transfer associate, terminal associate degrees. Founded 1967. *Setting:* 120-acre rural campus. *Educational spending 1994–95:* $1220 per undergrad. *Total enrollment:* 1,409. *Faculty:* 111 (37 full-time, 8% with terminal degrees, 74 part-time); student-faculty ratio is 12:1.
ENROLLMENT PROFILE 1,409 students from 2 states and territories. 75% women, 59% part-time, 92% state residents, 8% transferred in, 0% international, 52% 25 or older, 1% Native American, 2% African American, 1% Asian American. *Most popular recent majors:* liberal arts/general studies, nursing, business administration/commerce/management.
FIRST-YEAR CLASS 250 total; 850 applied, 99% were accepted, 30% of whom enrolled. 3 valedictorians.
ACADEMIC PROGRAM Core. Calendar: semesters. 400 courses offered in 1995–96. Academic remediation for entering students, services for LD students, advanced placement, summer session for credit, part-time degree program (daytime, evenings, summer), adult/continuing education programs, co-op programs and internships. Off-campus study at Northern Kentucky University.
GENERAL DEGREE REQUIREMENTS 60 credit hours; math/science requirements vary according to program; internship (some majors).
MAJORS Business administration/commerce/management, dental services, electrical engineering technology, liberal arts/general studies, nursing, retail management, secretarial studies/office management.
LIBRARY 30,398 books, 4,571 microform titles, 288 periodicals, 732 records, tapes, and CDs. Acquisition spending 1994–95: $33,144.
COMPUTERS ON CAMPUS 37 computers for student use in computer center, special math lab provide access to on-line services. Staffed computer lab on campus provides training in use of computers, software. Academic computing expenditure 1994–95: $34,409.
COLLEGE LIFE Choral group, student-run newspaper. 40% vote in student government elections. *Social organizations:* 4 eating clubs; 3% of eligible men and 15% of eligible women are members. *Most popular organizations:* Nursing Students Association, Math and Science Club. *Student services:* personal-psychological counseling.
HOUSING College housing not available.
CAREER PLANNING *Placement office:* 1 full-time staff. *Director:* Mr. John Lott, Counselor, 606-759-7141. *Services:* resume preparation, resume referral, career counseling, careers library, job bank, job interviews.
AFTER GRADUATION 90% of class of 1994 had job offers within 6 months. 42% of students completing a degree program went directly on to further study.
EXPENSES FOR 1996–97 State resident tuition: $1000 full-time, $42 per credit hour part-time. Nonresident tuition: $3000 full-time, $125 per credit hour part-time.
FINANCIAL AID *College-administered undergrad aid 1995–96:* 75 need-based scholarships (average $600), 15 non-need scholarships (average $800), low-interest long-term loans from external sources (average $1500), Federal Work-Study, 4 part-time jobs. *Required forms:* institutional, FAFSA. *Priority deadline:* 3/1. *Payment plan:* deferred payment. *Waivers:* full or partial for employees or children of employees and senior citizens. *Notification:* 7/1.
APPLYING Open admission except for nursing, dental hygiene programs. *Option:* early entrance. *Required:* 3 years of high school math and science, TOEFL for international students. *Recommended:* some high school foreign language. *Required for some:* ACT. Test scores used for counseling/placement. *Application deadline:* rolling. *Notification:* continuous.
APPLYING/TRANSFER *Required for some:* 3 years of high school math and science. *Entrance:* noncompetitive. *Application deadline:* rolling. *Notification:* continuous.
CONTACT Mr. John F. Meyers, Registrar and Admissions Officer, University of Kentucky, Maysville Community College, Maysville, KY 41056, 606-759-7141 Ext. 120. *E-mail:* ccsmayrg@ukcc.uky.edu. College video available.

UNIVERSITY OF KENTUCKY, PADUCAH COMMUNITY COLLEGE
Paducah, Kentucky

UG Enrollment: 2,833	Tuition & Fees (KY Res): $1000
Application Deadline: rolling	Room & Board: N/Avail

GENERAL State-supported, 2-year, coed. Part of University of Kentucky Community College System. Awards transfer associate, terminal associate degrees. Founded 1932. *Setting:* 117-acre small-town campus. *Total enrollment:* 2,833. *Faculty:* 143 (72 full-time, 100% with terminal degrees, 71 part-time).
ENROLLMENT PROFILE 2,833 students from 12 states and territories. 66% women, 34% men, 53% part-time, 99% state residents, 1% transferred in, 52% 25 or older, 1% Native American, 1% Hispanic, 4% African American, 1% Asian American. *Most popular recent majors:* nursing, computer information systems, business administration/commerce/management.
FIRST-YEAR CLASS 582 total; 771 applied, 100% were accepted, 75% of whom enrolled.
ACADEMIC PROGRAM Core. Calendar: semesters. Academic remediation for entering students, services for LD students, honors program, summer session for credit, part-time degree program (daytime, evenings, summer), adult/continuing education programs, co-op programs and internships.
GENERAL DEGREE REQUIREMENTS 60 credit hours; math/science requirements vary according to program; computer course; internship (some majors).
MAJORS Accounting, business administration/commerce/management, communication, computer information systems, electrical engineering technology, nursing, physical therapy, radiological technology, real estate, retail management, secretarial studies/office management.
LIBRARY Paducah Community College Library with 33,167 books, 55 microform titles, 155 periodicals, 18 CD-ROMs, 8,090 records, tapes, and CDs. Acquisition spending 1994–95: $60,706.
COMPUTERS ON CAMPUS 160 computers for student use in computer center, computer labs, learning resource center, classrooms, library provide access to Novell network. Staffed computer lab on campus provides training in use of computers, software.
COLLEGE LIFE Drama-theater group, choral group, student-run newspaper, radio station. 10% vote in student government elections. *Social organizations:* local fraternities, local sororities; 6% of eligible men and 5% of eligible women are members. *Student services:* women's center. *Campus security:* 14-hour patrols by trained security personnel.
HOUSING College housing not available.
ATHLETICS *Intramural:* basketball, golf, volleyball. *Contact:* Mr. Tony McClure, Athletic Director, 502-554-9200.
CAREER PLANNING *Service:* career counseling.
EXPENSES FOR 1996–97 State resident tuition: $1000 full-time, $42 per credit hour part-time. Nonresident tuition: $3000 full-time, $125 per credit hour part-time.
FINANCIAL AID *College-administered undergrad aid 1995–96:* 60 need-based scholarships (average $500), 150 non-need scholarships (average $500), low-interest long-term loans from external sources (average $2500), 20 Federal Work-Study (averaging $1400), 50 part-time jobs. *Required forms:* institutional, FAFSA. *Priority deadline:* 4/1. *Payment plan:* deferred payment. *Waivers:* full or partial for employees or children of employees and senior citizens. *Notification:* 7/1.
APPLYING Open admission. *Option:* early entrance. *Required:* TOEFL for international students. *Required for some:* school transcript, ACT. Test scores used for counseling/placement. *Application deadline:* rolling.
APPLYING/TRANSFER *Required for some:* standardized test scores, high school transcript. *Entrance:* noncompetitive. *Application deadline:* rolling. *Contact:* Mr. Jerry Anderson, Admissions Counselor, 502-554-9200 Ext. 113.
CONTACT Mr. Jerry Anderson, Admissions Counselor, University of Kentucky, Paducah Community College, Paducah, KY 42002-7380, 502-554-9200 Ext. 113.

UNIVERSITY OF KENTUCKY, PRESTONSBURG COMMUNITY COLLEGE
Prestonsburg, Kentucky

UG Enrollment: 2,798	Tuition & Fees (KY Res): $1346
Application Deadline: rolling	Room & Board: N/Avail

GENERAL State-supported, 2-year, coed. Part of University of Kentucky Community College System. Awards transfer associate, terminal associate degrees. Founded 1964. *Setting:* 50-acre rural campus. *Total enrollment:* 2,798. *Faculty:* 121 (78 full-time, 31% with terminal degrees, 43 part-time); student-faculty ratio is 28:1.
ENROLLMENT PROFILE 2,798 students from 3 states and territories, 1 other country. 70% women, 37% part-time, 99% state residents, 2% transferred in, 75% have need-based financial aid, 2% have non-need-based financial aid, 1% international, 40% 25 or older, 1% Native American, 1% Hispanic, 1% African American, 1% Asian American. *Areas of study chosen:* 20% education, 19% social sciences, 10% health professions and related sciences, 8% liberal arts/general studies, 5% business management and administrative services, 3% English language/literature/letters, 2% biological and life sciences, 2% computer and information sciences, 2% prelaw, 1% communications and journalism, 1% engineering and applied sciences, 1% fine arts, 1% library and information studies, 1% mathematics, 1% performing arts, 1% predentistry, 1% premed, 1% prevet, 1% psychology. *Most popular recent major:* nursing.
FIRST-YEAR CLASS 624 total; 923 applied, 100% were accepted, 68% of whom enrolled.
ACADEMIC PROGRAM Core, honor code. Calendar: semesters. Academic remediation for entering students, advanced placement, tutorials, summer session for credit, part-time degree program (evenings), adult/continuing education programs, co-op programs.
GENERAL DEGREE REQUIREMENTS 60 credit hours; 3 credit hours of math; 6 credit hours of science; computer course.
MAJORS Accounting, business administration/commerce/management, computer information systems, liberal arts/general studies, nursing, real estate.
LIBRARY Magoffin Learning Resource Center with 33,955 books, 61 microform titles, 308 periodicals, 8 on-line bibliographic services, 4 CD-ROMs, 2,872 records, tapes, and CDs.
COMPUTERS ON CAMPUS Computer purchase plan available. 71 computers for student use in computer labs, classrooms, library provide access to off-campus computing facilities, on-line services, Internet. Staffed computer lab on campus provides training in use of computers, software.
COLLEGE LIFE Orientation program (2 days, no cost). Drama-theater group, choral group, student-run newspaper. 7% vote in student government elections. *Most popular organizations:* Phi Theta Kappa, Baptist Student Union, Student Government Association. *Major annual events:* Mountain Dew Festival, College Day Fair, Disabilities Awareness Day. *Student services:* personal-psychological counseling. *Campus security:* 24-hour emergency response devices.
HOUSING College housing not available.
ATHLETICS *Intramural:* archery, badminton, basketball, bowling, football, softball, table tennis (Ping-Pong), tennis, volleyball.
CAREER PLANNING *Placement office:* 4 full-time staff. *Director:* Ms. Brenda C. Music, Counselor/Acting Dean of Student Affairs, 606-886-3863. *Services:* resume preparation, career counseling, careers library.
AFTER GRADUATION 35% of students completing a degree program in 1994–95 went directly on to further study.
EXPENSES FOR 1995–96 State resident tuition: $1260 full-time, $42 per credit hour part-time. Nonresident tuition: $3750 full-time, $125 per credit hour part-time. Part-time mandatory fees: $4 per credit hour. Full-time mandatory fees: $86.
FINANCIAL AID *College-administered undergrad aid 1995–96:* 50 need-based scholarships (averaging $340), non-need scholarships, short-term loans (averaging $200), low-interest long-term loans from external sources (averaging $2625), Federal Work-Study, 10 part-time jobs. *Required forms:* CSS Financial Aid PROFILE, institutional, FAFSA; required for some: state. *Priority deadline:* 4/1. *Payment plan:* installment. *Waivers:* full or partial for employees or children of employees and senior citizens.
APPLYING Open admission. *Options:* Common Application, early entrance, deferred entrance. *Required:* school transcript, ACT, TOEFL for international students. *Recommended:* 3 years of high school math. Test scores used for counseling/placement. *Application deadline:* rolling.

Kentucky–Louisiana

University of Kentucky, Prestonsburg Community College (continued)
APPLYING/TRANSFER *Required:* standardized test scores, high school transcript, college transcript. *Recommended:* 3 years of high school math. *Entrance:* noncompetitive. *Application deadline:* rolling. *Contact:* Ms. Gia Rae Hall, Admissions Officer/Registrar, 606-886-3863.
CONTACT Ms. Gia Rae Hall, Admissions Officer/Registrar, University of Kentucky, Prestonsburg Community College, Prestonsburg, KY 41653-1815, 606-886-3863. *Fax:* 606-886-6943. *E-mail:* ccsprerg@ukccs.edu. College video available.

UNIVERSITY OF KENTUCKY, SOMERSET COMMUNITY COLLEGE
Somerset, Kentucky

UG Enrollment: 2,647	Tuition & Fees (KY Res): $1080
Application Deadline: 7/29	Room & Board: N/Avail

GENERAL State-supported, 2-year, coed. Part of University of Kentucky Community College System. Awards transfer associate, terminal associate degrees. Founded 1965. *Setting:* 70-acre small-town campus. *Total enrollment:* 2,647. *Faculty:* 153 (55 full-time, 98 part-time); student-faculty ratio is 17:1.
ENROLLMENT PROFILE 2,647 students from 3 states and territories, 2 other countries. 70% women, 45% part-time, 99% state residents, 5% transferred in, 45% 25 or older, 1% Native American, 0% Hispanic, 1% African American, 0% Asian American. *Most popular recent majors:* business administration/commerce/management, nursing.
FIRST-YEAR CLASS 1,600 total; 2,100 applied, 100% were accepted.
ACADEMIC PROGRAM Core. Calendar: semesters. 412 courses offered in 1995–96. Academic remediation for entering students, services for LD students, advanced placement, summer session for credit, part-time degree program (daytime, evenings, summer), adult/continuing education programs, co-op programs and internships.
GENERAL DEGREE REQUIREMENTS 60 credit hours; 1 college algebra course, 2 science courses for associate of arts degree; 1 course each in college algebra and trigonometry, 4 science courses for associate of science degree; computer course.
MAJORS Accounting, business administration/commerce/management, computer information systems, medical laboratory technology, nursing, secretarial studies/office management.
LIBRARY Strunk Learning Resources Center with 43,604 books, 298 microform titles, 281 periodicals, 4 CD-ROMs, 3,606 records, tapes, and CDs.
COMPUTERS ON CAMPUS 175 computers for student use in computer labs, learning resource center, library provide access to main academic computer, e-mail, Internet.
COLLEGE LIFE Drama-theater group, choral group. *Social organizations:* 6 open to all. *Student services:* personal-psychological counseling. *Campus security:* late-night transport-escort service.
HOUSING College housing not available.
ATHLETICS *Intramural:* basketball, football, softball, volleyball.
CAREER PLANNING *Placement office:* 4 full-time, 1 part-time staff. *Director:* Dr. Alvis Brown, Director of Counseling Services, 606-679-8501 Ext. 3334. *Services:* job fairs, resume preparation, resume referral, career counseling, careers library, job interviews.
EXPENSES FOR 1996–97 State resident tuition: $1000 full-time, $42 per credit hour part-time. Nonresident tuition: $3000 full-time, $126 per credit hour part-time. Part-time mandatory fees: $4 per credit hour. Full-time mandatory fees: $80.
FINANCIAL AID *College-administered undergrad aid 1995–96:* 740 need-based scholarships (average $960), 40 non-need scholarships (average $960), low-interest long-term loans from college funds (average $1500), loans from external sources (average $2000), Federal Work-Study, 25 part-time jobs. *Required forms:* institutional, FAFSA. *Priority deadline:* 4/1. *Payment plan:* deferred payment. *Waivers:* full or partial for employees or children of employees and senior citizens. *Notification:* 4/15.
APPLYING Open admission except for nursing, clinical laboratory technology programs. *Option:* early entrance. *Required:* school transcript, ACT, TOEFL for international students. Test scores used for counseling/placement. *Application deadline:* 7/29. *Notification:* continuous.
APPLYING/TRANSFER *Required:* college transcript. *Required for some:* standardized test scores, high school transcript. *Application deadline:* 8/23. *Notification:* continuous. *Contact:* Ms. Tracy Casada, Registrar, 606-679-8501.
CONTACT Mr. Rodney Patton, Dean of Student Affairs, University of Kentucky, Somerset Community College, Somerset, KY 42501-2973, 606-679-8501 Ext. 3213.

UNIVERSITY OF KENTUCKY, SOUTHEAST COMMUNITY COLLEGE
Cumberland, Kentucky

UG Enrollment: 2,466	Tuition & Fees (KY Res): $980
Application Deadline: 8/20	Room & Board: N/Avail

GENERAL State-supported, 2-year, coed. Part of University of Kentucky Community College System. Awards diplomas, transfer associate, terminal associate degrees. Founded 1960. *Setting:* 150-acre small-town campus. *Total enrollment:* 2,466. *Faculty:* 107 (42 full-time, 90% with terminal degrees, 65 part-time); student-faculty ratio is 20:1.
ENROLLMENT PROFILE 2,466 students: 68% women, 35% part-time, 99% state residents, 3% transferred in, 0% international, 30% 25 or older, 0% Native American, 0% Hispanic, 2% African American, 0% Asian American. *Most popular recent majors:* business administration/commerce/management, nursing, liberal arts/general studies.
FIRST-YEAR CLASS 527 total. Of the students who applied, 100% were accepted, 84% of whom enrolled.
ACADEMIC PROGRAM Core. Calendar: semesters. Academic remediation for entering students, advanced placement, tutorials, summer session for credit, part-time degree program (daytime, evenings, summer), adult/continuing education programs, co-op programs and internships.
GENERAL DEGREE REQUIREMENTS 60 credit hours; 1 college algebra course, 6 credit hours of science for associate of arts degree; 2 math courses, 12 credit hours of science for associate of science degree; computer course.
MAJORS Business administration/commerce/management, computer technologies, data processing, liberal arts/general studies, management information systems, mining technology, nursing, secretarial studies/office management.

LIBRARY 25,921 books, 3,087 microform titles, 200 periodicals, 926 records, tapes, and CDs.
COMPUTERS ON CAMPUS Computer purchase plan available. 46 computers for student use in computer center, computer labs.
COLLEGE LIFE 20% vote in student government elections. *Student services:* personal-psychological counseling.
HOUSING College housing not available.
ATHLETICS *Intramural:* basketball, football, table tennis (Ping-Pong), volleyball.
CAREER PLANNING *Services:* resume preparation, career counseling.
AFTER GRADUATION 60% of students completing a degree program in 1994–95 went directly on to further study.
EXPENSES FOR 1995–96 State resident tuition: $980 full-time, $41 per credit hour part-time. Nonresident tuition: $2940 full-time, $123 per credit hour part-time.
FINANCIAL AID *College-administered undergrad aid 1995–96:* need-based scholarships, non-need scholarships, low-interest long-term loans from external sources (average $1000), Federal Work-Study, part-time jobs. *Required forms:* CSS Financial Aid PROFILE, institutional; required for some: state. *Priority deadline:* 4/15. *Waivers:* full or partial for senior citizens.
APPLYING Open admission. *Option:* early entrance. *Required:* school transcript, ACT, TOEFL for international students. Test scores used for counseling/placement. *Application deadline:* 8/20. *Notification:* continuous until 9/3.
APPLYING/TRANSFER *Required:* college transcript. *Entrance:* noncompetitive. *Application deadline:* 8/20. *Notification:* continuous until 9/3. *Contact:* Ms. Diane Fair, Counselor, 606-589-2145 Ext. 2110.
CONTACT Mr. Charles Sellars, Dean of Student Affairs, University of Kentucky, Southeast Community College, Cumberland, KY 40823-1099, 606-589-2145 Ext. 46.

LOUISIANA

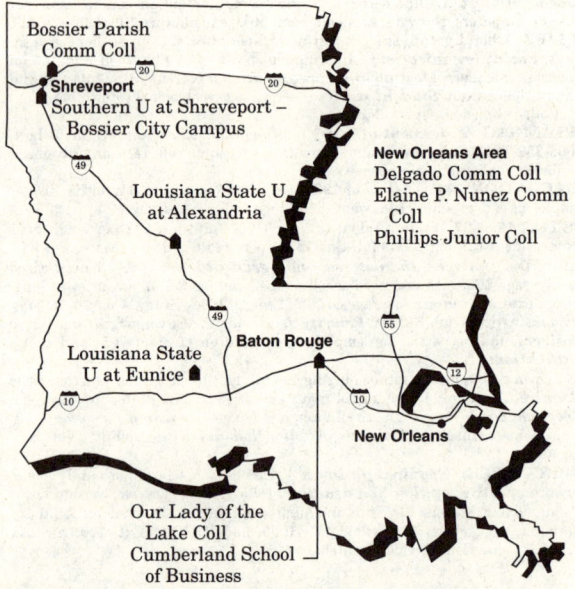

BOSSIER PARISH COMMUNITY COLLEGE
Bossier City, Louisiana

UG Enrollment: 4,687	Tuition & Fees (Area Res): $640
Application Deadline: 8/10	Room & Board: N/Avail

GENERAL State and locally supported, 2-year, coed. Part of Bossier Parish School Board. Awards certificates, transfer associate, terminal associate degrees. Founded 1967. *Setting:* 64-acre urban campus. *Total enrollment:* 4,687. *Faculty:* 134 (79 full-time, 55 part-time); student-faculty ratio is 35:1.
ENROLLMENT PROFILE 4,687 students: 65% women, 50% part-time, 99% state residents, 0% Native American, 1% Hispanic, 22% African American, 1% Asian American. *Areas of study chosen:* 27% interdisciplinary studies.
FIRST-YEAR CLASS 1,135 total. Of the students who applied, 100% were accepted.
ACADEMIC PROGRAM Core, interdisciplinary curriculum. Calendar: semesters. 1,400 courses offered in 1995–96. Academic remediation for entering students, services for LD students, advanced placement, summer session for credit, part-time degree program (daytime, evenings, summer), adult/continuing education programs.
GENERAL DEGREE REQUIREMENTS 66 semester hours; computer course.
MAJORS Business administration/commerce/management, computer information systems, corrections, data processing, drafting and design, electrical and electronics technologies, emergency medical technology, law enforcement/police sciences, liberal arts/general studies, medical assistant technologies, physical therapy, respiratory therapy, secretarial studies/office management, telecommunications.
LIBRARY Bossier Parish Community College Library with 24,800 books, 144 microform titles, 300 periodicals, 481 records, tapes, and CDs. Acquisition spending 1994–95: $94,509.

COMPUTERS ON CAMPUS 77 computers for student use in learning resource center, classrooms. Staffed computer lab on campus provides training in use of computers, software. Academic computing expenditure 1994–95: $2.7 million.
COLLEGE LIFE Drama-theater group, choral group, student-run newspaper. ***Most popular organizations:*** Student Government Association, Cavalier Players Drama Club, Data Processing Management Association. ***Major annual events:*** Basketball Homecoming, Halloween Dance, Doo Dah Parade. ***Student services:*** personal-psychological counseling. ***Campus security:*** student patrols.
HOUSING College housing not available.
ATHLETICS Member NJCAA. ***Intercollegiate:*** baseball M(s), basketball M(s), tennis W(s). ***Intramural:*** badminton, bowling, football, racquetball, softball, table tennis (Ping-Pong), volleyball. ***Contact:*** Mr. Mike McConathy, Athletic Director, 318-746-9851.
CAREER PLANNING ***Placement office:*** 3 full-time staff. ***Director:*** Mrs. Karen Musgrove, Director, Job Placement Office, 318-746-9851. ***Services:*** job fairs, resume preparation, resume referral, career counseling, careers library, job bank, job interviews.
EXPENSES FOR 1995–96 ***Application fee:*** $5. Area resident tuition: $640 full-time. State resident tuition: $712 full-time. Nonresident tuition: $1352 full-time. Part-time tuition per credit hour ranges from $170 to $295 for area residents, $195 to $328 for state residents, $365 to $623 for nonresidents.
FINANCIAL AID ***College-administered undergrad aid 1995–96:*** 100 need-based scholarships, 100 non-need scholarships, low-interest long-term loans from external sources, Federal Work-Study, part-time jobs. ***Required forms for some financial aid applicants:*** state, institutional, FAFSA. ***Priority deadline:*** 6/1. ***Payment plan:*** deferred payment. ***Waivers:*** full or partial for minority students, employees or children of employees, and senior citizens.
APPLYING Open admission. ***Options:*** Common Application, early entrance, midyear entrance. ***Required:*** school transcript, TOEFL for international students. ***Required for some:*** SAT I or ACT. Test scores used for counseling/placement. ***Application deadline:*** 8/10.
APPLYING/TRANSFER ***Required:*** high school transcript, college transcript. ***Entrance:*** noncompetitive. ***Application deadline:*** 8/10.
CONTACT Ms. Ann Jampole, Admissions Officer, Bossier Parish Community College, 2719 Airline Drive North, Bossier City, LA 71111-5801, 318-746-9851 Ext. 15. ***Fax:*** 318-742-8664.

CUMBERLAND SCHOOL OF TECHNOLOGY
Baton Rouge, Louisiana

UG Enrollment: 32	**Tuition & Fees: $4725**
Application Deadline: rolling	**Room & Board: N/Avail**

GENERAL Proprietary, 2-year, coed. Awards transfer associate degrees. Founded 1970. ***Setting:*** 4-acre urban campus. ***Total enrollment:*** 32. ***Faculty:*** 3 (all full-time).
ENROLLMENT PROFILE 32 students: 80% women, 20% men, 100% state residents. ***Areas of study chosen:*** 100% health professions and related sciences.
FIRST-YEAR CLASS 20 total.
ACADEMIC PROGRAM Calendar: quarters. Tutorials, internships.
GENERAL DEGREE REQUIREMENTS 90 quarter hours; 1 math course; computer course for secretarial studies majors.
MAJORS Medical laboratory technology, secretarial studies/office management.
CAREER PLANNING ***Placement office:*** 1 full-time, 2 part-time staff. ***Director:*** Mr. Mike Floyd, Director, 504-338-9085. ***Services:*** resume preparation, resume referral, career counseling, job bank, job interviews.
AFTER GRADUATION 85% of class of 1994 had job offers within 6 months.
EXPENSES FOR 1996–97 ***Application fee:*** $100. Tuition: $105 per quarter hour part-time. One-time mandatory fee: $100. Full-time tuition: $7403 for medical laboratory degree program, $4725 for secretarial studies program.
FINANCIAL AID ***College-administered undergrad aid 1995–96:*** need-based scholarships (average $300), low-interest long-term loans from external sources (average $6625). ***Required forms:*** FAFSA. ***Application deadline:*** continuous.
APPLYING ***Option:*** Common Application. ***Required:*** school transcript, interview. ***Recommended:*** minimum 2.0 GPA, recommendations, Wonderlic aptitude test. ***Application deadline:*** rolling. ***Notification:*** continuous.
APPLYING/TRANSFER ***Required:*** high school transcript, interview, college transcript. ***Recommended:*** standardized test scores, recommendations, minimum 2.0 college GPA, minimum 2.0 high school GPA. ***Application deadline:*** rolling. ***Notification:*** continuous.

DELGADO COMMUNITY COLLEGE
New Orleans, Louisiana

UG Enrollment: 13,937	**Tuition & Fees (LA Res): $1136**
Application Deadline: rolling	**Room & Board: N/Avail**

GENERAL State-supported, 2-year, coed. Awards certificates, transfer associate, terminal associate degrees. Founded 1921. ***Setting:*** 57-acre urban campus. ***Endowment:*** $513,604. ***Research spending 1994–95:*** $91,433. ***Educational spending 1994–95:*** $1100 per undergrad. ***Total enrollment:*** 13,937. ***Faculty:*** 1,015 (435 full-time, 20% with terminal degrees, 580 part-time); student-faculty ratio is 15:1. ***Notable Alumni:*** R. E. "Gus" Payne, author; Greg Sonnier, chef and restaurant owner; C. Maxine Holtry Daniels, civil rights leader; Clyde E. Butler, director of construction for the Aquarium of the Americas; Sylvia Parker, product manager for Angio Dynamics.
ENROLLMENT PROFILE 13,937 students from 36 states and territories, 52 other countries. 63% women, 37% men, 57% part-time, 90% state residents, 8% transferred in, 6% international, 44% 25 or older, 2% Native American, 6% Hispanic, 32% African American, 3% Asian American. ***Areas of study chosen:*** 39% health professions and related sciences, 18% liberal arts/general studies, 12% business management and administrative services, 9% engineering and applied sciences, 4% computer and information sciences, 4% education, 1% fine arts. ***Most popular recent majors:*** nursing, liberal arts/general studies, business administration/commerce/management.
FIRST-YEAR CLASS 1,983 total; 3,553 applied, 100% were accepted, 90% of whom enrolled.
ACADEMIC PROGRAM Core, honor code. Calendar: semesters. 1,255 courses offered in 1995–96; average class size 26 in required courses. Academic remediation for entering students, English as a second language program offered during academic year and summer, services for LD students, self-designed majors, honors program, summer session for credit, part-time degree program (daytime, evenings), co-op programs. Off-campus study at University of New Orleans, Southern University at New Orleans. ROTC: Army (c).
GENERAL DEGREE REQUIREMENTS 66 semester credit hours; 1 course in college algebra.
MAJORS Accounting, aircraft and missile maintenance, architectural technologies, art/fine arts, automotive technologies, biomedical technologies, business administration/commerce/management, carpentry, civil engineering technology, commercial art, computer information systems, computer science, construction management, criminal justice, culinary arts, dental services, dietetics, early childhood education, electrical and electronics technologies, electrical engineering technology, electronics engineering technology, emergency medical technology, engineering (general), engineering technology, fire science, funeral service, industrial arts, industrial design, interior design, liberal arts/general studies, machine and tool technologies, medical records services, music, nuclear medical technology, nursing, occupational therapy, painting/drawing, physical therapy, radiological technology, respiratory therapy, science, secretarial studies/office management, theater arts/drama, welding technology.
LIBRARY Moss Memorial Library with 88,941 books, 871 microform titles, 1,441 periodicals, 7,574 records, tapes, and CDs. Acquisition spending 1994–95: $486,257.
COMPUTERS ON CAMPUS 414 computers for student use in computer labs, learning resource center, library provide access to Internet. Staffed computer lab on campus (open 24 hours a day). Academic computing expenditure 1994–95: $1.4 million.
COLLEGE LIFE Drama-theater group, choral group, student-run newspaper. ***Social organizations:*** 50 open to all. ***Most popular organizations:*** Student Government, Circle K, International Club, Phi Theta Kappa, Lambda Phi Nu. ***Major annual events:*** Homecoming Week, Spring Fest, International Week. ***Student services:*** health clinic, personal-psychological counseling. ***Campus security:*** 24-hour patrols, student patrols.
HOUSING College housing not available.
ATHLETICS Member NJCAA. ***Intercollegiate:*** baseball M(s), basketball M(s). ***Intramural:*** football, soccer, tennis, volleyball. ***Contact:*** Mr. Tommy Smith, Athletic Director, 504-483-4381.
CAREER PLANNING ***Placement office:*** 9 full-time staff; $174,506 operating expenditure 1994–95. ***Director:*** Ms. Anne Alexander, Director of Career and Counseling Center, 504-483-4968. ***Services:*** job fairs, resume preparation, resume referral, career counseling, careers library, job bank, job interviews. 100 organizations recruited on campus 1994–95.
AFTER GRADUATION 37% of class of 1994 had job offers within 6 months.
EXPENSES FOR 1996–97 ***Application fee:*** $15. State resident tuition: $1116 full-time. Nonresident tuition: $2856 full-time. Part-time tuition per semester ranges from $225 to $521 for state residents, $225 to $1311 for nonresidents. Part-time mandatory fees: $10 per semester. Full-time mandatory fees: $20.
FINANCIAL AID ***College-administered undergrad aid 1995–96:*** 884 need-based scholarships (average $636), 148 non-need scholarships (average $698), short-term loans (average $85), low-interest long-term loans from college funds (average $200), loans from external sources (average $1330), Federal Work-Study, 240 part-time jobs. ***Required forms:*** FAFSA; required for some: state, institutional. ***Priority deadline:*** 5/1. ***Payment plan:*** deferred payment. ***Waivers:*** full or partial for children of alumni, employees or children of employees, and senior citizens.
APPLYING Open admission except for allied health, nursing, culinary arts programs. ***Option:*** midyear entrance. ***Required:*** TOEFL for international students. Test scores used for counseling/placement. ***Application deadline:*** rolling.
APPLYING/TRANSFER ***Entrance:*** noncompetitive. ***Application deadline:*** rolling. ***Contact:*** Ms. Anne Alexander, Director of Career and Counseling Center, 504-483-4968.
CONTACT Ms. Janice Bolden, Director of Admissions, Delgado Community College, 501 City Park Avenue, New Orleans, LA 70119-4399, 504-483-4004. College video available.

ELAINE P. NUNEZ COMMUNITY COLLEGE
Chalmette, Louisiana

UG Enrollment: 1,521	**Tuition & Fees (LA Res): $993**
Application Deadline: 8/1	**Room & Board: N/Avail**

GENERAL State-supported, 2-year, coed. Part of University of Louisiana System. Awards certificates, transfer associate, terminal associate degrees. Founded 1992. ***Setting:*** 20-acre suburban campus with easy access to New Orleans. ***Endowment:*** $100,904. ***Educational spending 1994–95:*** $1923 per undergrad. ***Total enrollment:*** 1,521. ***Faculty:*** 103 (46 full-time, 89% with terminal degrees, 57 part-time).
ENROLLMENT PROFILE 1,521 students from 11 states and territories, 8 other countries. 65% women, 35% men, 64% part-time, 98% state residents, 24% transferred in, 50% have need-based financial aid, 7% have non-need-based financial aid, 1% international, 57% 25 or older, 1% Native American, 3% Hispanic, 10% African American, 2% Asian American. ***Areas of study chosen:*** 28% liberal arts/general studies, 14% business management and administrative services, 9% engineering and applied sciences, 8% health professions and related sciences, 4% biological and life sciences, 4% computer and information sciences, 1% natural resource sciences. ***Most popular recent majors:*** liberal arts/general studies, business administration/commerce/management, science.
FIRST-YEAR CLASS 556 total; 569 applied, 100% were accepted, 98% of whom enrolled. 7% from top 10% of their high school class, 12% from top quarter, 40% from top half. 1 National Merit Scholar.
ACADEMIC PROGRAM Core, comprehensive curriculum, honor code. Calendar: semesters. 509 courses offered in 1995–96; average class size 20 in required courses. Academic remediation for entering students, English as a second language program offered during academic year, services for LD students, advanced placement, self-designed majors, Freshman Honors College, summer session for credit, part-time degree program (daytime, evenings, weekends, summer), external degree programs, adult/continuing education programs, co-op programs and internships. Off-campus study at University of New Orleans.
GENERAL DEGREE REQUIREMENTS 66 semester hours; 6 semester hours of college math; 3 semester hours of science; computer course for early childhood education, business administration, accounting, health services, office management, liberal arts majors; internship (some majors).

Peterson's Guide to Two-Year Colleges 1997

345

Elaine P. Nunez Community College (continued)

MAJORS Accounting, business administration/commerce/management, computer information systems, computer science, computer technologies, culinary arts, drafting and design, early childhood education, electronics engineering technology, emergency medical technology, environmental engineering technology, heating/refrigeration/air conditioning, industrial administration, liberal arts/general studies, medical records services, optical technologies, plastics technology, practical nursing, science, secretarial studies/office management.
LIBRARY Nunez Community College Library with 29,423 books, 239 microform titles, 140 periodicals, 6 on-line bibliographic services, 26 CD-ROMs, 998 records, tapes, and CDs. Acquisition spending 1994–95: $66,769.
COMPUTERS ON CAMPUS 87 computers for student use in computer labs, learning resource center, counseling and testing center, library, student center provide access to on-line services. Staffed computer lab on campus provides training in use of computers, software.
COLLEGE LIFE Drama-theater group, choral group, student-run newspaper. 20% vote in student government elections. ***Social organizations:*** 2 open to all; 1 national fraternity, 2 coed fraternities; 5% of eligible men and 6% of eligible women are members. ***Most popular organizations:*** Nunez Environmental Team, Rotoract. ***Major annual events:*** Spring Fling, Fall Fest. ***Student services:*** personal-psychological counseling. ***Campus security:*** 24-hour emergency response devices, late-night transport-escort service.
HOUSING College housing not available.
ATHLETICS ***Intramural:*** basketball, football, softball, volleyball. ***Contact:*** Mr. Jean Faust, Assistant Professor of Health and Physical Education, 504-278-7440 Ext. 241.
CAREER PLANNING ***Placement office:*** 2 full-time staff. ***Director:*** Ms. Marilyn Barefield, Counselor, 504-278-7440 Ext. 210. ***Services:*** resume preparation, career counseling, careers library, job bank. 7 organizations recruited on campus 1994–95.
AFTER GRADUATION 39% of class of 1994 had job offers within 6 months.
EXPENSES FOR 1996–97 ***Application fee:*** $10. State resident tuition: $976 full-time. Nonresident tuition: $3046 full-time. Part-time tuition per semester ranges from $65 to $468 for state residents, $682 to $1418 for nonresidents. Part-time mandatory fees: $17 per year. Full-time mandatory fees: $17.
FINANCIAL AID ***College-administered undergrad aid 1995–96:*** 30 need-based scholarships (average $1000), 20 non-need scholarships (average $1000), 32 Federal Work-Study (averaging $2550), 10 part-time jobs. ***Required forms:*** institutional; required for some: state; accepted: FAFSA. ***Priority deadline:*** 5/1. ***Payment plan:*** deferred payment. ***Waivers:*** full or partial for employees or children of employees and senior citizens. ***Notification:*** 8/1.
APPLYING Open admission. ***Options:*** early entrance, deferred entrance, midyear entrance. ***Recommended:*** minimum 2.0 GPA, ACT. ***Required for some:*** school transcript, recommendations, ACT COMPASS. Test scores used for counseling/placement. ***Application deadline:*** 8/1.
APPLYING/TRANSFER ***Required:*** college transcript. ***Required for some:*** essay, standardized test scores, high school transcript, minimum 2.0 college GPA, minimum 2.0 high school GPA. ***Entrance:*** noncompetitive. ***Application deadline:*** 8/1. ***Contact:*** Ms. Tanis Morse, Director, Recruiting and Admissions, 504-278-7350.
CONTACT Ms. Donna Clark, Registrar, Elaine P. Nunez Community College, Chalmette, LA 70043-1249, 504-278-7350. ***Fax:*** 504-278-7353.

LOUISIANA STATE UNIVERSITY AT ALEXANDRIA
Alexandria, Louisiana

UG Enrollment: 2,546	**Tuition & Fees (LA Res): $1110**
Application Deadline: rolling	**Room & Board: N/Avail**

GENERAL State-supported, 2-year, coed. Part of Louisiana State University System. Awards certificates, transfer associate, terminal associate degrees. Founded 1960. ***Setting:*** 3,114-acre rural campus. ***Total enrollment:*** 2,546. ***Faculty:*** 87 (67 full-time, 35% with terminal degrees, 20 part-time); student-faculty ratio is 30:1.
ENROLLMENT PROFILE 2,546 students: 69% women, 31% men, 58% part-time, 99% state residents, 8% transferred in, 1% international, 49% 25 or older, 1% Native American, 1% Hispanic, 9% African American.
FIRST-YEAR CLASS 554 total; 681 applied, 99% were accepted, 82% of whom enrolled.
ACADEMIC PROGRAM Calendar: semesters. Academic remediation for entering students, advanced placement, summer session for credit, part-time degree program (daytime, evenings, summer), adult/continuing education programs.
GENERAL DEGREE REQUIREMENTS 64 semester hours; 1 college math course or completion of math proficiency test.
MAJORS Business administration/commerce/management, computer science, education, liberal arts/general studies, nursing, science, secretarial studies/office management.
LIBRARY Bolton Library with 123,358 books, 91 microform titles, 940 periodicals, 870 records, tapes, and CDs.
COMPUTERS ON CAMPUS 100 computers for student use in labs, library provide access to Internet. Staffed computer lab on campus provides training in use of computers, software.
COLLEGE LIFE Choral group, student-run newspaper. ***Social organizations:*** 25 open to all. ***Most popular organizations:*** Circle K, Baptist Student Union, Catholic Student Center, Student Government Association, Gamma Beta. ***Student services:*** personal-psychological counseling. ***Campus security:*** 24-hour patrols.
HOUSING College housing not available.
ATHLETICS ***Intramural:*** archery, badminton, basketball, football, golf, tennis, volleyball.
CAREER PLANNING ***Placement office:*** 3 full-time staff. ***Director:*** Ms. Dee Slavant, Director, Counseling Center, 318-473-6545. ***Services:*** job fairs, career counseling, careers library, job interviews.
EXPENSES FOR 1995–96 ***Application fee:*** $20. State resident tuition: $1060 full-time, $40 per semester hour part-time. Nonresident tuition: $2164 full-time, $86 per semester hour part-time. Part-time mandatory fees: $50 per year. Full-time mandatory fees: $50.
FINANCIAL AID ***College-administered undergrad aid 1995–96:*** 79 need-based scholarships (averaging $1160), 110 non-need scholarships (averaging $544), low-interest long-term loans from external sources (averaging $1960), Federal Work-Study, 81 part-time jobs. ***Required forms:*** institutional, FAFSA. ***Priority deadline:*** 6/15. ***Payment plan:*** deferred payment. ***Waivers:*** full or partial for senior citizens.
APPLYING Open admission for state residents. ***Option:*** early entrance. ***Required:*** school transcript, ACT, TOEFL for international students. ***Recommended:*** 3 years of high school math and science, 2 years of high school foreign language. Test scores used for counseling/placement. ***Application deadline:*** rolling. ***Notification:*** continuous.
APPLYING/TRANSFER ***Required:*** college transcript. ***Required for some:*** standardized test scores. ***Entrance:*** minimally difficult. ***Application deadline:*** rolling. ***Notification:*** continuous. ***Contact:*** Mr. Richard Averitt, Registrar, 318-473-6413.
CONTACT Mr. Raymond Boswell, Director of Student Aid and Scholarships, Louisiana State University at Alexandria, Alexandria, LA 71302-9121, 318-473-6423.

LOUISIANA STATE UNIVERSITY AT EUNICE
Eunice, Louisiana

UG Enrollment: 2,861	**Tuition & Fees (LA Res): $1056**
Application Deadline: 8/9	**Room & Board: N/Avail**

GENERAL State-supported, 2-year, coed. Part of Louisiana State University System. Awards certificates, transfer associate, terminal associate degrees. Founded 1967. ***Setting:*** 199-acre small-town campus. ***Total enrollment:*** 2,861. ***Faculty:*** 120 (73 full-time, 47 part-time).
ENROLLMENT PROFILE 2,861 students from 5 states and territories. 67% women, 54% part-time, 99% state residents, 10% transferred in, 50% 25 or older, 1% Native American, 1% Hispanic, 10% African American, 0% Asian American. ***Areas of study chosen:*** 48% health professions and related sciences, 20% liberal arts/general studies, 12% biological and life sciences, 12% business management and administrative services, 7% engineering and applied sciences.
FIRST-YEAR CLASS 744 total; 1,070 applied, 99% were accepted, 70% of whom enrolled.
ACADEMIC PROGRAM Core, honor code. Calendar: semesters. Academic remediation for entering students, services for LD students, summer session for credit, part-time degree program (daytime, evenings, summer), adult/continuing education programs.
GENERAL DEGREE REQUIREMENTS 66 credit hours; math/science requirements vary according to program; computer course for most majors.
MAJORS Business administration/commerce/management, computer programming, criminal justice, fire science, law enforcement/police sciences, liberal arts/general studies, nursing, radiological technology, respiratory therapy, secretarial studies/office management.
LIBRARY Arnold LeDoux Library with 100,000 books, 31,584 microform titles, 253 periodicals, 20 CD-ROMs, 1,088 records, tapes, and CDs. Acquisition spending 1994–95: $248,670.
COMPUTERS ON CAMPUS 135 computers for student use in computer labs, library.
COLLEGE LIFE Student-run newspaper. 50% vote in student government elections. ***Social organizations:*** 14 open to all; 1 local fraternity, 1 local sorority; 3% of eligible men and 3% of eligible women are members. ***Most popular organizations:*** Student Government Association, Drama Club, Criminal Justice Society, Student Nurses Association, Phi Theta Kappa. ***Major annual events:*** Festival of the Arts, Annual Blood Drive, End-of-Semester Bash. ***Student services:*** personal-psychological counseling. ***Campus security:*** 24-hour emergency response devices and patrols.
HOUSING College housing not available.
ATHLETICS ***Intramural:*** basketball, golf, riflery, tennis, volleyball. ***Contact:*** Mr. Dan Harper, Coordinator of Student Activities, 318-457-7311.
CAREER PLANNING ***Services:*** job fairs, resume preparation, career counseling, job interviews.
AFTER GRADUATION 40% of students completing a degree program in 1994–95 went directly on to further study.
EXPENSES FOR 1995–96 State resident tuition: $1056 full-time, $44 per credit hour part-time. Nonresident tuition: $2256 full-time, $94 per credit hour part-time.
FINANCIAL AID ***College-administered undergrad aid 1995–96:*** need-based scholarships, 146 non-need scholarships (average $671), low-interest long-term loans from external sources (average $2600), Federal Work-Study, 80 part-time jobs. ***Required forms:*** institutional, FAFSA, nontaxable income verification; accepted: CSS Financial Aid PROFILE, state. ***Priority deadline:*** 7/1. ***Payment plan:*** deferred payment. ***Waivers:*** full or partial for senior citizens.
APPLYING Open admission. ***Options:*** Common Application, early entrance. ***Required:*** school transcript, TOEFL for international students. ***Recommended:*** ACT. ***Required for some:*** ACT. Test scores used for counseling/placement. ***Application deadline:*** 8/9.
APPLYING/TRANSFER ***Required:*** college transcript. ***Entrance:*** noncompetitive. ***Application deadline:*** 8/9. ***Contact:*** Mr. Dennis Hicks, Registrar/Director of Admissions, 318-457-7311 Ext. 303.
CONTACT Ms. Gracie Guillory, Director of Financial Aid, Louisiana State University at Eunice, Eunice, LA 70535-1129, 318-457-7311 Ext. 282.

OUR LADY OF THE LAKE COLLEGE
Baton Rouge, Louisiana

UG Enrollment: 768	**Tuition & Fees: $3675**
Application Deadline: rolling	**Room & Board: N/Avail**

GENERAL Independent Roman Catholic, 2-year, coed. Awards certificates, transfer associate, terminal associate degrees. Founded 1990. ***Setting:*** 5-acre suburban campus with easy access to New Orleans. ***Educational spending 1994–95:*** $3025 per undergrad. ***Total enrollment:*** 768. ***Faculty:*** 668 (265 full-time, 18% with terminal degrees, 403 part-time).
ENROLLMENT PROFILE 768 students: 83% women, 17% men, 65% part-time, 100% state residents, 10% have need-based financial aid, 10% have non-need-based financial aid, 65% 25 or older, 1% Native American, 1% Hispanic, 9% African American, 1% Asian American. ***Areas of study chosen:*** 100% health professions and related sciences.
FIRST-YEAR CLASS 66 total; 82 applied, 100% were accepted, 80% of whom enrolled.
ACADEMIC PROGRAM Core, health science curriculum. Calendar: semesters. 28 courses offered in 1995–96. Academic remediation for entering students, services for LD students, advanced placement, tutorials, summer session for credit.
GENERAL DEGREE REQUIREMENTS 69 credit hours; 1 college algebra course.
MAJORS Emergency medical technology, medical assistant technologies, nursing, operating room technology, radiological technology.

LIBRARY Learning Resources Center with 6,190 books, 272 periodicals, 3 on-line bibliographic services, 2 CD-ROMs, 829 records, tapes, and CDs.
COMPUTERS ON CAMPUS 25 computers for student use in learning resource center provide access to main academic computer, Internet. Staffed computer lab on campus provides training in use of computers, software. Academic computing expenditure 1994–95: $100,000.
COLLEGE LIFE 10% vote in student government elections. *Social organizations:* 2 open to all. *Most popular organizations:* Student Government Association, Cultural Arts Association. *Major annual events:* Welcoming Ceremony, Spring Student Social. *Student services:* health clinic, personal-psychological counseling. *Campus security:* 24-hour patrols.
HOUSING College housing not available.
CAREER PLANNING *Placement office:* 1 full-time staff; $60,000 operating expenditure 1994–95. *Director:* Dr. Mark Viator, Director, Counseling Services, 504-768-1700. *Services:* resume preparation, career counseling, careers library. 10 organizations recruited on campus 1994–95.
AFTER GRADUATION 90% of class of 1994 had job offers within 6 months.
EXPENSES FOR 1996–97 *Application fee:* $25. Tuition: $3600 full-time, $150 per credit hour part-time. Part-time mandatory fees: $50 per year. Full-time mandatory fees: $75.
FINANCIAL AID *College-administered undergrad aid 1995–96:* need-based scholarships, 7 non-need scholarships (average $1000), low-interest long-term loans from external sources. *Required forms:* institutional, FAFSA. *Priority deadline:* 4/1.
APPLYING Open admission except for professional programs. *Options:* Common Application, midyear entrance. *Required:* school transcript, minimum 2.0 GPA. *Required for some:* SAT I or ACT. Test scores used for admission. *Application deadline:* rolling.
APPLYING/TRANSFER *Required:* high school transcript, college transcript, minimum 2.0 college GPA, minimum 2.0 high school GPA. *Required for some:* essay, standardized test scores, recommendations, interview. *Entrance:* noncompetitive. *Application deadline:* rolling.
CONTACT Ms. Theresa Hay, Director of Admissions and Records, Our Lady of the Lake College, Baton Rouge, LA 70808, 504-768-1700 Ext. 1720.

PHILLIPS JUNIOR COLLEGE
New Orleans, Louisiana

GENERAL Proprietary, 2-year, coed. Awards transfer associate, terminal associate degrees. Founded 1970. *Total enrollment:* 300.
EXPENSES FOR 1995–96 *Application fee:* $25. Tuition: $10,848 per degree program. Tuition guaranteed not to increase for student's term of enrollment.
CONTACT Ms. Phyllis Forney, Director of Admissions, Phillips Junior College, New Orleans, LA 70123-3449, 504-734-0123.

SOUTHERN UNIVERSITY AT SHREVEPORT–BOSSIER CITY CAMPUS
Shreveport, Louisiana

UG Enrollment: 1,202	Tuition & Fees (LA Res): $1110
Application Deadline: rolling	Room & Board: N/Avail

GENERAL State-supported, 2-year, coed. Part of Southern University System. Awards transfer associate, terminal associate degrees. Founded 1964. *Setting:* 101-acre urban campus. *Research spending 1994–95:* $119,778. *Total enrollment:* 1,202. *Faculty:* 75 (60 full-time, 15 part-time); student-faculty ratio is 16:1.
ENROLLMENT PROFILE 1,202 students from 6 states and territories, 3 other countries. 71% women, 29% men, 13% part-time, 96% state residents, 24% transferred in, 95% have need-based financial aid, 93% have non-need-based financial aid, 42% 25 or older, 91% African American, 1% Asian American. *Areas of study chosen:* 40% health professions and related sciences, 9% education, 5% business management and administrative services, 3% computer and information sciences. *Most popular recent majors:* medical laboratory technology, respiratory therapy, radiologic technology.
FIRST-YEAR CLASS 440 total; 546 applied, 100% were accepted, 81% of whom enrolled. 10% from top 10% of their high school class, 30% from top quarter.
ACADEMIC PROGRAM Core. Calendar: semesters. Average class size 30 in required courses. Academic remediation for entering students, advanced placement, honors program, summer session for credit, part-time degree program (daytime, evenings, weekends, summer), co-op programs and internships. Off-campus study at Louisiana State University in Shreveport.
GENERAL DEGREE REQUIREMENTS 62 credits; 6 credits of math; computer course; internship (some majors).
MAJORS Accounting, art/fine arts, aviation technology, biology/biological sciences, business administration/commerce/management, chemistry, child care/child and family studies, computer science, early childhood education, electronics engineering technology, English, finance/banking, history, hotel and restaurant management, marketing/retailing/merchandising, mathematics, mechanical engineering technology, medical laboratory technology, medical records services, medical secretarial studies, mental health/rehabilitation counseling, natural sciences, operating room technology, paralegal studies, physics, radiological technology, respiratory therapy, social work, sociology, teacher aide studies, tourism and travel.
LIBRARY Southern University Library with 46,638 books, 24,308 microform titles, 396 periodicals, 2 on-line bibliographic services, 1,700 records, tapes, and CDs. Acquisition spending 1994–95: $33,196.
COMPUTERS ON CAMPUS 38 computers for student use in computer labs, classrooms, library. Staffed computer lab on campus provides training in use of computers, software. Academic computing expenditure 1994–95: $149,752.
COLLEGE LIFE Choral group, student-run newspaper. 12% vote in student government elections. *Social organizations:* 38 open to all. *Most popular organizations:* Afro-American Society, SUSBO Gospel Choir, Student Center Board, Allied Health, Engineering Club. *Major annual events:* Career Day, Homecoming, Crawfish Boil. *Student services:* personal-psychological counseling. *Campus security:* 24-hour patrols.
HOUSING College housing not available.
ATHLETICS Member NJCAA. *Intercollegiate:* basketball M/W. *Intramural:* basketball, football, volleyball. *Contact:* Mr. Roman Banks, Head Coach/Athletic Director, 318-674-3332.

CAREER PLANNING *Placement office:* $49,795 operating expenditure 1994–95. *Director:* Mr. S. Albert Gilliam, Vice Chancellor for Student Affairs, 318-674-3337. *Services:* job fairs, resume preparation, career counseling, careers library, job interviews. 30 organizations recruited on campus 1994–95.
AFTER GRADUATION 25% of students completing a degree program in 1994–95 went directly on to further study.
EXPENSES FOR 1996–97 State resident tuition: $1110 full-time. Nonresident tuition: $2240 full-time. Part-time tuition per semester ranges from $209 to $431 for state residents, $418 to $862 for nonresidents.
FINANCIAL AID *College-administered undergrad aid 1995–96:* need-based scholarships, non-need scholarships, low-interest long-term loans from college funds (average $501), loans from external sources (average $400), Federal Work-Study, 200 part-time jobs. *Required forms:* FAFSA; required for some: state; accepted: CSS Financial Aid PROFILE. *Priority deadline:* 7/15. *Payment plan:* deferred payment. *Waivers:* full or partial for employees or children of employees and senior citizens.
APPLYING Open admission. *Options:* early entrance, midyear entrance. *Required:* school transcript, interview, ACT. Test scores used for counseling/placement. *Application deadline:* rolling. *Notification:* continuous until 8/15.
APPLYING/TRANSFER *Entrance:* noncompetitive. *Application deadline:* rolling. *Notification:* continuous until 8/15.
CONTACT Dr. Anthony Molina, Vice Chancellor for Academic Affairs and Acting Registrar, Southern University at Shreveport–Bossier City Campus, 3050 Martin Luther King Drive, Shreveport, LA 71107, 318-674-3342. *Fax:* 318-674-3489.

MAINE

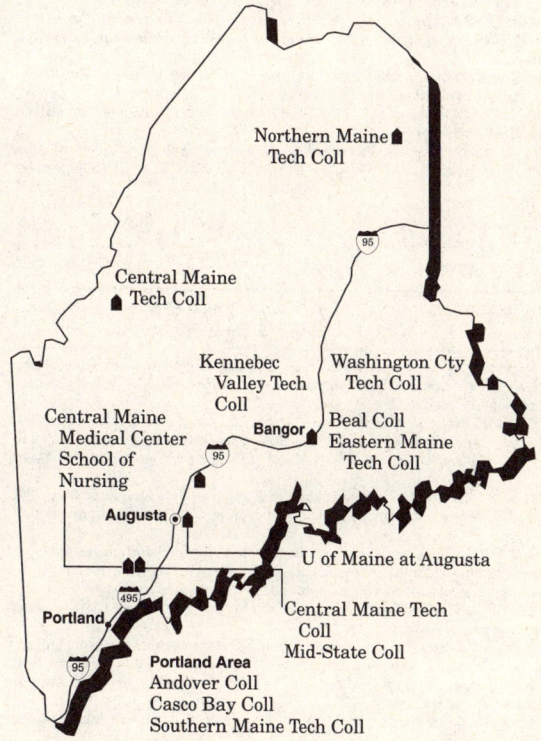

ANDOVER COLLEGE
Portland, Maine

UG Enrollment: 2,158	Tuition & Fees: $5050
Application Deadline: rolling	Room & Board: N/Avail

Four PC labs (Pentium/100 system, Pentium/60 system, 486/66 system, 486/33 system) with WordPerfect for Windows, PageMaker 5.0, Lotus 1-2-3 for Windows, and Microsoft Word. Associate degrees in 16 to 22 months in accounting, business administration, computer science, criminal justice, medical assisting, office management, and paralegal studies. Internships and placement services offered. Placement rate for graduates is 94%.

GENERAL Proprietary, 2-year, coed. Awards certificates, terminal associate degrees. Founded 1966. *Setting:* 2-acre urban campus. *Total enrollment:* 2,158. *Faculty:* 26 (11 full-time, 90% with terminal degrees, 15 part-time).
ENROLLMENT PROFILE 2,158 students from 4 states and territories, 3 other countries. 75% women, 25% men, 4% part-time, 98% state residents, 20% transferred in, 1% international, 60% 25 or older, 1% Native American, 0% Hispanic, 1% African American, 2% Asian American. *Most popular recent majors:* medical assistant technologies, business administration/commerce/management, criminal justice.
FIRST-YEAR CLASS 590 total; 778 applied, 86% were accepted, 88% of whom enrolled. 2% from top 10% of their high school class, 25% from top quarter, 40% from top half.

Andover College (continued)
ACADEMIC PROGRAM Core, honor code. Calendar: modular. 290 courses offered in 1995–96. Academic remediation for entering students, summer session for credit, part-time degree program (daytime, evenings), adult/continuing education programs, internships.
GENERAL DEGREE REQUIREMENTS 60 credit hours; computer course.
MAJORS Accounting, business administration/commerce/management, computer programming, computer science, criminal justice, legal secretarial studies, medical assistant technologies, medical secretarial studies, paralegal studies, secretarial studies/office management.
LIBRARY Andover Library with 6,000 books, 60 periodicals, 25 CD-ROMs, 20 records, tapes, and CDs.
COMPUTERS ON CAMPUS 81 computers for student use in computer center, computer labs, academic/administrative departments, library provide access to main academic computer. Staffed computer lab on campus provides training in use of computers, software.
COLLEGE LIFE ***Social organizations:*** 9 open to all. ***Most popular organizations:*** Student Senate, Andover Computer, Student Advisors Group, Honor Society, C.O.P.S. ***Major annual events:*** Campus Day, Career Day, Awards Banquet. ***Student services:*** personal-psychological counseling. ***Campus security:*** 24-hour emergency response devices.
HOUSING College housing not available.
CAREER PLANNING ***Placement office:*** 2 full-time staff. ***Director:*** Mrs. Charlotte A. Walker, Director of Career Planning and Placement, 207-774-6126. ***Services:*** job fairs, resume preparation, resume referral, career counseling, careers library, job bank, job interviews.
AFTER GRADUATION 3% of students completing a degree program in 1994–95 went directly on to further study.
EXPENSES FOR 1996–97 ***Application fee:*** $25. Tuition: $4400 full-time. Part-time tuition per course: $330 for evening classes, $450 for day classes. Full-time mandatory fees: $650. Tuition guaranteed not to increase for student's term of enrollment.
FINANCIAL AID ***College-administered undergrad aid 1995–96:*** need-based scholarships, 10 non-need scholarships (average $2100), low-interest long-term loans from external sources (average $2425), Federal Work-Study. ***Required forms:*** CSS Financial Aid PROFILE; accepted: FAFSA. ***Application deadline:*** continuous. ***Waivers:*** full or partial for employees or children of employees. ***Notification:*** continuous. ***Average indebtedness of graduates:*** $6125.
APPLYING Open admission. ***Options:*** early entrance, deferred entrance. ***Required:*** school transcript. ***Application deadline:*** rolling.
APPLYING/TRANSFER ***Required:*** college transcript. ***Entrance:*** noncompetitive. ***Application deadline:*** rolling.
CONTACT Mrs. Andrienne Amari, Vice President, Andover College, 901 Washington Avenue, Portland, ME 04103-2791, 207-774-6126 Ext. 36. ***Fax:*** 207-774-1715. College video available.

BEAL COLLEGE
Bangor, Maine

UG Enrollment: 455	**Tuition & Fees: $3865**
Application Deadline: rolling	**Room & Board: N/Avail**

GENERAL Proprietary, 2-year, coed. Awards terminal associate degrees. Founded 1891. ***Setting:*** 4-acre small-town campus. ***Total enrollment:*** 455. ***Faculty:*** 26 (9 full-time, 17 part-time); student-faculty ratio is 20:1.
ENROLLMENT PROFILE 455 students from 3 states and territories, 2 other countries. 89% women, 28% part-time, 98% state residents, 30% transferred in, 1% international, 59% 25 or older, 1% Native American, 0% Hispanic, 1% African American, 1% Asian American.
FIRST-YEAR CLASS 136 total. Of the students who applied, 91% were accepted, 79% of whom enrolled. 7% from top 10% of their high school class, 26% from top quarter, 68% from top half.
ACADEMIC PROGRAM Core. Calendar: modular. Academic remediation for entering students, summer session for credit, part-time degree program (daytime, evenings, summer), adult/continuing education programs, co-op programs and internships.
GENERAL DEGREE REQUIREMENTS 72 credit hours; 1 business math course; computer course; internship (some majors).
MAJORS Accounting, broadcasting, business administration/commerce/management, hospitality services, hotel and restaurant management, legal secretarial studies, medical assistant technologies, medical secretarial studies, paralegal studies, secretarial studies/office management, tourism and travel.
LIBRARY Beal College Library with 5,000 books, 100 periodicals, 1 on-line bibliographic service, 1 CD-ROM, 50 records, tapes, and CDs.
COMPUTERS ON CAMPUS 85 computers for student use in computer center, library provide access to on-line services.
COLLEGE LIFE Student-run newspaper. ***Most popular organizations:*** Sophomore Travel Club, Freshman Travel Club, College Yearbook Committee. ***Major annual events:*** Oktoberfest, Spring Fling, Christmas Buffet.
HOUSING College housing not available.
CAREER PLANNING ***Placement office:*** 2 full-time staff. ***Director:*** Ms. Louise G. Grant, Director of Career Services, 207-947-4951. ***Services:*** resume preparation, resume referral, career counseling, careers library, job bank, job interviews.
AFTER GRADUATION 3% of students completing a degree program in 1994–95 went directly on to further study.
EXPENSES FOR 1996–97 ***Application fee:*** $25. Tuition: $3840 full-time, $320 per course part-time. Part-time mandatory fees: $25 per year. Full-time mandatory fees: $25.
FINANCIAL AID ***College-administered undergrad aid 1995–96:*** 495 need-based scholarships (average $1950), 82 non-need scholarships (average $200), low-interest long-term loans from external sources (average $2625), 1 part-time job. ***Required forms:*** institutional; required for some: CSS Financial Aid PROFILE, FAFSA. ***Priority deadline:*** 7/1. ***Payment plan:*** installment. ***Waivers:*** full or partial for employees or children of employees. ***Notification:*** continuous.
APPLYING Open admission. ***Options:*** deferred entrance, midyear entrance. ***Required:*** school transcript, TOEFL for international students. ***Recommended:*** 3 years of high school math and science, some high school foreign language, campus interview. ***Application deadline:*** rolling.
APPLYING/TRANSFER ***Required:*** high school transcript, college transcript. ***Recommended:*** 3 years of high school math and science, some high school foreign language, campus interview. ***Entrance:*** noncompetitive. ***Application deadline:*** rolling.
CONTACT Ms. Louise G. Grant, Director of Admissions, Beal College, Bangor, ME 04401-6896, 207-947-4591 Ext. 12 or toll-free 800-660-7351 (in-state).

CASCO BAY COLLEGE
Portland, Maine

UG Enrollment: 350	**Tuition & Fees: $5775**
Application Deadline: rolling	**Room Only: $3120**

GENERAL Proprietary, 2-year, coed. Awards certificates, transfer associate, terminal associate degrees. Founded 1863. ***Setting:*** urban campus. ***Total enrollment:*** 350. ***Faculty:*** 28 (8 full-time, 20 part-time); student-faculty ratio is 14:1.
ENROLLMENT PROFILE 350 students from 6 states and territories, 2 other countries. 90% women, 20% part-time, 98% state residents, 1% transferred in, 1% international, 10% 25 or older, 0% Native American, 0% African American. ***Areas of study chosen:*** 100% business management and administrative services. ***Most popular recent majors:*** accounting, business administration/commerce/management, secretarial studies/office management.
FIRST-YEAR CLASS 140 total; 250 applied, 100% were accepted, 68% of whom enrolled. 5% from top 10% of their high school class, 25% from top quarter, 60% from top half.
ACADEMIC PROGRAM Core, honor code. Calendar: semesters (quarters for evening division). Academic remediation for entering students, summer session for credit, part-time degree program (daytime, evenings), adult/continuing education programs, internships.
GENERAL DEGREE REQUIREMENTS 60 credits; computer course; internship (some majors).
MAJORS Accounting, business administration/commerce/management, business education, child care/child and family studies, computer information systems, fashion merchandising, legal secretarial studies, medical secretarial studies, paralegal studies, real estate, secretarial studies/office management, tourism and travel.
LIBRARY Casco Bay College Library with 4,000 books, 85 periodicals.
COMPUTERS ON CAMPUS 60 computers for student use in computer center, library, student center provide access to on-line services.
COLLEGE LIFE Orientation program (2 days, no cost). ***Social organizations:*** 5 open to all. ***Student services:*** personal-psychological counseling. ***Campus security:*** 24-hour emergency response devices and patrols, controlled dormitory access.
HOUSING 60 college housing spaces available; all were occupied 1995–96. Freshmen given priority for college housing. On-campus residence required in freshman year except if living within commuting distance. ***Option:*** coed housing available.
ATHLETICS ***Intramural:*** basketball, cross-country running, golf, gymnastics, racquetball, sailing, skiing (cross-country), skiing (downhill), swimming and diving, tennis, volleyball, weight lifting.
CAREER PLANNING ***Placement office:*** 1 part-time staff. ***Director:*** Ms. Karyl Sylken, Director of the Learning Center, 207-772-0196. ***Services:*** job fairs, resume preparation, resume referral, career counseling, careers library, job bank, job interviews. Students must register freshman year.
AFTER GRADUATION 95% of class of 1994 had job offers within 6 months. 10% of students completing a degree program went directly on to further study.
EXPENSES FOR 1996–97 ***Application fee:*** $25. Tuition: $5700 full-time. Part-time tuition and fees: $190 per credit hour for day students, $350 per course for evening students. Full-time mandatory fees: $75. College room only: $3120.
FINANCIAL AID ***College-administered undergrad aid 1995–96:*** need-based scholarships, 4 non-need scholarships (average $500), short-term loans, low-interest long-term loans from external sources (average $2000), Federal Work-Study, 4 part-time jobs. ***Acceptable forms:*** CSS Financial Aid PROFILE, state, FAFSA. ***Application deadline:*** continuous. ***Payment plans:*** installment, deferred payment. ***Waivers:*** full or partial for employees or children of employees. ***Notification:*** continuous.
APPLYING Open admission. ***Option:*** deferred entrance. ***Application deadline:*** rolling.
APPLYING/TRANSFER ***Entrance:*** noncompetitive. ***Application deadline:*** rolling. ***Contact:*** Dr. Roberta Stearns, Dean, 207-772-0196.
CONTACT Ms. Sandra Glynn, Admissions Assistant, Casco Bay College, 477 Congress Street, Portland, ME 04101-3483, 207-772-0196. ***E-mail:*** cbcollege@aol.com. College video available.

❖ ***See page 716 for a narrative description.*** ❖

CENTRAL MAINE MEDICAL CENTER SCHOOL OF NURSING
Lewiston, Maine

UG Enrollment: 84	**Tuition & Fees: $2709**
Application Deadline: 6/1	**Room Only: $1320**

GENERAL Independent, 2-year, specialized, coed. Awards certificates, terminal associate degrees. Founded 1891. ***Setting:*** urban campus. ***Endowment:*** $83,374. ***Total enrollment:*** 84. ***Faculty:*** 11 (8 full-time, 3 part-time); student-faculty ratio is 8:1.
ENROLLMENT PROFILE 84 students from 2 states and territories. 89% women, 11% men, 12% part-time, 99% state residents, 8% live on campus, 0% transferred in, 0% international, 75% 25 or older, 0% Native American, 2% Hispanic, 0% African American, 0% Asian American. ***Areas of study chosen:*** 100% health professions and related sciences.
FIRST-YEAR CLASS 40 total; 213 applied, 31% were accepted, 60% of whom enrolled. 4% from top 10% of their high school class, 44% from top quarter, 72% from top half.
ACADEMIC PROGRAM Core, integrated curriculum. Calendar: semesters. 5 courses offered in 1995–96. Advanced placement. Off-campus study at University of Maine at Augusta, University of Southern Maine.
GENERAL DEGREE REQUIREMENTS 69 credits; 8 credits of anatomy and physiology, 4 credits of microbiology.
MAJOR Nursing.
LIBRARY Gerrish True Health Sciences Library with 1,700 books, 118 microform titles, 322 periodicals, 4 on-line bibliographic services, 3 CD-ROMs.
COMPUTERS ON CAMPUS 6 computers for student use in computer labs. Staffed computer lab on campus provides training in use of computers, software. Academic computing expenditure 1994–95: $90,266.
COLLEGE LIFE Orientation program (4 days, no cost). ***Social organizations:*** 3 open to all. ***Most popular organizations:*** Student Communication Council, Student Govern-

ment, Student Nurses Association. ***Major annual events:*** Alumni Banquet, President's Breakfast, Alumni Holiday Party. ***Student services:*** health clinic, personal-psychological counseling. ***Campus security:*** 24-hour emergency response devices and patrols, late-night transport-escort service, controlled dormitory access.
HOUSING 16 college housing spaces available; 6 were occupied 1995–96. No special consideration for freshman housing applicants. Off-campus living permitted. ***Option:*** coed (1 building) housing available.
CAREER PLANNING ***Service:*** job fairs.
EXPENSES FOR 1996–97 ***Application fee:*** $20. Tuition: $1974 full-time, $94 per credit part-time. Full-time mandatory fees: $735. College room only: $1320.
FINANCIAL AID ***College-administered undergrad aid 1995–96:*** 51 need-based scholarships (average $1149), non-need scholarships, low-interest long-term loans from college funds (average $1836), loans from external sources (average $3624), part-time jobs. ***Required forms:*** state, institutional, FAFSA, financial aid transcript (for transfers). ***Priority deadline:*** 3/15.
APPLYING ***Option:*** early decision. ***Required:*** essay, school transcript, 2 recommendations, SAT I, TOEFL for international students. ***Recommended:*** 3 years of high school math and science. Test scores used for admission. ***Application deadlines:*** 6/1, 1/1 for early decision. ***Notification:*** 3/15, continuous until 1/31 for early decision.
CONTACT Mrs. Kathleen C. Jacques, Registrar, Central Maine Medical Center School of Nursing, 300 Main Street, Lewiston, ME 04240-0305, 207-795-2858. ***Fax:*** 207-795-2849.

CENTRAL MAINE TECHNICAL COLLEGE
Auburn, Maine

UG Enrollment: 962 | **Tuition & Fees (ME Res): $2070**
Application Deadline: rolling | **Room & Board: $3350**

GENERAL State-supported, 2-year, coed. Part of Maine Technical College System. Awards certificates, diplomas, terminal associate degrees. Founded 1964. ***Setting:*** 110-acre small-town campus. ***Total enrollment:*** 962. ***Faculty:*** 47 (45 full-time, 42% with terminal degrees, 2 part-time); student-faculty ratio is 16:1.
ENROLLMENT PROFILE 962 students from 5 states and territories, 1 other country. 40% women, 40% part-time, 97% state residents, 10% live on campus, 32% 25 or older, 2% Native American, 0% Hispanic, 1% African American, 2% Asian American.
FIRST-YEAR CLASS 350 total; 778 applied, 50% were accepted, 91% of whom enrolled. 10% from top 10% of their high school class, 30% from top quarter, 60% from top half. 1 valedictorian.
ACADEMIC PROGRAM Core, honor code. Calendar: semesters. Academic remediation for entering students, services for LD students, advanced placement, summer session for credit, part-time degree program (daytime), adult/continuing education programs, co-op programs and internships.
GENERAL DEGREE REQUIREMENTS 66 credits; 9 credits of math/science; computer course.
MAJORS Automotive technologies, business administration/commerce/management, civil engineering technology, construction technologies, drafting and design, electromechanical technology, graphic arts, laboratory technologies, machine and tool technologies, mechanical design technology, medical laboratory technology, medical secretarial studies, nursing, occupational safety and health, radiological technology, secretarial studies/office management, welding technology.
LIBRARY Central Maine Technical College Library with 15,000 books, 850 microform titles, 240 periodicals. Acquisition spending 1994–95: $88,172.
COMPUTERS ON CAMPUS 150 computers for student use in computer center, computer labs, learning resource center, classrooms, library provide access to Internet. Staffed computer lab on campus provides training in use of computers, software. Academic computing expenditure 1994–95: $114,683.
COLLEGE LIFE ***Student services:*** health clinic, personal-psychological counseling. ***Campus security:*** 24-hour emergency response devices, controlled dormitory access, police patrols at night.
HOUSING 114 college housing spaces available; all were occupied 1995–96. Freshmen given priority for college housing. Off-campus living permitted. ***Option:*** single-sex (3 buildings) housing available. Resident assistants live in dorms.
ATHLETICS ***Intercollegiate:*** baseball M, basketball M, golf M/W, ice hockey M/W, soccer M/W, volleyball M. ***Intramural:*** bowling, field hockey, ice hockey, skiing (cross-country), skiing (downhill), swimming and diving, tennis, volleyball, weight lifting. ***Contact:*** Mr. Dave Gonyea, Athletic Director, 207-784-2385.
CAREER PLANNING ***Placement office:*** 1 full-time staff; $9345 operating expenditure 1994–95. ***Director:*** Ms. Anitra Crane, Personal and Career Counselor, 207-784-2385. ***Services:*** job fairs, resume preparation, career counseling, careers library, job interviews.
AFTER GRADUATION 84% of class of 1994 had job offers within 6 months.
EXPENSES FOR 1996–97 ***Application fee:*** $20. State resident tuition: $1920 full-time, $64 per credit part-time. Nonresident tuition: $4230 full-time, $141 per credit part-time. Tuition for nonresidents who are eligible for the New England Regional Student Program: $2400 full-time, $80 per credit part-time. Full-time mandatory fees: $150. College room and board: $3350.
FINANCIAL AID ***College-administered undergrad aid 1995–96:*** 200 need-based scholarships (average $400), short-term loans (average $165), low-interest long-term loans from college funds, loans from external sources (average $2370), Federal Work-Study, 50 part-time jobs. ***Required forms:*** institutional, FAFSA. ***Priority deadline:*** 5/1. ***Payment plan:*** installment. ***Waivers:*** full or partial for minority students, employees or children of employees, and senior citizens.
APPLYING ***Options:*** deferred entrance, midyear entrance. ***Required:*** essay, school transcript, SAT I. ***Recommended:*** minimum 2.0 GPA. ***Required for some:*** 3 years of high school math, 2 recommendations, interview, TOEFL for international students, MAPS. Test scores used for counseling/placement. ***Application deadline:*** rolling. ***Notification:*** continuous.
APPLYING/TRANSFER ***Required:*** high school transcript, college transcript. ***Recommended:*** minimum 2.0 college GPA, minimum 2.0 high school GPA. ***Required for some:*** 3 years of high school math. ***Entrance:*** minimally difficult. ***Application deadline:*** rolling. ***Notification:*** continuous. ***Contact:*** Mr. Ronald Bolstridge, Registrar, 207-784-2385 Ext. 246.
CONTACT Mr. Charlie Collins, Director of Admissions, Central Maine Technical College, Auburn, ME 04210-6436, 207-784-2385 Ext. 273. ***Fax:*** 207-777-7353. College video available.

EASTERN MAINE TECHNICAL COLLEGE
Bangor, Maine

UG Enrollment: 750 | **Tuition & Fees (ME Res): $2387**
Application Deadline: rolling | **Room & Board: $3400**

GENERAL State-supported, 2-year, coed. Part of Maine Technical College System. Awards transfer associate, terminal associate degrees. Founded 1966. ***Setting:*** 72-acre small-town campus. ***Total enrollment:*** 750. ***Faculty:*** 134 (54 full-time, 95% with terminal degrees, 80 part-time).
ENROLLMENT PROFILE 750 students from 4 states and territories, 2 other countries. 36% women, 7% part-time, 99% state residents, 30% live on campus, 28% transferred in, 26% 25 or older, 1% Native American.
FIRST-YEAR CLASS 263 total; 980 applied, 70% were accepted, 45% of whom enrolled.
ACADEMIC PROGRAM Honor code. Calendar: semesters. Academic remediation for entering students, advanced placement, summer session for credit, part-time degree program (daytime, evenings), adult/continuing education programs.
GENERAL DEGREE REQUIREMENTS 66 credit hours; 2 courses each in math and science.
MAJORS Automotive technologies, business administration/commerce/management, carpentry, construction technologies, electrical and electronics technologies, electrical engineering technology, electronics engineering technology, food services management, heating/refrigeration/air conditioning, industrial and heavy equipment maintenance, machine and tool technologies, medical laboratory technology, nursing, practical nursing, radiological technology, secretarial studies/office management, welding technology.
LIBRARY Eastern Maine Technical College Library plus 1 other, with 10,160 books, 31 microform titles, 192 periodicals, 7 CD-ROMs, 66 records, tapes, and CDs. Acquisition spending 1994–95: $63,409.
COMPUTERS ON CAMPUS 85 computers for student use in computer labs, learning resource center, labs, classrooms, library, dorms. Staffed computer lab on campus provides training in use of computers. Academic computing expenditure 1994–95: $49,450.
COLLEGE LIFE Orientation program (2 days, $30, parents included). Student-run newspaper. ***Social organizations:*** 12 open to all. ***Most popular organizations:*** Student Senate, Senior Council, Resident's Council, Associated General Contractors Student Chapter, American Welding Society Student Chapter. ***Major annual events:*** Technology Day, Winter Carnival, Harvest Breakfast. ***Student services:*** health clinic, personal-psychological counseling. ***Campus security:*** controlled dormitory access.
HOUSING 200 college housing spaces available; 140 were occupied 1995–96. No special consideration for freshman housing applicants. Off-campus living permitted. ***Option:*** coed housing available. Resident assistants live in dorms.
ATHLETICS ***Intercollegiate:*** basketball M, golf M/W, soccer M/W. ***Intramural:*** badminton, basketball, bowling, ice hockey, skiing (cross-country), skiing (downhill), soccer, table tennis (Ping-Pong), volleyball, weight lifting. ***Contact:*** Ms. Lisa E. Hanscam, Director of Athletics and Recreation, 207-941-4660.
CAREER PLANNING ***Placement office:*** 1 full-time staff. ***Director:*** Ms. Cathryn Marquez, Student Support Services Counselor, 207-941-4656. ***Services:*** job fairs, resume preparation, resume referral, career counseling, careers library, job bank, job interviews.
EXPENSES FOR 1996–97 ***Application fee:*** $15. State resident tuition: $2112 full-time, $64 per credit hour part-time. Nonresident tuition: $4554 full-time, $138 per credit hour part-time. Part-time mandatory fees per semester range from $35 to $137.50. Tuition for nonresidents who are eligible for the New England Regional Student Program: $2610 full-time, $87 per credit hour part-time. Full-time mandatory fees: $275. College room and board: $3400.
FINANCIAL AID ***College-administered undergrad aid 1995–96:*** 100 need-based scholarships (average $200), short-term loans (average $200), low-interest long-term loans from external sources (average $2000), Federal Work-Study, part-time jobs. ***Required forms:*** institutional, FAFSA; accepted: CSS Financial Aid PROFILE. ***Priority deadline:*** 4/1. ***Payment plan:*** installment. ***Waivers:*** full or partial for minority students, employees or children of employees, and senior citizens. ***Notification:*** continuous.
APPLYING ***Required:*** 3 years of high school math, TOEFL for international students. ***Required for some:*** 3 years of high school science, SAT I. Test scores used for admission and counseling/placement. ***Application deadline:*** rolling. ***Notification:*** continuous. Preference given to state residents.
APPLYING/TRANSFER ***Required:*** 3 years of high school math. ***Required for some:*** 3 years of high school science. ***Entrance:*** minimally difficult. ***Contact:*** Ms. Gina Toman, Assistant Academic Dean, 207-941-4600.
CONTACT Ms. Elizabeth Russell, Director of Admissions, Eastern Maine Technical College, Bangor, ME 04401-4206, 207-941-4680. ***Fax:*** 207-941-4608.

KENNEBEC VALLEY TECHNICAL COLLEGE
Fairfield, Maine

UG Enrollment: 701 | **Tuition & Fees (ME Res): $2155**
Application Deadline: rolling | **Room & Board: N/Avail**

GENERAL State-supported, 2-year, coed. Part of Maine Technical College System. Awards diplomas, terminal associate degrees. Founded 1970. ***Setting:*** 58-acre small-town campus. ***Total enrollment:*** 701. ***Faculty:*** 34 full-time.
ENROLLMENT PROFILE 701 students from 3 states and territories, 2 other countries. 65% women, 82% part-time, 95% state residents, 40% transferred in, 1% international, 40% 25 or older, 1% Native American, 0% Hispanic, 0% African American, 1% Asian American. ***Most popular recent majors:*** nursing, physical therapy, business administration/commerce/management.
FIRST-YEAR CLASS 761 applied, 49% were accepted, 90% of whom enrolled.
ACADEMIC PROGRAM Calendar: semesters. Academic remediation for entering students, services for LD students, part-time degree program (daytime, evenings, weekends, summer), adult/continuing education programs, internships.

Peterson's Guide to Two-Year Colleges 1997 349

Kennebec Valley Technical College (continued)
GENERAL DEGREE REQUIREMENTS 60 credits; math/science requirements vary according to program; computer course.
MAJORS Business administration/commerce/management, education, electrical and electronics technologies, emergency medical technology, medical records services, nursing, occupational therapy, physical therapy, respiratory therapy, secretarial studies/office management.
LIBRARY 12,500 books, 25 periodicals, 50 records, tapes, and CDs.
COMPUTERS ON CAMPUS 57 computers for student use in computer labs, learning center, labs.
COLLEGE LIFE ***Student services:*** personal-psychological counseling.
HOUSING College housing not available.
ATHLETICS ***Intramural:*** basketball, volleyball.
CAREER PLANNING ***Director:*** Ms. Pat Toto, Director of Placement, 207-453-9762. ***Service:*** career counseling.
EXPENSES FOR 1996–97 ***Application fee:*** $15. State resident tuition: $1830 full-time, $61 per credit hour part-time. Nonresident tuition: $4230 full-time, $141 per credit hour part-time. Part-time mandatory fees: $9 per credit hour (minimum). Tuition for nonresidents who are eligible for the New England Regional Student Program: $2880 full-time, $96 per credit hour part-time. Full-time mandatory fees: $325.
FINANCIAL AID ***College-administered undergrad aid 1995–96:*** need-based scholarships, non-need scholarships, short-term loans, low-interest long-term loans from external sources, Federal Work-Study. ***Required forms:*** CSS Financial Aid PROFILE, FAFSA. ***Application deadline:*** continuous.
APPLYING Open admission except for nursing, health programs. ***Required:*** school transcript, nursing exam. ***Required for some:*** recommendations, interview. Test scores used for admission and counseling/placement. ***Application deadline:*** rolling. ***Notification:*** continuous.
APPLYING/TRANSFER ***Required:*** high school transcript, college transcript. ***Required for some:*** recommendations, interview. ***Application deadline:*** rolling. ***Notification:*** continuous.
CONTACT Mr. Eric Hasenfus, Dean of Student Affairs, Kennebec Valley Technical College, Fairfield, ME 04937-1367, 207-453-5131.

MID-STATE COLLEGE
Auburn, Maine

UG Enrollment: 513	**Tuition & Fees: $3960**
Application Deadline: rolling	**Room Only: $1800**

The small college that means business, Mid-State has an atmosphere of close cooperation between students, staff members, and faculty members that gives students the benefit of personal attention. Mid-State offers an accelerated yet flexible program of study in a series of 8-week sessions with both day and evening classes. Studies begin at 6 points during the year. Its open admission policy attracts a diverse student body that enhances the learning environment.

GENERAL Proprietary, 2-year, coed. Awards certificates, diplomas, transfer associate, terminal associate degrees. Founded 1867. ***Setting:*** 20-acre suburban campus. ***Total enrollment:*** 513. ***Faculty:*** 25 (9 full-time, 10% with terminal degrees, 16 part-time); student-faculty ratio is 14:1.
ENROLLMENT PROFILE 513 students from 3 states and territories, 2 other countries. 86% women, 64% part-time, 99% state residents, 20% transferred in, 72% 25 or older, 0% Native American, 0% Hispanic, 3% African American, 2% Asian American. ***Areas of study chosen:*** 30% health professions and related sciences, 26% business management and administrative services, 10% computer and information sciences.
FIRST-YEAR CLASS 186 total; 225 applied, 100% were accepted, 83% of whom enrolled. 5% from top 10% of their high school class, 10% from top quarter, 70% from top half.
ACADEMIC PROGRAM Core. Calendar: modular. Academic remediation for entering students, advanced placement, summer session for credit, part-time degree program (daytime, evenings, summer), adult/continuing education programs, co-op programs and internships. Off-campus study at Beal College, Husson College, Thomas College.
GENERAL DEGREE REQUIREMENTS 72 credits; 1 college math course; computer course.
MAJORS Accounting, business administration/commerce/management, computer science, legal secretarial studies, medical assistant technologies, medical secretarial studies, secretarial studies/office management, tourism and travel.
LIBRARY 6,000 books, 75 periodicals, 100 records, tapes, and CDs.
COMPUTERS ON CAMPUS Computer purchase plan available. 65 computers for student use in computer center.
COLLEGE LIFE Student-run newspaper. 70% vote in student government elections. ***Social organizations:*** 3 open to all. ***Most popular organizations:*** Student Newspaper, Yearbook, Student Government. ***Student services:*** personal-psychological counseling. ***Campus security:*** 24-hour emergency response devices, student patrols.
HOUSING 20 college housing spaces available; 10 were occupied 1995–96. Freshmen given priority for college housing. Off-campus living permitted. ***Options:*** coed (1 building), international student housing available. Resident assistants live in dorms.
CAREER PLANNING ***Service:*** career counseling.
EXPENSES FOR 1995–96 Tuition: $3960 full-time, $330 per course part-time. College room only: $1800.
FINANCIAL AID ***College-administered undergrad aid 1995–96:*** 50 need-based scholarships (average $100), low-interest long-term loans from external sources (average $2625), Federal Work-Study, 2 part-time jobs. ***Required forms:*** CSS Financial Aid PROFILE, institutional, FAFSA; accepted: state. ***Application deadline:*** continuous. ***Payment plans:*** installment, deferred payment. ***Waivers:*** full or partial for employees or children of employees.
APPLYING Open admission. ***Options:*** early entrance, deferred entrance. ***Application deadline:*** rolling.
APPLYING/TRANSFER ***Entrance:*** noncompetitive. ***Application deadline:*** rolling. ***Contact:*** Ms. Marylin Newell, Academic Dean, 207-783-1478.
CONTACT Mr. Richard F. Gross, Director of Admissions, Mid-State College, Auburn, ME 04210-8888, 207-783-1478.

NORTHERN MAINE TECHNICAL COLLEGE
Presque Isle, Maine

UG Enrollment: 620	**Tuition & Fees (ME Res): $2183**
Application Deadline: rolling	**Room & Board: $3400**

GENERAL State-related, 2-year, coed. Part of Maine Technical College System. Awards terminal associate degrees. Founded 1963. ***Setting:*** 86-acre small-town campus. ***Total enrollment:*** 620. ***Faculty:*** 100 (50 full-time, 50 part-time).
ENROLLMENT PROFILE 620 students from 5 states and territories, 1 other country. 48% women, 23% part-time, 96% state residents, 9% transferred in, 10% 25 or older, 3% Native American, 0% Hispanic, 0% African American, 1% Asian American. ***Areas of study chosen:*** 10% engineering and applied sciences, 4% architecture.
FIRST-YEAR CLASS 420 total; 625 applied, 65% of whom enrolled. 75% from top half of their high school class.
ACADEMIC PROGRAM Calendar: semesters. Academic remediation for entering students, services for LD students, advanced placement, summer session for credit, part-time degree program (daytime, evenings, summer), adult/continuing education programs, co-op programs and internships. Off-campus study.
GENERAL DEGREE REQUIREMENTS 64 credit hours; 1 algebra course; computer course for business majors.
MAJORS Accounting, agricultural business, automotive technologies, business administration/commerce/management, carpentry, computer programming, computer technologies, data processing, drafting and design, electrical and electronics technologies, heating/refrigeration/air conditioning, legal secretarial studies, medical secretarial studies, nursing, plumbing, practical nursing, secretarial studies/office management.
LIBRARY 13,248 books, 30 microform titles, 200 periodicals, 28 CD-ROMs, 28 records, tapes, and CDs. Acquisition spending 1994–95: $20,000.
COMPUTERS ON CAMPUS Computers for student use in computer center, learning center, library, dorms provide access to main academic computer, e-mail.
COLLEGE LIFE ***Student services:*** health clinic, personal-psychological counseling.
HOUSING 255 college housing spaces available; 188 were occupied 1995–96. No special consideration for freshman housing applicants. Off-campus living permitted. ***Option:*** coed housing available. Resident assistants live in dorms.
ATHLETICS Member NSCAA. ***Intercollegiate:*** basketball M/W, golf M/W, ice hockey M/W, soccer M/W. ***Intramural:*** archery, basketball, football, golf, racquetball, soccer, table tennis (Ping-Pong), tennis, volleyball, weight lifting. ***Contact:*** Mr. William Casavant, 207-768-2786.
CAREER PLANNING ***Service:*** career counseling.
EXPENSES FOR 1996–97 ***Application fee:*** $15. State resident tuition: $2048 full-time, $64 per credit hour part-time. Nonresident tuition: $4512 full-time, $141 per credit hour part-time. Part-time mandatory fees: $30 per year. Tuition for nonresidents who are eligible for the New England Regional Student Program: $3072 full-time, $96 per credit hour part-time. Full-time mandatory fees: $135. College room and board: $3400. College room only: $1100.
FINANCIAL AID ***College-administered undergrad aid 1995–96:*** 425 need-based scholarships (average $150), short-term loans (average $25), Federal Work-Study, part-time jobs. ***Required forms:*** CSS Financial Aid PROFILE, institutional, FAFSA. ***Priority deadline:*** 4/1. ***Waivers:*** full or partial for employees or children of employees and senior citizens.
APPLYING Open admission except for nursing program. ***Option:*** early entrance. ***Required:*** school transcript, Assessment and Placement Services for Community Colleges. Test scores used for counseling/placement. ***Application deadline:*** rolling. Preference given to state residents.
APPLYING/TRANSFER ***Required:*** high school transcript, college transcript. ***Required for some:*** standardized test scores.
CONTACT Ms. Nancy Gagnon, Admissions Secretary, Northern Maine Technical College, Presque Isle, ME 04769-2016, 207-768-2785 Ext. 237 or toll-free 800-535-6682 (in-state). ***Fax:*** 207-764-8465.

SOUTHERN MAINE TECHNICAL COLLEGE
South Portland, Maine

UG Enrollment: 2,524	**Tuition & Fees (ME Res): $1766**
Application Deadline: rolling	**Room & Board: $3640**

GENERAL State-supported, 2-year, coed. Part of Maine Technical College System. Awards certificates, diplomas, transfer associate, terminal associate degrees. Founded 1946. ***Setting:*** 65-acre suburban campus. ***Total enrollment:*** 2,524. ***Faculty:*** 148 (98 full-time, 5% with terminal degrees, 50 part-time); student-faculty ratio is 12:1.
ENROLLMENT PROFILE 2,524 students from 14 states and territories, 1 other country. 41% women, 59% men, 20% part-time, 94% state residents, 10% live on campus, 47% transferred in, 60% have need-based financial aid, 0% have non-need-based financial aid, 1% international, 40% 25 or older, 1% Native American, 1% Hispanic, 1% African American, 1% Asian American. ***Most popular recent majors:*** law enforcement/police sciences, culinary arts, computer technologies.
FIRST-YEAR CLASS 877 total; 2,050 applied, 61% were accepted, 70% of whom enrolled. 5% from top 10% of their high school class, 30% from top quarter, 65% from top half.
ACADEMIC PROGRAM Core, honor code. Calendar: semesters. Academic remediation for entering students, services for LD students, advanced placement, summer session for credit, part-time degree program (daytime, evenings), external degree programs, adult/continuing education programs, co-op programs and internships. Off-campus study at University of Southern Maine, Southern Maine Admissions Consortium.
GENERAL DEGREE REQUIREMENTS 60 credits; math competence; computer course for allied health, hotel management, machine tool technology, drafting, medical assisting, culinary arts, marine biology majors; internship (some majors).
MAJORS Agronomy/soil and crop sciences, architectural technologies, automotive technologies, botany/plant sciences, business administration/commerce/management, business machine technologies, carpentry, child care/child and family studies, communication equipment technology, computer information systems, computer management, computer technolo-

Maine

gies, construction technologies, criminal justice, culinary arts, dietetics, drafting and design, early childhood education, electrical and electronics technologies, electrical engineering technology, electronics engineering technology, engineering design, environmental engineering technology, film and video production, fire science, food services management, food services technology, heating/refrigeration/air conditioning, horticulture, hospitality services, hotel and restaurant management, landscaping/grounds maintenance, law enforcement/police sciences, machine and tool technologies, management information systems, marine biology, medical assistant technologies, metallurgical technology, nursing, oceanography, operating room technology, plumbing, pollution control technologies, practical nursing, radiological technology, respiratory therapy.
LIBRARY Southern Maine Technical College Library with 15,000 books, 350 periodicals.
COMPUTERS ON CAMPUS 45 computers for student use in computer center, computer labs, campus center, study center, student center provide access to e-mail, on-line services, Internet. Staffed computer lab on campus provides training in use of computers, software.
COLLEGE LIFE Orientation program (5 days, no cost, parents included). Student-run newspaper. *Most popular organizations:* SEA Club, Student Government, Phi Theta Kappa, Honors Society, VICA. *Major annual events:* Earth Day, Christmas Gala, Awards Day. *Student services:* health clinic, personal-psychological counseling, women's center. *Campus security:* 24-hour emergency response devices, student patrols, late-night transport-escort service.
HOUSING 144 college housing spaces available; all were occupied 1995–96. Freshmen given priority for college housing. Off-campus living permitted. *Options:* freshmen-only, coed (2 buildings), single-sex (1 building) housing available. Resident assistants live in dorms.
ATHLETICS Member NSCAA. *Intercollegiate:* baseball M, basketball M/W, golf M/W, soccer M, softball W, volleyball M/W. *Intramural:* basketball, football, golf, skiing (cross-country), skiing (downhill), volleyball. *Contact:* Mr. John Dakin, Athletic Director, 207-767-9511.
CAREER PLANNING *Placement office:* 1 full-time, 1 part-time staff. *Director:* Ms. Joanne Raferty, Coordinator, 207-767-9500. *Services:* job fairs, resume preparation, career counseling, careers library, job bank.
AFTER GRADUATION 70% of class of 1994 had job offers within 6 months. 15% of students completing a degree program went directly on to further study.
EXPENSES FOR 1996–97 *Application fee:* $20. State resident tuition: $1536 full-time, $64 per credit hour part-time. Nonresident tuition: $3384 full-time, $141 per credit hour part-time. Part-time mandatory fees: $4 per credit hour. Tuition for nonresidents who are eligible for the New England Regional Student Program: $2400 full-time, $80 per credit part-time. Full-time mandatory fees: $230. College room and board: $3640 (minimum).
FINANCIAL AID *College-administered undergrad aid 1995–96:* need-based scholarships (average $500), low-interest long-term loans from external sources, Federal Work-Study, part-time jobs. *Required forms:* institutional, FAFSA; accepted: CSS Financial Aid PROFILE. *Priority deadline:* 4/1. *Payment plan:* installment. *Waivers:* full or partial for employees or children of employees and senior citizens.
APPLYING *Option:* midyear entrance. *Required:* essay, school transcript, TOEFL for international students. *Recommended:* minimum 2.0 GPA, 3 years of high school math. *Required for some:* 3 years of high school science, recommendations, campus interview, SAT I. Test scores used for admission. *Application deadline:* rolling. *Notification:* continuous. Preference given to state residents.
APPLYING/TRANSFER *Required:* essay, high school transcript, college transcript, minimum 2.0 college GPA. *Recommended:* minimum 3.0 college GPA, minimum 2.0 high school GPA. *Required for some:* standardized test scores, recommendations, campus interview. *Application deadline:* rolling. *Notification:* continuous. *Contact:* Mr. Robert A. Weimont, Director of Admissions, 207-767-9520.
CONTACT Mr. Robert A. Weimont, Director of Admissions, Southern Maine Technical College, South Portland, ME 04106, 207-767-9520. *Fax:* 207-767-2731. College video available.

UNIVERSITY OF MAINE AT AUGUSTA
Augusta, Maine

UG Enrollment: 6,123	Tuition & Fees (ME Res): $2685
Application Deadline: rolling	Room & Board: N/Avail

GENERAL State-supported, primarily 2-year, coed. Part of University of Maine System. Awards certificates, transfer associate, terminal associate, bachelor's degrees. Founded 1965. *Setting:* 165-acre small-town campus. Faculty: 272 (107 full-time, 28% with terminal degrees, 165 part-time); student-faculty ratio is 22:1.
ENROLLMENT PROFILE 6,123 students: 69% women, 31% men, 77% part-time, 99% state residents, 26% transferred in, 66% have need-based financial aid, 1% international, 60% 25 or older, 1% Native American, 1% African American. *Most popular recent majors:* business administration/commerce/management, nursing, social science.
FIRST-YEAR CLASS 685 total; 1,157 applied, 93% were accepted, 68% of whom enrolled.
ACADEMIC PROGRAM Core, interdisciplinary curriculum, honor code. Calendar: semesters. 501 courses offered in 1995–96. Academic remediation for entering students, services for LD students, advanced placement, honors program, summer session for credit, part-time degree program (daytime, evenings), adult/continuing education programs, co-op programs and internships. Off-campus study at other units of the University of Maine System.

GENERAL DEGREE REQUIREMENTS 60 credits for associate, 120 credits for bachelor's; 1 algebra course; computer course (varies by major); internship (some majors).
MAJORS Accounting (B), applied art, architectural technologies, business administration/commerce/management (B), computer information systems, criminal justice, English (B), graphic arts, human services, jazz (B), liberal arts/general studies, library science, mathematics (B), medical laboratory technology, nursing, photography, public administration (B), science (B), social science (B).
LIBRARY Learning Resources Center with 44,000 books, 4,200 microform titles, 560 periodicals, 1 on-line bibliographic service, 3 CD-ROMs, 5,500 records, tapes, and CDs.
COMPUTERS ON CAMPUS Computer purchase plan available. 88 computers for student use in computer center, computer labs, learning resource center, library provide access to main academic computer, off-campus computing facilities, e-mail, Internet. Staffed computer lab on campus provides training in use of computers, software.
COLLEGE LIFE *Most popular organizations:* Phi Theta Kappa, Student Government. *Major annual events:* UMA Day, Jazz Week. *Student services:* personal-psychological counseling. *Campus security:* 24-hour emergency response devices.
HOUSING College housing not available.
ATHLETICS Member NSCAA. *Intercollegiate:* basketball M/W(c), fencing M(c)/W(c), soccer M(c)/W(c). *Intramural:* golf, racquetball, skiing (cross-country), skiing (downhill), soccer, softball, volleyball. *Contact:* Mr. Ian MacKinnon, Director of Student Activities, 207-621-3442.
CAREER PLANNING *Placement office:* 2 full-time staff. *Director:* Ms. Sheri Cranston Fraser, Coordinator of Retention and Counselor, 207-621-3176. *Services:* job fairs, resume preparation, career counseling, careers library.
EXPENSES FOR 1995–96 State resident tuition: $2550 full-time, $85 per credit part-time. Nonresident tuition: $6210 full-time, $207 per credit part-time. Part-time mandatory fees: $4.50 per credit. Tuition for nonresidents who are eligible for the New England Regional Student Program: $3825 full-time, $127.50 per credit part-time. Full-time mandatory fees: $135.
FINANCIAL AID *College-administered undergrad aid 1995–96:* 580 need-based scholarships (average $575), 7 non-need scholarships (average $150), short-term loans (average $150), low-interest long-term loans from college funds (average $1370), loans from external sources (average $2100), 116 Federal Work-Study (averaging $1870), 40 part-time jobs. *Required forms:* FAFSA. *Priority deadline:* 3/1. *Payment plan:* installment. *Waivers:* full or partial for employees or children of employees and senior citizens.
APPLYING Open admission except for allied health, architectural studies, liberal arts, baccalaureate programs. *Options:* early entrance, early decision, deferred entrance, midyear entrance. *Required:* TOEFL for international students. *Recommended:* SAT I. *Required for some:* 3 years of high school math, SAT I. Test scores used for counseling/placement. *Application deadlines:* rolling, 11/1 for early decision. *Notification:* 12/1 for early decision.
APPLYING/TRANSFER *Required for some:* 3 years of high school math. *Application deadline:* rolling. *Contact:* Ms. Ann Corbett, Registrar, 207-621-3145.
CONTACT Mr. William Clark Ketcham, Director of Enrollment Services, University of Maine at Augusta, Augusta, ME 04330-9410, 207-621-3185 or toll-free 800-696-6000 (in-state). *Fax:* 207-621-3116. *E-mail:* umaar@maine.maine.edu. College video available.

WASHINGTON COUNTY TECHNICAL COLLEGE
Calais, Maine

UG Enrollment: 380	Tuition & Fees (ME Res): $2528
Application Deadline: rolling	Room Only: $690

GENERAL State-supported, 2-year, specialized, coed. Awards certificates, diplomas, transfer associate, terminal associate degrees. Founded 1969. *Setting:* 40-acre rural campus. *Total enrollment:* 380. *Faculty:* 40 (30 full-time, 10 part-time).
ENROLLMENT PROFILE 380 students.
FIRST-YEAR CLASS 256 total; 390 applied, 97% were accepted, 67% of whom enrolled.
ACADEMIC PROGRAM Calendar: semesters. Services for LD students, advanced placement, tutorials, part-time degree program (daytime, evenings, weekends, summer), adult/continuing education programs, co-op programs.
GENERAL DEGREE REQUIREMENTS 64 credits; math/science requirements vary according to program; computer course.
MAJORS Automotive technologies, construction technologies, engineering technology, marine technology.
COMPUTERS ON CAMPUS 100 computers for student use in computer labs, research center, learning resource center, business lab, library provide access to Internet.
EXPENSES FOR 1996–97 *Application fee:* $20. State resident tuition: $2048 full-time, $64 per credit part-time. Nonresident tuition: $4288 full-time, $134 per credit part-time. Part-time mandatory fees: $15 per credit. Full-time mandatory fees: $480. College room only: $690.
APPLYING Open admission. *Required:* school transcript. *Recommended:* minimum 2.0 GPA. *Application deadline:* rolling. *Notification:* continuous.
APPLYING/TRANSFER *Required:* high school transcript, college transcript. *Recommended:* minimum 2.0 college GPA, minimum 2.0 high school GPA. *Entrance:* noncompetitive.
CONTACT Ms. Pauli Caruncho, Director of Admissions, Washington County Technical College, Calais, ME 04619, 207-454-1010.

Maryland

MARYLAND

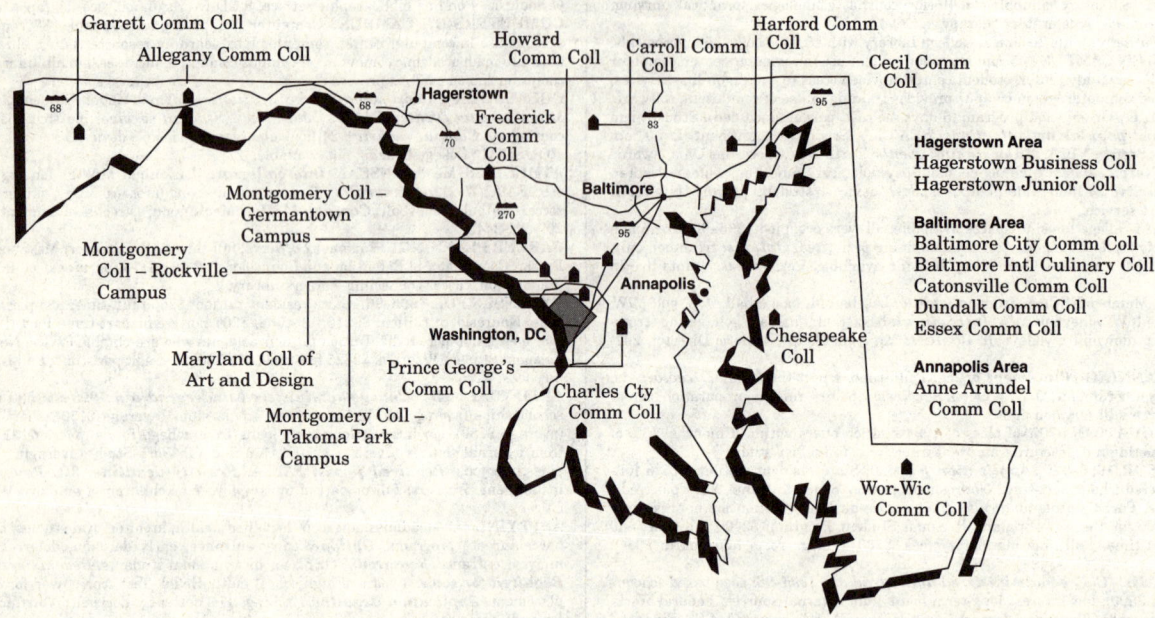

ALLEGANY COMMUNITY COLLEGE
Cumberland, Maryland

UG Enrollment: 2,844	Tuition & Fees (Area Res): $2170
Application Deadline: rolling	Room & Board: N/Avail

GENERAL State and locally supported, 2-year, coed. Part of Maryland State Community Colleges System. Awards certificates, transfer associate, terminal associate degrees. Founded 1961. *Setting:* 370-acre small-town campus. *Research spending 1994–95:* $50,187. *Educational spending 1994–95:* $2577 per undergrad. *Total enrollment:* 2,844. *Faculty:* 206 (87 full-time, 119 part-time); student-faculty ratio is 16:1.
ENROLLMENT PROFILE 2,844 students from 10 states and territories. 66% women, 34% men, 44% part-time, 62% state residents, 10% transferred in, 70% have need-based financial aid, 0% international, 41% 25 or older, 0% Native American, 1% Hispanic, 2% African American, 0% Asian American. *Areas of study chosen:* 35% liberal arts/general studies, 29% health professions and related sciences, 16% business management and administrative services, 5% computer and information sciences, 5% education, 3% natural resource sciences, 2% communications and journalism, 2% engineering and applied sciences, 2% psychology, 1% fine arts. *Most popular recent majors:* nursing, business administration/commerce/management, secretarial studies/office management.
FIRST-YEAR CLASS 664 total; 1,591 applied, 100% were accepted, 42% of whom enrolled.
ACADEMIC PROGRAM Interdisciplinary curriculum, honor code. Calendar: semesters. 550 courses offered in 1995–96. Academic remediation for entering students, advanced placement, honors program, summer session for credit, part-time degree program (daytime, evenings, summer), adult/continuing education programs, internships. ROTC: Army (c).
GENERAL DEGREE REQUIREMENTS 61 credits; 1 science course; computer course for most majors; internship (some majors).
MAJORS Accounting, art/fine arts, automotive technologies, biology/biological sciences, business administration/commerce/management, business education, chemistry, communication, communication equipment technology, computer programming, computer science, computer technologies, criminal justice, data processing, dental services, education, electromechanical technology, engineering (general), food services management, forestry, forest technology, hotel and restaurant management, legal secretarial studies, liberal arts/general studies, medical laboratory technology, medical secretarial studies, nursing, occupational therapy, psychology, radio and television studies, radiological technology, recreation and leisure services, respiratory therapy, secretarial studies/office management, social science, social work, sociology.
LIBRARY Allegany Community College Library with 51,189 books, 217 microform titles, 438 periodicals, 6 on-line bibliographic services, 6 CD-ROMs, 2,014 records, tapes, and CDs. Acquisition spending 1994–95: $38,251.
COMPUTERS ON CAMPUS Computer purchase plan available. 280 computers for student use in computer center, computer labs, learning resource center, humanities/science, continuing education buildings, library. Staffed computer lab on campus provides training in use of computers, software. Academic computing expenditure 1994–95: $334,590.

COLLEGE LIFE *Social organizations:* 24 open to all. *Most popular organizations:* SAHDA, Honors Club, EMT Club, Respiratory Therapy, Forestry Club. *Major annual events:* All College Awards Banquet, Welcome Back Picnic, Spring Fling Tension Breaker. *Student services:* personal-psychological counseling. *Campus security:* 24-hour patrols, late-night transport-escort service.
HOUSING College housing not available.
ATHLETICS Member NJCAA. *Intercollegiate:* baseball M, basketball M/W, soccer M, tennis M/W. *Intramural:* archery, badminton, baseball, basketball, bowling, racquetball, tennis, volleyball. *Contact:* Mr. Robert D. Kirk, Athletic Director, 301-724-7700 Ext. 265.
CAREER PLANNING *Placement office:* 1 full-time, 1 part-time staff; $15,858 operating expenditure 1994–95. *Director:* Mr. Rick Layman, Career Advising Specialist, 301-724-7700 Ext. 235. *Services:* job fairs, career counseling, careers library.
AFTER GRADUATION 50% of class of 1994 had job offers within 6 months. 50% of students completing a degree program went directly on to further study.
EXPENSES FOR 1995–96 Area resident tuition: $2070 full-time, $69 per credit part-time. State resident tuition: $2640 full-time, $88 per credit part-time. Nonresident tuition: $3450 full-time, $115 per credit part-time. Part-time mandatory fees per semester range from $30 to $50. Full-time mandatory fees: $100.
FINANCIAL AID *College-administered undergrad aid 1995–96:* 502 need-based scholarships (average $613), 57 non-need scholarships (average $901), short-term loans (average $100), 250 Federal Work-Study (averaging $1332). *Required forms:* institutional, FAFSA. *Priority deadline:* 3/15. *Payment plan:* deferred payment. *Waivers:* full or partial for employees or children of employees and senior citizens.
APPLYING Open admission. *Option:* early entrance. *Required:* TOEFL for international students. *Required for some:* ACT. Test scores used for counseling/placement. *Application deadline:* rolling.
APPLYING/TRANSFER *Required:* college transcript, minimum 2.0 college GPA. *Entrance:* noncompetitive. *Application deadline:* rolling. *Contact:* Mr. Bill Devlin, Director of Instructional Assistance, 301-724-7700 Ext. 168.
CONTACT Ms. Gloria Brooks-Broadwater, Director of Admissions and Registration, Allegany Community College, Cumberland, MD 21502, 301-724-7700 Ext. 202. *Fax:* 301-724-6892.

ANNE ARUNDEL COMMUNITY COLLEGE
Arnold, Maryland

UG Enrollment: 11,890	Tuition & Fees (Area Res): $1931
Application Deadline: rolling	Room & Board: N/Avail

GENERAL State and locally supported, 2-year, coed. Awards certificates, transfer associate, terminal associate degrees. Founded 1961. *Setting:* 230-acre suburban campus with easy access to Baltimore and Washington, DC. *Total enrollment:* 11,890. *Faculty:* 579 (198 full-time, 98% with terminal degrees, 381 part-time); student-faculty ratio is 21:1.

ENROLLMENT PROFILE 11,890 students from 6 states and territories, 19 other countries. 58% women, 42% men, 72% part-time, 98% state residents, 19% transferred in, 1% international, 50% 25 or older, 1% Native American, 2% Hispanic, 11% African American, 2% Asian American. ***Areas of study chosen:*** 41% liberal arts/general studies, 19% business management and administrative services, 12% health professions and related sciences, 11% computer and information sciences, 5% engineering and applied sciences, 4% education, 1% architecture, 1% fine arts. ***Most popular recent majors:*** nursing, liberal arts/general studies, computer technologies.
FIRST-YEAR CLASS 3,217 total. Of the students who applied, 100% were accepted, 100% of whom enrolled.
ACADEMIC PROGRAM Core, general education curriculum. Calendar: semesters. 782 courses offered in 1995–96. Academic remediation for entering students, English as a second language program offered during academic year and summer, services for LD students, advanced placement, self-designed majors, Freshman Honors College, tutorials, honors program, summer session for credit, part-time degree program (daytime, evenings, summer), adult/continuing education programs, co-op programs. ROTC: Army (c), Naval (c), Air Force (c).
GENERAL DEGREE REQUIREMENT 60 credit hours.
MAJORS Accounting, American studies, applied art, architectural technologies, art/fine arts, astronomy, behavioral sciences, biology/biological sciences, botany/plant sciences, broadcasting, business administration/commerce/management, business economics, chemistry, communication, communication equipment technology, computer information systems, computer management, computer programming, computer science, computer technologies, corrections, criminal justice, data processing, early childhood education, economics, education, electrical and electronics technologies, electrical engineering technology, elementary education, emergency medical technology, engineering technology, English, environmental sciences, European studies, film and video production, food services technology, health education, horticulture, hotel and restaurant management, humanities, human services, landscape architecture/design, law enforcement/police sciences, liberal arts/general studies, manufacturing technology, marine sciences, marketing/retailing/merchandising, mathematics, mechanical engineering technology, medical assistant technologies, medical technology, mental health/rehabilitation counseling, music, nursing, paralegal studies, photography, physical education, public administration, public affairs and policy studies, radiological technology, real estate, retail management, science, secretarial studies/office management, social science, telecommunications.
LIBRARY Andrew G. Truxal Library with 113,345 books, 27 microform titles, 525 periodicals, 4,222 records, tapes, and CDs. Acquisition spending 1994–95: $112,425.
COMPUTERS ON CAMPUS 250 computers for student use in computer center, computer labs, business department, library. Staffed computer lab on campus provides training in use of computers, software. Academic computing expenditure 1994–95: $1.3 million.
COLLEGE LIFE Drama-theater group, choral group, student-run newspaper. 8% vote in student government elections. ***Social organizations:*** 40 open to all. ***Most popular organizations:*** Dance Club, Student Association, Black Student Union, International Student Association, Chemistry Club. ***Major annual events:*** Lip Sync Contest, Spring Week, Dramatic/Theatrical Performances. ***Student services:*** health clinic, personal-psychological counseling. ***Campus security:*** 24-hour emergency response devices and patrols, student patrols, late-night transport-escort service.
HOUSING College housing not available.
ATHLETICS Member NJCAA. ***Intercollegiate:*** baseball M(s), basketball M(s)/W(s), cross-country running M(s)/W(s), golf M, lacrosse M(s)/W(s), soccer M(s)/W(s), softball W(s), tennis M(s), volleyball W. ***Intramural:*** badminton, basketball, soccer, softball, swimming and diving, table tennis (Ping-Pong), tennis, volleyball. ***Contact:*** Mr. Buddy Beardmore, Athletic Director, 410-647-7100.
CAREER PLANNING ***Placement office:*** 2 full-time, 2 part-time staff; $99,234 operating expenditure 1994–95. ***Director:*** Mr. Robert Schweriner, Director, Career Planning and Placement, 410-541-2787. ***Services:*** job fairs, resume preparation, resume referral, career counseling, careers library, job bank, job interviews.
EXPENSES FOR 1996–97 Area resident tuition: $1798 full-time, $58 per credit hour part-time. State resident tuition: $3286 full-time, $106 per credit hour part-time. Nonresident tuition: $6262 full-time, $202 per credit hour part-time. Part-time mandatory fees per semester range from $23 to $53. Full-time mandatory fees: $133.
FINANCIAL AID ***College-administered undergrad aid 1995–96:*** 67 need-based scholarships (averaging $613), 48 non-need scholarships (averaging $505), short-term loans (averaging $277), low-interest long-term loans from external sources (averaging $1113), 54 Federal Work-Study (averaging $2500), 44 part-time jobs. ***Required forms:*** state, institutional, FAFSA, financial aid transcript (for transfers). ***Priority deadline:*** 7/1. ***Payment plan:*** deferred payment. ***Waivers:*** full or partial for employees or children of employees.
APPLYING Open admission except for nursing, radiology programs, out-of-state applicants. ***Options:*** early entrance, deferred entrance. ***Recommended:*** 3 years of high school math and science, some high school foreign language, SAT I or ACT. ***Required for some:*** TOEFL for international students. Test scores used for counseling/placement. ***Application deadline:*** rolling.
APPLYING/TRANSFER ***Recommended:*** 3 years of high school math and science, some high school foreign language. ***Entrance:*** noncompetitive. ***Application deadline:*** rolling. ***Contact:*** Ms. Terry Clay, Director of Advising, 410-541-2305.
CONTACT Mr. Thomas McGinn, Director of Admissions, Anne Arundel Community College, Arnold, MD 21012-1895, 410-541-2240.

BALTIMORE CITY COMMUNITY COLLEGE
Baltimore, Maryland

UG Enrollment: 5,970	**Tuition & Fees (MD Res): $1961**
Application Deadline: 8/9	**Room & Board: N/Avail**

GENERAL State-supported, 2-year, coed. Awards certificates, transfer associate, terminal associate degrees. Founded 1947. ***Setting:*** 19-acre suburban campus. ***Total enrollment:*** 5,970. ***Faculty:*** 493 (143 full-time, 350 part-time).
ENROLLMENT PROFILE 5,970 students from 5 states and territories. 70% part-time, 98% state residents, 10% transferred in, 70% 25 or older, 2% Native American, 1% Hispanic, 74% African American, 1% Asian American. ***Most popular recent majors:*** liberal arts/general studies, accounting.
FIRST-YEAR CLASS 1,515 total. Of the students who applied, 100% were accepted, 50% of whom enrolled.
ACADEMIC PROGRAM Core. Calendar: semesters. Academic remediation for entering students, English as a second language program offered during academic year, services for LD students, honors program, summer session for credit, part-time degree program (daytime, evenings), adult/continuing education programs, co-op programs and internships. Study abroad in Israel.
GENERAL DEGREE REQUIREMENTS 62 credits; math/science requirements vary according to program; computer course for students without computer competency.
MAJORS Accounting, business administration/commerce/management, computer information systems, computer science, corrections, data processing, dental services, dietetics, drafting and design, early childhood education, electrical and electronics technologies, emergency medical technology, engineering (general), fashion design and technology, fashion merchandising, gerontology, human services, illustration, law enforcement/police sciences, legal secretarial studies, liberal arts/general studies, marketing/retailing/merchandising, medical records services, medical secretarial studies, nursing, operating room technology, paralegal studies, physical therapy, respiratory therapy, science, secretarial studies/office management.
LIBRARY 107,000 books, 500 microform titles, 760 periodicals, 6,000 records, tapes, and CDs.
COMPUTERS ON CAMPUS 57 computers for student use in computer center.
COLLEGE LIFE Student-run newspaper, radio station. ***Student services:*** health clinic, personal-psychological counseling.
HOUSING College housing not available.
ATHLETICS ***Intercollegiate:*** basketball M/W, cross-country running M/W, soccer M, track and field M/W. ***Contact:*** Mr. Vince Mumford, Director, Intercollegiate Athletics, 410-333-5372.
CAREER PLANNING ***Service:*** career counseling.
EXPENSES FOR 1996–97 State resident tuition: $1736 full-time, $56 per credit part-time. Nonresident tuition: $5642 full-time, $182 per credit part-time. Part-time mandatory fees: $7.50 per credit. Full-time mandatory fees: $225.
FINANCIAL AID ***College-administered undergrad aid 1995–96:*** 1,405 need-based scholarships (averaging $800), 476 non-need scholarships (averaging $417), short-term loans (averaging $450), low-interest long-term loans from external sources (averaging $2500), Federal Work-Study. ***Required forms:*** CSS Financial Aid PROFILE, institutional, FAFSA; accepted: state. ***Priority deadline:*** 5/31.
APPLYING Open admission except for allied health programs. ***Options:*** early entrance, deferred entrance. ***Required:*** school transcript. ***Application deadline:*** 8/9. ***Notification:*** continuous.
APPLYING/TRANSFER ***Required:*** high school transcript, college transcript. ***Entrance:*** noncompetitive. ***Application deadline:*** 8/9. ***Notification:*** continuous.
CONTACT Mr. DeWitt L. Powell, Director of Admissions, Baltimore City Community College, Baltimore, MD 21215-7893, 410-333-5393.

BALTIMORE INTERNATIONAL CULINARY COLLEGE
Baltimore, Maryland

UG Enrollment: 776	**Tuition & Fees: $10,746**
Application Deadline: rolling	**Room & Board: $4569**

GENERAL Independent, 2-year, specialized, coed. Awards certificates, transfer associate degrees. Founded 1972. ***Setting:*** 6-acre urban campus with easy access to Washington, DC. ***Total enrollment:*** 776. ***Faculty:*** 38 (24 full-time, 92% with terminal degrees, 14 part-time); student-faculty ratio is 13:1. ***Notable Alumni:*** Benny Gordon, Holly Forbes, Nancy Longo, Dawn Seiber.
ENROLLMENT PROFILE 776 students from 30 states and territories, 10 other countries. 35% women, 6% part-time, 66% state residents, 24% live on campus, 65% transferred in, 1% international, 40% 25 or older, 0% Native American, 3% Hispanic, 23% African American, 2% Asian American. ***Most popular recent major:*** culinary arts.
FIRST-YEAR CLASS 441 total; 1,160 applied, 95% were accepted.
ACADEMIC PROGRAM Core, honor code. Calendar: quarters. 64 courses offered in 1995–96. Academic remediation for entering students, advanced placement, honors program, co-op programs and internships. Study abroad in Ireland (70% of students participate).
GENERAL DEGREE REQUIREMENTS 69 credits; internship (some majors).
MAJORS Culinary arts, food services management, hotel and restaurant management.
LIBRARY George A. Piendak Library plus 1 other, with 8,300 books, 150 periodicals, 1 on-line bibliographic service, 12 CD-ROMs, 20 records, tapes, and CDs.
COMPUTERS ON CAMPUS 40 computers for student use in computer center, learning resource center, library, dorms provide access to main academic computer. Staffed computer lab on campus provides training in use of computers, software.
COLLEGE LIFE ***Student services:*** health clinic, personal-psychological counseling. ***Campus security:*** late-night transport-escort service, controlled dormitory access.
HOUSING 250 college housing spaces available; 180 were occupied 1995–96. Freshmen guaranteed college housing. On-campus residence required in freshman year. ***Options:*** freshmen-only, coed housing available. Resident assistants live in dorms.
CAREER PLANNING ***Placement office:*** 2 full-time staff. ***Director:*** Ms. Alicia Antone, Coordinator, Career Development, 410-752-0490. ***Services:*** job fairs, resume preparation, resume referral, career counseling, job bank, job interviews.
EXPENSES FOR 1995–96 ***Application fee:*** $25. Comprehensive fee of $15,315 includes full-time tuition ($9135), mandatory fees ($1611 minimum), and college room and board ($4569).
FINANCIAL AID ***College-administered undergrad aid 1995–96:*** 124 need-based scholarships (average $600), 655 non-need scholarships (average $992), short-term loans (average $3000), low-interest long-term loans from external sources (average $3313), Federal Work-Study, 18 part-time jobs. ***Required forms:*** institutional, FAFSA; accepted: CSS Financial Aid PROFILE, state. ***Priority deadline:*** 9/1. ***Payment plans:*** tuition prepayment, installment. ***Waivers:*** full or partial for employees or children of employees. ***Notification:*** continuous.
APPLYING ***Options:*** Common Application, deferred entrance. ***Recommended:*** SAT I or ACT, TOEFL for international students. Test scores used for admission and counseling/placement. ***Application deadline:*** rolling. ***Notification:*** continuous until 9/15.
APPLYING/TRANSFER ***Recommended:*** standardized test scores. ***Entrance:*** minimally difficult. ***Application deadline:*** rolling. ***Notification:*** continuous until 9/15. ***Contact:*** Ms. Lisa Rice, Director of Admissions, 410-752-4710.

Baltimore International Culinary College (continued)

CONTACT Mr. Raymond L. Joll, Vice President of Enrollment Management, Baltimore International Culinary College, 17 Commerce Street, Baltimore, MD 21202-3230, 410-752-4710 Ext. 13 or toll-free 800-624-9926. ***Fax:*** 410-752-3730. College video available.

❖ ***See page 700 for a narrative description.*** ❖

CARROLL COMMUNITY COLLEGE
Westminster, Maryland

UG Enrollment: 2,532 — **Tuition & Fees (Area Res): $2108**
Application Deadline: rolling — **Room & Board: N/Avail**

GENERAL State and locally supported, 2-year, coed. Part of Maryland Higher Education Commission. Awards certificates, transfer associate degrees. Founded 1996. ***Setting:*** 80-acre small-town campus with easy access to Baltimore. ***Total enrollment:*** 2,532. ***Faculty:*** 210 (60 full-time, 150 part-time).

ENROLLMENT PROFILE 2,532 students from 2 states and territories, 4 other countries. 63% women, 37% men, 67% part-time, 98% state residents, 10% transferred in, 1% international, 32% 25 or older, 1% Native American, 3% Hispanic, 2% African American, 1% Asian American.

FIRST-YEAR CLASS 350 total. Of the students who applied, 100% were accepted, 100% of whom enrolled.

ACADEMIC PROGRAM Calendar: semesters.

GENERAL DEGREE REQUIREMENTS 62 credits; 1 math course; 2 natural science courses; computer course.

COMPUTERS ON CAMPUS 250 computers for student use in computer center, computer labs, career center, classrooms, library, student rooms provide access to main academic computer, off-campus computing facilities, e-mail, on-line services, Internet. Staffed computer lab on campus provides training in use of computers, software.

HOUSING College housing not available.

EXPENSES FOR 1996–97 Area resident tuition: $2108 full-time, $68 per credit part-time. State resident tuition: $3968 full-time, $128 per credit part-time. Nonresident tuition: $6355 full-time, $205 per credit part-time.

APPLYING Open admission. ***Required:*** essay, school transcript. ***Recommended:*** SAT I or ACT. ***Application deadline:*** rolling. ***Notification:*** continuous.

APPLYING/TRANSFER ***Required:*** essay, high school transcript, college transcript. ***Recommended:*** standardized test scores. ***Application deadline:*** rolling. ***Notification:*** continuous.

CONTACT Ms. Dina-Athena S. Vakiaros, Director of Admissions, Carroll Community College, Westminster, MD 21157, 410-876-9602.

CATONSVILLE COMMUNITY COLLEGE
Catonsville, Maryland

UG Enrollment: 10,240 — **Tuition & Fees (Area Res): $1948**
Application Deadline: rolling — **Room & Board: N/Avail**

GENERAL County-supported, 2-year, coed. Awards certificates, transfer associate, terminal associate degrees. Founded 1957. ***Setting:*** 137-acre suburban campus with easy access to Baltimore. ***Total enrollment:*** 10,240. ***Faculty:*** 534 (208 full-time, 326 part-time).

ENROLLMENT PROFILE 10,240 students from 3 states and territories, 29 other countries. 56% women, 44% men, 72% part-time, 98% state residents, 8% transferred in, 1% international, 52% 25 or older, 1% Native American, 2% Hispanic, 24% African American, 5% Asian American. ***Most popular recent majors:*** nursing, accounting, computer information systems.

FIRST-YEAR CLASS 2,332 total; 4,244 applied, 100% were accepted, 55% of whom enrolled.

ACADEMIC PROGRAM Core, honor code. Calendar: 4-1-4. Academic remediation for entering students, English as a second language program offered during academic year and summer, services for LD students, honors program, summer session for credit, part-time degree program (daytime, evenings), adult/continuing education programs, internships. Off-campus study at Dundalk Community College, Essex Community College. ROTC: Naval (c).

GENERAL DEGREE REQUIREMENTS 62 semester hours; 3 semester hours of math; 4 semester hours of lab science.

MAJORS Accounting, air traffic control, applied art, architectural technologies, art/fine arts, automotive technologies, aviation administration, aviation technology, business administration/commerce/management, chemical engineering technology, civil engineering technology, commercial art, communication, computer graphics, computer information systems, computer management, computer programming, computer science, computer technologies, construction management, construction technologies, corrections, criminal justice, data processing, deaf interpreter training, drafting and design, early childhood education, education, electrical and electronics technologies, elementary education, engineering (general), engineering design, (pre)engineering sequence, engineering technology, fire science, flight training, funeral service, graphic arts, industrial engineering technology, interior design, international business, landscape architecture/design, law enforcement/police sciences, legal secretarial studies, legal studies, liberal arts/general studies, machine and tool technologies, manufacturing technology, marketing/retailing/merchandising, medical laboratory technology, medical secretarial studies, mental health/rehabilitation counseling, music, nursing, occupational safety and health, occupational therapy, photography, printing technologies, quality control technology, radio and television studies, real estate, recreation and leisure services, recreation therapy, science, secretarial studies/office management, social science, studio art, surveying technology, theater arts/drama, transportation technologies, zoology.

LIBRARY 100,000 books, 35,000 microform titles, 815 periodicals, 20,485 records, tapes, and CDs.

COMPUTERS ON CAMPUS 200 computers for student use in computer center, learning resource center, classrooms, library provide access to e-mail, Internet. Staffed computer lab on campus provides training in use of computers, software.

COLLEGE LIFE Drama-theater group, choral group, student-run newspaper, radio station. ***Social organizations:*** 51 open to all. ***Student services:*** health clinic, personal-psychological counseling. ***Campus security:*** 24-hour emergency response devices and patrols, late-night transport-escort service.

HOUSING College housing not available.

ATHLETICS Member NJCAA. ***Intercollegiate:*** baseball M, basketball M/W, bowling M/W, cross-country running M/W, lacrosse M(s), soccer M/W, softball W, swimming and diving M/W, tennis M/W, track and field M/W, volleyball W(s). ***Intramural:*** basketball, cross-country running, racquetball, skiing (cross-country), swimming and diving, table tennis (Ping-Pong), tennis, track and field, volleyball. ***Contact:*** Mr. Gary Keedy, Athletic Director, 410-455-4143.

CAREER PLANNING ***Director:*** Ms. Deborah Cuffie, Coordinator for Career Center, 410-455-4472. ***Services:*** job fairs, resume referral, career counseling, careers library.

EXPENSES FOR 1996–97 ***Application fee:*** $10. Area resident tuition: $1800 full-time, $60 per semester hour part-time. State resident tuition: $3180 full-time, $106 per semester hour part-time. Nonresident tuition: $4980 full-time, $166 per semester hour part-time. Part-time mandatory fees: $15 per semester hour. Full-time mandatory fees: $148.

FINANCIAL AID ***College-administered undergrad aid 1995–96:*** 691 need-based scholarships (average $1000), 63 non-need scholarships (average $429), short-term loans (average $25), low-interest long-term loans from external sources (average $2199), 128 Federal Work-Study (averaging $2402), 288 part-time jobs. ***Required forms:*** institutional, FAFSA; accepted: CSS Financial Aid PROFILE, state. ***Priority deadline:*** 6/1. ***Payment plan:*** deferred payment. ***Waivers:*** full or partial for employees or children of employees and senior citizens.

APPLYING Open admission. ***Option:*** early entrance. ***Recommended:*** 3 years of high school math and science, some high school foreign language. ***Required for some:*** SAT I or ACT, TOEFL for international students, CGP. Test scores used for counseling/placement. ***Application deadline:*** rolling.

APPLYING/TRANSFER ***Entrance:*** noncompetitive. ***Application deadline:*** rolling.

CONTACT Mrs. Marcia Amaimo, Director of Admissions, Catonsville Community College, Catonsville, MD 21228-5381, 410-455-4304. ***E-mail:*** aamo@catcc.bitnet. College video available.

CECIL COMMUNITY COLLEGE
North East, Maryland

UG Enrollment: 1,055 — **Tuition & Fees (Area Res): $1842**
Application Deadline: rolling — **Room & Board: N/Avail**

GENERAL County-supported, 2-year, coed. Awards certificates, diplomas, transfer associate, terminal associate degrees. Founded 1968. ***Setting:*** 100-acre rural campus with easy access to Baltimore. ***Total enrollment:*** 1,055. ***Faculty:*** 158 (47 full-time, 15% with terminal degrees, 111 part-time); student-faculty ratio is 12:1.

ENROLLMENT PROFILE 1,055 students from 4 states and territories. 64% women, 36% men, 71% part-time, 85% state residents, 20% transferred in, 22% have need-based financial aid, 15% have non-need-based financial aid, 1% international, 43% 25 or older, 1% Native American, 1% Hispanic, 3% African American, 2% Asian American. ***Areas of study chosen:*** 29% liberal arts/general studies, 22% health professions and related sciences, 16% business management and administrative services, 12% interdisciplinary studies, 9% computer and information sciences, 6% fine arts, 4% engineering and applied sciences, 2% social sciences. ***Most popular recent majors:*** nursing, liberal arts/general studies, electrical and electronics technologies.

FIRST-YEAR CLASS 238 total; 238 applied, 100% were accepted, 100% of whom enrolled.

ACADEMIC PROGRAM Interdisciplinary curriculum. Calendar: semesters. 283 courses offered in 1995–96. Academic remediation for entering students, English as a second language program offered during academic year and summer, advanced placement, summer session for credit, part-time degree program (daytime, evenings), adult/continuing education programs, co-op programs and internships.

GENERAL DEGREE REQUIREMENT 56 credit hours.

MAJORS Accounting, business administration/commerce/management, carpentry, computer graphics, computer programming, computer technologies, construction technologies, criminal justice, data processing, early childhood education, education, electrical and electronics technologies, elementary education, laboratory technologies, law enforcement/police sciences, liberal arts/general studies, marketing/retailing/merchandising, nursing, photography, plumbing, robotics, secretarial studies/office management, water resources, welding technology.

LIBRARY Cecil County Veteran's Memorial Library with 28,131 books, 51 microform titles, 142 periodicals, 8 CD-ROMs, 379 records, tapes, and CDs. Acquisition spending 1994–95: $257,533.

COMPUTERS ON CAMPUS Computer purchase plan available. 60 computers for student use in computer labs, learning resource center, classrooms, library provide access to e-mail, on-line services. Staffed computer lab on campus provides training in use of computers, software.

COLLEGE LIFE Drama-theater group, student-run newspaper. ***Social organizations:*** 12 open to all; 1 national fraternity; 2% of eligible men are members. ***Most popular organizations:*** Student Government, Non-Traditional Student Organization, Student Nurses Association, Student Newspaper. ***Major annual events:*** Welcome Back Event, Spring Fling, Easter Egg Hunt. ***Student services:*** personal-psychological counseling, women's center. ***Campus security:*** late-night transport-escort service.

HOUSING College housing not available.

ATHLETICS Member NJCAA. ***Intercollegiate:*** baseball M, basketball M(s)/W(s), field hockey W, soccer M(s), softball W, volleyball W(s). ***Intramural:*** basketball, bowling, golf, soccer, tennis, volleyball. ***Contact:*** Mr. Richard Brockell, Athletic Director, 410-287-6060.

CAREER PLANNING ***Placement office:*** 1 full-time staff. ***Director:*** Ms. Debbie Farris, Transfer Coordinator, 410-287-1000. ***Services:*** job fairs, resume preparation, career counseling, careers library, job bank.

EXPENSES FOR 1995–96 ***Application fee:*** $25. Area resident tuition: $1740 full-time, $58 per credit part-time. State resident tuition: $3450 full-time, $115 per credit part-time. Nonresident tuition: $4500 full-time, $150 per credit part-time. Part-time mandatory fees: $18 per semester. Full-time mandatory fees: $102.

FINANCIAL AID ***College-administered undergrad aid 1995–96:*** 225 need-based scholarships (averaging $627), 195 non-need scholarships (averaging $376), short-term loans, low-interest long-term loans from external sources (averaging $1224), 44 Federal

Work-Study (averaging $1035). ***Required forms:*** CSS Financial Aid PROFILE, institutional, FAFSA. ***Priority deadline:*** 8/31. ***Payment plan:*** installment. ***Waivers:*** full or partial for children of alumni and employees or children of employees. ***Notification:*** continuous.
APPLYING Open admission. ***Options:*** Common Application, early entrance, deferred entrance, midyear entrance. ***Required:*** school transcript, TOEFL for international students. Test scores used for counseling/placement. ***Application deadline:*** rolling. ***Notification:*** continuous.
APPLYING/TRANSFER ***Required:*** college transcript. ***Entrance:*** noncompetitive. ***Application deadline:*** rolling. ***Notification:*** continuous. ***Contact:*** Ms. Debbie Farris, Transfer Coordinator, 410-287-1000.
CONTACT Mr. Ray Perry, Computer Services Manager, Cecil Community College, North East, MD 21901-1999, 410-287-6060 Ext. 583. ***Fax:*** 410-287-1026.

CHARLES COUNTY COMMUNITY COLLEGE
La Plata, Maryland

UG Enrollment: 6,077	Tuition & Fees (Area Res): $1990
Application Deadline: rolling	Room & Board: N/Avail

GENERAL State and locally supported, 2-year, coed. Awards certificates, transfer associate, terminal associate degrees. Founded 1958. ***Setting:*** 175-acre rural campus with easy access to Washington, DC. ***Total enrollment:*** 6,077. ***Faculty:*** 355 (76 full-time, 279 part-time).
ENROLLMENT PROFILE 6,077 students from 3 states and territories, 1 other country. 65% women, 35% men, 75% part-time, 98% state residents, 2% international, 66% 25 or older, 1% Native American, 1% Hispanic, 11% African American, 2% Asian American. ***Most popular recent majors:*** liberal arts/general studies, business administration/commerce/management, nursing.
FIRST-YEAR CLASS 1,751 total.
ACADEMIC PROGRAM Honor code. Calendar: semesters. Academic remediation for entering students, English as a second language program offered during academic year, services for LD students, advanced placement, summer session for credit, part-time degree program (daytime, evenings, summer), adult/continuing education programs, co-op programs and internships. Study abroad in Spain.
GENERAL DEGREE REQUIREMENTS 62 credits; 1 math course.
MAJORS Accounting, biology/biological sciences, business administration/commerce/management, computer programming, computer technologies, data processing, early childhood education, education, electrical and electronics technologies, elementary education, engineering (general), (pre)engineering sequence, human services, liberal arts/general studies, nursing, paralegal studies, practical nursing.
LIBRARY Charles County Community College Library with 44,715 books, 3,000 microform titles, 568 periodicals, 3 on-line bibliographic services, 4,571 records, tapes, and CDs.
COMPUTERS ON CAMPUS Computer purchase plan available. 130 computers for student use in computer labs, learning resource center, library. Staffed computer lab on campus provides training in use of computers, software.
NOTEWORTHY RESEARCH FACILITIES Southern Maryland Studies Center.
COLLEGE LIFE Drama-theater group, choral group, student-run newspaper. ***Social organizations:*** 23 open to all. ***Most popular organizations:*** Spanish Club, Nursing Student Association, Science Club, Black Student Union, BACCHUS. ***Major annual events:*** Spring Fling Week, Fall Picnic. ***Student services:*** personal-psychological counseling, women's center. ***Campus security:*** 24-hour emergency response devices and patrols.
HOUSING College housing not available.
ATHLETICS Member NJCAA. ***Intercollegiate:*** baseball M, basketball M, golf M/W, soccer M, softball W, tennis M/W, volleyball W. ***Contact:*** Mr. Trevor Carpenter, Athletic Director, 301-934-2251 Ext. 228.
CAREER PLANNING ***Placement office:*** 5 full-time, 1 part-time staff. ***Director:*** Mrs. Joan Middleton, Director, 301-934-2251 Ext. 474. ***Services:*** job fairs, resume preparation, career counseling, careers library, job bank, job interviews.
AFTER GRADUATION 43% of students completing a degree program in 1994–95 went directly on to further study.
ESTIMATED EXPENSES FOR 1996–97 ***Application fee:*** $20. Area resident tuition: $1830 full-time, $61 per credit part-time. State resident tuition: $3660 full-time, $122 per credit part-time. Nonresident tuition: $5490 full-time, $183 per credit part-time. Part-time mandatory fees: $45 per semester (minimum). Full-time mandatory fees: $160 (minimum).
FINANCIAL AID ***College-administered undergrad aid 1995–96:*** 120 need-based scholarships (averaging $700), 75 non-need scholarships (averaging $500), low-interest long-term loans from external sources, 26 Federal Work-Study (averaging $1000), 80 part-time jobs. ***Required forms:*** institutional, FAFSA; accepted: CSS Financial Aid PROFILE. ***Priority deadline:*** 4/1. ***Waivers:*** full or partial for employees or children of employees and senior citizens.
APPLYING Open admission except for nursing program. ***Options:*** early entrance, deferred entrance. ***Required:*** TOEFL for international students. ***Recommended:*** school transcript. ***Required for some:*** ACT. Test scores used for admission. ***Application deadline:*** rolling. ***Notification:*** continuous.
APPLYING/TRANSFER ***Recommended:*** high school transcript. ***Required for some:*** college transcript. ***Application deadline:*** rolling. ***Notification:*** continuous.
CONTACT Ms. Charlotte Hill, Admissions Coordinator, Charles County Community College, PO Box 910, La Plata, MD 20646-0910, 301-934-2251 Ext. 544. ***Fax:*** 301-934-5255.

CHESAPEAKE COLLEGE
Wye Mills, Maryland

UG Enrollment: 2,068	Tuition & Fees (Area Res): $1886
Application Deadline: rolling	Room & Board: N/Avail

GENERAL State and locally supported, 2-year, coed. Awards certificates, transfer associate, terminal associate degrees. Founded 1965. ***Setting:*** 170-acre rural campus with easy access to Baltimore and Washington, DC. ***Total enrollment:*** 2,068. ***Faculty:*** 141 (41 full-time, 95% with terminal degrees, 100 part-time); student-faculty ratio is 18:1.
ENROLLMENT PROFILE 2,068 students from 3 states and territories. 69% women, 75% part-time, 99% state residents, 0% international, 55% 25 or older, 0% Native American, 0% Hispanic, 13% African American, 0% Asian American. ***Areas of study chosen:*** 39% liberal arts/general studies, 28% business management and administrative services, 10% education, 10% health professions and related sciences, 5% computer and information sciences, 4% engineering and applied sciences, 4% natural resource sciences.
FIRST-YEAR CLASS 654 total. 10% from top 10% of their high school class, 20% from top quarter, 50% from top half.
ACADEMIC PROGRAM Core. Calendar: semesters. 406 courses offered in 1995–96. Academic remediation for entering students, services for LD students, advanced placement, honors program, summer session for credit, part-time degree program (daytime, evenings, weekends, summer), adult/continuing education programs, co-op programs.
GENERAL DEGREE REQUIREMENT 63 credit hours.
MAJORS Accounting, architectural technologies, art/fine arts, aviation technology, business administration/commerce/management, computer programming, computer science, computer technologies, corrections, criminal justice, data processing, early childhood education, electrical and electronics technologies, elementary education, health education, humanities, human services, legal secretarial studies, liberal arts/general studies, mathematics, medical secretarial studies, music, physical education, physical sciences, radiological technology, recreation and leisure services, science, secretarial studies/office management, social science, sociology.
LIBRARY Learning Resource Center with 40,900 books, 800 microform titles, 350 periodicals, 700 records, tapes, and CDs.
COMPUTERS ON CAMPUS Computer purchase plan available. 200 computers for student use in computer center, computer labs, library provide access to e-mail, on-line services, Internet. Staffed computer lab on campus provides training in use of computers, software.
COLLEGE LIFE Drama-theater group, choral group. ***Social organizations:*** 6 open to all. ***Most popular organizations:*** Student Government Action Teams, Phi Theta Kappa Honor Society, Chesapeake Cheerleaders, UHURU, Chesapeake Players. ***Major annual events:*** Spring Fling, Fall Fest, Concert Series. ***Student services:*** personal-psychological counseling, women's center. ***Campus security:*** 24-hour patrols.
HOUSING College housing not available.
ATHLETICS Member NJCAA. ***Intercollegiate:*** basketball M/W, lacrosse M, soccer M, softball W, tennis M/W, volleyball W. ***Intramural:*** volleyball. ***Contact:*** Mr. Wayne Vashello, Athletic Director, 410-822-5400 Ext. 5818.
CAREER PLANNING ***Placement office:*** 1 full-time staff. ***Director:*** Ms. Kathy Petrichenko, Coordinator of Career Planning/Job Development, 410-822-5400 Ext. 5804. ***Services:*** job fairs, resume preparation, resume referral, career counseling, careers library, job bank, job interviews.
AFTER GRADUATION 45% of students completing a degree program in 1994–95 went directly on to further study.
EXPENSES FOR 1995–96 Area resident tuition: $1856 full-time, $58 per credit hour part-time. State resident tuition: $3712 full-time, $116 per credit hour part-time. Nonresident tuition: $5568 full-time, $174 per credit hour part-time. Part-time mandatory fees: $14 per semester. Full-time mandatory fees: $30.
FINANCIAL AID ***College-administered undergrad aid 1995–96:*** 135 need-based scholarships (averaging $375), 67 non-need scholarships (averaging $500), low-interest long-term loans from college funds (averaging $600), Federal Work-Study, 1 part-time job. ***Required forms:*** institutional, FAFSA. ***Priority deadline:*** 6/1. ***Payment plans:*** installment, deferred payment. ***Waivers:*** full or partial for employees or children of employees and senior citizens. ***Notification:*** 7/1. ***Average indebtedness of graduates:*** $1000.
APPLYING Open admission except for radiological technology, physical therapy assistant programs. ***Options:*** early entrance, deferred entrance, midyear entrance. ***Application deadline:*** rolling. ***Notification:*** continuous.
APPLYING/TRANSFER ***Entrance:*** noncompetitive. ***Application deadline:*** rolling. ***Notification:*** continuous. ***Contact:*** Mr. Richard Midcap, Director of Admissions, 410-822-5400 Ext. 455.
CONTACT Mr. Richard Midcap, Director of Admissions, Chesapeake College, Wye Mills, MD 21679-0008, 410-822-5400 Ext. 455. ***Fax:*** 410-827-9466. College video available.

DUNDALK COMMUNITY COLLEGE
Baltimore, Maryland

UG Enrollment: 3,203	Tuition & Fees (Area Res): $1880
Application Deadline: rolling	Room & Board: N/Avail

GENERAL County-supported, 2-year, coed. Awards transfer associate, terminal associate degrees. Founded 1970. ***Setting:*** 60-acre urban campus. ***Total enrollment:*** 3,203. ***Faculty:*** 230 (57 full-time, 18% with terminal degrees, 173 part-time); student-faculty ratio is 15:1.
ENROLLMENT PROFILE 3,203 students from 4 states and territories, 5 other countries. 57% women, 43% men, 82% part-time, 99% state residents, 8% transferred in, 68% 25 or older, 1% Native American, 1% Hispanic, 14% African American, 2% Asian American. ***Areas of study chosen:*** 25% interdisciplinary studies, 19% business management and administrative services, 12% engineering and applied sciences, 6% health professions and related sciences, 6% social sciences, 5% computer and information sciences, 3% vocational and home economics, 2% agriculture, 2% education, 2% performing arts, 1% communications and journalism. ***Most popular recent majors:*** liberal arts/general studies, paralegal studies, business administration/commerce/management.
FIRST-YEAR CLASS 624 total. Of the students who applied, 100% were accepted, 72% of whom enrolled.
ACADEMIC PROGRAM Core. Calendar: semesters. Academic remediation for entering students, English as a second language program offered during academic year, services for LD students, advanced placement, honors program, summer session for credit, part-time degree program (daytime, evenings, weekends, summer), external degree programs, adult/continuing education programs, co-op programs and internships.
GENERAL DEGREE REQUIREMENTS 60 credits; 2 math courses; 1 science course; computer course; internship (some majors).
MAJORS Accounting, business administration/commerce/management, child psychology/child development, communication equipment technology, computer information systems, early childhood education, electrical and electronics technologies, elementary education, engineering sciences, guidance and counseling, heating/refrigeration/air conditioning, industrial and heavy equipment maintenance, labor studies, legal secretarial studies,

Dundalk Community College (continued)
liberal arts/general studies, medical secretarial studies, mental health/rehabilitation counseling, ornamental horticulture, paralegal studies, photography, physical fitness/exercise science, real estate, secretarial studies/office management.
LIBRARY Dundalk Community College Library with 32,746 books, 109 microform titles, 285 periodicals, 3 CD-ROMs, 2,941 records, tapes, and CDs. Acquisition spending 1994–95: $438,059.
COMPUTERS ON CAMPUS 150 computers for student use in computer center, math, business labs provide access to off-campus computing facilities, Internet. Staffed computer lab on campus provides training in use of computers, software.
COLLEGE LIFE Drama-theater group, choral group, student-run newspaper. ***Most popular organizations:*** Student Government Association, Student Newspaper, Peer Counseling. ***Major annual events:*** Diversity Day, Activities Day, Annual Awards Ceremony. ***Student services:*** personal-psychological counseling, women's center. ***Campus security:*** 24-hour emergency response devices and patrols, late-night transport-escort service.
HOUSING College housing not available.
ATHLETICS Member NJCAA. ***Intercollegiate:*** baseball M(s), basketball M(s)/W(s), bowling M(s)/W(s), soccer M(s)/W(s), softball W(s), tennis M(s)/W(s), volleyball W(s). ***Contact:*** Mr. Kenneth MacLaughlin, Director of Athletics, 410-285-9713.
CAREER PLANNING ***Placement office:*** 1 full-time, 1 part-time staff. ***Director:*** Ms. Frances Smither, Director of Cooperative Education, 410-285-9956. ***Services:*** resume preparation, career counseling, careers library, job bank.
EXPENSES FOR 1996–97 ***Application fee:*** $10. Area resident tuition: $1800 full-time, $60 per credit part-time. State resident tuition: $3180 full-time, $106 per credit part-time. Nonresident tuition: $4890 full-time, $163 per credit part-time. Part-time mandatory fees: $5 per semester. Full-time mandatory fees: $80.
FINANCIAL AID ***College-administered undergrad aid 1995–96:*** need-based scholarships, short-term loans (average $100), Federal Work-Study, 15 part-time jobs. ***Required forms:*** institutional, FAFSA; accepted: CSS Financial Aid PROFILE. ***Priority deadline:*** 4/15. ***Payment plan:*** installment. ***Waivers:*** full or partial for employees or children of employees and senior citizens. ***Notification:*** 6/1.
APPLYING Open admission. ***Options:*** early entrance, midyear entrance. ***Required:*** school transcript. ***Recommended:*** TOEFL for international students. Test scores used for counseling/placement. ***Application deadline:*** rolling.
APPLYING/TRANSFER ***Required:*** high school transcript. ***Entrance:*** noncompetitive. ***Application deadline:*** rolling. ***Contact:*** Mr. Wayne Ching, Transfer Counselor, 410-285-9806.
CONTACT Mrs. Danielle Brookhart, Admissions Assistant, Dundalk Community College, 7200 Sollers Point Road, Baltimore, MD 21222-4694, 410-285-9802. College video available.

ESSEX COMMUNITY COLLEGE
Baltimore, Maryland

UG Enrollment: 9,252	**Tuition & Fees (Area Res): $1643**
Application Deadline: rolling	**Room & Board: N/Avail**

GENERAL State and locally supported, 2-year, coed. Awards certificates, transfer associate, terminal associate degrees. Founded 1957. ***Setting:*** 150-acre suburban campus with easy access to Baltimore and Washington, DC. ***Total enrollment:*** 9,252. ***Faculty:*** 525 (150 full-time, 35% with terminal degrees, 375 part-time).
ENROLLMENT PROFILE 9,252 students: 61% women, 39% men, 71% part-time, 99% state residents, 12% transferred in, 30% have need-based financial aid, 1% international, 50% 25 or older, 1% Native American, 1% Hispanic, 11% African American, 3% Asian American. ***Areas of study chosen:*** 33% interdisciplinary studies, 22% health professions and related sciences, 19% business management and administrative services, 6% social sciences, 5% computer and information sciences, 5% education, 4% engineering and applied sciences, 3% fine arts, 1% biological and life sciences, 1% mathematics, 1% prevet. ***Most popular recent majors:*** liberal arts/general studies, nursing, business administration/commerce/management.
FIRST-YEAR CLASS 1,407 total. Of the students who applied, 100% were accepted.
ACADEMIC PROGRAM Core. Calendar: semesters. Academic remediation for entering students, English as a second language program offered during academic year and summer, services for LD students, honors program, summer session for credit, part-time degree program (daytime, evenings, weekends, summer), adult/continuing education programs, co-op programs and internships. Off-campus study at Dundalk Community College, Catonsville Community College. ROTC: Army (c).
GENERAL DEGREE REQUIREMENTS 60 credits; 3 credits each of math and science.
MAJORS Accounting, anthropology, art education, art/fine arts, athletic training, biology/biological sciences, business administration/commerce/management, chemistry, computer information systems, computer science, criminal justice, dance, drafting and design, early childhood education, economics, emergency medical technology, engineering (general), English, geography, health services administration, history, human resources, liberal arts/general studies, marketing/retailing/merchandising, mathematics, medical laboratory technology, mental health/rehabilitation counseling, music, music education, nursing, philosophy, physical education, physical fitness/exercise science, physician's assistant studies, physics, political science/government, psychology, radiological technology, respiratory therapy, sociology, sports medicine, teacher aide studies, theater arts/drama, veterinary technology.
LIBRARY James Newpher Library with 92,416 books, 8,853 microform titles, 449 periodicals, 15 CD-ROMs, 7,639 records, tapes, and CDs. Acquisition spending 1994–95: $24,686.
COMPUTERS ON CAMPUS Computer purchase plan available. 300 computers for student use in computer center, computer labs, classrooms, library provide access to main academic computer. Staffed computer lab on campus provides training in use of computers, software.
COLLEGE LIFE Drama-theater group, student-run newspaper, radio station. ***Student services:*** personal-psychological counseling. ***Campus security:*** 24-hour emergency response devices and patrols, late-night transport-escort service.
HOUSING College housing not available.
ATHLETICS Member NJCAA. ***Intercollegiate:*** basketball M/W, bowling M/W, cross-country running M/W, field hockey W, golf M/W, lacrosse M/W, soccer M/W, tennis M/W, track and field M/W, volleyball M/W. ***Contact:*** Ms. Carol Eustis, Athletic Director, 410-780-6972.
CAREER PLANNING ***Director:*** Dr. Richard Lilley, Director of Counseling, 410-780-6368. ***Service:*** career counseling.
EXPENSES FOR 1996–97 ***Application fee:*** $10. Area resident tuition: $1500 full-time, $60 per credit part-time. State resident tuition: $2684 full-time, $106 per credit part-time. Nonresident tuition: $4124 full-time, $166 per credit part-time. Part-time mandatory fees per semester range from $15 to $67. Full-time mandatory fees: $143.
FINANCIAL AID ***College-administered undergrad aid 1995–96:*** 520 need-based scholarships (average $969), 135 non-need scholarships (average $473), short-term loans (average $350), low-interest long-term loans from external sources (average $2116), Federal Work-Study, 83 part-time jobs. ***Required forms:*** institutional; accepted: state, FAFSA. ***Priority deadline:*** 5/1.
APPLYING Open admission. ***Option:*** early entrance. ***Required:*** TOEFL for international students. ***Recommended:*** 3 years of high school math and science. Test scores used for counseling/placement. ***Application deadline:*** rolling. ***Notification:*** continuous until 9/8.
APPLYING/TRANSFER ***Recommended:*** 3 years of high school math and science. ***Entrance:*** noncompetitive. ***Application deadline:*** rolling. ***Notification:*** continuous until 9/8.
CONTACT Ms. Diane Lane, Director of Admissions, Essex Community College, Baltimore, MD 21237-3899, 410-780-6840 or toll-free 800-832-0262.

FREDERICK COMMUNITY COLLEGE
Frederick, Maryland

UG Enrollment: 4,378	**Tuition & Fees (Area Res): $1752**
Application Deadline: 9/1	**Room & Board: N/Avail**

GENERAL State and locally supported, 2-year, coed. Awards certificates, transfer associate, terminal associate degrees. Founded 1957. ***Setting:*** 125-acre small-town campus with easy access to Baltimore and Washington, DC. ***Total enrollment:*** 4,378. ***Faculty:*** 272 (72 full-time, 200 part-time); student-faculty ratio is 17:1.
ENROLLMENT PROFILE 4,378 students from 5 states and territories, 4 other countries. 61% women, 69% part-time, 98% state residents, 15% transferred in, 1% international, 60% 25 or older, 1% Native American, 1% Hispanic, 6% African American, 2% Asian American.
FIRST-YEAR CLASS 1,144 total. Of the students who applied, 100% were accepted.
ACADEMIC PROGRAM Core, honor code. Calendar: semesters. Academic remediation for entering students, English as a second language program offered during academic year and summer, services for LD students, advanced placement, honors program, summer session for credit, part-time degree program (daytime, evenings, summer), adult/continuing education programs, co-op programs. Off-campus study at Hood College, Mount Saint Mary's College. ROTC: Army (c).
GENERAL DEGREE REQUIREMENTS 60 credit hours; 1 course each in math and science; computer course for business majors.
MAJORS Accounting, agricultural business, agricultural sciences, art/fine arts, aviation technology, biology/biological sciences, business administration/commerce/management, chemistry, child care/child and family studies, communication, computer technologies, construction management, criminal justice, data processing, drafting and design, early childhood education, education, electrical and electronics technologies, elementary education, engineering (general), English, finance/banking, human services, international business, laboratory technologies, legal secretarial studies, liberal arts/general studies, marketing/retailing/merchandising, mathematics, medical secretarial studies, music education, nursing, paralegal studies, parks management, physical education, physical sciences, psychology, recreation and leisure services, respiratory therapy, secretarial studies/office management, wildlife management.
LIBRARY 41,000 books, 300 periodicals, 6,000 records, tapes, and CDs.
COMPUTERS ON CAMPUS 75 computers for student use in computer center, computer labs, learning resource center, writing center, classrooms, library. Staffed computer lab on campus.
COLLEGE LIFE Drama-theater group, student-run newspaper. ***Social organizations:*** 15 open to all. ***Student services:*** personal-psychological counseling. ***Campus security:*** 24-hour emergency response devices and patrols.
HOUSING College housing not available.
ATHLETICS Member NJCAA. ***Intercollegiate:*** basketball M/W, golf M, soccer M, volleyball W. ***Contact:*** Dr. Thomas Jandovitz, Athletic Director, 301-846-2500.
CAREER PLANNING ***Placement office:*** 2 full-time staff. ***Director:*** Ms. Sandy Smith, Director of Student Services, 301-846-2470. ***Services:*** job fairs, resume preparation, resume referral, career counseling, careers library, job bank, job interviews.
AFTER GRADUATION 39% of students completing a degree program in 1994–95 went directly on to further study.
EXPENSES FOR 1996–97 Area resident tuition: $1560 full-time, $65 per credit hour part-time. State resident tuition: $3120 full-time, $130 per credit hour part-time. Nonresident tuition: $4872 full-time, $203 per credit hour part-time. Full-time mandatory fees: $192.
FINANCIAL AID ***College-administered undergrad aid 1995–96:*** 18 need-based scholarships (average $150), 34 non-need scholarships (average $240), low-interest long-term loans from external sources (average $500), Federal Work-Study, part-time jobs. ***Acceptable forms:*** CSS Financial Aid PROFILE, FAFSA. ***Priority deadline:*** 7/15.
APPLYING Open admission except for nursing, aviation maintenance, respiratory therapy programs. ***Options:*** early entrance, deferred entrance. ***Required:*** TOEFL for international students. Test scores used for counseling/placement. ***Application deadline:*** 9/1.
APPLYING/TRANSFER ***Application deadline:*** 9/1. ***Contact:*** Ms. Debra Lee Martin, Transfer Counselor, 301-846-2470.
CONTACT Dr. James M. Holton, Associate Dean of Admissions and Registration, Frederick Community College, Frederick, MD 21702-2097, 301-846-2430.

GARRETT COMMUNITY COLLEGE
McHenry, Maryland

UG Enrollment: 722	**Tuition & Fees (Area Res): $1916**
Application Deadline: rolling	**Room & Board: N/R**

GENERAL State and locally supported, 2-year, coed. Awards certificates, transfer associate, terminal associate degrees. Founded 1966. ***Setting:*** 62-acre rural campus. ***Endow-***

ment: $500,000. ***Educational spending 1994–95:*** $2176 per undergrad. ***Total enrollment:*** 722. ***Faculty:*** 69 (17 full-time, 1% with terminal degrees, 52 part-time); student-faculty ratio is 15:1. ***Notable Alumni:*** Willetta Mateer, certified public accountant; Linda Buckel, principal of Red House Elementary School; Keith Harvey, principal of Crellin Elementary School; Linda Fike, director of personnel at Garrett Community College; Rob Michael owner of State Farm Insurance Agency.

ENROLLMENT PROFILE 722 students from 11 states and territories. 60% women, 40% men, 47% part-time, 72% state residents, 8% live on campus, 7% transferred in, 85% have need-based financial aid, 10% have non-need-based financial aid, 0% international, 44% 25 or older, 1% Native American, 1% Hispanic, 2% African American, 0% Asian American. ***Areas of study chosen:*** 31% business management and administrative services, 23% liberal arts/general studies, 12% education, 10% natural resource sciences, 7% social sciences, 4% agriculture, 3% mathematics, 2% fine arts. ***Most popular recent majors:*** business administration/commerce/management, liberal arts/general studies, education.

FIRST-YEAR CLASS 275 total; 381 applied, 100% were accepted, 72% of whom enrolled.

ACADEMIC PROGRAM Core, interdisciplinary curriculum, honor code. Calendar: semesters. 237 courses offered in 1995–96; average class size 15 in required courses. Academic remediation for entering students, services for LD students, self-designed majors, tutorials, summer session for credit, part-time degree program (daytime), external degree programs, adult/continuing education programs, internships.

GENERAL DEGREE REQUIREMENTS 64 credit hours; computer course for transfer associate degree students; internship (some majors).

MAJORS Agricultural technologies, art/fine arts, behavioral sciences, biology/biological sciences, business administration/commerce/management, education, elementary education, fish and game management, hotel and restaurant management, liberal arts/general studies, mathematics, music, natural resource management, parks management, physical education, psychology, recreation and leisure services, secretarial studies/office management, social science, sociology, wildlife biology, wildlife management.

LIBRARY Learning Resource Center with 26,000 books, 2 microform titles, 176 periodicals, 5 CD-ROMs, 450 records, tapes, and CDs. Acquisition spending 1994–95: $20,000.

COMPUTERS ON CAMPUS 60 computers for student use in computer center, departmental labs, library provide access to e-mail, on-line services. Staffed computer lab on campus provides training in use of computers, software.

COLLEGE LIFE Orientation program (3 days). Drama-theater group, student-run newspaper. ***Social organizations:*** 3 open to all; 1 national fraternity; 20% of eligible men are members. ***Most popular organizations:*** Wildlife Club, Raiders of the Lost Arts, Student Government. ***Major annual events:*** Back to College Event, GCC/ACC Basketball Game, Orientation. ***Student services:*** personal-psychological counseling.

HOUSING 60 college housing spaces available; all were occupied 1995–96. No special consideration for freshman housing applicants. Off-campus living permitted. ***Option:*** coed housing available. Resident assistants live in dorms.

ATHLETICS Member NJCAA. ***Intercollegiate:*** baseball M, basketball M(s)/W(s), golf M/W, skiing (downhill) M(c)/W(c), volleyball W(s). ***Intramural:*** badminton, basketball, bowling, golf, skiing (downhill), softball, table tennis (Ping-Pong), tennis, volleyball. ***Contact:*** Ms. Ann Wellham, Athletic Director, 301-387-3052.

CAREER PLANNING ***Placement office:*** 2 part-time staff; $403,210 operating expenditure 1994–95. ***Director:*** Ms. Sandy Major, Job Placement Coordinator, 301-387-3080. ***Services:*** job fairs, resume preparation, resume referral, career counseling, careers library, job bank, job interviews. 75 organizations recruited on campus 1994–95.

EXPENSES FOR 1995–96 Area resident tuition: $1856 full-time, $58 per credit hour part-time. State resident tuition: $2432 full-time, $76 per credit hour part-time. Nonresident tuition: $4032 full-time, $126 per credit hour part-time. Part-time mandatory fees: $10 per semester. Full-time mandatory fees: $60.

FINANCIAL AID ***College-administered undergrad aid 1995–96:*** 40 need-based scholarships (average $400), non-need scholarships, short-term loans, low-interest long-term loans from external sources (average $2625), Federal Work-Study, part-time jobs. ***Required forms:*** CSS Financial Aid PROFILE, institutional, FAFSA, verification worksheet; accepted: state. ***Priority deadline:*** 9/1.

APPLYING Open admission. ***Options:*** Common Application, early entrance, midyear entrance. ***Required:*** school transcript, interview, TOEFL for international students. ***Recommended:*** minimum 2.0 GPA, 3 years of high school math and science, SAT I or ACT. Test scores used for counseling/placement. ***Application deadline:*** rolling. ***Notification:*** continuous.

APPLYING/TRANSFER ***Required:*** high school transcript, college transcript, minimum 2.0 college GPA, minimum 2.0 high school GPA. ***Recommended:*** 3 years of high school math and science, interview. ***Entrance:*** noncompetitive. ***Application deadline:*** rolling. ***Notification:*** continuous. ***Contact:*** Ms. Darlene Reed, Administrative Assistant, Admissions, 301-387-3010.

CONTACT Ms. Darlene Reed, Administrative Assistant, Admissions, Garrett Community College, McHenry, MD 21541-0151, 301-387-3010.

HAGERSTOWN BUSINESS COLLEGE
Hagerstown, Maryland

UG Enrollment: 517	**Tuition & Fees: $4422**
Application Deadline: rolling	**Room Only: $2200**

GENERAL Proprietary, 2-year, primarily women. Awards certificates, terminal associate degrees. Founded 1938. ***Setting:*** 8-acre small-town campus with easy access to Baltimore and Washington, DC. ***Total enrollment:*** 517. ***Faculty:*** 32 (7 full-time, 25 part-time); student-faculty ratio is 16:1.

ENROLLMENT PROFILE 517 students from 5 states and territories. 91% women, 9% men, 42% part-time, 40% state residents, 3% live on campus, 3% transferred in, 63% have need-based financial aid, 5% have non-need-based financial aid, 0% international, 47% 25 or older, 1% Native American, 3% African American, 1% Asian American. ***Areas of study chosen:*** 48% health professions and related sciences, 22% business management and administrative services, 16% social sciences, 14% computer and information sciences. ***Most popular recent majors:*** medical secretarial studies, business administration/commerce/management, computer information systems.

FIRST-YEAR CLASS 186 total; 245 applied, 94% were accepted, 81% of whom enrolled.

ACADEMIC PROGRAM Honor code. Calendar: trimesters. 103 courses offered in 1995–96. Academic remediation for entering students, part-time degree program (daytime), adult/continuing education programs, internships.

GENERAL DEGREE REQUIREMENTS 68 credit hours; computer course; internship (some majors).

MAJORS Accounting, business administration/commerce/management, computer information systems, court reporting, data processing, legal secretarial studies, marketing/retailing/merchandising, medical assistant technologies, medical records services, medical secretarial studies, paralegal studies, secretarial studies/office management.

LIBRARY 6,418 books, 567 microform titles, 91 periodicals, 29 CD-ROMs, 407 records, tapes, and CDs.

COMPUTERS ON CAMPUS 84 computers for student use in computer labs, library. Staffed computer lab on campus.

COLLEGE LIFE 30% vote in student government elections. ***Social organizations:*** 5 open to all; 1 local sorority; 13% of eligible women are members. ***Student services:*** personal-psychological counseling. ***Campus security:*** 24-hour emergency response devices.

HOUSING 71 college housing spaces available; 18 were occupied 1995–96. No special consideration for freshman housing applicants. Off-campus living permitted. ***Option:*** coed (1 building) housing available. Resident assistants live in dorms.

CAREER PLANNING ***Placement office:*** 1 full-time staff. ***Director:*** Ms. Marci Dean, Director of Placement, 301-739-2670. ***Services:*** job fairs, resume preparation, resume referral, career counseling, job bank, job interviews.

AFTER GRADUATION 87% of class of 1994 had job offers within 6 months.

EXPENSES FOR 1995–96 ***Application fee:*** $25. Tuition: $4352 full-time, $128 per credit hour part-time. Part-time mandatory fees: $35 per trimester. Full-time mandatory fees: $70. College room only: $2200.

FINANCIAL AID ***College-administered undergrad aid 1995–96:*** 35 non-need scholarships (average $3000), low-interest long-term loans from external sources (average $2625), 15 Federal Work-Study (averaging $1200). ***Required forms:*** institutional, FAFSA; accepted: CSS Financial Aid PROFILE. ***Application deadline:*** continuous to 9/29. ***Payment plan:*** installment. ***Waivers:*** full or partial for employees or children of employees.

APPLYING Open admission. ***Options:*** early entrance, deferred entrance, midyear entrance. ***Required:*** school transcript, Assessment and Placement Services for Community Colleges. Test scores used for counseling/placement. ***Application deadline:*** rolling.

APPLYING/TRANSFER ***Required:*** high school transcript, college transcript. ***Entrance:*** noncompetitive. ***Application deadline:*** rolling. ***Contact:*** Ms. Teresa Adams, Director of Admissions, 301-739-2670.

CONTACT Mrs. Teresa Adams, Director of Admissions, Hagerstown Business College, Hagerstown, MD 21742-2797, 301-739-2670 or toll-free 800-422-2670. ***Fax:*** 301-791-7661.

HAGERSTOWN JUNIOR COLLEGE
Hagerstown, Maryland

UG Enrollment: 3,026	**Tuition & Fees (Area Res): $2164**
Application Deadline: rolling	**Room & Board: N/Avail**

GENERAL County-supported, 2-year, coed. Awards certificates, transfer associate, terminal associate degrees. Founded 1946. ***Setting:*** 187-acre small-town campus with easy access to Baltimore and Washington, DC. ***Endowment:*** $1.8 million. ***Educational spending 1994–95:*** $1541 per undergrad. ***Total enrollment:*** 3,026. ***Faculty:*** 177 (57 full-time, 21% with terminal degrees, 120 part-time); student-faculty ratio is 20:1. ***Notable Alumni:*** Mike Draper, major league baseball player; Charles Dutton, actor; John P. Corderman, judge; Charles "Tucker" Brugh, hospital executive administrator; Rev. A. Paul Harne, minister.

ENROLLMENT PROFILE 3,026 students from 12 states and territories, 1 other country. 62% women, 38% men, 64% part-time, 75% state residents, 10% transferred in, 30% have need-based financial aid, 1% have non-need-based financial aid, 1% international, 55% 25 or older, 1% Native American, 1% Hispanic, 6% African American, 1% Asian American. ***Areas of study chosen:*** 21% liberal arts/general studies, 17% business management and administrative services, 9% health professions and related sciences, 7% education, 6% engineering and applied sciences, 5% computer and information sciences, 5% social sciences, 2% biological and life sciences, 1% communications and journalism. ***Most popular recent majors:*** liberal arts/general studies, business administration/commerce/management, nursing.

FIRST-YEAR CLASS 729 total; 988 applied, 100% were accepted, 74% of whom enrolled. 10% from top 10% of their high school class, 90% from top half.

ACADEMIC PROGRAM Core, honor code. Calendar: semesters. 300 courses offered in 1995–96. Academic remediation for entering students, services for LD students, advanced placement, self-designed majors, tutorials, honors program, summer session for credit, part-time degree program (daytime, evenings, summer), adult/continuing education programs, co-op programs and internships. Off-campus study at Hood College.

GENERAL DEGREE REQUIREMENTS 64 credit hours; internship (some majors).

MAJORS Accounting, biology/biological sciences, business administration/commerce/management, chemistry, communication, computer information systems, computer science, early childhood education, education, electrical engineering technology, (pre)engineering sequence, human services, law enforcement/police sciences, liberal arts/general studies, marketing/retailing/merchandising, mathematics, mechanical engineering technology, nursing, paralegal studies, physical education, physics, radiological technology, secretarial studies/office management.

LIBRARY William Brish Library with 50,000 books, 450 periodicals, 3 CD-ROMs, 1,977 records, tapes, and CDs. Acquisition spending 1994–95: $74,106.

COMPUTERS ON CAMPUS Computer purchase plan available. 200 computers for student use in computer center, computer labs, learning resource center, satellite labs, classrooms, library provide access to main academic computer, off-campus computing facilities, e-mail, on-line services, Internet. Staffed computer lab on campus provides training in use of computers, software.

COLLEGE LIFE Drama-theater group, choral group, student-run newspaper. ***Social organizations:*** 16 open to all. ***Most popular organizations:*** Phi Theta Kappa, Drama Club, Health Occupations Association, Law Enforcement Association, Human Services Organization. ***Student services:*** health clinic, personal-psychological counseling. ***Campus security:*** 24-hour patrols.

HOUSING College housing not available.

ATHLETICS Member NJCAA. ***Intercollegiate:*** baseball M, basketball M(s)/W(s), cross-country running M(s)/W(s), soccer M, softball W, tennis M/W, track and field M(s)/W(s),

Peterson's Guide to Two-Year Colleges 1997 357

Hagerstown Junior College (continued)
volleyball W(s). ***Intramural:*** baseball, basketball, soccer, softball, table tennis (Ping-Pong), tennis, volleyball. ***Contact:*** Mr. James Brown, Athletic Director, 301-790-2800 Ext. 289.

CAREER PLANNING ***Placement office:*** 1 full-time, 2 part-time staff; $50,000 operating expenditure 1994–95. ***Director:*** Mr. Dave Cole, Director of Student Services, 301-790-2800. ***Services:*** resume preparation, resume referral, career counseling, careers library, job bank, job interviews.

AFTER GRADUATION 65% of students completing a degree program in 1994–95 went directly on to further study.

EXPENSES FOR 1995–96 ***Application fee:*** $10. Area resident tuition: $2048 full-time, $64 per credit hour part-time. State resident tuition: $2880 full-time, $90 per credit hour part-time. Nonresident tuition: $3744 full-time, $117 per credit hour part-time. Part-time mandatory fees per semester range from $13 to $43. Full-time mandatory fees: $116.

FINANCIAL AID ***College-administered undergrad aid 1995–96:*** 152 need-based scholarships (averaging $790), 33 non-need scholarships (averaging $637), short-term loans (averaging $75), low-interest long-term loans, Federal Work-Study, 75 part-time jobs. ***Required forms:*** institutional, FAFSA; accepted: CSS Financial Aid PROFILE. ***Priority deadline:*** 5/30. ***Payment plan:*** deferred payment. ***Waivers:*** full or partial for employees or children of employees and senior citizens. ***Average indebtedness of graduates:*** $3500.

APPLYING Open admission except for nursing, radiological technology programs. ***Options:*** Common Application, early entrance, deferred entrance. ***Required:*** school transcript, TOEFL for international students. ***Required for some:*** ACT. Test scores used for counseling/placement. ***Application deadline:*** rolling. ***Notification:*** 8/25.

APPLYING/TRANSFER ***Required:*** high school transcript, college transcript. ***Required for some:*** standardized test scores. ***Application deadline:*** rolling. ***Notification:*** 8/25. ***Contact:*** Dr. Marie Nowakowski, Transfer Counselor, 301-790-2800.

CONTACT Mr. Timothy R. Kennedy, Director of Enrollment Services, Hagerstown Junior College, Hagerstown, MD 21742-6590, 301-790-2800 Ext. 238. ***Fax:*** 301-739-0737.

HARFORD COMMUNITY COLLEGE
Bel Air, Maryland

UG Enrollment: 4,957	**Tuition & Fees (Area Res): $1878**
Application Deadline: rolling	**Room & Board: N/Avail**

GENERAL State and locally supported, 2-year, coed. Awards certificates, diplomas, transfer associate, terminal associate degrees. Founded 1957. ***Setting:*** 212-acre small-town campus with easy access to Baltimore. ***Endowment:*** $1.3 million. ***Total enrollment:*** 4,957. ***Faculty:*** 358 (84 full-time, 98% with terminal degrees, 274 part-time); student-faculty ratio is 19:1. ***Notable Alumni:*** James Harkins, Maryland State House of Delegates; Dale R. Bowles, Jr., chief of Risk Communications at U.S. Army Center for Health Promotion and Preventive Medicine; Chris Callis, accountant; Charles Ramsey, president of Famous and Spang Insurance Agency; Don Morrison, spokesperson for Hartford County public schools.

ENROLLMENT PROFILE 4,957 students from 4 states and territories, 9 other countries. 62% women, 38% men, 74% part-time, 98% state residents, 1% international, 54% 25 or older, 0% Native American, 2% Hispanic, 8% African American, 2% Asian American. ***Areas of study chosen:*** 31% liberal arts/general studies, 23% business management and administrative services, 16% health professions and related sciences, 7% education, 7% social sciences, 4% engineering and applied sciences, 4% interdisciplinary studies, 4% prelaw, 3% psychology, 2% architecture, 2% communications and journalism, 2% computer and information sciences, 1% physical sciences. ***Most popular recent majors:*** liberal arts/general studies, nursing, business administration/commerce/management.

FIRST-YEAR CLASS 1,029 total; 1,407 applied, 100% were accepted, 73% of whom enrolled. 5% from top 10% of their high school class, 50% from top half.

ACADEMIC PROGRAM Core, general education, career-oriented curriculum, honor code. Calendar: semesters. 423 courses offered in 1995–96. Academic remediation for entering students, English as a second language program offered during academic year, services for LD students, advanced placement, self-designed majors, summer session for credit, part-time degree program (daytime, evenings, weekends, summer), adult/continuing education programs, co-op programs and internships.

GENERAL DEGREE REQUIREMENTS 62 credits hours; 3 credit hours of math, 7 credit hours of science including at least 1 lab science course for associate of art and associate of science degree; 3 credit hours of math, 4 credits of science for associate of applied science degree.

MAJORS Accounting, art/fine arts, audio engineering, automotive technologies, behavioral sciences, biology/biological sciences, broadcasting, business administration/commerce/management, chemistry, child care/child and family studies, commercial art, communication, computer information systems, computer science, criminal justice, drafting and design, early childhood education, education, electrical and electronics technologies, elementary education, engineering (general), English, environmental engineering technology, environmental studies, health education, history, hospitality services, human development, humanities, information science, interior design, laboratory technologies, liberal arts/general studies, marketing/retailing/merchandising, mathematics, medical assistant technologies, medical laboratory technology, music, nursing, paralegal studies, philosophy, photography, physics, political science/government, psychology, public relations, retail management, science, secretarial studies/office management, social science, sociology.

LIBRARY Learning Resources Center with 53,032 books, 402 periodicals, 7 CD-ROMs, 3,878 records, tapes, and CDs. Acquisition spending 1994–95: $110,198.

COMPUTERS ON CAMPUS 244 computers for student use in computer center, computer labs, classrooms, library provide access to main academic computer. Staffed computer lab on campus provides training in use of computers, software.

COLLEGE LIFE Drama-theater group, choral group, student-run radio station. ***Social organizations:*** 18 open to all. ***Most popular organizations:*** Student Association, Paralegal Club, Multi-National Hispanics, Student Nursing Association, Video Club. ***Major annual events:*** Welcome Week Picnic, Octoberfest, Holiday Party. ***Student services:*** personal-psychological counseling. ***Campus security:*** 24-hour patrols, late-night transport-escort service.

HOUSING College housing not available.

ATHLETICS Member NJCAA. ***Intercollegiate:*** baseball M(s), basketball M/W(s), field hockey W(s), lacrosse M/W(s), soccer M, softball W(s), tennis M/W(s). ***Intramural:*** lacrosse. ***Contact:*** Mr. Jack Nichols, Athletic Director, 410-836-4321.

CAREER PLANNING ***Placement office:*** 1 full-time, 3 part-time staff. ***Director:*** Dr. Darwin Kysor, Coordinator, Cooperative Education and Placement, 410-836-4187. ***Services:*** job fairs, resume preparation, resume referral, career counseling, careers library, job bank, job interviews. 10 organizations recruited on campus 1994–95.

AFTER GRADUATION 45% of students completing a degree program in 1994–95 went directly on to further study.

EXPENSES FOR 1995–96 Area resident tuition: $1740 full-time, $58 per credit hour part-time. State resident tuition: $2760 full-time, $92 per credit hour part-time. Nonresident tuition: $4050 full-time, $135 per credit hour part-time. Part-time mandatory fees: $5.60 per credit hour. Full-time mandatory fees: $138.

FINANCIAL AID ***College-administered undergrad aid 1995–96:*** need-based scholarships (average $400), non-need scholarships (average $400), short-term loans (average $400), low-interest long-term loans from external sources (average $1000), Federal Work-Study. ***Required forms:*** institutional, FAFSA. ***Priority deadline:*** 5/1. ***Waivers:*** full or partial for employees or children of employees.

APPLYING Open admission. ***Options:*** Common Application, early entrance, midyear entrance. ***Required:*** TOEFL for international students. ***Application deadline:*** rolling.

APPLYING/TRANSFER ***Entrance:*** noncompetitive. ***Application deadline:*** rolling.

CONTACT Ms. Donna Youngberg, Admissions Advisor, Harford Community College, 401 Thomas Run Road, Bel Air, MD 21015-1698, 410-836-4220. ***Fax:*** 410-836-4197.

HOWARD COMMUNITY COLLEGE
Columbia, Maryland

UG Enrollment: 5,130	**Tuition & Fees (Area Res): $2592**
Application Deadline: rolling	**Room & Board: N/Avail**

GENERAL State and locally supported, 2-year, coed. Awards certificates, transfer associate, terminal associate degrees. Founded 1966. ***Setting:*** 122-acre suburban campus with easy access to Baltimore and Washington, DC. ***Endowment:*** $1.3 million. ***Total enrollment:*** 5,130. ***Faculty:*** 315 (94 full-time, 18% with terminal degrees, 221 part-time); student-faculty ratio is 20:1.

ENROLLMENT PROFILE 5,130 students: 60% women, 74% part-time, 99% state residents, 14% transferred in, 25% have need-based financial aid, 5% have non-need-based financial aid, 77% 25 or older, 1% Native American, 2% Hispanic, 17% African American, 6% Asian American. ***Most popular recent majors:*** nursing, business administration/commerce/management.

FIRST-YEAR CLASS 951 total; 951 applied, 100% were accepted, 100% of whom enrolled.

ACADEMIC PROGRAM Core, honor code. Calendar: semesters. 221 courses offered in 1995–96. Academic remediation for entering students, services for LD students, advanced placement, honors program, summer session for credit, part-time degree program (daytime, evenings, weekends, summer), adult/continuing education programs, co-op programs.

GENERAL DEGREE REQUIREMENTS 62 credit hours; math/science requirements vary according to program; computer course for business administration, engineering majors.

MAJORS Accounting, applied art, art/fine arts, biomedical technologies, business administration/commerce/management, child care/child and family studies, computer graphics, computer programming, computer science, computer technologies, criminal justice, data processing, drafting and design, drug and alcohol/substance abuse counseling, early childhood education, education, electrical and electronics technologies, electronics engineering technology, elementary education, engineering (general), fashion merchandising, finance/banking, health education, laboratory technologies, legal secretarial studies, liberal arts/general studies, medical secretarial studies, medical technology, music, nursing, pharmacy/pharmaceutical sciences, photography, physical sciences, practical nursing, psychology, retail management, science, secretarial studies/office management, social science, telecommunications, theater arts/drama, veterinary sciences.

LIBRARY Learning Resources Center with 36,956 books, 78 microform titles, 469 periodicals, 2 on-line bibliographic services, 25 CD-ROMs, 4,745 records, tapes, and CDs.

COMPUTERS ON CAMPUS 750 computers for student use in computer labs, learning resource center, counseling center, classrooms, library provide access to e-mail, on-line services, Internet. Staffed computer lab on campus provides training in use of computers, software.

COLLEGE LIFE Drama-theater group, choral group, student-run newspaper. ***Social organizations:*** 11 open to all. ***Most popular organizations:*** Secretarial Club, Nursing Club, Black Student Union, Student Newspaper, Student Government Association. ***Major annual events:*** Fall Cookout, Spring Fling, Weekly Block Time. ***Student services:*** personal-psychological counseling. ***Campus security:*** 24-hour emergency response devices and patrols, late-night transport-escort service.

HOUSING College housing not available.

ATHLETICS Member NJCAA. ***Intercollegiate:*** basketball M/W, cross-country running M/W, golf M/W, soccer M, tennis M/W, track and field M/W. ***Intramural:*** basketball, softball. ***Contact:*** Mr. Phil Chenier, Director of Student Activities, 410-964-4984.

CAREER PLANNING ***Placement office:*** 1 full-time, 1 part-time staff. ***Director:*** Dr. Brenda Lorick, Director of Counseling and Career Services, 410-992-4840. ***Services:*** job fairs, resume preparation, career counseling, careers library, job bank. 100 organizations recruited on campus 1994–95.

EXPENSES FOR 1996–97 ***Application fee:*** $10. Area resident tuition: $2356 full-time, $76 per credit hour part-time. State resident tuition: $3813 full-time, $123 per credit hour part-time. Nonresident tuition: $5425 full-time, $175 per credit hour part-time. Part-time mandatory fees per credit hour range from $7.60 to $17.50. Full-time mandatory fees: $236.

FINANCIAL AID ***College-administered undergrad aid 1995–96:*** 634 need-based scholarships (average $623), 10 non-need scholarships (average $1000), short-term loans, low-interest long-term loans from external sources (average $2200), 55 Federal Work-Study (averaging $642), 60 part-time jobs. ***Required forms:*** FAFSA; required for some: state, institutional. ***Priority deadline:*** 5/15. ***Waivers:*** full or partial for employees or children of employees and senior citizens. ***Notification:*** 7/1.

APPLYING Open admission. ***Options:*** early entrance, deferred entrance. ***Required:*** TOEFL for international students. ***Required for some:*** school transcript, SAT I or ACT. Test scores used for counseling/placement. ***Application deadline:*** rolling. ***Notification:*** continuous.

APPLYING/TRANSFER ***Required for some:*** high school transcript. ***Entrance:*** noncompetitive. ***Application deadline:*** rolling. ***Notification:*** continuous. ***Contact:*** Ms. Margaret R. Armitage, Transfer Coordinator, 410-992-4840.

CONTACT Ms. Barbara C. Greenfeld, Director of Admissions, Howard Community College, Columbia, MD 21044-3197, 410-992-4856.

MARYLAND COLLEGE OF ART AND DESIGN
Silver Spring, Maryland

UG Enrollment: 80	Tuition & Fees: $8830
Application Deadline: rolling	Room & Board: N/Avail

GENERAL Independent, 2-year, specialized, coed. Awards transfer associate degrees. Founded 1957. *Setting:* 5-acre suburban campus with easy access to Washington, DC. *Total enrollment:* 80. *Faculty:* 19 (3 full-time, 100% with terminal degrees, 16 part-time). *Notable Alumni:* Ty Wilson, artist; Tony Wade, artist; D. Claxton, illustrator.
ENROLLMENT PROFILE 80 students from 5 states and territories, 7 other countries. 40% women, 25% part-time, 72% state residents, 9% transferred in, 25% have need-based financial aid, 1% have non-need-based financial aid, 10% international, 35% 25 or older, 1% Native American, 1% Hispanic, 40% African American, 0% Asian American. *Areas of study chosen:* 10% fine arts.
FIRST-YEAR CLASS 36 total; 85 applied, 45% were accepted, 95% of whom enrolled. 3% from top quarter of their high school class, 95% from top half. 1 National Merit Scholar.
ACADEMIC PROGRAM Core, studio art curriculum, honor code. Calendar: semesters. 56 courses offered in 1995–96. Academic remediation for entering students, English as a second language program offered during academic year, services for LD students, advanced placement, tutorials, summer session for credit, part-time degree program (daytime, evenings, weekends, summer), adult/continuing education programs, internships. Off-campus study at Montgomery College–Rockville Campus.
GENERAL DEGREE REQUIREMENTS 63 credit hours; 1 math course; 2 science courses.
MAJORS Applied art, art/fine arts, commercial art, computer graphics, graphic arts, illustration, studio art.
LIBRARY Maryland College of Art and Design Library with 10,000 books, 38 periodicals. Acquisition spending 1994–95: $4000.
COMPUTERS ON CAMPUS 12 computers for student use in computer labs, library. Staffed computer lab on campus (open 24 hours a day) provides training in use of computers, software. Academic computing expenditure 1994–95: $23,921.
COLLEGE LIFE Student-run newspaper. 85% vote in student government elections. *Campus security:* 24-hour emergency response devices.
HOUSING College housing not available.
CAREER PLANNING *Placement office:* 1 full-time staff; $15,325 operating expenditure 1994–95. *Director:* Ms. Mary Post, Student Services, 301-649-4454. *Services:* resume preparation, resume referral, career counseling, careers library, job bank.
AFTER GRADUATION 80% of students completing a degree program in 1994–95 went directly on to further study.
EXPENSES FOR 1996–97 *Application fee:* $35. Tuition: $8400 full-time, $330 per credit hour part-time. Part-time mandatory fees: $155 per semester. Full-time mandatory fees: $430.
FINANCIAL AID *College-administered undergrad aid 1995–96:* 25 need-based scholarships (averaging $1000), 5 non-need scholarships (averaging $1500), low-interest long-term loans from external sources (averaging $2625), Federal Work-Study. *Required forms:* CSS Financial Aid PROFILE, institutional; accepted: state, FAFSA. *Priority deadline:* 7/1. *Payment plan:* deferred payment. *Waivers:* full or partial for minority students, employees or children of employees, and adult students.
APPLYING *Options:* early entrance, deferred entrance. *Required:* school transcript, minimum 2.0 GPA, recommendations, campus interview, TOEFL for international students. *Recommended:* SAT I. Test scores used for counseling/placement. *Application deadline:* rolling.
APPLYING/TRANSFER *Required:* high school transcript, college transcript, minimum 2.0 college GPA, minimum 2.0 high school GPA. *Recommended:* standardized test scores, recommendations, campus interview. *Entrance:* moderately difficult. *Application deadline:* rolling. *Contact:* Ms. Angela Looper, Registrar, 301-649-4454.
CONTACT Mr. Joe Kabriel, Director of Admissions, Maryland College of Art and Design, Silver Spring, MD 20902-4111, 301-649-4454.

MONTGOMERY COLLEGE–GERMANTOWN CAMPUS
Germantown, Maryland

UG Enrollment: 3,896	Tuition & Fees (Area Res): $2100
Application Deadline: rolling	Room & Board: N/Avail

GENERAL State and locally supported, 2-year, coed. Part of Montgomery College. Awards transfer associate, terminal associate degrees. Founded 1975. *Setting:* 196-acre small-town campus with easy access to Washington, DC. *Total enrollment:* 3,896. *Faculty:* 185 (60 full-time, 65% with terminal degrees, 125 part-time); student-faculty ratio is 19:1.
ENROLLMENT PROFILE 3,896 students: 61% women, 39% men, 78% part-time, 98% state residents, 4% transferred in, 5% have need-based financial aid, 2% international, 62% 25 or older, 1% Native American, 4% Hispanic, 13% African American, 9% Asian American.
FIRST-YEAR CLASS 490 total; 550 applied, 100% were accepted, 89% of whom enrolled.
ACADEMIC PROGRAM Core, general education curriculum, honor code. Calendar: semesters. Academic remediation for entering students, English as a second language program offered during academic year, services for LD students, advanced placement, self-designed majors, Freshman Honors College, tutorials, honors program, summer session for credit, part-time degree program (daytime, evenings, weekends), adult/continuing education programs, co-op programs and internships. Off-campus study at Hood College.
GENERAL DEGREE REQUIREMENTS 62 credit hours; math/science requirements vary according to program; computer course (varies by major); internship (some majors).
MAJORS Accounting, art/fine arts, business administration/commerce/management, business education, child care/child and family studies, computer science, data processing, drafting and design, education, electromechanical technology, elementary education, (pre)engineering sequence, finance/banking, information science, international business, liberal arts/general studies, marketing/retailing/merchandising, medical secretarial studies, retail management, secretarial studies/office management, telecommunications.
LIBRARY Germantown Library with 42,625 books, 273 microform titles, 497 periodicals, 2,139 records, tapes, and CDs.
COMPUTERS ON CAMPUS Computer purchase plan available. 150 computers for student use in computer center, computer labs, learning resource center, classrooms, library provide access to main academic computer, e-mail. Staffed computer lab on campus provides training in use of computers, software.
COLLEGE LIFE Drama-theater group, student-run newspaper, radio station. *Student services:* personal-psychological counseling, women's center. *Campus security:* 24-hour emergency response devices and patrols, student patrols, late-night transport-escort service.
HOUSING College housing not available.
ATHLETICS Member NJCAA. *Intercollegiate:* basketball M, tennis M/W. *Intramural:* badminton, basketball, golf, soccer, table tennis (Ping-Pong), tennis, volleyball, weight lifting.
CAREER PLANNING *Placement office:* 1 full-time, 1 part-time staff. *Director:* Ms. Yvonne Stephens, Career Center Coordinator, 301-353-7772. *Services:* job fairs, resume preparation, career counseling, careers library, job bank.
EXPENSES FOR 1995–96 *Application fee:* $25. Area resident tuition: $1830 full-time, $61 per credit part-time. State resident tuition: $3510 full-time, $117 per credit part-time. Nonresident tuition: $4950 full-time, $165 per credit part-time. Part-time mandatory fees per semester range from $41 to $257.40. Full-time mandatory fees per year: $270 for county residents, $486 for state residents, $673 for nonresidents.
FINANCIAL AID *College-administered undergrad aid 1995–96:* 184 need-based scholarships (average $406), 4 non-need scholarships (average $540), low-interest long-term loans from college funds (average $850), loans from external sources (average $1455), Federal Work-Study, 88 part-time jobs. *Required forms:* institutional, financial aid transcript (for transfers); accepted: CSS Financial Aid PROFILE, FAFSA. *Priority deadline:* 6/1. *Payment plan:* installment. *Waivers:* full or partial for employees or children of employees and senior citizens.
APPLYING Open admission except for foreign applicants. *Options:* early entrance, midyear entrance. *Required for some:* CELT. Test scores used for counseling/placement. *Application deadline:* rolling.
APPLYING/TRANSFER *Entrance:* noncompetitive. *Application deadline:* rolling. *Contact:* Mr. Harry Harden, Dean of Students, 301-353-7700.
CONTACT Mr. Tim Link, Registrar, Montgomery College–Germantown Campus, 20200 Observation Drive, Germantown, MD 20876, 301-353-7187. College video available.

MONTGOMERY COLLEGE–ROCKVILLE CAMPUS
Rockville, Maryland

UG Enrollment: 13,144	Tuition & Fees (Area Res): $2100
Application Deadline: rolling	Room & Board: N/Avail

GENERAL State and locally supported, 2-year, coed. Part of Montgomery College. Awards transfer associate, terminal associate degrees. Founded 1965. *Setting:* 88-acre suburban campus with easy access to Washington, DC. *Total enrollment:* 13,144. *Faculty:* 705 (254 full-time, 451 part-time); student-faculty ratio is 21:1.
ENROLLMENT PROFILE 13,144 students: 53% women, 47% men, 66% part-time, 95% state residents, 5% transferred in, 43% 25 or older, 1% Native American, 9% Hispanic, 17% African American, 18% Asian American.
FIRST-YEAR CLASS 6,000 total; 7,000 applied, 100% were accepted, 86% of whom enrolled.
ACADEMIC PROGRAM Calendar: semesters. Academic remediation for entering students, English as a second language program offered during academic year and summer, services for LD students, advanced placement, self-designed majors, honors program, summer session for credit, part-time degree program (daytime, evenings), adult/continuing education programs. Study abroad in England, Germany.
GENERAL DEGREE REQUIREMENTS 62 credit hours; math/science requirements vary according to program.
MAJORS Accounting, advertising, architectural technologies, art education, art history, automotive technologies, biology/biological sciences, business administration/commerce/management, cartography, child care/child and family studies, city/community/regional planning, civil engineering technology, commercial art, communication, computer science, computer technologies, construction management, corrections, criminal justice, dance, data processing, dietetics, early childhood education, education, electrical and electronics technologies, electronics engineering technology, engineering (general), (pre)engineering sequence, fire science, food services management, geography, gerontology, hotel and restaurant management, illustration, information science, interior design, law enforcement/police sciences, legal secretarial studies, liberal arts/general studies, marketing/retailing/merchandising, mathematics, mechanical design technology, mechanical engineering technology, music, photography, physical education, printing technologies, radio and television studies, recreation and leisure services, secretarial studies/office management, social science, studio art, theater arts/drama.
LIBRARY Rockville Library with 111,625 books, 392 microform titles, 800 periodicals, 9,071 records, tapes, and CDs.
COMPUTERS ON CAMPUS Computer purchase plan available. 260 computers for student use in computer center, labs provide access to main academic computer, e-mail. Staffed computer lab on campus provides training in use of computers, software.
COLLEGE LIFE Drama-theater group, student-run newspaper, radio station. *Student services:* personal-psychological counseling, women's center. *Campus security:* 24-hour patrols, late-night transport-escort service.
HOUSING College housing not available.
ATHLETICS Member NJCAA. *Intercollegiate:* baseball M/W, basketball M/W, cross-country running M/W, football M, golf M, soccer M/W, swimming and diving M/W, tennis M/W, track and field M/W, volleyball W. *Intramural:* baseball, basketball, bowling, cross-country running, fencing, football, golf, soccer, swimming and diving, tennis, volleyball.
CAREER PLANNING *Placement office:* 2 full-time staff. *Director:* Ms. Dana Baker, Career Center Coordinator, 301-279-5094. *Services:* job fairs, resume preparation, resume referral, career counseling, careers library, job bank, job interviews.
EXPENSES FOR 1995–96 *Application fee:* $25. Area resident tuition: $1830 full-time, $61 per credit part-time. State resident tuition: $3510 full-time, $117 per credit part-time. Nonresident tuition: $4950 full-time, $165 per credit part-time. Part-time

Montgomery College–Rockville Campus (continued)
mandatory fees per semester range from $41 to $257.40. Full-time mandatory fees per year: $270 for county residents, $486 for state residents, $673 for nonresidents.
FINANCIAL AID ***College-administered undergrad aid 1995–96:*** 1,322 need-based scholarships (average $406), 9 non-need scholarships (average $910), short-term loans (average $100), low-interest long-term loans from college funds (average $850), loans from external sources (average $1909), Federal Work-Study, 240 part-time jobs. ***Required forms:*** institutional, financial aid transcript (for transfers); accepted: CSS Financial Aid PROFILE, FAFSA. ***Priority deadline:*** 6/1. ***Payment plan:*** installment. ***Waivers:*** full or partial for senior citizens.
APPLYING Open admission except for foreign applicants. ***Option:*** early entrance. ***Required for some:*** CELT. Test scores used for counseling/placement. ***Application deadline:*** rolling.
APPLYING/TRANSFER ***Entrance:*** noncompetitive. ***Application deadline:*** rolling.
CONTACT Mr. Sherman Helberg, Director of Admissions, Registration, and Records, Montgomery College–Rockville Campus, Rockville, MD 20850-1196, 301-279-5033.

MONTGOMERY COLLEGE–TAKOMA PARK CAMPUS
Takoma Park, Maryland

UG Enrollment: 4,471	**Tuition & Fees (Area Res): $2100**
Application Deadline: rolling	**Room & Board: N/Avail**

GENERAL State and locally supported, 2-year, coed. Part of Montgomery College. Awards transfer associate, terminal associate degrees. Founded 1946. ***Setting:*** 13-acre small-town campus with easy access to Washington, DC. ***Total enrollment:*** 4,471. ***Faculty:*** 224 (85 full-time, 139 part-time); student-faculty ratio is 21:1.
ENROLLMENT PROFILE 4,471 students: 68% women, 32% men, 76% part-time, 94% state residents, 9% transferred in, 57% 25 or older, 1% Native American, 8% Hispanic, 53% African American, 12% Asian American.
FIRST-YEAR CLASS 678 total; 750 applied, 100% were accepted, 90% of whom enrolled.
ACADEMIC PROGRAM Core. Calendar: semesters. Average class size 22 in required courses. Academic remediation for entering students, English as a second language program offered during academic year, services for LD students, self-designed majors, honors program, summer session for credit, part-time degree program (daytime, evenings), adult/continuing education programs, internships.
GENERAL DEGREE REQUIREMENTS 62 credit hours; math/science requirements vary according to program; computer course (varies by major).
MAJORS Accounting, art/fine arts, biology/biological sciences, business administration/commerce/management, business education, child care/child and family studies, computer science, data processing, dental services, education, elementary education, engineering (general), (pre)engineering sequence, finance/banking, information science, legal secretarial studies, liberal arts/general studies, marketing/retailing/merchandising, mathematics, medical assistant technologies, medical laboratory technology, medical records services, medical secretarial studies, mental health/rehabilitation counseling, nursing, paralegal studies, radiological technology, real estate, secretarial studies/office management, social science.
LIBRARY Takoma Park Library with 57,154 books, 177 microform titles, 426 periodicals, 2,873 records, tapes, and CDs.
COMPUTERS ON CAMPUS Computer purchase plan available. 100 computers for student use in computer center provide access to main academic computer, e-mail. Staffed computer lab on campus provides training in use of computers, software.
COLLEGE LIFE Drama-theater group, student-run newspaper, radio station. ***Student services:*** personal-psychological counseling. ***Campus security:*** 24-hour patrols, late-night transport-escort service.
HOUSING College housing not available.
ATHLETICS Member NJCAA. ***Intercollegiate:*** basketball M, soccer M, swimming and diving M/W, tennis M/W, volleyball W. ***Intramural:*** basketball, racquetball, table tennis (Ping-Pong), tennis, volleyball.
CAREER PLANNING ***Placement office:*** 1 full-time, 1 part-time staff. ***Director:*** Ms. Joyce Fienstien, Career Center Coordinator, 301-650-1479. ***Services:*** job fairs, resume preparation, career counseling, careers library, job bank.
EXPENSES FOR 1995–96 ***Application fee:*** $25. Area resident tuition: $1830 full-time, $61 per credit part-time. State resident tuition: $3510 full-time, $117 per credit part-time. Nonresident tuition: $4950 full-time, $165 per credit part-time. Part-time mandatory fees per semester range from $41 to $257.40. Full-time mandatory fees per year: $270 for county residents, $486 for state residents, $673 for nonresidents.
FINANCIAL AID ***College-administered undergrad aid 1995–96:*** 72 need-based scholarships (average $486), 4 non-need scholarships (average $1044), low-interest long-term loans from college funds (average $850), loans from external sources (average $1836), Federal Work-Study, 64 part-time jobs. ***Required forms:*** institutional, financial aid transcript (for transfers); accepted: CSS Financial Aid PROFILE, FAFSA. ***Priority deadline:*** 6/1. ***Payment plan:*** installment. ***Waivers:*** full or partial for employees or children of employees and senior citizens.
APPLYING Open admission except for foreign applicants. ***Option:*** early entrance. ***Required for some:*** CELT. Test scores used for counseling/placement. ***Application deadline:*** rolling.
APPLYING/TRANSFER ***Entrance:*** noncompetitive. ***Application deadline:*** rolling.
CONTACT Mr. Marvin Logan, Campus Registrar, Montgomery College–Takoma Park Campus, Takoma Park, MD 20912, 301-650-1493.

PRINCE GEORGE'S COMMUNITY COLLEGE
Largo, Maryland

UG Enrollment: 12,050	**Tuition & Fees (Area Res): $2206**
Application Deadline: rolling	**Room & Board: N/Avail**

GENERAL County-supported, 2-year, coed. Awards certificates, transfer associate, terminal associate degrees. Founded 1958. ***Setting:*** 150-acre suburban campus with easy access to Washington, DC. ***Endowment:*** $933,667. ***Total enrollment:*** 12,050. ***Faculty:*** 554 (208 full-time, 33% with terminal degrees, 346 part-time); student-faculty ratio is 20:1.
ENROLLMENT PROFILE 12,050 students from 9 states and territories, 48 other countries. 63% women, 76% part-time, 97% state residents, 10% transferred in, 1% international, 54% 25 or older, 1% Native American, 3% Hispanic, 60% African American, 5% Asian American. ***Areas of study chosen:*** 29% liberal arts/general studies, 21% business management and administrative services, 15% health professions and related sciences, 9% computer and information sciences, 7% social sciences, 4% education, 4% engineering and applied sciences. ***Most popular recent majors:*** liberal arts/general studies, nursing, business administration/commerce/management.
FIRST-YEAR CLASS 2,397 total. Of the students who applied, 100% were accepted, 50% of whom enrolled.
ACADEMIC PROGRAM Core, honor code. Calendar: semesters plus 2 summer sessions. Academic remediation for entering students, English as a second language program offered during academic year, services for LD students, advanced placement, honors program, summer session for credit, part-time degree program (daytime, evenings, summer), adult/continuing education programs, co-op programs. ROTC: Army (c), Naval (c), Air Force (c).
GENERAL DEGREE REQUIREMENTS 62 credits; 1 course each in math and science; computer course.
MAJORS Accounting, aerospace engineering, art/fine arts, business administration/commerce/management, business education, computer information systems, computer management, computer programming, computer science, computer technologies, criminal justice, drafting and design, early childhood education, education, electronics engineering technology, elementary education, engineering (general), health education, legal secretarial studies, liberal arts/general studies, marketing/retailing/merchandising, medical records services, medical secretarial studies, music, nuclear medical technology, nursing, paralegal studies, physical education, quality control technology, radiological technology, respiratory therapy, secretarial studies/office management, word processing.
LIBRARY Accokeek Hall with 97,329 books, 754 periodicals, 6,682 records, tapes, and CDs.
COMPUTERS ON CAMPUS Computers for student use in computer center, computer labs, labs, classrooms, library provide access to main academic computer. Staffed computer lab on campus.
COLLEGE LIFE Drama-theater group, choral group, student-run newspaper. 10% vote in student government elections. ***Social organizations:*** 40 open to all. ***Most popular organizations:*** Student Government Association, Student Program Board, Union of Black Scholars. ***Major annual events:*** Spring Festival, Images Cultural Series, International Program. ***Student services:*** health clinic, personal-psychological counseling. ***Campus security:*** 24-hour emergency response devices and patrols, late-night transport-escort service.
HOUSING College housing not available.
ATHLETICS Member NJCAA. ***Intercollegiate:*** baseball M, basketball M(s)/W(s), bowling M(s)/W(s), golf M, soccer M, softball W(s), tennis M/W, volleyball W(s). ***Intramural:*** basketball, bowling, golf, soccer, softball, tennis, volleyball. ***Contact:*** Mr. Ronald Mann, Professor of Physical Education, 301-322-0513.
CAREER PLANNING ***Director:*** Dr. Margaret A. Taibi, Director, Career Assessment and Planning/Educ. Opportunities, 301-322-0886. ***Services:*** job fairs, resume preparation, resume referral, career counseling, careers library, job bank, job interviews.
AFTER GRADUATION 77% of students completing a degree program in 1994–95 went directly on to further study.
EXPENSES FOR 1995–96 Area resident tuition: $1656 full-time, $69 per credit part-time. State resident tuition: $3168 full-time, $132 per credit part-time. Nonresident tuition: $5112 full-time, $213 per credit part-time. Part-time mandatory fees: $20 per credit. Full-time mandatory fees: $550.
FINANCIAL AID ***College-administered undergrad aid 1995–96:*** need-based scholarships (average $250), low-interest long-term loans from external sources, Federal Work-Study, part-time jobs. ***Required forms:*** institutional, FAFSA; required for some: state. ***Application deadline:*** continuous to 5/31. ***Waivers:*** full or partial for employees or children of employees and senior citizens.
APPLYING Open admission. ***Options:*** early entrance, deferred entrance, midyear entrance. ***Required:*** school transcript. ***Recommended:*** minimum 2.0 GPA, 3 years of high school math. ***Required for some:*** Descriptive Test of Language Skills, Descriptive Test of Mathematic Skills, Michigan Test of English Language Proficiency. Test scores used for counseling/placement. ***Application deadline:*** rolling. ***Notification:*** continuous.
APPLYING/TRANSFER ***Required:*** college transcript. ***Entrance:*** noncompetitive.
CONTACT Ms. Vera Bagley, Director of Admissions and Records, Prince George's Community College, Largo, MD 20774-2199, 301-322-0801. College video available.

WOR-WIC COMMUNITY COLLEGE
Salisbury, Maryland

UG Enrollment: 1,963	**Tuition & Fees (Area Res): $1610**
Application Deadline: rolling	**Room & Board: N/Avail**

GENERAL State and locally supported, 2-year, coed. Part of Maryland State Community Colleges System. Awards transfer associate, terminal associate degrees. Founded 1976. ***Setting:*** small-town campus. ***Total enrollment:*** 1,963. ***Faculty:*** 103 (37 full-time, 66 part-time).
ENROLLMENT PROFILE 1,963 students from 3 states and territories. 76% women, 24% men, 82% part-time, 99% state residents, 21% transferred in, 50% 25 or older, 1% Native American, 1% Hispanic, 20% African American, 1% Asian American. ***Most popular recent majors:*** liberal arts/general studies, accounting, business administration/commerce/management.
FIRST-YEAR CLASS 687 total. Of the students who applied, 100% were accepted. 5% from top 10% of their high school class, 15% from top quarter, 50% from top half.
ACADEMIC PROGRAM Core. Calendar: semesters. Academic remediation for entering students, services for LD students, advanced placement, summer session for credit, part-time degree program (daytime, evenings), adult/continuing education programs. Off-campus study at Salisbury State University.
GENERAL DEGREE REQUIREMENT 60 credit hours.
MAJORS Accounting, business administration/commerce/management, computer programming, corrections, criminal justice, electronics engineering technology, hotel and restaurant

management, law enforcement/police sciences, liberal arts/general studies, mental health/rehabilitation counseling, nursing, radiological technology, secretarial studies/office management.
COMPUTERS ON CAMPUS 50 computers for student use in computer center, secretarial studies lab provide access to main academic computer.
COLLEGE LIFE *Student services:* personal-psychological counseling.
HOUSING College housing not available.
CAREER PLANNING *Director:* Ms. Shay Crowson, Director of Career Planning and Placement, 410-749-8181. *Service:* career counseling.
EXPENSES FOR 1996–97 Area resident tuition: $1590 full-time, $53 per credit hour part-time. State resident tuition: $3930 full-time, $131 per credit hour part-time. Nonresident tuition: $4500 full-time, $150 per credit hour part-time. Part-time mandatory fees: $10 per semester. Full-time mandatory fees: $20.

FINANCIAL AID *College-administered undergrad aid 1995–96:* need-based scholarships (average $250), non-need scholarships (average $350), short-term loans (average $150), low-interest long-term loans from external sources (average $2000), Federal Work-Study, 10 part-time jobs. *Acceptable forms:* CSS Financial Aid PROFILE, institutional, FAFSA. *Priority deadline:* 8/15.
APPLYING Open admission except for nursing, radiological technology programs. *Option:* deferred entrance. *Recommended:* school transcript. *Required for some:* ACT. Test scores used for admission. *Application deadline:* rolling. Preference given to state residents.
APPLYING/TRANSFER *Entrance:* noncompetitive. *Application deadline:* rolling.
CONTACT Mrs. Holly Foster, Director of Admissions, Wor-Wic Community College, Salisbury, MD 21804, 410-334-2895.

MASSACHUSETTS

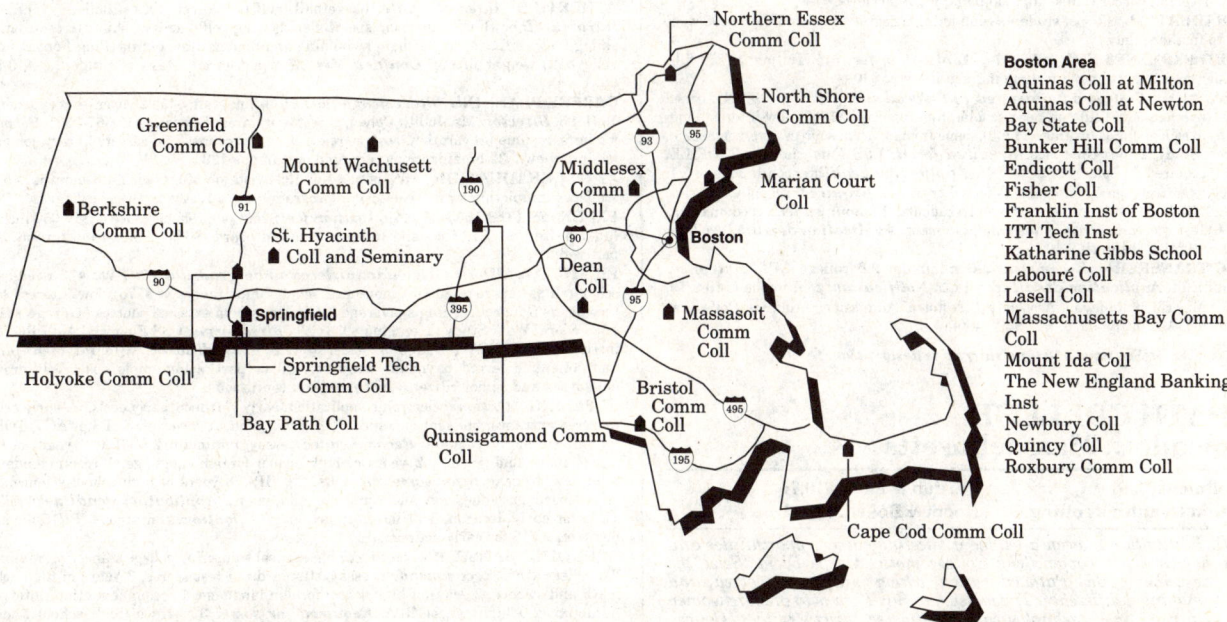

Boston Area
Aquinas Coll at Milton
Aquinas Coll at Newton
Bay State Coll
Bunker Hill Comm Coll
Endicott Coll
Fisher Coll
Franklin Inst of Boston
ITT Tech Inst
Katharine Gibbs School
Labouré Coll
Lasell Coll
Massachusetts Bay Comm Coll
Mount Ida Coll
The New England Banking Inst
Newbury Coll
Quincy Coll
Roxbury Comm Coll

AQUINAS COLLEGE AT MILTON
Milton, Massachusetts

UG Enrollment: 140	Tuition & Fees: $8350
Application Deadline: rolling	Room & Board: N/Avail

GENERAL Independent Roman Catholic, 2-year, women only. Awards certificates, transfer associate, terminal associate degrees. Founded 1956. *Setting:* 15-acre suburban campus with easy access to Boston. *Total enrollment:* 140. *Faculty:* 20 (16 full-time, 100% with terminal degrees, 4 part-time).
ENROLLMENT PROFILE 140 students: 100% women, 5% part-time, 100% state residents, 15% transferred in, 30% 25 or older, 2% Hispanic, 4% African American, 2% Asian American. *Areas of study chosen:* 78% business management and administrative services, 22% health professions and related sciences. *Most popular recent majors:* legal secretarial studies, business administration/commerce/management, secretarial studies/office management.
FIRST-YEAR CLASS 80 total; 180 applied. 5% from top quarter of their high school class, 90% from top half.
ACADEMIC PROGRAM Career-oriented curriculum. Calendar: modular. 120 courses offered in 1995–96. Academic remediation for entering students, English as a second language program offered during summer, part-time degree program (evenings), internships.
GENERAL DEGREE REQUIREMENTS 60 credits; internship (some majors).
MAJORS Accounting, business administration/commerce/management, computer information systems, court reporting, legal secretarial studies, liberal arts/general studies, medical assistant technologies, medical secretarial studies, recreation therapy, secretarial studies/office management.
LIBRARY 10,000 books, 22 microform titles, 106 periodicals, 2 CD-ROMs, 850 records, tapes, and CDs.
COMPUTERS ON CAMPUS 77 computers for student use in computer labs, classrooms, library.
COLLEGE LIFE Orientation program (2 days, no cost). *Social organizations:* 4 open to all. *Most popular organizations:* Red Key Club, Phi Theta Kappa, Campus Ministry, Student Government Association. *Major annual events:* Christmas Party, Class Night, Orientation Luncheon. *Student services:* personal-psychological counseling. *Campus security:* 24-hour emergency response devices.
HOUSING College housing not available.

Peterson's Guide to Two-Year Colleges 1997

CAREER PLANNING *Placement office:* 1 part-time staff. *Director:* Ms. Nancy Raby, Director of Career Services, 617-696-3100. *Services:* job fairs, resume preparation, career counseling, careers library, job bank, job interviews.
AFTER GRADUATION 18% of students completing a degree program in 1994–95 went directly on to further study.
EXPENSES FOR 1995–96 *Application fee:* $25. *Tuition:* $8150 full-time, $1018 per course part-time. Full-time mandatory fees: $200.
FINANCIAL AID *College-administered undergrad aid 1995–96:* need-based scholarships (average $5463), non-need scholarships, low-interest long-term loans from external sources (average $2625), Federal Work-Study. *Required forms:* CSS Financial Aid PROFILE, state, institutional, FAFSA. *Application deadline:* continuous. *Payment plans:* installment, deferred payment. *Waivers:* full or partial for employees or children of employees. *Notification:* continuous.
APPLYING *Option:* deferred entrance. *Required:* school transcript, interview. *Application deadline:* rolling.
APPLYING/TRANSFER *Required:* high school transcript, interview. *Entrance:* minimally difficult. *Application deadline:* rolling.
CONTACT Ms. Sandra Delaney, Director of Admissions, Aquinas College at Milton, Milton, MA 02186-4253, 617-696-3100. *Fax:* 617-696-8706.

AQUINAS COLLEGE AT NEWTON
Newton, Massachusetts

UG Enrollment: 225	Tuition & Fees: $7550
Application Deadline: rolling	Room & Board: N/Avail

GENERAL Independent Roman Catholic, 2-year, women only. Awards certificates, transfer associate, terminal associate degrees. Founded 1961. *Setting:* 14-acre suburban campus with easy access to Boston. *Total enrollment:* 225. *Faculty:* 22 (12 full-time, 8% with terminal degrees, 10 part-time); student-faculty ratio is 14:1.
ENROLLMENT PROFILE 225 students: 100% women, 8% part-time, 96% state residents, 13% transferred in, 4% international, 4% African American, 2% Asian American. *Most popular recent majors:* early childhood education, business administration/commerce/management, medical assistant technologies.

Aquinas College at Newton (continued)

FIRST-YEAR CLASS 100 total; 195 applied, 56% were accepted, 91% of whom enrolled. 10% from top 10% of their high school class, 30% from top quarter, 60% from top half.
ACADEMIC PROGRAM Core, honor code. Calendar: 4-1-4. Academic remediation for entering students, services for LD students, advanced placement, summer session for credit, part-time degree program (daytime, evenings, summer), adult/continuing education programs, internships.
GENERAL DEGREE REQUIREMENTS 60 credits; 3 math/science courses.
MAJORS Accounting, business administration/commerce/management, child care/child and family studies, early childhood education, legal secretarial studies, liberal arts/general studies, medical assistant technologies, medical secretarial studies, secretarial studies/office management.
LIBRARY 14,950 books, 110 periodicals.
COMPUTERS ON CAMPUS 40 computers for student use in computer center provide access to main academic computer. Staffed computer lab on campus.
COLLEGE LIFE Orientation program (3 days, no cost). ***Most popular organizations:*** Aquinas Student Association, Society for the Advancement of Management, Phi Theta Kappa. ***Major annual events:*** Cotillion, Senior Banquet, Christmas Party. ***Student services:*** personal-psychological counseling.
HOUSING College housing not available.
CAREER PLANNING ***Placement office:*** 1 full-time, 1 part-time staff. ***Director:*** Sr. Therese Dunn, Career Services Director, 617-969-4400. ***Services:*** job fairs, resume preparation, resume referral, career counseling, job bank, job interviews.
AFTER GRADUATION 30% of students completing a degree program in 1994–95 went directly on to further study.
ESTIMATED EXPENSES FOR 1996–97 ***Application fee:*** $15. Tuition: $7250 full-time, $233 per credit part-time. Full-time mandatory fees: $300.
FINANCIAL AID ***College-administered undergrad aid 1995–96:*** 89 need-based scholarships (average $600), 15 non-need scholarships (average $1000), low-interest long-term loans from college funds (average $1500), loans from external sources (average $2625), Federal Work-Study, 2 part-time jobs. ***Required forms:*** CSS Financial Aid PROFILE, institutional; required for some: state, FAFSA. ***Application deadline:*** continuous to 5/1.
APPLYING ***Options:*** early entrance, deferred entrance. ***Required:*** school transcript, minimum 2.0 GPA, TOEFL for international students. ***Recommended:*** recommendations, SAT I. Test scores used for counseling/placement. ***Application deadline:*** rolling. ***Notification:*** continuous until 9/10.
APPLYING/TRANSFER ***Recommended:*** minimum 2.0 college GPA. ***Entrance:*** minimally difficult. ***Application deadline:*** rolling. ***Notification:*** continuous until 9/10.
CONTACT Ms. Ellen Ronayne, Associate Director of Admissions, Aquinas College at Newton, Newton, MA 02158-9928, 617-969-4400.

❖ ***See page 690 for a narrative description.*** ❖

BAY PATH COLLEGE
Longmeadow, Massachusetts

UG Enrollment: 599	**Tuition & Fees: $10,700**
Application Deadline: rolling	**Room & Board: $6350**

Since 1897, Bay Path has been a leader in meeting career opportunities and expanding horizons for women. The College motto, Carpe Diem (Seize the Day), best describes a Bay Path education, which is active, involved, and dedicated to making a difference. The mission of Bay Path is to prepare women for leadership roles in a technological and diverse society, with a College emphasis on technological preparation, global understanding, community service, athletics and wellness, and lifelong learning. Bay Path expects a lot from its students because the students expect a lot from Bay Path. The College's challenging academic program, enhanced by dynamic internship opportunities, anticipates the career opportunities for women in the 21st century. Bay Path is known for its personalized learning environment, which guarantees individual attention and close interaction between students and faculty members. Bay Path's beautiful, suburban Longmeadow campus makes Bay Path a friendly, secure, and exciting place to live and learn.

GENERAL Independent, primarily 2-year, women only. Awards certificates, transfer associate, terminal associate, bachelor's degrees. Founded 1897. ***Setting:*** 32-acre suburban campus with easy access to Boston. ***Endowment:*** $17 million. ***Total enrollment:*** 599. ***Faculty:*** 44 (20 full-time, 37% with terminal degrees, 24 part-time); student-faculty ratio is 14:1. ***Notable Alumni:*** JoAnna Rhinehart, actress; Sue Venberg, director of National Holocaust Museum; Paige Turco, actress; Susan Kniep, mayor of East Hartford.
ENROLLMENT PROFILE 599 students from 14 states and territories, 10 other countries. 100% women, 25% part-time, 49% state residents, 65% live on campus, 14% transferred in, 82% have need-based financial aid, 10% have non-need-based financial aid, 9% international, 19% 25 or older, 0% Native American, 3% Hispanic, 4% African American, 2% Asian American. ***Areas of study chosen:*** 32% business management and administrative services, 23% education, 20% psychology, 10% liberal arts/general studies, 10% prelaw, 4% health professions and related sciences, 1% interdisciplinary studies. ***Most popular recent majors:*** business administration/commerce/management, early childhood education, criminal justice.
FIRST-YEAR CLASS 154 total; 524 applied, 73% were accepted, 41% of whom enrolled. 6% from top 10% of their high school class, 46% from top quarter, 76% from top half. 1 class president, 1 valedictorian.
ACADEMIC PROGRAM Core, interdisciplinary curriculum, honor code. Calendar: semesters. 159 courses offered in 1995–96. Academic remediation for entering students, English as a second language program offered during academic year and summer, advanced placement, self-designed majors, Freshman Honors College, tutorials, honors program, summer session for credit, part-time degree program (daytime, evenings), adult/continuing education programs, internships. Off-campus study at Cooperating Colleges of Greater Springfield. ROTC: Army (c).
GENERAL DEGREE REQUIREMENTS 63 credits for associate, 120 credits for bachelor's; 7 credits of math/science; computer course; internship (some majors).
MAJORS Accounting (B), business administration/commerce/management (B), criminal justice (B), early childhood education (B), elementary education (B), fashion merchandising (B), health services administration (B), hospitality services, human services (B), interior design (B), international business (B), legal studies (B), liberal arts/general studies (B), marketing/retailing/merchandising (B), occupational therapy, paralegal studies (B), psychology (B), tourism and travel (B).
LIBRARY Frank and Marion Hatch Library with 38,045 books, 266 periodicals, 3 on-line bibliographic services, 43 CD-ROMs, 2,347 records, tapes, and CDs. Acquisition spending 1994–95: $87,000.
COMPUTERS ON CAMPUS Computer purchase plan available. 85 computers for student use in computer center, computer labs, research center, classrooms, library provide access to main academic computer, e-mail, on-line services, Internet. Staffed computer lab on campus provides training in use of computers, software. Academic computing expenditure 1994–95: $160,000.
COLLEGE LIFE Orientation program (2 days, no cost, parents included). Drama-theater group, choral group. 70% vote in student government elections. ***Social organizations:*** 23 open to all. ***Most popular organizations:*** Student Government, Theater Club, Golden Z Service Club, Phi Beta Lambda, Law Club. ***Major annual events:*** Las Vegas Night, Campus Day, Musical Theater Productions. ***Student services:*** health clinic, personal-psychological counseling, women's center. ***Campus security:*** 24-hour emergency response devices and patrols, late-night transport-escort service, controlled dormitory access.
HOUSING 420 college housing spaces available; 341 were occupied 1995–96. Freshmen guaranteed college housing. On-campus residence required through sophomore year except if living within commuting distance. ***Option:*** single-sex (4 buildings) housing available. Resident assistants live in dorms.
ATHLETICS ***Intercollegiate:*** basketball, golf (s), soccer (s), softball (s), tennis (s). ***Intramural:*** bowling, equestrian sports, field hockey, golf, lacrosse, skiing (cross-country), skiing (downhill), soccer, softball, swimming and diving, table tennis (Ping-Pong), tennis, volleyball, weight lifting. ***Contact:*** Mrs. Marcia Conrad, Dean of Students, 413-567-0621.
CAREER PLANNING ***Placement office:*** 1 full-time staff; $45,226 operating expenditure 1994–95. ***Director:*** Ms. Judith Cohen, Director of Career Services, 413-567-0621. ***Services:*** job fairs, resume preparation, resume referral, career counseling, careers library, job bank, job interviews. 32 organizations recruited on campus 1994–95.
AFTER GRADUATION 85% of class of 1994 had job offers within 6 months. 48% of students completing transfer associate program went directly to 4-year colleges.
EXPENSES FOR 1995–96 ***Application fee:*** $25. Comprehensive fee of $17,050 includes full-time tuition ($10,700) and college room and board ($6350). Part-time tuition: $320 per credit.
FINANCIAL AID ***College-administered undergrad aid 1995–96:*** 422 need-based scholarships (average $2933), non-need scholarships (average $775), low-interest long-term loans from college funds (average $980), loans from external sources (average $3193), 166 Federal Work-Study (averaging $938). ***Required forms:*** CSS Financial Aid PROFILE, institutional, FAFSA; required for some: state. ***Priority deadline:*** 3/15. ***Payment plans:*** installment, deferred payment. ***Waivers:*** full or partial for employees or children of employees and senior citizens. ***Notification:*** continuous.
APPLYING ***Options:*** electronic application, early entrance, early decision, early action, deferred entrance, midyear entrance. ***Required:*** school transcript, SAT I or ACT, TOEFL for international students. ***Recommended:*** essay, minimum 2.0 GPA, 3 years of high school math and science, 2 years of high school foreign language, 1 recommendation, interview. ***Required for some:*** minimum 2.0 GPA, 3 years of high school science. Test scores used for admission and counseling/placement. ***Application deadlines:*** rolling, 11/15 for early decision, 11/1 for early action. ***Notification:*** continuous, 12/15 for early decision, 12/15 for early action.
APPLYING/TRANSFER ***Required:*** high school transcript, college transcript, minimum 2.0 college GPA. ***Recommended:*** essay, standardized test scores, 3 years of high school math and science, 2 years of high school foreign language, 1 recommendation, interview, minimum 2.0 high school GPA. ***Required for some:*** 3 years of high school science, minimum 3.0 college GPA, minimum 2.0 high school GPA. ***Entrance:*** moderately difficult. ***Application deadline:*** rolling. ***Notification:*** continuous. ***Contact:*** Mr. William Masi, Director of Admissions, 413-567-0621.
CONTACT Mr. Michael Backes, Dean of Admissions, Bay Path College, Longmeadow, MA 01106-2292, 413-567-0621 Ext. 331 or toll-free 800-782-7284 (out-of-state). ***Fax:*** 413-567-0501. ***E-mail:*** mbackes@baypath.edu. College video available.

BAY STATE COLLEGE
Boston, Massachusetts

UG Enrollment: 674	**Tuition & Fees: $9200**
Application Deadline: rolling	**Room & Board: $6700**

Bay State College, a private 2-year college, is located in the historic Back Bay section of Boston. Bay State College's Business Division offers programs in accounting, business administration, early childhood education, executive office administration, fashion merchandising, general business, hotel management, legal office administration, legal studies, medical office administration, office management, retail business management, and travel and tourism. The Allied Health Division offers programs in medical assistant studies, occupational therapy assistant studies, and physical therapist assistant studies.

GENERAL Independent, 2-year, coed. Awards terminal associate degrees. Founded 1946. ***Setting:*** urban campus. ***Total enrollment:*** 674. ***Faculty:*** 50 (20 full-time, 30 part-time); student-faculty ratio is 15:1.
ENROLLMENT PROFILE 674 students from 21 states and territories, 5 other countries. 81% women, 0% part-time, 83% state residents, 5% transferred in, 80% have need-based financial aid, 2% international, 5% 25 or older, 1% Native American, 11% Hispanic, 11% African American, 4% Asian American. ***Areas of study chosen:*** 67% business management and administrative services, 25% health professions and related sciences, 6% education, 2% liberal arts/general studies. ***Most popular recent majors:*** tourism and travel, business administration/commerce/management, fashion merchandising.
FIRST-YEAR CLASS 345 total; 1,300 applied, 86% were accepted, 31% of whom enrolled. 3% from top 10% of their high school class, 15% from top quarter, 40% from top half.
ACADEMIC PROGRAM Core. Calendar: semesters. 300 courses offered in 1995–96. Academic remediation for entering students, tutorials, part-time degree program (evenings), adult/continuing education programs, co-op programs and internships.

GENERAL DEGREE REQUIREMENTS 60 credits; computer course; internship (some majors).
MAJORS Accounting, business administration/commerce/management, early childhood education, fashion merchandising, hospitality services, hotel and restaurant management, legal secretarial studies, medical assistant technologies, medical secretarial studies, occupational therapy, physical therapy, retail management, secretarial studies/office management, tourism and travel.
LIBRARY Bay State College Library with 4,000 books, 19 microform titles, 250 periodicals, 12 CD-ROMs, 340 records, tapes, and CDs.
COMPUTERS ON CAMPUS 55 computers for student use in computer center, classrooms, library. Staffed computer lab on campus provides training in use of computers, software.
COLLEGE LIFE Orientation program (2 days, no cost, parents included). ***Social organizations:*** 7 open to all. ***Most popular organizations:*** Hospitality Marketing Association, Student Leader Organization, Fashion Club, Fine Arts Club, Student Medical Assisting Society. ***Student services:*** personal-psychological counseling. ***Campus security:*** late-night transport-escort service, 14-hour patrols by trained security personnel.
HOUSING 298 college housing spaces available; 294 were occupied 1995–96. Freshmen guaranteed college housing. Off-campus living permitted. ***Options:*** coed (1 building), single-sex (3 buildings) housing available. Resident assistants live in dorms.
CAREER PLANNING ***Placement office:*** 1 full-time staff. ***Director:*** Ms. Deborah Walsh, Director of Career Services, 617-236-8030. ***Services:*** job fairs, resume preparation, career counseling, careers library, job bank. 80 organizations recruited on campus 1994–95.
AFTER GRADUATION 98% of class of 1994 had job offers within 6 months.
EXPENSES FOR 1996–97 ***Application fee:*** $25. Comprehensive fee of $15,900 includes full-time tuition ($9200) and college room and board ($6700). Part-time tuition: $920 per course. Tuition for continuing education program: $580 per course.
FINANCIAL AID ***College-administered undergrad aid 1995–96:*** 50 need-based scholarships (averaging $1000), 10 non-need scholarships (averaging $500), low-interest long-term loans from college funds (averaging $1500), loans from external sources (averaging $3375), Federal Work-Study. ***Required forms:*** FAFSA; required for some: state. ***Priority deadline:*** 3/1. ***Payment plan:*** installment.
APPLYING ***Options:*** deferred entrance, midyear entrance. ***Required:*** school transcript, TOEFL for international students. ***Required for some:*** recommendations. ***Application deadline:*** rolling.
APPLYING/TRANSFER ***Required:*** college transcript. ***Application deadline:*** rolling. ***Contact:*** Mrs. Deborah Walsh, Director of Career Services, 617-236-8030.
CONTACT Ms. Ruth W. Carrigan, Director of Admissions, Bay State College, 122 Commonwealth Avenue, Boston, MA 02116-2975, 617-236-8000. ***Fax:*** 617-536-1735. College video available.

❖ *See page 702 for a narrative description.* ❖

BERKSHIRE COMMUNITY COLLEGE
Pittsfield, Massachusetts

UG Enrollment: 2,388 | **Tuition & Fees (MA Res): $2550**
Application Deadline: rolling | **Room & Board: N/Avail**

GENERAL State-supported, 2-year, coed. Part of Massachusetts Public Higher Education System. Awards certificates, transfer associate, terminal associate degrees. Founded 1960. ***Setting:*** 100-acre suburban campus. ***Total enrollment:*** 2,388. ***Faculty:*** 180 (75 full-time, 105 part-time); student-faculty ratio is 17:1.
ENROLLMENT PROFILE 2,388 students from 10 states and territories, 19 other countries. 62% women, 38% men, 62% part-time, 97% state residents, 20% transferred in, 2% international, 55% 25 or older, 1% Hispanic, 3% African American, 1% Asian American. ***Areas of study chosen:*** 23% health professions and related sciences, 21% liberal arts/general studies, 17% business management and administrative services, 12% social sciences, 10% engineering and applied sciences, 6% computer and information sciences, 4% natural resource sciences, 3% fine arts, 2% biological and life sciences, 2% performing arts. ***Most popular recent majors:*** liberal arts/general studies, nursing, business administration/commerce/management.
FIRST-YEAR CLASS 397 total; 625 applied, 100% were accepted, 64% of whom enrolled.
ACADEMIC PROGRAM Core, honor code. Calendar: semesters. Academic remediation for entering students, English as a second language program offered during academic year, services for LD students, advanced placement, tutorials, summer session for credit, part-time degree program (daytime, evenings, summer), adult/continuing education programs, internships. Off-campus study at North Adams State College, Williams College.
GENERAL DEGREE REQUIREMENTS 60 credit hours; math/science requirements vary according to program; internship (some majors).
MAJORS Accounting, animal sciences, art/fine arts, biology/biological sciences, biomedical technologies, business administration/commerce/management, computer information systems, computer science, conservation, criminal justice, culinary arts, data processing, ecology, electrical and electronics technologies, electrical engineering technology, electronics engineering technology, engineering (general), engineering and applied sciences, (pre)engineering sequence, engineering technology, environmental engineering technology, environmental sciences, environmental studies, finance/banking, fire science, food services management, hotel and restaurant management, human services, law enforcement/police sciences, liberal arts/general studies, marketing/retailing/merchandising, nursing, painting/drawing, peace studies, physical education, physical therapy, practical nursing, respiratory therapy, secretarial studies/office management, studio art, theater arts/drama.
LIBRARY Jonathan Edwards Library with 46,047 books, 88 microform titles, 343 periodicals, 2,478 records, tapes, and CDs.
COMPUTERS ON CAMPUS 100 computers for student use in computer center, computer labs, classrooms, library. Staffed computer lab on campus provides training in use of computers, software.
COLLEGE LIFE Drama-theater group, choral group. ***Social organizations:*** 15 open to all. ***Student services:*** health clinic, personal-psychological counseling. ***Campus security:*** 24-hour emergency response devices and patrols.
HOUSING College housing not available.
ATHLETICS Member NJCAA. ***Intercollegiate:*** basketball M/W, cross-country running M/W, soccer M/W. ***Intramural:*** basketball, tennis, volleyball. ***Contact:*** Mr. Dane Olsted, Athletic Director, 413-499-4660.
CAREER PLANNING ***Placement office:*** 1 full-time, 2 part-time staff. ***Director:*** Mr. Geoffrey Tabor, Career Counselor, 413-499-4660 Ext. 209. ***Services:*** job fairs, resume preparation, career counseling, careers library, job bank.
AFTER GRADUATION 50% of class of 1994 had job offers within 6 months. 66% of students completing a degree program went directly on to further study.
EXPENSES FOR 1995–96 ***Application fee:*** $10. State resident tuition: $1140 full-time, $38 per credit part-time. Nonresident tuition: $5640 full-time, $188 per credit part-time. Part-time mandatory fees: $47 per credit. Full-time mandatory fees: $1410.
FINANCIAL AID ***College-administered undergrad aid 1995–96:*** need-based scholarships, non-need scholarships, short-term loans, low-interest long-term loans from external sources, Federal Work-Study, part-time jobs. ***Required forms:*** institutional; required for some: CSS Financial Aid PROFILE, state, FAFSA. ***Priority deadline:*** 5/1. ***Payment plan:*** installment. ***Waivers:*** full or partial for employees or children of employees and senior citizens.
APPLYING Open admission except for allied health programs. ***Options:*** early entrance, deferred entrance, midyear entrance. ***Required:*** school transcript. ***Recommended:*** interview. ***Required for some:*** TOEFL for international students. Test scores used for counseling/placement. ***Application deadline:*** rolling. ***Notification:*** continuous.
APPLYING/TRANSFER ***Required:*** college transcript. ***Recommended:*** interview. ***Required for some:*** high school transcript. ***Entrance:*** noncompetitive. ***Application deadline:*** rolling. ***Notification:*** continuous. ***Contact:*** Ms. Naomi Gelfand, Transfer Counselor, 413-499-4660 Ext. 376.
CONTACT Mr. Michael Bullock, Director of Enrollment Services, Berkshire Community College, Pittsfield, MA 01201-5786, 413-499-4660 Ext. 387. College video available.

BRISTOL COMMUNITY COLLEGE
Fall River, Massachusetts

UG Enrollment: 5,223 | **Tuition & Fees (MA Res): $2460**
Application Deadline: N/R | **Room & Board: N/Avail**

GENERAL State-supported, 2-year, coed. Awards certificates, transfer associate, terminal associate degrees. Founded 1965. ***Setting:*** 105-acre urban campus with easy access to Boston. ***Total enrollment:*** 5,223. ***Faculty:*** 183 (93 full-time, 90 part-time).
ENROLLMENT PROFILE 5,223 students: 61% women, 26% part-time, 91% state residents, 3% transferred in, 1% international, 1% Native American, 2% Hispanic, 4% African American, 1% Asian American. ***Most popular recent majors:*** business administration/commerce/management, nursing, elementary education.
FIRST-YEAR CLASS 1,413 total; 2,575 applied, 95% were accepted, 58% of whom enrolled.
ACADEMIC PROGRAM Calendar: semesters. Academic remediation for entering students, English as a second language program offered during academic year, services for LD students, advanced placement, self-designed majors, honors program, summer session for credit, part-time degree program (daytime, evenings, weekends), adult/continuing education programs, co-op programs.
GENERAL DEGREE REQUIREMENT 60 credits.
MAJORS Accounting, applied art, art/fine arts, business administration/commerce/management, business education, child care/child and family studies, civil engineering technology, communication, computer programming, computer technologies, criminal justice, dental services, electrical engineering technology, electromechanical technology, electronics engineering technology, elementary education, engineering (general), fire science, human services, legal secretarial studies, liberal arts/general studies, marketing/retailing/merchandising, mathematics, mechanical engineering technology, medical laboratory technology, medical records services, medical secretarial studies, nursing, occupational therapy, retail management, secretarial studies/office management, theater arts/drama, word processing.
LIBRARY 57,425 books, 212 microform titles, 312 periodicals, 17,315 records, tapes, and CDs.
COMPUTERS ON CAMPUS 33 computers for student use in library.
COLLEGE LIFE Drama-theater group, student-run newspaper. ***Social organizations:*** 20 open to all. ***Major annual event:*** Honors Night. ***Student services:*** health clinic, personal-psychological counseling, women's center. ***Campus security:*** 24-hour emergency response devices and patrols, student patrols, late-night transport-escort service.
HOUSING College housing not available.
CAREER PLANNING ***Services:*** resume preparation, career counseling.
AFTER GRADUATION 20% of students completing a degree program in 1994–95 went directly on to further study.
EXPENSES FOR 1995–96 ***Application fee:*** $10. State resident tuition: $2460 full-time, $82 per credit part-time. Nonresident tuition: $6900 full-time, $230 per credit part-time.
FINANCIAL AID ***College-administered undergrad aid 1995–96:*** 885 need-based scholarships (average $500), 17 non-need scholarships (average $750), short-term loans (average $150), low-interest long-term loans from college funds (average $1150), loans from external sources (average $2100), Federal Work-Study, 50 part-time jobs. ***Required forms:*** institutional, FAFSA. ***Priority deadline:*** 4/15.
APPLYING Open admission except for nursing, dental hygiene, medical laboratory technology, occupational therapy assistant programs. ***Option:*** early entrance. ***Required for some:*** SAT I. Test scores used for admission. ***Notification:*** continuous. Preference given to state residents.
APPLYING/TRANSFER ***Contact:*** Ms. Eileen Shea, Transfer Counselor, 508-678-2811 Ext. 2227.
CONTACT Mr. Frank Noble, Director of Admissions, Bristol Community College, 777 Elsbree Street, Fall River, MA 02720-7395, 508-678-2811 Ext. 2179. College video available.

BUNKER HILL COMMUNITY COLLEGE
Boston, Massachusetts

UG Enrollment: 6,002 | **Tuition & Fees (MA Res): $2250**
Application Deadline: rolling | **Room & Board: N/Avail**

GENERAL State-supported, 2-year, coed. Awards certificates, transfer associate, terminal associate degrees. Founded 1973. ***Setting:*** 21-acre urban campus. ***Total enrollment:*** 6,002. ***Faculty:*** 145 (118 full-time, 27 part-time).

Bunker Hill Community College (continued)

ENROLLMENT PROFILE 6,002 students from 6 states and territories, 65 other countries. 60% women, 63% part-time, 93% state residents, 4% transferred in, 6% international, 41% 25 or older, 1% Native American, 7% Hispanic, 17% African American, 14% Asian American. ***Most popular recent majors:*** liberal arts/general studies, business administration/commerce/management, computer science.

FIRST-YEAR CLASS 1,534 total; 4,171 applied, 45% of whom enrolled.

ACADEMIC PROGRAM Core. Calendar: semesters. Academic remediation for entering students, English as a second language program offered during academic year and summer, advanced placement, honors program, summer session for credit, part-time degree program (daytime, evenings, weekends, summer), external degree programs, adult/continuing education programs, co-op programs. Off-campus study at University of Massachusetts, Massachusetts College of Art, Roxbury Community College. Study abroad in Italy, France, England, Czech Republic, Germany, Commonwealth of Independent States.

GENERAL DEGREE REQUIREMENT 62 credit hours.

MAJORS Accounting, behavioral sciences, business administration/commerce/management, communication equipment technology, community services, computer programming, computer science, computer technologies, criminal justice, culinary arts, educational media, electrical and electronics technologies, fire science, food services management, graphic arts, hotel and restaurant management, human services, illustration, labor studies, law enforcement/police sciences, legal secretarial studies, liberal arts/general studies, marketing/retailing/merchandising, medical secretarial studies, nuclear medical technology, nursing, optical technologies, radiological technology, retail management, secretarial studies/office management.

LIBRARY 46,000 books, 650 microform titles, 320 periodicals, 5,300 records, tapes, and CDs.

COMPUTERS ON CAMPUS 174 computers for student use in computer center.

COLLEGE LIFE Drama-theater group, student-run newspaper, radio station. 65% vote in student government elections. ***Social organizations:*** 1 national fraternity. ***Student services:*** health clinic, personal-psychological counseling. ***Campus security:*** 24-hour emergency response devices and patrols, late-night transport-escort service.

HOUSING College housing not available.

ATHLETICS ***Intercollegiate:*** basketball M, soccer M. ***Intramural:*** football, ice hockey, softball, tennis. ***Contact:*** Mr. Peter Siatta, Director of Athletics, 617-241-8600 Ext. 260.

CAREER PLANNING ***Service:*** career counseling.

EXPENSES FOR 1995–96 ***Application fee:*** $10. State resident tuition: $2250 full-time, $75 per credit hour part-time. Nonresident tuition: $6690 full-time, $223 per credit hour part-time.

FINANCIAL AID ***College-administered undergrad aid 1995–96:*** 381 need-based scholarships (average $500), low-interest long-term loans from external sources (average $1354), Federal Work-Study. ***Required forms:*** CSS Financial Aid PROFILE, institutional, FAFSA; required for some: nontaxable income verification; accepted: state. ***Priority deadline:*** 5/1.

APPLYING Open admission except for allied health programs. ***Options:*** Common Application, deferred entrance. ***Required:*** school transcript, TOEFL for international students. ***Required for some:*** nursing exam. Test scores used for counseling/placement. ***Application deadline:*** rolling. ***Notification:*** continuous. Preference given to state residents.

APPLYING/TRANSFER ***Required:*** high school transcript. ***Application deadline:*** rolling. ***Notification:*** continuous.

CONTACT Ms. Judy Benson, Admissions Recruiter, Bunker Hill Community College, 250 New Rutherford Avenue, Boston, MA 02129, 617-228-2238. ***Fax:*** 617-241-5535.

CAPE COD COMMUNITY COLLEGE
West Barnstable, Massachusetts

UG Enrollment: 3,640	**Tuition & Fees (MA Res): $2610**
Application Deadline: rolling	**Room & Board: N/Avail**

GENERAL State-supported, 2-year, coed. Part of Massachusetts Public Higher Education System. Awards transfer associate, terminal associate degrees. Founded 1961. ***Setting:*** 120-acre rural campus with easy access to Boston. ***Endowment:*** $360,314. ***Total enrollment:*** 3,640. ***Faculty:*** 259 (84 full-time, 175 part-time); student-faculty ratio is 16:1.

ENROLLMENT PROFILE 3,640 students: 66% women, 34% men, 53% part-time, 99% state residents, 35% transferred in, 54% 25 or older, 1% Hispanic, 2% African American, 1% Asian American. ***Areas of study chosen:*** 28% liberal arts/general studies, 24% health professions and related sciences, 7% education, 4% computer and information sciences, 3% social sciences, 2% communications and journalism, 2% fine arts, 1% engineering and applied sciences. ***Most popular recent majors:*** liberal arts/general studies, nursing.

FIRST-YEAR CLASS 1,136 total; 1,918 applied, 91% were accepted, 65% of whom enrolled. 7% from top quarter of their high school class, 32% from top half.

ACADEMIC PROGRAM Core, honor code. Calendar: semesters. Academic remediation for entering students, services for LD students, advanced placement, self-designed majors, summer session for credit, part-time degree program (daytime, evenings, summer), adult/continuing education programs, co-op programs and internships. Off-campus study at Bridgewater State College, Bristol Community College, Dean College, Massasoit Community College, Stonehill College, University of Massachusetts Dartmouth. Study abroad in England, Ireland, France, Germany, China, Italy, Portugal, Commonwealth of Independent States.

GENERAL DEGREE REQUIREMENTS 60 credit hours; 8 credit hours of science, 3 credit hours of math for associate of arts degree; 3 credit hours of math/science for associate of science degree; internship (some majors).

MAJORS Accounting, art/fine arts, business administration/commerce/management, computer information systems, computer science, construction management, criminal justice, dental services, early childhood education, education, engineering (general), (pre)engineering sequence, fire science, history, horticulture, hotel and restaurant management, legal secretarial studies, liberal arts/general studies, mathematics, medical secretarial studies, modern languages, music, nursing, paralegal studies, philosophy, physical education, physical therapy, psychology, recreation and leisure services, retail management, science, secretarial studies/office management, theater arts/drama.

LIBRARY Cape Cod Community College Learning Resource Center with 54,000 books, 385 microform titles, 425 periodicals, 2 on-line bibliographic services, 7 CD-ROMs, 1,560 records, tapes, and CDs. Acquisition spending 1994–95: $100,686.

COMPUTERS ON CAMPUS 125 computers for student use in computer center, Assessment Center. Staffed computer lab on campus provides training in use of computers. Academic computing expenditure 1994–95: $309,723.

COLLEGE LIFE Drama-theater group, choral group, student-run newspaper, radio station. ***Most popular organizations:*** Innkeepers Club, Adult Re-Entry Club, Student Senate, Ski Club, Ethnic Diversity. ***Major annual events:*** Women's Exposition, Minority Student Awareness Day. ***Student services:*** health clinic, personal-psychological counseling, women's center. ***Campus security:*** 24-hour patrols.

HOUSING College housing not available.

ATHLETICS ***Intramural:*** crew, racquetball, soccer, tennis, volleyball.

CAREER PLANNING ***Placement office:*** 1 full-time staff. ***Director:*** Ms. Pamela Carroll, Director, 508-362-2131 Ext. 4318. ***Services:*** resume preparation, career counseling, careers library, job bank.

EXPENSES FOR 1995–96 ***Application fee:*** $10. State resident tuition: $1200 full-time, $40 per credit hour part-time. Nonresident tuition: $5640 full-time, $188 per credit hour part-time. Part-time mandatory fees: $47 per credit hour. Full-time mandatory fees: $1410.

FINANCIAL AID ***College-administered undergrad aid 1995–96:*** 824 need-based scholarships (average $465), 15 non-need scholarships (average $2120), low-interest long-term loans from external sources (average $2445), Federal Work-Study. ***Required forms:*** FAFSA. ***Priority deadline:*** 4/1. ***Payment plans:*** installment, deferred payment. ***Waivers:*** full or partial for children of alumni, employees or children of employees, and senior citizens. ***Average indebtedness of graduates:*** $4900.

APPLYING Open admission except for nursing, dental hygiene, engineering, physical therapy, computer science programs. ***Options:*** deferred entrance, midyear entrance. ***Required:*** TOEFL for international students. Test scores used for admission. ***Application deadline:*** rolling. Preference given to state residents.

APPLYING/TRANSFER ***Entrance:*** noncompetitive. ***Application deadline:*** rolling.

CONTACT Ms. Susan Kline-Symington, Director of Admissions, Cape Cod Community College, West Barnstable, MA 02668, 508-362-2131 Ext. 4311. ***Fax:*** 508-362-8638.

DEAN COLLEGE
Franklin, Massachusetts

UG Enrollment: 1,950	**Tuition & Fees: $12,485**
Application Deadline: rolling	**Room & Board: $6300**

Dean College, one of the leading private 2-year residential colleges, promotes academic success and builds student confidence. With a safe, active, and attractive campus located less than 30 miles from Boston, the College enjoys a nearly ideal combination of facilities, programs, and dedicated teaching faculty members. Each year, 90% of graduating students transfer to complete their baccalaureate degree.

GENERAL Independent, 2-year, coed. Awards certificates, transfer associate, terminal associate degrees. Founded 1865. ***Setting:*** 100-acre small-town campus with easy access to Boston. ***Endowment:*** $8.6 million. ***Total enrollment:*** 1,950. ***Faculty:*** 92 (42 full-time, 6% with terminal degrees, 50 part-time); student-faculty ratio is 15:1. ***Notable Alumni:*** Michael J. Schumacher, chairman and president of Stasbourger Pearson Tulcin Wolff, Inc.; Robert J. Shook, senior associate in financial strategies group at Prudential Securities; Joseph Cortese, radio personality at WBMX-FM (Boston); R. Simon Bacal, entertainment journalist; Lynn Fischer, creative director at Walt Disney Company.

ENROLLMENT PROFILE 1,950 students from 22 states and territories, 24 other countries. 45% women, 44% part-time, 45% state residents, 5% transferred in, 65% have need-based financial aid, 11% have non-need-based financial aid, 5% international, 1% 25 or older, 1% Native American, 1% Hispanic, 4% African American. ***Most popular recent majors:*** business administration/commerce/management, liberal arts/general studies, communication.

FIRST-YEAR CLASS 504 total; 1,960 applied, 86% were accepted, 30% of whom enrolled. 3% from top quarter of their high school class, 7% from top half.

ACADEMIC PROGRAM Core, honor code. Calendar: semesters. Academic remediation for entering students, English as a second language program offered during academic year, services for LD students, advanced placement, self-designed majors, Freshman Honors College, honors program, summer session for credit, part-time degree program (daytime, evenings), adult/continuing education programs, internships.

GENERAL DEGREE REQUIREMENTS 60 credits; computer course for business, criminal justice, math, pre-engineering, science, paralegal majors; internship (some majors).

MAJORS Accounting, art/fine arts, athletic training, broadcasting, business administration/commerce/management, child care/child and family studies, communication, community services, computer information systems, computer science, corrections, criminal justice, dance, early childhood education, (pre)engineering sequence, fashion merchandising, humanities, human services, journalism, law enforcement/police sciences, liberal arts/general studies, marketing/retailing/merchandising, music, paralegal studies, physical education, physical fitness/exercise science, recreational facilities management, recreation and leisure services, retail management, science, social science, social work, sports administration, sports medicine, telecommunications, theater arts/drama.

LIBRARY E. Ross Anderson Library with 54,000 books, 297 microform titles, 350 periodicals, 8 CD-ROMs, 4,705 records, tapes, and CDs. Acquisition spending 1994–95: $92,775.

COMPUTERS ON CAMPUS 150 computers for student use in computer center, writing center, library provide access to Internet. Staffed computer lab on campus provides training in use of computers, software. Academic computing expenditure 1994–95: $103,000.

COLLEGE LIFE Orientation program (2 days, $200). Drama-theater group, choral group, student-run newspaper, radio station. 27% vote in student government elections. ***Social organizations:*** 30 open to all. ***Most popular organizations:*** Emerging Leaders, College Success Staff, Student Activities Committee, Student Government, Phi Theta Kappa. ***Major annual events:*** Homecoming, Harvest Weekend, Leadership Conference. ***Student services:*** health clinic, personal-psychological counseling. ***Campus security:*** 24-hour emergency response devices and patrols, late-night transport-escort service, controlled dormitory access.

HOUSING 830 college housing spaces available; 739 were occupied 1995–96. Freshmen given priority for college housing. On-campus residence required through sophomore year except if living with relatives. ***Options:*** coed, single-sex housing available. Resident assistants live in dorms.

ATHLETICS Member NJCAA. ***Intercollegiate:*** baseball M(s), basketball M(s), field hockey W(s), football M(s), lacrosse M(s), soccer M(s)/W(s), softball W(s), tennis M(s), volleyball W(s). ***Intramural:*** basketball, football, ice hockey, skiing (cross-country), skiing (downhill), swimming and diving, tennis, volleyball, water polo, weight lifting. ***Contact:*** Mr. John Jackson, Athletic Director, 508-541-1814.
CAREER PLANNING ***Placement office:*** 4 full-time, 3 part-time staff. ***Director:*** Mr. Kevin Clancy, Director of Counseling and Career Transfer Services, 508-541-1611. ***Services:*** job fairs, resume preparation, career counseling, careers library, job bank.
AFTER GRADUATION 90% of students completing a degree program in 1994–95 went directly on to further study.
EXPENSES FOR 1996–97 ***Application fee:*** $25. Comprehensive fee of $18,785 includes full-time tuition ($11,880), mandatory fees ($605), and college room and board ($6300). College room only: $4100. Part-time tuition: $130 per credit.
FINANCIAL AID ***College-administered undergrad aid 1995–96:*** 728 need-based scholarships (average $3757), 100 non-need scholarships (average $1000), low-interest long-term loans from college funds (average $500), loans from external sources (average $3000), 317 Federal Work-Study (averaging $800), 15 part-time jobs. ***Required forms:*** CSS Financial Aid PROFILE, FAFSA. ***Priority deadline:*** 2/15. ***Payment plan:*** installment. ***Waivers:*** full or partial for employees or children of employees and senior citizens. ***Notification:*** 3/1.
APPLYING ***Options:*** deferred entrance, midyear entrance. ***Required:*** school transcript, recommendations, TOEFL for international students. ***Recommended:*** minimum 2.0 GPA, 3 years of high school math and science, interview, SAT I or ACT. Test scores used for admission. ***Application deadline:*** rolling. ***Notification:*** continuous.
APPLYING/TRANSFER ***Required:*** college transcript. ***Recommended:*** 3 years of high school math and science. ***Entrance:*** minimally difficult. ***Application deadline:*** rolling. ***Notification:*** continuous. ***Contact:*** Ms. Linda Lyons, Director of Transfer and Career Development, 508-541-1603.
CONTACT Mr. Kevin Kelly, Vice President for Enrollment Services, Dean College, Franklin, MA 02038-1994, 508-541-1508 or toll-free 800-852-7702. ***Fax:*** 508-541-8726. College video available.

❖ *See page 732 for a narrative description.* ❖

ENDICOTT COLLEGE
Beverly, Massachusetts

UG Enrollment: 802	Tuition & Fees: $12,220
Application Deadline: rolling	Room & Board: $6400

Endicott College offers the best of both worlds: bachelor and associate degree programs with more than 45 4- and 2-year options. Located only 20 miles from Boston, the Endicott campus has been noted as one of the most scenic in the US. For more information on the 4-year offerings at the College, students should refer to Peterson's Guide to Four-Year Colleges 1997.

GENERAL Independent, primarily 2-year, coed. Awards certificates, transfer associate, terminal associate, bachelor's, master's degrees. Founded 1939. ***Setting:*** 150-acre suburban campus with easy access to Boston. ***Total enrollment:*** 802. ***Undergradu:*** 85 (42 full-time, 28% with terminal degrees, 43 part-time); student-faculty ratio is 11:1.
ENROLLMENT PROFILE 802 students from 25 states and territories, 43 other countries. 77% women, 23% men, 3% part-time, 53% state residents, 70% live on campus, 24% transferred in, 74% have need-based financial aid, 9% international, 14% 25 or older, 0% Native American, 4% Hispanic, 3% African American, 7% Asian American. ***Areas of study chosen:*** 28% liberal arts/general studies, 20% business management and administrative services, 15% health professions and related sciences, 12% education, 10% fine arts, 10% psychology, 5% communications and journalism. ***Most popular recent majors:*** nursing, psychology, education.
FIRST-YEAR CLASS 406 total; 1,378 applied, 81% were accepted, 36% of whom enrolled. 4% from top 10% of their high school class, 14% from top quarter, 48% from top half.
ACADEMIC PROGRAM Core. Calendar: 4-1-4. Academic remediation for entering students, English as a second language program offered during academic year and summer, advanced placement, self-designed majors, Freshman Honors College, tutorials, honors program, summer session for credit, part-time degree program (daytime), adult/continuing education programs, internships. Off-campus study at 10 members of the Northeast Consortium of Colleges and Universities in Massachusetts. Study abroad in Switzerland, Japan, Spain, Mexico.
GENERAL DEGREE REQUIREMENTS 64 credits for associate, 128 credits for bachelor's; internship.
MAJORS Advertising (B), art/fine arts (B), arts administration, athletic training (B), broadcasting (B), business administration/commerce/management (B), ceramic art and design, child care/child and family studies, commercial art (B), communication (B), computer programming, criminal justice (B), criminology, culinary arts, early childhood education (B), education (B), elementary education (B), fashion merchandising (B), food services management (B), food services technology (B), graphic arts (B), hospitality services (B), hotel and restaurant management (B), humanities, human services, interior design (B), jewelry and metalsmithing, journalism, liberal arts/general studies, marketing/retailing/merchandising (B), nursing (B), painting/drawing, paralegal studies, photography, physical education (B), physical therapy, psychology (B), public relations (B), radio and television studies (B), retail management (B), social science, social work, sports administration (B), sports medicine, studio art.
LIBRARY Fitz Memorial Library with 44,200 books, 4 microform titles, 950 periodicals, 1 on-line bibliographic service, 1 CD-ROM, 1,922 records, tapes, and CDs.
COMPUTERS ON CAMPUS Computer purchase plan available. Student rooms linked to a campus network. 80 computers for student use in computer center, computer labs, learning resource center, classrooms, library, dorms provide access to e-mail, on-line services, Internet. Staffed computer lab on campus provides training in use of computers, software.
COLLEGE LIFE Orientation program (3 days, parents included). Drama-theater group, choral group, student-run newspaper. ***Social organizations:*** 30 open to all. ***Most popular organizations:*** Fitness Club, Student Government, Sailing Club, Drama Club, Ski Club. ***Major annual events:*** Spring Week, Winter Holiday Festivities, Orientation. ***Student services:*** health clinic, personal-psychological counseling, women's center. ***Campus security:*** 24-hour emergency response devices and patrols, late-night transport-escort service, controlled dormitory access.
HOUSING 625 college housing spaces available; 525 were occupied 1995–96. Freshmen guaranteed college housing. except if over 23 or living with relatives. ***Option:*** single-sex (11 buildings) housing available. Resident assistants live in dorms.
ATHLETICS Member NCAA. All Division III. ***Intercollegiate:*** baseball M, basketball M/W, cross-country running M/W, field hockey W, lacrosse M/W, soccer M/W, softball W, tennis M/W, volleyball W. ***Intramural:*** basketball, cross-country running, field hockey, sailing, soccer, softball, tennis, volleyball. ***Contact:*** Mr. Larry Hiser, Director of Athletics, 508-927-0585 Ext. 2305.
CAREER PLANNING ***Director:*** Ms. Pat Makin, Internship Coordinator, 508-921-1000. ***Services:*** job fairs, resume preparation, resume referral, career counseling, careers library, job bank, job interviews.
EXPENSES FOR 1995–96 ***Application fee:*** $25. Comprehensive fee of $18,620 includes full-time tuition ($11,970), mandatory fees ($250), and college room and board ($6400). Part-time tuition: $365 per credit.
FINANCIAL AID ***College-administered undergrad aid 1995–96:*** 551 need-based scholarships (averaging $4000), low-interest long-term loans from college funds (averaging $800), loans from external sources (averaging $2625), 165 Federal Work-Study (averaging $800), 8 part-time jobs. Average total aid for freshmen: $8440. ***Required forms:*** CSS Financial Aid PROFILE, institutional, FAFSA. ***Priority deadline:*** 3/15. ***Payment plan:*** installment.
APPLYING ***Options:*** Common Application, electronic application, early entrance, early action, deferred entrance, midyear entrance. ***Required:*** essay, school transcript, minimum 2.0 GPA, recommendations, TOEFL for international students. ***Recommended:*** some high school foreign language, SAT I or ACT. ***Required for some:*** 3 years of high school math and science, interview, SAT I. Test scores used for counseling/placement. ***Application deadlines:*** rolling, 11/15 for early action. ***Notification:*** continuous, 12/1 for early action.
APPLYING/TRANSFER ***Required:*** essay, high school transcript, recommendations, college transcript, minimum 2.0 college GPA, minimum 2.0 high school GPA. ***Recommended:*** standardized test scores, some high school foreign language. ***Required for some:*** standardized test scores, 3 years of high school math and science, interview. ***Entrance:*** minimally difficult. ***Application deadline:*** rolling. ***Notification:*** continuous. ***Contact:*** Mr. Thomas J. Redman, Vice President of Admissions and Financial Aid, 508-921-1000.
CONTACT Mr. Thomas J. Redman, Vice President of Admissions and Financial Aid, Endicott College, Beverly, MA 01915-2096, 508-921-1000 or toll-free 800-325-1114 (out-of-state). ***Fax:*** 508-927-0084. College video available.

FISHER COLLEGE
Boston, Massachusetts

UG Enrollment: 420	Tuition & Fees: $11,900
Application Deadline: rolling	Room & Board: $6500

As the leading private 2-year college for women in Boston, Fisher College is the first in the country to include a free international trip each year as part of each student's education. The Fisher International Research Seminar Trip (F-I-R-S-T) is an international experience supported by academic preparation and instruction. Students will travel to Athens in 1996 and 1997.

GENERAL Independent, 2-year, women only. Awards transfer associate, terminal associate degrees. Founded 1903. ***Setting:*** 3-acre urban campus. ***Endowment:*** $20 million. ***Total enrollment:*** 420. ***Faculty:*** 36 (14 full-time, 22 part-time).
ENROLLMENT PROFILE 420 students from 15 states and territories, 12 other countries. 100% women, 1% part-time, 49% state residents, 49% live on campus, 12% transferred in, 15% international. ***Areas of study chosen:*** 48% business management and administrative services, 18% liberal arts/general studies, 13% social sciences, 11% education, 7% health professions and related sciences, 3% communications and journalism.
FIRST-YEAR CLASS 233 total; 715 applied, 83% were accepted, 39% of whom enrolled.
ACADEMIC PROGRAM Core. Calendar: semesters. Academic remediation for entering students, English as a second language program offered during academic year and summer, advanced placement, summer session for credit, part-time degree program (daytime, evenings), adult/continuing education programs, internships. Off-campus study at Emerson College.
GENERAL DEGREE REQUIREMENTS 60 credits; 1 course each in math and science; internship (some majors).
MAJORS Accounting, business administration/commerce/management, communication, criminal justice, early childhood education, fashion merchandising, hotel and restaurant management, international business, legal secretarial studies, liberal arts/general studies, medical assistant technologies, paralegal studies, physical therapy, secretarial studies/office management, tourism and travel.
LIBRARY Fisher College Library with 28,000 books, 47 microform titles, 109 periodicals, 200 records, tapes, and CDs.
COMPUTERS ON CAMPUS 112 computers for student use in computer center, learning resource center, dorms. Staffed computer lab on campus provides training in use of computers, software.
COLLEGE LIFE Orientation program (4 days, no cost, parents included). Drama-theater group, choral group. ***Major annual events:*** Parents' Weekend, Fisher Olympics, All College Outing. ***Student services:*** health clinic, personal-psychological counseling, women's center. ***Campus security:*** 24-hour emergency response devices and patrols.
HOUSING 200 college housing spaces available; all were occupied 1995–96. Freshmen guaranteed college housing. Off-campus living permitted. ***Option:*** single-sex housing available. Resident assistants live in dorms.
ATHLETICS ***Intercollegiate:*** basketball.
CAREER PLANNING ***Director:*** Ms. Sherri Zacardi, Director of Placement, 617-236-8800. ***Services:*** resume preparation, resume referral, career counseling, careers library, job interviews.
AFTER GRADUATION 50% of students completing a degree program in 1994–95 went directly on to further study.
EXPENSES FOR 1996–97 ***Application fee:*** $25. Comprehensive fee of $18,400 includes full-time tuition ($10,900), mandatory fees ($1000), and college room and board ($6500).
FINANCIAL AID ***College-administered undergrad aid 1995–96:*** 148 need-based scholarships (averaging $7085), 20 non-need scholarships (averaging $1200), low-interest long-term loans from external sources (averaging $2625), Federal Work-Study, 6 part-time jobs. ***Acceptable forms:*** FAFSA. ***Application deadline:*** continuous. ***Payment plan:*** installment. ***Waivers:*** full or partial for employees or children of employees.

Fisher College (continued)
APPLYING ***Options:*** Common Application, deferred entrance, midyear entrance. ***Required:*** school transcript, TOEFL for international students. ***Recommended:*** minimum 2.0 GPA, SAT I. Test scores used for admission. ***Application deadline:*** rolling.
APPLYING/TRANSFER ***Required:*** college transcript. ***Recommended:*** minimum 2.0 college GPA. ***Required for some:*** minimum 2.0 high school GPA. ***Entrance:*** minimally difficult. ***Application deadline:*** rolling. ***Contact:*** Ms. Marietta Baier, Associate Director of Admissions, 617-236-8800.
CONTACT Ms. Sandra M. Robbins, Director of Admissions, Fisher College, 118 Beacon Street, Boston, MA 02116-1500, 617-236-8800 Ext. 820 or toll-free 800-821-3050 (in-state), 800-446-1226 (out-of-state). ***Fax:*** 617-236-8858. College video available.

❖ *See page 738 for a narrative description.* ❖

FRANKLIN INSTITUTE OF BOSTON
Boston, Massachusetts

UG Enrollment: 302	**Tuition & Fees: $9050**
Application Deadline: rolling	**Room & Board: N/Avail**

GENERAL Independent, 2-year, primarily men. Awards certificates, terminal associate degrees. Founded 1908. ***Setting:*** 3-acre urban campus. ***Total enrollment:*** 302. ***Faculty:*** 37 (30 full-time, 2% with terminal degrees, 7 part-time); student-faculty ratio is 11:1.
ENROLLMENT PROFILE 302 students from 6 states and territories, 2 other countries. 3% women, 1% part-time, 85% state residents, 5% live on campus, 3% transferred in, 3% international, 20% 25 or older, 1% Native American, 8% Hispanic, 12% African American, 26% Asian American. ***Areas of study chosen:*** 50% engineering and applied sciences, 30% computer and information sciences, 10% architecture, 10% vocational and home economics. ***Most popular recent majors:*** automotive technologies, computer technologies, engineering technology.
FIRST-YEAR CLASS 145 total; 553 applied, 80% were accepted, 33% of whom enrolled.
ACADEMIC PROGRAM Hands-on technical education curriculum, honor code. Calendar: semesters. 146 courses offered in 1995–96. Academic remediation for entering students, English as a second language program offered during academic year, summer session for credit, part-time degree program (daytime), adult/continuing education programs, internships.
GENERAL DEGREE REQUIREMENTS 70 credits; math/science requirements vary according to program; computer course; internship (some majors).
MAJORS Architectural technologies, automotive technologies, civil engineering technology, computer science, computer technologies, drafting and design, electrical and electronics technologies, electrical engineering technology, engineering technology, mechanical engineering technology.
LIBRARY 13,000 books, 60 periodicals.
COMPUTERS ON CAMPUS 70 computers for student use in computer center, labs, classrooms, library. Staffed computer lab on campus provides training in use of computers, software.
COLLEGE LIFE 50% vote in student government elections. ***Social organizations:*** 3 open to all. ***Most popular organization:*** Society of Manufacturing Engineers. ***Major annual events:*** Engineering Week Competition, Ben Franklin's Birthday, Holiday Party. ***Campus security:*** 24-hour emergency response devices, student patrols.
HOUSING College housing not available.
ATHLETICS ***Intercollegiate:*** basketball M, soccer M. ***Intramural:*** volleyball.
CAREER PLANNING ***Placement office:*** 1 full-time staff. ***Director:*** Ms. Doreen White, Director of Student and Alumni Services, 617-423-4630. ***Services:*** resume preparation, resume referral, career counseling, job bank, job interviews.
EXPENSES FOR 1996–97 ***Application fee:*** $30. Tuition: $8850 full-time, $369 per credit part-time. Full-time mandatory fees: $200.
FINANCIAL AID ***College-administered undergrad aid 1995–96:*** 80 need-based scholarships (average $2700), low-interest long-term loans from college funds, loans from external sources, Federal Work-Study, part-time jobs. ***Required forms:*** institutional, FAFSA. ***Priority deadline:*** 3/1. ***Payment plan:*** installment. ***Waivers:*** full or partial for employees or children of employees.
APPLYING ***Option:*** midyear entrance. ***Required:*** school transcript, TOEFL for international students. ***Recommended:*** SAT I or ACT. Test scores used for counseling/placement. ***Application deadline:*** rolling. ***Notification:*** continuous.
APPLYING/TRANSFER ***Required:*** high school transcript, college transcript. ***Recommended:*** standardized test scores. ***Entrance:*** minimally difficult. ***Application deadline:*** rolling. ***Notification:*** continuous. ***Contact:*** Mr. Ed Connor, Admission Counselor, 617-423-4630.
CONTACT Mr. John J. Brady, Director of Admissions, Franklin Institute of Boston, 41 Berkeley Street, Boston, MA 02116-6296, 617-423-4630 Ext. 22. ***Fax:*** 617-482-3706. College video available.

❖ *See page 740 for a narrative description.* ❖

GREENFIELD COMMUNITY COLLEGE
Greenfield, Massachusetts

UG Enrollment: 1,863	**Tuition & Fees (MA Res): $2600**
Application Deadline: rolling	**Room & Board: N/Avail**

GENERAL State-supported, 2-year, coed. Awards certificates, transfer associate, terminal associate degrees. Founded 1962. ***Setting:*** 100-acre small-town campus. ***Total enrollment:*** 1,863. ***Faculty:*** 131 (61 full-time, 70 part-time); student-faculty ratio is 14:1.
ENROLLMENT PROFILE 1,863 students from 5 states and territories, 12 other countries. 60% women, 38% part-time, 93% state residents, 12% transferred in, 1% international, 48% 25 or older, 0% Native American, 2% Hispanic, 1% African American, 3% Asian American. ***Areas of study chosen:*** 43% interdisciplinary studies, 6% fine arts, 3% education, 3% engineering and applied sciences, 1% communications and journalism, 1% natural resource sciences. ***Most popular recent majors:*** liberal arts/general studies, business administration/commerce/management, nursing.
FIRST-YEAR CLASS 747 total. Of the students who applied, 90% were accepted, 56% of whom enrolled.
ACADEMIC PROGRAM Core. Calendar: semesters. 300 courses offered in 1995–96. Academic remediation for entering students, English as a second language program offered during academic year, services for LD students, advanced placement, tutorials, honors program, summer session for credit, part-time degree program (daytime, evenings, summer), adult/continuing education programs, co-op programs and internships.
GENERAL DEGREE REQUIREMENT 60 credits.
MAJORS Accounting, American studies, art/fine arts, behavioral sciences, business administration/commerce/management, communication, computer information systems, computer programming, criminal justice, early childhood education, education, engineering sciences, (pre)engineering sequence, fire science, food sciences, graphic arts, human ecology, humanities, human services, industrial engineering technology, liberal arts/general studies, marketing/retailing/merchandising, mathematics, natural resource management, nursing, photography, recreation and leisure services, science, secretarial studies/office management.
LIBRARY 52,690 books, 1,691 microform titles, 356 periodicals, 2,144 records, tapes, and CDs.
COMPUTERS ON CAMPUS 115 computers for student use in computer center, special labs, library provide access to off-campus computing facilities, e-mail, on-line services. Staffed computer lab on campus provides training in use of computers, software.
COLLEGE LIFE Drama-theater group, choral group. ***Major annual event:*** Spring Weekend. ***Student services:*** health clinic, personal-psychological counseling, women's center.
HOUSING College housing not available.
ATHLETICS Member NJCAA. ***Intercollegiate:*** baseball M, soccer M, softball W, volleyball W. ***Contact:*** Mr. John Palmer, Director of Athletics, 413-774-3131.
CAREER PLANNING ***Service:*** career counseling.
AFTER GRADUATION 50% of students completing a degree program in 1994–95 went directly on to further study.
EXPENSES FOR 1995–96 ***Application fee:*** $10. State resident tuition: $2600 full-time, $127 per credit part-time. Nonresident tuition: $7330 full-time, $277 per credit part-time. Tuition for nonresidents who are eligible for the New England Regional Student Program: $3400 full-time, $146 per credit hour part-time.
FINANCIAL AID ***College-administered undergrad aid 1995–96:*** 496 need-based scholarships (average $357), short-term loans (average $25), low-interest long-term loans from college funds (average $400), loans from external sources (average $1800), Federal Work-Study. ***Required forms:*** state, institutional, FAFSA, proof of Selective Service registration (for men). ***Priority deadline:*** 4/15. ***Waivers:*** full or partial for employees or children of employees and senior citizens.
APPLYING Open admission except for allied health, outdoor leadership programs. ***Options:*** early entrance, midyear entrance. ***Required:*** TOEFL for international students. ***Required for some:*** school transcript, Psychological Corporation Practical Nursing Entrance Examination. Test scores used for admission. ***Application deadline:*** rolling. Preference given to state residents.
APPLYING/TRANSFER ***Required for some:*** standardized test scores, high school transcript. ***Entrance:*** noncompetitive. ***Application deadline:*** rolling.
CONTACT Mr. Donald W. Brown, Director of Admissions, Greenfield Community College, Greenfield, MA 01301-9739, 413-774-3131 Ext. 237.

HOLYOKE COMMUNITY COLLEGE
Holyoke, Massachusetts

UG Enrollment: 3,558	**Tuition & Fees (MA Res): $2532**
Application Deadline: rolling	**Room & Board: N/Avail**

GENERAL State-supported, 2-year, coed. Part of Massachusetts Public Higher Education System. Awards certificates, transfer associate, terminal associate degrees (also offers continuing education program with significant enrollment not reflected in profile). Founded 1946. ***Setting:*** 135-acre suburban campus. ***Total enrollment:*** 3,558. ***Faculty:*** 235 (127 full-time, 25% with terminal degrees, 108 part-time); student-faculty ratio is 18:1.
ENROLLMENT PROFILE 3,558 students from 7 states and territories, 11 other countries. 60% women, 32% part-time, 98% state residents, 10% transferred in, 35% have need-based financial aid, 1% have non-need-based financial aid, 1% international, 35% 25 or older, 1% Native American, 12% Hispanic, 4% African American, 2% Asian American. ***Areas of study chosen:*** 48% interdisciplinary studies, 6% social sciences, 5% education, 3% engineering and applied sciences, 2% fine arts, 2% natural resource sciences, 2% prevet, 1% performing arts. ***Most popular recent majors:*** liberal arts/general studies, business administration/commerce/management, elementary education.
FIRST-YEAR CLASS 784 total; 1,874 applied, 100% were accepted, 42% of whom enrolled.
ACADEMIC PROGRAM Core, honor code. Calendar: semesters. Academic remediation for entering students, English as a second language program offered during academic year, services for LD students, advanced placement, self-designed majors, tutorials, honors program, summer session for credit, part-time degree program (daytime, evenings, summer), adult/continuing education programs, co-op programs and internships. Off-campus study at the Cooperating Colleges of Greater Springfield. Study abroad in 19 countries, including England, China, France, Germany. ROTC: Army (c), Air Force (c).
GENERAL DEGREE REQUIREMENTS 60 credit hours; 2 natural science lab courses; internship (some majors).
MAJORS Accounting, American studies, art/fine arts, biology/biological sciences, business administration/commerce/management, business education, chemistry, commercial art, communication, computer information systems, early childhood education, elementary education, engineering sciences, (pre)engineering sequence, environmental sciences, film and video production, home economics, hospitality services, hotel and restaurant management, human services, law enforcement/police sciences, legal secretarial studies, liberal arts/general studies, medical records services, medical technology, music, nursing, nutrition, photography, physics, radiological technology, retail management, secretarial studies/office management, sports administration, studio art, theater arts/drama, tourism and travel, veterinary sciences, veterinary technology, word processing.
LIBRARY Elaine Marieb Library with 68,965 books, 426 microform titles, 459 periodicals, 11 CD-ROMs, 4,528 records, tapes, and CDs. Acquisition spending 1994–95: $220,000.
COMPUTERS ON CAMPUS Computer purchase plan available. 275 computers for student use in computer center, computer labs, learning resource center, library provide access to main academic computer, e-mail, Internet. Staffed computer lab on campus provides training in use of computers, software. Academic computing expenditure 1994–95: $100,000.
COLLEGE LIFE Drama-theater group, choral group, student-run newspaper, radio station. ***Most popular organizations:*** Drama Club, Music Club, Student Advisory Board.

Major annual events: Spring Fling Week, Welcome Week, Black History Month. ***Student services:*** health clinic, personal-psychological counseling, women's center. ***Campus security:*** 24-hour emergency response devices and patrols, student patrols, late-night transport-escort service.

HOUSING College housing not available.

ATHLETICS Member NJCAA. ***Intercollegiate:*** baseball M, basketball M, golf M/W, skiing (downhill) M(c)/W(c), soccer M/W, softball W, tennis M/W. ***Contact:*** Mr. Richard Golas, Director of Athletics, 413-538-7000 Ext. 239.

CAREER PLANNING ***Placement office:*** 3 full-time, 2 part-time staff; $100,000 operating expenditure 1994–95. ***Director:*** Dr. Theresa Howard, Director of Cooperative Education and Career Services, 413-538-7000 Ext. 299. ***Services:*** job fairs, resume preparation, resume referral, career counseling, careers library, job bank, job interviews. 44 organizations recruited on campus 1994–95.

AFTER GRADUATION 56% of class of 1994 had job offers within 6 months. 45% of students completing a degree program went directly on to further study.

EXPENSES FOR 1995–96 ***Application fee:*** $10. State resident tuition: $2460 full-time, $82 per credit part-time. Nonresident tuition: $7230 full-time, $241 per credit part-time. Part-time mandatory fees per semester range from $24 to $36. Full-time mandatory fees: $72.

FINANCIAL AID ***College-administered undergrad aid 1995–96:*** need-based scholarships, non-need scholarships, short-term loans, low-interest long-term loans from external sources, Federal Work-Study. ***Required forms:*** institutional, FAFSA. ***Priority deadline:*** 5/15. ***Payment plan:*** installment. ***Waivers:*** full or partial for employees or children of employees and senior citizens.

APPLYING Open admission except for nursing, radiologic technology, ophthalmic technology programs. ***Options:*** early entrance, deferred entrance, midyear entrance. ***Required:*** school transcript. ***Recommended:*** campus interview. ***Required for some:*** TOEFL for international students, Assessment and Placement Services for Community Colleges, Health Occupations Exam. Test scores used for counseling/placement. ***Application deadline:*** rolling. ***Notification:*** continuous.

APPLYING/TRANSFER ***Required:*** college transcript. ***Recommended:*** high school transcript, campus interview. ***Required for some:*** standardized test scores. ***Entrance:*** noncompetitive. ***Application deadline:*** rolling. ***Notification:*** continuous.

CONTACT Mr. Dan Rosenfield, Director of Admissions, Holyoke Community College, Holyoke, MA 01040-1099, 413-538-7000 Ext. 241.

ITT TECHNICAL INSTITUTE
Framingham, Massachusetts

UG Enrollment: 267	**Tuition: $15,599/deg prog**
Application Deadline: rolling	**Room & Board: N/Avail**

GENERAL Proprietary, 2-year, coed. Part of ITT Educational Services, Inc. Awards transfer associate degrees. Founded 1990. ***Setting:*** suburban campus with easy access to Boston. ***Total enrollment:*** 267. ***Faculty:*** 14 (9 full-time, 5 part-time); student-faculty ratio is 19:1.

ENROLLMENT PROFILE 267 students. ***Areas of study chosen:*** 100% engineering and applied sciences. ***Most popular recent major:*** electronics engineering technology.

FIRST-YEAR CLASS 140 total; 226 applied, 91% were accepted, 68% of whom enrolled.

ACADEMIC PROGRAM Core, technical education curriculum, honor code. Calendar: quarters. Average class size 20 in required courses. Academic remediation for entering students, services for LD students, advanced placement, tutorials, internships.

GENERAL DEGREE REQUIREMENTS 114 credit hours; 1 course each in algebra, trigonometry and physics.

MAJORS Drafting and design, electronics engineering technology.

LIBRARY Main library plus 1 other, with 2,200 books, 28 periodicals, 40 records, tapes, and CDs.

COMPUTERS ON CAMPUS 50 computers for student use in computer labs, learning resource center. Staffed computer lab on campus provides training in use of computers, software.

COLLEGE LIFE 90% vote in student government elections. ***Social organizations:*** 3 open to all. ***Most popular organizations:*** Computer Club, Computer-Aided Drafting Club, Literary Club. ***Major annual events:*** College Summer Outing, Christmas Charity Event. ***Campus security:*** 24-hour emergency response devices.

HOUSING College housing not available.

CAREER PLANNING ***Placement office:*** 1 full-time, 1 part-time staff. ***Director:*** Ms. Lisa Brady, Director of Placement, 508-879-6266. ***Services:*** job fairs, resume preparation, resume referral, career counseling, careers library, job bank, job interviews. Students must register freshman year. 20 organizations recruited on campus 1994–95.

AFTER GRADUATION 100% of class of 1994 had job offers within 6 months. 6% of students completing a degree program went directly on to further study.

EXPENSES FOR 1996–97 ***Application fee:*** $100. Tuition per degree program ranges from $15,599 to $17,690. Full-time mandatory fees range from $540 to $720. Tuition guaranteed not to increase for student's term of enrollment.

FINANCIAL AID ***College-administered undergrad aid 1995–96:*** need-based scholarships, low-interest long-term loans from external sources, Federal Work-Study. ***Required forms:*** institutional, FAFSA; accepted: state. ***Priority deadline:*** 9/9. ***Payment plans:*** installment, deferred payment. ***Waivers:*** full or partial for employees or children of employees. ***Notification:*** continuous. ***Average indebtedness of graduates:*** $19,000.

APPLYING ***Option:*** deferred entrance. ***Required:*** essay, school transcript, 2 recommendations, interview, CPAt. Test scores used for admission. ***Application deadline:*** rolling.

APPLYING/TRANSFER ***Required:*** essay, standardized test scores, high school transcript, 2 recommendations, interview, college transcript, minimum 2.0 college GPA. ***Application deadline:*** rolling. ***Contact:*** Mr. Wayne Cardeiro, Director of Education, 508-879-6266.

CONTACT Ms. Kristen O'Leary, Special Services Coordinator, ITT Technical Institute, Framingham, MA 01701, 508-879-6266 or toll-free 800-879-8324 (in-state). ***Fax:*** 508-879-9745. College video available.

KATHARINE GIBBS SCHOOL
Boston, Massachusetts

UG Enrollment: 450	**Tuition & Fees: $8625**
Application Deadline: rolling	**Room & Board: N/Avail**

GENERAL Proprietary, 2-year, primarily women. Part of K-III Communications Corporation. Awards certificates, transfer associate, terminal associate degrees. Founded 1917. ***Setting:*** urban campus. ***Total enrollment:*** 450. ***Faculty:*** 37 (23 full-time, 25% with terminal degrees, 14 part-time). ***Notable Alumni:*** Dorothy Bush, Loretta Switt, Marilyn Jackson.

ENROLLMENT PROFILE 450 students from 15 states and territories, 6 other countries. 97% women, 32% part-time, 75% state residents, 15% transferred in, 10% international, 35% 25 or older, 0% Native American, 6% Hispanic, 13% African American, 8% Asian American. ***Areas of study chosen:*** 100% business management and administrative services.

FIRST-YEAR CLASS 400 total; 730 applied. 1% from top 10% of their high school class, 10% from top quarter, 30% from top half.

ACADEMIC PROGRAM Core, business curriculum, honor code. Calendar: quarters. 215 courses offered in 1995–96. Academic remediation for entering students, English as a second language program offered during academic year, summer session for credit, part-time degree program (evenings), adult/continuing education programs, internships.

GENERAL DEGREE REQUIREMENTS 96 credits; computer course; internship.

MAJORS Business administration/commerce/management, hospitality services, legal secretarial studies, medical secretarial studies, secretarial studies/office management.

LIBRARY William F. Reilly Library plus 1 other, with 3,800 books, 67 periodicals, 905 records, tapes, and CDs.

COMPUTERS ON CAMPUS 70 computers for student use in academic buildings provide access to main academic computer, e-mail. Staffed computer lab on campus provides training in use of computers, software.

COLLEGE LIFE ***Most popular organizations:*** Student Council, Yearbook, International Student Organization. ***Major annual events:*** Holiday Toys for Tots Drive, Spring Formal, Graduation Cruise. ***Student services:*** personal-psychological counseling.

HOUSING College housing not available.

CAREER PLANNING ***Placement office:*** 5 full-time staff. ***Director:*** Mrs. Theresa Alyward, Director of Placement, 617-578-7100. ***Services:*** job fairs, resume preparation, resume referral, career counseling, careers library, job bank, job interviews. Students must register freshman year.

EXPENSES FOR 1996–97 ***Application fee:*** $25. Tuition: $8600 full-time. Full-time mandatory fees: $25. Tuition guaranteed not to increase for student's term of enrollment.

FINANCIAL AID ***College-administered undergrad aid 1995–96:*** 30 need-based scholarships (average $1000), low-interest long-term loans from external sources (average $2625), Federal Work-Study, 10 part-time jobs. ***Required forms:*** institutional; required for some: FAFSA, nontaxable income verification; accepted: CSS Financial Aid PROFILE, state. ***Priority deadline:*** 9/1. ***Payment plan:*** installment.

APPLYING ***Option:*** midyear entrance. ***Required:*** school transcript, SAT I, CPAt. ***Recommended:*** TOEFL for international students. Test scores used for admission and counseling/placement. ***Application deadline:*** rolling.

APPLYING/TRANSFER ***Required:*** college transcript. ***Entrance:*** minimally difficult. ***Application deadline:*** rolling. ***Contact:*** Mrs. Kate Gjaja, Dean, 617-578-7100.

CONTACT Mr. Henry Ford, Director of Admissions, Katharine Gibbs School, 126 Newbury Street, Boston, MA 02116-2904, 617-578-7100 or toll-free 800-6SKILLS. ***Fax:*** 617-262-2610.

LABOURÉ COLLEGE
Boston, Massachusetts

UG Enrollment: 548	**Tuition & Fees: $10,713**
Application Deadline: rolling	**Room & Board: N/Avail**

Labouré's programs in health care are supported by its affiliations with more than 75 Boston-area health-care institutions. Each program offers career education and general education courses. The student-faculty ratio is 11:1. Opportunities for full- and part-time study, day or evening, and certificate programs are available. All 1995 graduates who elected to work found employment in their respective fields upon graduation.

GENERAL Independent Roman Catholic, 2-year, specialized, coed. Awards certificates, transfer associate, terminal associate degrees. Founded 1971. ***Setting:*** urban campus. ***Total enrollment:*** 548. ***Faculty:*** 57 (26 full-time, 31 part-time); student-faculty ratio is 11:1.

ENROLLMENT PROFILE 548 students from 5 states and territories. 80% women, 60% part-time, 95% state residents, 40% 25 or older. ***Most popular recent majors:*** nursing, radiological technology, medical records services.

FIRST-YEAR CLASS 204 total; 370 applied, 92% were accepted, 60% of whom enrolled. 4% from top 10% of their high school class, 20% from top quarter, 90% from top half.

ACADEMIC PROGRAM Core. Calendar: semesters. Academic remediation for entering students, summer session for credit, part-time degree program (daytime, evenings), adult/continuing education programs.

GENERAL DEGREE REQUIREMENTS 68 credits; 1 course each in anatomy and physiology; computer course for radiation therapy technology, medical information technology, clinical neurophysiological technology majors.

MAJORS Dietetics, medical records services, medical technology, nursing, radiological technology.

LIBRARY 10,000 books, 100 microform titles, 170 periodicals, 3 CD-ROMs, 1,000 records, tapes, and CDs.

COMPUTERS ON CAMPUS 20 computers for student use in computer center, computer labs, learning resource center. Staffed computer lab on campus provides training in use of computers, software.

COLLEGE LIFE ***Student services:*** health clinic, personal-psychological counseling. ***Campus security:*** 24-hour emergency response devices.

HOUSING College housing not available.

CAREER PLANNING ***Service:*** career counseling.

Peterson's Guide to Two-Year Colleges 1997 367

Labouré College (continued)
AFTER GRADUATION 25% of students completing a degree program in 1994–95 went directly on to further study.
EXPENSES FOR 1996–97 ***Application fee:*** $25. Tuition: $10,608 full-time, $312 per credit part-time. Part-time mandatory fees: $105 per year. Full-time mandatory fees: $105.
FINANCIAL AID ***College-administered undergrad aid 1995–96:*** 10 need-based scholarships (average $740), 23 non-need scholarships (average $715), short-term loans (average $700), low-interest long-term loans from external sources (average $640), Federal Work-Study, part-time jobs. ***Required forms:*** CSS Financial Aid PROFILE, state, institutional, FAFSA. ***Priority deadline:*** 5/1.
APPLYING ***Option:*** deferred entrance. ***Required:*** school transcript, recommendations, TOEFL for international students. ***Recommended:*** 3 years of high school math and science, interview. Test scores used for admission. ***Application deadline:*** rolling.
APPLYING/TRANSFER ***Required:*** high school transcript, recommendations, college transcript. ***Recommended:*** 3 years of high school math and science, interview. ***Application deadline:*** rolling.
CONTACT Ms. Robin Brady, Director of Admissions, Labouré College, 2120 Dorchester Avenue, Boston, MA 02124-5617, 617-296-8300 Ext. 4015.

LASELL COLLEGE
Newton, Massachusetts

UG Enrollment: 700	Tuition & Fees: $13,275
Application Deadline: rolling	Room & Board: $6425

The Lasell Plan of Education is distinguished by a philosophy called connected learning. In connected learning, students practice classroom theory in practical settings. In addition to off-campus internship sites, students gain practical experience in on-campus labs, which include 2 renowned child-study centers, a travel agency, a bed and breakfast, a fashion design and merchandising center, allied health labs, a CAD lab, and an art center.

GENERAL Independent, primarily 2-year, women only. Awards transfer associate, terminal associate, bachelor's degrees. Founded 1851. ***Setting:*** 50-acre suburban campus with easy access to Boston. ***Endowment:*** $5.1 million. ***Total enrollment:*** 700. ***Faculty:*** 138 (47 full-time, 38% with terminal degrees, 91 part-time); student-faculty ratio is 10:1.
ENROLLMENT PROFILE 700 students from 23 states and territories, 7 other countries. 100% women, 18% part-time, 64% state residents, 60% live on campus, 20% transferred in, 77% have need-based financial aid, 2% have non-need-based financial aid, 6% international, 7% 25 or older, 0% Native American, 6% Hispanic, 8% African American, 3% Asian American. ***Areas of study chosen:*** 19% health professions and related sciences, 18% education, 16% interdisciplinary studies, 12% liberal arts/general studies, 10% business management and administrative services, 1% fine arts. ***Most popular recent majors:*** education, fashion merchandising, physical therapy.
FIRST-YEAR CLASS 183 total; 656 applied, 86% were accepted, 33% of whom enrolled. 21% from top quarter of their high school class, 56% from top half.
ACADEMIC PROGRAM Core. Calendar: semesters. 390 courses offered in 1995–96; average class size 14 in required courses. Academic remediation for entering students, English as a second language program offered during academic year, services for LD students, advanced placement, self-designed majors, tutorials, honors program, part-time degree program (daytime), internships. Study abroad in England, Canada.
GENERAL DEGREE REQUIREMENTS 63 semester hours for associate, 128 semester hours for bachelor's; completion of math proficiency test; computer course; internship (some majors).
MAJORS Accounting, art/fine arts, business administration/commerce/management (B), child care/child and family studies (B), early childhood education (B), education (B), elementary education (B), fashion design and technology (B), fashion merchandising (B), health science, hotel and restaurant management (B), human services (B), interdisciplinary studies (B), interior design, liberal arts/general studies (B), marketing/retailing/merchandising (B), nursing, occupational therapy, physical fitness/exercise science (B), physical therapy, psychology (B), retail management (B), sociology (B), tourism and travel (B).
LIBRARY Brennan Library with 50,000 books, 134 microform titles, 400 periodicals, 1 on-line bibliographic service, 46 CD-ROMs, 1,187 records, tapes, and CDs. Acquisition spending 1994–95: $229,700.
COMPUTERS ON CAMPUS Computer purchase plan available. Student rooms linked to a campus network. 50 computers for student use in computer center, learning resource center, library provide access to e-mail, Internet. Staffed computer lab on campus provides training in use of computers, software. Academic computing expenditure 1994–95: $170,200.
COLLEGE LIFE Orientation program (3 days). Drama-theater group, choral group, student-run newspaper. ***Social organizations:*** 20 open to all. ***Most popular organization:*** Student Government Association. ***Major annual events:*** River Day/Family and Friends Weekend, Torchlight Parade, Spring/Winter Balls. ***Student services:*** health clinic, personal-psychological counseling, Women in Public Service Center. ***Campus security:*** 24-hour emergency response devices and patrols, late-night transport-escort service, controlled dormitory access.
HOUSING 320 college housing spaces available; 310 were occupied 1995–96. Freshmen guaranteed college housing. Off-campus living permitted. ***Option:*** single-sex housing available. Resident assistants live in dorms.
ATHLETICS ***Intercollegiate:*** basketball, cross-country running, soccer, softball, volleyball. ***Intramural:*** crew. ***Contact:*** Ms. Christine Walter, Athletic Director, 617-243-2147.
CAREER PLANNING ***Placement office:*** 1 full-time, 1 part-time staff; $39,400 operating expenditure 1994–95. ***Director:*** Ms. Marie Smith, Director of Career Services, 617-243-2307. ***Services:*** job fairs, resume preparation, resume referral, career counseling, careers library, job bank. Students must register sophomore year. 60 organizations recruited on campus 1994–95.
AFTER GRADUATION 90% of students completing transfer associate program in 1994–95 went directly to 4-year colleges.
EXPENSES FOR 1996–97 ***Application fee:*** $25. Comprehensive fee of $19,700 includes full-time tuition ($12,700), mandatory fees ($575), and college room and board ($6425). Part-time tuition: $420 per semester hour. Part-time mandatory fees: $140 per semester.
FINANCIAL AID ***College-administered undergrad aid 1995–96:*** 596 need-based scholarships (average $3926), 39 non-need scholarships (average $2000), low-interest long-term loans from external sources (average $3264), Federal Work-Study, 85 part-time jobs. Average total aid for freshmen: $11,399, meeting 81% of need. ***Required forms:*** FAFSA; required for some: state; accepted: CSS Financial Aid PROFILE, institutional. ***Priority deadline:*** 3/15. ***Payment plan:*** installment. ***Waivers:*** full or partial for employees or children of employees. ***Notification:*** continuous.
APPLYING ***Options:*** deferred entrance, midyear entrance. ***Required:*** school transcript, 1 recommendation, TOEFL for international students. ***Recommended:*** interview, SAT I. ***Required for some:*** 3 years of high school math and science. Test scores used for counseling/placement. ***Application deadline:*** rolling. ***Notification:*** continuous.
APPLYING/TRANSFER ***Required:*** 1 recommendation, college transcript. ***Recommended:*** interview. ***Required for some:*** high school transcript, 3 years of high school math and science. ***Application deadline:*** rolling. ***Notification:*** continuous. ***Contact:*** Ms. Eleanor Kinsella, Associate Director of Admissions, 617-243-2225.
CONTACT Ms. Adrienne Franciosi, Director of Admissions, Lasell College, Newton, MA 02166-2709, 617-243-2225. ***Fax:*** 617-243-2389.

❖ ***See page 752 for a narrative description.*** ❖

MARIAN COURT COLLEGE
Swampscott, Massachusetts

UG Enrollment: 220	Tuition & Fees: $8000
Application Deadline: rolling	Room & Board: N/Avail

GENERAL Independent Roman Catholic, 2-year, specialized, primarily women. Awards certificates, transfer associate degrees. Founded 1964. ***Setting:*** 6-acre suburban campus with easy access to Boston. ***Total enrollment:*** 220. ***Faculty:*** 34 (8 full-time, 3% with terminal degrees, 26 part-time); student-faculty ratio is 11:1.
ENROLLMENT PROFILE 220 students: 99% women, 28% part-time, 99% state residents, 12% transferred in, 79% have need-based financial aid, 0% have non-need-based financial aid, 1% international, 38% 25 or older, 0% Native American, 8% Hispanic, 2% African American, 1% Asian American. ***Areas of study chosen:*** 100% business management and administrative services. ***Most popular recent majors:*** legal secretarial studies, tourism and travel, accounting.
FIRST-YEAR CLASS 59 total; 132 applied, 80% were accepted, 56% of whom enrolled.
ACADEMIC PROGRAM Interdisciplinary curriculum, honor code. Calendar: semesters. 170 courses offered in 1995–96. Academic remediation for entering students, advanced placement, tutorials, honors program, summer session for credit, part-time degree program (daytime, evenings), adult/continuing education programs, internships. Off-campus study at members of the Northeast Consortium of Colleges and Universities in Massachusetts.
GENERAL DEGREE REQUIREMENTS 60 credits; computer course.
MAJORS Accounting, business administration/commerce/management, data processing, hospitality services, human resources, legal secretarial studies, liberal arts/general studies, medical secretarial studies, secretarial studies/office management, tourism and travel.
LIBRARY Lindsay Library with 4,600 books, 11 microform titles, 122 periodicals, 15 CD-ROMs, 344 records, tapes, and CDs. Acquisition spending 1994–95: $13,214.
COMPUTERS ON CAMPUS 43 computers for student use in computer center, classrooms, library, student center provide access to main academic computer. Staffed computer lab on campus provides training in use of computers, software.
COLLEGE LIFE Orientation program (2 days, no cost). 90% vote in student government elections. ***Most popular organizations:*** Travel and Tourism Club, Student Government, Hostess Club. ***Major annual events:*** International Supper, Christmas Dance, Spring Dance. ***Student services:*** personal-psychological counseling. ***Campus security:*** well-lit parking lots.
HOUSING College housing not available.
CAREER PLANNING ***Placement office:*** 1 full-time staff. ***Director:*** Ms. Carole Rich, Director of Placement, 617-595-6768. ***Services:*** job fairs, resume preparation, resume referral, career counseling, careers library, job bank, job interviews. 33 organizations recruited on campus 1994–95.
AFTER GRADUATION 98% of class of 1994 had job offers within 6 months. 20% of students completing a degree program went directly on to further study.
EXPENSES FOR 1996–97 ***Application fee:*** $25. Tuition: $7600 full-time. Full-time mandatory fees: $400.
FINANCIAL AID ***College-administered undergrad aid 1995–96:*** 109 need-based scholarships (average $638), short-term loans (average $3000), low-interest long-term loans from external sources (average $2500), Federal Work-Study, 1 part-time job. ***Required forms:*** institutional, FAFSA, nontaxable income verification; accepted: CSS Financial Aid PROFILE. ***Priority deadline:*** 4/1. ***Payment plan:*** installment. ***Waivers:*** full or partial for employees or children of employees, adult students, and senior citizens. ***Notification:*** continuous.
APPLYING ***Options:*** deferred entrance, midyear entrance. ***Required:*** school transcript, minimum 2.0 GPA, 2 recommendations, campus interview. ***Required for some:*** TOEFL for international students. ***Application deadline:*** rolling.
APPLYING/TRANSFER ***Required:*** high school transcript, 2 recommendations, campus interview, college transcript, minimum 2.0 high school GPA. ***Recommended:*** minimum 2.0 college GPA. ***Entrance:*** minimally difficult. ***Application deadline:*** rolling. ***Contact:*** Ms. Lisa Emerson, Director of Admissions, 617-595-6768 Ext. 16.
CONTACT Ms. Lisa Emerson, Director of Admissions, Marian Court College, Swampscott, MA 01907-2840, 617-595-6768 Ext. 16. ***Fax:*** 617-595-3560.

MASSACHUSETTS BAY COMMUNITY COLLEGE
Wellesley Hills, Massachusetts

UG Enrollment: 5,252	Tuition & Fees (MA Res): $2490
Application Deadline: rolling	Room & Board: N/Avail

GENERAL State-supported, 2-year, coed. Awards certificates, transfer associate, terminal associate degrees. Founded 1961. ***Setting:*** 84-acre suburban campus with easy access to Boston. ***Endowment:*** $1.5 million. ***Total enrollment:*** 5,252. ***Faculty:*** 274 (99 full-time, 90% with terminal degrees, 175 part-time); student-faculty ratio is 21:1.
ENROLLMENT PROFILE 5,252 students from 10 states and territories, 36 other countries. 59% women, 41% men, 58% part-time, 97% state residents, 20% transferred in, 21% have need-based financial aid, 2% international, 57% 25 or older, 1% Native American, 4% Hispanic, 12% African American, 3% Asian American. ***Areas of study***

chosen: 40% liberal arts/general studies, 28% health professions and related sciences, 14% business management and administrative services, 10% engineering and applied sciences, 4% education, 2% computer and information sciences, 1% fine arts, 1% social sciences. ***Most popular recent majors:*** business administration/commerce/management, liberal arts/general studies, nursing.
FIRST-YEAR CLASS 2,053 total; 3,647 applied, 100% were accepted, 56% of whom enrolled.
ACADEMIC PROGRAM Core, honor code. Calendar: semesters. Academic remediation for entering students, English as a second language program offered during academic year and summer, services for LD students, advanced placement, honors program, summer session for credit, part-time degree program (daytime, evenings, summer), adult/continuing education programs, co-op programs. Study-abroad program.
GENERAL DEGREE REQUIREMENTS 63 credits; computer course; internship (some majors).
MAJORS Accounting, automotive technologies, biotechnology, business administration/commerce/management, Canadian studies, chemical engineering technology, chemistry, communication, computer graphics, computer information systems, computer programming, computer science, computer technologies, construction management, court reporting, criminal justice, drafting and design, early childhood education, electrical and electronics technologies, electrical engineering technology, electronics engineering technology, emergency medical technology, engineering (general), engineering sciences, (pre)engineering sequence, engineering technology, environmental engineering technology, finance/banking, hospitality services, human services, information science, interior design, international studies, law enforcement/police sciences, liberal arts/general studies, marketing/retailing/merchandising, mechanical engineering technology, medical laboratory technology, medical records services, medical technology, nursing, occupational therapy, operating room technology, optometric/ophthalmic technologies, paralegal studies, pharmacy/pharmaceutical sciences, physical therapy, plastics technology, practical nursing, radiological technology, real estate, respiratory therapy, retail management, secretarial studies/office management, social work, theater arts/drama, tourism and travel, word processing.
LIBRARY Perkins Library with 43,644 books, 265 microform titles, 372 periodicals, 12 CD-ROMs, 1,454 records, tapes, and CDs. Acquisition spending 1994–95: $167,738.
COMPUTERS ON CAMPUS 330 computers for student use in computer center, learning resource center, academic offices, classrooms, library, student center provide access to main academic computer, e-mail, on-line services, Internet. Staffed computer lab on campus provides training in use of computers, software. Academic computing expenditure 1994–95: $325,000.
COLLEGE LIFE Drama-theater group, student-run newspaper. ***Student services:*** health clinic, personal-psychological counseling. ***Campus security:*** 24-hour emergency response devices and patrols.
HOUSING College housing not available.
ATHLETICS Member NJCAA. ***Intercollegiate:*** basketball M/W, soccer M, softball W. ***Intramural:*** baseball, basketball. ***Contact:*** Mr. Alan Harrison, Director of Athletics, 617-239-4065.
CAREER PLANNING ***Placement office:*** 3 full-time staff. ***Director:*** Ms. Trish Seddale, Director of Student Development, 617-237-1100. ***Services:*** job fairs, resume preparation, career counseling, careers library, job bank, job interviews.
EXPENSES FOR 1996–97 ***Application fee:*** $35. State resident tuition: $1200 full-time, $40 per credit hour part-time. Nonresident tuition: $5640 full-time, $188 per credit hour part-time. Part-time mandatory fees: $43 per credit hour. Part-time tuition and fees for evening division per credit hour: $83. Full-time mandatory fees: $1290.
FINANCIAL AID ***College-administered undergrad aid 1995–96:*** 464 need-based scholarships, 1 non-need scholarship, 12 Federal Work-Study (averaging $2000). ***Required forms:*** state, FAFSA; accepted: CSS Financial Aid PROFILE. ***Priority deadline:*** 5/1. ***Payment plan:*** installment. ***Waivers:*** full or partial for employees or children of employees and senior citizens. ***Notification:*** 7/1. ***Average indebtedness of graduates:*** $6000.
APPLYING Open admission except for nursing program. ***Option:*** early entrance. ***Required:*** ACT ASSET. Test scores used for counseling/placement. ***Application deadline:*** rolling. ***Notification:*** continuous.
APPLYING/TRANSFER ***Application deadline:*** rolling. ***Notification:*** continuous.
CONTACT Mr. James R. Regan, Director of Registration and Recruitment, Massachusetts Bay Community College, Wellesley Hills, MA 02181-5359, 617-237-1100 Ext. 163. ***Fax:*** 617-239-1047.

MASSASOIT COMMUNITY COLLEGE
Brockton, Massachusetts

UG Enrollment: 5,602	**Tuition & Fees (MA Res): $2490**
Application Deadline: rolling	**Room & Board: N/Avail**

GENERAL State-supported, 2-year, coed. Awards transfer associate, terminal associate degrees. Founded 1966. ***Setting:*** suburban campus with easy access to Boston. ***Total enrollment:*** 5,602. ***Faculty:*** 357 (153 full-time, 204 part-time); student-faculty ratio is 18:1.
ENROLLMENT PROFILE 5,602 students from 3 states and territories, 5 other countries. 56% women, 44% men, 50% part-time, 98% state residents, 12% transferred in, 34% have need-based financial aid, 1% international, 45% 25 or older, 1% Native American, 2% Hispanic, 6% African American, 1% Asian American. ***Areas of study chosen:*** 41% liberal arts/general studies, 22% business management and administrative services, 17% health professions and related sciences, 8% social sciences, 6% engineering and applied sciences, 4% computer and information sciences, 2% vocational and home economics, 1% architecture. ***Most popular recent majors:*** liberal arts/general studies, business administration/commerce/management.
FIRST-YEAR CLASS 1,002 total; 2,092 applied, 92% were accepted, 52% of whom enrolled. 5% from top 10% of their high school class, 15% from top quarter, 35% from top half.
ACADEMIC PROGRAM Core. Calendar: semesters. 2,500 courses offered in 1995–96. Academic remediation for entering students, English as a second language program offered during academic year and summer, services for LD students, summer session for credit, part-time degree program (daytime, evenings, summer), adult/continuing education programs, co-op programs. Off-campus study at 9 members of the Southeastern Association for Cooperation in Higher Education in Massachusetts.
GENERAL DEGREE REQUIREMENTS 60 credits; math/science requirements vary accorrding to program; computer course (varies by major); internship (some majors).
MAJORS Accounting, advertising, architectural technologies, automotive technologies, business administration/commerce/management, child care/child and family studies, civil engineering technology, commercial art, communication, computer information systems, corrections, court reporting, criminal justice, culinary arts, dental services, early childhood education, electrical and electronics technologies, electromechanical technology, fire science, heating/refrigeration/air conditioning, hospitality services, hotel and restaurant management, human services, law enforcement/police sciences, legal secretarial studies, liberal arts/general studies, marketing/retailing/merchandising, medical assistant technologies, medical laboratory technology, nursing, radiological technology, respiratory therapy, science, secretarial studies/office management, theater arts/drama, tourism and travel.
LIBRARY 71,022 books, 176 microform titles, 445 periodicals.
COMPUTERS ON CAMPUS 350 computers for student use in computer center, computer labs, learning resource center, classrooms, library, student center provide access to main academic computer, on-line services. Staffed computer lab on campus provides training in use of computers, software.
COLLEGE LIFE Drama-theater group, student-run newspaper, radio station. 10% vote in student government elections. ***Social organizations:*** 20 open to all. ***Most popular organizations:*** Drama Club, Student Newspaper, Phi Theta Kappa, International Student Group. ***Major annual events:*** Fall Fest, Spring Fest, Commencement. ***Student services:*** health clinic, personal-psychological counseling, women's center. ***Campus security:*** 24-hour patrols.
HOUSING College housing not available.
ATHLETICS Member NJCAA. ***Intercollegiate:*** baseball M, basketball M/W, soccer M/W, softball W, volleyball W. ***Intramural:*** basketball, volleyball. ***Contact:*** Mr. Nick Palantzas, Director of Physical Education and Athletics, 508-588-9100 Ext. 1430.
CAREER PLANNING ***Placement office:*** 1 full-time staff. ***Director:*** Ms. Maureen Thayer, Assistant Dean of Student Affairs, 508-588-9100 Ext. 1415. ***Services:*** job fairs, resume preparation, resume referral, career counseling, careers library, job bank, job interviews.
AFTER GRADUATION 32% of students completing a degree program in 1994–95 went directly on to further study.
EXPENSES FOR 1995–96 State resident tuition: $1200 full-time, $40 per credit part-time. Nonresident tuition: $5640 full-time, $188 per credit part-time. Part-time mandatory fees: $43 per credit. Full-time mandatory fees: $1290.
FINANCIAL AID ***College-administered undergrad aid 1995–96:*** need-based scholarships, Federal Work-Study. ***Required forms:*** CSS Financial Aid PROFILE, institutional, FAFSA. ***Priority deadline:*** 4/15. ***Waivers:*** full or partial for employees or children of employees and senior citizens.
APPLYING Open admission except for allied health programs. ***Option:*** midyear entrance. ***Recommended:*** TOEFL for international students. Test scores used for counseling/placement. ***Application deadline:*** rolling. ***Notification:*** continuous. Preference given to state residents.
APPLYING/TRANSFER ***Application deadline:*** rolling. ***Notification:*** continuous.
CONTACT Ms. Roberta Noodell, Director of Admissions, Massasoit Community College, Brockton, MA 02402-3996, 508-588-9100 Ext. 1410 or toll-free 800-CAREERS (in-state).

MIDDLESEX COMMUNITY COLLEGE
Bedford, Massachusetts

UG Enrollment: 5,984	**Tuition & Fees (MA Res): $2820**
Application Deadline: rolling	**Room & Board: N/Avail**

GENERAL State-supported, 2-year, coed. Part of Massachusetts Public Higher Education System. Awards certificates, transfer associate, terminal associate degrees. Founded 1970. ***Setting:*** 200-acre campus with easy access to Boston. ***Total enrollment:*** 5,984. ***Faculty:*** 377 (124 full-time, 94% with terminal degrees, 253 part-time); student-faculty ratio is 18:1.
ENROLLMENT PROFILE 5,984 students from 2 states and territories, 20 other countries. 62% women, 38% men, 56% part-time, 98% state residents, 14% transferred in, 30% have need-based financial aid, 6% have non-need-based financial aid, 1% international, 48% 25 or older, 1% Native American, 5% Hispanic, 3% African American, 6% Asian American. ***Areas of study chosen:*** 41% liberal arts/general studies, 19% business management and administrative services, 12% social sciences, 8% health professions and related sciences. ***Most popular recent majors:*** liberal arts/general studies, business administration/commerce/management.
FIRST-YEAR CLASS 1,995 total; 3,547 applied, 75% were accepted, 75% of whom enrolled.
ACADEMIC PROGRAM Core, interdisciplinary curriculum, honor code. Calendar: semesters. 518 courses offered in 1995–96. Academic remediation for entering students, English as a second language program offered during academic year, services for LD students, summer session for credit, part-time degree program (daytime, evenings), adult/continuing education programs, co-op programs and internships. Off-campus study at members of the Northeast Consortium of Colleges and Universities in Massachusetts. Study abroad in Ireland, Commonwealth of Independent States, China. ROTC: Air Force (c).
GENERAL DEGREE REQUIREMENTS 60 credits; 1 math course; computer course for most majors; internship (some majors).
MAJORS Accounting, art/fine arts, automotive technologies, biotechnology, business administration/commerce/management, business education, communication, computer programming, computer science, computer technologies, criminal justice, dental services, drafting and design, early childhood education, electronics engineering technology, (pre)engineering sequence, fashion merchandising, fire science, hotel and restaurant management, liberal arts/general studies, marketing/retailing/merchandising, medical assistant technologies, medical laboratory technology, mental health/rehabilitation counseling, nursing, radiological technology, retail management, secretarial studies/office management, theater arts/drama, word processing.
LIBRARY Main library plus 2 others, with 50,684 books, 5 microform titles, 393 periodicals, 1 on-line bibliographic service, 24 CD-ROMs, 1,200 records, tapes, and CDs.
COMPUTERS ON CAMPUS Computer purchase plan available. 100 computers for student use in computer center, computer labs, learning resource center, classrooms, library provide access to word processing, software, graphics prog. Staffed computer lab on campus provides training in use of computers, software.
COLLEGE LIFE Drama-theater group, student-run newspaper. 10% vote in student government elections. ***Social organizations:*** 25 open to all. ***Most popular organiza-***

Peterson's Guide to Two-Year Colleges 1997 369

Middlesex Community College (continued)
tions: Mental Health Club, International Club, Students Who Are Parents, Drama Club, Student Activities Board. ***Major annual events:*** Annual Speaker Series, Annual Recognition Banquet, Annual Semi-Formal. ***Student services:*** legal services, health clinic, personal-psychological counseling. ***Campus security:*** 24-hour emergency response devices and patrols.
HOUSING College housing not available.
ATHLETICS ***Intramural:*** basketball, softball, table tennis (Ping-Pong).
CAREER PLANNING ***Placement office:*** 2 full-time staff. ***Director:*** Dr. Evelyn Clements, Dean of Student Development, 617-280-3524. ***Services:*** job fairs, resume preparation, resume referral, career counseling, careers library, job bank. 70 organizations recruited on campus 1994–95.
AFTER GRADUATION 38% of students completing a degree program in 1994–95 went directly on to further study.
EXPENSES FOR 1995–96 State resident tuition: $2820 full-time, $94 per credit part-time. Nonresident tuition: $7260 full-time, $242 per credit part-time. Tuition for nonresidents who are eligible for the New England Regional Student Program: $3120 full-time, $104 per credit part-time.
FINANCIAL AID ***College-administered undergrad aid 1995–96:*** 1,300 need-based scholarships (average $400), 70 non-need scholarships (average $500), low-interest long-term loans from external sources (average $1600), 71 Federal Work-Study (averaging $1200), part-time jobs. ***Required forms:*** institutional, FAFSA. ***Application deadline:*** continuous. ***Payment plan:*** installment. ***Waivers:*** full or partial for employees or children of employees.
APPLYING Open admission for most programs. ***Option:*** early entrance. ***Required:*** TOEFL for international students. Test scores used for admission. ***Application deadline:*** rolling. ***Notification:*** continuous. Preference given to state residents.
APPLYING/TRANSFER ***Entrance:*** noncompetitive. ***Application deadline:*** rolling. ***Notification:*** continuous.
CONTACT Ms. Debra Regan, Director of Admissions, Middlesex Community College, 33 Kearney Square, Lowell, MA 01852, 508-656-3211 or toll-free 800-643-5739 (in-state). ***Fax:*** 508-441-1749. ***E-mail:*** middlesex@admin.mcc.mass.edu.

MOUNT IDA COLLEGE
Newton Centre, Massachusetts

UG Enrollment: 2,008 | **Tuition & Fees: $11,053**
Application Deadline: rolling | **Room & Board: $7718**

GENERAL Independent, primarily 2-year, coed. Awards certificates, diplomas, transfer associate, terminal associate, bachelor's degrees. Founded 1899. ***Setting:*** 85-acre suburban campus with easy access to Boston. ***Endowment:*** $5.9 million. ***Educational spending 1994–95:*** $2418 per undergrad. ***Total enrollment:*** 2,008. ***Faculty:*** 211 (66 full-time, 25% with terminal degrees, 145 part-time).
ENROLLMENT PROFILE 2,008 students from 29 states and territories, 50 other countries. 60% women, 40% men, 21% part-time, 64% state residents, 50% live on campus, 10% transferred in, 75% have need-based financial aid, 3% have non-need-based financial aid, 11% international, 8% 25 or older, 1% Native American, 4% Hispanic, 10% African American, 6% Asian American. ***Areas of study chosen:*** 19% health professions and related sciences, 16% business management and administrative services, 13% liberal arts/general studies, 9% engineering and applied sciences, 5% education, 4% communications and journalism, 1% computer and information sciences. ***Most popular recent majors:*** occupational therapy, liberal arts/general studies, veterinary technology.
FIRST-YEAR CLASS 830 total; 4,800 applied, 83% were accepted, 21% of whom enrolled.
ACADEMIC PROGRAM Core, professional studies curriculum. Calendar: semesters. 565 courses offered in 1995–96. Academic remediation for entering students, English as a second language program offered during academic year, services for LD students, advanced placement, self-designed majors, Freshman Honors College, tutorials, honors program, summer session for credit, part-time degree program (daytime, evenings), adult/continuing education programs, co-op programs and internships. Study abroad in England (2% of students participate).
GENERAL DEGREE REQUIREMENTS 60 credit hours for associate, 120 credit hours for bachelor's; math/science requirements vary according to program; computer course for most majors; internship (some majors).
MAJORS Accounting, advertising, animal sciences (B), applied art (B), art/fine arts (B), business administration/commerce/management (B), child care/child and family studies (B), child psychology/child development, commercial art (B), communication (B), computer programming, criminal justice (B), data processing, dental services, early childhood education (B), education (B), electrical engineering technology, (pre)engineering sequence, equestrian studies (B), fashion design and technology (B), fashion merchandising (B), funeral service (B), graphic arts (B), health science, hotel and restaurant management (B), human services, illustration, interior design (B), journalism (B), laboratory animal medicine, legal studies (B), liberal arts/general studies (B), marketing/retailing/merchandising (B), occupational therapy, paralegal studies, pharmacy/pharmaceutical sciences, physical fitness/exercise science, public administration (B), public affairs and policy studies (B), recreation and leisure services, retail management (B), science, secretarial studies/office management, social work, sports medicine, studio art (B), teacher aide studies, textiles and clothing, tourism and travel, veterinary technology (B).
LIBRARY Wadsworth Learning Resource Center plus 1 other, with 85,000 books, 2,740 microform titles, 530 periodicals, 1 on-line bibliographic service, 20 CD-ROMs, 1,500 records, tapes, and CDs. Acquisition spending 1994–95: $142,943.
COMPUTERS ON CAMPUS 80 computers for student use in computer center, computer labs, library provide access to main academic computer, on-line services. Staffed computer lab on campus provides training in use of computers, software. Academic computing expenditure 1994–95: $126,608.
NOTEWORTHY RESEARCH FACILITIES National Center for Death Education.
COLLEGE LIFE Orientation program (4 days, no cost, parents included). Drama-theater group, choral group, student-run newspaper, radio station. ***Social organizations:*** 25 open to all; 1 national fraternity, 1 national sorority; 4% of eligible men are members. ***Most popular organizations:*** Leadership Students, Student Government, Phi Theta Kappa, Residence Council, Alpha Chi. ***Major annual events:*** Parents' Weekend, Winter Fest, Spring Fling. ***Student services:*** health clinic, personal-psychological counseling. ***Campus security:*** 24-hour patrols, late-night transport-escort service, controlled residence hall entrances, secured campus entrance.
HOUSING 850 college housing spaces available; all were occupied 1995–96. Freshmen guaranteed college housing. Off-campus living permitted. ***Options:*** coed, single-sex (1 building), international student housing available. Resident assistants live in dorms.
ATHLETICS Member NJCAA. ***Intercollegiate:*** basketball W(s), equestrian sports M/W, lacrosse M(s), soccer M(s)/W(s), softball W(s), volleyball W(s). ***Intramural:*** badminton, baseball, basketball, equestrian sports, field hockey, football, golf, ice hockey, lacrosse, rugby, soccer, softball, tennis, volleyball, weight lifting, wrestling. ***Contact:*** Dr. Jackie Palmer, Athletic Director, 617-928-4549.
CAREER PLANNING ***Placement office:*** 1 full-time, 6 part-time staff; $2762 operating expenditure 1994–95. ***Director:*** Ms. Raye Robinson, Director of Career Services, 617-928-4611. ***Services:*** job fairs, resume preparation, career counseling, careers library, job bank. 80 organizations recruited on campus 1994–95.
AFTER GRADUATION 50% of students completing transfer associate program in 1994–95 went directly to 4-year colleges.
EXPENSES FOR 1995–96 ***Application fee:*** $25. Comprehensive fee of $18,771 includes full-time tuition ($10,888), mandatory fees ($165), and college room and board ($7718). Part-time tuition: $695 per course.
FINANCIAL AID ***College-administered undergrad aid 1995–96:*** need-based scholarships (averaging $6000), non-need scholarships, low-interest long-term loans from external sources, Federal Work-Study (averaging $1500), part-time jobs. ***Required forms:*** institutional, FAFSA. ***Application deadline:*** continuous to 9/13. ***Payment plan:*** installment. ***Waivers:*** full or partial for employees or children of employees. ***Notification:*** 10/13.
APPLYING ***Options:*** Common Application, electronic application, deferred entrance, midyear entrance. ***Required:*** school transcript, TOEFL for international students. ***Recommended:*** essay, minimum 2.0 GPA, 3 years of high school math and science, some high school foreign language, interview, SAT I. ***Required for some:*** recommendations. Test scores used for counseling/placement. ***Application deadline:*** rolling. ***Notification:*** continuous.
APPLYING/TRANSFER ***Required:*** high school transcript, college transcript, minimum 2.0 college GPA. ***Recommended:*** essay, standardized test scores, 3 years of high school math and science, some high school foreign language, interview, minimum 3.0 college GPA, minimum 2.0 high school GPA. ***Required for some:*** recommendations. ***Entrance:*** minimally difficult. ***Application deadline:*** rolling. ***Notification:*** continuous. ***Contact:*** Ms. Marie Kaden, Admissions Coordinator, 617-928-4553.
CONTACT Mr. Harold Duvall, Director of Admissions, Mount Ida College, Newton Centre, MA 02159-3310, 617-928-4506. ***Fax:*** 617-928-4760. College video available.

❖ ***See page 776 for a narrative description.*** ❖

MOUNT WACHUSETT COMMUNITY COLLEGE
Gardner, Massachusetts

UG Enrollment: 1,900 | **Tuition & Fees (MA Res): $3180**
Application Deadline: rolling | **Room & Board: N/Avail**

GENERAL State-supported, 2-year, coed. Part of Massachusetts Public Higher Education System. Awards certificates, transfer associate, terminal associate degrees. Founded 1963. ***Setting:*** 270-acre small-town campus with easy access to Boston. ***Total enrollment:*** 1,900. ***Faculty:*** 112 (72 full-time, 30% with terminal degrees, 40 part-time); student-faculty ratio is 20:1.
ENROLLMENT PROFILE 1,900 students: 61% women, 39% part-time, 93% state residents, 35% transferred in, 1% international, 42% 25 or older, 5% Native American, 3% Hispanic, 7% African American, 1% Asian American. ***Most popular recent majors:*** business administration/commerce/management, criminal justice.
FIRST-YEAR CLASS 1,428 total; 1,850 applied, 86% were accepted, 89% of whom enrolled.
ACADEMIC PROGRAM Core, interdisciplinary curriculum, honor code. Calendar: semesters. 400 courses offered in 1995–96. Academic remediation for entering students, English as a second language program offered during academic year and summer, services for LD students, advanced placement, Freshman Honors College, honors program, summer session for credit, part-time degree program (daytime, evenings, summer), adult/continuing education programs, co-op programs and internships. ROTC: Army (c), Naval (c), Air Force (c).
GENERAL DEGREE REQUIREMENTS 61 credits; computer course for business administration majors.
MAJORS Accounting, art/fine arts, automotive technologies, broadcasting, business administration/commerce/management, child care/child and family studies, computer information systems, corrections, criminal justice, data processing, electrical engineering technology, fire science, food services management, human services, liberal arts/general studies, marketing/retailing/merchandising, medical laboratory technology, nursing, physical therapy, plastics technology, secretarial studies/office management, studio art, telecommunications.
LIBRARY Mount Wachusett Community College Library with 60,944 books, 327 periodicals, 1,300 records, tapes, and CDs.
COMPUTERS ON CAMPUS 125 computers for student use in computer center.
COLLEGE LIFE Drama-theater group, student-run newspaper, radio station. ***Student services:*** health clinic, personal-psychological counseling, women's center. ***Campus security:*** 24-hour emergency response devices and patrols.
HOUSING College housing not available.
CAREER PLANNING ***Placement office:*** 1 full-time staff. ***Director:*** Mrs. Terry Andrews, Director of Career Planning and Placement, 508-632-6600 Ext. 288. ***Services:*** job fairs, resume preparation, career counseling, careers library.
AFTER GRADUATION 25% of students completing a degree program in 1994–95 went directly on to further study.
EXPENSES FOR 1995–96 ***Application fee:*** $10. State resident tuition: $3150 full-time, $105 per credit part-time. Nonresident tuition: $7590 full-time, $253 per credit part-time. Part-time mandatory fees: $30 per year. Full-time mandatory fees: $30.
FINANCIAL AID ***College-administered undergrad aid 1995–96:*** need-based scholarships, 26 non-need scholarships (averaging $354), short-term loans (averaging $50), low-interest long-term loans from external sources (averaging $700), Federal Work-Study, part-time jobs. ***Required forms:*** CSS Financial Aid PROFILE, institutional, FAFSA. ***Application deadline:*** continuous. ***Payment plan:*** installment. ***Waivers:*** full or partial for employees or children of employees and senior citizens.

APPLYING Open admission except for nursing, physical therapy assistant, clinical lab science programs. ***Options:*** early entrance, midyear entrance. Test scores used for counseling/placement. ***Application deadline:*** rolling. ***Notification:*** continuous. Preference given to state residents.
APPLYING/TRANSFER ***Application deadline:*** rolling. ***Notification:*** continuous. ***Contact:*** Ms. Ann Schmid, Transfer Coordinator, 508-632-6600 Ext. 238.
CONTACT Ms. Maria McCarthy, Director of Admission Services, Mount Wachusett Community College, Gardner, MA 01440-1000, 508-632-6600 Ext. 165. ***Fax:*** 508-632-1210. College video available.

NEWBURY COLLEGE
Brookline, Massachusetts

UG Enrollment: 1,088	**Tuition & Fees: $11,080**
Application Deadline: rolling	**Room & Board: $6040**

Just minutes from Boston, Newbury College features an ideal collegiate setting in a safe, elite neighborhood within easy walking distance of public transportation. Skilled, experienced faculty members and many hands-on training opportunities make Newbury graduates among the most employable.

GENERAL Independent, primarily 2-year, coed. Awards certificates, transfer associate, terminal associate, bachelor's degrees (also offers continuing education program with significant enrollment not reflected in profile). Founded 1962. ***Setting:*** 10-acre suburban campus with easy access to Boston. ***Endowment:*** $4.4 million. ***Educational spending 1994–95:*** $3411 per undergrad. ***Total enrollment:*** 1,088. ***Faculty:*** 105 (52 full-time, 15% with terminal degrees, 53 part-time).
ENROLLMENT PROFILE 1,088 students from 21 states and territories, 34 other countries. 55% women, 45% men, 4% part-time, 85% state residents, 35% live on campus, 9% transferred in, 75% have need-based financial aid, 25% have non-need-based financial aid, 24% 25 or older, 0% Native American, 9% Hispanic, 16% African American, 5% Asian American. ***Areas of study chosen:*** 22% vocational and home economics, 20% business management and administrative services, 16% health professions and related sciences, 7% communications and journalism, 7% prelaw, 2% computer and information sciences, 1% liberal arts/general studies, 1% psychology.
FIRST-YEAR CLASS 504 total; 1,249 applied, 96% were accepted, 44% of whom enrolled. 8% from top 10% of their high school class, 17% from top quarter, 47% from top half.
ACADEMIC PROGRAM Core, career-oriented curriculum, honor code. Calendar: semesters. 311 courses offered in 1995–96; average class size 20 in required courses. Academic remediation for entering students, English as a second language program offered during academic year and summer, services for LD students, advanced placement, tutorials, summer session for credit, part-time degree program (daytime, evenings, weekends, summer), adult/continuing education programs, co-op programs and internships.
GENERAL DEGREE REQUIREMENTS 65 credits for associate, 128 credits for bachelor's; computer course for business majors; internship (some majors).
MAJORS Accounting, business administration/commerce/management (B), communication, communication equipment technology, computer information systems, computer programming, criminal justice, culinary arts, environmental sciences, fashion design and technology, fashion merchandising, finance/banking, food services management, graphic arts, hotel and restaurant management, humanities, interior design, international business (B), legal studies (B), marketing/retailing/merchandising, medical assistant technologies, paralegal studies, physical therapy, psychology, radio and television studies, respiratory therapy, retail management, sociology, tourism and travel.
LIBRARY Newbury Library plus 1 other, with 27,796 books, 143 microform titles, 1,010 periodicals, 612 records, tapes, and CDs. Acquisition spending 1994–95: $155,893.
COMPUTERS ON CAMPUS Student rooms linked to a campus network. 55 computers for student use in computer labs, learning resource center, hospitality department lab, library provide access to on-line services, Internet. Staffed computer lab on campus provides training in use of computers, software. Academic computing expenditure 1994–95: $304,000.
COLLEGE LIFE Orientation program (3 days). Drama-theater group, student-run newspaper, radio station. ***Social organizations:*** 15 open to all. ***Most popular organizations:*** Innkeepers Club, Design Guild, Student Radio Station, Student Government, PAL Peer Activity Leaders. ***Major annual events:*** Fall Festival, Semiformal, Spring Festival. ***Student services:*** personal-psychological counseling. ***Campus security:*** 24-hour emergency response devices and patrols, controlled dormitory access.
HOUSING 320 college housing spaces available; 269 were occupied 1995–96. No special consideration for freshman housing applicants. Off-campus living permitted. ***Options:*** coed (7 buildings), international student housing available. Resident assistants live in dorms.
ATHLETICS Member NJCAA. ***Intercollegiate:*** baseball M, basketball M/W, cross-country running W, soccer M, softball W. ***Intramural:*** basketball, fencing, football, ice hockey, volleyball. ***Contact:*** Ms. Mary Beth Lamb, Director of Athletics, 617-730-7091.
CAREER PLANNING ***Placement office:*** 2 full-time, 2 part-time staff; $71,000 operating expenditure 1994–95. ***Director:*** Mrs. Maria Parsons, Director of Career Planning and Placement, 617-730-7072. ***Services:*** job fairs, resume preparation, career counseling, careers library, job bank, job interviews. 60 organizations recruited on campus 1994–95.
AFTER GRADUATION 96% of class of 1994 had job offers within 6 months. 24% of students completing transfer associate program went directly to 4-year colleges.
EXPENSES FOR 1995–96 ***Application fee:*** $30. Comprehensive fee of $17,120 includes full-time tuition ($10,580), mandatory fees ($500), and college room and board ($6040 minimum). Part-time tuition: $355 per credit.
FINANCIAL AID ***College-administered undergrad aid 1995–96:*** 960 need-based scholarships (average $1045), 470 non-need scholarships (average $975), low-interest long-term loans from external sources (average $3000), 320 Federal Work-Study (averaging $1500), part-time jobs. ***Required forms:*** institutional, FAFSA; required for some: state. ***Priority deadline:*** 5/1. ***Payment plan:*** installment.
APPLYING ***Options:*** deferred entrance, midyear entrance. ***Required:*** school transcript, TOEFL for international students. ***Recommended:*** minimum 2.0 GPA, 3 years of high school math and science, some high school foreign language, SAT I or ACT. Test scores used for admission. ***Application deadline:*** rolling. ***Notification:*** continuous until 9/1.
APPLYING/TRANSFER ***Required:*** high school transcript. ***Recommended:*** 3 years of high school math and science, some high school foreign language, minimum 2.0 high school GPA. ***Entrance:*** minimally difficult. ***Application deadline:*** rolling. ***Notification:*** continuous until 9/1.
CONTACT Ms. Kimberly Crone, Assistant Dean of Enrollment Management, Newbury College, Admission Center, 129 Fisher Avenue, Brookline, MA 02146-5750, 617-730-7007 or toll-free 800-NEWBURY. ***Fax:*** 617-731-9618. College video available.

❖ ***See page 780 for a narrative description.*** ❖

THE NEW ENGLAND BANKING INSTITUTE
Boston, Massachusetts

UG Enrollment: 1,744	**Tuition & Fees: $3720**
Application Deadline: rolling	**Room & Board: N/Avail**

GENERAL Independent, primarily 2-year, coed. Awards terminal associate, bachelor's degrees (offers primarily part-time evening degree programs; bachelor's degree offered jointly with Bentley College; has campuses in Glastonburg, CT and Providence, RI). Founded 1909. ***Setting:*** urban campus. ***Total enrollment:*** 1,744. ***Faculty:*** 360 (all part-time).
ENROLLMENT PROFILE 1,744 students from 3 states and territories. 78% women, 100% part-time, 99% state residents, 5% transferred in, 0% international, 81% 25 or older, 1% Native American, 3% Hispanic, 11% African American, 4% Asian American. ***Areas of study chosen:*** 100% business management and administrative services. ***Most popular recent majors:*** accounting, business administration/commerce/management, finance/banking.
FIRST-YEAR CLASS 583 total. Of the students accepted, 100% enrolled.
ACADEMIC PROGRAM Core, honor code. Calendar: semesters. 275 courses offered in 1995–96. Academic remediation for entering students, English as a second language program offered during academic year, tutorials, summer session for credit, part-time degree program (evenings), adult/continuing education programs, internships. Off-campus study.
GENERAL DEGREE REQUIREMENTS 63 credits for associate, 120 credits for bachelor's; 1 course each in algebra and environmental science; computer course.
MAJORS Accounting, business administration/commerce/management, computer science, finance/banking (B), management information systems, marketing/retailing/merchandising.
LIBRARY Sawyer Library with 4,500 books, 125 periodicals. Acquisition spending 1994–95: $6000.
COMPUTERS ON CAMPUS 10 computers for student use in computer center.
HOUSING College housing not available.
CAREER PLANNING ***Service:*** career counseling.
AFTER GRADUATION 45% of students completing transfer associate program in 1994–95 went directly to 4-year colleges.
EXPENSES FOR 1995–96 Part-time mandatory fees: $15 per semester. Tuition for members of the banking community: $3690 full-time, $123 per credit part-time. Tuition for all other students: $5280 full-time, $176 per credit part-time. Full-time mandatory fees: $30.
APPLYING ***Option:*** Common Application. ***Required:*** 1 recommendation, interview. ***Application deadline:*** rolling. ***Notification:*** continuous.
APPLYING/TRANSFER ***Required:*** 1 recommendation, interview, college transcript. ***Entrance:*** moderately difficult. ***Application deadline:*** rolling. ***Notification:*** continuous. ***Contact:*** Ms. Lynn Fitzgerald, Associate Dean, 617-951-2350.
CONTACT Ms. Deborah Pepper, Senior Vice President, The New England Banking Institute, 1 Lincoln Plaza, Boston, MA 02111-2671, 617-951-2350. ***Fax:*** 617-951-2533.

NEW ENGLAND INSTITUTE OF APPLIED ARTS AND SCIENCES
Massachusetts—See Mount Ida College

NORTHERN ESSEX COMMUNITY COLLEGE
Haverhill, Massachusetts

UG Enrollment: 6,359	**Tuition & Fees (MA Res): $2430**
Application Deadline: rolling	**Room & Board: N/Avail**

GENERAL State-supported, 2-year, coed. Awards certificates, transfer associate, terminal associate degrees. Founded 1960. ***Setting:*** 106-acre suburban campus with easy access to Boston. ***Total enrollment:*** 6,359. ***Faculty:*** 457 (124 full-time, 333 part-time).
ENROLLMENT PROFILE 6,359 students from 5 states and territories, 5 other countries. 66% women, 34% men, 60% part-time, 86% state residents, 5% transferred in, 50% have need-based financial aid, 1% international, 46% 25 or older, 1% Native American, 15% Hispanic, 1% African American, 3% Asian American. ***Areas of study chosen:*** 34% liberal arts/general studies, 17% business management and administrative services, 15% engineering and applied sciences, 14% social sciences, 9% health professions and related sciences, 8% computer and information sciences, 3% education. ***Most popular recent majors:*** liberal arts/general studies, business administration/commerce/management.
FIRST-YEAR CLASS 1,900 total; 2,300 applied, 88% were accepted, 94% of whom enrolled.
ACADEMIC PROGRAM Core. Calendar: semesters. 300 courses offered in 1995–96. Academic remediation for entering students, English as a second language program offered during academic year and summer, services for LD students, advanced placement, honors program, summer session for credit, part-time degree program (daytime, evenings, summer), adult/continuing education programs, co-op programs and internships. Off-campus study at Bradford College, members of the Northeast Consortium of Colleges and Universities in Massachusetts. Study abroad in England, Ireland, Italy, Germany, China, Cyprus, Denmark. ROTC: Air Force (c).

Northern Essex Community College (continued)
GENERAL DEGREE REQUIREMENTS 60 credits; math/science requirements vary according to program.
MAJORS Accounting, business administration/commerce/management, business education, civil engineering technology, commercial art, computer programming, computer science, computer technologies, criminal justice, dance, data processing, deaf interpreter training, early childhood education, education, electrical and electronics technologies, electrical engineering technology, electronics engineering technology, engineering sciences, finance/banking, history, hotel and restaurant management, information science, international studies, journalism, liberal arts/general studies, machine and tool technologies, marketing/retailing/merchandising, materials sciences, medical records services, medical secretarial studies, mental health/rehabilitation counseling, music, nursing, paralegal studies, physical education, political science/government, radiological technology, real estate, recreation and leisure services, respiratory therapy, science, secretarial studies/office management, theater arts/drama, tourism and travel, women's studies, word processing.
LIBRARY Bentley Library with 61,120 books, 261 microform titles, 598 periodicals. Acquisition spending 1994–95: $261,109.
COMPUTERS ON CAMPUS 250 computers for student use in computer center, classroom buildings. Staffed computer lab on campus provides training in use of computers, software.
COLLEGE LIFE Drama-theater group, student-run newspaper, radio station. ***Student services:*** health clinic, personal-psychological counseling. ***Campus security:*** 24-hour emergency response devices and patrols.
HOUSING College housing not available.
ATHLETICS Member NJCAA. ***Intercollegiate:*** baseball M, basketball M/W, golf M/W, soccer M/W, softball W. ***Intramural:*** basketball, cross-country running, football, golf, racquetball, skiing (cross-country), skiing (downhill), weight lifting. ***Contact:*** Mr. Carl Beal, Director of Intramurals, Recreation, and Athletics, 508-374-3820.
CAREER PLANNING ***Placement office:*** 2 full-time, 1 part-time staff. ***Director:*** Ms. M. J. Pernaa, Coordinator of Career Development, 508-374-3790. ***Services:*** job fairs, resume preparation, career counseling, careers library, job bank, job interviews.
AFTER GRADUATION 50% of students completing a degree program in 1994–95 went directly on to further study.
EXPENSES FOR 1995–96 State resident tuition: $2430 full-time, $81 per credit part-time. Nonresident tuition: $6720 full-time, $224 per credit part-time. Nonresidents who are eligible for the New England Regional Student Program: $2940 full-time, $98 per credit part-time.
FINANCIAL AID ***College-administered undergrad aid 1995–96:*** 1,500 need-based scholarships (average $800), 15 non-need scholarships (average $1056), low-interest long-term loans from external sources (average $2000), Federal Work-Study. ***Required forms:*** institutional, FAFSA. ***Priority deadline:*** 4/1. ***Payment plan:*** installment. ***Waivers:*** full or partial for employees or children of employees. ***Notification:*** 6/15.
APPLYING Open admission except for health, human services, technology programs. ***Options:*** early entrance, midyear entrance. ***Required:*** school transcript, TOEFL for international students, Psychological Corporation Aptitude Test for Practical Nursing. Test scores used for admission (for practical nursing program). ***Application deadline:*** rolling. ***Notification:*** continuous. Preference given to state residents.
APPLYING/TRANSFER ***Required:*** high school transcript, college transcript. ***Required for some:*** standardized test scores. ***Entrance:*** noncompetitive. ***Application deadline:*** rolling. ***Notification:*** continuous.
CONTACT Ms. Elizabeth Cole, Director of Admissions, Northern Essex Community College, Haverhill, MA 01830, 508-374-3605.

NORTH SHORE COMMUNITY COLLEGE
Danvers, Massachusetts

UG Enrollment: 5,163	**Tuition & Fees (MA Res): $1992**
Application Deadline: rolling	**Room & Board: N/Avail**

GENERAL State-supported, 2-year, coed. Awards certificates, diplomas, transfer associate, terminal associate degrees. Founded 1965. ***Setting:*** suburban campus with easy access to Boston. ***Total enrollment:*** 5,163. ***Faculty:*** 361 (118 full-time, 243 part-time). ***Notable Alumni:*** John Tudor, baseball player; Marie Balter, mental health advocate; Linda Harris, television news announcer.
ENROLLMENT PROFILE 5,163 students: 65% women, 35% men, 67% part-time, 98% state residents, 5% transferred in, 79% 25 or older, 0% Native American, 11% Hispanic, 5% African American, 2% Asian American. ***Most popular recent majors:*** liberal arts/general studies, business administration/commerce/management, nursing.
FIRST-YEAR CLASS 877 total; 1,940 applied, 94% were accepted, 48% of whom enrolled.
ACADEMIC PROGRAM Core. Calendar: semesters. Academic remediation for entering students, English as a second language program offered during academic year and summer, services for LD students, tutorials, honors program, summer session for credit, part-time degree program (daytime, evenings), external degree programs, adult/continuing education programs, co-op programs and internships. Off-campus study at Northeast Consortium of Colleges and Universities in Massachusetts.
GENERAL DEGREE REQUIREMENTS 60 credits; math competence; internship (some majors).
MAJORS Accounting, aviation technology, biotechnology, business administration/commerce/management, child care/child and family studies, computer information systems, computer programming, computer science, computer technologies, criminal justice, drug and alcohol/substance abuse counseling, early childhood education, engineering (general), engineering sciences, (pre)engineering sequence, fire science, flight training, gerontology, interdisciplinary studies, legal secretarial studies, liberal arts/general studies, manufacturing technology, marketing/retailing/merchandising, medical records services, medical secretarial studies, mental health/rehabilitation counseling, nursing, occupational therapy, paralegal studies, physical therapy, radiological technology, respiratory therapy, secretarial studies/office management, teacher aide studies, technical writing, tourism and travel.
LIBRARY Learning Resource Center plus 2 others, with 78,104 books, 135 microform titles, 401 periodicals, 4 on-line bibliographic services, 17 CD-ROMs, 4,889 records, tapes, and CDs.
COMPUTERS ON CAMPUS 300 computers for student use in computer labs, computer classrooms, student support center. Staffed computer lab on campus provides training in use of computers, software.
COLLEGE LIFE Drama-theater group, student-run newspaper. 10% vote in student government elections. ***Social organizations:*** 23 open to all. ***Most popular organizations:*** Program Council, Student Government, Performing Arts, Student Newspaper. ***Major annual events:*** Intercultural Fair, Student Activities Fair, Performing Arts Productions. ***Student services:*** health clinic, personal-psychological counseling, women's center. ***Campus security:*** 24-hour patrols.
HOUSING College housing not available.
ATHLETICS Member NJCAA. ***Intercollegiate:*** baseball M, basketball M, softball W. ***Intramural:*** table tennis (Ping-Pong), volleyball. ***Contact:*** Mr. F. Peter Della Monica, Director of Athletics and Recreation, 508-762-4000 Ext. 2122.
CAREER PLANNING ***Placement office:*** 14 full-time, 17 part-time staff. ***Director:*** Ms. Jean Keith, Director of the Student Support Center, 508-762-4000 Ext. 5547. ***Services:*** job fairs, career counseling.
AFTER GRADUATION 79% of students completing a degree program in 1994–95 went directly on to further study.
EXPENSES FOR 1995–96 State resident tuition: $960 full-time, $40 per credit part-time. Nonresident tuition: $4522 full-time, $188 per credit part-time. Part-time mandatory fees: $43 per credit. Full-time mandatory fees: $1032.
FINANCIAL AID ***College-administered undergrad aid 1995–96:*** need-based scholarships, low-interest long-term loans from external sources, 37 Federal Work-Study (averaging $1200). ***Required forms:*** institutional, FAFSA. ***Priority deadline:*** 5/1. ***Payment plan:*** installment. ***Waivers:*** full or partial for minority students, employees or children of employees, and senior citizens.
APPLYING Open admission except for nursing, engineering, health-related programs. ***Options:*** early entrance, midyear entrance. ***Required for some:*** school transcript, minimum 2.0 GPA, interview, TOEFL for international students, nursing exam. Test scores used for counseling/placement. ***Application deadline:*** rolling. ***Notification:*** continuous. Preference given to state residents.
APPLYING/TRANSFER ***Required for some:*** standardized test scores, high school transcript, interview, college transcript, minimum 2.0 college GPA, minimum 2.0 high school GPA. ***Application deadline:*** rolling. ***Notification:*** continuous. ***Contact:*** Mr. Peter Monaco, Coordinator of Transfer Services, 508-762-4000 Ext. 2132.
CONTACT Dr. Joanne Light, Staff Associate, Admissions Processing, North Shore Community College, Danvers, MA 01923-4093, 508-762-4000 Ext. 4356. College video available.

QUINCY COLLEGE
Quincy, Massachusetts

Enrollment: N/R	**Tuition & Fees: $2300**
Application Deadline: rolling	**Room & Board: N/Avail**

GENERAL City-supported, 2-year, coed. Awards certificates, transfer associate, terminal associate degrees. Founded 1958. ***Setting:*** 2-acre suburban campus with easy access to Boston. ***Faculty:*** 69 (44 full-time, 25 part-time); student-faculty ratio is 26:1.
ENROLLMENT PROFILE 70% women, 43% part-time, 89% state residents, 19% transferred in, 8% international, 45% 25 or older, 1% Native American, 2% Hispanic, 11% African American, 6% Asian American. ***Areas of study chosen:*** 38% liberal arts/general studies, 21% health professions and related sciences, 14% business management and administrative services, 10% prelaw, 5% education, 4% computer and information sciences, 3% communications and journalism, 3% vocational and home economics, 2% natural resource sciences. ***Most popular recent majors:*** nursing, business administration/commerce/management, liberal arts/general studies.
FIRST-YEAR CLASS 1,323 total. Of the students who applied, 100% were accepted, 70% of whom enrolled.
ACADEMIC PROGRAM Core. Calendar: semesters. 146 courses offered in 1995–96. Academic remediation for entering students, English as a second language program offered during academic year and summer, advanced placement, summer session for credit, part-time degree program (daytime, evenings, weekends, summer), adult/continuing education programs, internships.
GENERAL DEGREE REQUIREMENT 60 credits.
MAJORS Accounting, behavioral sciences, business administration/commerce/management, communication, computer programming, computer science, criminal justice, early childhood education, English, environmental sciences, food services management, hotel and restaurant management, humanities, law enforcement/police sciences, legal secretarial studies, liberal arts/general studies, marketing/retailing/merchandising, mathematics, medical secretarial studies, nursing, operating room technology, paralegal studies, physical sciences, physical therapy, practical nursing, psychology, retail management, science, secretarial studies/office management, social science, sociology, tourism and travel.
LIBRARY Anselmo Library plus 1 other, with 30,000 books, 305 periodicals, 250 records, tapes, and CDs.
COMPUTERS ON CAMPUS 80 computers for student use in computer center. Staffed computer lab on campus.
COLLEGE LIFE Student-run newspaper. ***Student services:*** women's center.
HOUSING College housing not available.
CAREER PLANNING ***Placement office:*** 1 full-time staff. ***Director:*** Ms. DeAnn Elliott, Director of Student Life, 617-984-1660. ***Services:*** job fairs, career counseling, job bank.
EXPENSES FOR 1995–96 ***Application fee:*** $15. Tuition: $1980 (minimum) full-time. Part-time tuition per credit ranges from $70 to $139. Part-time mandatory fees: $42 per credit. Full-time tuition ranges up to $4000 according to program. Full-time mandatory fees: $320.
FINANCIAL AID ***College-administered undergrad aid 1995–96:*** 30 need-based scholarships (averaging $500), low-interest long-term loans from external sources (averaging $2625), Federal Work-Study. ***Required forms:*** CSS Financial Aid PROFILE, state, institutional, FAFSA. ***Priority deadline:*** 4/1. ***Waivers:*** full or partial for senior citizens.
APPLYING Open admission except for nursing programs. ***Options:*** early entrance, deferred entrance, midyear entrance. ***Required:*** school transcript, TOEFL for international students, MAPS. Test scores used for counseling/placement. ***Application deadline:*** rolling.
APPLYING/TRANSFER ***Required:*** high school transcript. ***Entrance:*** noncompetitive. ***Application deadline:*** rolling.
CONTACT Ms. Carolyn A. Scott, Director of Admissions, Quincy College, Quincy, MA 02169-4522, 617-984-1700 or toll-free 800-698-1700 (in-state).

QUINSIGAMOND COMMUNITY COLLEGE
Worcester, Massachusetts

UG Enrollment: 4,680	Tuition & Fees (MA Res): $2670
Application Deadline: rolling	Room & Board: N/Avail

GENERAL State-supported, 2-year, coed. Awards certificates, transfer associate, terminal associate degrees. Founded 1963. *Setting:* 57-acre urban campus with easy access to Boston. *Total enrollment:* 4,680. *Faculty:* 224 (94 full-time, 130 part-time).
ENROLLMENT PROFILE 4,680 students from 3 states and territories, 13 other countries. 61% women, 62% part-time, 98% state residents, 6% transferred in, 47% 25 or older, 1% Native American, 7% Hispanic, 4% African American, 4% Asian American. *Most popular recent majors:* liberal arts/general studies, business administration/commerce/management, nursing.
FIRST-YEAR CLASS 1,105 total; 2,497 applied, 61% were accepted, 73% of whom enrolled. 18% from top quarter of their high school class, 82% from top half.
ACADEMIC PROGRAM Core. Calendar: semesters. Academic remediation for entering students, English as a second language program offered during academic year, services for LD students, tutorials, summer session for credit, part-time degree program (daytime, evenings, summer); adult/continuing education programs, co-op programs and internships. Off-campus study at members of the Worcester Consortium for Higher Education.
GENERAL DEGREE REQUIREMENTS 60 credits; computer course for business administration majors; internship (some majors).
MAJORS Accounting, art/fine arts, automotive technologies, business administration/commerce/management, computer information systems, computer programming, computer technologies, criminal justice, data processing, dental services, early childhood education, electrical and electronics technologies, (pre)engineering sequence, fire science, hotel and restaurant management, human services, liberal arts/general studies, nursing, occupational therapy, radiological technology, respiratory therapy, retail management, secretarial studies/office management, tourism and travel.
LIBRARY Quinsigamond Library with 63,720 books, 32 microform titles, 300 periodicals, 800 records, tapes, and CDs.
COMPUTERS ON CAMPUS 128 computers for student use in computer center, computer labs, learning resource center, classrooms. Staffed computer lab on campus provides training in use of computers, software.
COLLEGE LIFE Student-run newspaper. *Student services:* health clinic, personal-psychological counseling, women's center. *Campus security:* 24-hour emergency response devices and patrols.
HOUSING College housing not available.
ATHLETICS Member NJCAA. *Intercollegiate:* baseball M, basketball M/W, softball W. *Intramural:* archery, badminton, basketball, cross-country running, skiing (cross-country), skiing (downhill), swimming and diving, tennis, volleyball. *Contact:* Mr. Barry Glinski, Director of Athletics, 508-853-2300 Ext. 266.
CAREER PLANNING *Placement office:* 1 full-time staff. *Director:* Ms. Sarah Housepian, Coordinator of Placement and Career Counseling, 508-854-4315. *Services:* job fairs, resume preparation, resume referral, career counseling, careers library, job bank, job interviews.
AFTER GRADUATION 40% of students completing a degree program in 1994–95 went directly on to further study.
EXPENSES FOR 1995–96 *Application fee:* $10. State resident tuition: $1200 full-time, $40 per credit part-time. Nonresident tuition: $5640 full-time, $188 per credit part-time. Part-time mandatory fees per semester range from $61 to $505. Full-time mandatory fees: $1470.
FINANCIAL AID *College-administered undergrad aid 1995–96:* 200 need-based scholarships (average $300), 10 non-need scholarships (average $1000), low-interest long-term loans from external sources (average $2000), 100 Federal Work-Study (averaging $1000). *Required:* institutional, FAFSA; required for some: state; accepted: CSS Financial Aid PROFILE. *Priority deadline:* 7/1. *Payment plan:* deferred payment. *Waivers:* full or partial for employees or children of employees and senior citizens. *Notification:* continuous. *Average indebtedness of graduates:* $3244.
APPLYING *Options:* early entrance, midyear entrance. *Required:* TOEFL for international students. *Required for some:* 3 years of high school math. Test scores used for counseling/placement. *Application deadline:* rolling.
APPLYING/TRANSFER *Required for some:* 3 years of high school math. *Application deadline:* rolling.
CONTACT Dr. John A. Doon, Associate Dean of Student Affairs, Quinsigamond Community College, 670 West Boylston Street, Worcester, MA 01606-2092, 508-853-2300 Ext. 277. *Fax:* 508-852-6943.

ROXBURY COMMUNITY COLLEGE
Roxbury Crossing, Massachusetts

UG Enrollment: 3,000	Tuition & Fees (MA Res): $1920
Application Deadline: 9/1	Room & Board: N/Avail

GENERAL State-supported, 2-year, coed. Part of Massachusetts Public Higher Education System. Awards transfer associate, terminal associate degrees. Founded 1973. *Setting:* 12-acre urban campus with easy access to Boston. *Total enrollment:* 3,000. *Faculty:* 62 full-time; student-faculty ratio is 19:1.
ENROLLMENT PROFILE 3,000 students from 14 states and territories, 58 other countries. 65% women, 43% part-time, 90% state residents, 10% transferred in, 2% international, 75% 25 or older, 1% Native American, 26% Hispanic, 62% African American, 2% Asian American.
FIRST-YEAR CLASS 700 total; 1,500 applied, 100% were accepted, 47% of whom enrolled.
ACADEMIC PROGRAM Core. Calendar: semesters. Academic remediation for entering students, English as a second language program offered during academic year and summer, services for LD students, self-designed majors, honors program, summer session for credit, part-time degree program (daytime, evenings), adult/continuing education programs, internships. Off-campus study at University of Massachusetts.
GENERAL DEGREE REQUIREMENTS 60 credits; 1 course each in math and science; computer course for business majors.
MAJORS Accounting, architectural technologies, art/fine arts, biology/biological sciences, business administration/commerce/management, computer information systems, computer technologies, drafting and design, early childhood education, English, humanities, legal secretarial studies, liberal arts/general studies, mathematics, medical secretarial studies, nursing, physical sciences, retail management, secretarial studies/office management, social science, word processing.
LIBRARY Roxbury Community College Library with 12,800 books.
COMPUTERS ON CAMPUS 60 computers for student use in computer labs, teaching, learning labs.
COLLEGE LIFE Drama-theater group. *Student services:* personal-psychological counseling.
HOUSING College housing not available.
ATHLETICS Member NJCAA. *Intercollegiate:* basketball M/W, soccer M/W, tennis M/W. *Intramural:* basketball, racquetball. *Contact:* Mr. Ernest Austine, Director of Athletics, 617-541-5008.
CAREER PLANNING *Director:* Ms. Holly Guran, Director of Counseling, 617-541-5310 Ext. 5010. *Service:* career counseling.
EXPENSES FOR 1995–96 *Application fee:* $10. State resident tuition: $1920 full-time, $80 per credit part-time. Nonresident tuition: $5472 full-time, $228 per credit part-time.
FINANCIAL AID *College-administered undergrad aid 1995–96:* need-based scholarships, non-need scholarships, short-term loans (averaging $50), low-interest long-term loans from external sources, Federal Work-Study. *Required forms:* CSS Financial Aid PROFILE, institutional, FAFSA. *Priority deadline:* 4/15.
APPLYING Open admission. *Option:* deferred entrance. *Required:* ACT ASSET. *Application deadlines:* 9/1, 8/15 for nonresidents. Preference given to local residents.
APPLYING/TRANSFER *Application deadline:* 9/1.
CONTACT Mr. Michael Rice, Director of Admissions, Roxbury Community College, 1234 Columbus Avenue, Roxbury Crossing, MA 02120-3400, 617-541-5310 Ext. 5415.

ST. HYACINTH COLLEGE AND SEMINARY
Granby, Massachusetts

UG Enrollment: 40	Tuition & Fees: $4000
Application Deadline: rolling	Room & Board: N/Avail

GENERAL Independent Roman Catholic, 2-year, specialized, primarily men. Awards transfer associate, terminal associate degrees. Founded 1927. *Setting:* 600-acre small-town campus. *Total enrollment:* 40.
ENROLLMENT PROFILE 40 students from 7 states and territories, 1 other country. *Areas of study chosen:* 100% theology/religion.
FIRST-YEAR CLASS 10 total. Of the students who applied, 100% were accepted, 100% of whom enrolled. 40% from top 10% of their high school class, 50% from top quarter, 100% from top half.
ACADEMIC PROGRAM Core. Calendar: semesters. Academic remediation for entering students, services for LD students, advanced placement, tutorials, summer session for credit, part-time degree program (daytime).
GENERAL DEGREE REQUIREMENTS 60 semester hours; 6 semester hours of math/science.
MAJOR Religious studies.
LIBRARY Kolbe Memorial Library with 81,725 books, 157 periodicals, 784 records, tapes, and CDs. Acquisition spending 1994–95: $40,237.
COMPUTERS ON CAMPUS Students must have own computer. 4 computers for student use in computer center, library, student center.
COLLEGE LIFE Orientation program (2 days, no cost). Choral group, student-run newspaper. *Student services:* health clinic, personal-psychological counseling.
HOUSING College housing not available.
ATHLETICS *Intramural:* basketball, skiing (cross-country), skiing (downhill), soccer, softball, tennis, volleyball, weight lifting.
CAREER PLANNING *Service:* career counseling.
ESTIMATED EXPENSES FOR 1996–97 *Application fee:* $25. Tuition: $3800 full-time, $130 per semester hour part-time. Part-time mandatory fees: $20 per course. Full-time mandatory fees: $200.
FINANCIAL AID *College-administered undergrad aid 1995–96:* need-based scholarships, non-need scholarships, low-interest long-term loans from external sources (average $2800). *Required forms:* FAFSA; accepted: CSS Financial Aid PROFILE. *Priority deadline:* 5/1. *Payment plan:* installment. *Waivers:* full or partial for employees or children of employees. *Notification:* continuous.
APPLYING *Options:* Common Application, midyear entrance. *Required:* essay, school transcript, recommendations, campus interview, SAT I. Test scores used for counseling/placement. *Application deadline:* rolling.
APPLYING/TRANSFER *Required:* essay, standardized test scores, high school transcript, recommendations, campus interview, college transcript, minimum 2.0 college GPA. *Entrance:* moderately difficult. *Application deadline:* rolling. *Contact:* Fr. Gregory Moore, Director of Admissions, 413-467-7191.
CONTACT Fr. Gregory Moore, Director of Admissions, St. Hyacinth College and Seminary, Granby, MA 01033-9742, 413-467-7191. *Fax:* 413-467-9609.

SPRINGFIELD TECHNICAL COMMUNITY COLLEGE
Springfield, Massachusetts

UG Enrollment: 6,084	Tuition & Fees (MA Res): $1200
Application Deadline: rolling	Room & Board: N/Avail

GENERAL State-supported, 2-year, coed. Awards certificates, transfer associate, terminal associate degrees. Founded 1967. *Setting:* 34-acre urban campus. *Total enrollment:* 6,084. *Faculty:* 319 (174 full-time, 16% with terminal degrees, 145 part-time); student-faculty ratio is 16:1. *Notable Alumni:* Gary Cassarelli, chief of Springfield fire department; Marlene Goldstein, auditor; Jeannine Delchat, senior vice president of Regional Administration Fleet Bank; Willian Boyle, lawyer; James Gormally, police officer.

Massachusetts

Springfield Technical Community College (continued)

ENROLLMENT PROFILE 6,084 students from 6 states and territories, 21 other countries. 57% women, 43% men, 59% part-time, 98% state residents, 2% transferred in, 1% international, 64% 25 or older, 1% Native American, 7% Hispanic, 7% African American, 2% Asian American. *Areas of study chosen:* 28% interdisciplinary studies, 23% health professions and related sciences, 17% business management and administrative services, 14% engineering and applied sciences, 7% computer and information sciences, 4% vocational and home economics, 2% education, 2% performing arts, 2% physical sciences, 1% agriculture, 1% communications and journalism.

FIRST-YEAR CLASS 1,042 total; 2,003 applied, 95% were accepted, 55% of whom enrolled. 10% from top 10% of their high school class, 50% from top half.

ACADEMIC PROGRAM Core, career and transfer curriculum, honor code. Calendar: semesters. Academic remediation for entering students, English as a second language program offered during academic year and summer, services for LD students, advanced placement, tutorials, honors program, summer session for credit, part-time degree program (daytime, evenings, weekends, summer), adult/continuing education programs, co-op programs and internships. Off-campus study at the Cooperating Colleges of Greater Springfield.

GENERAL DEGREE REQUIREMENTS 60 credits; math/science requirements vary according to major; computer course for business administration majors.

MAJORS Accounting, architectural technologies, art/fine arts, automotive technologies, behavioral sciences, biomedical technologies, biotechnology, business administration/commerce/management, civil engineering technology, commercial art, computer information systems, computer technologies, cosmetology, court reporting, criminal justice, data processing, dental services, drafting and design, early childhood education, electrical engineering technology, electromechanical technology, electronics engineering technology, energy management technologies, engineering sciences, (pre)engineering sequence, environmental engineering technology, finance/banking, fire science, graphic arts, heating/refrigeration/air conditioning, humanities, human services, industrial engineering technology, landscape architecture/design, laser technologies, law enforcement/police sciences, legal secretarial studies, liberal arts/general studies, manufacturing technology, marketing/retailing/merchandising, mechanical design technology, mechanical engineering technology, medical assistant technologies, medical laboratory technology, medical secretarial studies, medical technology, nuclear medical technology, nursing, occupational therapy, operating room technology, painting/drawing, physical therapy, printing technologies, radiological technology, respiratory therapy, robotics, secretarial studies/office management, social science, telecommunications, word processing.

LIBRARY STCC Library with 60,862 books, 71 microform titles, 438 periodicals, 3 on-line bibliographic services, 8 CD-ROMs, 3,173 records, tapes, and CDs. Acquisition spending 1994–95: $132,299.

COMPUTERS ON CAMPUS Computer purchase plan available. 415 computers for student use in computer labs, learning resource center, classrooms, library provide access to off-campus computing facilities, e-mail, on-line services. Staffed computer lab on campus provides training in use of computers, software. Academic computing expenditure 1994–95: $350,000.

COLLEGE LIFE Drama-theater group, student-run newspaper. 10% vote in student government elections. *Most popular organizations:* African-American Culture Club, Ski Club, Cosmetology Club, Business Club, Gay/Lesbian Alliance. *Major annual events:* Earth Day, Spring Fling, Opening Picnic. *Student services:* health clinic, personal-psychological counseling, women's center. *Campus security:* 24-hour emergency response devices and patrols, late-night transport-escort service.

HOUSING College housing not available.

ATHLETICS Member NJCAA. *Intercollegiate:* baseball M, basketball M/W, golf M/W, soccer M/W, softball W, tennis M/W. *Intramural:* basketball, golf, softball, volleyball, weight lifting. *Contact:* Mr. J. Vincent Grassetti, Director of Athletics, 413-781-7822 Ext. 3929.

CAREER PLANNING *Placement office:* 3 full-time, 1 part-time staff; $106,514 operating expenditure 1994–95. *Director:* Ms. Louise Davis, Director, Co-op/Placement, 413-781-7822 Ext. 3470. *Services:* job fairs, resume preparation, resume referral, career counseling, careers library, job bank, job interviews. Students must register sophomore year. 45 organizations recruited on campus 1994–95.

AFTER GRADUATION 80% of class of 1994 had job offers within 6 months. 25% of students completing a degree program went directly on to further study.

EXPENSES FOR 1995-96 *Application fee:* $10. State resident tuition: $1200 full-time, $40 per credit part-time. Nonresident tuition: $5640 full-time, $188 per credit part-time. Tuition for nonresidents who are eligible for the New England Regional Student Program: $60 per credit.

FINANCIAL AID *College-administered undergrad aid 1995–96:* 1,253 need-based scholarships (average $591), low-interest long-term loans from college funds (average $1362), loans from external sources (average $1732), 98 Federal Work-Study (averaging $1500), 7 part-time jobs. *Required forms:* institutional, FAFSA. *Priority deadline:* 4/1. *Waivers:* full or partial for employees or children of employees and senior citizens. *Notification:* 7/15.

APPLYING Open admission except for certain vocational programs. *Options:* early entrance, midyear entrance. *Required:* school transcript, TOEFL for international students. *Required for some:* interview, SAT I. Test scores used for admission. *Application deadline:* rolling.

APPLYING/TRANSFER *Required:* high school transcript, college transcript. *Entrance:* noncompetitive. *Application deadline:* rolling. *Contact:* Mr. John D'Orazio, Director of Admissions, 413-781-7822 Ext. 3855.

CONTACT Mr. Patrick Tique, Asst. Dean of Enrollment Management/Director of Admissions, Springfield Technical Community College, 1 Armory Square, Springfield, MA 01105-1296, 413-781-7822 Ext. 3855.

Michigan

MICHIGAN

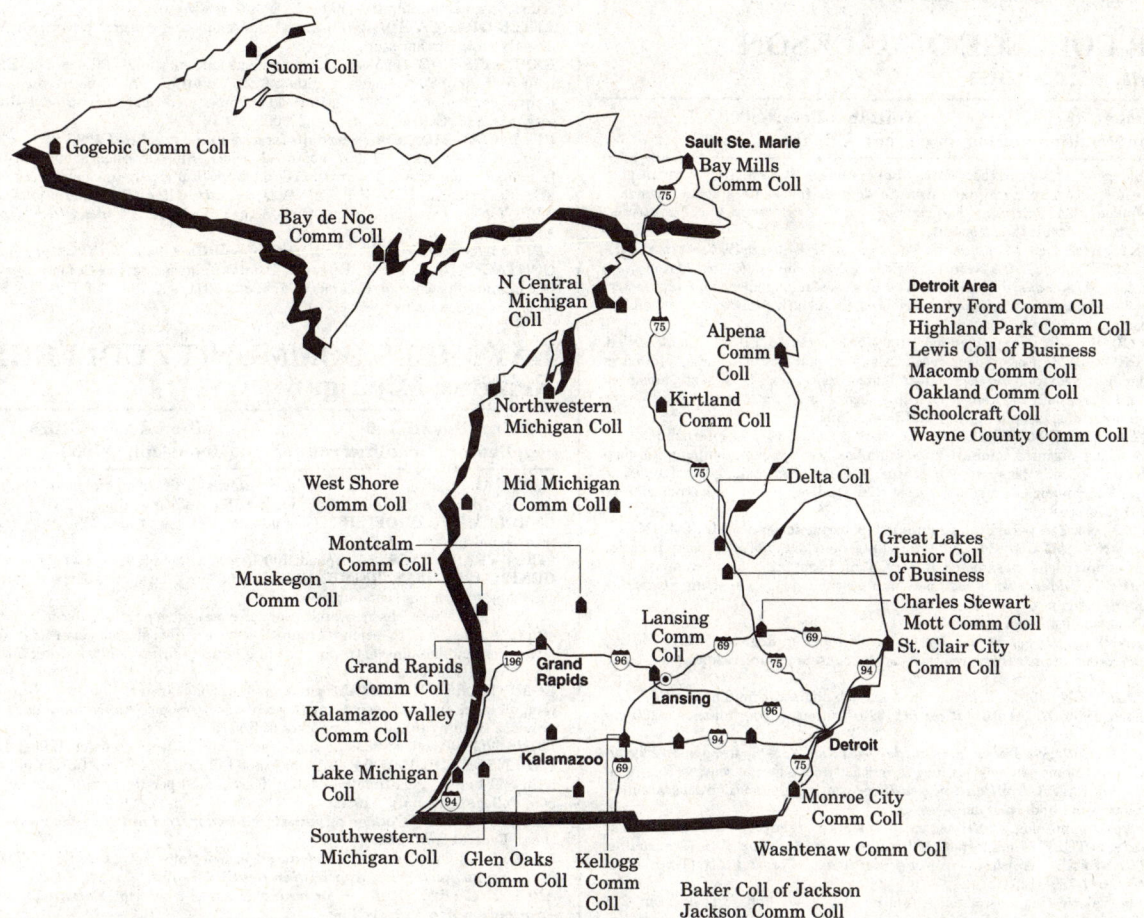

ALPENA COMMUNITY COLLEGE
Alpena, Michigan

UG Enrollment: 1,866	Tuition & Fees (Area Res): $1550
Application Deadline: rolling	Room & Board: N/Avail

GENERAL State and locally supported, 2-year, coed. Part of Michigan Department of Education. Awards certificates, transfer associate, terminal associate degrees. Founded 1952. *Setting:* 700-acre small-town campus. *Total enrollment:* 1,866. *Faculty:* 89 (49 full-time, 10% with terminal degrees, 40 part-time).
ENROLLMENT PROFILE 1,866 students from 3 states and territories, 2 other countries. 60% women, 40% men, 58% part-time, 99% state residents, 5% transferred in, 57% 25 or older, 1% Native American, 1% African American. *Most popular recent majors:* business administration/commerce/management, law enforcement/police sciences, liberal arts/general studies.
FIRST-YEAR CLASS 608 total; 950 applied, 100% were accepted, 64% of whom enrolled. 10% from top 10% of their high school class, 25% from top quarter, 50% from top half.
ACADEMIC PROGRAM Calendar: semesters. 250 courses offered in 1995–96. Academic remediation for entering students, services for LD students, advanced placement, summer session for credit, part-time degree program (daytime, evenings), internships.
GENERAL DEGREE REQUIREMENTS 60 semester hours; math/science requirements vary according to program; computer course for business, secretarial science majors.
MAJORS Accounting, automotive technologies, biology/biological sciences, business administration/commerce/management, chemical engineering technology, chemistry, data processing, drafting and design, electrical and electronics technologies, (pre)engineering sequence, English, graphic arts, law enforcement/police sciences, liberal arts/general studies, library science, machine and tool technologies, mathematics, nursing, practical nursing, secretarial studies/office management.
LIBRARY Alpena Community College Library plus 1 other, with 29,000 books, 135 microform titles, 183 periodicals, 456 records, tapes, and CDs. Acquisition spending 1994–95: $24,000.
COMPUTERS ON CAMPUS 65 computers for student use in computer center, computer labs, learning resource center, library provide access to main academic computer, on-line services, Internet. Staffed computer lab on campus provides training in use of computers, software. Academic computing expenditure 1994–95: $95,000.
COLLEGE LIFE Drama-theater group, student-run newspaper. 20% vote in student government elections. *Social organizations:* 8 open to all. *Most popular organizations:* Nursing Association, Student Senate, Phi Theta Kappa, Ski Club. *Major annual events:* Homecoming, Awards Night, Spring Fling. *Student services:* personal-psychological counseling, women's center. *Campus security:* 24-hour emergency response devices.
HOUSING College housing not available.
ATHLETICS Member NJCAA. *Intercollegiate:* basketball M(s)/W(s), cross-country running M(s), golf M, softball W(s). *Intramural:* basketball, bowling, football, riflery, softball, volleyball. *Contact:* Mr. Max Lindsay, Athletic Director, 517-356-9021 Ext. 200.
CAREER PLANNING *Placement office:* 3 full-time staff; $125,000 operating expenditure 1994–95. *Director:* Mr. Frank McCourt, Director of Career Guidance and Placement Office, 517-356-9021. *Services:* resume preparation, resume referral, career counseling, careers library, job bank, job interviews. 15 organizations recruited on campus 1994–95.
AFTER GRADUATION 65% of class of 1994 had job offers within 6 months. 35% of students completing a degree program went directly on to further study.
EXPENSES FOR 1995–96 Area resident tuition: $1380 full-time, $46 per contact hour part-time. State resident tuition: $2070 full-time, $69 per contact hour part-time. Nonresident tuition: $2760 full-time, $92 per contact hour part-time. Part-time mandatory fees: $6 per contact hour. Full-time mandatory fees: $170.
FINANCIAL AID *College-administered undergrad aid 1995–96:* 20 need-based scholarships (averaging $500), 20 non-need scholarships (averaging $500), low-interest long-term loans from external sources (averaging $1500), 100 Federal Work-Study (averaging $700), 25 part-time jobs. *Required forms:* FAFSA. *Priority deadline:* 8/15. *Waivers:* full or partial for employees or children of employees and senior citizens. *Notification:* continuous.
APPLYING Open admission except for nursing, utility technician programs. *Options:* early entrance, deferred entrance, midyear entrance. *Required:* school transcript, TOEFL for international students. *Required for some:* ACT ASSET. Test scores used for counseling/placement. *Application deadline:* rolling. *Notification:* continuous.

Peterson's Guide to Two-Year Colleges 1997

Michigan

Alpena Community College (continued)
APPLYING/TRANSFER *Required:* high school transcript, college transcript. *Required for some:* standardized test scores. *Entrance:* noncompetitive. *Application deadline:* rolling. *Notification:* continuous. *Contact:* Mr. Max P. Lindsay, Dean of Students, 517-356-9021 Ext. 200.
CONTACT Mr. Max P. Lindsay, Dean of Students, Alpena Community College, Alpena, MI 49707-1495, 517-356-9021 Ext. 200. *Fax:* 517-356-0980.

BAKER COLLEGE OF JACKSON
Jackson, Michigan

UG Enrollment: 461	Tuition & Fees: $6000
Application Deadline: rolling	Room & Board: N/Avail

GENERAL Independent, 2-year, coed. Part of Baker College System. Awards certificates, diplomas, transfer associate, terminal associate degrees (also offers some bachelor's programs). Founded 1994. *Setting:* urban campus. *Total enrollment:* 461. *Faculty:* 36 (all part-time); student-faculty ratio is 16:1.
ENROLLMENT PROFILE 461 students: 82% women, 18% men, 34% part-time, 100% state residents, 26% 25 or older, 0% Native American, 2% Hispanic, 13% African American, 1% Asian American. *Areas of study chosen:* 83% business management and administrative services, 8% computer and information sciences, 7% health professions and related sciences, 2% communications and journalism.
FIRST-YEAR CLASS 277 total; 340 applied, 100% were accepted, 81% of whom enrolled.
ACADEMIC PROGRAM Core, honor code. Calendar: quarters. 95 courses offered in 1995–96. Academic remediation for entering students, services for LD students, advanced placement, summer session for credit, part-time degree program (daytime, evenings), external degree programs, co-op programs and internships.
GENERAL DEGREE REQUIREMENTS 91 credits; 1 math course; internship.
MAJORS Accounting, business administration/commerce/management, computer information systems, data processing, legal secretarial studies, marketing/retailing/merchandising, medical assistant technologies, medical secretarial studies, secretarial studies/office management, word processing.
LIBRARY 2,038 books, 85 periodicals, 2 on-line bibliographic services, 5 CD-ROMs.
COMPUTERS ON CAMPUS Computer purchase plan available. 50 computers for student use in computer labs, classrooms, library. Staffed computer lab on campus.
COLLEGE LIFE *Student services:* personal-psychological counseling. *Campus security:* 24-hour emergency response devices.
HOUSING College housing not available.
CAREER PLANNING *Director:* Ms. Cynthia M. Van Gieson, Registrar, 517-789-6123. *Services:* resume preparation, resume referral, career counseling, careers library, job bank, job interviews.
AFTER GRADUATION 100% of class of 1994 had job offers within 6 months.
EXPENSES FOR 1996–97 *Application fee:* $20. Tuition: $6000 full-time, $130 per credit part-time.
FINANCIAL AID *College-administered undergrad aid 1995–96:* need-based scholarships, non-need scholarships, low-interest long-term loans from external sources. *Required forms:* institutional, FAFSA. *Application deadline:* continuous to 9/1. *Waivers:* full or partial for employees or children of employees.
APPLYING Open admission. *Options:* early entrance, deferred entrance, midyear entrance. *Required:* TOEFL for international students. *Application deadline:* rolling.
APPLYING/TRANSFER *Application deadline:* rolling. *Contact:* Ms. Cynthia Van Gieson, Registrar, 517-789-6123.
CONTACT Ms. Valerie Heldt, Director of Admissions, Baker College of Jackson, 338 South Mechanic Street, Jackson, MI 49202, 517-788-7800. *E-mail:* heldt_v@jackson.baker.edu. College video available.

BAY DE NOC COMMUNITY COLLEGE
Escanaba, Michigan

UG Enrollment: 2,229	Tuition & Fees (Area Res): $1668
Application Deadline: 8/15	Room Only: $1600

GENERAL County-supported, 2-year, coed. Part of Michigan Department of Education. Awards certificates, transfer associate, terminal associate degrees. Founded 1963. *Setting:* 150-acre rural campus. *Total enrollment:* 2,229. *Faculty:* 143 (43 full-time, 100 part-time).
ENROLLMENT PROFILE 2,229 students: 66% women, 44% part-time, 95% state residents, 8% transferred in, 63% have need-based financial aid, 10% have non-need-based financial aid, 1% international, 62% 25 or older, 3% Native American, 1% Hispanic, 1% African American, 1% Asian American. *Most popular recent majors:* business administration/commerce/management, accounting, liberal arts/general studies.
FIRST-YEAR CLASS 523 total; 743 applied, 100% were accepted, 70% of whom enrolled.
ACADEMIC PROGRAM Core, honor code. Calendar: semesters. Academic remediation for entering students, summer session for credit, part-time degree program (daytime, evenings, weekends, summer), adult/continuing education programs, co-op programs and internships.
GENERAL DEGREE REQUIREMENTS 62 credit hours; 4 credit hours each of math and lab science.
MAJORS Accounting, art education, automotive technologies, business administration/commerce/management, business machine technologies, construction technologies, criminal justice, drafting and design, early childhood education, economics, education, electrical and electronics technologies, electrical engineering technology, elementary education, (pre)engineering sequence, English, history, humanities, human services, journalism, law enforcement/police sciences, liberal arts/general studies, machine and tool technologies, marketing/retailing/merchandising, mathematics, nursing, paper and pulp sciences, physical education, political science/government, pollution control technologies, practical nursing, psychology, sanitation technology, social work, sociology, water resources, word processing.
LIBRARY Learning Resources Center plus 1 other, with 30,000 books, 2,000 microform titles, 200 periodicals, 1,000 records, tapes, and CDs.
COMPUTERS ON CAMPUS 150 computers for student use in computer labs, learning resource center, library, student center.

COLLEGE LIFE Student-run newspaper. *Campus security:* evening housing security personnel.
HOUSING 100 college housing spaces available; all were occupied 1995–96. Off-campus living permitted.
ATHLETICS *Intramural:* basketball, golf, skiing (cross-country), skiing (downhill), tennis, volleyball.
CAREER PLANNING *Services:* job fairs, resume preparation, resume referral, career counseling, careers library, job bank, job interviews.
AFTER GRADUATION 60% of students completing a degree program in 1994–95 went directly on to further study.
EXPENSES FOR 1995–96 Area resident tuition: $1620 full-time, $52.25 per credit hour part-time. State resident tuition: $2217 full-time, $71.50 per credit hour part-time. Nonresident tuition: $3542 full-time, $114.25 per credit hour part-time. Full-time mandatory fees: $48. College room only: $1600.
FINANCIAL AID *College-administered undergrad aid 1995–96:* 1,250 need-based scholarships (average $1200), non-need scholarships (average $500), low-interest long-term loans from external sources, Federal Work-Study, part-time jobs. *Acceptable forms:* CSS Financial Aid PROFILE, FAFSA. *Application deadline:* continuous to 4/1.
APPLYING Open admission. *Option:* early entrance. *Application deadline:* 8/15. *Notification:* continuous.
APPLYING/TRANSFER *Application deadline:* 8/15. *Notification:* continuous.
CONTACT Dr. K. James Peterson, Dean of Admissions and Student Services, Bay de Noc Community College, Escanaba, MI 49829-2511, 906-786-5802 Ext. 148. *Fax:* 906-786-6555. College video available.

BAY MILLS COMMUNITY COLLEGE
Brimley, Michigan

UG Enrollment: 180	Tuition & Fees: $1625
Application Deadline: rolling	Room Only: $1950

GENERAL District-supported, 2-year. Awards certificates, diplomas, transfer associate degrees. *Total enrollment:* 180. *Faculty:* 15 (9 full-time, 6 part-time).
ENROLLMENT PROFILE 180 students: 10% part-time, 98% state residents, 35% transferred in.
FIRST-YEAR CLASS 40 applied, 100% were accepted, 80% of whom enrolled.
GENERAL DEGREE REQUIREMENTS 63 credits; math/science requirements vary according to program; computer course.
MAJORS Business administration/commerce/management, computer information systems, ethnic studies, health science, human services, liberal arts/general studies, modern languages, public administration, reading education, secretarial studies/office management, social science.
COMPUTERS ON CAMPUS Students must have own computer. PCs are provided. 60 computers for student use in computer center, classrooms. Staffed computer lab on campus provides training in use of computers, software.
HOUSING 40 college housing spaces available; 12 were occupied 1995–96.
EXPENSES FOR 1995–96 Tuition: $1560 full-time. Part-time tuition per credit ranges from $50 to $65. Part-time mandatory fees: $32.50 per term. Full-time mandatory fees: $65. College room only: $1950.
FINANCIAL AID *College-administered undergrad aid 1995–96:* need-based scholarships, Federal Work-Study.
APPLYING Open admission. *Required:* school transcript, ACT ASSET. Test scores used for counseling/placement. *Application deadline:* rolling.
APPLYING/TRANSFER *Required:* high school transcript. *Entrance:* noncompetitive. *Application deadline:* rolling.
CONTACT Ms. Elaine Lehre, Admissions Officer, Bay Mills Community College, Brimley, MI 49715, 906-248-3354 Ext. 203.

CHARLES STEWART MOTT COMMUNITY COLLEGE
Flint, Michigan

UG Enrollment: 9,754	Tuition & Fees (Area Res): $1735
Application Deadline: 8/31	Room & Board: N/Avail

GENERAL District-supported, 2-year, coed. Part of Michigan Department of Education. Awards certificates, transfer associate, terminal associate degrees. Founded 1923. *Setting:* 20-acre urban campus with easy access to Detroit. *Endowment:* $22.5 million. *Educational spending 1994–95:* $1609 per undergrad. *Total enrollment:* 9,754. *Faculty:* 412 (158 full-time, 14% with terminal degrees, 254 part-time); student-faculty ratio is 24:1.
ENROLLMENT PROFILE 9,754 students: 61% women, 39% men, 73% part-time, 99% state residents, 3% transferred in, 1% international, 49% 25 or older, 2% Native American, 2% Hispanic, 16% African American, 1% Asian American.
FIRST-YEAR CLASS 1,903 total; 4,222 applied, 100% were accepted, 45% of whom enrolled.
ACADEMIC PROGRAM Core, general education curriculum. Calendar: semesters. Academic remediation for entering students, English as a second language program offered during academic year, services for LD students, advanced placement, honors program, summer session for credit, part-time degree program (daytime, evenings, weekends, summer), adult/continuing education programs, co-op programs.
GENERAL DEGREE REQUIREMENTS 62 credit hours; math/science requirements vary according to program; computer course (varies by major).
MAJORS Accounting, architectural technologies, art/fine arts, automotive technologies, biology/biological sciences, business administration/commerce/management, business education, chemistry, computer information systems, computer technologies, construction technologies, corrections, criminal justice, culinary arts, deaf interpreter training, dental services, drafting and design, electrical and electronics technologies, electrical engineering technology, emergency medical technology, (pre)engineering sequence, food services management, gerontology, industrial engineering technology, laboratory technologies, law enforcement/police sciences, legal secretarial studies, liberal arts/general studies, marketing/retailing/merchandising, mechanical engineering technology, medical technology, music, nursing, occupational therapy, paralegal studies, photography, practical nursing, quality

control technology, radiological technology, recreation and leisure services, respiratory therapy, robotics, secretarial studies/office management, social work, teacher aide studies.
LIBRARY Charles Stewart Mott Library with 111,359 books, 350 periodicals, 2 CD-ROMs, 924 records, tapes, and CDs. Acquisition spending 1994–95: $40,012.
COMPUTERS ON CAMPUS 250 computers for student use in computer center, computer labs, classrooms, library provide access to main academic computer, e-mail. Staffed computer lab on campus provides training in use of computers, software. Academic computing expenditure 1994–95: $926,163.
COLLEGE LIFE Choral group, student-run newspaper. ***Social organizations:*** 22 open to all. ***Student services:*** health clinic, personal-psychological counseling. ***Campus security:*** 24-hour emergency response devices and patrols, late-night transport-escort service.
HOUSING College housing not available.
ATHLETICS Member NJCAA. ***Intercollegiate:*** baseball M(s), basketball M(s)/W(s), golf M(s), softball W(s), volleyball W(s). ***Contact:*** Mr. Ernie Myers, Athletic Director, 810-762-0419.
CAREER PLANNING ***Placement office:*** 3 full-time, 3 part-time staff; $101,703 operating expenditure 1994–95. ***Director:*** Ms. Gail Ives, Executive Director of Career and Job Placement Center, 810-762-0250. ***Services:*** resume preparation, resume referral, career counseling, careers library, job bank, job interviews.
EXPENSES FOR 1996–97 Area resident tuition: $1654 full-time, $53.35 per hour part-time. State resident tuition: $2385 full-time, $76.95 per hour part-time. Nonresident tuition: $3181 full-time, $102.60 per hour part-time. Part-time mandatory fees: $40.52 per semester. Full-time mandatory fees: $81.
FINANCIAL AID ***College-administered undergrad aid 1995–96:*** 1,631 need-based scholarships (average $120), 281 non-need scholarships (average $338), short-term loans (average $500), low-interest long-term loans from external sources (average $1730), Federal Work-Study, part-time jobs. ***Required forms:*** institutional, FAFSA. ***Priority deadline:*** 6/25. ***Payment plan:*** deferred payment. ***Waivers:*** full or partial for employees or children of employees and senior citizens.
APPLYING Open admission. ***Options:*** early entrance, deferred entrance, midyear entrance. ***Required:*** school transcript, Michigan Test of English Language Proficiency. ***Recommended:*** SAT I or ACT. Test scores used for counseling/placement. ***Application deadline:*** 8/31.
APPLYING/TRANSFER ***Required:*** college transcript. ***Entrance:*** noncompetitive. ***Application deadline:*** 8/31. ***Contact:*** Ms. Anne Burns, Faculty/Counselor/Transfer Coordinator, 810-762-0359.
CONTACT Mrs. Angela Reeves, Executive Director of Admissions and Records, Charles Stewart Mott Community College, 1401 East Court Street, Flint, MI 48503-2089, 810-762-0245. ***Fax:*** 810-762-0257.

DELTA COLLEGE
University Center, Michigan

UG Enrollment: 10,446 | **Tuition & Fees (Area Res): $1706**
Application Deadline: rolling | **Room & Board: N/Avail**

GENERAL District-supported, 2-year, coed. Part of Michigan Department of Education. Awards certificates, transfer associate, terminal associate degrees. Founded 1961. ***Setting:*** 640-acre rural campus. ***Endowment:*** $2.2 million. ***Total enrollment:*** 10,446. ***Faculty:*** 515 (215 full-time, 300 part-time); student-faculty ratio is 20:1.
ENROLLMENT PROFILE 10,446 students from 7 states and territories, 13 other countries. 61% women, 67% part-time, 98% state residents, 2% transferred in, 1% international, 43% 25 or older, 1% Native American, 4% Hispanic, 8% African American, 1% Asian American.
FIRST-YEAR CLASS 2,287 total; 3,567 applied, 100% were accepted, 64% of whom enrolled.
ACADEMIC PROGRAM Core, honor code. Calendar: semesters. Academic remediation for entering students, English as a second language program offered during academic year, services for LD students, advanced placement, self-designed majors, tutorials, honors program, summer session for credit, part-time degree program (daytime, evenings, weekends), adult/continuing education programs, co-op programs.
GENERAL DEGREE REQUIREMENTS 62 semester hours; 8 semester hours of math/science including at least 1 lab science course; computer course (varies by major).
MAJORS Accounting, agricultural business, agricultural sciences, agricultural technologies, applied art, architectural technologies, art education, automotive technologies, aviation technology, biology/biological sciences, broadcasting, business administration/commerce/management, business education, carpentry, chemical engineering technology, chemistry, child care/child and family studies, computer information systems, computer management, computer programming, computer science, construction management, construction technologies, corrections, criminal justice, data processing, dental services, dietetics, drafting and design, electrical engineering technology, electronics engineering technology, elementary education, (pre)engineering sequence, engineering technology, English, environmental sciences, fashion merchandising, finance/banking, fire science, forestry, funeral service, geology, home economics, industrial arts, interior design, journalism, law enforcement/police sciences, legal secretarial studies, legal studies, liberal arts/general studies, machine and tool technologies, marketing/retailing/merchandising, mechanical design technology, mechanical engineering technology, medical assistant technologies, medical secretarial studies, medical technology, music, music education, natural resource management, nursing, operating room technology, paralegal studies, physical therapy, printing technologies, psychology, radio and television studies, radiological technology, real estate, respiratory therapy, retail management, secretarial studies/office management, social work, theater arts/drama, water resources, welding technology.
LIBRARY Learning Resources Center with 98,100 books, 740 periodicals, 12 CD-ROMs, 500 records, tapes, and CDs. Acquisition spending 1994–95: $130,589.
COMPUTERS ON CAMPUS 310 computers for student use in computer center, computer labs, learning resource center, various department labs, library provide access to off-campus computing facilities. Staffed computer lab on campus provides training in use of computers, software. Academic computing expenditure 1994–95: $377,401.
COLLEGE LIFE Drama-theater group, choral group, student-run newspaper. ***Social organizations:*** 1 national fraternity. ***Most popular organizations:*** Honors Society, Student Senate, Phi Theta Kappa, Intervarsity Christian Fellowship. ***Major annual events:*** Earth Day, Bienvenidos, Global Awareness Week. ***Student services:*** health clinic, personal-psychological counseling. ***Campus security:*** 24-hour emergency response devices and patrols, student patrols, late-night transport-escort service.
HOUSING College housing not available.
ATHLETICS Member NJCAA. ***Intercollegiate:*** basketball M(s)/W(s), golf M, soccer M(s), volleyball W(s). ***Intramural:*** baseball, basketball, cross-country running, football, golf, racquetball, soccer, table tennis (Ping-Pong), tennis, volleyball. ***Contact:*** Mr. Lyn Conway, Director of Athletics, 517-686-9023.
CAREER PLANNING ***Placement office:*** 4 full-time, 6 part-time staff; $279,343 operating expenditure 1994–95. ***Director:*** Ms. Nancy Nickerson, Director, Career Planning and Placement, 517-686-9074. ***Services:*** job fairs, resume preparation, resume referral, career counseling, careers library, job bank, job interviews.
EXPENSES FOR 1995–96 Area resident tuition: $1666 full-time, $53.75 per semester hour part-time. State resident tuition: $2170 full-time, $70 per semester hour part-time. Nonresident tuition: $3100 full-time, $100 per semester hour part-time. Part-time mandatory fees: $20 per semester. Full-time mandatory fees: $40.
FINANCIAL AID ***College-administered undergrad aid 1995–96:*** 314 need-based scholarships (average $445), 160 non-need scholarships (average $865), short-term loans (average $575), low-interest long-term loans from external sources (average $1500), Federal Work-Study, part-time jobs. ***Required forms:*** institutional, FAFSA; accepted: CSS Financial Aid PROFILE, state, SINGLEFILE Form of United Student Aid Funds. ***Priority deadline:*** 5/1. ***Waivers:*** full or partial for employees or children of employees and senior citizens. ***Notification:*** continuous.
APPLYING Open admission except for foreign applicants. ***Options:*** Common Application, early entrance, deferred entrance, midyear entrance. ***Required:*** TOEFL for international students, ACT ASSET. Test scores used for counseling/placement. ***Application deadline:*** rolling.
APPLYING/TRANSFER ***Entrance:*** noncompetitive. ***Application deadline:*** rolling.
CONTACT Dr. Pat Graves, Director of Admissions, Delta College, University Center, MI 48710, 517-686-9092 or toll-free 800-285-1704 (in-state). ***Fax:*** 517-686-8736. ***E-mail:*** elvina_sika@delta.edu.

GLEN OAKS COMMUNITY COLLEGE
Centreville, Michigan

UG Enrollment: 1,190 | **Tuition & Fees (Area Res): $1519**
Application Deadline: rolling | **Room & Board: N/Avail**

GENERAL State and locally supported, 2-year, coed. Part of Michigan Department of Education. Awards certificates, transfer associate, terminal associate degrees. Founded 1965. ***Setting:*** 300-acre rural campus. ***Total enrollment:*** 1,190. ***Faculty:*** 96 (31 full-time, 7% with terminal degrees, 65 part-time); student-faculty ratio is 16:1.
ENROLLMENT PROFILE 1,190 students from 3 states and territories, 4 other countries. 57% women, 63% part-time, 83% state residents, 9% transferred in, 1% international, 47% 25 or older, 1% Native American, 1% Hispanic, 2% African American, 2% Asian American. ***Areas of study chosen:*** 34% business management and administrative services, 30% liberal arts/general studies, 16% engineering and applied sciences, 10% health professions and related sciences, 5% physical sciences. ***Most popular recent majors:*** liberal arts/general studies, business administration/commerce/management, nursing.
FIRST-YEAR CLASS 262 total; 529 applied, 100% were accepted.
ACADEMIC PROGRAM Core, interdisciplinary curriculum, honor code. Calendar: semesters. Academic remediation for entering students, services for LD students, advanced placement, summer session for credit, part-time degree program (daytime, evenings), adult/continuing education programs, internships.
GENERAL DEGREE REQUIREMENTS 62 credit hours; math/science requirements vary according to program; computer course (varies by major).
MAJORS Automotive technologies, business administration/commerce/management, liberal arts/general studies, nursing, science.
LIBRARY E. J. Shaheen Library plus 1 other, with 37,087 books, 181 microform titles, 294 periodicals, 1 on-line bibliographic service, 6 CD-ROMs, 1,113 records, tapes, and CDs.
COMPUTERS ON CAMPUS 15 computers for student use in Academic Opportunity Center, media center provide access to software. Staffed computer lab on campus provides training in use of computers, software.
COLLEGE LIFE ***Social organizations:*** 5 open to all. ***Most popular organizations:*** Student Government, Choir, Band, Phi Theta Kappa. ***Major annual events:*** College Picnic, Olympics. ***Student services:*** personal-psychological counseling. ***Campus security:*** 24-hour emergency response devices.
HOUSING College housing not available.
ATHLETICS Member NJCAA. ***Intercollegiate:*** baseball M, basketball M(s)/W(s), golf M(s), volleyball W(s). ***Intramural:*** baseball, basketball, table tennis (Ping-Pong). ***Contact:*** Mr. Tom Horn, Athletic Director, 616-467-9945 Ext. 216.
CAREER PLANNING ***Placement office:*** 1 full-time, 4 part-time staff. ***Director:*** Mrs. Cheryl Hayden, Director of Career Planning and Placement, 616-467-9945. ***Services:*** job fairs, resume preparation, resume referral, career counseling, careers library, job bank.
EXPENSES FOR 1996–97 Area resident tuition: $1395 full-time, $45 per credit hour part-time. State resident tuition: $1643 full-time, $53 per credit hour part-time. Part-time mandatory fees: $4 per credit hour. Full-time mandatory fees: $124.
FINANCIAL AID ***College-administered undergrad aid 1995–96:*** 104 need-based scholarships (average $244), 125 non-need scholarships (average $790), short-term loans (average $863), low-interest long-term loans from external sources (average $2375), 22 Federal Work-Study (averaging $495), 23 part-time jobs. ***Required forms:*** institutional; accepted: CSS Financial Aid PROFILE, FAFSA. ***Priority deadline:*** 5/1. ***Payment plan:*** deferred payment. ***Waivers:*** full or partial for employees or children of employees and senior citizens.
APPLYING Open admission. ***Option:*** midyear entrance. ***Required:*** ACT ASSET. Test scores used for counseling/placement. ***Application deadline:*** rolling.
APPLYING/TRANSFER ***Entrance:*** noncompetitive. ***Application deadline:*** rolling. ***Contact:*** Ms. Beverly M. Andrews, Registrar and Coordinator of Institutional Research, 616-467-9945.
CONTACT Ms. Beverly M. Andrews, Registrar and Coordinator of Institutional Research, Glen Oaks Community College, Centreville, MI 49032-9719, 616-467-9945. ***Fax:*** 616-467-4114. College video available.

GOGEBIC COMMUNITY COLLEGE
Ironwood, Michigan

UG Enrollment: 1,399 **Tuition & Fees (Area Res): $1246**
Application Deadline: rolling **Room & Board: N/Avail**

GENERAL State and locally supported, 2-year, coed. Part of Michigan Department of Education. Awards certificates, transfer associate, terminal associate degrees. Founded 1932. ***Setting:*** 195-acre small-town campus. ***Educational spending 1994–95:*** $1690 per undergrad. ***Total enrollment:*** 1,399. ***Faculty:*** 91 (34 full-time, 100% with terminal degrees, 57 part-time); student-faculty ratio is 15:1.
ENROLLMENT PROFILE 1,399 students from 7 states and territories, 8 other countries. 61% women, 51% part-time, 83% state residents, 12% transferred in, 43% have need-based financial aid, 1% international, 46% 25 or older, 2% Native American, 1% Hispanic, 1% African American, 1% Asian American. ***Areas of study chosen:*** 13% interdisciplinary studies, 8% engineering and applied sciences, 8% social sciences, 6% education, 1% natural resource sciences, 1% premed, 1% prevet. ***Most popular recent majors:*** nursing, business administration/commerce/management, computer technologies.
FIRST-YEAR CLASS 563 total. Of the students who applied, 100% were accepted, 54% of whom enrolled. 8% from top 10% of their high school class, 40% from top quarter, 60% from top half.
ACADEMIC PROGRAM Core. Calendar: semesters. 693 courses offered in 1995–96. Academic remediation for entering students, English as a second language program, services for LD students, advanced placement, honors program, summer session for credit, part-time degree program (daytime, evenings), adult/continuing education programs, co-op programs and internships.
GENERAL DEGREE REQUIREMENTS 63 credit hours; computer course for most majors; internship (some majors).
MAJORS Accounting, automotive technologies, biology/biological sciences, business administration/commerce/management, child care/child and family studies, commercial art, computer graphics, computer science, computer technologies, construction technologies, corrections, cosmetology, court reporting, criminal justice, data processing, drafting and design, early childhood education, education, engineering and applied sciences, food services management, hotel and restaurant management, humanities, legal secretarial studies, liberal arts/general studies, mathematics, medical records services, medical secretarial studies, nursing, paralegal studies, practical nursing, printing technologies, secretarial studies/office management, social science, social work, word processing.
LIBRARY Alex D. Chisholm Learning Resources Center with 25,166 books, 75 microform titles, 228 periodicals, 1,691 records, tapes, and CDs. Acquisition spending 1994–95: $155,165.
COMPUTERS ON CAMPUS 210 computers for student use in computer center, learning resource center, labs provide access to e-mail, on-line services. Staffed computer lab on campus provides training in use of computers, software. Academic computing expenditure 1994–95: $180,089.
COLLEGE LIFE Orientation program (2 days, $30, parents included). Drama-theater group, choral group, student-run newspaper. ***Most popular organizations:*** Drama Club, Student Senate. ***Major annual event:*** Snow Week. ***Student services:*** personal-psychological counseling.
HOUSING College housing not available.
ATHLETICS Member NJCAA. ***Intercollegiate:*** basketball M(s)/W(s). ***Intramural:*** basketball, bowling, football, golf, skiing (cross-country), skiing (downhill), tennis, track and field, volleyball. ***Contact:*** Mr. Dennis Routheaux, Athletic Director, 906-932-4231 Ext. 287.
CAREER PLANNING ***Placement office:*** 1 full-time, 2 part-time staff; $86,277 operating expenditure 1994–95. ***Director:*** Ms. Pamela Peterson, Director of Counseling and Placement, 906-932-4231 Ext. 214. ***Services:*** job fairs, resume preparation, career counseling, careers library, job bank. Students must register sophomore year.
EXPENSES FOR 1996–97 ***Application fee:*** $5. Area resident tuition: $1116 full-time, $36 per credit hour part-time. Nonresident tuition: $1550 full-time, $50 per credit hour part-time. Part-time mandatory fees per semester range from $2 to $30. Full-time mandatory fees: $130.
FINANCIAL AID ***College-administered undergrad aid 1995–96:*** 71 need-based scholarships (averaging $250), 43 non-need scholarships (averaging $250), low-interest long-term loans from external sources (averaging $2022), Federal Work-Study, part-time jobs. ***Required forms for some financial aid applicants:*** state, institutional; accepted: CSS Financial Aid PROFILE, FAFSA. ***Priority deadline:*** 4/1. ***Waivers:*** full or partial for employees or children of employees and senior citizens.
APPLYING Open admission. ***Options:*** early entrance, deferred entrance, midyear entrance. ***Required:*** school transcript, TOEFL for international students. ***Recommended:*** ACT. Test scores used for counseling/placement. ***Application deadlines:*** rolling, 8/15 for nonresidents. ***Notification:*** continuous.
APPLYING/TRANSFER ***Required:*** high school transcript, college transcript. ***Recommended:*** standardized test scores. ***Entrance:*** noncompetitive. ***Application deadline:*** 8/15.
CONTACT Ms. Jeanne Wood, Admissions Coordinator, Gogebic Community College, Ironwood, MI 49938, 906-932-4231 Ext. 306 or toll-free 800-682-5910 (in-state). ***Fax:*** 906-932-0868.

GRAND RAPIDS COMMUNITY COLLEGE
Grand Rapids, Michigan

UG Enrollment: 13,934 **Tuition & Fees (Area Res): $1672**
Application Deadline: 8/23 **Room & Board: N/Avail**

GENERAL District-supported, 2-year, coed. Part of Michigan Department of Education. Awards certificates, transfer associate, terminal associate degrees. Founded 1914. ***Setting:*** 35-acre urban campus. ***Endowment:*** $5.3 million. ***Educational spending 1994–95:*** $1862 per undergrad. ***Total enrollment:*** 13,934. ***Faculty:*** 549 (244 full-time, 305 part-time); student-faculty ratio is 30:1. ***Notable Alumni:*** Dr. William F. LaPenna, cardiologist, administrator, and instructor; Gary J. Horton, executive vice president and director of Creative Services DMB&B Chicago; Doyle A. Hayes, vice president of human resources for Diesel Technology Company.
ENROLLMENT PROFILE 13,934 students: 49% women, 51% men, 68% part-time, 99% state residents, 0% live on campus, 5% transferred in, 1% international, 24% 25 or older, 1% Native American, 3% Hispanic, 6% African American, 3% Asian American.
FIRST-YEAR CLASS 3,719 total; 4,682 applied, 88% were accepted, 90% of whom enrolled.
ACADEMIC PROGRAM Core, honor code. Calendar: semesters. Average class size 30 in required courses. Academic remediation for entering students, English as a second language program offered during academic year, services for LD students, advanced placement, summer session for credit, part-time degree program (daytime, evenings, summer), adult/continuing education programs, co-op programs and internships. Study abroad in England, Italy.
GENERAL DEGREE REQUIREMENTS 62 credits; 8 credits each of math and natural science including at least 1 lab science course; computer course for health sciences, manufacturing, medical technology, natural resources management, nuclear medicine, packaging, physics, surveying majors.
MAJORS Accounting, architectural technologies, art/fine arts, automotive technologies, business administration/commerce/management, child care/child and family studies, communication, computer information systems, computer programming, computer science, computer technologies, corrections, criminal justice, culinary arts, data processing, dental services, drafting and design, electrical and electronics technologies, engineering sciences, (pre)engineering sequence, environmental health sciences, fashion design and technology, fashion merchandising, fire science, food services technology, forestry, geology, gerontology, health science, heating/refrigeration/air conditioning, hotel and restaurant management, interior design, law enforcement/police sciences, legal secretarial studies, liberal arts/general studies, manufacturing technology, marketing/retailing/merchandising, medical secretarial studies, music, nursing, occupational therapy, plastics technology, practical nursing, quality control technology, radiological technology, science, secretarial studies/office management, welding technology.
LIBRARY Arthur Andrews Memorial Library plus 1 other, with 53,000 books, 148 microform titles, 707 periodicals, 15 CD-ROMs, 310 records, tapes, and CDs. Acquisition spending 1994–95: $99,000.
COMPUTERS ON CAMPUS 600 computers for student use in computer labs, Applied Technology Center, classrooms, library provide access to main academic computer, Internet. Staffed computer lab on campus provides training in use of computers, software. Academic computing expenditure 1994–95: $808,000.
COLLEGE LIFE Orientation program (2 days, no cost, parents included). Drama-theater group, choral group, marching band, student-run newspaper. ***Social organizations:*** 28 open to all. ***Most popular organizations:*** Student Congress, Phi Theta Kappa, Christian Fellowship, Delta Pi Alpha, Service Learning Advisory Board. ***Major annual events:*** Finals Relaxer, Orientation Week, Entertainment Series. ***Student services:*** personal-psychological counseling. ***Campus security:*** 24-hour emergency response devices, late-night transport-escort service.
HOUSING College housing not available.
ATHLETICS Member NJCAA. ***Intercollegiate:*** baseball M/W(s), basketball M(s)/W(s), football M(s), golf M(s), softball W(s), swimming and diving M(s)/W(s), tennis M(s)/W(s), track and field M(s), volleyball W(s), wrestling M(s). ***Intramural:*** badminton, basketball, skiing (cross-country), skiing (downhill), soccer, swimming and diving, tennis, volleyball. ***Contact:*** Mr. Emil Caprara, Athletic Director, 616-771-3990.
CAREER PLANNING ***Placement office:*** 4 full-time staff; $164,500 operating expenditure 1994–95. ***Director:*** Mr. Paul Phifer, Director of Career Resource Center, 616-771-3891. ***Services:*** career counseling, careers library.
EXPENSES FOR 1995–96 ***Application fee:*** $20. Area resident tuition: $1612 full-time, $52 per credit part-time. State resident tuition: $2387 full-time, $77 per credit part-time. Nonresident tuition: $2821 full-time, $91 per credit part-time. Part-time mandatory fees per semester (6 to 11 credits): $20. Full-time mandatory fees: $60.
FINANCIAL AID ***College-administered undergrad aid 1995–96:*** need-based scholarships, non-need scholarships, short-term loans (average $150), low-interest long-term loans from external sources (average $1985), 272 Federal Work-Study, 186 part-time jobs. ***Required forms:*** FAFSA; accepted: CSS Financial Aid PROFILE, state. ***Priority deadline:*** 7/1.
APPLYING Open admission except for foreign students, allied health programs. ***Options:*** early entrance, deferred entrance, midyear entrance. ***Required:*** school transcript, TOEFL for international students. ***Recommended:*** 3 years of high school math and science, some high school foreign language, SAT I or ACT. ***Required for some:*** ACT ASSET. Test scores used for admission (TOEFL) and counseling/placement (ACT or ACT ASSET). ***Application deadline:*** 8/23. ***Notification:*** continuous.
APPLYING/TRANSFER ***Required:*** college transcript. ***Recommended:*** standardized test scores, 3 years of high school math and science, some high school foreign language. ***Required for some:*** standardized test scores. ***Entrance:*** noncompetitive. ***Application deadline:*** 8/23. ***Notification:*** continuous. ***Contact:*** Mr. Glenn Burgett, Chairperson, Counseling, 616-771-4130.
CONTACT Ms. Diane Defelice Patrick, Director of Admissions, Grand Rapids Community College, 143 Bostwick NE, Grand Rapids, MI 49503-3201, 616-771-4100. ***Fax:*** 616-771-4005.

GREAT LAKES JUNIOR COLLEGE OF BUSINESS
Saginaw, Michigan

UG Enrollment: 1,606 **Tuition & Fees: $5800**
Application Deadline: rolling **Room & Board: N/Avail**

GENERAL Independent, 2-year, coed. Awards certificates, transfer associate, terminal associate degrees. Founded 1907. ***Setting:*** urban campus. ***Total enrollment:*** 1,606. ***Faculty:*** 124 (36 full-time, 96% with terminal degrees, 88 part-time); student-faculty ratio is 18:1.
ENROLLMENT PROFILE 1,606 students: 83% women, 17% men, 74% part-time, 100% state residents, 30% transferred in, 0% international, 70% 25 or older, 0% Native American, 4% Hispanic, 10% African American, 0% Asian American. ***Areas of study chosen:*** 47% business management and administrative services, 39% health professions and related sciences, 10% computer and information sciences, 4% engineering and applied sciences. ***Most popular recent majors:*** business administration/commerce/management, paralegal studies, medical assistant technologies.
FIRST-YEAR CLASS 620 total; 1,200 applied, 90% were accepted, 57% of whom enrolled.

ACADEMIC PROGRAM Core, general education curriculum, honor code. Calendar: semesters. 823 courses offered in 1995–96. Academic remediation for entering students, summer session for credit, part-time degree program (daytime, evenings, summer), co-op programs and internships.
GENERAL DEGREE REQUIREMENTS 60 semester hours; 3 semester hours of math; computer course; internship (some majors).
MAJORS Accounting, biomedical technologies, business administration/commerce/management, computer programming, court reporting, data processing, electrical and electronics technologies, emergency medical technology, finance/banking, medical assistant technologies, medical secretarial studies, nursing, paralegal studies, secretarial studies/office management, word processing.
LIBRARY Great Lakes Junior College Library plus 5 others, with 35,200 books, 258 periodicals, 17 CD-ROMs, 3,609 records, tapes, and CDs. Acquisition spending 1994–95: $80,901.
COMPUTERS ON CAMPUS 197 computers for student use in computer center, computer labs, learning resource center, library provide access to on-line services. Staffed computer lab on campus provides training in use of computers, software. Academic computing expenditure 1994–95: $215,900.
COLLEGE LIFE ***Social organizations:*** 1 open to all. ***Major annual events:*** Honors Convocations, Commencement. ***Campus security:*** 24-hour emergency response devices.
HOUSING College housing not available.
CAREER PLANNING ***Placement office:*** 5 full-time, 1 part-time staff; $255,923 operating expenditure 1994–95. ***Director:*** Ms. Angela Rudy, Academic Dean, 517-755-3457. ***Services:*** resume preparation, resume referral, career counseling, careers library, job bank, job interviews.
AFTER GRADUATION 94% of class of 1994 had job offers within 6 months. 6% of students completing a degree program went directly on to further study.
EXPENSES FOR 1996–97 ***Application fee:*** $20. Tuition: $5760 full-time, $192 per semester hour part-time. Part-time mandatory fees: $20 per semester. Full-time mandatory fees: $40.
FINANCIAL AID ***College-administered undergrad aid 1995–96:*** need-based scholarships, 20 non-need scholarships (average $2400), low-interest long-term loans from college funds (average $2000), loans from external sources (average $2625), 44 Federal Work-Study (averaging $2531), 25 part-time jobs. ***Required forms:*** institutional, FAFSA; required for some: state. ***Priority deadline:*** 3/15. ***Payment plan:*** tuition prepayment.
APPLYING Open admission. ***Options:*** early entrance, deferred entrance, midyear entrance. ***Required:*** school transcript. Test scores used for counseling/placement. ***Application deadline:*** rolling.
APPLYING/TRANSFER ***Required:*** college transcript. ***Entrance:*** noncompetitive. ***Application deadline:*** rolling. ***Contact:*** Ms. Elizabeth Raabe, Registrar, 517-755-3457.
CONTACT Mr. William Guerriero, President, Great Lakes Junior College of Business, 320 South Washington Avenue, Saginaw, MI 48607-1158, 517-755-3457.

HENRY FORD COMMUNITY COLLEGE
Dearborn, Michigan

UG Enrollment: 13,300	Tuition & Fees (Area Res): $1982
Application Deadline: rolling	Room & Board: N/Avail

GENERAL District-supported, 2-year, coed. Awards certificates, transfer associate, terminal associate degrees. Founded 1938. ***Setting:*** 75-acre suburban campus with easy access to Detroit. ***Total enrollment:*** 13,300. ***Faculty:*** 994 (203 full-time, 791 part-time).
ENROLLMENT PROFILE 13,300 students from 3 states and territories, 35 other countries. 51% women, 49% men, 76% part-time, 98% state residents, 5% transferred in, 22% have need-based financial aid, 7% have non-need-based financial aid, 1% international, 44% 25 or older, 1% Native American, 3% Hispanic, 15% African American, 2% Asian American. ***Areas of study chosen:*** 18% liberal arts/general studies, 9% engineering and applied sciences, 5% business management and administrative services, 3% computer and information sciences, 3% health professions and related sciences, 2% architecture, 2% education, 2% fine arts, 1% biological and life sciences, 1% communications and journalism, 1% English language/literature/letters, 1% performing arts, 1% social sciences. ***Most popular recent majors:*** liberal arts/general studies, business administration/commerce/management.
FIRST-YEAR CLASS 3,259 total; 4,655 applied, 100% were accepted, 70% of whom enrolled.
ACADEMIC PROGRAM Core, liberal arts, pre-professional, and technical curriculum, honor code. Calendar: semesters. 1,700 courses offered in 1995–96. Academic remediation for entering students, English as a second language program offered during academic year, services for LD students, advanced placement, Freshman Honors College, tutorials, honors program, summer session for credit, part-time degree program (daytime, evenings, weekends, summer), adult/continuing education programs, co-op programs and internships. Study-abroad program.
GENERAL DEGREE REQUIREMENT 60 semester hours.
MAJORS Accounting, applied art, art/fine arts, automotive technologies, business administration/commerce/management, business machine technologies, ceramic art and design, commercial art, communication, computer information systems, computer science, construction technologies, corrections, criminal justice, culinary arts, data processing, drafting and design, electrical and electronics technologies, emergency medical technology, energy management technologies, (pre)engineering sequence, fire science, food services management, food services technology, graphic arts, heating/refrigeration/air conditioning, hospitality services, hotel and restaurant management, industrial engineering technology, information science, instrumentation technology, interior design, law enforcement/police sciences, legal secretarial studies, liberal arts/general studies, manufacturing technology, marketing/retailing/merchandising, materials sciences, medical assistant technologies, medical records services, medical secretarial studies, nursing, painting/drawing, paralegal studies, physical fitness/exercise science, quality control technology, real estate, respiratory therapy, robotics, secretarial studies/office management, theater arts/drama, transportation technologies.
LIBRARY Eshleman Library with 80,000 books, 600 microform titles, 650 periodicals, 9 CD-ROMs, 10,000 records, tapes, and CDs. Acquisition spending 1994–95: $135,776.
COMPUTERS ON CAMPUS 250 computers for student use in computer center, computer labs, learning resource center, business, automotive service technologies departments, library provide access to main academic computer, Internet. Staffed computer lab on campus (open 24 hours a day) provides training in use of computers, software. Academic computing expenditure 1994–95: $1 million.
COLLEGE LIFE Drama-theater group, choral group, student-run newspaper, radio station. ***Social organizations:*** 10 open to all. ***Most popular organizations:*** Phi Theta Kappa, Student Nurses, Future Teachers, ASAD (American Students of African Descent), Intervarsity Christian Fellowship. ***Major annual events:*** Theater/Concerts, Welcome Back Week. ***Student services:*** personal-psychological counseling, women's center. ***Campus security:*** 24-hour emergency response devices and patrols, late-night transport-escort service.
HOUSING College housing not available.
ATHLETICS Member NJCAA. ***Intercollegiate:*** baseball M(s), basketball M(s)/W(s), golf M(s), softball W(s), tennis M(s)/W(s), track and field M(s), volleyball W(s). ***Intramural:*** badminton, basketball, bowling, golf, racquetball, sailing, softball, tennis, volleyball, weight lifting. ***Contact:*** Mr. William Wilkinson, Coordinator of Registration/Records/Athletics, 313-845-9614 Ext. 9237.
CAREER PLANNING ***Placement office:*** 1 full-time staff; $82,510 operating expenditure 1994–95. ***Director:*** Mr. Gerald Olszewski, Director of Counseling, 313-845-9752. ***Services:*** job fairs, resume preparation, resume referral, career counseling, careers library, job bank, job interviews. 100 organizations recruited on campus 1994–95.
EXPENSES FOR 1995–96 ***Application fee:*** $20. Area resident tuition: $1702 full-time, $47 per credit hour part-time. State resident tuition: $2478 full-time, $73 per credit hour part-time. Nonresident tuition: $2777 full-time, $83 per credit hour part-time. Part-time mandatory fees: $7 per credit hour. Full-time mandatory fees: $280. Tuition guaranteed not to increase for student's term of enrollment.
FINANCIAL AID ***College-administered undergrad aid 1995–96:*** 2,587 need-based scholarships, short-term loans (averaging $100), low-interest long-term loans from external sources (averaging $1671), 249 Federal Work-Study (averaging $1024), 40 part-time jobs. ***Required forms:*** FAFSA. ***Priority deadline:*** 4/1. ***Waivers:*** full or partial for employees or children of employees and senior citizens. ***Notification:*** 4/2.
APPLYING Open admission except for nursing, allied health, honors programs. ***Options:*** early entrance, deferred entrance, midyear entrance. ***Required:*** TOEFL for international students. ***Recommended:*** school transcript, ACT. ***Required for some:*** ACT. Test scores used for counseling/placement. ***Application deadline:*** rolling. ***Notification:*** continuous.
APPLYING/TRANSFER ***Recommended:*** standardized test scores, high school transcript, college transcript. ***Entrance:*** noncompetitive. ***Application deadline:*** rolling. ***Notification:*** continuous.
CONTACT Ms. Dorothy A. Murphy, Coordinator of Recruitment, Henry Ford Community College, Dearborn, MI 48128-1495, 313-845-9766. ***Fax:*** 313-845-9658. ***E-mail:*** dorothy@mail.henryford.cc.mi.us. College video available.

HIGHLAND PARK COMMUNITY COLLEGE
Highland Park, Michigan

Enrollment: N/R	Tuition & Fees (MI Res): $1700
Application Deadline: rolling	Room & Board: N/Avail

GENERAL State and locally supported, 2-year, coed. Part of Michigan Department of Education. Awards certificates, diplomas, transfer associate, terminal associate degrees. Founded 1918. ***Setting:*** 3-acre small-town campus with easy access to Detroit. ***Faculty:*** 42. ***Notable Alumni:*** Jackie Vaughn III, Michigan state senator; Larry Wilkerson, certified public accountant; Comer Heath III, educator; Martha Scott, state representative; Elliott Hall, attorney.
ENROLLMENT PROFILE 70% women, 49% part-time, 98% state residents, 5% transferred in, 2% international, 50% 25 or older, 1% Native American, 1% Hispanic, 90% African American, 2% Asian American. ***Most popular recent majors:*** nursing, liberal arts/general studies.
FIRST-YEAR CLASS Of the students who applied, 100% were accepted, 38% of whom enrolled. 1% from top 10% of their high school class, 40% from top half.
ACADEMIC PROGRAM Core, honor code. Calendar: semesters. Academic remediation for entering students, summer session for credit, part-time degree program (daytime, evenings, summer), adult/continuing education programs.
GENERAL DEGREE REQUIREMENTS 60 semester hours; 1 math course; computer course (varies by major).
MAJORS Accounting, automotive technologies, child care/child and family studies, computer science, criminal justice, data processing, drafting and design, electrical and electronics technologies, (pre)engineering sequence, health services administration, hotel and restaurant management, legal secretarial studies, liberal arts/general studies, medical assistant technologies, medical laboratory technology, medical records services, medical secretarial studies, medical technology, nursing, operating room technology, practical nursing, secretarial studies/office management, welding technology.
LIBRARY 18,000 books, 150 periodicals, 2,187 records, tapes, and CDs.
COMPUTERS ON CAMPUS 60 computers for student use in computer center, learning resource center, library.
COLLEGE LIFE Drama-theater group, student-run newspaper. 15% vote in student government elections. ***Student services:*** personal-psychological counseling. ***Campus security:*** 24-hour emergency response devices and patrols.
HOUSING College housing not available.
ATHLETICS Member NJCAA. ***Intercollegiate:*** baseball M, basketball M(s)/W(s), cross-country running M. ***Intramural:*** cross-country running. ***Contact:*** Dr. Paul Merritt, Dean, 313-252-0475 Ext. 299.
CAREER PLANNING ***Director:*** Mr. Mosby Dixon, Director, 313-252-0475 Ext. 375. ***Service:*** career counseling.
EXPENSES FOR 1995–96 ***Application fee:*** $20. State resident tuition: $1650 full-time, $55 per semester hour part-time. Nonresident tuition: $1950 full-time, $65 per semester hour part-time. Full-time mandatory fees: $50.
FINANCIAL AID ***College-administered undergrad aid 1995–96:*** need-based scholarships, 10 non-need scholarships, low-interest long-term loans from external sources (averaging $2625), Federal Work-Study, part-time jobs. ***Required forms:*** FAFSA; accepted: CSS Financial Aid PROFILE. ***Application deadline:*** continuous to 8/15.
APPLYING Open admission except for nursing, respiratory care programs. ***Options:*** early entrance, deferred entrance. ***Recommended:*** TOEFL for international students. ***Required for some:*** TOEFL for international students. Test scores used for counseling/placement. ***Application deadline:*** rolling. ***Notification:*** continuous until 8/20. Preference given to local residents.
APPLYING/TRANSFER ***Application deadline:*** rolling. ***Notification:*** continuous until 8/20.

Highland Park Community College (continued)
CONTACT Mrs. Ameenah Omar, Director of Admissions and Records, Highland Park Community College, Highland Park, MI 48203, 313-252-0475 Ext. 240.

JACKSON COMMUNITY COLLEGE
Jackson, Michigan

UG Enrollment: 7,100 **Tuition & Fees (Area Res): $1513**
Application Deadline: rolling **Room & Board: N/Avail**

GENERAL County-supported, 2-year, coed. Part of Michigan Department of Education. Awards transfer associate, terminal associate degrees. Founded 1928. ***Setting:*** 580-acre suburban campus with easy access to Detroit. ***Total enrollment:*** 7,100. ***Faculty:*** 435 (110 full-time, 13% with terminal degrees, 325 part-time); student-faculty ratio is 18:1.
ENROLLMENT PROFILE 7,100 students from 4 states and territories. 62% women, 38% men, 73% part-time, 99% state residents, 8% transferred in, 0% international, 55% 25 or older, 1% Native American, 3% Hispanic, 5% African American, 1% Asian American.
FIRST-YEAR CLASS 1,100 total; 2,812 applied, 100% were accepted, 39% of whom enrolled.
ACADEMIC PROGRAM Core, interdisciplinary curriculum, honor code. Calendar: semesters. Academic remediation for entering students, English as a second language program offered during academic year, services for LD students, advanced placement, summer session for credit, part-time degree program (daytime, evenings, weekends, summer), external degree programs, adult/continuing education programs, co-op programs and internships.
GENERAL DEGREE REQUIREMENTS 63 credit hours; 3 credit hours of math; 4 credit hours of science; computer course.
MAJORS Accounting, advertising, automotive technologies, aviation technology, business administration/commerce/management, corrections, criminal justice, data processing, drafting and design, electrical engineering technology, electronics engineering technology, environmental engineering technology, finance/banking, flight training, hospitality services, industrial engineering technology, law enforcement/police sciences, legal secretarial studies, liberal arts/general studies, machine and tool technologies, manufacturing technology, marketing/retailing/merchandising, medical assistant technologies, medical secretarial studies, medical technology, nursing, practical nursing, radiological technology, robotics, secretarial studies/office management.
LIBRARY Atkinson Learning Resources Center with 52,000 books, 9,100 microform titles, 260 periodicals, 1 on-line bibliographic service, 12 CD-ROMs, 3,510 records, tapes, and CDs. Acquisition spending 1994–95: $22,300.
COMPUTERS ON CAMPUS Computer purchase plan available. 150 computers for student use in computer center, computer labs, writing lab, business lab, library provide access to e-mail, Internet. Academic computing expenditure 1994–95: $281,000.
COLLEGE LIFE Drama-theater group, choral group, student-run newspaper. ***Social organizations:*** 10 open to all. ***Most popular organizations:*** Student Senate, Nontraditional Student Association, Black Student Union. ***Major annual events:*** Halloween Happening, Dick Wendt Charity Event, Community Pow Wow. ***Student services:*** personal-psychological counseling. ***Campus security:*** 24-hour patrols.
HOUSING College housing not available.
ATHLETICS ***Intramural:*** baseball, basketball, golf, racquetball, soccer, softball, tennis, volleyball, weight lifting.
CAREER PLANNING ***Placement office:*** $220,000 operating expenditure 1994–95. ***Services:*** job fairs, resume preparation, resume referral, career counseling, careers library, job bank, job interviews.
EXPENSES FOR 1995–96 Area resident tuition: $1497 full-time, $47.50 per contact hour part-time. State resident tuition: $1922 full-time, $61 per contact hour part-time. Nonresident tuition: $2174 full-time, $69 per contact hour part-time. Part-time mandatory fees: $8 per semester. Full-time mandatory fees: $16.
FINANCIAL AID ***College-administered undergrad aid 1995–96:*** 441 need-based scholarships (average $338), 263 non-need scholarships (average $986), short-term loans, low-interest long-term loans from external sources (average $1415), Federal Work-Study, 146 part-time jobs. ***Required forms:*** CSS Financial Aid PROFILE, institutional, FAFSA. ***Priority deadline:*** 4/1. ***Waivers:*** full or partial for employees or children of employees.
APPLYING Open admission except for allied health programs. ***Option:*** early entrance. ***Recommended:*** ACT. Test scores used for counseling/placement. ***Application deadline:*** rolling. ***Notification:*** continuous. Preference given to county residents.
APPLYING/TRANSFER ***Application deadline:*** rolling. ***Notification:*** continuous.
CONTACT Mr. Mark Ulseth, Director of Enrollment Services, Jackson Community College, Jackson, MI 49201-8399, 517-787-0800 Ext. 122.

KALAMAZOO VALLEY COMMUNITY COLLEGE
Kalamazoo, Michigan

UG Enrollment: 11,027 **Tuition & Fees (Area Res): $1178**
Application Deadline: rolling **Room & Board: N/Avail**

GENERAL State and locally supported, 2-year, coed. Part of Michigan Department of Education. Awards certificates, transfer associate, terminal associate degrees. Founded 1966. ***Setting:*** 187-acre suburban campus. ***Total enrollment:*** 11,027. ***Faculty:*** 366 (114 full-time, 252 part-time).
ENROLLMENT PROFILE 11,027 students from 4 states and territories, 35 other countries. 56% women, 44% men, 76% part-time, 98% state residents, 3% transferred in, 1% international, 43% 25 or older, 1% Native American, 2% Hispanic, 8% African American, 1% Asian American. ***Areas of study chosen:*** 10% engineering and applied sciences.
FIRST-YEAR CLASS 2,120 total; 3,778 applied, 100% were accepted, 56% of whom enrolled.
ACADEMIC PROGRAM Core, honor code. Calendar: semesters. Academic remediation for entering students, English as a second language program offered during academic year and summer, services for LD students, self-designed majors, honors program, summer session for credit, part-time degree program (daytime, evenings), co-op programs and internships. Off-campus study at 5 members of the Kalamazoo Consortium. ROTC: Army (c).
GENERAL DEGREE REQUIREMENTS 62 semester hours; math/science requirements vary according to program; internship (some majors).
MAJORS Accounting, automotive technologies, biology/biological sciences, business administration/commerce/management, computer information systems, computer programming, data processing, dental services, drafting and design, education, electrical and electronics technologies, electronics engineering technology, emergency medical technology, (pre)engineering sequence, fire science, gerontology, health science, heating/refrigeration/air conditioning, international studies, law enforcement/police sciences, legal secretarial studies, liberal arts/general studies, machine and tool technologies, marketing/retailing/merchandising, materials sciences, mechanical engineering technology, medical assistant technologies, medical secretarial studies, nursing, plastics technology, respiratory therapy, science, secretarial studies/office management, welding technology.
LIBRARY 83,304 books, 3,044 microform titles, 470 periodicals.
COMPUTERS ON CAMPUS Computer purchase plan available. 350 computers for student use in computer center, computer labs, classrooms, library. Staffed computer lab on campus provides training in use of computers, software.
COLLEGE LIFE Choral group, student-run newspaper. ***Social organizations:*** 20 open to all. ***Student services:*** personal-psychological counseling, women's center. ***Campus security:*** 24-hour emergency response devices, late-night transport-escort service.
HOUSING College housing not available.
ATHLETICS Member NJCAA. ***Intercollegiate:*** baseball M(s), basketball M(s)/W(s), golf M(s), softball W(s), tennis M(s)/W(s), volleyball W(s). ***Intramural:*** softball, tennis, volleyball. ***Contact:*** Mr. Richard Shilts, Director of Athletics, 616-372-3395.
CAREER PLANNING ***Placement office:*** 2 full-time staff. ***Director:*** Mr. Richard Kabat, Assistant Vice President for Student Services, 616-372-5346. ***Services:*** job fairs, resume referral, career counseling, careers library, job bank.
EXPENSES FOR 1996–97 Area resident tuition: $1178 full-time, $38 per credit hour part-time. State resident tuition: $2201 full-time, $71 per credit hour part-time. Nonresident tuition: $3224 full-time, $104 per credit hour part-time.
FINANCIAL AID ***College-administered undergrad aid 1995–96:*** need-based scholarships, non-need scholarships, Federal Work-Study, part-time jobs. ***Required forms:*** institutional, FAFSA; accepted: CSS Financial Aid PROFILE. ***Priority deadline:*** 5/1. ***Waivers:*** full or partial for employees or children of employees and senior citizens.
APPLYING Open admission. ***Options:*** early entrance, deferred entrance, midyear entrance. ***Required:*** TOEFL for international students. Test scores used for counseling/placement. ***Application deadline:*** rolling. ***Notification:*** continuous.
APPLYING/TRANSFER ***Entrance:*** noncompetitive. ***Application deadline:*** rolling. ***Notification:*** continuous. ***Contact:*** Mr. Murray Maurer, Records Officer, 616-372-5357.
CONTACT Mr. Michael McCall, Director of Admissions and Registrar, Kalamazoo Valley Community College, Kalamazoo, MI 49003-4070, 616-372-5207.

KELLOGG COMMUNITY COLLEGE
Battle Creek, Michigan

UG Enrollment: 9,012 **Tuition & Fees (Area Res): $1427**
Application Deadline: 8/29 **Room & Board: N/Avail**

GENERAL State and locally supported, 2-year, coed. Part of Michigan Department of Education. Awards certificates, transfer associate, terminal associate degrees. Founded 1956. ***Setting:*** 120-acre urban campus. ***Endowment:*** $1.2 million. ***Total enrollment:*** 9,012. ***Faculty:*** 340 (99 full-time, 100% with terminal degrees, 241 part-time); student-faculty ratio is 30:1. ***Notable Alumni:*** Carole Finley Edmonds, Major General Fred A. Gorden, Dr. Virginia E. Keck.
ENROLLMENT PROFILE 9,012 students from 4 states and territories, 26 other countries. 57% women, 73% part-time, 98% state residents, 2% transferred in, 40% have need-based financial aid, 10% have non-need-based financial aid, 1% international, 51% 25 or older, 1% Native American, 2% Hispanic, 8% African American, 1% Asian American. ***Areas of study chosen:*** 10% education, 5% communications and journalism, 5% engineering and applied sciences, 5% fine arts, 5% performing arts, 5% premed, 5% prevet, 2% social sciences. ***Most popular recent majors:*** business administration/commerce/management, nursing, law enforcement/police sciences.
FIRST-YEAR CLASS 618 total; 1,743 applied, 100% were accepted.
ACADEMIC PROGRAM Core, honor code. Calendar: semesters. 1,499 courses offered in 1995–96. Academic remediation for entering students, English as a second language program offered during academic year and summer, services for LD students, advanced placement, Freshman Honors College, tutorials, honors program, summer session for credit, part-time degree program (daytime, evenings, weekends, summer), adult/continuing education programs, co-op programs and internships. Off-campus study at Kalamazoo Valley Community College, Southwestern Michigan College, Lake Michigan College, Jackson Community College.
GENERAL DEGREE REQUIREMENTS 62 credit hours; computer course for accounting, business management, chemical technology, human services, legal assistant, communications technology, secretarial studies majors.
MAJORS Accounting, anthropology, art education, art/fine arts, arts administration, biology/biological sciences, broadcasting, business administration/commerce/management, chemical engineering technology, chemistry, child care/child and family studies, commercial art, communication, computer information systems, computer programming, computer technologies, corrections, criminal justice, data processing, dental services, drafting and design, education, electrical and electronics technologies, electronics engineering technology, elementary education, emergency medical technology, (pre)engineering sequence, English, finance/banking, fire science, gerontology, graphic arts, history, human services, industrial engineering technology, international studies, journalism, law enforcement/police sciences, legal secretarial studies, legal studies, liberal arts/general studies, machine and tool technologies, manufacturing technology, mathematics, medical laboratory technology, medical secretarial studies, music, natural sciences, nursing, paralegal studies, pharmacy/pharmaceutical sciences, philosophy, physical education, physical therapy, physics, political science/government, practical nursing, psychology, public relations, radio and television studies, radiological technology, robotics, science, secretarial studies/office management, social work, sociology, speech/rhetoric/public address/debate, studio art, technical writing, theater arts/drama, veterinary sciences, welding technology.
LIBRARY Emory W. Morris Learning Resource Center with 48,442 books, 260 microform titles, 264 periodicals, 7 on-line bibliographic services, 15 CD-ROMs, 2,045 records, tapes, and CDs. Acquisition spending 1994–95: $37,268.

COMPUTERS ON CAMPUS Computer purchase plan available. 350 computers for student use in computer center, learning resource center, labs, classrooms, library. Staffed computer lab on campus provides training in use of computers, software. Academic computing expenditure 1994–95: $258,696.
COLLEGE LIFE Drama-theater group, choral group, student-run newspaper, radio station. 4% vote in student government elections. *Social organizations:* 23 open to all; 23 social clubs; 13% of eligible men and 25% of eligible women are members. *Most popular organizations:* Tech Club, Student Government, Bruin Christian Fellowship, Criminal Justice Association, Human Services Organization. *Major annual events:* Back to School Bash, Movies, Blood Drive. *Student services:* personal-psychological counseling. *Campus security:* 24-hour emergency response devices and patrols, late-night transport-escort service.
HOUSING College housing not available.
ATHLETICS Member NJCAA. *Intercollegiate:* baseball M(s), basketball M(s)/W(s), golf M, softball W(s), volleyball W(s). *Intramural:* basketball, bowling, racquetball, skiing (cross-country), soccer, tennis, volleyball, weight lifting. *Contact:* Mr. Douglas Dowdy, Director of Athletics, 616-965-3931.
CAREER PLANNING *Placement office:* 2 full-time, 1 part-time staff; $1.8 million operating expenditure 1994–95. *Director:* Ms. Lynnel Keresztesi, Director of Career Planning and Employment Services, 616-965-3931 Ext. 2632. *Services:* job fairs, resume preparation, resume referral, career counseling, careers library, job bank, job interviews. 16 organizations recruited on campus 1994–95.
AFTER GRADUATION 63% of students completing a degree program in 1994–95 went directly on to further study.
EXPENSES FOR 1996–97 Area resident tuition: $1287 full-time, $41.50 per credit hour part-time. State resident tuition: $2169 full-time, $69.96 per credit hour part-time. Nonresident tuition: $3415 full-time, $110.15 per credit hour part-time. Part-time mandatory fees: $4.50 per credit hour. Full-time mandatory fees: $140.
FINANCIAL AID *College-administered undergrad aid 1995–96:* 425 need-based scholarships (average $294), 171 non-need scholarships (average $525), short-term loans (average $50), 77 Federal Work-Study (averaging $1970), 125 part-time jobs. *Required forms:* institutional, FAFSA. *Priority deadline:* 5/1. *Payment plan:* deferred payment. *Waivers:* full or partial for employees or children of employees and senior citizens. *Notification:* continuous.
APPLYING Open admission except for allied health programs. *Options:* early entrance, midyear entrance. *Required:* TOEFL for international students. *Required for some:* minimum 2.0 GPA, ACT. Test scores used for admission (for allied health programs) and counseling/placement. *Application deadline:* 8/29. *Notification:* continuous.
APPLYING/TRANSFER *Required for some:* minimum 2.0 high school GPA. *Entrance:* noncompetitive. *Application deadline:* 8/29. *Notification:* continuous. *Contact:* Mr. Ken Behmer, Dean for Student Development, 616-965-4124.
CONTACT Mrs. Connie Speers, Director of Admissions, Kellogg Community College, 450 North Avenue, Battle Creek, MI 49017-3306, 616-965-3931 Ext. 2622. *Fax:* 616-965-4133. College video available.

KIRTLAND COMMUNITY COLLEGE
Roscommon, Michigan

UG Enrollment: 1,352	Tuition & Fees (Area Res): $1537
Application Deadline: rolling	Room & Board: N/Avail

GENERAL District-supported, 2-year, coed. Part of Michigan Department of Education. Awards certificates, transfer associate, terminal associate degrees. Founded 1966. *Setting:* 180-acre rural campus. *Educational spending 1994–95:* $1925 per undergrad. *Total enrollment:* 1,352. *Faculty:* 95 (39 full-time, 56 part-time); student-faculty ratio is 19:1.
ENROLLMENT PROFILE 1,352 students; 66% women, 65% part-time, 100% state residents, 20% transferred in, 45% 25 or older, 2% Native American, 1% Hispanic, 1% African American, 1% Asian American. *Areas of study chosen:* 25% liberal arts/general studies, 21% health professions and related sciences, 11% business management and administrative services, 9% engineering and applied sciences. *Most popular recent majors:* nursing, liberal arts/general studies, science.
FIRST-YEAR CLASS 296 total; 434 applied, 100% were accepted, 68% of whom enrolled.
ACADEMIC PROGRAM Core. Calendar: semesters. Academic remediation for entering students, services for LD students, advanced placement, summer session for credit, part-time degree program (daytime), adult/continuing education programs, co-op programs and internships.
GENERAL DEGREE REQUIREMENTS 60 credits; computer course for accounting, business management, real estate majors; internship (some majors).
MAJORS Accounting, art/fine arts, automotive technologies, business administration/commerce/management, computer information systems, corrections, cosmetology, creative writing, criminal justice, drafting and design, finance/banking, fire science, legal secretarial studies, liberal arts/general studies, manufacturing technology, marketing/retailing/merchandising, medical secretarial studies, nursing, practical nursing, science, secretarial studies/office management, welding technology, word processing.
LIBRARY Kirtland Community College Library with 35,000 books, 81 microform titles, 317 periodicals, 3 CD-ROMs, 500 records, tapes, and CDs. Acquisition spending 1994–95: $17,257.
COMPUTERS ON CAMPUS 125 computers for student use in computer center, labs, library.
COLLEGE LIFE Drama-theater group, choral group, student-run newspaper. 1% vote in student government elections. *Student services:* personal-psychological counseling. *Campus security:* student patrols, late-night transport-escort service.
HOUSING College housing not available.
CAREER PLANNING *Placement office:* 1 full-time, 1 part-time staff; $42,170 operating expenditure 1994–95. *Director:* Ms. Jennie Walker, Counselor/Coordinator, 517-275-5121. *Services:* resume preparation, resume referral, career counseling, careers library, job bank, job interviews.
EXPENSES FOR 1996–97 Area resident tuition: $1417 full-time, $47.25 per credit hour part-time. State resident tuition: $1942 full-time, $64.75 per credit hour part-time. Nonresident tuition: $2550 full-time, $85 per credit hour part-time. Part-time mandatory fees: $4 per credit hour. Full-time mandatory fees: $120.
FINANCIAL AID *College-administered undergrad aid 1995–96:* 602 need-based scholarships (averaging $363), 125 non-need scholarships (averaging $479), low-interest long-term loans from external sources (averaging $1948), Federal Work-Study, 87 part-time jobs. *Required forms:* institutional; required for some: FAFSA; accepted: CSS Financial Aid PROFILE. *Priority deadline:* 5/15. *Payment plan:* deferred payment. *Waivers:* full or partial for employees or children of employees and senior citizens.
APPLYING Open admission. *Options:* early entrance, deferred entrance, midyear entrance. *Required:* TOEFL for international students, ACT ASSET. *Recommended:* SAT I or ACT. *Required for some:* 3 years of high school math and science. Test scores used for counseling/placement. *Application deadline:* rolling. *Notification:* continuous until 8/22.
APPLYING/TRANSFER *Required:* standardized test scores. *Required for some:* 3 years of high school math and science. *Entrance:* noncompetitive. *Application deadline:* rolling. *Notification:* continuous until 8/22. *Contact:* Ms. Patricia B. Zielinski, Registrar, 517-275-5121 Ext. 248.
CONTACT Ms. Patricia B. Zielinski, Registrar, Kirtland Community College, Roscommon, MI 48653-9699, 517-275-5121 Ext. 248. College video available.

LAKE MICHIGAN COLLEGE
Benton Harbor, Michigan

UG Enrollment: 3,260	Tuition & Fees (Area Res): $1440
Application Deadline: rolling	Room & Board: N/Avail

GENERAL District-supported, 2-year, coed. Part of Michigan Department of Education. Awards transfer associate, terminal associate degrees. Founded 1946. *Setting:* 260-acre small-town campus. *Total enrollment:* 3,260. *Faculty:* 240 (60 full-time, 10% with terminal degrees, 180 part-time).
ENROLLMENT PROFILE 3,260 students from 5 states and territories. 75% part-time, 98% state residents, 20% transferred in, 28% have need-based financial aid, 3% have non-need-based financial aid, 56% 25 or older, 1% Native American, 1% Hispanic, 12% African American, 1% Asian American.
FIRST-YEAR CLASS 710 total; 710 applied, 100% were accepted, 100% of whom enrolled.
ACADEMIC PROGRAM Core. Calendar: semesters. Academic remediation for entering students, self-designed majors, honors program, summer session for credit, part-time degree program (daytime, evenings, summer), adult/continuing education programs.
GENERAL DEGREE REQUIREMENTS 61 credit hours; math/science requirements vary according to program; computer course for information systems, health sciences, business-related majors.
MAJORS Accounting, art/fine arts, biology/biological sciences, business administration/commerce/management, chemistry, computer programming, computer science, corrections, criminal justice, data processing, dental services, dietetics, drafting and design, economics, education, electrical and electronics technologies, electromechanical technology, elementary education, emergency medical technology, (pre)engineering sequence, English, finance/banking, food sciences, food services management, food services technology, geography, history, hospitality services, industrial administration, industrial arts, industrial engineering technology, laboratory technologies, law enforcement/police sciences, legal secretarial studies, liberal arts/general studies, machine and tool technologies, manufacturing technology, marketing/retailing/merchandising, mathematics, mechanical design technology, mechanical engineering technology, medical secretarial studies, music, nursing, philosophy, physical education, physical sciences, political science/government, practical nursing, psychology, radiological technology, sociology, teacher aide studies, theater arts/drama.
LIBRARY Lake Michigan College Library with 79,000 books, 206 microform titles, 280 periodicals, 1,800 records, tapes, and CDs. Acquisition spending 1994–95: $22,298.
COMPUTERS ON CAMPUS 124 computers for student use in computer center, computer labs. Academic computing expenditure 1994–95: $110,824.
COLLEGE LIFE Drama-theater group, student-run newspaper. *Social organizations:* 1 national sorority; 1% of eligible women are members. *Most popular organizations:* Hospitality Club, International Club, Pride Club II. *Major annual events:* Winner Within Scholarship Auction, Red and Gray Run. *Student services:* personal-psychological counseling, women's center.
HOUSING College housing not available.
ATHLETICS Member NJCAA. *Intercollegiate:* basketball M(s)/W(s), golf M(s), volleyball W(s). *Intramural:* basketball, volleyball. *Contact:* Ms. Kathy Leitke, Athletic Director, 616-927-2100 Ext. 8165.
CAREER PLANNING *Placement office:* 2 full-time staff; $50,955 operating expenditure 1994–95. *Director:* Ms. Phyllis Nelson, Director, Career Planning and Placement Center, 616-927-8100. *Services:* job fairs, resume preparation, resume referral, career counseling, careers library, job bank, job interviews.
EXPENSES FOR 1995–96 Area resident tuition: $1440 full-time, $48 per credit hour part-time. State resident tuition: $1740 full-time, $58 per credit hour part-time. Nonresident tuition: $2040 full-time, $68 per credit hour part-time.
FINANCIAL AID *College-administered undergrad aid 1995–96:* 1,000 need-based scholarships (average $1100), 50 non-need scholarships (average $500), low-interest long-term loans from external sources, Federal Work-Study, 50 part-time jobs. *Required forms:* institutional; accepted: CSS Financial Aid PROFILE, FAFSA. *Priority deadline:* 6/1.
APPLYING Open admission. *Options:* early entrance, deferred entrance. *Required:* school transcript, TOEFL for international students, ACT ASSET. *Recommended:* ACT. *Required for some:* interview. Test scores used for counseling/placement. *Application deadline:* rolling. *Notification:* continuous.
APPLYING/TRANSFER *Required:* standardized test scores, high school transcript. *Recommended:* college transcript. *Required for some:* interview. *Application deadline:* rolling. *Notification:* continuous.
CONTACT Ms. Sherry Hoadley-Pries, Director of Enrollment Management, Lake Michigan College, Benton Harbor, MI 49022-1899, 616-927-3571 Ext. 8139 or toll-free 800-252-1LMC (in-state).

LANSING COMMUNITY COLLEGE
Lansing, Michigan

UG Enrollment: 16,404	Tuition & Fees (Area Res): $1345
Application Deadline: rolling	Room & Board: N/Avail

GENERAL State and locally supported, 2-year, coed. Part of Michigan Department of Education. Awards certificates, transfer associate, terminal associate degrees. Founded

Lansing Community College (continued)

1957. ***Setting:*** 120-acre urban campus. ***Total enrollment:*** 16,404. ***Faculty:*** 1,085 (185 full-time, 900 part-time); student-faculty ratio is 13:1. ***Notable Alumni:*** Diane Byrum, senator; Charles F. Felice, chief justice; Dr. Richard J. Halik, superintendent of the Lansing School District; Dr. Jacqueline D. Taylor, vice president and executive dean of Community College of Allegheny County; Marion "Babe" Weyant Ruth, member of Aviation Hall of Fame.

ENROLLMENT PROFILE 16,404 students: 56% women, 44% men, 75% part-time, 98% state residents, 2% transferred in, 1% international, 1% Native American, 3% Hispanic, 7% African American, 3% Asian American. ***Most popular recent major:*** business administration/commerce/management.

FIRST-YEAR CLASS 3,853 total. Of the students who applied, 100% were accepted.

ACADEMIC PROGRAM Honor code. Calendar: semesters. 2,600 courses offered in 1995–96. Academic remediation for entering students, English as a second language program offered during academic year and summer, services for LD students, advanced placement, self-designed majors, tutorials, honors program, summer session for credit, part-time degree program (daytime, evenings, weekends, summer), external degree programs, adult/continuing education programs, co-op programs and internships. Study abroad in Japan, Mexico. ROTC: Army (c), Air Force (c).

GENERAL DEGREE REQUIREMENT 60 semester hours.

MAJORS Accounting, advertising, architectural technologies, art/fine arts, automotive technologies, aviation technology, biochemical technology, biology/biological sciences, biomedical technologies, broadcasting, business administration/commerce/management, carpentry, chemical engineering technology, child care/child and family studies, civil engineering technology, commercial art, communication, communication equipment technology, computer graphics, computer information systems, computer management, computer programming, computer technologies, construction technologies, corrections, court reporting, criminal justice, data processing, deaf interpreter training, dental services, drafting and design, drug and alcohol/substance abuse counseling, early childhood education, education, electrical and electronics technologies, electrical engineering technology, electromechanical technology, electronics engineering technology, elementary education, emergency medical technology, engineering (general), (pre)engineering sequence, engineering technology, film and video production, film studies, finance/banking, fire science, flight training, food services management, French, geography, geology, German, gerontology, heating/refrigeration/air conditioning, history, home economics, horticulture, hospitality services, hotel and restaurant management, human services, illustration, industrial and heavy equipment maintenance, industrial engineering technology, insurance, international business, journalism, landscape architecture/design, law enforcement/police sciences, legal secretarial studies, liberal arts/general studies, machine and tool technologies, management information systems, manufacturing technology, marketing/retailing/merchandising, mechanical design technology, mechanical engineering technology, medical assistant technologies, medical secretarial studies, military science, nursing, operating room technology, paralegal studies, photography, physical education, plumbing, practical nursing, quality control technology, radio and television studies, radiological technology, real estate, respiratory therapy, retail management, robotics, science, secretarial studies/office management, speech/rhetoric/public address/debate, studio art, surveying technology, teacher aide studies, telecommunications, tourism and travel, voice, welding technology, Western civilization and culture, word processing.

LIBRARY Arts and Sciences Library plus 2 others, with 106,575 books, 156 microform titles, 670 periodicals, 2 on-line bibliographic services, 20 CD-ROMs. Acquisition spending 1994–95: $148,025.

COMPUTERS ON CAMPUS 288 computers for student use in computer labs, classrooms. Staffed computer lab on campus provides training in use of computers, software.

COLLEGE LIFE Orientation program (2 days, no cost). Drama-theater group, choral group, student-run newspaper, radio station. ***Social organizations:*** 145 open to all; 1 national fraternity, 1 national sorority; 25% of eligible men and 75% of eligible women are members. ***Most popular organizations:*** Student Marketing Club, Legal Assistants Club, Student Nursing Club, Phi Theta Kappa, Student Advising Club. ***Major annual events:*** Graduation, Student Recognition Banquet, Fashion Show. ***Student services:*** women's center. ***Campus security:*** 24-hour emergency response devices and patrols, student patrols, late-night transport-escort service.

HOUSING College housing not available.

ATHLETICS Member NJCAA. ***Intercollegiate:*** basketball M(s)/W(s), cross-country running M(s)/W(s), golf M(s), volleyball W(s). ***Intramural:*** basketball, cross-country running, golf, volleyball. ***Contact:*** Mr. Richard Mull, Director of Athletics, 517-483-1624.

CAREER PLANNING ***Placement office:*** 2 full-time, 7 part-time staff; $178,325 operating expenditure 1994–95. ***Director:*** Dr. James Osborn, Director of Career Services, 517-483-1221. ***Services:*** job fairs, resume preparation, resume referral, career counseling, careers library, job interviews.

EXPENSES FOR 1995–96 ***Application fee:*** $10. Area resident tuition: $1290 full-time, $43 per semester hour part-time. State resident tuition: $2160 full-time, $72 per semester hour part-time. Nonresident tuition: $3030 full-time, $101 per semester hour part-time. Part-time mandatory fees per semester range from $21.50 to $27.50. Full-time mandatory fees: $55.

FINANCIAL AID ***College-administered undergrad aid 1995–96:*** need-based scholarships, non-need scholarships, short-term loans, low-interest long-term loans, Federal Work-Study, part-time jobs. ***Required forms:*** institutional, FAFSA. ***Application deadline:*** continuous to 9/1. ***Waivers:*** full or partial for employees or children of employees. ***Notification:*** continuous.

APPLYING Open admission except for allied health, aviation, fire science, automotive technologies, law enforcement programs and international students. ***Options:*** early entrance, deferred entrance, midyear entrance. ***Required:*** TOEFL for international students, Michigan Test of English Language Proficiency. ***Required for some:*** SAT I or ACT. Test scores used for counseling/placement. ***Application deadline:*** rolling. Preference given to district residents.

APPLYING/TRANSFER ***Entrance:*** noncompetitive. ***Application deadline:*** rolling. ***Contact:*** Ms. Joan Hartwig, Counselor/Coordinator of Transfer Programs, 517-483-1255.

CONTACT Ms. Rhoda Ritter, Registrar and Director of Entry Services, Lansing Community College, PO Box 40010, Lansing, MI 48901-7210, 517-483-1252. ***Fax:*** 517-483-9668. College video available.

LEWIS COLLEGE OF BUSINESS
Detroit, Michigan

UG Enrollment: 191	**Tuition & Fees: $2500**
Application Deadline: rolling	**Room & Board: N/Avail**

GENERAL Independent, 2-year, coed. Awards transfer associate, terminal associate degrees. Founded 1929. ***Setting:*** 11-acre urban campus. ***Total enrollment:*** 191. ***Faculty:*** 36 (9 full-time, 15% with terminal degrees, 27 part-time).

ENROLLMENT PROFILE 191 students: 77% women, 39% part-time, 98% state residents, 38% transferred in, 99% African American, 1% Asian American. ***Most popular recent majors:*** business administration/commerce/management, accounting, computer information systems.

FIRST-YEAR CLASS 48 applied, 81% were accepted.

ACADEMIC PROGRAM Honor code. Calendar: semesters. Academic remediation for entering students, summer session for credit, part-time degree program (daytime, evenings), co-op programs.

GENERAL DEGREE REQUIREMENTS 67 credit hours; math/science requirements vary according to program; computer course.

MAJORS Accounting, business administration/commerce/management, computer information systems, computer management, computer programming, computer science, data processing, legal secretarial studies, liberal arts/general studies, medical secretarial studies, secretarial studies/office management.

LIBRARY Main library plus 1 other, with 3,355 books, 680 microform titles, 90 periodicals, 81 records, tapes, and CDs.

COMPUTERS ON CAMPUS 54 computers for student use in computer labs, learning center, classrooms provide access to on-line services. Staffed computer lab on campus provides training in use of computers, software.

COLLEGE LIFE Orientation program (2 days, no cost, parents included). Student-run newspaper. 40% vote in student government elections. ***Social organizations:*** 5 open to all; 1 national sorority, local sororities; 10% of eligible women are members. ***Most popular organizations:*** Sister to Sister, Brother to Brother, The Voice, Student Government Association, Business Club. ***Student services:*** personal-psychological counseling. ***Campus security:*** parking lot security.

HOUSING College housing not available.

ATHLETICS ***Intercollegiate:*** basketball M.

CAREER PLANNING ***Placement office:*** 1 full-time, 1 part-time staff. ***Director:*** Ms. Phyllis Ponders, Director, Career Center, 313-862-6300. ***Services:*** job fairs, resume preparation, resume referral, career counseling, job bank, job interviews. Students must register sophomore year. 20 organizations recruited on campus 1994–95.

EXPENSES FOR 1996–97 ***Application fee:*** $15. Tuition: $2400 full-time, $215 per credit hour part-time. Full-time mandatory fees: $100.

FINANCIAL AID ***College-administered undergrad aid 1995–96:*** 60 need-based scholarships (average $1000), low-interest long-term loans from external sources (average $2625), Federal Work-Study, part-time jobs. ***Required forms:*** CSS Financial Aid PROFILE, state, FAFSA. ***Priority deadline:*** 7/15.

APPLYING Open admission. ***Options:*** Common Application, early entrance, deferred entrance. ***Required:*** school transcript, TOEFL for international students. Test scores used for counseling/placement. ***Application deadline:*** rolling. ***Notification:*** continuous until 8/30.

APPLYING/TRANSFER ***Required:*** high school transcript, college transcript. ***Application deadline:*** 8/1. ***Notification:*** continuous until 8/30.

CONTACT Ms. Frances Ambrose, Admissions Secretary, Lewis College of Business, 17370 Meyers Road, Detroit, MI 48235-1423, 313-862-6300.

MACOMB COMMUNITY COLLEGE
Warren, Michigan

UG Enrollment: 24,500	**Tuition & Fees (Area Res): $1581**
Application Deadline: rolling	**Room & Board: N/Avail**

GENERAL District-supported, 2-year, coed. Awards transfer associate, terminal associate degrees. Founded 1954. ***Setting:*** 384-acre suburban campus with easy access to Detroit. ***Total enrollment:*** 24,500. ***Faculty:*** 841 (346 full-time, 495 part-time).

ENROLLMENT PROFILE 24,500 students: 52% women, 76% part-time, 88% state residents, 5% transferred in, 0% international, 47% 25 or older, 1% Native American, 1% Hispanic, 2% African American, 2% Asian American.

FIRST-YEAR CLASS 4,898 total; 6,623 applied, 100% were accepted, 74% of whom enrolled.

ACADEMIC PROGRAM Calendar: semesters. Academic remediation for entering students, English as a second language program offered during academic year, services for LD students, advanced placement, self-designed majors, summer session for credit, part-time degree program (daytime, evenings, weekends, summer), adult/continuing education programs, co-op programs and internships. Off-campus study at Wayne State University, Wayne County Community College, Benjamin Davis Vocational Technical Center, Oakland Community College.

GENERAL DEGREE REQUIREMENTS 62 credits; computer course for accounting, business majors; internship (some majors).

MAJORS Accounting, architectural technologies, automotive technologies, aviation technology, behavioral sciences, business administration/commerce/management, child care/child and family studies, civil engineering technology, commercial art, communication equipment technology, computer information systems, computer technologies, construction technologies, criminal justice, culinary arts, drafting and design, early childhood education, electrical and electronics technologies, electrical engineering technology, electromechanical technology, electronics engineering technology, emergency medical technology, energy management technologies, engineering design, (pre)engineering sequence, fashion merchandising, finance/banking, fire science, gerontology, graphic arts, heating/refrigeration/air conditioning, illustration, international studies, labor and industrial relations, law enforcement/police sciences, legal secretarial studies, legal studies, liberal arts/general studies, machine and tool technologies, marketing/retailing/merchandising, materials sciences, mechanical design technology, medical secretarial studies, mental health/rehabilitation counseling, metallurgical technology, nursing, paralegal studies, photography, physical therapy, plastics technology, plumbing, printing technologies, quality control

technology, respiratory therapy, robotics, safety and security technologies, secretarial studies/office management, surveying technology, veterinary sciences, welding technology, word processing.
LIBRARY 131,199 books, 832 microform titles, 568 periodicals, 10,092 records, tapes, and CDs.
COMPUTERS ON CAMPUS 450 computers for student use in computer center, labs, classrooms, library.
COLLEGE LIFE Drama-theater group. ***Student services:*** health clinic, personal-psychological counseling.
HOUSING College housing not available.
ATHLETICS Member NJCAA. ***Intercollegiate:*** baseball M(s), basketball M(s), cross-country running M(s)/W(s), golf M(s), soccer M(s), softball W(s), tennis M(s)/W(s), track and field M(s)/W(s), volleyball W(s). ***Intramural:*** baseball, basketball, bowling, cross-country running, football, golf, gymnastics, racquetball, skiing (cross-country), skiing (downhill), tennis, volleyball. ***Contact:*** Mr. Ed Stanton, Athletic Director, 810-445-7476.
CAREER PLANNING ***Director:*** Mr. Richard Severance, Associate Dean, Student Development Services, 810-286-2216. ***Services:*** job fairs, resume preparation, resume referral, career counseling, careers library, job bank, job interviews.
EXPENSES FOR 1996–97 ***Application fee:*** $15. Area resident tuition: $1581 full-time, $51 per semester hour part-time. State resident tuition: $2372 full-time, $76.50 per semester hour part-time. Nonresident tuition: $2837 full-time, $91.50 per semester hour part-time.
FINANCIAL AID ***College-administered undergrad aid 1995–96:*** 200 need-based scholarships (average $400), 40 non-need scholarships (average $600), short-term loans (average $150), low-interest long-term loans from external sources, Federal Work-Study, part-time jobs. ***Required forms:*** CSS Financial Aid PROFILE, institutional; accepted: FAFSA. ***Priority deadline:*** 5/1. ***Waivers:*** full or partial for employees or children of employees and senior citizens.
APPLYING Open admission except for nursing, physical therapy programs. ***Options:*** early entrance, deferred entrance, midyear entrance. ***Required:*** TOEFL for international students. ***Required for some:*** ACT ASSET. Test scores used for counseling/placement. ***Application deadline:*** rolling.
APPLYING/TRANSFER ***Entrance:*** minimally difficult. ***Application deadline:*** rolling.
CONTACT Mr. Richard P. Stevens, Coordinator of Admissions and Assessment, Macomb Community College, Warren, MI 48093-3896, 810-445-7230. ***Fax:*** 810-445-7140.

MID MICHIGAN COMMUNITY COLLEGE
Harrison, Michigan

UG Enrollment: 3,304	Tuition & Fees (Area Res): $1160
Application Deadline: rolling	Room & Board: N/Avail

GENERAL State and locally supported, 2-year, coed. Part of Michigan Department of Education. Awards certificates, transfer associate, terminal associate degrees. Founded 1965. ***Setting:*** 560-acre rural campus. ***Educational spending 1994–95:*** $903 per undergrad. ***Total enrollment:*** 3,304. ***Faculty:*** 227 (39 full-time, 188 part-time).
ENROLLMENT PROFILE 3,304 students: 64% women, 60% part-time, 99% state residents, 5% transferred in, 1% international, 63% 25 or older, 1% Native American, 1% Hispanic, 1% African American, 1% Asian American. ***Most popular recent majors:*** nursing, business administration/commerce/management, art/fine arts.
FIRST-YEAR CLASS 460 total; 2,193 applied, 100% were accepted, 21% of whom enrolled.
ACADEMIC PROGRAM Core, honor code. Calendar: semesters. 356 courses offered in 1995–96. Academic remediation for entering students, services for LD students, advanced placement, honors program, summer session for credit, part-time degree program (daytime, evenings, summer), adult/continuing education programs, internships.
GENERAL DEGREE REQUIREMENTS 62 credit hours; 1 course each in math and science; computer course.
MAJORS Accounting, art/fine arts, automotive technologies, biochemical technology, biology/biological sciences, biotechnology, business administration/commerce/management, chemistry, child care/child and family studies, computer information systems, computer science, criminal justice, data processing, drafting and design, elementary education, (pre)engineering sequence, finance/banking, fire science, fish and game management, graphic arts, heating/refrigeration/air conditioning, history, hospitality services, legal secretarial studies, liberal arts/general studies, machine and tool technologies, marketing/retailing/merchandising, mathematics, mechanical engineering technology, nursing, pharmacy/pharmaceutical sciences, physical therapy, practical nursing, psychology, radiological technology, science, secretarial studies/office management, sociology, theater arts/drama, welding technology, word processing.
LIBRARY Charles A. Amble Library with 28,500 books, 2,950 microform titles, 200 periodicals, 2 on-line bibliographic services, 2 CD-ROMs, 314 records, tapes, and CDs. Acquisition spending 1994–95: $34,520.
COMPUTERS ON CAMPUS 150 computers for student use in computer center, computer labs, learning resource center provide access to on-line services. Staffed computer lab on campus provides training in use of computers. Academic computing expenditure 1994–95: $186,158.
COLLEGE LIFE Drama-theater group, choral group, student-run newspaper. 5% vote in student government elections. ***Most popular organizations:*** Commission of Student Activities Services, Phi Theta Kappa, Karate Club, CSAS Club. ***Major annual events:*** Spring Picnic, Fall Festival.
HOUSING College housing not available.
CAREER PLANNING ***Placement office:*** 2 full-time staff. ***Director:*** Mr. Jerry Hand, Career Counselor/Advisor, 517-386-6660. ***Services:*** job fairs, resume preparation, resume referral, career counseling, careers library, job bank, job interviews.
EXPENSES FOR 1995–96 Area resident tuition: $1080 full-time, $45 per semester part-time. State resident tuition: $1632 full-time, $68 per semester part-time. Nonresident tuition: $2160 full-time, $90 per semester part-time. Part-time mandatory fees: $20 per semester. Full-time mandatory fees: $80.
FINANCIAL AID ***College-administered undergrad aid 1995–96:*** 43 need-based scholarships (average $205), 182 non-need scholarships (average $190), low-interest long-term loans from external sources (average $1016), Federal Work-Study, 73 part-time jobs. ***Required forms:*** institutional, FAFSA; accepted: CSS Financial Aid PROFILE. ***Priority deadline:*** 7/1. ***Payment plan:*** deferred payment. ***Waivers:*** full or partial for minority students, employees or children of employees, adult students, and senior citizens.
APPLYING Open admission except for allied health programs. ***Options:*** early entrance, midyear entrance. ***Required:*** TOEFL for international students. ***Recommended:*** school transcript. ***Required for some:*** campus interview. Test scores used for counseling/placement. ***Application deadline:*** rolling. ***Notification:*** continuous.
APPLYING/TRANSFER ***Entrance:*** noncompetitive. ***Application deadline:*** rolling. ***Notification:*** continuous. ***Contact:*** Ms. Carol Santini, Transfer Counselor, 517-386-6623.
CONTACT Ms. Brenda Bishop, Admissions Specialist, Mid Michigan Community College, Harrison, MI 48625-9447, 517-386-6661. ***Fax:*** 517-386-9088.

MONROE COUNTY COMMUNITY COLLEGE
Monroe, Michigan

UG Enrollment: 3,923	Tuition & Fees (Area Res): $968
Application Deadline: rolling	Room & Board: N/Avail

GENERAL County-supported, 2-year, coed. Part of Michigan Department of Education. Awards certificates, transfer associate, terminal associate degrees. Founded 1964. ***Setting:*** 150-acre small-town campus with easy access to Detroit and Toledo. ***Total enrollment:*** 3,923. ***Faculty:*** 201 (54 full-time, 30% with terminal degrees, 147 part-time); student-faculty ratio is 25:1.
ENROLLMENT PROFILE 3,923 students from 3 states and territories, 5 other countries. 63% women, 72% part-time, 82% state residents, 7% transferred in, 42% have need-based financial aid, 12% have non-need-based financial aid, 1% international, 44% 25 or older, 1% Native American, 1% Hispanic, 1% African American, 1% Asian American. ***Areas of study chosen:*** 31% liberal arts/general studies, 17% business management and administrative services, 12% health professions and related sciences, 11% engineering and applied sciences, 6% education, 2% computer and information sciences, 2% prelaw, 2% psychology, 1% architecture, 1% biological and life sciences, 1% communications and journalism, 1% fine arts, 1% social sciences, 1% vocational and home economics. ***Most popular recent majors:*** liberal arts/general studies, nursing, business administration/commerce/management.
FIRST-YEAR CLASS 914 total. Of the students who applied, 100% were accepted.
ACADEMIC PROGRAM Core, transfer/occupational curriculum, honor code. Calendar: semesters. 460 courses offered in 1995–96. Academic remediation for entering students, services for LD students, advanced placement, summer session for credit, part-time degree program (daytime, evenings, summer), adult/continuing education programs.
GENERAL DEGREE REQUIREMENTS 60 credit hours; 1 math course; computer course for business majors.
MAJORS Accounting, architectural technologies, art/fine arts, automotive technologies, biology/biological sciences, business administration/commerce/management, child care/child and family studies, communication, computer technologies, culinary arts, data processing, drafting and design, electrical and electronics technologies, elementary education, (pre)engineering sequence, English, finance/banking, funeral service, industrial administration, journalism, law enforcement/police sciences, legal secretarial studies, liberal arts/general studies, manufacturing technology, marketing/retailing/merchandising, mathematics, medical secretarial studies, medical technology, nuclear technology, nursing, pharmacy/pharmaceutical sciences, physical therapy, psychology, radiological sciences, respiratory therapy, secretarial studies/office management, social work, speech/rhetoric/public address/debate, veterinary sciences, welding technology.
LIBRARY 47,352 books, 146 microform titles, 321 periodicals, 6 CD-ROMs, 6,196 records, tapes, and CDs. Acquisition spending 1994–95: $35,000.
COMPUTERS ON CAMPUS Computer purchase plan available. 140 computers for student use in computer labs. Staffed computer lab on campus provides training in use of computers, software.
COLLEGE LIFE Drama-theater group, choral group, student-run newspaper. 8% vote in student government elections. ***Most popular organizations:*** Student Council, Society of All Engineers, Delta Epsilon Chi, Oasis, Nursing Students Organization. ***Major annual events:*** Family Fun Night, Lunch with Santa, Honors Program. ***Campus security:*** patrols by police during open hours.
HOUSING College housing not available.
CAREER PLANNING ***Placement office:*** 1 part-time staff. ***Director:*** Dr. Joyce Haver, Professor of Counseling, 313-242-7300 Ext. 264. ***Services:*** career counseling, careers library.
EXPENSES FOR 1995–96 Area resident tuition: $888 full-time, $37 per credit hour part-time. State resident tuition: $1416 full-time, $59 per credit hour part-time. Nonresident tuition: $1584 full-time, $66 per credit hour part-time. Part-time mandatory fees: $40 per semester. Full-time mandatory fees: $80.
FINANCIAL AID ***College-administered undergrad aid 1995–96:*** 110 need-based scholarships (average $1100), 425 non-need scholarships (average $1100), short-term loans (average $250), low-interest long-term loans from external sources (average $2625), Federal Work-Study, 50 part-time jobs. ***Required forms:*** institutional, FAFSA; accepted: CSS Financial Aid PROFILE. ***Priority deadline:*** 6/1. ***Waivers:*** full or partial for employees or children of employees and senior citizens.
APPLYING Open admission except for allied health programs. ***Options:*** early entrance, deferred entrance, midyear entrance. ***Required:*** school transcript, TOEFL for international students, ACT ASSET. ***Required for some:*** ACT. Test scores used for admission (for allied health programs) and counseling/placement. ***Application deadline:*** rolling. ***Notification:*** continuous.
APPLYING/TRANSFER ***Required for some:*** standardized test scores, high school transcript. ***Entrance:*** noncompetitive. ***Application deadline:*** rolling. ***Notification:*** continuous.
CONTACT Mr. Randell W. Daniels, Director of Admissions and Guidance, Monroe County Community College, Monroe, MI 48161-9047, 313-242-7300 Ext. 205 or toll-free 800-462-5114 (in-state). ***Fax:*** 313-242-9711.

MONTCALM COMMUNITY COLLEGE
Sidney, Michigan

UG Enrollment: 1,753	Tuition & Fees (Area Res): $1421
Application Deadline: rolling	Room & Board: N/Avail

Peterson's Guide to Two-Year Colleges 1997 383

Montcalm Community College (continued)

GENERAL State and locally supported, 2-year, coed. Part of Michigan Department of Education. Awards certificates, transfer associate, terminal associate degrees. Founded 1965. ***Setting:*** 248-acre rural campus. ***Endowment:*** $47,401. ***Educational spending 1994–95:*** $1643 per undergrad. ***Total enrollment:*** 1,753. ***Faculty:*** 134 (27 full-time, 5% with terminal degrees, 107 part-time).

ENROLLMENT PROFILE 1,753 students: 63% women, 37% men, 74% part-time, 99% state residents, 8% transferred in, 56% 25 or older, 1% Native American, 2% Hispanic, 12% African American, 1% Asian American. ***Areas of study chosen:*** 24% liberal arts/general studies, 19% business management and administrative services, 16% health professions and related sciences, 11% engineering and applied sciences, 5% computer and information sciences, 4% vocational and home economics. ***Most popular recent majors:*** liberal arts/general studies, nursing, business administration/commerce/management.

FIRST-YEAR CLASS 358 total; 589 applied, 100% were accepted, 61% of whom enrolled.

ACADEMIC PROGRAM Core. Calendar: semesters. 695 courses offered in 1995–96. Academic remediation for entering students, services for LD students, advanced placement, summer session for credit, part-time degree program (daytime, evenings), adult/continuing education programs.

GENERAL DEGREE REQUIREMENTS 60 credit hours; computer course for industrial technology, electronics, drafting, business administration, accounting majors.

MAJORS Accounting, applied art, automotive technologies, business administration/commerce/management, child care/child and family studies, corrections, cosmetology, criminal justice, data processing, drafting and design, electrical and electronics technologies, emergency medical technology, food services technology, industrial engineering technology, legal secretarial studies, liberal arts/general studies, machine and tool technologies, medical secretarial studies, nursing, paralegal studies, practical nursing, radiological technology, secretarial studies/office management, welding technology, word processing.

LIBRARY Learning Resource Center with 28,000 books, 625 periodicals, 15 CD-ROMs, 935 records, tapes, and CDs. Acquisition spending 1994–95: $22,134.

COMPUTERS ON CAMPUS 400 computers for student use in computer center, computer labs, learning resource center, classrooms, library. Staffed computer lab on campus provides training in use of computers. Academic computing expenditure 1994–95: $188,402.

COLLEGE LIFE Drama-theater group, choral group, student-run newspaper. 9% vote in student government elections. ***Social organizations:*** 12 open to all. ***Most popular organizations:*** Student Government Association, Nursing Club, Sports Club, Phi Theta Kappa. ***Major annual events:*** Week on the Grass, Welcome Week, Heritage Village Festival. ***Student services:*** personal-psychological counseling.

HOUSING College housing not available.

ATHLETICS ***Intramural:*** basketball, bowling, skiing (cross-country), skiing (downhill), softball, swimming and diving, table tennis (Ping-Pong), tennis, volleyball, weight lifting.

CAREER PLANNING ***Placement office:*** 3 full-time staff. ***Director:*** Mr. Lon Holton, Dean of Student Services, 517-328-1276. ***Services:*** resume preparation, resume referral, career counseling, careers library, job bank, job interviews.

EXPENSES FOR 1995–96 Area resident tuition: $1385 full-time, $46.15 per credit hour part-time. State resident tuition: $2123 full-time, $70.75 per credit hour part-time. Nonresident tuition: $2708 full-time, $90.25 per credit hour part-time. Part-time mandatory fees: $1.50 per credit hour. Full-time mandatory fees: $36.

FINANCIAL AID ***College-administered undergrad aid 1995–96:*** 35 need-based scholarships (average $600), non-need scholarships (average $500), low-interest long-term loans from external sources (average $2200), 53 Federal Work-Study (averaging $2000), 5 part-time jobs. ***Required forms:*** institutional, FAFSA; accepted: CSS Financial Aid PROFILE. ***Priority deadline:*** 6/1. ***Payment plan:*** installment. ***Waivers:*** full or partial for employees or children of employees and senior citizens.

APPLYING Open admission except for nursing program. ***Options:*** early entrance, deferred entrance, midyear entrance. ***Required:*** school transcript, TOEFL for international students, ACT ASSET. ***Recommended:*** ACT. Test scores used for counseling/placement. ***Application deadline:*** rolling. ***Notification:*** continuous.

APPLYING/TRANSFER ***Recommended:*** college transcript. ***Entrance:*** noncompetitive. ***Application deadline:*** rolling. ***Notification:*** continuous. ***Contact:*** Mr. Jim Lucka, Counselor, 517-328-2111 Ext. 307.

CONTACT Ms. Kathie Lofts, Assistant Director of Admissions, Montcalm Community College, Sidney, MI 48885-0300, 517-328-1250. ***Fax:*** 517-328-2950. ***E-mail:*** admissions@montcalm.cc.mi.us.

MUSKEGON COMMUNITY COLLEGE
Muskegon, Michigan

UG Enrollment: 5,169	**Tuition & Fees (Area Res): $1302**
Application Deadline: rolling	**Room & Board: N/Avail**

GENERAL State and locally supported, 2-year, coed. Part of Michigan Department of Education. Awards transfer associate, terminal associate degrees. Founded 1926. ***Setting:*** 112-acre urban campus with easy access to Grand Rapids. ***Total enrollment:*** 5,169. ***Faculty:*** 150 (100 full-time, 50 part-time); student-faculty ratio is 33:1.

ENROLLMENT PROFILE 5,169 students from 3 states and territories, 5 other countries. 52% women, 57% part-time, 95% state residents, 8% transferred in, 2% international, 52% 25 or older, 2% Native American, 2% Hispanic, 10% African American. ***Most popular recent majors:*** nursing, business administration/commerce/management, liberal arts/general studies.

FIRST-YEAR CLASS 1,788 total. Of the students who applied, 100% were accepted.

ACADEMIC PROGRAM Core. Calendar: semesters. Academic remediation for entering students, self-designed majors, honors program, summer session for credit, part-time degree program (daytime, evenings, summer), adult/continuing education programs, co-op programs.

GENERAL DEGREE REQUIREMENT 62 credit hours.

MAJORS Accounting, advertising, anthropology, applied art, applied mathematics, art education, art/fine arts, art history, automotive technologies, biomedical technologies, biotechnology, business administration/commerce/management, business machine technologies, chemical engineering technology, child care/child and family studies, child psychology/child development, computer information systems, criminal justice, data processing, drafting and design, economics, education, electrical and electronics technologies, electromechanical technology, elementary education, emergency medical technology, engineering technology, finance/banking, food marketing, food services management, graphic arts, hospitality services, hotel and restaurant management, industrial arts, industrial engineering technology, legal secretarial studies, liberal arts/general studies, machine and tool technologies, marketing/retailing/merchandising, medical secretarial studies, nursing, recreation and leisure services, secretarial studies/office management, transportation technologies, welding technology.

LIBRARY 48,597 books, 366 microform titles, 450 periodicals, 10,200 records, tapes, and CDs.

COMPUTERS ON CAMPUS 30 computers for student use in computer center.

COLLEGE LIFE Drama-theater group, choral group. ***Student services:*** personal-psychological counseling.

HOUSING College housing not available.

ATHLETICS Member NJCAA. ***Intercollegiate:*** baseball M, basketball M(s)/W(s), golf M/W, softball W, volleyball W(s). ***Intramural:*** basketball, skiing (downhill).

CAREER PLANNING ***Service:*** career counseling.

EXPENSES FOR 1995–96 Area resident tuition: $1302 full-time, $42 per credit hour part-time. State resident tuition: $1860 full-time, $60 per credit hour part-time. Nonresident tuition: $2325 full-time, $75 per credit hour part-time.

FINANCIAL AID ***College-administered undergrad aid 1995–96:*** 50 need-based scholarships (averaging $300), 300 non-need scholarships (averaging $500), short-term loans (averaging $150), low-interest long-term loans from external sources (averaging $1750), Federal Work-Study, 150 part-time jobs. ***Required forms:*** CSS Financial Aid PROFILE, institutional, FAFSA. ***Priority deadline:*** 6/1. ***Payment plan:*** deferred payment. ***Waivers:*** full or partial for employees or children of employees and senior citizens.

APPLYING Open admission. ***Options:*** early entrance, deferred entrance. ***Required:*** TOEFL for international students. ***Recommended:*** SAT I or ACT. Test scores used for counseling/placement. ***Application deadline:*** rolling. ***Notification:*** continuous.

APPLYING/TRANSFER ***Entrance:*** noncompetitive. ***Application deadline:*** rolling. ***Notification:*** continuous.

CONTACT Ms. Lynda Schwartz, Admissions Coordinator, Muskegon Community College, 221 South Quarterline Road, Muskegon, MI 49442-1493, 616-773-9131 Ext. 366.

NORTH CENTRAL MICHIGAN COLLEGE
Petoskey, Michigan

UG Enrollment: 2,032	**Tuition & Fees (Area Res): $1440**
Application Deadline: rolling	**Room & Board: $3570**

GENERAL County-supported, 2-year, coed. Part of Michigan Department of Education. Awards certificates, transfer associate, terminal associate degrees. Founded 1958. ***Setting:*** 270-acre small-town campus. ***Educational spending 1994–95:*** $884 per undergrad. ***Total enrollment:*** 2,032. ***Faculty:*** 146 (28 full-time, 3% with terminal degrees, 118 part-time).

ENROLLMENT PROFILE 2,032 students from 4 states and territories, 2 other countries. 68% women, 32% men, 71% part-time, 98% state residents, 3% live on campus, 8% transferred in, 45% have need-based financial aid, 2% have non-need-based financial aid, 1% international, 55% 25 or older, 3% Native American, 1% Hispanic, 1% African American, 1% Asian American. ***Most popular recent majors:*** business administration/commerce/management, liberal arts/general studies, nursing.

FIRST-YEAR CLASS 472 total; 998 applied, 100% were accepted, 75% of whom enrolled. 10% from top 10% of their high school class, 80% from top half.

ACADEMIC PROGRAM Core, honor code. Calendar: semesters. 790 courses offered in 1995–96. Academic remediation for entering students, services for LD students, advanced placement, summer session for credit, part-time degree program (daytime, evenings), co-op programs and internships.

GENERAL DEGREE REQUIREMENTS 60 credit hours; 8 credit hours of math/science; computer course for business majors.

MAJORS Accounting, business administration/commerce/management, computer programming, criminal justice, data processing, drafting and design, (pre)engineering sequence, engineering technology, finance/banking, law enforcement/police sciences, legal secretarial studies, liberal arts/general studies, marketing/retailing/merchandising, nursing, secretarial studies/office management.

LIBRARY NCMC Library with 29,249 books, 66 microform titles, 325 periodicals, 15 on-line bibliographic services, 36 CD-ROMs, 467 records, tapes, and CDs. Acquisition spending 1994–95: $42,000.

COMPUTERS ON CAMPUS 133 computers for student use in computer center, computer labs, learning resource center, library provide access to main academic computer, e-mail, Internet. Staffed computer lab on campus provides training in use of computers, software. Academic computing expenditure 1994–95: $12,000.

COLLEGE LIFE Choral group. ***Student services:*** personal-psychological counseling. ***Campus security:*** 24-hour emergency response devices.

HOUSING 152 college housing spaces available; 60 were occupied 1995–96. Freshmen guaranteed college housing. Off-campus living permitted. ***Option:*** coed (1 building) housing available. Resident assistants live in dorms.

ATHLETICS ***Intramural:*** basketball, bowling, skiing (cross-country), skiing (downhill), tennis, volleyball.

CAREER PLANNING ***Placement office:*** $45,640 operating expenditure 1994–95. ***Services:*** resume preparation, career counseling, careers library.

AFTER GRADUATION 85% of students completing a degree program in 1994–95 went directly on to further study.

EXPENSES FOR 1996–97 Area resident tuition: $1380 full-time, $46 per credit hour part-time. State resident tuition: $1860 full-time, $62 per credit hour part-time. Nonresident tuition: $2310 full-time, $77 per credit hour part-time. Part-time mandatory fees: $2 per credit hour. Full-time mandatory fees: $60. College room and board: $3570. College room only: $1320.

FINANCIAL AID ***College-administered undergrad aid 1995–96:*** 20 need-based scholarships (average $250), 30 non-need scholarships (average $250), low-interest long-term loans from external sources (average $2000), 30 Federal Work-Study (averaging $950), 10 part-time jobs. ***Required forms:*** FAFSA; accepted: CSS Financial Aid PROFILE. ***Priority deadline:*** 5/15. ***Payment plan:*** installment. ***Waivers:*** full or partial for employees or children of employees and senior citizens. ***Notification:*** continuous.

APPLYING Open admission except for nursing program. ***Options:*** early entrance, deferred entrance. ***Required:*** TOEFL for international students. ***Recommended:*** ACT. Test scores used for counseling/placement. ***Application deadline:*** rolling. ***Notification:*** continuous. Preference given to county residents.

APPLYING/TRANSFER ***Entrance:*** noncompetitive. ***Application deadline:*** rolling. ***Notification:*** continuous. ***Contact:*** Mr. David Munger, Dean of Students/Registrar, 616-348-6605.
CONTACT Ms. Kathy Marek, Admissions Secretary, North Central Michigan College, Petoskey, MI 49770-8717, 616-348-6626.

NORTHWESTERN MICHIGAN COLLEGE
Traverse City, Michigan

UG Enrollment: 3,937	**Tuition & Fees (Area Res): $1700**
Application Deadline: rolling	**Room & Board: $4190**

GENERAL State and locally supported, 2-year, coed. Awards certificates, transfer associate, terminal associate degrees. Founded 1951. ***Setting:*** 180-acre small-town campus. ***Total enrollment:*** 3,937. ***Faculty:*** 97 (91 full-time, 100% with terminal degrees, 6 part-time); student-faculty ratio is 23:1.
ENROLLMENT PROFILE 3,937 students from 20 states and territories, 6 other countries. 59% women, 41% men, 63% part-time, 98% state residents, 10% live on campus, 9% transferred in, 1% international, 42% 25 or older, 2% Native American, 1% Hispanic, 1% African American, 1% Asian American. ***Areas of study chosen:*** 50% liberal arts/general studies, 20% health professions and related sciences, 10% business management and administrative services, 5% computer and information sciences. ***Most popular recent majors:*** liberal arts/general studies, business administration/commerce/management, nursing.
FIRST-YEAR CLASS 705 total; 1,068 applied, 100% were accepted, 66% of whom enrolled. 15% from top 10% of their high school class, 60% from top half.
ACADEMIC PROGRAM Core, honor code. Calendar: semesters. Academic remediation for entering students, English as a second language program offered during academic year, services for LD students, advanced placement, honors program, summer session for credit, part-time degree program (daytime, evenings, summer), adult/continuing education programs, co-op programs and internships.
GENERAL DEGREE REQUIREMENTS 62 credits; computer course for business administration majors; internship (some majors).
MAJORS Accounting, automotive technologies, aviation technology, business administration/commerce/management, business machine technologies, commercial art, computer information systems, computer programming, computer technologies, criminal justice, culinary arts, data processing, dental services, drafting and design, electrical and electronics technologies, (pre)engineering sequence, flight training, food services management, food services technology, hospitality services, hotel and restaurant management, law enforcement/police sciences, legal secretarial studies, liberal arts/general studies, manufacturing technology, maritime sciences, marketing/retailing/merchandising, medical assistant technologies, nursing, ornamental horticulture, paralegal studies, plastics technology, practical nursing, secretarial studies/office management, tourism and travel.
LIBRARY Mark and Helen Osterlin Library with 49,400 books, 61,000 microform titles, 594 periodicals, 2 on-line bibliographic services, 600 CD-ROMs, 1,171 records, tapes, and CDs.
COMPUTERS ON CAMPUS Computer purchase plan available. Student rooms linked to a campus network. 400 computers for student use in computer center, computer labs, learning resource center, classrooms, library, student center, dorms provide access to main academic computer, e-mail, on-line services. Staffed computer lab on campus provides training in use of computers, software.
COLLEGE LIFE Drama-theater group, choral group, student-run newspaper, radio station. ***Social organizations:*** 15 open to all. ***Most popular organizations:*** Student Government, Honors Fraternity, Student Newspaper, Student Magazine, Student Radio Station. ***Major annual events:*** Campus Clean-Up Day, Annual Barbecue, Graduation. ***Student services:*** health clinic, personal-psychological counseling. ***Campus security:*** 24-hour emergency response devices and patrols, controlled dormitory access, well-lit campus.
HOUSING 550 college housing spaces available; 500 were occupied 1995–96. Freshmen given priority for college housing. On-campus residence required in freshman year except if living with relatives. ***Options:*** coed (1 building), single-sex (3 buildings) housing available. Resident assistants live in dorms.
ATHLETICS ***Intramural:*** basketball, football, sailing, skiing (downhill), softball, volleyball.
CAREER PLANNING ***Placement office:*** 2 full-time, 2 part-time staff. ***Director:*** Ms. Wilemena Prinsen, Coordinator of Career and Student Employment Services, 616-922-1228. ***Services:*** job fairs, resume preparation, resume referral, career counseling, careers library, job bank, job interviews. 56 organizations recruited on campus 1994–95.
AFTER GRADUATION 98% of class of 1994 had job offers within 6 months. 50% of students completing a degree program went directly on to further study.
EXPENSES FOR 1995–96 ***Application fee:*** $15. Area resident tuition: $1576 full-time, $49.25 per credit part-time. State resident tuition: $2608 full-time, $81.50 per credit part-time. Nonresident tuition: $2928 full-time, $91.50 per credit part-time. Part-time mandatory fees per semester range from $10.25 to $51.25. Full-time mandatory fees: $124. College room and board: $4190. College room only: $2310.
FINANCIAL AID ***College-administered undergrad aid 1995–96:*** 576 need-based scholarships (averaging $623), 374 non-need scholarships (averaging $1212), short-term loans (averaging $400), low-interest long-term loans from college funds, loans from external sources (averaging $2296), 41 Federal Work-Study (averaging $1715), 227 part-time jobs. ***Required forms:*** FAFSA; accepted: CSS Financial Aid PROFILE. ***Priority deadline:*** 4/1. ***Payment plans:*** installment, deferred payment. ***Waivers:*** full or partial for employees or children of employees.
APPLYING Open admission for residents of sponsoring counties. ***Options:*** early entrance, deferred entrance, midyear entrance. ***Required:*** TOEFL for international students, ACT ASSET. ***Recommended:*** ACT. ***Required for some:*** ACT. Test scores used for counseling/placement. ***Application deadline:*** rolling. ***Notification:*** continuous until 8/28. Preference given to district residents.
APPLYING/TRANSFER ***Entrance:*** minimally difficult. ***Application deadline:*** rolling. ***Notification:*** continuous until 8/28. ***Contact:*** Ms. Avace Wildie, Counselor, 616-922-1040.
CONTACT Mr. Robert Warner, Director of Financial Aid and Admissions, Northwestern Michigan College, Traverse City, MI 49686-3061, 616-922-1034 or toll-free 800-748-0566. ***Fax:*** 616-922-1339. ***E-mail:*** bvance@nmc.edu. College video available.

OAKLAND COMMUNITY COLLEGE
Bloomfield Hills, Michigan

UG Enrollment: 26,144	**Tuition & Fees (Area Res): $1450**
Application Deadline: rolling	**Room & Board: N/Avail**

GENERAL State and locally supported, 2-year, coed. Part of Michigan Department of Education. Awards transfer associate, terminal associate degrees. Founded 1964. ***Setting:*** 540-acre suburban campus with easy access to Detroit. ***Total enrollment:*** 26,144. ***Faculty:*** 788 (290 full-time, 498 part-time).
ENROLLMENT PROFILE 26,144 students: 59% women, 41% men, 79% part-time, 87% state residents, 7% transferred in, 1% international, 51% 25 or older, 1% Native American, 2% Hispanic, 12% African American, 4% Asian American. ***Areas of study chosen:*** 51% vocational and home economics, 15% health professions and related sciences, 14% liberal arts/general studies, 10% business management and administrative services, 3% engineering and applied sciences, 2% computer and information sciences, 2% library and information studies, 1% fine arts, 1% natural resource sciences. ***Most popular recent majors:*** liberal arts/general studies, business administration/commerce/management.
FIRST-YEAR CLASS 7,456 applied.
ACADEMIC PROGRAM Core. Calendar: semesters. Academic remediation for entering students, English as a second language program offered during academic year, services for LD students, summer session for credit, part-time degree program (daytime, evenings, summer), adult/continuing education programs, co-op programs and internships. Off-campus study at Macomb Community College. Study abroad in England, Mexico.
GENERAL DEGREE REQUIREMENTS 62 credit hours; computer course (varies by major); internship (some majors).
MAJORS Accounting, architectural technologies, art/fine arts, automotive technologies, aviation technology, business administration/commerce/management, ceramic art and design, child care/child and family studies, commercial art, communication, computer information systems, computer programming, computer science, computer technologies, corrections, cosmetology, court reporting, criminal justice, culinary arts, dental services, dietetics, drafting and design, early childhood education, electrical and electronics technologies, electrical engineering technology, electromechanical technology, emergency medical technology, energy management technologies, (pre)engineering sequence, environmental engineering technology, environmental sciences, fashion design and technology, fashion merchandising, flight training, food sciences, food services management, food services technology, gerontology, graphic arts, health services administration, heating/refrigeration/air conditioning, hospitality services, hotel and restaurant management, illustration, industrial engineering technology, landscape architecture/design, law enforcement/police sciences, legal secretarial studies, liberal arts/general studies, library science, machine and tool technologies, manufacturing technology, marketing/retailing/merchandising, mechanical design technology, medical assistant technologies, medical laboratory technology, medical secretarial studies, medical technology, mental health/rehabilitation counseling, nuclear medical technology, nursing, pharmacy/pharmaceutical sciences, photography, physical fitness/exercise science, plastics technology, practical nursing, printing technologies, quality control technology, radiological technology, respiratory therapy, retail management, robotics, safety and security technologies, science, secretarial studies/office management, social work, solar technologies, studio art, welding technology.
LIBRARY 185,000 books, 2,100 microform titles, 1,200 periodicals, 3,500 records, tapes, and CDs.
COMPUTERS ON CAMPUS 60 computers for student use in computer labs, labs, library. Staffed computer lab on campus provides training in use of computers, software.
COLLEGE LIFE Drama-theater group, student-run newspaper, radio station. ***Student services:*** personal-psychological counseling, women's center. ***Campus security:*** 24-hour emergency response devices, late-night transport-escort service.
HOUSING College housing not available.
ATHLETICS Member NJCAA. ***Intercollegiate:*** basketball M(s)/W(s), cross-country running M(s)/W(s), golf M(s), softball W(s), tennis M(s)/W(s). ***Intramural:*** basketball, bowling, cross-country running, football, golf, racquetball, skiing (cross-country), skiing (downhill), softball, swimming and diving, tennis, volleyball.
CAREER PLANNING ***Placement office:*** 2 full-time staff. ***Director:*** Mr. Willie Lloyd, Director, Career Planning and Placement, Coop Ed, 810-340-6735. ***Services:*** job fairs, career counseling, careers library, job bank, job interviews.
EXPENSES FOR 1995–96 Area resident tuition: $1380 full-time, $46 per credit hour part-time. State resident tuition: $2340 full-time, $78 per credit hour part-time. Nonresident tuition: $3270 full-time, $109 per credit hour part-time. Part-time mandatory fees: $35 per semester. Full-time mandatory fees: $70.
FINANCIAL AID ***College-administered undergrad aid 1995–96:*** need-based scholarships, non-need scholarships, short-term loans, low-interest long-term loans from external sources, Federal Work-Study, part-time jobs. ***Required forms:*** CSS Financial Aid PROFILE, institutional, FAFSA. ***Priority deadline:*** 7/1. ***Waivers:*** full or partial for employees or children of employees and senior citizens.
APPLYING Open admission. ***Options:*** early entrance, deferred entrance, midyear entrance. ***Required:*** TOEFL for international students. Test scores used for counseling/placement. ***Application deadline:*** rolling. ***Notification:*** continuous.
APPLYING/TRANSFER ***Entrance:*** noncompetitive. ***Application deadline:*** rolling. ***Notification:*** continuous. ***Contact:*** Dr. Maurice H. McCall, Registrar/Director of Enrollment Services, 810-540-1589.
CONTACT Dr. Maurice H. McCall, Registrar/Director of Enrollment Services, Oakland Community College, Bloomfield Hills, MI 48304-2266, 810-540-1589.

ST. CLAIR COUNTY COMMUNITY COLLEGE
Port Huron, Michigan

UG Enrollment: 4,264	**Tuition & Fees (Area Res): $1714**
Application Deadline: rolling	**Room & Board: N/Avail**

GENERAL County-supported, 2-year, coed. Part of Michigan Department of Education. Awards certificates, transfer associate, terminal associate degrees. Founded 1923. ***Setting:*** 22-acre small-town campus with easy access to Detroit. ***Endowment:*** $1.3 million. ***Research spending 1994–95:*** $1425. ***Total enrollment:*** 4,264. ***Faculty:*** 279 (80 full-time, 100% with terminal degrees, 199 part-time); student-faculty ratio is 19:1.

St. Clair County Community College (continued)

ENROLLMENT PROFILE 4,264 students: 61% women, 69% part-time, 98% state residents, 8% transferred in, 32% have need-based financial aid, 27% have non-need-based financial aid, 1% international, 45% 25 or older, 1% Native American, 1% Hispanic, 2% African American, 1% Asian American. ***Most popular recent majors:*** nursing, liberal arts/general studies, business administration/commerce/management.

FIRST-YEAR CLASS 858 total; 1,131 applied, 100% were accepted, 76% of whom enrolled.

ACADEMIC PROGRAM Core, honor code. Calendar: semesters. Academic remediation for entering students, English as a second language program, services for LD students, advanced placement, self-designed majors, summer session for credit, part-time degree program (daytime), internships.

GENERAL DEGREE REQUIREMENTS 62 credits; math/science requirements vary according to program; internship (some majors).

MAJORS Accounting, advertising, agricultural business, agricultural sciences, agricultural technologies, architectural technologies, art/fine arts, broadcasting, business administration/commerce/management, child care/child and family studies, commercial art, communication, computer information systems, corrections, criminal justice, drafting and design, electrical and electronics technologies, fire science, horticulture, industrial engineering technology, journalism, legal secretarial studies, liberal arts/general studies, machine and tool technologies, manufacturing technology, marketing/retailing/merchandising, medical secretarial studies, mental health/rehabilitation counseling, nursing, pharmacy/pharmaceutical sciences, plastics technology, quality control technology, robotics, science, secretarial studies/office management, welding technology, word processing.

LIBRARY Learning Resources Center with 58,936 books, 145 microform titles, 496 periodicals, 3 CD-ROMs, 1,945 records, tapes, and CDs. Acquisition spending 1994–95: $141,747.

COMPUTERS ON CAMPUS Computer purchase plan available. 350 computers for student use in computer center, computer labs, classrooms, library. Academic computing expenditure 1994–95: $414,891.

COLLEGE LIFE Drama-theater group, choral group, student-run newspaper, radio station. ***Social organizations:*** social clubs. ***Student services:*** personal-psychological counseling. ***Campus security:*** security patrols until 10 p.m.

HOUSING College housing not available.

ATHLETICS Member NJCAA. ***Intercollegiate:*** baseball M(s), basketball M(s)/W(s), golf M(s), softball W. ***Contact:*** Mr. Dale Vos, Athletic Director, 810-989-5568.

CAREER PLANNING ***Placement office:*** 2 full-time, 1 part-time staff; $110,415 operating expenditure 1994–95. ***Director:*** Ms. Susan R. Boyd, Director of Career Planning and Placement, 810-989-5515. ***Services:*** job fairs, resume preparation, resume referral, career counseling, careers library, job bank, job interviews.

EXPENSES FOR 1995–96 ***Application fee:*** $10. Area resident tuition: $1674 full-time, $54 per credit part-time. State resident tuition: $2480 full-time, $80 per credit part-time. Nonresident tuition: $3348 full-time, $108 per credit part-time. Part-time mandatory fees: $40 per year. Full-time mandatory fees: $40.

FINANCIAL AID ***College-administered undergrad aid 1995–96:*** 679 need-based scholarships (average $250), 291 non-need scholarships (average $400), short-term loans (average $50), low-interest long-term loans from college funds (average $1530), loans from external sources (average $2900), 122 Federal Work-Study (averaging $1500), 10 part-time jobs. ***Required forms:*** institutional, FAFSA; accepted: CSS Financial Aid PROFILE. ***Priority deadline:*** 7/1. ***Payment plan:*** deferred payment. ***Waivers:*** full or partial for employees or children of employees and senior citizens.

APPLYING Open admission except for nursing program. ***Options:*** Common Application, early entrance, deferred entrance, midyear entrance. ***Required:*** TOEFL for international students. ***Recommended:*** SAT I or ACT. Test scores used for counseling/placement. ***Application deadline:*** rolling.

APPLYING/TRANSFER ***Required for some:*** standardized test scores. ***Entrance:*** noncompetitive. ***Application deadline:*** rolling. ***Contact:*** Mr. Robert Durkee, Registrar, 810-989-5552.

CONTACT Mrs. Michelle K. Mueller, Director of Admissions, St. Clair County Community College, Port Huron, MI 48061-5015, 810-989-5500. ***Fax:*** 810-984-4730.

SCHOOLCRAFT COLLEGE
Livonia, Michigan

UG Enrollment: 9,393	**Tuition & Fees (Area Res): $1535**
Application Deadline: rolling	**Room & Board: N/Avail**

GENERAL District-supported, 2-year, coed. Part of Michigan Department of Education. Awards certificates, transfer associate, terminal associate degrees. Founded 1961. ***Setting:*** 183-acre suburban campus with easy access to Detroit. ***Endowment:*** $104,068. ***Research spending 1994–95:*** $163,658. ***Educational spending 1994–95:*** $1512 per undergrad. ***Total enrollment:*** 9,393. ***Faculty:*** 421 (127 full-time, 96% with terminal degrees, 294 part-time); student-faculty ratio is 22:1. ***Notable Alumni:*** Geraldine Kiessel, retired school principal; Cheri Holman, professor at Schoolcraft College; Raymond Dreyfuss, advertising media executive at Chrysler Corporation; James Key, sales executive at Digital; Amelia S. Chan, dean at Eastern Michigan University Business School.

ENROLLMENT PROFILE 9,393 students: 58% women, 75% part-time, 99% state residents, 38% transferred in, 11% have need-based financial aid, 1% have non-need-based financial aid, 1% international, 45% 25 or older, 1% Native American, 1% Hispanic, 3% African American, 1% Asian American. ***Areas of study chosen:*** 12% engineering and applied sciences, 4% education, 2% fine arts, 1% architecture, 1% communications and journalism, 1% library and information studies, 1% natural resource sciences, 1% performing arts, 1% premed, 1% prevet, 1% social sciences. ***Most popular recent majors:*** science, liberal arts/general studies, business administration/commerce/management.

FIRST-YEAR CLASS 1,344 total; 2,104 applied, 100% were accepted, 64% of whom enrolled. 5% from top 10% of their high school class, 20% from top quarter, 70% from top half.

ACADEMIC PROGRAM Core. Calendar: semesters. Academic remediation for entering students, services for LD students, advanced placement, honors program, summer session for credit, part-time degree program (daytime, evenings, summer), adult/continuing education programs, co-op programs.

GENERAL DEGREE REQUIREMENTS 60 credit hours; math proficiency; computer course; internship (some majors).

MAJORS Accounting, art/fine arts, biomedical technologies, broadcasting, business administration/commerce/management, child care/child and family studies, child psychology/child development, commercial art, computer graphics, computer information systems, computer programming, computer science, computer technologies, corrections, criminal justice, culinary arts, drafting and design, early childhood education, electrical and electronics technologies, electronics engineering technology, (pre)engineering sequence, environmental engineering technology, food services management, liberal arts/general studies, manufacturing technology, marketing/retailing/merchandising, mechanical design technology, medical records services, metallurgy, nursing, occupational therapy, optical technologies, quality control technology, robotics, safety and security technologies, science, secretarial studies/office management, theater arts/drama, welding technology, word processing.

LIBRARY Bradner Library plus 1 other, with 69,500 books, 322 microform titles, 606 periodicals, 12 CD-ROMs. Acquisition spending 1994–95: $42,952.

COMPUTERS ON CAMPUS 600 computers for student use in computer center, computer labs, learning resource center, applied science building, classrooms, library. Staffed computer lab on campus. Academic computing expenditure 1994–95: $993,456.

COLLEGE LIFE Drama-theater group, choral group, student-run newspaper. ***Social organizations:*** 8 open to all; 1 national fraternity; 5% of eligible men are members. ***Most popular organizations:*** Student Activities Board, Ski Club, Student Newspaper, Music Club, Phi Theta Kappa. ***Major annual events:*** School Daze, Wildlife Education Program, Children's Safe Halloween Party. ***Student services:*** legal services, health clinic, women's center. ***Campus security:*** 24-hour emergency response devices and patrols, late-night transport-escort service.

HOUSING College housing not available.

ATHLETICS Member NJCAA. ***Intercollegiate:*** basketball M(s)/W(s), cross-country running W(s), golf M(s), soccer M(s)/W(s), volleyball W(s). ***Contact:*** Mr. Edward A. Kavanaugh, Athletic Director, 313-462-4400 Ext. 5249.

CAREER PLANNING ***Placement office:*** 6 full-time, 3 part-time staff; $276,516 operating expenditure 1994–95. ***Director:*** Dr. Jean E. Pike, Associate Dean of Student Services, 313-462-4421. ***Services:*** job fairs, resume preparation, career counseling, careers library, job bank, job interviews.

AFTER GRADUATION 65% of students completing a degree program in 1994–95 went directly on to further study.

ESTIMATED EXPENSES FOR 1996–97 ***Application fee:*** $10. Area resident tuition: $1440 full-time, $48 per credit hour part-time. State resident tuition: $2130 full-time, $71 per credit hour part-time. Nonresident tuition: $3150 full-time, $105 per credit hour part-time. Part-time mandatory fees per semester range from $31 to $33.50. Full-time mandatory fees: $95.

FINANCIAL AID ***College-administered undergrad aid 1995–96:*** 200 need-based scholarships (averaging $500), 100 non-need scholarships (averaging $800), short-term loans (averaging $200), low-interest long-term loans from external sources (averaging $2500), Federal Work-Study, 150 part-time jobs. ***Required forms:*** institutional, FAFSA. ***Priority deadline:*** 3/31. ***Waivers:*** full or partial for employees or children of employees and senior citizens.

APPLYING Open admission. ***Options:*** early entrance, deferred entrance, midyear entrance. ***Required for some:*** TOEFL for international students. Test scores used for counseling/placement. ***Application deadline:*** rolling.

APPLYING/TRANSFER ***Entrance:*** minimally difficult. ***Application deadline:*** rolling. ***Contact:*** Ms. Julieanne Ray Tobin, Director of Enrollment Management, 313-462-4426.

CONTACT Ms. Julieanne Ray Tobin, Director of Enrollment Management, Schoolcraft College, Livonia, MI 48152-2696, 313-462-4426. ***Fax:*** 313-462-4553. College video available.

SOUTHWESTERN MICHIGAN COLLEGE
Dowagiac, Michigan

UG Enrollment: 2,551	**Tuition & Fees (Area Res): $1612**
Application Deadline: rolling	**Room & Board: N/Avail**

GENERAL State and locally supported, 2-year, coed. Part of Michigan Department of Education. Awards certificates, transfer associate, terminal associate degrees. Founded 1964. ***Setting:*** 240-acre rural campus. ***Total enrollment:*** 2,551. ***Faculty:*** 180 (45 full-time, 13% with terminal degrees, 135 part-time); student-faculty ratio is 18:1.

ENROLLMENT PROFILE 2,551 students from 7 states and territories, 24 other countries. 64% women, 36% men, 67% part-time, 83% state residents, 9% transferred in, 3% international, 48% 25 or older, 1% Native American, 2% Hispanic, 8% African American, 1% Asian American. ***Areas of study chosen:*** 21% business management and administrative services, 21% health professions and related sciences, 13% liberal arts/general studies, 11% interdisciplinary studies, 9% engineering and applied sciences, 6% education, 3% computer and information sciences, 3% fine arts, 2% biological and life sciences, 2% communications and journalism, 2% physical sciences, 2% psychology, 1% performing arts, 1% prelaw, 1% premed, 1% social sciences, 1% vocational and home economics. ***Most popular recent majors:*** nursing, business administration/commerce/management, liberal arts/general studies.

FIRST-YEAR CLASS 663 total. Of the students who applied, 100% were accepted, 54% of whom enrolled.

ACADEMIC PROGRAM Core, interdisciplinary curriculum, honor code. Calendar: semesters. Academic remediation for entering students, English as a second language program offered during academic year and summer, services for LD students, advanced placement, self-designed majors, tutorials, summer session for credit, part-time degree program (daytime, evenings, weekends, summer), adult/continuing education programs, co-op programs and internships.

GENERAL DEGREE REQUIREMENTS 62 credit hours; algebra competence; computer course.

MAJORS Accounting, applied art, architectural technologies, automotive technologies, aviation technology, biochemical technology, biology/biological sciences, business administration/commerce/management, chemical engineering technology, commercial art, computer information systems, computer programming, data processing, drafting and design, early childhood education, education, electrical and electronics technologies, (pre)engineering sequence, engineering technology, fire science, graphic arts, health science, journalism, legal secretarial studies, liberal arts/general studies, machine and tool technologies, manufacturing technology, marketing/retailing/merchandising, mechanical design technology, medical secretarial studies, nursing, paralegal studies, pharmacy/pharmaceutical sciences, practical nursing, science, secretarial studies/office management, welding technology.

LIBRARY Fred L. Mathews Library with 34,000 books, 23,500 microform titles, 235 periodicals, 5 CD-ROMs, 920 records, tapes, and CDs.

COMPUTERS ON CAMPUS Computer purchase plan available. 200 computers for student use in computer center, computer labs, learning resource center, labs, classrooms provide access to main academic computer. Staffed computer lab on campus provides training in use of computers, software.
COLLEGE LIFE Drama-theater group, choral group, student-run newspaper. ***Most popular organization:*** Phi Theta Kappa. ***Major annual events:*** Fall Student/Staff Picnic, Winter "Beach Day". ***Campus security:*** 24-hour emergency response devices.
HOUSING College housing not available.
ATHLETICS Member NJCAA. ***Intercollegiate:*** baseball M(s), basketball M(s)/W(s), cross-country running M(s)/W(s), softball W(s), track and field M(s)/W(s), volleyball W(s). ***Intramural:*** archery, badminton, basketball, bowling, cross-country running, field hockey, golf, gymnastics, racquetball, skiing (cross-country), skiing (downhill), soccer, tennis, track and field, volleyball, weight lifting, wrestling. ***Contact:*** Mr. Ron Gunn, Dean, Sports Education, 800-456-8675.
CAREER PLANNING ***Placement office:*** 2 full-time staff. ***Director:*** Mr. Al Grashius, Director of Placement, 800-456-8675. ***Services:*** job fairs, resume preparation, resume referral, career counseling, careers library, job bank, job interviews. 70 organizations recruited on campus 1994–95.
EXPENSES FOR 1996–97 Area resident tuition: $1364 full-time, $44 per credit hour part-time. State resident tuition: $1736 full-time, $56 per credit hour part-time. Nonresident tuition: $2108 full-time, $68 per credit hour part-time. Part-time mandatory fees: $8 per credit hour. Full-time mandatory fees: $248.
FINANCIAL AID ***College-administered undergrad aid 1995–96:*** 900 need-based scholarships (average $1000), 350 non-need scholarships (average $300), low-interest long-term loans from external sources (average $1000), 150 Federal Work-Study (averaging $1000), 50 part-time jobs. ***Required forms:*** institutional, FAFSA; accepted: CSS Financial Aid PROFILE. ***Application deadline:*** continuous. ***Waivers:*** full or partial for employees or children of employees and senior citizens.
APPLYING Open admission except for nursing program. ***Options:*** early entrance, deferred entrance, midyear entrance. ***Required:*** school transcript. ***Recommended:*** SAT I or ACT. ***Required for some:*** recommendations, TOEFL for international students. Test scores used for counseling/placement. ***Application deadline:*** rolling. ***Notification:*** continuous until 9/17.
APPLYING/TRANSFER ***Entrance:*** noncompetitive. ***Application deadline:*** rolling. ***Notification:*** continuous until 9/17. ***Contact:*** Mrs. Karen Pugh, Dean of Admissions and Counseling, 616-782-5113 Ext. 310.
CONTACT Mrs. Karen Pugh, Dean of Admissions and Counseling, Southwestern Michigan College, Dowagiac, MI 49047-9793, 616-782-5113 Ext. 310 or toll-free 800-456-8675. ***Fax:*** 616-782-8414. College video available.

SUOMI COLLEGE
Hancock, Michigan

UG Enrollment: 336 — **Tuition & Fees: $9500**
Application Deadline: rolling — **Room & Board: $3700**

Entering its centennial year, Suomi College is excited to announce its approval to offer bachelor's degrees. Beginning in fall 1996, Suomi will offer 3-year (9-semester) bachelor's degrees in business, fine arts, and 4 design majors (ceramic, communications, industrial, and textile). The College will also continue to offer associate degrees.

GENERAL Independent, primarily 2-year, coed, affiliated with Evangelical Lutheran Church in America. Awards transfer associate, terminal associate, bachelor's degrees (part-time study available for associate degree only). Founded 1896. ***Setting:*** 25-acre small-town campus. ***Total enrollment:*** 336. ***Faculty:*** 30 (19 full-time, 100% with terminal degrees, 11 part-time); student-faculty ratio is 14:1.
ENROLLMENT PROFILE 336 students from 8 states and territories, 4 other countries. 66% women, 34% men, 11% part-time, 80% state residents, 30% live on campus, 11% transferred in, 92% have need-based financial aid, 6% international, 32% 25 or older, 2% Native American, 2% Hispanic, 8% African American, 1% Asian American. ***Areas of study chosen:*** 46% health professions and related sciences, 13% liberal arts/general studies, 12% business management and administrative services, 5% education, 2% fine arts, 2% social sciences, 1% engineering and applied sciences, 1% English language/literature/letters, 1% prelaw. ***Most popular recent major:*** business administration/commerce/management.
FIRST-YEAR CLASS 148 total; 336 applied, 81% were accepted, 54% of whom enrolled. 9% from top 10% of their high school class, 13% from top quarter.
ACADEMIC PROGRAM Core, liberal arts/competency based curriculum, honor code. Calendar: semesters. 168 courses offered in 1995–96. Academic remediation for entering students, English as a second language program offered during academic year, services for LD students, advanced placement, self-designed majors, summer session for credit, part-time degree program (daytime, evenings, summer), adult/continuing education programs, internships. Study abroad in Finland (1% of students participate). ROTC: Army (c), Air Force (c).
GENERAL DEGREE REQUIREMENTS 60 credits for associate, 129 credits for bachelor's; 1 year of math; internship (some majors).
MAJORS Applied art, art/fine arts (B), business administration/commerce/management (B), ceramic art and design (B), criminal justice, education, (pre)engineering sequence, English, health science, history, human services, industrial design (B), liberal arts/general studies, music, nursing, philosophy, physical therapy, religious studies, Scandinavian languages/studies, social science, studio art, textile arts (B), textiles and clothing (B), theater arts/drama, tourism and travel.
LIBRARY Suomi College Library with 31,323 books, 28 microform titles, 350 periodicals, 2 on-line bibliographic services, 2,865 records, tapes, and CDs. Acquisition spending 1994–95: $128,342.
COMPUTERS ON CAMPUS 40 computers for student use in computer center, teacher/learning center. Staffed computer lab on campus provides training in use of computers, software. Academic computing expenditure 1994–95: $60,909.
NOTEWORTHY RESEARCH FACILITIES Finnish American Heritage Center.
COLLEGE LIFE Orientation program (3 days, no cost). Drama-theater group, choral group. 15% vote in student government elections. ***Most popular organizations:*** Student Government, Community Service Club, African-American Student Association. ***Major annual events:*** Fall Fest, Winter Fest. ***Student services:*** health clinic, personal-psychological counseling. ***Campus security:*** 24-hour patrols, late-night transport-escort service.
HOUSING 400 college housing spaces available; 109 were occupied 1995–96. Freshmen guaranteed college housing. On-campus residence required through sophomore year. ***Option:*** coed (1 building) housing available. Resident assistants live in dorms.
ATHLETICS ***Intramural:*** basketball, bowling, equestrian sports, ice hockey, softball, tennis, volleyball, weight lifting. ***Contact:*** Ms. Carol Dolata, Physical Education Instructor, 906-487-7264.
CAREER PLANNING ***Placement office:*** 2 full-time staff; $33,268 operating expenditure 1994–95. ***Services:*** resume preparation, career counseling, careers library, job bank.
EXPENSES FOR 1995–96 ***Application fee:*** $20. Comprehensive fee of $13,200 includes full-time tuition ($9500 minimum) and college room and board ($3700). College room only: $2000. Part-time tuition per semester ranges from $2000 to $4400. Full-time tuition ranges up to $14,250 according to program.
FINANCIAL AID ***College-administered undergrad aid 1995–96:*** 91 need-based scholarships (averaging $558), 359 non-need scholarships (averaging $1814), low-interest long-term loans from external sources (averaging $2052), 270 Federal Work-Study (averaging $1137), 10 part-time jobs. ***Required forms:*** institutional, FAFSA; required for some: state; accepted: CSS Financial Aid PROFILE. ***Priority deadline:*** 5/1. ***Payment plan:*** installment. ***Waivers:*** full or partial for employees or children of employees.
APPLYING ***Options:*** early entrance, deferred entrance, midyear entrance. ***Recommended:*** minimum 2.0 GPA, 3 years of high school math and science, some high school foreign language, SAT I or ACT, TOEFL for international students. ***Required for some:*** recommendations, interview, ACT, Nelson Denny Reading Test. Test scores used for counseling/placement. ***Application deadline:*** rolling. ***Notification:*** continuous.
APPLYING/TRANSFER ***Required:*** college transcript. ***Recommended:*** 3 years of high school math and science, some high school foreign language, minimum 2.0 college GPA, minimum 2.0 high school GPA. ***Required for some:*** recommendations, interview. ***Application deadline:*** rolling. ***Notification:*** continuous.
CONTACT Ms. Elise Albrecht, Admissions Counselor, Suomi College, Hancock, MI 49930-1882, 906-487-7274 or toll-free 800-682-7604. ***Fax:*** 906-487-7300.

❖ ***See page 814 for a narrative description.*** ❖

WASHTENAW COMMUNITY COLLEGE
Ann Arbor, Michigan

UG Enrollment: 10,224 — **Tuition & Fees (Area Res): $1574**
Application Deadline: rolling — **Room & Board: N/Avail**

Washtenaw Community College is committed to offering learning experiences that develop skills for employment, provide for continuation at a 4-year college or university, and facilitate lifelong education. The College's benefits include a highly qualified faculty and staff, excellent facilities, state-of-the-art equipment, low tuition, and personalized instruction.

GENERAL State and locally supported, 2-year, coed. Awards certificates, transfer associate, terminal associate degrees. Founded 1965. ***Setting:*** 235-acre suburban campus with easy access to Detroit. ***Endowment:*** $1.7 million. ***Research spending 1994–95:*** $79,000. ***Educational spending 1994–95:*** $1458 per undergrad. ***Total enrollment:*** 10,224. ***Faculty:*** 759 (179 full-time, 10% with terminal degrees, 580 part-time); student-faculty ratio is 16:1.
ENROLLMENT PROFILE 10,224 students from 40 states and territories, 60 other countries. 56% women, 81% part-time, 94% state residents, 32% transferred in, 2% international, 38% 25 or older, 1% Native American, 1% Hispanic, 13% African American, 4% Asian American. ***Areas of study chosen:*** 29% liberal arts/general studies, 25% business management and administrative services, 18% health professions and related sciences, 16% engineering and applied sciences, 6% biological and life sciences, 6% mathematics. ***Most popular recent majors:*** nursing, business administration/commerce/management, liberal arts/general studies.
FIRST-YEAR CLASS 2,810 total; 3,260 applied, 100% were accepted, 86% of whom enrolled. 2% from top 10% of their high school class, 10% from top quarter, 24% from top half.
ACADEMIC PROGRAM Core, interdisciplinary curriculum, honor code. Calendar: semesters. 650 courses offered in 1995–96. Academic remediation for entering students, English as a second language program offered during academic year, services for LD students, advanced placement, self-designed majors, honors program, summer session for credit, part-time degree program (daytime, evenings, weekends, summer), external degree programs, adult/continuing education programs, co-op programs and internships. ROTC: Army (c), Naval (c), Air Force (c).
GENERAL DEGREE REQUIREMENTS 60 credits; 1 course each in math and science; computer course; internship (some majors).
MAJORS Accounting, applied art, architectural technologies, automotive technologies, biology/biological sciences, business administration/commerce/management, business machine technologies, child care/child and family studies, commercial art, computer graphics, computer information systems, computer programming, computer science, construction management, corrections, criminal justice, culinary arts, data processing, dental services, drafting and design, drug and alcohol/substance abuse counseling, electrical and electronics technologies, electrical engineering technology, electromechanical technology, electronics engineering technology, (pre)engineering sequence, engineering technology, fire science, food services management, food services technology, graphic arts, heating/refrigeration/air conditioning, hotel and restaurant management, illustration, industrial arts, industrial design, industrial engineering technology, law enforcement/police sciences, liberal arts/general studies, machine and tool technologies, manufacturing technology, marketing/retailing/merchandising, mechanical engineering technology, medical secretarial studies, nursing, pharmacy/pharmaceutical sciences, photography, printing technologies, quality control technology, radiological technology, respiratory therapy, robotics, secretarial studies/office management, technical writing, welding technology, word processing.
LIBRARY Learning Resource Center with 70,003 books, 579 periodicals, 79 CD-ROMs, 4,131 records, tapes, and CDs. Acquisition spending 1994–95: $189,000.
COMPUTERS ON CAMPUS 150 computers for student use in computer center, computer labs, classrooms, library provide access to main academic computer, on-line services. Staffed computer lab on campus provides training in use of computers, software.

Michigan

Washtenaw Community College (continued)

COLLEGE LIFE Drama-theater group, choral group, student-run newspaper. 4% vote in student government elections. *Social organizations:* 25 open to all. *Most popular organizations:* African-American Student Association, Delta Epsilon Chi, Business Professionals of America. *Student services:* personal-psychological counseling, women's center. *Campus security:* 24-hour emergency response devices and patrols, late-night transport-escort service.
HOUSING College housing not available.
CAREER PLANNING *Placement office:* 4 full-time, 2 part-time staff; $239,336 operating expenditure 1994–95. *Director:* Ms. Angelina Laycock, Director, Career Placement Center, 313-973-3551. *Services:* career counseling, careers library, job bank, job interviews. 27 organizations recruited on campus 1994–95.
AFTER GRADUATION 89% of students completing a degree program in 1994–95 went directly on to further study.
EXPENSES FOR 1995–96 *Application fee:* $15. Area resident tuition: $1530 full-time, $51 per credit hour part-time. State resident tuition: $2190 full-time, $73 per credit hour part-time. Nonresident tuition: $2760 full-time, $92 per credit hour part-time. Part-time mandatory fees: $22 per semester. Full-time mandatory fees: $44.
FINANCIAL AID *College-administered undergrad aid 1995–96:* 2,200 need-based scholarships (averaging $700), 150 non-need scholarships (averaging $500), short-term loans (averaging $210), low-interest long-term loans from college funds (averaging $500), loans from external sources (averaging $2100), Federal Work-Study, 25 part-time jobs. *Required forms:* institutional, FAFSA; accepted: CSS Financial Aid PROFILE, financial aid transcript (for transfers), affidavit of nonsupport. *Priority deadline:* 7/1. *Payment plan:* deferred payment. *Waivers:* full or partial for employees or children of employees and senior citizens.
APPLYING Open admission except for health occupations programs. *Options:* Common Application, early entrance, deferred entrance, midyear entrance. *Required:* TOEFL for international students. *Recommended:* SAT I or ACT. Test scores used for admission. *Application deadline:* rolling. *Notification:* continuous. Preference given to county residents.
APPLYING/TRANSFER *Entrance:* noncompetitive. *Application deadline:* rolling. *Notification:* continuous.
CONTACT Mr. David Placey, Director of Admissions, Washtenaw Community College, Ann Arbor, MI 48106, 313-973-3543. College video available.

WAYNE COUNTY COMMUNITY COLLEGE
Detroit, Michigan

UG Enrollment: 10,792	Tuition & Fees (Area Res): $1386
Application Deadline: rolling	Room & Board: N/Avail

GENERAL State and locally supported, 2-year, coed. Awards transfer associate, terminal associate degrees. Founded 1967. *Setting:* urban campus. *Total enrollment:* 10,792. *Faculty:* 400 (150 full-time, 250 part-time); student-faculty ratio is 24:1.
ENROLLMENT PROFILE 10,792 students: 71% women, 29% men, 70% part-time, 97% state residents, 5% transferred in, 1% international, 74% 25 or older, 1% Native American, 1% Hispanic, 66% African American, 1% Asian American. *Most popular recent majors:* liberal arts/general studies, nursing, business administration/commerce/management.
FIRST-YEAR CLASS 3,872 total; 6,525 applied, 100% were accepted, 59% of whom enrolled.
ACADEMIC PROGRAM Core, honor code. Calendar: semesters. Academic remediation for entering students, English as a second language program offered during academic year and summer, honors program, summer session for credit, part-time degree program (daytime, evenings, weekends), adult/continuing education programs, co-op programs.
GENERAL DEGREE REQUIREMENTS 60 credits; computer course (varies by major).
MAJORS Accounting, automotive technologies, aviation technology, business administration/commerce/management, child care/child and family studies, computer science, court reporting, criminal justice, culinary arts, data processing, dental services, dietetics, drafting and design, education, electrical engineering technology, emergency medical technology, engineering technology, environmental engineering technology, finance/banking, industrial engineering technology, labor studies, law enforcement/police sciences, legal secretarial studies, liberal arts/general studies, marketing/retailing/merchandising, medical laboratory technology, medical secretarial studies, natural resource management, Near and Middle Eastern studies, nursing, occupational therapy, secretarial studies/office management, veterinary technology, welding technology.
LIBRARY Learning Resource Center with 70,000 books, 525 records, tapes, and CDs.
COMPUTERS ON CAMPUS 118 computers for student use in learning labs, library.
COLLEGE LIFE Orientation program (2 days, $20). Student-run newspaper. *Social organizations:* national sororities, local sororities. *Campus security:* 24-hour emergency response devices.
HOUSING College housing not available.
CAREER PLANNING *Placement office:* 1 full-time, 4 part-time staff. *Director:* Mr. Richard Lightbody, Director of Career Planning and Placement, 313-496-2617. *Services:* job fairs, resume preparation, resume referral, career counseling, careers library, job bank, job interviews. 12 organizations recruited on campus 1994–95.
EXPENSES FOR 1995–96 *Application fee:* $10. Area resident tuition: $1296 full-time. State resident tuition: $1680 full-time. Nonresident tuition: $2136 full-time. Part-time tuition per semester ranges from $54 to $648 for area residents, $70 to $840 for state residents, $89 to $1068 for nonresidents. Part-time mandatory fees: $67 per semester. Full-time mandatory fees: $90.

FINANCIAL AID *College-administered undergrad aid 1995–96:* 1,337 need-based scholarships (average $495), low-interest long-term loans from external sources (average $2065), Federal Work-Study, 485 part-time jobs. *Required forms:* institutional, FAFSA; accepted: CSS Financial Aid PROFILE. *Priority deadline:* 6/1. *Payment plan:* installment. *Waivers:* full or partial for employees or children of employees and senior citizens. *Notification:* continuous.
APPLYING Open admission. *Options:* Common Application, early entrance, deferred entrance. *Required:* TOEFL for international students, ACT ASSET. Test scores used for counseling/placement. *Application deadline:* rolling.
APPLYING/TRANSFER *Entrance:* noncompetitive. *Application deadline:* rolling.
CONTACT Office of Admissions, Wayne County Community College, 801 West Fort Street, Detroit, MI 48226-9975, 313-496-2539. *Fax:* 313-961-2791. *E-mail:* caafjh@wccc.edu.

❖ *See page 828 for a narrative description.* ❖

WEST SHORE COMMUNITY COLLEGE
Scottville, Michigan

UG Enrollment: 1,617	Tuition & Fees (Area Res): $1406
Application Deadline: rolling	Room & Board: N/Avail

GENERAL District-supported, 2-year, coed. Part of Michigan Department of Education. Awards transfer associate, terminal associate degrees. Founded 1967. *Setting:* 375-acre rural campus. *Total enrollment:* 1,617. *Faculty:* 71 (26 full-time, 31% with terminal degrees, 45 part-time); student-faculty ratio is 24:1.
ENROLLMENT PROFILE 1,617 students from 3 states and territories, 1 other country. 62% women, 65% part-time, 99% state residents, 2% transferred in, 40% have need-based financial aid, 3% have non-need-based financial aid, 43% 25 or older, 2% Native American, 1% Hispanic, 3% African American, 1% Asian American. *Most popular recent majors:* liberal arts/general studies, nursing, criminal justice.
FIRST-YEAR CLASS 555 total. Of the students who applied, 100% were accepted.
ACADEMIC PROGRAM Core, general studies curriculum, honor code. Calendar: semesters. Average class size 30 in required courses. Academic remediation for entering students, services for LD students, advanced placement, self-designed majors, summer session for credit, part-time degree program (daytime, evenings, summer), adult/continuing education programs, co-op programs and internships.
GENERAL DEGREE REQUIREMENTS 60 credits; computer course for accounting, marketing management, data processing, office information systems, criminal justice majors.
MAJORS Accounting, art/fine arts, automotive technologies, behavioral sciences, business administration/commerce/management, business machine technologies, child care/child and family studies, communication, computer graphics, computer programming, computer technologies, corrections, criminal justice, data processing, education, electrical and electronics technologies, elementary education, emergency medical technology, (pre)engineering sequence, food services management, history, law enforcement/police sciences, legal secretarial studies, liberal arts/general studies, machine and tool technologies, manufacturing technology, marketing/retailing/merchandising, mathematics, medical secretarial studies, nursing, political science/government, practical nursing, psychology, retail management, science, secretarial studies/office management, social work, sociology, studio art, teacher aide studies, welding technology, word processing.
LIBRARY West Shore Library with 19,287 books, 1,500 microform titles, 198 periodicals, 2 CD-ROMs, 2,000 records, tapes, and CDs.
COMPUTERS ON CAMPUS 185 computers for student use in computer center, computer labs, learning resource center, classrooms, library. Staffed computer lab on campus provides training in use of computers, software.
COLLEGE LIFE Drama-theater group, choral group, student-run newspaper. *Social organizations:* 13 open to all. *Most popular organizations:* Teach Club, International Club, Campus Crusade for Christ, Law Enforcement Association, Science Club. *Student services:* personal-psychological counseling. *Campus security:* 24-hour emergency response devices and patrols.
HOUSING College housing not available.
ATHLETICS *Intramural:* basketball, football, racquetball, softball, swimming and diving, volleyball.
CAREER PLANNING *Placement office:* 2 part-time staff. *Services:* job fairs, resume preparation, resume referral, career counseling, careers library, job bank, job interviews. 60 organizations recruited on campus 1994–95.
EXPENSES FOR 1996–97 *Application fee:* $10. Area resident tuition: $1380 full-time, $46 per credit part-time. State resident tuition: $2130 full-time, $71 per credit part-time. Nonresident tuition: $2700 full-time, $90 per credit part-time. Part-time mandatory fees: $6 per semester. Full-time mandatory fees: $26.
FINANCIAL AID *College-administered undergrad aid 1995–96:* 30 need-based scholarships (average $350), 35 non-need scholarships (average $850), short-term loans (average $100), low-interest long-term loans from external sources (average $1000), Federal Work-Study. *Required forms:* institutional, FAFSA. *Priority deadline:* 4/1. *Payment plan:* deferred payment. *Waivers:* full or partial for employees or children of employees and senior citizens.
APPLYING Open admission. *Options:* early entrance, deferred entrance, midyear entrance. *Recommended:* school transcript, ACT. *Required for some:* school transcript, ACT, ACT ASSET. Test scores used for counseling/placement. *Application deadline:* rolling. *Notification:* continuous.
APPLYING/TRANSFER *Application deadline:* rolling. *Notification:* continuous. Contact: Ms. Mary LaDue, Director of Admissions, 616-845-6211 Ext. 3117.
CONTACT Ms. Mary LaDue, Director of Admissions, West Shore Community College, Scottville, MI 49454-9716, 616-845-6211 Ext. 3117. *Fax:* 616-845-0207.

MINNESOTA

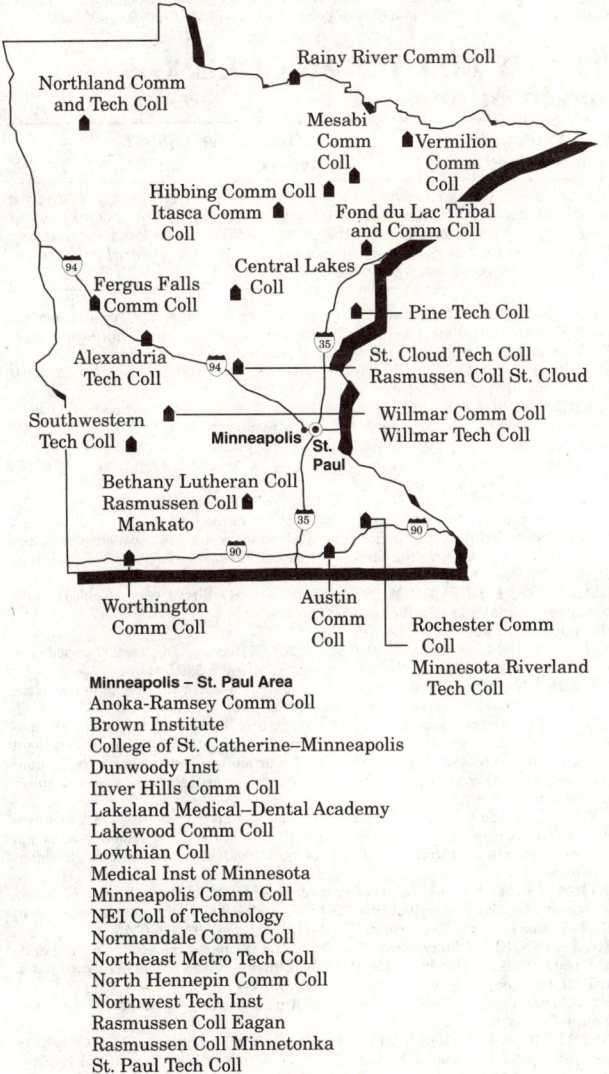

Minneapolis – St. Paul Area
Anoka-Ramsey Comm Coll
Brown Institute
College of St. Catherine–Minneapolis
Dunwoody Inst
Inver Hills Comm Coll
Lakeland Medical–Dental Academy
Lakewood Comm Coll
Lowthian Coll
Medical Inst of Minnesota
Minneapolis Comm Coll
NEI Coll of Technology
Normandale Comm Coll
Northeast Metro Tech Coll
North Hennepin Comm Coll
Northwest Tech Inst
Rasmussen Coll Eagan
Rasmussen Coll Minnetonka
St. Paul Tech Coll

ALEXANDRIA TECHNICAL COLLEGE
Alexandria, Minnesota

UG Enrollment: 1,630	Tuition & Fees (MN Res): $1950
Application Deadline: rolling	Room & Board: N/Avail

GENERAL State-supported, 2-year, coed. Part of Minnesota State Colleges and Universities System. Awards certificates, diplomas, transfer associate, terminal associate degrees. Founded 1961. *Setting:* 40-acre small-town campus. *Total enrollment:* 1,630. *Faculty:* 89 (79 full-time, 10 part-time).
ENROLLMENT PROFILE 1,630 students from 11 states and territories, 3 other countries. 40% women, 60% men, 13% part-time, 94% state residents, 4% transferred in, 85% have need-based financial aid, 1% international, 26% 25 or older, 1% Native American, 1% Hispanic, 1% African American, 1% Asian American. *Most popular recent majors:* law enforcement/police sciences, practical nursing, automotive technologies.
FIRST-YEAR CLASS 639 total.
ACADEMIC PROGRAM Technical/vocational curriculum. Calendar: quarters. 770 courses offered in 1995–96. Academic remediation for entering students, services for LD students, advanced placement, internships.
GENERAL DEGREE REQUIREMENTS 96 credits; internship (some majors).
MAJORS Accounting, automotive technologies, aviation technology, business machine technologies, carpentry, cartography, child care/child and family studies, communication equipment technology, computer information systems, computer programming, computer technologies, corrections, criminal justice, culinary arts, dietetics, fashion merchandising, finance/banking, fish and game management, geography, hotel and restaurant management, information science, interior design, law enforcement/police sciences, legal secretarial studies, machine and tool technologies, management information systems, manufacturing technology, marketing/retailing/merchandising, mechanical engineering technology, medical laboratory technology, medical secretarial studies, practical nursing, retail management, robotics, secretarial studies/office management, welding technology, word processing.
LIBRARY Learning Resource Center with 8,600 books, 120 periodicals, 800 records, tapes, and CDs.
COMPUTERS ON CAMPUS 273 computers for student use in computer center, library.
COLLEGE LIFE Student-run newspaper. 90% vote in student government elections. *Major annual events:* Open House, College for a Day, Sno-Daze. *Student services:* personal-psychological counseling. *Campus security:* 24-hour patrols, late-night transport-escort service.
HOUSING College housing not available.
ATHLETICS *Intercollegiate:* basketball M, volleyball M/W. *Intramural:* basketball, bowling, football, ice hockey, softball, tennis, volleyball. *Contact:* Mr. John Phillips, Vice President, 612-762-4469.
CAREER PLANNING *Placement office:* 2 full-time staff. *Director:* Mr. Dennis Rasmussen, Career Planning and Assessment Coordinator/Counselor, 612-762-4414. *Service:* career counseling.
EXPENSES FOR 1995–96 *Application fee:* $15. State resident tuition: $1920 full-time, $40 per credit part-time. Nonresident tuition: $3840 full-time, $80 per credit part-time. Part-time mandatory fees: $15 per quarter. Manitoba, South Dakota, and Wisconsin residents pay state resident tuition rates. Tuition for North Dakota residents: $2208 full-time, $46 part-time. Missouri residents pay 150% of state resident tuition. Kansas and Nebraska residents pay 150% of state resident tuition for associate of applied science program only. Full-time mandatory fees: $30.
FINANCIAL AID *College-administered undergrad aid 1995–96:* 313 need-based scholarships (average $541), short-term loans (average $150), low-interest long-term loans from external sources (average $2000), 157 Federal Work-Study (averaging $709). *Required forms for some financial aid applicants:* state, institutional; accepted: CSS Financial Aid PROFILE, FAFSA. *Priority deadline:* 5/1. *Payment plan:* deferred payment. *Waivers:* full or partial for senior citizens.
APPLYING *Option:* early entrance. *Required:* school transcript, interview. *Recommended:* ACT. *Required for some:* recommendations, TOEFL for international students, DAT, MMPI. Test scores used for counseling/placement. *Application deadline:* rolling.
APPLYING/TRANSFER *Required:* high school transcript, interview, college transcript. *Required for some:* standardized test scores, recommendations. *Entrance:* minimally difficult. *Contact:* Ms. Gloria Deick, Registrar, 612-762-4470.
CONTACT Mr. David Trites, Student Services Chairperson, Alexandria Technical College, Alexandria, MN 56308-3707, 612-762-0221 Ext. 4415 or toll-free 800-253-9884. *E-mail:* actinfo@alx.tec.mn.us. College video available.

ANOKA-RAMSEY COMMUNITY COLLEGE
Coon Rapids, Minnesota

UG Enrollment: 4,449	Tuition & Fees (MN Res): $2294
Application Deadline: 9/16	Room & Board: N/Avail

Students transferring to 4-year colleges and universities are the majority of degree-seeking students. Others earn a degree and start their careers in 2 years. Twenty associate degree career programs. Beautiful campus overlooking Mississippi River, 20 miles north of Minneapolis/St. Paul. Offers low cost, small classes, and personal attention.

GENERAL State-supported, 2-year, coed. Part of Minnesota State Colleges and Universities System. Awards transfer associate, terminal associate degrees. Founded 1965. *Setting:* 100-acre suburban campus with easy access to Minneapolis–St. Paul. *Research spending 1994–95:* $30,919. *Educational spending 1994–95:* $1384 per undergrad. *Total enrollment:* 4,449. *Faculty:* 179 (93 full-time, 98% with terminal degrees, 86 part-time); student-faculty ratio is 22:1.
ENROLLMENT PROFILE 4,449 students: 67% women, 60% part-time, 99% state residents, 15% transferred in, 1% international, 40% 25 or older, 1% Native American, 1% Hispanic, 1% African American, 2% Asian American. *Areas of study chosen:* 63% liberal arts/general studies, 7% health professions and related sciences, 6% business management and administrative services, 3% social sciences, 2% engineering and applied sciences, 1% agriculture, 1% architecture, 1% biological and life sciences, 1% communications and journalism, 1% computer and information sciences, 1% education, 1% English language/literature/letters, 1% fine arts, 1% library and information studies, 1% mathematics, 1% natural resource sciences, 1% performing arts, 1% physical sciences, 1% prelaw, 1% premed, 1% prevet, 1% psychology, 1% theology/religion, 1% vocational and home economics. *Most popular recent majors:* liberal arts/general studies, business administration/commerce/management, nursing.
FIRST-YEAR CLASS 1,596 total; 1,953 applied, 100% were accepted, 82% of whom enrolled.
ACADEMIC PROGRAM Core, honor code. Calendar: quarters. 394 courses offered in 1995–96. Academic remediation for entering students, English as a second language program offered during academic year, services for LD students, advanced placement, honors program, summer session for credit, part-time degree program (daytime, evenings, summer), co-op programs and internships. Off-campus study at other colleges in the Minnesota State Colleges and Universities System. ROTC: Army (c), Naval (c), Air Force (c).
GENERAL DEGREE REQUIREMENTS 96 quarter credits; computer course for business majors.
MAJORS Accounting, architectural technologies, automotive technologies, business administration/commerce/management, (pre)engineering sequence, horticulture, landscaping/grounds maintenance, legal secretarial studies, liberal arts/general studies, marketing/retailing/merchandising, mechanical design technology, medical records services, medical secretarial studies, nursing, occupational therapy, optometric/ophthalmic technologies, physical therapy, secretarial studies/office management, word processing.
LIBRARY 38,390 books, 130 microform titles, 268 periodicals, 2 on-line bibliographic services, 6 CD-ROMs, 968 records, tapes, and CDs. Acquisition spending 1994–95: $347,649.
COMPUTERS ON CAMPUS 200 computers for student use in computer center, computer labs, learning resource center, classrooms, library provide access to e-mail, Internet. Staffed computer lab on campus provides training in use of computers, software.
COLLEGE LIFE Drama-theater group, choral group, student-run newspaper. *Social organizations:* 11 open to all. *Most popular organizations:* Phi Theta Kappa, Student

Peterson's Guide to Two-Year Colleges 1997

Anoka-Ramsey Community College (continued)

Senate, Student Newspaper, Business Professionals of America, Intervarsity Christian Fellowship. ***Major annual events:*** Fall Picnic, Blahs Buster Week, Spring Picnic. ***Student services:*** personal-psychological counseling, women's center. ***Campus security:*** late-night transport-escort service.

HOUSING College housing not available.

ATHLETICS Member NJCAA. ***Intercollegiate:*** baseball M, basketball M/W, volleyball W. ***Intramural:*** basketball, cross-country running, football, ice hockey, racquetball, skiing (cross-country), skiing (downhill), soccer, softball, swimming and diving, tennis, track and field, volleyball, weight lifting. ***Contact:*** Mr. Harry Messick, Athletic Director, 612-422-3522.

CAREER PLANNING ***Placement office:*** 3 full-time, 2 part-time staff; $43,918 operating expenditure 1994–95. ***Director:*** Dr. Mary Ann Larios, Counselor, 612-427-2600. ***Services:*** job fairs, resume referral, career counseling, careers library, job bank.

EXPENSES FOR 1996–97 ***Application fee:*** $15. State resident tuition: $2143 full-time, $44.65 per credit part-time. Nonresident tuition: $4286 full-time, $89.30 per credit part-time. Part-time mandatory fees: $3.15 per credit. Wisconsin, North Dakota, and South Dakota residents pay tuition at the rate they would pay if attending a comparable state-supported institution in their home state. Full-time mandatory fees: $151.20.

FINANCIAL AID ***College-administered undergrad aid 1995–96:*** 1,300 need-based scholarships (averaging $580), 114 non-need scholarships (averaging $480), short-term loans (averaging $200), low-interest long-term loans from external sources (averaging $2000), 116 Federal Work-Study (averaging $1000), 110 part-time jobs. ***Required forms:*** institutional, FAFSA. ***Priority deadline:*** 6/1. ***Waivers:*** full or partial for employees or children of employees and senior citizens. ***Notification:*** 7/1.

APPLYING Open admission for state residents, except for nursing program. ***Options:*** Common Application, early entrance, deferred entrance. ***Recommended:*** ACT. ***Required for some:*** TOEFL for international students, nursing exam. Test scores used for counseling/placement. ***Application deadline:*** 9/16. ***Notification:*** continuous.

APPLYING/TRANSFER ***Recommended:*** standardized test scores. ***Required for some:*** standardized test scores. ***Application deadline:*** 9/16. ***Notification:*** continuous. ***Contact:*** Ms. Laurie Tralle, Director of Admissions, 612-422-3424.

CONTACT Ms. Laurie Tralle, Director of Admissions, Anoka-Ramsey Community College, Coon Rapids, MN 55433-3499, 612-422-3424. ***Fax:*** 612-422-3341. ***E-mail:*** trallela@an.cc.mn.us. College video and electronic viewbook available.

AUSTIN COMMUNITY COLLEGE
Austin, Minnesota

UG Enrollment: 1,420	**Tuition & Fees (MN Res): $2084**
Application Deadline: rolling	**Room & Board: N/Avail**

GENERAL State-supported, 2-year, coed. Part of Minnesota State Colleges and Universities System. Awards certificates, diplomas, transfer associate, terminal associate degrees. Founded 1940. ***Setting:*** 187-acre small-town campus with easy access to Minneapolis–St. Paul. ***Total enrollment:*** 1,420. ***Faculty:*** 73 (29 full-time, 44 part-time). ***Notable Alumni:*** Scott Heinzel, Nita Swendiman, Scott Leighton.

ENROLLMENT PROFILE 1,420 students from 7 states and territories, 4 other countries. 67% women, 33% men, 56% part-time, 97% state residents, 30% transferred in, 70% have need-based financial aid, 1% international, 50% 25 or older, 1% Native American, 1% Hispanic, 1% African American, 1% Asian American. ***Areas of study chosen:*** 50% liberal arts/general studies, 15% health professions and related sciences, 5% computer and information sciences, 2% business management and administrative services, 2% communications and journalism, 2% education.

FIRST-YEAR CLASS 500 total; 466 applied, 84% were accepted, 57% of whom enrolled. 50% from top half of their high school class.

ACADEMIC PROGRAM Core, honor code. Calendar: quarters. 300 courses offered in 1995–96. Academic remediation for entering students, services for LD students, advanced placement, summer session for credit, part-time degree program (daytime, evenings, summer), adult/continuing education programs, internships. Off-campus study at other colleges in the Minnesota State Community College System. Study abroad in England, France.

GENERAL DEGREE REQUIREMENTS 96 quarter hours; 12 quarter hours of math/science; computer course; internship (some majors).

MAJORS Business administration/commerce/management, child care/child and family studies, corrections, human services, law enforcement/police sciences, liberal arts/general studies, literature, nursing, occupational therapy, painting/drawing, physical therapy.

LIBRARY 20,000 books, 268 periodicals, 2,900 records, tapes, and CDs.

COMPUTERS ON CAMPUS 175 computers for student use in computer center, library. Staffed computer lab on campus provides training in use of computers.

COLLEGE LIFE Drama-theater group, choral group, student-run newspaper. 20% vote in student government elections. ***Social organizations:*** 8 open to all. ***Most popular organizations:*** College Choir, Student Newspaper, Student Activities Board, Phi Theta Kappa, Theater Club. ***Student services:*** personal-psychological counseling. ***Campus security:*** late-night transport-escort service.

HOUSING College housing not available.

ATHLETICS Member NJCAA. ***Intercollegiate:*** baseball M, basketball M/W, golf M/W, softball W, tennis M/W, volleyball W. ***Intramural:*** basketball. ***Contact:*** Mr. Dave Lillemon, Athletic Director, 507-433-0505; Ms. Pat Cornelius, Athletic Director, 507-433-0505.

CAREER PLANNING ***Services:*** job fairs, career counseling.

AFTER GRADUATION 55% of students completing a degree program in 1994–95 went directly on to further study.

EXPENSES FOR 1995–96 ***Application fee:*** $20. State resident tuition: $2028 full-time, $42.25 per quarter hour part-time. Nonresident tuition: $4056 full-time, $84.50 per quarter hour part-time. Part-time mandatory fees: $1.15 per quarter. Wisconsin, North Dakota, and South Dakota residents pay tuition at the rate they would pay if attending a comparable state-supported institution in their home state. Full-time mandatory fees: $56.

FINANCIAL AID ***College-administered undergrad aid 1995–96:*** 900 need-based scholarships, 75 non-need scholarships (averaging $200), short-term loans (averaging $50), low-interest long-term loans from college funds (averaging $1500), loans from external sources (averaging $2000), Federal Work-Study, 100 part-time jobs. ***Required forms:*** state, institutional, FAFSA. ***Priority deadline:*** 5/1. ***Payment plan:*** deferred payment. ***Waivers:*** full or partial for employees or children of employees, adult students, and senior citizens. ***Notification:*** 7/1.

APPLYING Open admission except for nursing, human services, occupational therapy assistant, law enforcement programs. ***Options:*** early entrance, midyear entrance. ***Required:*** school transcript, TOEFL for international students, Academic Skills Assessment Program. ***Recommended:*** ACT. Test scores used for counseling/placement. ***Application deadline:*** rolling.

APPLYING/TRANSFER ***Required:*** college transcript. ***Entrance:*** noncompetitive. ***Application deadline:*** rolling.

CONTACT Ms. Barbara Orcutt, Director of Admissions, Austin Community College, Austin, MN 55912-1407, 507-433-0517 or toll-free 800-747-6941. ***Fax:*** 507-433-0515.

BETHANY LUTHERAN COLLEGE
Mankato, Minnesota

UG Enrollment: 387	**Tuition & Fees: $8563**
Application Deadline: 8/1	**Room & Board: $3554**

Bethany Lutheran College, owned and operated by the Evangelical Lutheran Synod, is a private residential liberal arts junior college with a commitment to the teachings of the Bible as set forth in the Lutheran Confessions. Bethany provides studies in several preprofessional areas and general education, culminating in the Associate in Arts degree.

GENERAL Independent Lutheran, 2-year, coed. Awards transfer associate degrees. Founded 1927. ***Setting:*** 50-acre small-town campus with easy access to Minneapolis–St. Paul. ***Endowment:*** $7.7 million. ***Educational spending 1994–95:*** $2678 per undergrad. ***Total enrollment:*** 387. ***Faculty:*** 45 (20 full-time, 20% with terminal degrees, 25 part-time); student-faculty ratio is 13:1.

ENROLLMENT PROFILE 387 students from 20 states and territories, 4 other countries. 55% women, 2% part-time, 67% state residents, 78% live on campus, 1% transferred in, 75% have need-based financial aid, 1% international, 1% 25 or older, 1% Native American, 1% Hispanic, 2% African American, 1% Asian American. ***Areas of study chosen:*** 100% liberal arts/general studies.

FIRST-YEAR CLASS 211 total; 356 applied, 64% of whom enrolled. 8% from top 10% of their high school class, 24% from top quarter, 55% from top half.

ACADEMIC PROGRAM Core, honor code. Calendar: semesters. Academic remediation for entering students, services for LD students, advanced placement. Off-campus study at Mankato State University. ROTC: Army (c).

GENERAL DEGREE REQUIREMENTS 65 semester credits; 1 course each in math and lab science; computer course for business majors.

MAJOR Liberal arts/general studies.

LIBRARY Memorial Library with 30,000 books, 26,000 microform titles, 230 periodicals, 1,600 records, tapes, and CDs. Acquisition spending 1994–95: $36,594.

COMPUTERS ON CAMPUS 32 computers for student use in computer center, student center. Academic computing expenditure 1994–95: $55,190.

COLLEGE LIFE Orientation program (2 days, no cost, parents included). Drama-theater group, choral group, student-run newspaper. 70% vote in student government elections. ***Student services:*** personal-psychological counseling. ***Campus security:*** 24-hour emergency response devices and patrols, late-night transport-escort service, controlled dormitory access.

HOUSING 265 college housing spaces available; all were occupied 1995–96. Freshmen guaranteed college housing. On-campus residence required through sophomore year except if 21 or over or married. ***Option:*** single-sex (4 buildings) housing available. Resident assistants live in dorms.

ATHLETICS Member NJCAA. ***Intercollegiate:*** baseball M, basketball M(s)/W(s), soccer M(s), tennis M(c)/W(c), volleyball W(s). ***Intramural:*** basketball, football, soccer, tennis, volleyball. ***Contact:*** Mr. Art Westphal, Athletic Director, 507-386-5375.

CAREER PLANNING ***Placement office:*** 2 full-time, 1 part-time staff; $3064 operating expenditure 1994–95. ***Director:*** Mr. Mark Wiechmann, Career/Transfer Coordinator, 507-386-5329. ***Services:*** career counseling, careers library.

AFTER GRADUATION 87% of students completing a degree program in 1994–95 went directly on to further study.

EXPENSES FOR 1996–97 ***Application fee:*** $20. Comprehensive fee of $12,117 includes full-time tuition ($8380), mandatory fees ($183), and college room and board ($3554). College room only: $1242. Part-time tuition per credit ranges from $180 to $360.

FINANCIAL AID ***College-administered undergrad aid 1995–96:*** 200 need-based scholarships (average $5276), 225 non-need scholarships (average $1648), low-interest long-term loans from external sources (average $2709), 59 Federal Work-Study (averaging $800), 118 part-time jobs. ***Required forms:*** institutional, FAFSA. ***Priority deadline:*** 5/1. ***Payment plans:*** installment, deferred payment. ***Waivers:*** full or partial for employees or children of employees.

APPLYING ***Options:*** Common Application, early entrance, deferred entrance. ***Required:*** SAT I or ACT, TOEFL for international students. ***Recommended:*** minimum 2.0 GPA, 3 years of high school math and science, some high school foreign language. Test scores used for admission. ***Application deadline:*** 8/1.

APPLYING/TRANSFER ***Required:*** standardized test scores. ***Entrance:*** minimally difficult. ***Application deadline:*** rolling.

CONTACT Mr. Steven Jaeger, Dean of Admissions, Bethany Lutheran College, Mankato, MN 56001-4490, 507-386-5330 Ext. 331. ***Fax:*** 507-625-1849. ***E-mail:*** admiss@blc.edu.

BRAINERD COMMUNITY COLLEGE
Minnesota—See Central Lakes College

BROWN INSTITUTE
Minneapolis, Minnesota

UG Enrollment: 1,300	**Tuition: $7300/deg prog**
Application Deadline: rolling	**Room & Board: N/Avail**

GENERAL Proprietary, 2-year, coed. Awards transfer associate, terminal associate degrees. Founded 1946. ***Setting:*** 7-acre urban campus. ***Total enrollment:*** 1,300. ***Faculty:*** 96.

ENROLLMENT PROFILE 1,300 students from 15 states and territories. 28% women, 0% part-time, 90% state residents, 5% transferred in, 0% international, 1% Native American, 1% Hispanic, 2% African American, 2% Asian American. *Most popular recent majors:* advertising, broadcasting, electronics engineering technology.
FIRST-YEAR CLASS 140 total. Of the students who applied, 20% were accepted, 65% of whom enrolled.
ACADEMIC PROGRAM Career education curriculum, honor code. Calendar: quarters (modular for medical business clinical specialist program). Academic remediation for entering students, summer session for credit, part-time degree program (daytime, evenings), internships.
GENERAL DEGREE REQUIREMENTS 105 credits; computer course.
MAJORS Advertising, audio engineering, broadcasting, business administration/commerce/management, commercial art, communication equipment technology, computer information systems, computer programming, electronics engineering technology, medical assistant technologies.
LIBRARY Career Resource Center with 768 books, 33 periodicals.
COMPUTERS ON CAMPUS 60 computers for student use in computer center.
COLLEGE LIFE *Most popular organization:* Student Senate. *Major annual events:* Summer Fling, Portfolio Preview, Cultural Diversity Week. *Campus security:* 24-hour emergency response devices, student patrols, late-night transport-escort service.
HOUSING College housing not available.
CAREER PLANNING *Placement office:* 2 full-time, 3 part-time staff. *Director:* Mr. Robert Beringer, Director of Placement, 612-721-2481. *Services:* resume preparation, resume referral, career counseling, job interviews.
EXPENSES FOR 1995-96 *Application fee:* $50. Tuition per degree program ranges from $7300 to $19,200. Tuition guaranteed not to increase for student's term of enrollment.
FINANCIAL AID *College-administered undergrad aid 1995-96:* need-based scholarships, low-interest long-term loans from external sources (averaging $2500), Federal Work-Study, 175 part-time jobs. *Required forms:* institutional, FAFSA; required for some: state. *Priority deadline:* 9/1. *Payment plan:* installment.
APPLYING *Options:* deferred entrance, midyear entrance. *Required:* school transcript, interview, CPAt. *Recommended:* recommendations. *Required for some:* minimum 2.0 GPA. *Application deadline:* rolling.
APPLYING/TRANSFER *Required:* standardized test scores, high school transcript, interview, college transcript. *Recommended:* recommendations. *Required for some:* minimum 2.0 high school GPA. *Application deadline:* rolling.
CONTACT Mr. David Loughry, Director of Admissions, Brown Institute, 2225 East Lake Street, Minneapolis, MN 55407-1932, 612-721-2481. College video available.

CENTRAL LAKES COLLEGE
Brainerd, Minnesota

UG Enrollment: 1,961	Tuition & Fees (MN Res): $2129
Application Deadline: rolling	Room & Board: N/Avail

GENERAL State-supported, 2-year, coed. Part of Minnesota State Colleges and Universities System. Awards transfer associate, terminal associate degrees. Founded 1938. *Setting:* 1-acre small-town campus. *Total enrollment:* 1,961. *Faculty:* 98 (49 full-time, 1% with terminal degrees, 49 part-time).
ENROLLMENT PROFILE 1,961 students: 62% women, 38% men, 52% part-time, 99% state residents, 20% transferred in, 50% have need-based financial aid, 10% have non-need-based financial aid, 45% 25 or older, 1% Native American, 1% Hispanic, 1% African American, 1% Asian American.
FIRST-YEAR CLASS 770 total; 830 applied, 100% were accepted, 93% of whom enrolled.
ACADEMIC PROGRAM Core, honor code. Calendar: quarters. Academic remediation for entering students, advanced placement, summer session for credit, part-time degree program (daytime, evenings, weekends). Off-campus study at other colleges in the Minnesota State Colleges and Universities System.
GENERAL DEGREE REQUIREMENTS 96 credits; 4 credits of math.
MAJORS Accounting, business administration/commerce/management, child psychology/child development, horticulture, legal secretarial studies, liberal arts/general studies, marketing/retailing/merchandising, medical secretarial studies, nursing, secretarial studies/office management.
LIBRARY 16,052 books, 4,350 microform titles, 286 periodicals, 1,416 records, tapes, and CDs.
COMPUTERS ON CAMPUS 100 computers for student use in computer center provide access to main academic computer. Staffed computer lab on campus provides training in use of computers, software.
COLLEGE LIFE Drama-theater group, choral group, student-run newspaper. *Major annual events:* Homecoming, Snow Daze Festival. *Campus security:* late-night transport-escort service.
HOUSING College housing not available.
ATHLETICS Member NJCAA. *Intercollegiate:* baseball M, basketball M/W, football M, softball W, tennis M/W, volleyball W. *Intramural:* basketball, bowling, football, golf, softball, tennis, volleyball. *Contact:* Mr. Al Holmes II, Athletic Director, 218-828-2340; Ms. Jane Peterson, Athletic Director, 218-828-2274.
CAREER PLANNING *Placement office:* 1 full-time staff. *Director:* Ms. Sharon Boone, Coordinator, 218-828-2581. *Services:* job fairs, career counseling.
EXPENSES FOR 1995-96 *Application fee:* $20. State resident tuition: $2028 full-time, $42.25 per credit part-time. Nonresident tuition: $4056 full-time, $84.50 per credit part-time. Part-time mandatory fees: $2.10 per credit. Wisconsin, North Dakota, and South Dakota residents pay tuition at the rate they would pay if attending a comparable state-supported institution in their home state. Full-time mandatory fees: $101.
FINANCIAL AID *College-administered undergrad aid 1995-96:* 613 need-based scholarships (average $915), 76 non-need scholarships (average $300), short-term loans (average $127), low-interest long-term loans from college funds (average $2100), loans from external sources (average $1750), 130 Federal Work-Study (averaging $892), 81 part-time jobs. *Required forms:* institutional, FAFSA; accepted: CSS Financial Aid PROFILE, state. *Priority deadline:* 6/1. *Waivers:* full or partial for employees or children of employees and senior citizens.
APPLYING Open admission except for non-residents. *Options:* deferred entrance, midyear entrance. *Required:* TOEFL for international students. *Recommended:* ACT. Test scores used for counseling/placement. *Application deadline:* rolling.
APPLYING/TRANSFER *Recommended:* standardized test scores. *Application deadline:* rolling.

CONTACT Ms. Marilynn Stoxen, Registrar, Central Lakes College, Brainerd, MN 56401-3904, 218-828-2508. College video available.

COLLEGE OF ST. CATHERINE–MINNEAPOLIS
Minneapolis, Minnesota

UG Enrollment: 1,085	Tuition & Fees: $9880
Application Deadline: rolling	Room Only: $1540

GENERAL Independent Roman Catholic, 2-year, specialized, coed. Administratively affiliated with College of St. Catherine. Awards certificates, transfer associate, terminal associate, master's degrees. Founded 1964. *Setting:* 1-acre urban campus. *Educational spending 1994-95:* $4160 per undergrad. Faculty: 134 (63 full-time, 85% with terminal degrees, 71 part-time); student-faculty ratio is 14:1.
ENROLLMENT PROFILE 1,085 students from 16 states and territories. 86% women, 14% men, 78% part-time, 91% state residents, 7% live on campus, 84% transferred in, 75% have need-based financial aid, 3% have non-need-based financial aid, 0% international, 63% 25 or older, 1% Native American, 2% Hispanic, 6% African American, 3% Asian American. *Areas of study chosen:* 96% health professions and related sciences, 3% liberal arts/general studies, 1% education. *Most popular recent majors:* nursing, physical therapy.
FIRST-YEAR CLASS 470 total; 892 applied, 83% were accepted, 63% of whom enrolled.
ACADEMIC PROGRAM Core, liberal arts and technical curriculum. Calendar: 4-1-4. 236 courses offered in 1995-96. Academic remediation for entering students, services for LD students, summer session for credit, part-time degree program (daytime, evenings), adult/continuing education programs, internships.
GENERAL DEGREE REQUIREMENTS 60 semester credits; math/science requirements vary according to program; computer course; internship (some majors).
MAJORS Deaf interpreter training, drug and alcohol/substance abuse counseling, early childhood education, liberal arts/general studies, medical records services, medical technology, nursing, occupational therapy, physical therapy, radiological technology, respiratory therapy.
LIBRARY Minneapolis Campus Library with 31,425 books, 278 periodicals, 2 on-line bibliographic services, 5 CD-ROMs, 3,000 records, tapes, and CDs. Acquisition spending 1994-95: $46,000.
COMPUTERS ON CAMPUS 40 computers for student use in computer center, learning resource center, library, dorms provide access to main academic computer, off-campus computing facilities, e-mail, Internet. Staffed computer lab on campus provides training in use of computers, software. Academic computing expenditure 1994-95: $56,000.
COLLEGE LIFE *Social organizations:* 2 open to all. *Most popular organizations:* Christian Healthcare Fellowship, Occupational Therapy Club. *Student services:* health clinic, personal-psychological counseling. *Campus security:* 24-hour emergency response devices and patrols, late-night transport-escort service, controlled dormitory access.
HOUSING 83 college housing spaces available; 82 were occupied 1995-96. No special consideration for freshman housing applicants. Off-campus living permitted. *Option:* coed (1 building) housing available. Resident assistants live in dorms.
CAREER PLANNING *Placement office:* 1 full-time staff; $30,000 operating expenditure 1994-95. *Director:* Mr. Michael Peterson, Counselor, 612-690-7830. *Services:* career counseling, careers library, job bank.
EXPENSES FOR 1996-97 *Application fee:* $20. Tuition: $9840 full-time, $328 per semester hour part-time. Full-time mandatory fees: $40. College room only: $1540.
FINANCIAL AID *College-administered undergrad aid 1995-96:* 302 need-based scholarships (averaging $1283), 47 non-need scholarships (averaging $950), short-term loans (averaging $100), low-interest long-term loans from college funds (averaging $2200), loans from external sources (averaging $3000), 48 Federal Work-Study (averaging $950), 41 part-time jobs. *Required forms:* institutional, FAFSA; accepted: CSS Financial Aid PROFILE. *Priority deadline:* 6/1. *Payment plan:* installment. *Waivers:* full or partial for employees or children of employees. *Notification:* continuous.
APPLYING *Options:* deferred entrance, midyear entrance. *Required:* essay, school transcript, 2 recommendations, TOEFL for international students. *Recommended:* minimum 2.0 GPA, 3 years of high school math and science, interview, ACT. *Required for some:* minimum 3.0 GPA. Test scores used for counseling/placement. *Application deadline:* rolling. *Notification:* continuous.
APPLYING/TRANSFER *Required:* essay, high school transcript, 2 recommendations, college transcript. *Recommended:* 3 years of high school math and science, interview, minimum 2.0 college GPA, minimum 2.0 high school GPA. *Required for some:* standardized test scores, minimum 3.0 college GPA, minimum 3.0 high school GPA. *Entrance:* moderately difficult. *Application deadline:* rolling. *Notification:* continuous. *Contact:* Ms. Mary Brown, Registrar, 612-690-8107.
CONTACT Ms. Pamela Johnson, Director of Enrollment and Student Services, College of St. Catherine–Minneapolis, 601 25th Avenue South, Minneapolis, MN 55454-1494, 612-690-7800 or toll-free 800-945-4599. *Fax:* 612-690-7849. *E-mail:* careerinfo@admin.stkate.edu.

❖ *See page 724 for a narrative description.* ❖

DUNWOODY INSTITUTE
Minneapolis, Minnesota

UG Enrollment: 1,191	Tuition & Fees: $5500
Application Deadline: N/R	Room & Board: N/Avail

GENERAL Independent, 2-year, coed. Awards diplomas, transfer associate, terminal associate degrees. *Setting:* urban campus. *Total enrollment:* 1,191. *Faculty:* 75 (60 full-time, 15 part-time).
ENROLLMENT PROFILE 1,191 students.
FIRST-YEAR CLASS 449 total. Of the students who applied, 90% were accepted, 90% of whom enrolled.
ACADEMIC PROGRAM Calendar: quarters.
GENERAL DEGREE REQUIREMENTS 103 quarter hours; math/science requirements vary according to program; computer course.
MAJORS Automotive technologies, civil engineering technology, computer information systems, drafting and design, electrical engineering technology, electronics engineering

Dunwoody Institute (continued)
technology, engineering design, heating/refrigeration/air conditioning, machine and tool technologies, management information systems, printing technologies, systems science.
EXPENSES FOR 1996–97 Tuition: $5500 full-time. Part-time tuition per quarter hour ranges from $65 to $155.
APPLYING Open admission. ***Recommended:*** school transcript.
APPLYING/TRANSFER ***Required:*** college transcript. ***Recommended:*** high school transcript.
CONTACT Mr. Bernard Morgan, Director of Marketing and Admissions, Dunwoody Institute, 818 Dunwoody Boulevard, Minneapolis, MN 55403, 612-374-5800.

FERGUS FALLS COMMUNITY COLLEGE
Fergus Falls, Minnesota

UG Enrollment: 1,299 | **Tuition & Fees (MN Res): $2125**
Application Deadline: rolling | **Room & Board: N/Avail**

GENERAL State-supported, 2-year, coed. Part of Minnesota State Colleges and Universities System. Awards transfer associate, terminal associate degrees. Founded 1960. ***Setting:*** 146-acre rural campus. ***Total enrollment:*** 1,299. ***Faculty:*** 63 (35 full-time, 6% with terminal degrees, 28 part-time).
ENROLLMENT PROFILE 1,299 students from 7 states and territories, 6 other countries. 59% women, 41% men, 49% part-time, 92% state residents, 15% transferred in, 1% international, 36% 25 or older, 1% Native American, 1% Hispanic, 1% African American, 1% Asian American. ***Most popular recent majors:*** liberal arts/general studies, science.
FIRST-YEAR CLASS 644 total. Of the students who applied, 100% were accepted, 85% of whom enrolled. 5% from top 10% of their high school class, 14% from top quarter, 55% from top half. 4 valedictorians.
ACADEMIC PROGRAM Core, interdisciplinary curriculum. Calendar: quarters. 350 courses offered in 1995–96. Academic remediation for entering students, services for LD students, advanced placement, summer session for credit, part-time degree program (daytime, evenings). Off-campus study at other colleges in the Minnesota State Colleges and Universities System.
GENERAL DEGREE REQUIREMENT 96 credits.
MAJORS Business administration/commerce/management, (pre)engineering sequence, laboratory technologies, law enforcement/police sciences, legal secretarial studies, liberal arts/general studies, marketing/retailing/merchandising, medical laboratory technology, medical secretarial studies, nursing, practical nursing, science, secretarial studies/office management.
LIBRARY Fergus Falls Community College Library with 25,000 books, 48 microform titles, 170 periodicals, 4,300 records, tapes, and CDs. Acquisition spending 1994–95: $199,244.
COMPUTERS ON CAMPUS Computer purchase plan available. 60 computers for student use in computer center, resource center, library provide access to e-mail, on-line services, Internet. Staffed computer lab on campus provides training in use of computers, software. Academic computing expenditure 1994–95: $86,470.
COLLEGE LIFE Drama-theater group, choral group, student-run newspaper. ***Most popular organizations:*** Student Senate, Students In Free Enterprise, Phi Theta Kappa. ***Major annual events:*** Homecoming, "Minnesota Meltdown", Health Awareness Week. ***Student services:*** personal-psychological counseling, women's center. ***Campus security:*** late-night transport-escort service.
HOUSING College housing not available.
ATHLETICS Member NJCAA. ***Intercollegiate:*** baseball M, basketball M/W, football M, softball W, volleyball W, wrestling M. ***Intramural:*** badminton, basketball, bowling, football, golf, skiing (cross-country), skiing (downhill), softball, table tennis (Ping-Pong), tennis, volleyball, weight lifting. ***Contact:*** Mr. David Retzlaff, Athletic Director, 218-739-7538.
CAREER PLANNING ***Services:*** resume preparation, career counseling, careers library.
AFTER GRADUATION 70% of students completing a degree program in 1994–95 went directly on to further study.
EXPENSES FOR 1995–96 ***Application fee:*** $20. State resident tuition: $2028 full-time, $42.25 per credit part-time. Nonresident tuition: $4056 full-time, $84.50 per credit part-time. Part-time mandatory fees per credit range from $2.15 to $3.15. Full-time mandatory fees range from $97 to $142.
FINANCIAL AID ***College-administered undergrad aid 1995–96:*** 153 need-based scholarships (average $256), 160 non-need scholarships (average $461), low-interest long-term loans from external sources (average $2100), 120 Federal Work-Study (averaging $1500), 20 part-time jobs. ***Required forms:*** institutional, FAFSA. ***Priority deadline:*** 6/15. ***Waivers:*** full or partial for employees or children of employees and senior citizens.
APPLYING Open admission for state residents, except for nursing program. ***Options:*** Common Application, early entrance, deferred entrance. ***Required:*** school transcript, TOEFL for international students. ***Recommended:*** ACT. Test scores used for counseling/placement. ***Application deadline:*** rolling. ***Notification:*** continuous.
APPLYING/TRANSFER ***Required:*** high school transcript, college transcript, minimum 2.0 college GPA. ***Recommended:*** standardized test scores. ***Application deadline:*** rolling. ***Notification:*** continuous.
CONTACT Ms. Donna Tollefson, Director of Enrollment Management, Fergus Falls Community College, 1414 College Way, Fergus Falls, MN 56537-1009, 218-739-7425. ***Fax:*** 218-739-7475. College video available.

FOND DU LAC TRIBAL AND COMMUNITY COLLEGE
Cloquet, Minnesota

UG Enrollment: 833 | **Tuition & Fees (MN Res): $2025**
Application Deadline: N/R | **Room & Board: N/Avail**

GENERAL State-supported, 2-year, coed. Awards transfer associate, terminal associate degrees. Founded 1987. ***Setting:*** 31-acre rural campus. ***Educational spending 1994–95:*** $1833 per undergrad. ***Total enrollment:*** 833. ***Faculty:*** 57 (12 full-time, 15% with terminal degrees, 45 part-time).
ENROLLMENT PROFILE 833 students: 65% women, 35% men, 65% part-time, 98% state residents, 1% international, 84% 25 or older, 24% Native American, 1% Hispanic, 1% African American, 1% Asian American. ***Areas of study chosen:*** 100% liberal arts/general studies. ***Most popular recent majors:*** liberal arts/general studies, human services.
FIRST-YEAR CLASS 414 total; 414 applied, 100% were accepted, 100% of whom enrolled.
ACADEMIC PROGRAM Transfer curriculum, honor code. Calendar: quarters. Academic remediation for entering students, services for LD students, tutorials, summer session for credit, part-time degree program (daytime, evenings, summer), adult/continuing education programs, internships. Off-campus study.
GENERAL DEGREE REQUIREMENTS 96 credits; 4 credits of math; 9 credits of science; computer course for English majors; internship (some majors).
MAJORS Human services, law enforcement/police sciences, liberal arts/general studies.
COMPUTERS ON CAMPUS 100 computers for student use in computer center, computer labs, learning resource center, classrooms, library, student rooms provide access to off-campus computing facilities, e-mail, on-line services, Internet. Staffed computer lab on campus provides training in use of computers, software.
COLLEGE LIFE Student-run newspaper. ***Campus security:*** 24-hour emergency response devices, late-night transport-escort service.
HOUSING College housing not available.
CAREER PLANNING ***Placement office:*** 1 part-time staff. ***Director:*** Mr. Bill Kallis, Counselor, 218-879-0815.
EXPENSES FOR 1995–96 ***Application fee:*** $20. State resident tuition: $1901 full-time, $42.25 per credit part-time. Nonresident tuition: $4050 full-time, $90 per credit part-time. Part-time mandatory fees: $2.72 per credit. Full-time mandatory fees: $124.
FINANCIAL AID ***College-administered undergrad aid 1995–96:*** need-based scholarships (averaging $1000), short-term loans (averaging $50), low-interest long-term loans from external sources (averaging $2625), 64 Federal Work-Study. ***Acceptable forms:*** state, institutional, FAFSA. ***Application deadline:*** continuous. ***Payment plan:*** installment. ***Waivers:*** full or partial for employees or children of employees and senior citizens.
APPLYING Open admission. ***Options:*** Common Application, early entrance, deferred entrance, midyear entrance. ***Required:*** Academic Skills Assessment Program. Test scores used for counseling/placement.
APPLYING/TRANSFER ***Required:*** standardized test scores. ***Contact:*** Mr. Bill Kallis, Counselor, 218-879-0815.
CONTACT Mrs. Darla Klocke, Admissions Counselor, Fond du Lac Tribal and Community College, Cloquet, MN 55720, 218-879-0800. ***E-mail:*** darla@asab.fdl.cc.mn.us.

HIBBING COMMUNITY COLLEGE
Hibbing, Minnesota

UG Enrollment: 1,042 | **Tuition & Fees (MN Res): $2115**
Application Deadline: rolling | **Room & Board: N/Avail**

GENERAL State-supported, 2-year, coed. Part of Minnesota State Colleges and Universities System. Awards certificates, transfer associate, terminal associate degrees. Founded 1916. ***Setting:*** 100-acre small-town campus. ***Total enrollment:*** 1,042. ***Faculty:*** 65 (37 full-time, 28 part-time); student-faculty ratio is 22:1.
ENROLLMENT PROFILE 1,042 students from 5 states and territories, 1 other country. 58% women, 42% men, 51% part-time, 97% state residents, 5% transferred in, 1% international, 38% 25 or older, 4% Native American, 1% Hispanic, 1% African American, 1% Asian American. ***Most popular recent majors:*** liberal arts/general studies, (pre)engineering sequence, respiratory therapy.
FIRST-YEAR CLASS 401 total; 817 applied, 100% were accepted, 49% of whom enrolled. 7% from top 10% of their high school class, 54% from top half.
ACADEMIC PROGRAM Core, interdisciplinary curriculum, honor code. Calendar: quarters. Average class size 25 in required courses. Academic remediation for entering students, services for LD students, tutorials, summer session for credit, part-time degree program (daytime, evenings), adult/continuing education programs. Off-campus study at other colleges in the Minnesota State Colleges and Universities System.
GENERAL DEGREE REQUIREMENTS 96 credits; 1 math course; 2 lab science courses.
MAJORS Accounting, business administration/commerce/management, culinary arts, drafting and design, (pre)engineering sequence, history, law enforcement/police sciences, legal secretarial studies, liberal arts/general studies, medical laboratory technology, medical secretarial studies, nursing, respiratory therapy, secretarial studies/office management.
LIBRARY HCC Library with 19,536 books, 190 periodicals, 5 on-line bibliographic services, 250 records, tapes, and CDs.
COMPUTERS ON CAMPUS 150 computers for student use in computer center, computer labs, learning resource center, classrooms, library provide access to main academic computer, e-mail, Internet. Staffed computer lab on campus provides training in use of computers, software.
COLLEGE LIFE Drama-theater group, choral group. ***Most popular organizations:*** Phi Theta Kappa, Performing Music Ensembles Club, Student Senate, Engineering Club. ***Student services:*** personal-psychological counseling. ***Campus security:*** late-night transport-escort service.
HOUSING College housing not available.
ATHLETICS Member NJCAA. ***Intercollegiate:*** baseball M, basketball M/W, football M, ice hockey M, softball W, volleyball W. ***Intramural:*** basketball, bowling, field hockey, football, golf, skiing (cross-country), skiing (downhill), tennis, volleyball. ***Contact:*** Ms. Anna VanTassel, Athletic Director, 218-262-6700.
CAREER PLANNING ***Placement office:*** 1 part-time staff. ***Director:*** Ms. Bonnie Olson, Advisor, 218-262-6700. ***Services:*** resume preparation, career counseling, careers library.
ESTIMATED EXPENSES FOR 1996–97 ***Application fee:*** $20. State resident tuition: $2115 full-time, $47 per credit part-time. Nonresident tuition: $4050 full-time, $90 per credit part-time. Part-time mandatory fees: $2.15 per credit. Wisconsin, North Dakota, and South Dakota residents pay tuition at the rate they would pay if attending a comparable state-supported institution in their home state.
FINANCIAL AID ***College-administered undergrad aid 1995–96:*** 55 need-based scholarships (average $200), 20 non-need scholarships (average $100), low-interest long-term loans from college funds (average $1500), loans from external sources (average $1700), Federal Work-Study, 50 part-time jobs. ***Required forms:*** FAFSA. ***Priority deadline:*** 7/1. ***Waivers:*** full or partial for senior citizens. ***Notification:*** continuous.

APPLYING Open admission except for nursing program. *Options:* early entrance, deferred entrance, midyear entrance. *Required:* school transcript, TOEFL for international students. *Recommended:* 3 years of high school math and science, SAT I or ACT. Test scores used for counseling/placement. *Application deadline:* rolling. *Notification:* continuous.
APPLYING/TRANSFER *Required:* high school transcript, college transcript. *Recommended:* standardized test scores, 3 years of high school math and science. *Entrance:* minimally difficult. *Application deadline:* rolling. *Notification:* continuous. *Contact:* Ms. Carol Borich, Counselor, 218-262-6700.
CONTACT Ms. Teri McKusky, Director of Student Services, Hibbing Community College, Hibbing, MN 55746-3300, 218-262-6716. *E-mail:* admissions@hi.cc.mn.us. College video available.

INVER HILLS COMMUNITY COLLEGE
Inver Grove Heights, Minnesota

UG Enrollment: 5,161	Tuition & Fees (MN Res): $1953
Application Deadline: rolling	Room & Board: N/Avail

GENERAL State-supported, 2-year, coed. Part of Minnesota State Colleges and Universities System. Awards certificates, transfer associate, terminal associate degrees. Founded 1969. *Setting:* 100-acre suburban campus with easy access to Minneapolis–St. Paul. *Research spending 1994–95:* $83,000. *Educational spending 1994–95:* $1100 per undergrad. *Total enrollment:* 5,161. *Faculty:* 220 (100 full-time, 15% with terminal degrees, 120 part-time); student-faculty ratio is 24:1.
ENROLLMENT PROFILE 5,161 students from 6 states and territories, 14 other countries. 63% women, 37% men, 67% part-time, 97% state residents, 24% transferred in, 50% have need-based financial aid, 1% international, 50% 25 or older, 1% Native American, 2% Hispanic, 2% African American, 2% Asian American. *Most popular recent majors:* liberal arts/general studies, paralegal studies, nursing.
FIRST-YEAR CLASS 1,265 total; 1,373 applied, 100% were accepted, 92% of whom enrolled. 10% from top quarter of their high school class, 80% from top half.
ACADEMIC PROGRAM Core, honor code. Calendar: quarters. Average class size 30 in required courses. Academic remediation for entering students, English as a second language program offered during academic year, services for LD students, advanced placement, honors program, summer session for credit, part-time degree program (daytime, evenings), external degree programs, adult/continuing education programs, internships. Off-campus study at other colleges in the Minnesota State Colleges and Universities System. ROTC: Air Force (c).
GENERAL DEGREE REQUIREMENTS 96 credits; internship (some majors).
MAJORS Accounting, air traffic control, automotive technologies, aviation administration, business administration/commerce/management, child care/child and family studies, computer programming, computer technologies, construction technologies, deaf interpreter training, engineering and applied sciences, flight training, food services management, graphic arts, health services administration, human resources, human services, interior design, landscaping/grounds maintenance, law enforcement/police sciences, legal secretarial studies, liberal arts/general studies, machine and tool technologies, marketing/retailing/merchandising, medical secretarial studies, nursing, paralegal studies, secretarial studies/office management, telecommunications.
LIBRARY 42,073 books, 110 microform titles, 335 periodicals, 10 CD-ROMs, 2,500 records, tapes, and CDs. Acquisition spending 1994–95: $250,030.
COMPUTERS ON CAMPUS 195 computers for student use in computer center, computer labs, learning resource center, classrooms, library provide access to off-campus computing facilities, e-mail, on-line services. Staffed computer lab on campus provides training in use of computers, software. Academic computing expenditure 1994–95: $335,000.
COLLEGE LIFE Drama-theater group, choral group, student-run newspaper. *Social organizations:* 28 open to all. *Most popular organizations:* Student Activists for a Viable Environment, Math League, Christian Fellowship, Campus Activities Program, Aviation Club. *Major annual events:* Welcome Week, Snowtennial, Spring Fling. *Student services:* health clinic, personal-psychological counseling. *Campus security:* late-night transport-escort service, evening police patrol.
HOUSING College housing not available.
ATHLETICS *Intramural:* basketball, football, golf, ice hockey, skiing (cross-country), soccer, tennis, volleyball, weight lifting.
CAREER PLANNING *Placement office:* 2 part-time staff; $22,000 operating expenditure 1994–95. *Director:* Ms. Kathy Schur, Counselor, 612-450-8511. *Services:* resume preparation, resume referral, career counseling, careers library, job bank, job interviews. 40 organizations recruited on campus 1994–95.
EXPENSES FOR 1995–96 *Application fee:* $15. State resident tuition: $1953 full-time, $43.40 per credit part-time. Nonresident tuition: $3854 full-time, $85.65 per credit part-time. Wisconsin, North Dakota, and South Dakota residents pay tuition at the rate they would pay if attending a comparable state-supported institution in their home state.
FINANCIAL AID *College-administered undergrad aid 1995–96:* 112 need-based scholarships (average $600), 60 non-need scholarships (average $200), short-term loans (average $150), low-interest long-term loans from external sources (average $1865), 100 Federal Work-Study (averaging $1500), 130 part-time jobs. *Required forms:* institutional, FAFSA. *Priority deadline:* 5/1. *Waivers:* full or partial for employees or children of employees and senior citizens.
APPLYING Open admission except for nursing program. *Options:* early entrance, deferred entrance. *Required:* TOEFL for international students. *Recommended:* school transcript. *Required for some:* ACT. Test scores used for counseling/placement. *Application deadline:* rolling. *Notification:* continuous.
APPLYING/TRANSFER *Required:* college transcript. *Required for some:* standardized test scores. *Entrance:* noncompetitive. *Application deadline:* rolling. *Notification:* continuous. *Contact:* Mr. Jeff Greenwood, Counselor, 612-450-8513.
CONTACT Mrs. Darlene Magter, Clerk, Inver Hills Community College, 2500 East 80th Street, Inver Grove Heights, MN 55076-3209, 612-450-8503. *Fax:* 612-450-8679.

ITASCA COMMUNITY COLLEGE
Grand Rapids, Minnesota

UG Enrollment: 1,138	Tuition & Fees (MN Res): $2232
Application Deadline: rolling	Room & Board: N/Avail

GENERAL State-supported, 2-year, coed. Part of Minnesota State Colleges and Universities System. Awards certificates, diplomas, transfer associate, terminal associate degrees. Founded 1922. *Setting:* 24-acre rural campus. *Educational spending 1994–95:* $4585 per undergrad. *Total enrollment:* 1,138. *Faculty:* 73 (43 full-time, 30% with terminal degrees, 30 part-time).
ENROLLMENT PROFILE 1,138 students from 8 states and territories, 1 other country. 59% women, 31% part-time, 97% state residents, 7% transferred in, 1% international, 36% 25 or older, 4% Native American, 1% Hispanic, 1% African American, 1% Asian American. *Most popular recent majors:* liberal arts/general studies, practical nursing.
FIRST-YEAR CLASS 376 total; 516 applied, 100% were accepted, 73% of whom enrolled.
ACADEMIC PROGRAM Core, interdisciplinary curriculum, honor code. Calendar: quarters. 417 courses offered in 1995–96; average class size 24 in required courses. Academic remediation for entering students, services for LD students, advanced placement, summer session for credit, part-time degree program (daytime, evenings, summer), adult/continuing education programs, co-op programs and internships. Off-campus study at other colleges in the Minnesota State Colleges and Universities System.
GENERAL DEGREE REQUIREMENTS 96 credits; math/science requirements vary according to program; computer course for secretarial studies, accounting, forestry majors; internship (some majors).
MAJORS Accounting, business administration/commerce/management, child care/child and family studies, early childhood education, (pre)engineering sequence, forestry, forest technology, human services, legal secretarial studies, liberal arts/general studies, medical secretarial studies, Native American studies, paralegal studies, practical nursing, real estate, secretarial studies/office management, wildlife management.
LIBRARY Itasca Community College Library with 20,000 books, 40 microform titles, 320 periodicals, 6 CD-ROMs, 2,000 records, tapes, and CDs. Acquisition spending 1994–95: $17,729.
COMPUTERS ON CAMPUS 134 computers for student use in computer center, computer labs, learning resource center, classrooms, library, student center, dorms provide access to e-mail, on-line services, Internet. Staffed computer lab on campus (open 24 hours a day) provides training in use of computers, software. Academic computing expenditure 1994–95: $135,336.
COLLEGE LIFE 17% vote in student government elections. *Social organizations:* 7 open to all. *Most popular organizations:* Student Association, Circle K, Student Ambassadors. *Major annual events:* Christmas Dinner, Spring Fling, Halloween Dance. *Campus security:* student patrols, late-night transport-escort service, evening patrols by trained security personnel.
HOUSING College housing not available.
ATHLETICS Member NJCAA. *Intercollegiate:* baseball M, basketball W, football M, ice hockey M, softball W, volleyball W, wrestling M. *Intramural:* basketball, bowling, softball, table tennis (Ping-Pong), tennis, volleyball. *Contact:* Mr. Mike Rybak, Men's Athletic Director, 218-327-4305; Ms. Kathy Allen, Women's Athletic Director, 218-327-4307.
CAREER PLANNING *Placement office:* 1 full-time, 1 part-time staff; $10,000 operating expenditure 1994–95. *Director:* Ms. Pat Clarke, Counselor, 218-327-4467. *Services:* career counseling, careers library.
AFTER GRADUATION 80% of students completing a degree program in 1994–95 went directly on to further study.
EXPENSES FOR 1996–97 *Application fee:* $15. State resident tuition: $2052 full-time, $42.75 per credit part-time. Nonresident tuition: $4104 full-time, $85.50 per credit part-time. Part-time mandatory fees: $3.75 per credit. Wisconsin, North Dakota, and South Dakota residents pay tuition at the rate they would pay if attending a comparable state-supported institution in their home state. Full-time mandatory fees: $180.
FINANCIAL AID *College-administered undergrad aid 1995–96:* 1,040 need-based scholarships (averaging $505), 71 non-need scholarships (averaging $675), low-interest long-term loans from college funds (averaging $1810), loans from external sources (averaging $2060), 100 Federal Work-Study (averaging $825), 150 part-time jobs. *Required forms:* institutional, FAFSA. *Priority deadline:* 5/1. *Payment plans:* installment, deferred payment. *Waivers:* full or partial for employees or children of employees and senior citizens.
APPLYING Open admission except for practical nursing program. *Options:* Common Application, electronic application, early entrance, deferred entrance, midyear entrance. *Required:* school transcript, TOEFL for international students. *Recommended:* 3 years of high school math and science, some high school foreign language, ACT. Test scores used for counseling/placement. *Application deadline:* rolling. *Notification:* continuous.
APPLYING/TRANSFER *Required:* high school transcript. *Recommended:* standardized test scores. *Entrance:* noncompetitive. *Application deadline:* rolling. *Notification:* continuous. *Contact:* Ms. Candace Perry, Director of Enrollment Services, 218-327-4464.
CONTACT Ms. Candace Perry, Director of Enrollment Services, Itasca Community College, Grand Rapids, MN 55744, 218-327-4464. *E-mail:* info@it.cc.mn.us. College video available.

LAKELAND MEDICAL-DENTAL ACADEMY
Minneapolis, Minnesota

LAKEWOOD COMMUNITY COLLEGE
White Bear Lake, Minnesota

UG Enrollment: 5,290	Tuition & Fees (MN Res): $2275
Application Deadline: rolling	Room & Board: N/Avail

GENERAL State-supported, 2-year, coed. Part of Minnesota State Colleges and Universities System. Awards transfer associate, terminal associate degrees. Founded 1967. *Setting:* 90-acre suburban campus with easy access to Minneapolis–St. Paul. *Research spending 1994–95:* $35,000. *Total enrollment:* 5,290. *Faculty:* 189 (89 full-time, 15% with terminal degrees, 100 part-time); student-faculty ratio is 27:1.
ENROLLMENT PROFILE 5,290 students: 61% women, 64% part-time, 93% state residents, 38% transferred in, 1% international, 49% 25 or older, 1% Native American, 1% Hispanic, 2% African American, 4% Asian American. *Areas of study chosen:* 20% liberal arts/general studies, 6% business management and administrative services, 3%

Lakewood Community College (continued)
health professions and related sciences, 1% computer and information sciences. ***Most popular recent majors:*** liberal arts/general studies, business administration/commerce/management.
FIRST-YEAR CLASS 1,700 total; 2,500 applied, 100% were accepted, 68% of whom enrolled.
ACADEMIC PROGRAM Core, honor code. Calendar: quarters. Academic remediation for entering students, English as a second language program offered during academic year, services for LD students, advanced placement, self-designed majors, honors program, summer session for credit, part-time degree program (daytime, evenings, weekends, summer), external degree programs, adult/continuing education programs, co-op programs and internships. Off-campus study at other colleges in the Minnesota State Colleges and Universities System. ROTC: Army (c).
GENERAL DEGREE REQUIREMENTS 90 quarter hours; 6 quarter hours of math/science; computer course for accounting, business administration, business management, marketing majors; internship (some majors).
MAJORS Accounting, business administration/commerce/management, child psychology/child development, data processing, dietetics, emergency medical technology, environmental sciences, human services, liberal arts/general studies, marketing/retailing/merchandising, nursing, radiological technology, secretarial studies/office management.
LIBRARY Lakewood Community College Library with 34,767 books, 50 microform titles, 250 periodicals, 1 CD-ROM, 1,030 records, tapes, and CDs. Acquisition spending 1994–95: $99,039.
COMPUTERS ON CAMPUS 158 computers for student use in computer center. Staffed computer lab on campus provides training in use of computers, software. Academic computing expenditure 1994–95: $173,000.
COLLEGE LIFE Drama-theater group, choral group, student-run newspaper. ***Social organizations:*** 21 open to all. ***Most popular organizations:*** Student Senate, Phi Theta Kappa, Black Student Union, Flight Club, Asian Club. ***Major annual events:*** Senate Week, Sno Fest, Wood Duck Celebration. ***Student services:*** health clinic, personal-psychological counseling. ***Campus security:*** late-night transport-escort service, day and evening security.
HOUSING College housing not available.
ATHLETICS ***Intramural:*** basketball, cross-country running, golf, skiing (cross-country), skiing (downhill), soccer, softball, table tennis (Ping-Pong), tennis, volleyball.
CAREER PLANNING ***Placement office:*** 1 part-time staff; $18,000 operating expenditure 1994–95. ***Director:*** Ms. Charlotte Nordstrom, Counselor, 612-779-3285. ***Services:*** resume preparation, career counseling, careers library.
EXPENSES FOR 1996–97 State resident tuition: $2275 full-time, $47.40 per quarter hour part-time. Nonresident tuition: $4399 full-time, $91.65 per quarter hour part-time. Wisconsin, North Dakota, and South Dakota residents pay tuition at the rate they would pay if attending a comparable state-supported institution in their home state.
FINANCIAL AID ***College-administered undergrad aid 1995–96:*** 400 need-based scholarships (averaging $1500), 35 non-need scholarships (averaging $500), short-term loans (averaging $200), low-interest long-term loans from external sources (averaging $2000), Federal Work-Study, 150 part-time jobs. ***Required forms:*** institutional; accepted: CSS Financial Aid PROFILE, state, FAFSA. ***Priority deadline:*** 5/15. ***Payment plan:*** deferred payment. ***Waivers:*** full or partial for employees or children of employees and senior citizens. ***Notification:*** 7/1. ***Average indebtedness of graduates:*** $2500.
APPLYING Open admission except for nursing, medical imaging programs. ***Option:*** early entrance. ***Required:*** TOEFL for international students. ***Recommended:*** SAT I or ACT. Test scores used for counseling/placement. ***Application deadline:*** rolling. ***Notification:*** continuous.
APPLYING/TRANSFER ***Recommended:*** standardized test scores. ***Entrance:*** noncompetitive. ***Application deadline:*** rolling. ***Notification:*** continuous.
CONTACT Mr. Dan Thompson, Director of Admissions, Lakewood Community College, White Bear Lake, MN 55110-5697, 612-770-2351 Ext. 386.

LOWTHIAN COLLEGE
Minneapolis, Minnesota

UG Enrollment: 118	**Tuition & Fees: $4725**
Application Deadline: rolling	**Room & Board: N/Avail**

GENERAL Proprietary, 2-year, coed. Awards terminal associate degrees. Founded 1964. ***Setting:*** urban campus. ***Total enrollment:*** 118. ***Faculty:*** 22 (1 full-time, 21 part-time); student-faculty ratio is 9:1.
ENROLLMENT PROFILE 118 students from 6 states and territories, 2 other countries. 90% women, 10% men, 24% part-time, 86% state residents, 46% transferred in, 64% have need-based financial aid, 3% international, 31% 25 or older, 0% Native American, 1% Hispanic, 4% African American, 4% Asian American. ***Areas of study chosen:*** 81% vocational and home economics, 19% business management and administrative services. ***Most popular recent major:*** interior design.
FIRST-YEAR CLASS 54 total; 85 applied, 93% were accepted, 68% of whom enrolled.
ACADEMIC PROGRAM Core, interdisciplinary curriculum. Calendar: quarters. 150 courses offered in 1995–96. Academic remediation for entering students, services for LD students, advanced placement, tutorials, summer session for credit, part-time degree program (daytime, evenings), co-op programs and internships.
GENERAL DEGREE REQUIREMENT 90 credits.
MAJORS Fashion design and technology, fashion merchandising, interior design.
LIBRARY Vera Ochs Library with 1,450 books, 25 periodicals, 232 records, tapes, and CDs.
COMPUTERS ON CAMPUS 3 computers for student use in library.
COLLEGE LIFE Orientation program (4 days, no cost). ***Student services:*** personal-psychological counseling.
HOUSING College housing not available.
CAREER PLANNING ***Placement office:*** 1 full-time, 1 part-time staff. ***Director:*** Ms. Lynnae Otto, Director of Career Center, 612-332-3361. ***Services:*** resume preparation, resume referral, career counseling, careers library, job interviews.
AFTER GRADUATION 85% of class of 1994 had job offers within 6 months. 15% of students completing a degree program went directly on to further study.
EXPENSES FOR 1996–97 ***Application fee:*** $50. Tuition: $4725 full-time, $105 per credit part-time. Tuition guaranteed not to increase for student's term of enrollment.
FINANCIAL AID ***College-administered undergrad aid 1995–96:*** 4 need-based scholarships (average $700), short-term loans (average $300), low-interest long-term loans from external sources (average $2650), Federal Work-Study, 1 part-time job. ***Required forms:*** institutional, FAFSA; required for some: state; accepted: CSS Financial Aid PROFILE. ***Application deadline:*** continuous to 9/15. ***Payment plan:*** installment. ***Waivers:*** full or partial for employees or children of employees.
APPLYING ***Option:*** deferred entrance. ***Required:*** Thurston Mental Alertness Test. ***Recommended:*** 3 years of high school math, ACT. Test scores used for admission. ***Application deadline:*** rolling.
APPLYING/TRANSFER ***Required:*** standardized test scores. ***Recommended:*** 3 years of high school math. ***Entrance:*** minimally difficult. ***Application deadline:*** rolling. ***Contact:*** Mr. Michael Williams, Dean of Education, 612-332-3361.
CONTACT Ms. Ellen Yazbeck, Admissions Advisor, Lowthian College, 825 2nd Avenue South, Minneapolis, MN 55402-2836, 612-332-3361 or toll-free 800-777-FMID.

MEDICAL INSTITUTE OF MINNESOTA
Bloomington, Minnesota

UG Enrollment: 650	**Tuition & Fees: $6375**
Application Deadline: rolling	**Room & Board: N/Avail**

Founded in 1961, the Medical Institute of Minnesota is an accredited 2-year college offering associate degrees for entry into the following fields: diagnostic medical sonography, health information technology, histotechnology, medical assisting, medical laboratory technology, radiologic technology, and veterinary technology. Students receive general and technical education on campus, plus 4–6 month internships. Flexible schedules, financial aid, and on-site child care are available.

GENERAL Proprietary, 2-year, specialized, coed. Awards transfer associate, terminal associate degrees. Founded 1961. ***Setting:*** 4-acre suburban campus with easy access to Minneapolis. ***Educational spending 1994–95:*** $5800 per undergrad. ***Total enrollment:*** 650. ***Faculty:*** 44 (32 full-time, 68% with terminal degrees, 12 part-time); student-faculty ratio is 18:1.
ENROLLMENT PROFILE 650 students from 8 states and territories, 5 other countries. 85% women, 30% part-time, 75% state residents, 50% transferred in, 50% 25 or older, 1% Native American, 3% Hispanic, 10% African American, 2% Asian American. ***Areas of study chosen:*** 100% health professions and related sciences.
FIRST-YEAR CLASS 200 total; 392 applied, 87% were accepted, 59% of whom enrolled.
ACADEMIC PROGRAM Core, health care practice curriculum, honor code. Calendar: quarters. 64 courses offered in 1995–96. Academic remediation for entering students, services for LD students, tutorials, summer session for credit, part-time degree program (daytime, evenings, summer), internships.
GENERAL DEGREE REQUIREMENTS 95 credits; 1 math course; computer course; internship.
MAJORS Laboratory technologies, medical assistant technologies, medical laboratory technology, medical records services, medical technology, radiological sciences, radiological technology, veterinary technology.
LIBRARY 2,000 books, 15 periodicals, 30 records, tapes, and CDs. Acquisition spending 1994–95: $55,000.
COMPUTERS ON CAMPUS 50 computers for student use in computer center, computer labs, library, student center. Staffed computer lab on campus provides training in use of computers, software. Academic computing expenditure 1994–95: $45,000.
COLLEGE LIFE ***Campus security:*** 24-hour emergency response devices, late-night transport-escort service.
HOUSING College housing not available.
CAREER PLANNING ***Placement office:*** 1 full-time, 1 part-time staff; $18,000 operating expenditure 1994–95. ***Director:*** Ms. Lea Hunley, Student Placement Coordinator, 612-844-0064. ***Services:*** resume preparation, resume referral, career counseling, careers library, job bank.
AFTER GRADUATION 85% of class of 1994 had job offers within 6 months.
EXPENSES FOR 1995–96 ***Application fee:*** $25. Tuition: $6375 full-time, $157 per credit part-time.
FINANCIAL AID ***College-administered undergrad aid 1995–96:*** need-based scholarships, low-interest long-term loans from external sources (average $3500), 10 part-time jobs. ***Required forms:*** institutional, FAFSA; required for some: state; accepted: CSS Financial Aid PROFILE. ***Application deadline:*** continuous. ***Payment plans:*** installment, deferred payment. ***Waivers:*** full or partial for employees or children of employees. ***Average indebtedness of graduates:*** $6000.
APPLYING ***Options:*** deferred entrance, midyear entrance. ***Required:*** school transcript, Wonderlic aptitude test. Test scores used for admission and counseling/placement. ***Application deadline:*** rolling.
APPLYING/TRANSFER ***Required:*** standardized test scores, high school transcript. ***Entrance:*** moderately difficult. ***Application deadline:*** rolling. ***Contact:*** Dr. Bruce Cunliffe, Director of Education, 612-844-0064.
CONTACT Ms. O. Jeanne Stoneking, Director of Public Affairs, Medical Institute of Minnesota, Bloomington, MN 55437-1003, 612-844-0064 or toll-free 800-328-6795 Ext. 324 (in-state). ***Fax:*** 612-844-0671.

MESABI COMMUNITY COLLEGE
Virginia, Minnesota

UG Enrollment: 1,009	**Tuition & Fees (MN Res): $2292**
Application Deadline: rolling	**Room Only: $2115**

GENERAL State-supported, 2-year, coed. Part of Minnesota State Colleges and Universities System. Awards transfer associate, terminal associate degrees. Founded 1918. ***Setting:*** 30-acre small-town campus. ***Total enrollment:*** 1,009. ***Faculty:*** 71 (33 full-time, 9% with terminal degrees, 38 part-time).
ENROLLMENT PROFILE 1,009 students from 6 states and territories, 8 other countries. 60% women, 40% men, 42% part-time, 96% state residents, 10% live on campus, 5% transferred in, 1% international, 32% 25 or older, 4% Native American, 1% Hispanic, 2% African American. ***Areas of study chosen:*** 59% liberal arts/general studies, 5% business management and administrative services, 5% education, 5% health professions and related sciences, 4% social sciences, 3% engineering and applied sciences, 3% psychology, 2% vocational and home economics, 1% architecture, 1% area and ethnic studies, 1%

biological and life sciences, 1% communications and journalism, 1% computer and information sciences, 1% fine arts, 1% library and information studies, 1% mathematics, 1% natural resource sciences, 1% physical sciences, 1% predentistry, 1% prelaw, 1% premed, 1% prevet.
FIRST-YEAR CLASS 416 total; 341 applied, 100% were accepted, 82% of whom enrolled. 9% from top 10% of their high school class, 65% from top half.
ACADEMIC PROGRAM Core, honor code. Calendar: quarters. Academic remediation for entering students, English as a second language program, services for LD students, advanced placement, self-designed majors, tutorials, summer session for credit, part-time degree program (daytime, evenings), adult/continuing education programs, co-op programs and internships. Off-campus study at other colleges in the Minnesota State Colleges and Universities System.
GENERAL DEGREE REQUIREMENTS 96 credits; 1 math course; computer course; internship (some majors).
MAJORS Drug and alcohol/substance abuse counseling, (pre)engineering sequence, human services, law enforcement/police sciences, liberal arts/general studies, marketing/retailing/merchandising, optical technologies, paralegal studies, secretarial studies/office management.
LIBRARY Mesabi Library with 23,000 books, 22 microform titles, 167 periodicals, 2,000 records, tapes, and CDs.
COMPUTERS ON CAMPUS 80 computers for student use in computer center, computer labs, learning resource center, library provide access to e-mail, Internet. Staffed computer lab on campus provides training in use of computers, software.
COLLEGE LIFE Drama-theater group, choral group. *Social organizations:* 20 open to all. *Student services:* personal-psychological counseling. *Campus security:* late-night transport-escort service.
HOUSING 100 college housing spaces available; 90 were occupied 1995–96. Freshmen given priority for college housing. Off-campus living permitted. *Option:* coed (3 buildings) housing available. Resident assistants live in dorms.
ATHLETICS Member NJCAA. *Intercollegiate:* baseball M, basketball M/W, football M, softball W, volleyball W. *Intramural:* badminton, basketball, bowling, field hockey, football, golf, skiing (cross-country), skiing (downhill), tennis, volleyball. *Contact:* Mr. Bill Wirtanen, Athletic Director, 218-749-7756.
CAREER PLANNING *Director:* Ms. Pat Sterle, Student Support Services Director, 218-749-7788. *Services:* resume preparation, career counseling, careers library.
AFTER GRADUATION 80% of students completing a degree program in 1994–95 went directly on to further study.
EXPENSES FOR 1995–96 *Application fee:* $20. State resident tuition: $2160 full-time, $45 per credit part-time. Nonresident tuition: $4188 full-time, $87.25 per credit part-time. Part-time mandatory fees: $2.75 per credit. Wisconsin, North Dakota, and South Dakota residents pay tuition at the rate they would pay if attending a comparable state-supported institution in their home state. Full-time mandatory fees: $132. College room only: $2115.
FINANCIAL AID *College-administered undergrad aid 1995–96:* 363 need-based scholarships (average $548), 83 non-need scholarships (average $362), low-interest long-term loans from external sources (average $2000), Federal Work-Study, 100 part-time jobs. *Required forms:* state, institutional, FAFSA. *Application deadline:* continuous. *Waivers:* full or partial for employees or children of employees and senior citizens.
APPLYING Open admission for state residents. *Options:* early entrance, deferred entrance, midyear entrance. *Recommended:* ACT, TOEFL for international students. Test scores used for counseling/placement. *Application deadline:* rolling. *Notification:* continuous.
APPLYING/TRANSFER *Recommended:* standardized test scores. *Entrance:* noncompetitive. *Application deadline:* rolling. *Notification:* continuous. *Contact:* Ms. Donnie Gordon, Counselor, 218-749-7774.
CONTACT Ms. Brenda Kochevar, Enrollment Services Assistant, Mesabi Community College, Virginia, MN 55792-3448, 218-749-0314.

MINNEAPOLIS COMMUNITY COLLEGE
Minneapolis, Minnesota

UG Enrollment: 4,224	Tuition & Fees (MN Res): $2125
Application Deadline: 9/18	Room & Board: N/Avail

GENERAL State-supported, 2-year, coed. Part of Minnesota State Colleges and Universities System. Awards certificates, transfer associate, terminal associate degrees. Founded 1965. *Setting:* 4-acre urban campus. *Total enrollment:* 4,224. *Faculty:* 192 (102 full-time, 90 part-time).
ENROLLMENT PROFILE 4,224 students from 18 states and territories. 60% women, 40% men, 55% part-time, 95% state residents, 48% transferred in, 4% international, 50% 25 or older, 3% Native American, 2% Hispanic, 21% African American, 5% Asian American. *Most popular recent majors:* liberal arts/general studies, nursing, human services.
FIRST-YEAR CLASS 735 total.
ACADEMIC PROGRAM Core, honor code. Calendar: quarters. 530 courses offered in 1995–96. Academic remediation for entering students, English as a second language program offered during academic year, services for LD students, advanced placement, self-designed majors, honors program, summer session for credit, part-time degree program (daytime, evenings), adult/continuing education programs, internships. Off-campus study at Minneapolis Technical College, other colleges in the Minnesota State Colleges and Universities System.
GENERAL DEGREE REQUIREMENTS 96 quarter credits; math/science requirements vary according to program; internship (some majors).
MAJORS Accounting, business administration/commerce/management, child care/child and family studies, computer programming, computer technologies, drug and alcohol/substance abuse counseling, film and video production, human services, law enforcement/police sciences, liberal arts/general studies, mental health/rehabilitation counseling, nursing, postal management.
LIBRARY Minneapolis Community College Library with 42,000 books, 1 microform title, 415 periodicals, 4 on-line bibliographic services.
COMPUTERS ON CAMPUS 75 computers for student use in computer center, computer labs, learning resource center. Staffed computer lab on campus provides training in use of software.
COLLEGE LIFE Drama-theater group, choral group, student-run newspaper. *Most popular organizations:* Student Government, International Students Organization, Phi Theta Kappa, Women's Organization, African-American Support Club. *Major annual events:* College Activities Day, Transfer Fair Day, Health Fair/Earth Day. *Student services:* personal-psychological counseling, women's center. *Campus security:* late-night transport-escort service.
HOUSING College housing not available.
ATHLETICS Member NJCAA. *Intramural:* basketball, golf, volleyball. *Contact:* Mr. Jay Pivec, Athletic Director, 612-341-7070.
CAREER PLANNING *Placement office:* 1 part-time staff. *Director:* Ms. Jeanne Snaza, Director, 612-341-7598. *Services:* job fairs, resume preparation, career counseling, careers library, job bank.
EXPENSES FOR 1995–96 *Application fee:* $15. State resident tuition: $2028 full-time, $42.25 per credit part-time. Nonresident tuition: $4056 full-time, $84.50 per credit part-time. Part-time mandatory fees: $2.15 per credit. Wisconsin, North Dakota, and South Dakota residents pay tuition at the rate they would pay if attending a comparable state-supported institution in their home state. Full-time mandatory fees: $97.
FINANCIAL AID *College-administered undergrad aid 1995–96:* need-based scholarships, low-interest long-term loans from external sources (average $2035), Federal Work-Study, 130 part-time jobs. *Required forms:* institutional, FAFSA. *Priority deadline:* 3/1. *Payment plan:* deferred payment.
APPLYING Open admission except for nursing, law enforcement, human services programs. *Options:* early entrance, deferred entrance. *Required:* school transcript, TOEFL for international students. Test scores used for counseling/placement. *Application deadline:* 9/18. *Notification:* continuous. Preference given to state residents.
APPLYING/TRANSFER *Required:* high school transcript. *Entrance:* noncompetitive. *Application deadline:* rolling. *Notification:* continuous. *Contact:* Ms. Bonnie Wiger, Registrar, 612-341-7226.
CONTACT Ms. Bonnie Wiger, Registrar, Minneapolis Community College, 1501 Hennepin Avenue, Minneapolis, MN 55403-1779, 612-341-7226.

MINNESOTA RIVERLAND TECHNICAL COLLEGE
Rochester, Minnesota

Enrollment: N/R	Tuition & Fees: $1248
Application Deadline: rolling	Room & Board: N/Avail

GENERAL State-supported, 2-year, specialized, coed. Awards diplomas, transfer associate, terminal associate degrees.
ACADEMIC PROGRAM Calendar: quarters.
GENERAL DEGREE REQUIREMENT 96 quarter hours.
MAJOR Dental services.
ESTIMATED EXPENSES FOR 1996–97 *Application fee:* $20. Tuition: $1248 full-time, $41.60 per credit hour part-time.
APPLYING Open admission. *Required:* school transcript. *Recommended:* SAT I or ACT. Test scores used for counseling/placement. *Application deadline:* rolling.
APPLYING/TRANSFER *Required:* college transcript. *Recommended:* standardized test scores. *Application deadline:* rolling.
CONTACT Mr. Don Supalla, Vice President of Student Services, Minnesota Riverland Technical College, Rochester, MN 55904, 507-285-8631.

NEI COLLEGE OF TECHNOLOGY
Columbia Heights, Minnesota

UG Enrollment: 468	Tuition & Fees: $5400
Application Deadline: rolling	Room & Board: N/Avail

GENERAL Independent, 2-year, coed. Awards certificates, diplomas, transfer associate, terminal associate degrees. Founded 1930. *Setting:* 8-acre suburban campus with easy access to Minneapolis–St. Paul. *Total enrollment:* 468. *Faculty:* 28 (14 full-time, 10% with terminal degrees, 14 part-time); student-faculty ratio is 20:1.
ENROLLMENT PROFILE 468 students from 7 states and territories, 2 other countries. 8% women, 92% men, 37% part-time, 95% state residents, 1% transferred in, 82% have need-based financial aid, 10% have non-need-based financial aid, 1% international, 37% 25 or older, 1% Native American, 1% Hispanic, 4% African American, 5% Asian American.
FIRST-YEAR CLASS 76 total; 112 applied, 68% were accepted, 100% of whom enrolled.
ACADEMIC PROGRAM Core. Calendar: quarters. 90 courses offered in 1995–96. Tutorials, part-time degree program (daytime, evenings).
GENERAL DEGREE REQUIREMENTS 96 quarter hours; computer course (varies by major).
MAJORS Aviation technology, communication equipment technology, computer information systems, computer technologies, electrical and electronics technologies, electromechanical technology, electronics engineering technology, industrial engineering technology, information science, liberal arts/general studies, management information systems, radio and television studies, telecommunications.
LIBRARY Larson Library with 1,378 books, 60 periodicals, 90 records, tapes, and CDs.
COMPUTERS ON CAMPUS 52 computers for student use in computer labs. Staffed computer lab on campus provides training in use of computers, software.
COLLEGE LIFE *Major annual events:* Summer Picnic, Blood Drive. *Campus security:* 24-hour emergency response devices, late-night transport-escort service.
HOUSING College housing not available.
ATHLETICS *Intramural:* basketball, tennis, volleyball.
CAREER PLANNING *Placement office:* 1 full-time staff. *Director:* Ms. Eileen Weber, Placement Coordinator, 612-781-4881. *Services:* job fairs, resume preparation, resume referral, career counseling, careers library, job bank, job interviews. Students must register freshman year. 17 organizations recruited on campus 1994–95.
AFTER GRADUATION 95% of class of 1994 had job offers within 6 months. 10% of students completing a degree program went directly on to further study.
EXPENSES FOR 1995–96 *Application fee:* $40. Tuition: $5400 full-time, $150 per quarter hour part-time. Tuition guaranteed not to increase for student's term of enrollment.
FINANCIAL AID *College-administered undergrad aid 1995–96:* need-based scholarships, 25 non-need scholarships (average $200), low-interest long-term loans from external sources (average $2625), Federal Work-Study, 15 part-time jobs. *Required forms:* state, institutional, FAFSA. *Priority deadline:* 8/15. *Payment plans:* installment, deferred payment. *Waivers:* full or partial for employees or children of employees.

NEI College of Technology (continued)
APPLYING ***Option:*** midyear entrance. ***Required:*** school transcript, interview, Wonderlic aptitude test. ***Recommended:*** TOEFL for international students. Test scores used for admission. ***Application deadline:*** rolling.
APPLYING/TRANSFER ***Required:*** standardized test scores, high school transcript, interview, college transcript. ***Contact:*** Mr. RichardThomson, Director of Admissions, 612-781-4881.
CONTACT Mr. Chuck R. Nelson, Admissions Representative, NEI College of Technology, Columbia Heights, MN 55421-2910, 612-781-4881 Ext. 7 or toll-free 800-777-7634. ***Fax:*** 612-781-4884.

NORMANDALE COMMUNITY COLLEGE
Bloomington, Minnesota

UG Enrollment: 7,718	**Tuition & Fees (MN Res): $1953**
Application Deadline: rolling	**Room & Board: N/Avail**

GENERAL State-supported, 2-year, coed. Part of Minnesota State Colleges and Universities System. Awards transfer associate, terminal associate degrees. Founded 1968. ***Setting:*** 90-acre suburban campus with easy access to Minneapolis–St. Paul. ***Total enrollment:*** 7,718. ***Faculty:*** 281 (179 full-time, 12% with terminal degrees, 102 part-time); student-faculty ratio is 30:1.
ENROLLMENT PROFILE 7,718 students from 17 states and territories, 12 other countries. 59% women, 41% men, 55% part-time, 98% state residents, 6% transferred in, 1% international, 41% 25 or older, 1% Native American, 1% Hispanic, 3% African American, 4% Asian American. ***Areas of study chosen:*** 38% liberal arts/general studies, 7% business management and administrative services, 4% health professions and related sciences, 3% education, 3% engineering and applied sciences, 1% architecture, 1% communications and journalism, 1% computer and information sciences, 1% natural resource sciences, 1% premed.
FIRST-YEAR CLASS 2,326 total; 4,051 applied, 100% were accepted, 57% of whom enrolled. 4% from top 10% of their high school class, 23% from top quarter, 70% from top half.
ACADEMIC PROGRAM Core, honor code. Calendar: quarters. 479 courses offered in 1995–96. Academic remediation for entering students, English as a second language program offered during academic year, services for LD students, advanced placement, self-designed majors, tutorials, summer session for credit, part-time degree program (daytime, evenings, weekends), adult/continuing education programs, co-op programs and internships. Off-campus study at other colleges in the Minnesota State Colleges and Universities System. Study abroad in Japan, England, Mexico. ROTC: Army (c), Air Force (c).
GENERAL DEGREE REQUIREMENTS 90 quarter credits; computer course for accounting, business administration/management, hospitality services, mechanical engineering technology, office management majors; internship (some majors).
MAJORS Accounting, architectural technologies, biomedical technologies, business administration/commerce/management, child psychology/child development, dental services, dietetics, drafting and design, electromechanical technology, electronics engineering technology, (pre)engineering sequence, engineering technology, environmental sciences, hospitality services, hotel and restaurant management, law enforcement/police sciences, legal secretarial studies, liberal arts/general studies, marketing/retailing/merchandising, mechanical design technology, mechanical engineering technology, medical secretarial studies, nursing, nutrition, radiological technology, secretarial studies/office management.
LIBRARY 83,300 books, 1,500 microform titles, 800 periodicals, 30 CD-ROMs, 2,300 records, tapes, and CDs. Acquisition spending 1994–95: $147,000.
COMPUTERS ON CAMPUS Computer purchase plan available. 315 computers for student use in computer center, computer labs, learning resource center, classrooms, library provide access to main academic computer, e-mail, Internet. Staffed computer lab on campus provides training in use of computers, software. Academic computing expenditure 1994–95: $400,000.
COLLEGE LIFE Drama-theater group, choral group, student-run newspaper. ***Social organizations:*** 30 open to all. ***Most popular organizations:*** Normandale Entertainment and Arts Today (NEAT), Student Senate, Phi Theta Kappa, Speech/Forensics Club. ***Major annual events:*** Spring Fling, Fall Welcome Week, Chart Your Career Series. ***Student services:*** personal-psychological counseling. ***Campus security:*** 24-hour emergency response devices, student patrols, late-night transport-escort service.
HOUSING College housing not available.
ATHLETICS ***Intramural:*** badminton, basketball, bowling, field hockey, football, golf, ice hockey, racquetball, skiing (cross-country), skiing (downhill), soccer, table tennis (Ping-Pong), tennis, volleyball, weight lifting.
CAREER PLANNING ***Placement office:*** 1 full-time staff; $50,000 operating expenditure 1994–95. ***Director:*** Ms. Kathy Bednark, CRC Assistant, 612-832-6533. ***Services:*** job fairs, career counseling, careers library, job bank. 1,500 organizations recruited on campus 1994–95.
EXPENSES FOR 1995–96 ***Application fee:*** $20. State resident tuition: $1953 full-time, $43.40 per quarter hour part-time. Nonresident tuition: $3753 full-time, $83.40 per quarter hour part-time. Wisconsin, North Dakota, and South Dakota residents pay tuition at the rate they would pay if attending a comparable state-supported institution in their home state.
FINANCIAL AID ***College-administered undergrad aid 1995–96:*** 1,588 need-based scholarships (average $623), 50 non-need scholarships (average $350), short-term loans (average $350), low-interest long-term loans from external sources (average $2105), Federal Work-Study, 282 part-time jobs. ***Required forms:*** institutional, FAFSA. ***Priority deadline:*** 5/15. ***Waivers:*** full or partial for employees or children of employees. ***Average indebtedness of graduates:*** $6250.
APPLYING Open admission except for health programs. ***Options:*** Common Application, early entrance, deferred entrance, midyear entrance. ***Required:*** TOEFL for international students. ***Required for some:*** school transcript, ACT. Test scores used for admission. ***Application deadline:*** rolling. ***Notification:*** continuous.
APPLYING/TRANSFER ***Required for some:*** standardized test scores, high school transcript. ***Entrance:*** noncompetitive. ***Application deadline:*** rolling. ***Notification:*** continuous. ***Contact:*** Mr. Dennis Peterson, Director of Admissions, 612-832-6315.
CONTACT Mr. Dennis Peterson, Director of Admissions, Normandale Community College, Bloomington, MN 55431-4399, 612-832-6315. ***Fax:*** 612-832-6571.

NORTHEAST METRO TECHNICAL COLLEGE
White Bear Lake, Minnesota

UG Enrollment: 1,800	**Tuition & Fees (MN Res): $2300**
Application Deadline: rolling	**Room & Board: N/Avail**

GENERAL State-supported, 2-year, coed. Part of Minnesota State Colleges and Universities System. Awards certificates, diplomas, transfer associate, terminal associate degrees. Founded 1970. ***Setting:*** 80-acre suburban campus with easy access to Minneapolis–St. Paul. ***Total enrollment:*** 1,800. ***Faculty:*** 95 (90 full-time, 20% with terminal degrees, 5 part-time); student-faculty ratio is 18:1.
ENROLLMENT PROFILE 1,800 students: 55% women, 45% men, 40% part-time, 90% state residents, 1% international, 65% 25 or older, 2% Native American, 2% Hispanic, 2% African American, 2% Asian American.
FIRST-YEAR CLASS 650 total; 900 applied, 100% were accepted, 72% of whom enrolled.
ACADEMIC PROGRAM Calendar: quarters. 1,300 courses offered in 1995–96. Academic remediation for entering students, English as a second language program offered during academic year, services for LD students, summer session for credit, part-time degree program (daytime, evenings), adult/continuing education programs, internships.
GENERAL DEGREE REQUIREMENT 96 credits.
MAJORS Computer technologies, dietetics, emergency medical technology, environmental sciences, legal studies, quality control technology.
COMPUTERS ON CAMPUS 40 computers for student use in computer center provide access to main academic computer. Staffed computer lab on campus provides training in use of computers, software.
COLLEGE LIFE ***Campus security:*** late-night transport-escort service, daytime patrols.
HOUSING College housing not available.
EXPENSES FOR 1995–96 ***Application fee:*** $20. State resident tuition: $2300 full-time, $43.35 per credit part-time. Nonresident tuition: $4300 full-time, $83.35 per credit part-time.
FINANCIAL AID ***College-administered undergrad aid 1995–96:*** need-based scholarships, Federal Work-Study. ***Required forms:*** CSS Financial Aid PROFILE, FAFSA. ***Application deadline:*** 5/1.
APPLYING Open admission. ***Required:*** school transcript. ***Application deadline:*** rolling.
APPLYING/TRANSFER ***Required:*** high school transcript. ***Required for some:*** college transcript.
CONTACT Mr. Larry Uhlir, Director of Admissions/Records, Northeast Metro Technical College, White Bear Lake, MN 55110, 612-770-2351 Ext. 221 or toll-free 800-228-1978. ***Fax:*** 612-779-5810.

NORTH HENNEPIN COMMUNITY COLLEGE
Minneapolis, Minnesota

UG Enrollment: 5,527	**Tuition & Fees (MN Res): $2182**
Application Deadline: rolling	**Room & Board: N/Avail**

GENERAL State-supported, 2-year, coed. Part of Minnesota State Colleges and Universities System. Awards transfer associate, terminal associate degrees. Founded 1966. ***Setting:*** 80-acre suburban campus. ***Total enrollment:*** 5,527. ***Faculty:*** 220 (120 full-time, 20% with terminal degrees, 100 part-time); student-faculty ratio is 28:1.
ENROLLMENT PROFILE 5,527 students from 15 states and territories, 35 other countries. 62% women, 64% part-time, 98% state residents, 40% transferred in, 1% international, 46% 25 or older, 1% Native American, 1% Hispanic, 4% African American, 2% Asian American. ***Most popular recent majors:*** liberal arts/general studies, nursing, law enforcement/police sciences.
FIRST-YEAR CLASS 1,725 total; 2,700 applied, 97% were accepted, 66% of whom enrolled.
ACADEMIC PROGRAM Core. Calendar: quarters. 800 courses offered in 1995–96. Academic remediation for entering students, English as a second language program offered during academic year, services for LD students, advanced placement, tutorials, honors program, summer session for credit, part-time degree program (daytime, evenings), adult/continuing education programs. Off-campus study at Hennepin Technical Centers. Study abroad in Australia (1% of students participate). ROTC: Air Force (c).
GENERAL DEGREE REQUIREMENTS 96 credits; 12 credits of math/science; computer course for paralegal studies, business administration majors; internship (some majors).
MAJORS Accounting, automotive technologies, business administration/commerce/management, commercial art, construction management, electronics engineering technology, (pre)engineering sequence, fire science, graphic arts, law enforcement/police sciences, liberal arts/general studies, management information systems, manufacturing technology, marketing/retailing/merchandising, materials sciences, medical records services, nursing, paralegal studies, retail management, secretarial studies/office management, transportation technologies.
LIBRARY 33,000 books, 15 microform titles, 410 periodicals, 2,000 records, tapes, and CDs.
COMPUTERS ON CAMPUS 200 computers for student use in computer center, computer labs, learning resource center, various locations throughout campus, classrooms, library. Staffed computer lab on campus provides training in use of computers, software.
COLLEGE LIFE Drama-theater group, choral group, student-run newspaper. 5% vote in student government elections. ***Student services:*** personal-psychological counseling. ***Campus security:*** 24-hour patrols, late-night transport-escort service.
HOUSING College housing not available.
ATHLETICS Member NJCAA. ***Intercollegiate:*** baseball M, softball W. ***Intramural:*** basketball, bowling, football, golf, soccer, tennis, volleyball. ***Contact:*** Ms. Julie Zieminski, Athletic Director, 612-424-0796.
CAREER PLANNING ***Services:*** career counseling, careers library.
AFTER GRADUATION 60% of students completing a degree program in 1994–95 went directly on to further study.
EXPENSES FOR 1995–96 ***Application fee:*** $15. State resident tuition: $2179 full-time, $45.40 per credit part-time. Nonresident tuition: $4207 full-time, $87.65 per credit part-time. Part-time mandatory fees: $1 per quarter. Wisconsin, North Dakota, and South

Dakota residents pay tuition at the rate they would pay if attending a comparable state-supported institution in their home state. Full-time mandatory fees: $3.
FINANCIAL AID ***College-administered undergrad aid 1995–96:*** 1,304 need-based scholarships (average $585), non-need scholarships, short-term loans (average $100), low-interest long-term loans from college funds (average $2075), loans from external sources (average $671), 140 Federal Work-Study (averaging $899), 298 part-time jobs. ***Required forms:*** institutional; required for some: state; accepted: CSS Financial Aid PROFILE, FAFSA. ***Priority deadline:*** 5/1. ***Waivers:*** full or partial for employees or children of employees and senior citizens. ***Notification:*** continuous. ***Average indebtedness of graduates:*** $3250.
APPLYING Open admission except for nursing program, out-of-state applicants. ***Options:*** early entrance, deferred entrance, midyear entrance. ***Required for some:*** school transcript. Test scores used for counseling/placement. ***Application deadline:*** rolling. ***Notification:*** continuous.
APPLYING/TRANSFER ***Entrance:*** noncompetitive. ***Application deadline:*** rolling. ***Notification:*** continuous. ***Contact:*** Mr. Tom Wavrin, Registrar, 612-424-0713.
CONTACT Mr. Tom Wavrin, Registrar, North Hennepin Community College, Minneapolis, MN 55445-2231, 612-424-0713. College video available.

NORTHLAND COMMUNITY AND TECHNICAL COLLEGE
Thief River Falls, Minnesota

UG Enrollment: 1,150	**Tuition & Fees (MN Res): $2138**
Application Deadline: 9/15	**Room Only: $2025**

GENERAL State-supported, 2-year, coed. Part of Minnesota State Colleges and Universities System. Awards diplomas, transfer associate, terminal associate degrees. Founded 1965. ***Setting:*** rural campus. ***Total enrollment:*** 1,150. ***Faculty:*** 61 (47 full-time, 10% with terminal degrees, 14 part-time); student-faculty ratio is 22:1.
ENROLLMENT PROFILE 1,150 students from 17 states and territories, 3 other countries. 49% women, 51% men, 32% part-time, 94% state residents, 11% transferred in, 1% international, 32% 25 or older, 2% Native American, 1% Hispanic, 1% African American, 1% Asian American. ***Areas of study chosen:*** 30% vocational and home economics, 20% liberal arts/general studies, 12% education, 10% social sciences, 5% business management and administrative services, 3% health professions and related sciences, 2% interdisciplinary studies, 2% natural resource sciences, 1% communications and journalism, 1% computer and information sciences, 1% engineering and applied sciences, 1% fine arts, 1% premed, 1% prevet. ***Most popular recent majors:*** law enforcement/police sciences, nursing.
FIRST-YEAR CLASS 358 total; 467 applied, 100% were accepted, 77% of whom enrolled. 3% from top 10% of their high school class, 20% from top quarter, 54% from top half.
ACADEMIC PROGRAM Core, honor code. Calendar: quarters. 438 courses offered in 1995–96. Academic remediation for entering students, services for LD students, advanced placement, summer session for credit, part-time degree program (daytime, evenings), adult/continuing education programs, internships. Off-campus study at other colleges in the Minnesota State Colleges and Universities System.
GENERAL DEGREE REQUIREMENTS 96 credits; computer course for education, business administration, electrical and electronics technology majors.
MAJORS Accounting, aerospace sciences, athletic training, automotive technologies, aviation administration, aviation technology, broadcasting, business administration/commerce/management, child care/child and family studies, communication, computer science, computer technologies, cosmetology, criminal justice, criminology, drafting and design, drug and alcohol/substance abuse counseling, electrical and electronics technologies, human services, international business, law enforcement/police sciences, legal secretarial studies, legal studies, liberal arts/general studies, marketing/retailing/merchandising, medical records services, medical secretarial studies, nursing, paralegal studies, practical nursing, radio and television studies, retail management, secretarial studies/office management, social work, sports medicine, welding technology.
COMPUTERS ON CAMPUS 136 computers for student use in computer center, computer labs, learning resource center, classrooms, library provide access to off-campus computing facilities, e-mail, Internet. Staffed computer lab on campus.
COLLEGE LIFE Drama-theater group, choral group, student-run newspaper, radio station. 30% vote in student government elections. ***Most popular organizations:*** Law Enforcement Club, All-Nations Club, Business Club. ***Major annual events:*** Homecoming, Snow-Fest, Spring Fling. ***Student services:*** personal-psychological counseling, women's center. ***Campus security:*** late-night transport-escort service.
HOUSING 148 college housing spaces available. No special consideration for freshman housing applicants. Off-campus living permitted. ***Option:*** coed (4 buildings) housing available. Resident assistants live in dorms.
ATHLETICS Member NJCAA. ***Intercollegiate:*** baseball M, basketball M/W, softball W, volleyball W. ***Intramural:*** badminton, basketball, bowling, football, golf, racquetball, softball, tennis, volleyball. ***Contact:*** Mr. Rick Nelson, Athletic Coordinator, 218-681-0725.
CAREER PLANNING ***Placement office:*** 2 full-time staff. ***Director:*** Ms. Yolanda Martinez, Counselor, 218-681-0863. ***Services:*** job fairs, resume preparation, career counseling, careers library, job interviews. 138 organizations recruited on campus 1994–95.
AFTER GRADUATION 52% of students completing a degree program in 1994–95 went directly on to further study.
EXPENSES FOR 1995–96 ***Application fee:*** $20. State resident tuition: $1920 full-time, $40 per credit part-time. Nonresident tuition: $3840 full-time, $80 per credit part-time. Part-time mandatory fees: $3.40 per credit. Wisconsin, North Dakota, and South Dakota residents pay tuition at the rate they would pay if attending a comparable state-supported institution in their home state. Full-time mandatory fees: $218. College room only: $2025.
FINANCIAL AID ***College-administered undergrad aid 1995–96:*** need-based scholarships, non-need scholarships, short-term loans, low-interest long-term loans, Federal Work-Study, part-time jobs. ***Acceptable forms:*** CSS Financial Aid PROFILE, FAFSA. ***Priority deadline:*** 9/15. ***Payment plans:*** installment, deferred payment. ***Waivers:*** full or partial for employees or children of employees and senior citizens.
APPLYING Open admission for state residents, except for nursing program. ***Options:*** Common Application, early entrance, deferred entrance, midyear entrance. ***Required:*** school transcript, TOEFL for international students. ***Recommended:*** SAT I or ACT. Test scores used for counseling/placement. ***Application deadline:*** 9/15. ***Notification:*** continuous.
APPLYING/TRANSFER ***Required:*** high school transcript, college transcript. ***Recommended:*** standardized test scores. ***Entrance:*** noncompetitive. ***Application deadline:*** 9/15. ***Notification:*** continuous. ***Contact:*** Mr. Dennis L. Bendickson, Registrar, 218-681-0858.
CONTACT Ms. Becky Burda, Administrative Assistant, Northland Community and Technical College, Thief River Falls, MN 56701, 218-681-2181 Ext. 54 or toll-free 800-628-9918. ***Fax:*** 218-681-6405.

NORTHWEST TECHNICAL INSTITUTE
Eden Prairie, Minnesota

UG Enrollment: 180	**Tuition & Fees: $8450**
Application Deadline: rolling	**Room & Board: N/Avail**

GENERAL Proprietary, 2-year, specialized, coed. Awards transfer associate, terminal associate degrees. Founded 1957. ***Setting:*** suburban campus with easy access to Minneapolis–St. Paul. ***Total enrollment:*** 180. ***Faculty:*** 10 (all full-time, 70% with terminal degrees); student-faculty ratio is 15:1.
ENROLLMENT PROFILE 180 students from 4 states and territories. 20% women, 80% men, 0% part-time, 85% state residents, 25% transferred in, 0% international, 10% 25 or older, 1% Native American, 1% Hispanic, 2% African American, 3% Asian American. ***Areas of study chosen:*** 60% architecture, 40% engineering and applied sciences.
FIRST-YEAR CLASS 58 total. Of the students who applied, 100% were accepted, 87% of whom enrolled. 10% from top 10% of their high school class, 25% from top quarter, 50% from top half.
ACADEMIC PROGRAM Core. Calendar: semesters. Honors program.
GENERAL DEGREE REQUIREMENT 64 credits.
MAJOR Drafting and design.
LIBRARY 300 books, 28 periodicals.
COMPUTERS ON CAMPUS 75 computers for student use in computer center, labs. Staffed computer lab on campus provides training in use of computers, software.
HOUSING College housing not available.
CAREER PLANNING ***Service:*** career counseling.
AFTER GRADUATION 92% of class of 1994 had job offers within 6 months.
EXPENSES FOR 1996–97 ***Application fee:*** $25. Tuition: $8400 full-time. Full-time mandatory fees: $50. Tuition guaranteed not to increase for student's term of enrollment.
FINANCIAL AID ***College-administered undergrad aid 1995–96:*** need-based scholarships, low-interest long-term loans from external sources. ***Required forms:*** institutional, FAFSA. ***Application deadline:*** 10/1.
APPLYING Open admission. ***Required:*** school transcript, interview. ***Recommended:*** essay, SAT I or ACT. ***Application deadline:*** rolling. ***Notification:*** continuous.
APPLYING/TRANSFER ***Required:*** high school transcript, interview, college transcript. ***Recommended:*** essay. ***Entrance:*** noncompetitive. ***Application deadline:*** rolling. ***Notification:*** continuous.
CONTACT Mr. John Hartman, Career Consultant, Northwest Technical Institute, Eden Prairie, MN 55344-5351, 612-944-0080.

PINE TECHNICAL COLLEGE
Pine City, Minnesota

UG Enrollment: 700	**Tuition & Fees (MN Res): $2165**
Application Deadline: rolling	**Room & Board: N/Avail**

GENERAL State-supported, 2-year, coed. Part of Technical College System. Awards certificates, diplomas, transfer associate degrees. Founded 1965. ***Setting:*** 6-acre small-town campus with easy access to Minneapolis–St. Paul. ***Total enrollment:*** 700. ***Faculty:*** 44 (19 full-time, 25 part-time); student-faculty ratio is 14:1.
ENROLLMENT PROFILE 700 students from 5 states and territories. 53% part-time, 90% state residents, 8% transferred in, 92% have need-based financial aid, 0% international, 60% 25 or older, 2% Native American, 1% Hispanic, 1% African American, 0% Asian American.
FIRST-YEAR CLASS 390 total; 500 applied, 100% were accepted, 78% of whom enrolled. 10% from top 10% of their high school class, 30% from top quarter, 60% from top half.
ACADEMIC PROGRAM Core. Calendar: quarters. 600 courses offered in 1995–96; average class size 14 in required courses. Academic remediation for entering students, services for LD students, advanced placement, tutorials, summer session for credit, internships.
GENERAL DEGREE REQUIREMENTS 96 credits; math requirement varies according to program; computer course; internship (some majors).
MAJOR Secretarial studies/office management.
LIBRARY Media Center with 6,000 books, 30 periodicals.
COMPUTERS ON CAMPUS 150 computers for student use in computer center, computer labs, learning resource center, classrooms. Staffed computer lab on campus provides training in use of computers.
COLLEGE LIFE ***Student services:*** personal-psychological counseling, women's center. ***Campus security:*** late-night transport-escort service.
CAREER PLANNING ***Placement office:*** 1 full-time, 2 part-time staff. ***Director:*** Ms. Louise Speers, Counselor, 800-521-7463. ***Services:*** resume preparation, resume referral, career counseling, job interviews. Students must register freshman year.
AFTER GRADUATION 95% of class of 1994 had job offers within 6 months.
EXPENSES FOR 1995–96 ***Application fee:*** $20. State resident tuition: $1920 full-time, $40 per credit part-time. Nonresident tuition: $3840 full-time, $80 per credit part-time. Part-time mandatory fees: $4.70 per credit. Full-time mandatory fees: $245.
APPLYING Open admission. ***Options:*** Common Application, early entrance, midyear entrance. ***Required:*** school transcript, ACT ASSET. ***Required for some:*** recommendations. Test scores used for counseling/placement. ***Application deadline:*** rolling.
APPLYING/TRANSFER ***Required:*** high school transcript, college transcript, minimum 2.0 college GPA. ***Required for some:*** standardized test scores, recommendations. ***Entrance:*** noncompetitive. ***Application deadline:*** rolling. ***Contact:*** Mr. Jay Hutchins, Dean of Student Affairs, 612-629-6764.
CONTACT Mr. Jay Hutchins, Dean of Student Affairs, Pine Technical College, 1000 Fourth Street, Pine City, MN 55063, 612-629-6764 or toll-free 800-521-7463.

Minnesota

RAINY RIVER COMMUNITY COLLEGE
International Falls, Minnesota

UG Enrollment: 760	Tuition & Fees (MN Res): $2152
Application Deadline: rolling	Room & Board: $1980

GENERAL State-supported, 2-year, coed. Part of Minnesota State Colleges and Universities System. Awards certificates, transfer associate, terminal associate degrees. Founded 1967. *Setting:* 80-acre small-town campus. *Total enrollment:* 760. *Faculty:* 38 (28 full-time, 10 part-time).
ENROLLMENT PROFILE 760 students from 5 states and territories, 2 other countries. 68% women, 53% part-time, 80% state residents, 10% live on campus, 10% transferred in, 17% international, 45% 25 or older, 10% Native American, 1% Hispanic, 1% African American, 1% Asian American.
FIRST-YEAR CLASS 159 total; 243 applied, 77% of whom enrolled.
ACADEMIC PROGRAM Core, general education curriculum. Calendar: quarters. Academic remediation for entering students, services for LD students, advanced placement, honors program, summer session for credit, part-time degree program (daytime, evenings), adult/continuing education programs, co-op programs and internships.
GENERAL DEGREE REQUIREMENTS 96 credits; 5 credits of math; 12 credits of science; computer course.
MAJORS Accounting, business administration/commerce/management, (pre)engineering sequence, hospitality services, hotel and restaurant management, liberal arts/general studies, practical nursing, real estate, science, secretarial studies/office management.
LIBRARY 20,000 books.
COMPUTERS ON CAMPUS Computer purchase plan available. 65 computers for student use in computer center, computer labs, classrooms, library provide access to e-mail, on-line services, Internet. Staffed computer lab on campus (open 24 hours a day) provides training in use of computers, software.
COLLEGE LIFE Drama-theater group, choral group, student-run newspaper. 20% vote in student government elections. *Social organizations:* 3 open to all. *Most popular organizations:* Anishinaabe Student Coalition, Student Senate, Black Student Association. *Major annual events:* Awareness Week, Snow Week, Spring Olympics. *Student services:* personal-psychological counseling. *Campus security:* 24-hour emergency response devices, student patrols, late-night transport-escort service, controlled dormitory access.
HOUSING 80 college housing spaces available; 54 were occupied 1995–96. No special consideration for freshman housing applicants. Off-campus living permitted. *Option:* coed housing available. Resident assistants live in dorms.
ATHLETICS Member NJCAA. *Intercollegiate:* basketball M/W, ice hockey M, volleyball W. *Intramural:* archery, badminton, golf, skiing (cross-country), swimming and diving, tennis, volleyball, weight lifting. *Contact:* Mr. George Schlieff, Men's Athletic Director, 218-285-2240; Ms. Mel Millerbennd, Women's Athletic Director, 218-285-2240.
CAREER PLANNING *Director:* Ms. Suzanne Shomion, Counselor, 218-285-7722. *Services:* resume preparation, resume referral, career counseling, careers library, job bank. Students must register sophomore year.
AFTER GRADUATION 62% of students completing a degree program in 1994–95 went directly on to further study.
EXPENSES FOR 1995–96 *Application fee:* $20. State resident tuition: $2028 full-time, $42.25 per credit part-time. Nonresident tuition: $4056 full-time, $84.50 per credit part-time. Part-time mandatory fees: $1 per credit. Wisconsin, North Dakota, South Dakota, and Manitoba residents pay tuition at the rate they would pay if attending a comparable state-supported institution in their home state. Full-time mandatory fees: $124. College room and board: $1980. College room only: $1695.
FINANCIAL AID *College-administered undergrad aid 1995–96:* 10 need-based scholarships (average $200), 55 non-need scholarships (average $300), short-term loans (average $200), low-interest long-term loans from external sources (average $2000), 350 Federal Work-Study (averaging $1500), 40 part-time jobs. *Required forms:* state, institutional, FAFSA. *Priority deadline:* 7/1. *Payment plans:* installment, deferred payment. *Waivers:* full or partial for employees or children of employees and senior citizens. *Notification:* 7/1. *Average indebtedness of graduates:* $1700.
APPLYING Open admission. *Option:* early entrance. *Required:* school transcript, TOEFL for international students, Academic Skills Assessment Program. *Recommended:* ACT. Test scores used for counseling/placement. *Application deadline:* rolling. *Notification:* continuous.
APPLYING/TRANSFER *Required:* standardized test scores, high school transcript, college transcript. *Entrance:* noncompetitive. *Application deadline:* rolling. *Notification:* continuous. *Contact:* Mr. Richard Kangas, Counselor, 218-285-2206.
CONTACT Ms. Sue Collins, Director of Student Development, Rainy River Community College, International Falls, MN 56649, 218-285-2212 or toll-free 800-456-3996.

RASMUSSEN COLLEGE EAGAN
Eagan, Minnesota

UG Enrollment: 438	Tuition & Fees: $9010
Application Deadline: rolling	Room & Board: N/Avail

GENERAL Proprietary, 2-year, primarily women. Awards certificates, diplomas, terminal associate degrees. Founded 1900. *Setting:* 10-acre suburban campus with easy access to Minneapolis. *Educational spending 1994–95:* $1453 per undergrad. *Total enrollment:* 438. *Faculty:* 50 (7 full-time, 100% with terminal degrees, 43 part-time).
ENROLLMENT PROFILE 438 students from 3 states and territories, 1 other country. 81% women, 19% men, 34% part-time, 98% state residents, 21% transferred in, 77% have need-based financial aid, 33% have non-need-based financial aid, 1% international, 39% 25 or older, 1% Native American, 1% Hispanic, 1% African American, 1% Asian American. *Areas of study chosen:* 100% business management and administrative services. *Most popular recent majors:* business administration/commerce/management, court reporting.
FIRST-YEAR CLASS 239 total.
ACADEMIC PROGRAM Business, education curriculum. Calendar: quarters. 144 courses offered in 1995–96. Academic remediation for entering students, part-time degree program (evenings), adult/continuing education programs, internships.
GENERAL DEGREE REQUIREMENTS 113 credits; computer course for business administration majors; internship (some majors).
MAJORS Accounting, business administration/commerce/management, child care/child and family studies, court reporting, hotel and restaurant management, medical records services, medical secretarial studies, tourism and travel, word processing.
COMPUTERS ON CAMPUS Students must have own computer. PCs are provided. Computers for student use in computer labs, classrooms provide access to Internet. Staffed computer lab on campus provides training in use of computers, software.
COLLEGE LIFE *Campus security:* programs in safety and security.
HOUSING College housing not available.
CAREER PLANNING *Placement office:* 1 full-time staff; $85,274 operating expenditure 1994–95. *Services:* job fairs, resume preparation, resume referral, career counseling, careers library, job bank, job interviews. Students must register senior year. 35 organizations recruited on campus 1994–95.
AFTER GRADUATION 88% of class of 1994 had job offers within 6 months.
EXPENSES FOR 1996–97 *Application fee:* $60. Tuition: $8760 full-time, $4640 per year part-time. Part-time mandatory fees: $250 per year. Full-time mandatory fees: $250.
FINANCIAL AID *College-administered undergrad aid 1995–96:* 263 need-based scholarships (averaging $2470), 12 non-need scholarships (averaging $550), low-interest long-term loans from external sources (averaging $3500), 2 Federal Work-Study (averaging $1750), 5 part-time jobs. *Required forms:* state, institutional, FAFSA. *Priority deadline:* 8/15. *Payment plan:* installment. *Waivers:* full or partial for employees or children of employees.
APPLYING *Option:* Common Application. *Required:* school transcript, Otis Employment Test. Test scores used for admission. *Application deadlines:* rolling.
APPLYING/TRANSFER *Required:* standardized test scores, high school transcript, college transcript. *Entrance:* moderately difficult. *Application deadline:* rolling.
CONTACT Ms. Laurie Calies, Admissions Representative, Rasmussen College Eagan, Eagan, MN 55122, 612-687-9000. College video available.

RASMUSSEN COLLEGE MANKATO
Mankato, Minnesota

UG Enrollment: 280	Tuition & Fees: $7500
Application Deadline: N/R	Room & Board: N/Avail

GENERAL Proprietary, 2-year, primarily women. Awards certificates, diplomas, terminal associate degrees. Founded 1983. *Setting:* suburban campus with easy access to Minneapolis–St. Paul. *Endowment:* $100 million. *Total enrollment:* 280. *Faculty:* 23 (10 full-time, 21% with terminal degrees, 13 part-time); student-faculty ratio is 16:1. *Notable Alumni:* Paul Wilke, manager at River Hills Mall; Amy Ites, admissions officer at Rasmussen College.
ENROLLMENT PROFILE 280 students: 90% women, 10% men, 20% part-time, 80% state residents, 15% transferred in, 85% have need-based financial aid, 10% have non-need-based financial aid, 1% international, 40% 25 or older, 1% Native American, 1% Hispanic, 1% African American, 1% Asian American. *Areas of study chosen:* 70% business management and administrative services, 30% health professions and related sciences.
FIRST-YEAR CLASS 120 total; 180 applied, 94% were accepted, 71% of whom enrolled. 10% from top 10% of their high school class, 20% from top quarter, 60% from top half. 5 class presidents, 1 valedictorian.
ACADEMIC PROGRAM Core, liberal arts curriculum, honor code. Calendar: quarters. 140 courses offered in 1995–96; average class size 20 in required courses. Academic remediation for entering students, services for LD students, advanced placement, tutorials, summer session for credit, part-time degree program (daytime, evenings), co-op programs and internships.
GENERAL DEGREE REQUIREMENTS 64 credits; computer course for most majors; internship (some majors).
MAJORS Accounting, business administration/commerce/management, child care/child and family studies, data processing, fashion merchandising, legal secretarial studies, legal studies, marketing/retailing/merchandising, medical assistant technologies, medical records services, medical secretarial studies, paralegal studies, secretarial studies/office management, tourism and travel, word processing.
LIBRARY Media Center with 1,000 books, 3 periodicals, 200 records, tapes, and CDs.
COMPUTERS ON CAMPUS Students must have own computer. PCs are provided. 70 computers for student use in computer labs, learning resource center, classrooms provide access to off-campus computing facilities, on-line services, Internet. Staffed computer lab on campus provides training in use of computers, software.
COLLEGE LIFE 80% vote in student government elections. *Social organizations:* 1 open to all. *Most popular organization:* Student Government. *Major annual events:* Perfect Attendance Banquet, Awards Banquet, Graduation Ceremony. *Campus security:* limited access to buildings after hours.
HOUSING College housing not available.
CAREER PLANNING *Placement office:* 1 full-time staff. *Director:* Mr. Brian Koeneman, Career Services Director, 507-625-6556. *Services:* job fairs, resume preparation, resume referral, career counseling, careers library, job bank, job interviews. 10 organizations recruited on campus 1994–95.
AFTER GRADUATION 80% of class of 1994 had job offers within 6 months. 1% of students completing a degree program went directly on to further study.
EXPENSES FOR 1995–96 *Application fee:* $60. Tuition: $6750 full-time, $385 per course part-time. Full-time mandatory fees: $750.
FINANCIAL AID *College-administered undergrad aid 1995–96:* 68 need-based scholarships, low-interest long-term loans from college funds (averaging $1295), 3 Federal Work-Study (averaging $5264). *Required forms:* institutional, FAFSA; accepted: CSS Financial Aid PROFILE, state. *Priority deadline:* 8/1. *Payment plan:* tuition prepayment. *Waivers:* full or partial for employees or children of employees.
APPLYING *Options:* Common Application, deferred entrance, midyear entrance. *Required:* school transcript, campus interview, Otis-Lennon School Ability Test. *Required for some:* recommendations. Test scores used for admission.
APPLYING/TRANSFER *Required:* standardized test scores, high school transcript, campus interview, college transcript. *Recommended:* minimum 2.0 college GPA. *Required for some:* recommendations. *Entrance:* minimally difficult. *Contact:* Mr. Carter Leuthold, Admissions Officer, 507-625-6556.
CONTACT Mr. Carter Leuthold, Admissions Officer, Rasmussen College Mankato, 501 Holly Lane, Mankato, MN 56001-9938, 507-625-6556 or toll-free 800-657-6767 (in-state). *Fax:* 507-625-6557. *E-mail:* rascoll@ic.mankato.mn.us.

RASMUSSEN COLLEGE MINNETONKA
Minnetonka, Minnesota

UG Enrollment: 375	Tuition & Fees: $7635
Application Deadline: rolling	Room & Board: N/Avail

GENERAL Proprietary, 2-year, coed. Awards certificates, diplomas, terminal associate degrees. Founded 1900. *Setting:* 2-acre suburban campus with easy access to Minneapolis–St. Paul. *Total enrollment:* 375. *Faculty:* 44 (10 full-time, 100% with terminal degrees, 34 part-time).
ENROLLMENT PROFILE 375 students: 90% women, 10% men, 33% part-time, 99% state residents, 31% transferred in, 22% have need-based financial aid, 0% have non-need-based financial aid, 1% international, 80% 25 or older, 0% Native American, 0% Hispanic, 2% African American, 1% Asian American. *Areas of study chosen:* 100% business management and administrative services. *Most popular recent majors:* accounting, legal secretarial studies, secretarial studies/office management.
FIRST-YEAR CLASS 170 total; 320 applied, 83% were accepted, 64% of whom enrolled.
ACADEMIC PROGRAM Core, career-oriented curriculum, honor code. Calendar: quarters. 110 courses offered in 1995–96; average class size 30 in required courses. Academic remediation for entering students, tutorials, summer session for credit, part-time degree program (daytime, evenings, summer), internships.
GENERAL DEGREE REQUIREMENTS 116 credits; computer course; internship (some majors).
MAJORS Accounting, business administration/commerce/management, child care/child and family studies, court reporting, legal secretarial studies, marketing/retailing/merchandising, medical secretarial studies, secretarial studies/office management.
LIBRARY 3,400 books, 10 periodicals, 900 records, tapes, and CDs.
COMPUTERS ON CAMPUS Students must have own computer. PCs are provided. 300 computers for student use in computer labs, learning resource center, classrooms, library provide access to on-line services, Internet. Staffed computer lab on campus provides training in use of computers, software.
COLLEGE LIFE *Campus security:* late-night transport-escort service.
HOUSING College housing not available.
CAREER PLANNING *Placement office:* 1 full-time staff. *Director:* Ms. Kari Pastir-Smith, Director of Career Services, 612-545-2000. *Services:* job fairs, resume preparation, resume referral, career counseling, careers library, job bank, job interviews. 75 organizations recruited on campus 1994–95.
AFTER GRADUATION 92% of class of 1994 had job offers within 6 months.
EXPENSES FOR 1996–97 Tuition: $6810 full-time. Full-time mandatory fees: $825.
FINANCIAL AID *College-administered undergrad aid 1995–96:* 12 need-based scholarships (averaging $750), low-interest long-term loans. *Required forms:* institutional, FAFSA. *Application deadline:* continuous. *Payment plan:* installment. *Waivers:* full or partial for employees or children of employees.
APPLYING *Options:* early entrance, deferred entrance, midyear entrance. *Required:* school transcript, interview. *Application deadlines:* rolling, rolling for nonresidents.
APPLYING/TRANSFER *Required:* high school transcript, interview, college transcript. *Entrance:* moderately difficult. *Application deadline:* rolling.
CONTACT Ms. Mary Ellen Schmidt, Campus Director, Rasmussen College Minnetonka, Minnetonka, MN 55305-9845, 612-545-2000.

RASMUSSEN COLLEGE ST. CLOUD
St. Cloud, Minnesota

UG Enrollment: 198	Tuition & Fees: $4305
Application Deadline: rolling	Room & Board: N/Avail

GENERAL Proprietary, 2-year, primarily women. Awards certificates, diplomas, transfer associate, terminal associate degrees. Founded 1902. *Setting:* urban campus with easy access to Minneapolis. *Total enrollment:* 198. *Faculty:* 32 (11 full-time, 100% with terminal degrees, 21 part-time); student-faculty ratio is 10:1. *Notable Alumni:* Carol Daniel Klaphake; Barr Anderson; Will Hellmann; Linda Schwenzfeter; Mike McDonald.
ENROLLMENT PROFILE 198 students from 7 states and territories. 86% women, 14% men, 27% part-time, 97% state residents, 45% transferred in, 97% have need-based financial aid, 3% have non-need-based financial aid, 0% international, 35% 25 or older, 1% Native American, 1% Hispanic, 1% African American, 0% Asian American. *Areas of study chosen:* 26% business management and administrative services, 6% health professions and related sciences. *Most popular recent major:* business administration/commerce/management.
FIRST-YEAR CLASS 150 total; 201 applied, 95% were accepted, 79% of whom enrolled.
ACADEMIC PROGRAM Core, professional careers curriculum. Calendar: quarters. 110 courses offered in 1995–96. Self-designed majors, tutorials, summer session for credit, part-time degree program (daytime, evenings, summer), adult/continuing education programs, internships.
GENERAL DEGREE REQUIREMENTS 113 credits; computer course; internship (some majors).
MAJORS Accounting, business administration/commerce/management, court reporting, legal secretarial studies, marketing/retailing/merchandising, medical records services, medical secretarial studies, secretarial studies/office management, tourism and travel.
LIBRARY 494 books. Acquisition spending 1994–95: $40,000.
COMPUTERS ON CAMPUS Students must have own computer. PCs are provided. 75 computers for student use in computer center, computer labs, classrooms provide access to main academic computer, off-campus computing facilities, on-line services, Internet. Staffed computer lab on campus provides training in use of computers, software. Academic computing expenditure 1994–95: $207,100.
COLLEGE LIFE *Social organizations:* 1 open to all. *Most popular organization:* Student Senate. *Major annual events:* Awards Ceremony, Student Social, Advisory Meetings.
HOUSING College housing not available.
CAREER PLANNING *Placement office:* 1 full-time, 1 part-time staff; $33,200 operating expenditure 1994–95. *Director:* Ms. Nancy Myers, Career Services Director, 612-251-5600. *Services:* job fairs, resume preparation, resume referral, career counseling, job bank, job interviews. Students must register freshman year. 31 organizations recruited on campus 1994–95.

AFTER GRADUATION 83% of class of 1994 had job offers within 6 months. 1% of students completing a degree program went directly on to further study.
EXPENSES FOR 1996–97 *Application fee:* $60. Tuition: $2190 per quarter part-time. Part-time mandatory fees: $25 per quarter. Full-time tuition: $6570 for day program, $3480 for evening program. Full-time mandatory fees: $825. Tuition guaranteed not to increase for student's term of enrollment.
FINANCIAL AID *College-administered undergrad aid 1995–96:* 100 need-based scholarships (average $405), 18 non-need scholarships (average $450), low-interest long-term loans from external sources (average $2125), 18 Federal Work-Study (averaging $955), 15 part-time jobs. *Required forms:* institutional, FAFSA, Tax Returns. *Application deadline:* continuous. *Payment plan:* installment. *Waivers:* full or partial for employees or children of employees.
APPLYING *Options:* Common Application, early entrance, deferred entrance, midyear entrance. *Required:* school transcript, minimum 2.0 GPA, interview, Otis-Lennon School Ability Test. Test scores used for admission. *Application deadlines:* rolling, rolling for nonresidents.
APPLYING/TRANSFER *Required:* standardized test scores, high school transcript, interview, college transcript, minimum 2.0 high school GPA. *Recommended:* minimum 2.0 college GPA. *Entrance:* minimally difficult. *Application deadline:* rolling. *Contact:* Ms. Lynn Collen, Academic Dean, 612-251-5600.
CONTACT Ms. Stephanie Kadlec, Admissions Representative, Rasmussen College St. Cloud, 12450 Wayzata Boulevard, Suite 226, Minnetonka, MN 55305, 612-251-5600. College video available.

ROCHESTER COMMUNITY COLLEGE
Rochester, Minnesota

UG Enrollment: 3,593	Tuition & Fees (MN Res): $2206
Application Deadline: 9/1	Room & Board: N/Avail

GENERAL State-supported, 2-year, coed. Part of Minnesota State Colleges and Universities System. Awards certificates, transfer associate, terminal associate degrees. Founded 1915. *Setting:* 160-acre campus. *Endowment:* $437,000. *Total enrollment:* 3,593. *Faculty:* 225 (92 full-time, 133 part-time); student-faculty ratio is 18:1.
ENROLLMENT PROFILE 3,593 students from 18 states and territories, 36 other countries. 63% women, 37% men, 47% part-time, 95% state residents, 60% have need-based financial aid, 1% international, 41% 25 or older, 1% Native American, 1% Hispanic, 1% African American, 3% Asian American. *Areas of study chosen:* 58% interdisciplinary studies, 3% education, 3% engineering and applied sciences, 1% communications and journalism. *Most popular recent majors:* liberal arts/general studies, nursing, secretarial studies/office management.
FIRST-YEAR CLASS 1,238 total; 1,842 applied, 99% were accepted, 68% of whom enrolled.
ACADEMIC PROGRAM Core, honor code. Calendar: quarters. Academic remediation for entering students, English as a second language program offered during academic year, services for LD students, advanced placement, honors program, summer session for credit, part-time degree program (daytime, evenings, weekends, summer), adult/continuing education programs, internships. Off-campus study at other colleges in the Minnesota State Colleges and Universities System, Winona State University–Rochester Center.
GENERAL DEGREE REQUIREMENTS 96 quarter hours; computer course for business management majors; internship (some majors).
MAJORS Business administration/commerce/management, child psychology/child development, civil engineering technology, computer science, dental services, electronics engineering technology, (pre)engineering sequence, fashion merchandising, human services, law enforcement/police sciences, liberal arts/general studies, marketing/retailing/merchandising, mechanical engineering technology, medical assistant technologies, medical laboratory technology, medical secretarial studies, nursing, radiological technology, respiratory therapy, secretarial studies/office management.
LIBRARY Goddard Library with 62,000 books, 600 periodicals.
COMPUTERS ON CAMPUS 170 computers for student use in computer center, computer labs, learning resource center, writing center. Staffed computer lab on campus.
COLLEGE LIFE Orientation program (2 days). Drama-theater group, choral group, student-run newspaper. 5% vote in student government elections. *Student services:* health clinic. *Campus security:* student patrols, late-night transport-escort service.
HOUSING College housing not available.
ATHLETICS Member NJCAA. *Intercollegiate:* baseball M, basketball M/W, football M, golf M/W, softball W, tennis M/W, volleyball W, wrestling M. *Intramural:* basketball, football, softball, table tennis (Ping-Pong), tennis, track and field, volleyball. *Contact:* Ms. Jean Marconett, 507-285-7255.
CAREER PLANNING *Placement office:* 4 full-time staff. *Service:* career counseling.
EXPENSES FOR 1996–97 *Application fee:* $20. State resident tuition: $1997 full-time, $41.60 per quarter hour part-time. Nonresident tuition: $3994 full-time, $83.20 per quarter hour part-time. Part-time mandatory fees: $4.35 per quarter hour. Wisconsin, North Dakota, and South Dakota residents pay tuition at the rate they would pay if attending a comparable state-supported institution in their home state. Full-time mandatory fees: $209.
FINANCIAL AID *College-administered undergrad aid 1995–96:* 25 need-based scholarships (averaging $828), 96 non-need scholarships (averaging $765), short-term loans (averaging $50), low-interest long-term loans from college funds (averaging $395), loans from external sources (averaging $2156), Federal Work-Study, 260 part-time jobs. *Acceptable forms:* CSS Financial Aid PROFILE, FAFSA. *Application deadline:* continuous. *Waivers:* full or partial for employees or children of employees and senior citizens.
APPLYING Open admission except for allied health programs, non-residents. *Options:* early entrance, midyear entrance. *Required:* TOEFL for international students. *Recommended:* SAT I or ACT. *Required for some:* 3 years of high school math and science. Test scores used for counseling/placement. *Application deadline:* 9/1. *Notification:* continuous.
APPLYING/TRANSFER *Recommended:* standardized test scores. *Required for some:* 3 years of high school math and science. *Entrance:* noncompetitive. *Application deadline:* 9/1. *Notification:* continuous. *Contact:* Ms. Nancy Shumaker, Registrar, 507-285-7265.
CONTACT Mrs. Sue Slightam, Director of Enrollment Services, Rochester Community College, Rochester, MN 55904-4999, 507-285-7219.

ST. CLOUD TECHNICAL COLLEGE
St. Cloud, Minnesota

UG Enrollment: 2,431 **Tuition & Fees (MN Res): $2158**
Application Deadline: 8/1 **Room & Board: N/Avail**

GENERAL State-supported, 2-year, coed. Part of Minnesota State Colleges and Universities System. Awards diplomas, terminal associate degrees. Founded 1948. ***Setting:*** urban campus with easy access to Minneapolis–St. Paul. ***Total enrollment:*** 2,431. ***Faculty:*** 102 (84 full-time, 18 part-time); student-faculty ratio is 30:1.
ENROLLMENT PROFILE 2,431 students from 5 states and territories. 51% women, 49% men, 41% part-time, 98% state residents, 18% transferred in, 0% international, 47% 25 or older, 1% Native American, 1% Hispanic, 0% African American, 2% Asian American. ***Most popular recent majors:*** practical nursing, marketing/retailing/merchandising, business administration/commerce/management.
FIRST-YEAR CLASS 1,153 total; 1,790 applied, 100% of whom enrolled.
ACADEMIC PROGRAM Core. Calendar: quarters. Academic remediation for entering students, English as a second language program offered during academic year and summer, services for LD students, summer session for credit, part-time degree program (daytime), adult/continuing education programs, co-op programs and internships.
GENERAL DEGREE REQUIREMENTS 96 credits; 1 developmental math course; computer course for most majors; internship (some majors).
MAJORS Accounting, advertising, automotive technologies, business administration/commerce/management, carpentry, child care/child and family studies, civil engineering technology, computer programming, construction technologies, culinary arts, data processing, dental services, drafting and design, early childhood education, instrumentation technology, machine and tool technologies, marketing/retailing/merchandising, mechanical design technology, nursing, operating room technology, optometric/ophthalmic technologies, plumbing, practical nursing, real estate, respiratory therapy, retail management, secretarial studies/office management, teacher aide studies, welding technology, word processing.
LIBRARY 10,000 books, 500 microform titles, 500 periodicals, 1,500 records, tapes, and CDs.
COMPUTERS ON CAMPUS 175 computers for student use in computer center, computer labs, learning resource center, library.
COLLEGE LIFE Student-run newspaper. 15% vote in student government elections. ***Most popular organizations:*** Student Senate, Distributive Education Club of America, VICA, ADEED. ***Major annual events:*** Winter Fest, Annual Job Fair. ***Student services:*** personal-psychological counseling, women's center. ***Campus security:*** late-night transport-escort service.
HOUSING College housing not available.
ATHLETICS ***Intramural:*** basketball, softball, volleyball. ***Contact:*** Mr. Ron Osterman, Student Activities Director, 612-252-0101 Ext. 224.
CAREER PLANNING ***Placement office:*** 1 full-time, 2 part-time staff. ***Director:*** Mr. Terry Gruber, Placement Counselor, 612-654-5926. ***Services:*** job fairs, career counseling, careers library, job bank, job interviews. Students must register sophomore year.
EXPENSES FOR 1996–97 ***Application fee:*** $20. State resident tuition: $1997 full-time, $41.60 per credit part-time. Nonresident tuition: $3994 full-time, $83.20 per credit part-time. Part-time mandatory fees: $3.35 per credit. Tuition for North Dakota residents: $2208 full-time, $46 per credit part-time. Full-time mandatory fees: $161.
FINANCIAL AID ***College-administered undergrad aid 1995–96:*** need-based scholarships, non-need scholarships, short-term loans, low-interest long-term loans from college funds, loans from external sources, Federal Work-Study, part-time jobs. ***Required forms:*** institutional; accepted: FAFSA. ***Application deadline:*** continuous. ***Payment plan:*** installment. ***Waivers:*** full or partial for employees or children of employees and senior citizens.
APPLYING Open admission except for dental hygiene programs. ***Options:*** early entrance, deferred entrance. ***Required:*** school transcript, ACT ASSET. ***Required for some:*** TOEFL for international students. Test scores used for counseling/placement. ***Application deadline:*** 8/1. ***Notification:*** continuous until 8/25.
APPLYING/TRANSFER ***Required:*** high school transcript. ***Required for some:*** standardized test scores, college transcript. ***Entrance:*** noncompetitive. ***Contact:*** Ms. Cynthia Mehoves, Registrar, 612-654-5905.
CONTACT Admissions Office, St. Cloud Technical College, 1540 Northway Drive, St. Cloud, MN 56303-1240, 612-654-5061 or toll-free 800-222-1009 (in-state).

ST. PAUL TECHNICAL COLLEGE
St. Paul, Minnesota

UG Enrollment: 3,401 **Tuition & Fees (MN Res): $1850**
Application Deadline: rolling **Room & Board: N/Avail**

GENERAL State-related, 2-year, coed. Awards diplomas, terminal associate degrees. Founded 1922. ***Setting:*** urban campus. ***Total enrollment:*** 3,401. ***Faculty:*** 565 (115 full-time, 450 part-time).
ENROLLMENT PROFILE 3,401 students: 51% women, 27% part-time, 93% state residents, 21% transferred in, 0% international, 50% 25 or older, 1% Native American, 4% Hispanic, 11% African American, 12% Asian American.
FIRST-YEAR CLASS Of the students who applied, 100% were accepted.
ACADEMIC PROGRAM Calendar: quarters. Academic remediation for entering students, English as a second language program offered during academic year and summer, services for LD students, tutorials, adult/continuing education programs, internships.
GENERAL DEGREE REQUIREMENTS 110 credits; 4 credits of math/science; computer course for most majors; internship (some majors).
MAJORS Accounting, child care/child and family studies, computer programming, deaf interpreter training, electrical and electronics technologies, human resources, international business, manufacturing technology, medical laboratory technology, respiratory therapy, secretarial studies/office management.
LIBRARY St. Paul Technical College Library with 13,000 books, 1 microform title, 157 periodicals, 6 CD-ROMs, 240 records, tapes, and CDs.
COMPUTERS ON CAMPUS 520 computers for student use in computer center, computer labs, learning resource center, classrooms, library provide access to Internet. Staffed computer lab on campus.
COLLEGE LIFE ***Student services:*** health clinic, personal-psychological counseling, women's center. ***Campus security:*** late-night transport-escort service.
HOUSING College housing not available.
CAREER PLANNING ***Placement office:*** 3 full-time staff. ***Director:*** Ms. Merrily Karel, Marketing Specialist, 800-227-6029. ***Services:*** career counseling, job bank.
EXPENSES FOR 1995–96 ***Application fee:*** $15. State resident tuition: $1800 full-time, $40 per credit part-time. Nonresident tuition: $3600 full-time, $80 per credit part-time. Part-time mandatory fees: $1.10 per credit. Wisconsin residents pay state resident tuition. Tuition for North Dakota residents: $2070 full-time, $46 per credit part-time. Full-time mandatory fees: $50.
FINANCIAL AID ***College-administered undergrad aid 1995–96:*** 1,500 need-based scholarships (average $2400), 100 non-need scholarships (average $1000), short-term loans (average $200), low-interest long-term loans from external sources (average $2625), 46 Federal Work-Study (averaging $1500), 80 part-time jobs. ***Required forms:*** state, institutional; accepted: CSS Financial Aid PROFILE, FAFSA. ***Priority deadline:*** 8/1.
APPLYING Open admission. ***Option:*** early entrance. ***Required:*** ACT ASSET. ***Application deadline:*** rolling.
CONTACT Ms. Lisa Netzley, Admissions Counselor, St. Paul Technical College, 235 Marshall Avenue, St. Paul, MN 55102-1800, 612-221-1370 or toll-free 800-227-6029. College video available.

SOUTHWESTERN TECHNICAL COLLEGE
Granite Falls, Minnesota

UG Enrollment: 450 **Tuition & Fees (MN Res): $1997**
Application Deadline: rolling **Room & Board: N/Avail**

GENERAL State-supported, 2-year, coed. Awards certificates, diplomas, terminal associate degrees. Founded 1965. ***Setting:*** 15-acre small-town campus. ***Total enrollment:*** 450. ***Faculty:*** 38 (30 full-time, 8 part-time); student-faculty ratio is 15:1.
ENROLLMENT PROFILE 450 students. ***Most popular recent majors:*** mechanical engineering technology, robotics, machine and tool technologies.
FIRST-YEAR CLASS 200 total; 300 applied, 100% were accepted, 77% of whom enrolled.
ACADEMIC PROGRAM Occupational specific curriculum, honor code. Calendar: quarters. Services for LD students, internships.
GENERAL DEGREE REQUIREMENTS 96 quarter credits; internship (some majors).
MAJORS Accounting, automotive technologies, business administration/commerce/management, child care/child and family studies, computer information systems, consumer services, drafting and design, electronics engineering technology, engineering technology, insurance, legal secretarial studies, machine and tool technologies, manufacturing technology, mechanical engineering technology, medical secretarial studies, optometric/ophthalmic technologies, robotics.
COMPUTERS ON CAMPUS 100 computers for student use in computer labs, classrooms, library provide access to e-mail, on-line services. Staffed computer lab on campus provides training in use of computers, software.
COLLEGE LIFE 60% vote in student government elections. ***Student services:*** personal-psychological counseling.
HOUSING College housing not available.
ATHLETICS ***Intercollegiate:*** basketball M. ***Intramural:*** bowling, table tennis (Ping-Pong), volleyball.
CAREER PLANNING ***Services:*** job fairs, resume preparation, resume referral, career counseling, job bank.
EXPENSES FOR 1995–96 ***Application fee:*** $20. State resident tuition: $1920 full-time, $40 per credit part-time. Nonresident tuition: $3840 full-time, $80 per credit part-time. Part-time mandatory fees: $1.60 per credit. Full-time mandatory fees: $77.
FINANCIAL AID ***College-administered undergrad aid 1995–96:*** need-based scholarships, short-term loans (averaging $100), Federal Work-Study. ***Required forms:*** institutional, FAFSA. ***Priority deadline:*** 8/15. ***Payment plan:*** deferred payment.
APPLYING Open admission. ***Required:*** school transcript, ACT ASSET. ***Application deadline:*** rolling.
APPLYING/TRANSFER ***Required:*** standardized test scores, high school transcript. ***Application deadline:*** rolling.
CONTACT Ms. Michelle Pichaske, Campus Admissions, Southwestern Technical College, Granite Falls, MN 56241, 612-564-4511. College video available.

VERMILION COMMUNITY COLLEGE
Ely, Minnesota

UG Enrollment: 735 **Tuition & Fees (MN Res): $2160**
Application Deadline: rolling **Room & Board: $3420**

GENERAL State-supported, 2-year, coed. Part of Minnesota State Colleges and Universities System. Awards transfer associate, terminal associate degrees. Founded 1922. ***Setting:*** 5-acre rural campus. ***Total enrollment:*** 735. ***Faculty:*** 102 (32 full-time, 70 part-time); student-faculty ratio is 15:1.
ENROLLMENT PROFILE 735 students from 12 states and territories, 4 other countries. 35% women, 65% men, 13% part-time, 89% state residents, 1% international, 18% 25 or older, 8% Native American, 0% Hispanic, 1% African American. ***Areas of study chosen:*** 50% natural resource sciences, 10% biological and life sciences, 10% education, 10% liberal arts/general studies, 5% computer and information sciences, 5% engineering and applied sciences, 5% health professions and related sciences, 5% psychology. ***Most popular recent majors:*** law enforcement/police sciences, forestry, water resources.
FIRST-YEAR CLASS 390 total. Of the students who applied, 93% were accepted, 61% of whom enrolled.
ACADEMIC PROGRAM Core, honor code. Calendar: quarters. Academic remediation for entering students, services for LD students, advanced placement, honors program, summer session for credit, part-time degree program (daytime, evenings, summer), adult/continuing education programs, co-op programs and internships. Off-campus study at other colleges in the Minnesota State Colleges and Universities System.
GENERAL DEGREE REQUIREMENTS 96 quarter hours; math/science requirements vary according to program; computer course.

MAJORS Accounting, agricultural business, agricultural economics, agricultural education, agronomy/soil and crop sciences, architectural technologies, art education, art/fine arts, art history, aviation administration, biology/biological sciences, business administration/commerce/management, business economics, chemistry, communication, computer management, computer science, computer technologies, conservation, criminal justice, data processing, early childhood education, earth science, ecology, economics, education, elementary education, engineering (general), (pre)engineering sequence, environmental education, environmental sciences, environmental studies, finance/banking, fish and game management, food services management, forestry, forest technology, geography, health education, history, home economics, hospitality services, hotel and restaurant management, human ecology, industrial arts, industrial engineering technology, interdisciplinary studies, land use management and reclamation, law enforcement/police sciences, liberal arts/general studies, mathematics, medical records services, medical secretarial studies, music, natural resource management, painting/drawing, parks management, physical education, physical sciences, physics, political science/government, pollution control technologies, psychology, range management, recreation and leisure services, science, science education, sociology, soil conservation, speech/rhetoric/public address/debate, theater arts/drama, water resources, wildlife biology, wildlife management.
LIBRARY Vermilion Community College Library with 19,500 books, 100 periodicals.
COMPUTERS ON CAMPUS 30 computers for student use in computer labs, clerical lab provide access to e-mail, Internet. Staffed computer lab on campus provides training in use of computers, software.
COLLEGE LIFE ***Most popular organizations:*** Student Life Committee, Student Government, Drama Club. ***Major annual events:*** New Student Week, New Year's Dance, Karaoke Night. ***Student services:*** personal-psychological counseling, women's center. ***Campus security:*** student patrols, late-night transport-escort service.
HOUSING 174 college housing spaces available; all were occupied 1995–96. Freshmen given priority for college housing. Off-campus living permitted. ***Option:*** coed (3 buildings) housing available. Resident assistants live in dorms.
ATHLETICS Member NJCAA. ***Intercollegiate:*** baseball M, basketball M/W, football M, softball W, volleyball W. ***Intramural:*** basketball, bowling, football, skiing (cross-country), skiing (downhill), softball, tennis, volleyball, weight lifting, wrestling. ***Contact:*** Mr. Paul McDonald, Athletic Director, 218-365-7276; Mrs. Lynne Deadrick, Athletic Director, 218-365-7231.
CAREER PLANNING ***Director:*** Ms. Chris Braun, Academic Counselor/Advisor, 218-365-7237. ***Services:*** resume preparation, career counseling, careers library.
EXPENSES FOR 1995–96 ***Application fee:*** $15. State resident tuition: $2160 full-time, $45 per quarter hour part-time. Nonresident tuition: $4200 full-time, $87.50 per quarter hour part-time. College room and board: $3420 (minimum). College room only: $2040.
FINANCIAL AID ***College-administered undergrad aid 1995–96:*** 251 need-based scholarships, short-term loans, low-interest long-term loans from external sources, Federal Work-Study. ***Required forms for some financial aid applicants:*** state, institutional, FAFSA; accepted: CSS Financial Aid PROFILE. ***Priority deadline:*** 4/24. ***Payment plans:*** installment, deferred payment. ***Waivers:*** full or partial for employees or children of employees.
APPLYING Open admission. ***Options:*** early entrance, deferred entrance. ***Required:*** school transcript, TOEFL for international students. ***Recommended:*** 3 years of high school math and science, SAT I or ACT, SAT II Subject Tests. Test scores used for counseling/placement. ***Application deadline:*** rolling. ***Notification:*** continuous.
APPLYING/TRANSFER ***Required:*** high school transcript, college transcript. ***Recommended:*** standardized test scores, 3 years of high school math and science. ***Entrance:*** noncompetitive. ***Application deadline:*** rolling. ***Notification:*** continuous.
CONTACT Mr. Doug Furnstahl, Director of Enrollment Services, Vermilion Community College, Ely, MN 55731-1996, 218-365-7224 or toll-free 800-657-3608.

WILLMAR COMMUNITY COLLEGE
Willmar, Minnesota

UG Enrollment: 1,318 | **Tuition & Fees (MN Res): $2083**
Application Deadline: 9/1 | **Room & Board: N/Avail**

GENERAL State-supported, 2-year, coed. Part of Minnesota State Colleges and Universities System. Awards certificates, transfer associate, terminal associate degrees. Founded 1961. ***Setting:*** 83-acre small-town campus. ***Total enrollment:*** 1,318. ***Faculty:*** 68 (44 full-time, 2% with terminal degrees, 24 part-time); student-faculty ratio is 24:1.
ENROLLMENT PROFILE 1,318 students from 17 states and territories, 5 other countries. 61% women, 39% men, 39% part-time, 98% state residents, 46% transferred in, 81% have need-based financial aid, 1% international, 28% 25 or older, 1% Native American, 3% Hispanic, 1% African American, 1% Asian American. ***Areas of study chosen:*** 25% liberal arts/general studies, 17% business management and administrative services, 11% health professions and related sciences, 7% education, 2% agriculture, 2% computer and information sciences, 2% engineering and applied sciences, 2% psychology, 2% social sciences, 1% biological and life sciences, 1% communications and journalism, 1% English language/literature/letters, 1% fine arts, 1% natural resource sciences, 1% prelaw, 1% prevet. ***Most popular recent majors:*** law enforcement/police sciences, human services, business administration/commerce/management.
FIRST-YEAR CLASS 523 total; 570 applied, 100% were accepted, 92% of whom enrolled. 5% from top 10% of their high school class, 20% from top quarter, 51% from top half. 1 valedictorian.
ACADEMIC PROGRAM Core, liberal arts curriculum, honor code. Calendar: quarters. 295 courses offered in 1995–96. Academic remediation for entering students, English as a second language program, services for LD students, advanced placement, self-designed majors, tutorials, summer session for credit, part-time degree program (daytime, evenings, summer), adult/continuing education programs, co-op programs and internships. Off-campus study at Willmar Technical College, other colleges in the Minnesota State Colleges and Universities System.
GENERAL DEGREE REQUIREMENTS 96 quarter hours; 1 math course; 2 lab science courses; computer course for business administration, accounting, radiological technology majors; internship (some majors).
MAJORS Accounting, agricultural business, applied art, art/fine arts, broadcasting, business administration/commerce/management, child care/child and family studies, child psychology/child development, communication, community services, computer information systems, computer management, criminal justice, data processing, drafting and design, drug and alcohol/substance abuse counseling, electrical and electronics technologies, electronics engineering technology, engineering (general), (pre)engineering sequence, family services, gerontology, history, humanities, human services, interdisciplinary studies, journalism, law enforcement/police sciences, legal secretarial studies, liberal arts/general studies, mathematics, medical records services, medical secretarial studies, mental health/rehabilitation counseling, music, nursing, photography, physical education, physical sciences, psychology, radiological technology, real estate, retail management, science, secretarial studies/office management, social work, sociology, speech/rhetoric/public address/debate, theater arts/drama, tourism and travel, veterinary technology.
LIBRARY 25,000 books, 15,613 microform titles, 202 periodicals, 10 on-line bibliographic services, 16 CD-ROMs, 1,643 records, tapes, and CDs. Acquisition spending 1994–95: $60,000.
COMPUTERS ON CAMPUS 85 computers for student use in computer center, computer labs, learning resource center, counseling center, library. Staffed computer lab on campus provides training in use of computers, software. Academic computing expenditure 1994–95: $125,000.
COLLEGE LIFE Drama-theater group, choral group, student-run newspaper. 40% vote in student government elections. ***Social organizations:*** 4 open to all; 1 local fraternity; 1% of eligible men are members. ***Most popular organizations:*** Student Senate, Ski Club, Nontraditional Students Club, BACCHUS, Creative Writers, Unlimited. ***Major annual events:*** Homecoming, Snow Days, Spring Fling. ***Student services:*** personal-psychological counseling, women's center. ***Campus security:*** late-night transport-escort service.
HOUSING College housing not available.
ATHLETICS Member NJCAA. ***Intercollegiate:*** baseball M, basketball M/W, football M, softball W, tennis M/W, volleyball W, wrestling M. ***Intramural:*** basketball, football, racquetball, softball, weight lifting. ***Contact:*** Mr. Jack Denholm, Men's Athletic Director, 330-231-5122; Ms. Val Swanson, Women's Athletic Director, 330-231-5128.
CAREER PLANNING ***Placement office:*** 1 part-time staff; $14,000 operating expenditure 1994–95. ***Director:*** Ms. Sheila Pickrel Sjerven, Counselor, 330-231-5115. ***Services:*** resume preparation, career counseling, careers library, job interviews.
EXPENSES FOR 1995–96 ***Application fee:*** $20. State resident tuition: $2028 full-time, $42.25 per quarter hour part-time. Nonresident tuition: $4056 full-time, $84.50 per quarter hour part-time. Part-time mandatory fees: $1.15 per quarter hour. Wisconsin, North Dakota, and South Dakota residents pay tuition at the rate they would pay if attending a comparable state-supported institution in their home state. Full-time mandatory fees: $55.
FINANCIAL AID ***College-administered undergrad aid 1995–96:*** 825 need-based scholarships (average $1000), 40 non-need scholarships (average $1000), short-term loans (average $75), low-interest long-term loans from college funds (average $2250), loans from external sources (average $3500), 200 Federal Work-Study (averaging $2000), 50 part-time jobs. ***Required forms:*** FAFSA. ***Application deadline:*** continuous. ***Waivers:*** full or partial for employees or children of employees and senior citizens.
APPLYING Open admission except for nursing, chemical dependency practitioner, radiological technology programs. ***Options:*** early entrance, deferred entrance, midyear entrance. ***Required:*** school transcript, TOEFL for international students. ***Recommended:*** SAT I or ACT, PSAT. ***Required for some:*** recommendations. Test scores used for counseling/placement. ***Application deadline:*** 9/1. Preference given to state residents.
APPLYING/TRANSFER ***Required:*** high school transcript, college transcript. ***Recommended:*** standardized test scores. ***Required for some:*** standardized test scores, recommendations. ***Entrance:*** minimally difficult. ***Application deadline:*** 9/1. ***Contact:*** Mr. Arlen Sjerven, Director of Admissions, 330-231-5116.
CONTACT Ms. Sheila Pickrel Sjerven, Counselor, Willmar Community College, Willmar, MN 56201-0797, 330-231-5115. ***Fax:*** 330-231-6602.

WILLMAR TECHNICAL COLLEGE
Willmar, Minnesota

UG Enrollment: 1,340 | **Tuition & Fees (MN Res): $2121**
Application Deadline: rolling | **Room & Board: N/Avail**

GENERAL State-supported, 2-year, coed. Part of Minnesota State Colleges and Universities System. Awards diplomas, terminal associate degrees. Founded 1961. ***Setting:*** 15-acre small-town campus. ***Total enrollment:*** 1,340. ***Faculty:*** 90 (75 full-time, 70% with terminal degrees, 15 part-time); student-faculty ratio is 15:1.
ENROLLMENT PROFILE 1,340 students from 6 states and territories, 1 other country. 48% women, 34% part-time, 98% state residents, 3% transferred in, 1% international, 36% 25 or older, 1% Native American, 5% Hispanic. ***Areas of study chosen:*** 51% vocational and home economics, 21% business management and administrative services, 16% agriculture, 12% health professions and related sciences.
FIRST-YEAR CLASS 700 total; 1,440 applied, 85% were accepted, 57% of whom enrolled.
ACADEMIC PROGRAM Honor code. Calendar: quarters. 1,103 courses offered in 1995–96. Academic remediation for entering students, English as a second language program offered during academic year and summer, services for LD students, self-designed majors, part-time degree program (daytime, evenings, summer), adult/continuing education programs, co-op programs and internships.
GENERAL DEGREE REQUIREMENTS 96 credits; math/science requirments vary accordding to program; computer course for most majors; internship (some majors).
MAJORS Accounting, agricultural business, agronomy/soil and crop sciences, automotive technologies, carpentry, cosmetology, drafting and design, electrical and electronics technologies, electronics engineering technology, emergency medical technology, farm and ranch management, fashion merchandising, human services, illustration, legal secretarial studies, machine and tool technologies, marketing/retailing/merchandising, medical assistant technologies, medical records services, medical secretarial studies, photography, plastics technology, practical nursing, radio and television studies, secretarial studies/office management, veterinary technology, welding technology, word processing.
LIBRARY WCC Library with 1,725 books, 162 periodicals, 235 records, tapes, and CDs.
COMPUTERS ON CAMPUS Computer purchase plan available. 212 computers for student use in computer center, computer labs, classrooms, library. Staffed computer lab on campus provides training in use of computers.
COLLEGE LIFE Drama-theater group, choral group. 63% vote in student government elections. ***Social organizations:*** 9 open to all. ***Most popular organizations:*** Christian Students Together, Student Senate. ***Major annual events:*** School Dances, Snow Week, Conventions. ***Student services:*** health clinic, personal-psychological counseling, women's center. ***Campus security:*** late-night transport-escort service.

Peterson's Guide to Two-Year Colleges 1997 401

Minnesota–Mississippi

Willmar Technical College (continued)
HOUSING College housing not available.
ATHLETICS Member NJCAA. *Intercollegiate:* baseball M, basketball M/W, football M, softball W, tennis M/W, volleyball W, wrestling M. *Intramural:* basketball, bowling, football, racquetball, volleyball. *Contact:* Mr. Randy Fabel, Instructor, 612-235-5114.
CAREER PLANNING *Placement office:* 2 full-time staff. *Director:* Mr. Fred Hanson, Placement Coordinator, 612-235-5114. *Services:* job fairs, resume preparation, resume referral, career counseling, careers library, job bank, job interviews.
EXPENSES FOR 1995–96 *Application fee:* $20. State resident tuition: $1960 full-time, $40 per credit part-time. Nonresident tuition: $3865 full-time, $80 per credit part-time. Part-time mandatory fees: $3.35 per credit. Tuition for North Dakota residents: $2367 full-time, $49.31 per credit part-time. Wisconsin and South Dakota residents pay tuition at the rate they would pay if attending a comparable state supported institution in their home state. Full-time mandatory fees: $161.
FINANCIAL AID *College-administered undergrad aid 1995–96:* need-based scholarships, short-term loans (averaging $150), low-interest long-term loans from external sources (averaging $1847), Federal Work-Study. *Required forms:* state, FAFSA. *Priority deadline:* 5/1. *Payment plan:* deferred payment. *Waivers:* full or partial for senior citizens.
APPLYING Open admission except for practical nursing, accounting, electronics, physical damage appraisal and claims adjustment, veterinary technology majors. *Options:* Common Application, early entrance, deferred entrance. *Required:* school transcript, ACT ASSET. Test scores used for counseling/placement. *Application deadline:* rolling.
APPLYING/TRANSFER *Required:* high school transcript. *Required for some:* campus interview. *Application deadline:* rolling. *Contact:* Mr. Don Rinke, Admissions Coordinator, 612-235-5114 Ext. 2917.
CONTACT Ms. Linda Kamstra, Admissions Assistant, Willmar Technical College, P.O. Box 1097, Willmar, MN 56201-1097, 612-235-5114 Ext. 2914 or toll-free 800-722-1151. *Fax:* 612-231-7617. *E-mail:* drinke@hut.tec.mn.us. College video available.

WORTHINGTON COMMUNITY COLLEGE
Worthington, Minnesota

UG Enrollment: 882	Tuition & Fees (MN Res): $2263
Application Deadline: rolling	Room & Board: N/Avail

GENERAL State-supported, 2-year, coed. Part of Minnesota State Colleges and Universities System. Awards certificates, transfer associate, terminal associate degrees. Founded 1936. *Setting:* 70-acre small-town campus. *Educational spending 1994–95:* $1350 per undergrad. *Total enrollment:* 882. *Faculty:* 60 (29 full-time, 10% with terminal degrees, 31 part-time); student-faculty ratio is 18:1.
ENROLLMENT PROFILE 882 students from 6 states and territories, 2 other countries. 64% women, 49% part-time, 93% state residents, 5% transferred in, 1% international, 39% 25 or older, 0% Native American, 1% Hispanic, 2% African American, 2% Asian American. *Areas of study chosen:* 95% liberal arts/general studies, 1% agriculture. *Most popular recent majors:* liberal arts/general studies, business administration/commerce/management, nursing.
FIRST-YEAR CLASS 391 total. Of the students who applied, 98% were accepted, 81% of whom enrolled. 4% from top 10% of their high school class, 25% from top quarter, 60% from top half.
ACADEMIC PROGRAM Core. Calendar: quarters. Average class size 25 in required courses. Academic remediation for entering students, services for LD students, advanced placement, self-designed majors, summer session for credit, part-time degree program (daytime, evenings), adult/continuing education programs, co-op programs and internships. Off-campus study at other colleges in the Minnesota State Colleges and Universities System.
GENERAL DEGREE REQUIREMENTS 96 quarter credit hours; 1 math course; 2 science courses; computer course; internship (some majors).
MAJORS Agricultural business, agricultural sciences, agricultural technologies, business administration/commerce/management, (pre)engineering sequence, human services, liberal arts/general studies, nursing.
LIBRARY 31,000 books, 150 microform titles, 200 periodicals, 1 on-line bibliographic service, 650 records, tapes, and CDs. Acquisition spending 1994–95: $124,405.
COMPUTERS ON CAMPUS 50 computers for student use in computer center, study skills center. Staffed computer lab on campus provides training in use of computers, software.
COLLEGE LIFE Drama-theater group, choral group, student-run newspaper. 4% vote in student government elections. *Student services:* personal-psychological counseling. *Campus security:* late-night transport-escort service, patrols by police officers.
HOUSING College housing not available.
ATHLETICS Member NJCAA. *Intercollegiate:* basketball M(s)/W(s), football M(s), volleyball W(s), wrestling M(s). *Intramural:* basketball, bowling, football, skiing (cross-country), skiing (downhill), softball, tennis. *Contact:* Mr. Arlo Mogck, Athletic Director, 507-372-2107.
CAREER PLANNING *Director:* Mr. Jerry Jansen, Counselor, 507-372-2107. *Services:* resume preparation, career counseling, careers library.
AFTER GRADUATION 40% of students completing a degree program in 1994–95 went directly on to further study.
EXPENSES FOR 1996–97 *Application fee:* $20. State resident tuition: $2208 full-time, $46 per credit part-time. Nonresident tuition: $4205 full-time, $87.60 per credit part-time. Part-time mandatory fees per credit range from $1.15 to $2.30. Full-time mandatory fees range from $55 to $110.
FINANCIAL AID *College-administered undergrad aid 1995–96:* 15 need-based scholarships (average $300), 20 non-need scholarships (average $300), short-term loans (average $50), low-interest long-term loans from college funds (average $900), loans from external sources (average $2000), 35 Federal Work-Study (averaging $900), 45 part-time jobs. *Required forms:* state, institutional, FAFSA, accepted: CSS Financial Aid PROFILE. *Priority deadline:* 5/1. *Waivers:* full or partial for employees or children of employees and senior citizens.
APPLYING Open admission. *Options:* early entrance, deferred entrance. *Required:* school transcript, ACT. *Recommended:* TOEFL for international students. Test scores used for counseling/placement. *Application deadline:* rolling. *Notification:* continuous.
APPLYING/TRANSFER *Required:* standardized test scores, high school transcript. *Entrance:* noncompetitive. *Application deadline:* rolling. *Notification:* continuous. *Contact:* Mr. Jerry Jansen, Counselor, 507-372-2107.

CONTACT Mr. Donald A. Fleming, Dean of Student Services, Worthington Community College, 1450 College Way, Worthington, MN 56187-3024, 507-372-3406 or toll-free 800-657-3966 (in-state). *Fax:* 507-372-5803. *E-mail:* dfleming@ur.cc.mn.us.

MISSISSIPPI

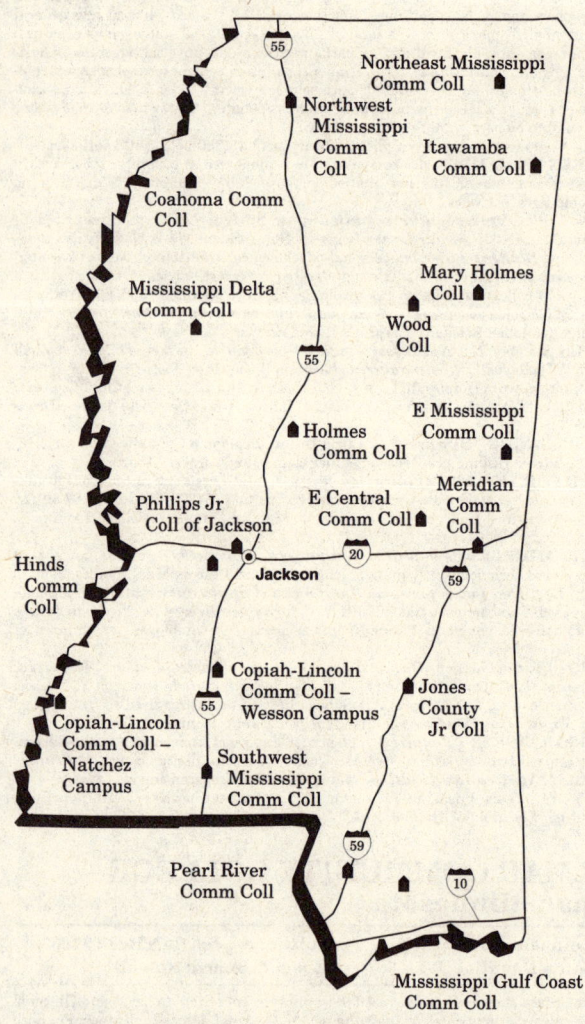

COAHOMA COMMUNITY COLLEGE
Clarksdale, Mississippi

UG Enrollment: 940	Tuition & Fees (Area Res): $1060
Application Deadline: rolling	Room & Board: $2036

GENERAL State and locally supported, 2-year, coed. Part of Mississippi State Board for Community and Junior Colleges. Awards transfer associate, terminal associate degrees. Founded 1949. *Setting:* 29-acre small-town campus with easy access to Memphis. *Total enrollment:* 940. *Faculty:* 85 (65 full-time, 20 part-time).
ENROLLMENT PROFILE 940 students from 8 states and territories. 68% women, 50% part-time, 93% state residents, 2% transferred in, 10% 25 or older, 90% African American.
FIRST-YEAR CLASS 562 total; 1,300 applied, 100% were accepted, 72% of whom enrolled.
ACADEMIC PROGRAM Core, honor code. Calendar: semesters. Part-time degree program (daytime, evenings, summer), adult/continuing education programs.
GENERAL DEGREE REQUIREMENTS 65 credit hours; 1 course in college algebra; computer course for most majors.
MAJORS Accounting, agricultural technologies, art/fine arts, biology/biological sciences, business administration/commerce/management, business economics, chemistry, computer programming, computer science, criminal justice, drafting and design, early childhood education, economics, electronics engineering technology, elementary education, English, graphic arts, health education, liberal arts/general studies, medical technology, radio and television studies, secretarial studies/office management, social work.
COMPUTERS ON CAMPUS 25 computers for student use in computer center, library.
COLLEGE LIFE Drama-theater group, choral group, marching band, student-run newspaper. *Most popular organizations:* Student Government Association, Vica, Phi

Theta Kappa Honor Society. ***Major annual events:*** High School Day, Coronation of Miss Coahoma Community College, Graduation. ***Student services:*** health clinic, personal-psychological counseling. ***Campus security:*** 24-hour patrols.

HOUSING 280 college housing spaces available; 179 were occupied 1995–96. Freshmen guaranteed college housing. ***Option:*** single-sex housing available. Resident assistants live in dorms.

ATHLETICS Member NJCAA. ***Intercollegiate:*** basketball M(s)/W(s), track and field M(s). ***Contact:*** Mr. George Green, Athletic Director, 601-627-2571 Ext. 171.

CAREER PLANNING ***Placement office:*** 2 full-time staff. ***Director:*** Mrs. Wanda Holmes, Director of Career Education, 601-627-2571 Ext. 155. ***Service:*** career counseling.

EXPENSES FOR 1995–96 Area resident tuition: $975 full-time, $40 per credit hour part-time. State resident tuition: $1824 full-time, $57 per credit hour part-time. Nonresident tuition: $3296 full-time, $103 per credit hour part-time. Full-time mandatory fees: $85. College room and board: $2036. College room only: $879.

FINANCIAL AID ***College-administered undergrad aid 1995–96:*** need-based scholarships, non-need scholarships, low-interest long-term loans from external sources, Federal Work-Study, part-time jobs. ***Required forms:*** CSS Financial Aid PROFILE, institutional. ***Application deadline:*** continuous. ***Payment plan:*** installment. ***Waivers:*** full or partial for employees or children of employees.

APPLYING Open admission. ***Option:*** Common Application. ***Required:*** school transcript, ACT. ***Required for some:*** some high school foreign language. Test scores used for admission and counseling/placement. ***Application deadline:*** rolling. ***Notification:*** continuous.

APPLYING/TRANSFER ***Required:*** high school transcript, college transcript, minimum 2.0 college GPA. ***Required for some:*** standardized test scores. ***Application deadline:*** rolling. ***Notification:*** continuous. ***Contact:*** Mrs. Rita S. Hanfor, Dean of Admissions and Records, 601-627-2571 Ext. 205.

CONTACT Mrs. Rita S. Hanfor, Dean of Admissions and Records, Coahoma Community College, Route 1, Box 616, Clarksdale, MS 38614-9799, 601-627-2571 Ext. 205 or toll-free 800-844-1222 (in-state). ***Fax:*** 800-844-1222.

COPIAH-LINCOLN COMMUNITY COLLEGE
Wesson, Mississippi

UG Enrollment: 1,805	**Tuition & Fees (MS Res): $1000**
Application Deadline: rolling	**Room & Board: $1800**

GENERAL State and locally supported, 2-year, coed. Part of Mississippi State Board for Community and Junior Colleges. Awards certificates, transfer associate, terminal associate degrees. Founded 1928. ***Setting:*** 525-acre rural campus. ***Total enrollment:*** 1,805. ***Faculty:*** 116 (76 full-time, 40 part-time); student-faculty ratio is 13:1.

ENROLLMENT PROFILE 1,805 students from 6 states and territories. 60% women, 40% men, 19% part-time, 98% state residents, 31% live on campus, 12% transferred in, 26% 25 or older, 25% African American.

FIRST-YEAR CLASS 700 total; 1,100 applied, 100% were accepted, 64% of whom enrolled.

ACADEMIC PROGRAM Honor code. Calendar: semesters. Academic remediation for entering students, advanced placement, self-designed majors, honors program, summer session for credit, part-time degree program (daytime, evenings, summer), adult/continuing education programs.

GENERAL DEGREE REQUIREMENTS 64 hours; 1 college algebra course; 2 lab science courses; computer course.

MAJORS Accounting, art education, biology/biological sciences, business administration/commerce/management, chemistry, child care/child and family studies, civil engineering technology, computer programming, cosmetology, data processing, drafting and design, economics, education, electrical and electronics technologies, electrical engineering technology, elementary education, engineering and applied sciences, English, food services management, French, health education, history, home economics education, journalism, law enforcement/police sciences, liberal arts/general studies, library science, medical laboratory technology, music education, nursing, physical education, radiological technology, science, vocational education.

LIBRARY Oswalt Memorial Library with 38,750 books, 70 microform titles, 250 periodicals. Acquisition spending 1994–95: $236,558.

COMPUTERS ON CAMPUS 250 computers for student use in computer center, computer labs, learning resource center, library. Staffed computer lab on campus provides training in use of computers.

COLLEGE LIFE Drama-theater group, choral group, marching band, student-run newspaper, radio station. ***Student services:*** health clinic, personal-psychological counseling. ***Campus security:*** 24-hour patrols.

HOUSING 640 college housing spaces available; 555 were occupied 1995–96. No special consideration for freshman housing applicants. Off-campus living permitted. ***Option:*** single-sex housing available. Resident assistants live in dorms.

ATHLETICS Member NJCAA. ***Intercollegiate:*** baseball M(s), basketball M(s)/W(s), football M(s), golf M/W, softball W, tennis M/W, track and field M. ***Intramural:*** basketball, football, golf, tennis, volleyball. ***Contact:*** Mr. Gwyn Young, Athletic Director, 601-643-8381.

CAREER PLANNING ***Services:*** career counseling, careers library.

EXPENSES FOR 1996–97 State resident tuition: $1000 full-time, $50 per semester hour part-time. Nonresident tuition: $2200 full-time, $100 per semester hour part-time. College room and board: $1800.

FINANCIAL AID ***College-administered undergrad aid 1995–96:*** need-based scholarships, 21 non-need scholarships (average $225), low-interest long-term loans from external sources, Federal Work-Study. ***Required forms:*** FAFSA. ***Priority deadline:*** 7/1. ***Payment plan:*** deferred payment. ***Waivers:*** full or partial for employees or children of employees and senior citizens.

APPLYING Open admission. ***Option:*** early entrance. ***Required:*** TOEFL for international students. ***Required for some:*** ACT. Test scores used for counseling/placement. ***Application deadline:*** rolling. Preference given to state residents.

APPLYING/TRANSFER ***Entrance:*** noncompetitive. ***Application deadline:*** rolling. ***Contact:*** Mr. Ralph Frazier, Registrar, 601-643-8307.

CONTACT Mr. Ralph Frazier, Registrar, Copiah-Lincoln Community College, PO Box 371, Wesson, MS 39191-0457, 601-643-8307.

COPIAH-LINCOLN COMMUNITY COLLEGE–NATCHEZ CAMPUS
Natchez, Mississippi

UG Enrollment: 655	**Tuition & Fees (MS Res): $1000**
Application Deadline: rolling	**Room & Board: N/Avail**

GENERAL State and locally supported, 2-year, coed. Part of Mississippi State Board for Community and Junior Colleges. Awards certificates, transfer associate, terminal associate degrees. Founded 1972. ***Setting:*** 24-acre small-town campus. ***Total enrollment:*** 655. ***Faculty:*** 42 (28 full-time, 7% with terminal degrees, 14 part-time); student-faculty ratio is 16:1.

ENROLLMENT PROFILE 655 students from 2 states and territories. 70% women, 40% part-time, 93% state residents, 20% transferred in, 0% international, 50% 25 or older, 0% Native American, 0% Hispanic, 25% African American.

FIRST-YEAR CLASS 250 total. Of the students who applied, 100% were accepted.

ACADEMIC PROGRAM Core. Calendar: semesters. Academic remediation for entering students, self-designed majors, honors program, summer session for credit, part-time degree program (daytime, evenings, summer), adult/continuing education programs.

GENERAL DEGREE REQUIREMENTS 64 semester hours; 1 math course; 2 lab science courses; computer course; internship (some majors).

MAJORS Elementary education, food services management, forestry, home economics, hotel and restaurant management, instrumentation technology, liberal arts/general studies, marketing/retailing/merchandising, political science/government, respiratory therapy, secretarial studies/office management.

LIBRARY Copiah-Lincoln Community College Library with 19,000 books, 47 microform titles, 112 periodicals, 2,384 records, tapes, and CDs.

COMPUTERS ON CAMPUS 480 computers for student use in learning resource center, classrooms. Staffed computer lab on campus provides training in use of computers, software.

COLLEGE LIFE Student-run newspaper. ***Most popular organization:*** Student Newspaper. ***Campus security:*** 24-hour patrols.

HOUSING College housing not available.

ATHLETICS Member NJCAA. ***Intramural:*** volleyball.

CAREER PLANNING ***Service:*** career counseling.

EXPENSES FOR 1996–97 State resident tuition: $1000 full-time, $50 per semester hour part-time. Nonresident tuition: $2200 full-time, $100 per semester hour part-time.

FINANCIAL AID ***College-administered undergrad aid 1995–96:*** need-based scholarships, 37 non-need scholarships (average $270), low-interest long-term loans from external sources (average $2000), Federal Work-Study. ***Required forms:*** FAFSA. ***Priority deadline:*** 7/1. ***Payment plan:*** deferred payment. ***Waivers:*** full or partial for employees or children of employees and senior citizens. ***Notification:*** continuous.

APPLYING Open admission. ***Option:*** early entrance. ***Required:*** school transcript, ACT, TOEFL for international students. ***Required for some:*** TABE. Test scores used for admission and counseling/placement. ***Application deadline:*** rolling. ***Notification:*** continuous.

APPLYING/TRANSFER ***Required:*** standardized test scores, high school transcript, college transcript. ***Entrance:*** noncompetitive. ***Application deadline:*** rolling. ***Notification:*** continuous.

CONTACT Mrs. Sandra Davidson, Director of Admissions and Records, Copiah-Lincoln Community College–Natchez Campus, Natchez, MS 39120-8446, 601-442-9111. ***Fax:*** 601-446-9967.

EAST CENTRAL COMMUNITY COLLEGE
Decatur, Mississippi

UG Enrollment: 1,699	**Tuition & Fees (MS Res): $1000**
Application Deadline: rolling	**Room & Board: $1830**

GENERAL State and locally supported, 2-year, coed. Part of Mississippi State Board for Community and Junior Colleges. Awards transfer associate, terminal associate degrees. Founded 1928. ***Setting:*** 200-acre rural campus. ***Total enrollment:*** 1,699. ***Faculty:*** 102 (62 full-time, 40 part-time); student-faculty ratio is 20:1.

ENROLLMENT PROFILE 1,699 students from 7 states and territories. 60% women, 30% part-time, 97% state residents, 29% live on campus, 2% transferred in, 0% international, 31% 25 or older, 8% Native American, 23% African American.

FIRST-YEAR CLASS 690 total. Of the students who applied, 99% were accepted.

ACADEMIC PROGRAM Core. Calendar: semesters. Academic remediation for entering students, services for LD students, advanced placement, honors program, summer session for credit, part-time degree program (daytime, evenings), adult/continuing education programs.

GENERAL DEGREE REQUIREMENTS 64 semester hours; 1 algebra course.

MAJORS Accounting, art education, art/fine arts, behavioral sciences, biology/biological sciences, business administration/commerce/management, carpentry, chemistry, computer science, cosmetology, data processing, drafting and design, early childhood education, economics, education, electrical and electronics technologies, elementary education, engineering (general), (pre)engineering sequence, English, health education, history, journalism, liberal arts/general studies, library science, literature, mathematics, medical records services, music, music education, nursing, occupational therapy, painting/drawing, pharmacy/pharmaceutical sciences, physical sciences, physical therapy, political science/government, psychology, science, science education, social science.

COMPUTERS ON CAMPUS 65 computers for student use in computer center, library provide access to main academic computer.

COLLEGE LIFE Drama-theater group, choral group, marching band, student-run newspaper. 30% vote in student government elections. ***Student services:*** health clinic, personal-psychological counseling. ***Campus security:*** 24-hour patrols.

HOUSING 500 college housing spaces available; 488 were occupied 1995–96. Off-campus living permitted. ***Options:*** freshmen-only, single-sex (5 buildings) housing available. Resident assistants live in dorms.

ATHLETICS Member NJCAA. ***Intercollegiate:*** baseball M, basketball M(s)/W(s), football M(s), golf M(s)/W, softball W(s), tennis M/W. ***Intramural:*** basketball, football, table tennis (Ping-Pong), volleyball. ***Contact:*** Mr. Sammy Pace, Athletic Director, 601-635-2111.

CAREER PLANNING ***Placement office:*** 1 full-time staff. ***Director:*** Ms. Lanette Hanna, Career Center Director, 601-635-2111. ***Service:*** career counseling.

East Central Community College (continued)

EXPENSES FOR 1996–97 State resident tuition: $1000 full-time, $50 per semester hour part-time. Nonresident tuition: $2200 full-time, $50 per semester hour part-time. College room and board: $1830.

FINANCIAL AID ***College-administered undergrad aid 1995–96:*** need-based scholarships, non-need scholarships, low-interest long-term loans from external sources, Federal Work-Study, part-time jobs. ***Required forms:*** institutional, FAFSA. ***Application deadline:*** continuous. ***Waivers:*** full or partial for employees or children of employees and senior citizens.

APPLYING Open admission. ***Options:*** Common Application, early entrance. ***Required:*** school transcript, ACT, TOEFL for international students. Test scores used for counseling/placement. ***Application deadline:*** rolling. ***Notification:*** continuous.

APPLYING/TRANSFER ***Required:*** standardized test scores, high school transcript, college transcript. ***Entrance:*** noncompetitive.

CONTACT Mr. Raymond McMullan, Director of Admissions, Records, and Research, East Central Community College, Decatur, MS 39327-0129, 601-635-2111 Ext. 206. ***Fax:*** 601-635-2150. College video available.

EAST MISSISSIPPI COMMUNITY COLLEGE
Scooba, Mississippi

UG Enrollment: 1,535 **Tuition & Fees (MS Res): $1000**
Application Deadline: rolling **Room & Board: $1850**

GENERAL State and locally supported, 2-year, coed. Part of Mississippi State Board for Community and Junior Colleges. Awards transfer associate, terminal associate degrees. Founded 1927. ***Setting:*** 25-acre rural campus. ***Total enrollment:*** 1,535. ***Faculty:*** 70 (40 full-time, 30 part-time).

ENROLLMENT PROFILE 1,535 students: 54% women, 40% part-time, 97% state residents, 12% transferred in, 0% international, 8% 25 or older, 48% African American. ***Most popular recent majors:*** business administration/commerce/management, nursing, funeral service.

FIRST-YEAR CLASS Of the students who applied, 100% were accepted.

ACADEMIC PROGRAM Core. Calendar: semesters. Academic remediation for entering students, services for LD students, advanced placement, tutorials, honors program, summer session for credit, part-time degree program (daytime, evenings, summer), adult/continuing education programs, co-op programs.

GENERAL DEGREE REQUIREMENTS 64 semester hours; 1 college algebra course; 2 lab science courses; computer course; internship (some majors).

MAJORS Accounting, agronomy/soil and crop sciences, art/fine arts, automotive technologies, aviation technology, biology/biological sciences, business administration/commerce/management, business education, chemistry, computer science, computer technologies, cosmetology, criminal justice, drafting and design, economics, education, electrical and electronics technologies, elementary education, (pre)engineering sequence, engineering technology, English, finance/banking, fire science, forestry, forest technology, funeral service, health education, history, instrumentation technology, law enforcement/police sciences, liberal arts/general studies, mathematics, music, nursing, optometric/ophthalmic technologies, psychology, reading education, real estate, science, secretarial studies/office management, social science, sociology.

LIBRARY Tubb-May Library with 22,138 books, 159 periodicals, 414 records, tapes, and CDs.

COMPUTERS ON CAMPUS 100 computers for student use in computer center, computer labs, classrooms, library. Staffed computer lab on campus provides training in use of computers, software.

COLLEGE LIFE Drama-theater group, choral group, marching band, student-run newspaper. 60% vote in student government elections. ***Social organizations:*** local fraternities. ***Student services:*** personal-psychological counseling. ***Campus security:*** 24-hour emergency response devices and patrols.

HOUSING 450 college housing spaces available; 400 were occupied 1995–96. No special consideration for freshman housing applicants. Off-campus living permitted.

ATHLETICS Member NJCAA. ***Intercollegiate:*** baseball M, basketball M(s)/W(s), football M(s), softball W. ***Intramural:*** basketball, football, gymnastics, tennis. ***Contact:*** Mr. Tom Goode, Athletic Director, 601-476-8442 Ext. 267.

EXPENSES FOR 1996–97 State resident tuition: $900 full-time, $55 per semester hour part-time. Nonresident tuition: $1000 full-time, $55 per semester hour part-time. Mandatory fees: $100 for stateresidents, $1000 for nonresidents full-time, $50 for state residents, $500 for nonresidents per semester part-time. College room and board: $1850.

FINANCIAL AID ***College-administered undergrad aid 1995–96:*** 20 need-based scholarships (average $300), 40 non-need scholarships (average $250), low-interest long-term loans from external sources, Federal Work-Study, part-time jobs. ***Required forms:*** FAFSA; accepted: CSS Financial Aid PROFILE. ***Application deadline:*** continuous. ***Payment plan:*** installment. ***Waivers:*** full or partial for employees or children of employees.

APPLYING Open admission. ***Options:*** Common Application, deferred entrance, midyear entrance. ***Required:*** school transcript, ACT. Test scores used for counseling/placement. ***Application deadline:*** rolling.

APPLYING/TRANSFER ***Required:*** college transcript. ***Entrance:*** noncompetitive. ***Application deadline:*** rolling. ***Contact:*** Ms. Melinda Sciple, Admissions Officer, 601-476-8442 Ext. 221.

CONTACT Ms. Melinda Sciple, Admissions Officer, East Mississippi Community College, PO Box 158, Scooba, MS 39358-0158, 601-476-8442 Ext. 221.

HINDS COMMUNITY COLLEGE
Raymond, Mississippi

UG Enrollment: 10,743 **Tuition & Fees (MS Res): $1070**
Application Deadline: rolling **Room & Board: $1070**

GENERAL State and locally supported, 2-year, coed. Part of Mississippi State Board for Community and Junior Colleges. Awards certificates, diplomas, transfer associate, terminal associate degrees. Founded 1917. ***Setting:*** 671-acre small-town campus. ***Endowment:*** $623,211. ***Total enrollment:*** 10,743. ***Faculty:*** 899 (386 full-time, 513 part-time). ***Notable Alumni:*** Ray Marshall, secretary of labor; Clifford Charlesworth, astronaut; Zig Ziglar, motivational speaker; Faith Hill, country singer; Patrick Smith, author.

ENROLLMENT PROFILE 10,743 students from 16 states and territories, 1 other country. 61% women, 28% part-time, 99% state residents, 15% live on campus, 10% transferred in, 66% have need-based financial aid, 16% have non-need-based financial aid, 43% 25 or older, 38% African American, 1% Asian American. ***Most popular recent majors:*** liberal arts/general studies, nursing, secretarial studies/office management.

FIRST-YEAR CLASS 3,098 total. Of the students who applied, 100% were accepted.

ACADEMIC PROGRAM Core, honor code. Calendar: semesters. 880 courses offered in 1995–96. Academic remediation for entering students, English as a second language program offered during academic year, services for LD students, advanced placement, honors program, summer session for credit, part-time degree program (daytime, evenings, summer), adult/continuing education programs, co-op programs. ROTC: Army (c).

GENERAL DEGREE REQUIREMENTS 64 semester hours; math/science requirements vary according to program; computer course for technology majors.

MAJORS Accounting, agricultural business, biology/biological sciences, carpentry, child psychology/child development, civil engineering technology, commercial art, communication, computer programming, criminal justice, data processing, dental services, dietetics, drafting and design, economics, electronics engineering technology, emergency medical technology, (pre)engineering sequence, English, fashion design and technology, finance/banking, food services management, home economics, hotel and restaurant management, industrial arts, journalism, landscaping/grounds maintenance, law enforcement/police sciences, liberal arts/general studies, machine and tool technologies, marketing/retailing/merchandising, mathematics, medical laboratory technology, medical records services, music, nursing, operating room technology, paralegal studies, political science/government, postal management, practical nursing, printing technologies, psychology, public administration, radiological technology, real estate, respiratory therapy, secretarial studies/office management, social science, sociology, textiles and clothing, theater arts/drama, veterinary sciences, welding technology.

LIBRARY McLendon Library with 162,680 books, 13,031 microform titles, 1,228 periodicals, 1 on-line bibliographic service, 8 CD-ROMs, 6,379 records, tapes, and CDs. Acquisition spending 1994–95: $1.2 million.

COMPUTERS ON CAMPUS 55 computers for student use in computer center, learning resource center, library provide access to main academic computer, independent study modules. Staffed computer lab on campus provides training in use of computers, software. Academic computing expenditure 1994–95: $55,000.

COLLEGE LIFE Drama-theater group, choral group, marching band, student-run newspaper. ***Social organizations:*** 51 open to all. ***Most popular organizations:*** Phi Theta Kappa, Baptist Student Union, Residence Hall Association, Hi-Steppers Dance Team, Band. ***Major annual events:*** Homecoming Week, Substance Abuse Week, Spring Fling. ***Student services:*** personal-psychological counseling, women's center. ***Campus security:*** 24-hour emergency response devices and patrols, controlled dormitory access.

HOUSING 1,750 college housing spaces available; 1,374 were occupied 1995–96. No special consideration for freshman housing applicants. Off-campus living permitted. ***Options:*** freshmen-only, single-sex housing available. Resident assistants live in dorms.

ATHLETICS Member NJCAA. ***Intercollegiate:*** baseball M(s), basketball M(s)/W(s), football M(s), golf M(s), soccer M(s), softball W(s), tennis M(s)/W(s), track and field M(s). ***Intramural:*** basketball, football, softball, volleyball. ***Contact:*** Mrs. Rene T. Warren, Athletic Director, 601-857-3362.

CAREER PLANNING ***Placement office:*** 8 full-time, 2 part-time staff; $119,865 operating expenditure 1994–95. ***Director:*** Mr. Clark Henderson, Director of Cooperative Education and Job Placement, 601-857-3427. ***Services:*** job fairs, resume preparation, resume referral, career counseling, careers library, job bank, job interviews.

EXPENSES FOR 1996–97 State resident tuition: $1020 full-time, $55 per semester hour part-time. Nonresident tuition: $3226 full-time, $135 per semester hour part-time. Part-time mandatory fees: $25 per semester. Full-time mandatory fees: $50. College room and board: $1070. College room only: $700.

FINANCIAL AID ***College-administered undergrad aid 1995–96:*** 3,883 need-based scholarships (average $1150), 984 non-need scholarships (average $500), low-interest long-term loans from external sources (average $2625), Federal Work-Study, 200 part-time jobs. ***Required forms:*** institutional, FAFSA; required for some: state, nontaxable income verification; accepted: CSS Financial Aid PROFILE. ***Priority deadline:*** 4/1.

APPLYING Open admission. ***Option:*** midyear entrance. ***Required:*** school transcript, 3 years of high school math and science, TOEFL for international students. ***Required for some:*** ACT. Test scores used for counseling/placement. ***Application deadline:*** rolling. ***Notification:*** continuous.

APPLYING/TRANSFER ***Required:*** college transcript. ***Application deadline:*** rolling. ***Notification:*** continuous. ***Contact:*** Mr. Bob Bain, Director of Admissions and Records, 601-857-3280.

CONTACT Mr. Bob Bain, Director of Admissions and Records, Hinds Community College, Raymond, MS 39154, 601-857-3280.

HOLMES COMMUNITY COLLEGE
Goodman, Mississippi

UG Enrollment: 2,553 **Tuition & Fees (MS Res): $1010**
Application Deadline: rolling **Room & Board: $1500**

GENERAL State and locally supported, 2-year, coed. Part of Mississippi State Board for Community and Junior Colleges. Awards certificates, transfer associate, terminal associate degrees. Founded 1928. ***Setting:*** 196-acre small-town campus. ***Endowment:*** $1.2 million. ***Educational spending 1994–95:*** $2100 per undergrad. ***Total enrollment:*** 2,553. ***Faculty:*** 125 (100 full-time, 10% with terminal degrees, 25 part-time); student-faculty ratio is 22:1. ***Notable Alumni:*** Shirlie Lobmiller, Mike Kennison, Donald E. Phillips, Dr. Alton B. Cobb, Dr. Ronald Doyle.

ENROLLMENT PROFILE 2,553 students from 7 states and territories, 4 other countries. 62% women, 47% part-time, 98% state residents, 20% transferred in, 65% have need-based financial aid, 20% have non-need-based financial aid, 1% Native American, 1% Hispanic, 23% African American, 1% Asian American. ***Areas of study chosen:*** 31% liberal arts/general studies, 23% health professions and related sciences, 20% vocational and home economics, 10% business management and administrative services, 8% education, 1% agriculture, 1% biological and life sciences, 1% computer and information sciences, 1% engineering and applied sciences, 1% mathematics, 1% prevet. ***Most popular recent majors:*** business administration/commerce/management, elementary education, secretarial studies/office management.

FIRST-YEAR CLASS 943 total. Of the students who applied, 70% were accepted.
ACADEMIC PROGRAM Core, interdisciplinary curriculum, honor code. Calendar: semesters. 375 courses offered in 1995–96. Academic remediation for entering students, services for LD students, advanced placement, summer session for credit, adult/continuing education programs, co-op programs.
GENERAL DEGREE REQUIREMENTS 64 semester hours; 1 college algebra course; 6 semester hours of lab science.
MAJORS Agricultural sciences, biology/biological sciences, business administration/commerce/management, business education, child care/child and family studies, computer science, data processing, drafting and design, elementary education, engineering (general), finance/banking, forestry, liberal arts/general studies, medical records services, medical technology, music education, nursing, pharmacy/pharmaceutical sciences, physical therapy, radio and television studies, respiratory therapy, science education, secretarial studies/office management, social work, veterinary sciences, wildlife biology.
LIBRARY McMorrough Library with 52,900 books, 247 microform titles, 471 periodicals, 1 CD-ROM, 2,665 records, tapes, and CDs. Acquisition spending 1994–95: $67,500.
COMPUTERS ON CAMPUS 120 computers for student use in computer labs, learning resource center, classrooms, library.
COLLEGE LIFE Drama-theater group, choral group, marching band, student-run newspaper, radio station. 30% vote in student government elections. *Social organizations:* 23 open to all. *Most popular organizations:* Student Government Association, Drama/Theater Club, Baptist Student Union, FCA, Vocational Industrial Clubs of America. *Major annual events:* Homecoming, Beauty Pageant, Spring Fling. *Student services:* personal-psychological counseling. *Campus security:* 24-hour emergency response devices and patrols.
HOUSING 514 college housing spaces available; 369 were occupied 1995–96. No special consideration for freshman housing applicants. Off-campus living permitted. *Option:* single-sex (5 buildings) housing available. Resident assistants live in dorms.
ATHLETICS Member NJCAA. *Intercollegiate:* baseball M(s), basketball M(s)/W, football M(s), golf M/W, softball W, tennis M/W, track and field M/W. *Intramural:* basketball, football, softball, volleyball. *Contact:* Mr. Robert Pool, Athletic Director, 601-472-2312.
CAREER PLANNING *Placement office:* 2 full-time staff. *Director:* Mrs. Janice Richardson, Counselor, 601-472-2312. *Services:* job fairs, resume preparation, resume referral, career counseling, careers library.
AFTER GRADUATION 65% of students completing a degree program in 1994–95 went directly on to further study.
EXPENSES FOR 1995–96 State resident tuition: $0 full-time. Nonresident tuition: $1200 full-time, $50 per semester hour part-time. Part-time mandatory fees: $42.08 per semester hour. Full-time mandatory fees: $1010. College room and board: $1500. College room only: $500.
FINANCIAL AID *College-administered undergrad aid 1995–96:* 286 need-based scholarships (average $400), 576 non-need scholarships (average $780), low-interest long-term loans from external sources (average $1860), Federal Work-Study. *Required forms for some financial aid applicants:* institutional, FAFSA. *Priority deadline:* 6/1. *Payment plan:* installment. *Waivers:* full or partial for senior citizens.
APPLYING *Option:* early entrance. *Required:* school transcript, ACT, TOEFL for international students. Test scores used for admission. *Application deadline:* rolling. *Notification:* continuous.
APPLYING/TRANSFER *Required:* standardized test scores, high school transcript, college transcript. *Entrance:* minimally difficult. *Application deadline:* rolling. *Notification:* continuous. *Contact:* Ms. Fedder Williams, Transfer Counselor, 601-472-2312 Ext. 89.
CONTACT Mr. Gene Richardson, Director of Admissions and Records, Holmes Community College, Goodman, MS 39079-0369, 601-472-2312 Ext. 23. *Fax:* 601-942-2566.

ITAWAMBA COMMUNITY COLLEGE
Fulton, Mississippi

UG Enrollment: 3,500	Tuition & Fees (Area Res): $910
Application Deadline: rolling	Room & Board: $1740

GENERAL State and locally supported, 2-year, coed. Part of Mississippi State Board for Community and Junior Colleges. Awards transfer associate, terminal associate degrees. Founded 1947. *Setting:* 300-acre small-town campus. *Total enrollment:* 3,500. *Faculty:* 102 (87 full-time, 15 part-time); student-faculty ratio is 34:1.
ENROLLMENT PROFILE 3,500 students from 9 states and territories, 3 other countries. 53% women, 35% part-time, 85% state residents, 35% transferred in, 1% international, 8% 25 or older, 0% Native American, 1% Hispanic, 22% African American, 1% Asian American.
FIRST-YEAR CLASS 2,177 total. Of the students who applied, 100% were accepted. 15% from top 10% of their high school class, 25% from top quarter, 70% from top half.
ACADEMIC PROGRAM Core. Calendar: semesters. Academic remediation for entering students, services for LD students, honors program, summer session for credit, part-time degree program (daytime, evenings), adult/continuing education programs. ROTC: Army.
GENERAL DEGREE REQUIREMENTS 63 semester hours; 1 college algebra course; 2 lab science courses; computer course for transfer associate degree.
MAJORS Accounting, agricultural business, art education, art/fine arts, biology/biological sciences, business administration/commerce/management, chemistry, child psychology/child development, civil engineering technology, computer science, computer technologies, construction technologies, data processing, drafting and design, early childhood education, economics, education, electrical and electronics technologies, elementary education, (pre)engineering sequence, English, fashion design and technology, forest technology, history, home economics, home economics education, human services, industrial arts, journalism, law enforcement/police sciences, liberal arts/general studies, library science, marketing/retailing/merchandising, mathematics, medical records services, modern languages, music, music education, nursing, physical education, piano/organ, political science/government, psychology, public administration, radiological technology, respiratory therapy, science, science education, secretarial studies/office management, social science, social work, sociology, speech/rhetoric/public address/debate, veterinary sciences, vocational education, wind and percussion instruments.
LIBRARY 36,816 books, 143 microform titles, 231 periodicals, 1,657 records, tapes, and CDs.
COMPUTERS ON CAMPUS 40 computers for student use in computer labs. Staffed computer lab on campus provides training in use of computers, software.

HOUSING 700 college housing spaces available; 440 were occupied 1995–96. Off-campus living permitted.
ATHLETICS Member NJCAA. *Intercollegiate:* basketball M(s)/W(s), football M(s), tennis M/W, track and field M. *Intramural:* badminton, basketball, football, tennis, volleyball. *Contact:* Mr. Mike Eaton, Athletic Director, 601-862-3101 Ext. 283.
CAREER PLANNING *Service:* career counseling.
EXPENSES FOR 1996–97 Area resident tuition: $850 full-time, $45 per semester hour part-time. State resident tuition: $860 full-time, $45 per semester hour part-time. Nonresident tuition: $2050 full-time, $45 per semester hour part-time. Part-time mandatory fees: $30 per semester. Full-time mandatory fees: $60. College room and board: $1740. College room only: $720.
FINANCIAL AID *College-administered undergrad aid 1995–96:* need-based scholarships, non-need scholarships, low-interest long-term loans from external sources, Federal Work-Study. *Application deadline:* continuous.
APPLYING Open admission except for allied health programs. *Option:* early entrance. *Required:* school transcript, ACT. Test scores used for counseling/placement. *Application deadline:* rolling. *Notification:* continuous.
APPLYING/TRANSFER *Required:* college transcript. *Application deadline:* rolling. *Notification:* continuous.
CONTACT Mr. Max Munn, Director of Recruiting, Itawamba Community College, Fulton, MS 38843-1099, 601-862-3101 Ext. 260. *Fax:* 601-862-9540. College video available.

JONES COUNTY JUNIOR COLLEGE
Ellisville, Mississippi

UG Enrollment: 4,430	Tuition & Fees (MS Res): $792
Application Deadline: 8/25	Room & Board: $1740

GENERAL State and locally supported, 2-year, coed. Part of Mississippi State Board for Community and Junior Colleges. Awards transfer associate, terminal associate degrees. Founded 1928. *Setting:* 360-acre small-town campus. *Total enrollment:* 4,430. *Faculty:* 175; student-faculty ratio is 26:1. *Notable Alumni:* Mr. Charles Pickering, federal judge.
ENROLLMENT PROFILE 4,430 students from 9 states and territories. 55% women, 22% part-time, 99% state residents, 20% live on campus, 14% transferred in, 0% international, 28% 25 or older, 18% African American.
FIRST-YEAR CLASS 2,800 total; 4,400 applied, 100% were accepted, 64% of whom enrolled.
ACADEMIC PROGRAM Core. Calendar: semesters. Advanced placement, honors program, summer session for credit, part-time degree program (daytime, evenings), co-op programs.
GENERAL DEGREE REQUIREMENTS 64 semester hours; 1 college algebra course.
MAJORS Accounting, agricultural sciences, applied art, art education, biology/biological sciences, business administration/commerce/management, chemistry, child care/child and family studies, data processing, drafting and design, economics, education, electrical and electronics technologies, emergency medical technology, engineering sciences, English, forest technology, home economics, home economics education, horticulture, law enforcement/police sciences, mathematics, music, music education, nursing, physical education, physical sciences, practical nursing, science, science education, voice.
LIBRARY Memorial Library with 62,349 books, 2,851 microform titles, 654 periodicals, 6,266 records, tapes, and CDs.
COMPUTERS ON CAMPUS 205 computers for student use in computer center, classrooms, library. Staffed computer lab on campus.
COLLEGE LIFE Drama-theater group, student-run newspaper. *Most popular organization:* Student Government. *Major annual events:* Homecoming, Spring Fever Week. *Student services:* health clinic, personal-psychological counseling. *Campus security:* 24-hour patrols.
HOUSING 536 college housing spaces available; all were occupied 1995–96. Off-campus living permitted. *Option:* single-sex housing available. Resident assistants live in dorms.
ATHLETICS Member NJCAA. *Intercollegiate:* baseball M, basketball M(s)/W(s), football M(s), golf M, softball W, tennis M/W, track and field M. *Intramural:* basketball, tennis, volleyball. *Contact:* Mr. Bobby Glaze, Athletic Director, 601-477-4091.
CAREER PLANNING *Service:* career counseling.
EXPENSES FOR 1995–96 State resident tuition: $744 full-time, $40 per semester hour part-time. Nonresident tuition: $1944 full-time, $95 per semester hour part-time. Part-time mandatory fees: $15 per semester. Full-time mandatory fees: $48. College room and board: $1740.
FINANCIAL AID *College-administered undergrad aid 1995–96:* need-based scholarships, 380 non-need scholarships (average $600), low-interest long-term loans from external sources (average $2000), Federal Work-Study, 80 part-time jobs. *Required forms:* FAFSA; accepted: CSS Financial Aid PROFILE. *Priority deadline:* 5/1.
APPLYING Open admission. *Options:* Common Application, early entrance. *Required:* school transcript, SAT I or ACT. *Recommended:* 3 years of high school math and science, some high school foreign language. Test scores used for admission and counseling/placement. *Application deadline:* 8/25. *Notification:* continuous. Preference given to district residents.
APPLYING/TRANSFER *Required:* standardized test scores, high school transcript, college transcript. *Entrance:* noncompetitive. *Application deadline:* 8/25. *Notification:* continuous.
CONTACT Mrs. Dianne Speed, Director of Admissions and Guidance, Jones County Junior College, Ellisville, MS 39437-3901, 601-477-4025.

MARY HOLMES COLLEGE
West Point, Mississippi

UG Enrollment: 375	Tuition & Fees: $4100
Application Deadline: rolling	Room & Board: $3890

GENERAL Independent Presbyterian, 2-year, coed. Awards certificates, diplomas, transfer associate, terminal associate degrees. Founded 1892. *Setting:* 192-acre rural campus. *Endowment:* $10,000. *Research spending 1994–95:* $500. *Educational spending 1994–95:* $267 per undergrad. *Total enrollment:* 375. *Faculty:* 29 (24 full-time, 21% with terminal degrees, 5 part-time). *Notable Alumni:* Bennie Turner, state senator; Dr. Mary

Mary Holmes College (continued)
Davidson, zoologist; Dr. Delores Janet Cooper, pharmacologist; Nettie Stewart, chairperson of board of trustees of Commonwealth National Bank; Aundrey Wilkins, interagency liasion for U.S. Department of Transportation.
ENROLLMENT PROFILE 375 students from 25 states and territories. 54% women, 46% men, 6% part-time, 65% state residents, 73% live on campus, 1% transferred in, 90% have need-based financial aid, 3% international, 10% 25 or older, 0% Native American, 1% Hispanic, 96% African American, 0% Asian American. ***Most popular recent majors:*** computer science, business administration/commerce/management, elementary education.
FIRST-YEAR CLASS 195 total; 400 applied, 63% were accepted, 78% of whom enrolled. 2% from top 10% of their high school class, 12% from top quarter, 60% from top half.
ACADEMIC PROGRAM Core, interdisciplinary curriculum, honor code. Calendar: semesters. 33 courses offered in 1995–96; average class size 20 in required courses. Academic remediation for entering students, advanced placement, honors program, part-time degree program (daytime, evenings).
GENERAL DEGREE REQUIREMENTS 64 credit hours; 1 course each in algebra and trigonometry; computer course.
MAJORS Accounting, business administration/commerce/management, business education, chemical engineering technology, child care/child and family studies, communication, computer science, early childhood education, education, elementary education, (pre)engineering sequence, liberal arts/general studies, mathematics, natural sciences, nursing, physical education, secretarial studies/office management, social science.
LIBRARY Sage Memorial Library with 24,888 books, 1,485 microform titles, 122 periodicals, 25 CD-ROMs, 166 records, tapes, and CDs. Acquisition spending 1994–95: $4000.
COMPUTERS ON CAMPUS 50 computers for student use in computer center, math, reading resource rooms, library, dorms. Staffed computer lab on campus provides training in use of computers, software. Academic computing expenditure 1994–95: $30,000.
NOTEWORTHY RESEARCH FACILITIES Walton Learning Resource Center.
COLLEGE LIFE Orientation program (4 days, no cost). Drama-theater group, choral group, student-run newspaper. 55% vote in student government elections. ***Social organizations:*** 10 open to all. ***Most popular organizations:*** Student Government Association, Student Christian Association, NAACP, Math and Science Club, Student Support Club. ***Major annual events:*** Coronation of Ms. MHC, Founder's Day, Graduation Exercises. ***Student services:*** personal-psychological counseling.
HOUSING 554 college housing spaces available; 241 were occupied 1995–96. Freshmen guaranteed college housing. Off-campus living permitted. ***Options:*** freshmen-only, single-sex (2 buildings) housing available. Resident assistants live in dorms.
ATHLETICS Member NJCAA. ***Intercollegiate:*** basketball M(s)/W(s), cross-country running M, soccer M, volleyball M/W. ***Intramural:*** archery, badminton, basketball, cross-country running, football, soccer, table tennis (Ping-Pong), track and field, volleyball, weight lifting. ***Contact:*** Mr. James Stewart, Athletic Director, 601-494-6820 Ext. 3220.
CAREER PLANNING ***Placement office:*** 1 full-time, 1 part-time staff; $40,000 operating expenditure 1994–95. ***Director:*** Mrs. Mary Kelley, Counselor, 601-494-6820 Ext. 3206. ***Services:*** resume preparation, career counseling, careers library.
AFTER GRADUATION 10% of class of 1994 had job offers within 6 months. 80% of students completing a degree program went directly on to further study.
EXPENSES FOR 1996–97 Comprehensive fee of $7990 includes full-time tuition ($4000), mandatory fees ($100), and college room and board ($3890). College room only: $1890. Part-time tuition: $134 per credit hour. Part-time mandatory fees: $50 per semester.
FINANCIAL AID ***College-administered undergrad aid 1995–96:*** 375 need-based scholarships (average $1590), non-need scholarships, low-interest long-term loans from external sources (average $2625), 150 Federal Work-Study (averaging $800). ***Required forms:*** CSS Financial Aid PROFILE, institutional, FAFSA. ***Priority deadline:*** 8/1. ***Payment plans:*** installment, deferred payment. ***Waivers:*** full or partial for employees or children of employees. ***Notification:*** continuous.
APPLYING Open admission. ***Options:*** Common Application, early entrance, deferred entrance, midyear entrance. ***Required:*** school transcript, 2 recommendations, TOEFL for international students. ***Recommended:*** 3 years of high school math and science. Test scores used for counseling/placement. ***Application deadline:*** rolling. ***Notification:*** continuous.
APPLYING/TRANSFER ***Required:*** high school transcript, college transcript. ***Entrance:*** minimally difficult. ***Application deadline:*** rolling. ***Notification:*** continuous. ***Contact:*** Ms. Brenda Carter, Director of Admissions, 601-494-6820 Ext. 3135.
CONTACT Ms. Brenda Carter, Director of Admissions, Mary Holmes College, West Point, MS 39773-1257, 601-494-6820 Ext. 3135 or toll-free 800-634-2749 (in-state). ***Fax:*** 601-494-1881. College video available.

MERIDIAN COMMUNITY COLLEGE
Meridian, Mississippi

UG Enrollment: 2,928	**Tuition & Fees (MS Res): $980**
Application Deadline: rolling	**Room & Board: $2200**

GENERAL State and locally supported, 2-year, coed. Part of Mississippi State Board for Community and Junior Colleges. Awards certificates, transfer associate, terminal associate degrees. Founded 1937. ***Setting:*** 62-acre small-town campus. ***Total enrollment:*** 2,928. ***Faculty:*** 236 (106 full-time, 6% with terminal degrees, 130 part-time).
ENROLLMENT PROFILE 2,928 students from 8 states and territories, 1 other country. 69% women, 39% part-time, 98% state residents, 12% live on campus, 30% transferred in, 43% 25 or older, 1% Native American, 1% Hispanic, 26% African American, 1% Asian American. ***Areas of study chosen:*** 21% health professions and related sciences, 5% business management and administrative services, 4% education, 1% communications and journalism, 1% computer and information sciences, 1% mathematics, 1% predentistry, 1% prelaw, 1% premed, 1% prevet, 1% psychology. ***Most popular recent majors:*** nursing, business administration/commerce/management, practical nursing.
FIRST-YEAR CLASS 1,036 total; 1,199 applied, 100% were accepted, 86% of whom enrolled.
ACADEMIC PROGRAM Core, honor code. Calendar: semesters. 420 courses offered in 1995–96. Academic remediation for entering students, advanced placement, self-designed majors, summer session for credit, part-time degree program (daytime, evenings, summer), adult/continuing education programs, co-op programs.
GENERAL DEGREE REQUIREMENTS 64 semester hours; 3 semester hours of math; 6 semester hours of science; computer course for marketing, medical records technology majors.
MAJORS Aviation administration, broadcasting, business administration/commerce/management, child psychology/child development, computer technologies, construction technologies, data processing, dental services, drafting and design, electrical and electronics technologies, electromechanical technology, elementary education, emergency medical technology, (pre)engineering sequence, fire science, food services management, horticulture, hotel and restaurant management, industrial engineering technology, laboratory technologies, law enforcement/police sciences, liberal arts/general studies, machine and tool technologies, manufacturing technology, marketing/retailing/merchandising, mechanical engineering technology, medical laboratory technology, medical records services, nursing, physical therapy, practical nursing, radiological technology, respiratory therapy, secretarial studies/office management.
LIBRARY L.O. Todd Library with 50,000 books, 80 microform titles, 600 periodicals, 6 CD-ROMs, 4,262 records, tapes, and CDs.
COMPUTERS ON CAMPUS 200 computers for student use in computer center, computer labs, academic building, classrooms. Staffed computer lab on campus provides training in use of computers, software.
NOTEWORTHY RESEARCH FACILITIES Southern Medical Library Consortium.
COLLEGE LIFE Choral group. ***Social organizations:*** 22 open to all. ***Most popular organizations:*** Phi Theta Kappa, Vocational Industrial Clubs of America, Health Occupations Students of America, Organization of Student Nurses, Distributive Education Clubs of America. ***Major annual events:*** Spring Fest, October Fest, Fall Picnic. ***Campus security:*** 24-hour patrols, student patrols.
HOUSING 168 college housing spaces available; all were occupied 1995–96. No special consideration for freshman housing applicants. Off-campus living permitted. ***Options:*** coed (2 buildings), single-sex (1 building) housing available. Resident assistants live in dorms.
ATHLETICS Member NJCAA. ***Intercollegiate:*** baseball M(s), basketball M(s)/W(s), golf M(s)/W, soccer M(s), softball W(s), tennis M(s)/W(s), track and field M(s)/W(s). ***Intramural:*** basketball, cross-country running, tennis. ***Contact:*** Ms. Michele Smith, Athletic and Fitness Center Director, 601-484-8773.
CAREER PLANNING ***Director:*** Ms. Dianne Walton, Director, College and Career Planning, 601-484-8895. ***Services:*** resume preparation, career counseling, careers library, job interviews.
AFTER GRADUATION 75% of students completing a degree program in 1994–95 went directly on to further study.
EXPENSES FOR 1995–96 State resident tuition: $960 full-time, $50 per semester hour part-time. Nonresident tuition: $2000 full-time, $100 per semester hour part-time. Part-time mandatory fees: $10 per semester hour. Full-time mandatory fees: $20. College room and board: $2200.
FINANCIAL AID ***College-administered undergrad aid 1995–96:*** need-based scholarships, 86 non-need scholarships (averaging $250), short-term loans, low-interest long-term loans from external sources, Federal Work-Study, 240 part-time jobs. ***Required forms:*** institutional, FAFSA; accepted: CSS Financial Aid PROFILE. ***Priority deadline:*** 4/1.
APPLYING Open admission. ***Option:*** early entrance. ***Required:*** school transcript, minimum 2.0 GPA, SAT I or ACT, TOEFL for international students. ***Required for some:*** essay. Test scores used for counseling/placement. ***Application deadline:*** rolling.
APPLYING/TRANSFER ***Required:*** high school transcript, college transcript, minimum 2.0 high school GPA. ***Application deadline:*** rolling. ***Contact:*** Ms. Dianne Walton, Director, College and Career Planning, 601-484-8895.
CONTACT Ms. Mary Faye Wilson, Admissions Director, Meridian Community College, Meridian, MS 39307, 601-484-8621 or toll-free 800-622-8731 (in-state).

MISSISSIPPI DELTA COMMUNITY COLLEGE
Moorhead, Mississippi

UG Enrollment: 2,403	**Tuition & Fees (MS Res): $770**
Application Deadline: 7/27	**Room & Board: $1450**

GENERAL District-supported, 2-year, coed. Part of Mississippi State Board for Community and Junior Colleges. Awards certificates, diplomas, transfer associate, terminal associate degrees. Founded 1926. ***Setting:*** 425-acre small-town campus. ***Total enrollment:*** 2,403. ***Faculty:*** 128 (90 full-time, 3% with terminal degrees, 38 part-time).
ENROLLMENT PROFILE 2,403 students from 6 states and territories. 54% women, 8% part-time, 99% state residents, 25% live on campus, 10% transferred in, 0% international, 5% 25 or older, 0% Native American, 1% Hispanic, 25% African American, 1% Asian American. ***Areas of study chosen:*** 28% business management and administrative services, 18% education, 13% biological and life sciences, 10% engineering and applied sciences, 10% health professions and related sciences, 3% agriculture, 3% liberal arts/general studies, 3% premed, 3% social sciences, 2% communications and journalism, 2% computer and information sciences, 2% prelaw, 1% mathematics, 1% predentistry, 1% prevet, 1% psychology.
FIRST-YEAR CLASS 1,008 total; 1,432 applied, 80% were accepted, 88% of whom enrolled. 4% from top 10% of their high school class, 20% from top quarter, 56% from top half. 10 class presidents, 11 valedictorians.
ACADEMIC PROGRAM Honor code. Calendar: semesters. Academic remediation for entering students, advanced placement, summer session for credit, part-time degree program (daytime, evenings), adult/continuing education programs.
GENERAL DEGREE REQUIREMENTS 64 semester hours; 1 college algebra course.
MAJORS Accounting, advertising, agricultural business, agricultural economics, American studies, applied art, art education, behavioral sciences, biology/biological sciences, business administration/commerce/management, business machine technologies, child psychology/child development, civil engineering technology, commercial art, computer technologies, construction technologies, criminal justice, data processing, drafting and design, economics, education, electrical and electronics technologies, elementary education, English, farm and ranch management, geography, health education, history, home economics, liberal arts/general studies, mathematics, medical laboratory technology, medical records services, music, music education, nursing, physical education, political science/government, radiological technology, science education, social work, theater arts/drama.
LIBRARY 30,000 books, 108 microform titles, 197 periodicals, 1,200 records, tapes, and CDs.
COMPUTERS ON CAMPUS 80 computers for student use in computer center, vo-tech center, library.

COLLEGE LIFE Drama-theater group, choral group, marching band, student-run newspaper. ***Student services:*** personal-psychological counseling. ***Campus security:*** 24-hour emergency response devices and patrols, late-night transport-escort service.
HOUSING 500 college housing spaces available; all were occupied 1995–96. No special consideration for freshman housing applicants. Off-campus living permitted. ***Option:*** single-sex (2 buildings) housing available. Resident assistants live in dorms.
ATHLETICS Member NJCAA. ***Intercollegiate:*** baseball M(s), basketball M(s)/W(s), football M(s), tennis M/W, track and field M. ***Intramural:*** badminton, basketball, football, tennis, track and field, volleyball. ***Contact:*** Mr. Jimmy Bellipanni, Athletic Director, 601-246-5631.
CAREER PLANNING ***Placement office:*** 5 full-time staff. ***Director:*** Mr. Ralph Ross, Director of Counseling Center, 601-246-5631. ***Service:*** career counseling.
AFTER GRADUATION 98% of students completing a degree program in 1994–95 went directly on to further study.
ESTIMATED EXPENSES FOR 1996–97 State resident tuition: $770 full-time, $45 per semester hour part-time. Nonresident tuition: $2050 full-time, $45 per semester hour part-time. College room and board: $1450.
FINANCIAL AID ***College-administered undergrad aid 1995–96:*** 1,033 need-based scholarships (average $800), 30 non-need scholarships (average $300), 178 Federal Work-Study (averaging $750). ***Required forms:*** FAFSA. ***Priority deadline:*** 8/20. ***Payment plans:*** installment, deferred payment.
APPLYING ***Option:*** deferred entrance. ***Required:*** school transcript. ***Required for some:*** ACT. Test scores used for admission. ***Application deadline:*** 7/27. Preference given to district residents.
APPLYING/TRANSFER ***Required:*** college transcript. ***Required for some:*** standardized test scores, high school transcript, minimum 2.0 college GPA. ***Application deadline:*** 7/27. ***Contact:*** Mr. Joseph F. Ray Jr., Dean of Admissions, Records, and Financial Aid, 601-246-6322.
CONTACT Mr. Joseph F. Ray Jr., Dean of Admissions, Records, and Financial Aid, Mississippi Delta Community College, Moorhead, MS 38761-0668, 601-246-6322.

MISSISSIPPI GULF COAST COMMUNITY COLLEGE
Perkinston, Mississippi

UG Enrollment: 9,858	**Tuition & Fees (MS Res): $880**
Application Deadline: rolling	**Room & Board: $948**

GENERAL District-supported, 2-year, coed. Part of Mississippi State Board for Community and Junior Colleges. Awards transfer associate, terminal associate degrees. Founded 1911. ***Setting:*** 1,000-acre small-town campus. ***Total enrollment:*** 9,858. ***Faculty:*** 753 (334 full-time, 419 part-time). ***Notable Alumni:*** Chuck Scarbrough, Fred Hayes, Greg Hibbard, Bill Holmes, Clare Sekul Hornsby.
ENROLLMENT PROFILE 9,858 students: 57% women, 43% men, 39% part-time, 98% state residents, 7% live on campus, 1% international, 43% 25 or older, 1% Native American, 1% Hispanic, 15% African American, 2% Asian American. ***Areas of study chosen:*** 25% liberal arts/general studies, 18% health professions and related sciences, 15% business management and administrative services, 9% education, 3% computer and information sciences, 3% engineering and applied sciences, 1% fine arts. ***Most popular recent majors:*** nursing, liberal arts/general studies, elementary education.
FIRST-YEAR CLASS 2,698 total. Of the students who applied, 100% were accepted, 99% of whom enrolled.
ACADEMIC PROGRAM Core, interdisciplinary curriculum. Calendar: semesters. Academic remediation for entering students, English as a second language program offered during academic year, services for LD students, advanced placement, tutorials, honors program, summer session for credit, part-time degree program (daytime, evenings, summer), adult/continuing education programs, co-op programs and internships.
GENERAL DEGREE REQUIREMENTS 64 semester hours; 8 semester hours of math/science for associate of arts degree; 4 semester hours of math/science for associate of applied sciences degree; computer course (varies by major).
MAJORS Accounting, advertising, agricultural business, art education, art/fine arts, automotive technologies, business administration/commerce/management, business education, chemical engineering technology, computer science, computer technologies, court reporting, criminal justice, drafting and design, early childhood education, education, electrical and electronics technologies, elementary education, emergency medical technology, (pre)engineering sequence, fashion merchandising, finance/banking, horticulture, hotel and restaurant management, human services, law enforcement/police sciences, liberal arts/general studies, marketing/retailing/merchandising, medical laboratory technology, nursing, ornamental horticulture, paralegal studies, postal management, radiological technology, respiratory therapy, science, secretarial studies/office management, welding technology.
LIBRARY 100,472 books, 933 periodicals. Acquisition spending 1994–95: $164,547.
COMPUTERS ON CAMPUS 435 computers for student use in computer center, learning resource center, labs. Staffed computer lab on campus provides training in use of computers, software.
COLLEGE LIFE Drama-theater group, choral group, marching band, student-run newspaper. 85% vote in student government elections. ***Social organizations:*** 33 open to all. ***Most popular organizations:*** VICA, SIFE, Student Government Association. ***Major annual events:*** Homecoming, Vocational Awareness Week. ***Student services:*** personal-psychological counseling, women's center. ***Campus security:*** 24-hour emergency response devices and patrols.
HOUSING 800 college housing spaces available; 650 were occupied 1995–96. No special consideration for freshman housing applicants. Off-campus living permitted. ***Option:*** single-sex (5 buildings) housing available. Resident assistants live in dorms.
ATHLETICS Member NJCAA. ***Intercollegiate:*** baseball M, basketball M/W, football M, golf M(s), softball W, tennis M(s)/W(s), track and field M. ***Intramural:*** basketball, football, softball, volleyball. ***Contact:*** Mr. J. C. Arban, Director of Athletics, 601-928-5211.
CAREER PLANNING ***Director:*** Ms. Nell Murray, Workforce Development, 601-928-6205. ***Service:*** career counseling.
EXPENSES FOR 1995–96 State resident tuition: $880 full-time, $52 per semester hour part-time. Nonresident tuition: $1900 full-time, $89.50 per semester hour part-time. College room and board: $948 (minimum). College room only: $350 (minimum).
FINANCIAL AID ***College-administered undergrad aid 1995–96:*** 4,830 need-based scholarships (averaging $1126), 3,028 non-need scholarships (averaging $942), short-term loans (averaging $126), low-interest long-term loans from external sources (averaging $2109), Federal Work-Study, 252 part-time jobs. ***Required forms:*** institutional, FAFSA, proof of Selective Service registration (for men). ***Priority deadline:*** 4/1. ***Payment plan:*** installment. ***Waivers:*** full or partial for employees or children of employees and senior citizens.
APPLYING Open admission except for allied health programs. ***Options:*** Common Application, early entrance, midyear entrance. ***Required:*** school transcript, TOEFL for international students. ***Required for some:*** ACT. Test scores used for counseling/placement. ***Application deadline:*** rolling. ***Notification:*** continuous. Preference given to district residents.
APPLYING/TRANSFER ***Required:*** high school transcript, college transcript. ***Required for some:*** standardized test scores. ***Application deadline:*** rolling. ***Notification:*** continuous.
CONTACT Mrs. Ann Provis, Director of Admissions, Mississippi Gulf Coast Community College, Perkinston, MS 39573-0047, 601-928-6264. ***Fax:*** 601-928-6386. College video available.

NORTHEAST MISSISSIPPI COMMUNITY COLLEGE
Booneville, Mississippi

UG Enrollment: 3,000	**Tuition & Fees (MS Res): $950**
Application Deadline: rolling	**Room & Board: $1900**

GENERAL State-supported, 2-year, coed. Part of Mississippi State Board for Community and Junior Colleges. Awards certificates, transfer associate, terminal associate degrees. Founded 1948. ***Setting:*** 100-acre small-town campus. ***Total enrollment:*** 3,000. ***Faculty:*** 126 (116 full-time, 10 part-time); student-faculty ratio is 19:1.
ENROLLMENT PROFILE 3,000 students from 18 states and territories. 9% part-time, 95% state residents, 25% live on campus, 4% transferred in, 20% 25 or older, 1% Native American, 0% Hispanic, 9% African American, 1% Asian American. ***Most popular recent majors:*** business administration/commerce/management, nursing, liberal arts/general studies.
FIRST-YEAR CLASS 1,500 total; 2,500 applied, 99% were accepted.
ACADEMIC PROGRAM Core, university parallel curriculum. Calendar: semesters. 480 courses offered in 1995–96. Academic remediation for entering students, services for LD students, advanced placement, self-designed majors, summer session for credit, part-time degree program (daytime, evenings, summer), adult/continuing education programs, co-op programs.
GENERAL DEGREE REQUIREMENTS 63 credits; 1 course in college algebra; computer course for most majors.
MAJORS Accounting, agricultural education, agricultural sciences, agronomy/soil and crop sciences, art education, art/fine arts, biblical studies, biology/biological sciences, broadcasting, business administration/commerce/management, business economics, business education, carpentry, chemistry, child care/child and family studies, child psychology/child development, civil engineering technology, commercial art, communication, computer information systems, computer management, computer programming, computer science, criminal justice, dairy sciences, data processing, dental services, drafting and design, early childhood education, economics, education, electrical and electronics technologies, electrical engineering technology, electronics engineering technology, elementary education, engineering (general), engineering and applied sciences, (pre)engineering sequence, engineering technology, English, entomology, fashion design and technology, fashion merchandising, food marketing, food sciences, food services management, forestry, forest technology, health education, health science, heating/refrigeration/air conditioning, history, home economics, home economics education, horticulture, hotel and restaurant management, industrial engineering technology, insurance, interior design, journalism, landscape architecture/design, law enforcement/police sciences, legal secretarial studies, liberal arts/general studies, library science, mathematics, medical assistant technologies, medical laboratory technology, medical secretarial studies, medical technology, music, music education, nursing, occupational therapy, oceanography, painting/drawing, paralegal studies, pharmacy/pharmaceutical sciences, photography, physical education, physical fitness/exercise science, physical therapy, political science/government, psychology, public administration, public relations, radio and television studies, radiological technology, recreation and leisure services, religious education, respiratory therapy, robotics, science, science education, secretarial studies/office management, social science, social work, speech therapy, teacher aide studies, theater arts/drama, theology, vocational education, wildlife biology, wildlife management, zoology.
LIBRARY Eula Dees Library with 29,879 books, 378 periodicals, 941 records, tapes, and CDs.
COMPUTERS ON CAMPUS 350 computers for student use in computer center, academic buildings, library. Staffed computer lab on campus.
COLLEGE LIFE Drama-theater group, choral group, marching band, student-run newspaper. 25% vote in student government elections. ***Student services:*** personal-psychological counseling. ***Campus security:*** 24-hour patrols, student patrols, controlled dormitory access.
HOUSING 700 college housing spaces available; all were occupied 1995–96. No special consideration for freshman housing applicants. Off-campus living permitted. ***Option:*** single-sex housing available. Resident assistants live in dorms.
ATHLETICS Member NJCAA. ***Intercollegiate:*** baseball M(s), basketball M(s)/W(s), football M(s), golf M, softball W, tennis M/W. ***Intramural:*** archery, badminton, basketball, soccer, softball, tennis, volleyball. ***Contact:*** Mr. David Carnell, Athletic Director, 601-728-7751 Ext. 240.
CAREER PLANNING ***Director:*** Mr. Donald G. Sweeney, Director of Counseling, 601-728-7751 Ext. 313. ***Services:*** career counseling, careers library, job bank, job interviews.
EXPENSES FOR 1996–97 State resident tuition: $950 full-time, $52 per semester hour part-time. Nonresident tuition: $2050 full-time, $97 per semester hour part-time. Part-time mandatory fees: $15 per semester. College room and board: $1900. College room only: $800.
FINANCIAL AID ***College-administered undergrad aid 1995–96:*** 300 need-based scholarships (average $950), 76 non-need scholarships (average $950), low-interest long-term loans from external sources (average $2625), 200 Federal Work-Study, 50 part-time jobs. ***Required forms:*** institutional, FAFSA; accepted: CSS Financial Aid PROFILE. ***Priority deadline:*** 5/1. ***Payment plan:*** installment. ***Waivers:*** full or partial for employees or children of employees and senior citizens. ***Notification:*** continuous.

Northeast Mississippi Community College (continued)

APPLYING Open admission. ***Options:*** early entrance, deferred entrance, midyear entrance. ***Required:*** TOEFL for international students. ***Recommended:*** 4 years of high school math and science. ***Required for some:*** SAT I or ACT. Test scores used for admission and counseling/placement. ***Application deadline:*** rolling. ***Notification:*** continuous.
APPLYING/TRANSFER ***Required for some:*** standardized test scores. ***Entrance:*** noncompetitive. ***Application deadline:*** rolling. ***Notification:*** continuous. ***Contact:*** Mr. Ronald M. Sweeney, Director of Admissions and Records, 601-728-7751 Ext. 239.
CONTACT Mr. Ronald M. Sweeney, Director of Admissions and Records, Northeast Mississippi Community College, Booneville, MS 38829, 601-728-7751 Ext. 239. ***Fax:*** 601-728-1165.

NORTHWEST MISSISSIPPI COMMUNITY COLLEGE
Senatobia, Mississippi

UG Enrollment: 4,200	**Tuition & Fees (MS Res): $1000**
Application Deadline: 9/7	**Room & Board: $1660**

GENERAL State and locally supported, 2-year, coed. Part of Mississippi State Board for Community and Junior Colleges. Awards transfer associate, terminal associate degrees. Founded 1927. ***Setting:*** 75-acre rural campus with easy access to Memphis. ***Total enrollment:*** 4,200. ***Faculty:*** 200 (99% of full-time faculty have terminal degrees); student-faculty ratio is 20:1. ***Notable Alumni:*** John Grisham, author.
ENROLLMENT PROFILE 4,200 students: 57% women, 43% men, 31% part-time, 91% state residents, 5% transferred in, 34% African American.
FIRST-YEAR CLASS 2,500 total; 4,200 applied, 100% were accepted, 60% of whom enrolled.
ACADEMIC PROGRAM Core. Calendar: semesters. Academic remediation for entering students, services for LD students, tutorials, honors program, summer session for credit, part-time degree program (daytime, evenings, summer), adult/continuing education programs. ROTC: Air Force.
GENERAL DEGREE REQUIREMENTS 66 semester hours; 1 course each in math and science.
MAJORS Accounting, agricultural economics, agricultural sciences, aircraft and missile maintenance, applied art, art/fine arts, automotive technologies, broadcasting, business administration/commerce/management, carpentry, child care/child and family studies, civil engineering technology, commercial art, computer science, computer technologies, cosmetology, data processing, dental services, drafting and design, education, electronics engineering technology, engineering and applied sciences, (pre)engineering sequence, fashion merchandising, forestry, funeral service, home economics education, hotel and restaurant management, journalism, law enforcement/police sciences, legal secretarial studies, liberal arts/general studies, library science, mathematics, mechanical design technology, medical records services, medical secretarial studies, medical technology, music education, nursing, paralegal studies, physical education, practical nursing, printmaking, radio and television studies, real estate, respiratory therapy, science, secretarial studies/office management, social work, sociology, telecommunications, vocational education.
LIBRARY R. C. Pugh Library with 38,000 books, 325 periodicals.
COMPUTERS ON CAMPUS 50 computers for student use in computer center, computer labs, learning resource center, classrooms, library provide access to main academic computer.
COLLEGE LIFE Drama-theater group, choral group, marching band, student-run newspaper, radio station. ***Major annual events:*** Homecoming, Career Week, Senior Round Ups. ***Student services:*** health clinic. ***Campus security:*** 24-hour emergency response devices, late-night transport-escort service.
HOUSING 938 college housing spaces available; all were occupied 1995–96. No special consideration for freshman housing applicants. Off-campus living permitted. ***Option:*** single-sex housing available.
ATHLETICS Member NJCAA. ***Intercollegiate:*** baseball M, basketball M(s)/W(s), equestrian sports M(s)/W(s), football M(s), golf M, softball W(s), tennis M(s)/W(s). ***Intramural:*** basketball, football. ***Contact:*** Mr. Jim Miles, Athletic Director, 601-562-3416.
CAREER PLANNING ***Placement office:*** 8 full-time staff. ***Director:*** Mr. Larry Simpson, Director of Counseling Center, 601-562-3200. ***Services:*** resume preparation, resume referral, career counseling, careers library, job interviews.
EXPENSES FOR 1996–97 State resident tuition: $1000 full-time, $45 per semester hour part-time. Nonresident tuition: $2050 full-time, $75 per semester hour part-time. College room and board: $1660 (minimum).
FINANCIAL AID ***College-administered undergrad aid 1995–96:*** 2,500 need-based scholarships (average $1200), 520 non-need scholarships (average $800), low-interest long-term loans, Federal Work-Study, 30 part-time jobs. ***Required forms:*** CSS Financial Aid PROFILE, institutional, FAFSA. ***Priority deadline:*** 3/1. ***Waivers:*** full or partial for employees or children of employees.
APPLYING Open admission. ***Options:*** Common Application, early entrance, deferred entrance. ***Required:*** school transcript, ACT, TOEFL for international students. Test scores used for counseling/placement. ***Application deadline:*** 9/7. ***Notification:*** continuous.
APPLYING/TRANSFER ***Required:*** standardized test scores, high school transcript, college transcript. ***Application deadline:*** 9/7. ***Notification:*** continuous.
CONTACT Ms. Deanna Ferguson, Director of Admissions and Recruiting, Northwest Mississippi Community College, Senatobia, MS 38668-1701, 601-562-3222. ***Fax:*** 601-562-3911. College video available.

PEARL RIVER COMMUNITY COLLEGE
Poplarville, Mississippi

UG Enrollment: 2,575	**Tuition & Fees (MS Res): $880**
Application Deadline: rolling	**Room & Board: $1560**

GENERAL State and locally supported, 2-year, coed. Part of Mississippi State Board for Community and Junior Colleges. Awards certificates, transfer associate, terminal associate degrees. Founded 1909. ***Setting:*** 240-acre rural campus with easy access to New Orleans. ***Educational spending 1994–95:*** $2027 per undergrad. ***Total enrollment:*** 2,575. ***Faculty:*** 167 (135 full-time, 36% with terminal degrees, 32 part-time).
ENROLLMENT PROFILE 2,575 students from 11 states and territories. 63% women, 37% men, 28% part-time, 95% state residents, 20% live on campus, 11% transferred in, 0% international, 27% 25 or older, 17% African American. ***Areas of study chosen:*** 40% health professions and related sciences, 30% liberal arts/general studies, 10% business management and administrative services, 5% biological and life sciences, 5% computer and information sciences, 5% education, 5% social sciences. ***Most popular recent majors:*** liberal arts/general studies, nursing, business administration/commerce/management.
FIRST-YEAR CLASS 998 total. Of the students who applied, 90% were accepted, 85% of whom enrolled. 8 class presidents, 13 valedictorians.
ACADEMIC PROGRAM Core, interdisciplinary curriculum. Calendar: semesters. 370 courses offered in 1995–96. Academic remediation for entering students, advanced placement, self-designed majors, summer session for credit, part-time degree program (daytime, evenings, summer), adult/continuing education programs, co-op programs.
GENERAL DEGREE REQUIREMENTS 64 credits; 1 college algebra course; 6 credit hours of lab science.
MAJORS Business administration/commerce/management, drafting and design, electrical and electronics technologies, liberal arts/general studies, marketing/retailing/merchandising, medical secretarial studies, nursing, respiratory therapy, secretarial studies/office management.
LIBRARY Pearl River Community College Library with 40,000 books, 1,000 microform titles, 340 periodicals, 2,100 records, tapes, and CDs. Acquisition spending 1994–95: $156,852.
COMPUTERS ON CAMPUS 90 computers for student use in computer center, computer labs, learning resource center, classrooms, library. Staffed computer lab on campus provides training in use of computers, software. Academic computing expenditure 1994–95: $73,156.
COLLEGE LIFE Drama-theater group, choral group, marching band, student-run newspaper. 20% vote in student government elections. ***Social organizations:*** 4 open to all. ***Major annual events:*** Homecoming, Fall Fest, Spring Fest. ***Student services:*** health clinic, personal-psychological counseling, women's center. ***Campus security:*** 24-hour patrols.
HOUSING 500 college housing spaces available; all were occupied 1995–96. No special consideration for freshman housing applicants. Off-campus living permitted. ***Option:*** single-sex housing available. Resident assistants live in dorms.
ATHLETICS Member NJCAA. ***Intercollegiate:*** baseball M(s), basketball M(s)/W(s), football M(s), golf M/W, softball W, tennis M/W. ***Intramural:*** badminton, basketball, football, golf, softball, tennis, volleyball, weight lifting. ***Contact:*** Mr. Mike Humphreys, Acting Athletic Director, 601-795-6801.
CAREER PLANNING ***Placement office:*** 2 full-time staff; $274,875 operating expenditure 1994–95. ***Director:*** Dr. Chris Lundy, Academic Counselor, 601-795-6801. ***Services:*** career counseling, careers library.
EXPENSES FOR 1996–97 State resident tuition: $850 full-time, $38 per semester hour part-time. Nonresident tuition: $1850 full-time, $80 per semester hour part-time. Part-time mandatory fees: $10 per course. Full-time mandatory fees: $30. College room and board: $1560 (minimum).
FINANCIAL AID ***College-administered undergrad aid 1995–96:*** 20 need-based scholarships (average $100), 50 non-need scholarships (average $500), low-interest long-term loans from external sources (average $800), Federal Work-Study, 30 part-time jobs. ***Required forms:*** institutional, FAFSA. ***Priority deadline:*** 6/1. ***Payment plans:*** installment, deferred payment. ***Waivers:*** full or partial for employees or children of employees and senior citizens.
APPLYING Open admission except for nursing, data processing programs. ***Options:*** early entrance, deferred entrance, midyear entrance. ***Required:*** school transcript, ACT, TOEFL for international students. Test scores used for counseling/placement. ***Application deadline:*** rolling. ***Notification:*** continuous until 8/15. Preference given to state residents.
APPLYING/TRANSFER ***Required:*** standardized test scores, high school transcript, college transcript, minimum 2.0 college GPA. ***Application deadline:*** rolling. ***Notification:*** continuous until 8/15. ***Contact:*** Dr. Chris Lundy, Academic Counselor, 601-795-6801.
CONTACT Mr. J. Dow Ford, Director of Admissions, Pearl River Community College, Poplarville, MS 39470, 601-795-6801 Ext. 216.

PHILLIPS JUNIOR COLLEGE OF JACKSON
Jackson, Mississippi

GENERAL Proprietary, 2-year, coed. Part of Phillips Colleges, Inc. Awards certificates, terminal associate degrees. Founded 1973. ***Setting:*** 1-acre urban campus. ***Total enrollment:*** 275. ***Faculty:*** 12 (9 full-time, 3 part-time).
EXPENSES FOR 1995–96 ***Application fee:*** $25. Tuition: $4950 (minimum) full-time. Full-time tuition ranges up to $12,250 according to program. Tuition guaranteed not to increase for student's term of enrollment.
CONTACT Mr. Bill Milstead, Director of Admissions, Phillips Junior College of Jackson, 2680 Insurance Center Drive, Jackson, MS 39216-4989, 601-362-6341 Ext. 21.

SOUTHWEST MISSISSIPPI COMMUNITY COLLEGE
Summit, Mississippi

UG Enrollment: 1,650	**Tuition & Fees (MS Res): $850**
Application Deadline: 8/1	**Room & Board: $1700**

GENERAL District-supported, 2-year, coed. Part of Mississippi State Board for Community and Junior Colleges. Awards transfer associate, terminal associate degrees. Founded 1918. ***Setting:*** 701-acre rural campus. ***Total enrollment:*** 1,650. ***Faculty:*** 89 (68 full-time, 21 part-time); student-faculty ratio is 17:1.
ENROLLMENT PROFILE 1,650 students from 6 states and territories. 60% women, 24% part-time, 89% state residents, 35% live on campus, 0% transferred in, 0% international, 31% 25 or older, 0% Native American, 0% Hispanic, 22% African American, 0% Asian American.
FIRST-YEAR CLASS 300 total. Of the students who applied, 100% were accepted, 88% of whom enrolled.

Mississippi–Missouri

ACADEMIC PROGRAM Core, honor code. Calendar: semesters. Academic remediation for entering students, summer session for credit, part-time degree program (daytime, evenings, summer), adult/continuing education programs.
GENERAL DEGREE REQUIREMENTS 64 credits; 1 college algebra course.
MAJORS Accounting, advertising, automotive technologies, biology/biological sciences, business administration/commerce/management, business education, carpentry, chemistry, computer science, construction technologies, cosmetology, education, electrical and electronics technologies, elementary education, emergency medical technology, engineering (general), English, fashion merchandising, finance/banking, health science, history, humanities, legal secretarial studies, liberal arts/general studies, machine and tool technologies, marketing/retailing/merchandising, music, music education, nursing, physical education, physical sciences, science, secretarial studies/office management, social science, welding technology.
LIBRARY 34,000 books, 375 microform titles, 150 periodicals, 575 records, tapes, and CDs.
COMPUTERS ON CAMPUS 100 computers for student use in library.
COLLEGE LIFE Choral group, marching band, student-run newspaper. 48% vote in student government elections. *Campus security:* 24-hour patrols.
HOUSING 450 college housing spaces available; all were occupied 1995–96. No special consideration for freshman housing applicants. Off-campus living permitted. *Option:* single-sex housing available. Resident assistants live in dorms.
ATHLETICS Member NJCAA. *Intercollegiate:* basketball M(s)/W(s), football M(s), golf M, tennis M/W. *Intramural:* basketball. *Contact:* Mr. Jerry Reid, Athletic Director, 601-276-2000.
CAREER PLANNING *Service:* career counseling.
EXPENSES FOR 1995–96 State resident tuition: $850 full-time, $40 per semester hour part-time. Nonresident tuition: $1900 full-time, $95 per semester hour part-time. College room and board: $1700.
FINANCIAL AID *College-administered undergrad aid 1995–96:* 30 non-need scholarships (average $330), short-term loans (average $175), low-interest long-term loans from external sources (average $2000), Federal Work-Study, 20 part-time jobs. *Priority deadline:* 8/1. *Waivers:* full or partial for senior citizens.
APPLYING Open admission. *Required:* school transcript. *Required for some:* ACT. Test scores used for counseling/placement. *Application deadline:* 8/1. Preference given to district residents.
APPLYING/TRANSFER *Required:* college transcript. *Required for some:* standardized test scores. *Contact:* Mr. William H. Johnson, Dean of Instruction, 601-226-3705.
CONTACT Mr. R. Glenn Shoemake, Registrar, Southwest Mississippi Community College, Summit, MS 39666, 601-276-2000.

WOOD COLLEGE
Mathiston, Mississippi

UG Enrollment: 1,500	Tuition & Fees: $3110
Application Deadline: rolling	Room & Board: $2200

GENERAL Independent Methodist, 2-year, coed. Awards transfer associate degrees. Founded 1886. *Setting:* 400-acre rural campus. *Total enrollment:* 1,500. *Faculty:* 35 (20 full-time, 15 part-time); student-faculty ratio is 22:1.
ENROLLMENT PROFILE 1,500 students: 57% women, 33% part-time, 98% state residents, 8% transferred in, 2% international, 25% 25 or older, 0% Native American, 0% Hispanic, 9% African American, 0% Asian American. *Most popular recent majors:* business administration/commerce/management, education.
FIRST-YEAR CLASS 300 total. Of the students who applied, 98% were accepted, 98% of whom enrolled. 5% from top 10% of their high school class, 15% from top quarter, 40% from top half.
ACADEMIC PROGRAM Core, honor code. Calendar: modular. Academic remediation for entering students, English as a second language program offered during academic year, summer session for credit, part-time degree program (daytime, evenings, summer).
GENERAL DEGREE REQUIREMENTS 64 semester hours; 9 semester hours of math/science.
MAJORS Business administration/commerce/management, education, elementary education, equestrian studies, liberal arts/general studies, ministries, physical education, secretarial studies/office management.
LIBRARY 26,000 books, 31 periodicals, 1,200 records, tapes, and CDs.
COMPUTERS ON CAMPUS 30 computers for student use in computer center, learning resource center.
COLLEGE LIFE Orientation program (2 days, no cost). Drama-theater group, choral group, student-run newspaper. *Campus security:* 24-hour patrols.
HOUSING 140 college housing spaces available; 84 were occupied 1995–96. Off-campus living permitted.
ATHLETICS *Intercollegiate:* equestrian sports M/W. *Intramural:* archery, basketball, equestrian sports, football, tennis, volleyball, weight lifting.
CAREER PLANNING *Service:* career counseling.
AFTER GRADUATION 83% of students completing a degree program in 1994–95 went directly on to further study.
EXPENSES FOR 1995–96 Comprehensive fee of $5310 includes full-time tuition ($3040), mandatory fees ($70), and college room and board ($2200). Part-time mandatory fees: $15 per term. Part-time tuition per semester hour: $115 for the first 4 semester hours, $105 for the next 7 semester hours.
FINANCIAL AID *College-administered undergrad aid 1995–96:* 40 need-based scholarships (average $300), 525 non-need scholarships (average $400), short-term loans (average $150), low-interest long-term loans from external sources (average $1500), Federal Work-Study, 25 part-time jobs. *Required forms:* institutional, FAFSA. *Priority deadline:* 6/1. *Payment plan:* installment. *Waivers:* full or partial for minority students, children of alumni, employees or children of employees, adult students, and senior citizens.
APPLYING *Options:* early entrance, deferred entrance. *Required:* school transcript. ACT. Test scores used for admission and counseling/placement. *Application deadline:* rolling. *Notification:* continuous.
APPLYING/TRANSFER *Required:* standardized test scores, high school transcript. *Entrance:* minimally difficult. *Application deadline:* rolling. *Notification:* continuous.
CONTACT Mrs. Bobbie R. Shaw, Director of Admissions, Wood College, Mathiston, MS 39752-0289, 601-263-5352 Ext. 25. *Fax:* 601-263-4964.

MISSOURI

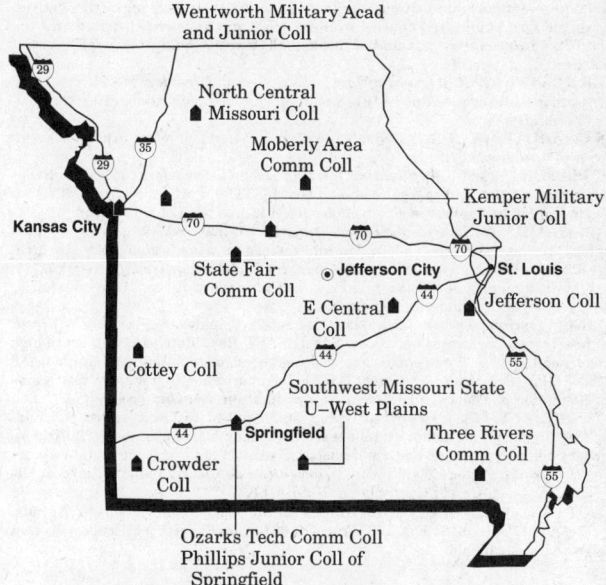

Kansas City Area
Maple Woods Comm Coll
Longview Comm Coll
Penn Valley Comm Coll
Sanford-Brown Coll

St. Louis Area
ITT Tech Inst
Jewish Hospital Coll of
  Nursing and Allied Health
Mineral Area Coll
Ranken Tech Coll
Saint Charles County Comm Coll
St. Louis Comm Coll at
  Florissant Valley
St. Louis Comm Coll at
  Forest Park
St. Louis Comm Coll at
  Meramec
Sanford-Brown Coll (Des Peres)
Sanford-Brown Coll (Hazelwood)
Sanford-Brown Coll (St. Charles)

COTTEY COLLEGE
Nevada, Missouri

UG Enrollment: 329	Tuition & Fees: $6700
Application Deadline: rolling	Room & Board: $3600

GENERAL Independent, 2-year, women only. Awards transfer associate degrees. Founded 1884. *Setting:* 51-acre small-town campus. *Total enrollment:* 329. *Faculty:* 36 (32 full-time, 97% with terminal degrees, 4 part-time); student-faculty ratio is 11:1.
ENROLLMENT PROFILE 329 students from 40 states and territories, 11 other countries. 100% women, 1% part-time, 8% state residents, 98% live on campus, 2% transferred in, 59% have need-based financial aid, 54% have non-need-based financial aid, 9% international, 2% 25 or older, 1% Native American, 2% Hispanic, 1% African American, 2% Asian American. *Areas of study chosen:* 100% liberal arts/general studies.
FIRST-YEAR CLASS 164 total. 322 applied, 80% were accepted, 63% of whom enrolled. 17% from top 10% of their high school class, 56% from top quarter, 87% from top half. 2 National Merit Scholars.
ACADEMIC PROGRAM Core, honor code. Calendar: semesters. 367 courses offered in 1995–96. Advanced placement, self-designed majors, part-time degree program (daytime).
GENERAL DEGREE REQUIREMENTS 62 credit hours; 3 credit hours of math; 4 credit hours of lab science.
MAJORS Liberal arts/general studies, science.
LIBRARY Blanche Skiff Ross Memorial Library with 49,720 books, 100 microform titles, 182 periodicals, 15 CD-ROMs, 2,302 records, tapes, and CDs.
COMPUTERS ON CAMPUS 50 computers for student use in computer labs, library, dorms. Staffed computer lab on campus.
COLLEGE LIFE Orientation program (4 days, no cost, parents included). Drama-theater group, choral group, student-run newspaper. 80% vote in student government elections. *Social organizations:* 13 open to all; 4 social clubs; 100% of eligible undergraduates are members. *Most popular organizations:* International Friendship Circle, Cottey Intramural Association, Ozarks Explorers Club, Intervarsity Club, Golden Keys. *Major annual events:* Hanging of the Greens, Quad C Week, Humanities Film Festival. *Student*

Peterson's Guide to Two-Year Colleges 1997

Cottey College (continued)
services: health clinic, personal-psychological counseling. ***Campus security:*** 24-hour emergency response devices and patrols, late-night transport-escort service, controlled dormitory access.
HOUSING 360 college housing spaces available. Freshmen guaranteed college housing. On-campus residence required through sophomore year except if living with relatives. ***Option:*** single-sex (3 buildings) housing available. Resident assistants live in dorms.
ATHLETICS ***Intramural:*** badminton, basketball, fencing, field hockey, golf, soccer, tennis, volleyball, water polo.
CAREER PLANNING ***Placement office:*** 1 full-time staff. ***Director:*** Ms. Shirley Wing, Transfer/Career Counselor, 417-667-8181. ***Services:*** resume preparation, career counseling, careers library.
AFTER GRADUATION 94% of students completing a degree program in 1994–95 went directly on to further study.
EXPENSES FOR 1996–97 ***Application fee:*** $20. Comprehensive fee of $10,300 includes full-time tuition ($6700) and college room and board ($3600). Part-time tuition: $279 per credit hour. Tuition guaranteed not to increase for student's term of enrollment.
FINANCIAL AID ***College-administered undergrad aid 1995–96:*** 225 need-based scholarships, 104 non-need scholarships, low-interest long-term loans from external sources (average $2410), Federal Work-Study, 104 part-time jobs. ***Required forms:*** FAFSA; accepted: state. ***Priority deadline:*** 5/1. ***Payment plan:*** installment. ***Waivers:*** full or partial for employees or children of employees.
APPLYING ***Options:*** early entrance, deferred entrance, midyear entrance. ***Required:*** essay, school transcript, recommendations, SAT I or ACT. ***Recommended:*** 3 years of high school math and science, 2 years of high school foreign language, interview, minimum 2.6 high school GPA. ***Required for some:*** TOEFL for international students. Test scores used for admission and counseling/placement. ***Application deadline:*** rolling.
APPLYING/TRANSFER ***Required:*** essay, standardized test scores, recommendations, college transcript, minimum 2.0 college GPA, minimum 2.0 high school GPA. ***Recommended:*** 3 years of high school math and science, 2 years of high school foreign language, interview. ***Entrance:*** moderately difficult. ***Application deadline:*** rolling. ***Contact:*** Ms. Shirley Wing, Transfer/Career Counselor, 417-667-8181.
CONTACT Mrs. Wendy Beckemeyer, Director of Admission, Cottey College, Nevada, MO 64772-2700, 417-667-8181 Ext. 107. ***Fax:*** 417-667-8103. ***E-mail:*** jchrisenbery@cottey.edu. College video available.

CROWDER COLLEGE
Neosho, Missouri

UG Enrollment: 1,698	**Tuition & Fees (Area Res): $1200**
Application Deadline: rolling	**Room & Board: $2700**

GENERAL State and locally supported, 2-year, coed. Part of Missouri Coordinating Board for Higher Education. Awards certificates, transfer associate, terminal associate degrees. Founded 1963. ***Setting:*** 608-acre rural campus. ***Total enrollment:*** 1,698. ***Faculty:*** 147 (61 full-time, 86 part-time).
ENROLLMENT PROFILE 1,698 students from 14 states and territories, 9 other countries. 59% women, 41% men, 57% part-time, 95% state residents, 10% transferred in, 1% international, 45% 25 or older, 2% Native American, 1% Hispanic, 1% African American, 1% Asian American. ***Areas of study chosen:*** 38% liberal arts/general studies, 15% business management and administrative services, 9% education, 9% health professions and related sciences, 7% agriculture, 7% engineering and applied sciences, 3% biological and life sciences, 2% computer and information sciences, 1% communications and journalism, 1% fine arts, 1% mathematics, 1% performing arts, 1% physical sciences.
FIRST-YEAR CLASS 750 total; 1,014 applied, 100% were accepted, 74% of whom enrolled.
ACADEMIC PROGRAM Core. Calendar: semesters. Academic remediation for entering students, advanced placement, Freshman Honors College, tutorials, honors program, summer session for credit, part-time degree program (daytime, evenings, summer), adult/continuing education programs, co-op programs and internships.
GENERAL DEGREE REQUIREMENTS 60 semester hours; 10 semester hours of science; 3 semester hours of college algebra; computer course (varies by major); internship (some majors).
MAJORS Agricultural business, agricultural sciences, art/fine arts, automotive technologies, biology/biological sciences, business administration/commerce/management, communication, computer science, construction technologies, drafting and design, education, electrical and electronics technologies, emergency medical technology, (pre)engineering sequence, environmental health sciences, farm and ranch management, fire science, industrial engineering technology, legal secretarial studies, liberal arts/general studies, marketing/retailing/merchandising, mathematics, medical secretarial studies, music, nursing, physical education, physical sciences, poultry sciences, recreation and leisure services, secretarial studies/office management.
LIBRARY Crowder College Library with 29,364 books, 34 microform titles, 274 periodicals, 2,430 records, tapes, and CDs.
COMPUTERS ON CAMPUS 65 computers for student use in computer labs, research center, learning resource center, office administration labs, classrooms, library provide access to main academic computer, Internet. Staffed computer lab on campus provides training in use of computers, software.
COLLEGE LIFE Choral group, student-run newspaper. 50% vote in student government elections. ***Student services:*** personal-psychological counseling.
HOUSING 245 college housing spaces available; all were occupied 1995–96. Off-campus living permitted. ***Option:*** single-sex housing available. Resident assistants live in dorms.
ATHLETICS Member NJCAA. ***Intercollegiate:*** basketball M(s)/W(s), bowling M, soccer M, volleyball M. ***Intramural:*** basketball, soccer, tennis.
CAREER PLANNING ***Director:*** Dr. Bob Foree, Director, Career Center, 417-451-3583. ***Services:*** job fairs, resume preparation, career counseling, careers library, job bank.
EXPENSES FOR 1995–96 Area resident tuition: $1080 full-time, $36 per semester hour part-time. State resident tuition: $1500 full-time, $50 per semester hour part-time. Nonresident tuition: $2190 full-time, $73 per semester hour part-time. Part-time mandatory fees: $4 per semester hour. Tuition for nursing program: $1650 full-time, $55 per semester hour part-time for area residents, $1950 full-time, $65 per semester hour part-time for state residents. Full-time mandatory fees: $120. College room and board: $2700.
FINANCIAL AID ***College-administered undergrad aid 1995–96:*** 195 need-based scholarships (average $280), non-need scholarships (average $280), 150 Federal Work-Study (averaging $1169), part-time jobs. ***Required forms:*** institutional, FAFSA. ***Priority deadline:*** 8/1. ***Payment plan:*** installment. ***Waivers:*** full or partial for employees or children of employees and senior citizens.
APPLYING Open admission. ***Options:*** early entrance, deferred entrance. ***Required:*** school transcript, ACT, TOEFL for international students. Test scores used for counseling/placement. ***Application deadline:*** rolling. ***Notification:*** continuous until 8/23.
APPLYING/TRANSFER ***Required:*** standardized test scores, high school transcript, college transcript. ***Entrance:*** noncompetitive. ***Application deadline:*** rolling. ***Notification:*** continuous until 8/23.
CONTACT Mrs. Cecilia Morris, Dean of Students, Crowder College, Neosho, MO 64850-9160, 417-451-3223 Ext. 204. Electronic viewbook available.

EAST CENTRAL COLLEGE
Union, Missouri

UG Enrollment: 2,990	**Tuition & Fees (Area Res): $1155**
Application Deadline: rolling	**Room & Board: N/Avail**

GENERAL District-supported, 2-year, coed. Part of Missouri Coordinating Board for Higher Education. Awards certificates, transfer associate, terminal associate degrees. Founded 1968. ***Setting:*** 114-acre rural campus with easy access to St. Louis. ***Endowment:*** $591,885. ***Educational spending 1994–95:*** $1389 per undergrad. ***Total enrollment:*** 2,990. ***Faculty:*** 181 (56 full-time, 22% with terminal degrees, 125 part-time); student-faculty ratio is 22:1. ***Notable Alumni:*** Jack Wagner, actor; Tom Henke, baseball player; John Griesheimer, state representative.
ENROLLMENT PROFILE 2,990 students from 3 states and territories, 3 other countries. 61% women, 53% part-time, 98% state residents, 21% transferred in, 24% have need-based financial aid, 38% have non-need-based financial aid, 1% international, 42% 25 or older, 0% Native American, 0% Hispanic, 1% African American, 0% Asian American. ***Areas of study chosen:*** 55% liberal arts/general studies, 22% education, 7% social sciences, 4% engineering and applied sciences, 4% fine arts, 2% health professions and related sciences, 1% architecture, 1% communications and journalism, 1% natural resource sciences, 1% performing arts, 1% premed. ***Most popular recent majors:*** business administration/commerce/management, education.
FIRST-YEAR CLASS 598 total; 678 applied, 100% were accepted, 88% of whom enrolled. 10% from top 10% of their high school class, 22% from top quarter, 60% from top half.
ACADEMIC PROGRAM Core, honor code. Calendar: semesters. 400 courses offered in 1995–96. Academic remediation for entering students, advanced placement, honors program, summer session for credit, part-time degree program (daytime, evenings, summer), adult/continuing education programs, internships.
GENERAL DEGREE REQUIREMENTS 64 semester hours; 3 semester hours of college algebra; computer course for business, education majors; internship (some majors).
MAJORS Accounting, anthropology, archaeology, art/fine arts, automotive technologies, biology/biological sciences, botany/plant sciences, business administration/commerce/management, chemistry, commercial art, communication, computer information systems, computer programming, computer science, construction technologies, criminal justice, data processing, drafting and design, ecology, economics, education, electrical and electronics technologies, elementary education, emergency medical technology, (pre)engineering sequence, English, fire science, fish and game management, food services management, forestry, French, geography, geology, German, heating/refrigeration/air conditioning, history, home economics, horticulture, hospitality services, hotel and restaurant management, humanities, interior design, journalism, law enforcement/police sciences, legal secretarial studies, liberal arts/general studies, library science, management information systems, marketing/retailing/merchandising, mathematics, medical secretarial studies, modern languages, music, nursing, pharmacy/pharmaceutical sciences, philosophy, physical education, physics, political science/government, psychology, public administration, recreation and leisure services, religious studies, respiratory therapy, secretarial studies/office management, social work, sociology, Spanish, speech/rhetoric/public address/debate, teacher aide studies, theater arts/drama, tourism and travel, welding technology, wildlife management, zoology.
LIBRARY 29,336 books, 38 microform titles, 324 periodicals, 1 CD-ROM, 176 records, tapes, and CDs. Acquisition spending 1994–95: $152,592.
COMPUTERS ON CAMPUS 150 computers for student use in computer center, computer labs, learning resource center, various campus facilities, classrooms provide access to Internet. Staffed computer lab on campus provides training in use of computers, software. Academic computing expenditure 1994–95: $222,202.
COLLEGE LIFE Drama-theater group, choral group, student-run newspaper. 30% vote in student government elections. ***Social organizations:*** 3 open to all. ***Most popular organizations:*** Student Government, Phi Theta Kappa, Amnesty International. ***Major annual events:*** Homecoming, All Campus Day, Blood Drive. ***Campus security:*** 24-hour emergency response devices, late-night transport-escort service.
HOUSING College housing not available.
ATHLETICS Member NJCAA. ***Intercollegiate:*** baseball M(s), basketball M(s)/W(s), soccer M(s), softball W(s), volleyball W(s). ***Intramural:*** basketball, table tennis (Ping-Pong), volleyball. ***Contact:*** Dr. Jim James, Athletic Director, 314-583-5195 Ext. 2215.
CAREER PLANNING ***Placement office:*** 2 full-time staff. ***Director:*** Ms. Sharon Hilburn, Career Services Coordinator, 314-583-5193. ***Services:*** job fairs, resume preparation, career counseling, careers library, job bank, job interviews. 325 organizations recruited on campus 1994–95.
AFTER GRADUATION 82% of class of 1994 had job offers within 6 months. 85% of students completing a degree program went directly on to further study.
ESTIMATED EXPENSES FOR 1996–97 Area resident tuition: $1080 full-time, $36 per semester hour part-time. State resident tuition: $1500 full-time, $50 per semester hour part-time. Nonresident tuition: $2310 full-time, $77 per semester hour part-time. Part-time mandatory fees: $2.50 per semester hour. Full-time mandatory fees: $75.
FINANCIAL AID ***College-administered undergrad aid 1995–96:*** 58 need-based scholarships (averaging $960), 120 non-need scholarships (averaging $960), short-term loans (averaging $200), low-interest long-term loans from external sources (averaging $2500), Federal Work-Study, 40 part-time jobs. ***Required forms:*** FAFSA; accepted: CSS Financial Aid PROFILE, state, institutional. ***Priority deadline:*** 4/15. ***Payment plan:*** installment. ***Waivers:*** full or partial for employees or children of employees and senior citizens. ***Average indebtedness of graduates:*** $3500.

APPLYING Open admission. *Options:* early entrance, deferred entrance. *Required:* school transcript, TOEFL for international students. *Recommended:* ACT. Test scores used for counseling/placement. *Application deadline:* rolling. Preference given to district residents.
APPLYING/TRANSFER *Recommended:* standardized test scores. *Entrance:* noncompetitive. *Application deadline:* rolling. *Contact:* Ms. Ina Hays, Academic Advisor, 314-583-5195 Ext. 2225.
CONTACT Mrs. Karen Wieda, Registrar, East Central College, Union, MO 63084-0529, 314-583-5195 Ext. 2220. *Fax:* 314-583-6637.

HEART OF THE OZARKS TECHNICAL COMMUNITY COLLEGE
Missouri—See Ozarks Technical Community College

ITT TECHNICAL INSTITUTE
Earth City, Missouri

UG Enrollment: 539	Tuition: $15,429/deg prog
Application Deadline: rolling	Room & Board: N/Avail

GENERAL Proprietary, primarily 2-year, coed. Part of ITT Educational Services, Inc. Awards transfer associate, terminal associate, bachelor's degrees. Founded 1936. *Setting:* 2-acre suburban campus with easy access to St. Louis. *Total enrollment:* 539. *Faculty:* 24 (22 full-time, 2 part-time); student-faculty ratio is 28:1.
ENROLLMENT PROFILE 539 students from 5 states and territories, 1 other country. 12% women, 88% men, 0% part-time, 68% state residents, 0% transferred in, 25% 25 or older, 0% Native American, 0% Hispanic, 16% African American, 1% Asian American. *Areas of study chosen:* 100% engineering and applied sciences. *Most popular recent major:* electronics engineering technology.
FIRST-YEAR CLASS 289 total; 475 applied, 100% were accepted, 61% of whom enrolled.
ACADEMIC PROGRAM Technical curriculum. Calendar: quarters. 81 courses offered in 1995–96. Academic remediation for entering students, tutorials, honors program, summer session for credit.
GENERAL DEGREE REQUIREMENTS 108 quarter hours for associate, 180 quarter hours for bachelor's; computer course.
MAJORS Drafting and design, electronics engineering technology (B).
LIBRARY 1,600 books, 31 periodicals.
COMPUTERS ON CAMPUS 52 computers for student use in learning resource center, labs provide access to Internet.
COLLEGE LIFE *Major annual events:* High Tech Fairs, Job Fairs, Very Special Arts Festival. *Campus security:* 24-hour emergency response devices.
HOUSING College housing not available.
CAREER PLANNING *Placement office:* 2 full-time staff. *Director:* Ms. Elizabeth McCuan, Director of Placement, 314-298-7800. *Services:* job fairs, resume preparation, resume referral, career counseling, careers library, job bank, job interviews. Students must register freshman year.
AFTER GRADUATION 88% of class of 1994 had job offers within 6 months.
EXPENSES FOR 1995-96 *Application fee:* $100. Tuition for associate degree program ranges from $15,429 to $17,690. Tuition for bachelor's degree program: $25,800. Full-time mandatory fees: $720. Tuition guaranteed not to increase for student's term of enrollment.
FINANCIAL AID *College-administered undergrad aid 1995–96:* need-based scholarships, non-need scholarships, low-interest long-term loans from external sources, Federal Work-Study, 8 part-time jobs. *Required forms:* institutional, FAFSA; accepted: CSS Financial Aid PROFILE. *Priority deadline:* 9/1. *Payment plan:* installment. *Waivers:* full or partial for employees or children of employees.
APPLYING *Option:* deferred entrance. *Required:* school transcript, CPAt. Test scores used for admission. *Application deadline:* rolling.
APPLYING/TRANSFER *Required:* standardized test scores, high school transcript. *Application deadline:* rolling. *Contact:* Ms. Susan M. Falzone, Director of Education, 314-298-7800.
CONTACT Ms. Patrice McMillon, Director of Recruitment, ITT Technical Institute, Earth City, MO 63045-1412, 314-298-7800 Ext. 19. College video available.

JEFFERSON COLLEGE
Hillsboro, Missouri

UG Enrollment: 3,783	Tuition & Fees (Area Res): $1302
Application Deadline: rolling	Room & Board: N/Avail

GENERAL State and locally supported, 2-year, coed. Part of Missouri Coordinating Board for Higher Education. Awards certificates, transfer associate, terminal associate degrees. Founded 1963. *Setting:* 480-acre rural campus with easy access to St. Louis. *Educational spending 1994–95:* $1825 per undergrad. *Total enrollment:* 3,783. *Faculty:* 190 (90 full-time, 17% with terminal degrees, 100 part-time); student-faculty ratio is 19:1.
ENROLLMENT PROFILE 3,783 students from 2 states and territories, 3 other countries. 60% women, 54% part-time, 98% state residents, 2% transferred in, 1% international, 50% 25 or older, 1% Native American, 1% Hispanic, 1% African American, 1% Asian American. *Areas of study chosen:* 26% liberal arts/general studies, 13% health professions and related sciences, 13% vocational and home economics, 10% business management and administrative services, 10% computer and information sciences, 7% social sciences, 5% biological and life sciences, 5% education, 3% performing arts, 2% engineering and applied sciences, 1% communications and journalism. *Most popular recent majors:* nursing, education, business administration/commerce/management.
FIRST-YEAR CLASS 1,315 total; 1,800 applied, 90% were accepted, 73% of whom enrolled. 11% from top 10% of their high school class, 35% from top quarter, 78% from top half.
ACADEMIC PROGRAM Core, general education/vocational curriculum, honor code. Calendar: semesters. 1,600 courses offered in 1995–96. Academic remediation for entering students, English as a second language program offered during academic year, services for LD students, advanced placement, Freshman Honors College, honors program, summer session for credit, part-time degree program (daytime, evenings, summer); adult/continuing education programs, internships.
GENERAL DEGREE REQUIREMENTS 62 semester hours; 3 semester hours of college algebra for associate of arts degree; 6 semester hours of math/science for associate of applied science degree; computer course.
MAJORS Accounting, architectural technologies, art/fine arts, automotive technologies, business administration/commerce/management, business education, child care/child and family studies, civil engineering technology, computer information systems, computer programming, criminal justice, data processing, drafting and design, early childhood education, education, electrical and electronics technologies, electrical engineering technology, elementary education, emergency medical technology, (pre)engineering sequence, English, fire science, forestry, geography, heating/refrigeration/air conditioning, history, hotel and restaurant management, information science, interdisciplinary studies, journalism, legal secretarial studies, liberal arts/general studies, machine and tool technologies, marketing/retailing/merchandising, mathematics, mechanical design technology, medical secretarial studies, music, nursing, physical education, physical sciences, political science/government, practical nursing, psychology, public administration, retail management, robotics, science, secretarial studies/office management, social work, sociology, Spanish, speech/rhetoric/public address/debate, telecommunications, theater arts/drama, veterinary technology, welding technology.
LIBRARY Jefferson College Library plus 1 other, with 54,000 books, 179 microform titles, 320 periodicals, 1 CD-ROM, 1,500 records, tapes, and CDs. Acquisition spending 1994–95: $13,252.
COMPUTERS ON CAMPUS 200 computers for student use in computer center, computer labs, library provide access to on-line services, Internet. Staffed computer lab on campus provides training in use of software. Academic computing expenditure 1994–95: $297,633.
COLLEGE LIFE Drama-theater group, choral group, student-run newspaper. 10% vote in student government elections. *Social organizations:* 9 open to all. *Most popular organizations:* Student Senate, Missouri Student Nursing Association, Baptist Student Union. *Major annual events:* Ice Cream Social, Shocktober Night, Spring Fling. *Campus security:* late-night transport-escort service.
HOUSING College housing not available.
ATHLETICS Member NJCAA. *Intercollegiate:* baseball M(s), basketball W(s), tennis M(s), volleyball W(s). *Intramural:* basketball, swimming and diving, volleyball. *Contact:* Mr. Harold Oetting, Director of Athletics, 314-789-3951 Ext. 380.
CAREER PLANNING *Placement office:* 2 full-time, 1 part-time staff; $111,816 operating expenditure 1994-95. *Director:* Mr. Bob Gross, Director of Career Services, 314-789-3951 Ext. 211. *Services:* job fairs, resume preparation, resume referral, career counseling, careers library, job bank, job interviews. 65 organizations recruited on campus 1994–95.
AFTER GRADUATION 95% of class of 1994 had job offers within 6 months.
EXPENSES FOR 1996-97 *Application fee:* $15. Area resident tuition: $1302 full-time, $42 per semester hour part-time. State resident tuition: $1643 full-time, $53 per semester hour part-time. Nonresident tuition: $2015 full-time, $65 per semester hour part-time.
FINANCIAL AID *College-administered undergrad aid 1995–96:* 150 need-based scholarships (average $300), 138 non-need scholarships (average $720), short-term loans (average $100), low-interest long-term loans from external sources (average $2000), Federal Work-Study, 52 part-time jobs. *Required forms:* institutional, FAFSA; accepted: CSS Financial Aid PROFILE, state, AFSSA-CSX. *Priority deadline:* 6/1. *Payment plan:* deferred payment. *Waivers:* full or partial for employees or children of employees.
APPLYING Open admission except for veterinary technology, electronics, nursing programs. *Options:* early entrance, midyear entrance. *Required:* school transcript, ACT, TOEFL for international students, ACT ASSET. *Recommended:* campus interview. Test scores used for counseling/placement. *Application deadline:* rolling. Preference given to district residents.
APPLYING/TRANSFER *Recommended:* high school transcript. *Required for some:* college transcript, minimum 2.0 college GPA. *Entrance:* noncompetitive. *Application deadline:* rolling. *Contact:* Mr. Sheldon Siegel, Director of Enrollment Services, 314-789-3951 Ext. 210.
CONTACT Ms. Deborah Below, Director of Admissions, Jefferson College, Hillsboro, MO 63050-2441, 314-789-3951 Ext. 217. *Fax:* 314-789-4012. College video available.

JEWISH HOSPITAL COLLEGE OF NURSING AND ALLIED HEALTH
St. Louis, Missouri

UG Enrollment: 470	Tuition & Fees: $8200
Application Deadline: rolling	Room Only: $1650

GENERAL Independent, primarily 2-year, primarily women. Awards certificates, transfer associate, bachelor's degrees. Founded 1902. *Setting:* urban campus. *Endowment:* $1.5 million. *Research spending 1994–95:* $5000. *Educational spending 1994–95:* $2457 per undergrad. *Total enrollment:* 470. *Faculty:* 32 (23 full-time, 19% with terminal degrees, 9 part-time); student-faculty ratio is 10:1.
ENROLLMENT PROFILE 470 students from 4 states and territories, 4 other countries. 88% women, 12% men, 45% part-time, 58% state residents, 80% transferred in, 75% have need-based financial aid, 2% international, 70% 25 or older, 1% Native American, 1% Hispanic, 9% African American, 2% Asian American. *Areas of study chosen:* 100% health professions and related sciences. *Most popular recent major:* nursing.
FIRST-YEAR CLASS 150 total; 298 applied, 56% were accepted, 90% of whom enrolled. 14% from top 10% of their high school class, 31% from top quarter, 59% from top half. 1 valedictorian.
ACADEMIC PROGRAM Core, health care curriculum, honor code. Calendar: semesters. 29 courses offered in 1995–96. Services for LD students, advanced placement, tutorials, summer session for credit, part-time degree program (daytime, evenings, weekends). Off-campus study at Washington University.
GENERAL DEGREE REQUIREMENTS 66 credit hours for associate, 126 credit hours for bachelor's; 1 microbiology course, 2 anatomy and physiology courses.
MAJORS Cytotechnology (B), medical technology (B), nursing (B).
LIBRARY George and Juanita Way Library plus 5 others, with 2,400 books, 145 periodicals, 1 on-line bibliographic service, 1 CD-ROM, 446 records, tapes, and CDs. Acquisition spending 1994–95: $53,319.

Jewish Hospital College of Nursing and Allied Health (continued)

COMPUTERS ON CAMPUS 21 computers for student use in computer labs, library provide access to off-campus computing facilities, on-line services, Internet, software. Academic computing expenditure 1994–95: $20,000.

COLLEGE LIFE Orientation program (2 days, no cost, parents included). Student-run newspaper. 30% vote in student government elections. ***Social organizations:*** 1 open to all. ***Most popular organization:*** Student Association. ***Major annual events:*** Holiday Party, Lobby Day, Dinner Dance. ***Student services:*** personal-psychological counseling. ***Campus security:*** 24-hour patrols, late-night transport-escort service, controlled dormitory access.

HOUSING 117 college housing spaces available; 57 were occupied 1995–96. Freshmen guaranteed college housing. Off-campus living permitted. ***Option:*** coed housing available. Resident assistants live in dorms.

ATHLETICS ***Intramural:*** basketball, soccer, volleyball.

CAREER PLANNING ***Director:*** Ms. Suzanne Sutterer, Director of Student Services, 314-454-8694. ***Services:*** resume preparation, career counseling, job bank.

AFTER GRADUATION 33% of class of 1994 had job offers within 6 months.

EXPENSES FOR 1996–97 ***Application fee:*** $25. Tuition: $8000 full-time, $250 per credit hour part-time. Part-time mandatory fees per semester range from $35 to $65. Full-time mandatory fees: $200. College room only: $1650 (minimum).

FINANCIAL AID ***College-administered undergrad aid 1995–96:*** 70 need-based scholarships (average $1100), 35 non-need scholarships (average $1200), low-interest long-term loans from college funds (average $1000), 10 Federal Work-Study (averaging $1000). ***Required forms:*** FAFSA; required for some: institutional; accepted: CSS Financial Aid PROFILE. ***Priority deadline:*** 4/15. ***Payment plans:*** installment, deferred payment.

APPLYING ***Options:*** early decision, deferred entrance, midyear entrance. ***Required:*** essay, school transcript, 3 years of high school math and science, recommendations, minimum 2.5 high school GPA; minimum 2.5 college GPA, SAT I or ACT, TOEFL for international students. ***Recommended:*** some high school foreign language. ***Required for some:*** campus interview, SCAT, Nelson Denny Reading Test. Test scores used for admission. ***Application deadlines:*** rolling, 11/1 for early decision. ***Notification:*** 12/1 for early decision.

APPLYING/TRANSFER ***Required:*** standardized test scores, 3 years of high school math and science, recommendations, college transcript, minimum 2.5 high school GPA; minimum 2.5 college GPA. ***Required for some:*** essay, high school transcript, campus interview. ***Entrance:*** moderately difficult. ***Application deadline:*** rolling. ***Contact:*** Ms. Susan Graves, Director of Administrative Services, 314-454-7058.

CONTACT Ms. Charlotte Lewinski, Chief Admissions Officer, Jewish Hospital College of Nursing and Allied Health, 306 South Kingshighway, St. Louis, MO 63110-1091, 314-454-7057 or toll-free 800-832-9009 (in-state). ***Fax:*** 314-454-5239. ***E-mail:*** cal7374@bjcmail.carenet.org.

KEMPER MILITARY JUNIOR COLLEGE
Boonville, Missouri

UG Enrollment: 202	Comprehensive Fee: $16,900
Application Deadline: rolling	**Room & Board: N/App**

GENERAL Independent, 2-year, coed. Awards diplomas, transfer associate degrees. Founded 1844. ***Setting:*** 140-acre small-town campus. ***Total enrollment:*** 202. ***Faculty:*** 20 (13 full-time, 10% with terminal degrees, 7 part-time); student-faculty ratio is 10:1. ***Notable Alumni:*** Don Tyson, CEO of Tyson Foods; Steve Raibbeck, actor; George Lindsey, actor; Hugh O'Brien, actor; Judge Bonner, former director of Drug Enforcement Agency.

ENROLLMENT PROFILE 202 students from 42 states and territories, 9 other countries. 29% women, 71% men, 13% part-time, 27% state residents, 1% transferred in, 8% 25 or older, 0% Native American, 3% Hispanic, 32% African American, 1% Asian American.

FIRST-YEAR CLASS 130 total; 170 applied, 100% were accepted, 76% of whom enrolled. 10% from top 10% of their high school class, 15% from top quarter, 33% from top half.

ACADEMIC PROGRAM Core, honor code. Calendar: semesters. Academic remediation for entering students, English as a second language program offered during academic year, advanced placement, honors program. ROTC: Army.

GENERAL DEGREE REQUIREMENT 62 credits.

MAJORS Biology/biological sciences, business administration/commerce/management, economics, English, environmental engineering technology, history, liberal arts/general studies, mathematics, military science, nursing, physical education, physical sciences, psychology, public administration, sociology.

LIBRARY Kemper Library with 23,000 books, 200 periodicals, 2 CD-ROMs, 100 records, tapes, and CDs.

COMPUTERS ON CAMPUS 60 computers for student use in computer labs, classrooms, library provide access to off-campus computing facilities, e-mail, on-line services. Staffed computer lab on campus provides training in use of computers, software.

COLLEGE LIFE Drama-theater group, marching band, student-run newspaper. ***Student services:*** health clinic, personal-psychological counseling. ***Campus security:*** 24-hour emergency response devices and patrols, student patrols, controlled dormitory access.

HOUSING 400 college housing spaces available; 110 were occupied 1995–96. Freshmen guaranteed college housing. On-campus residence required through sophomore year. Resident assistants live in dorms.

ATHLETICS Member NJCAA. ***Intercollegiate:*** basketball M(s), cross-country running M(s)/W(s), football M(s), golf M(s)/W(s), riflery M(s)/W(s), soccer M(s), tennis M(s)/W(s), track and field M(s)/W(s), volleyball W, wrestling M(s). ***Intramural:*** basketball, football, golf, riflery, soccer, swimming and diving, tennis, track and field, volleyball, weight lifting. ***Contact:*** Mr. Charlie Brown, Athletic Director, 816-882-5623.

CAREER PLANNING ***Service:*** career counseling. 27 organizations recruited on campus 1994–95.

AFTER GRADUATION 81% of students completing a degree program in 1994–95 went directly on to further study.

EXPENSES FOR 1995–96 Comprehensive fee: $16,900. Part-time tuition: $100 per semester hour.

FINANCIAL AID ***College-administered undergrad aid 1995–96:*** need-based scholarships, low-interest long-term loans from external sources, Federal Work-Study, 10 part-time jobs. ***Required forms:*** institutional; accepted: CSS Financial Aid PROFILE, state, FAFSA. ***Priority deadline:*** 8/1. ***Payment plan:*** tuition prepayment. ***Waivers:*** full or partial for employees or children of employees.

APPLYING ***Options:*** Common Application, early entrance, deferred entrance. ***Required:*** school transcript, 3 years of high school math, 2 recommendations, interview, SAT I or ACT. Test scores used for counseling/placement. ***Application deadline:*** rolling. ***Notification:*** continuous. Preference given to children of alumni.

APPLYING/TRANSFER ***Required:*** high school transcript, 3 years of high school math, 2 recommendations, interview. ***Application deadline:*** rolling. ***Notification:*** continuous. ***Contact:*** Mr. Jeff Venable, Registrar, 816-882-5623.

CONTACT Lt. Col. Michael J. Glass, Director of Admissions, Kemper Military Junior College, Boonville, MO 65233-1699, 816-882-5623 or toll-free 800-530-5600. ***Fax:*** 816-882-3332. College video available.

LONGVIEW COMMUNITY COLLEGE
Lee's Summit, Missouri

UG Enrollment: 8,388	Tuition & Fees (Area Res): $1350
Application Deadline: rolling	**Room & Board: N/Avail**

GENERAL State and locally supported, 2-year, coed. Part of Metropolitan Community Colleges System. Awards certificates, transfer associate, terminal associate degrees. Founded 1969. ***Setting:*** 147-acre suburban campus with easy access to Kansas City. ***Total enrollment:*** 8,388. ***Faculty:*** 396 (107 full-time, 98% with terminal degrees, 289 part-time); student-faculty ratio is 23:1.

ENROLLMENT PROFILE 8,388 students: 61% women, 39% men, 69% part-time, 99% state residents, 16% transferred in, 16% have need-based financial aid, 6% have non-need-based financial aid, 1% international, 50% 25 or older, 1% Native American, 2% Hispanic, 10% African American, 1% Asian American. ***Areas of study chosen:*** 61% liberal arts/general studies, 17% vocational and home economics, 8% business management and administrative services, 8% health professions and related sciences, 3% computer and information sciences, 3% engineering and applied sciences. ***Most popular recent majors:*** liberal arts/general studies, automotive technologies, business administration/commerce/management.

FIRST-YEAR CLASS 1,783 total. Of the students who applied, 100% were accepted.

ACADEMIC PROGRAM Core, college transfer and vocational curriculum, honor code. Calendar: semesters. 777 courses offered in 1995–96. Academic remediation for entering students, English as a second language program offered during academic year, services for LD students, advanced placement, honors program, summer session for credit, part-time degree program (daytime, evenings, summer), adult/continuing education programs, co-op programs and internships. Off-campus study at Johnson County Community College.

GENERAL DEGREE REQUIREMENTS 62 credit hours; 9 credit hours of math/science including at least 1 lab science course; computer course for business administration, most vocational majors; internship (some majors).

MAJORS Accounting, agricultural technologies, automotive technologies, biology/biological sciences, business administration/commerce/management, chemistry, computer programming, computer science, corrections, criminal justice, data processing, drafting and design, electrical and electronics technologies, electronics engineering technology, engineering (general), (pre)engineering sequence, human services, industrial and heavy equipment maintenance, law enforcement/police sciences, legal secretarial studies, liberal arts/general studies, marketing/retailing/merchandising, medical secretarial studies, postal management, quality control technology, science, secretarial studies/office management, word processing.

LIBRARY Longview Community College Library with 44,169 books, 6,474 microform titles, 247 periodicals, 1,282 records, tapes, and CDs. Acquisition spending 1994–95: $109,856.

COMPUTERS ON CAMPUS 500 computers for student use in computer center, computer labs, departmental labs, classrooms, library, student center provide access to main academic computer, Internet. Staffed computer lab on campus provides training in use of computers, software. Academic computing expenditure 1994–95: $498,600.

COLLEGE LIFE Drama-theater group, choral group, student-run newspaper. ***Social organizations:*** 1 national fraternity. ***Most popular organizations:*** Student Newspaper, Student Government, Phi Theta Kappa, Longview Mighty Voices Choir, Longview Broadcasting Network. ***Major annual events:*** Family Easter, Fall Dance, College Transfer Day. ***Student services:*** personal-psychological counseling. ***Campus security:*** 24-hour patrols.

HOUSING College housing not available.

ATHLETICS Member NJCAA. ***Intercollegiate:*** baseball M(s), volleyball W(s). ***Intramural:*** basketball, swimming and diving, volleyball. ***Contact:*** Mr. John O'Connell, Athletic Director, 816-767-0104.

CAREER PLANNING ***Placement office:*** 7 full-time, 2 part-time staff; $792,382 operating expenditure 1994–95. ***Director:*** Mr. Bruce Appel, Lead Counselor, 816-672-2235. ***Services:*** job fairs, career counseling, careers library, job bank, job interviews. 300 organizations recruited on campus 1994–95.

AFTER GRADUATION 61% of students completing a degree program in 1994–95 went directly on to further study.

EXPENSES FOR 1996–97 Area resident tuition: $1350 full-time, $45 per credit hour part-time. State resident tuition: $2250 full-time, $75 per credit hour part-time. Nonresident tuition: $3210 full-time, $107 per credit hour part-time.

FINANCIAL AID ***College-administered undergrad aid 1995–96:*** 331 need-based scholarships (average $515), 491 non-need scholarships (average $572), short-term loans (average $50), low-interest long-term loans from external sources (average $2065), 71 Federal Work-Study (averaging $1309), 152 part-time jobs. ***Required forms:*** institutional, FAFSA; required for some: state; accepted: CSS Financial Aid PROFILE. ***Priority deadline:*** 5/31. ***Waivers:*** full or partial for employees or children of employees and senior citizens. ***Notification:*** continuous.

APPLYING Open admission. ***Options:*** Common Application, early entrance, midyear entrance. ***Required:*** TOEFL for international students, ACT ASSET. ***Recommended:*** ACT. Test scores used for counseling/placement. ***Application deadline:*** rolling.

APPLYING/TRANSFER ***Required:*** standardized test scores. ***Recommended:*** college transcript. ***Entrance:*** noncompetitive. ***Application deadline:*** rolling. ***Contact:*** Mr. Richard Phelps, Registrar, 816-672-2247.

CONTACT Mr. Richard Phelps, Registrar, Longview Community College, Lee's Summit, MO 64081-2105, 816-672-2247.

MAPLE WOODS COMMUNITY COLLEGE
Kansas City, Missouri

UG Enrollment: 4,572	Tuition & Fees (Area Res): $1350
Application Deadline: rolling	Room & Board: N/Avail

GENERAL State and locally supported, 2-year, coed. Part of Metropolitan Community Colleges System. Awards certificates, transfer associate, terminal associate degrees. Founded 1969. *Setting:* 205-acre suburban campus. *Educational spending 1994–95:* $1428 per undergrad. *Total enrollment:* 4,572. *Faculty:* 175 (58 full-time, 98% with terminal degrees, 117 part-time); student-faculty ratio is 23:1.
ENROLLMENT PROFILE 4,572 students from 2 states and territories, 6 other countries. 60% women, 40% men, 69% part-time, 99% state residents, 21% transferred in, 18% have need-based financial aid, 6% have non-need-based financial aid, 1% international, 45% 25 or older, 1% Native American, 2% Hispanic, 2% African American, 1% Asian American. *Areas of study chosen:* 62% liberal arts/general studies, 13% vocational and home economics, 12% business management and administrative services, 7% health professions and related sciences, 4% computer and information sciences, 2% engineering and applied sciences. *Most popular recent majors:* liberal arts/general studies, secretarial studies/office management, veterinary technology.
FIRST-YEAR CLASS 720 total. Of the students who applied, 100% were accepted.
ACADEMIC PROGRAM Core, college transfer and vocational curriculum, honor code. Calendar: semesters. 702 courses offered in 1995–96. Academic remediation for entering students, English as a second language program offered during academic year, services for LD students, advanced placement, honors program, summer session for credit, part-time degree program (daytime, evenings), adult/continuing education programs, co-op programs and internships. Off-campus study at Johnson County Community College.
GENERAL DEGREE REQUIREMENTS 62 credit hours; 9 credit hours of math/science including at least 1 lab science course; computer course for business administration, most vocational majors; internship (some majors).
MAJORS Accounting, aviation technology, biology/biological sciences, business administration/commerce/management, chemistry, computer programming, computer science, criminal justice, data processing, electrical and electronics technologies, electronics engineering technology, (pre)engineering sequence, heating/refrigeration/air conditioning, law enforcement/police sciences, legal secretarial studies, liberal arts/general studies, machine and tool technologies, marketing/retailing/merchandising, medical secretarial studies, science, secretarial studies/office management, tourism and travel, veterinary technology.
LIBRARY Maple Woods Community College Library with 32,000 books, 43 microform titles, 253 periodicals, 27 CD-ROMs, 3,100 records, tapes, and CDs. Acquisition spending 1994–95: $63,325.
COMPUTERS ON CAMPUS 125 computers for student use in computer center, computer labs, learning resource center, academic labs, classrooms, library provide access to main academic computer, Internet. Staffed computer lab on campus provides training in use of computers, software. Academic computing expenditure 1994–95: $311,164.
COLLEGE LIFE Drama-theater group, choral group, student-run newspaper. *Social organizations:* 1 national fraternity. *Most popular organizations:* Student Activities Council, Art Club, Friends of All Cultures, Phi Theta Kappa, Engineering Club. *Major annual events:* Spring Fest, Family Christmas, Blood Drive. *Student services:* personal-psychological counseling. *Campus security:* 24-hour patrols, late-night transport-escort service.
HOUSING College housing not available.
ATHLETICS Member NJCAA. *Intercollegiate:* baseball M(s). *Intramural:* softball, volleyball. *Contact:* Mr. Bill Sharp, Athletic Director, 816-437-3177.
CAREER PLANNING *Placement office:* 7 full-time, 5 part-time staff; $376,641 operating expenditure 1994–95. *Director:* Ms. Christine Yanitelli, Counseling Chairperson, 816-437-3093. *Services:* job fairs, resume preparation, career counseling, careers library, job bank, job interviews. 200 organizations recruited on campus 1994–95.
AFTER GRADUATION 63% of students completing a degree program in 1994–95 went directly on to further study.
EXPENSES FOR 1996-97 Area resident tuition: $1350 full-time, $45 per credit hour part-time. State resident tuition: $2250 full-time, $75 per credit hour part-time. Nonresident tuition: $3210 full-time, $107 per credit hour part-time.
FINANCIAL AID *College-administered undergrad aid 1995–96:* 219 need-based scholarships (averaging $562), 289 non-need scholarships (averaging $553), short-term loans (averaging $50), low-interest long-term loans from external sources (averaging $2198), 40 Federal Work-Study (averaging $1089), 53 part-time jobs. *Required forms:* institutional, FAFSA; required for some: state; accepted: CSS Financial Aid PROFILE. *Priority deadline:* 5/31. *Waivers:* full or partial for employees or children of employees and senior citizens. *Notification:* continuous.
APPLYING Open admission except for veterinary technology. *Options:* early entrance, midyear entrance. *Required:* TOEFL for international students, ACT ASSET. Test scores used for counseling/placement. *Application deadline:* rolling. *Notification:* continuous.
APPLYING/TRANSFER *Required:* standardized test scores. *Recommended:* college transcript. *Entrance:* noncompetitive. *Application deadline:* rolling. *Notification:* continuous. *Contact:* Ms. Barbara Reinwald, Registrar, 816-437-3108.
CONTACT Ms. Barbara Reinwald, Registrar, Maple Woods Community College, Kansas City, MO 64156-1299, 816-437-3108.

MINERAL AREA COLLEGE
Park Hills, Missouri

UG Enrollment: 2,388	Tuition & Fees (Area Res): $840
Application Deadline: rolling	Room & Board: N/Avail

GENERAL District-supported, 2-year, coed. Part of Missouri Coordinating Board for Higher Education. Awards certificates, transfer associate, terminal associate degrees. Founded 1922. *Setting:* 200-acre rural campus with easy access to St. Louis. *Educational spending 1994–95:* $1467 per undergrad. *Total enrollment:* 2,388. *Faculty:* 154 (51 full-time, 103 part-time); student-faculty ratio is 20:1.
ENROLLMENT PROFILE 2,388 students from 15 states and territories. 66% women, 55% part-time, 99% state residents, 4% transferred in, 47% have need-based financial aid, 10% have non-need-based financial aid, 42% 25 or older, 0% Native American, 0% Hispanic, 1% African American, 0% Asian American. *Areas of study chosen:* 25% health professions and related sciences, 24% liberal arts/general studies, 21% education, 12% business management and administrative services, 8% social sciences, 5% engineering and applied sciences, 2% computer and information sciences, 1% biological and life sciences, 1% communications and journalism, 1% fine arts. *Most popular recent majors:* education, nursing, business administration/commerce/management.
FIRST-YEAR CLASS 949 total; 1,035 applied, 100% were accepted, 92% of whom enrolled. 20% from top 10% of their high school class, 22% from top quarter, 58% from top half.
ACADEMIC PROGRAM Core. Calendar: semesters. 275 courses offered in 1995–96. Academic remediation for entering students, services for LD students, honors program, summer session for credit, part-time degree program (daytime, evenings), internships. Off-campus study at East Central College, Jefferson College.
GENERAL DEGREE REQUIREMENTS 62 credit hours; computer course; internship (some majors).
MAJORS Art/fine arts, business administration/commerce/management, civil engineering technology, communication, construction technologies, criminal justice, drafting and design, education, electrical and electronics technologies, elementary education, engineering (general), (pre)engineering sequence, fashion merchandising, history, law enforcement/police sciences, liberal arts/general studies, manufacturing technology, marketing/retailing/merchandising, mathematics, medical laboratory technology, music, nursing, physical education, psychology, radiological technology, science, secretarial studies/office management, social science, social work, sociology.
LIBRARY Cozean Learning Resource Center with 30,773 books, 257 microform titles, 183 periodicals, 1,541 records, tapes, and CDs.
COMPUTERS ON CAMPUS 150 computers for student use in computer labs, learning resource center, classrooms, library provide access to e-mail. Staffed computer lab on campus. Academic computing expenditure 1994–95: $276,507.
COLLEGE LIFE Drama-theater group, choral group. *Most popular organization:* Student Senate. *Major annual events:* Spring Picnic, Summer Theatre. *Campus security:* 24-hour patrols.
HOUSING College housing not available.
ATHLETICS Member NJCAA. *Intercollegiate:* baseball M(s), basketball M(s)/W(s), tennis M(s)/W(s), volleyball W(s). *Intramural:* basketball, tennis, volleyball. *Contact:* Mr. Robert Sechrest, Athletic Director, 573-431-4593 Ext. 241.
CAREER PLANNING *Placement office:* 2 full-time staff. *Director:* Ms. Christine Landrum, Vocational Evaluator, 573-431-4593 Ext. 262. *Services:* job fairs, resume preparation, resume referral, career counseling, careers library, job bank, job interviews.
AFTER GRADUATION 74% of class of 1994 had job offers within 6 months. 28% of students completing a degree program went directly on to further study.
EXPENSES FOR 1995-96 Area resident tuition: $840 full-time, $35 per credit hour part-time. State resident tuition: $1200 full-time, $50 per credit hour part-time. Nonresident tuition: $1248 full-time, $50 per credit hour part-time.
FINANCIAL AID *College-administered undergrad aid 1995–96:* 313 need-based scholarships (averaging $575), 357 non-need scholarships (averaging $756), short-term loans (averaging $75), low-interest long-term loans from external sources (averaging $1854), Federal Work-Study. *Required forms:* FAFSA. *Priority deadline:* 7/30. *Waivers:* full or partial for employees or children of employees. *Notification:* continuous.
APPLYING Open admission except for allied health programs. *Options:* early entrance, midyear entrance. *Required:* ACT, TOEFL for international students. Test scores used for counseling/placement. *Application deadline:* rolling.
APPLYING/TRANSFER *Required:* college transcript. *Entrance:* noncompetitive. *Application deadline:* rolling. *Contact:* Mrs. Linda Huffman, Registrar, 573-431-4593 Ext. 259.
CONTACT Mrs. Linda Huffman, Registrar, Mineral Area College, Park Hills, MO 63601, 573-431-4593 Ext. 259.

MOBERLY AREA COMMUNITY COLLEGE
Moberly, Missouri

UG Enrollment: 2,014	Tuition & Fees (Area Res): $1133
Application Deadline: rolling	Room Only: $1200

GENERAL State and locally supported, 2-year, coed. Part of Missouri Coordinating Board for Higher Education. Awards certificates, transfer associate, terminal associate degrees. Founded 1927. *Setting:* 23-acre small-town campus. *Total enrollment:* 2,014. *Faculty:* 95 (34 full-time, 20% with terminal degrees, 61 part-time); student-faculty ratio is 20:1. *Notable Alumni:* Mitch Richmond, professional basketball player; Gerald Wilkins, professional basketball player, Cotton Fitzsimmons, NBA coach.
ENROLLMENT PROFILE 2,014 students from 6 states and territories, 7 other countries. 63% women, 37% men, 44% part-time, 99% state residents, 1% live on campus, 20% transferred in, 1% international, 44% 25 or older, 1% Native American, 1% Hispanic, 6% African American, 1% Asian American. *Most popular recent majors:* liberal arts/general studies, nursing, business administration/commerce/management.
FIRST-YEAR CLASS 876 total. Of the students who applied, 100% were accepted, 70% of whom enrolled. 25% from top 10% of their high school class, 40% from top quarter, 75% from top half.
ACADEMIC PROGRAM Core, honor code. Calendar: semesters. 800 courses offered in 1995–96. Academic remediation for entering students, services for LD students, self-designed majors, summer session for credit, part-time degree program (daytime, evenings, summer), adult/continuing education programs, co-op programs and internships.
GENERAL DEGREE REQUIREMENTS 64 credit hours; 1 course in college algebra; computer course.
MAJORS Accounting, art/fine arts, behavioral sciences, biology/biological sciences, business administration/commerce/management, business machine technologies, child care/child and family studies, computer information systems, data processing, education, electrical and electronics technologies, (pre)engineering sequence, history, law enforcement/police sciences, liberal arts/general studies, machine and tool technologies, marketing/retailing/merchandising, mathematics, metallurgical technology, music, nursing, painting/drawing, physical sciences, practical nursing, psychology, science, secretarial studies/office management, social science, welding technology.
LIBRARY Kate Stamper Wilhite Library with 20,400 books, 105 microform titles, 213 periodicals, 3 CD-ROMs, 475 records, tapes, and CDs. Acquisition spending 1994–95: $76,566.

Moberly Area Community College (continued)

COMPUTERS ON CAMPUS 48 computers for student use in computer center, learning resource center, library provide access to main academic computer, Internet. Academic computing expenditure 1994–95: $111,419.

COLLEGE LIFE Drama-theater group, choral group, student-run newspaper. 10% vote in student government elections. ***Social organizations:*** 7 open to all; 1 local fraternity, 1 local sorority; 10% of eligible men and 10% of eligible women are members. ***Most popular organizations:*** Phi Theta Kappa, Student Nurses Association, Child Care, Delta Epsilon Chi, Brother Ox. ***Major annual events:*** Singers/Jazz Ensemble, Theatrical Production, Alumni Weekend. ***Student services:*** personal-psychological counseling, women's center. ***Campus security:*** 24-hour emergency response devices and patrols, controlled dormitory access.

HOUSING 30 college housing spaces available; all were occupied 1995–96. No special consideration for freshman housing applicants. Housing for women and athletes only. ***Option:*** single-sex housing available. Resident assistants live in dorms.

ATHLETICS Member NJCAA. ***Intercollegiate:*** basketball M(s)/W(s). ***Intramural:*** basketball. ***Contact:*** Mr. Kenny Seifert, Athletic Director, 816-263-4110 Ext. 225; Mr. Kevin Bucher, Women's Head Coach, 816-263-4110 Ext. 284.

CAREER PLANNING ***Placement office:*** 27 full-time, 25 part-time staff; $47,142 operating expenditure 1994–95. ***Director:*** Mrs. Ruth Ann Finck, Dean of Vocational Education, 816-263-4110. ***Services:*** job fairs, resume preparation, resume referral, career counseling, careers library, job bank, job interviews. 25 organizations recruited on campus 1994–95.

AFTER GRADUATION 92% of class of 1994 had job offers within 6 months.

EXPENSES FOR 1996–97 Area resident tuition: $1088 full-time, $34 per credit hour part-time. State resident tuition: $1920 full-time, $60 per credit hour part-time. Nonresident tuition: $3520 full-time, $110 per credit hour part-time. Full-time mandatory fees: $45. College room only: $1200.

FINANCIAL AID ***College-administered undergrad aid 1995–96:*** 30 need-based scholarships (average $280), 379 non-need scholarships (average $275), low-interest long-term loans from external sources (average $1500), Federal Work-Study. ***Required forms:*** FAFSA; accepted: CSS Financial Aid PROFILE, state. ***Priority deadline:*** 6/30. ***Payment plans:*** installment, deferred payment. ***Waivers:*** full or partial for employees or children of employees and senior citizens.

APPLYING Open admission except for nursing program, nonresidents. ***Options:*** Common Application, early entrance, deferred entrance. ***Required:*** school transcript, TOEFL for international students. ***Recommended:*** SAT I. ***Required for some:*** ACT, ACT ASSET. Test scores used for counseling/placement. ***Application deadline:*** rolling. ***Notification:*** continuous until 9/5.

APPLYING/TRANSFER ***Recommended:*** standardized test scores. ***Entrance:*** minimally difficult. ***Application deadline:*** rolling. ***Notification:*** continuous until 9/15.

CONTACT Dr. James Grant, Dean of Student Services, Moberly Area Community College, Moberly, MO 65270-1392, 816-263-4110 Ext. 35 or toll-free 800-622-2070.

NORTH CENTRAL MISSOURI COLLEGE
Trenton, Missouri

UG Enrollment: 1,093 — **Tuition & Fees (Area Res): $1248**
Application Deadline: rolling — **Room & Board: $2340**

GENERAL District-supported, 2-year, coed. Part of Missouri Coordinating Board for Higher Education. Awards certificates, transfer associate, terminal associate degrees. Founded 1925. ***Setting:*** 1-acre small-town campus. ***Total enrollment:*** 1,093. ***Faculty:*** 69 (25 full-time, 20% with terminal degrees, 44 part-time); student-faculty ratio is 16:1.

ENROLLMENT PROFILE 1,093 students from 7 states and territories. 69% women, 59% part-time, 99% state residents, 6% transferred in, 0% international, 33% 25 or older, 0% Native American, 1% Hispanic, 1% African American, 0% Asian American. ***Most popular recent majors:*** liberal arts/general studies, nursing, accounting.

FIRST-YEAR CLASS 553 total. Of the students who applied, 100% were accepted, 70% of whom enrolled. 4% from top 10% of their high school class, 23% from top quarter, 50% from top half.

ACADEMIC PROGRAM Honor code. Calendar: semesters. Academic remediation for entering students, services for LD students, advanced placement, summer session for credit, part-time degree program (daytime, evenings), adult/continuing education programs, co-op programs and internships.

GENERAL DEGREE REQUIREMENTS 60 credit hours; computer course for accounting, office occupations, agriculture, business majors; internship (some majors).

MAJORS Accounting, agricultural business, automotive technologies, business administration/commerce/management, computer technologies, construction technologies, criminal justice, data processing, drafting and design, electrical and electronics technologies, emergency medical technology, farm and ranch management, fashion merchandising, liberal arts/general studies, marketing/retailing/merchandising, nursing, secretarial studies/office management.

LIBRARY 19,674 books, 1,693 microform titles, 110 periodicals, 1,352 records, tapes, and CDs. Acquisition spending 1994–95: $22,308.

COMPUTERS ON CAMPUS 48 computers for student use in computer center, Academic Reinforcement Center. Staffed computer lab on campus provides training in use of computers, software. Academic computing expenditure 1994–95: $63,425.

COLLEGE LIFE Drama-theater group. ***Social organizations:*** 1 local fraternity, 1 local sorority. ***Student services:*** personal-psychological counseling. ***Campus security:*** controlled dormitory access.

HOUSING 80 college housing spaces available; 76 were occupied 1995–96. No special consideration for freshman housing applicants. Off-campus living permitted. ***Option:*** single-sex housing available. Resident assistants live in dorms.

ATHLETICS Member NJCAA. ***Intercollegiate:*** baseball M(s), softball W(s). ***Intramural:*** football, swimming and diving, volleyball. ***Contact:*** Mr. Jack Derry, Athletic Director, 816-359-3948.

CAREER PLANNING ***Placement office:*** 1 part-time staff; $22,249 operating expenditure 1994–95. ***Director:*** Ms. Lynn Barron, Job Placement Coordinator, 816-359-3948 Ext. 278. ***Services:*** job fairs, resume referral, career counseling, careers library, job bank, job interviews. Students must register sophomore year.

EXPENSES FOR 1996–97 Area resident tuition: $1140 full-time, $38 per credit hour part-time. State resident tuition: $1770 full-time, $59 per credit hour part-time. Nonresident tuition: $2490 full-time, $83 per credit hour part-time. Part-time mandatory fees: $4.50 per credit hour. Full-time mandatory fees: $108. College room and board: $2340. College room only: $1350.

FINANCIAL AID ***College-administered undergrad aid 1995–96:*** 101 need-based scholarships (average $218), 143 non-need scholarships (average $470), short-term loans (average $300), low-interest long-term loans from external sources (average $2713), 16 Federal Work-Study (averaging $490), 19 part-time jobs. ***Required forms for some financial aid applicants:*** state, institutional, FAFSA. ***Priority deadline:*** 3/28. ***Payment plan:*** deferred payment. ***Waivers:*** full or partial for minority students, employees or children of employees, and senior citizens.

APPLYING Open admission except for health occupations programs. ***Options:*** early entrance, midyear entrance. ***Required:*** school transcript. ***Recommended:*** ACT, TOEFL for international students. ***Required for some:*** ACT, TOEFL for international students, nursing exam. Test scores used for counseling/placement. ***Application deadline:*** rolling.

APPLYING/TRANSFER ***Required:*** college transcript. ***Entrance:*** noncompetitive. ***Application deadline:*** rolling. ***Contact:*** Ms. Deanna Powell, Admissions Representative, 816-359-3948.

CONTACT Mr. Jack Derry, Director of Admissions, North Central Missouri College, Trenton, MO 64683-1824, 816-359-3948 Ext. 402. ***Fax:*** 800-880-6180 Ext. 401. College video available.

OZARKS TECHNICAL COMMUNITY COLLEGE
Springfield, Missouri

UG Enrollment: 3,507 — **Tuition & Fees (Area Res): $1338**
Application Deadline: N/R — **Room & Board: N/Avail**

GENERAL District-supported, 2-year, coed. Part of Missouri Coordinating Board for Higher Education. Awards certificates, diplomas, transfer associate, terminal associate degrees. ***Setting:*** 20-acre urban campus. ***Total enrollment:*** 3,507. ***Faculty:*** 150 (49 full-time, 95% with terminal degrees, 101 part-time); student-faculty ratio is 25:1.

ENROLLMENT PROFILE 3,507 students from 3 states and territories. 55% women, 45% men, 60% part-time, 98% state residents, 10% transferred in, 40% have need-based financial aid, 5% have non-need-based financial aid, 55% 25 or older, 1% Native American, 1% Hispanic, 2% African American, 2% Asian American. ***Areas of study chosen:*** 40% liberal arts/general studies, 16% computer and information sciences, 15% engineering and applied sciences, 15% health professions and related sciences, 14% business management and administrative services.

FIRST-YEAR CLASS 800 total; 1,000 applied, 100% were accepted, 80% of whom enrolled. 5% from top 10% of their high school class, 20% from top quarter, 30% from top half.

ACADEMIC PROGRAM Core, job training curriculum, honor code. Calendar: semesters. 345 courses offered in 1995–96; average class size 25 in required courses. Academic remediation for entering students, English as a second language program offered during academic year, services for LD students, tutorials, summer session for credit, part-time degree program (daytime, evenings, weekends, summer), adult/continuing education programs, co-op programs and internships. Off-campus study at Southwest Missouri State University. Study-abroad program.

GENERAL DEGREE REQUIREMENTS 62 credit hours; computer course for manufacturing technology, accounting, business administration, electronics, hospitality management, printing graphics technology majors.

MAJORS Accounting, automotive technologies, business administration/commerce/management, business machine technologies, computer information systems, construction technologies, dental services, early childhood education, electronics engineering technology, fire science, health services administration, heating/refrigeration/air conditioning, hospitality services, manufacturing technology, operating room technology, physical sciences, practical nursing, printing technologies, respiratory therapy, welding technology.

LIBRARY Learning Resource Center plus 1 other, with 6,000 books, 200 microform titles, 190 periodicals, 3 on-line bibliographic services, 30 CD-ROMs, 1,000 records, tapes, and CDs. Acquisition spending 1994–95: $50,000.

COMPUTERS ON CAMPUS Computer purchase plan available. 50 computers for student use in computer labs, classrooms, library provide access to on-line services, Internet. Staffed computer lab on campus provides training in use of computers, software. Academic computing expenditure 1994–95: $500,000.

COLLEGE LIFE Student-run newspaper. 5% vote in student government elections. ***Most popular organizations:*** Phi Theta Kappa, FBLA Phi Beta Lambda (Business). ***Major annual event:*** Annual Student Picnic. ***Student services:*** personal-psychological counseling. ***Campus security:*** 24-hour emergency response devices.

HOUSING College housing not available.

CAREER PLANNING ***Placement office:*** 3 full-time staff. ***Director:*** Ms. Sue Lawson, Placement Director, 417-895-7208. ***Services:*** resume preparation, resume referral, career counseling, job bank. 20 organizations recruited on campus 1994–95.

AFTER GRADUATION 94% of class of 1994 had job offers within 6 months.

EXPENSES FOR 1996–97 Area resident tuition: $1333 full-time, $43 per credit hour part-time. State resident tuition: $1953 full-time, $63 per credit hour part-time. Nonresident tuition: $2883 full-time, $93 per credit hour part-time. Part-time mandatory fees: $5 per year. Full-time mandatory fees: $5.

FINANCIAL AID ***College-administered undergrad aid 1995–96:*** 249 need-based scholarships (averaging $130), non-need scholarships, 37 Federal Work-Study (averaging $900). ***Required forms:*** CSS Financial Aid PROFILE, institutional, FAFSA. ***Priority deadline:*** 7/1. ***Payment plan:*** installment. ***Waivers:*** full or partial for senior citizens. ***Average indebtedness of graduates:*** $2400.

APPLYING Open admission. ***Options:*** Common Application, early entrance, midyear entrance. ***Required:*** school transcript, ACT ASSET. Test scores used for counseling/placement. ***Notification:*** continuous.

APPLYING/TRANSFER ***Required:*** college transcript. ***Required for some:*** standardized test scores, high school transcript. ***Notification:*** continuous. ***Contact:*** Mr. Bruce Renner, Assistant Dean for Student Development, 417-895-7310.

CONTACT Mr. Bruce Renner, Assistant Dean for Student Development, Ozarks Technical Community College, 1417 North Jefferson Avenue, Springfield, MO 65802, 417-895-7130. College video available.

PENN VALLEY COMMUNITY COLLEGE
Kansas City, Missouri

UG Enrollment: 4,432 **Tuition & Fees (Area Res): $1350**
Application Deadline: rolling **Room & Board: N/Avail**

GENERAL State and locally supported, 2-year, coed. Part of Metropolitan Community Colleges System. Awards certificates, transfer associate, terminal associate degrees. Founded 1969. ***Setting:*** 25-acre urban campus. ***Educational spending 1994–95:*** $2405 per undergrad. ***Total enrollment:*** 4,432. ***Faculty:*** 254 (106 full-time, 98% with terminal degrees, 148 part-time).
ENROLLMENT PROFILE 4,432 students: 66% women, 34% men, 73% part-time, 98% state residents, 15% transferred in, 29% have need-based financial aid, 9% have non-need-based financial aid, 2% international, 49% 25 or older, 1% Native American, 5% Hispanic, 36% African American, 4% Asian American. ***Areas of study chosen:*** 47% liberal arts/general studies, 25% health professions and related sciences, 16% vocational and home economics, 7% business management and administrative services, 3% computer and information sciences, 2% engineering and applied sciences. ***Most popular recent majors:*** liberal arts/general studies, nursing, physical therapy.
FIRST-YEAR CLASS 719 total. Of the students who applied, 100% were accepted.
ACADEMIC PROGRAM Core, college transfer and vocational curriculum, honor code. Calendar: semesters. 736 courses offered in 1995–96. Academic remediation for entering students, English as a second language program offered during academic year and summer, services for LD students, advanced placement, honors program, summer session for credit, part-time degree program (daytime, evenings, weekends, summer), adult/continuing education programs, co-op programs and internships. Off-campus study at Johnson County Community College.
GENERAL DEGREE REQUIREMENTS 62 credit hours; 1 algebra course; computer course for business administration, most vocational majors; internship (some majors).
MAJORS Accounting, biology/biological sciences, business administration/commerce/management, chemistry, commercial art, computer science, corrections, criminal justice, culinary arts, data processing, early childhood education, electrical and electronics technologies, electronics engineering technology, emergency medical technology, engineering (general), fashion design and technology, fashion merchandising, fire science, food services management, heating/refrigeration/air conditioning, home economics, hotel and restaurant management, law enforcement/police sciences, legal secretarial studies, liberal arts/general studies, marketing/retailing/merchandising, medical records services, medical secretarial studies, nursing, occupational therapy, paralegal studies, physical therapy, radiological technology, respiratory therapy, science, secretarial studies/office management.
LIBRARY Penn Valley Community College Library with 74,287 books, 2,255 microform titles, 194 periodicals, 32 CD-ROMs, 1,430 records, tapes, and CDs. Acquisition spending 1994–95: $77,433.
COMPUTERS ON CAMPUS 311 computers for student use in computer center, computer labs, learning resource center, labs, classrooms, library provide access to main academic computer, Internet. Staffed computer lab on campus provides training in use of computers, software. Academic computing expenditure 1994–95: $474,850.
COLLEGE LIFE Drama-theater group, choral group, student-run newspaper, radio station. ***Social organizations:*** 1 national fraternity. ***Most popular organizations:*** Black Student Association, Los Americanos, Phi Theta Kappa, Fashion Club. ***Major annual events:*** Black History Month, Spring Fling, Homecoming. ***Student services:*** personal-psychological counseling. ***Campus security:*** 24-hour patrols.
HOUSING College housing not available.
ATHLETICS Member NJCAA. ***Intercollegiate:*** basketball M(s), golf M(s). ***Contact:*** Mr. Fred Pohlman, Athletic Director, 816-759-4323.
CAREER PLANNING ***Placement office:*** 6 full-time staff; $455,739 operating expenditure 1994–95. ***Director:*** Mr. Tom Dewey, Counseling Department Chair, 816-759-4130. ***Services:*** job fairs, resume preparation, resume referral, career counseling, careers library, job bank, job interviews.
AFTER GRADUATION 61% of students completing a degree program in 1994–95 went directly on to further study.
EXPENSES FOR 1996–97 Area resident tuition: $1350 full-time, $45 per credit hour part-time. State resident tuition: $2250 full-time, $75 per credit hour part-time. Nonresident tuition: $3210 full-time, $107 per credit hour part-time.
FINANCIAL AID ***College-administered undergrad aid 1995–96:*** 332 need-based scholarships (averaging $533), 412 non-need scholarships (averaging $357), short-term loans (averaging $50), low-interest long-term loans from external sources (averaging $2006), 51 Federal Work-Study (averaging $1542), 123 part-time jobs. ***Required forms:*** institutional, FAFSA; required for some: state; accepted: CSS Financial Aid PROFILE. ***Priority deadline:*** 5/31. ***Payment plan:*** installment. ***Waivers:*** full or partial for employees or children of employees and senior citizens. ***Notification:*** continuous.
APPLYING Open admission except for allied health programs. ***Options:*** Common Application, early entrance, midyear entrance. ***Required:*** school transcript, TOEFL for international students, ACT ASSET. Test scores used for counseling/placement. ***Application deadline:*** rolling.
APPLYING/TRANSFER ***Recommended:*** high school transcript, college transcript. ***Required for some:*** standardized test scores. ***Entrance:*** noncompetitive. ***Application deadline:*** rolling. ***Contact:*** Mrs. Carroll O'Neal, Registrar, 816-759-4101.
CONTACT Mrs. Carroll O'Neal, Registrar, Penn Valley Community College, 3201 Southwest Trafficway, Kansas City, MO 64111, 816-759-4101.

PHILLIPS JUNIOR COLLEGE OF SPRINGFIELD
Springfield, Missouri

UG Enrollment: 360 **Tuition: $9995/deg prog**
Application Deadline: rolling **Room & Board: N/Avail**

GENERAL Proprietary, 2-year, coed. Part of Phillips Colleges, Inc. Awards terminal associate degrees. Founded 1976. ***Setting:*** 2-acre urban campus. ***Total enrollment:*** 360. ***Faculty:*** 15 (7 full-time, 100% with terminal degrees, 8 part-time); student-faculty ratio is 20:1.
ENROLLMENT PROFILE 360 students: 86% women, 14% men, 5% part-time, 100% state residents, 25% transferred in, 0% international, 60% 25 or older, 2% Native American, 2% Hispanic, 4% African American, 1% Asian American. ***Areas of study chosen:*** 60% business management and administrative services, 25% health professions and related sciences, 15% computer and information sciences. ***Most popular recent majors:*** business administration/commerce/management, paralegal studies, medical assistant technologies.
FIRST-YEAR CLASS 101 total; 207 applied, 96% were accepted, 51% of whom enrolled.
ACADEMIC PROGRAM Core, honor code. Calendar: quarters. 93 courses offered in 1995–96. Academic remediation for entering students, advanced placement, summer session for credit, part-time degree program (daytime, evenings, summer), internships.
GENERAL DEGREE REQUIREMENTS 96 credits; math/science requirements vary according to program; internship (some majors).
MAJORS Accounting, business administration/commerce/management, data processing, hospitality services, medical assistant technologies, paralegal studies, secretarial studies/office management.
LIBRARY Phillip Junior College Library with 2,500 books, 32 periodicals, 368 records, tapes, and CDs.
COMPUTERS ON CAMPUS 75 computers for student use in computer center, computer labs, classrooms, library. Staffed computer lab on campus provides training in use of computers, software.
COLLEGE LIFE Orientation program (2 days, no cost). ***Social organizations:*** 9 open to all; 1 local fraternity. ***Campus security:*** late-night transport-escort service.
HOUSING College housing not available.
CAREER PLANNING ***Placement office:*** 1 full-time, 1 part-time staff. ***Director:*** Ms. Carol Beckham, Director of Career Planning and Placement, 417-864-7220. ***Services:*** job fairs, resume preparation, resume referral, career counseling, job bank, job interviews.
EXPENSES FOR 1995–96 ***Application fee:*** $25. Tuition: $9995 per degree program. One-time mandatory fee: $100. Tuition guaranteed not to increase for student's term of enrollment.
FINANCIAL AID ***College-administered undergrad aid 1995–96:*** need-based scholarships, 3 non-need scholarships (averaging $500), low-interest long-term loans from external sources (averaging $600), Federal Work-Study, part-time jobs. ***Required forms:*** institutional, FAFSA; accepted: CSS Financial Aid PROFILE. ***Application deadline:*** continuous to 10/7. ***Payment plan:*** installment. ***Waivers:*** full or partial for employees or children of employees.
APPLYING Open admission. ***Options:*** deferred entrance, midyear entrance. ***Required:*** school transcript, interview, CPAt. Test scores used for admission and counseling/placement. ***Application deadline:*** rolling.
APPLYING/TRANSFER ***Required:*** college transcript. ***Entrance:*** noncompetitive. ***Application deadline:*** rolling. ***Contact:*** Ms. Kristee Buff, Director of Admissions, 417-864-7220.
CONTACT Ms. Kristee Buff, Director of Admissions, Phillips Junior College of Springfield, 1010 West Sunshine, Springfield, MO 65807-2488, 417-864-7220 or toll-free 800-864-5697 (in-state), 800-475-2669 (out-of-state). ***Fax:*** 417-865-5697.

RANKEN TECHNICAL COLLEGE
St. Louis, Missouri

UG Enrollment: 700 **Tuition & Fees: $3700**
Application Deadline: rolling **Room & Board: N/Avail**

GENERAL Independent, 2-year, coed. Awards terminal associate degrees. Founded 1907. ***Setting:*** 7-acre urban campus. ***Endowment:*** $24.6 million. ***Educational spending 1994–95:*** $2598 per undergrad. ***Total enrollment:*** 700. ***Faculty:*** 90 (58 full-time, 32 part-time).
ENROLLMENT PROFILE 700 students: 5% women, 0% part-time, 100% state residents, 0% international, 25% 25 or older, 0% Native American, 0% Hispanic, 17% African American, 1% Asian American. ***Most popular recent majors:*** automotive technologies, heating/refrigeration/air conditioning.
FIRST-YEAR CLASS 348 total.
ACADEMIC PROGRAM Honor code. Calendar: trimesters. Academic remediation for entering students, services for LD students, part-time degree program (evenings, weekends), adult/continuing education programs. Off-campus study.
GENERAL DEGREE REQUIREMENTS 92 hours; computer course.
MAJORS Automotive technologies, carpentry, communication equipment technology, computer technologies, electrical and electronics technologies, heating/refrigeration/air conditioning, instrumentation technology, machine and tool technologies, plumbing.
LIBRARY Learning Center with 8,707 books, 182 periodicals, 1 on-line bibliographic service, 1 CD-ROM, 225 records, tapes, and CDs. Acquisition spending 1994–95: $45,369.
COMPUTERS ON CAMPUS 53 computers for student use in computer center, computer labs, classrooms, library, student rooms. Staffed computer lab on campus provides training in use of computers, software. Academic computing expenditure 1994–95: $150,000.
COLLEGE LIFE Orientation program (2 days, no cost). Student-run newspaper. 50% vote in student government elections. ***Social organizations:*** 4 open to all. ***Most popular organizations:*** Student Government, Career Achievers, Phi Theta Kappa, Instrumentation Society of America. ***Major annual events:*** Dress Down Days, Wacky Olympics, Canned Food and Toy Drive. ***Student services:*** personal-psychological counseling. ***Campus security:*** 24-hour emergency response devices and patrols.
HOUSING College housing not available.
CAREER PLANNING ***Placement office:*** 1 full-time staff; $50,000 operating expenditure 1994–95. ***Director:*** Ms. Linda Dempsey, Placement Director, 314-371-0236. ***Services:*** job fairs, resume preparation, resume referral, career counseling, job bank.
AFTER GRADUATION 98% of class of 1994 had job offers within 6 months.
EXPENSES FOR 1996–97 Tuition: $3700 full-time, $515 per trimester part-time.
FINANCIAL AID ***College-administered undergrad aid 1995–96:*** 623 need-based scholarships (average $2625), short-term loans (average $500), Federal Work-Study. ***Required forms:*** institutional, FAFSA. ***Application deadline:*** continuous. ***Payment plan:*** installment. ***Waivers:*** full or partial for employees or children of employees. ***Average indebtedness of graduates:*** $6165.
APPLYING ***Options:*** Common Application, midyear entrance. ***Required:*** school transcript, campus interview. ***Recommended:*** SAT I, SAT II Subject Tests. Test scores used for admission. ***Application deadline:*** rolling.
APPLYING/TRANSFER ***Contact:*** Mr. Dave Kempfer, Registrar, 314-371-0233.
CONTACT Ms. Debra McPeak, Dean of Students, Ranken Technical College, 4431 Finney Avenue, St. Louis, MO 63113, 314-371-0233 Ext. 1080. College video available.

Peterson's Guide to Two-Year Colleges 1997

415

SAINT CHARLES COUNTY COMMUNITY COLLEGE
St. Peters, Missouri

UG Enrollment: 4,590 **Tuition & Fees (Area Res): $1536**
Application Deadline: rolling **Room & Board: N/Avail**

GENERAL State-supported, 2-year, coed. Part of Missouri Coordinating Board for Higher Education. Awards certificates, transfer associate, terminal associate degrees. Founded 1986. ***Setting:*** 135-acre small-town campus with easy access to St. Louis. ***Total enrollment:*** 4,590. ***Faculty:*** 206 (60 full-time, 17% with terminal degrees, 146 part-time); student-faculty ratio is 22:1.
ENROLLMENT PROFILE 4,590 students from 2 states and territories, 2 other countries. 65% women, 35% men, 72% part-time, 98% state residents, 8% transferred in, 22% have need-based financial aid, 4% have non-need-based financial aid, 1% international, 46% 25 or older, 1% Native American, 1% Hispanic, 2% African American, 1% Asian American. ***Areas of study chosen:*** 66% liberal arts/general studies, 14% business management and administrative services, 5% education, 5% health professions and related sciences, 3% computer and information sciences, 3% social sciences, 2% engineering and applied sciences, 1% biological and life sciences, 1% communications and journalism, 1% English language/literature/letters, 1% fine arts, 1% foreign language and literature, 1% mathematics, 1% performing arts, 1% physical sciences, 1% prelaw, 1% psychology, 1% vocational and home economics. ***Most popular recent majors:*** liberal arts/general studies, nursing, business administration/commerce/management.
FIRST-YEAR CLASS 941 total; 966 applied, 100% were accepted, 97% of whom enrolled. 2% from top 10% of their high school class, 14% from top quarter, 47% from top half.
ACADEMIC PROGRAM Core, general education curriculum, honor code. Calendar: semesters. 562 courses offered in 1995–96; average class size 18 in required courses. Academic remediation for entering students, English as a second language program offered during academic year and summer, services for LD students, honors program, summer session for credit, part-time degree program (daytime, evenings, summer), adult/continuing education programs.
GENERAL DEGREE REQUIREMENTS 64 semester hours; computer course for all majors except nursing.
MAJORS Accounting, business administration/commerce/management, child care/child and family studies, commercial art, computer science, criminal justice, drafting and design, electrical and electronics technologies, electronics engineering technology, (pre)engineering sequence, finance/banking, human services, law enforcement/police sciences, liberal arts/general studies, marketing/retailing/merchandising, medical records services, nursing, occupational therapy, robotics, secretarial studies/office management, word processing.
LIBRARY Instructional Resources Center with 35,493 books, 104 microform titles, 438 periodicals, 2 on-line bibliographic services, 10 CD-ROMs, 1,389 records, tapes, and CDs. Acquisition spending 1994–95: $144,365.
COMPUTERS ON CAMPUS 205 computers for student use in computer center, computer labs, learning resource center, classrooms provide access to e-mail. Staffed computer lab on campus provides training in use of computers, software.
COLLEGE LIFE ***Social organizations:*** 11 open to all. ***Most popular organizations:*** Phi Theta Kappa, Student Nurse Association, Environmental Club, Phi Beta Lambda. ***Major annual events:*** Spring Fling, Mid Rivers Kitchens Barbecues, Drawings. ***Student services:*** personal-psychological counseling. ***Campus security:*** 24-hour emergency response devices and patrols, late-night transport-escort service.
HOUSING College housing not available.
ATHLETICS ***Intercollegiate:*** baseball M, softball W. ***Intramural:*** basketball, football, soccer, softball, volleyball. ***Contact:*** Dr. Ron Shade, Vice President for Student Services, 314-922-8273.
CAREER PLANNING ***Placement office:*** 2 full-time, 1 part-time staff; $27,288 operating expenditure 1994–95. ***Director:*** Ms. Lisa Freise, Career Center Coordinator, 314-922-8244. ***Services:*** job fairs, resume preparation, resume referral, career counseling, careers library, job bank, job interviews. 102 organizations recruited on campus 1994–95.
AFTER GRADUATION 81% of class of 1994 had job offers within 6 months. 52% of students completing a degree program went directly on to further study.
EXPENSES FOR 1996–97 Area resident tuition: $1376 full-time, $43 per semester hour part-time. State resident tuition: $2016 full-time, $63 per semester hour part-time. Nonresident tuition: $3104 full-time, $97 per semester hour part-time. Part-time mandatory fees: $5 per semester hour. Full-time mandatory fees: $160.
FINANCIAL AID ***College-administered undergrad aid 1995–96:*** need-based scholarships, 35 non-need scholarships (average $1015), low-interest long-term loans from external sources (average $1856), 35 Federal Work-Study (averaging $1492). ***Required forms:*** institutional; accepted: CSS Financial Aid PROFILE, state, FAFSA. ***Priority deadline:*** 4/30. ***Waivers:*** full or partial for employees or children of employees and senior citizens. ***Average indebtedness of graduates:*** $2000.
APPLYING Open admission. ***Options:*** early entrance, deferred entrance. ***Required:*** ACT, TOEFL for international students. ***Required for some:*** school transcript. Test scores used for counseling/placement. ***Application deadline:*** rolling. ***Notification:*** continuous.
APPLYING/TRANSFER ***Required for some:*** high school transcript, college transcript, minimum 2.0 college GPA, minimum 2.0 high school GPA. ***Application deadline:*** rolling. ***Notification:*** continuous. ***Contact:*** Ms. Kathy Brockgreitens, Registrar, 314-922-8229.
CONTACT Mr. James B. Benedict, Dean of Students, Saint Charles County Community College, 4601 Mid Rivers Mall Drive, St. Peters, MO 63376-0975, 314-922-8000 Ext. 4271. ***Fax:*** 314-922-8236. ***E-mail:*** regist@chuck.stchas.edu.

ST. LOUIS COMMUNITY COLLEGE AT FLORISSANT VALLEY
St. Louis, Missouri

UG Enrollment: 8,160 **Tuition & Fees (Area Res): $1344**
Application Deadline: 8/19 **Room & Board: N/Avail**

GENERAL District-supported, 2-year, coed. Part of St. Louis Community College System. Awards certificates, transfer associate, terminal associate degrees. Founded 1963. ***Setting:*** 108-acre suburban campus. ***Total enrollment:*** 8,160. ***Faculty:*** 390 (140 full-time, 250 part-time); student-faculty ratio is 21:1.
ENROLLMENT PROFILE 8,160 students: 63% women, 37% men, 70% part-time, 97% state residents, 6% transferred in, 1% international, 48% 25 or older, 1% Native American, 1% Hispanic, 31% African American, 1% Asian American. ***Areas of study chosen:*** 39% interdisciplinary studies, 12% business management and administrative services, 8% communications and journalism, 7% engineering and applied sciences, 4% computer and information sciences, 4% fine arts, 2% education, 2% health professions and related sciences, 1% biological and life sciences, 1% mathematics.
FIRST-YEAR CLASS 1,475 total; 2,102 applied, 100% were accepted, 70% of whom enrolled.
ACADEMIC PROGRAM Core. Calendar: semesters. Academic remediation for entering students, English as a second language program offered during academic year, services for LD students, advanced placement, honors program, summer session for credit, part-time degree program (daytime, evenings, summer), adult/continuing education programs, co-op programs. Study abroad in England. ROTC: Army (c).
GENERAL DEGREE REQUIREMENT 64 credit hours.
MAJORS Accounting, art/fine arts, broadcasting, business administration/commerce/management, chemical engineering technology, child care/child and family studies, civil engineering technology, commercial art, communication, computer information systems, computer programming, computer science, computer technologies, construction technologies, corrections, criminal justice, data processing, deaf interpreter training, dietetics, electrical engineering technology, electronics engineering technology, elementary education, emergency medical technology, engineering (general), engineering sciences, (pre)engineering sequence, engineering technology, fashion merchandising, film and video production, finance/banking, fire science, food sciences, food services management, food services technology, human services, journalism, law enforcement/police sciences, legal studies, liberal arts/general studies, mathematics, mechanical engineering technology, music, nursing, photography, radio and television studies, real estate, secretarial studies/office management, telecommunications, theater arts/drama.
LIBRARY 90,021 books, 274 microform titles, 655 periodicals, 8 CD-ROMs, 3,704 records, tapes, and CDs.
COMPUTERS ON CAMPUS Computer purchase plan available. 400 computers for student use in computer center, computer labs, engineering-technical learning center.
COLLEGE LIFE Drama-theater group, student-run newspaper, radio station. 3% vote in student government elections. ***Social organizations:*** 20 open to all; 2 national fraternities, 1 national sorority; 20% of eligible men and 15% of eligible women are members. ***Most popular organizations:*** Phi Theta Kappa, Student Nurses Association, Women in New Goals, Florissant Valley Association of the Deaf, Student Government Association. ***Major annual events:*** Awareness Days Programs, School Spirit Days, Children's Christmas Party. ***Student services:*** health clinic, personal-psychological counseling. ***Campus security:*** 24-hour emergency response devices and patrols, late-night transport-escort service.
HOUSING College housing not available.
ATHLETICS Member NAIA, NJCAA. ***Intercollegiate:*** baseball M, basketball M(s)/W(s), cross-country running M(s)/W(s), soccer M(s)/W(s), softball W(s), track and field M(s)/W(s), volleyball W(s). ***Intramural:*** volleyball. ***Contact:*** Ms. Lea Plarski, Athletic Director, 314-595-4275.
CAREER PLANNING ***Placement office:*** 6 full-time staff. ***Director:*** Mr. Michael George, Manager, Career and Employment Services, 314-595-4218. ***Services:*** resume preparation, resume referral, career counseling, careers library, job bank, job interviews.
AFTER GRADUATION 26% of students completing a degree program in 1994–95 went directly on to further study.
EXPENSES FOR 1996–97 Area resident tuition: $1344 full-time, $42 per credit hour part-time. State resident tuition: $1696 full-time, $53 per credit hour part-time. Nonresident tuition: $2144 full-time, $67 per credit hour part-time.
FINANCIAL AID ***College-administered undergrad aid 1995–96:*** need-based scholarships, 45 non-need scholarships (averaging $640), short-term loans, low-interest long-term loans from external sources, Federal Work-Study, part-time jobs. ***Required forms:*** FAFSA. ***Priority deadline:*** 4/30. ***Waivers:*** full or partial for employees or children of employees and senior citizens.
APPLYING Open admission. ***Option:*** early entrance. ***Required:*** school transcript, TOEFL for international students. ***Recommended:*** SAT I or ACT. Test scores used for counseling/placement. ***Application deadline:*** 8/19. ***Notification:*** continuous.
APPLYING/TRANSFER ***Required:*** college transcript. ***Application deadline:*** 8/19. ***Notification:*** continuous. ***Contact:*** Ms. Bertha Brown, Manager for Advising, 314-595-4236.
CONTACT Mr. Mitchell Egeston, Manager of Admissions and Registration, St. Louis Community College at Florissant Valley, St. Louis, MO 63135-1499, 314-595-4250. College video available.

ST. LOUIS COMMUNITY COLLEGE AT FOREST PARK
St. Louis, Missouri

UG Enrollment: 8,197 **Tuition & Fees (Area Res): $1260**
Application Deadline: 8/22 **Room & Board: N/Avail**

GENERAL District-supported, 2-year, coed. Part of St. Louis Community College System. Awards transfer associate, terminal associate degrees. Founded 1962. ***Setting:*** 34-acre suburban campus. ***Total enrollment:*** 8,197. ***Faculty:*** 366 (131 full-time, 235 part-time).
ENROLLMENT PROFILE 8,197 students from 13 states and territories, 29 other countries. 61% women, 76% part-time, 95% state residents, 13% transferred in, 1% international, 62% 25 or older, 0% Native American, 0% Hispanic, 32% African American, 5% Asian American. ***Areas of study chosen:*** 27% business management and administrative services, 24% physical sciences, 20% engineering and applied sciences, 10% liberal arts/general studies, 8% computer and information sciences, 5% biological and life sciences, 5% mathematics, 1% fine arts.
FIRST-YEAR CLASS 1,722 applied, 100% were accepted.
ACADEMIC PROGRAM Core, honor code. Calendar: semesters. Academic remediation for entering students, English as a second language program offered during academic year, services for LD students, honors program, summer session for credit, part-time degree program (daytime, evenings, weekends, summer), adult/continuing education programs. Study-abroad program.
GENERAL DEGREE REQUIREMENTS 64 credit hours; math/science requirements vary according to program; computer course for business-related majors.

MAJORS Accounting, art/fine arts, automotive technologies, biology/biological sciences, biomedical technologies, black/African-American studies, business administration/commerce/management, child care/child and family studies, child psychology/child development, commercial art, communication, computer science, criminal justice, culinary arts, data processing, dental services, electrical engineering technology, electronics engineering technology, engineering and applied sciences, engineering sciences, (pre)engineering sequence, engineering technology, finance/banking, fire science, funeral service, hotel and restaurant management, human services, industrial engineering technology, international business, liberal arts/general studies, manufacturing technology, mathematics, mechanical engineering technology, medical laboratory technology, music, nursing, operating room technology, photography, plumbing, radiological technology, respiratory therapy, robotics, secretarial studies/office management, tourism and travel.
LIBRARY St. Louis Community College Library with 71,922 books, 452 microform titles, 503 periodicals, 8,672 records, tapes, and CDs.
COMPUTERS ON CAMPUS 302 computers for student use in computer center, library. Staffed computer lab on campus.
COLLEGE LIFE Drama-theater group, student-run newspaper. 7% vote in student government elections. ***Student services:*** personal-psychological counseling. ***Campus security:*** 24-hour patrols.
HOUSING College housing not available.
ATHLETICS Member NJCAA. ***Intercollegiate:*** basketball M/W, golf M, soccer M, volleyball W, wrestling M. ***Contact:*** Mr. Russ Dippold, Manager of Athletics, 314-644-9724.
CAREER PLANNING ***Service:*** career counseling.
EXPENSES FOR 1996–97 Area resident tuition: $1260 full-time, $42 per credit hour part-time. State resident tuition: $1590 full-time, $53 per credit hour part-time. Nonresident tuition: $2010 full-time, $67 per credit hour part-time.
FINANCIAL AID ***College-administered undergrad aid 1995–96:*** non-need scholarships (average $718), Federal Work-Study, part-time jobs. ***Required forms:*** FAFSA; accepted: CSS Financial Aid PROFILE. ***Application deadline:*** continuous to 4/1.
APPLYING Open admission except for allied medical programs. ***Option:*** early entrance. ***Required:*** TOEFL for international students. Test scores used for counseling/placement. ***Application deadline:*** 8/22. ***Notification:*** continuous. Preference given to district residents.
APPLYING/TRANSFER ***Entrance:*** minimally difficult. ***Application deadline:*** 2/28. ***Notification:*** continuous.
CONTACT Mr. Bart S. Devoti, Director of Admissions and Records, St. Louis Community College at Forest Park, St. Louis, MO 63110-1316, 314-644-9131.

ST. LOUIS COMMUNITY COLLEGE AT MERAMEC
Kirkwood, Missouri

UG Enrollment: 13,211	**Tuition & Fees (Area Res): $1320**
Application Deadline: rolling	**Room & Board: N/Avail**

GENERAL District-supported, 2-year, coed. Part of St. Louis Community College System. Awards transfer associate, terminal associate degrees. Founded 1963. ***Setting:*** 80-acre suburban campus with easy access to St. Louis. ***Educational spending 1994–95:*** $1304 per undergrad. ***Total enrollment:*** 13,211. ***Faculty:*** 570 (185 full-time, 14% with terminal degrees, 385 part-time).
ENROLLMENT PROFILE 13,211 students from 10 states and territories, 18 other countries. 59% women, 41% men, 65% part-time, 98% state residents, 7% transferred in, 1% international, 42% 25 or older, 1% Native American, 1% Hispanic, 3% African American, 2% Asian American. ***Areas of study chosen:*** 60% liberal arts/general studies, 14% business management and administrative services, 4% communications and journalism, 3% computer and information sciences, 3% education, 3% health professions and related sciences, 2% architecture, 2% engineering and applied sciences, 2% fine arts, 2% social sciences, 1% physical sciences, 1% vocational and home economics.
FIRST-YEAR CLASS 2,460 total. Of the students who applied, 100% were accepted.
ACADEMIC PROGRAM Core, honor code. Calendar: semesters. 605 courses offered in 1995–96. Academic remediation for entering students, English as a second language program offered during academic year, services for LD students, advanced placement, Freshman Honors College, tutorials, honors program, summer session for credit, part-time degree program (daytime, evenings, weekends, summer), adult/continuing education programs, internships. Off-campus study at The New England Banking Institute. Study abroad in England. ROTC: Army (c), Air Force (c).
GENERAL DEGREE REQUIREMENT 64 credit hours.
MAJORS Accounting, advertising, architectural technologies, art/fine arts, broadcasting, business administration/commerce/management, child care/child and family studies, computer information systems, computer programming, computer science, corrections, court reporting, creative writing, criminal justice, education, electrical engineering technology, elementary education, emergency medical technology, engineering sciences, film and video production, finance/banking, graphic arts, horticulture, human services, interior design, journalism, law enforcement/police sciences, legal secretarial studies, liberal arts/general studies, literature, materials sciences, mathematics, modern languages, music, nursing, occupational therapy, paralegal studies, photography, physical therapy, public relations, real estate, science, secretarial studies/office management, speech/rhetoric/public address/debate, theater arts/drama.
LIBRARY Meramec Library with 58,911 books, 500 periodicals, 2 on-line bibliographic services, 14 CD-ROMs, 5,480 records, tapes, and CDs. Acquisition spending 1994–95: $177,209.
COMPUTERS ON CAMPUS 420 computers for student use in computer center, computer labs, academic departments, classrooms, library, student center provide access to on-line services, Internet. Staffed computer lab on campus provides training in use of computers, software. Academic computing expenditure 1994–95: $186,380.
COLLEGE LIFE Drama-theater group, choral group, student-run newspaper. ***Social organizations:*** 50 open to all. ***Most popular organizations:*** Phi Theta Kappa, Scuba Club, International Club, Intervarsity Christian Fellowship, Horticulture Club. ***Major annual events:*** Las Vegas Night, Friday Night Movies, Barbecues. ***Student services:*** health clinic, personal-psychological counseling. ***Campus security:*** 24-hour emergency response devices and patrols.
HOUSING College housing not available.
ATHLETICS Member NJCAA. ***Intercollegiate:*** baseball M(s), basketball M(s), ice hockey M(c), soccer M(s)/W(s), softball W(s), volleyball W(s), wrestling M(s). ***Intramural:*** basketball, ice hockey, soccer, volleyball. ***Contact:*** Mr. Robert Bottger, Athletic Director, 314-984-7786.
CAREER PLANNING ***Placement office:*** 3 full-time, 1 part-time staff; $270,073 operating expenditure 1994–95. ***Director:*** Mr. Frank Gaal, Counselor/Coordinator, 314-984-7565. ***Services:*** job fairs, resume preparation, resume referral, career counseling, careers library, job bank, job interviews.
AFTER GRADUATION 43% of students completing a degree program in 1994–95 went directly on to further study.
EXPENSES FOR 1996–97 Area resident tuition: $1260 full-time, $42 per credit hour part-time. State resident tuition: $1590 full-time, $53 per credit hour part-time. Nonresident tuition: $2010 full-time, $67 per credit hour part-time. Part-time mandatory fees: $2 per credit hour. Full-time mandatory fees: $60.
FINANCIAL AID ***College-administered undergrad aid 1995–96:*** 41 need-based scholarships (average $912), 132 non-need scholarships (average $960), short-term loans (average $504), low-interest long-term loans from external sources (average $2600), Federal Work-Study, 168 part-time jobs. ***Required forms:*** institutional, FAFSA. ***Priority deadline:*** 4/30. ***Waivers:*** full or partial for employees or children of employees and senior citizens.
APPLYING Open admission except for nursing, paramedic, occupational therapy, physical therapy programs. ***Options:*** early entrance, deferred entrance, midyear entrance. ***Required:*** TOEFL for international students. ***Required for some:*** school transcript, interview, Michigan Test of English Language Proficiency. Test scores used for counseling/placement. ***Application deadline:*** rolling. ***Notification:*** continuous.
APPLYING/TRANSFER ***Required for some:*** standardized test scores, high school transcript, college transcript. ***Entrance:*** noncompetitive. ***Application deadline:*** rolling. ***Notification:*** continuous.
CONTACT Ms. Cheryl McCrary, Coordinator, Admissions, St. Louis Community College at Meramec, Kirkwood, MO 63122-5720, 314-984-7608. ***Fax:*** 314-984-7117. College video available.

SANFORD-BROWN COLLEGE
Des Peres, Missouri

UG Enrollment: 410	**Tuition & Fees: $15,100**
Application Deadline: N/R	**Room & Board: N/Avail**

GENERAL Proprietary, 2-year, coed. Awards certificates, diplomas, terminal associate degrees. Founded 1868. ***Setting:*** 6-acre suburban campus with easy access to St. Louis. ***Total enrollment:*** 410. ***Faculty:*** 35 (15 full-time, 20 part-time).
ENROLLMENT PROFILE 410 students from 2 states and territories. 75% women, 25% men, 0% part-time, 95% state residents, 25% transferred in, 85% have need-based financial aid, 15% have non-need-based financial aid, 2% international, 75% 25 or older, 2% Native American, 2% Hispanic, 20% African American, 2% Asian American. ***Areas of study chosen:*** 50% business management and administrative services, 50% health professions and related sciences.
FIRST-YEAR CLASS 325 total. Of the students who applied, 75% were accepted, 15% of whom enrolled.
ACADEMIC PROGRAM Core, business-health care curriculum. Calendar: quarters. 50 courses offered in 1995–96. Services for LD students, tutorials, adult/continuing education programs, internships.
GENERAL DEGREE REQUIREMENTS 91 credits; 1 course each in math and science; computer course.
MAJORS Accounting, computer science, nursing, occupational therapy, paralegal studies, physical therapy, secretarial studies/office management, tourism and travel.
COMPUTERS ON CAMPUS 40 computers for student use in computer center, learning resource center provide access to on-line services. Staffed computer lab on campus provides training in use of computers, software.
COLLEGE LIFE 20% vote in student government elections. ***Social organizations:*** 4 open to all. ***Most popular organizations:*** Paralegal Club, Peer Advisors, Student Council, Accounting Club. ***Major annual events:*** Christmas Party, Nursing Graduation Party, Summer Party. ***Student services:*** personal-psychological counseling. ***Campus security:*** late-night transport-escort service.
HOUSING College housing not available.
ATHLETICS ***Intercollegiate:*** basketball M. ***Contact:*** Mr. John Campbell, Athletic Director, 314-822-7100.
CAREER PLANNING ***Placement office:*** 1 full-time staff. ***Director:*** Ms. Sheryl Schulte, Placement Coordinator, 314-822-7100. ***Services:*** job fairs, resume preparation, resume referral, career counseling, careers library, job bank, job interviews. Students must register freshman year.
EXPENSES FOR 1996–97 Tuition: $15,000 full-time. Full-time mandatory fees: $100.
FINANCIAL AID ***College-administered undergrad aid 1995–96:*** 10 need-based scholarships, non-need scholarships, 10 part-time jobs. ***Required forms:*** state, institutional, FAFSA. ***Application deadline:*** continuous. ***Payment plans:*** tuition prepayment, installment, deferred pay. ***Waivers:*** full or partial for employees or children of employees.
APPLYING Open admission. ***Options:*** Common Application, deferred entrance, midyear entrance. ***Required:*** school transcript, Thurston Mental Alertness Test. Test scores used for admission.
CONTACT Ms. Judy Atkinson, Director of Admissions, Sanford-Brown College, Des Peres, MO 63131-4499, 314-822-7100.

SANFORD-BROWN COLLEGE
Hazelwood, Missouri

UG Enrollment: 348	**Tuition & Fees: $7980**
Application Deadline: rolling	**Room & Board: N/Avail**

GENERAL Proprietary, 2-year, coed. Awards diplomas, terminal associate degrees. Founded 1868. ***Setting:*** 1-acre campus with easy access to St. Louis. ***Total enrollment:*** 348. ***Faculty:*** 26 (8 full-time, 18 part-time); student-faculty ratio is 9:1.
ENROLLMENT PROFILE 348 students: 0% part-time, 0% state residents, 0% transferred in, 65% African American. ***Areas of study chosen:*** 51% business management and administrative services, 49% health professions and related sciences.
FIRST-YEAR CLASS 125 total; 175 applied, 71% were accepted, 100% of whom enrolled.

Missouri

Sanford-Brown College (continued)
ACADEMIC PROGRAM Core, interdisciplinary curriculum, honor code. Calendar: quarters. Average class size 12 in required courses. Academic remediation for entering students, services for LD students, part-time degree program (daytime, evenings), adult/continuing education programs, internships.
GENERAL DEGREE REQUIREMENTS 91 credits; internship (some majors).
MAJORS Accounting, business administration/commerce/management, computer programming, health education, paralegal studies, physical therapy, secretarial studies/office management.
COMPUTERS ON CAMPUS 32 computers for student use in computer labs, learning resource center. Staffed computer lab on campus provides training in use of computers, software.
COLLEGE LIFE 65% vote in student government elections. *Social organizations:* 4 open to all. *Most popular organizations:* Paralegal Club, Peer Advisors, Student Council, Accounting Club. *Major annual events:* Christmas Party, Nursing Graduation Party, Summer Party. *Student services:* personal-psychological counseling. *Campus security:* 24-hour emergency response devices and patrols.
ATHLETICS *Intercollegiate:* basketball M. *Contact:* Mr. John Campbell, Athletic Director, 314-731-1101.
CAREER PLANNING *Placement office:* 1 full-time staff. *Director:* Ms. Patricia Pou, Career Development Coordinator, 314-731-1101. *Services:* job fairs, resume preparation, resume referral, career counseling, job bank, job interviews. Students must register freshman year. 50 organizations recruited on campus 1994–95.
AFTER GRADUATION 83% of class of 1994 had job offers within 6 months.
EXPENSES FOR 1996–97 Tuition: $7680 (minimum) full-time. Part-time tuition per course ranges from $100 to $200. Full-time tuition ranges up to $16,500. Full-time mandatory fees range from $300 to $1500.
FINANCIAL AID *Payment plans:* installment, deferred payment. *Waivers:* full or partial for employees or children of employees.
APPLYING *Options:* Common Application, deferred entrance, midyear entrance. *Required:* school transcript, interview. Test scores used for admission. *Application deadline:* rolling.
APPLYING/TRANSFER *Required:* standardized test scores, high school transcript, interview, college transcript. *Contact:* Ms. Brenda Lee, Dean of Instruction, 314-731-1101.
CONTACT Mr. David Wood, Acting Chief Admissions Officer, Sanford-Brown College, Hazelwood, MO 63042, 314-731-1101.

SANFORD-BROWN COLLEGE
North Kansas City, Missouri

UG Enrollment: 277	Tuition: $10,000/deg prog
Application Deadline: rolling	Room & Board: N/Avail

GENERAL Proprietary, 2-year, coed. Awards diplomas, terminal associate degrees. Founded 1992. *Setting:* suburban campus. *Total enrollment:* 277. *Faculty:* 36.
ENROLLMENT PROFILE 277 students from 2 states and territories. 93% women, 7% men, 10% state residents, 90% transferred in. *Areas of study chosen:* 100% health professions and related sciences.
FIRST-YEAR CLASS Of the students who applied, 33% were accepted.
ACADEMIC PROGRAM Calendar: quarters. Services for LD students, tutorials, internships.
GENERAL DEGREE REQUIREMENTS 92 quarter hours; math/science requirements vary according to program; internship.
MAJORS Medical assistant technologies, physical therapy.
COMPUTERS ON CAMPUS 18 computers for student use in computer labs, learning resource center. Staffed computer lab on campus.
COLLEGE LIFE *Student services:* personal-psychological counseling. *Campus security:* 24-hour patrols.
CAREER PLANNING *Placement office:* 1 full-time staff. *Services:* job fairs, resume preparation, resume referral, career counseling, job bank, job interviews. Students must register freshman year.
EXPENSES FOR 1995–96 Tuition per degree program ranges from $10,000 to $16,000. Full-time mandatory fees: $300.
FINANCIAL AID *College-administered undergrad aid 1995–96:* 27 need-based scholarships (average $100), part-time jobs. *Required forms:* institutional, FAFSA; accepted: CSS Financial Aid PROFILE. *Application deadline:* continuous.
APPLYING *Options:* Common Application, deferred entrance, midyear entrance. Test scores used for admission. *Application deadline:* rolling. *Notification:* continuous.
APPLYING/TRANSFER *Required for some:* standardized test scores.
CONTACT Ms. Anita Barrow-Morrell, Director of Admissions, Sanford-Brown College, North Kansas City, MO 64117, 816-472-7400 or toll-free 800-456-7222.

SANFORD-BROWN COLLEGE
St. Charles, Missouri

Enrollment: N/R	Tuition & Fees: $10,700
Application Deadline: rolling	Room & Board: N/R

GENERAL Proprietary, 2-year, coed. Awards diplomas, transfer associate, terminal associate degrees. Founded 1868. *Setting:* 2-acre suburban campus with easy access to St. Louis. *Educational spending 1994–95:* $2500 per undergrad. *Faculty:* 25 (18 full-time, 5% with terminal degrees, 7 part-time); student-faculty ratio is 9:1.
ENROLLMENT PROFILE 80% women, 20% men, 2% part-time, 80% state residents, 5% live on campus, 20% transferred in, 80% have need-based financial aid, 0% have non-need-based financial aid, 0% international, 60% 25 or older, 1% Native American, 2% Hispanic, 10% African American, 1% Asian American. *Areas of study chosen:* 65% health professions and related sciences, 15% business management and administrative services.
FIRST-YEAR CLASS 400 total; 500 applied, 80% were accepted, 100% of whom enrolled.
ACADEMIC PROGRAM Business, nursing curriculum, honor code. Calendar: quarters. 15 courses offered in 1995–96. Academic remediation for entering students, services for LD students, tutorials, summer session for credit, part-time degree program (daytime, evenings), adult/continuing education programs, co-op programs and internships.
GENERAL DEGREE REQUIREMENTS 91 credits; math/science requirements vary according to program; computer course; internship (some majors).
MAJORS Accounting, business administration/commerce/management, computer programming, data processing, medical assistant technologies, nursing, paralegal studies, secretarial studies/office management.
LIBRARY Learning Resource Center with 1,350 books, 60 periodicals, 5 CD-ROMs. Acquisition spending 1994–95: $25,000.
COMPUTERS ON CAMPUS 40 computers for student use in computer labs, learning resource center, classrooms, library provide access to main academic computer, on-line services. Staffed computer lab on campus provides training in use of computers, software. Academic computing expenditure 1994–95: $50,000.
COLLEGE LIFE 5% vote in student government elections. *Social organizations:* 3 open to all. *Most popular organizations:* Student Council, PBL, Paralegal Club. *Major annual events:* Campus Bar-B-Que, Summer Picnic, Christmas Luncheon. *Student services:* personal-psychological counseling. *Campus security:* 24-hour emergency response devices.
HOUSING 50 college housing spaces available; 15 were occupied 1995–96. No special consideration for freshman housing applicants. Off-campus living permitted. *Option:* coed (2 buildings) housing available.
ATHLETICS *Intercollegiate:* basketball M. *Contact:* Mr. John Campbell, Athletic Director, 314-576-1267.
CAREER PLANNING *Placement office:* 1 full-time staff; $40,000 operating expenditure 1994–95. *Director:* Ms. Bonnie Rolte, Career Development Coordinator, 314-949-2620. *Services:* job fairs, resume preparation, resume referral, career counseling, careers library, job bank, job interviews. Students must register freshman year. 5 organizations recruited on campus 1994–95.
AFTER GRADUATION 90% of class of 1994 had job offers within 6 months.
EXPENSES FOR 1996–97 *Application fee:* $100. Tuition: $10,600 (minimum) full-time. Full-time tuition ranges up to $16,310. Full-time mandatory fees: $100. Tuition guaranteed not to increase for student's term of enrollment.
FINANCIAL AID *College-administered undergrad aid 1995–96:* 50 need-based scholarships (average $1000), low-interest long-term loans from external sources (average $6625), 3 part-time jobs. *Required forms:* FAFSA; accepted: state, institutional. *Application deadline:* continuous. *Payment plans:* tuition prepayment, installment, deferred pay. *Waivers:* full or partial for employees or children of employees.
APPLYING *Options:* Common Application, deferred entrance. *Required:* school transcript, campus interview. *Required for some:* Thurston Mental Alertness Test. Test scores used for admission. *Application deadline:* rolling.
APPLYING/TRANSFER *Required:* college transcript. *Required for some:* campus interview. *Entrance:* minimally difficult. *Application deadline:* rolling. *Contact:* Mr. Sam Dannoun, Dean, 314-949-2620.
CONTACT Mr. David Wood, Acting Corporate Director of Admissions, Sanford-Brown College, St. Charles, MO 63301, 314-949-2620 or toll-free 800-456-7222 (in-state).

SOUTHWEST MISSOURI STATE UNIVERSITY– WEST PLAINS
West Plains, Missouri

UG Enrollment: 1,018	Tuition & Fees (MO Res): $2573
Application Deadline: rolling	Room & Board: N/Avail

GENERAL State-supported, 2-year. Awards transfer associate, terminal associate degrees. Founded 1963. *Total enrollment:* 1,018. *Faculty:* 20.
ENROLLMENT PROFILE 1,018 students.
FIRST-YEAR CLASS 459 total. Of the students who applied, 100% were accepted, 100% of whom enrolled.
ACADEMIC PROGRAM Calendar: semesters.
GENERAL DEGREE REQUIREMENTS 62 credit hours; math/science requirements vary according to program.
MAJORS Accounting, biology/biological sciences, business administration/commerce/management, chemistry, drafting and design, history, manufacturing technology, nursing, paralegal studies, welding technology.
EXPENSES FOR 1996–97 State resident tuition: $2015 full-time, $65 per credit hour part-time. Nonresident tuition: $4030 full-time, $130 per credit hour part-time. Part-time mandatory fees per credit hour range from $18 to $25. Full-time mandatory fees: $558.
FINANCIAL AID *College-administered undergrad aid 1995–96:* need-based scholarships, non-need scholarships, low-interest long-term loans from external sources.
APPLYING Open admission. *Required:* school transcript, ACT. *Recommended:* 3 years of high school math and science. Test scores used for counseling/placement. *Application deadline:* rolling.
APPLYING/TRANSFER *Required:* high school transcript. *Application deadline:* rolling.
CONTACT Ms. Cheryl Caldwell, Coordinator, Southwest Missouri State University–West Plains, West Plains, MO 65775, 417-256-5533.

STATE FAIR COMMUNITY COLLEGE
Sedalia, Missouri

UG Enrollment: 2,277	Tuition & Fees (Area Res): $1312
Application Deadline: rolling	Room & Board: N/Avail

GENERAL District-supported, 2-year, coed. Part of Missouri Coordinating Board for Higher Education. Awards transfer associate, terminal associate degrees. Founded 1966. *Setting:* 128-acre small-town campus. *Total enrollment:* 2,277. *Faculty:* 98 (54 full-time, 44 part-time); student-faculty ratio is 22:1.
ENROLLMENT PROFILE 2,277 students from 4 states and territories, 2 other countries. 61% women, 57% part-time, 99% state residents, 10% transferred in, 52% 25 or older, 0% Native American, 1% Hispanic, 4% African American, 0% Asian American.
FIRST-YEAR CLASS 495 total; 550 applied, 98% were accepted, 92% of whom enrolled. 7% from top 10% of their high school class, 21% from top quarter, 55% from top half.

ACADEMIC PROGRAM Core. Calendar: semesters. 469 courses offered in 1995–96. Academic remediation for entering students, advanced placement, summer session for credit, part-time degree program (daytime, evenings), adult/continuing education programs, internships.
GENERAL DEGREE REQUIREMENTS 64 semester hours; 3 semester hours of college algebra; 8 semester hours of science including at least 1 lab science course; computer course; internship (some majors).
MAJORS Accounting, agricultural business, agricultural sciences, agricultural technologies, art/fine arts, automotive technologies, business administration/commerce/management, communication, computer information systems, computer technologies, construction technologies, court reporting, criminal justice, electrical and electronics technologies, finance/banking, food services management, law enforcement/police sciences, legal secretarial studies, liberal arts/general studies, machine and tool technologies, marketing/retailing/merchandising, medical records services, medical secretarial studies, nursing, practical nursing, retail management, secretarial studies/office management, welding technology.
LIBRARY Learning Resources Center with 36,000 books, 100 periodicals, 1,500 records, tapes, and CDs.
COMPUTERS ON CAMPUS Computer purchase plan available. 114 computers for student use in labs, classrooms.
COLLEGE LIFE Drama-theater group, choral group, student-run newspaper. 10% vote in student government elections. *Campus security:* security during evening class hours.
HOUSING College housing not available.
ATHLETICS Member NJCAA. *Intercollegiate:* basketball M(s)/W(s), soccer M(s). *Contact:* Mr. Keith Swanson, Associate Dean of Instruction, 816-530-5800.
CAREER PLANNING *Director:* Mr. Joe Horacek, Career Counselor, 816-530-5800. *Services:* resume preparation, resume referral, career counseling, careers library, job bank, job interviews. Students must register sophomore year.
EXPENSES FOR 1996–97 Area resident tuition: $1312 full-time, $41 per semester hour part-time. State resident tuition: $2016 full-time, $63 per semester hour part-time. Nonresident tuition: $3936 full-time, $123 per semester hour part-time.
FINANCIAL AID *College-administered undergrad aid 1995–96:* 50 need-based scholarships (average $200), 32 non-need scholarships (average $275), low-interest long-term loans from external sources (average $2120), Federal Work-Study, 15 part-time jobs. *Required forms:* institutional, FAFSA. *Priority deadline:* 8/1. *Waivers:* full or partial for employees or children of employees and senior citizens.
APPLYING Open admission except for allied health programs. *Options:* early entrance, midyear entrance. *Required:* school transcript, ACT, TOEFL for international students. *Recommended:* campus interview. Test scores used for counseling/placement. *Application deadline:* rolling.
APPLYING/TRANSFER *Required:* standardized test scores, high school transcript, college transcript, minimum 2.0 college GPA. *Recommended:* campus interview. *Entrance:* noncompetitive. *Application deadline:* rolling. *Contact:* Dr. Joyce Kimball, Dean of Student Services/Registrar, 816-530-5800.
CONTACT Dr. Joyce Kimball, Dean of Student Services/Registrar, State Fair Community College, Sedalia, MO 65301-2199, 816-530-5800. *Fax:* 816-827-4701. College video available.

THREE RIVERS COMMUNITY COLLEGE
Poplar Bluff, Missouri

UG Enrollment: 3,000	Tuition & Fees (Area Res): $1084
Application Deadline: 8/15	Room & Board: N/Avail

GENERAL State-supported, 2-year, coed. Part of Missouri Coordinating Board for Higher Education. Awards certificates, transfer associate, terminal associate degrees. Founded 1966. *Setting:* 70-acre rural campus. *Total enrollment:* 3,000. *Faculty:* 67 (52 full-time, 15 part-time); student-faculty ratio is 35:1. *Notable Alumni:* Latrell Sprewell, professional basketball player.
ENROLLMENT PROFILE 3,000 students from 2 states and territories, 8 other countries. 69% women, 46% part-time, 97% state residents, 3% transferred in, 1% international, 49% 25 or older, 1% Native American, 1% Hispanic, 3% African American, 0% Asian American. *Most popular recent majors:* education, business administration/commerce/management, nursing.
FIRST-YEAR CLASS 1,200 total. Of the students who applied, 100% were accepted, 75% of whom enrolled.
ACADEMIC PROGRAM Core, honor code. Calendar: semesters. Academic remediation for entering students, advanced placement, summer session for credit, part-time degree program (daytime, evenings, summer); adult/continuing education programs, internships.
GENERAL DEGREE REQUIREMENTS 62 credits; computer course for nursing majors; internship (some majors).
MAJORS Accounting, agricultural business, agricultural technologies, business administration/commerce/management, computer technologies, construction technologies, criminal justice, education, elementary education, engineering technology, industrial engineering technology, law enforcement/police sciences, liberal arts/general studies, marketing/retailing/merchandising, medical laboratory technology, music, nursing, secretarial studies/office management.
LIBRARY Rutland Library with 27,000 books, 150 microform titles, 385 periodicals, 500 records, tapes, and CDs.
COMPUTERS ON CAMPUS 21 computers for student use in computer labs provide access to Internet. Staffed computer lab on campus provides training in use of computers, software.
COLLEGE LIFE 40% vote in student government elections. *Campus security:* 24-hour patrols.
HOUSING College housing not available.
ATHLETICS Member NJCAA. *Intercollegiate:* baseball M, basketball M(s)/W(s), softball W(s), volleyball W(s). *Intramural:* baseball, basketball. *Contact:* Mr. Gene Bess, Director of Athletics, 314-840-9611.
CAREER PLANNING *Service:* career counseling.

AFTER GRADUATION 40% of students completing a degree program in 1994–95 went directly on to further study.
EXPENSES FOR 1996–97 *Application fee:* $20. Area resident tuition: $1054 full-time, $34 per credit part-time. State resident tuition: $1457 full-time, $47 per credit part-time. Nonresident tuition: $2635 full-time, $85 per credit part-time. Part-time mandatory fees: $5 per semester. Full-time mandatory fees: $30.
FINANCIAL AID *College-administered undergrad aid 1995–96:* need-based scholarships, 175 non-need scholarships (average $400), short-term loans (average $40), low-interest long-term loans from external sources (average $2000), Federal Work-Study. *Required forms:* CSS Financial Aid PROFILE. *Application deadline:* continuous. *Payment plan:* installment. *Waivers:* full or partial for employees or children of employees and senior citizens.
APPLYING Open admission. *Option:* early entrance. *Required:* school transcript. *Recommended:* ACT, ACT ASSET. Test scores used for counseling/placement. *Application deadline:* 8/15. *Notification:* continuous.
APPLYING/TRANSFER *Application deadline:* 8/15. *Notification:* continuous.
CONTACT Ms. Vida Stanard, Director, Three Rivers Community College, Poplar Bluff, MO 63901-2393, 314-840-9600.

WENTWORTH MILITARY ACADEMY AND JUNIOR COLLEGE
Lexington, Missouri

UG Enrollment: 247	Comprehensive Fee: $15,005
Application Deadline: rolling	Room & Board: N/App

Wentworth is located in Lexington, Missouri, 40 miles east of Kansas City. It is accredited by the North Central Association of Colleges and Schools and awards AA and AS degrees. A second lieutenant's commission may be earned in 2 years through the contract program. The College has small classes and excellent physical facilities; financial aid is available.

GENERAL Independent, 2-year, coed. Awards transfer associate degrees. Founded 1880. *Setting:* 130-acre small-town campus with easy access to Kansas City. *Total enrollment:* 247. *Faculty:* 51 (13 full-time, 2% with terminal degrees, 38 part-time). *Notable Alumni:* Ike Skelton, U.S. congressman.
ENROLLMENT PROFILE 247 students from 12 states and territories, 5 other countries. 64% women, 36% men, 35% part-time, 70% state residents, 6% transferred in, 95% have need-based financial aid, 3% international, 30% 25 or older, 1% Native American, 1% Hispanic, 5% African American, 1% Asian American. *Areas of study chosen:* 100% liberal arts/general studies.
FIRST-YEAR CLASS 56 total; 95 applied, 99% were accepted, 60% of whom enrolled. 7% from top 10% of their high school class, 25% from top quarter, 48% from top half.
ACADEMIC PROGRAM Core, general education curriculum, honor code. Calendar: semesters. 147 courses offered in 1995–96. Academic remediation for entering students, English as a second language program offered during academic year and summer, advanced placement, self-designed majors, tutorials, summer session for credit, part-time degree program (daytime, evenings, weekends, summer), adult/continuing education programs. ROTC: Army.
GENERAL DEGREE REQUIREMENTS 64 semester hours; 1 college algebra course; computer course.
MAJOR Liberal arts/general studies.
LIBRARY Seller Coombs Library with 21,000 books, 1,000 microform titles, 65 periodicals, 8 CD-ROMs, 12 records, tapes, and CDs. Acquisition spending 1994–95: $8874.
COMPUTERS ON CAMPUS 30 computers for student use in computer center, library. Staffed computer lab on campus.
COLLEGE LIFE Orientation program (2 days, no cost). Drama-theater group, choral group, marching band, student-run newspaper. *Social organizations:* 2 national fraternities; 10% of eligible men are members. *Major annual events:* Kansas City Symphony Concert, Artist Series, Field Days. *Student services:* health clinic, personal-psychological counseling. *Campus security:* 24-hour emergency response devices and patrols.
HOUSING 120 college housing spaces available; 110 were occupied 1995–96. Freshmen guaranteed college housing. On-campus residence required through sophomore year except if living with relatives within 30-mile radius. *Option:* single-sex housing available.
ATHLETICS Member NJCAA. *Intercollegiate:* baseball M, basketball M, cross-country running M, soccer M, tennis M. *Intramural:* racquetball, swimming and diving, table tennis (Ping-Pong), volleyball, weight lifting. *Contact:* Mr. Pat White, Athletics Director, 816-259-2221 Ext. 239.
CAREER PLANNING *Placement office:* 1 full-time staff. *Director:* Sgt. Maj. Marshell Foss, Guidance Counselor, 816-259-2221. *Services:* resume preparation, career counseling, careers library.
AFTER GRADUATION 82% of students completing a degree program in 1994–95 went directly on to further study.
EXPENSES FOR 1995–96 *Application fee:* $50. Comprehensive fee: $15,005. Day student tuition per semester hour: $75.
FINANCIAL AID *College-administered undergrad aid 1995–96:* 65 need-based scholarships, 48 non-need scholarships, low-interest long-term loans from external sources, 13 Federal Work-Study (averaging $535). *Required forms:* institutional, FAFSA; accepted: state. *Priority deadline:* 8/1. *Payment plans:* installment, deferred payment.
APPLYING *Option:* midyear entrance. *Required:* school transcript, recommendations, TOEFL for international students. *Recommended:* SAT I or ACT. Test scores used for admission. *Application deadline:* rolling.
APPLYING/TRANSFER *Required:* high school transcript, recommendations, college transcript. *Recommended:* standardized test scores. *Entrance:* moderately difficult. *Application deadline:* rolling. *Contact:* Mr. Michael W. Lierman, Dean of Admissions, 816-259-2221.
CONTACT Mr. Michael W. Lierman, Dean of Admissions, Wentworth Military Academy and Junior College, Lexington, MO 64067, 816-259-2221. *Fax:* 816-259-2677. College video available.

MONTANA

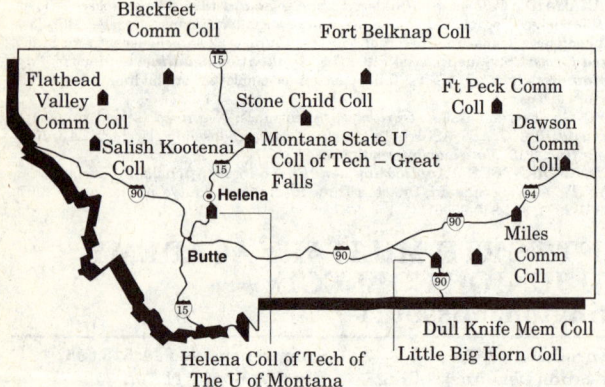

BLACKFEET COMMUNITY COLLEGE
Browning, Montana

UG Enrollment: 428	Tuition & Fees: $1371
Application Deadline: rolling	Room & Board: N/Avail

GENERAL Independent, 2-year, coed. Awards certificates, diplomas, transfer associate, terminal associate degrees. Founded 1974. *Setting:* 5-acre small-town campus. *Total enrollment:* 428. *Faculty:* 50 (30 full-time, 20 part-time).
ENROLLMENT PROFILE 428 students: 60% women, 60% part-time, 100% state residents, 10% transferred in, 73% 25 or older, 95% Native American.
FIRST-YEAR CLASS Of the students who applied, 100% were accepted, 100% of whom enrolled.
ACADEMIC PROGRAM Core. Calendar: quarters. Academic remediation for entering students, English as a second language program offered during academic year, part-time degree program (daytime, evenings), adult/continuing education programs. Off-campus study at members of the American Indian Higher Education Consortium.
GENERAL DEGREE REQUIREMENTS 99 credit hours; 1 course each in math and science; 1 course in Blackfeet; computer course.
MAJORS Business administration/commerce/management, early childhood education, human services, liberal arts/general studies, Native American studies, secretarial studies/office management, teacher aide studies.
LIBRARY 10,000 books, 175 periodicals.
COMPUTERS ON CAMPUS 55 computers for student use in classrooms. Staffed computer lab on campus provides training in use of computers, software.
COLLEGE LIFE Orientation program (2 days, no cost, parents included). *Student services:* health clinic, personal-psychological counseling.
HOUSING College housing not available.
ATHLETICS *Intramural:* basketball, cross-country running, golf, racquetball, skiing (cross-country), skiing (downhill), swimming and diving, tennis, volleyball, weight lifting.
CAREER PLANNING *Service:* career counseling.
EXPENSES FOR 1995–96 Tuition: $1050 full-time, $30 per credit hour part-time. Part-time mandatory fees per quarter range from $25 to $107. Full-time mandatory fees: $321.
FINANCIAL AID College-administered undergrad aid 1995–96: need-based scholarships, Federal Work-Study, 5 part-time jobs. *Required forms:* FAFSA; accepted: CSS Financial Aid PROFILE. *Priority deadline:* 3/30.
APPLYING Open admission. *Option:* early entrance. *Required:* school transcript, ACT ASSET. *Application deadline:* rolling. *Notification:* continuous.
APPLYING/TRANSFER *Required:* standardized test scores, high school transcript, college transcript. *Entrance:* noncompetitive. *Application deadline:* rolling. *Notification:* continuous.
CONTACT Ms. Deana McNabb, Registrar/Admissions Officer, Blackfeet Community College, Browning, MT 59417-0819, 406-338-5421 Ext. 243. *Fax:* 406-338-7808.

DAWSON COMMUNITY COLLEGE
Glendive, Montana

UG Enrollment: 535	Tuition & Fees (Area Res): $1400
Application Deadline: rolling	Room Only: $1215

GENERAL State and locally supported, 2-year, coed. Awards certificates, transfer associate, terminal associate degree. Founded 1940. *Setting:* 300-acre rural campus. *Endowment:* $259,561. *Total enrollment:* 535. *Faculty:* 68 (21 full-time, 5% with terminal degrees, 47 part-time).
ENROLLMENT PROFILE 535 students from 2 states and territories. 43% women, 57% men, 33% part-time, 97% state residents, 18% live on campus, 5% transferred in, 75% have need-based financial aid, 0% international, 24% 25 or older, 2% Native American, 1% Hispanic, 0% African American, 1% Asian American. *Areas of study chosen:* 26% liberal arts/general studies, 8% business management and administrative services, 7% agriculture, 4% health professions and related sciences, 2% computer and information sciences. *Most popular recent majors:* liberal arts/general studies, business administration/commerce/management, human services.
FIRST-YEAR CLASS 139 total; 217 applied, 100% were accepted, 64% of whom enrolled.
ACADEMIC PROGRAM Core. Calendar: semesters. Academic remediation for entering students, English as a second language program offered during academic year, services for LD students, self-designed majors, summer session for credit, part-time degree program (daytime, evenings), adult/continuing education programs, co-op programs and internships.
GENERAL DEGREE REQUIREMENTS 60 semester hours; computer course for agriculture, automotive, business, human services, office management majors, transfer associate degrees; internship (some majors).
MAJORS Agricultural business, automotive technologies, business administration/commerce/management, computer technologies, drug and alcohol/substance abuse counseling, equestrian studies, human services, law enforcement/police sciences, liberal arts/general studies, secretarial studies/office management.
LIBRARY Jane Carey Memorial Library with 18,404 books, 70 microform titles, 205 periodicals, 2 on-line bibliographic services, 8 CD-ROMs, 950 records, tapes, and CDs. Acquisition spending 1994–95: $27,390.
COMPUTERS ON CAMPUS 70 computers for student use in computer labs, learning resource center, library. Staffed computer lab on campus provides training in use of computers, software.
COLLEGE LIFE Orientation program (2 days, no cost). Drama-theater group, choral group. *Social organizations:* 6 open to all. *Most popular organizations:* Human Services Club, Law Enforcement Club, Associated Student Body, VICA, United Badlands Indian Club.
HOUSING 92 college housing spaces available; all were occupied 1995–96. No special consideration for freshman housing applicants. Off-campus living permitted. *Option:* coed (2 buildings) housing available. Resident assistants live in dorms.
ATHLETICS Member NJCAA. *Intercollegiate:* basketball M(s)/W(s), equestrian sports M(s)/W(s). *Intramural:* bowling, golf, racquetball, tennis, volleyball. *Contact:* Ms. Joyce Ayre, Athletic Director, 406-365-5525.
CAREER PLANNING *Placement office:* 1 part-time staff. *Director:* Ms. Trish Matteson, Career Advisor, 406-365-3396. *Services:* resume preparation, career counseling, careers library.
AFTER GRADUATION 48% of class of 1994 had job offers within 6 months. 60% of students completing a degree program went directly on to further study.
EXPENSES FOR 1996–97 *Application fee:* $30. Area resident tuition: $840 full-time, $30 per semester hour part-time. State resident tuition: $1442 full-time, $51.50 per semester hour part-time. Nonresident tuition: $3493 full-time, $124.75 per semester hour part-time. Part-time mandatory fees: $20 per semester hour. Nonresidents who are eligible for the Western Undergraduate Exchange Program pay state resident tuition rates. Full-time mandatory fees: $560. College room only: $1215.
FINANCIAL AID College-administered undergrad aid 1995–96: 69 need-based scholarships (average $750), 148 non-need scholarships (average $1442), short-term loans (average $100), low-interest long-term loans from external sources (average $2625), 70 Federal Work-Study (averaging $1000). *Required forms:* institutional, FAFSA. *Priority deadline:* 3/1. *Payment plan:* installment. *Waivers:* full or partial for employees or children of employees and senior citizens. *Notification:* 4/15.
APPLYING Open admission. *Options:* early entrance, deferred entrance. *Required:* school transcript, TOEFL for international students. *Recommended:* ACT. Test scores used for counseling/placement. *Application deadline:* rolling. *Notification:* continuous.
APPLYING/TRANSFER *Required:* high school transcript, college transcript. *Recommended:* standardized test scores. *Application deadline:* rolling. *Notification:* continuous. *Contact:* Mr. Daniel R. Bushnell, Director of Admissions, 406-365-3396 Ext. 31.
CONTACT Mr. Paul P. Fasting, Dean of Student Services, Dawson Community College, Glendive, MT 59330-0421, 406-365-3396 Ext. 28 or toll-free 800-821-8320. *Fax:* 406-365-8132.

DULL KNIFE MEMORIAL COLLEGE
Lame Deer, Montana

UG Enrollment: 328	Tuition & Fees: $1134
Application Deadline: rolling	Room & Board: N/Avail

GENERAL Independent, 2-year, coed. Awards certificates, transfer associate, terminal associate degrees. Founded 1975. *Setting:* 3-acre rural campus. *Total enrollment:* 328. *Faculty:* 30 (8 full-time, 25% with terminal degrees, 22 part-time); student-faculty ratio is 11:1.
ENROLLMENT PROFILE 328 students: 46% women, 80% part-time, 100% state residents, 8% transferred in, 0% international, 60% 25 or older, 85% Native American, 0% Hispanic, 0% African American, 0% Asian American. *Most popular recent majors:* liberal arts/general studies, mental health/rehabilitation counseling, secretarial studies/office management.
FIRST-YEAR CLASS 27 total; 27 applied, 100% were accepted, 100% of whom enrolled.
ACADEMIC PROGRAM Core, interdisciplinary curriculum, honor code. Calendar: semesters. 116 courses offered in 1995–96. Academic remediation for entering students, services for LD students, summer session for credit, part-time degree program (daytime, evenings), adult/continuing education programs, co-op programs and internships. Off-campus study at members of the American Indian Higher Education Consortium.
GENERAL DEGREE REQUIREMENTS 60 credit hours; 1 math course; computer course.
MAJORS Liberal arts/general studies, mental health/rehabilitation counseling, natural resource management, secretarial studies/office management.
LIBRARY 10,000 books, 431 microform titles, 128 periodicals, 200 records, tapes, and CDs.
COMPUTERS ON CAMPUS 25 computers for student use in computer center, learning resource center. Staffed computer lab on campus provides training in use of computers, software.
COLLEGE LIFE Student-run newspaper. 40% vote in student government elections. *Student services:* personal-psychological counseling.
HOUSING College housing not available.
ATHLETICS *Intramural:* basketball, volleyball.
CAREER PLANNING *Placement office:* 1 full-time staff. *Director:* Mr. Zane Spang, Counselor, 406-477-6215. *Services:* job fairs, resume preparation, career counseling, careers library.
AFTER GRADUATION 50% of students completing a degree program in 1994–95 went directly on to further study.
EXPENSES FOR 1996–97 Tuition: $960 full-time, $40 per credit hour part-time. Part-time mandatory fees per semester range from $6 to $81. Full-time mandatory fees: $174.

Montana

FINANCIAL AID *College-administered undergrad aid 1995–96:* 10 non-need scholarships (averaging $894). *Required forms:* FAFSA; required for some: CSS Financial Aid PROFILE. *Priority deadline:* 3/1. *Payment plans:* installment, deferred payment. *Waivers:* full or partial for employees or children of employees and senior citizens.
APPLYING Open admission. *Option:* early entrance. *Required:* school transcript, ACT ASSET. *Recommended:* ACT. Test scores used for counseling/placement. *Application deadline:* rolling. *Notification:* continuous.
APPLYING/TRANSFER *Entrance:* noncompetitive. *Application deadline:* rolling. *Notification:* continuous.
CONTACT Mr. William L. Wertman, Registrar/Director of Admissions, Dull Knife Memorial College, Lame Deer, MT 59043-0098, 406-477-6215. *Fax:* 406-477-6219. College video available.

FLATHEAD VALLEY COMMUNITY COLLEGE
Kalispell, Montana

UG Enrollment: 1,116	Tuition & Fees (Area Res): $1535
Application Deadline: rolling	Room & Board: N/Avail

GENERAL State and locally supported, 2-year, coed. Awards certificates, transfer associate, terminal associate degrees. Founded 1967. *Setting:* 40-acre small-town campus. *Educational spending 1994–95:* $1906 per undergrad. *Total enrollment:* 1,116. *Faculty:* 109 (34 full-time, 75 part-time).
ENROLLMENT PROFILE 1,116 students from 20 states and territories, 4 other countries. 50% women, 32% part-time, 96% state residents, 11% transferred in, 1% international, 65% 25 or older, 2% Native American, 1% Hispanic, 1% African American, 1% Asian American.
FIRST-YEAR CLASS 258 total; 288 applied, 100% were accepted, 90% of whom enrolled.
ACADEMIC PROGRAM Core, honor code. Calendar: semesters. 190 courses offered in 1995–96. Academic remediation for entering students, services for LD students, advanced placement, summer session for credit, part-time degree program (daytime, evenings), adult/continuing education programs, internships.
GENERAL DEGREE REQUIREMENTS 64 semester hours; 1 math course; computer course for associate of applied science degree; internship (some majors).
MAJORS Business administration/commerce/management, child psychology/child development, computer technologies, criminal justice, forest technology, hotel and restaurant management, human services, liberal arts/general studies, medical secretarial studies, secretarial studies/office management, surveying technology, wildlife management, word processing.
LIBRARY Flathead Valley Community College Library with 18,130 books, 800 microform titles, 150 periodicals, 8 CD-ROMs, 497 records, tapes, and CDs. Acquisition spending 1994–95: $41,483.
COMPUTERS ON CAMPUS 90 computers for student use in instructional labs. Staffed computer lab on campus. Academic computing expenditure 1994–95: $233,150.
COLLEGE LIFE Drama-theater group, student-run newspaper. *Social organizations:* 10 open to all. *Most popular organizations:* Human Services, Forestry Club, Gi-Ta. *Student services:* personal-psychological counseling.
HOUSING College housing not available.
ATHLETICS *Intercollegiate:* golf M/W, soccer M/W. *Intramural:* basketball, football, racquetball, soccer, tennis, volleyball, weight lifting. *Contact:* Mr. Mike McLean, Athletic Director, 406-756-3893.
CAREER PLANNING *Placement office:* 2 full-time, 1 part-time staff. *Director:* Ms. Charlene Herron, Career Counselor, 406-756-3890. *Services:* resume preparation, career counseling, careers library.
EXPENSES FOR 1996–97 Area resident tuition: $1505 full-time, $53.75 per semester hour part-time. State resident tuition: $2184 full-time, $78 per semester hour part-time. Nonresident tuition: $4599 full-time, $164.25 per semester hour part-time. Part-time mandatory fees: $16.25 per semester. Full-time mandatory fees: $30.
FINANCIAL AID *College-administered undergrad aid 1995–96:* 93 need-based scholarships (average $700), 145 non-need scholarships (average $764), short-term loans (average $50), low-interest long-term loans from external sources (average $2000), 48 Federal Work-Study (averaging $1200), 12 part-time jobs. *Required forms:* institutional, FAFSA; accepted: CSS Financial Aid PROFILE. *Priority deadline:* 5/1. *Payment plan:* deferred payment. *Waivers:* full or partial for employees or children of employees and senior citizens. *Notification:* continuous. *Average indebtedness of graduates:* $4400.
APPLYING Open admission. *Options:* early entrance, midyear entrance. *Required:* school transcript, ACT ASSET. Test scores used for counseling/placement. *Application deadline:* rolling.
APPLYING/TRANSFER *Required:* high school transcript, college transcript. *Entrance:* noncompetitive. *Application deadline:* rolling. *Contact:* Ms. Marlene C. Stoltz, Admissions/Graduation Coordinator, 406-756-3846.
CONTACT Ms. Marlene C. Stoltz, Admissions/Graduation Coordinator, Flathead Valley Community College, Kalispell, MT 59901-2622, 406-756-3846. *Fax:* 406-756-3815.

FORT BELKNAP COLLEGE
Harlem, Montana

UG Enrollment: 438	Tuition & Fees: $1440
Application Deadline: rolling	Room & Board: N/Avail

GENERAL Independent, 2-year, coed. Awards certificates, transfer associate degrees. Founded 1984. *Setting:* 3-acre rural campus. *Total enrollment:* 438. *Faculty:* 24 (10 full-time, 14 part-time).
ENROLLMENT PROFILE 438 students: 56% women, 44% men, 58% part-time, 100% state residents, 60% 25 or older, 91% Native American.
FIRST-YEAR CLASS Of the students who applied, 100% were accepted, 100% of whom enrolled.
ACADEMIC PROGRAM Core. Calendar: quarters. Academic remediation for entering students, part-time degree program (evenings, weekends), co-op programs.
GENERAL DEGREE REQUIREMENTS 92 credits; 2 courses each in math and science; computer course.
MAJORS Business administration/commerce/management, computer technologies, data processing, early childhood education, (pre)engineering sequence, human services, liberal arts/general studies, Native American studies, natural resource management, secretarial studies/office management.
LIBRARY 8,000 books, 50 periodicals.
COMPUTERS ON CAMPUS 34 computers for student use in computer center, computer labs, research center, learning resource center, library provide access to main academic computer, e-mail, Internet. Staffed computer lab on campus provides training in use of computers, software.
COLLEGE LIFE Student-run radio station.
HOUSING College housing not available.
ATHLETICS *Intercollegiate:* basketball M/W, cross-country running M/W, volleyball M/W. *Intramural:* basketball, cross-country running, volleyball.
CAREER PLANNING *Placement office:* 1 full-time staff. *Director:* Ms. Julia Doney, Transitional Counselor, 406-353-2607 Ext. 31. *Services:* resume preparation, career counseling, careers library.
EXPENSES FOR 1996–97 *Application fee:* $10. Tuition: $1440 full-time, $30 per credit part-time.
FINANCIAL AID *College-administered undergrad aid 1995–96:* 62 need-based scholarships (averaging $420), 19 non-need scholarships (averaging $962), Federal Work-Study, 2 part-time jobs. *Required forms:* CSS Financial Aid PROFILE; accepted: FAFSA. *Priority deadline:* 3/1. *Payment plan:* installment. *Waivers:* full or partial for senior citizens.
APPLYING Open admission. *Option:* early entrance. *Required:* school transcript, TABE. *Application deadline:* rolling. *Notification:* continuous.
APPLYING/TRANSFER *Required:* standardized test scores, high school transcript, college transcript. *Application deadline:* rolling. *Notification:* continuous.
CONTACT Ms. Nellie Main, Registrar/Admissions Officer, Fort Belknap College, Harlem, MT 59526-0159, 406-353-2607.

FORT PECK COMMUNITY COLLEGE
Poplar, Montana

UG Enrollment: 425	Tuition & Fees: $1230
Application Deadline: rolling	Room & Board: N/Avail

GENERAL Independent, 2-year, coed. Awards certificates, transfer associate, terminal associate degrees. Founded 1978. *Setting:* small-town campus. *Total enrollment:* 425. *Faculty:* 31 (17 full-time, 14 part-time).
ENROLLMENT PROFILE 425 students: 70% women, 33% part-time, 100% state residents, 20% transferred in, 0% international, 80% 25 or older, 95% Native American, 0% Hispanic, 0% African American, 0% Asian American.
FIRST-YEAR CLASS 98 total. Of the students who applied, 100% were accepted, 85% of whom enrolled.
ACADEMIC PROGRAM Core. Calendar: semesters. Summer session for credit, part-time degree program (daytime). Off-campus study at members of the American Indian Higher Education Consortium.
GENERAL DEGREE REQUIREMENTS 60 credit hours; 1 college algebra course; 4 credit hours of lab science; computer course.
MAJORS Agricultural technologies, automotive technologies, business administration/commerce/management, computer science, construction technologies, criminal justice, early childhood education, electrical and electronics technologies, human services, liberal arts/general studies, mental health/rehabilitation counseling, Native American studies, natural resource management, secretarial studies/office management.
COMPUTERS ON CAMPUS Computer purchase plan available. 50 computers for student use in computer labs, business department provide access to off-campus computing facilities, e-mail. Staffed computer lab on campus provides training in use of computers, software.
HOUSING College housing not available.
EXPENSES FOR 1996–97 *Application fee:* $15. Tuition: $1080 full-time, $45 per credit hour part-time. Full-time mandatory fees: $150.
FINANCIAL AID *College-administered undergrad aid 1995–96:* need-based scholarships, Federal Work-Study. *Required forms:* CSS Financial Aid PROFILE. *Application deadline:* continuous.
APPLYING Open admission. *Option:* electronic application. *Required:* ACT ASSET. Test scores used for counseling/placement. *Application deadline:* rolling.
APPLYING/TRANSFER *Required:* standardized test scores. *Entrance:* noncompetitive.
CONTACT Mr. Robert McAnally, Dean of Students, Fort Peck Community College, Poplar, MT 59255-0398, 406-768-5553.

HELENA COLLEGE OF TECHNOLOGY OF THE UNIVERSITY OF MONTANA
Helena, Montana

UG Enrollment: 634	Tuition & Fees (MT Res): $1880
Application Deadline: rolling	Room & Board: N/Avail

GENERAL State-supported, 2-year, coed. Part of University of Montana, Missoula. Awards certificates, terminal associate degrees. Founded 1939. *Setting:* small-town campus. *Total enrollment:* 634. *Faculty:* 43 (29 full-time, 14 part-time); student-faculty ratio is 16:1.
ENROLLMENT PROFILE 634 students: 0% international.
FIRST-YEAR CLASS 202 total; 325 applied, 100% were accepted, 63% of whom enrolled.
ACADEMIC PROGRAM Core. Calendar: semesters. Academic remediation for entering students, services for LD students, summer session for credit, part-time degree program (daytime), adult/continuing education programs.
GENERAL DEGREE REQUIREMENTS 68 credit hours; math/science requirements vary according to program; computer course.
MAJORS Accounting, aircraft and missile maintenance, automotive technologies, carpentry, computer programming, computer technologies, electrical and electronics technologies, legal secretarial studies, machine and tool technologies, medical secretarial studies, practical nursing, secretarial studies/office management, welding technology.
LIBRARY 1,600 books, 30 periodicals, 10 CD-ROMs.

Peterson's Guide to Two-Year Colleges 1997

Helena College of Technology of The University of Montana (continued)
COMPUTERS ON CAMPUS Computers for student use in learning resource center, library provide access to main academic computer, e-mail, on-line services, Internet. Staffed computer lab on campus provides training in use of computers, software.
COLLEGE LIFE ***Social organizations:*** 1 open to all. ***Most popular organization:*** Student Senate. ***Major annual events:*** Fall and Spring Barbecue, Christmas Party, Open House.
HOUSING College housing not available.
ATHLETICS ***Intramural:*** basketball, volleyball.
CAREER PLANNING ***Placement office:*** 1 full-time, 1 part-time staff. ***Director:*** Mr. David Vikander, Director of Placement, 406-444-6800. ***Services:*** resume preparation, resume referral, career counseling.
EXPENSES FOR 1995–96 ***Application fee:*** $30. State resident tuition: $1880 full-time. Nonresident tuition: $3920 full-time. Part-time tuition per semester ranges from $105 to $469 for state residents, $190 to $979 for nonresidents.
FINANCIAL AID ***Required forms:*** FAFSA. ***Priority deadline:*** 4/1.
APPLYING Open admission. ***Options:*** early entrance, deferred entrance, midyear entrance. ***Required:*** TOEFL for international students. Test scores used for counseling/placement. ***Application deadline:*** rolling.
APPLYING/TRANSFER ***Entrance:*** noncompetitive. ***Application deadline:*** rolling. ***Contact:*** Ms. Annette Walstad, Director of Admissions, 406-444-6800.
CONTACT Ms. Annette Walstad, Director of Admissions, Helena College of Technology of The University of Montana, Helena, MT 59601, 406-444-6800 or toll-free 800-241-4882 (in-state). ***Fax:*** 406-444-6892.

LITTLE BIG HORN COLLEGE
Crow Agency, Montana

UG Enrollment: 295 | **Tuition & Fees: $1335**
Application Deadline: rolling | **Room & Board: N/Avail**

GENERAL Independent, 2-year, coed. Awards certificates, transfer associate, terminal associate degrees. Founded 1980. ***Setting:*** 5-acre rural campus. ***Total enrollment:*** 295. ***Faculty:*** 19 (8 full-time, 11 part-time).
ENROLLMENT PROFILE 295 students: 60% women, 25% part-time, 100% state residents, 20% transferred in, 0% international, 50% 25 or older, 90% Native American, 0% Hispanic, 0% African American, 0% Asian American.
FIRST-YEAR CLASS 20 total. Of the students who applied, 100% were accepted.
ACADEMIC PROGRAM Core. Calendar: quarters. Part-time degree program (daytime). Off-campus study at members of the American Indian Higher Education Consortium.
GENERAL DEGREE REQUIREMENTS 92 quarter credits; 1 math course; 1 course in Crow.
MAJORS Business administration/commerce/management, carpentry, computer science, elementary education, liberal arts/general studies, mathematics, science.
COMPUTERS ON CAMPUS Computer purchase plan available. 30 computers for student use in classrooms. Staffed computer lab on campus provides training in use of computers, software.
COLLEGE LIFE Student-run newspaper.
HOUSING College housing not available.
ATHLETICS ***Intercollegiate:*** basketball M(s)/W(s). ***Intramural:*** basketball.
CAREER PLANNING ***Service:*** career counseling.
EXPENSES FOR 1995–96 Tuition: $1260 full-time, $35 per quarter hour part-time. Part-time mandatory fees: $25 per quarter. Full-time mandatory fees: $75.
FINANCIAL AID ***College-administered undergrad aid 1995–96:*** need-based scholarships, Federal Work-Study. ***Required forms:*** FAFSA. ***Priority deadline:*** 4/1.
APPLYING Open admission. ***Required:*** school transcript. ***Application deadline:*** rolling. ***Notification:*** continuous.
APPLYING/TRANSFER ***Required:*** high school transcript. ***Application deadline:*** rolling. ***Notification:*** continuous.
CONTACT Miss Ethel Big Medicine, Admissions Officer, Little Big Horn College, Crow Agency, MT 59022-0370, 406-638-2228.

MILES COMMUNITY COLLEGE
Miles City, Montana

UG Enrollment: 560 | **Tuition & Fees (Area Res): $1296**
Application Deadline: rolling | **Room & Board: $3020**

GENERAL State and locally supported, 2-year, coed. Part of Montana University System. Awards certificates, transfer associate, terminal associate degrees. Founded 1939. ***Setting:*** 8-acre small-town campus. ***Endowment:*** $500,000. ***Educational spending 1994–95:*** $1461 per undergrad. ***Total enrollment:*** 560. ***Faculty:*** 60 (25 full-time, 5% with terminal degrees, 35 part-time); student-faculty ratio is 14:1.
ENROLLMENT PROFILE 560 students from 5 states and territories, 5 other countries. 66% women, 34% men, 26% part-time, 87% state residents, 8% live on campus, 6% transferred in, 95% have need-based financial aid, 2% have non-need-based financial aid, 1% international, 26% 25 or older, 3% Native American, 1% Hispanic, 1% African American, 1% Asian American. ***Areas of study chosen:*** 25% liberal arts/general studies, 23% health professions and related sciences, 21% education, 15% business management and administrative services, 10% vocational and home economics, 3% psychology, 1% agriculture, 1% engineering and applied sciences, 1% mathematics. ***Most popular recent majors:*** liberal arts/general studies, nursing, business administration/commerce/management.
FIRST-YEAR CLASS 153 total; 203 applied, 100% were accepted, 75% of whom enrolled. 12% from top 10% of their high school class, 42% from top quarter, 60% from top half.
ACADEMIC PROGRAM Core, interdisciplinary curriculum, honor code. Calendar: semesters. 263 courses offered in 1995–96. Academic remediation for entering students, English as a second language program offered during academic year and summer, services for LD students, advanced placement, self-designed majors, tutorials, summer session for credit, part-time degree program (daytime, evenings, summer), adult/continuing education programs, co-op programs. Off-campus study at Dawson Community College.
GENERAL DEGREE REQUIREMENT 60 semester hours; computer course.
MAJORS Agricultural technologies, automotive technologies, business administration/commerce/management, computer management, electrical and electronics technologies, energy management technologies, fire science, graphic arts, liberal arts/general studies, marketing/retailing/merchandising, medical secretarial studies, nursing, retail management, secretarial studies/office management.
LIBRARY Library Resource Center with 17,396 books, 201 microform titles, 321 periodicals, 3 on-line bibliographic services, 95 CD-ROMs, 20,061 records, tapes, and CDs. Acquisition spending 1994–95: $126,373.
COMPUTERS ON CAMPUS 115 computers for student use in computer center, computer labs, learning resource center, classrooms, library provide access to main academic computer, on-line services. Staffed computer lab on campus provides training in use of computers, software.
COLLEGE LIFE Orientation program (2 days, no cost, parents included). Choral group, student-run newspaper. 47% vote in student government elections. ***Social organizations:*** 6 open to all. ***Most popular organizations:*** Campus Ministry, Multicultural Club, Student Nurses Association, Vocational Industrial Club, Western Club. ***Major annual events:*** Homecoming, Awards Banquets, All Campus Picnics. ***Student services:*** personal-psychological counseling. ***Campus security:*** 24-hour emergency response devices.
HOUSING 46 college housing spaces available; all were occupied 1995–96. No special consideration for freshman housing applicants. Off-campus living permitted. ***Option:*** coed housing available. Resident assistants live in dorms.
ATHLETICS Member NJCAA. ***Intercollegiate:*** basketball M(s)/W(s). ***Intramural:*** basketball, bowling, cross-country running, golf, ice hockey, racquetball, skiing (cross-country), skiing (downhill), soccer, softball, swimming and diving, table tennis (Ping-Pong), tennis, track and field, volleyball, weight lifting. ***Contact:*** Mr. Dennis Lordemann, Athletic Director, 406-232-3031.
CAREER PLANNING ***Placement office:*** 1 full-time staff. ***Director:*** Mrs. Jane Oberlander, Counselor, 406-232-3031. ***Services:*** resume preparation, resume referral, career counseling, careers library, job bank. 3 organizations recruited on campus 1994–95.
AFTER GRADUATION 76% of class of 1994 had job offers within 6 months. 96% of students completing a degree program went directly on to further study.
ESTIMATED EXPENSES FOR 1996–97 ***Application fee:*** $30. Area resident tuition: $792 full-time, $33 per credit part-time. State resident tuition: $1440 full-time, $81 per credit part-time. Nonresident tuition: $3384 full-time, $162 per credit part-time. Part-time mandatory fees: $21 per credit. Full-time mandatory fees: $504. College room and board: $3020.
FINANCIAL AID ***College-administered undergrad aid 1995–96:*** 503 need-based scholarships (average $2000), 103 non-need scholarships (average $1440), short-term loans (average $300), low-interest long-term loans from external sources (average $2625), 75 Federal Work-Study (averaging $1200). ***Required forms:*** institutional, FAFSA. ***Priority deadline:*** 3/1. ***Payment plan:*** deferred payment. ***Waivers:*** full or partial for employees or children of employees and senior citizens. ***Notification:*** 5/15.
APPLYING Open admission except for nursing program. ***Options:*** early entrance, deferred entrance, midyear entrance. ***Required:*** school transcript, TOEFL for international students. ***Recommended:*** SAT I or ACT. ***Required for some:*** SAT I or ACT. Test scores used for counseling/placement. ***Application deadline:*** rolling.
APPLYING/TRANSFER ***Required:*** high school transcript, college transcript. ***Entrance:*** noncompetitive. ***Application deadline:*** rolling.
CONTACT Ms. Brenda Richards, Admissions Counselor, Miles Community College, Miles City, MT 59301-4799, 406-232-3031 Ext. 13 or toll-free 800-541-9281. ***Fax:*** 406-232-5705. College video available.

MONTANA STATE UNIVERSITY COLLEGE OF TECHNOLOGY–GREAT FALLS
Great Falls, Montana

UG Enrollment: 961 | **Tuition & Fees (MT Res): $1700**
Application Deadline: rolling | **Room & Board: N/Avail**

GENERAL State-supported, 2-year, coed. Part of Montana University System. Awards certificates, terminal associate degrees. Founded 1969. ***Setting:*** 35-acre urban campus. ***Total enrollment:*** 961. ***Faculty:*** 65 (1% of full-time faculty have terminal degrees); student-faculty ratio is 15:1.
ENROLLMENT PROFILE 961 students: 66% women, 33% part-time, 1% transferred in, 80% have need-based financial aid, 4% Native American. ***Areas of study chosen:*** 60% business management and administrative services, 30% health professions and related sciences, 4% vocational and home economics. ***Most popular recent major:*** business administration/commerce/management.
FIRST-YEAR CLASS 760 total. Of the students who applied, 100% were accepted.
ACADEMIC PROGRAM Core. Calendar: semesters. Tutorials, summer session for credit, part-time degree program (daytime, evenings).
GENERAL DEGREE REQUIREMENTS 60 credits; computer course for business, allied health majors; internship (some majors).
MAJORS Accounting, automotive technologies, business administration/commerce/management, computer information systems, computer management, computer technologies, dental services, emergency medical technology, fire science, legal secretarial studies, medical assistant technologies, medical records services, medical secretarial studies, nursing, occupational therapy, physical therapy, practical nursing, respiratory therapy, secretarial studies/office management.
COMPUTERS ON CAMPUS Computer purchase plan available. 120 computers for student use in computer labs, classrooms, library, student rooms provide access to Internet. Staffed computer lab on campus provides training in use of computers, software.
COLLEGE LIFE ***Campus security:*** 24-hour emergency response devices.
HOUSING College housing not available.
CAREER PLANNING ***Placement office:*** 1 full-time staff. ***Director:*** Mrs. Diana Wyatt, Career Counselor, 406-771-4311. ***Services:*** job fairs, resume preparation, career counseling, careers library, job bank, job interviews.
EXPENSES FOR 1996–97 State resident tuition: $1700 full-time. Nonresident tuition: $4040 full-time. Part-time tuition per semester ranges from $95.75 to $703.25 for state residents, $180.35 to $1634 for nonresidents.
FINANCIAL AID ***College-administered undergrad aid 1995–96:*** need-based scholarships, Federal Work-Study. ***Acceptable forms:*** CSS Financial Aid PROFILE, FAFSA. ***Application deadline:*** continuous to 3/1.

APPLYING Open admission. *Options:* Common Application, deferred entrance, midyear entrance. *Required:* school transcript, ACT ASSET. *Required for some:* essay. Test scores used for counseling/placement. *Application deadline:* rolling.
APPLYING/TRANSFER *Required:* college transcript. *Contact:* Mr. David Farrington, Director of Admissions/Records, 406-771-4312.
CONTACT Mr. David Farrington, Director of Admissions/Records, Montana State University College of Technology–Great Falls, 2100 16th Avenue, South, Great Falls, MT 59405, 406-771-4312 or toll-free 800-446-2698 (in-state). *Fax:* 406-771-4317. College video available.

SALISH KOOTENAI COLLEGE
Pablo, Montana

UG Enrollment: 750	Tuition & Fees (MT Res): $2903
Application Deadline: rolling	Room & Board: N/Avail

GENERAL Independent, primarily 2-year, coed. Awards transfer associate, terminal associate, bachelor's degrees. Founded 1977. *Setting:* 4-acre rural campus. *Total enrollment:* 750. *Faculty:* 55 (20 full-time, 35 part-time); student-faculty ratio is 18:1.
ENROLLMENT PROFILE 750 students from 3 states and territories. 56% women, 50% part-time, 90% state residents, 30% transferred in, 0% international, 48% 25 or older, 65% Native American, 0% Hispanic, 0% African American, 0% Asian American. *Most popular recent majors:* nursing, human services, secretarial studies/office management.
FIRST-YEAR CLASS 150 total; 300 applied, 100% were accepted, 50% of whom enrolled. 50% from top half of their high school class.
ACADEMIC PROGRAM Core. Calendar: quarters. Academic remediation for entering students, services for LD students, summer session for credit, part-time degree program (daytime, evenings), adult/continuing education programs, co-op programs. Off-campus study at members of the American Indian Higher Education Consortium.
GENERAL DEGREE REQUIREMENTS 92 credits for associate, 180 credits for bachelor's; 1 college algebra course; computer course.
MAJORS Carpentry, child care/child and family studies, computer science, dental services, early childhood education, environmental sciences (B), forestry, forest technology, human services (B), liberal arts/general studies, Native American studies, natural resource management, natural sciences, nursing, secretarial studies/office management.
LIBRARY 24,000 books, 200 periodicals.
COMPUTERS ON CAMPUS 20 computers for student use in computer labs.
COLLEGE LIFE Drama-theater group, student-run newspaper. *Student services:* personal-psychological counseling.
HOUSING College housing not available.
ATHLETICS *Intramural:* baseball, basketball, skiing (cross-country), skiing (downhill), softball, tennis, volleyball, weight lifting.
CAREER PLANNING *Service:* career counseling.
EXPENSES FOR 1996–97 State resident tuition: $2432 full-time, $106 per credit part-time. Nonresident tuition: $6600 full-time, $205 per credit part-time. Part-time mandatory fees per quarter range from $63.25 to $195.75. Tuition for reservation residents: $1890 full-time, $91.25 per credit part-time. Full-time mandatory fees: $471.
FINANCIAL AID College-administered undergrad aid 1995–96: 300 need-based scholarships (average $1700), 10 non-need scholarships (average $750), low-interest long-term loans from external sources (average $2500), Federal Work-Study, 12 part-time jobs. *Priority deadline:* 3/15. *Payment plan:* installment. *Waivers:* full or partial for minority students, employees or children of employees, adult students, and senior citizens.
APPLYING Open admission. *Option:* deferred entrance. *Required:* school transcript, proof of immunization, tribal enrollment, ACT, TABE. Test scores used for counseling/placement. *Application deadline:* rolling. *Notification:* continuous. Preference given to Native Americans.
APPLYING/TRANSFER *Required:* college transcript. *Application deadline:* rolling. *Notification:* continuous.
CONTACT Ms. Jackie Noble, Admissions Officer, Salish Kootenai College, Pablo, MT 59855-0117, 406-675-4800. *Fax:* 406-675-4801.

STONE CHILD COLLEGE
Box Elder, Montana

UG Enrollment: 247	Tuition & Fees (MT Res): $1590
Application Deadline: N/R	Room & Board: N/Avail

GENERAL Independent, 2-year, coed. Awards transfer associate degrees. *Setting:* rural campus. *Total enrollment:* 247. *Faculty:* 25 (10 full-time, 15 part-time).
ENROLLMENT PROFILE 247 students.
FIRST-YEAR CLASS 97 total. Of the students who applied, 90% were accepted, 85% of whom enrolled.
ACADEMIC PROGRAM Calendar: trimesters.
GENERAL DEGREE REQUIREMENTS 64 semester credits; 1 course in math/science; computer course.
MAJORS Business administration/commerce/management, computer science, liberal arts/general studies, secretarial studies/office management.
EXPENSES FOR 1995–96 State resident tuition: $1400 full-time, $50 per credit part-time. Nonresident tuition: $1820 full-time, $65 per credit part-time. Part-time mandatory fees per trimester range from $47.50 to $95. Full-time mandatory fees: $190.
APPLYING Open admission. *Required:* school transcript.
APPLYING/TRANSFER *Required:* high school transcript.
CONTACT Mr. Ted Whitford, Registrar, Stone Child College, Box Elder, MT 59521, 406-395-4313.

NEBRASKA

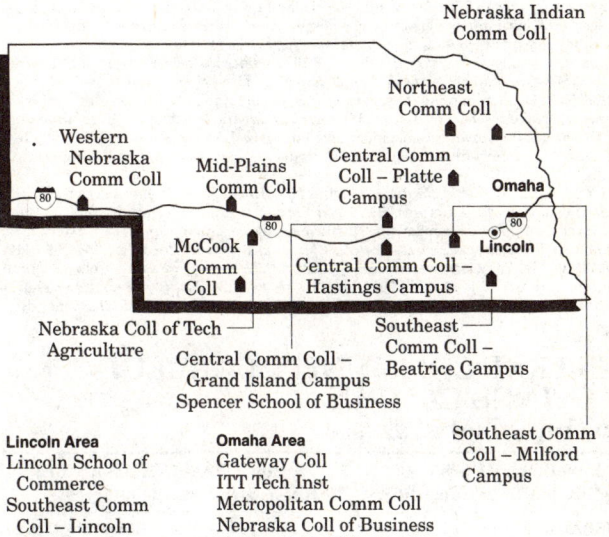

Lincoln Area
Lincoln School of Commerce
Southeast Comm Coll – Lincoln Campus

Omaha Area
Gateway Coll
ITT Tech Inst
Metropolitan Comm Coll
Nebraska Coll of Business
Omaha Coll of Health Careers

CENTRAL COMMUNITY COLLEGE–GRAND ISLAND CAMPUS
Grand Island, Nebraska

UG Enrollment: 1,602	Tuition & Fees (NE Res): $1312
Application Deadline: rolling	Room & Board: N/Avail

GENERAL State and locally supported, 2-year, coed. Part of Central Community College. Awards certificates, diplomas, transfer associate, terminal associate degrees. Founded 1976. *Setting:* 64-acre small-town campus. *Educational spending 1994–95:* $518 per undergrad. *Total enrollment:* 1,602. *Faculty:* 165 (39 full-time, 1% with terminal degrees, 126 part-time); student-faculty ratio is 15:1.
ENROLLMENT PROFILE 1,602 students from 18 states and territories. 67% women, 33% men, 92% part-time, 98% state residents, 1% transferred in, 1% international, 82% 25 or older, 1% Native American, 2% Hispanic, 1% African American, 1% Asian American. *Areas of study chosen:* 38% business management and administrative services, 20% health professions and related sciences, 15% engineering and applied sciences, 12% interdisciplinary studies, 8% computer and information sciences, 3% architecture, 3% vocational and home economics. *Most popular recent majors:* business administration/commerce/management, nursing, manufacturing technology.
FIRST-YEAR CLASS 133 total; 1,615 applied, 80% were accepted, 10% of whom enrolled. 3% from top 10% of their high school class, 13% from top quarter, 38% from top half.
ACADEMIC PROGRAM Core, interdisciplinary curriculum, honor code. Calendar: semesters plus 6-week summer session. 1,600 courses offered in 1995–96. Academic remediation for entering students, English as a second language program offered during academic year and summer, services for LD students, advanced placement, self-designed majors, summer session for credit, part-time degree program (daytime, evenings, summer), external degree programs, adult/continuing education programs, co-op programs and internships.
GENERAL DEGREE REQUIREMENTS 64 credits; computer course for accounting, office technology, business administration, electronics majors; internship (some majors).
MAJORS Accounting, automotive technologies, biology/biological sciences, business administration/commerce/management, child care/child and family studies, communication, computer information systems, computer programming, data processing, drafting and design, electrical and electronics technologies, heating/refrigeration/air conditioning, legal secretarial studies, manufacturing technology, mathematics, medical secretarial studies, nursing, paralegal studies, physical sciences, practical nursing, psychology, secretarial studies/office management, welding technology.
LIBRARY CCC-Grand Island Campus Library with 1,200 books, 20 microform titles, 60 periodicals, 8 CD-ROMs. Acquisition spending 1994–95: $1879.
COMPUTERS ON CAMPUS 156 computers for student use in computer center, computer labs, labs, classrooms, library, student center provide access to main academic computer, off-campus computing facilities, e-mail, Internet. Staffed computer lab on campus provides training in use of computers, software.
COLLEGE LIFE *Social organizations:* 3 open to all. *Most popular organizations:* Mid-Nebraska Users of Computers, Student Activities Organization, Intramurals. *Major annual events:* Christmas Party, Spring Picnic, Halloween Party. *Student services:* personal-psychological counseling.
HOUSING College housing not available.
ATHLETICS *Intramural:* bowling, softball, table tennis (Ping-Pong), volleyball.
CAREER PLANNING *Placement office:* 3 part-time staff; $53,228 operating expenditure 1994–95. *Director:* Ms. Virginia Ahlschwede, Placement Coordinator, 308-389-6421. *Services:* job fairs, resume preparation, resume referral, career counseling, careers library, job bank, job interviews.

Central Community College–Grand Island Campus (continued)
EXPENSES FOR 1996–97 State resident tuition: $1235 full-time, $38.60 per credit part-time. Nonresident tuition: $1853 full-time, $57.90 per credit part-time. Part-time mandatory fees: $2.40 per credit. Full-time mandatory fees: $77.
FINANCIAL AID ***College-administered undergrad aid 1995–96:*** 244 need-based scholarships (average $276), 104 non-need scholarships (average $371), short-term loans (average $105), low-interest long-term loans from external sources (average $2406), Federal Work-Study, part-time jobs. ***Required forms:*** institutional, FAFSA; required for some: verification worksheet. ***Priority deadline:*** 8/15. ***Payment plans:*** installment, deferred payment. ***Waivers:*** full or partial for employees or children of employees.
APPLYING Open admission. ***Options:*** electronic application, early entrance, midyear entrance. ***Required:*** school transcript, TOEFL for international students. ***Recommended:*** ACT. ***Required for some:*** recommendations, interview, SAT I or ACT, ACT ASSET. Test scores used for counseling/placement. ***Application deadline:*** rolling. ***Notification:*** continuous.
APPLYING/TRANSFER ***Required:*** high school transcript, college transcript. ***Recommended:*** standardized test scores. ***Required for some:*** standardized test scores, 3 years of high school math, recommendations. ***Entrance:*** noncompetitive. ***Application deadline:*** rolling. ***Notification:*** continuous. ***Contact:*** Mr. Don Richards, Registrar, 308-389-6412.
CONTACT Ms. Pamela Price, Admissions Director, Central Community College–Grand Island Campus, Grand Island, NE 68802-4903, 308-384-5220 Ext. 406 or toll-free 800-652-9177 (in-state). ***Fax:*** 308-389-6399. ***E-mail:*** prigsts@cccadm.gi.cccneb.edu. Electronic viewbook available.

CENTRAL COMMUNITY COLLEGE–HASTINGS CAMPUS
Hastings, Nebraska

UG Enrollment: 1,629	**Tuition & Fees (NE Res): $1312**
Application Deadline: rolling	**Room & Board: $2400**

GENERAL State and locally supported, 2-year, coed. Part of Central Community College. Awards certificates, diplomas, transfer associate, terminal associate degrees. Founded 1966. ***Setting:*** 600-acre small-town campus. ***Educational spending 1994–95:*** $1397 per undergrad. ***Total enrollment:*** 1,629. ***Faculty:*** 111 (60 full-time, 2% with terminal degrees, 51 part-time); student-faculty ratio is 15:1.
ENROLLMENT PROFILE 1,629 students from 17 states and territories, 2 other countries. 50% women, 50% men, 84% part-time, 99% state residents, 26% live on campus, 6% transferred in, 82% 25 or older, 1% Native American, 1% Hispanic, 1% African American, 1% Asian American. ***Areas of study chosen:*** 28% engineering and applied sciences, 23% business management and administrative services, 16% interdisciplinary studies, 15% health professions and related sciences, 6% agriculture, 6% computer and information sciences, 2% biological and life sciences, 2% communications and journalism, 2% vocational and home economics. ***Most popular recent majors:*** heating/refrigeration/air conditioning, business administration/commerce/management, horticulture.
FIRST-YEAR CLASS 358 total; 1,286 applied, 93% were accepted, 30% of whom enrolled. 3% from top 10% of their high school class, 13% from top quarter, 38% from top half.
ACADEMIC PROGRAM Core, interdisciplinary curriculum, honor code. Calendar: semesters plus 6-week summer session. Academic remediation for entering students, English as a second language program offered during academic year and summer, services for LD students, advanced placement, self-designed majors, summer session for credit, part-time degree program (daytime, evenings, summer), external degree programs, adult/continuing education programs, co-op programs and internships.
GENERAL DEGREE REQUIREMENTS 64 credits; computer course for accounting, office technology, business administration, electronics majors; internship (some majors).
MAJORS Accounting, agricultural business, agricultural technologies, architectural technologies, automotive technologies, biology/biological sciences, biotechnology, broadcasting, business administration/commerce/management, carpentry, child care/child and family studies, commercial art, communication, computer information systems, computer programming, construction technologies, data processing, dental services, dietetics, drafting and design, electrical and electronics technologies, electromechanical technology, food services management, food services technology, health services administration, heating/refrigeration/air conditioning, horticulture, hotel and restaurant management, human services, legal secretarial studies, machine and tool technologies, manufacturing technology, mathematics, medical assistant technologies, medical secretarial studies, physical sciences, printing technologies, psychology, secretarial studies/office management, welding technology.
LIBRARY Nuckolls Library with 17,678 books, 364 periodicals, 3 on-line bibliographic services, 6 CD-ROMs. Acquisition spending 1994–95: $14,184.
COMPUTERS ON CAMPUS 190 computers for student use in computer center, computer labs, learning resource center, classrooms, library provide access to main academic computer, off-campus computing facilities, e-mail, Internet. Staffed computer lab on campus provides training in use of computers, software.
COLLEGE LIFE Choral group, student-run radio station. ***Social organizations:*** 13 open to all. ***Most popular organizations:*** Student Senate, Central Dormitory Council, Judicial Board, Seeds and Soils, Young Farmers and Ranchers. ***Major annual events:*** Back to School Week Events, Christmas Party. ***Student services:*** personal-psychological counseling, women's center. ***Campus security:*** 24-hour patrols, controlled dormitory access.
HOUSING 238 college housing spaces available; 215 were occupied 1995–96. No special consideration for freshman housing applicants. Off-campus living permitted. ***Options:*** coed, single-sex housing available. Resident assistants live in dorms.
ATHLETICS Member NJCAA. ***Intramural:*** basketball, bowling, football, softball, table tennis (Ping-Pong), volleyball, weight lifting.
CAREER PLANNING ***Placement office:*** 1 full-time, 1 part-time staff; $44,373 operating expenditure 1994–95. ***Director:*** Mr. Ray Szlanda, Placement Director/Campus Center Director, 402-463-9811. ***Services:*** job fairs, resume referral, career counseling, careers library, job bank, job interviews.
EXPENSES FOR 1996–97 State resident tuition: $1235 full-time, $38.60 per credit part-time. Nonresident tuition: $1853 full-time, $57.90 per credit part-time. Part-time mandatory fees: $2.40 per credit. Full-time mandatory fees: $77. College room and board: $2400.
FINANCIAL AID ***College-administered undergrad aid 1995–96:*** 248 need-based scholarships (average $390), 168 non-need scholarships (average $293), short-term loans (average $130), low-interest long-term loans from external sources (average $2013), Federal Work-Study, 28 part-time jobs. ***Required forms:*** institutional, FAFSA; required for some: verification worksheet. ***Priority deadline:*** 8/15. ***Payment plans:*** installment, deferred payment. ***Waivers:*** full or partial for employees or children of employees.
APPLYING Open admission. ***Options:*** electronic application, early entrance, deferred entrance, midyear entrance. ***Required:*** school transcript, TOEFL for international students. ***Required for some:*** recommendations, SAT I or ACT, ACT ASSET. Test scores used for counseling/placement. ***Application deadline:*** rolling. ***Notification:*** continuous.
APPLYING/TRANSFER ***Required:*** high school transcript. ***Required for some:*** standardized test scores, 3 years of high school math, recommendations. ***Entrance:*** noncompetitive. ***Application deadline:*** rolling. ***Notification:*** continuous. ***Contact:*** Mr. Ken Rezac, Registrar, 402-564-7132.
CONTACT Mr. Robert Glenn, Admissions and Recruiting Director, Central Community College–Hastings Campus, Hastings, NE 68902-1024, 402-461-2428 or toll-free 800-742-7872 (in-state). ***E-mail:*** myehsts@cccadm.cccneb.edu. College video and electronic viewbook available.

CENTRAL COMMUNITY COLLEGE–PLATTE CAMPUS
Columbus, Nebraska

UG Enrollment: 1,511	**Tuition & Fees (NE Res): $1312**
Application Deadline: rolling	**Room & Board: $2400**

GENERAL State and locally supported, 2-year, coed. Part of Central Community College. Awards certificates, diplomas, transfer associate, terminal associate degrees. Founded 1968. ***Setting:*** 90-acre rural campus. ***Educational spending 1994–95:*** $737 per undergrad. ***Total enrollment:*** 1,511. ***Faculty:*** 100 (36 full-time, 6% with terminal degrees, 64 part-time); student-faculty ratio is 15:1.
ENROLLMENT PROFILE 1,511 students from 9 states and territories. 57% women, 43% men, 84% part-time, 98% state residents, 17% live on campus, 10% transferred in, 1% international, 82% 25 or older, 1% Native American, 1% Hispanic, 1% African American, 1% Asian American. ***Areas of study chosen:*** 25% business management and administrative services, 20% engineering and applied sciences, 12% interdisciplinary studies, 10% agriculture, 9% education, 5% health professions and related sciences, 4% architecture, 4% fine arts, 3% computer and information sciences, 2% psychology, 2% social sciences, 2% vocational and home economics, 1% biological and life sciences, 1% communications and journalism, 1% mathematics, 1% physical sciences. ***Most popular recent majors:*** business administration/commerce/management, agricultural business, data processing.
FIRST-YEAR CLASS 146 total; 524 applied, 95% were accepted, 29% of whom enrolled. 3% from top 10% of their high school class, 13% from top quarter, 38% from top half.
ACADEMIC PROGRAM Core, interdisciplinary curriculum, honor code. Calendar: semesters plus 6-week summer session. Academic remediation for entering students, English as a second language program offered during academic year and summer, services for LD students, advanced placement, self-designed majors, tutorials, summer session for credit, part-time degree program (daytime, evenings, summer), external degree programs, adult/continuing education programs, co-op programs and internships.
GENERAL DEGREE REQUIREMENTS 64 credits; computer course for accounting, office technology, business administration, electronics majors; internship (some majors).
MAJORS Accounting, agricultural business, agricultural economics, agricultural education, agronomy/soil and crop sciences, art education, art/fine arts, automotive technologies, behavioral sciences, biology/biological sciences, business administration/commerce/management, child care/child and family studies, commercial art, communication, computer technologies, data processing, drafting and design, economics, education, electrical and electronics technologies, electromechanical technology, (pre)engineering sequence, English, family and consumer studies, farm and ranch management, fashion merchandising, history, home economics, home economics education, interior design, legal secretarial studies, liberal arts/general studies, machine and tool technologies, marketing/retailing/merchandising, mathematics, medical records services, medical secretarial studies, music, music education, natural sciences, nursing, physical education, physical sciences, practical nursing, psychology, recreation and leisure services, science education, secretarial studies/office management, social work, sociology, teacher aide studies, theater arts/drama, welding technology.
LIBRARY Learning Resources Center with 30,000 books, 726 microform titles, 185 periodicals, 6 CD-ROMs, 741 records, tapes, and CDs. Acquisition spending 1994–95: $43,029.
COMPUTERS ON CAMPUS 100 computers for student use in computer center, computer labs, research center, learning resource center, classrooms, library, student rooms provide access to main academic computer, off-campus computing facilities, on-line services, Internet. Staffed computer lab on campus provides training in use of computers, software.
COLLEGE LIFE Choral group. ***Social organizations:*** 12 open to all. ***Most popular organizations:*** Phi Theta Kappa, Drama Club, Art Club, Cantari, Chorale. ***Major annual events:*** East Central Nebraska College Fair, Ethnic Festival, Plays. ***Student services:*** personal-psychological counseling, women's center. ***Campus security:*** late-night transport-escort service, controlled dormitory access, night security.
HOUSING 96 college housing spaces available; all were occupied 1995–96. No special consideration for freshman housing applicants. Off-campus living permitted. ***Option:*** coed housing available. Resident assistants live in dorms.
ATHLETICS Member NJCAA. ***Intercollegiate:*** basketball M(s), volleyball W(s). ***Intramural:*** basketball, football, golf, racquetball, softball, table tennis (Ping-Pong), volleyball. ***Contact:*** Mr. Jack Gutierrez, Recruiter/Athletic Director, 402-562-1234; Ms. Jenny Kosch, Women's Volleyball/Basketball, 402-562-1296.
CAREER PLANNING ***Placement office:*** 2 part-time staff; $27,738 operating expenditure 1994–95. ***Director:*** Ms. Beth Mierau, Career Planning/Placement Coordinator, 402-564-7132. ***Services:*** job fairs, resume preparation, resume referral, career counseling, careers library, job bank, job interviews.
AFTER GRADUATION 7% of students completing a degree program in 1994–95 went directly on to further study.
EXPENSES FOR 1996–97 State resident tuition: $1235 full-time, $38.60 per credit part-time. Nonresident tuition: $1853 full-time, $57.90 per credit part-time. Part-time mandatory fees: $2.40 per credit. Full-time mandatory fees: $77. College room and board: $2400.
FINANCIAL AID ***College-administered undergrad aid 1995–96:*** 132 need-based scholarships (average $447), 94 non-need scholarships (average $550), short-term loans (average $125), low-interest long-term loans from external sources (average $1346), Federal

Work-Study, 8 part-time jobs. ***Required forms:*** institutional, FAFSA; required for some: verification worksheet. ***Priority deadline:*** 8/15. ***Payment plans:*** installment, deferred payment. ***Waivers:*** full or partial for employees or children of employees.
APPLYING Open admission. ***Options:*** electronic application, early entrance, midyear entrance. ***Required:*** school transcript, TOEFL for international students. ***Required for some:*** recommendations, interview, SAT I or ACT, ACT ASSET. Test scores used for counseling/placement. ***Application deadline:*** rolling. ***Notification:*** continuous.
APPLYING/TRANSFER ***Required:*** high school transcript, 3 years of high school math, college transcript. ***Required for some:*** standardized test scores, recommendations, interview. ***Entrance:*** noncompetitive. ***Application deadline:*** rolling. ***Notification:*** continuous. ***Contact:*** Mr. Norris Augustin, Registrar/Admissions Officer, 402-564-7132 Ext. 278.
CONTACT Mr. Norris Augustin, Registrar/Admissions Officer, Central Community College–Platte Campus, Columbus, NE 68602-1027, 402-564-7132 Ext. 278 or toll-free 800-642-1083 (in-state). ***E-mail:*** augpsts@cccadm.gi.cccneb.edu. Electronic viewbook available.

GATEWAY COLLEGE
Omaha, Nebraska

UG Enrollment: 350	**Tuition: $10,980/deg prog**
Application Deadline: N/R	**Room & Board: N/Avail**

GENERAL Proprietary, 2-year, coed. Awards diplomas, transfer associate, terminal associate degrees. Founded 1970. ***Setting:*** suburban campus. ***Total enrollment:*** 350. ***Faculty:*** 36 (28 full-time, 8 part-time); student-faculty ratio is 14:1.
ENROLLMENT PROFILE 350 students: 25% women, 20% part-time, 95% state residents, 15% transferred in, 45% 25 or older, 10% African American. ***Areas of study chosen:*** 60% engineering and applied sciences. ***Most popular recent majors:*** electronics engineering technology, computer technologies, computer information systems.
FIRST-YEAR CLASS 285 total. Of the students who applied, 90% were accepted, 95% of whom enrolled.
ACADEMIC PROGRAM Calendar: semi-semester. Part-time degree program (evenings).
GENERAL DEGREE REQUIREMENTS 1800 contact hours; 1 course each in algebra, trigonometry and physics; computer course.
MAJORS Computer information systems, computer programming, computer science, computer technologies, drafting and design, electronics engineering technology, medical assistant technologies.
LIBRARY 3,000 books, 75 periodicals.
COMPUTERS ON CAMPUS 65 computers for student use in computer center.
HOUSING College housing not available.
CAREER PLANNING ***Services:*** job fairs, resume preparation, resume referral, career counseling, careers library, job bank, job interviews. Students must register freshman year.
EXPENSES FOR 1996–97 Tuition per degree program ranges from $10,980 to $12,200.
FINANCIAL AID ***College-administered undergrad aid 1995–96:*** need-based scholarships, low-interest long-term loans from external sources. ***Application deadline:*** continuous.
APPLYING ***Required:*** school transcript, campus interview, Wonderlic aptitude test. Test scores used for admission.
APPLYING/TRANSFER ***Required:*** standardized test scores, high school transcript, campus interview.
CONTACT Ms. Susan Shald, Director of Admissions and Marketing, Gateway College, 4862 South 96th Street, Omaha, NE 68114, 402-398-0900 or toll-free 800-786-3532. ***Fax:*** 402-593-0609.

ITT TECHNICAL INSTITUTE
Omaha, Nebraska

UG Enrollment: 203	**Tuition: $15,599/deg prog**
Application Deadline: rolling	**Room & Board: N/Avail**

GENERAL Proprietary, 2-year, coed. Part of ITT Educational Services, Inc. Awards terminal associate degrees. Founded 1991. ***Setting:*** 1-acre urban campus. ***Total enrollment:*** 203. ***Faculty:*** 12 (10 full-time, 90% with terminal degrees, 2 part-time).
ENROLLMENT PROFILE 203 students from 2 states and territories. ***Areas of study chosen:*** 100% engineering and applied sciences. ***Most popular recent major:*** electronics engineering technology.
FIRST-YEAR CLASS 113 total; 288 applied, 97% were accepted, 41% of whom enrolled.
ACADEMIC PROGRAM Core, honor code. Calendar: quarters. Academic remediation for entering students, services for LD students, advanced placement, tutorials.
GENERAL DEGREE REQUIREMENT 90 credit hours.
MAJORS Drafting and design, electronics engineering technology.
LIBRARY 100 books, 10 periodicals.
COMPUTERS ON CAMPUS 6 computers for student use in library.
COLLEGE LIFE Orientation program (2 days, no cost, parents included). ***Social organizations:*** 1 open to all. ***Most popular organization:*** Student Activity Committee. ***Major annual events:*** Summer Outing, Halloween Celebration. ***Campus security:*** 24-hour emergency response devices.
HOUSING College housing not available.
CAREER PLANNING ***Placement office:*** 1 full-time staff. ***Director:*** Ms. Regina Healy, Director of Placement, 402-331-2900. ***Services:*** job fairs, resume preparation, resume referral, career counseling, careers library, job bank, job interviews.
EXPENSES FOR 1996–97 ***Application fee:*** $100. Tuition per degree program ranges from $15,599 to $17,690. Full-time mandatory fees range from $540 to $720. Tuition guaranteed not to increase for student's term of enrollment.
FINANCIAL AID ***College-administered undergrad aid 1995–96:*** need-based scholarships, low-interest long-term loans from external sources, Federal Work-Study. ***Required forms:*** institutional, FAFSA; accepted: state. ***Application deadline:*** continuous. ***Payment plan:*** installment. ***Waivers:*** full or partial for employees or children of employees.
APPLYING ***Option:*** deferred entrance. ***Required:*** school transcript, TOEFL for international students, CPAt, DAT. Test scores used for admission. ***Application deadline:*** rolling.
APPLYING/TRANSFER ***Required:*** standardized test scores. ***Entrance:*** minimally difficult. ***Application deadline:*** rolling. ***Contact:*** Ms. Renee Spencer, Director of Education, 402-331-2900.
CONTACT Mr. Eddy Anthony, Director of Recruitment, ITT Technical Institute, 9814 M Street, Omaha, NE 68127-2056, 402-331-2900 or toll-free 800-677-9260. ***Fax:*** 402-331-9495. College video available.

LINCOLN SCHOOL OF COMMERCE
Lincoln, Nebraska

UG Enrollment: 450	**Tuition & Fees: $5625**
Application Deadline: rolling	**Room Only: $1760**

GENERAL Proprietary, 2-year, coed. Awards certificates, diplomas, transfer associate, terminal associate degrees. Founded 1884. ***Setting:*** 5-acre urban campus with easy access to Omaha. ***Total enrollment:*** 450. ***Faculty:*** 45 (15 full-time, 60% with terminal degrees, 30 part-time).
ENROLLMENT PROFILE 450 students from 3 states and territories, 1 other country. 80% women, 7% part-time, 95% state residents, 14% transferred in, 1% international, 40% 25 or older, 1% Native American, 1% Hispanic, 1% African American, 1% Asian American. ***Areas of study chosen:*** 16% business management and administrative services. ***Most popular recent majors:*** secretarial studies/office management, paralegal studies, tourism and travel.
FIRST-YEAR CLASS 190 total; 250 applied, 92% were accepted, 83% of whom enrolled. 10% from top 10% of their high school class, 40% from top quarter, 50% from top half.
ACADEMIC PROGRAM Core, honor code. Calendar: quarters. Academic remediation for entering students, tutorials, summer session for credit, co-op programs and internships.
GENERAL DEGREE REQUIREMENTS 110 credit hours; computer course.
MAJORS Accounting, business administration/commerce/management, computer programming, court reporting, legal secretarial studies, medical records services, medical secretarial studies, paralegal studies, secretarial studies/office management, tourism and travel.
LIBRARY Bennet Martin Library plus 1 other, with 1,800 books, 30 periodicals, 1,500 CD-ROMs, 500 records, tapes, and CDs.
COMPUTERS ON CAMPUS Computer purchase plan available. 100 computers for student use in computer center, computer labs, learning resource center, library provide access to on-line services, Internet. Staffed computer lab on campus provides training in use of computers, software.
COLLEGE LIFE Student-run newspaper. 20% vote in student government elections. ***Social organizations:*** 7 open to all. ***Most popular organizations:*** Travel Club, Secretarial Club, Business Club, Court Reporting Club, Legal Assisting Club. ***Major annual events:*** Spring Picnic, Fall Picnic, Spring Dance. ***Student services:*** personal-psychological counseling. ***Campus security:*** late-night transport-escort service.
HOUSING 142 college housing spaces available; 105 were occupied 1995–96. Freshmen given priority for college housing. Off-campus living permitted. ***Option:*** coed (1 building) housing available. Resident assistants live in dorms.
ATHLETICS ***Intramural:*** basketball, softball, volleyball.
CAREER PLANNING ***Placement office:*** 1 full-time, 1 part-time staff. ***Director:*** Mr. Kevin L. Sanderson, Director, Employment Services, 402-474-5315. ***Services:*** job fairs, resume preparation, resume referral, career counseling, careers library, job bank, job interviews. Students must register sophomore year. 50 organizations recruited on campus 1994–95.
AFTER GRADUATION 92% of class of 1994 had job offers within 6 months. 10% of students completing a degree program went directly on to further study.
EXPENSES FOR 1995–96 ***Application fee:*** $75. Tuition: $5550 full-time. Full-time mandatory fees: $75. College room only: $1760. Tuition guaranteed not to increase for student's term of enrollment.
FINANCIAL AID ***College-administered undergrad aid 1995–96:*** 15 need-based scholarships (average $750), 25 non-need scholarships (average $800), low-interest long-term loans from external sources (average $2625), Federal Work-Study, 5 part-time jobs. ***Acceptable forms:*** CSS Financial Aid PROFILE, state, FAFSA. ***Priority deadline:*** 8/1. ***Payment plan:*** installment.
APPLYING ***Options:*** early entrance, early decision, deferred entrance, midyear entrance. ***Required:*** TOEFL for international students, CPAt. ***Recommended:*** 3 years of high school math and science, some high school foreign language, SAT I or ACT, SAT II Subject Tests. Test scores used for admission and counseling/placement. ***Application deadlines:*** rolling, 12/15 for early decision. ***Notification:*** continuous, 1/15 for early decision.
APPLYING/TRANSFER ***Recommended:*** 3 years of high school math and science, some high school foreign language. ***Entrance:*** minimally difficult. ***Contact:*** Ms. Diane Bennett, Registrar, 402-474-5315.
CONTACT Mr. James Haga, Director of Admissions, Lincoln School of Commerce, 1821 K Street, PO Box 82826, Lincoln, NE 68501-2826, 402-474-5315 or toll-free 800-742-7738 (in-state). ***Fax:*** 402-474-5302. College video available.

McCOOK COMMUNITY COLLEGE
McCook, Nebraska

UG Enrollment: 951	**Tuition & Fees (NE Res): $960**
Application Deadline: rolling	**Room & Board: $2530**

GENERAL State and locally supported, 2-year, coed. Part of Mid-Plains Area Community Colleges. Awards certificates, transfer associate, terminal associate degrees. Founded 1926. ***Setting:*** 20-acre rural campus. ***Total enrollment:*** 951. ***Faculty:*** 62 (25 full-time, 10% with terminal degrees, 37 part-time); student-faculty ratio is 15:1.
ENROLLMENT PROFILE 951 students from 6 states and territories, 6 other countries. 59% women, 41% men, 61% part-time, 95% state residents, 1% transferred in, 1% international, 1% Native American, 1% Hispanic, 1% African American, 0% Asian American.
FIRST-YEAR CLASS 225 total; 293 applied, 100% were accepted, 77% of whom enrolled. 7% from top 10% of their high school class, 15% from top quarter, 60% from top half.
ACADEMIC PROGRAM Core. Calendar: semesters. 22 courses offered in 1995–96. Academic remediation for entering students, English as a second language program, advanced placement, self-designed majors, tutorials, summer session for credit, part-time degree program (daytime, evenings, summer), adult/continuing education programs, co-op programs. Off-campus study at Mid-Plains Community College.

Peterson's Guide to Two-Year Colleges 1997 425

McCook Community College (continued)
GENERAL DEGREE REQUIREMENTS 60 credit hours; computer course for transfer associate degree.
MAJORS Child care/child and family studies, legal secretarial studies, liberal arts/general studies, medical records services, paralegal studies, secretarial studies/office management.
LIBRARY Von Riesen Library with 30,400 books, 1,500 microform titles, 322 periodicals, 4,449 records, tapes, and CDs.
COMPUTERS ON CAMPUS 50 computers for student use in computer center, computer labs, learning resource center, labs, library provide access to e-mail, Internet. Staffed computer lab on campus provides training in use of computers, software.
COLLEGE LIFE Drama-theater group, student-run newspaper. ***Social organizations:*** 2 national fraternities, national sororities. ***Most popular organizations:*** Criminal Justice Club, Student Senate, Phi Theta Kappa. ***Major annual event:*** Homecoming. ***Student services:*** personal-psychological counseling. ***Campus security:*** 24-hour patrols, controlled dormitory access.
HOUSING 140 college housing spaces available; all were occupied 1995–96. No special consideration for freshman housing applicants. Off-campus living permitted. ***Option:*** coed housing available. Resident assistants live in dorms.
ATHLETICS Member NJCAA. ***Intercollegiate:*** basketball M(s)/W(s), golf M(s), volleyball W(s). ***Intramural:*** basketball, football, softball, table tennis (Ping-Pong), volleyball. ***Contact:*** Mr. Trace Bevell, Athletic Director, 308-345-6303 Ext. 12.
CAREER PLANNING ***Service:*** career counseling.
EXPENSES FOR 1995–96 ***Application fee:*** $40. State resident tuition: $900 full-time, $28 per credit hour part-time. Nonresident tuition: $1035 full-time, $32.50 per credit hour part-time. Part-time mandatory fees: $4 per credit hour. Room and board per year: $2530 for men, $2680 for women. Full-time mandatory fees: $60.
FINANCIAL AID ***College-administered undergrad aid 1995–96:*** need-based scholarships (average $285), non-need scholarships, short-term loans (average $25), low-interest long-term loans from external sources, Federal Work-Study, part-time jobs. ***Acceptable forms:*** CSS Financial Aid PROFILE, FAFSA. ***Priority deadline:*** 5/1.
APPLYING Open admission. ***Options:*** early entrance, deferred entrance, midyear entrance. ***Required:*** school transcript, TOEFL for international students, ACT ASSET. ***Recommended:*** 3 years of high school math and science. ***Required for some:*** SAT I or ACT. Test scores used for counseling/placement. ***Application deadline:*** rolling. ***Notification:*** continuous.
APPLYING/TRANSFER ***Recommended:*** 3 years of high school math and science. ***Entrance:*** noncompetitive. ***Application deadline:*** rolling. ***Notification:*** continuous. ***Contact:*** Dr. John Rucker, Dean of Instruction, 800-658-4348.
CONTACT Mrs. Marjorie Wilson, Registrar, McCook Community College, McCook, NE 69001-2631, 308-345-6303 Ext. 53 or toll-free 800-658-4348. ***E-mail:*** mwiemers@mcc.mccook.cc.ne.us.

METROPOLITAN COMMUNITY COLLEGE
Omaha, Nebraska

UG Enrollment: 10,686	Tuition & Fees (NE Res): $1147
Application Deadline: rolling	Room & Board: N/Avail

GENERAL State and locally supported, 2-year, coed. Part of Nebraska Coordinating Commission for Postsecondary Education. Awards certificates, diplomas, transfer associate, terminal associate degrees. Founded 1974. ***Setting:*** 172-acre urban campus. ***Total enrollment:*** 10,686. ***Faculty:*** 549 (149 full-time, 400 part-time).
ENROLLMENT PROFILE 10,686 students from 4 states and territories, 15 other countries. 60% women, 73% part-time, 98% state residents, 16% transferred in, 1% international, 65% 25 or older, 1% Native American, 3% Hispanic, 9% African American, 2% Asian American. ***Most popular recent majors:*** business administration/commerce/management, accounting, computer programming.
FIRST-YEAR CLASS 3,034 total. Of the students who applied, 100% were accepted, 100% of whom enrolled.
ACADEMIC PROGRAM Core. Calendar: quarters. 916 courses offered in 1995–96. Academic remediation for entering students, English as a second language program offered during academic year, services for LD students, advanced placement, summer session for credit, part-time degree program (daytime, evenings, weekends, summer), adult/continuing education programs, co-op programs and internships. ROTC: Army (c).
GENERAL DEGREE REQUIREMENTS 96 quarter hours; math/science requirements vary according to program; computer course (varies by major); internship (some majors).
MAJORS Accounting, architectural technologies, automotive technologies, business administration/commerce/management, child care/child and family studies, civil engineering technology, commercial art, computer programming, construction technologies, culinary arts, drafting and design, early childhood education, electrical and electronics technologies, (pre)engineering sequence, fashion merchandising, finance/banking, food services management, graphic arts, heating/refrigeration/air conditioning, horticulture, hotel and restaurant management, human services, industrial and heavy equipment maintenance, insurance, interior design, international business, law enforcement/police sciences, legal secretarial studies, legal studies, liberal arts/general studies, marketing/retailing/merchandising, medical secretarial studies, mental health/rehabilitation counseling, nursing, optometric/ophthalmic technologies, ornamental horticulture, paralegal studies, photography, physician's assistant studies, practical nursing, printing technologies, purchasing/inventory management, radiological technology, real estate, respiratory therapy, secretarial studies/office management, welding technology.
LIBRARY Main library plus 2 others, with 43,278 books, 3,232 microform titles, 790 periodicals, 1 on-line bibliographic service, 3,208 records, tapes, and CDs. Acquisition spending 1994–95: $151,953.
COMPUTERS ON CAMPUS 500 computers for student use in computer center, computer labs, learning resource center, classrooms provide access to main academic computer, on-line services. Staffed computer lab on campus provides training in use of computers, software. Academic computing expenditure 1994–95: $555,000.
COLLEGE LIFE ***Student services:*** personal-psychological counseling. ***Campus security:*** 24-hour emergency response devices and patrols, late-night transport-escort service.
HOUSING College housing not available.
ATHLETICS ***Intramural:*** basketball, bowling, softball, volleyball.
CAREER PLANNING ***Placement office:*** 20 full-time, 10 part-time staff; $153,492 operating expenditure 1994–95. ***Director:*** Mr. Steve Korenchen, Coordinator of Placement Services and Student Internships, 402-449-8421. ***Services:*** job fairs, resume preparation, resume referral, career counseling, job bank, job interviews.
AFTER GRADUATION 6% of students completing a degree program in 1994–95 went directly on to further study.
EXPENSES FOR 1996–97 State resident tuition: $1147 full-time, $25.50 per quarter hour part-time. Nonresident tuition: $1434 full-time, $31.88 per quarter hour part-time.
FINANCIAL AID ***College-administered undergrad aid 1995–96:*** 714 need-based scholarships (average $228), 186 non-need scholarships (average $1104), low-interest long-term loans from external sources (average $1943), Federal Work-Study, part-time jobs. ***Required forms:*** institutional, FAFSA. ***Priority deadline:*** 3/15. ***Waivers:*** full or partial for employees or children of employees and senior citizens.
APPLYING Open admission. ***Option:*** early entrance. ***Required:*** TOEFL for international students. ***Recommended:*** school transcript. Test scores used for counseling/placement. ***Application deadline:*** rolling. ***Notification:*** continuous.
APPLYING/TRANSFER ***Recommended:*** high school transcript, college transcript. ***Entrance:*** noncompetitive. ***Application deadline:*** rolling. ***Notification:*** continuous. ***Contact:*** Ms. Arlene Jordan, Coordinator of Enrollment Management, 402-449-8418.
CONTACT Mr. Jim Grotrian, Director of Enrollment Management, Metropolitan Community College, PO Box 3777, Omaha, NE 68103-0777, 402-449-8418 or toll-free 800-228-9553 (in-state). ***Fax:*** 402-449-8334.

MID-PLAINS COMMUNITY COLLEGE
North Platte, Nebraska

UG Enrollment: 1,824	Tuition & Fees (NE Res): $960
Application Deadline: rolling	Room Only: $900

GENERAL District-supported, 2-year, coed. Part of Mid-Plains Area Community Colleges. Awards certificates, diplomas, transfer associate, terminal associate degrees. Founded 1965. ***Setting:*** 160-acre rural campus. ***Total enrollment:*** 1,824. ***Faculty:*** 98 (57 full-time, 100% with terminal degrees, 41 part-time); student-faculty ratio is 18:1.
ENROLLMENT PROFILE 1,824 students from 7 states and territories, 2 other countries. 59% women, 41% men, 63% part-time, 97% state residents, 8% live on campus, 10% transferred in, 1% international, 20% 25 or older, 1% Native American, 4% Hispanic, 1% African American, 1% Asian American. ***Areas of study chosen:*** 18% health professions and related sciences, 16% business management and administrative services, 9% education, 7% social sciences, 4% computer and information sciences, 3% liberal arts/general studies, 2% agriculture, 2% engineering and applied sciences, 2% fine arts, 1% architecture, 1% biological and life sciences, 1% communications and journalism, 1% English language/literature/letters, 1% foreign language and literature, 1% mathematics, 1% performing arts, 1% physical sciences, 1% vocational and home economics. ***Most popular recent majors:*** nursing, business administration/commerce/management, secretarial studies/office management.
FIRST-YEAR CLASS 481 applied, 100% were accepted, 92% of whom enrolled. 5% from top 10% of their high school class, 20% from top quarter, 53% from top half.
ACADEMIC PROGRAM Core, honor code. Calendar: semesters. Academic remediation for entering students, honors program, summer session for credit, part-time degree program (daytime, evenings, summer), external degree programs, adult/continuing education programs, co-op programs and internships.
GENERAL DEGREE REQUIREMENTS 60 semester hours; 1 course each in college algebra and lab science; computer course; internship (some majors).
MAJORS Accounting, agricultural sciences, applied mathematics, art education, automotive technologies, behavioral sciences, biology/biological sciences, botany/plant sciences, business administration/commerce/management, business education, carpentry, chemistry, computer programming, construction technologies, criminal justice, data processing, dental services, drafting and design, early childhood education, education, electrical and electronics technologies, elementary education, emergency medical technology, (pre)engineering sequence, English, heating/refrigeration/air conditioning, legal secretarial studies, liberal arts/general studies, machine and tool technologies, mathematics, medical laboratory technology, medical secretarial studies, music, music education, natural sciences, nursing, optical technologies, physical education, physical sciences, physical therapy, political science/government, practical nursing, radiological technology, real estate, respiratory therapy, science, secretarial studies/office management, social science, sociology, theater arts/drama, veterinary sciences, vocational education, welding technology.
LIBRARY 23,000 books, 100 microform titles, 200 periodicals, 50 CD-ROMs, 500 records, tapes, and CDs. Acquisition spending 1994–95: $30,000.
COMPUTERS ON CAMPUS 250 computers for student use in computer center, classrooms, library provide access to off-campus computing facilities, e-mail, on-line services, Internet.
COLLEGE LIFE Drama-theater group, choral group. ***Social organizations:*** 10 open to all. ***Most popular organizations:*** Student Senate, Phi Theta Kappa, Vocational Industrial Clubs of America, Scribes. ***Student services:*** personal-psychological counseling. ***Campus security:*** patrols by trained security personnel.
HOUSING 64 college housing spaces available; all were occupied 1995–96. No special consideration for freshman housing applicants. Off-campus living permitted. ***Option:*** coed housing available. Resident assistants live in dorms.
ATHLETICS Member NJCAA. ***Intercollegiate:*** basketball M(s)/W(s), volleyball W(s). ***Intramural:*** basketball, football, tennis, volleyball. ***Contact:*** Mr. Kevin O'Connor, Athletic Director, 308-532-8980; Ms. Sally Thalken, Assistant Athletic Director, 308-532-8980.
CAREER PLANNING ***Placement office:*** 4 full-time staff. ***Director:*** Mr. Bill Eakins, Vocational Dean, 308-532-8740. ***Services:*** resume preparation, career counseling, careers library, job bank, job interviews.
AFTER GRADUATION 45% of students completing a degree program in 1994–95 went directly on to further study.
EXPENSES FOR 1996–97 ***Application fee:*** $30. State resident tuition: $900 full-time, $30 per semester hour part-time. Nonresident tuition: $1035 full-time, $34.50 per semester hour part-time. Part-time mandatory fees: $34 per semester. Full-time mandatory fees: $60. College room only: $900.
FINANCIAL AID ***College-administered undergrad aid 1995–96:*** 200 need-based scholarships (average $500), 300 non-need scholarships (average $800), short-term loans (average $50), low-interest long-term loans from external sources (average $180), Federal Work-Study (averaging $1000), 5 part-time jobs. ***Required forms:*** institutional, FAFSA;

accepted: CSS Financial Aid PROFILE. ***Priority deadline:*** 8/15. ***Payment plan:*** installment. ***Waivers:*** full or partial for employees or children of employees and senior citizens. ***Notification:*** continuous.
APPLYING Open admission except for nursing program. ***Options:*** early entrance, midyear entrance. ***Required:*** school transcript, ACT ASSET. ***Recommended:*** ACT. Test scores used for counseling/placement. ***Application deadline:*** rolling. ***Notification:*** continuous.
APPLYING/TRANSFER ***Required:*** high school transcript, college transcript. ***Application deadline:*** rolling. ***Notification:*** continuous. ***Contact:*** Dr. Darrel Hildebrand, Dean of Students, 308-532-8980.
CONTACT Ms. Angie Pacheco, Director Recruitment and Placement, Mid-Plains Community College, North Platte, NE 69101-9420, 308-532-8740 Ext. 233 or toll-free 800-658-4308 (in-state). ***Fax:*** 308-532-8590.

NEBRASKA COLLEGE OF BUSINESS
Omaha, Nebraska

UG Enrollment: 310	**Tuition & Fees: $5550**
Application Deadline: rolling	**Room & Board: N/Avail**

GENERAL Proprietary, 2-year, coed. Part of Educational Management, Inc. Awards certificates, diplomas, terminal associate degrees. Founded 1891. ***Setting:*** 12-acre urban campus. ***Total enrollment:*** 310. ***Faculty:*** 20 (13 full-time, 7 part-time).
ENROLLMENT PROFILE 310 students from 5 states and territories, 1 other country. 70% women, 0% part-time, 85% state residents, 20% transferred in, 60% 25 or older, 2% Native American, 2% Hispanic, 30% African American, 1% Asian American. ***Most popular recent majors:*** secretarial studies/office management, accounting, computer programming.
FIRST-YEAR CLASS 60 total; 200 applied, 80% were accepted, 80% of whom enrolled.
ACADEMIC PROGRAM Core, honor code. Calendar: modular. Academic remediation for entering students, advanced placement, summer session for credit, adult/continuing education programs, co-op programs and internships.
GENERAL DEGREE REQUIREMENTS 109 credit hours; 1 math course; computer course; internship (some majors).
MAJORS Accounting, business administration/commerce/management, computer programming, computer technologies, legal secretarial studies, legal studies, medical secretarial studies, secretarial studies/office management.
LIBRARY 250 books, 30 periodicals, 125 records, tapes, and CDs.
COMPUTERS ON CAMPUS 75 computers for student use in computer center, computer labs, classrooms provide access to on-line services. Staffed computer lab on campus provides training in use of computers, software.
COLLEGE LIFE Student-run newspaper. ***Student services:*** personal-psychological counseling. ***Campus security:*** late-night transport-escort service.
HOUSING College housing not available.
CAREER PLANNING ***Service:*** career counseling.
EXPENSES FOR 1995–96 ***Application fee:*** $75. Tuition: $5550 (minimum) full-time. Full-time tuition ranges up to $7400 according to class level. Tuition guaranteed not to increase for student's term of enrollment.
FINANCIAL AID ***College-administered undergrad aid 1995–96:*** need-based scholarships, 15 non-need scholarships (averaging $800), low-interest long-term loans from external sources (averaging $2500), Federal Work-Study, 12 part-time jobs. ***Acceptable forms:*** CSS Financial Aid PROFILE, FAFSA. ***Priority deadline:*** 9/1. ***Payment plan:*** installment. ***Waivers:*** full or partial for employees or children of employees.
APPLYING ***Options:*** early entrance, deferred entrance. ***Required:*** school transcript, minimum 3.0 GPA, interview, TOEFL for international students, CPAt. ***Recommended:*** 3 years of high school math and science, some high school foreign language, ACT. Test scores used for counseling/placement. ***Application deadline:*** rolling.
APPLYING/TRANSFER ***Required:*** standardized test scores, high school transcript, interview, minimum 3.0 high school GPA. ***Recommended:*** 3 years of high school math and science, some high school foreign language. ***Required for some:*** college transcript. ***Entrance:*** minimally difficult. ***Application deadline:*** rolling.
CONTACT Mrs. Natalie Guy, Director of Admissions, Nebraska College of Business, 3636 California Street, Omaha, NE 68131-1997, 402-553-8500 or toll-free 800-642-1456 (in-state). ***Fax:*** 402-553-0159. College video available.

NEBRASKA COLLEGE OF TECHNICAL AGRICULTURE
Curtis, Nebraska

UG Enrollment: 294	**Tuition & Fees (NE Res): $1647**
Application Deadline: rolling	**Room & Board: $2800**

GENERAL State-supported, 2-year, coed. Part of University of Nebraska System. Awards transfer associate, terminal associate degrees. Founded 1965. ***Setting:*** small-town campus. ***Endowment:*** $80,000. ***Total enrollment:*** 294. ***Faculty:*** 18 (15 full-time, 10% with terminal degrees, 3 part-time); student-faculty ratio is 10:1.
ENROLLMENT PROFILE 294 students from 6 states and territories. 43% women, 1% part-time, 94% state residents, 50% live on campus, 4% transferred in, 70% have need-based financial aid, 5% have non-need-based financial aid, 0% international, 26% 25 or older, 1% Hispanic, 0% African American, 0% Asian American. ***Areas of study chosen:*** 100% agriculture. ***Most popular recent majors:*** agricultural technologies, veterinary technology, horticulture.
FIRST-YEAR CLASS 169 total; 205 applied, 100% were accepted, 82% of whom enrolled. 10% from top 10% of their high school class, 20% from top quarter, 30% from top half.
ACADEMIC PROGRAM Core, agricultural curriculum, honor code. Calendar: semesters (4-week mandatory post-session). 113 courses offered in 1995–96. Academic remediation for entering students, tutorials, part-time degree program (daytime), adult/continuing education programs, internships.
GENERAL DEGREE REQUIREMENTS 72 semester hours; 1 course each in math and science; computer course; internship.
MAJORS Agricultural business, agricultural technologies, agronomy/soil and crop sciences, animal sciences, conservation, horticulture, industrial and heavy equipment maintenance, natural resource management, soil conservation, veterinary technology.
LIBRARY 5,500 books, 40 microform titles, 160 periodicals, 1 CD-ROM, 200 records, tapes, and CDs. Acquisition spending 1994–95: $11,580.
COMPUTERS ON CAMPUS Computer purchase plan available. 30 computers for student use in computer center, computer labs, student center, dorms. Staffed computer lab on campus provides training in use of computers, software. Academic computing expenditure 1994–95: $40,000.
COLLEGE LIFE ***Social organizations:*** 4 open to all; local fraternities; 10% of eligible men are members. ***Most popular organizations:*** Aggie Livestock Association, Student Technicians Veterinary Medicine Association, Activities Without Alcohol and Drugs, Business Club, Phi Theta Kappa. ***Major annual event:*** Annual Open House. ***Student services:*** health clinic, personal-psychological counseling. ***Campus security:*** 24-hour emergency response devices, controlled dormitory access.
HOUSING 160 college housing spaces available; 125 were occupied 1995–96. No special consideration for freshman housing applicants. Off-campus living permitted. ***Option:*** single-sex housing available. Resident assistants live in dorms.
ATHLETICS ***Intercollegiate:*** basketball M/W. ***Intramural:*** basketball, football, golf, soccer, softball, volleyball. ***Contact:*** Mr. Del VanDerWerff, Athletic Director, 308-367-4124.
CAREER PLANNING ***Placement office:*** 2 full-time staff; $28,000 operating expenditure 1994–95. ***Director:*** Ms. Susan Cull, Recruitment and Placement Coordinator, 800-328-7847.
AFTER GRADUATION 12% of students completing a degree program in 1994–95 went directly on to further study.
EXPENSES FOR 1995–96 ***Application fee:*** $10. State resident tuition: $1647 full-time, $45.75 per semester hour part-time. Nonresident tuition: $3294 full-time, $91.50 per semester hour part-time. College room and board: $2800. College room only: $1045.
FINANCIAL AID ***College-administered undergrad aid 1995–96:*** 30 need-based scholarships (average $100), 35 non-need scholarships (average $200), short-term loans (average $200), low-interest long-term loans from external sources (average $2500), 43 Federal Work-Study (averaging $800), 12 part-time jobs. ***Required forms:*** FAFSA; accepted: CSS Financial Aid PROFILE. ***Priority deadline:*** 5/1. ***Payment plan:*** installment.
APPLYING Open admission. ***Options:*** early entrance, midyear entrance. ***Required:*** school transcript, ACT. ***Recommended:*** 3 years of high school math and science, interview. Test scores used for counseling/placement. ***Application deadline:*** rolling.
APPLYING/TRANSFER ***Required:*** standardized test scores, high school transcript, college transcript, minimum 2.0 college GPA. ***Recommended:*** 3 years of high school math and science, interview. ***Contact:*** Mr. Gerald J. Huntwork, Assistant Dean, 308-367-4124.
CONTACT Mr. Gerald J. Huntwork, Assistant Dean, Nebraska College of Technical Agriculture, PO Box 69, Curtis, NE 69025-0069, 308-367-4124 Ext. 201. ***Fax:*** 308-367-5203. College video available.

NEBRASKA INDIAN COMMUNITY COLLEGE
Winnebago, Nebraska

UG Enrollment: 253	**Tuition & Fees: $2240**
Application Deadline: rolling	**Room & Board: N/Avail**

GENERAL Independent, 2-year, coed. Awards certificates, transfer associate, terminal associate degrees. Founded 1979. ***Setting:*** 2-acre rural campus. ***Total enrollment:*** 253. ***Faculty:*** 33 (12 full-time, 21 part-time).
ENROLLMENT PROFILE 253 students: 55% women, 45% part-time, 98% state residents, 10% transferred in, 0% international, 80% 25 or older, 95% Native American, 0% Hispanic, 0% African American, 0% Asian American. ***Most popular recent major:*** liberal arts/general studies.
FIRST-YEAR CLASS 47 total; 47 applied, 100% were accepted, 100% of whom enrolled. 100% from top half of their high school class.
ACADEMIC PROGRAM Core. Calendar: semesters. Academic remediation for entering students, summer session for credit, part-time degree program (daytime, evenings), adult/continuing education programs. Off-campus study at members of the American Indian Higher Education Consortium.
GENERAL DEGREE REQUIREMENTS 60 credit hours; internship (some majors).
MAJORS Business administration/commerce/management, carpentry, computer science, criminal justice, drug and alcohol/substance abuse counseling, early childhood education, education, electrical and electronics technologies, gerontology, human services, liberal arts/general studies, Native American studies, natural resource management, plumbing, public administration, secretarial studies/office management.
LIBRARY 14,000 books, 95 microform titles, 91 periodicals, 275 records, tapes, and CDs. Acquisition spending 1994–95: $29,006.
COMPUTERS ON CAMPUS 20 computers for student use in computer center, library. Staffed computer lab on campus provides training in use of computers, software.
COLLEGE LIFE ***Social organizations:*** national fraternities. ***Student services:*** personal-psychological counseling.
HOUSING College housing not available.
ATHLETICS ***Intercollegiate:*** basketball M/W, cross-country running M, volleyball W. ***Intramural:*** archery, bowling, skiing (cross-country), skiing (downhill).
CAREER PLANNING ***Service:*** career counseling.
EXPENSES FOR 1995–96 ***Application fee:*** $10. Tuition: $1800 full-time, $60 per credit hour part-time. Part-time mandatory fees per semester range from $40 to $160. Full-time mandatory fees: $440.
FINANCIAL AID ***College-administered undergrad aid 1995–96:*** need-based scholarships, Federal Work-Study. ***Required forms for some financial aid applicants:*** CSS Financial Aid PROFILE, FAFSA, Bureau of Indian Affairs form. ***Priority deadline:*** 9/1. ***Payment plan:*** installment. ***Waivers:*** full or partial for employees or children of employees and senior citizens.
APPLYING Open admission. ***Options:*** early entrance, deferred entrance. ***Required:*** school transcript, certificate of tribal enrollment. ***Application deadline:*** rolling. ***Notification:*** continuous.
APPLYING/TRANSFER ***Required:*** high school transcript, certificate of tribal enrollment. ***Entrance:*** noncompetitive. ***Application deadline:*** rolling. ***Notification:*** continuous.
CONTACT Ms. Karen Kemling, Director of Admissions/Registrar, Nebraska Indian Community College, Winnebago, NE 68071-0752, 402-878-2414. ***Fax:*** 402-878-2522.

NORTHEAST COMMUNITY COLLEGE
Norfolk, Nebraska

UG Enrollment: 3,413 — **Tuition & Fees (NE Res): $1185**
Application Deadline: rolling — **Room Only: $1460**

GENERAL State and locally supported, 2-year, coed. Part of Nebraska Coordinating Commission for Postsecondary Education. Awards diplomas, transfer associate, terminal associate degrees. Founded 1973. ***Setting:*** 205-acre small-town campus. ***Total enrollment:*** 3,413. ***Faculty:*** 122 (76 full-time, 46 part-time); student-faculty ratio is 18:1.
ENROLLMENT PROFILE 3,413 students from 13 states and territories, 5 other countries. 40% women, 60% men, 55% part-time, 98% state residents, 15% live on campus, 2% transferred in, 1% international, 15% 25 or older, 2% Native American, 2% Hispanic, 3% African American, 1% Asian American.
FIRST-YEAR CLASS 566 total; 1,080 applied, 100% were accepted, 52% of whom enrolled. 5% from top 10% of their high school class, 20% from top quarter, 60% from top half.
ACADEMIC PROGRAM Core, honor code. Calendar: semesters. 50 courses offered in 1995–96. Academic remediation for entering students, services for LD students, advanced placement, self-designed majors, tutorials, summer session for credit, part-time degree program (daytime, evenings, summer), adult/continuing education programs, internships.
GENERAL DEGREE REQUIREMENTS 60 credits; math/science requirements vary according to program; computer course for agriculture majors; internship (some majors).
MAJORS Accounting, agricultural business, agricultural technologies, agronomy/soil and crop sciences, art education, automotive technologies, biology/biological sciences, broadcasting, business administration/commerce/management, business education, carpentry, chemistry, child care/child and family studies, communication, computer programming, construction technologies, corrections, criminal justice, data processing, drafting and design, education, electrical and electronics technologies, electronics engineering technology, elementary education, English, farm and ranch management, French, heating/refrigeration/air conditioning, history, journalism, law enforcement/police sciences, legal secretarial studies, liberal arts/general studies, marketing/retailing/merchandising, mathematics, medical secretarial studies, music, nursing, physical education, physical therapy, physics, practical nursing, public administration, radio and television studies, real estate, secretarial studies/office management, speech/rhetoric/public address/debate, theater arts/drama, veterinary technology, welding technology.
LIBRARY Resource Center plus 1 other, with 27,623 books, 25 microform titles, 265 periodicals, 7 CD-ROMs, 579 records, tapes, and CDs. Acquisition spending 1994–95: $43,827.
COMPUTERS ON CAMPUS 150 computers for student use in computer center, agricultural buildings, electronics labs, library, dorms. Staffed computer lab on campus.
COLLEGE LIFE Drama-theater group, choral group, student-run newspaper, radio station. ***Student services:*** health clinic, personal-psychological counseling. ***Campus security:*** 24-hour patrols, controlled dormitory access.
HOUSING 204 college housing spaces available; all were occupied 1995–96. Freshmen given priority for college housing. Off-campus living permitted. ***Option:*** coed (3 buildings) housing available. Resident assistants live in dorms.
ATHLETICS Member NJCAA. ***Intercollegiate:*** basketball M(s)/W(s), golf M(s)/W(s), volleyball W(s). ***Intramural:*** basketball, bowling, football, skiing (cross-country), tennis, weight lifting, wrestling. ***Contact:*** Mr. Marlin Sekutera, Athletic Director, 402-644-0618.
CAREER PLANNING ***Placement office:*** 5 full-time, 6 part-time staff. ***Director:*** Dr. Karen Severson, Director, Career Achievement Center, 402-644-0435. ***Services:*** job fairs, resume preparation, career counseling, careers library.
AFTER GRADUATION 96% of class of 1994 had job offers within 6 months. 60% of students completing a degree program went directly on to further study.
EXPENSES FOR 1996–97 State resident tuition: $1080 full-time, $36 per semester hour part-time. Nonresident tuition: $1350 full-time, $45 per semester hour part-time. Part-time mandatory fees: $3.50 per semester hour. Full-time mandatory fees: $105. College room only: $1460 (minimum).
FINANCIAL AID ***College-administered undergrad aid 1995–96:*** need-based scholarships, non-need scholarships, short-term loans, Federal Work-Study. ***Required forms:*** FAFSA; accepted: CSS Financial Aid PROFILE. ***Priority deadline:*** 4/11. ***Waivers:*** full or partial for employees or children of employees.
APPLYING Open admission. ***Option:*** early entrance. ***Required:*** TOEFL for international students. ***Recommended:*** school transcript, ACT. Test scores used for counseling/placement. ***Application deadline:*** rolling. ***Notification:*** continuous.
APPLYING/TRANSFER ***Entrance:*** noncompetitive. ***Application deadline:*** rolling. ***Notification:*** continuous. ***Contact:*** Ms. Kathy Stover, Assistant Registrar, 402-644-0414.
CONTACT Mr. Eugene C. Hart, Director of Admissions, Northeast Community College, Norfolk, NE 68702-0469, 402-644-0459 or toll-free 800-348-9033 (in-state).

OMAHA COLLEGE OF HEALTH CAREERS
Omaha, Nebraska

UG Enrollment: 225 — **Tuition & Fees: $6795**
Application Deadline: rolling — **Room & Board: N/Avail**

GENERAL Proprietary, 2-year, coed. Awards diplomas, transfer associate degrees. Founded 1967. ***Setting:*** 1-acre urban campus. ***Total enrollment:*** 225. ***Faculty:*** 23 (13 full-time, 10 part-time).
ENROLLMENT PROFILE 225 students from 6 states and territories. 95% women, 5% men, 0% part-time, 70% state residents, 0% transferred in, 15% 25 or older, 2% Native American, 5% Hispanic, 20% African American. ***Areas of study chosen:*** 20% health professions and related sciences.
FIRST-YEAR CLASS 190 total; 287 applied, 85% were accepted, 78% of whom enrolled. 100% from top half of their high school class.
ACADEMIC PROGRAM Honor code. Calendar: modular. Summer session for credit.
GENERAL DEGREE REQUIREMENTS 100 quarter credits; internship.
MAJORS Commercial art, medical assistant technologies, medical secretarial studies, veterinary technology.
COMPUTERS ON CAMPUS Computer purchase plan available. 50 computers for student use in computer labs. Staffed computer lab on campus provides training in use of computers, software.
COLLEGE LIFE ***Campus security:*** 24-hour emergency response devices.
HOUSING College housing not available.
CAREER PLANNING ***Placement office:*** 1 full-time staff. ***Director:*** Ms. Myrna Feeken, Placement Director, 402-333-1400. ***Services:*** resume preparation, career counseling, job bank, job interviews. 30 organizations recruited on campus 1994–95.
AFTER GRADUATION 92% of class of 1994 had job offers within 6 months. 25% of students completing a degree program went directly on to further study.
EXPENSES FOR 1996–97 Tuition: $6795 full-time, $117 per credit hour part-time. Tuition guaranteed not to increase for student's term of enrollment.
FINANCIAL AID ***College-administered undergrad aid 1995–96:*** 2 need-based scholarships (average $3172), low-interest long-term loans from external sources (average $2625). ***Required forms:*** FAFSA. ***Application deadline:*** continuous. ***Payment plan:*** installment. ***Waivers:*** full or partial for employees or children of employees.
APPLYING ***Options:*** early entrance, deferred entrance. ***Required:*** school transcript, Wonderlic aptitude test. ***Recommended:*** SAT I or ACT. Test scores used for admission. ***Application deadline:*** rolling. ***Notification:*** continuous.
APPLYING/TRANSFER ***Required:*** standardized test scores. ***Entrance:*** moderately difficult. ***Application deadline:*** rolling. ***Notification:*** continuous.
CONTACT Dr. William J. Stuckey, Admissions Director, Omaha College of Health Careers, 10845 Harney Street, Omaha, NE 68154-2655, 402-333-1400.

SOUTHEAST COMMUNITY COLLEGE, BEATRICE CAMPUS
Beatrice, Nebraska

UG Enrollment: 920 — **Tuition & Fees (NE Res): $1163**
Application Deadline: rolling — **Room Only: $549**

GENERAL District-supported, 2-year, coed. Part of Southeast Community College System. Awards certificates, diplomas, transfer associate, terminal associate degrees. Founded 1976. ***Setting:*** 640-acre small-town campus with easy access to Omaha. ***Total enrollment:*** 920. ***Faculty:*** 65 (40 full-time, 5% with terminal degrees, 25 part-time); student-faculty ratio is 20:1.
ENROLLMENT PROFILE 920 students from 9 states and territories, 7 other countries. 60% women, 40% men, 36% part-time, 93% state residents, 20% live on campus, 4% transferred in, 1% international, 40% 25 or older, 1% Hispanic, 1% African American, 1% Asian American.
FIRST-YEAR CLASS 300 total; 600 applied, 100% were accepted, 50% of whom enrolled.
ACADEMIC PROGRAM Core, vocational/technical curriculum, honor code. Calendar: semesters. 110 courses offered in 1995–96. Academic remediation for entering students, services for LD students, summer session for credit, part-time degree program (daytime, evenings, summer), adult/continuing education programs, co-op programs and internships. Off-campus study at Peru State College.
GENERAL DEGREE REQUIREMENTS 60 credit hours; 3 credit hours of math; 1 lab science course; computer course; internship (some majors).
MAJORS Accounting, agricultural business, agricultural sciences, agricultural technologies, agronomy/soil and crop sciences, animal sciences, art/fine arts, biology/biological sciences, biotechnology, broadcasting, business administration/commerce/management, computer science, education, elementary education, finance/banking, journalism, legal secretarial studies, liberal arts/general studies, medical secretarial studies, physical sciences, practical nursing, science, secretarial studies/office management, soil conservation.
LIBRARY Learning Resource Center with 11,000 books, 45 microform titles, 225 periodicals, 450 records, tapes, and CDs.
COMPUTERS ON CAMPUS 75 computers for student use in computer center, computer labs, classrooms, library, dorms provide access to main academic computer, on-line services.
COLLEGE LIFE Orientation program (3 days, parents included). Drama-theater group, choral group, student-run newspaper, radio station. 35% vote in student government elections. ***Most popular organizations:*** Student Senate, Agricultural Club, Residence Hall Association, Licensed Practical Association of Nebraska, International Student Association. ***Major annual events:*** Homecoming, All Campus Spaghetti Feed. ***Student services:*** personal-psychological counseling. ***Campus security:*** 24-hour patrols, controlled dormitory access.
HOUSING 183 college housing spaces available; 165 were occupied 1995–96. No special consideration for freshman housing applicants. Off-campus living permitted. ***Option:*** coed housing available. Resident assistants live in dorms.
ATHLETICS Member NJCAA. ***Intercollegiate:*** basketball M(s)/W(s), golf M(s), volleyball W(s). ***Contact:*** Mr. Dan Johnson, Athletic Director, 402-228-3468 Ext. 232; Mr. Bill Campbell, Coach, 402-228-3468 Ext. 234.
CAREER PLANNING ***Placement office:*** 1 full-time staff. ***Director:*** Mr. Robert Kluge, Career/Information Specialist, 402-228-3468. ***Services:*** job fairs, resume preparation, resume referral, career counseling, job bank, job interviews. Students must register freshman year.
AFTER GRADUATION 87% of class of 1994 had job offers within 6 months. 80% of students completing a degree program went directly on to further study.
EXPENSES FOR 1995–96 State resident tuition: $1103 full-time, $36.75 per credit hour part-time. Nonresident tuition: $1283 full-time, $42.75 per credit hour part-time. Part-time mandatory fees: $2.50 per credit hour. Iowa, Kansas, Missouri, Wyoming, Colorado, and South Dakota residents pay state resident tuition rates. Full-time mandatory fees: $60. College room only: $549.
FINANCIAL AID ***College-administered undergrad aid 1995–96:*** need-based scholarships, 60 non-need scholarships (average $300), short-term loans (average $100), low-interest long-term loans from external sources (average $2125), Federal Work-Study, 10 part-time jobs. ***Required forms:*** institutional, FAFSA, financial aid transcript (for transfers); accepted: CSS Financial Aid PROFILE. ***Priority deadline:*** 7/1. ***Waivers:*** full or partial for minority students, employees or children of employees, and senior citizens. ***Notification:*** continuous.
APPLYING Open admission. ***Options:*** Common Application, early entrance, deferred entrance, midyear entrance. ***Required:*** school transcript, TOEFL for international students. ***Recommended:*** minimum 2.0 GPA, SAT I or ACT. ***Required for some:*** 3 years of high school math and science, ACT ASSET. Test scores used for admission (for practical nsing program) and counseling/placement. ***Application deadline:*** rolling.

APPLYING/TRANSFER ***Required:*** high school transcript, college transcript. ***Recommended:*** minimum 2.0 high school GPA. ***Required for some:*** standardized test scores. ***Entrance:*** noncompetitive. ***Application deadline:*** rolling.
CONTACT Dr. Joe R. Renteria, Dean of Student Services, Southeast Community College, Beatrice Campus, Beatrice, NE 68310-9683, 402-228-3468 Ext. 220 or toll-free 800-233-5027. ***Fax:*** 402-228-3468 Ext. 203.

SOUTHEAST COMMUNITY COLLEGE, LINCOLN CAMPUS
Lincoln, Nebraska

UG Enrollment: 4,555	**Tuition & Fees (NE Res): $1490**
Application Deadline: rolling	**Room & Board: N/Avail**

GENERAL District-supported, 2-year, coed. Part of Southeast Community College System. Awards certificates, diplomas, transfer associate, terminal associate degrees. Founded 1973. ***Setting:*** 115-acre suburban campus with easy access to Omaha. ***Educational spending 1994–95:*** $2930 per undergrad. ***Total enrollment:*** 4,555. ***Faculty:*** 545 (130 full-time, 2% with terminal degrees, 415 part-time).
ENROLLMENT PROFILE 4,555 students: 58% women, 42% men, 65% part-time, 99% state residents, 18% transferred in, 60% have need-based financial aid, 15% have non-need-based financial aid, 1% international, 50% 25 or older, 1% Native American, 1% Hispanic, 2% African American, 4% Asian American. ***Areas of study chosen:*** 30% health professions and related sciences, 25% engineering and applied sciences, 20% business management and administrative services, 15% liberal arts/general studies, 10% vocational and home economics. ***Most popular recent majors:*** business administration/commerce/management, nursing, human services.
FIRST-YEAR CLASS 1,280 total; 2,800 applied, 100% were accepted, 85% of whom enrolled.
ACADEMIC PROGRAM Vocational/technical curriculum, honor code. Calendar: quarters. Academic remediation for entering students, English as a second language program offered during academic year, services for LD students, tutorials, summer session for credit, part-time degree program (daytime, evenings, weekends, summer), adult/continuing education programs, co-op programs and internships.
GENERAL DEGREE REQUIREMENTS 96 quarter credits; internship (some majors).
MAJORS Accounting, automotive technologies, business administration/commerce/management, child care/child and family studies, computer technologies, culinary arts, dietetics, drafting and design, electrical and electronics technologies, environmental sciences, fire science, food services management, human services, liberal arts/general studies, machine and tool technologies, medical laboratory technology, medical secretarial studies, nursing, radiological technology, respiratory therapy, retail management, science, secretarial studies/office management, welding technology.
LIBRARY 15,575 books, 45 microform titles, 390 periodicals, 15 CD-ROMs, 2,230 records, tapes, and CDs. Acquisition spending 1994–95: $171,080.
COMPUTERS ON CAMPUS 200 computers for student use in computer labs, learning resource center, classrooms, library provide access to Internet. Staffed computer lab on campus provides training in use of computers, software. Academic computing expenditure 1994–95: $549,334.
COLLEGE LIFE ***Social organizations:*** 4 open to all. ***Most popular organizations:*** Student Senate, Phi Theta Kappa, Rainbow Club, Single Parents Club, Vocational Industrial Clubs of America. ***Student services:*** personal-psychological counseling. ***Campus security:*** late-night transport-escort service.
HOUSING College housing not available.
ATHLETICS ***Intramural:*** basketball, softball, table tennis (Ping-Pong), tennis, volleyball.
CAREER PLANNING ***Placement office:*** 5 full-time, 3 part-time staff; $254,975 operating expenditure 1994–95. ***Director:*** Mr. David Sonenberg, Director of Career Services, 402-437-2620. ***Services:*** job fairs, resume preparation, resume referral, career counseling, careers library, job bank, job interviews. 125 organizations recruited on campus 1994–95.
AFTER GRADUATION 90% of class of 1994 had job offers within 6 months. 50% of students completing a degree program went directly on to further study.
EXPENSES FOR 1996–97 State resident tuition: $1454 full-time, $25.50 per credit part-time. Nonresident tuition: $1710 full-time, $30 per credit part-time. Part-time mandatory fees: $1 per credit. Full-time mandatory fees: $36.
FINANCIAL AID ***College-administered undergrad aid 1995–96:*** 1,000 need-based scholarships (average $350), 175 non-need scholarships (average $365), short-term loans (average $150), low-interest long-term loans from external sources (average $2100), 50 Federal Work-Study (averaging $4000), 15 part-time jobs. ***Required forms:*** institutional, FAFSA; accepted: CSS Financial Aid PROFILE. ***Application deadline:*** continuous. ***Waivers:*** full or partial for minority students, employees or children of employees, and adult students. ***Notification:*** continuous. ***Average indebtedness of graduates:*** $4000.
APPLYING Open admission. ***Options:*** early entrance, deferred entrance, midyear entrance. ***Required:*** school transcript, TOEFL for international students. ***Recommended:*** 3 years of high school math and science. ***Required for some:*** ACT, ACT ASSET. Test scores used for counseling/placement. ***Application deadline:*** rolling.
APPLYING/TRANSFER ***Required:*** high school transcript, college transcript. ***Recommended:*** 3 years of high school math and science. ***Entrance:*** noncompetitive. ***Application deadline:*** rolling. ***Contact:*** Mr. Gerald D. Gruber, Dean of Student Services, 402-437-2619.
CONTACT Mrs. Robin Moore, Enrollment Management Specialist, Southeast Community College, Lincoln Campus, Lincoln, NE 68520-1299, 402-437-2604 or toll-free 800-642-4075 (in-state). College video available.

SOUTHEAST COMMUNITY COLLEGE, MILFORD CAMPUS
Milford, Nebraska

UG Enrollment: 920	**Tuition & Fees (NE Res): $1413**
Application Deadline: rolling	**Room & Board: $2085**

GENERAL District-supported, 2-year, coed. Part of Southeast Community College System. Awards diplomas, terminal associate degrees. Founded 1941. ***Setting:*** 50-acre small-town campus with easy access to Omaha. ***Total enrollment:*** 920. ***Faculty:*** 89 (86 full-time, 3 part-time).
ENROLLMENT PROFILE 920 students: 7% women, 3% part-time, 95% state residents, 33% live on campus, 5% transferred in, 1% international, 20% 25 or older, 0% Native American, 0% Hispanic, 0% African American, 0% Asian American. ***Most popular recent majors:*** architectural technologies, automotive technologies, construction technologies.
FIRST-YEAR CLASS 280 total; 380 applied, 100% were accepted, 74% of whom enrolled.
ACADEMIC PROGRAM Honor code. Calendar: quarters. Academic remediation for entering students, services for LD students, summer session for credit, co-op programs and internships.
GENERAL DEGREE REQUIREMENT 108 credits.
MAJORS Architectural technologies, automotive technologies, carpentry, civil engineering technology, commercial art, computer programming, computer technologies, construction technologies, data processing, drafting and design, electrical and electronics technologies, electrical engineering technology, electromechanical technology, electronics engineering technology, heating/refrigeration/air conditioning, industrial arts, industrial design, machine and tool technologies, manufacturing technology, mechanical design technology, mechanical engineering technology, metallurgical technology, metallurgy, plastics technology, plumbing, quality control technology, solar technologies, surveying technology, transportation technologies, welding technology.
LIBRARY 10,000 books, 300 periodicals.
COMPUTERS ON CAMPUS Computer purchase plan available. 72 computers for student use in computer center, library. Staffed computer lab on campus provides training in use of computers, software.
COLLEGE LIFE ***Major annual events:*** Convocations, Dances. ***Campus security:*** late-night transport-escort service.
HOUSING 330 college housing spaces available; 300 were occupied 1995–96. Off-campus living permitted. ***Option:*** single-sex housing available. Resident assistants live in dorms.
ATHLETICS ***Intramural:*** archery, basketball, bowling, football, golf, racquetball, swimming and diving, table tennis (Ping-Pong), tennis, volleyball, weight lifting, wrestling.
CAREER PLANNING ***Placement office:*** 1 full-time, 1 part-time staff. ***Director:*** Mr. Gerald Eigsti, Placement Director, 800-933-7223 Ext. 202. ***Services:*** job fairs, resume referral, career counseling, job bank, job interviews. Students must register sophomore year. 120 organizations recruited on campus 1994–95.
AFTER GRADUATION 99% of class of 1994 had job offers within 6 months.
EXPENSES FOR 1996–97 State resident tuition: $1377 (minimum) full-time, $25.50 per credit part-time. Nonresident tuition: $1647 (minimum) full-time, $30.50 per credit part-time. Part-time mandatory fees: $12 per quarter. Full-time tuition ranges up to $1454 for state residents, $1739 for non residents. Iowa, Kansas, Wyoming, Colorado, and South Dakota residents pay state resident tuition rates. Full-time mandatory fees: $36. College room and board: $2085.
FINANCIAL AID ***College-administered undergrad aid 1995–96:*** 50 need-based scholarships (averaging $200), 70 non-need scholarships (averaging $200), short-term loans (averaging $100), low-interest long-term loans from external sources (averaging $2000), Federal Work-Study, part-time jobs. ***Required forms:*** institutional, FAFSA; accepted: CSS Financial Aid PROFILE. ***Priority deadline:*** 4/1. ***Waivers:*** full or partial for minority students, employees or children of employees, adult students, and senior citizens. ***Average indebtedness of graduates:*** $4000.
APPLYING Open admission. ***Required:*** school transcript, ACT, TOEFL for international students, ACT ASSET. Test scores used for counseling/placement. ***Application deadline:*** rolling. ***Notification:*** continuous.
APPLYING/TRANSFER ***Required:*** college transcript. ***Application deadline:*** rolling. ***Notification:*** continuous. ***Contact:*** Ms. Donna Havener, Registrar, 402-761-2131.
CONTACT Mr. Larry E. Meyer, Dean of Students, Southeast Community College, Milford Campus, Milford, NE 68405-9397, 402-761-2131 Ext. 270 or toll-free 800-933-7223. College video available.

SPENCER SCHOOL OF BUSINESS
Grand Island, Nebraska

UG Enrollment: 136	**Tuition & Fees: $5985**
Application Deadline: 9/15	**Room Only: $2130**

GENERAL Proprietary, 2-year, primarily women. Awards certificates, diplomas, transfer associate, terminal associate degrees. Founded 1983. ***Setting:*** small-town campus. ***Research spending 1994–95:*** $2000. ***Total enrollment:*** 136. ***Faculty:*** 11 (7 full-time, 4 part-time); student-faculty ratio is 13:1.
ENROLLMENT PROFILE 136 students from 2 states and territories. 85% women, 1% part-time, 99% state residents, 50% live on campus, 31% transferred in, 100% have need-based financial aid, 0% international, 17% 25 or older, 0% Native American, 1% Hispanic, 0% African American, 0% Asian American. ***Areas of study chosen:*** 43% business management and administrative services, 37% health professions and related sciences, 20% computer and information sciences. ***Most popular recent majors:*** accounting, medical assistant technologies, secretarial studies/office management.
FIRST-YEAR CLASS 99 total; 163 applied, 99% were accepted, 61% of whom enrolled. 8% from top 10% of their high school class, 68% from top quarter, 90% from top half. 2 valedictorians.
ACADEMIC PROGRAM Core, honor code. Calendar: quarters. 70 courses offered in 1995–96. Academic remediation for entering students, services for LD students, advanced placement, part-time degree program (daytime), internships.
GENERAL DEGREE REQUIREMENTS 104 quarter credits; 1 college math course; computer course; internship.
MAJORS Accounting, business administration/commerce/management, computer information systems, computer technologies, fashion merchandising, finance/banking, legal secretarial studies, medical assistant technologies, medical secretarial studies, retail management, secretarial studies/office management, tourism and travel.
LIBRARY 950 books, 50 periodicals, 120 records, tapes, and CDs. Acquisition spending 1994–95: $5000.
COMPUTERS ON CAMPUS Computer purchase plan available. 36 computers for student use in computer center provide access to main academic computer, Internet. Staffed computer lab on campus provides training in use of computers, software. Academic computing expenditure 1994–95: $40,000.

Nebraska–Nevada

Spencer School of Business (continued)
HOUSING 74 college housing spaces available. Freshmen given priority for college housing. Off-campus living permitted. *Option:* coed housing available. Resident assistants live in dorms.
ATHLETICS *Intramural:* basketball, bowling, softball, volleyball.
CAREER PLANNING *Placement office:* $30,092 operating expenditure 1994–95. *Director:* Ms. Deb Stevens, Director of Student Employment, 308-382-8044. *Services:* job fairs, resume preparation, resume referral, career counseling, job bank, job interviews. Students must register freshman year.
AFTER GRADUATION 91% of class of 1994 had job offers within 6 months.
EXPENSES FOR 1996–97 *Application fee:* $35. Tuition: $5985 full-time, $92 per quarter hour part-time. One-time mandatory fee: $55. College room only: $2130 (minimum). Tuition guaranteed not to increase for student's term of enrollment.
FINANCIAL AID *College-administered undergrad aid 1995–96:* need-based scholarships, 40 non-need scholarships (average $500), low-interest long-term loans from external sources, 5 Federal Work-Study (averaging $1000). *Required forms:* institutional, FAFSA; accepted: CSS Financial Aid PROFILE. *Priority deadline:* 9/15. *Payment plan:* installment. *Waivers:* full or partial for employees or children of employees. *Average indebtedness of graduates:* $6125.
APPLYING *Options:* Common Application, deferred entrance. *Required:* school transcript, minimum 2.0 GPA. *Recommended:* SAT I or ACT. Test scores used for admission. *Application deadline:* 9/15.
APPLYING/TRANSFER *Required:* high school transcript, college transcript, minimum 2.0 high school GPA. *Recommended:* standardized test scores. *Entrance:* moderately difficult. *Application deadline:* 9/15.
CONTACT Ms. Melaine Schepers, Inside Interviewer, Spencer School of Business, Grand Island, NE 68802-0399, 308-382-8044. *Fax:* 308-382-5072. College video available.

WESTERN NEBRASKA COMMUNITY COLLEGE
Scottsbluff, Nebraska

UG Enrollment: 2,291	Tuition & Fees (NE Res): $1230
Application Deadline: rolling	Room & Board: $2560

GENERAL State and locally supported, 2-year, coed. Part of Western Community College Area System. Awards certificates, diplomas, transfer associate, terminal associate degrees. Founded 1921. *Setting:* 20-acre rural campus. *Endowment:* $454,300. *Educational spending 1994–95:* $1422 per undergrad. *Total enrollment:* 2,291. *Faculty:* 156 (69 full-time, 2% with terminal degrees, 87 part-time); student-faculty ratio is 18:1.
ENROLLMENT PROFILE 2,291 students from 17 states and territories, 4 other countries. 65% women, 35% men, 33% part-time, 96% state residents, 5% live on campus, 25% transferred in, 76% have need-based financial aid, 15% have non-need-based financial aid, 1% international, 54% 25 or older, 2% Native American, 11% Hispanic, 1% African American, 0% Asian American. *Areas of study chosen:* 38% liberal arts/general studies, 14% business management and administrative services, 14% health professions and related sciences, 13% vocational and home economics, 6% education, 2% agriculture, 2% computer and information sciences, 2% social sciences, 1% biological and life sciences, 1% fine arts, 1% natural resource sciences, 1% physical sciences, 1% psychology. *Most popular recent major:* aviation technology.
FIRST-YEAR CLASS 733 total. Of the students who applied, 100% were accepted. 10% from top 10% of their high school class, 50% from top half.
ACADEMIC PROGRAM Core. Calendar: semesters. 532 courses offered in 1995–96; average class size 19 in required courses. Academic remediation for entering students, English as a second language program offered during academic year and summer, services for LD students, summer session for credit, part-time degree program (daytime, evenings), co-op programs and internships.
GENERAL DEGREE REQUIREMENTS 60 semester hours; computer course for business administration, farm and ranch management, secretarial majors; internship (some majors).
MAJORS Accounting, anthropology, art education, automotive technologies, aviation technology, biology/biological sciences, business administration/commerce/management, chemistry, communication equipment technology, computer programming, computer science, computer technologies, cosmetology, criminal justice, early childhood education, economics, education, electrical and electronics technologies, electronics engineering technology, elementary education, emergency medical technology, English, environmental sciences, farm and ranch management, forestry, French, geography, German, guidance and counseling, history, human development, human services, journalism, liberal arts/general studies, marketing/retailing/merchandising, mathematics, music, nursing, physics, practical nursing, psychology, radiological technology, real estate, secretarial studies/office management, social work, sociology, Spanish, theater arts/drama, welding technology, wildlife management.
LIBRARY 28,000 books, 5 microform titles, 200 periodicals, 1 on-line bibliographic service, 50 CD-ROMs, 500 records, tapes, and CDs. Acquisition spending 1994–95: $61,326.
COMPUTERS ON CAMPUS 120 computers for student use in computer labs, learning resource center, classrooms, library, dorms provide access to main academic computer, off-campus computing facilities, e-mail, on-line services, Internet. Staffed computer lab on campus provides training in use of computers, software. Academic computing expenditure 1994–95: $162,323.
COLLEGE LIFE Drama-theater group, choral group, student-run newspaper. 20% vote in student government elections. *Social organizations:* 2 national sororities. *Student services:* personal-psychological counseling. *Campus security:* 24-hour emergency response devices, controlled dormitory access, patrols by trained security personnel from 12:30 a.m. to 6 a.m.
HOUSING 128 college housing spaces available; 117 were occupied 1995–96. No special consideration for freshman housing applicants. Off-campus living permitted. *Option:* coed (1 building) housing available. Resident assistants live in dorms.
ATHLETICS Member NJCAA. *Intercollegiate:* basketball M(s)/W(s), golf M(s), volleyball W(s). *Intramural:* basketball, bowling, football, table tennis (Ping-Pong), tennis, volleyball, weight lifting. *Contact:* Mr. Dave Campbell, Athletic Director, 308-635-6026.
CAREER PLANNING *Placement office:* 1 full-time, 3 part-time staff; $91,103 operating expenditure 1994–95. *Director:* Ms. Judy Smith, Director, Career Assessment Center, 308-635-6072. *Services:* resume preparation, career counseling, careers library, job bank. 11 organizations recruited on campus 1994–95.
AFTER GRADUATION 53% of class of 1994 had job offers within 6 months. 62% of students completing a degree program went directly on to further study.
EXPENSES FOR 1996–97 State resident tuition: $1095 full-time, $36.50 per semester hour part-time. Nonresident tuition: $1230 full-time, $41 per semester hour part-time. Part-time mandatory fees: $4.50 per semester hour. Full-time mandatory fees: $135. College room and board: $2560.
FINANCIAL AID *College-administered undergrad aid 1995–96:* 75 need-based scholarships (averaging $300), low-interest long-term loans from external sources (averaging $2625), 65 Federal Work-Study (averaging $2000). *Required forms:* institutional, FAFSA. *Priority deadline:* 3/15. *Waivers:* full or partial for employees or children of employees and senior citizens. *Notification:* 5/10.
APPLYING Open admission. *Options:* Common Application, electronic application, early entrance, midyear entrance. *Required:* TOEFL for international students, ACT ASSET. *Recommended:* ACT. Test scores used for counseling/placement. *Application deadline:* rolling.
APPLYING/TRANSFER *Recommended:* college transcript. *Entrance:* noncompetitive. *Application deadline:* rolling. *Contact:* Dr. Ernest Griffiths, Registrar, 308-635-6012.
CONTACT Mr. Roger Hovey, Director of Enrollment Marketing, Western Nebraska Community College, Scottsbluff, NE 69361, 308-635-6010 or toll-free 800-348-4435 (in-state). *E-mail:* rhovey@hannibal.wncc.cc.ne.us. Electronic viewbook available.

NEVADA

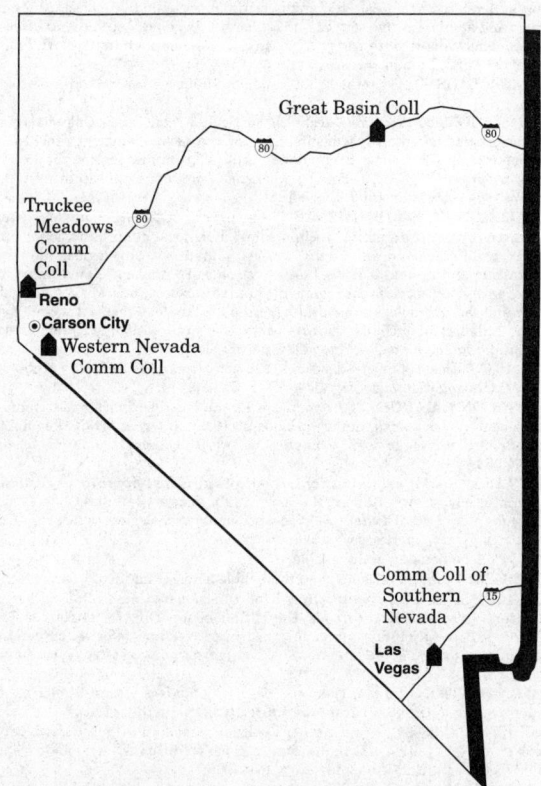

COMMUNITY COLLEGE OF SOUTHERN NEVADA
North Las Vegas, Nevada

UG Enrollment: 20,417	Tuition & Fees (NV Res): $1095
Application Deadline: 9/9	Room & Board: N/Avail

The Community College of Southern Nevada is an open-door comprehensive educational institution within the University and Community College System of Nevada. It serves 5 educational areas: continuing education, counseling and guidance, developmental education, occupational training, and university transfer preparation.

GENERAL State-supported, 2-year, coed. Part of University and Community College System of Nevada. Awards certificates, transfer associate degrees. Founded 1971. *Setting:* 89-acre suburban campus with easy access to Las Vegas. *Endowment:* $1.4 million. *Total enrollment:* 20,417. *Faculty:* 860 (222 full-time, 95% with terminal degrees, 638 part-time); student-faculty ratio is 21:1.
ENROLLMENT PROFILE 20,417 students: 55% women, 45% men, 87% part-time, 98% state residents, 10% transferred in, 1% international, 60% 25 or older, 1% Native American, 11% Hispanic, 9% African American, 7% Asian American. *Most popular recent majors:* liberal arts/general studies, practical nursing, business administration/commerce/management.
FIRST-YEAR CLASS 2,481 total. Of the students who applied, 100% were accepted, 100% of whom enrolled.

Peterson's Guide to Two-Year Colleges 1997

ACADEMIC PROGRAM Core. Calendar: semesters. Academic remediation for entering students, English as a second language program offered during academic year and summer, services for LD students, advanced placement, summer session for credit, part-time degree program (daytime, evenings, weekends, summer), adult/continuing education programs, co-op programs.
GENERAL DEGREE REQUIREMENTS 60 credit hours; computer course; internship (some majors).
MAJORS Accounting, anthropology, art/fine arts, automotive technologies, behavioral sciences, biology/biological sciences, business administration/commerce/management, chemistry, child care/child and family studies, communication, computer information systems, computer programming, computer science, computer technologies, construction management, construction technologies, corrections, court reporting, criminal justice, culinary arts, data processing, deaf interpreter training, dental services, drafting and design, early childhood education, economics, electrical and electronics technologies, electrical engineering technology, emergency medical technology, English, environmental studies, finance/banking, fire science, food services management, food services technology, graphic arts, heating/refrigeration/air conditioning, history, horticulture, hospitality services, hotel and restaurant management, industrial and heavy equipment maintenance, landscaping/grounds maintenance, legal secretarial studies, liberal arts/general studies, literature, marketing/retailing/merchandising, mathematics, mechanical design technology, mechanical engineering technology, medical laboratory technology, medical records services, medical technology, music, nursing, occupational therapy, ornamental horticulture, paralegal studies, pharmacy/pharmaceutical sciences, photography, practical nursing, printing technologies, radio and television studies, radiological sciences, radiological technology, real estate, recreation and leisure services, respiratory therapy, retail management, science, science education, secretarial studies/office management, social science, sociology, surveying technology, teacher aide studies, theater arts/drama, welding technology, word processing.
LIBRARY Learning Assistance Center with 49,606 books, 381 microform titles, 492 periodicals, 2 on-line bibliographic services, 5 CD-ROMs, 1,065 records, tapes, and CDs. Acquisition spending 1994–95: $265,607.
COMPUTERS ON CAMPUS Computer purchase plan available. 500 computers for student use in computer center, computer labs, learning resource center, classrooms, library provide access to off-campus computing facilities, e-mail, Internet. Academic computing expenditure 1994–95: $560,000.
COLLEGE LIFE Drama-theater group. ***Social organizations:*** 10 open to all. ***Most popular organizations:*** Culinary Club, Art Club, Black Student Association, Student Organization of Latinos, Student Nurses Club. ***Major annual events:*** Black History Week, Career Day, Cinco de Mayo. ***Student services:*** legal services, health clinic, personal-psychological counseling, women's center. ***Campus security:*** 24-hour emergency response devices and patrols.
HOUSING College housing not available.
ATHLETICS ***Intramural:*** basketball, bowling, golf, racquetball, tennis, weight lifting.
CAREER PLANNING ***Placement office:*** 2 full-time, 2 part-time staff; $77,055 operating expenditure 1994–95. ***Director:*** Ms. Rosmary Hall, Career Center Director, 702-651-4283. ***Services:*** job fairs, career counseling, careers library, job interviews.
EXPENSES FOR 1996–97 ***Application fee:*** $5. State resident tuition: $1095 full-time, $36.50 per credit hour part-time. Nonresident tuition: $4195 full-time. Nonresident part-time tuition per semester ranges from $52 to $951.50.
FINANCIAL AID ***College-administered undergrad aid 1995–96:*** 767 need-based scholarships (averaging $500), 24 non-need scholarships (averaging $500), short-term loans (averaging $100), low-interest long-term loans from external sources (averaging $2000), 72 Federal Work-Study, 13 part-time jobs. ***Required forms:*** institutional, FAFSA; accepted: state. ***Priority deadline:*** 4/15. ***Payment plan:*** deferred payment. ***Waivers:*** full or partial for employees or children of employees and senior citizens. ***Notification:*** 7/1. ***Average indebtedness of graduates:*** $3000.
APPLYING Open admission except for allied health programs. ***Option:*** early entrance. ***Required:*** student data form. ***Required for some:*** TOEFL for international students. Test scores used for counseling/placement. ***Application deadline:*** 9/9. ***Notification:*** continuous until 9/9.
APPLYING/TRANSFER ***Required:*** student data form. ***Entrance:*** noncompetitive. ***Application deadline:*** 8/30. ***Notification:*** continuous until 8/30. ***Contact:*** Ms. Joyce Ricci, Student Retention Manager, 702-651-4559.
CONTACT Mr. Arlie Stops, Associate Vice President for Admissions and Records, Community College of Southern Nevada, North Las Vegas, NV 89030-4296, 702-651-4060. ***E-mail:*** stops@ccmail.ccsn.nevada.edu. College video available.

GREAT BASIN COLLEGE
Elko, Nevada

UG Enrollment: 3,000	**Tuition & Fees (NV Res): $1005**
Application Deadline: rolling	**Room & Board: N/Avail**

GENERAL State-supported, 2-year, coed. Part of University and Community College System of Nevada. Awards transfer associate, terminal associate degrees. Founded 1967. ***Setting:*** 58-acre rural campus. ***Total enrollment:*** 3,000. ***Faculty:*** 333 (33 full-time, 75% with terminal degrees, 300 part-time).
ENROLLMENT PROFILE 3,000 students: 60% women, 40% men, 83% part-time, 99% state residents, 5% transferred in, 60% 25 or older, 10% Native American, 2% Hispanic, 1% African American. ***Areas of study chosen:*** 20% education, 20% fine arts, 20% liberal arts/general studies, 15% engineering and applied sciences, 5% business management and administrative services, 5% health professions and related sciences. ***Most popular recent majors:*** liberal arts/general studies, nursing.
FIRST-YEAR CLASS 608 total; 608 applied, 100% were accepted, 100% of whom enrolled.
ACADEMIC PROGRAM Core, honor code. Calendar: semesters. Academic remediation for entering students, English as a second language program offered during academic year and summer, services for LD students, summer session for credit, part-time degree program (daytime, evenings, weekends, summer), adult/continuing education programs, co-op programs.
GENERAL DEGREE REQUIREMENTS 60 semester hours; math/science requirements vary according to program; computer course for business administration, engineering, early childhood education, secretarial office administration majors.
MAJORS Accounting, art/fine arts, automotive technologies, business administration/commerce/management, business machine technologies, child care/child and family studies, child psychology/child development, computer information systems, computer technologies, criminal justice, electrical and electronics technologies, geology, liberal arts/general studies, metallurgical technology, mining technology, nursing, science, secretarial studies/office management, welding technology.
LIBRARY Learning Resources Center with 25,000 books, 585 microform titles, 250 periodicals, 150 CD-ROMs, 4,500 records, tapes, and CDs. Acquisition spending 1994–95: $87,499.
COMPUTERS ON CAMPUS Computer purchase plan available. 87 computers for student use in computer labs, learning resource center provide access to off-campus computing facilities, on-line services, Internet. Academic computing expenditure 1994–95: $254,000.
COLLEGE LIFE Orientation program (2 days, no cost). Drama-theater group, choral group. ***Social organizations:*** 1 local sorority; 1% of eligible women are members. ***Student services:*** personal-psychological counseling. ***Campus security:*** evening patrols by trained security personnel.
HOUSING College housing not available.
ATHLETICS ***Intramural:*** skiing (cross-country), skiing (downhill), weight lifting.
CAREER PLANNING ***Placement office:*** 1 full-time staff. ***Director:*** Mr. Phil Smith, Counselor, 702-753-2279. ***Services:*** resume preparation, career counseling, careers library.
EXPENSES FOR 1995–96 ***Application fee:*** $5. State resident tuition: $1005 full-time, $33.50 per semester hour part-time. Nonresident tuition: $4105 full-time. Nonresident part-time tuition per semester ranges from $33.50 to $1919.
FINANCIAL AID ***College-administered undergrad aid 1995–96:*** 150 need-based scholarships (average $300), 100 non-need scholarships (average $300), short-term loans (average $250), low-interest long-term loans from external sources (average $2625), Federal Work-Study, 50 part-time jobs. ***Required forms:*** institutional, FAFSA; accepted: CSS Financial Aid PROFILE, state. ***Priority deadline:*** 4/1.
APPLYING Open admission except for nursing program. ***Options:*** Common Application, early entrance, deferred entrance. ***Required:*** TOEFL for international students. Test scores used for counseling/placement. ***Application deadline:*** rolling. ***Notification:*** continuous.
APPLYING/TRANSFER ***Entrance:*** noncompetitive. ***Application deadline:*** rolling. ***Notification:*** continuous.
CONTACT Mr. Stan Aiazzi, Dean of Student Services, Great Basin College, Elko, NV 89801-3348, 702-738-8493 Ext. 271.

NORTHERN NEVADA COMMUNITY COLLEGE
Nevada—See Great Basin College

TRUCKEE MEADOWS COMMUNITY COLLEGE
Reno, Nevada

UG Enrollment: 8,346	**Tuition & Fees (NV Res): $1095**
Application Deadline: rolling	**Room & Board: N/Avail**

GENERAL State-supported, 2-year, coed. Part of University and Community College System of Nevada. Awards certificates, transfer associate, terminal associate degrees. Founded 1971. ***Setting:*** 63-acre suburban campus. ***Endowment:*** $3.5 million. ***Educational spending 1994–95:*** $1163 per undergrad. ***Total enrollment:*** 8,346. ***Faculty:*** 464 (111 full-time, 19% with terminal degrees, 353 part-time); student-faculty ratio is 18:1.
ENROLLMENT PROFILE 8,346 students from 15 states and territories, 2 other countries. 60% women, 40% men, 84% part-time, 94% state residents, 14% transferred in, 10% have need-based financial aid, 2% have non-need-based financial aid, 2% international, 64% 25 or older, 3% Native American, 6% Hispanic, 1% African American, 5% Asian American. ***Most popular recent majors:*** nursing, business administration/commerce/management, fire science.
FIRST-YEAR CLASS 2,563 total; 2,563 applied, 100% were accepted, 100% of whom enrolled.
ACADEMIC PROGRAM Core, honor code. Calendar: semesters. Academic remediation for entering students, English as a second language program offered during academic year, services for LD students, advanced placement, summer session for credit, part-time degree program (daytime, evenings, weekends, summer), adult/continuing education programs, co-op programs and internships. ROTC: Army (c).
GENERAL DEGREE REQUIREMENTS 60 credits; computer course for legal assistant, general studies majors; internship (some majors).
MAJORS Accounting, architectural technologies, automotive technologies, business administration/commerce/management, carpentry, child care/child and family studies, computer information systems, computer programming, computer technologies, construction technologies, corrections, criminal justice, culinary arts, data processing, dental services, drafting and design, drug and alcohol/substance abuse counseling, early childhood education, electrical and electronics technologies, engineering technology, environmental sciences, environmental studies, finance/banking, fire science, food services technology, graphic arts, heating/refrigeration/air conditioning, hospitality services, landscape architecture/design, law enforcement/police sciences, legal secretarial studies, liberal arts/general studies, marketing/retailing/merchandising, medical secretarial studies, nursing, occupational safety and health, plumbing, radiological technology, real estate, safety and security technologies, secretarial studies/office management, solar technologies, welding technology.
LIBRARY Learning Resource Center with 36,286 books, 125 microform titles, 6,701 periodicals, 5 on-line bibliographic services, 1,898 records, tapes, and CDs.
COMPUTERS ON CAMPUS 210 computers for student use in computer center, computer labs, department labs, library provide access to main academic computer, Internet. Staffed computer lab on campus. Academic computing expenditure 1994–95: $80,980.
COLLEGE LIFE Student-run newspaper. 2% vote in student government elections. ***Student services:*** health clinic, personal-psychological counseling. ***Campus security:*** 24-hour emergency response devices and patrols, late-night transport-escort service.
HOUSING College housing not available.
CAREER PLANNING ***Placement office:*** 9 full-time, 2 part-time staff. ***Director:*** Mr. Wirt Twitchell, Director of Counseling and Testing, 702-673-7060. ***Services:*** job fairs, resume preparation, resume referral, career counseling, careers library.

Peterson's Guide to Two-Year Colleges 1997

431

Nevada–New Hampshire

Truckee Meadows Community College (continued)
EXPENSES FOR 1996–97 *Application fee:* $5. State resident tuition: $1095 full-time, $36.50 per credit part-time. Nonresident tuition: $4295 full-time. Nonresident part-time tuition per semester ranges from $52 to $2001. Tuition for California residents who are eligible for the Good Neighbor Program: $54.75 per credit.
FINANCIAL AID *College-administered undergrad aid 1995–96:* need-based scholarships, 30 non-need scholarships (average $300), short-term loans (average $75), low-interest long-term loans from external sources (average $750), Federal Work-Study, 24 part-time jobs. *Required forms:* institutional, FAFSA; required for some: state. *Priority deadline:* 5/1. *Payment plan:* deferred payment. *Waivers:* full or partial for employees or children of employees.
APPLYING Open admission except for allied health programs. *Options:* early entrance, deferred entrance, midyear entrance. *Required:* TOEFL for international students. *Recommended:* SAT I or ACT. Test scores used for counseling/placement. *Application deadline:* rolling.
APPLYING/TRANSFER *Recommended:* standardized test scores. *Entrance:* noncompetitive. *Application deadline:* rolling. *Contact:* Ms. Kathy Lucchesi, Director of Admissions and Records, 702-673-7042.
CONTACT Ms. Kathy Lucchesi, Director of Admissions and Records, Truckee Meadows Community College, Mail Station #15, Reno, NV 89512-3901, 702-673-7042. *Fax:* 702-673-7028.

WESTERN NEVADA COMMUNITY COLLEGE
Carson City, Nevada

UG Enrollment: 4,498	Tuition & Fees (NV Res): $1095
Application Deadline: rolling	Room & Board: N/Avail

GENERAL State-supported, 2-year, coed. Part of University and Community College System of Nevada. Awards transfer associate, terminal associate degrees. Founded 1971. *Setting:* 200-acre small-town campus. *Total enrollment:* 4,498. *Faculty:* 358 (93 full-time, 265 part-time); student-faculty ratio is 16:1.
ENROLLMENT PROFILE 4,498 students from 21 states and territories, 4 other countries. 60% women, 91% part-time, 97% state residents, 11% transferred in, 1% international, 60% 25 or older, 3% Native American, 8% Hispanic, 1% African American, 2% Asian American.
FIRST-YEAR CLASS 1,372 applied, 100% were accepted.
ACADEMIC PROGRAM Core. Calendar: semesters. Academic remediation for entering students, English as a second language program offered during academic year and summer, services for LD students, advanced placement, tutorials, summer session for credit, part-time degree program (daytime, evenings), co-op programs and internships.
GENERAL DEGREE REQUIREMENTS 60 credits; computer course for most majors.
MAJORS Accounting, automotive technologies, biology/biological sciences, business administration/commerce/management, child care/child and family studies, computer information systems, corrections, criminal justice, drafting and design, electrical and electronics technologies, finance/banking, law enforcement/police sciences, liberal arts/general studies, machine and tool technologies, marketing/retailing/merchandising, mathematics, nursing, practical nursing, real estate, robotics, secretarial studies/office management, welding technology, word processing.
LIBRARY Western Nevada Community College Library with 20,208 books, 70 microform titles, 248 periodicals, 2,601 records, tapes, and CDs.
COMPUTERS ON CAMPUS 55 computers for student use in computer labs, library, student center.
COLLEGE LIFE Choral group. *Campus security:* late-night transport-escort service.
HOUSING College housing not available.
CAREER PLANNING *Service:* career counseling.
ESTIMATED EXPENSES FOR 1996–97 *Application fee:* $5. State resident tuition: $1095 full-time, $36.50 per credit part-time. Nonresident tuition: $4195 full-time. Nonresident part-time tuition per semester ranges from $52 to $1952.
FINANCIAL AID *College-administered undergrad aid 1995–96:* 480 need-based scholarships (average $500), 46 non-need scholarships (average $200), Federal Work-Study, part-time jobs. *Required forms:* institutional, FAFSA; accepted: CSS Financial Aid PROFILE. *Priority deadline:* 7/1. *Payment plan:* deferred payment. *Waivers:* full or partial for employees or children of employees and senior citizens.
APPLYING Open admission. *Options:* early entrance, midyear entrance. *Required:* TOEFL for international students. *Recommended:* ACT. Test scores used for counseling/placement. *Application deadline:* rolling.
APPLYING/TRANSFER *Required:* college transcript. *Entrance:* noncompetitive. *Application deadline:* rolling.
CONTACT Mr. Nick L. Paul II, Associate Dean of Student Services, Western Nevada Community College, Carson City, NV 89703-7316, 702-887-3138. *Fax:* 702-885-0642.

NEW HAMPSHIRE

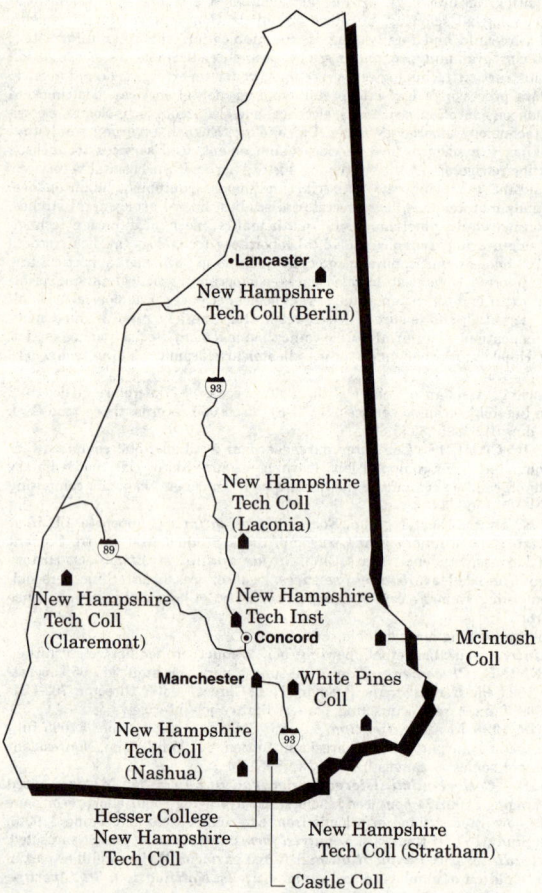

CASTLE COLLEGE
Windham, New Hampshire

UG Enrollment: 267	Tuition & Fees: $3975
Application Deadline: rolling	Room & Board: N/Avail

Students at Castle College find that classes are small and teachers genuinely care about them and their future. A low student-faculty ratio ensures personal and individualized instruction and academic support. While attending Castle College, students have the opportunity to explore career interests and acquire on-the-job training through an internship program.

GENERAL Independent, 2-year, coed. Awards certificates, transfer associate, terminal associate degrees. Founded 1963. *Setting:* 150-acre rural campus with easy access to Boston. *Educational spending 1994–95:* $1127 per undergrad. *Total enrollment:* 267. *Faculty:* 39 (7 full-time, 1% with terminal degrees, 32 part-time).
ENROLLMENT PROFILE 267 students from 2 states and territories. 93% women, 7% men, 16% part-time, 73% state residents, 20% transferred in, 86% have need-based financial aid, 9% have non-need-based financial aid, 0% international, 35% 25 or older, 0% Native American, 1% Hispanic, 0% African American, 0% Asian American. *Areas of study chosen:* 55% business management and administrative services, 29% health professions and related sciences, 14% education, 2% computer and information sciences, 2% interdisciplinary studies. *Most popular recent majors:* business administration/commerce/management, human services, early childhood education.
FIRST-YEAR CLASS 134 total; 206 applied, 74% were accepted, 88% of whom enrolled. 10% from top 10% of their high school class, 80% from top half.
ACADEMIC PROGRAM Core, job-oriented curriculum, honor code. Calendar: 4 eight-week terms and 1 five-week term for day division, 4 nine-week terms for evening division. 117 courses offered in 1995–96. Academic remediation for entering students, tutorials, summer session for credit, part-time degree program (daytime, evenings), external degree programs, adult/continuing education programs, co-op programs and internships.
GENERAL DEGREE REQUIREMENTS 60 credits; computer course for all business majors; internship (some majors).
MAJORS Accounting (B), business administration/commerce/management, business machine technologies, data processing, drug and alcohol/substance abuse counseling, early childhood education, human services, legal secretarial studies, medical secretarial studies, paralegal studies, recreation therapy, secretarial studies/office management, word processing.

432 Peterson's Guide to Two-Year Colleges 1997

LIBRARY Castle Library with 6,659 books, 6 microform titles, 86 periodicals, 4 CD-ROMs, 194 records, tapes, and CDs. Acquisition spending 1994–95: $16,000.
COMPUTERS ON CAMPUS 54 computers for student use in computer labs, classrooms, library. Staffed computer lab on campus provides training in use of computers, software. Academic computing expenditure 1994–95: $90,000.
COLLEGE LIFE ***Social organizations:*** 4 open to all. ***Most popular organizations:*** Student Activities Organization, Yearbook Committee, Student Ambassador Volunteers. ***Major annual events:*** Spring Dinner Dance, Spring Break Student Trip, Christmas Party. ***Student services:*** personal-psychological counseling.
HOUSING College housing not available.
CAREER PLANNING ***Placement office:*** 1 full-time staff; $55,000 operating expenditure 1994–95. ***Director:*** Ms. Maureen Jozwick, Job Placement Director, 603-893-6111. ***Services:*** resume preparation, resume referral, career counseling, job bank, job interviews.
AFTER GRADUATION 14% of students completing a degree program in 1994–95 went directly on to further study.
EXPENSES FOR 1996–97 ***Application fee:*** $25. Part-time mandatory fees: $50 per year. Full-time tuition: $5300 for day program, $3800 for evening program, $5000 for evening recreation program . Part-time tuition per course: $530 for day program, $385 for evening program, $500 for recreational therapy program. Full-time mandatory fees: $175.
FINANCIAL AID ***College-administered undergrad aid 1995–96:*** 150 need-based scholarships (average $600), 10 non-need scholarships (average $500), low-interest long-term loans from external sources (average $2296), Federal Work-Study. ***Required forms:*** institutional, FAFSA; accepted: CSS Financial Aid PROFILE, state. ***Priority deadline:*** 3/31. ***Payment plan:*** installment. ***Waivers:*** full or partial for employees or children of employees.
APPLYING ***Options:*** early entrance, deferred entrance, midyear entrance. ***Required:*** school transcript, recommendations, campus interview. ***Recommended:*** minimum 2.0 GPA. Test scores used for counseling/placement. ***Application deadline:*** rolling.
APPLYING/TRANSFER ***Required:*** high school transcript, campus interview, college transcript. ***Recommended:*** recommendations, minimum 2.0 high school GPA. ***Required for some:*** minimum 2.0 college GPA. ***Entrance:*** minimally difficult. ***Application deadline:*** rolling. ***Contact:*** Ms. Andrea Bard, Director of Admissions, 603-893-6111.
CONTACT Ms. Andrea Bard, Director of Admissions, Castle College, Windham, NH 03087-1297, 603-893-6111. ***Fax:*** 603-898-0547. College video available.

HESSER COLLEGE
Manchester, New Hampshire

UG Enrollment: 3,000 — **Tuition & Fees: $7360**
Application Deadline: rolling — **Room & Board: $3960**

GENERAL Proprietary, 2-year, coed. Awards diplomas, transfer associate, terminal associate degrees. Founded 1900. ***Setting:*** 1-acre urban campus with easy access to Boston. ***Total enrollment:*** 3,000. ***Faculty:*** 99 (23 full-time, 76 part-time). ***Notable Alumni:*** Holly Laramie, director of advertising and public relations at Hesser College; Maureen Blanchard, vice president and trust officer at First New Hampshire Bank; Maryellen MacKay, president of Foster Parent Association.
ENROLLMENT PROFILE 3,000 students from 12 states and territories, 10 other countries. 65% women, 35% men, 19% part-time, 60% state residents, 5% transferred in, 8% international, 25% 25 or older, 1% Native American, 1% Hispanic, 1% African American, 1% Asian American. ***Most popular recent majors:*** business administration/commerce/management, early childhood education, accounting.
FIRST-YEAR CLASS 605 total. Of the students who applied, 93% were accepted, 33% of whom enrolled. 12% from top 10% of their high school class, 20% from top quarter, 68% from top half.
ACADEMIC PROGRAM Core, career-oriented curriculum, honor code. Calendar: semesters. 236 courses offered in 1995–96; average class size 25 in required courses. Advanced placement, self-designed majors, tutorials, summer session for credit, part-time degree program (daytime, evenings), adult/continuing education programs, co-op programs and internships.
GENERAL DEGREE REQUIREMENTS 60 credits; computer course; internship (some majors).
MAJORS Accounting, broadcasting, business administration/commerce/management, communication, computer information systems, computer management, computer programming, computer science, computer technologies, construction management, corrections, criminal justice, early childhood education, fashion design and technology, fashion merchandising, film and video production, health education, hotel and restaurant management, human services, interior design, law enforcement/police sciences, legal secretarial studies, liberal arts/general studies, management information systems, marketing/retailing/merchandising, medical assistant technologies, medical records services, medical secretarial studies, occupational therapy, paralegal studies, physical therapy, psychology, retail management, secretarial studies/office management, social work, tourism and travel, word processing.
LIBRARY Kenneth W. Galeucia Memorial Library with 38,000 books, 150 periodicals.
COMPUTERS ON CAMPUS 60 computers for student use in computer labs, learning resource center, classrooms. Staffed computer lab on campus provides training in use of computers.
COLLEGE LIFE Student-run radio station. 60% vote in student government elections. ***Social organizations:*** 7 open to all. ***Most popular organizations:*** Student Government, Ski Club, Amnesty International, Yearbook, Aerobics Club. ***Major annual events:*** Job Fair, Orientation. ***Student services:*** health clinic, personal-psychological counseling. ***Campus security:*** 24-hour emergency response devices and patrols, student patrols, late-night transport-escort service, controlled dormitory access.
HOUSING 468 college housing spaces available; 400 were occupied 1995–96. No special consideration for freshman housing applicants. Off-campus living permitted. ***Option:*** coed (1 building) housing available. Resident assistants live in dorms.
ATHLETICS Member NJCAA. ***Intercollegiate:*** basketball M(s)/W(s), field hockey W, soccer M(s)/W, softball M(s)/W(s), volleyball M(s)/W(s). ***Intramural:*** basketball, bowling, skiing (downhill), volleyball, weight lifting. ***Contact:*** Ms. Kelly Bourbon, Athletic Director, 603-668-6660.
CAREER PLANNING ***Placement office:*** 2 full-time staff. ***Director:*** Mrs. Karen Diaz, Director of Placement, 603-668-6660 Ext. 311. ***Services:*** job fairs, resume preparation, career counseling, job interviews. 63 organizations recruited on campus 1994–95.
AFTER GRADUATION 97% of class of 1994 had job offers within 6 months. 40% of students completing a degree program went directly on to further study.
EXPENSES FOR 1996–97 ***Application fee:*** $10. Comprehensive fee of $11,320 includes full-time tuition ($7360) and college room and board ($3960). College room only: $2460. Part-time tuition per course: $756 for day classes, $408 for evening classes.
FINANCIAL AID ***College-administered undergrad aid 1995–96:*** 750 need-based scholarships (average $900), 320 non-need scholarships (average $750), low-interest long-term loans from external sources, 130 Federal Work-Study (averaging $650), 5 part-time jobs. ***Required forms:*** state, institutional, FAFSA; accepted: CSS Financial Aid PROFILE. ***Priority deadline:*** 5/1. ***Payment plans:*** installment, deferred payment. ***Waivers:*** full or partial for employees or children of employees. ***Notification:*** continuous. ***Average indebtedness of graduates:*** $10,000.
APPLYING ***Options:*** Common Application, deferred entrance, midyear entrance. ***Required:*** TOEFL for international students. ***Recommended:*** minimum 2.0 GPA, campus interview. ***Required for some:*** recommendations. Test scores used for admission. ***Application deadline:*** rolling. ***Notification:*** continuous.
APPLYING/TRANSFER ***Required:*** college transcript. ***Recommended:*** campus interview, minimum 2.0 college GPA. ***Required for some:*** recommendations. ***Entrance:*** moderately difficult. ***Application deadline:*** rolling. ***Notification:*** continuous. ***Contact:*** Ms. Ann Hetzel, Admissions Counselor, 603-668-6660 Ext. 180.
CONTACT Mr. Thomas Houle, Director of Recruitment, Hesser College, 3 Sundial Avenue, Manchester, NH 03103-7245, 603-668-6660 Ext. 120 or toll-free 800-526-9231. College video available.

❖ ***See page 744 for a narrative description.*** ❖

McINTOSH COLLEGE
Dover, New Hampshire

UG Enrollment: 1,050 — **Tuition & Fees: $4300**
Application Deadline: rolling — **Room & Board: $2900**

GENERAL Proprietary, 2-year, coed. Awards certificates, transfer associate degrees. Founded 1896. ***Setting:*** 11-acre small-town campus with easy access to Boston. ***Total enrollment:*** 1,050. ***Faculty:*** 27 (17 full-time, 25% with terminal degrees, 10 part-time); student-faculty ratio is 30:1.
ENROLLMENT PROFILE 1,050 students from 20 states and territories, 4 other countries. 65% women, 35% men, 43% part-time, 85% state residents, 15% transferred in, 2% international, 65% 25 or older, 0% Native American, 1% Hispanic, 1% African American, 1% Asian American. ***Areas of study chosen:*** 20% business management and administrative services, 20% computer and information sciences, 20% health professions and related sciences.
FIRST-YEAR CLASS 150 total. Of the students who applied, 85% were accepted, 90% of whom enrolled. 10% from top 10% of their high school class, 25% from top quarter, 65% from top half.
ACADEMIC PROGRAM Core, career-oriented curriculum, honor code. Calendar: modular. 360 courses offered in 1995–96. Services for LD students, advanced placement, tutorials, summer session for credit, part-time degree program (daytime, evenings, summer), adult/continuing education programs, internships.
GENERAL DEGREE REQUIREMENTS 66 credits; 1 business math course; computer course.
MAJORS Accounting, business administration/commerce/management, computer information systems, computer management, computer science, criminal justice, legal secretarial studies, legal studies, medical assistant technologies, medical secretarial studies, paralegal studies, secretarial studies/office management, tourism and travel.
LIBRARY 8,300 books, 78 periodicals, 20 CD-ROMs, 75 records, tapes, and CDs.
COMPUTERS ON CAMPUS 170 computers for student use in computer center, computer labs, library, student rooms provide access to Internet. Staffed computer lab on campus.
COLLEGE LIFE Drama-theater group, student-run newspaper. 50% vote in student government elections. ***Social organizations:*** 10 open to all. ***Most popular organizations:*** Student Activities Committee, Drama Club, Business Club, Culture Club, Collegiate Secretaries International. ***Major annual events:*** October Fest, Spring Fling, Graduation Dinner/Dance. ***Student services:*** personal-psychological counseling. ***Campus security:*** 24-hour emergency response devices and patrols, controlled dormitory access.
HOUSING 80 college housing spaces available; 20 were occupied 1995–96. Freshmen given priority for college housing. Off-campus living permitted. ***Options:*** freshmen-only, coed (1 building) housing available. Resident assistants live in dorms.
ATHLETICS ***Intercollegiate:*** softball M/W. ***Intramural:*** softball.
CAREER PLANNING ***Placement office:*** 1 full-time staff. ***Director:*** Ms. Connie Bardtosiewicz, Director of Career Development, 603-742-1234. ***Services:*** job fairs, resume preparation, resume referral, career counseling, careers library, job bank, job interviews.
AFTER GRADUATION 80% of class of 1994 had job offers within 6 months.
EXPENSES FOR 1996–97 ***Application fee:*** $15. Comprehensive fee of $7200 includes full-time tuition ($4125 minimum), mandatory fees ($175), and college room and board ($2900 minimum). Minimum part-time tuition per course ranges from $330 to $465. Part-time mandatory fees: $125 per year. Full-time tuition ranges up to $5035 according to program.
FINANCIAL AID ***College-administered undergrad aid 1995–96:*** 10 non-need scholarships (averaging $920), low-interest long-term loans from external sources, Federal Work-Study. ***Required forms:*** CSS Financial Aid PROFILE, FAFSA. ***Priority deadline:*** 8/1. ***Payment plan:*** deferred payment. ***Waivers:*** full or partial for employees or children of employees. ***Notification:*** continuous.
APPLYING Open admission. ***Options:*** early entrance, deferred entrance. ***Required:*** school transcript. ***Recommended:*** SAT I. ***Required for some:*** some high school foreign language. Test scores used for counseling/placement. ***Application deadline:*** rolling. ***Notification:*** continuous.
APPLYING/TRANSFER ***Required:*** college transcript. ***Required for some:*** high school transcript, some high school foreign language. ***Entrance:*** noncompetitive. ***Application deadline:*** rolling. ***Notification:*** continuous.
CONTACT Ms. Dorothy Johnsen, Dean of Enrollment Management, McIntosh College, Dover, NH 03820-3990, 603-742-1234. ***Fax:*** 603-742-7292.

❖ ***See page 768 for a narrative description.*** ❖

Peterson's Guide to Two-Year Colleges 1997 433

NEW HAMPSHIRE TECHNICAL COLLEGE
Berlin, New Hampshire

Enrollment: N/R **Tuition & Fees (NH Res): $2458**
Application Deadline: rolling **Room & Board: N/Avail**

GENERAL State-supported, 2-year, coed. Part of New Hampshire Post-Secondary Technical Education System. Awards transfer associate, terminal associate degrees. Founded 1966. ***Setting:*** 325-acre rural campus. ***Faculty:*** 45 (35 full-time, 10 part-time).
ENROLLMENT PROFILE 40% women, 28% part-time, 83% state residents, 5% transferred in, 18% 25 or older, 0% Native American, 0% African American.
FIRST-YEAR CLASS Of the students who applied, 58% were accepted, 100% of whom enrolled. 5% from top 10% of their high school class, 12% from top quarter, 65% from top half.
ACADEMIC PROGRAM Core. Calendar: semesters. Academic remediation for entering students, English as a second language program, advanced placement, summer session for credit, part-time degree program (daytime, evenings, summer), external degree programs, adult/continuing education programs, internships.
GENERAL DEGREE REQUIREMENTS 64 credits; 1 course each in math and science; computer course; internship (some majors).
MAJORS Accounting, automotive technologies, business administration/commerce/management, computer technologies, conservation, culinary arts, drafting and design, food services management, forestry, human services, machine and tool technologies, mechanical design technology, mental health/rehabilitation counseling, natural resource management, nursing, secretarial studies/office management, surveying technology, water resources.
LIBRARY 8,000 books, 50 microform titles, 145 periodicals, 6 CD-ROMs.
COMPUTERS ON CAMPUS 65 computers for student use in computer center, learning center, library.
COLLEGE LIFE Student-run newspaper. ***Most popular organization:*** Student Senate. ***Student services:*** personal-psychological counseling, women's center.
HOUSING College housing not available.
ATHLETICS ***Intercollegiate:*** basketball M/W, skiing (cross-country) M/W, skiing (downhill) M/W, soccer M/W. ***Intramural:*** basketball, bowling, golf, skiing (cross-country), volleyball. ***Contact:*** Ms. Martha LaFlamme, Athletic Director, 603-752-1113 Ext. 1010.
CAREER PLANNING ***Service:*** career counseling.
EXPENSES FOR 1995–96 ***Application fee:*** $10. State resident tuition: $2410 full-time, $101 per credit part-time. Nonresident tuition: $5678 full-time, $237 per credit part-time. Part-time mandatory fees: $2 per credit. Tuition for nonresidents who are eligible for the New England Regional Student Program: $3616 full-time, $151 per credit part-time. Full-time mandatory fees: $48.
FINANCIAL AID ***College-administered undergrad aid 1995–96:*** need-based scholarships, Federal Work-Study, part-time jobs. ***Required forms:*** CSS Financial Aid PROFILE, FAFSA. ***Priority deadline:*** 5/1. ***Payment plan:*** deferred payment.
APPLYING ***Recommended:*** 3 years of high school math and science. ***Required for some:*** CGP. Test scores used for counseling/placement. ***Application deadline:*** rolling. ***Notification:*** continuous. Preference given to state residents.
APPLYING/TRANSFER ***Recommended:*** 3 years of high school math. ***Entrance:*** minimally difficult. ***Application deadline:*** rolling. ***Notification:*** continuous.
CONTACT Ms. Kathleen M. Tremblay, Dean of Students, New Hampshire Technical College, 2020 Riverside Drive, Berlin, NH 03570-3717, 603-752-1113 Ext. 1004.

NEW HAMPSHIRE TECHNICAL COLLEGE
Claremont, New Hampshire

UG Enrollment: 519 **Tuition & Fees (NH Res): $2410**
Application Deadline: 8/1 **Room & Board: N/Avail**

GENERAL State-supported, 2-year, coed. Part of New Hampshire Post-Secondary Technical Education System. Awards terminal associate degrees. Founded 1967. ***Setting:*** 140-acre small-town campus. ***Total enrollment:*** 519. ***Faculty:*** 48 (36 full-time, 12 part-time); student-faculty ratio is 11:1.
ENROLLMENT PROFILE 519 students from 5 states and territories. 80% women, 38% part-time, 78% state residents, 45% transferred in, 0% international, 70% 25 or older, 0% Native American, 0% Hispanic, 0% African American, 1% Asian American.
FIRST-YEAR CLASS 420 total; 817 applied, 61% were accepted, 77% of whom enrolled. 5% from top 10% of their high school class, 20% from top quarter, 70% from top half.
ACADEMIC PROGRAM Core. Calendar: semesters. Academic remediation for entering students, summer session for credit, part-time degree program (daytime, evenings), adult/continuing education programs, internships.
GENERAL DEGREE REQUIREMENTS 64 credits; 1 course each in math and science.
MAJORS Accounting, business administration/commerce/management, computer management, computer technologies, electrical and electronics technologies, manufacturing technology, medical assistant technologies, medical laboratory technology, nursing, occupational therapy, physical therapy, respiratory therapy.
LIBRARY 11,000 books, 500 microform titles, 99 periodicals, 500 records, tapes, and CDs.
COMPUTERS ON CAMPUS 46 computers for student use in computer center, classrooms, library.
COLLEGE LIFE ***Student services:*** personal-psychological counseling.
HOUSING College housing not available.
ATHLETICS ***Intercollegiate:*** volleyball W. ***Intramural:*** skiing (cross-country), volleyball.
CAREER PLANNING ***Service:*** career counseling.
EXPENSES FOR 1995–96 ***Application fee:*** $10. State resident tuition: $2410 full-time, $101 per credit part-time. Nonresident tuition: $5678 full-time, $237 per credit part-time. Part-time mandatory fees: $2.50 per credit. Tuition for nonresidents who are eligible for the New England Regional Student Program: $3616 full-time, $151 per credit part-time.
FINANCIAL AID ***College-administered undergrad aid 1995–96:*** 40 need-based scholarships (average $1000), 10 non-need scholarships (average $750), short-term loans (average $200), low-interest long-term loans from college funds (average $1000), loans from external sources (average $2500), Federal Work-Study, 5 part-time jobs. ***Required forms:*** CSS Financial Aid PROFILE, institutional; required for some: state; accepted: FAFSA. ***Priority deadline:*** 5/1. ***Payment plans:*** installment, deferred payment. ***Waivers:*** full or partial for employees or children of employees.
APPLYING ***Required:*** school transcript, interview, TOEFL for international students, ACT ASSET. ***Required for some:*** 3 years of high school math and science. Test scores used for admission and counseling/placement. ***Application deadline:*** 8/1. ***Notification:*** continuous. Preference given to state residents.
APPLYING/TRANSFER ***Required:*** standardized test scores, high school transcript, interview, college transcript. ***Required for some:*** 3 years of high school math and science. ***Application deadline:*** 8/1. ***Notification:*** continuous.
CONTACT Ms. Marie T. Bender, Dean of Student Affairs, New Hampshire Technical College, Claremont, NH 03743-9707, 603-542-7744 Ext. 10.

NEW HAMPSHIRE TECHNICAL COLLEGE
Laconia, New Hampshire

UG Enrollment: 900 **Tuition & Fees (NH Res): $2458**
Application Deadline: rolling **Room & Board: N/Avail**

GENERAL State-supported, 2-year, coed. Part of New Hampshire Post-Secondary Technical Education System. Awards certificates, diplomas, transfer associate, terminal associate degrees. Founded 1967. ***Setting:*** 10-acre small-town campus. ***Total enrollment:*** 900. ***Faculty:*** 55 (35 full-time, 2% with terminal degrees, 20 part-time); student-faculty ratio is 13:1.
ENROLLMENT PROFILE 900 students from 8 states and territories, 2 other countries. 36% women, 64% men, 25% part-time, 80% state residents, 15% transferred in, 50% 25 or older, 1% Hispanic, 1% African American. ***Areas of study chosen:*** 70% vocational and home economics, 30% business management and administrative services. ***Most popular recent majors:*** fire science, graphic arts, business administration/commerce/management.
FIRST-YEAR CLASS 323 total; 360 applied, 95% were accepted, 94% of whom enrolled. 3% from top 10% of their high school class, 8% from top quarter, 33% from top half.
ACADEMIC PROGRAM Core, job skills curriculum, honor code. Calendar: semesters (quarters for automotive technologies, graphic arts). 225 courses offered in 1995–96. Academic remediation for entering students, services for LD students, tutorials, summer session for credit, part-time degree program (daytime, evenings), adult/continuing education programs, co-op programs and internships. Off-campus study at 6 members of the New Hampshire Postsecondary Technical Education System.
GENERAL DEGREE REQUIREMENTS 64 credits; 9 credits of math/science; computer course for graphics, automotive, marine, accounting, business, electrical majors; internship (some majors).
MAJORS Accounting, automotive technologies, aviation administration, business administration/commerce/management, computer technologies, early childhood education, electrical and electronics technologies, fire science, graphic arts, hospitality services, human services, manufacturing technology, marine technology, paralegal studies, real estate, secretarial studies/office management.
LIBRARY Technical College Library with 11,500 books, 35 microform titles, 120 periodicals, 4 on-line bibliographic services, 15 CD-ROMs, 255 records, tapes, and CDs. Acquisition spending 1994–95: $27,520.
COMPUTERS ON CAMPUS Computer purchase plan available. 75 computers for student use in computer center, computer labs, learning resource center, classrooms, library provide access to e-mail, on-line services, Internet. Staffed computer lab on campus provides training in use of computers, software. Academic computing expenditure 1994–95: $250,000.
COLLEGE LIFE 80% vote in student government elections. ***Social organizations:*** 4 open to all. ***Most popular organizations:*** Phi Theta Kappa, Student Senate, Fire Brigade, Chess Club. ***Major annual events:*** Winter Carnival, Halloween Dance, Spring Fling. ***Student services:*** personal-psychological counseling.
HOUSING College housing not available.
ATHLETICS ***Intercollegiate:*** baseball M, basketball M/W, softball W, volleyball M/W. ***Intramural:*** golf, ice hockey, skiing (downhill), soccer. ***Contact:*** Mr. Scott Bryant, Athletic Director, 603-524-3207.
CAREER PLANNING ***Placement office:*** 2 full-time, 1 part-time staff. ***Director:*** Mr. George Futch, Director of Co-op and Placement Services, 603-524-3207. ***Services:*** job fairs, resume preparation, career counseling, careers library, job interviews. 6 organizations recruited on campus 1994–95.
AFTER GRADUATION 68% of class of 1994 had job offers within 6 months. 11% of students completing a degree program went directly on to further study.
EXPENSES FOR 1995–96 ***Application fee:*** $10. State resident tuition: $2410 full-time, $101 per credit part-time. Nonresident tuition: $5678 full-time, $237 per credit part-time. Part-time mandatory fees: $2 per credit. Tuition for nonresidents who are eligible for the New England Regional Student Program: $3616 full-time, $151 per credit part-time. Full-time mandatory fees: $48.
FINANCIAL AID ***College-administered undergrad aid 1995–96:*** 423 need-based scholarships (average $1200), 9 non-need scholarships (average $900), short-term loans (average $500), low-interest long-term loans from college funds (average $800), loans from external sources (average $2800), Federal Work-Study. ***Required forms:*** institutional, FAFSA, verification worksheet; accepted: state. ***Priority deadline:*** 5/1. ***Payment plans:*** installment, deferred payment. ***Waivers:*** full or partial for employees or children of employees and senior citizens. ***Notification:*** 6/15. ***Average indebtedness of graduates:*** $6125.
APPLYING ***Options:*** early entrance, deferred entrance, midyear entrance. ***Required:*** school transcript, 1 recommendation. ***Recommended:*** minimum 2.0 GPA, SAT I. ***Required for some:*** interview, ACT ASSET. Test scores used for counseling/placement. ***Application deadline:*** rolling. ***Notification:*** continuous.
APPLYING/TRANSFER ***Required:*** high school transcript, college transcript. ***Recommended:*** standardized test scores, minimum 2.0 college GPA. ***Required for some:*** standardized test scores. ***Entrance:*** moderately difficult. ***Application deadline:*** rolling. ***Notification:*** continuous. ***Contact:*** Mr. Donald E. Morrissey, Dean of Students, 603-524-3207 Ext. 15.
CONTACT Mrs. Randi Provencal, Administrative Assistant, New Hampshire Technical College, Laconia, NH 03246, 603-524-3207 Ext. 40. ***Fax:*** 603-524-8084. ***E-mail:*** d_morris@tec.nh.us. College video available.

NEW HAMPSHIRE TECHNICAL COLLEGE
Manchester, New Hampshire

UG Enrollment: 676 | **Tuition & Fees (NH Res): $2595**
Application Deadline: rolling | **Room & Board: N/Avail**

GENERAL State-supported, 2-year, coed. Part of New Hampshire Post-Secondary Technical Education System. Awards transfer associate, terminal associate degrees. Founded 1945. ***Setting:*** 60-acre urban campus with easy access to Boston. ***Total enrollment:*** 676. ***Faculty:*** 200 (50 full-time, 10% with terminal degrees, 150 part-time).
ENROLLMENT PROFILE 676 students from 5 states and territories. 58% women, 35% part-time, 85% state residents, 20% transferred in, 35% 25 or older, 0% Native American, 2% Hispanic, 1% African American, 1% Asian American. ***Areas of study chosen:*** 8% communications and journalism.
FIRST-YEAR CLASS 389 total; 947 applied, 50% were accepted, 82% of whom enrolled.
ACADEMIC PROGRAM Core. Calendar: semesters. Academic remediation for entering students, English as a second language program, services for LD students, advanced placement, summer session for credit, part-time degree program (daytime, evenings, weekends, summer), external degree programs, adult/continuing education programs, co-op programs and internships.
GENERAL DEGREE REQUIREMENTS 64 credit hours; computer course (varies by major); internship (some majors).
MAJORS Accounting, automotive technologies, commercial art, community services, construction technologies, drafting and design, early childhood education, electrical and electronics technologies, electromechanical technology, electronics engineering technology, gerontology, heating/refrigeration/air conditioning, management information systems, marketing/retailing/merchandising, mechanical design technology, medical secretarial studies, nursing, physical fitness/exercise science, physical therapy, secretarial studies/office management, sports medicine, welding technology.
LIBRARY 15,000 books, 39 microform titles, 200 periodicals, 300 records, tapes, and CDs.
COMPUTERS ON CAMPUS 75 computers for student use in computer center, computer labs, library provide access to Internet. Staffed computer lab on campus provides training in use of computers, software.
COLLEGE LIFE Student-run newspaper. ***Social organizations:*** 4 open to all. ***Most popular organizations:*** Student Senate, Phi Theta Kappa, American Society of Welders, Student Nurses Association. ***Major annual events:*** System Ski Day, Spring Formal, Graduation. ***Student services:*** personal-psychological counseling. ***Campus security:*** trained security personnel.
HOUSING College housing not available.
ATHLETICS ***Intercollegiate:*** basketball M, golf M, ice hockey M/W, skiing (downhill) M/W, soccer M/W, softball W, volleyball M/W. ***Intramural:*** basketball, bowling, golf, ice hockey, skiing (cross-country), skiing (downhill), volleyball. ***Contact:*** Mr. David Pichette, Director of Athletics, 603-668-6706.
CAREER PLANNING ***Placement office:*** 1 part-time staff. ***Services:*** job fairs, resume preparation, career counseling, careers library, job interviews.
AFTER GRADUATION 9% of students completing a degree program in 1994–95 went directly on to further study.
EXPENSES FOR 1995–96 ***Application fee:*** $10. State resident tuition: $2500 full-time, $105 per credit hour part-time. Nonresident tuition: $5500 full-time, $250 per credit hour part-time. Tuition for nonresidents who are eligible for the New England Regional Student Program: $3750 full-time, $157 per credit hour part-time. Full-time mandatory fees: $95.
FINANCIAL AID ***College-administered undergrad aid 1995–96:*** need-based scholarships, short-term loans (average $50), low-interest long-term loans from college funds (average $500), loans from external sources, Federal Work-Study. ***Required forms:*** CSS Financial Aid PROFILE, institutional, FAFSA; required for some: state. ***Priority deadline:*** 8/15. ***Payment plans:*** installment, deferred payment. ***Waivers:*** full or partial for employees or children of employees and senior citizens.
APPLYING ***Options:*** early entrance, deferred entrance, midyear entrance. ***Required:*** school transcript, campus interview, TOEFL for international students. ***Recommended:*** recommendations. ***Required for some:*** 3 years of high school math, SAT I or ACT, Michigan Test of English Language Proficiency. Test scores used for counseling/placement. ***Application deadlines:*** rolling, rolling for nonresidents. ***Notification:*** continuous, continuous for nonresidents.
APPLYING/TRANSFER ***Required:*** high school transcript, campus interview. ***Recommended:*** recommendations. ***Required for some:*** standardized test scores. ***Application deadline:*** rolling. ***Notification:*** continuous. ***Contact:*** Mr. Kenneth R. McCann, Dean of Student Affairs, 603-668-6706 Ext. 202.
CONTACT Mr. Kenneth R. McCann, Dean of Student Affairs, New Hampshire Technical College, 1066 Front Street, Manchester, NH 03102-8528, 603-668-6706 Ext. 202.

NEW HAMPSHIRE TECHNICAL COLLEGE
Nashua, New Hampshire

UG Enrollment: 542 | **Tuition & Fees (NH Res): $2470**
Application Deadline: rolling | **Room & Board: N/Avail**

GENERAL State-supported, 2-year, coed. Part of New Hampshire Post-Secondary Technical Education System. Awards certificates, diplomas, transfer associate, terminal associate degrees. Founded 1967. ***Setting:*** 66-acre urban campus with easy access to Boston. ***Total enrollment:*** 542. ***Faculty:*** 63 (35 full-time, 28 part-time); student-faculty ratio is 15:1.
ENROLLMENT PROFILE 542 students from 6 states and territories, 2 other countries. 36% women, 17% part-time, 83% state residents, 25% transferred in, 1% international, 23% 25 or older, 1% Native American, 2% Hispanic, 2% African American, 2% Asian American. ***Areas of study chosen:*** 50% engineering and applied sciences, 40% business management and administrative services, 10% computer and information sciences.
FIRST-YEAR CLASS 322 total; 618 applied, 62% were accepted, 84% of whom enrolled. 5% from top 10% of their high school class, 12% from top quarter, 55% from top half.
ACADEMIC PROGRAM Core. Calendar: semesters. Academic remediation for entering students, English as a second language program offered during academic year and summer, services for LD students, advanced placement, summer session for credit, part-time degree program (daytime, evenings, summer), external degree programs, adult/continuing education programs, internships.
GENERAL DEGREE REQUIREMENTS 64 credits; 1 math course; computer course for most majors; internship (some majors).
MAJORS Accounting, automotive technologies, aviation technology, business administration/commerce/management, child care/child and family studies, computer information systems, computer technologies, drafting and design, early childhood education, electrical and electronics technologies, electromechanical technology, electronics engineering technology, engineering technology, human services, machine and tool technologies, manufacturing technology, marketing/retailing/merchandising, optometric/ophthalmic technologies, paralegal studies, quality control technology, robotics, telecommunications.
LIBRARY 10,000 books, 125 periodicals.
COMPUTERS ON CAMPUS 100 computers for student use in computer labs, learning resource center, classrooms, library provide access to e-mail, Internet. Staffed computer lab on campus.
COLLEGE LIFE Orientation program (2 days, $20, parents included). 65% vote in student government elections. ***Student services:*** personal-psychological counseling. ***Campus security:*** 24-hour emergency response devices.
HOUSING College housing not available.
ATHLETICS ***Intercollegiate:*** baseball M, basketball M/W, ice hockey M/W, soccer M/W, softball W, tennis M/W. ***Intramural:*** basketball, golf, skiing (cross-country), skiing (downhill), soccer, softball, tennis, volleyball. ***Contact:*** Dr. Kenneth Paradis, 603-882-6923.
CAREER PLANNING ***Services:*** resume preparation, career counseling, job bank, job interviews.
EXPENSES FOR 1995–96 ***Application fee:*** $10. State resident tuition: $2410 full-time, $101 per credit part-time. Nonresident tuition: $5678 full-time, $237 per credit part-time. Part-time mandatory fees: $5 per credit. Tuition for nonresidents who are eligible for the New England Regional Student Program: $3616 full-time, $151 per credit part-time. Full-time mandatory fees: $60.
FINANCIAL AID ***College-administered undergrad aid 1995–96:*** 98 need-based scholarships (average $500), short-term loans, low-interest long-term loans from college funds (average $1000), loans from external sources (average $2500), Federal Work-Study, 3 part-time jobs. ***Required forms:*** institutional, FAFSA. ***Priority deadline:*** 5/1. ***Payment plan:*** installment. ***Waivers:*** full or partial for employees or children of employees and senior citizens.
APPLYING ***Options:*** deferred entrance, midyear entrance. ***Required:*** school transcript, TOEFL for international students, ACT ASSET. Test scores used for counseling/placement. ***Application deadline:*** rolling. ***Notification:*** continuous.
APPLYING/TRANSFER ***Required:*** high school transcript. ***Application deadline:*** rolling. ***Notification:*** continuous.
CONTACT Mr. John T. Fischer, Dean of Student Affairs, New Hampshire Technical College, 505 Amherst Street, Nashua, NH 03061-2052, 603-882-6923. ***Fax:*** 603-882-8690. ***E-mail:*** nashua@tec.nh.us. College video available.

NEW HAMPSHIRE TECHNICAL COLLEGE
Stratham, New Hampshire

CONTACT Ms. Patricia Shay, Dean of Student Affairs, New Hampshire Technical College, Stratham, NH 03885-2297, 603-772-1194 Ext. 327 or toll-free 800-522-1194 (in-state). ***Fax:*** 603-772-1198. College video available.

NEW HAMPSHIRE TECHNICAL INSTITUTE
Concord, New Hampshire

UG Enrollment: 1,413 | **Tuition & Fees (NH Res): $2506**
Application Deadline: rolling | **Room & Board: $3966**

GENERAL State-supported, 2-year, coed. Part of New Hampshire Post-Secondary Technical Education System. Awards certificates, transfer associate degrees. Founded 1964. ***Setting:*** 225-acre small-town campus with easy access to Boston. ***Educational spending 1994–95:*** $6000 per undergrad. ***Total enrollment:*** 1,413. ***Faculty:*** 145 (110 full-time, 35 part-time); student-faculty ratio is 10:1.
ENROLLMENT PROFILE 1,413 students from 6 states and territories. 54% women, 30% part-time, 90% state residents, 43% transferred in, 45% have need-based financial aid, 70% 25 or older, 0% African American. ***Areas of study chosen:*** 30% health professions and related sciences, 20% business management and administrative services, 20% engineering and applied sciences, 10% computer and information sciences, 10% psychology, 10% social sciences. ***Most popular recent majors:*** nursing, engineering technology, business administration/commerce/management.
FIRST-YEAR CLASS 517 total. Of the students who applied, 58% were accepted, 47% of whom enrolled. 22% from top quarter of their high school class, 41% from top half.
ACADEMIC PROGRAM Calendar: semesters. 460 courses offered in 1995–96. Academic remediation for entering students, services for LD students, advanced placement, summer session for credit, part-time degree program (evenings), adult/continuing education programs, internships.
GENERAL DEGREE REQUIREMENTS 64 credits; computer course for business, criminal justice, radiology, engineering technology majors.
MAJORS Accounting, architectural technologies, business administration/commerce/management, computer information systems, criminal justice, dental services, early childhood education, electronics engineering technology, emergency medical technology, engineering technology, hotel and restaurant management, human resources, human services, industrial engineering technology, marketing/retailing/merchandising, mechanical engineering technology, mental health/rehabilitation counseling, nursing, radiological technology, tourism and travel.
LIBRARY Farnum Library with 32,000 books, 32 periodicals, 75 records, tapes, and CDs. Acquisition spending 1994–95: $200,000.
COMPUTERS ON CAMPUS 110 computers for student use in computer center, computer labs, library, dorms. Academic computing expenditure 1994–95: $606,000.

New Hampshire–New Jersey

New Hampshire Technical Institute *(continued)*

COLLEGE LIFE Drama-theater group. *Social organizations:* 2 local fraternities, 2 local sororities. *Major annual events:* Winter Carnival, Spring Weekend, Ski Day. *Student services:* health clinic, personal-psychological counseling. *Campus security:* late-night transport-escort service, controlled dormitory access.
HOUSING 400 college housing spaces available; all were occupied 1995–96. No special consideration for freshman housing applicants. Off-campus living permitted. *Options:* coed, single-sex housing available. Resident assistants live in dorms.
ATHLETICS Member NJCAA. *Intercollegiate:* basketball M/W, golf M/W, skiing (cross-country) M/W, skiing (downhill) M/W, soccer M/W, track and field M/W. *Intramural:* ice hockey, softball, volleyball. *Contact:* Mr. William Miller, Director of Athletics, 603-225-1859.
CAREER PLANNING *Placement office:* 1 full-time staff; $70,000 operating expenditure 1994–95. *Director:* Ms. Linda Schmidt, Director of Placement and Counseling, 603-225-1858. *Services:* job fairs, resume preparation, career counseling, careers library, job bank, job interviews.
AFTER GRADUATION 20% of students completing a degree program in 1994–95 went directly on to further study.
EXPENSES FOR 1995–96 *Application fee:* $10. State resident tuition: $2410 full-time, $101 per credit hour part-time. Nonresident tuition: $5678 full-time, $237 per credit hour part-time. Tuition for nonresidents who are eligible for the New England Regional Student Program: $3616 full-time, $151 per credit hour part-time. Full-time mandatory fees: $96. College room and board: $3966.
FINANCIAL AID *College-administered undergrad aid 1995–96:* 600 need-based scholarships, short-term loans (average $200), low-interest long-term loans from external sources, Federal Work-Study. *Required forms:* CSS Financial Aid PROFILE, state, institutional, FAFSA. *Priority deadline:* 5/1.
APPLYING *Option:* midyear entrance. *Required:* school transcript. *Recommended:* minimum 2.0 GPA, SAT I, TOEFL for international students. *Required for some:* essay, 3 years of high school math, recommendations, interview, National League of Nursing Exam. Test scores used for admission and counseling/placement. *Application deadline:* rolling. *Notification:* continuous.
APPLYING/TRANSFER *Required:* high school transcript, college transcript. *Recommended:* standardized test scores, minimum 2.0 high school GPA. *Required for some:* essay, 3 years of high school math, recommendations, interview. *Entrance:* moderately difficult. *Application deadline:* rolling. *Notification:* continuous. *Contact:* Ms. Linda Schmidt, Director of Placement, 603-225-1858.
CONTACT Mr. Francis P. Meyer, Director of Admissions, New Hampshire Technical Institute, Concord, NH 03301-7412, 603-225-1863 or toll-free 800-247-0179. College video available.

❖ *See page 782 for a narrative description.* ❖

WHITE PINES COLLEGE
Chester, New Hampshire

UG Enrollment: 55	Tuition & Fees: $7950
Application Deadline: rolling	Room & Board: $4000

GENERAL Independent, 2-year, coed. Awards transfer associate, terminal associate degrees. Founded 1965. *Setting:* 83-acre rural campus with easy access to Boston. *Total enrollment:* 55. *Faculty:* 17 (6 full-time, 85% with terminal degrees, 11 part-time); student-faculty ratio is 8:1.
ENROLLMENT PROFILE 55 students from 10 states and territories, 9 other countries. 55% women, 45% men, 5% part-time, 35% state residents, 10% transferred in, 85% have need-based financial aid, 28% international, 35% 25 or older, 0% Native American, 0% Hispanic, 10% African American, 0% Asian American. *Areas of study chosen:* 65% fine arts, 15% communications and journalism, 10% liberal arts/general studies, 10% social sciences. *Most popular recent major:* photography.
FIRST-YEAR CLASS 32 total; 76 applied, 89% were accepted, 47% of whom enrolled. 20% from top quarter of their high school class, 40% from top half.
ACADEMIC PROGRAM Core, honor code. Calendar: semesters. 28 courses offered in 1995–96. Academic remediation for entering students, English as a second language program offered during academic year and summer, services for LD students, advanced placement, honors program, part-time degree program (daytime, evenings), adult/continuing education programs, internships.
GENERAL DEGREE REQUIREMENTS 60 credits; 2 courses of math/natural science; computer course; internship (some majors).
MAJORS Advertising, art/fine arts, art history, broadcasting, child care/child and family studies, communication, journalism, liberal arts/general studies, photography, social work.
LIBRARY Wadleigh Library with 20,000 books, 100 periodicals, 600 records, tapes, and CDs.
COMPUTERS ON CAMPUS 5 computers for student use in library provide access to main academic computer. Staffed computer lab on campus provides training in use of computers, software.
COLLEGE LIFE Orientation program (2 days, no cost). *Social organizations:* 6 open to all. *Major annual events:* Vespers, Winter Carnival, Apple Festival. *Student services:* health clinic, personal-psychological counseling.
HOUSING 60 college housing spaces available; 40 were occupied 1995–96. Freshmen guaranteed college housing. On-campus residence required in freshman year. *Options:* coed (1 building), single-sex (2 buildings) housing available. Resident assistants live in dorms.
ATHLETICS *Intramural:* badminton, basketball, tennis, volleyball.
CAREER PLANNING *Service:* career counseling.
AFTER GRADUATION 100% of students completing a degree program in 1994–95 went directly on to further study.
EXPENSES FOR 1995–96 *Application fee:* $25. Comprehensive fee of $11,950 includes full-time tuition ($7800), mandatory fees ($150), and college room and board ($4000). Part-time tuition: $260 per credit. Part-time mandatory fees: $25 per course.
FINANCIAL AID *College-administered undergrad aid 1995–96:* 35 need-based scholarships (average $700), 10 non-need scholarships (average $1000), short-term loans (average $25), low-interest long-term loans from external sources (average $2615), Federal Work-Study, 3 part-time jobs. *Required forms:* CSS Financial Aid PROFILE, institutional; required for some: state; accepted: FAFSA. *Priority deadline:* 4/15. *Payment plan:* installment. *Waivers:* full or partial for employees or children of employees.

APPLYING *Option:* deferred entrance. *Required:* school transcript, TOEFL for international students. *Recommended:* minimum 2.0 GPA, SAT I or ACT, SAT II Subject Tests. Test scores used for counseling/placement. *Application deadline:* rolling.
APPLYING/TRANSFER *Required:* high school transcript, minimum 2.0 high school GPA. *Recommended:* standardized test scores. *Entrance:* minimally difficult. *Application deadline:* rolling. *Contact:* Ms. Joan Guild, Transfer/Career Planning, 603-887-4401.
CONTACT Mrs. Nancy Ouellette, Administrative Assistant, White Pines College, Chester, NH 03036-4331, 603-887-4401 Ext. 127 or toll-free 800-974-6372.

❖ *See page 830 for a narrative description.* ❖

NEW JERSEY

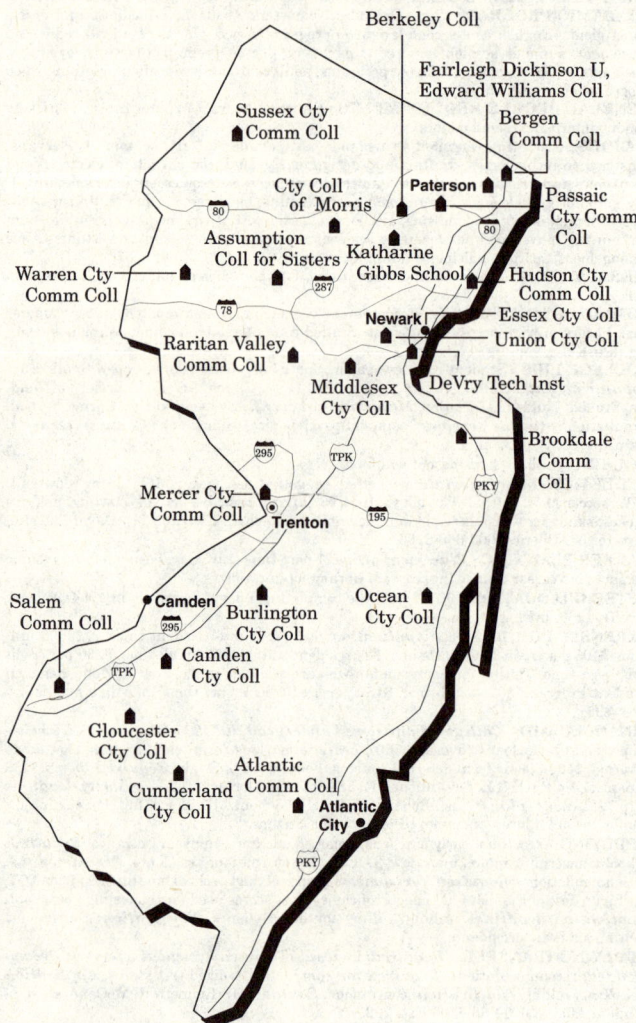

ASSUMPTION COLLEGE FOR SISTERS
Mendham, New Jersey

UG Enrollment: 32	Tuition & Fees: $1500
Application Deadline: rolling	Room & Board: N/R

GENERAL Independent Roman Catholic, 2-year, women only. Awards transfer associate degrees. Founded 1953. *Setting:* 112-acre rural campus with easy access to New York City. *Total enrollment:* 32. *Faculty:* 22 (100% of full-time faculty have terminal degrees); student-faculty ratio is 3:1.
ENROLLMENT PROFILE 32 students from 8 states and territories, 3 other countries. 100% women, 50% part-time, 0% state residents, 0% transferred in, 100% have need-based financial aid, 0% have non-need-based financial aid, 62% international, 37% 25 or older, 0% Native American, 3% Hispanic, 0% African American. *Areas of study chosen:* 100% liberal arts/general studies.
FIRST-YEAR CLASS 15 total; 15 applied, 100% were accepted, 100% of whom enrolled.
ACADEMIC PROGRAM Core, liberal arts and humanities curriculum. Calendar: semesters. 18 courses offered in 1995–96. Academic remediation for entering students, English as a second language program offered during academic year, services for LD students, advanced placement, summer session for credit, part-time degree program (daytime, evenings, summer).

Peterson's Guide to Two-Year Colleges 1997

GENERAL DEGREE REQUIREMENTS 66 credits; 3 credits of math; 8 credits of science; 6 credits of a foreign language.
MAJORS Liberal arts/general studies, theology.
LIBRARY Assumption College for Sisters Library with 27,672 books, 120 periodicals, 3,425 records, tapes, and CDs. Acquisition spending 1994–95: $9181.
COMPUTERS ON CAMPUS 10 computers for student use in computer center, science lab, classrooms, library. Staffed computer lab on campus provides training in use of computers. Academic computing expenditure 1994–95: $309,174.
COLLEGE LIFE Orientation program (2 days, no cost). Choral group. *Major annual events:* Orientation Program, Christmas Program. *Student services:* health clinic, personal-psychological counseling.
HOUSING 40 college housing spaces available; 6 were occupied 1995–96. Freshmen guaranteed college housing. On-campus residence required through sophomore year except if living in a convent of the student's religious congregation.
CAREER PLANNING *Service:* career counseling.
AFTER GRADUATION 100% of students completing a degree program in 1994–95 went directly on to further study.
EXPENSES FOR 1996–97 Tuition: $1500 full-time, $50 per credit part-time. Tuition guaranteed not to increase for student's term of enrollment.
FINANCIAL AID *College-administered undergrad aid 1995–96:* 21 need-based scholarships (average $600). *Required forms for some financial aid applicants:* FAFSA. *Priority deadline:* 8/1. *Payment plan:* installment.
APPLYING *Options:* deferred entrance, midyear entrance. *Required:* school transcript, 2 years of high school foreign language, recommendations, campus interview, intention of studying for Roman Catholic sisterhood. *Recommended:* SAT I or ACT. Test scores used for counseling/placement. *Application deadline:* rolling.
APPLYING/TRANSFER *Required:* high school transcript, 2 years of high school foreign language, recommendations, campus interview, college transcript, minimum 2.0 college GPA, intention of studying for Roman Catholic sisterhood. *Recommended:* standardized test scores. *Application deadline:* rolling. *Contact:* Sr. Catherine Kemper, SCC, Registrar/Treasurer, 201-543-6528.
CONTACT Sr. Mary Renée Nelson, SCC, Registrar, Assumption College for Sisters, 350 Bernardsville Road, Mendham, NJ 07945-0800, 201-543-6528. *Fax:* 201-543-9459.

ATLANTIC COMMUNITY COLLEGE
Mays Landing, New Jersey

UG Enrollment: 6,004	Tuition & Fees (Area Res): $1913
Application Deadline: 9/1	Room & Board: N/Avail

GENERAL County-supported, 2-year, coed. Awards transfer associate, terminal associate degrees. Founded 1966. *Setting:* 546-acre small-town campus with easy access to Philadelphia. *Total enrollment:* 6,004. *Faculty:* 331 (72 full-time, 21% with terminal degrees, 259 part-time); student-faculty ratio is 20:1.
ENROLLMENT PROFILE 6,004 students from 6 states and territories, 5 other countries. 62% women, 68% part-time, 98% state residents, 15% transferred in, 1% international, 48% 25 or older, 1% Native American, 5% Hispanic, 12% African American, 4% Asian American. *Most popular recent majors:* nursing, liberal arts/general studies, business administration/commerce/management.
FIRST-YEAR CLASS 2,200 total. Of the students who applied, 100% were accepted, 66% of whom enrolled. 5% from top 10% of their high school class, 15% from top quarter, 45% from top half.
ACADEMIC PROGRAM Core. Calendar: semesters. 1,200 courses offered in 1995–96. Academic remediation for entering students, English as a second language program offered during academic year, services for LD students, advanced placement, honors program, summer session for credit, part-time degree program (daytime, evenings, weekends, summer), adult/continuing education programs, co-op programs and internships.
GENERAL DEGREE REQUIREMENTS 64 credits; math/science requirements vary according to program; computer course for most majors.
MAJORS Accounting, biology/biological sciences, business administration/commerce/management, chemistry, child care/child and family studies, computer information systems, computer programming, computer technologies, construction management, corrections, criminal justice, culinary arts, education, electrical and electronics technologies, electronics engineering technology, history, hospitality services, humanities, law enforcement/police sciences, legal studies, liberal arts/general studies, literature, marine sciences, marketing/retailing/merchandising, mathematics, nursing, occupational therapy, paralegal studies, physical therapy, physiology, respiratory therapy, retail management, science, secretarial studies/office management, social science, social work, sociology, studio art, tourism and travel.
LIBRARY Daniel Leeds Library with 80,000 books, 350 periodicals, 2 on-line bibliographic services, 6 CD-ROMs, 1,000 records, tapes, and CDs.
COMPUTERS ON CAMPUS Computer purchase plan available. 220 computers for student use in computer center provide access to Internet.
COLLEGE LIFE Drama-theater group, student-run newspaper, radio station. 10% vote in student government elections. *Social organizations:* 22 open to all. *Most popular organizations:* Phi Theta Kappa, African-American Coalition, History/Government Club, International Club. *Major annual event:* Buccaneer Day. *Student services:* health clinic, personal-psychological counseling. *Campus security:* 24-hour emergency response devices and patrols.
HOUSING College housing not available.
ATHLETICS Member NJCAA. *Intercollegiate:* archery M/W, basketball M/W, tennis M/W. *Intramural:* basketball, soccer, tennis. *Contact:* Mr. Spike Edwards, Athletic Director, 609-343-5107.
CAREER PLANNING *Placement office:* 3 full-time staff. *Director:* Ms. Carmen Sanchez, Director of Counseling, 609-343-5087. *Services:* job fairs, resume preparation, career counseling, careers library, job bank, job interviews. 75 organizations recruited on campus 1994–95.
AFTER GRADUATION 63% of class of 1994 had job offers within 6 months.
EXPENSES FOR 1996–97 *Application fee:* $15. Area resident tuition: $1690 full-time, $54.15 per credit part-time. State resident tuition: $3380 full-time, $108.30 per credit part-time. Nonresident tuition: $5596 full-time, $188.90 per credit part-time. Full-time mandatory fees: $223.
FINANCIAL AID *College-administered undergrad aid 1995–96:* need-based scholarships (average $500), non-need scholarships (average $500), low-interest long-term loans from external sources (average $800), Federal Work-Study, part-time jobs. *Required forms:* CSS Financial Aid PROFILE, institutional, FAFSA. *Priority deadline:* 3/1. *Waivers:* full or partial for employees or children of employees and senior citizens.
APPLYING Open admission. *Option:* early entrance. *Required:* New Jersey Basic Skills Exam. *Required for some:* school transcript. Test scores used for counseling/placement. *Application deadline:* 9/1.
APPLYING/TRANSFER *Required:* college transcript. *Required for some:* high school transcript. *Application deadline:* 9/1.
CONTACT Mrs. Linda McLeod, College Recruiter, Atlantic Community College, Mays Landing, NJ 08330-2699, 609-343-5000 or toll-free 800-645-CHEF (in-state). *E-mail:* accadmit@nsvm.atlantic.edu. College video available.

❖ *See page 698 for a narrative description.* ❖

BERGEN COMMUNITY COLLEGE
Paramus, New Jersey

UG Enrollment: 13,207	Tuition & Fees (Area Res): $2227
Application Deadline: 7/31	Room & Board: N/Avail

For more than 25 years, Bergen Community College has offered its students a high-quality educational experience. BCC offers 3 types of degree programs in more than 70 fields of study. Students can earn an Associate in Arts, Associate in Science, or Associate in Applied Science degree. One-year certificate programs are also offered.

GENERAL County-supported, 2-year, coed. Awards certificates, transfer associate, terminal associate degrees. Founded 1965. *Setting:* 167-acre suburban campus with easy access to New York City. *Research spending 1994–95:* $241,540. *Total enrollment:* 13,207. *Faculty:* 681 (242 full-time, 35% with terminal degrees, 439 part-time).
ENROLLMENT PROFILE 13,207 students: 57% women, 43% men, 59% part-time, 4% transferred in, 10% international, 43% 25 or older, 1% Native American, 13% Hispanic, 5% African American, 9% Asian American. *Areas of study chosen:* 32% liberal arts/general studies, 16% business management and administrative services, 8% health professions and related sciences, 7% education, 4% computer and information sciences, 3% psychology, 2% biological and life sciences, 2% communications and journalism, 2% engineering and applied sciences, 2% social sciences, 1% fine arts. *Most popular recent majors:* liberal arts/general studies, business administration/commerce/management, nursing.
FIRST-YEAR CLASS 2,041 total; 2,551 applied, 100% were accepted, 80% of whom enrolled.
ACADEMIC PROGRAM Core. Calendar: semesters. Academic remediation for entering students, English as a second language program offered during academic year and summer, services for LD students, honors program, summer session for credit, part-time degree program (daytime, evenings, summer), adult/continuing education programs, co-op programs and internships. Study abroad in Spain.
GENERAL DEGREE REQUIREMENTS 64 credit hours; internship (some majors).
MAJORS Accounting, art/fine arts, automotive technologies, biology/biological sciences, broadcasting, business administration/commerce/management, chemistry, commercial art, communication, computer programming, computer science, computer technologies, criminal justice, dance, dental services, drafting and design, early childhood education, economics, education, electrical and electronics technologies, engineering sciences, finance/banking, history, hotel and restaurant management, legal secretarial studies, liberal arts/general studies, literature, manufacturing technology, mathematics, medical assistant technologies, medical laboratory technology, medical secretarial studies, music, nursing, ornamental horticulture, paralegal studies, philosophy, photography, physical fitness/exercise science, physics, political science/government, psychology, radiological technology, real estate, recreation and leisure services, respiratory therapy, retail management, secretarial studies/office management, sociology, theater arts/drama, women's studies, word processing.
LIBRARY Sidney Silverman Library and Learning Resources Center with 106,627 books, 707 periodicals, 7,336 records, tapes, and CDs.
COMPUTERS ON CAMPUS 225 computers for student use in computer center, computer labs, library, student center provide access to main academic computer. Staffed computer lab on campus.
COLLEGE LIFE Drama-theater group, choral group, student-run newspaper. *Social organizations:* 40 open to all. *Student services:* health clinic, personal-psychological counseling. *Campus security:* 24-hour patrols.
HOUSING College housing not available.
ATHLETICS Member NJCAA. *Intercollegiate:* baseball M, basketball M, cross-country running M/W, golf M/W, soccer M, softball W, track and field M/W, volleyball W, wrestling M. *Intramural:* basketball, tennis, volleyball.
CAREER PLANNING *Services:* job fairs, resume preparation, career counseling, careers library.
EXPENSES FOR 1995–96 *Application fee:* $20. Area resident tuition: $1936 full-time, $60.50 per credit part-time. State resident tuition: $4022 full-time, $125.70 per credit part-time. Nonresident tuition: $7744 full-time, $242 per credit part-time. Part-time mandatory fees per credit range from $9.08 to $36.30. Full-time mandatory fees range from $291 to $1162.
FINANCIAL AID *College-administered undergrad aid 1995–96:* 1,704 need-based scholarships (average $1500), 114 non-need scholarships (average $500), low-interest long-term loans from external sources (average $2000), Federal Work-Study, 75 part-time jobs. *Required forms:* institutional, FAFSA. *Priority deadline:* 6/15. *Waivers:* full or partial for employees or children of employees and senior citizens.
APPLYING Open admission except for allied health programs. *Application deadline:* 7/31. *Notification:* continuous. Preference given to county residents for nursing and dental hygiene programs.
APPLYING/TRANSFER *Application deadline:* 7/31. *Notification:* continuous.
CONTACT Ms. Josephine E. Figueras, Director of Admissions and Registration, Bergen Community College, Paramus, NJ 07652-1595, 201-447-7857. *Fax:* 201-444-7036.

❖ *See page 706 for a narrative description.* ❖

BERKELEY COLLEGE
West Paterson, New Jersey

UG Enrollment: 1,572 **Tuition & Fees: $10,750**
Application Deadline: rolling **Room Only: $4500**

GENERAL Proprietary, 2-year, coed. Awards certificates, transfer associate, terminal associate degrees (branch locations at 2 other New Jersey campuses in Bergen and Middlesex). Founded 1931. ***Setting:*** 16-acre suburban campus with easy access to New York City. ***Total enrollment:*** 1,572. ***Faculty:*** 102 (47 full-time, 10% with terminal degrees, 55 part-time); student-faculty ratio is 15:1.
ENROLLMENT PROFILE 1,572 students from 3 states and territories. 87% women, 13% men, 21% part-time, 94% state residents, 3% live on campus, 10% transferred in, 1% international, 30% 25 or older, 0% Native American, 22% Hispanic, 14% African American, 3% Asian American. ***Areas of study chosen:*** 70% business management and administrative services, 30% computer and information sciences. ***Most popular recent majors:*** business administration/commerce/management, secretarial studies/office management, paralegal studies.
FIRST-YEAR CLASS 764 total; 1,647 applied, 89% were accepted, 52% of whom enrolled. 5% from top 10% of their high school class, 16% from top quarter, 54% from top half.
ACADEMIC PROGRAM Core, business curriculum, honor code. Calendar: quarters. 160 courses offered in 1995–96. Academic remediation for entering students, advanced placement, tutorials, summer session for credit, part-time degree program (daytime, evenings), adult/continuing education programs, co-op programs and internships. Off-campus study at Berkeley College of New York, Berkeley College of White Plains. Study abroad in England (1% of students participate).
GENERAL DEGREE REQUIREMENTS 90 quarter hours; 4 quarter hours of math/science; computer course; internship (some majors).
MAJORS Accounting, business administration/commerce/management, fashion merchandising, health services administration, interior design, international business, paralegal studies, retail management, secretarial studies/office management, tourism and travel, word processing.
LIBRARY Walter A. Brower Library with 31,408 books, 11 microform titles, 238 periodicals, 613 records, tapes, and CDs.
COMPUTERS ON CAMPUS 275 computers for student use in computer center, computer labs, classrooms, library, student center provide access to on-line services, Internet. Staffed computer lab on campus provides training in use of computers, software.
COLLEGE LIFE ***Social organizations:*** 7 open to all; 1 local fraternity, 1 local sorority; 15% of eligible men and 3% of eligible women are members. ***Most popular organizations:*** Activity Club, Student Government, Phi Beta Lambda, Paralegal Club, Delta Epsilon Chi. ***Major annual events:*** Formal, International Day, Fashion Show. ***Student services:*** personal-psychological counseling. ***Campus security:*** security patrols during class hours.
HOUSING 17 college housing spaces available; all were occupied 1995–96. No special consideration for freshman housing applicants. Off-campus living permitted. ***Option:*** single-sex housing available.
CAREER PLANNING ***Placement office:*** 7 full-time staff. ***Director:*** Ms. Sally Grossberger, Director of Career Services, 201-278-5400. ***Services:*** job fairs, resume preparation, resume referral, career counseling, job bank, job interviews. 10 organizations recruited on campus 1994–95.
EXPENSES FOR 1996–97 ***Application fee:*** $35. Tuition: $10,650 full-time. Part-time tuition and fees per credit: $210 for evening classes, $280 for day classes. Full-time mandatory fees: $100. College room only: $4500.
FINANCIAL AID ***College-administered undergrad aid 1995–96:*** need-based scholarships, non-need scholarships, low-interest long-term loans from external sources (average $2625), Federal Work-Study, part-time jobs. ***Required forms:*** FAFSA; required for some: CSS Financial Aid PROFILE; accepted: state. ***Priority deadline:*** 10/1. ***Payment plan:*** installment. ***Waivers:*** full or partial for employees or children of employees.
APPLYING ***Options:*** deferred entrance, midyear entrance. ***Required:*** school transcript, campus interview, TOEFL for international students. ***Application deadline:*** rolling.
APPLYING/TRANSFER ***Required:*** high school transcript, campus interview. ***Recommended:*** college transcript. ***Entrance:*** minimally difficult. ***Application deadline:*** rolling. ***Contact:*** Ms. Tia Delouise, Senior Vice President and Academic Dean, 201-278-5400.
CONTACT Ms. Carol Allen, Director of Admissions, Berkeley College, 44 Rifle Camp Road, West Paterson, NJ 07424-3353, 201-278-5400 or toll-free 800-446-5400. ***Fax:*** 201-278-2242.

❖ *See page 708 for a narrative description.* ❖

BROOKDALE COMMUNITY COLLEGE
Lincroft, New Jersey

UG Enrollment: 12,446 **Tuition & Fees (Area Res): $2277**
Application Deadline: rolling **Room & Board: N/Avail**

GENERAL County-supported, 2-year, coed. Part of New Jersey Commission on Higher Education. Awards certificates, transfer associate, terminal associate degrees. Founded 1967. ***Setting:*** 221-acre small-town campus with easy access to New York City. ***Total enrollment:*** 12,446. ***Faculty:*** 443 (193 full-time, 250 part-time); student-faculty ratio is 22:1.
ENROLLMENT PROFILE 12,446 students from 6 states and territories, 37 other countries. 59% women, 62% part-time, 99% state residents, 5% transferred in, 8% have need-based financial aid, 12% have non-need-based financial aid, 48% 25 or older, 4% Hispanic, 8% African American, 4% Asian American. ***Areas of study chosen:*** 21% business management and administrative services, 15% biological and life sciences, 12% liberal arts/general studies, 9% education, 7% social sciences, 5% health professions and related sciences, 4% communications and journalism, 4% computer and information sciences, 4% vocational and home economics, 3% engineering and applied sciences, 2% fine arts, 1% agriculture, 1% architecture, 1% English language/literature/letters, 1% library and information studies, 1% mathematics, 1% performing arts, 1% physical sciences. ***Most popular recent majors:*** business administration/commerce/management, humanities, social science.
FIRST-YEAR CLASS 3,454 total; 4,609 applied, 100% were accepted, 75% of whom enrolled.
ACADEMIC PROGRAM Core, honor code. Calendar: semesters plus 1 twelve-week and 2 six-week summer terms. 600 courses offered in 1995–96. Academic remediation for entering students, English as a second language program offered during academic year, services for LD students, advanced placement, honors program, summer session for credit, part-time degree program (daytime, evenings, weekends, summer), adult/continuing education programs, co-op programs and internships. Study abroad in Ecuador, England, France, Israel, Spain. ROTC: Army (c), Air Force (c).
GENERAL DEGREE REQUIREMENTS 60 credits; math proficiency.
MAJORS Accounting, applied art, art/fine arts, automotive technologies, business administration/commerce/management, chemistry, communication, computer programming, computer science, criminal justice, drafting and design, early childhood education, education, electrical and electronics technologies, electrical engineering technology, electronics engineering technology, engineering (general), English, fashion merchandising, food services management, humanities, human services, insurance, liberal arts/general studies, library science, marketing/retailing/merchandising, mathematics, medical laboratory technology, music, nursing, paralegal studies, psychology, radiological sciences, recreation and leisure services, respiratory therapy, robotics, science, secretarial studies/office management, social science, sociology, speech/rhetoric/public address/debate, telecommunications, theater arts/drama.
LIBRARY Learning Resources Center with 97,733 books, 142 microform titles, 709 periodicals, 7 CD-ROMs, 25,206 records, tapes, and CDs.
COMPUTERS ON CAMPUS 700 computers for student use in computer center, computer labs, library. Staffed computer lab on campus.
COLLEGE LIFE Drama-theater group, student-run newspaper, radio station. ***Social organizations:*** 30 open to all. ***Most popular organizations:*** Ecology Club, Circle K, SAGE, Outdoor Club. ***Major annual events:*** Earth Week, May Fest, International Fair. ***Student services:*** personal-psychological counseling, women's center. ***Campus security:*** 24-hour emergency response devices and patrols.
HOUSING College housing not available.
ATHLETICS Member NJCAA. ***Intercollegiate:*** basketball M/W, cross-country running M/W, golf M/W, soccer M/W, tennis M/W, wrestling M. ***Intramural:*** basketball, fencing, volleyball. ***Contact:*** Mr. Robert Walsak, Athletic Director, 908-224-2378.
CAREER PLANNING ***Director:*** Mr. Harvey Schmelter-Davis, Director of Career Services, 908-224-2569. ***Services:*** job fairs, resume preparation, career counseling, careers library, job bank, job interviews.
AFTER GRADUATION 72% of students completing a degree program in 1994–95 went directly on to further study.
EXPENSES FOR 1995–96 Area resident tuition: $1980 full-time, $66 per credit part-time. State resident tuition: $3960 full-time, $132 per credit part-time. Nonresident tuition: $7920 full-time, $264 per credit part-time. Part-time mandatory fees: $9.90 per credit. Full-time mandatory fees: $297.
FINANCIAL AID ***College-administered undergrad aid 1995–96:*** 1,316 need-based scholarships (average $1201), 96 non-need scholarships (average $673), low-interest long-term loans from external sources (average $1768), 77 Federal Work-Study (averaging $1250), 167 part-time jobs. ***Required forms:*** institutional, FAFSA. ***Priority deadline:*** 5/1. ***Payment plan:*** deferred payment. ***Waivers:*** full or partial for employees or children of employees and senior citizens.
APPLYING Open admission. ***Options:*** early entrance, deferred entrance. ***Required:*** school transcript, TOEFL for international students. ***Application deadline:*** rolling. ***Notification:*** continuous. Preference given to county residents.
APPLYING/TRANSFER ***Required:*** high school transcript. ***Entrance:*** noncompetitive. ***Application deadline:*** rolling. ***Notification:*** continuous. ***Contact:*** Ms. Karen Abramski, Director of Articulation, 908-224-2777.
CONTACT Mr. Richard Pfeffer, Director of Enrollment Management, Brookdale Community College, Lincroft, NJ 07738, 908-224-2262. ***Fax:*** 908-576-1643.

BURLINGTON COUNTY COLLEGE
Pemberton, New Jersey

UG Enrollment: 6,433 **Tuition & Fees (Area Res): $1476**
Application Deadline: rolling **Room & Board: N/Avail**

GENERAL County-supported, 2-year, coed. Part of New Jersey Commission on Higher Education. Awards certificates, transfer associate, terminal associate degrees. Founded 1966. ***Setting:*** 225-acre suburban campus with easy access to Philadelphia. ***Endowment:*** $5.9 million. ***Total enrollment:*** 6,433. ***Faculty:*** 327 (66 full-time, 45% with terminal degrees, 261 part-time); student-faculty ratio is 20:1.
ENROLLMENT PROFILE 6,433 students from 2 states and territories, 8 other countries. 60% women, 40% men, 65% part-time, 99% state residents, 5% transferred in, 52% 25 or older, 1% Native American, 3% Hispanic, 14% African American, 3% Asian American. ***Areas of study chosen:*** 72% liberal arts/general studies, 11% health professions and related sciences, 3% business management and administrative services, 3% engineering and applied sciences, 2% computer and information sciences, 2% psychology, 2% social sciences, 1% architecture, 1% biological and life sciences, 1% communications and journalism, 1% English language/literature/letters, 1% performing arts. ***Most popular recent majors:*** liberal arts/general studies, business administration/commerce/management, nursing.
FIRST-YEAR CLASS 1,775 total. Of the students who applied, 100% were accepted, 59% of whom enrolled.
ACADEMIC PROGRAM Core, honor code. Calendar: semesters plus 2 summer terms. 300 courses offered in 1995–96. Academic remediation for entering students, English as a second language program offered during academic year, services for LD students, advanced placement, tutorials, honors program, summer session for credit, part-time degree program (daytime, evenings, weekends, summer), adult/continuing education programs, co-op programs and internships.
GENERAL DEGREE REQUIREMENTS 64 credit hours; computer course.
MAJORS Accounting, applied art, architectural technologies, art/fine arts, art therapy, automotive technologies, biology/biological sciences, business administration/commerce/management, business education, chemical engineering technology, chemistry, civil engineering technology, communication equipment technology, computer programming, computer science, criminal justice, data processing, drafting and design, early childhood education, ecology, electrical and electronics technologies, elementary education, engineering (general), (pre)engineering sequence, English, environmental sciences, finance/banking, food services management, food services technology, graphic arts, history, hotel and restaurant management, journalism, laboratory technologies, law enforcement/police sciences, legal secretarial

studies, liberal arts/general studies, medical assistant technologies, music, nursing, philosophy, physical education, physics, political science/government, psychology, radiological technology, science, secretarial studies/office management, sociology, theater arts/drama.
LIBRARY Burlington County College Library with 75,500 books, 1,100 microform titles, 595 periodicals, 8 CD-ROMs, 4,200 records, tapes, and CDs. Acquisition spending 1994–95: $102,505.
COMPUTERS ON CAMPUS 400 computers for student use in computer center, computer labs, classrooms, library. Staffed computer lab on campus provides training in use of computers, software.
COLLEGE LIFE Drama-theater group, student-run newspaper, radio station. *Major annual events:* AIDS Awareness Week, Drugs/Alcohol Awareness Week, Black History Month. *Student services:* personal-psychological counseling. *Campus security:* 24-hour emergency response devices and patrols, late-night transport-escort service.
HOUSING College housing not available.
ATHLETICS Member NJCAA. *Intercollegiate:* baseball M(s), basketball M(s)/W(s), golf M/W, soccer M(s)/W(s), softball W(s), swimming and diving M/W, tennis M(s)/W(s). *Intramural:* basketball, bowling, golf, soccer, swimming and diving, tennis, volleyball. *Contact:* Mr. Robert Seiler, Director of Athletics and Recreation, 609-894-9311 Ext. 434.
CAREER PLANNING *Director:* Ms. Judith Olsen, Director of Library Services, 609-894-9311 Ext. 222. *Services:* resume preparation, career counseling, careers library.
AFTER GRADUATION 60% of students completing a degree program in 1994–95 went directly on to further study.
EXPENSES FOR 1995–96 *Application fee:* $15. Area resident tuition: $1300 full-time, $50 per credit hour part-time. State resident tuition: $1856 full-time, $58 per credit hour part-time. Nonresident tuition: $3840 full-time, $120 per credit hour part-time. Part-time mandatory fees: $5.50 per credit hour. Full-time mandatory fees: $176.
FINANCIAL AID *College-administered undergrad aid 1995–96:* 30 need-based scholarships (averaging $350), 30 non-need scholarships (averaging $200), short-term loans (averaging $100), low-interest long-term loans from external sources (averaging $1300), Federal Work-Study, 70 part-time jobs. *Required forms:* state; accepted: FAFSA. *Application deadline:* continuous to 10/1. *Payment plans:* installment, deferred payment. *Waivers:* full or partial for employees or children of employees and senior citizens.
APPLYING Open admission except for nursing program. *Options:* early entrance, deferred entrance. *Required:* TOEFL for international students, New Jersey Basic Skills Exam. Test scores used for counseling/placement. *Application deadline:* rolling. *Notification:* continuous.
APPLYING/TRANSFER *Required:* standardized test scores. *Application deadline:* rolling. *Notification:* continuous. *Contact:* Dr. Douglas Devoll, Student Development Specialist, 609-894-9311 Ext. 342.
CONTACT Mr. Earl Teasley, Director of Admissions and Enrollment Management, Burlington County College, Pemberton, NJ 08068-1599, 609-894-9311 Ext. 7288. *Fax:* 609-894-0183. College video available.

CAMDEN COUNTY COLLEGE
Blackwood, New Jersey

UG Enrollment: 13,068	Tuition & Fees (Area Res): $1824
Application Deadline: rolling	Room & Board: N/Avail

GENERAL State and locally supported, 2-year, coed. Part of New Jersey Commission on Higher Education. Awards certificates, transfer associate, terminal associate degrees. Founded 1967. *Setting:* 320-acre suburban campus with easy access to Philadelphia. *Educational spending 1994–95:* $1063 per undergrad. *Total enrollment:* 13,068. *Faculty:* 701 (126 full-time, 21% with terminal degrees, 575 part-time).
ENROLLMENT PROFILE 13,068 students from 2 states and territories, 21 other countries. 60% women, 61% part-time, 98% state residents, 22% transferred in, 24% have need-based financial aid, 1% international, 39% 25 or older, 0% Native American, 4% Hispanic, 14% African American, 5% Asian American. *Areas of study chosen:* 30% liberal arts/general studies, 25% health professions and related sciences, 13% business management and administrative services, 10% engineering and applied sciences. *Most popular recent majors:* liberal arts/general studies, nursing, criminal justice.
FIRST-YEAR CLASS 2,786 total. Of the students who applied, 100% were accepted, 62% of whom enrolled.
ACADEMIC PROGRAM Core, honor code. Calendar: semesters. Academic remediation for entering students, English as a second language program offered during academic year, services for LD students, summer session for credit, part-time degree program (daytime, evenings), external degree programs, adult/continuing education programs, co-op programs. Study abroad in England (1% of students participate).
GENERAL DEGREE REQUIREMENTS 64 credits; 1 math course.
MAJORS Accounting, animal sciences, applied art, art/fine arts, automotive technologies, business administration/commerce/management, communication, computer programming, computer technologies, criminal justice, data processing, dental services, dietetics, early childhood education, electrical engineering technology, engineering sciences, environmental sciences, finance/banking, fire science, food services management, forestry, gerontology, human services, laboratory technologies, liberal arts/general studies, marketing/retailing/merchandising, mechanical engineering technology, medical laboratory technology, nursing, nutrition, occupational safety and health, optical technologies, physical fitness/exercise science, radiological technology, real estate, recreation and leisure services, respiratory therapy, robotics, secretarial studies/office management, theater arts/drama, word processing.
LIBRARY Learning Resource Center with 92,814 books, 448 periodicals, 4 CD-ROMs, 1,987 records, tapes, and CDs. Acquisition spending 1994–95: $94,908.
COMPUTERS ON CAMPUS 700 computers for student use in computer labs, classrooms, library. Staffed computer lab on campus.
COLLEGE LIFE Drama-theater group, choral group, student-run radio station. *Social organizations:* 45 open to all. *Most popular organizations:* Phi Theta Kappa, Circle K Club, Laser Club, Math Club, Chess Club. *Major annual events:* Welcome Back Barbecue, College Community Day, Military Career Day. *Campus security:* 24-hour emergency response devices.
HOUSING College housing not available.
ATHLETICS Member NJCAA. *Intercollegiate:* baseball M, basketball M/W, soccer M/W, softball W. *Intramural:* baseball, basketball, soccer, softball. *Contact:* Mr. Cliff Crispin, Director of Athletics and Facilities, 609-227-7200 Ext. 263.

CAREER PLANNING *Director:* Mr. Bernard Carlson, Director of Career Planning and Placement, 609-227-7200 Ext. 275. *Services:* job fairs, resume preparation, resume referral, career counseling, careers library, job bank, job interviews.
EXPENSES FOR 1996–97 *Application fee:* $15. Area resident tuition: $1728 full-time, $54 per credit part-time. Nonresident tuition: $1856 full-time, $58 per credit part-time. Part-time mandatory fees: $48 per semester. Tuition for international students: $3392 full-time, $106 per credit part-time. Full-time mandatory fees: $96.
FINANCIAL AID *College-administered undergrad aid 1995–96:* need-based scholarships, non-need scholarships, low-interest long-term loans, Federal Work-Study, part-time jobs. *Required forms:* CSS Financial Aid PROFILE, state, institutional, FAFSA. *Priority deadline:* 7/1. *Waivers:* full or partial for employees or children of employees and senior citizens.
APPLYING Open admission. *Option:* early entrance. *Required:* TOEFL for international students. *Required for some:* school transcript. Test scores used for counseling/placement. *Application deadline:* rolling.
APPLYING/TRANSFER *Required:* college transcript. *Required for some:* high school transcript. *Entrance:* noncompetitive. *Application deadline:* rolling. *Contact:* Ms. Joan Hacfle, Coordinator of Transfer Information, 609-227-7200 Ext. 227.
CONTACT Ms. Sharon Kohl, Director of Student Records and Registration, Camden County College, Blackwood, NJ 08012-0200, 609-227-7200 Ext. 347. College video available.

COUNTY COLLEGE OF MORRIS
Randolph, New Jersey

UG Enrollment: 9,342	Tuition & Fees (Area Res): $2464
Application Deadline: 9/1	Room & Board: N/Avail

GENERAL County-supported, 2-year, coed. Part of New Jersey Commission on Higher Education. Awards certificates, transfer associate, terminal associate degrees. Founded 1966. *Setting:* 218-acre rural campus with easy access to New York City. *Total enrollment:* 9,342. *Faculty:* 541 (190 full-time, 27% with terminal degrees, 351 part-time); student-faculty ratio is 21:1. *Notable Alumni:* John Monsport, vice-president of Sony/Loews Theatres; Dr. Lorrie Dixon; pediatrician; Dr. Robert DiPaola, oncologist and researcher; Peter Skurla, consultant; Joann Young, television producer.
ENROLLMENT PROFILE 9,342 students: 53% women, 47% men, 55% part-time, 99% state residents, 2% transferred in, 1% international, 41% 25 or older, 1% Native American, 7% Hispanic, 4% African American, 6% Asian American. *Areas of study chosen:* 23% liberal arts/general studies, 17% business management and administrative services, 7% health professions and related sciences, 4% computer and information sciences, 3% biological and life sciences, 3% engineering and applied sciences, 2% communications and journalism, 1% agriculture, 1% fine arts, 1% mathematics, 1% performing arts, 1% physical sciences. *Most popular recent majors:* business administration/commerce/management, liberal arts/general studies, nursing.
FIRST-YEAR CLASS 3,105 total; 5,101 applied, 100% were accepted, 61% of whom enrolled.
ACADEMIC PROGRAM Core, honor code. Calendar: semesters. Average class size 22 in required courses. Academic remediation for entering students, English as a second language program offered during academic year and summer, services for LD students, advanced placement, honors program, summer session for credit, part-time degree program (daytime, evenings, summer), adult/continuing education programs, co-op programs and internships.
GENERAL DEGREE REQUIREMENTS 62 credits; 6 credits of math/science; computer course for electronic engineering technology, manufacturing technology, biomedical technology, engineering science majors; internship (some majors).
MAJORS Accounting, advertising, agricultural business, art/fine arts, biology/biological sciences, biomedical technologies, broadcasting, business administration/commerce/management, chemical engineering technology, chemistry, communication, computer information systems, criminal justice, dance, drafting and design, electronics engineering technology, engineering sciences, (pre)engineering sequence, environmental sciences, finance/banking, graphic arts, hotel and restaurant management, humanities, human services, insurance, international studies, journalism, laboratory technologies, landscaping/grounds maintenance, liberal arts/general studies, manufacturing technology, marketing/retailing/merchandising, mathematics, mechanical engineering technology, medical laboratory technology, music, nursing, photography, public administration, respiratory therapy, retail management, science, secretarial studies/office management, social science, telecommunications, theater arts/drama, word processing.
LIBRARY Matsen Learning Resource Center with 105,000 books, 28,000 microform titles, 819 periodicals, 3 on-line bibliographic services, 25 CD-ROMs, 1,000 records, tapes, and CDs.
COMPUTERS ON CAMPUS 41 computers for student use in library. Staffed computer lab on campus provides training in use of computers, software.
COLLEGE LIFE Drama-theater group, choral group, student-run newspaper, radio station. 2% vote in student government elections. *Social organizations:* 25 open to all. *Most popular organizations:* Student Government Association, Student Activities Programming Board, Black Student Union, United Latino Organization, Student Newspaper. *Major annual event:* Spring Festival. *Student services:* health clinic, personal-psychological counseling, women's center. *Campus security:* 24-hour emergency response devices and patrols, late-night transport-escort service.
HOUSING College housing not available.
ATHLETICS Member NJCAA. *Intercollegiate:* baseball M(s), basketball M(s)/W(s), golf M/W, ice hockey M(s), soccer M, softball W(s), tennis M/W. *Intramural:* badminton, basketball, football, soccer, softball, tennis, volleyball, weight lifting, wrestling. *Contact:* Mr. Jack Martin, Athletic Director, 201-328-5252.
CAREER PLANNING *Placement office:* 6 full-time, 3 part-time staff. *Director:* Mr. Albert Foderaro, Director, Career Services, 201-328-5245. *Services:* resume preparation, resume referral, career counseling, careers library, job bank, job interviews. Students must register sophomore year. 66 organizations recruited on campus 1994–95.
EXPENSES FOR 1996–97 *Application fee:* $25. Area resident tuition: $2144 full-time, $67 per credit part-time. State resident tuition: $4288 full-time, $134 per credit part-time. Nonresident tuition: $5888 full-time, $184 per credit part-time. Part-time mandatory fees: $10 per credit. Full-time mandatory fees: $320.
FINANCIAL AID *College-administered undergrad aid 1995–96:* 150 need-based scholarships (average $500), 200 non-need scholarships (average $550), short-term loans, low-interest long-term loans from external sources (average $1500), Federal Work-Study,

County College of Morris (continued)
200 part-time jobs. ***Required forms:*** CSS Financial Aid PROFILE, FAFSA. ***Priority deadline:*** 5/15. ***Waivers:*** full or partial for employees or children of employees and senior citizens.
APPLYING Open admission. ***Options:*** Common Application, early entrance. ***Required:*** school transcript, TOEFL for international students, New Jersey Basic Skills Exam. ***Recommended:*** SAT I. ***Required for some:*** 3 years of high school math, SAT I. Test scores used for counseling/placement. ***Application deadline:*** 9/1. ***Notification:*** continuous.
APPLYING/TRANSFER ***Required:*** high school transcript. ***Required for some:*** standardized test scores, 3 years of high school math, college transcript. ***Entrance:*** noncompetitive. ***Application deadline:*** 9/1. ***Notification:*** continuous.
CONTACT Ms. Carolyn Holmfelt, Coordinator of Admissions, County College of Morris, Randolph, NJ 07869-2086, 201-328-5095. ***Fax:*** 201-328-1282.

CUMBERLAND COUNTY COLLEGE
Vineland, New Jersey

UG Enrollment: 2,484 | **Tuition & Fees (Area Res): $2376**
Application Deadline: rolling | **Room & Board: N/Avail**

GENERAL State and locally supported, 2-year, coed. Part of New Jersey Commision on Higher Education. Awards certificates, diplomas, transfer associate, terminal associate degrees. Founded 1963. ***Setting:*** 100-acre small-town campus with easy access to Philadelphia. ***Total enrollment:*** 2,484. ***Faculty:*** 118 (41 full-time, 77 part-time).
ENROLLMENT PROFILE 2,484 students: 64% women, 58% part-time, 99% state residents, 3% transferred in, 1% international, 50% 25 or older, 1% Native American, 9% Hispanic, 11% African American, 1% Asian American. ***Most popular recent majors:*** liberal arts/general studies, nursing.
FIRST-YEAR CLASS Of the students who applied, 100% were accepted, 62% of whom enrolled.
ACADEMIC PROGRAM Core. Calendar: semesters. Academic remediation for entering students, English as a second language program offered during academic year and summer, services for LD students, advanced placement, honors program, summer session for credit, part-time degree program (daytime, evenings), adult/continuing education programs, co-op programs.
GENERAL DEGREE REQUIREMENTS 64 credits; math proficiency or 1 math course; 1 science course; computer course.
MAJORS Accounting, agricultural business, agricultural sciences, aviation technology, broadcasting, business administration/commerce/management, community services, computer information systems, corrections, drafting and design, early childhood education, education, engineering and applied sciences, (pre)engineering sequence, film and video production, flight training, horticulture, human resources, industrial administration, industrial engineering technology, labor and industrial relations, law enforcement/police sciences, legal secretarial studies, liberal arts/general studies, marketing/retailing/merchandising, mathematics, nursing, ornamental horticulture, plastics technology, quality control technology, radiological technology, robotics, science, secretarial studies/office management, social work, theater arts/drama, word processing.
LIBRARY 51,000 books, 213 periodicals, 2,804 records, tapes, and CDs.
COMPUTERS ON CAMPUS 115 computers for student use in computer center. Staffed computer lab on campus provides training in use of computers, software.
COLLEGE LIFE ***Student services:*** personal-psychological counseling. ***Campus security:*** 24-hour emergency response devices.
HOUSING College housing not available.
CAREER PLANNING ***Service:*** career counseling.
EXPENSES FOR 1996–97 ***Application fee:*** $15. Area resident tuition: $2152 full-time, $67.25 per credit part-time. State resident tuition: $4304 full-time, $134.50 per credit part-time. Nonresident tuition: $8608 full-time, $269 per credit part-time. Part-time mandatory fees: $7 per credit. Full-time mandatory fees: $224.
FINANCIAL AID ***College-administered undergrad aid 1995–96:*** 50 need-based scholarships (average $400), 25 non-need scholarships (average $400), low-interest long-term loans from external sources, Federal Work-Study. ***Required forms:*** CSS Financial Aid PROFILE, state, institutional; required for some: FAFSA. ***Priority deadline:*** 7/1.
APPLYING Open admission except for nursing, radiography programs. ***Options:*** early entrance, deferred entrance. ***Required:*** school transcript. ***Application deadline:*** rolling. ***Notification:*** continuous.
APPLYING/TRANSFER ***Application deadline:*** rolling. ***Notification:*** continuous. ***Contact:*** Dr. Steven Stolar, Director of Advisement, 609-691-8600 Ext. 328.
CONTACT Ms. Maud Fried-Goodnight, Director of Enrollment Services, Cumberland County College, Vineland, NJ 08360-0517, 609-691-8600 Ext. 220.

DEVRY TECHNICAL INSTITUTE
Woodbridge, New Jersey

UG Enrollment: 2,536 | **Tuition & Fees: $6560**
Application Deadline: rolling | **Room & Board: N/Avail**

GENERAL Proprietary, 2-year, coed. Part of DeVry Inc./Keller Graduate School of Management. Awards diplomas, terminal associate degrees. Founded 1969. ***Setting:*** 10-acre urban campus with easy access to New York City. ***Total enrollment:*** 2,536. ***Faculty:*** 92 (52 full-time, 40 part-time); student-faculty ratio is 29:1.
ENROLLMENT PROFILE 2,536 students from 24 states and territories, 17 other countries. 17% women, 34% part-time, 74% state residents, 0% transferred in, 80% have need-based financial aid, 80% have non-need-based financial aid, 1% international, 45% 25 or older, 0% Native American, 14% Hispanic, 24% African American, 4% Asian American. ***Areas of study chosen:*** 59% engineering and applied sciences, 19% computer and information sciences, 15% business management and administrative services. ***Most popular recent majors:*** electrical and electronics technologies, telecommunications.
FIRST-YEAR CLASS 1,279 total; 1,571 applied, 91% were accepted, 89% of whom enrolled.
ACADEMIC PROGRAM Core, education, technology, and business curriculum, honor code. Calendar: semesters. 124 courses offered in 1995–96. Services for LD students, advanced placement, summer session for credit, part-time degree program (daytime, evenings, summer), adult/continuing education programs. ROTC: Army (c), Air Force (c).
GENERAL DEGREE REQUIREMENTS 88 credit hours; math/science requirements vary according to program; computer course.
MAJORS Computer information systems, electrical and electronics technologies, electronics engineering technology, telecommunications.
LIBRARY 15,295 books, 154 microform titles, 184 periodicals, 3 on-line bibliographic services, 19 CD-ROMs, 646 records, tapes, and CDs.
COMPUTERS ON CAMPUS 200 computers for student use in computer labs.
COLLEGE LIFE Student-run newspaper, radio station. ***Social organizations:*** 11 open to all. ***Most popular organizations:*** Big Sister/Little Sister, Tau Alpha Pi Honor Society, Black Student Union, Telecommunications Club, Institute for Electrical and Electronic Engineers. ***Major annual event:*** Student Appreciation Day. ***Campus security:*** 24-hour emergency response devices and patrols, late-night transport-escort service.
HOUSING College housing not available.
CAREER PLANNING ***Placement office:*** 7 full-time, 1 part-time staff. ***Director:*** Ms. Barbara Hurley, Dean of Student Affairs, 908-634-3460. ***Services:*** job fairs, resume preparation, resume referral, career counseling, careers library.
EXPENSES FOR 1996–97 ***Application fee:*** $25. Tuition: $6560 full-time, $295 per credit hour part-time.
FINANCIAL AID ***College-administered undergrad aid 1995–96:*** need-based scholarships, non-need scholarships, low-interest long-term loans from college funds (average $2000), loans from external sources (average $2195), Federal Work-Study, part-time jobs. ***Required forms:*** FAFSA. ***Priority deadline:*** 10/28. ***Payment plan:*** deferred payment. ***Waivers:*** full or partial for employees or children of employees. ***Notification:*** continuous.
APPLYING ***Options:*** deferred entrance, midyear entrance. ***Required:*** school transcript, interview, TOEFL for international students, CPT. ***Recommended:*** SAT I or ACT. Test scores used for admission. ***Application deadline:*** rolling. ***Notification:*** continuous.
APPLYING/TRANSFER ***Required:*** standardized test scores, high school transcript, interview, minimum 2.0 college GPA. ***Entrance:*** minimally difficult. ***Application deadline:*** rolling. ***Notification:*** continuous. ***Contact:*** Ms. Danielle DiNapoli, Director of Admission, 908-634-9510.
CONTACT Ms. Danielle DiNapoli, Director of Admission, DeVry Technical Institute, 479 Green Street, Woodbridge, NJ 07095-1407, 908-634-9510 or toll-free 800-333-3879.

ESSEX COUNTY COLLEGE
Newark, New Jersey

UG Enrollment: 8,952 | **Tuition & Fees (Area Res): $1800**
Application Deadline: 8/15 | **Room & Board: N/Avail**

GENERAL County-supported, 2-year, coed. Part of New Jersey Commission on Higher Education. Awards certificates, transfer associate, terminal associate degrees. Founded 1966. ***Setting:*** 22-acre urban campus with easy access to New York City. ***Total enrollment:*** 8,952. ***Faculty:*** 270 (146 full-time, 124 part-time).
ENROLLMENT PROFILE 8,952 students from 4 states and territories. 47% part-time, 93% state residents, 6% transferred in, 54% 25 or older, 0% Native American, 15% Hispanic, 52% African American, 1% Asian American. ***Most popular recent majors:*** business administration/commerce/management, nursing, computer science.
FIRST-YEAR CLASS 4,000 applied, 100% were accepted, 73% of whom enrolled.
ACADEMIC PROGRAM Core, honor code. Calendar: semesters. Academic remediation for entering students, English as a second language program offered during academic year and summer, services for LD students, advanced placement, honors program, summer session for credit, part-time degree program (daytime, evenings), adult/continuing education programs, co-op programs and internships. Off-campus study at New Jersey Institute of Technology, Rutgers, The State University of New Jersey, University of Medicine and Dentistry of New Jersey. ROTC: Army (c).
GENERAL DEGREE REQUIREMENTS 63 credits; math proficiency; computer course for most majors.
MAJORS Accounting, architectural technologies, art/fine arts, biology/biological sciences, business administration/commerce/management, business education, chemical engineering technology, chemistry, computer information systems, computer programming, computer science, criminal justice, data processing, dental services, early childhood education, education, electrical and electronics technologies, electronics engineering technology, elementary education, emergency medical technology, engineering (general), (pre)engineering sequence, engineering technology, fire science, health services administration, hotel and restaurant management, human services, law enforcement/police sciences, liberal arts/general studies, mathematics, medical secretarial studies, music, music education, nursing, optical technologies, physical education, physical therapy, radiological technology, secretarial studies/office management, social science.
LIBRARY 69,654 books, 4,114 microform titles, 627 periodicals, 3,962 records, tapes, and CDs.
COMPUTERS ON CAMPUS Computers for student use in computer center, computer labs, library.
COLLEGE LIFE Drama-theater group, student-run newspaper. ***Student services:*** legal services, health clinic, personal-psychological counseling, women's center. ***Campus security:*** 24-hour emergency response devices and patrols.
HOUSING College housing not available.
ATHLETICS Member NJCAA. ***Intercollegiate:*** basketball M(s)/W(s), cross-country running M(s)/W(s), soccer M, track and field M/W. ***Intramural:*** table tennis (Ping-Pong), weight lifting. ***Contact:*** Mr. Cleo Hill, Director of Athletics, 201-877-3306.
CAREER PLANNING ***Services:*** job fairs, resume preparation, resume referral, career counseling, careers library, job bank, job interviews.
EXPENSES FOR 1995–96 ***Application fee:*** $10. Area resident tuition: $1800 full-time, $75 per credit hour part-time. State resident tuition: $3360 full-time, $140 per credit hour part-time. Nonresident tuition: $4920 full-time, $205 per credit hour part-time.
FINANCIAL AID ***College-administered undergrad aid 1995–96:*** need-based scholarships, 25 non-need scholarships (average $540), short-term loans (average $100), low-interest long-term loans from external sources (average $2625), Federal Work-Study. ***Required forms:*** CSS Financial Aid PROFILE, institutional; required for some: FAFSA. ***Priority deadline:*** 6/1.
APPLYING Open admission except for allied health programs. ***Options:*** early entrance, deferred entrance. ***Required:*** school transcript, New Jersey Basic Skills Exam. Test scores used for counseling/placement. ***Application deadline:*** 8/15. ***Notification:*** continuous.

APPLYING/TRANSFER ***Required:*** standardized test scores, high school transcript. ***Entrance:*** noncompetitive. ***Application deadline:*** 8/15. ***Notification:*** continuous. ***Contact:*** Ms. Brenda Groomes, Associate Director, Transfer and Articulation, 201-877-1936.
CONTACT Mr. Steven Nash, Director of Admissions, Essex County College, 303 University Avenue, Newark, NJ 07102-1798, 201-877-3119. College video available.

FAIRLEIGH DICKINSON UNIVERSITY, EDWARD WILLIAMS COLLEGE
Hackensack, New Jersey

UG Enrollment: 746	**Tuition & Fees: $12,950**
Application Deadline: rolling	**Room & Board: $5864**

GENERAL Independent, 2-year, coed. Part of Fairleigh Dickinson University. Awards transfer associate degrees. Founded 1964. ***Setting:*** 125-acre suburban campus with easy access to New York City. ***Total enrollment:*** 746. ***Faculty:*** 60 (29 full-time, 41% with terminal degrees, 31 part-time); student-faculty ratio is 16:1. ***Notable Alumni:*** Dawn Ciallella, co-owner of Dynamics Special Advertising; Eleanor Kieliszek, former mayor of Madison, New Jersey; James P. Merriman, president of Database Software Technology; Dan Ficini, chairman, president and CEO of Duro-Test Corporation; William Macrone, editor of *PC Magazine*.
ENROLLMENT PROFILE 746 students: 58% women, 42% men, 30% part-time, 83% state residents, 1% transferred in, 34% have need-based financial aid, 3% have non-need-based financial aid, 7% international, 9% 25 or older, 1% Native American, 14% Hispanic, 33% African American, 5% Asian American. ***Areas of study chosen:*** 100% liberal arts/general studies.
FIRST-YEAR CLASS 314 total; 1,279 applied, 77% were accepted, 32% of whom enrolled. 4% from top 10% of their high school class, 11% from top quarter, 37% from top half.
ACADEMIC PROGRAM Core, liberal arts curriculum, honor code. Calendar: semesters. 388 courses offered in 1995–96. Academic remediation for entering students, English as a second language program offered during academic year, services for LD students, advanced placement, tutorials, summer session for credit, part-time degree program (daytime, evenings, weekends, summer), adult/continuing education programs, co-op programs. Study abroad in England (1% of students participate). ROTC: Army, Air Force.
GENERAL DEGREE REQUIREMENTS 60 credits; 6 credits each of math and science.
MAJOR Liberal arts/general studies.
LIBRARY Weiner Library plus 2 others, with 446,936 books, 2,505 periodicals, 3 on-line bibliographic services, 40 CD-ROMs, 6,251 records, tapes, and CDs.
COMPUTERS ON CAMPUS Computer purchase plan available. 300 computers for student use in computer center, academic buildings, library, dorms provide access to main academic computer, off-campus computing facilities, e-mail, on-line services, Internet. Staffed computer lab on campus provides training in use of computers, software.
NOTEWORTHY RESEARCH FACILITIES Center for Asian Studies.
COLLEGE LIFE Orientation program (2 days, $150, parents included). Drama-theater group, choral group, student-run newspaper, radio station. 18% vote in student government elections. ***Social organizations:*** 45 open to all; 6 national fraternities, 7 national sororities; 10% of eligible men and 10% of eligible women are members. ***Most popular organizations:*** Student Government, Program Board, Greek Council, Multi-Cultural Council, Media Organization. ***Major annual events:*** Homecoming, Spring Jam, Multi-Cultural Week. ***Student services:*** health clinic, personal-psychological counseling. ***Campus security:*** 24-hour emergency response devices and patrols, late-night transport-escort service, trained security personnel.
HOUSING 709 college housing spaces available; 695 were occupied 1995–96. Freshmen given priority for college housing. Off-campus living permitted. ***Options:*** freshmen-only, coed housing available. Resident assistants live in dorms.
ATHLETICS ***Intramural:*** basketball, bowling, cross-country running, softball, table tennis (Ping-Pong), tennis, track and field, volleyball. ***Contact:*** Mr. Gerald Oswald, Division I Athletic Director, 201-692-2208.
CAREER PLANNING ***Placement office:*** 5 full-time, 1 part-time staff. ***Director:*** Ms. Sharon Spaltro, Director, 201-692-2193. ***Services:*** job fairs, resume preparation, resume referral, career counseling, careers library, job bank, job interviews.
AFTER GRADUATION 90% of students completing a degree program in 1994–95 went directly on to further study.
EXPENSES FOR 1996–97 ***Application fee:*** $35. Comprehensive fee of $18,814 includes full-time tuition ($12,270), mandatory fees ($680), and college room and board ($5864). College room only: $3458. Part-time tuition: $409 per credit. Part-time mandatory fees: $87 per semester.
FINANCIAL AID ***College-administered undergrad aid 1995–96:*** 246 need-based scholarships (average $3840), 23 non-need scholarships (average $7780), low-interest long-term loans from external sources (average $2445), 110 Federal Work-Study (averaging $1204), 375 part-time jobs. ***Required forms:*** CSS Financial Aid PROFILE, institutional, FAFSA. ***Priority deadline:*** 3/15. ***Payment plans:*** installment, deferred payment. ***Waivers:*** full or partial for employees or children of employees. ***Notification:*** continuous.
APPLYING ***Options:*** Common Application, deferred entrance, midyear entrance. ***Required:*** SAT I or ACT, TOEFL for international students. ***Recommended:*** 3 years of high school math and science, some high school foreign language. Test scores used for admission. ***Application deadline:*** rolling.
APPLYING/TRANSFER ***Required:*** standardized test scores. ***Recommended:*** 3 years of high school math and science, some high school foreign language. ***Application deadline:*** rolling.
CONTACT Ms. Dale Herold, Dean of Enrollment Management, Fairleigh Dickinson University, Edward Williams College, Teaneck, NJ 07666-1914, 201-692-7304 or toll-free 800-338-8803. ***Fax:*** 201-692-7319.

GLOUCESTER COUNTY COLLEGE
Sewell, New Jersey

UG Enrollment: 5,047	**Tuition & Fees (Area Res): $1845**
Application Deadline: rolling	**Room & Board: N/Avail**

GENERAL County-supported, 2-year, coed. Part of New Jersey Commission on Higher Education. Awards certificates, transfer associate, terminal associate degrees (the college has been approved to award the degree of associate of applied science in diagnostic medical sonography (ultrasound)). Founded 1967. ***Setting:*** 270-acre rural campus with easy access to Philadelphia. ***Educational spending 1994–95:*** $1522 per undergrad. ***Total enrollment:*** 5,047. ***Faculty:*** 215 (70 full-time, 20% with terminal degrees, 145 part-time); student-faculty ratio is 18:1. ***Notable Alumni:*** Chuck Lamson, executive vice president of Tulsa Drillers; Lucinda Coleman Florio, former first lady of New Jersey; Joseph Mendolia, construction manager of Atlantic City Convention Center; Larry "Pretty Boy" Sharpe, former professional wrestler; Christopher Pallies, professional wrestler/actor.
ENROLLMENT PROFILE 5,047 students: 61% women, 58% part-time, 99% state residents, 2% transferred in, 20% have need-based financial aid, 1% have non-need-based financial aid, 1% international, 48% 25 or older, 0% Native American, 1% Hispanic, 6% African American, 2% Asian American. ***Areas of study chosen:*** 31% liberal arts/general studies, 9% education, 8% health professions and related sciences, 3% computer and information sciences, 2% engineering and applied sciences. ***Most popular recent majors:*** nursing, liberal arts/general studies.
FIRST-YEAR CLASS 1,635 total. Of the students who applied, 93% were accepted, 54% of whom enrolled.
ACADEMIC PROGRAM Core. Calendar: semesters. Academic remediation for entering students, services for LD students, summer session for credit, part-time degree program (daytime, evenings, weekends), co-op programs.
GENERAL DEGREE REQUIREMENTS 63 credit hours; computer course for most majors.
MAJORS Accounting, automotive technologies, biology/biological sciences, business administration/commerce/management, chemical engineering technology, chemistry, civil engineering technology, computer graphics, computer information systems, computer programming, computer science, computer technologies, data processing, drafting and design, education, engineering sciences, environmental engineering technology, finance/banking, human development, law enforcement/police sciences, legal secretarial studies, liberal arts/general studies, manufacturing technology, marketing/retailing/merchandising, medical secretarial studies, nuclear medical technology, nursing, physical education, physical sciences, respiratory therapy, retail management, secretarial studies/office management.
LIBRARY Gloucester County College Library with 51,186 books, 460 microform titles, 344 periodicals, 5 CD-ROMs, 2,361 records, tapes, and CDs. Acquisition spending 1994–95: $328,307.
COMPUTERS ON CAMPUS 120 computers for student use in computer labs, college center, library.
COLLEGE LIFE Drama-theater group, choral group, student-run newspaper, radio station. 19% vote in student government elections. ***Most popular organizations:*** Student Activities Board, Student Government, Accounting Club. ***Major annual events:*** St. Nicholas Day, Earth Day, Spring Fling. ***Student services:*** health clinic, personal-psychological counseling, women's center. ***Campus security:*** 24-hour emergency response devices and patrols, late-night transport-escort service.
HOUSING College housing not available.
ATHLETICS Member NJCAA. ***Intercollegiate:*** baseball M, basketball M, cross-country running M/W, soccer M/W, softball W, tennis M/W, track and field M/W, wrestling M. ***Intramural:*** volleyball. ***Contact:*** Mr. Ronald Case, Director of Athletics, 609-468-5000 Ext. 330.
CAREER PLANNING ***Placement office:*** $48,400 operating expenditure 1994–95. ***Director:*** Ms. Penny Britt, Director of Student Development, 609-464-4211. ***Services:*** job fairs, resume preparation, career counseling, job interviews.
EXPENSES FOR 1996–97 ***Application fee:*** $10. Area resident tuition: $1620 full-time, $54 per credit hour part-time. State resident tuition: $1650 full-time, $55 per credit hour part-time. Nonresident tuition: $6480 full-time, $216 per credit hour part-time. Part-time mandatory fees: $7.50 per credit hour. Full-time mandatory fees: $225.
FINANCIAL AID ***College-administered undergrad aid 1995–96:*** need-based scholarships, non-need scholarships, Federal Work-Study, part-time jobs. ***Required forms:*** CSS Financial Aid PROFILE, state, institutional, FAFSA. ***Application deadline:*** continuous to 10/1. ***Waivers:*** full or partial for employees or children of employees and senior citizens.
APPLYING Open admission except for nursing, respiratory therapy, nuclear medicine, ultrasound programs. ***Option:*** deferred entrance. ***Required:*** school transcript, TOEFL for international students. ***Required for some:*** SAT I or ACT. Test scores used for admission. ***Application deadline:*** rolling.
APPLYING/TRANSFER ***Required:*** high school transcript, college transcript. ***Required for some:*** standardized test scores. ***Entrance:*** noncompetitive. ***Application deadline:*** rolling.
CONTACT Ms. Carol L. Lange, Admissions and Recruitment Coordinator, Gloucester County College, Deptford Township, Tanyard Road, RR 4, Box 203, Sewell, NJ 08080, 609-468-5000 Ext. 341. ***Fax:*** 609-468-8498. College video available.

HUDSON COUNTY COMMUNITY COLLEGE
Jersey City, New Jersey

UG Enrollment: 4,249	**Tuition & Fees (Area Res): $2570**
Application Deadline: 9/1	**Room & Board: N/Avail**

GENERAL State and locally supported, 2-year, coed. Part of New Jersey Commission on Higher Education. Awards certificates, diplomas, transfer associate, terminal associate degrees. Founded 1974. ***Setting:*** urban campus with easy access to New York City. ***Endowment:*** $10,445. ***Total enrollment:*** 4,249. ***Faculty:*** 237 (49 full-time, 21% with terminal degrees, 188 part-time); student-faculty ratio is 16:1.
ENROLLMENT PROFILE 4,249 students from 2 states and territories, 1 other country. 60% women, 38% part-time, 99% state residents, 7% transferred in, 46% have need-based financial aid, 0% have non-need-based financial aid, 50% 25 or older, 1% Native American, 47% Hispanic, 18% African American, 12% Asian American. ***Areas of study chosen:*** 20% liberal arts/general studies, 10% health professions and related sciences, 8% business management and administrative services, 7% computer and information sciences, 5% education, 5% engineering and applied sciences, 5% vocational and home economics. ***Most popular recent majors:*** culinary arts, accounting, business administration/commerce/management.
FIRST-YEAR CLASS 1,596 total; 2,753 applied, 100% were accepted, 58% of whom enrolled.

Hudson County Community College (continued)
ACADEMIC PROGRAM Core. Calendar: semesters. 238 courses offered in 1995–96. Academic remediation for entering students, English as a second language program offered during academic year and summer, services for LD students, advanced placement, tutorials, summer session for credit, part-time degree program (daytime, evenings), adult/continuing education programs, internships. Off-campus study at Jersey City State College.
GENERAL DEGREE REQUIREMENTS 66 credits; 1 college algebra course; computer course; internship (some majors).
MAJORS Accounting, business administration/commerce/management, child care/child and family studies, computer science, computer technologies, criminal justice, culinary arts, data processing, electronics engineering technology, engineering (general), engineering sciences, (pre)engineering sequence, gerontology, human services, liberal arts/general studies, medical assistant technologies, medical records services, paralegal studies, public administration, safety and security technologies, secretarial studies/office management.
LIBRARY Hudson County Community College Library/Learning Resources Center with 12,100 books, 91 microform titles, 200 periodicals, 7 CD-ROMs, 166 records, tapes, and CDs. Acquisition spending 1994–95: $182,283.
COMPUTERS ON CAMPUS 500 computers for student use in computer labs, resource center, data processing room. Staffed computer lab on campus provides training in use of computers, software.
COLLEGE LIFE Drama-theater group, choral group, student-run newspaper. ***Social organizations:*** 1 local fraternity, 1 local sorority; 25% of eligible men and 30% of eligible women are members. ***Most popular organizations:*** Multicultural Club, Hospitality Club, Drama Club. ***Major annual events:*** International Festival, Senior Dinner Dance. ***Student services:*** personal-psychological counseling. ***Campus security:*** 24-hour emergency response devices.
HOUSING College housing not available.
ATHLETICS Member NJCAA. ***Intercollegiate:*** baseball M, basketball M/W, soccer M, softball W, volleyball W. ***Intramural:*** basketball, bowling, football, sailing, skiing (downhill), soccer, volleyball. ***Contact:*** Mr. Dennis McMullen, Assistant Dean of Students, 201-714-2210.
CAREER PLANNING ***Services:*** job fairs, resume preparation, resume referral, career counseling, careers library, job interviews.
AFTER GRADUATION 13% of students completing a degree program in 1994–95 went directly on to further study.
EXPENSES FOR 1996–97 ***Application fee:*** $10. Area resident tuition: $2063 full-time, $62.50 per credit part-time. State resident tuition: $4125 full-time, $125 per credit part-time. Nonresident tuition: $6188 full-time, $187.50 per credit part-time. Part-time mandatory fees per semester range from $24.75 to $172.25. Full-time mandatory fees: $507.
FINANCIAL AID ***College-administered undergrad aid 1995–96:*** 168 need-based scholarships (average $500), low-interest long-term loans from external sources, Federal Work-Study, 36 part-time jobs. ***Required forms:*** CSS Financial Aid PROFILE, FAFSA; accepted: state. ***Priority deadline:*** 6/1. ***Payment plan:*** deferred payment. ***Waivers:*** full or partial for employees or children of employees and senior citizens.
APPLYING Open admission. ***Option:*** midyear entrance. ***Required:*** school transcript, New Jersey Basic Skills Exam. Test scores used for counseling/placement. ***Application deadline:*** 9/1. ***Notification:*** continuous until 9/1. Preference given to county residents.
APPLYING/TRANSFER ***Required:*** college transcript. ***Application deadline:*** 9/1. ***Notification:*** continuous until 9/1.
CONTACT Mr. Michael Greenup, Counselor, Hudson County Community College, 168 Sip Avenue, Jersey City, NJ 07306, 201-714-2131. ***Fax:*** 201-656-8961.

KATHARINE GIBBS SCHOOL
Montclair, New Jersey

UG Enrollment: 400	**Tuition & Fees: $8095**
Application Deadline: rolling	**Room & Board: N/Avail**

GENERAL Proprietary, 2-year, coed. Awards certificates, transfer associate, terminal associate degrees. Founded 1950. ***Setting:*** 2-acre urban campus with easy access to New York City. ***Total enrollment:*** 400. ***Faculty:*** 20 (14 full-time, 6 part-time).
ENROLLMENT PROFILE 400 students.
FIRST-YEAR CLASS 100 total. Of the students who applied, 95% were accepted, 85% of whom enrolled.
ACADEMIC PROGRAM Calendar: quarters.
GENERAL DEGREE REQUIREMENTS 72 credit hours; computer course.
MAJOR Secretarial studies/office management.
HOUSING College housing not available.
EXPENSES FOR 1995–96 ***Application fee:*** $25. Tuition: $7995 full-time, $6450 per year part-time. Full-time mandatory fees: $100.
FINANCIAL AID ***College-administered undergrad aid 1995–96:*** low-interest long-term loans from external sources, Federal Work-Study, part-time jobs. ***Required forms:*** CSS Financial Aid PROFILE, FAFSA.
APPLYING ***Required:*** school transcript, CPAt. ***Application deadline:*** rolling.
APPLYING/TRANSFER ***Recommended:*** college transcript. ***Required for some:*** college transcript. ***Application deadline:*** rolling.
CONTACT Mr. Dave Dahlke, Director of Admissions, Katharine Gibbs School, 33 Plymouth Street, Montclair, NJ 07042-2699, 201-744-6967.

MERCER COUNTY COMMUNITY COLLEGE
Trenton, New Jersey

UG Enrollment: 6,936	**Tuition & Fees (Area Res): $2085**
Application Deadline: rolling	**Room & Board: N/Avail**

GENERAL State and locally supported, 2-year, coed. Awards certificates, transfer associate, terminal associate degrees. Founded 1966. ***Setting:*** 292-acre suburban campus with easy access to Philadelphia and New York City. ***Endowment:*** $2.2 million. ***Educational spending 1994–95:*** $1400 per undergrad. ***Total enrollment:*** 6,936. ***Faculty:*** 361 (113 full-time, 15% with terminal degrees, 248 part-time); student-faculty ratio is 23:1. ***Notable Alumni:*** Jake Jones, business owner; Kathy Wagner, radio personality for WYSP; James Branham, art director at Dana Communications; Sylvia Jessup, assistant vice president at Core States National Bank; Martha Goldman, Nursing Recognition Award recipient from New Jersey League of Nursing.
ENROLLMENT PROFILE 6,936 students from 5 states and territories. 55% women, 45% men, 60% part-time, 93% state residents, 7% transferred in, 2% international, 48% 25 or older, 0% Native American, 7% Hispanic, 16% African American, 2% Asian American. ***Areas of study chosen:*** 21% interdisciplinary studies, 20% business management and administrative services, 17% health professions and related sciences, 6% engineering and applied sciences, 4% fine arts, 1% agriculture, 1% architecture, 1% communications and journalism, 1% computer and information sciences. ***Most popular recent majors:*** humanities, nursing, business administration/commerce/management.
FIRST-YEAR CLASS 2,454 total; 3,474 applied, 81% were accepted, 88% of whom enrolled.
ACADEMIC PROGRAM Core, honor code. Calendar: semesters. 600 courses offered in 1995–96. Academic remediation for entering students, English as a second language program offered during academic year and summer, services for LD students, advanced placement, summer session for credit, part-time degree program (daytime, evenings), external degree programs, adult/continuing education programs, co-op programs. ROTC: Army (c), Air Force (c).
GENERAL DEGREE REQUIREMENTS 60 credits; math/science requirements vary according to program; computer course for most majors.
MAJORS Accounting, architectural technologies, art/fine arts, art history, automotive technologies, aviation administration, aviation technology, biology/biological sciences, botany/plant sciences, business administration/commerce/management, ceramic art and design, chemistry, civil engineering technology, commercial art, communication, community services, computer graphics, computer information systems, computer programming, computer science, computer technologies, construction technologies, corrections, criminal justice, dance, data processing, drafting and design, education, electrical and electronics technologies, electrical engineering technology, electronics engineering technology, engineering (general), engineering sciences, finance/banking, fire science, flight training, funeral service, graphic arts, heating/refrigeration/air conditioning, hotel and restaurant management, humanities, laboratory technologies, landscape architecture/design, law enforcement/police sciences, legal secretarial studies, liberal arts/general studies, mathematics, medical laboratory technology, music, nursing, ornamental horticulture, paralegal studies, photography, physics, radio and television studies, radiological technology, respiratory therapy, sculpture, secretarial studies/office management, surveying technology, teacher aide studies, telecommunications, theater arts/drama.
LIBRARY 65,386 books, 731 periodicals, 4 CD-ROMs, 4,719 records, tapes, and CDs. Acquisition spending 1994–95: $42,600.
COMPUTERS ON CAMPUS 800 computers for student use in computer labs, learning resource center, classrooms, library provide access to main academic computer, on-line services. Staffed computer lab on campus provides training in use of computers, software. Academic computing expenditure 1994–95: $569,728.
COLLEGE LIFE Drama-theater group, choral group, student-run newspaper, radio station. 20% vote in student government elections. ***Social organizations:*** 38 open to all. ***Most popular organizations:*** Student Government Association, Student Radio Station, African-American Student Organization, Student Activities Board, Phi Theta Kappa. ***Major annual events:*** NJCAA National Soccer Tournament, Computer Festival, Spring Day. ***Student services:*** personal-psychological counseling. ***Campus security:*** 24-hour emergency response devices and patrols.
HOUSING College housing not available.
ATHLETICS Member NJCAA. ***Intercollegiate:*** baseball M, basketball M(s)/W(s), soccer M(s)/W(s), softball W, tennis M(s)/W(s), track and field M(s)/W(s). ***Intramural:*** basketball, skiing (downhill), softball, volleyball. ***Contact:*** Mr. John Suarez, Director of Athletics, Recreation and Fitness, 609-586-4800 Ext. 741.
CAREER PLANNING ***Placement office:*** 2 full-time, 2 part-time staff; $89,879 operating expenditure 1994–95. ***Director:*** Mr. Jack Guarneri, Director, Career Services, 609-586-4800 Ext. 304. ***Services:*** job fairs, resume preparation, resume referral, career counseling, careers library, job bank, job interviews. 95 organizations recruited on campus 1994–95.
AFTER GRADUATION 64% of students completing a degree program in 1994–95 went directly on to further study.
EXPENSES FOR 1995–96 ***Application fee:*** $15. Area resident tuition: $1890 full-time, $63 per credit part-time. State resident tuition: $3105 full-time, $103.50 per credit part-time. Nonresident tuition: $5055 full-time, $168.50 per credit part-time. Part-time mandatory fees: $6.50 per credit. Full-time mandatory fees: $195.
FINANCIAL AID ***College-administered undergrad aid 1995–96:*** 200 need-based scholarships (average $500), 50 non-need scholarships (average $500), short-term loans (average $25), low-interest long-term loans from external sources (average $2600), 100 Federal Work-Study (averaging $1200), part-time jobs. ***Required forms:*** institutional, FAFSA; required for some: state, nontaxable income verification. ***Priority deadline:*** 5/1. ***Payment plan:*** deferred payment. ***Waivers:*** full or partial for employees or children of employees and senior citizens.
APPLYING Open admission. ***Options:*** early entrance, deferred entrance, midyear entrance. ***Required:*** school transcript, TOEFL for international students, New Jersey Basic Skills Exam. ***Recommended:*** recommendations, interview, SAT I. Test scores used for counseling/placement. ***Application deadline:*** rolling. ***Notification:*** continuous. Preference given to county residents.
APPLYING/TRANSFER ***Required:*** college transcript. ***Recommended:*** recommendations. ***Entrance:*** noncompetitive. ***Application deadline:*** rolling. ***Notification:*** continuous. ***Contact:*** Ms. Laurene Jones, Transfer Counselor, 609-586-4800 Ext. 307.
CONTACT Mr. Michael Glass, Director of Admissions, Mercer County Community College, Trenton, NJ 08690-1004, 609-586-0505 or toll-free 800-392-MCCC. ***Fax:*** 609-586-6944.

MIDDLESEX COUNTY COLLEGE
Edison, New Jersey

UG Enrollment: 12,500	**Tuition & Fees (Area Res): $2048**
Application Deadline: rolling	**Room & Board: N/Avail**

Middlesex County College received a $2.9-million grant from the National Science Foundation to lead a consortium of New Jersey colleges and universities, industries, high schools, and professional societies in creating a national *center of excellence in engineering technology education. The center is one of 6 advanced technology centers nationwide.*

GENERAL County-supported, 2-year, coed. Awards transfer associate, terminal associate degrees. Founded 1964. ***Setting:*** 200-acre suburban campus with easy access to New York City. ***Total enrollment:*** 12,500. ***Faculty:*** 538 (192 full-time, 346 part-time); student-faculty ratio is 21:1.

ENROLLMENT PROFILE 12,500 students from 4 states and territories, 60 other countries. 56% women, 44% men, 47% part-time, 92% state residents, 22% have need-based financial aid, 3% international, 44% 25 or older, 1% Native American, 13% Hispanic, 10% African American, 13% Asian American.

FIRST-YEAR CLASS 5,000 total. Of the students who applied, 94% were accepted, 70% of whom enrolled.

ACADEMIC PROGRAM Core. Calendar: semesters. Academic remediation for entering students, English as a second language program offered during academic year and summer, services for LD students, advanced placement, summer session for credit, part-time degree program (daytime, evenings, weekends, summer), adult/continuing education programs, co-op programs and internships. Study abroad in Spain, France, England. ROTC: Army (c), Air Force (c).

GENERAL DEGREE REQUIREMENTS 64 credits; 1 algebra course; computer course for business majors; internship (some majors).

MAJORS Accounting, advertising, applied art, art/fine arts, automotive technologies, biology/biological sciences, biotechnology, business administration/commerce/management, chemistry, child care/child and family studies, civil engineering technology, commercial art, computer graphics, computer information systems, computer programming, computer science, computer technologies, construction technologies, corrections, criminal justice, culinary arts, dance, dental services, dietetics, drafting and design, early childhood education, education, electrical and electronics technologies, electrical engineering technology, electronics engineering technology, engineering (general), engineering and applied sciences, engineering sciences, engineering technology, English, fashion design and technology, fashion merchandising, finance/banking, fire science, food services management, French, graphic arts, heating/refrigeration/air conditioning, history, hospitality services, hotel and restaurant management, industrial engineering technology, journalism, law enforcement/police sciences, legal secretarial studies, liberal arts/general studies, manufacturing technology, marketing/retailing/merchandising, mathematics, mechanical engineering technology, medical laboratory technology, modern languages, music, nursing, paralegal studies, photography, physical education, physical sciences, physics, political science/government, psychology, radiological technology, recreation and leisure services, rehabilitation therapy, retail management, robotics, Romance languages, science, secretarial studies/office management, social science, sociology, Spanish, studio art, surveying technology, teacher aide studies, theater arts/drama, transportation technologies.

LIBRARY 82,015 books, 9,879 microform titles, 727 periodicals, 2,200 records, tapes, and CDs.

COMPUTERS ON CAMPUS Computers for student use in computer center, computer labs, library. Staffed computer lab on campus.

COLLEGE LIFE Drama-theater group, choral group, student-run newspaper, radio station. ***Student services:*** health clinic, personal-psychological counseling. ***Campus security:*** 24-hour emergency response devices and patrols.

HOUSING College housing not available.

ATHLETICS Member NJCAA. ***Intercollegiate:*** baseball M, basketball M(s)/W(s), cross-country running M/W(s), field hockey W, golf M/W, soccer M/W, softball W(s), tennis M/W, track and field M/W, wrestling M(s). ***Intramural:*** bowling, gymnastics, tennis. ***Contact:*** Mr. Robert Zifchak, Director of Athletic Programs, 908-906-2558; Ms. Ilene Cohen, Assistant Director, 908-906-2558.

CAREER PLANNING ***Placement office:*** 12 full-time, 4 part-time staff. ***Director:*** Dr. John Herrling, Director of Counseling and Placement Services, 908-906-2456. ***Services:*** job fairs, resume preparation, resume referral, career counseling, careers library, job bank, job interviews.

EXPENSES FOR 1996–97 ***Application fee:*** $25. Area resident tuition: $2000 full-time, $62.50 per credit part-time. Nonresident tuition: $4000 full-time, $125 per credit part-time. Part-time mandatory fees: $24 per semester. Full-time mandatory fees: $48.

FINANCIAL AID ***College-administered undergrad aid 1995–96:*** need-based scholarships, non-need scholarships, short-term loans, low-interest long-term loans from external sources, Federal Work-Study, part-time jobs. ***Required forms:*** CSS Financial Aid PROFILE, institutional, FAFSA. ***Priority deadline:*** 5/1.

APPLYING Open admission except for dental hygiene, nursing, radiography, medical laboratory technology programs. ***Options:*** early entrance, deferred entrance. ***Required:*** TOEFL for international students. ***Required for some:*** 3 years of high school math and science, some high school foreign language, Dental Hygiene Candidate Admission Test, National League of Nursing Exam. Test scores used for admission and counseling/placement. ***Application deadline:*** rolling. ***Notification:*** continuous. Preference given to county residents.

APPLYING/TRANSFER ***Application deadline:*** rolling. ***Notification:*** continuous. ***Contact:*** Dr. Ken Maugle, Director of Transfer Programs, 908-906-2546.

CONTACT Ms. Diane Lemcoe, Director of Admissions, Middlesex County College, Edison, NJ 08818-3050, 908-906-2510.

❖ ***See page 772 for a narrative description.*** ❖

OCEAN COUNTY COLLEGE
Toms River, New Jersey

UG Enrollment: 8,122	**Tuition & Fees (Area Res): $1574**
Application Deadline: rolling	**Room & Board: N/Avail**

GENERAL County-supported, 2-year, coed. Part of New Jersey Commission on Higher Education. Awards certificates, diplomas, transfer associate, terminal associate degrees. Founded 1964. ***Setting:*** 275-acre small-town campus with easy access to Philadelphia. ***Total enrollment:*** 8,122. ***Faculty:*** 348 (128 full-time, 220 part-time); student-faculty ratio is 25:1.

ENROLLMENT PROFILE 8,122 students: 59% women, 41% men, 57% part-time, 6% transferred in, 1% international, 41% 25 or older, 1% Native American, 2% Hispanic, 3% African American, 2% Asian American. ***Most popular recent majors:*** liberal arts/general studies, business administration/commerce/management.

FIRST-YEAR CLASS 1,470 total; 3,274 applied, 100% were accepted, 45% of whom enrolled.

ACADEMIC PROGRAM Core. Calendar: semesters. 450 courses offered in 1995–96. Academic remediation for entering students, services for LD students, advanced placement, honors program, summer session for credit, part-time degree program (daytime, evenings, summer), adult/continuing education programs, co-op programs. Study abroad in Israel, England, Germany, Spain. ROTC: Army (c).

GENERAL DEGREE REQUIREMENTS 64 semester hours; 1 course each in math and science.

MAJORS Accounting, broadcasting, business administration/commerce/management, civil engineering technology, community services, computer science, construction technologies, criminal justice, electrical engineering technology, elementary education, engineering (general), engineering technology, finance/banking, fire science, gerontology, journalism, liberal arts/general studies, manufacturing technology, marketing/retailing/merchandising, medical laboratory technology, nursing, paralegal studies, real estate, retail management, secretarial studies/office management, surveying technology.

LIBRARY Ocean County College Library with 74,215 books, 215 microform titles, 428 periodicals, 77 CD-ROMs, 4,885 records, tapes, and CDs.

COMPUTERS ON CAMPUS 100 computers for student use in computer center, computer labs, various academic buildings. Staffed computer lab on campus.

COLLEGE LIFE Drama-theater group, choral group, student-run newspaper, radio station. ***Student services:*** health clinic, personal-psychological counseling. ***Campus security:*** 24-hour emergency response devices and patrols, late-night transport-escort service.

HOUSING College housing not available.

ATHLETICS Member NJCAA. ***Intercollegiate:*** basketball M/W, cross-country running M, field hockey W, golf M, soccer M, swimming and diving M/W, tennis M/W, track and field M/W, volleyball W. ***Intramural:*** cross-country running, wrestling.

CAREER PLANNING ***Director:*** Mr. Don Schultz, Director of Counseling, 908-255-0400 Ext. 300. ***Service:*** career counseling.

AFTER GRADUATION 65% of students completing a degree program in 1994–95 went directly on to further study.

EXPENSES FOR 1996–97 ***Application fee:*** $15. Area resident tuition: $1574 full-time, $65.60 per semester hour part-time. State resident tuition: $1826 full-time, $76.10 per semester hour part-time. Nonresident tuition: $2944 full-time, $122.65 per semester hour part-time.

FINANCIAL AID ***College-administered undergrad aid 1995–96:*** need-based scholarships, 45 non-need scholarships, Federal Work-Study, 80 part-time jobs. ***Required forms:*** CSS Financial Aid PROFILE, FAFSA. ***Priority deadline:*** 5/30. ***Payment plans:*** installment, deferred payment. ***Waivers:*** full or partial for employees or children of employees.

APPLYING Open admission except for nursing program. ***Options:*** early entrance, deferred entrance, midyear entrance. ***Required:*** TOEFL for international students. ***Required for some:*** SAT I or ACT. Test scores used for counseling/placement. ***Application deadline:*** rolling. ***Notification:*** continuous. Preference given to county residents for nursing program.

APPLYING/TRANSFER ***Required for some:*** standardized test scores. ***Application deadline:*** rolling. ***Notification:*** continuous.

CONTACT Mr. Carey Trevisan, Director of Admissions and Records, Ocean County College, Toms River, NJ 08754-2001, 908-255-0304 Ext. 2016.

PASSAIC COUNTY COMMUNITY COLLEGE
Paterson, New Jersey

UG Enrollment: 3,642	**Tuition & Fees (NJ Res): $1722**
Application Deadline: rolling	**Room & Board: N/Avail**

GENERAL County-supported, 2-year, coed. Awards certificates, diplomas, transfer associate, terminal associate degrees. Founded 1968. ***Setting:*** 6-acre urban campus with easy access to New York City. ***Research spending 1994–95:*** $100,046. ***Educational spending 1994–95:*** $1660 per undergrad. ***Total enrollment:*** 3,642. ***Faculty:*** 267 (67 full-time, 13% with terminal degrees, 200 part-time); student-faculty ratio is 14:1.

ENROLLMENT PROFILE 3,642 students: 62% women, 70% part-time, 99% state residents, 18% transferred in, 48% have need-based financial aid, 1% have non-need-based financial aid, 54% 25 or older, 1% Native American, 45% Hispanic, 25% African American, 6% Asian American. ***Areas of study chosen:*** 24% health professions and related sciences, 21% liberal arts/general studies, 14% business management and administrative services, 10% computer and information sciences, 3% education, 1% engineering and applied sciences. ***Most popular recent majors:*** humanities, criminal justice, nursing.

FIRST-YEAR CLASS 921 total; 1,978 applied, 100% were accepted, 47% of whom enrolled.

ACADEMIC PROGRAM Core, general education curriculum, honor code. Calendar: semesters. 212 courses offered in 1995–96. Academic remediation for entering students, English as a second language program offered during academic year and summer, advanced placement, honors program, summer session for credit, part-time degree program (daytime, evenings), co-op programs and internships. ROTC: Army (c).

GENERAL DEGREE REQUIREMENTS 64 credits; computer course for engineering majors.

MAJORS Accounting, business administration/commerce/management, computer information systems, criminal justice, early childhood education, (pre)engineering sequence, finance/banking, fire science, humanities, manufacturing technology, marketing/retailing/merchandising, mathematics, natural sciences, nursing, public administration, radiological technology, respiratory therapy, retail management, science, secretarial studies/office management.

LIBRARY Passaic County Community College Learning Resource Center plus 1 other, with 36,025 books, 84 microform titles, 166 periodicals, 1 on-line bibliographic service, 1 CD-ROM, 610 records, tapes, and CDs. Acquisition spending 1994–95: $464,575.

COMPUTERS ON CAMPUS 150 computers for student use in computer center, computer labs, special labs provide access to main academic computer. Staffed computer lab on campus provides training in use of computers, software.

COLLEGE LIFE Choral group, student-run newspaper. ***Student services:*** personal-psychological counseling. ***Campus security:*** late-night transport-escort service.

HOUSING College housing not available.

ATHLETICS Member NJCAA. ***Intramural:*** basketball, soccer, tennis, volleyball.

Peterson's Guide to Two-Year Colleges 1997 443

Passaic County Community College (continued)

CAREER PLANNING ***Placement office:*** 1 part-time staff. ***Director:*** Mr. Edward Casey, Counselor, 201-684-6085. ***Services:*** job fairs, career counseling, careers library, job bank, job interviews.

EXPENSES FOR 1995–96 ***Application fee:*** $15. State resident tuition: $1476 full-time, $61.50 per credit part-time. Nonresident tuition: $2952 full-time, $123 per credit part-time. Part-time mandatory fees: $9.25 per credit. Full-time mandatory fees: $246.

FINANCIAL AID ***College-administered undergrad aid 1995–96:*** 246 need-based scholarships (average $1000), 10 non-need scholarships (average $1000), low-interest long-term loans from external sources (average $1500), 76 Federal Work-Study (averaging $3000). ***Required forms:*** institutional, FAFSA, nontaxable income verification; required for some: state; accepted: CSS Financial Aid PROFILE. ***Priority deadline:*** 9/15. ***Payment plans:*** installment, deferred payment. ***Waivers:*** full or partial for employees or children of employees and senior citizens.

APPLYING Open admission except for nursing, respiratory therapy, radiological technology programs. ***Options:*** early entrance, deferred entrance, midyear entrance. Test scores used for counseling/placement. ***Application deadline:*** rolling. Preference given to county residents.

APPLYING/TRANSFER ***Entrance:*** noncompetitive. ***Application deadline:*** rolling. ***Contact:*** Mr. Edward Casey, Counselor, 201-684-6085.

CONTACT Mr. Brian Lewis, Dean of Admissions and Enrollment Management, Passaic County Community College, One College Boulevard, Paterson, NJ 07505-1179, 201-684-6304. College video available.

RARITAN VALLEY COMMUNITY COLLEGE
Somerville, New Jersey

UG Enrollment: 5,555 | **Tuition & Fees (Area Res): $2070**
Application Deadline: rolling | **Room & Board: N/Avail**

GENERAL County-supported, 2-year, coed. Awards transfer associate, terminal associate degrees. Founded 1965. ***Setting:*** 225-acre small-town campus with easy access to New York City and Philadelphia. ***Research spending 1994–95:*** $90,979. ***Total enrollment:*** 5,555. ***Faculty:*** 276 (88 full-time, 30% with terminal degrees, 188 part-time); student-faculty ratio is 18:1.

ENROLLMENT PROFILE 5,555 students from 2 states and territories, 14 other countries. 59% women, 58% part-time, 98% state residents, 8% transferred in, 1% international, 49% 25 or older, 1% Native American, 3% Hispanic, 4% African American, 4% Asian American. ***Areas of study chosen:*** 25% liberal arts/general studies, 21% business management and administrative services, 7% interdisciplinary studies, 4% health professions and related sciences, 4% performing arts, 3% computer and information sciences, 3% social sciences, 2% biological and life sciences, 2% education, 2% engineering and applied sciences, 2% fine arts, 1% communications and journalism. ***Most popular recent majors:*** business administration/commerce/management, liberal arts/general studies, nursing.

FIRST-YEAR CLASS 1,743 total; 2,241 applied, 92% were accepted, 84% of whom enrolled.

ACADEMIC PROGRAM Core, general liberal arts curriculum, honor code. Calendar: semesters. 450 courses offered in 1995–96. Academic remediation for entering students, English as a second language program offered during academic year and summer, services for LD students, advanced placement, honors program, summer session for credit, part-time degree program (daytime, evenings), adult/continuing education programs, co-op programs and internships. Off-campus study at Somerset County Technical Institute. ROTC: Air Force (c).

GENERAL DEGREE REQUIREMENTS 60 credits; proficiency in elementary algebra; internship (some majors).

MAJORS Accounting, art/fine arts, automotive technologies, biology/biological sciences, business administration/commerce/management, chemistry, child care/child and family studies, commercial art, communication, computer information systems, computer programming, computer science, construction technologies, criminal justice, data processing, drafting and design, early childhood education, education, electrical and electronics technologies, electromechanical technology, elementary education, engineering (general), (pre)engineering sequence, environmental sciences, graphic arts, heating/refrigeration/air conditioning, hotel and restaurant management, human services, international business, journalism, law enforcement/police sciences, liberal arts/general studies, management information systems, manufacturing technology, marketing/retailing/merchandising, mathematics, mechanical design technology, music, nursing, optometric/ophthalmic technologies, paralegal studies, psychology, real estate, respiratory therapy, retail management, robotics, science, secretarial studies/office management, social science, sociology, studio art, telecommunications, theater arts/drama, tourism and travel.

LIBRARY Evelyn S. Field Learning Resources Center with 84,150 books, 16,089 microform titles, 325 periodicals, 3 CD-ROMs, 4,161 records, tapes, and CDs. Acquisition spending 1994–95: $74,202.

COMPUTERS ON CAMPUS 120 computers for student use in computer center, computer labs, classrooms, library provide access to main academic computer, off-campus computing facilities, e-mail, Internet. Staffed computer lab on campus provides training in use of computers, software. Academic computing expenditure 1994–95: $647,013.

COLLEGE LIFE Drama-theater group, choral group, student-run newspaper, radio station. ***Social organizations:*** 20 open to all. ***Most popular organizations:*** Students for Environmental Awareness, Black Student Union, Student Nurses Association. ***Major annual events:*** International Festival, Spring Week. ***Student services:*** health clinic, personal-psychological counseling. ***Campus security:*** 24-hour emergency response devices and patrols, 24-hour outdoor surveillance cameras.

HOUSING College housing not available.

ATHLETICS Member NJCAA. ***Intercollegiate:*** baseball M, basketball M/W, cross-country running M/W, golf M/W, soccer M, tennis M/W. ***Intramural:*** archery, badminton, basketball, bowling, cross-country running, tennis, volleyball. ***Contact:*** Mr. Augie Eosso, Director of Athletics, 908-526-1200 Ext. 222.

CAREER PLANNING ***Placement office:*** 3 full-time, 2 part-time staff; $108,968 operating expenditure 1994–95. ***Director:*** Ms. Myra Swanson, Director, Career Development and Placement, 908-218-8860. ***Services:*** job fairs, resume preparation, career counseling, careers library, job bank, job interviews.

AFTER GRADUATION 65% of students completing a degree program in 1994–95 went directly on to further study.

EXPENSES FOR 1995–96 ***Application fee:*** $25. Area resident tuition: $1800 full-time, $60 per credit part-time. State resident tuition: $3600 full-time, $120 per credit part-time. Nonresident tuition: $7200 full-time, $240 per credit part-time. Part-time mandatory fees: $9 per credit. Full-time mandatory fees: $270.

FINANCIAL AID ***College-administered undergrad aid 1995–96:*** 100 need-based scholarships (averaging $400), short-term loans (averaging $100), low-interest long-term loans from external sources (averaging $1400), 25 Federal Work-Study (averaging $1000), 80 part-time jobs. ***Required forms:*** institutional, FAFSA; accepted: CSS Financial Aid PROFILE, state. ***Priority deadline:*** 4/1. ***Waivers:*** full or partial for employees or children of employees and senior citizens. ***Notification:*** 7/1.

APPLYING Open admission except for respiratory care, nursing program, foreign students. ***Options:*** early entrance, midyear entrance. ***Required:*** school transcript, TOEFL for international students. ***Recommended:*** 4 years of high school math, 3 years of high school science. Test scores used for admission. ***Application deadline:*** rolling. Preference given to county residents.

APPLYING/TRANSFER ***Recommended:*** 4 years of high school math, 3 years of high school science. ***Required for some:*** high school transcript, college transcript. ***Entrance:*** noncompetitive. ***Application deadline:*** rolling.

CONTACT Admissions Office, Raritan Valley Community College, PO Box 3300, Somerville, NJ 08876-1265, 908-218-8861. College video available.

SALEM COMMUNITY COLLEGE
Carneys Point, New Jersey

UG Enrollment: 1,228 | **Tuition & Fees (NJ Res): $2126**
Application Deadline: rolling | **Room & Board: N/Avail**

GENERAL County-supported, 2-year, coed. Part of New Jersey Commission on Higher Education. Awards transfer associate, terminal associate degrees. Founded 1971. ***Setting:*** 20-acre rural campus with easy access to Philadelphia. ***Total enrollment:*** 1,228. ***Faculty:*** 74 (28 full-time, 27% with terminal degrees, 46 part-time); student-faculty ratio is 18:1.

ENROLLMENT PROFILE 1,228 students from 6 states and territories, 17 other countries. 62% women, 62% part-time, 86% state residents, 3% transferred in, 1% international, 49% 25 or older, 1% Native American, 1% Hispanic, 14% African American, 2% Asian American. ***Areas of study chosen:*** 12% engineering and applied sciences, 7% social sciences, 5% fine arts, 4% education, 2% communications and journalism. ***Most popular recent majors:*** secretarial studies/office management, nursing, business administration/commerce/management.

FIRST-YEAR CLASS 641 total; 882 applied, 100% were accepted, 70% of whom enrolled.

ACADEMIC PROGRAM Core, honor code. Calendar: semesters. 178 courses offered in 1995–96. Academic remediation for entering students, English as a second language program offered during academic year, advanced placement, summer session for credit, part-time degree program (daytime, evenings), adult/continuing education programs, co-op programs.

GENERAL DEGREE REQUIREMENTS 60 credits; 6 credits of math; 8 credits of science; computer course.

MAJORS Accounting, architectural technologies, biology/biological sciences, business administration/commerce/management, chemistry, communication, community services, computer information systems, computer technologies, criminal justice, drafting and design, early childhood education, education, electrical and electronics technologies, electromechanical technology, English, health education, heating/refrigeration/air conditioning, history, humanities, industrial engineering technology, instrumentation technology, journalism, legal secretarial studies, liberal arts/general studies, marketing/retailing/merchandising, mathematics, medical assistant technologies, medical secretarial studies, nuclear technology, nursing, occupational safety and health, physical education, political science/government, public administration, retail management, science, secretarial studies/office management, social science, sociology.

LIBRARY Michael S. Cettei Memorial Library with 25,236 books, 325 microform titles, 240 periodicals, 1 on-line bibliographic service, 4 CD-ROMs, 180 records, tapes, and CDs.

COMPUTERS ON CAMPUS 125 computers for student use in computer center, classrooms, library. Staffed computer lab on campus provides training in use of computers, software.

COLLEGE LIFE Drama-theater group, choral group, student-run newspaper. 10% vote in student government elections. ***Most popular organizations:*** Drama Club, Science Club, Multicultural Exchange Club. ***Major annual events:*** Talent Show, Graduation Dinner Dance, Children's Christmas Party. ***Student services:*** personal-psychological counseling, women's center. ***Campus security:*** 24-hour emergency response devices and patrols, late-night transport-escort service.

HOUSING College housing not available.

ATHLETICS Member NJCAA. ***Intercollegiate:*** baseball M(s), basketball M(s)/W(s), softball W(s). ***Intramural:*** tennis. ***Contact:*** Mr. Nicholas J. DiCicco, Director of Athletics/Recreation, 609-299-2100 Ext. 525.

CAREER PLANNING ***Service:*** career counseling.

EXPENSES FOR 1996–97 ***Application fee:*** $15. State resident tuition: $1881 full-time, $62.71 per credit part-time. Nonresident tuition: $2108 full-time, $70.25 per credit part-time. Part-time mandatory fees per semester range from $42 to $112. Full-time mandatory fees: $245.

FINANCIAL AID ***College-administered undergrad aid 1995–96:*** need-based scholarships, non-need scholarships, low-interest long-term loans from external sources, Federal Work-Study, part-time jobs. ***Required forms:*** CSS Financial Aid PROFILE, institutional, FAFSA; required for some: state. ***Priority deadline:*** 3/1. ***Waivers:*** full or partial for employees or children of employees and senior citizens.

APPLYING Open admission. ***Options:*** Common Application, early entrance, deferred entrance, midyear entrance. ***Required:*** essay, New Jersey Basic Skills Exam. ***Recommended:*** school transcript. ***Required for some:*** ACT. Test scores used for counseling/placement. ***Application deadline:*** rolling. ***Notification:*** continuous.

APPLYING/TRANSFER ***Required:*** college transcript. ***Recommended:*** high school transcript. ***Required for some:*** essay, standardized test scores. ***Entrance:*** noncompetitive. ***Application deadline:*** rolling. ***Notification:*** continuous.

CONTACT Mr. Michael Burbine, Coordinator-Admissions, Information, and Veterans' Affairs, Salem Community College, Carneys Point, NJ 08069-2799, 609-351-2696. College video available.

SUSSEX COUNTY COMMUNITY COLLEGE
Newton, New Jersey

UG Enrollment: 2,293	Tuition & Fees (Area Res): $2243
Application Deadline: rolling	Room & Board: N/Avail

GENERAL State and locally supported, 2-year, coed. Part of New Jersey Commission on Higher Education. Awards certificates, diplomas, transfer associate, terminal associate degrees. Founded 1981. *Setting:* 130-acre small-town campus with easy access to New York City. *Endowment:* $75,000. *Educational spending 1994–95:* $1737 per undergrad. *Total enrollment:* 2,293. *Faculty:* 188 (38 full-time, 39% with terminal degrees, 150 part-time); student-faculty ratio is 18:1.
ENROLLMENT PROFILE 2,293 students: 63% women, 37% men, 62% part-time, 95% state residents, 7% transferred in, 67% have need-based financial aid, 0% international, 50% 25 or older, 1% Native American, 2% Hispanic, 1% African American, 1% Asian American. *Areas of study chosen:* 41% liberal arts/general studies, 9% business management and administrative services, 4% health professions and related sciences, 3% education, 1% communications and journalism, 1% computer and information sciences, 1% English language/literature/letters, 1% fine arts, 1% psychology, 1% social sciences. *Most popular recent majors:* liberal arts/general studies, business administration/commerce/management.
FIRST-YEAR CLASS 741 total; 860 applied, 100% were accepted, 86% of whom enrolled.
ACADEMIC PROGRAM Core. Calendar: 4-1-4. 200 courses offered in 1995–96. Academic remediation for entering students, English as a second language program offered during academic year and summer, services for LD students, advanced placement, tutorials, summer session for credit, part-time degree program (daytime, evenings, summer), internships.
GENERAL DEGREE REQUIREMENTS 60 credits; 6 credits of math; 4 credits of science; computer course; internship (some majors).
MAJORS Accounting, art/fine arts, biology/biological sciences, broadcasting, business administration/commerce/management, chemistry, computer information systems, criminal justice, English, environmental sciences, graphic arts, human services, information science, journalism, legal studies, liberal arts/general studies, mathematics, psychology, recreation and leisure services, respiratory therapy, retail management, secretarial studies/office management, social science.
LIBRARY Sussex County Community College Library with 40,000 books, 134 microform titles, 222 periodicals, 2 on-line bibliographic services, 8 CD-ROMs, 800 records, tapes, and CDs. Acquisition spending 1994–95: $75,887.
COMPUTERS ON CAMPUS 18 computers for student use in learning resource center. Staffed computer lab on campus provides training in use of computers, software. Academic computing expenditure 1994–95: $200,000.
COLLEGE LIFE Choral group, student-run newspaper. 10% vote in student government elections. *Social organizations:* 9 open to all. *Most popular organizations:* Student Government Association, Humanities, Fine Arts, Theater Arts, WHO. *Major annual events:* All-College Picnic, Talent Show, International Festival. *Student services:* personal-psychological counseling. *Campus security:* trained security personnel.
ATHLETICS Member NJCAA. *Intercollegiate:* baseball M, basketball M, soccer M/W, softball W. *Contact:* Mr. John Kuntz, Athletic Director, 201-300-2100.
CAREER PLANNING *Placement office:* 1 full-time, 1 part-time staff; $250,000 operating expenditure 1994–95. *Director:* Ms. Susan Rafter, Director of Counseling, 201-300-2100. *Services:* job fairs, resume preparation, career counseling, careers library, job bank, job interviews. 30 organizations recruited on campus 1994–95.
EXPENSES FOR 1996–97 *Application fee:* $15. Area resident tuition: $1973 full-time, $65.75 per credit part-time. State resident tuition: $3945 full-time, $131.50 per credit part-time. Nonresident tuition: $5918 full-time, $197.25 per credit part-time. Part-time mandatory fees: $9 per credit. Full-time mandatory fees: $270.
FINANCIAL AID *College-administered undergrad aid 1995–96:* 405 need-based scholarships (average $1214), 8 non-need scholarships (average $1000), low-interest long-term loans from external sources (average $2625), 48 Federal Work-Study (averaging $875). *Required forms:* institutional, FAFSA; accepted: CSS Financial Aid PROFILE. *Priority deadline:* 10/1. *Waivers:* full or partial for employees or children of employees and senior citizens. *Notification:* continuous. *Average indebtedness of graduates:* $2652.
APPLYING Open admission. *Option:* midyear entrance. *Application deadline:* rolling. *Notification:* continuous.
APPLYING/TRANSFER *Entrance:* noncompetitive. *Application deadline:* rolling. *Notification:* continuous.
CONTACT Mr. Harold H. Damato, Director of Admissions and Registrar, Sussex County Community College, Newton, NJ 07860, 201-300-2100.

UNION COUNTY COLLEGE
Cranford, New Jersey

UG Enrollment: 10,046	Tuition & Fees (Area Res): $2035
Application Deadline: 8/15	Room & Board: N/Avail

GENERAL State and locally supported, 2-year, coed. Part of New Jersey Commission on Higher Education. Awards certificates, diplomas, transfer associate, terminal associate degrees. Founded 1933. *Setting:* 48-acre suburban campus with easy access to New York City. *Endowment:* $217,047. *Total enrollment:* 10,046. *Faculty:* 422 (173 full-time, 28% with terminal degrees, 249 part-time); student-faculty ratio is 20:1.
ENROLLMENT PROFILE 10,046 students from 2 states and territories, 83 other countries. 63% women, 56% part-time, 99% state residents, 13% transferred in, 26% have need-based financial aid, 52% 25 or older, 1% Native American, 15% Hispanic, 23% African American, 5% Asian American. *Areas of study chosen:* 21% health professions and related sciences, 21% liberal arts/general studies, 10% English language/literature/letters, 9% business management and administrative services, 8% interdisciplinary studies, 4% education, 4% mathematics, 3% computer and information sciences, 3% engineering and applied sciences, 3% foreign language and literature, 3% military science, 3% social sciences, 2% biological and life sciences, 2% communications and journalism, 1% architecture, 1% fine arts, 1% performing arts, 1% physical sciences. *Most popular recent majors:* health science, business administration/commerce/management, liberal arts/general studies.
FIRST-YEAR CLASS 4,450 total; 6,792 applied, 95% were accepted, 70% of whom enrolled. 8% from top 10% of their high school class, 25% from top quarter, 58% from top half.
ACADEMIC PROGRAM Core, honor code. Calendar: semesters. 806 courses offered in 1995–96. Academic remediation for entering students, English as a second language program offered during academic year and summer, services for LD students, advanced placement, self-designed majors, honors program, summer session for credit, part-time degree program (daytime, evenings, weekends, summer), adult/continuing education programs, internships. Off-campus study at Rutgers, The State University of New Jersey, New Jersey Institute of Technology, Fairleigh Dickinson University, Kean College of New Jersey. ROTC: Air Force (c).
GENERAL DEGREE REQUIREMENTS 62 semester hours; internship (some majors).
MAJORS Accounting, architectural technologies, art/fine arts, biology/biological sciences, business administration/commerce/management, civil engineering technology, communication, computer information systems, computer science, criminal justice, data processing, deaf interpreter training, early childhood education, education, electromechanical technology, electronics engineering technology, engineering (general), finance/banking, fire science, gerontology, graphic arts, health science, illustration, international studies, liberal arts/general studies, marketing/retailing/merchandising, mechanical engineering technology, music, nursing, occupational therapy, photography, physical sciences, physical therapy, practical nursing, public administration, radiological technology, respiratory therapy, robotics, secretarial studies/office management, theater arts/drama, urban studies.
LIBRARY MacKay Library plus 2 others, with 116,671 books, 162 microform titles, 458 periodicals, 2 on-line bibliographic services, 9 CD-ROMs, 4,125 records, tapes, and CDs. Acquisition spending 1994–95: $94,985.
COMPUTERS ON CAMPUS 460 computers for student use in computer labs, learning resource center, labs, classrooms, library provide access to main academic computer, off-campus computing facilities, e-mail. Staffed computer lab on campus provides training in use of computers, software. Academic computing expenditure 1994–95: $382,752.
COLLEGE LIFE Drama-theater group, student-run newspaper, radio station. *Social organizations:* 21 open to all. *Most popular organizations:* SIGN, Spanish Club, Performing Arts Club, Business Club, Ski Club. *Major annual events:* New Student Mixers, International Cultural Festivals, Comedy Shows. *Student services:* personal-psychological counseling. *Campus security:* 24-hour emergency response devices and patrols, late-night transport-escort service.
HOUSING College housing not available.
ATHLETICS Member NJCAA. *Intercollegiate:* baseball M, basketball M/W(s), golf M/W, soccer M, softball W. *Intramural:* basketball, softball, table tennis (Ping-Pong), tennis, volleyball. *Contact:* Mr. Fred Perry, Director, Campus Center/Athletics, 908-709-7093.
CAREER PLANNING *Placement office:* 10 full-time, 1 part-time staff; $531,801 operating expenditure 1994–95. *Director:* Mr. Ron Nakashima, Director of Counseling Services, 908-965-6065. *Services:* resume preparation, career counseling, careers library, job bank.
AFTER GRADUATION 44% of students completing a degree program in 1994–95 went directly on to further study.
EXPENSES FOR 1995–96 *Application fee:* $20. Area resident tuition: $1755 full-time, $54.85 per credit part-time. State resident tuition: $3510 full-time, $109.70 per credit part-time. Nonresident tuition: $7020 full-time, $219.40 per credit part-time. Part-time mandatory fees: $9 per credit. Full-time mandatory fees: $280.
FINANCIAL AID *College-administered undergrad aid 1995–96:* 590 need-based scholarships (averaging $363), 168 non-need scholarships (averaging $1561), low-interest long-term loans from external sources (averaging $2167), Federal Work-Study, 102 part-time jobs. *Required forms:* institutional, FAFSA; required for some: state. *Priority deadline:* 6/1. *Payment plan:* deferred payment. *Waivers:* full or partial for employees or children of employees and senior citizens. *Notification:* continuous. *Average indebtedness of graduates:* $1925.
APPLYING Open admission. *Options:* early entrance, midyear entrance. *Required:* TOEFL for international students. *Recommended:* SAT I. *Required for some:* SAT I. Test scores used for counseling/placement. *Application deadline:* 8/15. *Notification:* continuous until 9/1.
APPLYING/TRANSFER *Required for some:* standardized test scores. *Entrance:* noncompetitive. *Application deadline:* 8/15. *Notification:* continuous until 9/1. *Contact:* Ms. Marilyn Flood, Transfer Counselor, 908-709-7027.
CONTACT Mr. Joseph Rugusa, Director of Admissions, Union County College, Cranford, NJ 07016-1528, 908-709-7121. *Fax:* 908-709-0527. College video available.

WARREN COUNTY COMMUNITY COLLEGE
Washington, New Jersey

UG Enrollment: 1,619	Tuition & Fees (Area Res): $1716
Application Deadline: rolling	Room & Board: N/Avail

GENERAL State and locally supported, 2-year, coed. Part of New Jersey Commission on Higher Education. Awards certificates, transfer associate, terminal associate degrees. Founded 1981. *Setting:* 77-acre rural campus. *Total enrollment:* 1,619. *Faculty:* 56 (14 full-time, 14% with terminal degrees, 42 part-time).
ENROLLMENT PROFILE 1,619 students from 4 states and territories. 64% women, 36% men, 77% part-time, 97% state residents, 16% transferred in, 0% international, 57% 25 or older, 0% Native American, 2% Hispanic, 3% African American, 0% Asian American. *Most popular recent majors:* liberal arts/general studies, business administration/commerce/management, paralegal studies.
FIRST-YEAR CLASS 607 total. Of the students who applied, 100% were accepted.
ACADEMIC PROGRAM Core. Calendar: semesters. 186 courses offered in 1995–96. Academic remediation for entering students, English as a second language program, services for LD students, advanced placement, summer session for credit, part-time degree program (evenings), co-op programs and internships. Off-campus study at Raritan Valley Community College, Union County College, Northampton County Area Community College.
GENERAL DEGREE REQUIREMENTS 64 credits; 3 credits of math/science.
MAJORS Accounting, biology/biological sciences, business administration/commerce/management, computer information systems, criminal justice, data processing, liberal arts/general studies, paralegal studies, respiratory therapy, secretarial studies/office management, social science.
LIBRARY 29,467 books, 78 microform titles, 225 periodicals, 14 CD-ROMs, 150 records, tapes, and CDs.

New Jersey–New Mexico

Warren County Community College (continued)

COMPUTERS ON CAMPUS 62 computers for student use in computer center, learning resource center, instrumentation lab, library provide access to main academic computer.
COLLEGE LIFE Drama-theater group, student-run newspaper. *Social organizations:* 1 national fraternity. *Student services:* personal-psychological counseling.
HOUSING College housing not available.
ATHLETICS *Intercollegiate:* softball W, wrestling M. *Intramural:* basketball, bowling, tennis, volleyball. *Contact:* Mr. Andrus Loigo, Director of Student Life, 908-689-7619.
CAREER PLANNING *Placement office:* 1 part-time staff. *Director:* Ms. Nancy Arzoumanian, Career Counselor, 908-689-1090. *Services:* resume preparation, career counseling, careers library, job bank. 5 organizations recruited on campus 1994–95.
EXPENSES FOR 1995–96 *Application fee:* $15. Area resident tuition: $1512 full-time, $63 per credit part-time. State resident tuition: $3024 full-time, $126 per credit part-time. Nonresident tuition: $4536 full-time, $189 per credit part-time. Part-time mandatory fees: $8.50 per credit. Full-time mandatory fees: $204.
FINANCIAL AID *College-administered undergrad aid 1995–96:* 46 need-based scholarships (average $500), 19 non-need scholarships (average $816), low-interest long-term loans from external sources (average $2029), Federal Work-Study. *Required forms:* CSS Financial Aid PROFILE, institutional. *Priority deadline:* 5/1. *Waivers:* full or partial for employees or children of employees and senior citizens.
APPLYING Open admission. *Options:* early entrance, deferred entrance. *Required:* New Jersey Basic Skills Exam. Test scores used for counseling/placement. *Application deadline:* rolling.
APPLYING/TRANSFER *Required:* standardized test scores. *Application deadline:* rolling.
CONTACT Ms. Lucila Haase, Admissions Counselor, Warren County Community College, 575 Route 57, Washington, NJ 07882-9605, 908-689-1090.

NEW MEXICO

Santa Fe Area
Inst of American Indian Arts
Santa Fe Comm Coll

Albuquerque Area
Albuquerque Technical Vocational Inst
Parks Coll
Pima Medical Inst
Southwestern Indian Polytechnic Inst

ALBUQUERQUE TECHNICAL VOCATIONAL INSTITUTE
Albuquerque, New Mexico

UG Enrollment: 15,021	Tuition & Fees (NM Res): $954
Application Deadline: rolling	Room & Board: N/Avail

GENERAL State-supported, 2-year, coed. Part of New Mexico Commission on Higher Education. Awards certificates, transfer associate, terminal associate degrees. Founded 1965. *Setting:* urban campus. *Endowment:* $982,404. *Total enrollment:* 15,021. *Faculty:* 601 (302 full-time, 299 part-time); student-faculty ratio is 25:1. *Notable Alumni:* Terance Mathis, wide receiver for the Atlanta Falcons; Eufemia Lucero, district manager for the United States Postal Service; William Tydeman, chief of police of Bernalillo, New Mexico; Peter Micono, senior technical associate for biophysics, Sadia National Laboratories.
ENROLLMENT PROFILE 15,021 students from 46 states and territories. 58% women, 42% men, 73% part-time, 97% state residents, 30% transferred in, 57% 25 or older, 6% Native American, 39% Hispanic, 3% African American, 2% Asian American. *Areas of study chosen:* 18% liberal arts/general studies, 15% business management and administrative services, 13% vocational and home economics, 9% health professions and related sciences. *Most popular recent majors:* liberal arts/general studies, nursing, paralegal studies.
FIRST-YEAR CLASS Of the students who applied, 100% were accepted.
ACADEMIC PROGRAM Interdisciplinary curriculum with technical/vocational emphasis. Calendar: trimesters. Academic remediation for entering students, English as a second language program offered during academic year and summer, services for LD students, summer session for credit, part-time degree program (daytime, evenings, weekends, summer), adult/continuing education programs, internships.
GENERAL DEGREE REQUIREMENTS 64 credit hours; 1 college math course; computer course; internship (some majors).
MAJORS Accounting, architectural technologies, business administration/commerce/management, child psychology/child development, computer programming, construction technologies, court reporting, criminal justice, criminology, culinary arts, drafting and design, electrical and electronics technologies, electrical engineering technology, electronics engineering technology, environmental engineering technology, fire science, instrumentation technology, liberal arts/general studies, medical laboratory technology, metallurgical technology, nursing, optical technologies, paralegal studies, respiratory therapy, secretarial studies/office management.
LIBRARY Main Campus Library plus 1 other, with 32,000 books, 498 microform titles, 1,350 periodicals, 1 on-line bibliographic service, 25 CD-ROMs. Acquisition spending 1994–95: $194,491.
COMPUTERS ON CAMPUS 900 computers for student use in computer labs, learning resource center, classrooms, library provide access to main academic computer, on-line services, Internet. Staffed computer lab on campus provides training in use of computers, software. Academic computing expenditure 1994–95: $1.2 million.
COLLEGE LIFE Student-run newspaper. 1% vote in student government elections. *Social organizations:* 17 open to all. *Most popular organizations:* Phi Theta Kappa, Student Government, Hispanic Club, DECA. *Major annual events:* Annual State-Wide Student Government Conference, Presidential Luncheons, Health Awareness Week. *Student services:* health clinic, personal-psychological counseling. *Campus security:* 24-hour patrols, student patrols, late-night transport-escort service.
HOUSING College housing not available.
CAREER PLANNING *Placement office:* 4 full-time staff; $123,576 operating expenditure 1994–95. *Director:* Ms. Gloria Hernandez, Director, Student Job Placement Services, 505-224-3060. *Services:* job fairs, resume preparation, resume referral, career counseling, careers library, job bank, job interviews. Students must register freshman year. 37 organizations recruited on campus 1994–95.
EXPENSES FOR 1995–96 *Application fee:* $20. State resident tuition: $954 full-time, $26.50 per credit hour part-time. Nonresident tuition: $2655 full-time, $73.75 per credit hour part-time.
FINANCIAL AID *Waivers:* full or partial for employees or children of employees.
APPLYING Open admission except for nursing, respiratory therapy, medical laboratory technology programs. *Option:* midyear entrance. *Recommended:* ACT. *Required for some:* school transcript. Test scores used for admission. *Application deadline:* rolling.
APPLYING/TRANSFER *Required:* college transcript. *Application deadline:* rolling.
Contact: Ms. Jane Campbell, Director of Admissions and Records, 505-224-3210.
CONTACT Ms. Jane Campbell, Director of Admissions and Records, Albuquerque Technical Vocational Institute, 525 Buena Vista, SE, Albuquerque, NM 87106-4096, 505-224-3210.

CLOVIS COMMUNITY COLLEGE
Clovis, New Mexico

UG Enrollment: 3,920	Tuition & Fees (Area Res): $520
Application Deadline: N/R	Room & Board: N/Avail

GENERAL State-supported, 2-year, coed. Part of Eastern New Mexico University System. Awards transfer associate, terminal associate degrees. Founded 1971. *Setting:* small-town campus. *Total enrollment:* 3,920. *Faculty:* 184 (49 full-time, 135 part-time).
ENROLLMENT PROFILE 3,920 students.
FIRST-YEAR CLASS Of the students who applied, 100% were accepted.
ACADEMIC PROGRAM Calendar: semesters. Services for LD students.
GENERAL DEGREE REQUIREMENTS 64 credit hours; 1 course each in math and science.
MAJORS Accounting, agricultural business, art/fine arts, automotive technologies, aviation technology, business administration/commerce/management, computer information systems, computer programming, construction technologies, criminal justice, electrical and electronics technologies, engineering technology, finance/banking, graphic arts, heating/refrigeration/air conditioning, human services, legal studies, liberal arts/general studies, library science, marketing/retailing/merchandising, nursing, physical education, psychology, radiological technology, real estate, secretarial studies/office management, word processing.
COMPUTERS ON CAMPUS Computers for student use in computer center.
HOUSING College housing not available.
CAREER PLANNING *Director:* Mr. Lupe Rosales, Career Services Coordinator, 505-769-4088.
EXPENSES FOR 1996–97 Area resident tuition: $520 full-time, $21 per credit hour part-time. State resident tuition: $544 full-time, $22 per credit hour part-time. Nonresident tuition: $1528 full-time, $63 per credit hour part-time.
FINANCIAL AID *College-administered undergrad aid 1995–96:* need-based scholarships, non-need scholarships, low-interest long-term loans from external sources.
APPLYING Open admission except for nursing, radiological technician programs. *Required:* school transcript. *Required for some:* TABE.
CONTACT Miss Victoria Quintella, Director of Enrollment Management, Clovis Community College, Clovis, NM 88101-8381, 505-769-4021.

DOÑA ANA BRANCH COMMUNITY COLLEGE
Las Cruces, New Mexico

UG Enrollment: 3,768	Tuition & Fees (Area Res): $768
Application Deadline: rolling	Room & Board: $3229

GENERAL State and locally supported, 2-year, coed. Part of New Mexico State University System. Awards terminal associate degrees. Founded 1973. *Setting:* 15-acre urban campus with easy access to El Paso and Ciudad Juárez. *Educational spending 1994–95:* $1444 per undergrad. *Total enrollment:* 3,768. *Faculty:* 168 (66 full-time, 6% with terminal degrees, 102 part-time); student-faculty ratio is 20:1.
ENROLLMENT PROFILE 3,768 students from 15 states and territories, 3 other countries. 51% women, 65% part-time, 84% state residents, 7% transferred in, 2% international, 46% 25 or older, 3% Native American, 48% Hispanic, 2% African American, 3% Asian American. *Areas of study chosen:* 12% business management and administrative services, 11% vocational and home economics, 4% computer and information sciences, 4% health professions and related sciences, 2% architecture, 2% natural resource sciences, 1% library and information studies. *Most popular recent majors:* secretarial studies/office management, water resources, computer technologies.
FIRST-YEAR CLASS 1,218 total. Of the students who applied, 100% were accepted, 80% of whom enrolled. 5% from top 10% of their high school class, 10% from top quarter, 85% from top half.
ACADEMIC PROGRAM Core, honor code. Calendar: semesters. Academic remediation for entering students, English as a second language program offered during academic year, services for LD students, advanced placement, Freshman Honors College, tutorials, honors program, summer session for credit, part-time degree program (daytime, evenings, weekends, summer), adult/continuing education programs, co-op programs and internships. ROTC: Army (c), Air Force (c).
GENERAL DEGREE REQUIREMENTS 66 credits; intermediate algebra competence or 1 intermediate algebra course; computer course; internship (some majors).
MAJORS Architectural technologies, automotive technologies, business administration/commerce/management, computer technologies, drafting and design, electrical and electronics technologies, emergency medical technology, fashion merchandising, finance/banking, fire science, heating/refrigeration/air conditioning, hospitality services, library science, nursing, paralegal studies, radiological technology, respiratory therapy, retail management, secretarial studies/office management, water resources, welding technology, word processing.
LIBRARY 10,500 books, 222 periodicals, 1 on-line bibliographic service, 11 CD-ROMs, 2,490 records, tapes, and CDs. Acquisition spending 1994–95: $57,522.
COMPUTERS ON CAMPUS 300 computers for student use in computer center, labs, classrooms provide access to e-mail, Internet. Staffed computer lab on campus provides training in use of computers, software. Academic computing expenditure 1994–95: $300,000.
COLLEGE LIFE Drama-theater group, student-run newspaper, radio station. 17% vote in student government elections. *Major annual events:* Homecoming, Spring Fling, Return to Campus. *Student services:* legal services, health clinic, personal-psychological counseling, women's center. *Campus security:* 24-hour emergency response devices and patrols, late-night transport-escort service.
HOUSING 4,000 college housing spaces available; 340 were occupied 1995–96. Freshmen guaranteed college housing. Off-campus living permitted. *Options:* coed, single-sex, international student housing available. Resident assistants live in dorms.
CAREER PLANNING *Placement office:* 3 full-time, 2 part-time staff; $155,000 operating expenditure 1994–95. *Director:* Mr. Richard Silva, Coordinator of Cooperative Education and Placement, 505-527-7538. *Services:* resume preparation, resume referral, career counseling, careers library, job interviews. Students must register freshman year.
EXPENSES FOR 1996–97 *Application fee:* $15. Area resident tuition: $768 full-time, $32 per credit part-time. State resident tuition: $864 full-time, $36 per credit part-time. Nonresident tuition: $1992 full-time, $83 per credit part-time. (Room and board are provided by New Mexico State University.) College room and board: $3229. College room only: $1669.
FINANCIAL AID College-administered undergrad aid 1995–96: need-based scholarships, short-term loans, low-interest long-term loans from external sources, Federal Work-Study, part-time jobs. *Required forms:* CSS Financial Aid PROFILE, state, FAFSA. *Priority deadline:* 5/1. *Payment plan:* installment. *Waivers:* full or partial for senior citizens.
APPLYING Open admission except for radiologic technology, nursing, respiratory care, paramedic, electrical apprenticeship, area vocational school programs. *Options:* deferred entrance, midyear entrance. *Required:* school transcript. *Recommended:* ACT ASSET or ACT. *Required for some:* 3 years of high school science, recommendations. Test scores used for counseling/placement. *Application deadline:* rolling.
APPLYING/TRANSFER *Required:* college transcript. *Contact:* Ms. Rosemary Gonzalez, Admissions Coordinator, 505-527-7532.
CONTACT Ms. Rosemary Gonzalez, Admissions Counselor, Doña Ana Branch Community College, Box 30001, Department 3DA, Las Cruces, NM 88003-8001, 505-527-7532.

EASTERN NEW MEXICO UNIVERSITY–ROSWELL
Roswell, New Mexico

UG Enrollment: 2,536	Tuition & Fees (Area Res): $888
Application Deadline: rolling	Room Only: $1086

GENERAL State-supported, 2-year, coed. Part of Eastern New Mexico University System. Awards certificates, transfer associate, terminal associate degrees. Founded 1958. *Setting:* 241-acre small-town campus. *Educational spending 1994–95:* $1400 per undergrad. *Total enrollment:* 2,536. *Faculty:* 150 (50 full-time, 2% with terminal degrees, 100 part-time); student-faculty ratio is 22:1. *Notable Alumni:* Steve Strain, Bobby Ramirez, Rudy Escamilla, Dr. Nora Hutto, Louis Brady.
ENROLLMENT PROFILE 2,536 students from 11 states and territories, 4 other countries. 64% women, 55% part-time, 98% state residents, 5% live on campus, 10% transferred in, 1% international, 50% 25 or older, 1% Native American, 33% Hispanic, 3% African American, 1% Asian American. *Most popular recent majors:* nursing, liberal arts/general studies, business administration/commerce/management.
FIRST-YEAR CLASS 240 total. Of the students who applied, 99% were accepted, 80% of whom enrolled.
ACADEMIC PROGRAM Core, honor code. Calendar: semesters. 350 courses offered in 1995–96. Academic remediation for entering students, services for LD students, tutorials, summer session for credit, part-time degree program (daytime, evenings), adult/continuing education programs, co-op programs and internships. Off-campus study at other units of the Eastern New Mexico University System. ROTC: Army (c), Naval (c), Air Force (c).
GENERAL DEGREE REQUIREMENTS 64 credit hours; internship (some majors).
MAJORS Automotive technologies, aviation technology, business administration/commerce/management, child care/child and family studies, child psychology/child development, computer information systems, computer science, criminal justice, drafting and design, electrical and electronics technologies, emergency medical technology, finance/banking, fire science, liberal arts/general studies, nursing, occupational therapy, paralegal studies, petroleum technology, secretarial studies/office management, welding technology.
LIBRARY Learning Resource Center with 30,000 books, 8,000 microform titles, 220 periodicals.
COMPUTERS ON CAMPUS 60 computers for student use in library. Staffed computer lab on campus provides training in use of computers, software.
COLLEGE LIFE Drama-theater group, choral group, student-run newspaper. 10% vote in student government elections. *Campus security:* 24-hour emergency response devices, student patrols.
HOUSING 120 college housing spaces available; 96 were occupied 1995–96. No special consideration for freshman housing applicants. Off-campus living permitted. *Option:* coed housing available. Resident assistants live in dorms.
ATHLETICS *Intramural:* basketball, football, racquetball, tennis, volleyball.
CAREER PLANNING *Placement office:* 2 full-time staff; $50,000 operating expenditure 1994–95. *Director:* Ms. Cheryl Franklin, Director, Placement Office, 505-624-4168. *Services:* job fairs, resume preparation, resume referral, career counseling, careers library, job bank, job interviews.
EXPENSES FOR 1996–97 Area resident tuition: $840 full-time, $26.25 per credit hour part-time. State resident tuition: $1872 full-time, $27.25 per credit hour part-time. Nonresident tuition: $2520 full-time, $78.75 per credit hour part-time. Part-time mandatory fees: $2 per credit hour. Full-time mandatory fees: $48. College room only: $1086.
FINANCIAL AID College-administered undergrad aid 1995–96: 231 need-based scholarships (average $580), 40 non-need scholarships (average $275), low-interest long-term loans from external sources (average $2000), Federal Work-Study. *Required forms:* CSS Financial Aid PROFILE, state; required for some: FAFSA. *Priority deadline:* 5/1. *Payment plans:* installment, deferred payment. *Waivers:* full or partial for employees or children of employees and senior citizens. *Notification:* continuous.
APPLYING Open admission. *Options:* early entrance, midyear entrance. *Required:* school transcript, TOEFL for international students. *Recommended:* ACT. Test scores used for admission and counseling/placement. *Application deadline:* rolling.
APPLYING/TRANSFER *Entrance:* noncompetitive. *Application deadline:* rolling. *Contact:* Mr. Mike Martinez, Assistant Dean, 505-624-7163.
CONTACT Ms. Ida Storer, Admission Specialist, Eastern New Mexico University–Roswell, Roswell, NM 88202-6000, 505-624-7149 or toll-free 800-243-6687 (in-state). *Fax:* 505-624-7119.

INSTITUTE OF AMERICAN INDIAN ARTS
Santa Fe, New Mexico

UG Enrollment: 240	Tuition & Fees: $9810
Application Deadline: 4/15	Room & Board: $3166

GENERAL Federally supported, 2-year, coed. Awards transfer associate degrees. Founded 1962. *Setting:* 100-acre urban campus. *Endowment:* $4 million. *Total enrollment:* 240. *Faculty:* 38 (10% of full-time faculty have terminal degrees); student-faculty ratio is 7:1. *Notable Alumni:* Linda Lomahaftewa, Charlene Teters, Dan Naminga, Earl Biss, Denise Wallace.
ENROLLMENT PROFILE 240 students from 29 states and territories, 3 other countries. 50% women, 22% part-time, 44% state residents, 30% transferred in, 70% have need-based financial aid, 6% international, 51% 25 or older, 90% Native American, 2% Hispanic, 0% African American, 0% Asian American. *Areas of study chosen:* 95% fine arts, 5% communications and journalism. *Most popular recent major:* art/fine arts.
FIRST-YEAR CLASS 34 total; 120 applied, 83% were accepted, 34% of whom enrolled. 5% from top 10% of their high school class, 7% from top quarter, 40% from top half. 1 valedictorian.
ACADEMIC PROGRAM Core, foundation arts curriculum, honor code. Calendar: semesters. 155 courses offered in 1995–96. Academic remediation for entering students, internships. Off-campus study at College of Santa Fe, Santa Fe Community College, University of Arizona, Haystack School of Crafts, University of New Mexico.
GENERAL DEGREE REQUIREMENT 65 credit hours.
MAJORS Art/fine arts, ceramic art and design, creative writing, jewelry and metalsmithing, museum studies, painting/drawing, photography, printmaking, sculpture, studio art, textile arts.
LIBRARY Fogelson Library with 15,200 books, 60 periodicals, 400 records, tapes, and CDs.
COMPUTERS ON CAMPUS 20 computers for student use in computer center, learning resource center, library, dorms provide access to Internet. Staffed computer lab on campus provides training in use of computers, software.
COLLEGE LIFE Orientation program (2 days, no cost). Drama-theater group, student-run newspaper. 50% vote in student government elections. *Social organizations:* 10 open to all; pow-wow club; 60% of eligible men and 60% of eligible women are members. *Most popular organizations:* Pow-Wow Club, Museum Club, Ski Club, Spring Break Club. *Major annual events:* Pow-Wow, Gallery Openings, Visit to Indian Reservations. *Student services:* personal-psychological counseling. *Campus security:* 24-hour patrols, late-night transport-escort service.
HOUSING 100 college housing spaces available; all were occupied 1995–96. No special consideration for freshman housing applicants. Off-campus living permitted. *Option:* coed housing available.
ATHLETICS *Intramural:* archery, basketball, bowling, cross-country running, skiing (cross-country), skiing (downhill), swimming and diving, table tennis (Ping-Pong), tennis, track and field, volleyball.

Institute of American Indian Arts (continued)
CAREER PLANNING ***Placement office:*** 1 part-time staff. ***Director:*** Ms. Juanita Barry, Director of Placement and Academic Advisor, 505-988-6498. ***Services:*** resume preparation, career counseling, careers library, job interviews. 7 organizations recruited on campus 1994–95.
AFTER GRADUATION 25% of students completing a degree program in 1994–95 went directly on to further study.
EXPENSES FOR 1995–96 Comprehensive fee of $12,976 includes full-time tuition ($9600), mandatory fees ($210), and college room and board ($3166). College room only: $1450. Part-time tuition: $300 per credit. Part-time mandatory fees: $150 per year.
FINANCIAL AID ***College-administered undergrad aid 1995–96:*** need-based scholarships, 187 non-need scholarships, Federal Work-Study, 30 part-time jobs. ***Required forms:*** FAFSA; accepted: CSS Financial Aid PROFILE. ***Priority deadline:*** 5/1.
APPLYING ***Options:*** deferred entrance, midyear entrance. ***Required:*** school transcript, minimum 2.0 GPA, 3 recommendations, TOEFL for international students. ***Recommended:*** 3 years of high school math and science, some high school foreign language, interview, ACT. Test scores used for counseling/placement. ***Application deadline:*** 4/15. ***Notification:*** continuous until 7/1.
APPLYING/TRANSFER ***Required:*** high school transcript, 3 recommendations, college transcript, minimum 2.0 college GPA, minimum 2.0 high school GPA. ***Recommended:*** 3 years of high school math and science, some high school foreign language, interview. ***Entrance:*** minimally difficult. ***Application deadline:*** 4/15. ***Notification:*** continuous until 7/1. ***Contact:*** Ms. Charlotte Tenorio, Registrar, 505-986-5512.
CONTACT Mr. Ramus Suina, Director of Recruitment, Institute of American Indian Arts, PO Box 20007, Santa Fe, NM 87504-0007, 505-988-6496 or toll-free 800-804-6422 (out-of-state). ***Fax:*** 505-988-6446.

LUNA VOCATIONAL TECHNICAL INSTITUTE
Las Vegas, New Mexico

NEW MEXICO JUNIOR COLLEGE
Hobbs, New Mexico

UG Enrollment: 2,752	**Tuition & Fees (Area Res): $496**
Application Deadline: rolling	**Room & Board: $3000**

GENERAL State and locally supported, 2-year, coed. Part of New Mexico Commission on Higher Education. Awards certificates, transfer associate, terminal associate degrees. Founded 1965. ***Setting:*** 185-acre small-town campus. ***Research spending 1994–95:*** $21,370. ***Total enrollment:*** 2,752. ***Faculty:*** 129 (68 full-time, 17% with terminal degrees, 61 part-time); student-faculty ratio is 18:1.
ENROLLMENT PROFILE 2,752 students from 21 states and territories, 6 other countries. 64% women, 36% men, 57% part-time, 90% state residents, 9% transferred in, 1% international, 52% 25 or older, 1% Native American, 27% Hispanic, 4% African American, 1% Asian American. ***Areas of study chosen:*** 23% liberal arts/general studies, 18% health professions and related sciences, 14% business management and administrative services, 12% education, 5% computer and information sciences, 3% engineering and applied sciences, 2% architecture, 1% agriculture, 1% biological and life sciences, 1% fine arts, 1% mathematics. ***Most popular recent majors:*** liberal arts/general studies, nursing, business administration/commerce/management.
FIRST-YEAR CLASS 805 total; 975 applied, 100% were accepted, 83% of whom enrolled. 9% from top 10% of their high school class, 24% from top quarter, 72% from top half. 4 valedictorians.
ACADEMIC PROGRAM Core, honor code. Calendar: semesters. 450 courses offered in 1995–96. Academic remediation for entering students, English as a second language program offered during academic year, services for LD students, advanced placement, tutorials, summer session for credit, part-time degree program (daytime, evenings, weekends, summer), adult/continuing education programs, co-op programs and internships.
GENERAL DEGREE REQUIREMENTS 64 semester hours; intermediate algebra competence; internship (some majors).
MAJORS Accounting, agricultural sciences, art education, art/fine arts, athletic training, automotive technologies, biology/biological sciences, business administration/commerce/management, business education, carpentry, chemistry, computer graphics, computer programming, computer science, construction technologies, cosmetology, data processing, drafting and design, education, elementary education, emergency medical technology, engineering (general), English, environmental education, environmental sciences, finance/banking, fire science, graphic arts, health science, history, industrial arts, law enforcement/police sciences, legal secretarial studies, liberal arts/general studies, machine and tool technologies, marketing/retailing/merchandising, mathematics, medical assistant technologies, medical laboratory technology, medical secretarial studies, music, nursing, petroleum technology, physical education, practical nursing, real estate, recreation and leisure services, science, secretarial studies/office management, sports medicine, theater arts/drama, vocational education, welding technology, word processing.
LIBRARY Pannell Library with 122,046 books, 203,940 microform titles, 440 periodicals, 1 on-line bibliographic service, 278 CD-ROMs, 1,500 records, tapes, and CDs. Acquisition spending 1994–95: $76,220.
COMPUTERS ON CAMPUS Computer purchase plan available. 275 computers for student use in computer labs, learning resource center, testing center, classrooms, library, student center, dorms provide access to main academic computer, on-line services. Staffed computer lab on campus provides training in use of computers.
COLLEGE LIFE Drama-theater group, choral group. 27% vote in student government elections. ***Most popular organizations:*** Student Nurses Association, Phi Theta Kappa, Fellowship of Christian Athletes. ***Major annual events:*** Cowboy Roundup Days, Southwest Poets Conference, New Mexico Junior College Rodeo. ***Student services:*** personal-psychological counseling. ***Campus security:*** 24-hour emergency response devices and patrols, controlled dormitory access.
HOUSING 200 college housing spaces available; all were occupied 1995–96. No special consideration for freshman housing applicants. On-campus residence required in freshman year except if living at home. ***Option:*** coed housing available. Resident assistants live in dorms.
ATHLETICS Member NJCAA. ***Intercollegiate:*** baseball M(s), basketball M(s)/W(s), golf M(s). ***Intramural:*** badminton, basketball, cross-country running, football, racquetball, skiing (cross-country), skiing (downhill), table tennis (Ping-Pong), tennis, volleyball, weight lifting. ***Contact:*** Mr. Richard Morris, Athletic Director, 505-392-5786.
CAREER PLANNING ***Placement office:*** 4 full-time staff. ***Director:*** Ms. Marilyn Jackson, Director, Learning and Career Services, 505-392-5499. ***Services:*** job fairs, resume preparation, resume referral, career counseling, careers library, job interviews. 22 organizations recruited on campus 1994–95.
AFTER GRADUATION 67% of students completing a degree program in 1994–95 went directly on to further study.
EXPENSES FOR 1996–97 Area resident tuition: $456 full-time, $19 per semester hour part-time. State resident tuition: $720 full-time, $30 per semester hour part-time. Nonresident tuition: $840 full-time, $35 per semester hour part-time. Part-time mandatory fees per semester range from $2 to $10. Full-time mandatory fees: $40. College room and board: $3000.
FINANCIAL AID ***College-administered undergrad aid 1995–96:*** 250 need-based scholarships (average $490), 275 non-need scholarships (average $500), short-term loans, low-interest long-term loans from external sources (average $1448), Federal Work-Study, 100 part-time jobs. ***Required forms:*** institutional; required for some: state, FAFSA. ***Priority deadline:*** 6/1. ***Payment plan:*** installment.
APPLYING Open admission. ***Options:*** early entrance, deferred entrance. ***Required:*** TOEFL for international students. ***Recommended:*** ACT. Test scores used for counseling/placement. ***Application deadline:*** rolling.
APPLYING/TRANSFER ***Entrance:*** noncompetitive. ***Application deadline:*** rolling. ***Contact:*** Mr. Robert Snow, Dean of Admissions and Records, 505-392-5092.
CONTACT Mr. Robert Snow, Dean of Admissions and Records, New Mexico Junior College, Hobbs, NM 88240-9123, 505-392-5092. ***Fax:*** 505-392-2527.

NEW MEXICO MILITARY INSTITUTE
Roswell, New Mexico

UG Enrollment: 460	**Tuition & Fees (NM Res): $1687**
Application Deadline: 8/11	**Room & Board: $1800**

New Mexico Military Institute, founded in 1891, is a state-supported military junior college (AA degree). Army ROTC. A preparatory school for the service academies. Approximately $15 million in cadet room renovations have allowed each cadet access to a state-of-the-art computer network.

GENERAL State-supported, 2-year, primarily men. Part of New Mexico Commission on Higher Education. Awards transfer associate degrees. Founded 1891. ***Setting:*** 262-acre small-town campus. ***Endowment:*** $16 million. ***Educational spending 1994–95:*** $4974 per undergrad. ***Total enrollment:*** 460. ***Faculty:*** 32 (all full-time, 20% with terminal degrees); student-faculty ratio is 13:1. ***Notable Alumni:*** Laquita Hamilton, special assistant attorney general of Texas; Chuck Roberts, anchor for CNN Headline News; Robert Junell, chairman of committee on appropriation for Texas House of Representatives; Rick Galles, president of Galles Racing; Waldo Freeman, U.S. Army commanding general.
ENROLLMENT PROFILE 460 students from 44 states and territories, 8 other countries. 20% women, 0% part-time, 39% state residents, 100% live on campus, 1% transferred in, 4% international, 0% 25 or older, 2% Native American, 15% Hispanic, 11% African American, 4% Asian American. ***Areas of study chosen:*** 21% business management and administrative services, 21% liberal arts/general studies, 17% premed, 16% engineering and applied sciences, 9% computer and information sciences, 7% biological and life sciences, 4% foreign language and literature, 3% mathematics, 2% social sciences. ***Most popular recent majors:*** engineering (general), military science, criminal justice.
FIRST-YEAR CLASS 250 total; 597 applied, 45% were accepted, 93% of whom enrolled.
ACADEMIC PROGRAM Core, liberal arts curriculum, honor code. Calendar: semesters. 95 courses offered in 1995–96. Academic remediation for entering students, English as a second language program offered during summer, advanced placement, summer session for credit. ROTC: Army.
GENERAL DEGREE REQUIREMENTS 68 hours; 1 intermediate algebra course.
MAJORS Accounting, art/fine arts, biology/biological sciences, business administration/commerce/management, chemistry, civil engineering technology, computer programming, computer science, criminal justice, economics, engineering (general), (pre)engineering sequence, English, finance/banking, French, German, history, humanities, law enforcement/police sciences, liberal arts/general studies, mathematics, military science, physical education, physics, science, social science, Spanish, sports administration.
LIBRARY Paul Horgan Library with 55,000 books, 250 microform titles, 150 periodicals, 2 on-line bibliographic services, 7 CD-ROMs, 500 records, tapes, and CDs. Acquisition spending 1994–95: $32,815.
COMPUTERS ON CAMPUS Computer purchase plan available. Student rooms linked to a campus network. 150 computers for student use in computer center, computer labs, classrooms, library, student center provide access to main academic computer, off-campus computing facilities, e-mail, Internet. Staffed computer lab on campus. Academic computing expenditure 1994–95: $301,370.
COLLEGE LIFE Orientation program (7 days, no cost). Drama-theater group, choral group, marching band, student-run newspaper. ***Major annual events:*** Parents' Weekend, Homecoming, Open House. ***Student services:*** health clinic, personal-psychological counseling. ***Campus security:*** 24-hour emergency response devices and patrols.
HOUSING 500 college housing spaces available; 458 were occupied 1995–96. Freshmen guaranteed college housing. On-campus residence required through sophomore year. ***Option:*** single-sex housing available. Resident assistants live in dorms.
ATHLETICS Member NJCAA. ***Intercollegiate:*** baseball M(s), basketball M(s), fencing M/W, football M(s), golf M(s), riflery M/W, tennis M(s)/W(s). ***Intramural:*** basketball, bowling, cross-country running, equestrian sports, fencing, football, golf, racquetball, riflery, skiing (cross-country), skiing (downhill), soccer, swimming and diving, tennis, track and field, volleyball, weight lifting, wrestling. ***Contact:*** Col. Richard Stecklein, Director of Athletics, 505-624-8271.
CAREER PLANNING ***Placement office:*** 7 full-time, 2 part-time staff. ***Director:*** Maj. John A. Schaffer, Director, Student Assistance Center, 505-624-8361. ***Services:*** career counseling, careers library.
AFTER GRADUATION 87% of students completing a degree program in 1994–95 went directly on to further study.
EXPENSES FOR 1996–97 ***Application fee:*** $60. State resident tuition: $727 full-time. Nonresident tuition: $2428 full-time. Students are required to deposit $1700 to defray the costs of uniforms, books, and supplies. Full-time mandatory fees: $960. College room and board: $1800. College room only: $1000.

FINANCIAL AID ***College-administered undergrad aid 1995–96:*** 41 need-based scholarships (average $500), 75 non-need scholarships (average $1000), low-interest long-term loans from external sources (average $1000), Federal Work-Study, 18 part-time jobs. ***Required forms:*** institutional, FAFSA; accepted: CSS Financial Aid PROFILE. ***Priority deadline:*** 5/1. ***Payment plan:*** deferred payment.
APPLYING ***Options:*** early entrance, deferred entrance, midyear entrance. ***Required:*** school transcript, minimum 2.0 GPA, SAT I or ACT, TOEFL for international students. Test scores used for admission. ***Application deadline:*** 8/11. ***Notification:*** continuous. Preference given to state residents.
APPLYING/TRANSFER ***Required:*** college transcript. ***Entrance:*** moderately difficult. ***Application deadline:*** 8/11. ***Notification:*** continuous. ***Contact:*** Maj. John Schaffer, Director, Student Assistance Center, 505-624-8361.
CONTACT Col. James H. Matchin, Director of Admissions, New Mexico Military Institute, Roswell, NM 88201-5173, 505-624-8050 or toll-free 800-421-5376. ***Fax:*** 505-624-8058. ***E-mail:*** admissions@yogi.nmmi.cc.nm.us. College video available.

❖ *See page 784 for a narrative description.* ❖

NEW MEXICO STATE UNIVERSITY–ALAMOGORDO
Alamogordo, New Mexico

UG Enrollment: 2,300	**Tuition & Fees (Area Res): $720**
Application Deadline: rolling	**Room & Board: N/Avail**

GENERAL State-supported, 2-year, coed. Part of New Mexico State University System. Awards transfer associate, terminal associate degrees. Founded 1958. ***Setting:*** 540-acre small-town campus. ***Total enrollment:*** 2,300. ***Faculty:*** 140 (54 full-time, 86 part-time).
ENROLLMENT PROFILE 2,300 students: 60% women, 79% part-time, 90% state residents, 14% transferred in, 0% international, 69% 25 or older, 4% Native American, 19% Hispanic, 6% African American, 2% Asian American.
FIRST-YEAR CLASS 350 total. Of the students who applied, 98% were accepted.
ACADEMIC PROGRAM Core. Calendar: semesters. Academic remediation for entering students, English as a second language program, services for LD students, advanced placement, self-designed majors, summer session for credit, part-time degree program (daytime, evenings), adult/continuing education programs, internships. Off-campus study at other branches of New Mexico State University.
GENERAL DEGREE REQUIREMENTS 66 credits; computer course.
MAJORS Business administration/commerce/management, data processing, engineering technology, law enforcement/police sciences, liberal arts/general studies, materials sciences, medical laboratory technology, nursing, real estate, secretarial studies/office management.
LIBRARY David H. Townsend Library with 35,000 books, 5 microform titles, 315 periodicals, 10 CD-ROMs, 2,000 records, tapes, and CDs.
COMPUTERS ON CAMPUS 42 computers for student use in computer center.
COLLEGE LIFE Drama-theater group. ***Campus security:*** 24-hour emergency response devices.
HOUSING College housing not available.
ATHLETICS ***Intramural:*** basketball, volleyball.
CAREER PLANNING ***Service:*** career counseling.
EXPENSES FOR 1995–96 ***Application fee:*** $10. Area resident tuition: $720 full-time, $30 per credit part-time. State resident tuition: $840 full-time, $35 per credit part-time. Nonresident tuition: $1944 full-time, $81 per credit part-time.
FINANCIAL AID ***College-administered undergrad aid 1995–96:*** need-based scholarships, non-need scholarships (average $264), short-term loans (average $50), low-interest long-term loans from external sources, Federal Work-Study, part-time jobs. ***Required forms:*** CSS Financial Aid PROFILE, FAFSA. ***Application deadline:*** continuous to 4/1.
APPLYING Open admission except for medical laboratory technology, nursing programs. ***Options:*** early entrance, deferred entrance. ***Required:*** school transcript, minimum 2.0 GPA, TOEFL for international students. Test scores used for counseling/placement. ***Application deadline:*** rolling. ***Notification:*** continuous.
APPLYING/TRANSFER ***Required:*** high school transcript, minimum 2.0 high school GPA. ***Entrance:*** noncompetitive. ***Application deadline:*** rolling. ***Notification:*** continuous.
CONTACT Ms. Joanne Bidal, Coordinator of Admissions and Records, New Mexico State University–Alamogordo, Alamogordo, NM 88310, 505-439-3700.

NEW MEXICO STATE UNIVERSITY–CARLSBAD
Carlsbad, New Mexico

UG Enrollment: 1,151	**Tuition & Fees (Area Res): $744**
Application Deadline: 8/25	**Room & Board: N/Avail**

GENERAL State-supported, 2-year, coed. Part of New Mexico State University System. Awards certificates, transfer associate, terminal associate degrees. Founded 1950. ***Setting:*** 40-acre small-town campus. ***Educational spending 1994–95:*** $3030 per undergrad. ***Total enrollment:*** 1,151. ***Faculty:*** 71 (28 full-time, 14% with terminal degrees, 43 part-time).
ENROLLMENT PROFILE 1,151 students from 6 states and territories. 62% women, 38% men, 61% part-time, 97% state residents, 6% transferred in, 2% have need-based financial aid, 9% have non-need-based financial aid, 0% international, 70% 25 or older, 4% Native American, 29% Hispanic, 1% African American, 1% Asian American. ***Areas of study chosen:*** 9% health professions and related sciences, 6% business management and administrative services, 4% engineering and applied sciences, 3% computer and information sciences, 3% education.
FIRST-YEAR CLASS 173 total; 173 applied, 100% were accepted, 100% of whom enrolled. 2% from top 10% of their high school class, 10% from top quarter, 40% from top half.
ACADEMIC PROGRAM Core. Calendar: semesters. 272 courses offered in 1995–96. Academic remediation for entering students, English as a second language program offered during academic year and summer, services for LD students, advanced placement, self-designed majors, summer session for credit, part-time degree program (daytime, evenings), adult/continuing education programs, co-op programs and internships.
GENERAL DEGREE REQUIREMENTS 66 credit hours; 1 math course; computer course (varies by major).
MAJORS Business administration/commerce/management, computer information systems, computer science, criminal justice, education, electrical and electronics technologies, engineering technology, fire science, liberal arts/general studies, nuclear technology, nursing, radiological sciences, radiological technology, secretarial studies/office management, welding technology, word processing.
LIBRARY Library and Media Center with 22,481 books, 17 microform titles, 259 periodicals, 1 on-line bibliographic service, 8 CD-ROMs, 1,195 records, tapes, and CDs. Acquisition spending 1994–95: $42,326.
COMPUTERS ON CAMPUS 145 computers for student use in computer center, computer labs, learning resource center, classrooms, library provide access to off-campus computing facilities, Internet. Staffed computer lab on campus provides training in use of computers, software. Academic computing expenditure 1994–95: $153,623.
COLLEGE LIFE Drama-theater group, student-run newspaper. 10% vote in student government elections. ***Social organizations:*** 10 open to all. ***Most popular organizations:*** Student Nurses Association, Alpha Sigma Phi-Criminal Justice. ***Major annual events:*** Haunted House, Race Across the Desert, Kramer Entertainment. ***Student services:*** health clinic, personal-psychological counseling, women's center. ***Campus security:*** 24-hour emergency response devices.
HOUSING College housing not available.
CAREER PLANNING ***Placement office:*** 3 full-time staff; $53,895 operating expenditure 1994–95. ***Director:*** Ms. Sigrid Walker, Coordinator, Career Development Center, 505-885-8831 Ext. 391. ***Services:*** job fairs, resume preparation, resume referral, career counseling, careers library, job interviews. 12 organizations recruited on campus 1994–95.
AFTER GRADUATION 52% of class of 1994 had job offers within 6 months. 12% of students completing a degree program went directly on to further study.
EXPENSES FOR 1996–97 ***Application fee:*** $15. Area resident tuition: $744 full-time, $31 per credit hour part-time. State resident tuition: $864 full-time, $36 per credit hour part-time. Nonresident tuition: $1968 full-time, $82 per credit hour part-time.
FINANCIAL AID ***College-administered undergrad aid 1995–96:*** 23 need-based scholarships (average $620), 23 non-need scholarships (average $620), low-interest long-term loans from external sources (average $2650), 3 Federal Work-Study, 35 part-time jobs. ***Required forms:*** institutional; required for some: FAFSA; accepted: CSS Financial Aid PROFILE. ***Priority deadline:*** 5/30. ***Payment plan:*** deferred payment. ***Waivers:*** full or partial for employees or children of employees and senior citizens.
APPLYING Open admission except for nursing, radiological technology programs. ***Options:*** early entrance, deferred entrance. ***Required:*** school transcript, 3 years of high school math. ***Recommended:*** 3 years of high school science, ACT. ***Required for some:*** some high school foreign language, ACT. Test scores used for counseling/placement. ***Application deadline:*** 8/25. ***Notification:*** continuous.
APPLYING/TRANSFER ***Required:*** college transcript. ***Recommended:*** standardized test scores, 3 years of high school science. ***Required for some:*** standardized test scores, high school transcript, 3 years of high school math. ***Entrance:*** noncompetitive. ***Application deadline:*** 8/25. ***Notification:*** continuous. ***Contact:*** Dr. Michael J. Cleary, Assistant Provost for Student Services, 505-887-7533.
CONTACT Ms. Everal Shannon, Records Technician II, New Mexico State University–Carlsbad, Carlsbad, NM 88220-3509, 505-887-7533. ***Fax:*** 505-885-4951.

NEW MEXICO STATE UNIVERSITY–GRANTS
Grants, New Mexico

UG Enrollment: 700	**Tuition & Fees (Area Res): $924**
Application Deadline: 7/30	**Room & Board: N/Avail**

GENERAL State-supported, 2-year, coed. Part of New Mexico State University System. Awards transfer associate, terminal associate degrees. Founded 1968. ***Setting:*** small-town campus. ***Total enrollment:*** 700. ***Faculty:*** 57 (12 full-time, 45 part-time); student-faculty ratio is 13:1.
ENROLLMENT PROFILE 700 students: 66% women, 62% part-time, 100% state residents, 20% transferred in.
FIRST-YEAR CLASS 400 total. Of the students who applied, 100% were accepted, 99% of whom enrolled.
ACADEMIC PROGRAM Core. Calendar: semesters. Summer session for credit, part-time degree program (daytime, evenings, summer).
GENERAL DEGREE REQUIREMENTS 66 credits; 1 course each in math and science; computer course.
MAJORS Business administration/commerce/management, criminal justice, data processing, education, electrical and electronics technologies, electronics engineering technology, liberal arts/general studies, paralegal studies, secretarial studies/office management.
LIBRARY 30,000 books, 20 periodicals.
COMPUTERS ON CAMPUS Computer purchase plan available. 150 computers for student use in computer labs, learning resource center provide access to e-mail. Staffed computer lab on campus provides training in use of computers, software.
HOUSING College housing not available.
EXPENSES FOR 1996–97 ***Application fee:*** $15. Area resident tuition: $924 full-time, $28 per credit part-time. State resident tuition: $1089 full-time, $33 per credit part-time. Nonresident tuition: $2607 full-time, $79 per credit part-time.
FINANCIAL AID ***Required forms:*** institutional; accepted: CSS Financial Aid PROFILE. ***Application deadline:*** continuous.
APPLYING Open admission. ***Option:*** early entrance. ***Required:*** school transcript, CPT. Test scores used for admission and counseling/placement. ***Application deadline:*** 7/30.
APPLYING/TRANSFER ***Required:*** high school transcript, college transcript.
CONTACT Ms. Bernadette Montoya, Director of Student Services, New Mexico State University–Grants, Grants, NM 87020-2025, 505-287-7981. ***E-mail:*** dwytsalu@grants.nmsu.edu.

NORTHERN NEW MEXICO COMMUNITY COLLEGE
Española, New Mexico

CONTACT Mr. Michael Costello, Registrar, Northern New Mexico Community College, Española, NM 87532, 505-747-2115.

Peterson's Guide to Two-Year Colleges 1997 449

PARKS COLLEGE
Albuquerque, New Mexico

UG Enrollment: 289 | **Tuition: $7629/deg prog**
Application Deadline: N/R | **Room & Board: N/Avail**

GENERAL Proprietary, 2-year, coed. Awards diplomas, transfer associate, terminal associate degrees. Founded 1978. ***Setting:*** 1-acre urban campus. ***Total enrollment:*** 289. ***Faculty:*** 16 (12 full-time, 100% with terminal degrees, 4 part-time); student-faculty ratio is 15:1.
ENROLLMENT PROFILE 289 students: 70% women, 5% part-time, 50% state residents, 10% transferred in, 85% have need-based financial aid, 20% 25 or older, 5% Native American, 70% Hispanic, 5% African American, 1% Asian American. ***Areas of study chosen:*** 75% vocational and home economics, 7% business management and administrative services, 6% computer and information sciences. ***Most popular recent majors:*** accounting, business administration/commerce/management, secretarial studies/office management.
FIRST-YEAR CLASS 125 total; 175 applied, 95% were accepted, 75% of whom enrolled. 10% from top 10% of their high school class, 20% from top quarter, 40% from top half.
ACADEMIC PROGRAM Honor code. Calendar: quarters. 45 courses offered in 1995–96. Summer session for credit, part-time degree program (daytime, evenings).
GENERAL DEGREE REQUIREMENTS 95 credits; computer course.
MAJORS Accounting, business administration/commerce/management, computer management, secretarial studies/office management.
LIBRARY Parks College Library plus 1 other, with 5,000 books, 73 periodicals, 240 records, tapes, and CDs. Acquisition spending 1994–95: $17,832.
COMPUTERS ON CAMPUS 33 computers for student use in computer center, computer labs, library provide access to Internet. Staffed computer lab on campus provides training in use of computers, software.
COLLEGE LIFE Orientation program (2 days, no cost). ***Student services:*** personal-psychological counseling. ***Campus security:*** 24-hour emergency response devices.
HOUSING College housing not available.
CAREER PLANNING ***Placement office:*** 1 full-time staff. ***Director:*** Ms. Inez Madeline, Director, Placement Office, 505-843-7500. ***Services:*** resume preparation, career counseling, job bank, job interviews. Students must register freshman year.
AFTER GRADUATION 5% of students completing a degree program in 1994–95 went directly on to further study.
EXPENSES FOR 1995–96 ***Application fee:*** $100. Tuition per degree program ranges from $7629 to $13,100.
FINANCIAL AID ***College-administered undergrad aid 1995–96:*** need-based scholarships, low-interest long-term loans from external sources (average $2625), Federal Work-Study, part-time jobs. ***Required forms:*** institutional, FAFSA. ***Priority deadline:*** 9/30. ***Waivers:*** full or partial for employees or children of employees.
APPLYING Open admission. ***Options:*** deferred entrance, midyear entrance. ***Required:*** school transcript, Wonderlic aptitude test. Test scores used for admission. ***Notification:*** continuous.
APPLYING/TRANSFER ***Required:*** college transcript. ***Entrance:*** noncompetitive. ***Notification:*** continuous. ***Contact:*** Mr. Robert A. Paper, Vice President of Administration, 505-843-7500 Ext. 24.
CONTACT Mr. Don Gray, Admissions Director, Parks College, 1023 Tijeras, NW, Albuquerque, NM 87102-2975, 505-843-7500 Ext. 19. College video available.

PIMA MEDICAL INSTITUTE
Albuquerque, New Mexico

UG Enrollment: 125 | **Tuition & Fees: $4500**
Application Deadline: rolling | **Room & Board: N/Avail**

GENERAL Proprietary, 2-year, specialized, coed. Awards certificates, diplomas, transfer associate, terminal associate degrees. Founded 1972. ***Setting:*** urban campus. ***Total enrollment:*** 125. ***Faculty:*** 28.
ENROLLMENT PROFILE 125 students.
ACADEMIC PROGRAM Calendar: modular.
GENERAL DEGREE REQUIREMENTS 90 hours; math/science requirements vary according to program; computer course for most majors; internship.
MAJORS Medical assistant technologies, medical records services, medical secretarial studies, radiological technology.
EXPENSES FOR 1996–97 Tuition: $4500 (minimum) full-time. Full-time tuition ranges up to $4950 according to program.
FINANCIAL AID ***College-administered undergrad aid 1995–96:*** need-based scholarships, Federal Work-Study.
APPLYING ***Required:*** campus interview, Wonderlic aptitude test. ***Required for some:*** school transcript. ***Application deadline:*** rolling.
APPLYING/TRANSFER ***Required:*** standardized test scores, campus interview. ***Required for some:*** high school transcript, college transcript. ***Application deadline:*** rolling.
CONTACT Ms. Popie White, Admissions Representative, Pima Medical Institute, 2201 San Pedro NE, Bldg 3, Ste 100, Albuquerque, NM 87110, 505-881-1234.

SAN JUAN COLLEGE
Farmington, New Mexico

UG Enrollment: 4,500 | **Tuition & Fees (NM Res): $360**
Application Deadline: rolling | **Room & Board: N/Avail**

GENERAL County-supported, 2-year, coed. Part of New Mexico Commission on Higher Education. Awards certificates, transfer associate, terminal associate degrees. Founded 1958. ***Setting:*** 698-acre small-town campus. ***Total enrollment:*** 4,500. ***Faculty:*** 243 (64 full-time, 25% with terminal degrees, 179 part-time).
ENROLLMENT PROFILE 4,500 students from 5 states and territories, 4 other countries. 65% women, 68% part-time, 96% state residents, 4% transferred in, 61% 25 or older, 26% Native American, 10% Hispanic, 2% Asian American. ***Areas of study chosen:*** 26% business management and administrative services, 15% health professions and related sciences, 15% liberal arts/general studies, 12% computer and information sciences, 5% education, 4% social sciences, 2% biological and life sciences, 2% communications and journalism, 2% engineering and applied sciences, 2% English language/literature/letters, 1% fine arts, 1% performing arts, 1% premed.
FIRST-YEAR CLASS 1,679 total; 1,935 applied, 100% were accepted, 87% of whom enrolled.
ACADEMIC PROGRAM Core, honor code. Calendar: semesters. Academic remediation for entering students, English as a second language program offered during academic year and summer, services for LD students, advanced placement, summer session for credit, part-time degree program (daytime, evenings, summer), adult/continuing education programs, co-op programs.
GENERAL DEGREE REQUIREMENT 64 credits.
MAJORS Accounting, anthropology, art/fine arts, automotive technologies, aviation technology, biology/biological sciences, business administration/commerce/management, business education, carpentry, chemical engineering technology, chemistry, child care/child and family studies, civil engineering technology, communication, computer science, dance, data processing, drafting and design, drug and alcohol/substance abuse counseling, early childhood education, education, electrical and electronics technologies, electrical engineering technology, electromechanical technology, electronics engineering technology, elementary education, engineering (general), engineering technology, English, finance/banking, geology, history, industrial arts, instrumentation technology, journalism, law enforcement/police sciences, legal studies, liberal arts/general studies, literature, machine and tool technologies, mathematics, mechanical engineering technology, modern languages, music, nursing, paralegal studies, philosophy, physical education, physical therapy, physics, political science/government, psychology, public administration, real estate, secretarial studies/office management, sociology, speech/rhetoric/public address/debate, theater arts/drama, welding technology.
LIBRARY San Juan College Library with 40,000 books, 322 periodicals, 3,064 records, tapes, and CDs.
COMPUTERS ON CAMPUS Computer purchase plan available. 200 computers for student use in computer center, computer labs, writing lab. Staffed computer lab on campus provides training in use of computers, software.
COLLEGE LIFE Drama-theater group, choral group, student-run newspaper, radio station. 15% vote in student government elections. ***Social organizations:*** 2 national fraternities; 1% of eligible men are members. ***Student services:*** personal-psychological counseling. ***Campus security:*** 24-hour patrols, late-night transport-escort service.
HOUSING College housing not available.
ATHLETICS ***Intramural:*** archery, badminton, basketball, bowling, cross-country running, football, golf, racquetball, skiing (cross-country), skiing (downhill), soccer, table tennis (Ping-Pong), tennis, volleyball.
CAREER PLANNING ***Services:*** job fairs, resume preparation, career counseling, careers library.
EXPENSES FOR 1996–97 ***Application fee:*** $10. State resident tuition: $360 full-time, $15 per credit part-time. Nonresident tuition: $600 full-time, $25 per credit part-time.
FINANCIAL AID ***College-administered undergrad aid 1995–96:*** 260 need-based scholarships (average $550), 140 non-need scholarships (average $500), short-term loans (average $75), low-interest long-term loans from external sources (average $2200), Federal Work-Study, 30 part-time jobs. ***Required forms:*** CSS Financial Aid PROFILE; required for some: state, institutional; accepted: FAFSA. ***Priority deadline:*** 5/1. ***Payment plan:*** tuition prepayment. ***Waivers:*** full or partial for senior citizens.
APPLYING Open admission. ***Option:*** early entrance. ***Required:*** school transcript, TOEFL for international students. ***Recommended:*** 3 years of high school math and science, some high school foreign language. Test scores used for counseling/placement. ***Application deadline:*** rolling. ***Notification:*** continuous.
APPLYING/TRANSFER ***Required:*** high school transcript, college transcript. ***Recommended:*** 3 years of high school math and science, some high school foreign language. ***Entrance:*** noncompetitive. ***Application deadline:*** rolling. ***Notification:*** continuous.
CONTACT Mr. Gary Golden, Dean of Student Services, San Juan College, Farmington, NM 87402-4699, 505-599-0318. ***Fax:*** 505-599-0385. College video available.

SANTA FE COMMUNITY COLLEGE
Santa Fe, New Mexico

Enrollment: N/R | **Tuition & Fees (Area Res): $439**
Application Deadline: rolling | **Room & Board: N/Avail**

GENERAL State and locally supported, 2-year, coed. Part of New Mexico Commission on Higher Education. Awards certificates, transfer associate, terminal associate degrees. Founded 1983. ***Setting:*** suburban campus. ***Faculty:*** 275 (46 full-time, 229 part-time); student-faculty ratio is 12:1.
ENROLLMENT PROFILE 49% part-time, 78% state residents, 12% transferred in, 78% 25 or older, 3% Native American, 40% Hispanic, 1% African American, 1% Asian American. ***Areas of study chosen:*** 6% liberal arts/general studies, 5% business management and administrative services, 3% health professions and related sciences, 2% computer and information sciences, 1% biological and life sciences, 1% communications and journalism, 1% education, 1% engineering and applied sciences, 1% social sciences, 1% vocational and home economics.
FIRST-YEAR CLASS Of the students who applied, 100% were accepted.
ACADEMIC PROGRAM Core. Calendar: semesters. Academic remediation for entering students, English as a second language program offered during academic year, services for LD students, advanced placement, self-designed majors, honors program, summer session for credit, part-time degree program (daytime, evenings, summer), adult/continuing education programs, co-op programs and internships.
GENERAL DEGREE REQUIREMENTS 64 credits; 3 credits of math; 8 credits of lab science; computer course; internship (some majors).
MAJORS Accounting, American studies, biology/biological sciences, business administration/commerce/management, chemistry, communication, communication equipment technology, computer information systems, computer programming, computer science, construction technologies, corrections, criminal justice, culinary arts, drafting and design, early childhood education, electrical and electronics technologies, electronics engineering technology, (pre)engineering sequence, finance/banking, health science, hotel and restaurant management, liberal arts/general studies, nuclear technology, nursing, paralegal studies, real estate, science, secretarial studies/office management, surveying technology.

LIBRARY 36,000 books, 56 microform titles, 200 periodicals, 6 CD-ROMs, 3,000 records, tapes, and CDs.
COMPUTERS ON CAMPUS 300 computers for student use in computer center, Academic Center for Enrichment provide access to Internet. Staffed computer lab on campus provides training in use of computers, software.
COLLEGE LIFE Student-run radio station. ***Student services:*** personal-psychological counseling, women's center. ***Campus security:*** 24-hour patrols, late-night transport-escort service.
HOUSING College housing not available.
CAREER PLANNING ***Service:*** career counseling.
EXPENSES FOR 1996–97 Area resident tuition: $408 full-time, $17 per credit part-time. State resident tuition: $552 full-time, $23 per credit part-time. Nonresident tuition: $1080 full-time, $45 per credit part-time. Full-time mandatory fees: $31.
FINANCIAL AID ***College-administered undergrad aid 1995–96:*** 100 need-based scholarships (average $220), 75 non-need scholarships (average $220), low-interest long-term loans from external sources (average $1250), 40 Federal Work-Study, 40 part-time jobs. ***Acceptable forms:*** CSS Financial Aid PROFILE, FAFSA, AFSSA-CSX. ***Priority deadline:*** 3/1.
APPLYING Open admission except for nursing program. ***Options:*** early entrance, deferred entrance. ***Required:*** school transcript, TOEFL for international students. Test scores used for counseling/placement. ***Application deadline:*** rolling.
APPLYING/TRANSFER ***Entrance:*** noncompetitive. ***Application deadline:*** rolling.
CONTACT Mrs. Anna Tupler, Director of Recruitment, Santa Fe Community College, Santa Fe, NM 87502-4187, 505-438-1262.

SOUTHWESTERN INDIAN POLYTECHNIC INSTITUTE
Albuquerque, New Mexico

UG Enrollment: 638	**Tuition & Fees: $60**
Application Deadline: 8/15	**Room & Board: N/R**

GENERAL Federally supported, 2-year, coed. Awards transfer associate, terminal associate degrees. Founded 1971. ***Setting:*** 174-acre suburban campus. ***Research spending 1994–95:*** $72,958. ***Total enrollment:*** 638. ***Faculty:*** 36 (34 full-time, 2% with terminal degrees, 2 part-time); student-faculty ratio is 16:1.
ENROLLMENT PROFILE 638 students from 33 states and territories. 45% women, 70% have need-based financial aid, 35% 25 or older, 100% Native American. ***Areas of study chosen:*** 35% natural resource sciences, 25% computer and information sciences, 20% business management and administrative services, 13% engineering and applied sciences, 7% liberal arts/general studies. ***Most popular recent majors:*** optical technologies, data processing, natural resource management.
FIRST-YEAR CLASS 273 total. Of the students who applied, 100% were accepted, 75% of whom enrolled. 3% from top 10% of their high school class, 11% from top quarter, 32% from top half.
ACADEMIC PROGRAM Core. Calendar: trimesters. 188 courses offered in 1995–96. Academic remediation for entering students, services for LD students, advanced placement, summer session for credit, part-time degree program, co-op programs and internships.
GENERAL DEGREE REQUIREMENTS 59 credit hours; computer course for most majors; internship (some majors).
MAJORS Accounting, business administration/commerce/management, business education, civil engineering technology, computer science, culinary arts, data processing, drafting and design, electronics engineering technology, engineering technology, graphic arts, liberal arts/general studies, marketing/retailing/merchandising, natural resource management, optical technologies, secretarial studies/office management.
LIBRARY 26,000 books, 120 periodicals, 100 records, tapes, and CDs. Acquisition spending 1994–95: $17,774.
COMPUTERS ON CAMPUS 124 computers for student use in computer center, learning resource center, academic building, classrooms, library, dorms. Staffed computer lab on campus provides training in use of computers, software. Academic computing expenditure 1994–95: $344,294.
COLLEGE LIFE Student-run newspaper. ***Student services:*** health clinic, personal-psychological counseling. ***Campus security:*** 24-hour emergency response devices, late-night transport-escort service.
HOUSING 512 college housing spaces available; all were occupied 1995–96. No special consideration for freshman housing applicants. Off-campus living permitted. ***Option:*** single-sex (2 buildings) housing available. Resident assistants live in dorms.
ATHLETICS Member NJCAA. ***Intercollegiate:*** cross-country running M/W. ***Contact:*** Mr. Tony Schuerch, Acting Athletic Director, 505-897-5336.
CAREER PLANNING ***Placement office:*** 1 full-time, 2 part-time staff; $243,552 operating expenditure 1994–95. ***Director:*** Ms. J. Wardlow, Placement Officer, 505-897-5325. ***Services:*** job fairs, resume preparation, resume referral, career counseling, careers library, job bank, job interviews. 20 organizations recruited on campus 1994–95.
EXPENSES FOR 1996–97 Tuition: $0 full-time. Part-time mandatory fees: $20 per trimester. Full-time mandatory fees: $60.
FINANCIAL AID ***College-administered undergrad aid 1995–96:*** 19 need-based scholarships. ***Required forms:*** institutional, FAFSA; required for some: state; accepted: CSS Financial Aid PROFILE. ***Priority deadline:*** 11/22.
APPLYING Open admission. ***Option:*** Common Application. ***Required:*** TABE. Test scores used for counseling/placement. ***Application deadline:*** 8/15. ***Notification:*** continuous. Preference given to Native Americans.
APPLYING/TRANSFER ***Required:*** standardized test scores, college transcript. ***Contact:*** Mr. James Lujan, Dean of Instruction, 505-897-5330.
CONTACT Recruitment Officer, Southwestern Indian Polytechnic Institute, Albuquerque, NM 87184-0146, 505-897-5348 or toll-free 800-586-7474. College video available.

UNIVERSITY OF NEW MEXICO–GALLUP BRANCH
Gallup, New Mexico

UG Enrollment: 3,000	**Tuition & Fees (NM Res): $720**
Application Deadline: rolling	**Room & Board: N/Avail**

GENERAL State-supported, primarily 2-year, coed. Part of University of New Mexico. Awards certificates, diplomas, transfer associate, terminal associate, bachelor's degrees. Founded 1968. ***Setting:*** 80-acre small-town campus. ***Total enrollment:*** 3,000. ***Faculty:*** 159 (75 full-time, 25% with terminal degrees, 84 part-time).
ENROLLMENT PROFILE 3,000 students from 10 states and territories, 4 other countries. 60% women, 40% men, 66% part-time, 86% state residents, 5% transferred in, 50% 25 or older, 69% Native American, 11% Hispanic, 1% African American, 1% Asian American. ***Areas of study chosen:*** 19% biological and life sciences, 18% business management and administrative services, 17% liberal arts/general studies, 15% vocational and home economics, 12% health professions and related sciences, 9% computer and information sciences, 6% education, 4% social sciences. ***Most popular recent majors:*** business administration/commerce/management, construction technologies, nursing.
FIRST-YEAR CLASS 814 total. Of the students who applied, 100% were accepted.
ACADEMIC PROGRAM Core. Calendar: semesters. 500 courses offered in 1995–96; average class size 20 in required courses. Academic remediation for entering students, English as a second language program offered during academic year and summer, services for LD students, advanced placement, self-designed majors, honors program, summer session for credit, part-time degree program (daytime, evenings, weekends, summer), adult/continuing education programs, co-op programs and internships.
GENERAL DEGREE REQUIREMENTS 60 credit hours for associate, 136 credit hours for bachelor's; computer course for business majors; internship (some majors).
MAJORS Accounting, art/fine arts, automotive technologies, business administration/commerce/management, business machine technologies, communication, computer graphics, computer technologies, construction technologies, corrections, cosmetology, criminal justice, early childhood education, education, elementary education (B), finance/banking, health education, human services, law enforcement/police sciences, legal secretarial studies, liberal arts/general studies, medical laboratory technology, nursing (B), physical education, physical fitness/exercise science, public administration, science, secretarial studies/office management, studio art, welding technology.
LIBRARY Zollinger Library plus 1 other, with 36,172 books, 105 microform titles, 354 periodicals, 14 CD-ROMs, 526 records, tapes, and CDs. Acquisition spending 1994–95: $126,966.
COMPUTERS ON CAMPUS Computer purchase plan available. 300 computers for student use in computer labs, classrooms provide access to on-line services, Internet. Staffed computer lab on campus provides training in use of computers, software.
COLLEGE LIFE Student-run newspaper. 10% vote in student government elections. ***Campus security:*** late-night transport-escort service.
HOUSING College housing not available.
CAREER PLANNING ***Director:*** Mr. Rodney Cole, Chairperson, College Learning Center, 505-863-7647. ***Service:*** career counseling.
AFTER GRADUATION 10% of students completing transfer associate program in 1994–95 went directly to 4-year colleges.
ESTIMATED EXPENSES FOR 1996–97 ***Application fee:*** $15. State resident tuition: $720 full-time, $30 per credit hour part-time. Nonresident tuition: $1490 full-time. Nonresident part-time tuition per credit hour: $30 for the first 6 credit hours, $62 for the next 5 credit hours.
FINANCIAL AID ***College-administered undergrad aid 1995–96:*** 29 need-based scholarships (average $348), 15 non-need scholarships (average $348), short-term loans (average $150), low-interest long-term loans from external sources (average $2000), 46 Federal Work-Study, 20 part-time jobs. ***Required forms:*** CSS Financial Aid PROFILE, FAFSA; required for some: state. ***Priority deadline:*** 3/1. ***Waivers:*** full or partial for minority students, employees or children of employees, and senior citizens. ***Notification:*** 7/15.
APPLYING Open admission except for associate of arts programs. ***Options:*** early entrance, midyear entrance. ***Required:*** TOEFL for international students. ***Required for some:*** ACT. Test scores used for admission and counseling/placement. ***Application deadline:*** rolling. ***Notification:*** continuous.
APPLYING/TRANSFER ***Entrance:*** noncompetitive. ***Application deadline:*** rolling. ***Notification:*** continuous.
CONTACT Mr. Tom Ray, Associate Director of Student Services, University of New Mexico–Gallup Branch, 200 College Road, Gallup, NM 87301-5603, 505-863-7508. ***Fax:*** 505-863-7532.

UNIVERSITY OF NEW MEXICO–LOS ALAMOS BRANCH
Los Alamos, New Mexico

UG Enrollment: 1,023	**Tuition & Fees (NM Res): $840**
Application Deadline: 8/12	**Room & Board: N/Avail**

GENERAL State-supported, 2-year, coed. Part of University of New Mexico. Awards certificates, transfer associate, terminal associate degrees. Founded 1980. ***Setting:*** 5-acre small-town campus. ***Total enrollment:*** 1,023. ***Faculty:*** 96 (all part-time); student-faculty ratio is 15:1.
ENROLLMENT PROFILE 1,023 students from 12 states and territories, 3 other countries. 65% women, 85% part-time, 98% state residents, 15% transferred in, 1% international, 40% 25 or older, 3% Native American, 20% Hispanic. ***Areas of study chosen:*** 24% engineering and applied sciences, 22% liberal arts/general studies, 20% computer and information sciences, 12% business management and administrative services, 12% interdisciplinary studies, 8% physical sciences, 2% biological and life sciences.
FIRST-YEAR CLASS 110 total. Of the students who applied, 100% were accepted, 80% of whom enrolled. 10% from top 10% of their high school class, 40% from top quarter, 50% from top half.
ACADEMIC PROGRAM Core, interdisciplinary curriculum, honor code. Calendar: semesters. Academic remediation for entering students, English as a second language program offered during academic year and summer, services for LD students, advanced placement, tutorials, summer session for credit, part-time degree program (daytime, evenings, summer), adult/continuing education programs, co-op programs and internships. Off-campus study at University of New Mexico, Northern New Mexico Community College, Santa Fe Community College.
GENERAL DEGREE REQUIREMENTS 64 credits; math/science requirements vary according to program; 1 course in foreign language.
MAJORS Accounting, applied art, business administration/commerce/management, computer programming, computer science, computer technologies, electrical and electron-

New Mexico

University of New Mexico–Los Alamos Branch (continued)
ics technologies, engineering (general), (pre)engineering sequence, environmental sciences, liberal arts/general studies, science, secretarial studies/office management, studio art.
LIBRARY 10,000 books, 100 microform titles, 160 periodicals, 1 CD-ROM, 500 records, tapes, and CDs. Acquisition spending 1994–95: $19,555.
COMPUTERS ON CAMPUS Computer purchase plan available. 60 computers for student use in computer center, computer labs, various buildings provide access to e-mail, on-line services. Staffed computer lab on campus provides training in use of computers, software. Academic computing expenditure 1994–95: $55,703.
COLLEGE LIFE Orientation program (2 days, parents included). Choral group, student-run newspaper. *Social organizations:* 4 open to all.
HOUSING College housing not available.
CAREER PLANNING *Placement office:* 1 part-time staff; $1259 operating expenditure 1994–95. *Director:* Ms. Susie Elliott, Career Center Coordinator, 505-662-5919. *Services:* job fairs, resume preparation, resume referral, career counseling, careers library, job bank, job interviews.
EXPENSES FOR 1996–97 *Application fee:* $15. State resident tuition: $744 full-time, $31 per semester hour part-time. Nonresident tuition: $1920 full-time, $80 per semester hour part-time. Part-time mandatory fees per semester range from $1 to $44. Full-time mandatory fees: $96.
FINANCIAL AID *College-administered undergrad aid 1995–96:* 50 need-based scholarships (average $612), 30 non-need scholarships (average $612), low-interest long-term loans from external sources (average $2625), Federal Work-Study, 14 part-time jobs. *Required forms:* state, institutional, FAFSA; accepted: CSS Financial Aid PROFILE. *Priority deadline:* 3/1. *Waivers:* full or partial for employees or children of employees and senior citizens. *Notification:* 6/1. *Average indebtedness of graduates:* $5500.
APPLYING Open admission. *Options:* early entrance, deferred entrance. *Required:* TOEFL for international students. *Recommended:* 3 years of high school math and science, some high school foreign language. *Required for some:* SAT I or ACT. Test scores used for counseling/placement. *Application deadline:* 8/12. *Notification:* continuous.
APPLYING/TRANSFER *Recommended:* 3 years of high school math and science, some high school foreign language. *Required for some:* standardized test scores. *Entrance:* noncompetitive. *Application deadline:* 8/12. *Notification:* continuous.
Contact: Mr. Jim A. Mariner, Registrar, 505-662-5919 Ext. 703.
CONTACT Mr. Jim A. Mariner, Registrar, University of New Mexico–Los Alamos Branch, Los Alamos, NM 87544-2233, 505-662-5919.

UNIVERSITY OF NEW MEXICO– VALENCIA CAMPUS
Los Lunas, New Mexico

UG Enrollment: 1,440	Tuition & Fees (NM Res): $720
Application Deadline: rolling	Room & Board: N/Avail

GENERAL State-supported, 2-year, coed. Part of University of New Mexico. Awards certificates, transfer associate, terminal associate degrees. Founded 1981. *Setting:* small-town campus with easy access to Albuquerque. *Total enrollment:* 1,440. *Faculty:* 93 (19 full-time, 80% with terminal degrees, 74 part-time).
ENROLLMENT PROFILE 1,440 students from 4 states and territories, 2 other countries. 68% women, 59% part-time, 97% state residents, 5% transferred in, 76% 25 or older, 4% Native American, 49% Hispanic, 1% African American, 0% Asian American. *Most popular recent majors:* liberal arts/general studies, education, secretarial studies/office management.
FIRST-YEAR CLASS 300 total. Of the students who applied, 100% were accepted, 95% of whom enrolled.
ACADEMIC PROGRAM Core. Calendar: semesters. 500 courses offered in 1995–96. Academic remediation for entering students, English as a second language program offered during academic year and summer, services for LD students, honors program, summer session for credit, part-time degree program (daytime, evenings), adult/continuing education programs.
GENERAL DEGREE REQUIREMENT 60 credits.
MAJORS Agricultural sciences, business administration/commerce/management, computer information systems, computer science, construction management, construction technologies, criminal justice, education, (pre)engineering sequence, human services, liberal arts/general studies, real estate, secretarial studies/office management, word processing.
LIBRARY 9,500 books, 150 periodicals, 350 records, tapes, and CDs.
COMPUTERS ON CAMPUS 65 computers for student use in computer labs, tutorial center provide access to e-mail, on-line services. Staffed computer lab on campus provides training in use of computers, software.
COLLEGE LIFE *Major annual events:* Halloween Carnival, Cultural Festival. *Student services:* personal-psychological counseling. *Campus security:* late-night transport-escort service.
HOUSING College housing not available.
CAREER PLANNING *Placement office:* 2 full-time, 1 part-time staff. *Director:* Mrs. Donna Romero, Career Services Coordinator, 505-865-9667. *Services:* job fairs, resume preparation, career counseling, careers library, job bank.
AFTER GRADUATION 50% of students completing a degree program in 1994–95 went directly on to further study.
EXPENSES FOR 1996–97 *Application fee:* $15. State resident tuition: $720 full-time, $30 per credit hour part-time. Nonresident tuition: $1776 full-time, $74 per credit hour part-time.
FINANCIAL AID *College-administered undergrad aid 1995–96:* 470 need-based scholarships, non-need scholarships, Federal Work-Study. *Required forms:* CSS Financial Aid PROFILE, FAFSA; required for some: institutional. *Priority deadline:* 8/1. *Payment plans:* installment, deferred payment. *Waivers:* full or partial for employees or children of employees and senior citizens.
APPLYING Open admission. *Options:* early entrance, deferred entrance. *Required for some:* minimum 2.0 GPA, 3 years of high school math, 1 year of high school foreign language, SAT I or ACT. Test scores used for counseling/placement. *Application deadline:* rolling.
APPLYING/TRANSFER *Required for some:* standardized test scores, minimum 2.0 high school GPA. *Entrance:* noncompetitive. *Application deadline:* rolling.
CONTACT Ms. Phyllis A. Pepin, Associate Director, University of New Mexico–Valencia Campus, Los Lunas, NM 87031-7633, 505-865-9667. *Fax:* 505-865-3095.

NEW YORK

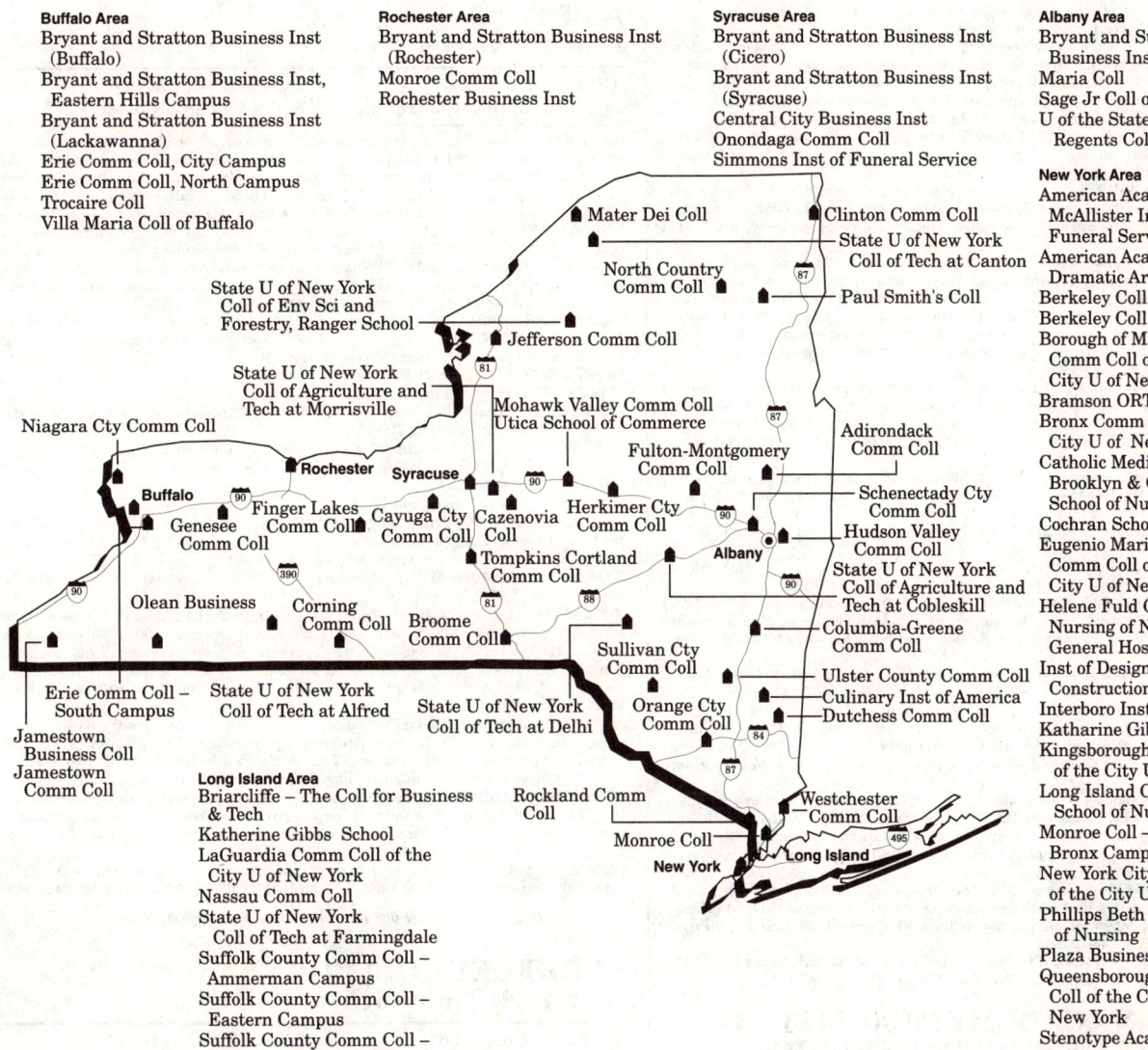

Buffalo Area
Bryant and Stratton Business Inst (Buffalo)
Bryant and Stratton Business Inst, Eastern Hills Campus
Bryant and Stratton Business Inst (Lackawanna)
Erie Comm Coll, City Campus
Erie Comm Coll, North Campus
Trocaire Coll
Villa Maria Coll of Buffalo

Rochester Area
Bryant and Stratton Business Inst (Rochester)
Monroe Comm Coll
Rochester Business Inst

Syracuse Area
Bryant and Stratton Business Inst (Cicero)
Bryant and Stratton Business Inst (Syracuse)
Central City Business Inst
Onondaga Comm Coll
Simmons Inst of Funeral Service

Albany Area
Bryant and Stratton Business Inst (Albany)
Maria Coll
Sage Jr Coll of Albany
U of the State of New York, Regents Coll

New York Area
American Academy McAllister Inst of Funeral Service
American Academy of Dramatic Arts
Berkeley Coll
Berkeley Coll (White Plains)
Borough of Manhattan Comm Coll of the City U of New York
Bramson ORT Tech Inst
Bronx Comm Coll of the City U of New York
Catholic Medical Ctr of Brooklyn & Queens School of Nursing
Cochran School of Nursing
Eugenio Maria de Hostos Comm Coll of the City U of New York
Helene Fuld Coll of Nursing of North General Hospital
Inst of Design and Construction
Interboro Institute
Katharine Gibbs School
Kingsborough Comm Coll of the City U of New York
Long Island Coll Hospital School of Nursing
Monroe Coll – Bronx Campus
New York City Tech Coll of the City U of New York
Phillips Beth Israel School of Nursing
Plaza Business Inst
Queensborough Comm Coll of the City U of New York
Stenotype Academy
Taylor Business Inst
Technical Career Inst
Westchester Business Inst
Wood Tobe – Coburn School

Long Island Area
Briarcliffe – The Coll for Business & Tech
Katherine Gibbs School
LaGuardia Comm Coll of the City U of New York
Nassau Comm Coll
State U of New York Coll of Tech at Farmingdale
Suffolk County Comm Coll – Ammerman Campus
Suffolk County Comm Coll – Eastern Campus
Suffolk County Comm Coll – Western Campus

ADIRONDACK COMMUNITY COLLEGE
Queensbury, New York

UG Enrollment: 3,602	**Tuition & Fees (NY Res):** $2200
Application Deadline: 8/15	**Room & Board:** N/Avail

Located in the Lake George–Saratoga Springs resort area. Most popular programs: accounting, business administration, criminal justice, data processing, drafting, engineering, liberal arts, nursing, secretarial studies, and tourism. Individualized scheduling, award-winning freshman experience program, dormitory-style housing adjacent to the campus, honors program, college survival program, writing center, math lab, academic computer center, extensive athletics and activities programs. Small classes, high-quality faculty, low cost, financial aid available.

GENERAL State and locally supported, 2-year, coed. Part of State University of New York System. Awards certificates, transfer associate, terminal associate degrees. Founded 1960. *Setting:* 141-acre small-town campus. *Endowment:* $670,000. *Total enrollment:* 3,602. *Faculty:* 233 (96 full-time, 25% with terminal degrees, 137 part-time); student-faculty ratio is 17:1.

ENROLLMENT PROFILE 3,602 students from 6 states and territories, 7 other countries. 63% women, 37% men, 53% part-time, 98% state residents, 6% transferred in, 49% have need-based financial aid, 2% have non-need-based financial aid, 1% international, 46% 25 or older, 1% Native American, 1% Hispanic, 1% African American, 1% Asian American. *Areas of study chosen:* 37% liberal arts/general studies, 22% business management and administrative services, 10% health professions and related sciences, 7% engineering and applied sciences, 7% mathematics, 6% social sciences, 4% biological and life sciences, 2% communications and journalism, 1% computer and information sciences, 1% vocational and home economics. *Most popular recent majors:* liberal arts/general studies, business administration/commerce/management, nursing.

FIRST-YEAR CLASS 934 total; 1,264 applied, 99% were accepted, 74% of whom enrolled. 7% from top 10% of their high school class, 23% from top quarter, 54% from top half. 1 valedictorian.

ACADEMIC PROGRAM Core, interdisciplinary curriculum, honor code. Calendar: semesters. 292 courses offered in 1995–96. Academic remediation for entering students, English as a second language program offered during academic year, services for LD

Peterson's Guide to Two-Year Colleges 1997

Adirondack Community College (continued)

students, advanced placement, tutorials, honors program, summer session for credit, part-time degree program (daytime, evenings), adult/continuing education programs, internships.
GENERAL DEGREE REQUIREMENTS 64 credit hours; 3 credit hours each of math and science; computer course for most majors.
MAJORS Accounting, broadcasting, business administration/commerce/management, communication, computer science, corrections, criminal justice, culinary arts, data processing, drafting and design, electrical engineering technology, engineering (general), engineering sciences, (pre)engineering sequence, environmental sciences, finance/banking, food services technology, forestry, forest technology, hospitality services, humanities, law enforcement/police sciences, liberal arts/general studies, marketing/retailing/merchandising, mathematics, mechanical design technology, medical records services, medical secretarial studies, nursing, photography, radio and television studies, science, secretarial studies/office management, social science, tourism and travel.
LIBRARY Adirondack Community College Library with 52,581 books, 177 microform titles, 376 periodicals, 4 on-line bibliographic services, 9 CD-ROMs, 1,466 records, tapes, and CDs. Acquisition spending 1994–95: $64,002.
COMPUTERS ON CAMPUS 125 computers for student use in computer labs, classrooms, library provide access to main academic computer. Staffed computer lab on campus provides training in use of computers, software. Academic computing expenditure 1994–95: $93,331.
COLLEGE LIFE Drama-theater group, choral group, student-run newspaper, radio station. 10% vote in student government elections. ***Social organizations:*** 25 open to all. ***Most popular organizations:*** New Horizons, Broadcasting Club, Humanities Club, College Activity Board, Sea and Ski Club. ***Major annual events:*** Hot Air Balloon Festival, Children's Holiday Party, Annual Beach Party. ***Student services:*** personal-psychological counseling. ***Campus security:*** patrols by trained security staff 8 a.m. to 10 p.m.
HOUSING College housing not available.
ATHLETICS Member NJCAA. ***Intercollegiate:*** baseball M(c), basketball M/W, bowling M/W, golf M, skiing (cross-country) M(c)/W(c), skiing (downhill) M(c)/W(c), soccer M/W, softball W, tennis M/W, volleyball W. ***Intramural:*** badminton, basketball, football, skiing (downhill), softball, tennis, volleyball, weight lifting. ***Contact:*** Mr. Robert Harris, Director of Athletics, 518-743-2269.
CAREER PLANNING ***Placement office:*** 2 full-time staff; $66,767 operating expenditure 1994–95. ***Director:*** Mr. Timothy Lahey, Director of Career Development and Placement, 518-743-2268. ***Services:*** job fairs, resume preparation, resume referral, career counseling, careers library, job bank, job interviews. 7 organizations recruited on campus 1994–95.
AFTER GRADUATION 42% of class of 1994 had job offers within 6 months. 80% of students completing a degree program went directly on to further study.
EXPENSES FOR 1995–96 ***Application fee:*** $30. State resident tuition: $2050 full-time, $73 per credit hour part-time. Nonresident tuition: $4100 full-time, $146 per credit hour part-time. Part-time mandatory fees: $3 per credit hour. Full-time mandatory fees: $150.
FINANCIAL AID ***College-administered undergrad aid 1995–96:*** 346 need-based scholarships (average $539), 71 non-need scholarships (average $576), short-term loans (average $200), low-interest long-term loans from external sources (average $2970), 61 Federal Work-Study (averaging $570), 92 part-time jobs. ***Required forms:*** state, institutional, FAFSA. ***Priority deadline:*** 6/15. ***Payment plan:*** installment. ***Waivers:*** full or partial for employees or children of employees and senior citizens. ***Notification:*** continuous.
APPLYING Open admission. ***Options:*** early entrance, deferred entrance, midyear entrance. ***Required:*** school transcript, TOEFL for international students. ***Recommended:*** SAT I or ACT. ***Required for some:*** 3 years of high school math and science. Test scores used for counseling/placement. ***Application deadline:*** 8/15. ***Notification:*** continuous until 9/1.
APPLYING/TRANSFER ***Required:*** high school transcript, college transcript. ***Required for some:*** 3 years of high school math and science. ***Entrance:*** noncompetitive. ***Application deadline:*** 8/15. ***Notification:*** continuous until 9/1. ***Contact:*** Dr. Frank Endieveri, Transfer Counselor, 518-743-2278.
CONTACT Mr. Levi H. Brown, Director of Admissions, Adirondack Community College, Queensbury, NY 12804, 518-743-2273. ***Fax:*** 518-745-1433.

AMERICAN ACADEMY MCALLISTER INSTITUTE OF FUNERAL SERVICE
New York, New York

UG Enrollment: 173	**Tuition & Fees: $5700**
Application Deadline: rolling	**Room & Board: N/Avail**

GENERAL Independent, 2-year, specialized, coed. Awards terminal associate degrees. Founded 1926. ***Setting:*** urban campus. ***Total enrollment:*** 173. ***Faculty:*** 15 (7 full-time, 8 part-time); student-faculty ratio is 13:1.
ENROLLMENT PROFILE 173 students from 9 states and territories, 2 other countries. 38% women, 62% men, 5% part-time, 80% state residents, 0% transferred in, 1% international, 97% 25 or older, 0% Native American, 3% Hispanic, 42% African American, 1% Asian American.
FIRST-YEAR CLASS 121 total; 198 applied, 72% of whom enrolled.
ACADEMIC PROGRAM Core, honor code. Calendar: semesters.
GENERAL DEGREE REQUIREMENT 74 credits.
MAJOR Funeral service.
LIBRARY American Academy MacAllister Institute Library with 2,075 books, 36 periodicals, 140 records, tapes, and CDs.
COMPUTERS ON CAMPUS 12 computers for student use in lab.
COLLEGE LIFE 95% vote in student government elections.
HOUSING College housing not available.
CAREER PLANNING ***Service:*** career counseling.
EXPENSES FOR 1996–97 ***Application fee:*** $25. Tuition: $5500 full-time, $166.67 per credit part-time. Full-time mandatory fees: $200.
FINANCIAL AID ***College-administered undergrad aid 1995–96:*** short-term loans (averaging $25), low-interest long-term loans from external sources (averaging $3500). ***Required forms:*** FAFSA; accepted: CSS Financial Aid PROFILE. ***Priority deadline:*** 7/15. ***Waivers:*** full or partial for employees or children of employees.
APPLYING Open admission. ***Required:*** school transcript, 2 recommendations. ***Application deadline:*** rolling.
APPLYING/TRANSFER ***Required:*** 2 recommendations, minimum 2.0 college GPA.
CONTACT Mr. Norman Provost, Registrar, American Academy McAllister Institute of Funeral Service, 450 West 56th Street, New York, NY 10019-3602, 212-757-1190. ***Fax:*** 212-765-5923.

AMERICAN ACADEMY OF DRAMATIC ARTS
New York, New York

UG Enrollment: 201	**Tuition & Fees: $9200**
Application Deadline: rolling	**Room & Board: N/Avail**

GENERAL Independent, 2-year, specialized, coed. Awards certificates, terminal associate degrees. Founded 1884. ***Setting:*** urban campus. ***Endowment:*** $1.5 million. ***Educational spending 1994–95:*** $2214 per undergrad. ***Total enrollment:*** 201. ***Faculty:*** 23 (10 full-time, 70% with terminal degrees, 13 part-time); student-faculty ratio is 9:1. ***Notable Alumni:*** Robert Redford, Danny DeVito, Anne Bancroft, Gena Rowlands, Jason Robards.
ENROLLMENT PROFILE 201 students from 30 states and territories, 9 other countries. 56% women, 44% men, 0% part-time, 15% state residents, 40% transferred in, 50% have need-based financial aid, 1% have non-need-based financial aid, 20% international, 26% 25 or older, 1% Native American, 6% Hispanic, 6% African American, 1% Asian American. ***Areas of study chosen:*** 100% performing arts.
FIRST-YEAR CLASS 138 total; 440 applied, 65% were accepted, 48% of whom enrolled.
ACADEMIC PROGRAM Core, professional actor training curriculum, honor code. Calendar: year-round. 21 courses offered in 1995–96.
GENERAL DEGREE REQUIREMENT 70 units.
MAJOR Theater arts/drama.
LIBRARY Academy/CBS Library with 7,100 books, 22 periodicals, 1,578 records, tapes, and CDs. Acquisition spending 1994–95: $4250.
COLLEGE LIFE ***Major annual events:*** Holiday Luncheon and Show, Graduation. ***Campus security:*** 24-hour emergency response devices and patrols, 8-hour patrols by trained security personnel.
HOUSING College housing not available.
CAREER PLANNING ***Placement office:*** 1 part-time staff; $5820 operating expenditure 1994–95. ***Director:*** Mr. Ernest A. Losso, Careers Consultant, 212-686-9244. ***Service:*** career counseling. 67 organizations recruited on campus 1994–95.
EXPENSES FOR 1996–97 ***Application fee:*** $35. Tuition: $9000 full-time. Full-time mandatory fees: $200.
FINANCIAL AID ***College-administered undergrad aid 1995–96:*** 117 need-based scholarships (average $1512), 3 non-need scholarships (average $500), short-term loans (average $250), low-interest long-term loans from external sources (average $6625), Federal Work-Study, 10 part-time jobs. ***Required forms:*** CSS Financial Aid PROFILE, state, institutional, FAFSA, financial aid transcript (for transfers). ***Priority deadline:*** 8/1. ***Payment plan:*** installment.
APPLYING ***Options:*** deferred entrance, midyear entrance. ***Required:*** 2 recommendations, interview, audition. ***Recommended:*** essay, minimum 2.0 GPA, SAT I or ACT. ***Required for some:*** school transcript. Test scores used for admission and counseling/placement. ***Application deadline:*** rolling. ***Notification:*** continuous.
APPLYING/TRANSFER ***Required:*** audition. ***Recommended:*** minimum 2.0 college GPA. ***Required for some:*** college transcript. ***Entrance:*** moderately difficult. ***Application deadline:*** rolling. ***Notification:*** continuous. ***Contact:*** Ms. Jeanne Gosselin, Director of Admissions, 212-686-9244.
CONTACT Ms. Jeanne Gosselin, Director of Admissions, American Academy of Dramatic Arts, 120 Madison Avenue, New York, NY 10016-7004, 212-686-9244. ***Fax:*** 212-545-7934.

❖ ***See page 688 for a narrative description.*** ❖

BERKELEY COLLEGE
New York, New York

UG Enrollment: 1,007	**Tuition & Fees: $10,750**
Application Deadline: rolling	**Room & Board: N/Avail**

GENERAL Proprietary, 2-year, coed. Awards certificates, transfer associate, terminal associate degrees. Founded 1945. ***Setting:*** urban campus. ***Total enrollment:*** 1,007. ***Faculty:*** 64 (12 full-time, 52 part-time).
ENROLLMENT PROFILE 1,007 students from 7 states and territories, 29 other countries. 77% women, 23% men, 18% part-time, 96% state residents, 10% transferred in, 5% 25 or older, 0% Native American, 37% Hispanic, 33% African American, 10% Asian American.
FIRST-YEAR CLASS 430 total; 1,200 applied, 46% were accepted, 78% of whom enrolled. 10% from top 10% of their high school class, 28% from top quarter, 60% from top half.
ACADEMIC PROGRAM Core, business curriculum, honor code. Calendar: quarters. 160 courses offered in 1995–96. Academic remediation for entering students, English as a second language program offered during academic year and summer, advanced placement, summer session for credit, part-time degree program (daytime, evenings, weekends), adult/continuing education programs, co-op programs and internships. Off-campus study at Berkeley College, White Plains, Berkeley College, West Paterson. Study abroad in England.
GENERAL DEGREE REQUIREMENTS 90 credits; computer course; internship (some majors).
MAJORS Accounting, business administration/commerce/management, fashion merchandising, health services administration, international business, marketing/retailing/merchandising, paralegal studies, retail management, secretarial studies/office management, tourism and travel, word processing.
LIBRARY 4,900 books, 70 periodicals, 352 records, tapes, and CDs.
COMPUTERS ON CAMPUS 120 computers for student use in computer labs, learning resource center, classrooms, library provide access to on-line services, Internet. Staffed computer lab on campus provides training in use of computers, software.
COLLEGE LIFE Drama-theater group. ***Social organizations:*** Berkeley Club; 33% of eligible men and 75% of eligible women are members. ***Most popular organizations:***

Student Government, International Club. ***Major annual events:*** International Day, Prom Fashion Show. ***Student services:*** personal-psychological counseling. ***Campus security:*** 24-hour emergency response devices.
HOUSING College housing not available.
CAREER PLANNING ***Placement office:*** 5 full-time staff. ***Director:*** Ms. Arlene Cohen, Vice President of Career Services, 212-986-3470. ***Services:*** resume preparation, resume referral, career counseling, job interviews.
EXPENSES FOR 1996–97 ***Application fee:*** $35. Tuition: $10,650 full-time. Part-time tuition and fees per credit: $210 for evening classes, $280 for day classes. Full-time mandatory fees: $100. Tuition guaranteed not to increase for student's term of enrollment.
FINANCIAL AID ***College-administered undergrad aid 1995–96:*** 10 need-based scholarships (average $1000), 12 non-need scholarships (average $4600), low-interest long-term loans from external sources (average $2625), 12 part-time jobs. ***Required forms:*** FAFSA, state income tax form; accepted: CSS Financial Aid PROFILE. ***Priority deadline:*** 9/15. ***Payment plan:*** installment. ***Waivers:*** full or partial for employees or children of employees.
APPLYING ***Options:*** deferred entrance, midyear entrance. ***Required:*** school transcript, campus interview, Berkeley Entrance Exam, TOEFL for international students. ***Application deadline:*** rolling.
APPLYING/TRANSFER ***Required:*** high school transcript, campus interview. ***Recommended:*** college transcript. ***Application deadline:*** rolling. ***Contact:*** Mr. Michael Perez, Director, Adult Admissions, 212-986-4343.
CONTACT Mr. Anthony Rolon, Director, High School Admissions, Berkeley College, 3 East 43rd Street, New York, NY 10017-4604, 212-986-4343 or toll-free 800-446-5400 (in-state). College video available.

❖ *See page 708 for a narrative description.* ❖

BERKELEY COLLEGE
White Plains, New York

UG Enrollment: 494	**Tuition & Fees: $10,750**
Application Deadline: rolling	**Room & Board: $4470**

GENERAL Proprietary, 2-year, coed. Awards certificates, transfer associate, terminal associate degrees. Founded 1945. ***Setting:*** 10-acre suburban campus with easy access to New York City. ***Total enrollment:*** 494. ***Faculty:*** 43 (14 full-time, 35% with terminal degrees, 29 part-time).
ENROLLMENT PROFILE 494 students from 6 states and territories, 11 other countries. 61% women, 90% state residents, 30% live on campus, 10% transferred in, 3% international, 4% 25 or older, 0% Native American, 18% Hispanic, 23% African American, 3% Asian American.
FIRST-YEAR CLASS 165 total; 334 applied, 94% were accepted, 53% of whom enrolled. 2% from top 10% of their high school class, 10% from top quarter, 40% from top half.
ACADEMIC PROGRAM Core, professional and business curriculum, honor code. Calendar: quarters. 160 courses offered in 1995–96. Academic remediation for entering students, English as a second language program offered during academic year and summer, services for LD students, advanced placement, tutorials, summer session for credit, part-time degree program (daytime, evenings, weekends, summer), adult/continuing education programs, co-op programs and internships. Off-campus study at Berkeley College, West Paterson, Berkeley College, New York. Study abroad in England (3% of students participate).
GENERAL DEGREE REQUIREMENTS 90 quarter credits; computer course; internship.
MAJORS Accounting, adult and continuing education, business administration/commerce/management, computer management, computer technologies, data processing, fashion merchandising, health services administration, hospitality services, hotel and restaurant management, international business, marketing/retailing/merchandising, medical records services, paralegal studies, retail management, secretarial studies/office management, tourism and travel, word processing.
LIBRARY 10,000 books, 125 periodicals, 500 records, tapes, and CDs.
COMPUTERS ON CAMPUS 104 computers for student use in computer center, learning resource center, classrooms, library, dorms provide access to e-mail, on-line services, Internet. Staffed computer lab on campus provides training in use of computers, software.
COLLEGE LIFE 50% vote in student government elections. ***Social organizations:*** 1 local fraternity, 1 local sorority; 5% of eligible men and 9% of eligible women are members. ***Most popular organizations:*** Student Government, International Club, Paralegal Club, DECA, Phi Theta Kappa. ***Major annual events:*** International Day, Fashion Show, National Business Education Month. ***Student services:*** personal-psychological counseling. ***Campus security:*** student patrols, night patrols by trained security personnel.
HOUSING College housing designed to accommodate 144 students; 150 undergraduates lived in college housing during 1995–96. Freshmen guaranteed college housing. Off-campus living permitted. ***Option:*** coed housing available. Resident assistants live in dorms.
CAREER PLANNING ***Placement office:*** 3 full-time staff. ***Director:*** Ms. Sandra Cohen, Director of Career Development, 914-694-1122. ***Services:*** job fairs, resume preparation, resume referral, career counseling, job bank, job interviews.
EXPENSES FOR 1996–97 ***Application fee:*** $35. Comprehensive fee of $15,220 includes full-time tuition ($10,650), mandatory fees ($100), and college room and board ($4470). Part-time tuition and fees per credit: $210 for evening classes, $280 for day classes. Tuition guaranteed not to increase for student's term of enrollment.
FINANCIAL AID ***College-administered undergrad aid 1995–96:*** 10 need-based scholarships (average $5400), 4 non-need scholarships (average $1400), low-interest long-term loans from external sources (average $2625), Federal Work-Study. ***Required forms:*** state, institutional, FAFSA; accepted: CSS Financial Aid PROFILE. ***Priority deadline:*** 9/15. ***Payment plan:*** installment. ***Waivers:*** full or partial for employees or children of employees. ***Notification:*** continuous.
APPLYING ***Options:*** deferred entrance, midyear entrance. ***Required:*** school transcript, interview, Berkeley Entrance Exam, TOEFL for international students. Test scores used for admission. ***Application deadline:*** rolling.
APPLYING/TRANSFER ***Required:*** high school transcript, interview, college transcript, Berkeley Entrance Exam. ***Entrance:*** minimally difficult. ***Application deadline:*** rolling. ***Contact:*** Mr. Sergio Messina, Director of Adult Admissions, 914-694-1122.
CONTACT Mr. Michael Talarico, Director of High School Admissions, Berkeley College, 100 West Prospect Street, Waldwick, NJ 07463, 914-694-1122. ***Fax:*** 800-446-5400.

❖ *See page 708 for a narrative description.* ❖

BOROUGH OF MANHATTAN COMMUNITY COLLEGE OF THE CITY UNIVERSITY OF NEW YORK
New York, New York

UG Enrollment: 16,334	**Tuition & Fees (NY Res): $2590**
Application Deadline: rolling	**Room & Board: N/Avail**

GENERAL State and locally supported, 2-year, coed. Part of City University of New York System. Awards transfer associate, terminal associate degrees. Founded 1963. ***Setting:*** urban campus. ***Endowment:*** $7000. ***Total enrollment:*** 16,334. ***Faculty:*** 1,204 (319 full-time, 80% with terminal degrees, 885 part-time).
ENROLLMENT PROFILE 16,334 students from 51 states and territories, 60 other countries. 62% women, 38% men, 53% part-time, 95% state residents, 11% transferred in, 47% 25 or older, 1% Native American, 26% Hispanic, 43% African American, 8% Asian American. ***Areas of study chosen:*** 29% liberal arts/general studies, 21% health professions and related sciences, 20% business management and administrative services, 10% computer and information sciences, 6% education, 3% engineering and applied sciences, 2% communications and journalism, 1% biological and life sciences, 1% physical sciences. ***Most popular recent majors:*** liberal arts/general studies, business administration/commerce/management, accounting.
FIRST-YEAR CLASS 3,009 total; 4,081 applied, 100% were accepted, 74% of whom enrolled. 2% from top 10% of their high school class, 10% from top quarter, 13% from top half.
ACADEMIC PROGRAM Core, honor code. Calendar: semesters. 681 courses offered in 1995–96. Academic remediation for entering students, English as a second language program offered during academic year and summer, services for LD students, advanced placement, honors program, summer session for credit, part-time degree program (daytime, evenings, weekends, summer), adult/continuing education programs, co-op programs and internships. Off-campus study at other units of the City University of New York System. Study abroad in Italy, Senegal (1% of students participate). ROTC: Army (c).
GENERAL DEGREE REQUIREMENTS Computer course for accounting, business administration/management, health, information technology, math, office automation, small business/entrepreneurship majors; internship (some majors).
MAJORS Accounting, business administration/commerce/management, child care/child and family studies, communication, community services, computer programming, dance, data processing, early childhood education, emergency medical technology, engineering sciences, finance/banking, health science, human services, liberal arts/general studies, marketing/retailing/merchandising, mathematics, music, nursing, physical education, public administration, real estate, recreation and leisure services, respiratory therapy, retail management, science, secretarial studies/office management, tourism and travel.
LIBRARY A. Philip Randolph Library with 77,848 books, 2,319 microform titles, 698 periodicals, 4 CD-ROMs, 847 records, tapes, and CDs. Acquisition spending 1994–95: $224,000.
COMPUTERS ON CAMPUS Computer purchase plan available. 650 computers for student use in computer center, computer labs, research center, learning resource center, classrooms, library provide access to main academic computer, off-campus computing facilities, e-mail, on-line services, Internet.
COLLEGE LIFE Orientation program (3 days, no cost, parents included). Drama-theater group, choral group, student-run newspaper. ***Social organizations:*** 50 open to all. ***Most popular organizations:*** Caribbean Students Association, Dominican Students Association, When One Voice is Not Enough (WOVINE), Students of Indian Descent Association, Asian Society. ***Major annual events:*** Club Fair, Women's History Month, Black History Month. ***Student services:*** health clinic, personal-psychological counseling, women's center. ***Campus security:*** 24-hour patrols.
HOUSING College housing not available.
ATHLETICS Member NJCAA. ***Intercollegiate:*** baseball M, basketball M/W, tennis M, volleyball W. ***Intramural:*** basketball, swimming and diving, table tennis (Ping-Pong), tennis, volleyball, weight lifting. ***Contact:*** Mr. Antonio Brimmer, Acting Athletic Director, 212-346-8266.
CAREER PLANNING ***Placement office:*** 10 full-time staff. ***Director:*** Mr. Brice Hargadon, Chairperson, Cooperative Education and Placement Department, 212-346-8360. ***Services:*** job fairs, resume preparation, career counseling.
AFTER GRADUATION 45% of students completing a degree program in 1994–95 went directly on to further study.
EXPENSES FOR 1995–96 State resident tuition: $2500 full-time, $105 per credit part-time. Nonresident tuition: $3076 full-time, $130 per credit part-time. Part-time mandatory fees: $24.85 per semester. Full-time mandatory fees: $90.
FINANCIAL AID ***College-administered undergrad aid 1995–96:*** 12 need-based scholarships (average $300), 7 non-need scholarships (average $1012), short-term loans (average $50), low-interest long-term loans from external sources (average $1000), Federal Work-Study, 450 part-time jobs. ***Required forms:*** FAFSA; required for some: state, institutional. ***Priority deadline:*** 7/1. ***Payment plan:*** installment. ***Waivers:*** full or partial for employees or children of employees and senior citizens.
APPLYING Open admission. ***Options:*** deferred entrance, midyear entrance. ***Required:*** TOEFL for international students. ***Recommended:*** 3 years of high school math and science, some high school foreign language. Test scores used for counseling/placement. ***Application deadline:*** rolling. ***Notification:*** continuous. Preference given to city residents.
APPLYING/TRANSFER ***Recommended:*** 3 years of high school math and science, some high school foreign language. ***Entrance:*** noncompetitive. ***Application deadline:*** rolling. ***Notification:*** continuous. ***Contact:*** Mr. Dwayne Wilson, Transfer Coordinator, 212-346-8896.
CONTACT Mr. Ramon P. Rivera, Director of Admissions, Borough of Manhattan Community College of the City University of New York, 199 Chambers Street, New York, NY 10007-1079, 212-346-8101. ***Fax:*** 212-346-8110. ***E-mail:*** bmadmrpr@cuny. College video available.

BRAMSON ORT TECHNICAL INSTITUTE
Forest Hills, New York

UG Enrollment: 1,200	**Tuition & Fees: $5820**
Application Deadline: rolling	**Room & Board: N/Avail**

Bramson ORT Technical Institute (continued)
GENERAL Independent, 2-year, coed. Awards certificates, terminal associate degrees. Founded 1977. ***Total enrollment:*** 1,200. ***Faculty:*** 57 (11 full-time, 46 part-time).
ENROLLMENT PROFILE 1,200 students from 3 states and territories, 5 other countries. 65% women, 10% part-time, 98% state residents, 5% transferred in, 1% international, 80% 25 or older, 0% Native American, 8% Hispanic, 2% African American.
FIRST-YEAR CLASS 500 total; 700 applied, 71% were accepted, 100% of whom enrolled. 1% from top 10% of their high school class, 5% from top quarter, 45% from top half.
ACADEMIC PROGRAM Calendar: semesters. Academic remediation for entering students, English as a second language program offered during academic year and summer, advanced placement, summer session for credit, part-time degree program (daytime, evenings), internships.
GENERAL DEGREE REQUIREMENTS 62 credits; math/science requirements vary according to program; computer course for most majors.
MAJORS Accounting, business administration/commerce/management, business education, business machine technologies, computer information systems, computer management, computer programming, computer science, computer technologies, electrical and electronics technologies, electromechanical technology, electronics engineering technology, legal secretarial studies, marketing/retailing/merchandising, secretarial studies/office management.
LIBRARY 8,000 books, 110 periodicals, 1,100 records, tapes, and CDs.
COMPUTERS ON CAMPUS 50 computers for student use in computer center.
COLLEGE LIFE Student-run newspaper. ***Student services:*** personal-psychological counseling, women's center.
HOUSING College housing not available.
CAREER PLANNING ***Service:*** career counseling.
EXPENSES FOR 1996–97 ***Application fee:*** $50. Tuition: $5520 full-time, $230 per credit part-time. Part-time mandatory fees: $150 per semester. Full-time mandatory fees: $300.
FINANCIAL AID ***College-administered undergrad aid 1995–96:*** 248 need-based scholarships (average $2100), low-interest long-term loans from external sources (average $2500), Federal Work-Study. ***Required forms:*** state, institutional, FAFSA; accepted: CSS Financial Aid PROFILE. ***Application deadline:*** continuous.
APPLYING Open admission. ***Options:*** early entrance, deferred entrance. ***Required:*** school transcript. ***Application deadline:*** rolling.
APPLYING/TRANSFER ***Required:*** high school transcript, college transcript. ***Entrance:*** noncompetitive. ***Application deadline:*** rolling.
CONTACT Admissions Office, Bramson ORT Technical Institute, Forest Hills, NY 11375-4239, 718-261-5800.

BRIARCLIFFE–THE COLLEGE FOR BUSINESS AND TECHNOLOGY
Woodbury, New York

UG Enrollment: 1,243	**Tuition & Fees: $7550**
Application Deadline: rolling	**Room & Board: N/Avail**

GENERAL Proprietary, 2-year, coed. Awards transfer associate, terminal associate degrees. Founded 1966. ***Setting:*** 5-acre suburban campus with easy access to New York City. ***Total enrollment:*** 1,243. ***Faculty:*** 101 (46 full-time, 8% with terminal degrees, 55 part-time); student-faculty ratio is 12:1.
ENROLLMENT PROFILE 1,243 students: 62% women, 38% men, 19% part-time, 100% state residents, 15% transferred in, 49% 25 or older, 9% Hispanic, 11% African American, 2% Asian American. ***Areas of study chosen:*** 65% business management and administrative services, 35% computer and information sciences. ***Most popular recent majors:*** paralegal studies, computer technologies, business administration/commerce/management.
FIRST-YEAR CLASS 382 total; 735 applied, 57% were accepted, 92% of whom enrolled. 15% from top 10% of their high school class, 30% from top quarter, 70% from top half.
ACADEMIC PROGRAM Career-focused curriculum, honor code. Calendar: semesters. 151 courses offered in 1995–96. Academic remediation for entering students, services for LD students, advanced placement, tutorials, summer session for credit, part-time degree program (daytime, evenings), adult/continuing education programs, internships.
GENERAL DEGREE REQUIREMENTS 60 credits; computer course for business administration majors.
MAJORS Business administration/commerce/management, computer information systems, computer technologies, electrical and electronics technologies, paralegal studies, secretarial studies/office management, telecommunications.
LIBRARY Briarcliffe Library with 11,834 books, 191 periodicals, 4 on-line bibliographic services, 20 CD-ROMs.
COMPUTERS ON CAMPUS 325 computers for student use in computer center, computer labs, classrooms, library. Staffed computer lab on campus provides training in use of computers, software.
NOTEWORTHY RESEARCH FACILITIES Center for Science and Technology.
COLLEGE LIFE Student-run newspaper. 33% vote in student government elections. ***Most popular organization:*** Student Government Association. ***Student services:*** personal-psychological counseling. ***Campus security:*** late-night transport-escort service.
HOUSING College housing not available.
ATHLETICS ***Intramural:*** basketball, volleyball.
CAREER PLANNING ***Placement office:*** 4 full-time, 1 part-time staff. ***Director:*** Ms. Marcy Hurowitz, Career Services Supervisor, 516-364-2055. ***Services:*** job fairs, resume preparation, resume referral, career counseling, careers library, job bank, job interviews. Students must register sophomore year. 62 organizations recruited on campus 1994–95.
AFTER GRADUATION 72% of class of 1994 had job offers within 6 months. 20% of students completing a degree program went directly on to further study.
EXPENSES FOR 1995–96 ***Application fee:*** $25. Tuition: $7200 full-time, $240 per credit part-time. Part-time mandatory fees per semester range from $17.50 to $175. Full-time mandatory fees: $350.
FINANCIAL AID ***College-administered undergrad aid 1995–96:*** 598 need-based scholarships (average $520), non-need scholarships, low-interest long-term loans from external sources (average $2625), 45 Federal Work-Study (averaging $1000). ***Required forms:*** institutional, FAFSA, state income tax form; accepted: CSS Financial Aid PROFILE, state. ***Priority deadline:*** 3/15. ***Payment plans:*** installment, deferred payment. ***Waivers:*** full or partial for employees or children of employees.
APPLYING ***Options:*** deferred entrance, midyear entrance. ***Required:*** school transcript, interview. Test scores used for counseling/placement. ***Application deadline:*** rolling. ***Notification:*** continuous.
APPLYING/TRANSFER ***Required:*** high school transcript, interview, college transcript. ***Entrance:*** minimally difficult. ***Application deadline:*** rolling. ***Notification:*** continuous. ***Contact:*** Ms. Roslyn Davis, Director of Transfer Evaluation, 516-364-2055.
CONTACT Ms. Gila Gevint, Associate Director of Admissions, Briarcliffe–The College for Business and Technology, Woodbury, NY 11797-2015, 516-364-2055. ***Fax:*** 516-931-9782.

BRONX COMMUNITY COLLEGE OF THE CITY UNIVERSITY OF NEW YORK
Bronx, New York

UG Enrollment: 8,450	**Tuition & Fees (NY Res): $3470**
Application Deadline: rolling	**Room & Board: N/Avail**

GENERAL State and locally supported, 2-year, coed. Part of City University of New York System. Awards certificates, transfer associate, terminal associate degrees. Founded 1959. ***Setting:*** 50-acre campus. ***Total enrollment:*** 8,450. ***Faculty:*** 390 (220 full-time, 170 part-time).
ENROLLMENT PROFILE 8,450 students: 66% women, 47% part-time, 99% state residents, 1% transferred in, 1% international, 1% Native American, 33% Hispanic, 53% African American.
FIRST-YEAR CLASS 1,605 total; 3,200 applied, 100% were accepted, 50% of whom enrolled.
ACADEMIC PROGRAM Calendar: semesters. Academic remediation for entering students, advanced placement, summer session for credit, part-time degree program (daytime, evenings, weekends, summer), adult/continuing education programs, co-op programs.
GENERAL DEGREE REQUIREMENT 64 credits.
MAJORS Accounting, art/fine arts, biology/biological sciences, black/African-American studies, business administration/commerce/management, business education, chemistry, child care/child and family studies, computer science, data processing, electrical engineering technology, (pre)engineering sequence, history, human services, international studies, liberal arts/general studies, marketing/retailing/merchandising, mathematics, medical laboratory technology, medical secretarial studies, music, nuclear medical technology, nursing, ornamental horticulture, paralegal studies, psychology, secretarial studies/office management.
LIBRARY 75,000 books, 800 periodicals.
COMPUTERS ON CAMPUS 300 computers for student use in computer labs, learning resource center, library provide access to main academic computer, off-campus computing facilities, on-line services.
COLLEGE LIFE Drama-theater group, student-run newspaper, radio station. ***Student services:*** personal-psychological counseling.
HOUSING College housing not available.
ATHLETICS Member NJCAA. ***Intercollegiate:*** basketball M/W, soccer M, tennis M/W, track and field M/W, volleyball W, wrestling M. ***Intramural:*** basketball, soccer, tennis, track and field, volleyball, wrestling.
CAREER PLANNING ***Service:*** career counseling.
EXPENSES FOR 1995–96 ***Application fee:*** $40. State resident tuition: $3360 full-time, $105 per credit part-time. Nonresident tuition: $4160 full-time, $130 per credit part-time. Part-time mandatory fees: $30 per semester. Full-time mandatory fees: $110.
FINANCIAL AID ***College-administered undergrad aid 1995–96:*** need-based scholarships, short-term loans, low-interest long-term loans from college funds, loans from external sources, Federal Work-Study, part-time jobs. ***Required forms:*** institutional. ***Application deadline:*** continuous.
APPLYING Open admission. ***Required:*** school transcript, TOEFL for international students. Test scores used for counseling/placement. ***Application deadline:*** rolling. ***Notification:*** continuous.
APPLYING/TRANSFER ***Required:*** high school transcript, college transcript. ***Application deadline:*** rolling. ***Notification:*** continuous.
CONTACT Ms. Alba Canceety, Admissions Officer, Bronx Community College of the City University of New York, Bronx, NY 10453, 718-289-5888.

BROOME COMMUNITY COLLEGE
Binghamton, New York

UG Enrollment: 5,986	**Tuition & Fees (NY Res): $2156**
Application Deadline: rolling	**Room & Board: N/Avail**

GENERAL State and locally supported, 2-year, coed. Part of State University of New York System. Awards certificates, transfer associate, terminal associate degrees. Founded 1946. ***Setting:*** 223-acre suburban campus. ***Educational spending 1994–95:*** $3005 per undergrad. ***Total enrollment:*** 5,986. ***Faculty:*** 379 (154 full-time, 17% with terminal degrees, 225 part-time); student-faculty ratio is 16:1. ***Notable Alumni:*** James Carrigg, president and chairman of the board at NYSEG; James McCoy, restauranteur; Robert Moppert, director at Department of Economic Development; Tom Libous, senator.
ENROLLMENT PROFILE 5,986 students from 8 states and territories, 34 other countries. 60% women, 41% part-time, 96% state residents, 5% transferred in, 2% international, 48% 25 or older, 0% Native American, 1% Hispanic, 3% African American, 2% Asian American. ***Areas of study chosen:*** 47% liberal arts/general studies, 12% business management and administrative services, 10% health professions and related sciences, 7% engineering and applied sciences, 3% computer and information sciences, 2% communications and journalism. ***Most popular recent majors:*** liberal arts/general studies, business administration/commerce/management.
FIRST-YEAR CLASS 1,408 total; 3,722 applied, 95% were accepted, 40% of whom enrolled. 3% from top 10% of their high school class, 29% from top quarter, 68% from top half.
ACADEMIC PROGRAM Core, honor code. Calendar: semesters. 851 courses offered in 1995–96. Academic remediation for entering students, English as a second language program offered during academic year, services for LD students, advanced placement, self-designed majors, summer session for credit, part-time degree program (daytime,

456

Peterson's Guide to Two-Year Colleges 1997

evenings, weekends, summer), external degree programs, adult/continuing education programs. Off-campus study at State University of New York at Binghamton, Keystone Junior College. Study abroad in England, Denmark, Egypt, Germany, Ghana, Switzerland, France, Ireland, Israel, Italy, Mexico, Spain.
GENERAL DEGREE REQUIREMENTS 62 credits; math/science requirements vary according to program.
MAJORS Accounting, business administration/commerce/management, chemical engineering technology, child care/child and family studies, civil engineering technology, computer science, criminal justice, data processing, dental services, electrical engineering technology, emergency medical technology, engineering sciences, fire science, hotel and restaurant management, information science, international business, liberal arts/general studies, marketing/retailing/merchandising, mechanical engineering technology, medical assistant technologies, medical laboratory technology, medical records services, nursing, occupational safety and health, paralegal studies, physical therapy, radiological technology, secretarial studies/office management, tourism and travel.
LIBRARY Cecil C. Tyrrell Learning ResourcesCenter with 65,056 books, 12,358 microform titles, 544 periodicals, 11 CD-ROMs, 1,291 records, tapes, and CDs.
COMPUTERS ON CAMPUS 400 computers for student use in computer center, computer labs, research center, learning resource center, business, applied technology buildings, classrooms, library, student center provide access to main academic computer, e-mail, on-line services, Internet. Staffed computer lab on campus provides training in use of computers, software.
COLLEGE LIFE Drama-theater group, student-run newspaper. ***Social organizations:*** 29 open to all. ***Most popular organizations:*** Broome Early Childhood Organization, Differentially Disabled Student Association, Ecology Club. ***Major annual events:*** Orientation, Convocation. ***Student services:*** health clinic, personal-psychological counseling. ***Campus security:*** 24-hour emergency response devices and patrols.
HOUSING College housing not available.
ATHLETICS Member NJCAA. ***Intercollegiate:*** baseball M/W, basketball M/W, cross-country running M/W, golf M, ice hockey M, soccer M, tennis M/W, volleyball W, wrestling M. ***Intramural:*** baseball, basketball, bowling, cross-country running, lacrosse, skiing (downhill), soccer, tennis, volleyball. ***Contact:*** Mr. Daniel Minch, Director of Athletics, 607-778-5003.
CAREER PLANNING ***Director:*** Mr. John Pagura, Head Career Counselor, 607-778-5210. ***Services:*** job fairs, resume preparation, career counseling, careers library.
AFTER GRADUATION 38% of students completing a degree program in 1994–95 went directly on to further study.
EXPENSES FOR 1995–96 ***Application fee:*** $10. State resident tuition: $2040 full-time, $85 per credit hour part-time. Nonresident tuition: $4080 full-time, $170 per credit hour part-time. Part-time mandatory fees: $5 per credit hour. Full-time mandatory fees: $116.
FINANCIAL AID ***College-administered undergrad aid 1995–96:*** 650 need-based scholarships (average $340), short-term loans (average $250), low-interest long-term loans from external sources (average $2000), Federal Work-Study, part-time jobs. ***Required forms:*** institutional; required for some: state; accepted: CSS Financial Aid PROFILE, FAFSA. ***Priority deadline:*** 4/1. ***Waivers:*** full or partial for senior citizens.
APPLYING Open admission except for allied health, engineering technology, computer science programs. ***Option:*** early entrance. ***Required for some:*** TOEFL for international students. Test scores used for admission. ***Application deadline:*** rolling. ***Notification:*** continuous. Preference given to county residents.
APPLYING/TRANSFER ***Application deadline:*** rolling. ***Notification:*** continuous.
CONTACT Mr. Anthony Fiorelli, Director of Admissions, Broome Community College, Binghamton, NY 13902-1017, 607-778-5001.

BRYANT AND STRATTON BUSINESS INSTITUTE
Albany, New York

UG Enrollment: 537	**Tuition & Fees: $6720**
Application Deadline: rolling	**Room & Board: N/Avail**

GENERAL Proprietary, 2-year, coed. Part of Bryant and Stratton Business Institute, Inc. Awards diplomas, transfer associate degrees. Founded 1857. ***Setting:*** suburban campus. ***Total enrollment:*** 537. ***Faculty:*** 48 (6 full-time, 2% with terminal degrees, 42 part-time); student-faculty ratio is 15:1. ***Notable Alumni:*** Barbara Thomas, Philip Parrish, Michael Cronin, Bridget O'Connor, Tamu Chambers.
ENROLLMENT PROFILE 537 students: 74% women, 26% men, 14% part-time, 100% state residents, 17% transferred in, 93% have need-based financial aid, 7% have non-need-based financial aid, 0% international, 49% 25 or older, 1% Native American, 2% Hispanic, 17% African American, 2% Asian American. ***Areas of study chosen:*** 23% computer and information sciences, 15% business management and administrative services, 13% health professions and related sciences. ***Most popular recent majors:*** computer information systems, business administration/commerce/management, accounting.
FIRST-YEAR CLASS 117 total; 179 applied, 98% were accepted, 67% of whom enrolled. 2% from top 10% of their high school class, 15% from top quarter, 52% from top half.
ACADEMIC PROGRAM Core, career-oriented curriculum, honor code. Calendar: quarters. 118 courses offered in 1995–96. Academic remediation for entering students, summer session for credit, part-time degree program (daytime, evenings), internships.
GENERAL DEGREE REQUIREMENTS 90 credit hours; 1 math course; computer course.
MAJORS Accounting, business administration/commerce/management, computer information systems, hotel and restaurant management, legal secretarial studies, marketing/retailing/merchandising, medical assistant technologies, medical secretarial studies, secretarial studies/office management, tourism and travel.
LIBRARY Resource Center with 2,237 books, 37 periodicals, 1 on-line bibliographic service, 20 CD-ROMs, 105 records, tapes, and CDs. Acquisition spending 1994–95: $15,000.
COMPUTERS ON CAMPUS 165 computers for student use in computer labs, learning resource center provide access to on-line services. Staffed computer lab on campus provides training in use of computers, software.
COLLEGE LIFE Student-run newspaper. 80% vote in student government elections. ***Student services:*** personal-psychological counseling. ***Campus security:*** 24-hour emergency response devices.
HOUSING College housing not available.
ATHLETICS ***Intramural:*** volleyball.
CAREER PLANNING ***Placement office:*** 2 full-time, 3 part-time staff; $64,000 operating expenditure 1994–95. ***Director:*** Mr. Bradford Peak, Director of Career Placement and Continuing Education, 518-437-1802. ***Services:*** job fairs, resume preparation, resume referral, career counseling, careers library, job bank, job interviews. Students must register sophomore year. 70 organizations recruited on campus 1994–95.
AFTER GRADUATION 90% of class of 1994 had job offers within 6 months.
EXPENSES FOR 1996–97 ***Application fee:*** $25. Tuition: $6720 full-time, $140 per credit hour part-time.
FINANCIAL AID ***College-administered undergrad aid 1995–96:*** 10 need-based scholarships (average $2200), 11 non-need scholarships (average $500), low-interest long-term loans from external sources (average $1500), Federal Work-Study, part-time jobs. ***Required forms:*** institutional, FAFSA; required for some: state; accepted: CSS Financial Aid PROFILE. ***Priority deadline:*** 10/1. ***Payment plan:*** installment. ***Waivers:*** full or partial for employees or children of employees.
APPLYING ***Option:*** deferred entrance. ***Required:*** school transcript, interview, TOEFL for international students, CPAt. ***Recommended:*** essay, SAT I or ACT. ***Required for some:*** recommendations. Test scores used for admission and counseling/placement. ***Application deadline:*** rolling.
APPLYING/TRANSFER ***Required:*** standardized test scores, interview, college transcript, minimum 2.0 college GPA. ***Recommended:*** essay. ***Required for some:*** high school transcript, recommendations. ***Entrance:*** minimally difficult. ***Application deadline:*** rolling. ***Contact:*** Ms. Sue Diehl-Peak, Academic Dean, 518-437-1802.
CONTACT Mr. Anthony Cascarano, Director of Admissions, Bryant and Stratton Business Institute, Albany, NY 12205-5230, 518-437-1802. ***Fax:*** 518-437-1048.

BRYANT AND STRATTON BUSINESS INSTITUTE
Buffalo, New York

UG Enrollment: 673	**Tuition & Fees: $6720**
Application Deadline: rolling	**Room & Board: N/Avail**

GENERAL Proprietary, 2-year, coed. Part of Bryant and Stratton Business Institute, Inc. Awards diplomas, transfer associate degrees. Founded 1854. ***Setting:*** 2-acre urban campus. ***Educational spending 1994–95:*** $1856 per undergrad. ***Total enrollment:*** 673. ***Faculty:*** 50 (18 full-time, 32 part-time); student-faculty ratio is 13:1.
ENROLLMENT PROFILE 673 students: 70% women, 30% men, 11% part-time, 99% state residents, 8% transferred in, 99% have need-based financial aid, 1% have non-need-based financial aid, 1% international, 44% 25 or older, 2% Native American, 5% Hispanic, 46% African American, 1% Asian American. ***Areas of study chosen:*** 53% business management and administrative services, 24% health professions and related sciences, 13% engineering and applied sciences, 10% computer and information sciences.
FIRST-YEAR CLASS 202 total. Of the students accepted, 85% enrolled. 0% from top 10% of their high school class, 10% from top quarter, 60% from top half.
ACADEMIC PROGRAM Honor code. Calendar: quarters. 110 courses offered in 1995–96. Academic remediation for entering students, summer session for credit, part-time degree program (daytime, evenings, summer), adult/continuing education programs, internships.
GENERAL DEGREE REQUIREMENTS 90 credit hours; 1 math course; computer course; internship (some majors).
MAJORS Accounting, business administration/commerce/management, computer programming, court reporting, electrical and electronics technologies, legal secretarial studies, marketing/retailing/merchandising, medical assistant technologies, medical secretarial studies, secretarial studies/office management, word processing.
LIBRARY Learning Center/Library with 2,290 books, 91 periodicals, 43 CD-ROMs, 450 records, tapes, and CDs. Acquisition spending 1994–95: $4900.
COMPUTERS ON CAMPUS Computer purchase plan available. 145 computers for student use in learning resource center, classrooms, library provide access to off-campus computing facilities, e-mail. Academic computing expenditure 1994–95: $81,000.
COLLEGE LIFE Student-run newspaper. ***Most popular organizations:*** Med Assisting Club, African-American Student Alliance, Secretarial Club, Accounting/Business Club, Student Council. ***Major annual events:*** Summer Carnival, Commencement.
HOUSING College housing not available.
CAREER PLANNING ***Placement office:*** 2 full-time, 1 part-time staff; $55,000 operating expenditure 1994–95. ***Director:*** Ms. Lisa August, Career Services Coordinator, 716-884-9120. ***Services:*** job fairs, resume preparation, resume referral, career counseling, careers library, job bank, job interviews. Students must register sophomore year.
EXPENSES FOR 1996–97 ***Application fee:*** $25. Tuition: $6720 full-time, $140 per credit hour part-time.
FINANCIAL AID ***College-administered undergrad aid 1995–96:*** 146 need-based scholarships (average $828), 25 non-need scholarships (average $1200), low-interest long-term loans from external sources (average $2000), Federal Work-Study. ***Required forms:*** FAFSA; required for some: state, institutional; accepted: CSS Financial Aid PROFILE. ***Priority deadline:*** 9/1. ***Payment plan:*** installment. ***Waivers:*** full or partial for employees or children of employees. ***Average indebtedness of graduates:*** $2000.
APPLYING ***Option:*** deferred entrance. ***Required:*** school transcript, interview, TOEFL for international students, TABE. ***Recommended:*** essay, minimum 2.0 GPA, SAT I or ACT. ***Required for some:*** recommendations. Test scores used for admission. ***Application deadline:*** rolling.
APPLYING/TRANSFER ***Required:*** standardized test scores, high school transcript, interview, college transcript, minimum 2.0 college GPA. ***Recommended:*** essay, minimum 2.0 high school GPA. ***Required for some:*** recommendations. ***Entrance:*** minimally difficult. ***Application deadline:*** rolling.
CONTACT Mr. Al Ciardi, Director of Admissions, Bryant and Stratton Business Institute, 1028 Main Street, Buffalo, NY 14202-1102, 716-884-9120 Ext. 640. College video available.

BRYANT AND STRATTON BUSINESS INSTITUTE
Cicero, New York

UG Enrollment: 678	**Tuition & Fees: $6720**
Application Deadline: rolling	**Room & Board: N/Avail**

Bryant and Stratton Business Institute (continued)

GENERAL Proprietary, 2-year, coed. Part of Bryant and Stratton Business Institute, Inc. Awards diplomas, transfer associate degrees. Founded 1983. ***Setting:*** 1-acre rural campus. ***Total enrollment:*** 678. ***Faculty:*** 47 (12 full-time, 35 part-time); student-faculty ratio is 16:1.

ENROLLMENT PROFILE 678 students: 67% women, 22% part-time, 99% state residents, 2% transferred in, 0% international, 40% 25 or older, 0% Native American, 1% Hispanic, 1% African American, 0% Asian American. ***Areas of study chosen:*** 70% business management and administrative services, 15% computer and information sciences, 15% engineering and applied sciences.

FIRST-YEAR CLASS 127 total; 273 applied, 96% were accepted, 48% of whom enrolled. 10% from top 10% of their high school class, 31% from top quarter, 59% from top half.

ACADEMIC PROGRAM Core, career-oriented curriculum, honor code. Calendar: quarters. 111 courses offered in 1995–96. Academic remediation for entering students, services for LD students, advanced placement, tutorials, summer session for credit, part-time degree program (daytime, evenings), adult/continuing education programs, internships.

GENERAL DEGREE REQUIREMENTS 90 credit hours; 1 math course; computer course; internship (some majors).

MAJORS Accounting, business administration/commerce/management, computer programming, electrical and electronics technologies, legal secretarial studies, paralegal studies, secretarial studies/office management, tourism and travel.

LIBRARY Resource Center plus 1 other, with 1,123 books, 30 periodicals, 2 CD-ROMs, 17 records, tapes, and CDs. Acquisition spending 1994–95: $27,563.

COMPUTERS ON CAMPUS 128 computers for student use in computer center, computer labs, learning resource center, classrooms, library provide access to main academic computer. Staffed computer lab on campus provides training in use of computers, software. Academic computing expenditure 1994–95: $90,000.

COLLEGE LIFE Student-run newspaper. ***Social organizations:*** 7 open to all. ***Most popular organizations:*** Institute of Managerial Accountants, Professional Secretaries International, Travel Club, Leadership Group, Computer Club. ***Major annual events:*** Job Fairs/Academic Day, Graduation Breakfast, Annual Picnic. ***Student services:*** personal-psychological counseling. ***Campus security:*** 24-hour emergency response devices.

HOUSING College housing not available.

CAREER PLANNING ***Placement office:*** 1 full-time, 1 part-time staff; $51,527 operating expenditure 1994–95. ***Director:*** Ms. Carol Hill, Career Services Director, 315-452-1105. ***Services:*** job fairs, resume preparation, resume referral, career counseling, careers library, job bank, job interviews. Students must register sophomore year. 80 organizations recruited on campus 1994–95.

AFTER GRADUATION 75% of class of 1994 had job offers within 6 months.

EXPENSES FOR 1996–97 ***Application fee:*** $25. Tuition: $6720 full-time, $140 per credit hour part-time.

FINANCIAL AID ***College-administered undergrad aid 1995–96:*** 71 need-based scholarships (average $900), 21 non-need scholarships (average $766), low-interest long-term loans from external sources (average $2050), Federal Work-Study, 10 part-time jobs. ***Required forms:*** FAFSA; required for some: state, institutional; accepted: CSS Financial Aid PROFILE. ***Priority deadline:*** 5/1. ***Payment plan:*** installment. ***Waivers:*** full or partial for employees or children of employees.

APPLYING ***Option:*** deferred entrance. ***Required:*** school transcript, interview, TOEFL for international students, CPAt. ***Recommended:*** essay, minimum 2.0 GPA, SAT I or ACT. ***Required for some:*** recommendations. Test scores used for admission. ***Application deadline:*** rolling. ***Notification:*** continuous.

APPLYING/TRANSFER ***Required:*** standardized test scores, high school transcript, interview, college transcript, minimum 2.0 college GPA. ***Recommended:*** essay, minimum 2.0 high school GPA. ***Required for some:*** recommendations. ***Entrance:*** minimally difficult. ***Application deadline:*** rolling. ***Notification:*** continuous.

CONTACT Mr. Michael Lynch, Director of Admissions, Bryant and Stratton Business Institute, Cicero, NY 13039-8698, 315-452-1105.

BRYANT AND STRATTON BUSINESS INSTITUTE
Lackawanna, New York

UG Enrollment: 427	**Tuition & Fees: $6720**
Application Deadline: rolling	**Room & Board: N/Avail**

GENERAL Proprietary, 2-year, coed. Part of Bryant and Stratton Business Institute, Inc. Awards diplomas, transfer associate degrees. Founded 1988. ***Setting:*** small-town campus with easy access to Buffalo. ***Total enrollment:*** 427. ***Faculty:*** 44 (7 full-time, 37 part-time).

ENROLLMENT PROFILE 427 students: 78% women, 23% part-time, 100% state residents, 10% transferred in, 0% international, 54% 25 or older, 2% Native American, 1% Hispanic, 1% African American, 1% Asian American. ***Most popular recent majors:*** secretarial studies/office management, accounting, medical secretarial studies.

FIRST-YEAR CLASS 127 total. Of the students who applied, 89% were accepted, 80% of whom enrolled. 5% from top 10% of their high school class, 25% from top quarter, 50% from top half.

ACADEMIC PROGRAM Core, honor code. Calendar: quarters. 500 courses offered in 1995–96. Academic remediation for entering students, advanced placement, summer session for credit, part-time degree program (daytime, evenings, summer), internships.

GENERAL DEGREE REQUIREMENTS 90 credit hours; 1 math course; computer course.

MAJORS Accounting, business administration/commerce/management, computer management, hotel and restaurant management, medical secretarial studies, secretarial studies/office management, tourism and travel.

LIBRARY 1,677 books, 40 periodicals, 8 CD-ROMs. Acquisition spending 1994–95: $1500.

COMPUTERS ON CAMPUS 102 computers for student use in computer center, computer labs, learning resource center provide access to Internet. Staffed computer lab on campus provides training in use of computers, software. Academic computing expenditure 1994–95: $100,000.

COLLEGE LIFE ***Social organizations:*** 5 open to all. ***Most popular organizations:*** Accounting/Business Club, Secretarial Club, Travel Club, Micro Club, Honor Society. ***Major annual events:*** Career Fest, Health Fair. ***Campus security:*** 24-hour emergency response devices.

HOUSING College housing not available.

CAREER PLANNING ***Placement office:*** 1 full-time staff; $32,000 operating expenditure 1994–95. ***Director:*** Mrs. Debbie Handzlik, Career Services Manager, 716-821-9331 Ext. 224. ***Services:*** job fairs, resume preparation, resume referral, career counseling, careers library, job bank, job interviews. Students must register sophomore year. 67 organizations recruited on campus 1994–95.

AFTER GRADUATION 86% of class of 1994 had job offers within 6 months.

EXPENSES FOR 1996–97 ***Application fee:*** $25. Tuition: $6720 full-time, $140 per credit hour part-time.

FINANCIAL AID ***College-administered undergrad aid 1995–96:*** 65 need-based scholarships (average $675), 30 non-need scholarships (average $1500), low-interest long-term loans from external sources (average $2625), 10 Federal Work-Study (averaging $1300), part-time jobs. ***Required forms:*** FAFSA; required for some: state; accepted: CSS Financial Aid PROFILE. ***Application deadline:*** continuous to 9/25. ***Payment plan:*** installment. ***Waivers:*** full or partial for employees or children of employees.

APPLYING ***Option:*** deferred entrance. ***Required:*** school transcript, interview, TOEFL for international students, CPAt. ***Recommended:*** essay, minimum 2.0 GPA, SAT I or ACT. ***Required for some:*** recommendations. Test scores used for admission and counseling/placement. ***Application deadline:*** rolling.

APPLYING/TRANSFER ***Required:*** standardized test scores, high school transcript, interview, college transcript, minimum 2.0 college GPA. ***Recommended:*** essay, minimum 2.0 high school GPA. ***Required for some:*** recommendations. ***Entrance:*** minimally difficult. ***Application deadline:*** rolling.

CONTACT Mr. Al Ciardi, Director of Admissions, Bryant and Stratton Business Institute, Lackawanna, NY 14218-1989, 716-821-9331 Ext. 203.

BRYANT AND STRATTON BUSINESS INSTITUTE
Rochester, New York

UG Enrollment: 314	**Tuition & Fees: $6720**
Application Deadline: rolling	**Room & Board: N/Avail**

GENERAL Proprietary, 2-year, coed. Part of Bryant and Stratton Business Institute, Inc. Awards diplomas, transfer associate degrees. Founded 1973. ***Setting:*** urban campus. ***Total enrollment:*** 314. ***Faculty:*** 38 (5 full-time, 33 part-time); student-faculty ratio is 12:1.

ENROLLMENT PROFILE 314 students from 4 states and territories, 2 other countries. 79% women, 21% men, 3% part-time, 98% state residents, 30% transferred in, 97% have need-based financial aid, 5% have non-need-based financial aid, 1% international, 30% 25 or older, 1% Native American, 10% Hispanic, 43% African American, 1% Asian American. ***Areas of study chosen:*** 98% business management and administrative services, 2% computer and information sciences.

FIRST-YEAR CLASS 114 total; 145 applied, 97% were accepted, 76% of whom enrolled. 10% from top 10% of their high school class, 25% from top quarter, 50% from top half.

ACADEMIC PROGRAM Career-oriented curriculum, honor code. Calendar: quarters. 488 courses offered in 1995–96. Academic remediation for entering students, services for LD students, summer session for credit, part-time degree program (daytime, evenings), adult/continuing education programs, internships.

GENERAL DEGREE REQUIREMENTS 90 credit hours; computer course; internship (some majors).

MAJORS Accounting, business administration/commerce/management, computer information systems, computer management, computer programming, consumer services, electrical and electronics technologies, hotel and restaurant management, legal secretarial studies, marketing/retailing/merchandising, medical assistant technologies, medical secretarial studies, secretarial studies/office management, word processing.

LIBRARY Rochester Campus Library with 250 books, 27 periodicals, 4 records, tapes, and CDs.

COMPUTERS ON CAMPUS 99 computers for student use in computer center, computer labs, research center, learning resource center, classrooms, library provide access to on-line services, Internet. Staffed computer lab on campus provides training in use of computers, software.

COLLEGE LIFE Student-run newspaper. ***Social organizations:*** 5 open to all. ***Major annual events:*** Holiday Party, Backyard Bar-B-Que. ***Student services:*** personal-psychological counseling. ***Campus security:*** 24-hour emergency response devices, late-night transport-escort service.

HOUSING College housing not available.

ATHLETICS ***Intramural:*** bowling, softball, volleyball.

CAREER PLANNING ***Placement office:*** 1 full-time staff. ***Director:*** Ms. Maria K. Pochalski, Director of Career Placement Services, 716-325-6010. ***Services:*** job fairs, resume preparation, resume referral, career counseling, careers library, job bank, job interviews. Students must register sophomore year. 232 organizations recruited on campus 1994–95.

AFTER GRADUATION 89% of class of 1994 had job offers within 6 months.

EXPENSES FOR 1996–97 ***Application fee:*** $25. Tuition: $6720 full-time, $140 per credit hour part-time.

FINANCIAL AID ***College-administered undergrad aid 1995–96:*** need-based scholarships, 22 non-need scholarships (averaging $2600), low-interest long-term loans from external sources (averaging $2500), Federal Work-Study. ***Required forms:*** state, FAFSA; accepted: CSS Financial Aid PROFILE. ***Priority deadline:*** 9/1.

APPLYING ***Options:*** deferred entrance, midyear entrance. ***Required:*** school transcript, interview, SAT I or ACT, TOEFL for international students, CPAt. ***Recommended:*** essay, minimum 2.0 GPA. ***Required for some:*** recommendations. Test scores used for admission. ***Application deadline:*** rolling.

APPLYING/TRANSFER ***Required:*** standardized test scores, high school transcript, interview, college transcript, minimum 2.0 college GPA. ***Recommended:*** essay, minimum 2.0 high school GPA. ***Required for some:*** recommendations. ***Entrance:*** minimally difficult. ***Application deadline:*** rolling. ***Contact:*** Mr. Jeff Tredo, Dean of Academic Affairs, 716-325-6010.

CONTACT Mr. William Bernys, Director of Admissions, Bryant and Stratton Business Institute, 82 St Paul Street, Rochester, NY 14604-1381, 716-325-6010.

BRYANT AND STRATTON BUSINESS INSTITUTE
Rochester, New York

UG Enrollment: 718	Tuition & Fees: $6720
Application Deadline: rolling	Room & Board: N/Avail

GENERAL Proprietary, 2-year, coed. Part of Bryant and Stratton Business Institute, Inc. Awards diplomas, transfer associate degrees. Founded 1985. *Setting:* 1-acre suburban campus. *Total enrollment:* 718. *Faculty:* 58 (15 full-time, 43 part-time).
ENROLLMENT PROFILE 718 students: 80% women, 20% men, 25% part-time, 100% state residents, 32% transferred in, 0% international, 68% 25 or older, 0% Native American, 2% Hispanic, 2% African American, 1% Asian American.
FIRST-YEAR CLASS 158 total. Of the students who applied, 80% were accepted, 80% of whom enrolled.
ACADEMIC PROGRAM Honor code. Calendar: quarters. Academic remediation for entering students, services for LD students, summer session for credit, part-time degree program (daytime, evenings), adult/continuing education programs, internships.
GENERAL DEGREE REQUIREMENTS 90 credit hours; 1 math course; computer course; internship (some majors).
MAJORS Accounting, business administration/commerce/management, commercial art, computer information systems, computer management, computer programming, electrical and electronics technologies, marketing/retailing/merchandising, medical assistant technologies, medical records services, medical secretarial studies, paralegal studies, secretarial studies/office management, tourism and travel, word processing.
LIBRARY Henrietta Campus Library with 1,600 books, 38 periodicals.
COMPUTERS ON CAMPUS 180 computers for student use in computer center, computer labs, research center, learning resource center, classrooms, library provide access to on-line services, Internet. Staffed computer lab on campus provides training in use of computers, software.
COLLEGE LIFE Student-run newspaper. *Social organizations:* 11 open to all. *Major annual events:* Student Christmas Party, Spring Fling, Student/Staff Halloween Contest. *Student services:* personal-psychological counseling. *Campus security:* late-night transport-escort service.
HOUSING College housing not available.
CAREER PLANNING *Placement office:* 4 full-time, 2 part-time staff. *Director:* Ms. Maria K. Pochalski, Director of Placement Services, 716-292-5627. *Services:* job fairs, resume preparation, resume referral, career counseling, careers library, job bank, job interviews. Students must register sophomore year. 232 organizations recruited on campus 1994–95.
AFTER GRADUATION 91% of class of 1994 had job offers within 6 months.
EXPENSES FOR 1996–97 *Application fee:* $25. Tuition: $6720 full-time, $140 per credit hour part-time.
FINANCIAL AID *College-administered undergrad aid 1995–96:* 205 need-based scholarships (average $675), 27 non-need scholarships (average $1677), low-interest long-term loans from college funds, loans from external sources (average $2625), Federal Work-Study, 6 part-time jobs. *Required forms:* state, FAFSA; accepted: CSS Financial Aid PROFILE. *Priority deadline:* 9/1. *Payment plan:* installment. *Waivers:* full or partial for employees or children of employees. *Notification:* continuous.
APPLYING *Options:* deferred entrance, midyear entrance. *Required:* school transcript, interview, TOEFL for international students, CPAt. *Recommended:* essay, minimum 2.0 GPA, SAT I or ACT. *Required for some:* recommendations. Test scores used for admission. *Application deadline:* rolling. *Notification:* continuous.
APPLYING/TRANSFER *Required:* standardized test scores, high school transcript, interview, college transcript, minimum 2.0 college GPA. *Recommended:* essay, minimum 2.0 high school GPA. *Required for some:* recommendations. *Entrance:* minimally difficult. *Application deadline:* rolling. *Notification:* continuous.
CONTACT Mr. James P. Paris, Director of Admissions, Bryant and Stratton Business Institute, Rochester, NY 14623-3136, 716-292-5627.

BRYANT AND STRATTON BUSINESS INSTITUTE
Syracuse, New York

UG Enrollment: 587	Tuition & Fees: $6720
Application Deadline: rolling	Room & Board: $3800

GENERAL Proprietary, 2-year, coed. Part of Bryant and Stratton Business Institute, Inc. Awards diplomas, transfer associate degrees. Founded 1854. *Setting:* urban campus. *Total enrollment:* 587. *Faculty:* 49 (12 full-time, 100% with terminal degrees, 37 part-time).
ENROLLMENT PROFILE 587 students: 80% women, 20% men, 13% part-time, 100% state residents, 7% live on campus, 8% transferred in, 8% international, 60% 25 or older, 3% Native American, 2% Hispanic, 18% African American, 1% Asian American.
FIRST-YEAR CLASS 182 total; 321 applied, 89% were accepted, 64% of whom enrolled. 2% from top 10% of their high school class, 8% from top quarter, 90% from top half.
ACADEMIC PROGRAM Core, honor code. Calendar: quarters. 640 courses offered in 1995–96; average class size 21 in required courses. Academic remediation for entering students, services for LD students, summer session for credit, part-time degree program (daytime, evenings), adult/continuing education programs, internships.
GENERAL DEGREE REQUIREMENTS 90 credits; 1 math course; computer course; internship (some majors).
MAJORS Accounting, business administration/commerce/management, computer programming, electrical and electronics technologies, hotel and restaurant management, legal secretarial studies, medical assistant technologies, medical secretarial studies, secretarial studies/office management, tourism and travel.
LIBRARY 631 books, 37 periodicals, 1 CD-ROM, 163 records, tapes, and CDs. Acquisition spending 1994–95: $15,000.
COMPUTERS ON CAMPUS 114 computers for student use in computer labs, learning resource center. Academic computing expenditure 1994–95: $115,000.
HOUSING 160 college housing spaces available; 60 were occupied 1995–96. Freshmen given priority for college housing. Off-campus living permitted. *Option:* coed housing available. Resident assistants live in dorms.
CAREER PLANNING *Placement office:* 1 full-time, 1 part-time staff; $45,000 operating expenditure 1994–95. *Director:* Mr. Philip Mazza, Career Services Director, 315-472-6603. *Services:* job fairs, resume referral, career counseling, careers library, job bank, job interviews. Students must register sophomore year. 45 organizations recruited on campus 1994–95.
AFTER GRADUATION 80% of class of 1994 had job offers within 6 months. 7% of students completing a degree program went directly on to further study.
EXPENSES FOR 1996–97 *Application fee:* $25. Comprehensive fee of $10,520 includes full-time tuition ($6720) and college room and board ($3800). College room only: $2400. Part-time tuition: $140 per credit.
FINANCIAL AID *College-administered undergrad aid 1995–96:* 117 need-based scholarships (average $705), 54 non-need scholarships (average $1887), 23 Federal Work-Study (averaging $634), 10 part-time jobs. *Required forms for some financial aid applicants:* institutional; accepted: CSS Financial Aid PROFILE, FAFSA. *Priority deadline:* 10/1. *Payment plan:* installment. *Waivers:* full or partial for employees or children of employees.
APPLYING *Options:* early entrance, deferred entrance. *Required:* school transcript, interview, TOEFL for international students, CPAt. *Recommended:* essay, minimum 2.0 GPA, SAT I or ACT. *Required for some:* recommendations. Test scores used for admission. *Application deadline:* rolling. *Notification:* continuous.
APPLYING/TRANSFER *Required:* standardized test scores, high school transcript, interview, college transcript, minimum 2.0 college GPA. *Recommended:* essay, minimum 2.0 high school GPA. *Required for some:* recommendations. *Application deadline:* rolling. *Notification:* continuous. *Contact:* Mr. Leonard Colella, Academic Dean, 315-472-6603.
CONTACT Ms. Susan Cumoletti, Director of Admissions, Bryant and Stratton Business Institute, 953 James Street, Syracuse, NY 13203-2502, 315-472-6603. College video available.

BRYANT AND STRATTON BUSINESS INSTITUTE, EASTERN HILLS CAMPUS
Clarence, New York

UG Enrollment: 550	Tuition & Fees: $6720
Application Deadline: rolling	Room & Board: N/Avail

GENERAL Proprietary, 2-year, coed. Part of Bryant and Stratton Business Institute, Inc. Awards diplomas, transfer associate degrees. Founded 1977. *Setting:* 12-acre suburban campus with easy access to Buffalo. *Total enrollment:* 550. *Faculty:* 51 (18 full-time, 33 part-time).
ENROLLMENT PROFILE 550 students: 55% women, 45% men, 11% part-time, 100% state residents, 30% transferred in, 0% international, 30% 25 or older, 0% Native American, 1% Hispanic, 1% African American, 1% Asian American.
FIRST-YEAR CLASS 180 total. Of the students who applied, 96% were accepted, 66% of whom enrolled. 14% from top 10% of their high school class, 42% from top quarter, 80% from top half.
ACADEMIC PROGRAM Core, honor code. Calendar: quarters. Academic remediation for entering students, summer session for credit, part-time degree program (daytime, evenings, weekends, summer), adult/continuing education programs, internships.
GENERAL DEGREE REQUIREMENTS 90 credit hours; 1 math course; computer course; internship (some majors).
MAJORS Accounting, business administration/commerce/management, commercial art, computer programming, data processing, fashion merchandising, interior design, legal secretarial studies, marketing/retailing/merchandising, medical assistant technologies, medical secretarial studies, paralegal studies, secretarial studies/office management, tourism and travel.
LIBRARY 1,500 books, 90 periodicals, 500 records, tapes, and CDs.
COMPUTERS ON CAMPUS 125 computers for student use in computer center, computer labs, labs, classrooms, library.
COLLEGE LIFE Student-run newspaper. *Social organizations:* 8 open to all.
HOUSING College housing not available.
ATHLETICS Intramural: volleyball.
CAREER PLANNING *Director:* Mrs. Wendy Rumrill, Career Services Manager, 716-631-0260. *Services:* resume referral, career counseling, careers library, job bank, job interviews. Students must register sophomore year.
AFTER GRADUATION 90% of class of 1994 had job offers within 6 months.
EXPENSES FOR 1996–97 *Application fee:* $25. Tuition: $6720 full-time, $140 per credit hour part-time.
FINANCIAL AID *College-administered undergrad aid 1995–96:* need-based scholarships, 12 non-need scholarships (averaging $4707), low-interest long-term loans from external sources (averaging $2000), Federal Work-Study, part-time jobs. *Required forms for some financial aid applicants:* FAFSA; accepted: CSS Financial Aid PROFILE, state. *Priority deadline:* 9/22. *Waivers:* full or partial for employees or children of employees.
APPLYING *Option:* deferred entrance. *Required:* school transcript, interview, TOEFL for international students. *Recommended:* essay, minimum 2.0 GPA, SAT I or ACT, CPAt. *Required for some:* recommendations, CPAt. Test scores used for admission. *Application deadline:* rolling.
APPLYING/TRANSFER *Required:* standardized test scores, high school transcript, interview, college transcript, minimum 2.0 college GPA. *Recommended:* essay, minimum 2.0 high school GPA. *Required for some:* recommendations. *Entrance:* moderately difficult. *Application deadline:* rolling.
CONTACT Ms. Lisa Kuloszewski, Director of Admissions, Bryant and Stratton Business Institute, Eastern Hills Campus, Williamsville, NY 14231, 716-631-0260.

CATHOLIC MEDICAL CENTER OF BROOKLYN AND QUEENS SCHOOL OF NURSING
Woodhaven, New York

UG Enrollment: 85 | **Tuition & Fees: $4680**
Application Deadline: 3/1 | **Room & Board: N/Avail**

GENERAL Independent, 2-year, specialized, coed. Awards terminal associate degrees. Founded 1969. ***Setting:*** 2-acre suburban campus. ***Total enrollment:*** 85. ***Faculty:*** 14 (9 full-time, 5 part-time); student-faculty ratio is 10:1.
ENROLLMENT PROFILE 85 students: 71% women, 29% men, 65% part-time, 100% state residents, 90% transferred in, 56% 25 or older, 0% Native American, 10% Hispanic, 21% African American, 8% Asian American. ***Areas of study chosen:*** 100% health professions and related sciences.
FIRST-YEAR CLASS 40 total; 306 applied, 18% were accepted, 74% of whom enrolled.
ACADEMIC PROGRAM Core, honor code. Calendar: semesters. Summer session for credit, part-time degree program (daytime).
GENERAL DEGREE REQUIREMENTS 34 credits; 1 course each in anatomy, physiology, microbiology and pharmacology; computer course.
MAJOR Nursing.
LIBRARY Crouse Library with 2,326 books, 42 periodicals, 324 records, tapes, and CDs.
COMPUTERS ON CAMPUS 6 computers for student use in library.
COLLEGE LIFE 100% vote in student government elections. ***Campus security:*** 24-hour patrols.
HOUSING College housing not available.
CAREER PLANNING ***Services:*** resume preparation, resume referral, career counseling.
EXPENSES FOR 1995–96 ***Application fee:*** $20. Tuition: $4480 full-time, $140 per credit part-time. Full-time mandatory fees: $200.
FINANCIAL AID ***College-administered undergrad aid 1995–96:*** 2 need-based scholarships (average $1500). ***Required forms:*** CSS Financial Aid PROFILE, state, FAFSA. ***Application deadline:*** continuous.
APPLYING ***Required:*** nursing exam. ***Recommended:*** 3 years of high school math and science. Test scores used for admission. ***Application deadline:*** 3/1.
APPLYING/TRANSFER ***Required:*** standardized test scores. ***Recommended:*** 3 years of high school math and science. ***Entrance:*** moderately difficult. ***Application deadline:*** 3/1. ***Contact:*** Ms. Mary E. Rohan, Director of Admissions, 718-805-5602.
CONTACT Ms. Mary E. Rohan, Director of Admissions, Catholic Medical Center of Brooklyn and Queens School of Nursing, Woodhaven, NY 11421-2698, 718-805-5602. ***Fax:*** 718-805-7094.

CAYUGA COUNTY COMMUNITY COLLEGE
Auburn, New York

UG Enrollment: 2,751 | **Tuition & Fees (NY Res): $2420**
Application Deadline: rolling | **Room & Board: N/Avail**

GENERAL State and locally supported, 2-year, coed. Part of State University of New York System. Awards certificates, transfer associate, terminal associate degrees. Founded 1953. ***Setting:*** 50-acre small-town campus with easy access to Syracuse and Rochester. ***Total enrollment:*** 2,751. ***Faculty:*** 171 (71 full-time, 7% with terminal degrees, 100 part-time). ***Notable Alumni:*** John Walsh, host of "America's Most Wanted"; William Komanecky, division chairman/professor at Cayuga Community College; Marilyn Higgins-Rhode, director of economic development at Niagara Mohawk Power Company; Kelly Connell, actor.
ENROLLMENT PROFILE 2,751 students: 53% women, 47% men, 51% part-time, 85% state residents, 8% transferred in, 1% Native American, 1% Hispanic, 2% African American, 1% Asian American. ***Areas of study chosen:*** 51% liberal arts/general studies, 23% business management and administrative services, 6% health professions and related sciences, 5% communications and journalism, 5% computer and information sciences, 5% education, 5% engineering and applied sciences.
FIRST-YEAR CLASS 1,924 total.
ACADEMIC PROGRAM Core, liberal arts curriculum, honor code. Calendar: semesters. 1,048 courses offered in 1995–96. Academic remediation for entering students, English as a second language program offered during academic year, services for LD students, advanced placement, tutorials, honors program, summer session for credit, part-time degree program (daytime, evenings, summer), adult/continuing education programs, internships. Study abroad in England, France, Italy (1% of students participate).
GENERAL DEGREE REQUIREMENTS 62 credits; 1 math/science course; computer course for liberal arts, business, engineering majors.
MAJORS Accounting, broadcasting, business administration/commerce/management, communication equipment technology, computer information systems, computer management, computer programming, computer science, corrections, criminal justice, data processing, drafting and design, early childhood education, electrical and electronics technologies, engineering and applied sciences, engineering sciences, humanities, information science, law enforcement/police sciences, liberal arts/general studies, marketing/retailing/merchandising, mathematics, mechanical design technology, nursing, radio and television studies, retail management, secretarial studies/office management, telecommunications.
LIBRARY Norman F. Bourke Memorial Library with 75,306 books, 1,720 microform titles, 511 periodicals, 4 on-line bibliographic services, 11 CD-ROMs, 6,203 records, tapes, and CDs. Acquisition spending 1994–95: $125,000.
COMPUTERS ON CAMPUS 150 computers for student use in computer center, learning resource center, library provide access to e-mail, on-line services, Internet. Staffed computer lab on campus provides training in use of computers, software.
COLLEGE LIFE Drama-theater group, choral group, student-run newspaper, radio station. 10% vote in student government elections. ***Social organizations:*** 5 open to all. ***Most popular organizations:*** Student Government Association, Student Activities Board, Radio and Television Guild, Tutor Club, Phi Beta Lambda. ***Major annual events:*** Folk Art Festival, Spring Fling, Transfer Day. ***Student services:*** health clinic, personal-psychological counseling. ***Campus security:*** security from 8 a.m. to 9 p.m.
HOUSING College housing not available.
ATHLETICS Member NJCAA. ***Intercollegiate:*** basketball M/W, cross-country running M/W, golf M/W, soccer M, softball W, tennis M/W, track and field M/W, volleyball W. ***Intramural:*** basketball, racquetball, volleyball. ***Contact:*** Mr. Ed Wagner, Director, 315-255-1743.
CAREER PLANNING ***Placement office:*** 6 full-time, 4 part-time staff. ***Director:*** Mr. John G. Battle, Director, Student Development Center, 315-255-1743. ***Services:*** resume preparation, career counseling, careers library.
AFTER GRADUATION 50% of class of 1994 had job offers within 6 months.
EXPENSES FOR 1995–96 State resident tuition: $2400 full-time, $82 per credit hour part-time. Nonresident tuition: $4800 full-time, $164 per credit hour part-time. Part-time mandatory fees: $10 per semester. Full-time mandatory fees: $20.
FINANCIAL AID ***College-administered undergrad aid 1995–96:*** need-based scholarships (average $400), non-need scholarships (average $705), short-term loans (average $125), low-interest long-term loans from external sources (average $2000), Federal Work-Study (averaging $1200), 126 part-time jobs. ***Required forms:*** FAFSA; required for some: state. ***Priority deadline:*** 5/15. ***Payment plan:*** installment. ***Waivers:*** full or partial for employees or children of employees. ***Notification:*** 6/1.
APPLYING Open admission. ***Options:*** early entrance, deferred entrance, midyear entrance. ***Required:*** school transcript, interview, TOEFL for international students. ***Recommended:*** SAT I or ACT. ***Required for some:*** 3 years of high school math and science. Test scores used for counseling/placement. ***Application deadline:*** rolling. ***Notification:*** continuous.
APPLYING/TRANSFER ***Required:*** high school transcript, interview, college transcript. ***Required for some:*** 3 years of high school math and science. ***Entrance:*** noncompetitive. ***Application deadline:*** rolling. ***Notification:*** continuous. ***Contact:*** Ms. Patricia A. Powers-Burdick, Director of Admissions, 315-255-1743 Ext. 241.
CONTACT Ms. Patricia A. Powers-Burdick, Director of Admissions, Cayuga County Community College, Auburn, NY 13021-3099, 315-255-1743 Ext. 241.

CAZENOVIA COLLEGE
Cazenovia, New York

UG Enrollment: 851 | **Tuition & Fees: $10,485**
Application Deadline: rolling | **Room & Board: $5100**

Cazenovia College offers bachelor's degrees as well as 24 career-oriented associate degrees. Discover why Money *magazine has consistently listed Cazenovia among its Best College Buys Now, and why* U.S. News & World Report *added Cazenovia to America's Best Colleges 1994. Students should contact the Help Desk for more information at 800-654-3210 Ext. 155. Students should also see the College's full description in* Peterson's Guide to Four-Year Colleges 1997.

GENERAL Independent, primarily 2-year, coed. Awards transfer associate, terminal associate, bachelor's degrees. Founded 1824. ***Setting:*** 40-acre small-town campus with easy access to Syracuse. ***Endowment:*** $33.1 million. ***Educational spending 1994–95:*** $4192 per undergrad. ***Total enrollment:*** 851. ***Faculty:*** 111 (46 full-time, 40% with terminal degrees, 65 part-time).
ENROLLMENT PROFILE 851 students from 13 states and territories, 1 other country. 63% women, 37% men, 3% part-time, 91% state residents, 86% live on campus, 5% transferred in, 87% have need-based financial aid, 13% have non-need-based financial aid, 1% international, 6% 25 or older, 1% Native American, 5% Hispanic, 15% African American, 1% Asian American. ***Areas of study chosen:*** 33% fine arts, 24% business management and administrative services, 24% liberal arts/general studies, 7% education, 4% interdisciplinary studies. ***Most popular recent majors:*** liberal arts/general studies, interior design.
FIRST-YEAR CLASS 299 total; 3,076 applied, 90% were accepted, 11% of whom enrolled. 2% from top 10% of their high school class, 9% from top quarter, 31% from top half.
ACADEMIC PROGRAM Core, competency-based career-oriented curriculum, honor code. Calendar: 12-12-6. 400 courses offered in 1995–96; average class size 20 in required courses. Academic remediation for entering students, services for LD students, advanced placement, self-designed majors, Freshman Honors College, tutorials, honors program, summer session for credit, part-time degree program (daytime, evenings), adult/continuing education programs, co-op programs and internships. Study abroad in England (1% of students participate). ROTC: Army (c), Air Force (c).
GENERAL DEGREE REQUIREMENTS 60 credits for associate, 126 credits for bachelor's; internship (some majors).
MAJORS Accounting, art/fine arts (B), business administration/commerce/management (B), child care/child and family studies, commercial art (B), community services, drafting and design (B), early childhood education, education, equestrian studies, farm and ranch management (B), fashion design and technology, graphic arts (B), human services, illustration (B), interior design (B), liberal arts/general studies, literature (B), retail management (B), science (B), social science (B), studio art.
LIBRARY Witheral Library with 60,576 books, 263 microform titles, 571 periodicals, 8 CD-ROMs, 2,326 records, tapes, and CDs. Acquisition spending 1994–95: $191,331.
COMPUTERS ON CAMPUS 70 computers for student use in computer center, learning resource center, learning center, library provide access to main academic computer. Staffed computer lab on campus provides training in use of computers, software. Academic computing expenditure 1994–95: $36,507.
COLLEGE LIFE Orientation program (3 days, $95, parents included). Drama-theater group, choral group, student-run newspaper, radio station. ***Social organizations:*** 22 open to all. ***Most popular organizations:*** Activities Board, Multicultural Student Group, Performing Arts, Student Radio Station, Yearbook. ***Major annual events:*** Spring Day, Parents' Weekend, Cultural Calendar Events. ***Student services:*** health clinic, personal-psychological counseling, women's center. ***Campus security:*** 24-hour emergency response devices and patrols, late-night transport-escort service, controlled dormitory access.
HOUSING 600 college housing spaces available; all were occupied 1995–96. Freshmen guaranteed college housing. On-campus residence required through sophomore year except if 20 or over or living with parents. ***Options:*** coed (6 buildings), single-sex (1 building) housing available. Resident assistants live in dorms.
ATHLETICS Member NCAA. ***Intercollegiate:*** baseball M, basketball M/W, equestrian sports M/W, golf M, soccer M/W, softball W, tennis M/W, volleyball W. ***Intramural:***

basketball, bowling, football, racquetball, soccer, swimming and diving, tennis, volleyball, weight lifting. ***Contact:*** Mr. Marvin Christopher, Athletic Director, 315-655-8005 Ext. 142.

CAREER PLANNING ***Placement office:*** 2 full-time staff; $48,345 operating expenditure 1994–95. ***Director:*** Ms. Patricia Durgin, Director of Career Services, 315-655-9446 Ext. 147. ***Services:*** job fairs, resume preparation, resume referral, career counseling, careers library, job bank, job interviews.

AFTER GRADUATION 30% of class of 1994 had job offers within 6 months. 70% of students completing transfer associate program went directly to 4-year colleges.

EXPENSES FOR 1995–96 ***Application fee:*** $25. Comprehensive fee of $15,585 includes full-time tuition ($9900), mandatory fees ($585), and college room and board ($5100). College room only: $2550. Part-time tuition: $264 per credit.

FINANCIAL AID ***College-administered undergrad aid 1995–96:*** 726 need-based scholarships (averaging $2691), 548 non-need scholarships (averaging $996), short-term loans (averaging $50), low-interest long-term loans from college funds (averaging $5035), loans from external sources (averaging $4019), 244 Federal Work-Study (averaging $896), 25 part-time jobs. ***Required forms:*** FAFSA; required for some: state; accepted: CSS Financial Aid PROFILE. ***Priority deadline:*** 3/15. ***Payment plan:*** installment. ***Waivers:*** full or partial for employees or children of employees.

APPLYING ***Options:*** early entrance, deferred entrance, midyear entrance. ***Required:*** school transcript, TOEFL for international students. ***Recommended:*** 3 years of high school math and science, SAT I or ACT, SAT II Subject Tests. Test scores used for counseling/placement. ***Application deadline:*** rolling. ***Notification:*** continuous.

APPLYING/TRANSFER ***Required:*** college transcript. ***Entrance:*** moderately difficult. ***Application deadline:*** rolling. ***Notification:*** continuous. ***Contact:*** Mr. Marc Schneeweiss, Assistant Director of Admissions, 315-655-8005 Ext. 269.

CONTACT Mr. Brian Mount, Director of Admissions and Financial Aid, Cazenovia College, Cazenovia, NY 13035, 315-655-8005 Ext. 158 or toll-free 800-654-3210 Ext. 155 (in-state). ***Fax:*** 315-655-2190. College video available.

❖ *See page 718 for a narrative description.* ❖

CENTRAL CITY BUSINESS INSTITUTE
Syracuse, New York

UG Enrollment: 326	**Tuition & Fees: $5420**
Application Deadline: 8/15	**Room & Board: N/Avail**

GENERAL Proprietary, 2-year, coed. Awards transfer associate, terminal associate degrees. Founded 1904. ***Setting:*** 1-acre urban campus. ***Total enrollment:*** 326. ***Faculty:*** 40 (10 full-time, 25% with terminal degrees, 30 part-time).

ENROLLMENT PROFILE 326 students from 5 states and territories, 1 other country. 83% women, 15% part-time, 98% state residents, 28% transferred in, 75% have need-based financial aid, 1% international, 25% 25 or older, 1% Native American, 2% Hispanic, 25% African American. ***Areas of study chosen:*** 50% business management and administrative services, 50% health professions and related sciences. ***Most popular recent majors:*** court reporting, secretarial studies/office management, business administration/commerce/management.

FIRST-YEAR CLASS 104 total. Of the students who applied, 90% were accepted, 88% of whom enrolled. 1% from top 10% of their high school class, 9% from top quarter, 90% from top half.

ACADEMIC PROGRAM Honor code. Calendar: semesters. 85 courses offered in 1995–96. Academic remediation for entering students, services for LD students, summer session for credit, part-time degree program (daytime, evenings), adult/continuing education programs, co-op programs and internships.

GENERAL DEGREE REQUIREMENTS 60 credit hours; computer course; internship (some majors).

MAJORS Accounting, business administration/commerce/management, court reporting, data processing, legal secretarial studies, legal studies, marketing/retailing/merchandising, medical assistant technologies, medical secretarial studies, retail management, secretarial studies/office management.

LIBRARY Victoria A. Nelli Library with 1,300 books, 100 periodicals, 250 records, tapes, and CDs.

COMPUTERS ON CAMPUS 100 computers for student use in computer center, computer labs, library. Staffed computer lab on campus provides training in use of computers, software.

COLLEGE LIFE Student-run newspaper. ***Social organizations:*** 10 open to all. ***Most popular organizations:*** Accounting Club, Secretarial Club, Medical Association. ***Major annual events:*** Semi-Formals, Holiday Parties. ***Student services:*** health clinic, personal-psychological counseling. ***Campus security:*** 24-hour patrols, late-night transport-escort service, voice activated car parking security system.

HOUSING College housing not available.

ATHLETICS ***Intramural:*** basketball, bowling, skiing (cross-country), volleyball.

CAREER PLANNING ***Placement office:*** 1 full-time staff. ***Director:*** Ms. Joan Yeomans, Director of Placement, 315-472-6233. ***Services:*** job fairs, resume preparation, resume referral, career counseling, careers library, job bank, job interviews. Students must register freshman year.

AFTER GRADUATION 12% of students completing a degree program in 1994–95 went directly on to further study.

EXPENSES FOR 1996–97 ***Application fee:*** $25. Tuition: $5200 full-time, $175 per credit hour part-time. Part-time mandatory fees per course: $35. Full-time mandatory fees: $220. Tuition guaranteed not to increase for student's term of enrollment.

FINANCIAL AID ***College-administered undergrad aid 1995–96:*** 200 need-based scholarships (averaging $600), 131 non-need scholarships (averaging $500), short-term loans (averaging $250), low-interest long-term loans from external sources (averaging $2000), Federal Work-Study, 20 part-time jobs. ***Required forms:*** CSS Financial Aid PROFILE, state, institutional, FAFSA. ***Priority deadline:*** 6/1. ***Payment plan:*** deferred payment. ***Waivers:*** full or partial for employees or children of employees.

APPLYING ***Options:*** early entrance, deferred entrance, midyear entrance. ***Required:*** school transcript, minimum 2.0 GPA, recommendations, interview, CPAt. ***Recommended:*** 3 years of high school math and science, some high school foreign language. Test scores used for admission. ***Application deadline:*** 8/15. ***Notification:*** continuous until 9/1.

APPLYING/TRANSFER ***Required:*** recommendations, interview, college transcript. ***Recommended:*** standardized test scores, high school transcript. ***Required for some:*** standardized test scores. ***Entrance:*** minimally difficult. ***Application deadline:*** 8/15. ***Notification:*** continuous until 9/1. ***Contact:*** Mr. Leonard Colella, Dean of Academic Affairs, 315-472-6233.

CONTACT Mr. Bob Flynn, Director of Admissions, Central City Business Institute, 224 Harrison Street, Syracuse, NY 13202-3052, 315-472-6233 or toll-free 800-945-CCBI.

CLINTON COMMUNITY COLLEGE
Plattsburgh, New York

UG Enrollment: 1,662	**Tuition & Fees (NY Res): $2185**
Application Deadline: 8/24	**Room & Board: N/Avail**

GENERAL State and locally supported, 2-year, coed. Part of State University of New York System. Awards certificates, transfer associate, terminal associate degrees. Founded 1969. ***Setting:*** 100-acre small-town campus. ***Total enrollment:*** 1,662. ***Faculty:*** 179 (43 full-time, 136 part-time); student-faculty ratio is 18:1. ***Notable Alumni:*** Bob Frenyea, Judy Jeffords, Kurt Tobrocke.

ENROLLMENT PROFILE 1,662 students from 10 states and territories, 2 other countries. 60% women, 40% men, 42% part-time, 78% state residents, 20% transferred in, 1% international, 40% 25 or older, 2% Native American, 2% Hispanic, 3% African American, 2% Asian American. ***Areas of study chosen:*** 49% liberal arts/general studies, 21% business management and administrative services, 8% health professions and related sciences, 3% education, 3% interdisciplinary studies. ***Most popular recent majors:*** liberal arts/general studies, business administration/commerce/management.

FIRST-YEAR CLASS 536 total; 864 applied, 85% of whom enrolled. 5% from top 10% of their high school class, 20% from top quarter, 75% from top half.

ACADEMIC PROGRAM Core, honor code. Calendar: semesters. 241 courses offered in 1995–96; average class size 18 in required courses. Academic remediation for entering students, English as a second language program offered during academic year, services for LD students, advanced placement, self-designed majors, summer session for credit, part-time degree program (daytime, evenings), adult/continuing education programs, co-op programs. Off-campus study at State University of New York College at Plattsburgh.

GENERAL DEGREE REQUIREMENTS 63 credits; math/science requirements vary according to program.

MAJORS Accounting, business administration/commerce/management, criminal justice, humanities, law enforcement/police sciences, liberal arts/general studies, medical laboratory technology, nursing, physical education, retail management, science, secretarial studies/office management, social science.

LIBRARY Clinton Community College Learning Resource Center with 50,000 books, 189 microform titles, 282 periodicals, 695 records, tapes, and CDs.

COMPUTERS ON CAMPUS Computer purchase plan available. 60 computers for student use in computer center, tutorial rooms, library. Staffed computer lab on campus provides training in use of computers, software.

COLLEGE LIFE Drama-theater group, choral group. ***Social organizations:*** 12 open to all; 1 local fraternity, 1 local sorority. ***Most popular organizations:*** Criminal Justice Club, Business Club, Tomorrow's New Teachers, Ski Club, Nursing Club. ***Major annual events:*** Fall Picnic, Christmas Buffet, Job Fair. ***Student services:*** health clinic, personal-psychological counseling. ***Campus security:*** 24-hour emergency response devices, security during class hours.

HOUSING College housing not available.

ATHLETICS Member NJCAA. ***Intercollegiate:*** baseball M, basketball M/W, soccer M/W, softball W. ***Intramural:*** bowling, football, golf, racquetball, skiing (cross-country), skiing (downhill), table tennis (Ping-Pong), tennis. ***Contact:*** Dr. Todd Roenbeck, Athletic Director, 518-562-4220.

CAREER PLANNING ***Placement office:*** 1 full-time, 1 part-time staff. ***Director:*** Ms. Tracey Cross-Baker, Director of Career Planning and Placement, 518-562-4103. ***Services:*** job fairs, resume preparation, resume referral, career counseling, careers library, job bank, job interviews.

EXPENSES FOR 1995–96 ***Application fee:*** $30. State resident tuition: $2075 full-time, $85 per credit part-time. Nonresident tuition: $4150 full-time, $170 per credit part-time. Full-time mandatory fees: $110.

FINANCIAL AID ***College-administered undergrad aid 1995–96:*** 75 need-based scholarships (average $300), 28 non-need scholarships (average $1000), low-interest long-term loans from external sources (average $2625), 38 Federal Work-Study (averaging $950), 20 part-time jobs. ***Required forms:*** state, FAFSA; required for some: institutional. ***Priority deadline:*** 6/1. ***Payment plan:*** deferred payment. ***Waivers:*** full or partial for employees or children of employees and senior citizens. ***Average indebtedness of graduates:*** $5250.

APPLYING Open admission except for nursing, medical laboratory technology, individual studies programs. ***Options:*** early entrance, deferred entrance, midyear entrance. ***Required:*** TOEFL for international students. Test scores used for counseling/placement. ***Application deadline:*** 8/24. ***Notification:*** continuous until 8/24. Preference given to county residents.

APPLYING/TRANSFER ***Application deadline:*** 8/24. ***Notification:*** continuous until 8/24. ***Contact:*** Mr. Robert Losser, Associate Dean, Enrollment Management, 518-562-4170.

CONTACT Mr. Bill Berman, Dean of Student Affairs, Clinton Community College, Plattsburgh, NY 12901-9573, 518-562-4120. College video available.

COCHRAN SCHOOL OF NURSING
Yonkers, New York

UG Enrollment: 142	**Tuition & Fees: $6000**
Application Deadline: rolling	**Room & Board: N/Avail**

GENERAL State-supported, 2-year, specialized, primarily women. Part of State University of New York System. Awards terminal associate degrees. Founded 1894. ***Setting:*** urban campus with easy access to New York City. ***Total enrollment:*** 142. ***Faculty:*** 23 (15 full-time, 8 part-time); student-faculty ratio is 8:1. ***Notable Alumni:*** Dr. Veronica O'Day, professor at Pace University; Cheryl Burke, director of nursing at Dobbs Ferry Hospital.

ENROLLMENT PROFILE 142 students: 90% women, 10% men, 100% state residents, 0% international, 68% 25 or older, 7% Hispanic, 20% African American, 6% Asian American. ***Areas of study chosen:*** 100% health professions and related sciences.

Cochran School of Nursing (continued)
FIRST-YEAR CLASS 64 total; 190 applied, 54% were accepted, 62% of whom enrolled. 10% from top 10% of their high school class, 30% from top quarter.
ACADEMIC PROGRAM Core, honor code. Calendar: semesters. Advanced placement, part-time degree program (daytime, evenings).
GENERAL DEGREE REQUIREMENT 74 credits.
MAJOR Nursing.
LIBRARY 3,037 books, 51 periodicals, 199 records, tapes, and CDs.
COMPUTERS ON CAMPUS 6 computers for student use in computer center.
COLLEGE LIFE 100% vote in student government elections. ***Student services:*** health clinic, personal-psychological counseling. ***Campus security:*** 24-hour emergency response devices and patrols, late-night transport-escort service.
HOUSING College housing not available.
CAREER PLANNING ***Service:*** career counseling.
ESTIMATED EXPENSES FOR 1996–97 Tuition: $6000 full-time. Part-time tuition per credit: $180 for nursing courses, $90 for academic courses.
FINANCIAL AID ***College-administered undergrad aid 1995–96:*** 12 need-based scholarships (averaging $500), non-need scholarships, low-interest long-term loans from external sources (averaging $2625), 8 part-time jobs. ***Required forms:*** CSS Financial Aid PROFILE, state, institutional, FAFSA. ***Application deadline:*** continuous.
APPLYING ***Option:*** deferred entrance. ***Required:*** SAT I. ***Recommended:*** 3 years of high school math and science. Test scores used for admission. ***Application deadline:*** rolling. ***Notification:*** continuous.
CONTACT Mrs. Carol Cataldi, Registrar, Cochran School of Nursing, 967 North Broadway, Yonkers, NY 10701, 914-964-4296.

COLUMBIA-GREENE COMMUNITY COLLEGE
Hudson, New York

UG Enrollment: 1,711	Tuition & Fees (NY Res): $2066
Application Deadline: rolling	Room & Board: N/Avail

GENERAL State and locally supported, 2-year, coed. Part of State University of New York System. Awards certificates, transfer associate, terminal associate degrees. Founded 1969. ***Setting:*** 143-acre rural campus. ***Total enrollment:*** 1,711. ***Faculty:*** 115 (48 full-time, 16% with terminal degrees, 67 part-time); student-faculty ratio is 15:1.
ENROLLMENT PROFILE 1,711 students from 4 states and territories, 12 other countries. 60% women, 48% part-time, 98% state residents, 20% transferred in, 80% have need-based financial aid, 2% have non-need-based financial aid, 1% international, 56% 25 or older, 1% Native American, 5% Hispanic, 12% African American, 1% Asian American. ***Areas of study chosen:*** 28% interdisciplinary studies, 25% health professions and related sciences, 20% social sciences, 10% business management and administrative services, 10% computer and information sciences, 2% fine arts. ***Most popular recent majors:*** nursing, criminal justice, interdisciplinary studies.
FIRST-YEAR CLASS 511 total; 920 applied, 83% of whom enrolled.
ACADEMIC PROGRAM Core, interdisciplinary curriculum. Calendar: semesters. 450 courses offered in 1995–96. Academic remediation for entering students, services for LD students, advanced placement, self-designed majors, tutorials, summer session for credit, part-time degree program (daytime, evenings, summer), adult/continuing education programs, internships.
GENERAL DEGREE REQUIREMENTS 62 credits; 1 course each in math and science; internship (some majors).
MAJORS Accounting, art/fine arts, automotive technologies, business administration/commerce/management, computer information systems, computer science, criminal justice, data processing, humanities, human services, insurance, interdisciplinary studies, liberal arts/general studies, mathematics, nursing, physical fitness/exercise science, real estate, science, secretarial studies/office management, social science.
LIBRARY 50,000 books, 640 periodicals, 100 CD-ROMs, 1,500 records, tapes, and CDs.
COMPUTERS ON CAMPUS 90 computers for student use in computer center, computer labs, learning resource center, library provide access to main academic computer, e-mail, on-line services. Staffed computer lab on campus provides training in use of computers, software.
COLLEGE LIFE Drama-theater group, choral group, student-run radio station. 50% vote in student government elections. ***Most popular organizations:*** Student Council/Government, Student Ambassadors, Nursing Club. ***Major annual event:*** Student Play Productions.
HOUSING College housing not available.
ATHLETICS Member NJCAA. ***Intercollegiate:*** baseball M, basketball M, bowling M/W, golf M, soccer W, softball W. ***Intramural:*** archery, badminton, baseball, basketball, bowling, fencing, soccer, table tennis (Ping-Pong), tennis, volleyball, weight lifting. ***Contact:*** Ms. Caroline Merritt, Athletic Director, 518-828-4181 Ext. 3211.
CAREER PLANNING ***Placement office:*** 1 full-time staff. ***Director:*** Mr. William Mathews, Counselor, 518-828-4181 Ext. 3396. ***Services:*** resume preparation, career counseling, careers library.
AFTER GRADUATION 75% of students completing a degree program in 1994–95 went directly on to further study.
EXPENSES FOR 1995–96 ***Application fee:*** $25. State resident tuition: $1940 full-time, $80 per credit part-time. Nonresident tuition: $3880 full-time, $160 per credit part-time. Part-time mandatory fees: $4 per credit. Full-time mandatory fees: $126.
FINANCIAL AID ***College-administered undergrad aid 1995–96:*** need-based scholarships, 43 non-need scholarships (average $500), Federal Work-Study, part-time jobs. ***Required forms:*** CSS Financial Aid PROFILE, institutional, FAFSA. ***Priority deadline:*** 5/1. ***Waivers:*** full or partial for employees or children of employees and senior citizens.
APPLYING Open admission except for nursing, automotive technology programs. ***Options:*** early entrance, deferred entrance, midyear entrance. ***Required:*** TOEFL for international students, College Qualifying Test. ***Recommended:*** SAT I or ACT. ***Required for some:*** 3 years of high school math and science. Test scores used for counseling/placement. ***Application deadline:*** rolling. ***Notification:*** continuous. Preference given to residents of sponsoring counties.
APPLYING/TRANSFER ***Entrance:*** minimally difficult. ***Application deadline:*** rolling. ***Notification:*** continuous.
CONTACT Mrs. Patricia Hallenbeck, Director of Admissions/Registrar, Columbia-Greene Community College, Hudson, NY 12534-0327, 518-828-4181 Ext. 5513. ***Fax:*** 518-828-8543. ***E-mail:*** hallenbeck@vaxa.cis.sunycgcc.edu.

CORNING COMMUNITY COLLEGE
Corning, New York

UG Enrollment: 3,295	Tuition & Fees (NY Res): $2466
Application Deadline: rolling	Room & Board: N/Avail

GENERAL State and locally supported, 2-year, coed. Part of State University of New York System. Awards certificates, transfer associate, terminal associate degrees. Founded 1956. ***Setting:*** 275-acre rural campus. ***Endowment:*** $884,575. ***Total enrollment:*** 3,295. ***Faculty:*** 176 (107 full-time, 95% with terminal degrees, 69 part-time); student-faculty ratio is 18:1. ***Notable Alumni:*** Lt. Col. Eileen M. Collins, astronaut; Dr. Alan Berry, genetic researcher; Steve Daley, journalist; Dr. Norman Walton, neurologist; Dr. Cassandra Runyon Coombs, astro-geologist.
ENROLLMENT PROFILE 3,295 students from 2 states and territories. 58% women, 42% men, 33% part-time, 96% state residents, 6% transferred in, 70% have need-based financial aid, 0% international, 40% 25 or older, 1% Native American, 1% Hispanic, 3% African American, 1% Asian American. ***Areas of study chosen:*** 29% health professions and related sciences, 18% business management and administrative services, 17% liberal arts/general studies, 14% social sciences, 7% computer and information sciences, 6% engineering and applied sciences, 5% mathematics, 1% vocational and home economics. ***Most popular recent majors:*** liberal arts/general studies, business administration/commerce/management, criminal justice.
FIRST-YEAR CLASS 956 total; 1,325 applied, 90% were accepted, 80% of whom enrolled. 2% from top 10% of their high school class, 15% from top quarter, 45% from top half.
ACADEMIC PROGRAM Honor code. Calendar: semesters. 918 courses offered in 1995–96. Academic remediation for entering students, services for LD students, advanced placement, self-designed majors, tutorials, honors program, summer session for credit, part-time degree program (daytime, evenings, summer), adult/continuing education programs, internships.
GENERAL DEGREE REQUIREMENTS 60 credits; 1 course each in math and science; computer course for most programs; internship (some majors).
MAJORS Accounting, automotive technologies, business administration/commerce/management, chemical engineering technology, child care/child and family studies, computer graphics, computer information systems, computer science, computer technologies, criminal justice, drafting and design, early childhood education, electrical and electronics technologies, emergency medical technology, (pre)engineering sequence, fire science, humanities, human services, industrial engineering technology, liberal arts/general studies, machine and tool technologies, mathematics, mechanical engineering technology, nursing, paralegal studies, science, secretarial studies/office management, social science, word processing.
LIBRARY Arthur A. Houghton, Jr. Library with 68,944 books, 23,500 microform titles, 900 periodicals, 6 on-line bibliographic services, 55 CD-ROMs, 2,697 records, tapes, and CDs. Acquisition spending 1994–95: $54,122.
COMPUTERS ON CAMPUS Computer purchase plan available. 350 computers for student use in computer labs, learning resource center, labs, classrooms, library provide access to main academic computer, off-campus computing facilities, e-mail, on-line services, Internet. Staffed computer lab on campus provides training in use of computers, software.
COLLEGE LIFE Drama-theater group, choral group, student-run newspaper, radio station. 10% vote in student government elections. ***Social organizations:*** 17 open to all. ***Most popular organizations:*** Student Government, WCEB, Two-Bit Players, Tech Guild, Nursing Society. ***Major annual events:*** Springfest, International Week, First Week Activities. ***Student services:*** legal services, health clinic, personal-psychological counseling. ***Campus security:*** late-night transport-escort service.
HOUSING College housing not available.
ATHLETICS Member NJCAA. ***Intercollegiate:*** baseball M, basketball M/W, lacrosse M, soccer M/W, softball W, volleyball W, wrestling M. ***Intramural:*** archery, badminton, basketball, bowling, cross-country running, golf, skiing (cross-country), soccer, swimming and diving, tennis, volleyball. ***Contact:*** Mr. Neil Bulkley, Director of Athletics, 607-962-9399.
CAREER PLANNING ***Placement office:*** 4 full-time staff. ***Director:*** Ms. Nancy L.E. Andrews, Director, Career Development, 607-962-9228. ***Services:*** job fairs, resume preparation, resume referral, career counseling, careers library, job interviews. 25 organizations recruited on campus 1994–95.
AFTER GRADUATION 54% of class of 1994 had job offers within 6 months. 66% of students completing a degree program went directly on to further study.
EXPENSES FOR 1995–96 ***Application fee:*** $25. State resident tuition: $2300 full-time, $96 per credit hour part-time. Nonresident tuition: $4600 full-time, $192 per credit hour part-time. Full-time mandatory fees: $166.
FINANCIAL AID ***College-administered undergrad aid 1995–96:*** 230 need-based scholarships (average $632), 20 non-need scholarships (average $500), low-interest long-term loans from external sources (average $2200), Federal Work-Study, 250 part-time jobs. ***Required forms:*** institutional, FAFSA. ***Priority deadline:*** 5/1. ***Waivers:*** full or partial for employees or children of employees.
APPLYING Open admission. ***Options:*** early entrance, midyear entrance. ***Required:*** TOEFL for international students. ***Required for some:*** 4 years of high school math and science. Test scores used for admission. ***Application deadline:*** rolling. ***Notification:*** continuous. Preference given to residents of sponsoring counties.
APPLYING/TRANSFER ***Required for some:*** standardized test scores, 4 years of high school math and science. ***Entrance:*** noncompetitive. ***Application deadline:*** rolling. ***Notification:*** continuous. ***Contact:*** Mr. David N. Biviano, Director of Admissions, 607-962-9220.
CONTACT Mr. David N. Biviano, Director of Admissions, Corning Community College, Corning, NY 14830-3297, 607-962-9221 Ext. 220 or toll-free 800-358-7171 (in-state). ***E-mail:*** admissions@sccvc.corning-cc.edu. College video available.

CULINARY INSTITUTE OF AMERICA
Hyde Park, New York

UG Enrollment: 2,000	Tuition & Fees: $13,140
Application Deadline: rolling	Room Only: $2800

GENERAL Independent, primarily 2-year, specialized, coed. Awards certificates, terminal associate, bachelor's degrees. Founded 1946. ***Setting:*** 150-acre small-town campus. ***Total enrollment:*** 2,000. ***Faculty:*** 124 (117 full-time, 7 part-time); student-faculty ratio is 18:1. ***Notable Alumni:*** John H. Bognette Jr., vice president and general manager of Hershey

462

Peterson's Guide to Two-Year Colleges 1997

Foods Corporation; Marcel DeSaulniers, executive chef and co-owner of Trellis Restaurant; John Doherty, executive chef for the Waldorf Astoria Hotel; Kenneth Gerver, corporate chef for SYSCO Foods.
ENROLLMENT PROFILE 2,000 students from 49 states and territories, 21 other countries. 22% women, 0% part-time, 1% transferred in, 85% have need-based financial aid, 2% international, 43% 25 or older, 1% Native American, 3% Hispanic, 3% African American, 3% Asian American.
FIRST-YEAR CLASS 1,905 applied, 95% were accepted, 71% of whom enrolled.
ACADEMIC PROGRAM Core. Calendar: semesters plus 18 or 21 week externship program. Academic remediation for entering students, services for LD students, adult/continuing education programs, co-op programs and internships. Off-campus study at the Associated Colleges of the Mid-Hudson Area.
GENERAL DEGREE REQUIREMENTS 72 credits for associate, 135 credits for bachelor's; 2 courses in math for bachelor's degree; 1 course in a foreign language for bachelor's degree; computer course; internship.
MAJOR Culinary arts (B).
LIBRARY Conrad N. Hilton Library with 45,000 books, 150 periodicals.
COMPUTERS ON CAMPUS Computer purchase plan available. 60 computers for student use in computer center, learning resource center, nutrition center. Staffed computer lab on campus provides training in use of computers, software.
COLLEGE LIFE Student-run newspaper. ***Student services:*** health clinic, personal-psychological counseling. ***Campus security:*** 24-hour emergency response devices and patrols, late-night transport-escort service, controlled dormitory access.
HOUSING 1,118 college housing spaces available; all were occupied 1995–96. Freshmen guaranteed college housing. Off-campus living permitted. ***Option:*** coed housing available. Resident assistants live in dorms.
ATHLETICS ***Intercollegiate:*** ice hockey M(c), soccer M(c). ***Intramural:*** basketball, bowling, softball, tennis, volleyball.
CAREER PLANNING ***Placement office:*** 7 full-time staff. ***Director:*** Mr. Raymond Wells, Director of Career Services, 914-452-9600. ***Services:*** job fairs, career counseling, careers library, job bank.
EXPENSES FOR 1996–97 ***Application fee:*** $30. Tuition: $12,390 full-time. Full-time mandatory fees: $750. College room only: $2800.
FINANCIAL AID ***College-administered undergrad aid 1995–96:*** 800 need-based scholarships (average $1500), 16 non-need scholarships (average $500), short-term loans (average $150), low-interest long-term loans from college funds (average $1000), loans from external sources (average $3000), Federal Work-Study, 552 part-time jobs. ***Required forms:*** institutional, FAFSA; required for some: state. ***Priority deadline:*** 7/1. ***Waivers:*** full or partial for minority students and employees or children of employees.
APPLYING ***Option:*** deferred entrance. ***Required:*** TOEFL for international students. ***Recommended:*** 3 years of high school math and science, some high school foreign language, SAT I or ACT. Test scores used for admission. ***Application deadline:*** rolling. ***Notification:*** continuous. Preference given to candidates with prior food service experience.
APPLYING/TRANSFER ***Recommended:*** standardized test scores, 3 years of high school math and science, some high school foreign language. ***Application deadline:*** rolling. ***Notification:*** continuous.
CONTACT Ms. Cathy Grande, Director of Admissions, Culinary Institute of America, Hyde Park, NY 12538-1499, 914-452-9600 Ext. 1327 or toll-free 800-CULINARY. ***Fax:*** 914-452-8629. College video available.

DUTCHESS COMMUNITY COLLEGE
Poughkeepsie, New York

UG Enrollment: 6,284	**Tuition & Fees (NY Res): $2095**
Application Deadline: rolling	**Room & Board: N/Avail**

GENERAL State and locally supported, 2-year, coed. Part of State University of New York System. Awards certificates, transfer associate, terminal associate degrees. Founded 1957. ***Setting:*** 130-acre suburban campus with easy access to New York City. ***Total enrollment:*** 6,284. ***Faculty:*** 420 (130 full-time, 15% with terminal degrees, 290 part-time); student-faculty ratio is 18:1.
ENROLLMENT PROFILE 6,284 students: 57% women, 43% men, 56% part-time, 99% state residents, 6% transferred in, 1% international, 48% 25 or older, 4% Hispanic, 9% African American, 2% Asian American. ***Areas of study chosen:*** 29% liberal arts/general studies, 23% business management and administrative services, 17% health professions and related sciences, 11% social sciences, 9% engineering and applied sciences, 5% computer and information sciences, 3% communications and journalism, 3% fine arts. ***Most popular recent majors:*** business administration/commerce/management, liberal arts/general studies, nursing.
FIRST-YEAR CLASS 1,161 total; 1,389 applied.
ACADEMIC PROGRAM Calendar: semesters. Academic remediation for entering students, English as a second language program offered during academic year, advanced placement, honors program, summer session for credit, part-time degree program (daytime, evenings, summer), adult/continuing education programs. Off-campus study at Marist College, Vassar College, State University of New York College at New Paltz, Culinary Institute of America, Bard College. Study-abroad program.
GENERAL DEGREE REQUIREMENTS 64 credits; math/science requirements vary according to program; computer course for accounting, business, architecture, engineering, medical laboratory technology majors.
MAJORS Accounting, architectural technologies, business administration/commerce/management, business machine technologies, child care/child and family studies, commercial art, communication, computer information systems, computer science, construction technologies, criminal justice, dietetics, early childhood education, electrical engineering technology, electromechanical technology, engineering sciences, food services management, humanities, liberal arts/general studies, mathematics, medical assistant technologies, medical laboratory technology, mental health/rehabilitation counseling, nursing, nutrition, recreation and leisure services, retail management, robotics, science, science education, secretarial studies/office management, social science.
LIBRARY Dutchess Library with 103,272 books, 988 microform titles, 540 periodicals, 3 on-line bibliographic services, 5 CD-ROMs, 3,394 records, tapes, and CDs.
COMPUTERS ON CAMPUS 50 computers for student use in computer center.
COLLEGE LIFE Drama-theater group, choral group, student-run newspaper, radio station. ***Major annual events:*** Fall Freshmen Day, Family Festival, Lyceum Series of Speakers. ***Student services:*** health clinic, personal-psychological counseling. ***Campus security:*** 24-hour emergency response devices and patrols, late-night transport-escort service.
HOUSING College housing not available.
ATHLETICS Member NJCAA. ***Intercollegiate:*** baseball M, basketball M/W, bowling M/W, golf M, soccer M/W, softball W, tennis M/W, volleyball W. ***Intramural:*** badminton, basketball, football, soccer, tennis, volleyball. ***Contact:*** Mr. Richard Skimin, Department Head-Health, Physical Education, and Athletics, 914-431-8460.
CAREER PLANNING ***Placement office:*** 5 full-time, 3 part-time staff. ***Director:*** Mrs. Carol Stevens, Assistant Dean of Student Personnel Services, 914-431-8040. ***Services:*** job fairs, resume preparation, resume referral, career counseling, careers library, job bank, job interviews.
AFTER GRADUATION 40% of students completing a degree program in 1994–95 went directly on to further study.
EXPENSES FOR 1995–96 State resident tuition: $2000 full-time, $78 per credit part-time. Nonresident tuition: $4000 full-time, $156 per credit part-time. Part-time mandatory fees: $11 per semester. Full-time mandatory fees: $95.
FINANCIAL AID ***College-administered undergrad aid 1995–96:*** 250 need-based scholarships (average $375), short-term loans (average $295), low-interest long-term loans from external sources (average $1300), Federal Work-Study, 210 part-time jobs. ***Required forms:*** CSS Financial Aid PROFILE, state, institutional. ***Priority deadline:*** 4/15. ***Payment plan:*** installment. ***Waivers:*** full or partial for employees or children of employees.
APPLYING Open admission for most programs. ***Options:*** early entrance, deferred entrance, midyear entrance. ***Recommended:*** SAT I or ACT, TOEFL for international students. Test scores used for counseling/placement. ***Application deadline:*** rolling. ***Notification:*** continuous. Preference given to county residents.
APPLYING/TRANSFER ***Entrance:*** noncompetitive. ***Application deadline:*** rolling. ***Notification:*** continuous. ***Contact:*** Mrs. Carol Stevens, Assistant Dean of Student Personnel Services, 914-431-8040.
CONTACT Ms. Rita Banner, Director of Admissions, Dutchess Community College, Poughkeepsie, NY 12601-1595, 914-431-8010 or toll-free 800-763-3933 (in-state). ***E-mail:*** banner@sunydutchess.edu.

ERIE COMMUNITY COLLEGE, CITY CAMPUS
Buffalo, New York

UG Enrollment: 3,112	**Tuition & Fees (Area Res): $2410**
Application Deadline: rolling	**Room & Board: N/Avail**

GENERAL State and locally supported, 2-year, coed. Part of State University of New York System. Awards certificates, diplomas, transfer associate, terminal associate degrees. Founded 1971. ***Setting:*** 1-acre urban campus. ***Total enrollment:*** 3,112. ***Faculty:*** 258 (115 full-time, 143 part-time); student-faculty ratio is 15:1.
ENROLLMENT PROFILE 3,112 students from 5 states and territories. 65% women, 33% part-time, 98% state residents, 4% transferred in, 0% international, 49% 25 or older, 1% Native American, 8% Hispanic, 27% African American, 1% Asian American. ***Areas of study chosen:*** 36% interdisciplinary studies, 28% business management and administrative services, 15% health professions and related sciences, 5% social sciences, 5% vocational and home economics, 3% computer and information sciences, 3% engineering and applied sciences. ***Most popular recent majors:*** business administration/commerce/management, child care/child and family studies.
FIRST-YEAR CLASS 609 total.
ACADEMIC PROGRAM Core, honor code. Calendar: semesters. Academic remediation for entering students, English as a second language program offered during academic year, services for LD students, summer session for credit, part-time degree program (daytime, evenings), adult/continuing education programs. ROTC: Army (c).
GENERAL DEGREE REQUIREMENTS 60 credits; computer course for recreation and leisure services majors; internship (some majors).
MAJORS Business administration/commerce/management, child care/child and family studies, computer information systems, computer science, criminal justice, culinary arts, data processing, engineering and applied sciences, English, fashion merchandising, forestry, forest technology, hospitality services, hotel and restaurant management, humanities, international business, liberal arts/general studies, manufacturing technology, marketing/retailing/merchandising, mental health/rehabilitation counseling, nursing, paralegal studies, radiological technology, recreation and leisure services, retail management, robotics, science, secretarial studies/office management, social science, word processing.
LIBRARY 24,451 books, 41 microform titles, 250 periodicals, 1 CD-ROM, 976 records, tapes, and CDs.
COMPUTERS ON CAMPUS 220 computers for student use in computer center, computer labs, learning resource center, library provide access to main academic computer, e-mail, on-line services, Internet. Staffed computer lab on campus.
COLLEGE LIFE Student-run newspaper, radio station. ***Student services:*** health clinic, personal-psychological counseling, women's center. ***Campus security:*** 24-hour emergency response devices and patrols, late-night transport-escort service.
HOUSING College housing not available.
ATHLETICS Member NJCAA. ***Intercollegiate:*** baseball M, basketball M/W, bowling M/W, cross-country running M/W, golf M/W, ice hockey M, lacrosse M, soccer M/W, softball W, tennis M, track and field M/W, volleyball W. ***Intramural:*** volleyball. ***Contact:*** Mr. Ralph Galante, Athletic Director, 716-851-1285.
CAREER PLANNING ***Director:*** Ms. Barbara Ware, Coordinator, Placement Services, 716-851-1184. ***Services:*** job fairs, resume preparation, resume referral, career counseling, careers library, job bank, job interviews.
AFTER GRADUATION 30% of students completing a degree program in 1994–95 went directly on to further study.
EXPENSES FOR 1995–96 ***Application fee:*** $25. Area resident tuition: $2340 full-time, $76 per credit hour part-time. Nonresident tuition: $4680 full-time, $152 per credit hour part-time. Part-time mandatory fees: $2.25 per credit hour. Full-time mandatory fees: $70.
FINANCIAL AID ***College-administered undergrad aid 1995–96:*** need-based scholarships, short-term loans, Federal Work-Study, part-time jobs. ***Acceptable forms:*** CSS Financial Aid PROFILE, FAFSA. ***Priority deadline:*** 8/21. ***Payment plan:*** deferred payment. ***Waivers:*** full or partial for senior citizens.
APPLYING Open admission except for nursing, manufacturing technology programs. ***Option:*** midyear entrance. ***Required:*** TOEFL for international students, ACT ASSET.

Erie Community College, City Campus (continued)
Required for some: 3 years of high school math. Test scores used for counseling/placement. ***Application deadline:*** rolling. ***Notification:*** continuous. Preference given to county residents.
APPLYING/TRANSFER ***Required:*** standardized test scores. ***Required for some:*** 3 years of high school math. ***Entrance:*** noncompetitive. ***Application deadline:*** rolling. ***Notification:*** continuous.
CONTACT Mr. B. Paul Hodan, Assistant Director of Student Services, Erie Community College, City Campus, Main Street and Youngs Road, Williamsville, NY 14221, 716-851-1588 Ext. 488. ***Fax:*** 716-842-1972.

ERIE COMMUNITY COLLEGE, NORTH CAMPUS
Williamsville, New York

UG Enrollment: 6,434	**Tuition & Fees (Area Res): $2410**
Application Deadline: rolling	**Room & Board: N/Avail**

GENERAL State and locally supported, 2-year, coed. Part of State University of New York System. Awards certificates, diplomas, transfer associate, terminal associate degrees. Founded 1946. ***Setting:*** 20-acre suburban campus. ***Total enrollment:*** 6,434. ***Faculty:*** 443 (209 full-time, 234 part-time); student-faculty ratio is 18:1.
ENROLLMENT PROFILE 6,434 students from 10 states and territories, 16 other countries. 50% women, 45% part-time, 98% state residents, 1% international, 0% Native American, 1% Hispanic, 1% Asian American. ***Areas of study chosen:*** 26% interdisciplinary studies, 21% health professions and related sciences, 16% engineering and applied sciences, 14% business management and administrative services, 10% liberal arts/general studies, 4% social sciences, 3% English language/literature/letters, 3% physical sciences, 2% computer and information sciences, 1% mathematics. ***Most popular recent majors:*** business administration/commerce/management, nursing, criminal justice.
FIRST-YEAR CLASS 609 total.
ACADEMIC PROGRAM Core, honor code. Calendar: semesters. Academic remediation for entering students, English as a second language program offered during academic year, services for LD students, summer session for credit, part-time degree program (daytime, evenings), adult/continuing education programs. ROTC: Army (c).
GENERAL DEGREE REQUIREMENTS 60 credits; computer course for criminal justice, respiratory care majors.
MAJORS Automotive technologies, business administration/commerce/management, chemical engineering technology, civil engineering technology, computer information systems, computer science, construction technologies, criminal justice, dental services, dietetics, electrical engineering technology, engineering sciences, environmental sciences, food services management, forest technology, humanities, industrial engineering technology, law enforcement/police sciences, liberal arts/general studies, materials sciences, mathematics, mechanical engineering technology, medical assistant technologies, medical laboratory technology, medical records services, metallurgical technology, nursing, occupational therapy, optometric/ophthalmic technologies, respiratory therapy, science, secretarial studies/office management, social science, word processing.
LIBRARY 79,763 books, 317 microform titles, 436 periodicals, 1 on-line bibliographic service, 2 CD-ROMs, 5,629 records, tapes, and CDs.
COMPUTERS ON CAMPUS 450 computers for student use in computer center, learning resource center, library.
COLLEGE LIFE Student-run newspaper, radio station. ***Student services:*** health clinic, personal-psychological counseling, women's center. ***Campus security:*** 24-hour emergency response devices and patrols, late-night transport-escort service.
HOUSING College housing not available.
ATHLETICS Member NJCAA. ***Intercollegiate:*** baseball M, basketball M/W, bowling M/W, cross-country running M/W, golf M/W, ice hockey M, lacrosse M, soccer M/W, softball W, tennis M, track and field M/W, volleyball W. ***Intramural:*** volleyball. ***Contact:*** Mr. Ralph Galante, Athletic Director, 716-851-1285.
CAREER PLANNING ***Placement office:*** 2 full-time staff. ***Director:*** Ms. Joan Eustace-Reeverts, Coordinator of Student Services, 716-851-1483. ***Services:*** job fairs, resume preparation, resume referral, career counseling, careers library, job bank, job interviews.
AFTER GRADUATION 32% of students completing a degree program in 1994–95 went directly on to further study.
EXPENSES FOR 1995–96 ***Application fee:*** $25. Area resident tuition: $2340 full-time, $76 per credit hour part-time. Nonresident tuition: $4680 full-time, $152 per credit hour part-time. Part-time mandatory fees: $2.25 per credit hour. Full-time mandatory fees: $70.
FINANCIAL AID ***College-administered undergrad aid 1995–96:*** need-based scholarships, short-term loans (average $100), Federal Work-Study, part-time jobs. ***Acceptable forms:*** CSS Financial Aid PROFILE, FAFSA. ***Priority deadline:*** 8/21.
APPLYING Open admission except for nursing, engineering science, occupational therapy programs. ***Option:*** midyear entrance. ***Required:*** TOEFL for international students, ACT ASSET. ***Required for some:*** 3 years of high school math. Test scores used for counseling/placement. ***Application deadline:*** rolling. ***Notification:*** continuous. Preference given to county residents.
APPLYING/TRANSFER ***Required:*** standardized test scores. ***Required for some:*** 3 years of high school math. ***Entrance:*** noncompetitive. ***Application deadline:*** rolling. ***Notification:*** continuous.
CONTACT Mr. B. Paul Hodan, Assistant Director of Student Services, Erie Community College, North Campus, Williamsville, NY 14221-7095, 716-851-1588. ***Fax:*** 716-634-3802.

ERIE COMMUNITY COLLEGE, SOUTH CAMPUS
Orchard Park, New York

UG Enrollment: 3,391	**Tuition & Fees (Area Res): $2410**
Application Deadline: rolling	**Room & Board: N/Avail**

GENERAL State and locally supported, 2-year, coed. Part of State University of New York System. Awards certificates, diplomas, transfer associate, terminal associate degrees. Founded 1974. ***Setting:*** 20-acre suburban campus with easy access to Buffalo. ***Total enrollment:*** 3,391. ***Faculty:*** 288 (95 full-time, 193 part-time); student-faculty ratio is 11:1.
ENROLLMENT PROFILE 3,391 students from 10 states and territories. 48% women, 43% part-time, 98% state residents, 4% transferred in, 0% international, 37% 25 or older, 1% Native American, 1% Hispanic, 1% African American, 0% Asian American. ***Areas of study chosen:*** 34% interdisciplinary studies, 25% business management and administrative services, 10% engineering and applied sciences, 8% social sciences, 6% architecture, 5% physical sciences, 4% English language/literature/letters, 3% computer and information sciences, 2% communications and journalism, 2% health professions and related sciences. ***Most popular recent majors:*** business administration/commerce/management, liberal arts/general studies.
FIRST-YEAR CLASS 981 total.
ACADEMIC PROGRAM Core, honor code. Calendar: semesters. Academic remediation for entering students, English as a second language program offered during academic year, services for LD students, summer session for credit, part-time degree program (daytime, evenings), adult/continuing education programs. ROTC: Army (c).
GENERAL DEGREE REQUIREMENTS 60 credits; computer course for recreation and leisure services majors.
MAJORS Architectural technologies, automotive technologies, biomedical technologies, business administration/commerce/management, communication equipment technology, computer information systems, computer technologies, dental services, drafting and design, emergency medical technology, English, environmental sciences, fire science, forestry, graphic arts, humanities, industrial engineering technology, liberal arts/general studies, printing technologies, recreation and leisure services, recreation therapy, science, secretarial studies/office management, telecommunications, word processing.
LIBRARY 45,182 books, 100 microform titles, 388 periodicals, 1,218 records, tapes, and CDs.
COMPUTERS ON CAMPUS 280 computers for student use in computer center, computer labs, learning resource center, library, student center provide access to main academic computer, e-mail, on-line services, Internet. Staffed computer lab on campus.
COLLEGE LIFE Student-run newspaper, radio station. ***Student services:*** health clinic, personal-psychological counseling. ***Campus security:*** 24-hour emergency response devices and patrols, late-night transport-escort service.
HOUSING College housing not available.
ATHLETICS Member NJCAA. ***Intercollegiate:*** baseball M, basketball M/W, bowling M/W, cross-country running M/W, golf M/W, ice hockey M, lacrosse M, soccer M/W, softball W, tennis M, track and field M/W, volleyball W. ***Intramural:*** riflery, volleyball. ***Contact:*** Mr. Ralph Galante, Athletic Director, 716-851-1285.
CAREER PLANNING ***Placement office:*** 1 full-time, 1 part-time staff. ***Director:*** Mr. Michael Golefiewski, Coordinator of Student Services, 716-851-1684. ***Services:*** job fairs, resume preparation, resume referral, career counseling, careers library, job bank, job interviews.
AFTER GRADUATION 32% of students completing a degree program in 1994–95 went directly on to further study.
EXPENSES FOR 1995–96 ***Application fee:*** $25. Area resident tuition: $2340 full-time, $76 per credit hour part-time. Nonresident tuition: $4680 full-time, $152 per credit hour part-time. Part-time mandatory fees: $2.25 per credit hour. Full-time mandatory fees: $70.
FINANCIAL AID ***College-administered undergrad aid 1995–96:*** need-based scholarships, Federal Work-Study, part-time jobs. ***Acceptable forms:*** CSS Financial Aid PROFILE, FAFSA. ***Priority deadline:*** 8/21. ***Waivers:*** full or partial for senior citizens.
APPLYING Open admission except for computer technology program. ***Option:*** midyear entrance. ***Required:*** TOEFL for international students, ACT ASSET. ***Required for some:*** 3 years of high school math. Test scores used for counseling/placement. ***Application deadline:*** rolling. ***Notification:*** continuous. Preference given to county residents.
APPLYING/TRANSFER ***Required:*** standardized test scores. ***Required for some:*** 3 years of high school math. ***Entrance:*** noncompetitive. ***Application deadline:*** rolling. ***Notification:*** continuous.
CONTACT Mr. B. Paul Hodan, Assistant Director of Student Services, Erie Community College, South Campus, Main Street and Youngs Road, Williamsville, NY 14221, 716-851-1588 Ext. 488. ***Fax:*** 716-648-9953.

EUGENIO MARÍA DE HOSTOS COMMUNITY COLLEGE OF THE CITY UNIVERSITY OF NEW YORK
Bronx, New York

UG Enrollment: 4,953	**Tuition & Fees (NY Res): $2552**
Application Deadline: rolling	**Room & Board: N/Avail**

GENERAL State and locally supported, 2-year, coed. Part of City University of New York System. Awards certificates, transfer associate, terminal associate degrees. Founded 1968. ***Setting:*** urban campus. ***Endowment:*** $76,500. ***Research spending 1994–95:*** $15,000. ***Educational spending 1994–95:*** $2303 per undergrad. ***Total enrollment:*** 4,953. ***Faculty:*** 403 (152 full-time, 65% with terminal degrees, 251 part-time); student-faculty ratio is 27:1. ***Notable Alumni:*** Geraldine Perri, Dr. Carolyn Shepard, Hector Diaz, Steve Delgado, Sharon Hill.
ENROLLMENT PROFILE 4,953 students: 77% women, 23% men, 22% part-time, 99% state residents, 6% transferred in, 1% international, 68% 25 or older, 0% Native American, 75% Hispanic, 20% African American, 2% Asian American. ***Areas of study chosen:*** 26% health professions and related sciences, 24% liberal arts/general studies, 14% social sciences, 13% business management and administrative services, 13% education, 10% computer and information sciences. ***Most popular recent majors:*** liberal arts/general studies, public administration, gerontology.
FIRST-YEAR CLASS 915 total; 2,179 applied, 52% of whom enrolled.
ACADEMIC PROGRAM Core, bilingual education curriculum, honor code. Calendar: semesters. 226 courses offered in 1995–96. Academic remediation for entering students, English as a second language program offered during academic year, services for LD students, tutorials, summer session for credit, part-time degree program (daytime, evenings, weekends), adult/continuing education programs, internships.
GENERAL DEGREE REQUIREMENTS 64 credits; math/science requirements vary according to program; computer course for most majors; internship (some majors).

MAJORS Accounting, business administration/commerce/management, data processing, dental services, early childhood education, gerontology, liberal arts/general studies, medical laboratory technology, medical secretarial studies, nursing, paralegal studies, public administration, radiological technology, secretarial studies/office management, word processing.
LIBRARY Hostos Community College Library with 54,451 books, 420 microform titles, 350 periodicals, 445 on-line bibliographic services, 134 CD-ROMs, 6,025 records, tapes, and CDs. Acquisition spending 1994–95: $121,173.
COMPUTERS ON CAMPUS Computer purchase plan available. 550 computers for student use in computer center, computer labs, research center, learning resource center, classrooms, library, student center provide access to main academic computer, off-campus computing facilities, e-mail, Internet. Staffed computer lab on campus provides training in use of computers. Academic computing expenditure 1994–95: $348,437.
COLLEGE LIFE 10% vote in student government elections. ***Social organizations:*** 25 open to all. ***Most popular organizations:*** Dominican Association, Puerto Rican Student Organization, Student Government Organization, Latin American Student Union, Black Student Union. ***Major annual events:*** Graduation, Ethnic Weeks, Prom Social. ***Student services:*** legal services, health clinic, personal-psychological counseling, women's center. ***Campus security:*** 24-hour patrols, late-night transport-escort service.
HOUSING College housing not available.
CAREER PLANNING ***Placement office:*** 2 full-time, 2 part-time staff; $88,407 operating expenditure 1994–95. ***Director:*** Ms. Virginia Paris, Director of Counseling, Department of Student Services, 718-518-6696. ***Services:*** job fairs, resume preparation, resume referral, career counseling, job bank, job interviews. 15 organizations recruited on campus 1994–95.
EXPENSES FOR 1995–96 ***Application fee:*** $40. State resident tuition: $2500 full-time, $105 per credit part-time. Nonresident tuition: $3076 full-time, $130 per credit part-time. Part-time mandatory fees: $13 per semester. Full-time mandatory fees: $52.
FINANCIAL AID ***College-administered undergrad aid 1995–96:*** need-based scholarships, 500 part-time jobs. ***Required forms:*** institutional, FAFSA. ***Priority deadline:*** 5/1. ***Payment plan:*** deferred payment. ***Waivers:*** full or partial for children of alumni, employees or children of employees, and senior citizens.
APPLYING Open admission. ***Required:*** school transcript. ***Recommended:*** 2 years of high school foreign language. ***Required for some:*** 3 years of high school math and science, TOEFL for international students. Test scores used for counseling/placement. ***Application deadline:*** rolling. ***Notification:*** continuous.
APPLYING/TRANSFER ***Required:*** high school transcript, college transcript, minimum 2.0 college GPA. ***Required for some:*** 3 years of high school math and science. ***Application deadline:*** rolling. ***Notification:*** continuous. ***Contact:*** Ms. Nydia Edgecombe, Director of Admissions, 718-518-6633.
CONTACT Ms. Nydia Edgecombe, Director of Admissions, Eugenio María de Hostos Community College of the City University of New York, 500 Grand Concourse, Bronx, NY 10451, 718-518-6633. ***E-mail:*** nreho@cunyvm.cuny.edu.

FINGER LAKES COMMUNITY COLLEGE
Canandaigua, New York

UG Enrollment: 3,848	**Tuition & Fees (NY Res): $2330**
Application Deadline: rolling	**Room & Board: N/Avail**

GENERAL State and locally supported, 2-year, coed. Part of State University of New York System. Awards certificates, transfer associate, terminal associate degrees. Founded 1965. ***Setting:*** 300-acre small-town campus with easy access to Rochester. ***Total enrollment:*** 3,848. ***Faculty:*** 234 (98 full-time, 136 part-time); student-faculty ratio is 18:1.
ENROLLMENT PROFILE 3,848 students: 58% women, 47% part-time, 99% state residents, 15% transferred in, 1% international, 24% 25 or older, 1% Hispanic, 2% African American. ***Most popular recent majors:*** business administration/commerce/management, criminal justice, conservation.
FIRST-YEAR CLASS 1,442 total; 2,192 applied, 98% were accepted, 64% of whom enrolled.
ACADEMIC PROGRAM Core, honor code. Calendar: semesters. Academic remediation for entering students, English as a second language program offered during academic year, services for LD students, advanced placement, honors program, summer session for credit, part-time degree program (daytime, evenings), internships. Off-campus study at the Rochester Area Colleges. ROTC: Army (c), Naval (c).
GENERAL DEGREE REQUIREMENTS 64 credit hours; computer course (varies by major); internship (some majors).
MAJORS Accounting, agricultural sciences, biology/biological sciences, biotechnology, broadcasting, business administration/commerce/management, chemical engineering technology, chemistry, commercial art, communication, computer science, computer technologies, conservation, criminal justice, data processing, drafting and design, early childhood education, electrical engineering technology, engineering (general), engineering sciences, (pre)engineering sequence, environmental sciences, fish and game management, horticulture, hotel and restaurant management, humanities, human services, landscape architecture/design, law enforcement/police sciences, legal secretarial studies, liberal arts/general studies, marketing/retailing/merchandising, mathematics, mechanical engineering technology, medical secretarial studies, music, natural resource management, nursing, ornamental horticulture, parks management, physical education, physics, political science/government, psychology, retail management, science, secretarial studies/office management, social science, social work, sociology, studio art, theater arts/drama, tourism and travel, wildlife management.
LIBRARY Charles Meder Library with 70,000 books, 246 microform titles, 450 periodicals, 7 CD-ROMs, 4,000 records, tapes, and CDs.
COMPUTERS ON CAMPUS 220 computers for student use in computer center, computer labs, learning resource center, academic departments, classrooms, library. Staffed computer lab on campus provides training in use of computers, software.
COLLEGE LIFE Drama-theater group, choral group, student-run newspaper, radio station. ***Social organizations:*** 30 open to all; 2 national fraternities, 2 national sororities; 3% of eligible men and 4% of eligible women are members. ***Student services:*** legal services, health clinic, personal-psychological counseling. ***Campus security:*** 24-hour emergency response devices and patrols, late-night transport-escort service.
HOUSING College housing not available.
ATHLETICS Member NJCAA. ***Intercollegiate:*** baseball M, basketball M/W, cross-country running M/W, soccer M/W, softball W. ***Intramural:*** basketball, tennis, volleyball. ***Contact:*** Mr. Dennis Moore, Athletic Director, 716-394-3500.
CAREER PLANNING ***Placement office:*** 3 full-time staff. ***Director:*** Ms. Ingrid Young, Director of Career Center, 716-394-3500. ***Services:*** job fairs, resume preparation, resume referral, career counseling, careers library, job bank, job interviews.
EXPENSES FOR 1995–96 ***Application fee:*** $30. State resident tuition: $2200 full-time, $87 per credit hour part-time. Nonresident tuition: $4400 full-time, $174 per credit hour part-time. Part-time mandatory fees: $3 per credit hour. Full-time mandatory fees: $130.
FINANCIAL AID ***College-administered undergrad aid 1995–96:*** need-based scholarships, 40 non-need scholarships (average $500), short-term loans (average $150), low-interest long-term loans from external sources (average $2000), 100 Federal Work-Study (averaging $1300), 40 part-time jobs. ***Required forms:*** state, institutional, FAFSA. ***Priority deadline:*** 4/1. ***Waivers:*** full or partial for senior citizens.
APPLYING Open admission except for nursing program. ***Options:*** early entrance, deferred entrance, midyear entrance. ***Recommended:*** SAT I or ACT. ***Required for some:*** 3 years of high school math and science. Test scores used for counseling/placement. ***Application deadline:*** rolling. ***Notification:*** continuous until 8/31. Preference given to state residents.
APPLYING/TRANSFER ***Required for some:*** 3 years of high school math and science. ***Application deadline:*** rolling. ***Notification:*** continuous until 8/31.
CONTACT Ms. Karen Schuhle-Williams, Assistant Dean for Enrollment Management, Finger Lakes Community College, Canandaigua, NY 14424-8395, 716-394-3500 Ext. 278.

FIORELLO H. LAGUARDIA COMMUNITY COLLEGE OF THE CITY UNIVERSITY OF NEW YORK
Long Island City, New York

UG Enrollment: 10,675	**Tuition & Fees (NY Res): $2612**
Application Deadline: rolling	**Room & Board: N/Avail**

Fiorello H. LaGuardia Community College, a branch of CUNY, is a dynamic community of teachers and learners. Founded in 1970, the College supports the principles of open access and equal opportunity for all. The College fosters innovative classroom teaching, strong support services for students, and professional development opportunities for faculty members. Its 27 degree programs and 2 professional certificates meet the needs of students who want to transfer to 4-year colleges as well as those who seek immediate employment.

GENERAL State and locally supported, 2-year, coed. Part of City University of New York System. Awards certificates, transfer associate, terminal associate degrees. Founded 1970. ***Setting:*** urban campus. ***Total enrollment:*** 10,675. ***Faculty:*** 914 (501 full-time, 25% with terminal degrees, 413 part-time).
ENROLLMENT PROFILE 10,675 students: 66% women, 38% part-time, 90% state residents, 14% transferred in, 43% have need-based financial aid, 0% have non-need-based financial aid, 47% 25 or older, 1% Native American, 35% Hispanic, 21% African American, 14% Asian American. ***Areas of study chosen:*** 28% health professions and related sciences, 24% business management and administrative services, 16% computer and information sciences, 16% liberal arts/general studies, 7% engineering and applied sciences. ***Most popular recent majors:*** accounting, business administration/commerce/management, tourism and travel.
FIRST-YEAR CLASS Of the students who applied, 100% were accepted, 50% of whom enrolled.
ACADEMIC PROGRAM Core, professional and humanistic learning curriculum. Calendar: modified semester. 448 courses offered in 1995–96. Academic remediation for entering students, English as a second language program offered during academic year, services for LD students, advanced placement, self-designed majors, tutorials, honors program, part-time degree program (daytime, evenings, weekends), adult/continuing education programs, co-op programs and internships. Off-campus study at Vassar College, other units of the City University of New York System. Study abroad in Dominican Republic.
GENERAL DEGREE REQUIREMENTS 64 units; internship (some majors).
MAJORS Accounting, business administration/commerce/management, business machine technologies, child psychology/child development, computer information systems, computer programming, computer science, computer technologies, data processing, dietetics, early childhood education, education, emergency medical technology, (pre)engineering sequence, finance/banking, food services management, funeral service, gerontology, human services, journalism, legal secretarial studies, liberal arts/general studies, mental health/rehabilitation counseling, natural sciences, nursing, occupational therapy, paralegal studies, photography, physical therapy, science, secretarial studies/office management, telecommunications, tourism and travel, veterinary technology.
LIBRARY Fiorello H. LaGuardia Community College Library Media Resources Center plus 1 other, with 78,360 books, 513 microform titles, 751 periodicals, 4 on-line bibliographic services, 3,760 records, tapes, and CDs. System-wide acquisition spending 1994–95: $300,000.
COMPUTERS ON CAMPUS Computer purchase plan available. 749 computers for student use in computer center, computer labs, classrooms, library provide access to off-campus computing facilities. System-wide academic computing expenditure 1994–95: $447,000.
COLLEGE LIFE Drama-theater group, student-run newspaper, radio station. ***Social organizations:*** 31 social clubs. ***Student services:*** health clinic, personal-psychological counseling, women's center.
HOUSING College housing not available.
ATHLETICS ***Intramural:*** badminton, basketball, bowling, soccer, softball, swimming and diving, table tennis (Ping-Pong), volleyball, weight lifting. ***Contact:*** Ms. Jane Corales, Director of Recreation, 718-482-5047.
CAREER PLANNING ***Director:*** Ms. Michelle Stewart, Director of Placement, 718-482-5238. ***Service:*** career counseling.
AFTER GRADUATION 49% of students completing a degree program in 1994–95 went directly on to further study.
EXPENSES FOR 1995–96 State resident tuition: $2500 full-time, $105 per unit part-time. Nonresident tuition: $3076 full-time, $130 per unit part-time. Part-time mandatory fees: $41.70 per year. Full-time mandatory fees: $112.
FINANCIAL AID ***College-administered undergrad aid 1995–96:*** need-based scholarships, low-interest long-term loans, Federal Work-Study, part-time jobs. ***Required forms:***

Fiorello H. LaGuardia Community College of the City University of New York (continued)

state, institutional, FAFSA; accepted: CSS Financial Aid PROFILE. ***Application deadline:*** continuous to 5/1. ***Payment plan:*** deferred payment. ***Waivers:*** full or partial for senior citizens. ***Average indebtedness of graduates:*** $4000.

APPLYING Open admission. ***Options:*** early entrance, deferred entrance, midyear entrance. ***Required:*** school transcript, TOEFL for international students. Test scores used for counseling/placement. ***Application deadline:*** rolling. ***Notification:*** continuous.

APPLYING/TRANSFER ***Required:*** high school transcript. ***Entrance:*** noncompetitive. ***Application deadline:*** rolling. ***Notification:*** continuous.

CONTACT Ms. Linda Tobash, Director of Admissions, Fiorello H. LaGuardia Community College of the City University of New York, 31-10 Thomson Avenue, Long Island City, NY 11101-3071, 718-482-5105. ***Fax:*** 718-482-5599. College video available.

FULTON-MONTGOMERY COMMUNITY COLLEGE
Johnstown, New York

UG Enrollment: 1,726	**Tuition & Fees (NY Res): $2217**
Application Deadline: 9/15	**Room & Board: N/Avail**

GENERAL State and locally supported, 2-year, coed. Part of State University of New York System. Awards transfer associate, terminal associate degrees. Founded 1964. ***Setting:*** 195-acre rural campus. ***Total enrollment:*** 1,726. ***Faculty:*** 94 (59 full-time, 90% with terminal degrees, 35 part-time).

ENROLLMENT PROFILE 1,726 students from 4 states and territories, 18 other countries. 60% women, 39% part-time, 90% state residents, 4% transferred in, 1% international, 40% 25 or older, 1% Native American, 3% Hispanic, 3% African American, 1% Asian American. ***Areas of study chosen:*** 30% liberal arts/general studies, 18% business management and administrative services, 5% biological and life sciences, 3% computer and information sciences, 3% engineering and applied sciences, 3% English language/literature/letters, 3% fine arts, 3% physical sciences, 2% communications and journalism, 2% mathematics, 2% natural resource sciences, 2% social sciences, 1% foreign language and literature. ***Most popular recent majors:*** liberal arts/general studies, business administration/commerce/management, nursing.

FIRST-YEAR CLASS 640 total; 1,040 applied, 94% were accepted, 66% of whom enrolled.

ACADEMIC PROGRAM Core. Calendar: 4-1-4 plus winter session. Academic remediation for entering students, English as a second language program offered during academic year and summer, services for LD students, advanced placement, self-designed majors, honors program, summer session for credit, part-time degree program (daytime, evenings, summer), external degree programs, adult/continuing education programs, co-op programs and internships. Off-campus study at 14 members of the Hudson-Mohawk Association of Colleges and Universities. ROTC: Army (c), Naval (c), Air Force (c).

GENERAL DEGREE REQUIREMENTS 60 credits; 1 unit of math; computer course; internship (some majors).

MAJORS Accounting, art/fine arts, automotive technologies, behavioral sciences, biology/biological sciences, business administration/commerce/management, carpentry, child psychology/child development, communication, computer information systems, computer science, computer technologies, conservation, construction technologies, criminal justice, data processing, early childhood education, elementary education, engineering sciences, English, finance/banking, flight training, food services management, forest technology, graphic arts, health education, history, humanities, human services, legal secretarial studies, liberal arts/general studies, mathematics, medical secretarial studies, natural resource management, nursing, physical education, printing technologies, psychology, science, secretarial studies/office management, social science, teacher aide studies, textile arts, theater arts/drama, word processing.

LIBRARY 61,000 books, 300 periodicals, 1,000 records, tapes, and CDs. Acquisition spending 1994–95: $249,474.

COMPUTERS ON CAMPUS 115 computers for student use in computer center, labs, library provide access to main academic computer. Academic computing expenditure 1994–95: $70,870.

NOTEWORTHY RESEARCH FACILITIES Natural Resources Research Boat.

COLLEGE LIFE Orientation program (2 days, parents included). Drama-theater group, choral group, marching band, student-run newspaper. ***Most popular organizations:*** Business Students Association, Criminal Justice Club, Adult Continuing Education Students Club. ***Major annual events:*** Spring Week, Anti-Substance Abuse Day, Orientation Week. ***Student services:*** personal-psychological counseling. ***Campus security:*** weekend and night security.

HOUSING College housing not available.

ATHLETICS Member NJCAA. ***Intercollegiate:*** baseball M, basketball M, bowling M/W, cross-country running M/W, soccer M, softball W, track and field M/W, volleyball W, wrestling M. ***Intramural:*** baseball, basketball, golf, soccer, volleyball. ***Contact:*** Mr. Dan Jarvis, Director of Athletics, 518-762-4651 Ext. 280.

CAREER PLANNING ***Service:*** careers library.

AFTER GRADUATION 47% of students completing a degree program in 1994–95 went directly on to further study.

EXPENSES FOR 1995–96 ***Application fee:*** $30. State resident tuition: $2100 full-time, $89 per credit part-time. Nonresident tuition: $4200 full-time, $188 per credit part-time. Part-time mandatory fees: $10 per term. Full-time mandatory fees: $117.

FINANCIAL AID ***College-administered undergrad aid 1995–96:*** 75 need-based scholarships (average $350), 25 non-need scholarships (average $675), low-interest long-term loans from external sources (average $1750), Federal Work-Study, 50 part-time jobs. ***Required forms:*** state, FAFSA; accepted: CSS Financial Aid PROFILE. ***Priority deadline:*** 6/1. ***Waivers:*** full or partial for employees or children of employees and senior citizens. ***Average indebtedness of graduates:*** $2089.

APPLYING Open admission except for nursing program. ***Options:*** early entrance, deferred entrance, midyear entrance. ***Application deadline:*** 9/15. ***Notification:*** continuous.

APPLYING/TRANSFER ***Application deadline:*** 9/15. ***Notification:*** continuous.

CONTACT Ms. C. Campbell Baker, Director of Admissions, Fulton-Montgomery Community College, Johnstown, NY 12095-3790, 518-762-4651 Ext. 200. ***Fax:*** 518-762-4334.

GENESEE COMMUNITY COLLEGE
Batavia, New York

UG Enrollment: 4,346	**Tuition & Fees (NY Res): $2300**
Application Deadline: rolling	**Room & Board: $3500**

GENERAL State and locally supported, 2-year, coed. Part of State University of New York System. Awards certificates, transfer associate, terminal associate degrees. Founded 1966. ***Setting:*** 256-acre small-town campus with easy access to Buffalo. ***Total enrollment:*** 4,346. ***Faculty:*** 291 (80 full-time, 10% with terminal degrees, 211 part-time); student-faculty ratio is 19:1.

ENROLLMENT PROFILE 4,346 students from 8 states and territories, 8 other countries. 62% women, 47% part-time, 98% state residents, 8% transferred in, 1% international, 42% 25 or older, 1% Native American, 1% Hispanic, 2% African American, 1% Asian American. ***Most popular recent majors:*** liberal arts/general studies, business administration/commerce/management, criminal justice.

FIRST-YEAR CLASS 1,188 total; 2,385 applied, 100% were accepted, 50% of whom enrolled.

ACADEMIC PROGRAM Core, honor code. Calendar: semesters. 1,660 courses offered in 1995–96. Academic remediation for entering students, services for LD students, advanced placement, honors program, summer session for credit, part-time degree program (daytime), adult/continuing education programs, co-op programs and internships.

GENERAL DEGREE REQUIREMENTS 1 math course or proficiency test; internship (some majors).

MAJORS Accounting, business administration/commerce/management, commercial art, communication, computer information systems, computer technologies, criminal justice, dietetics, drafting and design, drug and alcohol/substance abuse counseling, early childhood education, education, electrical and electronics technologies, elementary education, engineering sciences, fashion merchandising, gerontology, hotel and restaurant management, human services, liberal arts/general studies, marketing/retailing/merchandising, mathematics, medical laboratory technology, nursing, occupational therapy, paralegal studies, physical education, physical therapy, psychology, respiratory therapy, retail management, secretarial studies/office management, theater arts/drama, tourism and travel.

LIBRARY Alfred O'Connell Library with 72,600 books, 256 microform titles, 377 periodicals, 3 on-line bibliographic services, 9 CD-ROMs, 3,238 records, tapes, and CDs. Acquisition spending 1994–95: $391,145.

COMPUTERS ON CAMPUS 325 computers for student use in computer center, computer labs, learning resource center, classrooms, library provide access to main academic computer, e-mail. Staffed computer lab on campus provides training in use of computers, software. Academic computing expenditure 1994–95: $1 million.

COLLEGE LIFE Drama-theater group, choral group, student-run newspaper, radio station. 20% vote in student government elections. ***Social organizations:*** 25 open to all. ***Most popular organizations:*** Student Government Association, Phi Theta Kappa, DECA Club, Student Activities Council, Forum Players. ***Major annual events:*** Orientation Week, Rockfest, Fashion Show. ***Student services:*** health clinic, personal-psychological counseling. ***Campus security:*** 24-hour emergency response devices and patrols, late-night transport-escort service.

HOUSING 350 in college housing during 1995–96. Off-campus living permitted. ***Option:*** coed (7 buildings) housing available.

ATHLETICS Member NJCAA. ***Intercollegiate:*** baseball M(s), basketball M(s)/W(s), soccer M(s)/W(s), softball W(s), volleyball M(s)/W(s). ***Intramural:*** archery, badminton, basketball, football, golf, lacrosse, skiing (downhill), soccer, softball, table tennis (Ping-Pong), tennis, volleyball, water polo, weight lifting. ***Contact:*** Mr. Anthony Cory, Coordinator of Intercollegiate Athletics, 716-343-0055 Ext. 216.

CAREER PLANNING ***Placement office:*** 3 full-time staff; $123,415 operating expenditure 1994–95. ***Director:*** Ms. Priscilla DiRisio, Career Center Director, 716-343-0055 Ext. 423. ***Services:*** job fairs, resume preparation, career counseling, careers library.

EXPENSES FOR 1995–96 State resident tuition: $2300 full-time, $85 per credit hour part-time. Nonresident tuition: $2550 full-time, $94 per credit hour part-time. Part-time mandatory fees: $6 per semester. (Housing is available through a cooperative agreement between the institution and an area landlord.) College room and board: $3500.

FINANCIAL AID ***College-administered undergrad aid 1995–96:*** need-based scholarships (average $200), 25 non-need scholarships (average $200), short-term loans (average $100), low-interest long-term loans from external sources (average $200), 155 Federal Work-Study (averaging $1500), 30 part-time jobs. ***Required forms:*** state, FAFSA. ***Priority deadline:*** 5/1. ***Waivers:*** full or partial for employees or children of employees and senior citizens. ***Notification:*** continuous.

APPLYING Open admission except for nursing, physical therapy assistant, occupational therapy, respiratory care programs. ***Options:*** early entrance, midyear entrance. ***Required:*** ACT, TOEFL for international students. Test scores used for counseling/placement. ***Application deadline:*** rolling. ***Notification:*** continuous. Preference given to county residents.

APPLYING/TRANSFER ***Entrance:*** noncompetitive. ***Application deadline:*** rolling. ***Notification:*** continuous. ***Contact:*** Ms. Priscilla DiRisio, Transfer Counselor, 716-343-0055 Ext. 423.

CONTACT Mr. Malcolm T. Wormley, Director of Admissions, Genesee Community College, Batavia, NY 14020-9704, 716-343-0055 Ext. 215. College video available.

HELENE FULD COLLEGE OF NURSING OF NORTH GENERAL HOSPITAL
New York, New York

UG Enrollment: 202	**Tuition & Fees: $8981**
Application Deadline: rolling	**Room & Board: N/Avail**

GENERAL Independent, 2-year, specialized, coed. Awards transfer associate, terminal associate degrees. Founded 1945. ***Setting:*** urban campus. ***Total enrollment:*** 202. ***Faculty:*** 23 (14 full-time, 25% with terminal degrees, 9 part-time).

ENROLLMENT PROFILE 202 students from 4 states and territories, 4 other countries. 96% women, 60% part-time, 97% state residents, 25% transferred in, 93% 25 or older, 0% Native American, 6% Hispanic, 86% African American, 1% Asian American.

FIRST-YEAR CLASS 35 total.

466

Peterson's Guide to Two-Year Colleges 1997

ACADEMIC PROGRAM Honor code. Calendar: quarters. 7 courses offered in 1995–96. Academic remediation for entering students, part-time degree program (daytime, summer).
GENERAL DEGREE REQUIREMENTS 70 credits; 1 math course; 4 science courses.
MAJOR Nursing.
LIBRARY 7,000 books, 120 microform titles, 66 periodicals, 780 records, tapes, and CDs.
COMPUTERS ON CAMPUS 9 computers for student use in library. Staffed computer lab on campus.
COLLEGE LIFE ***Student services:*** health clinic. ***Campus security:*** security guard during open hours.
HOUSING College housing not available.
CAREER PLANNING ***Service:*** career counseling.
EXPENSES FOR 1995–96 Tuition: $8748 full-time, $162 per credit part-time. Part-time mandatory fees: $29.25 per quarter. Full-time mandatory fees: $233. Tuition guaranteed not to increase for student's term of enrollment.
FINANCIAL AID ***College-administered undergrad aid 1995–96:*** 95 need-based scholarships (averaging $1385), short-term loans (averaging $100), low-interest long-term loans from external sources (averaging $702). ***Required forms:*** institutional, FAFSA. ***Priority deadline:*** 10/31.
APPLYING ***Option:*** deferred entrance. ***Required:*** essay, school transcript, recommendations, interview, nursing exam, Nelson Denny Reading Test. Test scores used for admission and counseling/placement. ***Application deadline:*** rolling.
APPLYING/TRANSFER ***Required:*** essay, standardized test scores, recommendations, interview, college transcript. ***Entrance:*** moderately difficult. ***Application deadline:*** rolling. ***Contact:*** Ms. Gladys Tineda, Assistant Director of Student Services, 212-423-1000.
CONTACT Student Services, Helene Fuld College of Nursing of North General Hospital, 1879 Madison Avenue, New York, NY 10035-2709, 212-423-1000 Ext. 238. College video available.

HERKIMER COUNTY COMMUNITY COLLEGE
Herkimer, New York

UG Enrollment: 2,445	**Tuition & Fees (NY Res): $2220**
Application Deadline: 8/20	**Room & Board: N/Avail**

GENERAL State and locally supported, 2-year, coed. Part of State University of New York System. Awards certificates, transfer associate, terminal associate degrees. Founded 1966. ***Setting:*** 500-acre small-town campus. ***Educational spending 1994–95:*** $2276 per undergrad. ***Total enrollment:*** 2,445. ***Faculty:*** 123 (85 full-time, 85% with terminal degrees, 38 part-time); student-faculty ratio is 18:1.
ENROLLMENT PROFILE 2,445 students from 10 states and territories. 57% women, 43% men, 24% part-time, 99% state residents, 16% transferred in, 0% international, 28% 25 or older, 0% Native American, 1% Hispanic, 2% African American, 1% Asian American. ***Areas of study chosen:*** 25% business management and administrative services, 15% liberal arts/general studies, 10% biological and life sciences, 10% engineering and applied sciences, 9% fine arts, 8% health professions and related sciences, 7% computer and information sciences, 6% communications and journalism, 5% social sciences, 4% education, 1% mathematics. ***Most popular recent majors:*** liberal arts/general studies, business administration/commerce/management, tourism and travel.
FIRST-YEAR CLASS 950 total; 1,968 applied, 100% were accepted, 48% of whom enrolled.
ACADEMIC PROGRAM Liberal arts curriculum, honor code. Calendar: semesters. 380 courses offered in 1995–96. Academic remediation for entering students, English as a second language program, services for LD students, advanced placement, tutorials, honors program, summer session for credit, part-time degree program (daytime, summer), adult/continuing education programs, internships.
GENERAL DEGREE REQUIREMENTS 65 credit hours; computer course for telecommunications, health services, business administration majors; internship (some majors).
MAJORS Accounting, art/fine arts, biology/biological sciences, broadcasting, business administration/commerce/management, chemistry, child care/child and family studies, computer information systems, computer programming, computer science, conservation, construction technologies, corrections, court reporting, criminal justice, data processing, drafting and design, early childhood education, engineering sciences, (pre)engineering sequence, English, fashion merchandising, funeral service, health services administration, humanities, human services, journalism, laboratory technologies, law enforcement/police sciences, legal secretarial studies, liberal arts/general studies, marketing/retailing/merchandising, mathematics, medical laboratory technology, medical secretarial studies, occupational therapy, paralegal studies, photography, physical education, physical therapy, radio and television studies, science, secretarial studies/office management, social science, social work, sports administration, telecommunications, tourism and travel.
LIBRARY Herkimer County Community College Library with 71,115 books, 116 microform titles, 339 periodicals, 1 on-line bibliographic service, 9 CD-ROMs, 3,670 records, tapes, and CDs. Acquisition spending 1994–95: $88,102.
COMPUTERS ON CAMPUS Computer purchase plan available. 150 computers for student use in computer center, computer labs, learning resource center, classrooms, library provide access to main academic computer, on-line services, Internet. Staffed computer lab on campus provides training in use of computers, software. Academic computing expenditure 1994–95: $255,534.
COLLEGE LIFE Orientation program (2 days, no cost, parents included). Drama-theater group, choral group, student-run newspaper, radio station. 30% vote in student government elections. ***Social organizations:*** 36 open to all. ***Most popular organizations:*** Criminal Justice Club, Business Club, Student Senate. ***Major annual event:*** Arts and Crafts Show. ***Student services:*** personal-psychological counseling. ***Campus security:*** 24-hour emergency response devices and patrols.
HOUSING College housing not available.
ATHLETICS Member NJCAA. ***Intercollegiate:*** baseball M, basketball M/W, bowling M/W, cross-country running M/W, field hockey W, lacrosse M, soccer M/W, softball W, tennis W, track and field M/W, volleyball W. ***Intramural:*** baseball, basketball, lacrosse, soccer, softball, swimming and diving, tennis, volleyball. ***Contact:*** Mr. Sid Fox, Athletic Director, 315-866-0300 Ext. 255.
CAREER PLANNING ***Placement office:*** 1 full-time, 1 part-time staff; $63,243 operating expenditure 1994–95. ***Director:*** Mr. Robert M. Ichihana, Counselor, Career Services, 315-866-0300 Ext. 309. ***Services:*** job fairs, resume preparation, resume referral, career counseling, careers library, job bank, job interviews. 42 organizations recruited on campus 1994–95.
AFTER GRADUATION 44% of class of 1994 had job offers within 6 months. 70% of students completing a degree program went directly on to further study.
EXPENSES FOR 1995–96 ***Application fee:*** $25. State resident tuition: $2100 full-time, $80 per credit hour part-time. Nonresident tuition: $3450 full-time, $125 per credit hour part-time. Full-time mandatory fees: $120.
FINANCIAL AID ***College-administered undergrad aid 1995–96:*** 200 need-based scholarships, short-term loans (average $50), low-interest long-term loans from external sources (average $1900), Federal Work-Study, 20 part-time jobs. ***Required forms:*** FAFSA, financial aid transcript (for transfers); required for some: state; accepted: CSS Financial Aid PROFILE. ***Application deadline:*** continuous to 4/1. ***Payment plans:*** installment, deferred payment. ***Waivers:*** full or partial for employees or children of employees. ***Average indebtedness of graduates:*** $1400.
APPLYING Open admission except for engineering science, occupational therapy assistant, physical therapy assistant programs. ***Options:*** Common Application, early entrance, midyear entrance. ***Required:*** school transcript, TOEFL for international students. ***Recommended:*** SAT I or ACT. ***Required for some:*** 3 years of high school math. Test scores used for counseling/placement. ***Application deadline:*** 8/20. ***Notification:*** continuous. Preference given to county residents.
APPLYING/TRANSFER ***Required:*** college transcript. ***Required for some:*** 3 years of high school math. ***Entrance:*** noncompetitive. ***Application deadline:*** 8/20. ***Notification:*** continuous. ***Contact:*** Mrs. Katherine A. Schwabach, Counselor, Transfer Services, 315-866-0300 Ext. 308.
CONTACT Ms. Janet Tamburrino, Director of Admissions, Herkimer County Community College, Herkimer, NY 13350, 315-866-0300 Ext. 278 or toll-free 800-947-4432 (in-state). ***Fax:*** 315-866-7253. College video available.

HOSTOS COMMUNITY COLLEGE
New York—See Eugenio María de Hostos Community College of the City University of New York

HUDSON VALLEY COMMUNITY COLLEGE
Troy, New York

UG Enrollment: 10,102	**Tuition & Fees (NY Res): $2271**
Application Deadline: rolling	**Room & Board: N/Avail**

GENERAL State and locally supported, 2-year, coed. Part of State University of New York System. Awards transfer associate, terminal associate degrees. Founded 1953. ***Setting:*** 135-acre suburban campus. ***Total enrollment:*** 10,102. ***Faculty:*** 511 (268 full-time, 13% with terminal degrees, 243 part-time); student-faculty ratio is 20:1.
ENROLLMENT PROFILE 10,102 students from 21 states and territories, 18 other countries. 47% women, 17% part-time, 97% state residents, 5% transferred in, 1% international, 35% 25 or older, 1% Native American, 1% Hispanic, 5% African American, 1% Asian American. ***Most popular recent majors:*** liberal arts/general studies, criminal justice, accounting.
FIRST-YEAR CLASS 4,494 total; 5,973 applied, 80% were accepted, 94% of whom enrolled. 10% from top 10% of their high school class, 20% from top quarter, 50% from top half.
ACADEMIC PROGRAM Honor code. Calendar: semesters. Academic remediation for entering students, services for LD students, advanced placement, self-designed majors, summer session for credit, part-time degree program (daytime, evenings), external degree programs, adult/continuing education programs, co-op programs and internships. Off-campus study at 14 members of the Hudson-Mohawk Association of Colleges and Universities. ROTC: Army, Air Force (c).
GENERAL DEGREE REQUIREMENTS 60 credit hours; 1 year of math; internship (some majors).
MAJORS Accounting, automotive technologies, business administration/commerce/management, chemical engineering technology, chemistry, civil engineering technology, construction technologies, criminal justice, data processing, dental services, early childhood education, electrical and electronics technologies, electrical engineering technology, emergency medical technology, (pre)engineering sequence, environmental sciences, finance/banking, funeral service, heating/refrigeration/air conditioning, human services, industrial engineering technology, insurance, interdisciplinary studies, international business, liberal arts/general studies, machine and tool technologies, marketing/retailing/merchandising, mathematics, mechanical engineering technology, medical laboratory technology, medical secretarial studies, nursing, physical education, physician's assistant studies, radiological sciences, radiological technology, real estate, recreation and leisure services, respiratory therapy, safety and security technologies, secretarial studies/office management, telecommunications.
LIBRARY Marvia Library with 148,189 books, 41,272 microform titles, 691 periodicals, 4,671 records, tapes, and CDs.
COMPUTERS ON CAMPUS Computer purchase plan available. 300 computers for student use in computer center, terminal clusters, library. Staffed computer lab on campus (open 24 hours a day) provides training in use of computers, software.
COLLEGE LIFE Drama-theater group, student-run newspaper, radio station. 10% vote in student government elections. ***Student services:*** legal services, health clinic, personal-psychological counseling, women's center. ***Campus security:*** 24-hour emergency response devices and patrols, late-night transport-escort service.
HOUSING College housing not available.
ATHLETICS Member NJCAA. ***Intercollegiate:*** basketball M/W, bowling M/W, cross-country running M/W, football M, golf M/W, lacrosse M, soccer M, tennis M/W, track and field M/W, volleyball W. ***Intramural:*** archery, badminton, baseball, basketball, bowling, football, lacrosse, racquetball, softball, table tennis (Ping-Pong), tennis, track and field, volleyball. ***Contact:*** Mr. William Schieffelin, Director of Athletics, 518-270-7328.
CAREER PLANNING ***Director:*** Mr. Mark Schmideshoff, Director of Career Planning and Placement, 518-270-7326. ***Services:*** job fairs, career counseling, careers library, job bank, job interviews.

Hudson Valley Community College (continued)
AFTER GRADUATION 37% of students completing a degree program in 1994–95 went directly on to further study.
ESTIMATED EXPENSES FOR 1996–97 ***Application fee:*** $25. State resident tuition: $2150 full-time, $90 per credit part-time. Nonresident tuition: $4500 full-time, $180 per credit part-time. Part-time mandatory fees: $3 per credit. Full-time mandatory fees: $121.
FINANCIAL AID ***College-administered undergrad aid 1995–96:*** 50 need-based scholarships (average $100), 50 non-need scholarships (average $100), short-term loans (average $50), low-interest long-term loans from external sources (average $500), Federal Work-Study, 10 part-time jobs. ***Required forms:*** CSS Financial Aid PROFILE. ***Application deadline:*** continuous to 8/31. ***Waivers:*** full or partial for employees or children of employees and senior citizens.
APPLYING Open admission for individual studies program. ***Options:*** early entrance, deferred entrance. ***Required:*** school transcript, TOEFL for international students. ***Recommended:*** SAT I or ACT. ***Required for some:*** 3 years of high school math and science, SAT I or ACT. Test scores used for counseling/placement. ***Application deadline:*** rolling. ***Notification:*** continuous.
APPLYING/TRANSFER ***Recommended:*** standardized test scores. ***Required for some:*** standardized test scores, 3 years of high school math and science. ***Entrance:*** minimally difficult. ***Application deadline:*** rolling. ***Notification:*** continuous.
CONTACT Mr. Robert Gould, Director of Admissions, Hudson Valley Community College, Troy, NY 12180-6096, 518-270-7309. College video available.

INSTITUTE OF DESIGN AND CONSTRUCTION
Brooklyn, New York

UG Enrollment: 246 | **Tuition & Fees: $4255**
Application Deadline: rolling | **Room & Board: N/Avail**

GENERAL Independent, 2-year, coed. Awards transfer associate degrees. Founded 1947. ***Setting:*** urban campus. ***Total enrollment:*** 246. ***Faculty:*** 30 (all part-time).
ENROLLMENT PROFILE 246 students from 4 states and territories. 10% women, 50% part-time, 95% state residents, 4% international, 66% 25 or older, 10% Hispanic, 40% African American, 2% Asian American. ***Most popular recent majors:*** architectural technologies, construction technologies.
FIRST-YEAR CLASS 45 total; 127 applied, 80% were accepted, 44% of whom enrolled.
ACADEMIC PROGRAM Core. Calendar: semesters. 58 courses offered in 1995–96; average class size 18 in required courses. Academic remediation for entering students, advanced placement, tutorials, summer session for credit, part-time degree program (daytime, evenings), adult/continuing education programs, co-op programs.
GENERAL DEGREE REQUIREMENTS 66 credits; 1 applied math course.
MAJORS Architectural technologies, construction technologies, drafting and design, environmental design.
COMPUTERS ON CAMPUS 1 computers for student use in library.
COLLEGE LIFE ***Student services:*** personal-psychological counseling.
HOUSING College housing not available.
CAREER PLANNING ***Placement office:*** 1 full-time staff. ***Director:*** Miss Avino, Dean of Academic Affairs and Career Services, 718-855-3661 Ext. 12. ***Services:*** resume preparation, resume referral, career counseling, job bank, job interviews. Students must register sophomore year. 2 organizations recruited on campus 1994–95.
AFTER GRADUATION 85% of class of 1994 had job offers within 6 months. 20% of students completing a degree program went directly on to further study.
EXPENSES FOR 1996–97 ***Application fee:*** $30. Tuition: $4200 full-time, $140 per credit part-time. Full-time mandatory fees: $55.
FINANCIAL AID ***College-administered undergrad aid 1995–96:*** low-interest long-term loans from external sources. ***Required forms:*** institutional, FAFSA. ***Application deadline:*** continuous.
APPLYING Open admission. ***Option:*** Common Application. ***Required:*** school transcript. ***Application deadline:*** rolling. ***Notification:*** continuous until 9/30.
APPLYING/TRANSFER ***Required:*** high school transcript. ***Required for some:*** college transcript. ***Contact:*** Mr. Kevin Giannetti, Director of Admissions, 718-855-3661.
CONTACT Mr. Kevin Giannetti, Director of Admissions, Institute of Design and Construction, 141 Willoughby Street, Brooklyn, NY 11201-5317, 718-855-3661. ***Fax:*** 718-852-5889.

INTERBORO INSTITUTE
New York, New York

UG Enrollment: 1,147 | **Tuition & Fees: $5500**
Application Deadline: rolling | **Room & Board: N/Avail**

GENERAL Proprietary, 2-year, coed. Awards transfer associate, terminal associate degrees. Founded 1888. ***Setting:*** urban campus. ***Total enrollment:*** 1,147. ***Faculty:*** 47 (22 full-time, 33% with terminal degrees, 25 part-time); student-faculty ratio is 24:1.
ENROLLMENT PROFILE 1,147 students from 9 states and territories, 10 other countries. 63% women, 37% men, 3% part-time, 95% state residents, 2% transferred in, 90% have need-based financial aid, 0% have non-need-based financial aid, 1% international, 20% 25 or older, 0% Native American, 15% Hispanic, 80% African American, 2% Asian American. ***Most popular recent majors:*** business administration/commerce/management, legal secretarial studies, optometric/ophthalmic technologies.
FIRST-YEAR CLASS 570 total; 805 applied, 97% were accepted, 73% of whom enrolled.
ACADEMIC PROGRAM Core, business-oriented curriculum, honor code. Calendar: semesters. 104 courses offered in 1995–96. Academic remediation for entering students, advanced placement, tutorials, summer session for credit, adult/continuing education programs, co-op programs and internships.
GENERAL DEGREE REQUIREMENTS 60 credit hours; 1 math course; computer course.
MAJORS Accounting, business administration/commerce/management, legal secretarial studies, medical secretarial studies, optometric/ophthalmic technologies, paralegal studies, safety and security technologies, secretarial studies/office management.
LIBRARY Interboro Library with 5,986 books, 98 periodicals, 4 on-line bibliographic services, 175 records, tapes, and CDs.
COMPUTERS ON CAMPUS 78 computers for student use in computer center, computer labs, learning resource center provide access to on-line services, Internet. Staffed computer lab on campus provides training in use of computers, software.
COLLEGE LIFE Orientation program (2 days, no cost). Drama-theater group, student-run newspaper. ***Most popular organizations:*** Drama Club, Student Newspaper, OPT Society. ***Major annual events:*** Christmas Dance, Fashion Show, Interboro Day. ***Student services:*** personal-psychological counseling.
HOUSING College housing not available.
ATHLETICS ***Intramural:*** baseball.
CAREER PLANNING ***Placement office:*** 2 full-time staff. ***Director:*** Mrs. Erica Harrison, Placement Coordinator, 212-399-0091. ***Services:*** resume preparation, career counseling, job interviews.
EXPENSES FOR 1996–97 ***Application fee:*** $28. Tuition: $5500 full-time, $235 per credit part-time. Tuition for ophthalmic technology program: $5700 full-time, $240 per credit part-time.
FINANCIAL AID ***College-administered undergrad aid 1995–96:*** need-based scholarships, low-interest long-term loans from external sources, 15 part-time jobs. ***Required forms:*** state, FAFSA. ***Priority deadline:*** 8/31. ***Payment plan:*** installment.
APPLYING ***Options:*** deferred entrance, midyear entrance. ***Required:*** essay, interview, CPAt. ***Recommended:*** school transcript. Test scores used for admission. ***Application deadline:*** rolling. ***Notification:*** continuous.
APPLYING/TRANSFER ***Required:*** essay, interview, college transcript. ***Recommended:*** high school transcript. ***Required for some:*** standardized test scores. ***Entrance:*** noncompetitive. ***Application deadline:*** rolling. ***Notification:*** continuous. ***Contact:*** Ms. Geraldine Klass, Registrar, 212-399-0091.
CONTACT Ms. Cheryl Ryan, Director of Admissions, Interboro Institute, 450 West 56th Street, New York, NY 10019-3602, 212-399-0091 Ext. 115. ***Fax:*** 212-765-5772.

JAMESTOWN BUSINESS COLLEGE
Jamestown, New York

UG Enrollment: 315 | **Tuition & Fees: $6000**
Application Deadline: rolling | **Room & Board: N/Avail**

GENERAL Proprietary, 2-year, coed. Awards certificates, terminal associate degrees. Founded 1886. ***Setting:*** 1-acre small-town campus. ***Total enrollment:*** 315. ***Faculty:*** 15 (7 full-time, 100% with terminal degrees, 8 part-time); student-faculty ratio is 22:1.
ENROLLMENT PROFILE 315 students from 2 states and territories. 85% women, 15% men, 0% part-time, 85% state residents, 22% transferred in, 93% have need-based financial aid, 0% international, 33% 25 or older, 1% Native American, 4% Hispanic, 1% African American, 0% Asian American. ***Areas of study chosen:*** 100% business management and administrative services.
FIRST-YEAR CLASS 144 total; 232 applied, 94% were accepted, 66% of whom enrolled. 5% from top 10% of their high school class, 20% from top quarter, 50% from top half.
ACADEMIC PROGRAM Core, vocationally-centered business curriculum, honor code. Calendar: quarters. 34 courses offered in 1995–96; average class size 25 in required courses. Academic remediation for entering students, advanced placement, part-time degree program (daytime). Off-campus study at Jamestown Community College.
GENERAL DEGREE REQUIREMENTS 90 quarter credits; computer course.
MAJORS Accounting, business administration/commerce/management, information science, legal secretarial studies, marketing/retailing/merchandising, medical secretarial studies, secretarial studies/office management.
COMPUTERS ON CAMPUS 100 computers for student use in computer center, computer labs, learning resource center provide access to Internet. Staffed computer lab on campus provides training in use of computers, software.
COLLEGE LIFE ***Social organizations:*** 1 open to all. ***Most popular organization:*** Phi Beta Lambda. ***Major annual events:*** Trip to Toronto, Halloween Party, Christmas Party. ***Campus security:*** 24-hour emergency response devices.
HOUSING College housing not available.
ATHLETICS ***Intramural:*** bowling, racquetball, skiing (cross-country), skiing (downhill), softball, swimming and diving, table tennis (Ping-Pong), volleyball, weight lifting.
CAREER PLANNING ***Placement office:*** 1 full-time, 1 part-time staff. ***Director:*** Mrs. Sherrie Brookmire, Director of Admissions, Housing and Placement, 716-664-5100. ***Services:*** job fairs, resume preparation, resume referral, career counseling, careers library, job bank, job interviews. Students must register sophomore year.
AFTER GRADUATION 85% of class of 1994 had job offers within 6 months.
EXPENSES FOR 1996–97 ***Application fee:*** $25. Tuition: $5700 full-time. Full-time mandatory fees: $300.
FINANCIAL AID ***College-administered undergrad aid 1995–96:*** 17 need-based scholarships (average $578), 23 non-need scholarships (average $772), low-interest long-term loans from external sources (average $2192), part-time jobs. ***Acceptable forms:*** CSS Financial Aid PROFILE, state, FAFSA, AFSSA-CSX. ***Priority deadline:*** 8/15.
APPLYING ***Option:*** midyear entrance. ***Required:*** essay, school transcript, campus interview. ***Application deadline:*** rolling.
APPLYING/TRANSFER ***Required:*** college transcript. ***Application deadline:*** rolling. ***Contact:*** Ms. Donna Simmons, Dean, 716-664-5100.
CONTACT Mrs. Donna Simmons, Dean, Jamestown Business College, Jamestown, NY 14702-0429, 716-664-5100. ***Fax:*** 716-664-3144. ***E-mail:*** jbc@epix.net. College video available.

JAMESTOWN COMMUNITY COLLEGE
Jamestown, New York

UG Enrollment: 3,660 | **Tuition & Fees (NY Res): $2836**
Application Deadline: rolling | **Room & Board: N/Avail**

GENERAL State and locally supported, 2-year, coed. Part of State University of New York System. Awards certificates, transfer associate, terminal associate degrees. Founded 1950. ***Setting:*** 107-acre small-town campus. ***Educational spending 1994–95:*** $2938 per undergrad. ***Total enrollment:*** 3,660. Student-faculty ratio is 18:1. ***Notable Alumni:*** Roger Lexell, vice president of Asian operations for McDonald's Corporation; Dr. Peter Cala, biophysics researcher at University of California; Lawrence Igarashi, president of Beauwood California; Natalie Marker, national marketing director for Red Lobster; Natalie Merchant, musician and singer.

ENROLLMENT PROFILE 3,660 students from 4 states and territories, 13 other countries. 60% women, 47% part-time, 91% state residents, 6% transferred in, 1% international, 49% 25 or older, 1% Native American, 1% Hispanic, 2% African American, 1% Asian American. ***Most popular recent majors:*** business administration/commerce/management, criminal justice, nursing.
FIRST-YEAR CLASS 1,112 total; 1,138 applied, 99% were accepted, 98% of whom enrolled. 10% from top 10% of their high school class, 26% from top quarter, 52% from top half. 3 valedictorians.
ACADEMIC PROGRAM Core, interdisciplinary curriculum, honor code. Calendar: semesters. 1,600 courses offered in 1995–96. Academic remediation for entering students, services for LD students, advanced placement, self-designed majors, tutorials, honors program, summer session for credit, part-time degree program (daytime, evenings, summer), adult/continuing education programs, internships. Off-campus study at State University of New York College at Fredonia, Jamestown Business College. Study abroad in 16 countries, including Canada, Egypt, England, France, Ghana, India, Italy, Israel, Spain, Sweden (1% of students participate).
GENERAL DEGREE REQUIREMENTS 60 semester hours; 1 math course; computer course for engineering majors; internship (some majors).
MAJORS Accounting, business administration/commerce/management, communication, computer information systems, computer science, computer technologies, criminal justice, electrical engineering technology, engineering sciences, (pre)engineering sequence, humanities, human services, law enforcement/police sciences, liberal arts/general studies, mathematics, mechanical engineering technology, nursing, science, social science.
LIBRARY Hultquist Library plus 1 other, with 73,769 books, 176 microform titles, 628 periodicals, 10 CD-ROMs, 4,381 records, tapes, and CDs. Acquisition spending 1994–95: $193,509.
COMPUTERS ON CAMPUS Computer purchase plan available. 200 computers for student use in computer center, computer labs, research center, learning resource center, all academic buildings, classrooms, library provide access to main academic computer, off-campus computing facilities, e-mail, on-line services, Internet. Staffed computer lab on campus provides training in use of computers, software. Academic computing expenditure 1994–95: $292,000.
COLLEGE LIFE Drama-theater group, choral group, student-run newspaper, radio station. 85% vote in student government elections. ***Social organizations:*** 12 open to all. ***Most popular organizations:*** Nursing Club, Criminal Justice Club, Earth Awareness, Student Advisory Board, Intervarsity Christian Fellowship. ***Major annual events:*** Fall Open House, Spring Open House, New Student Orientation. ***Student services:*** health clinic, personal-psychological counseling.
HOUSING College housing not available.
ATHLETICS Member NJCAA. ***Intercollegiate:*** baseball M, basketball M(s)/W(s), golf M/W, soccer M, softball W(s), volleyball W(s). ***Intramural:*** basketball, bowling, football, racquetball, soccer, swimming and diving, table tennis (Ping-Pong), tennis, volleyball. ***Contact:*** Mr. Greg Fish, Athletic Director, 716-665-5220 Ext. 429.
CAREER PLANNING ***Placement office:*** 5 full-time, 2 part-time staff; $80,000 operating expenditure 1994–95. ***Director:*** Mr. Ron Turak, Career/Placement Counselor, 716-665-5220 Ext. 302. ***Services:*** job fairs, resume preparation, resume referral, career counseling, careers library, job bank, job interviews.
AFTER GRADUATION 82% of students completing a degree program in 1994–95 went directly on to further study.
EXPENSES FOR 1995–96 ***Application fee:*** $30. State resident tuition: $2600 full-time, $88 per semester hour part-time. Nonresident tuition: $5200 full-time, $154 per semester hour part-time. Part-time mandatory fees: $40.75 per semester. Full-time mandatory fees: $236.
FINANCIAL AID ***College-administered undergrad aid 1995–96:*** 159 need-based scholarships (average $765), 205 non-need scholarships (average $1380), short-term loans (average $133), low-interest long-term loans from college funds (average $388), loans from external sources (average $1543), Federal Work-Study, 191 part-time jobs. ***Required forms:*** FAFSA; required for some: state, institutional; accepted: CSS Financial Aid PROFILE. ***Priority deadline:*** 3/1. ***Payment plans:*** installment, deferred payment. ***Waivers:*** full or partial for employees or children of employees and senior citizens. ***Notification:*** continuous.
APPLYING Open admission except for nursing program. ***Options:*** early entrance, deferred entrance, midyear entrance. ***Required:*** TOEFL for international students, ACT ASSET. ***Required for some:*** 3 years of high school math. Test scores used for admission. ***Application deadline:*** rolling. ***Notification:*** continuous. Preference given to Chautauqua and Cattaraugus county residents.
APPLYING/TRANSFER ***Required for some:*** 3 years of high school math. ***Entrance:*** noncompetitive. ***Application deadline:*** rolling. ***Notification:*** continuous. ***Contact:*** Mr. Ron Turak, Counselor/Placement and Transfer Coordinator, 716-665-5220 Ext. 302.
CONTACT Mr. John Devney, Director of Admissions and Recruitment, Jamestown Community College, Jamestown, NY 14701-1999, 716-665-5220 Ext. 239 or toll-free 800-388-8557 (in-state). ***E-mail:*** devneyjf@jccw22.cc.sunyjcc.edu.

JEFFERSON COMMUNITY COLLEGE
Watertown, New York

UG Enrollment: 3,200	**Tuition & Fees (NY Res): $2232**
Application Deadline: rolling	**Room & Board: N/Avail**

GENERAL State and locally supported, 2-year, coed. Part of State University of New York System. Awards certificates, transfer associate, terminal associate degrees. Founded 1961. ***Setting:*** 75-acre small-town campus. ***Total enrollment:*** 3,200. ***Faculty:*** 193 (73 full-time, 11% with terminal degrees, 120 part-time); student-faculty ratio is 12:1.
ENROLLMENT PROFILE 3,200 students from 40 states and territories, 8 other countries. 56% women, 36% part-time, 97% state residents, 13% transferred in, 1% international, 48% 25 or older, 1% Native American, 3% Hispanic, 8% African American, 2% Asian American. ***Areas of study chosen:*** 41% liberal arts/general studies, 26% business management and administrative services, 21% vocational and home economics, 5% health professions and related sciences, 4% computer and information sciences, 3% engineering and applied sciences.
FIRST-YEAR CLASS 1,120 total; 1,558 applied, 76% were accepted, 95% of whom enrolled.
ACADEMIC PROGRAM Honor code. Calendar: semesters. Academic remediation for entering students, English as a second language program offered during academic year and summer, services for LD students, advanced placement, self-designed majors, honors program, summer session for credit, part-time degree program (daytime, evenings), adult/continuing education programs, internships. Off-campus study at members of the State University of New York North Country/Fort Drum Consortium.
GENERAL DEGREE REQUIREMENTS 62 credits; math/science requirements vary according to program; computer course for accounting, engineering, office technology majors; internship (some majors).
MAJORS Accounting, business administration/commerce/management, computer information systems, computer science, criminal justice, culinary arts, early childhood education, engineering sciences, (pre)engineering sequence, finance/banking, forest technology, hospitality services, hotel and restaurant management, humanities, human services, laboratory technologies, liberal arts/general studies, marketing/retailing/merchandising, mathematics, medical laboratory technology, medical secretarial studies, natural sciences, nursing, paralegal studies, retail management, science, secretarial studies/office management, tourism and travel, word processing.
LIBRARY Melvil Dewey Library with 53,109 books, 26 microform titles, 292 periodicals, 1 on-line bibliographic service, 19 CD-ROMs, 1,242 records, tapes, and CDs.
COMPUTERS ON CAMPUS Computer purchase plan available. 125 computers for student use in computer center, computer labs, learning resource center, classrooms, library provide access to e-mail, Internet. Staffed computer lab on campus provides training in use of computers, software.
COLLEGE LIFE Orientation program (2 days, $35, parents included). Drama-theater group, choral group, student-run newspaper. ***Social organizations:*** 23 open to all. ***Major annual events:*** Fall Fest, Spring Fest, Black History Month Program. ***Student services:*** health clinic, personal-psychological counseling. ***Campus security:*** 24-hour emergency response devices and patrols.
HOUSING College housing not available.
ATHLETICS Member NJCAA. ***Intercollegiate:*** baseball M, basketball M/W, cross-country running M/W, golf M, lacrosse M, soccer M/W, softball W, volleyball W. ***Intramural:*** basketball, skiing (cross-country), soccer, softball, tennis, volleyball. ***Contact:*** Mr. Robert Williams, Director of Athletics, 315-786-2248.
CAREER PLANNING ***Placement office:*** 1 full-time, 1 part-time staff. ***Director:*** Ms. Michelle Gefell, Career Counselor, 315-786-2269. ***Services:*** job fairs, resume preparation, resume referral, career counseling, careers library, job bank, job interviews.
AFTER GRADUATION 53% of students completing a degree program in 1994–95 went directly on to further study.
ESTIMATED EXPENSES FOR 1996–97 ***Application fee:*** $30. State resident tuition: $1992 full-time, $83 per credit hour part-time. Nonresident tuition: $3984 full-time, $166 per credit hour part-time. Part-time mandatory fees per semester range from $8.50 to $96. Full-time mandatory fees: $240.
FINANCIAL AID ***College-administered undergrad aid 1995–96:*** need-based scholarships (average $300), non-need scholarships (average $450), short-term loans (average $150), low-interest long-term loans from external sources (average $1200), Federal Work-Study, part-time jobs. ***Required forms:*** state, institutional, FAFSA. ***Priority deadline:*** 4/1. ***Payment plan:*** installment.
APPLYING ***Options:*** early entrance, deferred entrance, midyear entrance. ***Required:*** school transcript, TOEFL for international students. ***Required for some:*** 3 years of high school math and science, recommendations, interview, SAT I or ACT. Test scores used for counseling/placement. ***Application deadline:*** rolling. ***Notification:*** continuous. Preference given to county residents.
APPLYING/TRANSFER ***Recommended:*** college transcript. ***Required for some:*** high school transcript, 3 years of high school math and science. ***Entrance:*** minimally difficult. ***Application deadline:*** rolling. ***Notification:*** continuous. ***Contact:*** Ms. Roberta Lockwood, Transfer Counselor, 315-786-2227.
CONTACT Ms. Rosanne N. Weir, Director of Admissions, Jefferson Community College, Watertown, NY 13601, 315-786-2408. ***E-mail:*** admissions@ccmgate.sunyjefferson.edu.

JUNIOR COLLEGE OF ALBANY
New York—See Sage Junior College of Albany

KATHARINE GIBBS SCHOOL
Melville, New York

UG Enrollment: 430	**Tuition & Fees: $8546**
Application Deadline: rolling	**Room & Board: N/Avail**

GENERAL Proprietary, 2-year, primarily women. Part of K-III Communications Corporation. Awards transfer associate degrees. Founded 1971. ***Setting:*** suburban campus with easy access to New York City. ***Total enrollment:*** 430. ***Faculty:*** 37 (12 full-time, 25 part-time).
ENROLLMENT PROFILE 430 students: 99% women, 0% part-time, 100% state residents, 0% Native American. ***Most popular recent major:*** secretarial studies/office management.
FIRST-YEAR CLASS 41 total. Of the students who applied, 75% were accepted, 67% of whom enrolled.
ACADEMIC PROGRAM Honor code. Calendar: quarters. Internships. ROTC: Army (c).
GENERAL DEGREE REQUIREMENTS 91 credits; 1 business math course; computer course.
MAJORS Hotel and restaurant management, secretarial studies/office management.
COMPUTERS ON CAMPUS 120 computers for student use in computer labs, classrooms.
COLLEGE LIFE ***Campus security:*** security guard.
HOUSING College housing not available.
CAREER PLANNING ***Placement office:*** 4 full-time staff. ***Director:*** Ms. Monica Nydick, Director of Career Counseling and Placement, 516-293-1024. ***Services:*** job fairs, resume preparation, resume referral, career counseling, careers library, job bank, job interviews. 500 organizations recruited on campus 1994–95.
AFTER GRADUATION 80% of class of 1994 had job offers within 6 months.
EXPENSES FOR 1996–97 ***Application fee:*** $25. Tuition: $8496 (minimum) full-time. Full-time tuition ranges up to $16,992 according to program. Full-time mandatory fees range from $50 to $100.

New York

Katharine Gibbs School (continued)
FINANCIAL AID *College-administered undergrad aid 1995–96:* 145 need-based scholarships (average $425), 20 non-need scholarships (average $1000), low-interest long-term loans from external sources, 14 Federal Work-Study (averaging $1500). *Required forms:* FAFSA; required for some: state. *Priority deadline:* 5/31. *Payment plans:* tuition prepayment, installment. *Waivers:* full or partial for employees or children of employees. *Notification:* continuous.
APPLYING *Option:* deferred entrance. *Required:* school transcript, interview. *Recommended:* recommendations. *Required for some:* CPAt. Test scores used for admission. *Application deadline:* rolling. *Notification:* continuous.
APPLYING/TRANSFER *Required:* interview. *Recommended:* recommendations. *Required for some:* standardized test scores. *Entrance:* minimally difficult. *Application deadline:* rolling. *Notification:* continuous.
CONTACT Mr. Vincent J. Montera, Director of Admissions, Katharine Gibbs School, Melville, NY 11747-3785, 516-293-2460 Ext. 47. *Fax:* 516-293-2709.

KATHARINE GIBBS SCHOOL
New York, New York

CONTACT Ms. Liz Brannen, Admissions Director, Katharine Gibbs School, 200 Park Avenue, New York, NY 10166-0005, 212-867-9300 Ext. 4968.

KINGSBOROUGH COMMUNITY COLLEGE OF THE CITY UNIVERSITY OF NEW YORK
Brooklyn, New York

UG Enrollment: 15,464	Tuition & Fees (NY Res): $2600
Application Deadline: rolling	Room & Board: N/Avail

GENERAL State and locally supported, 2-year, coed. Part of City University of New York System. Awards transfer associate, terminal associate degrees. Founded 1963. *Setting:* 67-acre urban campus. *Total enrollment:* 15,464. *Faculty:* 842 (265 full-time, 82% with terminal degrees, 577 part-time).
ENROLLMENT PROFILE 15,464 students: 63% women, 52% part-time, 99% state residents, 17% transferred in, 17% 25 or older, 13% Hispanic, 23% African American, 3% Asian American.
FIRST-YEAR CLASS 2,477 total. Of the students who applied, 100% were accepted. 10% from top 10% of their high school class, 25% from top quarter, 60% from top half.
ACADEMIC PROGRAM Core. Calendar: 12-6-12-6. Academic remediation for entering students, English as a second language program offered during academic year and summer, services for LD students, advanced placement, self-designed majors, honors program, summer session for credit, part-time degree program (daytime, evenings), adult/continuing education programs. Off-campus study at other units of the City University of New York System.
GENERAL DEGREE REQUIREMENTS 60 credits; 11 credits of math/science; computer course for engineering science, acounting, business administration, marketing management majors.
MAJORS Accounting, applied art, art/fine arts, biology/biological sciences, broadcasting, business administration/commerce/management, chemistry, computer programming, computer science, data processing, early childhood education, (pre)engineering sequence, environmental health sciences, fashion merchandising, journalism, labor and industrial relations, liberal arts/general studies, marine technology, marketing/retailing/merchandising, medical records services, mental health/rehabilitation counseling, music, nursing, public health, recreation and leisure services, retail management, secretarial studies/office management, theater arts/drama, tourism and travel.
LIBRARY 147,860 books, 11,000 microform titles, 455 periodicals, 4,200 records, tapes, and CDs. Acquisition spending 1994–95: $73,000.
COMPUTERS ON CAMPUS 400 computers for student use in computer labs, library provide access to main academic computer, off-campus computing facilities, Internet. Staffed computer lab on campus provides training in use of computers, software.
COLLEGE LIFE Orientation program (2 days, no cost). Drama-theater group, student-run newspaper, radio station. *Student services:* health clinic, personal-psychological counseling. *Campus security:* 24-hour emergency response devices and patrols.
HOUSING College housing not available.
ATHLETICS Member NJCAA. *Intercollegiate:* basketball M/W, soccer M, tennis M/W, volleyball W. *Intramural:* basketball, bowling, cross-country running, football, golf, racquetball, soccer, swimming and diving, tennis, track and field, volleyball. *Contact:* Mr. Michael Aboussleman, Director of Athletics, 718-368-5696.
CAREER PLANNING *Director:* Professor Oliver Klapper, Director Career Counseling, Placement and Transfer, 718-368-5115. *Services:* job fairs, resume preparation, career counseling, careers library, job bank, job interviews.
AFTER GRADUATION 70% of students completing a degree program in 1994–95 went directly on to further study.
EXPENSES FOR 1995–96 State resident tuition: $2500 full-time, $120 per credit part-time. Nonresident tuition: $3076 full-time, $175 per credit part-time. Part-time mandatory fees: $25 per term. Full-time mandatory fees: $100.
FINANCIAL AID *College-administered undergrad aid 1995–96:* 5,000 need-based scholarships (averaging $1500), short-term loans (averaging $50), low-interest long-term loans from external sources (averaging $1300), Federal Work-Study, 40 part-time jobs. *Required forms:* state, institutional, FAFSA. *Priority deadline:* 8/1.
APPLYING Open admission. *Options:* early entrance, midyear entrance. *Required:* school transcript, TOEFL for international students. Test scores used for counseling/placement. *Application deadline:* rolling.
APPLYING/TRANSFER *Required:* high school transcript. *Entrance:* noncompetitive. *Application deadline:* rolling. *Contact:* Mr. Alan Wittes, Coordinator of Admissions Information Center, 718-368-5800.
CONTACT Mr. Alan Wittes, Coordinator of Admissions Information Center, Kingsborough Community College of the City University of New York, 2001 Oriental Blvd, Manhattan Beach, Brooklyn, NY 11235, 718-368-5800.

LAGUARDIA COMMUNITY COLLEGE
New York—See Fiorello H. LaGuardia Community College of the City University of New York

LONG ISLAND COLLEGE HOSPITAL SCHOOL OF NURSING
Brooklyn, New York

UG Enrollment: 185	Tuition & Fees: $8063
Application Deadline: rolling	Room & Board: N/Avail

GENERAL Independent, 2-year, specialized, coed. Awards transfer associate, terminal associate degrees. Founded 1883. *Total enrollment:* 185. *Faculty:* 15 (6 full-time, 9 part-time).
ENROLLMENT PROFILE 185 students from 2 states and territories. 84% women, 67% part-time, 99% state residents, 83% transferred in, 0% international, 81% 25 or older, 0% Native American, 13% Hispanic, 52% African American, 0% Asian American.
FIRST-YEAR CLASS 70 total; 300 applied, 33% were accepted, 70% of whom enrolled. 80% from top quarter of their high school class, 100% from top half.
ACADEMIC PROGRAM Core. Calendar: semesters. Summer session for credit, part-time degree program (daytime, evenings, summer), co-op programs and internships.
GENERAL DEGREE REQUIREMENTS 67 credits; 10 credits of science.
MAJOR Nursing.
LIBRARY 15,000 books.
COLLEGE LIFE *Student services:* health clinic, personal-psychological counseling.
HOUSING College housing not available.
EXPENSES FOR 1996–97 *Application fee:* $50. Tuition: $7498 full-time. Part-time tuition per credit ranges from $194 to $292. Part-time mandatory fees: $70 per semester. Full-time mandatory fees: $565.
FINANCIAL AID *College-administered undergrad aid 1995–96:* need-based scholarships, non-need scholarships, short-term loans, low-interest long-term loans from external sources, Federal Work-Study, part-time jobs. *Required forms:* state, FAFSA; accepted: CSS Financial Aid PROFILE. *Priority deadline:* 7/1.
APPLYING *Required:* essay, school transcript, 2 recommendations, interview, TOEFL for international students, nursing exam. *Recommended:* minimum 2.0 GPA, 3 years of high school math and science. Test scores used for admission. *Application deadline:* rolling. *Notification:* continuous.
APPLYING/TRANSFER *Required:* essay, standardized test scores, high school transcript, 2 recommendations, interview, college transcript. *Recommended:* 3 years of high school math and science, minimum 2.0 college GPA, minimum 2.0 high school GPA. *Entrance:* moderately difficult. *Application deadline:* rolling. *Notification:* continuous.
CONTACT Mr. Carlos Tonche, Director of Student Services and Registrar, Long Island College Hospital School of Nursing, Brooklyn, NY 11201-5940, 718-780-1898.

MARIA COLLEGE
Albany, New York

UG Enrollment: 829	Tuition & Fees: $5250
Application Deadline: rolling	Room & Board: N/Avail

Clinical facilities for nursing, physical therapy, and occupational therapy majors are among the institutional leaders. Exceptional laboratory school for education majors is among the finest in the Capital District. Liberal arts and business majors are highly transferable. The College recently added an associate degree program in legal assistant studies, as well as a 1-year certificate program for those who already hold an associate or bachelor's degree. 406770

GENERAL Independent, 2-year, coed. Awards certificates, transfer associate, terminal associate degrees. Founded 1958. *Setting:* 9-acre urban campus. *Total enrollment:* 829. *Faculty:* 66 (28 full-time, 100% with terminal degrees, 38 part-time); student-faculty ratio is 14:1.
ENROLLMENT PROFILE 829 students from 3 states and territories, 4 other countries. 80% women, 20% men, 57% part-time, 96% state residents, 73% transferred in, 46% have need-based financial aid, 0% have non-need financial aid, 1% international, 65% 25 or older, 1% Native American, 2% Hispanic, 9% African American, 2% Asian American.
Areas of study chosen: 72% health professions and related sciences, 10% business management and administrative services, 10% education, 8% liberal arts/general studies.
Most popular recent majors: nursing, physical therapy, liberal arts/general studies.
FIRST-YEAR CLASS 380 total; 779 applied, 64% were accepted, 76% of whom enrolled. 5% from top 10% of their high school class, 15% from top quarter, 55% from top half.
ACADEMIC PROGRAM Core, honor code. Calendar: semesters. Academic remediation for entering students, English as a second language program offered during academic year, services for LD students, advanced placement, summer session for credit, part-time degree program (daytime, evenings, weekends), adult/continuing education programs. Off-campus study at members of the Hudson-Mohawk Association of Colleges and Universities.
GENERAL DEGREE REQUIREMENTS 64 credits; computer course for business, legal assistant majors; internship (some majors).
MAJORS Accounting, business administration/commerce/management, early childhood education, legal studies, liberal arts/general studies, nursing, occupational therapy, physical therapy.
LIBRARY Maria College Library with 34,500 books, 700 microform titles, 200 periodicals, 1 on-line bibliographic service, 4 CD-ROMs, 900 records, tapes, and CDs.
COMPUTERS ON CAMPUS 17 computers for student use in computer center, computer labs, learning resource center, library provide access to Internet. Staffed computer lab on campus provides training in use of computers, software.
COLLEGE LIFE *Student services:* personal-psychological counseling. *Campus security:* late-night transport-escort service.
HOUSING College housing not available.

CAREER PLANNING ***Placement office:*** 1 full-time staff. ***Director:*** Sr. Renee Cudhea, Director of Placement, 518-489-7436 Ext. 58. ***Services:*** job fairs, resume preparation, resume referral, career counseling, careers library, job bank, job interviews. Students must register sophomore year. 30 organizations recruited on campus 1994–95.
AFTER GRADUATION 14% of students completing a degree program in 1994–95 went directly on to further study.
EXPENSES FOR 1996–97 ***Application fee:*** $20. Tuition: $5200 full-time. Part-time tuition per credit ranges from $190 to $195. Part-time mandatory fees: $15 per semester. Full-time mandatory fees: $50.
FINANCIAL AID ***College-administered undergrad aid 1995–96:*** 18 need-based scholarships (average $775), low-interest long-term loans from external sources (average $2500), Federal Work-Study. ***Required forms:*** state, institutional, FAFSA; accepted: CSS Financial Aid PROFILE. ***Priority deadline:*** 6/30. ***Payment plan:*** installment. ***Waivers:*** full or partial for employees or children of employees and senior citizens.
APPLYING ***Options:*** early entrance, midyear entrance. ***Required:*** essay, school transcript, minimum 2.0 GPA, recommendations, campus interview, SAT I or ACT, TOEFL for international students. ***Required for some:*** 3 years of high school math and science, ACT COMPASS. Test scores used for admission and counseling/placement. ***Application deadline:*** rolling. ***Notification:*** continuous until 8/30.
APPLYING/TRANSFER ***Required:*** essay, high school transcript, recommendations, campus interview, college transcript, minimum 2.0 high school GPA. ***Recommended:*** minimum 2.0 college GPA. ***Required for some:*** standardized test scores, 3 years of high school math and science. ***Entrance:*** minimally difficult. ***Application deadline:*** rolling. ***Notification:*** continuous until 8/30. ***Contact:*** Ms. Laurie Gilmore, Director of Admissions, 518-438-3111 Ext. 17.
CONTACT Ms. Laurie Gilmore, Director of Admissions, Maria College, 700 New Scotland Avenue, Albany, NY 12208-1798, 518-438-3111 Ext. 17.

❖ *See page 764 for a narrative description.* ❖

MATER DEI COLLEGE
Ogdensburg, New York

UG Enrollment: 394	Tuition & Fees: $6225
Application Deadline: rolling	Room & Board: $4020

Mater Dei is a private, coeducational, multicampus college offering 10 associate degree programs. A small, personable environment gives students of any religious faith individualized attention so that they receive the skills needed to transfer to a baccalaureate institution or to secure immediate employment. Through programs in liberal arts and professional studies, the College prepares students to pursue excellence in career development, personal growth, and social responsibility.

GENERAL Independent Roman Catholic, 2-year, coed. Awards certificates, transfer associate, terminal associate degrees. Founded 1960. ***Setting:*** 211-acre rural campus. ***Endowment:*** $1 million. ***Educational spending 1994–95:*** $2950 per undergrad. ***Total enrollment:*** 394. ***Faculty:*** 26 (21 full-time, 12% with terminal degrees, 5 part-time); student-faculty ratio is 14:1.
ENROLLMENT PROFILE 394 students from 4 states and territories, 2 other countries. 79% women, 21% men, 5% part-time, 99% state residents, 19% live on campus, 14% transferred in, 75% have need-based financial aid, 5% have non-need-based financial aid, 47% 25 or older, 10% Native American, 1% Hispanic, 1% African American, 1% Asian American. ***Areas of study chosen:*** 50% social sciences, 20% business management and administrative services, 15% education, 8% liberal arts/general studies, 7% health professions and related sciences. ***Most popular recent majors:*** business administration/commerce/management, social work, early childhood education.
FIRST-YEAR CLASS 104 total; 151 applied, 99% were accepted, 70% of whom enrolled.
ACADEMIC PROGRAM Core, honor code. Calendar: semesters. 192 courses offered in 1995–96. Academic remediation for entering students, services for LD students, advanced placement, summer session for credit, part-time degree program (daytime, evenings, summer), adult/continuing education programs, internships.
GENERAL DEGREE REQUIREMENTS 61 credit hours; internship (some majors).
MAJORS Accounting, business administration/commerce/management, court reporting, criminal justice, drug and alcohol/substance abuse counseling, early childhood education, legal secretarial studies, liberal arts/general studies, medical secretarial studies, optometric/ophthalmic technologies, religious studies, secretarial studies/office management, social work.
LIBRARY Augsbury Library with 63,249 books, 56 microform titles, 253 periodicals, 1 on-line bibliographic service, 2 CD-ROMs, 4,215 records, tapes, and CDs. Acquisition spending 1994–95: $28,000.
COMPUTERS ON CAMPUS 45 computers for student use in computer labs, learning resource center. Staffed computer lab on campus provides training in use of computers, software. Academic computing expenditure 1994–95: $44,700.
COLLEGE LIFE Orientation program (2 days, no cost). ***Social organizations:*** 13 open to all. ***Most popular organizations:*** Student Government Association, Student Optical Society, Court Reporter Club, Phi Theta Kappa, Early Childhood Education Association. ***Major annual events:*** Making Miracles Happen: Teddy Project, Christmas Party and Dance, Family Weekend. ***Student services:*** personal-psychological counseling. ***Campus security:*** evening patrols by trained security personnel.
HOUSING 180 college housing spaces available; 76 were occupied 1995–96. Freshmen guaranteed college housing. On-campus residence required through sophomore year. ***Option:*** coed (1 building) housing available. Resident assistants live in dorms.
ATHLETICS Member NJCAA. ***Intercollegiate:*** basketball W(s), soccer W. ***Intramural:*** badminton, basketball, skiing (cross-country), volleyball. ***Contact:*** Mr. David Burfeind, Athletic Director, 315-393-5930 Ext. 466.
CAREER PLANNING ***Placement office:*** $9000 operating expenditure 1994–95. ***Director:*** Mr. Tony Puccia, Career Planning and Placement Counselor, 315-393-5930 Ext. 429. ***Services:*** resume preparation, career counseling, careers library. 10 organizations recruited on campus 1994–95.
AFTER GRADUATION 52% of class of 1994 had job offers within 6 months. 19% of students completing a degree program went directly on to further study.
EXPENSES FOR 1995–96 ***Application fee:*** $25. Comprehensive fee of $10,245 includes full-time tuition ($5900), mandatory fees ($325), and college room and board ($4020). Part-time tuition: $246 per credit hour.
FINANCIAL AID ***College-administered undergrad aid 1995–96:*** 140 need-based scholarships (average $1250), 22 non-need scholarships (average $1100), low-interest long-term loans from external sources (average $2700), 42 Federal Work-Study (averaging $1000), part-time jobs. ***Required forms:*** state, FAFSA. ***Priority deadline:*** 4/1. ***Payment plans:*** installment, deferred payment. ***Waivers:*** full or partial for employees or children of employees.
APPLYING ***Options:*** early entrance, deferred entrance, midyear entrance. ***Required:*** school transcript, minimum 2.0 GPA, TOEFL for international students. ***Recommended:*** campus interview, SAT I or ACT. ***Required for some:*** essay. Test scores used for counseling/placement. ***Application deadline:*** rolling. ***Notification:*** continuous.
APPLYING/TRANSFER ***Required:*** high school transcript, college transcript. ***Recommended:*** standardized test scores, campus interview. ***Required for some:*** essay, standardized test scores. ***Entrance:*** minimally difficult. ***Application deadline:*** rolling. ***Notification:*** continuous. ***Contact:*** Mr. Mark J. Dougherty, Director of Admission Services, 315-393-5930 Ext. 409.
CONTACT Mr. Mark J. Dougherty, Director of Admission Services, Mater Dei College, Ogdensburg, NY 13669-9699, 315-393-5930 Ext. 409 or toll-free 800-724-4080 (in-state). ***Fax:*** 315-393-5930 Ext. 440. College video available.

❖ *See page 766 for a narrative description.* ❖

MOHAWK VALLEY COMMUNITY COLLEGE
Utica, New York

UG Enrollment: 6,328	Tuition & Fees (NY Res): $2465
Application Deadline: rolling	Room & Board: $3810

GENERAL State and locally supported, 2-year, coed. Part of State University of New York System. Awards certificates, transfer associate, terminal associate degrees. Founded 1946. ***Setting:*** 80-acre suburban campus. ***Total enrollment:*** 6,328. ***Faculty:*** 353 (170 full-time, 183 part-time); student-faculty ratio is 18:1.
ENROLLMENT PROFILE 6,328 students from 5 states and territories, 8 other countries. 51% women, 49% men, 12% part-time, 98% state residents, 4% live on campus, 6% transferred in, 1% international, 37% 25 or older, 1% Native American, 3% Hispanic, 7% African American, 1% Asian American. ***Areas of study chosen:*** 22% liberal arts/general studies, 14% business management and administrative services, 13% health professions and related sciences, 10% fine arts, 9% social sciences, 8% vocational and home economics, 6% engineering and applied sciences, 3% computer and information sciences, 1% biological and life sciences, 1% mathematics, 1% physical sciences. ***Most popular recent majors:*** business administration/commerce/management, liberal arts/general studies, nursing.
FIRST-YEAR CLASS 1,621 total; 2,825 applied, 93% were accepted, 62% of whom enrolled.
ACADEMIC PROGRAM Core, comprehensive curriculum. Calendar: semesters. 3,000 courses offered in 1995–96. Academic remediation for entering students, English as a second language program offered during academic year and summer, services for LD students, advanced placement, summer session for credit, part-time degree program (daytime, evenings, summer), adult/continuing education programs, internships. Off-campus study at Munson Williams Proctor Institute.
GENERAL DEGREE REQUIREMENTS 62 credits; computer course for graphic design, business, accounting, medical records, technologies, food service, restaurant management, hospitality majors; internship (some majors).
MAJORS Accounting, advertising, aircraft and missile maintenance, art/fine arts, biology/biological sciences, business administration/commerce/management, chemical engineering technology, chemistry, child care/child and family studies, civil engineering technology, commercial art, communication equipment technology, community services, computer information systems, computer programming, computer science, criminal justice, data processing, dietetics, drafting and design, drug and alcohol/substance abuse counseling, electrical and electronics technologies, electrical engineering technology, electronics engineering technology, engineering and applied sciences, engineering sciences, (pre)engineering sequence, environmental sciences, finance/banking, food services management, food services technology, graphic arts, heating/refrigeration/air conditioning, hospitality services, hotel and restaurant management, humanities, human services, illustration, insurance, international business, international studies, laboratory technologies, legal secretarial studies, liberal arts/general studies, machine and tool technologies, manufacturing technology, marketing/retailing/merchandising, mathematics, mechanical design technology, mechanical engineering technology, medical records services, medical secretarial studies, metallurgical technology, nursing, nutrition, physical education, physics, radiological technology, recreational facilities management, recreation and leisure services, respiratory therapy, retail management, science, secretarial studies/office management, social science, studio art, surveying technology, welding technology, word processing.
LIBRARY Mohawk Valley Community College Library with 65,000 books, 796 periodicals, 1,700 records, tapes, and CDs.
COMPUTERS ON CAMPUS 200 computers for student use in computer center, computer labs, learning resource center, classrooms, library provide access to main academic computer, off-campus computing facilities, on-line services. Staffed computer lab on campus provides training in use of computers, software.
COLLEGE LIFE Drama-theater group, student-run newspaper, radio station. ***Social organizations:*** 50 open to all. ***Most popular organizations:*** Drama Club, Student Congress, Returning Adult Student Association. ***Major annual events:*** Open House, Student Orientation. ***Student services:*** health clinic, personal-psychological counseling. ***Campus security:*** 24-hour emergency response devices and patrols, late-night transport-escort service, controlled dormitory access.
HOUSING 360 college housing spaces available; all were occupied 1995–96. Freshmen given priority for college housing. Off-campus living permitted. ***Option:*** coed housing available. Resident assistants live in dorms.
ATHLETICS Member NJCAA. ***Intercollegiate:*** baseball M, basketball M/W, bowling M/W, cross-country running M/W, golf M/W, ice hockey M, lacrosse M, soccer M/W, softball W, tennis M/W, track and field M/W, volleyball W, wrestling M. ***Intramural:*** basketball, cross-country running, football, racquetball, softball, swimming and diving. ***Contact:*** Mr. John Teller, Director, 315-792-5570.

Peterson's Guide to Two-Year Colleges 1997 471

Mohawk Valley Community College (continued)
CAREER PLANNING ***Placement office:*** 1 full-time staff. ***Director:*** Ms. Dawn DeBuvitz, Co-ordinator of Student Employment Services, 315-792-5488. ***Services:*** job fairs, resume preparation, resume referral, career counseling, careers library, job bank, job interviews.
AFTER GRADUATION 45% of students completing a degree program in 1994–95 went directly on to further study.
ESTIMATED EXPENSES FOR 1996–97 ***Application fee:*** $30. State resident tuition: $2350 full-time, $80 per credit part-time. Nonresident tuition: $4700 full-time, $160 per credit part-time. Part-time mandatory fees: $1 per credit. Full-time mandatory fees: $115. College room and board: $3810 (minimum). College room only: $2330.
FINANCIAL AID ***College-administered undergrad aid 1995–96:*** need-based scholarships, short-term loans (averaging $50), low-interest long-term loans from external sources (averaging $550), Federal Work-Study, 10 part-time jobs. ***Required forms:*** state, institutional, FAFSA. ***Priority deadline:*** 4/15. ***Waivers:*** full or partial for children of alumni, employees or children of employees, and senior citizens.
APPLYING Open admission. ***Options:*** electronic application, early entrance, deferred entrance, midyear entrance. ***Recommended:*** TOEFL for international students. ***Required for some:*** 2 years of high school foreign language. ***Application deadline:*** rolling.
APPLYING/TRANSFER ***Required for some:*** 2 years of high school foreign language. ***Entrance:*** noncompetitive. ***Application deadline:*** rolling. ***Contact:*** Mr. Robert Jastrab, Counselor, 315-792-5401.
CONTACT Mr. Denis J. Kennelty, Acting Assistant Dean of Enrollment Management, Mohawk Valley Community College, Utica, NY 13501-5394, 315-792-5357 or toll-free 800-SEE-MVCC (in-state). ***Fax:*** 315-792-5527. ***E-mail:*** dkennelty@mvcc.edu.

MONROE COLLEGE
Bronx, New York

UG Enrollment: 2,625	Tuition & Fees: $8460
Application Deadline: 8/26	Room & Board: N/Avail

GENERAL Proprietary, 2-year, coed. Awards transfer associate, terminal associate degrees. Founded 1933. ***Setting:*** urban campus. ***Total enrollment:*** 2,625. ***Faculty:*** 100 (55 full-time, 45 part-time); student-faculty ratio is 18:1.
ENROLLMENT PROFILE 2,625 students: 64% women, 2% part-time, 100% state residents, 30% transferred in, 0% international, 37% 25 or older, 0% Native American, 53% Hispanic, 43% African American, 1% Asian American. ***Areas of study chosen:*** 60% business management and administrative services, 20% computer and information sciences.
FIRST-YEAR CLASS 1,360 total; 2,236 applied, 80% were accepted, 76% of whom enrolled. 5 class presidents, 1 valedictorian.
ACADEMIC PROGRAM Core, business/corporate curriculum, honor code. Calendar: trimesters. 91 courses offered in 1995–96. Academic remediation for entering students, English as a second language program offered during academic year, tutorials, summer session for credit, part-time degree program (daytime, evenings, weekends), adult/continuing education programs, co-op programs and internships.
GENERAL DEGREE REQUIREMENTS 20 courses; 1 math course; computer course.
MAJORS Accounting, business administration/commerce/management, computer science, hospitality services, secretarial studies/office management, word processing.
LIBRARY Main library plus 1 other, with 16,000 books, 214 periodicals.
COMPUTERS ON CAMPUS 428 computers for student use in computer center, computer labs, research center, learning resource center, student center. Staffed computer lab on campus.
COLLEGE LIFE Drama-theater group, student-run newspaper. ***Social organizations:*** 5 open to all. ***Student services:*** personal-psychological counseling. ***Campus security:*** late-night transport-escort service.
HOUSING College housing not available.
ATHLETICS Member NJCAA. ***Intercollegiate:*** basketball M(s). ***Intramural:*** basketball, bowling, volleyball. ***Contact:*** Mr. Bert Shillingford, Athletic Director, 718-933-6700.
CAREER PLANNING ***Placement office:*** 4 full-time, 1 part-time staff. ***Director:*** Mrs. Carolyn Tabachnik, Director of Career Placement, 718-933-6700. ***Services:*** job fairs, resume preparation, resume referral, career counseling, careers library, job interviews. Students must register sophomore year. 18 organizations recruited on campus 1994–95.
AFTER GRADUATION 95% of class of 1994 had job offers within 6 months. 26% of students completing a degree program went directly on to further study.
EXPENSES FOR 1995–96 Tuition: $8160 full-time, $680 per course part-time. Part-time mandatory fees: $150 per trimester. Full-time mandatory fees: $300.
FINANCIAL AID ***College-administered undergrad aid 1995–96:*** need-based scholarships, non-need scholarships, short-term loans (average $100), low-interest long-term loans from external sources, Federal Work-Study, part-time jobs. ***Required forms:*** state, institutional, FAFSA; required for some: CSS Financial Aid PROFILE, statement of welfare benefits. ***Priority deadline:*** 8/26. ***Payment plans:*** installment, deferred payment.
APPLYING ***Options:*** early entrance, deferred entrance, midyear entrance. ***Required:*** ACT ASSET. Test scores used for counseling/placement. ***Application deadline:*** 8/26. ***Notification:*** continuous until 9/3.
APPLYING/TRANSFER ***Application deadline:*** 8/26. ***Contact:*** Dr. Donald E. Simon, Dean/Registrar, 718-933-6700.
CONTACT Mr. Anthony Allen, Dean of Admissions, Monroe College, Monroe College Way, Bronx, NY 10468-5407, 718-933-6700 Ext. 265. College video available.

MONROE COLLEGE
New Rochelle, New York

UG Enrollment: 562	Tuition & Fees: $8460
Application Deadline: 8/26	Room & Board: N/Avail

GENERAL Proprietary, 2-year, coed. Awards transfer associate, terminal associate degrees. Founded 1983. ***Setting:*** urban campus. ***Total enrollment:*** 562. ***Faculty:*** 25 (11 full-time, 14 part-time); student-faculty ratio is 17:1.
ENROLLMENT PROFILE 562 students from 2 states and territories, 3 other countries. 68% women, 1% part-time, 98% state residents, 14% transferred in, 70% have need-based financial aid, 2% international, 29% 25 or older, 0% Native American, 31% Hispanic, 52% African American, 2% Asian American. ***Areas of study chosen:*** 60% business management and administrative services, 20% computer and information sciences.
FIRST-YEAR CLASS 304 total; 427 applied, 81% were accepted, 88% of whom enrolled.
ACADEMIC PROGRAM Core, business and corporate curriculum, honor code. Calendar: trimesters. 38 courses offered in 1995–96; average class size 23 in required courses. Academic remediation for entering students, English as a second language program offered during academic year, tutorials, summer session for credit, part-time degree program (daytime, evenings, weekends), adult/continuing education programs, co-op programs and internships.
GENERAL DEGREE REQUIREMENTS 20 courses; 1 math course; computer course.
MAJORS Accounting, business administration/commerce/management, computer science, hospitality services, secretarial studies/office management, word processing.
LIBRARY 4,500 books, 200 periodicals.
COMPUTERS ON CAMPUS 126 computers for student use in computer center, computer labs, research center, learning resource center, student center. Staffed computer lab on campus.
COLLEGE LIFE Drama-theater group, student-run newspaper. ***Social organizations:*** 5 open to all. ***Student services:*** personal-psychological counseling. ***Campus security:*** late-night transport-escort service.
HOUSING College housing not available.
ATHLETICS Member NJCAA. ***Intercollegiate:*** basketball M(s). ***Intramural:*** basketball, bowling, volleyball. ***Contact:*** Mr. Edward Zanato, Director of Student Services, 914-632-5400.
CAREER PLANNING ***Placement office:*** 2 full-time staff. ***Director:*** Ms. Leslie Jerome, Director of Career Services, 914-632-5400. ***Services:*** job fairs, resume preparation, resume referral, career counseling, careers library, job interviews. Students must register sophomore year. 12 organizations recruited on campus 1994–95.
AFTER GRADUATION 95% of class of 1994 had job offers within 6 months. 26% of students completing a degree program went directly on to further study.
EXPENSES FOR 1995–96 Tuition: $8160 full-time, $680 per course part-time. Part-time mandatory fees: $150 per year. Full-time mandatory fees: $300.
FINANCIAL AID ***College-administered undergrad aid 1995–96:*** need-based scholarships, non-need scholarships, short-term loans (average $100), low-interest long-term loans from external sources, Federal Work-Study, part-time jobs. ***Required forms:*** state, institutional, FAFSA; required for some: CSS Financial Aid PROFILE, statement of welfare benefits. ***Priority deadline:*** 8/26. ***Payment plans:*** installment, deferred payment.
APPLYING ***Options:*** early entrance, deferred entrance, midyear entrance. ***Required:*** ACT ASSET. Test scores used for counseling/placement. ***Application deadline:*** 8/26. ***Notification:*** continuous until 9/3.
APPLYING/TRANSFER ***Application deadline:*** 8/26. ***Notification:*** continuous until 9/3. ***Contact:*** Dr. Donald E. Simon, Dean of Institutional Services, 718-933-6700.
CONTACT Mr. Marc Jerome, Branch Campus Director, Monroe College, 434 Main Street, New Rochelle, NY 10801, 914-632-5400. College video available.

MONROE COMMUNITY COLLEGE
Rochester, New York

UG Enrollment: 13,730	Tuition & Fees (NY Res): $2380
Application Deadline: rolling	Room & Board: N/Avail

GENERAL State and locally supported, 2-year, coed. Part of State University of New York System. Awards certificates, transfer associate, terminal associate degrees. Founded 1961. ***Setting:*** 314-acre suburban campus with easy access to Buffalo. ***Total enrollment:*** 13,730. ***Faculty:*** 642 (282 full-time, 20% with terminal degrees, 360 part-time); student-faculty ratio is 19:1.
ENROLLMENT PROFILE 13,730 students: 55% women, 45% men, 47% part-time, 99% state residents, 19% transferred in, 1% international, 1% Native American, 7% Hispanic, 16% African American, 4% Asian American. ***Most popular recent majors:*** liberal arts/general studies, business administration/commerce/management.
FIRST-YEAR CLASS 4,263 total; 6,995 applied.
ACADEMIC PROGRAM Honor code. Calendar: semesters. 930 courses offered in 1995–96. Academic remediation for entering students, English as a second language program offered during academic year, services for LD students, advanced placement, honors program, summer session for credit, part-time degree program (daytime, evenings, summer), adult/continuing education programs, co-op programs and internships. Off-campus study at the Rochester Area Colleges. Study-abroad program. ROTC: Army, Naval, Air Force.
GENERAL DEGREE REQUIREMENTS 64 credits; computer course for accounting, communication, marketing/retailing, interior design majors; internship (some majors).
MAJORS Accounting, art/fine arts, automotive technologies, behavioral sciences, biology/biological sciences, biotechnology, business administration/commerce/management, chemical engineering technology, chemistry, civil engineering technology, commercial art, communication, computer information systems, computer science, computer technologies, construction technologies, corrections, criminal justice, data processing, dental services, electrical engineering technology, engineering sciences, environmental sciences, fashion design and technology, fashion merchandising, fire science, food services management, food services technology, forestry, graphic arts, heating/refrigeration/air conditioning, history, hotel and restaurant management, human ecology, human services, instrumentation technology, interior design, international business, landscape architecture/design, law enforcement/police sciences, legal secretarial studies, liberal arts/general studies, manufacturing technology, marketing/retailing/merchandising, mathematics, mechanical engineering technology, medical records services, music, nursing, optical technologies, pharmacy/pharmaceutical sciences, physical education, physics, political science/government, printing technologies, quality control technology, radiological technology, recreation and leisure services, retail management, science, secretarial studies/office management, social science, tourism and travel.
LIBRARY LeRoy V. Good Library plus 1 other, with 108,000 books, 1,100 periodicals, 8 CD-ROMs, 1,707 records, tapes, and CDs.
COMPUTERS ON CAMPUS 150 computers for student use in computer center, learning resource center, library provide access to Internet. Staffed computer lab on campus.
NOTEWORTHY RESEARCH FACILITIES AIDS Resource Library.
COLLEGE LIFE Drama-theater group, choral group, student-run newspaper, radio station. ***Social organizations:*** 49 open to all. ***Most popular organizations:*** Student Newspaper, Phi Theta Kappa, Student Government. ***Student services:*** health clinic, personal-psychological counseling. ***Campus security:*** late-night transport-escort service.
HOUSING College housing not available.

ATHLETICS Member NJCAA. ***Intercollegiate:*** baseball M(s), basketball M(s)/W(s), cross-country running M/W, golf M/W, lacrosse M, soccer M(s)/W(s), swimming and diving M(s)/W(s), tennis M(s)/W(s), track and field M/W, volleyball W. ***Intramural:*** archery, basketball, bowling, cross-country running, field hockey, golf, gymnastics, lacrosse, racquetball, soccer, softball, swimming and diving, tennis, track and field, volleyball, water polo, wrestling. ***Contact:*** Mr. Bruce Shapiro, Director of Athletics, 716-292-2831.
CAREER PLANNING ***Placement office:*** 4 full-time staff. ***Director:*** Mr. G. Christopher Belle-Isle, Director of Transfer and Placement, 716-292-2270. ***Services:*** job fairs, resume preparation, resume referral, career counseling, careers library, job bank, job interviews.
AFTER GRADUATION 59% of students completing a degree program in 1994–95 went directly on to further study.
EXPENSES FOR 1995–96 ***Application fee:*** $20. State resident tuition: $2240 full-time, $94 per credit part-time. Nonresident tuition: $4480 full-time, $188 per credit part-time. Full-time mandatory fees: $140.
FINANCIAL AID ***College-administered undergrad aid 1995–96:*** 5,500 need-based scholarships (average $1000), non-need scholarships, short-term loans, Federal Work-Study, part-time jobs. ***Required forms:*** state, institutional, FAFSA. ***Priority deadline:*** 5/1. ***Payment plans:*** installment, deferred payment. ***Waivers:*** full or partial for employees or children of employees and senior citizens. ***Notification:*** continuous.
APPLYING Open admission except for allied health, business, engineering science programs. ***Options:*** electronic application, early entrance. ***Required:*** school transcript, TOEFL for international students. ***Required for some:*** 3 years of high school math and science. Test scores used for counseling/placement. ***Application deadline:*** rolling. ***Notification:*** continuous. Preference given to county residents.
APPLYING/TRANSFER ***Required for some:*** 3 years of high school math and science. ***Entrance:*** noncompetitive. ***Application deadline:*** rolling. ***Notification:*** continuous. ***Contact:*** Mr. G. Christopher Belle-Isle, Director of Transfer and Placement, 716-292-2270.
CONTACT Mr. Anthony Felicetti, Dean of Admissions and Financial Aid, Monroe Community College, Rochester, NY 14623-5780, 716-292-2000 Ext. 2221. ***Fax:*** 716-427-2749.

NASSAU COMMUNITY COLLEGE
Garden City, New York

UG Enrollment: 21,975	Tuition & Fees (NY Res): $2220
Application Deadline: 8/23	Room & Board: N/Avail

GENERAL State and locally supported, 2-year, coed. Part of State University of New York System. Awards certificates, transfer associate, terminal associate degrees. Founded 1959. ***Setting:*** 225-acre suburban campus with easy access to New York City. ***Total enrollment:*** 21,975. ***Faculty:*** 1,523 (512 full-time, 30% with terminal degrees, 1,011 part-time); student-faculty ratio is 21:1. ***Notable Alumni:*** Billy Crystal, Brian Baldinger.
ENROLLMENT PROFILE 21,975 students: 54% women, 46% men, 45% part-time, 99% state residents, 9% transferred in, 1% international, 32% 25 or older, 1% Native American, 9% Hispanic, 13% African American, 4% Asian American. ***Areas of study chosen:*** 48% liberal arts/general studies, 20% business management and administrative services, 7% health professions and related sciences, 2% communications and journalism, 2% computer and information sciences, 2% engineering and applied sciences, 2% fine arts, 1% performing arts. ***Most popular recent majors:*** liberal arts/general studies, business administration/commerce/management.
FIRST-YEAR CLASS 5,399 total; 8,364 applied, 88% were accepted, 74% of whom enrolled. 1% from top 10% of their high school class, 7% from top quarter, 26% from top half.
ACADEMIC PROGRAM Core, honor code. Calendar: semesters. 841 courses offered in 1995–96. Academic remediation for entering students, English as a second language program offered during academic year and summer, services for LD students, advanced placement, honors program, summer session for credit, part-time degree program (daytime, evenings, summer), adult/continuing education programs, co-op programs and internships. Off-campus study at members of the Long Island Regional Advisory Council for Higher Education. ROTC: Army (c).
GENERAL DEGREE REQUIREMENTS 64 credits; 3 credits of math; 4 credits of lab science; computer course for business, accounting, marketing majors; internship (some majors).
MAJORS Accounting, applied art, art/fine arts, audio engineering, black/African-American studies, business administration/commerce/management, child care/child and family studies, civil engineering technology, commercial art, communication, computer science, criminal justice, data processing, deaf interpreter training, early childhood education, electrical and electronics technologies, engineering sciences, fashion design and technology, fashion merchandising, finance/banking, food services management, funeral service, health education, hotel and restaurant management, humanities, interior design, legal secretarial studies, liberal arts/general studies, marketing/retailing/merchandising, mathematics, medical laboratory technology, medical secretarial studies, music, nursing, operating room technology, paralegal studies, physical education, radiological technology, respiratory therapy, retail management, science, secretarial studies/office management, social science, studio art, transportation technologies, word processing.
LIBRARY A. Holly Patterson Library with 183,160 books, 546 microform titles, 1,579 periodicals, 7,143 records, tapes, and CDs.
COMPUTERS ON CAMPUS 800 computers for student use in computer center, computer labs, learning resource center, classrooms, library provide access to main academic computer, e-mail. Staffed computer lab on campus provides training in use of computers, software.
COLLEGE LIFE Drama-theater group, choral group, marching band, student-run newspaper, radio station. 4% vote in student government elections. ***Social organizations:*** 1 local fraternity, 2 local sororities. ***Most popular organizations:*** Student Government Association, Engineering Society, Haraya, Vignette Newspaper. ***Major annual events:*** Spring Festival, Annual Ski Trip, Student Leaders' Awards Reception. ***Student services:*** health clinic, personal-psychological counseling, women's center. ***Campus security:*** 24-hour emergency response devices and patrols, late-night transport-escort service.
HOUSING College housing not available.
ATHLETICS Member NJCAA. ***Intercollegiate:*** baseball M, basketball M/W, bowling M/W, cross-country running M/W, football M, golf M/W, ice hockey M, lacrosse M, soccer M/W, softball W, tennis M/W, track and field M/W, volleyball W. ***Intramural:*** basketball, cross-country running, football, lacrosse, soccer, softball, tennis, volleyball. ***Contact:*** Mr. Michael Pelliccia, Athletic Director, 516-572-7538.
CAREER PLANNING ***Placement office:*** 2 full-time, 1 part-time staff. ***Director:*** Dr. John Dumas, Coordinator, Career Development, 516-572-7698. ***Services:*** job fairs, resume preparation, career counseling, careers library, job bank.
AFTER GRADUATION 65% of students completing a degree program in 1994–95 went directly on to further study.
EXPENSES FOR 1995–96 ***Application fee:*** $20. State resident tuition: $2120 full-time, $86 per credit part-time. Nonresident tuition: $4240 full-time, $172 per credit part-time. Part-time mandatory fees: $4 per credit. Full-time mandatory fees: $100.
FINANCIAL AID ***College-administered undergrad aid 1995–96:*** need-based scholarships, low-interest long-term loans from college funds, loans from external sources, Federal Work-Study, part-time jobs. ***Required forms:*** state, institutional, FAFSA. ***Priority deadline:*** 5/1. ***Waivers:*** full or partial for senior citizens. ***Notification:*** continuous.
APPLYING Open admission except for allied health, nursing, engineering science, engineering technology, mortuary science programs. ***Option:*** midyear entrance. ***Required:*** school transcript, TOEFL for international students. ***Required for some:*** minimum 2.0 GPA, 3 years of high school math and science, campus interview. Test scores used for counseling/placement. ***Application deadline:*** 8/23. ***Notification:*** continuous.
APPLYING/TRANSFER ***Required:*** high school transcript, college transcript. ***Required for some:*** 3 years of high school math and science, campus interview, minimum 2.0 high school GPA. ***Entrance:*** noncompetitive. ***Application deadline:*** 8/23. ***Notification:*** continuous. ***Contact:*** Ms. Evor Ingram, Coordinator, Transfer Counseling, 516-572-7128.
CONTACT Mr. Bernard Iantosca, Director of Admissions, Nassau Community College, Garden City, NY 11530-6793, 516-572-7210. College video available.

NEW YORK CITY TECHNICAL COLLEGE OF THE CITY UNIVERSITY OF NEW YORK
Brooklyn, New York

Enrollment: N/R	Tuition & Fees (NY Res): $3254
Application Deadline: rolling	Room & Board: N/Avail

GENERAL State and locally supported, primarily 2-year, coed. Part of City University of New York System. Awards transfer associate, terminal associate, bachelor's degrees. Founded 1946. ***Setting:*** urban campus. ***Faculty:*** 750 (300 full-time, 450 part-time); student-faculty ratio is 18:1.
ENROLLMENT PROFILE 42% part-time, 97% state residents, 4% transferred in, 45% 25 or older, 1% Native American, 21% Hispanic, 55% African American, 8% Asian American.
FIRST-YEAR CLASS Of the students who applied, 100% were accepted, 65% of whom enrolled.
ACADEMIC PROGRAM Core. Calendar: semesters. Academic remediation for entering students, English as a second language program offered during academic year and summer, services for LD students, advanced placement, summer session for credit, part-time degree program (daytime, evenings, weekends), adult/continuing education programs. Off-campus study at other units of the City University of New York System, Association of Graphic Arts. Study abroad in England, France, Germany, Italy. ROTC: Air Force (c).
GENERAL DEGREE REQUIREMENTS 64 credits for associate, 128 credits for bachelor's; math/science requirements vary according to major; computer course for marketing, engineering, electromechanical majors.
MAJORS Accounting, adult and continuing education (B), architectural technologies, automotive technologies, chemical engineering technology, civil engineering technology, commercial art, construction technologies, data processing, dental services, drafting and design, electrical engineering technology, electromechanical technology, engineering technology, environmental engineering technology, fashion merchandising, gerontology, graphic arts (B), heating/refrigeration/air conditioning, hotel and restaurant management (B), human services, legal secretarial studies, liberal arts/general studies, machine and tool technologies, marketing/retailing/merchandising, mechanical engineering technology, medical laboratory technology, nursing, optometric/ophthalmic technologies, paralegal studies, printing technologies (B), radiological technology, secretarial studies/office management, telecommunications.
LIBRARY 111,757 books, 7,337 microform titles, 870 periodicals, 1,954 records, tapes, and CDs.
COMPUTERS ON CAMPUS Computers for student use in computer center, labs, learning center, student center.
COLLEGE LIFE Drama-theater group, student-run newspaper. ***Social organizations:*** social clubs. ***Student services:*** health clinic, personal-psychological counseling.
HOUSING College housing not available.
ATHLETICS Member NJCAA. ***Intercollegiate:*** basketball M/W, soccer M, volleyball W. ***Intramural:*** basketball, volleyball.
CAREER PLANNING ***Service:*** career counseling.
EXPENSES FOR 1995–96 State resident tuition: $3200 full-time, $135 per semester part-time. Nonresident tuition: $6800 full-time, $285 per semester part-time. Part-time mandatory fees: $6.45 per semester. Full-time mandatory fees: $54.
FINANCIAL AID ***College-administered undergrad aid 1995–96:*** need-based scholarships, non-need scholarships, short-term loans, Federal Work-Study. ***Required forms:*** state, institutional, FAFSA. ***Priority deadline:*** 7/15.
APPLYING Open admission except for hotel and restaurant management, graphic arts and production management baccalaureate programs. ***Required:*** school transcript, TOEFL for international students. ***Recommended:*** 3 years of high school math and science. Test scores used for admission. ***Application deadline:*** rolling.
APPLYING/TRANSFER ***Required:*** high school transcript. ***Recommended:*** 3 years of high school math and science. ***Entrance:*** minimally difficult. ***Application deadline:*** rolling.
CONTACT Ms. Arlene M. Floyd, Director of Admissions, New York City Technical College of the City University of New York, 300 Jay Street, Brooklyn, NY 11201-2983, 718-260-5000.

NIAGARA COUNTY COMMUNITY COLLEGE
Sanborn, New York

UG Enrollment: 5,361 **Tuition & Fees (NY Res): $2354**
Application Deadline: rolling **Room & Board: N/Avail**

GENERAL State and locally supported, 2-year, coed. Part of State University of New York System. Awards certificates, transfer associate, terminal associate degrees. Founded 1962. ***Setting:*** 287-acre rural campus with easy access to Buffalo. ***Endowment:*** $900,000. ***Educational spending 1994–95:*** $2977 per undergrad. ***Total enrollment:*** 5,361. ***Faculty:*** 549 (225 full-time, 10% with terminal degrees, 324 part-time). ***Notable Alumni:*** Lessie Hamilton-Rose, project facilitator at Flower City School; Theresa Silvestre, 1994 Tonawanda Chamber of Commerce Citizen of the Year Award recipient; Charles Steiner, chairman of the board at Niagara Falls Chamber of Commerce; Joseph Ruffolo, CEO of Children's Hospital of Buffalo; George Maziarz, member of New York State Senate.

ENROLLMENT PROFILE 5,361 students from 2 states and territories, 15 other countries. 58% women, 42% men, 40% part-time, 98% state residents, 5% transferred in, 46% have need-based financial aid, 4% have non-need-based financial aid, 1% international, 42% 25 or older, 1% Native American, 1% Hispanic, 5% African American, 1% Asian American. ***Areas of study chosen:*** 35% liberal arts/general studies, 15% business management and administrative services, 15% health professions and related sciences, 15% social sciences, 8% engineering and applied sciences, 3% communications and journalism, 3% computer and information sciences, 3% fine arts, 1% biological and life sciences, 1% performing arts, 1% vocational and home economics. ***Most popular recent majors:*** liberal arts/general studies, social science, nursing.

FIRST-YEAR CLASS 1,458 total; 1,895 applied, 95% were accepted, 81% of whom enrolled. 6% from top 10% of their high school class, 22% from top quarter, 54% from top half.

ACADEMIC PROGRAM Honor code. Calendar: semesters. 2,725 courses offered in 1995–96. Academic remediation for entering students, services for LD students, advanced placement, self-designed majors, summer session for credit, part-time degree program (daytime, evenings, summer), adult/continuing education programs, co-op programs and internships. Off-campus study at 17 members of the Western New York Consortium. ROTC: Army (c).

GENERAL DEGREE REQUIREMENTS 62 credit hours; computer course for most majors; internship (some majors).

MAJORS Accounting, animal sciences, art/fine arts, biology/biological sciences, business administration/commerce/management, chemistry, communication, computer science, criminal justice, culinary arts, drafting and design, human services, liberal arts/general studies, mathematics, medical assistant technologies, medical secretarial studies, music, nursing, operating room technology, ornamental horticulture, physical therapy, practical nursing, radiological technology, retail management, science, secretarial studies/office management, social science, telecommunications, theater arts/drama, word processing.

LIBRARY Library Learning Center with 82,684 books, 178 microform titles, 532 periodicals, 7 CD-ROMs, 5,727 records, tapes, and CDs. Acquisition spending 1994–95: $210,508.

COMPUTERS ON CAMPUS 170 computers for student use in computer center, computer labs, learning resource center, learning labs, classrooms, library provide access to main academic computer. Staffed computer lab on campus provides training in use of computers, software. Academic computing expenditure 1994–95: $566,202.

COLLEGE LIFE Drama-theater group, choral group, student-run newspaper, radio station. 6% vote in student government elections. ***Social organizations:*** 40 open to all. ***Most popular organizations:*** Student Radio Station, Student Nurses Association, Phi Theta Kappa, Science Professionals. ***Major annual events:*** All College Picnics, Orientation, Theatrical/Musical Events. ***Student services:*** health clinic, personal-psychological counseling. ***Campus security:*** 24-hour emergency response devices and patrols, student patrols, late-night transport-escort service.

HOUSING College housing not available.

ATHLETICS Member NJCAA. ***Intercollegiate:*** baseball M, basketball M/W, bowling M/W, soccer M/W, softball W, volleyball W, wrestling M. ***Intramural:*** badminton, basketball, bowling, fencing, football, golf, lacrosse, racquetball, skiing (cross-country), skiing (downhill), soccer, squash, swimming and diving, table tennis (Ping-Pong), tennis, volleyball, weight lifting. ***Contact:*** Ms. Luann Ostranski, Coordinator of Athletics, 716-731-3271 Ext. 519.

CAREER PLANNING ***Placement office:*** 10 full-time staff; $532,980 operating expenditure 1994–95. ***Director:*** Ms. Carol Henschel, Professor/Counselor, 716-731-3271 Ext. 530. ***Services:*** job fairs, resume preparation, resume referral, career counseling, careers library, job bank, job interviews. 20 organizations recruited on campus 1994–95.

AFTER GRADUATION 46% of class of 1994 had job offers within 6 months. 56% of students completing a degree program went directly on to further study.

EXPENSES FOR 1995–96 State resident tuition: $2250 full-time, $80 per credit hour part-time. Nonresident tuition: $3375 full-time, $120 per credit hour part-time. Part-time mandatory fees: $2.50 per credit hour. Full-time mandatory fees: $104.

FINANCIAL AID ***College-administered undergrad aid 1995–96:*** 130 need-based scholarships (average $675), 5 non-need scholarships (average $1000), short-term loans (average $100), low-interest long-term loans from external sources (average $1622), 97 Federal Work-Study (averaging $960), 144 part-time jobs. ***Required forms:*** institutional; required for some: state, FAFSA; accepted: CSS Financial Aid PROFILE. ***Priority deadline:*** 4/1. ***Waivers:*** full or partial for employees or children of employees.

APPLYING Open admission. ***Options:*** Common Application, early entrance, midyear entrance. ***Required:*** school transcript, TOEFL for international students. ***Recommended:*** SAT I or ACT, SAT II Subject Tests. ***Required for some:*** minimum 2.0 GPA, 3 years of high school math, some high school foreign language. Test scores used for counseling/placement. ***Application deadline:*** rolling. ***Notification:*** continuous.

APPLYING/TRANSFER ***Required:*** college transcript. ***Required for some:*** 3 years of high school math, minimum 2.0 high school GPA. ***Application deadline:*** rolling. ***Notification:*** continuous. ***Contact:*** Mr. Joseph Colosi, Transfer Counselor, 716-731-3271.

CONTACT Ms. Laurie Ryan, Coordinator of Admissions, Niagara County Community College, Sanborn, NY 14132-9460, 716-731-3271 Ext. 112. ***Fax:*** 716-731-4053. College video available.

NORTH COUNTRY COMMUNITY COLLEGE
Saranac Lake, New York

UG Enrollment: 1,148 **Tuition & Fees (NY Res): $2235**
Application Deadline: rolling **Room & Board: N/Avail**

GENERAL State and locally supported, 2-year, coed. Part of State University of New York System. Awards certificates, transfer associate, terminal associate degrees. Founded 1967. ***Setting:*** 100-acre rural campus. ***Total enrollment:*** 1,148. ***Faculty:*** 140 (78 full-time, 62 part-time).

ENROLLMENT PROFILE 1,148 students from 13 states and territories. 64% women, 36% men, 19% part-time, 97% state residents, 98% transferred in, 41% 25 or older, 3% Native American, 1% Hispanic, 1% African American, 1% Asian American. ***Areas of study chosen:*** 20% liberal arts/general studies, 14% health professions and related sciences, 14% interdisciplinary studies, 13% business management and administrative services, 8% mathematics. ***Most popular recent majors:*** liberal arts/general studies, nursing, criminal justice.

FIRST-YEAR CLASS 346 total; 800 applied, 94% were accepted, 46% of whom enrolled. 6% from top 10% of their high school class, 13% from top quarter, 72% from top half. 8 class presidents.

ACADEMIC PROGRAM Core, interdisciplinary curriculum. Calendar: semesters. 458 courses offered in 1995–96. Academic remediation for entering students, services for LD students, advanced placement, self-designed majors, tutorials, summer session for credit, part-time degree program (daytime, evenings, summer), adult/continuing education programs, internships.

GENERAL DEGREE REQUIREMENTS 62 semester hours; math/science requirements vary according to program; computer course for business, retail management majors; internship (some majors).

MAJORS Business administration/commerce/management, criminal justice, forestry, forest technology, liberal arts/general studies, mathematics, mental health/rehabilitation counseling, nursing, radiological technology, recreational facilities management, recreation and leisure services, retail management, science, secretarial studies/office management.

LIBRARY North Country Community College Library with 38,174 books, 95 microform titles, 340 periodicals, 1,240 records, tapes, and CDs. Acquisition spending 1994–95: $142,694.

COMPUTERS ON CAMPUS Computers for student use in computer center, classroom building, learning lab, classrooms.

COLLEGE LIFE ***Most popular organizations:*** Student Government Association, Wilderness Recreation Club, Nursing Club, Astronomy Club. ***Major annual events:*** Winter Carnival, Homecoming, National Hockey Tournament. ***Student services:*** personal-psychological counseling.

HOUSING College housing not available.

ATHLETICS Member NJCAA. ***Intercollegiate:*** basketball M, ice hockey M/W, skiing (cross-country) M/W, skiing (downhill) M/W, soccer M/W, softball W. ***Intramural:*** archery, badminton, basketball, bowling, cross-country running, golf, skiing (cross-country), skiing (downhill), soccer, softball, swimming and diving, tennis, volleyball, weight lifting. ***Contact:*** Mr. Timothy Gerrish, Athletic Director, 518-891-2915.

CAREER PLANNING ***Placement office:*** 1 full-time, 2 part-time staff. ***Director:*** Ms. Roberta Karp, Career Planning/Placement Counselor, 518-891-2915. ***Services:*** job fairs, resume preparation, career counseling, careers library, job bank, job interviews.

AFTER GRADUATION 39% of students completing a degree program in 1994–95 went directly on to further study.

EXPENSES FOR 1995–96 State resident tuition: $2100 full-time, $75 per semester hour part-time. Nonresident tuition: $4200 full-time, $150 per semester hour part-time. Part-time mandatory fees: $4 per semester hour. Full-time mandatory fees: $135.

FINANCIAL AID ***College-administered undergrad aid 1995–96:*** need-based scholarships, low-interest long-term loans from external sources (averaging $2120), Federal Work-Study, 50 part-time jobs. ***Required forms for some financial aid applicants:*** institutional; accepted: CSS Financial Aid PROFILE, FAFSA. ***Priority deadline:*** 5/30. ***Waivers:*** full or partial for employees or children of employees and senior citizens.

APPLYING Open admission except for radiological technology, nursing programs. ***Options:*** early entrance, deferred entrance, midyear entrance. ***Required:*** school transcript, TOEFL for international students. ***Recommended:*** SAT I or ACT. ***Required for some:*** 3 years of high school math and science. Test scores used for counseling/placement. ***Application deadline:*** rolling. ***Notification:*** continuous. Preference given to residents of sponsoring counties.

APPLYING/TRANSFER ***Required:*** high school transcript, college transcript. ***Entrance:*** noncompetitive. ***Application deadline:*** rolling. ***Notification:*** continuous.

CONTACT Mr. George P. Maniates, Assistant Director of Admissions, North Country Community College, Saranac Lake, NY 12983-2046, 518-891-2915 Ext. 278 or toll-free 800-541-1021. ***Fax:*** 518-891-2915.

OLEAN BUSINESS INSTITUTE
Olean, New York

UG Enrollment: 173 **Tuition & Fees: $5400**
Application Deadline: 8/31 **Room & Board: N/Avail**

GENERAL Proprietary, 2-year, coed. Awards diplomas, terminal associate degrees. Founded 1961. ***Setting:*** small-town campus. ***Total enrollment:*** 173. ***Faculty:*** 12 (9 full-time, 3 part-time); student-faculty ratio is 15:1.

ENROLLMENT PROFILE 173 students from 2 states and territories. 90% women, 10% men, 5% part-time, 50% state residents, 10% transferred in, 80% have need-based financial aid, 50% 25 or older, 1% Native American, 1% African American. ***Areas of study chosen:*** 100% business management and administrative services. ***Most popular recent majors:*** medical secretarial studies, accounting, paralegal studies.

FIRST-YEAR CLASS 35 total.

ACADEMIC PROGRAM Honor code. Calendar: semesters. 35 courses offered in 1995–96. Tutorials, summer session for credit, part-time degree program (daytime, evenings), internships.

GENERAL DEGREE REQUIREMENTS 68 credit hours; computer course; internship (some majors).

MAJORS Accounting, business administration/commerce/management, legal secretarial studies, medical secretarial studies, paralegal studies, secretarial studies/office management.
LIBRARY 1,800 books.
COMPUTERS ON CAMPUS 70 computers for student use in computer center, computer labs, classrooms, student center provide access to main academic computer. Staffed computer lab on campus provides training in use of computers, software.
COLLEGE LIFE 100% vote in student government elections. ***Student services:*** personal-psychological counseling. ***Campus security:*** 24-hour emergency response devices, late-night transport-escort service.
HOUSING College housing not available.
ATHLETICS ***Intramural:*** bowling, tennis, volleyball.
CAREER PLANNING ***Placement office:*** 1 full-time staff. ***Director:*** Mrs. Jeanne Johnston, Director of Placement, 716-372-7978. ***Services:*** resume preparation, resume referral, career counseling, job interviews.
EXPENSES FOR 1996–97 ***Application fee:*** $25. Tuition: $5300 full-time, $175 per credit hour part-time. Full-time mandatory fees: $100.
FINANCIAL AID ***College-administered undergrad aid 1995–96:*** need-based scholarships, non-need scholarships, low-interest long-term loans from external sources. ***Required forms:*** CSS Financial Aid PROFILE, state, FAFSA. ***Application deadline:*** continuous to 5/1. ***Payment plan:*** installment.
APPLYING ***Required:*** school transcript. ***Required for some:*** essay, interview. ***Application deadline:*** 8/31. ***Notification:*** continuous until 9/1.
APPLYING/TRANSFER ***Required:*** high school transcript, college transcript. ***Required for some:*** essay, interview. ***Entrance:*** noncompetitive. ***Application deadline:*** 8/31. ***Notification:*** continuous until 9/1. ***Contact:*** Mr. Patrick McCarthy, Director, 716-372-7978.
CONTACT Mr. Patrick McCarthy, Director, Olean Business Institute, Olean, NY 14760-2691, 716-372-7978.

ONONDAGA COMMUNITY COLLEGE
Syracuse, New York

UG Enrollment: 7,400	**Tuition & Fees (Area Res): $2326**
Application Deadline: 8/10	**Room & Board: N/Avail**

GENERAL State and locally supported, 2-year, coed. Part of State University of New York System. Awards certificates, diplomas, transfer associate, terminal associate degrees. Founded 1962. ***Setting:*** 180-acre suburban campus. ***Total enrollment:*** 7,400. ***Faculty:*** 536 (200 full-time, 20% with terminal degrees, 336 part-time); student-faculty ratio is 15:1.
ENROLLMENT PROFILE 7,400 students from 9 states and territories, 37 other countries. 56% women, 50% part-time, 95% state residents, 4% transferred in, 1% international, 45% 25 or older, 2% Native American, 1% Hispanic, 6% African American, 2% Asian American. ***Most popular recent majors:*** humanities, human services.
FIRST-YEAR CLASS 1,249 total; 2,645 applied, 75% were accepted, 63% of whom enrolled. 10% from top 10% of their high school class, 20% from top quarter, 50% from top half.
ACADEMIC PROGRAM Core, honor code. Calendar: semesters. 1,793 courses offered in 1995–96. Academic remediation for entering students, English as a second language program offered during academic year, services for LD students, advanced placement, tutorials, summer session for credit, part-time degree program (daytime, evenings, weekends, summer), external degree programs, adult/continuing education programs, co-op programs and internships. ROTC: Army (c), Air Force (c).
GENERAL DEGREE REQUIREMENTS 62 credits; computer course for accounting, computer engineering technology, electrical engineering, engineering science, food services, hotel technology, insurance, office technology, word processing majors; internship (some majors).
MAJORS Accounting, architectural technologies, art/fine arts, automotive technologies, business administration/commerce/management, computer information systems, computer science, computer technologies, construction technologies, criminal justice, culinary arts, data processing, dental services, drafting and design, early childhood education, electrical and electronics technologies, electrical engineering technology, engineering sciences, finance/banking, fire science, food services management, graphic arts, hotel and restaurant management, humanities, human services, insurance, interior design, labor studies, landscape architecture/design, liberal arts/general studies, machine and tool technologies, mathematics, mechanical engineering technology, medical records services, music, nursing, photography, physical therapy, quality control technology, radio and television studies, recreation and leisure services, respiratory therapy, science, secretarial studies/office management, telecommunications, word processing.
LIBRARY Sidney B. Coulter Library with 95,960 books, 308 microform titles, 220 periodicals, 103 CD-ROMs, 4,387 records, tapes, and CDs. Acquisition spending 1994–95: $803,334.
COMPUTERS ON CAMPUS 150 computers for student use in computer center, business, math departments, library. Staffed computer lab on campus provides training in use of computers, software.
COLLEGE LIFE Choral group, student-run newspaper, radio station. 2% vote in student government elections. ***Social organizations:*** 22 open to all; 20 social clubs; 5% of eligible men and 5% of eligible women are members. ***Most popular organizations:*** Criminal Justice Club, Nursing Club, Photo Club, Outing Club. ***Major annual events:*** Party On the Quad, Orientation, Essay Contest and Dinner Dance. ***Student services:*** health clinic, personal-psychological counseling. ***Campus security:*** 24-hour patrols.
HOUSING College housing not available.
ATHLETICS Member NJCAA. ***Intercollegiate:*** baseball M(s), basketball M, lacrosse M, softball W, tennis M/W, volleyball W. ***Intramural:*** basketball, racquetball, tennis. ***Contact:*** Mr. Russell Thomas, Athletic Director, 315-469-2492.
CAREER PLANNING ***Placement office:*** 1 full-time staff. ***Director:*** Ms. Hilary Williams, Job Placement Counselor/Labor Services Representative, 315-469-2386. ***Services:*** resume preparation, career counseling, job interviews. Students must register sophomore year. 100 organizations recruited on campus 1994–95.
EXPENSES FOR 1995–96 ***Application fee:*** $25. Area resident tuition: $2230 full-time, $89 per credit part-time. State resident tuition: $4460 full-time, $178 per credit part-time. Nonresident tuition: $6690 full-time, $267 per credit part-time. Part-time mandatory fees: $15 per semester. Full-time mandatory fees: $96.
FINANCIAL AID ***College-administered undergrad aid 1995–96:*** 54 need-based scholarships, short-term loans, low-interest long-term loans from external sources (average $2000), Federal Work-Study. ***Required forms:*** state, FAFSA. ***Priority deadline:*** 3/1. ***Waivers:*** full or partial for employees or children of employees and senior citizens. ***Notification:*** 6/1.
APPLYING Open admission except for allied health, engineering, computer science, technology, art, music programs. ***Options:*** Common Application, early entrance, deferred entrance, midyear entrance. ***Required:*** TOEFL for international students. ***Recommended:*** 3 years of high school math and science, some high school foreign language, TSWE. ***Required for some:*** minimum 2.0 GPA, 3 years of high school math, some high school foreign language. Test scores used for admission and counseling/placement. ***Application deadline:*** 8/10. ***Notification:*** continuous. Preference given to county residents, members of the Armed Forces.
APPLYING/TRANSFER ***Entrance:*** noncompetitive. ***Application deadline:*** 8/10. ***Notification:*** continuous. ***Contact:*** Ms. Gloria Battaglia, Transfer Counselor, 315-469-2382.
CONTACT Mr. Monty R. Flynn, Associate Director of Admissions, Onondaga Community College, Syracuse, NY 13215, 315-469-2201. ***Fax:*** 315-469-6775.

ORANGE COUNTY COMMUNITY COLLEGE
Middletown, New York

UG Enrollment: 5,853	**Tuition & Fees (NY Res): $2085**
Application Deadline: 8/1	**Room & Board: N/Avail**

GENERAL State and locally supported, 2-year, coed. Part of State University of New York System. Awards certificates, transfer associate, terminal associate degrees. Founded 1950. ***Setting:*** 37-acre suburban campus with easy access to New York City. ***Educational spending 1994–95:*** $2657 per undergrad. ***Total enrollment:*** 5,853. ***Faculty:*** 336 (158 full-time, 15% with terminal degrees, 178 part-time); student-faculty ratio is 18:1.
ENROLLMENT PROFILE 5,853 students from 18 states and territories, 3 other countries. 62% women, 55% part-time, 99% state residents, 4% transferred in, 1% international, 44% 25 or older, 1% Native American, 7% Hispanic, 6% African American, 2% Asian American. ***Areas of study chosen:*** 18% liberal arts/general studies, 11% health professions and related sciences, 9% business management and administrative services, 8% physical sciences, 3% computer and information sciences, 3% engineering and applied sciences, 1% architecture, 1% education. ***Most popular recent majors:*** liberal arts/general studies, nursing, business administration/commerce/management.
FIRST-YEAR CLASS 1,531 total; 2,079 applied, 100% were accepted, 74% of whom enrolled. 7% from top 10% of their high school class, 33% from top quarter, 60% from top half.
ACADEMIC PROGRAM Core, honor code. Calendar: semesters. Academic remediation for entering students, English as a second language program offered during academic year, services for LD students, tutorials, honors program, summer session for credit, part-time degree program (daytime, evenings, weekends), external degree programs, adult/continuing education programs, internships.
GENERAL DEGREE REQUIREMENTS 60 credits; computer course (varies by major).
MAJORS Accounting, architectural technologies, biology/biological sciences, business administration/commerce/management, child care/child and family studies, computer information systems, computer programming, computer science, computer technologies, construction technologies, criminal justice, data processing, dental services, drafting and design, electrical and electronics technologies, electrical engineering technology, elementary education, engineering sciences, finance/banking, humanities, information science, law enforcement/police sciences, liberal arts/general studies, marketing/retailing/merchandising, medical laboratory technology, mental health/rehabilitation counseling, nursing, occupational therapy, physical fitness/exercise science, physical sciences, physical therapy, radiological technology, real estate, recreation and leisure services, retail management, science, secretarial studies/office management.
LIBRARY Learning Resource Center with 68,700 books, 200 microform titles, 361 periodicals, 6 CD-ROMs, 1,907 records, tapes, and CDs. Acquisition spending 1994–95: $117,669.
COMPUTERS ON CAMPUS 200 computers for student use in computer center, computer labs, learning resource center, writing, reading, math labs, business department, library provide access to main academic computer, on-line services, Internet. Staffed computer lab on campus provides training in use of computers, software.
COLLEGE LIFE Drama-theater group, choral group, student-run newspaper. ***Social organizations:*** 27 open to all. ***Student services:*** personal-psychological counseling. ***Campus security:*** student patrols, late-night transport-escort service.
HOUSING College housing not available.
ATHLETICS Member NJCAA. ***Intercollegiate:*** basketball M/W, golf M/W, soccer M/W, swimming and diving M/W, tennis M/W, volleyball W. ***Intramural:*** basketball, field hockey, racquetball, soccer, tennis, volleyball. ***Contact:*** Ms. Susan Deer, Athletic Director, 914-341-4215.
CAREER PLANNING ***Placement office:*** 2 full-time, 3 part-time staff. ***Director:*** Ms. Carole Wentzel, Coordinator of Career Development Center, 914-341-4444. ***Services:*** job fairs, resume preparation, resume referral, career counseling, careers library, job bank, job interviews. 87 organizations recruited on campus 1994–95.
AFTER GRADUATION 62% of students completing a degree program in 1994–95 went directly on to further study.
EXPENSES FOR 1995–96 ***Application fee:*** $20. State resident tuition: $2000 full-time, $80 per credit part-time. Nonresident tuition: $4000 full-time, $160 per credit part-time. Part-time mandatory fees: $3 per credit. Full-time mandatory fees: $85.
FINANCIAL AID ***College-administered undergrad aid 1995–96:*** 911 need-based scholarships (average $1100), short-term loans (average $25), low-interest long-term loans from external sources (average $1250), Federal Work-Study, 32 part-time jobs. ***Required forms:*** CSS Financial Aid PROFILE, institutional, FAFSA. ***Priority deadline:*** 5/1. ***Payment plan:*** installment. ***Waivers:*** full or partial for employees or children of employees.
APPLYING Open admission except for dental hygiene, engineering, occupational therapy, physical therapy, computer science programs. ***Options:*** early entrance, deferred entrance. ***Required:*** TOEFL for international students. ***Required for some:*** 3 years of high school math and science. Test scores used for counseling/placement. ***Application deadline:*** 8/1. ***Notification:*** continuous. Preference given to county residents.
APPLYING/TRANSFER ***Entrance:*** noncompetitive. ***Application deadline:*** 8/1. ***Notification:*** continuous.
CONTACT Ms. Margot St. Lawrence, Director of Admissions, Orange County Community College, Middletown, NY 10940-6437, 914-341-4030.

PAUL SMITH'S COLLEGE
Paul Smiths, New York

UG Enrollment: 771 **Tuition & Fees: $11,350**
Application Deadline: rolling **Room & Board: $4780**

Paul Smith's College is a private, 2-year, coeducational institution located in the heart of northern New York's Adirondack Mountains. Programs in culinary arts and baking, hospitality management, forestry, surveying technology, and ecology and environmental technology focus on experiential learning (learning by doing). Real-life labs include the 92-room Hotel Saranac and Lydia's Restaurant as well as 13,400 acres of College-owned lakes, streams, and mountain wilderness.

GENERAL Independent, 2-year, coed. Awards certificates, transfer associate, terminal associate degrees. Founded 1937. ***Setting:*** 13,400-acre rural campus. ***Endowment:*** $6 million. ***Total enrollment:*** 771. ***Faculty:*** 82 (67 full-time, 10% with terminal degrees, 15 part-time); student-faculty ratio is 14:1. ***Notable Alumni:*** Richard Cattani, president of Restaurant Services Division, Restaurant Associates; Richard Lewis, president of American Pulpwood Association; Sheldon Fox, general manager of Hyatt Regency at Hilton Head; John Dillon, executive vice president of International Paper; John Schaffer, president of Roush Gourmet Foods.

ENROLLMENT PROFILE 771 students from 31 states and territories, 5 other countries. 30% women, 3% part-time, 70% state residents, 85% live on campus, 6% transferred in, 4% international, 1% 25 or older, 2% Native American, 2% Hispanic, 2% African American, 1% Asian American. ***Most popular recent majors:*** ecology, hotel and restaurant management, forestry.

FIRST-YEAR CLASS 417 total; 1,223 applied, 94% were accepted, 36% of whom enrolled. 20% from top 10% of their high school class, 55% from top half.

ACADEMIC PROGRAM Core, honor code. Calendar: semesters. 253 courses offered in 1995–96. Academic remediation for entering students, English as a second language program offered during academic year and summer, services for LD students, advanced placement, self-designed majors, summer session for credit, adult/continuing education programs, co-op programs and internships.

GENERAL DEGREE REQUIREMENTS 60 credit hours; 2 semesters each of math and science; computer course for surveying, travel and tourism, hotel and restaurant management majors; internship (some majors).

MAJORS American studies, business administration/commerce/management, culinary arts, ecology, environmental sciences, forestry, forest technology, hospitality services, hotel and restaurant management, liberal arts/general studies, mathematics, parks management, science, surveying technology, technical writing, tourism and travel.

LIBRARY Frank C. Cubley Library with 52,570 books, 504 periodicals, 350 records, tapes, and CDs.

COMPUTERS ON CAMPUS 65 computers for student use in learning resource center provide access to main academic computer. Staffed computer lab on campus.

NOTEWORTHY RESEARCH FACILITIES Adirondack Aquatic Institute, Ecology and Environmental Technology Laboratory.

COLLEGE LIFE Orientation program (3 days, $60, parents included). Drama-theater group, student-run newspaper, radio station. 25% vote in student government elections. ***Most popular organizations:*** Forestry Club, Adirondack Experience Club, Student Radio Station, Emergency Wilderness Response Team, Junior American Culinary. ***Major annual events:*** Fall Weekend, Winter Carnival, Winter Weekend. ***Student services:*** health clinic, personal-psychological counseling. ***Campus security:*** 24-hour emergency response devices and patrols, late-night transport-escort service.

HOUSING 690 college housing spaces available; all were occupied 1995–96. Freshmen guaranteed college housing. On-campus residence required through sophomore year except if 22 or over, married, a veteran, living within commuting distance, or by special permission. ***Option:*** coed housing available. Resident assistants live in dorms.

ATHLETICS Member NJCAA. ***Intercollegiate:*** basketball M(s)/W(s), skiing (cross-country) M(s)/W(s), skiing (downhill) M(s)/W(s), soccer M(s)/W(s). ***Intramural:*** basketball, cross-country running, football, ice hockey, riflery, soccer, softball, swimming and diving, table tennis (Ping-Pong), tennis, volleyball. ***Contact:*** Mr. Mark Cartmill, Athletic Director, 518-327-6286.

CAREER PLANNING ***Placement office:*** 4 full-time, 1 part-time staff. ***Director:*** Ms. Cheryl Culotta, Director of Student Development, 518-327-6340. ***Services:*** job fairs, resume preparation, resume referral, career counseling, careers library, job bank, job interviews.

AFTER GRADUATION 25% of students completing a degree program in 1994–95 went directly on to further study.

EXPENSES FOR 1996–97 ***Application fee:*** $25. Comprehensive fee of $16,130 includes full-time tuition ($11,000 minimum), mandatory fees ($350 minimum), and college room and board ($4780 minimum). College room only: $2300 (minimum). Part-time tuition: $260 per credit hour. Part-time mandatory fees: $255 per semester. Full-time mandatory fees range up to $1150 according to program. Tuition guaranteed not to increase for student's term of enrollment.

FINANCIAL AID ***College-administered undergrad aid 1995–96:*** 650 need-based scholarships (average $2500), 25 non-need scholarships (average $2000), low-interest long-term loans from external sources (average $2500), Federal Work-Study, 100 part-time jobs. ***Required forms:*** CSS Financial Aid PROFILE, FAFSA. ***Priority deadline:*** 5/1. ***Payment plan:*** installment. ***Waivers:*** full or partial for employees or children of employees. ***Average indebtedness of graduates:*** $6000.

APPLYING ***Options:*** early entrance, deferred entrance, midyear entrance. ***Required:*** school transcript, SAT I or ACT, TOEFL for international students. ***Recommended:*** essay, recommendations. ***Required for some:*** 3 years of high school math and science. Test scores used for counseling/placement. ***Application deadline:*** rolling.

APPLYING/TRANSFER ***Required:*** standardized test scores, high school transcript, college transcript. ***Recommended:*** essay, recommendations. ***Required for some:*** 3 years of high school math and science. ***Entrance:*** minimally difficult. ***Application deadline:*** rolling.

CONTACT Mr. Duncan S. Adamson, Director of Admissions, Paul Smith's College, Paul Smiths, NY 12970, 518-327-6227 or toll-free 800-421-2605 (in-state). College video available.

❖ *See page 788 for a narrative description.* ❖

PHILLIPS BETH ISRAEL SCHOOL OF NURSING
New York, New York

UG Enrollment: 140 **Tuition & Fees: $6675**
Application Deadline: 4/1 **Room & Board: N/Avail**

GENERAL Independent, 2-year, specialized, coed. Awards transfer associate degrees. Founded 1904. ***Setting:*** urban campus. ***Total enrollment:*** 140. ***Faculty:*** 20 (15 full-time, 10% with terminal degrees, 5 part-time); student-faculty ratio is 9:1.

ENROLLMENT PROFILE 140 students from 5 states and territories, 5 other countries. 90% women, 10% men, 55% part-time, 96% state residents, 80% transferred in, 85% have need-based financial aid, 95% have non-need-based financial aid, 3% international, 75% 25 or older, 0% Native American, 5% Hispanic, 25% African American, 20% Asian American. ***Areas of study chosen:*** 100% health professions and related sciences.

FIRST-YEAR CLASS 70 total; 625 applied, 12% were accepted, 93% of whom enrolled. 15% from top 10% of their high school class, 65% from top quarter, 95% from top half. 1 class president.

ACADEMIC PROGRAM Core, nursing curriculum, honor code. Calendar: semesters. 17 courses offered in 1995–96; average class size 35 in required courses. Academic remediation for entering students, advanced placement, part-time degree program (daytime).

GENERAL DEGREE REQUIREMENTS 68 credits; 2 anatomy and physiology courses, 1 microbiology course.

MAJOR Nursing.

LIBRARY Phillips Health Science Library with 30,000 books, 650 periodicals, 4 on-line bibliographic services, 200 records, tapes, and CDs. Acquisition spending 1994–95: $150,000.

COMPUTERS ON CAMPUS 15 computers for student use in learning resource center, library. Staffed computer lab on campus provides training in use of computers, software.

COLLEGE LIFE Orientation program (3 days, no cost). Choral group, student-run newspaper. 100% vote in student government elections. ***Social organizations:*** 1 open to all. ***Most popular organization:*** National Student Nurses Association. ***Major annual events:*** Holiday Party, Senior Luncheon, Senior Gala. ***Student services:*** health clinic, personal-psychological counseling. ***Campus security:*** 24-hour emergency response devices.

HOUSING College housing not available.

CAREER PLANNING ***Service:*** career counseling.

AFTER GRADUATION 95% of class of 1994 had job offers within 6 months. 15% of students completing a degree program went directly on to further study.

EXPENSES FOR 1995–96 ***Application fee:*** $35. Tuition: $5445 (minimum) full-time, $170 per credit part-time. Full-time tuition ranges up to $8200 according to class level. Full-time mandatory fees: $1230.

FINANCIAL AID ***College-administered undergrad aid 1995–96:*** 140 non-need scholarships (average $1500), short-term loans (average $500), low-interest long-term loans from external sources (average $2625). ***Required forms:*** institutional, FAFSA; required for some: state. ***Priority deadline:*** 6/1. ***Payment plan:*** installment.

APPLYING ***Option:*** deferred entrance. ***Required:*** essay, school transcript, minimum 2.0 GPA, 2 recommendations, campus interview, nursing exam. ***Recommended:*** minimum 3.0 GPA, 3 years of high school math and science, 2 years of high school foreign language, SAT I. Test scores used for admission. ***Application deadline:*** 4/1.

APPLYING/TRANSFER ***Required:*** essay, standardized test scores, high school transcript, 2 recommendations, campus interview, college transcript, minimum 2.0 college GPA, minimum 2.0 high school GPA. ***Recommended:*** 3 years of high school math and science, 2 years of high school foreign language, minimum 3.0 college GPA, minimum 3.0 high school GPA. ***Entrance:*** moderately difficult. ***Application deadline:*** 4/1. ***Contact:*** Mrs. Bernice Pass-Stern, Coordinator of Student Services, 212-614-6108.

CONTACT Mrs. Bernice Pass-Stern, Coordinator of Student Services, Phillips Beth Israel School of Nursing, 310 East 22nd Street, 9th Floor, New York, NY 10010-5702, 212-614-6108.

PLAZA BUSINESS INSTITUTE
Jackson Heights, New York

CONTACT Ms. Sally Ann Weger, Director of Admissions, Plaza Business Institute, 74-09 37th Avenue, Jackson Heights, NY 11372-6300, 718-779-1430. ***Fax:*** 718-779-1456.

QUEENSBOROUGH COMMUNITY COLLEGE OF THE CITY UNIVERSITY OF NEW YORK
Bayside, New York

UG Enrollment: 12,000 **Tuition & Fees (NY Res): $2610**
Application Deadline: rolling **Room & Board: N/Avail**

GENERAL State and locally supported, 2-year, coed. Part of City University of New York System. Awards transfer associate, terminal associate degrees. Founded 1958. ***Setting:*** 34-acre urban campus. ***Total enrollment:*** 12,000. ***Faculty:*** 553 (300 full-time, 80% with terminal degrees, 253 part-time); student-faculty ratio is 14:1.

ENROLLMENT PROFILE 12,000 students: 57% women, 58% part-time, 99% state residents, 10% transferred in, 1% international, 39% 25 or older, 1% Native American, 17% Hispanic, 24% African American, 13% Asian American.

FIRST-YEAR CLASS 2,400 total; 4,000 applied, 100% were accepted, 60% of whom enrolled.

ACADEMIC PROGRAM Core. Calendar: semesters. Academic remediation for entering students, English as a second language program offered during academic year and summer, services for LD students, advanced placement, self-designed majors, honors program, summer session for credit, part-time degree program (daytime, evenings, summer), adult/continuing education programs, co-op programs and internships.

GENERAL DEGREE REQUIREMENTS 60 credits; 1 course in a foreign language or proficiency test.

MAJORS Accounting, art/fine arts, business administration/commerce/management, computer graphics, computer information systems, computer programming, computer technologies, drafting and design, electrical engineering technology, engineering sciences,

environmental health sciences, laser technologies, liberal arts/general studies, mechanical engineering technology, medical laboratory technology, musical instrument technology, nursing, secretarial studies/office management, theater arts/drama.
LIBRARY 126,412 books, 752 microform titles, 702 periodicals, 4,033 records, tapes, and CDs.
COMPUTERS ON CAMPUS 250 computers for student use in department labs, library. Staffed computer lab on campus provides training in use of computers, software.
COLLEGE LIFE Drama-theater group, choral group, student-run newspaper, radio station. 30% vote in student government elections. ***Social organizations:*** 42 open to all. ***Most popular organizations:*** Student Orientation Leaders, Student Nurses Association. ***Major annual events:*** Multicultural Festival, Transfer Day, Job Fair. ***Student services:*** health clinic, personal-psychological counseling. ***Campus security:*** 24-hour patrols, late-night transport-escort service.
HOUSING College housing not available.
ATHLETICS Member NJCAA. ***Intercollegiate:*** baseball M, basketball M/W, soccer M, softball W, tennis M/W. ***Intramural:*** archery, badminton, basketball, bowling, cross-country running, equestrian sports, fencing, football, racquetball, skiing (cross-country), soccer, softball, swimming and diving, table tennis (Ping-Pong), tennis, track and field, volleyball, weight lifting. ***Contact:*** Mr. Steve Weingard, Coordinator of Men's Athletics, 718-631-6322; Ms. Carol Bozek, Coordinator of Women's Athletics, 718-631-6322.
CAREER PLANNING ***Director:*** Ms. Arpy Coherain, Director of Job Placement Services, 718-631-6297. ***Services:*** job fairs, resume preparation, resume referral, career counseling, careers library, job bank, job interviews.
AFTER GRADUATION 58% of students completing a degree program in 1994–95 went directly on to further study.
EXPENSES FOR 1995–96 ***Application fee:*** $35. State resident tuition: $2500 full-time, $105 per credit part-time. Nonresident tuition: $3176 full-time, $130 per credit part-time. Part-time mandatory fees: $25 per semester. Full-time mandatory fees: $110.
FINANCIAL AID ***College-administered undergrad aid 1995–96:*** 2,500 need-based scholarships (average $1500), low-interest long-term loans from external sources, Federal Work-Study, part-time jobs. ***Required forms:*** CSS Financial Aid PROFILE, state, institutional, FAFSA. ***Priority deadline:*** 5/30.
APPLYING Open admission. ***Options:*** deferred entrance, midyear entrance. ***Required:*** TOEFL for international students. Test scores used for counseling/placement. ***Application deadline:*** rolling. ***Notification:*** continuous.
APPLYING/TRANSFER ***Application deadline:*** rolling. ***Notification:*** continuous. ***Contact:*** Dr. Martin Jacobs, Transfer Counselor, 718-631-6372.
CONTACT Dr. A. Calise, Director of Registration and Records, Queensborough Community College of the City University of New York, 222-05 56th Avenue, Bayside, NY 11364, 718-631-6307. College video available.

ROCHESTER BUSINESS INSTITUTE
Rochester, New York

UG Enrollment: 300 | **Tuition & Fees: $5700**
Application Deadline: N/R | **Room & Board: N/Avail**

GENERAL Proprietary, 2-year, coed. Part of Phillips Colleges, Inc. Awards certificates, diplomas, terminal associate degrees. Founded 1863. ***Setting:*** 2-acre suburban campus. ***Total enrollment:*** 300. ***Faculty:*** 21 (9 full-time, 12 part-time).
ENROLLMENT PROFILE 300 students from 2 states and territories, 2 other countries. 80% women, 5% part-time, 95% state residents, 30% transferred in, 3% international, 45% 25 or older, 1% Native American, 5% Hispanic, 38% African American, 1% Asian American.
FIRST-YEAR CLASS 125 total.
ACADEMIC PROGRAM Calendar: quarters. Academic remediation for entering students, advanced placement, summer session for credit, adult/continuing education programs.
GENERAL DEGREE REQUIREMENTS 96 quarter hours; math/science requirements vary according to program; computer course.
MAJORS Accounting, data processing, legal secretarial studies, marketing/retailing/merchandising, medical secretarial studies, secretarial studies/office management.
LIBRARY Rochester Business Institute Library with 4,800 books, 60 periodicals.
COMPUTERS ON CAMPUS 70 computers for student use in classrooms.
COLLEGE LIFE ***Campus security:*** late-night transport-escort service.
HOUSING College housing not available.
ATHLETICS ***Intramural:*** basketball, softball.
CAREER PLANNING ***Placement office:*** 2 full-time staff. ***Director:*** Ms. Lydia Dzus, Director of Graduate Placement, 716-266-0430. ***Services:*** job fairs, resume preparation, career counseling, careers library, job interviews.
EXPENSES FOR 1996–97 ***Application fee:*** $25. Tuition: $5400 full-time, $125 per quarter hour part-time. Full-time mandatory fees: $300.
FINANCIAL AID ***College-administered undergrad aid 1995–96:*** 6 need-based scholarships (average $300), 21 non-need scholarships (average $600), Federal Work-Study, 6 part-time jobs. ***Required forms:*** FAFSA. ***Priority deadline:*** 10/1.
APPLYING ***Options:*** early entrance, deferred entrance. ***Required:*** campus interview, CPAt. Test scores used for admission. ***Notification:*** continuous until 10/9.
APPLYING/TRANSFER ***Required:*** standardized test scores. ***Entrance:*** minimally difficult. ***Notification:*** continuous until 10/9.
CONTACT Mr. Carl Silvio, Director of Admissions, Rochester Business Institute, Rochester, NY 14622, 716-266-0430.

ROCKLAND COMMUNITY COLLEGE
Suffern, New York

UG Enrollment: 7,240 | **Tuition & Fees (NY Res): $2125**
Application Deadline: rolling | **Room & Board: N/Avail**

GENERAL State and locally supported, 2-year, coed. Part of State University of New York System. Awards transfer associate, terminal associate degrees. Founded 1959. ***Setting:*** 150-acre small-town campus with easy access to New York City. ***Research spending 1994–95:*** $1.3 million. ***Total enrollment:*** 7,240. ***Faculty:*** 792 (192 full-time, 20% with terminal degrees, 600 part-time); student-faculty ratio is 19:1.
ENROLLMENT PROFILE 7,240 students from 6 states and territories. 52% part-time, 96% state residents, 7% transferred in, 43% 25 or older, 7% Hispanic, 15% African American, 6% Asian American.
FIRST-YEAR CLASS 1,948 total; 2,705 applied, 100% were accepted, 72% of whom enrolled. 12% from top 10% of their high school class, 20% from top quarter, 68% from top half.
ACADEMIC PROGRAM Core. Calendar: semesters. Academic remediation for entering students, English as a second language program offered during academic year and summer, services for LD students, advanced placement, self-designed majors, honors program, summer session for credit, part-time degree program (daytime, evenings, weekends, summer), external degree programs, adult/continuing education programs, co-op programs and internships. Study abroad in England, Israel.
GENERAL DEGREE REQUIREMENTS 60 credits; 1 course in pharmacology; computer course for most majors.
MAJORS Accounting, advertising, applied art, art/fine arts, automotive technologies, business administration/commerce/management, child psychology/child development, commercial art, communication, computer programming, criminal justice, data processing, dietetics, drafting and design, electrical engineering technology, electromechanical technology, emergency medical technology, environmental sciences, finance/banking, fire science, food services management, forestry, graphic arts, insurance, liberal arts/general studies, marketing/retailing/merchandising, mathematics, mechanical engineering technology, medical laboratory technology, medical records services, nursing, occupational therapy, real estate, respiratory therapy, science, secretarial studies/office management, theater arts/drama, tourism and travel.
LIBRARY 135,959 books, 512 periodicals, 430 records, tapes, and CDs.
COMPUTERS ON CAMPUS 177 computers for student use in computer center. Academic computing expenditure 1994–95: $195,519.
COLLEGE LIFE Drama-theater group, student-run newspaper, radio station. ***Student services:*** legal services, personal-psychological counseling.
HOUSING College housing not available.
ATHLETICS Member NJCAA. ***Intercollegiate:*** baseball M(s), basketball M(s)/W(s), golf M(s), soccer M/W, softball W, tennis M/W, volleyball W. ***Intramural:*** basketball, bowling, field hockey, football, golf, racquetball, skiing (cross-country), soccer, softball, swimming and diving, tennis, track and field, volleyball. ***Contact:*** Mr. Howard Pierson, Director of Athletics, 914-574-4769.
CAREER PLANNING ***Director:*** Ms. Mickie Carlson, Assistant Dean, 914-574-4307. ***Service:*** career counseling.
AFTER GRADUATION 50% of students completing a degree program in 1994–95 went directly on to further study.
EXPENSES FOR 1995–96 State resident tuition: $2047 full-time, $85.50 per credit part-time. Nonresident tuition: $4094 full-time, $171 per credit part-time. Full-time mandatory fees: $78.
FINANCIAL AID ***College-administered undergrad aid 1995–96:*** 500 need-based scholarships (average $400), 120 non-need scholarships (average $490), short-term loans (average $100), low-interest long-term loans from external sources (average $1800), Federal Work-Study, 250 part-time jobs. ***Required forms:*** CSS Financial Aid PROFILE, state, institutional, FAFSA. ***Priority deadline:*** 6/15.
APPLYING Open admission. ***Options:*** early entrance, deferred entrance. ***Recommended:*** SAT I or ACT. Test scores used for counseling/placement. ***Application deadline:*** rolling.
APPLYING/TRANSFER ***Application deadline:*** rolling.
CONTACT Mr. Charles Connolly, Director of Recruitment and Entry Services, Rockland Community College, Suffern, NY 10901-3699, 914-574-4237. ***Fax:*** 914-574-4224.

SAGE JUNIOR COLLEGE OF ALBANY
Albany, New York

UG Enrollment: 655 | **Tuition & Fees: $7700**
Application Deadline: 8/1 | **Room & Board: $5840**

Sage Junior College of Albany welcomes visits from prospective students. Students can meet people who make up the Sage JCA community, get a closer look at the campus, visit the art gallery, sit in on a class, talk to students and professors, and have a chance to feel the spirit of Sage JCA. To schedule a campus visit, students should call 518-445-1730 or 800-999-9522 (toll-free). Students may also e-mail Sage JCA (jcaadm@sage.edu) or visit the College's World Wide Web site (http://www.sage.edu).

GENERAL Independent, 2-year, coed. Part of The Sage Colleges. Awards transfer associate, terminal associate degrees. Founded 1957. ***Setting:*** 15-acre small-town campus. ***Total enrollment:*** 655. ***Faculty:*** 85 (50 full-time, 35 part-time); student-faculty ratio is 12:1.
ENROLLMENT PROFILE 655 students from 8 states and territories, 2 other countries. 69% women, 31% men, 9% part-time, 96% state residents, 13% transferred in, 85% have need-based financial aid, 1% international, 10% 25 or older, 1% Native American, 4% Hispanic, 13% African American, 2% Asian American. ***Areas of study chosen:*** 30% fine arts, 17% business management and administrative services, 14% liberal arts/general studies, 12% social sciences, 6% education, 6% health professions and related sciences, 3% communications and journalism, 2% computer and information sciences. ***Most popular recent majors:*** art/fine arts, humanities, social science.
FIRST-YEAR CLASS 295 total; 705 applied, 76% were accepted, 55% of whom enrolled.
ACADEMIC PROGRAM Core. Calendar: semesters. Academic remediation for entering students, advanced placement, self-designed majors, Freshman Honors College, tutorials, honors program, summer session for credit, part-time degree program (daytime, evenings, weekends, summer), adult/continuing education programs, internships. Off-campus study at members of the Hudson-Mohawk Association of Colleges and Universities. Study abroad in France, Italy, England (1% of students participate). ROTC: Army (c), Air Force (c).
GENERAL DEGREE REQUIREMENTS 60 credits; math competence; computer course for graphic design, office information management, photography majors; internship (some majors).
MAJORS Accounting, art/fine arts, business administration/commerce/management, child care/child and family studies, communication, computer information systems, drug and alcohol/substance abuse counseling, elementary education, graphic arts, humanities,

Sage Junior College of Albany (continued)
interior design, international studies, legal studies, liberal arts/general studies, marketing/retailing/merchandising, photography, physical sciences, science, secretarial studies/office management, social science, sociology.
LIBRARY Albany Campus Library with 83,908 books, 1,759 microform titles, 679 periodicals, 630 records, tapes, and CDs.
COMPUTERS ON CAMPUS 37 computers for student use in computer labs provide access to main academic computer, off-campus computing facilities, e-mail, on-line services, Internet, SUNY VAX. Staffed computer lab on campus.
COLLEGE LIFE Drama-theater group, student-run newspaper. ***Social organizations:*** 16 open to all. ***Most popular organizations:*** Student Government, Art Club, Delta Epsilon Chi, Phi Theta Kappa, Science Club. ***Major annual events:*** Earth Day, Career Conference, Student Art Show. ***Student services:*** health clinic, personal-psychological counseling, women's center. ***Campus security:*** 24-hour emergency response devices and patrols, controlled dormitory access.
HOUSING 200 college housing spaces available. Freshmen guaranteed college housing. Off-campus living permitted. ***Options:*** coed (1 building), single-sex (1 building) housing available. Resident assistants live in dorms.
ATHLETICS Member NJCAA. ***Intercollegiate:*** basketball M(s), golf M/W, volleyball W(s). ***Intramural:*** basketball, volleyball. ***Contact:*** Mr. Bill Toomey, Athletic Director, 518-445-1774.
CAREER PLANNING ***Placement office:*** 3 full-time, 3 part-time staff. ***Director:*** Dr. Richard Naylor, Director of Career Services, 518-445-1793. ***Services:*** job fairs, resume preparation, resume referral, career counseling, careers library, job bank, job interviews. 50 organizations recruited on campus 1994–95.
AFTER GRADUATION 85% of class of 1994 had job offers within 6 months. 61% of students completing a degree program went directly on to further study.
EXPENSES FOR 1995–96 ***Application fee:*** $20. Comprehensive fee of $13,540 includes full-time tuition ($7480), mandatory fees ($220), and college room and board ($5840). College room only: $2770. Part-time tuition: $255 per credit.
FINANCIAL AID ***College-administered undergrad aid 1995–96:*** 463 need-based scholarships (average $1821), 99 non-need scholarships (average $3706), low-interest long-term loans from external sources (average $3200), 40 Federal Work-Study (averaging $1443), 24 part-time jobs. ***Required forms:*** state, FAFSA; accepted: CSS Financial Aid PROFILE. ***Priority deadline:*** 3/15. ***Payment plan:*** installment. ***Waivers:*** full or partial for employees or children of employees.
APPLYING ***Options:*** electronic application, early entrance, deferred entrance, midyear entrance. ***Required:*** school transcript, 1 recommendation, TOEFL for international students. ***Recommended:*** essay. ***Required for some:*** 3 years of high school math and science, SAT I. Test scores used for admission. ***Application deadline:*** 8/1. ***Notification:*** continuous until 8/15.
APPLYING/TRANSFER ***Required:*** high school transcript, college transcript, minimum 2.0 college GPA. ***Recommended:*** essay. ***Required for some:*** 3 years of high school math and science. ***Entrance:*** minimally difficult. ***Application deadline:*** 8/1. ***Notification:*** continuous until 8/15. ***Contact:*** Ms. Kristine Duffy, Director of Admissions, 518-445-1730.
CONTACT Ms. Kristine Duffy, Director of Admissions, Sage Junior College of Albany, Albany, NY 12208-3425, 518-445-1730 or toll-free 800-999-9522. ***Fax:*** 518-436-0539. ***E-mail:*** jcaadm@sage.edu. College video available.

❖ ***See page 800 for a narrative description.*** ❖

SCHENECTADY COUNTY COMMUNITY COLLEGE
Schenectady, New York

UG Enrollment: 3,692	**Tuition & Fees (NY Res): $2193**
Application Deadline: rolling	**Room & Board: N/Avail**

GENERAL State and locally supported, 2-year, coed. Part of State University of New York System. Awards transfer associate, terminal associate degrees. Founded 1968. ***Setting:*** 50-acre urban campus. ***Total enrollment:*** 3,692. ***Faculty:*** 208 (59 full-time, 5% with terminal degrees, 149 part-time); student-faculty ratio is 23:1.
ENROLLMENT PROFILE 3,692 students from 6 states and territories. 57% women, 43% men, 52% part-time, 99% state residents, 10% transferred in, 75% have need-based financial aid, 0% international, 50% 25 or older, 1% Native American, 2% Hispanic, 7% African American, 1% Asian American. ***Most popular recent majors:*** hotel and restaurant management, humanities, business administration/commerce/management.
FIRST-YEAR CLASS 792 total; 1,557 applied, 59% of whom enrolled. 2% from top 10% of their high school class, 7% from top quarter, 100% from top half.
ACADEMIC PROGRAM Core, general education and career preparatory curriculum. Calendar: semesters. Academic remediation for entering students, English as a second language program offered during academic year and summer, services for LD students, advanced placement, honors program, summer session for credit, part-time degree program (daytime, evenings), adult/continuing education programs, internships. Off-campus study at 14 members of the Hudson-Mohawk Association of Colleges and Universities. ROTC: Army (c), Naval (c), Air Force (c).
GENERAL DEGREE REQUIREMENTS 60 credit hours; computer course (varies by major); internship (some majors).
MAJORS Accounting, business administration/commerce/management, chemical engineering technology, computer science, criminal justice, culinary arts, data processing, education, electrical and electronics technologies, fire science, hotel and restaurant management, humanities, human services, industrial engineering technology, liberal arts/general studies, materials sciences, mathematics, music, music business, paralegal studies, plastics technology, quality control technology, science, secretarial studies/office management, social science, telecommunications, theater arts/drama, tourism and travel.
LIBRARY Begley Library with 71,421 books, 66,476 microform titles, 712 periodicals, 1 on-line bibliographic service, 9 CD-ROMs, 3,528 records, tapes, and CDs. Acquisition spending 1994–95: $390,247.
COMPUTERS ON CAMPUS Computers for student use in computer center, learning resource center, library. Staffed computer lab on campus provides training in use of computers, software. Academic computing expenditure 1994–95: $95,800.
COLLEGE LIFE Drama-theater group, choral group. ***Social organizations:*** 22 open to all; 1 local fraternity, 1 local sorority; 1% of eligible men and 2% of eligible women are members. ***Most popular organizations:*** Black and Latino Student Alliance, Culinary Arts Club, Student Government Association, Spanish Club, Rhythms Literary Magazine. ***Major annual events:*** SCCC Foundation Dinner, Honors Convocation, Annual Dinner Theater. ***Student services:*** personal-psychological counseling. ***Campus security:*** 24-hour emergency response devices and patrols.
HOUSING College housing not available.
ATHLETICS Member NJCAA. ***Intercollegiate:*** baseball M, basketball M, bowling M/W, softball W. ***Intramural:*** soccer, volleyball. ***Contact:*** Mr. David Gonzales, Athletic Director, 518-346-6211 Ext. 156.
CAREER PLANNING ***Placement office:*** 2 full-time staff; $53,987 operating expenditure 1994–95. ***Director:*** Mr. Robert Frederick, Coordinator of Job Services, 518-346-6211. ***Services:*** job fairs, resume preparation, resume referral, career counseling, careers library, job bank, job interviews.
AFTER GRADUATION 70% of students completing a degree program in 1994–95 went directly on to further study.
EXPENSES FOR 1995–96 ***Application fee:*** $25. State resident tuition: $2090 full-time, $87 per credit hour part-time. Nonresident tuition: $4180 full-time, $174 per credit hour part-time. Full-time mandatory fees: $103.
FINANCIAL AID ***College-administered undergrad aid 1995–96:*** 325 need-based scholarships (averaging $425), 30 non-need scholarships (averaging $350), short-term loans (averaging $25), low-interest long-term loans from external sources (averaging $2000), Federal Work-Study, 20 part-time jobs. ***Required forms:*** institutional; required for some: state, FAFSA; accepted: CSS Financial Aid PROFILE. ***Priority deadline:*** 5/1. ***Waivers:*** full or partial for employees or children of employees and senior citizens.
APPLYING Open admission. ***Options:*** early entrance, deferred entrance. ***Required:*** TOEFL for international students. ***Recommended:*** 3 years of high school math and science, some high school foreign language, SAT I or ACT. Test scores used for counseling/placement. ***Application deadline:*** rolling. ***Notification:*** continuous. Preference given to county residents.
APPLYING/TRANSFER ***Required:*** college transcript, minimum 2.0 college GPA. ***Recommended:*** standardized test scores. ***Application deadline:*** rolling. ***Notification:*** continuous. ***Contact:*** Mr. Robert Dinello, Director of Admissions, 518-346-6211.
CONTACT Mr. Robert Dinello, Director of Admissions, Schenectady County Community College, 78 Washington Avenue, Schenectady, NY 12305-2294, 518-346-6211 Ext. 166.

SIMMONS INSTITUTE OF FUNERAL SERVICE
Syracuse, New York

UG Enrollment: 74	**Tuition & Fees: $3790**
Application Deadline: N/R	**Room & Board: N/Avail**

GENERAL Proprietary, 2-year, specialized, coed. Awards terminal associate degrees. Founded 1900. ***Setting:*** 1-acre urban campus. ***Total enrollment:*** 74. ***Faculty:*** 14; student-faculty ratio is 7:1.
ENROLLMENT PROFILE 74 students: 38% women, 62% men, 100% transferred in, 0% Native American, 0% Hispanic, 16% African American, 0% Asian American.
ACADEMIC PROGRAM Honor code. Calendar: semesters. Part-time degree program (daytime, weekends, summer).
GENERAL DEGREE REQUIREMENT 64 semester credits.
MAJOR Funeral service.
COMPUTERS ON CAMPUS 18 computers for student use.
COLLEGE LIFE 90% vote in student government elections. ***Social organizations:*** 1 national fraternity. ***Campus security:*** 24-hour emergency response devices.
HOUSING College housing not available.
EXPENSES FOR 1996–97 ***Application fee:*** $50. Tuition: $3750 full-time. Full-time mandatory fees: $40.
FINANCIAL AID ***College-administered undergrad aid 1995–96:*** 51 need-based scholarships, 3 non-need scholarships.
APPLYING/TRANSFER ***Required:*** campus interview, minimum 2.0 high school GPA, minimum 2.0 high school GPA or significant background in funeral service, and letter of interest. ***Entrance:*** minimally difficult. ***Application deadline:*** rolling. ***Notification:*** continuous.

STATE UNIVERSITY OF NEW YORK COLLEGE OF AGRICULTURE AND TECHNOLOGY AT COBLESKILL
Cobleskill, New York

UG Enrollment: 2,410	**Tuition & Fees (NY Res): $3884**
Application Deadline: rolling	**Room & Board: $5240**

GENERAL State-supported, primarily 2-year, coed. Part of State University of New York System. Awards certificates, transfer associate, terminal associate, bachelor's degrees. Founded 1916. ***Setting:*** 750-acre rural campus. ***Total enrollment:*** 2,410. ***Faculty:*** 145 (125 full-time, 10% with terminal degrees, 20 part-time); student-faculty ratio is 20:1.
ENROLLMENT PROFILE 2,410 students from 13 states and territories, 2 other countries. 51% women, 49% men, 8% part-time, 95% state residents, 4% transferred in, 1% international, 10% 25 or older, 1% Native American, 4% Hispanic, 4% African American, 2% Asian American. ***Areas of study chosen:*** 30% agriculture, 15% liberal arts/general studies, 15% social sciences, 12% education, 10% business management and administrative services, 5% biological and life sciences, 3% computer and information sciences, 3% health professions and related sciences, 2% mathematics. ***Most popular recent majors:*** business administration/commerce/management, early childhood education.
FIRST-YEAR CLASS 997 total; 3,500 applied, 63% were accepted, 45% of whom enrolled. 4% from top 10% of their high school class, 30% from top quarter, 45% from top half.
ACADEMIC PROGRAM Core, honor code. Calendar: semesters. Academic remediation for entering students, English as a second language program offered during academic year, services for LD students, advanced placement, Freshman Honors College, tutorials, honors program, summer session for credit, part-time degree program (daytime, weekends),

adult/continuing education programs, internships. Off-campus study at other units of the State University of New York System. Study abroad in England (2% of students participate).
GENERAL DEGREE REQUIREMENTS 66 credit hours for associate, 126 credit hours for bachelor's; algebra competence.
MAJORS Accounting, agricultural business (B), agricultural economics, agricultural education, agricultural sciences (B), agricultural technologies (B), agronomy/soil and crop sciences, animal sciences (B), applied mathematics, automotive technologies, biology/biological sciences, botany/plant sciences (B), business administration/commerce/management, chemistry, computer information systems, computer programming, computer science, computer technologies, culinary arts, dairy sciences, data processing, early childhood education, equestrian studies, fish and game management, food services management, food services technology, forest technology, horticulture (B), hotel and restaurant management, humanities, landscaping/grounds maintenance, legal secretarial studies, liberal arts/general studies, mathematics, medical laboratory technology, ornamental horticulture, parks management, recreational facilities management, science, secretarial studies/office management, social science, sociology, tourism and travel, wildlife biology, wildlife management.
LIBRARY Jared Van Wagenor Library with 85,955 books, 438 microform titles, 958 periodicals, 5,088 records, tapes, and CDs.
COMPUTERS ON CAMPUS Student rooms linked to a campus network. 100 computers for student use in computer center, computer labs, learning resource center, classrooms, library, dorms, student rooms provide access to main academic computer, e-mail, Internet. Staffed computer lab on campus provides training in use of computers, software.
COLLEGE LIFE Orientation program (2 days, $85, parents included). Drama-theater group, choral group, student-run newspaper, radio station. 25% vote in student government elections. ***Social organizations:*** 60 open to all; 1 local fraternity, 1 local sorority; 1% of eligible men and 1% of eligible women are members. ***Student services:*** health clinic, personal-psychological counseling. ***Campus security:*** 24-hour emergency response devices and patrols, late-night transport-escort service, controlled dormitory access, bicycle patrols.
HOUSING College housing designed to accommodate 1,782 students; 2,033 undergraduates lived in college housing during 1995–96. Freshmen guaranteed college housing. On-campus residence required in freshman year. ***Options:*** coed (8 buildings), single-sex (2 buildings) housing available. Resident assistants live in dorms.
ATHLETICS Member NJCAA. ***Intercollegiate:*** basketball M/W, cross-country running M/W, equestrian sports M/W, golf M, lacrosse M, skiing (downhill) M/W, soccer M/W, tennis M/W, track and field M/W, volleyball W, wrestling M. ***Intramural:*** archery, badminton, baseball, basketball, bowling, field hockey, football, skiing (cross-country), skiing (downhill), tennis, volleyball. ***Contact:*** Mr. Kevin McCarthy, Athletic Director, 518-234-5127.
CAREER PLANNING ***Placement office:*** 3 full-time, 2 part-time staff. ***Director:*** Mr. Wayne Morris, Director of Counseling Services, 518-234-5211. ***Services:*** resume preparation, resume referral, career counseling, job bank, job interviews. Students must register sophomore year. 65 organizations recruited on campus 1994–95.
AFTER GRADUATION 35% of class of 1994 had job offers within 6 months. 95% of students completing transfer associate program went directly to 4-year colleges.
EXPENSES FOR 1995–96 ***Application fee:*** $30. State resident tuition: $3400 full-time, $137 per credit hour part-time. Nonresident tuition: $8300 full-time, $346 per credit hour part-time. Part-time mandatory fees: $16.95 per credit hour. Full-time mandatory fees: $484. College room and board: $5240.
FINANCIAL AID ***College-administered undergrad aid 1995–96:*** 265 need-based scholarships (average $755), 110 non-need scholarships (average $390), short-term loans (average $25), low-interest long-term loans from college funds, loans from external sources (average $1487), Federal Work-Study, 600 part-time jobs. ***Required forms:*** CSS Financial Aid PROFILE, institutional; required for some: state. ***Priority deadline:*** 4/1.
APPLYING ***Options:*** early entrance, deferred entrance. ***Required:*** school transcript, minimum 2.0 GPA, TOEFL for international students. ***Recommended:*** SAT I or ACT. ***Required for some:*** 3 years of high school math and science, interview. Test scores used for admission. ***Application deadline:*** rolling. ***Notification:*** continuous.
APPLYING/TRANSFER ***Required:*** college transcript, minimum 2.0 college GPA, minimum 2.0 high school GPA. ***Recommended:*** standardized test scores. ***Required for some:*** high school transcript, 3 years of high school math and science, interview. ***Entrance:*** moderately difficult. ***Application deadline:*** rolling. ***Notification:*** continuous. ***Contact:*** Mrs. Margaret Pearson, Transfer Counselor, 518-234-5624.
CONTACT Dr. Carol Eaton, Director of Admissions, State University of New York College of Agriculture and Technology at Cobleskill, Cobleskill, NY 12043, 518-234-5525 or toll-free 800-295-8988 (in-state). ***E-mail:*** admissions@snycob.cobleskill.edu. College video available.

❖ *See page 804 for a narrative description.* ❖

STATE UNIVERSITY OF NEW YORK COLLEGE OF AGRICULTURE AND TECHNOLOGY AT MORRISVILLE
Morrisville, New York

UG Enrollment: 2,890	**Tuition & Fees (NY Res): $3520**
Application Deadline: rolling	**Room & Board: $5080**

GENERAL State-supported, 2-year, coed. Part of State University of New York System. Awards certificates, transfer associate, terminal associate degrees. Founded 1908. ***Setting:*** 740-acre rural campus with easy access to Syracuse. ***Research spending 1994–95:*** $57,654. ***Educational spending 1994–95:*** $2408 per undergrad. ***Total enrollment:*** 2,890. ***Faculty:*** 171 (126 full-time, 17% with terminal degrees, 45 part-time); student-faculty ratio is 19:1. ***Notable Alumni:*** Alfred J. Tector, cardiovascular surgeon; Michael J. Billoni, vice president of Rich Baseball Operations; Richard T. McGuire, former agriculture and markets commissioner; Rick Bowley, vice president and general manager of Computer-Generated Imagery; Gail Doer, manager of Canandaigua Wine Company.
ENROLLMENT PROFILE 2,890 students from 14 states and territories, 11 other countries. 51% women, 49% men, 18% part-time, 98% state residents, 60% live on campus, 4% transferred in, 1% international, 23% 25 or older, 1% Native American, 4% Hispanic, 11% African American, 1% Asian American. ***Areas of study chosen:*** 20% liberal arts/general studies, 16% business management and administrative services, 14% agriculture, 12% interdisciplinary studies, 9% engineering and applied sciences, 8% social sciences, 7% health professions and related sciences, 5% natural resource sciences, 4% vocational and home economics, 3% communications and journalism, 2% computer and information sciences. ***Most popular recent majors:*** business administration/commerce/management, nursing, liberal arts/general studies.
FIRST-YEAR CLASS 1,243 total; 3,871 applied, 81% were accepted, 40% of whom enrolled. 8% from top 10% of their high school class, 20% from top quarter, 52% from top half. 6 National Merit Scholars.
ACADEMIC PROGRAM Core, technical/agricultural curriculum, honor code. Calendar: semesters. 600 courses offered in 1995–96. Academic remediation for entering students, English as a second language program offered during academic year, services for LD students, advanced placement, self-designed majors, summer session for credit, part-time degree program (daytime, evenings, weekends), adult/continuing education programs, internships. Off-campus study at other units of the State University of New York System.
GENERAL DEGREE REQUIREMENT Internship (some majors).
MAJORS Accounting, agricultural business, agricultural sciences, agricultural technologies, agronomy/soil and crop sciences, animal sciences, architectural technologies, automotive technologies, biology/biological sciences, biotechnology, business administration/commerce/management, chemistry, computer information systems, computer programming, computer science, computer technologies, conservation, construction technologies, dairy sciences, data processing, dietetics, drafting and design, electrical and electronics technologies, electrical engineering technology, engineering and applied sciences, engineering sciences, (pre)engineering sequence, engineering technology, environmental sciences, equestrian studies, farm and ranch management, finance/banking, fish and game management, food services management, food services technology, forestry, forest technology, horticulture, hospitality services, hotel and restaurant management, humanities, industrial engineering technology, journalism, landscape architecture/design, landscaping/grounds maintenance, legal secretarial studies, liberal arts/general studies, manufacturing technology, marine biology, marine sciences, marketing/retailing/merchandising, mathematics, mechanical engineering technology, medical laboratory technology, medical secretarial studies, natural resource management, nursing, parks management, physics, recreational facilities management, secretarial studies/office management, social science, tourism and travel, wildlife management, wood sciences, word processing.
LIBRARY SUNY Morrisville Library plus 1 other, with 99,258 books, 320 microform titles, 568 periodicals, 1 on-line bibliographic service, 2 CD-ROMs, 2,330 records, tapes, and CDs. Acquisition spending 1994–95: $567,856.
COMPUTERS ON CAMPUS Computer purchase plan available. Student rooms linked to a campus network. 90 computers for student use in computer center, computer labs, library, dorms provide access to main academic computer, e-mail, Internet. Staffed computer lab on campus provides training in use of computers, software. Academic computing expenditure 1994–95: $450,123.
NOTEWORTHY RESEARCH FACILITIES Automotive Performance Center, Dairy Barn and Laboratories, Equine Arena, Spader Greenhouses, Computer Science Laboratory.
COLLEGE LIFE Orientation program (3 days, parents included). Drama-theater group, choral group, student-run newspaper, radio station. ***Social organizations:*** 40 open to all; 3 local fraternities, 2 local sororities; 15% of eligible men and 15% of eligible women are members. ***Most popular organizations:*** African Student Union Black Alliance, Student Government Organization, Agriculture Club, Latino American Student Association, WCVM Student Radio Station. ***Major annual events:*** College/Community Picnic, Parents' Weekend, Alumni Weekend. ***Student services:*** health clinic, personal-psychological counseling. ***Campus security:*** 24-hour emergency response devices and patrols, late-night transport-escort service, controlled dormitory access.
HOUSING 1,915 college housing spaces available; 1,692 were occupied 1995–96. Freshmen guaranteed college housing. On-campus residence required in freshman year. ***Options:*** freshmen-only, coed (9 buildings) housing available. Resident assistants live in dorms.
ATHLETICS Member NJCAA. ***Intercollegiate:*** baseball M, basketball M/W, cross-country running M/W, equestrian sports M/W, lacrosse M, skiing (downhill) M/W, soccer M/W, softball W, swimming and diving M/W, track and field M/W, volleyball W, wrestling M. ***Intramural:*** basketball, bowling, riflery, soccer, softball, tennis, volleyball. ***Contact:*** Mr. Barry Cavanaugh, Athletic Director, 315-684-6072.
CAREER PLANNING ***Placement office:*** 2 full-time staff; $61,711 operating expenditure 1994–95. ***Director:*** Mr. Bruce Duncan, Director of Placement and Transfer Center, 315-684-6275. ***Services:*** job fairs, resume preparation, resume referral, career counseling, careers library, job bank, job interviews. Students must register sophomore year.
AFTER GRADUATION 44% of students completing a degree program in 1994–95 went directly on to further study.
EXPENSES FOR 1995–96 ***Application fee:*** $25. State resident tuition: $3200 full-time, $128 per credit part-time. Nonresident tuition: $8300 full-time, $346 per credit part-time. Part-time mandatory fees: $19.50 per credit (minimum). Full-time mandatory fees: $320 (minimum). College room and board: $5080.
FINANCIAL AID ***College-administered undergrad aid 1995–96:*** need-based scholarships, 36 non-need scholarships (average $2000), short-term loans (average $250), low-interest long-term loans from external sources (average $3100), 202 Federal Work-Study (averaging $1000), 200 part-time jobs. ***Required forms:*** state, FAFSA. ***Priority deadline:*** 2/1. ***Payment plan:*** deferred payment.
APPLYING ***Options:*** early entrance, deferred entrance, midyear entrance. ***Required:*** TOEFL for international students. ***Recommended:*** SAT I or ACT, SAT II Subject Tests. ***Required for some:*** 3 years of high school math and science. Test scores used for admission. ***Application deadline:*** rolling. ***Notification:*** continuous.
APPLYING/TRANSFER ***Required for some:*** 3 years of high school math and science. ***Entrance:*** minimally difficult. ***Application deadline:*** rolling. ***Notification:*** continuous. ***Contact:*** Mr. Bruce Duncan, Director of Placement and Transfer Center, 315-684-6275.
CONTACT Mr. Thomas Fletcher, Director of Admissions, State University of New York College of Agriculture and Technology at Morrisville, Morrisville, NY 13408, 315-684-6046 or toll-free 800-258-0111 (in-state). ***Fax:*** 315-684-6116. College video available.

❖ *See page 806 for a narrative description.* ❖

STATE UNIVERSITY OF NEW YORK COLLEGE OF ENVIRONMENTAL SCIENCE & FORESTRY, RANGER SCHOOL
Wanakena, New York

UG Enrollment: 48 **Tuition & Fees (NY Res): $3880**
Application Deadline: rolling **Room & Board: $6340**

GENERAL State-supported, 2-year, specialized, coed. Part of State University of New York College of Environmental Science and Forestry. Awards terminal associate degrees. Founded 1912. ***Setting:*** 2,800-acre rural campus. ***Total enrollment:*** 48. ***Faculty:*** 5 (all full-time); student-faculty ratio is 10:1. ***Notable Alumni:*** Joel Howard, forester and professor.
ENROLLMENT PROFILE 48 students from 2 states and territories. 11% women, 0% part-time, 92% state residents, 100% transferred in, 0% international, 10% 25 or older, 0% Native American, 2% Hispanic, 0% African American, 0% Asian American. ***Areas of study chosen:*** 100% natural resource sciences.
FIRST-YEAR CLASS 48 total; 113 applied, 60% were accepted, 71% of whom enrolled.
ACADEMIC PROGRAM Core, forest technology curriculum, honor code. Calendar: semesters. 25 courses offered in 1995–96. Advanced placement.
GENERAL DEGREE REQUIREMENTS 75 credit hours; 3 credit hours of trigonometry; 6 credit hours of natural science.
MAJOR Forest technology.
LIBRARY 5,000 books, 60 periodicals.
COMPUTERS ON CAMPUS 20 computers for student use in computer center, library.
COLLEGE LIFE ***Major annual events:*** Earth Day, Winter Weekend, Open House. ***Student services:*** legal services, health clinic, personal-psychological counseling.
HOUSING 92 college housing spaces available; 40 were occupied 1995–96. Off-campus living permitted. ***Option:*** coed housing available.
CAREER PLANNING ***Placement office:*** 1 full-time staff. ***Director:*** Mr. Thomas O. Slocum, Director, 315-470-6660. ***Services:*** job fairs, resume preparation, resume referral, career counseling, careers library, job interviews.
AFTER GRADUATION 31% of students completing a degree program in 1994–95 went directly on to further study.
EXPENSES FOR 1995–96 State resident tuition: $3400 full-time. Nonresident tuition: $8300 full-time. Full-time mandatory fees: $480. College room and board: $6340.
FINANCIAL AID ***College-administered undergrad aid 1995–96:*** 15 need-based scholarships (averaging $5000), 5 non-need scholarships (averaging $3000), short-term loans (averaging $200), low-interest long-term loans from external sources (averaging $800), Federal Work-Study, 15 part-time jobs. ***Required forms:*** state, institutional, FAFSA. ***Priority deadline:*** 3/1. ***Payment plans:*** installment, deferred payment.
APPLYING ***Option:*** deferred entrance. ***Required:*** TOEFL for international students. ***Required for some:*** SAT I or ACT. Test scores used for admission. ***Application deadline:*** rolling.
APPLYING/TRANSFER ***Recommended:*** 3 years of high school math and science. ***Entrance:*** minimally difficult. ***Application deadline:*** rolling.
CONTACT Ms. Susan Sanford, Associate Director of Admissions, State University of New York College of Environmental Science & Forestry, Ranger School, SUNY College of Environmental Science and Forestry, Bray 106, Syracuse, NY 13210-2779, 315-470-6600 or toll-free 800-777-7ESF. ***Fax:*** 315-470-6933.

❖ *See page 808 for a narrative description.* ❖

STATE UNIVERSITY OF NEW YORK COLLEGE OF TECHNOLOGY AT ALFRED
Alfred, New York

UG Enrollment: 3,319 **Tuition & Fees (NY Res): $3537**
Application Deadline: rolling **Room & Board: $4684**

GENERAL State-supported, primarily 2-year, coed. Part of State University of New York System. Awards certificates, transfer associate, terminal associate, bachelor's degrees. Founded 1908. ***Setting:*** 175-acre rural campus. ***Research spending 1994–95:*** $210,865. ***Total enrollment:*** 3,319. ***Faculty:*** 176; student-faculty ratio is 19:1. ***Notable Alumni:*** Tom Galisano, CEO of Paychex, Inc.; Erund E. Kailbroune, chairman and CEO of Fleet Bank; Howard S. Wertheimer, architect at Lord, Aeck Sargent and Company, Inc.
ENROLLMENT PROFILE 3,319 students from 6 states and territories, 2 other countries. 37% women, 63% men, 6% part-time, 98% state residents, 61% live on campus, 5% transferred in, 1% international, 17% 25 or older, 1% Native American, 1% Hispanic, 5% African American, 1% Asian American. ***Areas of study chosen:*** 23% vocational and home economics, 19% engineering and applied sciences, 11% social sciences, 9% business management and administrative services, 9% liberal arts/general studies, 7% health professions and related sciences, 6% biological and life sciences, 6% computer and information sciences, 5% agriculture. ***Most popular recent majors:*** nursing, liberal arts/general studies, human services.
FIRST-YEAR CLASS 1,574 total; 4,132 applied, 75% were accepted, 51% of whom enrolled. 5% from top 10% of their high school class, 21% from top quarter, 50% from top half.
ACADEMIC PROGRAM Core, honor code. Calendar: semesters. Academic remediation for entering students, services for LD students, advanced placement, self-designed majors, tutorials, summer session for credit, part-time degree program (daytime, evenings, weekends), adult/continuing education programs. Off-campus study at Alfred University. ROTC: Army (c).
GENERAL DEGREE REQUIREMENTS 60 credit hours for associate, 120 credit hours for bachelor's; computer course (varies by major).
MAJORS Accounting, agricultural business, agricultural sciences, animal sciences, architectural technologies, automotive technologies, biotechnology, business administration/commerce/management, carpentry, chemical engineering technology, civil engineering technology, computer graphics, computer information systems, computer science, computer technologies, construction technologies, court reporting, culinary arts, dairy sciences, data processing, drafting and design, electrical and electronics technologies, electrical engineering technology (B), electromechanical technology (B), engineering sciences, (pre)engineering sequence, environmental sciences, finance/banking, food marketing, heating/refrigeration/air conditioning, horticulture, humanities, human services, industrial and heavy equipment maintenance, landscaping/grounds maintenance, liberal arts/general studies, marketing/retailing/merchandising, mathematics, mechanical design technology, mechanical engineering technology (B), medical assistant technologies, medical laboratory technology, medical records services, nursing (B), ornamental horticulture, plumbing, retail management, science, secretarial studies/office management, social science, surveying technology (B), word processing.
LIBRARY Walter C. Hinkle Memorial Library plus 1 other, with 56,950 books, 478 microform titles, 673 periodicals, 2 on-line bibliographic services, 8 CD-ROMs, 1,538 records, tapes, and CDs. Acquisition spending 1994–95: $104,193.
COMPUTERS ON CAMPUS Student rooms linked to a campus network. 1,400 computers for student use in computer center, computer labs, learning resource center, academic buildings, classrooms, library, dorms, student rooms provide access to main academic computer, off-campus computing facilities, e-mail, on-line services, Internet. Staffed computer lab on campus provides training in use of computers, software. Academic computing expenditure 1994–95: $335,936.
COLLEGE LIFE Orientation program (2 days, $70, parents included). Drama-theater group, choral group, student-run newspaper, radio station. 10% vote in student government elections. ***Social organizations:*** 50 open to all; 2 local fraternities, 3 local sororities; 3% of eligible men and 2% of eligible women are members. ***Most popular organizations:*** Outdoor Activity Club, BACCHUS, Sondai Society, Drama Club, Choir. ***Major annual events:*** Freshman Carnival, Ag Day. ***Student services:*** health clinic, personal-psychological counseling. ***Campus security:*** 24-hour emergency response devices and patrols, late-night transport-escort service, dormitory door guards.
HOUSING 2,348 college housing spaces available; 2,139 were occupied 1995–96. Freshmen guaranteed college housing. On-campus residence required through sophomore year except by special permission. ***Option:*** coed (10 buildings) housing available. Resident assistants live in dorms.
ATHLETICS Member NJCAA. ***Intercollegiate:*** baseball M, basketball M(s)/W(s), cross-country running M(s)/W(s), football M(s), lacrosse M(s), soccer M(s)/W(s), softball W(s), swimming and diving M/W, track and field M(s)/W(s), volleyball W, wrestling M. ***Intramural:*** basketball, bowling, cross-country running, football, golf, lacrosse, racquetball, rugby, skiing (cross-country), soccer, softball, table tennis (Ping-Pong), tennis, volleyball, water polo. ***Contact:*** Ms. Kathy Feldman, Director of Athletics, 607-587-4360.
CAREER PLANNING ***Placement office:*** 2 full-time staff; $66,504 operating expenditure 1994–95. ***Director:*** Ms. Carol Woughter, Career Planning Officer, 607-587-4385. ***Services:*** job fairs, resume preparation, resume referral, career counseling, careers library, job bank, job interviews.
AFTER GRADUATION 86% of class of 1994 had job offers within 6 months. 38% of students completing transfer associate program went directly to 4-year colleges.
EXPENSES FOR 1995–96 ***Application fee:*** $30. State resident tuition: $3200 (minimum) full-time, $128 per credit hour part-time. Nonresident tuition: $8300 full-time, $346 per credit hour part-time. Part-time mandatory fees per semester range from $15.25 to $101.25. Full-time mandatory fees: $337. College room and board: $4684.
FINANCIAL AID ***College-administered undergrad aid 1995–96:*** 8 need-based scholarships (average $125), 100 non-need scholarships (average $600), short-term loans (average $40), low-interest long-term loans from college funds (average $800), loans from external sources (average $1700), Federal Work-Study, 350 part-time jobs. ***Required forms for some financial aid applicants:*** FAFSA; accepted: CSS Financial Aid PROFILE, state. ***Priority deadline:*** 3/31. ***Payment plan:*** installment. ***Waivers:*** full or partial for employees or children of employees.
APPLYING ***Options:*** electronic application, deferred entrance, midyear entrance. ***Required:*** school transcript. ***Recommended:*** essay, recommendations, interview, SAT I or ACT. ***Required for some:*** minimum 2.0 GPA, 3 years of high school math and science, TOEFL for international students. Test scores used for counseling/placement. ***Application deadline:*** rolling. ***Notification:*** continuous.
APPLYING/TRANSFER ***Required:*** high school transcript, college transcript, minimum 2.0 college GPA. ***Recommended:*** essay, standardized test scores, recommendations, interview, minimum 2.0 high school GPA. ***Required for some:*** 3 years of high school math and science. ***Entrance:*** moderately difficult. ***Application deadline:*** rolling. ***Notification:*** continuous. ***Contact:*** Ms. Merry Coburn, Transfer Counselor, 607-587-4500.
CONTACT Ms. Deborah J. Goodrich, Director of Admissions, State University of New York College of Technology at Alfred, Alfred, NY 14802, 607-587-4215 or toll-free 800-4-ALFRED. ***Fax:*** 607-587-4299. ***E-mail:*** admissions@asc.alfredtech.edu. College video and electronic viewbook available.

STATE UNIVERSITY OF NEW YORK COLLEGE OF TECHNOLOGY AT CANTON
Canton, New York

UG Enrollment: 2,004 **Tuition & Fees (NY Res): $3595**
Application Deadline: rolling **Room & Board: $4715**

The State University of New York College of Technology at Canton offers a variety of associate degree and 1-year certificate programs in 4 Centers of Excellence—Business and Public Service, Engineering and Technology, Health and Medical Technologies, and Liberal Arts and Science. These programs lead to excellent transfer and career opportunities.

GENERAL State-supported, 2-year, coed. Part of State University of New York System. Awards transfer associate, terminal associate degrees. Founded 1906. ***Setting:*** 555-acre small-town campus. ***Research spending 1994–95:*** $42,119. ***Educational spending 1994–95:*** $2995 per undergrad. ***Total enrollment:*** 2,004. ***Faculty:*** 107 (92 full-time, 11% with terminal degrees, 15 part-time); student-faculty ratio is 22:1.
ENROLLMENT PROFILE 2,004 students from 11 states and territories, 3 other countries. 45% women, 16% part-time, 99% state residents, 55% live on campus, 7% transferred in, 26% 25 or older, 1% Native American, 2% Hispanic, 5% African American, 1% Asian American. ***Areas of study chosen:*** 24% business management and administra-

tive services, 21% liberal arts/general studies, 20% interdisciplinary studies, 19% engineering and applied sciences, 8% health professions and related sciences, 2% computer and information sciences, 2% social sciences. ***Most popular recent majors:*** interdisciplinary studies, business administration/commerce/management, nursing.

FIRST-YEAR CLASS 800 total; 2,000 applied, 83% were accepted, 48% of whom enrolled. 3% from top 10% of their high school class, 12% from top quarter, 40% from top half.

ACADEMIC PROGRAM Core. Calendar: semesters. Academic remediation for entering students, services for LD students, advanced placement, self-designed majors, summer session for credit, part-time degree program (daytime, evenings), adult/continuing education programs, internships. Off-campus study at the Associated Colleges of the St. Lawrence Valley. ROTC: Army (c), Air Force (c).

GENERAL DEGREE REQUIREMENTS 61 credit hours; math/science requirements vary according to program; computer course; internship (some majors).

MAJORS Accounting, automotive technologies, biology/biological sciences, business administration/commerce/management, carpentry, chemistry, civil engineering technology, computer information systems, construction technologies, corrections, criminal justice, early childhood education, ecology, electrical and electronics technologies, electrical engineering technology, engineering sciences, engineering technology, environmental sciences, forest technology, funeral service, heating/refrigeration/air conditioning, humanities, human services, industrial engineering technology, interdisciplinary studies, landscape architecture/design, law enforcement/police sciences, liberal arts/general studies, manufacturing technology, marketing/retailing/merchandising, mechanical engineering technology, medical laboratory technology, nursing, paper and pulp sciences, physical sciences, physics, plumbing, real estate, retail management, science, secretarial studies/office management, social science, veterinary technology.

LIBRARY Southworth Library with 62,256 books, 146 microform titles, 8,043 periodicals, 10 on-line bibliographic services, 3 CD-ROMs, 790 records, tapes, and CDs. Acquisition spending 1994–95: $331,293.

COMPUTERS ON CAMPUS Computer purchase plan available. Student rooms linked to a campus network. 215 computers for student use in computer center, academic buildings, library provide access to main academic computer, off-campus computing facilities, e-mail, on-line services, Internet. Staffed computer lab on campus provides training in use of computers, software. Academic computing expenditure 1994–95: $166,064.

COLLEGE LIFE Orientation program (2 days, $51, parents included). Drama-theater group, choral group, student-run newspaper, radio station. 55% vote in student government elections. ***Social organizations:*** 53 open to all; 3 local fraternities, 3 local sororities; 10% of eligible men and 5% of eligible women are members. ***Most popular organizations:*** Karate Club, Alpha Theta Gamma. ***Major annual events:*** Family Weekend, Mardis Gras, National Shakespeare Theater. ***Student services:*** legal services, health clinic, personal-psychological counseling. ***Campus security:*** 24-hour emergency response devices and patrols, late-night transport-escort service, controlled dormitory access.

HOUSING College housing designed to accommodate 864 students; 1,015 undergraduates lived in college housing during 1995–96. Freshmen given priority for college housing. On-campus residence required through sophomore year. ***Options:*** coed, single-sex housing available. Resident assistants live in dorms.

ATHLETICS Member NJCAA. ***Intercollegiate:*** basketball M/W, football M, ice hockey M, lacrosse M, soccer M/W, softball W, volleyball W. ***Intramural:*** badminton, basketball, cross-country running, football, golf, lacrosse, skiing (cross-country), skiing (downhill), soccer, softball, tennis, volleyball, water polo, weight lifting. ***Contact:*** Ms. Diane Para, Director of Athletics, 315-386-7335.

CAREER PLANNING ***Placement office:*** 1 full-time, 2 part-time staff; $79,795 operating expenditure 1994–95. ***Director:*** Mr. Joel Bixby, Director, Career Services, 315-386-7119. ***Services:*** resume preparation, career counseling, job bank, job interviews. Students must register freshman year. 40 organizations recruited on campus 1994–95.

AFTER GRADUATION 40% of class of 1994 had job offers within 6 months. 81% of students completing a degree program went directly on to further study.

EXPENSES FOR 1996–97 ***Application fee:*** $25. State resident tuition: $3200 full-time, $105 per credit hour part-time. Nonresident tuition: $8300 full-time, $274 per credit hour part-time. Part-time mandatory fees: $10.45 per credit hour. Full-time mandatory fees: $395. College room and board: $4715. College room only: $2818.

FINANCIAL AID ***College-administered undergrad aid 1995–96:*** 80 need-based scholarships (average $300), 20 non-need scholarships (average $200), short-term loans (average $300), low-interest long-term loans from external sources (average $2100), 200 Federal Work-Study (averaging $1500), 210 part-time jobs. ***Required forms:*** institutional; required for some: state; accepted: FAFSA. ***Priority deadline:*** 3/1. ***Payment plan:*** installment.

APPLYING ***Options:*** electronic application, early entrance, deferred entrance, midyear entrance. ***Required:*** ACT, TOEFL for international students. ***Recommended:*** minimum 2.0 GPA, SAT I. ***Required for some:*** 3 years of high school math and science. Test scores used for counseling/placement. ***Application deadline:*** rolling. ***Notification:*** continuous.

APPLYING/TRANSFER ***Required for some:*** 3 years of high school math and science. ***Application deadline:*** rolling. ***Notification:*** continuous. ***Contact:*** Mr. Harry Podgurski, Director of Counseling, 315-386-7122.

CONTACT Mr. Michael Brophy, Dean of Enrollment Management, State University of New York College of Technology at Canton, Canton, NY 13617, 315-386-7123 or toll-free 800-388-7123. ***Fax:*** 315-386-7930. College video available.

❖ ***See page 810 for a narrative description.*** ❖

STATE UNIVERSITY OF NEW YORK COLLEGE OF TECHNOLOGY AT DELHI
Delhi, New York

UG Enrollment: 2,098	**Tuition & Fees (NY Res): $3647**
Application Deadline: rolling	**Room & Board: $4942**

GENERAL State-supported, 2-year, coed. Part of State University of New York System. Awards certificates, transfer associate, terminal associate degrees. Founded 1913. ***Setting:*** 1,100-acre small-town campus. ***Total enrollment:*** 2,098. Student-faculty ratio is 17:1.

ENROLLMENT PROFILE 2,098 students from 7 states and territories. 42% women, 7% part-time, 98% state residents, 61% live on campus, 12% transferred in, 68% have need-based financial aid, 0% have non-need-based financial aid, 0% international, 15% 25 or older, 1% Native American, 6% Hispanic, 9% African American, 2% Asian American. ***Areas of study chosen:*** 23% business management and administrative services, 23% liberal arts/general studies, 21% vocational and home economics, 17% agriculture, 5% health professions and related sciences, 4% architecture, 4% engineering and applied sciences, 1% computer and information sciences. ***Most popular recent majors:*** business administration/commerce/management, carpentry.

FIRST-YEAR CLASS 778 total; 3,100 applied, 81% were accepted, 31% of whom enrolled. 1% from top 10% of their high school class, 12% from top quarter, 53% from top half.

ACADEMIC PROGRAM Core, general studies curriculum. Calendar: semesters. 235 courses offered in 1995–96. Academic remediation for entering students, services for LD students, advanced placement, self-designed majors, honors program, summer session for credit, part-time degree program (daytime, evenings), adult/continuing education programs, internships.

GENERAL DEGREE REQUIREMENTS 60 credit hours; computer course (varies by major); internship (some majors).

MAJORS Accounting, architectural technologies, automotive technologies, business administration/commerce/management, carpentry, computer information systems, construction management, construction technologies, culinary arts, drafting and design, engineering sciences, (pre)engineering sequence, food services management, forestry, forest technology, heating/refrigeration/air conditioning, horticulture, hotel and restaurant management, interdisciplinary studies, laboratory animal medicine, landscape architecture/design, landscaping/grounds maintenance, legal secretarial studies, liberal arts/general studies, marketing/retailing/merchandising, nursing, parks management, physical education, plumbing, recreational facilities management, recreation and leisure services, secretarial studies/office management, tourism and travel, veterinary technology, welding technology, word processing.

LIBRARY Resnick Library with 47,909 books, 131 microform titles, 384 periodicals, 23 CD-ROMs, 663 records, tapes, and CDs.

COMPUTERS ON CAMPUS 350 computers for student use in computer labs, learning resource center, classrooms, library provide access to main academic computer, e-mail, on-line services, Internet. Staffed computer lab on campus provides training in use of computers, software.

COLLEGE LIFE Orientation program (2 days, $65, parents included). Drama-theater group, student-run newspaper, radio station. ***Social organizations:*** 40 open to all; 1 national fraternity, 2 local fraternities, 2 local sororities; 3% of eligible men and 2% of eligible women are members. ***Most popular organizations:*** Latin American Student Organization, Hotel Sales Management Association, Student Radio Station, Phi Theta Kappa, Student Programming Board. ***Major annual events:*** Fall Weekend, Winter Weekend, Spring Weekend. ***Student services:*** legal services, health clinic, personal-psychological counseling. ***Campus security:*** 24-hour emergency response devices and patrols.

HOUSING College housing designed to accommodate 1,238 students; 1,280 undergraduates lived in college housing during 1995–96. Freshmen given priority for college housing. On-campus residence required through sophomore year except if 21 or over. ***Option:*** coed (5 buildings) housing available. Resident assistants live in dorms.

ATHLETICS Member NJCAA. ***Intercollegiate:*** basketball M/W, cross-country running M/W, golf M/W, soccer M/W, tennis M/W, track and field M/W. ***Intramural:*** basketball, bowling, cross-country running, football, golf, racquetball, skiing (cross-country), skiing (downhill), swimming and diving, tennis, volleyball, weight lifting. ***Contact:*** Mr. Robert Backus, Director of Athletics, 607-746-4675.

CAREER PLANNING ***Placement office:*** 2 full-time, 1 part-time staff. ***Director:*** Mr. Louis M. Shields, Director Career Services, 607-746-4648. ***Services:*** job fairs, resume preparation, resume referral, career counseling, careers library, job bank, job interviews.

AFTER GRADUATION 82% of students completing a degree program in 1994–95 went directly on to further study.

EXPENSES FOR 1995–96 ***Application fee:*** $30. State resident tuition: $3250 full-time, $135 per credit hour part-time. Nonresident tuition: $8300 full-time, $345 per credit hour part-time. Part-time mandatory fees: $8.10 per credit hour. Full-time mandatory fees: $397. College room and board: $4942.

FINANCIAL AID ***College-administered undergrad aid 1995–96:*** 62 need-based scholarships (averaging $488), short-term loans (averaging $300), low-interest long-term loans from external sources (averaging $2100), 127 Federal Work-Study (averaging $1000), 85 part-time jobs. ***Required forms:*** CSS Financial Aid PROFILE, FAFSA; required for some: state. ***Priority deadline:*** 2/15. ***Payment plans:*** installment, deferred payment.

APPLYING ***Options:*** early entrance, deferred entrance. ***Required:*** school transcript, TOEFL for international students. ***Recommended:*** SAT I or ACT. ***Required for some:*** minimum 2.0 GPA, 3 years of high school math. Test scores used for counseling/placement. ***Application deadline:*** rolling. ***Notification:*** continuous.

APPLYING/TRANSFER ***Required:*** college transcript. ***Required for some:*** high school transcript, 3 years of high school math. ***Entrance:*** moderately difficult. ***Application deadline:*** rolling. ***Notification:*** continuous. ***Contact:*** Mr. John Ellis, Senior Admissions Advisor, 607-746-4550.

CONTACT Mr. Richard Cardoza, Director of Admissions, State University of New York College of Technology at Delhi, Delhi, NY 13753, 607-746-4246. ***Fax:*** 607-746-4208. College video available.

STATE UNIVERSITY OF NEW YORK COLLEGE OF TECHNOLOGY AT FARMINGDALE
Farmingdale, New York

UG Enrollment: 6,209	**Tuition & Fees (NY Res): $3621**
Application Deadline: rolling	**Room & Board: $5491**

GENERAL State-supported, primarily 2-year, coed. Part of State University of New York System. Awards certificates, transfer associate, terminal associate, bachelor's degrees (bachelor's is upper-level). Founded 1912. ***Setting:*** 380-acre small-town campus with easy access to New York City. ***Endowment:*** $250,400. ***Research spending 1994–95:*** $1.1 million. ***Total enrollment:*** 6,209. ***Faculty:*** 390 (200 full-time, 37% with terminal degrees, 190 part-time); student-faculty ratio is 17:1. ***Notable Alumni:*** Donald Shelansky, chief operating officer of Lone Star Crowers; Robert W. Gray, president of Allstate Insurance Company Personal Lines Division; William A. Barabino, managing general partner of Mass Light General Group; David Gura, president of Ethos Development Corporation; Robert B. Peters, consultant for the Scott Company.

State University of New York College of Technology at Farmingdale (continued)

ENROLLMENT PROFILE 6,209 students from 9 states and territories, 2 other countries. 45% women, 55% men, 46% part-time, 99% state residents, 8% live on campus, 60% have need-based financial aid, 28% 25 or older, 1% Native American, 9% Hispanic, 13% African American, 5% Asian American. ***Areas of study chosen:*** 30% business management and administrative services, 27% liberal arts/general studies, 22% engineering and applied sciences, 9% health professions and related sciences, 5% computer and information sciences, 4% biological and life sciences. ***Most popular recent majors:*** liberal arts/general studies, business administration/commerce/management.

FIRST-YEAR CLASS 1,302 total; 4,020 applied, 51% were accepted, 63% of whom enrolled. 10% from top 10% of their high school class, 20% from top quarter, 70% from top half.

ACADEMIC PROGRAM Core, specialized study curriculum, honor code. Calendar: semesters. 830 courses offered in 1995–96. Academic remediation for entering students, English as a second language program offered during academic year, services for LD students, advanced placement, summer session for credit, part-time degree program (daytime, evenings), internships. ROTC: Army (c), Air Force (c).

GENERAL DEGREE REQUIREMENTS 60 credits for associate, 127 credits for bachelor's; 6 credits of math/science for associate degree; 12 credits of math/science for bachelor's degree; computer course for business administration, engineering, horticulture, nutrition majors.

MAJORS Accounting, aerospace sciences (B), applied mathematics, architectural technologies, automotive technologies, aviation administration (B), aviation technology, biomedical technologies, business administration/commerce/management, commercial art (B), computer information systems, computer programming, computer science, construction management (B), construction technologies, criminal justice, data processing, dental services, electrical and electronics technologies (B), electrical engineering technology (B), electronics engineering technology (B), engineering (general), engineering sciences, flight training (B), horticulture, industrial administration (B), landscape architecture/design, law enforcement/police sciences, liberal arts/general studies, management information systems, manufacturing technology (B), mechanical engineering technology, medical laboratory technology, nursing, nutrition, ornamental horticulture, purchasing/inventory management (B), quality control technology (B).

LIBRARY Greenley Hall with 128,000 books, 258 microform titles, 1,000 periodicals, 20 CD-ROMs, 5,000 records, tapes, and CDs. Acquisition spending 1994–95: $255,920.

COMPUTERS ON CAMPUS Computer purchase plan available. 285 computers for student use in computer labs, learning resource center, writing center, classrooms, library, student center, dorms provide access to main academic computer, off-campus computing facilities, e-mail, on-line services, Internet. Staffed computer lab on campus provides training in use of computers, software.

COLLEGE LIFE Orientation program ($50, parents included). Drama-theater group, choral group, student-run newspaper, radio station. ***Social organizations:*** 44 open to all. ***Most popular organizations:*** Inter-Residence Council, Student Nurses Association, Student Government Association, Backstage Theater, Rambler Newspaper. ***Major annual events:*** Orientation, Welcome Week Activities. ***Student services:*** health clinic, personal-psychological counseling. ***Campus security:*** 24-hour emergency response devices and patrols, student patrols.

HOUSING 656 college housing spaces available; 507 were occupied 1995–96. Freshmen given priority for college housing. Off-campus living permitted. ***Options:*** coed, single-sex housing available. Resident assistants live in dorms.

ATHLETICS Member NJCAA. ***Intercollegiate:*** baseball M, basketball M/W, cross-country running M/W, golf M, lacrosse M, soccer M/W, softball W, track and field M/W, volleyball W, wrestling M. ***Intramural:*** archery, badminton, basketball, field hockey, football, ice hockey, racquetball, squash, tennis, volleyball, wrestling. ***Contact:*** Mr. Bruce Robbins, Athletic Director, 516-420-2053.

CAREER PLANNING ***Placement office:*** 2 full-time, 1 part-time staff; $103,425 operating expenditure 1994–95. ***Director:*** Ms. Malka Edelman, Director of Career Placement, 516-420-2296. ***Services:*** job fairs, resume preparation, career counseling, job bank, job interviews. 82 organizations recruited on campus 1994–95.

AFTER GRADUATION 50% of students completing transfer associate program in 1994–95 went directly to 4-year colleges.

EXPENSES FOR 1995–96 ***Application fee:*** $30. State resident tuition: $3200 (minimum) full-time, $128 per credit (minimum) part-time. Nonresident tuition: $8300 (minimum) full-time, $346 per credit (minimum) part-time. Part-time mandatory fees: $7.85 per credit. Full-time mandatory fees: $421. College room and board: $5491. College room only: $2700.

FINANCIAL AID ***College-administered undergrad aid 1995–96:*** 1,999 need-based scholarships (averaging $1119), 95 non-need scholarships (averaging $1000), Federal Work-Study, 190 part-time jobs. ***Required forms:*** state, institutional, FAFSA; accepted: CSS Financial Aid PROFILE. ***Priority deadline:*** 4/1. ***Payment plans:*** installment, deferred payment. ***Waivers:*** full or partial for senior citizens. ***Notification:*** 6/1. ***Average indebtedness of graduates:*** $1200.

APPLYING ***Options:*** early entrance, midyear entrance. ***Required:*** school transcript, TOEFL for international students. ***Recommended:*** 2 years of high school foreign language, SAT I or ACT, SAT II Subject Tests. ***Required for some:*** minimum 2.0 GPA, 3 years of high school math. Test scores used for counseling/placement. ***Application deadline:*** rolling.

APPLYING/TRANSFER ***Required:*** college transcript. ***Recommended:*** standardized test scores, 2 years of high school foreign language. ***Required for some:*** high school transcript, 3 years of high school math, campus interview, minimum 2.0 college GPA. ***Entrance:*** minimally difficult. ***Application deadline:*** rolling. ***Contact:*** Mr. Jeffrey Stein, Director of Admissions, 516-420-2200.

CONTACT Mr. Jeffrey Stein, Director of Admissions, State University of New York College of Technology at Farmingdale, Farmingdale, NY 11735, 516-420-2200.

❖ ***See page 812 for a narrative description.*** ❖

STENOTYPE ACADEMY
New York, New York

UG Enrollment: 800	**Tuition & Fees: $4400**
Application Deadline: rolling	**Room & Board: N/Avail**

GENERAL Proprietary, 2-year, coed. Awards terminal associate degrees. Founded 1942. ***Setting:*** urban campus. ***Total enrollment:*** 800. ***Faculty:*** 35 (20 full-time, 15 part-time).

ENROLLMENT PROFILE 800 students: 93% women, 22% part-time, 98% state residents, 5% transferred in, 0% international, 35% 25 or older, 0% Native American, 25% Hispanic, 30% African American, 5% Asian American.

FIRST-YEAR CLASS 200 total. Of the students who applied, 100% were accepted, 50% of whom enrolled.

ACADEMIC PROGRAM Core. Calendar: trimesters (semesters for evening division). Academic remediation for entering students, services for LD students, summer session for credit, part-time degree program (evenings), internships.

GENERAL DEGREE REQUIREMENTS 60 credits; computer course.

MAJORS Court reporting, paralegal studies.

LIBRARY 5,010 books, 23 periodicals, 300 records, tapes, and CDs.

COMPUTERS ON CAMPUS 50 computers for student use in computer center. Staffed computer lab on campus provides training in use of computers, software.

COLLEGE LIFE Student-run newspaper.

HOUSING College housing not available.

CAREER PLANNING ***Service:*** career counseling.

EXPENSES FOR 1995–96 ***Application fee:*** $25. Full-time tuition: $6600 for day program, $4400 for evening program.

FINANCIAL AID ***College-administered undergrad aid 1995–96:*** need-based scholarships, low-interest long-term loans from external sources. ***Required forms:*** state, FAFSA. ***Priority deadline:*** 7/15. ***Payment plan:*** installment.

APPLYING Open admission. ***Required:*** school transcript, interview. ***Required for some:*** recommendations. ***Application deadline:*** rolling. ***Notification:*** continuous.

APPLYING/TRANSFER ***Required:*** high school transcript, interview, college transcript. ***Required for some:*** recommendations. ***Application deadline:*** rolling. ***Notification:*** continuous.

CONTACT Ms. Alice DeWalt, Director of Admissions, Stenotype Academy, 15 Park Row, 4th Floor, New York, NY 10038-2301, 212-962-0002.

SUFFOLK COUNTY COMMUNITY COLLEGE–AMMERMAN CAMPUS
Selden, New York

UG Enrollment: 13,154	**Tuition & Fees (NY Res): $2206**
Application Deadline: rolling	**Room & Board: N/Avail**

GENERAL State and locally supported, 2-year, coed. Part of State University of New York System. Awards transfer associate, terminal associate degrees. Founded 1962. ***Setting:*** 200-acre small-town campus with easy access to New York City. ***Total enrollment:*** 13,154. ***Faculty:*** 782 (287 full-time, 495 part-time).

ENROLLMENT PROFILE 13,154 students: 61% women, 53% part-time, 100% state residents, 5% transferred in, 37% 25 or older, 4% Hispanic, 4% African American.

FIRST-YEAR CLASS 3,645 total; 5,602 applied, 89% were accepted, 73% of whom enrolled.

ACADEMIC PROGRAM Core. Calendar: semesters. Academic remediation for entering students, English as a second language program offered during academic year and summer, services for LD students, honors program, summer session for credit, part-time degree program (daytime, evenings, weekends, summer), adult/continuing education programs, internships. Off-campus study at members of the Long Island Regional Advisory Council for Higher Education.

GENERAL DEGREE REQUIREMENTS 68 credits; math/science requirements vary according to program; computer course for business administration majors; internship (some majors).

MAJORS Accounting, art/fine arts, automotive technologies, biology/biological sciences, broadcasting, business administration/commerce/management, chemistry, child care/child and family studies, civil engineering technology, community services, computer information systems, computer programming, computer science, computer technologies, construction technologies, criminal justice, data processing, deaf interpreter training, drafting and design, early childhood education, electrical and electronics technologies, electrical engineering technology, engineering (general), engineering sciences, English, humanities, insurance, journalism, law enforcement/police sciences, legal secretarial studies, liberal arts/general studies, manufacturing technology, marine technology, marketing/retailing/merchandising, mathematics, mechanical engineering technology, music, nursing, paralegal studies, physical therapy, real estate, recreation and leisure services, recreation therapy, retail management, science, secretarial studies/office management, social science, telecommunications, theater arts/drama, women's studies.

LIBRARY 119,161 books, 3,181 microform titles, 711 periodicals, 2 on-line bibliographic services, 3 CD-ROMs, 18,442 records, tapes, and CDs. Acquisition spending 1994–95: $2 million.

COMPUTERS ON CAMPUS 200 computers for student use in computer center, computer labs, learning resource center, library. Academic computing expenditure 1994–95: $499,443.

COLLEGE LIFE Drama-theater group, student-run newspaper, radio station. ***Student services:*** health clinic, personal-psychological counseling, women's center. ***Campus security:*** 24-hour patrols.

HOUSING College housing not available.

ATHLETICS Member NAIA, NJCAA. ***Intercollegiate:*** basketball M/W, cross-country running M/W, golf M, lacrosse M, soccer M, tennis M/W, track and field M/W, volleyball M, wrestling M. ***Contact:*** Mr. Eugene J. Farry, Director of Athletics, 516-451-4380.

CAREER PLANNING ***Placement office:*** 2 full-time, 3 part-time staff; $142,905 operating expenditure 1994–95. ***Director:*** Ms. Sylvia E. Camacho, Director, Career Placement Center, 516-451-4049. ***Services:*** job fairs, resume preparation, career counseling, job bank.

AFTER GRADUATION 60% of students completing a degree program in 1994–95 went directly on to further study.

EXPENSES FOR 1995–96 ***Application fee:*** $25. State resident tuition: $2100 full-time, $90 per credit part-time. Nonresident tuition: $4200 full-time, $180 per credit part-time. Part-time mandatory fees: $4.50 per credit. Full-time mandatory fees: $106.

FINANCIAL AID ***College-administered undergrad aid 1995–96:*** 540 need-based scholarships (average $562), 79 non-need scholarships (average $245), short-term loans (average $200), Federal Work-Study, 50 part-time jobs. ***Required forms:*** institutional, FAFSA; accepted: CSS Financial Aid PROFILE. ***Priority deadline:*** 6/1. ***Waivers:*** full or partial for employees or children of employees.

APPLYING Open admission except for engineering, physical therapy assistant, nursing, computer science, early childhood education, paralegal programs. ***Option:*** early entrance. ***Required:*** TOEFL for international students. ***Recommended:*** SAT I or ACT.

Required for some: 3 years of high school math, SAT I or ACT. Test scores used for counseling/placement. ***Application deadline:*** rolling. ***Notification:*** continuous. Preference given to county residents.
APPLYING/TRANSFER ***Entrance:*** noncompetitive. ***Application deadline:*** rolling. ***Notification:*** continuous. ***Contact:*** Ms. Linda Reiser, Dean of Students, 516-451-4043.
CONTACT Ms. Pat Southard, Campus Director of Admissions, Suffolk County Community College–Ammerman Campus, Selden, NY 11784-2851, 516-451-4022. College video available.

SUFFOLK COUNTY COMMUNITY COLLEGE–EASTERN CAMPUS
Riverhead, New York

UG Enrollment: 2,680 **Tuition & Fees (NY Res): $2226**
Application Deadline: rolling **Room & Board: N/Avail**

GENERAL State and locally supported, 2-year, coed. Part of State University of New York System. Awards transfer associate, terminal associate degrees. Founded 1977. ***Setting:*** 192-acre small-town campus. ***Total enrollment:*** 2,680. ***Faculty:*** 216 (42 full-time, 174 part-time).
ENROLLMENT PROFILE 2,680 students: 68% women, 68% part-time, 100% state residents, 40% transferred in, 0% international, 51% 25 or older, 1% Native American, 3% Hispanic, 3% African American, 1% Asian American. ***Most popular recent majors:*** liberal arts/general studies, business administration/commerce/management, accounting.
FIRST-YEAR CLASS 741 total. 2% from top 10% of their high school class, 19% from top quarter, 43% from top half.
ACADEMIC PROGRAM Core. Calendar: semesters. Academic remediation for entering students, English as a second language program offered during academic year and summer, services for LD students, advanced placement, honors program, summer session for credit, part-time degree program (daytime, evenings, weekends, summer), adult/continuing education programs, co-op programs. Off-campus study at members of the Long Island Regional Advisory Council for Higher Education. ROTC: Army (c), Naval (c).
GENERAL DEGREE REQUIREMENTS 66 credits; math/science requirements vary according to program; computer course for most majors; internship (some majors).
MAJORS Accounting, business administration/commerce/management, criminal justice, dietetics, early childhood education, food services management, graphic arts, horticulture, hotel and restaurant management, interior design, law enforcement/police sciences, legal secretarial studies, liberal arts/general studies, marine technology, marketing/retailing/merchandising, real estate, retail management, secretarial studies/office management, tourism and travel.
LIBRARY Eastern Campus Library with 32,342 books, 271 periodicals, 2 on-line bibliographic services, 1 CD-ROM, 6,217 records, tapes, and CDs. Acquisition spending 1994–95: $350,858.
COMPUTERS ON CAMPUS 45 computers for student use in computer center, learning resource center, library. Academic computing expenditure 1994–95: $87,130.
COLLEGE LIFE Drama-theater group, student-run newspaper. 20% vote in student government elections. ***Student services:*** health clinic, personal-psychological counseling, women's center. ***Campus security:*** 24-hour patrols.
HOUSING College housing not available.
ATHLETICS Member NJCAA. ***Intercollegiate:*** baseball M, basketball M/W, cross-country running M/W, golf M, gymnastics M/W, lacrosse M, sailing M/W, softball W, tennis M/W, volleyball W. ***Contact:*** Mr. Gene Farry, Director of Athletics, 516-548-4380.
CAREER PLANNING ***Placement office:*** 1 full-time, 1 part-time staff; $26,330 operating expenditure 1994–95. ***Director:*** Mr. George J. Hiltner, Professor of Counseling/Career Counselor, 516-548-2520. ***Services:*** job fairs, resume preparation, career counseling, careers library, job bank.
AFTER GRADUATION 75% of students completing a degree program in 1994–95 went directly on to further study.
EXPENSES FOR 1995–96 ***Application fee:*** $25. State resident tuition: $2100 full-time, $90 per credit part-time. Nonresident tuition: $4200 full-time, $180 per credit part-time. Part-time mandatory fees: $4.50 per credit. Full-time mandatory fees: $126.
FINANCIAL AID ***College-administered undergrad aid 1995–96:*** 162 need-based scholarships (average $563), 14 non-need scholarships (average $155), short-term loans (average $200), low-interest long-term loans from external sources (average $2000), Federal Work-Study, 9 part-time jobs. ***Required forms:*** institutional; accepted: CSS Financial Aid PROFILE, FAFSA. ***Priority deadline:*** 6/1. ***Waivers:*** full or partial for employees or children of employees.
APPLYING Open admission. ***Option:*** early entrance. ***Required:*** TOEFL for international students. ***Recommended:*** SAT I or ACT. ***Required for some:*** 3 years of high school math, SAT I or ACT. Test scores used for counseling/placement. ***Application deadline:*** rolling. ***Notification:*** continuous. Preference given to county residents.
APPLYING/TRANSFER ***Entrance:*** noncompetitive. ***Application deadline:*** rolling. ***Notification:*** continuous. ***Contact:*** Ms. Joanne Braxton, Dean of Students, 516-451-2515.
CONTACT Mr. Charles Bartolotta, Assistant Director of Admissions and Financial Aid, Suffolk County Community College–Eastern Campus, Riverhead, NY 11901, 516-548-2513. College video available.

SUFFOLK COUNTY COMMUNITY COLLEGE–WESTERN CAMPUS
Brentwood, New York

UG Enrollment: 6,097 **Tuition & Fees (NY Res): $2402**
Application Deadline: rolling **Room & Board: N/Avail**

GENERAL State and locally supported, 2-year, coed. Part of State University of New York System. Awards transfer associate, terminal associate degrees. Founded 1974. ***Setting:*** 206-acre suburban campus with easy access to New York City. ***Total enrollment:*** 6,097. ***Faculty:*** 349 (94 full-time, 255 part-time); student-faculty ratio is 18:1.
ENROLLMENT PROFILE 6,097 students: 66% women, 70% part-time, 99% state residents, 12% transferred in, 46% 25 or older, 8% Hispanic, 7% African American, 1% Asian American.
FIRST-YEAR CLASS 919 total; 1,865 applied, 65% of whom enrolled.
ACADEMIC PROGRAM Core. Calendar: semesters. Academic remediation for entering students, English as a second language program offered during academic year and summer, services for LD students, advanced placement, honors program, summer session for credit, part-time degree program (daytime, evenings, weekends, summer), co-op programs. Off-campus study at members of the Long Island Regional Advisory Council for Higher Education.
GENERAL DEGREE REQUIREMENTS 62 credits; math/science requirements vary according to program; computer course for business majors.
MAJORS Accounting, business administration/commerce/management, criminal justice, data processing, drug and alcohol/substance abuse counseling, early childhood education, electrical and electronics technologies, finance/banking, legal secretarial studies, liberal arts/general studies, marketing/retailing/merchandising, medical secretarial studies, medical technology, nursing, real estate, retail management, secretarial studies/office management, veterinary sciences.
LIBRARY Western Campus Library with 39,171 books, 6,746 microform titles, 321 periodicals, 2 on-line bibliographic services, 1 CD-ROM, 1,894 records, tapes, and CDs. Acquisition spending 1994–95: $784,162.
COMPUTERS ON CAMPUS 270 computers for student use. Academic computing expenditure 1994–95: $139,448.
COLLEGE LIFE Drama-theater group, student-run newspaper, radio station. ***Student services:*** health clinic, personal-psychological counseling, women's center. ***Campus security:*** 24-hour patrols.
HOUSING College housing not available.
ATHLETICS Member NJCAA. ***Intercollegiate:*** baseball M, basketball M, bowling M/W, golf M, soccer M, softball W.
CAREER PLANNING ***Placement office:*** 1 full-time, 2 part-time staff; $34,551 operating expenditure 1994–95. ***Director:*** Ms. Donna Della Rocca, Career/Placement Counselor, 516-434-6717. ***Services:*** job fairs, resume preparation, career counseling, careers library, job bank, job interviews.
AFTER GRADUATION 60% of students completing a degree program in 1994–95 went directly on to further study.
EXPENSES FOR 1995–96 ***Application fee:*** $25. State resident tuition: $2220 full-time, $90 per credit part-time. Nonresident tuition: $4456 full-time, $180 per credit part-time. Part-time mandatory fees: $4.50 per credit. Full-time mandatory fees: $182.
FINANCIAL AID ***College-administered undergrad aid 1995–96:*** 380 need-based scholarships (average $586), 77 non-need scholarships (average $125), short-term loans (average $200), Federal Work-Study, 8 part-time jobs. ***Required forms:*** institutional, FAFSA; accepted: CSS Financial Aid PROFILE. ***Priority deadline:*** 6/1.
APPLYING Open admission except for nursing, chemical dependency counseling, veterinary science technology programs. ***Option:*** early entrance. ***Required:*** TOEFL for international students. ***Recommended:*** SAT I or ACT. ***Required for some:*** 3 years of high school math and science, SAT I or ACT. Test scores used for counseling/placement. ***Application deadline:*** rolling. ***Notification:*** continuous. Preference given to county residents.
APPLYING/TRANSFER ***Required for some:*** 3 years of high school math and science. ***Entrance:*** noncompetitive. ***Application deadline:*** rolling. ***Notification:*** continuous. ***Contact:*** Ms. Allie Parrish, Dean of Students, 516-451-6502.
CONTACT Miss Kathryn Reinauer, Campus Director of Admissions, Suffolk County Community College–Western Campus, Brentwood, NY 11717, 516-434-6704. College video and electronic viewbook available.

SULLIVAN COUNTY COMMUNITY COLLEGE
Loch Sheldrake, New York

UG Enrollment: 2,085 **Tuition & Fees (NY Res): $2356**
Application Deadline: rolling **Room & Board: N/Avail**

More than 35 career-oriented or college transfer programs are offered in hospitality, travel and tourism, environmental studies, surveying technology, photography, commercial art, engineering science, home child care / nanny studies, business administration, and liberal arts. Study-abroad opportunities in Japan. Housing and financial aid available.

GENERAL State and locally supported, 2-year, coed. Part of State University of New York System. Awards certificates, transfer associate, terminal associate degrees. Founded 1962. ***Setting:*** 405-acre rural campus. ***Endowment:*** $759,333. ***Educational spending 1994–95:*** $2942 per undergrad. ***Total enrollment:*** 2,085. ***Faculty:*** 106 (56 full-time, 23% with terminal degrees, 50 part-time); student-faculty ratio is 18:1.
ENROLLMENT PROFILE 2,085 students from 4 states and territories, 7 other countries. 56% women, 33% part-time, 95% state residents, 9% transferred in, 3% international, 43% 25 or older, 0% Native American, 8% Hispanic, 18% African American, 2% Asian American. ***Most popular recent majors:*** liberal arts/general studies, hospitality services, commercial art.
FIRST-YEAR CLASS 554 total; 2,100 applied, 98% were accepted, 27% of whom enrolled. 28% from top half of their high school class.
ACADEMIC PROGRAM Core, honor code. Calendar: 4-1-4. Average class size 35 in required courses. Academic remediation for entering students, English as a second language program offered during academic year, services for LD students, advanced placement, tutorials, honors program, summer session for credit, part-time degree program (daytime, evenings, summer), adult/continuing education programs, internships. Study abroad in Japan.
GENERAL DEGREE REQUIREMENTS 63 credits; 8 credits of science; internship (some majors).
MAJORS Accounting, behavioral sciences, biology/biological sciences, broadcasting, business administration/commerce/management, child care/child and family studies, commercial art, communication, computer information systems, computer technologies, corrections, criminal justice, culinary arts, data processing, drug and alcohol/substance abuse counseling, early childhood education, education, elementary education, engineering (general), engineering sciences, (pre)engineering sequence, English, food services technology, forestry, forest technology, graphic arts, hospitality services, hotel and restaurant management, humanities, human services, insurance, law enforcement/police sciences, liberal arts/general studies, marketing/retailing/merchandising, mental health/rehabilitation counseling, natural sciences, nursing, paralegal studies, photography, physical sciences, psychology, radio and television studies, recreational facilities management, retail manage-

Sullivan County Community College (continued)
ment, science, secretarial studies/office management, social science, social work, sports administration, surveying technology, tourism and travel, word processing.
LIBRARY Hermann Memorial Library with 62,000 books, 10,000 microform titles, 600 periodicals, 4,000 records, tapes, and CDs. Acquisition spending 1994–95: $107,803.
COMPUTERS ON CAMPUS 80 computers for student use in computer center, science labs, library. Staffed computer lab on campus provides training in use of computers, software. Academic computing expenditure 1994–95: $249,151.
COLLEGE LIFE Orientation program (1 weekend, parents included). Student-run radio station. 10% vote in student government elections. ***Social organizations:*** 15 open to all. ***Most popular organizations:*** Science Alliance, Black Student Union, Drama Club, Baking Club, Honor Society. ***Major annual events:*** Talent Show, Kite Day. ***Student services:*** legal services, health clinic, personal-psychological counseling. ***Campus security:*** 24-hour emergency response devices and patrols.
HOUSING College housing not available.
ATHLETICS Member NJCAA. ***Intercollegiate:*** basketball M, golf M/W, softball W, volleyball W. ***Intramural:*** badminton, basketball, bowling, equestrian sports, football, racquetball, skiing (downhill), softball, table tennis (Ping-Pong), tennis, volleyball, weight lifting. ***Contact:*** Mr. Michael McGuire, Athletic Director, 914-434-5750.
CAREER PLANNING ***Placement office:*** 2 full-time, 1 part-time staff. ***Director:*** Mr. Richard M. Sush, Director of Student Life Services, 914-434-5750. ***Services:*** resume preparation, career counseling, careers library.
AFTER GRADUATION 48% of students completing a degree program in 1994–95 went directly on to further study.
EXPENSES FOR 1995–96 ***Application fee:*** $30. State resident tuition: $2200 full-time, $75 per credit hour part-time. Nonresident tuition: $4400 full-time, $155 per credit hour part-time. Part-time mandatory fees: $5.25 per credit. Full-time mandatory fees: $156.
FINANCIAL AID ***College-administered undergrad aid 1995–96:*** 143 need-based scholarships (average $522), non-need scholarships, low-interest long-term loans from external sources (average $2609), 65 Federal Work-Study (averaging $1033), 47 part-time jobs. ***Required forms:*** institutional, FAFSA; accepted: CSS Financial Aid PROFILE, state. ***Priority deadline:*** 4/15. ***Waivers:*** full or partial for employees or children of employees. ***Notification:*** 5/15. ***Average indebtedness of graduates:*** $5218.
APPLYING Open admission. ***Options:*** Common Application, early entrance, deferred entrance, midyear entrance. ***Required:*** school transcript, TOEFL for international students. ***Recommended:*** SAT I or ACT. ***Required for some:*** 3 years of high school math and science. Test scores used for counseling/placement. ***Application deadline:*** rolling. ***Notification:*** continuous. Preference given to county residents.
APPLYING/TRANSFER ***Recommended:*** college transcript. ***Required for some:*** college transcript. ***Application deadline:*** rolling. ***Notification:*** continuous. ***Contact:*** Ms. Helen Rados, Counseling, Career and Transfer Center, 914-434-5750.
CONTACT Mr. Lawrence G. Appel, Director of Admissions, Sullivan County Community College, Loch Sheldrake, NY 12759-4002, 914-434-5750 Ext. 287. ***Fax:*** 914-434-4806. College video available.

TAYLOR BUSINESS INSTITUTE
New York, New York

UG Enrollment: 525	**Tuition & Fees: $7500**
Application Deadline: rolling	**Room & Board: N/Avail**

GENERAL Proprietary, 2-year, coed. Part of Phillips Colleges, Inc. Awards transfer associate, terminal associate degrees. Founded 1961. ***Setting:*** urban campus. ***Total enrollment:*** 525. ***Faculty:*** 19 (11 full-time, 8 part-time); student-faculty ratio is 25:1.
ENROLLMENT PROFILE 525 students: 0% part-time, 99% state residents, 25% transferred in, 20% 25 or older, 40% Hispanic, 49% African American, 4% Asian American.
FIRST-YEAR CLASS Of the students who applied, 80% were accepted, 80% of whom enrolled.
ACADEMIC PROGRAM Calendar: quarters. Academic remediation for entering students, honors program, summer session for credit.
GENERAL DEGREE REQUIREMENTS 97 credits; computer course.
MAJORS Accounting, business administration/commerce/management, secretarial studies/office management, tourism and travel.
LIBRARY 2,873 books, 83 periodicals, 70 records, tapes, and CDs.
COMPUTERS ON CAMPUS 35 computers for student use in classrooms.
COLLEGE LIFE 80% vote in student government elections. ***Student services:*** personal-psychological counseling. ***Campus security:*** student patrols, 12-hour campus security.
HOUSING College housing not available.
CAREER PLANNING ***Service:*** career counseling.
EXPENSES FOR 1995–96 Tuition: $7200 full-time. Full-time mandatory fees: $300. Tuition guaranteed not to increase for student's term of enrollment.
FINANCIAL AID ***College-administered undergrad aid 1995–96:*** 500 need-based scholarships (averaging $1750), low-interest long-term loans from external sources, Federal Work-Study. ***Required forms:*** institutional, FAFSA. ***Priority deadline:*** 7/1. ***Payment plan:*** installment. ***Waivers:*** full or partial for employees or children of employees.
APPLYING ***Option:*** deferred entrance. ***Required:*** school transcript, CPAt. ***Required for some:*** TOEFL for international students. Test scores used for admission and counseling/placement. ***Application deadline:*** rolling.
APPLYING/TRANSFER ***Required:*** standardized test scores, high school transcript. ***Required for some:*** college transcript. ***Entrance:*** minimally difficult. ***Application deadline:*** rolling.
CONTACT Ms. Sheryl R. Caro, Admissions Director, Taylor Business Institute, 120 W. 30th Street, New York, NY 10001, 212-279-0510.

TECHNICAL CAREER INSTITUTES
New York, New York

UG Enrollment: 3,300	**Tuition & Fees: $7820**
Application Deadline: rolling	**Room & Board: N/Avail**

GENERAL Proprietary, 2-year, coed. Awards terminal associate degrees. Founded 1974. ***Setting:*** urban campus. ***Total enrollment:*** 3,300. ***Faculty:*** 152 (72 full-time, 80 part-time); student-faculty ratio is 25:1.
ENROLLMENT PROFILE 3,300 students: 25% women, 30% part-time, 93% state residents, 10% transferred in, 7% international, 2% Native American, 21% Hispanic, 25% African American, 39% Asian American.
FIRST-YEAR CLASS 1,500 total. Of the students who applied, 95% were accepted.
ACADEMIC PROGRAM Core, honor code. Calendar: semesters. Academic remediation for entering students, English as a second language program, summer session for credit, part-time degree program (evenings), co-op programs and internships.
GENERAL DEGREE REQUIREMENTS 65 semester hours; math/science requirements vary according to program; computer course.
MAJORS Computer technologies, electrical and electronics technologies, electrical engineering technology, secretarial studies/office management.
LIBRARY 5,000 books, 100 periodicals.
COMPUTERS ON CAMPUS 312 computers for student use in computer labs, classrooms provide access to on-line services. Staffed computer lab on campus provides training in use of computers, software.
COLLEGE LIFE Choral group, student-run newspaper. ***Student services:*** personal-psychological counseling. ***Campus security:*** 24-hour patrols.
HOUSING College housing not available.
CAREER PLANNING ***Service:*** career counseling.
EXPENSES FOR 1995–96 Tuition: $7820 full-time, $170 per credit part-time.
FINANCIAL AID ***College-administered undergrad aid 1995–96:*** need-based scholarships, low-interest long-term loans from external sources (average $1000), 30 part-time jobs. ***Required forms:*** state, FAFSA; accepted: CSS Financial Aid PROFILE. ***Application deadline:*** continuous. ***Payment plan:*** installment. ***Waivers:*** full or partial for employees or children of employees.
APPLYING Open admission. ***Options:*** Common Application, deferred entrance. ***Required:*** Assessment and Placement Services for Community Colleges. Test scores used for counseling/placement. ***Application deadline:*** rolling. ***Notification:*** continuous.
APPLYING/TRANSFER ***Entrance:*** noncompetitive. ***Application deadline:*** rolling. ***Notification:*** continuous.
CONTACT Ms. Ellen Devens, Director of Admissions Marketing, Technical Career Institutes, 320 West 31st Street, New York, NY 10001-2705, 212-594-4001. ***Fax:*** 212-629-3937.

TOMPKINS CORTLAND COMMUNITY COLLEGE
Dryden, New York

UG Enrollment: 2,754	**Tuition & Fees (NY Res): $2529**
Application Deadline: rolling	**Room & Board: N/Avail**

GENERAL State and locally supported, 2-year, coed. Part of State University of New York System. Awards certificates, transfer associate, terminal associate degrees. Founded 1968. ***Setting:*** 250-acre rural campus with easy access to Syracuse. ***Total enrollment:*** 2,754. ***Faculty:*** 196 (61 full-time, 135 part-time); student-faculty ratio is 17:1.
ENROLLMENT PROFILE 2,754 students from 10 states and territories. 63% women, 48% part-time, 97% state residents, 15% transferred in, 88% have need-based financial aid, 2% international, 51% 25 or older, 1% Native American, 2% Hispanic, 4% African American, 2% Asian American. ***Areas of study chosen:*** 22% social sciences, 5% engineering and applied sciences, 2% architecture, 2% communications and journalism. ***Most popular recent majors:*** business administration/commerce/management, liberal arts/general studies, secretarial studies/office management.
FIRST-YEAR CLASS 564 total; 825 applied, 95% were accepted, 72% of whom enrolled.
ACADEMIC PROGRAM Core, honor code. Calendar: semesters. Academic remediation for entering students, English as a second language program offered during academic year, services for LD students, advanced placement, honors program, summer session for credit, part-time degree program (daytime, evenings), adult/continuing education programs, co-op programs and internships. Off-campus study at State University of New York College at Cortland. ROTC: Army (c).
GENERAL DEGREE REQUIREMENTS 62 credits; math/science requirements vary according to program; computer course for most majors; internship (some majors).
MAJORS Accounting, business administration/commerce/management, communication, computer graphics, computer information systems, computer science, construction technologies, criminal justice, electrical and electronics technologies, engineering sciences, graphic arts, hotel and restaurant management, humanities, human services, international business, labor studies, liberal arts/general studies, marketing/retailing/merchandising, mathematics, medical laboratory technology, nursing, paralegal studies, radio and television studies, recreation and leisure services, science, secretarial studies/office management, social science, tourism and travel, women's studies.
LIBRARY 43,133 books, 115 microform titles, 535 periodicals, 1,690 records, tapes, and CDs. Acquisition spending 1994–95: $449,859.
COMPUTERS ON CAMPUS 160 computers for student use in computer center, computer labs, labs, CAD room. Staffed computer lab on campus provides training in use of computers, software.
COLLEGE LIFE Choral group, student-run newspaper. ***Student services:*** personal-psychological counseling. ***Campus security:*** 24-hour emergency response devices and patrols.
HOUSING College housing not available.
ATHLETICS Member NJCAA. ***Intercollegiate:*** basketball M, golf M, soccer M, softball W, volleyball W. ***Intramural:*** basketball, bowling, football, golf, racquetball, skiing (cross-country), skiing (downhill), soccer, softball, swimming and diving, table tennis (Ping-Pong), tennis, volleyball, water polo. ***Contact:*** Mr. Larry Hinkle, Athletic Director, 607-844-8211 Ext. 4495.
CAREER PLANNING ***Placement office:*** 2 full-time, 1 part-time staff. ***Director:*** Mr. James Hull, Director of Counseling, 607-844-8211 Ext. 4263. ***Services:*** job fairs, resume preparation, resume referral, career counseling, careers library, job bank, job interviews.
AFTER GRADUATION 59% of students completing a degree program in 1994–95 went directly on to further study.
EXPENSES FOR 1995–96 ***Application fee:*** $15. State resident tuition: $2400 full-time, $85 per credit part-time. Nonresident tuition: $4800 full-time, $170 per credit part-time. Part-time mandatory fees: $4 per credit. Full-time mandatory fees: $129.
FINANCIAL AID ***College-administered undergrad aid 1995–96:*** 520 need-based scholarships (average $600), short-term loans (average $150), low-interest long-term loans from external sources (average $2025), Federal Work-Study, 100 part-time jobs. ***Required***

forms: institutional, FAFSA; required for some: state. *Priority deadline:* 6/1. *Payment plan:* deferred payment. *Waivers:* full or partial for employees or children of employees and senior citizens.
APPLYING Open admission except for nursing program. *Options:* early entrance, deferred entrance. *Required:* TOEFL for international students. *Recommended:* ACT. *Required for some:* 3 years of high school math and science, SAT I or ACT. Test scores used for counseling/placement. *Application deadline:* rolling. *Notification:* continuous.
APPLYING/TRANSFER *Required for some:* 3 years of high school math and science. *Entrance:* noncompetitive. *Application deadline:* rolling. *Notification:* continuous.
CONTACT Mr. Michael McGraw, Director of Recruitment, Admissions, and Financial Aid, Tompkins Cortland Community College, Dryden, NY 13053-9533, 607-844-8211 Ext. 4445. *Fax:* 607-844-9665.

TROCAIRE COLLEGE
Buffalo, New York

UG Enrollment: 1,044	Tuition & Fees: $5770
Application Deadline: rolling	Room & Board: N/Avail

Trocaire College, a small, private, values-oriented, urban 2-year college, is celebrating more than 35 years of helping dreams happen. High-quality programs in liberal arts, business, health sciences, and education are offered. Trocaire is committed to educational excellence and to the needs of its students as individuals.

GENERAL Independent, 2-year, coed. Awards certificates, transfer associate, terminal associate degrees. Founded 1958. *Setting:* 5-acre urban campus. *Endowment:* $2.4 million. *Total enrollment:* 1,044. *Faculty:* 113 (43 full-time, 5% with terminal degrees, 70 part-time); student-faculty ratio is 11:1.
ENROLLMENT PROFILE 1,044 students: 87% women, 13% men, 50% part-time, 99% state residents, 11% transferred in, 80% have need-based financial aid, 0% have non-need-based financial aid, 1% international, 64% 25 or older, 1% Native American, 1% Hispanic, 8% African American, 1% Asian American. *Areas of study chosen:* 59% health professions and related sciences, 29% liberal arts/general studies, 8% business management and administrative services, 4% education. *Most popular recent majors:* nursing, radiological technology, medical records services.
FIRST-YEAR CLASS 350 total; 717 applied, 73% were accepted, 67% of whom enrolled. 6% from top 10% of their high school class, 18% from top quarter, 47% from top half.
ACADEMIC PROGRAM Core, honor code. Calendar: semesters. Academic remediation for entering students, services for LD students, advanced placement, summer session for credit, part-time degree program (daytime, evenings, weekends), adult/continuing education programs, internships. Off-campus study at members of the Western New York Consortium.
GENERAL DEGREE REQUIREMENTS 60 credit hours; computer course for medical assistant, radiologic technology, hotel management, health information technology, business administration majors; internship (some majors).
MAJORS Accounting, business administration/commerce/management, early childhood education, hotel and restaurant management, legal secretarial studies, liberal arts/general studies, marketing/retailing/merchandising, medical assistant technologies, medical laboratory technology, medical records services, medical secretarial studies, nursing, operating room technology, radiological technology, secretarial studies/office management.
LIBRARY Trocaire College Library plus 2 others, with 21,530 books, 52 microform titles, 220 periodicals, 1 on-line bibliographic service, 3 CD-ROMs, 2,080 records, tapes, and CDs. Acquisition spending 1994–95: $30,303.
COMPUTERS ON CAMPUS 55 computers for student use in computer center, computer labs, learning resource center. Staffed computer lab on campus provides training in use of computers, software. Academic computing expenditure 1994–95: $28,000.
COLLEGE LIFE Orientation program (2 days, no cost). Student-run newspaper. *Social organizations:* 3 open to all; 1 national fraternity. *Most popular organizations:* Student Government Association, Student Newspaper, Student Yearbook. *Student services:* health clinic, personal-psychological counseling. *Campus security:* 24-hour patrols, late-night transport-escort service.
HOUSING College housing not available.
CAREER PLANNING *Placement office:* 1 full-time staff; $28,000 operating expenditure 1994–95. *Director:* Ms. Claire Darstein, Director of Career Planning and Placement, 716-826-1200 Ext. 282. *Services:* job fairs, resume preparation, resume referral, career counseling, careers library, job bank, job interviews.
AFTER GRADUATION 70% of class of 1994 had job offers within 6 months. 8% of students completing a degree program went directly on to further study.
EXPENSES FOR 1995–96 *Application fee:* $15. Tuition: $5550 full-time, $160 per credit hour part-time. Part-time mandatory fees: $10 per credit hour. Full-time mandatory fees: $220 (minimum).
FINANCIAL AID *College-administered undergrad aid 1995–96:* need-based scholarships, short-term loans, low-interest long-term loans from external sources, Federal Work-Study. *Required forms:* state, FAFSA; accepted: CSS Financial Aid PROFILE. *Priority deadline:* 3/1. *Payment plan:* installment. *Waivers:* full or partial for employees or children of employees and senior citizens.
APPLYING *Options:* deferred entrance, midyear entrance. *Required:* school transcript, 1 recommendation. *Recommended:* campus interview, TOEFL for international students. *Required for some:* SAT I or ACT. Test scores used for admission and counseling/placement. *Application deadline:* rolling.
APPLYING/TRANSFER *Required:* high school transcript, 1 recommendation, college transcript, minimum 2.0 college GPA. *Recommended:* campus interview. *Application deadline:* rolling. *Contact:* Mrs. Claire Darstein, Director of Career Planning and Placement, 716-826-1200 Ext. 282.
CONTACT Mrs. Kathleen A. Hahn, Dean of Admissions, Trocaire College, 110 Red Jacket Parkway, Buffalo, NY 14220-2094, 716-826-1200 Ext. 218. *Fax:* 716-826-4704.

ULSTER COUNTY COMMUNITY COLLEGE
Stone Ridge, New York

UG Enrollment: 2,642	Tuition & Fees (Area Res): $2346
Application Deadline: rolling	Room & Board: N/Avail

GENERAL State and locally supported, 2-year, coed. Part of State University of New York System. Awards diplomas, transfer associate, terminal associate degrees. Founded 1961. *Setting:* 165-acre rural campus. *Research spending 1994–95:* $1.1 million. *Total enrollment:* 2,642. *Faculty:* 162 (64 full-time, 10% with terminal degrees, 98 part-time); student-faculty ratio is 21:1.
ENROLLMENT PROFILE 2,642 students from 2 states and territories. 54% women, 50% part-time, 99% state residents, 3% transferred in, 0% international, 47% 25 or older, 2% Hispanic, 3% African American, 1% Asian American. *Areas of study chosen:* 36% social sciences, 18% liberal arts/general studies, 14% business management and administrative services, 10% health professions and related sciences, 5% communications and journalism, 5% education, 4% engineering and applied sciences, 3% mathematics, 3% natural resource sciences, 2% computer and information sciences. *Most popular recent majors:* liberal arts/general studies, nursing, mathematics.
FIRST-YEAR CLASS 696 total; 1,417 applied, 100% were accepted, 49% of whom enrolled.
ACADEMIC PROGRAM Core. Calendar: semesters. Academic remediation for entering students, English as a second language program offered during academic year, services for LD students, advanced placement, self-designed majors, honors program, summer session for credit, part-time degree program (daytime, evenings), adult/continuing education programs, co-op programs and internships. Off-campus study at State University of New York College at New Paltz.
GENERAL DEGREE REQUIREMENTS 62 credits; math/science requirements vary according to major.
MAJORS Accounting, business administration/commerce/management, communication, community services, computer information systems, computer science, criminal justice, data processing, drafting and design, elementary education, engineering (general), engineering technology, graphic arts, humanities, human services, industrial engineering technology, journalism, liberal arts/general studies, marketing/retailing/merchandising, mathematics, nursing, physical sciences, pollution control technologies, recreation and leisure services, retail management, science, secretarial studies/office management, social science.
LIBRARY 77,858 books, 184 microform titles, 529 periodicals, 13 CD-ROMs, 2,546 records, tapes, and CDs. Acquisition spending 1994–95: $64,042.
COMPUTERS ON CAMPUS 243 computers for student use in computer labs, learning resource center, library provide access to Internet. Staffed computer lab on campus provides training in use of computers, software.
COLLEGE LIFE Drama-theater group, choral group, student-run newspaper, radio station. *Most popular organizations:* Ski Club, Basic Club. *Major annual events:* Earth Day, Annual Dance, Welcome Back BBQ. *Student services:* health clinic, personal-psychological counseling.
HOUSING College housing not available.
ATHLETICS Member NJCAA. *Intercollegiate:* baseball M, basketball M/W, bowling M/W, cross-country running M, golf M/W, skiing (cross-country) M/W, skiing (downhill) M/W, soccer M, softball W, tennis M/W, volleyball W. *Intramural:* badminton, baseball, field hockey, skiing (cross-country), skiing (downhill), tennis, volleyball. *Contact:* Mr. Mark Cranfield, Director of Athletics, 914-687-5278; Ms. Christine Zettler, Professor of Physical Education, 914-361-1575.
CAREER PLANNING *Placement office:* 1 full-time staff. *Director:* Ms. Karen Robinson, Coordinator of Career Services, 914-687-5091. *Services:* job fairs, resume preparation, career counseling, careers library, job bank, job interviews.
AFTER GRADUATION 48% of students completing a degree program in 1994–95 went directly on to further study.
EXPENSES FOR 1995–96 Area resident tuition: $2220 full-time, $87 per credit hour part-time. Nonresident tuition: $4440 full-time, $174 per credit hour part-time. Part-time mandatory fees: $15 per semester. Full-time mandatory fees: $126.
FINANCIAL AID *College-administered undergrad aid 1995–96:* 76 non-need scholarships (average $325), low-interest long-term loans from external sources (average $1900), 90 Federal Work-Study (averaging $650), 200 part-time jobs. *Required forms:* institutional, FAFSA, nontaxable income verification; required for some: state. *Priority deadline:* 6/1. *Payment plans:* installment, deferred payment. *Waivers:* full or partial for employees or children of employees and senior citizens.
APPLYING Open admission. *Options:* early entrance, deferred entrance. *Required:* TOEFL for international students. Test scores used for admission and counseling/placement. *Application deadline:* rolling. *Notification:* continuous.
APPLYING/TRANSFER *Entrance:* noncompetitive. *Application deadline:* rolling. *Notification:* continuous.
CONTACT Admissions Office, Ulster County Community College, Stone Ridge, NY 12484, 914-687-5022 or toll-free 800-724-0833. College video available.

UNIVERSITY OF THE STATE OF NEW YORK, REGENTS COLLEGE
Albany, New York

UG Enrollment: 19,443	Tuition & Fees: N/R
Application Deadline: rolling	Room & Board: N/Avail

GENERAL Independent, primarily 2-year, coed. Awards transfer associate, terminal associate, bachelor's degrees (offers only external degree programs). Founded 1970. *Setting:* urban campus. *Total enrollment:* 19,443.
ENROLLMENT PROFILE 19,443 students from 52 states and territories, 39 other countries. 62% women, 38% men, 100% part-time, 16% state residents, 1% international, 94% 25 or older, 1% Native American, 4% Hispanic, 14% African American, 4% Asian American. *Areas of study chosen:* 64% health professions and related sciences, 24% liberal arts/general studies, 7% business management and administrative services, 5% engineering and applied sciences. *Most popular recent majors:* liberal arts/general studies, nursing, business administration/commerce/management.

University of the State of New York, Regents College (continued)

ACADEMIC PROGRAM Core, honor code. Calendar: year-round. Advanced placement, self-designed majors, part-time degree program, external degree programs, adult/continuing education programs.

GENERAL DEGREE REQUIREMENTS 60 credits for associate, 120 credits for bachelor's; 6 credits of math/science; computer course for electronics, nuclear technology, technology majors.

MAJORS Accounting (B), biology/biological sciences (B), business administration/commerce/management (B), chemical engineering technology (B), chemistry (B), communication (B), computer information systems (B), computer science (B), computer technologies (B), economics (B), electrical and electronics technologies (B), electromechanical technology (B), finance/banking (B), geography (B), geology (B), history (B), human resources (B), international business (B), liberal arts/general studies (B), literature (B), management information systems (B), manufacturing technology (B), marketing/retailing/merchandising (B), mathematics (B), mechanical engineering technology (B), music (B), nuclear technology (B), nursing (B), operations research (B), optical technologies (B), philosophy (B), physics (B), political science/government (B), psychology (B), sociology (B), welding technology (B).

COLLEGE LIFE ***Major annual event:*** Commencement.

HOUSING College housing not available.

EXPENSES FOR 1995–96 Tuition and fees vary according to degree program.

FINANCIAL AID ***College-administered undergrad aid 1995–96:*** 190 need-based scholarships (averaging $620), 2 non-need scholarships (averaging $700). ***Required forms:*** institutional; required for some: state, FAFSA. ***Priority deadline:*** 7/1. ***Payment plan:*** installment. ***Waivers:*** full or partial for employees or children of employees. ***Notification:*** continuous.

APPLYING Open admission except for applicants to nursing program without certain health care experience. ***Options:*** early entrance, midyear entrance. ***Application deadline:*** rolling.

APPLYING/TRANSFER ***Required for some:*** college transcript. ***Application deadline:*** rolling.

CONTACT Dean of Enrollment Management, University of the State of New York, Regents College, 7 Columbia Circle, Albany, NY 12203-5159, 518-464-8500. ***Fax:*** 518-464-8777.

❖ *See page 818 for a narrative description.* ❖

UTICA SCHOOL OF COMMERCE
Utica, New York

UG Enrollment: 605 | **Tuition & Fees: $5550**
Application Deadline: rolling | **Room & Board: N/Avail**

GENERAL Proprietary, 2-year, coed. Awards certificates, diplomas, transfer associate, terminal associate degrees. Founded 1896. ***Setting:*** urban campus. ***Total enrollment:*** 605. ***Faculty:*** 70 (2% of full-time faculty have terminal degrees).

ENROLLMENT PROFILE 605 students: 83% women, 19% part-time, 100% state residents, 21% transferred in, 0% international, 29% 25 or older, 2% Hispanic, 2% African American. ***Most popular recent majors:*** business administration/commerce/management, data processing, accounting.

FIRST-YEAR CLASS 248 total; 420 applied. 15% from top 10% of their high school class, 50% from top half.

ACADEMIC PROGRAM Honor code. Calendar: quarters. 70 courses offered in 1995–96. Academic remediation for entering students, services for LD students, advanced placement, tutorials, summer session for credit, part-time degree program (daytime, evenings, weekends, summer), adult/continuing education programs, internships.

GENERAL DEGREE REQUIREMENTS 99 credit hours; 1 semester of math; computer course.

MAJORS Accounting, business administration/commerce/management, computer information systems, data processing, real estate, secretarial studies/office management, word processing.

LIBRARY Utica School of Commerce Library plus 3 others, with 2,000 books, 135 periodicals, 100 records, tapes, and CDs.

COMPUTERS ON CAMPUS 123 computers for student use in learning resource center, labs, classrooms, library. Staffed computer lab on campus provides training in use of computers, software.

COLLEGE LIFE Orientation program (2½ days). Student-run newspaper. 40% vote in student government elections. ***Campus security:*** security during class hours.

HOUSING College housing not available.

ATHLETICS ***Intramural:*** bowling, soccer, swimming and diving, table tennis (Ping-Pong).

CAREER PLANNING ***Placement office:*** 1 full-time, 1 part-time staff. ***Director:*** Ms. Wendy Cary, Director of Placement, 315-733-2307. ***Services:*** resume preparation, resume referral, career counseling, job interviews. Students must register freshman year.

EXPENSES FOR 1996–97 ***Application fee:*** $20. Tuition: $5550 full-time, $125 per credit hour part-time. Tuition guaranteed not to increase for student's term of enrollment.

FINANCIAL AID ***College-administered undergrad aid 1995–96:*** 42 non-need scholarships (average $650), low-interest long-term loans from external sources. ***Required forms:*** FAFSA; accepted: CSS Financial Aid PROFILE, state. ***Priority deadline:*** 8/15.

APPLYING ***Options:*** electronic application, early entrance, deferred entrance, midyear entrance. ***Required:*** school transcript, interview, ACT. ***Recommended:*** essay, recommendations. ***Required for some:*** Nelson Denny Reading Test. Test scores used for counseling/placement. ***Application deadline:*** rolling.

APPLYING/TRANSFER ***Entrance:*** minimally difficult. ***Contact:*** Mr. Thomas Finch, Dean of Students, 315-733-2307.

CONTACT Ms. Tracy Berie-Pratt, Director of Admissions, Utica School of Commerce, 201 Bleecker Street, Utica, NY 13501-2280, 315-733-2307 Ext. 17 or toll-free 800-321-4USC. ***Fax:*** 315-733-9281. College video available.

VILLA MARIA COLLEGE OF BUFFALO
Buffalo, New York

UG Enrollment: 312 | **Tuition & Fees: $6480**
Application Deadline: rolling | **Room & Board: N/Avail**

GENERAL Independent Roman Catholic, 2-year, coed. Awards certificates, transfer associate, terminal associate degrees. Founded 1960. ***Setting:*** 9-acre suburban campus. ***Endowment:*** $571,631. ***Total enrollment:*** 312. ***Faculty:*** 40 (16 full-time, 24 part-time); student-faculty ratio is 11:1. ***Notable Alumni:*** Michael Muscarella, Buffalo Management of Housing; Ralfa Musialowski, co-owner of RJM Associates; Deborah Romana Navarro, president and owner of Denore; John Bernard Thuersom, president and owner of Shoreline Design Group; Dr. Paul Horst, chiropractor.

ENROLLMENT PROFILE 312 students: 77% women, 23% men, 27% part-time, 99% state residents, 12% transferred in, 65% have need-based financial aid, 35% have non-need-based financial aid, 1% international, 44% 25 or older, 1% Native American, 1% Hispanic, 12% African American. ***Areas of study chosen:*** 21% education, 19% architecture, 18% business management and administrative services, 18% liberal arts/general studies, 9% communications and journalism, 8% performing arts, 4% computer and information sciences, 1% fine arts. ***Most popular recent majors:*** early childhood education, interior design, liberal arts/general studies.

FIRST-YEAR CLASS 112 total; 268 applied, 66% were accepted, 64% of whom enrolled. 7% from top 10% of their high school class, 13% from top quarter, 41% from top half.

ACADEMIC PROGRAM Core, liberal arts curriculum, honor code. Calendar: semesters. 194 courses offered in 1995–96; average class size 12 in required courses. Academic remediation for entering students, services for LD students, advanced placement, tutorials, summer session for credit, part-time degree program (daytime, evenings), co-op programs and internships. Off-campus study at members of the Western New York Consortium.

GENERAL DEGREE REQUIREMENTS 61 credits; math/science requirements vary according to program; computer course for graphic design, interior design, photography, business majors; internship (some majors).

MAJORS Art/fine arts, business administration/commerce/management, computer management, early childhood education, education, graphic arts, interior design, liberal arts/general studies, music, music business, photography, secretarial studies/office management.

LIBRARY Villa Maria College Library with 45,804 books, 65 microform titles, 196 periodicals, 1 on-line bibliographic service, 5 CD-ROMs, 4,915 records, tapes, and CDs.

COMPUTERS ON CAMPUS Computer purchase plan available. 67 computers for student use in computer labs, classrooms, library provide access to main academic computer, e-mail, Internet. Staffed computer lab on campus provides training in use of computers, software.

COLLEGE LIFE Drama-theater group, choral group, student-run newspaper, radio station. ***Social organizations:*** 19 open to all. ***Most popular organizations:*** Design and Beyond, Teachers Love Children, Multicultural Group, Phi Theta Kappa, Helping Adults New Dreams Succeed. ***Major annual events:*** Spring Arts Festival, Lawn Fete, Formal Dinner Dance. ***Student services:*** health clinic, personal-psychological counseling. ***Campus security:*** late-night transport-escort service.

HOUSING College housing not available.

CAREER PLANNING ***Placement office:*** 1 part-time staff. ***Director:*** Ms. Nicole Rivera-Dugan, Coordinator, 716-896-0700 Ext. 402. ***Services:*** job fairs, resume preparation, career counseling, careers library, job bank. Students must register freshman year. 30 organizations recruited on campus 1994–95.

AFTER GRADUATION 48% of students completing a degree program in 1994–95 went directly on to further study.

EXPENSES FOR 1995–96 ***Application fee:*** $25. Tuition: $6300 full-time, $210 per credit part-time. Full-time mandatory fees: $180.

FINANCIAL AID ***College-administered undergrad aid 1995–96:*** 26 need-based scholarships (average $1538), 88 non-need scholarships (average $900), low-interest long-term loans from external sources (average $2065), 62 Federal Work-Study (averaging $800), part-time jobs. ***Required forms:*** state, FAFSA; required for some: institutional; accepted: CSS Financial Aid PROFILE. ***Priority deadline:*** 5/1. ***Payment plans:*** installment, deferred payment. ***Waivers:*** full or partial for employees or children of employees and senior citizens. ***Average indebtedness of graduates:*** $4000.

APPLYING ***Options:*** Common Application, deferred entrance, midyear entrance. ***Required:*** essay, interview, TOEFL for international students, CGP (math section), Nelson Denny Reading Test. ***Recommended:*** 3 years of high school science, SAT I or ACT. ***Required for some:*** 3 years of high school math. Test scores used for counseling/placement. ***Application deadline:*** rolling. ***Notification:*** continuous.

APPLYING/TRANSFER ***Required:*** standardized test scores, college transcript. ***Recommended:*** 3 years of high school science. ***Required for some:*** 3 years of high school math. ***Entrance:*** minimally difficult. ***Application deadline:*** rolling. ***Notification:*** continuous. ***Contact:*** Sister Mary Mark Janik, Director of Admissions, 716-896-0700 Ext. 339.

CONTACT Sister Mary Mark Janik, Director of Admissions, Villa Maria College of Buffalo, Buffalo, NY 14225-3999, 716-896-0700 Ext. 339. ***Fax:*** 716-896-0705.

WESTCHESTER BUSINESS INSTITUTE
White Plains, New York

UG Enrollment: 975 | **Tuition & Fees: $10,494**
Application Deadline: rolling | **Room & Board: N/Avail**

GENERAL Proprietary, 2-year, coed. Awards diplomas, transfer associate, terminal associate degrees. Founded 1915. ***Setting:*** suburban campus with easy access to New York City. ***Total enrollment:*** 975. ***Faculty:*** 35 (14 full-time, 21 part-time).

ENROLLMENT PROFILE 975 students from 3 states and territories, 4 other countries. 62% women, 6% part-time, 94% state residents, 9% transferred in, 2% international, 45% 25 or older, 0% Native American, 7% Hispanic, 25% African American, 0% Asian American. ***Most popular recent majors:*** accounting, business administration/commerce/management, computer information systems.

FIRST-YEAR CLASS 296 total. Of the students who applied, 76% were accepted, 47% of whom enrolled. 3% from top 10% of their high school class, 22% from top quarter, 53% from top half.

New York

ACADEMIC PROGRAM Core. Calendar: quarters for day division, semesters for evening and weekend divisions. Academic remediation for entering students, self-designed majors, summer session for credit, part-time degree program (evenings, weekends, summer), adult/continuing education programs, co-op programs.
GENERAL DEGREE REQUIREMENTS 66 credits; computer course.
MAJORS Accounting, business administration/commerce/management, computer information systems, computer programming, data processing, management information systems, marketing/retailing/merchandising, medical secretarial studies, secretarial studies/office management, word processing.
LIBRARY Westchester Business Institute Resource Center with 7,800 books, 26 periodicals, 70 records, tapes, and CDs.
COMPUTERS ON CAMPUS 108 computers for student use in computer center, computer labs, learning resource center. Staffed computer lab on campus provides training in use of computers, software.
HOUSING College housing not available.
CAREER PLANNING *Placement office:* 2 full-time, 2 part-time staff. *Director:* Ms. Nancy Sutkowski, College Placement Coordinator, 914-948-4442. *Services:* job fairs, resume preparation, resume referral, career counseling, careers library, job bank, job interviews.
AFTER GRADUATION 95% of class of 1994 had job offers within 6 months.
EXPENSES FOR 1996–97 *Application fee:* $25. Tuition: $10,494 full-time, $318 per credit part-time. Tuition guaranteed not to increase for student's term of enrollment.
FINANCIAL AID *College-administered undergrad aid 1995–96:* 85 need-based scholarships (averaging $1000), 44 non-need scholarships (averaging $2207), 12 part-time jobs. *Required forms for some financial aid applicants:* state; accepted: CSS Financial Aid PROFILE, institutional, FAFSA. *Priority deadline:* 8/1. *Waivers:* full or partial for employees or children of employees.
APPLYING *Option:* Common Application. *Recommended:* SAT I or ACT. Test scores used for counseling/placement. *Application deadline:* rolling.
APPLYING/TRANSFER *Recommended:* standardized test scores. *Application deadline:* rolling. *Contact:* Ms. Lynne Vahey, Assistant Dean/Registrar, 914-948-4442.
CONTACT Mr. Dale T. Smith, Vice President and Dean of Admissions, Westchester Business Institute, White Plains, NY 10602, 914-948-4442 or toll-free 800-333-4924.

WESTCHESTER COMMUNITY COLLEGE
Valhalla, New York

UG Enrollment: 16,914	Tuition & Fees (NY Res): $2583
Application Deadline: rolling	Room & Board: N/Avail

GENERAL State and locally supported, 2-year, coed. Part of State University of New York System. Awards certificates, transfer associate, terminal associate degrees. Founded 1946. *Setting:* 218-acre suburban campus with easy access to New York City. *Endowment:* $2.4 million. *Total enrollment:* 16,914. *Faculty:* 716 (162 full-time, 23% with terminal degrees, 554 part-time); student-faculty ratio is 24:1. *Notable Alumni:* Walter Anderson, Wayne Cilento.
ENROLLMENT PROFILE 16,914 students from 6 states and territories, 10 other countries. 56% women, 44% men, 59% part-time, 90% state residents, 8% transferred in, 29% have need-based financial aid, 1% have non-need-based financial aid, 1% international, 46% 25 or older, 1% Native American, 11% Hispanic, 15% African American, 5% Asian American. *Areas of study chosen:* 18% engineering and applied sciences, 15% business management and administrative services, 10% social sciences, 6% liberal arts/general studies, 4% health professions and related sciences, 2% communications and journalism, 2% library and information studies, 1% computer and information sciences, 1% fine arts, 1% interdisciplinary studies, 1% natural resource sciences, 1% performing arts.
FIRST-YEAR CLASS 4,081 total; 5,670 applied, 100% were accepted, 72% of whom enrolled.
ACADEMIC PROGRAM Core, interdisciplinary curriculum, honor code. Calendar: semesters. 980 courses offered in 1995–96. Academic remediation for entering students, English as a second language program offered during academic year and summer, services for LD students, self-designed majors, tutorials, honors program, summer session for credit, part-time degree program (daytime, evenings), adult/continuing education programs, internships.
GENERAL DEGREE REQUIREMENTS 64 credits; internship (some majors).
MAJORS Accounting, applied art, art/fine arts, automotive technologies, biomedical technologies, business administration/commerce/management, chemical engineering technology, child care/child and family studies, civil engineering technology, communication, computer information systems, computer science, corrections, criminal justice, culinary arts, dance, data processing, dietetics, drug and alcohol/substance abuse counseling, electrical engineering technology, engineering sciences, engineering technology, environmental engineering technology, environmental sciences, finance/banking, food services management, food services technology, hotel and restaurant management, humanities, human services, information science, insurance, international business, law enforcement/police sciences, legal secretarial studies, liberal arts/general studies, machine and tool technologies, marketing/retailing/merchandising, mechanical engineering technology, medical laboratory technology, medical technology, music, nursing, paralegal studies, pharmacy/pharmaceutical sciences, pollution control technologies, public administration, radiological technology, real estate, respiratory therapy, retail management, science, secretarial studies/office management, social science, tourism and travel.
LIBRARY Westchester Community College Library with 108,199 books, 123 microform titles, 693 periodicals, 71 CD-ROMs, 5,482 records, tapes, and CDs. Acquisition spending 1994–95: $194,500.

COMPUTERS ON CAMPUS 525 computers for student use in computer center, computer labs, learning resource center, classrooms, library provide access to main academic computer, on-line services. Staffed computer lab on campus provides training in use of computers, software. Academic computing expenditure 1994–95: $2.1 million.
COLLEGE LIFE Drama-theater group, choral group, student-run newspaper, radio station. *Social organizations:* 50 open to all. *Most popular organizations:* Student Senate, African Culture Club, Italian Club, International Friendship Club, Alpha Beta Gamma. *Major annual events:* Cultural Solidarity Week, D.J. Contest, Hypnosis Demo. *Student services:* health clinic, personal-psychological counseling, women's center. *Campus security:* 24-hour emergency response devices and patrols, late-night transport-escort service.
HOUSING College housing not available.
ATHLETICS Member NJCAA. *Intercollegiate:* baseball M, basketball M/W, bowling M/W, golf M, lacrosse M, soccer M, softball W, tennis M/W, volleyball W. *Intramural:* badminton, basketball, football, racquetball, skiing (cross-country), softball, swimming and diving, tennis, volleyball, water polo, weight lifting. *Contact:* Mr. Anthony Mezzatesta, Director of Athletics, 914-785-6954.
CAREER PLANNING *Placement office:* 2 full-time, 2 part-time staff; $150,000 operating expenditure 1994–95. *Director:* Mr. Richard L. Putnam, Director, Job and Career Center, 914-785-6783. *Services:* job fairs, resume preparation, resume referral, career counseling, careers library, job bank, job interviews. 2,000 organizations recruited on campus 1994–95.
AFTER GRADUATION 63% of students completing a degree program in 1994–95 went directly on to further study.
EXPENSES FOR 1996–97 *Application fee:* $25. State resident tuition: $2350 full-time, $98 per credit part-time. Nonresident tuition: $5374 full-time, $245 per credit part-time. Part-time mandatory fees: $45.50 per credit. Full-time mandatory fees: $233.
FINANCIAL AID *College-administered undergrad aid 1995–96:* 1,667 need-based scholarships (average $400), short-term loans (average $600), low-interest long-term loans from external sources (average $2275), 80 Federal Work-Study (averaging $750), 170 part-time jobs. *Required forms:* state, institutional, FAFSA. *Priority deadline:* 7/1. *Waivers:* full or partial for employees or children of employees. *Average indebtedness of graduates:* $900.
APPLYING Open admission except for nursing, radiologic technology, respiratory care programs. *Options:* early entrance, midyear entrance. *Required:* TOEFL for international students. *Recommended:* SAT I or ACT. Test scores used for counseling/placement. *Application deadline:* rolling. *Notification:* continuous.
APPLYING/TRANSFER *Required for some:* college transcript. *Entrance:* noncompetitive. *Application deadline:* rolling. *Notification:* continuous. *Contact:* Ms. Terri Weisel, Director of Admissions, 914-785-6735.
CONTACT Ms. Terri Weisel, Director of Admissions, Westchester Community College, Valhalla, NY 10595-1698, 914-785-6735. College video available.

WOOD TOBE–COBURN SCHOOL
New York, New York

UG Enrollment: 223	Tuition & Fees: $8640
Application Deadline: rolling	Room & Board: N/Avail

GENERAL Proprietary, 2-year, specialized, women only. Part of Bradford Schools, Inc. Awards diplomas, terminal associate degrees. Founded 1879. *Setting:* urban campus. *Total enrollment:* 223. *Faculty:* 20 (10 full-time, 10 part-time).
ENROLLMENT PROFILE 223 students from 3 states and territories. 100% women, 0% part-time, 95% state residents, 13% transferred in, 0% international, 1% 25 or older, 0% Native American, 50% Hispanic, 26% African American, 2% Asian American.
FIRST-YEAR CLASS Of the students who applied, 94% were accepted. 5% from top 10% of their high school class, 26% from top quarter, 47% from top half.
ACADEMIC PROGRAM Calendar: semesters. Academic remediation for entering students, summer session for credit, co-op programs and internships.
GENERAL DEGREE REQUIREMENTS 60 credits; computer course; internship (some majors).
MAJORS Accounting, computer programming, fashion design and technology, fashion merchandising, secretarial studies/office management.
LIBRARY 698 books, 18 periodicals, 263 records, tapes, and CDs.
COMPUTERS ON CAMPUS 117 computers for student use in computer center provide access to main academic computer, off-campus computing facilities, e-mail, on-line services. Staffed computer lab on campus provides training in use of computers, software.
HOUSING College housing not available.
CAREER PLANNING *Service:* career counseling.
EXPENSES FOR 1995–96 Tuition: $8640 (minimum) full-time. Tuition for fashion programs: $9440.
FINANCIAL AID *College-administered undergrad aid 1995–96:* need-based scholarships, 25 non-need scholarships (averaging $1000), low-interest long-term loans from external sources (averaging $2500), Federal Work-Study, part-time jobs. *Required forms:* FAFSA; required for some: state; accepted: CSS Financial Aid PROFILE. *Application deadline:* continuous to 8/26.
APPLYING *Required:* school transcript, interview. *Required for some:* Otis-Lennon School Ability Test. Test scores used for admission. *Application deadline:* rolling.
APPLYING/TRANSFER *Required:* interview. *Recommended:* college transcript. *Required for some:* standardized test scores. *Application deadline:* rolling.
CONTACT Ms. Sandy Gruninger, Director of Admissions, Wood Tobe–Coburn School, 8 East 40th Street, New York, NY 10016-0102, 212-686-9040 Ext. 37.

North Carolina

NORTH CAROLINA

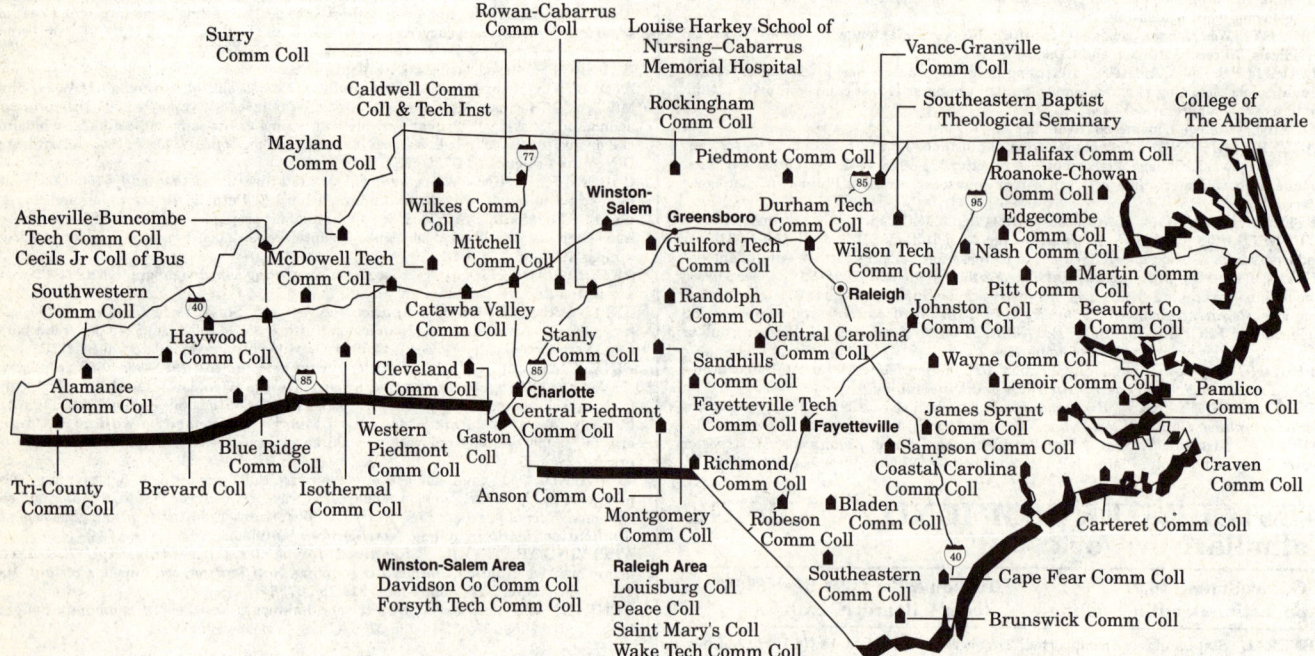

ALAMANCE COMMUNITY COLLEGE
Graham, North Carolina

UG Enrollment: 3,340	**Tuition & Fees (NC Res): $572**
Application Deadline: rolling	**Room & Board: N/Avail**

GENERAL State-supported, 2-year, coed. Part of North Carolina Community College System. Awards transfer associate, terminal associate degrees. Founded 1959. *Setting:* 48-acre small-town campus. *Total enrollment:* 3,340. *Faculty:* 145 (65 full-time, 80 part-time); student-faculty ratio is 22:1.
ENROLLMENT PROFILE 3,340 students from 11 states and territories, 11 other countries. 60% women, 64% part-time, 98% state residents, 6% transferred in, 1% international, 50% 25 or older, 17% African American. *Areas of study chosen:* 32% business management and administrative services, 18% engineering and applied sciences, 15% health professions and related sciences, 9% social sciences, 7% computer and information sciences, 6% vocational and home economics, 4% performing arts, 3% biological and life sciences, 2% agriculture, 2% education. *Most popular recent majors:* nursing, business administration/commerce/management, accounting.
FIRST-YEAR CLASS 1,127 total; 2,747 applied, 100% were accepted, 41% of whom enrolled.
ACADEMIC PROGRAM Calendar: quarters. Academic remediation for entering students, summer session for credit, part-time degree program (daytime, evenings, summer), adult/continuing education programs, co-op programs. Off-campus study at University of North Carolina at Greensboro.
GENERAL DEGREE REQUIREMENTS 114 quarter hours; computer course (varies by major).
MAJORS Accounting, animal sciences, automotive technologies, biomedical technologies, biotechnology, business administration/commerce/management, business machine technologies, carpentry, child care/child and family studies, commercial art, computer programming, computer technologies, corrections, cosmetology, criminal justice, dental services, drafting and design, early childhood education, educational media, electrical and electronics technologies, electromechanical technology, electronics engineering technology, fashion merchandising, fire science, food sciences, food services management, food services technology, heating/refrigeration/air conditioning, horticulture, industrial administration, law enforcement/police sciences, liberal arts/general studies, machine and tool technologies, mechanical design technology, medical laboratory technology, medical secretarial studies, nursing, real estate, teacher aide studies, welding technology.
LIBRARY 26,000 books, 110 microform titles, 212 periodicals, 12 CD-ROMs, 625 records, tapes, and CDs.
COMPUTERS ON CAMPUS 100 computers for student use in computer center, computer labs, classrooms, library provide access to on-line services.
COLLEGE LIFE Student-run newspaper. *Social organizations:* 5 open to all. *Student services:* personal-psychological counseling. *Campus security:* 24-hour emergency response devices and patrols, student patrols, late-night transport-escort service.
HOUSING College housing not available.
ATHLETICS *Intramural:* basketball, bowling, golf, tennis, volleyball.

CAREER PLANNING *Placement office:* 1 full-time staff. *Director:* Mr. Steve Reinhartson, Coordinator of Placement, 910-578-2002. *Service:* career counseling. 50 organizations recruited on campus 1994–95.
AFTER GRADUATION 95% of class of 1994 had job offers within 6 months.
EXPENSES FOR 1995–96 State resident tuition: $557 full-time, $13.25 per quarter hour part-time. Nonresident tuition: $4515 full-time, $107.50 per quarter hour part-time. Part-time mandatory fees: $5.05 per quarter. Full-time mandatory fees: $15.
FINANCIAL AID *College-administered undergrad aid 1995–96:* need-based scholarships (average $300), 10 non-need scholarships (average $300), low-interest long-term loans from external sources, 25 Federal Work-Study, 15 part-time jobs. *Required forms:* institutional; required for some: FAFSA; accepted: CSS Financial Aid PROFILE. *Priority deadline:* 8/15. *Waivers:* full or partial for senior citizens. *Notification:* continuous. *Average indebtedness of graduates:* $100.
APPLYING Open admission except for nursing, dental, medical laboratory technology programs. *Option:* early entrance. *Required:* school transcript, TOEFL for international students. Test scores used for counseling/placement. *Application deadline:* rolling. *Notification:* continuous.
APPLYING/TRANSFER *Required:* high school transcript, college transcript. *Entrance:* minimally difficult. *Application deadline:* rolling. *Notification:* continuous. *Contact:* Ms. Janice Reaves, Coordinator of Counseling, 910-578-2002.
CONTACT Ms. Suzanne Mintz, Coordinator of Admissions and Records, Alamance Community College, Graham, NC 27253-8000, 910-578-2002 Ext. 138. College video available.

ANSON COMMUNITY COLLEGE
Polkton, North Carolina

UG Enrollment: 1,379	**Tuition & Fees (NC Res): $579**
Application Deadline: rolling	**Room & Board: N/Avail**

GENERAL State-supported, 2-year, coed. Part of North Carolina Community College System. Awards certificates, diplomas, transfer associate, terminal associate degrees. Founded 1962. *Setting:* 97-acre rural campus. *Total enrollment:* 1,379. *Faculty:* 84 (34 full-time, 50 part-time); student-faculty ratio is 11:1. *Notable Alumni:* Michael Freeman, principal; Eric Tillman, manager of FinanceCorporation; Billy Jordan, politician and businessman; Carolyn Hilliard, elementary teacher; Elizabeth Kersey, secretary to dean of instruction at Anson Community College.
ENROLLMENT PROFILE 1,379 students: 60% women, 59% part-time, 98% state residents, 5% transferred in, 1% international, 65% 25 or older, 1% Native American, 1% Hispanic, 40% African American, 1% Asian American.
FIRST-YEAR CLASS 435 total; 575 applied, 100% were accepted, 76% of whom enrolled. 5% from top 10% of their high school class, 10% from top quarter, 35% from top half.
ACADEMIC PROGRAM Core, honor code. Calendar: quarters. Academic remediation for entering students, services for LD students, summer session for credit, part-time degree program (daytime, evenings, summer), adult/continuing education programs, co-op programs. Off-campus study at Anson-Stanly Community College–Union Branch.

488   Peterson's Guide to Two-Year Colleges 1997

GENERAL DEGREE REQUIREMENTS 116 quarter hours; math/science requirements vary according to program; computer course for most majors.
MAJORS Accounting, automotive technologies, business administration/commerce/management, carpentry, computer technologies, construction technologies, cosmetology, criminal justice, data processing, drafting and design, electrical and electronics technologies, food services technology, heating/refrigeration/air conditioning, industrial and heavy equipment maintenance, industrial arts, legal secretarial studies, liberal arts/general studies, machine and tool technologies, marketing/retailing/merchandising, mechanical design technology, medical assistant technologies, medical secretarial studies, secretarial studies/office management, social work, welding technology.
LIBRARY Martin Learning Resource Center with 18,553 books, 111 microform titles, 170 periodicals, 1 on-line bibliographic service, 18 CD-ROMs, 996 records, tapes, and CDs. Acquisition spending 1994–95: $14,544.
COMPUTERS ON CAMPUS 50 computers for student use in computer center, learning resource center, classrooms, library. Staffed computer lab on campus provides training in use of computers, software.
COLLEGE LIFE Choral group. 50% vote in student government elections. ***Most popular organizations:*** Student Association, Phi Beta Lambda, Phi Theta Kappa, Social Services Club, Criminal Justice Club. ***Major annual events:*** Spring Fling, Career Day, Christmas Party. ***Student services:*** personal-psychological counseling, women's center. ***Campus security:*** 24-hour emergency response devices and patrols, evening security.
HOUSING College housing not available.
CAREER PLANNING ***Placement office:*** $3500 operating expenditure 1994–95. ***Director:*** Ms. Gloria Walton, Counselor, 704-272-7635 Ext. 30. ***Services:*** job fairs, career counseling.
EXPENSES FOR 1995–96 State resident tuition: $557 full-time, $13.25 per quarter hour part-time. Nonresident tuition: $4515 full-time, $107.50 per quarter hour part-time. Part-time mandatory fees per quarter range from $1.85 to $7.25. Full-time mandatory fees: $22.
FINANCIAL AID ***College-administered undergrad aid 1995–96:*** 25 need-based scholarships (average $500), 5 non-need scholarships (average $500), low-interest long-term loans, Federal Work-Study. ***Required forms:*** FAFSA; required for some: institutional; accepted: CSS Financial Aid PROFILE. ***Application deadline:*** continuous. ***Payment plan:*** deferred payment. ***Waivers:*** full or partial for employees or children of employees and senior citizens.
APPLYING Open admission. ***Options:*** early entrance, deferred entrance. ***Required:*** school transcript, TOEFL for international students. ***Recommended:*** CAT, CPT. ***Required for some:*** CAT, CPT. Test scores used for counseling/placement. ***Application deadline:*** rolling. ***Notification:*** continuous.
APPLYING/TRANSFER ***Required:*** high school transcript, college transcript. ***Entrance:*** noncompetitive. ***Application deadline:*** rolling. ***Notification:*** continuous. ***Contact:*** Dr. Algie C. Gatewood, Dean of Students, 704-272-7635.
CONTACT Ms. Pat Taylor, Admissions Coordinator, Anson Community College, Polkton, NC 28135-0126, 704-272-7635. ***E-mail:*** abavcom@vnet.net.

ASHEVILLE-BUNCOMBE TECHNICAL COMMUNITY COLLEGE
Asheville, North Carolina

UG Enrollment: 4,021 — **Tuition & Fees (NC Res): $597**
Application Deadline: rolling — **Room & Board: N/Avail**

GENERAL State-supported, 2-year, coed. Part of North Carolina Community College System. Awards certificates, diplomas, transfer associate, terminal associate degrees. Founded 1959. ***Setting:*** 126-acre urban campus. ***Total enrollment:*** 4,021. ***Faculty:*** 407 (94 full-time, 313 part-time).
ENROLLMENT PROFILE 4,021 students from 27 states and territories, 14 other countries. 58% women, 42% men, 65% part-time, 98% state residents, 36% transferred in, 1% international, 52% 25 or older, 1% Native American, 1% Hispanic, 6% African American. ***Most popular recent majors:*** business administration/commerce/management, nursing, liberal arts/general studies.
FIRST-YEAR CLASS 2,591 total.
ACADEMIC PROGRAM Core. Calendar: quarters. 390 courses offered in 1995–96; average class size 25 in required courses. Academic remediation for entering students, English as a second language program offered during academic year and summer, services for LD students, advanced placement, summer session for credit, part-time degree program (daytime, evenings), adult/continuing education programs, co-op programs.
GENERAL DEGREE REQUIREMENTS 96 quarter hours; math/science requirements vary according to program; computer course for most majors.
MAJORS Accounting, automotive technologies, business administration/commerce/management, child care/child and family studies, civil engineering technology, computer programming, culinary arts, dental services, drafting and design, electronics engineering technology, emergency medical technology, food services management, hotel and restaurant management, law enforcement/police sciences, liberal arts/general studies, machine and tool technologies, marketing/retailing/merchandising, mechanical engineering technology, medical laboratory technology, nursing, radiological technology, secretarial studies/office management, social work, surveying technology.
LIBRARY 29,631 books, 35,154 microform titles, 298 periodicals, 3,987 records, tapes, and CDs.
COMPUTERS ON CAMPUS 414 computers for student use in computer center, computer labs, classrooms, library. Staffed computer lab on campus provides training in use of computers, software.
COLLEGE LIFE Student-run newspaper. ***Major annual events:*** Spring Fling, Welcome Freshmen Picnic, July 4th Ice Cream/Watermelon Cutting. ***Student services:*** personal-psychological counseling. ***Campus security:*** 24-hour emergency response devices and patrols.
HOUSING College housing not available.
CAREER PLANNING ***Service:*** career counseling.
ESTIMATED EXPENSES FOR 1996–97 State resident tuition: $576 full-time, $13.25 per quarter hour part-time. Nonresident tuition: $4515 full-time, $107.50 per quarter hour part-time. Part-time mandatory fees per quarter range from $7.75 to $10.25. Full-time mandatory fees: $21.
FINANCIAL AID ***College-administered undergrad aid 1995–96:*** 123 need-based scholarships (average $334), 265 non-need scholarships (average $404), short-term loans (average $200), low-interest long-term loans from college funds (average $750), loans from external sources (average $1866), Federal Work-Study, 79 part-time jobs. ***Priority deadline:*** 3/1. ***Payment plan:*** installment. ***Waivers:*** full or partial for senior citizens.
APPLYING Open admission. ***Option:*** deferred entrance. ***Required:*** SAT I or ACT, TOEFL for international students, CPT. ***Recommended:*** school transcript. ***Required for some:*** 3 years of high school math, recommendations, interview. Test scores used for admission and counseling/placement. ***Application deadline:*** rolling. ***Notification:*** continuous.
APPLYING/TRANSFER ***Recommended:*** high school transcript, college transcript. ***Required for some:*** standardized test scores, 3 years of high school math. ***Application deadline:*** rolling. ***Notification:*** continuous. ***Contact:*** Ms. Connie S. Buckner, Director of Admissions, 704-254-1921 Ext. 149.
CONTACT Ms. Connie S. Buckner, Director of Admissions, Asheville-Buncombe Technical Community College, 340 Victoria Road, Asheville, NC 28801-4897, 704-254-1921 Ext. 149.

BEAUFORT COUNTY COMMUNITY COLLEGE
Washington, North Carolina

UG Enrollment: 1,154 — **Tuition & Fees (NC Res): $575**
Application Deadline: rolling — **Room & Board: N/Avail**

GENERAL State-supported, 2-year, coed. Part of North Carolina Community College System. Awards transfer associate, terminal associate degrees. Founded 1967. ***Setting:*** 67-acre rural campus. ***Total enrollment:*** 1,154. ***Faculty:*** 110 (40 full-time, 70 part-time); student-faculty ratio is 15:1.
ENROLLMENT PROFILE 1,154 students: 64% women, 48% part-time, 99% state residents, 5% transferred in, 57% 25 or older, 1% Hispanic, 20% African American. ***Most popular recent majors:*** business administration/commerce/management, nursing, liberal arts/general studies.
FIRST-YEAR CLASS 640 applied, 100% were accepted. 6% from top 10% of their high school class, 51% from top half.
ACADEMIC PROGRAM Core, honor code. Calendar: quarters. Academic remediation for entering students, services for LD students, advanced placement, summer session for credit, part-time degree program (daytime, evenings, summer), adult/continuing education programs, co-op programs.
GENERAL DEGREE REQUIREMENTS 114 quarter hours; 1 math course; computer course for allied health, engineering majors; internship (some majors).
MAJORS Accounting, agricultural technologies, automotive technologies, business administration/commerce/management, computer programming, computer technologies, drafting and design, early childhood education, electrical engineering technology, electronics engineering technology, elementary education, law enforcement/police sciences, liberal arts/general studies, medical laboratory technology, medical secretarial studies, nursing, secretarial studies/office management, social work.
LIBRARY Beaufort Community College Library with 25,734 books, 1,285 microform titles, 214 periodicals, 8 CD-ROMs, 2,979 records, tapes, and CDs.
COMPUTERS ON CAMPUS 60 computers for student use in computer center, computer labs, learning resource center, classrooms, library provide access to main academic computer, Internet. Staffed computer lab on campus provides training in use of computers, software.
COLLEGE LIFE ***Most popular organizations:*** Student Government Association, Data Processing Management Association. ***Major annual events:*** Christmas, Thanksgiving, Field Day. ***Student services:*** personal-psychological counseling. ***Campus security:*** 24-hour emergency response devices and patrols.
HOUSING College housing not available.
CAREER PLANNING ***Services:*** resume preparation, career counseling, job bank.
AFTER GRADUATION 75% of students completing a degree program in 1994–95 went directly on to further study.
EXPENSES FOR 1995–96 State resident tuition: $557 full-time, $13.25 per quarter hour part-time. Nonresident tuition: $4515 full-time, $107.50 per quarter hour part-time. Part-time mandatory fees per quarter range from $1 to $3. Full-time mandatory fees: $18.
FINANCIAL AID ***College-administered undergrad aid 1995–96:*** 84 need-based scholarships (average $600), low-interest long-term loans from external sources (average $2500), 30 Federal Work-Study (averaging $800), 9 part-time jobs. ***Required forms:*** FAFSA; accepted: CSS Financial Aid PROFILE. ***Priority deadline:*** 8/15. ***Waivers:*** full or partial for employees or children of employees and senior citizens.
APPLYING Open admission except for nursing, medical laboratory technology programs. ***Options:*** early entrance, deferred entrance. ***Required:*** school transcript, CGP. ***Required for some:*** essay, recommendations, interview. Test scores used for admission and counseling/placement. ***Application deadline:*** rolling. ***Notification:*** continuous.
APPLYING/TRANSFER ***Required:*** standardized test scores, high school transcript, college transcript. ***Required for some:*** essay, recommendations, interview. ***Application deadline:*** rolling. ***Notification:*** continuous.
CONTACT Mr. Gary Burbage, Director of Admissions, Beaufort County Community College, PO Box 1069, Washington, NC 27889-1069, 919-946-6194 Ext. 233. ***Fax:*** 919-946-0271. College video available.

BLADEN COMMUNITY COLLEGE
Dublin, North Carolina

UG Enrollment: 692 — **Tuition & Fees (NC Res): $588**
Application Deadline: 9/1 — **Room & Board: N/Avail**

GENERAL State and locally supported, 2-year, coed. Part of North Carolina Community College System. Awards transfer associate, terminal associate degrees. Founded 1967. ***Setting:*** 45-acre rural campus. ***Research spending 1994–95:*** $10,000. ***Total enrollment:*** 692. ***Faculty:*** 61 (26 full-time, 10% with terminal degrees, 35 part-time); student-faculty ratio is 12:1.
ENROLLMENT PROFILE 692 students from 2 states and territories. 64% women, 44% part-time, 99% state residents, 4% transferred in, 31% have need-based financial aid, 1% have non-need-based financial aid, 0% international, 42% 25 or older, 2% Native American, 0% Hispanic, 34% African American, 1% Asian American. ***Areas of study***

Peterson's Guide to Two-Year Colleges 1997

489

Bladen Community College (continued)
chosen: 20% education, 10% communications and journalism, 5% engineering and applied sciences, 1% fine arts. ***Most popular recent majors:*** liberal arts/general studies, business administration/commerce/management, law enforcement/police sciences.
FIRST-YEAR CLASS 275 total; 309 applied, 100% were accepted, 89% of whom enrolled. 10% from top 10% of their high school class, 15% from top quarter, 75% from top half. 2 class presidents, 1 valedictorian.
ACADEMIC PROGRAM Core, general studies curriculum. Calendar: quarters. 130 courses offered in 1995–96. Academic remediation for entering students, services for LD students, tutorials, summer session for credit, part-time degree program (daytime, evenings), adult/continuing education programs.
GENERAL DEGREE REQUIREMENTS 96 quarter hours; 1 course each in math and science; computer course for technology, business-related majors.
MAJORS Business administration/commerce/management, computer programming, electrical and electronics technologies, law enforcement/police sciences, liberal arts/ general studies, secretarial studies/office management.
LIBRARY 17,000 books, 8,000 microform titles, 100 periodicals, 2,000 records, tapes, and CDs. Acquisition spending 1994–95: $24,830.
COMPUTERS ON CAMPUS 75 computers for student use in computer center, computer labs provide access to e-mail, Internet. Staffed computer lab on campus provides training in use of computers, software. Academic computing expenditure 1994–95: $110,000.
COLLEGE LIFE ***Most popular organization:*** Student Government Association. ***Major annual events:*** Mister and Miss BCC, Spring Field Day. ***Student services:*** personal-psychological counseling.
HOUSING College housing not available.
ATHLETICS ***Intercollegiate:*** golf M/W, tennis M/W, volleyball M/W. ***Intramural:*** table tennis (Ping-Pong).
CAREER PLANNING ***Placement office:*** 1 full-time, 1 part-time staff; $75,000 operating expenditure 1994–95. ***Director:*** Ms. Linda Leach, Counselor, 910-862-2164. ***Services:*** resume preparation, resume referral, career counseling, careers library, job bank.
AFTER GRADUATION 65% of students completing a degree program in 1994–95 went directly on to further study.
EXPENSES FOR 1996–97 State resident tuition: $557 full-time, $13.25 per quarter hour part-time. Nonresident tuition: $4515 full-time, $107.50 per quarter hour part-time. Part-time mandatory fees per quarter range from $4.25 to $7.25. Full-time mandatory fees: $31.
FINANCIAL AID ***College-administered undergrad aid 1995–96:*** 20 need-based scholarships (averaging $500), 3 non-need scholarships (averaging $500), low-interest long-term loans from external sources (averaging $1500), Federal Work-Study. ***Required forms:*** FAFSA. ***Priority deadline:*** 9/1.
APPLYING Open admission. ***Options:*** deferred entrance, midyear entrance. ***Required:*** school transcript, interview, Assessment and Placement Services for Community Colleges. ***Recommended:*** minimum 2.0 GPA, 3 years of high school math. Test scores used for counseling/placement. ***Application deadline:*** 9/1. ***Notification:*** continuous until 9/15.
APPLYING/TRANSFER ***Required:*** standardized test scores, high school transcript, interview, college transcript. ***Recommended:*** 3 years of high school math, minimum 2.0 high school GPA. ***Entrance:*** noncompetitive. ***Application deadline:*** 9/1. ***Notification:*** continuous until 9/15.
CONTACT Mr. James H. Oxendine, Dean of Students, Bladen Community College, Dublin, NC 28332-0266, 910-862-2164 Ext. 207.

BLUE RIDGE COMMUNITY COLLEGE
Flat Rock, North Carolina

UG Enrollment: 2,529	**Tuition & Fees (NC Res): $588**
Application Deadline: rolling	**Room & Board: N/Avail**

GENERAL State and locally supported, 2-year, coed. Part of North Carolina Community College System. Awards certificates, diplomas, transfer associate, terminal associate degrees. Founded 1969. ***Setting:*** 109-acre small-town campus. ***Total enrollment:*** 2,529. ***Faculty:*** 176 (44 full-time, 66% with terminal degrees, 132 part-time).
ENROLLMENT PROFILE 2,529 students: 54% women, 46% men, 60% part-time, 99% state residents, 3% transferred in, 61% 25 or older, 1% Native American, 1% Hispanic, 4% African American, 1% Asian American. ***Most popular recent majors:*** business administration/commerce/management, liberal arts/general studies, computer programming.
FIRST-YEAR CLASS 633 total. Of the students who applied, 100% were accepted.
ACADEMIC PROGRAM Core, honor code. Calendar: quarters. Academic remediation for entering students, services for LD students, part-time degree program (daytime, evenings, summer), adult/continuing education programs.
GENERAL DEGREE REQUIREMENTS 100 credit hours; 1 math course; computer course for business majors.
MAJORS Art/fine arts, business administration/commerce/management, carpentry, child care/child and family studies, computer programming, cosmetology, data processing, drafting and design, electrical and electronics technologies, electronics engineering technology, heating/refrigeration/air conditioning, horticulture, industrial engineering technology, liberal arts/general studies, machine and tool technologies, manufacturing technology, marketing/retailing/merchandising, mechanical engineering technology, nursing, secretarial studies/office management, tourism and travel, vocational education, welding technology.
LIBRARY 25,581 books, 156 periodicals, 707 records, tapes, and CDs.
COMPUTERS ON CAMPUS 40 computers for student use in computer labs, library provide access to on-line services, Internet. Staffed computer lab on campus provides training in use of computers, software.
COLLEGE LIFE 20% vote in student government elections. ***Student services:*** personal-psychological counseling. ***Campus security:*** security during class hours.
HOUSING College housing not available.
CAREER PLANNING ***Placement office:*** 1 full-time staff. ***Director:*** Ms. Julie Thompson, Counselor/Job Placement Officer, 704-692-3572 Ext. 216. ***Services:*** job fairs, resume preparation, resume referral, career counseling, careers library, job bank, job interviews.
EXPENSES FOR 1995–96 State resident tuition: $557 full-time, $13.25 per credit hour part-time. Nonresident tuition: $4515 full-time, $107.50 per credit hour part-time. Part-time mandatory fees per quarter range from $7.25 to $10.25. Full-time mandatory fees: $31.
FINANCIAL AID ***College-administered undergrad aid 1995–96:*** 15 need-based scholarships (average $300), 6 non-need scholarships (average $200), short-term loans (average $100), Federal Work-Study, 5 part-time jobs. ***Required forms for some financial aid applicants:*** CSS Financial Aid PROFILE, institutional, FAFSA. ***Priority deadline:*** 8/15. ***Waivers:*** full or partial for senior citizens.
APPLYING Open admission. ***Options:*** Common Application, early entrance, midyear entrance. ***Required:*** school transcript, TOEFL for international students. Test scores used for counseling/placement. ***Application deadline:*** rolling. ***Notification:*** continuous until 10/1.
APPLYING/TRANSFER ***Required:*** high school transcript, college transcript. ***Entrance:*** noncompetitive. ***Application deadline:*** rolling. ***Notification:*** continuous until 10/1.
CONTACT Mr. Donald L. Shoemaker, Dean for Student and Administrative Services, Blue Ridge Community College, Flat Rock, NC 28731, 704-692-3572. ***Fax:*** 704-692-2441. ***E-mail:*** sarahj@blueridge.cc.nc.us. College video available.

BREVARD COLLEGE
Brevard, North Carolina

UG Enrollment: 636	**Tuition & Fees: $9125**
Application Deadline: rolling	**Room & Board: $3900**

Brevard College has a beautiful 140-acre campus located in the heart of the Blue Ridge Mountains near Asheville, North Carolina. Eighty-nine percent of the students reside on campus, and the student body represents more than 30 states and 11 countries. Intercollegiate athletics include baseball, basketball, cross-country and track, golf, soccer, tennis, and volleyball. Skiing, bicycling on the Blue Ridge Parkway, white-water canoeing, camping, and hiking and backpacking on the Appalachian Trail are all part of the Brevard College experience. The academic program is designed principally for students who plan to go on to a 4-year university. Ninety-two percent of the students in the associate degree university-parallel curriculum continue their education as juniors at some of the nation's leading universities.

GENERAL Independent Methodist, primarily 2-year, coed. Awards transfer associate, bachelor's degrees (bachelor's in music and art only). Founded 1853. ***Setting:*** 140-acre small-town campus. ***Total enrollment:*** 636. ***Faculty:*** 99 (68 full-time, 85% with terminal degrees, 31 part-time).
ENROLLMENT PROFILE 636 students from 31 states and territories, 11 other countries. 45% women, 55% men, 7% part-time, 52% state residents, 4% transferred in, 60% have need-based financial aid, 40% have non-need-based financial aid, 10% international, 3% 25 or older, 3% Native American, 1% Hispanic, 12% African American, 1% Asian American. ***Most popular recent majors:*** art/fine arts, environmental studies, business administration/commerce/management.
FIRST-YEAR CLASS 401 total; 862 applied, 90% were accepted, 52% of whom enrolled.
ACADEMIC PROGRAM Core, interdisciplinary curriculum, honor code. Calendar: semesters. Academic remediation for entering students, English as a second language program offered during academic year, services for LD students, advanced placement, Freshman Honors College, honors program, summer session for credit, part-time degree program (daytime), adult/continuing education programs, internships. Off-campus study at 5 members of the Smoky Mountain Consortium. Study abroad in Austria.
GENERAL DEGREE REQUIREMENTS 66 semester hours for associate, 124 semester hours for bachelor's; 1 course in math; computer course for students without computer competency.
MAJORS Accounting, agricultural sciences, anatomy, applied art, art education (B), art/ fine arts (B), art history (B), arts administration (B), art therapy (B), behavioral sciences, biblical studies, biology/biological sciences, botany/plant sciences, broadcasting, business administration/commerce/management, business economics, business education, ceramic art and design, chemical engineering technology, chemistry, child psychology/child development, commercial art, communication, community services, computer graphics, computer information systems, computer management, computer programming, computer science, computer technologies, conservation, creative writing, dance, drama therapy, early childhood education, earth science, ecology, economics, education, educational administration, engineering (general), engineering and applied sciences, engineering design, engineering sciences, (pre)engineering sequence, English, environmental design, environmental education, environmental health sciences, environmental sciences, environmental studies, equestrian studies, European studies, family services, forestry, forest technology, French, geology, German, graphic arts, guidance and counseling, health education, health science, health services administration, history, human ecology, humanities, interdisciplinary studies, interior design, international business, international studies, jazz, journalism, liberal arts/general studies, literature, marine biology, marketing/retailing/merchandising, mathematics, medical technology, ministries, music (B), musical instrument technology, music business (B), music education (B), music history (B), music therapy (B), Native American studies, natural sciences, nursing, occupational therapy, painting/drawing (B), parks management, pastoral studies, philosophy, photography, physical education, physical fitness/exercise science, physical sciences, physical therapy, physics, piano/organ, political science/government, printmaking, psychology, public administration, public relations, recreational facilities management, recreation and leisure services, recreation therapy, religious education, religious studies, sacred music (B), science, science education, sculpture (B), social science, social work, sociology, Spanish, sports administration, sports medicine, statistics, studio art, theater arts/drama, theology, veterinary sciences, voice (B), Western civilization and culture, wildlife biology, wildlife management, wind and percussion instruments (B).
LIBRARY Jones Library with 49,000 books, 200 periodicals, 900 records, tapes, and CDs.
COMPUTERS ON CAMPUS 52 computers for student use in computer center, computer labs, learning resource center, library, student center provide access to e-mail, Internet. Staffed computer lab on campus (open 24 hours a day) provides training in use of computers, software.
COLLEGE LIFE Orientation program (4 days, no cost, parents included). Drama-theater group, choral group, student-run newspaper. ***Social organizations:*** 23 open to all. ***Most popular organizations:*** Fine Arts Organization, Outdoor/Skiing Club, Environmental Awareness Club, Student Ambassadors, Student Government. ***Major annual events:*** Derby Day, Homecoming, Spring Fling. ***Student services:*** health clinic, personal-psychological counseling. ***Campus security:*** 24-hour emergency response devices and patrols, late-night transport-escort service, controlled dormitory access.

HOUSING 660 college housing spaces available; 600 were occupied 1995–96. Freshmen guaranteed college housing. On-campus residence required through sophomore year except if living with relatives. ***Option:*** single-sex (6 buildings) housing available.
ATHLETICS Member NJCAA. ***Intercollegiate:*** baseball M, basketball M(s)/W(s), cross-country running M(s)/W(s), golf M(s), soccer M(s)/W(s), tennis W(s), track and field M(s)/W(s), volleyball W. ***Intramural:*** archery, badminton, basketball, bowling, cross-country running, equestrian sports, football, golf, gymnastics, racquetball, skiing (cross-country), skiing (downhill), soccer, softball, swimming and diving, tennis, track and field, volleyball, weight lifting. ***Contact:*** Mr. Dave Rinker, Athletic Director, 704-883-8292.
CAREER PLANNING ***Placement office:*** 1 full-time staff. ***Director:*** Ms. Adelaide Hart, Director of Connection Center, 704-883-8292. ***Services:*** job fairs, resume preparation, career counseling, careers library, job bank, job interviews.
AFTER GRADUATION 93% of students completing transfer associate program in 1994–95 went directly to 4-year colleges.
EXPENSES FOR 1996–97 Comprehensive fee of $13,025 includes full-time tuition ($8500), mandatory fees ($625), and college room and board ($3900). College room only: $1700. Part-time tuition: $130 per semester hour.
FINANCIAL AID ***College-administered undergrad aid 1995–96:*** 375 need-based scholarships (average $2500), 218 non-need scholarships (average $2000), low-interest long-term loans from college funds (average $1100), loans from external sources (average $2600), Federal Work-Study (averaging $1000), 75 part-time jobs. Average total aid for freshmen: $7652, meeting 85% of need. ***Acceptable forms:*** CSS Financial Aid PROFILE, FAFSA. ***Priority deadline:*** 8/1. ***Payment plan:*** installment. ***Waivers:*** full or partial for employees or children of employees and senior citizens.
APPLYING ***Options:*** early entrance, deferred entrance, midyear entrance. ***Required:*** school transcript, SAT I or ACT, TOEFL for international students. ***Recommended:*** essay, 3 years of high school math and science, 2 years of high school foreign language. ***Required for some:*** minimum 2.0 GPA, minimum 3.0 GPA, recommendations, interview. Test scores used for admission and counseling/placement. ***Application deadline:*** rolling.
APPLYING/TRANSFER ***Required:*** high school transcript, college transcript. ***Recommended:*** essay, 3 years of high school math and science, 2 years of high school foreign language, minimum 2.0 college GPA. ***Required for some:*** standardized test scores, recommendations, interview, minimum 2.0 high school GPA. ***Application deadline:*** rolling. ***Contact:*** Mr. Robert G. McLendon, Dean of Admissions, 704-884-8300.
CONTACT Mr. Robert G. McLendon, Dean of Admissions, Brevard College, Brevard, NC 28712-3306, 704-884-8300. ***E-mail:*** admissions@lightnin.brevard.edu. College video available.

❖ ***See page 712 for a narrative description.*** ❖

BRUNSWICK COMMUNITY COLLEGE
Supply, North Carolina

UG Enrollment: 829 **Tuition & Fees (NC Res): $581**
Application Deadline: rolling **Room & Board: N/Avail**

GENERAL State-supported, 2-year, coed. Part of North Carolina Community College System. Awards certificates, diplomas, transfer associate, terminal associate degrees. Founded 1979. ***Setting:*** 179-acre rural campus. ***Total enrollment:*** 829. ***Faculty:*** 70 (21 full-time, 10% with terminal degrees, 49 part-time); student-faculty ratio is 15:1.
ENROLLMENT PROFILE 829 students: 70% women, 51% part-time, 98% state residents, 23% transferred in, 0% international, 79% 25 or older, 0% Native American, 0% Hispanic, 16% African American, 0% Asian American. ***Most popular recent majors:*** cosmetology, business administration/commerce/management, nursing.
FIRST-YEAR CLASS 312 total. Of the students who applied, 100% were accepted.
ACADEMIC PROGRAM Core, honor code. Calendar: quarters. Academic remediation for entering students, services for LD students, part-time degree program (daytime, evenings), adult/continuing education programs, internships.
GENERAL DEGREE REQUIREMENTS 96 quarter hours; computer course; internship (some majors).
MAJORS Business administration/commerce/management, computer programming, cosmetology, electronics engineering technology, heating/refrigeration/air conditioning, landscaping/grounds maintenance, liberal arts/general studies, medical records services, nursing, occupational therapy, real estate, recreational facilities management, secretarial studies/office management.
LIBRARY 10,000 books, 20 microform titles, 125 periodicals, 200 records, tapes, and CDs.
COMPUTERS ON CAMPUS 58 computers for student use in computer center, learning resource center.
COLLEGE LIFE 1% vote in student government elections. ***Social organizations:*** 1 open to all. ***Most popular organization:*** Student Government Association. ***Student services:*** personal-psychological counseling, women's center.
HOUSING College housing not available.
ATHLETICS ***Intercollegiate:*** baseball M, golf M/W, tennis M/W, volleyball M/W. ***Contact:*** Mr. Joe Moorefield, Athletic Director, 910-754-6900.
CAREER PLANNING ***Services:*** resume preparation, resume referral, career counseling, careers library, job interviews.
EXPENSES FOR 1995–96 State resident tuition: $557 full-time, $13.25 per quarter hour part-time. Nonresident tuition: $4515 full-time, $107.50 per quarter hour part-time. Part-time mandatory fees per quarter range from $1.10 to $6.05. Full-time mandatory fees: $24.
FINANCIAL AID ***College-administered undergrad aid 1995–96:*** 110 need-based scholarships (averaging $92), Federal Work-Study. ***Required forms:*** institutional, FAFSA; accepted: CSS Financial Aid PROFILE, state. ***Priority deadline:*** 8/1. ***Waivers:*** full or partial for senior citizens.
APPLYING Open admission. ***Option:*** Common Application. ***Required:*** school transcript. ***Recommended:*** TOEFL for international students. ***Required for some:*** recommendations, interview, ACT ASSET. Test scores used for counseling/placement. ***Application deadline:*** rolling. ***Notification:*** continuous.
APPLYING/TRANSFER ***Required:*** high school transcript, college transcript. ***Required for some:*** recommendations, interview. ***Application deadline:*** rolling. ***Notification:*** continuous. ***Contact:*** Mr. Johnnie Simpson, Vice President for Academics, 910-754-6900.
CONTACT Ms. Matlynn Bryant, Vice President for Student Development, Brunswick Community College, Supply, NC 28462-0030, 910-754-6900.

CALDWELL COMMUNITY COLLEGE AND TECHNICAL INSTITUTE
Hudson, North Carolina

UG Enrollment: 3,162 **Tuition & Fees (NC Res): $578**
Application Deadline: rolling **Room & Board: N/Avail**

GENERAL State-supported, 2-year, coed. Part of North Carolina Community College System. Awards certificates, diplomas, transfer associate, terminal associate degrees. Founded 1964. ***Setting:*** 50-acre small-town campus. ***Total enrollment:*** 3,162. ***Faculty:*** 189 (74 full-time, 8% with terminal degrees, 115 part-time); student-faculty ratio is 15:1.
ENROLLMENT PROFILE 3,162 students: 52% women, 56% part-time, 95% state residents, 32% transferred in, 1% international, 36% 25 or older, 4% African American.
FIRST-YEAR CLASS 1,130 total; 1,947 applied, 94% were accepted.
ACADEMIC PROGRAM Core, honor code. Calendar: quarters. Academic remediation for entering students, services for LD students, advanced placement, summer session for credit, part-time degree program (daytime, evenings, weekends), adult/continuing education programs, co-op programs.
GENERAL DEGREE REQUIREMENTS 96 quarter hours; math/science requirements vary according to major; computer course for most majors.
MAJORS Accounting, biomedical technologies, business administration/commerce/management, data processing, drafting and design, electrical and electronics technologies, (pre)engineering sequence, industrial engineering technology, liberal arts/general studies, medical secretarial studies, music, nuclear medical technology, nursing, occupational therapy, paralegal studies, physical therapy, radiological technology, science, secretarial studies/office management.
LIBRARY Broyhill Center for Learning Resources with 40,226 books, 71 microform titles, 537 periodicals, 2 on-line bibliographic services, 18 CD-ROMs, 8,105 records, tapes, and CDs.
COMPUTERS ON CAMPUS 100 computers for student use in labs. Staffed computer lab on campus provides training in use of computers, software.
COLLEGE LIFE Orientation program (2 days, $15). Drama-theater group, choral group. 30% vote in student government elections. ***Campus security:*** trained security personnel during open hours.
HOUSING College housing not available.
ATHLETICS ***Intramural:*** badminton, basketball, tennis, volleyball.
CAREER PLANNING ***Placement office:*** 2 full-time, 5 part-time staff. ***Director:*** Ms. Doris Conn, Director, Career Services, 704-726-2270. ***Services:*** job fairs, resume preparation, resume referral, career counseling, careers library, job bank, job interviews. 82 organizations recruited on campus 1994–95.
ESTIMATED EXPENSES FOR 1996–97 State resident tuition: $557 full-time, $13.25 per quarter hour part-time. Nonresident tuition: $4515 full-time, $107.50 per quarter hour part-time. Part-time mandatory fees per quarter range from $1.75 to $7. Full-time mandatory fees: $21.
FINANCIAL AID ***College-administered undergrad aid 1995–96:*** 200 need-based scholarships (average $400), 6 non-need scholarships (average $500), low-interest long-term loans from external sources (average $2500), Federal Work-Study, 40 part-time jobs. ***Required forms:*** FAFSA. ***Priority deadline:*** 4/15.
APPLYING Open admission except for allied health programs. ***Options:*** early entrance, midyear entrance. ***Required:*** TOEFL for international students. Test scores used for counseling/placement. ***Application deadline:*** rolling. ***Notification:*** continuous.
APPLYING/TRANSFER ***Entrance:*** noncompetitive. ***Application deadline:*** rolling. ***Notification:*** continuous. ***Contact:*** Mrs. Janice Van Osdol, Director of Admissions, 704-726-2245.
CONTACT Mrs. Janice Van Osdol, Director of Admissions, Caldwell Community College and Technical Institute, Hudson, NC 28638-2397, 704-726-2245.

CAPE FEAR COMMUNITY COLLEGE
Wilmington, North Carolina

UG Enrollment: 3,700 **Tuition & Fees (NC Res): $575**
Application Deadline: rolling **Room & Board: N/Avail**

GENERAL State-supported, 2-year, coed. Part of North Carolina Community College System. Awards certificates, diplomas, transfer associate, terminal associate degrees. Founded 1959. ***Setting:*** 3-acre urban campus. ***Endowment:*** $238,334. ***Total enrollment:*** 3,700. ***Faculty:*** 205 (86 full-time, 99% with terminal degrees, 119 part-time); student-faculty ratio is 18:1.
ENROLLMENT PROFILE 3,700 students from 23 states and territories, 5 other countries. 55% women, 50% part-time, 96% state residents, 4% transferred in, 16% have need-based financial aid, 1% international, 40% 25 or older, 1% Native American, 1% Hispanic, 17% African American, 1% Asian American. ***Most popular recent majors:*** business administration/commerce/management, nursing.
FIRST-YEAR CLASS 1,255 total; 2,750 applied, 100% were accepted, 46% of whom enrolled. 8% from top 10% of their high school class, 32% from top quarter, 60% from top half.
ACADEMIC PROGRAM Core, honor code. Calendar: quarters. Academic remediation for entering students, English as a second language program, services for LD students, part-time degree program (daytime, evenings), adult/continuing education programs, co-op programs and internships.
GENERAL DEGREE REQUIREMENTS 96 quarter hours; math/science requirements vary according to program; computer course; internship (some majors).
MAJORS Accounting, automotive technologies, business administration/commerce/management, carpentry, chemical engineering technology, computer technologies, criminal justice, drafting and design, early childhood education, electrical and electronics technologies, electronics engineering technology, heating/refrigeration/air conditioning, hotel and restaurant management, instrumentation technology, liberal arts/general studies, machine and tool technologies, manufacturing technology, marine technology, mechanical design technology, medical records services, nursing, paralegal studies, secretarial studies/office management.
LIBRARY 30,091 books, 1,942 microform titles, 599 periodicals, 1 on-line bibliographic service, 15 CD-ROMs, 523 records, tapes, and CDs. Acquisition spending 1994–95: $142,877.

Peterson's Guide to Two-Year Colleges 1997 491

North Carolina

Cape Fear Community College (continued)
COMPUTERS ON CAMPUS 80 computers for student use in computer center, learning resource center. Staffed computer lab on campus provides training in use of computers, software.
COLLEGE LIFE Choral group, student-run newspaper. *Campus security:* 24-hour emergency response devices, late-night transport-escort service, 14-hour patrols by trained security personnel.
HOUSING College housing not available.
ATHLETICS *Intercollegiate:* basketball M, golf M/W, softball M/W, tennis M/W, volleyball M/W. *Intramural:* bowling. *Contact:* Mr. Rick Stewart, Director of Student Activities, 910-251-5142.
CAREER PLANNING *Placement office:* 2 full-time staff. *Director:* Dr. Mary B. Rea-Poteat, Director, Career and Testing Services, 910-251-5143. *Services:* job fairs, resume preparation, resume referral, career counseling, careers library, job bank, job interviews.
AFTER GRADUATION 85% of students completing a degree program in 1994–95 went directly on to further study.
EXPENSES FOR 1995–96 State resident tuition: $557 full-time, $13.25 per quarter hour part-time. Nonresident tuition: $4515 full-time, $107.50 per quarter hour part-time. Part-time mandatory fees per quarter range from $1 to $6. Full-time mandatory fees: $18.
FINANCIAL AID *College-administered undergrad aid 1995–96:* 50 need-based scholarships (average $500), 30 non-need scholarships (average $500), low-interest long-term loans from external sources (average $2300), Federal Work-Study, 5 part-time jobs. *Required forms:* institutional, FAFSA, income verification; accepted: CSS Financial Aid PROFILE. *Priority deadline:* 3/15. *Waivers:* full or partial for employees or children of employees.
APPLYING Open admission. *Required:* school transcript, TOEFL for international students. Test scores used for counseling/placement. *Application deadline:* rolling. *Notification:* continuous.
APPLYING/TRANSFER *Required:* high school transcript, college transcript. *Application deadline:* rolling. *Notification:* continuous.
CONTACT Mr. Chris Zingelmann, Director of Enrollment Management, Cape Fear Community College, 411 North Front Street, Wilmington, NC 28401-3993, 910-251-5154. *Fax:* 910-251-5180.

CARTERET COMMUNITY COLLEGE
Morehead City, North Carolina

UG Enrollment: 1,428	Tuition & Fees (NC Res): $762
Application Deadline: rolling	Room & Board: N/Avail

GENERAL State-supported, 2-year, coed. Part of North Carolina Community College System. Awards certificates, diplomas, transfer associate, terminal associate degrees. Founded 1963. *Setting:* 25-acre small-town campus. *Total enrollment:* 1,428. *Faculty:* 93 (41 full-time, 52 part-time); student-faculty ratio is 16:1.
ENROLLMENT PROFILE 1,428 students from 22 states and territories. 62% women, 59% part-time, 96% state residents, 22% transferred in, 0% international, 53% 25 or older, 1% Native American, 1% Hispanic, 8% African American, 1% Asian American. *Most popular recent majors:* criminal justice, business administration/commerce/management, paralegal studies.
FIRST-YEAR CLASS 1,051 total; 1,093 applied, 99% of whom enrolled.
ACADEMIC PROGRAM Honor code. Calendar: quarters. Academic remediation for entering students, services for LD students, tutorials, summer session for credit, part-time degree program (daytime, evenings), adult/continuing education programs, co-op programs and internships.
GENERAL DEGREE REQUIREMENTS 110 quarter hours; 1 math course.
MAJORS Business administration/commerce/management, computer technologies, criminal justice, interior design, legal secretarial studies, liberal arts/general studies, medical assistant technologies, paralegal studies, photography, practical nursing, radiological technology, recreation therapy, respiratory therapy, secretarial studies/office management, teacher aide studies.
LIBRARY 21,000 books, 193 microform titles, 165 periodicals, 1,500 records, tapes, and CDs.
COMPUTERS ON CAMPUS 150 computers for student use in computer labs, classrooms, library.
COLLEGE LIFE Student-run newspaper.
HOUSING College housing not available.
ATHLETICS *Intercollegiate:* softball M/W, volleyball M/W.
CAREER PLANNING *Placement office:* 1 part-time staff. *Director:* Ms. Beth Belcher, Counselor, 919-247-6000. *Services:* resume preparation, resume referral, career counseling, careers library.
EXPENSES FOR 1995–96 State resident tuition: $729 full-time, $13.25 per quarter hour part-time. Nonresident tuition: $5913 full-time, $107.50 per quarter hour part-time. Part-time mandatory fees per quarter hour range from $5.25 to $8.25. Full-time mandatory fees: $33.
FINANCIAL AID *College-administered undergrad aid 1995–96:* 600 need-based scholarships (average $1500), 50 non-need scholarships (average $500), short-term loans (average $300), low-interest long-term loans from external sources (average $2000), 50 Federal Work-Study (averaging $600), 3 part-time jobs. *Required forms:* CSS Financial Aid PROFILE, institutional, FAFSA. *Priority deadline:* 8/31. *Waivers:* full or partial for senior citizens.
APPLYING Open admission except for health-related programs. *Option:* early entrance. *Required:* school transcript. *Recommended:* SAT I. Test scores used for counseling/placement. *Application deadline:* rolling. *Notification:* continuous.
APPLYING/TRANSFER *Required:* college transcript. *Required for some:* high school transcript. *Entrance:* minimally difficult. *Application deadline:* rolling. *Notification:* continuous.
CONTACT Mr. Don Thompson, Director of Student Services, Carteret Community College, Morehead City, NC 28557-2989, 919-247-4142 Ext. 149.

CATAWBA VALLEY COMMUNITY COLLEGE
Hickory, North Carolina

UG Enrollment: 3,499	Tuition & Fees (NC Res): $640
Application Deadline: rolling	Room & Board: N/Avail

GENERAL State and locally supported, 2-year, coed. Part of North Carolina Community College System. Awards transfer associate, terminal associate degrees. Founded 1960. *Setting:* 50-acre small-town campus with easy access to Charlotte. *Total enrollment:* 3,499. *Faculty:* 235 (85 full-time, 150 part-time); student-faculty ratio is 19:1.
ENROLLMENT PROFILE 3,499 students from 10 states and territories. 51% women, 74% part-time, 98% state residents, 10% transferred in, 54% 25 or older, 1% Native American, 1% Hispanic, 6% African American, 1% Asian American. *Most popular recent majors:* nursing, electronics engineering technology, accounting.
FIRST-YEAR CLASS 987 total; 2,000 applied, 100% were accepted, 49% of whom enrolled.
ACADEMIC PROGRAM Core. Calendar: quarters. Academic remediation for entering students, services for LD students, summer session for credit, part-time degree program (daytime, evenings), adult/continuing education programs, co-op programs.
GENERAL DEGREE REQUIREMENTS 96 quarter hours; 1 course each in math and lab science; computer course for students without computer competency.
MAJORS Accounting, architectural technologies, business administration/commerce/management, computer programming, computer science, computer technologies, data processing, drafting and design, electrical and electronics technologies, electronics engineering technology, emergency medical technology, finance/banking, horticulture, industrial administration, industrial engineering technology, liberal arts/general studies, mechanical engineering technology, medical technology, nursing, operating room technology, real estate, recreational facilities management, robotics, secretarial studies/office management, teacher aide studies, transportation technologies.
LIBRARY 32,256 books, 1,192 microform titles, 185 periodicals, 3,222 records, tapes, and CDs.
COMPUTERS ON CAMPUS 40 computers for student use in computer center provide access to off-campus computing facilities, on-line services. Staffed computer lab on campus.
COLLEGE LIFE *Student services:* personal-psychological counseling, women's center.
HOUSING College housing not available.
ATHLETICS Member NJCAA. *Intercollegiate:* golf M, tennis M/W. *Intramural:* table tennis (Ping-Pong).
CAREER PLANNING *Service:* career counseling.
AFTER GRADUATION 60% of students completing a degree program in 1994–95 went directly on to further study.
EXPENSES FOR 1995–96 State resident tuition: $557 full-time, $13.25 per quarter hour part-time. Nonresident tuition: $4515 full-time, $107.50 per quarter hour part-time. Part-time mandatory fees: $1.55 per quarter hour. Full-time mandatory fees: $83.
FINANCIAL AID *College-administered undergrad aid 1995–96:* 30 need-based scholarships (averaging $250), low-interest long-term loans from external sources (averaging $2625), Federal Work-Study. *Acceptable forms:* FAFSA. *Application deadline:* continuous. *Waivers:* full or partial for senior citizens.
APPLYING Open admission except for nursing, emergency medical services programs. *Options:* early entrance, deferred entrance. *Required:* school transcript, TOEFL for international students, ACT ASSET. Test scores used for counseling/placement. *Application deadline:* rolling. *Notification:* continuous.
APPLYING/TRANSFER *Required:* high school transcript, college transcript. *Application deadline:* rolling. *Notification:* continuous.
CONTACT Ms. Louise M. Garrison, Director of Admissions and Records, Catawba Valley Community College, Hickory, NC 28602-9699, 704-327-7009. *Fax:* 704-327-7000 Ext. 301.

CECILS JUNIOR COLLEGE OF BUSINESS
Asheville, North Carolina

UG Enrollment: 150	Tuition & Fees: $4525
Application Deadline: rolling	Room & Board: N/Avail

GENERAL Proprietary, 2-year, coed. Awards transfer associate degrees. Founded 1905. *Setting:* 8-acre urban campus. *Total enrollment:* 150. *Faculty:* 15 (8 full-time, 25% with terminal degrees, 7 part-time).
ENROLLMENT PROFILE 150 students: 83% women, 35% part-time, 99% state residents, 45% transferred in, 0% international, 80% 25 or older, 0% Native American, 1% Hispanic, 13% African American, 0% Asian American. *Most popular recent majors:* paralegal studies, medical assistant technologies, business administration/commerce/management.
FIRST-YEAR CLASS 50 total. Of the students accepted, 80% enrolled.
ACADEMIC PROGRAM Core. Calendar: quarters. Academic remediation for entering students, summer session for credit, part-time degree program (daytime, evenings, summer), adult/continuing education programs, internships.
GENERAL DEGREE REQUIREMENTS 115 credits; 1 course each in algebra and geology; computer course.
MAJORS Business administration/commerce/management, medical assistant technologies, paralegal studies, secretarial studies/office management.
LIBRARY 10,094 books, 74 periodicals, 276 records, tapes, and CDs.
COMPUTERS ON CAMPUS 20 computers for student use in computer center.
COLLEGE LIFE 50% vote in student government elections.
HOUSING College housing not available.
CAREER PLANNING *Placement office:* 1 part-time staff. *Director:* Ms. Marie Lombardo, Job Placement Director, 704-252-2486. *Services:* resume preparation, career counseling, job interviews. Students must register sophomore year.
EXPENSES FOR 1995–96 *Application fee:* $25. Tuition: $4350 full-time, $525 per course part-time. Part-time mandatory fees: $175 per year. One-time mandatory fee: $100. Full-time mandatory fees: $175.
FINANCIAL AID *College-administered undergrad aid 1995–96:* 112 need-based scholarships (average $600), 1 non-need scholarship ($1000), low-interest long-term loans

from external sources, Federal Work-Study. *Required forms:* institutional, FAFSA; accepted: CSS Financial Aid PROFILE, state. *Priority deadline:* 9/22. *Payment plan:* installment.
APPLYING Open admission. *Option:* deferred entrance. *Required:* essay, school transcript, CPAt. Test scores used for counseling/placement. *Application deadline:* rolling.
APPLYING/TRANSFER *Required:* essay, standardized test scores, high school transcript, college transcript. *Application deadline:* rolling.
CONTACT Mr. Toney McFadden, Director of Admissions, Cecils Junior College of Business, 1567 Patton Avenue, PO Box 6407, Asheville, NC 28816-6407, 704-252-2486 Ext. 14.

CENTRAL CAROLINA COMMUNITY COLLEGE
Sanford, North Carolina

UG Enrollment: 3,140	Tuition & Fees (NC Res): $584
Application Deadline: rolling	Room & Board: N/Avail

GENERAL State and locally supported, 2-year, coed. Part of North Carolina Community College System. Awards certificates, diplomas, transfer associate, terminal associate degrees. Founded 1962. *Setting:* 32-acre small-town campus. *Total enrollment:* 3,140. *Faculty:* 171 (106 full-time, 90% with terminal degrees, 65 part-time); student-faculty ratio is 15:1.
ENROLLMENT PROFILE 3,140 students from 18 states and territories, 7 other countries. 59% women, 52% part-time, 98% state residents, 22% transferred in, 52% 25 or older, 1% Native American, 2% Hispanic, 24% African American, 1% Asian American. *Areas of study chosen:* 17% liberal arts/general studies, 13% business management and administrative services, 10% health professions and related sciences, 5% engineering and applied sciences, 4% social sciences, 3% computer and information sciences, 2% communications and journalism, 2% vocational and home economics. *Most popular recent majors:* business administration/commerce/management, electrical and electronics technologies, computer programming.
FIRST-YEAR CLASS 1,295 total; 2,047 applied, 87% were accepted, 72% of whom enrolled. 2% from top 10% of their high school class, 10% from top quarter, 80% from top half.
ACADEMIC PROGRAM Core, honor code. Calendar: quarters for terminal associate degree, semesters for transfer associate degree. Academic remediation for entering students, English as a second language program offered during academic year, summer session for credit, part-time degree program (daytime, evenings, summer), adult/continuing education programs, internships.
GENERAL DEGREE REQUIREMENTS 106 quarter hours; computer course for most majors; internship (some majors).
MAJORS Accounting, automotive technologies, business administration/commerce/management, child care/child and family studies, computer programming, corrections, criminal justice, drafting and design, early childhood education, education, electrical and electronics technologies, industrial administration, instrumentation technology, laser technologies, law enforcement/police sciences, legal secretarial studies, liberal arts/general studies, marketing/retailing/merchandising, medical assistant technologies, medical secretarial studies, nursing, paralegal studies, quality control technology, radio and television studies, secretarial studies/office management, social work, telecommunications, veterinary technology.
LIBRARY 49,559 books, 109 microform titles, 330 periodicals, 23 CD-ROMs, 937 records, tapes, and CDs.
COMPUTERS ON CAMPUS 120 computers for student use in computer center.
COLLEGE LIFE Student-run radio station. 5% vote in student government elections. *Social organizations:* 1 open to all. *Most popular organization:* Student Government Association. *Major annual events:* Activity Day, Ms. CCCC Pageant, Spring Dance. *Student services:* personal-psychological counseling.
HOUSING College housing not available.
ATHLETICS *Intramural:* basketball, bowling, golf, softball, tennis, volleyball. *Contact:* Mr. Mike Neal, Student Activities Director, 919-775-5401 Ext. 337.
CAREER PLANNING *Placement office:* 1 part-time staff. *Director:* Ms. Teresa Sutton, Job Placement Officer, 919-775-5401. *Services:* job fairs, resume preparation, resume referral, career counseling, job bank, job interviews.
EXPENSES FOR 1995-96 State resident tuition: $557 full-time, $13.25 per quarter hour part-time. Nonresident tuition: $4515 full-time, $107.50 per quarter hour part-time. Part-time mandatory fees: $4.50 per quarter. Full-time mandatory fees: $27.
FINANCIAL AID *College-administered undergrad aid 1995-96:* 25 need-based scholarships (average $500), 9 non-need scholarships (average $578), short-term loans (average $100), low-interest long-term loans from external sources (average $2625), 57 Federal Work-Study (averaging $1463), 12 part-time jobs. *Required forms:* institutional, FAFSA; accepted: CSS Financial Aid PROFILE, state. *Priority deadline:* 3/31. *Waivers:* full or partial for employees or children of employees and senior citizens.
APPLYING Open admission except for nursing program. *Options:* early entrance, deferred entrance. *Required:* school transcript, TOEFL for international students, CGP, CTBS. Test scores used for admission (for nursing program) and counseling/placement. *Application deadline:* rolling. *Notification:* continuous. Preference given to residents of sponsoring counties.
APPLYING/TRANSFER *Required:* high school transcript. *Required for some:* standardized test scores. *Contact:* Mr. Sam Cope, College Transfer Counselor, 919-775-5401.
CONTACT Ms. Donna A. Hunt, Director of Admissions, Central Carolina Community College, Sanford, NC 27330-9000, 919-775-5401 Ext. 234 or toll-free 800-682-8353 (in-state). *Fax:* 919-775-1221. College video available.

CENTRAL PIEDMONT COMMUNITY COLLEGE
Charlotte, North Carolina

UG Enrollment: 15,614	Tuition & Fees (NC Res): $572
Application Deadline: rolling	Room & Board: N/Avail

GENERAL State and locally supported, 2-year, coed. Part of North Carolina Community College System. Awards certificates, diplomas, transfer associate, terminal associate degrees. Founded 1963. *Setting:* 37-acre urban campus. *Endowment:* $4.4 million. *Total enrollment:* 15,614. *Faculty:* 1,630 (630 full-time, 1,000 part-time); student-faculty ratio is 10:1.
ENROLLMENT PROFILE 15,614 students from 21 states and territories, 14 other countries. 57% women, 43% men, 70% part-time, 85% state residents, 1% transferred in, 2% international, 62% 25 or older, 1% Native American, 1% Hispanic, 22% African American, 2% Asian American. *Most popular recent majors:* nursing, medical assistant technologies.
FIRST-YEAR CLASS 800 total; 800 applied, 100% were accepted, 100% of whom enrolled.
ACADEMIC PROGRAM Core, honor code. Calendar: quarters. Academic remediation for entering students, English as a second language program offered during academic year and summer, services for LD students, advanced placement, self-designed majors, honors program, summer session for credit, part-time degree program (daytime, evenings, summer), adult/continuing education programs, co-op programs. Off-campus study at members of the Charlotte Area Educational Consortium.
GENERAL DEGREE REQUIREMENTS 96 quarter hours; 1 course each in math and science.
MAJORS Accounting, advertising, applied art, architectural technologies, art/fine arts, automotive technologies, biology/biological sciences, business administration/commerce/management, business machine technologies, child care/child and family studies, civil engineering technology, commercial art, computer programming, computer science, computer technologies, criminal justice, culinary arts, dance, data processing, deaf interpreter training, dental services, drafting and design, early childhood education, electrical and electronics technologies, electrical engineering technology, electromechanical technology, electronics engineering technology, engineering technology, environmental engineering technology, fashion merchandising, finance/banking, fire science, food sciences, food services management, food services technology, graphic arts, health services administration, horticulture, hospitality services, hotel and restaurant management, human services, insurance, interior design, law enforcement/police sciences, legal secretarial studies, liberal arts/general studies, machine and tool technologies, manufacturing technology, marketing/retailing/merchandising, mechanical engineering technology, medical assistant technologies, medical laboratory technology, medical records services, medical secretarial studies, medical technology, music, nursing, paralegal studies, physical therapy, postal management, practical nursing, printing technologies, real estate, respiratory therapy, retail management, secretarial studies/office management, social work, surveying technology, tourism and travel, transportation technologies, welding technology.
LIBRARY Hagemyer Learning Center with 92,285 books, 107,999 microform titles, 731 periodicals, 10,087 records, tapes, and CDs. Acquisition spending 1994-95: $345,096.
COMPUTERS ON CAMPUS Computers for student use in computer center, learning resource center, library, student center provide access to on-line services, Internet. Staffed computer lab on campus provides training in use of computers, software.
COLLEGE LIFE Drama-theater group, choral group, student-run newspaper. 3% vote in student government elections. *Social organizations:* 22 open to all; 1 local fraternity. *Most popular organizations:* Phi Theta Kappa, Black Students Organization, Students for Environmental Sanity, Sierra Club, Nursing Club. *Major annual events:* Fall Fest, Spring Fling, World Games. *Student services:* personal-psychological counseling. *Campus security:* 24-hour emergency response devices and patrols.
HOUSING College housing not available.
ATHLETICS Member NJCAA. *Intercollegiate:* basketball M/W, fencing M/W, golf M. *Intramural:* basketball, fencing, golf, soccer, softball, tennis, volleyball. *Contact:* Mr. John Toms, Athletic Director, 704-342-6512.
CAREER PLANNING *Placement office:* 8 full-time, 1 part-time staff. *Director:* Mrs. Debbie Bouton, Director, 704-342-6241. *Services:* job fairs, resume preparation, resume referral, career counseling, careers library, job bank, job interviews.
AFTER GRADUATION 29% of students completing a degree program in 1994-95 went directly on to further study.
EXPENSES FOR 1995-96 State resident tuition: $557 full-time, $13.25 per quarter hour part-time. Nonresident tuition: $4515 full-time, $107.50 per quarter hour part-time. Part-time mandatory fees: $5 per quarter. Full-time mandatory fees: $15.
FINANCIAL AID *College-administered undergrad aid 1995-96:* 426 need-based scholarships (averaging $150), 70 non-need scholarships (averaging $600), short-term loans (averaging $50), low-interest long-term loans from external sources (averaging $2487), 82 Federal Work-Study (averaging $4200). *Acceptable forms:* CSS Financial Aid PROFILE, FAFSA. *Priority deadline:* 4/1. *Waivers:* full or partial for employees or children of employees and senior citizens.
APPLYING Open admission. *Required:* TOEFL for international students. *Required for some:* Nelson Denny Reading Test or CPT. Test scores used for counseling/placement. *Application deadline:* rolling. *Notification:* continuous.
APPLYING/TRANSFER *Required:* college transcript. *Entrance:* noncompetitive. *Application deadline:* rolling. *Notification:* continuous. *Contact:* Mr. Don Flowers, Director, 704-342-6867.
CONTACT Dr. Mel Gay, Dean of Student Development, Central Piedmont Community College, PO Box 35009, Charlotte, NC 28235-5009, 704-342-6888.

CLEVELAND COMMUNITY COLLEGE
Shelby, North Carolina

UG Enrollment: 1,873	Tuition & Fees (NC Res): $587
Application Deadline: rolling	Room & Board: N/Avail

GENERAL State-supported, 2-year, coed. Part of North Carolina Community College System. Awards certificates, diplomas, transfer associate, terminal associate degrees. Founded 1965. *Setting:* 35-acre small-town campus with easy access to Charlotte. *Total enrollment:* 1,873. *Faculty:* 91 (45 full-time, 46 part-time); student-faculty ratio is 19:1.
ENROLLMENT PROFILE 1,873 students: 55% women, 45% men, 67% part-time, 99% state residents, 6% transferred in, 1% international, 75% 25 or older, 18% African American, 1% Asian American.
FIRST-YEAR CLASS 648 total; 663 applied, 100% were accepted, 98% of whom enrolled.
ACADEMIC PROGRAM Core, honor code. Calendar: quarters. Academic remediation for entering students, English as a second language program offered during academic year and summer, advanced placement, summer session for credit, part-time degree program (daytime, evenings), adult/continuing education programs, co-op programs.

Cleveland Community College (continued)

GENERAL DEGREE REQUIREMENTS 96 quarter hours; math requirement varies according to program; computer course for technology majors.
MAJORS Accounting, business administration/commerce/management, communication equipment technology, computer technologies, criminal justice, electronics engineering technology, fashion merchandising, industrial administration, liberal arts/general studies, medical secretarial studies, radiological technology, science, secretarial studies/office management.
LIBRARY 29,118 books, 2,524 microform titles, 243 periodicals, 5,660 records, tapes, and CDs.
COMPUTERS ON CAMPUS 100 computers for student use in labs, classrooms provide access to main academic computer, Internet. Staffed computer lab on campus provides training in use of computers, software.
COLLEGE LIFE Drama-theater group, student-run newspaper. 33% vote in student government elections. *Student services:* personal-psychological counseling. *Campus security:* security personnel during open hours.
HOUSING College housing not available.
ATHLETICS *Intramural:* basketball, volleyball.
CAREER PLANNING *Service:* career counseling.
EXPENSES FOR 1995–96 State resident tuition: $557 full-time, $13.25 per quarter hour part-time. Nonresident tuition: $4515 full-time, $107.50 per quarter hour part-time. Part-time mandatory fees per quarter range from $5 to $10. Full-time mandatory fees: $30.
FINANCIAL AID *College-administered undergrad aid 1995–96:* 16 need-based scholarships (averaging $325), low-interest long-term loans from external sources, Federal Work-Study. *Required forms:* institutional, FAFSA, ACT Institutional Verification Form; accepted: CSS Financial Aid PROFILE, state. *Priority deadline:* 5/1.
APPLYING Open admission. *Options:* early entrance, deferred entrance. *Required:* school transcript, TOEFL for international students. Test scores used for counseling/placement. *Application deadline:* rolling. *Notification:* continuous.
APPLYING/TRANSFER *Required:* high school transcript, college transcript. *Entrance:* noncompetitive. *Application deadline:* rolling. *Notification:* continuous.
CONTACT Ms. Caroline Moore, Director of Admissions, Cleveland Community College, Shelby, NC 28152, 704-484-4073.

COASTAL CAROLINA COMMUNITY COLLEGE
Jacksonville, North Carolina

UG Enrollment: 3,491	Tuition & Fees (NC Res): $578
Application Deadline: rolling	Room & Board: N/Avail

GENERAL State and locally supported, 2-year, coed. Part of North Carolina Community College System. Awards certificates, diplomas, transfer associate, terminal associate degrees. Founded 1964. *Setting:* 98-acre small-town campus. *Endowment:* $2.3 million. *Total enrollment:* 3,491. *Faculty:* 195 (105 full-time, 10% with terminal degrees, 90 part-time); student-faculty ratio is 19:1.
ENROLLMENT PROFILE 3,491 students from 45 states and territories. 61% women, 39% men, 46% part-time, 75% state residents, 15% transferred in, 50% 25 or older, 1% Native American, 5% Hispanic, 17% African American, 2% Asian American. *Most popular recent majors:* liberal arts/general studies, nursing.
FIRST-YEAR CLASS 2,098 total; 3,122 applied, 100% were accepted, 67% of whom enrolled.
ACADEMIC PROGRAM Core, comprehensive curriculum. Calendar: quarters. 380 courses offered in 1995–96. Academic remediation for entering students, English as a second language program offered during academic year, services for LD students, advanced placement, summer session for credit, part-time degree program (daytime, evenings), adult/continuing education programs, internships.
GENERAL DEGREE REQUIREMENTS 96 quarter hours; computer course.
MAJORS Accounting, architectural technologies, art/fine arts, business administration/commerce/management, business education, child care/child and family studies, computer programming, computer technologies, cosmetology, criminal justice, dental services, elementary education, emergency medical technology, (pre)engineering sequence, fire science, heating/refrigeration/air conditioning, legal secretarial studies, liberal arts/general studies, medical laboratory technology, medical secretarial studies, music, nursing, operating room technology, paralegal studies, practical nursing, science, secretarial studies/office management, welding technology.
LIBRARY 40,105 books, 2,982 microform titles, 314 periodicals, 6,552 records, tapes, and CDs. Acquisition spending 1994–95: $392,643.
COMPUTERS ON CAMPUS 450 computers for student use in computer labs, learning resource center, tutorial center, classrooms, library. Staffed computer lab on campus provides training in use of computers, software. Academic computing expenditure 1994–95: $565,847.
COLLEGE LIFE Drama-theater group. 10% vote in student government elections. *Student services:* personal-psychological counseling. *Campus security:* 24-hour emergency response devices and patrols, late-night transport-escort service.
HOUSING College housing not available.
ATHLETICS *Intercollegiate:* golf M/W, tennis M/W, volleyball M/W. *Intramural:* archery, bowling, football, racquetball, soccer, table tennis (Ping-Pong), tennis, volleyball, weight lifting.
CAREER PLANNING *Placement office:* 1 full-time staff. *Director:* Mr. Jeff Nardo, Director, Career Center, 910-938-6373. *Services:* job fairs, resume preparation, resume referral, career counseling, careers library, job bank, job interviews.
EXPENSES FOR 1995–96 State resident tuition: $557 full-time, $13.25 per quarter hour part-time. Nonresident tuition: $4515 full-time, $107.50 per quarter hour part-time. Part-time mandatory fees: $2 per quarter. Full-time mandatory fees: $21.
FINANCIAL AID *College-administered undergrad aid 1995–96:* 15 need-based scholarships (average $350), 100 non-need scholarships (average $200), short-term loans (average $200), 27 Federal Work-Study (averaging $260), 3 part-time jobs. *Required forms:* FAFSA, required for some: institutional. *Priority deadline:* 8/15. *Waivers:* full or partial for senior citizens.
APPLYING Open admission. *Options:* deferred entrance, midyear entrance. *Required:* school transcript, TOEFL for international students, ACT ASSET. *Required for some:* 2 recommendations, campus interview. Test scores used for counseling/placement. *Application deadline:* rolling. *Notification:* continuous.
APPLYING/TRANSFER *Required:* standardized test scores, high school transcript, college transcript. *Required for some:* 2 recommendations, campus interview. *Application deadline:* rolling. *Notification:* continuous.
CONTACT Mr. Jerry W. Snead, Director of Enrollment Management, Coastal Carolina Community College, Jacksonville, NC 28546-6877, 910-938-6246. *Fax:* 910-455-2767.

COLLEGE OF THE ALBEMARLE
Elizabeth City, North Carolina

UG Enrollment: 1,894	Tuition & Fees (NC Res): $586
Application Deadline: rolling	Room & Board: N/Avail

GENERAL State-supported, 2-year, coed. Part of North Carolina Community College System. Awards certificates, diplomas, transfer associate, terminal associate degrees. Founded 1960. *Setting:* 40-acre small-town campus. *Total enrollment:* 1,894. *Faculty:* 118 (56 full-time, 3% with terminal degrees, 62 part-time); student-faculty ratio is 18:1.
ENROLLMENT PROFILE 1,894 students from 17 states and territories, 4 other countries. 69% women, 31% men, 55% part-time, 94% state residents, 14% transferred in, 31% have need-based financial aid, 10% have non-need-based financial aid, 1% international, 56% 25 or older, 1% Native American, 1% Hispanic, 19% African American, 1% Asian American. *Areas of study chosen:* 13% health professions and related sciences, 7% business management and administrative services, 6% vocational and home economics, 4% computer and information sciences, 4% engineering and applied sciences, 4% liberal arts/general studies, 3% education, 1% agriculture, 1% fine arts, 1% physical sciences, 1% prelaw, 1% premed, 1% social sciences. *Most popular recent majors:* nursing, medical secretarial studies, business administration/commerce/management.
FIRST-YEAR CLASS 689 total; 1,000 applied, 100% were accepted, 69% of whom enrolled.
ACADEMIC PROGRAM Calendar: quarters. Academic remediation for entering students, English as a second language program, services for LD students, advanced placement, summer session for credit, part-time degree program (daytime, evenings, summer), adult/continuing education programs, co-op programs.
GENERAL DEGREE REQUIREMENTS 96 quarter hours; computer course for business majors.
MAJORS Art/fine arts, business administration/commerce/management, computer programming, computer technologies, criminal justice, electronics engineering technology, elementary education, (pre)engineering sequence, finance/banking, legal secretarial studies, liberal arts/general studies, mechanical design technology, medical secretarial studies, music, nursing, paralegal studies, science, secretarial studies/office management, theater arts/drama.
LIBRARY 48,400 books, 3,000 microform titles, 280 periodicals, 4,500 records, tapes, and CDs.
COMPUTERS ON CAMPUS 85 computers for student use in computer center, library. Staffed computer lab on campus.
COLLEGE LIFE Drama-theater group, choral group. *Social organizations:* 18 open to all. *Most popular organizations:* Phi Beta Lambda, Phi Theta Kappa. *Major annual events:* Welcome Back Student Day, Club Day, Career Day. *Student services:* personal-psychological counseling. *Campus security:* 24-hour patrols.
HOUSING College housing not available.
ATHLETICS *Intercollegiate:* soccer M. *Intramural:* archery, badminton, basketball, football, soccer, softball, table tennis (Ping-Pong), tennis, volleyball. *Contact:* Mr. John M. Wells, Assistant Dean of Admissions and Testing, 919-335-0821 Ext. 220.
CAREER PLANNING *Placement office:* 1 full-time staff. *Director:* Mrs. Deborah Williams, Director of Coop and Job Placement, 919-335-0821. *Services:* job fairs, resume preparation, resume referral, career counseling, careers library, job bank, job interviews.
AFTER GRADUATION 84% of students completing a degree program in 1994–95 went directly on to further study.
EXPENSES FOR 1995–96 State resident tuition: $557 full-time, $13.25 per quarter hour part-time. Nonresident tuition: $4515 full-time, $107.50 per quarter hour part-time. Part-time mandatory fees: $5 per quarter. Full-time mandatory fees: $29.
FINANCIAL AID *College-administered undergrad aid 1995–96:* 656 need-based scholarships (averaging $1631), 173 non-need scholarships (averaging $751), low-interest long-term loans from external sources (averaging $2625), Federal Work-Study, 67 part-time jobs. *Required forms:* institutional, FAFSA; accepted: CSS Financial Aid PROFILE, state. *Priority deadline:* 6/1. *Waivers:* full or partial for senior citizens.
APPLYING Open admission except for nursing and allied health programs. *Options:* early entrance, deferred entrance, midyear entrance. *Required:* school transcript, TOEFL for international students. *Recommended:* 3 years of high school math and science, some high school foreign language, SAT I or ACT. Test scores used for counseling/placement. *Application deadline:* rolling. *Notification:* continuous.
APPLYING/TRANSFER *Required:* high school transcript, college transcript. *Recommended:* standardized test scores, 3 years of high school math and science, some high school foreign language. *Entrance:* noncompetitive. *Application deadline:* rolling. *Notification:* continuous.
CONTACT Mr. John M. Wells, Assistant Dean of Admissions and Testing, College of The Albemarle, Elizabeth City, NC 27906-2327, 919-335-0821 Ext. 220. *Fax:* 919-335-2011.

CRAVEN COMMUNITY COLLEGE
New Bern, North Carolina

UG Enrollment: 2,254	Tuition & Fees (NC Res): $584
Application Deadline: rolling	Room & Board: N/Avail

GENERAL State-supported, 2-year, coed. Part of North Carolina Community College System. Awards transfer associate, terminal associate degrees. Founded 1965. *Setting:* 100-acre suburban campus. *Endowment:* $329,951. *Educational spending 1994–95:* $1976 per undergrad. *Total enrollment:* 2,254. *Faculty:* 211 (61 full-time, 7% with terminal degrees, 150 part-time); student-faculty ratio is 12:1.
ENROLLMENT PROFILE 2,254 students from 38 states and territories, 1 other country. 63% women, 37% men, 45% part-time, 92% state residents, 18% transferred in, 25% have need-based financial aid, 1% have non-need-based financial aid, 54% 25 or older, 1% Native American, 2% Hispanic, 25% African American, 1% Asian American. *Areas of study chosen:* 40% liberal arts/general studies, 9% business management and

administrative services, 6% engineering and applied sciences, 5% computer and information sciences, 4% education, 3% health professions and related sciences. ***Most popular recent majors:*** liberal arts/general studies, nursing, secretarial studies/office management.

FIRST-YEAR CLASS 438 total; 629 applied, 81% of whom enrolled.

ACADEMIC PROGRAM Core, interdisciplinary curriculum, honor code. Calendar: quarters. 575 courses offered in 1995–96. Academic remediation for entering students, English as a second language program offered during academic year and summer, services for LD students, advanced placement, summer session for credit, part-time degree program (daytime, evenings), adult/continuing education programs, co-op programs and internships.

GENERAL DEGREE REQUIREMENTS 96 quarter hours; 1 math course; computer course for most majors.

MAJORS Accounting, business administration/commerce/management, computer information systems, computer programming, computer technologies, criminal justice, drafting and design, early childhood education, electrical engineering technology, electronics engineering technology, heating/refrigeration/air conditioning, industrial engineering technology, legal secretarial studies, liberal arts/general studies, marketing/retailing/merchandising, medical secretarial studies, nursing, science, secretarial studies/office management, teacher aide studies.

LIBRARY R. C. Godwin Memorial Library with 26,398 books, 110 microform titles, 299 periodicals, 4 CD-ROMs, 2,025 records, tapes, and CDs. Acquisition spending 1994–95: $14,720.

COMPUTERS ON CAMPUS 350 computers for student use in computer center, computer labs, learning resource center, classrooms, library provide access to main academic computer, Internet. Staffed computer lab on campus provides training in use of computers, software. Academic computing expenditure 1994–95: $275,000.

COLLEGE LIFE Choral group. 2% vote in student government elections. ***Social organizations:*** 12 open to all. ***Most popular organizations:*** Phi Beta Lambda, Data Processing Management Association, Machinist Association, Cosmetology Club, Sign Language Club. ***Major annual events:*** Pizza Pizza, Diversity Fair, Job Fair. ***Student services:*** personal-psychological counseling. ***Campus security:*** 24-hour patrols.

HOUSING College housing not available.

ATHLETICS Member NJCAA. ***Intercollegiate:*** basketball M(s), golf M(s)/W(s), tennis M(s)/W(s). ***Contact:*** Mr. John Fonville, Dean of Students, 919-638-7222.

CAREER PLANNING ***Services:*** job fairs, resume preparation, resume referral, career counseling, job interviews. 42 organizations recruited on campus 1994–95.

EXPENSES FOR 1995–96 State resident tuition: $557 full-time, $13.25 per quarter hour part-time. Nonresident tuition: $4515 full-time, $107.50 per quarter hour part-time. Part-time mandatory fees: $9 per quarter. Full-time mandatory fees: $27.

FINANCIAL AID ***College-administered undergrad aid 1995–96:*** 177 need-based scholarships (average $942), 32 non-need scholarships (average $463), short-term loans (average $214), low-interest long-term loans from external sources, 38 Federal Work-Study, part-time jobs. ***Required forms:*** FAFSA. ***Priority deadline:*** 4/1. ***Waivers:*** full or partial for employees or children of employees and senior citizens. ***Notification:*** continuous. ***Average indebtedness of graduates:*** $1664.

APPLYING Open admission except for nursing program. ***Option:*** midyear entrance. ***Required:*** interview, TOEFL for international students, CGP, ACT ASSET. ***Recommended:*** school transcript, SAT I or ACT. Test scores used for counseling/placement. ***Application deadline:*** rolling.

APPLYING/TRANSFER ***Required:*** standardized test scores, interview, minimum 2.0 college GPA. ***Recommended:*** high school transcript. ***Required for some:*** college transcript. ***Entrance:*** noncompetitive. ***Application deadline:*** rolling. ***Contact:*** Mr. Nett Williams, Articulation Specialist, 919-638-7297.

CONTACT Ms. Millicent Fulford, Recruiter, Craven Community College, 800 College Court, New Bern, NC 28562-4984, 919-638-7232. ***Fax:*** 919-638-4232.

DAVIDSON COUNTY COMMUNITY COLLEGE
Lexington, North Carolina

UG Enrollment: 2,301	**Tuition & Fees (NC Res): $584**
Application Deadline: rolling	**Room & Board: N/Avail**

GENERAL State and locally supported, 2-year, coed. Part of North Carolina Community College System. Awards certificates, diplomas, transfer associate, terminal associate degrees. Founded 1958. ***Setting:*** 83-acre rural campus. ***Educational spending 1994–95:*** $2911 per undergrad. ***Total enrollment:*** 2,301. ***Faculty:*** 140 (66 full-time, 23% with terminal degrees, 74 part-time); student-faculty ratio is 21:1.

ENROLLMENT PROFILE 2,301 students: 62% women, 52% part-time, 99% state residents, 1% transferred in, 51% have need-based financial aid, 1% have non-need-based financial aid, 1% international, 35% 25 or older, 1% Native American, 1% Hispanic, 12% African American, 1% Asian American. ***Most popular recent majors:*** business administration/commerce/management, computer programming, liberal arts/general studies.

FIRST-YEAR CLASS 917 total; 1,401 applied, 100% were accepted, 65% of whom enrolled.

ACADEMIC PROGRAM Core. Calendar: quarters. 300 courses offered in 1995–96. Academic remediation for entering students, services for LD students, advanced placement, summer session for credit, part-time degree program (daytime, evenings), adult/continuing education programs, internships. Off-campus study at Rowan-Cabarrus Community College, Forsyth Technical Community College, Guilford Technical Community College, Rockingham Community College.

GENERAL DEGREE REQUIREMENTS 96 quarter hours; math/science requirements vary according to program.

MAJORS Accounting, business administration/commerce/management, computer programming, computer technologies, corrections, criminal justice, data processing, electrical and electronics technologies, electronics engineering technology, (pre)engineering sequence, engineering technology, fire science, law enforcement/police sciences, liberal arts/general studies, medical assistant technologies, medical laboratory technology, medical records services, nursing, paralegal studies, plastics technology, science, secretarial studies/office management.

LIBRARY Grady E. Love Learning Resource Center plus 1 other, with 53,922 books, 142 microform titles, 337 periodicals, 2 on-line bibliographic services, 6 CD-ROMs, 1,238 records, tapes, and CDs. Acquisition spending 1994–95: $83,798.

COMPUTERS ON CAMPUS Computer purchase plan available. 400 computers for student use in computer center, computer labs, learning resource center, classrooms, library. Staffed computer lab on campus provides training in use of computers, software. Academic computing expenditure 1994–95: $208,286.

COLLEGE LIFE ***Social organizations:*** 1 open to all. ***Most popular organization:*** Alpha B. ***Major annual events:*** Fall Fest, Spring Fling, G. E. Love Lecture Series. ***Campus security:*** late-night transport-escort service, security guards.

HOUSING College housing not available.

ATHLETICS ***Intramural:*** basketball, golf.

CAREER PLANNING ***Placement office:*** 1 full-time staff. ***Director:*** Mr. Joe McIntosh, Admissions and Minority Services Officer, 704-249-8186 Ext. 242. ***Services:*** resume preparation, resume referral, career counseling, careers library, job bank, job interviews. 86 organizations recruited on campus 1994–95.

AFTER GRADUATION 67% of students completing a degree program in 1994–95 went directly on to further study.

EXPENSES FOR 1995–96 State resident tuition: $557 full-time, $13.25 per quarter hour part-time. Nonresident tuition: $4515 full-time, $107.50 per quarter hour part-time. Part-time mandatory fees per quarter range from $4 to $6.50. Full-time mandatory fees: $27.

FINANCIAL AID ***College-administered undergrad aid 1995–96:*** 1,189 need-based scholarships (average $736), 8 non-need scholarships (average $708), low-interest long-term loans from external sources (average $2788), 41 Federal Work-Study (averaging $865), 58 part-time jobs. ***Required forms:*** institutional, FAFSA; accepted: CSS Financial Aid PROFILE. ***Priority deadline:*** 7/1. ***Waivers:*** full or partial for senior citizens.

APPLYING Open admission except for nursing, computer programming, allied health, electronic engineering technology, paralegal programs. ***Options:*** early entrance, deferred entrance, midyear entrance. ***Required:*** school transcript, TOEFL for international students, ACT ASSET. ***Required for some:*** campus interview. Test scores used for counseling/placement. ***Application deadline:*** rolling. ***Notification:*** continuous.

APPLYING/TRANSFER ***Required:*** standardized test scores, high school transcript, college transcript. ***Required for some:*** campus interview. ***Entrance:*** noncompetitive. ***Application deadline:*** rolling. ***Notification:*** continuous. ***Contact:*** Ms. Judith Lee Cottrell, Director of Admissions and Student Records, 704-249-8186 Ext. 234.

CONTACT Ms. Judith Lee Cottrell, Director of Admissions and Student Records, Davidson County Community College, Lexington, NC 27293-1287, 704-249-8186 Ext. 234. ***Fax:*** 704-249-0379.

DURHAM TECHNICAL COMMUNITY COLLEGE
Durham, North Carolina

UG Enrollment: 4,694	**Tuition & Fees (NC Res): $575**
Application Deadline: 8/16	**Room & Board: N/Avail**

GENERAL State-supported, 2-year, coed. Part of North Carolina Community College System. Awards certificates, diplomas, transfer associate, terminal associate degrees. Founded 1961. ***Setting:*** 20-acre urban campus. ***Total enrollment:*** 4,694. ***Faculty:*** 443 (109 full-time, 334 part-time).

ENROLLMENT PROFILE 4,694 students: 64% women, 36% men, 70% part-time, 97% state residents, 1% international, 64% 25 or older, 1% Native American, 1% Hispanic, 41% African American, 2% Asian American. ***Areas of study chosen:*** 30% health professions and related sciences, 29% liberal arts/general studies, 22% business management and administrative services, 7% engineering and applied sciences. ***Most popular recent majors:*** business administration/commerce/management, paralegal studies, nursing.

FIRST-YEAR CLASS 1,306 total; 1,826 applied, 100% were accepted, 72% of whom enrolled.

ACADEMIC PROGRAM Core. Calendar: quarters. 578 courses offered in 1995–96. Academic remediation for entering students, English as a second language program offered during academic year and summer, services for LD students, advanced placement, self-designed majors, summer session for credit, part-time degree program (daytime, evenings), adult/continuing education programs, co-op programs and internships.

GENERAL DEGREE REQUIREMENTS 96 quarter hours; 1 math/science course; computer course for most majors.

MAJORS Accounting, automotive technologies, business administration/commerce/management, carpentry, child care/child and family studies, computer programming, computer technologies, construction management, construction technologies, criminal justice, data processing, dental services, drafting and design, early childhood education, electrical and electronics technologies, electronics engineering technology, fire science, industrial administration, insurance, law enforcement/police sciences, liberal arts/general studies, machine and tool technologies, medical records services, medical secretarial studies, nursing, occupational therapy, optical technologies, paralegal studies, pharmacy/pharmaceutical sciences, practical nursing, real estate, respiratory therapy, secretarial studies/office management, word processing.

LIBRARY Educational Resources Center with 33,711 books, 442 microform titles, 349 periodicals, 4 on-line bibliographic services, 8 CD-ROMs, 1,715 records, tapes, and CDs. Acquisition spending 1994–95: $108,447.

COMPUTERS ON CAMPUS 600 computers for student use in computer labs, learning resource center, classrooms, library provide access to main academic computer. Staffed computer lab on campus provides training in use of computers, software.

COLLEGE LIFE ***Social organizations:*** 17 open to all. ***Most popular organizations:*** Phi Beta Lambda, Gamma Beta Phi, Student Senate, Student Nurses Organization, Practical Nurses Students Club. ***Major annual events:*** Campus Fund Drive and Barbecue, Native American Festival, "Pops on the Plaza" Summer Concert. ***Student services:*** personal-psychological counseling. ***Campus security:*** 24-hour patrols, late-night transport-escort service.

HOUSING College housing not available.

ATHLETICS ***Intramural:*** softball.

CAREER PLANNING ***Placement office:*** 1 full-time, 1 part-time staff; $60,000 operating expenditure 1994–95. ***Director:*** Mr. Tom Russo, Coordinator, Career Services Center, 919-686-3652. ***Services:*** job fairs, resume preparation, career counseling, careers library, job bank. 2,500 organizations recruited on campus 1994–95.

EXPENSES FOR 1995–96 State resident tuition: $557 full-time, $13.25 per quarter hour part-time. Nonresident tuition: $4515 full-time, $107.50 per quarter hour part-time. Full-time mandatory fees: $18.

Durham Technical Community College (continued)

FINANCIAL AID ***College-administered undergrad aid 1995–96:*** 438 need-based scholarships (averaging $250), short-term loans (averaging $100), 20 Federal Work-Study (averaging $1650). ***Required forms:*** FAFSA. ***Priority deadline:*** 5/1. ***Waivers:*** full or partial for employees or children of employees and senior citizens. ***Notification:*** 6/30.

APPLYING Open admission. ***Options:*** deferred entrance, midyear entrance. ***Required:*** school transcript, ACT ASSET. ***Recommended:*** interview. ***Required for some:*** essay. Test scores used for counseling/placement. ***Application deadline:*** 8/16. ***Notification:*** continuous.

APPLYING/TRANSFER ***Recommended:*** interview. ***Required for some:*** standardized test scores, high school transcript, college transcript. ***Entrance:*** noncompetitive. ***Application deadline:*** 8/16. ***Notification:*** continuous. ***Contact:*** Mr. Jerry McDaniel, Admissions Counselor, 919-686-3627.

CONTACT Dr. Jane Ellen Austin, Coordinator of Admissions, Durham Technical Community College, 1637 Lawson Street, Durham, NC 27703-5023, 919-686-3629. College video available.

EDGECOMBE COMMUNITY COLLEGE
Tarboro, North Carolina

UG Enrollment: 1,978 | **Tuition & Fees (NC Res): $568**
Application Deadline: rolling | **Room & Board: N/Avail**

GENERAL State and locally supported, 2-year, coed. Part of North Carolina Community College System. Awards certificates, diplomas, transfer associate, terminal associate degrees. Founded 1968. ***Setting:*** 90-acre small-town campus. ***Endowment:*** $650,000. ***Educational spending 1994–95:*** $4000 per undergrad. ***Total enrollment:*** 1,978. ***Faculty:*** 135 (70 full-time, 65 part-time); student-faculty ratio is 16:1.

ENROLLMENT PROFILE 1,978 students from 3 states and territories. 71% women, 29% men, 61% part-time, 99% state residents, 8% transferred in, 55% have need-based financial aid, 5% have non-need-based financial aid, 65% 25 or older, 0% Native American, 1% Hispanic, 53% African American, 0% Asian American. ***Areas of study chosen:*** 25% health professions and related sciences, 18% liberal arts/general studies, 15% social sciences, 11% business management and administrative services, 9% computer and information sciences, 6% engineering and applied sciences, 5% education. ***Most popular recent majors:*** business administration/commerce/management, nursing, radiological technology.

FIRST-YEAR CLASS 178 total; 625 applied, 83% were accepted, 34% of whom enrolled.

ACADEMIC PROGRAM Calendar: quarters. 400 courses offered in 1995–96. Academic remediation for entering students, English as a second language program offered during academic year, services for LD students, advanced placement, tutorials, summer session for credit, part-time degree program (daytime, evenings, summer), adult/continuing education programs, co-op programs. Off-campus study.

GENERAL DEGREE REQUIREMENTS 96 quarter hours; computer course.

MAJORS Accounting, business administration/commerce/management, computer programming, computer technologies, criminal justice, data processing, early childhood education, electrical and electronics technologies, engineering (general), liberal arts/general studies, mechanical design technology, mechanical engineering technology, medical assistant technologies, medical records services, medical secretarial studies, nursing, operating room technology, paralegal studies, radiological technology, real estate, respiratory therapy, science, secretarial studies/office management, social work.

LIBRARY 33,000 books, 160 periodicals, 3,000 records, tapes, and CDs. Acquisition spending 1994–95: $60,000.

COMPUTERS ON CAMPUS 135 computers for student use in computer center, computer labs, business lab, library provide access to main academic computer. Staffed computer lab on campus provides training in use of computers, software. Academic computing expenditure 1994–95: $75,000.

COLLEGE LIFE 10% vote in student government elections. ***Social organizations:*** 1 open to all. ***Most popular organizations:*** Student Government Association, Phi Theta Kappa. ***Major annual events:*** Annual Dance, Spring Fling, Halloween Festival.

HOUSING College housing not available.

ATHLETICS ***Intercollegiate:*** golf M, tennis M, volleyball M/W. ***Intramural:*** golf, softball, table tennis (Ping-Pong), tennis, volleyball. ***Contact:*** Mr. Johnny Williams, Athletic Director, 919-823-5166.

CAREER PLANNING ***Placement office:*** 2 full-time staff; $55,000 operating expenditure 1994–95. ***Director:*** Dr. Travis Martin, Career Development Counselor, 919-446-0436. ***Services:*** job fairs, resume preparation, career counseling, careers library, job bank, job interviews. 52 organizations recruited on campus 1994–95.

AFTER GRADUATION 85% of class of 1994 had job offers within 6 months. 65% of students completing a degree program went directly on to further study.

ESTIMATED EXPENSES FOR 1996–97 State resident tuition: $557 full-time, $13.25 per quarter hour part-time. Nonresident tuition: $4515 full-time, $107.50 per quarter hour part-time. Full-time mandatory fees: $11.

FINANCIAL AID ***College-administered undergrad aid 1995–96:*** 140 need-based scholarships (averaging $400), 12 non-need scholarships (averaging $500), low-interest long-term loans from college funds (averaging $800), loans from external sources, Federal Work-Study, 2 part-time jobs. ***Required forms:*** institutional, FAFSA. ***Priority deadline:*** 8/15. ***Waivers:*** full or partial for senior citizens.

APPLYING Open admission except for radiological technology, nursing, respiratory therapy, surgical technology, computer programming, business programs. ***Option:*** deferred entrance. ***Required:*** school transcript, minimum 2.0 GPA. ***Recommended:*** MAPS. ***Required for some:*** recommendations. Test scores used for counseling/placement. ***Application deadline:*** rolling. ***Notification:*** continuous.

APPLYING/TRANSFER ***Required:*** high school transcript, college transcript, minimum 2.0 college GPA, minimum 2.0 high school GPA. ***Recommended:*** standardized test scores. ***Required for some:*** recommendations. ***Entrance:*** noncompetitive. ***Application deadline:*** rolling. ***Notification:*** continuous. ***Contact:*** Mr. Michael Jordan, Coordinator of College Transfer Programs, 919-823-5166.

CONTACT Mr. Thomas B. Anderson, Vice President of Student Services, Edgecombe Community College, Tarboro, NC 27886-9399, 919-823-5166 Ext. 242. ***Fax:*** 919-823-6817. College video available.

FAYETTEVILLE TECHNICAL COMMUNITY COLLEGE
Fayetteville, North Carolina

UG Enrollment: 7,118 | **Tuition & Fees (NC Res): $569**
Application Deadline: rolling | **Room & Board: N/Avail**

GENERAL State-supported, 2-year, coed. Part of North Carolina Community College System. Awards certificates, diplomas, transfer associate, terminal associate degrees. Founded 1961. ***Setting:*** 112-acre suburban campus with easy access to Raleigh. ***Total enrollment:*** 7,118. ***Faculty:*** 736 (209 full-time, 6% with terminal degrees, 527 part-time); student-faculty ratio is 14:1. ***Notable Alumni:*** Karen Barefoot, physician; Teresa Engel, electronics engineering technician, Randall Fraley, cable communications.

ENROLLMENT PROFILE 7,118 students from 47 states and territories, 3 other countries. 58% women, 50% part-time, 72% state residents, 1% transferred in, 1% international, 58% 25 or older, 1% Native American, 5% Hispanic, 36% African American, 1% Asian American. ***Most popular recent majors:*** business administration/commerce/management, computer programming, nursing.

FIRST-YEAR CLASS 3,279 total; 12,000 applied, 99% were accepted, 28% of whom enrolled.

ACADEMIC PROGRAM Core. Calendar: quarters. Academic remediation for entering students, English as a second language program offered during academic year and summer, advanced placement, summer session for credit, part-time degree program (daytime, evenings, summer), adult/continuing education programs, co-op programs.

GENERAL DEGREE REQUIREMENTS 100 quarter hours; computer course for most majors.

MAJORS Accounting, architectural technologies, automotive technologies, business administration/commerce/management, carpentry, civil engineering technology, commercial art, computer programming, cosmetology, criminal justice, dental services, early childhood education, electronics engineering technology, finance/banking, food services management, funeral service, heating/refrigeration/air conditioning, horticulture, insurance, liberal arts/general studies, machine and tool technologies, marketing/retailing/merchandising, nursing, paralegal studies, pharmacy/pharmaceutical sciences, physical therapy, plumbing, postal management, practical nursing, public administration, radiological technology, real estate, recreation and leisure services, respiratory therapy, science education, secretarial studies/office management, welding technology.

LIBRARY 55,000 books, 4,643 microform titles, 333 periodicals, 2,422 records, tapes, and CDs.

COMPUTERS ON CAMPUS 400 computers for student use in department labs, library. Staffed computer lab on campus (open 24 hours a day) provides training in use of computers, software.

COLLEGE LIFE ***Major annual events:*** Fall Fling, Spring Fling. ***Student services:*** health clinic, personal-psychological counseling. ***Campus security:*** 24-hour emergency response devices and patrols, late-night transport-escort service, call boxes on campus.

HOUSING College housing not available.

ATHLETICS ***Intramural:*** basketball, table tennis (Ping-Pong).

CAREER PLANNING ***Placement office:*** 2 full-time staff. ***Director:*** Ms. Mary Knutson, Supervisor, Career Center, 910-678-8205. ***Services:*** career counseling, careers library.

EXPENSES FOR 1995–96 State resident tuition: $557 full-time, $13.25 per quarter hour part-time. Nonresident tuition: $4515 full-time, $107.50 per quarter hour part-time. Part-time mandatory fees: $4 per quarter. Full-time mandatory fees: $12.

FINANCIAL AID ***College-administered undergrad aid 1995–96:*** need-based scholarships, short-term loans (average $75), low-interest long-term loans from external sources, Federal Work-Study. ***Required forms:*** institutional, FAFSA. ***Priority deadline:*** 8/1. ***Waivers:*** full or partial for senior citizens.

APPLYING Open admission except for allied health programs. ***Required:*** school transcript, TOEFL for international students, ACT ASSET. Test scores used for counseling/placement. ***Application deadline:*** rolling. ***Notification:*** continuous.

APPLYING/TRANSFER ***Required:*** standardized test scores, high school transcript, college transcript. ***Application deadline:*** rolling. ***Notification:*** continuous. ***Contact:*** Mr. John Wheelous, Counselor, 910-678-8411.

CONTACT Mr. Donald W. LaHuffman, Director of Admissions, Fayetteville Technical Community College, Fayetteville, NC 28303-0236, 910-678-8274. ***Fax:*** 910-484-6600. ***E-mail:*** lahuffmd@sunmis2.faytech.cc.nc.us. College video available.

FORSYTH TECHNICAL COMMUNITY COLLEGE
Winston-Salem, North Carolina

UG Enrollment: 4,895 | **Tuition & Fees (NC Res): $572**
Application Deadline: 9/1 | **Room & Board: N/Avail**

GENERAL State-supported, 2-year, coed. Part of North Carolina Community College System. Awards certificates, diplomas, transfer associate, terminal associate degrees. Founded 1964. ***Setting:*** 38-acre suburban campus. ***Total enrollment:*** 4,895. ***Faculty:*** 535 (123 full-time, 412 part-time).

ENROLLMENT PROFILE 4,895 students from 10 states and territories. 65% women, 66% part-time, 99% state residents, 4% transferred in, 51% 25 or older, 21% African American. ***Most popular recent majors:*** business administration/commerce/management, data processing, accounting.

FIRST-YEAR CLASS 2,704 total; 4,653 applied, 75% of whom enrolled.

ACADEMIC PROGRAM Honor code. Calendar: quarters. Academic remediation for entering students, English as a second language program offered during academic year and summer, services for LD students, summer session for credit, part-time degree program (daytime, evenings), adult/continuing education programs.

GENERAL DEGREE REQUIREMENTS 98 quarter hours; computer course for technology majors; internship (some majors).

MAJORS Accounting, architectural technologies, automotive technologies, business administration/commerce/management, carpentry, child care/child and family studies, computer science, computer technologies, construction technologies, criminal justice, data processing, drafting and design, early childhood education, electrical and electronics technologies, electromechanical technology, electronics engineering technology, engineering technology, finance/banking, funeral service, graphic arts, heating/refrigeration/air

conditioning, horticulture, industrial administration, law enforcement/police sciences, machine and tool technologies, manufacturing technology, marketing/retailing/merchandising, mechanical design technology, medical assistant technologies, nuclear medical technology, nursing, ornamental horticulture, paralegal studies, plumbing, printing technologies, radiological technology, real estate, respiratory therapy, secretarial studies/office management, welding technology.
LIBRARY Forsyth Technical Community College Library plus 1 other, with 41,606 books, 82 microform titles, 358 periodicals, 3,966 records, tapes, and CDs.
COMPUTERS ON CAMPUS 450 computers for student use in computer labs, classrooms, library. Staffed computer lab on campus.
COLLEGE LIFE Student-run newspaper. 60% vote in student government elections. ***Student services:*** personal-psychological counseling. ***Campus security:*** 24-hour patrols.
HOUSING College housing not available.
ATHLETICS ***Intramural:*** basketball, bowling, volleyball.
CAREER PLANNING ***Director:*** Mr. Ben Howell, Director of Counseling, 910-723-0371 Ext. 239. ***Services:*** career counseling, careers library.
EXPENSES FOR 1995–96 State resident tuition: $557 full-time, $13.25 per quarter hour part-time. Nonresident tuition: $4515 full-time, $107.50 per quarter hour part-time. Part-time mandatory fees: $5 per quarter. Full-time mandatory fees: $15.
FINANCIAL AID ***College-administered undergrad aid 1995–96:*** 521 need-based scholarships (average $400), 127 non-need scholarships (average $225), short-term loans (average $125), low-interest long-term loans from college funds (average $1000), loans from external sources (average $1000), Federal Work-Study, 106 part-time jobs. ***Required forms:*** institutional, FAFSA; accepted: CSS Financial Aid PROFILE. ***Priority deadline:*** 5/1. ***Waivers:*** full or partial for senior citizens.
APPLYING Open admission except for allied health, engineering technology programs. ***Required:*** school transcript, Assessment and Placement Services for Community Colleges. ***Recommended:*** SAT I or ACT. Test scores used for counseling/placement. ***Application deadline:*** 9/1. ***Notification:*** continuous until 9/8.
APPLYING/TRANSFER ***Required:*** high school transcript, college transcript. ***Recommended:*** standardized test scores. ***Entrance:*** noncompetitive. ***Application deadline:*** 9/1. ***Notification:*** continuous until 9/8. ***Contact:*** Ms. Sandra Suggs, Transfer Counselor, 910-723-0371 Ext. 254.
CONTACT Mr. George McLendon, Director of Admissions, Forsyth Technical Community College, Winston-Salem, NC 27103-5197, 910-723-0371 Ext. 260. College video available.

GASTON COLLEGE
Dallas, North Carolina

UG Enrollment: 4,046 | **Tuition & Fees (NC Res): $569**
Application Deadline: rolling | **Room & Board: N/Avail**

GENERAL State and locally supported, 2-year, coed. Part of North Carolina Community College System. Awards certificates, diplomas, transfer associate, terminal associate degrees. Founded 1963. ***Setting:*** 166-acre small-town campus with easy access to Charlotte. ***Total enrollment:*** 4,046. ***Faculty:*** 370 (113 full-time, 99% with terminal degrees, 257 part-time).
ENROLLMENT PROFILE 4,046 students from 10 states and territories. 60% women, 53% part-time, 99% state residents, 2% transferred in, 72% have need-based financial aid, 8% have non-need-based financial aid, 0% international, 55% 25 or older, 0% Native American, 1% Hispanic, 10% African American, 1% Asian American. ***Areas of study chosen:*** 40% liberal arts/general studies, 17% business management and administrative services, 17% health professions and related sciences, 12% vocational and home economics, 8% engineering and applied sciences, 6% computer and information sciences, 4% biological and life sciences, 2% education, 1% architecture, 1% communications and journalism, 1% fine arts, 1% prevet.
FIRST-YEAR CLASS 772 total; 1,169 applied, 100% were accepted, 66% of whom enrolled. 5% from top 10% of their high school class, 39% from top quarter, 51% from top half.
ACADEMIC PROGRAM Core, honor code. Calendar: quarters. 350 courses offered in 1995–96. Academic remediation for entering students, English as a second language program offered during academic year, services for LD students, advanced placement, summer session for credit, part-time degree program (daytime, evenings, summer), adult/continuing education programs, co-op programs. Off-campus study at 10 members of the Charlotte Area Educational Consortium. Study abroad in 40 countries.
GENERAL DEGREE REQUIREMENTS 101 credit hours; computer course for business, engineering technology majors; internship (some majors).
MAJORS Accounting, architectural technologies, art/fine arts, automotive technologies, broadcasting, business administration/commerce/management, child care/child and family studies, civil engineering technology, computer programming, criminal justice, drafting and design, early childhood education, electronics engineering technology, emergency medical technology, (pre)engineering sequence, fire science, industrial administration, industrial engineering technology, legal secretarial studies, liberal arts/general studies, marketing/retailing/merchandising, mechanical engineering technology, medical assistant technologies, nursing, radio and television studies, secretarial studies/office management, social work, welding technology.
LIBRARY Gaston College Library with 42,927 books, 37,199 microform titles, 218 periodicals, 10 CD-ROMs, 2,992 records, tapes, and CDs. Acquisition spending 1994–95: $110,307.
COMPUTERS ON CAMPUS Computer purchase plan available. 250 computers for student use in computer center, computer labs, learning resource center, classroom buildings, classrooms, library provide access to main academic computer. Staffed computer lab on campus provides training in use of computers, software.
COLLEGE LIFE Drama-theater group, choral group, student-run radio station. ***Social organizations:*** 15 open to all. ***Most popular organization:*** Student Government Association. ***Major annual events:*** Fall Week, Spring Week. ***Campus security:*** 24-hour patrols.
HOUSING College housing not available.
CAREER PLANNING ***Placement office:*** 5 full-time staff; $329,100 operating expenditure 1994–95. ***Director:*** Dr. Dale Gunter, Director, Enrollment Management, 704-922-6220. ***Services:*** job fairs, resume preparation, resume referral, career counseling, careers library, job bank. 64 organizations recruited on campus 1994–95.
AFTER GRADUATION 67% of class of 1994 had job offers within 6 months. 28% of students completing a degree program went directly on to further study.
EXPENSES FOR 1995–96 State resident tuition: $557 full-time, $13.25 per credit hour part-time. Nonresident tuition: $4515 full-time, $107.50 per credit hour part-time. Full-time mandatory fees: $12.
FINANCIAL AID ***College-administered undergrad aid 1995–96:*** 438 need-based scholarships (average $400), 225 non-need scholarships (average $200), low-interest long-term loans from external sources (average $2300), Federal Work-Study, 900 part-time jobs. ***Required forms:*** institutional; accepted: CSS Financial Aid PROFILE, state, FAFSA. ***Priority deadline:*** 3/15. ***Payment plan:*** deferred payment. ***Waivers:*** full or partial for employees or children of employees and senior citizens. ***Average indebtedness of graduates:*** $1500.
APPLYING Open admission except for nursing, allied health programs. ***Option:*** midyear entrance. ***Required:*** ACT ASSET. ***Required for some:*** school transcript, ACT, TOEFL for international students. Test scores used for counseling/placement. ***Application deadline:*** rolling. ***Notification:*** continuous.
APPLYING/TRANSFER ***Required:*** college transcript. ***Application deadline:*** rolling. ***Notification:*** continuous. ***Contact:*** Dr. Dale Gunter, Director of Enrollment Management, 704-922-6219.
CONTACT Mrs. Alice Hopper, Admissions Specialist, Gaston College, Dallas, NC 28034-1499, 704-922-6214. College video available.

GUILFORD TECHNICAL COMMUNITY COLLEGE
Jamestown, North Carolina

UG Enrollment: 6,647 | **Tuition & Fees (NC Res): $585**
Application Deadline: rolling | **Room & Board: N/Avail**

GENERAL State and locally supported, 2-year, coed. Part of North Carolina Community College System. Awards certificates, diplomas, transfer associate, terminal associate degrees. Founded 1958. ***Setting:*** 158-acre suburban campus. ***Total enrollment:*** 6,647. ***Faculty:*** 385 (185 full-time, 8% with terminal degrees, 200 part-time); student-faculty ratio is 18:1.
ENROLLMENT PROFILE 6,647 students from 16 states and territories, 17 other countries. 54% women, 64% part-time, 98% state residents, 16% transferred in, 1% international, 44% 25 or older, 1% Native American, 1% Hispanic, 19% African American. ***Most popular recent majors:*** nursing, dental services, commercial art.
FIRST-YEAR CLASS 2,684 total; 5,500 applied, 100% were accepted, 49% of whom enrolled.
ACADEMIC PROGRAM Core. Calendar: quarters. Academic remediation for entering students, English as a second language program, advanced placement, self-designed majors, summer session for credit, part-time degree program (daytime, evenings), adult/continuing education programs, co-op programs. Off-campus study at members of the Greater Greensboro Consortium. ROTC: Army (c), Air Force (c).
GENERAL DEGREE REQUIREMENTS 96 quarter hours; math/science requirements vary according to program; computer course for most majors.
MAJORS Accounting, aircraft and missile maintenance, architectural technologies, automotive technologies, aviation administration, aviation technology, business administration/commerce/management, child care/child and family studies, civil engineering technology, commercial art, computer information systems, computer programming, consumer services, corrections, criminal justice, culinary arts, dental services, drafting and design, early childhood education, electrical and electronics technologies, electronics engineering technology, emergency medical technology, fire science, flight training, food services management, industrial administration, industrial and heavy equipment maintenance, law enforcement/police sciences, liberal arts/general studies, marketing/retailing/merchandising, medical assistant technologies, medical secretarial studies, nursing, paralegal studies, science, secretarial studies/office management, surveying technology, theater arts/drama, vocational education.
LIBRARY 55,664 books, 256 microform titles, 484 periodicals, 8,493 records, tapes, and CDs.
COMPUTERS ON CAMPUS 200 computers for student use in computer center, classroom labs, library provide access to main academic computer, off-campus computing facilities, on-line services. Staffed computer lab on campus.
COLLEGE LIFE Drama-theater group, student-run newspaper.
HOUSING College housing not available.
CAREER PLANNING ***Service:*** career counseling.
AFTER GRADUATION 50% of students completing a degree program in 1994–95 went directly on to further study.
EXPENSES FOR 1995–96 State resident tuition: $557 full-time, $13.25 per quarter hour part-time. Nonresident tuition: $4494 full-time, $107.25 per quarter hour part-time. Part-time mandatory fees: $6.25 per quarter. Full-time mandatory fees: $28.
FINANCIAL AID ***College-administered undergrad aid 1995–96:*** 29 need-based scholarships (average $400), 17 non-need scholarships (average $200), low-interest long-term loans from external sources (average $2000), Federal Work-Study, 70 part-time jobs. ***Required forms:*** institutional; accepted: CSS Financial Aid PROFILE. ***Priority deadline:*** 7/1. ***Waivers:*** full or partial for employees or children of employees and senior citizens.
APPLYING Open admission except for health-related, aviation maintenance programs. ***Options:*** early entrance, deferred entrance. ***Required:*** school transcript, ACT ASSET. ***Required for some:*** campus interview, TOEFL for international students. Test scores used for counseling/placement. ***Application deadline:*** rolling. ***Notification:*** continuous.
APPLYING/TRANSFER ***Required:*** high school transcript, college transcript. ***Required for some:*** standardized test scores, campus interview. ***Entrance:*** noncompetitive. ***Application deadline:*** rolling. ***Notification:*** continuous.
CONTACT Mr. Herbert Curkin, Director of Admissions, Guilford Technical Community College, Jamestown, NC 27282-0309, 910-334-4822 Ext. 2338.

HALIFAX COMMUNITY COLLEGE
Weldon, North Carolina

UG Enrollment: 1,360 | **Tuition & Fees (NC Res): $572**
Application Deadline: rolling | **Room & Board: N/Avail**

Halifax Community College (continued)

GENERAL State and locally supported, 2-year, coed. Part of North Carolina Community College System. Awards certificates, diplomas, transfer associate degrees. Founded 1967. ***Setting:*** 109-acre rural campus. ***Total enrollment:*** 1,360. ***Faculty:*** 68 (39 full-time, 29 part-time); student-faculty ratio is 25:1.

ENROLLMENT PROFILE 1,360 students from 2 states and territories. 60% women, 46% part-time, 97% state residents, 11% transferred in, 1% Native American, 0% Hispanic, 44% African American, 0% Asian American.

FIRST-YEAR CLASS 437 total; 680 applied, 100% were accepted, 64% of whom enrolled.

ACADEMIC PROGRAM Core. Calendar: quarters. Academic remediation for entering students, summer session for credit, part-time degree program (daytime, evenings, summer), adult/continuing education programs, co-op programs.

GENERAL DEGREE REQUIREMENTS 96 quarter hours; math/science requirements vary according to program.

MAJORS Art education, business administration/commerce/management, business education, commercial art, corrections, education, industrial engineering technology, interior design, law enforcement/police sciences, liberal arts/general studies, marketing/retailing/merchandising, medical laboratory technology, medical secretarial studies, nursing, secretarial studies/office management, social work.

LIBRARY Halifax Community College Library with 26,527 books, 113 microform titles, 122 periodicals, 2,137 records, tapes, and CDs.

COMPUTERS ON CAMPUS 100 computers for student use in computer center. Staffed computer lab on campus.

COLLEGE LIFE Student-run newspaper. ***Campus security:*** 12-hour patrols by trained security personnel.

HOUSING College housing not available.

CAREER PLANNING ***Placement office:*** 2 full-time staff. ***Director:*** Ms. Emily Holmes, Counselor, 919-536-7207. ***Service:*** career counseling.

EXPENSES FOR 1995–96 State resident tuition: $557 full-time, $13.25 per quarter hour part-time. Nonresident tuition: $4515 full-time, $107.50 per quarter hour part-time. Part-time mandatory fees: $5 per quarter. Full-time mandatory fees: $15.

FINANCIAL AID ***College-administered undergrad aid 1995–96:*** 60 need-based scholarships (average $75), 45 non-need scholarships (average $50), short-term loans (average $50), low-interest long-term loans from college funds (average $75), Federal Work-Study, part-time jobs. ***Required forms:*** state, institutional, FAFSA; accepted: CSS Financial Aid PROFILE. ***Priority deadline:*** 6/30.

APPLYING Open admission. ***Option:*** deferred entrance. ***Required:*** school transcript. ***Application deadline:*** rolling. ***Notification:*** continuous.

APPLYING/TRANSFER ***Required:*** college transcript. ***Required for some:*** high school transcript. ***Entrance:*** noncompetitive. ***Application deadline:*** rolling. ***Notification:*** continuous. ***Contact:*** Ms. Kim Robinson Faison, Counselor, 919-536-7296.

CONTACT Mrs. Scottie Dickens, Director of Admissions, Halifax Community College, Weldon, NC 27890-0809, 919-536-2551 Ext. 220. College video available.

HAYWOOD COMMUNITY COLLEGE
Clyde, North Carolina

UG Enrollment: 1,322	**Tuition & Fees (NC Res): $577**
Application Deadline: rolling	**Room & Board: N/Avail**

GENERAL State and locally supported, 2-year, coed. Part of North Carolina Community College System. Awards certificates, diplomas, transfer associate, terminal associate degrees. Founded 1964. ***Setting:*** 85-acre rural campus. ***Educational spending 1994–95:*** $3100 per undergrad. ***Total enrollment:*** 1,322. ***Faculty:*** 118 (57 full-time, 3% with terminal degrees, 61 part-time).

ENROLLMENT PROFILE 1,322 students from 20 states and territories. 52% women, 48% men, 47% part-time, 96% state residents, 8% transferred in, 20% have need-based financial aid, 18% have non-need-based financial aid, 0% international, 45% 25 or older, 1% Native American, 1% Hispanic, 1% African American, 1% Asian American. ***Areas of study chosen:*** 18% liberal arts/general studies, 13% natural resource sciences, 11% engineering and applied sciences, 10% business management and administrative services, 10% vocational and home economics, 6% health professions and related sciences, 5% fine arts, 3% computer and information sciences, 3% social sciences. ***Most popular recent majors:*** liberal arts/general studies, business administration/commerce/management, fish and game management.

FIRST-YEAR CLASS 442 total; 720 applied, 81% were accepted, 76% of whom enrolled.

ACADEMIC PROGRAM Honor code. Calendar: quarters. 630 courses offered in 1995–96. Academic remediation for entering students, English as a second language program offered during academic year, services for LD students, advanced placement, part-time degree program (daytime, evenings), adult/continuing education programs, co-op programs and internships.

GENERAL DEGREE REQUIREMENTS 96 quarter hours; 1 math course; computer course for all associate degree programs; internship (some majors).

MAJORS Automotive technologies, business administration/commerce/management, ceramic art and design, computer technologies, cosmetology, criminal justice, electronics engineering technology, fish and game management, forest technology, horticulture, jewelry and metalsmithing, liberal arts/general studies, machine and tool technologies, manufacturing technology, medical assistant technologies, nursing, plumbing, real estate, secretarial studies/office management, textile arts, welding technology, wildlife management, wood sciences.

LIBRARY Freedlander Learning Resource Center with 26,788 books, 120 microform titles, 167 periodicals, 97 CD-ROMs, 485 records, tapes, and CDs. Acquisition spending 1994–95: $114,580.

COMPUTERS ON CAMPUS 7 computers for student use in library provide access to word processing.

COLLEGE LIFE 20% vote in student government elections. ***Social organizations:*** 10 open to all. ***Most popular organizations:*** Student Government Association, Phi Theta Kappa, Phi Beta Lambda, Outdoors Club, Cosmetology Club. ***Major annual event:*** Ski Day. ***Student services:*** personal-psychological counseling. ***Campus security:*** 24-hour patrols.

HOUSING College housing not available.

ATHLETICS ***Intramural:*** basketball, bowling, football, softball, volleyball.

CAREER PLANNING ***Placement office:*** 1 full-time, 1 part-time staff; $42,000 operating expenditure 1994–95. ***Director:*** Ms. Sherry Thompson, Career Counselor, 704-627-4504. ***Services:*** resume preparation, career counseling, careers library.

EXPENSES FOR 1995–96 State resident tuition: $557 full-time, $13.25 per quarter hour part-time. Nonresident tuition: $4515 full-time, $107.50 per quarter hour part-time. Full-time mandatory fees: $20.

FINANCIAL AID ***College-administered undergrad aid 1995–96:*** 61 need-based scholarships (average $496), non-need scholarships, short-term loans (average $176), low-interest long-term loans from external sources (average $1925), 20 Federal Work-Study (averaging $1800), 100 part-time jobs. ***Required forms:*** institutional, FAFSA; accepted: CSS Financial Aid PROFILE. ***Priority deadline:*** 4/1. ***Waivers:*** full or partial for employees or children of employees and senior citizens. ***Notification:*** 7/15.

APPLYING Open admission except for nursing, some technical programs. ***Option:*** midyear entrance. ***Required:*** school transcript, Assessment and Placement Services for Community Colleges. Test scores used for admission (for nursing, some technical programs) and counseling/placement. ***Application deadline:*** rolling.

APPLYING/TRANSFER ***Required:*** high school transcript, college transcript. ***Entrance:*** noncompetitive. ***Application deadline:*** rolling. ***Contact:*** Ms. Carol Smith, Director of Enrollment Management, 704-627-4505.

CONTACT Ms. Carol Smith, Director of Enrollment Management, Haywood Community College, Clyde, NC 28721-9453, 704-627-4505. ***Fax:*** 704-627-3606. ***E-mail:*** csmith@daystrom.haywood.cc.nc.us. College video available.

ISOTHERMAL COMMUNITY COLLEGE
Spindale, North Carolina

UG Enrollment: 1,747	**Tuition & Fees (NC Res): $664**
Application Deadline: rolling	**Room & Board: N/Avail**

GENERAL State-supported, 2-year, coed. Part of North Carolina Community College System. Awards certificates, diplomas, transfer associate, terminal associate degrees. Founded 1965. ***Setting:*** 120-acre rural campus. ***Total enrollment:*** 1,747. ***Faculty:*** 92 (51 full-time, 41 part-time).

ENROLLMENT PROFILE 1,747 students: 60% women, 75% part-time, 98% state residents, 4% transferred in, 1% international, 49% 25 or older, 0% Native American, 0% Hispanic, 9% African American.

FIRST-YEAR CLASS 443 total; 953 applied, 100% were accepted, 46% of whom enrolled.

ACADEMIC PROGRAM Core. Calendar: quarters. Academic remediation for entering students, English as a second language program offered during academic year and summer, services for LD students, advanced placement, self-designed majors, honors program, summer session for credit, part-time degree program (daytime, evenings, summer), external degree programs, adult/continuing education programs, co-op programs.

GENERAL DEGREE REQUIREMENTS 96 quarter hours; math requirement varies according to program; computer course.

MAJORS Automotive technologies, broadcasting, business administration/commerce/management, business education, commercial art, computer programming, computer science, cosmetology, criminal justice, drafting and design, early childhood education, education, electrical and electronics technologies, electrical engineering technology, electronics engineering technology, elementary education, (pre)engineering sequence, graphic arts, insurance, law enforcement/police sciences, liberal arts/general studies, machine and tool technologies, marketing/retailing/merchandising, mechanical design technology, mechanical engineering technology, music, pharmacy/pharmaceutical sciences, practical nursing, radio and television studies, real estate, science, secretarial studies/office management, teacher aide studies, veterinary sciences, vocational education, welding technology.

LIBRARY 35,200 books, 2,333 microform titles, 289 periodicals, 3,635 records, tapes, and CDs.

COLLEGE LIFE Orientation program (2 days). Student-run newspaper, radio station. ***Student services:*** personal-psychological counseling.

HOUSING College housing not available.

ATHLETICS ***Intramural:*** basketball, football, golf, swimming and diving, tennis, volleyball.

CAREER PLANNING ***Service:*** career counseling.

EXPENSES FOR 1995–96 State resident tuition: $636 full-time, $13.25 per quarter hour part-time. Nonresident tuition: $5160 full-time, $107.50 per quarter hour part-time. Part-time mandatory fees: $28 per year. Full-time mandatory fees: $28.

FINANCIAL AID ***College-administered undergrad aid 1995–96:*** need-based scholarships, short-term loans, Federal Work-Study, part-time jobs. ***Required forms:*** FAFSA; accepted: CSS Financial Aid PROFILE. ***Application deadline:*** continuous.

APPLYING Open admission. ***Options:*** early entrance, deferred entrance. ***Required:*** school transcript, TOEFL for international students, ACT ASSET. Test scores used for counseling/placement. ***Application deadline:*** rolling. ***Notification:*** continuous.

APPLYING/TRANSFER ***Required:*** college transcript. ***Application deadline:*** rolling. ***Notification:*** continuous.

CONTACT Ms. Betty Gabriel, Director of Counseling, Isothermal Community College, Spindale, NC 28160-0804, 704-286-3636 Ext. 243.

JAMES SPRUNT COMMUNITY COLLEGE
Kenansville, North Carolina

UG Enrollment: 1,021	**Tuition & Fees (NC Res): $581**
Application Deadline: rolling	**Room & Board: N/Avail**

GENERAL State-supported, 2-year, coed. Part of North Carolina Community College System. Awards certificates, diplomas, transfer associate, terminal associate degrees. Founded 1964. ***Setting:*** 51-acre rural campus. ***Endowment:*** $15,856. ***Total enrollment:*** 1,021. ***Faculty:*** 77 (43 full-time, 34 part-time); student-faculty ratio is 15:1.

ENROLLMENT PROFILE 1,021 students from 5 states and territories. 67% women, 33% men, 48% part-time, 99% state residents, 28% transferred in, 0% international, 56% 25 or older, 0% Native American, 1% Hispanic, 33% African American, 0% Asian American. ***Areas of study chosen:*** 14% health professions and related sciences, 11% liberal arts/general studies, 9% business management and administrative services, 4% agriculture, 4% computer and information sciences, 3% education. ***Most popular recent majors:*** nursing, liberal arts/general studies, business administration/commerce/management.

FIRST-YEAR CLASS 366 total; 556 applied, 89% were accepted, 74% of whom enrolled. 5% from top 10% of their high school class, 22% from top quarter, 40% from top half.

ACADEMIC PROGRAM Core, honor code. Calendar: quarters. 437 courses offered in 1995–96. Academic remediation for entering students, English as a second language program offered during academic year and summer, advanced placement, summer session for credit, part-time degree program (daytime, evenings), adult/continuing education programs, internships.
GENERAL DEGREE REQUIREMENTS 96 quarter hours; 1 math course; computer course.
MAJORS Accounting, agricultural business, animal sciences, business administration/commerce/management, business education, commercial art, computer technologies, criminal justice, early childhood education, education, elementary education, liberal arts/general studies, medical assistant technologies, medical records services, nursing, science, secretarial studies/office management.
LIBRARY James Sprunt Community College Library with 19,000 books, 42 microform titles, 231 periodicals, 12 CD-ROMs, 1,245 records, tapes, and CDs. Acquisition spending 1994–95: $32,923.
COMPUTERS ON CAMPUS 100 computers for student use in computer center, computer labs, Academic Support Center, classrooms, library, student center. Staffed computer lab on campus provides training in use of computers, software.
COLLEGE LIFE Student-run newspaper. ***Social organizations:*** 3 open to all. ***Most popular organizations:*** Student Nurses Association, Art Club, Alumni Association, National Technical-Vocational Honor Society. ***Major annual events:*** Christmas Dance/Coronation, Activity Day, Halloween Day. ***Campus security:*** trained security personnel.
HOUSING College housing not available.
ATHLETICS ***Intercollegiate:*** softball W. ***Contact:*** Ms. Sonya Smith, Director of Student Activities, 910-296-2508.
CAREER PLANNING ***Placement office:*** 1 part-time staff. ***Director:*** Ms. Sonya Smith, Career Placement Officer, 910-296-2508. ***Services:*** job fairs, resume preparation, resume referral, career counseling, careers library, job bank, job interviews.
AFTER GRADUATION 90% of students completing a degree program in 1994–95 went directly on to further study.
EXPENSES FOR 1995–96 State resident tuition: $557 full-time, $13.25 per quarter hour part-time. Nonresident tuition: $4515 full-time, $107.50 per quarter hour part-time. Part-time mandatory fees per quarter range from $4 to $8. Full-time mandatory fees: $24.
FINANCIAL AID ***College-administered undergrad aid 1995–96:*** 77 need-based scholarships (average $500), 72 non-need scholarships (average $449), short-term loans (average $150), low-interest long-term loans from external sources (average $2000), Federal Work-Study (averaging $1400), 10 part-time jobs. ***Required forms:*** institutional, FAFSA. ***Priority deadline:*** 7/1. ***Waivers:*** full or partial for employees or children of employees and senior citizens.
APPLYING Open admission except for allied health programs. ***Options:*** early entrance, deferred entrance. ***Required:*** school transcript, TOEFL for international students, Assessment and Placement Services for Community Colleges. Test scores used for counseling/placement. ***Application deadline:*** rolling. ***Notification:*** continuous.
APPLYING/TRANSFER ***Required:*** high school transcript, college transcript. ***Required for some:*** standardized test scores. ***Application deadline:*** rolling. ***Notification:*** continuous. ***Contact:*** Mrs. Rita B. Brown, Director of Admissions and Records, 910-296-2500.
CONTACT Mrs. Rita B. Brown, Director of Admissions and Records, James Sprunt Community College, Kenansville, NC 28349-0398, 910-296-2500. ***Fax:*** 910-296-1636. College video available.

JOHNSTON COMMUNITY COLLEGE
Smithfield, North Carolina

UG Enrollment: 2,655	**Tuition & Fees (NC Res): $578**
Application Deadline: rolling	**Room & Board: N/Avail**

GENERAL State-supported, 2-year, coed. Part of North Carolina Community College System. Awards certificates, diplomas, transfer associate, terminal associate degrees. Founded 1969. ***Setting:*** 100-acre rural campus. ***Total enrollment:*** 2,655. ***Faculty:*** 269 (118 full-time, 151 part-time).
ENROLLMENT PROFILE 2,655 students from 7 states and territories. 57% women, 43% men, 48% part-time, 99% state residents, 10% transferred in, 46% 25 or older, 1% Native American, 1% Hispanic, 21% African American. ***Areas of study chosen:*** 38% business management and administrative services, 37% liberal arts/general studies, 37% library and information studies, 7% health professions and related sciences, 6% computer and information sciences, 5% fine arts, 4% vocational and home economics, 2% engineering and applied sciences. ***Most popular recent majors:*** business administration/commerce/management, computer programming, accounting.
FIRST-YEAR CLASS 1,096 total; 1,803 applied, 73% of whom enrolled.
ACADEMIC PROGRAM Calendar: quarters. Academic remediation for entering students, services for LD students, advanced placement, summer session for credit, part-time degree program (daytime, evenings), adult/continuing education programs.
GENERAL DEGREE REQUIREMENTS 96 quarter hours; 1 math course; computer course for accounting, business, electronics, secretarial majors.
MAJORS Accounting, business administration/commerce/management, child care/child and family studies, commercial art, computer programming, early childhood education, electronics engineering technology, industrial administration, law enforcement/police sciences, liberal arts/general studies, medical secretarial studies, nursing, paralegal studies, radiological technology, secretarial studies/office management.
LIBRARY Johnston Community College Library plus 1 other, with 25,115 books, 156 microform titles, 348 periodicals, 17 CD-ROMs, 806 records, tapes, and CDs. Acquisition spending 1994–95: $250,229.
COMPUTERS ON CAMPUS 186 computers for student use in computer center, labs. Academic computing expenditure 1994–95: $175,000.
COLLEGE LIFE ***Student services:*** personal-psychological counseling. ***Campus security:*** 24-hour patrols.
HOUSING College housing not available.
ATHLETICS ***Intercollegiate:*** golf M/W, softball W, volleyball M/W. ***Intramural:*** basketball. ***Contact:*** Mr. Gregory Thompson, Activity Director, 919-934-3051.
CAREER PLANNING ***Service:*** career counseling.
EXPENSES FOR 1995–96 State resident tuition: $557 full-time, $13.25 per quarter hour part-time. Nonresident tuition: $4515 full-time, $107.50 per quarter hour part-time. Full-time mandatory fees: $21.
FINANCIAL AID ***College-administered undergrad aid 1995–96:*** 116 need-based scholarships (averaging $550), 121 non-need scholarships (averaging $578), short-term loans (averaging $151), low-interest long-term loans from external sources (averaging $2013), 16 Federal Work-Study (averaging $2103), 2 part-time jobs. ***Required forms:*** FAFSA; required for some: state, institutional; accepted: CSS Financial Aid PROFILE. ***Priority deadline:*** 6/30.
APPLYING Open admission except for nursing, radiological technology programs. ***Option:*** early entrance. ***Required:*** school transcript. ***Required for some:*** CGP. Test scores used for counseling/placement. ***Application deadline:*** rolling. ***Notification:*** continuous.
APPLYING/TRANSFER ***Entrance:*** noncompetitive. ***Application deadline:*** rolling. ***Notification:*** continuous.
CONTACT Mr. James H. O'Neal Jr., Director of Admissions and Records, Johnston Community College, PO Box 2350, Smithfield, NC 27577-2350, 919-934-3051 Ext. 229. ***Fax:*** 919-934-2823.

LENOIR COMMUNITY COLLEGE
Kinston, North Carolina

UG Enrollment: 2,069	**Tuition & Fees (NC Res): $584**
Application Deadline: rolling	**Room & Board: N/Avail**

GENERAL State-supported, 2-year, coed. Part of North Carolina Community College System. Awards certificates, diplomas, transfer associate, terminal associate degrees. Founded 1960. ***Setting:*** 86-acre small-town campus. ***Total enrollment:*** 2,069. ***Faculty:*** 163 (80 full-time, 83 part-time). ***Notable Alumni:*** Michael Moye, television network writer; Dr. Lonnie Blizzard, president of Lenoir Community College; Dr. Young D. T. Nguyen, mechanical engineer; Paul Jones, aeroservice flight instructor; Dr. Paul Stroud, pharmacist.
ENROLLMENT PROFILE 2,069 students: 57% women, 47% part-time, 99% state residents, 21% transferred in, 1% international, 0% Native American, 1% Hispanic, 30% African American, 1% Asian American. ***Most popular recent majors:*** liberal arts/general studies, nursing, business administration/commerce/management.
FIRST-YEAR CLASS 957 total; 1,640 applied, 86% were accepted, 68% of whom enrolled.
ACADEMIC PROGRAM Core, honor code. Calendar: quarters. Academic remediation for entering students, English as a second language program offered during academic year, advanced placement, summer session for credit, part-time degree program (daytime, evenings, summer), adult/continuing education programs, co-op programs.
GENERAL DEGREE REQUIREMENTS 96 quarter hours; math/science requirements vary according to program; computer course.
MAJORS Accounting, agricultural business, agricultural sciences, art/fine arts, aviation administration, aviation technology, business administration/commerce/management, computer programming, cosmetology, court reporting, criminal justice, drafting and design, electrical and electronics technologies, electronics engineering technology, elementary education, (pre)engineering sequence, finance/banking, fire science, flight training, food services technology, graphic arts, horticulture, industrial administration, industrial and heavy equipment maintenance, industrial engineering technology, instrumentation technology, insurance, landscape architecture/design, law enforcement/police sciences, legal secretarial studies, liberal arts/general studies, library science, marketing/retailing/merchandising, mechanical design technology, medical assistant technologies, medical secretarial studies, mental health/rehabilitation counseling, nursing, ornamental horticulture, postal management, printing technologies, retail management, secretarial studies/office management, vocational education, welding technology.
LIBRARY Learning Resources Center plus 1 other, with 55,053 books, 10,533 microform titles, 381 periodicals, 1,850 records, tapes, and CDs.
COMPUTERS ON CAMPUS Computer purchase plan available. 116 computers for student use in computer center, library. Staffed computer lab on campus provides training in use of computers, software.
COLLEGE LIFE Choral group, student-run newspaper. 15% vote in student government elections. ***Social organizations:*** 19 open to all. ***Most popular organizations:*** Student Government Association, Automotive Club, Electronics Club, Drafting Club, Cosmetology Club. ***Major annual events:*** Fall Festival, Spring Joust, Fall Get-Together. ***Student services:*** personal-psychological counseling. ***Campus security:*** 24-hour emergency response devices and patrols, student patrols.
HOUSING College housing not available.
ATHLETICS Member NJCAA. ***Intercollegiate:*** baseball M, basketball M(s), golf M(s)/W(s), softball W. ***Intramural:*** basketball, softball, volleyball. ***Contact:*** Mr. Pete Barnes, Athletics Director, 919-527-6223 Ext. 200; Ms. Sue Smith, College Union Staff Assistant, 919-527-6233 Ext. 209.
CAREER PLANNING ***Director:*** Ms. Joan Callaway, Director of Counseling, 919-527-6223 Ext. 369. ***Services:*** job fairs, career counseling, job bank.
EXPENSES FOR 1995–96 State resident tuition: $557 full-time, $13.50 per quarter hour part-time. Nonresident tuition: $4515 full-time, $107.50 per quarter hour part-time. Part-time mandatory fees: $5 per quarter. Full-time mandatory fees: $27.
FINANCIAL AID ***College-administered undergrad aid 1995–96:*** 486 need-based scholarships (averaging $1006), 167 non-need scholarships (averaging $360), short-term loans (averaging $100), Federal Work-Study, 121 part-time jobs. ***Required forms:*** CSS Financial Aid PROFILE. ***Priority deadline:*** 4/30. ***Waivers:*** full or partial for employees or children of employees and senior citizens.
APPLYING Open admission except for allied health programs. ***Option:*** early entrance. ***Required:*** school transcript, TOEFL for international students, Assessment and Placement Services for Community Colleges. ***Recommended:*** 3 years of high school math and science, SAT I or ACT. Test scores used for counseling/placement. ***Application deadline:*** rolling. ***Notification:*** continuous.
APPLYING/TRANSFER ***Required:*** college transcript. ***Recommended:*** minimum 2.0 college GPA. ***Application deadline:*** rolling. ***Notification:*** continuous.
CONTACT Mr. Mark Hollar, Director of Admissions, Lenoir Community College, Kinston, NC 28501, 919-527-6223 Ext. 309.

LOUISBURG COLLEGE
Louisburg, North Carolina

UG Enrollment: 560	**Tuition & Fees: $7530**
Application Deadline: rolling	**Room & Board: $3815**

Peterson's Guide to Two-Year Colleges 1997

499

Louisburg College (continued)

GENERAL Independent United Methodist, 2-year, coed. Awards transfer associate, terminal associate degrees. Founded 1787. ***Setting:*** 75-acre small-town campus with easy access to Raleigh. ***Total enrollment:*** 560. ***Faculty:*** 42 (37 full-time, 20% with terminal degrees, 5 part-time); student-faculty ratio is 12:1.

ENROLLMENT PROFILE 560 students from 17 states and territories, 4 other countries. 45% women, 55% men, 2% part-time, 76% state residents, 85% live on campus, 10% transferred in, 50% have need-based financial aid, 10% have non-need-based financial aid, 1% international, 5% 25 or older, 0% Native American, 1% Hispanic, 22% African American, 1% Asian American.

FIRST-YEAR CLASS 333 total; 734 applied, 86% were accepted, 53% of whom enrolled. 2% from top 10% of their high school class, 10% from top quarter, 35% from top half.

ACADEMIC PROGRAM Core, transfer curriculum, honor code. Calendar: semesters. 150 courses offered in 1995–96. Academic remediation for entering students, English as a second language program offered during academic year, services for LD students, advanced placement, tutorials, summer session for credit, part-time degree program (daytime, weekends, summer), adult/continuing education programs.

GENERAL DEGREE REQUIREMENTS 64 semester hours; 6 semester hours of math; computer course.

MAJORS Business administration/commerce/management, (pre)engineering sequence, liberal arts/general studies, science, secretarial studies/office management.

LIBRARY Robbins Library with 64,000 books, 1,700 microform titles, 150 periodicals, 3 on-line bibliographic services, 8 CD-ROMs, 4,000 records, tapes, and CDs.

COMPUTERS ON CAMPUS 30 computers for student use in computer center, computer labs provide access to e-mail, on-line services, Internet. Staffed computer lab on campus.

COLLEGE LIFE Orientation program (3 days, $10). Drama-theater group, choral group, student-run newspaper, radio station. ***Social organizations:*** 12 open to all. ***Most popular organizations:*** Student Government Association, Workers Actively Volunteering Energetic Services, Drama Club, Christian Life Council, Ecological Concerns Club. ***Major annual events:*** Homecoming, Mud-Volleyball, Spring Dance Formal. ***Student services:*** health clinic, personal-psychological counseling. ***Campus security:*** 24-hour emergency response devices and patrols, controlled dormitory access.

HOUSING 650 college housing spaces available; 500 were occupied 1995–96. Freshmen guaranteed college housing. On-campus residence required through sophomore year except for foreign students, if 21 or over, married, or living with relatives within commuting distance. ***Option:*** single-sex (5 buildings) housing available. Resident assistants live in dorms.

ATHLETICS Member NJCAA. ***Intercollegiate:*** baseball M(s), basketball M(s)/W(s), golf M/W, soccer M(s)/W(s), softball W(s), tennis M(s)/W(s). ***Intramural:*** basketball, football, soccer, softball, table tennis (Ping-Pong), tennis, volleyball. ***Contact:*** Mr. Russell W. Frazier, Athletic Director, 919-496-2521 Ext. 245.

CAREER PLANNING ***Placement office:*** 1 full-time staff. ***Director:*** Dr. Becky Ansted, Director of Counseling Services, 919-496-2521 Ext. 234. ***Services:*** career counseling, careers library.

AFTER GRADUATION 90% of students completing a degree program in 1994–95 went directly on to further study.

EXPENSES FOR 1995–96 ***Application fee:*** $15. Comprehensive fee of $11,345 includes full-time tuition ($7000), mandatory fees ($530), and college room and board ($3815). Part-time tuition: $235 per semester hour.

FINANCIAL AID ***College-administered undergrad aid 1995–96:*** 290 need-based scholarships (average $2945), 82 non-need scholarships (average $2014), low-interest long-term loans from college funds (average $2041), loans from external sources (average $3238), 113 Federal Work-Study (averaging $1029), 16 part-time jobs. ***Required forms:*** institutional, FAFSA; required for some: state. ***Priority deadline:*** 3/15. ***Payment plan:*** installment. ***Waivers:*** full or partial for employees or children of employees.

APPLYING ***Options:*** deferred entrance, midyear entrance. ***Required:*** school transcript, SAT I or ACT, TOEFL for international students. ***Required for some:*** recommendations, interview. Test scores used for counseling/placement. ***Application deadline:*** rolling. ***Notification:*** continuous.

APPLYING/TRANSFER ***Required:*** standardized test scores, high school transcript, college transcript. ***Recommended:*** 3 years of high school math and science, some high school foreign language. ***Required for some:*** recommendations, interview. ***Entrance:*** minimally difficult. ***Application deadline:*** rolling. ***Notification:*** continuous.

CONTACT Mr. Rick Lowe, Director of Admissions, Louisburg College, 501 North Main Street, Louisburg, NC 27549-2399, 919-496-2521 Ext. 237 or toll-free 800-775-0208. ***Fax:*** 919-496-1788. College video available.

LOUISE HARKEY SCHOOL OF NURSING –CABARRUS MEMORIAL HOSPITAL
Concord, North Carolina

UG Enrollment: 139	**Tuition & Fees: $4150**
Application Deadline: rolling	**Room & Board: N/Avail**

GENERAL Independent, 2-year, specialized, primarily women. Awards terminal associate degrees. Founded 1942. ***Setting:*** small-town campus with easy access to Charlotte. ***Educational spending 1994–95:*** $4425 per undergrad. ***Total enrollment:*** 139. ***Faculty:*** 22 (13 full-time, 15% with terminal degrees, 9 part-time); student-faculty ratio is 11:1. ***Notable Alumni:*** Dr. Kay Jackson Smith, director at Mercy School of Nursing; Gayle Deal, director of business health services at Cabarrus Memorial Hospital; Emily Troutman Love, administrator at The Country Home.

ENROLLMENT PROFILE 139 students from 3 states and territories. 91% women, 9% men, 23% part-time, 98% state residents, 81% transferred in, 47% have need-based financial aid, 5% have non-need-based financial aid, 0% international, 45% 25 or older, 1% Native American, 1% Hispanic, 4% African American, 1% Asian American. ***Areas of study chosen:*** 100% health professions and related sciences. ***Most popular recent major:*** nursing.

FIRST-YEAR CLASS 68 total; 207 applied, 44% were accepted, 75% of whom enrolled. 13% from top 10% of their high school class, 54% from top quarter, 95% from top half.

ACADEMIC PROGRAM Core, integrated nursing curriculum, honor code. Calendar: semesters. 18 courses offered in 1995–96; average class size 30 in required courses. Tutorials, part-time degree program (daytime).

GENERAL DEGREE REQUIREMENTS 71 semester hours; math/science requirements vary according to program.

MAJOR Nursing.

LIBRARY Cabarrus Memorial Hospital Library with 6,272 books, 207 periodicals, 1 on-line bibliographic service, 2 CD-ROMs, 110 records, tapes, and CDs. Acquisition spending 1994–95: $37,215.

COMPUTERS ON CAMPUS 20 computers for student use in computer labs, library provide access to main academic computer. Staffed computer lab on campus provides training in use of computers, software.

COLLEGE LIFE Orientation program (5 days, no cost, parents included). 50% vote in student government elections. ***Social organizations:*** 3 open to all. ***Most popular organizations:*** Student Nurse Association, Christian Student Union, Student Government. ***Major annual events:*** Welcome Picnic, Spring Family Day. ***Student services:*** health clinic, personal-psychological counseling. ***Campus security:*** 24-hour emergency response devices.

HOUSING College housing not available.

CAREER PLANNING ***Service:*** career counseling.

AFTER GRADUATION 100% of class of 1994 had job offers within 6 months.

EXPENSES FOR 1995–96 ***Application fee:*** $25. Tuition: $3850 (minimum) full-time. Full-time tuition ranges up to $4180 according to class level. Full-time mandatory fees: $300.

FINANCIAL AID ***College-administered undergrad aid 1995–96:*** 45 need-based scholarships (averaging $1077), non-need scholarships, low-interest long-term loans from external sources (averaging $3000). ***Required forms:*** FAFSA. ***Priority deadline:*** 5/1.

APPLYING ***Options:*** early action, deferred entrance, midyear entrance. ***Required:*** essay, school transcript, minimum 2.0 GPA, 3 recommendations, campus interview, SAT I or ACT. ***Recommended:*** minimum 3.0 GPA, 3 years of high school math and science. Test scores used for admission. ***Application deadlines:*** rolling, 8/31 for early action. ***Notification:*** 12/15 for early action.

APPLYING/TRANSFER ***Required:*** essay, standardized test scores, high school transcript, 3 recommendations, campus interview, college transcript, minimum 2.0 college GPA, minimum 2.0 high school GPA. ***Recommended:*** 3 years of high school math and science, minimum 3.0 college GPA, minimum 3.0 high school GPA. ***Entrance:*** moderately difficult. ***Application deadline:*** rolling. ***Contact:*** Ms. Kim Thompson, Admissions Coordinator, 704-783-1616.

CONTACT Ms. Kim Thompson, Admissions Coordinator, Louise Harkey School of Nursing –Cabarrus Memorial Hospital, Concord, NC 28025-2405, 704-783-1616. ***Fax:*** 704-783-1764.

MARTIN COMMUNITY COLLEGE
Williamston, North Carolina

UG Enrollment: 702	**Tuition & Fees (NC Res): $585**
Application Deadline: rolling	**Room & Board: N/Avail**

GENERAL State-supported, 2-year, coed. Part of North Carolina Community College System. Awards certificates, diplomas, transfer associate, terminal associate degrees. Founded 1968. ***Setting:*** 65-acre rural campus. ***Endowment:*** $28,402. ***Educational spending 1994–95:*** $2066 per undergrad. ***Total enrollment:*** 702. ***Faculty:*** 48 (24 full-time, 2% with terminal degrees, 24 part-time); student-faculty ratio is 15:1.

ENROLLMENT PROFILE 702 students from 6 states and territories. 76% women, 24% men, 39% part-time, 99% state residents, 10% transferred in, 40% have need-based financial aid, 1% have non-need-based financial aid, 0% international, 51% 25 or older, 1% Native American, 0% Hispanic, 41% African American, 0% Asian American. ***Areas of study chosen:*** 22% business management and administrative services, 20% liberal arts/general studies, 15% vocational and home economics, 14% health professions and related sciences, 13% computer and information sciences, 6% education, 4% agriculture, 3% engineering and applied sciences, 3% social sciences. ***Most popular recent majors:*** liberal arts/general studies, computer information systems, secretarial studies/office management.

FIRST-YEAR CLASS 656 applied, 91% were accepted, 59% of whom enrolled. 5% from top 10% of their high school class, 20% from top quarter, 40% from top half.

ACADEMIC PROGRAM Honor code. Calendar: quarters. 285 courses offered in 1995–96. Academic remediation for entering students, English as a second language program, advanced placement, summer session for credit, part-time degree program (daytime, evenings), co-op programs and internships.

GENERAL DEGREE REQUIREMENTS 96 quarter hours; computer course for most majors; internship (some majors).

MAJORS Accounting, automotive technologies, business administration/commerce/management, computer information systems, equestrian studies, heating/refrigeration/air conditioning, laboratory technologies, liberal arts/general studies, physical therapy, secretarial studies/office management.

LIBRARY Martin Community College Learning Resources Center with 29,500 books, 1,300 microform titles, 254 periodicals, 3 CD-ROMs, 1,950 records, tapes, and CDs. Acquisition spending 1994–95: $157,110.

COMPUTERS ON CAMPUS 90 computers for student use in computer labs, classrooms, library. Staffed computer lab on campus provides training in use of computers, software. Academic computing expenditure 1994–95: $123,735.

COLLEGE LIFE 20% vote in student government elections. ***Most popular organizations:*** Physical Therapist Assistant Club, Phi Theta Kappa, Equine Club, Student Government Association, Alpha Beta Gamma. ***Major annual events:*** Stampede in the Park, Spring Fling, Fall Festival. ***Student services:*** personal-psychological counseling. ***Campus security:*** 24-hour emergency response devices, part-time patrols by trained security personnel.

HOUSING College housing not available.

ATHLETICS ***Intramural:*** softball, table tennis (Ping-Pong), volleyball.

CAREER PLANNING ***Placement office:*** 1 part-time staff. ***Director:*** Mr. Charles Askew, Counselor, 919-792-1521. ***Services:*** job fairs, career counseling, careers library, job bank, job interviews. 25 organizations recruited on campus 1994–95.

AFTER GRADUATION 50% of students completing a degree program in 1994–95 went directly on to further study.

EXPENSES FOR 1995–96 State resident tuition: $557 full-time, $13.25 per quarter hour part-time. Nonresident tuition: $4515 full-time, $107.50 per quarter hour part-time. Part-time mandatory fees: $4.25 per quarter. Full-time mandatory fees: $28.

FINANCIAL AID ***College-administered undergrad aid 1995–96:*** 40 need-based scholarships (average $600), 8 non-need scholarships (average $500), short-term loans (average $200), low-interest long-term loans from external sources (average $2600), 34 Federal Work-Study (averaging $750), 20 part-time jobs. ***Required forms:*** FAFSA;

accepted: CSS Financial Aid PROFILE. ***Priority deadline:*** 8/1. ***Waivers:*** full or partial for employees or children of employees and senior citizens. ***Notification:*** continuous. ***Average indebtedness of graduates:*** $2232.
APPLYING Open admission except for physical therapy assistant program. ***Options:*** early entrance, midyear entrance. ***Required:*** school transcript, TOEFL for international students. ***Required for some:*** campus interview, Assessment and Placement Services for Community Colleges. Test scores used for counseling/placement. ***Application deadline:*** rolling.
APPLYING/TRANSFER ***Required:*** high school transcript, college transcript. ***Required for some:*** standardized test scores, campus interview. ***Entrance:*** noncompetitive. ***Application deadline:*** rolling. ***Contact:*** Ms. Carolyn H. Mills, Registrar/Admissions Officer, 919-792-1521.
CONTACT Ms. Carolyn H. Mills, Registrar/Admissions Officer, Martin Community College, Williamston, NC 27892, 919-792-1521 Ext. 243. ***Fax:*** 919-792-4425. College video available.

MAYLAND COMMUNITY COLLEGE
Spruce Pine, North Carolina

UG Enrollment: 798 | **Tuition & Fees (NC Res): $572**
Application Deadline: rolling | **Room & Board: N/Avail**

GENERAL State and locally supported, 2-year, coed. Part of North Carolina Community College System. Awards certificates, diplomas, transfer associate degrees. Founded 1971. ***Setting:*** 38-acre rural campus. ***Total enrollment:*** 798. ***Faculty:*** 35 (15 full-time, 20 part-time); student-faculty ratio is 23:1.
ENROLLMENT PROFILE 798 students from 3 states and territories. 62% women, 38% men, 60% part-time, 99% state residents, 14% transferred in, 0% international, 46% 25 or older, 1% Native American, 0% Hispanic, 3% African American, 1% Asian American. ***Areas of study chosen:*** 20% liberal arts/general studies, 15% business management and administrative services, 15% health professions and related sciences, 4% computer and information sciences, 3% engineering and applied sciences. ***Most popular recent majors:*** business administration/commerce/management, medical secretarial studies, nursing.
FIRST-YEAR CLASS 257 total; 366 applied, 96% were accepted, 73% of whom enrolled.
ACADEMIC PROGRAM Calendar: quarters. Academic remediation for entering students, services for LD students, advanced placement, summer session for credit, part-time degree program (daytime, evenings, summer), adult/continuing education programs.
GENERAL DEGREE REQUIREMENT 116 quarter hours.
MAJORS Accounting, architectural technologies, business administration/commerce/management, computer programming, criminal justice, early childhood education, electrical and electronics technologies, electronics engineering technology, finance/banking, horticulture, law enforcement/police sciences, liberal arts/general studies, medical secretarial studies, nursing, postal management, real estate, secretarial studies/office management, tourism and travel.
LIBRARY 17,620 books, 215 microform titles, 246 periodicals, 572 records, tapes, and CDs.
COMPUTERS ON CAMPUS 70 computers for student use in computer labs, classrooms.
COLLEGE LIFE 60% vote in student government elections. ***Student services:*** personal-psychological counseling.
HOUSING College housing not available.
CAREER PLANNING ***Service:*** career counseling.
EXPENSES FOR 1995–96 State resident tuition: $557 full-time, $13.25 per quarter hour part-time. Nonresident tuition: $4515 full-time, $107.50 per quarter hour part-time. Part-time mandatory fees per quarter range from $2 to $4.90. Full-time mandatory fees: $15.
FINANCIAL AID ***College-administered undergrad aid 1995–96:*** need-based scholarships, low-interest long-term loans from external sources, Federal Work-Study. ***Required forms:*** FAFSA; accepted: CSS Financial Aid PROFILE. ***Priority deadline:*** 3/31. ***Waivers:*** full or partial for senior citizens.
APPLYING Open admission. ***Option:*** deferred entrance. ***Required:*** school transcript, TOEFL for international students, Assessment and Placement Services for Community Colleges (for nursing studies), CGP. Test scores used for admission (for nursing program) and counseling/placement. ***Application deadline:*** rolling. ***Notification:*** continuous.
APPLYING/TRANSFER ***Required:*** standardized test scores, high school transcript, college transcript. ***Entrance:*** noncompetitive. ***Application deadline:*** rolling. ***Notification:*** continuous. ***Contact:*** Mr. John Saparilas, Transfer Counselor, 704-765-7351.
CONTACT Mrs. Brenda Wilcox, Registrar, Mayland Community College, Spruce Pine, NC 28777-0547, 704-765-7356 Ext. 226.

McDOWELL TECHNICAL COMMUNITY COLLEGE
Marion, North Carolina

UG Enrollment: 939 | **Tuition & Fees (NC Res): $572**
Application Deadline: rolling | **Room & Board: N/Avail**

GENERAL State-supported, 2-year, coed. Part of North Carolina Community College System. Awards certificates, diplomas, transfer associate, terminal associate degrees. Founded 1964. ***Setting:*** 31-acre rural campus. ***Total enrollment:*** 939. ***Faculty:*** 50 (36 full-time, 90% with terminal degrees, 14 part-time); student-faculty ratio is 17:1.
ENROLLMENT PROFILE 939 students: 65% women, 35% men, 54% part-time, 99% state residents, 9% transferred in, 0% international, 1% Native American, 0% Hispanic, 4% African American, 1% Asian American. ***Areas of study chosen:*** 8% health professions and related sciences, 5% computer and information sciences. ***Most popular recent majors:*** nursing, electrical and electronics technologies, accounting.
FIRST-YEAR CLASS 518 total; 652 applied, 88% were accepted, 91% of whom enrolled.
ACADEMIC PROGRAM Core, honor code. Calendar: quarters. Academic remediation for entering students, services for LD students, tutorials, summer session for credit, part-time degree program (daytime, evenings, summer), adult/continuing education programs, co-op programs.
GENERAL DEGREE REQUIREMENTS 96 quarter hours; 1 math course; computer course for most majors.
MAJORS Accounting, automotive technologies, business administration/commerce/management, child care/child and family studies, commercial art, computer programming, construction technologies, cosmetology, criminal justice, electrical and electronics technologies, industrial administration, industrial and heavy equipment maintenance, liberal arts/general studies, machine and tool technologies, marketing/retailing/merchandising, nursing, photography, secretarial studies/office management, teacher aide studies, welding technology.
LIBRARY 18,055 books, 1,636 microform titles, 156 periodicals, 21,316 records, tapes, and CDs.
COMPUTERS ON CAMPUS 53 computers for student use in computer center, computer labs, learning resource center, career center, library. Staffed computer lab on campus provides training in use of computers, software.
COLLEGE LIFE 40% vote in student government elections. ***Student services:*** personal-psychological counseling. ***Campus security:*** 24-hour emergency response devices.
HOUSING College housing not available.
ATHLETICS ***Intercollegiate:*** tennis M. ***Intramural:*** basketball, table tennis (Ping-Pong), tennis, volleyball.
CAREER PLANNING ***Placement office:*** 2 full-time staff. ***Director:*** Dr. Jim Robinson, Director, Career Center, 704-652-6021. ***Services:*** job fairs, resume preparation, resume referral, career counseling, careers library, job bank, job interviews. 30 organizations recruited on campus 1994–95.
AFTER GRADUATION 60% of students completing a degree program in 1994–95 went directly on to further study.
EXPENSES FOR 1995–96 State resident tuition: $557 full-time, $13.25 per quarter hour part-time. Nonresident tuition: $4515 full-time, $107.50 per quarter hour part-time. Part-time mandatory fees: $5 per quarter. Full-time mandatory fees: $15.
FINANCIAL AID ***College-administered undergrad aid 1995–96:*** 294 need-based scholarships, 65 non-need scholarships, low-interest long-term loans from external sources, 9 Federal Work-Study (averaging $781). ***Required forms:*** institutional, FAFSA; accepted: CSS Financial Aid PROFILE. ***Priority deadline:*** 7/15. ***Payment plans:*** installment, deferred payment. ***Waivers:*** full or partial for employees or children of employees and senior citizens.
APPLYING Open admission except for registered nursing, licensed practical nursing programs. ***Options:*** early entrance, deferred entrance, midyear entrance. ***Required:*** TOEFL for international students. ***Required for some:*** school transcript, CPT. Test scores used for counseling/placement. ***Application deadline:*** rolling. ***Notification:*** continuous.
APPLYING/TRANSFER ***Required for some:*** standardized test scores, high school transcript, college transcript. ***Application deadline:*** rolling. ***Notification:*** continuous. ***Contact:*** Mr. Jim L. Biddix, Dean of Students, 704-652-6021 Ext. 401.
CONTACT Mr. Jim L. Biddix, Dean of Students, McDowell Technical Community College, Marion, NC 28752-9724, 704-652-6021 Ext. 401. ***Fax:*** 704-652-1014. College video available.

MITCHELL COMMUNITY COLLEGE
Statesville, North Carolina

UG Enrollment: 1,550 | **Tuition & Fees (NC Res): $582**
Application Deadline: rolling | **Room & Board: N/Avail**

GENERAL State-supported, 2-year, coed. Part of North Carolina Community College System. Awards certificates, diplomas, transfer associate, terminal associate degrees. Founded 1852. ***Setting:*** 8-acre small-town campus with easy access to Charlotte. ***Total enrollment:*** 1,550. ***Faculty:*** 90 (47 full-time, 98% with terminal degrees, 43 part-time); student-faculty ratio is 19:1.
ENROLLMENT PROFILE 1,550 students from 7 states and territories. 61% women, 50% part-time, 99% state residents, 3% transferred in, 0% international, 30% 25 or older, 0% Native American, 1% Hispanic, 11% African American, 1% Asian American. ***Most popular recent majors:*** liberal arts/general studies, nursing, business administration/commerce/management.
FIRST-YEAR CLASS Of the students who applied, 100% were accepted, 75% of whom enrolled.
ACADEMIC PROGRAM Core, honor code. Calendar: quarters. Academic remediation for entering students, English as a second language program offered during academic year and summer, services for LD students, advanced placement, summer session for credit, part-time degree program (daytime, evenings, summer), adult/continuing education programs, co-op programs. ROTC: Army (c).
GENERAL DEGREE REQUIREMENTS 96 quarter hours; math/science requirements vary according to program; computer course for most majors; internship (some majors).
MAJORS Accounting, agricultural sciences, art/fine arts, automotive technologies, business administration/commerce/management, computer science, criminal justice, data processing, drafting and design, electronics engineering technology, human services, liberal arts/general studies, nursing, science, secretarial studies/office management.
LIBRARY Main library plus 1 other, with 30,000 books, 60 periodicals, 1,159 records, tapes, and CDs.
COMPUTERS ON CAMPUS 40 computers for student use in computer labs, vocational building. Staffed computer lab on campus provides training in use of computers, software.
COLLEGE LIFE Choral group. ***Social organizations:*** 10 open to all. ***Most popular organizations:*** Circle K Club, Phi Beta Lambda, Medical Assisting Club, Ebony Kinship. ***Major annual events:*** May (Spring) Week, Intramural Activities, Christmas Activities. ***Student services:*** personal-psychological counseling. ***Campus security:*** day and evening security guards.
HOUSING College housing not available.
ATHLETICS ***Intercollegiate:*** golf M/W. ***Intramural:*** basketball, bowling, softball, tennis, volleyball.
CAREER PLANNING ***Placement office:*** 1 full-time staff. ***Director:*** Mr. Bill Jennings, Director of Testing/Career Center, 704-878-3242. ***Services:*** job fairs, career counseling, careers library, job interviews.
EXPENSES FOR 1995–96 State resident tuition: $557 full-time, $13.25 per quarter hour part-time. Nonresident tuition: $4515 full-time, $107.50 per quarter hour part-time. Part-time mandatory fees: $8.40 per quarter. Full-time mandatory fees: $25.
FINANCIAL AID ***College-administered undergrad aid 1995–96:*** need-based scholarships, part-time jobs. ***Required forms:*** institutional, FAFSA. ***Application deadline:*** continuous. ***Waivers:*** full or partial for senior citizens.

Mitchell Community College (continued)
APPLYING Open admission. ***Required:*** school transcript, TOEFL for international students. ***Application deadline:*** rolling. ***Notification:*** continuous.
APPLYING/TRANSFER ***Required:*** high school transcript, college transcript. ***Entrance:*** noncompetitive. ***Application deadline:*** rolling. ***Notification:*** continuous.
CONTACT Ms. Judy Hamilton, Recruiter, Mitchell Community College, Statesville, NC 28677-5293, 704-878-3280 or toll-free 800-448-4590 (in-state). ***Fax:*** 704-878-0872.

MONTGOMERY COMMUNITY COLLEGE
Troy, North Carolina

UG Enrollment: 551 — **Tuition & Fees (NC Res): $770**
Application Deadline: rolling — **Room & Board: N/Avail**

GENERAL State-supported, 2-year, coed. Part of North Carolina Community College System. Awards certificates, diplomas, transfer associate, terminal associate degrees. Founded 1967. ***Setting:*** 159-acre rural campus. ***Educational spending 1994–95:*** $3025 per undergrad. ***Total enrollment:*** 551. ***Faculty:*** 50 (25 full-time, 1% with terminal degrees, 25 part-time); student-faculty ratio is 13:1. ***Notable Alumni:*** Becky C. Wallace, Wayne Wooten, George Bowden, Dana Hatley, Carol Shue.
ENROLLMENT PROFILE 551 students from 10 states and territories. 51% women, 49% men, 41% part-time, 96% state residents, 19% transferred in, 58% have need-based financial aid, 1% international, 63% 25 or older, 1% Native American, 0% Hispanic, 25% African American, 0% Asian American.
FIRST-YEAR CLASS 207 total; 328 applied, 78% were accepted, 81% of whom enrolled. 3% from top 10% of their high school class, 25% from top quarter, 30% from top half.
ACADEMIC PROGRAM Core, honor code. Calendar: quarters. 297 courses offered in 1995–96; average class size 15 in required courses. Academic remediation for entering students, English as a second language program offered during academic year and summer, tutorials, summer session for credit, part-time degree program (daytime, evenings, summer), adult/continuing education programs, co-op programs.
GENERAL DEGREE REQUIREMENTS 96 quarter hours; 1 math course; computer course.
MAJORS Accounting, automotive technologies, business administration/commerce/management, computer science, criminal justice, early childhood education, electrical and electronics technologies, emergency medical technology, forest technology, law enforcement/police sciences, liberal arts/general studies, medical assistant technologies, science, secretarial studies/office management.
LIBRARY 16,500 books, 200 periodicals, 1 on-line bibliographic service, 3 CD-ROMs. Acquisition spending 1994–95: $34,976.
COMPUTERS ON CAMPUS 51 computers for student use in computer center, learning resource center. Academic computing expenditure 1994–95: $89,782.
COLLEGE LIFE ***Social organizations:*** 3 open to all. ***Most popular organizations:*** Archery Club, Gunsmithing Club, Student Government Association. ***Campus security:*** 24-hour emergency response devices, late-night transport-escort service, 24-hour maintenance/security.
HOUSING College housing not available.
ATHLETICS ***Intramural:*** archery, riflery, volleyball.
CAREER PLANNING ***Placement office:*** 1 full-time staff; $40,001 operating expenditure 1994–95. ***Director:*** Ms. Margo Gaddy, Counselor, 910-576-6222. ***Services:*** job fairs, resume preparation, career counseling, job interviews. 25 organizations recruited on campus 1994–95.
AFTER GRADUATION 79% of class of 1994 had job offers within 6 months.
EXPENSES FOR 1996–97 State resident tuition: $742 full-time, $13.25 per quarter hour part-time. Nonresident tuition: $6020 full-time, $107.50 per quarter hour part-time. Part-time mandatory fees: $7 per quarter. Full-time mandatory fees: $28.
FINANCIAL AID ***College-administered undergrad aid 1995–96:*** 165 need-based scholarships (average $900), 10 Federal Work-Study (averaging $510). ***Required forms:*** FAFSA. ***Priority deadline:*** 10/1. ***Payment plan:*** deferred payment.
APPLYING Open admission except for nursing program. ***Options:*** early entrance, deferred entrance, midyear entrance. ***Required:*** school transcript, TOEFL for international students, ACT ASSET. Test scores used for counseling/placement. ***Application deadline:*** rolling. ***Notification:*** continuous. Preference given to residents of Montgomery and adjacent counties.
APPLYING/TRANSFER ***Required:*** high school transcript, college transcript. ***Entrance:*** noncompetitive. ***Application deadline:*** rolling. ***Notification:*** continuous. ***Contact:*** Ms. Margo Gaddy, Counselor, 910-576-6222.
CONTACT Ms. Beth Smith, Admissions Office, Montgomery Community College, Troy, NC 27371-0787, 910-576-6222 Ext. 225. College video available.

NASH COMMUNITY COLLEGE
Rocky Mount, North Carolina

UG Enrollment: 1,880 — **Tuition & Fees (NC Res): $578**
Application Deadline: rolling — **Room & Board: N/Avail**

GENERAL State-supported, 2-year, coed. Part of North Carolina Community College System. Awards certificates, diplomas, transfer associate, terminal associate degrees. Founded 1967. ***Setting:*** 69-acre rural campus. ***Total enrollment:*** 1,880. ***Faculty:*** 106 (46 full-time, 100% with terminal degrees, 60 part-time); student-faculty ratio is 21:1.
ENROLLMENT PROFILE 1,880 students from 2 states and territories. 66% women, 63% part-time, 99% state residents, 5% transferred in, 0% international, 45% 25 or older, 2% Native American, 0% Hispanic, 28% African American, 0% Asian American. ***Areas of study chosen:*** 23% liberal arts/general studies, 13% business management and administrative services, 9% interdisciplinary studies, 8% vocational and home economics, 7% health professions and related sciences, 6% computer and information sciences, 3% engineering and applied sciences, 2% architecture, 2% education. ***Most popular recent majors:*** nursing, business administration/commerce/management.
FIRST-YEAR CLASS 551 total; 680 applied, 100% were accepted, 81% of whom enrolled.
ACADEMIC PROGRAM Calendar: quarters. 500 courses offered in 1995–96. Academic remediation for entering students, services for LD students, advanced placement, summer session for credit, part-time degree program (daytime, evenings, summer), adult/continuing education programs.
GENERAL DEGREE REQUIREMENTS 96 quarter hours; 1 math course.
MAJORS Accounting, architectural technologies, business administration/commerce/management, cosmetology, early childhood education, electronics engineering technology, law enforcement/police sciences, legal secretarial studies, liberal arts/general studies, marketing/retailing/merchandising, medical secretarial studies, nursing, physical therapy, secretarial studies/office management, teacher aide studies.
LIBRARY 34,000 books, 60 microform titles, 110 periodicals, 3 CD-ROMs, 200 records, tapes, and CDs. Acquisition spending 1994–95: $40,586.
COMPUTERS ON CAMPUS 110 computers for student use in computer center provide access to main academic computer. Academic computing expenditure 1994–95: $39,000.
COLLEGE LIFE Student-run newspaper. 2% vote in student government elections. ***Social organizations:*** 2 open to all. ***Campus security:*** 24-hour emergency response devices, late-night transport-escort service.
HOUSING College housing not available.
CAREER PLANNING ***Placement office:*** 1 full-time staff; $25,000 operating expenditure 1994–95. ***Director:*** Ms. Georgia Roberson, Job Placement, 919-443-4011 Ext. 297. ***Services:*** job fairs, resume preparation, career counseling, careers library, job bank, job interviews. Students must register freshman year. 30 organizations recruited on campus 1994–95.
AFTER GRADUATION 90% of students completing a degree program in 1994–95 went directly on to further study.
EXPENSES FOR 1995–96 State resident tuition: $557 full-time, $13.25 per quarter hour part-time. Nonresident tuition: $4515 full-time, $107.50 per quarter hour part-time. Full-time mandatory fees: $21.
FINANCIAL AID ***College-administered undergrad aid 1995–96:*** 84 need-based scholarships (averaging $500), 4 non-need scholarships (averaging $500), short-term loans (averaging $100), low-interest long-term loans from external sources (averaging $1000), Federal Work-Study, 24 part-time jobs. ***Required forms:*** institutional, FAFSA; accepted: CSS Financial Aid PROFILE. ***Priority deadline:*** 7/1. ***Waivers:*** full or partial for employees or children of employees and senior citizens. ***Notification:*** continuous.
APPLYING Open admission except for nursing, physical therapy assistant, cosmetology, phlebotomy programs. ***Options:*** Common Application, deferred entrance. ***Required:*** TOEFL for international students, Assessment and Placement Services for Community Colleges. ***Recommended:*** SAT I. ***Required for some:*** 3 years of high school math and science. Test scores used for counseling/placement. ***Application deadline:*** rolling. ***Notification:*** continuous.
APPLYING/TRANSFER ***Required for some:*** 3 years of high school math and science. ***Entrance:*** noncompetitive. ***Application deadline:*** rolling. ***Notification:*** continuous. ***Contact:*** Ms. Anne H. Gregg, Registrar, 919-443-4011 Ext. 274.
CONTACT Ms. Mary Blunt, Admissions Officer, Nash Community College, Rocky Mount, NC 27804-0488, 919-443-4011 Ext. 300. ***Fax:*** 919-443-0828.

PAMLICO COMMUNITY COLLEGE
Grantsboro, North Carolina

UG Enrollment: 205 — **Tuition & Fees (NC Res): $572**
Application Deadline: rolling — **Room & Board: N/Avail**

GENERAL State-supported, 2-year, coed. Part of North Carolina Community College System. Awards certificates, diplomas, terminal associate degrees. Founded 1963. ***Setting:*** 44-acre rural campus. ***Total enrollment:*** 205. ***Faculty:*** 10 (6 full-time, 4 part-time); student-faculty ratio is 10:1.
ENROLLMENT PROFILE 205 students: 73% women, 27% men, 43% part-time, 100% state residents, 18% transferred in, 56% 25 or older, 1% Hispanic, 18% African American, 1% Asian American.
FIRST-YEAR CLASS 45 total; 64 applied, 100% were accepted, 70% of whom enrolled.
ACADEMIC PROGRAM Core, honor code. Calendar: quarters. Academic remediation for entering students, services for LD students, summer session for credit, part-time degree program (daytime, evenings, summer), adult/continuing education programs, co-op programs.
GENERAL DEGREE REQUIREMENTS 110 quarter hours; math/science requirements vary according to program; computer course.
MAJORS Accounting, automotive technologies, business administration/commerce/management, computer technologies, electrical engineering technology, environmental sciences, liberal arts/general studies, medical assistant technologies, medical laboratory technology, secretarial studies/office management.
LIBRARY 18,950 books, 16,300 microform titles, 190 periodicals, 2,900 records, tapes, and CDs.
COMPUTERS ON CAMPUS 43 computers for student use in computer center, Student Development Services department, library.
COLLEGE LIFE Student-run newspaper. 100% vote in student government elections. ***Student services:*** personal-psychological counseling. ***Campus security:*** evening security guard.
HOUSING College housing not available.
ATHLETICS ***Intramural:*** softball, volleyball.
CAREER PLANNING ***Services:*** resume preparation, resume referral, career counseling, careers library, job interviews.
ESTIMATED EXPENSES FOR 1996–97 State resident tuition: $557 full-time, $13.25 per quarter hour part-time. Nonresident tuition: $4515 full-time, $107.50 per quarter hour part-time. Part-time mandatory fees per quarter range from $2.50 to $3.75. Full-time mandatory fees: $15.
FINANCIAL AID ***College-administered undergrad aid 1995–96:*** 12 need-based scholarships (average $700), 1 non-need scholarship ($300), short-term loans (average $47), low-interest long-term loans from external sources (average $1000), Federal Work-Study, 3 part-time jobs. ***Required forms:*** FAFSA. ***Priority deadline:*** 9/1.
APPLYING Open admission. ***Options:*** early entrance, deferred entrance. ***Required:*** school transcript, ACT ASSET. Test scores used for counseling/placement. ***Application deadline:*** rolling. ***Notification:*** continuous.
APPLYING/TRANSFER ***Required:*** high school transcript, college transcript. ***Required for some:*** standardized test scores. ***Entrance:*** noncompetitive. ***Application deadline:*** rolling. ***Notification:*** continuous. ***Contact:*** Mr. Floyd Hardison, Admission Counselor, 919-249-1851.
CONTACT Mr. John T. Jones, Dean of Student Services, Pamlico Community College, Grantsboro, NC 28529-0185, 919-249-1851 Ext. 28.

PEACE COLLEGE
Raleigh, North Carolina

UG Enrollment: 424	**Tuition & Fees: $6778**
Application Deadline: rolling	**Room & Board: $5020**

GENERAL Independent, primarily 2-year, women only, affiliated with Presbyterian Church (U.S.A.) Awards transfer associate, bachelor's degrees. Founded 1857. ***Setting:*** 16-acre urban campus. ***Endowment:*** $32.9 million. ***Educational spending 1994–95:*** $4775 per undergrad. ***Total enrollment:*** 424. ***Faculty:*** 52 (27 full-time, 73% with terminal degrees, 25 part-time); student-faculty ratio is 13:1.
ENROLLMENT PROFILE 424 students: 100% women, 4% part-time, 87% state residents, 95% live on campus, 5% transferred in, 44% have need-based financial aid, 37% have non-need-based financial aid, 1% international, 1% 25 or older, 0% Native American, 1% Hispanic, 3% African American, 1% Asian American.
FIRST-YEAR CLASS 188 total; 389 applied, 77% were accepted, 63% of whom enrolled.
ACADEMIC PROGRAM Core, liberal arts and sciences curriculum, honor code. Calendar: semesters. Academic remediation for entering students, services for LD students, advanced placement, Freshman Honors College, tutorials, honors program, adult/continuing education programs, internships. Off-campus study at members of the Cooperating Raleigh Colleges. Study abroad in England, Mexico. ROTC: Army (c), Naval (c), Air Force (c).
GENERAL DEGREE REQUIREMENTS 63 semester hours for associate, 124 semester hours for bachelor's; 1 course in math/science; 1 course in a foreign language.
MAJORS Biology/biological sciences (B), business administration/commerce/management (B), communication (B), human resources (B), liberal arts/general studies (B), music.
LIBRARY Lucy Cooper Finch Library with 50,000 books, 25 microform titles, 140 periodicals, 1 on-line bibliographic service, 20 CD-ROMs, 800 records, tapes, and CDs. Acquisition spending 1994–95: $52,250.
COMPUTERS ON CAMPUS 35 computers for student use in computer center, computer labs provide access to main academic computer, on-line services, Internet. Staffed computer lab on campus provides training in use of computers, software.
COLLEGE LIFE Drama-theater group, choral group, student-run newspaper. 95% vote in student government elections. ***Social organizations:*** 15 open to all. ***Most popular organizations:*** Student Government Association, Peace Student Christian Association, Recreation Association, Young Democrats, Future Business Women. ***Major annual events:*** Fall Festival, Spring Fling, Stunt Night. ***Student services:*** health clinic, personal-psychological counseling. ***Campus security:*** 24-hour emergency response devices and patrols, late-night transport-escort service, controlled dormitory access.
HOUSING 435 college housing spaces available; 360 were occupied 1995–96. Freshmen guaranteed college housing. On-campus residence required through sophomore year except if living with relatives. ***Option:*** single-sex housing available. Resident assistants live in dorms.
ATHLETICS Member NJCAA. ***Intercollegiate:*** basketball, tennis, volleyball. ***Intramural:*** badminton, soccer, softball, swimming and diving, table tennis (Ping-Pong), tennis, volleyball. ***Contact:*** Ms. Deb Houser, Athletic Director, 919-508-2000 Ext. 2279.
CAREER PLANNING ***Placement office:*** 1 full-time, 1 part-time staff. ***Director:*** Ms. Judy Woodson-Bruhn, Director of Counseling Center, 919-508-2000 Ext. 2303. ***Services:*** resume preparation, career counseling, careers library, job bank.
EXPENSES FOR 1996–97 ***Application fee:*** $25. Comprehensive fee of $11,798 includes full-time tuition ($6640), mandatory fees ($138), and college room and board ($5020). Part-time tuition: $150 per semester hour.
FINANCIAL AID ***College-administered undergrad aid 1995–96:*** 176 need-based scholarships (average $3946), 150 non-need scholarships (average $3533), low-interest long-term loans from external sources (average $2732), Federal Work-Study, 74 part-time jobs. ***Required forms:*** FAFSA. ***Priority deadline:*** 4/1. ***Payment plans:*** installment, deferred payment. ***Waivers:*** full or partial for employees or children of employees.
APPLYING ***Options:*** early entrance, deferred entrance, midyear entrance. ***Required:*** essay, school transcript, minimum 2.0 GPA, 3 years of high school math, 1 year of high school foreign language, 2 recommendations, SAT I or ACT, TOEFL for international students. ***Recommended:*** 3 years of high school science, 2 years of high school foreign language, interview. Test scores used for admission. ***Application deadline:*** rolling. ***Notification:*** continuous.
APPLYING/TRANSFER ***Required:*** essay, 3 years of high school math, 1 year of high school foreign language, 2 recommendations, college transcript, minimum 2.0 college GPA, minimum 2.0 high school GPA. ***Recommended:*** 3 years of high school science, 2 years of high school foreign language, interview. ***Required for some:*** standardized test scores, high school transcript. ***Application deadline:*** rolling. ***Notification:*** continuous. ***Contact:*** Mrs. Christie Hill, Associate Director of Admissions, 919-508-2214.
CONTACT Mrs. Cynthia Wyatt, Dean of Admissions, Peace College, 15 East Peace Street, Raleigh, NC 27604-1194, 919-508-2000 Ext. 2214 or toll-free 800-PEACE-47. College video available.

PIEDMONT COMMUNITY COLLEGE
Roxboro, North Carolina

UG Enrollment: 600	**Tuition & Fees (NC Res): $593**
Application Deadline: rolling	**Room & Board: N/Avail**

GENERAL State-supported, 2-year, coed. Part of North Carolina Community College System. Awards certificates, diplomas, transfer associate, terminal associate degrees. Founded 1970. ***Setting:*** 178-acre small-town campus. ***Endowment:*** $782,359. ***Total enrollment:*** 600. ***Faculty:*** 95 (47 full-time, 73% with terminal degrees, 48 part-time).
ENROLLMENT PROFILE 600 students: 54% women, 46% men, 61% part-time, 89% state residents, 5% transferred in, 0% international, 1% Native American, 1% Hispanic, 36% African American, 1% Asian American. ***Areas of study chosen:*** 30% business management and administrative services, 22% liberal arts/general studies, 19% computer and information sciences, 18% social sciences, 11% health professions and related sciences.
FIRST-YEAR CLASS 417 total. Of the students who applied, 100% were accepted.
ACADEMIC PROGRAM Core, honor code. Calendar: quarters. Academic remediation for entering students, advanced placement, summer session for credit, part-time degree program (daytime, evenings, summer), adult/continuing education programs, co-op programs. Off-campus study at other technical institutes and community colleges in North Carolina.
GENERAL DEGREE REQUIREMENTS 118 quarter hours; 1 math course; computer course for most majors.
MAJORS Accounting, business administration/commerce/management, community services, computer programming, legal secretarial studies, liberal arts/general studies, medical secretarial studies, nursing, secretarial studies/office management, social science, vocational education, welding technology.
LIBRARY Learning Resource Center with 24,707 books, 23 microform titles, 271 periodicals, 54 CD-ROMs, 2,389 records, tapes, and CDs. Acquisition spending 1994–95: $69,507.
COMPUTERS ON CAMPUS 75 computers for student use in computer labs, learning resource center, classrooms provide access to main academic computer, off-campus computing facilities. Staffed computer lab on campus provides training in use of computers, software.
COLLEGE LIFE ***Major annual events:*** Family Day, Valentine Dance, Blood Drive. ***Student services:*** personal-psychological counseling. ***Campus security:*** security guard during certain evening and weekend hours.
HOUSING College housing not available.
ATHLETICS ***Intramural:*** volleyball.
CAREER PLANNING ***Director:*** Ms. Dianne Wright, Career and Job Placement Counselor, 910-599-1181 Ext. 210. ***Services:*** job fairs, resume preparation, career counseling, job bank, job interviews.
EXPENSES FOR 1995–96 State resident tuition: $557 full-time, $13.25 per quarter hour part-time. Nonresident tuition: $4515 full-time, $107.50 per quarter hour part-time. Full-time mandatory fees: $36.
FINANCIAL AID ***College-administered undergrad aid 1995–96:*** 110 need-based scholarships (average $1500), non-need scholarships, short-term loans, Federal Work-Study, 16 part-time jobs. ***Acceptable forms:*** CSS Financial Aid PROFILE, FAFSA. ***Priority deadline:*** 8/1.
APPLYING Open admission except for nursing program. ***Options:*** early entrance, deferred entrance. ***Required:*** school transcript, ACT ASSET. ***Required for some:*** TOEFL for international students. Test scores used for counseling/placement. ***Application deadline:*** rolling. ***Notification:*** continuous until 9/29.
APPLYING/TRANSFER ***Required:*** standardized test scores, high school transcript. ***Required for some:*** college transcript. ***Entrance:*** noncompetitive. ***Application deadline:*** rolling. ***Notification:*** continuous until 9/29.
CONTACT Mr. Ken Whitehurst, Dean of Student Affairs, Piedmont Community College, Roxboro, NC 27573-1197, 910-599-1181 Ext. 272.

PITT COMMUNITY COLLEGE
Greenville, North Carolina

UG Enrollment: 4,712	**Tuition & Fees (NC Res): $588**
Application Deadline: rolling	**Room & Board: N/Avail**

GENERAL State and locally supported, 2-year, coed. Part of North Carolina Community College System. Awards certificates, diplomas, transfer associate, terminal associate degrees. Founded 1961. ***Setting:*** 171-acre small-town campus. ***Endowment:*** $226,370. ***Total enrollment:*** 4,712. ***Faculty:*** 240 (119 full-time, 97% with terminal degrees, 121 part-time); student-faculty ratio is 19:1.
ENROLLMENT PROFILE 4,712 students: 59% women, 41% men, 53% part-time, 99% state residents, 24% transferred in, 37% 25 or older, 0% Native American, 1% Hispanic, 27% African American, 1% Asian American. ***Areas of study chosen:*** 28% business management and administrative services, 23% interdisciplinary studies, 21% health professions and related sciences, 10% computer and information sciences, 10% engineering and applied sciences, 8% education. ***Most popular recent majors:*** nursing, paralegal studies, radiological technology.
FIRST-YEAR CLASS 289 total; 3,627 applied, 100% were accepted.
ACADEMIC PROGRAM Core, honor code. Calendar: quarters. 906 courses offered in 1995–96. Academic remediation for entering students, services for LD students, advanced placement, summer session for credit, part-time degree program (daytime, evenings), adult/continuing education programs, co-op programs and internships.
GENERAL DEGREE REQUIREMENTS 97 quarter hours; computer course for most majors; internship (some majors).
MAJORS Accounting, architectural technologies, automotive technologies, business administration/commerce/management, child psychology/child development, commercial art, computer programming, corrections, criminal justice, early childhood education, electrical and electronics technologies, elementary education, heating/refrigeration/air conditioning, human services, industrial engineering technology, law enforcement/police sciences, liberal arts/general studies, manufacturing technology, marketing/retailing/merchandising, medical assistant technologies, medical records services, medical secretarial studies, nursing, occupational therapy, paralegal studies, radiological sciences, radiological technology, respiratory therapy, secretarial studies/office management.
LIBRARY Learning Resource Center with 40,456 books, 198 microform titles, 403 periodicals, 1 on-line bibliographic service, 20 CD-ROMs, 891 records, tapes, and CDs. Acquisition spending 1994–95: $591,895.
COMPUTERS ON CAMPUS 98 computers for student use in learning resource center, academic departments. Staffed computer lab on campus provides training in use of computers, software. Academic computing expenditure 1994–95: $369,832.
COLLEGE LIFE ***Student services:*** personal-psychological counseling. ***Campus security:*** 24-hour patrols, student patrols, late-night transport-escort service, patrols during campus hours.
HOUSING College housing not available.
ATHLETICS Member NJCAA. ***Intercollegiate:*** baseball M, golf M, tennis M/W, volleyball M/W. ***Contact:*** Mr. George Whitfield, Athletic Director, 919-321-4212.
CAREER PLANNING ***Placement office:*** 2 full-time, 1 part-time staff; $98,674 operating expenditure 1994–95. ***Director:*** Ms. Leslie Rogers, Director, Career Planning and Placement, 919-321-4322. ***Services:*** job fairs, resume preparation, resume referral, career counseling, careers library, job interviews. 50 organizations recruited on campus 1994–95.
AFTER GRADUATION 92% of class of 1994 had job offers within 6 months.
EXPENSES FOR 1995–96 State resident tuition: $557 full-time, $13.25 per quarter hour part-time. Nonresident tuition: $4515 full-time, $107.50 per quarter hour part-time. Part-time mandatory fees: $8 per quarter. Full-time mandatory fees: $31.
FINANCIAL AID ***College-administered undergrad aid 1995–96:*** 326 need-based scholarships (average $417), short-term loans (average $175), low-interest long-term loans

Pitt Community College (continued)
from external sources (average $2008), Federal Work-Study, 82 part-time jobs. ***Acceptable forms:*** CSS Financial Aid PROFILE, FAFSA. ***Priority deadline:*** 3/15. ***Waivers:*** full or partial for senior citizens.
APPLYING Open admission except for all health science programs. ***Options:*** deferred entrance, midyear entrance. ***Required:*** school transcript, TOEFL for international students. Test scores used for counseling/placement. ***Application deadline:*** rolling.
APPLYING/TRANSFER ***Required:*** high school transcript, college transcript. ***Entrance:*** noncompetitive. ***Application deadline:*** rolling.
CONTACT Ms. Norma Barrett, Director of Counseling, Pitt Community College, Greenville, NC 27835-7007, 919-321-4245. ***Fax:*** 919-321-4401.

RANDOLPH COMMUNITY COLLEGE
Asheboro, North Carolina

UG Enrollment: 1,343	**Tuition & Fees (NC Res): $582**
Application Deadline: rolling	**Room & Board: N/Avail**

GENERAL State-supported, 2-year, coed. Part of North Carolina Community College System. Awards certificates, diplomas, transfer associate, terminal associate degrees. Founded 1962. ***Setting:*** 27-acre small-town campus. ***Total enrollment:*** 1,343. ***Faculty:*** 73 (43 full-time, 30 part-time); student-faculty ratio is 22:1.
ENROLLMENT PROFILE 1,343 students from 7 states and territories. 62% women, 38% men, 51% part-time, 99% state residents, 10% transferred in, 47% 25 or older, 0% Native American, 1% Hispanic, 6% African American, 0% Asian American. ***Areas of study chosen:*** 21% business management and administrative services, 20% liberal arts/general studies, 11% health professions and related sciences, 9% computer and information sciences. ***Most popular recent majors:*** photography, interior design, business administration/commerce/management.
FIRST-YEAR CLASS 164 total.
ACADEMIC PROGRAM Core, honor code. Calendar: quarters for terminal associate degree, semesters for transfer associate degree. Academic remediation for entering students, services for LD students, advanced placement, summer session for credit, part-time degree program (daytime, evenings, summer), adult/continuing education programs, internships. Off-campus study at other members of the North Carolina Community College System.
GENERAL DEGREE REQUIREMENTS 96 credit hours; computer course for photography, accounting, commercial graphics, business administration, criminal justice majors; internship (some majors).
MAJORS Accounting, automotive technologies, business administration/commerce/management, commercial art, computer programming, computer science, computer technologies, criminal justice, data processing, electrical and electronics technologies, horticulture, interior design, liberal arts/general studies, machine and tool technologies, nursing, photography, secretarial studies/office management, welding technology.
LIBRARY 30,000 books, 650 microform titles, 250 periodicals, 10 CD-ROMs, 4,000 records, tapes, and CDs.
COMPUTERS ON CAMPUS Computer purchase plan available. 125 computers for student use in computer center, learning resource center, labs, library provide access to Internet, Novell network. Staffed computer lab on campus provides training in use of computers, software.
COLLEGE LIFE ***Student services:*** personal-psychological counseling.
HOUSING College housing not available.
CAREER PLANNING ***Placement office:*** 1 full-time, 1 part-time staff. ***Director:*** Ms. Mary S. Morgan, Counselor, Career Center, 910-629-1471. ***Services:*** job fairs, resume preparation, resume referral, career counseling, careers library, job interviews.
AFTER GRADUATION 70% of students completing a degree program in 1994–95 went directly on to further study.
EXPENSES FOR 1995–96 State resident tuition: $557 full-time, $13.25 per quarter hour part-time. Nonresident tuition: $4515 full-time, $107.50 per quarter hour part-time. Part-time mandatory fees per quarter hour range from $1.80 to $8.40. Full-time mandatory fees: $25.
FINANCIAL AID ***College-administered undergrad aid 1995–96:*** 160 need-based scholarships (average $570), 2 non-need scholarships (average $563), short-term loans (average $50), low-interest long-term loans from external sources (average $2186), Federal Work-Study, 12 part-time jobs. ***Required forms:*** institutional, FAFSA; accepted: CSS Financial Aid PROFILE. ***Priority deadline:*** 5/1.
APPLYING Open admission. ***Options:*** deferred entrance, midyear entrance. ***Required:*** school transcript, TOEFL for international students. ***Recommended:*** SAT I. Test scores used for counseling/placement. ***Application deadline:*** rolling. ***Notification:*** continuous.
APPLYING/TRANSFER ***Required:*** high school transcript, college transcript. ***Entrance:*** noncompetitive. ***Application deadline:*** rolling. ***Notification:*** continuous.
CONTACT Mrs. Carol M. Elmore, Registrar, Randolph Community College, Asheboro, NC 27204-1009, 910-629-1471. ***Fax:*** 910-629-4695.

RICHMOND COMMUNITY COLLEGE
Hamlet, North Carolina

UG Enrollment: 1,146	**Tuition & Fees (NC Res): $584**
Application Deadline: rolling	**Room & Board: N/Avail**

GENERAL State-supported, 2-year, coed. Part of North Carolina Community College System. Awards diplomas, transfer associate, terminal associate degrees. Founded 1964. ***Setting:*** 163-acre rural campus. ***Total enrollment:*** 1,146. ***Faculty:*** 100 (50 full-time, 50 part-time).
ENROLLMENT PROFILE 1,146 students from 2 states and territories, 1 other country. 67% women, 33% men, 47% part-time, 98% state residents, 6% transferred in, 1% international, 55% 25 or older, 7% Native American, 1% Hispanic, 25% African American, 1% Asian American. ***Most popular recent majors:*** business administration/commerce/management, human services, liberal arts/general studies.
FIRST-YEAR CLASS 337 total; 711 applied, 73% were accepted, 65% of whom enrolled.
ACADEMIC PROGRAM Honor code. Calendar: quarters. Academic remediation for entering students, English as a second language program offered during academic year, advanced placement, self-designed majors, tutorials, summer session for credit, part-time degree program (daytime, evenings), adult/continuing education programs, co-op programs and internships.
GENERAL DEGREE REQUIREMENTS 96 quarter hours; 1 course each in math and science; computer course; internship (some majors).
MAJORS Accounting, business administration/commerce/management, criminal justice, data processing, electronics engineering technology, human services, liberal arts/general studies, machine and tool technologies, mechanical engineering technology, nursing, practical nursing, secretarial studies/office management.
LIBRARY Richmond Community College Library plus 1 other, with 23,620 books, 10,200 microform titles, 203 periodicals, 4 CD-ROMs, 658 records, tapes, and CDs. Acquisition spending 1994–95: $28,707.
COMPUTERS ON CAMPUS 150 computers for student use in computer center, computer labs, learning resource center, classrooms, library provide access to off-campus computing facilities.
COLLEGE LIFE 10% vote in student government elections. ***Most popular organizations:*** Criminal Justice Club, Human Services Club, Native American Club. ***Major annual events:*** Native American Pow Wow, Field Day. ***Student services:*** personal-psychological counseling. ***Campus security:*** 24-hour emergency response devices, security guard during evening hours.
HOUSING College housing not available.
CAREER PLANNING ***Placement office:*** 4 full-time staff. ***Director:*** Mr. Gerald T. Melton, Director of Counseling and Career Development, 910-582-7103. ***Services:*** job fairs, resume preparation, resume referral, career counseling, careers library, job bank, job interviews.
EXPENSES FOR 1995–96 State resident tuition: $557 full-time, $13.25 per quarter hour part-time. Nonresident tuition: $4515 full-time, $107.50 per quarter hour part-time. Part-time mandatory fees: $4.50 per quarter. Full-time mandatory fees: $27.
FINANCIAL AID ***College-administered undergrad aid 1995–96:*** 75 need-based scholarships (average $500), 30 non-need scholarships (average $750), short-term loans (average $195), low-interest long-term loans from external sources (average $2625), 30 Federal Work-Study (averaging $900), 25 part-time jobs. ***Required forms:*** institutional, FAFSA. ***Priority deadline:*** 7/15. ***Payment plan:*** deferred payment. ***Waivers:*** full or partial for employees or children of employees and senior citizens. ***Notification:*** continuous.
APPLYING Open admission except for nursing program. ***Option:*** deferred entrance. ***Required:*** school transcript, TOEFL for international students. Test scores used for admission. ***Application deadline:*** rolling. ***Notification:*** continuous until 9/1.
APPLYING/TRANSFER ***Required:*** college transcript. ***Recommended:*** high school transcript. ***Application deadline:*** rolling. ***Notification:*** continuous until 9/1.
CONTACT Ms. Teri P. Jacobs, Director of Admissions/Registrar, Richmond Community College, Hamlet, NC 28345-1189, 910-582-7113. ***Fax:*** 910-582-7028.

ROANOKE-CHOWAN COMMUNITY COLLEGE
Ahoskie, North Carolina

UG Enrollment: 855	**Tuition & Fees (NC Res): $581**
Application Deadline: rolling	**Room & Board: N/Avail**

GENERAL State-supported, 2-year, coed. Part of North Carolina Community College System. Awards transfer associate, terminal associate degrees. Founded 1967. ***Setting:*** 39-acre rural campus. ***Total enrollment:*** 855. ***Faculty:*** 54 (24 full-time, 30 part-time).
ENROLLMENT PROFILE 855 students: 71% women, 47% part-time, 98% state residents, 4% transferred in, 73% 25 or older, 49% African American.
FIRST-YEAR CLASS 249 total. Of the students who applied, 100% were accepted.
ACADEMIC PROGRAM Core. Calendar: quarters. Academic remediation for entering students, summer session for credit, part-time degree program (daytime, evenings, summer), adult/continuing education programs, co-op programs.
GENERAL DEGREE REQUIREMENT 105 credits.
MAJORS Architectural technologies, automotive technologies, business administration/commerce/management, computer programming, construction technologies, cosmetology, criminal justice, early childhood education, education, electrical and electronics technologies, heating/refrigeration/air conditioning, liberal arts/general studies, nursing, secretarial studies/office management, welding technology.
LIBRARY 29,268 books, 7,223 microform titles, 207 periodicals, 5,203 records, tapes, and CDs.
COMPUTERS ON CAMPUS 70 computers for student use in computer center, academic labs, library.
HOUSING College housing not available.
ATHLETICS ***Intramural:*** basketball, volleyball.
CAREER PLANNING ***Service:*** career counseling.
EXPENSES FOR 1995–96 State resident tuition: $557 full-time, $13.25 per credit hour part-time. Nonresident tuition: $4515 full-time, $107.50 per credit hour part-time. Part-time mandatory fees: $4.60 per credit hour. Full-time mandatory fees: $24.
FINANCIAL AID ***College-administered undergrad aid 1995–96:*** need-based scholarships, short-term loans (averaging $61), low-interest long-term loans from external sources (averaging $673), Federal Work-Study. ***Required forms:*** FAFSA; accepted: CSS Financial Aid PROFILE. ***Application deadline:*** continuous.
APPLYING Open admission except for nursing program. ***Option:*** early entrance. ***Required:*** ACT ASSET. ***Required for some:*** campus interview. Test scores used for counseling/placement. ***Application deadline:*** rolling. ***Notification:*** continuous.
APPLYING/TRANSFER ***Required:*** standardized test scores. ***Required for some:*** campus interview. ***Entrance:*** noncompetitive. ***Application deadline:*** rolling. ***Notification:*** continuous.
CONTACT Miss Sandra Copeland, Admissions Counselor, Roanoke-Chowan Community College, Ahoskie, NC 27910, 919-332-5921 Ext. 225.

ROBESON COMMUNITY COLLEGE
Lumberton, North Carolina

UG Enrollment: 1,322	**Tuition & Fees (NC Res): $578**
Application Deadline: rolling	**Room & Board: N/Avail**

GENERAL State-supported, 2-year, coed. Part of North Carolina Community College System. Awards transfer associate, terminal associate degrees. Founded 1965. *Setting:* 78-acre small-town campus. *Total enrollment:* 1,322. *Faculty:* 114 (44 full-time, 70 part-time).
ENROLLMENT PROFILE 1,322 students: 60% women, 50% part-time, 34% Native American, 24% African American. *Most popular recent majors:* nursing, computer programming, business administration/commerce/management.
FIRST-YEAR CLASS 700 total. Of the students who applied, 100% were accepted.
ACADEMIC PROGRAM Calendar: semesters. Services for LD students, adult/continuing education programs.
GENERAL DEGREE REQUIREMENTS 117 credit hours; 3 credit hours of math; 4 credit hours of science; computer course for business majors.
MAJORS Accounting, agricultural sciences, business administration/commerce/management, computer programming, education, finance/banking, industrial and heavy equipment maintenance, law enforcement/police sciences, nursing, practical nursing, secretarial studies/office management, teacher aide studies.
LIBRARY 39,000 books, 2,400 microform titles, 225 periodicals.
COMPUTERS ON CAMPUS 100 computers for student use in classrooms. Staffed computer lab on campus.
COLLEGE LIFE *Student services:* personal-psychological counseling.
HOUSING College housing not available.
CAREER PLANNING *Service:* career counseling.
AFTER GRADUATION 82% of students completing a degree program in 1994–95 went directly on to further study.
EXPENSES FOR 1996–97 State resident tuition: $557 full-time, $13.25 per credit hour part-time. Nonresident tuition: $4515 full-time, $107.50 per credit hour part-time. Part-time mandatory fees per credit hour range from $4 to $7. Full-time mandatory fees: $21.
FINANCIAL AID *College-administered undergrad aid 1995–96:* need-based scholarships, low-interest long-term loans from external sources, Federal Work-Study. *Required forms:* FAFSA. *Application deadline:* continuous to 5/1. *Waivers:* full or partial for senior citizens. *Notification:* continuous.
APPLYING Open admission. *Option:* early entrance. *Required:* ACT ASSET. *Application deadline:* rolling. *Notification:* continuous.
APPLYING/TRANSFER *Required:* standardized test scores. *Application deadline:* rolling. *Notification:* continuous.
CONTACT Ms. Judy Revels, Director of Admissions, Robeson Community College, Lumberton, NC 28359-1420, 910-738-7101 Ext. 251. *Fax:* 910-671-4143.

ROCKINGHAM COMMUNITY COLLEGE
Wentworth, North Carolina

UG Enrollment: 1,907	Tuition & Fees (NC Res): $584
Application Deadline: rolling	Room & Board: N/Avail

GENERAL State-supported, 2-year, coed. Part of North Carolina Community College System. Awards transfer associate, terminal associate degrees. Founded 1964. *Setting:* 257-acre rural campus. *Educational spending 1994–95:* $1247 per undergrad. *Total enrollment:* 1,907. *Faculty:* 114 (47 full-time, 100% with terminal degrees, 67 part-time); student-faculty ratio is 22:1.
ENROLLMENT PROFILE 1,907 students from 6 states and territories, 1 other country. 65% women, 49% part-time, 98% state residents, 8% transferred in, 1% international, 53% 25 or older, 1% Native American, 1% Hispanic, 17% African American, 0% Asian American. *Areas of study chosen:* 35% liberal arts/general studies, 19% fine arts, 16% vocational and home economics, 5% computer and information sciences, 3% health professions and related sciences. *Most popular recent majors:* liberal arts/general studies, nursing, business administration/commerce/management.
FIRST-YEAR CLASS 595 total; 595 applied, 100% were accepted, 100% of whom enrolled.
ACADEMIC PROGRAM Calendar: quarters. Academic remediation for entering students, advanced placement, self-designed majors, summer session for credit, part-time degree program (daytime, evenings), adult/continuing education programs, co-op programs.
GENERAL DEGREE REQUIREMENTS 90 credits; computer course.
MAJORS Accounting, art/fine arts, business administration/commerce/management, business machine technologies, carpentry, child care/child and family studies, computer information systems, construction technologies, consumer services, cosmetology, criminal justice, electromechanical technology, heating/refrigeration/air conditioning, horticulture, human resources, industrial arts, labor and industrial relations, law enforcement/police sciences, legal secretarial studies, liberal arts/general studies, medical assistant technologies, medical secretarial studies, nursing, paralegal studies, practical nursing, science, secretarial studies/office management, teacher aide studies, tourism and travel.
LIBRARY Gerald B. James Library with 35,000 books, 217 periodicals, 2,012 records, tapes, and CDs. Acquisition spending 1994–95: $248,270.
COMPUTERS ON CAMPUS Computer purchase plan available. 93 computers for student use in computer center, classrooms, library, student center. Staffed computer lab on campus.
COLLEGE LIFE Student-run newspaper. *Social organizations:* 19 open to all. *Most popular organizations:* Phi Theta Kappa, Cultural Diversity Club, Paralegal Club. *Major annual events:* Rockingham County Folk Festival, Cultural Diversity Day. *Student services:* personal-psychological counseling. *Campus security:* late-night transport-escort service.
HOUSING College housing not available.
ATHLETICS *Intramural:* archery, badminton, basketball, golf, table tennis (Ping-Pong), tennis, volleyball.
CAREER PLANNING *Placement office:* 1 full-time staff. *Director:* Ms. Jane Norwood, Career Counselor, 910-342-4261 Ext. 177. *Services:* job fairs, career counseling, careers library, job bank, job interviews.
EXPENSES FOR 1995–96 State resident tuition: $557 full-time, $13.25 per quarter hour part-time. Nonresident tuition: $4515 full-time, $107.50 per quarter hour part-time. Part-time mandatory fees per quarter range from $2 to $9. Full-time mandatory fees: $27.
FINANCIAL AID *College-administered undergrad aid 1995–96:* 1,128 need-based scholarships, 16 non-need scholarships, short-term loans (average $174), low-interest long-term loans from college funds, loans from external sources (average $2186), Federal Work-Study, 42 part-time jobs. *Required forms:* CSS Financial Aid PROFILE, FAFSA. *Priority deadline:* 5/1. *Waivers:* full or partial for senior citizens.

APPLYING Open admission except for nursing, electromechanical technology programs. *Options:* early entrance, deferred entrance. *Required:* TOEFL for international students. *Required for some:* CGP. Test scores used for counseling/placement. *Application deadline:* rolling. *Notification:* continuous.
APPLYING/TRANSFER *Required for some:* standardized test scores. *Entrance:* noncompetitive. *Application deadline:* rolling. *Notification:* continuous.
CONTACT Dr. LaCheata Hall, Director of Enrollment Management, Rockingham Community College, Wentworth, NC 27375-0038, 910-342-4261 Ext. 117.

ROWAN-CABARRUS COMMUNITY COLLEGE
Salisbury, North Carolina

UG Enrollment: 3,500	Tuition & Fees (NC Res): $584
Application Deadline: rolling	Room & Board: N/Avail

GENERAL State-supported, 2-year, coed. Part of North Carolina Community College System. Awards transfer associate, terminal associate degrees. Founded 1963. *Setting:* 100-acre small-town campus. *Total enrollment:* 3,500. *Faculty:* 130 (60 full-time, 99% with terminal degrees, 70 part-time); student-faculty ratio is 20:1.
ENROLLMENT PROFILE 3,500 students: 55% women, 45% men, 45% part-time, 99% state residents, 15% transferred in, 1% international, 55% 25 or older, 1% Native American, 1% Hispanic, 15% African American. *Areas of study chosen:* 20% liberal arts/general studies, 15% business management and administrative services, 5% computer and information sciences, 4% health professions and related sciences. *Most popular recent majors:* business administration/commerce/management, computer programming, nursing.
FIRST-YEAR CLASS 800 total; 2,000 applied, 100% were accepted, 40% of whom enrolled. 5% from top 10% of their high school class, 50% from top half.
ACADEMIC PROGRAM Honor code. Calendar: quarters. Academic remediation for entering students, services for LD students, advanced placement, summer session for credit, part-time degree program (daytime, evenings, summer), adult/continuing education programs.
GENERAL DEGREE REQUIREMENTS 96 credits; 1 math/science course; computer course for most majors.
MAJORS Accounting, automotive technologies, business administration/commerce/management, child care/child and family studies, computer programming, criminal justice, data processing, drafting and design, early childhood education, electrical and electronics technologies, electrical engineering technology, industrial administration, liberal arts/general studies, manufacturing technology, medical secretarial studies, nursing, paralegal studies, radiological technology, science.
LIBRARY 23,005 books, 22,907 microform titles, 313 periodicals, 1,488 records, tapes, and CDs.
COMPUTERS ON CAMPUS 200 computers for student use in computer center, classrooms, library, student center. Staffed computer lab on campus provides training in use of computers, software.
COLLEGE LIFE *Student services:* personal-psychological counseling.
HOUSING College housing not available.
ATHLETICS *Intramural:* basketball.
CAREER PLANNING *Director:* Mr. Reg Boland, Director of Counseling, 704-637-0760. *Services:* job fairs, resume preparation, career counseling.
AFTER GRADUATION 95% of students completing a degree program in 1994–95 went directly on to further study.
EXPENSES FOR 1995–96 State resident tuition: $557 full-time, $13.25 per credit part-time. Nonresident tuition: $4515 full-time, $107.50 per credit part-time. Part-time mandatory fees per quarter range from $3.25 to $5.25. Full-time mandatory fees: $27. Tuition guaranteed not to increase for student's term of enrollment.
FINANCIAL AID *College-administered undergrad aid 1995–96:* need-based scholarships, short-term loans, low-interest long-term loans from external sources, part-time jobs. *Required forms:* FAFSA. *Application deadline:* continuous.
APPLYING Open admission. *Required:* school transcript, TOEFL for international students, ACT ASSET. Test scores used for counseling/placement. *Application deadline:* rolling.
APPLYING/TRANSFER *Required:* college transcript. *Required for some:* standardized test scores. *Application deadline:* rolling. *Contact:* Mr. Reg Boland, Director of Counseling, 704-637-0760.
CONTACT Mr. Eddie H. Myers, Vice President of Student Services, Rowan-Cabarrus Community College, Salisbury, NC 28145-1595, 704-637-0760 Ext. 271. *Fax:* 704-637-6642.

SAINT MARY'S COLLEGE
Raleigh, North Carolina

UG Enrollment: 136	Tuition & Fees: $7880
Application Deadline: rolling	Room & Board: $6500

GENERAL Independent Episcopal, 2-year, women only. Awards transfer associate degrees. Founded 1842. *Setting:* 24-acre urban campus. *Endowment:* $12 million. *Total enrollment:* 136. *Faculty:* 34 (27 full-time, 32% with terminal degrees, 7 part-time). *Notable Alumni:* Betty Ray McCain, secretary of North Carolina Department of Cultural Resources; Betty Debnam Hunt, creator and editor of *The Mini Page*; Jeanne Smith Piland, opera singer; Marie Watters Colton, first woman speaker pro tempore of North Carolina House of Representatives.
ENROLLMENT PROFILE 136 students from 15 states and territories, 4 other countries. 100% women, 4% part-time, 63% state residents, 0% transferred in, 65% have need-based financial aid, 35% have non-need-based financial aid, 3% international, 0% 25 or older, 0% Native American, 1% Hispanic, 1% African American, 1% Asian American. *Areas of study chosen:* 100% liberal arts/general studies.
FIRST-YEAR CLASS 80 total; 137 applied, 93% were accepted, 63% of whom enrolled. 8% from top 10% of their high school class, 27% from top quarter, 54% from top half. 2 class presidents.
ACADEMIC PROGRAM Core, liberal arts curriculum, honor code. Calendar: semesters. 147 courses offered in 1995–96; average class size 20 in required courses. English as a

Saint Mary's College (continued)
second language program offered during academic year, advanced placement, honors program, summer session for credit. Off-campus study at members of the Cooperating Raleigh Colleges.
GENERAL DEGREE REQUIREMENTS 62 semester hours; 6 semester hours of math; 4 semester hours of science; 6 semester hours of a foreign language.
MAJOR Liberal arts/general studies.
LIBRARY Kenan Library with 40,000 books, 85 microform titles, 205 periodicals, 1 on-line bibliographic service, 1 CD-ROM, 300 records, tapes, and CDs. Acquisition spending 1994–95: $24,801.
COMPUTERS ON CAMPUS 42 computers for student use in computer center, library, student center provide access to main academic computer, e-mail, on-line services, Internet. Staffed computer lab on campus provides training in use of computers, software. Academic computing expenditure 1994–95: $159,805.
COLLEGE LIFE Orientation program (1 week, no cost). Drama-theater group, choral group, student-run newspaper. ***Student services:*** health clinic, personal-psychological counseling. ***Campus security:*** 24-hour emergency response devices and patrols, late-night transport-escort service, controlled dormitory access.
HOUSING 138 college housing spaces available; 108 were occupied 1995–96. Freshmen guaranteed college housing. On-campus residence required through sophomore year except if living with relatives. ***Options:*** freshmen-only, single-sex housing available. Resident assistants live in dorms.
ATHLETICS Member NJCAA. ***Intercollegiate:*** soccer, tennis. ***Intramural:*** badminton, basketball, bowling, equestrian sports, softball, swimming and diving, tennis. ***Contact:*** Mr. Davis Dillon, Director of Athletics, 919-839-4020.
CAREER PLANNING ***Placement office:*** $89,521 operating expenditure 1994–95. ***Service:*** career counseling.
AFTER GRADUATION 99% of students completing a degree program in 1994–95 went directly on to further study.
EXPENSES FOR 1996–97 ***Application fee:*** $25. Comprehensive fee of $14,380 includes full-time tuition ($7730), mandatory fees ($150), and college room and board ($6500).
FINANCIAL AID ***College-administered undergrad aid 1995–96:*** 47 need-based scholarships (average $6340), 26 non-need scholarships (average $4538), low-interest long-term loans from external sources (average $2625), 45 part-time jobs. ***Required forms:*** institutional; accepted: CSS Financial Aid PROFILE. ***Priority deadline:*** 4/1. ***Payment plan:*** installment.
APPLYING ***Options:*** Common Application, early entrance, deferred entrance, midyear entrance. ***Required:*** school transcript, minimum 2.0 GPA, 3 years of high school math, 2 years of high school foreign language, 2 recommendations, SAT I or ACT, TOEFL for international students. ***Recommended:*** 3 years of high school science, SAT II Subject Tests. Test scores used for admission. ***Application deadline:*** rolling.
APPLYING/TRANSFER ***Required:*** standardized test scores, high school transcript, 3 years of high school math, some high school foreign language, 2 recommendations, college transcript, minimum 2.0 college GPA, minimum 2.0 high school GPA. ***Recommended:*** 3 years of high school science. ***Entrance:*** minimally difficult. ***Application deadline:*** rolling.
CONTACT Mrs. Jennette C. Herbert, Director of Admissions, Saint Mary's College, 900 Hillsborough Street, Raleigh, NC 27603-1610, 919-839-4001. ***Fax:*** 919-839-4137. College video available.

SAMPSON COMMUNITY COLLEGE
Clinton, North Carolina

UG Enrollment: 993 | **Tuition & Fees (NC Res): $587**
Application Deadline: rolling | **Room & Board: N/Avail**

GENERAL State and locally supported, 2-year, coed. Part of North Carolina Community College System. Awards certificates, diplomas, transfer associate, terminal associate degrees. Founded 1965. ***Setting:*** 55-acre rural campus. ***Total enrollment:*** 993. ***Faculty:*** 102 (47 full-time, 4% with terminal degrees, 55 part-time).
ENROLLMENT PROFILE 993 students: 69% women, 50% part-time, 98% state residents, 13% transferred in, 55% 25 or older, 3% Native American, 2% Hispanic, 32% African American. ***Areas of study chosen:*** 43% business management and administrative services, 15% liberal arts/general studies, 14% education, 13% health professions and related sciences, 8% computer and information sciences, 4% agriculture, 3% engineering and applied sciences. ***Most popular recent majors:*** business administration/commerce/management, nursing, liberal arts/general studies.
FIRST-YEAR CLASS 298 total; 449 applied, 82% were accepted, 81% of whom enrolled.
ACADEMIC PROGRAM Core. Calendar: quarters. Average class size 25 in required courses. Academic remediation for entering students, services for LD students, summer session for credit, part-time degree program (daytime, evenings), adult/continuing education programs, co-op programs and internships.
GENERAL DEGREE REQUIREMENTS 115 quarter hours; computer course for nursing, welding, horticulture majors; internship (some majors).
MAJORS Accounting, business administration/commerce/management, computer programming, criminal justice, horticulture, industrial engineering technology, liberal arts/general studies, nursing, practical nursing, secretarial studies/office management.
LIBRARY 22,000 books, 108 periodicals, 2,100 records, tapes, and CDs.
COMPUTERS ON CAMPUS 78 computers for student use in computer center, classrooms.
COLLEGE LIFE 40% vote in student government elections. ***Most popular organizations:*** Student Government Association, Criminal Justice Club, Nursing Student Association, Cosmetology Alliance Club, Phi Beta Lambda. ***Major annual event:*** Field Day. ***Student services:*** personal-psychological counseling. ***Campus security:*** local police patrol.
HOUSING College housing not available.
ATHLETICS ***Intramural:*** basketball, golf, volleyball. ***Contact:*** Mr. Terry Norris, Student Activities Coordinator, 910-592-8084.
CAREER PLANNING ***Placement office:*** 4 part-time staff. ***Director:*** Ms. Linda Combs, Career Counselor, 910-592-8084 Ext. 249. ***Services:*** career counseling, careers library.
AFTER GRADUATION 23% of students completing a degree program in 1994–95 went directly on to further study.
EXPENSES FOR 1995–96 State resident tuition: $557 full-time, $13.25 per quarter hour part-time. Nonresident tuition: $4515 full-time, $107.50 per quarter hour part-time. Part-time mandatory fees per quarter range from $6.20 to $10. Full-time mandatory fees: $30.
FINANCIAL AID ***College-administered undergrad aid 1995–96:*** 201 need-based scholarships (average $578), 53 non-need scholarships (average $793), short-term loans (average $130), low-interest long-term loans from external sources (average $1886), 26 Federal Work-Study (averaging $1011), 52 part-time jobs. ***Required forms:*** FAFSA. ***Priority deadline:*** 8/15. ***Waivers:*** full or partial for employees or children of employees and senior citizens. ***Notification:*** continuous.
APPLYING Open admission except for nursing programs. ***Option:*** deferred entrance. ***Required:*** school transcript, interview, Assessment and Placement Services for Community Colleges. ***Recommended:*** minimum 2.0 GPA. Test scores used for counseling/placement. ***Application deadline:*** rolling. ***Notification:*** continuous.
APPLYING/TRANSFER ***Required:*** high school transcript, interview, college transcript. ***Recommended:*** minimum 2.0 high school GPA. ***Required for some:*** standardized test scores. ***Entrance:*** noncompetitive. ***Application deadline:*** rolling. ***Notification:*** continuous. ***Contact:*** Ms. Cynthia Barber, Transfer Counselor, 910-592-8084.
CONTACT Mr. William R. Jordan, Director of Admissions, Sampson Community College, Clinton, NC 28329-0318, 910-592-8084. ***Fax:*** 910-592-8048.

SANDHILLS COMMUNITY COLLEGE
Pinehurst, North Carolina

UG Enrollment: 2,396 | **Tuition & Fees (NC Res): $578**
Application Deadline: rolling | **Room & Board: N/Avail**

GENERAL State and locally supported, 2-year, coed. Part of North Carolina Community College System. Awards certificates, diplomas, transfer associate, terminal associate degrees. Founded 1963. ***Setting:*** 230-acre small-town campus. ***Educational spending 1994–95:*** $3292 per undergrad. ***Total enrollment:*** 2,396. ***Faculty:*** 147 (98 full-time, 6% with terminal degrees, 49 part-time); student-faculty ratio is 17:1.
ENROLLMENT PROFILE 2,396 students from 20 states and territories, 15 other countries. 65% women, 35% men, 43% part-time, 98% state residents, 13% transferred in, 40% have need-based financial aid, 5% have non-need-based financial aid, 1% international, 39% 25 or older, 3% Native American, 1% Hispanic, 21% African American, 1% Asian American. ***Areas of study chosen:*** 23% health professions and related sciences, 15% business management and administrative services, 14% liberal arts/general studies, 9% vocational and home economics, 7% social sciences, 6% computer and information sciences, 5% engineering and applied sciences, 3% education, 2% agriculture, 2% biological and life sciences, 2% fine arts, 1% architecture, 1% communications and journalism, 1% English language/literature/letters, 1% mathematics, 1% natural resource sciences, 1% performing arts, 1% physical sciences, 1% predentistry, 1% prelaw, 1% premed, 1% prevet, 1% psychology. ***Most popular recent majors:*** liberal arts/general studies, nursing, business administration/commerce/management.
FIRST-YEAR CLASS 492 total; 1,029 applied, 100% were accepted, 48% of whom enrolled.
ACADEMIC PROGRAM Core, liberal arts and technical/vocational curriculum, honor code. Calendar: quarters. 691 courses offered in 1995–96; average class size 17 in required courses. Academic remediation for entering students, English as a second language program offered during academic year and summer, services for LD students, advanced placement, honors program, summer session for credit, part-time degree program (daytime, evenings), adult/continuing education programs, co-op programs and internships.
GENERAL DEGREE REQUIREMENTS 96 quarter hours; computer course for most majors; internship (some majors).
MAJORS Accounting, architectural technologies, art/fine arts, automotive technologies, business administration/commerce/management, child care/child and family studies, civil engineering technology, computer programming, computer technologies, cosmetology, criminal justice, culinary arts, data processing, drug and alcohol/substance abuse counseling, early childhood education, electrical and electronics technologies, electronics engineering technology, (pre)engineering sequence, engineering technology, hotel and restaurant management, human services, landscaping/grounds maintenance, law enforcement/police sciences, liberal arts/general studies, manufacturing technology, mathematics, medical laboratory technology, medical secretarial studies, mental health/rehabilitation counseling, music, music education, nursing, operating room technology, painting/drawing, paralegal studies, practical nursing, radiological technology, respiratory therapy, science, science education, secretarial studies/office management, studio art, surveying technology, teacher aide studies.
LIBRARY Boyd Library with 75,973 books, 97,182 microform titles, 558 periodicals, 1 on-line bibliographic service, 15 CD-ROMs, 839 records, tapes, and CDs. Acquisition spending 1994–95: $506,744.
COMPUTERS ON CAMPUS 275 computers for student use in computer center, computer labs, learning resource center, labs, writing center, classrooms, library provide access to e-mail, Internet. Staffed computer lab on campus provides training in use of computers, software. Academic computing expenditure 1994–95: $129,115.
COLLEGE LIFE Choral group, student-run newspaper. ***Social organizations:*** 6 open to all. ***Most popular organizations:*** Student Government Association, Minority Students for Academic and Cultural Enrichment, Circle K. ***Major annual events:*** Spring Fling, College Day, Health Career Day. ***Student services:*** personal-psychological counseling. ***Campus security:*** 24-hour emergency response devices, security on duty until 12 a.m.
HOUSING College housing not available.
ATHLETICS ***Intramural:*** basketball, golf, racquetball, softball, table tennis (Ping-Pong), tennis, volleyball. ***Contact:*** Mr. Jim Reid, Director of Athletics, 910-695-3786; Ms. Cindy Kennedy, Physical Education Professor, 910-695-3787.
CAREER PLANNING ***Placement office:*** 1 full-time staff; $41,000 operating expenditure 1994–95. ***Director:*** Mr. Stephen Athans, Career Counselor, 910-695-3732. ***Services:*** job fairs, resume preparation, resume referral, career counseling, careers library, job bank, job interviews.
AFTER GRADUATION 87% of class of 1994 had job offers within 6 months. 69% of students completing a degree program went directly on to further study.
ESTIMATED EXPENSES FOR 1996–97 State resident tuition: $557 full-time, $13.25 per quarter hour part-time. Nonresident tuition: $4515 full-time, $107.50 per quarter hour part-time. Part-time mandatory fees: $7 per quarter. Full-time mandatory fees: $21.
FINANCIAL AID ***College-administered undergrad aid 1995–96:*** 175 need-based scholarships (averaging $850), 50 non-need scholarships (averaging $600), short-term loans (averaging $138), low-interest long-term loans from external sources (averaging $2000), 31 Federal Work-Study (averaging $1400). ***Required forms:*** institutional, FAFSA. ***Priority deadline:*** 8/15. ***Waivers:*** full or partial for employees or children of employees and senior citizens. ***Notification:*** continuous.

APPLYING Open admission except for landscaping, medical programs. *Options:* deferred entrance, midyear entrance. *Required:* school transcript, TOEFL for international students. *Required for some:* 3 years of high school science, ACT ASSET. Test scores used for counseling/placement. *Application deadline:* rolling. *Notification:* continuous.
APPLYING/TRANSFER *Required:* high school transcript, college transcript. *Required for some:* standardized test scores, 3 years of high school science. *Entrance:* noncompetitive. *Application deadline:* rolling. *Notification:* continuous. *Contact:* Ms. Sharon Ashburn, Transfer Counselor, 910-695-3731.
CONTACT Ms. Beverly Offutt, Admissions Counselor, Sandhills Community College, Pinehurst, NC 28374-8299, 910-695-3729 or toll-free 800-338-3944 (in-state). *Fax:* 910-695-1823.

SOUTHEASTERN BAPTIST THEOLOGICAL SEMINARY
Wake Forest, North Carolina

UG Enrollment: 142	Tuition & Fees: $1100
Application Deadline: 7/20	Room Only: $1080

GENERAL Independent Southern Baptist, 2-year, specialized, coed. Awards transfer associate, terminal associate, master's, doctoral, first professional degrees. Founded 1950. *Setting:* 450-acre small-town campus with easy access to Raleigh. Faculty: 32 (23 full-time, 100% with terminal degrees, 9 part-time); student-faculty ratio is 30:1.
ENROLLMENT PROFILE 142 students from 22 states and territories, 5 other countries. 10% women, 20% part-time, 50% state residents, 30% live on campus, 65% transferred in, 75% have need-based financial aid, 2% international, 100% 25 or older, 6% African American. *Areas of study chosen:* 100% theology/religion.
FIRST-YEAR CLASS 77 total; 110 applied, 80% were accepted, 88% of whom enrolled.
ACADEMIC PROGRAM Core, theological curriculum, honor code. Calendar: semesters. Academic remediation for entering students, summer session for credit, part-time degree program (daytime), internships.
GENERAL DEGREE REQUIREMENT 56 credits.
MAJORS Ministries, pastoral studies, theology.
LIBRARY 191,734 books, 103,915 microform titles, 1,014 periodicals, 1 on-line bibliographic service, 8 CD-ROMs, 1,000 records, tapes, and CDs. Acquisition spending 1994–95: $101,000.
COMPUTERS ON CAMPUS 7 computers for student use in library provide access to main academic computer. Staffed computer lab on campus.
COLLEGE LIFE Drama-theater group, choral group, student-run newspaper. *Student services:* health clinic, personal-psychological counseling. *Campus security:* 24-hour emergency response devices and patrols, late-night transport-escort service.
HOUSING 175 college housing spaces available; 50 were occupied 1995–96. No special consideration for freshman housing applicants. Off-campus living permitted. *Options:* single-sex (2 buildings), international student housing available.
ATHLETICS *Intramural:* basketball, football, golf, racquetball, table tennis (Ping-Pong), tennis, volleyball, weight lifting.
CAREER PLANNING *Placement office:* 2 full-time, 2 part-time staff; $68,047 operating expenditure 1994–95. *Director:* Dr. Gerald Cowen, Director, Student Field Ministries, 919-556-3101 Ext. 315. *Services:* resume referral, career counseling, job bank, job interviews. 50 organizations recruited on campus 1994–95.
EXPENSES FOR 1996–97 *Application fee:* $25. Part-time mandatory fees: $65 per hour. Tuition for Southern Baptists: $1000 full-time, $250 per semester part-time. Tuition for all other students: $2000 full-time, $500 per semester part-time. Full-time mandatory fees: $100. College room only: $1080.
FINANCIAL AID *College-administered undergrad aid 1995–96:* need-based scholarships, non-need scholarships, short-term loans, low-interest long-term loans from college funds, Federal Work-Study, part-time jobs. *Required forms:* institutional. *Application deadline:* 9/15.
APPLYING Open admission. *Option:* Common Application. *Required:* 3 recommendations, TOEFL for international students. *Required for some:* interview. Test scores used for admission. *Application deadline:* 7/20. *Notification:* continuous until 8/20.
APPLYING/TRANSFER *Required:* 3 recommendations, college transcript. *Required for some:* interview. *Entrance:* noncompetitive. *Application deadline:* 7/20. *Notification:* continuous until 8/20. *Contact:* Mr. Sheldon H. Alexander, Registrar/Assistant to the Dean, 919-556-3101.
CONTACT Mr. L. Russ Bush III, Vice President for Academic Affairs/Dean of Faculty, Southeastern Baptist Theological Seminary, Wake Forest, NC 27588-1889, 919-556-3101 Ext. 249 or toll-free 800-284-6317.

SOUTHEASTERN COMMUNITY COLLEGE
Whiteville, North Carolina

UG Enrollment: 1,750	Tuition & Fees (NC Res): $589
Application Deadline: rolling	Room & Board: N/Avail

GENERAL State-supported, 2-year, coed. Part of North Carolina Community College System. Awards certificates, diplomas, transfer associate, terminal associate degrees. Founded 1964. *Setting:* 106-acre rural campus. *Total enrollment:* 1,750. *Faculty:* 145 (52 full-time, 40% with terminal degrees, 93 part-time); student-faculty ratio is 12:1.
ENROLLMENT PROFILE 1,750 students from 2 states and territories, 10 other countries. 66% women, 40% part-time, 98% state residents, 5% transferred in, 40% have need-based financial aid, 5% have non-need-based financial aid, 1% international, 45% 25 or older, 3% Native American, 0% Hispanic, 20% African American. *Areas of study chosen:* 35% health professions and related sciences, 10% education, 10% engineering and applied sciences, 5% biological and life sciences, 5% business management and administrative services, 5% computer and information sciences, 5% fine arts, 5% liberal arts/general studies, 5% performing arts, 5% social sciences.
FIRST-YEAR CLASS 460 total; 980 applied, 100% were accepted, 70% of whom enrolled. 10% from top 10% of their high school class, 25% from top quarter, 50% from top half.
ACADEMIC PROGRAM Core, honor code. Calendar: quarters. 150 courses offered in 1995–96; average class size 12 in required courses. Academic remediation for entering students, English as a second language program, services for LD students, advanced placement, tutorials, honors program, summer session for credit, part-time degree program (daytime, evenings, summer), adult/continuing education programs, co-op programs and internships. ROTC: Army (c).
GENERAL DEGREE REQUIREMENTS 96 quarter hours; computer course for business, criminal justice, forestry majors; internship (some majors).
MAJORS Art/fine arts, business administration/commerce/management, computer technologies, cosmetology, criminal justice, early childhood education, electrical engineering technology, forest technology, liberal arts/general studies, medical laboratory technology, music, nursing, recreation and leisure services, science, secretarial studies/office management, teacher aide studies, welding technology.
LIBRARY Southeastern Community College Library with 50,297 books, 769 microform titles, 192 periodicals, 3 on-line bibliographic services, 1 CD-ROM, 4,699 records, tapes, and CDs.
COMPUTERS ON CAMPUS 80 computers for student use in computer center, business lab.
COLLEGE LIFE Drama-theater group, choral group. *Social organizations:* 6 open to all. *Most popular organizations:* Student Government Association, Forestry Club, Nursing Club. *Major annual events:* High School Senior Day, 8th Grader Day. *Student services:* personal-psychological counseling. *Campus security:* 24-hour emergency response devices.
HOUSING College housing not available.
ATHLETICS Member NJCAA. *Intercollegiate:* baseball M. *Contact:* Mr. Joe Nance, Athletic Director, 910-642-7141.
CAREER PLANNING *Placement office:* 1 full-time staff. *Director:* Ms. Maggie Chepul, Job Development/Placement, 910-642-7141 Ext. 311. *Services:* job fairs, resume preparation, career counseling, careers library, job bank, job interviews. Students must register sophomore year. 2 organizations recruited on campus 1994–95.
EXPENSES FOR 1995–96 State resident tuition: $557 full-time, $13.25 per quarter hour part-time. Nonresident tuition: $4515 full-time, $107.50 per quarter hour part-time. Part-time mandatory fees: $10.75 per quarter. Full-time mandatory fees: $32.
FINANCIAL AID *College-administered undergrad aid 1995–96:* 147 need-based scholarships (average $215), 19 non-need scholarships (average $342), short-term loans (average $105), low-interest long-term loans from college funds (average $481), loans from external sources (average $1356), Federal Work-Study, 26 part-time jobs. *Required forms:* CSS Financial Aid PROFILE, FAFSA; accepted: state, institutional. *Priority deadline:* 4/15.
APPLYING Open admission except for nursing, phlebotomy, medical laboratory technology programs. *Options:* Common Application, early entrance, deferred entrance, midyear entrance. *Required:* school transcript, TOEFL for international students. Test scores used for counseling/placement. *Application deadline:* rolling.
APPLYING/TRANSFER *Required:* high school transcript. *Required for some:* standardized test scores, college transcript. *Application deadline:* rolling. *Contact:* Mr. James Fowler, Dean of Students, 910-642-7141.
CONTACT Ms. Judy Young, Admissions Secretary, Southeastern Community College, Whiteville, NC 28472-0151, 910-642-7141 Ext. 264.

SOUTHWESTERN COMMUNITY COLLEGE
Sylva, North Carolina

UG Enrollment: 1,517	Tuition & Fees (NC Res): $746
Application Deadline: rolling	Room & Board: N/Avail

GENERAL State-supported, 2-year, coed. Part of North Carolina Community College System. Awards certificates, diplomas, transfer associate, terminal associate degrees. Founded 1964. *Setting:* 55-acre small-town campus. *Total enrollment:* 1,517. *Faculty:* 202 (40 full-time, 156 part-time); student-faculty ratio is 10:1.
ENROLLMENT PROFILE 1,517 students: 61% women, 48% part-time, 95% state residents, 7% transferred in, 60% have need-based financial aid, 0% international, 46% 25 or older, 11% Native American, 0% Hispanic, 2% African American, 0% Asian American.
FIRST-YEAR CLASS 543 total. Of the students who applied, 75% were accepted.
ACADEMIC PROGRAM Core, honor code. Calendar: quarters year-round. Academic remediation for entering students, services for LD students, summer session for credit, part-time degree program (daytime, evenings), adult/continuing education programs, co-op programs. Off-campus study at Haywood Community College.
GENERAL DEGREE REQUIREMENTS 96 credit hours; 1 math course; computer course.
MAJORS Accounting, automotive technologies, business administration/commerce/management, commercial art, computer information systems, computer technologies, cosmetology, early childhood education, electrical and electronics technologies, food services management, law enforcement/police sciences, liberal arts/general studies, medical laboratory technology, mental health/rehabilitation counseling, nursing, occupational therapy, paralegal studies, physical therapy, radio and television studies, radiological technology, respiratory therapy, secretarial studies/office management.
LIBRARY Learning Resources Center with 24,000 books, 210 periodicals, 810 records, tapes, and CDs.
COMPUTERS ON CAMPUS 75 computers for student use in computer center, computer labs, learning resource center, classrooms provide access to on-line services. Staffed computer lab on campus.
COLLEGE LIFE Student-run radio station. *Student services:* personal-psychological counseling.
HOUSING College housing not available.
CAREER PLANNING *Placement office:* 1 full-time staff. *Director:* Ms. Shirley Kool, Career Planning and Placement Officer, 704-586-4091 Ext. 279. *Services:* job fairs, resume preparation, resume referral, career counseling, careers library, job bank, job interviews.
EXPENSES FOR 1996–97 State resident tuition: $722 full-time, $15.05 per quarter hour part-time. Nonresident tuition: $5160 full-time, $107.50 per quarter hour part-time. Part-time mandatory fees per quarter range from $1.50 to $5.50. Full-time mandatory fees: $24.
FINANCIAL AID *College-administered undergrad aid 1995–96:* 46 need-based scholarships (average $250), low-interest long-term loans from external sources (average $1366), Federal Work-Study. *Required forms:* FAFSA. *Priority deadline:* 6/1. *Payment plan:* deferred payment. *Waivers:* full or partial for senior citizens. *Notification:* continuous.

Southwestern Community College(continued)

APPLYING Open admission except for allied health programs. ***Options:*** early entrance, deferred entrance. ***Required:*** school transcript, SAT I or ACT, TOEFL for international students, CPT. Test scores used for counseling/placement. ***Application deadline:*** rolling. ***Notification:*** continuous.

APPLYING/TRANSFER ***Required:*** college transcript. ***Application deadline:*** rolling. ***Notification:*** continuous. ***Contact:*** Mr. David McClure, Registrar, 704-586-4091.

CONTACT Ms. Myrna Campbell, Director of Admissions, Southwestern Community College, Sylva, NC 28779, 704-586-4091 Ext. 253. ***Fax:*** 704-586-4093 Ext. 293. College video available.

STANLY COMMUNITY COLLEGE
Albemarle, North Carolina

UG Enrollment: 1,660	**Tuition & Fees (NC Res): $578**
Application Deadline: rolling	**Room & Board: N/Avail**

GENERAL State-supported, 2-year, coed. Part of North Carolina Community College System. Awards certificates, diplomas, transfer associate, terminal associate degrees. Founded 1971. ***Setting:*** 150-acre small-town campus. ***Total enrollment:*** 1,660. ***Faculty:*** 76 (38 full-time, 38 part-time); student-faculty ratio is 21:1.

ENROLLMENT PROFILE 1,660 students from 5 states and territories, 2 other countries. 62% women, 57% part-time, 98% state residents, 10% transferred in, 1% international, 55% 25 or older, 1% Native American, 1% Hispanic, 10% African American, 1% Asian American.

FIRST-YEAR CLASS 533 total. Of the students who applied, 75% were accepted, 83% of whom enrolled.

ACADEMIC PROGRAM Calendar: quarters. Academic remediation for entering students, English as a second language program offered during academic year, summer session for credit, part-time degree program (daytime, evenings), adult/continuing education programs, co-op programs. Off-campus study at Anson-Stanly Community College–Union Branch.

GENERAL DEGREE REQUIREMENTS 118 quarter hours; computer course.

MAJORS Accounting, biomedical technologies, business administration/commerce/management, computer programming, criminal justice, drafting and design, early childhood education, electrical and electronics technologies, legal secretarial studies, medical assistant technologies, medical secretarial studies, nursing, occupational therapy, physical therapy, respiratory therapy, secretarial studies/office management.

LIBRARY 20,781 books, 55 microform titles, 173 periodicals, 1,350 records, tapes, and CDs.

COMPUTERS ON CAMPUS 100 computers for student use in computer labs, learning resource center, classrooms. Staffed computer lab on campus provides training in use of computers, software.

COLLEGE LIFE Student-run newspaper. 65% vote in student government elections. ***Student services:*** personal-psychological counseling.

HOUSING College housing not available.

CAREER PLANNING ***Service:*** career counseling.

EXPENSES FOR 1995–96 State resident tuition: $557 full-time, $13.25 per quarter hour part-time. Nonresident tuition: $4515 full-time, $107.50 per quarter hour part-time. Full-time mandatory fees: $21.

FINANCIAL AID ***College-administered undergrad aid 1995–96:*** 78 need-based scholarships (average $411), 20 non-need scholarships (average $500), short-term loans (average $125), low-interest long-term loans from external sources (average $1880), Federal Work-Study, part-time jobs. ***Required forms:*** institutional; required for some: CSS Financial Aid PROFILE, state, FAFSA. ***Priority deadline:*** 5/1.

APPLYING Open admission except for allied health programs. ***Options:*** early entrance, deferred entrance. ***Required:*** school transcript, TOEFL for international students, ACT ASSET. ***Recommended:*** SAT I. Test scores used for counseling/placement. ***Application deadline:*** rolling. ***Notification:*** continuous.

APPLYING/TRANSFER ***Required:*** standardized test scores, high school transcript, college transcript. ***Application deadline:*** rolling. ***Notification:*** continuous.

CONTACT Mr. Ronnie Hinson, Director of Admissions and Placement, Stanly Community College, Albemarle, NC 28001-7458, 704-982-0121 Ext. 233.

SURRY COMMUNITY COLLEGE
Dobson, North Carolina

UG Enrollment: 3,036	**Tuition & Fees (NC Res): $578**
Application Deadline: 8/31	**Room & Board: N/Avail**

GENERAL State-supported, 2-year, coed. Part of North Carolina Community College System. Awards certificates, diplomas, transfer associate, terminal associate degrees. Founded 1965. ***Setting:*** 100-acre rural campus. ***Total enrollment:*** 3,036. ***Faculty:*** 98 (84 full-time, 8% with terminal degrees, 14 part-time).

ENROLLMENT PROFILE 3,036 students from 3 states and territories, 2 other countries. 60% women, 35% part-time, 75% state residents, 5% transferred in, 60% 25 or older, 15% African American. ***Areas of study chosen:*** 40% liberal arts/general studies, 20% health professions and related sciences, 15% business management and administrative services, 15% computer and information sciences, 5% engineering and applied sciences, 4% agriculture, 1% vocational and home economics. ***Most popular recent majors:*** liberal arts/general studies, nursing, business administration/commerce/management.

FIRST-YEAR CLASS 1,354 total; 1,510 applied, 100% were accepted, 90% of whom enrolled. 20% from top 10% of their high school class, 70% from top half.

ACADEMIC PROGRAM Core, honor code. Calendar: quarters. Academic remediation for entering students, English as a second language program offered during academic year, advanced placement, summer session for credit, part-time degree program (daytime, evenings, summer), adult/continuing education programs, co-op programs and internships.

GENERAL DEGREE REQUIREMENTS 96 quarter hours; computer course for business, accounting, secretarial majors; internship (some majors).

MAJORS Accounting, agricultural business, agricultural sciences, agricultural technologies, automotive technologies, business administration/commerce/management, carpentry, construction technologies, criminal justice, drafting and design, electrical and electronics technologies, electronics engineering technology, horticulture, legal secretarial studies, liberal arts/general studies, medical secretarial studies, nursing, paralegal studies, practical nursing, real estate, retail management, secretarial studies/office management, welding technology.

LIBRARY Resource Center with 20,000 books.

COMPUTERS ON CAMPUS 50 computers for student use in computer center, computer labs, learning resource center, classrooms. Staffed computer lab on campus provides training in use of computers, software.

COLLEGE LIFE Choral group, student-run newspaper. 10% vote in student government elections. ***Social organizations:*** 7 open to all. ***Most popular organizations:*** Student Government Association, Phi Beta Lambda, Phi Theta Kappa, BSU. ***Major annual events:*** Student Appreciation Day, New Student Orientation, Christmas Dance. ***Student services:*** personal-psychological counseling. ***Campus security:*** security guard during evening hours.

HOUSING College housing not available.

ATHLETICS ***Intramural:*** basketball, golf, softball, tennis, volleyball, wrestling. ***Contact:*** Mr. Tony Searcy, Technical Programs Counselor, 910-386-8121 Ext. 246.

CAREER PLANNING ***Placement office:*** 1 full-time staff. ***Director:*** Ms. Anne Marie Woodruff, Counselor, 910-386-8121 Ext. 247. ***Services:*** resume preparation, career counseling, careers library.

AFTER GRADUATION 90% of students completing a degree program in 1994–95 went directly on to further study.

EXPENSES FOR 1995–96 State resident tuition: $557 full-time, $13.25 per quarter hour part-time. Nonresident tuition: $4515 full-time, $107.50 per quarter hour part-time. Part-time mandatory fees: $7 per quarter. Full-time mandatory fees: $21.

FINANCIAL AID ***College-administered undergrad aid 1995–96:*** need-based scholarships, non-need scholarships, low-interest long-term loans from external sources, Federal Work-Study. ***Required forms:*** institutional, FAFSA; accepted: CSS Financial Aid PROFILE. ***Priority deadline:*** 6/15. ***Waivers:*** full or partial for senior citizens.

APPLYING Open admission except for nursing program. ***Options:*** early entrance, deferred entrance, midyear entrance. ***Required:*** school transcript. ***Recommended:*** TOEFL for international students. Test scores used for counseling/placement. ***Application deadline:*** 8/31.

APPLYING/TRANSFER ***Required:*** college transcript. ***Application deadline:*** 8/31. ***Contact:*** Ms. Melissa Key White, College Transfer Counselor, 910-386-8121 Ext. 262.

CONTACT Mr. Greg Stanley, Registrar, Surry Community College, PO Box 304, Dobson, NC 27017-0304, 910-386-8121 Ext. 208. ***Fax:*** 910-386-8951. College video available.

TRI-COUNTY COMMUNITY COLLEGE
Murphy, North Carolina

UG Enrollment: 919	**Tuition & Fees (NC Res): $573**
Application Deadline: rolling	**Room & Board: N/Avail**

GENERAL State-supported, 2-year, coed. Part of North Carolina Community College System. Awards certificates, diplomas, transfer associate, terminal associate degrees. Founded 1964. ***Setting:*** 40-acre rural campus. ***Total enrollment:*** 919. ***Faculty:*** 55 (20 full-time, 35 part-time).

ENROLLMENT PROFILE 919 students from 6 states and territories. 65% women, 63% part-time, 95% state residents, 9% transferred in, 0% international, 62% 25 or older, 1% Native American, 1% Hispanic, 1% African American, 0% Asian American. ***Most popular recent majors:*** liberal arts/general studies, business administration/commerce/management, nursing.

FIRST-YEAR CLASS 295 total; 299 applied, 100% were accepted, 99% of whom enrolled. 10% from top 10% of their high school class, 35% from top quarter, 55% from top half.

ACADEMIC PROGRAM Core. Calendar: quarters. Academic remediation for entering students, services for LD students, summer session for credit, part-time degree program (daytime, evenings, summer), adult/continuing education programs.

GENERAL DEGREE REQUIREMENTS 97 quarter hours; 9 quarter hours of math; 12 quarter hours of science; computer course for most majors.

MAJORS Accounting, automotive technologies, business administration/commerce/management, computer management, electrical and electronics technologies, liberal arts/general studies, medical assistant technologies, nursing, secretarial studies/office management.

LIBRARY 16,224 books, 94 microform titles, 306 periodicals, 1,000 records, tapes, and CDs.

COMPUTERS ON CAMPUS 33 computers for student use in computer center, library.

COLLEGE LIFE Student-run newspaper. 40% vote in student government elections. ***Student services:*** personal-psychological counseling.

HOUSING College housing not available.

CAREER PLANNING ***Service:*** career counseling.

AFTER GRADUATION 40% of students completing a degree program in 1994–95 went directly on to further study.

EXPENSES FOR 1995–96 State resident tuition: $557 full-time, $13.25 per quarter hour part-time. Nonresident tuition: $4515 full-time, $107.50 per quarter hour part-time. Part-time mandatory fees: $5.25 per quarter. Full-time mandatory fees: $16.

FINANCIAL AID ***College-administered undergrad aid 1995–96:*** 52 need-based scholarships (average $210), 3 non-need scholarships (average $1000), Federal Work-Study, 8 part-time jobs. ***Acceptable forms:*** CSS Financial Aid PROFILE, institutional, FAFSA. ***Priority deadline:*** 8/1. ***Waivers:*** full or partial for senior citizens.

APPLYING Open admission except for nursing, medical assistant programs. ***Required:*** school transcript. ***Recommended:*** SAT I. ***Required for some:*** Assessment and Placement Services for Community Colleges. Test scores used for counseling/placement. ***Application deadline:*** rolling. ***Notification:*** continuous. Preference given to state residents.

APPLYING/TRANSFER ***Required:*** college transcript. ***Required for some:*** standardized test scores. ***Entrance:*** moderately difficult. ***Application deadline:*** rolling. ***Notification:*** continuous.

CONTACT Mr. Robert Jordan, Director of Admissions, Tri-County Community College, Murphy, NC 28906-7919, 704-837-6810 Ext. 225.

VANCE-GRANVILLE COMMUNITY COLLEGE
Henderson, North Carolina

UG Enrollment: 2,434 **Tuition & Fees (NC Res): $584**
Application Deadline: rolling **Room & Board: N/Avail**

GENERAL State-supported, 2-year, coed. Part of North Carolina Community College System. Awards certificates, diplomas, transfer associate, terminal associate degrees. Founded 1969. ***Setting:*** 83-acre rural campus with easy access to Raleigh. ***Endowment:*** $1.4 million. ***Educational spending 1994–95:*** $2003 per undergrad. ***Total enrollment:*** 2,434. ***Faculty:*** 194 (73 full-time, 4% with terminal degrees, 121 part-time); student-faculty ratio is 18:1. ***Notable Alumni:*** James Wheeler, chairperson of college vocational training division.

ENROLLMENT PROFILE 2,434 students from 7 states and territories. 66% women, 34% men, 52% part-time, 99% state residents, 4% transferred in, 55% have need-based financial aid, 8% have non-need-based financial aid, 0% international, 52% 25 or older, 1% Native American, 1% Hispanic, 43% African American, 0% Asian American. ***Areas of study chosen:*** 30% business management and administrative services, 22% vocational and home economics, 21% liberal arts/general studies, 11% health professions and related sciences, 8% computer and information sciences, 5% education, 3% engineering and applied sciences. ***Most popular recent majors:*** computer programming, business administration/commerce/management, liberal arts/general studies.

FIRST-YEAR CLASS 792 total; 1,254 applied, 95% were accepted, 66% of whom enrolled. 4% from top 10% of their high school class, 35% from top quarter, 61% from top half.

ACADEMIC PROGRAM Core, honor code. Calendar: quarters. 386 courses offered in 1995–96; average class size 18 in required courses. Academic remediation for entering students, English as a second language program offered during academic year, services for LD students, advanced placement, tutorials, summer session for credit, part-time degree program (daytime, evenings), adult/continuing education programs.

GENERAL DEGREE REQUIREMENTS 96 quarter hours; 1 math course; internship (some majors).

MAJORS Accounting, automotive technologies, business administration/commerce/management, carpentry, child care/child and family studies, computer programming, computer technologies, construction technologies, corrections, cosmetology, criminal justice, data processing, early childhood education, education, electrical and electronics technologies, electronics engineering technology, elementary education, heating/refrigeration/air conditioning, industrial administration, industrial engineering technology, labor and industrial relations, law enforcement/police sciences, legal secretarial studies, liberal arts/general studies, medical secretarial studies, nursing, practical nursing, radiological technology, recreation and leisure services, recreation therapy, secretarial studies/office management, teacher aide studies, welding technology.

LIBRARY 33,000 books, 200 microform titles, 235 periodicals, 2,050 records, tapes, and CDs. Acquisition spending 1994–95: $202,137.

COMPUTERS ON CAMPUS 135 computers for student use in computer center, computer labs, library provide access to main academic computer. Staffed computer lab on campus provides training in use of computers, software. Academic computing expenditure 1994–95: $218,396.

COLLEGE LIFE Drama-theater group. 60% vote in student government elections. ***Most popular organizations:*** Vocational Club, Phi Beta Kappa, Computer Club. ***Major annual events:*** Spring Sports Day, College-Wide Olympic Games, Career Day. ***Student services:*** personal-psychological counseling. ***Campus security:*** 24-hour emergency response devices and patrols.

HOUSING College housing not available.

ATHLETICS ***Intramural:*** basketball, soccer, tennis, track and field, volleyball.

CAREER PLANNING ***Placement office:*** 1 full-time staff; $40,000 operating expenditure 1994–95. ***Director:*** Ms. Barbara Smith, Career Specialist, 919-492-2061. ***Services:*** job fairs, resume preparation, resume referral, career counseling, careers library, job bank, job interviews. Students must register sophomore year. 120 organizations recruited on campus 1994–95.

AFTER GRADUATION 65% of class of 1994 had job offers within 6 months. 92% of students completing a degree program went directly on to further study.

EXPENSES FOR 1995–96 State resident tuition: $557 full-time, $13.25 per quarter hour part-time. Nonresident tuition: $4515 full-time, $107.50 per quarter hour part-time. Part-time mandatory fees: $9 per quarter. Full-time mandatory fees: $27.

FINANCIAL AID ***College-administered undergrad aid 1995–96:*** 30 need-based scholarships (average $500), 70 non-need scholarships (average $500), short-term loans (average $250), low-interest long-term loans from external sources (average $2500), 35 Federal Work-Study, 40 part-time jobs. ***Required forms:*** institutional; accepted: CSS Financial Aid PROFILE. ***Priority deadline:*** 8/15. ***Waivers:*** full or partial for employees or children of employees and senior citizens. ***Notification:*** 8/30. ***Average indebtedness of graduates:*** $2000.

APPLYING Open admission except for nursing, radiology programs. ***Options:*** early entrance, deferred entrance, midyear entrance. ***Required for some:*** 3 years of high school math and science, some high school foreign language, ACT, nursing exam, Health Occupations Exam. Test scores used for counseling/placement. ***Application deadline:*** rolling. ***Notification:*** continuous. Preference given to district and then state residents.

APPLYING/TRANSFER ***Required for some:*** 3 years of high school math and science, some high school foreign language. ***Entrance:*** noncompetitive. ***Application deadline:*** rolling. ***Notification:*** continuous. ***Contact:*** Ms. Mary Jo Wilson, Director of Counseling Services, 919-492-2061.

CONTACT Ms. Brenda W. Beck, Admissions Officer, Vance-Granville Community College, Henderson, NC 27536-0917, 919-492-2061 Ext. 267. ***Fax:*** 919-430-0460.

WAKE TECHNICAL COMMUNITY COLLEGE
Raleigh, North Carolina

UG Enrollment: 7,340 **Tuition & Fees (NC Res): $587**
Application Deadline: rolling **Room & Board: N/Avail**

GENERAL State and locally supported, 2-year, coed. Part of North Carolina Community College System. Awards certificates, diplomas, transfer associate, terminal associate degrees. Founded 1958. ***Setting:*** 79-acre suburban campus. ***Total enrollment:*** 7,340. ***Faculty:*** 405 (190 full-time, 215 part-time).

ENROLLMENT PROFILE 7,340 students: 55% women, 63% part-time, 98% state residents, 59% transferred in, 1% international, 56% 25 or older, 0% Native American, 1% Hispanic, 17% African American, 3% Asian American. ***Areas of study chosen:*** 36% business management and administrative services, 25% liberal arts/general studies, 16% engineering and applied sciences, 13% health professions and related sciences, 7% vocational and home economics, 3% computer and information sciences. ***Most popular recent majors:*** nursing, civil engineering technology, criminal justice.

FIRST-YEAR CLASS 2,911 total; 7,770 applied, 100% were accepted, 37% of whom enrolled. 4% from top 10% of their high school class, 22% from top quarter, 47% from top half.

ACADEMIC PROGRAM Core. Calendar: quarters. 631 courses offered in 1995–96. Academic remediation for entering students, English as a second language program offered during academic year and summer, services for LD students, summer session for credit, part-time degree program (daytime, evenings, summer), adult/continuing education programs, co-op programs.

GENERAL DEGREE REQUIREMENTS 96 quarter hours; math/science requirements vary according to program; computer course.

MAJORS Accounting, architectural technologies, business administration/commerce/management, child care/child and family studies, civil engineering technology, computer graphics, computer programming, computer technologies, criminal justice, culinary arts, data processing, dental services, drafting and design, early childhood education, electrical and electronics technologies, electronics engineering technology, emergency medical technology, (pre)engineering sequence, environmental engineering technology, hotel and restaurant management, industrial and heavy equipment maintenance, industrial engineering technology, landscape architecture/design, law enforcement/police sciences, legal secretarial studies, liberal arts/general studies, machine and tool technologies, manufacturing technology, mechanical engineering technology, medical assistant technologies, medical laboratory technology, medical secretarial studies, nursing, pharmacy/pharmaceutical sciences, plumbing, radiological technology, real estate, robotics, science, secretarial studies/office management, surveying technology, telecommunications.

LIBRARY Wake Technical Main Library with 52,930 books, 415 microform titles, 551 periodicals, 8 CD-ROMs, 788 records, tapes, and CDs.

COMPUTERS ON CAMPUS Computer purchase plan available. 675 computers for student use in computer center, learning resource center, labs, classrooms.

COLLEGE LIFE Student-run newspaper. 24% vote in student government elections. ***Student services:*** personal-psychological counseling. ***Campus security:*** 24-hour patrols.

HOUSING College housing not available.

CAREER PLANNING ***Service:*** career counseling.

AFTER GRADUATION 100% of students completing a degree program in 1994–95 went directly on to further study.

ESTIMATED EXPENSES FOR 1996–97 State resident tuition: $557 full-time, $13.25 per quarter hour part-time. Nonresident tuition: $4515 full-time, $107.50 per quarter hour part-time. Part-time mandatory fees: $10 per quarter. Full-time mandatory fees: $30.

FINANCIAL AID ***College-administered undergrad aid 1995–96:*** 710 need-based scholarships, low-interest long-term loans from external sources, Federal Work-Study, 27 part-time jobs. ***Required forms:*** institutional, FAFSA; accepted: CSS Financial Aid PROFILE. ***Priority deadline:*** 3/15. ***Waivers:*** full or partial for employees or children of employees and senior citizens. ***Notification:*** 7/15.

APPLYING Open admission except for nursing program. ***Option:*** early entrance. ***Required:*** school transcript, ACT ASSET. ***Recommended:*** 3 years of high school science, some high school foreign language, SAT I, TOEFL for international students. ***Required for some:*** 3 years of high school math. Test scores used for counseling/placement. ***Application deadline:*** rolling.

APPLYING/TRANSFER ***Required:*** standardized test scores, high school transcript, college transcript. ***Recommended:*** 3 years of high school science, some high school foreign language. ***Required for some:*** 3 years of high school math. ***Entrance:*** noncompetitive. ***Application deadline:*** rolling.

CONTACT Mr. Robert L. Brown, Acting Vice President for Student Services, Wake Technical Community College, Raleigh, NC 27603-5696, 919-662-3343. ***Fax:*** 919-779-3360.

WAYNE COMMUNITY COLLEGE
Goldsboro, North Carolina

UG Enrollment: 2,639 **Tuition & Fees (NC Res): $584**
Application Deadline: rolling **Room & Board: N/Avail**

GENERAL State and locally supported, 2-year, coed. Part of North Carolina Community College System. Awards transfer associate, terminal associate degrees. Founded 1957. ***Setting:*** 125-acre small-town campus. ***Total enrollment:*** 2,639. ***Faculty:*** 153 (89 full-time, 6% with terminal degrees, 64 part-time).

ENROLLMENT PROFILE 2,639 students from 3 states and territories, 3 other countries. 61% women, 34% part-time, 88% state residents, 25% transferred in, 95% have need-based financial aid, 44% 25 or older, 1% Hispanic, 27% African American, 1% Asian American. ***Most popular recent majors:*** liberal arts/general studies, business administration/commerce/management, nursing.

FIRST-YEAR CLASS 827 total; 1,126 applied, 100% were accepted, 73% of whom enrolled.

ACADEMIC PROGRAM Core. Calendar: quarters. Academic remediation for entering students, services for LD students, advanced placement, summer session for credit, part-time degree program (daytime, evenings), adult/continuing education programs, co-op programs.

GENERAL DEGREE REQUIREMENTS 96 quarter hours; math/science requirements vary according to program; computer course.

MAJORS Accounting, agricultural sciences, automotive technologies, aviation technology, business administration/commerce/management, computer information systems, computer programming, corrections, criminal justice, dental services, drafting and design, early childhood education, electronics engineering technology, engineering (general), fashion merchandising, fish and game management, forest technology, gerontology, human services, law enforcement/police sciences, legal secretarial studies, liberal arts/general studies,

Peterson's Guide to Two-Year Colleges 1997 509

Wayne Community College (continued)
marketing/retailing/merchandising, medical assistant technologies, medical secretarial studies, mental health/rehabilitation counseling, nursing, poultry sciences, science, secretarial studies/office management, wildlife management.
LIBRARY 37,000 books, 514 microform titles, 306 periodicals, 2 CD-ROMs, 2,312 records, tapes, and CDs. Acquisition spending 1994–95: $562,474.
COMPUTERS ON CAMPUS 130 computers for student use in labs, library provide access to main academic computer.
COLLEGE LIFE Orientation program (2 days, $14). Choral group, student-run newspaper. ***Social organizations:*** 2 national fraternities; 10% of eligible men are members. ***Most popular organizations:*** Student Government, Phi Beta Lambda. ***Major annual events:*** Homecoming, Spring Fling, Faculty Appreciation Day. ***Student services:*** health clinic, personal-psychological counseling.
HOUSING College housing not available.
ATHLETICS ***Intercollegiate:*** basketball M, golf M/W, softball M/W, tennis M/W, volleyball M/W. ***Intramural:*** football, table tennis (Ping-Pong), volleyball. ***Contact:*** Mr. Jerry Kornegay, Director of Student Activities and Recruiting, 919-735-5151.
CAREER PLANNING ***Placement office:*** 1 full-time staff. ***Director:*** Ms. Norma Dawson, Counselor, Career Training Center, 919-735-5151. ***Services:*** job fairs, resume preparation, resume referral, career counseling, careers library, job bank, job interviews.
AFTER GRADUATION 25% of students completing a degree program in 1994–95 went directly on to further study.
EXPENSES FOR 1996–97 State resident tuition: $557 full-time, $13.25 per credit hour part-time. Nonresident tuition: $4515 full-time, $107.50 per credit hour part-time. Part-time mandatory fees per quarter range from $4.50 to $9. Full-time mandatory fees: $27.
FINANCIAL AID ***College-administered undergrad aid 1995–96:*** 26 need-based scholarships (average $400), low-interest long-term loans from external sources (average $992), Federal Work-Study, 12 part-time jobs. ***Required forms:*** CSS Financial Aid PROFILE, institutional, FAFSA. ***Priority deadline:*** 7/1. ***Waivers:*** full or partial for employees or children of employees and senior citizens. ***Notification:*** continuous.
APPLYING Open admission except for nursing, dental services programs. ***Options:*** deferred entrance, midyear entrance. ***Required:*** school transcript, campus interview, TOEFL for international students. ***Required for some:*** ACT ASSET. Test scores used for counseling/placement. ***Application deadline:*** rolling. ***Notification:*** continuous.
APPLYING/TRANSFER ***Required:*** high school transcript, campus interview, college transcript. ***Entrance:*** noncompetitive. ***Application deadline:*** rolling. ***Notification:*** continuous.
CONTACT Ms. Susan Mooring Sasser, Director of Admissions and Records, Wayne Community College, Goldsboro, NC 27533-8002, 919-735-5151 Ext. 216. ***Fax:*** 919-736-3204.

WESTERN PIEDMONT COMMUNITY COLLEGE
Morganton, North Carolina

UG Enrollment: 2,562	**Tuition & Fees (NC Res): $578**
Application Deadline: rolling	**Room & Board: N/Avail**

GENERAL State-supported, 2-year, coed. Part of North Carolina Community College System. Awards transfer associate, terminal associate degrees. Founded 1964. ***Setting:*** 130-acre small-town campus. ***Total enrollment:*** 2,562. ***Faculty:*** 132 (59 full-time, 73 part-time); student-faculty ratio is 20:1.
ENROLLMENT PROFILE 2,562 students from 5 states and territories. 59% women, 63% part-time, 99% state residents, 10% transferred in, 0% international, 6% African American. ***Most popular recent majors:*** liberal arts/general studies, nursing, business administration/commerce/management.
FIRST-YEAR CLASS 400 total; 800 applied, 100% were accepted, 50% of whom enrolled.
ACADEMIC PROGRAM Core. Calendar: quarters. Academic remediation for entering students, advanced placement, summer session for credit, part-time degree program (daytime, evenings, summer), adult/continuing education programs, co-op programs.
GENERAL DEGREE REQUIREMENTS 96 quarter hours; 10 quarter hours of math; 12 quarter hours of science; computer course.
MAJORS Accounting, art/fine arts, business administration/commerce/management, civil engineering technology, computer programming, computer technologies, criminal justice, drafting and design, electrical engineering technology, (pre)engineering sequence, finance/banking, horticulture, industrial arts, industrial engineering technology, interior design, law enforcement/police sciences, legal secretarial studies, liberal arts/general studies, marketing/retailing/merchandising, medical assistant technologies, medical laboratory technology, medical secretarial studies, nursing, paralegal studies, recreation therapy, secretarial studies/office management.
LIBRARY 31,195 books, 200 periodicals, 6,480 records, tapes, and CDs.
COMPUTERS ON CAMPUS 60 computers for student use in computer center.
COLLEGE LIFE Drama-theater group, student-run newspaper. ***Student services:*** personal-psychological counseling, women's center.
HOUSING College housing not available.
ATHLETICS ***Intramural:*** basketball, volleyball.
CAREER PLANNING ***Service:*** career counseling.
ESTIMATED EXPENSES FOR 1996–97 State resident tuition: $557 full-time, $13.25 per quarter hour part-time. Nonresident tuition: $4515 full-time, $107.50 per quarter hour part-time. Part-time mandatory fees: $7 per quarter. Full-time mandatory fees: $21.
FINANCIAL AID ***College-administered undergrad aid 1995–96:*** need-based scholarships, 10 non-need scholarships (average $300), low-interest long-term loans from external sources, Federal Work-Study. ***Required forms:*** FAFSA; accepted: CSS Financial Aid PROFILE. ***Priority deadline:*** 4/30.
APPLYING Open admission. ***Required:*** school transcript, TOEFL for international students, ACT ASSET. Test scores used for counseling/placement. ***Application deadline:*** rolling. ***Notification:*** continuous.
APPLYING/TRANSFER ***Required:*** high school transcript, college transcript. ***Required for some:*** standardized test scores. ***Entrance:*** noncompetitive. ***Application deadline:*** rolling. ***Notification:*** continuous.
CONTACT Mr. Jim Reed, Director of Admissions, Western Piedmont Community College, Morganton, NC 28655-9978, 704-438-6051. ***Fax:*** 704-438-6015. Electronic viewbook available.

WILKES COMMUNITY COLLEGE
Wilkesboro, North Carolina

UG Enrollment: 2,178	**Tuition & Fees (NC Res): $583**
Application Deadline: rolling	**Room & Board: N/Avail**

GENERAL State-supported, 2-year, coed. Part of North Carolina Community College System. Awards certificates, diplomas, transfer associate, terminal associate degrees. Founded 1965. ***Setting:*** 140-acre small-town campus. ***Educational spending 1994–95:*** $2875 per undergrad. ***Total enrollment:*** 2,178. ***Faculty:*** 221 (58 full-time, 163 part-time); student-faculty ratio is 12:1.
ENROLLMENT PROFILE 2,178 students from 9 states and territories, 3 other countries. 68% women, 32% men, 55% part-time, 98% state residents, 1% transferred in, 60% have need-based financial aid, 40% have non-need-based financial aid, 1% international, 50% 25 or older, 1% Native American, 1% Hispanic, 6% African American, 1% Asian American. ***Areas of study chosen:*** 29% liberal arts/general studies, 20% business management and administrative services, 18% health professions and related sciences, 6% education, 6% engineering and applied sciences, 4% computer and information sciences, 1% architecture, 1% communications and journalism, 1% fine arts, 1% performing arts, 1% vocational and home economics. ***Most popular recent majors:*** liberal arts/general studies, business administration/commerce/management.
FIRST-YEAR CLASS 794 total; 1,207 applied, 100% were accepted, 66% of whom enrolled.
ACADEMIC PROGRAM Core, honor code. Calendar: quarters. Academic remediation for entering students, English as a second language program offered during academic year, services for LD students, advanced placement, tutorials, summer session for credit, part-time degree program (daytime, evenings), adult/continuing education programs, co-op programs and internships.
GENERAL DEGREE REQUIREMENTS 96 quarter hours; 1 math course; computer course; internship (some majors).
MAJORS Accounting, automotive technologies, business administration/commerce/management, computer programming, computer science, construction technologies, criminal justice, dental services, drafting and design, early childhood education, electromechanical technology, electronics engineering technology, food services management, hotel and restaurant management, liberal arts/general studies, mathematics, medical assistant technologies, music, nursing, radio and television studies, science, secretarial studies/office management, social work, theater arts/drama.
LIBRARY 51,682 books, 140 microform titles, 114 periodicals, 6 CD-ROMs, 1,898 records, tapes, and CDs.
COMPUTERS ON CAMPUS 100 computers for student use in computer center, computer labs, learning resource center, classrooms, library provide access to Internet.
COLLEGE LIFE Drama-theater group, choral group, student-run newspaper, radio station. 15% vote in student government elections. ***Social organizations:*** 12 open to all. ***Most popular organizations:*** Student Government Association, Students Against Drunk Drivers (SADD), Yearbook, Camera Club, Baptist Student Union. ***Major annual events:*** Talent Show, Winter Fest, Spring Fling. ***Student services:*** personal-psychological counseling. ***Campus security:*** 24-hour emergency response devices, student patrols, late-night transport-escort service.
HOUSING College housing not available.
ATHLETICS Member NJCAA. ***Intercollegiate:*** baseball M, basketball M. ***Intramural:*** basketball, football, softball, table tennis (Ping-Pong), tennis, volleyball.
CAREER PLANNING ***Placement office:*** 1 full-time staff. ***Director:*** Ms. Cathy Annas, Counselor, 910-838-6147. ***Services:*** job fairs, resume preparation, career counseling, job interviews. 3 organizations recruited on campus 1994–95.
AFTER GRADUATION 71% of students completing a degree program in 1994–95 went directly on to further study.
EXPENSES FOR 1995–96 State resident tuition: $557 full-time, $13.25 per quarter hour part-time. Nonresident tuition: $4515 full-time, $107.50 per quarter hour part-time. Full-time mandatory fees: $26.
FINANCIAL AID ***College-administered undergrad aid 1995–96:*** 180 need-based scholarships (average $600), 40 non-need scholarships (average $2500), low-interest long-term loans from external sources (average $2400), 45 Federal Work-Study (averaging $1100), 90 part-time jobs. ***Required forms:*** FAFSA; required for some: institutional. ***Priority deadline:*** 3/1. ***Waivers:*** full or partial for employees or children of employees and senior citizens. ***Notification:*** 6/1. ***Average indebtedness of graduates:*** $4900.
APPLYING Open admission. ***Options:*** deferred entrance, midyear entrance. ***Required:*** school transcript, TOEFL for international students, ACT ASSET. Test scores used for counseling/placement. ***Application deadline:*** rolling. ***Notification:*** continuous.
APPLYING/TRANSFER ***Required:*** high school transcript. ***Required for some:*** standardized test scores. ***Application deadline:*** rolling. ***Notification:*** continuous. ***Contact:*** Mr. Larry Caudill, Director of Guidance, 910-838-6148.
CONTACT Dr. Bob C. Thompson, Dean for Student Development, Wilkes Community College, Wilkesboro, NC 28697, 910-838-6138. ***Fax:*** 910-838-6277.

WILSON TECHNICAL COMMUNITY COLLEGE
Wilson, North Carolina

UG Enrollment: 1,416	**Tuition & Fees (NC Res): $578**
Application Deadline: rolling	**Room & Board: N/Avail**

GENERAL State-supported, 2-year, coed. Part of North Carolina Community College System. Awards certificates, diplomas, transfer associate, terminal associate degrees. Founded 1958. ***Setting:*** 35-acre small-town campus. ***Endowment:*** $495,000. ***Total enrollment:*** 1,416. ***Faculty:*** 79 (47 full-time, 32 part-time); student-faculty ratio is 18:1.
ENROLLMENT PROFILE 1,416 students from 5 states and territories. 64% women, 36% men, 53% part-time, 99% state residents, 22% transferred in, 27% have need-based financial aid, 2% have non-need-based financial aid, 0% international, 57% 25 or older, 0% Native American, 1% Hispanic, 32% African American, 0% Asian American. ***Areas of study chosen:*** 26% business management and administrative services, 18% vocational and home economics, 10% engineering and applied sciences, 9% computer and information sciences, 9% liberal arts/general studies, 7% health professions and related sciences, 3% education. ***Most popular recent majors:*** nursing, business administration/commerce/management, accounting.

FIRST-YEAR CLASS 442 total; 710 applied, 76% were accepted, 81% of whom enrolled.
ACADEMIC PROGRAM Core. Calendar: quarters. Academic remediation for entering students, English as a second language program, services for LD students, summer session for credit, part-time degree program (daytime, evenings), co-op programs and internships.
GENERAL DEGREE REQUIREMENTS 96 quarter hours; math/science requirements vary according to program; computer course for most majors.
MAJORS Accounting, business administration/commerce/management, computer programming, criminal justice, deaf interpreter training, drafting and design, early childhood education, electrical and electronics technologies, electronics engineering technology, emergency medical technology, fire science, industrial administration, liberal arts/general studies, manufacturing technology, nursing, paralegal studies, practical nursing, secretarial studies/office management.
LIBRARY 25,347 books, 76 microform titles, 345 periodicals, 2 on-line bibliographic services, 2 CD-ROMs, 2,159 records, tapes, and CDs. Acquisition spending 1994–95: $156,362.
COMPUTERS ON CAMPUS 150 computers for student use in computer center, labs, classrooms, library provide access to on-line services.
COLLEGE LIFE *Student services:* personal-psychological counseling. *Campus security:* 11-hour patrols by trained security personnel.
HOUSING College housing not available.
CAREER PLANNING *Placement office:* 1 part-time staff. *Director:* Mr. Patrick J. Williams, Job Placement Counselor, 919-291-1195 Ext. 228. *Services:* job fairs, resume preparation, resume referral, career counseling, careers library, job interviews. 36 organizations recruited on campus 1994–95.
EXPENSES FOR 1995–96 State resident tuition: $557 full-time, $13.25 per credit hour part-time. Nonresident tuition: $4515 full-time, $107.50 per credit hour part-time. Full-time mandatory fees: $21.
FINANCIAL AID *College-administered undergrad aid 1995–96:* need-based scholarships, non-need scholarships, short-term loans (averaging $75), low-interest long-term loans from external sources (averaging $1200), 39 Federal Work-Study (averaging $498), part-time jobs. *Required forms for some financial aid applicants:* institutional, FAFSA; accepted: CSS Financial Aid PROFILE. *Priority deadline:* 8/15. *Waivers:* full or partial for employees or children of employees and senior citizens.
APPLYING Open admission except for nursing education program. *Options:* deferred entrance, midyear entrance. *Required:* school transcript, TOEFL for international students. Test scores used for counseling/placement. *Application deadline:* rolling. *Notification:* continuous.
APPLYING/TRANSFER *Required:* standardized test scores, high school transcript, college transcript. *Application deadline:* rolling. *Notification:* continuous. *Contact:* Ms. Brenda Thorne, Counselor, 919-291-1195 Ext. 257.
CONTACT Ms. Denise L. Sessons, Dean of Student Services, Wilson Technical Community College, Wilson, NC 27893-3310, 919-291-1195 Ext. 275. *Fax:* 919-243-7148.

NORTH DAKOTA

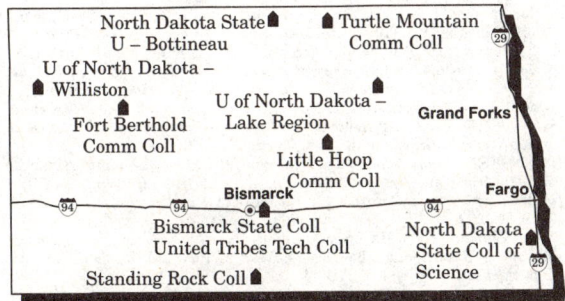

BISMARCK STATE COLLEGE
Bismarck, North Dakota

UG Enrollment: 2,313	**Tuition & Fees (ND Res):** $1760
Application Deadline: 8/15	**Room & Board:** $2330

GENERAL State-supported, 2-year, coed. Part of North Dakota University System. Awards transfer associate, terminal associate degrees. Founded 1939. *Setting:* 95-acre suburban campus. *Total enrollment:* 2,313. *Faculty:* 117 (82 full-time, 35 part-time); student-faculty ratio is 22:1.
ENROLLMENT PROFILE 2,313 students from 10 states and territories, 2 other countries. 51% women, 31% part-time, 97% state residents, 10% live on campus, 10% transferred in, 66% have need-based financial aid, 1% international, 30% 25 or older, 3% Native American. *Areas of study chosen:* 42% liberal arts/general studies, 17% business management and administrative services, 11% health professions and related sciences, 8% social sciences, 5% agriculture, 3% education, 3% engineering and applied sciences, 2% mathematics, 1% computer and information sciences. *Most popular recent major:* business administration/commerce/management.
FIRST-YEAR CLASS 672 total. Of the students who applied, 100% were accepted.
ACADEMIC PROGRAM Core. Calendar: semesters. Academic remediation for entering students, services for LD students, summer session for credit, part-time degree program (daytime, evenings, summer), adult/continuing education programs, co-op programs and internships. ROTC: Army (c), Air Force (c).
GENERAL DEGREE REQUIREMENTS 60 semester hours; 1 course each in math and science.
MAJORS Agricultural business, automotive technologies, biology/biological sciences, business administration/commerce/management, business education, carpentry, chemical engineering technology, chemistry, commercial art, computer science, criminal justice,

education, electrical and electronics technologies, elementary education, energy management technologies, engineering (general), English, farm and ranch management, health education, heating/refrigeration/air conditioning, history, hotel and restaurant management, journalism, legal secretarial studies, liberal arts/general studies, marketing/retailing/merchandising, mathematics, medical laboratory technology, medical secretarial studies, medical technology, music, nursing, pharmacy/pharmaceutical sciences, physical education, political science/government, psychology, public administration, retail management, secretarial studies/office management, social science, speech/rhetoric/public address/debate, theater arts/drama, welding technology.
LIBRARY Bismarck State College Library with 35,000 books, 350 periodicals, 2,400 records, tapes, and CDs.
COMPUTERS ON CAMPUS Computer purchase plan available. 90 computers for student use in computer labs, faculty offices, library, student center provide access to main academic computer, on-line services, Internet. Staffed computer lab on campus provides training in use of software.
COLLEGE LIFE Drama-theater group, choral group. *Most popular organizations:* Rodeo Club, Older Than Average Club. *Major annual events:* Fall Fantasy Week, Snow Fest Week. *Student services:* legal services, health clinic.
HOUSING 240 college housing spaces available; all were occupied 1995–96. No special consideration for freshman housing applicants. Off-campus living permitted. *Option:* coed housing available. Resident assistants live in dorms.
ATHLETICS Member NJCAA. *Intercollegiate:* basketball M(s)/W(s); golf M, tennis M/W, track and field M(s)/W(s), volleyball W(s), wrestling M(s). *Intramural:* basketball, softball, volleyball. *Contact:* Mr. Edroy Kringstad, Athletic Director, 701-224-5456.
CAREER PLANNING *Placement office:* 1 full-time staff. *Director:* Mr. Mike Lenhardt, Counselor, 701-224-5400. *Services:* resume preparation, career counseling, careers library.
EXPENSES FOR 1995–96 *Application fee:* $25. State resident tuition: $1760 full-time, $73.36 per credit part-time. Nonresident tuition: $4352 full-time, $181.34 per credit part-time. Tuition for Minnesota, South Dakota, Montana, Manitoba and Saskatchewan residents: $2148 full-time, $89.53 per credit part-time. College room and board: $2330.
FINANCIAL AID *College-administered undergrad aid 1995–96:* 407 need-based scholarships (averaging $571), 168 non-need scholarships (averaging $935), low-interest long-term loans from college funds (averaging $1381), loans from external sources (averaging $2415), Federal Work-Study, 16 part-time jobs. *Required forms:* institutional, FAFSA; accepted: state. *Priority deadline:* 4/15. *Payment plan:* installment. *Waivers:* full or partial for minority students and employees or children of employees. *Notification:* 6/15.
APPLYING Open admission. *Options:* early entrance, deferred entrance. *Required:* TOEFL for international students. *Recommended:* 3 years of high school math and science. *Required for some:* school transcript, SAT I or ACT. Test scores used for counseling/placement. *Application deadline:* 8/15. *Notification:* continuous.
APPLYING/TRANSFER *Recommended:* 3 years of high school math and science. *Required for some:* standardized test scores. *Application deadline:* 8/15. *Notification:* continuous.
CONTACT Mr. Tom Leno, Registrar, Bismarck State College, Bismarck, ND 58501-1299, 701-224-5497. College video available.

FORT BERTHOLD COMMUNITY COLLEGE
New Town, North Dakota

UG Enrollment: 423	**Tuition & Fees:** $1600
Application Deadline: rolling	**Room & Board:** N/Avail

GENERAL Independent, 2-year, coed. Awards certificates, transfer associate degrees. Founded 1973. *Setting:* small-town campus. *Total enrollment:* 423. *Faculty:* 45 (9 full-time, 1% with terminal degrees, 36 part-time).
ENROLLMENT PROFILE 423 students: 68% women, 32% men, 52% part-time, 100% state residents, 28% transferred in, 0% international, 57% 25 or older, 74% Native American, 1% Hispanic, 0% African American, 0% Asian American. *Areas of study chosen:* 38% liberal arts/general studies, 20% health professions and related sciences, 16% business management and administrative services, 13% education, 5% biological and life sciences, 3% agriculture, 1% computer and information sciences, 1% mathematics. *Most popular recent majors:* nursing, liberal arts/general studies, business administration/commerce/management.
FIRST-YEAR CLASS 194 total; 194 applied, 100% were accepted, 100% of whom enrolled. 4% from top 10% of their high school class, 20% from top quarter, 50% from top half.
ACADEMIC PROGRAM Core, honor code. Calendar: semesters. 126 courses offered in 1995–96. Academic remediation for entering students, English as a second language program, tutorials, summer session for credit, part-time degree program (daytime), co-op programs and internships. Off-campus study at University of North Dakota, Minot State University.
GENERAL DEGREE REQUIREMENTS 64 semester hours; 2 courses each in math and science; computer course for liberal arts majors; internship (some majors).
MAJORS Accounting, business administration/commerce/management, carpentry, computer information systems, early childhood education, environmental sciences, farm and ranch management, human services, liberal arts/general studies, marketing/retailing/merchandising, mathematics, medical records technology, nursing, public administration, science, secretarial studies/office management.
LIBRARY 10,000 books, 300 periodicals.
COMPUTERS ON CAMPUS 50 computers for student use in classrooms provide access to e-mail.
COLLEGE LIFE Drama-theater group, student-run newspaper. 30% vote in student government elections. *Student services:* legal services, health clinic, personal-psychological counseling.
HOUSING College housing not available.
ATHLETICS *Intercollegiate:* basketball M/W, cross-country running M/W. *Intramural:* basketball, football, softball, volleyball, weight lifting.
CAREER PLANNING *Placement office:* 1 full-time staff. *Director:* Ms. Mavis Young Bear, Vocational Education Counselor, 701-627-4738. *Services:* resume preparation, career counseling. 3 organizations recruited on campus 1994–95.
AFTER GRADUATION 70% of class of 1994 had job offers within 6 months. 42% of students completing a degree program went directly on to further study.

Fort Berthold Community College (continued)
EXPENSES FOR 1996–97 ***Application fee:*** $10. Tuition: $1440 full-time, $60 per semester hour part-time. Part-time mandatory fees: $70 per semester. Full-time mandatory fees: $160.
FINANCIAL AID ***College-administered undergrad aid 1995–96:*** need-based scholarships, Federal Work-Study. ***Required forms:*** FAFSA. ***Priority deadline:*** 10/1. ***Payment plan:*** deferred payment. ***Waivers:*** full or partial for employees or children of employees and senior citizens.
APPLYING Open admission except for nursing program. ***Options:*** Common Application, deferred entrance. ***Recommended:*** 3 years of high school math and science. ***Required for some:*** some high school foreign language, TOEFL for international students. Test scores used for counseling/placement. ***Application deadline:*** rolling.
APPLYING/TRANSFER ***Recommended:*** 3 years of high school math and science. ***Required for some:*** some high school foreign language. ***Entrance:*** noncompetitive. ***Contact:*** Mr. RussellMason Jr., Registrar/Admissions Director, 701-627-3665.
CONTACT Mr. Russell Mason Jr., Registrar/Admissions Director, Fort Berthold Community College, New Town, ND 58763-0490, 701-627-3665. ***Fax:*** 701-627-3609.

LITTLE HOOP COMMUNITY COLLEGE
Fort Totten, North Dakota

UG Enrollment: 120	**Tuition & Fees: $1160**
Application Deadline: 8/22	**Room & Board: N/Avail**

GENERAL Federally supported, 2-year, coed. Awards transfer associate degrees. Founded 1974. ***Setting:*** 1-acre small-town campus. ***Total enrollment:*** 120. ***Faculty:*** 15 (8 full-time, 7 part-time).
ENROLLMENT PROFILE 120 students from 5 states and territories. 65% women, 41% part-time, 98% state residents, 0% international, 50% 25 or older, 98% Native American, 0% Hispanic, 0% African American, 0% Asian American.
FIRST-YEAR CLASS 65 total. Of the students who applied, 100% were accepted, 100% of whom enrolled.
ACADEMIC PROGRAM Core, honor code. Calendar: semesters. Academic remediation for entering students, services for LD students, self-designed majors, summer session for credit, part-time degree program (daytime, evenings), adult/continuing education programs, co-op programs. Off-campus study at members of the American Indian Higher Education Consortium.
GENERAL DEGREE REQUIREMENTS 61 credits; 2 courses each in math and lab science; computer course.
MAJORS Accounting, art/fine arts, art history, business administration/commerce/management, business education, carpentry, chemistry, child psychology/child development, computer science, English, geography, health education, history, liberal arts/general studies, marketing/retailing/merchandising, mathematics, recreation and leisure services, secretarial studies/office management, vocational education.
LIBRARY 7,500 books, 48 periodicals, 30 records, tapes, and CDs.
COMPUTERS ON CAMPUS 50 computers for student use in computer center, secretarial classroom.
COLLEGE LIFE Drama-theater group. 98% vote in student government elections. ***Student services:*** personal-psychological counseling. ***Campus security:*** late-night transport-escort service.
HOUSING College housing not available.
ATHLETICS ***Intramural:*** basketball, bowling, volleyball, weight lifting.
CAREER PLANNING ***Service:*** career counseling.
AFTER GRADUATION 10% of students completing a degree program in 1994–95 went directly on to further study.
EXPENSES FOR 1995–96 Tuition: $1080 full-time, $45 per credit hour part-time. Part-time mandatory fees: $10 per semester. Full-time mandatory fees: $80.
FINANCIAL AID ***College-administered undergrad aid 1995–96:*** need-based scholarships, Federal Work-Study. ***Required forms:*** institutional, FAFSA; accepted: state. ***Application deadline:*** 10/15. ***Payment plans:*** tuition prepayment, installment.
APPLYING Open admission. ***Options:*** early entrance, deferred entrance. ***Required:*** TABE. Test scores used for counseling/placement. ***Application deadline:*** 8/22. ***Notification:*** continuous.
APPLYING/TRANSFER ***Entrance:*** noncompetitive. ***Application deadline:*** 8/22. ***Notification:*** continuous.
CONTACT Ms. Renita Delorne, Admissions Registrar, Little Hoop Community College, Fort Totten, ND 58335-0269, 701-766-4415.

NORTH DAKOTA STATE COLLEGE OF SCIENCE
Wahpeton, North Dakota

UG Enrollment: 2,492	**Tuition & Fees (ND Res): $1701**
Application Deadline: rolling	**Room & Board: $2010**

GENERAL State-supported, 2-year, coed. Awards certificates, diplomas, transfer associate, terminal associate degrees. Founded 1903. ***Setting:*** 125-acre rural campus. ***Endowment:*** $4000. ***Educational spending 1994–95:*** $3546 per undergrad. ***Total enrollment:*** 2,492. ***Faculty:*** 156 (140 full-time, 2% with terminal degrees, 16 part-time); student-faculty ratio is 17:1.
ENROLLMENT PROFILE 2,492 students from 25 states and territories, 8 other countries. 38% women, 62% men, 9% part-time, 69% state residents, 57% live on campus, 31% transferred in, 1% international, 17% 25 or older, 1% Native American, 0% Hispanic, 1% African American, 0% Asian American. ***Areas of study chosen:*** 57% engineering and applied sciences, 24% liberal arts/general studies, 15% health professions and related sciences, 4% agriculture. ***Most popular recent majors:*** liberal arts/general studies, practical nursing, automotive technologies.
FIRST-YEAR CLASS 919 total; 1,130 applied, 94% were accepted, 87% of whom enrolled.
ACADEMIC PROGRAM Core. Calendar: semesters. 736 courses offered in 1995–96. Academic remediation for entering students, English as a second language program offered during academic year and summer, services for LD students, advanced placement, self-designed majors, summer session for credit, part-time degree program (daytime), adult/continuing education programs, co-op programs and internships.
GENERAL DEGREE REQUIREMENTS 64 semester hours; computer course for most majors; internship (some majors).
MAJORS Accounting, agricultural business, agricultural technologies, architectural technologies, automotive technologies, civil engineering technology, communication equipment technology, computer programming, computer science, computer technologies, construction technologies, culinary arts, dental services, drafting and design, electrical and electronics technologies, electrical engineering technology, electronics engineering technology, (pre)engineering sequence, food services technology, graphic arts, heating/refrigeration/air conditioning, industrial engineering technology, instrumentation technology, insurance, law enforcement/police sciences, legal secretarial studies, liberal arts/general studies, machine and tool technologies, manufacturing technology, mechanical design technology, medical records services, medical secretarial studies, medical technology, nursing, occupational therapy, physical education, physical sciences, practical nursing, real estate, science, secretarial studies/office management, welding technology.
LIBRARY Mildred Johnson Library with 79,555 books, 715 microform titles, 927 periodicals, 5 CD-ROMs, 3,352 records, tapes, and CDs. Acquisition spending 1994–95: $152,396.
COMPUTERS ON CAMPUS Computer purchase plan available. 450 computers for student use in computer center, learning resource center, classrooms, library, student center provide access to on-line services. Staffed computer lab on campus provides training in use of computers, software. Academic computing expenditure 1994–95: $328,792.
COLLEGE LIFE Drama-theater group, choral group. 15% vote in student government elections. ***Major annual event:*** Homecoming. ***Student services:*** legal services, health clinic, personal-psychological counseling. ***Campus security:*** 24-hour emergency response devices and patrols, student patrols, controlled dormitory access.
HOUSING 1,760 college housing spaces available; 1,411 were occupied 1995–96. Freshmen guaranteed college housing. On-campus residence required in freshman year. ***Options:*** coed (1 building), single-sex (10 buildings) housing available. Resident assistants live in dorms.
ATHLETICS Member NJCAA. ***Intercollegiate:*** basketball M(s)/W(s), cross-country running M(s)/W(s), football M(s), track and field M(s)/W(s), volleyball W(s). ***Intramural:*** basketball, football, racquetball, softball, volleyball. ***Contact:*** Mr. Don Engen, Athletic Director, 701-671-2283.
CAREER PLANNING ***Placement office:*** 2 full-time, 1 part-time staff; $594,472 operating expenditure 1994–95. ***Director:*** Mr. Richard Hauck, Director of Counseling Center, 701-671-2319. ***Services:*** resume preparation, resume referral, career counseling, careers library, job interviews. 83 organizations recruited on campus 1994–95.
AFTER GRADUATION 96% of class of 1994 had job offers within 6 months. 85% of students completing a degree program went directly on to further study.
EXPENSES FOR 1995–96 ***Application fee:*** $20. State resident tuition: $1552 full-time, $70.88 per credit part-time. Nonresident tuition: $4144 full-time, $172.67 per credit part-time. Part-time mandatory fees: $6.21 per credit. Minnesota, South Dakota, Montana, Manitoba, and Saskatchewan resident tuition: $1940 full-time, $87.05 per credit part-time. Full-time mandatory fees: $149. College room and board: $2010. College room only: $800 (minimum).
FINANCIAL AID ***College-administered undergrad aid 1995–96:*** 61 need-based scholarships (average $415), 165 non-need scholarships (average $375), short-term loans (average $105), low-interest long-term loans from college funds (average $2102), loans from external sources (average $2384), Federal Work-Study, 178 part-time jobs. ***Required forms:*** FAFSA; required for some: state; accepted: CSS Financial Aid PROFILE, institutional. ***Priority deadline:*** 4/15. ***Payment plans:*** installment, deferred payment. ***Waivers:*** full or partial for employees or children of employees. ***Notification:*** 6/15.
APPLYING Open admission. ***Options:*** Common Application, early entrance. ***Required:*** school transcript, ACT, TOEFL for international students. Test scores used for counseling/placement. ***Application deadline:*** rolling. ***Notification:*** continuous.
APPLYING/TRANSFER ***Required:*** college transcript. ***Required for some:*** standardized test scores, high school transcript. ***Entrance:*** noncompetitive. ***Application deadline:*** rolling. ***Notification:*** continuous. ***Contact:*** Mr. Richard L. Holm, Director of Admissions and Records, 701-671-2203.
CONTACT Mr. Richard L. Holm, Director of Admissions and Records, North Dakota State College of Science, Wahpeton, ND 58076, 701-671-2203. ***Fax:*** 701-671-2332. ***E-mail:*** rlholm@plains.nodak.edu. College video available.

NORTH DAKOTA STATE UNIVERSITY–BOTTINEAU
Bottineau, North Dakota

UG Enrollment: 356	**Tuition & Fees (ND Res): $1757**
Application Deadline: rolling	**Room & Board: $2340**

GENERAL State-supported, 2-year, coed. Part of North Dakota University System. Awards transfer associate, terminal associate degrees. Founded 1907. ***Setting:*** 35-acre rural campus. ***Total enrollment:*** 356. ***Faculty:*** 28 (22 full-time, 25% with terminal degrees, 6 part-time); student-faculty ratio is 15:1.
ENROLLMENT PROFILE 356 students from 31 states and territories, 1 other country. 40% women, 60% men, 6% part-time, 67% state residents, 75% live on campus, 14% transferred in, 65% have need-based financial aid, 15% have non-need-based financial aid, 10% international, 14% 25 or older, 5% Native American, 1% Hispanic, 1% African American, 0% Asian American. ***Areas of study chosen:*** 38% natural resource sciences, 22% interdisciplinary studies, 6% education, 4% agriculture. ***Most popular recent majors:*** wildlife biology, liberal arts/general studies, business administration/commerce/management.
FIRST-YEAR CLASS 232 total; 302 applied, 100% were accepted, 77% of whom enrolled.
ACADEMIC PROGRAM Calendar: semesters. Academic remediation for entering students, services for LD students, part-time degree program (daytime), adult/continuing education programs, co-op programs and internships.
GENERAL DEGREE REQUIREMENTS 61 semester hours; 1 course each in math and lab science; computer course; internship (some majors).
MAJORS Biology/biological sciences, botany/plant sciences, business administration/commerce/management, business education, computer programming, computer science, computer technologies, conservation, ecology, education, engineering (general), (pre)engineering sequence, environmental sciences, farm and ranch management, fish and game manage-

ment, forestry, forest technology, home economics, horticulture, landscape architecture/design, legal secretarial studies, liberal arts/general studies, marketing/retailing/merchandising, mathematics, medical assistant technologies, medical laboratory technology, medical secretarial studies, natural resource management, natural sciences, parks management, physical education, range management, retail management, science, secretarial studies/office management, wildlife biology, wildlife management.

LIBRARY North Dakota State University-Bottineau Library plus 1 other, with 45,000 books, 260 periodicals.

COMPUTERS ON CAMPUS 55 computers for student use in computer center, library.

COLLEGE LIFE Orientation program (2 days, no cost, parents included). Drama-theater group. ***Major annual events:*** Smokey's Week, Luau Week, Valentine's Dance/Party. ***Student services:*** personal-psychological counseling.

HOUSING 296 college housing spaces available; 208 were occupied 1995–96. No special consideration for freshman housing applicants. On-campus residence required through sophomore year. ***Option:*** single-sex housing available. Resident assistants live in dorms.

ATHLETICS Member NJCAA. ***Intercollegiate:*** basketball M(s)/W(s), ice hockey M(s), volleyball W(s). ***Intramural:*** archery, basketball, football, ice hockey, skiing (cross-country), skiing (downhill), tennis, track and field, volleyball, wrestling. ***Contact:*** Dr. David Agnes, Athletic Director, 701-228-5452.

AFTER GRADUATION 58% of students completing a degree program in 1994–95 went directly on to further study.

EXPENSES FOR 1995–96 ***Application fee:*** $25. State resident tuition: $1757 full-time, $73.21 per credit part-time. Nonresident tuition: $4349 full-time, $181.21 per credit part-time. Tuition for South Dakota, Montana, Manitoba, and Saskatchewan residents: $2145 full-time, $89.38 per credit part-time. Tuition for Minnesota residents: $1991 full-time, $82.96 per credit part-time. Tuition for students eligible for the Western Undergraduate Exchange: $2553 full-time, $106.38 per credit part-time. College room and board: $2340.

FINANCIAL AID ***College-administered undergrad aid 1995–96:*** 80 need-based scholarships (average $500), 25 non-need scholarships (average $500), short-term loans (average $150), low-interest long-term loans from college funds (average $1200), loans from external sources (average $2600), Federal Work-Study, 15 part-time jobs. ***Required forms:*** FAFSA; required for some: state, institutional, affidavit of nonsupport; accepted: CSS Financial Aid PROFILE. ***Priority deadline:*** 4/15.

APPLYING Open admission. ***Options:*** early entrance, deferred entrance, midyear entrance. ***Required:*** school transcript, ACT. Test scores used for counseling/placement. ***Application deadline:*** rolling. ***Notification:*** continuous until 8/23. Preference given to state residents.

APPLYING/TRANSFER ***Required:*** college transcript. ***Entrance:*** noncompetitive. ***Application deadline:*** rolling. ***Notification:*** continuous until 8/23.

CONTACT Mr. Tom Berube, Admissions Counselor, North Dakota State University–Bottineau, Bottineau, ND 58318-1198, 701-228-5426 Ext. 426 or toll-free 800-542-6866 (in-state). ***Fax:*** 701-228-5499. College video available.

STANDING ROCK COLLEGE
Fort Yates, North Dakota

UG Enrollment: 204	**Tuition & Fees: $1870**
Application Deadline: 9/6	**Room & Board: N/Avail**

GENERAL Independent, 2-year, coed. Awards transfer associate, terminal associate degrees. Founded 1973. ***Setting:*** rural campus. ***Educational spending 1994–95:*** $2001 per undergrad. ***Total enrollment:*** 204. ***Faculty:*** 21 (14 full-time, 7 part-time); student-faculty ratio is 7:1. ***Notable Alumni:*** Tom Condon, dean at Standing Rock College; John Buckley, director of Healthy Start Program; Wynona Flying Earth, director of Tribal Education Program; Donna Wuitschick, financial aid officer at Standing Rock College; Laurel Vermillion, academic dean at Standing Rock College.

ENROLLMENT PROFILE 204 students from 2 states and territories. 64% women, 36% men, 19% part-time, 10% transferred in, 40% 25 or older, 92% Native American.

FIRST-YEAR CLASS 38 total. Of the students who applied, 100% were accepted, 100% of whom enrolled.

ACADEMIC PROGRAM Core. Calendar: semesters. Academic remediation for entering students, tutorials, part-time degree program (daytime, evenings), adult/continuing education programs. Off-campus study at members of the American Indian Higher Education Consortium.

GENERAL DEGREE REQUIREMENTS 61 credit hours; math/science requirements vary according to program.

MAJORS Education, human services, liberal arts/general studies, marketing/retailing/merchandising, Native American studies, secretarial studies/office management.

LIBRARY Standing Rock College Library with 8,000 books, 130 periodicals, 10 CD-ROMs, 125 records, tapes, and CDs. Acquisition spending 1994–95: $48,059.

COMPUTERS ON CAMPUS Computer purchase plan available. 16 computers for student use in computer center. Staffed computer lab on campus provides training in use of computers, software. Academic computing expenditure 1994–95: $100,000.

COLLEGE LIFE Student-run newspaper. ***Most popular organizations:*** Student Government, Future Teachers Club, Ikce Oyate Culture Club, Phi Beta Lambda, Ski Club. ***Major annual events:*** Homecoming, Thanksgiving Dinner, Student Awards Night. ***Student services:*** personal-psychological counseling.

HOUSING College housing not available.

ATHLETICS ***Intercollegiate:*** basketball M/W. ***Intramural:*** basketball. ***Contact:*** Mr. Bill Ruter, Instructor, 701-854-7317.

CAREER PLANNING ***Placement office:*** 1 full-time staff; $25,000 operating expenditure 1994–95. ***Services:*** resume preparation, career counseling.

AFTER GRADUATION 40% of students completing a degree program in 1994–95 went directly on to further study.

EXPENSES FOR 1995–96 Tuition: $1800 full-time, $60 per credit hour part-time. Part-time mandatory fees: $30 per semester. Full-time mandatory fees: $70 (minimum).

FINANCIAL AID ***College-administered undergrad aid 1995–96:*** 47 need-based scholarships (average $1543), 90 non-need scholarships (average $462), 5 Federal Work-Study (averaging $2400). ***Required forms:*** institutional, FAFSA; accepted: CSS Financial Aid PROFILE, state. ***Priority deadline:*** 5/15.

APPLYING Open admission. ***Options:*** early entrance, midyear entrance. ***Required:*** school transcript, medical questionnaire, TABE. ***Application deadline:*** 9/6. ***Notification:*** continuous.

APPLYING/TRANSFER ***Required:*** high school transcript, college transcript, medical questionnaire. ***Application deadline:*** 9/6. ***Notification:*** continuous.

CONTACT Director of Admissions, Standing Rock College, Fort Yates, ND 58538-9701, 701-854-3864 Ext. 214. College video available.

TURTLE MOUNTAIN COMMUNITY COLLEGE
Belcourt, North Dakota

UG Enrollment: 404	**Tuition & Fees: $1176**
Application Deadline: rolling	**Room & Board: N/Avail**

GENERAL Independent, 2-year, coed. Awards transfer associate, terminal associate degrees. Founded 1972. ***Setting:*** 10-acre rural campus. ***Total enrollment:*** 404. ***Faculty:*** 41 (20 full-time, 21 part-time).

ENROLLMENT PROFILE 404 students: 72% women, 28% men, 44% part-time, 100% state residents, 16% transferred in, 75% 25 or older, 92% Native American. ***Areas of study chosen:*** 32% liberal arts/general studies, 20% computer and information sciences, 11% education, 9% vocational and home economics, 8% business management and administrative services, 7% health professions and related sciences, 3% biological and life sciences, 3% natural resource sciences, 3% social sciences, 1% engineering and applied sciences, 1% mathematics, 1% prelaw, 1% premed, 1% prevet.

FIRST-YEAR CLASS 225 total. Of the students who applied, 100% were accepted.

ACADEMIC PROGRAM Core, honor code. Calendar: semesters. 100 courses offered in 1995–96. Academic remediation for entering students, tutorials, part-time degree program (daytime, evenings), adult/continuing education programs, internships.

GENERAL DEGREE REQUIREMENTS 63 semester hours; 2 courses each in math and lab science; computer course for business majors; internship (some majors).

MAJORS Art/fine arts, biology/biological sciences, business administration/commerce/management, computer science, early childhood education, elementary education, (pre)engineering sequence, English, environmental sciences, history, human services, journalism, liberal arts/general studies, mathematics, medical records services, medical technology, natural resource management, nursing, pharmacy/pharmaceutical sciences, physical therapy, science, secretarial studies/office management, social science, social work, veterinary technology, vocational education, wildlife management.

LIBRARY Turtle Mountain Community College Library with 20,500 books, 144 microform titles, 150 periodicals, 10 CD-ROMs, 1,150 records, tapes, and CDs.

COMPUTERS ON CAMPUS 147 computers for student use in computer center, classrooms. Staffed computer lab on campus provides training in use of computers, software.

COLLEGE LIFE 70% vote in student government elections. ***Most popular organization:*** Student Government. ***Major annual events:*** College Awareness Week, Student Picnic, Annual Pow-Wow. ***Student services:*** personal-psychological counseling.

HOUSING College housing not available.

ATHLETICS ***Intramural:*** basketball, softball, tennis, volleyball. ***Contact:*** Mr. Steven DeCoteau, Student Support Services Director, 701-477-5605 Ext. 214.

CAREER PLANNING ***Placement office:*** 1 full-time staff. ***Director:*** Mr. Dave Garcia, Career Counselor, 701-477-5605. ***Services:*** resume preparation, career counseling.

EXPENSES FOR 1996–97 Tuition: $984 full-time, $41 per semester hour part-time. Part-time mandatory fees: $8 per semester hour. Full-time mandatory fees: $192.

FINANCIAL AID ***College-administered undergrad aid 1995–96:*** need-based scholarships (averaging $1150), non-need scholarships, Federal Work-Study. ***Required forms:*** institutional, FAFSA; required for some: state. ***Priority deadline:*** 4/15. ***Payment plan:*** installment. ***Waivers:*** full or partial for minority students and adult students.

APPLYING Open admission. ***Options:*** early entrance, deferred entrance, midyear entrance. ***Required:*** school transcript, ACT. Test scores used for admission. ***Application deadline:*** rolling.

APPLYING/TRANSFER ***Required:*** standardized test scores, high school transcript, college transcript, minimum 2.0 college GPA. ***Entrance:*** noncompetitive. ***Application deadline:*** rolling. ***Contact:*** Mr. Dave Garcia, Career Counselor, 701-477-5605.

CONTACT Ms. Joni LaFontaine, Admissions/Records Officer, Turtle Mountain Community College, Belcourt, ND 58316-0340, 701-477-5605 Ext. 217. ***Fax:*** 701-477-5028.

UNITED TRIBES TECHNICAL COLLEGE
Bismarck, North Dakota

UG Enrollment: 250	**Tuition & Fees: $3800**
Application Deadline: rolling	**Room & Board: $2400**

GENERAL Federally supported, 2-year, coed. Awards certificates, diplomas, transfer associate, terminal associate degrees. Founded 1969. ***Setting:*** 105-acre small-town campus. ***Total enrollment:*** 250. ***Faculty:*** 23 (22 full-time, 1 part-time).

ENROLLMENT PROFILE 250 students: 65% women, 0% part-time, 75% state residents, 10% transferred in, 95% Native American.

FIRST-YEAR CLASS 118 total; 150 applied, 89% were accepted, 88% of whom enrolled.

ACADEMIC PROGRAM Calendar: 1-4-4. Academic remediation for entering students, honors program, summer session for credit, part-time degree program (daytime, summer).

GENERAL DEGREE REQUIREMENTS 60 credit hours; 6 credit hours of math.

MAJORS Automotive technologies, business administration/commerce/management, child psychology/child development, criminal justice, early childhood education, medical records services, nursing.

LIBRARY 6,000 books, 86 periodicals.

COMPUTERS ON CAMPUS 210 computers for student use in learning center, business-clerical room, classrooms. Staffed computer lab on campus provides training in use of computers, software.

COLLEGE LIFE Student-run newspaper. ***Student services:*** personal-psychological counseling. ***Campus security:*** 24-hour emergency response devices and patrols.

HOUSING 146 college housing spaces available; 140 were occupied 1995–96. Off-campus living permitted.

ATHLETICS Member NJCAA. ***Intercollegiate:*** basketball M, cross-country running M/W. ***Intramural:*** basketball, volleyball.

CAREER PLANNING ***Service:*** career counseling.

United Tribes Technical College (continued)

EXPENSES FOR 1996–97 Comprehensive fee of $6200 includes full-time tuition ($3100), mandatory fees ($700), and college room and board ($2400 minimum). Part-time tuition: $87.50 per credit hour. Tuition guaranteed not to increase for student's term of enrollment.
FINANCIAL AID ***College-administered undergrad aid 1995–96:*** 2 need-based scholarships (average $1000), short-term loans (average $150), Federal Work-Study, part-time jobs. ***Required forms:*** institutional, FAFSA, Bureau of Indian Affairs form; required for some: state; accepted: CSS Financial Aid PROFILE. ***Application deadline:*** continuous.
APPLYING Open admission. ***Required:*** school transcript. ***Recommended:*** ACT. Test scores used for admission. ***Application deadline:*** rolling.
APPLYING/TRANSFER ***Required:*** high school transcript, college transcript. ***Recommended:*** standardized test scores. ***Application deadline:*** rolling.
CONTACT Mr. T. J. McLaughlin, Admissions Coordinator, United Tribes Technical College, Bismarck, ND 58504-7596, 701-255-3285 Ext. 334.

UNIVERSITY OF NORTH DAKOTA–LAKE REGION
Devils Lake, North Dakota

UG Enrollment: 723 | **Tuition & Fees (ND Res): $1752**
Application Deadline: rolling | **Room & Board: $2370**

GENERAL State-supported, 2-year, coed. Part of North Dakota University System. Awards certificates, diplomas, transfer associate, terminal associate degrees. Founded 1941. ***Setting:*** 15-acre small-town campus. ***Total enrollment:*** 723. ***Faculty:*** 54 (26 full-time, 8% with terminal degrees, 28 part-time).
ENROLLMENT PROFILE 723 students from 4 states and territories. 54% women, 45% part-time, 98% state residents, 19% live on campus, 11% transferred in, 0% international, 39% 25 or older, 4% Native American, 0% Hispanic, 0% African American, 0% Asian American. ***Most popular recent majors:*** liberal arts/general studies, agricultural business, marketing/retailing/merchandising.
FIRST-YEAR CLASS 283 total; 298 applied, 100% were accepted, 95% of whom enrolled.
ACADEMIC PROGRAM Core. Calendar: semesters. 450 courses offered in 1995–96. Academic remediation for entering students, English as a second language program offered during academic year and summer, Freshman Honors College, summer session for credit, part-time degree program (daytime, evenings), adult/continuing education programs, co-op programs and internships.
GENERAL DEGREE REQUIREMENTS 60 semester hours; internship (some majors).
MAJORS Agricultural business, agricultural sciences, agricultural technologies, automotive technologies, aviation technology, business administration/commerce/management, child care/child and family studies, computer technologies, data processing, electrical and electronics technologies, farm and ranch management, fashion merchandising, law enforcement/police sciences, legal secretarial studies, liberal arts/general studies, marketing/retailing/merchandising, medical secretarial studies, paralegal studies, secretarial studies/office management, telecommunications.
LIBRARY Paul Hoghaug Library plus 1 other, with 30,000 books, 24 microform titles, 500 periodicals, 3 on-line bibliographic services, 10 CD-ROMs, 1,537 records, tapes, and CDs. Acquisition spending 1994–95: $20,000.
COMPUTERS ON CAMPUS 127 computers for student use in computer labs, classrooms, dorms provide access to main academic computer, e-mail, on-line services, Internet. Staffed computer lab on campus provides training in use of computers, software. Academic computing expenditure 1994–95: $205,000.
COLLEGE LIFE Drama-theater group. 45% vote in student government elections. ***Most popular organizations:*** Drama Club, Students Older Than Average. ***Major annual events:*** Sno Daze, Fall Fling, Spring Blast. ***Student services:*** personal-psychological counseling. ***Campus security:*** 24-hour emergency response devices.
HOUSING 200 college housing spaces available; 136 were occupied 1995–96. No special consideration for freshman housing applicants. Off-campus living permitted. ***Option:*** single-sex housing available. Resident assistants live in dorms.
ATHLETICS Member NJCAA. ***Intercollegiate:*** basketball M(s)/W(s), volleyball W(s). ***Intramural:*** basketball, bowling, football, table tennis (Ping-Pong), volleyball. ***Contact:*** Mr. Terry Porter, Athletic Director, 701-662-1523.
CAREER PLANNING ***Placement office:*** 1 full-time staff; $44,000 operating expenditure 1994–95. ***Director:*** Dr. Randall Fixen, Director of Counseling, 701-662-1518. ***Services:*** resume preparation, career counseling, careers library, job bank, job interviews. 8 organizations recruited on campus 1994–95.
EXPENSES FOR 1995–96 ***Application fee:*** $25. State resident tuition: $1552 full-time, $65 per semester hour part-time. Nonresident tuition: $4144 full-time, $173 per semester hour part-time. Part-time mandatory fees: $7 per semester hour. Full-time mandatory fees: $200. College room and board: $2370.
FINANCIAL AID ***College-administered undergrad aid 1995–96:*** 15 need-based scholarships (average $250), 130 non-need scholarships (average $450), low-interest long-term loans from external sources (average $2500), 75 Federal Work-Study (averaging $900), 10 part-time jobs. ***Required forms:*** FAFSA. ***Priority deadline:*** 4/15. ***Payment plans:*** installment, deferred payment. ***Waivers:*** full or partial for minority students.
APPLYING Open admission. ***Options:*** Common Application, electronic application, midyear entrance. ***Required:*** school transcript, SAT I or ACT, TOEFL for international students. Test scores used for counseling/placement. ***Application deadline:*** rolling.
APPLYING/TRANSFER ***Required:*** college transcript. ***Entrance:*** noncompetitive. ***Application deadline:*** rolling. ***Contact:*** Mr. Dan Johnson, Registrar, 701-662-1556.
CONTACT Mrs. Laurel Goulding, Dean of Student Services, University of North Dakota–Lake Region, Devils Lake, ND 58301-1598, 701-662-1514 or toll-free 800-443-1313. ***Fax:*** 701-662-1570. ***E-mail:*** wagners@shorelines.und-lr.nodak.edu.

UNIVERSITY OF NORTH DAKOTA–WILLISTON
Williston, North Dakota

UG Enrollment: 919 | **Tuition & Fees (ND Res): $1802**
Application Deadline: rolling | **Room & Board: $1080**

GENERAL State-supported, 2-year, coed. Part of North Dakota University System. Awards certificates, diplomas, transfer associate, terminal associate degrees. Founded 1957. ***Setting:*** 80-acre small-town campus. ***Educational spending 1994–95:*** $2462 per undergrad. ***Total enrollment:*** 919. ***Faculty:*** 59 (30 full-time, 3% with terminal degrees, 29 part-time); student-faculty ratio is 15:1.
ENROLLMENT PROFILE 919 students from 12 states and territories, 3 other countries. 61% women, 39% men, 28% part-time, 80% state residents, 13% live on campus, 10% transferred in, 65% have need-based financial aid, 15% have non-need-based financial aid, 4% international, 40% 25 or older, 4% Native American, 0% African American, 0% Asian American. ***Areas of study chosen:*** 45% liberal arts/general studies, 11% health professions and related sciences, 6% business management and administrative services, 3% agriculture. ***Most popular recent majors:*** liberal arts/general studies, practical nursing.
FIRST-YEAR CLASS 282 total; 300 applied, 96% were accepted, 98% of whom enrolled.
ACADEMIC PROGRAM Core. Calendar: semesters. 350 courses offered in 1995–96; average class size 30 in required courses. Academic remediation for entering students, services for LD students, advanced placement, self-designed majors, part-time degree program (daytime, evenings), co-op programs and internships. Off-campus study at Dickinson State University, University of North Dakota-Lake Region, University of North Dakota.
GENERAL DEGREE REQUIREMENTS 62 credits; 1 math/science course; computer course for most majors; internship (some majors).
MAJORS Agricultural technologies, automotive technologies, environmental health sciences, liberal arts/general studies, marketing/retailing/merchandising, physical therapy, practical nursing, secretarial studies/office management.
LIBRARY UND-Williston Library with 13,370 books, 15 microform titles, 177 periodicals, 4 on-line bibliographic services, 2 CD-ROMs, 323 records, tapes, and CDs. Acquisition spending 1994–95: $15,692.
COMPUTERS ON CAMPUS 100 computers for student use in computer center, computer labs, learning resource center, classrooms, library, dorms provide access to off-campus computing facilities, e-mail, on-line services, Internet. Staffed computer lab on campus provides training in use of computers, software. Academic computing expenditure 1994–95: $1.1 million.
COLLEGE LIFE Choral group. ***Social organizations:*** 4 open to all; 2 national sororities; 15% of eligible women are members. ***Most popular organizations:*** Student Senate, Phi Theta Kappa, Computer Club. ***Major annual events:*** Winter Carnival, Spring Luau, Honors Brunch. ***Student services:*** personal-psychological counseling. ***Campus security:*** controlled dormitory access.
HOUSING 116 college housing spaces available; 115 were occupied 1995–96. No special consideration for freshman housing applicants. Off-campus living permitted. ***Options:*** coed (1 building), single-sex (4 buildings) housing available. Resident assistants live in dorms.
ATHLETICS Member NJCAA. ***Intercollegiate:*** baseball M(s), basketball M(s)/W(s), volleyball W(s). ***Intramural:*** basketball, golf, softball, tennis, volleyball. ***Contact:*** Mr. Terry Olson, Athletic Director, 701-774-4242.
CAREER PLANNING ***Placement office:*** 2 part-time staff. ***Director:*** Mr. Pat Riley, Career Counselor, Educational Opportunity Center, 701-774-4216. ***Services:*** resume preparation, resume referral, career counseling, careers library, job bank, job interviews.
AFTER GRADUATION 80% of students completing a degree program in 1994–95 went directly on to further study.
EXPENSES FOR 1996–97 ***Application fee:*** $25. State resident tuition: $1552 full-time, $73.26 per credit hour part-time. Nonresident tuition: $4144 full-time, $181.26 per credit hour part-time. Part-time mandatory fees: $10.59 per credit hour. Tuition for Minnesota residents: $1800 full-time, $83.59 per credit hour part-time. Tuition for South Dakota, Montana, Manitoba, and Saskatchewan residents: $1940 full-time, $86.51 per credit hour part-time. Tuition for nonresidents who are eligible for the Western Undergraduate Exchange Program: $2328 full-time, $105.56 per credit hour part-time. Full-time mandatory fees: $250. College room and board: $1080. College room only: $680.
FINANCIAL AID ***College-administered undergrad aid 1995–96:*** 200 need-based scholarships (averaging $500), 50 non-need scholarships (averaging $500), short-term loans (averaging $100), low-interest long-term loans from external sources (averaging $2000), 42 Federal Work-Study (averaging $900), 25 part-time jobs. ***Required forms:*** FAFSA; accepted: CSS Financial Aid PROFILE, state, institutional. ***Priority deadline:*** 4/15. ***Waivers:*** full or partial for employees or children of employees and senior citizens. ***Notification:*** 5/15.
APPLYING Open admission. ***Options:*** early entrance, deferred entrance, midyear entrance. ***Required:*** school transcript, TOEFL for international students. ***Required for some:*** ACT. Test scores used for counseling/placement. ***Application deadline:*** rolling. ***Notification:*** continuous. Preference given to state residents.
APPLYING/TRANSFER ***Required:*** good standing at previous institution. ***Required for some:*** high school transcript, college transcript. ***Entrance:*** noncompetitive. ***Application deadline:*** rolling. ***Notification:*** continuous. ***Contact:*** Ms. Jan Solem, Director of Admission/Registrar, 701-774-4212.
CONTACT Ms. Jan Solem, Director of Admissions/Registrar, University of North Dakota–Williston, Williston, ND 58802-1326, 701-774-4212. ***E-mail:*** jclark@basin.und-w.nodak.edu.

OHIO

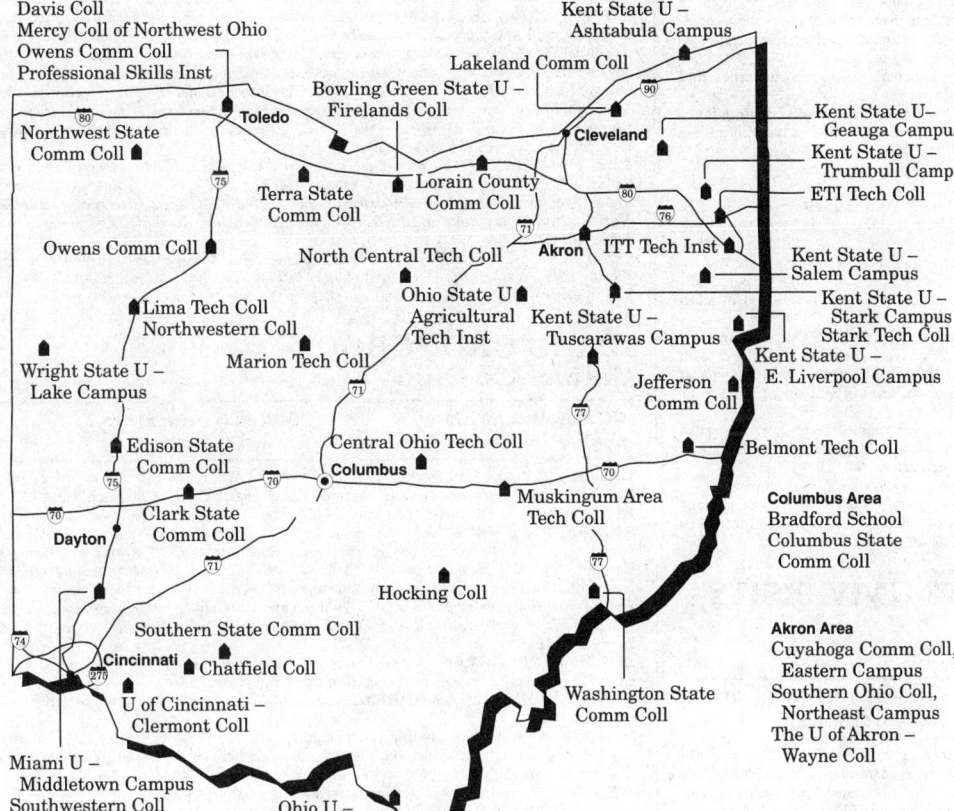

ANTONELLI COLLEGE
Cincinnati, Ohio

UG Enrollment: 175	Tuition & Fees: $7690
Application Deadline: 9/1	Room & Board: N/Avail

GENERAL Proprietary, 2-year, coed. Awards diplomas, terminal associate degrees. Founded 1947. *Setting:* urban campus. *Total enrollment:* 175. *Faculty:* 29 (16 full-time, 13 part-time).
ENROLLMENT PROFILE 175 students from 5 states and territories, 2 other countries. 65% women, 0% part-time, 99% state residents, 25% transferred in, 20% 25 or older, 5% African American. *Most popular recent majors:* commercial art, interior design, photography.
FIRST-YEAR CLASS 68 total; 83 applied, 100% were accepted, 82% of whom enrolled.
ACADEMIC PROGRAM Core, honor code. Calendar: semesters. 96 courses offered in 1995–96. English as a second language program, honors program, summer session for credit, part-time degree program (daytime).
GENERAL DEGREE REQUIREMENTS 65 credits; computer course.
MAJORS Commercial art, computer technologies, fashion merchandising, interior design, photography.
LIBRARY 2,000 books, 30 periodicals.
COMPUTERS ON CAMPUS 25 computers for student use in computer center, computer labs. Staffed computer lab on campus provides training in use of computers, software.
COLLEGE LIFE *Student services:* personal-psychological counseling. *Campus security:* 24-hour emergency response devices.
HOUSING College housing not available.
CAREER PLANNING *Placement office:* 1 full-time staff. *Director:* Mr. Greg Bartell, Director, Placement, 513-241-4338. *Services:* resume preparation, resume referral, career counseling, job bank, job interviews. Students must register freshman year.
AFTER GRADUATION 88% of class of 1994 had job offers within 6 months.
EXPENSES FOR 1995–96 *Application fee:* $50. Tuition: $7690 (minimum) full-time. Full-time tuition ranges up to $8740 according to program.
FINANCIAL AID College-administered undergrad aid 1995–96: need-based scholarships, low-interest long-term loans from external sources (averaging $2600), Federal Work-Study. *Required forms:* institutional, FAFSA; required for some: Stafford Student Loan form; accepted: CSS Financial Aid PROFILE, state. *Application deadline:* continuous. *Payment plan:* installment.
APPLYING Open admission. *Options:* early entrance, deferred entrance, midyear entrance. *Required:* campus interview, TOEFL for international students. *Recommended:* recommendations. *Required for some:* art portfolio. *Application deadline:* 9/1. *Notification:* continuous until 9/17.
APPLYING/TRANSFER *Entrance:* noncompetitive. *Application deadline:* 9/1. *Notification:* continuous until 9/17. *Contact:* Mr. Bob Wilson, Director of Admissions, 513-241-4338.
CONTACT Mr. Bob Wilson, Director of Admissions, Antonelli College, 124 East Seventh Street, Cincinnati, OH 45202-2539, 513-241-4338 or toll-free 800-505-4338. College video available.

BELMONT TECHNICAL COLLEGE
St. Clairsville, Ohio

UG Enrollment: 1,694	Tuition & Fees (OH Res): $2519
Application Deadline: rolling	Room & Board: N/Avail

GENERAL State-supported, 2-year, coed. Part of Ohio Board of Regents. Awards diplomas, terminal associate degrees. Founded 1971. *Setting:* 55-acre rural campus. *Total enrollment:* 1,694. *Faculty:* 101 (41 full-time, 51% with terminal degrees, 60 part-time).
ENROLLMENT PROFILE 1,694 students from 10 states and territories. 61% women, 39% men, 34% part-time, 81% state residents, 7% transferred in, 0% international, 55% 25 or older, 0% Native American, 0% Hispanic, 2% African American, 0% Asian American. *Areas of study chosen:* 38% health professions and related sciences, 9% engineering and applied sciences, 7% business management and administrative services, 7% computer and information sciences. *Most popular recent majors:* accounting, business administration/commerce/management, nursing.
FIRST-YEAR CLASS 454 total; 751 applied, 100% were accepted, 60% of whom enrolled.

Peterson's Guide to Two-Year Colleges 1997

Belmont Technical College (continued)
ACADEMIC PROGRAM Core. Calendar: quarters. 350 courses offered in 1995–96. Academic remediation for entering students, summer session for credit, part-time degree program (daytime, evenings).
GENERAL DEGREE REQUIREMENTS 90 credit hours; 1 quarter of college level math; 1 quarter of science; computer course for most majors.
MAJORS Accounting, business administration/commerce/management, civil engineering technology, computer programming, computer technologies, corrections, electrical and electronics technologies, electromechanical technology, emergency medical technology, heating/refrigeration/air conditioning, historic preservation, mechanical engineering technology, medical assistant technologies, mental health/rehabilitation counseling, nursing, practical nursing, secretarial studies/office management, welding technology.
LIBRARY 5,612 books, 616 microform titles, 217 periodicals, 1,375 records, tapes, and CDs.
COMPUTERS ON CAMPUS 85 computers for student use in computer center, computer labs, learning resource center. Staffed computer lab on campus provides training in use of computers, software.
COLLEGE LIFE ***Student services:*** personal-psychological counseling.
HOUSING College housing not available.
CAREER PLANNING ***Placement office:*** 1 full-time staff. ***Director:*** Mr. Mark S. Farmer, Placement Coordinator, 614-695-9500. ***Services:*** resume referral, career counseling, job interviews. Students must register sophomore year.
EXPENSES FOR 1995–96 ***Application fee:*** $20. State resident tuition: $2519 full-time, $46.64 per credit part-time. Nonresident tuition: $3132 full-time, $58 per credit part-time. West Virginia residents of Brooke, Ohio, Hancock, Marshall, and Wetzel counties pay state resident tuition rates.
FINANCIAL AID ***College-administered undergrad aid 1995–96:*** 40 non-need scholarships (average $760), Federal Work-Study. ***Required forms:*** FAFSA; accepted: CSS Financial Aid PROFILE. ***Application deadline:*** continuous. ***Payment plan:*** installment. ***Waivers:*** full or partial for employees or children of employees and senior citizens.
APPLYING Open admission except for nursing, emergency medical technology programs. ***Option:*** early entrance. ***Required:*** TOEFL for international students, ACT ASSET. Test scores used for counseling/placement. ***Application deadline:*** rolling.
APPLYING/TRANSFER ***Required:*** college transcript. ***Entrance:*** noncompetitive.
CONTACT Mr. Thomas J. Tarowsky, Assistant Dean of Student Services, Belmont Technical College, St. Clairsville, OH 43950-9766, 614-695-9500 Ext. 64 or toll-free 800-423-1188 (in-state). ***E-mail:*** ttarowsk@belmont.tech.oh.us.

BOWLING GREEN STATE UNIVERSITY–FIRELANDS COLLEGE
Huron, Ohio

UG Enrollment: 1,379	**Tuition & Fees (OH Res): $3014**
Application Deadline: 8/1	**Room & Board: N/Avail**

GENERAL State-supported, primarily 2-year, coed. Part of Bowling Green State University System. Awards certificates, transfer associate, terminal associate, bachelor's degrees (also offers some upper-level and graduate courses). Founded 1968. ***Setting:*** 216-acre rural campus with easy access to Cleveland and Toledo. ***Educational spending 1994–95:*** $3415 per undergrad. Faculty: 81 (37 full-time, 68% with terminal degrees, 44 part-time); student-faculty ratio is 16:1.
ENROLLMENT PROFILE 1,379 students from 7 states and territories. 68% women, 48% part-time, 99% state residents, 6% transferred in, 55% have need-based financial aid, 2% have non-need-based financial aid, 47% 25 or older, 1% Hispanic, 5% African American. ***Areas of study chosen:*** 25% health professions and related sciences, 21% liberal arts/general studies, 15% engineering and applied sciences, 13% business management and administrative services, 12% education, 5% interdisciplinary studies, 4% computer and information sciences, 2% biological and life sciences, 1% communications and journalism, 1% English language/literature/letters, 1% social sciences.
FIRST-YEAR CLASS 273 total; 459 applied, 99% were accepted, 60% of whom enrolled. 3% from top 10% of their high school class, 23% from top quarter, 72% from top half.
ACADEMIC PROGRAM Core, honor code. Calendar: semesters. 450 courses offered in 1995–96. Academic remediation for entering students, services for LD students, advanced placement, self-designed majors, tutorials, summer session for credit, part-time degree program (daytime, evenings), adult/continuing education programs, internships. Off-campus study at University of Toledo. ROTC: Army (c), Air Force (c).
GENERAL DEGREE REQUIREMENTS 62 credit hours for associate, 122 credit hours for bachelor's; 1 intermediate algebra course or high school equivalent; computer course; internship (some majors).
MAJORS Accounting, business administration/commerce/management, computer programming, computer technologies, criminal justice, education, electrical and electronics technologies, elementary education, (pre)engineering sequence, humanities, human services, industrial administration, interdisciplinary studies, liberal arts/general studies, manufacturing technology, marketing/retailing/merchandising, mechanical design technology, medical records services, nursing, physical sciences, quality control technology, respiratory therapy, retail management, science, secretarial studies/office management, social science, social work.
LIBRARY 29,946 books, 23 microform titles, 220 periodicals, 1,692 records, tapes, and CDs. Acquisition spending 1994–95: $32,958.
COMPUTERS ON CAMPUS 250 computers for student use in computer center, computer labs, learning center, classrooms, library provide access to e-mail, on-line services, Internet. Staffed computer lab on campus provides training in use of computers, software. Academic computing expenditure 1994–95: $132,989.
COLLEGE LIFE Drama-theater group. 3% vote in student government elections. ***Social organizations:*** 20 open to all. ***Most popular organizations:*** Speech Activities Organization, Allied Health Club, Student Government, Intramural Club, Campus Fellowship. ***Major annual events:*** Beggars Banquet, Welcome Back Cookout, Recognition Banquet. ***Campus security:*** patrols by trained security personnel.
HOUSING College housing not available.
ATHLETICS ***Intramural:*** basketball, football, skiing (downhill), softball, volleyball, weight lifting.
CAREER PLANNING ***Placement office:*** 1 full-time, 1 part-time staff; $32,619 operating expenditure 1994–95. ***Director:*** Mr. John Clark, Coordinator of Career Services, 419-433-5560. ***Services:*** job fairs, resume preparation, resume referral, career counseling, careers library, job bank, job interviews. 13 organizations recruited on campus 1994–95.
AFTER GRADUATION 69% of class of 1994 had job offers within 6 months.
EXPENSES FOR 1995–96 ***Application fee:*** $30. State resident tuition: $3014 full-time, $148 per credit hour part-time. Nonresident tuition: $7572 full-time, $217 per credit hour part-time.
FINANCIAL AID ***College-administered undergrad aid 1995–96:*** 74 non-need scholarships (average $660), short-term loans (average $300), low-interest long-term loans from college funds, loans from external sources (average $3500), 19 Federal Work-Study (averaging $2000), 38 part-time jobs. ***Acceptable forms:*** CSS Financial Aid PROFILE, institutional, FAFSA. ***Priority deadline:*** 4/1. ***Payment plan:*** installment. ***Waivers:*** full or partial for employees or children of employees. ***Notification:*** continuous.
APPLYING Open admission. ***Options:*** early entrance, deferred entrance, midyear entrance. ***Required:*** school transcript, TOEFL for international students. ***Recommended:*** 3 years of high school math and science, 2 years of high school foreign language. ***Required for some:*** SAT I or ACT. Test scores used for counseling/placement. ***Application deadline:*** 8/1. ***Notification:*** continuous until 8/15.
APPLYING/TRANSFER ***Required:*** high school transcript, college transcript, minimum 2.0 college GPA. ***Recommended:*** 3 years of high school math and science, 2 years of high school foreign language. ***Entrance:*** minimally difficult. ***Application deadline:*** 8/1. ***Notification:*** continuous until 8/15. ***Contact:*** Ms. Arlene Hazlett, Director of Admissions, 419-433-5560.
CONTACT Ms. Arlene Hazlett, Director of Admissions, Bowling Green State University–Firelands College, Huron, OH 44839-9791, 419-433-5560 or toll-free 800-322-4787 (in-state). ***E-mail:*** ahazlet@bgnet.bgsu.edu. College video available.

BRADFORD SCHOOL
Columbus, Ohio

UG Enrollment: 214	**Tuition & Fees: $7320**
Application Deadline: rolling	**Room Only: $2940**

GENERAL Proprietary, 2-year, primarily women. Awards transfer associate degrees. Founded 1911. ***Setting:*** suburban campus. ***Total enrollment:*** 214. ***Faculty:*** 8 (3 full-time, 5 part-time); student-faculty ratio is 25:1.
ENROLLMENT PROFILE 214 students: 96% women, 0% part-time, 100% state residents, 0% transferred in, 0% international, 0% 25 or older, 0% Native American, 0% Hispanic, 6% African American, 0% Asian American. ***Most popular recent majors:*** accounting, secretarial studies/office management, medical assistant technologies.
FIRST-YEAR CLASS 167 total. Of the students who applied, 90% were accepted, 60% of whom enrolled. 6% from top 10% of their high school class, 11% from top quarter, 83% from top half.
ACADEMIC PROGRAM Core, honor code. Calendar: semesters. Tutorials, adult/continuing education programs, co-op programs and internships.
GENERAL DEGREE REQUIREMENTS 1400 hours; computer course; internship (some majors).
MAJORS Accounting, computer programming, graphic arts, legal secretarial studies, medical assistant technologies, paralegal studies, secretarial studies/office management, tourism and travel.
LIBRARY 50 books, 5 periodicals, 30 records, tapes, and CDs.
COMPUTERS ON CAMPUS 77 computers for student use in computer labs.
COLLEGE LIFE ***Social organizations:*** 2 open to all. ***Most popular organizations:*** Student Senate, Bradford Byline. ***Campus security:*** 24-hour patrols.
HOUSING 200 college housing spaces available; 70 were occupied 1995–96. Freshmen given priority for college housing. Off-campus living permitted. ***Option:*** single-sex housing available.
CAREER PLANNING ***Services:*** resume referral, career counseling, job interviews.
EXPENSES FOR 1996–97 ***Application fee:*** $50. Tuition: $7320 full-time. College room only: $2940. Tuition guaranteed not to increase for student's term of enrollment.
FINANCIAL AID ***College-administered undergrad aid 1995–96:*** need-based scholarships, 16 non-need scholarships (averaging $650), low-interest long-term loans from college funds (averaging $2500), loans from external sources (averaging $2625), Federal Work-Study. ***Required forms:*** FAFSA; required for some: state, institutional; accepted: CSS Financial Aid PROFILE. ***Priority deadline:*** 8/29. ***Payment plan:*** installment. ***Waivers:*** full or partial for employees or children of employees.
APPLYING ***Option:*** Common Application. ***Required for some:*** school transcript, campus interview. ***Application deadline:*** rolling.
APPLYING/TRANSFER ***Required:*** college transcript. ***Required for some:*** campus interview. ***Entrance:*** moderately difficult. ***Application deadline:*** rolling.
CONTACT Ms. Beverly Denney, Director of Admissions, Bradford School, Columbus, OH 43229-2507, 614-846-9410.

BRYANT AND STRATTON COLLEGE
Parma, Ohio

UG Enrollment: 493	**Tuition & Fees: $6720**
Application Deadline: rolling	**Room & Board: N/Avail**

GENERAL Proprietary, 2-year, coed. Part of Bryant and Stratton Business Institute, Inc. Awards diplomas, transfer associate degrees. Founded 1981. ***Setting:*** 4-acre suburban campus with easy access to Cleveland. ***Total enrollment:*** 493. ***Faculty:*** 47 (7 full-time, 40 part-time); student-faculty ratio is 14:1.
ENROLLMENT PROFILE 493 students: 75% women, 25% men, 28% part-time, 100% state residents, 35% transferred in, 0% international, 45% 25 or older, 1% Native American, 5% Hispanic, 5% African American, 3% Asian American. ***Areas of study chosen:*** 20% business management and administrative services, 20% computer and information sciences.
FIRST-YEAR CLASS 230 total; 265 applied, 92% were accepted, 77% of whom enrolled. 1% from top 10% of their high school class, 20% from top quarter, 45% from top half.
ACADEMIC PROGRAM Core, business curriculum, honor code. Calendar: quarters. 74 courses offered in 1995–96. Academic remediation for entering students, tutorials, summer session for credit, part-time degree program (daytime, evenings), internships.
GENERAL DEGREE REQUIREMENTS 90 quarter hours; 1 math course; computer course; internship (some majors).

MAJORS Accounting, business administration/commerce/management, computer management, computer programming, computer science, hotel and restaurant management, legal secretarial studies, marketing/retailing/merchandising, medical assistant technologies, medical secretarial studies, secretarial studies/office management.
LIBRARY 500 books, 12 periodicals.
COMPUTERS ON CAMPUS 96 computers for student use in computer center, computer labs, learning resource center, library. Staffed computer lab on campus provides training in use of computers, software.
COLLEGE LIFE Student-run newspaper. ***Social organizations:*** 4 open to all. ***Most popular organizations:*** Student Activities Council, Student Newspaper, Professional Secretaries International. ***Student services:*** personal-psychological counseling. ***Campus security:*** 24-hour emergency response devices.
HOUSING College housing not available.
ATHLETICS ***Intramural:*** softball.
CAREER PLANNING ***Placement office:*** 1 full-time, 1 part-time staff. ***Services:*** job fairs, resume preparation, resume referral, career counseling, careers library, job bank, job interviews. Students must register sophomore year. 24 organizations recruited on campus 1994–95.
AFTER GRADUATION 80% of class of 1994 had job offers within 6 months. 10% of students completing a degree program went directly on to further study.
EXPENSES FOR 1996–97 ***Application fee:*** $25. Tuition: $6720 full-time, $140 per quarter hour part-time.
FINANCIAL AID ***College-administered undergrad aid 1995–96:*** 40 need-based scholarships (average $200), 8 non-need scholarships (average $1600), low-interest long-term loans from external sources (average $2625), Federal Work-Study, 1 part-time job. ***Required forms:*** institutional, FAFSA; required for some: state; accepted: CSS Financial Aid PROFILE. ***Priority deadline:*** 9/25. ***Waivers:*** full or partial for employees or children of employees.
APPLYING ***Options:*** Common Application, deferred entrance, midyear entrance. ***Required:*** school transcript, interview, TOEFL for international students, CPAt. ***Recommended:*** essay, minimum 2.0 GPA, SAT I or ACT. ***Required for some:*** recommendations. Test scores used for admission. ***Application deadline:*** rolling.
APPLYING/TRANSFER ***Required:*** standardized test scores, high school transcript, interview, college transcript, minimum 2.0 college GPA. ***Recommended:*** essay, minimum 2.0 high school GPA. ***Required for some:*** recommendations. ***Entrance:*** minimally difficult. ***Application deadline:*** rolling. ***Contact:*** Ms. Christiane Hoelle, Academic Dean, 216-265-3151.
CONTACT Mr. Alan Hyers, Campus Director, Bryant and Stratton College, Parma, OH 44130-1013, 216-265-3151 or toll-free 800-327-3151 (in-state). ***Fax:*** 216-265-0325. College video available.

BRYANT AND STRATTON COLLEGE
Richmond Heights, Ohio

UG Enrollment: 234	**Tuition & Fees: $6720**
Application Deadline: rolling	**Room & Board: N/Avail**

GENERAL Proprietary, 2-year, coed. Part of Bryant and Stratton Business Institute, Inc. Awards diplomas, transfer associate degrees. Founded 1987. ***Setting:*** suburban campus with easy access to Cleveland. ***Total enrollment:*** 234. ***Faculty:*** 30 (7 full-time, 23 part-time).
ENROLLMENT PROFILE 234 students: 77% women, 23% men, 43% part-time, 100% state residents, 0% international, 1% Hispanic, 58% African American.
FIRST-YEAR CLASS 66 total; 97 applied, 92% were accepted, 74% of whom enrolled. 10% from top half of their high school class.
ACADEMIC PROGRAM Core, honor code. Calendar: quarters. Academic remediation for entering students, tutorials, summer session for credit, part-time degree program (daytime, evenings, summer), adult/continuing education programs, internships.
GENERAL DEGREE REQUIREMENTS 90 credit hours; 1 math course; computer course; internship (some majors).
MAJORS Accounting, business administration/commerce/management, computer technologies, medical assistant technologies, secretarial studies/office management.
LIBRARY Main library plus 1 other, with 2,100 books, 31 periodicals. Acquisition spending 1994–95: $2600.
COMPUTERS ON CAMPUS 90 computers for student use in computer center, classrooms, library, student center. Academic computing expenditure 1994–95: $179,454.
COLLEGE LIFE Student-run newspaper. ***Social organizations:*** 5 open to all. ***Most popular organizations:*** Student Advisory Committee, Professional Secretaries International, Accounting Club, Micro Club, Health Careers Club. ***Major annual events:*** Career Day, Christmas Potluck, Halloween Party. ***Student services:*** personal-psychological counseling. ***Campus security:*** 24-hour emergency response devices, late-night transport-escort service.
HOUSING College housing not available.
CAREER PLANNING ***Placement office:*** 1 full-time staff; $40,000 operating expenditure 1994–95. ***Director:*** Mrs. Louanne Chung, Director, Career Placement Services, 216-461-3151 Ext. 118. ***Services:*** resume preparation, resume referral, career counseling, careers library, job bank, job interviews. Students must register sophomore year.
AFTER GRADUATION 3% of students completing a degree program in 1994–95 went directly on to further study.
EXPENSES FOR 1996–97 ***Application fee:*** $25. Tuition: $6720 full-time, $140 per credit hour part-time.
FINANCIAL AID ***College-administered undergrad aid 1995–96:*** need-based scholarships, non-need scholarships, low-interest long-term loans from external sources, Federal Work-Study. ***Required forms:*** state, institutional, FAFSA. ***Priority deadline:*** 10/1. ***Payment plan:*** installment. ***Waivers:*** full or partial for employees or children of employees. ***Notification:*** 10/2.
APPLYING ***Options:*** deferred entrance, midyear entrance. ***Required:*** school transcript, interview, TOEFL for international students, CPAt. ***Recommended:*** essay, minimum 2.0 GPA, SAT I or ACT. ***Required for some:*** recommendations. Test scores used for admission. ***Application deadline:*** rolling.
APPLYING/TRANSFER ***Required:*** standardized test scores, high school transcript, interview, college transcript, minimum 2.0 college GPA. ***Recommended:*** essay, minimum 2.0 high school GPA. ***Required for some:*** recommendations. ***Application deadline:*** rolling. ***Contact:*** Ms. Jeanne A. Hitch, Dean, 216-461-3151.
CONTACT Mr. Vic Hart, Director of Admissions, Bryant and Stratton College, Richmond Heights, OH 44143-2900, 216-461-3151. College video available.

CENTRAL OHIO TECHNICAL COLLEGE
Newark, Ohio

UG Enrollment: 1,664	**Tuition & Fees (OH Res): $3182**
Application Deadline: rolling	**Room & Board: N/R**

GENERAL State-supported, 2-year, coed. Part of Ohio Board of Regents. Awards certificates, terminal associate degrees. Founded 1971. ***Setting:*** 155-acre small-town campus with easy access to Columbus. ***Total enrollment:*** 1,664. ***Faculty:*** 103 (45 full-time, 6% with terminal degrees, 58 part-time); student-faculty ratio is 15:1.
ENROLLMENT PROFILE 1,664 students: 67% women, 55% part-time, 99% state residents, 8% transferred in, 1% international, 81% 25 or older, 1% Native American, 1% Hispanic, 2% African American, 1% Asian American. ***Areas of study chosen:*** 39% health professions and related sciences, 31% business management and administrative services, 12% engineering and applied sciences, 10% social sciences, 8% computer and information sciences. ***Most popular recent majors:*** nursing, business administration/commerce/management, accounting.
FIRST-YEAR CLASS 422 total; 659 applied, 100% were accepted, 64% of whom enrolled.
ACADEMIC PROGRAM Core, honor code. Calendar: quarters. 350 courses offered in 1995–96. Academic remediation for entering students, services for LD students, summer session for credit, part-time degree program (daytime, evenings), adult/continuing education programs, co-op programs and internships. Off-campus study at Ohio State University–Newark Campus.
GENERAL DEGREE REQUIREMENTS 101 quarter credit hours; computer course for business, accounting, engineering, criminal justice, secretarial science, nursing majors.
MAJORS Accounting, business administration/commerce/management, computer programming, corrections, criminal justice, drafting and design, early childhood education, electromechanical technology, electronics engineering technology, human services, industrial engineering technology, law enforcement/police sciences, manufacturing technology, mechanical engineering technology, nursing, physical therapy, radiological technology, secretarial studies/office management.
LIBRARY Newark Campus Library with 45,000 books, 7,285 microform titles, 500 periodicals, 2,900 records, tapes, and CDs.
COMPUTERS ON CAMPUS 300 computers for student use in computer center, computer labs, learning resource center provide access to main academic computer, e-mail, Internet. Staffed computer lab on campus provides training in use of computers, software.
COLLEGE LIFE Drama-theater group, choral group. 5% vote in student government elections. ***Social organizations:*** 15 open to all. ***Most popular organizations:*** Student Senate, Phi Theta Kappa, Student Nursing Organization, Campus Chorus, Physical Therapy Assistants Organization. ***Major annual events:*** Spring Fling, Annual "Blood Battle" Blood Drive, Campus Artists and Performers Series. ***Student services:*** personal-psychological counseling. ***Campus security:*** 24-hour emergency response devices, student patrols, late-night transport-escort service.
HOUSING 150 college housing spaces available; 100 were occupied 1995–96. No special consideration for freshman housing applicants. Off-campus living permitted. ***Option:*** coed (2 buildings) housing available. Resident assistants live in dorms.
ATHLETICS ***Intercollegiate:*** baseball M, basketball M/W, golf M/W, soccer M, softball W, tennis M/W, volleyball M/W. ***Intramural:*** baseball, basketball, bowling, football, golf, skiing (downhill), soccer, softball, table tennis (Ping-Pong), tennis, volleyball, weight lifting. ***Contact:*** Mr. John Kaminsky, Athletic Coordinator, 614-366-9245.
CAREER PLANNING ***Placement office:*** 1 full-time, 1 part-time staff. ***Services:*** job fairs, resume preparation, resume referral, career counseling, careers library, job bank, job interviews.
AFTER GRADUATION 89% of class of 1994 had job offers within 6 months.
ESTIMATED EXPENSES FOR 1996–97 ***Application fee:*** $15. State resident tuition: $3182 full-time, $63 per quarter hour part-time. Nonresident tuition: $4495 full-time, $89 per quarter hour part-time.
FINANCIAL AID ***College-administered undergrad aid 1995–96:*** 700 need-based scholarships (average $2200), 100 non-need scholarships (average $465), short-term loans (average $100), low-interest long-term loans from external sources (average $2625), Federal Work-Study, 30 part-time jobs. ***Required forms:*** CSS Financial Aid PROFILE, state, institutional, FAFSA. ***Priority deadline:*** 4/15. ***Payment plan:*** deferred payment. ***Waivers:*** full or partial for employees or children of employees and senior citizens.
APPLYING Open admission except for health programs. ***Options:*** Common Application, early entrance, deferred entrance. ***Required:*** school transcript, ACT, ACT ASSET. Test scores used for counseling/placement. ***Application deadline:*** rolling.
APPLYING/TRANSFER ***Required:*** college transcript. ***Entrance:*** noncompetitive. ***Application deadline:*** rolling. ***Contact:*** Mr. John K. Merrin, Coordinator of Admissions, 614-366-9222.
CONTACT Ms. Kelly Gienger, Admissions Representative, Central Ohio Technical College, 1179 University Drive, Newark, OH 43055-1767, 614-366-9222 or toll-free 800-9NEWARK (in-state). ***Fax:*** 614-366-5047 Ext. 222. ***E-mail:*** lnelson@bigvax.newark.ohio-state.edu. College video available.

CHATFIELD COLLEGE
St. Martin, Ohio

UG Enrollment: 226	**Tuition & Fees: $4620**
Application Deadline: rolling	**Room & Board: N/Avail**

GENERAL Independent, 2-year, coed. Awards transfer associate degrees. Founded 1970. ***Setting:*** 200-acre rural campus with easy access to Dayton and Cincinnati. ***Total enrollment:*** 226. ***Faculty:*** 42 (all part-time); student-faculty ratio is 8:1.
ENROLLMENT PROFILE 226 students: 80% women, 20% men, 68% part-time, 100% state residents, 8% transferred in, 65% have need-based financial aid, 2% have non-need-based financial aid, 0% international, 86% 25 or older, 0% Native American, 0% Hispanic, 2% African American. ***Areas of study chosen:*** 100% liberal arts/general studies. ***Most popular recent majors:*** liberal arts/general studies, child psychology/child development, business administration/commerce/management.
FIRST-YEAR CLASS 75 total; 104 applied, 100% were accepted, 72% of whom enrolled. 12% from top 10% of their high school class, 34% from top quarter.
ACADEMIC PROGRAM Core, liberal arts curriculum, honor code. Calendar: semesters. 80 courses offered in 1995–96. Academic remediation for entering students, advanced

Peterson's Guide to Two-Year Colleges 1997 517

Chatfield College (continued)
placement, summer session for credit, part-time degree program (daytime, evenings), adult/continuing education programs, internships. Off-campus study at 13 members of the Greater Cincinnati Consortium of Colleges and Universities.
GENERAL DEGREE REQUIREMENTS 62 semester credits; 1 course each in math and science; internship (some majors).
MAJORS Business administration/commerce/management, child psychology/child development, commercial art, human services, liberal arts/general studies.
LIBRARY Chatfield College Library with 14,200 books, 57 periodicals, 250 records, tapes, and CDs. Acquisition spending 1994–95: $1826.
COMPUTERS ON CAMPUS 16 computers for student use in computer center, library. Staffed computer lab on campus provides training in use of computers, software.
COLLEGE LIFE Student-run newspaper. ***Social organizations:*** 1 open to all. ***Most popular organizations:*** Earth Awareness Group, Bible Study Group. ***Student services:*** personal-psychological counseling. ***Campus security:*** 12-hour night security patrol.
HOUSING College housing not available.
CAREER PLANNING ***Service:*** career counseling.
AFTER GRADUATION 41% of students completing a degree program in 1994–95 went directly on to further study.
EXPENSES FOR 1995–96 ***Application fee:*** $10. Tuition: $4590 full-time, $153 per credit part-time. Part-time mandatory fees: $15 per semester. Full-time mandatory fees: $30.
FINANCIAL AID ***College-administered undergrad aid 1995–96:*** 120 need-based scholarships (average $635), non-need scholarships, short-term loans (average $125), low-interest long-term loans from college funds (average $1100), loans from external sources (average $1700), 8 Federal Work-Study (averaging $400). ***Required forms:*** institutional, FAFSA. ***Priority deadline:*** 7/1. ***Payment plan:*** installment. ***Waivers:*** full or partial for employees or children of employees and senior citizens. ***Notification:*** continuous.
APPLYING Open admission. ***Options:*** Common Application, early entrance, deferred entrance, midyear entrance. ***Required:*** school transcript. ***Recommended:*** 3 years of high school math and science, 2 years of high school foreign language. Test scores used for counseling/placement. ***Application deadline:*** rolling. ***Notification:*** continuous.
APPLYING/TRANSFER ***Required:*** college transcript. ***Recommended:*** 3 years of high school math and science, 2 years of high school foreign language. ***Entrance:*** noncompetitive. ***Application deadline:*** rolling. ***Notification:*** continuous. ***Contact:*** Mr. John Cooper, Director of Enrollment Services, 513-875-3344.
CONTACT Mr. John Cooper, Director of Enrollment Services, Chatfield College, St. Martin, OH 45118-9705, 513-875-3344.

CINCINNATI STATE TECHNICAL AND COMMUNITY COLLEGE
Cincinnati, Ohio

UG Enrollment: 5,790	**Tuition & Fees (OH Res): $3540**
Application Deadline: rolling	**Room & Board: N/Avail**

GENERAL State-supported, 2-year, coed. Part of Ohio Board of Regents. Awards certificates, transfer associate, terminal associate degrees. Founded 1966. ***Setting:*** 46-acre urban campus. ***Total enrollment:*** 5,790. ***Faculty:*** 351 (145 full-time, 206 part-time).
ENROLLMENT PROFILE 5,790 students from 6 states and territories, 16 other countries. 47% women, 53% men, 55% part-time, 88% state residents, 17% transferred in, 1% international, 41% 25 or older, 1% Native American, 2% Hispanic, 20% African American, 1% Asian American. ***Most popular recent majors:*** business administration/commerce/management, nursing, electronics engineering technology.
FIRST-YEAR CLASS 1,901 total. Of the students who applied, 100% were accepted, 60% of whom enrolled.
ACADEMIC PROGRAM Core, honor code. Calendar: 5 ten-week terms. 46 courses offered in 1995–96. Academic remediation for entering students, services for LD students, advanced placement, self-designed majors, summer session for credit, part-time degree program (daytime, evenings), adult/continuing education programs, co-op programs and internships. Off-campus study at 12 members of the Greater Cincinnati Consortium of Colleges and Universities. ROTC: Army (c), Air Force (c).
GENERAL DEGREE REQUIREMENTS 110 quarter hours; computer course for all associate of science and associate of applied science degree students; internship (some majors).
MAJORS Accounting, applied art, architectural technologies, art/fine arts, automotive technologies, aviation technology, biomedical technologies, business administration/commerce/management, civil engineering technology, computer information systems, computer programming, computer technologies, construction technologies, culinary arts, data processing, dietetics, electrical engineering technology, electromechanical technology, electronics engineering technology, (pre)engineering sequence, environmental engineering technology, horticulture, hotel and restaurant management, international business, laser technologies, management information systems, manufacturing technology, marketing/retailing/merchandising, mechanical engineering technology, medical assistant technologies, medical laboratory technology, medical records services, nursing, occupational therapy, operating room technology, ornamental horticulture, physical sciences, printing technologies, purchasing/inventory management, real estate, respiratory therapy, science, secretarial studies/office management, surveying technology, technical writing, word processing.
LIBRARY Johnnie Mae Berry Library with 17,799 books, 106 microform titles, 380 periodicals, 450 records, tapes, and CDs.
COMPUTERS ON CAMPUS 750 computers for student use in computer labs, classrooms, library provide access to e-mail, Internet. Staffed computer lab on campus provides training in use of computers, software.
COLLEGE LIFE Choral group, student-run newspaper. 2% vote in student government elections. ***Most popular organizations:*** Student Government, Student Newspaper, Minority Affairs. ***Major annual event:*** Homecoming. ***Student services:*** personal-psychological counseling. ***Campus security:*** 24-hour emergency response devices and patrols, late-night transport-escort service.
HOUSING College housing not available.
ATHLETICS Member NJCAA. ***Intercollegiate:*** basketball M/W. ***Intramural:*** golf. ***Contact:*** Mr. John Hurley, Director of Activities, 513-569-1500.
CAREER PLANNING ***Placement office:*** 4 full-time, 1 part-time staff. ***Director:*** Ms. Linda Meador, Counselor, 513-569-1500. ***Services:*** career counseling, careers library.
AFTER GRADUATION 8% of students completing a degree program in 1994–95 went directly on to further study.
EXPENSES FOR 1995–96 State resident tuition: $3540 full-time, $59 per credit part-time. Nonresident tuition: $7080 full-time, $118 per credit part-time. Residents of Northern Kentucky pay state resident tuition rates for all programs except nursing, respiratory therapy and certificate programs.
FINANCIAL AID ***College-administered undergrad aid 1995–96:*** need-based scholarships, non-need scholarships, low-interest long-term loans from external sources, Federal Work-Study, part-time jobs. ***Required forms:*** state, institutional, FAFSA; accepted: CSS Financial Aid PROFILE. ***Priority deadline:*** 3/1.
APPLYING Open admission. ***Options:*** deferred entrance, midyear entrance. ***Required:*** school transcript, TOEFL for international students, ACT COMPASS. ***Required for some:*** 3 years of high school math and science. Test scores used for counseling/placement. ***Application deadline:*** rolling. ***Notification:*** continuous until 10/1.
APPLYING/TRANSFER ***Required:*** high school transcript, college transcript. ***Required for some:*** 3 years of high school math and science. ***Entrance:*** noncompetitive. ***Application deadline:*** rolling. ***Notification:*** continuous until 10/1.
CONTACT Ms. Gabriele Boeckermann, Coordinator of Educational Relations, Cincinnati State Technical and Community College, 3520 Central Parkway, Cincinnati, OH 45223-2690, 513-569-1550.

CLARK STATE COMMUNITY COLLEGE
Springfield, Ohio

UG Enrollment: 2,746	**Tuition & Fees (OH Res): $2351**
Application Deadline: rolling	**Room & Board: N/Avail**

GENERAL State-supported, 2-year, coed. Part of Ohio Board of Regents. Awards certificates, transfer associate, terminal associate degrees. Founded 1962. ***Setting:*** 60-acre suburban campus with easy access to Dayton and Columbus. ***Total enrollment:*** 2,746. ***Faculty:*** 186 (57 full-time, 16% with terminal degrees, 129 part-time).
ENROLLMENT PROFILE 2,746 students: 68% women, 32% men, 63% part-time, 99% state residents, 1% Native American, 1% Hispanic, 7% African American, 1% Asian American. ***Areas of study chosen:*** 27% health professions and related sciences, 23% business management and administrative services, 18% interdisciplinary studies, 18% social sciences, 5% computer and information sciences, 5% engineering and applied sciences, 3% agriculture, 2% performing arts. ***Most popular recent majors:*** nursing, accounting, business administration/commerce/management.
FIRST-YEAR CLASS 890 total; 1,055 applied, 100% were accepted, 84% of whom enrolled. 7% from top 10% of their high school class, 25% from top quarter, 58% from top half.
ACADEMIC PROGRAM Core. Calendar: quarters. Academic remediation for entering students, services for LD students, advanced placement, self-designed majors, summer session for credit, part-time degree program (daytime, evenings), adult/continuing education programs, co-op programs and internships. Off-campus study at 17 members of the Southwestern Ohio Council for Higher Education. ROTC: Army (c).
GENERAL DEGREE REQUIREMENTS 90 credit hours; computer course for most majors; internship (some majors).
MAJORS Accounting, agricultural business, agricultural sciences, agricultural technologies, business administration/commerce/management, civil engineering technology, commercial art, computer information systems, computer programming, corrections, court reporting, criminal justice, drafting and design, early childhood education, electrical engineering technology, electronics engineering technology, emergency medical technology, finance/banking, forensic sciences, horticulture, human services, industrial engineering technology, landscaping/grounds maintenance, law enforcement/police sciences, liberal arts/general studies, manufacturing technology, mechanical engineering technology, medical laboratory technology, medical secretarial studies, nursing, paralegal studies, photography, practical nursing, secretarial studies/office management, social work, theater arts/drama.
LIBRARY Clark State Community College Library with 31,437 books, 30 microform titles, 375 periodicals, 2 on-line bibliographic services, 12 CD-ROMs, 810 records, tapes, and CDs.
COMPUTERS ON CAMPUS Computer purchase plan available. 350 computers for student use in computer center, computer labs, open labs, library provide access to off-campus computing facilities, e-mail, on-line services, Internet. Staffed computer lab on campus provides training in use of computers, software.
COLLEGE LIFE Drama-theater group, choral group, student-run newspaper. ***Social organizations:*** 1 local fraternity, 1 local sorority. ***Most popular organizations:*** Student Government Association, Minority Student Forum. ***Major annual event:*** Multicultural Day. ***Student services:*** health clinic, personal-psychological counseling. ***Campus security:*** late-night transport-escort service.
HOUSING College housing not available.
ATHLETICS Member NJCAA. ***Intercollegiate:*** basketball M/W, golf M, volleyball W. ***Intramural:*** basketball, golf, tennis, volleyball. ***Contact:*** Mr. Todd Jones, Athletic Coordinator, 513-328-6084.
CAREER PLANNING ***Placement office:*** 1 full-time, 1 part-time staff. ***Director:*** Ms. Jean Chepp, Career Placement Officer, 513-328-6091. ***Services:*** job fairs, resume preparation, resume referral, career counseling, careers library.
EXPENSES FOR 1996–97 ***Application fee:*** $15. State resident tuition: $2081 full-time, $46.25 per credit hour part-time. Nonresident tuition: $4163 full-time, $92.50 per credit hour part-time. Part-time mandatory fees: $6 per credit hour. Full-time mandatory fees: $270.
FINANCIAL AID ***College-administered undergrad aid 1995–96:*** need-based scholarships, non-need scholarships, short-term loans, low-interest long-term loans from external sources, Federal Work-Study, part-time jobs. ***Required forms for some financial aid applicants:*** institutional; accepted: CSS Financial Aid PROFILE, state, FAFSA. ***Priority deadline:*** 8/1. ***Payment plan:*** installment. ***Waivers:*** full or partial for employees or children of employees and senior citizens. ***Notification:*** continuous.
APPLYING Open admission. ***Option:*** early entrance. ***Required:*** school transcript, TOEFL for international students. ***Recommended:*** SAT I or ACT. Test scores used for counseling/placement. ***Application deadline:*** rolling. ***Notification:*** continuous.
APPLYING/TRANSFER ***Required:*** college transcript. ***Entrance:*** noncompetitive. ***Application deadline:*** rolling. ***Notification:*** continuous.
CONTACT Mr. Todd Jones, Director of Admissions, Clark State Community College, Springfield, OH 45501-0570, 513-328-6027. College video available.

CLERMONT COLLEGE
Ohio—See University of Cincinnati Clermont College

CLEVELAND INSTITUTE OF ELECTRONICS
Cleveland, Ohio

UG Enrollment: 2,300	Tuition & Fees: $2400
Application Deadline: rolling	Room & Board: N/Avail

GENERAL Proprietary, 2-year, specialized, primarily men. Awards terminal associate degrees (offers only external degree programs conducted through home study). Founded 1934. *Setting:* urban campus. *Total enrollment:* 2,300. *Faculty:* 6 (4 full-time, 2 part-time).
ENROLLMENT PROFILE 2,300 students from 52 states and territories, 70 other countries. 4% women, 96% men, 100% part-time, 5% state residents, 12% international, 87% 25 or older, 2% Native American, 7% Hispanic, 12% African American, 6% Asian American. *Areas of study chosen:* 100% engineering and applied sciences. *Most popular recent major:* electronics engineering technology.
FIRST-YEAR CLASS Of the students who applied, 100% were accepted, 100% of whom enrolled.
ACADEMIC PROGRAM Calendar: year-round. Part-time degree program, external degree programs, adult/continuing education programs.
GENERAL DEGREE REQUIREMENT 106 quarter credit hours.
MAJOR Electronics engineering technology.
LIBRARY 5,000 books, 38 periodicals.
HOUSING College housing not available.
CAREER PLANNING *Service:* resume preparation.
EXPENSES FOR 1996–97 Tuition: $2400 per year part-time.
FINANCIAL AID College-administered undergrad aid 1995–96: need-based scholarships, non-need scholarships, low-interest long-term loans from college funds. *Required forms:* institutional; required for some: FAFSA. *Payment plans:* installment, deferred payment.
APPLYING Open admission. *Option:* early entrance. *Application deadline:* rolling. *Notification:* continuous.
APPLYING/TRANSFER *Application deadline:* rolling. *Notification:* continuous. *Contact:* Ms. Mary Jane McEachin, Director of Student Management, 216-781-9400.
CONTACT Mr. Jeff Dodge, Admissions Representative, Cleveland Institute of Electronics, 1776 East Seventeenth Street, Cleveland, OH 44114-3636, 216-781-9400 Ext. 238 or toll-free 800-243-6446.

COLUMBUS STATE COMMUNITY COLLEGE
Columbus, Ohio

UG Enrollment: 16,500	Tuition & Fees (OH Res): $2622
Application Deadline: rolling	Room & Board: N/Avail

GENERAL State-supported, 2-year, coed. Part of Ohio Board of Regents. Awards transfer associate, terminal associate degrees. Founded 1963. *Setting:* 60-acre urban campus. *Educational spending 1994–95:* $1183 per undergrad. *Total enrollment:* 16,500. *Faculty:* 897 (191 full-time, 12% with terminal degrees, 706 part-time); student-faculty ratio is 20:1.
ENROLLMENT PROFILE 16,500 students: 58% women, 63% part-time, 97% state residents, 3% transferred in, 34% have need-based financial aid, 10% have non-need-based financial aid, 3% international, 48% 25 or older, 1% Native American, 1% Hispanic, 16% African American, 2% Asian American. *Areas of study chosen:* 17% health professions and related sciences, 15% business management and administrative services, 14% liberal arts/general studies, 10% engineering and applied sciences, 6% computer and information sciences, 1% architecture. *Most popular recent majors:* nursing, business administration/commerce/management, accounting.
FIRST-YEAR CLASS 4,739 total; 5,763 applied, 100% were accepted, 82% of whom enrolled. 5% from top 10% of their high school class, 18% from top quarter, 44% from top half.
ACADEMIC PROGRAM Core. Calendar: quarters. 1,210 courses offered in 1995–96; average class size 20 in required courses. Academic remediation for entering students, English as a second language program offered during academic year and summer, services for LD students, self-designed majors, tutorials, summer session for credit, part-time degree program (daytime, evenings, summer), adult/continuing education programs, co-op programs and internships. Off-campus study at members of the Higher Education Council of Columbus. ROTC: Army (c).
GENERAL DEGREE REQUIREMENTS 92 quarter credit hours; computer course for most technical majors; internship (some majors).
MAJORS Accounting, aircraft and missile maintenance, architectural technologies, automotive technologies, aviation technology, business administration/commerce/management, child care/child and family studies, child psychology/child development, civil engineering technology, computer programming, computer science, computer technologies, construction management, construction technologies, corrections, culinary arts, data processing, deaf interpreter training, dietetics, drug and alcohol/substance abuse counseling, early childhood education, electromechanical technology, electronics engineering technology, emergency medical technology, engineering technology, environmental engineering technology, finance/banking, food services management, food services technology, gerontology, graphic arts, heating/refrigeration/air conditioning, hospitality services, hotel and restaurant management, landscape architecture/design, law enforcement/police sciences, legal secretarial studies, liberal arts/general studies, marketing/retailing/merchandising, mechanical design technology, mechanical engineering technology, medical laboratory technology, medical records services, medical secretarial studies, medical technology, mental health/rehabilitation counseling, nursing, operating room technology, paralegal studies, printing technologies, purchasing/inventory management, quality control technology, radiological technology, real estate, respiratory therapy, retail management, safety and security technologies, secretarial studies/office management, social work, sports administration, technical writing, tourism and travel, veterinary technology.
LIBRARY Main library plus 1 other, with 27,372 books, 118 microform titles, 455 periodicals, 3 on-line bibliographic services, 12 CD-ROMs, 2,434 records, tapes, and CDs. Acquisition spending 1994–95: $153,720.
COMPUTERS ON CAMPUS 402 computers for student use in computer center, classrooms, library. Academic computing expenditure 1994–95: $1 million.
COLLEGE LIFE Choral group. *Social organizations:* 15 open to all. *Most popular organizations:* Greek Service and Scholastic Organizations, Technology-Related Organizations. *Major annual events:* Welcome Back, May Day, Homecoming. *Student services:* health clinic, personal-psychological counseling. *Campus security:* 24-hour emergency response devices and patrols, late-night transport-escort service.
HOUSING College housing not available.
ATHLETICS Member NJCAA. *Intercollegiate:* baseball M, basketball M, cross-country running M/W, equestrian sports W, golf M/W, soccer M, softball W, volleyball W. *Intramural:* badminton, basketball, golf, soccer, table tennis (Ping-Pong), volleyball, weight lifting. *Contact:* Mr. Eric Welch, Coordinator, Student Activities, 614-227-2445.
CAREER PLANNING *Placement office:* 4 full-time, 4 part-time staff; $220,407 operating expenditure 1994–95. *Director:* Mr. Charles Dawson, Director, Career and Placement Office, 614-227-2651. *Services:* job fairs, resume preparation, resume referral, career counseling, careers library, job bank, job interviews.
AFTER GRADUATION 28% of students completing a degree program in 1994–95 went directly on to further study.
EXPENSES FOR 1996–97 *Application fee:* $10. State resident tuition: $2622 full-time, $57 per quarter hour part-time. Nonresident tuition: $5750 full-time, $125 per quarter hour part-time. Tuition for international students: $152 per quarter hour.
FINANCIAL AID College-administered undergrad aid 1995–96: 403 need-based scholarships (average $600), 109 non-need scholarships (average $731), short-term loans (average $150), low-interest long-term loans from external sources (average $2585), Federal Work-Study, part-time jobs. *Required forms:* institutional, FAFSA. *Priority deadline:* 4/1. *Waivers:* full or partial for employees or children of employees and senior citizens. *Notification:* 5/15. *Average indebtedness of graduates:* $6076.
APPLYING Open admission. *Options:* early entrance, deferred entrance. *Required:* school transcript, TOEFL for international students, ACT COMPASS. Test scores used for counseling/placement. *Application deadline:* rolling. *Notification:* continuous.
APPLYING/TRANSFER *Required:* high school transcript, college transcript. *Entrance:* noncompetitive. *Application deadline:* rolling. *Notification:* continuous. *Contact:* Mr. Brian Seegar, Academic Transfer Advisor/Coordinator, 614-227-2668.
CONTACT Ms. Mary Jo Deerwester, Director of Admissions, Columbus State Community College, Box 1609, Columbus, OH 43216-1609, 614-227-2453 or toll-free 800-621-6407. *Fax:* 614-227-5117. College video available.

❖ *See page 728 for a narrative description.* ❖

CUYAHOGA COMMUNITY COLLEGE, EASTERN CAMPUS
Highland Hills, Ohio

UG Enrollment: 5,382	Tuition & Fees (Area Res): $1643
Application Deadline: rolling	Room & Board: N/Avail

GENERAL State and locally supported, 2-year, coed. Part of Cuyahoga Community College District System. Awards certificates, transfer associate, terminal associate degrees. Founded 1971. *Setting:* 25-acre suburban campus with easy access to Cleveland. *Total enrollment:* 5,382. *Faculty:* 240 (81 full-time, 23% with terminal degrees, 159 part-time); student-faculty ratio is 20:1.
ENROLLMENT PROFILE 5,382 students: 70% women, 30% men, 73% part-time, 98% state residents, 42% transferred in, 20% have need-based financial aid, 1% international, 65% 25 or older, 0% Native American, 1% Hispanic, 46% African American, 2% Asian American. *Areas of study chosen:* 37% liberal arts/general studies, 20% health professions and related sciences, 16% business management and administrative services, 2% engineering and applied sciences. *Most popular recent major:* liberal arts/general studies.
FIRST-YEAR CLASS 791 total. Of the students who applied, 100% were accepted, 69% of whom enrolled.
ACADEMIC PROGRAM Core, honor code. Calendar: quarters. Academic remediation for entering students, English as a second language program offered during academic year and summer, services for LD students, advanced placement, self-designed majors, summer session for credit, part-time degree program (daytime, evenings, summer), co-op programs and internships. Off-campus study at members of the Cleveland Commission on Higher Education. ROTC: Air Force (c).
GENERAL DEGREE REQUIREMENTS 93 credit hours; math/science requirements vary according to program; computer course for office administration, word processing, finance, business administration, accounting, agricultural technology, marketing, real estate, pharmacy majors; internship (some majors).
MAJORS Accounting, agricultural technologies, business administration/commerce/management, commercial art, computer technologies, early childhood education, engineering technology, finance/banking, health science, interior design, landscaping/grounds maintenance, liberal arts/general studies, marketing/retailing/merchandising, nursing, pharmacy/pharmaceutical sciences, real estate, secretarial studies/office management, word processing.
LIBRARY 34,698 books, 416 periodicals, 2 on-line bibliographic services.
COMPUTERS ON CAMPUS 200 computers for student use in computer labs, classrooms provide access to main academic computer, off-campus computing facilities, e-mail. Staffed computer lab on campus provides training in use of computers, software.
COLLEGE LIFE Drama-theater group, choral group, student-run newspaper. *Social organizations:* 12 open to all. *Most popular organizations:* Phi Theta Kappa, Theater Club, Interior Design Organization, Veterans' Organization, International Club. *Major annual events:* Annual Welcome Back, Black History Month Events, Diversity Day. *Student services:* health clinic, personal-psychological counseling. *Campus security:* 24-hour emergency response devices and patrols, late-night transport-escort service.
HOUSING College housing not available.
ATHLETICS Member NJCAA. *Intercollegiate:* basketball W(s), volleyball W(s). *Intramural:* archery, basketball, golf, tennis. *Contact:* Ms. Janet Schmid, Director of Athletics/Physical Education, 216-987-2075.

Cuyahoga Community College, Eastern Campus (continued)

CAREER PLANNING ***Placement office:*** 3 full-time staff. ***Director:*** Mr. Ronald Moss, Dean of Student Development, 216-987-2202. ***Services:*** job fairs, resume preparation, resume referral, career counseling, careers library, job bank, job interviews. 100 organizations recruited on campus 1994–95.

EXPENSES FOR 1995–96 ***Application fee:*** $10. Area resident tuition: $1643 full-time, $36.50 per credit hour part-time. State resident tuition: $2183 full-time, $48.50 per credit hour part-time. Nonresident tuition: $4354 full-time, $96.75 per credit hour part-time.

FINANCIAL AID ***College-administered undergrad aid 1995–96:*** 3,576 need-based scholarships (average $883), 29 non-need scholarships (average $616), low-interest long-term loans from external sources (average $2136), 110 Federal Work-Study (averaging $1413), part-time jobs. ***Required forms:*** FAFSA; accepted: CSS Financial Aid PROFILE. ***Application deadline:*** continuous. ***Payment plans:*** installment, deferred payment. ***Waivers:*** full or partial for employees or children of employees and senior citizens.

APPLYING Open admission except for allied health, early childhood education, agricultural technology programs. ***Option:*** early entrance. ***Required:*** TOEFL for international students. ***Required for some:*** school transcript. Test scores used for counseling/placement. ***Application deadline:*** rolling. ***Notification:*** continuous.

APPLYING/TRANSFER ***Required:*** college transcript. ***Required for some:*** high school transcript. ***Entrance:*** noncompetitive. ***Application deadline:*** rolling. ***Notification:*** continuous. ***Contact:*** Ms. Joanna Bacik, Director of Counseling, 216-987-2283.

CONTACT Mr. David Puffer, Director of Admissions and Records, Cuyahoga Community College, Eastern Campus, 4250 Richmond Road, Highland Hills, OH 44122-6104, 216-987-2019. College video available.

CUYAHOGA COMMUNITY COLLEGE, METROPOLITAN CAMPUS
Cleveland, Ohio

UG Enrollment: 6,015	**Tuition & Fees (Area Res): $1643**
Application Deadline: rolling	**Room & Board: N/Avail**

GENERAL State and locally supported, 2-year, coed. Part of Cuyahoga Community College District System. Awards certificates, transfer associate, terminal associate degrees. Founded 1963. ***Setting:*** 42-acre urban campus. ***Total enrollment:*** 6,015. ***Faculty:*** 351 (144 full-time, 30% with terminal degrees, 207 part-time); student-faculty ratio is 18:1.

ENROLLMENT PROFILE 6,015 students: 65% women, 35% men, 57% part-time, 96% state residents, 27% transferred in, 41% have need-based financial aid, 4% international, 64% 25 or older, 1% Native American, 4% Hispanic, 55% African American, 4% Asian American. ***Areas of study chosen:*** 34% liberal arts/general studies, 25% health professions and related sciences, 14% business management and administrative services, 6% engineering and applied sciences. ***Most popular recent major:*** liberal arts/general studies.

FIRST-YEAR CLASS 881 total. Of the students who applied, 100% were accepted, 69% of whom enrolled.

ACADEMIC PROGRAM Core, honor code. Calendar: quarters. Academic remediation for entering students, English as a second language program offered during academic year and summer, services for LD students, advanced placement, self-designed majors, summer session for credit, part-time degree program (daytime, evenings, summer), co-op programs and internships. Off-campus study at members of the Cleveland Commission on Higher Education. ROTC: Air Force (c).

GENERAL DEGREE REQUIREMENTS 93 quarter hours; math/science requirements vary according to program; computer course for accounting, office administration, word processing, medical records, postal management, hotel/restaurant management, food services, law enforcement, marketing, real estate majors; internship (some majors).

MAJORS Accounting, architectural technologies, business administration/commerce/management, computer technologies, court reporting, culinary arts, dental services, early childhood education, electrical and electronics technologies, emergency medical technology, engineering and applied sciences, engineering technology, food services management, health science, hospitality services, hotel and restaurant management, industrial engineering technology, interior design, law enforcement/police sciences, liberal arts/general studies, marketing/retailing/merchandising, mechanical engineering technology, medical assistant technologies, medical laboratory technology, medical records services, mental health/rehabilitation counseling, nursing, occupational therapy, optometric/ophthalmic technologies, physical therapy, postal management, real estate, secretarial studies/office management, telecommunications, word processing.

LIBRARY 59,577 books, 508 periodicals, 2 on-line bibliographic services.

COMPUTERS ON CAMPUS 120 computers for student use in computer center, computer labs, classrooms, library provide access to main academic computer, off-campus computing facilities, e-mail. Staffed computer lab on campus provides training in use of computers, software.

COLLEGE LIFE Drama-theater group, choral group, student-run newspaper. ***Social organizations:*** 30 open to all; 1 national fraternity. ***Most popular organizations:*** Phi Theta Kappa, Nursing Student Organization, Veterans' Education Task Force, Dietetic Technology Club, Physical Therapy Club. ***Major annual events:*** Annual Welcome Back Picnic, Annual Community Halloween, Diversity Day. ***Student services:*** health clinic, personal-psychological counseling. ***Campus security:*** 24-hour emergency response devices and patrols, student patrols, late-night transport-escort service.

HOUSING College housing not available.

ATHLETICS Member NJCAA. ***Intercollegiate:*** basketball M(s), wrestling M(s). ***Intramural:*** archery, basketball, fencing, football, racquetball, swimming and diving, table tennis (Ping-Pong), tennis, volleyball, weight lifting. ***Contact:*** Mr. Elijah Whitter, Dean of Physical Education, 216-987-4475.

CAREER PLANNING ***Placement office:*** 2 full-time, 1 part-time staff. ***Director:*** Mr. Ronald Moss, Dean of Student Development, 216-987-2202. ***Services:*** job fairs, resume preparation, resume referral, career counseling, careers library, job bank, job interviews. 100 organizations recruited on campus 1994–95.

EXPENSES FOR 1995–96 ***Application fee:*** $10. Area resident tuition: $1643 full-time, $36.50 per quarter hour part-time. State resident tuition: $2183 full-time, $48.50 per quarter hour part-time. Nonresident tuition: $4354 full-time, $96.75 per quarter hour part-time.

FINANCIAL AID ***College-administered undergrad aid 1995–96:*** 6,988 need-based scholarships (averaging $930), 39 non-need scholarships (averaging $408), low-interest long-term loans from external sources (averaging $1976), 230 Federal Work-Study (averaging $1229). ***Required forms:*** FAFSA; accepted: CSS Financial Aid PROFILE. ***Application deadline:*** continuous. ***Payment plans:*** installment, deferred payment. ***Waivers:*** full or partial for employees or children of employees and senior citizens.

APPLYING Open admission except for allied health, some technical programs. ***Option:*** early entrance. ***Required:*** TOEFL for international students. ***Required for some:*** school transcript. Test scores used for counseling/placement. ***Application deadline:*** rolling. ***Notification:*** continuous.

APPLYING/TRANSFER ***Required:*** college transcript. ***Required for some:*** high school transcript. ***Entrance:*** noncompetitive. ***Application deadline:*** rolling. ***Notification:*** continuous. ***Contact:*** Mr. Tom Schick, Director of Counseling, 216-987-4623.

CONTACT Dr. Sammie Tyree Cox, Campus Director of Admissions and Records, Cuyahoga Community College, Metropolitan Campus, 2900 Community College Avenue, Cleveland, OH 44115-3123, 216-987-4030 or toll-free 800-954-TRIC. College video available.

CUYAHOGA COMMUNITY COLLEGE, WESTERN CAMPUS
Parma, Ohio

UG Enrollment: 12,228	**Tuition & Fees (Area Res): $1643**
Application Deadline: rolling	**Room & Board: N/Avail**

GENERAL State and locally supported, 2-year, coed. Part of Cuyahoga Community College District System. Awards certificates, transfer associate, terminal associate degrees. Founded 1966. ***Setting:*** 183-acre suburban campus with easy access to Cleveland. ***Total enrollment:*** 12,228. ***Faculty:*** 513 (101 full-time, 27% with terminal degrees, 412 part-time); student-faculty ratio is 20:1.

ENROLLMENT PROFILE 12,228 students: 62% women, 38% men, 71% part-time, 99% state residents, 31% transferred in, 39% have need-based financial aid, 0% international, 52% 25 or older, 0% Native American, 2% Hispanic, 3% African American, 2% Asian American. ***Areas of study chosen:*** 31% liberal arts/general studies, 17% health professions and related sciences, 15% business management and administrative services, 3% engineering and applied sciences. ***Most popular recent major:*** liberal arts/general studies.

FIRST-YEAR CLASS 2,024 total. Of the students who applied, 100% were accepted, 69% of whom enrolled.

ACADEMIC PROGRAM Core, honor code. Calendar: quarters. Academic remediation for entering students, English as a second language program offered during academic year and summer, services for LD students, advanced placement, self-designed majors, summer session for credit, part-time degree program (daytime, evenings, summer), co-op programs and internships. Off-campus study at Cleveland Commission on Higher Education. ROTC: Air Force (c).

GENERAL DEGREE REQUIREMENTS 93 credit hours; math/science requirements vary according to program; computer course for office administration, word processing, finance, veterinary technology, accounting, aviation, law enforcement, marketing, real estate, radiological technology, cardiovascular technology majors; internship (some majors).

MAJORS Accounting, automotive technologies, aviation technology, business administration/commerce/management, commercial art, computer technologies, court reporting, early childhood education, engineering technology, finance/banking, fire science, graphic arts, health science, law enforcement/police sciences, liberal arts/general studies, marketing/retailing/merchandising, medical technology, nursing, operating room technology, paralegal studies, pharmacy/pharmaceutical sciences, photography, physician's assistant studies, radiological technology, real estate, respiratory therapy, safety and security technologies, secretarial studies/office management, veterinary technology.

LIBRARY 53,042 books, 488 periodicals, 2 on-line bibliographic services.

COMPUTERS ON CAMPUS 120 computers for student use in computer labs, classrooms, library provide access to main academic computer, off-campus computing facilities, e-mail, Internet. Staffed computer lab on campus provides training in use of computers, software.

COLLEGE LIFE Drama-theater group, choral group, student-run newspaper. ***Social organizations:*** 21 open to all. ***Most popular organizations:*** Student Senate, T-CEAG, Business Focus, Phi Theta Kappa, Physician's Assistant/Surgical Assistant Group. ***Major annual events:*** Welcome Back, Diversity Day. ***Student services:*** health clinic, personal-psychological counseling. ***Campus security:*** 24-hour emergency response devices and patrols, late-night transport-escort service.

HOUSING College housing not available.

ATHLETICS Member NJCAA. ***Intercollegiate:*** baseball M(s), cross-country running M(s)/W(s), soccer M(s), softball W(s). ***Intramural:*** basketball, tennis, track and field, volleyball. ***Contact:*** Mr. Mark Rodriguez, Campus Director, 216-987-5458.

CAREER PLANNING ***Placement office:*** 3 full-time, 2 part-time staff. ***Director:*** Mr. Ronald Moss, Dean of Students Development, 216-987-2202. ***Services:*** job fairs, resume preparation, resume referral, career counseling, careers library, job bank, job interviews. 100 organizations recruited on campus 1994–95.

EXPENSES FOR 1995–96 ***Application fee:*** $10. Area resident tuition: $1643 full-time, $36.50 per credit hour part-time. State resident tuition: $2183 full-time, $48.50 per credit hour part-time. Nonresident tuition: $4354 full-time, $96.75 per credit hour part-time.

FINANCIAL AID ***College-administered undergrad aid 1995–96:*** 5,986 need-based scholarships (averaging $777), 79 non-need scholarships (averaging $506), low-interest long-term loans from external sources (averaging $1952), 135 Federal Work-Study (averaging $1604), part-time jobs. ***Required forms:*** FAFSA; accepted: CSS Financial Aid PROFILE. ***Application deadline:*** continuous. ***Payment plans:*** installment, deferred payment. ***Waivers:*** full or partial for employees or children of employees and senior citizens.

APPLYING Open admission except for allied health, automotive service, paralegal, aviation, court reporting, law enforcement, graphics, photography programs. ***Option:*** early entrance. ***Required:*** TOEFL for international students. ***Required for some:*** school transcript. Test scores used for counseling/placement. ***Application deadline:*** rolling. ***Notification:*** continuous.

APPLYING/TRANSFER ***Required:*** college transcript. ***Required for some:*** high school transcript. ***Entrance:*** noncompetitive. ***Application deadline:*** rolling. ***Notification:*** continuous. ***Contact:*** Mr. Pete Ross, Director of Counseling, 216-987-5200.

CONTACT Ms. Sandy Harper, Admissions Supervisor, Cuyahoga Community College, Western Campus, Parma, OH 44130-5199, 216-987-5154 or toll-free 800-954-TRIC. College video available.

DAVIS COLLEGE
Toledo, Ohio

UG Enrollment: 466 **Tuition & Fees: $5964**
Application Deadline: rolling **Room & Board: N/Avail**

GENERAL Proprietary, 2-year, coed. Awards certificates, diplomas, terminal associate degrees. Founded 1858. ***Setting:*** 1-acre urban campus with easy access to Detroit. ***Total enrollment:*** 466. ***Faculty:*** 44 (17 full-time, 35% with terminal degrees, 27 part-time); student-faculty ratio is 15:1.
ENROLLMENT PROFILE 466 students from 2 states and territories. 74% women, 50% part-time, 91% state residents, 75% have need-based financial aid, 70% 25 or older, 1% Native American, 1% Hispanic, 14% African American. ***Areas of study chosen:*** 23% business management and administrative services, 17% health professions and related sciences, 15% fine arts, 3% computer and information sciences. ***Most popular recent majors:*** medical assistant technologies, computer technologies, secretarial studies/office management.
FIRST-YEAR CLASS 138 total; 195 applied, 100% were accepted, 71% of whom enrolled. 10% from top 10% of their high school class, 20% from top quarter, 35% from top half.
ACADEMIC PROGRAM Core, honor code. Calendar: quarters. 180 courses offered in 1995–96; average class size 20 in required courses. Academic remediation for entering students, advanced placement, summer session for credit, part-time degree program (daytime, evenings, summer), adult/continuing education programs, internships.
GENERAL DEGREE REQUIREMENTS 92 credits; computer course; internship (some majors).
MAJORS Accounting, aviation administration, business administration/commerce/management, computer technologies, data processing, fashion merchandising, graphic arts, illustration, interior design, legal secretarial studies, medical assistant technologies, medical secretarial studies, secretarial studies/office management, tourism and travel, word processing.
LIBRARY Davis College Resource Center with 3,000 books, 155 periodicals, 25 CD-ROMs, 125 records, tapes, and CDs. Acquisition spending 1994–95: $12,207.
COMPUTERS ON CAMPUS 60 computers for student use in computer center, computer labs, learning resource center. Staffed computer lab on campus provides training in use of computers, software. Academic computing expenditure 1994–95: $726,642.
COLLEGE LIFE ***Social organizations:*** 1 open to all. ***Most popular organization:*** Student Advisory Board. ***Major annual events:*** Hay Ride, Christmas Party, MS Fund Raiser. ***Student services:*** personal-psychological counseling. ***Campus security:*** 24-hour emergency response devices.
HOUSING College housing not available.
CAREER PLANNING ***Placement office:*** 1 full-time, 2 part-time staff; $494,251 operating expenditure 1994–95. ***Director:*** Ms. Barbara Kennedy, Director of Placement, 419-473-2700. ***Services:*** job fairs, resume preparation, resume referral, career counseling, job bank, job interviews. 11 organizations recruited on campus 1994–95.
AFTER GRADUATION 84% of class of 1994 had job offers within 6 months. 10% of students completing a degree program went directly on to further study.
EXPENSES FOR 1995–96 ***Application fee:*** $10. Tuition: $5964 full-time, $124 per credit hour part-time.
FINANCIAL AID ***College-administered undergrad aid 1995–96:*** 85 need-based scholarships (averaging $900), 6 non-need scholarships (averaging $300), low-interest long-term loans from external sources (averaging $2625), 6 Federal Work-Study (averaging $400), 2 part-time jobs. ***Required forms:*** institutional, FAFSA. ***Application deadline:*** continuous. ***Payment plan:*** installment. ***Waivers:*** full or partial for employees or children of employees. ***Notification:*** 9/11.
APPLYING ***Options:*** early entrance, deferred entrance, midyear entrance. ***Required:*** school transcript, interview, CPAt. Test scores used for admission. ***Application deadline:*** rolling. ***Notification:*** continuous.
APPLYING/TRANSFER ***Required:*** standardized test scores, high school transcript, interview, college transcript, minimum 2.0 college GPA. ***Entrance:*** minimally difficult. ***Application deadline:*** rolling. ***Notification:*** continuous. ***Contact:*** Ms. Marsha Klingbeil, Registrar, 419-473-2700.
CONTACT Ms. Diane Brunner, President, Davis College, 4747 Monroe Street, Toledo, OH 43623-4307, 419-473-2700.

EDISON STATE COMMUNITY COLLEGE
Piqua, Ohio

UG Enrollment: 3,297 **Tuition & Fees (OH Res): $2258**
Application Deadline: rolling **Room & Board: N/Avail**

GENERAL State-supported, 2-year, coed. Part of Ohio Board of Regents. Awards certificates, transfer associate, terminal associate degrees. Founded 1973. ***Setting:*** 130-acre small-town campus. ***Total enrollment:*** 3,297. ***Faculty:*** 183 (42 full-time, 141 part-time); student-faculty ratio is 22:1.
ENROLLMENT PROFILE 3,297 students from 2 states and territories, 3 other countries. 65% women, 69% part-time, 99% state residents, 7% transferred in, 1% international, 53% 25 or older, 1% Native American, 1% Hispanic, 2% African American, 1% Asian American.
FIRST-YEAR CLASS 1,118 total; 1,251 applied, 100% were accepted, 89% of whom enrolled. 4% from top 10% of their high school class, 12% from top quarter, 24% from top half.
ACADEMIC PROGRAM Core. Calendar: semesters. Academic remediation for entering students, English as a second language program offered during academic year, services for LD students, summer session for credit, part-time degree program (daytime, evenings, summer), adult/continuing education programs. ROTC: Army (c), Air Force (c).
GENERAL DEGREE REQUIREMENTS 60 credit hours; math/science requirements vary according to program; computer course for students without computer competency.
MAJORS Accounting, art/fine arts, aviation technology, business administration/commerce/management, civil engineering technology, commercial art, community services, computer programming, computer science, construction management, criminal justice, data processing, drafting and design, early childhood education, electrical and electronics technologies, electrical engineering technology, electromechanical technology, elementary education, emergency medical technology, engineering and applied sciences, engineering design, (pre)engineering sequence, engineering technology, English, human services, industrial engineering technology, law enforcement/police sciences, legal studies, liberal arts/general studies, marketing/retailing/merchandising, mathematics, nursing, paralegal studies, real estate, retail management, secretarial studies/office management.
LIBRARY 32,000 books, 86,000 microform titles, 365 periodicals, 1,137 records, tapes, and CDs.
COMPUTERS ON CAMPUS 100 computers for student use in labs, Tutor Center, library.
COLLEGE LIFE Drama-theater group, student-run newspaper. ***Student services:*** personal-psychological counseling. ***Campus security:*** late-night transport-escort service, 16-hour patrols by trained security personnel.
HOUSING College housing not available.
ATHLETICS Member NJCAA. ***Intercollegiate:*** baseball M, basketball M/W, golf M/W. ***Intramural:*** tennis. ***Contact:*** Mr. Larry Leffel, Athletic Director, 513-778-8600; Ms. Lori May, Women's Basketball Coach, 513-778-8600.
CAREER PLANNING ***Services:*** job fairs, resume preparation, resume referral, career counseling, careers library, job bank.
EXPENSES FOR 1996–97 ***Application fee:*** $15. State resident tuition: $1958 full-time, $65.25 per credit hour part-time. Nonresident tuition: $3915 full-time, $130.50 per credit hour part-time. Part-time mandatory fees: $10 per credit hour. Full-time mandatory fees: $300.
FINANCIAL AID ***College-administered undergrad aid 1995–96:*** Federal Work-Study, part-time jobs. ***Acceptable forms:*** CSS Financial Aid PROFILE, FAFSA. ***Application deadline:*** continuous. ***Payment plan:*** deferred payment. ***Waivers:*** full or partial for employees or children of employees and senior citizens.
APPLYING Open admission except for nursing program. ***Options:*** early entrance, deferred entrance. ***Recommended:*** 3 years of high school math and science, 2 years of high school foreign language, TOEFL for international students. ***Required for some:*** SAT I or ACT, ACT COMPASS. Test scores used for counseling/placement. ***Application deadline:*** rolling. Preference given to district residents for nursing program.
APPLYING/TRANSFER ***Entrance:*** noncompetitive. ***Application deadline:*** rolling. ***Contact:*** Ms. Suzanne Wegmiller, Transfer Coordinator, 513-778-8600.
CONTACT Ms. Beth Iams Culbertson, Director of Admissions, Edison State Community College, Piqua, OH 45356-9253, 513-778-8600 Ext. 317 or toll-free 800-922-3722 (in-state). ***Fax:*** 513-778-1920. ***E-mail:*** info@edison.cc.oh.us.

ETI TECHNICAL COLLEGE
Niles, Ohio

UG Enrollment: 246 **Tuition & Fees: $3938**
Application Deadline: rolling **Room & Board: N/Avail**

GENERAL Proprietary, 2-year, coed. Awards diplomas, terminal associate degrees. Founded 1989. ***Setting:*** small-town campus with easy access to Cleveland and Pittsburgh. ***Total enrollment:*** 246. ***Faculty:*** 26 (16 full-time, 10 part-time); student-faculty ratio is 15:1.
ENROLLMENT PROFILE 246 students from 2 states and territories. 60% women, 85% state residents, 10% transferred in, 70% 25 or older, 1% Native American, 1% Hispanic, 10% African American. ***Areas of study chosen:*** 34% engineering and applied sciences. ***Most popular recent majors:*** paralegal studies, electronics engineering technology.
FIRST-YEAR CLASS 92 total; 130 applied, 77% were accepted, 92% of whom enrolled.
ACADEMIC PROGRAM Core, honor code. Calendar: semesters. Academic remediation for entering students, services for LD students, advanced placement, part-time degree program (daytime, evenings, summer), adult/continuing education programs.
GENERAL DEGREE REQUIREMENTS 72 credits; internship (some majors).
MAJORS Computer programming, electronics engineering technology, medical assistant technologies, paralegal studies.
COMPUTERS ON CAMPUS 50 computers for student use in computer center, classrooms. Staffed computer lab on campus provides training in use of computers, software.
COLLEGE LIFE Student-run newspaper. 80% vote in student government elections. ***Student services:*** personal-psychological counseling. ***Campus security:*** 24-hour emergency response devices.
HOUSING College housing not available.
CAREER PLANNING ***Services:*** resume preparation, resume referral, career counseling, careers library, job interviews.
EXPENSES FOR 1995–96 ***Application fee:*** $50. Tuition: $3888 (minimum) full-time. Full-time tuition ranges up to $6156 according to program. Full-time mandatory fees: $50. Tuition guaranteed not to increase for student's term of enrollment.
FINANCIAL AID ***College-administered undergrad aid 1995–96:*** 166 need-based scholarships (average $2300), non-need scholarships, low-interest long-term loans from external sources (average $2000). ***Required forms for some financial aid applicants:*** state, institutional, FAFSA; accepted: CSS Financial Aid PROFILE. ***Priority deadline:*** 9/9. ***Payment plan:*** installment. ***Waivers:*** full or partial for employees or children of employees.
APPLYING ***Options:*** early entrance, deferred entrance. ***Application deadline:*** rolling. ***Notification:*** continuous.
APPLYING/TRANSFER ***Application deadline:*** rolling. ***Notification:*** continuous.
CONTACT Ms. Diane Marsteller, Director of Admissions, ETI Technical College, Niles, OH 44446-4398, 330-652-9919 or toll-free 800-362-9380 (in-state). ***Fax:*** 330-652-4399.

HOCKING COLLEGE
Nelsonville, Ohio

UG Enrollment: 6,200 **Tuition & Fees (OH Res): $2625**
Application Deadline: rolling **Room & Board: $3600**

GENERAL State-supported, 2-year, coed. Part of Ohio Board of Regents. Awards terminal associate degrees. Founded 1968. ***Setting:*** 250-acre rural campus with easy access to Columbus. ***Total enrollment:*** 6,200. ***Faculty:*** 265 (149 full-time, 98% with terminal degrees, 116 part-time).
ENROLLMENT PROFILE 6,200 students from 23 states and territories, 30 other countries. 40% women, 29% part-time, 86% state residents, 9% transferred in, 51% have need-based financial aid, 9% have non-need-based financial aid, 1% international, 48%

Peterson's Guide to Two-Year Colleges 1997 521

Hocking College (continued)
25 or older, 0% Native American, 1% Hispanic, 1% African American, 0% Asian American. ***Areas of study chosen:*** 34% agriculture, 23% health professions and related sciences, 15% engineering and applied sciences, 13% business management and administrative services, 2% computer and information sciences. ***Most popular recent majors:*** nursing, wildlife management, law enforcement/police sciences.
FIRST-YEAR CLASS 1,261 total; 2,825 applied, 67% were accepted, 66% of whom enrolled.
ACADEMIC PROGRAM Core, hands-on training curriculum. Calendar: quarters. Academic remediation for entering students, services for LD students, advanced placement, self-designed majors, summer session for credit, part-time degree program (daytime, evenings, summer), adult/continuing education programs, co-op programs and internships. ROTC: Army (c).
GENERAL DEGREE REQUIREMENTS 90 credit hours; computer course for most majors.
MAJORS Accounting, automotive technologies, broadcasting, business administration/commerce/management, ceramic sciences, computer programming, computer science, computer technologies, corrections, criminal justice, culinary arts, data processing, dietetics, drafting and design, electrical and electronics technologies, electrical engineering technology, emergency medical technology, energy management technologies, finance/banking, fire science, fish and game management, food sciences, food services management, forestry, forest technology, hospitality services, hotel and restaurant management, industrial engineering technology, law enforcement/police sciences, legal secretarial studies, marketing/retailing/merchandising, medical assistant technologies, medical records services, medical secretarial studies, natural resource management, nursing, parks management, petroleum technology, physical fitness/exercise science, retail management, secretarial studies/office management, telecommunications, tourism and travel, wildlife management.
LIBRARY 16,800 books, 149 microform titles, 300 periodicals, 5 CD-ROMs, 4,000 records, tapes, and CDs.
COMPUTERS ON CAMPUS 280 computers for student use in computer center, computer labs, classrooms, student center, dorms provide access to main academic computer. Staffed computer lab on campus.
COLLEGE LIFE Orientation program (3 days). Student-run newspaper. ***Social organizations:*** 20 open to all; 1 national fraternity, social clubs; 5% of eligible men and 5% of eligible women are members. ***Most popular organizations:*** Phi Theta Kappa, Outdoor Club, Student Senate, Circle K. ***Major annual event:*** Paul Bunyan Show. ***Student services:*** health clinic, personal-psychological counseling. ***Campus security:*** 24-hour patrols, student patrols, late-night transport-escort service.
HOUSING 326 college housing spaces available; all were occupied 1995–96. No special consideration for freshman housing applicants. Off-campus living permitted. ***Option:*** coed housing available.
ATHLETICS ***Intramural:*** archery, basketball, cross-country running, football, golf, soccer, softball, tennis, volleyball, weight lifting. ***Contact:*** Mr. Chris McDade, Activities Director, 614-753-3591.
CAREER PLANNING ***Placement office:*** 2 full-time staff. ***Director:*** Mr. Randy Light, Career Counselor, 614-753-3591. ***Services:*** job fairs, resume preparation, resume referral, career counseling, careers library, job interviews.
EXPENSES FOR 1996–97 ***Application fee:*** $15. State resident tuition: $2610 full-time, $58 per credit hour part-time. Nonresident tuition: $5220 full-time, $116 per credit hour part-time. Part-time mandatory fees: $5 per quarter. Full-time mandatory fees: $15. College room and board: $3600.
FINANCIAL AID ***College-administered undergrad aid 1995–96:*** 30 need-based scholarships (average $300), 40 non-need scholarships (average $500), short-term loans (average $35), Federal Work-Study, 250 part-time jobs. ***Required forms:*** CSS Financial Aid PROFILE, state, institutional; accepted: FAFSA. ***Priority deadline:*** 4/30. ***Payment plan:*** installment. ***Waivers:*** full or partial for employees or children of employees and senior citizens.
APPLYING Open admission except for nursing program. ***Options:*** early entrance, midyear entrance. ***Required:*** school transcript. ***Recommended:*** TOEFL for international students. ***Required for some:*** nursing exam. Test scores used for counseling/placement. ***Application deadline:*** rolling. ***Notification:*** continuous.
APPLYING/TRANSFER ***Required:*** college transcript. ***Application deadline:*** rolling. ***Notification:*** continuous. ***Contact:*** Ms. Lynn Lynch, Academic Advisor, 614-753-3591.
CONTACT Dr. Candace Vancko, Vice President for Enrollment Services, Hocking College, Nelsonville, OH 45764-9588, 614-753-3591 Ext. 2150 or toll-free 800-282-4163 (in-state). ***E-mail:*** canvan@hocking.cc.oh.us. College video available.

ITT TECHNICAL INSTITUTE
Dayton, Ohio

UG Enrollment: 547	**Tuition: $15,599/deg prog**
Application Deadline: rolling	**Room & Board: N/Avail**

GENERAL Proprietary, 2-year, coed. Part of ITT Educational Services, Inc. Awards terminal associate degrees. Founded 1935. ***Setting:*** 7-acre suburban campus. ***Total enrollment:*** 547. ***Faculty:*** 27 (26 full-time, 1 part-time).
ENROLLMENT PROFILE 547 students from 3 states and territories. 0% part-time, 99% state residents, 0% transferred in, 22% 25 or older. ***Most popular recent majors:*** electronics engineering technology, architectural technologies, machine and tool technologies.
FIRST-YEAR CLASS 444 total; 718 applied, 67% were accepted, 86% of whom enrolled. 2% from top 10% of their high school class, 7% from top quarter, 58% from top half.
ACADEMIC PROGRAM Calendar: quarters. Academic remediation for entering students, tutorials, summer session for credit.
GENERAL DEGREE REQUIREMENT 90 credit hours.
MAJORS Architectural technologies, drafting and design, electronics engineering technology, heating/refrigeration/air conditioning, machine and tool technologies.
COMPUTERS ON CAMPUS 44 computers for student use in computer room, library. Staffed computer lab on campus provides training in use of computers, software.
COLLEGE LIFE ***Campus security:*** 24-hour emergency response devices.
HOUSING College housing not available.
CAREER PLANNING ***Placement office:*** 2 full-time, 1 part-time staff. ***Director:*** Ms. Priscilla Jones, Director of Placement, 513-454-2267. ***Services:*** job fairs, resume preparation, resume referral, careers library, job bank, job interviews. 31 organizations recruited on campus 1994–95.
AFTER GRADUATION 73% of class of 1994 had job offers within 6 months.
EXPENSES FOR 1996–97 ***Application fee:*** $100. Tuition per degree program ranges from $15,599 to $17,690. Full-time mandatory fees range from $540 to $720. Tuition guaranteed not to increase for student's term of enrollment.
FINANCIAL AID ***College-administered undergrad aid 1995–96:*** need-based scholarships, low-interest long-term loans from external sources, Federal Work-Study, part-time jobs. ***Required forms:*** institutional, FAFSA; accepted: CSS Financial Aid PROFILE. ***Priority deadline:*** 9/1. ***Payment plan:*** installment. ***Waivers:*** full or partial for employees or children of employees.
APPLYING ***Option:*** deferred entrance. ***Required:*** TOEFL for international students, CPAt. ***Recommended:*** 3 years of high school math and science. Test scores used for admission. ***Application deadline:*** rolling.
APPLYING/TRANSFER ***Recommended:*** 3 years of high school math and science. ***Application deadline:*** rolling. ***Contact:*** Mr. William Hughes, Director of Education, 513-454-2267.
CONTACT Mr. Roy Kimble, Director of Recruitment, ITT Technical Institute, Dayton, OH 45414-3425, 513-454-2267. College video available.

ITT TECHNICAL INSTITUTE
Youngstown, Ohio

UG Enrollment: 269	**Tuition: $15,429/deg prog**
Application Deadline: rolling	**Room & Board: N/Avail**

GENERAL Proprietary, 2-year, coed. Part of ITT Educational Services, Inc. Awards terminal associate degrees. Founded 1967. ***Setting:*** suburban campus with easy access to Cleveland and Pittsburgh. ***Total enrollment:*** 269. ***Faculty:*** 13 (12 full-time, 1 part-time).
ENROLLMENT PROFILE 269 students: 0% part-time, 100% state residents, 0% transferred in. ***Most popular recent majors:*** electronics engineering technology, drafting and design.
FIRST-YEAR CLASS 159 total.
ACADEMIC PROGRAM Technical curriculum, honor code. Calendar: quarters. 83 courses offered in 1995–96. Academic remediation for entering students, summer session for credit.
GENERAL DEGREE REQUIREMENTS 110 credit hours; 2 math courses; computer course for computer-aided drafting technology, business management, accounting majors.
MAJORS Accounting, business administration/commerce/management, drafting and design, electronics engineering technology.
LIBRARY 1,472 books, 37 periodicals, 141 records, tapes, and CDs.
COMPUTERS ON CAMPUS 125 computers for student use in computer labs, learning resource center, classrooms provide access to main academic computer. Staffed computer lab on campus (open 24 hours a day) provides training in use of computers.
COLLEGE LIFE ***Campus security:*** 24-hour emergency response devices.
HOUSING College housing not available.
CAREER PLANNING ***Placement office:*** 1 full-time staff. ***Director:*** Ms. Brenda Spencer, Director of Placement, 216-270-1600. ***Services:*** job fairs, resume preparation, resume referral, career counseling, careers library, job bank, job interviews. Students must register freshman year. 75 organizations recruited on campus 1994–95.
AFTER GRADUATION 100% of class of 1994 had job offers within 6 months.
EXPENSES FOR 1995–96 Tuition per degree program ranges from $15,429 to $17,690. Full-time mandatory fees: $720. Tuition guaranteed not to increase for student's term of enrollment.
FINANCIAL AID ***College-administered undergrad aid 1995–96:*** need-based scholarships, low-interest long-term loans from external sources, Federal Work-Study. ***Required forms:*** institutional, FAFSA; accepted: CSS Financial Aid PROFILE, state. ***Priority deadline:*** 9/5. ***Payment plan:*** installment. ***Waivers:*** full or partial for employees or children of employees.
APPLYING ***Option:*** deferred entrance. ***Required:*** CPAt (DAT also required for drafting program). Test scores used for counseling/placement. ***Application deadline:*** rolling. ***Notification:*** continuous.
APPLYING/TRANSFER ***Application deadline:*** rolling. ***Contact:*** Ms. Sara Sofia, Director of Education, 216-270-1600.
CONTACT Mr. Frank Quartini, Director of Recruitment, ITT Technical Institute, 1030 N. Meridian Rd., Youngstown, OH 44509-4098, 216-270-1600 Ext. 14. ***Fax:*** 216-270-8333. College video available.

JEFFERSON COMMUNITY COLLEGE
Steubenville, Ohio

UG Enrollment: 1,437	**Tuition & Fees (Area Res): $1710**
Application Deadline: 9/20	**Room & Board: N/Avail**

GENERAL State and locally supported, 2-year, coed. Part of Ohio Board of Regents. Awards transfer associate, terminal associate degrees. Founded 1966. ***Setting:*** 83-acre small-town campus with easy access to Pittsburgh. ***Total enrollment:*** 1,437. ***Faculty:*** 114 (40 full-time, 74 part-time); student-faculty ratio is 15:1.
ENROLLMENT PROFILE 1,437 students from 6 states and territories. 64% women, 36% men, 47% part-time, 84% state residents, 0% international, 54% 25 or older, 0% Native American, 0% Hispanic, 4% African American, 0% Asian American. ***Most popular recent majors:*** business administration/commerce/management, practical nursing, accounting.
FIRST-YEAR CLASS 532 total; 769 applied, 100% were accepted, 69% of whom enrolled.
ACADEMIC PROGRAM Core, honor code. Calendar: semesters. Academic remediation for entering students, services for LD students, summer session for credit, part-time degree program (daytime, evenings), adult/continuing education programs, internships. Off-campus study at members of the Southeastern Ohio Technical Education Consortium.
GENERAL DEGREE REQUIREMENTS 60 semester hours; computer course for medical assistant, law enforcement, engineering majors; internship.
MAJORS Accounting, business administration/commerce/management, child psychology/child development, corrections, data processing, dental services, drafting and design, electrical and electronics technologies, electrical engineering technology, electronics engineering technology, emergency medical technology, finance/banking, food services management, industrial engineering technology, law enforcement/police sciences, legal secretarial stud-

ies, manufacturing technology, mechanical engineering technology, medical assistant technologies, medical laboratory technology, medical secretarial studies, practical nursing, radiological technology, real estate, respiratory therapy, retail management, secretarial studies/office management, welding technology.
LIBRARY Jefferson Community College Library with 12,000 books, 80 microform titles, 180 periodicals, 6 CD-ROMs.
COMPUTERS ON CAMPUS 200 computers for student use in computer center, learning skills lab, library.
COLLEGE LIFE *Student services:* health clinic, personal-psychological counseling. *Campus security:* student patrols.
HOUSING College housing not available.
ATHLETICS *Intramural:* basketball, tennis, volleyball.
CAREER PLANNING *Placement office:* 1 full-time staff. *Director:* Mr. Robert Mackey, Career Counselor, 614-264-5591. *Services:* job fairs, resume preparation, resume referral, career counseling, job bank, job interviews. 30 organizations recruited on campus 1994–95.
EXPENSES FOR 1996–97 *Application fee:* $15. Area resident tuition: $1710 full-time, $57 per semester hour part-time. State resident tuition: $1860 full-time, $62 per semester hour part-time. Nonresident tuition: $2400 full-time, $80 per semester hour part-time. Tuition for West Virginia residents of Marshall, Ohio, Brooke, Hancock, and Wetzel counties pay state resident tuition.
FINANCIAL AID *College-administered undergrad aid 1995–96:* need-based scholarships, 18 non-need scholarships (average $260), short-term loans (average $180), Federal Work-Study. *Required forms:* institutional, FAFSA; required for some: state; accepted: CSS Financial Aid PROFILE. *Priority deadline:* 6/1.
APPLYING Open admission except for allied health programs. *Options:* early entrance, deferred entrance. *Required:* TOEFL for international students. *Required for some:* SAT I or ACT. Test scores used for admission and counseling/placement. *Application deadline:* 9/20. *Notification:* continuous until 9/20.
APPLYING/TRANSFER *Required for some:* college transcript. *Entrance:* noncompetitive. *Application deadline:* 9/20. *Notification:* continuous until 9/20.
CONTACT Mr. Charles Mascellino, Director of Admissions, Jefferson Community College, Steubenville, OH 43952-3598, 614-264-5591 Ext. 108. *Fax:* 614-264-1338.

KENT STATE UNIVERSITY, ASHTABULA CAMPUS
Ashtabula, Ohio

UG Enrollment: 1,100	Tuition & Fees (OH Res): $2942
Application Deadline: 8/1	Room & Board: N/Avail

GENERAL State-supported, 2-year, coed. Part of Kent State University System. Awards transfer associate, terminal associate degrees (also offers some upper-level and graduate courses). Founded 1958. *Setting:* 120-acre small-town campus with easy access to Cleveland. *Research spending 1994–95:* $87,132. *Total enrollment:* 1,100. *Faculty:* 74 (30 full-time, 30% with terminal degrees, 44 part-time); student-faculty ratio is 17:1.
ENROLLMENT PROFILE 1,100 students from 2 states and territories, 1 other country. 70% women, 52% part-time, 98% state residents, 6% transferred in, 75% have need-based financial aid, 25% have non-need-based financial aid, 40% 25 or older, 1% Native American, 1% Hispanic, 1% African American. *Areas of study chosen:* 15% education, 15% health professions and related sciences, 15% social sciences, 10% communications and journalism, 10% computer and information sciences, 10% liberal arts/general studies, 5% business management and administrative services, 5% engineering and applied sciences, 5% natural resource sciences, 5% premed, 5% prevet.
FIRST-YEAR CLASS 234 total; 340 applied, 100% were accepted, 69% of whom enrolled. 10% from top 10% of their high school class, 32% from top quarter, 82% from top half.
ACADEMIC PROGRAM Honor code. Calendar: semesters. Academic remediation for entering students, advanced placement, self-designed majors, Freshman Honors College, honors program, summer session for credit, part-time degree program (daytime, evenings), internships. ROTC: Army (c).
GENERAL DEGREE REQUIREMENTS 66 semester hours; computer course for engineering, business management majors; internship (some majors).
MAJORS Accounting, business administration/commerce/management, computer technologies, early childhood education, electrical and electronics technologies, electrical engineering technology, engineering technology, environmental studies, finance/banking, human services, industrial engineering technology, law enforcement/police sciences, legal secretarial studies, liberal arts/general studies, manufacturing technology, marketing/retailing/merchandising, materials sciences, mechanical engineering technology, nursing, physical therapy, real estate, secretarial studies/office management.
LIBRARY 51,884 books, 323 microform titles, 225 periodicals, 1 on-line bibliographic service, 2 CD-ROMs, 624 records, tapes, and CDs. Acquisition spending 1994–95: $34,678.
COMPUTERS ON CAMPUS Students must have own computer. PCs are provided. 25 computers for student use in computer center provide access to Internet. Staffed computer lab on campus provides training in use of computers, software. Academic computing expenditure 1994–95: $103,886.
COLLEGE LIFE Drama-theater group, student-run newspaper. 20% vote in student government elections. *Most popular organizations:* Student Government, Student Newspaper, Student Nurses Association. *Campus security:* 24-hour emergency response devices.
HOUSING College housing not available.
CAREER PLANNING *Placement office:* 1 part-time staff; $37,313 operating expenditure 1994–95. *Director:* Mrs. Roxana Christopher, Coordinator of Developmental Education, 216-964-4233. *Services:* career counseling, careers library.
AFTER GRADUATION 95% of class of 1994 had job offers within 6 months.
EXPENSES FOR 1995–96 State resident tuition: $2942 full-time, $133.75 per semester hour part-time. Nonresident tuition: $6869 full-time, $312.25 per semester hour part-time.
FINANCIAL AID *College-administered undergrad aid 1995–96:* 21 need-based scholarships (average $400), 26 non-need scholarships (average $450), low-interest long-term loans from external sources (average $1950), 15 Federal Work-Study, 14 part-time jobs. *Required forms:* state, institutional, FAFSA; accepted: CSS Financial Aid PROFILE. *Priority deadline:* 4/1.
APPLYING Open admission except for nursing program. *Options:* early entrance, deferred entrance. *Required:* SAT I or ACT. *Recommended:* 3 years of high school math

and science, some high school foreign language. Test scores used for counseling/placement. *Application deadlines:* 8/1, 7/15 for nonresidents. *Notification:* continuous until 8/1, continuous until 7/15 for nonresidents.
APPLYING/TRANSFER *Required for some:* 3 years of high school math and science, some high school foreign language. *Entrance:* noncompetitive. *Application deadline:* 7/15. *Notification:* continuous until 7/15.
CONTACT Mr. Edward G. Robinson, Admissions Counselor, Kent State University, Ashtabula Campus, Ashtabula, OH 44004-2299, 216-964-4240.

KENT STATE UNIVERSITY, EAST LIVERPOOL CAMPUS
East Liverpool, Ohio

UG Enrollment: 817	Tuition & Fees (OH Res): $2999
Application Deadline: rolling	Room & Board: N/Avail

GENERAL State-supported, 2-year, coed. Part of Kent State University System. Awards transfer associate, terminal associate degrees (also offers some upper-level and graduate courses). Founded 1967. *Setting:* 4-acre small-town campus with easy access to Pittsburgh. *Total enrollment:* 817. *Faculty:* 77 (25 full-time, 42% with terminal degrees, 52 part-time); student-faculty ratio is 11:1.
ENROLLMENT PROFILE 817 students from 2 states and territories. 75% women, 25% men, 49% part-time, 99% state residents, 8% transferred in, 71% have need-based financial aid, 51% 25 or older, 1% African American. *Areas of study chosen:* 55% health professions and related sciences, 33% liberal arts/general studies, 6% business management and administrative services, 6% education. *Most popular recent majors:* nursing, physical therapy, occupational therapy.
FIRST-YEAR CLASS 121 total; 230 applied, 100% were accepted, 53% of whom enrolled.
ACADEMIC PROGRAM Core, honor code. Calendar: semesters. 104 courses offered in 1995–96. Academic remediation for entering students, services for LD students, advanced placement, self-designed majors, summer session for credit, part-time degree program (daytime, evenings), adult/continuing education programs, internships. ROTC: Army (c), Naval (c), Air Force (c).
GENERAL DEGREE REQUIREMENTS 65 semester hours; computer course for accounting technology, business management technology majors.
MAJORS Accounting, business administration/commerce/management, computer technologies, criminal justice, data processing, finance/banking, legal secretarial studies, liberal arts/general studies, nursing, occupational therapy, physical therapy.
LIBRARY East Liverpool Campus Library with 30,000 books, 131 periodicals, 2 on-line bibliographic services, 1 CD-ROM.
COMPUTERS ON CAMPUS 50 computers for student use in computer center, computer labs, learning resource center, library provide access to main academic computer, off-campus computing facilities, e-mail, Internet. Staffed computer lab on campus provides training in use of computers, software.
COLLEGE LIFE Student-run newspaper. *Social organizations:* 8 open to all. *Most popular organizations:* Student Senate, Student Nurses Association, Alpha Beta Gamma, Occupational Therapist Assistant Club, Physical Therapist Assistant Club. *Major annual events:* Christmas on Campus, Spring Fling, Wall of Fame Dinner. *Campus security:* student patrols, late-night transport-escort service.
HOUSING College housing not available.
ATHLETICS *Intramural:* basketball, bowling, golf, racquetball, tennis, volleyball.
CAREER PLANNING *Placement office:* 1 full-time, 1 part-time staff. *Director:* Mrs. Doris R. Buzzard, Director of Career Services, 216-385-3805. *Services:* job fairs, resume preparation, resume referral, career counseling, careers library, job bank, job interviews. 22 organizations recruited on campus 1994–95.
AFTER GRADUATION 80% of class of 1994 had job offers within 6 months. 50% of students completing a degree program went directly on to further study.
EXPENSES FOR 1996–97 *Application fee:* $25. State resident tuition: $2999 full-time, $136.50 per semester hour part-time. Nonresident tuition: $7287 full-time, $331.50 per semester hour part-time.
FINANCIAL AID *College-administered undergrad aid 1995–96:* 84 need-based scholarships (average $300), 64 non-need scholarships (average $628), short-term loans (average $1056), low-interest long-term loans from college funds, loans from external sources (average $1649), 28 Federal Work-Study (averaging $818), 48 part-time jobs. *Required forms:* CSS Financial Aid PROFILE, institutional, FAFSA. *Priority deadline:* 2/15. *Payment plan:* installment. *Waivers:* full or partial for employees or children of employees and senior citizens. *Notification:* continuous.
APPLYING Open admission except for nursing, physical therapy assistant, occupational therapy assistant programs. *Options:* early entrance, deferred entrance, midyear entrance. *Required:* TOEFL for international students. *Recommended:* some high school foreign language, ACT. *Required for some:* 3 years of high school math and science, ACT. Test scores used for counseling/placement. *Application deadline:* rolling. *Notification:* continuous until 9/1.
APPLYING/TRANSFER *Recommended:* some high school foreign language. *Required for some:* 3 years of high school math and science. *Entrance:* noncompetitive. *Application deadline:* rolling. *Notification:* continuous until 9/1. *Contact:* Mr. Darwin K. Smith, Assistant to the Dean, 216-385-3805 Ext. 14.
CONTACT Mr. Darwin K. Smith, Assistant to the Dean, Kent State University, East Liverpool Campus, East Liverpool, OH 43920-3497, 216-385-3805 Ext. 14. *Fax:* 216-385-3757. *E-mail:* admissions@eliv.kenteliv.kent.edu.

KENT STATE UNIVERSITY, GEAUGA CAMPUS
Burton, Ohio

UG Enrollment: 474	Tuition & Fees (OH Res): $2942
Application Deadline: rolling	Room & Board: N/Avail

GENERAL State-supported, 2-year, coed. Part of Kent State University System. Awards transfer associate degrees (also offers some graduate courses). Founded 1964. *Setting:* 87-acre rural campus with easy access to Cleveland. Faculty: 54 (9 full-time, 30% with terminal degrees, 45 part-time).

Kent State University, Geauga Campus (continued)

ENROLLMENT PROFILE 474 students: 63% women, 60% part-time, 100% state residents, 15% transferred in, 55% 25 or older, 1% Hispanic, 13% African American, 0% Asian American. ***Areas of study chosen:*** 32% business management and administrative services, 15% education, 10% computer and information sciences, 10% fine arts, 7% psychology, 5% communications and journalism, 5% English language/literature/letters, 3% liberal arts/general studies, 2% mathematics, 2% prelaw, 2% premed. ***Most popular recent majors:*** business administration/commerce/management, computer technologies, accounting.

FIRST-YEAR CLASS 69 total; 69 applied, 100% were accepted, 100% of whom enrolled. 2% from top 10% of their high school class, 10% from top quarter, 60% from top half. 2 class presidents, 1 valedictorian.

ACADEMIC PROGRAM Core, honor code. Calendar: semesters. Academic remediation for entering students, English as a second language program, services for LD students, advanced placement, self-designed majors, tutorials, summer session for credit, part-time degree program (daytime, evenings), adult/continuing education programs, internships. ROTC: Army (c), Naval (c), Air Force (c).

GENERAL DEGREE REQUIREMENTS 65 semester hours; math/science requirements vary according to program.

MAJORS Accounting, business administration/commerce/management, computer programming, computer technologies, data processing, economics, (pre)engineering sequence, industrial engineering technology, liberal arts/general studies.

LIBRARY Kent State University Library with 14,000 books, 150 periodicals, 100 records, tapes, and CDs. Acquisition spending 1994–95: $75,000.

COMPUTERS ON CAMPUS 50 computers for student use in computer center, learning resource center, library provide access to e-mail. Staffed computer lab on campus provides training in use of computers. Academic computing expenditure 1994–95: $85,000.

COLLEGE LIFE Student-run newspaper. ***Social organizations:*** 5 open to all. ***Most popular organizations:*** Computer Club, Student Senate. ***Major annual events:*** Computer Software Fair, Faculty Colloquium. ***Campus security:*** 24-hour emergency response devices.

HOUSING College housing not available.

ATHLETICS ***Intramural:*** skiing (downhill).

CAREER PLANNING ***Placement office:*** 1 full-time staff; $25,000 operating expenditure 1994–95. ***Director:*** Ms. Louise Senra, Coordinator of Developmental Education, 216-834-4187. ***Services:*** resume preparation, career counseling, careers library, job bank.

AFTER GRADUATION 65% of students completing a degree program in 1994–95 went directly on to further study.

EXPENSES FOR 1996–97 State resident tuition: $2942 full-time, $133.75 per semester hour part-time. Nonresident tuition: $7026 full-time, $319.50 per semester hour part-time.

FINANCIAL AID ***College-administered undergrad aid 1995–96:*** 30 need-based scholarships (averaging $600), 3 non-need scholarships (averaging $300), short-term loans (averaging $400), low-interest long-term loans from external sources (averaging $2600), Federal Work-Study, 25 part-time jobs. ***Required forms:*** state, institutional, FAFSA, FARE; accepted: CSS Financial Aid PROFILE. ***Priority deadline:*** 3/1. ***Payment plan:*** installment. ***Waivers:*** full or partial for employees or children of employees and senior citizens. ***Notification:*** 4/1.

APPLYING Open admission. ***Options:*** early entrance, deferred entrance, midyear entrance. ***Required:*** school transcript, interview, TOEFL for international students. ***Recommended:*** minimum 2.0 GPA, 3 years of high school math and science, some high school foreign language, ACT. Test scores used for counseling/placement. ***Application deadline:*** rolling.

APPLYING/TRANSFER ***Required:*** high school transcript, interview, college transcript. ***Recommended:*** standardized test scores, 3 years of high school math and science, some high school foreign language, minimum 2.0 high school GPA. ***Application deadline:*** rolling. ***Contact:*** Dr. Mary Ann Schneider, Director of Academic Affairs, 216-834-4187.

CONTACT Ms. Betty Landrus, Admissions and Records Secretary, Kent State University, Geauga Campus, Burton, OH 44021-9500, 216-834-4187. ***Fax:*** 216-834-0919.

KENT STATE UNIVERSITY, SALEM CAMPUS
Salem, Ohio

UG Enrollment: 924	**Tuition & Fees (OH Res): $2942**
Application Deadline: rolling	**Room & Board: N/Avail**

GENERAL State-supported, 2-year, coed. Part of Kent State University System. Awards transfer associate, terminal associate degrees (also offers some upper-level and graduate courses). Founded 1966. ***Setting:*** 98-acre rural campus. ***Total enrollment:*** 924. ***Faculty:*** 71 (37 full-time, 49% with terminal degrees, 34 part-time); student-faculty ratio is 14:1.

ENROLLMENT PROFILE 924 students from 2 states and territories. 70% women, 30% men, 52% part-time, 99% state residents, 23% transferred in, 0% international, 47% 25 or older, 0% Hispanic, 1% African American, 0% Asian American. ***Most popular recent majors:*** radiological technology, business administration/commerce/management, horticulture.

FIRST-YEAR CLASS 154 total; 228 applied, 100% were accepted, 68% of whom enrolled.

ACADEMIC PROGRAM Core. Calendar: semesters. Academic remediation for entering students, services for LD students, advanced placement, tutorials, summer session for credit, part-time degree program (daytime, evenings), adult/continuing education programs, internships. ROTC: Army (c), Air Force (c).

GENERAL DEGREE REQUIREMENTS 65 semester hours; math/science requirements vary according to program; internship (some majors).

MAJORS Accounting, business administration/commerce/management, computer technologies, early childhood education, environmental sciences, horticulture, human services, liberal arts/general studies, manufacturing technology, radiological technology, secretarial studies/office management.

LIBRARY 18,531 books, 2 microform titles, 152 periodicals, 2 CD-ROMs, 611 records, tapes, and CDs.

COMPUTERS ON CAMPUS 100 computers for student use in computer center, computer labs, learning resource center, writing lab, library provide access to e-mail. Staffed computer lab on campus provides training in use of computers, software.

COLLEGE LIFE Drama-theater group. ***Social organizations:*** 11 open to all. ***Most popular organizations:*** Student Government, NEXUS, Ski Club, Art Club, Drama Club. ***Major annual events:*** Awards Banquet, Movie Nights. ***Student services:*** personal-psychological counseling, women's center. ***Campus security:*** late-night transport-escort service.

HOUSING College housing not available.

ATHLETICS ***Intramural:*** badminton, basketball, bowling, football, racquetball, skiing (downhill), softball, table tennis (Ping-Pong), tennis, volleyball.

CAREER PLANNING ***Placement office:*** 1 full-time staff. ***Director:*** Ms. Donna Walker, Coordinator of Career Planning, 216-332-0361. ***Services:*** job fairs, resume preparation, resume referral, career counseling, careers library, job bank.

EXPENSES FOR 1995–96 ***Application fee:*** $25. State resident tuition: $2942 full-time, $134 per semester hour part-time. Nonresident tuition: $7026 full-time, $319 per semester hour part-time.

FINANCIAL AID ***College-administered undergrad aid 1995–96:*** need-based scholarships, short-term loans (average $300), low-interest long-term loans from external sources (average $1000), Federal Work-Study, 16 part-time jobs. ***Required forms:*** FAFSA. ***Priority deadline:*** 2/15. ***Payment plans:*** tuition prepayment, installment, deferred pay. ***Waivers:*** full or partial for employees or children of employees.

APPLYING Open admission except for radiological technology, human services programs. ***Options:*** early entrance, deferred entrance. ***Recommended:*** 3 years of high school math and science, 3 years of high school foreign language, SAT I or ACT. ***Required for some:*** SAT I or ACT, TOEFL for international students. Test scores used for counseling/placement. ***Application deadline:*** rolling.

APPLYING/TRANSFER ***Recommended:*** standardized test scores, 3 years of high school math and science, 3 years of high school foreign language. ***Required for some:*** standardized test scores. ***Entrance:*** noncompetitive. ***Application deadline:*** rolling. ***Contact:*** Ms. Marilyn Ward, Director of Enrollment Management, 216-332-0361.

CONTACT Ms. Martha Bowker, Admissions Secretary, Kent State University, Salem Campus, Salem, OH 44460-9412, 216-332-0361. ***Fax:*** 216-332-9256. ***E-mail:*** ask-us@salem-1.salem.kent.edu. College video available.

KENT STATE UNIVERSITY, STARK CAMPUS
Canton, Ohio

UG Enrollment: 2,464	**Tuition & Fees (OH Res): $2942**
Application Deadline: rolling	**Room & Board: N/Avail**

GENERAL State-supported, 2-year, coed. Part of Kent State University System. Awards transfer associate degrees (also offers some upper-level and graduate courses). Founded 1967. ***Setting:*** 200-acre suburban campus with easy access to Cleveland. Faculty: 105 (60 full-time, 60% with terminal degrees, 45 part-time); student-faculty ratio is 26:1.

ENROLLMENT PROFILE 2,464 students from 2 states and territories. 60% women, 40% men, 46% part-time, 99% state residents, 10% transferred in, 30% have need-based financial aid, 0% international, 1% Native American, 1% Hispanic, 7% African American, 1% Asian American. ***Areas of study chosen:*** 100% liberal arts/general studies.

FIRST-YEAR CLASS 553 total; 709 applied, 100% were accepted, 78% of whom enrolled. 6% from top 10% of their high school class, 22% from top quarter, 60% from top half.

ACADEMIC PROGRAM Core, liberal arts curriculum. Calendar: semesters. 268 courses offered in 1995–96. Academic remediation for entering students, English as a second language program offered during academic year and summer, services for LD students, advanced placement, self-designed majors, Freshman Honors College, tutorials, honors program, summer session for credit, part-time degree program (daytime, evenings, summer), adult/continuing education programs, co-op programs and internships. Off-campus study at Stark Technical College. ROTC: Army (c), Air Force (c).

GENERAL DEGREE REQUIREMENTS 65 semester hours; 1 course in math/logic; computer course for business administration majors; internship (some majors).

MAJORS Art/fine arts, business administration/commerce/management, education, liberal arts/general studies, science.

LIBRARY Kent Stark Library with 59,897 books, 4,624 microform titles, 343 periodicals, 2 CD-ROMs, 1,002 records, tapes, and CDs.

COMPUTERS ON CAMPUS 76 computers for student use in computer center, learning resource center, Writing Skills Center, English lab, library provide access to e-mail, Internet. Staffed computer lab on campus provides training in use of computers, software.

COLLEGE LIFE Drama-theater group, choral group, student-run newspaper. ***Social organizations:*** 15 open to all. ***Most popular organizations:*** Political Science Forum, Pan African Student Alliance, Kent Stark Student Education Association, Kent Stark Choral Society, History Club. ***Major annual events:*** New Student Day, Featured Speaker Series. ***Student services:*** personal-psychological counseling. ***Campus security:*** 24-hour emergency response devices, late-night transport-escort service.

HOUSING College housing not available.

ATHLETICS ***Intramural:*** baseball, basketball, bowling, football, golf, racquetball, tennis, volleyball, weight lifting.

CAREER PLANNING ***Placement office:*** 1 full-time, 1 part-time staff. ***Director:*** Ms. Diane Hoffman, Coordinator of Advising and Student Services, 216-499-9600. ***Services:*** job fairs, resume preparation, career counseling, careers library.

EXPENSES FOR 1995–96 ***Application fee:*** $25. State resident tuition: $2942 full-time, $133.75 per semester hour part-time. Nonresident tuition: $7026 full-time, $319.50 per semester hour part-time. Tuition guaranteed not to increase for student's term of enrollment.

FINANCIAL AID ***College-administered undergrad aid 1995–96:*** 7 need-based scholarships (average $250), 15 non-need scholarships (average $500), short-term loans (average $250), low-interest long-term loans from external sources (average $1500), Federal Work-Study, 70 part-time jobs. ***Required forms:*** FAFSA; accepted: CSS Financial Aid PROFILE. ***Priority deadline:*** 2/15. ***Payment plan:*** installment. ***Waivers:*** full or partial for employees or children of employees and senior citizens.

APPLYING Open admission. ***Options:*** early entrance, deferred entrance, midyear entrance. ***Required:*** school transcript, 3 years of high school math and science, 3 years of high school foreign language, SAT I or ACT. Test scores used for counseling/placement. ***Application deadline:*** rolling.

APPLYING/TRANSFER ***Required:*** standardized test scores, college transcript. ***Application deadline:*** rolling. ***Contact:*** Ms. Diane Hoffman, Coordinator of Advising and Student Services, 216-499-9600.

CONTACT Ms. Mary Southards, Registrar and Director of Admissions, Kent State University, Stark Campus, Canton, OH 44720-7599, 216-499-9600 Ext. 240. ***Fax:*** 216-494-6121.

KENT STATE UNIVERSITY, TRUMBULL CAMPUS
Warren, Ohio

UG Enrollment: 1,918 **Tuition & Fees (OH Res): $2942**
Application Deadline: 7/30 **Room & Board: N/Avail**

GENERAL State-supported, 2-year, coed. Part of Kent State University System. Awards transfer associate, terminal associate degrees (also offers some upper-level and graduate courses). Founded 1954. ***Setting:*** 200-acre suburban campus with easy access to Cleveland. ***Total enrollment:*** 1,918. ***Faculty:*** 100 (50 full-time, 50 part-time); student-faculty ratio is 19:1.
ENROLLMENT PROFILE 1,918 students from 4 states and territories. 64% women, 36% men, 60% part-time, 99% state residents, 4% transferred in, 54% 25 or older, 1% Native American, 1% Hispanic, 7% African American, 1% Asian American. ***Most popular recent majors:*** liberal arts/general studies, business administration/commerce/management.
FIRST-YEAR CLASS 673 total; 723 applied, 93% were accepted, 100% of whom enrolled.
ACADEMIC PROGRAM Core. Calendar: semesters. 450 courses offered in 1995–96. Academic remediation for entering students, services for LD students, advanced placement, self-designed majors, Freshman Honors College, tutorials, honors program, summer session for credit, part-time degree program (daytime, evenings, weekends, summer), adult/continuing education programs, co-op programs and internships. ROTC: Army (c), Air Force (c).
GENERAL DEGREE REQUIREMENTS 65 credit hours; computer course for most majors; internship (some majors).
MAJORS Accounting, automotive technologies, business administration/commerce/management, computer technologies, criminal justice, electrical and electronics technologies, engineering (general), environmental engineering technology, finance/banking, industrial engineering technology, liberal arts/general studies, marketing/retailing/merchandising, mechanical engineering technology, real estate, secretarial studies/office management, tourism and travel.
LIBRARY Trumbull Campus Library with 65,951 books, 35,923 microform titles, 759 periodicals, 2 on-line bibliographic services, 5,490 records, tapes, and CDs.
COMPUTERS ON CAMPUS Computer purchase plan available. 300 computers for student use in computer center, computer labs, learning resource center, multimedia room, distance education room, classrooms, library provide access to main academic computer, off-campus computing facilities, e-mail, Internet. Staffed computer lab on campus provides training in use of computers, software.
COLLEGE LIFE Orientation program (no cost, parents included). Drama-theater group, student-run newspaper. 15% vote in student government elections. ***Social organizations:*** 10 open to all. ***Most popular organizations:*** Student Senate, Trumbull Environmental Club, Union Activities Board, Gamemasters, Kent Christian Fellowship. ***Campus security:*** 24-hour emergency response devices, late-night transport-escort service, patrols by trained security personnel during open hours.
HOUSING College housing not available.
ATHLETICS ***Intramural:*** basketball, bowling, golf, skiing (downhill), volleyball.
CAREER PLANNING ***Placement office:*** 1 full-time staff. ***Director:*** Ms. Verna Williams, Coordinator, 216-847-0571. ***Services:*** job fairs, resume preparation, resume referral, career counseling, careers library, job bank, job interviews.
EXPENSES FOR 1995–96 ***Application fee:*** $25. State resident tuition: $2942 full-time, $133.75 per credit hour part-time. Nonresident tuition: $7026 full-time, $319.50 per credit hour part-time.
FINANCIAL AID ***College-administered undergrad aid 1995–96:*** 1,000 need-based scholarships (average $1650), short-term loans (average $550), low-interest long-term loans from external sources (average $2000), Federal Work-Study, 90 part-time jobs. ***Required forms:*** FAFSA; accepted: CSS Financial Aid PROFILE. ***Priority deadline:*** 5/1. ***Payment plan:*** installment. ***Waivers:*** full or partial for employees or children of employees and senior citizens.
APPLYING Open admission except for nursing program. ***Options:*** early entrance, deferred entrance, midyear entrance. ***Required:*** school transcript, BSAT. ***Required for some:*** SAT I or ACT, TOEFL for international students. Test scores used for counseling/placement. ***Application deadline:*** 7/30. ***Notification:*** continuous until 8/30.
APPLYING/TRANSFER ***Required:*** high school transcript, college transcript. ***Recommended:*** standardized test scores, minimum 2.0 college GPA. ***Required for some:*** standardized test scores. ***Entrance:*** minimally difficult. ***Application deadline:*** rolling. ***Notification:*** continuous until 8/30. ***Contact:*** Mr. Mel Anthony May, Director of Student Affairs, 216-847-0571.
CONTACT Ms. Kerrianne Kacik, Admissions Clerk, Kent State University, Trumbull Campus, Warren, OH 44483-1998, 216-847-0571 Ext. 367. ***E-mail:*** info@lyceum.trumbull.kent.edu.

KENT STATE UNIVERSITY, TUSCARAWAS CAMPUS
New Philadelphia, Ohio

UG Enrollment: 1,133 **Tuition & Fees (OH Res): $2942**
Application Deadline: 8/14 **Room & Board: N/Avail**

GENERAL State-supported, 2-year, coed. Part of Kent State University System. Awards certificates, transfer associate, terminal associate degrees (also offers some graduate courses). Founded 1962. ***Setting:*** 168-acre small-town campus with easy access to Cleveland. ***Endowment:*** $927,656. ***Total enrollment:*** 1,133. ***Faculty:*** 86 (31 full-time, 52% with terminal degrees, 55 part-time); student-faculty ratio is 15:1.
ENROLLMENT PROFILE 1,133 students: 65% women, 35% men, 49% part-time, 100% state residents, 5% transferred in, 65% have need-based financial aid, 2% have non-need-based financial aid, 0% international, 43% 25 or older, 1% Native American, 1% Hispanic, 1% African American, 1% Asian American. ***Areas of study chosen:*** 26% liberal arts/general studies, 21% business management and administrative services, 9% health professions and related sciences, 8% engineering and applied sciences, 6% education, 3% computer and information sciences, 3% psychology, 2% social sciences, 1% biological and life sciences, 1% communications and journalism, 1% fine arts, 1% foreign language and literature, 1% prevet, 1% vocational and home economics.
FIRST-YEAR CLASS 249 total; 350 applied, 100% were accepted, 71% of whom enrolled. 12% from top 10% of their high school class, 29% from top quarter, 59% from top half.
ACADEMIC PROGRAM Core, liberal education curriculum. Calendar: semesters. 247 courses offered in 1995–96. Academic remediation for entering students, services for LD students, advanced placement, self-designed majors, Freshman Honors College, tutorials, honors program, summer session for credit, part-time degree program (evenings), adult/continuing education programs, internships. ROTC: Army (c), Air Force (c).
GENERAL DEGREE REQUIREMENTS 65 semester hours; math/science requirements vary according to program.
MAJORS Accounting, business administration/commerce/management, computer technologies, electrical engineering technology, electronics engineering technology, engineering technology, environmental sciences, industrial engineering technology, law enforcement/police sciences, liberal arts/general studies, mechanical engineering technology, nursing, secretarial studies/office management.
LIBRARY Tuscarawas Campus Library with 52,768 books, 58 microform titles, 375 periodicals, 3 CD-ROMs, 1,800 records, tapes, and CDs. Acquisition spending 1994–95: $58,900.
COMPUTERS ON CAMPUS 98 computers for student use in computer center, computer labs, library provide access to e-mail, on-line services. Staffed computer lab on campus provides training in use of computers, software. Academic computing expenditure 1994–95: $89,249.
COLLEGE LIFE Choral group. 13% vote in student government elections. ***Social organizations:*** 5 open to all. ***Most popular organizations:*** Society of Mechanical Engineers, Student Government, Business Club, Data Processing Management Association. ***Major annual events:*** Spring Dinner Dance, Halloween Dance, Commencement. ***Campus security:*** maintenance security.
HOUSING College housing not available.
ATHLETICS ***Intramural:*** basketball, football, volleyball.
CAREER PLANNING ***Placement office:*** 2 part-time staff; $1836 operating expenditure 1994–95. ***Director:*** Mr. James Kinsey, Coordinator, Career Services, 216-339-3391 Ext. 262. ***Services:*** resume preparation, career counseling, careers library.
AFTER GRADUATION 80% of students completing a degree program in 1994–95 went directly on to further study.
EXPENSES FOR 1995–96 ***Application fee:*** $25. State resident tuition: $2942 full-time, $133.25 per semester hour part-time. Nonresident tuition: $7026 full-time, $319.50 per semester hour part-time.
FINANCIAL AID ***College-administered undergrad aid 1995–96:*** 77 need-based scholarships (average $565), 55 non-need scholarships (average $894), low-interest long-term loans from college funds (average $757), loans from external sources (average $2706), Federal Work-Study, 30 part-time jobs. ***Required forms:*** FAFSA; required for some: Stafford Student Loan form. ***Priority deadline:*** 2/15. ***Payment plans:*** installment, deferred payment. ***Waivers:*** full or partial for employees or children of employees. ***Notification:*** 4/1.
APPLYING Open admission except for business administration, education, nursing, fine and performing arts programs. ***Options:*** early entrance, deferred entrance, midyear entrance. ***Required:*** TOEFL for international students. ***Recommended:*** 3 years of high school math and science, 3 years of high school foreign language. ***Required for some:*** SAT I or ACT. Test scores used for counseling/placement. ***Application deadline:*** 8/14. ***Notification:*** continuous.
APPLYING/TRANSFER ***Required for some:*** standardized test scores. ***Application deadline:*** 8/14. ***Notification:*** continuous. ***Contact:*** Ms. Connie Espenschied, Director of Admissions, 216-339-3391 Ext. 235.
CONTACT Ms. Connie Espenschied, Director of Admissions, Kent State University, Tuscarawas Campus, New Philadelphia, OH 44663-9447, 216-339-3391 Ext. 235. ***Fax:*** 216-339-3321. ***E-mail:*** cespenschied@ksu.tusc.kent.edu.

KETTERING COLLEGE OF MEDICAL ARTS
Kettering, Ohio

UG Enrollment: 599 **Tuition & Fees: $5948**
Application Deadline: rolling **Room & Board: $3001**

GENERAL Independent Seventh-day Adventist, 2-year, coed. Awards certificates, transfer associate, terminal associate degrees. Founded 1967. ***Setting:*** 35-acre urban campus. ***Total enrollment:*** 599. ***Faculty:*** 47 (32 full-time, 100% with terminal degrees, 15 part-time); student-faculty ratio is 10:1.
ENROLLMENT PROFILE 599 students from 26 states and territories, 2 other countries. 70% women, 51% part-time, 82% state residents, 21% live on campus, 69% transferred in, 47% 25 or older, 1% Native American, 2% Hispanic, 4% African American, 3% Asian American. ***Areas of study chosen:*** 99% health professions and related sciences, 1% predentistry, 1% premed. ***Most popular recent majors:*** nursing, physician's assistant studies, respiratory therapy.
FIRST-YEAR CLASS 83 total; 139 applied, 91% were accepted, 65% of whom enrolled. 10% from top 10% of their high school class, 39% from top quarter, 72% from top half.
ACADEMIC PROGRAM Core, honor code. Calendar: semesters. Academic remediation for entering students, advanced placement, summer session for credit, part-time degree program (daytime, evenings), internships. Off-campus study at members of the Southwestern Ohio Council for Higher Education.
GENERAL DEGREE REQUIREMENTS 64 credits; completion of math proficiency test; computer course for nursing majors; internship (some majors).
MAJORS Biomedical technologies, electrical and electronics technologies, liberal arts/general studies, nuclear medical technology, nursing, physician's assistant studies, radiological sciences, radiological technology, respiratory therapy.
LIBRARY Learning Resources Center plus 1 other, with 27,013 books, 206 microform titles, 263 periodicals, 2 on-line bibliographic services, 5 CD-ROMs, 890 records, tapes, and CDs.
COMPUTERS ON CAMPUS Student rooms linked to a campus network. 25 computers for student use in computer center, computer labs.
COLLEGE LIFE Choral group, student-run newspaper. ***Social organizations:*** 3 open to all. ***Most popular organization:*** Student Nurses Association. ***Major annual events:*** Weeks of Spiritual Emphasis, Nursing Dedication Ceremony, Christmas Party. ***Student services:*** health clinic, personal-psychological counseling. ***Campus security:*** 24-hour emergency response devices and patrols, late-night transport-escort service.

Kettering College of Medical Arts (continued)

HOUSING 150 college housing spaces available; all were occupied 1995–96. No special consideration for freshman housing applicants. Off-campus living permitted. ***Options:*** coed, single-sex housing available. Resident assistants live in dorms.

ATHLETICS ***Intramural:*** basketball, tennis, volleyball. ***Contact:*** Mr. Tim Willsey, Professor of Physical Education, 513-296-7201.

CAREER PLANNING ***Services:*** job fairs, career counseling, job interviews.

EXPENSES FOR 1996–97 ***Application fee:*** $25. Comprehensive fee of $8949 includes full-time tuition ($5760), mandatory fees ($188), and college room and board ($3001). College room only: $1600. Part-time tuition: $180 per credit.

FINANCIAL AID ***College-administered undergrad aid 1995–96:*** need-based scholarships, non-need scholarships, low-interest long-term loans from college funds (average $1500), loans from external sources (average $2625), Federal Work-Study, 54 part-time jobs. ***Required forms:*** institutional, FAFSA; accepted: CSS Financial Aid PROFILE, state. ***Priority deadline:*** 3/31. ***Payment plan:*** installment. ***Waivers:*** full or partial for employees or children of employees. ***Notification:*** continuous. ***Average indebtedness of graduates:*** $6125.

APPLYING ***Options:*** early entrance, midyear entrance. ***Required:*** school transcript, minimum 2.0 GPA, 3 recommendations, ACT, TOEFL for international students. ***Recommended:*** minimum 3.0 GPA, 3 years of high school math and science, interview, SAT I. Test scores used for admission. ***Application deadline:*** rolling. ***Notification:*** continuous.

APPLYING/TRANSFER ***Required:*** high school transcript, 3 recommendations, college transcript, minimum 2.0 college GPA. ***Recommended:*** interview. ***Entrance:*** moderately difficult. ***Application deadline:*** rolling. ***Notification:*** continuous. ***Contact:*** Ms. Judi Grigsby, Director of Admissions, 513-296-7228.

CONTACT Ms. Judi Grigsby, Director of Admissions, Kettering College of Medical Arts, 3737 Southern Boulevard, Kettering, OH 45429-1299, 513-296-7228. ***Fax:*** 513-296-4238. College video available.

LAKELAND COMMUNITY COLLEGE
Kirtland, Ohio

UG Enrollment: 8,515	**Tuition & Fees (Area Res): $2002**
Application Deadline: 9/21	**Room & Board: N/Avail**

GENERAL State and locally supported, 2-year, coed. Part of Ohio Board of Regents. Awards certificates, transfer associate, terminal associate degrees. Founded 1967. ***Setting:*** 380-acre suburban campus with easy access to Cleveland. ***Endowment:*** $267,012. ***Total enrollment:*** 8,515. ***Faculty:*** 544 (130 full-time, 414 part-time); student-faculty ratio is 16:1.

ENROLLMENT PROFILE 8,515 students: 61% women, 39% men, 72% part-time, 99% state residents, 8% transferred in, 19% have need-based financial aid, 8% have non-need-based financial aid, 53% 25 or older, 1% Native American, 1% Hispanic, 2% African American, 1% Asian American. ***Areas of study chosen:*** 27% business management and administrative services, 26% liberal arts/general studies, 15% health professions and related sciences, 8% engineering and applied sciences, 1% vocational and home economics. ***Most popular recent majors:*** nursing, business administration/commerce/management.

FIRST-YEAR CLASS 2,088 total; 2,643 applied, 100% were accepted, 79% of whom enrolled.

ACADEMIC PROGRAM Core, honor code. Calendar: quarters. 760 courses offered in 1995–96. Academic remediation for entering students, services for LD students, advanced placement, summer session for credit, part-time degree program (daytime, evenings, summer), external degree programs, adult/continuing education programs, co-op programs and internships.

GENERAL DEGREE REQUIREMENTS 96 credit hours; math/science requirements vary according to program; computer course for most majors.

MAJORS Accounting, business administration/commerce/management, civil engineering technology, computer information systems, corrections, criminal justice, data processing, dental services, early childhood education, electrical and electronics technologies, electronics engineering technology, emergency medical technology, engineering technology, fire science, graphic arts, hospitality services, human services, industrial engineering technology, law enforcement/police sciences, liberal arts/general studies, machine and tool technologies, manufacturing technology, mechanical engineering technology, medical laboratory technology, nursing, optometric/ophthalmic technologies, paralegal studies, radiological technology, respiratory therapy, safety and security technologies, science, secretarial studies/office management, tourism and travel.

LIBRARY Lakeland Community College Library with 57,529 books, 176 microform titles, 452 periodicals, 10 CD-ROMs, 760 records, tapes, and CDs. Acquisition spending 1994–95: $121,434.

COMPUTERS ON CAMPUS 500 computers for student use in computer center, computer labs, learning resource center, classrooms, library provide access to off-campus computing facilities, on-line services, Internet. Staffed computer lab on campus provides training in use of computers, software.

COLLEGE LIFE Drama-theater group, choral group, student-run newspaper, radio station. 15% vote in student government elections. ***Social organizations:*** 25 open to all. ***Most popular organizations:*** Campus Activities Board, Gamers Guild, United Students of African Descent, Federation of Lakeland Trekkers, Aikido Club. ***Major annual events:*** Spring Fling, Jazz Festival, Health Educational Programming. ***Student services:*** health clinic, personal-psychological counseling, women's center. ***Campus security:*** 24-hour emergency response devices, student patrols, late-night transport-escort service.

HOUSING College housing not available.

ATHLETICS Member NJCAA. ***Intercollegiate:*** basketball M(s)/W(s), golf M(s), soccer M(s), softball W, tennis M, volleyball W(s). ***Intramural:*** basketball, volleyball, wrestling. ***Contact:*** Mr. Don Delaney, Athletic Director, 216-953-7302.

CAREER PLANNING ***Placement office:*** 2 full-time, 3 part-time staff; $113,500 operating expenditure 1994–95. ***Director:*** Ms. Rebecca Turbok, Director, Career Services, 216-953-7207. ***Services:*** job fairs, resume preparation, resume referral, career counseling, careers library, job bank, job interviews. 95 organizations recruited on campus 1994–95.

AFTER GRADUATION 80% of class of 1994 had job offers within 6 months.

EXPENSES FOR 1995–96 ***Application fee:*** $15. Area resident tuition: $2002 full-time, $41.70 per credit hour part-time. State resident tuition: $2455 full-time, $51.15 per credit hour part-time. Nonresident tuition: $5239 full-time, $109.15 per credit hour part-time.

FINANCIAL AID ***College-administered undergrad aid 1995–96:*** 592 need-based scholarships (average $243), non-need scholarships, short-term loans (average $346), low-interest long-term loans from college funds (average $1481), loans from external sources (average $1884), 76 Federal Work-Study (averaging $1822), part-time jobs. ***Required forms:*** institutional, FAFSA; accepted: CSS Financial Aid PROFILE. ***Priority deadline:*** 7/1. ***Waivers:*** full or partial for employees or children of employees and senior citizens.

APPLYING Open admission except for allied health programs. ***Options:*** early entrance, deferred entrance. ***Required:*** school transcript, TOEFL for international students. ***Required for some:*** SAT I or ACT, ACT ASSET. Test scores used for counseling/placement. ***Application deadline:*** 9/21. ***Notification:*** continuous until 9/21.

APPLYING/TRANSFER ***Required:*** college transcript. ***Entrance:*** noncompetitive. ***Application deadline:*** 9/21. ***Notification:*** continuous until 9/21. ***Contact:*** Ms. Carol Larson, Dean of Counseling, 216-953-7200.

CONTACT Mr. William Kraus, Director for Admissions/Registrar, Lakeland Community College, Kirtland, OH 44094-5198, 216-953-7106. ***Fax:*** 216-953-1692. ***E-mail:*** wkraus@lcc2.lakeland.cc.oh.us.

LIMA TECHNICAL COLLEGE
Lima, Ohio

UG Enrollment: 2,591	**Tuition & Fees (OH Res): $2175**
Application Deadline: rolling	**Room & Board: N/Avail**

LTC, a 2-year public technical college, has 2,600 students. The suburban campus is located an hour from 3 major metropolitan Ohio cities. Degree programs include majors in business, health, public services, and engineering and industrial technologies. Student activities, athletics, and support services are available. Articulation agreements exist with several colleges and universities.

GENERAL State-supported, 2-year, coed. Awards certificates, transfer associate, terminal associate degrees. Founded 1971. ***Setting:*** 565-acre suburban campus. ***Total enrollment:*** 2,591. ***Faculty:*** 167 (100 full-time, 10% with terminal degrees, 67 part-time).

ENROLLMENT PROFILE 2,591 students: 69% women, 50% part-time, 99% state residents, 8% transferred in, 60% have need-based financial aid, 10% have non-need-based financial aid, 0% international, 54% 25 or older, 0% Native American, 1% Hispanic, 6% African American, 0% Asian American. ***Areas of study chosen:*** 31% liberal arts/general studies, 22% business management and administrative services, 20% health professions and related sciences, 14% social sciences, 13% engineering and applied sciences.

FIRST-YEAR CLASS 509 total. Of the students who applied, 100% were accepted, 68% of whom enrolled. 5% from top 10% of their high school class, 20% from top quarter, 40% from top half.

ACADEMIC PROGRAM Core. Calendar: quarters. Academic remediation for entering students, services for LD students, advanced placement, self-designed majors, tutorials, summer session for credit, part-time degree program (daytime, evenings, weekends), external degree programs, adult/continuing education programs, co-op programs and internships.

GENERAL DEGREE REQUIREMENTS 1 math course; computer course; internship (some majors).

MAJORS Accounting, business administration/commerce/management, child care/child and family studies, computer programming, corrections, dental services, dietetics, drafting and design, electronics engineering technology, emergency medical technology, engineering technology, fashion merchandising, finance/banking, human services, industrial administration, industrial engineering technology, law enforcement/police sciences, legal secretarial studies, manufacturing technology, marketing/retailing/merchandising, mechanical design technology, mechanical engineering technology, medical secretarial studies, nursing, paralegal studies, physical therapy, quality control technology, radiological technology, respiratory therapy, retail management, robotics, secretarial studies/office management.

LIBRARY 80,000 books.

COMPUTERS ON CAMPUS 130 computers for student use in computer center, learning resource center, business lab, offices, Discover/Career Center, library provide access to e-mail. Staffed computer lab on campus provides training in use of computers, software.

COLLEGE LIFE Drama-theater group, choral group, student-run newspaper, radio station. ***Most popular organizations:*** Student Senate, Social Activities Board, Ski Club. ***Major annual events:*** May Week, Battle of the Bands, Almost-All-Nighter. ***Campus security:*** late-night transport-escort service.

HOUSING College housing not available.

ATHLETICS ***Intercollegiate:*** basketball M/W, golf M, tennis M/W, volleyball W. ***Intramural:*** basketball, bowling, cross-country running, football, golf, racquetball, skiing (cross-country), skiing (downhill), tennis, volleyball, weight lifting. ***Contact:*** Mr. Rob Livchak, Athletic Director, 419-221-1112 Ext. 281.

CAREER PLANNING ***Director:*** Mr. John Upshaw, Career Counselor, 419-221-1112. ***Services:*** resume preparation, career counseling, careers library, job bank. Students must register sophomore year.

AFTER GRADUATION 12% of students completing a degree program in 1994–95 went directly on to further study.

EXPENSES FOR 1995–96 ***Application fee:*** $10. State resident tuition: $2115 full-time, $58.75 per credit hour part-time. Nonresident tuition: $4230 full-time, $117.50 per credit hour part-time. Part-time mandatory fees: $20 per quarter. Full-time mandatory fees: $60.

FINANCIAL AID ***College-administered undergrad aid 1995–96:*** 50 need-based scholarships (averaging $400), 100 non-need scholarships (averaging $400), low-interest long-term loans from college funds (averaging $200), Federal Work-Study, 50 part-time jobs. ***Required forms:*** CSS Financial Aid PROFILE; accepted: FAFSA. ***Priority deadline:*** 4/15. ***Payment plan:*** deferred payment. ***Waivers:*** full or partial for employees or children of employees.

APPLYING Open admission except for allied health programs. ***Options:*** Common Application, electronic application, early entrance, deferred entrance. ***Recommended:*** 3 years of high school math and science. ***Required for some:*** ACT. Test scores used for counseling/placement. ***Application deadline:*** rolling. ***Notification:*** continuous until 9/22.

APPLYING/TRANSFER ***Recommended:*** 3 years of high school math and science. ***Application deadline:*** rolling. ***Notification:*** continuous until 9/22.

CONTACT Mrs. Julia Candler, Admissions Counselor, Lima Technical College, 4240 Campus Drive, Lima, OH 45804-3597, 419-221-1112 Ext. 317. ***Fax:*** 419-221-0450. ***E-mail:*** petersl@hc.tech.oh.us.

LORAIN COUNTY COMMUNITY COLLEGE
Elyria, Ohio

UG Enrollment: 7,047	Tuition & Fees (Area Res): $2103
Application Deadline: rolling	Room & Board: N/Avail

GENERAL State and locally supported, 2-year, coed. Part of Ohio Board of Regents. Awards certificates, transfer associate, terminal associate degrees. Founded 1963. *Setting:* 480-acre suburban campus with easy access to Cleveland. *Total enrollment:* 7,047. *Faculty:* 347 (112 full-time, 235 part-time); student-faculty ratio is 19:1.
ENROLLMENT PROFILE 7,047 students: 65% women, 66% part-time, 99% state residents, 11% transferred in, 1% international, 54% 25 or older, 1% Native American, 5% Hispanic, 6% African American, 1% Asian American. *Most popular recent majors:* nursing, business administration/commerce/management, elementary education.
FIRST-YEAR CLASS 1,930 total; 2,100 applied, 100% were accepted, 92% of whom enrolled.
ACADEMIC PROGRAM Core. Calendar: quarters. Academic remediation for entering students, English as a second language program offered during academic year, services for LD students, advanced placement, self-designed majors, honors program, summer session for credit, part-time degree program (daytime, evenings), adult/continuing education programs, co-op programs.
GENERAL DEGREE REQUIREMENTS 93 quarter credits; computer course for technology majors.
MAJORS Accounting, art/fine arts, biology/biological sciences, business administration/commerce/management, chemistry, civil engineering technology, communication, computer information systems, computer programming, computer science, computer technologies, corrections, drafting and design, early childhood education, education, electrical and electronics technologies, electronics engineering technology, elementary education, engineering (general), (pre)engineering sequence, engineering technology, finance/banking, fire science, history, journalism, law enforcement/police sciences, liberal arts/general studies, machine and tool technologies, manufacturing technology, marketing/retailing/merchandising, mathematics, mechanical design technology, medical laboratory technology, music, nuclear medical technology, nursing, operating room technology, pharmacy/pharmaceutical sciences, physical education, physics, plastics technology, political science/government, psychology, quality control technology, radiological technology, real estate, retail management, robotics, science, secretarial studies/office management, social science, social work, sociology, sports medicine, theater arts/drama, tourism and travel, urban studies, veterinary sciences.
LIBRARY 104,131 books, 305 microform titles, 750 periodicals, 3,296 records, tapes, and CDs.
COMPUTERS ON CAMPUS 300 computers for student use in academic buildings, library.
COLLEGE LIFE Drama-theater group, choral group, student-run newspaper. 4% vote in student government elections. *Student services:* health clinic, personal-psychological counseling, women's center. *Campus security:* 24-hour emergency response devices and patrols.
HOUSING College housing not available.
ATHLETICS *Intramural:* archery, basketball, volleyball, weight lifting, wrestling.
CAREER PLANNING *Service:* career counseling.
AFTER GRADUATION 80% of students completing a degree program in 1994-95 went directly on to further study.
EXPENSES FOR 1995-96 *Application fee:* $10. Area resident tuition: $2103 full-time, $48.30 per credit part-time. State resident tuition: $2554 full-time, $58.30 per credit part-time. Nonresident tuition: $5300 full-time, $119.30 per credit part-time.
FINANCIAL AID *College-administered undergrad aid 1995-96:* 4,550 need-based scholarships (average $2400), 350 non-need scholarships (average $1250), short-term loans (average $87), low-interest long-term loans from external sources (average $2200), Federal Work-Study, 421 part-time jobs. *Required forms:* state, institutional, FAFSA. *Priority deadline:* 9/20. *Waivers:* full or partial for employees or children of employees and senior citizens.
APPLYING Open admission. *Options:* early entrance, deferred entrance. *Required:* TOEFL for international students. *Recommended:* SAT I or ACT. *Required for some:* school transcript, 3 years of high school math and science, some high school foreign language, Michigan English Language Assessment Battery, ACT ASSET. Test scores used for counseling/placement. *Application deadline:* rolling. *Notification:* continuous.
APPLYING/TRANSFER *Required:* college transcript. *Required for some:* 3 years of high school math and science, some high school foreign language. *Entrance:* noncompetitive. *Application deadline:* rolling. *Notification:* continuous.
CONTACT Dr. John Thrash, Director of Student Development, Lorain County Community College, Elyria, OH 44035, 216-365-4191 Ext. 7525. *Fax:* 216-365-6519. College video available.

MARION TECHNICAL COLLEGE
Marion, Ohio

UG Enrollment: 1,800	Tuition & Fees (OH Res): $2992
Application Deadline: rolling	Room & Board: N/Avail

GENERAL State-related, 2-year, coed. Part of Ohio Board of Regents. Awards certificates, transfer associate, terminal associate degrees. Founded 1971. *Setting:* 180-acre small-town campus with easy access to Columbus. *Total enrollment:* 1,800. *Faculty:* 105 (36 full-time, 100% with terminal degrees, 69 part-time); student-faculty ratio is 17:1. *Notable Alumni:* Linda Pullins, vice president of patient care at Marion General Hospital; Alicia Robinson, distribution estimator for Ohio Edison; James Posegate, medical laboratory technician at South Arizona Medical Center.
ENROLLMENT PROFILE 1,800 students from 4 states and territories, 3 other countries. 68% women, 57% part-time, 98% state residents, 4% transferred in, 1% international, 65% 25 or older, 1% Native American, 1% Hispanic, 5% African American, 1% Asian American. *Areas of study chosen:* 37% business management and administrative services, 26% health professions and related sciences, 17% computer and information sciences, 15% engineering and applied sciences, 5% social sciences. *Most popular recent majors:* nursing, business administration/commerce/management, accounting.
FIRST-YEAR CLASS 456 total; 720 applied, 91% of whom enrolled.
ACADEMIC PROGRAM Hands-on experience curriculum, honor code. Calendar: quarters. 860 courses offered in 1995-96. Academic remediation for entering students, services for LD students, self-designed majors, summer session for credit, part-time degree program (daytime, evenings, weekends, summer), adult/continuing education programs, co-op programs and internships.
GENERAL DEGREE REQUIREMENTS 98 quarter credit hours; computer course.
MAJORS Accounting, business administration/commerce/management, data processing, drafting and design, electrical and electronics technologies, electrical engineering technology, engineering technology, finance/banking, human services, industrial engineering technology, marketing/retailing/merchandising, mechanical engineering technology, medical laboratory technology, medical secretarial studies, nursing, paralegal studies, radiological technology, secretarial studies/office management.
LIBRARY 30,000 books, 200 periodicals. Acquisition spending 1994-95: $14,187.
COMPUTERS ON CAMPUS 100 computers for student use in computer center, student resource center, classrooms provide access to main academic computer, on-line services. Staffed computer lab on campus provides training in use of computers, software.
COLLEGE LIFE *Most popular organization:* Student Admission Committee. *Major annual events:* May Day, Scarlet and Gray Party, Beach Party in Winter. *Campus security:* 24-hour emergency response devices.
HOUSING College housing not available.
ATHLETICS *Intramural:* basketball, football, rugby, skiing (cross-country), skiing (downhill), tennis, volleyball. *Contact:* Mr. Dave Beckel, Director of Student Activities and Recreation, 614-389-6786.
CAREER PLANNING *Placement office:* 2 part-time staff; $34,296 operating expenditure 1994-95. *Director:* Mr. Joel Liles, Director of Admissions and Career Services, 614-389-4636 Ext. 249. *Services:* resume preparation, resume referral, career counseling, careers library, job bank, job interviews.
AFTER GRADUATION 89% of class of 1994 had job offers within 6 months.
EXPENSES FOR 1996-97 *Application fee:* $20. State resident tuition: $2842 full-time, $58 per credit hour part-time. Nonresident tuition: $5047 full-time, $103 per credit hour part-time. Full-time mandatory fees: $150.
FINANCIAL AID *College-administered undergrad aid 1995-96:* 50 need-based scholarships (average $150), 75 non-need scholarships (average $300), short-term loans (average $300), low-interest long-term loans from external sources (average $2000), Federal Work-Study, 48 part-time jobs. *Required forms:* institutional, FAFSA; required for some: state; accepted: CSS Financial Aid PROFILE. *Priority deadline:* 7/15. *Payment plan:* deferred payment. *Waivers:* full or partial for employees or children of employees and senior citizens. *Average indebtedness of graduates:* $4000.
APPLYING Open admission except for nursing, medical laboratory technology, paralegal, human services, radiological technology programs. *Options:* early entrance, deferred entrance, midyear entrance. *Required:* school transcript, TOEFL for international students. *Required for some:* ACT. Test scores used for counseling/placement. *Application deadline:* rolling. *Notification:* continuous.
APPLYING/TRANSFER *Required:* high school transcript, college transcript. *Required for some:* standardized test scores. *Application deadline:* rolling. *Notification:* continuous. *Contact:* Mr. Dennis Budkowski, Vice President of Instruction, 614-389-4636.
CONTACT Mr. Joel O. Liles, Director of Admissions and Career Services, Marion Technical College, Marion, OH 43302-5694, 614-389-4636 Ext. 249. *Fax:* 614-389-6136. College video available.

MERCY COLLEGE OF NORTHWEST OHIO
Toledo, Ohio

Enrollment: N/R	Tuition & Fees: $4467
Application Deadline: 5/1	Room & Board: N/R

GENERAL Independent, 2-year, coed. Awards transfer associate, terminal associate degrees. Founded 1993. *Setting:* urban campus with easy access to Detroit. *Faculty:* 15 (13 full-time, 2 part-time).
ENROLLMENT PROFILE *Areas of study chosen:* 100% health professions and related sciences.
ACADEMIC PROGRAM Core, applied health technologies curriculum. Calendar: quarters. 18 courses offered in 1995-96; average class size 15 in required courses. Academic remediation for entering students, advanced placement, tutorials, summer session for credit, part-time degree program (daytime, evenings, summer), internships. Off-campus study at University of Toledo.
GENERAL DEGREE REQUIREMENTS 108 credit hours; math/science requirements vary according to program; computer course; internship.
MAJORS Nursing, pharmacy/pharmaceutical sciences.
COLLEGE LIFE Student-run newspaper. *Student services:* health clinic, personal-psychological counseling. *Campus security:* 24-hour emergency response devices and patrols, late-night transport-escort service, controlled dormitory access.
HOUSING No special consideration for freshman housing applicants. Off-campus living permitted.
EXPENSES FOR 1995-96 *Application fee:* $25. Tuition: $4392 (minimum) full-time, $122 per credit hour part-time. Part-time mandatory fees: $25 per quarter. Full-time tuition ranges up to $6954 according to class level. Full-time mandatory fees: $75.
APPLYING *Required:* essay, SAT I or ACT. *Required for some:* school transcript, minimum 2.0 GPA, 3 years of high school math and science. Test scores used for admission. *Application deadline:* 5/1. *Notification:* continuous.
APPLYING/TRANSFER *Required:* essay, standardized test scores, college transcript, minimum 2.0 college GPA. *Required for some:* high school transcript, 3 years of high school math and science, minimum 2.0 high school GPA. *Entrance:* moderately difficult. *Application deadline:* 5/1. *Notification:* continuous. *Contact:* Ms. Shelly McCoy, Registrar/Admissions Coordinator, 419-259-1313.
CONTACT Ms. Shelly McCoy, Registrar/Admissions Coordinator, Mercy College of Northwest Ohio, 2238 Jefferson Avenue, Toledo, OH 43624-1197, 419-259-1313.

MIAMI-JACOBS COLLEGE
Dayton, Ohio

UG Enrollment: 410 **Tuition & Fees: $6650**
Application Deadline: 8/15 **Room & Board: N/Avail**

GENERAL Proprietary, 2-year, primarily women. Awards diplomas, terminal associate degrees. Founded 1860. ***Setting:*** small-town campus. ***Total enrollment:*** 410. ***Faculty:*** 30 (6 full-time, 24 part-time); student-faculty ratio is 14:1.
ENROLLMENT PROFILE 410 students: 86% women, 23% part-time, 100% state residents, 7% transferred in, 48% 25 or older, 0% Native American, 0% Hispanic, 14% African American. ***Areas of study chosen:*** 60% business management and administrative services, 40% health professions and related sciences.
FIRST-YEAR CLASS 467 applied, 94% were accepted, 84% of whom enrolled.
ACADEMIC PROGRAM Core. Calendar: quarters. Academic remediation for entering students, honors program, summer session for credit, part-time degree program (daytime, evenings), internships. Off-campus study at Southern Ohio Council for Higher Education.
GENERAL DEGREE REQUIREMENTS 102 credits; 6 credits of math; computer course; internship.
MAJORS Accounting, business administration/commerce/management, legal secretarial studies, marketing/retailing/merchandising, medical assistant technologies, medical secretarial studies, secretarial studies/office management.
LIBRARY 5,000 books, 60 periodicals, 265 records, tapes, and CDs.
COMPUTERS ON CAMPUS 67 computers for student use in computer labs. Staffed computer lab on campus provides training in use of computers, software.
COLLEGE LIFE ***Social organizations:*** 5 open to all. ***Most popular organizations:*** Student Governing Board, Business Technologies Club, Collegiate Secretaries International, Dayton Legal Secretary's Association. ***Major annual events:*** Spring Fling, Fall Party, Christmas Party. ***Student services:*** personal-psychological counseling. ***Campus security:*** late-night transport-escort service.
HOUSING College housing not available.
CAREER PLANNING ***Placement office:*** 1 full-time, 1 part-time staff. ***Director:*** Ms. Angela Vance, Career Resources Director, 513-461-5174 Ext. 147. ***Service:*** career counseling.
EXPENSES FOR 1996–97 ***Application fee:*** $25. Tuition: $6650 full-time, $135 per credit part-time. Tuition guaranteed not to increase for student's term of enrollment.
FINANCIAL AID ***College-administered undergrad aid 1995–96:*** need-based scholarships, low-interest long-term loans, Federal Work-Study, 25 part-time jobs. ***Required forms:*** state, institutional; accepted: CSS Financial Aid PROFILE. ***Priority deadline:*** 8/15. ***Payment plans:*** installment, deferred payment. ***Waivers:*** full or partial for employees or children of employees.
APPLYING ***Options:*** early entrance, deferred entrance. ***Required:*** essay, school transcript, interview, TOEFL for international students, Wonderlic aptitude test. ***Recommended:*** recommendations, SAT I or ACT. ***Required for some:*** ACT. Test scores used for admission and counseling/placement. ***Application deadline:*** 8/15. ***Notification:*** continuous until 8/25.
APPLYING/TRANSFER ***Required:*** essay, standardized test scores, high school transcript, interview. ***Recommended:*** recommendations, college transcript. ***Entrance:*** minimally difficult. ***Application deadline:*** rolling. ***Notification:*** continuous until 8/24. ***Contact:*** Ms. Darlene R. Waite, Vice President of Academic and Student Affairs, 513-461-5174.
CONTACT Ms. Darlene R. Waite, Vice President of Academic and Student Affairs, Miami-Jacobs College, Dayton, OH 45401-1433, 513-461-5174.

MIAMI UNIVERSITY–HAMILTON CAMPUS
Hamilton, Ohio

UG Enrollment: 2,324 **Tuition & Fees (OH Res): $3368**
Application Deadline: rolling **Room & Board: N/Avail**

GENERAL State-supported, 2-year, coed. Part of Miami University System. Awards certificates, transfer associate, terminal associate degrees (also offers up to 2 years of most baccalaureate programs offered at Miami University main campus). Founded 1968. ***Setting:*** 78-acre suburban campus with easy access to Cincinnati. Faculty: 140 (75 full-time, 65 part-time).
ENROLLMENT PROFILE 2,324 students from 3 states and territories, 1 other country. 62% women, 38% men, 61% part-time, 99% state residents, 4% transferred in, 38% 25 or older, 1% Native American, 1% Hispanic, 3% African American, 1% Asian American. ***Most popular recent majors:*** nursing, business administration/commerce/management.
FIRST-YEAR CLASS 458 total. Of the students who applied, 100% were accepted, 68% of whom enrolled. 25% from top 10% of their high school class, 77% from top half.
ACADEMIC PROGRAM Core, honor code. Calendar: semesters summer sessions. Academic remediation for entering students, services for LD students, advanced placement, self-designed majors, summer session for credit, part-time degree program (daytime, evenings, summer), adult/continuing education programs, co-op programs and internships. Study abroad in Luxembourg. ROTC: Naval (c), Air Force (c).
GENERAL DEGREE REQUIREMENTS 64 credits; math/science requirements vary according to program.
MAJORS Accounting, business administration/commerce/management, computer technologies, electrical and electronics technologies, electrical engineering technology, electromechanical technology, engineering technology, finance/banking, insurance, liberal arts/general studies, manufacturing technology, nursing, real estate, secretarial studies/office management.
LIBRARY Rentschler Library with 66,000 books, 280 microform titles, 377 periodicals, 1 on-line bibliographic service, 10 CD-ROMs, 455 records, tapes, and CDs.
COMPUTERS ON CAMPUS 100 computers for student use in computer center, computer labs, learning resource center provide access to main academic computer, e-mail, on-line services.
COLLEGE LIFE Drama-theater group, choral group. 20% vote in student government elections. ***Social organizations:*** 17 open to all. ***Most popular organizations:*** Student Government, Campus Activities Committee, Organization for Wiser Learners, Community Empowerment Committee, Minority Action Committee. ***Major annual events:*** New Student Orientation, Springfest, Fall Picnic. ***Student services:*** personal-psychological counseling. ***Campus security:*** 24-hour patrols, late-night transport-escort service.
HOUSING College housing not available.
ATHLETICS ***Intercollegiate:*** baseball M, basketball M/W, golf M/W, tennis M/W, volleyball W. ***Intramural:*** basketball, bowling, golf, skiing (cross-country), soccer, softball, tennis, volleyball, weight lifting. ***Contact:*** Ms. Karen Murray, Coordinator of Recreational Sports and Athletics, 513-785-3120.
CAREER PLANNING ***Placement office:*** 2 full-time, 1 part-time staff. ***Director:*** Dr. Shelley Cassady, Placement Coordinator and Co-op Director, 513-785-3113 Ext. 313. ***Services:*** job fairs, resume preparation, resume referral, career counseling, careers library, job bank, job interviews. 15 organizations recruited on campus 1994–95.
EXPENSES FOR 1995–96 ***Application fee:*** $25. State resident tuition: $3066 full-time. Nonresident tuition: $9876 full-time. Part-time mandatory fees per semester range from $19 to $139. Part-time tuition per credit hour ranges from $116 to $133 for state residents, $343 to $360 for nonresidents according to course load. Full-time mandatory fees: $302.
FINANCIAL AID ***College-administered undergrad aid 1995–96:*** 152 need-based scholarships (average $1374), 72 non-need scholarships (average $3148), short-term loans, low-interest long-term loans from college funds (average $828), loans from external sources (average $2939), 74 Federal Work-Study (averaging $1381), 80 part-time jobs. ***Required forms:*** FAFSA. ***Priority deadline:*** 2/15. ***Payment plan:*** installment. ***Waivers:*** full or partial for employees or children of employees. ***Notification:*** 3/15. ***Average indebtedness of graduates:*** $9487.
APPLYING Open admission except for nursing program, transfer students. ***Option:*** early entrance. ***Required:*** school transcript. ***Recommended:*** 3 years of high school math and science, some high school foreign language. ***Required for some:*** SAT I or ACT, TOEFL for international students. Test scores used for counseling/placement. ***Application deadline:*** rolling. ***Notification:*** continuous.
APPLYING/TRANSFER ***Required:*** high school transcript. ***Recommended:*** 3 years of high school math and science, some high school foreign language. ***Required for some:*** standardized test scores. ***Entrance:*** minimally difficult. ***Application deadline:*** rolling. ***Notification:*** continuous.
CONTACT Mr. Archie Nelson, Assistant Director of Admissions, Miami University–Hamilton Campus, Hamilton, OH 45011-3399, 513-863-8833 Ext. 208.

MIAMI UNIVERSITY–MIDDLETOWN CAMPUS
Middletown, Ohio

UG Enrollment: 2,296 **Tuition & Fees (OH Res): $3368**
Application Deadline: rolling **Room & Board: N/Avail**

GENERAL State-supported, 2-year, coed. Part of Miami University System. Awards certificates, transfer associate, terminal associate degrees (also offers up to 2 years of most baccalaureate programs offered at Miami University main campus). Founded 1966. ***Setting:*** 141-acre small-town campus with easy access to Cincinnati and Dayton. Faculty: 165 (65 full-time, 70% with terminal degrees, 100 part-time); student-faculty ratio is 19:1.
ENROLLMENT PROFILE 2,296 students: 65% women, 35% men, 55% part-time, 100% state residents, 5% transferred in, 0% international, 40% 25 or older, 1% Native American, 1% Hispanic, 2% African American, 1% Asian American. ***Areas of study chosen:*** 18% health professions and related sciences, 17% education, 13% business management and administrative services, 5% social sciences, 4% biological and life sciences, 4% computer and information sciences, 4% engineering and applied sciences, 3% psychology, 1% communications and journalism.
FIRST-YEAR CLASS 468 total; 508 applied, 100% were accepted, 92% of whom enrolled. 27% from top 10% of their high school class, 28% from top quarter, 40% from top half.
ACADEMIC PROGRAM Core, liberal education curriculum. Calendar: semesters. Academic remediation for entering students, English as a second language program, services for LD students, advanced placement, self-designed majors, Freshman Honors College, tutorials, honors program, summer session for credit, part-time degree program (daytime, evenings, summer), adult/continuing education programs, co-op programs and internships. Off-campus study at members of the Greater Cincinnati Consortium of Colleges and Universities. Study abroad in Luxembourg. ROTC: Naval (c), Air Force (c).
GENERAL DEGREE REQUIREMENTS 64 semester hours; 1 math/science course.
MAJORS Accounting, anthropology, art/fine arts, botany/plant sciences, business administration/commerce/management, business economics, business machine technologies, chemical engineering technology, chemistry, communication, computer information systems, computer science, computer technologies, early childhood education, economics, education, electrical engineering technology, electromechanical technology, elementary education, engineering and applied sciences, (pre)engineering sequence, engineering technology, English, finance/banking, geography, geology, history, industrial engineering technology, information science, legal secretarial studies, liberal arts/general studies, manufacturing technology, marketing/retailing/merchandising, mathematics, mechanical engineering technology, medical secretarial studies, nursing, philosophy, physics, political science/government, psychology, radiological technology, real estate, science, secretarial studies/office management, sociology, systems science, zoology.
LIBRARY Gardner-Harvey Library with 79,100 books, 7,362 microform titles, 473 periodicals, 20 CD-ROMs, 6,175 records, tapes, and CDs. Acquisition spending 1994–95: $113,500.
COMPUTERS ON CAMPUS 150 computers for student use in computer center, computer labs, learning resource center, academic buildings, classrooms, library provide access to main academic computer, off-campus computing facilities, e-mail, on-line services, Internet. Staffed computer lab on campus provides training in use of computers, software. Academic computing expenditure 1994–95: $250,000.
NOTEWORTHY RESEARCH FACILITIES Center for Applied Research.
COLLEGE LIFE Drama-theater group, choral group, student-run newspaper, radio station. ***Social organizations:*** 28 open to all. ***Most popular organizations:*** Student Radio Station, Student Newspaper, Student Nurses Association, Model United Nations, Program Board. ***Student services:*** personal-psychological counseling, women's center. ***Campus security:*** 24-hour patrols, late-night transport-escort service.
HOUSING College housing not available.
ATHLETICS ***Intercollegiate:*** baseball M(c), basketball M(c)/W(c), golf M(c)/W(c), tennis M(c)/W(c), volleyball W(c). ***Intramural:*** basketball, football, golf, racquetball, skiing (cross-country), skiing (downhill), soccer, softball, table tennis (Ping-Pong), tennis, volleyball, weight lifting. ***Contact:*** Mr. James Sliger, Director of Athletics, 513-727-3317.

CAREER PLANNING *Placement office:* 2 full-time staff; $32,000 operating expenditure 1994–95. *Director:* Ms. Kim Ernsting, Coordinator of Placement and Cooperative Education, 513-727-3431. *Services:* resume preparation, career counseling, careers library, job bank, job interviews.
EXPENSES FOR 1995–96 *Application fee:* $25. State resident tuition: $3066 (minimum) full-time. Nonresident tuition: $8496 (minimum) full-time. Part-time tuition per semester hour ranges from $116 to $133 for state residents, $343 to $360 for nonresidents. Part-time mandatory fees per semester hour range from $19 to $139. Full-time tuition ranges up to $3460 for residents, $8890 for nonresidents according to class level. Full-time mandatory fees: $302.
FINANCIAL AID *College-administered undergrad aid 1995–96:* 199 need-based scholarships (averaging $815), 40 non-need scholarships (averaging $561), short-term loans (averaging $507), low-interest long-term loans from college funds (averaging $1342), loans from external sources (averaging $2188), Federal Work-Study, 118 part-time jobs. *Required forms:* FAFSA; accepted: CSS Financial Aid PROFILE, state, institutional. *Priority deadline:* 2/15. *Payment plan:* installment. *Waivers:* full or partial for employees or children of employees and senior citizens.
APPLYING Open admission except for nursing program. *Options:* early entrance, deferred entrance, midyear entrance. *Required:* school transcript, SAT I or ACT, TOEFL for international students. Test scores used for counseling/placement. *Application deadline:* rolling. *Notification:* continuous.
APPLYING/TRANSFER *Required:* standardized test scores, high school transcript, college transcript, minimum 2.0 college GPA. *Entrance:* noncompetitive. *Application deadline:* rolling. *Notification:* continuous. *Contact:* Mr. David Johnson, Director of Records and Registration, 513-727-3217.
CONTACT Mrs. Mary Lu Flynn, Director of Enrollment Services, Miami University–Middletown Campus, Middletown, OH 45042-3497, 513-727-7216. *Fax:* 513-727-3223. *E-mail:* mlflynn@miavx3.mid.muohio.edu.

MUSKINGUM AREA TECHNICAL COLLEGE
Zanesville, Ohio

UG Enrollment: 2,135	Tuition & Fees (OH Res): $2145
Application Deadline: rolling	Room & Board: N/Avail

GENERAL State and locally supported, 2-year, coed. Awards terminal associate degrees. Founded 1969. *Setting:* 170-acre small-town campus with easy access to Columbus. *Total enrollment:* 2,135. *Faculty:* 104 (40 full-time, 64 part-time).
ENROLLMENT PROFILE 2,135 students: 63% women, 65% part-time, 99% state residents, 5% transferred in, 45% 25 or older, 1% Native American, 1% Hispanic, 3% African American, 1% Asian American. *Most popular recent majors:* criminal justice, accounting, business administration/commerce/management.
FIRST-YEAR CLASS 895 applied, 100% were accepted.
ACADEMIC PROGRAM Core. Calendar: quarters. Academic remediation for entering students, services for LD students, self-designed majors, honors program, summer session for credit, part-time degree program (daytime, evenings, summer), adult/continuing education programs, co-op programs and internships. Off-campus study at Ohio University–Zanesville.
GENERAL DEGREE REQUIREMENTS 110 credits; math/science requirements vary according to program; computer course.
MAJORS Accounting, automotive technologies, business administration/commerce/management, child psychology/child development, criminal justice, data processing, electrical and electronics technologies, environmental sciences, fashion merchandising, manufacturing technology, marketing/retailing/merchandising, medical assistant technologies, mental health/rehabilitation counseling, occupational therapy, paralegal studies, parks management, radiological technology, recreation and leisure services, secretarial studies/office management, social work, tourism and travel.
COMPUTERS ON CAMPUS 110 computers for student use in computer labs, business lab. Staffed computer lab on campus.
COLLEGE LIFE Student-run newspaper. *Student services:* personal-psychological counseling.
HOUSING College housing not available.
ATHLETICS *Intramural:* basketball, bowling, football, volleyball.
CAREER PLANNING *Director:* Mr. Herb Davis, Director of Career Services, 614-454-2501 Ext. 222. *Service:* career counseling.
EXPENSES FOR 1995–96 *Application fee:* $25. State resident tuition: $2115 full-time, $47 per credit hour part-time. Nonresident tuition: $3465 full-time, $77 per credit hour part-time. Full-time mandatory fees: $30.
FINANCIAL AID *College-administered undergrad aid 1995–96:* need-based scholarships, short-term loans, low-interest long-term loans from college funds, loans from external sources, Federal Work-Study. *Required forms:* CSS Financial Aid PROFILE, state, institutional. *Priority deadline:* 6/15.
APPLYING Open admission except for health technology programs. *Option:* early entrance. *Required:* school transcript, CPPT. *Recommended:* 3 years of high school math and science, SAT I or ACT. *Required for some:* recommendations, interview, SAT II Subject Tests, TOEFL for international students. Test scores used for admission (ACT, SAT) and counseling/placement (CPPT). *Application deadline:* rolling. *Notification:* continuous.
APPLYING/TRANSFER *Required:* standardized test scores, high school transcript, college transcript. *Recommended:* 3 years of high school math and science. *Required for some:* recommendations, interview. *Entrance:* noncompetitive. *Application deadline:* rolling. *Notification:* continuous.
CONTACT Mr. Tim L. Shepfer, Director of Admissions/Alumni Officer, Muskingum Area Technical College, Zanesville, OH 43701-2694, 614-454-2501 Ext. 225 or toll-free 800-686-TECH (in-state).

NORTH CENTRAL TECHNICAL COLLEGE
Mansfield, Ohio

UG Enrollment: 2,601	Tuition & Fees (OH Res): $2590
Application Deadline: rolling	Room & Board: N/Avail

GENERAL State-supported, 2-year, coed. Part of Ohio Board of Regents. Awards certificates, terminal associate degrees. Founded 1961. *Setting:* 600-acre suburban campus with easy access to Cleveland and Columbus. *Educational spending 1994–95:* $1580 per undergrad. *Total enrollment:* 2,601. *Faculty:* 182 (78 full-time, 9% with terminal degrees, 104 part-time).
ENROLLMENT PROFILE 2,601 students: 66% women, 34% men, 57% part-time, 100% state residents, 8% transferred in, 56% have need-based financial aid, 1% have non-need-based financial aid, 0% international, 60% 25 or older, 1% Native American, 1% Hispanic, 5% African American, 1% Asian American. *Areas of study chosen:* 29% health professions and related sciences, 26% business management and administrative services, 19% social sciences, 15% engineering and applied sciences, 8% computer and information sciences, 3% education. *Most popular recent majors:* nursing, criminal justice, business administration/commerce/management.
FIRST-YEAR CLASS 440 total; 667 applied, 100% were accepted, 66% of whom enrolled.
ACADEMIC PROGRAM Honor code. Calendar: quarters. 555 courses offered in 1995–96. Academic remediation for entering students, services for LD students, advanced placement, self-designed majors, summer session for credit, part-time degree program (daytime, evenings), adult/continuing education programs, internships.
GENERAL DEGREE REQUIREMENTS 100 quarter hours; computer course for business, engineering, early childhood, therapeutic recreation majors; internship (some majors).
MAJORS Accounting, biomedical technologies, business administration/commerce/management, child care/child and family studies, computer information systems, computer programming, criminal justice, drafting and design, early childhood education, electrical and electronics technologies, electronics engineering technology, finance/banking, food services management, heating/refrigeration/air conditioning, hotel and restaurant management, human services, machine and tool technologies, manufacturing technology, mechanical engineering technology, nursing, paralegal studies, pharmacy/pharmaceutical sciences, physical therapy, quality control technology, radiological technology, recreation therapy, respiratory therapy, secretarial studies/office management.
LIBRARY 52,700 books, 106 microform titles, 450 periodicals, 15,000 records, tapes, and CDs. Acquisition spending 1994–95: $159,120.
COMPUTERS ON CAMPUS 144 computers for student use in computer center, Comprehensive Learning Center. Staffed computer lab on campus. Academic computing expenditure 1994–95: $304,128.
COLLEGE LIFE Choral group. *Social organizations:* 2 open to all. *Most popular organizations:* Student Programming Board, Choral Group. *Major annual event:* May Daze. *Student services:* personal-psychological counseling. *Campus security:* 24-hour emergency response devices and patrols, late-night transport-escort service.
HOUSING College housing not available.
ATHLETICS *Intramural:* basketball, football, golf, softball, table tennis (Ping-Pong), tennis, volleyball.
CAREER PLANNING *Placement office:* 1 full-time, 1 part-time staff; $30,275 operating expenditure 1994–95. *Director:* Ms. Peg Moir, Director of Counseling and Career Services, 419-755-4896. *Services:* job fairs, resume preparation, resume referral, career counseling, careers library, job bank, job interviews. 55 organizations recruited on campus 1994–95.
AFTER GRADUATION 94% of class of 1994 had job offers within 6 months.
EXPENSES FOR 1995–96 *Application fee:* $35. State resident tuition: $2590 full-time, $51.80 per quarter hour part-time. Nonresident tuition: $4865 full-time, $97.30 per quarter hour part-time.
FINANCIAL AID *College-administered undergrad aid 1995–96:* 16 need-based scholarships (average $600), 21 non-need scholarships (average $2050), low-interest long-term loans from external sources (average $2187), Federal Work-Study. *Required forms:* institutional; accepted: CSS Financial Aid PROFILE, FAFSA. *Priority deadline:* 9/1. *Payment plan:* deferred payment. *Waivers:* full or partial for employees or children of employees and senior citizens. *Notification:* continuous.
APPLYING Open admission. *Options:* early entrance, deferred entrance, midyear entrance. *Required:* TOEFL for international students, ACT ASSET. *Required for some:* school transcript. Test scores used for counseling/placement. *Application deadline:* rolling. *Notification:* continuous.
APPLYING/TRANSFER *Recommended:* college transcript. *Required for some:* college transcript. *Entrance:* noncompetitive. *Application deadline:* rolling. *Notification:* continuous. *Contact:* Mr. Mark J. Monnes, Director of Admissions, 419-755-4824.
CONTACT Ms. Stevi Bowler, Admission Secretary, North Central Technical College, PO Box 698, Mansfield, OH 44901-0698, 419-755-4888. College video available.

NORTHWESTERN COLLEGE
Lima, Ohio

UG Enrollment: 1,800	Tuition & Fees: $5130
Application Deadline: rolling	Room Only: $1800

GENERAL Independent, 2-year, coed. Awards transfer associate degrees. Founded 1920. *Setting:* 35-acre small-town campus with easy access to Toledo and Dayton. *Total enrollment:* 1,800. *Faculty:* 59 (43 full-time, 16 part-time).
ENROLLMENT PROFILE 1,800 students from 10 states and territories. 50% women, 11% part-time, 99% state residents, 55% live on campus, 1% transferred in, 0% international, 14% 25 or older, 1% Hispanic, 10% African American. *Most popular recent majors:* automotive technologies, secretarial studies/office management.
FIRST-YEAR CLASS 1,200 total. Of the students who applied, 98% were accepted, 58% of whom enrolled. 5% from top 10% of their high school class, 20% from top quarter, 75% from top half.
ACADEMIC PROGRAM Core. Calendar: quarters. 26 courses offered in 1995–96. Academic remediation for entering students, advanced placement, tutorials, summer session for credit, part-time degree program (daytime, evenings, weekends), adult/continuing education programs, co-op programs.
GENERAL DEGREE REQUIREMENTS 108 credits; 1 math course; computer course.

Ohio

Northwestern College (continued)
MAJORS Accounting, automotive technologies, business administration/commerce/management, computer technologies, legal secretarial studies, marketing/retailing/merchandising, medical assistant technologies, medical secretarial studies, secretarial studies/office management.
LIBRARY 4,000 books, 80 periodicals. Acquisition spending 1994–95: $25,000.
COMPUTERS ON CAMPUS 55 computers for student use in computer center, auto school classroom. Staffed computer lab on campus provides training in use of computers, software. Academic computing expenditure 1994–95: $75,000.
COLLEGE LIFE Orientation program (2 days, no cost). *Social organizations:* 10 open to all. *Major annual events:* Mud Volleyball, Car Show. *Student services:* personal-psychological counseling. *Campus security:* 24-hour emergency response devices and patrols.
HOUSING 750 college housing spaces available; all were occupied 1995–96. Freshmen given priority for college housing. On-campus residence required through sophomore year except if living with relatives. *Option:* coed housing available. Resident assistants live in dorms.
ATHLETICS *Intramural:* basketball, bowling, skiing (downhill), volleyball, weight lifting.
CAREER PLANNING *Placement office:* 2 full-time staff. *Director:* Mr. Tom Frail, Director of Career Services, 419-227-3141. *Services:* resume preparation, resume referral, career counseling, job bank, job interviews. Students must register freshman year.
AFTER GRADUATION 40% of students completing a degree program in 1994–95 went directly on to further study.
EXPENSES FOR 1995–96 *Application fee:* $50. Tuition: $5130 (minimum) full-time, $95 per credit part-time. Full-time tuition ranges up to $7495. College room only: $1800. Tuition guaranteed not to increase for student's term of enrollment.
FINANCIAL AID *College-administered undergrad aid 1995–96:* need-based scholarships, non-need scholarships, Federal Work-Study, part-time jobs. *Acceptable forms:* CSS Financial Aid PROFILE, state, FAFSA. *Priority deadline:* 8/16. *Payment plan:* installment. *Waivers:* full or partial for employees or children of employees.
APPLYING Open admission. *Options:* early entrance, deferred entrance, midyear entrance. *Required:* school transcript, TOEFL for international students. *Recommended:* SAT I or ACT. Test scores used for counseling/placement. *Application deadline:* rolling.
APPLYING/TRANSFER *Required:* high school transcript, college transcript. *Recommended:* standardized test scores. *Application deadline:* rolling.
CONTACT Mr. Jack Fitzgerald, Senior Vice President, Northwestern College, Lima, OH 45805-1498, 419-227-3141. *Fax:* 419-229-6926. College video available.

NORTHWEST STATE COMMUNITY COLLEGE
Archbold, Ohio

UG Enrollment: 1,991	Tuition & Fees (OH Res): $2914
Application Deadline: rolling	Room & Board: N/Avail

GENERAL State-supported, 2-year, coed. Part of Ohio Board of Regents. Awards certificates, transfer associate, terminal associate degrees. Founded 1968. *Setting:* 87-acre rural campus with easy access to Toledo. *Total enrollment:* 1,991. *Faculty:* 115 (41 full-time, 10% with terminal degrees, 74 part-time); student-faculty ratio is 15:1.
ENROLLMENT PROFILE 1,991 students from 4 states and territories. 65% women, 35% men, 68% part-time, 98% state residents, 26% transferred in, 0% international, 52% 25 or older, 1% Native American, 5% Hispanic, 1% African American, 1% Asian American. *Areas of study chosen:* 29% health professions and related sciences, 26% business management and administrative services, 11% engineering and applied sciences, 6% social sciences, 5% liberal arts/general studies, 4% computer and information sciences. *Most popular recent majors:* accounting, nursing, business administration/commerce/management.
FIRST-YEAR CLASS 702 total; 1,136 applied, 100% were accepted, 62% of whom enrolled. 9% from top 10% of their high school class, 28% from top quarter, 61% from top half.
ACADEMIC PROGRAM Core. Calendar: semesters. 332 courses offered in 1995–96; average class size 17 in required courses. Academic remediation for entering students, services for LD students, self-designed majors, summer session for credit, part-time degree program (daytime, evenings, weekends, summer), external degree programs, adult/continuing education programs, co-op programs and internships.
GENERAL DEGREE REQUIREMENTS 62 semester hours; 1 college algebra course; computer course; internship (some majors).
MAJORS Accounting, business administration/commerce/management, child care/child and family studies, computer programming, computer technologies, criminal justice, drafting and design, early childhood education, electrical engineering technology, finance/banking, human services, industrial engineering technology, legal secretarial studies, marketing/retailing/merchandising, mechanical engineering technology, medical records services, medical secretarial studies, nursing, paralegal studies, quality control technology, real estate, secretarial studies/office management, word processing.
LIBRARY 16,748 books, 58 microform titles, 284 periodicals, 2,426 records, tapes, and CDs. Acquisition spending 1994–95: $166,709.
COMPUTERS ON CAMPUS 214 computers for student use in computer center, computer labs, learning resource center, classrooms, library provide access to main academic computer, e-mail, on-line services, Internet. Staffed computer lab on campus provides training in use of computers, software. Academic computing expenditure 1994–95: $239,921.
COLLEGE LIFE *Social organizations:* 2 open to all. *Most popular organizations:* Student Body Organization, Student Nurses Association. *Major annual events:* Spring Fling, Student Appreciation Days, Graduate Luncheon. *Student services:* personal-psychological counseling. *Campus security:* evening security patrols.
HOUSING College housing not available.
ATHLETICS *Intramural:* basketball, bowling, volleyball. *Contact:* Mr. Keith Van Horn, Coordinator of Student Activities, 419-267-5511.
CAREER PLANNING *Placement office:* 2 full-time staff; $254,168 operating expenditure 1994–95. *Director:* Ms. Natalie Brandon, Coordinator of Career Services, 419-267-5511 Ext. 330. *Services:* job fairs, resume preparation, resume referral, career counseling, careers library, job bank, job interviews. 270 organizations recruited on campus 1994–95.
AFTER GRADUATION 94% of class of 1994 had job offers within 6 months.

EXPENSES FOR 1996–97 *Application fee:* $10. State resident tuition: $2914 full-time, $94 per semester hour part-time. Nonresident tuition: $5487 full-time, $177 per semester hour part-time.
FINANCIAL AID *College-administered undergrad aid 1995–96:* 245 need-based scholarships (average $200), 100 non-need scholarships (average $2700), low-interest long-term loans from external sources (average $2625), 30 Federal Work-Study (averaging $900). *Required forms:* institutional, FAFSA. *Priority deadline:* 6/1. *Payment plan:* deferred payment. *Waivers:* full or partial for employees or children of employees and senior citizens.
APPLYING Open admission. *Options:* early entrance, deferred entrance, midyear entrance. *Required:* school transcript, TOEFL for international students, ACT ASSET. *Recommended:* 3 years of high school math and science. Test scores used for counseling/placement. *Application deadline:* rolling.
APPLYING/TRANSFER *Required:* high school transcript, college transcript. *Recommended:* 3 years of high school math and science. *Entrance:* noncompetitive. *Application deadline:* rolling. *Contact:* Mr. Dennis Gable, Dean of Student Services, 419-267-5511 Ext. 318.
CONTACT Mr. Dennis Gable, Dean of Student Services, Northwest State Community College, Archbold, OH 43502-9542, 419-267-5511 Ext. 318. *Fax:* 419-267-3688.

OHIO INSTITUTE OF PHOTOGRAPHY AND TECHNOLOGY
Dayton, Ohio

UG Enrollment: 373	Tuition & Fees: $7110
Application Deadline: rolling	Room & Board: N/Avail

GENERAL Proprietary, 2-year, coed. Awards diplomas, terminal associate degrees. Founded 1971. *Setting:* 2-acre urban campus with easy access to Columbus and Cincinnati. *Total enrollment:* 373. *Faculty:* 30 (12 full-time, 18 part-time); student-faculty ratio is 14:1. *Notable Alumni:* Dawn Meifert; Tim Courlas; Terry Walburg; Mark Heatley.
ENROLLMENT PROFILE 373 students from 14 states and territories, 2 other countries. 69% women, 31% men, 19% part-time, 70% state residents, 15% transferred in, 78% have need-based financial aid, 1% have non-need-based financial aid, 1% international, 23% 25 or older, 1% Native American, 1% Hispanic, 8% African American, 0% Asian American. *Areas of study chosen:* 65% performing arts, 35% health professions and related sciences.
FIRST-YEAR CLASS 299 total; 499 applied, 99% were accepted, 60% of whom enrolled. 10% from top 10% of their high school class, 30% from top quarter, 85% from top half.
ACADEMIC PROGRAM Core, honor code. Calendar: quarters. Average class size 15 in required courses. Self-designed majors, tutorials, summer session for credit, part-time degree program (daytime, evenings), co-op programs and internships.
GENERAL DEGREE REQUIREMENTS 96 credit hours; computer course; internship (some majors).
MAJORS Computer graphics, medical assistant technologies, photography.
LIBRARY 640 books, 35 periodicals, 6 CD-ROMs, 43 records, tapes, and CDs. Acquisition spending 1994–95: $5400.
COMPUTERS ON CAMPUS 35 computers for student use in computer labs, library. Staffed computer lab on campus provides training in use of computers, software. Academic computing expenditure 1994–95: $35,000.
COLLEGE LIFE *Major annual events:* Welcome Picnic, Annual Rib-Off. *Campus security:* 24-hour emergency response devices.
HOUSING College housing not available.
CAREER PLANNING *Placement office:* 1 full-time staff. *Director:* Ms. Helen Morris, Director of Education, 513-294-6155. *Services:* resume preparation, career counseling, careers library, job bank.
AFTER GRADUATION 63% of class of 1994 had job offers within 6 months.
EXPENSES FOR 1995–96 *Application fee:* $100. Tuition: $7110 (minimum) full-time. Full-time tuition ranges up to $13,818 according to program. Part-time tuition and fees per credit hour: $102 for general studies, $250 for lab courses.
FINANCIAL AID *College-administered undergrad aid 1995–96:* need-based scholarships, 2 non-need scholarships (averaging $500), low-interest long-term loans from external sources (averaging $2500), 6 Federal Work-Study (averaging $480), 24 part-time jobs. *Acceptable forms:* CSS Financial Aid PROFILE, state, institutional, FAFSA. *Priority deadline:* 8/15. *Payment plan:* installment.
APPLYING *Options:* early entrance, deferred entrance. *Required:* interview, TOEFL for international students, CPAt. *Application deadline:* rolling. *Notification:* continuous.
APPLYING/TRANSFER *Required:* college transcript. *Entrance:* moderately difficult. *Application deadline:* rolling. *Notification:* continuous.
CONTACT Mr. David Evans, Executive Director, Ohio Institute of Photography and Technology, 2029 Edgefield Road, Dayton, OH 45439-1917, 513-294-6155 or toll-free 800-932-9698. *Fax:* 513-294-2259. College video available.

OHIO STATE UNIVERSITY AGRICULTURAL TECHNICAL INSTITUTE
Wooster, Ohio

UG Enrollment: 783	Tuition & Fees (OH Res): $3156
Application Deadline: 8/15	Room Only: $2325

GENERAL State-supported, 2-year, coed. Part of Ohio State University. Awards terminal associate degrees. Founded 1971. *Setting:* 136-acre small-town campus with easy access to Cleveland and Columbus. *Total enrollment:* 783. *Faculty:* 61 (34 full-time, 27 part-time); student-faculty ratio is 12:1.
ENROLLMENT PROFILE 783 students from 11 states and territories, 1 other country. 26% women, 74% men, 14% part-time, 98% state residents, 24% live on campus, 11% transferred in, 1% international, 26% 25 or older, 1% Native American, 1% Hispanic, 4% African American, 0% Asian American. *Areas of study chosen:* 100% agriculture.
FIRST-YEAR CLASS 250 total; 373 applied, 94% were accepted, 71% of whom enrolled. 5% from top 10% of their high school class, 19% from top quarter, 50% from top half.

ACADEMIC PROGRAM Core, honor code. Calendar: quarters. Academic remediation for entering students, services for LD students, advanced placement, self-designed majors, tutorials, honors program, summer session for credit, part-time degree program (daytime), adult/continuing education programs, co-op programs and internships. ROTC: Army (c), Naval (c), Air Force (c).
GENERAL DEGREE REQUIREMENTS 100 quarter hours; math/science requirements vary according to programs; computer course for most majors.
MAJORS Agricultural business, agricultural economics, agricultural sciences, agricultural technologies, agronomy/soil and crop sciences, animal sciences, botany/plant sciences, business machine technologies, construction technologies, dairy sciences, environmental sciences, equestrian studies, food marketing, horticulture, laboratory technologies, landscaping/grounds maintenance, manufacturing technology, natural resource management, ornamental horticulture, soil conservation, technology and public affairs.
LIBRARY Agricultural Technical Institute Library with 18,354 books, 27,829 microform titles, 588 periodicals.
COMPUTERS ON CAMPUS 85 computers for student use in computer center, learning resource center, library, dorms.
COLLEGE LIFE Orientation program (2 days, $40, parents included). ***Student services:*** health clinic, personal-psychological counseling. ***Campus security:*** 24-hour emergency response devices and patrols.
HOUSING 185 college housing spaces available; all were occupied 1995–96. No special consideration for freshman housing applicants. Off-campus living permitted. ***Option:*** coed (1 building) housing available. Resident assistants live in dorms.
ATHLETICS ***Intramural:*** basketball, football, racquetball, softball, volleyball. ***Contact:*** Ms. Kathy Maksymicz, Program Assistant, 216-264-3911.
CAREER PLANNING ***Services:*** job fairs, resume preparation, career counseling, job interviews.
EXPENSES FOR 1995–96 ***Application fee:*** $30. State resident tuition: $3156 full-time. Nonresident tuition: $9696 full-time. Part-time tuition per quarter ranges from $88 to $965 for state residents, $179 to $2963 for nonresidents. College room only: $2325.
FINANCIAL AID ***College-administered undergrad aid 1995–96:*** need-based scholarships, non-need scholarships, short-term loans, low-interest long-term loans from college funds, loans from external sources, Federal Work-Study, part-time jobs. ***Required forms:*** institutional, FAFSA; required for some: state. ***Priority deadline:*** 2/15. ***Payment plan:*** installment. ***Waivers:*** full or partial for employees or children of employees. ***Notification:*** 6/1.
APPLYING Open admission for state residents. ***Options:*** early entrance, midyear entrance. ***Required:*** TOEFL for international students. ***Recommended:*** 3 years of high school math and science. ***Required for some:*** SAT I or ACT. Test scores used for admission (for nonresidents) and counseling/placement. ***Application deadline:*** 8/15. ***Notification:*** continuous until 9/15.
APPLYING/TRANSFER ***Recommended:*** 3 years of high school math and science, minimum 2.0 high school GPA. ***Entrance:*** moderately difficult. ***Application deadline:*** 8/15. ***Notification:*** continuous until 9/15. ***Contact:*** Dr. Arnold Mokma, Assistant Director for Academic Affairs/Coordinator, 216-264-3911 Ext. 211.
CONTACT Ms. Veronica Thomas, Admissions Coordinator, Ohio State University Agricultural Technical Institute, Wooster, OH 44691, 216-264-3911 or toll-free 800-647-8283 (in-state). College video available.

OHIO UNIVERSITY–SOUTHERN CAMPUS
Ironton, Ohio

UG Enrollment: 2,102 | **Tuition & Fees (OH Res): $2658**
Application Deadline: rolling | **Room & Board: N/Avail**

GENERAL State-supported, primarily 2-year, coed. Part of Ohio University System. Awards transfer associate, terminal associate, bachelor's degrees (offers first 2 years of most baccalaureate programs available at the main campus in Athens; also offers some upper-level and graduate courses). Founded 1956. ***Setting:*** 9-acre small-town campus. Faculty: 125 (15 full-time, 110 part-time).
ENROLLMENT PROFILE 2,102 students from 3 states and territories. 62% women, 38% men, 45% part-time, 86% state residents, 6% transferred in, 0% international, 56% 25 or older, 0% Native American, 0% Hispanic, 2% African American, 0% Asian American.
FIRST-YEAR CLASS 642 total; 642 applied, 100% were accepted, 100% of whom enrolled.
ACADEMIC PROGRAM Core. Calendar: quarters. Academic remediation for entering students, self-designed majors, summer session for credit, part-time degree program (evenings), adult/continuing education programs.
GENERAL DEGREE REQUIREMENTS 96 quarter hours for associate, 192 quarter hours for bachelor's; 1 course each in math and science.
MAJORS Business administration/commerce/management (B), computer science, education (B), liberal arts/general studies, science.
LIBRARY Ohio University-Southern Campus Library with 16,300 books, 4 microform titles, 230 periodicals, 200 records, tapes, and CDs.
COMPUTERS ON CAMPUS 32 computers for student use in computer center, computer labs, library, student center.
COLLEGE LIFE Choral group. ***Student services:*** legal services.
HOUSING College housing not available.
ATHLETICS ***Intramural:*** archery, golf, skiing (downhill), swimming and diving, tennis, volleyball.
CAREER PLANNING ***Director:*** Mr. Don Baker, Student Services Advisor, 614-533-4545.
EXPENSES FOR 1995–96 ***Application fee:*** $15. State resident tuition: $2658 full-time, $82 per quarter hour part-time. Nonresident tuition: $2772 full-time, $85 per quarter hour part-time.
FINANCIAL AID ***College-administered undergrad aid 1995–96:*** need-based scholarships, non-need scholarships, Federal Work-Study. ***Required forms:*** CSS Financial Aid PROFILE, state, institutional. ***Priority deadline:*** 5/1. ***Waivers:*** full or partial for employees or children of employees and senior citizens. ***Notification:*** continuous.
APPLYING Open admission. ***Options:*** early entrance, deferred entrance, midyear entrance. ***Recommended:*** 3 years of high school math and science, 2 years of high school foreign language, SAT I or ACT. Test scores used for counseling/placement. ***Application deadline:*** rolling.
APPLYING/TRANSFER ***Entrance:*** noncompetitive. ***Application deadline:*** rolling.
CONTACT Dr. Charles W. Jarrett, Coordinator of Admissions, Ohio University–Southern Campus, Ironton, OH 45638-2214, 614-533-4600. ***Fax:*** 614-533-4632.

OWENS COMMUNITY COLLEGE
Findlay, Ohio

UG Enrollment: 1,767 | **Tuition & Fees (OH Res): $1808**
Application Deadline: rolling | **Room & Board: N/Avail**

GENERAL State-supported, 2-year, coed. Part of Owens Community College System. Awards certificates, transfer associate, terminal associate degrees. Founded 1983. ***Setting:*** suburban campus with easy access to Toledo. ***Total enrollment:*** 1,767. ***Faculty:*** 102 (12 full-time, 15% with terminal degrees, 90 part-time); student-faculty ratio is 15:1.
ENROLLMENT PROFILE 1,767 students from 2 states and territories, 2 other countries. 58% women, 67% part-time, 98% state residents, 10% transferred in, 1% international, 50% 25 or older, 1% Native American, 3% Hispanic, 4% African American, 1% Asian American. ***Areas of study chosen:*** 33% engineering and applied sciences, 24% business management and administrative services, 20% health professions and related sciences, 20% liberal arts/general studies. ***Most popular recent majors:*** nursing, computer programming, electromechanical technology.
FIRST-YEAR CLASS 591 total. Of the students who applied, 100% were accepted. 5% from top 10% of their high school class, 10% from top quarter, 50% from top half.
ACADEMIC PROGRAM Core. Calendar: semesters. Academic remediation for entering students, services for LD students, tutorials, summer session for credit, part-time degree program (daytime, evenings), adult/continuing education programs, co-op programs and internships. ROTC: Army (c), Air Force.
GENERAL DEGREE REQUIREMENTS 65 credit hours; computer course for engineering technology, industrial technology majors.
MAJORS Accounting, agricultural business, automotive technologies, behavioral sciences, biology/biological sciences, biomedical technologies, business administration/commerce/management, child care/child and family studies, civil engineering technology, computer programming, drafting and design, early childhood education, electrical engineering technology, electromechanical technology, electronics engineering technology, environmental engineering technology, fashion merchandising, food services technology, industrial engineering technology, law enforcement/police sciences, liberal arts/general studies, marketing/retailing/merchandising, mathematics, mechanical engineering technology, nuclear medical technology, nursing, optometric/ophthalmic technologies, physical therapy, psychology, quality control technology, radiological technology, robotics, secretarial studies/office management, social science, telecommunications, welding technology.
LIBRARY Learning Resource Media Center with 41,250 books, 500 microform titles, 700 periodicals, 1 on-line bibliographic service, 1 CD-ROM.
COMPUTERS ON CAMPUS 83 computers for student use in computer center, computer labs, classrooms provide access to on-line services. Staffed computer lab on campus provides training in use of computers, software.
COLLEGE LIFE ***Most popular organizations:*** Intramurals, Student Senate, Photography Club, Snow Ski Club. ***Student services:*** personal-psychological counseling. ***Campus security:*** 24-hour emergency response devices and patrols, student patrols.
HOUSING College housing not available.
ATHLETICS Member NJCAA. ***Intercollegiate:*** baseball M, basketball M/W, volleyball W. ***Intramural:*** baseball, basketball, football, golf, skiing (cross-country), skiing (downhill), softball, tennis, volleyball, weight lifting. ***Contact:*** Mr. Michael Rickard, Coordinator of Athletics and Intramurals, 419-661-7409.
CAREER PLANNING ***Placement office:*** 7 full-time, 3 part-time staff. ***Director:*** Mr. Lindsey Whitehead, Director of Counseling, 419-661-7500. ***Services:*** job fairs, resume preparation, resume referral, career counseling, careers library, job interviews. Students must register sophomore year.
AFTER GRADUATION 80% of class of 1994 had job offers within 6 months.
EXPENSES FOR 1995–96 State resident tuition: $1788 full-time, $74.50 per credit hour part-time. Nonresident tuition: $3336 full-time, $139 per credit hour part-time. Part-time mandatory fees: $10 per semester. Full-time mandatory fees: $20.
FINANCIAL AID ***College-administered undergrad aid 1995–96:*** 600 need-based scholarships (average $900), short-term loans (average $500), low-interest long-term loans from external sources, Federal Work-Study, 15 part-time jobs. ***Required forms:*** institutional; accepted: CSS Financial Aid PROFILE, state, FAFSA. ***Priority deadline:*** 3/15. ***Payment plan:*** installment. ***Waivers:*** full or partial for employees or children of employees and senior citizens.
APPLYING Open admission except for health technology, peace officer academy programs. ***Options:*** early entrance, deferred entrance, midyear entrance. ***Required:*** school transcript, TOEFL for international students. ***Recommended:*** essay, 3 years of high school math and science, some high school foreign language, recommendations, interview, ACT, ACT ASSET. ***Required for some:*** minimum 2.0 GPA, minimum 3.0 GPA, ACT. Test scores used for counseling/placement. ***Application deadline:*** rolling. ***Notification:*** continuous.
APPLYING/TRANSFER ***Required:*** high school transcript, college transcript. ***Recommended:*** essay, standardized test scores, 3 years of high school math and science, some high school foreign language, recommendations, interview, minimum 2.0 college GPA, minimum 2.0 high school GPA. ***Required for some:*** standardized test scores, minimum 3.0 high school GPA. ***Entrance:*** noncompetitive. ***Application deadline:*** rolling. ***Notification:*** continuous. ***Contact:*** Mr. Cesar Hernandez, Manager of New Student Advising and Assessment, 419-661-7504.
CONTACT Mr. Gary Ulrich, Student Services Representative, Owens Community College, Findlay, OH 45840, 419-423-6827. ***Fax:*** 419-423-6827 Ext. 250.

OWENS COMMUNITY COLLEGE
Toledo, Ohio

UG Enrollment: 9,682 | **Tuition & Fees (OH Res): $1808**
Application Deadline: rolling | **Room & Board: N/Avail**

GENERAL State-supported, 2-year, coed. Part of Owens Community College System. Awards certificates, transfer associate, terminal associate degrees. Founded 1966. ***Setting:*** 100-acre suburban campus. ***Total enrollment:*** 9,682. ***Faculty:*** 752 (133 full-time, 15% with terminal degrees, 619 part-time).
ENROLLMENT PROFILE 9,682 students from 2 states and territories, 2 other countries. 50% women, 50% men, 66% part-time, 98% state residents, 10% transferred

Peterson's Guide to Two-Year Colleges 1997 531

Owens Community College (continued)

in, 1% international, 48% 25 or older, 1% Native American, 4% Hispanic, 8% African American, 1% Asian American. ***Areas of study chosen:*** 46% engineering and applied sciences, 23% health professions and related sciences, 17% business management and administrative services, 14% liberal arts/general studies. ***Most popular recent majors:*** nursing, business administration/commerce/management.

FIRST-YEAR CLASS 2,907 total. Of the students who applied, 100% were accepted. 5% from top 10% of their high school class, 10% from top quarter, 50% from top half.

ACADEMIC PROGRAM Core. Calendar: semesters. Academic remediation for entering students, English as a second language program offered during academic year, services for LD students, tutorials, summer session for credit, part-time degree program (daytime, evenings), adult/continuing education programs, co-op programs and internships. ROTC: Army (c), Air Force.

GENERAL DEGREE REQUIREMENTS 65 semester hours; computer course for engineering technology, industrial technology majors.

MAJORS Accounting, agricultural business, architectural technologies, automotive technologies, behavioral sciences, biology/biological sciences, biomedical technologies, business administration/commerce/management, child care/child and family studies, civil engineering technology, computer programming, computer technologies, dental services, dietetics, drafting and design, early childhood education, electrical and electronics technologies, electrical engineering technology, electromechanical technology, electronics engineering technology, environmental engineering technology, fashion merchandising, finance/banking, fire science, food services technology, hotel and restaurant management, industrial and heavy equipment maintenance, industrial engineering technology, landscaping/grounds maintenance, law enforcement/police sciences, liberal arts/general studies, machine and tool technologies, manufacturing technology, marketing/retailing/merchandising, mathematics, mechanical design technology, mechanical engineering technology, nuclear medical technology, nursing, nutrition, operating room technology, optometric/ophthalmic technologies, physical therapy, psychology, quality control technology, radiological technology, robotics, secretarial studies/office management, social science, telecommunications, welding technology.

LIBRARY Learning Resource Media Center with 41,250 books, 500 microform titles, 700 periodicals, 1 on-line bibliographic service, 1 CD-ROM.

COMPUTERS ON CAMPUS 200 computers for student use in computer center, computer labs, learning resource center, classrooms, library provide access to on-line services. Staffed computer lab on campus provides training in use of computers, software.

COLLEGE LIFE ***Social organizations:*** 18 open to all. ***Most popular organizations:*** Intramurals, Student Senate, Photography Club, Snow Ski Club, Derobies. ***Student services:*** personal-psychological counseling. ***Campus security:*** 24-hour emergency response devices and patrols, student patrols.

HOUSING College housing not available.

ATHLETICS Member NJCAA. ***Intercollegiate:*** baseball M, basketball M(s)/W(s), volleyball W. ***Intramural:*** baseball, basketball, football, golf, sailing, skiing (cross-country), skiing (downhill), softball, tennis, volleyball, weight lifting. ***Contact:*** Mr. Michael Rickard, Coordinator of Athletics and Intramurals, 419-661-7409.

CAREER PLANNING ***Placement office:*** 7 full-time, 3 part-time staff. ***Director:*** Mr. Lindsey Whitehead, Director of Counseling, 419-661-7500. ***Services:*** job fairs, resume preparation, resume referral, career counseling, careers library, job interviews. Students must register sophomore year.

AFTER GRADUATION 80% of class of 1994 had job offers within 6 months.

EXPENSES FOR 1995–96 State resident tuition: $1788 full-time, $74.50 per semester hour part-time. Nonresident tuition: $3336 full-time, $139 per semester hour part-time. Part-time mandatory fees: $10 per semester. Full-time mandatory fees: $20.

FINANCIAL AID ***College-administered undergrad aid 1995–96:*** 4,000 need-based scholarships (average $1800), short-term loans (average $500), low-interest long-term loans from external sources, Federal Work-Study, 100 part-time jobs. ***Required forms:*** institutional; accepted: CSS Financial Aid PROFILE, state, FAFSA. ***Priority deadline:*** 3/15. ***Payment plan:*** installment. ***Waivers:*** full or partial for employees or children of employees and senior citizens.

APPLYING Open admission except for health technology, peace officer academy programs. ***Option:*** early entrance. ***Required:*** school transcript. ***Recommended:*** essay, 3 years of high school math and science, some high school foreign language, recommendations, interview, SAT I or ACT, TOEFL for international students, ACT ASSET. ***Required for some:*** minimum 2.0 GPA, minimum 3.0 GPA, SAT I or ACT. Test scores used for counseling/placement. ***Application deadline:*** rolling. ***Notification:*** continuous.

APPLYING/TRANSFER ***Required:*** high school transcript, college transcript. ***Recommended:*** essay, standardized test scores, 3 years of high school math and science, some high school foreign language, recommendations, interview, minimum 2.0 college GPA, minimum 2.0 high school GPA. ***Required for some:*** standardized test scores, minimum 3.0 high school GPA. ***Entrance:*** noncompetitive. ***Application deadline:*** rolling. ***Notification:*** continuous. ***Contact:*** Mr. Cesar Hernandez, Manager of New Student Advising and Assessment, 419-661-7504.

CONTACT Mr. Jim Welling, Admissions Coordinator, Owens Community College, Toledo, OH 43699-1947, 419-661-7225 or toll-free 800-GO-OWENS (in-state).

PROFESSIONAL SKILLS INSTITUTE
Toledo, Ohio

UG Enrollment: 120	**Tuition: $18,477/deg prog**
Application Deadline: 2/8	**Room & Board: N/Avail**

GENERAL Proprietary, 2-year, primarily women. Awards certificates, terminal associate degrees. Founded 1984. ***Setting:*** urban campus. ***Total enrollment:*** 120. ***Faculty:*** 12 (6 full-time, 100% with terminal degrees, 6 part-time).

ENROLLMENT PROFILE 120 students from 3 states and territories. 81% women, 19% men, 8% part-time, 60% 25 or older, 1% Native American, 5% Hispanic, 16% African American, 4% Asian American. ***Areas of study chosen:*** 100% health professions and related sciences.

FIRST-YEAR CLASS 27 total. Of the students accepted, 100% enrolled.

ACADEMIC PROGRAM Core, interdisciplinary curriculum. Calendar: quarters. Services for LD students, part-time degree program (daytime), internships. Off-campus study at Lourdes College.

GENERAL DEGREE REQUIREMENTS 119 quarter credit hours; computer course; internship.

MAJOR Physical therapy.

LIBRARY PSI Library plus 1 other, with 2,000 books, 50 periodicals, 1 on-line bibliographic service, 1 CD-ROM, 114 records, tapes, and CDs.

COMPUTERS ON CAMPUS 28 computers for student use in computer labs, library provide access to main academic computer. Staffed computer lab on campus provides training in use of computers, software.

COLLEGE LIFE ***Student services:*** health clinic.

HOUSING College housing not available.

CAREER PLANNING ***Placement office:*** 1 part-time staff. ***Director:*** Ms. Patricia Bell, Placement Coordinator, 419-531-9610 Ext. 116. ***Services:*** job fairs, resume preparation, resume referral, career counseling.

AFTER GRADUATION 100% of class of 1994 had job offers within 6 months.

EXPENSES FOR 1996–97 ***Application fee:*** $100. Tuition: $18,477 per degree program.

FINANCIAL AID ***Required forms:*** FAFSA; required for some: state, Veterans Administration Form. ***Application deadline:*** continuous. ***Payment plan:*** installment. ***Waivers:*** full or partial for employees or children of employees.

APPLYING Open admission except for physical therapist assistant program. ***Required:*** school transcript, Wonderlic aptitude test. ***Required for some:*** minimum 2.0 GPA, recommendations, campus interview. Test scores used for admission. ***Application deadline:*** 2/8. ***Notification:*** 8/3.

APPLYING/TRANSFER ***Required:*** standardized test scores, high school transcript. ***Required for some:*** recommendations, campus interview, college transcript, minimum 2.0 college GPA, minimum 2.0 high school GPA. ***Contact:*** Ms. Stephanie Homan, Director of Admissions, 419-531-9610.

CONTACT Ms. Stephanie Homan, Director of Admissions, Professional Skills Institute, 20 Arco Drive, Toledo, OH 43607, 419-531-9610. ***Fax:*** 419-531-4732.

RAYMOND WALTERS COLLEGE
Ohio—See University of Cincinnati Raymond Walters College

RETS TECH CENTER
Centerville, Ohio

UG Enrollment: 443	**Tuition & Fees: $5395**
Application Deadline: rolling	**Room & Board: N/Avail**

GENERAL Proprietary, 2-year, coed. Awards diplomas, transfer associate, terminal associate degrees. Founded 1953. ***Setting:*** 4-acre suburban campus. ***Total enrollment:*** 443. ***Faculty:*** 35 (12 full-time, 23 part-time); student-faculty ratio is 15:1.

ENROLLMENT PROFILE 443 students from 3 states and territories. 50% women, 50% men, 0% part-time, 99% state residents, 5% transferred in, 85% have need-based financial aid, 0% have non-need-based financial aid, 0% international, 50% 25 or older, 0% Native American, 1% Hispanic, 15% African American, 1% Asian American. ***Areas of study chosen:*** 45% health professions and related sciences, 35% engineering and applied sciences, 15% computer and information sciences, 5% business management and administrative services.

FIRST-YEAR CLASS 187 total. Of the students who applied, 85% were accepted, 100% of whom enrolled.

ACADEMIC PROGRAM Honor code. Calendar: semesters. 6 courses offered in 1995–96. Summer session for credit, internships.

GENERAL DEGREE REQUIREMENTS 63 credit hours; internship (some majors).

MAJORS Computer programming, computer science, computer technologies, electrical and electronics technologies, electronics engineering technology, heating/refrigeration/air conditioning, medical assistant technologies, paralegal studies, secretarial studies/office management, tourism and travel.

LIBRARY RETS Library with 970 books, 19 periodicals, 35 records, tapes, and CDs.

COMPUTERS ON CAMPUS 70 computers for student use in computer labs, various locations throughout campus, classrooms.

COLLEGE LIFE ***Student services:*** personal-psychological counseling. ***Campus security:*** 24-hour emergency response devices.

HOUSING College housing not available.

CAREER PLANNING ***Placement office:*** 1 full-time staff. ***Director:*** Ms. Lisa Treffinger, Director, Career Services, 513-433-3410. ***Services:*** resume preparation, resume referral, career counseling, job interviews. 10 organizations recruited on campus 1994–95.

AFTER GRADUATION 50% of class of 1994 had job offers within 6 months.

EXPENSES FOR 1996–97 Tuition: $5395 full-time. One-time mandatory fee: $100. Tuition guaranteed not to increase for student's term of enrollment.

FINANCIAL AID ***College-administered undergrad aid 1995–96:*** need-based scholarships, low-interest long-term loans from external sources (average $2500). ***Required forms:*** state, institutional; required for some: FAFSA; accepted: CSS Financial Aid PROFILE. ***Application deadline:*** continuous.

APPLYING Open admission. ***Options:*** early entrance, deferred entrance. ***Required:*** programming aptitude tests. Test scores used for counseling/placement. ***Application deadline:*** rolling.

APPLYING/TRANSFER ***Required:*** standardized test scores. ***Entrance:*** noncompetitive. ***Application deadline:*** rolling.

CONTACT Mr. Ken Miller, Director, RETS Tech Center, Centerville, OH 45459-4815, 513-433-3410.

SAWYER COLLEGE OF BUSINESS
Cleveland, Ohio

UG Enrollment: 212	**Tuition & Fees: $6580**
Application Deadline: rolling	**Room & Board: N/Avail**

GENERAL Proprietary, 2-year, primarily women. Awards transfer associate degrees. Founded 1978. ***Setting:*** 1-acre urban campus. ***Total enrollment:*** 212. ***Faculty:*** 25 (all part-time); student-faculty ratio is 8:1.

ENROLLMENT PROFILE 212 students: 92% women, 0% part-time, 100% state residents, 5% transferred in, 2% Hispanic, 10% African American. ***Areas of study chosen:*** 30% computer and information sciences, 30% health professions and related sciences.

FIRST-YEAR CLASS Of the students who applied, 82% were accepted. 5% from top 10% of their high school class, 30% from top quarter, 90% from top half.
ACADEMIC PROGRAM Honor code. Calendar: quarters. Part-time degree program (evenings), internships.
GENERAL DEGREE REQUIREMENTS 90 credits; computer course for most majors.
MAJORS Accounting, business administration/commerce/management, computer programming, cosmetology, data processing, economics, medical assistant technologies, secretarial studies/office management.
LIBRARY 1,200 books, 20 periodicals. Acquisition spending 1994–95: $500.
COMPUTERS ON CAMPUS 30 computers for student use in computer center, classrooms. Academic computing expenditure 1994–95: $50,000.
COLLEGE LIFE ***Campus security:*** 24-hour emergency response devices.
HOUSING College housing not available.
CAREER PLANNING ***Placement office:*** 1 full-time, 1 part-time staff; $1000 operating expenditure 1994–95. ***Director:*** Mrs. Kate Cherney, Placement Director, 216-941-7666. ***Services:*** job fairs, resume preparation, resume referral, career counseling, job interviews. Students must register freshman year.
AFTER GRADUATION 83% of class of 1994 had job offers within 6 months.
EXPENSES FOR 1995–96 Tuition: $6580 full-time. One-time mandatory fee: $75.
FINANCIAL AID ***College-administered undergrad aid 1995–96:*** non-need scholarships, low-interest long-term loans from external sources. ***Required forms:*** institutional. ***Application deadline:*** continuous. ***Payment plan:*** installment.
APPLYING ***Required:*** school transcript, CPAt. Test scores used for admission. ***Application deadline:*** rolling.
APPLYING/TRANSFER ***Required:*** high school transcript, college transcript. ***Entrance:*** minimally difficult.
CONTACT Ms. Marion Hearns, Admissions Secretary and Representative, Sawyer College of Business, 13027 Lorain Avenue, Cleveland, OH 44111-2623, 216-941-7666.

SAWYER COLLEGE OF BUSINESS
Cleveland Heights, Ohio

UG Enrollment: 223 | **Tuition & Fees: $4980**
Application Deadline: rolling | **Room & Board: N/Avail**

GENERAL Proprietary, 2-year, primarily women. Awards terminal associate degrees. Founded 1970. ***Setting:*** 1-acre suburban campus. ***Total enrollment:*** 223. ***Faculty:*** 31 (all part-time); student-faculty ratio is 12:1.
ENROLLMENT PROFILE 223 students: 85% women, 5% part-time, 99% state residents, 30% transferred in, 50% 25 or older, 0% Native American, 2% Hispanic, 60% African American, 1% Asian American.
FIRST-YEAR CLASS 106 total. Of the students who applied, 80% were accepted. 10% from top 10% of their high school class, 20% from top quarter, 65% from top half.
ACADEMIC PROGRAM Calendar: quarters.
GENERAL DEGREE REQUIREMENTS 94 credit hours; math/science requirements vary according to program; computer course.
MAJORS Accounting, business administration/commerce/management, data processing, medical assistant technologies, paralegal studies.
LIBRARY 250 books, 4 periodicals, 200 records, tapes, and CDs.
COMPUTERS ON CAMPUS 40 computers for student use in computer center, classrooms.
HOUSING College housing not available.
CAREER PLANNING ***Service:*** career counseling.
EXPENSES FOR 1996–97 Tuition: $4980 full-time, $103 per quarter hour part-time. One-time mandatory fee: $25. Tuition guaranteed not to increase for student's term of enrollment.
FINANCIAL AID ***College-administered undergrad aid 1995–96:*** 3 non-need scholarships (average $3300), low-interest long-term loans from external sources (average $1500), 5 part-time jobs. ***Required forms:*** CSS Financial Aid PROFILE, institutional, FAFSA. ***Priority deadline:*** 8/15.
APPLYING ***Required:*** school transcript, SRA adaptability test, CPAt. Test scores used for admission. ***Application deadline:*** rolling.
APPLYING/TRANSFER ***Required:*** standardized test scores, high school transcript. ***Entrance:*** moderately difficult. ***Application deadline:*** rolling.
CONTACT Mr. Gary Cappy, Director of Admissions, Sawyer College of Business, Cleveland Heights, OH 44118-1763, 216-932-0911 Ext. 13.

SINCLAIR COMMUNITY COLLEGE
Dayton, Ohio

UG Enrollment: 19,817 | **Tuition & Fees (Area Res): $1395**
Application Deadline: rolling | **Room & Board: N/Avail**

GENERAL State and locally supported, 2-year, coed. Part of Ohio Board of Regents. Awards certificates, transfer associate, terminal associate degrees. Founded 1887. ***Setting:*** 50-acre urban campus. ***Total enrollment:*** 19,817. ***Faculty:*** 975 (395 full-time, 580 part-time); student-faculty ratio is 22:1. ***Notable Alumni:*** Jim Baldridge, television news anchor; Debbie Schrubb, president of Ohio Health Information Management Association; Alan Bomar Jones, actor, director, and producer.
ENROLLMENT PROFILE 19,817 students from 12 states and territories. 63% women, 69% part-time, 99% state residents, 6% transferred in, 32% have need-based financial aid, 6% have non-need-based financial aid, 0% international, 60% 25 or older, 1% Native American, 1% Hispanic, 16% African American, 2% Asian American. ***Areas of study chosen:*** 21% health professions and related sciences, 16% liberal arts/general studies, 11% engineering and applied sciences, 8% business management and administrative services, 3% communications and journalism, 3% computer and information sciences, 1% architecture, 1% fine arts, 1% performing arts. ***Most popular recent majors:*** nursing, liberal arts/general studies, business administration/commerce/management.
FIRST-YEAR CLASS 5,531 applied, 100% were accepted, 72% of whom enrolled.
ACADEMIC PROGRAM Core. Calendar: quarters. 1,700 courses offered in 1995–96. Academic remediation for entering students, English as a second language program offered during academic year and summer, services for LD students, self-designed majors, tutorials, honors program, summer session for credit, part-time degree program (daytime, evenings, weekends, summer), external degree programs, adult/continuing education programs, co-op programs and internships. Off-campus study at 17 members of the Southwestern Ohio Council for Higher Education. ROTC: Army (c).
GENERAL DEGREE REQUIREMENTS Math requirement varies according to program; computer course for students without computer competency.
MAJORS Accounting, African studies, applied art, architectural technologies, art/fine arts, automotive technologies, aviation administration, business administration/commerce/management, child care/child and family studies, civil engineering technology, commercial art, communication, computer information systems, corrections, criminal justice, culinary arts, dance, deaf interpreter training, dental services, dietetics, drafting and design, early childhood education, education, electrical and electronics technologies, electromechanical technology, electronics engineering technology, emergency medical technology, engineering and applied sciences, finance/banking, fire science, food services management, gerontology, graphic arts, hotel and restaurant management, human services, industrial engineering technology, interior design, labor and industrial relations, labor studies, law enforcement/police sciences, legal secretarial studies, liberal arts/general studies, machine and tool technologies, manufacturing technology, marketing/retailing/merchandising, mechanical engineering technology, medical assistant technologies, medical records services, medical secretarial studies, mental health/rehabilitation counseling, music, nursing, nutrition, occupational therapy, paralegal studies, physical education, physical therapy, printing technologies, public administration, quality control technology, radiological technology, real estate, respiratory therapy, retail management, robotics, secretarial studies/office management, studio art, surveying technology, theater arts/drama, tourism and travel, transportation technologies.
LIBRARY Learning Resources Center with 135,828 books, 287 microform titles, 678 periodicals, 3 on-line bibliographic services, 75 CD-ROMs, 2,370 records, tapes, and CDs. Acquisition spending 1994–95: $1.6 million.
COMPUTERS ON CAMPUS 700 computers for student use in computer labs, learning resource center, classrooms, library provide access to Internet. Staffed computer lab on campus. Academic computing expenditure 1994–95: $843,876.
COLLEGE LIFE Drama-theater group, choral group, student-run newspaper, radio station. 2% vote in student government elections. ***Social organizations:*** 55 open to all. ***Most popular organizations:*** African-American Men of the Future, Ohio Fellows, Phi Theta Kappa, Student Government, Student Newspaper. ***Major annual events:*** Welcome Week, Spring Fling, Student Health Fair. ***Student services:*** personal-psychological counseling, women's center. ***Campus security:*** 24-hour emergency response devices and patrols, late-night transport-escort service.
HOUSING College housing not available.
ATHLETICS Member NJCAA. ***Intercollegiate:*** baseball M(s), basketball M(s)/W(s), golf M(s), tennis M(s)/W(s), volleyball W(s). ***Intramural:*** basketball, bowling, gymnastics, racquetball, squash, tennis, volleyball. ***Contact:*** Dr. Patrick Hodges, Chairperson, Department of Physical Education, 513-226-2860.
CAREER PLANNING ***Placement office:*** 6 full-time, 6 part-time staff; $122,957 operating expenditure 1994–95. ***Director:*** Mr. Del Vaughan, Director, Career Planning and Placement, 513-226-2772. ***Services:*** job fairs, resume preparation, resume referral, career counseling, careers library, job bank, job interviews. 130 organizations recruited on campus 1994–95.
EXPENSES FOR 1996–97 ***Application fee:*** $10. Area resident tuition: $1395 full-time, $31 per quarter hour part-time. State resident tuition: $2205 full-time, $49 per quarter hour part-time. Nonresident tuition: $3600 full-time, $80 per quarter hour part-time.
FINANCIAL AID ***College-administered undergrad aid 1995–96:*** 3,500 need-based scholarships (average $450), 436 non-need scholarships (average $600), short-term loans (average $1750), low-interest long-term loans from external sources, 130 Federal Work-Study (averaging $2000). ***Required forms:*** state, institutional; accepted: CSS Financial Aid PROFILE, FAFSA. ***Priority deadline:*** 4/15. ***Waivers:*** full or partial for employees or children of employees and senior citizens. ***Notification:*** 8/1.
APPLYING Open admission. ***Options:*** early entrance, midyear entrance. ***Required:*** TOEFL for international students. ***Required for some:*** minimum 2.0 GPA, ACT COMPASS. Test scores used for counseling/placement. ***Application deadline:*** rolling. ***Notification:*** continuous.
APPLYING/TRANSFER ***Required for some:*** college transcript. ***Entrance:*** noncompetitive. ***Application deadline:*** rolling. ***Notification:*** continuous.
CONTACT Ms. Sara Porter Smith, Director of Admissions, Sinclair Community College, 444 West Third Street, Dayton, OH 45402-1453, 513-226-3000. ***E-mail:*** ssmith@sinclair.edu. College video available.

SOUTHERN OHIO COLLEGE, CINCINNATI CAMPUS
Cincinnati, Ohio

UG Enrollment: 440 | **Tuition & Fees: $6750**
Application Deadline: rolling | **Room & Board: N/Avail**

GENERAL Proprietary, 2-year, coed. Part of American Education Centers, Inc. Awards terminal associate degrees. Founded 1927. ***Setting:*** 3-acre suburban campus. ***Total enrollment:*** 440. ***Faculty:*** 32 (10 full-time, 50% with terminal degrees, 22 part-time); student-faculty ratio is 15:1.
ENROLLMENT PROFILE 440 students from 3 states and territories, 1 other country. 70% women, 18% part-time, 99% state residents, 20% transferred in, 65% 25 or older, 39% African American. ***Most popular recent majors:*** audio engineering, medical assistant technologies, business administration/commerce/management.
FIRST-YEAR CLASS 3% from top 10% of their high school class, 40% from top half.
ACADEMIC PROGRAM Core, honor code. Calendar: quarters. Academic remediation for entering students, advanced placement, summer session for credit, part-time degree program (daytime, evenings), adult/continuing education programs, internships.
GENERAL DEGREE REQUIREMENTS 102 credits; computer course; internship (some majors).
MAJORS Audio engineering, business administration/commerce/management, computer science, electrical and electronics technologies, medical assistant technologies, medical secretarial studies, optical technologies, real estate, secretarial studies/office management, tourism and travel.
LIBRARY 5,000 books, 80 periodicals, 50 records, tapes, and CDs.
COMPUTERS ON CAMPUS 50 computers for student use in computer labs, classrooms, library.

Peterson's Guide to Two-Year Colleges 1997

533

Southern Ohio College, Cincinnati Campus (continued)

COLLEGE LIFE Student-run newspaper. ***Campus security:*** 24-hour emergency response devices.
HOUSING College housing not available.
CAREER PLANNING ***Director:*** Ms. Elizabeth Shepard, Employment Assistance Director, 513-242-3791. ***Service:*** career counseling. Students must register sophomore year.
EXPENSES FOR 1995–96 Tuition: $6630 full-time, $130 per credit hour part-time. Full-time mandatory fees: $120.
FINANCIAL AID ***College-administered undergrad aid 1995–96:*** need-based scholarships, 10 non-need scholarships (averaging $2000), low-interest long-term loans from college funds, loans from external sources (averaging $2625), Federal Work-Study. ***Required forms:*** institutional, FAFSA; required for some: state; accepted: CSS Financial Aid PROFILE. ***Application deadline:*** continuous.
APPLYING ***Options:*** early entrance, deferred entrance, midyear entrance. ***Required:*** campus interview, TOEFL for international students, CAPt. Test scores used for admission and counseling/placement. ***Application deadline:*** rolling.
APPLYING/TRANSFER ***Application deadline:*** rolling.
CONTACT Mr. T. Humphrey, School Director, Southern Ohio College, Cincinnati Campus, Cincinnati, OH 45215, 513-242-3791 or toll-free 800-582-2629 (in-state).

SOUTHERN OHIO COLLEGE, NORTHEAST CAMPUS
Akron, Ohio

UG Enrollment: 300	**Tuition & Fees: $6954**
Application Deadline: rolling	**Room & Board: N/Avail**

GENERAL Proprietary, 2-year, coed. Administratively affiliated with Southern Ohio College. Awards certificates, diplomas, terminal associate degrees. Founded 1968. ***Setting:*** 3-acre suburban campus with easy access to Cleveland. ***Total enrollment:*** 300. ***Faculty:*** 33 (8 full-time, 25 part-time).
ENROLLMENT PROFILE 300 students: 66% women, 40% part-time, 99% state residents, 12% transferred in, 67% have need-based financial aid, 70% 25 or older, 0% Native American, 1% Hispanic, 11% African American, 1% Asian American. ***Areas of study chosen:*** 60% business management and administrative services, 22% health professions and related sciences, 17% computer and information sciences, 1% liberal arts/general studies.
FIRST-YEAR CLASS 89 total; 114 applied, 87% were accepted, 90% of whom enrolled. 1% from top 10% of their high school class, 18% from top quarter, 65% from top half.
ACADEMIC PROGRAM Core, modern business practices curriculum, honor code. Calendar: quarters. 88 courses offered in 1995–96. Academic remediation for entering students, advanced placement, tutorials, summer session for credit, part-time degree program (daytime, evenings, summer), co-op programs and internships.
GENERAL DEGREE REQUIREMENTS 102 quarter hours; computer course; internship (some majors).
MAJORS Accounting, business administration/commerce/management, business machine technologies, computer science, secretarial studies/office management.
LIBRARY 3,725 books, 56 periodicals, 1 on-line bibliographic service, 1 CD-ROM, 145 records, tapes, and CDs. Acquisition spending 1994–95: $8000.
COMPUTERS ON CAMPUS 51 computers for student use in computer labs, labs, classrooms, library provide access to on-line services, software. Staffed computer lab on campus provides training in use of computers, software.
COLLEGE LIFE Student-run newspaper. 50% vote in student government elections. ***Social organizations:*** 3 open to all. ***Most popular organizations:*** Phi Beta Lambda, Student Advisory Board, Collegiate Secretaries International. ***Major annual events:*** National Medical Assisting Week, Holiday Food Drives, Campus Blood Drives. ***Student services:*** personal-psychological counseling. ***Campus security:*** late-night transport-escort service.
HOUSING College housing not available.
CAREER PLANNING ***Placement office:*** 1 full-time, 1 part-time staff. ***Director:*** Ms. Patricia A. May, Employer Relations Director, 330-733-8766. ***Services:*** resume preparation, resume referral, career counseling, careers library, job bank, job interviews. Students must register sophomore year.
AFTER GRADUATION 9% of students completing a degree program in 1994–95 went directly on to further study.
EXPENSES FOR 1996–97 ***Application fee:*** $100. Tuition: $6864 full-time, $143 per credit part-time. Part-time mandatory fees: $30 per quarter. Full-time mandatory fees: $90.
FINANCIAL AID ***College-administered undergrad aid 1995–96:*** need-based scholarships, 12 non-need scholarships (average $1500), low-interest long-term loans from external sources, Federal Work-Study. ***Required forms:*** CSS Financial Aid PROFILE, institutional, FAFSA; accepted: state. ***Priority deadline:*** 10/1. ***Payment plan:*** installment. ***Waivers:*** full or partial for employees or children of employees and senior citizens.
APPLYING ***Options:*** early entrance, deferred entrance, midyear entrance. ***Required:*** TOEFL for international students, CCAP. ***Recommended:*** minimum 2.0 GPA, 3 years of high school math, SAT I or ACT. ***Required for some:*** 3 years of high school science. Test scores used for counseling/placement. ***Application deadline:*** rolling. ***Notification:*** continuous.
APPLYING/TRANSFER ***Required:*** standardized test scores. ***Recommended:*** 3 years of high school math, minimum 2.0 high school GPA. ***Required for some:*** 3 years of high school science. ***Entrance:*** minimally difficult. ***Application deadline:*** rolling. ***Notification:*** continuous. ***Contact:*** Ms. Christine Montini, Registrar, 330-733-8766.
CONTACT Ms. Bonnie Binns, Senior Admissions Officer, Southern Ohio College, Northeast Campus, Akron, OH 44312-1596, 330-733-8766.

SOUTHERN STATE COMMUNITY COLLEGE
Hillsboro, Ohio

UG Enrollment: 1,468	**Tuition & Fees (OH Res): $2907**
Application Deadline: rolling	**Room & Board: N/Avail**

GENERAL State-supported, 2-year, coed. Part of Ohio Board of Regents. Awards certificates, transfer associate, terminal associate degrees. Founded 1975. ***Setting:*** 40-acre rural campus. ***Endowment:*** $12,046. ***Research spending 1994–95:*** $55,180. ***Educational spending 1994–95:*** $1600 per undergrad. ***Total enrollment:*** 1,468. ***Faculty:*** 117 (42 full-time, 10% with terminal degrees, 75 part-time); student-faculty ratio is 16:1.
ENROLLMENT PROFILE 1,468 students: 73% women, 49% part-time, 100% state residents, 4% transferred in, 48% 25 or older, 1% Native American, 1% Hispanic, 1% African American, 1% Asian American. ***Areas of study chosen:*** 61% interdisciplinary studies, 15% business management and administrative services, 10% health professions and related sciences, 6% education, 4% computer and information sciences, 3% engineering and applied sciences, 1% agriculture. ***Most popular recent majors:*** liberal arts/general studies, nursing, business administration/commerce/management.
FIRST-YEAR CLASS 419 total; 560 applied, 100% were accepted, 75% of whom enrolled.
ACADEMIC PROGRAM Core, interdisciplinary curriculum, honor code. Calendar: quarters. 554 courses offered in 1995–96. Academic remediation for entering students, services for LD students, advanced placement, self-designed majors, tutorials, summer session for credit, part-time degree program (daytime, evenings), internships. Off-campus study at 15 members of the Southwestern Ohio Council for Higher Education.
GENERAL DEGREE REQUIREMENTS 90 quarter hours; math/science requirements vary according to program; computer course for allied health, business, medical assistant majors; internship (some majors).
MAJORS Accounting, agricultural technologies, business administration/commerce/management, computer programming, computer technologies, drafting and design, early childhood education, electrical and electronics technologies, elementary education, industrial engineering technology, liberal arts/general studies, medical assistant technologies, nursing, practical nursing, real estate, robotics, secretarial studies/office management.
LIBRARY Learning Resources Center plus 3 others, with 34,625 books, 850 periodicals, 4 on-line bibliographic services, 1,500 records, tapes, and CDs. Acquisition spending 1994–95: $6104.
COMPUTERS ON CAMPUS 145 computers for student use in computer center, computer labs, learning resource center, classrooms, library provide access to e-mail, on-line services, Internet. Staffed computer lab on campus provides training in use of computers, software. Academic computing expenditure 1994–95: $9463.
COLLEGE LIFE Drama-theater group, choral group. ***Social organizations:*** 3 open to all; national fraternities. ***Most popular organizations:*** Student Government Association, BACCHUS, Drama Club. ***Major annual event:*** Spring Fling. ***Student services:*** personal-psychological counseling.
HOUSING College housing not available.
ATHLETICS Member NJCAA. ***Intercollegiate:*** basketball M/W, golf M(s), soccer M(s), softball W(s), volleyball W(s). ***Intramural:*** basketball, bowling, football, golf, softball, table tennis (Ping-Pong), tennis, volleyball. ***Contact:*** Mr. Ken Holliday, Coordinator of Recruitment and Student Activities, 513-393-3431.
CAREER PLANNING ***Placement office:*** 1 part-time staff; $136,325 operating expenditure 1994–95. ***Director:*** Ms. Sherry Stout, South Campus Director and Placement Coordinator, 513-695-0307. ***Services:*** job fairs, resume preparation, resume referral, career counseling, careers library, job bank.
EXPENSES FOR 1996–97 ***Application fee:*** $15. State resident tuition: $2880 full-time, $64 per quarter hour part-time. Nonresident tuition: $5400 full-time, $120 per quarter hour part-time. Part-time mandatory fees: $9 per quarter. Full-time mandatory fees: $27.
FINANCIAL AID ***College-administered undergrad aid 1995–96:*** 650 need-based scholarships (average $267), 334 non-need scholarships (average $639), low-interest long-term loans from external sources (average $2625), Federal Work-Study. ***Required forms:*** institutional, FAFSA. ***Priority deadline:*** 7/1. ***Payment plan:*** deferred payment. ***Waivers:*** full or partial for employees or children of employees and senior citizens. ***Average indebtedness of graduates:*** $5000.
APPLYING Open admission. ***Options:*** early entrance, deferred entrance. ***Required:*** school transcript, TOEFL for international students. ***Recommended:*** SAT I or ACT. ***Required for some:*** SAT I or ACT. Test scores used for counseling/placement. ***Application deadline:*** rolling.
APPLYING/TRANSFER ***Required:*** college transcript. ***Entrance:*** noncompetitive. ***Application deadline:*** rolling. ***Contact:*** Ms. Sharon Purvis, Registrar, 513-393-3431.
CONTACT Mr. Ken Holliday, Coordinator of Recruitment and Student Activities, Southern State Community College, Hillsboro, OH 45133-9487, 513-393-3431 Ext. 695 or toll-free 800-628-7722 (in-state). ***Fax:*** 513-393-9370. ***E-mail:*** khollida@soucc.southern.cc.oh.us. College video available.

SOUTHWESTERN COLLEGE OF BUSINESS
Cincinnati, Ohio

UG Enrollment: 190	**Tuition & Fees: $4800**
Application Deadline: rolling	**Room & Board: N/Avail**

GENERAL Proprietary, 2-year, coed. Awards terminal associate degrees. Founded 1972. ***Setting:*** suburban campus. ***Total enrollment:*** 190. ***Faculty:*** 19 (8 full-time, 11 part-time).
ENROLLMENT PROFILE 190 students: 85% women, 6% part-time, 100% state residents, 0% transferred in, 0% Native American, 1% Hispanic, 35% African American, 64% Asian American.
FIRST-YEAR CLASS 52 total. Of the students who applied, 97% were accepted, 80% of whom enrolled.
ACADEMIC PROGRAM Core. Calendar: quarters. Academic remediation for entering students, summer session for credit, external degree programs, co-op programs.
GENERAL DEGREE REQUIREMENT 96 quarter hours.
MAJORS Accounting, business administration/commerce/management, computer information systems, computer programming, computer science, labor studies, medical assistant technologies, medical laboratory technology, medical secretarial studies, real estate, secretarial studies/office management.
COMPUTERS ON CAMPUS 50 computers for student use in computer center, classrooms. Staffed computer lab on campus provides training in use of computers, software.
COLLEGE LIFE ***Student services:*** personal-psychological counseling.
HOUSING College housing not available.
CAREER PLANNING ***Service:*** career counseling.

Ohio

EXPENSES FOR 1995–96 Tuition: $4400 full-time, $50 per credit part-time. Full-time mandatory fees: $400.
FINANCIAL AID *College-administered undergrad aid 1995–96:* need-based scholarships, low-interest long-term loans from college funds, loans from external sources. *Required forms:* state, institutional, FAFSA. *Application deadline:* continuous.
APPLYING *Option:* deferred entrance. *Required for some:* CPAt. Test scores used for admission and counseling/placement. *Application deadline:* rolling. *Notification:* continuous.
APPLYING/TRANSFER *Required for some:* standardized test scores. *Entrance:* minimally difficult. *Application deadline:* rolling. *Notification:* continuous.
CONTACT Ms. Gail Rizzo, Office of Admissions and Marketing, Southwestern College of Business, Cincinnati, OH 45246-1122, 513-874-0432.

SOUTHWESTERN COLLEGE OF BUSINESS
Cincinnati, Ohio

UG Enrollment: 252	Tuition & Fees: $3600
Application Deadline: rolling	Room & Board: N/Avail

GENERAL Proprietary, 2-year, coed. Awards transfer associate, terminal associate degrees. Founded 1972. *Setting:* urban campus. *Total enrollment:* 252. *Faculty:* 17 (all part-time); student-faculty ratio is 15:1.
ENROLLMENT PROFILE 252 students: 92% women, 4% part-time, 10% transferred in, 95% have need-based financial aid, 0% international, 41% 25 or older, 0% Native American, 0% Hispanic, 89% African American, 0% Asian American.
FIRST-YEAR CLASS 100 total; 162 applied, 90% were accepted, 68% of whom enrolled.
ACADEMIC PROGRAM Calendar: quarters. Tutorials, summer session for credit, part-time degree program (daytime, evenings), co-op programs and internships.
GENERAL DEGREE REQUIREMENTS 99 credit hours; computer course; internship (some majors).
MAJORS Accounting, business administration/commerce/management, computer science, medical assistant technologies, secretarial studies/office management.
COMPUTERS ON CAMPUS 54 computers for student use in computer center.
HOUSING College housing not available.
CAREER PLANNING *Services:* resume preparation, resume referral, career counseling, job interviews.
EXPENSES FOR 1996–97 Tuition: $3300 full-time, $92 per credit hour part-time. Part-time mandatory fees: $100 per quarter. Full-time mandatory fees: $300.
FINANCIAL AID *College-administered undergrad aid 1995–96:* need-based scholarships, low-interest long-term loans from external sources. *Required forms:* institutional, FAFSA. *Priority deadline:* 9/1. *Payment plans:* installment, deferred payment.
APPLYING *Option:* deferred entrance. *Required for some:* CPAt. Test scores used for admission and counseling/placement. *Application deadline:* rolling. *Notification:* continuous.
APPLYING/TRANSFER *Required for some:* standardized test scores. *Entrance:* minimally difficult. *Application deadline:* rolling. *Notification:* continuous.
CONTACT Ms. Sue Hatfield, Director of Education, Southwestern College of Business, 632 Vine Street, Suite 200, Cincinnati, OH 45202-4304, 513-421-3212.

SOUTHWESTERN COLLEGE OF BUSINESS
Dayton, Ohio

UG Enrollment: 200	Tuition & Fees: $3600
Application Deadline: rolling	Room & Board: N/Avail

GENERAL Proprietary, 2-year, coed. Awards terminal associate degrees. Founded 1972. *Setting:* urban campus. *Total enrollment:* 200. *Faculty:* 20.
ENROLLMENT PROFILE 200 students: 90% women, 1% part-time, 99% state residents, 25% transferred in, 1% Hispanic, 50% African American.
FIRST-YEAR CLASS 60 total. Of the students who applied, 90% were accepted, 75% of whom enrolled.
ACADEMIC PROGRAM Core. Calendar: quarters. Academic remediation for entering students, summer session for credit, external degree programs, co-op programs.
GENERAL DEGREE REQUIREMENT 96 quarter hours.
MAJORS Accounting, business administration/commerce/management, computer science, medical assistant technologies, secretarial studies/office management.
COMPUTERS ON CAMPUS 30 computers for student use in computer center.
COLLEGE LIFE *Student services:* personal-psychological counseling.
HOUSING College housing not available.
CAREER PLANNING *Service:* career counseling.
EXPENSES FOR 1995–96 Tuition: $3300 full-time, $50 per credit part-time. Full-time mandatory fees: $300.
FINANCIAL AID *College-administered undergrad aid 1995–96:* need-based scholarships, low-interest long-term loans from external sources, Federal Work-Study. *Required forms:* state, institutional, FAFSA. *Application deadline:* continuous.
APPLYING *Option:* deferred entrance. *Required for some:* CPAt. *Application deadline:* rolling. *Notification:* continuous.
APPLYING/TRANSFER *Required for some:* standardized test scores. *Entrance:* minimally difficult. *Application deadline:* rolling. *Notification:* continuous.
CONTACT Director of Admissions and Marketing, Southwestern College of Business, 225 West First Street, Dayton, OH 45402-3003, 513-874-0432.

SOUTHWESTERN COLLEGE OF BUSINESS
Middletown, Ohio

UG Enrollment: 187	Tuition & Fees: $4800
Application Deadline: rolling	Room & Board: N/Avail

GENERAL Proprietary, 2-year, coed. Awards certificates, diplomas, terminal associate degrees. Founded 1981. *Setting:* suburban campus with easy access to Dayton and Cincinnati. *Total enrollment:* 187. *Faculty:* 19 (all part-time).
ENROLLMENT PROFILE 187 students: 87% women, 10% part-time, 100% state residents, 5% transferred in, 0% international, 75% 25 or older, 1% Native American, 0% Hispanic, 5% African American, 0% Asian American.
FIRST-YEAR CLASS 118 total. Of the students who applied, 71% were accepted.
ACADEMIC PROGRAM Core. Calendar: quarters.
GENERAL DEGREE REQUIREMENTS 99 credit hours; 2 math courses; computer course.
MAJORS Business administration/commerce/management, computer science, medical secretarial studies, secretarial studies/office management.
COMPUTERS ON CAMPUS 33 computers for student use in classrooms.
HOUSING College housing not available.
CAREER PLANNING *Service:* career counseling.
EXPENSES FOR 1996–97 Tuition: $4400 full-time. Part-time tuition per quarter ranges from $92 to $1000. Full-time mandatory fees: $400.
APPLYING *Required:* school transcript, campus interview. *Application deadline:* rolling. *Notification:* continuous.
APPLYING/TRANSFER *Required:* high school transcript, campus interview.
CONTACT Mr. Darrell Brown, Admissions Director, Southwestern College of Business, Middletown, OH 45044-5113, 513-423-3346.

STARK TECHNICAL COLLEGE
Canton, Ohio

UG Enrollment: 4,164	Tuition & Fees (OH Res): $2490
Application Deadline: rolling	Room & Board: N/Avail

GENERAL State and locally supported, 2-year, coed. Part of Ohio Board of Regents. Awards terminal associate degrees. Founded 1970. *Setting:* 97-acre suburban campus with easy access to Cleveland. *Total enrollment:* 4,164. *Faculty:* 210 (100 full-time, 110 part-time); student-faculty ratio is 20:1.
ENROLLMENT PROFILE 4,164 students from 4 states and territories. 66% women, 61% part-time, 99% state residents, 15% transferred in, 0% international, 62% 25 or older, 1% Native American, 1% Hispanic, 7% African American, 1% Asian American.
FIRST-YEAR CLASS Of the students who applied, 100% were accepted, 80% of whom enrolled. 5% from top 10% of their high school class, 15% from top quarter, 60% from top half.
ACADEMIC PROGRAM Honor code. Calendar: semesters. Academic remediation for entering students, self-designed majors, summer session for credit, part-time degree program (daytime, evenings, summer), external degree programs, adult/continuing education programs, co-op programs. Off-campus study at Malone College, University of Akron, Walsh College, Kent State University, Stark Campus.
GENERAL DEGREE REQUIREMENTS 70 semester hours; computer course for most majors; internship (some majors).
MAJORS Accounting, architectural technologies, automotive technologies, biomedical technologies, business administration/commerce/management, civil engineering technology, computer programming, computer technologies, construction technologies, court reporting, drafting and design, early childhood education, electrical and electronics technologies, electrical engineering technology, electronics engineering technology, fire science, food services technology, human services, industrial engineering technology, interdisciplinary studies, legal secretarial studies, management information systems, marketing/retailing/merchandising, mechanical engineering technology, medical assistant technologies, medical laboratory technology, medical records services, nursing, occupational therapy, physical therapy, respiratory therapy, secretarial studies/office management.
LIBRARY Learning Resource Center with 70,000 books, 4,000 microform titles, 425 periodicals, 1,600 records, tapes, and CDs.
COMPUTERS ON CAMPUS 190 computers for student use in computer center, computer labs, classrooms provide access to main academic computer. Staffed computer lab on campus.
COLLEGE LIFE Student-run newspaper. 3% vote in student government elections. *Student services:* personal-psychological counseling. *Campus security:* 24-hour emergency response devices, late-night transport-escort service.
HOUSING College housing not available.
ATHLETICS *Intramural:* basketball, bowling, golf, skiing (cross-country), skiing (downhill), tennis, volleyball.
CAREER PLANNING *Placement office:* 3 full-time, 1 part-time staff. *Director:* Mr. Charles Koehler, Director, Career Services, 216-966-5459. *Services:* job fairs, resume preparation, resume referral, career counseling, careers library, job bank, job interviews.
EXPENSES FOR 1996–97 *Application fee:* $35. State resident tuition: $2490 full-time, $83 per semester hour part-time. Nonresident tuition: $3390 full-time, $113 per semester hour part-time.
FINANCIAL AID *College-administered undergrad aid 1995–96:* 2,500 need-based scholarships (average $3400), 50 non-need scholarships (average $2500), Federal Work-Study, 70 part-time jobs. *Required forms:* state, institutional, FAFSA; accepted: CSS Financial Aid PROFILE. *Priority deadline:* 5/1. *Payment plans:* installment, deferred payment. *Waivers:* full or partial for employees or children of employees and senior citizens. *Notification:* 7/1.
APPLYING Open admission. *Options:* early entrance, deferred entrance, midyear entrance. *Required:* school transcript, TOEFL for international students. *Recommended:* SAT I or ACT. Test scores used for counseling/placement. *Application deadline:* rolling.
APPLYING/TRANSFER *Required:* high school transcript, college transcript. *Recommended:* standardized test scores. *Entrance:* noncompetitive. *Application deadline:* rolling. *Contact:* Mr. Wallace Hoffer, Associate Dean of Student Services, 216-966-5450.
CONTACT Mr. Wallace Hoffer, Associate Dean of Student Services, Stark Technical College, Canton, OH 44720-7299, 216-966-5450 or toll-free 800-797-8275. *Fax:* 216-497-6313. College video available.

TERRA STATE COMMUNITY COLLEGE
Fremont, Ohio

UG Enrollment: 2,628 | **Tuition & Fees (OH Res): $2688**
Application Deadline: rolling | **Room & Board: N/Avail**

GENERAL State-supported, 2-year, coed. Part of Ohio Board of Regents. Awards certificates, transfer associate, terminal associate degrees. Founded 1968. ***Setting:*** 100-acre small-town campus with easy access to Toledo. ***Total enrollment:*** 2,628. ***Faculty:*** 148 (48 full-time, 10% with terminal degrees, 100 part-time); student-faculty ratio is 19:1.
ENROLLMENT PROFILE 2,628 students from 5 states and territories. 48% women, 56% part-time, 90% state residents, 6% transferred in, 0% international, 50% 25 or older, 4% Hispanic, 2% African American. ***Most popular recent majors:*** law enforcement/police sciences, business administration/commerce/management, computer information systems.
FIRST-YEAR CLASS 853 total. Of the students who applied, 100% were accepted.
ACADEMIC PROGRAM Core, honor code. Calendar: quarters. Academic remediation for entering students, services for LD students, self-designed majors, tutorials, summer session for credit, part-time degree program (daytime, evenings, weekends), adult/continuing education programs.
GENERAL DEGREE REQUIREMENTS 90 credits; 1 math course; computer course.
MAJORS Accounting, architectural technologies, automotive technologies, business administration/commerce/management, chemistry, child care/child and family studies, computer information systems, construction management, deaf interpreter training, drafting and design, early childhood education, electrical and electronics technologies, electromechanical technology, engineering (general), finance/banking, graphic arts, heating/refrigeration/air conditioning, industrial administration, industrial engineering technology, law enforcement/police sciences, legal secretarial studies, manufacturing technology, marketing/retailing/merchandising, mathematics, mechanical engineering technology, medical secretarial studies, nuclear technology, physics, plastics technology, printing technologies, quality control technology, real estate, secretarial studies/office management, surveying technology, technical writing, welding technology.
LIBRARY 18,442 books, 42,518 microform titles, 411 periodicals, 3,184 records, tapes, and CDs.
COMPUTERS ON CAMPUS 300 computers for student use in computer center, computer labs, classrooms, library provide access to main academic computer. Staffed computer lab on campus provides training in use of computers, software.
COLLEGE LIFE Student-run newspaper. ***Social organizations:*** 1 national fraternity, 1 national sorority; 3% of eligible men and 3% of eligible women are members. ***Student services:*** personal-psychological counseling. ***Campus security:*** 24-hour emergency response devices, late-night transport-escort service.
HOUSING College housing not available.
ATHLETICS ***Intramural:*** basketball, football, golf, skiing (cross-country), skiing (downhill), softball, table tennis (Ping-Pong), volleyball.
CAREER PLANNING ***Placement office:*** 1 full-time staff. ***Director:*** Ms. Bobbie Walmer, Placement Coordinator, 419-334-8400 Ext. 341. ***Services:*** job fairs, resume preparation, resume referral, career counseling, job interviews.
EXPENSES FOR 1995–96 State resident tuition: $2100 full-time, $45 per credit hour part-time. Nonresident tuition: $5082 full-time, $116 per credit hour part-time. Part-time mandatory fees: $14 per credit hour. Full-time mandatory fees: $588.
FINANCIAL AID ***College-administered undergrad aid 1995–96:*** 5 non-need scholarships (average $500), low-interest long-term loans from college funds (average $400), loans from external sources (average $2625), 30 part-time jobs. ***Required forms:*** institutional, FAFSA; required for some: state; accepted: CSS Financial Aid PROFILE. ***Priority deadline:*** 6/15. ***Payment plan:*** installment. ***Waivers:*** full or partial for employees or children of employees and senior citizens.
APPLYING Open admission. ***Options:*** early entrance, deferred entrance, midyear entrance. ***Required:*** TOEFL for international students, ACT ASSET. ***Recommended:*** SAT I or ACT. Test scores used for counseling/placement. ***Application deadline:*** rolling.
APPLYING/TRANSFER ***Required:*** standardized test scores. ***Entrance:*** noncompetitive. ***Application deadline:*** rolling.
CONTACT Ms. Maryjo Jay, Admissions Counselor, Terra State Community College, Fremont, OH 43420-9670, 419-334-8400 Ext. 350 or toll-free 800-334-3886 (in-state). ***Fax:*** 419-334-9414.

THE UNIVERSITY OF AKRON–WAYNE COLLEGE
Orrville, Ohio

UG Enrollment: 1,458 | **Tuition & Fees (OH Res): $3590**
Application Deadline: 8/28 | **Room & Board: N/Avail**

GENERAL State-supported, 2-year, coed. Part of University of Akron. Awards transfer associate, terminal associate degrees. Founded 1972. ***Setting:*** 163-acre rural campus. ***Total enrollment:*** 1,458. ***Faculty:*** 109 (24 full-time, 85 part-time).
ENROLLMENT PROFILE 1,458 students: 51% women, 56% part-time, 100% state residents, 9% transferred in, 61% 25 or older, 1% Native American, 0% Hispanic, 1% African American. ***Most popular recent majors:*** business administration/commerce/management, science, social work.
FIRST-YEAR CLASS 194 total. Of the students who applied, 98% were accepted, 91% of whom enrolled. 1 National Merit Scholar.
ACADEMIC PROGRAM Core. Calendar: early semester. Academic remediation for entering students, services for LD students, summer session for credit, part-time degree program (daytime, evenings, weekends, summer), adult/continuing education programs, co-op programs. ROTC: Army (c), Naval (c), Air Force (c).
GENERAL DEGREE REQUIREMENTS 64 credits; math/science requirements vary according to program.
MAJORS Accounting, business administration/commerce/management, computer science, computer technologies, data processing, interdisciplinary studies, liberal arts/general studies, science, secretarial studies/office management, social work.
LIBRARY 20,000 books, 9,500 microform titles, 240 periodicals, 424 records, tapes, and CDs.
COMPUTERS ON CAMPUS 223 computers for student use in computer center, various campus facilities, library.
COLLEGE LIFE Drama-theater group, student-run newspaper. ***Student services:*** legal services, personal-psychological counseling.
HOUSING College housing not available.
ATHLETICS ***Intercollegiate:*** basketball M(s)/W, golf M, tennis M/W, volleyball W. ***Intramural:*** volleyball.
CAREER PLANNING ***Placement office:*** 1 full-time staff. ***Service:*** career counseling.
EXPENSES FOR 1995–96 ***Application fee:*** $25. State resident tuition: $3485 full-time, $116.15 per credit part-time. Nonresident tuition: $7970 full-time, $265.65 per credit part-time. Part-time mandatory fees: $3.50 per credit. Full-time mandatory fees: $105.
FINANCIAL AID ***College-administered undergrad aid 1995–96:*** need-based scholarships, non-need scholarships, short-term loans, low-interest long-term loans from external sources, Federal Work-Study, 20 part-time jobs. ***Required forms:*** CSS Financial Aid PROFILE, institutional, FAFSA. ***Priority deadline:*** 4/1.
APPLYING Open admission. ***Options:*** early entrance, deferred entrance. ***Recommended:*** 3 years of high school math and science, some high school foreign language, SAT I or ACT. ***Required for some:*** SAT I or ACT. Test scores used for counseling/placement. ***Application deadline:*** 8/28. ***Notification:*** continuous until 8/28.
APPLYING/TRANSFER ***Recommended:*** 3 years of high school math and science, some high school foreign language. ***Required for some:*** standardized test scores. ***Entrance:*** minimally difficult. ***Application deadline:*** 8/28. ***Notification:*** continuous until 8/28.
CONTACT Mrs. Peggy J. Shallenberger, Admissions Coordinator, The University of Akron–Wayne College, Orrville, OH 44667-9192, 216-683-2010 or toll-free 800-221-8308.

UNIVERSITY OF CINCINNATI CLERMONT COLLEGE
Batavia, Ohio

UG Enrollment: 1,997 | **Tuition & Fees (OH Res): $2961**
Application Deadline: rolling | **Room & Board: N/Avail**

GENERAL State-supported, 2-year, coed. Part of University of Cincinnati System. Awards transfer associate, terminal associate degrees. Founded 1972. ***Setting:*** 65-acre rural campus with easy access to Cincinnati. ***Total enrollment:*** 1,997. ***Faculty:*** 143 (36 full-time, 107 part-time).
ENROLLMENT PROFILE 1,997 students from 3 states and territories. 66% women, 34% men, 54% part-time, 99% state residents, 17% transferred in, 0% international, 50% 25 or older, 2% Native American, 1% Hispanic, 4% African American, 1% Asian American. ***Areas of study chosen:*** 29% business management and administrative services, 18% liberal arts/general studies, 15% education, 7% biological and life sciences, 5% computer and information sciences, 4% engineering and applied sciences, 1% predentistry, 1% prelaw, 1% premed, 1% prevet. ***Most popular recent majors:*** business administration/commerce/management, liberal arts/general studies, elementary education.
FIRST-YEAR CLASS 877 total. 8% from top 10% of their high school class, 28% from top quarter, 46% from top half.
ACADEMIC PROGRAM Calendar: quarters. Academic remediation for entering students, advanced placement, self-designed majors, summer session for credit, part-time degree program (daytime, evenings, weekends), adult/continuing education programs, co-op programs and internships. Off-campus study at 11 members of the Greater Cincinnati Consortium of Colleges and Universities. ROTC: Air Force (c).
GENERAL DEGREE REQUIREMENTS 93 quarter hours; math proficiency; computer course for business management, electrical engineering, pre-business, business and office administration, accounting, information science majors.
MAJORS Accounting, aviation technology, business administration/commerce/management, computer graphics, computer information systems, computer programming, court reporting, criminal justice, electrical engineering technology, elementary education, hospitality services, information science, legal secretarial studies, liberal arts/general studies, medical secretarial studies, paralegal studies, pharmacy/pharmaceutical sciences, secretarial studies/office management, social work.
LIBRARY 19,235 books, 552 microform titles, 174 periodicals, 209 records, tapes, and CDs.
COMPUTERS ON CAMPUS 104 computers for student use in computer center, computer labs, classrooms provide access to Internet.
COLLEGE LIFE Drama-theater group. ***Student services:*** personal-psychological counseling. ***Campus security:*** 12-hour patrols by trained security personnel.
HOUSING College housing not available.
ATHLETICS ***Intramural:*** basketball, bowling, golf, table tennis (Ping-Pong), tennis, volleyball. ***Contact:*** Mr. Philip Sinkovich, Coach/Academic Advisor, 513-732-5200.
CAREER PLANNING ***Placement office:*** 1 full-time, 1 part-time staff. ***Director:*** Mrs. Carol Pleuss, Director/Counselor, Career and Placement, 513-732-5221. ***Service:*** career counseling. 50 organizations recruited on campus 1994–95.
EXPENSES FOR 1995–96 State resident tuition: $2961 full-time, $81 per quarter hour part-time. Nonresident tuition: $7245 full-time, $200 per quarter hour part-time.
FINANCIAL AID ***College-administered undergrad aid 1995–96:*** 157 need-based scholarships (average $1018), 50 non-need scholarships (average $1000), short-term loans, low-interest long-term loans from external sources (average $1790), Federal Work-Study, 26 part-time jobs. ***Required forms:*** CSS Financial Aid PROFILE, state, FAFSA. ***Priority deadline:*** 3/1. ***Payment plan:*** installment. ***Waivers:*** full or partial for employees or children of employees and senior citizens.
APPLYING Open admission. ***Option:*** deferred entrance. ***Required:*** school transcript. ***Recommended:*** SAT I or ACT. ***Required for some:*** SAT I or ACT. Test scores used for counseling/placement. ***Application deadline:*** rolling. ***Notification:*** continuous.
APPLYING/TRANSFER ***Required:*** high school transcript, college transcript. ***Recommended:*** standardized test scores. ***Required for some:*** standardized test scores. ***Entrance:*** noncompetitive. ***Application deadline:*** rolling. ***Notification:*** continuous. ***Contact:*** Mr. Robert W. Neel, Director of Enrollment Management, 513-732-5247.
CONTACT Ms. Tanya Bohart, Admissions Assistant, University of Cincinnati Clermont College, Batavia, OH 45103-1785, 513-732-5202. ***E-mail:*** tanya.bohart@uc.edu.

UNIVERSITY OF CINCINNATI RAYMOND WALTERS COLLEGE
Cincinnati, Ohio

UG Enrollment: 2,838 **Tuition & Fees (OH Res): $3684**
Application Deadline: rolling **Room & Board: N/Avail**

GENERAL State-supported, 2-year, coed. Part of University of Cincinnati System. Awards certificates, transfer associate, terminal associate degrees. Founded 1967. ***Setting:*** 120-acre suburban campus. ***Endowment:*** $32,399. ***Research spending 1994–95:*** $5000. ***Total enrollment:*** 2,838. ***Faculty:*** 236 (91 full-time, 41% with terminal degrees, 145 part-time); student-faculty ratio is 12:1.

ENROLLMENT PROFILE 2,838 students from 4 states and territories, 4 other countries. 71% women, 29% men, 61% part-time, 98% state residents, 10% transferred in, 45% have need-based financial aid, 5% have non-need-based financial aid, 1% international, 55% 25 or older, 1% Native American, 1% Hispanic, 10% African American, 1% Asian American. ***Areas of study chosen:*** 38% health professions and related sciences, 28% business management and administrative services, 8% liberal arts/general studies, 5% computer and information sciences, 5% education, 4% social sciences, 3% engineering and applied sciences, 3% fine arts, 2% natural resource sciences, 1% library and information studies, 1% prelaw, 1% premed.

FIRST-YEAR CLASS 491 total; 759 applied, 93% were accepted, 70% of whom enrolled. 2% from top 10% of their high school class, 8% from top quarter, 23% from top half.

ACADEMIC PROGRAM Calendar: quarters. 659 courses offered in 1995–96. Academic remediation for entering students, English as a second language program offered during academic year, services for LD students, advanced placement, self-designed majors, summer session for credit, part-time degree program (daytime, evenings), adult/continuing education programs, co-op programs and internships. Off-campus study at 12 members of the Greater Cincinnati Consortium of Colleges and Universities. Study abroad in Great Britain. ROTC: Army (c), Air Force (c).

GENERAL DEGREE REQUIREMENT 90 credit hours.

MAJORS Accounting, automotive technologies, biochemical technology, biology/biological sciences, business administration/commerce/management, chemistry, commercial art, computer information systems, computer programming, computer science, computer technologies, dental services, dietetics, economics, education, emergency medical technology, (pre)engineering sequence, environmental sciences, humanities, industrial administration, laboratory technologies, legal secretarial studies, liberal arts/general studies, library science, management information systems, manufacturing technology, marketing/retailing/merchandising, medical secretarial studies, medical technology, nuclear medical technology, nursing, radiological technology, real estate, secretarial studies/office management, social work, urban studies, veterinary technology.

LIBRARY Raymond Walters College Library with 54,934 books, 11,520 microform titles, 600 periodicals, 3 on-line bibliographic services, 3 CD-ROMs, 1,285 records, tapes, and CDs. Acquisition spending 1994–95: $111,516.

COMPUTERS ON CAMPUS Computer purchase plan available. 231 computers for student use in computer center, computer labs, library provide access to main academic computer, off-campus computing facilities, e-mail, on-line services, Internet. Staffed computer lab on campus provides training in use of computers, software. Academic computing expenditure 1994–95: $100,000.

COLLEGE LIFE Student-run newspaper. ***Social organizations:*** 15 open to all; national fraternities, national sororities, local fraternities, local sororities; 2% of eligible men and 2% of eligible women are members. ***Most popular organizations:*** Student Government, African-American Cultural Association, Phi Theta Kappa, College Secretaries International, American Dental Hygiene Students Association. ***Major annual events:*** Honors Ceremony, End of Year Picnic, Holiday Party for Needy Families. ***Student services:*** health clinic. ***Campus security:*** 24-hour emergency response devices and patrols, student patrols, late-night transport-escort service.

HOUSING College housing not available.

ATHLETICS ***Intercollegiate:*** basketball M(s)/W(s), cross-country running M(s)/W(s), football M(s), gymnastics M(s)/W(s), ice hockey M(s), swimming and diving M(s)/W(s), tennis M(s)/W(s), track and field M(s)/W(s), wrestling M(s). ***Intramural:*** basketball, cross-country running, equestrian sports, fencing, football, gymnastics, ice hockey, sailing, soccer, swimming and diving, tennis, track and field, volleyball, wrestling. ***Contact:*** Mr. Gerald K. O'Dell, Director of Athletics, 513-556-4603.

CAREER PLANNING ***Placement office:*** 2 full-time staff; $70,000 operating expenditure 1994–95. ***Director:*** Ms. Pam Lineback, Director, Career Services, 513-745-5670. ***Services:*** job fairs, resume preparation, resume referral, career counseling, careers library, job interviews.

EXPENSES FOR 1995–96 ***Application fee:*** $30. State resident tuition: $3339 full-time, $91 per credit hour part-time. Nonresident tuition: $8241 full-time, $233 per credit hour part-time. Full-time mandatory fees: $345.

FINANCIAL AID ***College-administered undergrad aid 1995–96:*** need-based scholarships, non-need scholarships, short-term loans, low-interest long-term loans from external sources, Federal Work-Study, part-time jobs. ***Required forms:*** state, FAFSA. ***Application deadline:*** continuous to 7/1. ***Payment plan:*** installment. ***Waivers:*** full or partial for employees or children of employees and senior citizens.

APPLYING Open admission except for allied health programs. ***Options:*** early entrance, deferred entrance, midyear entrance. ***Required:*** school transcript, TOEFL for international students, ACT ASSET. ***Recommended:*** SAT I or ACT. ***Required for some:*** SAT I or ACT. Test scores used for counseling/placement. ***Application deadline:*** rolling. ***Notification:*** continuous. Preference given to state residents.

APPLYING/TRANSFER ***Required:*** high school transcript, college transcript, good standing at previous institution. ***Recommended:*** standardized test scores. ***Required for some:*** standardized test scores. ***Application deadline:*** rolling. ***Notification:*** continuous. ***Contact:*** Ms. Dana Freer, Acting Director of Enrollment Management, 513-745-5700.

CONTACT Ms. Dana Freer, Acting Director of Enrollment Management, University of Cincinnati Raymond Walters College, 9555 Plainfield Road, Cincinnati, OH 45236-1007, 513-745-5700. ***Fax:*** 513-745-5780.

VIRGINIA MARTI COLLEGE OF FASHION AND ART
Lakewood, Ohio

UG Enrollment: 200 **Tuition & Fees: $9020**
Application Deadline: rolling **Room & Board: N/Avail**

GENERAL Proprietary, 2-year, coed. Awards diplomas, terminal associate degrees. Founded 1966. ***Setting:*** urban campus with easy access to Cleveland. ***Total enrollment:*** 200. ***Faculty:*** 30 (5 full-time, 25 part-time); student-faculty ratio is 10:1.

ENROLLMENT PROFILE 200 students from 2 states and territories, 4 other countries. 60% women, 37% part-time, 95% state residents, 20% transferred in, 40% 25 or older, 1% Native American, 4% Hispanic, 30% African American, 3% Asian American. ***Most popular recent majors:*** fashion design and technology, interior design.

FIRST-YEAR CLASS 32 total; 44 applied, 86% were accepted, 84% of whom enrolled.

ACADEMIC PROGRAM Honor code. Calendar: quarters. Academic remediation for entering students, English as a second language program offered during academic year and summer, self-designed majors, summer session for credit, part-time degree program (daytime, evenings, weekends, summer), adult/continuing education programs, co-op programs and internships. Study abroad in France, Italy, England.

GENERAL DEGREE REQUIREMENTS 105 quarter hours; 1 course in math; computer course.

MAJORS Commercial art, fashion design and technology, fashion merchandising, interior design, jewelry and metalsmithing.

COMPUTERS ON CAMPUS 12 computers for student use in computer center, student center.

COLLEGE LIFE Student-run newspaper. ***Student services:*** personal-psychological counseling. ***Campus security:*** 24-hour emergency response devices.

HOUSING College housing not available.

CAREER PLANNING ***Services:*** job fairs, resume preparation, resume referral, career counseling, careers library, job bank, job interviews. Students must register freshman year.

EXPENSES FOR 1995–96 ***Application fee:*** $20. Tuition: $8840 full-time, $170 per quarter hour part-time. Full-time mandatory fees: $180. Tuition guaranteed not to increase for student's term of enrollment.

FINANCIAL AID ***College-administered undergrad aid 1995–96:*** 3 need-based scholarships (average $3000), low-interest long-term loans from external sources (average $2500), Federal Work-Study, 2 part-time jobs. ***Required forms:*** institutional, FAFSA; required for some: CSS Financial Aid PROFILE, state. ***Priority deadline:*** 9/1. ***Payment plan:*** installment. ***Waivers:*** full or partial for employees or children of employees.

APPLYING ***Options:*** early entrance, deferred entrance, midyear entrance. ***Required:*** minimum 2.0 GPA, campus interview, TOEFL for international students, CAPS. Test scores used for admission. ***Application deadline:*** rolling.

APPLYING/TRANSFER ***Required:*** standardized test scores, campus interview, college transcript. ***Entrance:*** minimally difficult. ***Application deadline:*** rolling. ***Contact:*** Ms. Sue Hoban, Registrar, 216-221-7574.

CONTACT Mr. Dennis Marti, Director of Admissions, Virginia Marti College of Fashion and Art, 11724 Detroit Avenue, PO Box 580, Lakewood, OH 44107-3002, 216-221-8584 Ext. 21. College video available.

❖ ***See page 826 for a narrative description.*** ❖

WASHINGTON STATE COMMUNITY COLLEGE
Marietta, Ohio

UG Enrollment: 2,019 **Tuition & Fees (OH Res): $2464**
Application Deadline: rolling **Room & Board: N/Avail**

GENERAL State-supported, 2-year, coed. Part of Ohio Board of Regents. Awards certificates, transfer associate, terminal associate degrees. Founded 1971. ***Setting:*** small-town campus. ***Total enrollment:*** 2,019. ***Faculty:*** 132 (61 full-time, 71 part-time).

ENROLLMENT PROFILE 2,019 students from 5 states and territories. 60% women, 40% men, 46% part-time, 90% state residents, 5% transferred in, 0% international, 51% 25 or older, 1% Native American, 1% Hispanic, 2% African American, 1% Asian American. ***Areas of study chosen:*** 16% business management and administrative services, 12% engineering and applied sciences, 10% health professions and related sciences, 4% computer and information sciences, 4% education, 4% liberal arts/general studies, 3% social sciences, 2% biological and life sciences, 2% communications and journalism, 1% mathematics, 1% physical sciences. ***Most popular recent majors:*** automotive technologies, nursing, secretarial studies/office management.

FIRST-YEAR CLASS 659 total; 915 applied, 100% were accepted, 72% of whom enrolled.

ACADEMIC PROGRAM Core. Calendar: quarters. Academic remediation for entering students, services for LD students, self-designed majors, summer session for credit, part-time degree program (daytime, evenings), adult/continuing education programs, internships.

GENERAL DEGREE REQUIREMENTS 90 credit hours; computer course.

MAJORS Accounting, automotive technologies, biology/biological sciences, business administration/commerce/management, chemical engineering technology, computer technologies, data processing, drafting and design, early childhood education, education, electrical and electronics technologies, electrical engineering technology, engineering (general), engineering and applied sciences, heating/refrigeration/air conditioning, liberal arts/general studies, manufacturing technology, marketing/retailing/merchandising, mathematics, mechanical engineering technology, medical laboratory technology, medical secretarial studies, nursing, physical sciences, practical nursing, radio and television studies, science, secretarial studies/office management, social work.

LIBRARY 15,000 books, 68 microform titles, 200 periodicals, 300 records, tapes, and CDs.

COMPUTERS ON CAMPUS 175 computers for student use in computer center, computer labs, learning resource center, classrooms, library provide access to Internet. Staffed computer lab on campus.

Peterson's Guide to Two-Year Colleges 1997 537

Ohio–Oklahoma

Washington State Community College (continued)
COLLEGE LIFE Choral group. 5% vote in student government elections. *Social organizations:* 14 open to all. *Most popular organizations:* Student Senate, Phi Theta Kappa, Practical Nursing Club, Business Lunch Club, Beta Club. *Student services:* personal-psychological counseling.
HOUSING College housing not available.
ATHLETICS *Intramural:* basketball, softball, volleyball.
CAREER PLANNING *Placement office:* 1 full-time staff. *Director:* Mr. Kraig Curry, Student Services Advisor, 614-374-8716. *Services:* job fairs, career counseling, careers library, job bank, job interviews.
AFTER GRADUATION 95% of class of 1994 had job offers within 6 months. 90% of students completing a degree program went directly on to further study.
EXPENSES FOR 1996–97 State resident tuition: $2419 full-time, $53.75 per credit part-time. Nonresident tuition: $4838 full-time, $107.50 per credit part-time. Part-time mandatory fees: $45 per year. Full-time mandatory fees: $45.
FINANCIAL AID *College-administered undergrad aid 1995–96:* need-based scholarships, non-need scholarships, 33 Federal Work-Study (averaging $903). *Required forms:* institutional; accepted: CSS Financial Aid PROFILE, state, FAFSA. *Payment plan:* installment. *Waivers:* full or partial for employees or children of employees and senior citizens.
APPLYING Open admission except for medical laboratory technology, nursing programs. *Options:* early entrance, deferred entrance, midyear entrance. *Required:* TOEFL for international students, ACT ASSET. *Recommended:* school transcript. *Required for some:* school transcript. Test scores used for counseling/placement. *Application deadline:* rolling. *Notification:* continuous.
APPLYING/TRANSFER *Recommended:* college transcript. *Required for some:* college transcript. *Entrance:* noncompetitive. *Application deadline:* rolling. *Notification:* continuous. *Contact:* Ms. Gloria Norris, Transfer Coordinator, 614-374-8716.
CONTACT Mr. Kevin Conley, Director of Admissions, Washington State Community College, Marietta, OH 45750-9225, 614-374-8716. *Fax:* 614-373-7496.

WEST SIDE INSTITUTE OF TECHNOLOGY
Cleveland, Ohio

GENERAL Proprietary, 2-year, specialized, primarily men. Awards transfer associate, terminal associate degrees. Founded 1958. *Setting:* 4-acre urban campus. *Total enrollment:* 14. *Faculty:* 18 (6 full-time, 12 part-time).
EXPENSES FOR 1995–96 Tuition: $4545 full-time. One-time mandatory fee: $100. Tuition guaranteed not to increase for student's term of enrollment.
CONTACT Mr. Luerue Dickerson, Admissions Representative, West Side Institute of Technology, 9801 Walford Avenue, Cleveland, OH 44102-4797, 216-651-1656.

WRIGHT STATE UNIVERSITY, LAKE CAMPUS
Celina, Ohio

UG Enrollment: 650	Tuition & Fees (OH Res): $3074
Application Deadline: rolling	Room & Board: N/Avail

GENERAL State-supported, 2-year, coed. Part of Wright State University. Awards certificates, transfer associate, terminal associate degrees. Founded 1969. *Setting:* 173-acre rural campus. *Total enrollment:* 650. *Faculty:* 48 (18 full-time, 30 part-time).
ENROLLMENT PROFILE 650 students from 3 states and territories, 1 other country. 60% women, 40% men, 52% part-time, 99% state residents, 6% transferred in, 46% have need-based financial aid, 3% have non-need-based financial aid, 52% 25 or older, 1% Native American, 0% Hispanic, 0% African American, 1% Asian American. *Areas of study chosen:* 27% business management and administrative services, 19% education, 13% engineering and applied sciences, 5% social sciences, 3% biological and life sciences, 3% health professions and related sciences, 2% communications and journalism, 2% psychology, 1% computer and information sciences, 1% English language/literature/letters, 1% fine arts, 1% foreign language and literature, 1% mathematics, 1% physical sciences. *Most popular recent majors:* business administration/commerce/management, secretarial studies/office management, accounting.
FIRST-YEAR CLASS 179 total; 231 applied, 99% were accepted, 78% of whom enrolled.
ACADEMIC PROGRAM Core, interdisciplinary curriculum, honor code. Calendar: quarters. 403 courses offered in 1995–96. Academic remediation for entering students, services for LD students, advanced placement, self-designed majors, honors program, summer session for credit, part-time degree program (daytime, evenings), adult/continuing education programs. Off-campus study at members of the Southwestern Ohio Council for Higher Education.
GENERAL DEGREE REQUIREMENT 94 credit hours.
MAJORS Accounting, biology/biological sciences, business administration/commerce/management, chemistry, communication, drafting and design, electrical engineering technology, electronics engineering technology, elementary education, engineering (general), engineering design, (pre)engineering sequence, engineering technology, English, finance/banking, geography, history, industrial engineering technology, legal secretarial studies, liberal arts/general studies, management information systems, manufacturing technology, marketing/retailing/merchandising, mechanical engineering technology, medical secretarial studies, psychology, retail management, secretarial studies/office management, social work, sociology, word processing.
LIBRARY Wright State University, Lake Campus Library with 26,000 books, 25 microform titles, 347 periodicals, 2 on-line bibliographic services, 1 CD-ROM, 200 records, tapes, and CDs.
COMPUTERS ON CAMPUS 105 computers for student use in computer center, computer labs, learning resource center, library provide access to e-mail, on-line services. Staffed computer lab on campus provides training in use of computers, software.
COLLEGE LIFE Drama-theater group, student-run newspaper. *Social organizations:* 2 open to all. *Most popular organizations:* Business Professionals of America, Student Manufacturing Association. *Student services:* personal-psychological counseling. *Campus security:* 24-hour emergency response devices.
HOUSING College housing not available.

ATHLETICS *Intercollegiate:* basketball M/W, golf M, volleyball W. *Contact:* Mr. Vaughn Schellhause, Athletic Director, 419-586-0329.
CAREER PLANNING *Director:* Mr. Gregory Schumm, Assistant Dean, 419-586-0330. *Services:* resume referral, career counseling, job interviews.
EXPENSES FOR 1995–96 *Application fee:* $30. State resident tuition: $3069 full-time, $96 per credit hour part-time. Nonresident tuition: $6498 full-time, $203 per credit hour part-time. Full-time mandatory fees: $5.
FINANCIAL AID *College-administered undergrad aid 1995–96:* need-based scholarships, 10 non-need scholarships (averaging $1800), short-term loans (averaging $300), low-interest long-term loans from college funds (averaging $1420), loans from external sources (averaging $2200), Federal Work-Study, 25 part-time jobs. *Required forms:* institutional, FAFSA; accepted: CSS Financial Aid PROFILE, state. *Priority deadline:* 6/1. *Payment plans:* installment, deferred payment. *Waivers:* full or partial for employees or children of employees and senior citizens. *Average indebtedness of graduates:* $2000.
APPLYING Open admission for state residents. *Options:* early entrance, deferred entrance, midyear entrance. *Required:* school transcript, 2 years of high school foreign language, SAT I or ACT, TOEFL for international students. *Recommended:* minimum 2.0 GPA, 3 years of high school math and science. Test scores used for counseling/placement. *Application deadline:* rolling. *Notification:* continuous.
APPLYING/TRANSFER *Recommended:* 3 years of high school math and science. *Entrance:* noncompetitive. *Application deadline:* rolling. *Notification:* continuous. *Contact:* Mrs. B.J. Hobler, Coordinator of Registration and Admissions, 419-586-0324.
CONTACT Mrs. B.J. Hobler, Coordinator of Registration and Admissions, Wright State University, Lake Campus, Celina, OH 45822-2921, 419-586-0324 or toll-free 800-237-1477 (in-state). *Fax:* 419-586-0358.

OKLAHOMA

[Map of Oklahoma showing colleges: Northeastern Oklahoma Agricultural & Mechanical Coll, Northern Oklahoma Coll, Rogers State Coll, Bacone Coll, Tulsa, Rose State Coll, Redlands Comm Coll, Oklahoma City, Connors St Coll, Seminole Jr Coll, E Oklahoma State Coll, Southwestern Oklahoma State U at Sayre, Western Oklahoma State Coll, Murray State Coll, St. Gregory's Coll, Carl Albert State Coll, Oklahoma State U, Okmulgee.]

Oklahoma City Area
Oklahoma City Comm Coll
Oklahoma State U, Oklahoma City

Tulsa Area
Natl Educ Ctr – Spartan Sch of Aeronautics Campus
Tulsa Jr Coll

BACONE COLLEGE
Muskogee, Oklahoma

UG Enrollment: 386	Tuition & Fees: $3830
Application Deadline: rolling	Room & Board: $3470

GENERAL Independent, 2-year, coed, affiliated with American Baptist Churches in the U.S.A. Awards certificates, diplomas, transfer associate, terminal associate degrees. Founded 1880. *Setting:* 160-acre small-town campus with easy access to Tulsa. *Total enrollment:* 386. *Faculty:* 30 (22 full-time, 8 part-time); student-faculty ratio is 12:1.
ENROLLMENT PROFILE 386 students from 29 states and territories, 2 other countries. 69% women, 30% part-time, 89% state residents, 21% transferred in, 2% international, 50% 25 or older, 53% Native American, 1% Hispanic, 17% African American, 2% Asian American.
FIRST-YEAR CLASS 155 total. Of the students who applied, 100% were accepted, 33% of whom enrolled. 10% from top 10% of their high school class, 25% from top quarter, 50% from top half.
ACADEMIC PROGRAM Core. Calendar: semesters. Academic remediation for entering students, English as a second language program offered during academic year and summer, services for LD students, advanced placement, self-designed majors, summer session for credit, part-time degree program (daytime, evenings, weekends, summer), adult/continuing education programs, co-op programs.
GENERAL DEGREE REQUIREMENTS 62 semester hours; 3 semester hours of college algebra; 8 semester hours of science.
MAJORS Art/fine arts, business administration/commerce/management, business education, computer science, home economics, horticulture, journalism, liberal arts/general studies, Native American studies, natural resource management, nursing, radiological technology, secretarial studies/office management.
LIBRARY 33,250 books, 11,250 microform titles, 147 periodicals, 850 records, tapes, and CDs.
COMPUTERS ON CAMPUS 46 computers for student use in computer labs, library provide access to on-line services. Staffed computer lab on campus provides training in use of computers, software.

COLLEGE LIFE Orientation program (5 days, no cost, parents included). Drama-theater group, student-run newspaper. ***Most popular organizations:*** Native American Club, Phi Beta Kappa, Christian Nurses Fellowship. ***Student services:*** health clinic, personal-psychological counseling. ***Campus security:*** controlled dormitory access, 8-hour patrols by trained security personnel.

HOUSING 170 college housing spaces available; 80 were occupied 1995–96. No special consideration for freshman housing applicants. Off-campus living permitted. ***Option:*** coed housing available. Resident assistants live in dorms.

ATHLETICS Member NJCAA. ***Intercollegiate:*** baseball M(s), basketball M(s)/W(s), softball M/W(s). ***Intramural:*** badminton, basketball, football, racquetball, softball, table tennis (Ping-Pong), tennis, volleyball. ***Contact:*** Mr. David Baker, Athletics Director, 918-683-4581 Ext. 286.

CAREER PLANNING ***Service:*** career counseling.

AFTER GRADUATION 80% of students completing a degree program in 1994–95 went directly on to further study.

EXPENSES FOR 1996–97 ***Application fee:*** $10. Comprehensive fee of $7300 includes full-time tuition ($3470), mandatory fees ($360), and college room and board ($3470). Part-time tuition per semester hour ranges from $105 to $125. Part-time mandatory fees: $180 per semester.

FINANCIAL AID ***College-administered undergrad aid 1995–96:*** 100 need-based scholarships (average $1000), 28 non-need scholarships (average $1500), short-term loans (average $170), low-interest long-term loans from external sources (average $2625), Federal Work-Study. ***Required forms:*** institutional, FAFSA; required for some: state, IVF. ***Priority deadline:*** 8/20. ***Payment plan:*** installment. ***Waivers:*** full or partial for employees or children of employees. ***Notification:*** continuous.

APPLYING Open admission except for nursing, radiological technology programs. ***Options:*** early entrance, deferred entrance. ***Required:*** school transcript, SAT I or ACT, TOEFL for international students. ***Required for some:*** 3 years of high school math and science. Test scores used for counseling/placement. ***Application deadline:*** rolling.

APPLYING/TRANSFER ***Required:*** standardized test scores, high school transcript, college transcript. ***Required for some:*** 3 years of high school math. ***Entrance:*** noncompetitive. ***Application deadline:*** rolling. ***Contact:*** Mr. Yahola Tiger, Director of Student Support Services, 918-683-4581 Ext. 258.

CONTACT Ms. Jean Kay, Administrative Assistant, Bacone College, Muskogee, OK 74403-1597, 918-683-4581 Ext. 340. ***Fax:*** 918-682-5514. College video available.

CARL ALBERT STATE COLLEGE
Poteau, Oklahoma

UG Enrollment: 1,933	**Tuition & Fees (OK Res): $1213**
Application Deadline: 8/15	**Room & Board: $1800**

GENERAL State-supported, 2-year, coed. Part of Oklahoma State Regents for Higher Education. Awards transfer associate, terminal associate degrees. Founded 1934. ***Setting:*** 78-acre small-town campus. ***Total enrollment:*** 1,933. ***Faculty:*** 160 (42 full-time, 118 part-time); student-faculty ratio is 10:1.

ENROLLMENT PROFILE 1,933 students: 64% women, 60% part-time, 90% state residents, 2% transferred in, 0% international, 13% Native American, 1% Hispanic, 2% African American, 1% Asian American. ***Most popular recent major:*** business administration/commerce/management.

FIRST-YEAR CLASS 518 total. Of the students who applied, 100% were accepted, 95% of whom enrolled. 5% from top 10% of their high school class, 30% from top half.

ACADEMIC PROGRAM Core. Calendar: semesters. Academic remediation for entering students, English as a second language program offered during academic year, part-time degree program (daytime, evenings, summer), adult/continuing education programs, co-op programs.

GENERAL DEGREE REQUIREMENTS 62 credit hours; 3 credit hours of college algebra; 8 credit hours of science; computer course.

MAJORS Accounting, agricultural business, art education, biology/biological sciences, business administration/commerce/management, business education, computer science, early childhood education, elementary education, (pre)engineering sequence, English, hotel and restaurant management, industrial arts, journalism, legal secretarial studies, mathematics, medical secretarial studies, music, nursing, physical education, physical sciences, psychology, secretarial studies/office management, social science, zoology.

LIBRARY 21,508 books, 692 microform titles, 241 periodicals, 1,023 records, tapes, and CDs.

COMPUTERS ON CAMPUS 15 computers for student use in computer labs. Staffed computer lab on campus provides training in use of computers, software.

COLLEGE LIFE Drama-theater group, student-run newspaper. ***Social organizations:*** 1 local sorority. ***Student services:*** personal-psychological counseling.

HOUSING 76 college housing spaces available; all were occupied 1995–96. Off-campus living permitted.

ATHLETICS Member NJCAA. ***Intercollegiate:*** basketball M(s)/W(s). ***Intramural:*** tennis, volleyball, weight lifting.

CAREER PLANNING ***Service:*** career counseling.

EXPENSES FOR 1996–97 State resident tuition: $868 full-time, $28 per credit hour part-time. Nonresident tuition: $2728 full-time, $88 per credit hour part-time. Part-time mandatory fees: $11.50 per credit hour. Full-time mandatory fees: $345. College room and board: $1800.

FINANCIAL AID ***College-administered undergrad aid 1995–96:*** need-based scholarships, non-need scholarships, short-term loans, low-interest long-term loans from external sources, Federal Work-Study, part-time jobs. ***Required forms:*** institutional, FAFSA. ***Priority deadline:*** 7/31.

APPLYING Open admission. ***Required:*** school transcript, ACT, TOEFL for international students. Test scores used for counseling/placement. ***Application deadline:*** 8/15. ***Notification:*** continuous.

APPLYING/TRANSFER ***Required:*** high school transcript, college transcript. ***Entrance:*** noncompetitive. ***Application deadline:*** 8/15. ***Notification:*** continuous.

CONTACT Mrs. Lynda Hooper, Director of Admissions, Carl Albert State College, Poteau, OK 74953-5208, 918-647-1300. College video available.

CONNORS STATE COLLEGE
Warner, Oklahoma

UG Enrollment: 2,317	**Tuition & Fees (OK Res): $1163**
Application Deadline: rolling	**Room & Board: $2054**

GENERAL State-supported, 2-year, coed. Part of Oklahoma State Regents for Higher Education. Awards transfer associate, terminal associate degrees. Founded 1908. ***Setting:*** 1,658-acre rural campus. ***Total enrollment:*** 2,317. ***Faculty:*** 121 (53 full-time, 4% with terminal degrees, 68 part-time); student-faculty ratio is 22:1.

ENROLLMENT PROFILE 2,317 students from 17 states and territories. 67% women, 33% men, 35% part-time, 98% state residents, 12% live on campus, 21% transferred in, 45% 25 or older, 20% Native American, 1% Hispanic, 9% African American, 1% Asian American. ***Areas of study chosen:*** 35% liberal arts/general studies, 16% health professions and related sciences, 11% business management and administrative services, 6% education, 5% agriculture, 4% premed, 3% social sciences, 2% computer and information sciences, 2% psychology, 1% predentistry, 1% prelaw. ***Most popular recent majors:*** liberal arts/general studies, business administration/commerce/management, nursing.

FIRST-YEAR CLASS 511 total; 563 applied, 100% were accepted, 91% of whom enrolled. 9% from top 10% of their high school class, 23% from top quarter, 58% from top half. 9 valedictorians.

ACADEMIC PROGRAM Core, honor code. Calendar: semesters. Academic remediation for entering students, advanced placement, summer session for credit, part-time degree program (daytime, evenings, summer), adult/continuing education programs, internships.

GENERAL DEGREE REQUIREMENTS 60 semester hours; 1 college algebra course or 6 hours of science.

MAJORS Accounting, agricultural education, agricultural technologies, animal sciences, art education, biology/biological sciences, business administration/commerce/management, chemistry, child care/child and family studies, child psychology/child development, computer programming, computer science, criminal justice, data processing, drafting and design, education, engineering (general), English, finance/banking, gerontology, history, home economics, journalism, law enforcement/police sciences, liberal arts/general studies, mathematics, music, nursing, physical education, postal management, psychology, secretarial studies/office management, social work, sociology, speech/rhetoric/public address/debate, zoology.

LIBRARY Carl Westbrook Library with 58,371 books, 19,429 microform titles, 326 periodicals, 4,793 records, tapes, and CDs.

COMPUTERS ON CAMPUS 153 computers for student use in computer center, computer labs, learning resource center, classrooms, library provide access to on-line services. Staffed computer lab on campus provides training in use of computers, software.

COLLEGE LIFE Drama-theater group, student-run newspaper. 35% vote in student government elections. ***Social organizations:*** 21 open to all. ***Most popular organizations:*** Aggie Club, CD Club, Twilight Angels, McClarren Club, Library Club. ***Major annual events:*** Welcome Back Hamburger Cookout, Aggie Rodeo, Co-Ed Softball. ***Student services:*** health clinic. ***Campus security:*** late-night transport-escort service, trained security personnel.

HOUSING 355 college housing spaces available; 286 were occupied 1995–96. No special consideration for freshman housing applicants. Off-campus living permitted. ***Option:*** single-sex (2 buildings) housing available. Resident assistants live in dorms.

ATHLETICS Member NJCAA. ***Intercollegiate:*** baseball M(s), basketball M(s)/W(s), softball W(s), tennis M/W. ***Intramural:*** basketball, football, softball, tennis, volleyball. ***Contact:*** Mr. Monty Madewell, Athletic Director, 918-463-6246.

CAREER PLANNING ***Placement office:*** 1 full-time, 1 part-time staff. ***Director:*** Mr. John Turnbull, Counselor and Job Placement Officer, 918-463-6298. ***Services:*** career counseling, careers library.

EXPENSES FOR 1996–97 State resident tuition: $1163 full-time, $38.75 per semester hour part-time. Nonresident tuition: $2963 full-time, $98.75 per semester hour part-time. College room and board: $2054.

FINANCIAL AID ***College-administered undergrad aid 1995–96:*** 340 need-based scholarships (average $400), 150 non-need scholarships (average $350), short-term loans (average $25), low-interest long-term loans from external sources (average $1800), 80 Federal Work-Study (averaging $1200), 200 part-time jobs. ***Required forms:*** institutional, FAFSA. ***Priority deadline:*** 5/1. ***Waivers:*** full or partial for employees or children of employees and senior citizens. ***Average indebtedness of graduates:*** $3000.

APPLYING Open admission. ***Options:*** early entrance, deferred entrance. ***Required:*** 3 years of high school math, TOEFL for international students. ***Required for some:*** school transcript, SAT I or ACT, CPT. Test scores used for counseling/placement. ***Application deadline:*** rolling.

APPLYING/TRANSFER ***Required:*** 3 years of high school math, college transcript. ***Required for some:*** standardized test scores, high school transcript. ***Entrance:*** noncompetitive. ***Application deadline:*** rolling. ***Contact:*** Mr. Paul D. Wells, Director of Admissions and Registrar, 918-463-6233.

CONTACT Mr. Paul D. Wells, Director of Admissions and Registrar, Connors State College, Warner, OK 74469-9700, 918-463-6233.

EASTERN OKLAHOMA STATE COLLEGE
Wilburton, Oklahoma

UG Enrollment: 2,474	**Tuition & Fees (OK Res): $1224**
Application Deadline: rolling	**Room & Board: $2224**

GENERAL State-supported, 2-year, coed. Part of Oklahoma State Regents for Higher Education. Awards transfer associate, terminal associate degrees. Founded 1908. ***Setting:*** 4,000-acre rural campus. ***Total enrollment:*** 2,474. ***Faculty:*** 54 (48 full-time, 6 part-time). ***Notable Alumni:*** Charles Hardt, J. D. Wiliams, E. T. Dunlap, George Nigh, Henry Migor.

ENROLLMENT PROFILE 2,474 students from 8 states and territories, 2 other countries. 63% women, 43% part-time, 98% state residents, 20% live on campus, 13% transferred in, 1% international, 31% 25 or older, 20% Native American, 1% Hispanic, 4% African American. ***Areas of study chosen:*** 18% education, 15% social sciences, 13% engineering and applied sciences, 9% agriculture, 2% communications and journalism, 2% premed, 1% fine arts, 1% performing arts, 1% prevet.

Peterson's Guide to Two-Year Colleges 1997

539

Eastern Oklahoma State College (continued)
FIRST-YEAR CLASS 563 total; 602 applied, 100% were accepted, 94% of whom enrolled. 12% from top 10% of their high school class, 18% from top quarter, 52% from top half.
ACADEMIC PROGRAM Core, general education curriculum. Calendar: semesters. 1,020 courses offered in 1995–96. Academic remediation for entering students, advanced placement, tutorials, honors program, summer session for credit, part-time degree program (daytime), adult/continuing education programs, co-op programs and internships. Off-campus study at E. T. Dunlap Higher Education Center.
GENERAL DEGREE REQUIREMENTS 64 semester hours; 3 semester hours of math; computer course (varies by major); internship (some majors).
MAJORS Accounting, agricultural business, agricultural economics, agricultural education, agronomy/soil and crop sciences, animal sciences, art education, art/fine arts, biology/biological sciences, business administration/commerce/management, business education, chemistry, computer science, computer technologies, corrections, economics, education, electrical engineering technology, elementary education, (pre)engineering sequence, English, farm and ranch management, fashion merchandising, forestry, forest technology, history, horticulture, industrial arts, journalism, legal secretarial studies, marketing/retailing/merchandising, mathematics, medical assistant technologies, medical laboratory technology, medical technology, music, nursing, physical education, physical sciences, political science/government, psychology, range management, science education, secretarial studies/office management, sociology, speech/rhetoric/public address/debate, surveying technology, theater arts/drama, veterinary sciences, wildlife management.
LIBRARY 39,994 books, 4,905 microform titles, 212 periodicals, 1 on-line bibliographic service, 25 CD-ROMs, 2,702 records, tapes, and CDs.
COMPUTERS ON CAMPUS 100 computers for student use in computer labs, learning resource center, lab, library. Staffed computer lab on campus provides training in use of software.
COLLEGE LIFE Orientation program (2 days, $33). Drama-theater group, choral group, student-run newspaper. 10% vote in student government elections. ***Most popular organizations:*** Student Senate, Aggie Club, Phi Beta Lambda. ***Major annual events:*** Homecoming Week, Mudbowl. ***Student services:*** personal-psychological counseling. ***Campus security:*** late-night transport-escort service.
HOUSING 520 college housing spaces available; 264 were occupied 1995–96. Freshmen guaranteed college housing. On-campus residence required through sophomore year except if 21 or over, married, or living with relatives. ***Option:*** single-sex housing available. Resident assistants live in dorms.
ATHLETICS Member NJCAA. ***Intercollegiate:*** baseball M(s), basketball M(s)/W(s), softball W(s). ***Intramural:*** baseball, basketball, football, golf, soccer, softball, swimming and diving, tennis, track and field, volleyball. ***Contact:*** Mr. Ron Robison, Director of Athletics, 918-465-2361.
CAREER PLANNING ***Placement office:*** 3 full-time, 1 part-time staff. ***Director:*** Mr. John Garofoli, Director of Counseling, 918-465-2361 Ext. 298. ***Services:*** resume preparation, resume referral, career counseling, careers library, job interviews.
AFTER GRADUATION 80% of students completing a degree program in 1994–95 went directly on to further study.
EXPENSES FOR 1995–96 ***Application fee:*** $15. State resident tuition: $1152 full-time, $36 per semester hour part-time. Nonresident tuition: $3072 full-time, $96 per semester hour part-time. Part-time mandatory fees: $36 per semester. Full-time mandatory fees: $72. College room and board: $2224.
FINANCIAL AID ***College-administered undergrad aid 1995–96:*** 169 need-based scholarships (averaging $350), 185 non-need scholarships (averaging $250), short-term loans (averaging $25), 150 Federal Work-Study (averaging $1360), 131 part-time jobs. ***Required forms:*** FAFSA. ***Application deadline:*** continuous. ***Payment plan:*** deferred payment. ***Waivers:*** full or partial for employees or children of employees and senior citizens. ***Notification:*** continuous.
APPLYING Open admission for state residents. ***Options:*** Common Application, early entrance, deferred entrance, midyear entrance. ***Required:*** school transcript, 3 years of high school math, ACT, TOEFL for international students. Test scores used for counseling/placement. ***Application deadline:*** rolling.
APPLYING/TRANSFER ***Required:*** standardized test scores, high school transcript, 3 years of high school math, college transcript. ***Entrance:*** minimally difficult. ***Application deadline:*** rolling. ***Contact:*** Mr. Jerry Smith, Registrar, 918-465-2361 Ext. 339.
CONTACT Mr. Jerry Smith, Registrar, Eastern Oklahoma State College, Wilburton, OK 74578-4999, 918-465-2361 Ext. 339.

MURRAY STATE COLLEGE
Tishomingo, Oklahoma

UG Enrollment: 1,701	**Tuition & Fees (OK Res): $1354**
Application Deadline: rolling	**Room & Board: $2340**

GENERAL State-supported, 2-year, coed. Part of Oklahoma State Regents for Higher Education. Awards transfer associate, terminal associate degrees. Founded 1908. ***Setting:*** 120-acre rural campus. ***Total enrollment:*** 1,701. ***Faculty:*** 70 (40 full-time, 1% with terminal degrees, 30 part-time); student-faculty ratio is 20:1.
ENROLLMENT PROFILE 1,701 students from 15 states and territories, 5 other countries. 62% women, 38% men, 44% part-time, 97% state residents, 5% live on campus, 5% transferred in, 1% international, 13% Native American, 1% Hispanic, 4% African American, 1% Asian American. ***Areas of study chosen:*** 41% liberal arts/general studies, 12% business management and administrative services, 3% computer and information sciences, 2% agriculture, 2% engineering and applied sciences, 1% biological and life sciences, 1% English language/literature/letters, 1% mathematics, 1% predentistry, 1% premed, 1% prevet.
FIRST-YEAR CLASS 466 total; 466 applied, 100% were accepted, 100% of whom enrolled. 5% from top 10% of their high school class, 10% from top quarter, 55% from top half.
ACADEMIC PROGRAM Core. Calendar: semesters. Academic remediation for entering students, advanced placement, honors program, summer session for credit, part-time degree program (daytime, evenings, summer), internships.
GENERAL DEGREE REQUIREMENTS 63 credit hours; internship (some majors).
MAJORS Agricultural education, agricultural sciences, animal sciences, art/fine arts, business administration/commerce/management, business education, chemistry, child care/child and family studies, computer information systems, computer science, conservation, drafting and design, electrical and electronics technologies, elementary education, engineering (general), (pre)engineering sequence, engineering technology, English, equestrian studies, health science, history, liberal arts/general studies, mathematics, metallurgical technology, nursing, physical education, science, secretarial studies/office management, veterinary sciences, veterinary technology, wildlife management.
LIBRARY Murray State College Library plus 1 other, with 20,000 books, 75 microform titles, 160 periodicals, 1 on-line bibliographic service, 25 CD-ROMs, 500 records, tapes, and CDs.
COMPUTERS ON CAMPUS 100 computers for student use in library, student center. Staffed computer lab on campus provides training in use of computers, software.
COLLEGE LIFE Orientation program (3 days, no cost, parents included). Drama-theater group, choral group, student-run newspaper. 25% vote in student government elections. ***Student services:*** personal-psychological counseling. ***Campus security:*** 24-hour patrols.
HOUSING 100 college housing spaces available; 85 were occupied 1995–96. No special consideration for freshman housing applicants. Off-campus living permitted. ***Option:*** coed (1 building) housing available. Resident assistants live in dorms.
ATHLETICS Member NJCAA. ***Intercollegiate:*** baseball M, basketball M(s)/W(s). ***Intramural:*** basketball, football, golf, swimming and diving, tennis, volleyball, weight lifting. ***Contact:*** Mr. Mike St. John, Athletic Director, 405-371-2371 Ext. 161.
CAREER PLANNING ***Service:*** career counseling.
EXPENSES FOR 1996–97 State resident tuition: $1354 full-time, $42.30 per credit hour part-time. Nonresident tuition: $3274 full-time, $102.30 per credit hour part-time. College room and board: $2340.
FINANCIAL AID ***College-administered undergrad aid 1995–96:*** 320 need-based scholarships (averaging $875), non-need scholarships, short-term loans, low-interest long-term loans from external sources (averaging $800), Federal Work-Study, 80 part-time jobs. ***Required forms for some financial aid applicants:*** state, institutional, FAFSA; accepted: CSS Financial Aid PROFILE. ***Priority deadline:*** 5/1.
APPLYING Open admission. ***Options:*** Common Application, early entrance, deferred entrance, midyear entrance. ***Required:*** school transcript, 3 years of high school math, ACT, TOEFL for international students. Test scores used for counseling/placement. ***Application deadline:*** rolling. ***Notification:*** continuous.
APPLYING/TRANSFER ***Required:*** college transcript. ***Application deadline:*** rolling. ***Notification:*** continuous.
CONTACT Mrs. Mary Golloway, Dean of Students/Registrar, Murray State College, Tishomingo, OK 73460-3130, 405-371-2371 Ext. 171.

NATIONAL EDUCATION CENTER–SPARTAN SCHOOL OF AERONAUTICS CAMPUS
Tulsa, Oklahoma

UG Enrollment: 1,110	**Tuition: $12,690/deg prog**
Application Deadline: rolling	**Room & Board: N/Avail**

GENERAL Proprietary, 2-year, primarily men. Part of National Education Centers, Inc. Awards certificates, terminal associate degrees. Founded 1928. ***Setting:*** 26-acre urban campus. ***Total enrollment:*** 1,110. ***Faculty:*** 150 (120 full-time, 28% with terminal degrees, 30 part-time).
ENROLLMENT PROFILE 1,110 students from 52 states and territories, 40 other countries. 5% women, 15% state residents, 3% transferred in, 8% international, 32% 25 or older, 1% Native American, 5% Hispanic, 20% African American, 1% Asian American. ***Most popular recent majors:*** aviation technology, electrical and electronics technologies, flight training.
FIRST-YEAR CLASS 318 total. Of the students who applied, 85% were accepted, 100% of whom enrolled. 5% from top 10% of their high school class, 30% from top quarter, 65% from top half.
ACADEMIC PROGRAM Calendar: quarters. 53 courses offered in 1995–96. Academic remediation for entering students, English as a second language program offered during academic year, advanced placement.
GENERAL DEGREE REQUIREMENTS 42 credit hours; math/science requirements vary according to program.
MAJORS Aerospace sciences, aviation technology, communication equipment technology, electrical and electronics technologies, flight training, instrumentation technology, quality control technology.
LIBRARY 18,000 books, 300 microform titles, 160 periodicals, 225 records, tapes, and CDs.
COMPUTERS ON CAMPUS 75 computers for student use in avionics lab, classrooms, library provide access to off-campus computing facilities. Staffed computer lab on campus provides training in use of computers, software.
COLLEGE LIFE ***Most popular organization:*** Student Executive Association. ***Major annual event:*** Annual Barbecue.
HOUSING College housing not available.
ATHLETICS ***Intercollegiate:*** softball W. ***Intramural:*** archery, basketball, bowling, football, golf, soccer, volleyball.
CAREER PLANNING ***Placement office:*** 4 full-time, 2 part-time staff. ***Director:*** Dr. Cheryl J. Marrs, Director, Career Center, 918-831-5302. ***Services:*** job fairs, resume preparation, resume referral, career counseling, careers library, job bank, job interviews. Students must register sophomore year.
AFTER GRADUATION 2% of students completing a degree program in 1994–95 went directly on to further study.
EXPENSES FOR 1996–97 ***Application fee:*** $100. Tuition per degree program ranges from $12,690 to $24,576.
FINANCIAL AID ***College-administered undergrad aid 1995–96:*** need-based scholarships, 3 non-need scholarships (average $4800), low-interest long-term loans from external sources, Federal Work-Study. ***Required forms:*** institutional, FAFSA. ***Application deadline:*** continuous. ***Waivers:*** full or partial for employees or children of employees.
APPLYING Open admission. ***Option:*** deferred entrance. ***Required:*** school transcript, ACT ASSET. ***Recommended:*** 3 years of high school math and science, interview. Test scores used for counseling/placement. ***Application deadline:*** rolling.
APPLYING/TRANSFER ***Required:*** standardized test scores, high school transcript, college transcript. ***Recommended:*** 3 years of high school math and science, interview. ***Entrance:*** noncompetitive. ***Application deadline:*** rolling.

CONTACT Mr. John Buck, Vice President of Marketing, National Education Center–Spartan School of Aeronautics Campus, 8820 East Pine St, PO Box 582833, Tulsa, OK 74158-2833, 918-836-6886. College video available.

NORTHEASTERN OKLAHOMA AGRICULTURAL AND MECHANICAL COLLEGE
Miami, Oklahoma

UG Enrollment: 2,200 **Tuition & Fees (OK Res): $1125**
Application Deadline: rolling **Room & Board: $2214**

GENERAL State-supported, 2-year, coed. Part of Oklahoma State Regents for Higher Education. Awards transfer associate, terminal associate degrees. Founded 1919. ***Setting:*** small-town campus. ***Total enrollment:*** 2,200. ***Faculty:*** 100 (80 full-time, 20 part-time); student-faculty ratio is 23:1.
ENROLLMENT PROFILE 2,200 students from 12 states and territories, 19 other countries. 55% women, 45% men, 25% part-time, 80% state residents, 33% live on campus, 7% transferred in, 35% 25 or older, 17% Native American, 1% Hispanic, 10% African American.
FIRST-YEAR CLASS 900 total; 1,500 applied, 100% were accepted, 60% of whom enrolled. 5% from top 10% of their high school class, 80% from top half. 10 valedictorians.
ACADEMIC PROGRAM Core. Calendar: semesters. Academic remediation for entering students, advanced placement, Freshman Honors College, honors program, summer session for credit, part-time degree program (daytime, evenings, weekends, summer), adult/continuing education programs.
GENERAL DEGREE REQUIREMENTS 60 credit hours; 2 credit hours of math; 8 credit hours of science.
MAJORS Accounting, agricultural business, agricultural economics, agronomy/soil and crop sciences, animal sciences, art education, art/fine arts, automotive technologies, botany/plant sciences, broadcasting, business administration/commerce/management, chemistry, child care/child and family studies, computer programming, computer science, construction technologies, criminal justice, dairy sciences, drafting and design, economics, electrical and electronics technologies, elementary education, (pre)engineering sequence, farm and ranch management, fashion design and technology, fashion merchandising, forestry, home economics, horticulture, hotel and restaurant management, industrial arts, interior design, journalism, legal secretarial studies, marketing/retailing/merchandising, mathematics, mechanical engineering technology, medical secretarial studies, music, Native American studies, nursing, philosophy, photography, physical education, physical therapy, piano/organ, plastics technology, political science/government, printing technologies, psychology, range management, real estate, secretarial studies/office management, social science, social work, sociology, textiles and clothing, theater arts/drama, veterinary sciences, vocational education, welding technology, wildlife biology, wildlife management.
LIBRARY Learning Resource Center with 51,103 books, 50 periodicals, 2,800 records, tapes, and CDs.
COMPUTERS ON CAMPUS 65 computers for student use in computer center, computer labs, learning resource center, various locations throughout campus, library, student center provide access to on-line services, Internet. Staffed computer lab on campus provides training in use of computers, software.
COLLEGE LIFE Drama-theater group, choral group, marching band, student-run newspaper. 50% vote in student government elections. ***Social organizations:*** 50 open to all. ***Student services:*** legal services, health clinic, personal-psychological counseling, women's center. ***Campus security:*** 24-hour patrols.
HOUSING 1,050 college housing spaces available; 900 were occupied 1995–96. No special consideration for freshman housing applicants. On-campus residence required through sophomore year except by special permission. ***Options:*** single-sex (7 buildings), international student housing available. Resident assistants live in dorms.
ATHLETICS Member NJCAA. ***Intercollegiate:*** baseball M(s), basketball M(s)/W(s), football M(s), softball W(s), volleyball W(s). ***Intramural:*** basketball, football, softball, tennis. ***Contact:*** Mr. Robert Maxwell, Athletic Director, 918-542-8441 Ext. 265.
CAREER PLANNING ***Placement office:*** 4 full-time staff. ***Director:*** Ms. Cheryl Butler, Director of Counseling, 918-540-6236. ***Services:*** job fairs, career counseling, careers library, job interviews.
AFTER GRADUATION 70% of students completing a degree program in 1994–95 went directly on to further study.
EXPENSES FOR 1995–96 State resident tuition: $1125 full-time, $37.50 per credit hour part-time. Nonresident tuition: $2925 full-time, $97.50 per credit hour part-time. College room and board: $2214. College room only: $800.
FINANCIAL AID ***College-administered undergrad aid 1995–96:*** 400 need-based scholarships (average $1000), non-need scholarships, short-term loans, low-interest long-term loans from external sources, Federal Work-Study, part-time jobs. ***Acceptable forms:*** CSS Financial Aid PROFILE, institutional. ***Application deadline:*** continuous to 3/1. ***Payment plan:*** installment. ***Waivers:*** full or partial for employees or children of employees and senior citizens.
APPLYING Open admission. ***Options:*** early entrance, midyear entrance. ***Required:*** school transcript, ACT, TOEFL for international students. ***Recommended:*** 3 years of high school math and science. Test scores used for counseling/placement. ***Application deadline:*** rolling. ***Notification:*** continuous.
APPLYING/TRANSFER ***Required:*** college transcript. ***Recommended:*** 3 years of high school math and science. ***Entrance:*** noncompetitive. ***Application deadline:*** rolling. ***Notification:*** continuous.
CONTACT Mr. Dale Patterson, Dean of Admissions and Records, Northeastern Oklahoma Agricultural and Mechanical College, Miami, OK 74354-6434, 918-540-6210 or toll-free 800-234-4727 (in-state). ***Fax:*** 918-542-9759. College video available.

NORTHERN OKLAHOMA COLLEGE
Tonkawa, Oklahoma

UG Enrollment: 2,350 **Tuition & Fees (OK Res): $1128**
Application Deadline: rolling **Room & Board: $1880**

GENERAL State-supported, 2-year, coed. Part of Oklahoma State Regents for Higher Education. Awards transfer associate, terminal associate degrees. Founded 1901. ***Setting:*** 10-acre rural campus. ***Total enrollment:*** 2,350. ***Faculty:*** 80 (45 full-time, 35 part-time); student-faculty ratio is 25:1.
ENROLLMENT PROFILE 2,350 students: 60% women, 40% men, 44% part-time, 99% state residents, 20% live on campus, 13% transferred in, 1% international, 40% 25 or older, 8% Native American, 1% Hispanic, 2% African American. ***Most popular recent majors:*** business administration/commerce/management, nursing, liberal arts/general studies.
FIRST-YEAR CLASS 541 total. Of the students who applied, 100% were accepted, 90% of whom enrolled.
ACADEMIC PROGRAM Honor code. Calendar: semesters. Academic remediation for entering students, English as a second language program, services for LD students, advanced placement, summer session for credit, part-time degree program (daytime, evenings), adult/continuing education programs.
GENERAL DEGREE REQUIREMENTS 60 credit hours; 1 algebra course; computer course for business majors.
MAJORS Accounting, agricultural business, broadcasting, business administration/commerce/management, computer information systems, computer science, construction technologies, criminal justice, drafting and design, elementary education, engineering (general), graphic arts, liberal arts/general studies, nursing, printing technologies, science, secretarial studies/office management.
LIBRARY Vineyard Library with 34,458 books, 93 microform titles, 211 periodicals, 2 CD-ROMs, 1,693 records, tapes, and CDs.
COMPUTERS ON CAMPUS 150 computers for student use in computer center, computer labs, learning resource center, academic labs, classrooms, library, dorms, student rooms provide access to on-line services, Internet. Staffed computer lab on campus.
COLLEGE LIFE Drama-theater group, choral group, student-run newspaper, radio station. ***Social organizations:*** 15 open to all. ***Most popular organizations:*** Phi Theta Kappa, Law Enforcement Club, Fellowship of Christian Athletes, Student Nurses Association, Young Republicans. ***Major annual events:*** Homecoming, Drug Awareness Week. ***Student services:*** health clinic, personal-psychological counseling. ***Campus security:*** 24-hour emergency response devices and patrols.
HOUSING 400 college housing spaces available; 345 were occupied 1995–96. No special consideration for freshman housing applicants. On-campus residence required through sophomore year except if living with relatives, 22 or over, or married. ***Option:*** single-sex housing available. Resident assistants live in dorms.
ATHLETICS Member NJCAA. ***Intercollegiate:*** baseball W(s), basketball M(s)/W(s). ***Intramural:*** badminton, basketball, football, racquetball, softball, tennis, volleyball, water polo. ***Contact:*** Mr. Robert Zweiacher, Athletic Director, 405-628-6760; Ms. Nevona Kegans, Dean of Women, 405-628-6763.
CAREER PLANNING ***Placement office:*** 3 full-time, 1 part-time staff. ***Services:*** career counseling, careers library. Students must register freshman year.
EXPENSES FOR 1996–97 ***Application fee:*** $15. State resident tuition: $1104 full-time, $36 per credit hour part-time. Nonresident tuition: $2904 full-time, $98 per credit hour part-time. Full-time mandatory fees: $24. College room and board: $1880 (minimum).
FINANCIAL AID ***College-administered undergrad aid 1995–96:*** 195 need-based scholarships (average $429), 95 non-need scholarships (average $442), short-term loans (average $120), low-interest long-term loans from external sources (average $2500), Federal Work-Study, 80 part-time jobs. ***Required forms:*** institutional, FAFSA; accepted: CSS Financial Aid PROFILE. ***Priority deadline:*** 8/1.
APPLYING Open admission except for nursing program. ***Options:*** Common Application, early entrance. ***Required:*** school transcript, 3 years of high school math, ACT, TOEFL for international students. Test scores used for counseling/placement. ***Application deadline:*** rolling.
APPLYING/TRANSFER ***Required:*** standardized test scores, high school transcript, college transcript. ***Entrance:*** noncompetitive. ***Contact:*** Ms. Wanda Webb, Registrar, 405-628-6220.
CONTACT Ms. Cara Freund, Director of College Relations, Northern Oklahoma College, Tonkawa, OK 74653-0310, 405-628-6290.

OKLAHOMA CITY COMMUNITY COLLEGE
Oklahoma City, Oklahoma

UG Enrollment: 10,586 **Tuition & Fees (OK Res): $1248**
Application Deadline: rolling **Room & Board: N/Avail**

GENERAL State-supported, 2-year, coed. Part of Oklahoma State Regents for Higher Education. Awards certificates, transfer associate, terminal associate degrees. Founded 1969. ***Setting:*** 143-acre urban campus. ***Total enrollment:*** 10,586. ***Faculty:*** 342 (101 full-time, 20% with terminal degrees, 241 part-time); student-faculty ratio is 20:1.
ENROLLMENT PROFILE 10,586 students from 10 states and territories, 12 other countries. 59% women, 68% part-time, 93% state residents, 8% transferred in, 27% have need-based financial aid, 20% have non-need-based financial aid, 6% international, 50% 25 or older, 5% Native American, 3% Hispanic, 6% African American, 6% Asian American. ***Areas of study chosen:*** 27% business management and administrative services, 24% health professions and related sciences, 15% engineering and applied sciences, 10% biological and life sciences, 7% computer and information sciences, 2% communications and journalism, 2% fine arts, 2% interdisciplinary studies, 2% liberal arts/general studies, 2% mathematics, 2% social sciences, 1% foreign language and literature, 1% psychology. ***Most popular recent majors:*** business administration/commerce/management, nursing, emergency medical technology.
FIRST-YEAR CLASS 3,370 total; 3,465 applied, 97% were accepted, 100% of whom enrolled. 11 valedictorians.
ACADEMIC PROGRAM Core, interdisciplinary curriculum, honor code. Calendar: semesters. 500 courses offered in 1995–96; average class size 28 in required courses. Academic remediation for entering students, English as a second language program offered during academic year and summer, advanced placement, self-designed majors, Freshman Honors College, honors program, summer session for credit, part-time degree program (daytime, evenings, weekends, summer), external degree programs, co-op programs.
GENERAL DEGREE REQUIREMENTS 60 credit hours; 1 course in college algebra/lab science.
MAJORS Accounting, aircraft and missile maintenance, applied art, art/fine arts, automotive technologies, aviation technology, biology/biological sciences, broadcasting, business

Peterson's Guide to Two-Year Colleges 1997 541

Oklahoma City Community College (continued)
administration/commerce/management, chemistry, child care/child and family studies, commercial art, communication, computer science, computer technologies, drafting and design, electrical and electronics technologies, emergency medical technology, engineering (general), (pre)engineering sequence, finance/banking, gerontology, graphic arts, history, humanities, insurance, literature, machine and tool technologies, mathematics, mechanical design technology, medical records services, modern languages, music, nursing, occupational therapy, physical therapy, physics, political science/government, psychology, real estate, science, sociology, theater arts/drama, tourism and travel.
LIBRARY 53,000 books, 245 microform titles, 450 periodicals, 28 CD-ROMs, 8,350 records, tapes, and CDs. Acquisition spending 1994–95: $564,849.
COMPUTERS ON CAMPUS 190 computers for student use in computer labs, classrooms, library provide access to main academic computer. Staffed computer lab on campus provides training in use of computers, software.
COLLEGE LIFE Drama-theater group, choral group, student-run newspaper. ***Social organizations:*** 20 open to all. ***Most popular organizations:*** Phi Theta Kappa, College Republicans, Future Teachers, Hispanic Organization to Promote Education, Student Activities Board. ***Major annual events:*** Arts Festival, Dinner Theatre, SAB Film Series. ***Campus security:*** 24-hour emergency response devices and patrols.
HOUSING College housing not available.
ATHLETICS ***Intramural:*** basketball, bowling, football, golf, racquetball, soccer, softball, swimming and diving, tennis, volleyball, weight lifting.
CAREER PLANNING ***Placement office:*** 2 full-time, 2 part-time staff. ***Director:*** Ms. Sally Edwards, Director of Career Services, 405-682-7576. ***Services:*** job fairs, career counseling, job bank. 60 organizations recruited on campus 1994–95.
AFTER GRADUATION 40% of class of 1994 had job offers within 6 months. 30% of students completing a degree program went directly on to further study.
EXPENSES FOR 1996–97 ***Application fee:*** $25. State resident tuition: $840 full-time, $28 per credit hour part-time. Nonresident tuition: $2640 full-time, $88 per credit hour part-time. Part-time mandatory fees: $13.60 per credit hour. Full-time mandatory fees: $408.
FINANCIAL AID ***College-administered undergrad aid 1995–96:*** 983 need-based scholarships, 150 non-need scholarships (average $500), short-term loans (average $150), low-interest long-term loans from college funds (average $800), loans from external sources (average $3062), Federal Work-Study. ***Required forms:*** institutional, FAFSA. ***Priority deadline:*** 5/31. ***Payment plan:*** installment. ***Waivers:*** full or partial for employees or children of employees and senior citizens.
APPLYING Open admission. ***Options:*** early entrance, deferred entrance, midyear entrance. ***Required:*** TOEFL for international students. ***Required for some:*** ACT, CPT. Test scores used for admission (TOEFL) and counseling/placement (ACT, CPT). ***Application deadline:*** rolling.
APPLYING/TRANSFER ***Required:*** college transcript. ***Required for some:*** standardized test scores. ***Entrance:*** noncompetitive. ***Application deadline:*** rolling.
CONTACT Ms. Gloria Barton, Dean of Admissions/Registrar, Oklahoma City Community College, 7777 South May Avenue, Oklahoma City, OK 73159-4419, 405-682-7515.

OKLAHOMA STATE UNIVERSITY, OKLAHOMA CITY
Oklahoma City, Oklahoma

UG Enrollment: 4,357 | **Tuition & Fees (OK Res): $1574**
Application Deadline: rolling | **Room & Board: N/Avail**

GENERAL State-supported, 2-year, coed. Part of Oklahoma State University. Awards certificates, transfer associate, terminal associate degrees. Founded 1961. ***Setting:*** 80-acre urban campus. ***Educational spending 1994–95:*** $1044 per undergrad. ***Total enrollment:*** 4,357. ***Faculty:*** 205 (61 full-time, 1% with terminal degrees, 144 part-time); student-faculty ratio is 18:1.
ENROLLMENT PROFILE 4,357 students from 18 states and territories, 15 other countries. 52% women, 70% part-time, 98% state residents, 24% transferred in, 1% international, 80% 25 or older, 3% Native American, 2% Hispanic, 6% African American, 3% Asian American. ***Most popular recent major:*** nursing.
FIRST-YEAR CLASS 1,151 total; 1,250 applied, 99% were accepted, 93% of whom enrolled. 10% from top 10% of their high school class, 15% from top half.
ACADEMIC PROGRAM Core, honor code. Calendar: semesters. Academic remediation for entering students, services for LD students, advanced placement, honors program, summer session for credit, part-time degree program (daytime, evenings, weekends, summer), adult/continuing education programs.
GENERAL DEGREE REQUIREMENTS 60 semester hours; math/science requirements vary according to program; computer course for architectural technology, environment systems technology, technical communications majors.
MAJORS Accounting, architectural technologies, aviation technology, business administration/commerce/management, civil engineering technology, computer programming, computer science, computer technologies, construction management, construction technologies, data processing, deaf interpreter training, drafting and design, drug and alcohol/substance abuse counseling, electrical and electronics technologies, electronics engineering technology, engineering (general), engineering technology, environmental engineering technology, fire science, heating/refrigeration/air conditioning, horticulture, industrial design, industrial engineering technology, instrumentation technology, international business, landscape architecture/design, law enforcement/police sciences, nursing, petroleum technology, quality control technology, surveying technology, technical writing, transportation technologies.
LIBRARY OSU-OKC Library with 13,192 books, 156 microform titles, 232 periodicals, 1 on-line bibliographic service, 2 CD-ROMs, 1,975 records, tapes, and CDs. Acquisition spending 1994–95: $33,735.
COMPUTERS ON CAMPUS 55 computers for student use in computer center, library provide access to Internet. Staffed computer lab on campus. Academic computing expenditure 1994–95: $312,315.
COLLEGE LIFE ***Social organizations:*** 20 open to all. ***Major annual event:*** Howdy Week. ***Student services:*** personal-psychological counseling. ***Campus security:*** 24-hour patrols, late-night transport-escort service.
HOUSING College housing not available.
ATHLETICS ***Intramural:*** soccer.
CAREER PLANNING ***Placement office:*** 1 full-time staff. ***Director:*** Ms. Sharon Johnson, Career Counseling, 405-945-3224. ***Services:*** job fairs, resume preparation, career counseling, careers library, job bank, job interviews.
AFTER GRADUATION 30% of students completing a degree program in 1994–95 went directly on to further study.
EXPENSES FOR 1995–96 State resident tuition: $1539 full-time, $51.30 per semester hour part-time. Nonresident tuition: $3714 full-time, $123.80 per semester hour part-time. Part-time mandatory fees: $25 per semester. Full-time mandatory fees: $35.
FINANCIAL AID ***College-administered undergrad aid 1995–96:*** 175 need-based scholarships (average $250), 190 non-need scholarships (average $400), short-term loans (average $100), low-interest long-term loans from college funds (average $1125), loans from external sources (average $1313), Federal Work-Study, 15 part-time jobs. ***Required forms:*** institutional, FAFSA. ***Priority deadline:*** 7/1. ***Waivers:*** full or partial for minority students, employees or children of employees, adult students, and senior citizens.
APPLYING Open admission except for nursing program. ***Options:*** early entrance, midyear entrance. ***Required:*** TOEFL for international students. ***Required for some:*** SAT I or ACT. Test scores used for counseling/placement. ***Application deadline:*** rolling. ***Notification:*** continuous.
APPLYING/TRANSFER ***Application deadline:*** rolling. ***Notification:*** continuous. ***Contact:*** Ms. Jeanne Kubier, Assistant Registrar, 405-945-3252.
CONTACT Ms. Jo Ella Fields, Assistant Director of Admissions, Oklahoma State University, Oklahoma City, 900 North Portland, Oklahoma City, OK 73107-6120, 405-945-3270. ***Fax:*** 405-945-3277.

OKLAHOMA STATE UNIVERSITY, OKMULGEE
Okmulgee, Oklahoma

UG Enrollment: 2,188 | **Tuition & Fees (OK Res): $1656**
Application Deadline: rolling | **Room & Board: $2024**

GENERAL State-supported, 2-year, coed. Part of Oklahoma State University. Awards diplomas, terminal associate degrees. Founded 1946. ***Setting:*** 160-acre small-town campus with easy access to Tulsa. ***Total enrollment:*** 2,188. ***Faculty:*** 138 (135 full-time, 3 part-time); student-faculty ratio is 20:1.
ENROLLMENT PROFILE 2,188 students from 24 states and territories, 1 other country. 38% women, 62% men, 30% part-time, 97% state residents, 25% live on campus, 23% transferred in, 70% have need-based financial aid, 5% have non-need-based financial aid, 1% international, 40% 25 or older, 13% Native American, 1% Hispanic, 8% African American, 1% Asian American. ***Areas of study chosen:*** 3% architecture, 3% computer and information sciences, 2% business management and administrative services. ***Most popular recent majors:*** electrical and electronics technologies, commercial art, heating/refrigeration/air conditioning.
FIRST-YEAR CLASS 845 total; 1,100 applied, 100% were accepted, 77% of whom enrolled.
ACADEMIC PROGRAM Core, hands-on lab experience curriculum, honor code. Calendar: trimesters. 500 courses offered in 1995–96. Academic remediation for entering students, services for LD students, advanced placement, tutorials, summer session for credit, part-time degree program (daytime), adult/continuing education programs, internships.
GENERAL DEGREE REQUIREMENTS 84 credit hours; 1 math course; computer course; internship (some majors).
MAJORS Accounting, architectural technologies, automotive technologies, aviation technology, business administration/commerce/management, commercial art, computer graphics, computer information systems, construction technologies, culinary arts, dietetics, drafting and design, electrical and electronics technologies, electrical engineering technology, food services management, food services technology, heating/refrigeration/air conditioning, hospitality services, illustration, industrial and heavy equipment maintenance, jewelry and metalsmithing, legal secretarial studies, machine and tool technologies, manufacturing technology, marketing/retailing/merchandising, medical secretarial studies, photography, plumbing, printing technologies, robotics, secretarial studies/office management.
LIBRARY Learning Resource Center with 9,965 books, 128 microform titles, 474 periodicals, 11 CD-ROMs.
COMPUTERS ON CAMPUS 360 computers for student use in computer center, computer labs, learning resource center, academic departments, classrooms, library, dorms provide access to main academic computer, off-campus computing facilities, e-mail, on-line services. Staffed computer lab on campus provides training in use of computers, software.
COLLEGE LIFE Student-run newspaper. 30% vote in student government elections. ***Social organizations:*** 30 open to all. ***Most popular organizations:*** Student Senate, Junior Ambassadors, Phi Theta Kappa, Departmental Clubs. ***Major annual events:*** Super Weekend, Okmulgee College and Career Day, Auto Show. ***Student services:*** health clinic, personal-psychological counseling. ***Campus security:*** 24-hour emergency response devices and patrols, late-night transport-escort service.
HOUSING 831 college housing spaces available; 598 were occupied 1995–96. No special consideration for freshman housing applicants. On-campus residence required in freshman year except if living within commuting distance, 21 or over, married with dependents, or living with parents or legal guardian. ***Options:*** coed, single-sex housing available. Resident assistants live in dorms.
ATHLETICS ***Intramural:*** basketball, football, table tennis (Ping-Pong), volleyball.
CAREER PLANNING ***Placement office:*** 2 full-time staff. ***Director:*** Ms. Wanda Blackwell, Psychometrist for Career Profiling, 918-756-6211 Ext. 401. ***Services:*** resume preparation, career counseling, careers library, job bank. 70 organizations recruited on campus 1994–95.
AFTER GRADUATION 95% of class of 1994 had job offers within 6 months.
EXPENSES FOR 1995–96 State resident tuition: $1656 full-time, $46 per credit hour part-time. Nonresident tuition: $4230 full-time, $117.50 per credit hour part-time. College room and board: $2024.
FINANCIAL AID ***College-administered undergrad aid 1995–96:*** 414 need-based scholarships (average $500), 292 non-need scholarships (average $500), short-term loans (average $25), low-interest long-term loans from college funds (average $500), loans from external sources (average $875), 208 Federal Work-Study, 62 part-time jobs. ***Required forms:*** institutional, FAFSA. ***Priority deadline:*** 4/15. ***Waivers:*** full or partial for employees or children of employees and senior citizens.

APPLYING Open admission. ***Options:*** Common Application, deferred entrance, midyear entrance. ***Required:*** school transcript, SAT I or ACT, TOEFL for international students. ***Recommended:*** 3 years of high school math and science. Test scores used for counseling/placement. ***Application deadline:*** rolling.
APPLYING/TRANSFER ***Required:*** high school transcript, college transcript. ***Recommended:*** 3 years of high school math and science. ***Required for some:*** standardized test scores. ***Entrance:*** noncompetitive. ***Application deadline:*** rolling. ***Contact:*** Mr. Cary Fox, Registrar, 918-756-6211 Ext. 345.
CONTACT Mrs. Susan Hill, Director of Admissions, Oklahoma State University, Okmulgee, Okmulgee, OK 74447-3901, 918-756-6211 Ext. 251 or toll-free 800-722-4471. ***Fax:*** 918-756-4175. ***E-mail:*** shill@okway.okstate.edu. College video available.

REDLANDS COMMUNITY COLLEGE
El Reno, Oklahoma

UG Enrollment: 1,901	**Tuition & Fees (OK Res): $1328**
Application Deadline: rolling	**Room & Board: N/Avail**

GENERAL State-supported, 2-year, coed. Part of Oklahoma State Regents for Higher Education. Awards certificates, transfer associate, terminal associate degrees. Founded 1938. ***Setting:*** 55-acre suburban campus with easy access to Oklahoma City. ***Educational spending 1994–95:*** $910 per undergrad. ***Total enrollment:*** 1,901. ***Faculty:*** 131 (26 full-time, 12% with terminal degrees, 105 part-time).
ENROLLMENT PROFILE 1,901 students from 5 states and territories, 1 other country. 58% women, 42% men, 51% part-time, 98% state residents, 11% transferred in, 47% have need-based financial aid, 23% have non-need-based financial aid, 1% international, 37% 25 or older, 7% Native American, 2% Hispanic, 6% African American, 1% Asian American. ***Areas of study chosen:*** 50% liberal arts/general studies, 17% health professions and related sciences, 12% business management and administrative services, 5% education, 4% agriculture, 4% social sciences, 3% psychology, 2% computer and information sciences, 1% communications and journalism, 1% physical sciences, 1% premed. ***Most popular recent majors:*** nursing, liberal arts/general studies.
FIRST-YEAR CLASS 533 total; 576 applied, 99% were accepted, 93% of whom enrolled. 7% from top 10% of their high school class, 25% from top quarter, 49% from top half.
ACADEMIC PROGRAM Core, interdisciplinary curriculum. Calendar: semesters. 324 courses offered in 1995–96; average class size 25 in required courses. Academic remediation for entering students, English as a second language program offered during academic year, services for LD students, advanced placement, tutorials, honors program, summer session for credit, part-time degree program (daytime, evenings, weekends, summer), adult/continuing education programs, co-op programs and internships.
GENERAL DEGREE REQUIREMENTS 64 semester hours; 1 math course; computer course.
MAJORS Accounting, agricultural business, agricultural economics, agricultural education, agricultural sciences, agricultural technologies, American studies, animal sciences, applied art, art/fine arts, behavioral sciences, biology/biological sciences, botany/plant sciences, business administration/commerce/management, chemistry, child care/child and family studies, child psychology/child development, commercial art, communication, community services, computer information systems, computer programming, computer science, construction technologies, corrections, criminal justice, drafting and design, early childhood education, economics, education, electrical and electronics technologies, elementary education, emergency medical technology, (pre)engineering sequence, English, equestrian studies, farm and ranch management, finance/banking, health science, history, humanities, human services, journalism, laboratory animal medicine, law enforcement/police sciences, liberal arts/general studies, literature, mathematics, medical laboratory technology, music, natural sciences, nursing, physical education, physical sciences, physics, political science/government, psychology, science, secretarial studies/office management, social science, sociology, speech/rhetoric/public address/debate, zoology.
LIBRARY Learning Resource Center with 21,266 books, 89 microform titles, 274 periodicals, 2 CD-ROMs, 3,819 records, tapes, and CDs. Acquisition spending 1994–95: $17,181.
COMPUTERS ON CAMPUS 65 computers for student use in computer labs, classrooms. Academic computing expenditure 1994–95: $54,522.
COLLEGE LIFE Drama-theater group, choral group, student-run newspaper. ***Social organizations:*** 11 open to all. ***Most popular organizations:*** Nursing Club, Aggie Club, Baptist Student Union, Phi Theta Kappa, Drama Club. ***Major annual events:*** Back to School Bash, End of Year Party, Career Fair. ***Student services:*** personal-psychological counseling. ***Campus security:*** 24-hour patrols.
HOUSING College housing not available.
ATHLETICS Member NJCAA. ***Intercollegiate:*** baseball M(s), basketball M(s)/W(s). ***Intramural:*** basketball. ***Contact:*** Mr. Kevin Steele, Athletic Director, 405-262-2552 Ext. 1280.
CAREER PLANNING ***Placement office:*** 2 full-time, 2 part-time staff. ***Director:*** Mr. James Mauldin, Coordinator/Job Developer, 405-262-2552. ***Services:*** job fairs, resume preparation, career counseling, careers library.
AFTER GRADUATION 54% of students completing a degree program in 1994–95 went directly on to further study.
EXPENSES FOR 1995–96 State resident tuition: $1328 full-time, $44.25 per semester hour part-time. Nonresident tuition: $3008 full-time, $100.25 per semester hour part-time.
FINANCIAL AID ***College-administered undergrad aid 1995–96:*** 910 need-based scholarships (average $1200), 380 non-need scholarships (average $500), low-interest long-term loans from external sources (average $2000), 15 Federal Work-Study (averaging $1500), 1,500 part-time jobs. ***Acceptable forms:*** CSS Financial Aid PROFILE, state, institutional, FAFSA. ***Priority deadline:*** 4/1. ***Waivers:*** full or partial for minority students, children of alumni, employees or children of employees, adult students, and senior citizens. ***Average indebtedness of graduates:*** $5000.
APPLYING Open admission except for nursing, medical laboratory technology programs. ***Options:*** Common Application, early entrance, deferred entrance, midyear entrance. ***Required:*** school transcript, ACT, TOEFL for international students. ***Recommended:*** 3 years of high school math and science. Test scores used for counseling/placement. ***Application deadline:*** rolling. ***Notification:*** continuous.
APPLYING/TRANSFER ***Required:*** college transcript. ***Entrance:*** noncompetitive. ***Application deadline:*** rolling. ***Notification:*** continuous. ***Contact:*** Ms. Tricia Hobson, Admission Coordinator, 405-262-2552.
CONTACT Mr. Curt E. Luttrell, Director, Enrollment Management/Registrar, Redlands Community College, El Reno, OK 73036, 405-262-2552 Ext. 2342.

ROGERS STATE COLLEGE
Claremore, Oklahoma

UG Enrollment: 3,204	**Tuition & Fees (OK Res): $1409**
Application Deadline: rolling	**Room & Board: N/R**

GENERAL State-supported, 2-year, coed. Part of Oklahoma State Regents for Higher Education. Awards certificates, diplomas, transfer associate, terminal associate degrees. Founded 1909. ***Setting:*** small-town campus with easy access to Tulsa. ***Endowment:*** $2.1 million. ***Research spending 1994–95:*** $13,227. ***Total enrollment:*** 3,204. ***Faculty:*** 270 (200 full-time, 70 part-time). ***Notable Alumni:*** Senator Stratton Taylor; Dwayne Studley; Colonel Ed Ramsey; General William E. Potts; John Starks.
ENROLLMENT PROFILE 3,204 students: 66% women, 64% part-time, 97% state residents, 14% transferred in, 3% international, 58% 25 or older, 13% Native American, 1% Hispanic, 1% African American, 1% Asian American.
FIRST-YEAR CLASS 1,005 total; 4,150 applied, 100% were accepted, 93% of whom enrolled.
ACADEMIC PROGRAM Core, honor code. Calendar: semesters. Academic remediation for entering students, services for LD students, advanced placement, summer session for credit, part-time degree program (daytime, evenings, summer), adult/continuing education programs, co-op programs and internships.
GENERAL DEGREE REQUIREMENTS 60 credit hours; 1 college algebra course; 6 credit hours of science; internship (some majors).
MAJORS Accounting, agricultural business, art/fine arts, aviation technology, biology/biological sciences, broadcasting, business administration/commerce/management, chemistry, computer programming, computer science, computer technologies, court reporting, criminal justice, dental services, drug and alcohol/substance abuse counseling, elementary education, emergency medical technology, engineering (general), engineering technology, English, equestrian studies, farm and ranch management, graphic arts, history, industrial arts, law enforcement/police sciences, legal secretarial studies, liberal arts/general studies, mathematics, Native American studies, nursing, paralegal studies, pharmacy/pharmaceutical sciences, physical sciences, physical therapy, political science/government, radio and television studies, secretarial studies/office management.
LIBRARY Thunderbird Library with 31,000 books, 51,000 microform titles, 425 periodicals, 1 on-line bibliographic service, 46 CD-ROMs, 1,675 records, tapes, and CDs. Acquisition spending 1994–95: $369,325.
COMPUTERS ON CAMPUS 150 computers for student use in computer center, computer labs, learning resource center, classrooms, library, student center provide access to e-mail, on-line services. Staffed computer lab on campus. Academic computing expenditure 1994–95: $181,000.
COLLEGE LIFE Student-run radio station. ***Social organizations:*** 19 open to all. ***Most popular organizations:*** Phi Theta Kappa, Adult Students Aspiring to Prosper, FBLA, International Student Organization, Student Association of Legal Assistants. ***Campus security:*** 24-hour patrols.
HOUSING 70 college housing spaces available; all were occupied 1995–96. No special consideration for freshman housing applicants. Off-campus living permitted. ***Option:*** coed (2 buildings) housing available. Resident assistants live in dorms.
ATHLETICS ***Intramural:*** riflery.
CAREER PLANNING ***Placement office:*** 1 full-time staff; $55,000 operating expenditure 1994–95. ***Director:*** Dr. Jay Caldwell, Vice President for Student Services, 918-341-7510 Ext. 313. ***Service:*** career counseling.
EXPENSES FOR 1995–96 State resident tuition: $1409 full-time, $46.95 per credit hour part-time. Nonresident tuition: $3209 full-time, $106.95 per credit hour part-time.
FINANCIAL AID ***College-administered undergrad aid 1995–96:*** 800 need-based scholarships (averaging $1100), 100 non-need scholarships (averaging $350), low-interest long-term loans from external sources (averaging $2500), 123 Federal Work-Study (averaging $970). ***Required forms:*** institutional, FAFSA; required for some: state. ***Priority deadline:*** 6/15.
APPLYING Open admission. ***Option:*** Common Application. ***Required:*** school transcript, 3 years of high school math, ACT, TOEFL for international students. Test scores used for counseling/placement. ***Application deadline:*** rolling.
APPLYING/TRANSFER ***Required:*** college transcript. ***Required for some:*** standardized test scores. ***Entrance:*** noncompetitive. ***Application deadline:*** rolling. ***Contact:*** Ms. Jane Summerlin, Director of Admissions and Records, 918-343-7546.
CONTACT Ms. Jane Summerlin, Director of Admissions and Records, Rogers State College, Claremore, OK 74017-3252, 918-343-7546. ***E-mail:*** rscsummer@aol.com. College video available.

ROSE STATE COLLEGE
Midwest City, Oklahoma

UG Enrollment: 9,083	**Tuition & Fees (OK Res): $1101**
Application Deadline: rolling	**Room & Board: N/Avail**

GENERAL State and locally supported, 2-year, coed. Part of Oklahoma State Regents for Higher Education. Awards certificates, transfer associate, terminal associate degrees. Founded 1968. ***Setting:*** 100-acre suburban campus with easy access to Oklahoma City. ***Total enrollment:*** 9,083. ***Faculty:*** 402 (130 full-time, 25% with terminal degrees, 272 part-time); student-faculty ratio is 25:1.
ENROLLMENT PROFILE 9,083 students from 15 states and territories, 26 other countries. 59% women, 41% men, 68% part-time, 98% state residents, 36% transferred in, 1% international, 60% 25 or older, 5% Native American, 3% Hispanic, 15% African American, 3% Asian American. ***Areas of study chosen:*** 18% health professions and related sciences, 14% business management and administrative services, 10% liberal arts/general studies, 8% education, 4% engineering and applied sciences, 4% psychology, 3% computer and information sciences, 2% communications and journalism, 2% physical sciences, 1% biological and life sciences, 1% English language/literature/letters, 1% foreign language and literature, 1% library and information studies, 1% mathematics, 1% performing arts, 1% predentistry, 1% prelaw, 1% premed, 1% social sciences, 1% vocational and home economics. ***Most popular recent majors:*** business administration/commerce/management, liberal arts/general studies, nursing.

Rose State College (continued)

FIRST-YEAR CLASS 10% from top 10% of their high school class, 15% from top quarter, 55% from top half.

ACADEMIC PROGRAM Core, transfer and career curriculum, honor code. Calendar: semesters. 808 courses offered in 1995–96. Academic remediation for entering students, services for LD students, summer session for credit, part-time degree program (daytime, evenings, weekends, summer), adult/continuing education programs, internships. ROTC: Army (c), Naval (c), Air Force (c).

GENERAL DEGREE REQUIREMENTS 62 credit hours; 3 credit hours of math; computer course for business, health science majors; internship (some majors).

MAJORS Accounting, art/fine arts, aviation technology, biology/biological sciences, broadcasting, business administration/commerce/management, chemistry, child psychology/child development, computer information systems, court reporting, criminal justice, dental services, drafting and design, early childhood education, electrical and electronics technologies, elementary education, (pre)engineering sequence, English, environmental sciences, history, home economics, journalism, legal secretarial studies, liberal arts/general studies, library science, mathematics, medical laboratory technology, medical records services, modern languages, music, nursing, physical education, physics, political science/government, psychology, radiological technology, respiratory therapy, secretarial studies/office management, sociology, speech/rhetoric/public address/debate, theater arts/drama.

LIBRARY Rose State College Learning Resources Center with 86,931 books, 103 microform titles, 426 periodicals, 2 on-line bibliographic services, 6 CD-ROMs, 2,967 records, tapes, and CDs.

COMPUTERS ON CAMPUS Computer purchase plan available. 390 computers for student use in computer center, computer labs, learning resource center, various locations throughout campus, library provide access to main academic computer, e-mail, Internet. Staffed computer lab on campus provides training in use of computers, software.

COLLEGE LIFE Drama-theater group, choral group, student-run newspaper. 5% vote in student government elections. ***Student services:*** health clinic, personal-psychological counseling, women's center. ***Campus security:*** 24-hour patrols.

HOUSING College housing not available.

ATHLETICS Member NJCAA. ***Intercollegiate:*** baseball M(s), basketball M(s)/W(s). ***Intramural:*** basketball, bowling, soccer, tennis, volleyball, water polo. ***Contact:*** Mr. Les Berryhill, Director of Recreation and Intercollegiate Athletics, 405-733-7350; Mr. Glenn Chilcoat, Coordinator of Intramurals and Women's Basketball, 405-733-7351.

CAREER PLANNING ***Placement office:*** 2 full-time, 2 part-time staff. ***Director:*** Ms. Karla Derrick, Director of Student Placement, 405-733-7377. ***Services:*** job fairs, resume preparation, resume referral, career counseling, careers library, job bank.

EXPENSES FOR 1995–96 ***Application fee:*** $15. State resident tuition: $868 full-time, $28 per credit hour part-time. Nonresident tuition: $2728 full-time, $88 per credit hour part-time. Part-time mandatory fees: $7.50 per credit hour. Full-time mandatory fees: $233.

FINANCIAL AID ***College-administered undergrad aid 1995–96:*** need-based scholarships, non-need scholarships, short-term loans, low-interest long-term loans, Federal Work-Study, part-time jobs. ***Required forms:*** FAFSA. ***Priority deadline:*** 9/15. ***Waivers:*** full or partial for employees or children of employees.

APPLYING Open admission except for health occupations programs. ***Options:*** Common Application, early entrance, deferred entrance. ***Required:*** school transcript, TOEFL for international students. ***Recommended:*** SAT I or ACT. Test scores used for counseling/placement. ***Application deadline:*** rolling. ***Notification:*** continuous.

APPLYING/TRANSFER ***Required:*** college transcript. ***Recommended:*** standardized test scores. ***Application deadline:*** rolling. ***Notification:*** continuous.

CONTACT Ms. Evelyn K. Hutchings, Registrar and Director of Admissions, Rose State College, 6420 S.E. 15th Street, Midwest City, OK 73110-2799, 405-733-7308. ***Fax:*** 405-736-0309. ***E-mail:*** ekhutchings@ms.rose.cc.ok.us. College video available.

ST. GREGORY'S COLLEGE
Shawnee, Oklahoma

UG Enrollment: 335	**Tuition & Fees: $5860**
Application Deadline: rolling	**Room & Board: $3764**

GENERAL Independent Roman Catholic, 2-year, coed. Awards transfer associate, terminal associate degrees. Founded 1875. ***Setting:*** 640-acre small-town campus with easy access to Oklahoma City. ***Endowment:*** $3.2 million. ***Educational spending 1994–95:*** $1315 per undergrad. ***Total enrollment:*** 335. ***Faculty:*** 30 (12 full-time, 30% with terminal degrees, 18 part-time); student-faculty ratio is 16:1.

ENROLLMENT PROFILE 335 students from 11 states and territories, 7 other countries. 54% women, 46% men, 26% part-time, 86% state residents, 18% transferred in, 6% international, 16% 25 or older, 11% Native American, 3% Hispanic, 4% African American, 2% Asian American. ***Areas of study chosen:*** 35% liberal arts/general studies, 21% social sciences, 13% business management and administrative services, 9% education, 3% engineering and applied sciences, 2% communications and journalism, 2% English language/literature/letters, 2% fine arts, 2% physical sciences, 1% theology/religion. ***Most popular recent majors:*** business administration/commerce/management, natural sciences, engineering sciences.

FIRST-YEAR CLASS 161 total; 217 applied, 100% were accepted, 74% of whom enrolled. 20% from top 10% of their high school class, 38% from top quarter, 78% from top half.

ACADEMIC PROGRAM Core, honor code. Calendar: semesters. Academic remediation for entering students, English as a second language program offered during academic year, advanced placement, part-time degree program (evenings, summer), adult/continuing education programs. Off-campus study at Oklahoma Baptist University. ROTC: Air Force (c).

GENERAL DEGREE REQUIREMENTS 64 credit hours; 3 credit hours of math; 8 credit hours of natural science; computer course for business majors.

MAJORS Art/fine arts, biology/biological sciences, botany/plant sciences, business administration/commerce/management, chemistry, child psychology/child development, early childhood education, engineering sciences, English, history, humanities, liberal arts/general studies, mathematics, natural sciences, philosophy, photography, sculpture, social science, theology.

LIBRARY 42,574 books, 1,200 microform titles, 284 periodicals, 180 records, tapes, and CDs. Acquisition spending 1994–95: $70,109.

COMPUTERS ON CAMPUS Computer purchase plan available. 35 computers for student use in computer labs, learning resource center, dorms provide access to on-line services, Internet. Staffed computer lab on campus provides training in use of computers, software. Academic computing expenditure 1994–95: $41,302.

COLLEGE LIFE Orientation program (2 days, parents included). Drama-theater group, choral group, student-run newspaper. ***Social organizations:*** 27 open to all. ***Most popular organizations:*** Residence Halls Association, Rainbow Coalition, Phi Theta Kappa, Campus Ministry, This is My Environment (TIME). ***Major annual events:*** Orientation, Dean's Activity Night, Winter/Spring Formals. ***Student services:*** health clinic, personal-psychological counseling. ***Campus security:*** 24-hour emergency response devices, student patrols, late-night transport-escort service, controlled dormitory access.

HOUSING 500 college housing spaces available; 184 were occupied 1995–96. Freshmen guaranteed college housing. On-campus residence required through sophomore year. ***Option:*** single-sex (2 buildings) housing available. Resident assistants live in dorms.

ATHLETICS Member NJCAA. ***Intercollegiate:*** basketball M(s)/W(s), fencing M/W, golf M/W. ***Intramural:*** basketball, equestrian sports, football, golf, racquetball, skiing (cross-country), skiing (downhill), soccer, softball, swimming and diving, tennis, volleyball, weight lifting. ***Contact:*** Mr. Don Sumner, Athletic Director, 405-878-5172.

CAREER PLANNING ***Placement office:*** 2 full-time, 1 part-time staff; $135,142 operating expenditure 1994–95. ***Director:*** Sr. Veronica Sokolosky, Counselor, Career Services, 405-878-5170. ***Services:*** resume preparation, resume referral, career counseling, careers library, job bank.

AFTER GRADUATION 91% of students completing a degree program in 1994–95 went directly on to further study.

EXPENSES FOR 1996–97 ***Application fee:*** $25. Comprehensive fee of $9624 includes full-time tuition ($5310), mandatory fees ($550), and college room and board ($3764). Part-time tuition: $160 per credit hour. Part-time mandatory fees: $30 per credit hour.

FINANCIAL AID ***College-administered undergrad aid 1995–96:*** 130 need-based scholarships (average $964), 94 non-need scholarships (average $4513), low-interest long-term loans from college funds (average $2619), loans from external sources (average $2282), 35 Federal Work-Study (averaging $1000), 70 part-time jobs. ***Required forms:*** institutional, FAFSA; accepted: CSS Financial Aid PROFILE, state. ***Priority deadline:*** 7/15. ***Payment plans:*** installment, deferred payment. ***Waivers:*** full or partial for employees or children of employees and senior citizens. ***Notification:*** continuous. ***Average indebtedness of graduates:*** $4587.

APPLYING ***Options:*** early entrance, deferred entrance. ***Required:*** school transcript, SAT I or ACT, TOEFL for international students. ***Recommended:*** 3 years of high school math and science, some high school foreign language. ***Required for some:*** essay, recommendations, interview. Test scores used for admission. ***Application deadline:*** rolling. ***Notification:*** continuous.

APPLYING/TRANSFER ***Required:*** high school transcript, college transcript. ***Recommended:*** minimum 2.0 college GPA. ***Required for some:*** essay, standardized test scores, recommendations. ***Entrance:*** minimally difficult. ***Application deadline:*** rolling. ***Notification:*** continuous.

CONTACT Mrs. Kay Stith, Director of Admission, St. Gregory's College, Shawnee, OK 74801-2499, 405-878-5447. ***Fax:*** 405-878-5198.

SEMINOLE JUNIOR COLLEGE
Seminole, Oklahoma

UG Enrollment: 1,700	**Tuition & Fees (OK Res): $1095**
Application Deadline: rolling	**Room & Board: $1830**

GENERAL State-supported, 2-year, coed. Part of Oklahoma State Regents for Higher Education. Awards transfer associate, terminal associate degrees. Founded 1931. ***Setting:*** 40-acre small-town campus. ***Educational spending 1994–95:*** $1398 per undergrad. ***Total enrollment:*** 1,700. ***Faculty:*** 85 (46 full-time, 20% with terminal degrees, 39 part-time).

ENROLLMENT PROFILE 1,700 students from 11 states and territories, 4 other countries. 64% women, 38% part-time, 94% state residents, 5% transferred in, 1% international, 42% 25 or older, 15% Native American, 1% Hispanic, 5% African American, 1% Asian American. ***Areas of study chosen:*** 40% liberal arts/general studies, 12% health professions and related sciences, 10% business management and administrative services, 8% education, 4% psychology, 2% computer and information sciences, 2% social sciences, 1% biological and life sciences, 1% communications and journalism, 1% English language/literature/letters, 1% fine arts, 1% mathematics, 1% physical sciences.

FIRST-YEAR CLASS 781 total. Of the students who applied, 100% were accepted, 100% of whom enrolled.

ACADEMIC PROGRAM Core, honor code. Calendar: semesters. Academic remediation for entering students, services for LD students, advanced placement, self-designed majors, honors program, summer session for credit, part-time degree program (daytime, evenings, summer), adult/continuing education programs, co-op programs.

GENERAL DEGREE REQUIREMENT 60 credits.

MAJORS Accounting, art/fine arts, behavioral sciences, biology/biological sciences, business administration/commerce/management, computer science, elementary education, law enforcement/police sciences, liberal arts/general studies, medical laboratory technology, nursing, physical education, secretarial studies/office management.

LIBRARY Boren Library with 21,827 books, 50 periodicals, 524 records, tapes, and CDs. Acquisition spending 1994–95: $61,323.

COMPUTERS ON CAMPUS 50 computers for student use in computer labs provide access to main academic computer. Staffed computer lab on campus provides training in use of computers, software. Academic computing expenditure 1994–95: $54,713.

COLLEGE LIFE Student-run newspaper. 25% vote in student government elections. ***Social organizations:*** 1 local fraternity. ***Student services:*** personal-psychological counseling. ***Campus security:*** security patrols from 8 a.m.-10 a.m. and 4 p.m.-10 p.m.

HOUSING 48 college housing spaces available; all were occupied 1995–96. No special consideration for freshman housing applicants. Off-campus living permitted.

ATHLETICS Member NJCAA. ***Intercollegiate:*** baseball M, basketball M(s)/W(s).

CAREER PLANNING ***Services:*** resume preparation, career counseling.

EXPENSES FOR 1996–97 ***Application fee:*** $15. State resident tuition: $840 full-time, $28 per credit hour part-time. Nonresident tuition: $2640 full-time, $88 per credit hour part-time. Part-time mandatory fees: $8.50 per credit hour. Full-time mandatory fees: $255. College room and board: $1830.

FINANCIAL AID ***College-administered undergrad aid 1995–96:*** 100 need-based scholarships (averaging $1000), 70 non-need scholarships (averaging $550), short-term

loans (averaging $100), low-interest long-term loans from external sources, Federal Work-Study, part-time jobs. ***Required forms:*** institutional, FAFSA; accepted: CSS Financial Aid PROFILE. ***Priority deadline:*** 7/31.
APPLYING Open admission. ***Options:*** early entrance, deferred entrance, midyear entrance. ***Required:*** 3 years of high school math, TOEFL for international students. ***Required for some:*** ACT. Test scores used for counseling/placement. ***Application deadline:*** rolling. ***Notification:*** continuous.
APPLYING/TRANSFER ***Required:*** 3 years of high school math. ***Required for some:*** standardized test scores. ***Application deadline:*** rolling. ***Notification:*** continuous. ***Contact:*** Mr. Wayne M. Day, Vice President for Student Affairs, 405-382-9950 Ext. 231.
CONTACT Mr. Wayne M. Day, Vice President for Student Affairs, Seminole Junior College, Seminole, OK 74818-0351, 405-382-9950 Ext. 231.

SOUTHWESTERN OKLAHOMA STATE UNIVERSITY AT SAYRE
Sayre, Oklahoma

UG Enrollment: 623	**Tuition & Fees (OK Res): $1680**
Application Deadline: rolling	**Room & Board: N/Avail**

GENERAL State and locally supported, 2-year, coed. Part of Southwestern Oklahoma State University. Awards transfer associate, terminal associate degrees. Founded 1938. ***Setting:*** 6-acre rural campus. ***Total enrollment:*** 623. ***Faculty:*** 30 (20 full-time, 90% with terminal degrees, 10 part-time).
ENROLLMENT PROFILE 623 students: 72% women, 35% part-time, 97% state residents, 5% transferred in, 75% have need-based financial aid, 45% 25 or older, 1% Native American, 1% Hispanic, 1% African American. ***Most popular recent majors:*** medical technology, radiological technology.
FIRST-YEAR CLASS 160 total. Of the students who applied, 100% were accepted, 100% of whom enrolled. 11% from top 10% of their high school class, 22% from top quarter, 55% from top half.
ACADEMIC PROGRAM Core. Calendar: semesters. 110 courses offered in 1995–96. Academic remediation for entering students, adult/continuing education programs.
GENERAL DEGREE REQUIREMENTS 64 credit hours; 3 credit hours of math; 8 credit hours of science; computer course.
MAJORS Business administration/commerce/management, computer programming, liberal arts/general studies, medical laboratory technology, medical secretarial studies, medical technology, nursing, radiological technology.
LIBRARY Oscar McMahan Library with 9,975 books, 22 microform titles, 38 periodicals, 1,000 records, tapes, and CDs.
COMPUTERS ON CAMPUS 60 computers for student use in computer center provide access to main academic computer. Staffed computer lab on campus provides training in use of computers, software.
HOUSING College housing not available.
ATHLETICS ***Intramural:*** basketball, bowling, golf, tennis, volleyball.
CAREER PLANNING ***Placement office:*** 1 full-time staff. ***Director:*** Dr. Nancy Ryan, Counselor and Director, Career Information Center, 405-928-5533. ***Service:*** career counseling.
AFTER GRADUATION 75% of students completing a degree program in 1994–95 went directly on to further study.
EXPENSES FOR 1995–96 State resident tuition: $1376 full-time, $43 per credit hour part-time. Nonresident tuition: $3616 full-time, $113 per credit hour part-time. Part-time mandatory fees: $9.50 per credit hour. Full-time mandatory fees: $304.
FINANCIAL AID ***College-administered undergrad aid 1995–96:*** 17 need-based scholarships (average $300), 15 non-need scholarships (average $300), short-term loans (average $30), low-interest long-term loans from external sources (average $1500), Federal Work-Study, 10 part-time jobs. ***Required forms:*** FAFSA. ***Priority deadline:*** 5/1. ***Payment plan:*** installment.
APPLYING Open admission. ***Options:*** early entrance, deferred entrance. ***Required:*** school transcript, 3 years of high school math, ACT, TOEFL for international students. Test scores used for counseling/placement. ***Application deadline:*** rolling.
APPLYING/TRANSFER ***Required:*** standardized test scores, high school transcript, college transcript. ***Entrance:*** noncompetitive. ***Application deadline:*** rolling.
CONTACT Mrs. Pat Tignor, Registrar, Southwestern Oklahoma State University at Sayre, Sayre, OK 73662-1236, 405-928-5533 Ext. 101.

TULSA JUNIOR COLLEGE
Tulsa, Oklahoma

UG Enrollment: 21,147	**Tuition & Fees (OK Res): $1080**
Application Deadline: 8/20	**Room & Board: N/Avail**

GENERAL State-supported, 2-year, coed. Part of Oklahoma State Regents for Higher Education. Awards transfer associate, terminal associate degrees. Founded 1968. ***Setting:*** 160-acre urban campus. ***Total enrollment:*** 21,147. ***Faculty:*** 1,102 (240 full-time, 862 part-time).
ENROLLMENT PROFILE 21,147 students: 78% part-time, 99% state residents, 24% transferred in, 50% 25 or older, 3% Native American, 1% Hispanic, 6% African American, 1% Asian American.
FIRST-YEAR CLASS 3,352 total. Of the students who applied, 100% were accepted.
ACADEMIC PROGRAM Core. Calendar: semesters. Academic remediation for entering students, services for LD students, advanced placement, honors program, summer session for credit, part-time degree program (daytime, evenings, summer), adult/continuing education programs, co-op programs.
GENERAL DEGREE REQUIREMENTS 60 credit hours; 6 credit hours of science including at least 1 lab science course; 3 credit hours of math.
MAJORS Accounting, advertising, agricultural business, agricultural sciences, American studies, art education, art/fine arts, automotive technologies, aviation technology, biology/biological sciences, botany/plant sciences, business administration/commerce/management, business education, chemistry, child care/child and family studies, communication, computer information systems, computer management, computer programming, computer science, computer technologies, construction technologies, corrections, creative writing, criminal justice, data processing, deaf interpreter training, dental services, drafting and design, earth science, ecology, economics, education, electrical and electronics technologies, electromechanical technology, electronics engineering technology, elementary education, energy management technologies, engineering (general), engineering and applied sciences, (pre)engineering sequence, English, fashion design and technology, finance/banking, fire science, food services management, forestry, French, geography, geology, German, health science, heating/refrigeration/air conditioning, history, horticulture, hotel and restaurant management, humanities, industrial administration, information science, insurance, interior design, international business, international economics, international studies, Italian, Japanese, journalism, labor and industrial relations, labor studies, landscape architecture/design, Latin, law enforcement/police sciences, legal secretarial studies, liberal arts/general studies, management information systems, marketing/retailing/merchandising, materials sciences, mathematics, mechanical engineering technology, medical assistant technologies, medical laboratory technology, medical records services, medical secretarial studies, music, music education, nursing, occupational therapy, paralegal studies, petroleum technology, philosophy, physical education, physical therapy, physician's assistant studies, political science/government, psychology, purchasing/inventory management, radiological technology, real estate, respiratory therapy, retail management, robotics, Russian, secretarial studies/office management, social science, social work, sociology, Spanish, surveying technology, telecommunications, theater arts/drama, tourism and travel, transportation technologies, vocational education, zoology.
LIBRARY 100,000 books.
COMPUTERS ON CAMPUS 650 computers for student use in computer center, various labs, library.
COLLEGE LIFE Drama-theater group, student-run newspaper. ***Student services:*** personal-psychological counseling, women's center. ***Campus security:*** 24-hour patrols, student patrols, late-night transport-escort service.
HOUSING College housing not available.
ATHLETICS ***Intramural:*** basketball, bowling, cross-country running, football, golf, racquetball, soccer, tennis, track and field, volleyball.
CAREER PLANNING ***Service:*** career counseling.
EXPENSES FOR 1995–96 ***Application fee:*** $15. State resident tuition: $1050 full-time, $35 per credit part-time. Nonresident tuition: $2888 full-time, $96.25 per credit part-time. Part-time mandatory fees: $15 per semester. Full-time mandatory fees: $30.
FINANCIAL AID ***College-administered undergrad aid 1995–96:*** need-based scholarships, non-need scholarships, short-term loans, low-interest long-term loans from college funds, loans from external sources, Federal Work-Study, part-time jobs. ***Required forms:*** institutional, FAFSA; accepted: CSS Financial Aid PROFILE. ***Application deadline:*** continuous to 7/31.
APPLYING Open admission except for honors, allied health programs. ***Option:*** early entrance. ***Required:*** 3 years of high school science, 2 years of high school lab science, SAT I or ACT, TOEFL for international students, CPT. ***Recommended:*** 2 years of high school foreign language. Test scores used for counseling/placement. ***Application deadline:*** 8/20.
APPLYING/TRANSFER ***Required:*** standardized test scores, 3 years of high school science, 2 years of high school foreign language, 2 years of high school lab science. ***Entrance:*** noncompetitive. ***Application deadline:*** 8/20.
CONTACT Ms. Barbara Childers, Registrar, Tulsa Junior College, 6111 East Skelly Drive, Tulsa, OK 74135-6198, 918-595-7526.

WESTERN OKLAHOMA STATE COLLEGE
Altus, Oklahoma

UG Enrollment: 1,718	**Tuition & Fees (OK Res): $1110**
Application Deadline: rolling	**Room & Board: N/Avail**

GENERAL State-supported, 2-year, coed. Part of Oklahoma State Regents for Higher Education. Awards certificates, transfer associate, terminal associate degrees. Founded 1926. ***Setting:*** 142-acre rural campus. ***Total enrollment:*** 1,718. ***Faculty:*** 78 (46 full-time, 1% with terminal degrees, 32 part-time).
ENROLLMENT PROFILE 1,718 students from 30 states and territories, 3 other countries. 54% women, 46% men, 45% part-time, 98% state residents, 30% transferred in, 1% international, 50% 25 or older, 2% Native American, 7% Hispanic, 7% African American, 2% Asian American. ***Most popular recent majors:*** business administration/commerce/management, nursing, liberal arts/general studies.
FIRST-YEAR CLASS 324 total; 324 applied, 100% were accepted, 100% of whom enrolled. 10% from top 10% of their high school class, 20% from top quarter, 50% from top half.
ACADEMIC PROGRAM Core, honor code. Calendar: semesters. Academic remediation for entering students, English as a second language program, services for LD students, advanced placement, self-designed majors, honors program, summer session for credit, part-time degree program (daytime, evenings, summer), adult/continuing education programs. Off-campus study at all state institutions in the Oklahoma Higher Education Televised Instructional System.
GENERAL DEGREE REQUIREMENT 64 credits.
MAJORS Accounting, agricultural business, art education, aviation administration, behavioral sciences, biology/biological sciences, business administration/commerce/management, child care/child and family studies, commercial art, construction technologies, corrections, data processing, drafting and design, economics, education, elementary education, engineering (general), English, fire science, graphic arts, humanities, journalism, law enforcement/police sciences, liberal arts/general studies, library science, mathematics, music education, nursing, physical education, physical sciences, retail management, social science, sociology, Spanish, speech/rhetoric/public address/debate, welding technology.
COMPUTERS ON CAMPUS 40 computers for student use in computer center, learning resource center, library. Staffed computer lab on campus provides training in use of computers, software.
COLLEGE LIFE Drama-theater group, choral group. ***Social organizations:*** 1 national fraternity; 1% of eligible men are members. ***Student services:*** personal-psychological counseling. ***Campus security:*** 24-hour emergency response devices.
HOUSING College housing not available.
ATHLETICS Member NJCAA. ***Intercollegiate:*** baseball M(s), basketball M(s)/W(s). ***Intramural:*** basketball, football, golf, tennis, volleyball. ***Contact:*** Mr. Bob Pearson, Athletic Director, 405-477-2000.

Oklahoma–Oregon

Western Oklahoma State College (continued)
CAREER PLANNING *Placement office:* 1 full-time, 1 part-time staff. *Director:* Dr. Glyna Olson, Director of Counseling and Assessment, 405-477-2000 Ext. 232. *Service:* career counseling. 25 organizations recruited on campus 1994–95.
EXPENSES FOR 1995-96 *Application fee:* $15. State resident tuition: $1110 full-time, $37 per credit part-time. Nonresident tuition: $2910 full-time, $97 per credit part-time.
FINANCIAL AID *College-administered undergrad aid 1995-96:* 93 need-based scholarships (average $550), 135 non-need scholarships (average $500), low-interest long-term loans from external sources (average $3000), Federal Work-Study, 40 part-time jobs. *Acceptable forms:* CSS Financial Aid PROFILE, FAFSA. *Priority deadline:* 4/1. *Waivers:* full or partial for employees or children of employees and senior citizens. *Notification:* 7/1.
APPLYING Open admission. *Option:* early entrance. *Required:* school transcript, 3 years of high school math, TOEFL for international students. *Required for some:* ACT. Test scores used for admission and counseling/placement. *Application deadline:* rolling. *Notification:* continuous.
APPLYING/TRANSFER *Required:* high school transcript, 3 years of high school math, college transcript. *Required for some:* standardized test scores. *Application deadline:* rolling. *Notification:* continuous.
CONTACT Mr. Larry Paxton, Director of Admissions/Registrar, Western Oklahoma State College, Altus, OK 73521-1397, 405-477-2000 Ext. 213. *Fax:* 405-521-6154. College video available.

OREGON

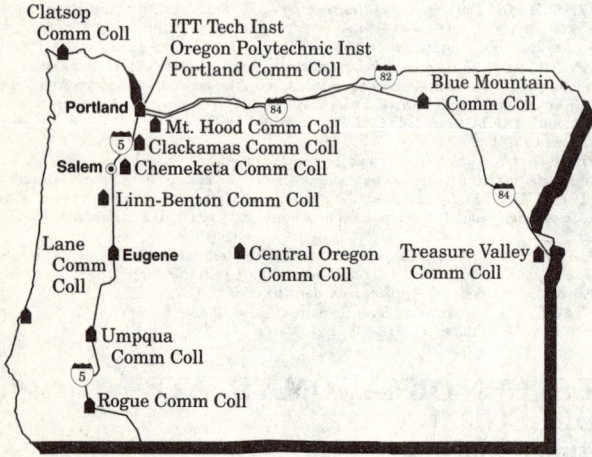

BLUE MOUNTAIN COMMUNITY COLLEGE
Pendleton, Oregon

UG Enrollment: 3,808	Tuition & Fees (OR Res): $1272
Application Deadline: rolling	Room & Board: N/Avail

GENERAL State and locally supported, 2-year, coed. Awards certificates, transfer associate, terminal associate degrees. Founded 1962. *Setting:* 170-acre rural campus. *Total enrollment:* 3,808. *Faculty:* 245 (74 full-time, 171 part-time); student-faculty ratio is 15:1.
ENROLLMENT PROFILE 3,808 students from 11 states and territories, 3 other countries. 50% women, 50% men, 71% part-time, 95% state residents, 10% transferred in, 1% international, 59% 25 or older, 2% Native American, 7% Hispanic, 1% African American, 1% Asian American. *Areas of study chosen:* 29% liberal arts/general studies, 24% business management and administrative services, 16% social sciences, 12% health professions and related sciences, 9% engineering and applied sciences, 7% vocational and home economics, 3% agriculture.
FIRST-YEAR CLASS 360 total. Of the students who applied, 100% were accepted.
ACADEMIC PROGRAM Core. Calendar: quarters. Academic remediation for entering students, English as a second language program offered during academic year, services for LD students, advanced placement, summer session for credit, part-time degree program (daytime, evenings), adult/continuing education programs.
GENERAL DEGREE REQUIREMENTS 90 credit hours; math/science requirements vary according to program.
MAJORS Accounting, agricultural business, agronomy/soil and crop sciences, animal sciences, automotive technologies, broadcasting, business administration/commerce/management, civil engineering technology, criminal justice, drafting and design, electrical and electronics technologies, (pre)engineering sequence, farm and ranch management, human services, law enforcement/police sciences, liberal arts/general studies, marketing/retailing/merchandising, medical secretarial studies, nursing, practical nursing, secretarial studies/office management.
LIBRARY 36,737 books, 433 periodicals.
COMPUTERS ON CAMPUS 180 computers for student use in computer center, academic buildings. Staffed computer lab on campus.

COLLEGE LIFE Drama-theater group, choral group, student-run radio station. *Social organizations:* 3 open to all. *Student services:* personal-psychological counseling.
HOUSING College housing not available.
ATHLETICS *Intercollegiate:* baseball M(s), basketball M(s)/W(s), cross-country running M(s)/W(s), track and field M(s)/W(s), volleyball W(s). *Intramural:* basketball, skiing (cross-country), skiing (downhill).
CAREER PLANNING *Service:* career counseling.
EXPENSES FOR 1995-96 State resident tuition: $1248 full-time, $32 per credit hour part-time. Nonresident tuition: $3744 full-time, $32 per credit hour (minimum) part-time. Full-time mandatory fees: $24.
FINANCIAL AID *College-administered undergrad aid 1995-96:* need-based scholarships, short-term loans (average $75), low-interest long-term loans from external sources. *Required forms:* CSS Financial Aid PROFILE, FAFSA. *Priority deadline:* 3/30. *Waivers:* full or partial for employees or children of employees and senior citizens.
APPLYING Open admission. *Required:* school transcript, TOEFL for international students, ACT ASSET. Test scores used for counseling/placement. *Application deadline:* rolling. *Notification:* continuous.
APPLYING/TRANSFER *Required:* college transcript. *Entrance:* noncompetitive. *Application deadline:* rolling. *Notification:* continuous.
CONTACT Mr. C. Dorwin Lovell, Registrar, Blue Mountain Community College, Pendleton, OR 97801-1000, 541-276-1260 Ext. 289.

CENTRAL OREGON COMMUNITY COLLEGE
Bend, Oregon

UG Enrollment: 3,240	Tuition & Fees (Area Res): $1710
Application Deadline: rolling	Room & Board: $4000

COCC's 193-acre campus is situated on the pine- and juniper-studded West Hills of Bend, with spectacular views of the nearby Oregon Cascade mountains. Approximately 3,200 students pursue courses, certificates, and associate degrees for university transfer and for professional/technical training. Coed Juniper Residence Hall houses 100 students.

GENERAL District-supported, 2-year, coed. Part of Oregon Community College Association. Awards certificates, transfer associate, terminal associate degrees. Founded 1949. *Setting:* 193-acre small-town campus. *Endowment:* $266,726. *Total enrollment:* 3,240. *Faculty:* 184 (84 full-time, 83% with terminal degrees, 100 part-time); student-faculty ratio is 18:1.
ENROLLMENT PROFILE 3,240 students from 15 states and territories, 6 other countries. 59% women, 41% men, 62% part-time, 98% state residents, 3% live on campus, 15% transferred in, 36% have need-based financial aid, 1% international, 53% 25 or older, 4% Native American, 2% Hispanic, 0% African American, 1% Asian American.
FIRST-YEAR CLASS 731 total; 1,400 applied, 100% were accepted, 52% of whom enrolled.
ACADEMIC PROGRAM Core, transfer, professional, and technical curriculum, honor code. Calendar: quarters. 659 courses offered in 1995–96. Academic remediation for entering students, English as a second language program offered during academic year and summer, services for LD students, advanced placement, self-designed majors, summer session for credit, part-time degree program (daytime, evenings, summer), external degree programs, adult/continuing education programs, co-op programs and internships. Study abroad in Mexico, Spain, England (2% of students participate).
GENERAL DEGREE REQUIREMENTS 93 credits; internship (some majors).
MAJORS Accounting, art/fine arts, automotive technologies, business administration/commerce/management, business machine technologies, civil engineering technology, computer graphics, computer information systems, computer science, computer technologies, criminal justice, culinary arts, drafting and design, education, electrical and electronics technologies, electrical engineering technology, engineering (general), engineering and applied sciences, (pre)engineering sequence, engineering technology, fire science, fish and game management, forest technology, hospitality services, hotel and restaurant management, humanities, legal secretarial studies, liberal arts/general studies, machine and tool technologies, manufacturing technology, marketing/retailing/merchandising, mathematics, mechanical engineering technology, medical records services, medical secretarial studies, nursing, physical education, physical sciences, practical nursing, robotics, science, secretarial studies/office management, social science, welding technology.
LIBRARY Main library plus 1 other, with 44,481 books, 6,726 microform titles, 393 periodicals, 1 on-line bibliographic service, 121 CD-ROMs, 793 records, tapes, and CDs. Acquisition spending 1994–95: $80,000.
COMPUTERS ON CAMPUS Computer purchase plan available. Student rooms linked to a campus network. 300 computers for student use in computer labs, library, dorms provide access to e-mail, Internet. Staffed computer lab on campus provides training in use of computers, software. Academic computing expenditure 1994–95: $111,625.
COLLEGE LIFE Drama-theater group, choral group, student-run newspaper. 16% vote in student government elections. *Most popular organizations:* Student Government, Magic Circle Theatre, Phi Theta Kappa, DEC, Business Club. *Major annual events:* Earth Day, Women's History Week. *Student services:* health clinic, personal-psychological counseling. *Campus security:* 24-hour emergency response devices, late-night transport-escort service.
HOUSING 102 college housing spaces available; all were occupied 1995–96. No special consideration for freshman housing applicants. Off-campus living permitted. *Option:* coed (1 building) housing available. Resident assistants live in dorms.
ATHLETICS *Intercollegiate:* archery M(c)/W(c), basketball W(c), golf M(c)/W(c), racquetball M(c)/W(c), soccer M(c)/W(c), softball M(c)/W(c), tennis M(c)/W(c), volleyball W(c). *Intramural:* archery, badminton, baseball, basketball, bowling, cross-country running, equestrian sports, football, golf, racquetball, skiing (downhill), soccer, softball, tennis, track and field, volleyball.
CAREER PLANNING *Placement office:* 4 full-time, 1 part-time staff. *Director:* Ms. Mary Ostrander, Director of Counseling, 541-383-7580. *Services:* job fairs, resume preparation, resume referral, career counseling, careers library, job bank, job interviews.
AFTER GRADUATION 50% of students completing a degree program in 1994–95 went directly on to further study.
EXPENSES FOR 1996-97 Area resident tuition: $1656 full-time, $36 per credit part-time. State resident tuition: $2162 full-time, $47 per credit part-time. Nonresident tuition:

$5934 full-time, $129 per credit part-time. Part-time mandatory fees per quarter range from $1.50 to $18. Full-time mandatory fees: $54. College room and board: $4000.
FINANCIAL AID ***College-administered undergrad aid 1995–96:*** 912 need-based scholarships (average $988), 200 non-need scholarships (average $1005), short-term loans (average $150), low-interest long-term loans from external sources (average $3587), 179 Federal Work-Study (averaging $828). ***Required forms:*** institutional, FAFSA; accepted: CSS Financial Aid PROFILE. ***Priority deadline:*** 2/28. ***Payment plans:*** installment, deferred payment. ***Waivers:*** full or partial for employees or children of employees and senior citizens. ***Average indebtedness of graduates:*** $4187.
APPLYING Open admission for state residents. ***Options:*** Common Application, early entrance, deferred entrance, midyear entrance. ***Required:*** TOEFL for international students. ***Recommended:*** school transcript. Test scores used for counseling/placement. ***Application deadline:*** rolling. ***Notification:*** continuous. Preference given to district residents for nursing program.
APPLYING/TRANSFER ***Recommended:*** high school transcript. ***Entrance:*** noncompetitive. ***Application deadline:*** rolling. ***Notification:*** continuous. ***Contact:*** Ms. Christine Kerlin, Director of Admissions and Records, 541-383-7500.
CONTACT Ms. Christine Kerlin, Director of Admissions and Records, Central Oregon Community College, Bend, OR 97701-5998, 541-383-7500 or toll-free 800-422-3041 (in-state). ***Fax:*** 541-383-7506. ***E-mail:*** welcome@metolius.cocc.edu.

CHEMEKETA COMMUNITY COLLEGE
Salem, Oregon

UG Enrollment: 9,784	**Tuition & Fees (OR Res): $1530**
Application Deadline: rolling	**Room & Board: N/Avail**

GENERAL State and locally supported, 2-year, coed. Awards certificates, transfer associate, terminal associate degrees. Founded 1955. ***Setting:*** 72-acre urban campus with easy access to Portland. ***Total enrollment:*** 9,784. ***Faculty:*** 883 (241 full-time, 642 part-time); student-faculty ratio is 15:1.
ENROLLMENT PROFILE 9,784 students from 5 states and territories, 17 other countries. 57% women, 43% men, 80% part-time, 98% state residents, 50% have need-based financial aid, 1% have non-need-based financial aid, 61% 25 or older, 2% Native American, 10% Hispanic, 1% African American, 3% Asian American. ***Areas of study chosen:*** 42% liberal arts/general studies, 10% business management and administrative services, 10% vocational and home economics, 9% health professions and related sciences, 6% social sciences, 4% computer and information sciences, 4% education, 3% engineering and applied sciences, 2% communications and journalism, 1% natural resource sciences, 1% physical sciences. ***Most popular recent majors:*** liberal arts/general studies, nursing, practical nursing.
FIRST-YEAR CLASS 10,572 applied, 100% were accepted.
ACADEMIC PROGRAM Honor code. Calendar: quarters. 1,235 courses offered in 1995–96. Academic remediation for entering students, English as a second language program offered during academic year and summer, services for LD students, advanced placement, summer session for credit, part-time degree program (daytime, evenings), adult/continuing education programs, co-op programs and internships.
GENERAL DEGREE REQUIREMENTS 92 credits; 1 math course; computer course; internship (some majors).
MAJORS Accounting, agricultural sciences, automotive technologies, botany/plant sciences, business administration/commerce/management, chemistry, child care/child and family studies, child psychology/child development, civil engineering technology, communication equipment technology, computer programming, computer science, computer technologies, construction technologies, corrections, criminal justice, data processing, dental services, drafting and design, drug and alcohol/substance abuse counseling, early childhood education, economics, education, electrical and electronics technologies, electromechanical technology, electronics engineering technology, emergency medical technology, engineering (general), English, entomology, finance/banking, fire science, forestry, forest technology, geography, geology, gerontology, graphic arts, health education, history, home economics, hospitality services, hotel and restaurant management, humanities, human resources, human services, industrial engineering technology, journalism, law enforcement/police sciences, legal secretarial studies, liberal arts/general studies, machine and tool technologies, manufacturing technology, mathematics, mechanical design technology, medical assistant technologies, medical records services, medical secretarial studies, mental health/rehabilitation counseling, nursing, philosophy, physical education, physics, political science/government, practical nursing, printing technologies, psychology, real estate, science, secretarial studies/office management, social science, social work, sociology, speech/rhetoric/public address/debate, surveying technology, teacher aide studies, welding technology, zoology.
LIBRARY Chemeketa Community College Library with 57,588 books, 147 microform titles, 721 periodicals, 10 CD-ROMs, 4,923 records, tapes, and CDs.
COMPUTERS ON CAMPUS Computer purchase plan available. 325 computers for student use in computer center, computer labs, classrooms, library provide access to main academic computer, off-campus computing facilities. Staffed computer lab on campus provides training in use of computers, software.
COLLEGE LIFE Drama-theater group, choral group, student-run newspaper. 5% vote in student government elections. ***Social organizations:*** 30 open to all. ***Most popular organizations:*** Health Occupations Students of America, International Conference of Building Officials, Ski Club, Christian Fellowship. ***Major annual events:*** International Food Fair, Holiday Crafts Fair, Ski Ball. ***Student services:*** personal-psychological counseling, women's center. ***Campus security:*** 24-hour emergency response devices and patrols, late-night transport-escort service.
HOUSING College housing not available.
ATHLETICS ***Intercollegiate:*** baseball M(s), basketball M(s)/W(s), cross-country running M(s)/W(s), soccer M(c)/W(c), track and field M(s)/W(s), volleyball W(s). ***Intramural:*** skiing (downhill). ***Contact:*** Mr. George Libbon, Athletic Director, 503-399-6248.
CAREER PLANNING ***Placement office:*** 11 full-time, 1 part-time staff. ***Director:*** Mr. Ray Phipps, Director of CWE and Placement, 503-399-6540. ***Services:*** job fairs, resume preparation, resume referral, career counseling, careers library, job bank. 12 organizations recruited on campus 1994–95.
EXPENSES FOR 1995–96 State resident tuition: $1530 full-time, $34 per credit hour part-time. Nonresident tuition: $5400 full-time, $120 per credit hour part-time.
FINANCIAL AID ***College-administered undergrad aid 1995–96:*** 10 need-based scholarships (averaging $1188), 30 non-need scholarships (averaging $1188), short-term loans (averaging $100), low-interest long-term loans from external sources (averaging $1500), 700 Federal Work-Study (averaging $1500), 200 part-time jobs. ***Required forms:*** state, institutional, FAFSA; accepted: CSS Financial Aid PROFILE. ***Priority deadline:*** 4/1. ***Payment plan:*** installment. ***Waivers:*** full or partial for employees or children of employees and senior citizens.
APPLYING Open admission except for nursing, allied health, fire science, building inspection, construction technology, dental assisting, emergency medical technology, human services, instructional assistant, professional technical teacher preparation, visual communications programs. ***Option:*** early entrance. ***Required:*** TOEFL for international students. ***Required for some:*** ACT ASSET. Test scores used for counseling/placement. ***Application deadline:*** rolling. ***Notification:*** continuous.
APPLYING/TRANSFER ***Entrance:*** noncompetitive. ***Application deadline:*** rolling. ***Notification:*** continuous. ***Contact:*** Ms. Karen Weiss, Admissions Specialist, 503-399-5006.
CONTACT Ms. Carolyn Brownell, Admissions Specialist, Chemeketa Community College, 4000 Lancaster Drive, NE, Salem, OR 97309-7070, 503-399-5006. ***Fax:*** 503-399-3918. ***E-mail:*** broc@chemek.cc.or.us.

CLACKAMAS COMMUNITY COLLEGE
Oregon City, Oregon

UG Enrollment: 6,933	**Tuition & Fees (OR Res): $1512**
Application Deadline: rolling	**Room & Board: N/Avail**

GENERAL District-supported, 2-year, coed. Awards certificates, diplomas, transfer associate, terminal associate degrees. Founded 1966. ***Setting:*** 175-acre suburban campus with easy access to Portland. ***Endowment:*** $885,456. ***Total enrollment:*** 6,933. ***Faculty:*** 506 (144 full-time, 6% with terminal degrees, 362 part-time); student-faculty ratio is 17:1.
ENROLLMENT PROFILE 6,933 students from 11 states and territories, 11 other countries. 47% women, 53% men, 69% part-time, 97% state residents, 13% transferred in, 1% international, 51% 25 or older, 1% Native American, 3% Hispanic, 1% African American, 3% Asian American. ***Areas of study chosen:*** 41% liberal arts/general studies, 15% business management and administrative services, 13% biological and life sciences, 10% social sciences, 7% education, 7% mathematics, 5% fine arts, 4% English language/literature/letters. ***Most popular recent majors:*** business administration/commerce/management, science, social science.
FIRST-YEAR CLASS 1,627 total. Of the students who applied, 100% were accepted, 100% of whom enrolled.
ACADEMIC PROGRAM Core. Calendar: quarters. 445 courses offered in 1995–96. Academic remediation for entering students, English as a second language program offered during academic year, services for LD students, advanced placement, tutorials, honors program, summer session for credit, part-time degree program (daytime, evenings), adult/continuing education programs, co-op programs and internships. Study abroad in Spain.
GENERAL DEGREE REQUIREMENTS 93 credit hours; math/science requirements vary according to program; computer course; internship (some majors).
MAJORS Accounting, anthropology, art/fine arts, automotive technologies, biology/biological sciences, business administration/commerce/management, chemistry, computer science, construction technologies, criminal justice, drafting and design, economics, education, elementary education, engineering and applied sciences, English, geography, geology, history, human services, industrial engineering technology, international studies, journalism, law enforcement/police sciences, liberal arts/general studies, manufacturing technology, marketing/retailing/merchandising, mathematics, mechanical engineering technology, music, nursing, nutrition, ornamental horticulture, philosophy, physical education, physics, political science/government, psychology, religious studies, science, secretarial studies/office management, social science, sociology, theater arts/drama, water resources.
LIBRARY Dye Learning Resource Center plus 1 other, with 48,916 books, 169 microform titles, 306 periodicals, 1,570 records, tapes, and CDs. Acquisition spending 1994–95: $64,041.
COMPUTERS ON CAMPUS 135 computers for student use in computer labs, learning resource center, classrooms provide access to e-mail, on-line services, Internet. Staffed computer lab on campus provides training in use of computers, software.
COLLEGE LIFE Drama-theater group, choral group, student-run newspaper. 1% vote in student government elections. ***Social organizations:*** 1 national fraternity. ***Student services:*** personal-psychological counseling, women's center. ***Campus security:*** 24-hour emergency response devices and patrols, student patrols, late-night transport-escort service.
HOUSING College housing not available.
ATHLETICS Member NJCAA. ***Intercollegiate:*** baseball M(s), basketball M(s)/W(s), cross-country running M(s)/W(s), softball W(s), track and field M(s)/W(s), volleyball W(s), wrestling M(s). ***Intramural:*** basketball, softball, tennis, volleyball. ***Contact:*** Mr. Jim Jackson, Director of Athletics, Physical Education and Health, 503-657-6958 Ext. 2295.
CAREER PLANNING ***Placement office:*** 3 full-time staff. ***Director:*** Ms. Jan Godfrey, Associate Dean, Student Services and Counseling, 503-657-6958 Ext. 2552. ***Services:*** job fairs, resume preparation, career counseling, careers library, job bank, job interviews.
EXPENSES FOR 1995–96 State resident tuition: $1440 full-time, $32 per credit hour part-time. Nonresident tuition: $5040 full-time, $112 per credit hour part-time. Part-time mandatory fees: $2 per credit hour. Full-time mandatory fees: $72.
FINANCIAL AID ***College-administered undergrad aid 1995–96:*** 566 need-based scholarships (averaging $568), 391 non-need scholarships (averaging $616), short-term loans (averaging $128), low-interest long-term loans from external sources (averaging $2202), 142 Federal Work-Study (averaging $1414), 200 part-time jobs. ***Required forms:*** FAFSA; required for some: institutional. ***Priority deadline:*** 4/1. ***Payment plan:*** deferred payment. ***Waivers:*** full or partial for employees or children of employees and senior citizens.
APPLYING Open admission except for nursing program. ***Options:*** early entrance, midyear entrance. ***Required:*** TOEFL for international students. ***Recommended:*** school transcript, SAT I or ACT. Test scores used for counseling/placement. ***Application deadline:*** rolling.
APPLYING/TRANSFER ***Recommended:*** standardized test scores, college transcript. ***Entrance:*** noncompetitive. ***Application deadline:*** rolling. ***Contact:*** Ms. Mary Bezodis, Evaluation Specialist, 503-657-6958 Ext. 2264.
CONTACT Ms. Mary Dykes, Associate Dean of Student Services/Registrar, Clackamas Community College, Oregon City, OR 97045-7998, 503-657-6958 Ext. 2425. ***Fax:*** 503-650-6654. ***E-mail:*** suem@clackamas.cc.or.us.

CLATSOP COMMUNITY COLLEGE
Astoria, Oregon

UG Enrollment: 2,474	**Tuition & Fees (OR Res): $1260**
Application Deadline: 9/16	**Room & Board: N/Avail**

GENERAL County-supported, 2-year, coed. Awards transfer associate degrees. Founded 1958. ***Setting:*** 20-acre small-town campus. ***Total enrollment:*** 2,474. ***Faculty:*** 165 (40 full-time, 100% with terminal degrees, 125 part-time); student-faculty ratio is 12:1.
ENROLLMENT PROFILE 2,474 students from 7 states and territories, 2 other countries. 42% men, 83% part-time, 93% state residents, 10% transferred in, 1% international, 66% 25 or older, 1% Native American, 1% Hispanic, 1% African American, 1% Asian American. ***Most popular recent majors:*** liberal arts/general studies, nursing, business administration/commerce/management.
FIRST-YEAR CLASS 402 applied, 100% were accepted, 99% of whom enrolled.
ACADEMIC PROGRAM Core. Calendar: quarters. 285 courses offered in 1995–96. Academic remediation for entering students, English as a second language program offered during academic year, services for LD students, self-designed majors, summer session for credit, part-time degree program (daytime), adult/continuing education programs, co-op programs.
GENERAL DEGREE REQUIREMENTS 90 credits; math/science requirements vary according to program; computer course for all associate of applied science degree students.
MAJORS Accounting, automotive technologies, business administration/commerce/management, criminal justice, data processing, fire science, legal secretarial studies, liberal arts/general studies, medical secretarial studies, nursing, secretarial studies/office management, welding technology.
LIBRARY Dora Badollet Library with 42,741 books, 93 microform titles, 670 periodicals, 3,800 records, tapes, and CDs. Acquisition spending 1994–95: $22,294.
COMPUTERS ON CAMPUS 76 computers for student use in computer labs. Staffed computer lab on campus.
COLLEGE LIFE Drama-theater group. ***Most popular organizations:*** Lives in Transition, Phi Beta Kappa, Nursing Club, Spanish Club. ***Major annual events:*** Blood Drive, Graduation Festival, End of Year Awards Ceremony. ***Student services:*** personal-psychological counseling. ***Campus security:*** 24-hour emergency response devices.
HOUSING College housing not available.
ATHLETICS ***Intercollegiate:*** fencing M/W. ***Intramural:*** archery, basketball, fencing, skiing (cross-country), skiing (downhill), volleyball.
CAREER PLANNING ***Service:*** career counseling.
EXPENSES FOR 1996–97 State resident tuition: $1260 full-time, $35 per credit part-time. Nonresident tuition: $3600 full-time, $100 per credit part-time.
FINANCIAL AID ***College-administered undergrad aid 1995–96:*** 298 need-based scholarships (averaging $739), 75 non-need scholarships (averaging $281), short-term loans (averaging $270), low-interest long-term loans from external sources (averaging $2532), 214 Federal Work-Study (averaging $937), 60 part-time jobs. ***Required forms:*** institutional, FAFSA. ***Priority deadline:*** 8/1. ***Waivers:*** full or partial for employees or children of employees, adult students, and senior citizens.
APPLYING Open admission. ***Options:*** early entrance, deferred entrance, midyear entrance. ***Required:*** TOEFL for international students, ACT ASSET. Test scores used for admission (TOEFL) and counseling/placement (ACT ASSET). ***Application deadline:*** 9/16. ***Notification:*** continuous.
APPLYING/TRANSFER ***Required for some:*** standardized test scores. ***Entrance:*** noncompetitive. ***Application deadline:*** 9/16. ***Notification:*** continuous. ***Contact:*** Ms. Linda Oldenkamp, Director of Admissions, 503-325-2411.
CONTACT Mrs. Linda Gallino, Associate Dean of Student Services, Clatsop Community College, Astoria, OR 97103, 503-325-0910 Ext. 2211. ***Fax:*** 503-325-5738.

ITT TECHNICAL INSTITUTE
Portland, Oregon

UG Enrollment: 498	**Tuition: $15,429/deg prog**
Application Deadline: rolling	**Room & Board: N/Avail**

GENERAL Proprietary, primarily 2-year, coed. Part of ITT Educational Services, Inc. Awards terminal associate, bachelor's degrees. Founded 1971. ***Setting:*** 4-acre urban campus. ***Total enrollment:*** 498. ***Faculty:*** 32 (23 full-time, 100% with terminal degrees, 9 part-time); student-faculty ratio is 20:1.
ENROLLMENT PROFILE 498 students from 10 states and territories, 5 other countries. 21% women, 0% part-time, 85% state residents, 11% transferred in, 31% 25 or older, 1% Native American, 2% Hispanic, 3% African American, 4% Asian American. ***Most popular recent majors:*** electronics engineering technology, drafting and design.
FIRST-YEAR CLASS 248 applied, 97% were accepted, 74% of whom enrolled. 5% from top 10% of their high school class, 10% from top quarter, 48% from top half.
ACADEMIC PROGRAM Core, honor code. Calendar: quarters. 136 courses offered in 1995–96. Academic remediation for entering students, summer session for credit, co-op programs and internships.
GENERAL DEGREE REQUIREMENTS 91 quarter credits for associate, 198 quarter credits for bachelor's; 1 math course; computer course; internship (some majors).
MAJORS Drafting and design, electronics engineering technology, hotel and restaurant management (B), robotics (B).
LIBRARY 3,400 books, 45 periodicals, 6 CD-ROMs, 101 records, tapes, and CDs.
COMPUTERS ON CAMPUS 80 computers for student use in computer center, computer labs, research center, learning resource center, library provide access to main academic computer, e-mail, Internet. Staffed computer lab on campus.
COLLEGE LIFE Orientation program (2 days, no cost, parents included). Student-run newspaper. ***Major annual events:*** Technical Fest, School Picnic. ***Campus security:*** 24-hour emergency response devices, student patrols.
HOUSING College housing not available.
ATHLETICS ***Intramural:*** basketball, golf, volleyball.
CAREER PLANNING ***Placement office:*** 2 full-time staff. ***Director:*** Ms. Heidi Hall, Director of Placement, 503-255-6500 Ext. 311. ***Services:*** job fairs, resume preparation, resume referral, career counseling, careers library, job bank, job interviews. 104 organizations recruited on campus 1994–95.
AFTER GRADUATION 86% of class of 1994 had job offers within 6 months. 3% of students completing transfer associate program went directly to 4-year colleges.
EXPENSES FOR 1995–96 ***Application fee:*** $100. Full-time tuition per degree program: $15,429 to $17,690 for associate, $29,064 to $31,110 for bachelor's. Tuition guaranteed not to increase for student's term of enrollment.
FINANCIAL AID ***College-administered undergrad aid 1995–96:*** need-based scholarships, low-interest long-term loans from external sources, Federal Work-Study, 2 part-time jobs. ***Required forms:*** institutional, FAFSA; required for some: CSS Financial Aid PROFILE. ***Priority deadline:*** 9/9. ***Payment plan:*** installment. ***Waivers:*** full or partial for employees or children of employees.
APPLYING ***Option:*** deferred entrance. ***Required:*** TOEFL for international students, CPAt. ***Recommended:*** 3 years of high school math and science. Test scores used for admission. ***Application deadline:*** rolling.
APPLYING/TRANSFER ***Recommended:*** 3 years of high school math and science. ***Entrance:*** minimally difficult. ***Application deadline:*** rolling. ***Contact:*** Mr. Galen Rose, Director of Education, 503-255-6500 Ext. 316.
CONTACT Mr. Cliff Custer, Director of Recruitment, ITT Technical Institute, 6035 Northeast 78th Court, Portland, OR 97218-2854, 503-255-6500 Ext. 314 or toll-free 800-234-5488. ***Fax:*** 503-255-6135. College video available.

LANE COMMUNITY COLLEGE
Eugene, Oregon

UG Enrollment: 9,533	**Tuition & Fees (OR Res): $1547**
Application Deadline: rolling	**Room & Board: N/Avail**

GENERAL State and locally supported, 2-year, coed. Awards certificates, transfer associate, terminal associate degrees. Founded 1964. ***Setting:*** 240-acre suburban campus. ***Endowment:*** $3 million. ***Total enrollment:*** 9,533. ***Faculty:*** 528 (282 full-time, 91% with terminal degrees, 246 part-time).
ENROLLMENT PROFILE 9,533 students from 28 states and territories, 25 other countries. 55% women, 59% part-time, 96% state residents, 18% transferred in, 26% have need-based financial aid, 9% have non-need-based financial aid, 3% international, 51% 25 or older, 2% Native American, 2% Hispanic, 1% African American, 5% Asian American. ***Most popular recent majors:*** nursing, business administration/commerce/management.
FIRST-YEAR CLASS 3,532 total; 4,923 applied, 100% were accepted, 72% of whom enrolled.
ACADEMIC PROGRAM Core, college transfer and vocational curriculum, honor code. Calendar: quarters. 1,404 courses offered in 1995–96. Academic remediation for entering students, English as a second language program offered during academic year and summer, services for LD students, advanced placement, summer session for credit, part-time degree program (daytime, evenings), adult/continuing education programs, co-op programs and internships.
GENERAL DEGREE REQUIREMENTS 93 credits; math/science requirements vary according to program; computer course for most majors; internship (some majors).
MAJORS Accounting, agricultural technologies, automotive technologies, aviation technology, broadcasting, business administration/commerce/management, child care/child and family studies, community services, computer programming, computer technologies, construction technologies, criminal justice, culinary arts, dental services, drafting and design, drug and alcohol/substance abuse counseling, early childhood education, electrical and electronics technologies, electrical engineering technology, electronics engineering technology, energy management technologies, film and video production, flight training, food services management, food services technology, graphic arts, heating/refrigeration/air conditioning, hospitality services, hotel and restaurant management, industrial and heavy equipment maintenance, legal secretarial studies, liberal arts/general studies, manufacturing technology, nursing, radio and television studies, real estate, respiratory therapy, secretarial studies/office management, welding technology.
LIBRARY Lane Community College Library plus 1 other, with 64,950 books, 227 microform titles, 496 periodicals, 1 on-line bibliographic service, 26 CD-ROMs, 2,955 records, tapes, and CDs. Acquisition spending 1994–95: $140,109.
COMPUTERS ON CAMPUS Computer purchase plan available. 450 computers for student use in computer center, computer labs, classrooms, library provide access to main academic computer, on-line services. Staffed computer lab on campus. Academic computing expenditure 1994–95: $1.1 million.
COLLEGE LIFE Drama-theater group, choral group, student-run newspaper. 10% vote in student government elections. ***Social organizations:*** 15 open to all. ***Most popular organizations:*** Associated Students of Lane, Multicultural Center Club, Native American Students Club, Lane Writing Club, Forensics Club. ***Major annual events:*** Fall Welcome Week, Martin Luther King, Jr. Celebration. ***Student services:*** legal services, health clinic, personal-psychological counseling, women's center. ***Campus security:*** 24-hour emergency response devices and patrols, student patrols, late-night transport-escort service.
HOUSING College housing not available.
ATHLETICS ***Intercollegiate:*** baseball M(s), basketball M(s)/W(s), cross-country running M(s)/W(s), track and field M(s)/W(s), volleyball W(s). ***Intramural:*** badminton, basketball, bowling, football, golf, skiing (cross-country), skiing (downhill), soccer, softball, tennis, volleyball, weight lifting. ***Contact:*** Mr. Harland Yriarte, Athletic Director, 541-726-2215.
CAREER PLANNING ***Placement office:*** 1 full-time, 18 part-time staff; $177,893 operating expenditure 1994–95. ***Director:*** Ms. Geri Meyers, Assessment and Testing Specialist, 541-747-4501 Ext. 2296. ***Services:*** job fairs, resume preparation, career counseling, careers library, job bank, job interviews. 62 organizations recruited on campus 1994–95.
EXPENSES FOR 1995–96 State resident tuition: $1472 full-time, $32 per credit hour part-time. Nonresident tuition: $5014 full-time, $109 per credit hour part-time. Part-time mandatory fees: $25 per quarter. Full-time mandatory fees: $75.
FINANCIAL AID ***College-administered undergrad aid 1995–96:*** 1,193 need-based scholarships (average $615), 222 non-need scholarships (average $584), short-term loans (average $50), 354 Federal Work-Study (averaging $1709). ***Required forms:*** institutional. ***Priority deadline:*** 4/30. ***Payment plan:*** installment. ***Waivers:*** full or partial for employees or children of employees and senior citizens. ***Notification:*** 5/25.
APPLYING Open admission. ***Options:*** Common Application, early entrance. ***Required:*** TOEFL for international students. ***Required for some:*** nursing exam. Test scores used for counseling/placement. ***Application deadline:*** rolling. ***Notification:*** continuous. Preference given to district residents.
APPLYING/TRANSFER ***Required for some:*** standardized test scores, high school transcript, college transcript. ***Entrance:*** noncompetitive. ***Application deadline:*** rolling. ***Notification:*** continuous.

CONTACT Ms. Sharon K. Williams, Director of Admissions and Registration, Lane Community College, Eugene, OR 97405-0640, 541-747-4501 Ext. 2686 or 541-726-2207. ***Fax:*** 541-744-3995. ***E-mail:*** williamss@lanecc.edu.

LINN-BENTON COMMUNITY COLLEGE
Albany, Oregon

UG Enrollment: 5,453 **Tuition & Fees (OR Res): $1530**
Application Deadline: rolling **Room & Board: N/Avail**

GENERAL State and locally supported, 2-year, coed. Awards certificates, transfer associate, terminal associate degrees. Founded 1966. ***Setting:*** 104-acre small-town campus. ***Endowment:*** $378,944. ***Research spending 1994–95:*** $42,285. ***Total enrollment:*** 5,453. ***Faculty:*** 472 (177 full-time, 295 part-time).
ENROLLMENT PROFILE 5,453 students: 54% women, 46% men, 61% part-time, 98% state residents, 1% international, 57% 25 or older, 2% Native American, 2% Hispanic, 1% African American, 2% Asian American.
FIRST-YEAR CLASS 1,652 total; 1,978 applied, 100% were accepted, 84% of whom enrolled.
ACADEMIC PROGRAM Core. Calendar: quarters. 621 courses offered in 1995–96. Academic remediation for entering students, English as a second language program offered during academic year and summer, services for LD students, advanced placement, self-designed majors, tutorials, summer session for credit, part-time degree program (daytime, evenings), adult/continuing education programs, co-op programs and internships. ROTC: Army (c), Air Force (c).
GENERAL DEGREE REQUIREMENTS 90 quarter credit hours; 1 math course; computer course.
MAJORS Accounting, agricultural business, agricultural education, agricultural sciences, animal sciences, art/fine arts, automotive technologies, biology/biological sciences, business administration/commerce/management, computer graphics, computer programming, computer science, criminal justice, culinary arts, drafting and design, economics, education, electronics engineering technology, elementary education, (pre)engineering sequence, graphic arts, heating/refrigeration/air conditioning, home economics, horticulture, hospitality services, journalism, legal secretarial studies, liberal arts/general studies, manufacturing technology, mathematics, medical secretarial studies, metallurgical technology, nursing, physical education, secretarial studies/office management, theater arts/drama, water resources, welding technology.
LIBRARY Linton Benton Community College Library with 38,642 books, 373 microform titles, 211 periodicals, 1 on-line bibliographic service, 10 CD-ROMs, 1,982 records, tapes, and CDs. Acquisition spending 1994–95: $337,821.
COMPUTERS ON CAMPUS 500 computers for student use in computer labs, learning resource center, classrooms. Staffed computer lab on campus provides training in use of computers, software. Academic computing expenditure 1994–95: $490,800.
COLLEGE LIFE Drama-theater group, choral group, student-run newspaper. 4% vote in student government elections. ***Social organizations:*** 17 open to all. ***Most popular organizations:*** EBOP Club, Phi Theta Kappa, Campus Family Co-op, Horticulture Club, Soccer Club. ***Major annual events:*** Martin Luther King Celebration, Valentine Flower Sale, Children's Winter Festival. ***Student services:*** personal-psychological counseling, women's center. ***Campus security:*** 24-hour emergency response devices and patrols, late-night transport-escort service.
HOUSING College housing not available.
ATHLETICS ***Intercollegiate:*** baseball M(s), basketball M(s)/W(s), track and field M(s)/W(s), volleyball W(s). ***Intramural:*** basketball, volleyball. ***Contact:*** Mr. Greg Hawk, Athletic Director, 503-967-6109.
CAREER PLANNING ***Placement office:*** 12 full-time, 8 part-time staff; $233,410 operating expenditure 1994–95. ***Director:*** Ms. Marlene Propst, Director of Career Center and Entry Center Services, 503-917-4780. ***Services:*** job fairs, resume preparation, resume referral, career counseling, careers library, job interviews.
EXPENSES FOR 1995–96 ***Application fee:*** $20. State resident tuition: $1530 full-time, $34 per credit part-time. Nonresident tuition: $5445 full-time, $121 per credit part-time. Tuition for international students: $136 per credit.
FINANCIAL AID ***College-administered undergrad aid 1995–96:*** 100 need-based scholarships (averaging $500), 250 non-need scholarships (averaging $500), short-term loans (averaging $100), low-interest long-term loans from external sources (averaging $2625), 220 Federal Work-Study (averaging $1500), 50 part-time jobs. ***Required forms:*** institutional, FAFSA. ***Priority deadline:*** 4/1. ***Payment plan:*** installment. ***Waivers:*** full or partial for employees or children of employees and senior citizens. ***Notification:*** 5/15.
APPLYING Open admission except for nursing, dental assistant, emergency medical technology, water resources, electronics programs. ***Options:*** deferred entrance, midyear entrance. ***Required:*** TOEFL for international students, CPT. Test scores used for counseling/placement. ***Application deadline:*** rolling. Preference given to district residents.
APPLYING/TRANSFER ***Required:*** standardized test scores. ***Entrance:*** noncompetitive. ***Application deadline:*** rolling.
CONTACT Dr. Diane Watson, Director of Admissions and Records, Linn-Benton Community College, Albany, OR 97321, 503-967-6105. ***Fax:*** 503-928-6352. ***E-mail:*** watsond@gw.lbcc.cc.or.us.

MT. HOOD COMMUNITY COLLEGE
Gresham, Oregon

UG Enrollment: 7,171 **Tuition & Fees (OR Res): $1485**
Application Deadline: rolling **Room & Board: N/Avail**

GENERAL State and locally supported, 2-year, coed. Awards certificates, transfer associate, terminal associate degrees. Founded 1966. ***Setting:*** 212-acre suburban campus with easy access to Portland. ***Research spending 1994–95:*** $75,611. ***Total enrollment:*** 7,171. ***Faculty:*** 547 (167 full-time, 95% with terminal degrees, 380 part-time).
ENROLLMENT PROFILE 7,171 students from 16 states and territories, 6 other countries. 60% women, 70% part-time, 80% state residents, 10% transferred in, 25% have need-based financial aid, 1% have non-need-based financial aid, 1% international, 56% 25 or older, 1% Native American, 2% Hispanic, 2% African American, 3% Asian American. ***Most popular recent majors:*** liberal arts/general studies, nursing, physical therapy.
FIRST-YEAR CLASS 2,198 total. Of the students who applied, 100% were accepted.
ACADEMIC PROGRAM Core. Calendar: quarters. Academic remediation for entering students, English as a second language program offered during academic year, services for LD students, advanced placement, summer session for credit, part-time degree program (daytime, evenings, summer), adult/continuing education programs, co-op programs and internships. Study abroad in Hong Kong, Peru, Mexico, Costa Rica, England.
GENERAL DEGREE REQUIREMENTS 90 credits; math/science requirements vary according to program; computer course (varies by major); internship (some majors).
MAJORS Accounting, architectural technologies, automotive technologies, aviation technology, broadcasting, business administration/commerce/management, business education, civil engineering technology, commercial art, computer technologies, cosmetology, dental services, early childhood education, electrical and electronics technologies, fire science, fish and game management, food sciences, forest technology, funeral service, graphic arts, horticulture, hospitality services, industrial engineering technology, journalism, legal secretarial studies, liberal arts/general studies, manufacturing technology, marketing/retailing/merchandising, mechanical engineering technology, medical assistant technologies, medical secretarial studies, mental health/rehabilitation counseling, nursing, occupational therapy, operating room technology, ornamental horticulture, physical therapy, radio and television studies, respiratory therapy, safety and security technologies, tourism and travel, word processing.
LIBRARY Library Resource Center with 64,000 books, 31 microform titles, 412 periodicals, 2 CD-ROMs, 6,500 records, tapes, and CDs. Acquisition spending 1994–95: $441,649.
COMPUTERS ON CAMPUS 100 computers for student use in computer center, computer labs, art lab, writing lab, classrooms, library provide access to main academic computer, on-line services, Internet. Staffed computer lab on campus provides training in use of computers, software. Academic computing expenditure 1994–95: $200,000.
COLLEGE LIFE Drama-theater group, student-run newspaper, radio station. ***Student services:*** health clinic, personal-psychological counseling, women's center. ***Campus security:*** 24-hour emergency response devices and patrols, student patrols, late-night transport-escort service.
HOUSING College housing not available.
ATHLETICS ***Intercollegiate:*** basketball M(s)/W(s), cross-country running M(s)/W(s), golf M(s), tennis M(s)/W(s), track and field M(s)/W(s), volleyball W(s), wrestling M(s). ***Intramural:*** archery, badminton, basketball, bowling, cross-country running, fencing, field hockey, football, golf, racquetball, skiing (cross-country), skiing (downhill), soccer, swimming and diving, tennis, track and field, volleyball, wrestling. ***Contact:*** Mr. Bruce Turner, Athletic Director, 503-667-7451.
CAREER PLANNING ***Placement office:*** 3 full-time, 1 part-time staff; $108,464 operating expenditure 1994–95. ***Director:*** Mr. Skip Paynter, 503-667-7418. ***Services:*** job fairs, resume preparation, resume referral, career counseling, careers library, job bank, job interviews.
EXPENSES FOR 1995–96 State resident tuition: $1440 full-time, $32 per credit part-time. Nonresident tuition: $4950 full-time, $110 per credit part-time. Part-time mandatory fees: $1 per credit. Tuition for international students: $125 per credit. Full-time mandatory fees: $45.
FINANCIAL AID ***College-administered undergrad aid 1995–96:*** 1,500 need-based scholarships (averaging $441), 350 non-need scholarships (averaging $441), short-term loans (averaging $100), low-interest long-term loans from external sources (averaging $1600), Federal Work-Study, part-time jobs. ***Required forms:*** institutional; accepted: CSS Financial Aid PROFILE, FAFSA. ***Priority deadline:*** 4/1. ***Payment plans:*** installment, deferred payment. ***Waivers:*** full or partial for employees or children of employees. ***Notification:*** continuous.
APPLYING Open admission except for allied health, some professional-technical programs. ***Options:*** early entrance, deferred entrance. ***Required for some:*** minimum 2.0 GPA, TOEFL for international students, CPT. Test scores used for counseling/placement. ***Application deadline:*** rolling. ***Notification:*** continuous. Preference given to state residents.
APPLYING/TRANSFER ***Required for some:*** standardized test scores, minimum 2.0 high school GPA. ***Application deadline:*** rolling. ***Notification:*** continuous.
CONTACT Mrs. Marilyn Kennedy, Registrar/Director of Admissions, Mt. Hood Community College, Gresham, OR 97030-3300, 503-667-7368. ***Fax:*** 503-667-7388.

OREGON POLYTECHNIC INSTITUTE
Portland, Oregon

UG Enrollment: 200 **Tuition: $12,150/deg prog**
Application Deadline: rolling **Room & Board: N/Avail**

GENERAL Proprietary, 2-year, specialized, coed. Awards diplomas, terminal associate degrees. Founded 1947. ***Setting:*** 2-acre urban campus. ***Total enrollment:*** 200. ***Faculty:*** 12 (7 full-time, 100% with terminal degrees, 5 part-time); student-faculty ratio is 20:1.
ENROLLMENT PROFILE 200 students from 2 states and territories, 2 other countries. 17% women, 1% part-time, 98% state residents, 0% transferred in, 1% international, 65% 25 or older, 0% Native American, 2% Hispanic, 2% African American, 1% Asian American. ***Areas of study chosen:*** 100% engineering and applied sciences.
FIRST-YEAR CLASS 33 total; 42 applied, 100% were accepted, 79% of whom enrolled.
ACADEMIC PROGRAM Honor code. Calendar: quarters. 70 courses offered in 1995–96. Academic remediation for entering students, tutorials, summer session for credit.
GENERAL DEGREE REQUIREMENTS 90 credits; 1 math course; computer course.
MAJORS Computer programming, drafting and design, electronics engineering technology.
LIBRARY The Loft plus 1 other, with 1,600 books, 25 periodicals, 50 records, tapes, and CDs.
COMPUTERS ON CAMPUS Computer purchase plan available. 48 computers for student use in computer center. Staffed computer lab on campus provides training in use of computers, software.
COLLEGE LIFE ***Campus security:*** 24-hour emergency response devices.
HOUSING College housing not available.
CAREER PLANNING ***Placement office:*** 1 full-time staff. ***Director:*** Ms. Kathi Costa, Graduate Placement Director, 503-234-9333. ***Services:*** job fairs, resume preparation, resume referral, career counseling, job interviews.
ESTIMATED EXPENSES FOR 1996–97 ***Application fee:*** $25. Tuition: $12,150 per degree program.
FINANCIAL AID ***College-administered undergrad aid 1995–96:*** need-based scholarships, low-interest long-term loans from external sources (average $2625), Federal Work-

Oregon Polytechnic Institute (continued)
Study. ***Required forms:*** CSS Financial Aid PROFILE; required for some: FAFSA. ***Priority deadline:*** 6/15. ***Payment plans:*** tuition prepayment, installment, deferred pay. ***Waivers:*** full or partial for employees or children of employees.
APPLYING Open admission. ***Required:*** school transcript, CPAt. Test scores used for admission. ***Application deadline:*** rolling.
APPLYING/TRANSFER ***Recommended:*** college transcript. ***Required for some:*** college transcript. ***Application deadline:*** rolling.
CONTACT Ms. Mardall Lanfranco, Director, Oregon Polytechnic Institute, 900 Southeast Sandy Boulevard, Portland, OR 97214-1395, 503-234-9333.

PORTLAND COMMUNITY COLLEGE
Portland, Oregon

UG Enrollment: 22,840 | **Tuition & Fees (OR Res): $1440**
Application Deadline: rolling | **Room & Board: N/Avail**

GENERAL State and locally supported, 2-year, coed. Awards certificates, diplomas, transfer associate, terminal associate degrees. Founded 1961. ***Setting:*** 400-acre urban campus. ***Total enrollment:*** 22,840. ***Faculty:*** 1,215 (390 full-time, 825 part-time).
ENROLLMENT PROFILE 22,840 students from 18 states and territories, 73 other countries. 56% women, 44% men, 68% part-time, 98% state residents, 1% international, 67% 25 or older, 1% Native American, 5% Hispanic, 4% African American, 8% Asian American. ***Most popular recent majors:*** science, nursing, radiological technology.
FIRST-YEAR CLASS Of the students who applied, 100% were accepted.
ACADEMIC PROGRAM Calendar: quarters. Academic remediation for entering students, English as a second language program offered during academic year and summer, services for LD students, advanced placement, summer session for credit, part-time degree program (daytime, evenings, weekends), external degree programs, adult/continuing education programs, co-op programs and internships. Off-campus study at Concordia College (OR), Marylhurst College, members of the Oregon State System of Higher Education.
GENERAL DEGREE REQUIREMENTS 90 credits; internship (some majors).
MAJORS Accounting, automotive technologies, aviation technology, biotechnology, business administration/commerce/management, carpentry, child care/child and family studies, civil engineering technology, computer information systems, computer programming, computer technologies, construction technologies, criminal justice, deaf interpreter training, dental services, dietetics, drafting and design, educational media, electrical and electronics technologies, electrical engineering technology, electronics engineering technology, elementary education, engineering (general), (pre)engineering sequence, engineering technology, family and consumer studies, fire science, graphic arts, home economics, industrial design, laboratory technologies, landscape architecture/design, legal secretarial studies, liberal arts/general studies, library science, machine and tool technologies, marketing/retailing/merchandising, mechanical engineering technology, medical assistant technologies, medical laboratory technology, medical records services, medical secretarial studies, nursing, optical technologies, optometric/ophthalmic technologies, paralegal studies, physical sciences, radiological technology, real estate, science, secretarial studies/office management, vocational education, welding technology.
LIBRARY 83,355 books, 815 periodicals, 9,298 records, tapes, and CDs.
COMPUTERS ON CAMPUS 200 computers for student use in computer center, computer labs, learning resource center, library. Staffed computer lab on campus provides training in use of computers, software.
COLLEGE LIFE Drama-theater group, student-run newspaper. ***Student services:*** personal-psychological counseling, women's center. ***Campus security:*** 24-hour emergency response devices and patrols, late-night transport-escort service.
HOUSING College housing not available.
ATHLETICS ***Intercollegiate:*** basketball M/W. ***Intramural:*** archery, badminton, basketball, bowling, cross-country running, golf, racquetball, skiing (cross-country), skiing (downhill), soccer, swimming and diving, track and field, volleyball, weight lifting, wrestling. ***Contact:*** Mr. Craig Bell, Athletic Director, 503-244-6111; Ms. Penny Wills, Athletic Director, 503-244-6111.
CAREER PLANNING ***Service:*** career counseling.
EXPENSES FOR 1996–97 State resident tuition: $1440 full-time, $32 per credit hour part-time. Nonresident tuition: $5625 full-time, $125 per credit hour part-time.
FINANCIAL AID ***College-administered undergrad aid 1995–96:*** 337 need-based scholarships (average $582), short-term loans (average $150), low-interest long-term loans from college funds (average $120), Federal Work-Study, part-time jobs. ***Acceptable forms:*** CSS Financial Aid PROFILE, FAFSA, SINGLEFILE Form of United Student Aid Funds. ***Priority deadline:*** 3/1. ***Payment plan:*** deferred payment. ***Waivers:*** full or partial for employees or children of employees and senior citizens.
APPLYING Open admission. ***Option:*** early entrance. ***Required:*** TOEFL for international students. Test scores used for counseling/placement. ***Application deadline:*** rolling.
CONTACT Mr. G. Frost Johnson, Director of Enrollment Services, Portland Community College, PO Box 19000, Portland, OR 97280-0990, 503-414-2227 or toll-free 800-634-7999. ***Fax:*** 503-452-4988.

ROGUE COMMUNITY COLLEGE
Grants Pass, Oregon

UG Enrollment: 1,804 | **Tuition & Fees (Area Res): $1224**
Application Deadline: rolling | **Room & Board: N/Avail**

GENERAL State and locally supported, 2-year, coed. Awards certificates, diplomas, transfer associate, terminal associate degrees. Founded 1970. ***Setting:*** 90-acre rural campus. ***Total enrollment:*** 1,804. ***Faculty:*** 279 (57 full-time, 222 part-time).
ENROLLMENT PROFILE 1,804 students from 3 states and territories. 56% women, 60% part-time, 99% state residents, 70% have need-based financial aid, 0% international, 57% 25 or older, 2% Native American, 8% Hispanic, 1% African American, 2% Asian American. ***Areas of study chosen:*** 14% liberal arts/general studies, 13% health professions and related sciences, 12% business management and administrative services, 10% engineering and applied sciences, 5% computer and information sciences, 5% social sciences, 4% psychology, 3% education, 2% fine arts, 1% agriculture, 1% biological and life sciences, 1% English language/literature/letters, 1% premed, 1% vocational and home economics. ***Most popular recent majors:*** liberal arts/general studies, business administration/commerce/management, nursing.
FIRST-YEAR CLASS 125 total. Of the students who applied, 100% were accepted, 100% of whom enrolled.
ACADEMIC PROGRAM Core, vocational and health sciences curriculum, honor code. Calendar: quarters. 350 courses offered in 1995–96. Academic remediation for entering students, English as a second language program offered during academic year and summer, services for LD students, advanced placement, summer session for credit, part-time degree program (daytime), adult/continuing education programs, co-op programs and internships.
GENERAL DEGREE REQUIREMENTS 90 credits; 6 credits of math, 8 credits of science; computer course for business administration, office technology majors.
MAJORS Accounting, art history, automotive technologies, business administration/commerce/management, child care/child and family studies, computer science, criminal justice, drug and alcohol/substance abuse counseling, electrical and electronics technologies, fire science, humanities, human services, industrial and heavy equipment maintenance, liberal arts/general studies, manufacturing technology, mathematics, nursing, respiratory therapy, science, secretarial studies/office management, social science.
LIBRARY Rogue Community College Library with 33,000 books, 7 microform titles, 275 periodicals, 2 on-line bibliographic services, 250 CD-ROMs, 250 records, tapes, and CDs. Acquisition spending 1994–95: $24,010.
COMPUTERS ON CAMPUS 96 computers for student use in computer center, computer labs, learning resource center, student center provide access to e-mail, on-line services, Internet. Staffed computer lab on campus. Academic computing expenditure 1994–95: $337,856.
COLLEGE LIFE Drama-theater group, choral group, student-run newspaper. ***Student services:*** personal-psychological counseling, women's center. ***Campus security:*** 24-hour patrols, late-night transport-escort service.
HOUSING College housing not available.
ATHLETICS ***Intramural:*** badminton, basketball, skiing (cross-country), tennis, volleyball.
CAREER PLANNING ***Placement office:*** 7 full-time, 7 part-time staff; $141,927 operating expenditure 1994–95. ***Director:*** Mr. Edward Risser, Director of Enrollment and Student Employment Services, 503-471-3500 Ext. 301. ***Services:*** resume preparation, resume referral, career counseling, careers library, job bank.
EXPENSES FOR 1995–96 Area resident tuition: $1224 full-time, $34 per credit part-time. State resident tuition: $1872 full-time, $52 per credit part-time. Nonresident tuition: $3816 full-time, $106 per credit part-time. Part-time mandatory fees: $10 per quarter.
FINANCIAL AID ***College-administered undergrad aid 1995–96:*** 60 need-based scholarships (average $500), 50 non-need scholarships (average $525), low-interest long-term loans from external sources (average $2000), Federal Work-Study, 100 part-time jobs. ***Required forms:*** institutional; accepted: CSS Financial Aid PROFILE, FAFSA. ***Priority deadline:*** 4/1. ***Waivers:*** full or partial for employees or children of employees.
APPLYING Open admission except for respiratory therapy, nursing, emergency medical technology programs. ***Option:*** early entrance. ***Required:*** TOEFL for international students, ACT ASSET. Test scores used for counseling/placement. ***Application deadline:*** rolling. Preference given to local residents.
APPLYING/TRANSFER ***Entrance:*** noncompetitive. ***Application deadline:*** rolling.
CONTACT Mr. Edward Risser, Director of Enrollment and Student Employment Services, Rogue Community College, 3345 Redwood Highway, Grants Pass, OR 97527-9298, 503-471-3500 Ext. 301.

SOUTHWESTERN OREGON COMMUNITY COLLEGE
Coos Bay, Oregon

UG Enrollment: 1,534 | **Tuition & Fees: $1644**
Application Deadline: rolling | **Room & Board: N/Avail**

GENERAL State and locally supported, 2-year, coed. Awards certificates, transfer associate, terminal associate degrees. Founded 1961. ***Setting:*** 125-acre small-town campus. ***Total enrollment:*** 1,534. ***Faculty:*** 250 (80 full-time, 14% with terminal degrees, 170 part-time).
ENROLLMENT PROFILE 1,534 students: 57% women, 43% men, 51% part-time, 98% state residents, 12% transferred in, 41% have non-need-based financial aid, 2% international, 46% 25 or older, 4% Native American, 3% Hispanic, 1% African American, 2% Asian American. ***Areas of study chosen:*** 56% liberal arts/general studies, 14% business management and administrative services, 11% health professions and related sciences, 8% social sciences, 6% vocational and home economics, 2% computer and information sciences, 2% natural resource sciences, 1% education. ***Most popular recent major:*** business administration/commerce/management.
FIRST-YEAR CLASS 406 total. Of the students who applied, 100% were accepted.
ACADEMIC PROGRAM Core. Calendar: quarters. Academic remediation for entering students, English as a second language program offered during academic year and summer, advanced placement, summer session for credit, part-time degree program (daytime, evenings), adult/continuing education programs, co-op programs and internships.
GENERAL DEGREE REQUIREMENT 93 credits.
MAJORS Accounting, automotive technologies, business administration/commerce/management, child care/child and family studies, computer information systems, criminal justice, early childhood education, electrical and electronics technologies, finance/banking, fire science, forest technology, gerontology, human services, industrial engineering technology, liberal arts/general studies, machine and tool technologies, marketing/retailing/merchandising, medical secretarial studies, nursing, secretarial studies/office management, welding technology.
LIBRARY Southwestern Oregon Community College Library with 53,459 books, 37 microform titles, 448 periodicals, 2 on-line bibliographic services, 24 CD-ROMs, 6,552 records, tapes, and CDs.
COMPUTERS ON CAMPUS 60 computers for student use in computer center, computer labs, library. Staffed computer lab on campus provides training in use of computers, software.
COLLEGE LIFE Drama-theater group, choral group, student-run newspaper. ***Student services:*** personal-psychological counseling.
HOUSING College housing not available.
ATHLETICS ***Intercollegiate:*** baseball M(s), basketball M(s)/W(s), soccer M(s)/W(s), softball W(s), track and field M, volleyball W(s). ***Intramural:*** basketball, volleyball.
CAREER PLANNING ***Service:*** career counseling.

EXPENSES FOR 1996–97 *Application fee:* $20. Tuition: $1620 full-time, $36 per credit hour part-time. Part-time mandatory fees: $8 per quarter. Tuition for international students: $123 per credit hour. Full-time mandatory fees: $24.
FINANCIAL AID *College-administered undergrad aid 1995–96:* need-based scholarships, non-need scholarships, short-term loans, low-interest long-term loans from external sources, Federal Work-Study, part-time jobs. *Required forms:* FAFSA; required for some: institutional. *Priority deadline:* 2/1. *Payment plan:* deferred payment. *Waivers:* full or partial for employees or children of employees and senior citizens. *Notification:* 6/1.
APPLYING Open admission except for nursing, emergency medical technology programs. *Option:* early entrance. *Required:* TOEFL for international students. *Required for some:* school transcript. Test scores used for counseling/placement. *Application deadline:* rolling. *Notification:* continuous.
APPLYING/TRANSFER *Required for some:* high school transcript, college transcript. *Application deadline:* rolling. *Notification:* continuous.
CONTACT Ms. Joanna Blount, Registrar/Associate Dean of Student Services, Southwestern Oregon Community College, Coos Bay, OR 97420-2911, 541-888-7339.

TREASURE VALLEY COMMUNITY COLLEGE
Ontario, Oregon

UG Enrollment: 2,348	Tuition & Fees (OR Res): $1635
Application Deadline: rolling	Room & Board: $3261

GENERAL State and locally supported, 2-year, coed. Awards certificates, transfer associate, terminal associate degrees. Founded 1962. *Setting:* 95-acre small-town campus. *Total enrollment:* 2,348. *Faculty:* 110 (42 full-time, 68 part-time); student-faculty ratio is 20:1.
ENROLLMENT PROFILE 2,348 students from 8 states and territories, 3 other countries. 60% women, 40% men, 75% part-time, 92% state residents, 6% live on campus, 2% transferred in, 1% international, 45% 25 or older, 1% Native American, 5% Hispanic, 1% African American, 1% Asian American. *Most popular recent majors:* liberal arts/general studies, education, business administration/commerce/management.
FIRST-YEAR CLASS 421 total; 780 applied, 100% were accepted, 54% of whom enrolled.
ACADEMIC PROGRAM Core. Calendar: quarters. Academic remediation for entering students, English as a second language program offered during academic year, services for LD students, advanced placement, summer session for credit, part-time degree program (daytime, evenings), adult/continuing education programs, co-op programs.
GENERAL DEGREE REQUIREMENTS 90 credits; 1 college algebra course; computer course for business majors.
MAJORS Agricultural business, agricultural sciences, agricultural technologies, agronomy/soil and crop sciences, art/fine arts, biology/biological sciences, business administration/commerce/management, chemistry, commercial art, communication, computer science, criminal justice, drafting and design, economics, education, engineering (general), English, forestry, forest technology, history, humanities, law enforcement/police sciences, legal secretarial studies, liberal arts/general studies, mathematics, music, music education, natural resource management, nursing, physical education, physical sciences, political science/government, range management, science, secretarial studies/office management, social science, sociology, surveying technology, theater arts/drama, welding technology, wildlife management.
LIBRARY 28,000 books, 150 periodicals, 250 records, tapes, and CDs.
COMPUTERS ON CAMPUS 70 computers for student use in computer center, computer labs, library provide access to e-mail. Staffed computer lab on campus.
COLLEGE LIFE Drama-theater group, choral group. 20% vote in student government elections. *Social organizations:* 6 open to all. *Student services:* health clinic, personal-psychological counseling. *Campus security:* student patrols, controlled dormitory access.
HOUSING 200 college housing spaces available; 135 were occupied 1995–96. No special consideration for freshman housing applicants. Off-campus living permitted. *Option:* single-sex housing available. Resident assistants live in dorms.
ATHLETICS Member NJCAA. *Intercollegiate:* baseball M(s), basketball M(s)/W(s), volleyball W(s). *Intramural:* basketball, softball, volleyball. *Contact:* Mr. Gary Farnworth, Athletic Director, 503-889-6493.
CAREER PLANNING *Service:* career counseling.
EXPENSES FOR 1996–97 State resident tuition: $1575 full-time, $35 per credit part-time. Nonresident tuition: $2340 full-time, $52 per credit part-time. Part-time mandatory fees: $10 per quarter. Full-time mandatory fees: $60. College room and board: $3261.
FINANCIAL AID *College-administered undergrad aid 1995–96:* need-based scholarships (average $500), low-interest long-term loans from external sources (average $600), Federal Work-Study, part-time jobs. *Required forms:* CSS Financial Aid PROFILE, institutional, FAFSA. *Priority deadline:* 3/15. *Payment plan:* installment. *Waivers:* full or partial for employees or children of employees and senior citizens.
APPLYING Open admission. *Options:* early entrance, deferred entrance. *Required:* TOEFL for international students. Test scores used for counseling/placement. *Application deadline:* rolling. *Notification:* continuous.
APPLYING/TRANSFER *Entrance:* noncompetitive. *Application deadline:* rolling. *Notification:* continuous. *Contact:* Mr. Ron Kulm, Director of Admissions and Student Services, 503-889-6493 Ext. 232.
CONTACT Mr. Ron Kulm, Director of Admissions and Student Services, Treasure Valley Community College, Ontario, OR 97914-3423, 503-889-6493 Ext. 232. *Fax:* 503-889-3017.

UMPQUA COMMUNITY COLLEGE
Roseburg, Oregon

UG Enrollment: 2,100	Tuition & Fees (OR Res): $1564
Application Deadline: 10/1	Room & Board: N/Avail

GENERAL State and locally supported, 2-year, coed. Awards transfer associate, terminal associate degrees. Founded 1964. *Setting:* 100-acre rural campus. *Endowment:* $1.3 million. *Educational spending 1994–95:* $2395 per undergrad. *Total enrollment:* 2,100. *Faculty:* 145 (70 full-time, 25% with terminal degrees, 75 part-time).
ENROLLMENT PROFILE 2,100 students from 5 states and territories, 6 other countries. 53% women, 47% men, 40% part-time, 98% state residents, 10% transferred in, 56% have need-based financial aid, 12% have non-need-based financial aid, 1% international, 1% Native American, 1% Hispanic, 1% African American, 1% Asian American. *Areas of study chosen:* 58% library and information studies, 20% vocational and home economics, 5% business management and administrative services, 5% education, 5% health professions and related sciences, 5% psychology, 2% engineering and applied sciences. *Most popular recent majors:* liberal arts/general studies, nursing, business administration/commerce/management.
FIRST-YEAR CLASS 1,350 total; 1,700 applied, 100% were accepted, 79% of whom enrolled.
ACADEMIC PROGRAM Core, liberal arts curriculum. Calendar: quarters. Academic remediation for entering students, English as a second language program offered during academic year and summer, services for LD students, advanced placement, self-designed majors, tutorials, honors program, summer session for credit, part-time degree program (daytime, evenings), adult/continuing education programs, co-op programs.
GENERAL DEGREE REQUIREMENTS 93 credits; math/science requirements vary according to program; computer course for office technology, business, automation and digital systems majors.
MAJORS Accounting, agricultural sciences, anthropology, art education, art/fine arts, art history, automotive technologies, behavioral sciences, biology/biological sciences, business administration/commerce/management, chemistry, child care/child and family studies, civil engineering technology, computer science, computer technologies, cosmetology, criminal justice, early childhood education, economics, education, electrical and electronics technologies, elementary education, emergency medical technology, engineering (general), (pre)engineering sequence, English, fire science, forestry, health education, history, humanities, human resources, journalism, legal secretarial studies, liberal arts/general studies, marketing/retailing/merchandising, mathematics, medical secretarial studies, music, music education, natural sciences, nursing, physical education, physical sciences, political science/government, practical nursing, psychology, science, secretarial studies/office management, social science, social work, sociology, technical writing, theater arts/drama, welding technology.
LIBRARY Umpqua Community College Library with 41,000 books, 20 periodicals, 800 records, tapes, and CDs. Acquisition spending 1994–95: $36,200.
COMPUTERS ON CAMPUS Computer purchase plan available. 200 computers for student use in computer center, labs, library provide access to main academic computer. Staffed computer lab on campus. Academic computing expenditure 1994–95: $130,000.
COLLEGE LIFE Drama-theater group, choral group, student-run newspaper. *Most popular organizations:* Phi Theta Kappa, Computer Club, Phi Beta Lambda, Nursing Club, Umpqua Accounting Associates. *Student services:* personal-psychological counseling.
HOUSING College housing not available.
ATHLETICS *Intercollegiate:* basketball M(s)/W(s), cross-country running M/W, track and field M(s)/W(s), volleyball W(s). *Intramural:* basketball. *Contact:* Dr. William Bachman, Athletic Director, 541-440-4627.
CAREER PLANNING *Placement office:* 3 full-time, 3 part-time staff; $5500 operating expenditure 1994–95. *Director:* Dr. Leon Young, Director of Counseling, 541-440-4609. *Services:* job fairs, resume preparation, career counseling, careers library, job bank, job interviews.
AFTER GRADUATION 35% of students completing a degree program in 1994–95 went directly on to further study.
EXPENSES FOR 1996–97 State resident tuition: $1564 full-time, $34 per credit part-time. Nonresident tuition: $4600 full-time, $100 per credit part-time.
FINANCIAL AID *College-administered undergrad aid 1995–96:* 900 need-based scholarships (average $800), 130 non-need scholarships (average $560), short-term loans (average $325), 125 Federal Work-Study (averaging $800), 24 part-time jobs. *Required forms:* institutional, FAFSA. *Priority deadline:* 3/1. *Waivers:* full or partial for employees or children of employees and senior citizens. *Average indebtedness of graduates:* $1400.
APPLYING Open admission except for nursing and emergency medical technology programs. *Options:* early entrance, deferred entrance, midyear entrance. *Required:* TOEFL for international students. *Recommended:* school transcript. Test scores used for counseling/placement. *Application deadline:* 10/1.
APPLYING/TRANSFER *Required:* college transcript. *Entrance:* noncompetitive. *Application deadline:* 10/1. *Contact:* Dr. Larry Shipley, Director of Admissions and Records, 541-440-4616.
CONTACT Dr. Larry Shipley, Director of Admissions and Records, Umpqua Community College, Roseburg, OR 97470-0226, 541-440-4616. *Fax:* 541-440-4612.

Pennsylvania

PENNSYLVANIA

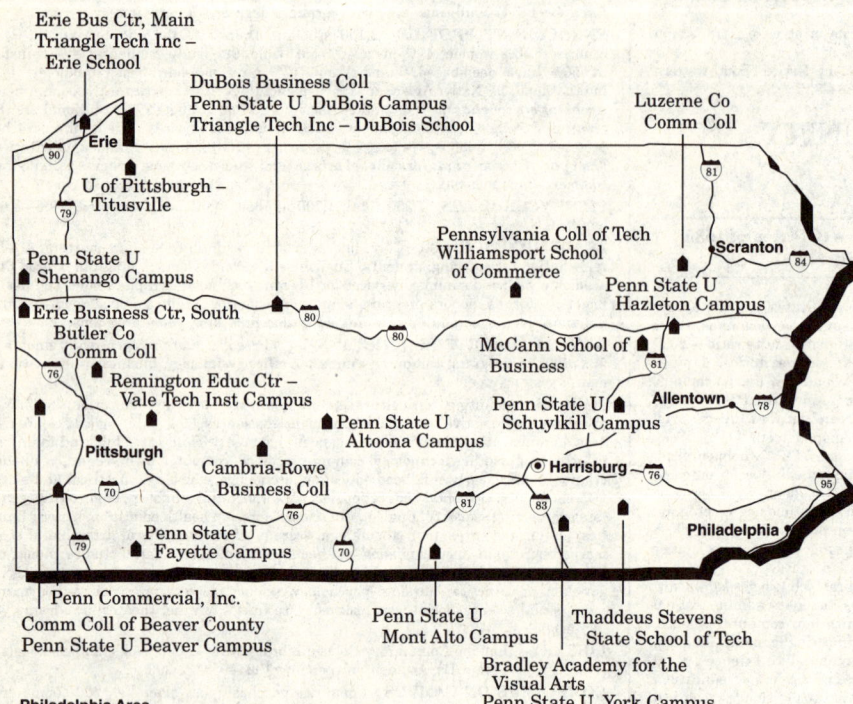

Allentown Area
Allentown Bus School
Churchman Business School
Lehigh Carbon Comm Coll
Lincoln Tech Inst
Northampton Co Area Comm Coll
Penn State U Allentown Campus
Welder Training & Testing Inst

Pittsburgh Area
Art Inst of Pittsburgh
Comm Coll of Allegheny Co
 Allegheny Campus
Comm Coll of Allegheny Co
 Boyce Campus
Comm Coll of Allegheny Co
 North Campus
Comm Coll of Allegheny Co
 South Campus
Dean Inst of Tech
Duff's Business Inst
Electronic Inst
ICM School of Business
Median School of Allied
 Health Careers
Newport Business Inst
Penn State U
 McKeesport Campus
Penn State U
 New Kensington Campus
Penn Tech Inst
Pittsburgh Inst of Aeronautics
Pittsburgh Inst of Mortuary
 Science, Inc.
Pittsburgh Tech Inst
Triangle Tech Inc –
 Greensburg Ctr
Triangle Tech Inc
 (Pittsburgh)
Westmoreland County Comm Coll

Harrisburg Area
Central Pennsylvania Business School
Electronic Inst
Harrisburg Area Comm Coll
Thompson Inst

Philadelphia Area
American Inst of Design
Antonelli Inst
The Art Inst of Philadelphia
Berean Inst
Bucks Co Comm Coll
CHI Inst
CHI Inst, RETS Campus
Comm Coll of Philadelphia
Delaware Co Comm Coll
Harcum Coll
Hussian School of Art
Lansdale School of Business
Lincoln Tech Inst
Manor Jr Coll
McCarrie Schools of Health
 Science & Tech
Montgomery Co Comm Coll

Peirce Coll
Penn State U Abington–
 Ogontz Campus
Penn State U
 Berks Campus
Penn State U
 Delaware Co Campus
Pennco Tech
Pennsylvania Inst of Tech
Reading Area Comm Coll
Valley Forge Military Coll
The Williamson Free School
 of Mechanical Trades

Scranton Area
ICS Ctr for Degree Studies
Johnson Tech Inst
Keystone Coll
Lackawanna Jr Coll
Penn State U
 Wilkes-Barre Campus
Penn State U
 Worthington Scranton Campus

ALLENTOWN BUSINESS SCHOOL
Allentown, Pennsylvania

UG Enrollment: 1,000	**Tuition:** $6400/deg prog
Application Deadline: rolling	**Room & Board:** N/Avail

GENERAL Proprietary, 2-year, coed. Part of Career Education Corporation. Awards diplomas, transfer associate, terminal associate degrees. Founded 1869. *Setting:* urban campus. *Total enrollment:* 1,000. *Faculty:* 50; student-faculty ratio is 25:1.
ENROLLMENT PROFILE 1,000 students from 5 states and territories. 70% women, 0% part-time, 90% state residents, 5% transferred in, 0% international, 20% 25 or older, 0% Native American, 10% Hispanic, 5% African American, 0% Asian American. *Areas of study chosen:* 100% business management and administrative services.
FIRST-YEAR CLASS 250 total. Of the students who applied, 95% were accepted, 80% of whom enrolled. 1% from top 10% of their high school class, 10% from top quarter, 45% from top half.
ACADEMIC PROGRAM Core, business and career-oriented curriculum, honor code. Calendar: quarters. Academic remediation for entering students, English as a second language program, adult/continuing education programs, co-op programs and internships.

GENERAL DEGREE REQUIREMENTS 90 credits; math/science requirements vary according to program; computer course; internship (some majors).
MAJORS Accounting, business administration/commerce/management, fashion merchandising, legal secretarial studies, marketing/retailing/merchandising, medical secretarial studies, secretarial studies/office management, tourism and travel.
COMPUTERS ON CAMPUS 100 computers for student use in computer labs, learning resource center, classrooms. Staffed computer lab on campus.
COLLEGE LIFE *Social organizations:* Better Late Than Never (for students 21 or over); 3% of eligible men and 15% of eligible women are members. *Campus security:* evening security guard.
HOUSING College housing not available.
CAREER PLANNING *Placement office:* 2 full-time staff. *Director:* Ms. Kathy Bennicoff, Director of Career Development, 610-791-5100. *Services:* job fairs, resume preparation, resume referral, career counseling, job interviews.
EXPENSES FOR 1996–97 *Application fee:* $50. Tuition per degree program ranges from $6400 to $11,880. Tuition guaranteed not to increase for student's term of enrollment.
FINANCIAL AID *College-administered undergrad aid 1995–96:* need-based scholarships, non-need scholarships, low-interest long-term loans from external sources. *Required forms:* institutional, FAFSA; required for some: state. *Priority deadline:* 10/23. *Payment plan:* installment.

552   Peterson's Guide to Two-Year Colleges 1997

Pennsylvania

APPLYING Open admission. *Option:* deferred entrance. *Required for some:* SRA achievement series, reading and math. Test scores used for admission. *Application deadline:* rolling. *Notification:* continuous.
APPLYING/TRANSFER *Entrance:* noncompetitive. *Application deadline:* rolling. *Notification:* continuous.
CONTACT Mrs. Jean Vokes, Director of Admissions, Allentown Business School, 1501 Lehigh Street, Allentown, PA 18103-3880, 610-791-5100. *Fax:* 610-791-7810. College video available.

AMERICAN INSTITUTE OF DESIGN
Philadelphia, Pennsylvania

UG Enrollment: 350	Tuition: $15,950/deg prog
Application Deadline: rolling	Room & Board: N/Avail

GENERAL Proprietary, 2-year, coed. Awards terminal associate degrees. Founded 1966. *Setting:* urban campus. *Total enrollment:* 350. *Faculty:* 20 (15 full-time, 5 part-time); student-faculty ratio is 20:1.
ENROLLMENT PROFILE 350 students from 5 states and territories. 15% women, 5% part-time, 85% state residents, 5% transferred in, 10% 25 or older, 0% Native American, 1% Hispanic, 35% African American, 1% Asian American. *Areas of study chosen:* 90% architecture.
FIRST-YEAR CLASS Of the students who applied, 90% were accepted, 85% of whom enrolled. 15% from top 10% of their high school class, 25% from top quarter, 45% from top half.
ACADEMIC PROGRAM Honor code. Calendar: semesters continuous.
GENERAL DEGREE REQUIREMENTS 2100 clock hours; computer course for drafting and design majors.
MAJORS Architectural technologies, drafting and design, electromechanical technology, interior design, mechanical design technology.
LIBRARY 1,500 books, 15 periodicals, 10 records, tapes, and CDs.
COMPUTERS ON CAMPUS 10 computers for student use in computer center.
COLLEGE LIFE Orientation program (2 days, no cost). *Student services:* personal-psychological counseling.
HOUSING College housing not available.
ATHLETICS *Intramural:* basketball, bowling.
CAREER PLANNING *Placement office:* 1 full-time staff. *Services:* job fairs, resume preparation, resume referral, career counseling, job bank, job interviews.
EXPENSES FOR 1996–97 *Application fee:* $90. Tuition: $15,950 per degree program. Full-time mandatory fees: $90.
FINANCIAL AID *College-administered undergrad aid 1995–96:* need-based scholarships, 3 non-need scholarships (average $6525), low-interest long-term loans from external sources, part-time jobs. *Required forms:* state, FAFSA. *Priority deadline:* 8/1. *Payment plan:* tuition prepayment.
APPLYING *Option:* deferred entrance. *Required:* TOEFL for international students. *Recommended:* school transcript. *Required for some:* 3 years of high school math. Test scores used for admission. *Application deadline:* rolling.
APPLYING/TRANSFER *Required:* college transcript. *Recommended:* high school transcript. *Entrance:* minimally difficult. *Application deadline:* rolling.
CONTACT Ms. Dorothy Miller, Director of Admissions, American Institute of Design, 1616 Orthodox Street, Philadelphia, PA 19124-3799, 215-288-8200.

ANTONELLI INSTITUTE
Erdenheim, Pennsylvania

UG Enrollment: 200	Tuition & Fees: $7600
Application Deadline: 8/30	Room Only: $3200

GENERAL Proprietary, 2-year, coed. Awards diplomas, transfer associate, terminal associate degrees. Founded 1938. *Setting:* 15-acre suburban campus with easy access to Philadelphia. *Total enrollment:* 200. *Faculty:* 37 (5 full-time, 32 part-time).
ENROLLMENT PROFILE 200 students from 4 states and territories. 55% women, 5% part-time, 80% state residents, 20% live on campus, 5% transferred in, 65% have need-based financial aid, 0% international, 17% 25 or older, 0% Native American, 0% Hispanic, 4% African American, 1% Asian American. *Areas of study chosen:* 100% fine arts. *Most popular recent major:* commercial art.
FIRST-YEAR CLASS 118 total; 262 applied, 58% of whom enrolled. 25% from top 10% of their high school class, 70% from top half.
ACADEMIC PROGRAM Core, classic skills and creative curriculum, honor code. Calendar: semesters. Tutorials, adult/continuing education programs.
GENERAL DEGREE REQUIREMENTS 60 credits; computer course.
MAJORS Commercial art, graphic arts, interior design, photography.
LIBRARY 5,000 books, 1,000 periodicals.
COMPUTERS ON CAMPUS 15 computers for student use in computer labs, classrooms provide access to Bulletin Board Service. Staffed computer lab on campus provides training in use of computers, software.
COLLEGE LIFE 70% vote in student government elections. *Major annual events:* Antonelli Day Barbecue, School Dance, Halloween Party. *Student services:* personal-psychological counseling. *Campus security:* 24-hour emergency response devices, controlled dormitory access.
HOUSING 50 college housing spaces available; 40 were occupied 1995–96. Freshmen guaranteed college housing. Off-campus living permitted. *Option:* single-sex housing available. Resident assistants live in dorms.
CAREER PLANNING *Placement office:* 2 part-time staff. *Director:* Mr. Dan Fione, Coordinator, 610-275-3040. *Services:* resume preparation, resume referral, career counseling, job bank, job interviews.
AFTER GRADUATION 84% of class of 1994 had job offers within 6 months.
EXPENSES FOR 1995–96 *Application fee:* $25. Tuition for day division ranges from $7600 to $9200 full-time, $275 to $310 per credit hour part-time. Tuition for evening division: $7800 full-time, $325 per credit hour part-time. One-time mandatory fee of $125. College room only: $3200.
FINANCIAL AID *College-administered undergrad aid 1995–96:* need-based scholarships, low-interest long-term loans from external sources (average $2500), 2 part-time jobs. *Required forms for some financial aid applicants:* state, FAFSA. *Priority*

deadline: 8/1. *Payment plan:* installment. *Waivers:* full or partial for employees or children of employees. *Notification:* 8/15. *Average indebtedness of graduates:* $5000.
APPLYING Open admission. *Options:* deferred entrance, midyear entrance. *Required:* school transcript, campus interview. *Recommended:* 1 recommendation, TOEFL for international students. *Application deadline:* 8/30.
APPLYING/TRANSFER *Required:* high school transcript, campus interview. *Required for some:* college transcript. *Application deadline:* 8/30. *Contact:* Ms. Maryann McQuaid, Transfer Coordinator, 610-275-3040.
CONTACT Mr. Anthony Detore, Admissions Director, Antonelli Institute, Erdenheim, PA 19038, 610-275-3040 or toll-free 800-722-7871. *Fax:* 610-275-5630.

THE ART INSTITUTE OF PHILADELPHIA
Philadelphia, Pennsylvania

UG Enrollment: 1,700	Tuition & Fees: $9325
Application Deadline: rolling	Room Only: $3525

The Art Institute of Philadelphia is a 2-year postsecondary institution offering career education that leads to a specialized associate degree or to a diploma. The Institute is committed to the professional and personal development of its students, and its curriculum balances a technical education with experience in the arts and sciences.

GENERAL Proprietary, 2-year, coed. Part of Education Management Corporation. Awards transfer associate, terminal associate degrees. Founded 1966. *Setting:* urban campus. *Total enrollment:* 1,700. *Faculty:* 90 (50 full-time, 40 part-time); student-faculty ratio is 20:1.
ENROLLMENT PROFILE 1,700 students from 15 states and territories, 10 other countries. 52% women, 2% part-time, 75% state residents, 5% transferred in, 1% international, 5% 25 or older, 1% Native American, 1% Hispanic, 18% African American, 2% Asian American.
FIRST-YEAR CLASS 590 total; 900 applied, 97% were accepted, 68% of whom enrolled. 5% from top 10% of their high school class, 20% from top quarter, 60% from top half.
ACADEMIC PROGRAM Core. Calendar: quarters. Summer session for credit, adult/continuing education programs. Off-campus study at The Art Institutes.
GENERAL DEGREE REQUIREMENTS 98 credit hours; math proficiency or 1 college math course; computer course.
MAJORS Commercial art, fashion design and technology, fashion merchandising, illustration, industrial design, interior design, music business, photography.
LIBRARY 5,000 books, 80 periodicals.
COMPUTERS ON CAMPUS 50 computers for student use in computer center.
COLLEGE LIFE Orientation program (2 days, parents included). *Student services:* personal-psychological counseling.
HOUSING 280 college housing spaces available; all were occupied 1995–96. Freshmen given priority for college housing. Off-campus living permitted. *Option:* coed housing available.
CAREER PLANNING *Services:* resume preparation, career counseling, job bank, job interviews.
EXPENSES FOR 1995–96 *Application fee:* $50. Tuition: $9000 (minimum) full-time. Full-time tuition ranges up to $9,270 according to program. One time enrollment fee: $275. Full-time mandatory fees: $325. College room only: $3525.
FINANCIAL AID *College-administered undergrad aid 1995–96:* need-based scholarships, 5 non-need scholarships, low-interest long-term loans from external sources (average $2625), Federal Work-Study, 12 part-time jobs. *Required forms:* institutional, FAFSA; accepted: CSS Financial Aid PROFILE, state. *Application deadline:* continuous.
APPLYING *Options:* Common Application, deferred entrance. *Required:* school transcript. *Recommended:* interview, TOEFL for international students. *Required for some:* TOEFL for international students. Test scores used for admission. *Application deadline:* rolling. *Notification:* continuous.
APPLYING/TRANSFER *Required:* high school transcript, college transcript. *Recommended:* interview. *Entrance:* minimally difficult. *Application deadline:* rolling. *Notification:* continuous.
CONTACT Mr. James Palermo, Director of Admissions, The Art Institute of Philadelphia, 1622 Chestnut Street, Philadelphia, PA 19103-5198, 215-567-7080 Ext. 3320 or toll-free 800-275-2474. College video available.

❖ *See page 696 for a narrative description.* ❖

ART INSTITUTE OF PITTSBURGH
Pittsburgh, Pennsylvania

UG Enrollment: 2,100	Tuition & Fees: $9550
Application Deadline: rolling	Room & Board: $5205

In addition to art, design, FX, video, and fashion programs, career training is now offered in computer animation. The Computer Animation/Multimedia Program trains students in 3-D modeling, interactive modeling, and cell and stop-motion animation. Graduates are prepared to enter the television, video, film, and advertising industries. Artisan Technology is another new program, in which students learn techniques for ceramic, metal works, and jewelry design for mass production and marketing.

GENERAL Proprietary, 2-year, coed. Part of Education Management Corporation. Awards diplomas, transfer associate, terminal associate degrees. Founded 1921. *Setting:* urban campus. *Total enrollment:* 2,100. *Faculty:* 107 (80 full-time, 27 part-time); student-faculty ratio is 23:1. *Notable Alumni:* Mark Stutzman, Phil Wilson, Jim Allan, Tom Wilson, Will Finn.
ENROLLMENT PROFILE 2,100 students from 28 states and territories, 13 other countries. 55% women, 0% part-time, 54% state residents, 25% live on campus, 20% transferred in, 1% international, 1% Native American, 2% Hispanic, 8% African American, 2% Asian American. *Most popular recent majors:* communication, music business, industrial design.

Peterson's Guide to Two-Year Colleges 1997

Art Institute of Pittsburgh (continued)

FIRST-YEAR CLASS 800 total. Of the students who applied, 98% were accepted.
ACADEMIC PROGRAM Core. Calendar: quarters. Academic remediation for entering students, self-designed majors, tutorials, summer session for credit, part-time degree program (evenings).
GENERAL DEGREE REQUIREMENTS Math/science requirements vary according to program; computer course.
MAJORS Advertising, applied art, audio engineering, ceramic art and design, commercial art, communication, communication equipment technology, computer graphics, drafting and design, environmental design, fashion design and technology, fashion merchandising, film and video production, graphic arts, illustration, industrial arts, industrial design, interior design, jewelry and metalsmithing, landscape architecture/design, marketing/retailing/merchandising, music business, photography, radio and television studies, retail management.
LIBRARY Student Resource Center with 5,291 books, 173 periodicals.
COMPUTERS ON CAMPUS 145 computers for student use in computer labs, classrooms. Staffed computer lab on campus provides training in use of computers, software.
COLLEGE LIFE Orientation program (2 days, no cost, parents included). Student-run radio station. ***Most popular organizations:*** American Society of Interior Designers, Distributive Education Club of America, Music Video Rockers, Production Monsters, International Student Club. ***Major annual events:*** Health and Wellness Week, Welcome Week, School Tour Day. ***Student services:*** personal-psychological counseling.
HOUSING 610 college housing spaces available; 608 were occupied 1995–96. Freshmen given priority for college housing. Off-campus living permitted. ***Option:*** coed housing available. Resident assistants live in dorms.
CAREER PLANNING ***Placement office:*** 16 full-time staff. ***Director:*** Ms. Diana Frye, Director, Employment Assistance, 800-275-2470. ***Services:*** job fairs, resume preparation, resume referral, career counseling, careers library, job bank, job interviews.
EXPENSES FOR 1995–96 ***Application fee:*** $50. Comprehensive fee of $14,755 includes full-time tuition ($9300), mandatory fees ($250 minimum), and college room and board ($5205 minimum). College room only: $2970. Full-time mandatory fees range from $250 to $275.
FINANCIAL AID ***College-administered undergrad aid 1995–96:*** need-based scholarships, 6 non-need scholarships (average $9000), low-interest long-term loans from external sources (average $2625). ***Required forms:*** state, institutional, FAFSA; accepted: CSS Financial Aid PROFILE. ***Priority deadline:*** 4/1. ***Payment plans:*** installment, deferred payment. ***Waivers:*** full or partial for employees or children of employees.
APPLYING Open admission. ***Option:*** deferred entrance. ***Required:*** essay, school transcript, TOEFL for international students. Test scores used for admission. ***Application deadline:*** rolling. ***Notification:*** continuous.
APPLYING/TRANSFER ***Required:*** essay, college transcript. ***Entrance:*** noncompetitive. ***Application deadline:*** rolling. ***Notification:*** continuous. ***Contact:*** Ms. Jan Sieff, Associate Director of Admission, 412-263-6600.
CONTACT Mr. Lee Colker, Vice President and Director of Admissions, Art Institute of Pittsburgh, 526 Penn Avenue, Pittsburgh, PA 15222-3269, 412-263-6600 Ext. 238 or toll-free 800-275-2470. College video available.

BEREAN INSTITUTE
Philadelphia, Pennsylvania

UG Enrollment: 319 | **Tuition: $6000/deg prog**
Application Deadline: rolling | **Room & Board: N/Avail**

GENERAL Independent, 2-year, coed. Awards terminal associate degrees. Founded 1899. ***Setting:*** 3-acre urban campus. ***Total enrollment:*** 319. ***Faculty:*** 17 (13 full-time, 4 part-time); student-faculty ratio is 17:1.
ENROLLMENT PROFILE 319 students from 3 states and territories. 76% women, 20% part-time, 97% state residents, 29% transferred in, 1% international, 25% 25 or older, 0% Native American, 1% Hispanic, 97% African American, 1% Asian American.
FIRST-YEAR CLASS 150 total. Of the students who applied, 100% were accepted, 75% of whom enrolled. 1% from top 10% of their high school class, 8% from top quarter, 15% from top half.
ACADEMIC PROGRAM Calendar: trimesters. Academic remediation for entering students, advanced placement, honors program, part-time degree program (daytime, evenings), adult/continuing education programs, internships.
GENERAL DEGREE REQUIREMENT 1575 hours.
MAJORS Accounting, computer science, court reporting, electrical and electronics technologies, legal secretarial studies, medical secretarial studies, secretarial studies/office management.
LIBRARY 3,500 books, 48 periodicals, 300 records, tapes, and CDs.
COMPUTERS ON CAMPUS 30 computers for student use in computer center, office machine classroom.
COLLEGE LIFE Orientation program (5 days, no cost). Drama-theater group, student-run newspaper. ***Social organizations:*** 1 local fraternity. ***Student services:*** personal-psychological counseling.
HOUSING College housing not available.
ATHLETICS ***Intramural:*** basketball.
CAREER PLANNING ***Service:*** career counseling.
EXPENSES FOR 1996–97 ***Application fee:*** $20. Tuition: $6000 per degree program. Part-time tuition per credit: $100. Mandatory fees for all students per course: $150.
FINANCIAL AID ***College-administered undergrad aid 1995–96:*** need-based scholarships, short-term loans (average $50), low-interest long-term loans from external sources (average $1019), Federal Work-Study. ***Required forms:*** state, institutional, FAFSA. ***Priority deadline:*** 8/1.
APPLYING Open admission. ***Option:*** deferred entrance. ***Required:*** school transcript, interview. Test scores used for counseling/placement. ***Application deadline:*** rolling. ***Notification:*** continuous.
APPLYING/TRANSFER ***Required:*** high school transcript, interview. ***Recommended:*** college transcript. ***Application deadline:*** rolling. ***Notification:*** continuous.
CONTACT Mr. John Spruill, Admissions Coordinator, Berean Institute, 1901 West Girard Avenue, Philadelphia, PA 19130-1599, 215-763-4833.

BRADLEY ACADEMY FOR THE VISUAL ARTS
York, Pennsylvania

UG Enrollment: 266 | **Tuition & Fees: $9180**
Application Deadline: rolling | **Room & Board: N/Avail**

GENERAL Proprietary, 2-year, coed. Awards terminal associate degrees. Founded 1952. ***Setting:*** 1-acre small-town campus with easy access to Baltimore. ***Total enrollment:*** 266. ***Faculty:*** 29 (8 full-time, 21 part-time); student-faculty ratio is 8:1.
ENROLLMENT PROFILE 266 students from 6 states and territories. 65% women, 5% part-time, 99% state residents, 10% transferred in, 35% have need-based financial aid, 45% have non-need-based financial aid, 0% international, 18% 25 or older, 2% Hispanic, 2% African American, 0% Asian American. ***Areas of study chosen:*** 65% communications and journalism, 20% architecture, 15% business management and administrative services. ***Most popular recent majors:*** graphic arts, interior design, fashion merchandising.
FIRST-YEAR CLASS 140 total; 250 applied, 90% were accepted, 62% of whom enrolled. 10% from top 10% of their high school class, 15% from top quarter, 75% from top half.
ACADEMIC PROGRAM Core, hands-on career training curriculum, honor code. Calendar: semesters. 72 courses offered in 1995–96. Tutorials, summer session for credit, part-time degree program (daytime), adult/continuing education programs, internships.
GENERAL DEGREE REQUIREMENTS 72 credits; computer course.
MAJORS Advertising, art/fine arts, commercial art, computer graphics, fashion merchandising, graphic arts, interior design, textiles and clothing.
LIBRARY Bradley Academy Library with 1,200 books, 38 periodicals, 2 CD-ROMs, 50 records, tapes, and CDs.
COMPUTERS ON CAMPUS Computer purchase plan available. 29 computers for student use in computer center, library. Staffed computer lab on campus provides training in use of computers, software.
COLLEGE LIFE ***Major annual events:*** Senior Portfolio Exhibition, Annual Halloween Bash, Fall Open House. ***Student services:*** personal-psychological counseling.
HOUSING College housing not available.
CAREER PLANNING ***Placement office:*** 1 full-time, 1 part-time staff. ***Director:*** Mr. William K. Gutshall, Director of Student and Graduate Services, 717-848-1447. ***Services:*** job fairs, resume preparation, resume referral, career counseling, job bank, job interviews.
AFTER GRADUATION 100% of class of 1994 had job offers within 6 months.
EXPENSES FOR 1996–97 ***Application fee:*** $25. Tuition: $9180 full-time, $255 per credit hour part-time.
FINANCIAL AID ***College-administered undergrad aid 1995–96:*** 40 need-based scholarships (average $400), 5 non-need scholarships (average $4000), low-interest long-term loans from external sources, Federal Work-Study, 2 part-time jobs. ***Required forms:*** state, institutional, FAFSA; accepted: CSS Financial Aid PROFILE. ***Application deadline:*** continuous to 8/1. ***Payment plan:*** installment. ***Waivers:*** full or partial for employees or children of employees. ***Notification:*** 9/1. ***Average indebtedness of graduates:*** $5250.
APPLYING ***Options:*** deferred entrance, midyear entrance. ***Required:*** school transcript, 2 recommendations, interview, TOEFL for international students. ***Recommended:*** minimum 2.0 GPA, SAT I. ***Required for some:*** portfolio. Test scores used for counseling/placement. ***Application deadline:*** rolling.
APPLYING/TRANSFER ***Required:*** 2 recommendations, interview, college transcript. ***Recommended:*** minimum 2.0 high school GPA. ***Required for some:*** portfolio. ***Application deadline:*** rolling. ***Contact:*** Ms. Janet M. Stevens, Director of Admissions, 717-848-1447.
CONTACT Ms. Janet M. Stevens, Director of Admissions, Bradley Academy for the Visual Arts, 625 East Philadelphia Street, York, PA 17403-1625, 717-848-1447 or toll-free 800-864-7725 (out-of-state). ***Fax:*** 717-848-1447. College video available.

❖ *See page 710 for a narrative description.* ❖

BUCKS COUNTY COMMUNITY COLLEGE
Newtown, Pennsylvania

UG Enrollment: 9,500 | **Tuition & Fees (Area Res): $2280**
Application Deadline: 5/1 | **Room & Board: N/Avail**

GENERAL County-supported, 2-year, coed. Awards certificates, transfer associate, terminal associate degrees. Founded 1964. ***Setting:*** 200-acre small-town campus with easy access to Philadelphia. ***Total enrollment:*** 9,500. ***Faculty:*** 452 (184 full-time, 268 part-time); student-faculty ratio is 25:1.
ENROLLMENT PROFILE 9,500 students from 2 states and territories. 61% women, 72% part-time, 99% state residents, 15% transferred in, 0% international, 49% 25 or older, 1% Native American, 1% Hispanic, 1% African American, 2% Asian American. ***Most popular recent majors:*** business administration/commerce/management, liberal arts/general studies.
FIRST-YEAR CLASS 1,800 total. Of the students who applied, 100% were accepted.
ACADEMIC PROGRAM Core, honor code. Calendar: semesters. Academic remediation for entering students, English as a second language program offered during academic year and summer, services for LD students, advanced placement, self-designed majors, summer session for credit, part-time degree program (daytime, evenings, weekends, summer), adult/continuing education programs, co-op programs and internships. Study abroad in 16 countries, including India, Ireland, Israel, Sweden, Egypt, Italy, Malaysia, Mexico, Kenya, France.
GENERAL DEGREE REQUIREMENTS 60 credits; 1 math/science course; computer course for business, math, graphic arts majors; internship (some majors).
MAJORS Accounting, American studies, art/fine arts, biology/biological sciences, broadcasting, business administration/commerce/management, chemical engineering technology, chemistry, child care/child and family studies, communication, computer information systems, computer programming, computer science, computer technologies, corrections, criminal justice, culinary arts, data processing, dietetics, drafting and design, early childhood education, education, electrical and electronics technologies, engineering (general), finance/banking, food sciences, food services management, graphic arts, health education, health science, hospitality services, hotel and restaurant management, humanities,

human services, industrial arts, information science, journalism, laboratory technologies, labor studies, law enforcement/police sciences, legal secretarial studies, liberal arts/general studies, marketing/retailing/merchandising, mathematics, medical assistant technologies, medical secretarial studies, music, nursing, paralegal studies, physical education, psychology, radio and television studies, real estate, retail management, secretarial studies/office management, social science, teacher aide studies, telecommunications, theater arts/drama, word processing.
LIBRARY 152,000 books, 285,607 microform titles, 437 periodicals, 10,000 records, tapes, and CDs.
COMPUTERS ON CAMPUS Computer purchase plan available. 275 computers for student use in computer center, classrooms, library. Staffed computer lab on campus.
COLLEGE LIFE Drama-theater group, choral group, student-run newspaper, radio station. ***Major annual event:*** Open House. ***Student services:*** personal-psychological counseling. ***Campus security:*** 24-hour emergency response devices and patrols, late-night transport-escort service.
HOUSING College housing not available.
ATHLETICS Member NJCAA. ***Intercollegiate:*** basketball M/W, cross-country running M/W, equestrian sports M/W, field hockey W, golf M/W, soccer M/W, tennis M/W, volleyball W. ***Intramural:*** archery, baseball, basketball, equestrian sports, football, skiing (cross-country), skiing (downhill), soccer, swimming and diving, volleyball, water polo. ***Contact:*** Mr. Lou Pacchioli, Athletic Director, 215-968-8450.
CAREER PLANNING ***Placement office:*** 2 full-time, 1 part-time staff. ***Director:*** Ms. Cheryl Bonner, Coordinator of Career Center, 215-968-8196. ***Services:*** job fairs, resume preparation, career counseling, careers library.
AFTER GRADUATION 90% of students completing a degree program in 1994–95 went directly on to further study.
EXPENSES FOR 1996–97 ***Application fee:*** $30. Area resident tuition: $1980 full-time, $66 per credit part-time. State resident tuition: $3960 full-time, $132 per credit part-time. Nonresident tuition: $5940 full-time, $198 per credit part-time. Full-time mandatory fees per year: $300 for state residents, $600 for nonresidents.
FINANCIAL AID ***College-administered undergrad aid 1995–96:*** need-based scholarships, 104 non-need scholarships (average $628), short-term loans (average $75), low-interest long-term loans from external sources (average $2000), Federal Work-Study, 150 part-time jobs. ***Required forms:*** state, institutional; accepted: CSS Financial Aid PROFILE. ***Priority deadline:*** 5/1. ***Payment plan:*** deferred payment. ***Waivers:*** full or partial for employees or children of employees and senior citizens.
APPLYING Open admission except for nursing, fine arts, fine woodworking, chef's apprentice programs. ***Options:*** Common Application, early entrance. ***Recommended:*** ACT. ***Required for some:*** SAT I. Test scores used for counseling/placement. ***Application deadline:*** 5/1. Preference given to county residents for nursing program.
APPLYING/TRANSFER ***Application deadline:*** 5/1.
CONTACT Ms. Beth Benson, Assistant Director of Admissions, Bucks County Community College, Newtown, PA 18940-1525, 215-968-8119. ***Fax:*** 215-968-8110.

BUTLER COUNTY COMMUNITY COLLEGE
Butler, Pennsylvania

UG Enrollment: 3,133	**Tuition & Fees (Area Res): $1248**
Application Deadline: 8/15	**Room & Board: N/Avail**

GENERAL County-supported, 2-year, coed. Awards certificates, diplomas, transfer associate, terminal associate degrees. Founded 1965. ***Setting:*** 300-acre rural campus with easy access to Pittsburgh. ***Total enrollment:*** 3,133. ***Faculty:*** 220 (70 full-time, 20% with terminal degrees, 150 part-time); student-faculty ratio is 19:1.
ENROLLMENT PROFILE 3,133 students from 8 states and territories, 2 other countries. 64% women, 36% men, 52% part-time, 98% state residents, 20% transferred in, 50% have need-based financial aid, 5% have non-need-based financial aid, 1% international, 40% 25 or older, 0% Native American, 1% Hispanic, 1% African American, 1% Asian American. ***Areas of study chosen:*** 20% business management and administrative services, 20% engineering and applied sciences, 20% health professions and related sciences, 15% liberal arts/general studies, 5% biological and life sciences, 5% communications and journalism, 5% computer and information sciences, 5% education, 5% social sciences. ***Most popular recent majors:*** liberal arts/general studies, business administration/commerce/management, nursing.
FIRST-YEAR CLASS 1,124 total; 1,198 applied, 100% were accepted, 94% of whom enrolled.
ACADEMIC PROGRAM Core. Calendar: semesters. 944 courses offered in 1995–96. Academic remediation for entering students, English as a second language program offered during academic year, services for LD students, advanced placement, tutorials, summer session for credit, part-time degree program (daytime, evenings, summer), adult/continuing education programs, co-op programs and internships.
GENERAL DEGREE REQUIREMENTS 63 credits; 1 math course; computer course for all business majors; internship (some majors).
MAJORS Accounting, architectural technologies, biology/biological sciences, business administration/commerce/management, civil engineering technology, communication, computer information systems, computer programming, computer technologies, criminology, data processing, drafting and design, early childhood education, education, electrical and electronics technologies, elementary education, (pre)engineering sequence, English, food services management, food services technology, graphic arts, hospitality services, humanities, industrial administration, instrumentation technology, legal secretarial studies, liberal arts/general studies, marketing/retailing/merchandising, mathematics, mechanical design technology, medical assistant technologies, medical secretarial studies, nursing, parks management, physical education, physical fitness/exercise science, physical sciences, physical therapy, quality control technology, retail management, secretarial studies/office management, sports administration, word processing.
LIBRARY John A. Beck, Jr. Library with 63,000 books, 305 periodicals, 1,100 records, tapes, and CDs.
COMPUTERS ON CAMPUS 350 computers for student use in computer center, computer labs, learning resource center, academic areas, classrooms, library. Staffed computer lab on campus provides training in use of computers, software.
COLLEGE LIFE Drama-theater group, choral group, student-run newspaper, radio station. ***Social organizations:*** 35 open to all. ***Most popular organizations:*** Student Government, Ski Club, Drama Club, Outdoor Recreation Club. ***Major annual events:*** Spring Dinner Theatre, Spring Dinner Dance, Ice Cream Festival. ***Student services:*** personal-psychological counseling. ***Campus security:*** 24-hour emergency response devices, late-night transport-escort service.
HOUSING College housing not available.
ATHLETICS Member NJCAA. ***Intercollegiate:*** baseball M, basketball M, golf M/W, softball W, volleyball W. ***Intramural:*** badminton, basketball, racquetball, soccer, softball, table tennis (Ping-Pong), tennis, volleyball, weight lifting. ***Contact:*** Mr. Charles Dunaway, Athletic Director, 412-287-8711.
CAREER PLANNING ***Placement office:*** 1 full-time staff. ***Director:*** Mr. Fred Kinnick, Counselor, 412-287-8711. ***Services:*** job fairs, resume preparation, resume referral, career counseling, careers library, job interviews.
EXPENSES FOR 1996–97 ***Application fee:*** $10. Area resident tuition: $1200 full-time, $50 per credit part-time. State resident tuition: $2400 full-time, $100 per credit part-time. Nonresident tuition: $3600 full-time, $150 per credit part-time. Part-time mandatory fees: $2 per credit. Full-time mandatory fees: $48.
FINANCIAL AID ***College-administered undergrad aid 1995–96:*** 55 need-based scholarships (average $500), 10 non-need scholarships (average $1000), short-term loans (average $100), low-interest long-term loans from external sources (average $1800), Federal Work-Study, 16 part-time jobs. ***Acceptable forms:*** CSS Financial Aid PROFILE, state, FAFSA. ***Priority deadline:*** 5/1. ***Waivers:*** full or partial for employees or children of employees and senior citizens.
APPLYING Open admission except for nursing, metrology, physical therapy, medical assistant technologies programs. ***Options:*** early entrance, deferred entrance, midyear entrance. ***Required:*** TOEFL for international students, ACT ASSET. Test scores used for counseling/placement. ***Application deadline:*** 8/15. ***Notification:*** continuous until 8/15.
APPLYING/TRANSFER ***Entrance:*** noncompetitive. ***Application deadline:*** 8/15. ***Notification:*** continuous until 8/15. ***Contact:*** Mrs. Sue Bennitt, Transfer Counselor, 412-287-8711.
CONTACT Mr. William Miller, Director of Admissions, Butler County Community College, Butler, PA 16003-1203, 412-287-8711 Ext. 344. College video available.

CAMBRIA-ROWE BUSINESS COLLEGE
Johnstown, Pennsylvania

UG Enrollment: 235	**Tuition & Fees: $4875**
Application Deadline: rolling	**Room & Board: N/Avail**

GENERAL Proprietary, 2-year, coed. Awards transfer associate, terminal associate degrees. Founded 1891. ***Setting:*** small-town campus with easy access to Pittsburgh. ***Total enrollment:*** 235. ***Faculty:*** 11 (10 full-time, 100% with terminal degrees, 1 part-time); student-faculty ratio is 23:1.
ENROLLMENT PROFILE 235 students: 70% women, 1% part-time, 100% state residents, 15% transferred in, 40% 25 or older, 3% African American. ***Areas of study chosen:*** 100% business management and administrative services. ***Most popular recent majors:*** accounting, business administration/commerce/management, medical secretarial studies.
FIRST-YEAR CLASS 85 total.
ACADEMIC PROGRAM Core, specialized study curriculum. Calendar: quarters. 62 courses offered in 1995–96; average class size 20 in required courses. Summer session for credit, part-time degree program (daytime).
GENERAL DEGREE REQUIREMENTS 90 credits; 1 business math course; computer course.
MAJORS Accounting, business administration/commerce/management, legal secretarial studies, medical secretarial studies, secretarial studies/office management.
COMPUTERS ON CAMPUS 80 computers for student use in computer center, computer labs, research center provide access to main academic computer.
COLLEGE LIFE Student-run newspaper. ***Student services:*** personal-psychological counseling.
HOUSING College housing not available.
CAREER PLANNING ***Placement office:*** 1 full-time staff. ***Director:*** Miss Patricia Kiniry, Director of Career Services, 814-536-5168. ***Services:*** job fairs, resume preparation, resume referral, career counseling, careers library, job bank, job interviews. Students must register freshman year.
AFTER GRADUATION 85% of class of 1994 had job offers within 6 months. 2% of students completing a degree program went directly on to further study.
EXPENSES FOR 1995–96 ***Application fee:*** $15. Tuition: $4800 full-time, $420 per course part-time. Full-time mandatory fees: $75.
FINANCIAL AID ***College-administered undergrad aid 1995–96:*** 4 non-need scholarships (average $4800), low-interest long-term loans from external sources (average $2625), 1 part-time job. ***Required forms:*** state, FAFSA. ***Application deadline:*** continuous to 8/1.
APPLYING ***Options:*** Common Application, early entrance. ***Required:*** school transcript. ***Recommended:*** minimum 2.0 GPA, interview. ***Required for some:*** recommendations. ***Application deadline:*** rolling. ***Notification:*** continuous.
APPLYING/TRANSFER ***Required:*** high school transcript, college transcript. ***Recommended:*** interview, minimum 2.0 high school GPA. ***Entrance:*** minimally difficult. ***Contact:*** Ms. Linda Wess, Director of Admissions, 814-536-5168.
CONTACT Mrs. Linda Wess, Director of Admissions, Cambria-Rowe Business College, Johnstown, PA 15902-2494, 814-536-5168. ***Fax:*** 814-536-5160.

CENTRAL PENNSYLVANIA BUSINESS SCHOOL
Summerdale, Pennsylvania

UG Enrollment: 574	**Tuition & Fees: $5990**
Application Deadline: 8/31	**Room Only: $2500**

GENERAL Proprietary, 2-year, coed. Awards diplomas, transfer associate, terminal associate degrees. Founded 1922. ***Setting:*** 20-acre small-town campus. ***Total enrollment:*** 574. ***Faculty:*** 49 (23 full-time, 100% with terminal degrees, 26 part-time); student-faculty ratio is 12:1.
ENROLLMENT PROFILE 574 students from 7 states and territories. 81% women, 19% men, 11% part-time, 97% state residents, 60% live on campus, 20% transferred in,

Central Pennsylvania Business School (continued)
0% international, 3% 25 or older, 1% Native American, 1% Hispanic, 2% African American, 1% Asian American. ***Areas of study chosen:*** 65% business management and administrative services, 31% health professions and related sciences, 2% communications and journalism, 2% computer and information sciences. ***Most popular recent majors:*** physical therapy, court reporting, business administration/commerce/management.
FIRST-YEAR CLASS 298 total; 809 applied, 87% were accepted, 43% of whom enrolled.
ACADEMIC PROGRAM Career-related curriculum, honor code. Calendar: trimesters. 196 courses offered in 1995–96. Academic remediation for entering students, advanced placement, tutorials, summer session for credit, part-time degree program (daytime, summer), adult/continuing education programs, internships.
GENERAL DEGREE REQUIREMENTS 75 credit hours; computer course; internship (some majors).
MAJORS Accounting, business administration/commerce/management, child care/child and family studies, communication, computer information systems, court reporting, finance/banking, hotel and restaurant management, legal secretarial studies, marketing/retailing/merchandising, medical assistant technologies, medical secretarial studies, paralegal studies, physical therapy, retail management, secretarial studies/office management, tourism and travel.
LIBRARY Learning Resource Center with 4,600 books, 133 periodicals, 6 CD-ROMs, 1,171 records, tapes, and CDs.
COMPUTERS ON CAMPUS 110 computers for student use in computer center, classrooms, library provide access to on-line services. Staffed computer lab on campus provides training in use of computers, software.
COLLEGE LIFE Orientation program (2 days, no cost). Student-run newspaper. 15% vote in student government elections. ***Social organizations:*** 15 open to all. ***Most popular organizations:*** Campus Christian Fellowship, Ski Club, Student Ambassadors, Phi Beta Lambda, Travel Club. ***Major annual events:*** Break Away Weekend, Fashion Show. ***Student services:*** personal-psychological counseling. ***Campus security:*** 24-hour emergency response devices and patrols.
HOUSING 434 college housing spaces available; 342 were occupied 1995–96. No special consideration for freshman housing applicants. Off-campus living permitted. ***Option:*** coed (11 buildings) housing available. Resident assistants live in dorms.
ATHLETICS ***Intercollegiate:*** basketball M, golf M/W, volleyball W. ***Intramural:*** basketball, bowling, football, softball, tennis, volleyball. ***Contact:*** Mr. Tony DeStadio, Coordinator of Activities and Athletics, 717-728-2209.
CAREER PLANNING ***Placement office:*** 1 full-time staff. ***Director:*** Mrs. Ada Emmert, Coordinator of Career Services, 800-759-CPBS Ext. 2262. ***Services:*** job fairs, resume preparation, resume referral, career counseling, careers library, job bank, job interviews. Students must register sophomore year. 49 organizations recruited on campus 1994–95.
AFTER GRADUATION 77% of class of 1994 had job offers within 6 months. 4% of students completing a degree program went directly on to further study.
EXPENSES FOR 1996–97 Tuition: $5710 (minimum) full-time. Part-time tuition per credit ranges from $190 to $212. Part-time mandatory fees: $140 per trimester. Full-time tuition ranges up to $6350 according to program. Full-time mandatory fees: $280 (minimum). College room only: $2500 (minimum).
FINANCIAL AID ***College-administered undergrad aid 1995–96:*** 150 need-based scholarships (average $1000), low-interest long-term loans from external sources (average $2725), 45 Federal Work-Study (averaging $700), 10 part-time jobs. ***Required forms:*** institutional; accepted: state, FAFSA. ***Priority deadline:*** 5/1. ***Payment plan:*** deferred payment. ***Waivers:*** full or partial for employees or children of employees.
APPLYING Open admission except for physical therapy, legal secretary programs. ***Options:*** early entrance, deferred entrance, midyear entrance. ***Required:*** essay, school transcript, TOEFL for international students. ***Recommended:*** campus interview. ***Required for some:*** minimum 2.0 GPA, 3 years of high school math and science, campus interview, SAT I. Test scores used for counseling/placement. ***Application deadline:*** 8/31. ***Notification:*** continuous.
APPLYING/TRANSFER ***Required:*** essay, high school transcript, college transcript. ***Recommended:*** campus interview. ***Required for some:*** standardized test scores, 3 years of high school math and science, campus interview, minimum 2.0 college GPA, minimum 2.0 high school GPA. ***Entrance:*** noncompetitive. ***Application deadline:*** 8/31. ***Notification:*** continuous. ***Contact:*** Mrs. Karen Weikel, Registrar, 717-728-2205.
CONTACT Mr. Jon Tobin, Director of Admissions, Central Pennsylvania Business School, Summerdale, PA 17093-0309, 717-732-0702 Ext. 266 or toll-free 800-759-CPBS. ***Fax:*** 717-732-5254. College video available.

CHI INSTITUTE
Southampton, Pennsylvania

UG Enrollment: 550	Tuition & Fees: $7990
Application Deadline: rolling	Room & Board: N/Avail

GENERAL Proprietary, 2-year, specialized, coed. Awards terminal associate degrees. Founded 1981. ***Setting:*** 6-acre small-town campus with easy access to Philadelphia. ***Total enrollment:*** 550. ***Faculty:*** 35 (22 full-time, 13 part-time); student-faculty ratio is 20:1.
ENROLLMENT PROFILE 550 students: 10% women, 33% part-time, 90% state residents, 0% transferred in, 0% international, 50% 25 or older, 0% Native American, 2% Hispanic, 5% African American, 2% Asian American. ***Areas of study chosen:*** 25% computer and information sciences. ***Most popular recent majors:*** computer technologies, electrical and electronics technologies, heating/refrigeration/air conditioning.
FIRST-YEAR CLASS 275 total; 325 applied, 92% were accepted, 92% of whom enrolled.
ACADEMIC PROGRAM Core. Calendar: quarters. Academic remediation for entering students, tutorials, adult/continuing education programs.
GENERAL DEGREE REQUIREMENT 1800 hours.
MAJORS Computer technologies, electrical and electronics technologies, heating/refrigeration/air conditioning, telecommunications, word processing.
LIBRARY 2,500 books, 25 periodicals.
COMPUTERS ON CAMPUS Computer purchase plan available. 50 computers for student use in computer labs.
COLLEGE LIFE ***Student services:*** personal-psychological counseling.
HOUSING College housing not available.
CAREER PLANNING ***Placement office:*** 1 full-time, 1 part-time staff. ***Director:*** Ms. Nancy Mills, Job Placement Director, 215-357-5100. ***Services:*** job fairs, resume preparation, resume referral, career counseling, careers library, job bank, job interviews. Students must register freshman year.
EXPENSES FOR 1996–97 Tuition: $7740 full-time, $3870 per year part-time. Part-time mandatory fees: $250 per year. Full-time mandatory fees: $250.
FINANCIAL AID ***College-administered undergrad aid 1995–96:*** low-interest long-term loans from external sources. ***Required forms:*** FAFSA; required for some: state. ***Application deadline:*** continuous to 9/15. ***Payment plans:*** tuition prepayment, installment. ***Waivers:*** full or partial for employees or children of employees. ***Notification:*** continuous.
APPLYING ***Option:*** deferred entrance. ***Required for some:*** school transcript. ***Application deadline:*** rolling.
APPLYING/TRANSFER ***Application deadline:*** rolling.
CONTACT Mr. Kevin Quinn, Director of Marketing, CHI Institute, Southampton, PA 18966-3747, 215-357-5100. College video available.

CHI INSTITUTE, RETS CAMPUS
Broomall, Pennsylvania

UG Enrollment: 440	Tuition & Fees: $5780
Application Deadline: rolling	Room & Board: N/Avail

GENERAL Proprietary, 2-year, coed. Awards transfer associate, terminal associate degrees. Founded 1958. ***Setting:*** small-town campus with easy access to Philadelphia. ***Total enrollment:*** 440. ***Faculty:*** 20.
ENROLLMENT PROFILE 440 students: 6% women, 0% part-time, 95% state residents, 10% transferred in, 2% international, 30% 25 or older, 1% Native American, 2% Hispanic, 20% African American, 4% Asian American.
ACADEMIC PROGRAM Calendar: quarters. Academic remediation for entering students, advanced placement, self-designed majors, honors program, adult/continuing education programs.
GENERAL DEGREE REQUIREMENTS 600 hours; math/science requirements vary according to program.
MAJOR Electronics engineering technology.
COMPUTERS ON CAMPUS 35 computers for student use in classrooms.
COLLEGE LIFE Orientation program (2 days, no cost, parents included). ***Student services:*** personal-psychological counseling.
HOUSING College housing not available.
CAREER PLANNING ***Service:*** career counseling.
EXPENSES FOR 1996–97 ***Application fee:*** $100. Tuition: $5530 (minimum) full-time. Full-time tuition ranges up to $13,770 according to program. Full-time mandatory fees: $250.
FINANCIAL AID ***College-administered undergrad aid 1995–96:*** low-interest long-term loans from external sources, 10 part-time jobs. ***Required forms:*** state, institutional, FAFSA.
APPLYING ***Option:*** deferred entrance. ***Required:*** school transcript, ABLE. Test scores used for counseling/placement. ***Application deadline:*** rolling.
APPLYING/TRANSFER ***Required:*** standardized test scores, high school transcript. ***Entrance:*** minimally difficult.
CONTACT Ms. Connie Pickhaver, Admissions Coordinator, CHI Institute, RETS Campus, Broomall, PA 19008, 610-353-7630.

CHURCHMAN BUSINESS SCHOOL
Easton, Pennsylvania

UG Enrollment: 205	Tuition & Fees: $5520
Application Deadline: rolling	Room & Board: N/Avail

GENERAL Proprietary, 2-year, coed. Awards diplomas, transfer associate, terminal associate degrees. Founded 1911. ***Setting:*** small-town campus. ***Total enrollment:*** 205. ***Faculty:*** 9 (8 full-time, 100% with terminal degrees, 1 part-time); student-faculty ratio is 23:1.
ENROLLMENT PROFILE 205 students from 2 states and territories. 60% women, 3% part-time, 64% state residents, 2% transferred in, 1% 25 or older, 1% African American. ***Most popular recent majors:*** accounting, secretarial studies/office management, finance/banking.
FIRST-YEAR CLASS 105 total; 127 applied, 95% were accepted, 98% of whom enrolled. 6% from top 10% of their high school class, 16% from top quarter, 63% from top half.
ACADEMIC PROGRAM Core, honor code. Calendar: trimesters. English as a second language program offered during academic year, part-time degree program (daytime, evenings), adult/continuing education programs.
GENERAL DEGREE REQUIREMENTS 84 credits; 2 business math courses; computer course.
MAJORS Accounting, business administration/commerce/management, finance/banking, legal secretarial studies, medical secretarial studies, secretarial studies/office management.
LIBRARY 5,000 books, 15 periodicals.
COMPUTERS ON CAMPUS 48 computers for student use in computer center provide access to off-campus computing facilities. Staffed computer lab on campus provides training in use of computers, software.
COLLEGE LIFE 75% vote in student government elections. ***Social organizations:*** 2 open to all. ***Campus security:*** 24-hour emergency response devices.
HOUSING College housing not available.
CAREER PLANNING ***Service:*** career counseling.
EXPENSES FOR 1996–97 ***Application fee:*** $25. Tuition: $5385 full-time, $75 per credit part-time. Full-time mandatory fees: $135.
FINANCIAL AID ***College-administered undergrad aid 1995–96:*** low-interest long-term loans from external sources (average $2300). ***Acceptable forms:*** state, FAFSA. ***Priority deadline:*** 8/1. ***Payment plan:*** installment.
APPLYING ***Options:*** early entrance, deferred entrance, midyear entrance. ***Required:*** school transcript. ***Recommended:*** recommendations, interview. ***Application deadline:*** rolling. ***Notification:*** continuous until 7/30.
APPLYING/TRANSFER ***Required:*** high school transcript, college transcript. ***Recommended:*** recommendations, interview. ***Entrance:*** minimally difficult. ***Application deadline:*** rolling. ***Notification:*** continuous until 7/30. ***Contact:*** Mr. Scott Castone, Admissions Counselor, 610-258-5345.
CONTACT Mr. Dale W. Houck Jr., Director of Admissions, Churchman Business School, Easton, PA 18042-3592, 610-258-5345.

COMMUNITY COLLEGE OF ALLEGHENY COUNTY ALLEGHENY CAMPUS
Pittsburgh, Pennsylvania

UG Enrollment: 5,701	Tuition & Fees (Area Res): $2167
Application Deadline: rolling	Room & Board: N/Avail

The Community College of Allegheny County (CCAC), a comprehensive 2-year public institution in Pennsylvania, offers programs to meet a wide range of needs. More than 200 academic programs lead to the Associate in Arts, Associate in Science, and Associate in Applied Science degrees and the certificate.

GENERAL County-supported, 2-year, coed. Part of Community Colleges of Allegheny County System. Awards certificates, transfer associate, terminal associate degrees. Founded 1966. *Setting:* 15-acre urban campus. *Total enrollment:* 5,701. *Faculty:* 710 (141 full-time, 91% with terminal degrees, 569 part-time).
ENROLLMENT PROFILE 5,701 students: 63% women, 37% men, 56% part-time, 95% state residents, 15% transferred in, 1% international, 45% 25 or older, 1% Native American, 1% Hispanic, 27% African American, 2% Asian American. *Areas of study chosen:* 43% liberal arts/general studies, 26% health professions and related sciences, 13% business management and administrative services, 7% education, 3% physical sciences, 3% social sciences, 2% engineering and applied sciences, 1% agriculture, 1% performing arts, 1% vocational and home economics. *Most popular recent majors:* liberal arts/general studies, business administration/commerce/management.
FIRST-YEAR CLASS 2,172 total; 3,166 applied, 98% were accepted, 70% of whom enrolled.
ACADEMIC PROGRAM Core. Calendar: semesters. 201 courses offered in 1995–96; average class size 17 in required courses. Academic remediation for entering students, English as a second language program offered during academic year and summer, services for LD students, advanced placement, self-designed majors, honors program, summer session for credit, part-time degree program (daytime, evenings, weekends, summer); adult/continuing education programs, co-op programs and internships. Off-campus study at members of the Pittsburgh Council on Higher Education. Study abroad in England, Italy, France (1% of students participate). ROTC: Army (c), Air Force (c).
GENERAL DEGREE REQUIREMENT 63 credits.
MAJORS Accounting, art/fine arts, aviation administration, aviation technology, behavioral sciences, biochemical technology, biology/biological sciences, business administration/commerce/management, chemical engineering technology, chemistry, child care/child and family studies, child psychology/child development, commercial art, communication, computer information systems, computer programming, computer science, corrections, court reporting, culinary arts, data processing, dietetics, early childhood education, economics, education, elementary education, emergency medical technology, engineering (general), (pre)engineering sequence, engineering technology, English, flight training, food services management, food services technology, French, German, graphic arts, health education, history, human development, humanities, human services, industrial design, information science, interdisciplinary studies, Italian, journalism, labor and industrial relations, labor studies, legal secretarial studies, liberal arts/general studies, marketing/retailing/merchandising, mathematics, medical assistant technologies, medical laboratory technology, medical records services, medical technology, modern languages, music, music education, nuclear medical technology, nursing, nutrition, paralegal studies, physical education, physics, psychology, public administration, purchasing/inventory management, radiological technology, real estate, respiratory therapy, retail management, Russian, science, secretarial studies/office management, social science, social work, sociology, Spanish, theater arts/drama.
LIBRARY 80,000 books, 131 microform titles, 637 periodicals, 7 CD-ROMs, 3,500 records, tapes, and CDs. Acquisition spending 1994–95: $1.6 million.
COMPUTERS ON CAMPUS 500 computers for student use in computer center, computer labs, learning resource center, various departments, classrooms, library provide access to main academic computer, on-line services. Staffed computer lab on campus provides training in use of computers, software. Academic computing expenditure 1994–95: $1.5 million.
COLLEGE LIFE Drama-theater group, choral group, student-run newspaper. 15% vote in student government elections. *Student services:* health clinic, personal-psychological counseling, women's center. *Campus security:* 24-hour emergency response devices, late-night transport-escort service.
HOUSING College housing not available.
ATHLETICS Member NJCAA. *Intercollegiate:* baseball M, basketball M/W, soccer M, softball W. *Intramural:* basketball, soccer, swimming and diving, volleyball, weight lifting.
CAREER PLANNING *Placement office:* 2 full-time staff. *Director:* Mr. John Wallace, Coordinator/Career Counselor, 412-237-2764. *Services:* job fairs, resume preparation, resume referral, career counseling, careers library, job bank, job interviews.
AFTER GRADUATION 28% of students completing a degree program in 1994–95 went directly on to further study.
EXPENSES FOR 1996–97 Area resident tuition: $2040 full-time, $68 per credit part-time. State resident tuition: $4080 full-time, $136 per credit part-time. Nonresident tuition: $6120 full-time, $204 per credit part-time. Part-time mandatory fees: $74 per year. Full-time mandatory fees: $127.
FINANCIAL AID *College-administered undergrad aid 1995–96:* 1,953 need-based scholarships (average $345), non-need scholarships (average $550), low-interest long-term loans from college funds, Federal Work-Study, part-time jobs. *Required forms:* state, institutional, FAFSA; accepted: CSS Financial Aid PROFILE. *Priority deadline:* 5/1. *Payment plan:* deferred payment. *Waivers:* full or partial for employees or children of employees.
APPLYING Open admission except for health-related programs. *Options:* Common Application, early entrance, deferred entrance. *Recommended:* school transcript. *Application deadline:* rolling. *Notification:* continuous.
APPLYING/TRANSFER *Recommended:* high school transcript, college transcript. *Entrance:* noncompetitive. *Application deadline:* rolling. *Notification:* continuous. *Contact:* Mr. Walter Milinski, Director of Transfers, 412-237-2747.

CONTACT Ms. Colleen O'Neil, Acting Director of Admissions, Community College of Allegheny County Allegheny Campus, 808 Ridge Avenue, Pittsburgh, PA 15212-6003, 412-237-2511. College video available.

❖ *See page 730 for a narrative description.* ❖

COMMUNITY COLLEGE OF ALLEGHENY COUNTY BOYCE CAMPUS
Monroeville, Pennsylvania

UG Enrollment: 3,725	Tuition & Fees (Area Res): $2167
Application Deadline: rolling	Room & Board: N/Avail

GENERAL County-supported, 2-year, coed. Part of Community Colleges of Allegheny County System. Awards certificates, transfer associate, terminal associate degrees. Founded 1966. *Setting:* 25-acre suburban campus with easy access to Pittsburgh. *Total enrollment:* 3,725. *Faculty:* 321 (71 full-time, 91% with terminal degrees, 250 part-time).
ENROLLMENT PROFILE 3,725 students: 61% women, 39% men, 61% part-time, 99% state residents, 25% transferred in, 1% international, 55% 25 or older, 1% Native American, 1% Hispanic, 6% African American, 1% Asian American. *Areas of study chosen:* 43% liberal arts/general studies, 26% health professions and related sciences, 13% business management and administrative services, 7% education, 3% physical sciences, 3% social sciences, 2% engineering and applied sciences, 1% agriculture, 1% performing arts, 1% vocational and home economics. *Most popular recent majors:* liberal arts/general studies, business administration/commerce/management.
FIRST-YEAR CLASS 1,565 total; 2,282 applied, 98% were accepted, 70% of whom enrolled.
ACADEMIC PROGRAM Core. Calendar: semesters. 201 courses offered in 1995–96; average class size 16 in required courses. Academic remediation for entering students, English as a second language program offered during academic year and summer, services for LD students, advanced placement, self-designed majors, honors program, summer session for credit, part-time degree program (daytime, evenings, weekends, summer); adult/continuing education programs, co-op programs and internships. Off-campus study at members of the Pittsburgh Council on Higher Education. Study abroad in England, Italy, France (1% of students participate). ROTC: Army (c), Air Force (c).
GENERAL DEGREE REQUIREMENT 63 credits.
MAJORS Accounting, art/fine arts, behavioral sciences, broadcasting, business administration/commerce/management, chemistry, civil engineering technology, communication, computer information systems, computer science, criminal justice, data processing, drafting and design, education, engineering (general), engineering design, engineering sciences, (pre)engineering sequence, engineering technology, English, finance/banking, fire science, food services management, food services technology, heating/refrigeration/air conditioning, hotel and restaurant management, humanities, information science, journalism, law enforcement/police sciences, liberal arts/general studies, marketing/retailing/merchandising, mathematics, mechanical design technology, mechanical engineering technology, medical secretarial studies, music, natural sciences, nursing, occupational therapy, operating room technology, paralegal studies, physical therapy, physics, political science/government, radiological technology, real estate, retail management, secretarial studies/office management, surveying technology, theater arts/drama.
LIBRARY 63,992 books, 104 microform titles, 351 periodicals, 1,315 records, tapes, and CDs. Acquisition spending 1994–95: $1 million.
COMPUTERS ON CAMPUS 200 computers for student use in computer center, computer labs, learning resource center, labs, classrooms, library provide access to main academic computer, on-line services. Staffed computer lab on campus provides training in use of computers, software. Academic computing expenditure 1994–95: $964,405.
COLLEGE LIFE Drama-theater group, student-run newspaper. 15% vote in student government elections. *Student services:* health clinic, women's center. *Campus security:* 24-hour emergency response devices, late-night transport-escort service.
HOUSING College housing not available.
ATHLETICS Member NJCAA. *Intercollegiate:* golf M/W, softball W, tennis M/W, volleyball W.
CAREER PLANNING *Placement office:* 1 full-time staff. *Director:* Dr. Charles P. Bostaph, Director of Career and Counseling Center, 412-325-6770. *Services:* job fairs, resume preparation, resume referral, career counseling, careers library, job bank, job interviews. Students must register freshman year.
AFTER GRADUATION 28% of students completing a degree program in 1994–95 went directly on to further study.
EXPENSES FOR 1996–97 Area resident tuition: $2040 full-time, $68 per credit part-time. State resident tuition: $4080 full-time, $136 per credit part-time. Nonresident tuition: $6120 full-time, $204 per credit part-time. Part-time mandatory fees: $74 per year. Full-time mandatory fees: $127.
FINANCIAL AID *College-administered undergrad aid 1995–96:* 1,299 need-based scholarships (average $506), Federal Work-Study, part-time jobs. *Required forms:* state, institutional, FAFSA. *Priority deadline:* 5/1. *Payment plan:* deferred payment. *Waivers:* full or partial for employees or children of employees.
APPLYING Open admission except for health-related programs. *Options:* Common Application, early entrance, deferred entrance. *Recommended:* school transcript. *Application deadline:* rolling. *Notification:* continuous.
APPLYING/TRANSFER *Recommended:* high school transcript, college transcript. *Entrance:* noncompetitive. *Application deadline:* rolling. *Notification:* continuous. *Contact:* Dr. Dan O'bara, Dean of Instruction, 412-325-6550.
CONTACT Ms. Mary Ellen Gray, Director of Admissions, Community College of Allegheny County Boyce Campus, 595 Beatty Road, Monroeville, PA 15146-1348, 412-327-1327 Ext. 215. *Fax:* 412-733-4397. College video available.

❖ *See page 730 for a narrative description.* ❖

COMMUNITY COLLEGE OF ALLEGHENY COUNTY NORTH CAMPUS
Pittsburgh, Pennsylvania

UG Enrollment: 4,374	Tuition & Fees (Area Res): $2167
Application Deadline: rolling	Room & Board: N/Avail

Community College of Allegheny County North Campus (continued)

GENERAL County-supported, 2-year, coed. Part of Community Colleges of Allegheny County System. Awards certificates, transfer associate, terminal associate degrees. Founded 1972. ***Setting:*** 2-acre suburban campus. ***Total enrollment:*** 4,374. ***Faculty:*** 632 (44 full-time, 91% with terminal degrees, 588 part-time).

ENROLLMENT PROFILE 4,374 students: 48% women, 52% men, 71% part-time, 99% state residents, 25% transferred in, 50% 25 or older, 1% Native American, 1% Hispanic, 2% African American, 1% Asian American. ***Areas of study chosen:*** 43% liberal arts/general studies, 26% health professions and related sciences, 13% business management and administrative services, 7% education, 3% physical sciences, 3% social sciences, 2% engineering and applied sciences, 1% agriculture, 1% performing arts, 1% vocational and home economics. ***Most popular recent majors:*** liberal arts/general studies, business administration/commerce/management.

FIRST-YEAR CLASS 1,104 total; 1,609 applied, 98% were accepted, 70% of whom enrolled.

ACADEMIC PROGRAM Core. Calendar: semesters. 201 courses offered in 1995–96; average class size 18 in required courses. Academic remediation for entering students, English as a second language program offered during academic year and summer, services for LD students, advanced placement, self-designed majors, honors program, summer session for credit, part-time degree program (daytime, evenings, weekends, summer), adult/continuing education programs, co-op programs. Off-campus study at members of the Pittsburgh Council on Higher Education. Study abroad in England, Italy, France (1% of students participate). ROTC: Army (c), Air Force (c).

GENERAL DEGREE REQUIREMENT 63 credits.

MAJORS Accounting, anthropology, art/fine arts, automotive technologies, behavioral sciences, business administration/commerce/management, child psychology/child development, community services, computer information systems, computer management, computer programming, computer science, computer technologies, construction technologies, data processing, deaf interpreter training, drafting and design, early childhood education, economics, education, electrical and electronics technologies, electromechanical technology, electronics engineering technology, elementary education, English, family services, finance/banking, gerontology, heating/refrigeration/air conditioning, hotel and restaurant management, humanities, human services, legal secretarial studies, liberal arts/general studies, machine and tool technologies, manufacturing technology, marketing/retailing/merchandising, mathematics, medical secretarial studies, mental health/rehabilitation counseling, nursing, plumbing, psychology, quality control technology, real estate, retail management, secretarial studies/office management, social science, social work, sports administration, vocational education, welding technology.

LIBRARY 15,978 books, 161 microform titles, 217 periodicals, 7 CD-ROMs, 1,103 records, tapes, and CDs. Acquisition spending 1994–95: $1.3 million.

COMPUTERS ON CAMPUS 207 computers for student use in computer center, computer labs, learning resource center, classrooms, library provide access to main academic computer, on-line services. Staffed computer lab on campus provides training in use of computers, software. Academic computing expenditure 1994–95: $1.4 million.

COLLEGE LIFE 15% vote in student government elections. ***Student services:*** personal-psychological counseling, women's center. ***Campus security:*** 24-hour emergency response devices, late-night transport-escort service.

HOUSING College housing not available.

ATHLETICS Member NJCAA. ***Intercollegiate:*** golf M/W, tennis M/W. ***Intramural:*** basketball, bowling, equestrian sports, field hockey, football, golf, skiing (cross-country), skiing (downhill), swimming and diving, volleyball.

CAREER PLANNING ***Placement office:*** 1 full-time, 2 part-time staff. ***Director:*** Dr. David A. Young, Director of Placement and Transfer Services, 412-369-3631. ***Services:*** job fairs, resume preparation, resume referral, career counseling, careers library, job bank, job interviews.

AFTER GRADUATION 28% of students completing a degree program in 1994–95 went directly on to further study.

EXPENSES FOR 1996–97 Area resident tuition: $2040 full-time, $68 per credit part-time. State resident tuition: $4080 full-time, $136 per credit part-time. Nonresident tuition: $6120 full-time, $204 per credit part-time. Part-time mandatory fees: $74 per year. Full-time mandatory fees: $127.

FINANCIAL AID ***College-administered undergrad aid 1995–96:*** 794 need-based scholarships (average $454), 21 non-need scholarships (average $450), low-interest long-term loans from external sources (average $1500), Federal Work-Study, part-time jobs. ***Required forms:*** state, institutional, FAFSA; accepted: CSS Financial Aid PROFILE. ***Priority deadline:*** 5/1. ***Payment plan:*** deferred payment. ***Waivers:*** full or partial for employees or children of employees.

APPLYING Open admission except for nursing program. ***Options:*** Common Application, early entrance, deferred entrance. ***Recommended:*** school transcript. ***Application deadline:*** rolling. ***Notification:*** continuous.

APPLYING/TRANSFER ***Recommended:*** high school transcript, college transcript. ***Entrance:*** noncompetitive. ***Application deadline:*** rolling. ***Notification:*** continuous. ***Contact:*** Dr. David Young, Director of Placement and Transfer, 412-369-3631.

CONTACT Mr. Ray Oyler, Director of Admissions, Community College of Allegheny County North Campus, Pittsburgh, PA 15237-5353, 412-369-3641. College video available.

❖ *See page 730 for a narrative description.* ❖

COMMUNITY COLLEGE OF ALLEGHENY COUNTY SOUTH CAMPUS
West Mifflin, Pennsylvania

UG Enrollment: 4,567	**Tuition & Fees (Area Res): $2167**
Application Deadline: rolling	**Room & Board: N/Avail**

GENERAL County-supported, 2-year, coed. Part of Community Colleges of Allegheny County System. Awards certificates, transfer associate, terminal associate degrees. Founded 1967. ***Setting:*** 200-acre small-town campus with easy access to Pittsburgh. ***Total enrollment:*** 4,567. ***Faculty:*** 428 (82 full-time, 91% with terminal degrees, 346 part-time).

ENROLLMENT PROFILE 4,567 students: 60% women, 40% men, 61% part-time, 99% state residents, 11% transferred in, 1% international, 40% 25 or older, 1% Native American, 1% Hispanic, 3% African American, 1% Asian American. ***Areas of study chosen:*** 43% liberal arts/general studies, 26% health professions and related sciences, 13% business management and administrative services, 7% education, 3% physical sciences, 3% social sciences, 2% engineering and applied sciences, 1% agriculture, 1% performing arts, 1% vocational and home economics. ***Most popular recent majors:*** liberal arts/general studies, business administration/commerce/management.

FIRST-YEAR CLASS 1,645 total; 2,398 applied, 98% were accepted, 70% of whom enrolled.

ACADEMIC PROGRAM Core. Calendar: semesters. 201 courses offered in 1995–96; average class size 19 in required courses. Academic remediation for entering students, English as a second language program offered during academic year and summer, services for LD students, advanced placement, self-designed majors, honors program, summer session for credit, part-time degree program (daytime, evenings, weekends, summer), adult/continuing education programs, co-op programs. Off-campus study at members of the Pittsburgh Council on Higher Education. Study abroad in England, Italy, France (1% of students participate). ROTC: Army (c), Air Force (c).

GENERAL DEGREE REQUIREMENT 63 credits.

MAJORS Accounting, advertising, anthropology, applied art, architectural technologies, art education, art/fine arts, automotive technologies, behavioral sciences, biology/biological sciences, botany/plant sciences, business administration/commerce/management, business education, business machine technologies, chemical engineering technology, chemistry, child care/child and family studies, child psychology/child development, civil engineering technology, commercial art, communication, communication equipment technology, computer information systems, computer management, computer programming, computer science, computer technologies, construction management, construction technologies, corrections, creative writing, criminal justice, data processing, drafting and design, early childhood education, earth science, economics, education, electrical and electronics technologies, electrical engineering technology, electromechanical technology, electronics engineering technology, elementary education, energy management technologies, engineering (general), engineering and applied sciences, engineering design, engineering sciences, (pre)engineering sequence, engineering technology, English, environmental engineering technology, fashion merchandising, finance/banking, graphic arts, heating/refrigeration/air conditioning, history, horticulture, human development, humanities, human resources, human services, industrial arts, industrial design, industrial engineering technology, information science, instrumentation technology, interdisciplinary studies, journalism, laboratory technologies, landscape architecture/design, landscaping/grounds maintenance, law enforcement/police sciences, legal secretarial studies, liberal arts/general studies, literature, management information systems, manufacturing technology, marketing/retailing/merchandising, mathematics, mechanical design technology, mechanical engineering technology, medical assistant technologies, medical laboratory technology, medical secretarial studies, medical technology, music, nursing, optometric/ophthalmic technologies, ornamental horticulture, painting/drawing, pharmacy/pharmaceutical sciences, philosophy, photography, physical fitness/exercise science, physics, political science/government, printing technologies, psychology, public administration, real estate, retail management, robotics, science, science education, secretarial studies/office management, social science, social work, sociology, solar technologies, surveying technology, teacher aide studies, technical writing, theater arts/drama, vocational education, welding technology, Western civilization and culture.

LIBRARY E.R. Crawford Library with 56,896 books, 654 microform titles, 433 periodicals, 1 on-line bibliographic service, 16 CD-ROMs, 3,468 records, tapes, and CDs. Acquisition spending 1994–95: $1.2 million.

COMPUTERS ON CAMPUS 460 computers for student use in computer center, computer labs, learning resource center, various locations throughout campus, classrooms, library provide access to main academic computer, on-line services. Staffed computer lab on campus provides training in use of computers, software. Academic computing expenditure 1994–95: $980,839.

COLLEGE LIFE Drama-theater group, choral group, student-run newspaper, radio station. 15% vote in student government elections. ***Student services:*** health clinic, personal-psychological counseling, women's center. ***Campus security:*** 24-hour emergency response devices, late-night transport-escort service.

HOUSING College housing not available.

ATHLETICS Member NJCAA. ***Intercollegiate:*** basketball M/W, golf M/W, volleyball M/W. ***Intramural:*** badminton, bowling, football, racquetball, tennis, volleyball, weight lifting.

CAREER PLANNING ***Placement office:*** 2 full-time staff. ***Director:*** Ms. Judy McAdoo, Dir. of Career Planning, Placement and Cooperative Ed., 412-469-6213. ***Services:*** job fairs, resume preparation, resume referral, career counseling, careers library, job bank, job interviews.

AFTER GRADUATION 28% of students completing a degree program in 1994–95 went directly on to further study.

EXPENSES FOR 1996–97 Area resident tuition: $2040 full-time, $68 per credit part-time. State resident tuition: $4080 full-time, $136 per credit part-time. Nonresident tuition: $6120 full-time, $204 per credit part-time. Part-time mandatory fees: $74 per year. Full-time mandatory fees: $127.

FINANCIAL AID ***College-administered undergrad aid 1995–96:*** 1,257 need-based scholarships (average $407), non-need scholarships (average $300), low-interest long-term loans from external sources, Federal Work-Study. ***Required forms:*** state, institutional, FAFSA; accepted: CSS Financial Aid PROFILE. ***Priority deadline:*** 5/1. ***Payment plan:*** deferred payment. ***Waivers:*** full or partial for employees or children of employees. ***Notification:*** continuous.

APPLYING Open admission except for engineering, allied health programs. ***Options:*** Common Application, early entrance, deferred entrance. ***Recommended:*** school transcript. ***Application deadline:*** rolling. ***Notification:*** continuous.

APPLYING/TRANSFER ***Recommended:*** high school transcript, college transcript. ***Entrance:*** noncompetitive. ***Application deadline:*** rolling. ***Notification:*** continuous. ***Contact:*** Ms. Pam Young, Transfer Counselor, 412-469-6346.

CONTACT Ms. Olga Ellsworth, Acting Director of Admissions, Community College of Allegheny County South Campus, West Mifflin, PA 15122-3029, 412-469-4301. College video available.

❖ *See page 730 for a narrative description.* ❖

COMMUNITY COLLEGE OF BEAVER COUNTY
Monaca, Pennsylvania

UG Enrollment: 2,497	**Tuition & Fees (Area Res): $2030**
Application Deadline: rolling	**Room & Board: N/Avail**

GENERAL State-supported, 2-year, coed. Awards certificates, diplomas, transfer associate, terminal associate degrees. Founded 1966. ***Setting:*** 75-acre small-town campus with easy access to Pittsburgh. ***Total enrollment:*** 2,497. ***Faculty:*** 150 (60 full-time, 90 part-time); student-faculty ratio is 20:1.
ENROLLMENT PROFILE 2,497 students from 19 states and territories, 1 other country. 55% women, 49% part-time, 94% state residents, 5% transferred in, 1% international, 56% 25 or older, 1% Native American, 0% Hispanic, 5% African American, 0% Asian American. ***Most popular recent majors:*** nursing, aviation technology, liberal arts/general studies.
FIRST-YEAR CLASS 807 total; 958 applied, 100% were accepted, 84% of whom enrolled. 10% from top 10% of their high school class, 20% from top quarter, 50% from top half.
ACADEMIC PROGRAM Core. Calendar: semesters. Academic remediation for entering students, services for LD students, summer session for credit, part-time degree program (daytime, evenings, summer), adult/continuing education programs, internships. Off-campus study at Geneva College, Pennsylvania State University Beaver Campus, La Roche College, Robert Morris College.
GENERAL DEGREE REQUIREMENTS 60 credits; math/science requirements vary according to program; internship (some majors).
MAJORS Accounting, aerospace sciences, air traffic control, architectural technologies, aviation technology, biology/biological sciences, business administration/commerce/management, communication equipment technology, computer information systems, computer programming, criminal justice, culinary arts, data processing, drafting and design, education, electrical and electronics technologies, environmental studies, flight training, industrial arts, information science, law enforcement/police sciences, liberal arts/general studies, manufacturing technology, marketing/retailing/merchandising, medical laboratory technology, medical secretarial studies, nursing, practical nursing, public relations, robotics, secretarial studies/office management, surveying technology, telecommunications, word processing.
LIBRARY 60,000 books, 322 periodicals, 1,200 records, tapes, and CDs.
COMPUTERS ON CAMPUS 66 computers for student use in computer center, learning resource center, library provide access to main academic computer. Staffed computer lab on campus provides training in use of computers, software.
COLLEGE LIFE ***Social organizations:*** 2 local fraternities, 1 local sorority; 1% of eligible men and 2% of eligible women are members.
HOUSING College housing not available.
ATHLETICS Member NJCAA. ***Intercollegiate:*** baseball M, basketball M, golf M/W, softball W, tennis M/W, volleyball W. ***Intramural:*** basketball, golf, table tennis (Ping-Pong), volleyball.
CAREER PLANNING ***Placement office:*** 1 full-time staff. ***Director:*** Ms. Ann Bender, Assistant to the Director of Career Planning, 412-775-8561 Ext. 276. ***Services:*** resume preparation, resume referral, career counseling, careers library, job bank.
AFTER GRADUATION 59% of students completing a degree program in 1994–95 went directly on to further study.
EXPENSES FOR 1996–97 ***Application fee:*** $25. Area resident tuition: $1980 full-time, $66 per credit part-time. State resident tuition: $4260 full-time, $142 per credit part-time. Nonresident tuition: $6540 full-time, $218 per credit part-time. Part-time mandatory fees: $25 per semester. Full-time mandatory fees: $50.
FINANCIAL AID ***College-administered undergrad aid 1995–96:*** need-based scholarships, 48 non-need scholarships (average $1200), short-term loans (average $200), low-interest long-term loans from external sources (average $2000), Federal Work-Study, part-time jobs. ***Required forms:*** state, institutional; accepted: CSS Financial Aid PROFILE, FAFSA. ***Application deadline:*** continuous. ***Payment plan:*** deferred payment. ***Waivers:*** full or partial for senior citizens.
APPLYING Open admission except for nursing, medical laboratory technology programs. ***Option:*** early entrance. ***Recommended:*** school transcript. ***Required for some:*** 3 years of high school math and science, ACT, nursing exam. Test scores used for counseling/placement. ***Application deadline:*** rolling. ***Notification:*** continuous.
APPLYING/TRANSFER ***Required:*** high school transcript. ***Entrance:*** noncompetitive. ***Application deadline:*** rolling. ***Notification:*** continuous.
CONTACT Mr. Scott Ensworth, Director of Admissions, Community College of Beaver County, One Campus Drive, Monaca, PA 15061-2588, 412-775-8561 Ext. 101.

COMMUNITY COLLEGE OF PHILADELPHIA
Philadelphia, Pennsylvania

UG Enrollment: 18,713	Tuition & Fees (Area Res): $2025
Application Deadline: rolling	Room & Board: N/Avail

GENERAL State and locally supported, 2-year, coed. Awards certificates, diplomas, transfer associate, terminal associate degrees. Founded 1964. ***Setting:*** 14-acre urban campus. ***Total enrollment:*** 18,713. ***Faculty:*** 1,182 (372 full-time, 810 part-time); student-faculty ratio is 22:1.
ENROLLMENT PROFILE 18,713 students: 66% women, 71% part-time, 99% state residents, 3% transferred in, 38% have need-based financial aid, 53% 25 or older, 1% Native American, 5% Hispanic, 42% African American, 7% Asian American. ***Most popular recent majors:*** liberal arts/general studies, nursing, business administration/commerce/management.
FIRST-YEAR CLASS 4,125 total; 8,018 applied, 100% were accepted, 51% of whom enrolled.
ACADEMIC PROGRAM Core. Calendar: semesters. Academic remediation for entering students, English as a second language program offered during academic year and summer, services for LD students, self-designed majors, honors program, summer session for credit, part-time degree program (daytime, evenings, weekends, summer), adult/continuing education programs, internships.
GENERAL DEGREE REQUIREMENTS 62 credits; 1 math course; computer course for most majors.
MAJORS Accounting, architectural technologies, art/fine arts, automotive technologies, biomedical technologies, business administration/commerce/management, business education, chemical engineering technology, communication equipment technology, community services, computer science, computer technologies, construction technologies, criminal justice, culinary arts, data processing, deaf interpreter training, dental services, dietetics, drafting and design, early childhood education, education, electronics engineering technology, engineering (general), (pre)engineering sequence, engineering technology, environmental engineering technology, fashion merchandising, finance/banking, fire science, food services management, gerontology, hotel and restaurant management, international business, legal secretarial studies, liberal arts/general studies, library science, marketing/retailing/merchandising, medical assistant technologies, medical laboratory technology, medical records services, medical secretarial studies, mental health/rehabilitation counseling, music, nursing, nutrition, paralegal studies, photography, radiological technology, real estate, respiratory therapy, retail management, science, secretarial studies/office management.
LIBRARY 92,698 books, 27,240 microform titles, 376 periodicals, 579 records, tapes, and CDs. Acquisition spending 1994–95: $832,022.
COMPUTERS ON CAMPUS 350 computers for student use in learning lab, classrooms, library provide access to off-campus computing facilities. Staffed computer lab on campus provides training in use of computers.
COLLEGE LIFE Drama-theater group, choral group, student-run newspaper, radio station. ***Social organizations:*** 40 open to all. ***Student services:*** health clinic, personal-psychological counseling, women's center. ***Campus security:*** 24-hour emergency response devices and patrols.
HOUSING College housing not available.
ATHLETICS ***Intercollegiate:*** baseball M, basketball M/W, cross-country running M/W, soccer M, softball W, tennis M/W, volleyball W. ***Intramural:*** basketball, soccer, tennis, track and field, volleyball. ***Contact:*** Mr. James J. Burton, Director of Athletics, 215-751-8965.
CAREER PLANNING ***Placement office:*** 2 full-time staff. ***Director:*** Mr. Chet Rispoli, Director of Career Planning and Placement, 215-751-8165. ***Services:*** job fairs, resume preparation, resume referral, career counseling, careers library, job interviews.
EXPENSES FOR 1995–96 Area resident tuition: $1980 full-time, $66 per credit hour part-time. State resident tuition: $3960 full-time, $132 per credit hour part-time. Nonresident tuition: $5940 full-time, $198 per credit hour part-time. Part-time mandatory fees: $1.50 per credit hour. Full-time mandatory fees: $45.
FINANCIAL AID ***College-administered undergrad aid 1995–96:*** 1,972 need-based scholarships (average $991), 89 non-need scholarships (average $1438), short-term loans (average $393), low-interest long-term loans from external sources (average $1637), Federal Work-Study, 371 part-time jobs. ***Required forms:*** institutional, FAFSA; accepted: CSS Financial Aid PROFILE, state. ***Priority deadline:*** 5/1. ***Waivers:*** full or partial for employees or children of employees and senior citizens.
APPLYING Open admission except for allied health, mental health/social service, engineering science programs. ***Options:*** early entrance, deferred entrance. ***Required for some:*** school transcript. Test scores used for admission. ***Application deadline:*** rolling. ***Notification:*** continuous. Preference given to city residents.
APPLYING/TRANSFER ***Required for some:*** high school transcript. ***Application deadline:*** rolling. ***Notification:*** continuous.
CONTACT Mr. Gordon K. Holly, Director of Admissions and Recruitment, Community College of Philadelphia, 1700 Spring Garden Street, Philadelphia, PA 19130-3991, 215-751-8233. ***Fax:*** 215-972-6361. College video available.

DEAN INSTITUTE OF TECHNOLOGY
Pittsburgh, Pennsylvania

UG Enrollment: 200	Tuition: $9720/deg prog
Application Deadline: rolling	Room & Board: N/Avail

GENERAL Proprietary, 2-year, coed. Awards terminal associate degrees. Founded 1947. ***Setting:*** 2-acre urban campus. ***Total enrollment:*** 200. ***Faculty:*** 18 (50% of full-time faculty have terminal degrees); student-faculty ratio is 10:1.

ENROLLMENT PROFILE 200 students from 3 states and territories, 1 other country. 10% women, 36% part-time, 98% state residents, 10% transferred in, 90% have need-based financial aid, 0% have non-need-based financial aid, 15% 25 or older, 15% African American.

FIRST-YEAR CLASS 100 total. Of the students who applied, 96% were accepted, 95% of whom enrolled. 10% from top half of their high school class.

ACADEMIC PROGRAM Core. Calendar: quarters. English as a second language program, part-time degree program (evenings).

GENERAL DEGREE REQUIREMENTS 30 courses; 1 math course; computer course.

MAJORS Drafting and design, electromechanical technology.

LIBRARY 2,500 books, 25 periodicals, 50 records, tapes, and CDs. Acquisition spending 1994–95: $4940.

COMPUTERS ON CAMPUS 10 computers for student use in computer center. Academic computing expenditure 1994–95: $21,350.

COLLEGE LIFE ***Campus security:*** 24-hour emergency response devices.

HOUSING College housing not available.

CAREER PLANNING ***Placement office:*** $12,800 operating expenditure 1994–95. ***Service:*** career counseling.

AFTER GRADUATION 2% of students completing a degree program in 1994–95 went directly on to further study.

EXPENSES FOR 1996–97 ***Application fee:*** $50. Tuition: $9720 per degree program. One-time mandatory fee: $50. Part-time tuition: $4500 per year. Tuition guaranteed not to increase for student's term of enrollment.

FINANCIAL AID ***College-administered undergrad aid 1995–96:*** 38 need-based scholarships (average $2300), low-interest long-term loans from external sources (average $2625). ***Required forms:*** institutional; required for some: state, FAFSA. ***Priority deadline:*** 7/1. ***Payment plan:*** installment.

APPLYING Open admission. ***Options:*** early entrance, deferred entrance, midyear entrance. ***Application deadline:*** rolling.

APPLYING/TRANSFER ***Application deadline:*** rolling. ***Contact:*** Mr. William C. Nichie, Admissions Director, 412-531-4433.

CONTACT Mr. William C. Nichie, Admissions Director, Dean Institute of Technology, 1501 West Liberty Avenue, Pittsburgh, PA 15226-1103, 412-531-4433. ***Fax:*** 412-531-4435.

DELAWARE COUNTY COMMUNITY COLLEGE
Media, Pennsylvania

UG Enrollment: 9,807	**Tuition & Fees (Area Res): $2040**
Application Deadline: rolling	**Room & Board: N/Avail**

DCCC is a large college (about 10,000 students) with a warm small-college atmosphere. State-of-the-art information technology on campus; outstanding labs for electronic design, math/science, computer-aided drafting, and other areas. More than 50 programs of study in both university transfer and career areas. Special transfer agreements with 40 colleges.

GENERAL State and locally supported, 2-year, coed. Awards certificates, transfer associate, terminal associate degrees. Founded 1967. ***Setting:*** 125-acre suburban campus with easy access to Philadelphia. ***Total enrollment:*** 9,807. ***Faculty:*** 438 (123 full-time, 14% with terminal degrees, 315 part-time); student-faculty ratio is 24:1.
ENROLLMENT PROFILE 9,807 students: 54% women, 46% men, 68% part-time, 99% state residents, 20% have need-based financial aid, 4% have non-need-based financial aid, 1% international, 48% 25 or older, 1% Native American, 1% Hispanic, 9% African American, 3% Asian American. ***Most popular recent majors:*** liberal arts/general studies, business administration/commerce/management, nursing.
FIRST-YEAR CLASS 3,046 total; 4,029 applied, 100% were accepted, 76% of whom enrolled.
ACADEMIC PROGRAM Honor code. Calendar: semesters. Academic remediation for entering students, English as a second language program offered during academic year, services for LD students, advanced placement, self-designed majors, tutorials, summer session for credit, part-time degree program (daytime, evenings, weekends), adult/continuing education programs, co-op programs and internships. Study-abroad program.
GENERAL DEGREE REQUIREMENT 60 credit hours.
MAJORS Accounting, architectural technologies, biomedical technologies, business administration/commerce/management, computer information systems, computer programming, computer science, computer technologies, construction technologies, criminal justice, drafting and design, early childhood education, electrical and electronics technologies, energy management technologies, (pre)engineering sequence, finance/banking, fire science, graphic arts, health services administration, heating/refrigeration/air conditioning, hotel and restaurant management, insurance, liberal arts/general studies, management information systems, mechanical engineering technology, medical assistant technologies, natural sciences, nursing, operating room technology, plastics technology, respiratory therapy, retail management, robotics, secretarial studies/office management, telecommunications.
LIBRARY 72,905 books, 23,000 microform titles, 480 periodicals, 5 CD-ROMs, 3,000 records, tapes, and CDs. Acquisition spending 1994–95: $548,629.
COMPUTERS ON CAMPUS Computer purchase plan available. 250 computers for student use in computer center, computer labs, learning resource center, labs, classrooms, library provide access to main academic computer, off-campus computing facilities, e-mail, on-line services, Internet. Staffed computer lab on campus provides training in use of computers, software. Academic computing expenditure 1994–95: $452,869.
COLLEGE LIFE Drama-theater group, choral group, student-run radio station. ***Social organizations:*** 15 open to all. ***Most popular organizations:*** Student Government, Student Radio Station. ***Major annual events:*** Springfest, Health Fair, Career Fairs. ***Student services:*** health clinic, personal-psychological counseling. ***Campus security:*** 24-hour emergency response devices and patrols, late-night transport-escort service.
HOUSING College housing not available.
ATHLETICS Member NJCAA. ***Intercollegiate:*** baseball M, basketball M/W, golf M/W, soccer M, softball W, tennis M/W, volleyball M/W. ***Intramural:*** basketball, bowling, cross-country running, tennis, volleyball. ***Contact:*** Ms. Cheryl Massaro, Coordinator of Athletics, 610-359-5047.
CAREER PLANNING ***Placement office:*** 4 full-time staff; $858,605 operating expenditure 1994–95. ***Director:*** Dr. Grant S. Snyder, Director of Career and Counseling Center, 610-359-5060. ***Services:*** job fairs, resume preparation, resume referral, career counseling, careers library, job bank. Students must register sophomore year.
AFTER GRADUATION 71% of students completing a degree program in 1994–95 went directly on to further study.
EXPENSES FOR 1996–97 ***Application fee:*** $20. Area resident tuition: $2010 full-time, $67 per credit hour part-time. State resident tuition: $3900 full-time, $130 per credit hour part-time. Nonresident tuition: $6420 full-time, $214 per credit hour part-time. Part-time mandatory fees: $15 per semester. Full-time mandatory fees: $30.
FINANCIAL AID ***College-administered undergrad aid 1995–96:*** need-based scholarships (average $400), 25 non-need scholarships (average $750), short-term loans, low-interest long-term loans from external sources (average $2500), 100 Federal Work-Study (averaging $1600), 140 part-time jobs. ***Required forms:*** state, institutional, FAFSA; accepted: CSS Financial Aid PROFILE. ***Priority deadline:*** 5/1. ***Payment plan:*** deferred payment. ***Waivers:*** full or partial for employees or children of employees and senior citizens. ***Notification:*** continuous.
APPLYING Open admission except for allied health programs, international students. ***Options:*** early entrance, deferred entrance, midyear entrance. ***Required:*** school transcript. ***Recommended:*** TOEFL for international students. Test scores used for counseling/placement. ***Application deadline:*** rolling. ***Notification:*** continuous. Preference given to residents of sponsoring school districts.
APPLYING/TRANSFER ***Required:*** high school transcript. ***Entrance:*** noncompetitive. ***Application deadline:*** rolling. ***Notification:*** continuous.
CONTACT Ms. Betty Brown, Director of Admissions, Delaware County Community College, Media, PA 19063-1094, 610-359-5333. ***E-mail:*** admiss@dcccnet.dccc.edu.

❖ *See page 734 for a narrative description.* ❖

DUBOIS BUSINESS COLLEGE
DuBois, Pennsylvania

UG Enrollment: 230	**Tuition & Fees: $5425**
Application Deadline: rolling	**Room & Board: N/Avail**

GENERAL Proprietary, 2-year, primarily women. Awards diplomas, terminal associate degrees. Founded 1885. ***Setting:*** 4-acre small-town campus. ***Total enrollment:*** 230. ***Faculty:*** 18 (13 full-time, 5 part-time); student-faculty ratio is 15:1. ***Notable Alumni:*** William Mauthe, CPA; Gary Vetro, owner of Developac; Jakki Strickland, general manager of Hampton Inn; Terry LaBorde, owner of Keystone Financial Services; Wendy Sperling, personnel manager of United Electric.
ENROLLMENT PROFILE 230 students: 80% women, 1% part-time, 98% state residents, 4% transferred in, 40% 25 or older, 0% Native American, 0% Hispanic, 0% African American, 2% Asian American. ***Areas of study chosen:*** 100% business management and administrative services. ***Most popular recent majors:*** medical secretarial studies, accounting, computer management.
FIRST-YEAR CLASS 80 total. 20% from top 10% of their high school class, 40% from top half.
ACADEMIC PROGRAM Core, honor code. Calendar: quarters. Academic remediation for entering students, summer session for credit, part-time degree program (daytime).
GENERAL DEGREE REQUIREMENTS 78 credits; computer course.
MAJORS Accounting, computer management, legal secretarial studies, medical secretarial studies, secretarial studies/office management.
LIBRARY 2,100 books, 10 periodicals, 40 records, tapes, and CDs.
COMPUTERS ON CAMPUS 110 computers for student use in 5 information processing centers provide access to main academic computer, e-mail, on-line services, Internet. Staffed computer lab on campus provides training in use of computers, software.
COLLEGE LIFE Student-run newspaper. 100% vote in student government elections. ***Social organizations:*** 1 local fraternity, 1 local sorority; 50% of eligible men and 50% of eligible women are members. ***Major annual events:*** Presidents Day Picnic, Annual Christmas Party, Academic Field Trip Day. ***Student services:*** personal-psychological counseling.
HOUSING College housing not available.
ATHLETICS ***Intramural:*** badminton, volleyball.
CAREER PLANNING ***Placement office:*** 1 full-time staff. ***Director:*** Ms. Robin Polohonki, Placement Director, 814-371-6920. ***Services:*** job fairs, resume preparation, resume referral, career counseling, careers library, job bank, job interviews. Students must register sophomore year. 50 organizations recruited on campus 1994–95.
AFTER GRADUATION 97% of class of 1994 had job offers within 6 months.
EXPENSES FOR 1996–97 ***Application fee:*** $25. Tuition: $5100 full-time, $135 per credit part-time. Full-time mandatory fees: $325.
FINANCIAL AID ***College-administered undergrad aid 1995–96:*** need-based scholarships, low-interest long-term loans from external sources. ***Required forms for some financial aid applicants:*** state, FAFSA. ***Application deadline:*** continuous to 8/1. ***Payment plan:*** installment. ***Waivers:*** full or partial for employees or children of employees.
APPLYING ***Options:*** Common Application, deferred entrance. ***Required:*** school transcript, campus interview. ***Recommended:*** recommendations. ***Application deadline:*** rolling. ***Notification:*** continuous.
APPLYING/TRANSFER ***Required:*** high school transcript, campus interview, college transcript. ***Recommended:*** recommendations. ***Required for some:*** minimum 2.0 college GPA. ***Entrance:*** minimally difficult. ***Application deadline:*** rolling. ***Notification:*** continuous. ***Contact:*** Mrs. Jackie Syktich, Director, 814-371-6920.
CONTACT Mr. Joe Jacob, Admissions Representative, DuBois Business College, DuBois, PA 15801-2401, 814-371-6920 or toll-free 800-692-6213 (in-state). College video available.

DUFF'S BUSINESS INSTITUTE
Pittsburgh, Pennsylvania

UG Enrollment: 600	**Tuition: $11,700/deg prog**
Application Deadline: rolling	**Room & Board: N/Avail**

GENERAL Proprietary, 2-year, primarily women. Part of Phillips Colleges, Inc. Awards diplomas, transfer associate, terminal associate degrees. Founded 1840. ***Setting:*** urban campus. ***Total enrollment:*** 600. ***Faculty:*** 21 (15 full-time, 6 part-time); student-faculty ratio is 21:1.
ENROLLMENT PROFILE 600 students from 3 states and territories. 87% women, 15% part-time, 95% state residents, 10% transferred in, 40% 25 or older, 35% African American.
FIRST-YEAR CLASS 125 total. Of the students who applied, 85% were accepted, 93% of whom enrolled. 10% from top 10% of their high school class, 20% from top quarter, 45% from top half.
ACADEMIC PROGRAM Core. Calendar: quarters. Academic remediation for entering students, advanced placement, tutorials, summer session for credit, part-time degree program (daytime, evenings), adult/continuing education programs, co-op programs and internships.
GENERAL DEGREE REQUIREMENTS 103 credits; internship (some majors).
MAJORS Accounting, business administration/commerce/management, computer programming, court reporting, fashion merchandising, legal secretarial studies, medical assistant technologies, medical secretarial studies, paralegal studies, secretarial studies/office management.
LIBRARY Main library plus 1 other, with 7,500 books, 30 periodicals, 300 records, tapes, and CDs.
COMPUTERS ON CAMPUS 80 computers for student use in classrooms.
COLLEGE LIFE Orientation program (2 days). ***Student services:*** personal-psychological counseling. ***Campus security:*** 24-hour emergency response devices.
HOUSING College housing not available.
ATHLETICS ***Intramural:*** basketball.
CAREER PLANNING ***Placement office:*** 2 full-time, 1 part-time staff. ***Director:*** Ms. Ann Hummel, Director of Graduate Placement, 412-261-4526. ***Services:*** job fairs, resume preparation, resume referral, career counseling, careers library, job bank, job interviews. Students must register sophomore year.
AFTER GRADUATION 10% of students completing a degree program in 1994–95 went directly on to further study.
EXPENSES FOR 1995–96 ***Application fee:*** $25. Tuition per degree program ranges from $11,700 to $18,000. Part-time tuition per course: $375. Tuition guaranteed not to increase for student's term of enrollment.
FINANCIAL AID ***College-administered undergrad aid 1995–96:*** 6 need-based scholarships (average $3500), low-interest long-term loans from external sources, Federal Work-Study, 30 part-time jobs. ***Required forms:*** state, institutional; accepted: CSS Financial Aid PROFILE. ***Priority deadline:*** 9/1. ***Payment plan:*** installment.

APPLYING ***Options:*** deferred entrance, midyear entrance. ***Required:*** CPAt. Test scores used for admission. ***Application deadline:*** rolling.
APPLYING/TRANSFER ***Application deadline:*** rolling.
CONTACT Mr. Marc Scott, Director of School, Duff's Business Institute, 110 Ninth Street, Pittsburgh, PA 15222-3618, 412-261-4528 or toll-free 800-222-DUFF (in-state). ***Fax:*** 412-261-4546.

ELECTRONIC INSTITUTE
Middletown, Pennsylvania

UG Enrollment: 109	**Tuition & Fees: $5430**
Application Deadline: rolling	**Room & Board: N/Avail**

GENERAL Independent, 2-year, coed. Awards transfer associate, terminal associate degrees. Founded 1959. ***Setting:*** small-town campus. ***Total enrollment:*** 109. ***Faculty:*** 8 (all full-time); student-faculty ratio is 15:1.
ENROLLMENT PROFILE 109 students: 3% women, 97% men, 0% part-time, 100% state residents, 2% transferred in, 0% international, 14% 25 or older, 0% Native American, 1% Hispanic, 1% African American, 2% Asian American. ***Areas of study chosen:*** 100% engineering and applied sciences.
FIRST-YEAR CLASS 28 total; 35 applied, 89% were accepted, 90% of whom enrolled.
ACADEMIC PROGRAM Core. Calendar: trimesters. Academic remediation for entering students.
GENERAL DEGREE REQUIREMENTS 152 credits; 16 credits of math; 8 credits of science; computer course.
MAJORS Computer technologies, electronics engineering technology.
COMPUTERS ON CAMPUS 32 computers for student use in computer center, computer labs, library. Staffed computer lab on campus provides training in use of computers, software.
COLLEGE LIFE ***Student services:*** personal-psychological counseling.
HOUSING College housing not available.
CAREER PLANNING ***Placement office:*** 1 full-time staff. ***Director:*** Mr. Joseph Schauerman, Placement Director, 717-944-2731. ***Services:*** job fairs, resume preparation, resume referral, career counseling, job bank, job interviews.
AFTER GRADUATION 98% of class of 1994 had job offers within 6 months.
EXPENSES FOR 1996–97 Tuition: $5280 full-time. Full-time mandatory fees: $150. Tuition guaranteed not to increase for student's term of enrollment.
FINANCIAL AID ***College-administered undergrad aid 1995–96:*** need-based scholarships, 10 non-need scholarships (average $3375), low-interest long-term loans from external sources. ***Required forms:*** state, FAFSA. ***Application deadline:*** continuous to 8/1. ***Waivers:*** full or partial for employees or children of employees.
APPLYING ***Options:*** deferred entrance, midyear entrance. ***Required:*** school transcript, 1 year of high school algebra. ***Application deadline:*** rolling.
APPLYING/TRANSFER ***Required:*** college transcript. ***Application deadline:*** rolling. ***Contact:*** Mr. William F. Margut, Director, 717-944-2731.
CONTACT Mr. Robert Nickoloff, Admissions Officer, Electronic Institute, Middletown, PA 17057-4851, 717-944-2731 or toll-free 800-884-2731. ***Fax:*** 717-944-2734.

ELECTRONIC INSTITUTES
Pittsburgh, Pennsylvania

UG Enrollment: 113	**Tuition & Fees: $5430**
Application Deadline: rolling	**Room & Board: N/Avail**

GENERAL Independent, 2-year, primarily men. Awards transfer associate, terminal associate degrees. Founded 1955. ***Setting:*** urban campus. ***Total enrollment:*** 113. ***Faculty:*** 8 (all full-time); student-faculty ratio is 12:1.
ENROLLMENT PROFILE 113 students from 3 states and territories. 6% women, 94% men, 0% part-time, 99% state residents, 2% transferred in, 0% international, 25% 25 or older, 0% Native American, 0% Hispanic, 16% African American, 0% Asian American.
FIRST-YEAR CLASS 57 total; 116 applied, 89% were accepted, 55% of whom enrolled. 2% from top 10% of their high school class, 15% from top quarter, 60% from top half.
ACADEMIC PROGRAM Core, honor code. Calendar: trimesters. Academic remediation for entering students, tutorials.
GENERAL DEGREE REQUIREMENT 152 credit hours.
MAJORS Computer technologies, electrical and electronics technologies, electronics engineering technology.
LIBRARY 3,000 books, 28 periodicals, 50 records, tapes, and CDs.
COMPUTERS ON CAMPUS 60 computers for student use in computer center, computer labs, classrooms, library. Staffed computer lab on campus provides training in use of computers, software.
COLLEGE LIFE Student-run newspaper. ***Major annual events:*** Christmas Blood Drive, Memorial Day Blood Drive. ***Student services:*** personal-psychological counseling. ***Campus security:*** 24-hour emergency response devices.
HOUSING College housing not available.
CAREER PLANNING ***Placement office:*** 2 full-time staff. ***Director:*** Mr. Matthew G. Wierzchowski, Director of Education, 412-521-8686. ***Services:*** resume preparation, resume referral, career counseling, careers library, job interviews. 45 organizations recruited on campus 1994–95.
AFTER GRADUATION 94% of class of 1994 had job offers within 6 months.
EXPENSES FOR 1996–97 ***Application fee:*** $10. Tuition: $5280 full-time. Full-time mandatory fees: $150. Tuition guaranteed not to increase for student's term of enrollment.
FINANCIAL AID ***College-administered undergrad aid 1995–96:*** need-based scholarships, low-interest long-term loans from external sources. ***Required forms:*** state. ***Priority deadline:*** 8/1. ***Waivers:*** full or partial for employees or children of employees.
APPLYING ***Options:*** deferred entrance, midyear entrance. ***Required:*** school transcript, campus interview, 1 course in high school algebra, Otis Employment Test. Test scores used for admission. ***Application deadline:*** rolling.
APPLYING/TRANSFER ***Required:*** high school transcript, campus interview, college transcript, 1 course in high school algebra. ***Application deadline:*** rolling. ***Contact:*** Mr. Ronald Kubitz, Director of Admissions, 412-521-8686.
CONTACT Mr. Ronald Kubitz, Director of Admissions, Electronic Institutes, 4634 Browns Hill Road, Pittsburgh, PA 15217-2919, 412-521-8686 or toll-free 800-721-8686 (in-state). ***Fax:*** 412-521-9277.

ERIE BUSINESS CENTER, MAIN
Erie, Pennsylvania

UG Enrollment: 353	**Tuition & Fees: $8685**
Application Deadline: rolling	**Room & Board: $4125**

GENERAL Proprietary, 2-year, coed. Awards terminal associate degrees. Founded 1884. ***Setting:*** 1-acre urban campus. ***Educational spending 1994–95:*** $1092 per undergrad. ***Total enrollment:*** 353. ***Faculty:*** 28 (15 full-time, 13 part-time); student-faculty ratio is 15:1. ***Notable Alumni:*** Marie Ednie, medical transcriptionist at Hamot Medical Center; Carol Salzer, medical assistant at Medicor Associates, Inc.; Judy Lyons, computer program specialist at Columbus Community College; Jennifer Funk, executive administrative assistant at Evans, Salata Architects.
ENROLLMENT PROFILE 353 students: 90% women, 10% men, 4% part-time, 95% state residents, 10% transferred in, 20% 25 or older, 0% Native American, 2% Hispanic, 11% African American, 0% Asian American. ***Areas of study chosen:*** 50% business management and administrative services, 40% education, 10% computer and information sciences. ***Most popular recent majors:*** accounting, medical secretarial studies, business administration/commerce/management.
FIRST-YEAR CLASS 210 total; 225 applied, 93% were accepted, 89% of whom enrolled. 5% from top 10% of their high school class, 25% from top quarter, 50% from top half.
ACADEMIC PROGRAM Core, business curriculum, honor code. Calendar: trimesters. 26 courses offered in 1995–96; average class size 20 in required courses. Academic remediation for entering students, tutorials, summer session for credit, part-time degree program (daytime, evenings), adult/continuing education programs, co-op programs and internships.
GENERAL DEGREE REQUIREMENTS 78 credits; 1 math course; computer course; internship.
MAJORS Accounting, business administration/commerce/management, computer information systems, computer science, equestrian studies, legal secretarial studies, marketing/retailing/merchandising, medical assistant technologies, medical secretarial studies, paralegal studies, secretarial studies/office management, tourism and travel.
LIBRARY EBC Blackmer Library with 338 books, 80 periodicals. Acquisition spending 1994–95: $2545.
COMPUTERS ON CAMPUS 44 computers for student use in computer center, labs. Staffed computer lab on campus provides training in use of computers, software. Academic computing expenditure 1994–95: $68,000.
COLLEGE LIFE Orientation program (2 days, parents included). Drama-theater group, student-run newspaper. 75% vote in student government elections. ***Social organizations:*** 1 open to all; 1 local sorority; 20% of eligible women are members. ***Most popular organization:*** Drama Club. ***Major annual event:*** Pre-Registration Activities. ***Student services:*** personal-psychological counseling. ***Campus security:*** 24-hour emergency response devices, trained security guard.
HOUSING 72 college housing spaces available; 36 were occupied 1995–96. Freshmen guaranteed college housing. On-campus residence required through sophomore year except if living with relatives. ***Option:*** coed (3 buildings) housing available. Resident assistants live in dorms.
CAREER PLANNING ***Placement office:*** 1 full-time staff; $23,000 operating expenditure 1994–95. ***Director:*** Ms. Joan Knobloch, Placement and Public Relations Coordinator, 814-456-7504. ***Services:*** resume preparation, resume referral, career counseling. 1 organization recruited on campus 1994–95.
AFTER GRADUATION 80% of class of 1994 had job offers within 6 months. 5% of students completing a degree program went directly on to further study.
EXPENSES FOR 1996–97 ***Application fee:*** $25. Comprehensive fee of $12,810 includes full-time tuition ($8100), mandatory fees ($585), and college room and board ($4125). College room only: $2850. Part-time tuition: $540 per course. Part-time mandatory fees: $30 per course.
FINANCIAL AID ***College-administered undergrad aid 1995–96:*** 50 need-based scholarships (average $600), 5 non-need scholarships (average $1650), low-interest long-term loans from external sources (average $2625), 10 Federal Work-Study (averaging $1350), 2 part-time jobs. ***Required forms:*** state, FAFSA; accepted: CSS Financial Aid PROFILE. ***Priority deadline:*** 8/1. ***Payment plans:*** installment, deferred payment.
APPLYING ***Options:*** deferred entrance, midyear entrance. ***Required:*** essay, school transcript, minimum 2.0 GPA, 3 years of high school math, interview, SAT I or ACT. ***Required for some:*** Wonderlic aptitude test. Test scores used for admission and counseling/placement. ***Application deadline:*** rolling. ***Notification:*** continuous.
APPLYING/TRANSFER ***Required:*** standardized test scores, high school transcript, 3 years of high school math, interview, college transcript, minimum 2.0 college GPA, minimum 2.0 high school GPA. ***Required for some:*** essay. ***Application deadline:*** rolling. ***Notification:*** continuous. ***Contact:*** Ms. Amy Tevis, Head of New Student Enrollments, 814-456-7504.
CONTACT Mr. Tony Piccirillo, Director of Personnel and Admissions, Erie Business Center, Main, 246 West Ninth Street, Erie, PA 16501-1392, 814-456-7504 or toll-free 800-352-ERIE. ***Fax:*** 814-456-4882. College video available.

ERIE BUSINESS CENTER SOUTH
New Castle, Pennsylvania

UG Enrollment: 80	**Tuition & Fees: $4360**
Application Deadline: rolling	**Room & Board: N/Avail**

GENERAL Proprietary, 2-year, coed. Awards transfer associate, terminal associate degrees. Founded 1894. ***Setting:*** 1-acre small-town campus with easy access to Pittsburgh. ***Total enrollment:*** 80. ***Faculty:*** 7 (4 full-time, 3 part-time); student-faculty ratio is 13:1.
ENROLLMENT PROFILE 80 students: 2% part-time. ***Areas of study chosen:*** 85% business management and administrative services, 15% computer and information sciences. ***Most popular recent majors:*** accounting, secretarial studies/office management, tourism and travel.
FIRST-YEAR CLASS 28 total.
ACADEMIC PROGRAM Core. Calendar: quarters. 116 courses offered in 1995–96. Academic remediation for entering students, tutorials, part-time degree program (daytime, summer), adult/continuing education programs, internships.
GENERAL DEGREE REQUIREMENTS 88 credit hours; 1 math course; computer course; internship.

Peterson's Guide to Two-Year Colleges 1997 561

Erie Business Center South (continued)
MAJORS Accounting, advertising, business administration/commerce/management, computer science, legal secretarial studies, marketing/retailing/merchandising, medical records services, medical secretarial studies, secretarial studies/office management, tourism and travel.
LIBRARY 1,606 books, 20 periodicals.
COMPUTERS ON CAMPUS 26 computers for student use in computer center, library.
COLLEGE LIFE ***Social organizations:*** 6 open to all. ***Most popular organizations:*** Student Government, Business Club, Medical Club, Travel Club, Ambassadors Club. ***Major annual events:*** Winter Formal, Christmas Party, Kennywood Park Fun Day. ***Student services:*** personal-psychological counseling. ***Campus security:*** 24-hour patrols.
HOUSING College housing not available.
ATHLETICS ***Intramural:*** basketball, bowling, softball, volleyball.
CAREER PLANNING ***Placement office:*** 2 part-time staff. ***Director:*** Ms. Irene G. Marburger, Director, 412-658-9066. ***Services:*** job fairs, resume preparation, resume referral, career counseling, job interviews.
EXPENSES FOR 1996–97 Tuition: $4140 full-time, $115 per credit part-time. Full-time mandatory fees: $220. Tuition guaranteed not to increase for student's term of enrollment.
FINANCIAL AID ***College-administered undergrad aid 1995–96:*** low-interest long-term loans from external sources (averaging $2625), part-time jobs. ***Required forms:*** state, institutional, FAFSA. ***Priority deadline:*** 8/1. ***Payment plan:*** installment. ***Waivers:*** full or partial for employees or children of employees.
APPLYING ***Options:*** Common Application, deferred entrance. ***Recommended:*** SAT I or ACT, SAT II Subject Tests. Test scores used for admission and counseling/placement. ***Application deadline:*** rolling.
APPLYING/TRANSFER ***Application deadline:*** rolling. ***Contact:*** Ms. Irene G. Marburger, Director, 412-658-9066.
CONTACT Mr. Dan Bickel, Admissions Director, Erie Business Center South, 700 Moravia Street, New Castle, PA 16101-3950, 412-658-9066. College video available.

HARCUM COLLEGE
Bryn Mawr, Pennsylvania

UG Enrollment: 661	**Tuition & Fees: $8450**
Application Deadline: rolling	**Room & Board: $4884**

Harcum College is a private college located 12 miles west of Philadelphia that enrolls more than 650 students, 94% of whom are women, in more than 16 degree-granting programs. Approximately 70% of Harcum students receive some sort of financial aid. Small class size and a faculty committed to teaching enable Harcum College to emphasize personal attention.

GENERAL Independent, 2-year, primarily women. Awards certificates, transfer associate, terminal associate degrees. Founded 1915. ***Setting:*** 12-acre suburban campus with easy access to Philadelphia. ***Endowment:*** $5.2 million. ***Research spending 1994–95:*** $14,624. ***Total enrollment:*** 661. ***Faculty:*** 91 (37 full-time, 54 part-time); student-faculty ratio is 12:1.
ENROLLMENT PROFILE 661 students from 11 states and territories, 8 other countries. 94% women, 6% men, 29% part-time, 78% state residents, 28% live on campus, 15% transferred in, 51% have need-based financial aid, 25% have non-need-based financial aid, 6% international, 23% 25 or older, 0% Native American, 1% Hispanic, 9% African American, 2% Asian American. ***Areas of study chosen:*** 63% health professions and related sciences, 16% interdisciplinary studies, 7% liberal arts/general studies, 6% education, 3% business management and administrative services, 3% fine arts, 1% communications and journalism, 1% computer and information sciences. ***Most popular recent majors:*** veterinary technology, physical therapy, occupational therapy.
FIRST-YEAR CLASS 107 total; 851 applied, 70% were accepted, 18% of whom enrolled. 40% from top half of their high school class.
ACADEMIC PROGRAM Core, honor code. Calendar: semesters. 350 courses offered in 1995–96; average class size 20 in required courses. Academic remediation for entering students, English as a second language program offered during academic year and summer, services for LD students, advanced placement, self-designed majors, summer session for credit, part-time degree program (daytime, evenings), adult/continuing education programs, internships.
GENERAL DEGREE REQUIREMENTS 60 credits; 1 course each in math and science; computer course; internship (some majors).
MAJORS Animal sciences, applied art, business administration/commerce/management, computer information systems, dental services, early childhood education, fashion design and technology, fashion merchandising, health science, hospitality services, illustration, interdisciplinary studies, interior design, laboratory technologies, liberal arts/general studies, marketing/retailing/merchandising, medical assistant technologies, medical laboratory technology, medical secretarial studies, occupational therapy, physical therapy, retail management, tourism and travel, veterinary technology.
LIBRARY 38,400 books, 23 microform titles, 225 periodicals, 2 CD-ROMs. Acquisition spending 1994–95: $26,839.
COMPUTERS ON CAMPUS Student rooms linked to a campus network. 65 computers for student use in computer center, classrooms, library provide access to e-mail, on-line services, Internet. Staffed computer lab on campus. Academic computing expenditure 1994–95: $76,481.
COLLEGE LIFE Orientation program (3 days, no cost, parents included). Student-run newspaper. 50% vote in student government elections. ***Social organizations:*** 10 open to all. ***Most popular organizations:*** Student Government, Dental Hygiene Club, College Newspaper. ***Major annual events:*** Family Day, Thanksgiving Dinner. ***Student services:*** health clinic, personal-psychological counseling. ***Campus security:*** 24-hour patrols.
HOUSING 500 college housing spaces available; 190 were occupied 1995–96. Freshmen guaranteed college housing. Off-campus living permitted. ***Option:*** single-sex (2 buildings) housing available. Resident assistants live in dorms.
ATHLETICS ***Intercollegiate:*** badminton W, baseball W, field hockey W, volleyball W. ***Intramural:*** badminton, field hockey, volleyball. ***Contact:*** Ms. Kathy Wright, Athletic Director, 610-526-6091.
CAREER PLANNING ***Placement office:*** 1 full-time staff; $20,289 operating expenditure 1994–95. ***Director:*** Ms. Patricia Connolly, Director of Career Services, 610-526-6033. ***Services:*** job fairs, resume preparation, career counseling, careers library, job interviews.
AFTER GRADUATION 37% of students completing a degree program in 1994–95 went directly on to further study.
EXPENSES FOR 1995–96 ***Application fee:*** $35. Comprehensive fee of $13,334 includes full-time tuition ($7990), mandatory fees ($460 minimum), and college room and board ($4884). Full-time mandatory fees range from $460 to $582. Part-time tuition: $266 per credit. Part-time mandatory fees: $25 per credit.
FINANCIAL AID ***College-administered undergrad aid 1995–96:*** 172 need-based scholarships (average $1933), non-need scholarships, low-interest long-term loans from external sources (average $2460), Federal Work-Study, part-time jobs. ***Required forms:*** state, institutional; accepted: CSS Financial Aid PROFILE, FAFSA. ***Priority deadline:*** 5/1. ***Payment plan:*** installment. ***Waivers:*** full or partial for employees or children of employees.
APPLYING ***Options:*** early entrance, deferred entrance. ***Required:*** school transcript, TOEFL for international students. ***Recommended:*** SAT I. ***Required for some:*** 3 years of high school math and science, recommendations, interview, SAT I. Test scores used for counseling/placement. ***Application deadline:*** rolling. ***Notification:*** continuous.
APPLYING/TRANSFER ***Required:*** high school transcript, college transcript. ***Required for some:*** 3 years of high school math and science, recommendations, interview. ***Entrance:*** minimally difficult. ***Application deadline:*** rolling. ***Notification:*** continuous. ***Contact:*** Ms. Kris Romel, Director of Student Transfers, 610-526-6045.
CONTACT Ms. Lori Tomassetti, Dean of Enrollment Services, Harcum College, Bryn Mawr, PA 19010-3476, 610-526-6105 or toll-free 800-345-2600. College video available.

❖ ***See page 742 for a narrative description.*** ❖

HARRISBURG AREA COMMUNITY COLLEGE
Harrisburg, Pennsylvania

UG Enrollment: 10,726	**Tuition & Fees (Area Res): $1398**
Application Deadline: rolling	**Room & Board: N/Avail**

GENERAL State and locally supported, 2-year, coed. Awards certificates, diplomas, transfer associate, terminal associate degrees. Founded 1964. ***Setting:*** 212-acre urban campus. ***Total enrollment:*** 10,726. ***Faculty:*** 589 (192 full-time, 15% with terminal degrees, 397 part-time); student-faculty ratio is 22:1.
ENROLLMENT PROFILE 10,726 students: 60% women, 63% part-time, 99% state residents, 5% transferred in, 1% international, 47% 25 or older, 1% Native American, 2% Hispanic, 6% African American, 3% Asian American. ***Areas of study chosen:*** 19% business management and administrative services, 16% interdisciplinary studies, 14% education, 10% computer and information sciences, 8% social sciences, 7% health professions and related sciences, 5% communications and journalism, 4% biological and life sciences, 4% engineering and applied sciences, 4% psychology, 3% vocational and home economics, 1% fine arts, 1% mathematics, 1% natural resource sciences, 1% performing arts, 1% physical sciences. ***Most popular recent majors:*** business administration/commerce/management, nursing, criminal justice.
FIRST-YEAR CLASS 4,528 total; 5,588 applied, 99% were accepted, 82% of whom enrolled.
ACADEMIC PROGRAM Core, career and transfer curriculum, honor code. Calendar: semesters. Academic remediation for entering students, English as a second language program offered during academic year and summer, services for LD students, advanced placement, self-designed majors, honors program, summer session for credit, part-time degree program (daytime, evenings, weekends, summer), adult/continuing education programs, co-op programs and internships. Study abroad in Denmark, Egypt, England, Germany, Switzerland, Ireland, Israel, Italy, Mexico, Spain, Canada, India, France. ROTC: Army.
GENERAL DEGREE REQUIREMENT 61 semester units.
MAJORS Accounting, actuarial science, architectural technologies, art/fine arts, automotive technologies, biology/biological sciences, business administration/commerce/management, business education, chemistry, commercial art, communication, computer information systems, computer programming, computer science, computer technologies, construction technologies, criminal justice, culinary arts, data processing, dental services, dietetics, early childhood education, education, electrical and electronics technologies, electrical engineering technology, electronics engineering technology, elementary education, emergency medical technology, engineering (general), engineering technology, environmental sciences, fire science, food services management, graphic arts, hotel and restaurant management, human services, industrial engineering technology, information science, law enforcement/police sciences, legal secretarial studies, liberal arts/general studies, management information systems, manufacturing technology, marketing/retailing/merchandising, mathematics, mechanical engineering technology, medical laboratory technology, music, nuclear medical technology, nursing, paralegal studies, photography, physical education, physical sciences, practical nursing, psychology, radiological technology, real estate, respiratory therapy, retail management, science education, secretarial studies/office management, social science, social work, theater arts/drama, tourism and travel.
LIBRARY McCormick Library with 92,288 books, 397 microform titles, 717 periodicals, 5,139 records, tapes, and CDs. Acquisition spending 1994–95: $2 million.
COMPUTERS ON CAMPUS Computer purchase plan available. 260 computers for student use in computer center, labs, library provide access to main academic computer, e-mail, Internet.
COLLEGE LIFE Drama-theater group, student-run newspaper, radio station. 5% vote in student government elections. ***Social organizations:*** local fraternities. ***Student services:*** personal-psychological counseling. ***Campus security:*** 24-hour emergency response devices and patrols, late-night transport-escort service.
HOUSING College housing not available.
ATHLETICS ***Intramural:*** basketball, football, golf, racquetball, skiing (downhill), soccer, softball, squash, swimming and diving, tennis, volleyball.
CAREER PLANNING ***Placement office:*** 3 full-time staff. ***Director:*** Ms. Mary Fourlas, Director of Career and Transfer Services, 717-780-2404. ***Services:*** job fairs, resume preparation, career counseling, careers library, job bank, job interviews. 75 organizations recruited on campus 1994–95.
AFTER GRADUATION 73% of students completing a degree program in 1994–95 went directly on to further study.

Pennsylvania

EXPENSES FOR 1995–96 *Application fee:* $25. Area resident tuition: $1398 full-time, $58.25 per credit hour part-time. State resident tuition: $2796 full-time, $116.50 per credit hour part-time. Nonresident tuition: $4194 full-time, $174.75 per credit hour part-time.
FINANCIAL AID *College-administered undergrad aid 1995–96:* 800 need-based scholarships, 100 non-need scholarships, short-term loans (average $232), low-interest long-term loans from college funds, loans from external sources (average $3000), 300 Federal Work-Study (averaging $1400), 310 part-time jobs. *Required forms:* state, institutional, FAFSA. *Priority deadline:* 5/15.
APPLYING Open admission except for allied health, chef's apprenticeship programs. *Option:* early entrance. *Required:* school transcript, TOEFL for international students. *Required for some:* ACT. Test scores used for counseling/placement. *Application deadline:* rolling.
APPLYING/TRANSFER *Required:* high school transcript. *Required for some:* standardized test scores. *Entrance:* noncompetitive. *Application deadline:* rolling.
CONTACT Mrs. Vanita Cowan, Administrative Clerk, Admissions, Harrisburg Area Community College, 1 HACC Drive, Harrisburg, PA 17110-2999, 717-780-2406 or toll-free 800-ABC-HACC (in-state). *Fax:* 717-231-7674. College video available.

HUSSIAN SCHOOL OF ART
Philadelphia, Pennsylvania

UG Enrollment: 130	Tuition & Fees: $7695
Application Deadline: rolling	Room & Board: N/Avail

GENERAL Proprietary, 2-year, specialized, coed. Awards terminal associate degrees. Founded 1946. *Setting:* 1-acre urban campus. *Total enrollment:* 130. *Faculty:* 25 (2 full-time, 23 part-time).
ENROLLMENT PROFILE 130 students from 4 states and territories. 25% women, 3% part-time, 75% state residents, 1% transferred in, 0% international, 2% 25 or older, 1% Native American, 3% Hispanic, 16% African American, 0% Asian American.
FIRST-YEAR CLASS 50 total; 100 applied, 95% were accepted, 53% of whom enrolled.
ACADEMIC PROGRAM Core. Calendar: semesters. Part-time degree program (daytime), co-op programs.
GENERAL DEGREE REQUIREMENT 120 credits.
MAJORS Advertising, illustration.
LIBRARY 8,000 books, 10 periodicals, 74 records, tapes, and CDs.
COMPUTERS ON CAMPUS 15 computers for student use in computer center provide access to main academic computer. Staffed computer lab on campus provides training in use of computers, software.
COLLEGE LIFE *Student services:* personal-psychological counseling.
HOUSING College housing not available.
CAREER PLANNING *Director:* Ms. Teresa Mak, Job Placement Director, 215-981-0900. *Service:* career counseling.
EXPENSES FOR 1996–97 *Application fee:* $25. Tuition: $7600 full-time. Full-time mandatory fees: $95.
FINANCIAL AID *College-administered undergrad aid 1995–96:* 3 need-based scholarships, non-need scholarships, short-term loans (averaging $100), low-interest long-term loans from college funds, loans from external sources, Federal Work-Study, 6 part-time jobs. *Required forms:* FAFSA; required for some: state, institutional. *Application deadline:* continuous to 8/1. *Payment plan:* installment.
APPLYING *Option:* deferred entrance. *Required:* school transcript, art portfolio. *Application deadline:* rolling.
APPLYING/TRANSFER *Required:* art portfolio. *Entrance:* moderately difficult. *Application deadline:* rolling.
CONTACT Ms. Joan Rafferty, Admissions Director, Hussian School of Art, 1118 Market Street, Philadelphia, PA 19107-3679, 215-981-0900. *Fax:* 215-238-0848. College video available.

ICM SCHOOL OF BUSINESS
Pittsburgh, Pennsylvania

UG Enrollment: 493	Tuition: $12,225/deg prog
Application Deadline: rolling	Room & Board: N/Avail

GENERAL Proprietary, 2-year, coed. Awards certificates, diplomas, transfer associate, terminal associate degrees. Founded 1963. *Setting:* urban campus. *Total enrollment:* 493. *Faculty:* 45 (25 full-time, 20 part-time).
ENROLLMENT PROFILE 493 students from 3 states and territories, 4 other countries. 55% women, 45% men, 0% part-time, 80% state residents, 2% transferred in, 1% international, 45% 25 or older, 0% Native American, 1% Hispanic, 30% African American, 1% Asian American. *Most popular recent majors:* secretarial studies/office management, computer management, medical secretarial studies.
FIRST-YEAR CLASS 240 total. 1% from top 10% of their high school class, 35% from top half.
ACADEMIC PROGRAM Core, honor code. Calendar: year-round. Academic remediation for entering students, advanced placement, tutorials, summer session for credit, co-op programs and internships.
GENERAL DEGREE REQUIREMENTS 1500 clock hours; computer course; internship (some majors).
MAJORS Accounting, business administration/commerce/management, computer management, computer programming, computer science, computer technologies, fashion merchandising, hotel and restaurant management, legal secretarial studies, medical assistant technologies, medical secretarial studies, secretarial studies/office management, tourism and travel.
LIBRARY ICM School Library with 1,250 books, 48 periodicals, 1 CD-ROM, 40 records, tapes, and CDs.
COMPUTERS ON CAMPUS 120 computers for student use in learning resource center, labs provide access to Internet. Staffed computer lab on campus provides training in use of computers, software.
COLLEGE LIFE Orientation program (no cost). 20% vote in student government elections. *Most popular organizations:* Data Processing Management Association, Collegiate Secretaries International, Student Activities Association, American Association of Medical Assistants, Travel and Tourism Club. *Campus security:* 24-hour emergency response devices, evening security personnel.

HOUSING College housing not available.
CAREER PLANNING *Placement office:* 2 full-time staff. *Director:* Ms. Patricia Salopek, Career Advisor, 412-261-2647. *Services:* job fairs, resume preparation, resume referral, career counseling, careers library, job bank, job interviews. Students must register sophomore year. 10 organizations recruited on campus 1994–95.
AFTER GRADUATION 95% of class of 1994 had job offers within 6 months.
EXPENSES FOR 1995–96 *Application fee:* $100. Tuition: $12,225 per degree program. Full-time mandatory fees: $100.
FINANCIAL AID *College-administered undergrad aid 1995–96:* 4 need-based scholarships, 4 non-need scholarships, low-interest long-term loans from external sources, Federal Work-Study. *Required forms:* institutional, FAFSA; required for some: state. *Priority deadline:* 8/1. *Payment plans:* installment, deferred payment. *Waivers:* full or partial for employees or children of employees.
APPLYING *Options:* Common Application, midyear entrance. *Required:* essay, school transcript, Wonderlic aptitude test. Test scores used for admission. *Application deadline:* rolling. *Notification:* continuous.
APPLYING/TRANSFER *Required:* essay, standardized test scores, high school transcript, college transcript. *Entrance:* moderately difficult. *Application deadline:* rolling. *Notification:* continuous. *Contact:* Mrs. Carla M. Ryba, Director of Education, 412-261-2647.
CONTACT Ms. Judy Shanahan, Director of Admissions, ICM School of Business, 10 Wood Street, Pittsburgh, PA 15222, 412-261-2647 or toll-free 800-441-5222. College video available.

ICS CENTER FOR DEGREE STUDIES
Scranton, Pennsylvania

Enrollment: N/R	Tuition: $2956/deg prog
Application Deadline: rolling	Room & Board: N/Avail

GENERAL Proprietary, 2-year, coed. Part of National Education Centers, Inc. Awards terminal associate degrees (offers only external degree programs conducted through home study). Founded 1975. *Faculty:* 50 (22 full-time, 28 part-time).
ENROLLMENT PROFILE 54% women, 46% men, 11% state residents, 15% transferred in, 5% international, 80% 25 or older. *Most popular recent majors:* business administration/commerce/management, accounting.
FIRST-YEAR CLASS Of the students who applied, 100% were accepted.
ACADEMIC PROGRAM Core. Calendar: semesters. Academic remediation for entering students, summer session for credit, part-time degree program (daytime, evenings, weekends, summer), external degree programs.
GENERAL DEGREE REQUIREMENT 60 credits.
MAJORS Accounting, business administration/commerce/management, civil engineering technology, computer science, electrical and electronics technologies, electrical engineering technology, finance/banking, hospitality services, industrial engineering technology, marketing/retailing/merchandising, mechanical engineering technology.
HOUSING College housing not available.
EXPENSES FOR 1996–97 Tuition per degree program ranges from $2956 to $3566. Tuition guaranteed not to increase for student's term of enrollment.
FINANCIAL AID *Payment plan:* installment.
APPLYING Open admission. *Option:* Common Application. *Required:* school transcript. *Application deadline:* rolling.
APPLYING/TRANSFER *Required:* high school transcript. *Application deadline:* rolling.
CONTACT Ms. Connie Dempsey, Director of Education, ICS Center for Degree Studies, Scranton, PA 18515, 717-342-7701.

JOHNSON TECHNICAL INSTITUTE
Scranton, Pennsylvania

UG Enrollment: 308	Tuition & Fees: $6036
Application Deadline: rolling	Room Only: $2600

GENERAL Independent, 2-year, primarily men. Awards terminal associate degrees. Founded 1912. *Setting:* 65-acre urban campus. *Total enrollment:* 308. *Faculty:* 23 (21 full-time, 2 part-time); student-faculty ratio is 19:1.
ENROLLMENT PROFILE 308 students from 6 states and territories. 7% women, 3% part-time, 92% state residents, 9% live on campus, 9% transferred in, 0% international, 11% 25 or older, 0% Native American, 1% Hispanic, 1% African American, 1% Asian American. *Most popular recent majors:* carpentry, biomedical technologies, electrical and electronics technologies.
FIRST-YEAR CLASS 144 total; 320 applied, 88% were accepted, 51% of whom enrolled. 6% from top 10% of their high school class, 12% from top quarter, 45% from top half.
ACADEMIC PROGRAM Core, honor code. Calendar: semesters. Academic remediation for entering students, services for LD students, summer session for credit, part-time degree program (daytime, evenings), adult/continuing education programs, internships.
GENERAL DEGREE REQUIREMENTS 76 credits; 1 algebra course; internship (some majors).
MAJORS Architectural technologies, automotive technologies, biomedical technologies, carpentry, construction technology, drafting and design, electrical and electronics technologies, electromechanical technology, machine and tool technologies, mechanical design technology, transportation technologies, veterinary technology, welding technology.
LIBRARY Johnson Technical Institute Library with 4,473 books, 118 periodicals, 3 CD-ROMs, 101 records, tapes, and CDs.
COMPUTERS ON CAMPUS 70 computers for student use in computer labs, learning resource center, counseling office, library, student center provide access to on-line services, Internet.
COLLEGE LIFE Orientation program (2 days, no cost, parents included). *Social organizations:* 1 national fraternity; 7% of eligible men are members. *Most popular organizations:* Student Government, Social Force Club. *Major annual events:* Activity Day, Career Day, Parents' Day. *Student services:* personal-psychological counseling. *Campus security:* 24-hour emergency response devices, patrols by college staff.
HOUSING 32 college housing spaces available. No special consideration for freshman housing applicants. Off-campus living permitted. *Option:* coed housing available.

Peterson's Guide to Two-Year Colleges 1997

Johnson Technical Institute (continued)
ATHLETICS ***Intramural:*** basketball, skiing (downhill), softball, table tennis (Ping-Pong), volleyball, weight lifting. ***Contact:*** Ms. Tyonia Crawford, Director of Student Services, 717-342-6404.
CAREER PLANNING ***Placement office:*** 1 full-time staff. ***Director:*** Ms. Carolyn L. Brozzetti, Placement Director, 717-342-6404. ***Services:*** job fairs, resume preparation, resume referral, career counseling, careers library, job bank, job interviews. Students must register freshman year. 20 organizations recruited on campus 1994–95.
AFTER GRADUATION 82% of class of 1994 had job offers within 6 months.
EXPENSES FOR 1995–96 ***Application fee:*** $25. Tuition: $5936 (minimum) full-time. Part-time tuition per credit ranges from $100 to $210. Part-time mandatory fees: $100 per year. Full-time tuition ranges up to $6300 according to program. Full-time mandatory fees: $100. College room only: $2600.
FINANCIAL AID ***College-administered undergrad aid 1995–96:*** need-based scholarships, 8 non-need scholarships (average $1406), low-interest long-term loans from external sources (average $2625), 10 part-time jobs. ***Required forms:*** state; accepted: CSS Financial Aid PROFILE, FAFSA. ***Application deadline:*** continuous. ***Payment plan:*** installment. ***Waivers:*** full or partial for employees or children of employees.
APPLYING ***Options:*** Common Application, deferred entrance. ***Required:*** school transcript, recommendations, campus interview, TOEFL for international students. ***Recommended:*** minimum 2.0 GPA, 3 years of high school math, SAT I. ***Required for some:*** 3 years of high school science, College Qualifying Test. Test scores used for admission. ***Application deadline:*** rolling.
APPLYING/TRANSFER ***Required:*** college transcript, minimum 2.0 college GPA. ***Entrance:*** minimally difficult. ***Application deadline:*** rolling. ***Contact:*** Mr. Harry R. Dickinson, Vice President for Enrollment Management, 717-342-6404 Ext. 15.
CONTACT Mr. Harry R. Dickinson, Vice President for Enrollment Management, Johnson Technical Institute, 3427 North Main Avenue, Scranton, PA 18508-1495, 717-342-6404 Ext. 15. ***Fax:*** 717-348-2181. College video available.

KEYSTONE COLLEGE
La Plume, Pennsylvania

UG Enrollment: 875	Tuition & Fees: $8970
Application Deadline: rolling	Room & Board: $5240

Keystone College is a residential private institution that offers a diverse curriculum supported by a strong liberal arts base leading to real career opportunities for students. Keystone is located 15 miles north of Scranton, PA, in the beautiful northeastern Pocono region. Sixty-five percent of graduates transfer to 4-year colleges and universities with full junior status. Others go directly on to careers. The academic strength of the institution lies in its emphasis on high-quality instruction and genuine concern for the individual student. Keystone's small-college atmosphere provides for an interaction between professors and students that extends far beyond the classroom. Recently, Keystone was selected as one of the top 2-year colleges in the country by Rugg's Recommendations on Colleges.

GENERAL Independent, 2-year, coed. Awards transfer associate, terminal associate degrees. Founded 1868. ***Setting:*** 260-acre rural campus. ***Total enrollment:*** 875. ***Faculty:*** 77 (29 full-time, 30% with terminal degrees, 48 part-time); student-faculty ratio is 13:1. ***Notable Alumni:*** Diane Paparo, administrator and partner of Diane Paparo Associates, LTD; Peter Moylan, investment banker; John Butler, Jr., owner of Butler Trucking; Elmer Hawk, owner of Gertrude Hawk Chocolates; Anthony Mercuri, podiatrist.
ENROLLMENT PROFILE 875 students from 11 states and territories, 10 other countries. 60% women, 40% men, 44% part-time, 89% state residents, 27% live on campus, 28% transferred in, 54% have need-based financial aid, 32% have non-need-based financial aid, 3% international, 41% 25 or older, 1% Native American, 1% Hispanic, 4% African American, 1% Asian American. ***Areas of study chosen:*** 29% liberal arts/general studies, 19% business management and administrative services, 11% education, 11% health professions and related sciences, 6% fine arts, 6% social sciences, 5% computer and information sciences, 4% communications and journalism, 4% engineering and applied sciences, 3% natural resource sciences, 1% architecture, 1% biological and life sciences. ***Most popular recent majors:*** liberal arts/general studies, business administration/commerce/management, early childhood education.
FIRST-YEAR CLASS 330 total; 625 applied, 91% were accepted, 58% of whom enrolled. 2% from top 10% of their high school class, 9% from top quarter, 38% from top half.
ACADEMIC PROGRAM Core. Calendar: semesters. 231 courses offered in 1995–96. Academic remediation for entering students, English as a second language program offered during academic year and summer, advanced placement, self-designed majors, summer session for credit, part-time degree program (daytime, evenings, weekends, summer), adult/continuing education programs, co-op programs and internships. Off-campus study at Pennsylvania State University, Wilkes University, Mansfield University of Pennsylvania, Luzerne County Community College, Lackawanna Junior College, West Chester University of Pennsylvania. ROTC: Army (c), Air Force (c).
GENERAL DEGREE REQUIREMENTS 67 credit hours; 6 credit hours each of math and science; computer course for most majors; internship.
MAJORS Accounting, art/fine arts, biology/biological sciences, business administration/commerce/management, chemistry, child care/child and family studies, communication, computer information systems, criminal justice, culinary arts, cytotechnology, early childhood education, environmental engineering technology, environmental studies, food services management, forestry, hospitality services, hotel and restaurant management, human services, international business, landscape architecture/design, liberal arts/general studies, medical technology, nursing, occupational therapy, physical therapy, radiological technology, tourism and travel, wood sciences.
LIBRARY Miller Library with 39,000 books, 95 microform titles, 234 periodicals, 3 on-line bibliographic services, 13 CD-ROMs, 2,293 records, tapes, and CDs.
COMPUTERS ON CAMPUS Computer purchase plan available. 80 computers for student use in computer labs, counseling center, library. Staffed computer lab on campus provides training in use of computers, software.
COLLEGE LIFE Orientation program (5 days, $156, parents included). Drama-theater group, choral group, student-run newspaper, radio station. ***Social organizations:*** 21 open to all. ***Most popular organizations:*** Campus Activity Board, Student Senate, Students Against Drunk Drivers (SADD). ***Major annual events:*** Homecoming, Quality of Life Day, Spring Weekend. ***Student services:*** health clinic, personal-psychological counseling, women's center. ***Campus security:*** 24-hour emergency response devices and patrols, late-night transport-escort service, controlled dormitory access.
HOUSING 519 college housing spaces available; 235 were occupied 1995–96. Freshmen guaranteed college housing. Off-campus living permitted. ***Options:*** coed (7 buildings), single-sex (1 building), international student housing available. Resident assistants live in dorms.
ATHLETICS Member NJCAA. ***Intercollegiate:*** baseball M, basketball M/W, soccer M/W, softball W, volleyball W. ***Intramural:*** archery, badminton, basketball, bowling, cross-country running, football, racquetball, soccer, softball, table tennis (Ping-Pong), tennis, volleyball, weight lifting. ***Contact:*** Ms. Terry Wise, Director of Athletics, 717-945-5141 Ext. 3901.
CAREER PLANNING ***Placement office:*** 2 full-time, 4 part-time staff. ***Director:*** Mrs. Maria V. Fanning, Coordinator of Career Planning and Placement, 717-945-5141 Ext. 3500. ***Services:*** job fairs, resume preparation, resume referral, career counseling, careers library, job bank, job interviews. Students must register freshman year. 30 organizations recruited on campus 1994–95.
EXPENSES FOR 1995–96 ***Application fee:*** $25. Comprehensive fee of $14,210 includes full-time tuition ($8200), mandatory fees ($770), and college room and board ($5240). Part-time tuition: $210 per credit hour. Part-time mandatory fees: $25 per credit hour. Tuition guaranteed not to increase for student's term of enrollment.
FINANCIAL AID ***College-administered undergrad aid 1995–96:*** 321 need-based scholarships (average $3270), 99 non-need scholarships (average $3676), low-interest long-term loans from external sources (average $3021), 203 Federal Work-Study (averaging $950), 31 part-time jobs. ***Required forms:*** state, institutional, FAFSA. ***Priority deadline:*** 5/1. ***Payment plan:*** installment. ***Waivers:*** full or partial for employees or children of employees. ***Notification:*** continuous.
APPLYING ***Options:*** early entrance, deferred entrance, midyear entrance. ***Required:*** TOEFL for international students. ***Recommended:*** SAT I or ACT. ***Required for some:*** 3 years of high school math and science, some high school foreign language. Test scores used for admission. ***Application deadline:*** rolling.
APPLYING/TRANSFER ***Recommended:*** standardized test scores. ***Required for some:*** 3 years of high school math and science, some high school foreign language. ***Entrance:*** minimally difficult. ***Application deadline:*** rolling. ***Contact:*** Ms. Sharon Clark, Coordinator of Academic and Transfer Advising, 717-945-5141 Ext. 2800.
CONTACT Mr. Thomas LoBasso, Director of Admissions, Keystone College, La Plume, PA 18440-0200, 717-945-5141 Ext. 6004 or toll-free 800-824-2764. College video available.

❖ ***See page 750 for a narrative description.*** ❖

LACKAWANNA JUNIOR COLLEGE
Scranton, Pennsylvania

UG Enrollment: 740	Tuition & Fees: $6880
Application Deadline: rolling	Room & Board: N/Avail

GENERAL Independent, 2-year, coed. Awards certificates, transfer associate degrees. Founded 1894. ***Setting:*** 4-acre urban campus. ***Endowment:*** $20,300. ***Research spending 1994–95:*** $18,475. ***Total enrollment:*** 740. ***Faculty:*** 52 (24 full-time, 28 part-time); student-faculty ratio is 15:1. ***Notable Alumni:*** Robert Mellow, Pennsylvania senator; Frank Eagen, judge; Steve Nocilla, director of Catholic Social Services of Scranton.
ENROLLMENT PROFILE 740 students from 4 states and territories, 3 other countries. 60% women, 35% part-time, 88% state residents, 13% transferred in, 1% international, 43% 25 or older, 0% Native American, 0% Hispanic, 5% African American, 0% Asian American. ***Most popular recent majors:*** business administration/commerce/management, accounting, human services.
FIRST-YEAR CLASS 330 total; 641 applied, 99% were accepted, 52% of whom enrolled. 10% from top 10% of their high school class, 20% from top quarter, 45% from top half.
ACADEMIC PROGRAM Core, general education curriculum, honor code. Calendar: semesters. 547 courses offered in 1995–96. Academic remediation for entering students, services for LD students, advanced placement, tutorials, summer session for credit, part-time degree program (daytime, evenings, summer), adult/continuing education programs, co-op programs. ROTC: Air Force (c).
GENERAL DEGREE REQUIREMENTS 64 credits; math/science requirements vary according to program; computer course.
MAJORS Accounting, business administration/commerce/management, computer information systems, criminal justice, education, environmental sciences, hotel and restaurant management, human services, legal secretarial studies, liberal arts/general studies, marketing/retailing/merchandising, medical secretarial studies, secretarial studies/office management.
LIBRARY Sealey Memorial Library with 26,000 books, 1 microform title, 65 periodicals, 22 CD-ROMs, 907 records, tapes, and CDs. Acquisition spending 1994–95: $31,540.
COMPUTERS ON CAMPUS 92 computers for student use in computer center, reference learning center, typing lab provide access to main academic computer, on-line services. Staffed computer lab on campus provides training in use of computers, software. Academic computing expenditure 1994–95: $1.2 million.
COLLEGE LIFE Drama-theater group, student-run newspaper. 50% vote in student government elections. ***Social organizations:*** social clubs; 20% of eligible women are members. ***Most popular organizations:*** Student Government, Student/Alumni Association. ***Major annual events:*** Groundhog Day Cookout, Graduation Dinner Dance, Homecoming. ***Student services:*** personal-psychological counseling. ***Campus security:*** late-night transport-escort service.
HOUSING College housing not available.
ATHLETICS Member NJCAA. ***Intercollegiate:*** baseball M, basketball M(s)/W(s), football M, golf M(s)/W(s), softball W, volleyball W. ***Intramural:*** volleyball, weight lifting. ***Contact:*** Mr. Tim Dempsey, Athletic Director, 717-961-7818.
CAREER PLANNING ***Placement office:*** 6 full-time, 4 part-time staff; $424,182 operating expenditure 1994–95. ***Director:*** Mr. Jay J. Mannion, Director of Admissions, 717-961-7841. ***Services:*** job fairs, resume preparation, career counseling, careers library, job bank, job interviews.
AFTER GRADUATION 80% of students completing a degree program in 1994–95 went directly on to further study.
EXPENSES FOR 1996–97 ***Application fee:*** $20. Tuition: $6880 full-time, $215 per credit part-time.
FINANCIAL AID ***College-administered undergrad aid 1995–96:*** 195 need-based scholarships (averaging $698), 105 non-need scholarships (averaging $2063), Federal Work-Study. ***Required forms:*** state, institutional, FAFSA. ***Priority deadline:*** 8/1. ***Payment***

plans: installment, deferred payment. ***Waivers:*** full or partial for employees or children of employees and senior citizens. ***Average indebtedness of graduates:*** $6125.
APPLYING Open admission. ***Options:*** early entrance, deferred entrance, midyear entrance. ***Required:*** school transcript, interview. ***Recommended:*** recommendations, SAT I or ACT, TOEFL for international students. Test scores used for counseling/placement. ***Application deadline:*** rolling.
APPLYING/TRANSFER ***Required:*** high school transcript, interview, college transcript. ***Recommended:*** standardized test scores, recommendations. ***Entrance:*** noncompetitive. ***Application deadline:*** rolling. ***Contact:*** Mrs. Suellen Musewicz, Director of Counseling, 717-961-7812.
CONTACT Mrs. Diane Lang, Registrar, Lackawanna Junior College, 901 Prospect Avenue, Scranton, PA 18505-1845, 717-961-7840 or toll-free 800-458-2050 (in-state). ***Fax:*** 717-961-7858.

LANSDALE SCHOOL OF BUSINESS
North Wales, Pennsylvania

UG Enrollment: 350 **Tuition & Fees: $6250**
Application Deadline: rolling **Room & Board: N/Avail**

GENERAL Proprietary, 2-year, coed. Awards terminal associate degrees. Founded 1918. ***Setting:*** small-town campus with easy access to Philadelphia. ***Total enrollment:*** 350. ***Faculty:*** 33 (8 full-time, 25 part-time); student-faculty ratio is 15:1.
ENROLLMENT PROFILE 350 students: 80% women, 60% part-time, 100% state residents, 20% transferred in, 0% international, 50% 25 or older, 0% Native American, 2% Hispanic, 5% African American, 2% Asian American.
FIRST-YEAR CLASS 125 total; 147 applied, 90% were accepted, 95% of whom enrolled. 10% from top quarter of their high school class, 40% from top half.
ACADEMIC PROGRAM Core, honor code. Calendar: semesters. Summer session for credit, part-time degree program (daytime, evenings), adult/continuing education programs.
GENERAL DEGREE REQUIREMENTS 68 credits; computer course.
MAJORS Accounting, computer technologies, data processing, fashion merchandising, hospitality services, medical assistant technologies, medical secretarial studies, paralegal studies, secretarial studies/office management, word processing.
LIBRARY LSB Library with 2,000 books, 75 periodicals, 25 CD-ROMs.
COMPUTERS ON CAMPUS 48 computers for student use in computer center, library. Staffed computer lab on campus provides training in use of computers, software.
HOUSING College housing not available.
CAREER PLANNING ***Placement office:*** 2 full-time staff. ***Director:*** Mrs. Janice Weaver, Director of Student Services, 215-699-5700. ***Services:*** resume preparation, resume referral, career counseling, careers library, job bank, job interviews.
EXPENSES FOR 1996–97 ***Application fee:*** $20. Tuition: $6250 full-time. Part-time tuition per credit: $156 for day division, $125 for evening division.
FINANCIAL AID ***College-administered undergrad aid 1995–96:*** low-interest long-term loans from external sources (average $2625). ***Required forms:*** state. ***Application deadline:*** continuous. ***Payment plans:*** installment, deferred payment. ***Waivers:*** full or partial for employees or children of employees.
APPLYING ***Application deadline:*** rolling.
APPLYING/TRANSFER ***Entrance:*** minimally difficult. ***Application deadline:*** rolling.
CONTACT Ms. Marianne H. Johnson, Director of Admissions, Lansdale School of Business, North Wales, PA 19454-4148, 215-699-5700.

LEHIGH CARBON COMMUNITY COLLEGE
Schnecksville, Pennsylvania

UG Enrollment: 4,397 **Tuition & Fees (Area Res): $2040**
Application Deadline: rolling **Room & Board: N/Avail**

GENERAL State and locally supported, 2-year, coed. Awards certificates, transfer associate, terminal associate degrees. Founded 1967. ***Setting:*** 100-acre rural campus. ***Total enrollment:*** 4,397. ***Faculty:*** 257 (73 full-time, 184 part-time); student-faculty ratio is 20:1.
ENROLLMENT PROFILE 4,397 students from 5 states and territories, 15 other countries. 50% women, 55% part-time, 98% state residents, 16% transferred in, 2% international, 54% 25 or older, 0% Native American, 3% Hispanic, 1% African American, 3% Asian American. ***Areas of study chosen:*** 32% liberal arts/general studies, 14% vocational and home economics, 13% business management and administrative services, 8% social sciences, 7% computer and information sciences, 7% health professions and related sciences, 5% education, 2% biological and life sciences, 2% engineering and applied sciences, 1% mathematics. ***Most popular recent majors:*** liberal arts/general studies, accounting, business administration/commerce/management.
FIRST-YEAR CLASS 1,453 total; 2,198 applied, 91% were accepted, 73% of whom enrolled.
ACADEMIC PROGRAM Core, honor code. Calendar: semesters. Academic remediation for entering students, English as a second language program offered during academic year, services for LD students, advanced placement, summer session for credit, part-time degree program (daytime, evenings), adult/continuing education programs, co-op programs and internships. ROTC: Army (c).
GENERAL DEGREE REQUIREMENTS 60 credits; computer course for business majors.
MAJORS Accounting, automotive technologies, aviation administration, aviation technology, biomedical technologies, broadcasting, business administration/commerce/management, computer information systems, computer programming, computer science, computer technologies, criminal justice, drafting and design, early childhood education, education, electrical and electronics technologies, electrical engineering technology, electronics engineering technology, engineering (general), (pre)engineering sequence, engineering technology, heating/refrigeration/air conditioning, hotel and restaurant management, humanities, industrial administration, law enforcement/police sciences, legal secretarial studies, liberal arts/general studies, mathematics, mechanical engineering technology, medical assistant technologies, medical records services, natural sciences, nursing, occupational therapy, paralegal studies, physical therapy, practical nursing, public administration, real estate, respiratory therapy, science, secretarial studies/office management, social science, tourism and travel, word processing.
LIBRARY Learning Resource Center with 48,000 books, 81 microform titles, 450 periodicals, 3,660 records, tapes, and CDs.
COMPUTERS ON CAMPUS Computer purchase plan available. 175 computers for student use in computer center, computer labs, learning resource center, library provide access to main academic computer. Staffed computer lab on campus.
COLLEGE LIFE Student-run newspaper, radio station. 1% vote in student government elections. ***Social organizations:*** 18 open to all. ***Most popular organizations:*** Phi Theta Kappa, Returning Adults Organization, Student Radio Station, Student Government, Student Newspaper. ***Major annual events:*** Spring Awards Program, Dances, Film Festival. ***Student services:*** health clinic, personal-psychological counseling. ***Campus security:*** 24-hour emergency response devices and patrols, student patrols, late-night transport-escort service.
HOUSING College housing not available.
ATHLETICS ***Intercollegiate:*** basketball M, golf M/W, tennis M/W, volleyball W. ***Intramural:*** archery, badminton, baseball, basketball, bowling, field hockey, football, golf, racquetball, skiing (downhill), soccer, softball, swimming and diving, table tennis (Ping-Pong), tennis, track and field, volleyball, weight lifting. ***Contact:*** Mr. Douglas Stewart, Director of Student Activities, 610-799-1155.
CAREER PLANNING ***Placement office:*** 1 full-time staff. ***Services:*** job fairs, resume preparation, resume referral, career counseling.
AFTER GRADUATION 53% of students completing a degree program in 1994–95 went directly on to further study.
EXPENSES FOR 1996–97 ***Application fee:*** $25. Area resident tuition: $1890 full-time, $63 per credit part-time. State resident tuition: $3960 full-time, $132 per credit part-time. Nonresident tuition: $6030 full-time, $201 per credit part-time. Part-time mandatory fees: $5 per credit. Full-time mandatory fees: $150.
FINANCIAL AID ***College-administered undergrad aid 1995–96:*** 479 need-based scholarships (average $681), low-interest long-term loans from college funds (average $1385), loans from external sources (average $2180), 76 Federal Work-Study (averaging $1065), 40 part-time jobs. ***Required forms:*** state, FAFSA. ***Priority deadline:*** 5/1. ***Waivers:*** full or partial for employees or children of employees and senior citizens.
APPLYING Open admission except for allied health, aviation, auto technician, veterinary technicial programs. ***Recommended:*** TOEFL for international students. ***Required for some:*** school transcript. Test scores used for counseling/placement. ***Application deadline:*** rolling. ***Notification:*** continuous.
APPLYING/TRANSFER ***Required:*** college transcript. ***Required for some:*** high school transcript. ***Application deadline:*** rolling. ***Notification:*** continuous. ***Contact:*** Ms. Ginny Mihalik, Transfer Counselor, 610-799-1178.
CONTACT Mr. David F. Moyer, Director of Admissions, Lehigh Carbon Community College, Schnecksville, PA 18078-2598, 610-799-1134. ***Fax:*** 610-799-1527.

LINCOLN TECHNICAL INSTITUTE
Allentown, Pennsylvania

UG Enrollment: 650 **Tuition & Fees: $6600**
Application Deadline: rolling **Room & Board: N/Avail**

GENERAL Proprietary, 2-year, coed. Part of Lincoln Technical Institute, Inc. Awards terminal associate degrees. Founded 1949. ***Setting:*** 10-acre suburban campus with easy access to Philadelphia. ***Total enrollment:*** 650. ***Faculty:*** 30 (25 full-time, 5 part-time); student-faculty ratio is 16:1.
ENROLLMENT PROFILE 650 students: 5% women, 0% part-time, 2% Hispanic, 2% African American.
FIRST-YEAR CLASS 175 total.
ACADEMIC PROGRAM Core. Calendar: trimesters. Summer session for credit.
GENERAL DEGREE REQUIREMENTS 97 credits; math/science requirements vary according to program; computer course.
MAJORS Drafting and design, electrical and electronics technologies.
COMPUTERS ON CAMPUS 60 computers for student use in computer center, classrooms, library.
COLLEGE LIFE Orientation program (2 days).
HOUSING College housing not available.
CAREER PLANNING ***Service:*** career counseling.
EXPENSES FOR 1996–97 ***Application fee:*** $100. Tuition: $6600 (minimum) full-time. Full-time tuition ranges up to $16,600 according to program.
FINANCIAL AID ***College-administered undergrad aid 1995–96:*** need-based scholarships, non-need scholarships, low-interest long-term loans from external sources, Federal Work-Study. ***Required forms:*** state, FAFSA. ***Application deadline:*** continuous. ***Payment plans:*** installment, deferred payment. ***Waivers:*** full or partial for employees or children of employees.
APPLYING Open admission. ***Option:*** early entrance. ***Required:*** school transcript, interview. ***Recommended:*** 3 years of high school math, recommendations. ***Application deadline:*** rolling.
APPLYING/TRANSFER ***Required:*** high school transcript, interview. ***Recommended:*** 3 years of high school math, recommendations. ***Required for some:*** college transcript. ***Contact:*** Mr. Joe Carretta, Director of Admissions, 610-398-5301.
CONTACT Admissions Office, Lincoln Technical Institute, Allentown, PA 18104-3298, 610-398-5301.

LINCOLN TECHNICAL INSTITUTE
Philadelphia, Pennsylvania

UG Enrollment: 200 **Tuition: $13,000/deg prog**
Application Deadline: rolling **Room & Board: N/Avail**

GENERAL Proprietary, 2-year, specialized, primarily men. Part of Lincoln Technical Institute, Inc. Awards terminal associate degrees. Founded 1946. ***Setting:*** 3-acre suburban campus. ***Total enrollment:*** 200. ***Faculty:*** 19 (13 full-time, 6 part-time).
ENROLLMENT PROFILE 200 students: 5% women, 60% state residents, 15% transferred in.
FIRST-YEAR CLASS 150 total. Of the students who applied, 100% were accepted.

Lincoln Technical Institute (continued)

ACADEMIC PROGRAM Core. Calendar: modular. Part-time degree program (evenings), adult/continuing education programs, co-op programs.
GENERAL DEGREE REQUIREMENT 76 credits.
MAJORS Automotive technologies, drafting and design.
COMPUTERS ON CAMPUS 6 computers for student use in classrooms.
COLLEGE LIFE Student-run newspaper. ***Campus security:*** 16-hour patrols by trained security personnel.
HOUSING College housing not available.
CAREER PLANNING ***Director:*** Mr. Dan Henkel, Employment Assistance Officer, 215-335-0800. ***Services:*** job fairs, resume preparation, career counseling, job interviews.
EXPENSES FOR 1996–97 ***Application fee:*** $25. Tuition per degree program ranges from $13,000 to $16,000. Tuition guaranteed not to increase for student's term of enrollment.
FINANCIAL AID ***College-administered undergrad aid 1995–96:*** need-based scholarships, non-need scholarships, low-interest long-term loans from external sources, Federal Work-Study. ***Required forms:*** institutional, FAFSA; required for some: state. ***Application deadline:*** continuous.
APPLYING Open admission. ***Option:*** deferred entrance. ***Required:*** school transcript, minimum 2.0 GPA, interview. ***Required for some:*** 3 years of high school math and science, some high school foreign language. ***Application deadline:*** rolling.
APPLYING/TRANSFER ***Required:*** high school transcript, interview, minimum 2.0 high school GPA. ***Entrance:*** noncompetitive. ***Application deadline:*** rolling.
CONTACT Mr. Leo Urso, Director of Admissions, Lincoln Technical Institute, Philadelphia, PA 19136-1595, 215-335-0800. College video available.

LUZERNE COUNTY COMMUNITY COLLEGE
Nanticoke, Pennsylvania

UG Enrollment: 6,407	**Tuition & Fees (Area Res): $1590**
Application Deadline: rolling	**Room & Board: N/Avail**

GENERAL County-supported, 2-year, coed. Awards certificates, transfer associate, terminal associate degrees. Founded 1966. ***Setting:*** 122-acre suburban campus. ***Total enrollment:*** 6,407. ***Faculty:*** 495 (150 full-time, 7% with terminal degrees, 345 part-time).
ENROLLMENT PROFILE 6,407 students: 60% women, 40% men, 62% part-time, 99% state residents, 3% transferred in, 60% have need-based financial aid, 5% have non-need-based financial aid, 1% international, 51% 25 or older, 1% Native American, 1% Hispanic, 2% African American, 1% Asian American. ***Areas of study chosen:*** 32% liberal arts/general studies, 20% business management and administrative services, 7% health professions and related sciences, 6% computer and information sciences, 6% education, 4% engineering and applied sciences, 4% fine arts, 3% premed, 2% communications and journalism, 2% social sciences, 1% architecture, 1% English language/literature/letters, 1% mathematics.
FIRST-YEAR CLASS 1,951 total; 2,864 applied, 100% were accepted, 68% of whom enrolled.
ACADEMIC PROGRAM Core, interdisciplinary curriculum. Calendar: semesters. 535 courses offered in 1995–96; average class size 24 in required courses. Academic remediation for entering students, services for LD students, advanced placement, summer session for credit, part-time degree program (daytime, evenings), external degree programs, internships. ROTC: Air Force (c).
GENERAL DEGREE REQUIREMENTS 60 semester hours; 3 semester hours of math; internship (some majors).
MAJORS Accounting, architectural technologies, automotive technologies, aviation administration, aviation technology, broadcasting, business administration/commerce/management, commercial art, computer science, computer technologies, criminal justice, culinary arts, data processing, dental services, drafting and design, early childhood education, education, electrical and electronics technologies, electronics engineering technology, emergency medical technology, finance/banking, fire science, food services technology, health services administration, heating/refrigeration/air conditioning, horticulture, hotel and restaurant management, humanities, human services, information science, international business, journalism, liberal arts/general studies, mathematics, mechanical design technology, medical secretarial studies, nuclear technology, nursing, operating room technology, painting/drawing, paralegal studies, pharmacy/pharmaceutical sciences, photography, physical education, plumbing, printing technologies, real estate, recreation and leisure services, respiratory therapy, robotics, science, secretarial studies/office management, social science, systems science, tourism and travel, word processing.
LIBRARY Learning Resources Center plus 1 other, with 57,358 books, 30,066 microform titles, 549 periodicals, 11 on-line bibliographic services, 25 CD-ROMs, 857 records, tapes, and CDs. Acquisition spending 1994–95: $53,963.
COMPUTERS ON CAMPUS 200 computers for student use in computer center, computer labs, learning resource center, classrooms, library provide access to main academic computer. Staffed computer lab on campus provides training in use of computers, software. Academic computing expenditure 1994–95: $264,897.
COLLEGE LIFE Choral group, student-run newspaper, radio station. ***Social organizations:*** 25 open to all. ***Most popular organizations:*** Student Government, Circle K, Nursing Forum, Science Club, SADAH. ***Major annual events:*** Alumni Career Fair, College Night, Craft Festival. ***Campus security:*** patrols during campus hours.
HOUSING College housing not available.
ATHLETICS Member NJCAA. ***Intercollegiate:*** baseball M, basketball M/W, cross-country running M/W, golf M/W, softball W, volleyball W. ***Intramural:*** badminton, basketball, bowling, tennis, volleyball. ***Contact:*** Mr. James Atherton, Director of Student Activities, 717-829-7429.
CAREER PLANNING ***Placement office:*** 3 full-time, 2 part-time staff; $100,340 operating expenditure 1994–95. ***Director:*** Dr. Barbara Price, Director, Career Planning and Placement, 717-740-0456. ***Services:*** job fairs, resume preparation, resume referral, career counseling, careers library, job bank, job interviews. Students must register sophomore year. 54 organizations recruited on campus 1994–95.
AFTER GRADUATION 40% of students completing a degree program in 1994–95 went directly on to further study.
EXPENSES FOR 1995–96 ***Application fee:*** $20. Area resident tuition: $1440 full-time, $48 per semester hour part-time. State resident tuition: $2880 full-time, $96 per semester hour part-time. Nonresident tuition: $4320 full-time, $144 per semester hour part-time. Part-time mandatory fees: $5 per semester hour. Full-time mandatory fees: $150.
FINANCIAL AID ***College-administered undergrad aid 1995–96:*** 250 need-based scholarships (average $400), 15 non-need scholarships, low-interest long-term loans from external sources (average $1265), 135 Federal Work-Study (averaging $1200). ***Required forms:*** FAFSA; required for some: institutional. ***Priority deadline:*** 7/1. ***Waivers:*** full or partial for employees or children of employees and senior citizens.
APPLYING Open admission except for allied health programs. ***Options:*** early entrance, deferred entrance, midyear entrance. ***Required:*** TOEFL for international students. ***Recommended:*** school transcript. Test scores used for counseling/placement. ***Application deadline:*** rolling.
APPLYING/TRANSFER ***Recommended:*** college transcript. ***Entrance:*** noncompetitive. ***Application deadline:*** rolling. ***Contact:*** Mr. Thomas P. Leary, Dean of Admissions and Student Affairs, 717-740-0336.
CONTACT Mr. Thomas P. Leary, Dean of Admissions and Student Affairs, Luzerne County Community College, Nanticoke, PA 18634-9804, 717-829-0336 or toll-free 800-377-5222 (in-state).

MANOR JUNIOR COLLEGE
Jenkintown, Pennsylvania

UG Enrollment: 659	**Tuition & Fees: $6990**
Application Deadline: rolling	**Room & Board: $3600**

Manor Junior College, located in Jenkintown, a suburb of Philadelphia, offers associate degree and transfer programs in the allied health, business, and liberal arts fields. Areas of study include accounting; allied health; business administration; court reporting; early child care/human services; dental hygiene; expanded functions dental assisting; health-care management; medical laboratory technology; medical, legal, and administrative secretarial studies; paralegal studies; psychology; and veterinary technology.405990

GENERAL Independent Byzantine Catholic, 2-year, coed. Awards transfer associate, terminal associate degrees. Founded 1947. ***Setting:*** 35-acre small-town campus with easy access to Philadelphia. ***Total enrollment:*** 659. ***Faculty:*** 97 (20 full-time, 77 part-time); student-faculty ratio is 7:1.
ENROLLMENT PROFILE 659 students from 4 states and territories, 7 other countries. 78% women, 23% part-time, 90% state residents, 17% transferred in, 7% international, 14% 25 or older, 0% Native American, 1% Hispanic, 9% African American, 2% Asian American. ***Most popular recent majors:*** health science, liberal arts/general studies, business administration/commerce/management.
FIRST-YEAR CLASS 243 total; 439 applied, 72% were accepted, 77% of whom enrolled. 14% from top 10% of their high school class, 37% from top quarter, 72% from top half.
ACADEMIC PROGRAM Core. Calendar: semesters. Academic remediation for entering students, English as a second language program offered during academic year, advanced placement, honors program, part-time degree program (daytime, evenings, summer), adult/continuing education programs, internships.
GENERAL DEGREE REQUIREMENTS 60 credit hours; 3 credit hours each of math and science; computer course.
MAJORS Accounting, animal sciences, business administration/commerce/management, child care/child and family studies, court reporting, cytotechnology, dental services, early childhood education, education, elementary education, health science, human services, laboratory animal medicine, legal secretarial studies, liberal arts/general studies, medical laboratory technology, medical secretarial studies, nursing, occupational therapy, paralegal studies, physical therapy, psychology, science, secretarial studies/office management, veterinary sciences.
LIBRARY Basileiad Library with 40,900 books, 225 periodicals.
COMPUTERS ON CAMPUS 32 computers for student use in computer center, classrooms, library.
COLLEGE LIFE Orientation program (2 days, $20, parents included). Choral group. ***Student services:*** personal-psychological counseling.
HOUSING 94 college housing spaces available; 59 were occupied 1995–96. Freshmen guaranteed college housing. Off-campus living permitted. ***Option:*** coed housing available.
ATHLETICS ***Intercollegiate:*** basketball M(s)/W(s), soccer M(s)/W(s), volleyball W(s). ***Intramural:*** basketball, soccer, volleyball.
CAREER PLANNING ***Service:*** career counseling.
AFTER GRADUATION 54% of students completing a degree program in 1994–95 went directly on to further study.
EXPENSES FOR 1995–96 ***Application fee:*** $20. Comprehensive fee of $10,590 includes full-time tuition ($6790 minimum), mandatory fees ($200), and college room and board ($3600). Part-time tuition per credit hour ranges from $176 to $259. Full-time tuition ranges up to $7084 according to program.
FINANCIAL AID ***College-administered undergrad aid 1995–96:*** 183 need-based scholarships (averaging $700), 49 non-need scholarships (averaging $1780), low-interest long-term loans from external sources (averaging $2625), Federal Work-Study. ***Required forms:*** state, institutional, FAFSA. ***Priority deadline:*** 5/1. ***Payment plan:*** deferred payment. ***Waivers:*** full or partial for employees or children of employees and senior citizens.
APPLYING ***Options:*** early entrance, deferred entrance. ***Required:*** school transcript, 3 years of high school math and science, interview, TOEFL for international students. ***Recommended:*** recommendations. ***Required for some:*** SAT I or ACT. Test scores used for admission. ***Application deadline:*** rolling. ***Notification:*** continuous.
APPLYING/TRANSFER ***Required:*** high school transcript, 3 years of high school math and science, interview, college transcript. ***Recommended:*** recommendations. ***Required for some:*** standardized test scores. ***Entrance:*** minimally difficult. ***Application deadline:*** rolling. ***Notification:*** continuous.
CONTACT Mr. I. Jerry Czenstuch, Dean of Admissions, Manor Junior College, Jenkintown, PA 19046-3399, 215-885-2360 Ext. 213.

❖ ***See page 762 for a narrative description.*** ❖

Pennsylvania

McCANN SCHOOL OF BUSINESS
Mahanoy City, Pennsylvania

UG Enrollment: 205	Tuition: $12,150/deg prog
Application Deadline: rolling	Room & Board: N/Avail

GENERAL Proprietary, 2-year, coed. Awards certificates, diplomas, transfer associate, terminal associate degrees. Founded 1897. *Setting:* small-town campus. *Total enrollment:* 205. *Faculty:* 21 (6 full-time, 15 part-time).
ENROLLMENT PROFILE 205 students: 92% women, 8% men, 32% part-time, 100% state residents, 1% transferred in, 36% 25 or older, 2% African American. *Most popular recent majors:* accounting, secretarial studies/office management, paralegal studies.
FIRST-YEAR CLASS 88 total; 112 applied, 96% were accepted, 77% of whom enrolled. 8% from top 10% of their high school class, 33% from top quarter, 52% from top half. 1 valedictorian.
ACADEMIC PROGRAM Core. Calendar: quarters. 84 courses offered in 1995–96. Academic remediation for entering students, summer session for credit, part-time degree program (daytime, evenings), internships.
GENERAL DEGREE REQUIREMENTS 90 credits; computer course; internship (some majors).
MAJORS Accounting, business administration/commerce/management, computer science, marketing/retailing/merchandising, paralegal studies, secretarial studies/office management.
LIBRARY 1,850 books, 24 periodicals, 95 records, tapes, and CDs.
COMPUTERS ON CAMPUS 20 computers for student use in computer labs. Staffed computer lab on campus provides training in use of computers, software.
COLLEGE LIFE *Social organizations:* 2 open to all. *Most popular organizations:* Student Council, Circle K.
HOUSING College housing not available.
CAREER PLANNING *Services:* job fairs, resume preparation, resume referral, career counseling, job interviews. Students must register sophomore year. 35 organizations recruited on campus 1994–95.
AFTER GRADUATION 83% of class of 1994 had job offers within 6 months.
EXPENSES FOR 1996–97 *Application fee:* $25. Tuition: $12,150 per degree program. Part-time tuition per credit: $135.
FINANCIAL AID *College-administered undergrad aid 1995–96:* non-need scholarships, low-interest long-term loans from external sources (average $2000). *Required forms:* state, FAFSA; accepted: CSS Financial Aid PROFILE. *Application deadline:* continuous to 8/1.
APPLYING *Option:* Common Application. *Required:* school transcript, minimum 2.0 GPA, campus interview. *Application deadline:* rolling.
APPLYING/TRANSFER *Required:* high school transcript, campus interview, college transcript, minimum 2.0 college GPA, minimum 2.0 high school GPA. *Application deadline:* rolling. *Contact:* Ms. Linda Walinsky, Admissions Director, 717-773-1820.
CONTACT Mr. Tom Fletcher, Director, McCann School of Business, 47 South Main Street, Mahanoy City, PA 17948, 717-773-1820.

McCARRIE SCHOOLS OF HEALTH SCIENCES AND TECHNOLOGY
Philadelphia, Pennsylvania

UG Enrollment: 427	Tuition: $9455/deg prog
Application Deadline: rolling	Room & Board: N/Avail

GENERAL Proprietary, 2-year, coed. Awards terminal associate degrees. Founded 1917. *Setting:* urban campus. *Total enrollment:* 427. *Faculty:* 20; student-faculty ratio is 25:1.
ENROLLMENT PROFILE 427 students from 3 states and territories, 9 other countries. 60% women, 90% state residents, 1% transferred in, 6% international, 30% 25 or older, 9% Hispanic, 38% African American, 16% Asian American.
FIRST-YEAR CLASS Of the students who applied, 80% were accepted, 90% of whom enrolled.
ACADEMIC PROGRAM Calendar: semesters. Internships.
GENERAL DEGREE REQUIREMENT Internship.
MAJORS Dental services, medical assistant technologies, medical laboratory technology, nursing, operating room technology, optical technologies.
LIBRARY 750 books, 25 periodicals.
HOUSING College housing not available.
CAREER PLANNING *Service:* career counseling.
EXPENSES FOR 1995–96 Tuition per degree program ranges from $9455 to $9905.
FINANCIAL AID *College-administered undergrad aid 1995–96:* need-based scholarships, low-interest long-term loans from external sources (average $2000). *Required forms:* institutional; accepted: CSS Financial Aid PROFILE, state, FAFSA. *Priority deadline:* 5/1. *Payment plans:* tuition prepayment, installment.
APPLYING *Option:* deferred entrance. *Required for some:* CPAt. Test scores used for admission. *Application deadline:* rolling. *Notification:* continuous.
CONTACT Mr. Wally McKenzie, Director of Admissions, McCarrie Schools of Health Sciences and Technology, 512 South Broad Street, Philadelphia, PA 19146-1613, 215-545-7772.

MEDIAN SCHOOL OF ALLIED HEALTH CAREERS
Pittsburgh, Pennsylvania

UG Enrollment: 83	Tuition & Fees: N/R
Application Deadline: rolling	Room & Board: N/Avail

GENERAL Proprietary, 2-year, coed. Awards terminal associate degrees. Founded 1958. *Setting:* urban campus. *Total enrollment:* 83. *Faculty:* 25 (14 full-time, 11 part-time).
ENROLLMENT PROFILE 83 students from 7 states and territories, 1 other country. 57% women, 43% men, 0% part-time, 90% state residents, 1% international, 84% have need-based financial aid, 1% international, 37% 25 or older, 0% Native American, 0% Hispanic, 17% African American, 0% Asian American. *Areas of study chosen:* 100% health professions and related sciences. *Most popular recent major:* medical assistant technologies.
FIRST-YEAR CLASS 29 total; 29 applied, 87% were accepted, 100% of whom enrolled.
ACADEMIC PROGRAM Calendar: quarters. Internships.
GENERAL DEGREE REQUIREMENTS 1800 clock hours; computer course for medical assisting, medical billing, veterinary assisting majors; internship (some majors).
MAJOR Medical assistant technologies.
LIBRARY Median Resource Center with 1,403 books, 43 periodicals, 135 records, tapes, and CDs.
COMPUTERS ON CAMPUS 25 computers for student use in computer center. Staffed computer lab on campus provides training in use of computers, software.
COLLEGE LIFE *Student services:* personal-psychological counseling. *Campus security:* security during class hours.
HOUSING College housing not available.
CAREER PLANNING *Placement office:* 1 full-time staff. *Director:* Ms. Cindy Laspina, Placement Director, 412-391-7021. *Services:* resume preparation, resume referral, career counseling, job interviews. 20 organizations recruited on campus 1994–95.
AFTER GRADUATION 94% of class of 1994 had job offers within 6 months.
EXPENSES FOR 1996–97 *Application fee:* $75. Full-time tuition varies according to program.
FINANCIAL AID *College-administered undergrad aid 1995–96:* need-based scholarships, 7 non-need scholarships (average $1000), low-interest long-term loans from external sources, Federal Work-Study. *Required forms for some financial aid applicants:* state, FAFSA. *Payment plans:* tuition prepayment, installment.
APPLYING *Options:* deferred entrance, midyear entrance. *Required:* essay, school transcript, interview, Wonderlic aptitude test. *Recommended:* minimum 2.0 GPA, 3 years of high school math and science. Test scores used for admission. *Application deadline:* rolling.
APPLYING/TRANSFER *Required:* essay, standardized test scores, high school transcript, college transcript. *Recommended:* 3 years of high school math and science, minimum 2.0 college GPA, minimum 2.0 high school GPA. *Contact:* Ms. Ginger Serafini, Director of Admissions, 412-391-7021.
CONTACT Ms. Ginger Serafini, Director of Admissions, Median School of Allied Health Careers, 125 Seventh Street, Pittsburgh, PA 15222-3400, 412-391-7021 or toll-free 800-570-0693 (in-state). *Fax:* 412-232-4348.

MONTGOMERY COUNTY COMMUNITY COLLEGE
Blue Bell, Pennsylvania

UG Enrollment: 8,751	Tuition & Fees (Area Res): $2010
Application Deadline: rolling	Room & Board: N/Avail

GENERAL County-supported, 2-year, coed. Awards certificates, transfer associate, terminal associate degrees. Founded 1964. *Setting:* 186-acre suburban campus with easy access to Philadelphia. *Educational spending 1994–95:* $1751 per undergrad. *Total enrollment:* 8,751. *Faculty:* 514 (130 full-time, 24% with terminal degrees, 384 part-time); student-faculty ratio is 22:1.
ENROLLMENT PROFILE 8,751 students from 3 states and territories. 58% women, 42% men, 71% part-time, 99% state residents, 8% transferred in, 18% have need-based financial aid, 47% 25 or older, 1% Native American, 1% Hispanic, 6% African American, 4% Asian American. *Areas of study chosen:* 44% liberal arts/general studies, 15% business management and administrative services, 9% health professions and related sciences, 5% education, 4% computer and information sciences, 4% engineering and applied sciences, 3% fine arts, 2% biological and life sciences, 2% social sciences, 1% communications and journalism, 1% mathematics, 1% physical sciences. *Most popular recent majors:* liberal arts/general studies, nursing, business administration/commerce/management.
FIRST-YEAR CLASS 2,804 total. Of the students who applied, 100% were accepted. 4% from top 10% of their high school class, 35% from top quarter, 46% from top half.
ACADEMIC PROGRAM Core. Calendar: semesters. 650 courses offered in 1995–96. Academic remediation for entering students, English as a second language program offered during academic year, services for LD students, advanced placement, self-designed majors, tutorials, honors program, summer session for credit, part-time degree program (daytime, evenings, weekends, summer), adult/continuing education programs, internships. Off-campus study.
GENERAL DEGREE REQUIREMENTS 63 credits; computer course for most majors; internship (some majors).
MAJORS Accounting, art/fine arts, automotive technologies, biology/biological sciences, business administration/commerce/management, chemistry, communication, communication equipment technology, computer information systems, computer science, criminal justice, data processing, dental services, drafting and design, early childhood education, education, electrical and electronics technologies, elementary education, engineering (general), engineering technology, English, environmental engineering technology, fire science, gerontology, graphic arts, hotel and restaurant management, humanities, human services, law enforcement/police sciences, liberal arts/general studies, marketing/retailing/merchandising, mathematics, medical laboratory technology, nursing, physical education, physical sciences, psychology, real estate, secretarial studies/office management, social science, teacher aide studies, technology and public affairs, telecommunications.
LIBRARY Learning Resource Center with 86,814 books, 429 periodicals, 110 CD-ROMs, 10,140 records, tapes, and CDs. Acquisition spending 1994–95: $142,825.
COMPUTERS ON CAMPUS 225 computers for student use in computer center, computer labs, learning resource center, classrooms, library provide access to main academic computer, e-mail, Internet. Staffed computer lab on campus provides training in use of computers, software. Academic computing expenditure 1994–95: $806,351.
COLLEGE LIFE Choral group, student-run newspaper, radio station. *Social organizations:* 20 open to all. *Most popular organizations:* Student Government, Meridians Non-traditional Age Club, Student Radio Station. *Major annual events:* Volleyball Benefit, Spring Fling/Fun Day, Cultural Fair. *Student services:* health clinic, personal-psychological counseling. *Campus security:* 24-hour emergency response devices and patrols, late-night transport-escort service.
HOUSING College housing not available.

Peterson's Guide to Two-Year Colleges 1997

Montgomery County Community College (continued)

ATHLETICS ***Intramural:*** archery, badminton, basketball, bowling, cross-country running, field hockey, football, golf, racquetball, soccer, softball, table tennis (Ping-Pong), volleyball, weight lifting. ***Contact:*** Ms. Pam Famous, Director of Athletics, 215-641-6514.

CAREER PLANNING ***Placement office:*** 7 full-time, 6 part-time staff; $763,732 operating expenditure 1994–95. ***Director:*** Ms. Cynthia Love, Director of Counseling and Career Development, 215-641-6577. ***Services:*** resume preparation, career counseling, careers library, job bank.

EXPENSES FOR 1995–96 ***Application fee:*** $20. Area resident tuition: $1920 full-time. State resident tuition: $3840 full-time. Nonresident tuition: $5760 full-time. Tuition per semester ranges from $64 to $704 for area residents, $128 to $1408 for state residents, $192 to $2112 for nonresidents. Part-time mandatory fees: $3 per credit hour. Full-time mandatory fees: $90.

FINANCIAL AID ***College-administered undergrad aid 1995–96:*** 73 need-based scholarships (average $800), 37 non-need scholarships (average $1000), short-term loans (average $125), low-interest long-term loans from external sources (average $2625), Federal Work-Study, 33 part-time jobs. ***Required forms:*** state, institutional; accepted: CSS Financial Aid PROFILE, FAFSA. ***Priority deadline:*** 3/15. ***Payment plan:*** deferred payment. ***Waivers:*** full or partial for employees or children of employees and senior citizens. ***Notification:*** continuous.

APPLYING Open admission except for dental hygiene, nursing, medical laboratory technology, automotive technology programs. ***Options:*** early entrance, deferred entrance, midyear entrance. Test scores used for counseling/placement. ***Application deadline:*** rolling. ***Notification:*** continuous. Preference given to county residents.

APPLYING/TRANSFER ***Application deadline:*** rolling. ***Notification:*** continuous. ***Contact:*** Mr. Peter Cubbage, Counselor, 215-641-6568.

CONTACT Mr. Dennis Murphy, Director of Admissions and Records, Montgomery County Community College, Blue Bell, PA 19422-0796, 215-641-6550. ***Fax:*** 215-653-0585. College video available.

NATIONAL EDUCATION CENTER–VALE TECHNICAL INSTITUTE CAMPUS

Pennsylvania—See Remington Education Center–Vale Campus

NEW KENSINGTON COMMERCIAL SCHOOL

Pennsylvania—See Newport Business Institute

NEWPORT BUSINESS INSTITUTE

Lower Burrell, Pennsylvania

UG Enrollment: 215	**Tuition & Fees: $4975**
Application Deadline: rolling	**Room & Board: N/Avail**

GENERAL Proprietary, 2-year, coed. Awards terminal associate degrees. Founded 1895. ***Setting:*** 4-acre small-town campus with easy access to Pittsburgh. ***Research spending 1994–95:*** $2000. ***Educational spending 1994–95:*** $200 per undergrad. ***Total enrollment:*** 215. ***Faculty:*** 12 (10 full-time, 2 part-time).

ENROLLMENT PROFILE 215 students: 80% women, 1% part-time, 100% state residents, 20% transferred in, 0% international, 25% 25 or older, 1% Native American, 0% Hispanic, 2% African American, 0% Asian American. ***Areas of study chosen:*** 40% business management and administrative services, 30% computer and information sciences, 30% health professions and related sciences. ***Most popular recent majors:*** medical secretarial studies, business administration/commerce/management, accounting.

FIRST-YEAR CLASS 75 total; 95 applied, 95% were accepted, 83% of whom enrolled. 15% from top 10% of their high school class, 35% from top quarter, 65% from top half.

ACADEMIC PROGRAM Honor code. Calendar: quarters. Self-designed majors.

GENERAL DEGREE REQUIREMENTS 75 credits; computer course.

MAJORS Accounting, business administration/commerce/management, computer programming, data processing, fashion merchandising, legal secretarial studies, medical assistant technologies, medical records services, medical secretarial studies, retail management, secretarial studies/office management, tourism and travel.

LIBRARY 100 books, 40 microform titles, 10 periodicals, 30 records, tapes, and CDs. Acquisition spending 1994–95: $2000.

COMPUTERS ON CAMPUS 85 computers for student use in computer center, computer labs, classrooms. Staffed computer lab on campus provides training in use of computers, software. Academic computing expenditure 1994–95: $100,000.

COLLEGE LIFE Student-run newspaper. ***Social organizations:*** 4 open to all. ***Most popular organizations:*** Student Government, Data Processing Management Association, Professional Secretaries International. ***Major annual events:*** Blood Drive, Commencement Exercise, Bring-a-Friend Day. ***Student services:*** personal-psychological counseling. ***Campus security:*** security system.

HOUSING College housing not available.

CAREER PLANNING ***Placement office:*** $10,000 operating expenditure 1994–95. ***Director:*** Mr. Michael Choma, Director of Academic Affairs, 412-339-7542. ***Services:*** job fairs, resume preparation, resume referral, career counseling, job interviews. Students must register sophomore year. 10 organizations recruited on campus 1994–95.

AFTER GRADUATION 97% of class of 1994 had job offers within 6 months. 4% of students completing a degree program went directly on to further study.

EXPENSES FOR 1996–97 ***Application fee:*** $15. Tuition: $4675 full-time, $390 per course part-time. Full-time mandatory fees: $300.

FINANCIAL AID ***College-administered undergrad aid 1995–96:*** 140 need-based scholarships (average $1100), low-interest long-term loans from external sources (average $1500). ***Required forms:*** state. ***Priority deadline:*** 9/1. ***Payment plan:*** installment. ***Waivers:*** full or partial for employees or children of employees. ***Notification:*** continuous.

APPLYING Open admission. ***Option:*** Common Application. ***Required:*** school transcript. ***Application deadline:*** rolling. ***Notification:*** continuous.

APPLYING/TRANSFER ***Required:*** high school transcript, college transcript. ***Application deadline:*** rolling. ***Notification:*** continuous. ***Contact:*** Mr. Michael Choma, Director of Academic Affairs, 412-339-7542.

CONTACT Mr. Robert Kaiser, Director of Admissions, Newport Business Institute, Lower Burrell, PA 15068-3929, 412-339-7542 or toll-free 800-752-7695. ***Fax:*** 412-339-7542. College video available.

NORTHAMPTON COUNTY AREA COMMUNITY COLLEGE

Bethlehem, Pennsylvania

UG Enrollment: 5,857	**Tuition & Fees (Area Res): $1950**
Application Deadline: rolling	**Room & Board: $3820**

GENERAL State and locally supported, 2-year, coed. Awards certificates, diplomas, transfer associate, terminal associate degrees. Founded 1967. ***Setting:*** 165-acre suburban campus with easy access to Philadelphia. ***Endowment:*** $5.1 million. ***Total enrollment:*** 5,857. ***Faculty:*** 311 (73 full-time, 238 part-time); student-faculty ratio is 19:1. ***Notable Alumni:*** James R. Bartholomew, senior vice president of PNC Bank; Ms. Carol Guzy, photographer for the Washington Post; R. Charles Stehly, president of Signcorp; Jesse Johnson, funeral director; Jim Palmer, funeral director.

ENROLLMENT PROFILE 5,857 students from 12 states and territories, 20 other countries. 60% women, 40% men, 64% part-time, 95% state residents, 3% live on campus, 22% transferred in, 40% have need-based financial aid, 10% have non-need-based financial aid, 1% international, 48% 25 or older, 0% Native American, 5% Hispanic, 3% African American, 2% Asian American. ***Areas of study chosen:*** 35% liberal arts/general studies, 22% business management and administrative services, 11% health professions and related sciences, 8% education, 5% social sciences, 4% computer and information sciences, 4% engineering and applied sciences, 2% architecture, 2% biological and life sciences, 2% communications and journalism, 2% vocational and home economics, 1% fine arts, 1% library and information studies, 1% physical sciences. ***Most popular recent majors:*** liberal arts/general studies, education, criminal justice.

FIRST-YEAR CLASS 1,296 total; 1,995 applied, 99% were accepted, 66% of whom enrolled.

ACADEMIC PROGRAM Core, foundational skills and studies curriculum, honor code. Calendar: semesters. 824 courses offered in 1995–96; average class size 21 in required courses. Academic remediation for entering students, English as a second language program offered during academic year, services for LD students, advanced placement, self-designed majors, summer session for credit, part-time degree program (daytime, evenings, summer), adult/continuing education programs, co-op programs and internships.

GENERAL DEGREE REQUIREMENTS 60 credit hours; computer course for most majors; internship (some majors).

MAJORS Accounting, architectural technologies, art/fine arts, automotive technologies, biology/biological sciences, business administration/commerce/management, chemical engineering technology, chemistry, commercial art, computer information systems, computer science, criminal justice, data processing, dental services, drafting and design, early childhood education, education, electrical and electronics technologies, electromechanical technology, emergency medical technology, engineering (general), environmental health sciences, finance/banking, funeral service, hotel and restaurant management, interior design, legal secretarial studies, liberal arts/general studies, manufacturing technology, mathematics, medical secretarial studies, nursing, occupational safety and health, physics, plastics technology, radio and television studies, radiological technology, secretarial studies/office management, social work, sports administration, tourism and travel.

LIBRARY Learning Resources Center with 70,000 books, 61 microform titles, 448 periodicals, 10 CD-ROMs, 2,093 records, tapes, and CDs. Acquisition spending 1994–95: $125,293.

COMPUTERS ON CAMPUS 441 computers for student use in computer labs, learning resource center, off-campus centers, classrooms, library. Academic computing expenditure 1994–95: $208,806.

COLLEGE LIFE Drama-theater group, choral group, student-run newspaper, radio station. 4% vote in student government elections. ***Social organizations:*** 39 open to all. ***Most popular organizations:*** Phi Theta Kappa, Nursing Student Organization, Video Waves, Student American Dental Hygiene Association, International Student Organization. ***Major annual events:*** Family Day, Club Fair, Casino Day. ***Student services:*** health clinic, personal-psychological counseling. ***Campus security:*** 24-hour emergency response devices and patrols.

HOUSING 149 college housing spaces available; all were occupied 1995–96. Freshmen given priority for college housing. Off-campus living permitted. ***Option:*** coed (2 buildings) housing available. Resident assistants live in dorms.

ATHLETICS ***Intercollegiate:*** baseball M, basketball M/W, bowling M/W, golf M/W, softball W, tennis M/W, volleyball W. ***Intramural:*** basketball, bowling, football, golf, racquetball, softball, volleyball. ***Contact:*** Mr. William Bearse, Athletic Director, 610-861-5368.

CAREER PLANNING ***Placement office:*** 5 full-time, 4 part-time staff; $91,075 operating expenditure 1994–95. ***Director:*** Ms. Linda Arra, Director of Counseling and Placement, 610-861-5344. ***Services:*** job fairs, resume preparation, resume referral, career counseling, careers library, job bank, job interviews. 30 organizations recruited on campus 1994–95.

AFTER GRADUATION 56% of students completing a degree program in 1994–95 went directly on to further study.

EXPENSES FOR 1995–96 ***Application fee:*** $25. Area resident tuition: $1740 full-time, $58 per credit hour part-time. State resident tuition: $3480 full-time, $116 per credit hour part-time. Nonresident tuition: $5220 full-time, $174 per credit hour part-time. Full-time mandatory fees: $210 for area residents, $600 for state residents, $990 for nonresidents. Part-time mandatory fees per credit hour: $7 for area residents, $20 for state residents, $33 for nonresidents. College room and board: $3820. College room only: $2400.

FINANCIAL AID ***College-administered undergrad aid 1995–96:*** 450 need-based scholarships (average $400), short-term loans (average $100), low-interest long-term loans from external sources (average $2000), 223 Federal Work-Study (averaging $800), 55 part-time jobs. ***Required forms:*** state, institutional, FAFSA; accepted: CSS Financial Aid PROFILE. ***Priority deadline:*** 3/31. ***Waivers:*** full or partial for employees or children of employees and senior citizens. ***Notification:*** continuous.

APPLYING Open admission except for allied health, advertising design programs. ***Options:*** Common Application, early entrance, deferred entrance, midyear entrance. ***Required:*** school transcript. ***Required for some:*** campus interview, art evaluation for advertising design program. ***Application deadline:*** rolling. ***Notification:*** continuous.
APPLYING/TRANSFER ***Required:*** high school transcript, college transcript. ***Required for some:*** campus interview, art evaluation for advertising design program. ***Entrance:*** noncompetitive. ***Application deadline:*** rolling. ***Notification:*** continuous. ***Contact:*** Ms. Maria Teresa Donate, Director of Admissions, 610-861-5500.
CONTACT Ms. Maria Teresa Donate, Director of Admissions, Northampton County Area Community College, Bethlehem, PA 18017-7599, 610-861-5500. ***E-mail:*** adminfo@pmail.nhrm.cc.pa.us. College video available.

PEIRCE COLLEGE
Philadelphia, Pennsylvania

UG Enrollment: 1,154	**Tuition & Fees: $6692**
Application Deadline: rolling	**Room Only: $3400**

Peirce's goal is to provide the knowledge and skills necessary for employment. Peirce maintains strong ties to the business community and continually updates its courses to reflect hiring trends. New programs include computer network technologies and microcomputing. The paralegal studies program is approved by the American Bar Association.

GENERAL Independent, 2-year, coed. Awards transfer associate, terminal associate degrees. Founded 1865. ***Setting:*** 2-acre urban campus. ***Total enrollment:*** 1,154. ***Faculty:*** 57 (25 full-time, 16% with terminal degrees, 32 part-time); student-faculty ratio is 19:1. ***Notable Alumni:*** J. Linford Snyder, Thomas Heck, William H. Duron.
ENROLLMENT PROFILE 1,154 students from 9 states and territories, 13 other countries. 76% women, 32% part-time, 81% state residents, 3% live on campus, 5% transferred in, 75% have need-based financial aid, 15% have non-need-based financial aid, 3% international, 35% 25 or older, 1% Native American, 3% Hispanic, 55% African American, 2% Asian American.
FIRST-YEAR CLASS 520 total; 706 applied, 92% were accepted, 80% of whom enrolled.
ACADEMIC PROGRAM Core, business curriculum, honor code. Calendar: semesters. Academic remediation for entering students, English as a second language program offered during academic year, services for LD students, advanced placement, self-designed majors, honors program, summer session for credit, part-time degree program (daytime, evenings, weekends, summer), adult/continuing education programs, co-op programs and internships.
GENERAL DEGREE REQUIREMENTS 60 credits; 1 math course; internship (some majors).
MAJORS Accounting, business administration/commerce/management, computer information systems, court reporting, hotel and restaurant management, liberal arts/general studies, medical secretarial studies, paralegal studies, secretarial studies/office management.
LIBRARY 40,000 books, 82 microform titles, 135 periodicals, 5 CD-ROMs, 4,010 records, tapes, and CDs.
COMPUTERS ON CAMPUS 150 computers for student use in computer center, computer labs, learning resource center provide access to main academic computer. Staffed computer lab on campus provides training in use of computers, software.
COLLEGE LIFE ***Social organizations:*** 12 open to all; 1 local fraternity, 2 local sororities; 8% of eligible men and 16% of eligible women are members. ***Most popular organizations:*** Phi Theta Kappa, Paralegal Association, Success, Peirce Ambassadors, Black Student Union. ***Major annual events:*** Unity Day, Career Day, Peirce Pride. ***Student services:*** personal-psychological counseling. ***Campus security:*** 24-hour patrols.
HOUSING 40 college housing spaces available; all were occupied 1995–96. No special consideration for freshman housing applicants. Off-campus living permitted. ***Option:*** coed (2 buildings) housing available. Resident assistants live in dorms.
CAREER PLANNING ***Placement office:*** 4 full-time staff. ***Director:*** Ms. Barbara Zelino, Director, Career Services, 215-545-6400 Ext. 278. ***Services:*** job fairs, resume preparation, resume referral, career counseling, careers library, job bank, job interviews. Students must register freshman year.
AFTER GRADUATION 25% of students completing a degree program in 1994–95 went directly on to further study.
EXPENSES FOR 1995–96 ***Application fee:*** $20. Tuition: $6500 full-time. Part-time mandatory fees per semester range from $39 to $102. Part-time tuition per credit: $181 for evening classes, $231 for day classes. Full-time mandatory fees: $192. College room only: $3400.
FINANCIAL AID ***College-administered undergrad aid 1995–96:*** 125 need-based scholarships (averaging $760), 30 non-need scholarships (averaging $1500), short-term loans (averaging $200), low-interest long-term loans from external sources (averaging $1300), Federal Work-Study, part-time jobs. ***Required forms:*** state, institutional; accepted: FAFSA. ***Priority deadline:*** 7/31. ***Payment plan:*** deferred payment. ***Waivers:*** full or partial for children of alumni and employees or children of employees.
APPLYING ***Options:*** early entrance, deferred entrance, midyear entrance. ***Recommended:*** minimum 2.0 GPA, 3 years of high school math and science, SAT I, TOEFL for international students. Test scores used for counseling/placement. ***Application deadline:*** rolling. ***Notification:*** continuous.
APPLYING/TRANSFER ***Recommended:*** standardized test scores, 3 years of high school math and science, minimum 2.0 high school GPA. ***Entrance:*** minimally difficult. ***Application deadline:*** rolling. ***Notification:*** continuous.
CONTACT Mr. Steven Bird, Director of Admissions, Peirce College, 1420 Pine Street, Philadelphia, PA 19102-4603, 215-545-6400 Ext. 212. ***Fax:*** 215-546-5996.

❖ ***See page 790 for a narrative description.*** ❖

PENN COMMERCIAL, INC.
Washington, Pennsylvania

UG Enrollment: 230	**Tuition: $5000/deg prog**
Application Deadline: rolling	**Room & Board: N/Avail**

GENERAL Proprietary, 2-year, coed. Awards diplomas, transfer associate degrees. Founded 1929. ***Setting:*** 1-acre small-town campus with easy access to Pittsburgh. ***Total enrollment:*** 230. ***Faculty:*** 18 (all full-time).
ENROLLMENT PROFILE 230 students from 3 states and territories. 60% women, 40% men, 4% part-time, 95% state residents, 3% transferred in, 0% international, 50% 25 or older, 0% Native American, 0% Hispanic, 10% African American, 0% Asian American. ***Most popular recent major:*** business administration/commerce/management.
FIRST-YEAR CLASS 83 total; 106 applied, 100% of whom enrolled. 3% from top 10% of their high school class, 37% from top quarter, 60% from top half.
ACADEMIC PROGRAM Calendar: quarters. Academic remediation for entering students, summer session for credit.
GENERAL DEGREE REQUIREMENTS 1500 clock hours; internship (some majors).
MAJORS Business administration/commerce/management, legal secretarial studies, medical assistant technologies, medical secretarial studies, secretarial studies/office management.
LIBRARY 400 books, 10 periodicals, 30 records, tapes, and CDs.
COMPUTERS ON CAMPUS 60 computers for student use in computer labs, classrooms, library provide access to main academic computer. Staffed computer lab on campus provides training in use of computers, software.
COLLEGE LIFE Student-run newspaper.
HOUSING College housing not available.
CAREER PLANNING ***Placement office:*** 3 full-time staff. ***Director:*** Ms. Alice Kozikoski, Educational Director, 412-222-5330. ***Services:*** resume preparation, resume referral, career counseling, careers library, job interviews.
AFTER GRADUATION 90% of class of 1994 had job offers within 6 months.
EXPENSES FOR 1996–97 ***Application fee:*** $25. Tuition per degree program ranges from $5000 to $13,600. One-time mandatory fee: $100.
FINANCIAL AID ***College-administered undergrad aid 1995–96:*** need-based scholarships, low-interest long-term loans from external sources (average $2000). ***Acceptable forms:*** state. ***Application deadline:*** continuous. ***Payment plan:*** installment.
APPLYING Open admission. ***Options:*** early entrance, deferred entrance. ***Required:*** school transcript. ***Application deadline:*** rolling. ***Notification:*** continuous.
APPLYING/TRANSFER ***Required:*** high school transcript, college transcript. ***Application deadline:*** rolling. ***Notification:*** continuous.
CONTACT Ms. Debbie Husarchik, Admissions Representative, Penn Commercial, Inc., Washington, PA 15301-6822, 412-222-5330 Ext. 40. College video available.

PENNCO TECH
Bristol, Pennsylvania

Enrollment: N/R	**Tuition: $5000/deg prog**
Application Deadline: rolling	**Room & Board: N/Avail**

GENERAL Proprietary, 2-year, coed. Part of Pennco Institutes, Inc. Awards transfer associate, terminal associate degrees. Founded 1961. ***Setting:*** 7-acre small-town campus with easy access to Philadelphia. ***Faculty:*** 100 (60 full-time, 40 part-time).
ENROLLMENT PROFILE 0% part-time, 86% state residents, 7% transferred in, 2% Hispanic, 22% African American, 4% Asian American.
FIRST-YEAR CLASS Of the students who applied, 80% were accepted, 80% of whom enrolled.
ACADEMIC PROGRAM Calendar: modular. Academic remediation for entering students, advanced placement, adult/continuing education programs, co-op programs.
GENERAL DEGREE REQUIREMENT 1900 hours.
MAJORS Automotive technologies, computer programming, drafting and design, electrical and electronics technologies.
LIBRARY 6,000 books, 10 periodicals.
COLLEGE LIFE Student-run newspaper.
HOUSING College housing not available.
CAREER PLANNING ***Service:*** career counseling.
EXPENSES FOR 1995–96 Tuition and fees per degree program range from $5000 to $19000 for day program, $5000 to $13,000 for evenining program.
FINANCIAL AID ***College-administered undergrad aid 1995–96:*** need-based scholarships, 6 non-need scholarships, low-interest long-term loans from external sources (average $2500), Federal Work-Study, 5 part-time jobs. ***Acceptable forms:*** CSS Financial Aid PROFILE, state, institutional, FAFSA. ***Application deadline:*** continuous.
APPLYING ***Recommended:*** TOEFL for international students. ***Required for some:*** IBM Aptitude Test. Test scores used for admission. ***Application deadline:*** rolling.
APPLYING/TRANSFER ***Entrance:*** minimally difficult. ***Application deadline:*** rolling.
CONTACT Mr. Michael Hobyak, Director of Admissions, Pennco Tech, Bristol, PA 19007-3696, 215-824-3200.

PENNSYLVANIA COLLEGE OF TECHNOLOGY
Williamsport, Pennsylvania

UG Enrollment: 4,729	**Tuition & Fees (PA Res): $6306**
Application Deadline: rolling	**Room & Board: N/Avail**

Pennsylvania College of Technology is Pennsylvania's premier technical college. An affiliate of Pennsylvania State University (Penn State), Penn College has a national reputation for quality and diversity of instruction in traditional and advanced technologies and for its hands-on approach to learning. Baccalaureate, associate degree, and certificate programs range from business, computer, and industrial technologies to health sciences, construction, transportation, and natural resources management. Programs for transfer students are offered as well. New facilities opened since 1993 include a $6-million Aviation Center, an $11-million Community Arts Center, a $12-million Campus Center, and a Diesel Center located at the Earth Science Center.

GENERAL State-related, primarily 2-year, coed. Part of Pennsylvania State University. Awards certificates, transfer associate, terminal associate, bachelor's degrees. Founded 1965. ***Setting:*** 899-acre small-town campus. ***Total enrollment:*** 4,729. ***Faculty:*** 350 (222 full-time, 77% with terminal degrees, 128 part-time); student-faculty ratio is 18:1. ***Notable Alumni:*** Thomas A. Marino, district attorney for Lycoming County; Frederick T. Gilmour, III, director of instructional media at Penn College; Louisa Forsa, president of Hope Intermediate Residence; David and Mary McGravey, owners of B & S Frames, Inc.

Pennsylvania College of Technology (continued)

ENROLLMENT PROFILE 4,729 students from 14 states and territories, 4 other countries. 43% women, 57% men, 24% part-time, 97% state residents, 6% transferred in, 1% international, 35% 25 or older, 1% Native American, 1% Hispanic, 3% African American, 1% Asian American. ***Areas of study chosen:*** 17% health professions and related sciences, 12% engineering and applied sciences, 9% business management and administrative services, 4% liberal arts/general studies, 3% computer and information sciences, 2% architecture, 2% natural resource sciences, 1% communications and journalism. ***Most popular recent majors:*** heating/refrigeration/air conditioning, automotive technologies, nursing.

FIRST-YEAR CLASS 985 total; 1,977 applied, 96% were accepted, 52% of whom enrolled. 7% from top 10% of their high school class, 17% from top quarter, 38% from top half.

ACADEMIC PROGRAM Core, honor code. Calendar: semesters. 105 courses offered in 1995–96. Academic remediation for entering students, services for LD students, advanced placement, self-designed majors, summer session for credit, part-time degree program (daytime, evenings), co-op programs and internships. Off-campus study at Lycoming College, Pennsylvania State University.

GENERAL DEGREE REQUIREMENTS 60 credits for associate, 120 credits for bachelor's; math/science requirements vary according to program; computer course (varies by major); internship (some majors).

MAJORS Accounting, advertising, architectural technologies, automotive engineering, automotive technologies (B), aviation technology, biology/biological sciences, broadcasting, business administration/commerce/management (B), civil engineering technology, communication, computer information systems, computer science, computer technologies, construction management (B), construction technologies, culinary arts, dental services (B), drafting and design, early childhood education, educational media (B), electrical and electronics technologies, electrical engineering, electronics engineering, electronics engineering technology (B), (pre)engineering sequence, environmental engineering technology, food services management, food services technology, forest technology, graphic arts (B), heating/refrigeration/air conditioning (B), hotel and restaurant management, human services (B), industrial administration (B), industrial and heavy equipment maintenance, industrial engineering technology, landscaping/grounds maintenance, legal studies (B), liberal arts/general studies, manufacturing engineering (B), manufacturing technology, natural resource management, nursing, occupational therapy, optical technologies, ornamental horticulture, paralegal studies, physical sciences, plastics technology (B), practical nursing, quality control technology, radiological technology, retail management, robotics, secretarial studies/office management, surveying technology, vocational education, welding technology (B), wood sciences.

LIBRARY Penn College Library plus 2 others, with 65,000 books, 462 microform titles, 941 periodicals, 3 on-line bibliographic services, 15 CD-ROMs, 3,750 records, tapes, and CDs. Acquisition spending 1994–95: $972,030.

COMPUTERS ON CAMPUS Computer purchase plan available. 1,000 computers for student use in computer center, computer labs, classrooms, library provide access to main academic computer, Internet. Staffed computer lab on campus provides training in use of computers, software.

COLLEGE LIFE Orientation program (3 days, parents included). Student-run newspaper, radio station. ***Social organizations:*** 25 open to all; 2 local fraternities; 2% of eligible men are members. ***Most popular organizations:*** Student Government Association, Horticultural Organization, Occupational Therapy Assisting Club, Human Services Club, Phi Beta Lambda. ***Major annual events:*** Fall Visitation Days, Career Days, Welcome Day. ***Student services:*** personal-psychological counseling, women's center. ***Campus security:*** 24-hour emergency response devices and patrols, late-night transport-escort service, campus police.

HOUSING College housing not available.

ATHLETICS ***Intercollegiate:*** baseball M, cross-country running M/W, golf M/W, softball W, tennis M/W. ***Intramural:*** archery, badminton, basketball, bowling, football, golf, racquetball, skiing (cross-country), skiing (downhill), soccer, softball, table tennis (Ping-Pong), tennis, volleyball, weight lifting, wrestling. ***Contact:*** Mr. Michael Stanzione, Coordinator of Athletics, 717-327-4537.

CAREER PLANNING ***Placement office:*** 9 full-time, 1 part-time staff. ***Director:*** Ms. Sharon K. Waters, Director of Counseling and Career Services, 717-327-4765. ***Services:*** job fairs, resume preparation, resume referral, career counseling, careers library, job bank, job interviews. Students must register sophomore year. 135 organizations recruited on campus 1994–95.

AFTER GRADUATION 80% of class of 1994 had job offers within 6 months.

ESTIMATED EXPENSES FOR 1996–97 ***Application fee:*** $35. State resident tuition: $6000 full-time, $180.70 per credit part-time. Nonresident tuition: $7000 full-time, $214.90 per credit part-time. Part-time mandatory fees: $10.20 per credit. Full-time mandatory fees: $306.

FINANCIAL AID ***College-administered undergrad aid 1995–96:*** need-based scholarships, 62 non-need scholarships (average $500), short-term loans (average $300), low-interest long-term loans from external sources (average $2500), Federal Work-Study, 100 part-time jobs. ***Required forms:*** state, institutional; required for some: FAFSA. ***Priority deadline:*** 5/1. ***Payment plan:*** deferred payment. ***Waivers:*** full or partial for employees or children of employees.

APPLYING Open admission. ***Options:*** Common Application, electronic application, early entrance. ***Required:*** school transcript, campus interview, TOEFL for international students. ***Required for some:*** 3 years of high school math and science, SAT I. Test scores used for admission. ***Application deadline:*** rolling.

APPLYING/TRANSFER ***Entrance:*** noncompetitive. ***Application deadline:*** rolling.

CONTACT Mr. Chester Schuman, Director of Admissions, Pennsylvania College of Technology, Williamsport, PA 17701-5778, 717-327-4761 or toll-free 800-367-9222 (in-state). ***Fax:*** 717-321-5536. ***E-mail:*** cschuman@pct.edu. College video and electronic viewbook available.

❖ ***See page 792 for a narrative description.*** ❖

PENNSYLVANIA INSTITUTE OF TECHNOLOGY
Media, Pennsylvania

UG Enrollment: 540	**Tuition & Fees: $7320**
Application Deadline: rolling	**Room & Board: N/Avail**

GENERAL Independent, 2-year, coed. Awards transfer associate, terminal associate degrees. Founded 1953. ***Setting:*** 12-acre small-town campus with easy access to Philadelphia. ***Total enrollment:*** 540. ***Faculty:*** 29 (15 full-time, 14 part-time).

ENROLLMENT PROFILE 540 students from 4 states and territories, 3 other countries. 22% women, 40% part-time, 95% state residents, 34% transferred in, 16% 25 or older, 0% Native American, 1% Hispanic, 25% African American, 3% Asian American.

FIRST-YEAR CLASS 210 total; 350 applied, 100% of whom enrolled.

ACADEMIC PROGRAM Core. Calendar: quarters. Academic remediation for entering students, English as a second language program, advanced placement, summer session for credit, part-time degree program (daytime, evenings), adult/continuing education programs, co-op programs.

GENERAL DEGREE REQUIREMENTS 63 credits; 1 calculus course; 2 physical science courses; computer course.

MAJORS Architectural technologies, civil engineering technology, computer technologies, drafting and design, electrical and electronics technologies, electronics engineering technology, manufacturing technology, mechanical design technology, mechanical engineering technology, medical records services, medical secretarial studies, secretarial studies/office management.

LIBRARY 10,000 books, 206 periodicals.

COMPUTERS ON CAMPUS 85 computers for student use in computer center, labs, classrooms, library.

COLLEGE LIFE ***Student services:*** personal-psychological counseling. ***Campus security:*** 24-hour emergency response devices.

HOUSING College housing not available.

ATHLETICS ***Intramural:*** basketball.

CAREER PLANNING ***Placement office:*** 1 full-time staff. ***Director:*** Mr. Dennis T. Shannon, Director of Career Services, 610-892-1511. ***Services:*** job fairs, resume preparation, resume referral, career counseling, careers library, job bank, job interviews.

EXPENSES FOR 1996–97 ***Application fee:*** $25. Tuition: $7200 full-time, $199 per credit part-time. Part-time mandatory fees: $4 per credit. Full-time mandatory fees: $120.

FINANCIAL AID ***College-administered undergrad aid 1995–96:*** need-based scholarships, low-interest long-term loans, Federal Work-Study, 30 part-time jobs. ***Required forms:*** institutional, FAFSA; required for some: CSS Financial Aid PROFILE. ***Priority deadline:*** 8/1.

APPLYING Open admission. ***Option:*** deferred entrance. ***Required:*** school transcript, TOEFL for international students. ***Recommended:*** SAT I or ACT. Test scores used for counseling/placement. ***Application deadline:*** rolling.

APPLYING/TRANSFER ***Required:*** high school transcript, college transcript. ***Recommended:*** standardized test scores. ***Entrance:*** noncompetitive. ***Application deadline:*** rolling.

CONTACT Mr. John Founds, Director of Institutional Advancement, Pennsylvania Institute of Technology, Media, PA 19063-4036, 610-565-7900 Ext. 1550 or toll-free 800-422-0025.

PENNSYLVANIA STATE UNIVERSITY ABINGTON–OGONTZ CAMPUS
Abington, Pennsylvania

UG Enrollment: 3,149	**Tuition & Fees (PA Res): $5094**
Application Deadline: rolling	**Room & Board: N/Avail**

GENERAL State-related, 2-year, coed. Part of Pennsylvania State University. Awards terminal associate degrees (also offers up to 2 years of most baccalaureate programs offered at University Park campus; of students entering the associate degree program, 25% complete the degree and an additional 35% change to a baccalaureate program). Founded 1950. ***Setting:*** 45-acre small-town campus with easy access to Philadelphia. ***Research spending 1994–95:*** $987. Faculty: 173 (93 full-time, 83% with terminal degrees, 80 part-time); student-faculty ratio is 23:1.

ENROLLMENT PROFILE 3,149 students from 11 states and territories. 52% women, 48% men, 38% part-time, 98% state residents, 3% transferred in, 0% international, 25% 25 or older, 0% Native American, 2% Hispanic, 9% African American, 6% Asian American. ***Areas of study chosen:*** 25% engineering and applied sciences, 19% business management and administrative services, 17% interdisciplinary studies, 9% education, 9% health professions and related sciences, 6% agriculture, 4% communications and journalism, 3% social sciences, 2% natural resource sciences, 2% performing arts, 1% computer and information sciences, 1% physical sciences.

FIRST-YEAR CLASS 924 total; 2,390 applied, 87% were accepted, 45% of whom enrolled. 8% from top 10% of their high school class, 55% from top quarter, 82% from top half.

ACADEMIC PROGRAM Core, honor code. Calendar: semesters. Academic remediation for entering students, services for LD students, advanced placement, summer session for credit, adult/continuing education programs, internships. ROTC: Army, Air Force (c).

GENERAL DEGREE REQUIREMENTS 60 credits; computer course for engineering, technology, business, science majors; internship (some majors).

MAJORS Agricultural business, biomedical technologies, business administration/commerce/management, electrical engineering technology, liberal arts/general studies, manufacturing technology, mechanical engineering technology.

LIBRARY 51,290 books, 6,273 microform titles, 362 periodicals, 3,680 records, tapes, and CDs. Acquisition spending 1994–95: $1.2 million.

COMPUTERS ON CAMPUS 128 computers for student use in computer labs.

COLLEGE LIFE Orientation program (2 days, no cost, parents included). Drama-theater group, student-run newspaper. ***Campus security:*** 24-hour patrols, late-night transport-escort service.

HOUSING College housing not available.

ATHLETICS ***Intercollegiate:*** basketball M/W, field hockey M/W, golf M, soccer M, softball M/W, tennis M/W, volleyball W. ***Intramural:*** basketball, bowling, ice hockey, riflery, skiing (downhill), swimming and diving, tennis, volleyball, weight lifting.

CAREER PLANNING ***Service:*** career counseling.

EXPENSES FOR 1995–96 ***Application fee:*** $35. State resident tuition: $5024 full-time, $201 per credit part-time. Nonresident tuition: $7808 full-time, $326 per credit part-time. Part-time mandatory fees per semester range from $12 to $25. Full-time mandatory fees: $70.

FINANCIAL AID ***College-administered undergrad aid 1995–96:*** need-based scholarships, non-need scholarships, low-interest long-term loans from external sources, Federal

Work-Study, part-time jobs. ***Required forms:*** FAFSA. ***Priority deadline:*** 2/15. ***Payment plan:*** deferred payment. ***Waivers:*** full or partial for employees or children of employees and senior citizens.
APPLYING ***Options:*** Common Application, electronic application, midyear entrance. ***Required:*** school transcript, 3 years of high school math and science, SAT I or ACT, TOEFL for international students. ***Required for some:*** some high school foreign language. Test scores used for admission. ***Application deadline:*** rolling. ***Notification:*** continuous.
APPLYING/TRANSFER ***Application deadline:*** rolling. ***Notification:*** continuous. ***Contact:*** Mr. Richard Mullen, Admissions Officer, 215-881-7600 Ext. 266.
CONTACT Mr. Richard Mullen, Admissions Officer, Pennsylvania State University Abington–Ogontz Campus, Abington, PA 19001-3918, 215-881-7600 Ext. 266.

PENNSYLVANIA STATE UNIVERSITY ALLENTOWN CAMPUS
Fogelsville, Pennsylvania

UG Enrollment: 583	**Tuition & Fees (PA Res): $5094**
Application Deadline: rolling	**Room & Board: N/Avail**

GENERAL State-related, 2-year, coed. Part of Pennsylvania State University. Awards terminal associate degrees (also offers up to 2 years of most baccalaureate programs offered at University Park campus). Founded 1912. ***Setting:*** 42-acre small-town campus. Faculty: 49 (22 full-time, 80% with terminal degrees, 27 part-time).
ENROLLMENT PROFILE 583 students from 4 states and territories. 41% women, 59% men, 24% part-time, 96% state residents, 3% transferred in, 0% international, 13% 25 or older, 0% Native American, 4% Hispanic, 2% African American, 5% Asian American. ***Areas of study chosen:*** 25% engineering and applied sciences, 19% business management and administrative services, 17% interdisciplinary studies, 9% education, 9% health professions and related sciences, 6% agriculture, 4% communications and journalism, 3% social sciences, 2% natural resource sciences, 2% performing arts, 1% computer and information sciences, 1% physical sciences.
FIRST-YEAR CLASS 196 total; 507 applied, 89% were accepted, 43% of whom enrolled. 8% from top 10% of their high school class, 55% from top quarter, 82% from top half.
ACADEMIC PROGRAM Core, honor code. Calendar: semesters. Academic remediation for entering students, services for LD students, advanced placement, summer session for credit, adult/continuing education programs, internships. ROTC: Army (c), Air Force (c).
GENERAL DEGREE REQUIREMENTS 60 credits; computer course for engineering, technology, business, science majors; internship (some majors).
MAJOR Liberal arts/general studies.
LIBRARY 33,204 books, 3,076 microform titles, 171 periodicals, 5,775 records, tapes, and CDs. Acquisition spending 1994–95: $312,288.
COMPUTERS ON CAMPUS 39 computers for student use in computer labs.
COLLEGE LIFE Orientation program (2 days, no cost, parents included).
HOUSING College housing not available.
ATHLETICS ***Intercollegiate:*** cross-country running M. ***Intramural:*** basketball, bowling, golf, racquetball, soccer, tennis, volleyball.
CAREER PLANNING ***Service:*** career counseling.
EXPENSES FOR 1995–96 ***Application fee:*** $35. State resident tuition: $5024 full-time, $201 per credit part-time. Nonresident tuition: $7808 full-time, $326 per credit part-time. Part-time mandatory fees per semester range from $12 to $25. Full-time mandatory fees: $70.
FINANCIAL AID ***College-administered undergrad aid 1995–96:*** need-based scholarships, non-need scholarships, low-interest long-term loans from external sources, Federal Work-Study, part-time jobs. ***Required forms:*** FAFSA. ***Priority deadline:*** 2/15. ***Payment plan:*** deferred payment. ***Waivers:*** full or partial for employees or children of employees and senior citizens.
APPLYING ***Options:*** Common Application, electronic application, midyear entrance. ***Required:*** school transcript, 3 years of high school math and science, SAT I or ACT, TOEFL for international students. ***Required for some:*** some high school foreign language. Test scores used for admission. ***Application deadline:*** rolling.
APPLYING/TRANSFER ***Application deadline:*** rolling. ***Contact:*** Mrs. Judith A. Cary, Admissions Officer, 610-821-6577.
CONTACT Mrs. Judith A. Cary, Admissions Officer, Pennsylvania State University Allentown Campus, Fogelsville, PA 18051-9999, 610-821-6577.

PENNSYLVANIA STATE UNIVERSITY ALTOONA CAMPUS
Altoona, Pennsylvania

UG Enrollment: 2,895	**Tuition & Fees (PA Res): $5094**
Application Deadline: rolling	**Room & Board: $4040**

GENERAL State-related, 2-year, coed. Part of Pennsylvania State University. Awards terminal associate degrees (also offers up to 2 years of most baccalaureate programs offered at University Park campus; of students entering the associate degree program, 25% complete the degree and an additional 35% change to a baccalaureate program). Founded 1929. ***Setting:*** 81-acre suburban campus. Faculty: 150 (80 full-time, 85% with terminal degrees, 70 part-time).
ENROLLMENT PROFILE 2,895 students from 24 states and territories. 47% women, 53% men, 12% part-time, 91% state residents, 3% transferred in, 0% international, 14% 25 or older, 0% Native American, 1% Hispanic, 3% African American, 2% Asian American. ***Areas of study chosen:*** 25% engineering and applied sciences, 19% business management and administrative services, 17% interdisciplinary studies, 9% education, 9% health professions and related sciences, 6% agriculture, 4% communications and journalism, 3% social sciences, 2% natural resource sciences, 2% performing arts, 1% computer and information sciences, 1% physical sciences.
FIRST-YEAR CLASS 1,283 total; 3,439 applied, 94% were accepted, 40% of whom enrolled. 8% from top 10% of their high school class, 55% from top quarter, 82% from top half.
ACADEMIC PROGRAM Core, honor code. Calendar: semesters. Academic remediation for entering students, services for LD students, advanced placement, summer session for credit, adult/continuing education programs, internships. ROTC: Army.
GENERAL DEGREE REQUIREMENTS 60 credits; computer course for engineering, technology, business, science majors; internship (some majors).
MAJORS Agricultural business, biology/biological sciences, biomedical technologies, business administration/commerce/management, computer technologies, electrical engineering technology, liberal arts/general studies, manufacturing technology, mechanical engineering technology, nursing.
LIBRARY 49,931 books, 49,070 microform titles, 332 periodicals, 4,921 records, tapes, and CDs. Acquisition spending 1994–95: $1.1 million.
COMPUTERS ON CAMPUS 123 computers for student use in computer labs.
COLLEGE LIFE Orientation program (2 days, no cost, parents included). Drama-theater group, student-run newspaper, radio station. ***Campus security:*** 24-hour emergency response devices and patrols, student patrols, late-night transport-escort service, controlled dormitory access.
HOUSING College housing designed to accommodate 577 students; 629 undergraduates lived in college housing during 1995–96. Freshmen given priority for college housing. Off-campus living permitted. ***Option:*** single-sex housing available. Resident assistants live in dorms.
ATHLETICS ***Intercollegiate:*** basketball M/W, volleyball W. ***Intramural:*** basketball, racquetball, skiing (downhill), soccer, swimming and diving, tennis, volleyball.
CAREER PLANNING ***Service:*** career counseling.
EXPENSES FOR 1995–96 ***Application fee:*** $35. State resident tuition: $5024 full-time, $201 per credit part-time. Nonresident tuition: $7808 full-time, $326 per credit part-time. Part-time mandatory fees per semester range from $12 to $25. Full-time mandatory fees: $70. College room and board: $4040.
FINANCIAL AID ***College-administered undergrad aid 1995–96:*** need-based scholarships, non-need scholarships, low-interest long-term loans, Federal Work-Study, part-time jobs. ***Required forms:*** FAFSA. ***Priority deadline:*** 2/15. ***Payment plan:*** deferred payment. ***Waivers:*** full or partial for employees or children of employees and senior citizens.
APPLYING ***Options:*** Common Application, electronic application, midyear entrance. ***Required:*** school transcript, 3 years of high school math and science, SAT I or ACT, TOEFL for international students. ***Required for some:*** some high school foreign language. Test scores used for admission. ***Application deadline:*** rolling.
APPLYING/TRANSFER ***Application deadline:*** rolling. ***Contact:*** Ms. Fredina Ingold, Admissions Officer, 814-949-5466.
CONTACT Ms. Fredina Ingold, Admissions Officer, Pennsylvania State University Altoona Campus, Altoona, PA 16601-3760, 814-949-5466.

PENNSYLVANIA STATE UNIVERSITY BEAVER CAMPUS
Monaca, Pennsylvania

UG Enrollment: 836	**Tuition & Fees (PA Res): $5094**
Application Deadline: rolling	**Room & Board: $4040**

GENERAL State-related, 2-year, coed. Part of Pennsylvania State University. Awards terminal associate degrees (also offers up to 2 years of most baccalaureate programs offered at University Park campus; of students entering the associate degree program, 25% complete the degree and an additional 35% change to a baccalaureate program). Founded 1964. ***Setting:*** 90-acre small-town campus with easy access to Pittsburgh. Faculty: 59 (37 full-time, 66% with terminal degrees, 22 part-time); student-faculty ratio is 20:1.
ENROLLMENT PROFILE 836 students from 17 states and territories. 37% women, 63% men, 8% part-time, 92% state residents, 3% transferred in, 0% international, 6% 25 or older, 0% Native American, 2% Hispanic, 5% African American, 1% Asian American. ***Areas of study chosen:*** 25% engineering and applied sciences, 19% business management and administrative services, 17% interdisciplinary studies, 9% education, 9% health professions and related sciences, 6% agriculture, 4% communications and journalism, 3% social sciences, 2% natural resource sciences, 2% performing arts, 1% computer and information sciences, 1% physical sciences.
FIRST-YEAR CLASS 365 total; 823 applied, 92% were accepted, 48% of whom enrolled. 8% from top 10% of their high school class, 55% from top quarter, 82% from top half.
ACADEMIC PROGRAM Core, honor code. Calendar: semesters. Academic remediation for entering students, services for LD students, advanced placement, summer session for credit, adult/continuing education programs.
GENERAL DEGREE REQUIREMENTS 60 credits; computer course for engineering, technology, business, science majors; internship (some majors).
MAJORS Agricultural business, biology/biological sciences, biomedical technologies, electrical engineering technology, hotel and restaurant management, liberal arts/general studies, manufacturing technology, mechanical engineering technology, physical sciences.
LIBRARY 35,920 books, 9,356 microform titles, 206 periodicals, 5,953 records, tapes, and CDs. Acquisition spending 1994–95: $371,937.
COMPUTERS ON CAMPUS 85 computers for student use in computer labs.
COLLEGE LIFE Orientation program (2 days, no cost, parents included). Drama-theater group, student-run newspaper, radio station. ***Campus security:*** 24-hour patrols, controlled dormitory access.
HOUSING 310 college housing spaces available; 309 were occupied 1995–96. Freshmen given priority for college housing. Off-campus living permitted. ***Option:*** single-sex housing available. Resident assistants live in dorms.
ATHLETICS Member NJCAA. ***Intercollegiate:*** baseball M, golf M/W, softball W, volleyball W. ***Intramural:*** basketball, bowling, fencing, golf, ice hockey, racquetball, skiing (downhill), tennis, track and field, volleyball.
CAREER PLANNING ***Service:*** career counseling.
EXPENSES FOR 1995–96 ***Application fee:*** $35. State resident tuition: $5024 full-time, $201 per credit part-time. Nonresident tuition: $7808 full-time, $326 per credit part-time. Part-time mandatory fees per semester range from $12 to $25. Full-time mandatory fees: $70. College room and board: $4040.
FINANCIAL AID ***College-administered undergrad aid 1995–96:*** need-based scholarships, non-need scholarships, low-interest long-term loans from external sources, Federal Work-Study, part-time jobs. ***Required forms:*** FAFSA. ***Priority deadline:*** 2/15. ***Payment plan:*** deferred payment. ***Waivers:*** full or partial for employees or children of employees and senior citizens.
APPLYING ***Options:*** Common Application, electronic application, midyear entrance. ***Required:*** school transcript, 3 years of high school math and science, SAT I or ACT, TOEFL for international students. ***Required for some:*** some high school foreign language. Test scores used for admission. ***Application deadline:*** rolling.

Pennsylvania State University Beaver Campus (continued)

APPLYING/TRANSFER ***Application deadline:*** rolling. ***Contact:*** Ms. Cheryl Vuich, Admissions Officer, 412-773-3800.

CONTACT Ms. Cheryl Vuich, Admissions Officer, Pennsylvania State University Beaver Campus, Monaca, PA 15061-2799, 412-773-3800.

PENNSYLVANIA STATE UNIVERSITY BERKS CAMPUS
Reading, Pennsylvania

UG Enrollment: 1,708	Tuition & Fees (PA Res): $5094
Application Deadline: rolling	Room & Board: $4040

GENERAL State-related, 2-year, coed. Part of Pennsylvania State University. Awards terminal associate degrees (also offers up to 2 years of most baccalaureate programs offered at University Park campus; of students entering the associate degree program, 25% complete the degree and an additional 35% change to a baccalaureate program). Founded 1924. ***Setting:*** 241-acre suburban campus with easy access to Philadelphia. ***Research spending 1994–95:*** $30,855. Faculty: 107 (49 full-time, 82% with terminal degrees, 58 part-time).

ENROLLMENT PROFILE 1,708 students from 14 states and territories. 41% women, 59% men, 19% part-time, 95% state residents, 3% transferred in, 0% international, 14% 25 or older, 0% Native American, 3% Hispanic, 3% African American, 3% Asian American. ***Areas of study chosen:*** 25% engineering and applied sciences, 19% business management and administrative services, 17% interdisciplinary studies, 9% education, 9% health professions and related sciences, 6% agriculture, 4% communications and journalism, 3% social sciences, 2% natural resource sciences, 2% performing arts, 1% computer and information sciences, 1% physical sciences.

FIRST-YEAR CLASS 662 total; 1,818 applied, 86% were accepted, 43% of whom enrolled. 8% from top 10% of their high school class, 55% from top quarter, 82% from top half.

ACADEMIC PROGRAM Core, honor code. Calendar: semesters. Academic remediation for entering students, services for LD students, advanced placement, summer session for credit, adult/continuing education programs. ROTC: Army.

GENERAL DEGREE REQUIREMENTS 60 credits; computer course for engineering, technology, business, science majors; internship (some majors).

MAJORS Agricultural business, biomedical technologies, business administration/commerce/management, electrical engineering technology, hotel and restaurant management, liberal arts/general studies, manufacturing technology, mechanical engineering technology, occupational therapy.

LIBRARY 38,162 books, 1,960 microform titles, 362 periodicals, 1,146 records, tapes, and CDs. Acquisition spending 1994–95: $733,511.

COMPUTERS ON CAMPUS 20 computers for student use in computer labs.

COLLEGE LIFE Orientation program (2 days, no cost, parents included). Drama-theater group, student-run newspaper. ***Campus security:*** 24-hour emergency response devices and patrols, controlled dormitory access.

HOUSING 390 college housing spaces available; all were occupied 1995–96. Freshmen given priority for college housing. Off-campus living permitted. ***Option:*** single-sex housing available. Resident assistants live in dorms.

ATHLETICS Member NAIA. ***Intercollegiate:*** baseball M, basketball M, soccer M, softball W, volleyball W. ***Intramural:*** basketball, bowling, fencing, tennis, volleyball.

CAREER PLANNING ***Service:*** career counseling.

EXPENSES FOR 1995–96 ***Application fee:*** $35. State resident tuition: $5024 full-time, $201 per credit part-time. Nonresident tuition: $7808 full-time, $326 per credit part-time. Part-time mandatory fees per semester range from $12 to $25. Full-time mandatory fees: $70. College room and board: $4040.

FINANCIAL AID ***College-administered undergrad aid 1995–96:*** need-based scholarships, non-need scholarships, low-interest long-term loans from external sources, Federal Work-Study, part-time jobs. ***Required forms:*** FAFSA. ***Priority deadline:*** 2/15. ***Payment plan:*** deferred payment. ***Waivers:*** full or partial for employees or children of employees and senior citizens.

APPLYING ***Options:*** Common Application, electronic application, midyear entrance. ***Required:*** school transcript, 3 years of high school math and science, SAT I or ACT, TOEFL for international students. ***Required for some:*** some high school foreign language. Test scores used for admission. ***Application deadline:*** rolling.

APPLYING/TRANSFER ***Application deadline:*** rolling. ***Contact:*** Mr. John W. Gemmell, Admissions Officer, 610-320-4864.

CONTACT Mr. John W. Gemmell, Admissions Officer, Pennsylvania State University Berks Campus, Reading, PA 19610-6009, 610-320-4864.

PENNSYLVANIA STATE UNIVERSITY DELAWARE COUNTY CAMPUS
Media, Pennsylvania

UG Enrollment: 1,531	Tuition & Fees (PA Res): $5094
Application Deadline: rolling	Room & Board: N/Avail

GENERAL State-related, primarily 2-year, coed. Part of Pennsylvania State University. Awards transfer associate, terminal associate, bachelor's degrees (also offers up to 2 years of most baccalaureate programs offered at University Park campus; of students entering the associate degree program, 25% complete the degree and an additional 35% change to a baccalaureate program). Founded 1966. ***Setting:*** 87-acre small-town campus with easy access to Philadelphia. ***Research spending 1994–95:*** $41,998. Faculty: 90 (46 full-time, 95% with terminal degrees, 44 part-time); student-faculty ratio is 24:1.

ENROLLMENT PROFILE 1,531 students from 5 states and territories. 46% women, 54% men, 27% part-time, 97% state residents, 3% transferred in, 1% international, 20% 25 or older, 0% Native American, 1% Hispanic, 9% African American, 4% Asian American. ***Areas of study chosen:*** 25% engineering and applied sciences, 19% business management and administrative services, 17% interdisciplinary studies, 9% education, 9% health professions and related sciences, 6% agriculture, 4% communications and journalism, 3% social sciences, 2% natural resource sciences, 2% performing arts, 1% computer and information sciences, 1% physical sciences.

FIRST-YEAR CLASS 544 total; 1,381 applied, 86% were accepted, 46% of whom enrolled. 8% from top 10% of their high school class, 55% from top quarter, 82% from top half.

ACADEMIC PROGRAM Core, honor code. Calendar: semesters. Academic remediation for entering students, services for LD students, advanced placement, summer session for credit, adult/continuing education programs. ROTC: Army, Air Force (c).

GENERAL DEGREE REQUIREMENTS 60 credits for associate, 120 credits for bachelor's; computer course for some engineering majors; internship (some majors).

MAJORS Agricultural business, business administration/commerce/management, liberal arts/general studies.

LIBRARY 44,019 books, 4,431 microform titles, 233 periodicals, 1,707 records, tapes, and CDs. Acquisition spending 1994–95: $647,401.

COMPUTERS ON CAMPUS 70 computers for student use in computer labs.

COLLEGE LIFE Orientation program (2 days, no cost, parents included). Drama-theater group, student-run newspaper. ***Campus security:*** late-night transport-escort service, part-time trained security personnel.

HOUSING College housing not available.

ATHLETICS Member NJCAA. ***Intercollegiate:*** baseball M, basketball M/W, soccer M/W, tennis M/W, volleyball W. ***Intramural:*** basketball, bowling, ice hockey, racquetball, riflery, skiing (downhill), soccer, tennis, volleyball.

CAREER PLANNING ***Service:*** career counseling.

EXPENSES FOR 1995–96 ***Application fee:*** $35. State resident tuition: $5024 full-time, $201 per credit part-time. Nonresident tuition: $7808 full-time, $326 per credit part-time. Part-time mandatory fees per semester range from $12 to $25. Full-time mandatory fees: $70.

FINANCIAL AID ***College-administered undergrad aid 1995–96:*** need-based scholarships, non-need scholarships, low-interest long-term loans from external sources, Federal Work-Study, part-time jobs. ***Required forms:*** FAFSA. ***Priority deadline:*** 2/15. ***Payment plan:*** deferred payment. ***Waivers:*** full or partial for employees or children of employees and senior citizens.

APPLYING ***Options:*** Common Application, electronic application, midyear entrance. ***Required:*** 3 years of high school math and science, SAT I or ACT, TOEFL for international students. ***Required for some:*** some high school foreign language. Test scores used for admission. ***Application deadline:*** rolling.

APPLYING/TRANSFER ***Application deadline:*** rolling. ***Contact:*** Ms. Carolyn Boswell, Admissions Officer, 610-892-1200.

CONTACT Ms. Carolyn Boswell, Admissions Officer, Pennsylvania State University Delaware County Campus, Media, PA 19063-5596, 610-892-1200.

PENNSYLVANIA STATE UNIVERSITY DUBOIS CAMPUS
DuBois, Pennsylvania

UG Enrollment: 915	Tuition & Fees (PA Res): $5094
Application Deadline: rolling	Room & Board: N/Avail

GENERAL State-related, 2-year, coed. Part of Pennsylvania State University. Awards terminal associate degrees (also offers up to 2 years of most baccalaureate programs offered at University Park campus; of students entering the associate degree program, 25% complete the degree and an additional 35% change to a baccalaureate program). Founded 1935. ***Setting:*** 12-acre small-town campus. ***Research spending 1994–95:*** $21,666. Faculty: 57 (42 full-time, 79% with terminal degrees, 15 part-time); student-faculty ratio is 17:1.

ENROLLMENT PROFILE 915 students from 9 states and territories. 50% women, 50% men, 27% part-time, 98% state residents, 2% transferred in, 0% international, 32% 25 or older, 0% Native American, 0% Hispanic, 1% African American, 1% Asian American. ***Areas of study chosen:*** 25% engineering and applied sciences, 19% business management and administrative services, 17% interdisciplinary studies, 9% education, 9% health professions and related sciences, 6% agriculture, 4% communications and journalism, 3% social sciences, 2% natural resource sciences, 2% performing arts, 1% computer and information sciences, 1% physical sciences.

FIRST-YEAR CLASS 218 total; 412 applied, 84% were accepted, 63% of whom enrolled. 8% from top 10% of their high school class, 55% from top quarter, 82% from top half.

ACADEMIC PROGRAM Core, honor code. Calendar: semesters. Academic remediation for entering students, services for LD students, advanced placement, summer session for credit, adult/continuing education programs, internships.

GENERAL DEGREE REQUIREMENTS 60 credits; computer course for engineering, technology, business, science majors; internship (some majors).

MAJORS Agricultural business, biology/biological sciences, biomedical technologies, business administration/commerce/management, electrical engineering technology, family and consumer studies, liberal arts/general studies, manufacturing technology, mechanical engineering technology, medical laboratory technology, physical therapy, wildlife management.

LIBRARY 38,843 books, 9,306 microform titles, 241 periodicals, 616 records, tapes, and CDs. Acquisition spending 1994–95: $375,667.

COMPUTERS ON CAMPUS 53 computers for student use in computer labs.

COLLEGE LIFE Orientation program (2 days, no cost, parents included). Drama-theater group, student-run newspaper, radio station.

HOUSING College housing not available.

ATHLETICS ***Intercollegiate:*** basketball M, golf M, volleyball W. ***Intramural:*** basketball, bowling, skiing (cross-country), tennis, volleyball, weight lifting.

CAREER PLANNING ***Service:*** career counseling.

EXPENSES FOR 1995–96 ***Application fee:*** $35. State resident tuition: $5024 full-time, $201 per credit part-time. Nonresident tuition: $7808 full-time, $326 per credit part-time. Part-time mandatory fees per semester range from $12 to $25. Full-time mandatory fees: $70.

FINANCIAL AID ***College-administered undergrad aid 1995–96:*** need-based scholarships, non-need scholarships, low-interest long-term loans from external sources, Federal Work-Study, part-time jobs. ***Required forms:*** FAFSA. ***Priority deadline:*** 2/15. ***Payment plan:*** installment. ***Waivers:*** full or partial for employees or children of employees.

APPLYING ***Options:*** Common Application, electronic application, midyear entrance. ***Required:*** school transcript, 3 years of high school math and science, SAT I or ACT, TOEFL for international students. ***Required for some:*** some high school foreign language. Test scores used for admission. ***Application deadline:*** rolling.

APPLYING/TRANSFER ***Application deadline:*** rolling. ***Contact:*** Mr. Thomas D. Hewitt, Admissions Officer, 814-375-4720.

CONTACT Mr. Thomas D. Hewitt, Admissions Officer, Pennsylvania State University DuBois Campus, DuBois, PA 15801-3199, 814-375-4720.

PENNSYLVANIA STATE UNIVERSITY FAYETTE CAMPUS
Uniontown, Pennsylvania

UG Enrollment: 994	Tuition & Fees (PA Res): $5094
Application Deadline: rolling	Room & Board: N/Avail

GENERAL State-related, 2-year, coed. Part of Pennsylvania State University. Awards terminal associate degrees (also offers up to 2 years of most baccalaureate programs offered at University Park campus; of students entering the associate degree program, 25% complete the degree and an additional 35% change to a baccalaureate program). Founded 1934. *Setting:* 193-acre small-town campus. *Research spending 1994–95:* $10,638. *Total enrollment:* 994. *Faculty:* 72 (45 full-time, 81% with terminal degrees, 27 part-time); student-faculty ratio is 17:1.
ENROLLMENT PROFILE 994 students from 6 states and territories. 55% women, 45% men, 28% part-time, 99% state residents, 2% transferred in, 0% international, 33% 25 or older, 0% Native American, 0% Hispanic, 4% African American, 1% Asian American. *Areas of study chosen:* 25% engineering and applied sciences, 19% business management and administrative services, 17% interdisciplinary studies, 9% education, 9% health professions and related sciences, 6% agriculture, 4% communications and journalism, 3% social sciences, 2% natural resource sciences, 2% performing arts, 1% computer and information sciences, 1% physical sciences.
FIRST-YEAR CLASS 200 total; 372 applied, 87% were accepted, 62% of whom enrolled. 8% from top 10% of their high school class, 55% from top quarter, 82% from top half.
ACADEMIC PROGRAM Core, honor code. Calendar: semesters. Academic remediation for entering students, services for LD students, advanced placement, summer session for credit, adult/continuing education programs. ROTC: Army (c).
GENERAL DEGREE REQUIREMENTS 60 credits; computer course for engineering, technology, business, science majors; internship (some majors).
MAJORS Agricultural business, biomedical technologies, business administration/commerce/management, electrical engineering technology, family and consumer studies, liberal arts/general studies, manufacturing technology, mechanical engineering technology, nursing.
LIBRARY 46,903 books, 6,398 microform titles, 194 periodicals, 4,872 records, tapes, and CDs. Acquisition spending 1994–95: $399,866.
COMPUTERS ON CAMPUS 52 computers for student use in computer labs.
COLLEGE LIFE Orientation program (2 days, no cost, parents included). Drama-theater group, student-run newspaper. *Campus security:* student patrols, 8-hour patrols by trained security personnel.
HOUSING College housing not available.
ATHLETICS *Intramural:* basketball, fencing, racquetball, skiing (downhill), soccer, tennis, track and field, volleyball, weight lifting.
CAREER PLANNING *Service:* career counseling.
EXPENSES FOR 1995–96 *Application fee:* $35. State resident tuition: $5024 full-time, $201 per credit part-time. Nonresident tuition: $7808 full-time, $326 per credit part-time. Part-time mandatory fees per semester range from $12 to $25. Full-time mandatory fees: $70.
FINANCIAL AID *College-administered undergrad aid 1995–96:* need-based scholarships, non-need scholarships, low-interest long-term loans from external sources, Federal Work-Study, part-time jobs. *Required forms:* FAFSA. *Priority deadline:* 2/15. *Payment plan:* deferred payment. *Waivers:* full or partial for employees or children of employees and senior citizens.
APPLYING *Options:* Common Application, electronic application, midyear entrance. *Required:* school transcript, 3 years of high school math and science, SAT I or ACT, TOEFL for international students. *Required for some:* some high school foreign language. Test scores used for admission. *Application deadline:* rolling.
APPLYING/TRANSFER *Application deadline:* rolling. *Contact:* Mr. Louis E. Ridgley, Admissions Officer, 412-430-4130.
CONTACT Mr. Louis E. Ridgley, Admissions Officer, Pennsylvania State University Fayette Campus, Uniontown, PA 15401-0519, 412-430-4130.

PENNSYLVANIA STATE UNIVERSITY HAZLETON CAMPUS
Hazleton, Pennsylvania

UG Enrollment: 1,314	Tuition & Fees (PA Res): $5094
Application Deadline: rolling	Room & Board: $4040

GENERAL State-related, 2-year, coed. Part of Pennsylvania State University. Awards terminal associate degrees (also offers up to 2 years of most baccalaureate programs offered at University Park campus; of students entering the associate degree program, 25% complete the degree and an additional 35% change to a baccalaureate program). Founded 1934. *Setting:* 73-acre small-town campus. *Research spending 1994–95:* $14,909. Faculty: 75 (51 full-time, 74% with terminal degrees, 24 part-time); student-faculty ratio is 23:1.
ENROLLMENT PROFILE 1,314 students from 15 states and territories. 44% women, 56% men, 8% part-time, 88% state residents, 3% transferred in, 0% international, 7% 25 or older, 0% Native American, 2% Hispanic, 3% African American, 3% Asian American. *Areas of study chosen:* 25% engineering and applied sciences, 19% business management and administrative services, 17% interdisciplinary studies, 9% education, 9% health professions and related sciences, 6% agriculture, 4% communications and journalism, 3% social sciences, 2% natural resource sciences, 2% performing arts, 1% computer and information sciences, 1% physical sciences.
FIRST-YEAR CLASS 622 total; 1,754 applied, 91% were accepted, 39% of whom enrolled. 8% from top 10% of their high school class, 55% from top quarter, 82% from top half.
ACADEMIC PROGRAM Core, honor code. Calendar: semesters. Academic remediation for entering students, services for LD students, advanced placement, summer session for credit, adult/continuing education programs, co-op programs and internships. ROTC: Army, Air Force (c).
GENERAL DEGREE REQUIREMENTS 60 credits; computer course for engineering, technology, business, science majors; internship (some majors).
MAJORS Agricultural business, biomedical technologies, business administration/commerce/management, electrical engineering technology, liberal arts/general studies, manufacturing technology, mechanical engineering technology, medical laboratory technology, physical therapy, sociology.
LIBRARY 78,140 books, 7,280 microform titles, 423 periodicals, 3,963 records, tapes, and CDs. Acquisition spending 1994–95: $534,901.
COMPUTERS ON CAMPUS 43 computers for student use in computer labs.
COLLEGE LIFE Orientation program (2 days, no cost, parents included). Drama-theater group, student-run newspaper, radio station. *Campus security:* 24-hour patrols, late-night transport-escort service, controlled dormitory access.
HOUSING College housing designed to accommodate 465 students; 469 undergraduates lived in college housing during 1995–96. Freshmen given priority for college housing. Off-campus living permitted. *Option:* single-sex housing available. Resident assistants live in dorms.
ATHLETICS *Intercollegiate:* baseball M, basketball M, soccer M, softball W, tennis M/W, volleyball W. *Intramural:* bowling, racquetball, skiing (downhill), soccer, swimming and diving, tennis, volleyball, weight lifting.
CAREER PLANNING *Service:* career counseling.
EXPENSES FOR 1995–96 *Application fee:* $35. State resident tuition: $5024 full-time, $201 per credit part-time. Nonresident tuition: $7808 full-time, $326 per credit part-time. Part-time mandatory fees per semester range from $12 to $25. Full-time mandatory fees: $70. College room and board: $4040.
FINANCIAL AID *College-administered undergrad aid 1995–96:* need-based scholarships, non-need scholarships, low-interest long-term loans from external sources, Federal Work-Study, part-time jobs. *Required forms:* FAFSA. *Priority deadline:* 2/15. *Payment plan:* deferred payment. *Waivers:* full or partial for employees or children of employees and senior citizens. *Notification:* continuous.
APPLYING *Options:* Common Application, electronic application, midyear entrance. *Required:* school transcript, 3 years of high school math and science, SAT I or ACT, TOEFL for international students. *Required for some:* some high school foreign language. Test scores used for admission. *Application deadline:* rolling.
APPLYING/TRANSFER *Application deadline:* rolling. *Contact:* Mr. Joseph L. McCallus, Admissions Officer, 717-450-3142.
CONTACT Mr. Joseph L. McCallus, Admissions Officer, Pennsylvania State University Hazleton Campus, Hazleton, PA 18201-1291, 717-450-3142.

PENNSYLVANIA STATE UNIVERSITY McKEESPORT CAMPUS
McKeesport, Pennsylvania

UG Enrollment: 876	Tuition & Fees (PA Res): $5094
Application Deadline: rolling	Room & Board: $4040

GENERAL State-related, 2-year, coed. Part of Pennsylvania State University. Awards terminal associate degrees (also offers up to 2 years of most baccalaureate programs offered at University Park campus; of students entering the associate degree program, 25% complete the degree and an additional 35% change to a baccalaureate program). Founded 1947. *Setting:* 40-acre small-town campus with easy access to Pittsburgh. Faculty: 62 (31 full-time, 85% with terminal degrees, 31 part-time); student-faculty ratio is 21:1.
ENROLLMENT PROFILE 876 students from 18 states and territories. 42% women, 58% men, 21% part-time, 93% state residents, 2% transferred in, 0% international, 21% 25 or older, 0% Native American, 2% Hispanic, 15% African American, 1% Asian American. *Areas of study chosen:* 25% engineering and applied sciences, 19% business management and administrative services, 17% interdisciplinary studies, 9% education, 9% health professions and related sciences, 6% agriculture, 4% communications and journalism, 3% social sciences, 2% natural resource sciences, 2% performing arts, 1% computer and information sciences, 1% physical sciences.
FIRST-YEAR CLASS 314 total; 635 applied, 90% were accepted, 55% of whom enrolled. 8% from top 10% of their high school class, 55% from top quarter, 82% from top half.
ACADEMIC PROGRAM Core, honor code. Calendar: semesters. Academic remediation for entering students, services for LD students, advanced placement, summer session for credit, adult/continuing education programs, internships. ROTC: Army.
GENERAL DEGREE REQUIREMENTS 60 credits; computer course for engineering, technology, business, science majors; internship (some majors).
MAJORS Agricultural business, biology/biological sciences, biomedical technologies, business administration/commerce/management, electrical engineering technology, liberal arts/general studies, manufacturing technology, mechanical engineering technology, physical sciences.
LIBRARY 36,399 books, 8,059 microform titles, 313 periodicals, 1,201 records, tapes, and CDs. Acquisition spending 1994–95: $345,189.
COMPUTERS ON CAMPUS 61 computers for student use in computer labs.
COLLEGE LIFE Orientation program (2 days, no cost, parents included). Student-run newspaper, radio station. *Campus security:* 24-hour patrols, controlled dormitory access.
HOUSING 210 college housing spaces available; 158 were occupied 1995–96. Freshmen given priority for college housing. Off-campus living permitted. *Option:* single-sex housing available. Resident assistants live in dorms.
ATHLETICS *Intramural:* basketball, bowling, fencing, golf, ice hockey, racquetball, skiing (downhill), soccer, swimming and diving, tennis, track and field, volleyball, weight lifting.
CAREER PLANNING *Service:* career counseling.
EXPENSES FOR 1995–96 *Application fee:* $35. State resident tuition: $5024 full-time, $201 per credit part-time. Nonresident tuition: $7808 full-time, $326 per credit part-time. Part-time mandatory fees per semester range from $12 to $25. Full-time mandatory fees: $70. College room and board: $4040.
FINANCIAL AID *College-administered undergrad aid 1995–96:* need-based scholarships, non-need scholarships, low-interest long-term loans, Federal Work-Study, part-time jobs. *Required forms:* FAFSA. *Priority deadline:* 2/15. *Payment plan:* deferred payment. *Waivers:* full or partial for employees or children of employees and senior citizens.
APPLYING *Options:* Common Application, electronic application, midyear entrance. *Required:* school transcript, 3 years of high school math and science, SAT I or ACT, TOEFL for international students. *Required for some:* some high school foreign language. Test scores used for admission. *Application deadline:* rolling.

Pennsylvania State University McKeesport Campus (continued)
APPLYING/TRANSFER ***Application deadline:*** rolling. ***Contact:*** Mr. Thomas J. Riley, Admissions Officer, 412-675-9010.
CONTACT Mr. Thomas J. Riley, Admissions Officer, Pennsylvania State University McKeesport Campus, McKeesport, PA 15132-7698, 412-675-9010.

PENNSYLVANIA STATE UNIVERSITY MONT ALTO CAMPUS
Mont Alto, Pennsylvania

UG Enrollment: 1,127	Tuition & Fees (PA Res): $5094
Application Deadline: rolling	Room & Board: $4040

GENERAL State-related, 2-year, coed. Part of Pennsylvania State University. Awards terminal associate degrees (also offers up to 2 years of most baccalaureate programs offered at University Park campus; of students entering the associate degree program, 25% complete the degree and an additional 35% change to a baccalaureate program). Founded 1929. ***Setting:*** 62-acre small-town campus. ***Research spending 1994–95:*** $17,555. Faculty: 66 (47 full-time, 71% with terminal degrees, 19 part-time); student-faculty ratio is 21:1.
ENROLLMENT PROFILE 1,127 students from 12 states and territories. 53% women, 47% men, 22% part-time, 92% state residents, 4% transferred in, 0% international, 23% 25 or older, 0% Native American, 2% Hispanic, 3% African American, 2% Asian American. ***Areas of study chosen:*** 25% engineering and applied sciences, 19% business management and administrative services, 17% interdisciplinary studies, 9% education, 9% health professions and related sciences, 6% agriculture, 4% communications and journalism, 3% social sciences, 2% natural resource sciences, 2% performing arts, 1% computer and information sciences, 1% physical sciences.
FIRST-YEAR CLASS 374 total; 824 applied, 83% were accepted, 55% of whom enrolled. 8% from top 10% of their high school class, 55% from top quarter, 82% from top half.
ACADEMIC PROGRAM Core, honor code. Calendar: semesters. Academic remediation for entering students, services for LD students, advanced placement, summer session for credit, adult/continuing education programs, internships. ROTC: Army.
GENERAL DEGREE REQUIREMENTS 60 credits; computer course for engineering, technology, business, science majors; internship (some majors).
MAJORS Agricultural business, business administration/commerce/management, family and consumer studies, forest technology, liberal arts/general studies, nursing, occupational therapy, physical therapy.
LIBRARY 32,243 books, 12,689 microform titles, 299 periodicals, 854 records, tapes, and CDs. Acquisition spending 1994–95: $520,059.
COMPUTERS ON CAMPUS 25 computers for student use in computer labs.
COLLEGE LIFE Orientation program (2 days, no cost, parents included). Drama-theater group, student-run radio station. ***Campus security:*** 24-hour patrols, controlled dormitory access.
HOUSING College housing designed to accommodate 428 students; 446 undergraduates lived in college housing during 1995–96. Freshmen given priority for college housing. Off-campus living permitted. ***Option:*** single-sex housing available. Resident assistants live in dorms.
ATHLETICS ***Intercollegiate:*** basketball M/W, soccer M, tennis M/W. ***Intramural:*** basketball, skiing (downhill), soccer.
CAREER PLANNING ***Service:*** career counseling.
EXPENSES FOR 1995–96 ***Application fee:*** $35. State resident tuition: $5024 full-time, $201 per credit part-time. Nonresident tuition: $7808 full-time, $326 per credit part-time. Part-time mandatory fees per semester range from $12 to $25. Full-time mandatory fees: $70. College room and board: $4040.
FINANCIAL AID ***College-administered undergrad aid 1995–96:*** need-based scholarships, non-need scholarships, low-interest long-term loans from external sources, Federal Work-Study, part-time jobs. ***Required forms:*** FAFSA. ***Priority deadline:*** 2/15. ***Payment plan:*** deferred payment. ***Waivers:*** full or partial for employees or children of employees and senior citizens.
APPLYING ***Options:*** Common Application, electronic application, midyear entrance. ***Required:*** school transcript, 3 years of high school math and science, SAT I or ACT, TOEFL for international students. ***Required for some:*** some high school foreign language. Test scores used for admission. ***Application deadline:*** rolling.
APPLYING/TRANSFER ***Application deadline:*** rolling. ***Contact:*** Mr. Charles Wharton, Admissions Officer, 717-749-6130.
CONTACT Mr. Charles Wharton, Admissions Officer, Pennsylvania State University Mont Alto Campus, Mont Alto, PA 17237-9703, 717-749-6130.

PENNSYLVANIA STATE UNIVERSITY NEW KENSINGTON CAMPUS
New Kensington, Pennsylvania

UG Enrollment: 980	Tuition & Fees (PA Res): $5094
Application Deadline: rolling	Room & Board: N/Avail

GENERAL State-related, 2-year, coed. Part of Pennsylvania State University. Awards terminal associate degrees (also offers up to 2 years of most baccalaureate programs offered at University Park campus; of students entering the associate degree program, 25% complete the degree and an additional 35% change to a baccalaureate program). Founded 1958. ***Setting:*** 71-acre small-town campus with easy access to Pittsburgh. Faculty: 70 (40 full-time, 76% with terminal degrees, 30 part-time); student-faculty ratio is 17:1.
ENROLLMENT PROFILE 980 students from 7 states and territories. 45% women, 55% men, 35% part-time, 99% state residents, 4% transferred in, 0% international, 36% 25 or older, 0% Native American, 1% Hispanic, 1% African American, 1% Asian American. ***Areas of study chosen:*** 25% engineering and applied sciences, 19% business management and administrative services, 17% interdisciplinary studies, 9% education, 9% health professions and related sciences, 6% agriculture, 4% communications and journalism, 3% social sciences, 2% natural resource sciences, 2% performing arts, 1% computer and information sciences, 1% physical sciences.
FIRST-YEAR CLASS 219 total; 502 applied, 88% were accepted, 50% of whom enrolled. 8% from top 10% of their high school class, 55% from top quarter, 82% from top half.
ACADEMIC PROGRAM Core, honor code. Calendar: semesters. Academic remediation for entering students, services for LD students, advanced placement, summer session for credit, adult/continuing education programs, internships.
GENERAL DEGREE REQUIREMENTS 60 credits; computer course for engineering, technology, business, science majors; internship (some majors).
MAJORS Agricultural business, biology/biological sciences, biomedical technologies, business administration/commerce/management, computer science, electrical engineering technology, liberal arts/general studies, manufacturing technology, mechanical engineering technology, medical laboratory technology, physical sciences.
LIBRARY 28,651 books, 4,435 microform titles, 207 periodicals, 4,068 records, tapes, and CDs. Acquisition spending 1994–95: $379,450.
COMPUTERS ON CAMPUS 70 computers for student use in computer labs.
COLLEGE LIFE Orientation program (2 days, no cost, parents included). Drama-theater group, student-run radio station. ***Campus security:*** part-time trained security personnel.
HOUSING College housing not available.
ATHLETICS ***Intercollegiate:*** baseball M, basketball M, volleyball M/W. ***Intramural:*** basketball, ice hockey, racquetball, tennis, volleyball.
CAREER PLANNING ***Service:*** career counseling.
EXPENSES FOR 1995–96 ***Application fee:*** $35. State resident tuition: $5024 full-time, $201 per credit part-time. Nonresident tuition: $7808 full-time, $326 per credit part-time. Part-time mandatory fees per semester range from $12 to $25. Full-time mandatory fees: $70.
FINANCIAL AID ***College-administered undergrad aid 1995–96:*** need-based scholarships, non-need scholarships, low-interest long-term loans from external sources, Federal Work-Study, part-time jobs. ***Required forms:*** FAFSA. ***Priority deadline:*** 2/15. ***Payment plan:*** deferred payment. ***Waivers:*** full or partial for employees or children of employees and senior citizens.
APPLYING ***Options:*** Common Application, electronic application, midyear entrance. ***Required:*** school transcript, 3 years of high school math and science, SAT I or ACT, TOEFL for international students. ***Required for some:*** some high school foreign language. Test scores used for admission. ***Application deadline:*** rolling.
APPLYING/TRANSFER ***Application deadline:*** rolling. ***Contact:*** Mr. Jeffrey E. Arnold, Admissions Officer, 412-339-5400.
CONTACT Mr. Jeffrey E. Arnold, Admissions Officer, Pennsylvania State University New Kensington Campus, New Kensington, PA 15068-1798, 412-339-5400.

PENNSYLVANIA STATE UNIVERSITY SCHUYLKILL CAMPUS
Schuylkill Haven, Pennsylvania

UG Enrollment: 1,040	Tuition & Fees (PA Res): $5094
Application Deadline: rolling	Room & Board: $4040

GENERAL State-related, 2-year, coed. Part of Pennsylvania State University. Awards terminal associate degrees (also offers up to 2 years of most baccalaureate programs offered at University Park campus; of students entering the associate degree program, 25% complete the degree and an additional 35% change to a baccalaureate program). Founded 1934. ***Setting:*** 58-acre small-town campus. Faculty: 62 (36 full-time, 82% with terminal degrees, 26 part-time); student-faculty ratio is 21:1.
ENROLLMENT PROFILE 1,040 students from 9 states and territories. 60% women, 40% men, 31% part-time, 94% state residents, 2% transferred in, 0% international, 24% 25 or older, 0% Native American, 2% Hispanic, 5% African American, 2% Asian American. ***Areas of study chosen:*** 25% engineering and applied sciences, 19% business management and administrative services, 17% interdisciplinary studies, 9% education, 9% health professions and related sciences, 6% agriculture, 4% communications and journalism, 3% social sciences, 2% natural resource sciences, 2% performing arts, 1% computer and information sciences, 1% physical sciences.
FIRST-YEAR CLASS 255 total; 556 applied, 90% were accepted, 51% of whom enrolled. 8% from top 10% of their high school class, 55% from top quarter, 82% from top half.
ACADEMIC PROGRAM Core, honor code. Calendar: semesters. Academic remediation for entering students, services for LD students, advanced placement, summer session for credit, adult/continuing education programs, internships. ROTC: Army.
GENERAL DEGREE REQUIREMENTS 60 credits; computer course for engineering, technology, business, science majors; internship (some majors).
MAJORS Agricultural business, biology/biological sciences, biomedical technologies, business administration/commerce/management, computer science, electrical engineering technology, family and consumer studies, liberal arts/general studies, manufacturing technology, mechanical engineering technology, physical sciences.
LIBRARY 32,662 books, 15,338 microform titles, 248 periodicals, 484 records, tapes, and CDs. Acquisition spending 1994–95: $393,550.
COMPUTERS ON CAMPUS 60 computers for student use in computer labs.
COLLEGE LIFE Orientation program (2 days, no cost, parents included). Drama-theater group, student-run newspaper, radio station. ***Campus security:*** 24-hour patrols, controlled dormitory access.
HOUSING 176 college housing spaces available. Freshmen given priority for college housing. Off-campus living permitted. ***Option:*** single-sex housing available. Resident assistants live in dorms.
ATHLETICS ***Intercollegiate:*** basketball M/W, cross-country running M/W, softball M/W, tennis M/W, volleyball M/W. ***Intramural:*** basketball, bowling, racquetball, riflery, skiing (downhill), swimming and diving, tennis, track and field, volleyball, weight lifting.
CAREER PLANNING ***Service:*** career counseling.
EXPENSES FOR 1995–96 ***Application fee:*** $35. State resident tuition: $5024 full-time, $201 per credit part-time. Nonresident tuition: $7808 full-time, $326 per credit part-time. Part-time mandatory fees per semester range from $12 to $25. Full-time mandatory fees: $70. College room and board: $4040.
FINANCIAL AID ***College-administered undergrad aid 1995–96:*** need-based scholarships, non-need scholarships, low-interest long-term loans from external sources, Federal Work-Study, part-time jobs. ***Required forms:*** FAFSA. ***Priority deadline:*** 2/15. ***Payment plan:*** deferred payment. ***Waivers:*** full or partial for employees or children of employees and senior citizens.
APPLYING ***Options:*** Common Application, electronic application, midyear entrance. ***Required:*** school transcript, 3 years of high school math and science, SAT I or ACT, TOEFL for international students. ***Required for some:*** some high school foreign language. Test scores used for admission. ***Application deadline:*** rolling.

APPLYING/TRANSFER *Application deadline:* rolling. *Contact:* Ms. Linda Walinsky, Director of Student Programs and Services, 717-385-6252.
CONTACT Ms. Linda Walinsky, Director of Student Programs and Services, Pennsylvania State University Schuylkill Campus, Schuylkill Haven, PA 17972-2208, 717-385-6252.

PENNSYLVANIA STATE UNIVERSITY SHENANGO CAMPUS
Sharon, Pennsylvania

UG Enrollment: 976	Tuition & Fees (PA Res): $5094
Application Deadline: rolling	Room & Board: N/Avail

GENERAL State-related, 2-year, coed. Part of Pennsylvania State University. Awards terminal associate degrees (also offers up to 2 years of most baccalaureate programs offered at University Park campus; of students entering the associate degree program, 25% complete the degree and an additional 35% change to a baccalaureate program). Founded 1965. *Setting:* 14-acre small-town campus. *Research spending 1994–95:* $26,999. Faculty: 76 (28 full-time, 88% with terminal degrees, 48 part-time).
ENROLLMENT PROFILE 976 students from 3 states and territories. 64% women, 36% men, 44% part-time, 88% state residents, 3% transferred in, 0% international, 52% 25 or older, 1% Native American, 0% Hispanic, 8% African American, 0% Asian American. *Areas of study chosen:* 25% engineering and applied sciences, 19% business management and administrative services, 17% interdisciplinary studies, 9% education, 9% health professions and related sciences, 6% agriculture, 4% communications and journalism, 3% social sciences, 2% natural resource sciences, 2% performing arts, 1% computer and information sciences, 1% physical sciences.
FIRST-YEAR CLASS 134 total; 235 applied, 89% were accepted, 64% of whom enrolled. 8% from top 10% of their high school class, 55% from top quarter, 82% from top half.
ACADEMIC PROGRAM Core, honor code. Calendar: semesters. Academic remediation for entering students, services for LD students, advanced placement, summer session for credit, adult/continuing education programs, internships.
GENERAL DEGREE REQUIREMENTS 60 credits; computer course for engineering, technology, business, science majors; internship (some majors).
MAJORS Agricultural business, biology/biological sciences, biomedical technologies, business administration/commerce/management, electrical engineering technology, liberal arts/general studies, manufacturing technology, mechanical engineering technology, medical laboratory technology, physical sciences, physical therapy.
LIBRARY 26,014 books, 3,603 microform titles, 147 periodicals, 1,850 records, tapes, and CDs. Acquisition spending 1994–95: $384,566.
COMPUTERS ON CAMPUS 36 computers for student use in computer labs.
COLLEGE LIFE Orientation program (2 days, no cost, parents included). Student-run newspaper. *Campus security:* part-time trained security personnel.
HOUSING College housing not available.
ATHLETICS *Intramural:* basketball, bowling, golf, racquetball, tennis, volleyball.
CAREER PLANNING *Service:* career counseling.
EXPENSES FOR 1995–96 *Application fee:* $35. State resident tuition: $5024 full-time, $201 per credit part-time. Nonresident tuition: $7808 full-time, $326 per credit part-time. Part-time mandatory fees per semester range from $12 to $25. Full-time mandatory fees: $70.
FINANCIAL AID *College-administered undergrad aid 1995–96:* need-based scholarships, non-need scholarships, low-interest long-term loans from external sources, Federal Work-Study, part-time jobs. *Required forms:* FAFSA. *Priority deadline:* 2/15. *Payment plan:* deferred payment. *Waivers:* full or partial for employees or children of employees and senior citizens.
APPLYING *Options:* Common Application, electronic application, midyear entrance. *Required:* school transcript, 3 years of high school math and science, SAT I or ACT, TOEFL for international students. *Required for some:* some high school foreign language. Test scores used for admission. *Application deadline:* rolling.
APPLYING/TRANSFER *Application deadline:* rolling. *Contact:* Ms. Gail Gilchrest, Admissions Officer, 412-983-5830.
CONTACT Ms. Gail Gilchrest, Admissions Officer, Pennsylvania State University Shenango Campus, Sharon, PA 16146-1537, 412-983-5830 or toll-free 800-367-2211 (in-state).

PENNSYLVANIA STATE UNIVERSITY WILKES-BARRE CAMPUS
Lehman, Pennsylvania

UG Enrollment: 777	Tuition & Fees (PA Res): $5094
Application Deadline: rolling	Room & Board: N/Avail

GENERAL State-related, 2-year, coed. Part of Pennsylvania State University. Awards terminal associate degrees (also offers up to 2 years of most baccalaureate programs offered at University Park campus; of students entering the associate degree program, 25% complete the degree and an additional 35% change to a baccalaureate program). Founded 1916. *Setting:* 58-acre rural campus. *Research spending 1994–95:* $51,488. Faculty: 70 (34 full-time, 77% with terminal degrees, 36 part-time).
ENROLLMENT PROFILE 777 students from 6 states and territories. 34% women, 66% men, 21% part-time, 96% state residents, 4% transferred in, 0% international, 18% 25 or older, 0% Native American, 1% Hispanic, 5% African American, 2% Asian American. *Areas of study chosen:* 25% engineering and applied sciences, 19% business management and administrative services, 17% interdisciplinary studies, 9% education, 9% health professions and related sciences, 6% agriculture, 4% communications and journalism, 3% social sciences, 2% natural resource sciences, 2% performing arts, 1% computer and information sciences, 1% physical sciences.
FIRST-YEAR CLASS 228 total; 527 applied, 88% were accepted, 49% of whom enrolled. 8% from top 10% of their high school class, 55% from top quarter, 82% from top half.
ACADEMIC PROGRAM Core, honor code. Calendar: semesters. Academic remediation for entering students, services for LD students, advanced placement, summer session for credit, adult/continuing education programs. ROTC: Army (c), Air Force (c).
GENERAL DEGREE REQUIREMENTS 60 credits; computer course for engineering, technology, business, science majors; internship (some majors).
MAJORS Agricultural business, biomedical technologies, business administration/commerce/management, electrical engineering technology, liberal arts/general studies, manufacturing technology, mechanical engineering technology, surveying technology.
LIBRARY 29,215 books, 1,682 microform titles, 512 periodicals, 265 records, tapes, and CDs. Acquisition spending 1994–95: $352,432.
COMPUTERS ON CAMPUS 33 computers for student use in computer labs.
COLLEGE LIFE Orientation program (2 days, no cost, parents included). Student-run newspaper. *Campus security:* part-time trained security personnel.
HOUSING College housing not available.
ATHLETICS *Intercollegiate:* baseball M, golf M, soccer M, volleyball M/W. *Intramural:* basketball, skiing (downhill), volleyball.
CAREER PLANNING *Service:* career counseling.
EXPENSES FOR 1995–96 *Application fee:* $35. State resident tuition: $5024 full-time, $201 per credit part-time. Nonresident tuition: $7808 full-time, $326 per credit part-time. Part-time mandatory fees per semester range from $12 to $25. Full-time mandatory fees: $70.
FINANCIAL AID *College-administered undergrad aid 1995–96:* need-based scholarships, non-need scholarships, low-interest long-term loans from external sources, Federal Work-Study, part-time jobs. *Required forms:* FAFSA. *Priority deadline:* 2/15. *Payment plan:* deferred payment. *Waivers:* full or partial for employees or children of employees and senior citizens.
APPLYING *Options:* Common Application, electronic application, midyear entrance. *Required:* school transcript, 3 years of high school math and science, SAT I or ACT, TOEFL for international students. *Required for some:* some high school foreign language. Test scores used for admission. *Application deadline:* rolling.
APPLYING/TRANSFER *Application deadline:* rolling. *Contact:* Mr. John S. Barnes Jr., Director of Student Programs and Services, 717-675-9238.
CONTACT Mr. John S. Barnes Jr., Director of Student Programs and Services, Pennsylvania State University Wilkes-Barre Campus, Lehman, PA 18627-0217, 717-675-9238 or toll-free 800-426-2358.

PENNSYLVANIA STATE UNIVERSITY WORTHINGTON SCRANTON CAMPUS
Dunmore, Pennsylvania

UG Enrollment: 1,115	Tuition & Fees (PA Res): $5094
Application Deadline: rolling	Room & Board: N/Avail

GENERAL State-related, 2-year, coed. Part of Pennsylvania State University. Awards terminal associate degrees (also offers up to 2 years of most baccalaureate programs offered at University Park campus; of students entering the associate degree program, 25% complete the degree and an additional 35% change to a baccalaureate program). Founded 1923. *Setting:* 43-acre small-town campus. *Research spending 1994–95:* $112. Faculty: 80 (44 full-time, 77% with terminal degrees, 36 part-time).
ENROLLMENT PROFILE 1,115 students from 7 states and territories. 46% women, 54% men, 23% part-time, 99% state residents, 5% transferred in, 0% international, 21% 25 or older, 0% Native American, 1% Hispanic, 1% African American, 1% Asian American. *Areas of study chosen:* 25% engineering and applied sciences, 19% business management and administrative services, 17% interdisciplinary studies, 9% education, 9% health professions and related sciences, 6% agriculture, 4% communications and journalism, 3% social sciences, 2% natural resource sciences, 2% performing arts, 1% computer and information sciences, 1% physical sciences.
FIRST-YEAR CLASS 269 total; 644 applied, 84% were accepted, 50% of whom enrolled. 8% from top 10% of their high school class, 55% from top quarter, 82% from top half.
ACADEMIC PROGRAM Core, honor code. Calendar: semesters. Academic remediation for entering students, services for LD students, advanced placement, summer session for credit, adult/continuing education programs, internships. ROTC: Army (c), Air Force (c).
GENERAL DEGREE REQUIREMENTS 60 credits; computer course for engineering, technology, business, science majors; internship (some majors).
MAJORS Agricultural business, architectural technologies, business administration/commerce/management, liberal arts/general studies, manufacturing technology, nursing.
LIBRARY 42,901 books, 33,328 microform titles, 222 periodicals, 1,663 records, tapes, and CDs. Acquisition spending 1994–95: $529,554.
COMPUTERS ON CAMPUS 61 computers for student use in computer labs.
COLLEGE LIFE Orientation program (2 days, no cost, parents included). Drama-theater group, student-run newspaper. *Campus security:* part-time trained security personnel.
HOUSING College housing not available.
ATHLETICS *Intercollegiate:* baseball M, basketball M, cross-country running M, soccer M, volleyball W. *Intramural:* basketball, bowling, skiing (downhill), soccer, tennis, volleyball.
CAREER PLANNING *Service:* career counseling.
EXPENSES FOR 1995–96 *Application fee:* $35. State resident tuition: $5024 full-time, $201 per credit part-time. Nonresident tuition: $7808 full-time, $326 per credit part-time. Part-time mandatory fees per semester range from $12 to $25. Full-time mandatory fees: $70.
FINANCIAL AID *College-administered undergrad aid 1995–96:* need-based scholarships, non-need scholarships, low-interest long-term loans from external sources, Federal Work-Study, part-time jobs. *Required forms:* FAFSA. *Priority deadline:* 2/15. *Payment plan:* deferred payment. *Waivers:* full or partial for employees or children of employees and senior citizens.
APPLYING *Options:* Common Application, electronic application, midyear entrance. *Required:* school transcript, 3 years of high school math and science, SAT I or ACT, TOEFL for international students. *Required for some:* some high school foreign language. Test scores used for admission. *Application deadline:* rolling.
APPLYING/TRANSFER *Application deadline:* rolling. *Contact:* Dr. Ralph Mastriani, Admissions Officer, 717-963-4757.
CONTACT Dr. Ralph Mastriani, Admissions Officer, Pennsylvania State University Worthington Scranton Campus, Dunmore, PA 18512-1699, 717-963-4757.

Pennsylvania

PENNSYLVANIA STATE UNIVERSITY YORK CAMPUS
York, Pennsylvania

UG Enrollment: 1,896	Tuition & Fees (PA Res): $5094
Application Deadline: rolling	Room & Board: N/Avail

GENERAL State-related, 2-year, coed. Part of Pennsylvania State University. Awards terminal associate degrees (also offers up to 2 years of most baccalaureate programs offered at University Park campus; of students entering the associate degree program, 25% complete the degree and an additional 35% change to a baccalaureate program). Founded 1926. *Setting:* 52-acre suburban campus. Faculty: 116 (48 full-time, 87% with terminal degrees, 68 part-time); student-faculty ratio is 21:1.
ENROLLMENT PROFILE 1,896 students from 8 states and territories. 41% women, 59% men, 55% part-time, 98% state residents, 2% transferred in, 0% international, 46% 25 or older, 0% Native American, 1% Hispanic, 3% African American, 3% Asian American.
Areas of study chosen: 25% engineering and applied sciences, 19% business management and administrative services, 17% interdisciplinary studies, 9% education, 9% health professions and related sciences, 6% agriculture, 4% communications and journalism, 3% social sciences, 2% natural resource sciences, 2% performing arts, 1% computer and information sciences, 1% physical sciences.
FIRST-YEAR CLASS 322 total; 677 applied, 92% were accepted, 52% of whom enrolled. 8% from top 10% of their high school class, 55% from top quarter, 82% from top half.
ACADEMIC PROGRAM Core, honor code. Calendar: semesters. Academic remediation for entering students, services for LD students, advanced placement, summer session for credit, adult/continuing education programs. ROTC: Army (c).
GENERAL DEGREE REQUIREMENTS 60 credits; computer course for engineering, technology, business, science majors; internship (some majors).
MAJORS Agricultural business, biomedical technologies, business administration/commerce/management, computer science, electrical engineering technology, liberal arts/general studies, manufacturing technology, mechanical engineering technology.
LIBRARY 38,250 books, 3,600 microform titles, 255 periodicals, 2,013 records, tapes, and CDs. Acquisition spending 1994–95: $731,674.
COMPUTERS ON CAMPUS 74 computers for student use in computer labs.
COLLEGE LIFE Orientation program (2 days, no cost, parents included). Student-run newspaper. *Campus security:* part-time trained security personnel.
HOUSING College housing not available.
ATHLETICS *Intercollegiate:* basketball M, soccer M, tennis M/W, volleyball W. *Intramural:* bowling, golf, racquetball, skiing (downhill), tennis, track and field, volleyball.
CAREER PLANNING *Service:* career counseling.
EXPENSES FOR 1995–96 *Application fee:* $35. State resident tuition: $5024 full-time, $201 per credit part-time. Nonresident tuition: $7808 full-time, $326 per credit part-time. Part-time mandatory fees per semester range from $12 to $25. Full-time mandatory fees: $70.
FINANCIAL AID *College-administered undergrad aid 1995–96:* need-based scholarships, non-need scholarships, low-interest long-term loans from external sources, Federal Work-Study, part-time jobs. *Required forms:* FAFSA. *Priority deadline:* 2/15. *Payment plan:* deferred payment. *Waivers:* full or partial for employees or children of employees and senior citizens.
APPLYING *Options:* Common Application, electronic application, midyear entrance. *Required:* school transcript, 3 years of high school math and science, SAT I or ACT, TOEFL for international students. *Required for some:* some high school foreign language. Test scores used for admission. *Application deadline:* rolling.
APPLYING/TRANSFER *Application deadline:* rolling. *Contact:* Ms. Nan L. Flesher, Admissions Officer, 717-771-4040.
CONTACT Ms. Nan L. Flesher, Admissions Officer, Pennsylvania State University York Campus, York, PA 17403-3298, 717-771-4040.

PENN TECHNICAL INSTITUTE
Pittsburgh, Pennsylvania

UG Enrollment: 150	Tuition & Fees: $7785
Application Deadline: rolling	Room & Board: N/Avail

GENERAL Proprietary, 2-year, specialized, primarily men. Awards transfer associate, terminal associate degrees. Founded 1947. *Setting:* urban campus. *Total enrollment:* 150. *Faculty:* 11 (all full-time).
ENROLLMENT PROFILE 150 students: 2% women, 20% part-time, 100% state residents, 2% transferred in, 0% international, 2% African American.
FIRST-YEAR CLASS 32 total. Of the students who applied, 95% were accepted.
ACADEMIC PROGRAM Core. Calendar: quarters. Summer session for credit, part-time degree program (evenings).
GENERAL DEGREE REQUIREMENTS 104 quarter hours; 26 quarter hours of math; computer course.
MAJOR Electrical and electronics technologies.
LIBRARY 1,200 books, 20 periodicals.
COMPUTERS ON CAMPUS 50 computers for student use in computer center, lab. Staffed computer lab on campus provides training in use of computers, software.
HOUSING College housing not available.
EXPENSES FOR 1996–97 Tuition: $7785 full-time, $3893 per quarter part-time.
FINANCIAL AID *College-administered undergrad aid 1995–96:* need-based scholarships, low-interest long-term loans from external sources. *Required forms:* state, institutional, FAFSA. *Application deadline:* continuous. *Waivers:* full or partial for employees or children of employees.
APPLYING *Options:* deferred entrance, midyear entrance. *Application deadline:* rolling.
APPLYING/TRANSFER *Entrance:* minimally difficult.
CONTACT Mr. Louis A. Dimasi, Admissions Director, Penn Technical Institute, 110 Ninth Street, Pittsburgh, PA 15222-3618, 412-355-0455.

PITTSBURGH INSTITUTE OF AERONAUTICS
Pittsburgh, Pennsylvania

UG Enrollment: 350	Tuition & Fees: $7452
Application Deadline: rolling	Room & Board: N/Avail

GENERAL Independent, 2-year, specialized, primarily men. Awards transfer associate, terminal associate degrees. Founded 1929. *Setting:* suburban campus. *Total enrollment:* 350. *Faculty:* 17 (16 full-time, 1 part-time); student-faculty ratio is 14:1.
ENROLLMENT PROFILE 350 students from 12 states and territories, 4 other countries. 2% women, 0% part-time, 57% state residents, 1% transferred in, 4% international, 45% 25 or older, 1% Hispanic, 1% African American, 1% Asian American.
FIRST-YEAR CLASS 75 total. Of the students who applied, 95% were accepted, 100% of whom enrolled. 3% from top 10% of their high school class, 8% from top quarter, 27% from top half.
ACADEMIC PROGRAM Core, aviation technology curriculum. Calendar: quarters. 12 courses offered in 1995–96. Academic remediation for entering students.
GENERAL DEGREE REQUIREMENTS 2520 hours; 2 math courses; 1 science course; computer course.
MAJORS Aircraft and missile maintenance, aviation technology, electrical and electronics technologies.
LIBRARY Technical Library with 15,000 books, 35 periodicals.
COLLEGE LIFE *Student services:* personal-psychological counseling.
HOUSING College housing not available.
CAREER PLANNING *Services:* resume preparation, resume referral, career counseling, job bank, job interviews.
EXPENSES FOR 1996–97 *Application fee:* $150. Tuition: $7452 full-time.
FINANCIAL AID *College-administered undergrad aid 1995–96:* need-based scholarships, low-interest long-term loans from external sources. *Required forms:* state, FAFSA; required for some: CSS Financial Aid PROFILE. *Application deadline:* continuous. *Payment plans:* tuition prepayment, installment. *Waivers:* full or partial for employees or children of employees.
APPLYING Open admission. *Option:* deferred entrance. *Required:* TOEFL for international students. *Recommended:* 3 years of high school math and science. Test scores used for admission. *Application deadline:* rolling. *Notification:* continuous.
APPLYING/TRANSFER *Application deadline:* rolling. *Notification:* continuous.
CONTACT Mrs. Sundae L. Kerr, Admissions Director, Pittsburgh Institute of Aeronautics, Pittsburgh, PA 15236-0897, 412-462-9011 Ext. 114 or toll-free 800-444-1440. *Fax:* 412-466-0513.

PITTSBURGH INSTITUTE OF MORTUARY SCIENCE, INCORPORATED
Pittsburgh, Pennsylvania

UG Enrollment: 130	Tuition & Fees: $8260
Application Deadline: rolling	Room & Board: N/Avail

GENERAL Independent, 2-year, specialized, coed. Awards transfer associate, terminal associate degrees. Founded 1939. *Setting:* urban campus. *Total enrollment:* 130. *Faculty:* 20 (4 full-time, 25% with terminal degrees, 16 part-time); student-faculty ratio is 4:1.
ENROLLMENT PROFILE 130 students from 10 states and territories, 4 other countries. 31% women, 4% part-time, 90% transferred in, 50% 25 or older, 10% African American.
FIRST-YEAR CLASS 73 total. Of the students who applied, 100% were accepted, 90% of whom enrolled.
ACADEMIC PROGRAM Core, honor code. Calendar: trimesters. Academic remediation for entering students, part-time degree program (daytime), co-op programs and internships.
GENERAL DEGREE REQUIREMENTS 96 credits; computer course; internship.
MAJOR Funeral service.
COMPUTERS ON CAMPUS 10 computers for student use in computer center. Staffed computer lab on campus provides training in use of computers, software.
COLLEGE LIFE 95% vote in student government elections. *Campus security:* 24-hour emergency response devices.
HOUSING College housing not available.
CAREER PLANNING *Director:* Mr. Eugene C. Ogrodnik, President and CEO, 412-362-8500. *Services:* resume preparation, resume referral, career counseling, job interviews. 4 organizations recruited on campus 1994–95.
AFTER GRADUATION 100% of class of 1994 had job offers within 6 months.
EXPENSES FOR 1995–96 *Application fee:* $30. Tuition: $7500 full-time, $200 per credit part-time. Full-time mandatory fees: $760.
FINANCIAL AID *College-administered undergrad aid 1995–96:* need-based scholarships, low-interest long-term loans from external sources, part-time jobs. *Required forms:* FAFSA; required for some: Pennsylvania Higher Educational Assistance Agency Form. *Application deadline:* continuous. *Payment plans:* installment, deferred payment.
APPLYING Open admission. *Required:* school transcript. *Application deadline:* rolling. *Notification:* continuous.
APPLYING/TRANSFER *Required:* college transcript. *Application deadline:* rolling. *Notification:* continuous.
CONTACT Ms. Jeanette G. Matthews, Registrar, Pittsburgh Institute of Mortuary Science, Incorporated, 5808 Baum Boulevard, Pittsburgh, PA 15206-3706, 412-362-8500 or toll-free 800-933-5808 (out-of-state). *Fax:* 412-362-1684.

PITTSBURGH TECHNICAL INSTITUTE
Pittsburgh, Pennsylvania

UG Enrollment: 657	Tuition: $15,600/deg prog
Application Deadline: rolling	Room & Board: N/Avail

GENERAL Proprietary, 2-year, coed. Awards diplomas, terminal associate degrees. Founded 1946. *Setting:* urban campus. *Total enrollment:* 657. *Faculty:* 31 (all full-time, 100% with terminal degrees). *Notable Alumni:* Keith Zecchini, manager at Trafalgar House; Thomas Naser, president and owner of I.M. Solutions; Steve Taylor, vice president at Structural Engineering; Rob Wilson, graphic designer at Page Imaging; Brian Gross, store manager at Options Incorporated.
ENROLLMENT PROFILE 657 students from 5 states and territories. 20% women, 80% men, 0% part-time, 88% state residents, 7% transferred in, 75% have need-based financial aid, 20% have non-need-based financial aid, 8% 25 or older, 1% Hispanic, 7% African American, 1% Asian American. *Areas of study chosen:* 90% vocational and home economics, 5% business management and administrative services, 5% computer and information sciences. *Most popular recent majors:* drafting and design, graphic arts, business administration/commerce/management.
FIRST-YEAR CLASS 352 total; 711 applied, 97% were accepted, 51% of whom enrolled. 7% from top 10% of their high school class, 17% from top quarter, 40% from top half.
ACADEMIC PROGRAM Vocational/occupational curriculum, honor code. Calendar: quarters. Academic remediation for entering students, tutorials, internships.
GENERAL DEGREE REQUIREMENTS 98 credit hours; computer course; internship.
MAJORS Business administration/commerce/management, commercial art, computer graphics, computer management, computer programming, drafting and design, graphic arts.
LIBRARY Learning Resources Center with 2,150 books, 85 periodicals, 2 on-line bibliographic services, 2 CD-ROMs, 15 records, tapes, and CDs.
COMPUTERS ON CAMPUS Computer purchase plan available. 95 computers for student use in computer center, learning resource center provide access to e-mail, on-line services, Internet. Staffed computer lab on campus provides training in use of computers, software.
COLLEGE LIFE *Most popular organizations:* Student Council, Student Activities Club. *Student services:* personal-psychological counseling. *Campus security:* electronically operated building access after hours.
HOUSING College housing not available.
ATHLETICS *Intramural:* basketball, softball, volleyball.
CAREER PLANNING *Placement office:* 4 full-time staff. *Director:* Ms. Carol Brooks, Director of Graduate Services, 412-471-1011. *Services:* job fairs, resume preparation, resume referral, career counseling, careers library, job bank, job interviews. Students must register sophomore year. 200 organizations recruited on campus 1994-95.
AFTER GRADUATION 98% of class of 1994 had job offers within 6 months.
EXPENSES FOR 1995-96 *Application fee:* $40. Tuition per degree program ranges from $15,600 to $18,000. Tuition guaranteed not to increase for student's term of enrollment.
FINANCIAL AID *College-administered undergrad aid 1995-96:* 120 need-based scholarships (average $600), 3 non-need scholarships (average $4850), low-interest long-term loans from external sources (average $3000), 5 part-time jobs. *Required forms:* state, institutional, FAFSA; required for some: financial aid transcript (for transfers); accepted: CSS Financial Aid PROFILE. *Priority deadline:* 8/1.
APPLYING *Options:* deferred entrance, midyear entrance. *Required:* school transcript, campus interview, TOEFL for international students. *Recommended:* SAT I or ACT, SAT II Subject Tests. Test scores used for counseling/placement. *Application deadline:* rolling.
APPLYING/TRANSFER *Required:* high school transcript, campus interview, college transcript. *Application deadline:* rolling.
CONTACT Ms. Laurel Black, Admissions Systems Manager, Pittsburgh Technical Institute, 635 Smithfield Street, Pittsburgh, PA 15222-2560, 412-471-1011. *Fax:* 412-471-9014.

READING AREA COMMUNITY COLLEGE
Reading, Pennsylvania

UG Enrollment: 3,000	Tuition & Fees (Area Res): $1803
Application Deadline: rolling	Room & Board: N/Avail

GENERAL County-supported, 2-year, coed. Awards transfer associate, terminal associate degrees. Founded 1971. *Setting:* urban campus with easy access to Philadelphia. *Total enrollment:* 3,000. *Faculty:* 249 (59 full-time, 190 part-time).
ENROLLMENT PROFILE 3,000 students: 69% women, 31% men, 73% part-time, 99% state residents, 35% transferred in, 1% international, 56% 25 or older, 1% Native American, 7% Hispanic, 8% African American, 2% Asian American.
FIRST-YEAR CLASS 489 total; 1,084 applied, 100% were accepted, 45% of whom enrolled.
ACADEMIC PROGRAM Core. Calendar: 3 ten-week semesters. Academic remediation for entering students, English as a second language program offered during academic year, services for LD students, self-designed majors, summer session for credit, part-time degree program (daytime, evenings), external degree programs, adult/continuing education programs, co-op programs.
GENERAL DEGREE REQUIREMENTS 60 credits; 1 course each in math and science; computer course for business majors; internship (some majors).
MAJORS Accounting, behavioral sciences, biology/biological sciences, business administration/commerce/management, business education, chemistry, child care/child and family studies, communication equipment technology, computer information systems, computer programming, computer science, data processing, dental services, early childhood education, education, electrical and electronics technologies, electrical engineering technology, electronics engineering technology, elementary education, engineering (general), engineering and applied sciences, engineering sciences, (pre)engineering sequence, engineering technology, finance/banking, gerontology, humanities, human resources, human services, industrial administration, industrial engineering technology, laboratory technologies, legal secretarial studies, legal studies, liberal arts/general studies, machine and tool technologies, marketing/retailing/merchandising, mechanical engineering technology, medical laboratory technology, medical records services, medical secretarial studies, medical technology, mental health/rehabilitation counseling, nursing, pharmacy/pharmaceutical sciences, political science/government, practical nursing, psychology, public administration, radiological technology, respiratory therapy, retail management, secretarial studies/office management, social science, social work, telecommunications, tourism and travel, veterinary sciences.
LIBRARY 25,541 books, 6,500 microform titles, 284 periodicals, 1,377 records, tapes, and CDs.
COMPUTERS ON CAMPUS 10 computers for student use in computer center, computer labs, learning resource center, classrooms, library.
COLLEGE LIFE Student-run newspaper. *Student services:* personal-psychological counseling, women's center. *Campus security:* 24-hour patrols.
HOUSING College housing not available.
ATHLETICS *Intercollegiate:* basketball M, cross-country running M/W, soccer M, volleyball W. *Intramural:* cross-country running.
CAREER PLANNING *Director:* Ms. Linda Matthews, Director of Center for Counseling and Academic Development, 610-372-4721 Ext. 215. *Services:* resume preparation, career counseling, careers library.
EXPENSES FOR 1995-96 *Application fee:* $10. Area resident tuition: $1740 full-time, $58 per credit part-time. State resident tuition: $3480 full-time, $116 per credit part-time. Nonresident tuition: $6960 full-time, $232 per credit part-time. Part-time mandatory fees per term range from $2 to $44. Full-time mandatory fees: $63 for county residents, $126 for state residents and nonresidents.
FINANCIAL AID *College-administered undergrad aid 1995-96:* 35 need-based scholarships (average $300), 5 non-need scholarships (average $600), short-term loans (average $100), low-interest long-term loans from external sources (average $2000), Federal Work-Study, 30 part-time jobs. *Required forms:* state, institutional; accepted: CSS Financial Aid PROFILE, FAFSA. *Priority deadline:* 8/1. *Waivers:* full or partial for employees or children of employees and senior citizens.
APPLYING Open admission. *Options:* early entrance, deferred entrance. *Required:* TOEFL for international students. *Required for some:* 3 years of high school science. Test scores used for counseling/placement. *Application deadline:* rolling.
APPLYING/TRANSFER *Required for some:* 3 years of high school science. *Application deadline:* rolling.
CONTACT Mr. Kenneth P. Mross, Admissions Coordinator, Reading Area Community College, PO Box 1706, Reading, PA 19603-1706, 610-372-4721 Ext. 236 or toll-free 800-626-1665 (in-state). *Fax:* 610-375-8255.

REMINGTON EDUCATION CENTER–VALE CAMPUS
Blairsville, Pennsylvania

UG Enrollment: 298	Tuition: $13,350/deg prog
Application Deadline: rolling	Room Only: $2080

GENERAL Independent, 2-year, primarily men. Part of Remington Education Center. Awards certificates, diplomas, transfer associate, terminal associate degrees. Founded 1946. *Setting:* 5-acre small-town campus with easy access to Pittsburgh. *Total enrollment:* 298. *Faculty:* 17.
ENROLLMENT PROFILE 298 students from 8 states and territories, 3 other countries. 3% women, 0% part-time, 80% state residents, 10% transferred in, 30% 25 or older, 1% Hispanic, 1% African American, 1% Asian American.
FIRST-YEAR CLASS 165 total; 695 applied, 72% were accepted, 33% of whom enrolled.
ACADEMIC PROGRAM Automotive technology curriculum. Calendar: modular. Academic remediation for entering students, advanced placement, tutorials, summer session for credit, adult/continuing education programs.
GENERAL DEGREE REQUIREMENT 1950 hours.
MAJOR Automotive technologies.
LIBRARY 689 books, 15 periodicals, 7 CD-ROMs, 190 records, tapes, and CDs.
COMPUTERS ON CAMPUS 50 computers for student use in computer center, computer labs, learning resource center, library, student center. Staffed computer lab on campus.
COLLEGE LIFE *Major annual events:* Student Appreciation Day, Day at the Races. *Campus security:* 24-hour emergency response devices and patrols.
HOUSING 53 college housing spaces available; 50 were occupied 1995-96. No special consideration for freshman housing applicants. Off-campus living permitted. Resident assistants live in dorms.
CAREER PLANNING *Placement office:* 1 full-time staff; $355,457 operating expenditure 1994-95. *Director:* Mrs. Nancy Baker, Placement Director, 412-459-9500 Ext. 316. *Services:* resume preparation, resume referral, career counseling, job interviews.
EXPENSES FOR 1996-97 *Application fee:* $50. Tuition: $13,350 per degree program. Full-time mandatory fees: $95. College room only: $2080.
FINANCIAL AID *College-administered undergrad aid 1995-96:* need-based scholarships, low-interest long-term loans from external sources, Federal Work-Study. *Required forms:* state, institutional, FAFSA. *Priority deadline:* 7/1. *Payment plans:* tuition prepayment, installment.
APPLYING *Options:* Common Application, early entrance, deferred entrance, midyear entrance. *Required:* school transcript, TOEFL for international students. *Required for some:* CPAt. Test scores used for admission. *Application deadline:* rolling. *Notification:* continuous.
APPLYING/TRANSFER *Required:* high school transcript, college transcript. *Entrance:* minimally difficult. *Application deadline:* rolling. *Notification:* continuous.
CONTACT Ms. Holly Derringer, Director of Admissions, Remington Education Center–Vale Campus, Blairsville, PA 15717-1389, 412-459-9500 or toll-free 800-822-8253 (in-state).

THADDEUS STEVENS STATE SCHOOL OF TECHNOLOGY
Lancaster, Pennsylvania

UG Enrollment: 427	Tuition & Fees: $4570
Application Deadline: 7/30	Room & Board: $4025

GENERAL State-supported, 2-year, primarily men. Awards certificates, terminal associate degrees. Founded 1905. *Setting:* 33-acre urban campus with easy access to Philadelphia. *Total enrollment:* 427. *Faculty:* 42 (39 full-time, 3 part-time).
ENROLLMENT PROFILE 427 students: 5% women, 0% part-time, 100% state residents, 75% live on campus, 5% transferred in, 20% have need-based financial aid, 20% have non-need-based financial aid, 25% 25 or older, 1% Native American, 4% Hispanic, 13% African American, 2% Asian American. *Areas of study chosen:* 100% vocational and home economics. *Most popular recent majors:* carpentry, automotive technologies, architectural technologies.

Pennsylvania

Thaddeus Stevens State School of Technology *(continued)*
FIRST-YEAR CLASS 281 total; 830 applied. 5% from top 10% of their high school class, 10% from top quarter, 40% from top half.
ACADEMIC PROGRAM Core, interdisciplinary curriculum. Calendar: semesters. Academic remediation for entering students, English as a second language program offered during academic year, services for LD students.
GENERAL DEGREE REQUIREMENTS 60 credits; 1 course each in math and science; computer course for electrical technology, heating/refrigeration/air conditioning, printing technology majors.
MAJORS Architectural technologies, automotive technologies, carpentry, construction technologies, drafting and design, electrical and electronics technologies, electrical engineering technology, electronics engineering technology, heating/refrigeration/air conditioning, industrial arts, legal secretarial studies, machine and tool technologies, mechanical design technology, plumbing, printing technologies.
LIBRARY Schuler Library with 26,000 books, 1,000 microform titles, 450 periodicals, 3,000 records, tapes, and CDs.
COMPUTERS ON CAMPUS 100 computers for student use in computer center, library. Staffed computer lab on campus.
COLLEGE LIFE Orientation program (3 days, no cost). Student-run newspaper. *Social organizations:* local fraternities. *Student services:* health clinic, personal-psychological counseling. *Campus security:* 24-hour emergency response devices.
HOUSING 320 college housing spaces available; 290 were occupied 1995–96. Freshmen given priority for college housing. Off-campus living permitted. *Option:* single-sex housing available. Resident assistants live in dorms.
ATHLETICS Member NJCAA. *Intercollegiate:* basketball M, cross-country running M, football M, track and field M, wrestling M. *Intramural:* archery, baseball, basketball, bowling, cross-country running, football, soccer, softball, table tennis (Ping-Pong), tennis, track and field, volleyball, weight lifting, wrestling. *Contact:* Mr. Todd Blankenstine, Director of Athletics, 717-299-7774.
CAREER PLANNING *Placement office:* 1 full-time staff. *Director:* Ms. Deb Schuch, Counselor, 717-299-7408. *Services:* job fairs, resume preparation, career counseling.
AFTER GRADUATION 15% of students completing a degree program in 1994–95 went directly on to further study.
EXPENSES FOR 1996–97 *Application fee:* $25. Comprehensive fee of $8595 includes full-time tuition ($4400), mandatory fees ($170), and college room and board ($4025). College room only: $1650. Tuition, room and board, and books are free for needy state residents.
FINANCIAL AID *College-administered undergrad aid 1995–96:* need-based scholarships, non-need scholarships, low-interest long-term loans from external sources, part-time jobs. *Required forms:* state, FAFSA. *Priority deadline:* 7/1.
APPLYING *Option:* deferred entrance. *Required:* minimum 2.0 GPA, 3 years of high school math and science, ACT ASSET. Test scores used for admission and counseling/placement. *Application deadline:* 7/30. *Notification:* continuous until 8/30. Preference given to needy students, indigent orphans.
APPLYING/TRANSFER *Required:* 3 years of high school math and science, minimum 2.0 high school GPA. *Entrance:* moderately difficult. *Application deadline:* 7/30. *Notification:* continuous until 8/30.
CONTACT Mr. George Burke, Director of Enrollment Services, Thaddeus Stevens State School of Technology, 750 East King Street, Lancaster, PA 17602-3198, 717-299-7772.

THOMPSON INSTITUTE
Harrisburg, Pennsylvania

UG Enrollment: 400 | **Tuition: $8000/deg prog**
Application Deadline: rolling | **Room Only: $2400**

GENERAL Proprietary, 2-year, coed. Part of Thompson Learning Corporation. Awards terminal associate degrees. Founded 1934. *Setting:* 5-acre suburban campus. *Total enrollment:* 400. *Faculty:* 25; student-faculty ratio is 20:1.
ENROLLMENT PROFILE 400 students from 3 states and territories, 2 other countries. 49% women, 18% part-time, 96% state residents, 15% transferred in, 25% 25 or older, 0% Native American, 5% Hispanic, 8% African American, 5% Asian American.
FIRST-YEAR CLASS 150 total. Of the students who applied, 95% were accepted, 70% of whom enrolled. 10% from top 10% of their high school class, 30% from top quarter, 75% from top half.
ACADEMIC PROGRAM Calendar: quarters. Academic remediation for entering students, services for LD students, summer session for credit, adult/continuing education programs, co-op programs.
GENERAL DEGREE REQUIREMENTS 72 credits; computer course.
MAJORS Accounting, business administration/commerce/management, computer management, computer programming, drafting and design, electrical and electronics technologies, medical assistant technologies.
LIBRARY 950 books, 20 periodicals, 50 records, tapes, and CDs.
COMPUTERS ON CAMPUS 60 computers for student use in computer center, computer labs, learning resource center, classrooms provide access to main academic computer, e-mail, on-line services.
COLLEGE LIFE *Social organizations:* 1 national sorority; 5% of eligible women are members. *Student services:* personal-psychological counseling.
HOUSING 85 college housing spaces available; 77 were occupied 1995–96. Freshmen given priority for college housing. Off-campus living permitted. *Option:* coed housing available.
ATHLETICS *Intramural:* basketball, football, golf, volleyball.
CAREER PLANNING *Services:* job fairs, resume preparation, resume referral, career counseling. Students must register sophomore year. 25 organizations recruited on campus 1994–95.
EXPENSES FOR 1995–96 *Application fee:* $50. Tuition per degree program ranges from $8000 to $9000. College room only: $2400.
FINANCIAL AID *College-administered undergrad aid 1995–96:* need-based scholarships, low-interest long-term loans from external sources (average $2500), 3 part-time jobs. *Required forms for some financial aid applicants:* state, institutional, FAFSA; accepted: CSS Financial Aid PROFILE. *Priority deadline:* 10/1.
APPLYING Open admission. *Options:* Common Application, electronic application, deferred entrance. *Required:* school transcript. *Recommended:* 3 years of high school math. *Application deadline:* rolling.

APPLYING/TRANSFER *Required:* high school transcript, college transcript. *Application deadline:* rolling.
CONTACT Mr. Tom Bogush, High School Supervisor, Thompson Institute, Harrisburg, PA 17111-3518, 717-564-4112 or toll-free 800-272-4632 (in-state). *Fax:* 717-564-3779.

TRIANGLE TECH, INC.
Pittsburgh, Pennsylvania

UG Enrollment: 360 | **Tuition & Fees: $6000**
Application Deadline: rolling | **Room & Board: N/Avail**

GENERAL Proprietary, 2-year, coed. Part of Triangle Tech, Inc. Awards certificates, diplomas, terminal associate degrees. Founded 1944. *Setting:* 5-acre urban campus. *Total enrollment:* 360. *Faculty:* 30 (20 full-time, 10 part-time).
ENROLLMENT PROFILE 360 students from 3 states and territories. 12% women, 0% part-time, 97% state residents, 2% transferred in, 18% African American.
FIRST-YEAR CLASS 113 total. Of the students who applied, 98% were accepted, 96% of whom enrolled. 9% from top 10% of their high school class, 55% from top half.
ACADEMIC PROGRAM Core. Calendar: semesters. Academic remediation for entering students.
GENERAL DEGREE REQUIREMENTS 70 credits; 1 math course; computer course for most majors.
MAJORS Architectural technologies, drafting and design, electrical engineering technology, heating/refrigeration/air conditioning, mechanical design technology.
LIBRARY 2,000 books, 30 periodicals.
COMPUTERS ON CAMPUS 50 computers for student use in computer labs. Staffed computer lab on campus provides training in use of computers, software.
HOUSING College housing not available.
CAREER PLANNING *Service:* career counseling.
EXPENSES FOR 1995–96 Tuition: $5850 full-time. Full-time mandatory fees: $150.
FINANCIAL AID *College-administered undergrad aid 1995–96:* 50 need-based scholarships (average $300), 5 non-need scholarships (average $2500), low-interest long-term loans from college funds (average $1000), loans from external sources (average $2625), Federal Work-Study. *Required forms:* state, institutional, FAFSA; accepted: CSS Financial Aid PROFILE. *Application deadline:* continuous to 8/1. *Payment plan:* installment. *Waivers:* full or partial for employees or children of employees.
APPLYING *Options:* early entrance, deferred entrance. *Application deadline:* rolling.
APPLYING/TRANSFER *Application deadline:* rolling.
CONTACT Mr. John A. Mazzarese, Corporate Director of Admissions, Triangle Tech, Inc., 1940 Perrysville Avenue, Pittsburgh, PA 15214-3897, 412-359-1000 Ext. 174. *Fax:* 412-359-1012.

TRIANGLE TECH, INC.–DUBOIS SCHOOL
DuBois, Pennsylvania

UG Enrollment: 325 | **Tuition & Fees: $6000**
Application Deadline: rolling | **Room & Board: N/Avail**

GENERAL Proprietary, 2-year, primarily men. Part of Triangle Tech, Inc. Awards certificates, diplomas, terminal associate degrees. Founded 1944. *Setting:* 5-acre small-town campus. *Total enrollment:* 325. *Faculty:* 20 (all full-time, 5% with terminal degrees).
ENROLLMENT PROFILE 325 students from 4 states and territories. 4% women, 0% part-time, 2% transferred in, 0% international, 18% 25 or older, 1% Native American, 1% Hispanic, 1% African American, 1% Asian American.
FIRST-YEAR CLASS 135 total. Of the students who applied, 98% were accepted, 96% of whom enrolled.
ACADEMIC PROGRAM Core, honor code. Calendar: semesters. Academic remediation for entering students. Off-campus study at all other campuses of Triangle Tech, Inc.
GENERAL DEGREE REQUIREMENTS 70 credits; 1 math course; computer course for most majors.
MAJORS Carpentry, drafting and design, electrical and electronics technologies, welding technology.
LIBRARY 1,200 books, 10 periodicals.
COMPUTERS ON CAMPUS 40 computers for student use in computer labs, library. Staffed computer lab on campus provides training in use of computers, software.
HOUSING College housing not available.
CAREER PLANNING *Placement office:* 1 full-time, 1 part-time staff. *Director:* Ms. Denise Ehrewsberger, Career Advisor, 814-371-2090. *Services:* resume referral, career counseling, careers library.
EXPENSES FOR 1995–96 Tuition: $5850 full-time. Full-time mandatory fees: $150.
FINANCIAL AID *College-administered undergrad aid 1995–96:* need-based scholarships, 5 non-need scholarships (average $2500), low-interest long-term loans from external sources, Federal Work-Study. *Required forms:* institutional, FAFSA. *Application deadline:* continuous. *Payment plan:* installment. *Waivers:* full or partial for employees or children of employees.
APPLYING *Option:* deferred entrance. *Application deadline:* rolling.
APPLYING/TRANSFER *Entrance:* minimally difficult. *Application deadline:* rolling.
CONTACT Mrs. Karen L. Kemmer, Director of Admissions, Triangle Tech, Inc.–DuBois School, DuBois, PA 15801-0551, 814-371-2090 or toll-free 800-472-4351. *Fax:* 814-371-9227.

TRIANGLE TECH, INC.–ERIE SCHOOL
Erie, Pennsylvania

UG Enrollment: 215 | **Tuition & Fees: $6740**
Application Deadline: rolling | **Room & Board: N/Avail**

GENERAL Proprietary, 2-year, primarily men. Part of Triangle Tech, Inc. Awards transfer associate, terminal associate degrees. Founded 1976. *Setting:* 1-acre urban campus. *Total enrollment:* 215. *Faculty:* 16 (14 full-time, 2 part-time); student-faculty ratio is 15:1.

ENROLLMENT PROFILE 215 students from 3 states and territories. 1% women, 99% men, 0% part-time, 95% state residents, 1% transferred in, 40% 25 or older, 2% African American. ***Areas of study chosen:*** 55% engineering and applied sciences. ***Most popular recent majors:*** architectural technologies, mechanical design technology.
FIRST-YEAR CLASS 72 total. Of the students who applied, 97% were accepted, 81% of whom enrolled. 15% from top 10% of their high school class, 60% from top half.
ACADEMIC PROGRAM Core. Calendar: semesters. Academic remediation for entering students, summer session for credit.
GENERAL DEGREE REQUIREMENTS 72 credits; math requirement varies according to program; computer course for drafting majors.
MAJORS Architectural technologies, drafting and design, electrical and electronics technologies, mechanical design technology.
LIBRARY 400 books, 15 periodicals.
COMPUTERS ON CAMPUS Computer purchase plan available. 32 computers for student use in classrooms. Staffed computer lab on campus provides training in use of computers, software.
COLLEGE LIFE ***Social organizations:*** 1 open to all. ***Most popular organization:*** Student Advisory Council.
HOUSING College housing not available.
ATHLETICS ***Intramural:*** basketball, bowling, football, golf, skiing (downhill).
CAREER PLANNING ***Service:*** career counseling.
AFTER GRADUATION 2% of students completing a degree program in 1994–95 went directly on to further study.
EXPENSES FOR 1995–96 Tuition: $5850 full-time. Full-time mandatory fees: $150.
FINANCIAL AID ***College-administered undergrad aid 1995–96:*** need-based scholarships, non-need scholarships, low-interest long-term loans from external sources (average $2500), Federal Work-Study. ***Required forms:*** institutional, FAFSA; required for some: state. ***Application deadline:*** continuous. ***Payment plan:*** installment. ***Waivers:*** full or partial for employees or children of employees.
APPLYING Open admission. ***Options:*** deferred entrance, midyear entrance. ***Required:*** school transcript, interview, Nelson Denny Reading Test. Test scores used for counseling/placement. ***Application deadline:*** rolling.
APPLYING/TRANSFER ***Required:*** standardized test scores, high school transcript, interview, college transcript. ***Application deadline:*** rolling. ***Contact:*** Ms. Kimberly Woodle, Career Services Advisor, 814-453-6016.
CONTACT Ms. Polly Bihler, Admissions Representative, Triangle Tech, Inc.–Erie School, 2000 Liberty Street, Erie, PA 16502-2594, 814-453-6016.

TRIANGLE TECH, INC.–GREENSBURG CENTER
Greensburg, Pennsylvania

UG Enrollment: 225	**Tuition & Fees: $6000**
Application Deadline: rolling	**Room & Board: N/Avail**

GENERAL Proprietary, 2-year, coed. Part of Triangle Tech, Inc. Awards certificates, diplomas, terminal associate degrees. Founded 1944. ***Setting:*** small-town campus with easy access to Pittsburgh. ***Total enrollment:*** 225. ***Faculty:*** 16 (12 full-time, 4 part-time).
ENROLLMENT PROFILE 225 students from 4 states and territories, 1 other country. 3% women, 1% part-time, 99% state residents, 0% transferred in, 20% 25 or older, 0% Native American, 0% Hispanic, 1% African American, 0% Asian American.
FIRST-YEAR CLASS 71 total. Of the students who applied, 94% were accepted, 92% of whom enrolled. 4% from top 10% of their high school class, 10% from top quarter, 80% from top half.
ACADEMIC PROGRAM Core. Calendar: semesters. Academic remediation for entering students, summer session for credit, adult/continuing education programs.
GENERAL DEGREE REQUIREMENTS 70 credits; 1 math course; computer course for most majors.
MAJORS Architectural technologies, drafting and design, heating/refrigeration/air conditioning, mechanical design technology.
LIBRARY 330 books, 8 periodicals.
COMPUTERS ON CAMPUS Students must have own computer. 40 computers for student use in computer center. Staffed computer lab on campus provides training in use of computers, software.
COLLEGE LIFE ***Student services:*** personal-psychological counseling.
HOUSING College housing not available.
CAREER PLANNING ***Service:*** career counseling.
EXPENSES FOR 1995–96 Tuition: $5850 full-time. Full-time mandatory fees: $150.
FINANCIAL AID ***College-administered undergrad aid 1995–96:*** need-based scholarships, 2 non-need scholarships (average $2500), low-interest long-term loans from college funds (average $500), loans from external sources (average $2625), Federal Work-Study. ***Required forms:*** state, institutional, FAFSA. ***Application deadline:*** continuous to 8/1. ***Payment plan:*** installment. ***Waivers:*** full or partial for employees or children of employees.
APPLYING ***Option:*** deferred entrance. ***Required:*** TOEFL for international students. Test scores used for admission. ***Application deadline:*** rolling.
APPLYING/TRANSFER ***Application deadline:*** rolling.
CONTACT Mr. John A. Mazzarese, Corporate Director of Admissions, Triangle Tech, Inc.–Greensburg Center, Greensburg, PA 15601-2012, 412-359-1000.

UNIVERSITY OF PITTSBURGH–TITUSVILLE
Titusville, Pennsylvania

UG Enrollment: 299	**Tuition & Fees (PA Res): $5414**
Application Deadline: rolling	**Room & Board: $4336**

GENERAL State-related, 2-year, coed. Part of University of Pittsburgh System. Awards transfer associate, terminal associate degrees. Founded 1963. ***Setting:*** 10-acre small-town campus with easy access to Pittsburgh. ***Endowment:*** $30,305. ***Research spending 1994–95:*** $6754. ***Educational spending 1994–95:*** $4300 per undergrad. ***Total enrollment:*** 299. ***Faculty:*** 38 (21 full-time, 73% with terminal degrees, 17 part-time); student-faculty ratio is 10:1.
ENROLLMENT PROFILE 299 students from 6 states and territories. 60% women, 40% men, 20% part-time, 96% state residents, 35% live on campus, 20% transferred in, 80% have need-based financial aid, 10% have non-need-based financial aid, 30% 25 or older, 1% Native American, 3% Hispanic, 1% African American, 3% Asian American. ***Areas of study chosen:*** 34% liberal arts/general studies, 30% health professions and related sciences, 15% business management and administrative services, 4% education, 4% engineering and applied sciences, 2% English language/literature/letters, 2% fine arts, 2% mathematics, 2% natural resource sciences, 2% psychology, 2% social sciences, 1% physical sciences. ***Most popular recent major:*** liberal arts/general studies.
FIRST-YEAR CLASS 128 total; 606 applied, 98% were accepted, 22% of whom enrolled. 3% from top 10% of their high school class, 12% from top quarter, 45% from top half.
ACADEMIC PROGRAM Core, liberal arts curriculum. Calendar: semesters. 36 courses offered in 1995–96. Academic remediation for entering students, advanced placement, tutorials, summer session for credit, part-time degree program (daytime, evenings, weekends, summer), adult/continuing education programs, co-op programs and internships. ROTC: Army (c), Air Force (c).
GENERAL DEGREE REQUIREMENTS 60 credits; computer course for business, health sciences majors; internship (some majors).
MAJORS Accounting, business administration/commerce/management, liberal arts/general studies, natural sciences, occupational therapy, physical therapy.
LIBRARY Hoskel Memorial Library plus 1 other, with 45,000 books, 1,200 microform titles, 200 periodicals, 155 records, tapes, and CDs. Acquisition spending 1994–95: $32,168.
COMPUTERS ON CAMPUS Student rooms linked to a campus network. 55 computers for student use in computer center, library provide access to main academic computer, e-mail, on-line services, Internet. Staffed computer lab on campus provides training in use of computers, software. Academic computing expenditure 1994–95: $101,218.
COLLEGE LIFE Orientation program (2 days, $35, parents included). Drama-theater group, choral group. ***Social organizations:*** 20 open to all. ***Most popular organizations:*** Admissions Advisory Board, Wilderness Club, Student Government Association, Theater Club, Travel Club. ***Major annual events:*** Semi-Formal Ball, Winter Carnival, Kick-off Dance. ***Student services:*** health clinic, personal-psychological counseling. ***Campus security:*** 24-hour emergency response devices and patrols.
HOUSING 346 college housing spaces available; 110 were occupied 1995–96. Freshmen guaranteed college housing. On-campus residence required through sophomore year except if living with relatives, married, or 21 or over. ***Option:*** coed (2 buildings) housing available. Resident assistants live in dorms.
ATHLETICS ***Intercollegiate:*** basketball M, volleyball W. ***Intramural:*** badminton, basketball, bowling, football, golf, racquetball, skiing (cross-country), skiing (downhill), softball, swimming and diving, table tennis (Ping-Pong), tennis, volleyball, weight lifting.
CAREER PLANNING ***Placement office:*** 1 full-time staff. ***Director:*** Ms. Judy Berneburg, Counseling and Student Development, 814-827-3113. ***Services:*** resume preparation, career counseling, careers library.
EXPENSES FOR 1995–96 ***Application fee:*** $35. State resident tuition: $4974 full-time, $169 per credit part-time. Nonresident tuition: $10,816 full-time, $359 per credit part-time. Part-time mandatory fees: $33 per semester. Full-time mandatory fees: $440. College room and board: $4336. College room only: $2340.
FINANCIAL AID ***College-administered undergrad aid 1995–96:*** need-based scholarships, non-need scholarships, low-interest long-term loans from external sources, Federal Work-Study, part-time jobs. ***Required forms:*** state, institutional, FAFSA; accepted: CSS Financial Aid PROFILE. ***Priority deadline:*** 5/1. ***Payment plans:*** installment, deferred payment. ***Waivers:*** full or partial for employees or children of employees and senior citizens.
APPLYING ***Options:*** early entrance, deferred entrance, midyear entrance. ***Required:*** school transcript, minimum 2.0 GPA, SAT I or ACT, TOEFL for international students. ***Recommended:*** essay, 3 years of high school math and science, 3 years of high school foreign language, 3 recommendations, interview. ***Required for some:*** essay, 3 recommendations. Test scores used for admission. ***Application deadline:*** rolling.
APPLYING/TRANSFER ***Required:*** high school transcript, college transcript, minimum 2.0 college GPA. ***Recommended:*** essay, 3 years of high school math and science, 3 years of high school foreign language, 3 recommendations, interview. ***Required for some:*** essay, standardized test scores, 3 recommendations, minimum 2.0 high school GPA. ***Entrance:*** minimally difficult. ***Application deadline:*** rolling. ***Contact:*** Mr. Robert Kvidt, Director of Admissions and Financial Aid, 814-827-4427.
CONTACT Mr. Robert Kvidt, Director of Admissions and Financial Aid, University of Pittsburgh–Titusville, Titusville, PA 16354, 814-827-4427. ***Fax:*** 814-827-4448. ***E-mail:*** uptadm@pitt.edu.

VALLEY FORGE MILITARY COLLEGE
Wayne, Pennsylvania

UG Enrollment: 182	**Comprehensive Fee: $18,800**
Application Deadline: rolling	**Room & Board: N/App**

The College's primary goal is to prepare young men to transfer to and succeed at the 4-year college or university of their choice. For more than 90% of the graduates, that goal is achieved through challenging academic programs; a structured environment that builds confidence and character and fosters academic success; and personal transfer counseling and transfer agreements with major universities. The only 2-year Army ROTC commissioning program in the Northeast US, with full scholarships for qualified applicants.

GENERAL Independent, 2-year, men only. Awards transfer associate degrees. Founded 1928. ***Setting:*** 115-acre suburban campus with easy access to Philadelphia. ***Total enrollment:*** 182. ***Faculty:*** 31 (14 full-time, 21% with terminal degrees, 17 part-time). ***Notable Alumni:*** Norman Schwarzkopf, Warren Rudman, J. D. Salinger.
ENROLLMENT PROFILE 182 students from 25 states and territories, 12 other countries. 0% women, 0% part-time, 25% state residents, 2% transferred in, 13% international, 1% 25 or older, 0% Native American, 4% Hispanic, 16% African American, 3% Asian American. ***Areas of study chosen:*** 29% business management and administrative services, 23% liberal arts/general studies, 15% engineering and applied sciences, 12% biological and life sciences.
FIRST-YEAR CLASS 120 total; 227 applied, 96% were accepted, 55% of whom enrolled.

Peterson's Guide to Two-Year Colleges 1997 579

Valley Forge Military College (continued)
ACADEMIC PROGRAM Core, honor code. Calendar: 4-1-4. 93 courses offered in 1995–96; average class size 12 in required courses. Academic remediation for entering students, English as a second language program offered during academic year and summer, advanced placement, honors program. ROTC: Army, Air Force (c).
GENERAL DEGREE REQUIREMENTS 60 credits; 2 semesters each of math and science; computer course.
MAJORS Business administration/commerce/management, criminal justice, engineering (general), liberal arts/general studies, science.
LIBRARY Baker Library with 60,644 books, 56,915 microform titles, 90 periodicals.
COMPUTERS ON CAMPUS 36 computers for student use in computer labs, classrooms, library provide access to main academic computer, off-campus computing facilities, e-mail, on-line services. Staffed computer lab on campus provides training in use of computers, software.
COLLEGE LIFE Orientation program (4 days, no cost). Drama-theater group, choral group, marching band, student-run newspaper. ***Social organizations:*** national fraternities. ***Student services:*** health clinic, personal-psychological counseling. ***Campus security:*** 24-hour patrols.
HOUSING 225 college housing spaces available; 100 were occupied 1995–96. Freshmen guaranteed college housing. On-campus residence required through sophomore year.
ATHLETICS ***Intercollegiate:*** basketball (s), cross-country running, equestrian sports, football (s), golf, riflery, soccer (s), tennis. ***Intramural:*** football, water polo, weight lifting. ***Contact:*** Mr. Jim Burner, Director of Athletics, 610-989-1341.
CAREER PLANNING ***Director:*** Ms. Barbara Parker, Transfer Advisor, 610-989-1453. ***Service:*** career counseling. Students must register freshman year.
AFTER GRADUATION 96% of students completing a degree program in 1994–95 went directly on to further study.
EXPENSES FOR 1996–97 Comprehensive fee: $18,800.
FINANCIAL AID ***College-administered undergrad aid 1995–96:*** 94 need-based scholarships (average $4390), 35 non-need scholarships (average $3745), low-interest long-term loans from external sources (average $2767), Federal Work-Study, 28 part-time jobs. ***Required forms:*** institutional; accepted: CSS Financial Aid PROFILE. ***Priority deadline:*** 6/1. ***Payment plans:*** installment, deferred payment. ***Waivers:*** full or partial for employees or children of employees.
APPLYING ***Options:*** early entrance, deferred entrance. ***Required:*** school transcript, 3 years of high school math and science, SAT I or ACT. ***Recommended:*** minimum 2.0 GPA, some high school foreign language, recommendations, interview. ***Required for some:*** TOEFL for international students. Test scores used for admission. ***Application deadline:*** rolling. ***Notification:*** continuous.
APPLYING/TRANSFER ***Required:*** standardized test scores, high school transcript, 3 years of high school math and science, college transcript. ***Recommended:*** some high school foreign language, recommendations, interview, minimum 2.0 college GPA, minimum 2.0 high school GPA. ***Entrance:*** moderately difficult. ***Application deadline:*** rolling. ***Notification:*** continuous.
CONTACT LTC Fred A. Serino, Director of Admissions, Valley Forge Military College, Wayne, PA 19087-3695, 610-989-1301 or toll-free 800-234-8362. ***Fax:*** 610-688-1545. College video available.

❖ ***See page 820 for a narrative description.*** ❖

WELDER TRAINING AND TESTING INSTITUTE
Allentown, Pennsylvania

UG Enrollment: 300	**Tuition & Fees: $6300**
Application Deadline: rolling	**Room & Board: N/Avail**

GENERAL Proprietary, 2-year, primarily men. Awards terminal associate degrees. Founded 1922. ***Setting:*** suburban campus with easy access to Philadelphia. ***Total enrollment:*** 300. ***Faculty:*** 18 (9 full-time, 9 part-time); student-faculty ratio is 15:1.
ENROLLMENT PROFILE 300 students: 5% women, 31% part-time, 85% state residents.
FIRST-YEAR CLASS 191 total. Of the students who applied, 82% were accepted, 95% of whom enrolled.
ACADEMIC PROGRAM Core. Calendar: 4-1-4. Part-time degree program (daytime), adult/continuing education programs.
GENERAL DEGREE REQUIREMENT 1600 hours.
MAJOR Welding technology.
HOUSING College housing not available.
CAREER PLANNING ***Service:*** career counseling.
EXPENSES FOR 1996–97 ***Application fee:*** $75. Tuition: $6300 full-time, $7 per hour part-time. Tuition guaranteed not to increase for student's term of enrollment.
FINANCIAL AID ***College-administered undergrad aid 1995–96:*** need-based scholarships, 6 non-need scholarships (average $3330), low-interest long-term loans from external sources (average $2500). ***Required forms:*** institutional, FAFSA. ***Priority deadline:*** 8/1.
APPLYING ***Options:*** early entrance, deferred entrance. ***Required:*** SRA Test of Mechanical Skills, Wonderlic aptitude test. Test scores used for admission. ***Application deadline:*** rolling.
APPLYING/TRANSFER ***Required:*** standardized test scores. ***Entrance:*** noncompetitive.
CONTACT Mr. Vincent Castellucci, Administrator Representatives, Welder Training and Testing Institute, Allentown, PA 18103-1263, 610-820-9551 or toll-free 800-223-9884.

WESTMORELAND COUNTY COMMUNITY COLLEGE
Youngwood, Pennsylvania

UG Enrollment: 6,026	**Tuition & Fees (Area Res): $1350**
Application Deadline: rolling	**Room & Board: N/Avail**

GENERAL County-supported, 2-year, coed. Awards certificates, diplomas, transfer associate, terminal associate degrees. Founded 1970. ***Setting:*** 85-acre rural campus with easy access to Pittsburgh. ***Total enrollment:*** 6,026. ***Faculty:*** 390 (85 full-time, 25% with terminal degrees, 305 part-time); student-faculty ratio is 17:1.
ENROLLMENT PROFILE 6,026 students from 3 states and territories, 3 other countries. 62% women, 38% men, 55% part-time, 99% state residents, 8% transferred in, 55% 25 or older, 1% Native American, 0% Hispanic, 2% African American, 0% Asian American. ***Areas of study chosen:*** 44% liberal arts/general studies, 12% health professions and related sciences, 10% computer and information sciences, 10% vocational and home economics, 8% business management and administrative services, 8% engineering and applied sciences, 3% education. ***Most popular recent majors:*** nursing, business administration/commerce/management, paralegal studies.
FIRST-YEAR CLASS 1,727 total; 2,084 applied, 100% were accepted, 83% of whom enrolled.
ACADEMIC PROGRAM Core, honor code. Calendar: semesters. Academic remediation for entering students, services for LD students, advanced placement, honors program, summer session for credit, part-time degree program (daytime, evenings, weekends, summer), adult/continuing education programs, co-op programs and internships. Off-campus study at Seton Hill College, University of Pittsburgh.
GENERAL DEGREE REQUIREMENTS 60 credits; internship (some majors).
MAJORS Accounting, architectural technologies, business administration/commerce/management, child care/child and family studies, commercial art, computer graphics, computer information systems, computer science, computer technologies, criminal justice, culinary arts, data processing, dental services, dietetics, drafting and design, electrical and electronics technologies, electronics engineering technology, engineering (general), environmental engineering technology, fashion design and technology, fashion merchandising, finance/banking, fire science, food services management, graphic arts, health education, heating/refrigeration/air conditioning, horticulture, hospitality services, hotel and restaurant management, human services, information science, law enforcement/police sciences, legal secretarial studies, liberal arts/general studies, marketing/retailing/merchandising, mechanical design technology, mechanical engineering technology, medical records services, medical secretarial studies, nuclear technology, nursing, optometric/ophthalmic technologies, paralegal studies, photography, practical nursing, printing technologies, public administration, publishing, real estate, retail management, robotics, secretarial studies/office management, tourism and travel, welding technology.
LIBRARY 34,522 books, 38,885 microform titles, 643 periodicals, 2,333 records, tapes, and CDs.
COMPUTERS ON CAMPUS Computer purchase plan available. 240 computers for student use in computer center, computer labs, learning resource center, classrooms, library provide access to off-campus computing facilities, e-mail, on-line services. Staffed computer lab on campus provides training in use of computers, software.
COLLEGE LIFE Orientation program (5 days, no cost). Choral group, student-run newspaper, radio station. ***Social organizations:*** 25 open to all. ***Student services:*** personal-psychological counseling. ***Campus security:*** 24-hour emergency response devices and patrols.
HOUSING College housing not available.
ATHLETICS Member NJCAA. ***Intercollegiate:*** baseball M, golf M/W, softball W, tennis M/W, volleyball W. ***Intramural:*** basketball, bowling, football, racquetball, skiing (downhill), softball, table tennis (Ping-Pong), volleyball, weight lifting. ***Contact:*** Mr. Robert Kostelink, Director of Student Life, 412-925-4129.
CAREER PLANNING ***Placement office:*** 1 full-time staff. ***Director:*** Ms. Sandra Montemurro, Director of Student Development, 412-925-4050. ***Services:*** job fairs, resume preparation, resume referral, career counseling, careers library, job bank, job interviews.
AFTER GRADUATION 91% of class of 1994 had job offers within 6 months.
EXPENSES FOR 1996–97 Area resident tuition: $1290 full-time, $43 per credit part-time. State resident tuition: $2580 full-time, $86 per credit part-time. Nonresident tuition: $3870 full-time, $129 per credit part-time. Part-time mandatory fees: $2 per credit. Full-time mandatory fees: $60.
FINANCIAL AID ***College-administered undergrad aid 1995–96:*** 15 need-based scholarships (average $250), 88 non-need scholarships (average $1000), Federal Work-Study, part-time jobs. ***Required forms:*** state, FAFSA. ***Priority deadline:*** 5/1. ***Waivers:*** full or partial for employees or children of employees and senior citizens.
APPLYING Open admission except for nursing, dental services programs. ***Option:*** early entrance. ***Required:*** TOEFL for international students, ACT ASSET. ***Required for some:*** 3 years of high school math and science. Test scores used for counseling/placement. ***Application deadline:*** rolling. ***Notification:*** continuous. Preference given to county residents for nursing program.
APPLYING/TRANSFER ***Required for some:*** 3 years of high school math and science. ***Application deadline:*** rolling. ***Notification:*** continuous. ***Contact:*** Mr. Richard Capozzi, Transfer Counselor, 412-925-4059.
CONTACT Mr. Randal M. Finfrock, Director of Enrollment Management, Westmoreland County Community College, Youngwood, PA 15697, 412-925-4060. ***Fax:*** 412-925-1150. ***E-mail:*** kuhnsl@wccc.westmoreland.cc.pa.us. College video available.

THE WILLIAMSON FREE SCHOOL OF MECHANICAL TRADES
Media, Pennsylvania

UG Enrollment: 254	**Tuition & Fees: $155**
Application Deadline: 3/31	**Room & Board: N/R**

GENERAL Independent, 2-year, men only. Awards diplomas, terminal associate degrees. Founded 1888. ***Setting:*** 240-acre small-town campus with easy access to Philadelphia. ***Educational spending 1994–95:*** $2375 per undergrad. ***Total enrollment:*** 254. ***Faculty:*** 24 (14 full-time, 43% with terminal degrees, 10 part-time); student-faculty ratio is 14:1.
ENROLLMENT PROFILE 254 students from 5 states and territories. 0% women, 0% part-time, 90% state residents, 100% live on campus, 4% transferred in, 0% international, 0% 25 or older, 0% Native American, 1% Hispanic, 3% African American, 0% Asian American. ***Areas of study chosen:*** 83% engineering and applied sciences, 7% agriculture. ***Most popular recent majors:*** electrical and electronics technologies, construction technologies, machine and tool technologies.
FIRST-YEAR CLASS 104 total. Of the students accepted, 100% enrolled. 5% from top 10% of their high school class, 20% from top quarter, 60% from top half.
ACADEMIC PROGRAM Core, trade and technical curriculum, honor code. Calendar: semesters. 168 courses offered in 1995–96. Academic remediation for entering students, internships. Off-campus study at Delaware County Community College.
GENERAL DEGREE REQUIREMENTS 148 credit hours; computer course; internship (some majors).

MAJORS Carpentry, construction technologies, electrical and electronics technologies, energy management technologies, horticulture, machine and tool technologies, ornamental horticulture.
LIBRARY Shrigley Library plus 3 others, with 1,600 books, 70 periodicals. Acquisition spending 1994–95: $3101.
COMPUTERS ON CAMPUS 20 computers for student use in computer labs, shops provide access to on-line services. Staffed computer lab on campus provides training in use of computers, software. Academic computing expenditure 1994–95: $75,316.
COLLEGE LIFE Orientation program (2 days, no cost, parents included). Choral group. *Most popular organizations:* Campus Crusade for Christ, Vocational Industrial Clubs of America. *Major annual events:* Homecoming, Alumni Day. *Student services:* health clinic, personal-psychological counseling. *Campus security:* evening patrols, gate security.
HOUSING 265 college housing spaces available; 244 were occupied 1995–96. Freshmen guaranteed college housing. Resident assistants live in dorms.
ATHLETICS *Intercollegiate:* baseball, basketball, cross-country running, football, soccer, wrestling. *Intramural:* archery, badminton, baseball, basketball, cross-country running, football, racquetball, soccer, table tennis (Ping-Pong), volleyball, weight lifting, wrestling. *Contact:* Mr. Dale Plummer, Athletic Director, 610-566-2815.
CAREER PLANNING *Placement office:* 1 part-time staff; $5300 operating expenditure 1994–95. *Director:* Mrs. Margaret Kingham, Placement Director, 610-566-1776. *Services:* job fairs, resume preparation, career counseling, careers library, job interviews. Students must register sophomore year.
EXPENSES FOR 1996–97 Tuition: $0 full-time. Tuition, room and board, and books are provided by the school. One-time mandatory fee: $195. Full-time mandatory fees: $155.
APPLYING *Required:* minimum 2.0 GPA, Armed Services Vocational Aptitude Battery. *Recommended:* 3 years of high school math and science. Test scores used for admission. *Application deadline:* 3/31. Preference given to needy students.
APPLYING/TRANSFER *Required:* standardized test scores.
CONTACT Mr. Edward D. Bailey, Director of Admissions, The Williamson Free School of Mechanical Trades, Media, PA 19063, 610-566-1776. *Fax:* 610-566-6502. College video available.

WILLIAMSPORT SCHOOL OF COMMERCE
Williamsport, Pennsylvania

UG Enrollment: 134	Tuition & Fees: $4525
Application Deadline: rolling	Room & Board: N/Avail

GENERAL Proprietary, 2-year, primarily women. Awards terminal associate degrees. Founded 1955. *Setting:* small-town campus. *Total enrollment:* 134. *Faculty:* 6 (all full-time).
ENROLLMENT PROFILE 134 students: 93% women, 1% part-time, 100% state residents, 7% transferred in, 0% international, 0% Native American, 0% Hispanic, 1% African American, 0% Asian American.
FIRST-YEAR CLASS 49 total. Of the students who applied, 98% were accepted, 65% of whom enrolled.
ACADEMIC PROGRAM Calendar: quarters. Summer session for credit, part-time degree program (daytime, summer).
GENERAL DEGREE REQUIREMENTS 90 quarter credits; 1 math course.
MAJORS Business administration/commerce/management, legal secretarial studies, medical secretarial studies, secretarial studies/office management.
COMPUTERS ON CAMPUS 22 computers for student use in computer center provide access to on-line services. Staffed computer lab on campus provides training in use of computers, software.
HOUSING College housing not available.
CAREER PLANNING *Service:* career counseling.
EXPENSES FOR 1995–96 *Application fee:* $15. Tuition: $4525 full-time, $375 per course part-time.
FINANCIAL AID *College-administered undergrad aid 1995–96:* low-interest long-term loans from external sources. *Required forms:* institutional, FAFSA. *Application deadline:* continuous to 8/1. *Payment plan:* installment. *Waivers:* full or partial for employees or children of employees.
APPLYING *Option:* deferred entrance. *Application deadline:* rolling.
APPLYING/TRANSFER *Application deadline:* rolling.
CONTACT Mr. Benjamin H. Comfort III, Director of Admissions, Williamsport School of Commerce, Williamsport, PA 17701-5855, 717-326-2869 or toll-free 800-962-6971. *Fax:* 717-326-2136.

RHODE ISLAND

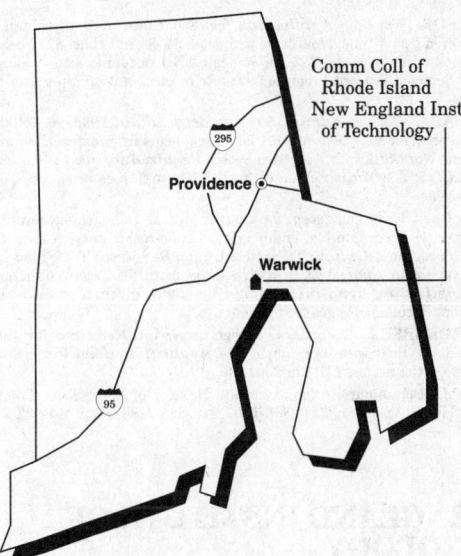

COMMUNITY COLLEGE OF RHODE ISLAND
Warwick, Rhode Island

UG Enrollment: 12,184	Tuition & Fees (RI Res): $1646
Application Deadline: rolling	Room & Board: N/Avail

GENERAL State-supported, 2-year, coed. Part of Community College of Rhode Island System. Awards transfer associate, terminal associate degrees. Founded 1964. *Setting:* 205-acre suburban campus with easy access to Boston. *Total enrollment:* 12,184. *Faculty:* 697 (293 full-time, 20% with terminal degrees, 404 part-time).
ENROLLMENT PROFILE 12,184 students from 3 states and territories, 9 other countries. 63% women, 62% part-time, 95% state residents, 6% transferred in, 1% international, 55% 25 or older, 1% Native American, 6% Hispanic, 4% African American, 2% Asian American. *Most popular recent majors:* liberal arts/general studies, business administration/commerce/management, nursing.
FIRST-YEAR CLASS 3,643 total; 5,790 applied, 87% were accepted, 73% of whom enrolled.
ACADEMIC PROGRAM Core, honor code. Calendar: semesters. Academic remediation for entering students, English as a second language program offered during academic year and summer, services for LD students, advanced placement, honors program, summer session for credit, part-time degree program (daytime, evenings, weekends, summer), external degree programs, adult/continuing education programs, co-op programs and internships. Off-campus study at Rhode Island College, University of Rhode Island. ROTC: Army (c).
GENERAL DEGREE REQUIREMENTS 60 credits; 1 course in math/science; internship (some majors).
MAJORS Accounting, art/fine arts, business administration/commerce/management, chemical engineering technology, child psychology/child development, computer programming, computer science, corrections, dental services, drug and alcohol/substance abuse counseling, early childhood education, education, electrical and electronics technologies, electronics engineering technology, elementary education, engineering (general), fashion merchandising, fire science, gerontology, human services, instrumentation technology, jazz, labor studies, law enforcement/police sciences, legal secretarial studies, liberal arts/general studies, machine and tool technologies, marketing/retailing/merchandising, mechanical design technology, mechanical engineering technology, medical laboratory technology, medical secretarial studies, mental health/rehabilitation counseling, music, nursing, paralegal studies, physical therapy, radiological technology, real estate, respiratory therapy, retail management, science, secretarial studies/office management, social work, theater arts/drama, urban studies.
LIBRARY Community College of Rhode Island Learning Resources Center with 84,344 books, 968 microform titles, 905 periodicals, 4 on-line bibliographic services, 11 CD-ROMs, 3,602 records, tapes, and CDs. Acquisition spending 1994–95: $1.5 million.
COMPUTERS ON CAMPUS 260 computers for student use in computer labs, open labs, math, accounting, nursing, English labs, office administration, community services departments, library, student center provide access to main academic computer, e-mail, on-line services. Staffed computer lab on campus.
COLLEGE LIFE Drama-theater group, choral group, student-run newspaper. *Social organizations:* 54 open to all. *Most popular organizations:* Distributive Education Clubs of America, Theater Group, ABLE. *Major annual events:* Christmas Dinner Theater, Springfest. *Student services:* health clinic, personal-psychological counseling. *Campus security:* 24-hour emergency response devices and patrols.
HOUSING College housing not available.
ATHLETICS Member NJCAA. *Intercollegiate:* baseball M, basketball M/W, cross-country running M/W, golf M/W, ice hockey M, soccer M, softball W, tennis M/W, track and field M/W, volleyball W. *Intramural:* badminton, basketball, golf, soccer, softball, swimming and diving, tennis, volleyball, water polo, weight lifting. *Contact:* Mr. Vincent Cullen, Director of Athletics, 401-825-2200.

Rhode Island–South Carolina

Community College of Rhode Island (continued)

CAREER PLANNING *Placement office:* 1 full-time staff. *Director:* Ms. Marcia Allen, Coordinator, Career Services, 401-825-7254. *Services:* job fairs, resume preparation, resume referral, career counseling, careers library, job bank, job interviews. 35 organizations recruited on campus 1994–95.
EXPENSES FOR 1995–96 *Application fee:* $20. State resident tuition: $1566 full-time, $73 per credit part-time. Nonresident tuition: $4584 full-time, $217 per credit part-time. Part-time mandatory fees: $25 per semester. Nonresidents who are eligible for the New England Regional Student Program pay state resident tuition rates. Full-time mandatory fees: $80.
FINANCIAL AID *College-administered undergrad aid 1995–96:* 1,400 need-based scholarships (average $800), low-interest long-term loans from external sources (average $1250), Federal Work-Study, 225 part-time jobs. *Required forms:* institutional, FAFSA. *Priority deadline:* 3/1. *Waivers:* full or partial for employees or children of employees and senior citizens.
APPLYING Open admission except for nursing, dental, radiography, physical therapist assistant, computer programming, engineering, cardio-respiratory care, medical laboratory technician programs. *Option:* deferred entrance. *Required:* TOEFL for international students. *Required for some:* 3 years of high school math. Test scores used for counseling/placement. *Application deadline:* rolling. Preference given to state residents, New England Regional Student Program applicants.
APPLYING/TRANSFER *Required:* college transcript. *Required for some:* 3 years of high school math. *Entrance:* noncompetitive. *Application deadline:* rolling. *Contact:* Mr. Ira Schaeffer, Counselor, 401-825-2301.
CONTACT Ms. Donnamarie Allen, Associate Director of Admissions, Community College of Rhode Island, Warwick, RI 02886-1807, 401-825-2285. *Fax:* 401-825-2418. College video available.

NEW ENGLAND INSTITUTE OF TECHNOLOGY
Warwick, Rhode Island

UG Enrollment: 2,354	Tuition: $18,300/deg prog
Application Deadline: rolling	Room & Board: N/Avail

GENERAL Independent, primarily 2-year, coed. Awards transfer associate, terminal associate, bachelor's degrees. Founded 1940. *Setting:* 10-acre suburban campus with easy access to Boston. *Total enrollment:* 2,354. *Faculty:* 168 (71 full-time, 97 part-time).
ENROLLMENT PROFILE 2,354 students from 8 states and territories, 6 other countries. 22% women, 80% state residents, 1% transferred in, 2% international, 36% 25 or older, 0% Native American, 2% Hispanic, 3% African American, 1% Asian American. *Most popular recent majors:* electrical and electronics technologies, automotive technologies.
FIRST-YEAR CLASS 800 total.
ACADEMIC PROGRAM Core, technical curriculum, honor code. Calendar: quarters. 431 courses offered in 1995–96. Academic remediation for entering students, English as a second language program offered during academic year and summer, services for LD students, advanced placement, summer session for credit, adult/continuing education programs, internships.
GENERAL DEGREE REQUIREMENTS 90 credits for associate, 180 credits for bachelor's; math/science requirements vary according to program; computer course for business-related, medical assistant majors; internship (some majors).
MAJORS Automotive technologies, business administration/commerce/management (B), carpentry, computer information systems, computer programming (B), computer technologies (B), construction technologies, drafting and design, electrical and electronics technologies (B), electronics engineering (B), heating/refrigeration/air conditioning, interior design, machine and tool technologies (B), marine technology, medical assistant technologies, operating room technology, plumbing, radio and television studies, secretarial studies/office management, telecommunications (B).
LIBRARY Learning Resources Center with 19,937 books, 32 microform titles, 211 periodicals, 1 on-line bibliographic service, 935 records, tapes, and CDs.
COMPUTERS ON CAMPUS 175 computers for student use in computer center, computer labs, learning resource center, classrooms provide access to main academic computer. Staffed computer lab on campus provides training in use of computers, software.
COLLEGE LIFE Choral group. *Student services:* personal-psychological counseling. *Campus security:* security personnel during open hours.
HOUSING College housing not available.
CAREER PLANNING *Placement office:* 3 full-time, 1 part-time staff. *Director:* Ms. Catherine B. Kennedy, Director of Career Services, 401-739-5000. *Services:* resume preparation, resume referral, career counseling, careers library, job interviews. Students must register sophomore year.
EXPENSES FOR 1996–97 *Application fee:* $25. Tuition: $18,300 per degree program. Full-time mandatory fees: $300. Tuition guaranteed not to increase for student's term of enrollment.
FINANCIAL AID *College-administered undergrad aid 1995–96:* 398 need-based scholarships (average $1200), low-interest long-term loans from external sources (average $2500), Federal Work-Study. *Required forms:* institutional, FAFSA; accepted: CSS Financial Aid PROFILE, state. *Priority deadline:* 10/1. *Payment plans:* installment, deferred payment. *Waivers:* full or partial for employees or children of employees. *Notification:* continuous.
APPLYING Open admission. *Options:* early entrance, deferred entrance, midyear entrance. *Required:* school transcript. *Recommended:* TOEFL for international students. Test scores used for counseling/placement. *Application deadline:* rolling.
APPLYING/TRANSFER *Required:* high school transcript, college transcript. *Application deadline:* rolling. *Contact:* Mr. Michael Kwiatkowski, Director of Admissions, 401-739-5000.
CONTACT Mr. Michael Kwiatkowski, Director of Admissions, New England Institute of Technology, Warwick, RI 02886-2244, 401-739-5000. College video available.

SOUTH CAROLINA

Map of South Carolina showing:
Spartanburg Methodist Coll, Spartanburg Tech Coll, York Tech Coll, U of South Carolina at Lancaster, Greenville Tech Coll, Chesterfield-Marlboro Tech Coll, Forrest Junior Coll, U of South Carolina at Union, Piedmont Tech Coll, Florence-Darlington Tech Coll, Tri-County Tech Coll, Columbia, Sumter, Horry-Georgetown Tech Coll, Aiken Tech Coll, Orangeburg-Calhoun Tech Coll, Williamsburg Tech Coll, Denmark Tech Coll, U of South Carolina Salkehatchie Reg Campus, Nielsen Electronics Inst, Trident Tech Coll, Charleston, Tech Coll of the Lowcountry, U of South Carolina at Beaufort

Sumter Area
Central Carolina Tech Coll
U of South Carolina at Sumter

Columbia Area
Columbia Jr Coll of Business
Midlands Tech Coll

AIKEN TECHNICAL COLLEGE
Aiken, South Carolina

UG Enrollment: 2,258	Tuition & Fees (SC Res): $941
Application Deadline: rolling	Room & Board: N/Avail

GENERAL State and locally supported, 2-year, coed. Part of South Carolina State Board for Technical and Comprehensive Education. Awards certificates, diplomas, transfer associate, terminal associate degrees. Founded 1972. *Setting:* 88-acre rural campus. *Endowment:* $5521. *Educational spending 1994–95:* $1702 per undergrad. *Total enrollment:* 2,258. *Faculty:* 119 (50 full-time, 100% with terminal degrees, 69 part-time); student-faculty ratio is 19:1. *Notable Alumni:* John Miano, Gwendolyn Jones, Allison Eigle.
ENROLLMENT PROFILE 2,258 students from 6 states and territories. 57% women, 43% men, 57% part-time, 88% state residents, 8% transferred in, 30% have need-based financial aid, 1% have non-need-based financial aid, 0% international, 49% 25 or older, 1% Native American, 1% Hispanic, 31% African American, 1% Asian American. *Areas of study chosen:* 25% engineering and applied sciences, 18% business management and administrative services, 18% liberal arts/general studies, 13% health professions and related sciences, 9% interdisciplinary studies, 8% computer and information sciences, 6% social sciences, 3% vocational and home economics. *Most popular recent majors:* computer technologies, nuclear technology.
FIRST-YEAR CLASS 538 total; 900 applied, 100% were accepted, 60% of whom enrolled. 3% from top 10% of their high school class, 12% from top quarter, 39% from top half.
ACADEMIC PROGRAM Core, honor code. Calendar: semesters. 951 courses offered in 1995–96. Academic remediation for entering students, services for LD students, advanced placement, tutorials, summer session for credit, part-time degree program (daytime, evenings, summer), adult/continuing education programs, co-op programs and internships. Off-campus study at University of South Carolina-Aiken.
GENERAL DEGREE REQUIREMENTS 64 semester hours; computer course (varies by major).
MAJORS Accounting, business administration/commerce/management, computer technologies, electrical engineering technology, electromechanical technology, electronics engineering technology, engineering technology, human services, interdisciplinary studies, liberal arts/general studies, machine and tool technologies, manufacturing technology, marketing/retailing/merchandising, nuclear technology, science, secretarial studies/office management, social work.
LIBRARY Aiken Technical College Library with 32,118 books, 11,741 microform titles, 425 periodicals, 5 CD-ROMs. Acquisition spending 1994–95: $417,943.
COMPUTERS ON CAMPUS 200 computers for student use in computer labs, classrooms, library provide access to main academic computer, on-line services, Internet. Staffed computer lab on campus provides training in use of computers, software.
COLLEGE LIFE Student-run newspaper. *Most popular organizations:* Student Government, Phi Theta Kappa, Student Newspaper. *Major annual events:* Field Day, Health Fair, Orientation. *Student services:* personal-psychological counseling. *Campus security:* 24-hour patrols, late-night transport-escort service.
HOUSING College housing not available.
ATHLETICS Member NJCAA. *Intercollegiate:* basketball M, golf M. *Intramural:* softball. *Contact:* Mr. Charles Welch, Instructor, 803-593-9231.
CAREER PLANNING *Placement office:* 2 full-time staff. *Director:* Ms. Margaret Topp, Coordinator, Career Planning and Placement, 803-593-9231 Ext. 1522. *Services:* job fairs, resume preparation, resume referral, career counseling, careers library, job bank, job interviews.
AFTER GRADUATION 30% of students completing a degree program in 1994–95 went directly on to further study.

EXPENSES FOR 1996–97 ***Application fee:*** $15. State resident tuition: $912 full-time, $38 per semester hour part-time. Nonresident tuition: $1248 full-time, $52 per semester hour part-time. Tuition for Georgia residents of Columbia and Richmond counties: $942 full-time, $38 per semester hour part-time. Full-time mandatory fees: $29.
FINANCIAL AID ***College-administered undergrad aid 1995–96:*** 130 need-based scholarships (average $500), 20 non-need scholarships (average $1000), short-term loans (average $200), low-interest long-term loans, 30 Federal Work-Study, 50 part-time jobs. ***Required forms:*** institutional, FAFSA. ***Priority deadline:*** 5/1. ***Waivers:*** full or partial for senior citizens. ***Notification:*** 6/1.
APPLYING Open admission except for nursing program. ***Options:*** deferred entrance, midyear entrance. ***Required:*** school transcript, TOEFL for international students. ***Recommended:*** SAT I. ***Required for some:*** essay, ACT, ACT ASSET. Test scores used for counseling/placement. ***Application deadline:*** rolling.
APPLYING/TRANSFER ***Required:*** high school transcript. ***Required for some:*** essay, college transcript. ***Entrance:*** noncompetitive. ***Application deadline:*** rolling.
CONTACT Ms. Carol Dozier, Director of Admissions, Aiken Technical College, Aiken, SC 29802-0600, 803-593-9231 Ext. 1295. ***E-mail:*** dozier@aik.tec.sc.us. College video available.

CENTRAL CAROLINA TECHNICAL COLLEGE
Sumter, South Carolina

UG Enrollment: 2,189	**Tuition & Fees (Area Res): $800**
Application Deadline: rolling	**Room & Board: N/Avail**

GENERAL State-supported, 2-year, coed. Part of South Carolina Technical and Comprehensive Education System. Awards certificates, diplomas, transfer associate, terminal associate degrees. Founded 1963. ***Setting:*** 29-acre small-town campus. ***Total enrollment:*** 2,189. ***Faculty:*** 144 (64 full-time, 10% with terminal degrees, 80 part-time).
ENROLLMENT PROFILE 2,189 students: 61% women, 54% part-time, 100% state residents, 2% transferred in, 80% have need-based financial aid, 20% have non-need-based financial aid, 0% international, 47% 25 or older, 1% Native American, 1% Hispanic, 35% African American, 1% Asian American. ***Areas of study chosen:*** 35% engineering and applied sciences, 30% health professions and related sciences, 10% business management and administrative services, 10% computer and information sciences, 10% natural resource sciences, 5% liberal arts/general studies. ***Most popular recent majors:*** computer technologies, criminal justice, nursing.
FIRST-YEAR CLASS 600 total; 1,400 applied, 100% were accepted, 45% of whom enrolled. 1% from top 10% of their high school class, 10% from top quarter, 25% from top half.
ACADEMIC PROGRAM Core, technical curriculum, honor code. Calendar: semesters. 800 courses offered in 1995–96. Academic remediation for entering students, advanced placement, self-designed majors, tutorials, summer session for credit, part-time degree program (daytime, evenings, summer), external degree programs, adult/continuing education programs, co-op programs.
GENERAL DEGREE REQUIREMENTS 60 semester hours; math/science requirements vary according to program; computer course for students without computer competency.
MAJORS Accounting, automotive technologies, business administration/commerce/management, civil engineering technology, computer technologies, criminal justice, electrical and electronics technologies, environmental engineering technology, machine and tool technologies, marketing/retailing/merchandising, natural resource management, nursing, paralegal studies, secretarial studies/office management.
LIBRARY Central Carolina Technical College Library with 19,143 books, 33 microform titles, 239 periodicals, 1,228 records, tapes, and CDs.
COMPUTERS ON CAMPUS 60 computers for student use in computer center, computer labs, learning resource center. Staffed computer lab on campus provides training in use of computers, software.
COLLEGE LIFE Drama-theater group, choral group. 40% vote in student government elections. ***Social organizations:*** 18 open to all. ***Most popular organizations:*** Earth Club, Electronics Club, Office Systems Association, Paralegal-Criminal Justice, Nursing Clubs. ***Major annual event:*** Student Appreciation Days. ***Student services:*** personal-psychological counseling. ***Campus security:*** 24-hour emergency response devices.
HOUSING College housing not available.
CAREER PLANNING ***Placement office:*** 1 full-time staff. ***Director:*** Dr. James Williamson, Dean of Student Affairs, 803-778-1961 Ext. 222. ***Services:*** job fairs, resume preparation, resume referral, career counseling, careers library, job bank, job interviews.
AFTER GRADUATION 10% of students completing a degree program in 1994–95 went directly on to further study.
EXPENSES FOR 1995–96 ***Application fee:*** $20. Area resident tuition: $800 full-time, $33.35 per semester hour part-time. State resident tuition: $1000 full-time, $42.50 per semester hour part-time. Nonresident tuition: $1430 full-time, $59.60 per semester hour part-time. State residents enrolled in environmental engineering technology and natural resources management programs pay county resident tuition. Tuition for residents of Kershow county: $960 full-time, $40 per semester hour part-time.
FINANCIAL AID ***College-administered undergrad aid 1995–96:*** need-based scholarships, non-need scholarships, short-term loans, low-interest long-term loans from external sources, Federal Work-Study, part-time jobs. ***Acceptable forms:*** CSS Financial Aid PROFILE, institutional, FAFSA. ***Application deadline:*** continuous. ***Waivers:*** full or partial for employees or children of employees and senior citizens. ***Notification:*** continuous. ***Average indebtedness of graduates:*** $2000.
APPLYING Open admission except for nursing program. ***Options:*** electronic application, early entrance, deferred entrance, midyear entrance. ***Required:*** school transcript, TOEFL for international students, CPT. ***Required for some:*** SAT I. Test scores used for counseling/placement. ***Application deadline:*** rolling.
APPLYING/TRANSFER ***Required:*** college transcript. ***Required for some:*** standardized test scores. ***Application deadline:*** rolling. ***Contact:*** Ms. Deborah Calhoun, Registrar/Admissions, 803-778-1961 Ext. 457.
CONTACT Ms. Lisa Mills, Recruitment/Admissions, Central Carolina Technical College, Sumter, SC 29150-2499, 803-778-1961 Ext. 296 or toll-free 800-221-8711 (in-state). ***Fax:*** 803-773-4859. College video available.

CHESTERFIELD-MARLBORO TECHNICAL COLLEGE
Cheraw, South Carolina

UG Enrollment: 1,030	**Tuition & Fees (Area Res): $816**
Application Deadline: rolling	**Room & Board: $2000**

GENERAL State and locally supported, 2-year, coed. Part of South Carolina State Board for Technical and Comprehensive Education. Awards certificates, diplomas, transfer associate, terminal associate degrees. Founded 1967. ***Setting:*** 59-acre rural campus. ***Total enrollment:*** 1,030. ***Faculty:*** 66 (25 full-time, 41 part-time); student-faculty ratio is 20:1.
ENROLLMENT PROFILE 1,030 students from 2 states and territories, 2 other countries. 71% women, 29% men, 67% part-time, 98% state residents, 7% transferred in, 26% have need-based financial aid, 1% international, 50% 25 or older, 1% Native American, 0% Hispanic, 34% African American, 1% Asian American. ***Areas of study chosen:*** 24% liberal arts/general studies, 21% business management and administrative services, 15% health professions and related sciences, 13% vocational and home economics, 10% computer and information sciences. ***Most popular recent majors:*** liberal arts/general studies, business administration/commerce/management, nursing.
FIRST-YEAR CLASS 215 total; 380 applied, 100% were accepted, 57% of whom enrolled.
ACADEMIC PROGRAM Core. Calendar: semesters. Academic remediation for entering students, advanced placement, summer session for credit, part-time degree program (daytime), adult/continuing education programs.
GENERAL DEGREE REQUIREMENTS 60 semester hours; 1 math course; computer course.
MAJORS Accounting, business administration/commerce/management, computer programming, computer science, data processing, electrical and electronics technologies, liberal arts/general studies, machine and tool technologies, marketing/retailing/merchandising, mechanical design technology, nursing, secretarial studies/office management.
LIBRARY Chesterfield-Marlboro Technical College Library with 19,912 books, 159 periodicals, 1 CD-ROM. Acquisition spending 1994–95: $17,357.
COMPUTERS ON CAMPUS Computer purchase plan available. 125 computers for student use in computer center, computer labs, learning resource center, classrooms, library, student center provide access to main academic computer, off-campus computing facilities, e-mail, on-line services, Internet. Staffed computer lab on campus provides training in use of computers, software. Academic computing expenditure 1994–95: $20,852.
COLLEGE LIFE 50% vote in student government elections. ***Student services:*** personal-psychological counseling. ***Campus security:*** 24-hour emergency response devices.
CAREER PLANNING ***Placement office:*** 1 full-time staff; $39,356 operating expenditure 1994–95. ***Director:*** Ms. Jean Alison, Career Center Coordinator, 803-921-6936. ***Services:*** resume preparation, resume referral, career counseling, careers library, job bank, job interviews. 50 organizations recruited on campus 1994–95.
AFTER GRADUATION 14% of students completing a degree program in 1994–95 went directly on to further study.
EXPENSES FOR 1996–97 Area resident tuition: $816 full-time, $35 per semester hour part-time. State resident tuition: $878 full-time, $37 per semester hour part-time. Nonresident tuition: $1188 full-time, $50 per semester hour part-time. College room and board: $2000 (minimum).
FINANCIAL AID ***College-administered undergrad aid 1995–96:*** need-based scholarships, short-term loans, Federal Work-Study. ***Required forms:*** institutional, FAFSA. ***Priority deadline:*** 6/15. ***Waivers:*** full or partial for senior citizens. ***Notification:*** continuous.
APPLYING Open admission except for nursing program. ***Option:*** early entrance. ***Required:*** school transcript, interview, TOEFL for international students, ACT ASSET. ***Required for some:*** SAT I. Test scores used for admission (for nursing program) and counseling/placement. ***Application deadline:*** rolling.
APPLYING/TRANSFER ***Required:*** standardized test scores, high school transcript, interview, college transcript. ***Entrance:*** noncompetitive. ***Application deadline:*** rolling. ***Contact:*** Mrs. Mary K. Newton, Assistant Dean of Students, 803-921-6935.
CONTACT Mrs. Mary K. Newton, Assistant Dean of Students, Chesterfield-Marlboro Technical College, Cheraw, SC 29520-1007, 803-921-6935. ***Fax:*** 803-537-6148. ***E-mail:*** mpace@cmt.chm.tec.sc.us.

COLUMBIA JUNIOR COLLEGE OF BUSINESS
Columbia, South Carolina

UG Enrollment: 400	**Tuition & Fees: $2875**
Application Deadline: rolling	**Room & Board: $4185**

GENERAL Proprietary, 2-year, coed. Awards diplomas, terminal associate degrees. Founded 1935. ***Setting:*** 2-acre urban campus. ***Total enrollment:*** 400. ***Faculty:*** 47 (15 full-time, 32 part-time).
ENROLLMENT PROFILE 400 students from 6 states and territories, 4 other countries. 85% women, 21% part-time, 95% state residents, 15% transferred in, 60% have need-based financial aid, 5% have non-need-based financial aid, 1% international, 14% 25 or older, 1% Native American, 1% Hispanic, 85% African American, 0% Asian American. ***Areas of study chosen:*** 50% health professions and related sciences, 25% business management and administrative services, 25% computer and information sciences.
FIRST-YEAR CLASS 200 total; 300 applied, 99% were accepted, 67% of whom enrolled. 2% from top 10% of their high school class, 12% from top quarter, 51% from top half.
ACADEMIC PROGRAM Core, career-preparation curriculum, honor code. Calendar: quarters. 93 courses offered in 1995–96; average class size 25 in required courses. Academic remediation for entering students, summer session for credit, part-time degree program (daytime, evenings), adult/continuing education programs, internships.
GENERAL DEGREE REQUIREMENTS 100 quarter hours; 1 business math course; computer course for medical assistant, medical transcription majors; internship (some majors).
MAJORS Accounting, business administration/commerce/management, computer information systems, data processing, marketing/retailing/merchandising, medical records services, medical secretarial studies, paralegal studies, secretarial studies/office management.
LIBRARY 5,000 books, 35 periodicals.

Peterson's Guide to Two-Year Colleges 1997

583

Columbia Junior College of Business (continued)

COMPUTERS ON CAMPUS 35 computers for student use in computer center, classrooms.
COLLEGE LIFE Orientation program (2 days, no cost, parents included). Choral group, student-run newspaper. ***Social organizations:*** 10 open to all; 1 local fraternity, 1 local sorority. ***Most popular organization:*** Phi Beta Lambda. ***Student services:*** personal-psychological counseling. ***Campus security:*** 24-hour emergency response devices.
HOUSING 350 college housing spaces available; 250 were occupied 1995–96. Freshmen given priority for college housing. Off-campus living permitted. ***Options:*** coed, single-sex housing available.
CAREER PLANNING ***Placement office:*** 1 full-time staff. ***Director:*** Ms. Rachel Haynie, Director of Career Development and Placement, 803-799-9082. ***Services:*** job fairs, resume preparation, resume referral, career counseling, careers library, job bank, job interviews. 50 organizations recruited on campus 1994–95.
AFTER GRADUATION 75% of class of 1994 had job offers within 6 months.
EXPENSES FOR 1996–97 ***Application fee:*** $35. Comprehensive fee of $7060 includes full-time tuition ($2850 minimum), mandatory fees ($25), and college room and board ($4185). College room only: $1485. Full-time tuition: $3585 for day program, $2850 for evening program. Part-time tuition per quarter hour: $100 for day program, $80 for evening program.
FINANCIAL AID ***College-administered undergrad aid 1995–96:*** 250 need-based scholarships (average $600), 20 non-need scholarships (average $1000), low-interest long-term loans from external sources, 90 Federal Work-Study (averaging $1044), part-time jobs. ***Required forms:*** FAFSA. ***Priority deadline:*** 7/1. ***Payment plan:*** installment. ***Waivers:*** full or partial for senior citizens.
APPLYING Open admission except for paralegal program. ***Options:*** Common Application, deferred entrance, midyear entrance. ***Required:*** school transcript, minimum 2.0 GPA, interview, TOEFL for international students. ***Recommended:*** SAT I. Test scores used for counseling/placement. ***Application deadline:*** rolling.
APPLYING/TRANSFER ***Required:*** high school transcript, interview, college transcript, minimum 2.0 high school GPA. ***Recommended:*** minimum 2.0 college GPA. ***Entrance:*** noncompetitive. ***Application deadline:*** rolling. ***Contact:*** Mr. Fred A. Evans, Dean of Academic Affairs, 803-799-9082.
CONTACT Ms. Jackie Dorsey, Admissions Representative, Columbia Junior College of Business, PO Box 1196, Columbia, SC 29203-6400, 803-799-9082.

DENMARK TECHNICAL COLLEGE
Denmark, South Carolina

UG Enrollment: 842	**Tuition & Fees (SC Res): $1160**
Application Deadline: rolling	**Room & Board: $2782**

GENERAL State-supported, 2-year, coed. Part of South Carolina State Board for Technical and Comprehensive Education. Awards certificates, diplomas, transfer associate degrees. Founded 1948. ***Setting:*** 53-acre rural campus. ***Total enrollment:*** 842. ***Faculty:*** 44 (23 full-time, 7% with terminal degrees, 21 part-time); student-faculty ratio is 21:1.
ENROLLMENT PROFILE 842 students from 8 states and territories. 51% women, 24% part-time, 96% state residents, 3% transferred in, 98% have need-based financial aid, 0% international, 20% 25 or older, 0% Native American, 0% Hispanic, 96% African American, 0% Asian American. ***Areas of study chosen:*** 11% business management and administrative services, 7% computer and information sciences, 7% vocational and home economics, 5% liberal arts/general studies, 2% engineering and applied sciences. ***Most popular recent majors:*** human services, criminal justice, computer technologies.
FIRST-YEAR CLASS 389 total; 825 applied, 100% were accepted, 47% of whom enrolled. 2% from top 10% of their high school class, 25% from top quarter.
ACADEMIC PROGRAM Honor code. Calendar: semesters. Academic remediation for entering students, advanced placement, tutorials, summer session for credit, part-time degree program (daytime), adult/continuing education programs, co-op programs and internships. Off-campus study at Voorhees College, South Carolina State College. ROTC: Army (c).
GENERAL DEGREE REQUIREMENTS 60 credit hours; 6 credit hours of math/science for associate of arts degree; 23 credit hours of math/science for associate of science degree; computer course; internship (some majors).
MAJORS Automotive technologies, business administration/commerce/management, computer technologies, criminal justice, engineering technology, human services, secretarial studies/office management.
LIBRARY Denmark Technical College Learning Resources Center with 15,437 books, 62 microform titles, 200 periodicals, 3 CD-ROMs, 364 records, tapes, and CDs. Acquisition spending 1994–95: $25,900.
COMPUTERS ON CAMPUS 105 computers for student use in computer labs provide access to main academic computer. Staffed computer lab on campus provides training in use of computers, software. Academic computing expenditure 1994–95: $100,343.
COLLEGE LIFE Orientation program (1 week, no cost, parents included). Choral group, student-run newspaper. 45% vote in student government elections. ***Social organizations:*** 2 national fraternities, national sororities, 2 local fraternities, 1 local sorority; 25% of eligible men and 30% of eligible women are members. ***Most popular organizations:*** Phi Beta Lambda, Denmark Technical College Gospel Choir, Denmark Technical College Drama Club. ***Major annual events:*** Homecoming, Family Day, Annual Honors Day Convocation. ***Student services:*** health clinic, personal-psychological counseling. ***Campus security:*** 24-hour patrols.
HOUSING College housing designed to accommodate 244 students; 323 undergraduates lived in college housing during 1995–96. Freshmen given priority for college housing. Off-campus living permitted. ***Option:*** single-sex housing available. Resident assistants live in dorms.
ATHLETICS ***Intercollegiate:*** baseball M, basketball M/W, softball W. ***Intramural:*** basketball, tennis, volleyball. ***Contact:*** Mr. Theodore Chaplin Jr., Director of Athletics, 803-793-5160.
CAREER PLANNING ***Placement office:*** 1 full-time staff; $31,696 operating expenditure 1994–95. ***Services:*** job fairs, resume preparation, resume referral, career counseling, careers library, job bank, job interviews. Students must register freshman year. 10 organizations recruited on campus 1994–95.
AFTER GRADUATION 10% of students completing a degree program in 1994–95 went directly on to further study.
EXPENSES FOR 1995–96 ***Application fee:*** $10. State resident tuition: $960 full-time, $40 per credit hour part-time. Nonresident tuition: $2040 full-time, $85 per credit hour part-time. Part-time mandatory fees: $30 per semester. Full-time mandatory fees: $200. College room and board: $2782.
FINANCIAL AID ***College-administered undergrad aid 1995–96:*** 15 need-based scholarships (averaging $500), low-interest long-term loans from external sources (averaging $2000), Federal Work-Study. ***Required forms:*** institutional, FAFSA; accepted: CSS Financial Aid PROFILE. ***Priority deadline:*** 6/1. ***Payment plan:*** tuition prepayment. ***Waivers:*** full or partial for senior citizens. ***Notification:*** 7/1. ***Average indebtedness of graduates:*** $3100.
APPLYING Open admission. ***Options:*** early entrance, deferred entrance. ***Required:*** school transcript, TOEFL for international students, ACT ASSET. Test scores used for counseling/placement. ***Application deadline:*** rolling.
APPLYING/TRANSFER ***Required:*** standardized test scores, college transcript. ***Entrance:*** noncompetitive. ***Application deadline:*** rolling.
CONTACT Ms. Geraldine Brantley, Director of Recruitment, Denmark Technical College, Denmark, SC 29042-0327, 803-793-5175. ***Fax:*** 803-793-5942. College video available.

FLORENCE-DARLINGTON TECHNICAL COLLEGE
Florence, South Carolina

UG Enrollment: 3,125	**Tuition & Fees (Area Res): $1010**
Application Deadline: 8/1	**Room & Board: N/Avail**

GENERAL State-supported, 2-year, coed. Awards certificates, diplomas, transfer associate, terminal associate degrees. Founded 1963. ***Setting:*** 100-acre small-town campus with easy access to Columbia. ***Educational spending 1994–95:*** $1668 per undergrad. ***Total enrollment:*** 3,125. ***Faculty:*** 184 (94 full-time, 6% with terminal degrees, 90 part-time); student-faculty ratio is 12:1.
ENROLLMENT PROFILE 3,125 students from 6 states and territories, 3 other countries. 67% women, 53% part-time, 98% state residents, 38% 25 or older, 31% African American. ***Most popular recent major:*** nursing.
FIRST-YEAR CLASS 600 total; 1,447 applied, 100% were accepted, 41% of whom enrolled.
ACADEMIC PROGRAM Core, honor code. Calendar: semesters. Average class size 30 in required courses. Academic remediation for entering students, advanced placement, summer session for credit, part-time degree program (daytime, evenings), adult/continuing education programs, internships. ROTC: Army (c).
GENERAL DEGREE REQUIREMENTS 61 credit hours; computer course for most majors; internship (some majors).
MAJORS Accounting, aircraft and missile maintenance, automotive technologies, business administration/commerce/management, chemical engineering technology, civil engineering technology, computer technologies, criminal justice, dental services, drafting and design, electrical and electronics technologies, electronics engineering technology, engineering technology, funeral service, heating/refrigeration/air conditioning, human services, machine and tool technologies, marketing/retailing/merchandising, medical laboratory technology, medical records services, nursing, paralegal studies, physical therapy, radiological technology, respiratory therapy, secretarial studies/office management, vocational education.
LIBRARY 33,956 books, 349 periodicals, 4 on-line bibliographic services, 7 CD-ROMs, 261 records, tapes, and CDs. Acquisition spending 1994–95: $63,348.
COMPUTERS ON CAMPUS 220 computers for student use in computer center, learning resource center, classrooms, library provide access to main academic computer, off-campus computing facilities, on-line services, Internet. Staffed computer lab on campus provides training in use of computers, software. Academic computing expenditure 1994–95: $65,433.
COLLEGE LIFE Choral group, student-run newspaper. 12% vote in student government elections. ***Major annual event:*** Spring Fling. ***Student services:*** personal-psychological counseling. ***Campus security:*** 24-hour emergency response devices and patrols, late-night transport-escort service.
HOUSING College housing not available.
CAREER PLANNING ***Placement office:*** 4 full-time staff; $170,190 operating expenditure 1994–95. ***Director:*** Ms. Vivian Gallman, Director of Career services, 803-661-8029. ***Services:*** job fairs, resume preparation, resume referral, career counseling, careers library, job bank, job interviews. 50 organizations recruited on campus 1994–95.
EXPENSES FOR 1995–96 ***Application fee:*** $15. Area resident tuition: $1000 full-time, $42 per credit hour part-time. State resident tuition: $1150 full-time, $48 per credit hour part-time. Nonresident tuition: $1376 full-time, $58 per credit hour part-time. Part-time mandatory fees: $10 per year. Full-time mandatory fees: $10.
FINANCIAL AID ***College-administered undergrad aid 1995–96:*** 250 need-based scholarships (average $400), 50 non-need scholarships (average $500), low-interest long-term loans from college funds, loans from external sources, 110 Federal Work-Study. ***Required forms:*** institutional, FAFSA; accepted: CSS Financial Aid PROFILE. ***Priority deadline:*** 4/1. ***Waivers:*** full or partial for employees or children of employees and senior citizens.
APPLYING Open admission. ***Options:*** Common Application, deferred entrance, midyear entrance. ***Required:*** TOEFL for international students. ***Required for some:*** school transcript, SAT I or ACT. Test scores used for admission and counseling/placement. ***Application deadline:*** 8/1.
APPLYING/TRANSFER ***Required:*** college transcript. ***Required for some:*** standardized test scores, high school transcript. ***Entrance:*** noncompetitive. ***Application deadline:*** 8/1. ***Contact:*** Ms. Perry T. Kirven, Director of Enrollment Services, 803-661-8153.
CONTACT Ms. Perry T. Kirven, Director of Enrollment Services, Florence-Darlington Technical College, Florence, SC 29501-0548, 803-661-8153 or toll-free 800-228-5745 (in-state). ***Fax:*** 803-661-8041. ***E-mail:*** kirven@fdtc.flo.tec.sc.us.

FORREST JUNIOR COLLEGE
Anderson, South Carolina

UG Enrollment: 104	**Tuition & Fees: $3432**
Application Deadline: N/R	**Room & Board: N/Avail**

GENERAL Proprietary, 2-year. Awards terminal associate degrees. Founded 1946. ***Total enrollment:*** 104.

ENROLLMENT PROFILE 104 students.

FIRST-YEAR CLASS 20 total. Of the students who applied, 90% were accepted, 95% of whom enrolled.

ACADEMIC PROGRAM Calendar: quarters.

GENERAL DEGREE REQUIREMENTS 108 quarter hours; 1 math course; computer course.

EXPENSES FOR 1996–97 ***Application fee:*** $15. Tuition: $3432 full-time, $88 per quarter hour part-time. Tuition for international students: $4872 full-time.

CONTACT Ms. Merridy Lanzy, Director of Admissions, Forrest Junior College, Anderson, SC 29624, 803-225-7653.

GREENVILLE TECHNICAL COLLEGE
Greenville, South Carolina

UG Enrollment: 8,734 **Tuition & Fees (Area Res): $1030**
Application Deadline: rolling **Room & Board: N/Avail**

GENERAL State-supported, 2-year, coed. Part of South Carolina State Board for Technical and Comprehensive Education. Awards certificates, diplomas, transfer associate, terminal associate degrees. Founded 1962. ***Setting:*** 407-acre urban campus. ***Total enrollment:*** 8,734. ***Faculty:*** 539 (223 full-time, 316 part-time).

ENROLLMENT PROFILE 8,734 students: 56% women, 56% part-time, 99% state residents, 31% have need-based financial aid, 2% have non-need-based financial aid, 1% international, 42% 25 or older, 1% Native American, 1% Hispanic, 15% African American, 1% Asian American. ***Most popular recent majors:*** liberal arts/general studies, business administration/commerce/management, nursing.

FIRST-YEAR CLASS 2,664 total. Of the students who applied, 100% were accepted, 80% of whom enrolled.

ACADEMIC PROGRAM Core. Calendar: semesters. 1,000 courses offered in 1995–96. Academic remediation for entering students, advanced placement, summer session for credit, part-time degree program (daytime, evenings, summer), adult/continuing education programs, co-op programs.

GENERAL DEGREE REQUIREMENTS 60 semester hours; 1 math course; 4 semester hours of science; computer course for emergency medical technology, business majors.

MAJORS Accounting, aircraft and missile maintenance, architectural technologies, automotive technologies, aviation technology, business administration/commerce/management, computer programming, computer technologies, construction technologies, criminal justice, dental services, drafting and design, electronics engineering technology, emergency medical technology, engineering (general), engineering and applied sciences, (pre)engineering sequence, fire science, food services management, health science, heating/refrigeration/air conditioning, hospitality services, industrial engineering technology, law enforcement/police sciences, legal studies, liberal arts/general studies, machine and tool technologies, manufacturing technology, marketing/retailing/merchandising, materials sciences, mechanical engineering technology, medical laboratory technology, nursing, paralegal studies, physical therapy, radiological technology, respiratory therapy, science, secretarial studies/office management.

LIBRARY Vern Smith Library/Technical Resource Center with 49,500 books, 1,511 microform titles, 658 periodicals, 1 on-line bibliographic service, 17 CD-ROMs. Acquisition spending 1994–95: $97,941.

COMPUTERS ON CAMPUS Computer purchase plan available. 830 computers for student use in computer center, computer labs, labs, classrooms. Staffed computer lab on campus provides training in use of computers, software. Academic computing expenditure 1994–95: $575,161.

COLLEGE LIFE ***Social organizations:*** 12 open to all. ***Most popular organizations:*** Student Government Association, Phi Theta Kappa, Student Nurses Association, Christians on Campus, International and Friends Organization. ***Major annual events:*** Spring Picnic, Red Ribbon Week, Student Leadership Conference. ***Campus security:*** 24-hour emergency response devices and patrols, student patrols, late-night transport-escort service.

HOUSING College housing not available.

ATHLETICS ***Intramural:*** bowling, tennis, volleyball.

CAREER PLANNING ***Placement office:*** 4 full-time, 5 part-time staff. ***Director:*** Ms. Yvonne Duckett, Director of the Career Direction Center, 864-250-8142. ***Services:*** job fairs, resume preparation, resume referral, career counseling, careers library, job bank.

ESTIMATED EXPENSES FOR 1996–97 ***Application fee:*** $25. Area resident tuition: $1000 full-time, $42 per semester hour part-time. State resident tuition: $1080 full-time, $45 per semester hour part-time. Nonresident tuition: $1600 full-time, $67 per semester hour part-time. Part-time mandatory fees: $15 per semester. Full-time mandatory fees: $30.

FINANCIAL AID ***College-administered undergrad aid 1995–96:*** need-based scholarships, 190 non-need scholarships (average $1000), short-term loans (average $375), low-interest long-term loans from external sources (average $2625), Federal Work-Study. ***Required forms:*** institutional, FAFSA; accepted: CSS Financial Aid PROFILE. ***Priority deadline:*** 5/1. ***Waivers:*** full or partial for minority students and senior citizens. ***Notification:*** continuous.

APPLYING Open admission. ***Options:*** early entrance, deferred entrance, midyear entrance. ***Required:*** TOEFL for international students. ***Recommended:*** 3 years of high school math and science, SAT I or ACT, ACT ASSET. ***Required for some:*** ACT ASSET. Test scores used for admission and counseling/placement. ***Application deadline:*** rolling. ***Notification:*** continuous until 8/20.

APPLYING/TRANSFER ***Recommended:*** standardized test scores, 3 years of high school math and science. ***Entrance:*** noncompetitive. ***Application deadline:*** rolling. ***Notification:*** continuous until 8/20.

CONTACT Mrs. Nancy Hagan, Director of Admissions, Greenville Technical College, PO Box 5616, Greenville, SC 29606-5616, 864-250-8359. College video available.

HORRY-GEORGETOWN TECHNICAL COLLEGE
Conway, South Carolina

UG Enrollment: 3,194 **Tuition & Fees (Area Res): $1015**
Application Deadline: rolling **Room & Board: N/Avail**

GENERAL State and locally supported, 2-year, coed. Part of South Carolina State Board for Technical and Comprehensive Education. Awards certificates, diplomas, transfer associate, terminal associate degrees. Founded 1965. ***Setting:*** small-town campus. ***Total enrollment:*** 3,194. ***Faculty:*** 215 (80 full-time, 5% with terminal degrees, 135 part-time); student-faculty ratio is 15:1.

ENROLLMENT PROFILE 3,194 students from 5 states and territories, 8 other countries. 57% women, 37% part-time, 97% state residents, 20% transferred in, 15% African American. ***Areas of study chosen:*** 35% interdisciplinary studies, 20% liberal arts/general studies, 14% business management and administrative services, 12% health professions and related sciences, 7% agriculture, 6% engineering and applied sciences, 5% computer and information sciences, 1% education. ***Most popular recent majors:*** business administration/commerce/management, criminal justice.

FIRST-YEAR CLASS 1,557 total; 1,849 applied, 100% were accepted, 84% of whom enrolled. 1% from top 10% of their high school class, 5% from top quarter, 35% from top half.

ACADEMIC PROGRAM Core. Calendar: semesters. 465 courses offered in 1995–96. Academic remediation for entering students, services for LD students, advanced placement, tutorials, summer session for credit, part-time degree program (daytime, evenings), adult/continuing education programs, co-op programs and internships.

GENERAL DEGREE REQUIREMENTS 63 semester hours; math/science requirements vary according to program; computer course; internship (some majors).

MAJORS Agricultural sciences, business administration/commerce/management, civil engineering technology, computer technologies, criminal justice, culinary arts, electrical and electronics technologies, electronics engineering technology, (pre)engineering sequence, forest technology, heating/refrigeration/air conditioning, hotel and restaurant management, landscaping/grounds maintenance, machine and tool technologies, nursing, paralegal studies, parks management, practical nursing, radiological technology, secretarial studies/office management.

LIBRARY Conway Campus Learning Resource Center plus 2 others, with 42,500 books, 12,550 microform titles, 425 periodicals, 2 on-line bibliographic services, 25 CD-ROMs, 85 records, tapes, and CDs. Acquisition spending 1994–95: $328,163.

COMPUTERS ON CAMPUS 300 computers for student use in computer labs, Learning Success Center, classrooms, library provide access to main academic computer, on-line services, Internet. Staffed computer lab on campus provides training in use of computers, software.

COLLEGE LIFE ***Student services:*** personal-psychological counseling.

HOUSING College housing not available.

ATHLETICS ***Intercollegiate:*** golf M(c).

CAREER PLANNING ***Placement office:*** 6 full-time, 1 part-time staff. ***Director:*** Ms. Maureen Arneman, Director of Counseling and Student Development, 803-347-3186 Ext. 258. ***Services:*** resume preparation, resume referral, career counseling, careers library, job bank, job interviews.

AFTER GRADUATION 10% of students completing a degree program in 1994–95 went directly on to further study.

EXPENSES FOR 1995–96 ***Application fee:*** $15. Area resident tuition: $1000 full-time, $42 per semester hour part-time. State resident tuition: $1104 full-time, $46 per semester hour part-time. Nonresident tuition: $2208 full-time, $92 per semester hour part-time. Part-time mandatory fees per semester range from $3.75 to $7.50. Full-time mandatory fees: $15.

FINANCIAL AID ***College-administered undergrad aid 1995–96:*** 20 need-based scholarships (average $1000), short-term loans (average $200), low-interest long-term loans from external sources (average $2625), Federal Work-Study, 100 part-time jobs. ***Required forms:*** institutional, FAFSA; accepted: CSS Financial Aid PROFILE. ***Priority deadline:*** 4/1. ***Payment plan:*** deferred payment. ***Waivers:*** full or partial for senior citizens. ***Notification:*** 6/1.

APPLYING Open admission. ***Options:*** early entrance, midyear entrance. ***Required:*** SAT I or ACT, TOEFL for international students, CPT. ***Required for some:*** school transcript. Test scores used for admission and counseling/placement. ***Application deadline:*** rolling. ***Notification:*** continuous.

APPLYING/TRANSFER ***Required:*** standardized test scores, college transcript. ***Required for some:*** high school transcript. ***Entrance:*** noncompetitive. ***Application deadline:*** rolling. ***Notification:*** continuous.

CONTACT Ms. Teresa Hilburn, Director of Admissions, Horry-Georgetown Technical College, Conway, SC 29526, 803-347-3186 Ext. 238.

MIDLANDS TECHNICAL COLLEGE
Columbia, South Carolina

UG Enrollment: 9,834 **Tuition & Fees (Area Res): $990**
Application Deadline: 7/26 **Room & Board: N/Avail**

GENERAL State and locally supported, 2-year, coed. Part of South Carolina State Board for Technical and Comprehensive Education. Awards certificates, diplomas, transfer associate, terminal associate degrees. Founded 1974. ***Setting:*** 113-acre suburban campus. ***Total enrollment:*** 9,834. ***Faculty:*** 675 (225 full-time, 1% with terminal degrees, 450 part-time); student-faculty ratio is 18:1.

ENROLLMENT PROFILE 9,834 students from 15 states and territories. 60% women, 40% men, 58% part-time, 98% state residents, 5% transferred in, 1% international, 46% 25 or older, 1% Native American, 1% Hispanic, 32% African American, 1% Asian American. ***Areas of study chosen:*** 27% liberal arts/general studies, 22% health professions and related sciences, 16% business management and administrative services, 8% computer and information sciences, 8% engineering and applied sciences, 5% interdisciplinary studies, 1% performing arts. ***Most popular recent majors:*** nursing, criminal justice, business administration/commerce/management.

FIRST-YEAR CLASS 2,450 total; 2,800 applied, 91% were accepted, 96% of whom enrolled.

Peterson's Guide to Two-Year Colleges 1997

585

Midlands Technical College (continued)

ACADEMIC PROGRAM Honor code. Calendar: semesters. 425 courses offered in 1995–96. Academic remediation for entering students, English as a second language program offered during academic year and summer, services for LD students, advanced placement, self-designed majors, tutorials, summer session for credit, part-time degree program (daytime, evenings, summer), adult/continuing education programs, co-op programs and internships.

GENERAL DEGREE REQUIREMENTS 60 semester hours; 14 semester hours of math/science; internship (some majors).

MAJORS Accounting, architectural technologies, business administration/commerce/management, civil engineering technology, computer technologies, court reporting, criminal justice, data processing, dental services, electrical and electronics technologies, electrical engineering technology, engineering technology, finance/banking, graphic arts, heating/refrigeration/air conditioning, human services, legal studies, liberal arts/general studies, machine and tool technologies, marketing/retailing/merchandising, mechanical engineering technology, medical laboratory technology, medical records services, medical secretarial studies, nursing, radiological technology, respiratory therapy, secretarial studies/office management, telecommunications.

LIBRARY 65,000 books, 4,000 microform titles, 500 periodicals. Acquisition spending 1994–95: $128,343.

COMPUTERS ON CAMPUS 125 computers for student use in computer labs, learning resource center, classrooms, library provide access to main academic computer, e-mail, on-line services, Internet. Staffed computer lab on campus provides training in use of computers, software. Academic computing expenditure 1994–95: $427,058.

COLLEGE LIFE Student-run newspaper. ***Student services:*** personal-psychological counseling, women's center. ***Campus security:*** 24-hour emergency response devices and patrols.

HOUSING College housing not available.

ATHLETICS ***Intramural:*** basketball, football, softball, volleyball.

CAREER PLANNING ***Placement office:*** 9 full-time, 2 part-time staff; $944,065 operating expenditure 1994–95. ***Director:*** Mrs. Cathy Wooldridge, Director of Counseling Services, 803-882-3508. ***Services:*** job fairs, resume preparation, resume referral, career counseling, careers library, job bank, job interviews.

EXPENSES FOR 1996–97 ***Application fee:*** $20. Area resident tuition: $990 full-time, $42 per semester hour part-time. State resident tuition: $1238 full-time, $52 per semester hour part-time. Nonresident tuition: $1980 full-time, $83 per semester hour part-time.

FINANCIAL AID ***College-administered undergrad aid 1995–96:*** need-based scholarships, non-need scholarships, short-term loans, low-interest long-term loans from external sources, Federal Work-Study. ***Required forms:*** CSS Financial Aid PROFILE, institutional, FAFSA. ***Application deadline:*** continuous to 5/1. ***Waivers:*** full or partial for employees or children of employees and senior citizens. ***Notification:*** continuous.

APPLYING ***Options:*** Common Application, early entrance, deferred entrance, midyear entrance. ***Required:*** TOEFL for international students, ACT ASSET. ***Recommended:*** school transcript, SAT I or ACT. ***Required for some:*** 3 years of high school math and science. Test scores used for admission. ***Application deadline:*** 7/26. ***Notification:*** continuous.

APPLYING/TRANSFER ***Recommended:*** high school transcript, college transcript. ***Required for some:*** standardized test scores, 3 years of high school math and science. ***Application deadline:*** rolling. ***Notification:*** continuous. ***Contact:*** Ms. Joan Sallenger, Transfer Coordinator, 803-822-3344.

CONTACT Mr. Richard Tinneny, Director of Admissions, Midlands Technical College, West Cola, SC 29171, 803-738-7764. ***Fax:*** 803-738-7784. College video available.

NIELSEN ELECTRONICS INSTITUTE
Charleston, South Carolina

UG Enrollment: 260	**Tuition & Fees: $9840**
Application Deadline: rolling	**Room Only: $2700**

GENERAL Proprietary, 2-year, specialized, coed. Awards certificates, terminal associate degrees. Founded 1965. ***Setting:*** 3-acre urban campus. ***Total enrollment:*** 260. ***Faculty:*** 8 (all full-time); student-faculty ratio is 20:1.

ENROLLMENT PROFILE 260 students from 2 states and territories. 4% women, 0% part-time, 99% state residents, 15% transferred in, 29% 25 or older, 61% African American, 3% Asian American.

FIRST-YEAR CLASS 40 total. Of the students who applied, 80% were accepted, 60% of whom enrolled. 5% from top 10% of their high school class, 10% from top quarter, 45% from top half.

ACADEMIC PROGRAM Core. Calendar: quarters. Summer session for credit, internships.

GENERAL DEGREE REQUIREMENTS 96 quarter hours; computer course.

MAJOR Electrical and electronics technologies.

LIBRARY 2,000 books.

COMPUTERS ON CAMPUS 30 computers for student use in computer center.

COLLEGE LIFE ***Social organizations:*** 1 local fraternity; 35% of eligible men are members. ***Student services:*** personal-psychological counseling.

HOUSING 86 college housing spaces available; all were occupied 1995–96. Off-campus living permitted.

ATHLETICS ***Intramural:*** basketball.

CAREER PLANNING ***Service:*** career counseling.

EXPENSES FOR 1996–97 ***Application fee:*** $25. Tuition: $9840 full-time. College room only: $2700.

FINANCIAL AID ***College-administered undergrad aid 1995–96:*** 29 need-based scholarships (average $656). ***Priority deadline:*** 9/1.

APPLYING ***Option:*** deferred entrance. ***Recommended:*** SAT I or ACT. Test scores used for admission. ***Application deadline:*** rolling. ***Notification:*** continuous.

APPLYING/TRANSFER ***Recommended:*** standardized test scores. ***Entrance:*** minimally difficult. ***Application deadline:*** rolling. ***Notification:*** continuous.

CONTACT Mr. James Brown, Director of Admissions/Registrar, Nielsen Electronics Institute, 1600 Meeting Street, Charleston, SC 29405-9417, 803-722-2344.

ORANGEBURG-CALHOUN TECHNICAL COLLEGE
Orangeburg, South Carolina

UG Enrollment: 1,768	**Tuition & Fees (Area Res): $1260**
Application Deadline: rolling	**Room & Board: N/Avail**

GENERAL State and locally supported, 2-year, coed. Awards certificates, diplomas, transfer associate, terminal associate degrees. Founded 1968. ***Setting:*** 100-acre small-town campus. ***Total enrollment:*** 1,768. ***Faculty:*** 120 (56 full-time, 64 part-time); student-faculty ratio is 15:1.

ENROLLMENT PROFILE 1,768 students from 5 states and territories, 3 other countries. 69% women, 43% part-time, 99% state residents, 7% transferred in, 65% have need-based financial aid, 37% 25 or older, 48% African American. ***Most popular recent majors:*** nursing, computer technologies, liberal arts/general studies.

FIRST-YEAR CLASS 655 total; 1,900 applied, 95% were accepted, 36% of whom enrolled.

ACADEMIC PROGRAM Core, honor code. Calendar: semesters. Academic remediation for entering students, English as a second language program offered during academic year, services for LD students, advanced placement, summer session for credit, part-time degree program (daytime, evenings, summer), adult/continuing education programs, co-op programs and internships.

GENERAL DEGREE REQUIREMENTS 62 semester hours; math/science requirements vary according to program; computer course (varies by major); internship (some majors).

MAJORS Accounting, agricultural sciences, art/fine arts, automotive technologies, business administration/commerce/management, computer technologies, criminal justice, drafting and design, electrical and electronics technologies, electronics engineering technology, engineering (general), finance/banking, forest technology, instrumentation technology, law enforcement/police sciences, legal secretarial studies, liberal arts/general studies, machine and tool technologies, mechanical engineering technology, medical assistant technologies, medical laboratory technology, medical secretarial studies, nursing, paralegal studies, radiological technology, real estate, respiratory therapy, science, secretarial studies/office management.

LIBRARY Gressett Learning Center plus 1 other, with 30,989 books, 388 periodicals, 1,400 records, tapes, and CDs.

COMPUTERS ON CAMPUS 100 computers for student use in computer center, labs, library provide access to e-mail, Internet.

COLLEGE LIFE 50% vote in student government elections. ***Student services:*** personal-psychological counseling, women's center. ***Campus security:*** 24-hour patrols.

HOUSING College housing not available.

ATHLETICS ***Intramural:*** basketball, football, golf, tennis, track and field, volleyball.

CAREER PLANNING ***Director:*** Ms. Marolyn Blanton, Career Center Director, 803-535-1223. ***Services:*** career counseling, careers library.

EXPENSES FOR 1995–96 Area resident tuition: $1260 full-time, $36 per semester hour part-time. State resident tuition: $1539 full-time, $44 per semester hour part-time. Nonresident tuition: $1854 full-time, $53 per semester hour part-time.

FINANCIAL AID ***College-administered undergrad aid 1995–96:*** 25 need-based scholarships (average $500), Federal Work-Study. ***Required forms:*** FAFSA. ***Priority deadline:*** 8/1.

APPLYING Open admission. ***Options:*** Common Application, early entrance. ***Required:*** TOEFL for international students. ***Recommended:*** SAT I or ACT, SAT II Subject Tests. Test scores used for counseling/placement. ***Application deadline:*** rolling. ***Notification:*** continuous.

APPLYING/TRANSFER ***Application deadline:*** rolling. ***Notification:*** continuous. ***Contact:*** Mr. Mike Hammond, Arts and Sciences Division Chairman, 803-535-1267.

CONTACT Mrs. Bobbie Felder, Director of Enrollment Management, Orangeburg-Calhoun Technical College, Orangeburg, SC 29115-8299, 803-535-1218. ***Fax:*** 803-531-4364.

PIEDMONT TECHNICAL COLLEGE
Greenwood, South Carolina

UG Enrollment: 3,148	**Tuition & Fees (Area Res): $1380**
Application Deadline: rolling	**Room & Board: N/Avail**

GENERAL State-supported, 2-year, coed. Awards transfer associate, terminal associate degrees. Founded 1966. ***Setting:*** 60-acre small-town campus. ***Research spending 1994–95:*** $133,740. ***Educational spending 1994–95:*** $1880 per undergrad. ***Total enrollment:*** 3,148. ***Faculty:*** 127 (74 full-time, 53 part-time); student-faculty ratio is 17:1.

ENROLLMENT PROFILE 3,148 students from 6 states and territories, 4 other countries. 62% women, 52% part-time, 99% state residents, 8% transferred in, 44% 25 or older, 30% African American.

FIRST-YEAR CLASS 349 total. Of the students who applied, 99% were accepted.

ACADEMIC PROGRAM Core. Calendar: semesters. Academic remediation for entering students, advanced placement, summer session for credit, part-time degree program (daytime, evenings), adult/continuing education programs, co-op programs.

GENERAL DEGREE REQUIREMENTS 60 credits; 6 credits of math/science; computer course for most majors.

MAJORS Accounting, art/fine arts, automotive technologies, business administration/commerce/management, carpentry, child care/child and family studies, computer programming, construction management, criminal justice, drafting and design, electrical and electronics technologies, electronics engineering technology, engineering (general), engineering design, engineering technology, fashion merchandising, graphic arts, heating/refrigeration/air conditioning, human services, industrial engineering technology, machine and tool technologies, manufacturing technology, marketing/retailing/merchandising, mechanical design technology, mechanical engineering technology, medical assistant technologies, nursing, radiological technology, respiratory therapy, robotics, science, secretarial studies/office management.

LIBRARY Piedmont Technical College Library with 30,000 books, 191 microform titles, 328 periodicals, 1 on-line bibliographic service, 1 CD-ROM, 2,717 records, tapes, and CDs. Acquisition spending 1994–95: $175,810.

COMPUTERS ON CAMPUS 205 computers for student use in computer center, developmental labs, classrooms. Staffed computer lab on campus provides training in use of computers, software. Academic computing expenditure 1994–95: $298,435.
COLLEGE LIFE Choral group, student-run newspaper. ***Social organizations:*** 16 open to all. ***Most popular organizations:*** Phi Theta Kappa, Student Government Association. ***Major annual events:*** Spring Activities Day, Fall Convocation. ***Student services:*** personal-psychological counseling, women's center. ***Campus security:*** 24-hour emergency response devices and patrols, late-night transport-escort service.
HOUSING College housing not available.
ATHLETICS ***Intramural:*** basketball, football, volleyball.
CAREER PLANNING ***Placement office:*** 5 full-time staff. ***Director:*** Mr. Andy Omundson, Director, 864-941-8376. ***Services:*** job fairs, resume preparation, resume referral, career counseling, careers library, job bank, job interviews.
AFTER GRADUATION 10% of students completing a degree program in 1994–95 went directly on to further study.
EXPENSES FOR 1996–97 ***Application fee:*** $25. Area resident tuition: $1350 full-time, $45 per credit hour part-time. State resident tuition: $1680 full-time, $56 per credit hour part-time. Nonresident tuition: $2070 (minimum) full-time, $69 per credit hour part-time. Tuition for international students: $2300. Full-time mandatory fees: $30.
FINANCIAL AID ***College-administered undergrad aid 1995–96:*** 475 need-based scholarships (average $1250), 98 non-need scholarships (average $334), low-interest long-term loans from external sources (average $2000), Federal Work-Study, 33 part-time jobs. ***Required forms for some financial aid applicants:*** FAFSA; accepted: CSS Financial Aid PROFILE. ***Priority deadline:*** 6/1. ***Waivers:*** full or partial for senior citizens.
APPLYING Open admission except for nursing, health sciences programs. ***Options:*** early entrance, deferred entrance. ***Required:*** school transcript, TOEFL for international students, ACT ASSET. ***Recommended:*** SAT I. Test scores used for counseling/placement. ***Application deadline:*** rolling. ***Notification:*** continuous until 8/20.
APPLYING/TRANSFER ***Required:*** high school transcript. ***Recommended:*** college transcript. ***Entrance:*** noncompetitive. ***Application deadline:*** rolling. ***Notification:*** continuous until 8/20.
CONTACT Mr. Gavin Bethea, Admissions Counselor, Piedmont Technical College, Greenwood, SC 29648-1467, 864-941-8371 or toll-free 800-868-5528 (in-state). ***Fax:*** 864-941-8555.

SPARTANBURG METHODIST COLLEGE
Spartanburg, South Carolina

UG Enrollment: 878	**Tuition & Fees: $6700**
Application Deadline: rolling	**Room & Board: $3850**

GENERAL Independent Methodist, 2-year, coed. Awards transfer associate, terminal associate degrees. Founded 1911. ***Setting:*** 111-acre urban campus with easy access to Charlotte. ***Endowment:*** $8 million. ***Total enrollment:*** 878. ***Faculty:*** 51 (41 full-time, 17% with terminal degrees, 10 part-time); student-faculty ratio is 20:1.
ENROLLMENT PROFILE 878 students from 8 states and territories, 11 other countries. 44% women, 18% part-time, 85% state residents, 3% transferred in, 4% international, 1% 25 or older, 0% Native American, 0% Hispanic, 24% African American, 0% Asian American. ***Areas of study chosen:*** 100% liberal arts/general studies.
FIRST-YEAR CLASS 442 total; 1,206 applied, 75% were accepted, 49% of whom enrolled. 6% from top 10% of their high school class, 29% from top quarter, 47% from top half. 3 class presidents, 4 valedictorians.
ACADEMIC PROGRAM Core, liberal arts curriculum, honor code. Calendar: semesters. 164 courses offered in 1995–96. Academic remediation for entering students, English as a second language program offered during academic year and summer, advanced placement, tutorials, honors program, summer session for credit, part-time degree program (daytime, evenings, weekends, summer). ROTC: Army.
GENERAL DEGREE REQUIREMENTS 60 credits; 8 credits of math/science; computer course.
MAJORS Criminal justice, law enforcement/police sciences, liberal arts/general studies, retail management, science, secretarial studies/office management.
LIBRARY Marie Blair Burgess Learning Resource Center with 37,429 books, 52 microform titles, 180 periodicals, 2,500 records, tapes, and CDs. Acquisition spending 1994–95: $150,000.
COMPUTERS ON CAMPUS 30 computers for student use in computer labs, library. Staffed computer lab on campus provides training in use of computers, software.
COLLEGE LIFE Drama-theater group, choral group, student-run newspaper. ***Social organizations:*** 5 open to all; 2 national fraternities. ***Most popular organizations:*** College Christian Movement, Alpha Phi Omega, Student Government. ***Major annual events:*** Homecoming, Miss Spartanburg Methodist College Pageant, Spartanburg Methodist College Spirit Blitz. ***Student services:*** health clinic, personal-psychological counseling. ***Campus security:*** 24-hour emergency response devices and patrols.
HOUSING 447 college housing spaces available; 394 were occupied 1995–96. Freshmen guaranteed college housing. Off-campus living permitted. ***Options:*** single-sex, international student housing available. Resident assistants live in dorms.
ATHLETICS Member NJCAA. ***Intercollegiate:*** baseball M(s), basketball M(s)/W(s), golf M(s)/W(s), soccer M(s)/W(s), softball W(s), tennis W(s), volleyball W(s). ***Intramural:*** basketball, football, golf, racquetball, soccer, softball, table tennis (Ping-Pong), tennis, volleyball. ***Contact:*** Mr. Tim Wallace, Athletic Director, 864-587-4267.
CAREER PLANNING ***Placement office:*** 4 full-time staff; $138,000 operating expenditure 1994–95. ***Director:*** Mr. Pete Aylor, Director of Counseling, 864-587-4229. ***Service:*** career counseling.
AFTER GRADUATION 91% of students completing a degree program in 1994–95 went directly on to further study.
EXPENSES FOR 1995–96 ***Application fee:*** $20. Comprehensive fee of $10,550 includes full-time tuition ($6100), mandatory fees ($600), and college room and board ($3850). Part-time tuition: $161 per credit.
FINANCIAL AID ***College-administered undergrad aid 1995–96:*** need-based scholarships (average $2500), non-need scholarships (average $1100), low-interest long-term loans from external sources (average $2500), Federal Work-Study, part-time jobs. ***Required forms:*** state, institutional, FAFSA; accepted: CSS Financial Aid PROFILE. ***Application deadline:*** continuous to 6/1. ***Payment plan:*** installment. ***Waivers:*** full or partial for employees or children of employees and senior citizens.
APPLYING ***Options:*** deferred entrance, midyear entrance. ***Required:*** SAT I or ACT, TOEFL for international students. ***Recommended:*** 3 years of high school math. Test scores used for admission. ***Application deadline:*** rolling. ***Notification:*** continuous.
APPLYING/TRANSFER ***Required:*** standardized test scores. ***Application deadline:*** rolling. ***Notification:*** continuous. ***Contact:*** Mr. Pete Aylor, Director of Counseling, 864-587-4229.
CONTACT Mr. Darrell Brockway, Assistant Vice President for Enrollment Management, Spartanburg Methodist College, 1200 Textile Road, Spartanburg, SC 29301-0009, 864-587-4231 or toll-free 800-772-7286 (in-state). ***Fax:*** 864-574-6919. College video available.

SPARTANBURG TECHNICAL COLLEGE
Spartanburg, South Carolina

UG Enrollment: 2,500	**Tuition & Fees (Area Res): $878**
Application Deadline: rolling	**Room & Board: N/Avail**

GENERAL State-supported, 2-year, coed. Part of South Carolina State Board for Technical and Comprehensive Education. Awards certificates, diplomas, transfer associate, terminal associate degrees. Founded 1961. ***Setting:*** 104-acre urban campus. ***Total enrollment:*** 2,500. ***Faculty:*** 98 full-time, 100% with terminal degrees; student-faculty ratio is 25:1.
ENROLLMENT PROFILE 2,500 students from 4 states and territories. 53% women, 50% part-time, 99% state residents, 1% transferred in, 41% 25 or older, 1% Native American, 1% Hispanic, 20% African American, 1% Asian American.
FIRST-YEAR CLASS 1,878 applied, 100% were accepted, 87% of whom enrolled.
ACADEMIC PROGRAM Core, honor code. Calendar: semesters plus summer sessions. Academic remediation for entering students, services for LD students, advanced placement, summer session for credit, part-time degree program (daytime, evenings, summer), adult/continuing education programs, co-op programs.
GENERAL DEGREE REQUIREMENTS 60 semester hours; 1 math/science course; computer course.
MAJORS Accounting, architectural technologies, automotive technologies, business administration/commerce/management, civil engineering technology, computer technologies, electrical and electronics technologies, electronics engineering technology, engineering technology, horticulture, machine and tool technologies, marketing/retailing/merchandising, mechanical engineering technology, medical laboratory technology, medical secretarial studies, radiological technology, respiratory therapy, vocational education.
COMPUTERS ON CAMPUS 40 computers for student use in computer labs. Staffed computer lab on campus provides training in use of computers, software.
COLLEGE LIFE Drama-theater group, student-run newspaper. ***Student services:*** personal-psychological counseling, women's center. ***Campus security:*** 24-hour patrols.
HOUSING College housing not available.
CAREER PLANNING ***Director:*** Mr. Art Decker, Coordinator of Career Planning and Placement, 803-591-3820 Ext. 2. ***Services:*** resume preparation, resume referral, career counseling, careers library.
EXPENSES FOR 1995–96 ***Application fee:*** $10. Area resident tuition: $878 full-time, $37 per semester hour part-time. State resident tuition: $1100 full-time, $46 per semester hour part-time. Nonresident tuition: $1756 full-time, $74 per semester hour part-time.
FINANCIAL AID ***College-administered undergrad aid 1995–96:*** need-based scholarships, non-need scholarships, Federal Work-Study. ***Required forms:*** institutional; accepted: CSS Financial Aid PROFILE, FAFSA. ***Priority deadline:*** 7/1.
APPLYING Open admission except for allied health, engineering programs. ***Option:*** early entrance. ***Required:*** school transcript, TOEFL for international students, ACT ASSET. Test scores used for counseling/placement. ***Application deadline:*** rolling. ***Notification:*** continuous.
APPLYING/TRANSFER ***Required:*** college transcript. ***Required for some:*** standardized test scores. ***Application deadline:*** rolling. ***Notification:*** continuous.
CONTACT Ms. Pam Hagan, Director of Admissions and Counseling, Spartanburg Technical College, PO Box 4386, Spartanburg, SC 29305-4386, 803-591-3800 or toll-free 800-922-3679 (in-state).

TECHNICAL COLLEGE OF THE LOWCOUNTRY
Beaufort, South Carolina

GENERAL State-supported, 2-year, coed. Part of South Carolina Technical and Comprehensive Education System. Awards transfer associate, terminal associate degrees. Founded 1972. ***Setting:*** 12-acre small-town campus. ***Total enrollment:*** 1,600. ***Faculty:*** 69 (41 full-time, 28 part-time); student-faculty ratio is 20:1.
EXPENSES FOR 1995–96 ***Application fee:*** $10. State resident tuition: $1000 full-time, $42 per credit hour part-time. Nonresident tuition: $1500 full-time, $63 per credit hour part-time. Tuition for Georgia residents: $1200 full-time, $50 per credit hour part-time.
CONTACT Mr. Les Brediger, Interim Director of Admissions, Technical College of the Lowcountry, Beaufort, SC 29901-1288, 803-525-8207.

TRI-COUNTY TECHNICAL COLLEGE
Pendleton, South Carolina

UG Enrollment: 3,179	**Tuition & Fees (SC Res): $900**
Application Deadline: rolling	**Room & Board: N/Avail**

GENERAL State-supported, 2-year, coed. Part of South Carolina State Board for Technical and Comprehensive Education. Awards certificates, diplomas, transfer associate, terminal associate degrees. Founded 1962. ***Setting:*** 100-acre rural campus. ***Total enrollment:*** 3,179. ***Faculty:*** 250 (100 full-time, 150 part-time).
ENROLLMENT PROFILE 3,179 students from 3 states and territories, 9 other countries. 54% women, 46% men, 51% part-time, 96% state residents, 7% transferred in, 30% have need-based financial aid, 30% have non-need-based financial aid, 1% international, 52% 25 or older, 1% Native American, 1% Hispanic, 10% African American, 1% Asian American. ***Areas of study chosen:*** 24% health professions and related sciences, 20%

Peterson's Guide to Two-Year Colleges 1997 587

Tri-County Technical College (continued)
engineering and applied sciences, 7% business management and administrative services, 6% computer and information sciences, 1% communications and journalism. ***Most popular recent majors:*** electrical and electronics technologies, nursing.
FIRST-YEAR CLASS 1,458 applied, 76% were accepted, 77% of whom enrolled. 12% from top 10% of their high school class, 30% from top quarter, 75% from top half.
ACADEMIC PROGRAM Honor code. Calendar: semesters. Academic remediation for entering students, English as a second language program offered during academic year, advanced placement, summer session for credit, part-time degree program (daytime, evenings), adult/continuing education programs, co-op programs and internships. Study abroad in Germany. ROTC: Army (c), Air Force (c).
GENERAL DEGREE REQUIREMENTS 60 credits; 3 credits of math; computer course (varies by major); internship (some majors).
MAJORS Accounting, business administration/commerce/management, child care/child and family studies, computer programming, computer technologies, criminal justice, data processing, drafting and design, electrical and electronics technologies, electromechanical technology, electronics engineering technology, heating/refrigeration/air conditioning, liberal arts/general studies, machine and tool technologies, medical laboratory technology, nursing, quality control technology, radio and television studies, secretarial studies/office management, textiles and clothing, veterinary technology, welding technology.
LIBRARY Tri-County Technical College Library with 35,287 books, 261 microform titles, 276 periodicals, 7 CD-ROMs, 4,178 records, tapes, and CDs. Acquisition spending 1994–95: $47,000.
COMPUTERS ON CAMPUS 450 computers for student use in computer center, computer labs, learning resource center, classrooms, library. Staffed computer lab on campus.
COLLEGE LIFE Student-run newspaper. ***Social organizations:*** 14 open to all. ***Major annual events:*** Welcome Back Bash, Annual Talent Show, Martin Luther King, Jr. Celebration. ***Student services:*** personal-psychological counseling. ***Campus security:*** 24-hour emergency response devices and patrols.
HOUSING College housing not available.
CAREER PLANNING ***Placement office:*** 3 full-time, 2 part-time staff; $92,000 operating expenditure 1994–95. ***Director:*** Mr. Glenn Hellenga, Director of Counseling, 864-646-8361 Ext. 2165. ***Services:*** resume preparation, resume referral, career counseling, careers library, job bank, job interviews.
EXPENSES FOR 1995–96 ***Application fee:*** $15. State resident tuition: $900 full-time, $38 per credit part-time. Nonresident tuition: $1728 full-time, $72 per credit part-time.
FINANCIAL AID ***College-administered undergrad aid 1995–96:*** need-based scholarships, non-need scholarships, short-term loans (average $200), low-interest long-term loans from external sources, Federal Work-Study. ***Required forms:*** FAFSA; accepted: CSS Financial Aid PROFILE. ***Priority deadline:*** 7/1. ***Waivers:*** full or partial for senior citizens.
APPLYING Open admission except for allied health programs. ***Option:*** early entrance. ***Required:*** TOEFL for international students. ***Required for some:*** SAT I, National League of Nursing Exam. Test scores used for counseling/placement. ***Application deadline:*** rolling. ***Notification:*** continuous.
APPLYING/TRANSFER ***Entrance:*** noncompetitive. ***Application deadline:*** rolling. ***Notification:*** continuous. ***Contact:*** Mr. David Shirley, Director of Admissions, 864-646-8641.
CONTACT Mr. David Shirley, Director of Admissions, Tri-County Technical College, PO Box 587, Pendleton, SC 29670-0587, 864-646-8641. College video available.

TRIDENT TECHNICAL COLLEGE
Charleston, South Carolina

UG Enrollment: 9,110	**Tuition & Fees (Area Res): $1034**
Application Deadline: 8/3	**Room & Board: N/Avail**

GENERAL State and locally supported, 2-year, coed. Part of South Carolina Technical and Comprehensive Education System. Awards certificates, diplomas, transfer associate, terminal associate degrees. Founded 1964. ***Setting:*** urban campus. ***Total enrollment:*** 9,110. ***Faculty:*** 497 (210 full-time, 287 part-time).
ENROLLMENT PROFILE 9,110 students: 56% women, 65% part-time, 98% state residents, 50% have need-based financial aid, 10% have non-need-based financial aid, 1% international, 50% 25 or older, 1% Native American, 1% Hispanic, 20% African American, 2% Asian American. ***Areas of study chosen:*** 12% health professions and related sciences, 10% business management and administrative services, 10% engineering and applied sciences, 5% computer and information sciences, 2% vocational and home economics.
FIRST-YEAR CLASS 1,638 total. Of the students who applied, 99% were accepted.
ACADEMIC PROGRAM Core. Calendar: semesters. Academic remediation for entering students, English as a second language program offered during academic year and summer, services for LD students, advanced placement, summer session for credit, part-time degree program (daytime, evenings), co-op programs.
GENERAL DEGREE REQUIREMENTS 60 credits; computer course.
MAJORS Accounting, aircraft and missile maintenance, automotive technologies, broadcasting, business administration/commerce/management, chemical engineering technology, civil engineering technology, commercial art, computer technologies, criminal justice, culinary arts, dental services, early childhood education, electrical and electronics technologies, electrical engineering technology, electronics engineering technology, horticulture, hotel and restaurant management, industrial administration, industrial engineering technology, legal studies, machine and tool technologies, manufacturing technology, marketing/retailing/merchandising, mechanical engineering technology, medical laboratory technology, medical secretarial studies, nursing, occupational therapy, physical therapy, radiological technology, respiratory therapy, science, secretarial studies/office management.
LIBRARY Main library plus 2 others, with 68,462 books, 839 microform titles, 868 periodicals, 6 on-line bibliographic services, 25 CD-ROMs, 3,614 records, tapes, and CDs. Acquisition spending 1994–95: $123,445.
COMPUTERS ON CAMPUS Computer purchase plan available. 500 computers for student use in computer center, computer labs, learning resource center, classrooms, library provide access to main academic computer, on-line services. Staffed computer lab on campus provides training in use of computers, software. Academic computing expenditure 1994–95: $592,424.
COLLEGE LIFE Student-run newspaper. ***Major annual events:*** Holiday Drop-in, Big Band Concert, Spring Week. ***Student services:*** personal-psychological counseling. ***Campus security:*** 24-hour emergency response devices and patrols, late-night transport-escort service.
HOUSING College housing not available.
CAREER PLANNING ***Placement office:*** 2 full-time, 2 part-time staff. ***Director:*** Ms. Jean Chandler, Director of Career Placement, 803-572-6011. ***Services:*** job fairs, resume preparation, resume referral, career counseling, job bank, job interviews.
EXPENSES FOR 1995–96 ***Application fee:*** $20. Area resident tuition: $1010 full-time, $42 per credit hour part-time. State resident tuition: $1178 full-time, $49 per credit hour part-time. Nonresident tuition: $1606 full-time, $70 per credit hour part-time. Part-time mandatory fees: $12 per semester. Full-time mandatory fees: $24.
FINANCIAL AID ***College-administered undergrad aid 1995–96:*** 2 need-based scholarships (average $210), 25 non-need scholarships (average $210), short-term loans (average $158), low-interest long-term loans from external sources (average $1003), Federal Work-Study, 64 part-time jobs. ***Required forms for some financial aid applicants:*** CSS Financial Aid PROFILE, FAFSA. ***Priority deadline:*** 6/30.
APPLYING Open admission except for nursing, allied health programs. ***Options:*** early entrance, midyear entrance. ***Required:*** SAT I or ACT, TOEFL for international students, National League of Nursing Exam. Test scores used for counseling/placement. ***Application deadline:*** 8/3. ***Notification:*** continuous.
APPLYING/TRANSFER ***Required:*** standardized test scores. ***Application deadline:*** 8/3. ***Notification:*** continuous.
CONTACT Ms. Jeanie Norris, Director of Admissions and Records, Trident Technical College, 7000 Rivers Avenue, Charleston, SC 29423-8067, 803-572-6325.

UNIVERSITY OF SOUTH CAROLINA AT BEAUFORT
Beaufort, South Carolina

UG Enrollment: 1,223	**Tuition & Fees (SC Res): $1786**
Application Deadline: rolling	**Room & Board: N/Avail**

GENERAL State-supported, 2-year, coed. Part of University of South Carolina System. Awards transfer associate degrees (offers courses for bachelor's degrees awarded at other University of South Carolina campuses). Founded 1959. ***Setting:*** 5-acre small-town campus. ***Total enrollment:*** 1,223. ***Faculty:*** 81 (26 full-time, 72% with terminal degrees, 55 part-time); student-faculty ratio is 19:1.
ENROLLMENT PROFILE 1,223 students: 60% women, 40% men, 65% part-time, 98% state residents, 10% transferred in, 50% 25 or older, 1% Native American, 4% Hispanic, 17% African American, 2% Asian American.
FIRST-YEAR CLASS 112 total; 203 applied, 100% were accepted, 55% of whom enrolled. 15% from top 10% of their high school class, 75% from top half.
ACADEMIC PROGRAM Core, liberal arts curriculum, honor code. Calendar: semesters. 275 courses offered in 1995–96. Academic remediation for entering students, services for LD students, advanced placement, Freshman Honors College, tutorials, honors program, summer session for credit, part-time degree program (daytime, evenings, summer), adult/continuing education programs. Off-campus study at Technical College of the Lowcountry. Study abroad in Costa Rica, France.
GENERAL DEGREE REQUIREMENTS 60 semester hours; 6 semester hours of math; 7 semester hours of science; computer course for business administration majors.
MAJORS Liberal arts/general studies, science.
LIBRARY University of South Carolina at Beaufort Library with 50,000 books, 395 periodicals, 9 on-line bibliographic services, 15 CD-ROMs.
COMPUTERS ON CAMPUS 50 computers for student use in computer center, computer labs, classrooms, library provide access to main academic computer, e-mail, Internet. Staffed computer lab on campus provides training in use of computers, software.
COLLEGE LIFE Student-run newspaper. 10% vote in student government elections. ***Social organizations:*** 7 open to all. ***Most popular organizations:*** Student Government Association, Gamma Beta Phi, Black Student Organization, Business Club, Spanish Club. ***Major annual events:*** Student Cookouts, Christmas Party, Spring Fling. ***Student services:*** personal-psychological counseling. ***Campus security:*** 24-hour emergency response devices, evening security service.
HOUSING College housing not available.
ATHLETICS ***Intramural:*** bowling, golf, tennis, weight lifting.
CAREER PLANNING ***Director:*** Mr. Vince Mesaric, Associate Dean of Students, 803-521-4117. ***Services:*** resume preparation, career counseling, careers library.
EXPENSES FOR 1995–96 ***Application fee:*** $25. State resident tuition: $1786 full-time, $77 per semester hour part-time. Nonresident tuition: $4480 full-time, $187 per semester hour part-time.
FINANCIAL AID ***College-administered undergrad aid 1995–96:*** 6 need-based scholarships (average $1000), 20 non-need scholarships (average $1370), short-term loans (average $300), low-interest long-term loans from external sources, 20 Federal Work-Study (averaging $1600), 10 part-time jobs. ***Required forms:*** institutional, FAFSA; accepted: CSS Financial Aid PROFILE. ***Priority deadline:*** 4/15. ***Waivers:*** full or partial for senior citizens. ***Notification:*** continuous.
APPLYING Open admission. ***Options:*** deferred entrance, midyear entrance. ***Required:*** school transcript, TOEFL for international students. ***Recommended:*** minimum 2.0 GPA, 3 years of high school math and science, some high school foreign language. ***Required for some:*** SAT I or ACT. Test scores used for admission and counseling/placement. ***Application deadline:*** rolling.
APPLYING/TRANSFER ***Required:*** college transcript, minimum 2.0 college GPA. ***Recommended:*** 3 years of high school math and science, some high school foreign language. ***Required for some:*** standardized test scores, high school transcript. ***Entrance:*** minimally difficult. ***Application deadline:*** rolling.
CONTACT Ms. Tinker Folsom, Director of Admissions, University of South Carolina at Beaufort, Beaufort, SC 29902-4601, 803-521-4100 Ext. 4101. ***E-mail:*** ibfrt36@univscvm.sc.edu.

UNIVERSITY OF SOUTH CAROLINA AT LANCASTER
Lancaster, South Carolina

UG Enrollment: 1,153	Tuition & Fees (SC Res): $1888
Application Deadline: rolling	Room & Board: N/Avail

GENERAL State-supported, 2-year, coed. Part of University of South Carolina System. Awards transfer associate, terminal associate degrees. Founded 1959. *Setting:* 17-acre small-town campus with easy access to Charlotte. *Total enrollment:* 1,153. *Faculty:* 52 (22 full-time, 30 part-time).
ENROLLMENT PROFILE 1,153 students from 3 states and territories, 1 other country. 63% women, 37% men, 62% part-time, 99% state residents, 5% transferred in, 37% 25 or older, 1% Native American, 0% Hispanic, 16% African American, 1% Asian American. *Areas of study chosen:* 17% business management and administrative services, 5% liberal arts/general studies, 4% interdisciplinary studies, 2% psychology, 1% biological and life sciences, 1% communications and journalism, 1% computer and information sciences.
FIRST-YEAR CLASS 204 total; 302 applied, 98% were accepted, 69% of whom enrolled. 10% from top 10% of their high school class, 25% from top quarter, 50% from top half. 3 valedictorians.
ACADEMIC PROGRAM Calendar: semesters. Academic remediation for entering students, advanced placement, honors program, summer session for credit, part-time degree program (evenings, weekends), adult/continuing education programs.
GENERAL DEGREE REQUIREMENTS 60 semester hours; 3 semester hours each of math and science for associate of art degree; 6 semester hours of math, 7 semester hours of science for associate of science degree.
MAJORS Business administration/commerce/management, criminal justice, education, liberal arts/general studies, nursing, science, secretarial studies/office management.
LIBRARY Medford Library with 68,192 books, 454 periodicals, 2,272 records, tapes, and CDs.
COMPUTERS ON CAMPUS 25 computers for student use in computer labs, learning center.
COLLEGE LIFE Orientation program (2 days, no cost, parents included). Choral group, student-run newspaper. *Student services:* personal-psychological counseling, women's center.
HOUSING College housing not available.
ATHLETICS *Intercollegiate:* basketball M/W. *Intramural:* golf, racquetball, soccer, tennis, volleyball, weight lifting.
CAREER PLANNING *Service:* career counseling.
AFTER GRADUATION 42% of students completing a degree program in 1994–95 went directly on to further study.
EXPENSES FOR 1995–96 *Application fee:* $35. State resident tuition: $1888 full-time, $82 per semester hour part-time. Nonresident tuition: $4484 full-time, $187 per semester hour part-time. One-time mandatory fee: $25.
FINANCIAL AID *College-administered undergrad aid 1995–96:* need-based scholarships, 52 non-need scholarships, low-interest long-term loans from external sources, Federal Work-Study, part-time jobs. *Required forms:* institutional, FAFSA; accepted: CSS Financial Aid PROFILE. *Priority deadline:* 4/15. *Waivers:* full or partial for senior citizens.
APPLYING Open admission. *Options:* Common Application, early entrance. *Required:* school transcript, SAT I or ACT, TOEFL for international students. *Required for some:* 3 years of high school math and science, some high school foreign language. Test scores used for admission and counseling/placement. *Application deadline:* rolling. *Notification:* continuous.
APPLYING/TRANSFER *Required:* high school transcript, college transcript. *Required for some:* standardized test scores. *Application deadline:* rolling. *Notification:* continuous.
CONTACT Ms. Rebecca Parker, Director of Admissions, University of South Carolina at Lancaster, Lancaster, SC 29721-0889, 803-285-7471 Ext. 7073. *E-mail:* bparker@scarolina.edu. College video available.

UNIVERSITY OF SOUTH CAROLINA AT SUMTER
Sumter, South Carolina

UG Enrollment: 1,396	Tuition & Fees (SC Res): $1786
Application Deadline: 8/6	Room & Board: N/Avail

GENERAL State-supported, 2-year, coed. Part of University of South Carolina System. Awards transfer associate, terminal associate degrees. Founded 1966. *Setting:* 35-acre urban campus. *Total enrollment:* 1,396. *Faculty:* 73 (42 full-time, 67% with terminal degrees, 31 part-time).
ENROLLMENT PROFILE 1,396 students from 6 states and territories, 14 other countries. 62% women, 38% men, 48% part-time, 98% state residents, 26% transferred in, 69% have need-based financial aid, 31% have non-need-based financial aid, 1% international, 41% 25 or older, 1% Native American, 2% Hispanic, 19% African American, 2% Asian American.
FIRST-YEAR CLASS 168 total; 1,105 applied, 57% of whom enrolled. 15% from top 10% of their high school class, 41% from top quarter, 75% from top half. 1 valedictorian.
ACADEMIC PROGRAM Honor code. Calendar: semesters. 235 courses offered in 1995–96; average class size 17 in required courses. English as a second language program offered during academic year, services for LD students, advanced placement, Freshman Honors College, honors program, summer session for credit, part-time degree program (daytime, evenings, summer), adult/continuing education programs. Off-campus study at Central Carolina Technical College. ROTC: Army (c), Air Force (c).
GENERAL DEGREE REQUIREMENTS 60 semester hours; 3 semester hours of math, 7 semester hours of natural science for associate of art degree; 6 semester hours of math, 7 semester hours of natural science for associate of science degree; computer course (varies by major).
MAJORS Liberal arts/general studies, science.
LIBRARY University of South Carolina at Sumter Library with 45,736 books, 17,667 microform titles, 488 periodicals, 21 CD-ROMs, 1,756 records, tapes, and CDs.
COMPUTERS ON CAMPUS 210 computers for student use in computer center, computer labs, classrooms, library, student center provide access to main academic computer, e-mail, on-line services, Internet. Staffed computer lab on campus provides training in use of computers.
COLLEGE LIFE Orientation program (2 days, no cost). Choral group, student-run newspaper, radio station. 60% vote in student government elections. *Most popular organizations:* Association of African-American Students, Baptist Student Union, Student Education Association, Roller Hockey, Young Republicans. *Major annual events:* Opening Convocation, Alcohol Awareness Week Festival, Martin Luther King, Jr. Festivities. *Student services:* personal-psychological counseling. *Campus security:* late-night transport-escort service.
HOUSING College housing not available.
ATHLETICS Member NSCAA. *Intramural:* badminton, basketball, bowling, football, golf, racquetball, soccer, softball, table tennis (Ping-Pong), tennis, volleyball.
CAREER PLANNING *Placement office:* 1 part-time staff. *Director:* Ms. Susan Jarvie, Academic Advisor, 803-775-6341. *Services:* career counseling, job bank.
AFTER GRADUATION 68% of students completing a degree program in 1994–95 went directly on to further study.
EXPENSES FOR 1995–96 *Application fee:* $35. State resident tuition: $1786 full-time, $77 per semester hour part-time. Nonresident tuition: $4480 full-time, $187 per semester hour part-time.
FINANCIAL AID *College-administered undergrad aid 1995–96:* 141 need-based scholarships (average $1000), 60 non-need scholarships (average $600), low-interest long-term loans from external sources (average $2000), 56 Federal Work-Study (averaging $1624). *Acceptable forms:* CSS Financial Aid PROFILE, institutional, FAFSA. *Priority deadline:* 4/15. *Payment plan:* deferred payment. *Waivers:* full or partial for senior citizens.
APPLYING *Option:* midyear entrance. *Required:* school transcript, minimum 2.0 GPA, 3 years of high school math, 2 years of high school foreign language, SAT I or ACT, TOEFL for international students. Test scores used for admission and counseling/placement. *Application deadline:* 8/6.
APPLYING/TRANSFER *Required:* college transcript. *Required for some:* standardized test scores, high school transcript, 3 years of high school math, 2 years of high school foreign language. *Entrance:* moderately difficult. *Application deadline:* 8/6.
CONTACT Dr. William R. Ferrell III, Director of Enrollment Management, University of South Carolina at Sumter, 200 Miller Road, Sumter, SC 29150-2498, 803-775-6341. Electronic viewbook available.

UNIVERSITY OF SOUTH CAROLINA AT UNION
Union, South Carolina

UG Enrollment: 400	Tuition & Fees (SC Res): $1786
Application Deadline: rolling	Room & Board: N/Avail

GENERAL State-supported, 2-year, coed. Part of University of South Carolina System. Awards transfer associate degrees. Founded 1965. *Setting:* small-town campus. *Total enrollment:* 400. *Faculty:* 34 (18 full-time, 16 part-time); student-faculty ratio is 10:1.
ENROLLMENT PROFILE 400 students: 72% women, 44% part-time, 97% state residents, 25% transferred in, 0% international, 48% 25 or older.
FIRST-YEAR CLASS 150 total; 200 applied, 100% were accepted, 75% of whom enrolled.
ACADEMIC PROGRAM Calendar: semesters. Part-time degree program (daytime, evenings).
GENERAL DEGREE REQUIREMENTS 60 semester hours; 3 semester hours each of math and science for associate of arts degree; 6 semester hours each of math and science for associate of science degree.
MAJORS Liberal arts/general studies, science.
COMPUTERS ON CAMPUS 30 computers for student use in computer labs, library.
COLLEGE LIFE *Social organizations:* 12 open to all.
HOUSING College housing not available.
EXPENSES FOR 1995–96 *Application fee:* $25. State resident tuition: $1786 full-time, $77 per semester hour part-time. Nonresident tuition: $4480 full-time, $187 per semester hour part-time.
FINANCIAL AID *College-administered undergrad aid 1995–96:* need-based scholarships, non-need scholarships, short-term loans, low-interest long-term loans from external sources, Federal Work-Study. *Acceptable forms:* CSS Financial Aid PROFILE. *Priority deadline:* 6/15.
APPLYING Open admission. *Required:* school transcript, SAT I or ACT. *Application deadline:* rolling.
APPLYING/TRANSFER *Required:* high school transcript, college transcript. *Required for some:* standardized test scores. *Contact:* Mr. Terry E. Young, Enrollment Manager, 803-429-8728.
CONTACT Mr. Terry E. Young, Enrollment Manager, University of South Carolina at Union, Union, SC 29379-0729, 803-429-8728.

UNIVERSITY OF SOUTH CAROLINA SALKEHATCHIE REGIONAL CAMPUS
Allendale, South Carolina

UG Enrollment: 908	Tuition & Fees (SC Res): $1786
Application Deadline: rolling	Room & Board: N/Avail

GENERAL State-supported, 2-year, coed. Part of University of South Carolina System. Awards transfer associate degrees. Founded 1965. *Setting:* 95-acre rural campus. *Research spending 1994–95:* $12,000. *Educational spending 1994–95:* $1660 per undergrad. *Total enrollment:* 908. *Faculty:* 40 (18 full-time, 40% with terminal degrees, 22 part-time).
ENROLLMENT PROFILE 908 students from 4 states and territories, 3 other countries. 65% women, 35% men, 54% part-time, 98% state residents, 10% transferred in, 1% international, 32% 25 or older, 0% Native American, 0% Hispanic, 35% African American, 0% Asian American. *Areas of study chosen:* 100% liberal arts/general studies.
FIRST-YEAR CLASS 176 total; 221 applied, 100% were accepted, 80% of whom enrolled. 10% from top 10% of their high school class, 20% from top quarter, 60% from top half.

South Carolina

University of South Carolina Salkehatchie Regional Campus *(continued)*
ACADEMIC PROGRAM Core, interdisciplinary curriculum, honor code. Calendar: semesters. 400 courses offered in 1995–96. Academic remediation for entering students, advanced placement, self-designed majors, summer session for credit, part-time degree program (daytime, evenings), adult/continuing education programs.
GENERAL DEGREE REQUIREMENTS 60 semester hours; 3 semester hours each of analytical reasoning and science.
MAJORS Liberal arts/general studies, mathematics, science.
LIBRARY Salkehatchie Learning Resource Center with 30,800 books, 300 periodicals, 1 on-line bibliographic service, 600 records, tapes, and CDs. Acquisition spending 1994–95: $56,436.
COMPUTERS ON CAMPUS 70 computers for student use in computer center, computer labs, library provide access to e-mail, Internet. Staffed computer lab on campus provides training in use of computers, software. Academic computing expenditure 1994–95: $67,595.
COLLEGE LIFE Student-run newspaper. *Social organizations:* 3 open to all. *Most popular organizations:* Student Government Association, Minority Student Organization, Gamma Beta Phi. *Major annual event:* Feast Day. *Campus security:* 24-hour emergency response devices.
HOUSING College housing not available.
ATHLETICS Member NJCAA. *Intercollegiate:* golf M. *Intramural:* basketball, football, tennis, volleyball. *Contact:* Mr. Joe Baxter, Athletic Director, 803-584-3446.
CAREER PLANNING *Service:* career counseling.
AFTER GRADUATION 60% of students completing a degree program in 1994–95 went directly on to further study.
EXPENSES FOR 1995–96 *Application fee:* $25. State resident tuition: $1786 full-time, $77 per semester hour part-time. Nonresident tuition: $4480 full-time, $187 per semester hour part-time.
FINANCIAL AID *College-administered undergrad aid 1995–96:* need-based scholarships, non-need scholarships, low-interest long-term loans from external sources (average $2652), 59 Federal Work-Study (averaging $1243), 46 part-time jobs. *Required forms:* institutional; accepted: CSS Financial Aid PROFILE, FAFSA. *Priority deadline:* 4/15. *Waivers:* full or partial for senior citizens. *Notification:* 6/1.
APPLYING Open admission. *Option:* midyear entrance. *Required:* school transcript, minimum 2.0 GPA, 3 years of high school math and science, 2 years of high school foreign language, SAT I or ACT, TOEFL for international students. Test scores used for counseling/placement. *Application deadline:* rolling.
APPLYING/TRANSFER *Required:* college transcript, minimum 2.0 college GPA. *Entrance:* noncompetitive. *Application deadline:* rolling. *Contact:* Ms. Jane T. Brewer, Associate Dean for Student Services, 803-584-3446.
CONTACT Ms. Jane T. Brewer, Associate Dean for Student Services, University of South Carolina Salkehatchie Regional Campus, PO Box 617, Allendale, SC 29810-0617, 803-584-3446 or toll-free 800-922-5500 (in-state). College video available.

WILLIAMSBURG TECHNICAL COLLEGE
Kingstree, South Carolina

UG Enrollment: 625	Tuition & Fees: $768
Application Deadline: rolling	Room & Board: N/Avail

GENERAL State-supported, 2-year, coed. Part of South Carolina State Board for Technical and Comprehensive Education. Awards certificates, diplomas, transfer associate, terminal associate degrees. Founded 1969. *Setting:* 41-acre rural campus. *Endowment:* $32,021. *Educational spending 1994–95:* $1268 per undergrad. *Total enrollment:* 625. *Faculty:* 42 (10 full-time, 1% with terminal degrees, 32 part-time).
ENROLLMENT PROFILE 625 students: 77% women, 23% men, 77% part-time, 100% state residents, 1% transferred in, 0% international, 60% 25 or older, 0% Native American, 1% Hispanic, 54% African American, 1% Asian American. *Areas of study chosen:* 40% fine arts, 8% interdisciplinary studies.
FIRST-YEAR CLASS 116 total; 268 applied, 100% were accepted, 43% of whom enrolled. 10% from top 10% of their high school class, 25% from top quarter, 65% from top half.
ACADEMIC PROGRAM Core, honor code. Calendar: semesters. 405 courses offered in 1995–96. Academic remediation for entering students, services for LD students, advanced placement, self-designed majors, honors program, summer session for credit, part-time degree program (daytime, evenings, summer), adult/continuing education programs.
GENERAL DEGREE REQUIREMENTS 60 semester hours; computer course.
MAJORS Business administration/commerce/management, engineering technology, liberal arts/general studies, science, secretarial studies/office management.
LIBRARY 24,115 books, 30 microform titles, 113 periodicals, 14 CD-ROMs, 1,277 records, tapes, and CDs. Acquisition spending 1994–95: $44,089.
COMPUTERS ON CAMPUS 60 computers for student use in computer center, computer labs, library, student center provide access to main academic computer, e-mail, Internet. Staffed computer lab on campus provides training in use of computers, software. Academic computing expenditure 1994–95: $128,736.
COLLEGE LIFE Choral group, student-run newspaper. 50% vote in student government elections. *Social organizations:* 9 open to all; 2 national fraternities, 2 national sororities; 30% of eligible men and 30% of eligible women are members. *Most popular organizations:* Student Government Association, National Vocational-Technical Honor Society, Phi Theta Kappa International Honor Society. *Major annual events:* Tech Fest, Ms. Tech Pageant, Christmas Party. *Student services:* personal-psychological counseling, women's center. *Campus security:* late-night transport-escort service.
HOUSING College housing not available.
ATHLETICS *Intramural:* badminton, basketball, cross-country running, gymnastics, softball, volleyball. *Contact:* Mr. Donald W. Melton, Admissions Coordinator, 803-354-2021 Ext. 162; Mrs. Lynn A. Selph, Dean of Student Services, 803-354-2021 Ext. 170.
CAREER PLANNING *Placement office:* 1 full-time, 1 part-time staff. *Director:* Mr. Donald W. Melton, Admissions Coordinator, 803-354-2021 Ext. 162. *Services:* job fairs, resume preparation, career counseling, careers library, job bank, job interviews. Students must register freshman year. 30 organizations recruited on campus 1994–95.
AFTER GRADUATION 70% of class of 1994 had job offers within 6 months. 23% of students completing a degree program went directly on to further study.
EXPENSES FOR 1996–97 *Application fee:* $10. Tuition: $768 full-time, $32 per semester hour part-time.
FINANCIAL AID *College-administered undergrad aid 1995–96:* 131 need-based scholarships (averaging $100), 3 non-need scholarships (averaging $748), 41 Federal Work-Study (averaging $1600), part-time jobs. *Required forms:* institutional, FAFSA. *Priority deadline:* 8/15. *Payment plan:* deferred payment. *Waivers:* full or partial for senior citizens. *Notification:* continuous.
APPLYING Open admission. *Options:* early entrance, deferred entrance, midyear entrance. *Required:* ACT COMPASS. *Recommended:* SAT I. Test scores used for counseling/placement. *Application deadline:* rolling. *Notification:* continuous until 9/1.
APPLYING/TRANSFER *Application deadline:* rolling. *Notification:* continuous until 9/1. *Contact:* Mr. Donald W. Melton, Admissions Coordinator, 803-354-2021 Ext. 162.
CONTACT Mr. Donald W. Melton, Admissions Coordinator, Williamsburg Technical College, Kingstree, SC 29556-4197, 803-354-2021 Ext. 162 or toll-free 800-768-2021. *Fax:* 803-354-7269.

YORK TECHNICAL COLLEGE
Rock Hill, South Carolina

UG Enrollment: 3,342	Tuition & Fees (Area Res): $1085
Application Deadline: rolling	Room & Board: N/Avail

GENERAL State-supported, 2-year, coed. Part of South Carolina State Board for Technical and Comprehensive Education. Awards certificates, diplomas, transfer associate, terminal associate degrees. Founded 1961. *Setting:* 110-acre small-town campus. *Total enrollment:* 3,342. *Faculty:* 236 (93 full-time, 98% with terminal degrees, 143 part-time).
ENROLLMENT PROFILE 3,342 students: 61% women, 39% men, 57% part-time, 99% state residents, 5% transferred in, 46% have need-based financial aid, 0% international, 47% 25 or older, 1% Native American, 1% Hispanic, 19% African American, 1% Asian American.
FIRST-YEAR CLASS 690 total.
ACADEMIC PROGRAM Core, honor code. Calendar: semesters. 58 courses offered in 1995–96. Academic remediation for entering students, services for LD students, advanced placement, summer session for credit, part-time degree program (daytime, evenings, summer), adult/continuing education programs, co-op programs and internships. Off-campus study at Charlotte Area Educational Consortium.
GENERAL DEGREE REQUIREMENTS 62 semester hours; 3 semester hours of math; computer course for most majors.
MAJORS Accounting, automotive technologies, business administration/commerce/management, child psychology/child development, civil engineering technology, computer programming, computer technologies, dental services, drafting and design, electrical and electronics technologies, electromechanical technology, electronics engineering technology, engineering technology, heating/refrigeration/air conditioning, industrial administration, industrial and heavy equipment maintenance, industrial engineering technology, liberal arts/general studies, machine and tool technologies, mechanical engineering technology, medical laboratory technology, nursing, operating room technology, radiological technology, science, secretarial studies/office management, welding technology.
LIBRARY Ann Springs Close Library with 26,947 books, 286 periodicals, 13 CD-ROMs, 2,785 records, tapes, and CDs.
COMPUTERS ON CAMPUS 180 computers for student use in computer center, computer labs, learning resource center, library provide access to Internet. Staffed computer lab on campus provides training in use of computers, software.
COLLEGE LIFE Choral group, student-run newspaper. *Major annual event:* Tech Fest. *Student services:* personal-psychological counseling, women's center. *Campus security:* 24-hour patrols.
HOUSING College housing not available.
CAREER PLANNING *Services:* job fairs, resume preparation, resume referral, career counseling, careers library, job bank, job interviews.
EXPENSES FOR 1995–96 Area resident tuition: $1085 full-time, $35 per semester hour part-time. State resident tuition: $1302 full-time, $42 per semester hour part-time. Nonresident tuition: $2170 full-time, $70 per semester hour part-time.
FINANCIAL AID *College-administered undergrad aid 1995–96:* 185 need-based scholarships (averaging $1050), 38 non-need scholarships (averaging $775), Federal Work-Study. *Required forms:* institutional, FAFSA. *Priority deadline:* 7/1. *Waivers:* full or partial for senior citizens. *Notification:* continuous.
APPLYING Open admission. *Option:* midyear entrance. *Required:* TOEFL for international students, SAT I, ACT, or ACT ASSET. Test scores used for admission and counseling/placement. *Application deadline:* rolling. *Notification:* continuous.
APPLYING/TRANSFER *Entrance:* noncompetitive. *Application deadline:* rolling. *Notification:* continuous.
CONTACT Mr. Kenny Aldridge, Admissions Department Manager, York Technical College, Rock Hill, SC 29730-3395, 803-327-8008 Ext. 8223 or toll-free 800-922-8324 (in-state). *Fax:* 803-327-8059. College video available.

SOUTH DAKOTA

[Map showing South Dakota with locations: Sisseton-Wahpeton Comm Coll, Southeast Tech Inst, Central Indian Bible Coll, Lake Area Vo-Tech Inst, Western Dakota Tech Inst, Rapid City, Pierre, Mitchell Tech Inst, Sioux Falls, Kilian Comm Coll, Nettleton Career Coll]

CENTRAL INDIAN BIBLE COLLEGE
Mobridge, South Dakota

UG Enrollment: 25	Tuition & Fees: $1050
Application Deadline: 7/31	Room & Board: $1000

GENERAL Independent, 2-year, coed, affiliated with Assemblies of God. Awards diplomas, transfer associate, terminal associate degrees. Founded 1970. *Setting:* 12-acre small-town campus. *Total enrollment:* 25. *Faculty:* 6 (5 full-time, 1 part-time).
ENROLLMENT PROFILE 25 students: 50% women, 3% transferred in, 100% have need-based financial aid, 0% have non-need-based financial aid, 0% international, 95% 25 or older, 82% Native American, 0% Hispanic, 0% African American, 0% Asian American.
FIRST-YEAR CLASS 4 total.
ACADEMIC PROGRAM Honor code. Calendar: semesters. Part-time degree program (daytime).
GENERAL DEGREE REQUIREMENT 64 credits.
MAJOR Biblical studies.
COLLEGE LIFE *Campus security:* controlled dormitory access.
HOUSING 200 college housing spaces available; 8 were occupied 1995–96. Freshmen guaranteed college housing. On-campus residence required in freshman year. *Option:* single-sex (2 buildings) housing available.
EXPENSES FOR 1995–96 Comprehensive fee of $2050 includes full-time tuition ($1050) and college room and board ($1000). College room only: $600. Tuition guaranteed not to increase for student's term of enrollment.
FINANCIAL AID *College-administered undergrad aid 1995–96:* need-based scholarships, low-interest long-term loans from external sources, Federal Work-Study. *Required forms:* institutional, FAFSA. *Priority deadline:* 5/1. *Payment plan:* installment. *Waivers:* full or partial for employees or children of employees. *Notification:* continuous.
APPLYING *Options:* deferred entrance, midyear entrance. *Required:* school transcript. *Application deadline:* 7/31.
APPLYING/TRANSFER *Required:* high school transcript. *Entrance:* noncompetitive. *Application deadline:* 7/31.
CONTACT Ms. Kathleen Wadhams, Interim Admissions and Recruitment Officer, Central Indian Bible College, Mobridge, SD 57601, 605-845-7801.

KILIAN COMMUNITY COLLEGE
Sioux Falls, South Dakota

UG Enrollment: 202	Tuition & Fees: $4700
Application Deadline: rolling	Room & Board: N/Avail

GENERAL Independent, 2-year, coed. Awards certificates, transfer associate, terminal associate degrees. Founded 1977. *Setting:* 1-acre urban campus. *Endowment:* $1510. *Educational spending 1994–95:* $1189 per undergrad. *Total enrollment:* 202. *Faculty:* 75 (3 full-time, 100% with terminal degrees, 72 part-time).
ENROLLMENT PROFILE 202 students from 3 states and territories. 67% women, 33% men, 64% part-time, 97% state residents, 22% transferred in, 90% have need-based financial aid, 10% have non-need-based financial aid, 62% 25 or older, 13% Native American, 0% Hispanic, 2% African American, 1% Asian American. *Areas of study chosen:* 30% health professions and related sciences, 22% business management and administrative services, 17% vocational and home economics, 16% interdisciplinary studies, 9% computer and information sciences, 6% liberal arts/general studies. *Most popular recent majors:* criminal justice, human services, legal secretarial studies.
FIRST-YEAR CLASS 42 total; 47 applied, 100% were accepted, 89% of whom enrolled.
ACADEMIC PROGRAM Core, comprehensive curriculum, honor code. Calendar: trimesters. 250 courses offered in 1995–96. Academic remediation for entering students, English as a second language program offered during academic year, services for LD students, tutorials, summer session for credit, part-time degree program (daytime, evenings, weekends, summer), external degree programs, adult/continuing education programs, co-op programs and internships.

GENERAL DEGREE REQUIREMENTS 60 credit hours; 1 math course; computer course; internship (some majors).
MAJORS Accounting, business administration/commerce/management, computer science, computer technologies, criminal justice, fire science, human services, interdisciplinary studies, legal secretarial studies, legal studies, medical secretarial studies, secretarial studies/office management, word processing.
LIBRARY University of Sioux Falls Mears Library with 78,000 books, 590 microform titles, 395 periodicals, 4,785 records, tapes, and CDs. Acquisition spending 1994–95: $5000.
COMPUTERS ON CAMPUS 30 computers for student use in computer labs, classrooms, library provide access to off-campus computing facilities, on-line services. Staffed computer lab on campus. Academic computing expenditure 1994–95: $16,993.
COLLEGE LIFE *Social organizations:* 1 open to all. *Campus security:* late-night transport-escort service.
HOUSING College housing not available.
CAREER PLANNING *Placement office:* 2 full-time staff; $35,000 operating expenditure 1994–95. *Director:* Ms. Sandy Garber, Director of Student Services, 605-336-1711. *Services:* job fairs, resume preparation, career counseling, careers library, job bank, job interviews. 1 organization recruited on campus 1994–95.
AFTER GRADUATION 88% of class of 1994 had job offers within 6 months. 10% of students completing a degree program went directly on to further study.
EXPENSES FOR 1995–96 *Application fee:* $25. Tuition: $4500 full-time, $125 per credit hour part-time. Part-time mandatory fees: $100 per year. Full-time mandatory fees: $200.
FINANCIAL AID *College-administered undergrad aid 1995–96:* 120 need-based scholarships (average $140), 20 non-need scholarships (average $150), low-interest long-term loans from external sources (average $3400), 8 Federal Work-Study (averaging $1000), 1 part-time job. *Required forms:* institutional, FAFSA; required for some: state; accepted: CSS Financial Aid PROFILE. *Priority deadline:* 6/1. *Payment plans:* installment, deferred payment. *Waivers:* full or partial for employees or children of employees and senior citizens. *Average indebtedness of graduates:* $5000.
APPLYING Open admission. *Options:* early entrance, deferred entrance, midyear entrance. *Required:* school transcript. *Required for some:* TOEFL for international students. Test scores used for counseling/placement. *Application deadline:* rolling.
APPLYING/TRANSFER *Required:* high school transcript. *Recommended:* college transcript, minimum 2.0 college GPA. *Entrance:* noncompetitive. *Application deadline:* rolling. *Contact:* Ms. LeAnne Van Regenmorter, Registrar, 605-336-1711.
CONTACT Ms. Sandy Garber, Director of Student Services, Kilian Community College, 224 North Phillips Avenue, Sioux Falls, SD 57102, 605-336-1711 or toll-free 800-888-1147 (in-state). *Fax:* 605-336-2606. College video available.

LAKE AREA VOCATIONAL-TECHNICAL INSTITUTE
Watertown, South Dakota

UG Enrollment: 1,044	Tuition & Fees: $2110
Application Deadline: N/R	Room & Board: N/Avail

GENERAL State-supported, 2-year, coed. Awards diplomas, transfer associate, terminal associate degrees. Founded 1964. *Setting:* 16-acre small-town campus. *Total enrollment:* 1,044. *Faculty:* 65; student-faculty ratio is 15:1.
ENROLLMENT PROFILE 1,044 students.
FIRST-YEAR CLASS 654 total; 800 applied, 84% were accepted, 97% of whom enrolled.
ACADEMIC PROGRAM Core. Calendar: semesters. Academic remediation for entering students.
GENERAL DEGREE REQUIREMENT 70 credits.
MAJORS Accounting, agricultural business, automotive technologies, aviation technology, biotechnology, carpentry, child psychology/child development, computer programming, cosmetology, dental services, drafting and design, electronics engineering technology, finance/banking, human services, machine and tool technologies, marketing/retailing/merchandising, medical assistant technologies, medical laboratory technology, occupational therapy, physical therapy, practical nursing, secretarial studies/office management, welding technology.
COMPUTERS ON CAMPUS 150 computers for student use in computer center, computer labs, learning resource center, library provide access to main academic computer, Internet. Staffed computer lab on campus provides training in use of computers, software.
HOUSING College housing not available.
CAREER PLANNING *Director:* Ms. Sue Bogen, Placement Coordinator, 605-882-5284. *Services:* job fairs, resume preparation, resume referral, career counseling, job bank.
AFTER GRADUATION 95% of class of 1994 had job offers within 6 months.
EXPENSES FOR 1996–97 Tuition: $1800 (minimum) full-time, $50 per credit part-time. Full-time tuition ranges up to $2400. Full-time mandatory fees: $310 (minimum).
FINANCIAL AID *College-administered undergrad aid 1995–96:* 150 need-based scholarships (averaging $500), 25 non-need scholarships (averaging $250), short-term loans (averaging $100), low-interest long-term loans from external sources (averaging $2500), 200 Federal Work-Study (averaging $600), part-time jobs. *Required forms:* FAFSA. *Priority deadline:* 5/1.
APPLYING *Option:* electronic application. *Required:* school transcript. *Required for some:* ACT. Test scores used for admission.
APPLYING/TRANSFER *Required:* high school transcript. *Required for some:* standardized test scores. *Entrance:* minimally difficult.
CONTACT Ms. Debra Shephard, Assistant Director, Lake Area Vocational-Technical Institute, Watertown, SD 57201, 605-882-5284. *E-mail:* latiinfo@lati.tec.sd.us. College video available.

MITCHELL TECHNICAL INSTITUTE
Mitchell, South Dakota

Enrollment: N/R	Tuition & Fees: $2856
Application Deadline: rolling	Room & Board: N/Avail

GENERAL District-supported, 2-year, specialized, coed. Awards certificates, diplomas, transfer associate degrees. Founded 1968.
ACADEMIC PROGRAM Core. Calendar: semesters.
GENERAL DEGREE REQUIREMENTS 60 credits; computer course.

South Dakota

Mitchell Technical Institute (continued)
MAJORS Accounting, agricultural technologies.
EXPENSES FOR 1996-97 *Application fee:* $25. Tuition: $1500 (minimum) full-time. Part-time tuition per credit ranges from $50 to $64. Part-time mandatory fees: $678 per semester. Full-time tuition ranges up to $1900 according to program. Full-time mandatory fees: $1356 (minimum).
APPLYING *Required:* school transcript, ACT, TABE. *Recommended:* minimum 2.0 GPA. *Application deadline:* rolling. *Notification:* continuous.
APPLYING/TRANSFER *Required:* standardized test scores, college transcript. *Application deadline. Notification:* continuous.
CONTACT Mr. Lance Carter, Director of Admissions, Mitchell Technical Institute, Mitchell, SD 57301, 605-995-3024.

NETTLETON CAREER COLLEGE
Sioux Falls, South Dakota

UG Enrollment: 134	Tuition: $11,500/deg prog
Application Deadline: rolling	Room & Board: N/Avail

GENERAL Proprietary, 2-year, coed. Awards terminal associate degrees. Founded 1919. *Setting:* 1-acre urban campus. *Total enrollment:* 134. *Faculty:* 18 (7 full-time, 100% with terminal degrees, 11 part-time). *Notable Alumni:* Rick Knobe, former mayor; Gene Rieholt, former college owner; Jerry Noonan, business owner; Deb Ludens Jorgensen, retail store manager.
ENROLLMENT PROFILE 134 students from 5 states and territories, 2 other countries. 78% women, 9% part-time, 60% state residents, 36% transferred in, 78% have need-based financial aid, 10% have non-need-based financial aid, 4% international, 30% 25 or older, 1% Native American, 0% Hispanic, 3% African American, 1% Asian American. *Areas of study chosen:* 51% business management and administrative services, 24% health professions and related sciences, 18% prelaw, 7% computer and information sciences.
FIRST-YEAR CLASS 58 total; 250 applied, 90% were accepted, 26% of whom enrolled. 0% from top 10% of their high school class, 2% from top quarter, 3% from top half.
ACADEMIC PROGRAM Core. Calendar: quarters. Academic remediation for entering students, tutorials, part-time degree program (daytime, evenings, weekends), co-op programs and internships.
GENERAL DEGREE REQUIREMENTS 96 credits; math/science requirements vary according to program; computer course; internship (some majors).
MAJORS Accounting, business administration/commerce/management, computer information systems, data processing, fashion merchandising, medical assistant technologies, paralegal studies, secretarial studies/office management, tourism and travel.
LIBRARY Learning Resource Center with 10,000 books, 1 microform title, 75 periodicals, 1 on-line bibliographic service, 200 records, tapes, and CDs.
COMPUTERS ON CAMPUS 45 computers for student use in computer labs, research center, learning resource center, classrooms, library, student rooms. Staffed computer lab on campus provides training in use of computers, software.
COLLEGE LIFE *Social organizations:* 1 open to all. *Most popular organization:* Student Senate. *Major annual event:* Graduation.
HOUSING College housing not available.
CAREER PLANNING *Placement office:* 1 full-time staff. *Director:* Ms. Gladys Daniels, Placement Director, 605-336-1837. *Services:* job fairs, resume preparation, career counseling, job bank, job interviews.
EXPENSES FOR 1995–96 Tuition per degree program ranges from $11,500 to $14,640. Full-time mandatory fees: $25. Tuition guaranteed not to increase for student's term of enrollment.
FINANCIAL AID *College-administered undergrad aid 1995–96:* 200 need-based scholarships (average $300), non-need scholarships, low-interest long-term loans from external sources (average $2625), Federal Work-Study. *Required forms:* institutional, FAFSA. *Application deadline:* continuous. *Waivers:* full or partial for employees or children of employees.
APPLYING *Options:* deferred entrance, midyear entrance. *Required:* school transcript, interview, SAT I, SAT II Subject Tests, CPAt. Test scores used for admission. *Application deadline:* rolling.
APPLYING/TRANSFER *Required:* standardized test scores, high school transcript, interview, college transcript. *Entrance:* minimally difficult. *Application deadline:* rolling. *Contact:* Mr. Richard Odens, Academic Dean, 605-336-1837.
CONTACT Ms. Pam Baccus, Director of Admissions, Nettleton Career College, 100 South Spring Avenue, Sioux Falls, SD 57104, 605-336-1837 or toll-free 800-727-1837. *Fax:* 605-336-7626.

SISSETON-WAHPETON COMMUNITY COLLEGE
Sisseton, South Dakota

UG Enrollment: 224	Tuition & Fees: $2750
Application Deadline: rolling	Room & Board: N/Avail

GENERAL Federally supported, 2-year, coed. Awards certificates, transfer associate, terminal associate degrees. Founded 1979. *Setting:* 2-acre rural campus. *Endowment:* $134,448. *Total enrollment:* 224. *Faculty:* 28 (13 full-time, 15 part-time); student-faculty ratio is 10:1. *Notable Alumni:* Elden Lawrence, dean of instruction at Sisseton-Wahpeton Community College; Nancy Harles, associate professor at University of North Dakota; Gene Heminga, tenant services coordinator; Nola DuMarce, nursing instructor.
ENROLLMENT PROFILE 224 students from 2 states and territories, 2 other countries. 58% women, 25% part-time, 3% transferred in, 75% 25 or older, 70% Native American.
FIRST-YEAR CLASS 55 total; 78 applied, 100% were accepted, 71% of whom enrolled. 5% from top quarter of their high school class, 5% from top half.
ACADEMIC PROGRAM Core, interdisciplinary curriculum, honor code. Calendar: semesters. 183 courses offered in 1995-96. Academic remediation for entering students, summer session for credit, part-time degree program (daytime, summer), adult/continuing education programs, internships. Off-campus study at members of the American Indian Higher Education Consortium.

GENERAL DEGREE REQUIREMENTS 64 semester credits; 1 semester each of college algebra and natural science; 1 semester of Dakota; computer course; internship (some majors).
MAJORS Accounting, business administration/commerce/management, carpentry, computer information systems, drug and alcohol/substance abuse counseling, early childhood education, electrical and electronics technologies, hospitality services, liberal arts/general studies, Native American studies, natural sciences, nursing, plumbing.
LIBRARY Sisseton-Wahpeton Community College Library with 8,000 books, 155 periodicals, 2 on-line bibliographic services, 6 CD-ROMs, 340 records, tapes, and CDs. Acquisition spending 1994-95: $12,250.
COMPUTERS ON CAMPUS 26 computers for student use in computer center, learning resource center, library provide access to e-mail, Internet. Staffed computer lab on campus provides training in use of computers. Academic computing expenditure 1994–95: $106,157.
NOTEWORTHY RESEARCH FACILITIES Institute for Dakota Studies.
COLLEGE LIFE 50% vote in student government elections. *Social organizations:* 1 open to all. *Most popular organization:* Student Senate. *Major annual event:* Dakota Awareness Days. *Student services:* personal-psychological counseling. *Campus security:* 24-hour emergency response devices.
HOUSING College housing not available.
CAREER PLANNING *Placement office:* 1 full-time, 1 part-time staff; $15,000 operating expenditure 1994–95. *Director:* Ms. Susan Brooks, Librarian, 605-698-3966. *Services:* resume preparation, career counseling, careers library.
AFTER GRADUATION 65% of class of 1994 had job offers within 6 months.
EXPENSES FOR 1995–96 Tuition: $2400 full-time, $80 per semester hour part-time. Part-time mandatory fees: $40 per semester hour. Full-time mandatory fees: $350.
FINANCIAL AID *College-administered undergrad aid 1995–96:* 26 need-based scholarships (average $650), 12 non-need scholarships (average $300), low-interest long-term loans from external sources (average $2625), Federal Work-Study. *Required forms:* institutional, FAFSA; required for some: affidavit of nonsupport. *Priority deadline:* 8/1. *Payment plan:* installment. *Waivers:* full or partial for employees or children of employees and senior citizens.
APPLYING Open admission. *Option:* midyear entrance. *Required:* school transcript, Assessment and Placement Services for Community Colleges. *Recommended:* minimum 2.0 GPA, 3 years of high school math and science, some high school foreign language, recommendations, interview. Test scores used for counseling/placement. *Application deadline:* rolling.
APPLYING/TRANSFER *Required:* high school transcript, college transcript. *Recommended:* standardized test scores, 3 years of high school math and science, some high school foreign language, recommendations, interview, minimum 2.0 college GPA, minimum 2.0 high school GPA. *Entrance:* noncompetitive. *Contact:* Mr. William R. Montgomery, Director of Student Services, 605-698-3966.
CONTACT Ms. Darlene Redday, Registrar, Sisseton-Wahpeton Community College, Sisseton, SD 57262-0689, 605-698-3966 Ext. 10. *E-mail:* william@daknet.com.

SOUTHEAST TECHNICAL INSTITUTE
Sioux Falls, South Dakota

UG Enrollment: 2,581	Tuition & Fees: $1944
Application Deadline: N/R	Room & Board: N/Avail

GENERAL State-supported, 2-year, coed. Awards transfer associate degrees. *Setting:* urban campus. *Total enrollment:* 2,581. *Faculty:* 105.
ENROLLMENT PROFILE 2,581 students.
FIRST-YEAR CLASS 600 total. Of the students who applied, 90% were accepted.
ACADEMIC PROGRAM Calendar: semesters.
GENERAL DEGREE REQUIREMENTS 62 credits; math/science requirements vary according to program; computer course.
MAJORS Business administration/commerce/management, engineering technology, graphic arts, health science.
EXPENSES FOR 1996-97 Tuition: $1550 full-time, $50 per credit part-time. Part-time mandatory fees: $26.25 per credit. Full-time mandatory fees: $394.
APPLYING/TRANSFER *Required:* college transcript.
CONTACT Mr. Darrell Borgen, Head of Student Services, Southeast Technical Institute, 2301 Career Place, Sioux Falls, SD 57107, 605-367-7624 Ext. 263.

WESTERN DAKOTA TECHNICAL INSTITUTE
Rapid City, South Dakota

UG Enrollment: 842	Tuition & Fees: $1800
Application Deadline: 8/1	Room & Board: N/Avail

GENERAL State-supported, 2-year, coed. Awards certificates, diplomas, terminal associate degrees. Founded 1968. *Setting:* 5-acre small-town campus. *Educational spending 1994–95:* $2961 per undergrad. *Total enrollment:* 842. *Faculty:* 88 (48 full-time, 40 part-time).
ENROLLMENT PROFILE 842 students from 8 states and territories. 50% women, 50% men, 17% part-time, 92% state residents, 24% transferred in, 72% have need-based financial aid, 9% have non-need-based financial aid, 0% international, 38% 25 or older, 9% Native American, 1% Hispanic, 1% African American, 1% Asian American. *Areas of study chosen:* 17% business management and administrative services, 7% agriculture, 4% computer and information sciences. *Most popular recent major:* drafting and design.
FIRST-YEAR CLASS 684 applied, 75% were accepted.
ACADEMIC PROGRAM Core, technical curriculum, honor code. Calendar: semesters. 341 courses offered in 1995-96; average class size 20 in required courses. Academic remediation for entering students, English as a second language program, services for LD students, advanced placement, summer session for credit, part-time degree program (daytime, evenings), internships.
GENERAL DEGREE REQUIREMENTS 71 credits; 1 math course; computer course (varies by major); internship.
MAJORS Accounting, agricultural business, automotive technologies, business administration/commerce/management, drafting and design, electrical and electronics

technologies, equestrian studies, farm and ranch management, law enforcement/police sciences, medical records services, paralegal studies, secretarial studies/office management.
LIBRARY Western Dakota Technical Institute Media Center with 6,238 books, 14 microform titles, 120 periodicals, 2 on-line bibliographic services, 12 CD-ROMs, 20 records, tapes, and CDs. Acquisition spending 1994–95: $11,442.
COMPUTERS ON CAMPUS 120 computers for student use in computer labs, learning resource center, classrooms, library provide access to software. Staffed computer lab on campus provides training in use of computers, software. Academic computing expenditure 1994–95: $22,337.
COLLEGE LIFE Orientation program (4 days, $50). *Social organizations:* 3 open to all. *Most popular organizations:* Student Council, Rodeo Club, Ski Club. *Major annual events:* Christmas Party with Santa, Fall Picnic, Valentine Carnation/Candy Day. *Student services:* personal-psychological counseling.
HOUSING College housing not available.
CAREER PLANNING *Placement office:* 1 full-time staff; $42,061 operating expenditure 1994–95. *Director:* Mr. Bruce Lail, Placement Coordinator, 605-394-4034 Ext. 102. *Services:* resume referral, career counseling, job bank, job interviews. 12 organizations recruited on campus 1994–95.
AFTER GRADUATION 90% of class of 1994 had job offers within 6 months. 4% of students completing a degree program went directly on to further study.

EXPENSES FOR 1995–96 *Application fee:* $10. Tuition: $1800 full-time. One-time mandatory fee: $807.
FINANCIAL AID *College-administered undergrad aid 1995–96:* 90 need-based scholarships (average $450), 6 non-need scholarships (average $500), short-term loans (average $25), 48 Federal Work-Study (averaging $750). *Required forms:* FAFSA; accepted: state, institutional. *Priority deadline:* 4/15. *Payment plan:* deferred payment. *Waivers:* full or partial for employees or children of employees.
APPLYING Open admission. *Options:* Common Application, midyear entrance. *Required:* essay, school transcript, TOEFL for international students, TABE. *Recommended:* minimum 2.0 GPA. *Required for some:* campus interview. Test scores used for counseling/placement. *Application deadline:* 8/1. *Notification:* continuous until 8/15.
APPLYING/TRANSFER *Required:* essay, standardized test scores, high school transcript, college transcript. *Recommended:* minimum 2.0 college GPA, minimum 2.0 high school GPA. *Required for some:* campus interview. *Entrance:* noncompetitive. *Application deadline:* 8/1. *Notification:* continuous until 8/15. *Contact:* Mr. Jeff Bailie, Admissions Counselor, 605-394-4034 Ext. 110.
CONTACT Mr. Jeff Bailie, Admissions Counselor, Western Dakota Technical Institute, 800 Mickelson Drive, Rapid City, SD 57701, 605-394-4034 Ext. 110 or toll-free 800-544-8765 (in-state).

TENNESSEE

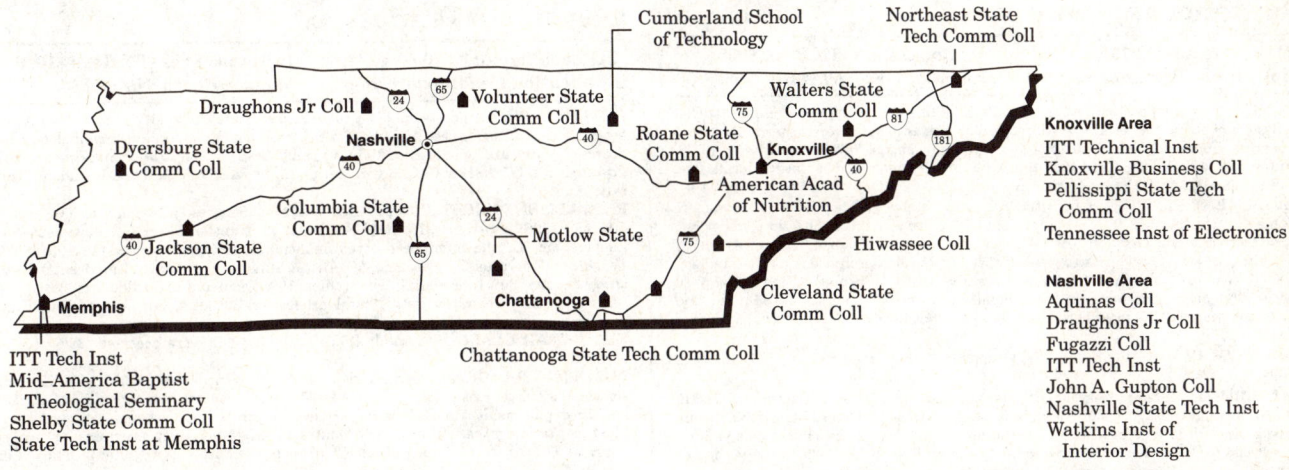

AMERICAN ACADEMY OF NUTRITION
Knoxville, Tennessee

UG Enrollment: 150	Tuition & Fees: $2570
Application Deadline: rolling	Room & Board: N/Avail

GENERAL Proprietary, 2-year, coed. Awards certificates, diplomas, transfer associate degrees (offers only external degree programs through home study). Founded 1984. *Setting:* suburban campus. *Research spending 1994–95:* $10,000. *Educational spending 1994–95:* $1150 per undergrad. *Total enrollment:* 150. *Faculty:* 5 (3 full-time, 100% with terminal degrees, 2 part-time). *Notable Alumni:* Dr. E. S. Kapadia, physician; Larry Brown, co-chairman of AT&T/IBEW training program; William P. Davenport, professor; Ze'ev Sieradski, rabbi.
ENROLLMENT PROFILE 150 students from 41 states and territories, 9 other countries. 83% women, 17% men, 91% part-time, 5% transferred in, 15% international, 87% 25 or older. *Areas of study chosen:* 100% health professions and related sciences.
FIRST-YEAR CLASS 75 total. Of the students accepted, 100% enrolled.
ACADEMIC PROGRAM Core, nutrition science curriculum, honor code. 22 courses offered in 1995–96. Academic remediation for entering students, self-designed majors, honors program, summer session for credit, part-time degree program (daytime, evenings, weekends, summer), external degree programs, adult/continuing education programs.
GENERAL DEGREE REQUIREMENTS 60 credit hours; 1 math course; 4 science courses.
MAJOR Nutrition.
COMPUTERS ON CAMPUS Academic computing expenditure 1994–95: $25,000.
EXPENSES FOR 1996–97 Tuition: $2570 full-time, $1285 per term part-time.
FINANCIAL AID *Payment plans:* tuition prepayment, installment.
APPLYING Open admission. *Options:* Common Application, electronic application, deferred entrance, midyear entrance. *Recommended:* minimum 2.0 GPA. *Required for some:* school transcript. *Application deadline:* rolling. *Notification:* continuous.
APPLYING/TRANSFER *Required:* minimum 2.0 college GPA. *Required for some:* high school transcript, college transcript. *Contact:* Dr. Wina Haynes, Registrar, 423-524-8079.

CONTACT Dr. Wina Haynes, Registrar, American Academy of Nutrition, Knoxville, TN 37919, 423-524-8079 or toll-free 800-290-4226. *Fax:* 423-524-6118. *E-mail:* aantn@aol.com. Electronic viewbook available.

AQUINAS COLLEGE
Nashville, Tennessee

UG Enrollment: 408	Tuition & Fees: $6050
Application Deadline: 7/31	Room & Board: N/Avail

GENERAL Independent Roman Catholic, 2-year, coed. Awards transfer associate, terminal associate degrees (bachelor's in elementary education only). Founded 1961. *Setting:* 90-acre suburban campus. *Total enrollment:* 408. *Faculty:* 41 (22 full-time, 19 part-time); student-faculty ratio is 13:1.
ENROLLMENT PROFILE 408 students from 3 states and territories, 2 other countries. 69% women, 56% part-time, 95% state residents, 33% transferred in, 1% international, 41% 25 or older, 0% Native American, 5% Hispanic, 10% African American, 4% Asian American. *Areas of study chosen:* 50% health professions and related sciences, 40% liberal arts/general studies, 10% education. *Most popular recent major:* liberal arts/general studies.
FIRST-YEAR CLASS 160 total; 289 applied, 81% were accepted, 68% of whom enrolled.
ACADEMIC PROGRAM Core, liberal arts curriculum, honor code. Calendar: semesters. 249 courses offered in 1995–96. Academic remediation for entering students, advanced placement, summer session for credit, part-time degree program (daytime, evenings, summer). ROTC: Army (c), Air Force (c).
GENERAL DEGREE REQUIREMENTS 64 semester hours; 6 semester hours of math; 8 semester hours of science.
MAJORS Elementary education (B), liberal arts/general studies, nursing.
LIBRARY 25,000 books, 901 microform titles, 148 periodicals, 2,500 records, tapes, and CDs.
COMPUTERS ON CAMPUS Computer purchase plan available. 42 computers for student use in computer center, computer labs, library.
COLLEGE LIFE Student-run newspaper. *Social organizations:* 1 open to all. *Student services:* personal-psychological counseling. *Campus security:* 24-hour patrols.
HOUSING College housing not available.

Aquinas College (continued)

ATHLETICS Member NJCAA. ***Intercollegiate:*** baseball M(s), basketball M(s). ***Contact:*** Mr. Charles Anderson, Athletic Director, 615-297-7653.

CAREER PLANNING ***Director:*** Dr. Dick Seay, Dean of Students, 615-383-3230. ***Services:*** career counseling, job bank.

EXPENSES FOR 1996–97 ***Application fee:*** $20. Tuition: $5760 full-time, $180 per semester hour part-time. Part-time mandatory fees: $30 per semester. Full-time mandatory fees: $290.

FINANCIAL AID ***College-administered undergrad aid 1995–96:*** 27 need-based scholarships (average $544), 38 non-need scholarships (average $2618), low-interest long-term loans from external sources (average $5659), 13 Federal Work-Study (averaging $850). ***Required forms:*** institutional, FAFSA; accepted: state. ***Priority deadline:*** 5/31. ***Payment plan:*** installment. ***Waivers:*** full or partial for employees or children of employees.

APPLYING ***Option:*** deferred entrance. ***Required:*** school transcript, minimum 2.0 GPA, SAT I or ACT, TOEFL for international students. ***Recommended:*** some high school foreign language. ***Required for some:*** essay. Test scores used for admission and counseling/placement. ***Application deadline:*** 7/31. ***Notification:*** continuous.

APPLYING/TRANSFER ***Required:*** standardized test scores, high school transcript, college transcript, minimum 2.0 college GPA, minimum 2.0 high school GPA. ***Required for some:*** essay. ***Entrance:*** moderately difficult. ***Application deadline:*** 8/6. ***Notification:*** continuous.

CONTACT Ms. Swapna Chinniah, Director of Enrollment Management, Aquinas College, Nashville, TN 37205-2005, 615-297-7545.

CHATTANOOGA STATE TECHNICAL COMMUNITY COLLEGE
Chattanooga, Tennessee

UG Enrollment: 8,676 | **Tuition & Fees (TN Res): $2084**
Application Deadline: rolling | **Room & Board: N/Avail**

GENERAL State-supported, 2-year, coed. Part of State University and Community College System of Tennessee. Awards certificates, diplomas, transfer associate, terminal associate degrees. Founded 1965. ***Setting:*** 100-acre urban campus. ***Total enrollment:*** 8,676. ***Faculty:*** 599 (199 full-time, 400 part-time). ***Notable Alumni:*** Ellen Hardy, Norma Lee, Clifford Skiles, Joyce Stakely, Glenda Varner.

ENROLLMENT PROFILE 8,676 students from 5 states and territories. 61% women, 39% men, 63% part-time, 94% state residents, 13% transferred in, 50% 25 or older, 0% Native American, 1% Hispanic, 12% African American, 1% Asian American. ***Areas of study chosen:*** 40% liberal arts/general studies, 22% health professions and related sciences, 7% business management and administrative services, 7% engineering and applied sciences, 7% physical sciences, 6% vocational and home economics, 3% computer and information sciences, 3% interdisciplinary studies, 1% education, 1% fine arts, 1% social sciences.

FIRST-YEAR CLASS 1,098 total; 1,233 applied, 100% were accepted, 89% of whom enrolled.

ACADEMIC PROGRAM Core, honor code. Calendar: semesters. 463 courses offered in 1995–96; average class size 30 in required courses. Academic remediation for entering students, English as a second language program offered during academic year and summer, services for LD students, honors program, summer session for credit, part-time degree program (daytime, evenings), adult/continuing education programs, co-op programs and internships.

GENERAL DEGREE REQUIREMENTS 64 semester hours; 1 math/science course; computer course; internship (some majors).

MAJORS Accounting, advertising, applied art, automotive technologies, aviation administration, aviation technology, biology/biological sciences, broadcasting, business administration/commerce/management, chemical engineering technology, chemistry, child care/child and family studies, civil engineering technology, commercial art, communication, computer information systems, computer programming, computer science, computer technologies, criminal justice, data processing, deaf interpreter training, dental services, drafting and design, early childhood education, electrical and electronics technologies, electrical engineering technology, electronics engineering technology, emergency medical technology, energy management technologies, engineering design, environmental engineering technology, finance/banking, fire science, fish and game management, flight training, food services technology, forestry, forest technology, graphic arts, heating/refrigeration/air conditioning, hotel and restaurant management, instrumentation technology, legal secretarial studies, liberal arts/general studies, machine and tool technologies, mechanical design technology, mechanical engineering technology, medical records services, medical secretarial studies, nuclear medical technology, nuclear technology, nursing, occupational therapy, physical therapy, printing technologies, radio and television studies, radiological technology, respiratory therapy, retail management, robotics, secretarial studies/office management, surveying technology, transportation technologies, welding technology, wildlife management.

LIBRARY Augusta R. Kolwyck Library with 73,954 books, 103,721 microform titles, 808 periodicals, 1 on-line bibliographic service, 25 CD-ROMs, 1,051 records, tapes, and CDs. Acquisition spending 1994–95: $183,320.

COMPUTERS ON CAMPUS 500 computers for student use in computer labs, learning resource center, various departments, classrooms, library provide access to main academic computer, off-campus computing facilities, e-mail, Internet. Staffed computer lab on campus (open 24 hours a day) provides training in use of computers. Academic computing expenditure 1994–95: $982,078.

COLLEGE LIFE Choral group, student-run newspaper, radio station. 5% vote in student government elections. ***Social organizations:*** 35 open to all. ***Most popular organizations:*** Accounting Club, Student Government Association, Student Nurses Association, Concert Choir, Activities Programming Board. ***Major annual events:*** Fun In The Sun, Oktoberfest, Wellness Festival. ***Student services:*** personal-psychological counseling, women's center. ***Campus security:*** 24-hour patrols, late-night transport-escort service.

HOUSING College housing not available.

ATHLETICS Member NJCAA. ***Intercollegiate:*** baseball M(s), basketball M(s)/W(s), softball W(s), tennis W(c). ***Intramural:*** soccer, softball, tennis. ***Contact:*** Mrs. Kim Weams Smith, Athletic Director, 423-697-4707.

CAREER PLANNING ***Placement office:*** 4 full-time, 4 part-time staff; $85,839 operating expenditure 1994–95. ***Director:*** Ms. Betty Soward, Director, Student Development, 423-697-4202. ***Services:*** job fairs, resume preparation, resume referral, career counseling, careers library, job bank, job interviews.

EXPENSES FOR 1995–96 ***Application fee:*** $5. State resident tuition: $1563 full-time, $44 per semester hour part-time. Nonresident tuition: $5880 full-time, $172 per semester hour part-time. Part-time mandatory fees per semester range from $12 to $22. Full-time mandatory fees: $521.

FINANCIAL AID ***College-administered undergrad aid 1995–96:*** 850 need-based scholarships (averaging $500), 600 non-need scholarships (averaging $521), low-interest long-term loans from external sources (averaging $2625), 75 Federal Work-Study (averaging $2000), 300 part-time jobs. ***Required forms:*** institutional, FAFSA; required for some: state; accepted: CSS Financial Aid PROFILE. ***Priority deadline:*** 6/1. ***Waivers:*** full or partial for employees or children of employees and senior citizens.

APPLYING Open admission. ***Options:*** early entrance, deferred entrance. ***Required:*** school transcript, TOEFL for international students. ***Required for some:*** 3 years of high school math, 2 years of high school foreign language, SAT I or ACT. Test scores used for counseling/placement. ***Application deadline:*** rolling. ***Notification:*** continuous.

APPLYING/TRANSFER ***Required:*** college transcript. ***Required for some:*** standardized test scores, 3 years of high school math, 2 years of high school foreign language. ***Entrance:*** noncompetitive. ***Application deadline:*** rolling. ***Notification:*** continuous. ***Contact:*** Ms. Julie Bennett, Assistant Director of Student Services/Registrar, 423-697-4404.

CONTACT Ms. Julie Bennett, Assistant Director of Student Services/Registrar, Chattanooga State Technical Community College, 4501 Amnicola Highway, Chattanooga, TN 37406-1018, 423-697-4404.

CLEVELAND STATE COMMUNITY COLLEGE
Cleveland, Tennessee

UG Enrollment: 3,670 | **Tuition & Fees (TN Res): $1010**
Application Deadline: rolling | **Room & Board: N/Avail**

GENERAL State-supported, 2-year, coed. Part of State University and Community College System of Tennessee. Awards certificates, transfer associate, terminal associate degrees. Founded 1967. ***Setting:*** 105-acre small-town campus. ***Total enrollment:*** 3,670. ***Faculty:*** 182 (77 full-time, 18% with terminal degrees, 105 part-time); student-faculty ratio is 22:1.

ENROLLMENT PROFILE 3,670 students from 13 states and territories. 60% women, 40% men, 59% part-time, 97% state residents, 4% transferred in, 30% have need-based financial aid, 12% have non-need-based financial aid, 0% international, 48% 25 or older, 1% Native American, 1% Hispanic, 5% African American, 1% Asian American. ***Areas of study chosen:*** 30% interdisciplinary studies, 10% architecture, 5% fine arts, 2% premed. ***Most popular recent majors:*** liberal arts/general studies, business administration/commerce/management, nursing.

FIRST-YEAR CLASS 541 total; 1,691 applied, 100% were accepted, 32% of whom enrolled.

ACADEMIC PROGRAM Core, transfer and career curriculum, honor code. Calendar: semesters. 250 courses offered in 1995–96. Academic remediation for entering students, advanced placement, tutorials, summer session for credit, part-time degree program (daytime, evenings), adult/continuing education programs, co-op programs. Off-campus study at University of Tennessee at Chattanooga, Chattanooga State Technical Community College.

GENERAL DEGREE REQUIREMENTS 64 credits; math/science requirements vary according to program; computer course; internship (some majors).

MAJORS Accounting, business administration/commerce/management, computer information systems, construction technologies, drug and alcohol/substance abuse counseling, health services administration, human services, industrial engineering technology, law enforcement/police sciences, liberal arts/general studies, medical laboratory technology, nursing, paralegal studies, secretarial studies/office management.

LIBRARY 61,092 books, 368 microform titles, 365 periodicals, 1 on-line bibliographic service, 16 CD-ROMs, 2,627 records, tapes, and CDs. Acquisition spending 1994–95: $373,795.

COMPUTERS ON CAMPUS 200 computers for student use in computer labs, learning resource center, labs, classrooms, library, student center provide access to main academic computer, off-campus computing facilities, e-mail, Internet. Staffed computer lab on campus provides training in use of computers, software. Academic computing expenditure 1994–95: $479,459.

COLLEGE LIFE Choral group, student-run newspaper. ***Social organizations:*** 4 open to all. ***Most popular organizations:*** Student Senate, Circle K, Phi Theta Kappa, Student Hosts. ***Major annual events:*** Career Fair, Health Fair. ***Student services:*** personal-psychological counseling. ***Campus security:*** 24-hour emergency response devices and patrols, late-night transport-escort service.

HOUSING College housing not available.

ATHLETICS Member NJCAA. ***Intercollegiate:*** baseball M(s), basketball M(s)/W(s), softball W(s). ***Intramural:*** archery, badminton, basketball, bowling, softball, table tennis (Ping-Pong), volleyball. ***Contact:*** Mr. Jim Cigliano, Vice President for Student Services, 423-478-6211.

CAREER PLANNING ***Placement office:*** 5 full-time staff; $420,905 operating expenditure 1994–95. ***Director:*** Dr. Michael Stokes, Director of Student Development, 423-472-7141. ***Services:*** job fairs, resume preparation, resume referral, career counseling, careers library, job bank, job interviews. Students must register sophomore year.

AFTER GRADUATION 30% of students completing a degree program in 1994–95 went directly on to further study.

EXPENSES FOR 1995–96 ***Application fee:*** $5. State resident tuition: $994 full-time, $44 per semester hour part-time. Nonresident tuition: $3920 full-time, $172 per semester hour part-time. Part-time mandatory fees: $8 per semester. Full-time mandatory fees: $16.

FINANCIAL AID ***College-administered undergrad aid 1995–96:*** 23 need-based scholarships (averaging $966), 72 non-need scholarships (averaging $966), low-interest long-term loans from external sources (averaging $1816), 50 Federal Work-Study (averaging $1500). ***Required forms:*** institutional, FAFSA; accepted: CSS Financial Aid PROFILE. ***Priority deadline:*** 6/1. ***Waivers:*** full or partial for employees or children of employees and senior citizens.

APPLYING Open admission except for nursing, medical laboratory technology programs. *Options:* early entrance, deferred entrance, midyear entrance. *Required:* school transcript, TOEFL for international students. *Recommended:* 3 years of high school math. *Required for some:* 3 years of high school math, 2 years of high school foreign language, ACT Test scores used for counseling/placement. *Application deadline:* rolling. *Notification:* continuous.

APPLYING/TRANSFER *Required:* college transcript. *Required for some:* standardized test scores, high school transcript, 3 years of high school math, 2 years of high school foreign language. *Entrance:* noncompetitive. *Application deadline:* rolling. *Notification:* continuous. *Contact:* Mrs. Marcia Owens, Registrar, 423-478-6212.

CONTACT Ms. Jodi Johnson, Director of Admissions, Cleveland State Community College, Cleveland, TN 37320-3570, 423-478-6208 or toll-free 800-604-2722 (in-state). *Fax:* 423-478-6255.

COLUMBIA STATE COMMUNITY COLLEGE
Columbia, Tennessee

UG Enrollment: 3,755	Tuition & Fees (TN Res): $1034
Application Deadline: rolling	Room & Board: N/Avail

GENERAL State-supported, 2-year, coed. Awards certificates, transfer associate, terminal associate degrees. Founded 1966. *Setting:* 150-acre small-town campus with easy access to Nashville. *Educational spending 1994–95:* $1547 per undergrad. *Total enrollment:* 3,755. *Faculty:* 217 (95 full-time, 86% with terminal degrees, 122 part-time).

ENROLLMENT PROFILE 3,755 students from 7 states and territories, 3 other countries. 67% women, 33% men, 54% part-time, 97% state residents, 15% transferred in, 1% international, 38% 25 or older, 1% Native American, 1% Hispanic, 7% African American, 1% Asian American. *Areas of study chosen:* 46% liberal arts/general studies, 25% health professions and related sciences, 7% engineering and applied sciences, 1% computer and information sciences.

FIRST-YEAR CLASS 771 total. Of the students who applied, 100% were accepted.

ACADEMIC PROGRAM Core, interdisciplinary curriculum, honor code. Calendar: semesters. 304 courses offered in 1995–96. Academic remediation for entering students, advanced placement, tutorials, honors program, summer session for credit, part-time degree program (daytime, evenings), adult/continuing education programs.

GENERAL DEGREE REQUIREMENTS 66 semester hours; computer course for liberal arts, accounting, electronic technology, veterinary technology majors.

MAJORS Accounting, agricultural business, art/fine arts, biology/biological sciences, business education, chemistry, communication, computer information systems, dental services, economics, electronics engineering technology, elementary education, emergency medical technology, (pre)engineering sequence, English, geography, health education, history, liberal arts/general studies, marketing/retailing/merchandising, mathematics, medical laboratory technology, music, nursing, pharmacy/pharmaceutical sciences, physical education, physical therapy, physics, political science/government, psychology, radiological technology, respiratory therapy, secretarial studies/office management, sociology, speech/rhetoric/public address/debate, veterinary technology.

LIBRARY John W. Finney Memorial Learning Resources Center with 57,408 books, 338 microform titles, 342 periodicals, 2 on-line bibliographic services, 1,715 records, tapes, and CDs. Acquisition spending 1994–95: $154,719.

COMPUTERS ON CAMPUS 200 computers for student use in computer labs, advising center provide access to on-line services, Internet. Staffed computer lab on campus provides training in use of computers. Academic computing expenditure 1994–95: $400,000.

COLLEGE LIFE Drama-theater group. 60% vote in student government elections. *Social organizations:* 12 open to all. *Most popular organizations:* Student Government Association, Student Tennessee Education Association, Circle K Club, Gamma Beta Phi, Students In Free Enterprise. *Major annual events:* Homecoming, Multi-Cultural Festival, Drug Awareness Week. *Student services:* health clinic, personal-psychological counseling, women's center. *Campus security:* 24-hour patrols.

HOUSING College housing not available.

ATHLETICS Member NJCAA. *Intercollegiate:* baseball M(s), basketball M(s)/W(s), golf M, softball W(s). *Intramural:* basketball, table tennis (Ping-Pong), volleyball. *Contact:* Mr. Dave Hall, Director of Athletics, 615-540-2632.

CAREER PLANNING *Placement office:* 5 full-time staff. *Director:* Dr. Johnny Williams, Vice President of Student Services, 615-540-2566. *Services:* job fairs, resume preparation, resume referral, career counseling, careers library, job bank. 10 organizations recruited on campus 1994–95.

EXPENSES FOR 1995–96 *Application fee:* $5. State resident tuition: $994 full-time, $44 per semester hour part-time. Nonresident tuition: $3920 full-time, $172 per semester hour part-time. Part-time mandatory fees per semester range from $6.25 to $20. Full-time mandatory fees: $40.

FINANCIAL AID *College-administered undergrad aid 1995–96:* 50 need-based scholarships (averaging $500), 200 non-need scholarships (averaging $1000), low-interest long-term loans from external sources (averaging $2000), 35 Federal Work-Study, 40 part-time jobs. *Required forms:* state, FAFSA; required for some: institutional; accepted: CSS Financial Aid PROFILE. *Priority deadline:* 4/1. *Waivers:* full or partial for employees or children of employees and senior citizens. *Notification:* 6/15.

APPLYING Open admission. *Options:* early entrance, deferred entrance, midyear entrance. *Required:* school transcript, TOEFL for international students. *Recommended:* 4 years of high school math, 2 years of high school foreign language. *Required for some:* SAT I or ACT. Test scores used for counseling/placement. *Application deadline:* rolling.

APPLYING/TRANSFER *Required:* college transcript. *Required for some:* standardized test scores, high school transcript. *Entrance:* noncompetitive. *Application deadline:* rolling. *Contact:* Ms. Sharon Bowen, Director of Admissions, 615-540-2548.

CONTACT Mrs. Sharon Bowen, Director of Admissions, Columbia State Community College, Columbia, TN 38402-1315, 615-540-2548. *E-mail:* scruggs@coscc.cc.tn.us. College video available.

CUMBERLAND SCHOOL OF TECHNOLOGY
Cookeville, Tennessee

UG Enrollment: 47	Tuition & Fees: $4725
Application Deadline: rolling	Room & Board: N/Avail

GENERAL Proprietary, 2-year, coed. Awards certificates, diplomas, transfer associate degrees. Founded 1970. *Setting:* 4-acre small-town campus. *Total enrollment:* 47. *Faculty:* 7 (2 full-time, 5 part-time). *Notable Alumni:* Dr. Roger M. Duke, Dr. Steven Richardson.

ENROLLMENT PROFILE 47 students: 100% state residents. *Areas of study chosen:* 85% health professions and related sciences, 15% business management and administrative services.

FIRST-YEAR CLASS 15 total.

ACADEMIC PROGRAM Calendar: quarters. Tutorials, internships.

GENERAL DEGREE REQUIREMENTS 90 quarter hours; 1 math course; computer course for secretarial studies majors.

MAJORS Medical laboratory technology, secretarial studies/office management.

COMPUTERS ON CAMPUS 24 computers for student use in computer labs. Staffed computer lab on campus provides training in use of computers, software.

CAREER PLANNING *Placement office:* 1 full-time, 2 part-time staff. *Director:* Ms. Judy Maxwell, Student Services Director, 615-526-3660. *Services:* resume preparation, resume referral, career counseling, job bank, job interviews.

AFTER GRADUATION 94% of class of 1994 had job offers within 6 months.

EXPENSES FOR 1996–97 *Application fee:* $100. Tuition: $105 per quarter hour part-time. One-time mandatory fee: $100. Full-time tuition: $7403 for medical laboratory technology program, $4725 for secretarial studies program.

FINANCIAL AID *College-administered undergrad aid 1995–96:* 63 need-based scholarships (average $300), low-interest long-term loans from external sources (average $6625). *Required forms:* FAFSA. *Application deadline:* continuous.

APPLYING *Option:* Common Application. *Required:* school transcript, interview. *Recommended:* minimum 2.0 GPA, recommendations, Wonderlic Aptitude test. *Application deadline:* rolling. *Notification:* continuous.

APPLYING/TRANSFER *Required:* high school transcript, interview, college transcript. *Recommended:* standardized test scores, recommendations, minimum 2.0 college GPA, minimum 2.0 high school GPA. *Application deadline:* rolling. *Notification:* continuous.

CONTACT Ms. Elizabeth McDonald, Director of Enrollment Management, Cumberland School of Technology, Cookeville, TN 38501, 615-526-3660.

DRAUGHONS JUNIOR COLLEGE
Clarksville, Tennessee

UG Enrollment: 300	Tuition & Fees: $4440
Application Deadline: rolling	Room & Board: N/Avail

GENERAL Proprietary, 2-year, coed. Awards terminal associate degrees. Founded 1987. *Total enrollment:* 300. *Faculty:* 26.

ENROLLMENT PROFILE 300 students.

ACADEMIC PROGRAM Core. Calendar: semesters. Part-time degree program (daytime, evenings).

GENERAL DEGREE REQUIREMENTS 60 semester hours; computer course.

EXPENSES FOR 1996–97 Tuition: $4350 full-time, $145 per semester hour part-time. Full-time mandatory fees: $90.

APPLYING Open admission. *Required:* school transcript, interview. *Recommended:* SAT I. *Application deadline:* rolling. *Notification:* continuous.

APPLYING/TRANSFER *Required:* high school transcript, interview, college transcript. *Recommended:* standardized test scores. *Entrance:* noncompetitive. *Application deadline:* rolling. *Notification:* continuous.

CONTACT Mr. William Greene, Director of Admissions, Draughons Junior College, Clarksville, TN 37040, 615-361-7555.

DRAUGHONS JUNIOR COLLEGE
Nashville, Tennessee

UG Enrollment: 440	Tuition & Fees: $4440
Application Deadline: rolling	Room & Board: N/Avail

GENERAL Proprietary, 2-year, coed. Awards transfer associate, terminal associate degrees. Founded 1884. *Setting:* 5-acre suburban campus. *Total enrollment:* 440. *Faculty:* 45 (20 full-time, 25 part-time).

ENROLLMENT PROFILE 440 students: 75% women, 25% men, 20% part-time, 97% state residents, 10% transferred in, 1% international, 50% 25 or older, 0% Native American, 0% Hispanic, 18% African American, 2% Asian American. *Areas of study chosen:* 30% health professions and related sciences, 25% business management and administrative services, 20% computer and information sciences. *Most popular recent majors:* business administration/commerce/management, computer science, secretarial studies/office management.

FIRST-YEAR CLASS 180 total; 200 applied, 90% were accepted, 100% of whom enrolled. 5% from top 10% of their high school class, 30% from top half.

ACADEMIC PROGRAM Core, honor code. Calendar: semesters. Academic remediation for entering students, tutorials, summer session for credit, part-time degree program (daytime, evenings), internships.

GENERAL DEGREE REQUIREMENTS 60 semester hours; computer course; internship (some majors).

MAJORS Accounting, broadcasting, business administration/commerce/management, computer information systems, computer programming, computer science, fashion merchandising, legal studies, medical assistant technologies, medical records services, radio and television studies, secretarial studies/office management.

LIBRARY 3,250 books, 20 periodicals, 30 records, tapes, and CDs.

Peterson's Guide to Two-Year Colleges 1997

Draughons Junior College (continued)
COMPUTERS ON CAMPUS 50 computers for student use in classrooms provide access to Internet. Staffed computer lab on campus provides training in use of computers, software.
COLLEGE LIFE Student-run newspaper. ***Campus security:*** 24-hour emergency response devices.
HOUSING College housing not available.
CAREER PLANNING ***Services:*** resume preparation, career counseling, job bank, job interviews. 10 organizations recruited on campus 1994–95.
AFTER GRADUATION 92% of class of 1994 had job offers within 6 months.
EXPENSES FOR 1996–97 ***Application fee:*** $10. Tuition: $4350 full-time, $145 per semester hour part-time. Full-time mandatory fees: $90.
FINANCIAL AID ***College-administered undergrad aid 1995–96:*** need-based scholarships, low-interest long-term loans from external sources (average $2000), Federal Work-Study. ***Required forms:*** FAFSA; required for some: CSS Financial Aid PROFILE, state; accepted: institutional. ***Priority deadline:*** 10/1.
APPLYING Open admission. ***Option:*** deferred entrance. ***Required:*** school transcript, TOEFL for international students. ***Recommended:*** SAT I. ***Application deadline:*** rolling. ***Notification:*** continuous.
APPLYING/TRANSFER ***Required:*** high school transcript, college transcript. ***Recommended:*** standardized test scores. ***Entrance:*** noncompetitive. ***Application deadline:*** rolling. ***Notification:*** continuous. ***Contact:*** Mr. William R. Greene, Director of Admissions, 615-361-7555.
CONTACT Mr. William R. Greene, Director of Admissions, Draughons Junior College, Nashville, TN 37217, 615-361-7555

DYERSBURG STATE COMMUNITY COLLEGE
Dyersburg, Tennessee

UG Enrollment: 2,079	**Tuition & Fees (TN Res): $1086**
Application Deadline: rolling	**Room & Board: N/Avail**

GENERAL State-supported, 2-year, coed. Part of State University and Community College System of Tennessee. Awards transfer associate, terminal associate degrees. Founded 1969. ***Setting:*** 100-acre small-town campus with easy access to Memphis. ***Endowment:*** $562,565. ***Educational spending 1994–95:*** $1894 per undergrad. ***Total enrollment:*** 2,079. ***Faculty:*** 153 (51 full-time, 25% with terminal degrees, 102 part-time).
ENROLLMENT PROFILE 2,079 students from 4 states and territories, 5 other countries. 68% women, 32% men, 44% part-time, 96% state residents, 24% transferred in, 1% international, 39% 25 or older, 0% Native American, 0% Hispanic, 15% African American, 0% Asian American. ***Areas of study chosen:*** 16% education, 12% health professions and related sciences, 6% liberal arts/general studies, 5% business management and administrative services, 2% psychology, 1% computer and information sciences. ***Most popular recent majors:*** liberal arts/general studies, business administration/commerce/management, nursing.
FIRST-YEAR CLASS 428 total; 727 applied, 100% were accepted, 59% of whom enrolled. 1% from top 10% of their high school class, 17% from top quarter, 44% from top half.
ACADEMIC PROGRAM Core, honor code. Calendar: semesters. Academic remediation for entering students, advanced placement, summer session for credit, part-time degree program (daytime), adult/continuing education programs.
GENERAL DEGREE REQUIREMENTS 64 semester hours; 3 semester hours of math; 4 semester hours of science; computer course.
MAJORS Business administration/commerce/management, electrical and electronics technologies, law enforcement/police sciences, liberal arts/general studies, nursing.
LIBRARY Learning Resource Center with 36,056 books, 341 microform titles, 252 periodicals, 2 on-line bibliographic services, 20 CD-ROMs, 2,126 records, tapes, and CDs. Acquisition spending 1994–95: $51,437.
COMPUTERS ON CAMPUS 110 computers for student use in computer labs, learning resource center, library provide access to main academic computer, e-mail. Staffed computer lab on campus. Academic computing expenditure 1994–95: $214,960.
COLLEGE LIFE Drama-theater group, choral group, student-run newspaper. ***Social organizations:*** 6 open to all. ***Most popular organizations:*** Student Government, Phi Theta Kappa, Minority Association for Successful Students, Video Club, Psychology Club. ***Major annual events:*** Fall Festival, Spring Fling, Homecoming. ***Student services:*** personal-psychological counseling. ***Campus security:*** 24-hour patrols.
HOUSING College housing not available.
ATHLETICS Member NJCAA. ***Intercollegiate:*** basketball M(s)/W(s). ***Intramural:*** basketball, volleyball. ***Contact:*** Mr. Alan Barnett, Athletic Director, 901-286-3259.
CAREER PLANNING ***Placement office:*** 1 part-time staff. ***Director:*** Ms. Pam Dahl, Counselor, 901-286-3242. ***Services:*** job fairs, resume preparation, career counseling, careers library, job bank.
EXPENSES FOR 1995–96 ***Application fee:*** $5. State resident tuition: $1040 full-time, $44 per semester hour part-time. Nonresident tuition: $3966 full-time, $172 per semester hour part-time. Part-time mandatory fees per semester range from $5 to $23. Full-time mandatory fees: $46.
FINANCIAL AID ***College-administered undergrad aid 1995–96:*** 175 need-based scholarships (average $453), 290 non-need scholarships (average $643), short-term loans (average $500), low-interest long-term loans from external sources (average $2075), Federal Work-Study, 53 part-time jobs. ***Required forms:*** institutional, FAFSA; accepted: CSS Financial Aid PROFILE. ***Priority deadline:*** 3/15. ***Waivers:*** full or partial for employees or children of employees and senior citizens. ***Notification:*** continuous.
APPLYING Open admission except for nursing program. ***Options:*** Common Application, early entrance, midyear entrance. ***Required:*** school transcript, TOEFL for international students. ***Required for some:*** 3 years of high school math and science, 2 years of high school foreign language, ACT. Test scores used for counseling/placement. ***Application deadline:*** rolling. ***Notification:*** continuous. Preference given to state residents.
APPLYING/TRANSFER ***Required:*** high school transcript, college transcript. ***Entrance:*** noncompetitive. ***Application deadline:*** rolling. ***Notification:*** continuous.
CONTACT Mrs. Vida McClure, Technical Clerk, Admissions, Dyersburg State Community College, 1510 Lake Road, Dyersburg, TN 38024, 901-286-3330.

FUGAZZI COLLEGE
Nashville, Tennessee

UG Enrollment: 150	**Tuition & Fees: $5526**
Application Deadline: N/R	**Room & Board: N/Avail**

GENERAL Proprietary, 2-year. Awards diplomas, terminal associate degrees. Founded 1991. ***Total enrollment:*** 150.
ENROLLMENT PROFILE 150 students.
FIRST-YEAR CLASS Of the students who applied, 100% were accepted, 40% of whom enrolled.
ACADEMIC PROGRAM Calendar: quarters.
GENERAL DEGREE REQUIREMENTS 96 credit hours; 1 math course; computer course.
HOUSING College housing not available.
EXPENSES FOR 1996–97 Tuition: $5496 full-time, $114.50 per credit hour part-time. Part-time mandatory fees: $10 per quarter. Full-time mandatory fees: $30.
CONTACT Mrs. Cindy Weaver, Director of Admissions, Fugazzi College, Nashville, TN 37211, 615-333-3344.

HIWASSEE COLLEGE
Madisonville, Tennessee

UG Enrollment: 479	**Tuition & Fees: $5380**
Application Deadline: rolling	**Room & Board: $3510**

GENERAL Independent Methodist, 2-year, coed. Awards transfer associate, terminal associate degrees. Founded 1849. ***Setting:*** 410-acre rural campus. ***Endowment:*** $6.8 million. ***Research spending 1994–95:*** $7004. ***Educational spending 1994–95:*** $2488 per undergrad. ***Total enrollment:*** 479. ***Faculty:*** 30 (17 full-time, 47% with terminal degrees, 13 part-time); student-faculty ratio is 15:1. ***Notable Alumni:*** Donald R. Youell, president of American Corrugated Products; Allen O. Kinzer, president of BMW Manufacturing Corporation; Rev. Eddie Fox, director of World Evangelism; Marvin G. White, district manager of South Central Bell; Rocky Young, judge on general sessions court.
ENROLLMENT PROFILE 479 students from 21 states and territories, 8 other countries. 63% women, 37% men, 31% part-time, 88% state residents, 40% live on campus, 7% transferred in, 80% have need-based financial aid, 20% have non-need-based financial aid, 4% international, 13% 25 or older, 1% Native American, 1% Hispanic, 7% African American, 4% Asian American. ***Areas of study chosen:*** 33% health professions and related sciences, 26% liberal arts/general studies, 13% education, 9% business management and administrative services, 2% agriculture, 2% philosophy, 2% theology/religion, 1% biological and life sciences, 1% communications and journalism, 1% computer and information sciences, 1% engineering and applied sciences, 1% psychology, 1% social sciences. ***Most popular recent majors:*** health science, education, business administration/commerce/management.
FIRST-YEAR CLASS 165 total; 394 applied, 99% were accepted, 42% of whom enrolled. 15% from top 10% of their high school class, 26% from top quarter, 56% from top half.
ACADEMIC PROGRAM Core, liberal arts curriculum, honor code. Calendar: semesters. 176 courses offered in 1995–96. Academic remediation for entering students, English as a second language program offered during academic year, advanced placement, self-designed majors, honors program, summer session for credit, part-time degree program (daytime, evenings, summer), adult/continuing education programs.
GENERAL DEGREE REQUIREMENT 66 semester hours.
MAJORS Accounting, agricultural business, animal sciences, art/fine arts, biblical studies, biology/biological sciences, business administration/commerce/management, business education, chemistry, child care/child and family studies, child psychology/child development, communication, computer programming, computer science, computer technologies, dairy sciences, data processing, dental services, drafting and design, early childhood education, economics, education, elementary education, engineering (general), (pre)engineering sequence, English, family and consumer studies, family services, fashion design and technology, fashion merchandising, finance/banking, food services management, food services technology, forestry, forest technology, health science, history, home economics, home economics education, humanities, human services, interior design, liberal arts/general studies, marriage and family counseling, mathematics, medical assistant technologies, medical records services, medical secretarial studies, ministries, music, music education, nursing, parks management, pastoral studies, pharmacy/pharmaceutical sciences, physical education, physical therapy, political science/government, psychology, secretarial studies/office management, social work, sociology, textile arts, textiles and clothing, veterinary sciences, wildlife management, wood sciences.
LIBRARY Hardwick-Johnston Library with 40,000 books, 250 periodicals. Acquisition spending 1994–95: $11,709.
COMPUTERS ON CAMPUS 61 computers for student use in computer center, computer labs, learning resource center, classrooms, library provide access to e-mail, software. Staffed computer lab on campus provides training in use of computers, software. Academic computing expenditure 1994–95: $30,000.
COLLEGE LIFE Orientation program (2 days, no cost). Drama-theater group, choral group. 45% vote in student government elections. ***Most popular organizations:*** Baptist Student Union, Christian Student Movement, FFA/Agriculture Club, Theatre Hiwassee, Student Government Association. ***Major annual events:*** Homecoming Week, Welcome Week, Spring Festival. ***Campus security:*** 24-hour emergency response devices, controlled dormitory access, late night trained security personnel.
HOUSING 336 college housing spaces available; 192 were occupied 1995–96. No special consideration for freshman housing applicants. On-campus residence required through sophomore year except if living with relatives. Resident assistants live in dorms.
ATHLETICS Member NJCAA. ***Intercollegiate:*** baseball M(s), basketball M(s)/W(s), softball W(s). ***Intramural:*** basketball, football, swimming and diving, table tennis (Ping-Pong), tennis, volleyball, weight lifting. ***Contact:*** Mr. Rick Hughes, Athletic Director, 423-442-2001 Ext. 290.
CAREER PLANNING ***Placement office:*** 1 full-time staff. ***Director:*** Ms. Barbara Butler, Registrar, 423-442-2001 Ext. 215. ***Services:*** career counseling, careers library.
AFTER GRADUATION 90% of students completing a degree program in 1994–95 went directly on to further study.

EXPENSES FOR 1996–97 ***Application fee:*** $25. Comprehensive fee of $8890 includes full-time tuition ($5280), mandatory fees ($100), and college room and board ($3510). College room only: $1550. Part-time tuition: $220 per semester hour.
FINANCIAL AID ***College-administered undergrad aid 1995–96:*** 250 need-based scholarships (average $1950), 148 non-need scholarships (average $2385), low-interest long-term loans from college funds (average $500), loans from external sources (average $2300), 185 Federal Work-Study (averaging $800), 65 part-time jobs. ***Required forms:*** state, institutional, FAFSA; accepted: CSS Financial Aid PROFILE. ***Priority deadline:*** 5/1. ***Payment plan:*** installment. ***Waivers:*** full or partial for employees or children of employees. ***Notification:*** continuous.
APPLYING ***Options:*** early entrance, deferred entrance. ***Required:*** school transcript, SAT I or ACT. ***Recommended:*** 3 years of high school math and science, some high school foreign language. ***Required for some:*** TOEFL for international students. Test scores used for counseling/placement. ***Application deadline:*** rolling.
APPLYING/TRANSFER ***Required:*** standardized test scores, high school transcript, college transcript. ***Entrance:*** minimally difficult. ***Application deadline:*** rolling. ***Contact:*** Mr. James R. Hemphill, Vice President of Admissions and Financial Aid, 423-442-3283.
CONTACT Mr. Ron Hemphill, Associate Director of Admissions and Financial Aid, Hiwassee College, Madisonville, TN 37354, 423-442-3283 Ext. 205. ***Fax:*** 423-442-3520. College video available.

ITT TECHNICAL INSTITUTE
Knoxville, Tennessee

UG Enrollment: 364	**Tuition: $9688/deg prog**
Application Deadline: rolling	**Room & Board: N/Avail**

GENERAL Proprietary, primarily 2-year, coed. Part of ITT Educational Services, Inc. Awards terminal associate, bachelor's degrees. Founded 1988. ***Setting:*** 5-acre suburban campus. ***Total enrollment:*** 364. ***Faculty:*** 12 (all full-time, 86% with terminal degrees); student-faculty ratio is 26:1.
ENROLLMENT PROFILE 364 students: 9% women, 0% Hispanic, 6% African American, 1% Asian American.
FIRST-YEAR CLASS 236 total; 454 applied, 95% were accepted, 55% of whom enrolled.
ACADEMIC PROGRAM Core, honor code. Calendar: quarters. Academic remediation for entering students.
MAJOR Electronics engineering technology.
COMPUTERS ON CAMPUS 47 computers for student use in computer labs, library.
COLLEGE LIFE ***Campus security:*** 24-hour emergency response devices.
HOUSING College housing not available.
CAREER PLANNING ***Placement office:*** 1 full-time, 1 part-time staff. ***Director:*** Ms. Mary Sonner, Director of Placement, 423-671-2800. ***Services:*** job fairs, resume preparation, resume referral, career counseling, careers library, job bank, job interviews. 37 organizations recruited on campus 1994–95.
AFTER GRADUATION 79% of class of 1994 had job offers within 6 months.
EXPENSES FOR 1996–97 ***Application fee:*** $100. Tuition per degree program ranges from $9688 to $17,690.
FINANCIAL AID ***Required forms:*** institutional, FAFSA; required for some: state; accepted: CSS Financial Aid PROFILE. ***Payment plan:*** installment. ***Waivers:*** full or partial for employees or children of employees.
APPLYING ***Option:*** deferred entrance. ***Required:*** CPAt. Test scores used for admission. ***Application deadline:*** rolling.
APPLYING/TRANSFER ***Application deadline:*** rolling. ***Contact:*** Mr. Roger Kelley, Director of Education, 423-671-2800.
CONTACT Mr. Larry Lehmann, Director of Recruitment, ITT Technical Institute, Knoxville, TN 37932, 423-671-2800 or toll-free 800-952-9004 (in-state). ***Fax:*** 423-691-0337. College video available.

ITT TECHNICAL INSTITUTE
Memphis, Tennessee

UG Enrollment: 170	**Tuition: $15,599/deg prog**
Application Deadline: rolling	**Room & Board: N/Avail**

GENERAL Proprietary, 2-year, coed. Part of ITT Educational Services, Inc. Awards terminal associate degrees. Founded 1994. ***Setting:*** 1-acre suburban campus. ***Total enrollment:*** 170. ***Faculty:*** 13 (all full-time, 100% with terminal degrees); student-faculty ratio is 15:1.
ENROLLMENT PROFILE 170 students from 5 states and territories. 20% women, 80% men, 0% part-time, 75% state residents, 5% transferred in, 0% international, 28% 25 or older, 0% Native American, 1% Hispanic, 74% African American, 0% Asian American. ***Most popular recent major:*** electronics engineering technology.
FIRST-YEAR CLASS 120 total; 250 applied, 85% were accepted. 5% from top 10% of their high school class, 15% from top quarter, 50% from top half.
ACADEMIC PROGRAM Calendar: quarters. Academic remediation for entering students.
GENERAL DEGREE REQUIREMENT 90 credit hours.
MAJORS Drafting and design, electronics engineering technology.
COMPUTERS ON CAMPUS 25 computers for student use in computer labs, learning resource center. Staffed computer lab on campus provides training in use of computers, software.
COLLEGE LIFE Student-run newspaper. 90% vote in student government elections. ***Campus security:*** 24-hour emergency response devices and patrols, late-night transport-escort service.
HOUSING College housing not available.
CAREER PLANNING ***Placement office:*** 1 full-time staff. ***Director:*** Ms. Gretchen Higgins, Director of Placement, 901-762-0556. ***Services:*** job fairs, resume preparation, resume referral, career counseling, careers library, job bank, job interviews. Students must register freshman year. 10 organizations recruited on campus 1994–95.
EXPENSES FOR 1996–97 ***Application fee:*** $100. Tuition per degree program ranges from $15,599 to $17,690. Full-time mandatory fees range from $540 to $720. Tuition guaranteed not to increase for student's term of enrollment.
FINANCIAL AID ***College-administered undergrad aid 1995–96:*** Federal Work-Study. ***Application deadline:*** continuous. ***Payment plans:*** installment, deferred payment.
APPLYING ***Option:*** deferred entrance. ***Required:*** school transcript, minimum 2.0 GPA, recommendations, CPAt. ***Required for some:*** interview. Test scores used for admission. ***Application deadline:*** rolling.
APPLYING/TRANSFER ***Contact:*** Mr. Bobby Reese, Director of Education, 901-762-0556.
CONTACT Mr. David Bowden, Director, ITT Technical Institute, Memphis, TN 38119, 901-762-0556. College video available.

ITT TECHNICAL INSTITUTE
Nashville, Tennessee

UG Enrollment: 475	**Tuition: $15,599/deg prog**
Application Deadline: rolling	**Room & Board: N/Avail**

GENERAL Proprietary, primarily 2-year, coed. Part of ITT Educational Services, Inc. Awards transfer associate, terminal associate, bachelor's degrees. Founded 1984. ***Setting:*** 21-acre urban campus. ***Total enrollment:*** 475. ***Faculty:*** 25 (all full-time, 90% with terminal degrees).
ENROLLMENT PROFILE 475 students from 2 states and territories. 14% women, 0% part-time, 8% transferred in, 0% international, 29% 25 or older, 1% Native American, 1% Hispanic, 13% African American, 0% Asian American. ***Areas of study chosen:*** 100% engineering and applied sciences. ***Most popular recent major:*** drafting and design.
FIRST-YEAR CLASS 258 total; 632 applied, 100% were accepted, 41% of whom enrolled. 5% from top 10% of their high school class, 25% from top quarter, 85% from top half.
ACADEMIC PROGRAM Calendar: quarters. 53 courses offered in 1995–96. Academic remediation for entering students, summer session for credit.
GENERAL DEGREE REQUIREMENTS 90 credit hours for associate, 162 credit hours for bachelor's.
MAJORS Drafting and design, electronics engineering technology.
LIBRARY Learning Resource Center with 870 books.
COMPUTERS ON CAMPUS 65 computers for student use in computer labs, classrooms, library.
COLLEGE LIFE ***Major annual event:*** Student Picnic.
HOUSING College housing not available.
CAREER PLANNING ***Placement office:*** 2 full-time, 1 part-time staff. ***Director:*** Ms. Laura Key, Director of Placement, 615-889-8700. ***Services:*** resume preparation, resume referral, career counseling, job interviews. Students must register freshman year.
EXPENSES FOR 1996–97 ***Application fee:*** $100. Tuition per degree program ranges from $15,599 to $17,690. Tuition guaranteed not to increase for student's term of enrollment.
FINANCIAL AID ***College-administered undergrad aid 1995–96:*** need-based scholarships, low-interest long-term loans from external sources, Federal Work-Study, 5 part-time jobs. ***Required forms:*** FAFSA. ***Application deadline:*** continuous. ***Payment plan:*** installment. ***Waivers:*** full or partial for employees or children of employees.
APPLYING ***Option:*** deferred entrance. ***Required:*** school transcript, SRA achievement series, reading. ***Recommended:*** 3 years of high school math. ***Required for some:*** TOEFL for international students. Test scores used for admission. ***Application deadline:*** rolling.
APPLYING/TRANSFER ***Application deadline:*** rolling. ***Contact:*** Mr. Robert Hammes Fahr, Director of Education, 615-889-8700.
CONTACT Mr. James Eller, Director of Recruitment, ITT Technical Institute, 441 Donelson Pike, PO Box 148029, Nashville, TN 37214-8029, 615-889-8700. College video available.

JACKSON STATE COMMUNITY COLLEGE
Jackson, Tennessee

UG Enrollment: 3,438	**Tuition & Fees (TN Res): $1010**
Application Deadline: 9/8	**Room & Board: N/Avail**

GENERAL State-supported, 2-year, coed. Part of State University and Community College System of Tennessee. Awards transfer associate, terminal associate degrees. Founded 1967. ***Setting:*** 104-acre small-town campus. ***Total enrollment:*** 3,438. ***Faculty:*** 188 (86 full-time, 20% with terminal degrees, 102 part-time); student-faculty ratio is 19:1.
ENROLLMENT PROFILE 3,438 students: 61% women, 39% men, 55% part-time, 99% state residents, 4% transferred in, 32% have need-based financial aid, 3% have non-need-based financial aid, 46% 25 or older, 16% African American. ***Areas of study chosen:*** 51% liberal arts/general studies, 29% health professions and related sciences, 12% business management and administrative services, 5% computer and information sciences, 3% agriculture. ***Most popular recent majors:*** liberal arts/general studies, radiological technology, business administration/commerce/management.
FIRST-YEAR CLASS 507 total. Of the students who applied, 100% were accepted. 5% from top 10% of their high school class, 40% from top half.
ACADEMIC PROGRAM Core. Calendar: semesters. Academic remediation for entering students, advanced placement, summer session for credit, part-time degree program (daytime, evenings, summer), adult/continuing education programs, co-op programs.
GENERAL DEGREE REQUIREMENTS 64 semester hours; 1 college algebra course; 2 natural science courses; computer course.
MAJORS Accounting, agronomy/soil and crop sciences, art/fine arts, biology/biological sciences, broadcasting, business administration/commerce/management, chemistry, communication, computer programming, computer science, data processing, economics, education, elementary education, emergency medical technology, engineering (general), (pre)engineering sequence, engineering technology, English, finance/banking, geography, history, home economics, human resources, industrial engineering technology, liberal arts/general studies, literature, marketing/retailing/merchandising, mathematics, medical technology, music, natural sciences, nursing, physical education, physical sciences, physical therapy, piano/organ, political science/government, psychology, radiological technology, real estate, respiratory therapy, science, secretarial studies/office management, social science, social work, sociology, transportation technologies, voice, wind and percussion instruments, zoology.
LIBRARY 60,401 books, 32,000 microform titles, 350 periodicals, 1,501 records, tapes, and CDs.

Peterson's Guide to Two-Year Colleges 1997

597

Tennessee

Jackson State Community College *(continued)*
COMPUTERS ON CAMPUS 60 computers for student use in computer center, open labs, library, student center.
COLLEGE LIFE Choral group, student-run newspaper. *Student services:* health clinic, personal-psychological counseling. *Campus security:* 24-hour patrols.
HOUSING College housing not available.
ATHLETICS Member NJCAA. *Intercollegiate:* baseball M(s), basketball M(s)/W(s). *Intramural:* basketball, football, tennis, volleyball. *Contact:* Mr. Jack Martin, Athletic Director, 901-424-3520.
CAREER PLANNING *Service:* career counseling. 20 organizations recruited on campus 1994–95.
AFTER GRADUATION 80% of students completing a degree program in 1994–95 went directly on to further study.
EXPENSES FOR 1995–96 *Application fee:* $5. State resident tuition: $994 full-time, $44 per semester hour part-time. Nonresident tuition: $3930 full-time, $172 per semester hour part-time. Part-time mandatory fees: $8 per semester. Full-time mandatory fees: $16.
FINANCIAL AID *College-administered undergrad aid 1995–96:* need-based scholarships, 85 non-need scholarships (average $925), Federal Work-Study, 47 part-time jobs. *Required forms:* institutional, FAFSA; required for some: state; accepted: CSS Financial Aid PROFILE. *Priority deadline:* 4/1. *Waivers:* full or partial for minority students, employees or children of employees, and senior citizens. *Notification:* 7/1.
APPLYING Open admission except for allied health programs. *Options:* Common Application, early entrance, deferred entrance. *Required:* TOEFL for international students. *Required for some:* school transcript, 3 years of high school math, 2 years of high school foreign language, SAT I or ACT. Test scores used for counseling/placement. *Application deadlines:* 9/8, 9/1 for nonresidents. *Notification:* continuous, continuous for nonresidents. Preference given to state residents.
APPLYING/TRANSFER *Required:* college transcript. *Required for some:* standardized test scores, high school transcript. *Entrance:* minimally difficult. *Application deadline:* rolling. *Notification:* continuous.
CONTACT Mr. John L. Johnson, Director of Admissions and Records, Jackson State Community College, Jackson, TN 38301-3797, 901-425-2644. *Fax:* 901-425-2647.

JOHN A. GUPTON COLLEGE
Nashville, Tennessee

UG Enrollment: 78	Tuition & Fees: $4000
Application Deadline: rolling	Room & Board: N/Avail

GENERAL Independent, 2-year, specialized, coed. Awards transfer associate degrees. Founded 1946. *Setting:* 1-acre urban campus. *Endowment:* $35,594. *Total enrollment:* 78. *Faculty:* 14 (4 full-time, 10 part-time); student-faculty ratio is 7:1.
ENROLLMENT PROFILE 78 students: 15% women, 0% part-time, 60% state residents, 15% African American.
FIRST-YEAR CLASS 20 total. Of the students who applied, 100% were accepted, 100% of whom enrolled.
ACADEMIC PROGRAM Calendar: semesters.
GENERAL DEGREE REQUIREMENTS 65 semester hours; 1 course each in anatomy, physiology, chemistry, microbiology, pathology and math; internship.
MAJOR Funeral service.
LIBRARY Memorial Library with 4,000 books, 54 periodicals, 3 CD-ROMs, 21 records, tapes, and CDs. Acquisition spending 1994–95: $5193.
COMPUTERS ON CAMPUS 3 computers for student use in library provide access to e-mail, Internet. Staffed computer lab on campus provides training in use of computers, software. Academic computing expenditure 1994–95: $10,602.
COLLEGE LIFE *Campus security:* daytime patrols.
HOUSING College housing not available.
CAREER PLANNING *Service:* career counseling.
EXPENSES FOR 1996–97 *Application fee:* $20. Tuition: $3840 full-time, $120 per semester hour part-time. Full-time mandatory fees: $160.
FINANCIAL AID *College-administered undergrad aid 1995–96:* low-interest long-term loans from external sources (average $2500). *Required forms:* FAFSA; required for some: institutional. *Application deadline:* continuous.
APPLYING *Options:* Common Application, deferred entrance, midyear entrance. *Required:* essay, school transcript, 2 recommendations, health forms, ACT. Test scores used for admission. *Application deadline:* rolling.
APPLYING/TRANSFER *Required:* essay, standardized test scores, high school transcript, 2 recommendations, college transcript, health forms. *Entrance:* minimally difficult. *Application deadline:* rolling. *Contact:* Ms. Lisa Bolin, Registrar, 615-327-3927.
CONTACT Ms. Lisa Bolin, Registrar, John A. Gupton College, 1616 Church Street, Nashville, TN 37203-2920, 615-327-3927.

KNOXVILLE BUSINESS COLLEGE
Knoxville, Tennessee

UG Enrollment: 711	Tuition & Fees: $6800
Application Deadline: 10/3	Room & Board: N/Avail

GENERAL Proprietary, 2-year, coed. Awards transfer associate, terminal associate degrees. Founded 1882. *Setting:* 2-acre urban campus. *Total enrollment:* 711. *Faculty:* 28 (8 full-time, 25% with terminal degrees, 20 part-time).
ENROLLMENT PROFILE 711 students from 2 states and territories. 5% part-time, 98% state residents, 8% transferred in, 60% 25 or older, 0% Native American, 0% Hispanic, 20% African American, 2% Asian American. *Areas of study chosen:* 50% business management and administrative services, 30% health professions and related sciences, 20% computer and information sciences. *Most popular recent majors:* paralegal studies, medical secretarial studies, legal secretarial studies.
FIRST-YEAR CLASS 326 total.
ACADEMIC PROGRAM Calendar: quarters. Academic remediation for entering students, advanced placement, summer session for credit, part-time degree program (daytime, evenings), adult/continuing education programs, internships.
GENERAL DEGREE REQUIREMENTS 100 quarter hours; computer course; internship (some majors).
MAJORS Accounting, business administration/commerce/management, computer information systems, computer management, computer science, hotel and restaurant management, legal secretarial studies, medical assistant technologies, medical secretarial studies, paralegal studies, secretarial studies/office management.
LIBRARY Knoxville Business College Library with 6,000 books, 75 periodicals, 2 on-line bibliographic services, 125 records, tapes, and CDs.
COMPUTERS ON CAMPUS 50 computers for student use in computer center, computer labs, library.
COLLEGE LIFE Student-run newspaper. *Social organizations:* 5 open to all. *Most popular organizations:* College Secretaries International, Institute of Management Accountants, Hotel/Restaurant Association, Paralegal Club. *Major annual event:* College Picnic. *Student services:* personal-psychological counseling.
HOUSING College housing not available.
CAREER PLANNING *Placement office:* 1 full-time staff. *Director:* Mr. Gary Taylor, Placement Coordinator, 423-524-3043. *Services:* job fairs, resume preparation, resume referral, career counseling, careers library, job interviews. Students must register sophomore year.
AFTER GRADUATION 9% of students completing a degree program in 1994–95 went directly on to further study.
EXPENSES FOR 1995–96 *Application fee:* $25. Tuition: $6800 full-time, $95 per quarter hour part-time.
FINANCIAL AID *College-administered undergrad aid 1995–96:* need-based scholarships, low-interest long-term loans from college funds (average $900), loans from external sources (average $2400), Federal Work-Study. *Required forms:* institutional, FAFSA; accepted: CSS Financial Aid PROFILE, state. *Application deadline:* continuous to 10/9.
APPLYING *Options:* Common Application, early entrance, deferred entrance, midyear entrance. *Required:* school transcript, interview, TOEFL for international students. *Recommended:* CPAt, SAT I, or ACT. Test scores used for counseling/placement. *Application deadline:* 10/3. *Notification:* continuous until 10/3.
APPLYING/TRANSFER *Required:* high school transcript, interview, college transcript. *Recommended:* standardized test scores. *Entrance:* moderately difficult. *Application deadline:* 10/3. *Contact:* Ms. Kimberely Hall, Dean of Academic Affairs, 423-524-3043.
CONTACT Mr. Nelson Bridge, Head of Admissions, Knoxville Business College, 720 North Fifth Avenue, Knoxville, TN 37917, 423-524-3043. *Fax:* 423-637-0127. College video available.

MID-AMERICA BAPTIST THEOLOGICAL SEMINARY
Germantown, Tennessee

CONTACT Mrs. Louise Burnett, Registrar, Mid-America Baptist Theological Seminary, Germantown, TN 38183-1528, 901-751-8453.

MOTLOW STATE COMMUNITY COLLEGE
Tullahoma, Tennessee

UG Enrollment: 3,129	Tuition & Fees (TN Res): $994
Application Deadline: rolling	Room & Board: N/Avail

GENERAL State-supported, 2-year, coed. Part of State University and Community College System of Tennessee. Awards diplomas, transfer associate, terminal associate degrees. Founded 1969. *Setting:* 187-acre small-town campus with easy access to Nashville. *Total enrollment:* 3,129. *Faculty:* 205 (71 full-time, 10% with terminal degrees, 134 part-time); student-faculty ratio is 19:1.
ENROLLMENT PROFILE 3,129 students: 67% women, 33% men, 48% part-time, 99% state residents, 5% transferred in, 1% international, 43% 25 or older, 1% Native American, 1% Hispanic, 6% African American, 1% Asian American. *Most popular recent majors:* liberal arts/general studies, nursing.
FIRST-YEAR CLASS 700 total; 2,000 applied, 100% were accepted, 35% of whom enrolled. 12% from top 10% of their high school class, 33% from top quarter, 42% from top half.
ACADEMIC PROGRAM Core, honor code. Calendar: semesters. 376 courses offered in 1995–96. Academic remediation for entering students, services for LD students, advanced placement, honors program, summer session for credit, part-time degree program (daytime, evenings, summer), adult/continuing education programs, co-op programs.
GENERAL DEGREE REQUIREMENTS 66 credits; 2 science courses; computer course.
MAJORS Accounting, biology/biological sciences, business administration/commerce/management, computer information systems, computer programming, computer science, computer technologies, early childhood education, economics, education, electrical and electronics technologies, electrical engineering technology, engineering (general), (pre)engineering sequence, engineering technology, English, geography, health education, history, information science, insurance, liberal arts/general studies, mathematics, medical records services, music, nursing, physical education, physical sciences, physical therapy, physics, psychology, real estate, secretarial studies/office management, social science, social work, sociology.
LIBRARY Crouch Learning Center with 54,000 books, 860 microform titles, 310 periodicals, 1 on-line bibliographic service, 6 CD-ROMs, 2,001 records, tapes, and CDs.
COMPUTERS ON CAMPUS 245 computers for student use in computer center, computer labs, math lab, library. Staffed computer lab on campus (open 24 hours a day).
COLLEGE LIFE Drama-theater group, student-run newspaper. *Student services:* health clinic, personal-psychological counseling, women's center. *Campus security:* 24-hour patrols, late-night transport-escort service.
HOUSING College housing not available.
ATHLETICS Member NJCAA. *Intercollegiate:* baseball M, basketball M(s)/W(s), golf M, softball W. *Intramural:* basketball, volleyball. *Contact:* Mr. Don Rhoton, Athletic Director, 615-393-1500 Ext. 1614.
CAREER PLANNING *Director:* Mr. Monty Thomas, Dean of Career Education, 615-393-1627. *Service:* career counseling.
EXPENSES FOR 1995–96 *Application fee:* $5. State resident tuition: $994 full-time, $44 per semester hour part-time. Nonresident tuition: $3920 full-time, $172 per semester hour part-time.

FINANCIAL AID ***College-administered undergrad aid 1995–96:*** 40 need-based scholarships (average $500), 50 non-need scholarships (average $225), short-term loans (average $467), Federal Work-Study, 40 part-time jobs. ***Required forms for some financial aid applicants:*** state, institutional, FAFSA; accepted: CSS Financial Aid PROFILE. ***Priority deadline:*** 5/1. ***Waivers:*** full or partial for employees or children of employees and senior citizens.
APPLYING Open admission except for nursing program. ***Options:*** early entrance, deferred entrance. ***Required:*** school transcript, TOEFL for international students. ***Required for some:*** 3 years of high school math, 2 years of high school foreign language, ACT. Test scores used for counseling/placement. ***Application deadline:*** rolling. ***Notification:*** continuous.
APPLYING/TRANSFER ***Required:*** college transcript. ***Required for some:*** 3 years of high school math, some high school foreign language. ***Application deadline:*** rolling. ***Notification:*** continuous.
CONTACT Ms. Wanda N. Fruehaut, Director of Admissions and Records, Motlow State Community College, Tullahoma, TN 37388-8100, 615-393-1500 Ext. 1530 or toll-free 800-654-4877 (in-state).

NASHVILLE STATE TECHNICAL INSTITUTE
Nashville, Tennessee

UG Enrollment: 6,386	Tuition & Fees (TN Res): $1002
Application Deadline: rolling	Room & Board: N/Avail

GENERAL State-supported, 2-year, coed. Part of State University and Community College System of Tennessee. Awards terminal associate degrees. Founded 1970. ***Setting:*** 60-acre urban campus. ***Total enrollment:*** 6,386. ***Faculty:*** 294 (94 full-time, 200 part-time); student-faculty ratio is 19:1.
ENROLLMENT PROFILE 6,386 students: 48% women, 81% part-time, 99% state residents, 9% transferred in, 1% international, 71% 25 or older, 0% Native American, 1% Hispanic, 17% African American, 2% Asian American. ***Areas of study chosen:*** 7% engineering and applied sciences, 5% communications and journalism, 2% architecture.
FIRST-YEAR CLASS 2,778 total. Of the students who applied, 100% were accepted, 90% of whom enrolled.
ACADEMIC PROGRAM Core. Calendar: semesters. Academic remediation for entering students, services for LD students, advanced placement, tutorials, summer session for credit, part-time degree program (daytime, evenings), adult/continuing education programs, co-op programs.
GENERAL DEGREE REQUIREMENTS 65 credits; 1 course each in math and science; computer course.
MAJORS Accounting, architectural technologies, automotive technologies, business administration/commerce/management, civil engineering technology, computer information systems, computer technologies, data processing, electrical engineering technology, electronics engineering technology, graphic arts, industrial engineering technology, mechanical engineering technology, occupational therapy, photography, robotics, secretarial studies/office management.
LIBRARY 38,502 books, 241 microform titles, 275 periodicals, 1 on-line bibliographic service, 15 CD-ROMs, 5,240 records, tapes, and CDs.
COMPUTERS ON CAMPUS 518 computers for student use in labs, classrooms.
COLLEGE LIFE ***Student services:*** personal-psychological counseling. ***Campus security:*** 24-hour emergency response devices and patrols, late-night transport-escort service.
HOUSING College housing not available.
ATHLETICS ***Intramural:*** table tennis (Ping-Pong), volleyball.
CAREER PLANNING ***Placement office:*** 1 full-time staff. ***Director:*** Ms. Evelyn Hadley, Admissions Career Counselor, 615-353-3233. ***Services:*** job fairs, resume preparation, resume referral, career counseling, careers library, job bank, job interviews. Students must register sophomore year.
EXPENSES FOR 1995–96 ***Application fee:*** $5. State resident tuition: $994 full-time, $44 per semester hour part-time. Nonresident tuition: $3920 full-time, $172 per semester hour part-time. Part-time mandatory fees: $4 per semester. Full-time mandatory fees: $8.
FINANCIAL AID ***College-administered undergrad aid 1995–96:*** 225 need-based scholarships (average $708), 168 non-need scholarships (average $848), short-term loans (average $380), low-interest long-term loans from external sources (average $2100), Federal Work-Study, part-time jobs. ***Required forms:*** institutional; accepted: CSS Financial Aid PROFILE, FAFSA. ***Priority deadline:*** 5/1. ***Waivers:*** full or partial for employees or children of employees and senior citizens.
APPLYING Open admission except for occupational therapy, automotive services technology, surgical technology programs. ***Options:*** deferred entrance, midyear entrance. ***Required:*** school transcript, TOEFL for international students. ***Required for some:*** 3 years of high school math, some high school foreign language, SAT I or ACT. Test scores used for counseling/placement. ***Application deadline:*** rolling. ***Notification:*** continuous. Preference given to state residents.
APPLYING/TRANSFER ***Required:*** college transcript. ***Required for some:*** standardized test scores. ***Entrance:*** noncompetitive. ***Application deadline:*** rolling. ***Notification:*** continuous.
CONTACT Mrs. Nancy Jewell, Assistant Director of Admissions, Nashville State Technical Institute, 120 White Bridge Road, Nashville, TN 37209-4515, 615-353-3214. ***Fax:*** 615-353-3243.

NORTHEAST STATE TECHNICAL COMMUNITY COLLEGE
Blountville, Tennessee

UG Enrollment: 3,488	Tuition & Fees (TN Res): $1024
Application Deadline: rolling	Room & Board: N/Avail

GENERAL State-supported, 2-year, coed. Part of State University and Community College System of Tennessee. Awards certificates, transfer associate, terminal associate degrees. Founded 1966. ***Setting:*** 100-acre small-town campus. ***Educational spending 1994–95:*** $1880 per undergrad. ***Total enrollment:*** 3,488. ***Faculty:*** 246 (90 full-time, 1% with terminal degrees, 156 part-time).
ENROLLMENT PROFILE 3,488 students from 2 states and territories. 44% women, 56% men, 50% part-time, 96% state residents, 12% transferred in, 0% international, 40% 25 or older, 2% African American. ***Areas of study chosen:*** 44% liberal arts/general studies, 30% engineering and applied sciences, 14% business management and administrative services, 7% interdisciplinary studies, 5% computer and information sciences. ***Most popular recent majors:*** electronics engineering technology, drafting and design, data processing.
FIRST-YEAR CLASS 1,196 total; 1,636 applied, 100% were accepted, 73% of whom enrolled. 10% from top 10% of their high school class, 20% from top quarter, 40% from top half.
ACADEMIC PROGRAM Core. Calendar: semesters. 387 courses offered in 1995–96; average class size 20 in required courses. Academic remediation for entering students, services for LD students, advanced placement, honors program, summer session for credit, part-time degree program (daytime, evenings), co-op programs.
GENERAL DEGREE REQUIREMENTS 64 credits; 1 math course; computer course.
MAJORS Accounting, automotive technologies, chemistry, computer programming, data processing, drafting and design, electrical and electronics technologies, electronics engineering technology, emergency medical technology, engineering technology, industrial and heavy equipment maintenance, instrumentation technology, liberal arts/general studies, machine and tool technologies, manufacturing technology, secretarial studies/office management, welding technology.
LIBRARY Learning Resource Center with 23,000 books, 110 microform titles, 415 periodicals, 13 CD-ROMs, 1,886 records, tapes, and CDs. Acquisition spending 1994–95: $142,912.
COMPUTERS ON CAMPUS 511 computers for student use in computer center, computer labs, math, writing labs, library provide access to main academic computer, e-mail, Internet. Staffed computer lab on campus provides training in use of computers, software. Academic computing expenditure 1994–95: $462,271.
COLLEGE LIFE 15% vote in student government elections. ***Social organizations:*** 15 open to all. ***Most popular organizations:*** Phi Theta Kappa, Student Government Association, Wordsmith Literary Society, Business Society, Computer Science Club. ***Major annual events:*** Spring Fling, Cultural Events, Fall Finale. ***Campus security:*** 24-hour patrols, late-night transport-escort service.
HOUSING College housing not available.
CAREER PLANNING ***Placement office:*** 1 full-time, 1 part-time staff; $48,895 operating expenditure 1994–95. ***Director:*** Ms. Kathy Webster, Career Life Counselor, 423-323-3191. ***Services:*** resume preparation, resume referral, career counseling, job interviews. 14 organizations recruited on campus 1994–95.
AFTER GRADUATION 87% of class of 1994 had job offers within 6 months. 85% of students completing a degree program went directly on to further study.
EXPENSES FOR 1995–96 ***Application fee:*** $5. State resident tuition: $994 full-time, $44 per semester hour part-time. Nonresident tuition: $3920 full-time, $172 per semester hour part-time. Part-time mandatory fees per semester range from $7 to $15. Full-time mandatory fees: $30.
FINANCIAL AID ***College-administered undergrad aid 1995–96:*** need-based scholarships, 129 non-need scholarships (average $1100), low-interest long-term loans from external sources (average $1200), 50 Federal Work-Study (averaging $750). ***Required forms:*** FAFSA; accepted: CSS Financial Aid PROFILE. ***Priority deadline:*** 7/1. ***Waivers:*** full or partial for employees or children of employees and senior citizens.
APPLYING Open admission. ***Options:*** early entrance, deferred entrance. ***Required:*** school transcript, SAT I or ACT. ***Recommended:*** 3 years of high school math and science. ***Required for some:*** TOEFL for international students. Test scores used for counseling/placement. ***Application deadline:*** rolling. ***Notification:*** continuous. Preference given to state residents.
APPLYING/TRANSFER ***Required:*** college transcript. ***Application deadline:*** rolling. ***Notification:*** continuous. ***Contact:*** Ms. Susan Allen, Director of Admissions, 423-323-3191.
CONTACT Mr. Patrick H. Sweeney, Dean of Student Services, Northeast State Technical Community College, Blountville, TN 37617-0246, 423-323-3191 Ext. 324. ***Fax:*** 423-323-3083.

PELLISSIPPI STATE TECHNICAL COMMUNITY COLLEGE
Knoxville, Tennessee

UG Enrollment: 7,468	Tuition & Fees (TN Res): $1145
Application Deadline: rolling	Room & Board: N/Avail

GENERAL State-supported, 2-year, coed. Part of State University and Community College System of Tennessee. Awards certificates, transfer associate, terminal associate degrees. Founded 1974. ***Setting:*** 144-acre suburban campus. ***Endowment:*** $838,685. ***Total enrollment:*** 7,468. ***Faculty:*** 448 (159 full-time, 289 part-time); student-faculty ratio is 19:1.
ENROLLMENT PROFILE 7,468 students from 17 states and territories, 37 other countries. 55% women, 52% part-time, 98% state residents, 9% transferred in, 28% have need-based financial aid, 2% have non-need-based financial aid, 1% international, 41% 25 or older, 1% Native American, 1% Hispanic, 4% African American, 2% Asian American. ***Areas of study chosen:*** 57% liberal arts/general studies, 7% business management and administrative services, 5% engineering and applied sciences, 4% computer and information sciences.
FIRST-YEAR CLASS 1,200 total. Of the students who applied, 100% were accepted, 90% of whom enrolled.
ACADEMIC PROGRAM Core. Calendar: semesters. 1,437 courses offered in 1995–96. Academic remediation for entering students, English as a second language program offered during academic year, services for LD students, advanced placement, honors program, summer session for credit, part-time degree program (daytime, evenings, summer), adult/continuing education programs, co-op programs and internships.
GENERAL DEGREE REQUIREMENTS 64 credit hours; computer course; internship (some majors).
MAJORS Accounting, automotive technologies, business administration/commerce/management, business machine technologies, chemical engineering technology, civil engineering technology, commercial art, computer programming, computer science, computer

Peterson's Guide to Two-Year Colleges 1997

599

Pellissippi State Technical Community College (continued)
technologies, construction technologies, data processing, drafting and design, electrical engineering technology, electronics engineering technology, environmental engineering technology, finance/banking, information science, interior design, legal secretarial studies, liberal arts/general studies, machine and tool technologies, manufacturing technology, marketing/retailing/merchandising, mechanical engineering technology, paralegal studies, secretarial studies/office management.
LIBRARY Educational Resource Center with 34,000 books, 636 microform titles, 527 periodicals, 3 on-line bibliographic services, 47 CD-ROMs, 2,222 records, tapes, and CDs. Acquisition spending 1994–95: $150,000.
COMPUTERS ON CAMPUS Computer purchase plan available. 700 computers for student use in computer center, computer labs, learning resource center, labs, classrooms, library provide access to e-mail, Internet. Staffed computer lab on campus provides training in use of computers. Academic computing expenditure 1994–95: $24.6 million.
COLLEGE LIFE Drama-theater group, choral group, student-run newspaper. 2% vote in student government elections. ***Social organizations:*** 27 open to all. ***Most popular organizations:*** Student Government Association, Progressive Student Alliance, Collegiate Secretaries International, Baptist Student Union, Vision. ***Major annual events:*** Spring Fling, Round Up, Breakfast With Santa. ***Student services:*** personal-psychological counseling. ***Campus security:*** 24-hour patrols.
HOUSING College housing not available.
ATHLETICS ***Intramural:*** basketball, bowling, golf, softball, tennis, volleyball. ***Contact:*** Mr. Bob Hoppe, Director, Student Recreation Center, 423-694-6576.
CAREER PLANNING ***Placement office:*** 7 full-time, 2 part-time staff; $222,665 operating expenditure 1994–95. ***Director:*** Dr. Phyllis Pace, Director of Student Development, 423-694-6547. ***Services:*** job fairs, resume preparation, resume referral, career counseling, careers library, job interviews. 26 organizations recruited on campus 1994–95.
AFTER GRADUATION 92% of class of 1994 had job offers within 6 months. 45% of students completing a degree program went directly on to further study.
EXPENSES FOR 1995–96 ***Application fee:*** $5. State resident tuition: $1068 full-time, $44 per credit hour part-time. Nonresident tuition: $3994 full-time, $128 per credit hour part-time. Part-time mandatory fees: $77 per year. Full-time mandatory fees: $77.
FINANCIAL AID ***College-administered undergrad aid 1995–96:*** 425 need-based scholarships (averaging $520), 135 non-need scholarships (averaging $1037), short-term loans (averaging $200), Federal Work-Study, part-time jobs. ***Required forms:*** FAFSA; required for some: state; accepted: CSS Financial Aid PROFILE. ***Priority deadline:*** 5/1. ***Payment plan:*** deferred payment. ***Waivers:*** full or partial for employees or children of employees and senior citizens. ***Notification:*** continuous.
APPLYING Open admission. ***Options:*** early entrance, deferred entrance, midyear entrance. ***Required:*** school transcript, TOEFL for international students. ***Recommended:*** 3 years of high school math and science, ACT. ***Required for some:*** 3 years of high school math, some high school foreign language, ACT. Test scores used for counseling/placement. ***Application deadline:*** rolling. ***Notification:*** continuous.
APPLYING/TRANSFER ***Required:*** high school transcript, 3 years of high school math, college transcript. ***Recommended:*** standardized test scores, 3 years of high school science. ***Required for some:*** standardized test scores, some high school foreign language. ***Entrance:*** noncompetitive. ***Application deadline:*** rolling. ***Notification:*** continuous. ***Contact:*** Ms. Jane Johnson, Director of Admissions, 423-694-6570.
CONTACT Dr. Harris Moeller, Dean of Student Affairs, Pellissippi State Technical Community College, Knoxville, TN 37933-0990, 423-694-6552. ***E-mail:*** jjohnson@pstcc.cc.tn.us.

ROANE STATE COMMUNITY COLLEGE
Harriman, Tennessee

UG Enrollment: 5,803	**Tuition & Fees (TN Res): $1460**
Application Deadline: rolling	**Room & Board: N/Avail**

GENERAL State-supported, 2-year, coed. Awards transfer associate, terminal associate degrees. Founded 1971. ***Setting:*** 104-acre rural campus with easy access to Knoxville. ***Endowment:*** $18,123. ***Educational spending 1994–95:*** $1817 per undergrad. ***Total enrollment:*** 5,803. ***Faculty:*** 337 (138 full-time, 100% with terminal degrees, 199 part-time); student-faculty ratio is 19:1. ***Notable Alumni:*** Bernadette Locke-Maddox, head coach of womens basketball at University of Kentucky; E. Scott Sills, physician; Michael Freeman, civil engineer and coordinator of traffic for 1996 Olympics; Christopher Whaley, attorney; Tom Hassler, acting director of materials management at Methodist Medical Center.
ENROLLMENT PROFILE 5,803 students: 58% women, 50% part-time, 99% state residents, 4% transferred in, 1% international, 52% 25 or older, 1% Native American, 1% Hispanic, 3% African American, 1% Asian American. ***Most popular recent majors:*** liberal arts/general studies, nursing.
FIRST-YEAR CLASS 814 total; 2,799 applied, 100% were accepted, 29% of whom enrolled. 13% from top 10% of their high school class, 22% from top quarter, 75% from top half.
ACADEMIC PROGRAM Core, honor code. Calendar: semesters. Average class size 30 in required courses. Academic remediation for entering students, services for LD students, advanced placement, Freshman Honors College, honors program, summer session for credit, part-time degree program (daytime, evenings, weekends, summer), adult/continuing education programs, co-op programs and internships. ROTC: Army (c).
GENERAL DEGREE REQUIREMENTS 64 semester hours; 1 course each in college algebra and lab science; computer course; internship (some majors).
MAJORS Accounting, art education, art/fine arts, biology/biological sciences, business administration/commerce/management, business education, chemistry, computer science, computer technologies, corrections, criminal justice, dental services, early childhood education, education, elementary education, emergency medical technology, engineering (general), (pre)engineering sequence, environmental health sciences, law enforcement/police sciences, legal secretarial studies, liberal arts/general studies, mathematics, medical laboratory technology, medical records services, medical secretarial studies, music education, nursing, occupational therapy, optical technologies, physical education, physical sciences, physical therapy, radiological technology, respiratory therapy, secretarial studies/office management, social science.
LIBRARY 52,422 books, 9,241 microform titles, 560 periodicals, 3,581 records, tapes, and CDs. Acquisition spending 1994–95: $71,189.
COMPUTERS ON CAMPUS Computer purchase plan available. 550 computers for student use in computer center, computer labs, learning resource center, classrooms, library provide access to main academic computer, off-campus computing facilities, e-mail, on-line services, Internet. Staffed computer lab on campus provides training in use of computers, software. Academic computing expenditure 1994–95: $1.2 million.
COLLEGE LIFE Drama-theater group, choral group, student-run newspaper. 20% vote in student government elections. ***Social organizations:*** 21 open to all. ***Most popular organizations:*** Baptist Student Union, American Chemical Society, Physical Therapy Student Association, Student Artists At Roane State (S.T.A.R.S.), Phi Theta Kappa. ***Major annual events:*** Thanksgiving Feast, Spring Fling, Children's Egg Hunt. ***Student services:*** health clinic, personal-psychological counseling. ***Campus security:*** 24-hour patrols.
HOUSING College housing not available.
ATHLETICS Member NJCAA. ***Intercollegiate:*** baseball M(s), basketball M(s)/W(s), softball W(s). ***Intramural:*** basketball, football, softball. ***Contact:*** Mr. Randy Nesbit, Athletic Director, 423-354-3000.
CAREER PLANNING ***Placement office:*** 1 full-time staff; $393,920 operating expenditure 1994–95. ***Director:*** Mr. Tom Gutridge, Director, Career Planning and Placement, 423-354-3000. ***Services:*** resume preparation, career counseling, careers library.
EXPENSES FOR 1995–96 ***Application fee:*** $5. State resident tuition: $1408 full-time, $44 per semester hour part-time. Nonresident tuition: $5504 full-time, $172 per semester hour part-time. Part-time mandatory fees: $10 per year. Full-time mandatory fees: $52.
FINANCIAL AID ***College-administered undergrad aid 1995–96:*** 350 non-need scholarships (average $500), short-term loans (average $391), 85 Federal Work-Study (averaging $1500). ***Required forms:*** institutional, FAFSA; accepted: CSS Financial Aid PROFILE. ***Priority deadline:*** 5/1. ***Waivers:*** full or partial for employees or children of employees and senior citizens.
APPLYING Open admission except for allied health, nursing, computer technology programs. ***Options:*** early entrance, deferred entrance. ***Required:*** school transcript, TOEFL for international students. ***Recommended:*** 3 years of high school math, 2 years of high school foreign language. ***Required for some:*** SAT I or ACT. Test scores used for counseling/placement. ***Application deadline:*** rolling. ***Notification:*** continuous. Preference given to state residents.
APPLYING/TRANSFER ***Required:*** college transcript. ***Required for some:*** standardized test scores, high school transcript. ***Entrance:*** noncompetitive. ***Application deadline:*** rolling. ***Notification:*** continuous. ***Contact:*** Ms. Joyce Perry, Coordinator of Records, 423-882-4367.
CONTACT Mr. A. Odell Fearn, Assistant to the Director, Roane State Community College, Harriman, TN 37748-5011, 423-354-3000 Ext. 4328 or toll-free 800-343-9104 (in-state). ***Fax:*** 423-354-3000 Ext. 4462. ***E-mail:*** richardson_a@a1.rscc.cc.tn.us.

SHELBY STATE COMMUNITY COLLEGE
Memphis, Tennessee

UG Enrollment: 6,350	**Tuition & Fees (TN Res): $1020**
Application Deadline: rolling	**Room & Board: N/Avail**

GENERAL State-supported, 2-year, coed. Part of State University and Community College System of Tennessee. Awards certificates, diplomas, transfer associate degrees. Founded 1970. ***Setting:*** 22-acre urban campus. ***Educational spending 1994–95:*** $1600 per undergrad. ***Total enrollment:*** 6,350. ***Faculty:*** 342 (134 full-time, 19% with terminal degrees, 208 part-time); student-faculty ratio is 21:1.
ENROLLMENT PROFILE 6,350 students from 15 states and territories. 69% women, 31% men, 52% part-time, 99% state residents, 7% transferred in, 63% have need-based financial aid, 1% have non-need-based financial aid, 0% international, 46% 25 or older, 0% Native American, 1% Hispanic, 63% African American, 1% Asian American. ***Areas of study chosen:*** 52% liberal arts/general studies, 40% health professions and related sciences, 5% business management and administrative services, 4% social sciences, 1% education. ***Most popular recent majors:*** emergency medical technology, nursing, liberal arts/general studies.
FIRST-YEAR CLASS 966 total; 2,930 applied, 100% were accepted, 33% of whom enrolled.
ACADEMIC PROGRAM Core. Calendar: semesters. 288 courses offered in 1995–96. Academic remediation for entering students, English as a second language program, services for LD students, advanced placement, summer session for credit, part-time degree program (daytime, evenings), co-op programs. ROTC: Army (c), Air Force (c).
GENERAL DEGREE REQUIREMENTS 64 semester hours; science requirement varies according to program; 1 college algebra course; computer course.
MAJORS Accounting, business administration/commerce/management, criminal justice, dietetics, early childhood education, emergency medical technology, fashion merchandising, liberal arts/general studies, marketing/retailing/merchandising, medical assistant technologies, medical laboratory technology, medical secretarial studies, nursing, physical therapy, radiological technology, secretarial studies/office management.
LIBRARY Shelby State Community College Library with 41,514 books, 369 periodicals, 4,663 records, tapes, and CDs. Acquisition spending 1994–95: $136,300.
COMPUTERS ON CAMPUS 200 computers for student use in labs, classrooms.
COLLEGE LIFE Drama-theater group, choral group, student-run newspaper. ***Social organizations:*** 19 open to all. ***Most popular organizations:*** Phi Theta Kappa, Police Science Association, Baptist Student Union, Medical Lab Technology Association, Radiological Technology Student Association. ***Major annual events:*** Homecoming/Coronation, Family Day, Job Fairs. ***Student services:*** personal-psychological counseling. ***Campus security:*** 24-hour emergency response devices and patrols, late-night transport-escort service.
HOUSING College housing not available.
ATHLETICS Member NJCAA. ***Intercollegiate:*** baseball M(s), basketball M(s)/W(s), softball W(s). ***Contact:*** Mr. Verties Sails, Athletic Director, 901-544-5143.
CAREER PLANNING ***Placement office:*** 4 full-time staff. ***Director:*** Mr. Terrance Johns, Director of Job Placement and Student Activities, 901-544-5380. ***Services:*** job fairs, resume preparation, resume referral, career counseling, careers library, job bank, job interviews. 44 organizations recruited on campus 1994–95.
AFTER GRADUATION 95% of class of 1994 had job offers within 6 months.
EXPENSES FOR 1995–96 ***Application fee:*** $5. State resident tuition: $1020 full-time, $44 per semester hour part-time. Nonresident tuition: $2926 full-time, $128 per semester hour part-time. Part-time mandatory fees: $13 per semester hour. Full-time mandatory fees: $26.
FINANCIAL AID ***College-administered undergrad aid 1995–96:*** 220 need-based scholarships (averaging $510), 407 non-need scholarships (averaging $510), short-term

loans, low-interest long-term loans from external sources (averaging $2625), 239 Federal Work-Study (averaging $2700), part-time jobs. ***Required forms:*** institutional, FAFSA; required for some: state. ***Priority deadline:*** 4/15. ***Waivers:*** full or partial for senior citizens. ***Notification:*** 6/1.

APPLYING Open admission except for allied health programs. ***Options:*** early entrance, deferred entrance. ***Required:*** school transcript, TOEFL for international students. ***Required for some:*** 3 years of high school math and science, some high school foreign language, ACT. Test scores used for counseling/placement. ***Application deadline:*** rolling. ***Notification:*** continuous. Preference given to state residents in allied health or other special programs.

APPLYING/TRANSFER ***Required:*** college transcript. ***Required for some:*** standardized test scores. ***Entrance:*** noncompetitive. ***Application deadline:*** rolling. ***Notification:*** continuous. ***Contact:*** Mrs. June Chinn-Jones, Director of Admissions, 901-544-5931.

CONTACT Ms. Verna S. Crockett, Dean of Admissions and Records, Shelby State Community College, PO Box 40568, Memphis, TN 38174-0568, 901-544-5900. ***E-mail:*** chinnjones@sscc.cc.tn.us.

STATE TECHNICAL INSTITUTE AT MEMPHIS
Memphis, Tennessee

UG Enrollment: 10,569	**Tuition & Fees (TN Res): $994**
Application Deadline: 9/1	**Room & Board: N/Avail**

GENERAL State-supported, 2-year, coed. Part of State University and Community College System of Tennessee. Awards diplomas, terminal associate degrees. Founded 1967. ***Setting:*** 100-acre suburban campus. ***Educational spending 1994–95:*** $1668 per undergrad. ***Total enrollment:*** 10,569. ***Faculty:*** 620 (161 full-time, 14% with terminal degrees, 459 part-time); student-faculty ratio is 18:1.

ENROLLMENT PROFILE 10,569 students from 7 states and territories. 46% women, 54% men, 74% part-time, 95% state residents, 16% transferred in, 16% have need-based financial aid, 5% have non-need-based financial aid, 66% 25 or older, 0% Native American, 1% Hispanic, 29% African American, 1% Asian American. ***Areas of study chosen:*** 15% engineering and applied sciences. ***Most popular recent majors:*** electronics engineering technology, accounting, secretarial studies/office management.

FIRST-YEAR CLASS 1,013 total; 5,182 applied, 100% were accepted, 20% of whom enrolled. 5% from top 10% of their high school class, 25% from top quarter, 40% from top half.

ACADEMIC PROGRAM Core, career-oriented/technical curriculum. Calendar: semesters. 617 courses offered in 1995–96; average class size 20 in required courses. Academic remediation for entering students, services for LD students, advanced placement, tutorials, summer session for credit, part-time degree program (daytime, evenings, weekends, summer), adult/continuing education programs, co-op programs and internships. ROTC: Air Force (c).

GENERAL DEGREE REQUIREMENTS 60 credits; 2 math courses; computer course; internship (some majors).

MAJORS Accounting, architectural technologies, automotive technologies, biomedical technologies, business administration/commerce/management, chemical engineering technology, civil engineering technology, computer information systems, computer science, computer technologies, data processing, electrical and electronics technologies, electrical engineering technology, electronics engineering technology, engineering technology, finance/banking, hotel and restaurant management, industrial administration, industrial engineering technology, legal secretarial studies, mechanical engineering technology, secretarial studies/office management, telecommunications.

LIBRARY Freeman Library with 50,801 books, 466 microform titles, 230 periodicals, 16 CD-ROMs. Acquisition spending 1994–95: $123,320.

COMPUTERS ON CAMPUS Computer purchase plan available. 800 computers for student use in computer center, computer labs, labs provide access to Internet. Academic computing expenditure 1994–95: $816,225.

COLLEGE LIFE Student-run newspaper. ***Social organizations:*** 19 open to all. ***Most popular organizations:*** Student Newspaper, NAACP, Phi Beta Lambda, Phi Theta Kappa, Society of Manufacturing. ***Major annual events:*** Tech Fest, International Night, Career Day. ***Student services:*** personal-psychological counseling, women's center. ***Campus security:*** 24-hour emergency response devices and patrols, late-night transport-escort service.

HOUSING College housing not available.

CAREER PLANNING ***Placement office:*** 14 full-time staff; $373,908 operating expenditure 1994–95. ***Director:*** Mr. William J. Cavanaugh, Director, Student Employment/Career Counseling, 901-383-4180. ***Services:*** job fairs, resume preparation, resume referral, career counseling, careers library, job bank, job interviews. Students must register sophomore year.

AFTER GRADUATION 89% of class of 1994 had job offers within 6 months.

EXPENSES FOR 1995–96 State resident tuition: $994 full-time, $44 per semester hour part-time. Nonresident tuition: $3920 full-time, $172 per semester hour part-time.

FINANCIAL AID ***College-administered undergrad aid 1995–96:*** 450 non-need scholarships (averaging $1100), 150 Federal Work-Study (averaging $2400), 100 part-time jobs. ***Required forms:*** institutional, FAFSA; accepted: CSS Financial Aid PROFILE, state. ***Priority deadline:*** 3/15. ***Waivers:*** full or partial for employees or children of employees and senior citizens. ***Notification:*** 6/15.

APPLYING Open admission. ***Options:*** early entrance, deferred entrance, midyear entrance. ***Required:*** TOEFL for international students. ***Recommended:*** SAT I, SAT II Subject Tests. ***Required for some:*** ACT. Test scores used for counseling/placement. ***Application deadline:*** 9/1. ***Notification:*** continuous until 9/1. Preference given to state residents.

APPLYING/TRANSFER ***Entrance:*** noncompetitive. ***Application deadline:*** 9/1. ***Notification:*** continuous until 9/1.

CONTACT Ms. Cindy Meziere, Assistant Director of Admissions, State Technical Institute at Memphis, Memphis, TN 38134-7693, 901-383-4195. ***Fax:*** 901-383-4503. ***E-mail:*** jturner@stim.tec.tn.us. College video available.

TENNESSEE INSTITUTE OF ELECTRONICS
Knoxville, Tennessee

UG Enrollment: 90	**Tuition: $8355/deg prog**
Application Deadline: rolling	**Room & Board: N/Avail**

GENERAL Proprietary, 2-year, specialized, coed. Awards terminal associate degrees. Founded 1947. ***Setting:*** 1-acre suburban campus. ***Total enrollment:*** 90. ***Faculty:*** 4; student-faculty ratio is 18:1.

ENROLLMENT PROFILE 90 students: 6% women, 30% part-time, 100% state residents, 5% transferred in, 0% international, 20% 25 or older, 0% Native American, 0% Hispanic, 2% African American, 0% Asian American.

FIRST-YEAR CLASS 20 total. Of the students who applied, 100% were accepted, 100% of whom enrolled.

ACADEMIC PROGRAM Core. Calendar: quarters. Summer session for credit, part-time degree program (evenings).

GENERAL DEGREE REQUIREMENT 162 credits.

MAJORS Communication equipment technology, computer technologies, electrical and electronics technologies, industrial engineering technology.

LIBRARY 1,200 books, 1,000 periodicals, 12 records, tapes, and CDs.

COMPUTERS ON CAMPUS 15 computers for student use in library.

HOUSING College housing not available.

EXPENSES FOR 1995–96 ***Application fee:*** $75. Tuition: $8355 per degree program.

FINANCIAL AID ***College-administered undergrad aid 1995–96:*** low-interest long-term loans from external sources. ***Required forms:*** FAFSA. ***Application deadline:*** continuous.

APPLYING Open admission. ***Required for some:*** school transcript. ***Application deadline:*** rolling. ***Notification:*** continuous.

APPLYING/TRANSFER ***Required for some:*** high school transcript. ***Application deadline:*** rolling. ***Notification:*** continuous.

CONTACT Mr. Ronald R. Rackley, Director, Tennessee Institute of Electronics, 3203 Tazewell Pike, Knoxville, TN 37918-2530, 423-688-9422.

VOLUNTEER STATE COMMUNITY COLLEGE
Gallatin, Tennessee

UG Enrollment: 6,583	**Tuition & Fees (TN Res): $1020**
Application Deadline: 7/31	**Room & Board: N/Avail**

GENERAL State-supported, 2-year, coed. Part of State University and Community College System of Tennessee. Awards certificates, transfer associate, terminal associate degrees. Founded 1970. ***Setting:*** 100-acre small-town campus with easy access to Nashville. ***Endowment:*** $68,149. ***Total enrollment:*** 6,583. ***Faculty:*** 404 (144 full-time, 24% with terminal degrees, 260 part-time); student-faculty ratio is 20:1.

ENROLLMENT PROFILE 6,583 students from 8 states and territories. 65% women, 35% men, 58% part-time, 94% state residents, 11% transferred in, 34% have need-based financial aid, 34% have non-need-based financial aid, 48% 25 or older, 0% Native American, 1% Hispanic, 7% African American, 1% Asian American. ***Areas of study chosen:*** 29% interdisciplinary studies, 26% health professions and related sciences, 18% business management and administrative services, 10% liberal arts/general studies, 10% library and information studies, 7% education, 3% premed, 2% communications and journalism, 2% engineering and applied sciences, 1% mathematics, 1% natural resource sciences, 1% prelaw. ***Most popular recent majors:*** liberal arts/general studies, business administration/commerce/management, medical records services.

FIRST-YEAR CLASS 1,050 total; 2,122 applied, 100% were accepted, 49% of whom enrolled.

ACADEMIC PROGRAM Core, interdisciplinary curriculum. Calendar: semesters. Academic remediation for entering students, services for LD students, advanced placement, self-designed majors, tutorials, honors program, summer session for credit, part-time degree program (daytime, evenings), adult/continuing education programs.

GENERAL DEGREE REQUIREMENTS 68 semester hours; 1 semester of math; 2 semesters of science; computer course.

MAJORS Business administration/commerce/management, dental services, elementary education, emergency medical technology, health education, interdisciplinary studies, liberal arts/general studies, medical records services, paralegal studies, physical therapy, radiological technology, respiratory therapy, secretarial studies/office management.

LIBRARY Learning Resource Center with 44,088 books, 150 microform titles, 320 periodicals, 3 on-line bibliographic services, 97 records, tapes, and CDs. Acquisition spending 1994–95: $83,585.

COMPUTERS ON CAMPUS 325 computers for student use in computer labs, research center, learning resource center, classrooms, library provide access to main academic computer, off-campus computing facilities, e-mail, Internet. Staffed computer lab on campus provides training in use of computers, software.

COLLEGE LIFE Drama-theater group, choral group, student-run newspaper, radio station. ***Social organizations:*** 18 open to all. ***Most popular organizations:*** Gamma Beta Phi, Returning Women's Organization, African-American Student Union, Student Government Association, The Settler. ***Major annual events:*** Homecoming, Pioneer Field Day, Fall Fling. ***Student services:*** health clinic, personal-psychological counseling. ***Campus security:*** 24-hour emergency response devices and patrols.

HOUSING College housing not available.

ATHLETICS Member NJCAA. ***Intercollegiate:*** baseball M(s), basketball M(s)/W(s). ***Intramural:*** basketball, volleyball. ***Contact:*** Mr. Richard Moore, Athletic Director, 615-452-8600 Ext. 244.

CAREER PLANNING ***Service:*** career counseling.

ESTIMATED EXPENSES FOR 1996–97 ***Application fee:*** $5. State resident tuition: $1000 full-time, $50 per semester hour part-time. Nonresident tuition: $3912 full-time, $180 per semester hour part-time. Part-time mandatory fees: $10 per semester. Full-time mandatory fees: $20.

FINANCIAL AID ***College-administered undergrad aid 1995–96:*** 137 need-based scholarships (average $626), 647 non-need scholarships (average $495), low-interest long-term loans from external sources (average $2041), 72 Federal Work-Study (averaging

Peterson's Guide to Two-Year Colleges 1997 601

Tennessee

Volunteer State Community College (continued)
$650), 24 part-time jobs. *Required forms:* institutional; accepted: FAFSA. *Priority deadline:* 4/15. *Waivers:* full or partial for employees or children of employees and senior citizens. *Average indebtedness of graduates:* $5250.
APPLYING Open admission. *Options:* Common Application, early entrance, deferred entrance. *Required:* school transcript, 3 years of high school math, some high school foreign language. *Required for some:* minimum 2.0 GPA, minimum 3.0 GPA, ACT, TOEFL for international students. Test scores used for counseling/placement. *Application deadline:* 7/31. *Notification:* continuous.
APPLYING/TRANSFER *Required:* high school transcript, 3 years of high school math, some high school foreign language. *Required for some:* standardized test scores, interview, college transcript, minimum 3.0 college GPA, minimum 2.0 high school GPA, minimum 3.0 high school GPA. *Entrance:* noncompetitive. *Application deadline:* 7/31. *Notification:* continuous. *Contact:* Mrs. Janice R. Roark, Director of Admission and Records, 615-452-8600 Ext. 460.
CONTACT Mrs. Janice R. Roark, Director of Admission and Records, Volunteer State Community College, 1360 Nashville Pike, Gallatin, TN 37066-3146, 615-452-8600 Ext. 460. *Fax:* 615-230-3577. College video available.

WALTERS STATE COMMUNITY COLLEGE
Morristown, Tennessee

UG Enrollment: 5,824	Tuition & Fees (TN Res): $1034
Application Deadline: rolling	Room & Board: N/Avail

GENERAL State-supported, 2-year, coed. Part of State University and Community College System of Tennessee. Awards transfer associate, terminal associate degrees. Founded 1970. *Setting:* 100-acre small-town campus. *Total enrollment:* 5,824. *Faculty:* 253 (111 full-time, 142 part-time); student-faculty ratio is 25:1.
ENROLLMENT PROFILE 5,824 students from 5 states and territories. 63% women, 37% men, 56% part-time, 99% state residents, 5% transferred in, 45% 25 or older, 3% African American. *Areas of study chosen:* 56% interdisciplinary studies, 28% health professions and related sciences, 5% social sciences, 4% business management and administrative services, 3% engineering and applied sciences, 2% computer and information sciences, 1% agriculture, 1% vocational and home economics. *Most popular recent majors:* liberal arts/general studies, nursing.
FIRST-YEAR CLASS 913 total; 1,930 applied, 100% were accepted, 47% of whom enrolled. 5% from top 10% of their high school class, 20% from top quarter, 50% from top half.
ACADEMIC PROGRAM Core, honor code. Calendar: semesters. 200 courses offered in 1995–96. Academic remediation for entering students, advanced placement, summer session for credit, part-time degree program (daytime, evenings, summer), adult/continuing education programs.
GENERAL DEGREE REQUIREMENTS 64 semester hours; 3 semester hours of math; computer course.
MAJORS Agricultural technologies, art education, art/fine arts, business administration/commerce/management, child care/child and family studies, computer science, criminal justice, education, (pre)engineering sequence, interdisciplinary studies, liberal arts/general studies, medical laboratory technology, medical secretarial studies, music education, nursing, physical education, radiological technology, secretarial studies/office management.
LIBRARY 55,904 books, 350 microform titles, 430 periodicals, 3,862 records, tapes, and CDs.
COMPUTERS ON CAMPUS 212 computers for student use in computer center, computer labs, accounting, math labs, library.
COLLEGE LIFE Student-run newspaper. 25% vote in student government elections. *Student services:* health clinic. *Campus security:* 24-hour emergency response devices.
HOUSING College housing not available.
ATHLETICS Member NJCAA. *Intercollegiate:* basketball M(s)/W(s). *Intramural:* basketball. *Contact:* Mr. Ron Carr, Director of Athletics, 423-587-9722 Ext. 254.
CAREER PLANNING *Service:* career counseling.
AFTER GRADUATION 85% of students completing a degree program in 1994–95 went directly on to further study.
EXPENSES FOR 1995–96 *Application fee:* $5. State resident tuition: $1034 full-time, $44 per semester hour part-time. Nonresident tuition: $3960 full-time, $179 per semester hour part-time.
FINANCIAL AID *College-administered undergrad aid 1995–96:* 50 need-based scholarships (averaging $250), 63 non-need scholarships (averaging $252), short-term loans (averaging $65), low-interest long-term loans from external sources (averaging $1866), Federal Work-Study, 40 part-time jobs. *Required forms:* institutional, FAFSA, financial aid transcript (for transfers); accepted: CSS Financial Aid PROFILE. *Priority deadline:* 3/31. *Waivers:* full or partial for minority students and employees or children of employees.
APPLYING Open admission. *Options:* early entrance, deferred entrance, midyear entrance. *Required:* 3 years of high school math, 2 years of high school foreign language, SAT I or ACT, TOEFL for international students. Test scores used for admission. *Application deadline:* rolling. *Notification:* continuous.
APPLYING/TRANSFER *Required:* 3 years of high school math, 2 years of high school foreign language. *Required for some:* standardized test scores. *Entrance:* noncompetitive. *Application deadline:* rolling. *Notification:* continuous. *Contact:* Mr. James D. Wilder, Director, Student Information Systems/Admission Service, 423-585-2683.
CONTACT Mr. James D. Wilder, Director, Student Information Systems/Admissions Service, Walters State Community College, Morristown, TN 37813-6899, 423-585-2683 or toll-free 800-225-4770 (in-state).

WATKINS INSTITUTE OF INTERIOR DESIGN
Nashville, Tennessee

Enrollment: N/R	Tuition & Fees (TN Res): $2800
Application Deadline: 8/20	Room & Board: N/Avail

GENERAL Independent, 2-year, coed. Awards certificates, transfer associate degrees. Founded 1885. *Setting:* urban campus.
ACADEMIC PROGRAM Core. Calendar: semesters. Internships.
GENERAL DEGREE REQUIREMENTS 66 credit hours; computer course; internship (some majors).
MAJORS Art/fine arts, film studies, graphic arts, interior design, photography.
HOUSING College housing not available.
ESTIMATED EXPENSES FOR 1996–97 *Application fee:* $35. State resident tuition: $2800 full-time, $240 per course part-time. Nonresident tuition: $7400 full-time, $360 per course part-time.
FINANCIAL AID *College-administered undergrad aid 1995–96:* need-based scholarships, part-time jobs. *Required forms:* institutional. *Application deadline:* continuous to 8/13.
APPLYING Open admission. *Required:* school transcript. *Recommended:* recommendations. *Required for some:* campus interview, portfolio. *Application deadline:* 8/20. *Notification:* continuous.
APPLYING/TRANSFER *Required:* college transcript, minimum 2.0 college GPA. *Recommended:* recommendations. *Required for some:* campus interview, portfolio. *Entrance:* noncompetitive. *Application deadline:* 8/20. *Notification:* continuous.
CONTACT Ms. Kim Hutto, Director of Admissions, Watkins Institute of Interior Design, 601 Church Street, Nashville, TN 37219-2390, 615-242-1851.

TEXAS

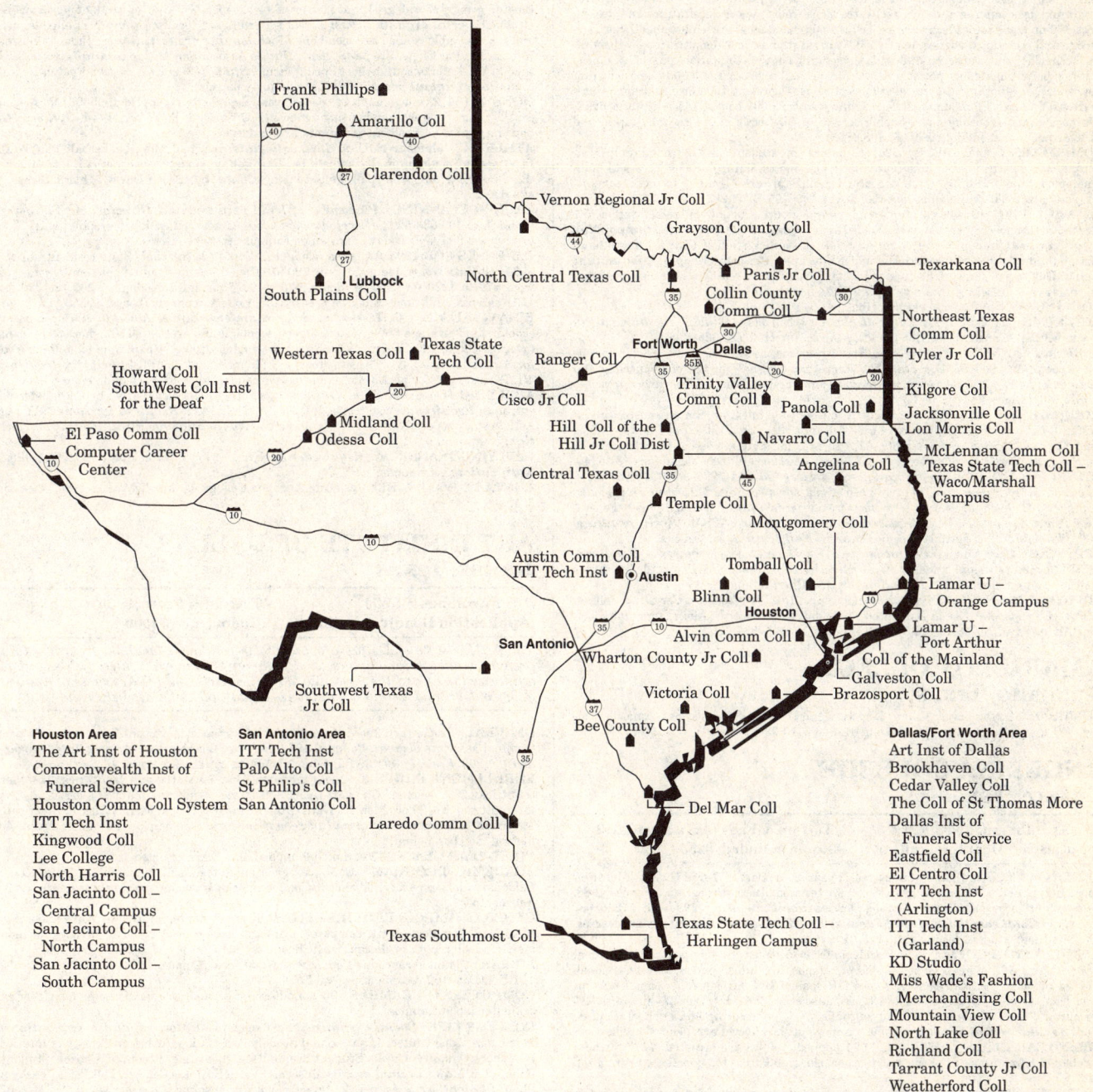

ALVIN COMMUNITY COLLEGE
Alvin, Texas

UG Enrollment: 3,864	**Tuition & Fees (Area Res):** $508
Application Deadline: rolling	**Room & Board:** N/Avail

GENERAL State and locally supported, 2-year, coed. Part of Texas Higher Education Coordinating Board. Awards transfer associate, terminal associate degrees. Founded 1949.

Setting: 113-acre small-town campus with easy access to Houston. *Total enrollment:* 3,864. *Faculty:* 141 (102 full-time, 20% with terminal degrees, 39 part-time); student-faculty ratio is 20:1.

ENROLLMENT PROFILE 3,864 students: 55% women, 63% part-time, 99% state residents, 26% transferred in, 1% international, 48% 25 or older, 1% Native American, 13% Hispanic, 8% African American, 2% Asian American. *Most popular recent majors:* liberal arts/general studies, nursing, business administration/commerce/management.

FIRST-YEAR CLASS 679 total; 892 applied, 96% were accepted, 79% of whom enrolled.

Peterson's Guide to Two-Year Colleges 1997   603

Alvin Community College (continued)
ACADEMIC PROGRAM Core, honor code. Calendar: semesters. 702 courses offered in 1995–96. Academic remediation for entering students, English as a second language program offered during academic year, services for LD students, advanced placement, self-designed majors, summer session for credit, part-time degree program (daytime, evenings), adult/continuing education programs, internships.
GENERAL DEGREE REQUIREMENTS 64 credits; 1 college algebra course; computer course; internship (some majors).
MAJORS Accounting, aerospace sciences, art/fine arts, biology/biological sciences, business administration/commerce/management, child care/child and family studies, computer programming, computer technologies, corrections, court reporting, drafting and design, electrical and electronics technologies, fashion merchandising, law enforcement/police sciences, legal secretarial studies, liberal arts/general studies, mathematics, medical laboratory technology, medical secretarial studies, mental health/rehabilitation counseling, music, nursing, paralegal studies, physical education, physical sciences, radio and television studies, respiratory therapy, secretarial studies/office management, theater arts/drama, voice.
LIBRARY Alvin Community College Library with 27,000 books, 186 microform titles, 200 periodicals, 1 on-line bibliographic service, 2 CD-ROMs, 2,381 records, tapes, and CDs. Acquisition spending 1994–95: $38,336.
COMPUTERS ON CAMPUS 200 computers for student use in computer center, computer labs, learning resource center, labs, classrooms, library provide access to main academic computer. Staffed computer lab on campus provides training in use of computers, software. Academic computing expenditure 1994–95: $251,291.
COLLEGE LIFE Drama-theater group, choral group, student-run radio station. 5% vote in student government elections. ***Social organizations:*** 33 open to all. ***Most popular organizations:*** Student Government Association, Baptist Student Union, International African Student Society, Hispanics United for Education, Phi Theta Kappa. ***Major annual events:*** Halloween Carnival, Festival of Lights, Spring Dance. ***Student services:*** personal-psychological counseling. ***Campus security:*** 24-hour patrols.
HOUSING College housing not available.
ATHLETICS Member NJCAA. ***Intercollegiate:*** baseball M(s), volleyball W(s). ***Intramural:*** soccer, softball. ***Contact:*** Mr. Don Childs, Athletic Director, 713-388-4706.
CAREER PLANNING ***Placement office:*** 1 full-time, 1 part-time staff; $68,673 operating expenditure 1994–95. ***Director:*** Mr. James Ray Couser, Director of Counseling and Testing, 713-388-4631. ***Services:*** job fairs, resume preparation, resume referral, career counseling, careers library, job bank.
EXPENSES FOR 1996–97 Area resident tuition: $468 full-time. State resident tuition: $708 full-time. Nonresident tuition: $1332 full-time. Part-time tuition per course ranges from $117 to $217 for area residents, $127 to $327 for state residents, $243 to $613 for nonresidents. Part-time mandatory fees: $20 per semester. Full-time mandatory fees: $40.
FINANCIAL AID ***College-administered undergrad aid 1995–96:*** 671 need-based scholarships (average $1250), 377 non-need scholarships (average $422), short-term loans (average $100), low-interest long-term loans from external sources (average $1370), Federal Work-Study, 80 part-time jobs. ***Required forms:*** institutional, FAFSA. ***Priority deadline:*** 6/30. ***Waivers:*** full or partial for senior citizens. ***Notification:*** continuous.
APPLYING Open admission. ***Options:*** early entrance, midyear entrance. ***Required:*** TOEFL for international students, TASP. ***Required for some:*** SAT I or ACT. Test scores used for counseling/placement. ***Application deadline:*** rolling.
APPLYING/TRANSFER ***Entrance:*** noncompetitive. ***Application deadline:*** rolling.
CONTACT Ms. JoAn Anderson, Director of Admissions/Records, Alvin Community College, Alvin, TX 77511-4898, 713-388-4615. ***Fax:*** 713-388-4895.

AMARILLO COLLEGE
Amarillo, Texas

CONTACT Mr. Dennis McMillan, Registrar and Director of Admissions, Amarillo College, PO Box 447, Amarillo, TX 79178-0001, 806-371-5024. ***Fax:*** 806-371-5370.

ANGELINA COLLEGE
Lufkin, Texas

UG Enrollment: 3,984	**Tuition & Fees (Area Res): $552**
Application Deadline: rolling	**Room & Board: $2550**

GENERAL State and locally supported, 2-year, coed. Part of Texas Higher Education Coordinating Board. Awards transfer associate, terminal associate degrees. Founded 1968. ***Setting:*** 140-acre small-town campus. ***Educational spending 1994–95:*** $1296 per undergrad. ***Total enrollment:*** 3,984. ***Faculty:*** 201 (98 full-time, 7% with terminal degrees, 103 part-time); student-faculty ratio is 23:1.
ENROLLMENT PROFILE 3,984 students from 15 states and territories. 61% women, 50% part-time, 99% state residents, 1% live on campus, 16% transferred in, 0% international, 58% 25 or older, 1% Native American, 4% Hispanic, 16% African American, 1% Asian American. ***Areas of study chosen:*** 13% social sciences, 7% education, 2% fine arts, 1% agriculture, 1% communications and journalism, 1% engineering and applied sciences. ***Most popular recent majors:*** nursing, criminal justice, liberal arts/general studies.
FIRST-YEAR CLASS 1,370 total; 1,924 applied, 100% were accepted, 71% of whom enrolled. 6% from top 10% of their high school class, 20% from top quarter, 40% from top half.
ACADEMIC PROGRAM Core, honor code. Calendar: semesters. 120 courses offered in 1995–96. Academic remediation for entering students, English as a second language program, services for LD students, advanced placement, self-designed majors, tutorials, honors program, summer session for credit, part-time degree program (daytime, evenings, summer), adult/continuing education programs, co-op programs and internships. ROTC: Army (c).
GENERAL DEGREE REQUIREMENTS 70 semester hours; internship (some majors).
MAJORS Accounting, agricultural business, agricultural sciences, art education, art/fine arts, automotive technologies, biology/biological sciences, business administration/commerce/management, chemistry, child care/child and family studies, child psychology/child development, computer programming, computer science, computer technologies, criminal justice, data processing, drafting and design, electrical and electronics technologies, electromechanical technology, elementary education, emergency medical technology, engineering (general), engineering and applied sciences, English, health education, history, humanities, human services, journalism, liberal arts/general studies, mathematics, medical laboratory technology, medical technology, music, music education, nursing, pharmacy/pharmaceutical sciences, physical education, physical sciences, physical therapy, piano/organ, postal management, practical nursing, radiological technology, real estate, respiratory therapy, science, science education, secretarial studies/office management, social science, social work, teacher aide studies, voice, welding technology.
LIBRARY Angelina College Library with 37,000 books, 270 periodicals, 3,000 records, tapes, and CDs. Acquisition spending 1994–95: $265,024.
COMPUTERS ON CAMPUS 200 computers for student use in computer center, various labs, library, student center provide access to off-campus computing facilities. Staffed computer lab on campus provides training in use of computers, software. Academic computing expenditure 1994–95: $400,000.
COLLEGE LIFE Orientation program (2 days, no cost, parents included). Drama-theater group, choral group, student-run newspaper. 9% vote in student government elections. ***Social organizations:*** 2 local fraternities, 1 local sorority; 6% of eligible men and 8% of eligible women are members. ***Most popular organizations:*** Students in Free Enterprise, Phi Theta Kappa, Student Nurses Association. ***Major annual events:*** Red Ribbon Week, Smokeout, School Spring Picnic. ***Student services:*** personal-psychological counseling. ***Campus security:*** evening security patrols.
HOUSING 112 college housing spaces available; all were occupied 1995–96. No special consideration for freshman housing applicants. Off-campus living permitted. ***Option:*** coed housing available. Resident assistants live in dorms.
ATHLETICS Member NJCAA. ***Intercollegiate:*** baseball M(s), basketball M(s)/W(s). ***Intramural:*** badminton, basketball, bowling, golf, gymnastics, racquetball, table tennis (Ping-Pong), tennis, volleyball, weight lifting. ***Contact:*** Mr. Guy Davis, Athletic Director, 409-639-1301.
CAREER PLANNING ***Placement office:*** 1 part-time staff. ***Director:*** Mr. Bill Berry, Counselor, 409-633-5292. ***Services:*** job fairs, career counseling, careers library, job interviews. 5 organizations recruited on campus 1994–95.
EXPENSES FOR 1995–96 Area resident tuition: $420 full-time. State resident tuition: $570 full-time. Nonresident tuition: $720 full-time. Part-time tuition per semester ranges from $79 to $220 for area residents, $79 to $275 for state residents, $209 to $330 for nonresidents. Full-time mandatory fees: $132. College room and board: $2550.
FINANCIAL AID ***College-administered undergrad aid 1995–96:*** 100 need-based scholarships (average $500), 120 non-need scholarships (average $250), short-term loans (average $300), 120 Federal Work-Study (averaging $1006), 6 part-time jobs. ***Required forms:*** institutional, FAFSA; accepted: CSS Financial Aid PROFILE. ***Priority deadline:*** 4/1. ***Waivers:*** full or partial for employees or children of employees and senior citizens.
APPLYING Open admission. ***Options:*** Common Application, early entrance, deferred entrance. ***Required:*** school transcript, ACT ASSET, TASP. ***Required for some:*** SAT I or ACT. Test scores used for counseling/placement. ***Application deadline:*** rolling. ***Notification:*** continuous.
APPLYING/TRANSFER ***Required:*** college transcript. ***Application deadline:*** rolling. ***Notification:*** continuous.
CONTACT Ms. J. A. Hill, Registrar, Angelina College, Lufkin, TX 75902-1768, 409-633-5212.

ART INSTITUTE OF DALLAS
Dallas, Texas

UG Enrollment: 1,200	**Tuition & Fees: $9630**
Application Deadline: rolling	**Room Only: $3900**

The Art Institute of Dallas provides postsecondary education programs that prepare students for careers in design- and business-related fields and is authorized to award the Associate of Applied Arts and the Associate of Applied Science degrees. Curricula emphasize actual job skills needed in the field.

GENERAL Proprietary, 2-year, coed. Part of Education Management Corporation. Awards terminal associate degrees. Founded 1978. ***Setting:*** 2-acre urban campus. ***Total enrollment:*** 1,200. ***Faculty:*** 84 (36 full-time, 100% with terminal degrees, 48 part-time).
ENROLLMENT PROFILE 1,200 students from 32 states and territories, 15 other countries. 55% women, 0% part-time, 85% state residents, 5% transferred in, 2% international, 5% 25 or older, 1% Native American, 16% Hispanic, 11% African American, 4% Asian American. ***Most popular recent majors:*** commercial art, music business, fashion merchandising.
FIRST-YEAR CLASS 436 total; 750 applied, 95% were accepted.
ACADEMIC PROGRAM Core, career-oriented/technical curriculum, honor code. Calendar: quarters. Academic remediation for entering students, summer session for credit, internships.
GENERAL DEGREE REQUIREMENTS 90 credit hours; internship (some majors).
MAJORS Commercial art, computer graphics, fashion design and technology, fashion merchandising, interior design, music business, photography.
LIBRARY Main library plus 1 other, with 5,300 books, 2 microform titles, 111 periodicals, 11 CD-ROMs, 162 records, tapes, and CDs.
COMPUTERS ON CAMPUS 96 computers for student use in computer labs. Staffed computer lab on campus.
COLLEGE LIFE ***Social organizations:*** 6 open to all. ***Most popular organizations:*** Music and Video United, International Student Association, American Society of Interior Designers, Quality Circle Student Committee, Learning Resource Center Student Committee. ***Major annual events:*** Music and Video Business Concert, Fall Picnic, Fashion Show. ***Student services:*** personal-psychological counseling. ***Campus security:*** 24-hour emergency response devices and patrols, late-night transport-escort service.
HOUSING 44 college housing spaces available; 37 were occupied 1995–96. No special consideration for freshman housing applicants. Off-campus living permitted. ***Option:*** coed (1 building) housing available.
CAREER PLANNING ***Placement office:*** 5 full-time staff. ***Director:*** Mrs. Peggy Sindelar, Director, 214-692-8080 Ext. 660. ***Services:*** job fairs, resume preparation, resume referral, career counseling, job bank, job interviews.
EXPENSES FOR 1996–97 ***Application fee:*** $50. Tuition: $9630 full-time, $214 per credit hour part-time. One-time mandatory fee: $250. College room only: $3900.
FINANCIAL AID ***College-administered undergrad aid 1995–96:*** need-based scholarships, 20 non-need scholarships (averaging $2300), low-interest long-term loans from external sources, Federal Work-Study, part-time jobs. ***Required forms:*** institutional, FAFSA; accepted: CSS Financial Aid PROFILE. ***Priority deadline:*** 9/19.
APPLYING Open admission. ***Option:*** deferred entrance. ***Required:*** essay, school transcript, interview, TOEFL for international students, ACT ASSET. Test scores used for counseling/placement. ***Application deadline:*** rolling.

APPLYING/TRANSFER *Required:* essay, standardized test scores, high school transcript, interview, college transcript. *Entrance:* noncompetitive.
CONTACT Mr. Randy McKinley, Director of Admissions, Art Institute of Dallas, 8080 Park Lane, Dallas, TX 75231-9959, 214-692-8080 Ext. 620 or toll-free 800-275-4243. *Fax:* 214-692-6541.

❖ *See page 692 for a narrative description.* ❖

THE ART INSTITUTE OF HOUSTON
Houston, Texas

UG Enrollment: 1,189	Tuition: $21,480/deg prog
Application Deadline: rolling	Room Only: $3393

GENERAL Proprietary, 2-year, coed. Awards transfer associate, terminal associate degrees. Founded 1978. *Setting:* urban campus. *Total enrollment:* 1,189. *Faculty:* 78 (20 full-time, 58 part-time).
ENROLLMENT PROFILE 1,189 students: 40% women, 0% part-time, 80% state residents, 85% have need-based financial aid, 7% international, 2% Native American, 20% Hispanic, 20% African American, 5% Asian American. *Most popular recent majors:* commercial art, culinary arts.
FIRST-YEAR CLASS 450 total. Of the students who applied, 95% were accepted.
ACADEMIC PROGRAM Honor code. Calendar: quarters. Academic remediation for entering students, advanced placement, summer session for credit, adult/continuing education programs, co-op programs and internships. Off-campus study at 9 members of The Art Institutes.
GENERAL DEGREE REQUIREMENTS 90 credits; 1 course each in math and science; computer course; internship (some majors).
MAJORS Art/fine arts, commercial art, culinary arts, drafting and design, film and video production, food services management, interior design, photography.
LIBRARY Resource Center with 9,000 books, 128 periodicals, 158 CD-ROMs, 606 records, tapes, and CDs.
COMPUTERS ON CAMPUS 177 computers for student use in computer center, computer labs, learning resource center provide access to main academic computer. Staffed computer lab on campus provides training in use of computers, software.
COLLEGE LIFE Orientation program (2 days, no cost, parents included). *Most popular organizations:* Texas Chef's Association, Association of Interior Designers. *Student services:* personal-psychological counseling. *Campus security:* 24-hour emergency response devices.
HOUSING 120 college housing spaces available; 105 were occupied 1995-96. No special consideration for freshman housing applicants. Off-campus living permitted. *Option:* coed housing available.
CAREER PLANNING *Placement office:* 6 full-time, 1 part-time staff. *Director:* Mr. Lee Schnell, Director of Employment Assistance and Housing Services, 713-623-2040 Ext. 740. *Services:* job fairs, resume preparation, resume referral, career counseling, careers library, job bank, job interviews. Students must register freshman year.
EXPENSES FOR 1995-96 *Application fee:* $50. Tuition per degree program ranges from $21,480 to $25,560. College room only: $3393.
FINANCIAL AID *College-administered undergrad aid 1995-96:* need-based scholarships, 5 non-need scholarships (average $4500), low-interest long-term loans from external sources, Federal Work-Study, part-time jobs. *Required forms for some financial aid applicants:* state, FAFSA. *Priority deadline:* 6/1.
APPLYING *Required:* essay, school transcript, interview. *Recommended:* minimum 2.0 GPA, recommendations, SAT I or ACT, SAT II Subject Tests. *Required for some:* TOEFL for international students. Test scores used for counseling/placement. *Application deadline:* rolling.
APPLYING/TRANSFER *Application deadline:* rolling.
CONTACT Mr. Rick Simmons, Director of Admissions, The Art Institute of Houston, 1900 Yorktown, Houston, TX 77056-4115, 713-623-2040 Ext. 720 or toll-free 800-231-6093 (out-of-state). *Fax:* 713-966-2700. College video available.

AUSTIN COMMUNITY COLLEGE
Austin, Texas

UG Enrollment: 25,275	Tuition & Fees (Area Res): $960
Application Deadline: rolling	Room & Board: N/Avail

GENERAL District-supported, 2-year, coed. Part of Texas Higher Education Coordinating Board. Awards certificates, diplomas, transfer associate, terminal associate degrees. Founded 1972. *Setting:* urban campus. *Total enrollment:* 25,275. *Faculty:* 1,388 (270 full-time, 1,118 part-time); student-faculty ratio is 17:1.
ENROLLMENT PROFILE 25,275 students: 53% women, 75% part-time, 98% state residents, 45% transferred in, 1% international, 28% 25 or older, 1% Native American, 15% Hispanic, 6% African American, 4% Asian American.
FIRST-YEAR CLASS 6,849 total; 7,000 applied, 100% were accepted, 98% of whom enrolled. 70 National Merit Scholars.
ACADEMIC PROGRAM Core. Calendar: semesters. Academic remediation for entering students, English as a second language program offered during academic year, services for LD students, self-designed majors, summer session for credit, part-time degree program (daytime, evenings, summer), adult/continuing education programs, co-op programs. Off-campus study at 2 members of the Austin Consortium. ROTC: Army (c), Air Force (c).
GENERAL DEGREE REQUIREMENTS 62 semester hours; math/science requirements vary according to program.
MAJORS Accounting, art/fine arts, astronomy, automotive technologies, biology/biological sciences, business administration/commerce/management, chemistry, child psychology/child development, commercial art, communication, computer information systems, computer programming, computer science, construction technologies, criminal justice, deaf interpreter training, drafting and design, economics, electrical and electronics technologies, electrical engineering technology, emergency medical technology, (pre)engineering sequence, English, fashion merchandising, finance/banking, fire science, food marketing, French, geology, German, heating/refrigeration/air conditioning, history, hotel and restaurant management, human services, insurance, Japanese, journalism, law enforcement/police sciences, legal secretarial studies, liberal arts/general studies, manufacturing technology, marketing/retailing/merchandising, mathematics, medical assistant technologies, medical laboratory technology, music, nursing, occupational therapy, operating room technology, paralegal studies, photography, physical sciences, physics, political science/government, printing technologies, psychology, quality control technology, radio and television studies, radiological technology, real estate, retail management, Russian, secretarial studies/office management, social work, sociology, Spanish, speech/rhetoric/public address/debate, surveying technology, technical writing, welding technology.
LIBRARY 91,000 books, 192 microform titles, 931 periodicals, 4,737 records, tapes, and CDs.
COMPUTERS ON CAMPUS 74 computers for student use in computer center.
COLLEGE LIFE Drama-theater group, student-run newspaper. *Student services:* personal-psychological counseling.
HOUSING College housing not available.
ATHLETICS *Intramural:* basketball, football, racquetball, volleyball, weight lifting.
CAREER PLANNING *Director:* Ms. Gerrie Shook, Manager, ACES Office, 512-223-7007. *Service:* career counseling.
EXPENSES FOR 1996-97 Area resident tuition: $660 full-time, $22 per semester hour part-time. State resident tuition: $1230 full-time, $41 per semester hour part-time. Nonresident tuition: $3570 full-time, $119 per semester hour part-time. Part-time mandatory fees: $10 per semester hour. Full-time mandatory fees: $300.
FINANCIAL AID *College-administered undergrad aid 1995-96:* 950 need-based scholarships (average $700), non-need scholarships, low-interest long-term loans, Federal Work-Study. *Required forms:* CSS Financial Aid PROFILE, FAFSA. *Priority deadline:* 2/16.
APPLYING Open admission. *Option:* early entrance. *Required:* TOEFL for international students. *Recommended:* school transcript, SAT I or ACT. Test scores used for admission. *Application deadline:* rolling.
APPLYING/TRANSFER *Required:* college transcript. *Recommended:* standardized test scores. *Entrance:* noncompetitive. *Application deadline:* rolling.
CONTACT Mr. Clifton Van Dyke, Director of Admissions and Records, Austin Community College, 5930 Middle Fiskville Road, Austin, TX 78752-4342, 512-223-7000. *Fax:* 512-223-7791.

BEE COUNTY COLLEGE
Beeville, Texas

UG Enrollment: 2,417	Tuition & Fees (Area Res): $574
Application Deadline: 8/15	Room & Board: $2220

GENERAL County-supported, 2-year, coed. Part of Texas Higher Education Coordinating Board. Awards transfer associate, terminal associate degrees. Founded 1965. *Setting:* 100-acre rural campus. *Total enrollment:* 2,417. *Faculty:* 134 (92 full-time, 10% with terminal degrees, 42 part-time); student-faculty ratio is 18:1.
ENROLLMENT PROFILE 2,417 students: 59% women, 41% men, 43% part-time, 99% state residents, 22% transferred in, 48% have need-based financial aid, 1% international, 45% 25 or older, 0% Native American, 54% Hispanic, 5% African American, 1% Asian American. *Most popular recent majors:* nursing, dental services, child care/child and family studies.
FIRST-YEAR CLASS 610 total; 610 applied, 100% were accepted, 100% of whom enrolled. 5% from top 10% of their high school class, 40% from top half.
ACADEMIC PROGRAM Honor code. Calendar: semesters. Academic remediation for entering students, services for LD students, advanced placement, summer session for credit, part-time degree program (daytime), adult/continuing education programs, co-op programs and internships. Off-campus study.
GENERAL DEGREE REQUIREMENTS 62 semester hours; math/science requirements vary according to program; computer course; internship (some majors).
MAJORS Accounting, agricultural sciences, applied art, art education, art/fine arts, automotive technologies, biology/biological sciences, business administration/commerce/management, chemistry, child care/child and family studies, child psychology/child development, commercial art, computer science, computer technologies, cosmetology, criminal justice, data processing, dental services, drafting and design, economics, education, elementary education, engineering (general), English, finance/banking, French, geology, German, health education, history, journalism, law enforcement/police sciences, legal secretarial studies, liberal arts/general studies, mathematics, music, music education, nursing, petroleum technology, pharmacy/pharmaceutical sciences, physical education, physics, political science/government, practical nursing, psychology, public relations, recreation and leisure services, science, secretarial studies/office management, sociology, speech/rhetoric/public address/debate, studio art, theater arts/drama, voice, welding technology.
LIBRARY Grady C. Hogue Learning Resource Center with 46,000 books, 326 periodicals, 1,550 records, tapes, and CDs.
COMPUTERS ON CAMPUS 220 computers for student use in computer center, computer labs, learning resource center, learning assistance center, classrooms, library. Staffed computer lab on campus provides training in use of computers, software.
COLLEGE LIFE Drama-theater group, choral group. *Student services:* personal-psychological counseling. *Campus security:* 24-hour emergency response devices, controlled dormitory access.
HOUSING 140 college housing spaces available; all were occupied 1995-96. No special consideration for freshman housing applicants. Off-campus living permitted. *Option:* coed housing available.
ATHLETICS *Intramural:* archery, badminton, basketball, bowling, golf, gymnastics, softball, swimming and diving, table tennis (Ping-Pong), tennis, track and field.
CAREER PLANNING *Placement office:* 1 full-time, 1 part-time staff. *Director:* Mr. Richardo Gaujardo, Career Placement Officer/Counselor, 512-358-3130 Ext. 720. *Services:* job fairs, resume preparation, resume referral, career counseling, careers library, job bank, job interviews.
EXPENSES FOR 1996-97 Area resident tuition: $574 full-time. State resident tuition: $958 full-time. Nonresident tuition: $1374 full-time. Part-time tuition per semester hour ranges from $92 to $202 for area residents, $104 to $334 for state residents, $217 to $477 for nonresidents. College room and board: $2220. College room only: $1060.
FINANCIAL AID *College-administered undergrad aid 1995-96:* need-based scholarships, 225 non-need scholarships (average $700), Federal Work-Study, 20 part-time jobs. *Required forms:* CSS Financial Aid PROFILE, institutional, FAFSA. *Priority deadline:* 4/1. *Waivers:* full or partial for senior citizens.
APPLYING Open admission. *Options:* early entrance, deferred entrance. *Required:* school transcript, TOEFL for international students. *Recommended:* SAT I or ACT. *Required for some:* SAT I or ACT, TASP. Test scores used for counseling/placement. *Application deadline:* 8/15.

Bee County College (continued)
APPLYING/TRANSFER ***Required:*** college transcript. ***Application deadline:*** 8/15.
CONTACT Mr. Pedro Martinez, Registrar, Bee County College, 3800 Charco Road, Beeville, TX 78102-2197, 512-358-3130 Ext. 2245. College video available.

BLINN COLLEGE
Brenham, Texas

UG Enrollment: 9,165 **Tuition & Fees (Area Res): $958**
Application Deadline: rolling **Room & Board: $2750**

GENERAL State and locally supported, 2-year, coed. Part of Texas Higher Education Coordinating Board. Awards transfer associate, terminal associate degrees. Founded 1883. ***Setting:*** 100-acre small-town campus with easy access to Houston. ***Total enrollment:*** 9,165. ***Faculty:*** 370 (137 full-time, 16% with terminal degrees, 233 part-time); student-faculty ratio is 25:1.
ENROLLMENT PROFILE 9,165 students from 36 states and territories, 57 other countries. 49% women, 48% part-time, 96% state residents, 9% live on campus, 38% transferred in, 2% international, 18% 25 or older, 1% Native American, 10% Hispanic, 7% African American, 2% Asian American.
FIRST-YEAR CLASS 2,566 total. Of the students who applied, 99% were accepted.
ACADEMIC PROGRAM Core, general curriculum. Calendar: semesters. 375 courses offered in 1995–96. Academic remediation for entering students, English as a second language program offered during academic year, services for LD students, tutorials, summer session for credit, part-time degree program (daytime, evenings, summer), adult/continuing education programs.
GENERAL DEGREE REQUIREMENTS 62 credit hours; 1 college algebra course; 4 credit hours of science.
MAJORS Agricultural sciences, biology/biological sciences, business administration/commerce/management, chemistry, child psychology/child development, communication, computer science, criminal justice, English, fire science, health education, history, legal secretarial studies, literature, mathematics, music, nursing, physical education, physical sciences, physics, practical nursing, radiological technology, real estate, science, secretarial studies/office management, Spanish, speech/rhetoric/public address/debate, theater arts/drama.
LIBRARY W. L. Moody, Jr. Library with 126,000 books, 800 microform titles, 900 periodicals, 3 CD-ROMs, 2,200 records, tapes, and CDs.
COMPUTERS ON CAMPUS 420 computers for student use in computer center, computer labs, classrooms. Staffed computer lab on campus.
COLLEGE LIFE Drama-theater group, choral group, marching band, student-run newspaper. 20% vote in student government elections. ***Social organizations:*** 38 open to all. ***Most popular organizations:*** Student Government Association, Phi Theta Kappa, Baptist Student Ministries, Blinn Ethnic Student Organization, Circle K International. ***Major annual events:*** Homecoming, Blinnfest, Transfer Day. ***Student services:*** personal-psychological counseling. ***Campus security:*** 24-hour emergency response devices and patrols, controlled dormitory access.
HOUSING 830 college housing spaces available; all were occupied 1995–96. No special consideration for freshman housing applicants. On-campus residence required through sophomore year except if married or living with relatives. ***Option:*** single-sex (15 buildings) housing available. Resident assistants live in dorms.
ATHLETICS Member NJCAA. ***Intercollegiate:*** baseball M(s), basketball M(s)/W(s), football M(s), softball W, volleyball W. ***Intramural:*** basketball, football, softball, table tennis (Ping-Pong), tennis, track and field, volleyball, weight lifting. ***Contact:*** Mr. Don Wilhelm, Athletic Director, 409-830-4171.
CAREER PLANNING ***Service:*** career counseling.
AFTER GRADUATION 55% of students completing a degree program in 1994–95 went directly on to further study.
EXPENSES FOR 1996–97 Area resident tuition: $558 full-time. State resident tuition: $837 full-time. Nonresident tuition: $2790 full-time. Part-time tuition per semester hour ranges from $54 to $198 for area residents, $81 to $297 for state residents, $270 to $990 for nonresidents. Part-time mandatory fees per semester range from $170 to $338. Full-time mandatory fees: $400. College room and board: $2750.
FINANCIAL AID ***College-administered undergrad aid 1995–96:*** need-based scholarships, low-interest long-term loans from external sources, part-time jobs. ***Required forms:*** FAFSA; required for some: institutional. ***Priority deadline:*** 7/1. ***Waivers:*** full or partial for employees or children of employees.
APPLYING Open admission. ***Options:*** early entrance, deferred entrance. ***Required:*** school transcript. ***Recommended:*** SAT I or ACT, SAT II Subject Tests. ***Required for some:*** TOEFL for international students, TASP, MAPS. Test scores used for counseling/placement. ***Application deadline:*** rolling.
APPLYING/TRANSFER ***Required:*** college transcript. ***Recommended:*** minimum 2.0 college GPA. ***Required for some:*** standardized test scores, high school transcript. ***Entrance:*** noncompetitive. ***Application deadline:*** rolling. ***Contact:*** Dr. Don R. Stafford, Dean, Admissions and Records, 409-830-4140.
CONTACT Dr. Don R. Stafford, Dean, Admissions and Records, Blinn College, Brenham, TX 77833-4049, 409-830-4140.

BRAZOSPORT COLLEGE
Lake Jackson, Texas

UG Enrollment: 3,104 **Tuition & Fees (Area Res): $460**
Application Deadline: 8/15 **Room & Board: N/Avail**

GENERAL State and locally supported, 2-year, coed. Awards certificates, transfer associate, terminal associate degrees. Founded 1948. ***Setting:*** 160-acre small-town campus with easy access to Houston. ***Endowment:*** $3.8 million. ***Total enrollment:*** 3,104. ***Faculty:*** 157 (61 full-time, 96 part-time); student-faculty ratio is 18:1.
ENROLLMENT PROFILE 3,104 students from 12 states and territories, 6 other countries. 50% women, 50% men, 73% part-time, 95% state residents, 5% transferred in, 1% international, 48% 25 or older, 0% Native American, 19% Hispanic, 6% African American, 1% Asian American. ***Most popular recent majors:*** computer technologies, education, business administration/commerce/management.
FIRST-YEAR CLASS 764 total.
ACADEMIC PROGRAM Honor code. Calendar: semesters. 400 courses offered in 1995–96. Academic remediation for entering students, English as a second language program offered during academic year and summer, advanced placement, summer session for credit, part-time degree program (daytime, evenings, summer), adult/continuing education programs, co-op programs and internships.
GENERAL DEGREE REQUIREMENTS 62 semester hours; 1 college algebra course; 4 semester hours of lab science; computer course (varies by major); internship (some majors).
MAJORS Art education, art/fine arts, automotive technologies, biology/biological sciences, business administration/commerce/management, carpentry, chemical engineering technology, chemistry, child care/child and family studies, computer information systems, computer technologies, construction technologies, criminal justice, drafting and design, early childhood education, education, electrical and electronics technologies, elementary education, engineering (general), engineering design, (pre)engineering sequence, English, French, heating/refrigeration/air conditioning, history, industrial and heavy equipment maintenance, industrial engineering technology, instrumentation technology, law enforcement/police sciences, legal secretarial studies, liberal arts/general studies, marketing/retailing/merchandising, mathematics, medical secretarial studies, music, nursing, physics, political science/government, practical nursing, psychology, real estate, science, secretarial studies/office management, social science, sociology, Spanish, speech/rhetoric/public address/debate, welding technology, word processing.
LIBRARY Brazosport College Library with 57,517 books, 395 microform titles, 434 periodicals, 1 on-line bibliographic service. Acquisition spending 1994–95: $329,786.
COMPUTERS ON CAMPUS Computer purchase plan available. 375 computers for student use in computer center, computer labs, learning resource center, classrooms, library provide access to main academic computer, e-mail, on-line services. Academic computing expenditure 1994–95: $268,009.
COLLEGE LIFE Orientation program (2 days, no cost). Drama-theater group, choral group. 10% vote in student government elections. ***Most popular organizations:*** Phi Theta Kappa, Baptist Student Union, African-American Club, Hispanic Club, Student Senate. ***Major annual events:*** Gator Day, Senior College Day, Fair Parade. ***Campus security:*** 24-hour patrols.
HOUSING College housing not available.
ATHLETICS ***Intramural:*** football, softball, tennis, track and field, volleyball.
CAREER PLANNING ***Director:*** Mr. George Barnett, Supervisor, Occupational Counseling and Placement, 409-266-3000. ***Services:*** resume preparation, resume referral, career counseling, careers library, job bank, job interviews.
EXPENSES FOR 1995–96 Area resident tuition: $460 full-time. State resident tuition: $610 full-time. Nonresident tuition: $2110 full-time. Part-time tuition per semester ranges from $39 to $168 for area residents, $44 to $223 for state residents, $219 to $773 for nonresidents.
FINANCIAL AID ***College-administered undergrad aid 1995–96:*** 357 need-based scholarships (average $123), 410 non-need scholarships (average $330), short-term loans (average $194), 128 part-time jobs. ***Required forms:*** institutional, FAFSA; accepted: CSS Financial Aid PROFILE. ***Priority deadline:*** 8/1. ***Waivers:*** full or partial for employees or children of employees.
APPLYING Open admission. ***Options:*** early entrance, deferred entrance. ***Required:*** TOEFL for international students. Test scores used for counseling/placement. ***Application deadline:*** 8/15.
APPLYING/TRANSFER ***Entrance:*** minimally difficult. ***Application deadline:*** 8/15. ***Contact:*** Mr. James Barta, Director of Admissions and Registrar, 409-266-3217.
CONTACT Mr. James Barta, Director of Admissions and Registrar, Brazosport College, Lake Jackson, TX 77566-3199, 409-266-3217. ***Fax:*** 409-265-2944.

BROOKHAVEN COLLEGE
Farmers Branch, Texas

UG Enrollment: 9,060 **Tuition & Fees (Area Res): $570**
Application Deadline: rolling **Room & Board: N/Avail**

GENERAL County-supported, 2-year, coed. Part of Dallas County Community College District System. Awards transfer associate, terminal associate degrees. Founded 1978. ***Setting:*** 200-acre small-town campus with easy access to Dallas–Fort Worth. ***Total enrollment:*** 9,060. ***Faculty:*** 525 (100 full-time, 24% with terminal degrees, 425 part-time).
ENROLLMENT PROFILE 9,060 students: 56% women, 75% part-time, 96% state residents, 41% transferred in, 1% international, 52% 25 or older, 1% Native American, 10% Hispanic, 8% African American, 7% Asian American. ***Most popular recent major:*** liberal arts/general studies.
FIRST-YEAR CLASS 4,042 total. Of the students who applied, 100% were accepted.
ACADEMIC PROGRAM Core, honor code. Calendar: semesters. Academic remediation for entering students, English as a second language program offered during academic year and summer, services for LD students, advanced placement, self-designed majors, tutorials, honors program, summer session for credit, part-time degree program (daytime, evenings, weekends, summer), adult/continuing education programs, internships. Off-campus study. Study-abroad program. ROTC: Army (c).
GENERAL DEGREE REQUIREMENTS 60 semester hours; computer course for accounting, automotive technologies, fashion merchandising, secretarial science, administrative management majors; internship (some majors).
MAJORS Accounting, automotive technologies, business administration/commerce/management, child care/child and family studies, child psychology/child development, commercial art, computer information systems, electromechanical technology, engineering technology, fashion merchandising, liberal arts/general studies, manufacturing technology, marketing/retailing/merchandising, nursing, retail management, secretarial studies/office management.
LIBRARY 43,000 books, 1,793 microform titles, 417 periodicals, 2,703 records, tapes, and CDs.
COMPUTERS ON CAMPUS 250 computers for student use in computer center, computer labs, learning resource center, classrooms, library.
COLLEGE LIFE Drama-theater group, choral group, student-run newspaper. ***Social organizations:*** 23 open to all; eating clubs. ***Student services:*** health clinic, personal-psychological counseling. ***Campus security:*** 24-hour emergency response devices and patrols, late-night transport-escort service.
HOUSING College housing not available.

ATHLETICS Member NJCAA. ***Intercollegiate:*** golf M/W, tennis M/W, volleyball W. ***Intramural:*** archery, basketball, bowling, gymnastics, racquetball, soccer, weight lifting. ***Contact:*** Ms. Lynn Levesque, Athletic Director, 214-860-4120.
CAREER PLANNING ***Placement office:*** 1 full-time, 3 part-time staff. ***Director:*** Ms. Patricia Harrison, Coordinator, 214-860-4892. ***Services:*** job fairs, resume preparation, resume referral, career counseling, careers library, job bank, job interviews.
EXPENSES FOR 1996–97 Area resident tuition: $520 full-time. State resident tuition: $900 full-time. Nonresident tuition: $2010 full-time. Part-time tuition per semester ranges from $54 to $196 for area residents, $111 to $386 for state residents, $201 to $737 for nonresidents. Part-time mandatory fees: $25 per semester. Full-time mandatory fees: $50.
FINANCIAL AID ***College-administered undergrad aid 1995–96:*** 5 need-based scholarships (average $125), 75 non-need scholarships (average $188), short-term loans (average $150), low-interest long-term loans from external sources (average $1442), Federal Work-Study, 84 part-time jobs. ***Required forms:*** CSS Financial Aid PROFILE, institutional, FAFSA. ***Application deadline:*** continuous to 6/1.
APPLYING Open admission. ***Options:*** Common Application, early entrance, deferred entrance. ***Required:*** TOEFL for international students, TASP. ***Recommended:*** SAT I or ACT. Test scores used for counseling/placement. ***Application deadline:*** rolling.
APPLYING/TRANSFER ***Recommended:*** standardized test scores. ***Required for some:*** standardized test scores. ***Application deadline:*** rolling. ***Contact:*** Ms. Shelia McCoy, Transfer Advisor, 214-860-4616.
CONTACT Ms. Barbara B. Burke, Registrar, Brookhaven College, Farmers Branch, TX 75244-4997, 214-860-4604. ***Fax:*** 214-860-4897. ***E-mail:*** bhc2310@dcccd.edu. College video available.

CEDAR VALLEY COLLEGE
Lancaster, Texas

UG Enrollment: 3,136 | **Tuition & Fees (Area Res): $610**
Application Deadline: rolling | **Room & Board: N/Avail**

GENERAL State-supported, 2-year, coed. Part of Dallas County Community College District System. Awards transfer associate, terminal associate degrees. Founded 1977. ***Setting:*** 353-acre small-town campus with easy access to Dallas–Fort Worth. ***Total enrollment:*** 3,136. ***Faculty:*** 130 (57 full-time, 73 part-time); student-faculty ratio is 25:1.
ENROLLMENT PROFILE 3,136 students from 2 states and territories, 1 other country. 57% women, 74% part-time, 98% state residents, 32% transferred in, 1% international, 1% Native American, 7% Hispanic, 42% African American, 1% Asian American. ***Most popular recent majors:*** liberal arts/general studies, veterinary technology, automotive technologies.
FIRST-YEAR CLASS 2,314 total. Of the students who applied, 100% were accepted.
ACADEMIC PROGRAM Core. Calendar: semesters. Academic remediation for entering students, services for LD students, advanced placement, part-time degree program (daytime, evenings, weekends), adult/continuing education programs, co-op programs.
GENERAL DEGREE REQUIREMENTS 61 semester hours; 3 semester hours of college math; 8 semester hours of lab science.
MAJORS Accounting, automotive technologies, fashion merchandising, legal secretarial studies, liberal arts/general studies, marketing/retailing/merchandising, music, veterinary technology.
COMPUTERS ON CAMPUS 50 computers for student use in computer labs.
COLLEGE LIFE ***Student services:*** health clinic, personal-psychological counseling. ***Campus security:*** 24-hour emergency response devices and patrols.
HOUSING College housing not available.
ATHLETICS ***Intercollegiate:*** baseball M, basketball M, volleyball W. ***Contact:*** Mr. Tony Airhart, 214-860-8178; Ms. Debby Yoder, 214-860-8177.
CAREER PLANNING ***Service:*** career counseling.
EXPENSES FOR 1996–97 Area resident tuition: $520 full-time. State resident tuition: $900 full-time. Nonresident tuition: $2010 full-time. Part-time tuition per semester ranges from $54 to $196 for area residents, $110 to $386 for state residents, $201 to $737 for nonresidents. Part-time mandatory fees per semester range from $25 to $37. Full-time mandatory fees: $90.
FINANCIAL AID ***College-administered undergrad aid 1995–96:*** need-based scholarships, 20 non-need scholarships (average $150), short-term loans (average $100), low-interest long-term loans from external sources, Federal Work-Study, 15 part-time jobs. ***Acceptable forms:*** CSS Financial Aid PROFILE, FAFSA. ***Application deadline:*** continuous. ***Waivers:*** full or partial for employees or children of employees.
APPLYING Open admission. ***Option:*** early entrance. ***Required:*** TOEFL for international students. ***Recommended:*** school transcript, SAT I or ACT. ***Required for some:*** recommendations, interview. Test scores used for admission and counseling/placement. ***Application deadline:*** rolling. ***Notification:*** continuous.
APPLYING/TRANSFER ***Required:*** college transcript. ***Application deadline:*** rolling. ***Notification:*** continuous. ***Contact:*** Mr. John W. Williamson, Director of Admissions and Registrar, 214-860-8201.
CONTACT Mr. John W. Williamson, Director of Admissions and Registrar, Cedar Valley College, Lancaster, TX 75134-3799, 214-860-8201.

CENTRAL TEXAS COLLEGE
Killeen, Texas

UG Enrollment: 8,600 | **Tuition & Fees (TX Res): $672**
Application Deadline: 9/6 | **Room & Board: $2652**

GENERAL State and locally supported, 2-year, coed. Part of Texas Higher Education Coordinating Board. Awards transfer associate, terminal associate degrees. Founded 1967. ***Setting:*** 500-acre small-town campus with easy access to Austin. ***Total enrollment:*** 8,600. ***Faculty:*** 328 (120 full-time, 20% with terminal degrees, 208 part-time); student-faculty ratio is 27:1.
ENROLLMENT PROFILE 8,600 students from 48 states and territories, 19 other countries. 48% women, 70% part-time, 77% state residents, 1% live on campus, 17% transferred in, 2% international, 55% 25 or older, 1% Native American, 11% Hispanic, 27% African American, 4% Asian American. ***Areas of study chosen:*** 36% liberal arts/general studies, 20% business management and administrative services, 9% health professions and related sciences, 5% social sciences, 4% computer and information sciences, 2% education, 2% engineering and applied sciences, 1% agriculture, 1% communications and journalism.
FIRST-YEAR CLASS 1,043 total. Of the students who applied, 100% were accepted, 75% of whom enrolled.
ACADEMIC PROGRAM Interdisciplinary curriculum, honor code. Calendar: semesters. Academic remediation for entering students, English as a second language program offered during academic year and summer, services for LD students, advanced placement, self-designed majors, summer session for credit, part-time degree program (daytime, evenings, weekends, summer), external degree programs, adult/continuing education programs, internships.
GENERAL DEGREE REQUIREMENTS 64 semester hours; 1 college algebra course; computer course; internship (some majors).
MAJORS Agricultural sciences, agricultural technologies, agronomy/soil and crop sciences, animal sciences, art/fine arts, automotive technologies, aviation administration, aviation technology, behavioral sciences, biology/biological sciences, broadcasting, business administration/commerce/management, business economics, chemistry, child care/child and family studies, civil engineering technology, commercial art, communication, communication equipment technology, computer information systems, computer programming, computer science, computer technologies, construction technologies, corrections, cosmetology, criminal justice, data processing, drafting and design, drug and alcohol/substance abuse counseling, education, electrical and electronics technologies, engineering (general), engineering design, engineering sciences, (pre)engineering sequence, engineering technology, English, equestrian studies, farm and ranch management, fashion design and technology, fashion merchandising, finance/banking, flight training, food services management, food services technology, geology, health education, heating/refrigeration/air conditioning, history, hospitality services, hotel and restaurant management, humanities, interdisciplinary studies, journalism, law enforcement/police sciences, legal secretarial studies, legal studies, liberal arts/general studies, marketing/retailing/merchandising, mathematics, medical laboratory technology, medical records services, medical secretarial studies, medical technology, modern languages, music, natural sciences, nursing, painting/drawing, paralegal studies, physical education, physical sciences, physics, political science/government, practical nursing, printing technologies, psychology, radio and television studies, range management, real estate, retail management, robotics, science, secretarial studies/office management, social science, sociology, Spanish, telecommunications, welding technology, wildlife management, word processing.
LIBRARY Oveta Culp Hobby Memorial Library with 73,737 books, 94,623 microform titles, 527 periodicals, 4 on-line bibliographic services, 13 CD-ROMs, 640 records, tapes, and CDs.
COMPUTERS ON CAMPUS 80 computers for student use in computer center, computer labs, learning resource center, library. Staffed computer lab on campus provides training in use of computers, software.
COLLEGE LIFE Student-run radio station. ***Social organizations:*** 22 open to all. ***Most popular organizations:*** We Can Do It Club, Career Pilot, Criminal Justice Club. ***Major annual events:*** Graduation, New Student Orientation, Student Fun Day. ***Campus security:*** 24-hour emergency response devices and patrols.
HOUSING 200 college housing spaces available; all were occupied 1995–96. No special consideration for freshman housing applicants. Off-campus living permitted. ***Option:*** coed housing available. Resident assistants live in dorms.
ATHLETICS ***Intramural:*** badminton, basketball, bowling, football, golf, soccer, softball, table tennis (Ping-Pong), tennis, volleyball, weight lifting.
CAREER PLANNING ***Placement office:*** 2 full-time, 3 part-time staff. ***Director:*** Mr. David McClure, Director, Placement and Follow-up, 817-526-1106. ***Services:*** job fairs, resume preparation, resume referral, career counseling, careers library, job bank, job interviews.
EXPENSES FOR 1995–96 State resident tuition: $576 full-time. Nonresident tuition: $2000 full-time. Part-time mandatory fees: $3 per semester hour. Part-time tuition per semester ranges from $54 to $198 for state residents, $250 to $650 for nonresidents. Full-time mandatory fees: $96. College room and board: $2652.
FINANCIAL AID ***College-administered undergrad aid 1995–96:*** 75 need-based scholarships (average $300), 60 non-need scholarships (average $2000), short-term loans (average $150), low-interest long-term loans from external sources (average $2000), Federal Work-Study. ***Required forms:*** institutional, FAFSA; accepted: CSS Financial Aid PROFILE. ***Priority deadline:*** 8/1. ***Waivers:*** full or partial for employees or children of employees. ***Notification:*** continuous.
APPLYING Open admission. ***Options:*** early entrance, deferred entrance. ***Required:*** essay, school transcript, minimum 2.0 GPA, TOEFL for international students. ***Recommended:*** SAT I or ACT. ***Required for some:*** ACT. Test scores used for counseling/placement. ***Application deadline:*** 9/6. ***Notification:*** continuous.
APPLYING/TRANSFER ***Required:*** essay, high school transcript, college transcript, minimum 2.0 college GPA, minimum 2.0 high school GPA. ***Recommended:*** standardized test scores. ***Application deadline:*** 9/6. ***Notification:*** continuous.
CONTACT Mr. Bill Alexander, Dean of Guidance and Counseling, Central Texas College, PO Box 1800, Killeen, TX 76542-4199, 817-526-1104 or toll-free 800-792-3348. College video available.

CISCO JUNIOR COLLEGE
Cisco, Texas

UG Enrollment: 2,553 | **Tuition & Fees (Area Res): $830**
Application Deadline: rolling | **Room & Board: $2200**

GENERAL State and locally supported, 2-year, coed. Part of Texas Higher Education Coordinating Board. Awards certificates, transfer associate, terminal associate degrees. Founded 1940. ***Setting:*** 40-acre rural campus. ***Total enrollment:*** 2,553. ***Faculty:*** 98 (55 full-time, 43 part-time).
ENROLLMENT PROFILE 2,553 students from 21 states and territories. 54% women, 46% men, 44% part-time, 99% state residents, 12% live on campus, 15% transferred in, 0% international, 45% 25 or older, 1% Native American, 9% Hispanic, 9% African American, 2% Asian American. ***Most popular recent majors:*** law enforcement/police sciences, education, nursing.
FIRST-YEAR CLASS 847 total; 847 applied, 100% were accepted, 100% of whom enrolled. 20% from top quarter of their high school class, 40% from top half.

Cisco Junior College (continued)

ACADEMIC PROGRAM Core, honor code. Calendar: semesters. Academic remediation for entering students, advanced placement, summer session for credit, part-time degree program (daytime, evenings). ROTC: Army (c).

GENERAL DEGREE REQUIREMENTS 63 credit hours; computer course.

MAJORS Accounting, agricultural business, agricultural sciences, automotive technologies, biology/biological sciences, business administration/commerce/management, business education, chemistry, child care/child and family studies, child psychology/child development, computer programming, computer science, construction technologies, cosmetology, dairy sciences, data processing, drafting and design, early childhood education, education, electrical and electronics technologies, finance/banking, fire science, French, history, human services, law enforcement/police sciences, marketing/retailing/merchandising, mathematics, medical technology, nursing, physical education, psychology, real estate, retail management, welding technology.

LIBRARY Maner Library with 34,000 books, 515 microform titles, 173 periodicals, 2,250 records, tapes, and CDs.

COMPUTERS ON CAMPUS 36 computers for student use in computer center, computer labs, learning resource center, library provide access to on-line services, Internet. Staffed computer lab on campus provides training in use of computers.

COLLEGE LIFE Orientation program (2 days). Drama-theater group, marching band. ***Most popular organizations:*** Christian Athletes Association, Agricultural Club. ***Major annual events:*** Homecoming, Ranch Day. ***Campus security:*** late-night transport-escort service.

HOUSING 325 college housing spaces available; all were occupied 1995–96. No special consideration for freshman housing applicants. On-campus residence required through sophomore year. ***Option:*** single-sex housing available. Resident assistants live in dorms.

ATHLETICS Member NJCAA. ***Intercollegiate:*** basketball M(s)/W(s), football M(s), softball W, volleyball W. ***Intramural:*** badminton, basketball, bowling, football, volleyball. ***Contact:*** Mr. Chuck Lawerence, Athletic Director, 817-442-2567.

CAREER PLANNING ***Service:*** career counseling. 35 organizations recruited on campus 1994–95.

EXPENSES FOR 1995–96 Area resident tuition: $830 full-time. State resident tuition: $950 full-time. Nonresident tuition: $1256 full-time. Part-time tuition per semester hour ranges from $67 to $327 for area residents, $71 to $371 for state residents, $224 to $524 for nonresidents. Room and board per year: $2200 for men, $2400 for women. College room and board: $2200 (minimum).

FINANCIAL AID ***College-administered undergrad aid 1995–96:*** 325 non-need scholarships (average $250), low-interest long-term loans from external sources (average $1250), 15 part-time jobs. ***Priority deadline:*** 8/15. ***Payment plan:*** installment. ***Waivers:*** full or partial for employees or children of employees.

APPLYING Open admission. ***Options:*** early entrance, deferred entrance. ***Recommended:*** SAT I or ACT, SAT II Subject Tests. Test scores used for counseling/placement. ***Application deadline:*** rolling.

APPLYING/TRANSFER ***Entrance:*** noncompetitive. ***Application deadline:*** rolling.

CONTACT Mr. Olin O. Odom III, Dean of Admission/Registrar, Cisco Junior College, Cisco, TX 76437-9321, 817-442-2567 Ext. 130.

CLARENDON COLLEGE
Clarendon, Texas

UG Enrollment: 811 | **Tuition & Fees (Area Res): $800**
Application Deadline: rolling | **Room & Board: $1980**

GENERAL State and locally supported, 2-year, coed. Part of Texas Higher Education Coordinating Board. Awards certificates, transfer associate, terminal associate degrees. Founded 1898. ***Setting:*** 88-acre rural campus. ***Total enrollment:*** 811. ***Faculty:*** 61 (32 full-time, 29 part-time).

ENROLLMENT PROFILE 811 students: 56% women, 44% part-time, 87% state residents, 10% transferred in, 43% 25 or older, 2% Native American, 4% Hispanic, 5% African American, 0% Asian American. ***Most popular recent majors:*** agricultural sciences, business administration/commerce/management, liberal arts/general studies.

FIRST-YEAR CLASS 289 total; 345 applied, 99% were accepted, 85% of whom enrolled. 3% from top 10% of their high school class, 7% from top quarter, 80% from top half.

ACADEMIC PROGRAM Core. Calendar: semesters. Academic remediation for entering students, summer session for credit, part-time degree program (daytime, evenings, summer), adult/continuing education programs.

GENERAL DEGREE REQUIREMENTS 62 semester hours; 3 semester hours of math; 8 semester hours of science; computer course.

MAJORS Agricultural sciences, art education, art/fine arts, automotive technologies, business administration/commerce/management, business economics, business education, child care/child and family studies, education, electrical and electronics technologies, farm and ranch management, history, liberal arts/general studies, radio and television studies.

LIBRARY 20,000 books.

COMPUTERS ON CAMPUS 30 computers for student use in business department provide access to main academic computer. Staffed computer lab on campus provides training in use of computers, software.

COLLEGE LIFE Orientation program (2 days, $8). Drama-theater group.

HOUSING 190 college housing spaces available; all were occupied 1995–96. No special consideration for freshman housing applicants. On-campus residence required through sophomore year.

ATHLETICS Member NJCAA. ***Intercollegiate:*** basketball M(s)/W(s). ***Intramural:*** badminton, basketball, football, golf, tennis, track and field, volleyball. ***Contact:*** Mr. Joe Mondragon, Athletic Director, 806-874-3571.

CAREER PLANNING ***Director:*** Mr. Nelson Christie, Counselor, 806-874-3571. ***Service:*** career counseling.

EXPENSES FOR 1996–97 Area resident tuition: $480 full-time. State resident tuition: $510 full-time. Nonresident tuition: $520 full-time, $200 per semester part-time. Part-time tuition per semester ranges from $50 to $180 for area residents, $50 to $180 for state residents. Full-time mandatory fees: $320. College room and board: $1980.

FINANCIAL AID ***College-administered undergrad aid 1995–96:*** need-based scholarships (average $150), non-need scholarships (average $100), short-term loans (average $300), Federal Work-Study, part-time jobs. ***Required forms:*** FAFSA; accepted: CSS Financial Aid PROFILE. ***Priority deadline:*** 8/1.

APPLYING Open admission. ***Options:*** early entrance, deferred entrance. ***Required:*** school transcript, ACT, TOEFL for international students. ***Required for some:*** recommendations, interview. Test scores used for counseling/placement. ***Application deadline:*** rolling. ***Notification:*** continuous.

APPLYING/TRANSFER ***Required:*** standardized test scores, high school transcript, college transcript. ***Required for some:*** recommendations, interview. ***Entrance:*** noncompetitive. ***Application deadline:*** rolling. ***Notification:*** continuous.

CONTACT Mr. L. D. Selvidge, Dean of Student Life/Registrar, Clarendon College, Clarendon, TX 79226-0968, 806-874-3571.

THE COLLEGE OF SAINT THOMAS MORE
Fort Worth, Texas

UG Enrollment: 15 | **Tuition & Fees: $5400**
Application Deadline: rolling | **Room & Board: N/Avail**

GENERAL Independent, 2-year, coed, affiliated with Roman Catholic Church. Awards transfer associate, terminal associate degrees. Founded 1981. ***Setting:*** urban campus. ***Total enrollment:*** 15. ***Faculty:*** 7 (4 full-time, 3 part-time).

ENROLLMENT PROFILE 15 students.

FIRST-YEAR CLASS 8 total; 8 applied, 100% were accepted, 100% of whom enrolled.

ACADEMIC PROGRAM Core, traditional classics curriculum. Calendar: semesters. 20 courses offered in 1995–96. Study abroad in England, Italy.

GENERAL DEGREE REQUIREMENTS 63 courses; 9 hours of math; 12 hours of Greek or Latin.

MAJORS Classics, literature, philosophy, theology.

HOUSING College housing not available.

EXPENSES FOR 1996–97 ***Application fee:*** $25. Tuition: $5200 full-time, $525 per course part-time. Full-time mandatory fees: $200.

FINANCIAL AID ***College-administered undergrad aid 1995–96:*** need-based scholarships, non-need scholarships.

APPLYING Open admission. ***Required:*** essay, school transcript, minimum 2.0 GPA, 1 recommendation, SAT I or ACT. ***Recommended:*** 2 years of high school foreign language, campus interview. Test scores used for counseling/placement. ***Application deadline:*** rolling.

APPLYING/TRANSFER ***Required:*** college transcript. ***Recommended:*** standardized test scores. ***Entrance:*** minimally difficult. ***Application deadline:*** rolling.

CONTACT Mr. Lloyd Newton, Dean of Students, The College of Saint Thomas More, 3001 Lubbock Avenue, Fort Worth, TX 76109, 817-923-8459 or toll-free 800-583-6489.

COLLEGE OF THE MAINLAND
Texas City, Texas

UG Enrollment: 3,564 | **Tuition & Fees (Area Res): $538**
Application Deadline: rolling | **Room & Board: N/Avail**

GENERAL State and locally supported, 2-year, coed. Part of Texas Higher Education Coordinating Board. Awards certificates, transfer associate, terminal associate degrees. Founded 1967. ***Setting:*** 120-acre small-town campus with easy access to Houston. ***Total enrollment:*** 3,564. ***Faculty:*** 180 (62 full-time, 118 part-time); student-faculty ratio is 25:1.

ENROLLMENT PROFILE 3,564 students from 2 states and territories, 6 other countries. 61% women, 39% men, 70% part-time, 98% state residents, 24% transferred in, 1% international, 60% 25 or older, 14% Hispanic, 16% African American, 2% Asian American. ***Most popular recent majors:*** nursing, computer science.

FIRST-YEAR CLASS 800 total; 1,000 applied, 100% were accepted, 80% of whom enrolled.

ACADEMIC PROGRAM Core. Calendar: semesters. Academic remediation for entering students, English as a second language program, services for LD students, honors program, summer session for credit, part-time degree program (daytime, evenings, summer), adult/continuing education programs, co-op programs.

GENERAL DEGREE REQUIREMENTS 62 hours; 6 hours of math; 12 hours of lab science.

MAJORS Accounting, architectural technologies, automotive technologies, business administration/commerce/management, child care/child and family studies, computer science, cosmetology, criminal justice, drafting and design, electrical and electronics technologies, emergency medical technology, finance/banking, heating/refrigeration/air conditioning, industrial engineering technology, labor studies, nursing, real estate, science.

LIBRARY 40,000 books, 300 microform titles, 325 periodicals. Acquisition spending 1994–95: $362,803.

COMPUTERS ON CAMPUS 275 computers for student use in computer center, computer labs, classrooms. Staffed computer lab on campus provides training in use of computers, software.

COLLEGE LIFE Drama-theater group, choral group, student-run newspaper. 20% vote in student government elections. ***Student services:*** personal-psychological counseling, women's center. ***Campus security:*** 24-hour emergency response devices and patrols, student patrols.

HOUSING College housing not available.

ATHLETICS ***Intramural:*** basketball, field hockey, football, gymnastics, tennis, track and field, volleyball.

CAREER PLANNING ***Services:*** job fairs, career counseling.

EXPENSES FOR 1995–96 Area resident tuition: $538 full-time. State resident tuition: $1014 full-time. Nonresident tuition: $1314 full-time. Part-time tuition per course ranges from $100 to $200 for area residents, $200 to $365 for state residents, $215 to $481.50 for nonresidents.

FINANCIAL AID ***College-administered undergrad aid 1995–96:*** need-based scholarships (average $150), low-interest long-term loans, Federal Work-Study, part-time jobs. ***Required forms:*** CSS Financial Aid PROFILE, FAFSA. ***Application deadline:*** continuous. ***Waivers:*** full or partial for employees or children of employees.

APPLYING Open admission. ***Options:*** early entrance, deferred entrance. ***Required:*** TOEFL for international students. ***Required for some:*** 3 years of high school math and

science, some high school foreign language, SAT I or ACT, TASP. Test scores used for counseling/placement. *Application deadline:* rolling. *Notification:* continuous.
APPLYING/TRANSFER *Entrance:* noncompetitive. *Application deadline:* rolling. *Notification:* continuous.
CONTACT Mr. William L. Peace, Registrar, College of the Mainland, Texas City, TX 77591-2499, 409-938-1211 Ext. 263. *Fax:* 409-938-1306.

COLLIN COUNTY COMMUNITY COLLEGE
McKinney, Texas

UG Enrollment: 10,300	Tuition & Fees (Area Res): $705
Application Deadline: rolling	Room & Board: N/Avail

GENERAL State and locally supported, 2-year, coed. Part of Texas Higher Education Coordinating Board. Awards certificates, transfer associate, terminal associate degrees. Founded 1985. *Setting:* 100-acre suburban campus with easy access to Dallas–Fort Worth. *Total enrollment:* 10,300. *Faculty:* 594 (124 full-time, 81% with terminal degrees, 470 part-time); student-faculty ratio is 21:1.
ENROLLMENT PROFILE 10,300 students from 17 states and territories, 37 other countries. 57% women, 43% men, 69% part-time, 96% state residents, 16% transferred in, 35% have need-based financial aid, 1% international, 48% 25 or older, 1% Native American, 6% Hispanic, 4% African American, 5% Asian American. *Areas of study chosen:* 16% business management and administrative services, 6% computer and information sciences, 5% health professions and related sciences, 4% engineering and applied sciences, 3% fine arts, 3% psychology, 2% biological and life sciences, 2% education, 1% social sciences, 1% agriculture, 1% communications and journalism, 1% English language/literature/letters, 1% foreign language and literature, 1% liberal arts/general studies, 1% mathematics, 1% vocational and home economics. *Most popular recent majors:* business administration/commerce/management, nursing, data processing.
FIRST-YEAR CLASS 1,897 total; 2,157 applied, 100% were accepted, 88% of whom enrolled.
ACADEMIC PROGRAM Core, honor code. Calendar: semesters. 708 courses offered in 1995–96. Academic remediation for entering students, English as a second language program offered during academic year and summer, services for LD students, advanced placement, honors program, summer session for credit, part-time degree program (daytime, evenings), adult/continuing education programs, co-op programs and internships. Study abroad in France, England.
GENERAL DEGREE REQUIREMENTS 60 credit hours; math/science requirements vary according to program; computer course.
MAJORS Accounting, advertising, anthropology, art/fine arts, biology/biological sciences, business administration/commerce/management, chemistry, child care/child and family studies, child psychology/child development, commercial art, computer information systems, computer programming, computer science, criminal justice, data processing, deaf interpreter training, drafting and design, drama therapy, early childhood education, economics, education, electrical and electronics technologies, electrical engineering technology, electronics engineering technology, emergency medical technology, engineering and applied sciences, (pre)engineering sequence, engineering technology, English, fashion merchandising, fire science, French, geography, geology, German, health science, history, horticulture, journalism, landscaping/grounds maintenance, legal secretarial studies, liberal arts/general studies, marketing/retailing/merchandising, mathematics, medical secretarial studies, music, nursing, ornamental horticulture, philosophy, photography, physical therapy, physics, political science/government, psychology, real estate, respiratory therapy, science, secretarial studies/office management, sociology, Spanish, speech/rhetoric/public address/debate, theater arts/drama, word processing.
LIBRARY 111,444 books, 460 microform titles, 675 periodicals, 35 on-line bibliographic services, 17 CD-ROMs, 6,500 records, tapes, and CDs. Acquisition spending 1994–95: $1.2 million.
COMPUTERS ON CAMPUS 800 computers for student use in computer center, computer labs, learning resource center, classrooms, library, student center provide access to main academic computer, off-campus computing facilities, e-mail, on-line services, Internet. Staffed computer lab on campus provides training in use of computers, software.
COLLEGE LIFE Drama-theater group, choral group, student-run newspaper. *Student services:* personal-psychological counseling. *Campus security:* 24-hour emergency response devices and patrols.
HOUSING College housing not available.
ATHLETICS Member NJCAA. *Intercollegiate:* baseball M(s), basketball M(s), tennis M(s)/W(s), volleyball W(s). *Intramural:* basketball, bowling, football, racquetball, softball, tennis, volleyball. *Contact:* Mr. Rex Parcells, Dean, 214-881-5790.
CAREER PLANNING *Placement office:* 6 full-time, 1 part-time staff. *Director:* Mrs. Barbara Money, Director, 214-881-5790. *Services:* job fairs, resume preparation, career counseling, job bank, job interviews. Students must register freshman year.
AFTER GRADUATION 36% of students completing a degree program in 1994–95 went directly on to further study.
EXPENSES FOR 1996–97 Area resident tuition: $435 full-time, $14.50 per credit hour part-time. State resident tuition: $645 full-time, $21.50 per credit hour part-time. Nonresident tuition: $1695 full-time, $56.50 per credit hour part-time. Part-time mandatory fees: $9 per credit hour. Full-time mandatory fees: $270.
FINANCIAL AID *College-administered undergrad aid 1995–96:* 1,300 need-based scholarships (average $2800), 55 non-need scholarships (average $600), short-term loans (average $300), low-interest long-term loans from external sources (average $2500). *Required forms:* CSS Financial Aid PROFILE, state, institutional, FAFSA. *Priority deadline:* 5/1. *Payment plan:* deferred payment. *Waivers:* full or partial for employees or children of employees and senior citizens. *Notification:* continuous.
APPLYING Open admission except for nursing, respiratory care, fire science, physical therapy programs. *Option:* early entrance. *Required:* school transcript, TOEFL for international students. *Required for some:* TASP. Test scores used for counseling/placement. *Application deadline:* rolling.
APPLYING/TRANSFER *Required:* college transcript. *Entrance:* noncompetitive. *Application deadline:* rolling. *Contact:* Mrs. Billie Collins, Director of Articulation, 214-548-6790.
CONTACT Ms. Vicki Woolverton, Admissions Supervisor, Collin County Community College, 2200 West University Drive, McKinney, TX 75070-2906, 214-881-5710. *Fax:* 214-548-6702. *E-mail:* zsbhill@express.cccd.edu. College video available.

COMMONWEALTH INSTITUTE OF FUNERAL SERVICE
Houston, Texas

UG Enrollment: 130	Tuition: $6000/deg prog
Application Deadline: rolling	Room & Board: N/Avail

GENERAL Independent, 2-year, specialized, coed. Awards certificates, diplomas, terminal associate degrees. Founded 1988. *Setting:* urban campus. *Total enrollment:* 130. *Faculty:* 6 (17% of full-time faculty have terminal degrees).
ENROLLMENT PROFILE 130 students from 11 states and territories. 36% women, 64% men, 86% state residents, 30% 25 or older, 1% Native American, 12% Hispanic, 30% African American, 1% Asian American.
ACADEMIC PROGRAM Core. Calendar: quarters. Average class size 70 in required courses.
GENERAL DEGREE REQUIREMENTS 99 quarter hours; computer course.
MAJOR Funeral service.
COMPUTERS ON CAMPUS 6 computers for student use in computer labs. Staffed computer lab on campus provides training in use of computers, software.
COLLEGE LIFE *Campus security:* 24-hour emergency response devices.
HOUSING College housing not available.
CAREER PLANNING *Services:* resume preparation, resume referral, career counseling, job bank, job interviews.
AFTER GRADUATION 89% of class of 1994 had job offers within 6 months.
EXPENSES FOR 1995-96 *Application fee:* $25. Tuition: $6000 per degree program. Full-time mandatory fees: $75.
FINANCIAL AID *College-administered undergrad aid 1995–96:* low-interest long-term loans from external sources (average $2625). *Required forms:* FAFSA; required for some: institutional. *Priority deadline:* 7/15. *Payment plan:* installment.
APPLYING *Option:* Common Application. *Required:* school transcript. *Recommended:* SAT I or ACT. Test scores used for admission. *Application deadline:* rolling. *Notification:* continuous.
APPLYING/TRANSFER *Required:* high school transcript, college transcript, minimum 2.0 college GPA. *Recommended:* standardized test scores. *Contact:* Mr. Stuart Moen, Dean, 713-873-0262.
CONTACT Ms. Patricia Moreno, Registrar, Commonwealth Institute of Funeral Service, 415 Barren Springs Drive, Houston, TX 77090, 713-873-0262 or toll-free 800-628-1580. *Fax:* 713-873-5232. College video available.

COMPUTER CAREER CENTER
El Paso, Texas

UG Enrollment: 230	Tuition & Fees: $4100
Application Deadline: N/R	Room & Board: N/Avail

GENERAL Proprietary, 2-year, coed. Awards diplomas, transfer associate degrees. *Setting:* urban campus. *Total enrollment:* 230. *Faculty:* 12 (9 full-time, 3 part-time).
ENROLLMENT PROFILE 230 students.
FIRST-YEAR CLASS 100 total. Of the students accepted, 90% enrolled.
ACADEMIC PROGRAM Calendar: 8 6-week terms.
GENERAL DEGREE REQUIREMENTS 68 units; 1 college algebra course; computer course.
MAJOR Accounting.
EXPENSES FOR 1996-97 Tuition: $4000 (minimum) full-time. Full-time tuition ranges up to $8000 according to program. Full-time mandatory fees: $100.
APPLYING Open admission. *Required:* TABE.
CONTACT Ms. Camille Medelline, Admissions Representative, Computer Career Center, 6101 Montana Avenue, El Paso, TX 79925, 915-779-8031.

DALLAS INSTITUTE OF FUNERAL SERVICE
Dallas, Texas

UG Enrollment: 225	Tuition: $7500/deg prog
Application Deadline: N/R	Room & Board: N/Avail

GENERAL Independent, 2-year, specialized, coed. Awards transfer associate, terminal associate degrees. *Setting:* urban campus. *Total enrollment:* 225. *Faculty:* 13 (6 full-time, 7 part-time).
ENROLLMENT PROFILE 225 students.
FIRST-YEAR CLASS 123 total. Of the students who applied, 100% were accepted, 90% of whom enrolled.
ACADEMIC PROGRAM Calendar: quarters.
GENERAL DEGREE REQUIREMENTS 101 quarter hours; 1 math course; computer course.
MAJOR Funeral service.
EXPENSES FOR 1996-97 Tuition: $7500 per degree program. Full-time mandatory fees: $25.
APPLYING Open admission.
CONTACT Mr. James Shoemake, President, Dallas Institute of Funeral Service, 3909 South Buckner Boulevard, Dallas, TX 75227, 214-388-5466.

DEL MAR COLLEGE
Corpus Christi, Texas

UG Enrollment: 10,757	Tuition & Fees (Area Res): $512
Application Deadline: rolling	Room & Board: N/Avail

Del Mar College (continued)

GENERAL State and locally supported, 2-year, coed. Part of Texas Higher Education Coordinating Board. Awards certificates, transfer associate, terminal associate degrees. Founded 1935. ***Setting:*** 159-acre urban campus. ***Total enrollment:*** 10,757. ***Faculty:*** 514.

ENROLLMENT PROFILE 10,757 students: 59% women, 66% part-time, 99% state residents, 7% transferred in, 68% 25 or older, 1% Native American, 49% Hispanic, 2% African American, 1% Asian American.

FIRST-YEAR CLASS 1,970 total. Of the students who applied, 99% were accepted. 2% from top 10% of their high school class, 30% from top half.

ACADEMIC PROGRAM Core, honor code. Calendar: semesters. Academic remediation for entering students, English as a second language program offered during academic year, Freshman Honors College, honors program, summer session for credit, part-time degree program (daytime, evenings, summer), adult/continuing education programs, co-op programs and internships. Off-campus study. ROTC: Army.

GENERAL DEGREE REQUIREMENTS 61 semester hours; math/science requirements vary according to program; computer course (varies by major).

MAJORS Accounting, agricultural technologies, applied art, architectural technologies, art education, art/fine arts, art history, automotive technologies, biology/biological sciences, business administration/commerce/management, chemistry, child care/child and family studies, community services, computer information systems, computer programming, computer science, cosmetology, court reporting, criminal justice, culinary arts, dental services, drafting and design, early childhood education, education, electrical and electronics technologies, electrical engineering technology, electronics engineering technology, (pre)engineering sequence, English, finance/banking, fire science, food services management, geography, geology, health education, heating/refrigeration/air conditioning, history, hotel and restaurant management, industrial and heavy equipment maintenance, interdisciplinary studies, journalism, law enforcement/police sciences, legal secretarial studies, legal studies, liberal arts/general studies, machine and tool technologies, mathematics, medical laboratory technology, medical technology, mental health/rehabilitation counseling, music, music education, music history, nursing, pharmacy/pharmaceutical sciences, physical education, physics, political science/government, psychology, public administration, public affairs and policy studies, radio and television studies, radiological technology, real estate, recreation and leisure services, respiratory therapy, retail management, secretarial studies/office management, social work, sociology, speech/rhetoric/public address/debate, studio art, theater arts/drama, veterinary sciences, vocational education, voice, welding technology, word processing.

LIBRARY 127,717 books, 739 periodicals, 6,559 records, tapes, and CDs.

COMPUTERS ON CAMPUS 450 computers for student use in computer center, computer labs, learning resource center, business building, English department, classrooms, library, student center.

COLLEGE LIFE Drama-theater group, student-run newspaper, radio station. ***Campus security:*** 24-hour emergency response devices and patrols.

HOUSING College housing not available.

ATHLETICS ***Intramural:*** archery, badminton, basketball, bowling, fencing, football, golf, gymnastics, sailing, swimming and diving, tennis, track and field, volleyball, weight lifting. ***Contact:*** Dr. Patricia A. Schmitt, Director, Department of Kinesiology, 512-886-1334.

CAREER PLANNING ***Services:*** job fairs, resume preparation, resume referral, career counseling, careers library, job bank, job interviews.

EXPENSES FOR 1995–96 Area resident tuition: $360 full-time, $180 per semester part-time. State resident tuition: $540 full-time, $270 per semester part-time. Nonresident tuition: $960 full-time, $480 per semester part-time. Part-time mandatory fees: $40 per semester. Full-time mandatory fees: $152.

FINANCIAL AID ***College-administered undergrad aid 1995–96:*** 150 need-based scholarships (average $350), 350 non-need scholarships (average $350), short-term loans (average $150), low-interest long-term loans from external sources (average $1600), Federal Work-Study, part-time jobs. ***Required forms:*** CSS Financial Aid PROFILE, state, institutional, FAFSA, financial aid transcript (for transfers). ***Priority deadline:*** 5/1. ***Waivers:*** full or partial for employees or children of employees and senior citizens.

APPLYING Open admission except for allied health programs. ***Options:*** early entrance, deferred entrance. ***Required:*** TOEFL for international students, TASP and SAT, ACT or ACT ASSET. Test scores used for counseling/placement. ***Application deadline:*** rolling.

APPLYING/TRANSFER ***Entrance:*** noncompetitive. ***Application deadline:*** rolling.

CONTACT Ms. Frances P. Jordan, Director of Admissions/Registrar, Del Mar College, Baldwin and Ayres, Corpus Christi, TX 78404-3897, 512-886-1248. College video available.

EASTFIELD COLLEGE
Mesquite, Texas

UG Enrollment: 8,458 | **Tuition & Fees (Area Res): $610**
Application Deadline: rolling | **Room & Board: N/Avail**

GENERAL State and locally supported, 2-year, coed. Part of Dallas County Community College District System. Awards certificates, transfer associate, terminal associate degrees. Founded 1970. ***Setting:*** 244-acre suburban campus with easy access to Dallas–Fort Worth. ***Total enrollment:*** 8,458. ***Faculty:*** 105 (all full-time).

ENROLLMENT PROFILE 8,458 students: 57% women, 71% part-time, 99% state residents, 25% transferred in, 1% international, 51% 25 or older, 1% Native American, 15% Hispanic, 15% African American, 6% Asian American. ***Most popular recent majors:*** liberal arts/general studies, computer programming, electrical and electronics technologies.

FIRST-YEAR CLASS 1,688 total; 1,688 applied, 100% were accepted, 100% of whom enrolled.

ACADEMIC PROGRAM Core, honor code. Calendar: semesters. Academic remediation for entering students, English as a second language program offered during academic year, services for LD students, advanced placement, honors program, summer session for credit, part-time degree program (daytime, evenings, summer), adult/continuing education programs, co-op programs.

GENERAL DEGREE REQUIREMENTS 61 credit hours; math/science requirements vary according to program.

MAJORS Accounting, automotive technologies, business administration/commerce/management, child psychology/child development, computer information systems, computer programming, deaf interpreter training, drafting and design, drug and alcohol/substance abuse counseling, early childhood education, electrical and electronics technologies, graphic arts, heating/refrigeration/air conditioning, legal secretarial studies, liberal arts/general studies, secretarial studies/office management, social work.

COMPUTERS ON CAMPUS 50 computers for student use in computer labs, library. Staffed computer lab on campus provides training in use of computers, software.

COLLEGE LIFE Drama-theater group, choral group, student-run newspaper. ***Student services:*** health clinic, personal-psychological counseling, women's center. ***Campus security:*** 24-hour emergency response devices and patrols.

HOUSING College housing not available.

ATHLETICS Member NJCAA. ***Intercollegiate:*** baseball M, basketball M, golf M, tennis M/W, volleyball M/W. ***Intramural:*** basketball, football, softball, volleyball. ***Contact:*** Mr. Robert E. Flickner, Athletic Director/Physical Education Coordinator, 214-860-7140.

CAREER PLANNING ***Placement office:*** 4 full-time, 1 part-time staff. ***Services:*** job fairs, resume preparation, career counseling, careers library, job bank, job interviews.

EXPENSES FOR 1996–97 Area resident tuition: $520 full-time. State resident tuition: $900 full-time. Nonresident tuition: $2010 full-time. Part-time tuition per semester ranges from $54 to $196 for area residents, $110 to $386 for state residents, $200 to $737 for nonresidents. Part-time mandatory fees per semester range from $25 to $37. Full-time mandatory fees: $90.

FINANCIAL AID ***College-administered undergrad aid 1995–96:*** 721 need-based scholarships (average $350), short-term loans (average $200), Federal Work-Study, 82 part-time jobs. ***Acceptable forms:*** CSS Financial Aid PROFILE, FAFSA. ***Priority deadline:*** 5/1. ***Waivers:*** full or partial for employees or children of employees. ***Average indebtedness of graduates:*** $3932.

APPLYING Open admission. ***Options:*** early entrance, deferred entrance. ***Required:*** TOEFL for international students. ***Recommended:*** 3 years of high school math and science. Test scores used for counseling/placement. ***Application deadline:*** rolling. ***Notification:*** continuous.

APPLYING/TRANSFER ***Required:*** college transcript. ***Recommended:*** 3 years of high school math and science. ***Entrance:*** noncompetitive. ***Application deadline:*** rolling. ***Notification:*** continuous.

CONTACT Miss Bobbie Trout, Director of Admissions and Registrar, Eastfield College, Mesquite, TX 75150-2099, 214-860-7005.

EL CENTRO COLLEGE
Dallas, Texas

UG Enrollment: 4,593 | **Tuition & Fees (Area Res): $948**
Application Deadline: rolling | **Room & Board: N/Avail**

GENERAL County-supported, 2-year, coed. Part of Dallas County Community College District System. Awards transfer associate, terminal associate degrees. Founded 1966. ***Setting:*** 2-acre urban campus. ***Total enrollment:*** 4,593. ***Faculty:*** 397 (121 full-time, 23% with terminal degrees, 276 part-time); student-faculty ratio is 18:1.

ENROLLMENT PROFILE 4,593 students from 38 states and territories, 54 other countries. 68% women, 32% men, 74% part-time, 98% state residents, 12% transferred in, 32% have need-based financial aid, 1% international, 51% 25 or older, 1% Native American, 17% Hispanic, 44% African American, 3% Asian American. ***Areas of study chosen:*** 17% interdisciplinary studies, 8% fine arts, 3% education. ***Most popular recent majors:*** nursing, paralegal studies, food services management.

FIRST-YEAR CLASS 779 total; 6,247 applied, 100% were accepted, 12% of whom enrolled.

ACADEMIC PROGRAM Core. Calendar: semesters. 107 courses offered in 1995–96; average class size 25 in required courses. Academic remediation for entering students, English as a second language program offered during academic year and summer, services for LD students, advanced placement, Freshman Honors College, tutorials, honors program, summer session for credit, part-time degree program (daytime, evenings, weekends, summer), adult/continuing education programs, co-op programs. Study abroad in Germany, England. ROTC: Army (c).

GENERAL DEGREE REQUIREMENTS 62 credit hours; 3 credit hours of math; computer course for business majors.

MAJORS Accounting, computer information systems, computer programming, computer science, criminal justice, culinary arts, data processing, drafting and design, fashion design and technology, fire science, food sciences, food services management, food services technology, hospitality services, hotel and restaurant management, interior design, law enforcement/police sciences, legal studies, liberal arts/general studies, medical assistant technologies, medical laboratory technology, medical records services, medical technology, nursing, operating room technology, paralegal studies, practical nursing, radiological sciences, radiological technology, respiratory therapy, textiles and clothing.

LIBRARY 71,765 books, 254 periodicals, 1,500 records, tapes, and CDs.

COMPUTERS ON CAMPUS Computers for student use in computer center, classrooms, library provide access to main academic computer, Internet. Staffed computer lab on campus provides training in use of computers, software.

COLLEGE LIFE Drama-theater group, student-run newspaper. ***Student services:*** health clinic, personal-psychological counseling. ***Campus security:*** 24-hour patrols, late-night transport-escort service.

HOUSING College housing not available.

ATHLETICS ***Intramural:*** basketball, softball, volleyball.

CAREER PLANNING ***Placement office:*** 1 part-time staff. ***Director:*** Mr. Michael Jackson, Job Placement Supervisor, 214-860-2148. ***Services:*** job fairs, resume preparation, career counseling, careers library, job bank, job interviews. 26 organizations recruited on campus 1994–95.

AFTER GRADUATION 34% of students completing a degree program in 1994–95 went directly on to further study.

EXPENSES FOR 1995–96 Area resident tuition: $948 full-time, $79 per course part-time. State resident tuition: $1632 full-time, $136 per course part-time. Nonresident tuition: $2700 full-time, $226 per course part-time.

FINANCIAL AID ***College-administered undergrad aid 1995–96:*** 163 need-based scholarships (average $750), 373 non-need scholarships (average $150), short-term loans (average $100), low-interest long-term loans, Federal Work-Study, 184 part-time jobs. ***Required forms:*** institutional, FAFSA; required for some: CSS Financial Aid PROFILE. ***Priority deadline:*** 8/1.

APPLYING Open admission except for allied health programs. ***Option:*** early entrance. ***Required:*** school transcript, TOEFL for international students. ***Recommended:*** SAT I or ACT. Test scores used for counseling/placement. ***Application deadline:*** rolling.

APPLYING/TRANSFER *Entrance:* noncompetitive. *Application deadline:* rolling.
CONTACT Mr. Robert C. Bennett, Registrar/Director of Admissions, El Centro College, Main and Lamar Streets, Dallas, TX 75202-3604, 214-860-2311. *E-mail:* rcb@dcccd.edu.

EL PASO COMMUNITY COLLEGE
El Paso, Texas

UG Enrollment: 22,264	Tuition & Fees (TX Res): $916
Application Deadline: 7/25	Room & Board: N/Avail

GENERAL County-supported, 2-year, coed. Part of Texas Higher Education Coordinating Board. Awards certificates, transfer associate, terminal associate degrees. Founded 1969. *Setting:* urban campus. *Educational spending 1994–95:* $1122 per undergrad. *Total enrollment:* 22,264. *Faculty:* 1,307 (323 full-time, 12% with terminal degrees, 984 part-time); student-faculty ratio is 17:1.
ENROLLMENT PROFILE 22,264 students from 33 states and territories, 43 other countries. 61% women, 55% part-time, 95% state residents, 4% transferred in, 1% international, 48% 25 or older, 1% Native American, 80% Hispanic, 3% African American, 1% Asian American. *Areas of study chosen:* 18% health professions and related sciences, 17% English language/literature/letters, 15% business management and administrative services, 10% engineering and applied sciences, 8% interdisciplinary studies, 6% education, 5% computer and information sciences, 4% social sciences, 2% biological and life sciences, 2% communications and journalism, 2% psychology, 1% architecture, 1% fine arts, 1% foreign language and literature, 1% liberal arts/general studies, 1% natural resource sciences, 1% performing arts, 1% physical sciences. *Most popular recent majors:* liberal arts/general studies, business administration/commerce/management, nursing.
FIRST-YEAR CLASS 3,510 total; 5,000 applied, 100% were accepted.
ACADEMIC PROGRAM Honor code. Calendar: semesters. 1,062 courses offered in 1995–96. Academic remediation for entering students, English as a second language program offered during academic year and summer, services for LD students, advanced placement, tutorials, honors program, summer session for credit, part-time degree program (daytime, evenings, weekends, summer), external degree programs, adult/continuing education programs, co-op programs. Off-campus study at University of Texas at El Paso. ROTC: Army (c).
GENERAL DEGREE REQUIREMENTS 60 credit hours; math/science requirements vary according to program; computer course.
MAJORS Accounting, architectural technologies, art/fine arts, automotive technologies, biology/biological sciences, broadcasting, business administration/commerce/management, chemistry, child care/child and family studies, commercial art, communication, computer programming, construction management, corrections, court reporting, deaf interpreter training, dental services, dietetics, drafting and design, education, electrical and electronics technologies, elementary education, (pre)engineering sequence, English, fashion design and technology, fashion merchandising, finance/banking, fire science, geology, health education, health science, heating/refrigeration/air conditioning, history, human services, industrial arts, information science, interior design, international business, law enforcement/police sciences, liberal arts/general studies, mathematics, medical assistant technologies, medical laboratory technology, medical records services, mental health/rehabilitation counseling, music, nursing, optometric/ophthalmic technologies, pharmacy/pharmaceutical sciences, photography, physical therapy, physics, political science/government, psychology, radiological technology, real estate, respiratory therapy, secretarial studies/office management, social science, sociology, speech/rhetoric/public address/debate, theater arts/drama, tourism and travel, welding technology.
LIBRARY EPCC Learning Resource Center with 87,562 books, 338 microform titles, 611 periodicals, 18 CD-ROMs, 4,422 records, tapes, and CDs.
COMPUTERS ON CAMPUS 1,200 computers for student use in computer center, computer labs, learning resource center, classrooms, library provide access to on-line services. Staffed computer lab on campus provides training in use of computers, software. Academic computing expenditure 1994–95: $600,000.
COLLEGE LIFE Drama-theater group, student-run newspaper, radio station. *Social organizations:* 52 open to all. *Most popular organizations:* African-American Coalition, Art Student Society, Phi Theta Kappa, Architecture Club, Social Science Club. *Major annual events:* National Alcohol Prevention Awareness Week, Intramural Sports Festival, Hispanic Heritage Month. *Student services:* personal-psychological counseling. *Campus security:* 24-hour patrols, late-night transport-escort service.
HOUSING College housing not available.
ATHLETICS Member NJCAA. *Intercollegiate:* baseball M, softball W. *Intramural:* basketball, bowling, cross-country running, softball, table tennis (Ping-Pong), tennis, volleyball, weight lifting. *Contact:* Mr. Robert Femat, Athletic Director, 915-594-2622.
CAREER PLANNING *Placement office:* 13 full-time, 3 part-time staff; $225,955 operating expenditure 1994–95. *Director:* Dr. Harvey Ideus, Director of Co-op, Job Placement and Career Planning, 915-594-2638. *Services:* job fairs, resume preparation, resume referral, career counseling, careers library, job bank, job interviews. 28 organizations recruited on campus 1994–95.
AFTER GRADUATION 79% of class of 1994 had job offers within 6 months. 39% of students completing a degree program went directly on to further study.
EXPENSES FOR 1995–96 *Application fee:* $10. State resident tuition: $916 full-time. Nonresident tuition: $3086 full-time. Part-time tuition per semester ranges from $94 to $354 for state residents, $259 to $1119 for nonresidents.
FINANCIAL AID *College-administered undergrad aid 1995–96:* 5,871 need-based scholarships (average $400), 603 non-need scholarships (average $372), short-term loans (average $150), low-interest long-term loans from external sources (average $2625), 755 Federal Work-Study (averaging $1930). *Required forms:* institutional, FAFSA; required for some: state; accepted: CSS Financial Aid PROFILE. *Priority deadline:* 6/1. *Waivers:* full or partial for employees or children of employees and senior citizens. *Notification:* 7/1.
APPLYING Open admission. *Options:* early entrance, deferred entrance, midyear entrance. *Required:* TOEFL for international students. *Recommended:* school transcript, SAT I or ACT. Test scores used for counseling/placement. *Application deadline:* 7/25.
APPLYING/TRANSFER *Recommended:* standardized test scores, high school transcript. *Entrance:* noncompetitive. *Application deadline:* 7/25. *Contact:* Mr. Tim Nugent, Director of Admissions, 915-594-2150.
CONTACT Mr. Tim Nugent, Director of Admissions, El Paso Community College, PO Box 20500, El Paso, TX 79998-0500, 915-594-2150. *Fax:* 915-594-2161.

FRANK PHILLIPS COLLEGE
Borger, Texas

UG Enrollment: 1,108	Tuition & Fees (Area Res): $686
Application Deadline: 8/25	Room & Board: $2050

GENERAL State and locally supported, 2-year, coed. Part of Texas Higher Education Coordinating Board. Awards transfer associate, terminal associate degrees. Founded 1948. *Setting:* 60-acre small-town campus. *Total enrollment:* 1,108. *Faculty:* 93 (25 full-time, 68 part-time).
ENROLLMENT PROFILE 1,108 students from 6 states and territories, 6 other countries. 55% women, 25% part-time, 95% state residents, 10% transferred in, 45% 25 or older, 1% Native American, 5% Hispanic, 5% African American, 1% Asian American. *Most popular recent majors:* nursing, business administration/commerce/management, education.
FIRST-YEAR CLASS 462 total. Of the students who applied, 100% were accepted. 25% from top 10% of their high school class, 75% from top half.
ACADEMIC PROGRAM Calendar: semesters. Academic remediation for entering students, self-designed majors, honors program, summer session for credit, part-time degree program (daytime, evenings, weekends, summer), adult/continuing education programs, co-op programs and internships. ROTC: Army (c).
GENERAL DEGREE REQUIREMENTS 62 credit hours; math/science requirements vary according to program; computer course.
MAJORS Accounting, agricultural business, agricultural economics, agricultural education, agricultural technologies, agronomy/soil and crop sciences, anatomy, art education, art/fine arts, biology/biological sciences, botany/plant sciences, broadcasting, business administration/commerce/management, business economics, business education, business machine technologies, chemistry, child psychology/child development, computer programming, computer science, computer technologies, cosmetology, data processing, economics, education, electrical engineering technology, elementary education, engineering (general), (pre)engineering sequence, engineering technology, English, farm and ranch management, finance/banking, fire science, flight training, heating/refrigeration/air conditioning, history, horticulture, law enforcement/police sciences, legal secretarial studies, liberal arts/general studies, mathematics, music, music education, natural resource management, nursing, petroleum technology, pharmacy/pharmaceutical sciences, physical education, physical sciences, piano/organ, political science/government, postal management, psychology, science, secretarial studies/office management, sociology, surveying technology, welding technology, zoology.
LIBRARY Frank Phillips College Learning Resource Center with 28,000 books, 1,975 microform titles, 196 periodicals, 1,553 records, tapes, and CDs.
COMPUTERS ON CAMPUS 29 computers for student use in computer center, administration building. Staffed computer lab on campus provides training in use of computers, software.
COLLEGE LIFE *Student services:* personal-psychological counseling. *Campus security:* 24-hour emergency response devices and patrols.
HOUSING 200 college housing spaces available; 150 were occupied 1995–96. No special consideration for freshman housing applicants. Off-campus living permitted. *Option:* single-sex housing available. Resident assistants live in dorms.
ATHLETICS Member NJCAA. *Intercollegiate:* baseball M(s), basketball M(s)/W(s), volleyball W(s). *Intramural:* basketball, racquetball, volleyball. *Contact:* Mr. Garry McGregor, Athletic Director, 806-274-5311 Ext. 24.
CAREER PLANNING *Director:* Ms. Traci Keisling, Counselor, 806-274-5311 Ext. 51. *Services:* job fairs, resume preparation, career counseling, careers library.
EXPENSES FOR 1996–97 Area resident tuition: $496 full-time. State resident tuition: $713 full-time. Nonresident tuition: $775 full-time. Part-time tuition per semester ranges from $50 to $240 for area residents, $70 to $345 for state residents, $200 to $375 for nonresidents. Part-time mandatory fees: $190 per year. Full-time mandatory fees: $190. College room and board: $2050.
FINANCIAL AID *College-administered undergrad aid 1995–96:* 85 need-based scholarships (averaging $850), 200 non-need scholarships (averaging $200), low-interest long-term loans from external sources (averaging $2000), Federal Work-Study, part-time jobs. *Required forms:* institutional; accepted: CSS Financial Aid PROFILE, state, FAFSA. *Priority deadline:* 8/25.
APPLYING Open admission. *Options:* early entrance, deferred entrance. *Required:* school transcript, TOEFL for international students, TASP. Test scores used for counseling/placement. *Application deadline:* 8/25. *Notification:* continuous until 8/25.
APPLYING/TRANSFER *Required:* high school transcript, college transcript. *Entrance:* noncompetitive.
CONTACT Ms. Glenda Guyton, Dean of Student Life, Frank Phillips College, Borger, TX 79008-5118, 806-274-5311 Ext. 20.

GALVESTON COLLEGE
Galveston, Texas

UG Enrollment: 2,218	Tuition & Fees (TX Res): $740
Application Deadline: rolling	Room & Board: N/Avail

GENERAL State and locally supported, 2-year, coed. Part of Texas Higher Education Coordinating Board. Awards certificates, transfer associate, terminal associate degrees. Founded 1967. *Setting:* 11-acre urban campus with easy access to Houston. *Educational spending 1994–95:* $1945 per undergrad. *Total enrollment:* 2,218. *Faculty:* 146 (48 full-time, 100% with terminal degrees, 98 part-time); student-faculty ratio is 19:1.
ENROLLMENT PROFILE 2,218 students from 84 states and territories, 31 other countries. 66% women, 34% men, 71% part-time, 95% state residents, 12% transferred in, 1% international, 50% 25 or older, 1% Native American, 20% Hispanic, 17% African American, 3% Asian American. *Most popular recent majors:* nursing, radiological technology, business administration/commerce/management.
FIRST-YEAR CLASS 342 total; 342 applied, 100% were accepted, 100% of whom enrolled.
ACADEMIC PROGRAM Core. Calendar: semesters. 521 courses offered in 1995–96. Academic remediation for entering students, English as a second language program offered during academic year, services for LD students, advanced placement, summer session for

Galveston College (continued)
credit, part-time degree program (daytime, evenings, weekends, summer), adult/continuing education programs, co-op programs and internships. Off-campus study at Brazosport College, College of the Mainland.
GENERAL DEGREE REQUIREMENTS 60 credit hours; math/science requirements vary according to program; computer course for business, technology majors; internship (some majors).
MAJORS Art/fine arts, behavioral sciences, business administration/commerce/ management, computer science, culinary arts, education, English, fire science, history, hotel and restaurant management, humanities, law enforcement/police sciences, liberal arts/general studies, mathematics, modern languages, music, natural sciences, nuclear medical technology, nursing, physical education, physical sciences, practical nursing, radiological technology, science, secretarial studies/office management, social science, social work, theater arts/drama.
LIBRARY David Glenn Hunt Memorial Library with 41,211 books, 181 microform titles, 403 periodicals, 5 CD-ROMs, 1,787 records, tapes, and CDs. Acquisition spending 1994–95: $57,552.
COMPUTERS ON CAMPUS 190 computers for student use in computer center, computer labs, learning resource center, classrooms, library provide access to main academic computer, e-mail. Staffed computer lab on campus provides training in use of computers, software. Academic computing expenditure 1994–95: $89,922.
COLLEGE LIFE Drama-theater group, choral group, student-run newspaper. ***Social organizations:*** 12 open to all. ***Most popular organizations:*** Student Government, Phi Theta Kappa, Student Nurses Association. ***Major annual events:*** College Night, Back-to-School Activity, Business Symposium. ***Student services:*** personal-psychological counseling. ***Campus security:*** 24-hour emergency response devices, late-night transport-escort service.
HOUSING College housing not available.
ATHLETICS Member NJCAA. ***Intercollegiate:*** baseball M(s), volleyball W(s). ***Intramural:*** bowling, golf, racquetball, volleyball. ***Contact:*** Mr. Dick Smith, Athletic Director, 409-763-6551.
CAREER PLANNING ***Placement office:*** 1 full-time, 1 part-time staff; $40,000 operating expenditure 1994–95. ***Director:*** Ms. Susan Rush, Career Counselor, 409-763-6551 Ext. 222. ***Services:*** job fairs, resume preparation, resume referral, career counseling, careers library, job bank, job interviews.
EXPENSES FOR 1995–96 State resident tuition: $240 full-time. Nonresident tuition: $600 full-time. Part-time tuition per semester ranges from $50 to $88 for state residents, $200 to $220 for nonresidents. Part-time mandatory fees per semester range from $35 to $190. Full-time mandatory fees: $500.
FINANCIAL AID ***College-administered undergrad aid 1995–96:*** need-based scholarships, 82 non-need scholarships, short-term loans (average $100), low-interest long-term loans from external sources (average $2435), Federal Work-Study. ***Required forms:*** institutional, FAFSA. ***Application deadline:*** continuous to 5/15. ***Waivers:*** full or partial for employees or children of employees and senior citizens. ***Average indebtedness of graduates:*** $4000.
APPLYING Open admission. ***Option:*** early entrance. ***Required:*** TOEFL for international students, TASP. ***Required for some:*** school transcript. Test scores used for counseling/placement. ***Application deadline:*** rolling.
APPLYING/TRANSFER ***Required:*** college transcript. ***Entrance:*** noncompetitive. ***Application deadline:*** rolling. ***Contact:*** Dr. Gaynelle Hayes, Vice President/Dean of Student Development Services, 409-763-6551 Ext. 205.
CONTACT Dr. Gaynelle Hayes, Vice President/Dean of Student Development Services, Galveston College, 4015 Avenue Q, Galveston, TX 77550-7496, 409-763-6551 Ext. 205. ***Fax:*** 409-762-9367.

GRAYSON COUNTY COLLEGE
Denison, Texas

UG Enrollment: 3,286	Tuition & Fees (Area Res): $864
Application Deadline: 8/31	Room & Board: $1860

GENERAL State and locally supported, 2-year, coed. Part of Texas Higher Education Coordinating Board. Awards certificates, diplomas, transfer associate, terminal associate degrees. Founded 1964. ***Setting:*** 500-acre rural campus. ***Total enrollment:*** 3,286. ***Faculty:*** 176 (96 full-time, 80 part-time).
ENROLLMENT PROFILE 3,286 students from 3 states and territories, 2 other countries. 55% women, 67% part-time, 98% state residents, 1% international, 53% 25 or older, 1% Native American, 1% Hispanic, 4% African American, 1% Asian American. ***Most popular recent majors:*** nursing, liberal arts/general studies, business administration/commerce/management.
FIRST-YEAR CLASS 537 total. Of the students who applied, 100% were accepted, 85% of whom enrolled.
ACADEMIC PROGRAM Core. Calendar: semesters. Academic remediation for entering students, English as a second language program offered during academic year, advanced placement, honors program, summer session for credit, part-time degree program (daytime, evenings, summer), adult/continuing education programs.
GENERAL DEGREE REQUIREMENTS 65 semester hours; math/science requirements vary according to program; computer course for students without computer competency.
MAJORS Accounting, agricultural business, agricultural education, agricultural sciences, art education, art/fine arts, automotive technologies, biology/biological sciences, business administration/commerce/management, chemistry, computer science, computer technologies, conservation, cosmetology, criminal justice, drafting and design, education, electrical and electronics technologies, electrical engineering technology, elementary education, (pre)engineering sequence, finance/banking, geology, heating/refrigeration/air conditioning, home economics, industrial and heavy equipment maintenance, journalism, landscape architecture/design, landscaping/grounds maintenance, law enforcement/police sciences, legal secretarial studies, liberal arts/general studies, machine and tool technologies, management information systems, mathematics, mechanical engineering technology, medical laboratory technology, medical technology, music, nursing, physical education, physics, psychology, real estate, secretarial studies/office management, sociology, speech/rhetoric/public address/debate, theater arts/drama, veterinary sciences, welding technology.
LIBRARY 51,500 books, 310 periodicals, 900 records, tapes, and CDs.
COMPUTERS ON CAMPUS 25 computers for student use in computer center, learning assistance center, library provide access to off-campus computing facilities, e-mail. Staffed computer lab on campus provides training in use of computers, software.
COLLEGE LIFE Drama-theater group.
HOUSING 400 college housing spaces available; 250 were occupied 1995–96. No special consideration for freshman housing applicants. Off-campus living permitted.
ATHLETICS Member NJCAA. ***Intercollegiate:*** basketball M(s)/W(s), golf M(s)/W(s), tennis M(s)/W(s). ***Intramural:*** basketball, golf, tennis. ***Contact:*** Mr. Tim Williams, Director of Athletics, 903-453-8641.
CAREER PLANNING ***Director:*** Dr. Paul Bowers, Director of Guidance, 903-463-8695. ***Service:*** career counseling.
EXPENSES FOR 1995–96 Area resident tuition: $864 full-time, $27 per semester hour part-time. State resident tuition: $992 full-time, $31 per semester hour part-time. Nonresident tuition: $2144 full-time, $67 per semester hour part-time. College room and board: $1860. College room only: $890.
FINANCIAL AID ***College-administered undergrad aid 1995–96:*** 75 need-based scholarships (average $330), 43 non-need scholarships (average $862), short-term loans (average $195), low-interest long-term loans from external sources (average $1800), 35 part-time jobs. ***Required forms:*** CSS Financial Aid PROFILE, FAFSA; accepted: institutional. ***Priority deadline:*** 8/1.
APPLYING Open admission. ***Options:*** early entrance, deferred entrance. ***Required:*** TOEFL for international students. ***Recommended:*** SAT I or ACT. ***Required for some:*** TASP. Test scores used for counseling/placement. ***Application deadline:*** 8/31. ***Notification:*** continuous.
APPLYING/TRANSFER ***Recommended:*** standardized test scores. ***Required for some:*** standardized test scores. ***Entrance:*** noncompetitive. ***Notification:*** continuous.
CONTACT Dr. David Petrash, Associate Vice President for Admissions and Records, Grayson County College, Denison, TX 75020-8299, 903-463-8650.

HILL COLLEGE OF THE HILL JUNIOR COLLEGE DISTRICT
Hillsboro, Texas

UG Enrollment: 2,500	Tuition & Fees (Area Res): $720
Application Deadline: rolling	Room & Board: $2500

GENERAL District-supported, 2-year, coed. Part of Texas Higher Education Coordinating Board. Awards transfer associate, terminal associate degrees. Founded 1923. ***Setting:*** 80-acre small-town campus with easy access to Dallas–Fort Worth. ***Total enrollment:*** 2,500. ***Faculty:*** 80 (60 full-time, 5% with terminal degrees, 20 part-time); student-faculty ratio is 25:1. ***Notable Alumni:*** Scott Hill, certified public accountant; Dr. James Prescher, veterinarian; Gary Kemp, pharmacist; Bob Bullock, lieutenant governor of Texas; Dr. Clifford Auten, dentist.
ENROLLMENT PROFILE 2,500 students from 16 states and territories, 3 other countries. 61% women, 40% part-time, 95% state residents, 20% live on campus, 6% transferred in, 1% international, 40% 25 or older, 1% Native American, 6% Hispanic, 8% African American, 1% Asian American.
FIRST-YEAR CLASS 1,200 total. Of the students who applied, 100% were accepted, 100% of whom enrolled.
ACADEMIC PROGRAM Core. Calendar: semesters. Academic remediation for entering students, services for LD students, summer session for credit, part-time degree program (daytime, evenings, summer), adult/continuing education programs, co-op programs and internships. Off-campus study.
GENERAL DEGREE REQUIREMENT 62 credit hours.
MAJORS Accounting, agricultural business, agricultural economics, agricultural sciences, animal sciences, applied art, art education, art/fine arts, art history, automotive technologies, behavioral sciences, biology/biological sciences, botany/plant sciences, business administration/commerce/management, business economics, ceramic art and design, chemistry, child care/child and family studies, child psychology/child development, civil engineering technology, commercial art, communication, computer information systems, computer programming, computer science, cosmetology, criminal justice, dairy sciences, data processing, drafting and design, economics, education, electrical and electronics technologies, electrical engineering technology, elementary education, engineering and applied sciences, engineering sciences, (pre)engineering sequence, English, farm and ranch management, finance/banking, geography, geology, health education, health science, history, home economics, horticulture, humanities, journalism, law enforcement/police sciences, liberal arts/general studies, machine and tool technologies, mathematics, music, music education, music history, music therapy, nursing, photography, physical education, physical sciences, physics, piano/organ, political science/government, practical nursing, psychology, public affairs and policy studies, public health, real estate, robotics, science, secretarial studies/office management, social science, social work, sociology, Spanish, speech/rhetoric/public address/debate, theater arts/drama, voice, welding technology, word processing, zoology.
LIBRARY Hill College Library with 40,000 books, 300 periodicals, 775 records, tapes, and CDs.
COMPUTERS ON CAMPUS 150 computers for student use in computer center, computer labs, learning resource center. Staffed computer lab on campus provides training in use of computers, software.
NOTEWORTHY RESEARCH FACILITIES H. B. Simpson History Complex, Audie Murphy Gun Museum, Confederate Research Center.
COLLEGE LIFE Orientation program (2 days, no cost). Drama-theater group, choral group, student-run newspaper. ***Most popular organizations:*** Business Professionals of America, Sigma Phi Omega. ***Major annual events:*** Western Day, Career Day, Job Fair. ***Student services:*** personal-psychological counseling. ***Campus security:*** security officers.
HOUSING 250 college housing spaces available; all were occupied 1995–96. Freshmen given priority for college housing. On-campus residence required through sophomore year except if living with relatives. ***Options:*** coed (1 building), single-sex (3 buildings) housing available. Resident assistants live in dorms.
ATHLETICS Member NJCAA. ***Intercollegiate:*** baseball M, basketball M(s)/W(s), golf M/W, soccer M/W, softball W, volleyball W(s). ***Intramural:*** basketball, volleyball. ***Contact:*** Mr. Ray Roberts, Athletic Director, 817-582-2555.
CAREER PLANNING ***Placement office:*** 6 full-time staff. ***Director:*** Ms. Pam Boehm, Career Center Director, 817-582-2555. ***Services:*** job fairs, resume preparation, career counseling, careers library, job interviews.

AFTER GRADUATION 60% of students completing a degree program in 1994–95 went directly on to further study.
EXPENSES FOR 1995–96 Area resident tuition: $720 full-time. State resident tuition: $960 full-time. Nonresident tuition: $1168 full-time. Part-time tuition per semester hour ranges from $96 to $264 for area residents, $128 to $352 for state residents, $328 to $552 for nonresidents. College room and board: $2500.
FINANCIAL AID ***College-administered undergrad aid 1995–96:*** need-based scholarships, non-need scholarships, short-term loans, low-interest long-term loans, Federal Work-Study, part-time jobs. ***Required forms:*** institutional, FAFSA; accepted: CSS Financial Aid PROFILE. ***Priority deadline:*** 8/1. ***Waivers:*** full or partial for senior citizens.
APPLYING Open admission. ***Options:*** early entrance, deferred entrance. ***Required:*** TOEFL for international students. ***Recommended:*** ACT. Test scores used for counseling/placement. ***Application deadline:*** rolling.
APPLYING/TRANSFER ***Entrance:*** noncompetitive. ***Application deadline:*** rolling.
CONTACT Mrs. Diane Hudson, Registrar, Hill College of the Hill Junior College District, Hillsboro, TX 76645-0619, 817-582-2555 Ext. 205.

HOUSTON COMMUNITY COLLEGE SYSTEM
Houston, Texas

UG Enrollment: 39,541	Tuition & Fees (Area Res): $840
Application Deadline: rolling	Room & Board: N/Avail

GENERAL State and locally supported, 2-year, coed. Part of Texas Higher Education Coordinating Board. Awards certificates, transfer associate, terminal associate degrees. Founded 1971. ***Setting:*** urban campus. ***Total enrollment:*** 39,541. ***Faculty:*** 2,387 (579 full-time, 20% with terminal degrees, 1,808 part-time).
ENROLLMENT PROFILE 39,541 students from 44 states and territories, 87 other countries. 57% women, 73% part-time, 96% state residents, 1% transferred in, 1% international, 61% 25 or older, 1% Native American, 20% Hispanic, 13% African American, 14% Asian American. ***Most popular recent majors:*** nursing, business administration/commerce/management, secretarial studies/office management.
FIRST-YEAR CLASS 4,739 total; 4,739 applied, 100% were accepted, 100% of whom enrolled.
ACADEMIC PROGRAM Core, general education, liberal arts, and occupational curriculum, honor code. Calendar: semesters. Average class size 25 in required courses. Academic remediation for entering students, English as a second language program offered during academic year and summer, advanced placement, summer session for credit, part-time degree program (daytime, evenings, weekends, summer), adult/continuing education programs, co-op programs. ROTC: Army (c).
GENERAL DEGREE REQUIREMENTS 60 semester hours; 3 semester hours of math or science; internship (some majors).
MAJORS Accounting, agricultural sciences, art/fine arts, audio engineering, business administration/commerce/management, child care/child and family studies, civil engineering technology, commercial art, communication, computer science, construction technologies, court reporting, criminal justice, deaf interpreter training, dietetics, drafting and design, electromechanical technology, electronics engineering technology, engineering technology, fashion design and technology, fashion merchandising, fire science, graphic arts, home economics, horticulture, hotel and restaurant management, human resources, illustration, interior design, law enforcement/police sciences, liberal arts/general studies, manufacturing technology, marketing/retailing/merchandising, medical laboratory technology, medical records services, mental health/rehabilitation counseling, music, musical instrument technology, music business, nuclear medical technology, nursing, occupational therapy, paralegal studies, photography, physical fitness/exercise science, physical therapy, radiological technology, real estate, respiratory therapy, science, secretarial studies/office management, social science, technical writing, theater arts/drama, tourism and travel, word processing.
LIBRARY Main library plus 23 others, with 154,106 books, 515 microform titles, 1,870 periodicals, 1 on-line bibliographic service, 28 CD-ROMs, 302 records, tapes, and CDs. Acquisition spending 1994–95: $489,476.
COMPUTERS ON CAMPUS 750 computers for student use in computer labs, library. Staffed computer lab on campus.
COLLEGE LIFE Drama-theater group, choral group, student-run newspaper. ***Social organizations:*** 49 open to all. ***Most popular organizations:*** Phi Theta Kappa, Association of Latin American Students, Eagle's Club, Society of Hispanic Engineers, International Student Association. ***Major annual events:*** International Festival, Cinco de Mayo, Black History Month. ***Student services:*** personal-psychological counseling, women's center. ***Campus security:*** 24-hour emergency response devices and patrols, late-night transport-escort service.
HOUSING College housing not available.
ATHLETICS ***Intramural:*** basketball, bowling, football, golf, racquetball, skiing (downhill), soccer, softball, squash, table tennis (Ping-Pong), tennis, volleyball. ***Contact:*** Mr. Norman Hanks, Intramural Coordinator, 713-718-8530.
CAREER PLANNING ***Placement office:*** 6 full-time, 8 part-time staff. ***Director:*** Mr. Rudy Soliz, Acting Coordinator Career Development and Placement, 713-718-8541. ***Services:*** job fairs, resume preparation, career counseling, careers library, job bank, job interviews.
AFTER GRADUATION 22% of students completing a degree program in 1994–95 went directly on to further study.
EXPENSES FOR 1995–96 Area resident tuition: $840 full-time. State resident tuition: $1200 full-time. Nonresident tuition: $2610 full-time. Part-time tuition per semester hour ranges from $102 to $308 for area residents, $129 to $440 for state residents, $330 to $957 for nonresidents.
FINANCIAL AID ***College-administered undergrad aid 1995–96:*** 2,014 need-based scholarships (average $432), 546 non-need scholarships (average $525), low-interest long-term loans from external sources (average $2200), 87 Federal Work-Study (averaging $1591). ***Required forms:*** institutional, FAFSA; accepted: CSS Financial Aid PROFILE, state. ***Priority deadline:*** 4/15.
APPLYING Open admission except for allied health programs. ***Option:*** early entrance. ***Recommended:*** SAT I. ***Required for some:*** ACT, TOEFL for international students. Test scores used for counseling/placement. ***Application deadline:*** rolling. ***Notification:*** continuous.
APPLYING/TRANSFER ***Application deadline:*** rolling. ***Notification:*** continuous. ***Contact:*** Mr. Mark Tengler, Transfer Counselor, 713-718-8535.
CONTACT Dr. Dona G. Harris, Associate Vice Chancellor for Enrollment Services, Houston Community College System, PO Box 7849, Houston, TX 77270-7849, 713-718-8615.

HOWARD COLLEGE
Big Spring, Texas

UG Enrollment: 2,400	Tuition & Fees (Area Res): $628
Application Deadline: rolling	Room & Board: $2000

GENERAL State and locally supported, 2-year, coed. Part of Howard County Junior College District System. Awards certificates, transfer associate, terminal associate degrees. Founded 1945. ***Setting:*** 120-acre small-town campus. ***Total enrollment:*** 2,400. ***Faculty:*** 165 (60 full-time, 10% with terminal degrees, 105 part-time); student-faculty ratio is 10:1.
ENROLLMENT PROFILE 2,400 students from 28 states and territories, 4 other countries. 60% women, 40% men, 57% part-time, 94% state residents, 15% live on campus, 22% transferred in, 1% international, 26% 25 or older, 1% Native American, 23% Hispanic, 4% African American, 1% Asian American. ***Areas of study chosen:*** 30% health professions and related sciences, 16% business management and administrative services, 7% vocational and home economics, 6% education, 5% physical sciences, 4% computer and information sciences, 4% psychology, 3% biological and life sciences, 2% agriculture, 1% communications and journalism, 1% engineering and applied sciences, 1% English language/literature/letters, 1% fine arts, 1% mathematics, 1% performing arts, 1% predentistry, 1% prelaw, 1% premed, 1% social sciences. ***Most popular recent majors:*** nursing, business administration/commerce/management.
FIRST-YEAR CLASS 700 total; 700 applied, 100% were accepted, 100% of whom enrolled. 2 valedictorians.
ACADEMIC PROGRAM Core. Calendar: semesters. Academic remediation for entering students, services for LD students, advanced placement, summer session for credit, part-time degree program (daytime, evenings, summer), adult/continuing education programs, co-op programs.
GENERAL DEGREE REQUIREMENTS 62 credit hours; internship (some majors).
MAJORS Accounting, agricultural sciences, art/fine arts, automotive technologies, behavioral sciences, biology/biological sciences, business administration/commerce/management, chemistry, child care/child and family studies, computer programming, computer science, cosmetology, dental services, drafting and design, drug and alcohol/substance abuse counseling, (pre)engineering sequence, English, finance/banking, fire science, geology, industrial arts, journalism, law enforcement/police sciences, mathematics, medical records services, medical secretarial studies, music education, nursing, ornamental horticulture, pharmacy/pharmaceutical sciences, physical education, physical therapy, practical nursing, respiratory therapy, social science, speech/rhetoric/public address/debate, theater arts/drama.
LIBRARY Howard College Library with 27,481 books, 19,006 microform titles, 232 periodicals, 20 CD-ROMs.
COMPUTERS ON CAMPUS 40 computers for student use in computer center. Staffed computer lab on campus provides training in use of computers, software.
COLLEGE LIFE Drama-theater group, choral group. 30% vote in student government elections. ***Student services:*** personal-psychological counseling. ***Campus security:*** 24-hour patrols.
HOUSING 250 college housing spaces available; all were occupied 1995–96. No special consideration for freshman housing applicants. On-campus residence required in freshman year except if living with relatives. ***Option:*** single-sex housing available. Resident assistants live in dorms.
ATHLETICS Member NJCAA. ***Intercollegiate:*** baseball M(s), basketball M(s)/W(s). ***Intramural:*** basketball, bowling, golf, racquetball, tennis. ***Contact:*** Mr. Tommy Collins, Athletic Director, 915-264-5040.
CAREER PLANNING ***Service:*** career counseling.
EXPENSES FOR 1995–96 Area resident tuition: $420 full-time. State resident tuition: $430 full-time. Nonresident tuition: $830 full-time. Part-time tuition per semester hour ranges from $71 to $270 for area residents, $91 to $290 for state residents, $271 to $670 for nonresidents. Full-time mandatory fees: $208. College room and board: $2000. College room only: $700.
FINANCIAL AID ***College-administered undergrad aid 1995–96:*** 200 need-based scholarships (averaging $250), 450 non-need scholarships (averaging $100), short-term loans, low-interest long-term loans from external sources (averaging $2000), Federal Work-Study, 50 part-time jobs. ***Required forms:*** institutional, FAFSA; required for some: state; accepted: CSS Financial Aid PROFILE. ***Priority deadline:*** 4/1.
APPLYING Open admission. ***Option:*** early entrance. ***Required:*** school transcript, TOEFL for international students. ***Recommended:*** 3 years of high school math and science, some high school foreign language. ***Required for some:*** SAT I or ACT. Test scores used for counseling/placement. ***Application deadline:*** rolling. ***Notification:*** continuous until 8/31.
APPLYING/TRANSFER ***Required for some:*** standardized test scores. ***Entrance:*** noncompetitive. ***Application deadline:*** rolling. ***Notification:*** continuous until 8/31.
CONTACT Mr. Mike Evans, Registrar, Howard College, 1001 Birdwell Lane, Big Spring, TX 79720-3702, 915-264-5106. ***Fax:*** 915-264-5082.

ITT TECHNICAL INSTITUTE
Arlington, Texas

UG Enrollment: 336	Tuition: $15,599/deg prog
Application Deadline: rolling	Room & Board: N/Avail

GENERAL Proprietary, 2-year, coed. Part of ITT Educational Services, Inc. Awards terminal associate degrees. Founded 1982. ***Setting:*** suburban campus with easy access to Dallas–Fort Worth. ***Total enrollment:*** 336. ***Faculty:*** 19 (16 full-time, 3 part-time).
ENROLLMENT PROFILE 336 students: 14% women, 0% part-time, 99% state residents, 0% transferred in, 72% 25 or older, 12% Hispanic, 13% African American, 2% Asian American. ***Areas of study chosen:*** 100% engineering and applied sciences. ***Most popular recent major:*** electronics engineering technology.
FIRST-YEAR CLASS 195 total; 400 applied, 84% were accepted, 58% of whom enrolled.
ACADEMIC PROGRAM Calendar: quarters. Academic remediation for entering students, tutorials.
GENERAL DEGREE REQUIREMENT 90 credit hours.

Peterson's Guide to Two-Year Colleges 1997 613

Texas

ITT Technical Institute (continued)
MAJORS Drafting and design, electronics engineering technology.
LIBRARY 517 books, 148 periodicals.
COMPUTERS ON CAMPUS 75 computers for student use in computer labs, learning resource center, library. Staffed computer lab on campus (open 24 hours a day) provides training in use of computers, software.
COLLEGE LIFE *Campus security:* 24-hour emergency response devices.
HOUSING College housing not available.
CAREER PLANNING *Placement office:* 1 full-time staff. *Director:* Ms. Sandy Raska, Director of Placement, 817-640-7100. *Services:* resume preparation, resume referral, career counseling, job bank, job interviews. Students must register sophomore year.
EXPENSES FOR 1996–97 Tuition per degree program ranges from $15,599 to $17,690. Full-time mandatory fees range from $540 to $720. Tuition guaranteed not to increase for student's term of enrollment.
FINANCIAL AID *College-administered undergrad aid 1995–96:* need-based scholarships, low-interest long-term loans from external sources. *Required forms:* institutional, FAFSA; accepted: CSS Financial Aid PROFILE. *Priority deadline:* 8/1.
APPLYING *Option:* deferred entrance. *Required:* CPAt. Test scores used for admission. *Application deadline:* rolling. *Notification:* continuous.
APPLYING/TRANSFER *Entrance:* minimally difficult. *Application deadline:* rolling. *Notification:* continuous. *Contact:* Mr. Frank Cave, Director of Education, 817-640-7100.
CONTACT Mr. Tommy Marley, Director, ITT Technical Institute, Arlington, TX 76011-6319, 817-640-7100. College video available.

ITT TECHNICAL INSTITUTE
Austin, Texas

UG Enrollment: 465	Tuition: $15,599/deg prog
Application Deadline: rolling	Room & Board: N/Avail

GENERAL Proprietary, 2-year, coed. Part of ITT Educational Services, Inc. Awards terminal associate degrees. Founded 1985. *Setting:* urban campus. *Total enrollment:* 465. *Faculty:* 27 (19 full-time, 10% with terminal degrees, 8 part-time); student-faculty ratio is 20:1.
ENROLLMENT PROFILE 465 students: 15% women, 3% transferred in, 0% international, 30% 25 or older, 25% Hispanic, 25% African American, 1% Asian American. *Most popular recent major:* electronics engineering technology.
FIRST-YEAR CLASS 289 total; 586 applied, 85% were accepted, 95% of whom enrolled.
ACADEMIC PROGRAM Core. Calendar: quarters. Academic remediation for entering students, tutorials.
GENERAL DEGREE REQUIREMENTS 90 credit hours; 1 course each in algebra and physics; computer course.
MAJORS Drafting and design, electronics engineering technology.
COMPUTERS ON CAMPUS 6 computers for student use in learning resource center provide access to main academic computer. Staffed computer lab on campus provides training in use of computers, software.
HOUSING College housing not available.
CAREER PLANNING *Placement office:* 2 full-time staff. *Director:* Ms. Linda Hodges, Director of Placement, 512-467-6800. *Services:* job fairs, resume preparation, career counseling, job interviews. Students must register freshman year. 25 organizations recruited on campus 1994–95.
AFTER GRADUATION 94% of class of 1994 had job offers within 6 months.
EXPENSES FOR 1996–97 *Application fee:* $100. Tuition per degree program ranges from $15,599 to $17,690. Full-time mandatory fees range from $540 to $720.
FINANCIAL AID *College-administered undergrad aid 1995–96:* need-based scholarships, Federal Work-Study. *Required forms:* FAFSA. *Payment plan:* installment. *Waivers:* full or partial for employees or children of employees.
APPLYING *Option:* deferred entrance. *Required:* school transcript, interview, CPAt. Test scores used for admission. *Application deadline:* rolling. *Notification:* continuous.
APPLYING/TRANSFER *Required:* college transcript. *Application deadline:* rolling. *Notification:* continuous. *Contact:* Dr. Thomas Creola, Director of Education, 512-467-6800.
CONTACT Mr. John A. Byers, Director, ITT Technical Institute, 6330 East Highway 290, Suite 150, Austin, TX 78723-1061, 512-467-6800. College video available.

ITT TECHNICAL INSTITUTE
Garland, Texas

UG Enrollment: 379	Tuition: $15,599/deg prog
Application Deadline: rolling	Room & Board: N/Avail

GENERAL Proprietary, 2-year, coed. Part of ITT Educational Services, Inc. Awards terminal associate degrees. Founded 1989. *Setting:* suburban campus with easy access to Dallas. *Total enrollment:* 379. *Faculty:* 14 (all full-time, 93% with terminal degrees); student-faculty ratio is 27:1.
ENROLLMENT PROFILE 379 students.
FIRST-YEAR CLASS 241 total; 567 applied.
ACADEMIC PROGRAM Calendar: quarters. 41 courses offered in 1995–96. Advanced placement, tutorials.
GENERAL DEGREE REQUIREMENTS 90 credit hours; 1 course each in algebra and physics; computer course.
MAJORS Drafting and design, electronics engineering technology.
LIBRARY Learning Resource Center with 890 books, 68 periodicals, 10 CD-ROMs, 520 records, tapes, and CDs.
COMPUTERS ON CAMPUS 23 computers for student use in learning resource center. Staffed computer lab on campus provides training in use of computers, software.
COLLEGE LIFE Student-run newspaper. *Most popular organizations:* Student Council, MVTHS. *Major annual event:* Student Appreciation Day. *Campus security:* 24-hour emergency response devices.
HOUSING College housing not available.
CAREER PLANNING *Placement office:* 2 full-time staff. *Director:* Ms. Carrie D. Austin, Director of Placement, 214-279-0500. *Services:* job fairs, resume preparation, resume referral, career counseling, careers library, job bank, job interviews. 63 organizations recruited on campus 1994–95.
AFTER GRADUATION 83% of class of 1994 had job offers within 6 months.
EXPENSES FOR 1996–97 *Application fee:* $100. Tuition per degree program ranges from $15,599 to $17,690. Full-time mandatory fees range from $540 to $720. Tuition guaranteed not to increase for student's term of enrollment.
FINANCIAL AID *College-administered undergrad aid 1995–96:* need-based scholarships, low-interest long-term loans from college funds, Federal Work-Study, part-time jobs. *Required forms:* institutional, FAFSA, tax forms. *Application deadline:* continuous. *Payment plan:* installment. *Waivers:* full or partial for employees or children of employees.
APPLYING *Option:* deferred entrance. *Required:* school transcript, interview, CPAt. Test scores used for admission. *Application deadline:* rolling.
APPLYING/TRANSFER *Application deadline:* rolling. *Contact:* Mr. Travis Lunsfond, Director of Education, 214-279-0500.
CONTACT Dr. Lesly Massey, Director of Recruitment, ITT Technical Institute, Garland, TX 75041-5509, 214-279-0500 or toll-free 800-683-4888 (in-state). *Fax:* 214-613-4523. College video available.

ITT TECHNICAL INSTITUTE
Houston, Texas

UG Enrollment: 316	Tuition: $15,599/deg prog
Application Deadline: rolling	Room & Board: N/Avail

GENERAL Proprietary, 2-year, coed. Part of ITT Educational Services, Inc. Awards transfer associate, terminal associate degrees. Founded 1985. *Setting:* 1-acre suburban campus. *Total enrollment:* 316. *Faculty:* 16 (11 full-time, 100% with terminal degrees, 5 part-time).
ENROLLMENT PROFILE 316 students: 15% women, 85% men, 0% part-time, 100% state residents, 10% transferred in, 82% have need-based financial aid, 0% international, 22% 25 or older, 0% Native American, 26% Hispanic, 19% African American, 5% Asian American. *Areas of study chosen:* 100% engineering and applied sciences. *Most popular recent major:* electronics engineering technology.
FIRST-YEAR CLASS 152 total; 411 applied, 81% were accepted, 46% of whom enrolled. 0% from top 10% of their high school class, 5% from top quarter, 15% from top half.
ACADEMIC PROGRAM Core, technical curriculum, honor code. Calendar: quarters. Academic remediation for entering students.
GENERAL DEGREE REQUIREMENTS 90 units; 2 courses each in algebra and physics; computer course.
MAJORS Drafting and design, electronics engineering technology.
LIBRARY Learning Resource Center with 650 books, 20 periodicals, 10 CD-ROMs.
COMPUTERS ON CAMPUS 76 computers for student use in computer labs, learning resource center, labs, library. Staffed computer lab on campus provides training in use of computers, software.
COLLEGE LIFE *Social organizations:* 2 open to all. *Most popular organizations:* National Vocational/Technical Honor Society, American Drafting and Design Association. *Major annual events:* Spring and Summer Activity Days, Fall Sports Day, Christmas Food Drive. *Student services:* personal-psychological counseling. *Campus security:* 24-hour emergency response devices, evening patrols by trained security personnel.
HOUSING College housing not available.
ATHLETICS *Intramural:* bowling, football, softball.
CAREER PLANNING *Placement office:* 1 full-time staff. *Director:* Ms. Evelyn Corey, Director of Placement, 713-873-0512. *Services:* job fairs, resume preparation, resume referral, career counseling, job bank, job interviews. Students must register freshman year. 46 organizations recruited on campus 1994–95.
AFTER GRADUATION 83% of class of 1994 had job offers within 6 months. 7% of students completing a degree program went directly on to further study.
EXPENSES FOR 1996–97 *Application fee:* $100. Tuition per degree program ranges from $15,599 to $17,690. Full-time mandatory fees range from $540 to $720. Tuition guaranteed not to increase for student's term of enrollment.
FINANCIAL AID *College-administered undergrad aid 1995–96:* need-based scholarships, low-interest long-term loans from external sources, Federal Work-Study, part-time jobs. *Required forms:* institutional, FAFSA. *Application deadline:* continuous to 9/1. *Payment plan:* installment. *Waivers:* full or partial for employees or children of employees.
APPLYING *Option:* deferred entrance. *Required:* interview, CPAt. *Required for some:* school transcript. Test scores used for admission. *Application deadline:* rolling.
APPLYING/TRANSFER *Required:* interview, college transcript. *Required for some:* high school transcript. *Application deadline:* rolling. *Contact:* Mr. Hamid Rahighi, Director of Education, 713-873-0512.
CONTACT Mr. Robert Dowdy, Director of Recruitment, ITT Technical Institute, Houston, TX 77090-5818, 713-873-0512 or toll-free 800-879-6486 (in-state). *Fax:* 713-873-0518. College video available.

ITT TECHNICAL INSTITUTE
Houston, Texas

UG Enrollment: 600	Tuition: $15,599/deg prog
Application Deadline: rolling	Room & Board: N/Avail

GENERAL Proprietary, 2-year, coed. Part of ITT Educational Services, Inc. Awards terminal associate degrees. Founded 1983. *Setting:* 4-acre urban campus. *Total enrollment:* 600. *Faculty:* 26 (23 full-time, 100% with terminal degrees, 3 part-time); student-faculty ratio is 20:1.
ENROLLMENT PROFILE 600 students from 5 states and territories, 12 other countries. 12% women, 88% men, 0% part-time, 0% transferred in, 16% international, 44% 25 or older, 0% Native American, 34% Hispanic, 18% African American, 9% Asian American. *Areas of study chosen:* 100% engineering and applied sciences. *Most popular recent major:* electronics engineering technology.
FIRST-YEAR CLASS 470 total; 710 applied, 90% were accepted, 74% of whom enrolled. 0% from top 10% of their high school class, 5% from top quarter, 50% from top half.

Texas

ACADEMIC PROGRAM Technical curriculum, honor code. Calendar: quarters. 58 courses offered in 1995–96. Academic remediation for entering students, tutorials.
GENERAL DEGREE REQUIREMENTS 90 credit hours; computer course.
MAJORS Chemical engineering technology, drafting and design, electronics engineering technology.
COMPUTERS ON CAMPUS 75 computers for student use in computer center, computer labs, learning resource center, library provide access to Internet. Staffed computer lab on campus provides training in use of computers, software.
COLLEGE LIFE Orientation program (3 weeks, no cost). Student-run newspaper. 50% vote in student government elections. *Campus security:* 24-hour patrols, late-night transport-escort service.
HOUSING College housing not available.
CAREER PLANNING *Placement office:* 2 full-time staff. *Director:* Ms. Peggy Payne, Director of Placement, 713-952-2294. *Services:* job fairs, resume preparation, resume referral, career counseling, careers library, job bank, job interviews. Students must register freshman year. 85 organizations recruited on campus 1994–95.
AFTER GRADUATION 92% of class of 1994 had job offers within 6 months.
EXPENSES FOR 1996–97 *Application fee:* $100. Tuition per degree program ranges from $15,599 to $17,690. Full-time mandatory fees range from $540 to $720.
FINANCIAL AID *College-administered undergrad aid 1995–96:* need-based scholarships, 2 non-need scholarships, low-interest long-term loans from external sources, 15 Federal Work-Study. *Required forms:* institutional, FAFSA; accepted: CSS Financial Aid PROFILE. *Priority deadline:* 9/1. *Payment plan:* installment. *Waivers:* full or partial for employees or children of employees.
APPLYING *Option:* deferred entrance. *Required:* CPAt. Test scores used for admission. *Application deadline:* rolling. *Notification:* continuous.
APPLYING/TRANSFER *Application deadline:* rolling. *Notification:* continuous. *Contact:* Mr. Donald Montgomery, Director of Education, 713-952-2294.
CONTACT Mr. Gary Updike, Marketing Director, ITT Technical Institute, 2950 South Gessner, Houston, TX 77063-3751, 713-952-2294. *Fax:* 713-270-8251. College video available.

ITT TECHNICAL INSTITUTE
San Antonio, Texas

UG Enrollment: 464	Tuition: $15,599/deg prog
Application Deadline: rolling	Room & Board: N/Avail

GENERAL Proprietary, 2-year, coed. Part of ITT Educational Services, Inc. Awards transfer associate degrees. Founded 1988. *Setting:* urban campus. *Total enrollment:* 464. *Faculty:* 21 (18 full-time, 3 part-time). *Notable Alumni:* Rafael Mendoza, designer; Ramon Perez, technical representative; Carrolton Boles, waferfab technican; Alexander Rojas, computer analyst; Edward Anevalos, linekeeper.
ENROLLMENT PROFILE 464 students. *Areas of study chosen:* 100% computer and information sciences.
FIRST-YEAR CLASS 226 total; 534 applied.
ACADEMIC PROGRAM Technical curriculum. Calendar: quarters. Academic remediation for entering students, tutorials.
GENERAL DEGREE REQUIREMENTS 90 credit hours; 1 algebra course; computer course.
MAJORS Drafting and design, electronics engineering technology.
LIBRARY Learning Resource Center with 540 books, 12 periodicals, 8 records, tapes, and CDs.
COMPUTERS ON CAMPUS 70 computers for student use in computer labs, library provide access to main academic computer, Internet. Staffed computer lab on campus provides training in use of computers, software.
COLLEGE LIFE Student-run newspaper. *Most popular organizations:* National Vocation Honor Society, Computer Club, FCC License Club, Sci-Fi Club. *Major annual events:* Annual Summer Picnic, Quarterly Activity Days. *Campus security:* 24-hour emergency response devices and patrols.
HOUSING College housing not available.
CAREER PLANNING *Placement office:* 1 full-time, 1 part-time staff. *Director:* Ms. Kathy Masiker, Director of Placement, 210-737-1881. *Services:* resume preparation, career counseling, job interviews. Students must register freshman year. 20 organizations recruited on campus 1994–95.
AFTER GRADUATION 87% of class of 1994 had job offers within 6 months.
EXPENSES FOR 1996–97 Tuition per degree program ranges from $15,599 to $17,690. Full-time mandatory fees range from $540 to $720.
FINANCIAL AID *Required forms:* institutional, FAFSA. *Application deadline:* continuous. *Payment plan:* installment. *Waivers:* full or partial for employees or children of employees.
APPLYING *Option:* deferred entrance. *Required:* school transcript, CPAt, DAT. Test scores used for admission. *Application deadline:* rolling.
APPLYING/TRANSFER *Required:* standardized test scores, high school transcript. *Application deadline:* rolling. *Contact:* Mr. Robert E. Montz, Director of Education, 210-737-1881.
CONTACT Mr. Doug Howard, Director of Admissions, ITT Technical Institute, 4242 Piedras Drive East, San Antonio, TX 78228, 210-737-1881. College video available.

JACKSONVILLE COLLEGE
Jacksonville, Texas

UG Enrollment: 325	Tuition & Fees: $3410
Application Deadline: 7/1	Room & Board: $2628

GENERAL Independent Baptist, 2-year, coed. Awards certificates, diplomas, transfer associate, terminal associate degrees. Founded 1899. *Setting:* 20-acre small-town campus. *Total enrollment:* 325. *Faculty:* 30 (14 full-time, 16 part-time).
ENROLLMENT PROFILE 325 students from 9 states and territories, 6 other countries. 60% women, 19% part-time, 95% state residents, 34% live on campus, 33% transferred in, 3% international, 20% 25 or older, 1% Native American, 4% Hispanic, 15% African American, 0% Asian American.
FIRST-YEAR CLASS 154 total; 200 applied, 100% were accepted, 77% of whom enrolled.

ACADEMIC PROGRAM Core. Calendar: semesters. 100 courses offered in 1995–96. Academic remediation for entering students, advanced placement, summer session for credit, part-time degree program (daytime, summer), adult/continuing education programs.
GENERAL DEGREE REQUIREMENTS 64 semester hours; 1 math course; computer course.
MAJORS Liberal arts/general studies, science.
LIBRARY Weatherby Memorial Building plus 1 other, with 22,000 books, 170 periodicals, 1,200 records, tapes, and CDs.
COMPUTERS ON CAMPUS 20 computers for student use in computer center, computer labs, library provide access to Internet. Staffed computer lab on campus.
COLLEGE LIFE Drama-theater group, choral group, student-run newspaper. 50% vote in student government elections. *Social organizations:* 6 open to all. *Most popular organizations:* Drama Club, Ministerial Alliance, Mission Band, Volleyball Club, Commuters In Action. *Major annual events:* Homecoming, College Preview Day, Family Day. *Student services:* health clinic, personal-psychological counseling. *Campus security:* 24-hour emergency response devices, evening security personnel.
HOUSING 125 college housing spaces available; 105 were occupied 1995–96. No special consideration for freshman housing applicants. On-campus residence required through sophomore year except if living within commuting distance. *Option:* single-sex housing available. Resident assistants live in dorms.
ATHLETICS Member NJCAA. *Intercollegiate:* basketball M(s), volleyball W. *Intramural:* basketball, table tennis (Ping-Pong), tennis, volleyball. *Contact:* Mr. Joe Shidler, Athletic Director, 903-586-2518.
CAREER PLANNING *Service:* career counseling.
AFTER GRADUATION 85% of students completing a degree program in 1994–95 went directly on to further study.
EXPENSES FOR 1996–97 *Application fee:* $10. Comprehensive fee of $6038 includes full-time tuition ($3000), mandatory fees ($410), and college room and board ($2628). Part-time tuition: $100 per semester hour.
FINANCIAL AID *College-administered undergrad aid 1995–96:* need-based scholarships, non-need scholarships, low-interest long-term loans from external sources. *Required forms:* institutional; accepted: FAFSA. *Priority deadline:* 8/1. *Payment plan:* installment.
APPLYING Open admission. *Option:* early entrance. *Required:* TOEFL for international students, TASP. Test scores used for counseling/placement. *Application deadline:* 7/1. *Notification:* continuous until 7/1.
APPLYING/TRANSFER *Entrance:* noncompetitive. *Application deadline:* 7/1. *Notification:* continuous until 7/1.
CONTACT Mr. Brent Thompson, Director of Admissions, Jacksonville College, Jacksonville, TX 75766-4759, 903-586-2518 Ext. 225 or toll-free 800-256-8522.

KD STUDIO
Dallas, Texas

Enrollment: N/R	Tuition & Fees: $6000
Application Deadline: rolling	Room & Board: N/Avail

GENERAL Proprietary, 2-year, specialized, coed. Awards terminal associate degrees. Founded 1979. *Setting:* urban campus. *Educational spending 1994–95:* $2405 per undergrad. *Faculty:* 23 (all part-time). *Notable Alumni:* Toby Metcalf, actor; George Eads, actor; Helen Cates, actress; Emily Courtney, actress; Julio Cedillo, actor.
ENROLLMENT PROFILE 55% women, 45% men, 0% part-time, 95% state residents, 39% transferred in, 2% international, 24% 25 or older, 1% Native American, 7% Hispanic, 8% African American, 1% Asian American. *Areas of study chosen:* 100% performing arts.
FIRST-YEAR CLASS 220 total; 270 applied, 99% were accepted, 82% of whom enrolled. 100% from top half of their high school class.
ACADEMIC PROGRAM Core, dramatic arts curriculum. Calendar: semesters. 25 courses offered in 1995–96; average class size 15 in required courses. Tutorials, co-op programs.
GENERAL DEGREE REQUIREMENT 70 credits.
MAJOR Theater arts/drama.
LIBRARY KD Studio Library with 800 books, 15 periodicals, 50 records, tapes, and CDs. Acquisition spending 1994–95: $25,000.
COMPUTERS ON CAMPUS Academic computing expenditure 1994–95: $870,242.
COLLEGE LIFE *Campus security:* 24-hour emergency response devices and patrols.
HOUSING College housing not available.
CAREER PLANNING *Services:* resume preparation, career counseling, careers library. 40 organizations recruited on campus 1994–95.
AFTER GRADUATION 95% of class of 1994 had job offers within 6 months. 4% of students completing a degree program went directly on to further study.
EXPENSES FOR 1996–97 *Application fee:* $100. Tuition: $6000 full-time.
FINANCIAL AID *Required forms:* institutional, FAFSA. *Priority deadline:* 10/1. *Payment plan:* installment. *Waivers:* full or partial for employees or children of employees. *Average indebtedness of graduates:* $10,000.
APPLYING Open admission. *Options:* Common Application, deferred entrance, midyear entrance. *Required:* school transcript, interview. *Required for some:* recommendations. *Application deadlines:* rolling, rolling for nonresidents.
APPLYING/TRANSFER *Required:* high school transcript, interview. *Required for some:* recommendations, college transcript. *Entrance:* noncompetitive. *Application deadline:* rolling. *Contact:* Ms. Colleen O'Connor, Director of Education, 214-638-0484.
CONTACT Ms. Colleen O'Connor, Director of Education, KD Studio, 2600 Stemmons Freeway, #117, Dallas, TX 75207, 214-638-0484. *Fax:* 214-630-5140. *E-mail:* acting@onramp.net.

KILGORE COLLEGE
Kilgore, Texas

CONTACT Mr. William Holda, Dean of Admissions and Registrar, Kilgore College, Kilgore, TX 75662-3299, 903-983-8200. *Fax:* 903-983-8607. College video available.

KINGWOOD COLLEGE
Kingwood, Texas

UG Enrollment: 3,400 | **Tuition & Fees (Area Res): $714**
Application Deadline: rolling | **Room & Board: N/Avail**

GENERAL State and locally supported, 2-year, coed. Part of North Harris Montgomery Community College District. Awards transfer associate, terminal associate degrees. Founded 1984. ***Setting:*** 224-acre suburban campus with easy access to Houston. ***Educational spending 1994–95:*** $1338 per undergrad. ***Total enrollment:*** 3,400. ***Faculty:*** 194 (54 full-time, 18% with terminal degrees, 140 part-time); student-faculty ratio is 15:1.
ENROLLMENT PROFILE 3,400 students: 63% women, 37% men, 66% part-time, 98% state residents, 37% transferred in, 1% international, 57% 25 or older, 1% Native American, 7% Hispanic, 4% African American, 2% Asian American. ***Areas of study chosen:*** 3% health professions and related sciences.
FIRST-YEAR CLASS 723 total; 723 applied, 100% were accepted, 100% of whom enrolled.
ACADEMIC PROGRAM Core. Calendar: semesters. Academic remediation for entering students, English as a second language program offered during academic year, services for LD students, advanced placement, honors program, summer session for credit, part-time degree program (daytime, evenings, weekends), co-op programs.
GENERAL DEGREE REQUIREMENTS 60 credit hours; computer course for all associate of science degree students; internship (some majors).
MAJORS Accounting, business administration/commerce/management, computer graphics, computer technologies, data processing, practical nursing, real estate, word processing.
LIBRARY Kingswood College Library with 30,706 books, 1,165 microform titles, 290 periodicals, 1 on-line bibliographic service, 35 CD-ROMs, 165 records, tapes, and CDs. Acquisition spending 1994–95: $120,687.
COMPUTERS ON CAMPUS 350 computers for student use in computer labs, classrooms provide access to off-campus computing facilities, e-mail, on-line services, Internet. Staffed computer lab on campus provides training in use of computers, software. Academic computing expenditure 1994–95: $240,862.
COLLEGE LIFE Drama-theater group, choral group, student-run newspaper. 1% vote in student government elections. ***Most popular organizations:*** Phi Theta Kappa, Office Administration Club, Black Student Alliance, Student Government Association. ***Major annual events:*** Fall Festival, Spring Fling. ***Student services:*** personal-psychological counseling. ***Campus security:*** 24-hour patrols, late-night transport-escort service.
HOUSING College housing not available.
CAREER PLANNING ***Placement office:*** 3 full-time staff; $198,627 operating expenditure 1994–95. ***Director:*** Ms. Suann Bailey, Director of Counseling, 713-359-1604. ***Services:*** resume preparation, career counseling, careers library.
EXPENSES FOR 1996–97 Area resident tuition: $714 full-time, $60 per credit hour part-time. State resident tuition: $1764 full-time, $95 per credit hour part-time. Nonresident tuition: $2064 full-time, $200 per credit hour part-time.
FINANCIAL AID ***College-administered undergrad aid 1995–96:*** 900 need-based scholarships (average $500), short-term loans (average $200). ***Required forms:*** institutional, FAFSA. ***Priority deadline:*** 4/15.
APPLYING Open admission. ***Option:*** early entrance. ***Recommended:*** SAT I or ACT, ACT ASSET. Test scores used for counseling/placement. ***Application deadline:*** rolling.
APPLYING/TRANSFER ***Entrance:*** noncompetitive. ***Application deadline:*** rolling.
CONTACT Mr. Peter Barbatis, Dean of Student Development, Kingwood College, Kingwood, TX 77339-3801, 713-359-0444.

LAMAR UNIVERSITY–ORANGE
Orange, Texas

UG Enrollment: 1,489 | **Tuition & Fees (TX Res): $1626**
Application Deadline: rolling | **Room & Board: N/Avail**

GENERAL State-supported, 2-year, coed. Part of Lamar University. Awards certificates, transfer associate, terminal associate degrees. Founded 1969. ***Setting:*** small-town campus. ***Total enrollment:*** 1,489. ***Faculty:*** 63 (37 full-time, 26 part-time).
ENROLLMENT PROFILE 1,489 students: 72% women, 28% men, 60% part-time.
FIRST-YEAR CLASS 396 total. Of the students who applied, 100% were accepted, 75% of whom enrolled.
ACADEMIC PROGRAM Core. Calendar: semesters.
GENERAL DEGREE REQUIREMENTS 82 credit hours; 1 course each in math and science.
MAJORS Accounting, architectural technologies, business administration/commerce/management, communication, computer information systems, computer science, data processing, liberal arts/general studies, literature, mathematics, medical laboratory technology, nursing, real estate, secretarial studies/office management, social science.
COMPUTERS ON CAMPUS 100 computers for student use in computer center, library provide access to Internet.
COLLEGE LIFE Student-run newspaper. 15% vote in student government elections. ***Campus security:*** 24-hour emergency response devices.
HOUSING College housing not available.
CAREER PLANNING ***Service:*** career counseling.
EXPENSES FOR 1996–97 State resident tuition: $960 full-time. Nonresident tuition: $7380 full-time, $246 per semester part-time. State resident part-time tuition per semester ranges from $120 to $352. Part-time mandatory fees per semester range from $56 to $319. Full-time mandatory fees: $666.
FINANCIAL AID ***College-administered undergrad aid 1995–96:*** need-based scholarships, short-term loans, 100 Federal Work-Study (averaging $2000), part-time jobs. ***Required forms:*** CSS Financial Aid PROFILE, institutional, FAFSA. ***Application deadline:*** continuous.
APPLYING Open admission. ***Option:*** Common Application. ***Required:*** school transcript, 3 years of high school math and science, TASP. ***Recommended:*** minimum 2.0 GPA, SAT I or ACT. ***Application deadline:*** rolling. ***Notification:*** continuous.
APPLYING/TRANSFER ***Required:*** high school transcript, college transcript. ***Recommended:*** standardized test scores, minimum 2.0 college GPA, minimum 2.0 high school GPA. ***Required for some:*** 3 years of high school math and science. ***Application deadline:*** rolling. ***Notification:*** continuous.
CONTACT Ms. Myra Miller, Registrar, Lamar University–Orange, Orange, TX 77630-5899, 409-883-7750 Ext. 3318.

LAMAR UNIVERSITY–PORT ARTHUR
Port Arthur, Texas

UG Enrollment: 2,233 | **Tuition & Fees (TX Res): $1772**
Application Deadline: rolling | **Room & Board: N/Avail**

GENERAL State-supported, 2-year, coed. Part of Lamar University. Awards certificates, transfer associate, terminal associate degrees. Founded 1909. ***Setting:*** 34-acre suburban campus. ***Total enrollment:*** 2,233. ***Faculty:*** 129 (57 full-time, 9% with terminal degrees, 72 part-time).
ENROLLMENT PROFILE 2,233 students from 6 states and territories. 65% women, 59% part-time, 99% state residents, 5% transferred in, 36% have need-based financial aid, 5% have non-need-based financial aid, 0% international, 45% 25 or older, 1% Native American, 6% Hispanic, 28% African American, 4% Asian American. ***Areas of study chosen:*** 49% vocational and home economics. ***Most popular recent majors:*** nursing, computer technologies, drug and alcohol/substance abuse counseling.
FIRST-YEAR CLASS 417 total; 600 applied, 100% were accepted, 70% of whom enrolled.
ACADEMIC PROGRAM Core. Calendar: semesters. 175 courses offered in 1995–96. Academic remediation for entering students, English as a second language program offered during academic year, services for LD students, advanced placement, tutorials, honors program, summer session for credit, part-time degree program (daytime, evenings, weekends, summer), adult/continuing education programs, co-op programs and internships. Off-campus study at Lamar University-Beaumont, Lamar University-Orange. ROTC: Army (c).
GENERAL DEGREE REQUIREMENTS 62 credit hours; computer course for accounting, automotive technology, child care technology, electronics technology, hazardous material technology, legal assistant, management development, secretarial majors; internship (some majors).
MAJORS Accounting, automotive technologies, child care/child and family studies, computer programming, computer technologies, cosmetology, criminal justice, drug and alcohol/substance abuse counseling, electronics engineering technology, heating/refrigeration/air conditioning, home economics, legal secretarial studies, liberal arts/general studies, medical secretarial studies, nursing, paralegal studies, science, secretarial studies/office management, social science, word processing.
LIBRARY Gates Memorial Library with 36,902 books, 100 microform titles, 326 periodicals, 4 CD-ROMs, 588 records, tapes, and CDs.
COMPUTERS ON CAMPUS 160 computers for student use in computer center, computer labs, learning resource center, classrooms, library provide access to main academic computer. Staffed computer lab on campus provides training in use of computers, software.
COLLEGE LIFE Drama-theater group, choral group. 11% vote in student government elections. ***Social organizations:*** 4 open to all. ***Most popular organizations:*** Chi Alpha, Historical Society, Phi Theta Kappa, Student Government Association, Criminal Justice Association. ***Major annual events:*** Highway Clean-up, Walk America, Food Drive. ***Student services:*** personal-psychological counseling. ***Campus security:*** 24-hour emergency response devices, student patrols, late-night transport-escort service.
HOUSING College housing not available.
CAREER PLANNING ***Placement office:*** 3 full-time staff. ***Director:*** Ms. Bette Beshears, Career/Job Placement Counselor, 409-984-6239. ***Services:*** job fairs, resume preparation, resume referral, career counseling, careers library, job bank, job interviews.
AFTER GRADUATION 75% of class of 1994 had job offers within 6 months.
EXPENSES FOR 1995–96 State resident tuition: $960 full-time. Nonresident tuition: $5492 full-time. Part-time tuition per semester ranges from $100 to $330 for state residents, $176 to $1886 for nonresidents. Part-time mandatory fees per semester range from $52 to $277. Full-time mandatory fees: $812.
FINANCIAL AID ***College-administered undergrad aid 1995–96:*** 500 need-based scholarships (averaging $700), non-need scholarships, short-term loans (averaging $500), 20 Federal Work-Study (averaging $2400), 65 part-time jobs. ***Required forms:*** institutional, FAFSA. ***Priority deadline:*** 4/1. ***Payment plan:*** installment. ***Waivers:*** full or partial for senior citizens.
APPLYING Open admission. ***Options:*** Common Application, early entrance, deferred entrance, midyear entrance. ***Required:*** school transcript, TOEFL for international students. ***Required for some:*** interview, TASP. Test scores used for counseling/placement. ***Application deadline:*** rolling. ***Notification:*** continuous.
APPLYING/TRANSFER ***Required:*** high school transcript, college transcript. ***Required for some:*** interview. ***Entrance:*** noncompetitive. ***Application deadline:*** rolling. ***Notification:*** continuous. ***Contact:*** Ms. Connie Nicholas, Registrar, 409-984-6165.
CONTACT Mr. Tom Neal, Dean of Student Services, Lamar University–Port Arthur, PO Box 310, Port Arthur, TX 77641-0310, 409-984-6156. ***Fax:*** 409-984-6000.

LAREDO COMMUNITY COLLEGE
Laredo, Texas

UG Enrollment: 6,919 | **Tuition & Fees (Area Res): $766**
Application Deadline: rolling | **Room Only: $1660**

GENERAL State and locally supported, 2-year, coed. Awards transfer associate, terminal associate degrees. Founded 1946. ***Setting:*** 186-acre urban campus. ***Total enrollment:*** 6,919. ***Faculty:*** 308 (177 full-time, 131 part-time); student-faculty ratio is 17:1.
ENROLLMENT PROFILE 6,919 students from 5 states and territories, 6 other countries. 58% women, 57% part-time, 93% state residents, 15% transferred in, 1% international, 92% Hispanic, 1% African American, 1% Asian American.
FIRST-YEAR CLASS 1,471 total; 1,475 applied, 100% were accepted, 99% of whom enrolled.
ACADEMIC PROGRAM Core. Calendar: semesters. Academic remediation for entering students, English as a second language program offered during academic year and summer, services for LD students, advanced placement, honors program, summer session for credit, part-time degree program (daytime, evenings), adult/continuing education programs, internships.
GENERAL DEGREE REQUIREMENTS 60 credit hours; 1 year of lab science; 1 course in algebra; computer course for most majors.

616 Peterson's Guide to Two-Year Colleges 1997

MAJORS Child care/child and family studies, computer information systems, computer programming, construction technologies, data processing, electrical and electronics technologies, emergency medical technology, fashion merchandising, fire science, hotel and restaurant management, international business, law enforcement/police sciences, liberal arts/general studies, marketing/retailing/merchandising, medical assistant technologies, medical laboratory technology, nursing, physical therapy, radiological sciences, radiological technology, real estate, secretarial studies/office management, social science.
LIBRARY Yeary Library with 70,423 books, 298 periodicals.
COMPUTERS ON CAMPUS Computers for student use in learning center, various buildings.
COLLEGE LIFE Drama-theater group, choral group, student-run newspaper. ***Student services:*** personal-psychological counseling, women's center. ***Campus security:*** 24-hour emergency response devices and patrols.
HOUSING 120 college housing spaces available. Off-campus living permitted. ***Option:*** coed housing available. Resident assistants live in dorms.
ATHLETICS Member NJCAA. ***Intercollegiate:*** baseball M(s), tennis M(s)/W(s), volleyball W(s). ***Intramural:*** cross-country running, golf, gymnastics, swimming and diving, tennis, track and field, volleyball. ***Contact:*** Mr. Troy Van Burunt, Director of Intramurals, 210-721-5178.
CAREER PLANNING ***Placement office:*** 2 full-time, 2 part-time staff. ***Director:*** Ms. Caroline Jurgens, Director of Placement, 210-721-5461. ***Services:*** job fairs, resume preparation, career counseling, careers library, job bank, job interviews.
EXPENSES FOR 1995–96 Area resident tuition: $420 full-time. State resident tuition: $1260 full-time. Nonresident tuition: $2100 full-time. Part-time tuition per semester ranges from $25 to $154 for area residents, $42 to $462 for state residents, $200 to $770 for nonresidents. Part-time mandatory fees per semester range from $47 to $137. Full-time mandatory fees: $346. College room only: $1660 (minimum).
FINANCIAL AID ***College-administered undergrad aid 1995–96:*** 3,500 need-based scholarships (averaging $800), short-term loans, Federal Work-Study. ***Required forms:*** CSS Financial Aid PROFILE, FAFSA. ***Application deadline:*** 5/1. ***Waivers:*** full or partial for employees or children of employees and senior citizens.
APPLYING Open admission. ***Options:*** Common Application, early entrance, deferred entrance. ***Required:*** school transcript. ***Recommended:*** ACT. Test scores used for counseling/placement. ***Application deadline:*** rolling.
APPLYING/TRANSFER ***Required:*** college transcript. ***Application deadline:*** rolling.
CONTACT Dr. Kenneth A. Wolfe, Registrar/Director of Admissions, Laredo Community College, West End Washington Street, Laredo, TX 78040-4395, 210-721-5109. ***Fax:*** 210-721-5493. ***E-mail:*** wolfelcc@icsi.net.

LEE COLLEGE
Baytown, Texas

UG Enrollment: 5,753	**Tuition & Fees (Area Res): $355**
Application Deadline: rolling	**Room & Board: N/Avail**

GENERAL District-supported, 2-year, coed. Part of Texas Higher Education Coordinating Board. Awards certificates, transfer associate, terminal associate degrees. Founded 1934. ***Setting:*** 35-acre suburban campus with easy access to Houston. ***Total enrollment:*** 5,753. ***Faculty:*** 333 (156 full-time, 177 part-time); student-faculty ratio is 22:1.
ENROLLMENT PROFILE 5,753 students: 55% women, 45% men, 64% part-time, 99% state residents, 3% transferred in, 1% international, 52% 25 or older, 1% Native American, 16% Hispanic, 12% African American, 1% Asian American. ***Most popular recent majors:*** liberal arts/general studies, nursing.
FIRST-YEAR CLASS 1,026 total. Of the students who applied, 100% were accepted.
ACADEMIC PROGRAM Core, honor code. Calendar: semesters. Academic remediation for entering students, English as a second language program, advanced placement, honors program, summer session for credit, part-time degree program (daytime, evenings, summer), adult/continuing education programs, co-op programs. Study abroad in China (1% of students participate). ROTC: Army (c).
GENERAL DEGREE REQUIREMENTS 60 credit hours; math/science requirements vary according to program; computer course.
MAJORS Accounting, aerospace sciences, art/fine arts, aviation technology, biology/biological sciences, business administration/commerce/management, chemistry, communication, computer information systems, criminal justice, data processing, drafting and design, drug and alcohol/substance abuse counseling, electrical and electronics technologies, (pre)engineering sequence, fashion merchandising, flight training, French, German, graphic arts, heating/refrigeration/air conditioning, law enforcement/police sciences, legal secretarial studies, liberal arts/general studies, machine and tool technologies, mathematics, medical records services, music, nursing, paralegal studies, physical education, science, secretarial studies/office management, Spanish, telecommunications, theater arts/drama, welding technology.
LIBRARY Erma Wood Carlson Learning Resource Center with 94,509 books, 504 periodicals, 10,367 records, tapes, and CDs.
COLLEGE LIFE Drama-theater group, choral group, student-run newspaper. ***Social organizations:*** 10 open to all. ***Most popular organizations:*** Student Congress, Health Information Student Association, Lee College Awareness, Medical Professions Club, ASHRAE- Air Conditioning Society of Heat and Refrigeration Engineers. ***Major annual events:*** Fall Fiesta, Spring Fling, Annual Blood Drive. ***Student services:*** personal-psychological counseling. ***Campus security:*** 24-hour patrols, late-night transport-escort service, emergency telephones.
HOUSING College housing not available.
ATHLETICS Member NJCAA. ***Intercollegiate:*** baseball M(s), basketball M(s), tennis W(s), volleyball W(s). ***Intramural:*** basketball, bowling, football, racquetball, table tennis (Ping-Pong), volleyball. ***Contact:*** Ms. Karen Guthmiller, Director of Athletics, 713-425-6437.
CAREER PLANNING ***Director:*** Dr. Dennis Dressler, Director of Counseling, 713-425-6384. ***Services:*** job fairs, resume preparation, career counseling, careers library, job bank, job interviews.
AFTER GRADUATION 5% of students completing a degree program in 1994–95 went directly on to further study.
ESTIMATED EXPENSES FOR 1996–97 Area resident tuition: $288 full-time. State resident tuition: $576 full-time. Nonresident tuition: $960 full-time. Part-time tuition per semester ranges from $72 to $144 for area residents, $144 to $288 for state residents, $240 to $480 for nonresidents. Part-time mandatory fees: $48 per semester. Full-time mandatory fees: $67.
FINANCIAL AID ***College-administered undergrad aid 1995–96:*** 114 need-based scholarships (average $717), 629 non-need scholarships (average $347), short-term loans (average $150), 24 Federal Work-Study, 84 part-time jobs. ***Required forms:*** institutional; accepted: CSS Financial Aid PROFILE, FAFSA. ***Priority deadline:*** 6/1. ***Waivers:*** full or partial for employees or children of employees and senior citizens.
APPLYING Open admission except for nursing program. ***Options:*** early entrance, deferred entrance, midyear entrance. ***Required:*** TOEFL for international students. ***Required for some:*** school transcript, TASP. Test scores used for counseling/placement. ***Application deadline:*** rolling. ***Notification:*** continuous.
APPLYING/TRANSFER ***Required for some:*** college transcript. ***Entrance:*** noncompetitive. ***Application deadline:*** rolling. ***Notification:*** continuous. ***Contact:*** Dr. Dennis Dressler, Director of Counseling, 713-425-6384.
CONTACT Ms. Charlotte Scott, Registrar, Lee College, PO Box 818, Baytown, TX 77522-0818, 713-425-6399. ***Fax:*** 713-425-6831.

LON MORRIS COLLEGE
Jacksonville, Texas

UG Enrollment: 350	**Tuition & Fees: $6590**
Application Deadline: 8/15	**Room & Board: $3690**

GENERAL Independent United Methodist, 2-year, coed. Awards transfer associate degrees. Founded 1873. ***Setting:*** 76-acre small-town campus. ***Total enrollment:*** 350. ***Faculty:*** 30 (16 full-time, 14 part-time).
ENROLLMENT PROFILE 350 students from 11 states and territories, 9 other countries. 39% women, 4% part-time, 85% state residents, 2% transferred in, 12% international, 4% 25 or older, 0% Native American, 2% Hispanic, 9% African American, 0% Asian American.
FIRST-YEAR CLASS 190 total; 240 applied, 94% were accepted, 84% of whom enrolled. 10% from top 10% of their high school class, 30% from top quarter, 70% from top half.
ACADEMIC PROGRAM Core. Calendar: semesters. Academic remediation for entering students, advanced placement, honors program.
GENERAL DEGREE REQUIREMENTS 62 credits; math/science requirements vary according to program; computer course.
MAJORS Accounting, applied art, art education, art/fine arts, art history, biblical studies, biology/biological sciences, botany/plant sciences, business administration/commerce/management, business machine technologies, chemistry, commercial art, communication, computer science, creative writing, dance, economics, education, elementary education, engineering (general), (pre)engineering sequence, English, French, history, humanities, liberal arts/general studies, literature, mathematics, ministries, modern languages, music, music education, painting/drawing, philosophy, physical education, physics, piano/organ, political science/government, psychology, religious education, religious studies, Romance languages, social science, sociology, Spanish, speech/rhetoric/public address/debate, studio art, theater arts/drama, theology, voice, Western civilization and culture.
LIBRARY 26,000 books, 135 microform titles, 265 periodicals, 1,640 records, tapes, and CDs.
COMPUTERS ON CAMPUS 20 computers for student use in computer center, library.
COLLEGE LIFE Orientation program (3 days, no cost, parents included). Drama-theater group, student-run newspaper. ***Social organizations:*** 2 local fraternities, 2 local sororities; 19% of eligible men and 29% of eligible women are members. ***Student services:*** personal-psychological counseling.
HOUSING 340 college housing spaces available; 298 were occupied 1995–96. Freshmen guaranteed college housing. On-campus residence required through sophomore year.
ATHLETICS Member NJCAA. ***Intercollegiate:*** basketball M(s), golf M(s). ***Intramural:*** basketball, cross-country running, football, soccer, tennis, volleyball, weight lifting.
CAREER PLANNING ***Service:*** career counseling.
EXPENSES FOR 1996–97 Comprehensive fee of $10,280 includes full-time tuition ($5900), mandatory fees ($690), and college room and board ($3690). College room only: $1700. Part-time tuition per semester ranges from $750 to $2250.
FINANCIAL AID ***College-administered undergrad aid 1995–96:*** need-based scholarships, non-need scholarships, low-interest long-term loans from external sources, Federal Work-Study, part-time jobs. ***Required forms:*** CSS Financial Aid PROFILE, state, institutional; required for some: FAFSA. ***Priority deadline:*** 5/15.
APPLYING ***Options:*** early entrance, deferred entrance. ***Required:*** school transcript, SAT I or ACT, TOEFL for international students. Test scores used for counseling/placement. ***Application deadline:*** 8/15. ***Notification:*** continuous until 8/15.
APPLYING/TRANSFER ***Required:*** college transcript. ***Entrance:*** minimally difficult. ***Application deadline:*** 8/15. ***Notification:*** continuous until 8/15.
CONTACT Mr. David Hubbard, Director of Admissions, Lon Morris College, Jacksonville, TX 75766-9983, 903-589-4005 or toll-free 800-594-2201.

McLENNAN COMMUNITY COLLEGE
Waco, Texas

UG Enrollment: 5,561	**Tuition & Fees (Area Res): $870**
Application Deadline: rolling	**Room & Board: N/Avail**

GENERAL County-supported, 2-year, coed. Part of Texas Higher Education Coordinating Board. Awards certificates, transfer associate, terminal associate degrees. Founded 1965. ***Setting:*** 200-acre urban campus. ***Total enrollment:*** 5,561. ***Faculty:*** 284 (179 full-time, 10% with terminal degrees, 105 part-time); student-faculty ratio is 22:1.
ENROLLMENT PROFILE 5,561 students: 64% women, 36% men, 54% part-time, 98% state residents, 7% transferred in, 2% international, 55% 25 or older, 1% Native American, 10% Hispanic, 15% African American, 1% Asian American.
FIRST-YEAR CLASS 1,255 total; 2,528 applied, 100% were accepted, 50% of whom enrolled.
ACADEMIC PROGRAM Core. Calendar: semesters. Academic remediation for entering students, English as a second language program offered during academic year, services for LD students, advanced placement, self-designed majors, honors program, summer session for credit, part-time degree program (daytime, evenings, summer), adult/continuing education programs, co-op programs and internships. Off-campus study at Baylor University. Study abroad in England, Mexico, Czech Republic. ROTC: Air Force (c).
GENERAL DEGREE REQUIREMENTS 60 semester hours; computer course for most majors; internship (some majors).

Peterson's Guide to Two-Year Colleges 1997

617

McLennan Community College (continued)

MAJORS Accounting, art education, business administration/commerce/management, child psychology/child development, computer information systems, computer technologies, criminal justice, deaf interpreter training, early childhood education, finance/banking, journalism, law enforcement/police sciences, legal secretarial studies, liberal arts/general studies, medical laboratory technology, medical records services, medical secretarial studies, mental health/rehabilitation counseling, music, nursing, paralegal studies, philosophy, physical education, physical sciences, physical therapy, radiological technology, real estate, respiratory therapy, secretarial studies/office management.

LIBRARY McLennan Community College Library with 92,600 books, 473 microform titles, 387 periodicals, 364 records, tapes, and CDs.

COMPUTERS ON CAMPUS 425 computers for student use in computer center, computer labs, research center, learning resource center, learning center, accounting lab, classrooms, library provide access to e-mail, Internet. Staffed computer lab on campus provides training in use of computers, software.

COLLEGE LIFE Drama-theater group, choral group, student-run newspaper. ***Student services:*** personal-psychological counseling. ***Campus security:*** 24-hour patrols.

HOUSING College housing not available.

ATHLETICS Member NJCAA. ***Intercollegiate:*** baseball M(s), basketball M(s)/W(s), golf M(s), tennis W(s). ***Intramural:*** basketball, football, gymnastics, volleyball. ***Contact:*** Mr. Stan Mitchell, Athletics Director, 817-750-3492.

CAREER PLANNING ***Placement office:*** 8 full-time staff. ***Director:*** Ms. Lynn Abernathy, Director of Student Success Service, 817-750-3614. ***Services:*** job fairs, resume preparation, resume referral, career counseling, careers library, job bank, job interviews.

EXPENSES FOR 1996–97 Area resident tuition: $600 full-time, $20 per semester hour part-time. State resident tuition: $750 full-time, $25 per semester hour part-time. Nonresident tuition: $2400 full-time, $80 per semester hour part-time. Full-time mandatory fees: $270.

FINANCIAL AID ***College-administered undergrad aid 1995–96:*** 250 need-based scholarships (average $200), 50 non-need scholarships (average $260), short-term loans (average $250), low-interest long-term loans from external sources (average $2600), Federal Work-Study, 130 part-time jobs. ***Required forms:*** state; required for some: institutional; accepted: CSS Financial Aid PROFILE, FAFSA. ***Priority deadline:*** 6/1. ***Waivers:*** full or partial for employees or children of employees.

APPLYING Open admission except for health careers programs. ***Option:*** early entrance. ***Required:*** school transcript, TOEFL for international students. ***Required for some:*** SAT I or ACT. Test scores used for counseling/placement. ***Application deadline:*** rolling. ***Notification:*** continuous until 9/2.

APPLYING/TRANSFER ***Required:*** college transcript. ***Application deadline:*** rolling. ***Notification:*** continuous until 9/2. ***Contact:*** Ms. Marie Thibodeaux, Transfer Advisor, 817-756-6551.

CONTACT Ms. Karen L. Clark, Coordinator of Student Admissions, McLennan Community College, 1400 College Drive, Waco, TX 76708-1499, 817-750-3529.

MIDLAND COLLEGE
Midland, Texas

UG Enrollment: 3,763 | **Tuition & Fees (Area Res): $675**
Application Deadline: rolling | **Room & Board: N/Avail**

GENERAL State and locally supported, 2-year, coed. Part of Texas Higher Education Coordinating Board. Awards certificates, transfer associate, terminal associate degrees. Founded 1969. ***Setting:*** 163-acre suburban campus. ***Total enrollment:*** 3,763. ***Faculty:*** 194 (86 full-time, 67% with terminal degrees, 108 part-time); student-faculty ratio is 20:1. ***Notable Alumni:*** David Ward, medical doctor; Arnulfo Carrasco, medical doctor; "Spud" Webb, professional basketball player; "Mookie" Blaylock, professional basketball player.

ENROLLMENT PROFILE 3,763 students from 20 states and territories, 19 other countries. 60% women, 40% men, 65% part-time, 97% state residents, 25% transferred in, 42% have need-based financial aid, 9% have non-need-based financial aid, 1% international, 55% 25 or older, 1% Native American, 18% Hispanic, 5% African American, 1% Asian American. ***Most popular recent majors:*** nursing, business administration/commerce/management, paralegal studies.

FIRST-YEAR CLASS 1,330 total; 1,400 applied, 100% were accepted, 95% of whom enrolled. 10% from top 10% of their high school class, 20% from top quarter, 50% from top half.

ACADEMIC PROGRAM Core, honor code. Calendar: semesters. Academic remediation for entering students, English as a second language program offered during academic year, services for LD students, advanced placement, self-designed majors, honors program, summer session for credit, part-time degree program (daytime, evenings, summer), adult/continuing education programs, co-op programs and internships.

GENERAL DEGREE REQUIREMENTS 62 semester hours; 3 semester hours of math/science; computer course for anthropology, automotive technology, biology, business administration, chemistry, law enforcement, drafting, history majors; internship (some majors).

MAJORS Accounting, art education, art/fine arts, automotive technologies, aviation technology, behavioral sciences, biology/biological sciences, business administration/commerce/management, chemistry, child care/child and family studies, child psychology/child development, commercial art, communication, computer programming, computer science, criminal justice, dance, data processing, drafting and design, electrical and electronics technologies, emergency medical technology, engineering (general), engineering sciences, (pre)engineering sequence, English, environmental engineering technology, environmental sciences, fire science, French, geology, German, graphic arts, heating/refrigeration/air conditioning, journalism, law enforcement/police sciences, legal secretarial studies, liberal arts/general studies, literature, mathematics, mental health/rehabilitation counseling, modern languages, music, music education, nursing, painting/drawing, paralegal studies, petroleum technology, physical education, physical sciences, practical nursing, psychology, radiological technology, respiratory therapy, retail management, science, secretarial studies/office management, social science, Spanish, speech/rhetoric/public address/debate, studio art, veterinary technology, welding technology.

LIBRARY Murry Fasken Learning Center with 39,100 books, 196 microform titles, 335 periodicals, 931 records, tapes, and CDs.

COMPUTERS ON CAMPUS 25 computers for student use in computer labs, learning resource center, library. Staffed computer lab on campus provides training in use of computers.

COLLEGE LIFE Orientation program (2 days, no cost). Drama-theater group, choral group, student-run newspaper. 20% vote in student government elections. ***Social organizations:*** 20 open to all. ***Most popular organizations:*** Students in Free Enterprise, Midland College Latin American Student Society, Student Government Association. ***Major annual events:*** Homecoming Night, Carol of Lights Christmas Celebration, Halloween Spook House. ***Student services:*** personal-psychological counseling. ***Campus security:*** 24-hour patrols.

HOUSING College housing not available.

ATHLETICS Member NJCAA. ***Intercollegiate:*** basketball M(s)/W(s), golf M(s). ***Intramural:*** basketball, football, soccer, table tennis (Ping-Pong), tennis, volleyball. ***Contact:*** Mr. Joe Williams, Director of Athletics, 915-685-4575.

CAREER PLANNING ***Placement office:*** 1 full-time, 3 part-time staff. ***Director:*** Mr. Terry Clemmer, Vocational Career Counselor, 915-685-4695. ***Services:*** job fairs, resume preparation, career counseling. 30 organizations recruited on campus 1994–95.

AFTER GRADUATION 80% of students completing a degree program in 1994–95 went directly on to further study.

EXPENSES FOR 1995–96 Area resident tuition: $675 full-time. State resident tuition: $723 full-time. Nonresident tuition: $1042 full-time. Part-time tuition per semester hour ranges from $100 to $301 for area residents, $108 to $323 for state residents, $232 to $389 for nonresidents.

FINANCIAL AID ***College-administered undergrad aid 1995–96:*** 500 need-based scholarships, 1,250 non-need scholarships (average $500), short-term loans (average $300), 60 Federal Work-Study. ***Required forms:*** FAFSA; accepted: CSS Financial Aid PROFILE. ***Priority deadline:*** 6/1. ***Waivers:*** full or partial for employees or children of employees.

APPLYING Open admission except for nursing, respiratory therapy, radiological technology programs. ***Options:*** early entrance, deferred entrance, midyear entrance. ***Required:*** school transcript, TOEFL for international students, TASP. ***Recommended:*** ACT. Test scores used for counseling/placement. ***Application deadline:*** rolling. ***Notification:*** continuous.

APPLYING/TRANSFER ***Required:*** college transcript, minimum 2.0 college GPA. ***Entrance:*** noncompetitive. ***Application deadline:*** rolling. ***Notification:*** continuous. ***Contact:*** Dr. Elizabeth Robinett, Transfer Counselor, 915-685-4506.

CONTACT Mr. Camal C. Dakil, Vice President, Student Services, Midland College, Midland, TX 79705-6399, 915-685-4503.

MISS WADE'S FASHION MERCHANDISING COLLEGE
Dallas, Texas

UG Enrollment: 226 | **Tuition & Fees: $6105**
Application Deadline: rolling | **Room Only: $1990**

GENERAL Proprietary, 2-year, coed. Awards transfer associate degrees. Founded 1965. ***Setting:*** 175-acre urban campus. ***Total enrollment:*** 226. ***Faculty:*** 12 (8 full-time, 40% with terminal degrees, 4 part-time); student-faculty ratio is 20:1. ***Notable Alumni:*** Christi Harris, businesswoman; Julie Esping, fashion designer.

ENROLLMENT PROFILE 226 students from 17 states and territories, 6 other countries. 93% women, 7% men, 0% part-time, 75% state residents, 32% transferred in, 85% have need-based financial aid, 0% have non-need-based financial aid, 3% international, 27% 25 or older, 1% Native American, 20% Hispanic, 30% African American, 5% Asian American. ***Areas of study chosen:*** 100% interdisciplinary studies.

FIRST-YEAR CLASS 105 total; 570 applied, 85% were accepted, 22% of whom enrolled. 15% from top 10% of their high school class, 25% from top quarter, 75% from top half.

ACADEMIC PROGRAM Core, professional curriculum, honor code. Calendar: trimesters. 24 courses offered in 1995–96. Academic remediation for entering students, services for LD students, self-designed majors, honors program, summer session for credit, co-op programs and internships. Study abroad in England, France, Italy, Switzerland.

GENERAL DEGREE REQUIREMENTS 76 credits; 4 credits of math; computer course; internship.

MAJORS Business administration/commerce/management, fashion design and technology, fashion merchandising, interior design, marketing/retailing/merchandising.

LIBRARY College Library with 12,171 books, 50 microform titles, 152 periodicals, 5 CD-ROMs, 702 records, tapes, and CDs.

COMPUTERS ON CAMPUS 50 computers for student use in computer center, learning resource center, library provide access to Internet. Staffed computer lab on campus provides training in use of computers, software.

COLLEGE LIFE Orientation program (2 days, no cost, parents included). Student-run newspaper. 90% vote in student government elections. ***Social organizations:*** 4 open to all; 1 national fraternity, 1 national sorority; 50% of eligible men and 50% of eligible women are members. ***Most popular organizations:*** Fashion Group, Phi Theta Kappa, Phi Beta Lambda, Interior Design Student Group. ***Major annual events:*** Annual Banquet, Women's Apparel Market, Men's Apparel Market. ***Student services:*** personal-psychological counseling, women's center. ***Campus security:*** 24-hour emergency response devices and patrols, late-night transport-escort service.

HOUSING 250 college housing spaces available; 80 were occupied 1995–96. Freshmen guaranteed college housing. Off-campus living permitted. ***Options:*** coed, single-sex housing available. Resident assistants live in dorms.

CAREER PLANNING ***Placement office:*** 4 full-time staff. ***Director:*** Miss Suzane Wade, Executive Director, 214-637-3530. ***Services:*** job fairs, resume preparation, resume referral, career counseling, careers library, job bank, job interviews. Students must register freshman year. 50 organizations recruited on campus 1994–95.

AFTER GRADUATION 90% of class of 1994 had job offers within 6 months. 35% of students completing a degree program went directly on to further study.

EXPENSES FOR 1996–97 Tuition: $5980 full-time. Full-time mandatory fees: $125. College room only: $1990.

FINANCIAL AID ***College-administered undergrad aid 1995–96:*** 100 need-based scholarships (average $400), low-interest long-term loans from college funds (average $3000), loans from external sources (average $3000), 5 Federal Work-Study (averaging $5000), 200 part-time jobs. ***Required forms:*** institutional, FAFSA; accepted: CSS Financial Aid PROFILE. ***Application deadline:*** continuous. ***Payment plan:*** installment.

APPLYING ***Option:*** Common Application. ***Required:*** school transcript. ***Application deadline:*** rolling.

APPLYING/TRANSFER ***Required:*** high school transcript, college transcript. ***Entrance:*** minimally difficult. ***Application deadline:*** rolling. ***Contact:*** Dr. Charles L. Restivo, Executive Vice President, 214-637-3530.

CONTACT Dr. Charles L. Restivo, Executive Vice President, Miss Wade's Fashion Merchandising College, M-5120 Apparel Mart, PO Box 586343, Dallas, TX 75258-6343, 214-637-3530 or toll-free 800-624-4850. College video available.

MONTGOMERY COLLEGE
Conroe, Texas

UG Enrollment: 3,196 **Tuition & Fees (Area Res): $856**
Application Deadline: rolling **Room & Board: N/Avail**

GENERAL State and locally supported, 2-year, coed. Part of North Harris Montgomery Community College District. Awards certificates, transfer associate, terminal associate degrees. ***Setting:*** suburban campus with easy access to Houston. ***Total enrollment:*** 3,196. ***Faculty:*** 179 (38 full-time, 141 part-time).
ENROLLMENT PROFILE 3,196 students: 20% have need-based financial aid, 5% have non-need-based financial aid.
ACADEMIC PROGRAM Core, interdisciplinary curriculum. Calendar: semesters. 350 courses offered in 1995–96; average class size 20 in required courses. Academic remediation for entering students, English as a second language program offered during academic year, services for LD students, advanced placement, summer session for credit, part-time degree program (daytime, evenings, weekends, summer), adult/continuing education programs, internships.
GENERAL DEGREE REQUIREMENTS 62 credit hours; computer course for accounting, office administration, travel and tourism, legal assisting, criminal justice, geologic technology, food service, management, real estate, records management majors.
MAJORS Accounting, biotechnology, business administration/commerce/management, computer graphics, computer information systems, computer programming, computer technologies, criminal justice, drafting and design, emergency medical technology, human services, information science, medical records services, nursing, practical nursing, real estate, secretarial studies/office management, vocational education.
LIBRARY Library/Learning Resources Center with 3,000 books, 300 microform titles, 350 periodicals, 20 on-line bibliographic services, 100 CD-ROMs, 200 records, tapes, and CDs.
COMPUTERS ON CAMPUS 600 computers for student use in computer center, computer labs, research center, learning resource center, classrooms, library, student center, student rooms provide access to off-campus computing facilities, e-mail, on-line services, Internet. Staffed computer lab on campus provides training in use of computers, software.
COLLEGE LIFE ***Most popular organizations:*** Campus Crusade for Christ, Student Government, Phi Theta Kappa. ***Student services:*** personal-psychological counseling. ***Campus security:*** 24-hour emergency response devices and patrols.
HOUSING College housing not available.
CAREER PLANNING ***Placement office:*** 1 full-time, 1 part-time staff. ***Director:*** Ms. Karen Murphy, Assistant Dean of Student Development, 409-273-7236. ***Services:*** resume preparation, career counseling, careers library, job bank.
EXPENSES FOR 1995–96 Area resident tuition: $760 full-time. State resident tuition: $1880 full-time. Nonresident tuition: $2200 full-time. Part-time tuition per semester hour ranges from $75 to $265 for area residents, $110 to $650 for state residents, $215 to $760 for nonresidents. Part-time mandatory fees: $3 per credit hour. Full-time mandatory fees: $96.
FINANCIAL AID ***College-administered undergrad aid 1995–96:*** 400 need-based scholarships (averaging $700), 3 non-need scholarships (averaging $500), short-term loans (averaging $500), low-interest long-term loans from external sources (averaging $2000), 6 Federal Work-Study (averaging $1000). ***Acceptable forms:*** FAFSA. ***Priority deadline:*** 6/1. ***Waivers:*** full or partial for employees or children of employees. ***Notification:*** continuous.
APPLYING Open admission. ***Options:*** Common Application, early entrance. ***Required:*** CELT (for foreign students). Test scores used for counseling/placement. ***Application deadlines:*** rolling.
APPLYING/TRANSFER ***Entrance:*** noncompetitive. ***Application deadline:*** rolling. ***Contact:*** Mr. Earl Godfrey, Admissions Advising Coordinator, 409-273-2900.
CONTACT Dr. Linda Stegall, Vice Chancellor for Educational and Student Development, Montgomery College, Conroe, TX 77384, 713-591-3523. ***E-mail:*** earlg@me.nhmccd.cc.tx.us.

MOUNTAIN VIEW COLLEGE
Dallas, Texas

UG Enrollment: 6,027 **Tuition & Fees (Area Res): $474**
Application Deadline: rolling **Room & Board: N/Avail**

GENERAL County-supported, 2-year, coed. Part of Dallas County Community College District System. Awards certificates, transfer associate, terminal associate degrees. Founded 1970. ***Setting:*** 200-acre urban campus. ***Total enrollment:*** 6,027. ***Faculty:*** 264 (79 full-time, 185 part-time); student-faculty ratio is 25:1.
ENROLLMENT PROFILE 6,027 students: 56% women, 70% part-time, 98% state residents, 24% transferred in, 1% international, 40% 25 or older, 1% Native American, 25% Hispanic, 24% African American, 5% Asian American. ***Most popular recent majors:*** liberal arts/general studies, aviation technology, accounting.
FIRST-YEAR CLASS 1,261 total; 1,560 applied, 100% were accepted, 81% of whom enrolled.
ACADEMIC PROGRAM Core. Calendar: semesters. Academic remediation for entering students, English as a second language program offered during academic year and summer, services for LD students, advanced placement, honors program, summer session for credit, part-time degree program (daytime, evenings, summer), external degree programs, adult/continuing education programs, co-op programs and internships. ROTC: Army (c).
GENERAL DEGREE REQUIREMENTS 61 credit hours; 1 math course.
MAJORS Accounting, aviation administration, aviation technology, computer information systems, computer programming, drafting and design, electrical and electronics technologies, electrical engineering technology, electromechanical technology, electronics engineering technology, engineering technology, legal secretarial studies, liberal arts/general studies, quality control technology, robotics, welding technology.
COMPUTERS ON CAMPUS 188 computers for student use in computer center, computer labs, learning resource center, classrooms, library, student center. Staffed computer lab on campus provides training in use of computers, software.
COLLEGE LIFE Drama-theater group, choral group. 10% vote in student government elections. ***Social organizations:*** local fraternities, local sororities. ***Student services:*** health clinic, personal-psychological counseling, women's center. ***Campus security:*** 24-hour patrols, late-night transport-escort service.
HOUSING College housing not available.
ATHLETICS Member NJCAA. ***Intercollegiate:*** basketball M, soccer M, squash W, volleyball W. ***Intramural:*** basketball, football.
CAREER PLANNING ***Director:*** Ms. Corina Gardea, Vice President of Student Development, 214-860-8696. ***Services:*** career counseling, careers library.
EXPENSES FOR 1996–97 Area resident tuition: $424 full-time. State resident tuition: $804 full-time. Nonresident tuition: $1608 full-time. Part-time mandatory fees: $25 per semester. Part-time tuition per 6 credit hours: $108 for area residents, $222 for state residents, $402 for nonresidents. Full-time mandatory fees: $50.
FINANCIAL AID ***College-administered undergrad aid 1995–96:*** 45 need-based scholarships (averaging $1250), short-term loans (averaging $75), low-interest long-term loans from external sources, Federal Work-Study, 175 part-time jobs. ***Required forms:*** FAFSA; accepted: CSS Financial Aid PROFILE. ***Application deadline:*** continuous. ***Waivers:*** full or partial for employees or children of employees.
APPLYING Open admission. ***Options:*** electronic application, early entrance, deferred entrance, midyear entrance. ***Required:*** TOEFL for international students. ***Recommended:*** SAT I or ACT. ***Required for some:*** school transcript. Test scores used for counseling/placement. ***Application deadline:*** rolling. ***Notification:*** continuous.
APPLYING/TRANSFER ***Required:*** college transcript. ***Recommended:*** standardized test scores. ***Entrance:*** noncompetitive. ***Application deadline:*** rolling. ***Notification:*** continuous.
CONTACT Mr. Juan C. Torres, Registrar/Director of Admissions, Mountain View College, 4849 West Illinois Avenue, Dallas, TX 75211-6599, 214-860-8603. ***Fax:*** 214-860-8570. ***E-mail:*** jctorres@dcccd.edu.

NAVARRO COLLEGE
Corsicana, Texas

UG Enrollment: 3,211 **Tuition & Fees (Area Res): $1125**
Application Deadline: 9/1 **Room & Board: $2670**

GENERAL State and locally supported, 2-year, coed. Part of Texas Higher Education Coordinating Board. Awards certificates, transfer associate, terminal associate degrees. Founded 1946. ***Setting:*** 275-acre small-town campus with easy access to Dallas. ***Total enrollment:*** 3,211. ***Faculty:*** 175 (78 full-time, 7% with terminal degrees, 97 part-time); student-faculty ratio is 20:1.
ENROLLMENT PROFILE 3,211 students from 22 states and territories, 30 other countries. 60% women, 40% men, 47% part-time, 91% state residents, 25% live on campus, 16% transferred in, 4% international, 35% 25 or older, 1% Native American, 7% Hispanic, 15% African American, 3% Asian American.
FIRST-YEAR CLASS 1,075 total; 1,075 applied, 100% were accepted. 10% from top 10% of their high school class, 40% from top half.
ACADEMIC PROGRAM Core. Calendar: semesters. Academic remediation for entering students, English as a second language program offered during academic year, services for LD students, advanced placement, self-designed majors, tutorials, honors program, summer session for credit, part-time degree program (daytime, evenings, summer), adult/continuing education programs, co-op programs.
GENERAL DEGREE REQUIREMENTS 63 semester hours; 6 semester hours of math/science; computer course.
MAJORS Accounting, agricultural technologies, art/fine arts, aviation technology, biology/biological sciences, broadcasting, business administration/commerce/management, chemistry, child psychology/child development, commercial art, computer graphics, computer programming, computer science, corrections, criminal justice, dance, data processing, dental services, drafting and design, education, elementary education, engineering (general), (pre)engineering sequence, English, fire science, flight training, industrial design, industrial engineering technology, journalism, law enforcement/police sciences, legal secretarial studies, legal studies, marketing/retailing/merchandising, mathematics, medical laboratory technology, music, nursing, occupational therapy, paralegal studies, pharmacy/pharmaceutical sciences, physical education, physical sciences, physics, practical nursing, psychology, radio and television studies, real estate, retail management, science, secretarial studies/office management, social science, sociology, speech/rhetoric/public address/debate, theater arts/drama, veterinary sciences, voice.
LIBRARY Gaston T. Gooch Learning Resource Center with 40,000 books, 68 microform titles, 250 periodicals, 27 CD-ROMs, 1,700 records, tapes, and CDs. Acquisition spending 1994–95: $86,681.
COMPUTERS ON CAMPUS 80 computers for student use in computer labs, learning resource center, library. Staffed computer lab on campus provides training in use of computers, software. Academic computing expenditure 1994–95: $262,600.
COLLEGE LIFE Drama-theater group, choral group, marching band. 25% vote in student government elections. ***Social organizations:*** 35 open to all; 1 local sorority. ***Most popular organizations:*** Student Government Association, Phi Theta Kappa, Soccer Club, Ebony Club, Que Pasa. ***Major annual events:*** Homecoming, Bulldog Bash, "Mr. NC" Contest. ***Student services:*** personal-psychological counseling. ***Campus security:*** 24-hour patrols.
HOUSING 550 college housing spaces available; all were occupied 1995–96. Freshmen given priority for college housing. Off-campus living permitted. ***Option:*** single-sex (14 buildings) housing available. Resident assistants live in dorms.
ATHLETICS Member NJCAA. ***Intercollegiate:*** baseball M(s), basketball M(s), football M(s), golf M(s), tennis M(s)/W(s), volleyball W(s). ***Intramural:*** basketball, bowling, football, soccer, softball, volleyball. ***Contact:*** Dr. Bill Malloy, Athletic Director, 903-874-6501.
CAREER PLANNING ***Placement office:*** 4 full-time, 3 part-time staff. ***Director:*** Ms. Robbye Nesmith, Director, Carl Perkins Career Center, 903-874-6501. ***Services:*** job fairs, resume preparation, resume referral, career counseling, careers library, job bank, job interviews.
EXPENSES FOR 1995–96 Area resident tuition: $860 full-time. State resident tuition: $1130 full-time. Nonresident tuition: $1290 full-time. Full-time mandatory fees: $265. College room and board: $2670 (minimum).

Peterson's Guide to Two-Year Colleges 1997 619

Navarro College (continued)
FINANCIAL AID ***College-administered undergrad aid 1995–96:*** 400 need-based scholarships (average $800), 250 non-need scholarships (average $800), low-interest long-term loans from external sources (average $2625), 98 Federal Work-Study (averaging $765). ***Required forms:*** institutional, FAFSA. ***Priority deadline:*** 6/1. ***Waivers:*** full or partial for employees or children of employees.
APPLYING Open admission. ***Options:*** early entrance, midyear entrance. ***Required:*** TOEFL for international students. ***Recommended:*** SAT I or ACT. Test scores used for counseling/placement. ***Application deadline:*** 9/1. ***Notification:*** continuous until 9/1.
APPLYING/TRANSFER ***Application deadline:*** 9/1. ***Notification:*** continuous until 9/1.
CONTACT Ms. Donna Wald, Director of Recruiting, Navarro College, 3200 West 7th Avenue, Corsicana, TX 75110-4899, 903-874-6501 Ext. 291 or toll-free 800-628-2776.

NORTH CENTRAL TEXAS COLLEGE
Gainesville, Texas

UG Enrollment: 4,133	Tuition & Fees (TX Res): $651
Application Deadline: rolling	Room & Board: $1960

GENERAL County-supported, 2-year, coed. Part of Texas Higher Education Coordinating Board. Awards certificates, transfer associate, terminal associate degrees. Founded 1924. ***Setting:*** 132-acre rural campus with easy access to Dallas–Fort Worth. ***Total enrollment:*** 4,133. ***Faculty:*** 175 (74 full-time, 30% with terminal degrees, 101 part-time); student-faculty ratio is 20:1.
ENROLLMENT PROFILE 4,133 students from 14 states and territories, 21 other countries. 60% women, 74% part-time, 95% state residents, 2% live on campus, 25% transferred in, 25% have need-based financial aid, 2% international, 49% 25 or older, 1% Native American, 4% Hispanic, 4% African American, 1% Asian American. ***Most popular recent major:*** nursing.
FIRST-YEAR CLASS 1,250 total; 1,300 applied, 100% were accepted, 96% of whom enrolled.
ACADEMIC PROGRAM Core. Calendar: semesters. 275 courses offered in 1995–96; average class size 20 in required courses. Academic remediation for entering students, services for LD students, tutorials, summer session for credit, part-time degree program (daytime, evenings), adult/continuing education programs, internships.
GENERAL DEGREE REQUIREMENTS 62 credit hours; 2 courses in math/science; computer course.
MAJORS Agricultural technologies, automotive technologies, business administration/commerce/management, computer information systems, computer management, computer programming, computer science, computer technologies, criminal justice, data processing, drafting and design, electrical and electronics technologies, electrical engineering technology, electronics engineering technology, emergency medical technology, (pre)engineering sequence, equestrian studies, farm and ranch management, law enforcement/police sciences, legal secretarial studies, liberal arts/general studies, machine and tool technologies, medical records services, nursing, occupational therapy, paralegal studies, real estate, science, secretarial studies/office management, welding technology.
LIBRARY NCTC Library plus 1 other, with 44,260 books, 410 microform titles, 370 periodicals, 1,901 records, tapes, and CDs.
COMPUTERS ON CAMPUS 60 computers for student use in computer center, computer labs, learning resource center, library. Staffed computer lab on campus.
COLLEGE LIFE Drama-theater group, choral group. ***Student services:*** personal-psychological counseling. ***Campus security:*** late-night transport-escort service, late night security personnel.
HOUSING 106 college housing spaces available; 89 were occupied 1995–96. No special consideration for freshman housing applicants. Off-campus living permitted. ***Option:*** coed housing available. Resident assistants live in dorms.
ATHLETICS Member NJCAA. ***Intercollegiate:*** baseball M(s), equestrian sports M(s)/W(s), tennis W(s), volleyball W(s). ***Intramural:*** basketball, bowling, football, golf, table tennis (Ping-Pong), tennis, volleyball. ***Contact:*** Mr. Kevin Darwin, Athletics Director, 817-668-7731.
CAREER PLANNING ***Service:*** career counseling.
EXPENSES FOR 1995–96 State resident tuition: $496 full-time, $16 per credit hour part-time. Nonresident tuition: $806 full-time, $26 per credit hour part-time. Full-time mandatory fees per year: $155 for state residents, $372 for nonresidents. Part-time mandatory fees per credit hour: $5 for state residents, $12 for nonresidents. Oklahoma residents pay state resident tuition rates. College room and board: $1960.
FINANCIAL AID ***College-administered undergrad aid 1995–96:*** 147 need-based scholarships (averaging $430), 509 non-need scholarships (averaging $205), short-term loans (averaging $100), low-interest long-term loans from external sources (averaging $2325), Federal Work-Study, 44 part-time jobs. ***Required forms:*** state; required for some: institutional; accepted: FAFSA. ***Priority deadline:*** 6/1. ***Waivers:*** full or partial for employees or children of employees.
APPLYING Open admission except for allied health, legal assistant, equine technology, occupational therapy assistant programs. ***Options:*** early entrance, midyear entrance. ***Required:*** TOEFL for international students. ***Recommended:*** ACT. ***Required for some:*** ACT, TASP. Test scores used for counseling/placement. ***Application deadline:*** rolling.
APPLYING/TRANSFER ***Entrance:*** noncompetitive. ***Application deadline:*** rolling.
CONTACT Ms. Janie Neighbors, Director of Admissions/Registrar, North Central Texas College, Gainesville, TX 76240-4699, 817-668-7731 Ext. 415. ***Fax:*** 817-668-6049. College video available.

NORTHEAST TEXAS COMMUNITY COLLEGE
Mount Pleasant, Texas

UG Enrollment: 1,952	Tuition & Fees (Area Res): $860
Application Deadline: rolling	Room & Board: $2700

GENERAL State and locally supported, 2-year, coed. Part of Texas Higher Education Coordinating Board. Awards transfer associate, terminal associate degrees. Founded 1985. ***Setting:*** 175-acre rural campus. ***Research spending 1994–95:*** $7500. ***Total enrollment:*** 1,952. ***Faculty:*** 114 (48 full-time, 82% with terminal degrees, 66 part-time); student-faculty ratio is 16:1.
ENROLLMENT PROFILE 1,952 students from 13 states and territories, 1 other country. 62% women, 54% part-time, 99% state residents, 3% live on campus, 7% transferred in, 48% 25 or older, 0% Native American, 3% Hispanic, 7% African American, 0% Asian American. ***Areas of study chosen:*** 23% liberal arts/general studies, 7% business management and administrative services, 6% education, 5% agriculture, 4% computer and information sciences, 2% fine arts, 1% English language/literature/letters, 1% mathematics. ***Most popular recent majors:*** criminal justice, nursing, computer science.
FIRST-YEAR CLASS 255 total.
ACADEMIC PROGRAM Core. Calendar: semesters. 675 courses offered in 1995–96. Academic remediation for entering students, English as a second language program offered during academic year, services for LD students, advanced placement, summer session for credit, part-time degree program (daytime, evenings, summer), adult/continuing education programs, co-op programs.
GENERAL DEGREE REQUIREMENTS 62 credit hours; 1 college algebra course; computer course.
MAJORS Accounting, agricultural sciences, automotive technologies, computer information systems, computer science, cosmetology, criminal justice, dairy sciences, finance/banking, food services technology, legal secretarial studies, medical secretarial studies, nursing, poultry sciences, range management, real estate, secretarial studies/office management.
LIBRARY Learning Resource Center with 24,501 books, 40 microform titles, 325 periodicals, 13 CD-ROMs, 2,272 records, tapes, and CDs. Acquisition spending 1994–95: $84,750.
COMPUTERS ON CAMPUS 126 computers for student use in computer labs, learning resource center. Staffed computer lab on campus provides training in use of computers, software.
COLLEGE LIFE Drama-theater group, choral group, student-run newspaper. ***Social organizations:*** 12 open to all. ***Most popular organizations:*** Student Coordinating Board, Student Nurses Association, Criminal Justice Organization (COPSS), Baptist Student Union, Computer Club. ***Major annual events:*** Intercollegiate Rodeo, Carol of Lights, Health Fair. ***Student services:*** personal-psychological counseling, women's center. ***Campus security:*** 24-hour patrols.
HOUSING 64 college housing spaces available; 58 were occupied 1995–96. No special consideration for freshman housing applicants. Off-campus living permitted. ***Option:*** single-sex (1 building) housing available. Resident assistants live in dorms.
ATHLETICS Member NJCAA. ***Intercollegiate:*** baseball M(s), golf M, softball W. ***Intramural:*** tennis, volleyball. ***Contact:*** Dr. Jerry Wesson, Athletic Director, 903-572-1911.
CAREER PLANNING ***Placement office:*** 4 full-time staff; $15,492 operating expenditure 1994–95. ***Director:*** Mr. John Baker, Director of Counseling and Testing, 903-572-1911. ***Services:*** resume preparation, career counseling, careers library.
EXPENSES FOR 1996–97 Area resident tuition: $860 full-time. State resident tuition: $1160 full-time. Nonresident tuition: $1670 full-time. Part-time tuition per credit hour ranges from $48 to $318 for area residents, $58 to $428 for state residents, $223 to $615 for nonresidents. College room and board: $2700. College room only: $1300.
FINANCIAL AID ***College-administered undergrad aid 1995–96:*** 29 need-based scholarships (average $235), 300 non-need scholarships (average $250), short-term loans (average $200), low-interest long-term loans, Federal Work-Study, 51 part-time jobs. ***Required forms:*** institutional, FAFSA; required for some: state. ***Priority deadline:*** 6/1. ***Waivers:*** full or partial for employees or children of employees and senior citizens.
APPLYING Open admission. ***Options:*** early entrance, midyear entrance. ***Required:*** TOEFL for international students. ***Required for some:*** SAT I or ACT. Test scores used for counseling/placement. ***Application deadline:*** rolling.
APPLYING/TRANSFER ***Entrance:*** noncompetitive. ***Application deadline:*** rolling.
CONTACT Mr. Phil Ebensberger, Dean of Admissions/Registrar, Northeast Texas Community College, Mount Pleasant, TX 75456-1307, 903-572-1911 Ext. 213. ***Fax:*** 903-572-6712.

NORTH HARRIS COLLEGE
Houston, Texas

UG Enrollment: 3,080	Tuition & Fees (Area Res): $714
Application Deadline: rolling	Room & Board: N/Avail

GENERAL State and locally supported, 2-year, coed. Part of North Harris Montgomery Community College District. Awards certificates, transfer associate, terminal associate degrees. Founded 1972. ***Setting:*** 185-acre suburban campus. ***Total enrollment:*** 3,080. ***Faculty:*** 196 (56 full-time, 140 part-time); student-faculty ratio is 20:1.
ENROLLMENT PROFILE 3,080 students from 41 states and territories, 25 other countries. 60% women, 70% part-time, 98% state residents, 12% transferred in, 1% international, 48% 25 or older, 1% Native American, 9% Hispanic, 6% African American, 4% Asian American.
FIRST-YEAR CLASS Of the students who applied, 100% were accepted.
ACADEMIC PROGRAM Core, honor code. Calendar: semesters. Academic remediation for entering students, English as a second language program offered during academic year and summer, services for LD students, summer session for credit, part-time degree program (daytime, evenings, summer), adult/continuing education programs, co-op programs. ROTC: Army (c).
GENERAL DEGREE REQUIREMENTS 62 credits; computer course for most majors; internship (some majors).
MAJORS Accounting, art education, art/fine arts, automotive technologies, biotechnology, business administration/commerce/management, child care/child and family studies, computer science, cosmetology, criminal justice, data processing, drafting and design, education, electrical and electronics technologies, (pre)engineering sequence, finance/banking, heating/refrigeration/air conditioning, human services, information science, interior design, journalism, law enforcement/police sciences, legal studies, liberal arts/general studies, marketing/retailing/merchandising, mathematics, music, nursing, photography, physical education, political science/government, real estate, respiratory therapy, science, secretarial studies/office management, sociology, speech/rhetoric/public address/debate, theater arts/drama, tourism and travel, veterinary sciences, welding technology.
LIBRARY 85,538 books, 586 microform titles, 1,010 periodicals, 3,631 records, tapes, and CDs.

COMPUTERS ON CAMPUS 39 computers for student use in lab, library. Staffed computer lab on campus provides training in use of computers, software.
COLLEGE LIFE Choral group, student-run newspaper. ***Social organizations:*** 33 open to all. ***Most popular organizations:*** Phi Theta Kappa, Student Ambassadors, African-American Student Association, Vietnamese Student Association, Earth Alliance. ***Major annual events:*** Oktoberfest, Spring Fling. ***Student services:*** personal-psychological counseling, women's center. ***Campus security:*** 24-hour patrols.
HOUSING College housing not available.
ATHLETICS ***Intramural:*** badminton, basketball, bowling, football, gymnastics, racquetball, tennis, volleyball.
CAREER PLANNING ***Placement office:*** 3 full-time, 2 part-time staff. ***Director:*** Mr. Robert Winter, Career Counselor, 713-443-5471. ***Services:*** resume preparation, resume referral, career counseling, careers library, job bank, job interviews.
EXPENSES FOR 1996–97 Area resident tuition: $714 full-time, $60 per semester part-time. State resident tuition: $1764 full-time, $95 per semester part-time. Nonresident tuition: $2064 full-time, $200 per semester part-time.
FINANCIAL AID ***College-administered undergrad aid 1995–96:*** 1,300 need-based scholarships (average $650), 700 non-need scholarships (average $350), short-term loans (average $150), low-interest long-term loans from external sources (average $1700), Federal Work-Study, 495 part-time jobs. ***Required forms:*** institutional, FAFSA; accepted: CSS Financial Aid PROFILE. ***Priority deadline:*** 4/15. ***Payment plans:*** installment, deferred payment.
APPLYING Open admission except for nursing, respiratory therapy programs. ***Options:*** Common Application, early entrance. ***Required:*** school transcript, SAT I or ACT, TOEFL for international students, ACT ASSET. Test scores used for counseling/placement. ***Application deadline:*** rolling. ***Notification:*** continuous until 7/28.
APPLYING/TRANSFER ***Required:*** standardized test scores, high school transcript, college transcript. ***Entrance:*** noncompetitive. ***Application deadline:*** rolling. ***Notification:*** continuous until 7/28.
CONTACT Dr. Raquel Henry, Vice President for Student and Organizational Development, North Harris College, 20000 Kingwood Drive, Kingwood, TX 77339, 713-359-1611. ***Fax:*** 713-359-1612.

NORTH LAKE COLLEGE
Irving, Texas

UG Enrollment: 6,400	**Tuition & Fees (Area Res): $610**
Application Deadline: 8/24	**Room & Board: N/Avail**

GENERAL County-supported, 2-year, coed. Part of Dallas County Community College District System. Awards transfer associate, terminal associate degrees. Founded 1977. ***Setting:*** 250-acre suburban campus with easy access to Dallas. ***Total enrollment:*** 6,400. ***Faculty:*** 280 (80 full-time, 200 part-time).
ENROLLMENT PROFILE 6,400 students: 52% women, 48% men, 75% part-time, 98% state residents, 12% transferred in, 1% international, 53% 25 or older, 1% Native American, 12% Hispanic, 10% African American, 7% Asian American. ***Most popular recent majors:*** liberal arts/general studies, electrical and electronics technologies, business administration/commerce/management.
FIRST-YEAR CLASS 1,900 total. Of the students who applied, 99% were accepted. 2% from top 10% of their high school class, 85% from top half.
ACADEMIC PROGRAM Core. Calendar: semesters. Academic remediation for entering students, English as a second language program, services for LD students, advanced placement, part-time degree program (daytime, evenings, summer), co-op programs.
GENERAL DEGREE REQUIREMENTS 62 semester hours; 1 math course.
MAJORS Accounting, business administration/commerce/management, carpentry, communication equipment technology, computer information systems, computer programming, construction technologies, data processing, electrical and electronics technologies, electronics engineering technology, heating/refrigeration/air conditioning, legal secretarial studies, liberal arts/general studies, physical fitness/exercise science, real estate, secretarial studies/office management.
LIBRARY North Lake College Library with 34,000 books, 2,600 microform titles, 400 periodicals, 3,600 records, tapes, and CDs.
COMPUTERS ON CAMPUS 65 computers for student use in computer center.
COLLEGE LIFE Drama-theater group, choral group. ***Student services:*** health clinic, personal-psychological counseling, women's center. ***Campus security:*** late-night transport-escort service.
HOUSING College housing not available.
ATHLETICS Member NJCAA. ***Intercollegiate:*** baseball M, basketball M, softball W, volleyball W.
CAREER PLANNING ***Director:*** Ms. Zena Jackson, Director of Career Services, 214-273-3146. ***Service:*** career counseling.
EXPENSES FOR 1996–97 Area resident tuition: $610 full-time. State resident tuition: $990 full-time. Nonresident tuition: $2100 full-time. Part-time tuition per semester ranges from $79 to $233 for area residents, $136 to $423 for state residents, $226 to $774 for nonresidents.
FINANCIAL AID ***College-administered undergrad aid 1995–96:*** 150 need-based scholarships (average $200), 50 non-need scholarships (average $125), short-term loans (average $60), low-interest long-term loans from external sources (average $1000), Federal Work-Study, 200 part-time jobs. ***Required forms:*** institutional; accepted: CSS Financial Aid PROFILE, FAFSA. ***Application deadline:*** continuous. ***Waivers:*** full or partial for employees or children of employees.
APPLYING Open admission. ***Option:*** early entrance. ***Recommended:*** school transcript. ***Application deadline:*** 8/24. ***Notification:*** continuous.
APPLYING/TRANSFER ***Required:*** college transcript. ***Recommended:*** high school transcript. ***Application deadline:*** 8/24. ***Notification:*** continuous.
CONTACT Mr. Steve Twenge, Director of Admissions and Registration, North Lake College, Irving, TX 75038-3899, 214-273-3109.

ODESSA COLLEGE
Odessa, Texas

UG Enrollment: 4,679	**Tuition & Fees (Area Res): $778**
Application Deadline: rolling	**Room & Board: $1225**

GENERAL State and locally supported, 2-year, coed. Awards certificates, diplomas, transfer associate, terminal associate degrees. Founded 1946. ***Setting:*** 87-acre urban campus. ***Endowment:*** $521,784. ***Total enrollment:*** 4,679. ***Faculty:*** 206 (113 full-time, 15% with terminal degrees, 93 part-time); student-faculty ratio is 19:1.
ENROLLMENT PROFILE 4,679 students from 19 states and territories, 2 other countries. 58% women, 42% men, 67% part-time, 99% state residents, 3% live on campus, 4% transferred in, 20% have need-based financial aid, 11% have non-need-based financial aid, 44% 25 or older, 1% Native American, 29% Hispanic, 4% African American, 1% Asian American. ***Most popular recent majors:*** liberal arts/general studies, business administration/commerce/management, law enforcement/police sciences.
FIRST-YEAR CLASS 1,285 total; 1,665 applied, 100% were accepted, 77% of whom enrolled.
ACADEMIC PROGRAM Core, comprehensive curriculum, honor code. Calendar: semesters. Academic remediation for entering students, services for LD students, advanced placement, self-designed majors, tutorials, summer session for credit, part-time degree program (daytime), adult/continuing education programs, co-op programs and internships.
GENERAL DEGREE REQUIREMENTS 62 semester hours; computer course (varies by major); internship (some majors).
MAJORS Accounting, applied art, art/fine arts, athletic training, automotive technologies, biology/biological sciences, business administration/commerce/management, chemistry, child care/child and family studies, computer information systems, computer science, construction technologies, cosmetology, criminal justice, culinary arts, data processing, drafting and design, drug and alcohol/substance abuse counseling, early childhood education, education, electrical and electronics technologies, emergency medical technology, (pre)engineering sequence, English, fashion merchandising, fire science, geology, heating/refrigeration/air conditioning, history, human services, law enforcement/police sciences, legal secretarial studies, liberal arts/general studies, machine and tool technologies, mathematics, medical laboratory technology, modern languages, music, nursing, operating room technology, petroleum technology, photography, physical education, physical therapy, physics, political science/government, psychology, radio and television studies, radiological technology, respiratory therapy, secretarial studies/office management, social science, sociology, speech/rhetoric/public address/debate, teacher aide studies, welding technology.
LIBRARY Murray H. Fly Learning Resource Center with 79,882 books, 238 microform titles, 496 periodicals, 9 CD-ROMs, 4,880 records, tapes, and CDs. Acquisition spending 1994–95: $125,654.
COMPUTERS ON CAMPUS Computer purchase plan available. 275 computers for student use in computer center, computer labs, learning resource center, classrooms. Staffed computer lab on campus provides training in use of computers, software. Academic computing expenditure 1994–95: $75,679.
COLLEGE LIFE Choral group. 7% vote in student government elections. ***Social organizations:*** 13 open to all. ***Most popular organizations:*** Baptist Student Union, American Chemical Society, CAHOOTS, Physical Therapy Assistant Club, Rodeo Club. ***Major annual events:*** Back-to-School Picnic, Homecoming, Spring Fest. ***Student services:*** personal-psychological counseling. ***Campus security:*** 24-hour emergency response devices and patrols, late-night transport-escort service.
HOUSING 130 college housing spaces available; 125 were occupied 1995–96. No special consideration for freshman housing applicants. Off-campus living permitted. ***Options:*** coed (1 building), single-sex (1 building) housing available. Resident assistants live in dorms.
ATHLETICS Member NJCAA. ***Intercollegiate:*** baseball M(s), basketball M(s)/W(s), crew W(s), golf M(s), track and field W(s). ***Intramural:*** basketball, bowling, football, racquetball, softball, table tennis (Ping-Pong), volleyball, weight lifting. ***Contact:*** Mr. Jim Carlson, Athletic Director, 915-335-6574.
CAREER PLANNING ***Placement office:*** 1 full-time, 1 part-time staff; $51,575 operating expenditure 1994–95. ***Director:*** Ms. Laura Volkmann, Director of Career Services, 915-335-6980. ***Services:*** job fairs, resume preparation, career counseling, careers library, job bank. 673 organizations recruited on campus 1994–95.
AFTER GRADUATION 42% of students completing a degree program in 1994–95 went directly on to further study.
EXPENSES FOR 1995–96 Area resident tuition: $364 full-time. State resident tuition: $494 full-time. Nonresident tuition: $620 full-time, $310 per semester part-time. Part-time tuition per semester ranges from $42 to $154 for area residents, $57 to $209 for state residents. Part-time mandatory fees per semester range from $15 to $155. Full-time mandatory fees: $414. College room and board: $1225.
FINANCIAL AID ***College-administered undergrad aid 1995–96:*** need-based scholarships (average $403), non-need scholarships (average $605), short-term loans (average $303), low-interest long-term loans from external sources (average $1755), 66 Federal Work-Study (averaging $2148), 170 part-time jobs. ***Required forms:*** institutional; required for some: state; accepted: CSS Financial Aid PROFILE, FAFSA. ***Priority deadline:*** 3/15.
APPLYING Open admission except for allied health programs. ***Options:*** Common Application, electronic application, early entrance, deferred entrance. ***Required:*** TOEFL for international students. Test scores used for counseling/placement. ***Application deadline:*** rolling. ***Notification:*** continuous.
APPLYING/TRANSFER ***Application deadline:*** rolling. ***Notification:*** continuous. ***Contact:*** Mr. Robert Sturges, Dean of Admissions, 915-335-6404.
CONTACT Dr. Robert Sturges, Dean of Admissions, Odessa College, 201 West University, Odessa, TX 79764-7127, 915-335-6404. ***E-mail:*** regrs@odessa.edu.

PALO ALTO COLLEGE
San Antonio, Texas

UG Enrollment: 7,499	**Tuition & Fees (Area Res): $734**
Application Deadline: rolling	**Room & Board: N/Avail**

GENERAL State and locally supported, 2-year, coed. Part of Alamo Community College District System. Awards transfer associate, terminal associate degrees. Founded 1987. ***Setting:*** urban campus. ***Total enrollment:*** 7,499. ***Faculty:*** 317 (67 full-time, 250 part-time).
ENROLLMENT PROFILE 7,499 students from 50 states and territories. 61% women, 70% part-time, 88% state residents, 20% transferred in, 46% 25 or older, 2% Native American, 57% Hispanic, 6% African American, 1% Asian American.
FIRST-YEAR CLASS 3,000 total. Of the students who applied, 100% were accepted, 99% of whom enrolled.

Peterson's Guide to Two-Year Colleges 1997 621

Palo Alto College (continued)
ACADEMIC PROGRAM Core. Calendar: semesters. Academic remediation for entering students, English as a second language program offered during academic year and summer, summer session for credit, part-time degree program (daytime, evenings, weekends, summer), adult/continuing education programs, co-op programs.
GENERAL DEGREE REQUIREMENTS 60 semester hours; 1 college algebra course for associate of arts degree; 2 algebra courses, 6 hours of science for associate of science degree; computer course.
MAJORS Agricultural sciences, architectural technologies, art/fine arts, aviation administration, aviation technology, biology/biological sciences, business administration/commerce/management, business machine technologies, chemistry, computer information systems, computer management, computer science, computer technologies, economics, education, engineering and applied sciences, English, finance/banking, geology, health science, history, horticulture, journalism, legal studies, liberal arts/general studies, library science, mathematics, modern languages, music, nursing, philosophy, physical education, physics, psychology, sociology, speech/rhetoric/public address/debate, veterinary sciences, vocational education.
COMPUTERS ON CAMPUS Computer purchase plan available. 100 computers for student use in computer center, Student Learning Assistance Center, library provide access to main academic computer. Staffed computer lab on campus provides training in use of computers, software.
COLLEGE LIFE Drama-theater group, student-run newspaper. ***Student services:*** health clinic, personal-psychological counseling.
HOUSING College housing not available.
CAREER PLANNING ***Service:*** career counseling.
EXPENSES FOR 1996–97 Area resident tuition: $576 full-time. State resident tuition: $1104 full-time. Nonresident tuition: $2208 full-time. Part-time tuition per semester ranges from $120 to $264 for area residents, $230 to $506 for state residents, $460 to $1012 for nonresidents. Part-time mandatory fees: $79 per semester. Full-time mandatory fees: $158.
FINANCIAL AID ***College-administered undergrad aid 1995–96:*** 20 need-based scholarships (averaging $500), 500 non-need scholarships (averaging $50), short-term loans (averaging $250), low-interest long-term loans from external sources (averaging $2625), Federal Work-Study. ***Required forms:*** institutional, FAFSA. ***Application deadline:*** 6/1.
APPLYING Open admission. ***Option:*** early entrance. ***Required:*** school transcript, ACT ASSET. ***Required for some:*** SAT I or ACT. Test scores used for counseling/placement. ***Application deadline:*** rolling.
APPLYING/TRANSFER ***Required:*** college transcript. ***Entrance:*** noncompetitive.
CONTACT Mr. F. Patrick Terrell, Director of Records and Admissions, Palo Alto College, 1400 West Villaret, San Antonio, TX 78224-2499, 210-921-5279.

PANOLA COLLEGE
Carthage, Texas

CONTACT Ms. Betsy Wheat, Dean of Student Affairs, Panola College, 1109 West Panola Street, Carthage, TX 75633-2397, 903-693-2036.

PARIS JUNIOR COLLEGE
Paris, Texas

UG Enrollment: 2,450	**Tuition & Fees (Area Res): $848**
Application Deadline: rolling	**Room & Board: $2556**

GENERAL State and locally supported, 2-year, coed. Part of Texas Higher Education Coordinating Board. Awards transfer associate, terminal associate degrees. Founded 1924. ***Setting:*** 54-acre rural campus. ***Total enrollment:*** 2,450. ***Faculty:*** 117 (89 full-time, 28 part-time); student-faculty ratio is 20:1.
ENROLLMENT PROFILE 2,450 students from 16 states and territories, 9 other countries. 60% women, 50% part-time, 95% state residents, 1% transferred in, 1% international, 41% 25 or older, 1% Native American, 1% Hispanic, 12% African American, 1% Asian American. ***Most popular recent majors:*** nursing, jewelry and metalsmithing, liberal arts/general studies.
FIRST-YEAR CLASS 1,680 total. Of the students who applied, 100% were accepted.
ACADEMIC PROGRAM Calendar: semesters. Academic remediation for entering students, English as a second language program offered during academic year and summer, summer session for credit, part-time degree program (daytime, evenings, summer), external degree programs, adult/continuing education programs.
GENERAL DEGREE REQUIREMENTS 64 semester hours; 6 semester hours of lab science.
MAJORS Agricultural technologies, art/fine arts, business administration/commerce/management, business education, computer information systems, computer technologies, construction management, cosmetology, drafting and design, education, electrical and electronics technologies, elementary education, engineering (general), engineering and applied sciences, heating/refrigeration/air conditioning, jewelry and metalsmithing, liberal arts/general studies, mathematics, nursing, real estate, science, welding technology.
LIBRARY 38,150 books, 224 microform titles, 404 periodicals, 6,954 records, tapes, and CDs.
COMPUTERS ON CAMPUS 82 computers for student use in computer center, library.
COLLEGE LIFE Drama-theater group, choral group. ***Student services:*** personal-psychological counseling, women's center. ***Campus security:*** 24-hour emergency response devices, late-night transport-escort service.
HOUSING 231 college housing spaces available; 202 were occupied 1995–96. Freshmen guaranteed college housing. On-campus residence required in freshman year except if living with relatives or within commuting distance.
ATHLETICS Member NJCAA. ***Intercollegiate:*** basketball M(s)/W(s), golf M(s). ***Intramural:*** badminton, basketball, football, table tennis (Ping-Pong), tennis, volleyball.
CAREER PLANNING ***Services:*** job fairs, career counseling, careers library, job bank.
EXPENSES FOR 1995–96 Area resident tuition: $848 full-time, $20 per semester hour part-time. State resident tuition: $1178 full-time, $30 per semester hour part-time. Nonresident tuition: $1898 full-time, $53 per semester hour part-time. College room and board: $2556 (minimum).
FINANCIAL AID ***College-administered undergrad aid 1995–96:*** need-based scholarships, Federal Work-Study, part-time jobs. ***Required forms:*** institutional, FAFSA. ***Priority deadline:*** 6/1. ***Waivers:*** full or partial for employees or children of employees.
APPLYING Open admission except for nursing program. ***Option:*** early entrance. ***Required:*** school transcript, TOEFL for international students. ***Recommended:*** ACT. ***Required for some:*** ACT. Test scores used for counseling/placement. ***Application deadline:*** rolling.
APPLYING/TRANSFER ***Required:*** high school transcript, college transcript. ***Entrance:*** noncompetitive. ***Application deadline:*** rolling.
CONTACT Ms. Mary Catherine Kincaid, Director of Admissions, Paris Junior College, Paris, TX 75460-6298, 903-784-9431 or toll-free 800-232-5804 (out-of-state).

RANGER COLLEGE
Ranger, Texas

UG Enrollment: 856	**Tuition & Fees (TX Res): $948**
Application Deadline: rolling	**Room & Board: $2528**

GENERAL State-related, 2-year, coed. Part of Texas Higher Education Coordinating Board. Awards transfer associate, terminal associate degrees. Founded 1926. ***Setting:*** 100-acre rural campus with easy access to Dallas–Fort Worth. ***Total enrollment:*** 856. ***Faculty:*** 51 (28 full-time, 16% with terminal degrees, 23 part-time); student-faculty ratio is 15:1.
ENROLLMENT PROFILE 856 students from 7 states and territories, 4 other countries. 52% women, 30% part-time, 97% state residents, 45% live on campus, 3% transferred in, 38% have need-based financial aid, 54% have non-need-based financial aid, 1% international, 10% Hispanic, 18% African American. ***Areas of study chosen:*** 7% education.
FIRST-YEAR CLASS 719 total. Of the students who applied, 100% were accepted, 67% of whom enrolled. 15% from top 10% of their high school class, 75% from top half.
ACADEMIC PROGRAM Core, honor code. Calendar: semesters. Academic remediation for entering students, advanced placement, self-designed majors, Freshman Honors College, honors program, summer session for credit, part-time degree program (daytime, evenings, summer), adult/continuing education programs.
GENERAL DEGREE REQUIREMENTS 62 credits; math/science requirements vary according to program; computer course.
MAJORS Automotive technologies, computer technologies, liberal arts/general studies, science education, secretarial studies/office management, welding technology.
LIBRARY Golemon Library with 24,211 books, 544 microform titles, 133 periodicals.
COMPUTERS ON CAMPUS 35 computers for student use in computer labs, learning resource center, labs provide access to off-campus computing facilities, e-mail, on-line services. Staffed computer lab on campus provides training in use of computers, software.
COLLEGE LIFE Choral group, marching band. ***Student services:*** health clinic, personal-psychological counseling. ***Campus security:*** controlled dormitory access.
HOUSING 440 college housing spaces available; 401 were occupied 1995–96. No special consideration for freshman housing applicants. Off-campus living permitted. ***Option:*** single-sex (10 buildings) housing available. Resident assistants live in dorms.
ATHLETICS Member NJCAA. ***Intercollegiate:*** baseball M(s), basketball M(s)/W(s), cross-country running M(s)/W(s), football M(s), softball W(s), track and field M(s)/W(s). ***Intramural:*** basketball, football, track and field, volleyball. ***Contact:*** Mr. Ron Butler, Athletic Director, 817-647-3234 Ext. 106.
CAREER PLANNING ***Placement office:*** 2 full-time, 1 part-time staff. ***Director:*** Mr. John Slaughter, Vocational Counselor, 817-647-3234. ***Services:*** resume preparation, career counseling.
EXPENSES FOR 1996–97 State resident tuition: $564 full-time, $27 per semester hour part-time. Nonresident tuition: $1020 full-time. Nonresident part-time tuition per semester hour ranges from $210 to $310. Part-time mandatory fees: $12 per semester hour. Full-time mandatory fees: $384. College room and board: $2528.
FINANCIAL AID ***College-administered undergrad aid 1995–96:*** need-based scholarships (average $250), low-interest long-term loans, Federal Work-Study. ***Acceptable forms:*** CSS Financial Aid PROFILE, FAFSA. ***Priority deadline:*** 8/15.
APPLYING Open admission. ***Option:*** early entrance. ***Required:*** TOEFL for international students. ***Recommended:*** SAT I or ACT, SAT II Subject Tests. Test scores used for counseling/placement. ***Application deadline:*** rolling. ***Notification:*** continuous.
APPLYING/TRANSFER ***Recommended:*** standardized test scores. ***Entrance:*** noncompetitive. ***Application deadline:*** rolling. ***Notification:*** continuous.
CONTACT Dr. Jim Davis, Dean of Students, Ranger College, Ranger, TX 76470, 817-647-3234 Ext. 110.

RICHLAND COLLEGE
Dallas, Texas

UG Enrollment: 13,391	**Tuition & Fees (Area Res): $598**
Application Deadline: rolling	**Room & Board: N/Avail**

GENERAL State and locally supported, 2-year, coed. Part of Dallas County Community College District System. Awards transfer associate, terminal associate degrees. Founded 1972. ***Setting:*** 250-acre suburban campus. ***Total enrollment:*** 13,391. ***Faculty:*** 665 (165 full-time, 500 part-time); student-faculty ratio is 19:1.
ENROLLMENT PROFILE 13,391 students from 24 states and territories, 21 other countries. 55% women, 73% part-time, 97% state residents, 35% transferred in, 2% international, 47% 25 or older, 1% Native American, 7% Hispanic, 9% African American, 7% Asian American. ***Most popular recent majors:*** liberal arts/general studies, business administration/commerce/management.
FIRST-YEAR CLASS 9,871 total.
ACADEMIC PROGRAM Core, honor code. Calendar: semesters. Academic remediation for entering students, English as a second language program offered during academic year and summer, services for LD students, advanced placement, Freshman Honors College, honors program, summer session for credit, part-time degree program (daytime, evenings, weekends, summer), adult/continuing education programs, co-op programs. Study abroad in England, Italy, Scotland, Wales, France, Germany, Commonwealth of Independent States.
GENERAL DEGREE REQUIREMENTS 61 credits; 3 credit hours of math; 8 credit hours of lab science; computer course.
MAJORS Accounting, business administration/commerce/management, computer programming, data processing, electronics engineering technology, engineering and applied sciences, horticulture, international business, liberal arts/general studies, manufacturing

technology, mechanical design technology, mechanical engineering technology, ornamental horticulture, real estate, robotics, secretarial studies/office management.
LIBRARY Richland College Library with 63,000 books, 2,309 microform titles, 350 periodicals, 8 CD-ROMs, 4,000 records, tapes, and CDs.
COMPUTERS ON CAMPUS 400 computers for student use in computer center, computer labs.
COLLEGE LIFE Drama-theater group, choral group, student-run newspaper. ***Student services:*** health clinic, personal-psychological counseling, women's center. ***Campus security:*** 24-hour emergency response devices and patrols, late-night transport-escort service, emergency call boxes.
HOUSING College housing not available.
ATHLETICS Member NJCAA. ***Intercollegiate:*** baseball M, basketball M, soccer M/W, volleyball W. ***Intramural:*** badminton, basketball, bowling, cross-country running, football, soccer, softball, tennis, track and field, volleyball, weight lifting. ***Contact:*** Mr. Louis Stone, Dean of Physical Education, 214-238-6260.
CAREER PLANNING ***Placement office:*** 3 full-time, 2 part-time staff. ***Director:*** Ms. Gilda Jones, Career Information and Placement Services, 214-238-6921. ***Services:*** job fairs, resume preparation, resume referral, career counseling, careers library, job bank, job interviews.
EXPENSES FOR 1996–97 Area resident tuition: $520 full-time. State resident tuition: $900 full-time. Nonresident tuition: $2010 full-time. Part-time tuition per semester hour ranges from $54 to $196 for area residents, $111 to $386 for state residents, $201 to $737 for nonresidents. Part-time mandatory fees: $25 per semester. Full-time mandatory fees: $78.
FINANCIAL AID ***College-administered undergrad aid 1995–96:*** 450 need-based scholarships (average $600), non-need scholarships (average $150), short-term loans (average $175), low-interest long-term loans from external sources (average $2200), Federal Work-Study, part-time jobs. ***Required forms:*** institutional; accepted: FAFSA. ***Priority deadline:*** 6/1.
APPLYING Open admission. ***Options:*** early entrance, midyear entrance. ***Required:*** TOEFL for international students. ***Recommended:*** SAT I or ACT. ***Required for some:*** school transcript. Test scores used for counseling/placement. ***Application deadline:*** rolling. ***Notification:*** continuous.
APPLYING/TRANSFER ***Required:*** college transcript. ***Recommended:*** standardized test scores. ***Entrance:*** noncompetitive. ***Application deadline:*** rolling. ***Notification:*** continuous. ***Contact:*** Ms. Anna Garcia, Academic Advisor, 214-238-6332.
CONTACT Ms. Carol McKinney, Department Assistant, Richland College, Dallas, TX 75243-2199, 214-238-6100. ***Fax:*** 214-238-6149.

ST. PHILIP'S COLLEGE
San Antonio, Texas

UG Enrollment: 72,128	**Tuition & Fees (Area Res): $734**
Application Deadline: N/R	**Room & Board: N/Avail**

GENERAL District-supported, 2-year, coed. Part of Alamo Community College District System. Awards transfer associate, terminal associate degrees. Founded 1898. ***Setting:*** 16-acre urban campus. ***Total enrollment:*** 72,128. ***Faculty:*** 334 (191 full-time, 143 part-time).
ENROLLMENT PROFILE 72,128 students from 50 states and territories. 51% women, 66% part-time, 86% state residents, 14% transferred in, 58% 25 or older, 1% Native American, 40% Hispanic, 22% African American, 2% Asian American.
FIRST-YEAR CLASS 1,875 total; 1,875 applied, 100% were accepted, 100% of whom enrolled.
ACADEMIC PROGRAM Core, honor code. Calendar: semesters. 950 courses offered in 1995–96. Academic remediation for entering students, English as a second language program offered during academic year and summer, services for LD students, advanced placement, self-designed majors, Freshman Honors College, tutorials, honors program, summer session for credit, part-time degree program (daytime, evenings, weekends, summer), adult/continuing education programs, co-op programs and internships. ROTC: Army (c).
GENERAL DEGREE REQUIREMENTS 60 credits; computer course for business administration majors.
MAJORS Accounting, aircraft and missile maintenance, architectural technologies, art/fine arts, automotive technologies, aviation technology, biology/biological sciences, biomedical technologies, business administration/commerce/management, carpentry, chemistry, communication equipment technology, computer information systems, construction technologies, culinary arts, data processing, drafting and design, electrical and electronics technologies, electronics engineering technology, (pre)engineering sequence, English, fashion design and technology, food services management, health education, heating/refrigeration/air conditioning, history, hotel and restaurant management, interior design, legal secretarial studies, legal studies, liberal arts/general studies, machine and tool technologies, mathematics, medical laboratory technology, medical records services, medical secretarial studies, medical technology, modern languages, music, natural sciences, nursing, occupational therapy, operating room technology, paralegal studies, pharmacy/pharmaceutical sciences, physical education, physical therapy, plumbing, political science/government, practical nursing, psychology, radiological technology, respiratory therapy, secretarial studies/office management, sociology, Spanish, speech/rhetoric/public address/debate, teacher aide studies, textiles and clothing, theater arts/drama, welding technology.
LIBRARY Main library plus 1 other, with 60,595 books, 6,188 microform titles, 1,124 periodicals, 2,254 records, tapes, and CDs.
COMPUTERS ON CAMPUS Computer purchase plan available. 150 computers for student use in learning resource center, library, student center.
COLLEGE LIFE Choral group, student-run newspaper. 40% vote in student government elections. ***Student services:*** women's center. ***Campus security:*** 24-hour emergency response devices.
HOUSING College housing not available.
CAREER PLANNING ***Services:*** job fairs, resume preparation, resume referral, career counseling, careers library, job bank.
EXPENSES FOR 1996–97 Area resident tuition: $734 full-time, $24 per credit part-time. State resident tuition: $1262 full-time, $46 per credit part-time. Nonresident tuition: $2366 full-time, $92 per credit part-time. Part-time mandatory fees: $79 per semester.
FINANCIAL AID ***College-administered undergrad aid 1995–96:*** 2,400 need-based scholarships (average $300), 150 non-need scholarships (average $250), short-term loans (average $300), low-interest long-term loans from external sources (average $2625), Federal Work-Study, part-time jobs. ***Required forms:*** institutional, FAFSA; accepted: CSS Financial Aid PROFILE. ***Priority deadline:*** 6/1. ***Waivers:*** full or partial for employees or children of employees and senior citizens.
APPLYING Open admission. ***Options:*** Common Application, early entrance. ***Required:*** school transcript, TOEFL for international students. ***Recommended:*** SAT I or ACT. Test scores used for counseling/placement. ***Notification:*** continuous until 8/31.
APPLYING/TRANSFER ***Required:*** college transcript. ***Notification:*** continuous until 8/31.
CONTACT Mr. Harry Stine, Director of Admissions and Records, St. Philip's College, 1801 Martin Luther King Drive, San Antonio, TX 78203-2098, 210-531-3290. ***Fax:*** 210-531-3235.

SAN ANTONIO COLLEGE
San Antonio, Texas

UG Enrollment: 21,238	**Tuition & Fees (Area Res): $710**
Application Deadline: rolling	**Room & Board: N/Avail**

GENERAL State and locally supported, 2-year, coed. Part of Alamo Community College District System. Awards transfer associate, terminal associate degrees. Founded 1925. ***Setting:*** 45-acre urban campus. ***Total enrollment:*** 21,238. ***Faculty:*** 896; student-faculty ratio is 30:1. ***Notable Alumni:*** Henry B. Gonzales, congressman; Bill Hayden, Dell Computers; Lisa Brown, archaeologist; Frank Gonzalez, oceanographer; Patsy Torres, entertainer.
ENROLLMENT PROFILE 21,238 students from 52 states and territories, 53 other countries. 58% women, 42% men, 64% part-time, 97% state residents, 8% transferred in, 1% international, 54% 25 or older, 50% Hispanic, 5% African American, 2% Asian American.
FIRST-YEAR CLASS Of the students who applied, 100% were accepted, 100% of whom enrolled.
ACADEMIC PROGRAM Core. Calendar: semesters. Academic remediation for entering students, English as a second language program offered during academic year and summer, services for LD students, advanced placement, honors program, summer session for credit, part-time degree program (daytime, evenings, weekends, summer), adult/continuing education programs, co-op programs and internships. ROTC: Army (c), Air Force (c).
GENERAL DEGREE REQUIREMENTS 66 credits; computer course.
MAJORS Business administration/commerce/management, business machine technologies, child care/child and family studies, child psychology/child development, civil engineering technology, commercial art, computer programming, computer technologies, corrections, court reporting, criminal justice, data processing, dental services, drafting and design, electrical and electronics technologies, engineering technology, fire science, funeral service, industrial engineering technology, jewelry and metalsmithing, law enforcement/police sciences, legal secretarial studies, liberal arts/general studies, manufacturing technology, mechanical engineering technology, medical assistant technologies, nursing, postal management, psychology, public administration, radio and television studies, real estate, science.
LIBRARY 225,285 books, 18,852 microform titles, 1,496 periodicals, 11,871 records, tapes, and CDs.
COMPUTERS ON CAMPUS Computers for student use in classrooms.
COLLEGE LIFE Orientation program (3 days, $17). Drama-theater group, choral group, student-run newspaper, radio station. ***Student services:*** health clinic, personal-psychological counseling, women's center. ***Campus security:*** 24-hour patrols, late-night transport-escort service.
HOUSING College housing not available.
ATHLETICS ***Intramural:*** basketball, cross-country running, fencing, football, soccer, swimming and diving, tennis, volleyball, weight lifting.
CAREER PLANNING ***Service:*** career counseling.
EXPENSES FOR 1995–96 Area resident tuition: $552 full-time. State resident tuition: $1056 full-time. Nonresident tuition: $2112 full-time. Part-time tuition per semester ranges from $115 to $320 for area residents, $220 to $551 for state residents, $440 to $1035 for nonresidents. Part-time mandatory fees: $74 per semester. Full-time mandatory fees: $158.
FINANCIAL AID ***College-administered undergrad aid 1995–96:*** 350 need-based scholarships (average $400), 300 non-need scholarships (average $400), short-term loans (average $200), low-interest long-term loans from external sources (average $1000), Federal Work-Study, 315 part-time jobs. ***Required forms:*** institutional, FAFSA, SINGLEFILE Form of United Student Aid Funds; accepted: CSS Financial Aid PROFILE. ***Priority deadline:*** 5/1.
APPLYING Open admission. ***Option:*** early entrance. ***Required:*** minimum 2.0 GPA. ***Recommended:*** SAT I or ACT, TOEFL for international students, ACT ASSET, TASP. ***Required for some:*** ACT ASSET, TASP. Test scores used for counseling/placement. ***Application deadline:*** rolling.
APPLYING/TRANSFER ***Required:*** college transcript. ***Application deadline:*** rolling. ***Notification:*** continuous.
CONTACT Ms. Rosemarie Hoopes, Director of Admissions and Records, San Antonio College, 1300 San Pedro Avenue, San Antonio, TX 78212-4299, 210-733-2582.

SAN JACINTO COLLEGE–CENTRAL CAMPUS
Pasadena, Texas

Enrollment: N/R	**Tuition & Fees (Area Res): $584**
Application Deadline: rolling	**Room & Board: N/Avail**

GENERAL State and locally supported, 2-year, coed. Part of San Jacinto College District. Awards certificates, transfer associate, terminal associate degrees. Founded 1961. ***Setting:*** 141-acre suburban campus with easy access to Houston. ***Faculty:*** 539 (282 full-time, 257 part-time).
ENROLLMENT PROFILE 67% part-time, 67% state residents, 17% transferred in, 48% 25 or older, 0% Native American, 13% Hispanic, 4% African American, 3% Asian American. ***Areas of study chosen:*** 30% vocational and home economics, 11% education, 9% business management and administrative services, 9% health professions and related sciences, 8% interdisciplinary studies, 7% social sciences, 4% psychology, 3% computer and information sciences, 3% engineering and applied sciences, 3% English language/literature/letters, 2% biological and life sciences, 2% communications and journalism, 2%

San Jacinto College–Central Campus (continued)
fine arts, 2% premed, 1% architecture, 1% foreign language and literature, 1% mathematics, 1% predentistry, 1% prelaw. ***Most popular recent majors:*** nursing, business administration/commerce/management, computer science.
FIRST-YEAR CLASS 6,500 applied, 99% were accepted, 100% of whom enrolled.
ACADEMIC PROGRAM Honor code. Calendar: semesters. Academic remediation for entering students, English as a second language program offered during academic year and summer, services for LD students, summer session for credit, part-time degree program (daytime, evenings, weekends, summer), adult/continuing education programs, internships.
GENERAL DEGREE REQUIREMENTS 62 credit hours; 1 math course; computer course; internship (some majors).
MAJORS Accounting, aerospace sciences, anatomy, anthropology, art/fine arts, audio engineering, automotive technologies, aviation technology, behavioral sciences, biblical studies, biology/biological sciences, botany/plant sciences, business administration/commerce/management, chemistry, child care/child and family studies, child psychology/child development, commercial art, communication, computer programming, computer science, cosmetology, creative writing, criminal justice, data processing, dietetics, drafting and design, early childhood education, economics, electrical and electronics technologies, electrical engineering technology, emergency medical technology, engineering (general), (pre)engineering sequence, engineering technology, English, fashion design and technology, fashion merchandising, finance/banking, fire science, flight training, food services management, geology, German, history, home economics, horticulture, hotel and restaurant management, industrial and heavy equipment maintenance, interior design, journalism, law enforcement/police sciences, legal secretarial studies, liberal arts/general studies, literature, marketing/retailing/merchandising, mathematics, medical laboratory technology, medical secretarial studies, modern languages, music, music business, nursing, nutrition, occupational safety and health, operating room technology, painting/drawing, paralegal studies, philosophy, physical sciences, political science/government, printing technologies, psychology, radiological technology, real estate, respiratory therapy, safety and security technologies, science, secretarial studies/office management, sociology, Spanish, studio art, surveying technology, theater arts/drama, welding technology, zoology.
LIBRARY Lee Davis Library with 100,000 books, 400 periodicals, 2,000 records, tapes, and CDs.
COMPUTERS ON CAMPUS 58 computers for student use in computer center, computer labs, learning resource center.
COLLEGE LIFE Drama-theater group, student-run newspaper. ***Social organizations:*** 31 open to all. ***Campus security:*** 24-hour emergency response devices and patrols.
HOUSING College housing not available.
ATHLETICS Member NJCAA. ***Intercollegiate:*** basketball M(s)/W(s), golf M(s), tennis M(s)/W(s), track and field M(s)/W(s), volleyball W(s). ***Intramural:*** basketball, football, racquetball, volleyball. ***Contact:*** Mr. Scott Gernander, Athletic Director, 713-476-1849.
CAREER PLANNING ***Placement office:*** 8 full-time staff. ***Director:*** Mr. Bill Wood, Director of Counseling and Guidance, 713-476-1813. ***Services:*** job fairs, resume preparation, resume referral, career counseling, careers library, job bank, job interviews.
EXPENSES FOR 1995–96 Area resident tuition: $584 full-time. State resident tuition: $944 full-time. Nonresident tuition: $1814 full-time. Part-time tuition per semester ranges from $116 to $238 for area residents, $152 to $382 for state residents, $281 to $730 for nonresidents.
FINANCIAL AID ***College-administered undergrad aid 1995–96:*** need-based scholarships, non-need scholarships, short-term loans, low-interest long-term loans from external sources, part-time jobs. ***Required forms:*** FAFSA. ***Priority deadline:*** 7/1.
APPLYING Open admission except for nursing program. ***Option:*** early entrance. ***Required:*** school transcript, TOEFL for international students. ***Recommended:*** SAT I or ACT. ***Required for some:*** SAT I or ACT. Test scores used for counseling/placement. ***Application deadline:*** rolling.
APPLYING/TRANSFER ***Required:*** high school transcript. ***Recommended:*** standardized test scores. ***Required for some:*** standardized test scores. ***Entrance:*** noncompetitive. ***Application deadline:*** rolling.
CONTACT Dr. Delwin Long, Director of Admissions, San Jacinto College–Central Campus, Pasadena, TX 77501-2007, 713-476-1819.

SAN JACINTO COLLEGE–NORTH CAMPUS
Houston, Texas

UG Enrollment: 4,211	**Tuition & Fees (Area Res): $508**
Application Deadline: rolling	**Room & Board: N/Avail**

GENERAL State and locally supported, 2-year, coed. Part of San Jacinto College District. Awards transfer associate, terminal associate degrees. Founded 1974. ***Setting:*** 105-acre suburban campus. ***Total enrollment:*** 4,211. ***Faculty:*** 196 (85 full-time, 111 part-time).
ENROLLMENT PROFILE 4,211 students from 14 states and territories, 46 other countries. 57% women, 43% men, 69% part-time, 99% state residents, 14% transferred in, 39% 25 or older, 1% Native American, 22% Hispanic, 17% African American, 2% Asian American. ***Most popular recent majors:*** nursing, computer information systems, drafting and design.
FIRST-YEAR CLASS 894 total. Of the students who applied, 100% were accepted, 100% of whom enrolled.
ACADEMIC PROGRAM Core. Calendar: semesters. Academic remediation for entering students, services for LD students, advanced placement, honors program, summer session for credit, part-time degree program (daytime, evenings, weekends, summer), adult/continuing education programs, internships.
GENERAL DEGREE REQUIREMENTS 62 credits; 1 college algebra course; internship (some majors).
MAJORS Accounting, art/fine arts, automotive technologies, business administration/commerce/management, carpentry, chemistry, child care/child and family studies, computer information systems, computer science, construction technologies, corrections, cosmetology, criminal justice, culinary arts, data processing, dietetics, drafting and design, early childhood education, economics, electrical and electronics technologies, electrical engineering technology, emergency medical technology, English, fashion design and technology, fashion merchandising, food sciences, home economics, interior design, law enforcement/police sciences, legal secretarial studies, music, music business, nursing, painting/drawing, physical education, piano/organ, real estate, sociology, Spanish, theater arts/drama, voice, welding technology.
LIBRARY Edwin E. Lehr Library with 48,461 books, 546 microform titles, 471 periodicals, 1 on-line bibliographic service, 4 CD-ROMs.
COMPUTERS ON CAMPUS 400 computers for student use in computer labs, classrooms, library provide access to main academic computer. Staffed computer lab on campus provides training in use of computers, software.
COLLEGE LIFE Drama-theater group, choral group, student-run newspaper. ***Campus security:*** 24-hour emergency response devices and patrols.
HOUSING College housing not available.
ATHLETICS Member NJCAA. ***Intercollegiate:*** baseball M(s), basketball W(s), golf M(s)/W(s). ***Intramural:*** basketball, tennis, volleyball. ***Contact:*** Mr. Gene Moore, Athletic Director, 713-458-4050 Ext. 7292.
CAREER PLANNING ***Placement office:*** 1 full-time, 1 part-time staff. ***Director:*** Ms. Margaret Black, Job Placement Coordinator, 713-459-7156 Ext. 7156. ***Services:*** job fairs, resume preparation, career counseling, careers library, job bank, job interviews. 40 organizations recruited on campus 1994–95.
AFTER GRADUATION 50% of class of 1994 had job offers within 6 months.
EXPENSES FOR 1996–97 Area resident tuition: $384 full-time. State resident tuition: $704 full-time. Nonresident tuition: $1280 full-time. Part-time tuition per semester ranges from $72 to $132 for area residents, $132 to $242 for state residents, $240 to $440 for nonresidents. Part-time mandatory fees: $42 per semester. Full-time mandatory fees: $124.
FINANCIAL AID ***College-administered undergrad aid 1995–96:*** 687 need-based scholarships (average $1387), 267 non-need scholarships (average $517), short-term loans (average $145), low-interest long-term loans from external sources (average $2607), Federal Work-Study, 78 part-time jobs. ***Required forms:*** institutional; accepted: FAFSA. ***Priority deadline:*** 6/1.
APPLYING Open admission. ***Option:*** early entrance. ***Required:*** TOEFL for international students. ***Recommended:*** SAT I or ACT. Test scores used for counseling/placement. ***Application deadline:*** rolling.
APPLYING/TRANSFER ***Entrance:*** noncompetitive. ***Application deadline:*** rolling. ***Contact:*** Ms. Wanda Simpson, Registrar, 713-458-4050.
CONTACT Ms. Wanda Simpson, Registrar, San Jacinto College–North Campus, Houston, TX 77049-4599, 713-458-4050.

SAN JACINTO COLLEGE–SOUTH CAMPUS
Houston, Texas

UG Enrollment: 5,411	**Tuition & Fees (Area Res): $456**
Application Deadline: rolling	**Room & Board: N/Avail**

GENERAL State and locally supported, 2-year, coed. Part of San Jacinto College District. Awards certificates, transfer associate, terminal associate degrees. Founded 1979. ***Setting:*** 114-acre suburban campus. ***Total enrollment:*** 5,411. ***Faculty:*** 220 (109 full-time, 12% with terminal degrees, 111 part-time); student-faculty ratio is 23:1.
ENROLLMENT PROFILE 5,411 students from 26 states and territories, 57 other countries. 55% women, 75% part-time, 97% state residents, 24% transferred in, 2% international, 50% 25 or older, 0% Native American, 16% Hispanic, 7% African American, 7% Asian American.
FIRST-YEAR CLASS 365 applied, 100% were accepted, 100% of whom enrolled.
ACADEMIC PROGRAM Core. Calendar: semesters. 895 courses offered in 1995–96. Academic remediation for entering students, services for LD students, summer session for credit, part-time degree program (daytime, evenings, summer), adult/continuing education programs, internships.
GENERAL DEGREE REQUIREMENTS 62 credit hours; 1 course in college algebra; internship (some majors).
MAJORS Accounting, art/fine arts, automotive technologies, behavioral sciences, biology/biological sciences, business administration/commerce/management, chemistry, commercial art, computer information systems, computer science, cosmetology, data processing, drafting and design, electrical and electronics technologies, (pre)engineering sequence, English, environmental sciences, fashion design and technology, fashion merchandising, finance/banking, heating/refrigeration/air conditioning, history, legal secretarial studies, mathematics, mechanical engineering technology, music, natural sciences, nursing, occupational therapy, physical education, physical therapy, practical nursing, psychology, real estate, science, secretarial studies/office management, social science, sociology.
LIBRARY San Jacinto College South Library plus 1 other, with 40,000 books, 731 microform titles, 320 periodicals, 6 CD-ROMs, 550 records, tapes, and CDs.
COMPUTERS ON CAMPUS 370 computers for student use in computer labs, classrooms, library provide access to main academic computer. Staffed computer lab on campus provides training in use of computers, software.
COLLEGE LIFE Drama-theater group, choral group. ***Major annual event:*** Coyote Day Carnival. ***Campus security:*** 24-hour patrols.
HOUSING College housing not available.
ATHLETICS Member NJCAA. ***Intercollegiate:*** soccer M. ***Intramural:*** badminton, basketball, bowling, football, golf, racquetball, soccer, softball, tennis, volleyball.
CAREER PLANNING ***Placement office:*** 5 full-time staff. ***Director:*** Dr. William Raffetto, Dean of Student Services, 713-922-3402. ***Services:*** job fairs, career counseling, careers library, job bank.
EXPENSES FOR 1996–97 Area resident tuition: $384 full-time. State resident tuition: $706 full-time. Nonresident tuition: $1440 full-time. Part-time tuition per semester ranges from $86 to $168 for area residents, $96 to $278 for state residents, $236 to $531 for nonresidents. Full-time mandatory fees: $72.
FINANCIAL AID ***College-administered undergrad aid 1995–96:*** need-based scholarships, 44 non-need scholarships (average $400), short-term loans (average $85), low-interest long-term loans from external sources (average $1850), 55 part-time jobs. ***Required forms:*** institutional, FAFSA; accepted: CSS Financial Aid PROFILE. ***Priority deadline:*** 6/1. ***Payment plan:*** deferred payment.
APPLYING Open admission except for health science programs. ***Options:*** Common Application, early entrance. ***Required:*** TOEFL for international students, TASP. Test scores used for counseling/placement. ***Application deadline:*** rolling.
APPLYING/TRANSFER ***Entrance:*** noncompetitive. ***Application deadline:*** rolling.
CONTACT Dr. Rhea Oglesbee, Registrar, San Jacinto College–South Campus, Houston, TX 77089-6099, 713-922-3431. ***E-mail:*** season@sjcd.cc.tx.us.

SOUTH PLAINS COLLEGE
Levelland, Texas

UG Enrollment: 5,703	Tuition & Fees (Area Res): $578
Application Deadline: rolling	Room & Board: $2200

GENERAL State and locally supported, 2-year, coed. Part of Texas Higher Education Coordinating Board. Awards transfer associate, terminal associate degrees. Founded 1958. *Setting:* 177-acre small-town campus. *Endowment:* $2 million. *Total enrollment:* 5,703. *Faculty:* 356 (257 full-time, 100% with terminal degrees, 99 part-time); student-faculty ratio is 22:1.
ENROLLMENT PROFILE 5,703 students from 21 states and territories, 8 other countries. 55% women, 45% men, 47% part-time, 95% state residents, 10% live on campus, 40% transferred in, 40% have need-based financial aid, 20% have non-need-based financial aid, 1% international, 45% 25 or older, 1% Native American, 24% Hispanic, 6% African American, 1% Asian American. *Most popular recent majors:* nursing, education, law enforcement/police sciences.
FIRST-YEAR CLASS 1,964 total; 2,030 applied, 100% were accepted, 97% of whom enrolled. 10% from top 10% of their high school class, 32% from top quarter, 60% from top half.
ACADEMIC PROGRAM Core, honor code. Calendar: semesters. 1,250 courses offered in 1995–96. Academic remediation for entering students, advanced placement, self-designed majors, summer session for credit, part-time degree program (daytime, evenings, summer), adult/continuing education programs.
GENERAL DEGREE REQUIREMENTS 62 semester hours; math/science requirements vary according to major; computer course for students without computer competency.
MAJORS Accounting, advertising, agricultural economics, agricultural sciences, agronomy/soil and crop sciences, art/fine arts, audio engineering, automotive technologies, biology/biological sciences, business administration/commerce/management, carpentry, chemistry, child care/child and family studies, child psychology/child development, commercial art, communication, computer programming, computer science, computer technologies, cosmetology, criminal justice, data processing, dietetics, drafting and design, education, electrical and electronics technologies, engineering (general), (pre)engineering sequence, fashion merchandising, fire science, food services management, health services administration, heating/refrigeration/air conditioning, journalism, law enforcement/police sciences, legal secretarial studies, liberal arts/general studies, machine and tool technologies, marketing/retailing/merchandising, medical records services, medical secretarial studies, mental health/rehabilitation counseling, music, nursing, operating room technology, petroleum technology, physical education, physical therapy, postal management, practical nursing, radiological technology, real estate, respiratory therapy, retail management, science, secretarial studies/office management, social work, telecommunications, welding technology.
LIBRARY 70,000 books, 310 periodicals.
COMPUTERS ON CAMPUS 24 computers for student use in library, student center. Staffed computer lab on campus provides training in use of computers, software.
COLLEGE LIFE Orientation program (2 days, no cost). Drama-theater group, choral group, student-run newspaper. *Most popular organizations:* Student Government, Phi Beta Kappa, Bleacher Bums, Law Enforcement Association. *Major annual events:* Homecoming, Spring Fling, Miss Cap Rock Pageant. *Student services:* health clinic. *Campus security:* 24-hour emergency response devices and patrols.
HOUSING 600 college housing spaces available; 590 were occupied 1995–96. No special consideration for freshman housing applicants. On-campus residence required through sophomore year except if married or living with relatives. *Option:* single-sex housing available. Resident assistants live in dorms.
ATHLETICS Member NJCAA. *Intercollegiate:* basketball M(s)/W(s), cross-country running M(s)/W, track and field M(s)/W(s). *Intramural:* basketball, cross-country running, football, racquetball, softball, table tennis (Ping-Pong), tennis, volleyball. *Contact:* Mr. Joe Tubb, Director of Athletics, 806-894-9611 Ext. 220.
CAREER PLANNING *Placement office:* 5 full-time, 2 part-time staff. *Director:* Mrs. Claudine Oliver, Director of Guidance and Counseling, 806-894-9611 Ext. 363. *Services:* resume preparation, career counseling, careers library, job bank.
AFTER GRADUATION 90% of students completing a degree program in 1994–95 went directly on to further study.
EXPENSES FOR 1995–96 Area resident tuition: $480 full-time. State resident tuition: $750 full-time. Nonresident tuition: $1230 full-time. Part-time tuition per semester ranges from $45 to $160 for area residents, $47 to $250 for state residents, $250 to $410 for nonresidents. Part-time mandatory fees per semester range from $31 to $55. Full-time mandatory fees: $98. College room and board: $2200.
FINANCIAL AID *College-administered undergrad aid 1995–96:* need-based scholarships, non-need scholarships, low-interest long-term loans, part-time jobs. *Required forms:* institutional, FAFSA. *Priority deadline:* 6/1.
APPLYING Open admission. *Options:* early entrance, midyear entrance. *Required:* TOEFL for international students. *Recommended:* ACT. Test scores used for counseling/placement. *Application deadline:* rolling.
APPLYING/TRANSFER *Entrance:* noncompetitive. *Application deadline:* rolling. *Contact:* Mr. Bobby James, Dean of Admissions and Records, 806-894-9611 Ext. 2370.
CONTACT Mr. Bobby James, Dean of Admissions and Records, South Plains College, Levelland, TX 79336-6595, 806-894-9611 Ext. 2370. *Fax:* 806-894-5274.

SOUTHWEST COLLEGIATE INSTITUTE FOR THE DEAF
Big Spring, Texas

UG Enrollment: 100	Tuition & Fees (TX Res): $558
Application Deadline: rolling	Room & Board: $2652

GENERAL State-supported, 2-year, coed. Part of Howard County Junior College District System. Awards certificates, transfer associate, terminal associate degrees (The main telephone number is accessible by TTY for the hearing impaired). Founded 1980. *Setting:* 60-acre small-town campus. *Total enrollment:* 100. *Faculty:* 23 (16 full-time, 7 part-time); student-faculty ratio is 6:1.
ENROLLMENT PROFILE 100 students from 15 states and territories. 55% women, 7% part-time, 73% state residents, 11% transferred in, 21% 25 or older, 10% Hispanic, 10% African American, 1% Asian American.
FIRST-YEAR CLASS 37 total; 60 applied, 100% were accepted, 62% of whom enrolled. 0% from top 10% of their high school class, 5% from top quarter, 45% from top half.
ACADEMIC PROGRAM Core. Calendar: semesters. Academic remediation for entering students, services for LD students, honors program, summer session for credit, part-time degree program (daytime), adult/continuing education programs, internships.
GENERAL DEGREE REQUIREMENTS 62 credits; 3 credits of math; science requirement varies according to program; computer course.
MAJORS Accounting, art/fine arts, automotive technologies, biology/biological sciences, business education, carpentry, chemistry, child care/child and family studies, computer programming, computer science, deaf interpreter training, dental services, drafting and design, economics, education, (pre)engineering sequence, English, food sciences, health education, history, human development, journalism, mathematics, medical laboratory technology, philosophy, photography, physical education, physics, political science/government, psychology, social science, welding technology.
LIBRARY 33,197 books, 20 microform titles, 225 periodicals, 1,129 records, tapes, and CDs.
COMPUTERS ON CAMPUS 25 computers for student use in computer center, learning resource center.
COLLEGE LIFE Orientation program (2 weeks, $500, parents included). Drama-theater group, student-run newspaper. *Student services:* personal-psychological counseling.
HOUSING 152 college housing spaces available; 87 were occupied 1995–96. Freshmen given priority for college housing. On-campus residence required in freshman year.
ATHLETICS *Intercollegiate:* equestrian sports M(s)/W(s). *Intramural:* basketball, bowling, football, soccer, volleyball.
CAREER PLANNING *Service:* career counseling.
AFTER GRADUATION 10% of students completing a degree program in 1994–95 went directly on to further study.
EXPENSES FOR 1996–97 State resident tuition: $558 full-time, $18 per credit part-time. Nonresident tuition: $3782 full-time, $122 per credit part-time. College room and board: $2652.
FINANCIAL AID *College-administered undergrad aid 1995–96:* need-based scholarships, 15 non-need scholarships (average $500), short-term loans (average $150), Federal Work-Study, 5 part-time jobs. *Required forms:* institutional; accepted: CSS Financial Aid PROFILE, state, FAFSA. *Priority deadline:* 6/1.
APPLYING Open admission. *Options:* early entrance, deferred entrance. *Required:* school transcript, TOEFL for international students, Stanford Achievement Test for the Hearing Impaired. Test scores used for counseling/placement. *Application deadline:* rolling. *Notification:* continuous. Preference given to state residents.
APPLYING/TRANSFER *Required:* standardized test scores, college transcript. *Application deadline:* rolling. *Notification:* continuous.
CONTACT Ms. Rhonda Smith, Director of College Relations, SouthWest Collegiate Institute for the Deaf, Big Spring, TX 79720-7298, 915-264-3700 Ext. 227.

SOUTHWEST TEXAS JUNIOR COLLEGE
Uvalde, Texas

UG Enrollment: 3,256	Tuition & Fees (Area Res): $864
Application Deadline: rolling	Room & Board: $2120

GENERAL State and locally supported, 2-year, coed. Part of Texas Higher Education Coordinating Board. Awards transfer associate, terminal associate degrees. Founded 1946. *Setting:* 97-acre small-town campus with easy access to San Antonio. *Total enrollment:* 3,256. *Faculty:* 166 (66 full-time, 100 part-time); student-faculty ratio is 22:1.
ENROLLMENT PROFILE 3,256 students; 59% women, 35% part-time, 98% state residents, 9% live on campus, 2% transferred in, 75% Hispanic, 1% African American. *Areas of study chosen:* 36% education, 10% premed, 5% agriculture, 2% engineering and applied sciences. *Most popular recent majors:* liberal arts/general studies, criminal justice, data processing.
FIRST-YEAR CLASS Of the students who applied, 100% were accepted, 98% of whom enrolled.
ACADEMIC PROGRAM Core, honor code. Calendar: semesters. Academic remediation for entering students, English as a second language program offered during academic year, advanced placement, honors program, summer session for credit, part-time degree program (daytime, evenings), external degree programs, adult/continuing education programs.
GENERAL DEGREE REQUIREMENTS 62 credits; 1 math course; 2 science courses; computer course.
MAJORS Agricultural technologies, automotive technologies, aviation technology, business administration/commerce/management, computer technologies, cosmetology, criminal justice, data processing, education, engineering and applied sciences, farm and ranch management, liberal arts/general studies, science, teacher aide studies.
LIBRARY Will C. Miller Memorial Library with 30,890 books, 344,979 microform titles, 285 periodicals, 1,664 records, tapes, and CDs.
COMPUTERS ON CAMPUS 300 computers for student use in computer center, math, writing labs, library provide access to main academic computer, off-campus computing facilities, on-line services. Staffed computer lab on campus provides training in use of computers, software.
COLLEGE LIFE Orientation program (2 days, no cost). *Most popular organizations:* Catholic Students Club, Business Administration Club. *Major annual event:* Spring Palms Festival. *Student services:* health clinic, personal-psychological counseling. *Campus security:* 24-hour patrols, controlled dormitory access.
HOUSING 250 college housing spaces available; all were occupied 1995–96. No special consideration for freshman housing applicants. Off-campus living permitted. *Option:* coed housing available. Resident assistants live in dorms.
ATHLETICS *Intercollegiate:* equestrian sports M/W. *Intramural:* basketball, equestrian sports, football, golf, racquetball, swimming and diving, tennis.
CAREER PLANNING *Placement office:* 1 full-time staff. *Director:* Mr. Sotero Alviar, Coordinator of Student Recruitment and Job Placement, 210-278-4401 Ext. 226. *Services:* resume preparation, resume referral, career counseling, careers library, job bank, job interviews.
EXPENSES FOR 1996–97 Area resident tuition: $864 full-time. State resident tuition: $1104 full-time. Nonresident tuition: $2268 full-time. Part-time tuition per credit ranges from $93 to $311 for area residents, $117 to $399 for state residents, $243 to $817 for nonresidents. College room and board: $2120.

Southwest Texas Junior College (continued)

FINANCIAL AID ***College-administered undergrad aid 1995–96:*** need-based scholarships, non-need scholarships, short-term loans, Federal Work-Study, part-time jobs. ***Required forms:*** institutional, FAFSA; accepted: CSS Financial Aid PROFILE. ***Application deadline:*** continuous.

APPLYING Open admission. ***Options:*** electronic application, early entrance, deferred entrance. ***Required:*** TOEFL for international students. Test scores used for counseling/placement. ***Application deadline:*** rolling. ***Notification:*** continuous. Preference given to local residents.

APPLYING/TRANSFER ***Application deadline:*** rolling. ***Notification:*** continuous.

CONTACT Mr. Ismael Sosa Jr., Dean of Admissions and Student Services, Southwest Texas Junior College, Uvalde, TX 78801-6296, 210-278-4401 Ext. 277.

TARRANT COUNTY JUNIOR COLLEGE
Fort Worth, Texas

UG Enrollment: 26,584	**Tuition & Fees (Area Res): $672**
Application Deadline: rolling	**Room & Board: N/Avail**

GENERAL County-supported, 2-year, coed. Part of Texas Higher Education Coordinating Board. Awards transfer associate, terminal associate degrees. Founded 1967. ***Setting:*** 667-acre urban campus. ***Total enrollment:*** 26,584. ***Faculty:*** 1,122 (451 full-time, 17% with terminal degrees, 671 part-time); student-faculty ratio is 22:1.

ENROLLMENT PROFILE 26,584 students: 57% women, 43% men, 72% part-time, 99% state residents, 11% transferred in, 8% have need-based financial aid, 15% have non-need-based financial aid, 0% international, 48% 25 or older, 1% Native American, 10% Hispanic, 10% African American, 4% Asian American. ***Most popular recent majors:*** business administration/commerce/management, paralegal studies, computer science.

FIRST-YEAR CLASS 4,647 total. Of the students who applied, 100% were accepted.

ACADEMIC PROGRAM Core. Calendar: semesters. 779 courses offered in 1995–96. Academic remediation for entering students, English as a second language program offered during academic year and summer, services for LD students, advanced placement, honors program, summer session for credit, part-time degree program (daytime, evenings, summer), adult/continuing education programs. ROTC: Army (c), Air Force (c).

GENERAL DEGREE REQUIREMENT 64 semester hours.

MAJORS Accounting, architectural technologies, automotive technologies, aviation technology, business administration/commerce/management, child psychology/child development, computer programming, computer science, construction technologies, criminal justice, deaf interpreter training, dental services, dietetics, drafting and design, educational media, electrical and electronics technologies, electromechanical technology, emergency medical technology, fashion merchandising, fire science, food services technology, heating/refrigeration/air conditioning, horticulture, liberal arts/general studies, machine and tool technologies, marketing/retailing/merchandising, mechanical engineering technology, medical laboratory technology, medical records services, medical technology, mental health/rehabilitation counseling, nursing, operating room technology, paralegal studies, physical therapy, postal management, printing technologies, quality control technology, radiological technology, respiratory therapy, retail management, secretarial studies/office management, welding technology.

LIBRARY 157,422 books, 837 microform titles, 747 periodicals, 2 on-line bibliographic services, 13 CD-ROMs, 12,298 records, tapes, and CDs. Acquisition spending 1994–95: $314,266.

COMPUTERS ON CAMPUS 1,500 computers for student use in computer labs, labs, classrooms, library. Staffed computer lab on campus provides training in use of computers, software.

COLLEGE LIFE Drama-theater group, choral group, student-run newspaper. ***Social organizations:*** 48 open to all. ***Student services:*** health clinic, personal-psychological counseling. ***Campus security:*** 24-hour emergency response devices and patrols.

HOUSING College housing not available.

ATHLETICS ***Intramural:*** football, sailing, table tennis (Ping-Pong), tennis, volleyball.

CAREER PLANNING ***Placement office:*** 4 full-time, 4 part-time staff. ***Director:*** Dr. Paula Harbour, Associate Professor of Psychology/Counselor, 817-534-4861 Ext. 4551. ***Services:*** job fairs, resume preparation, resume referral, career counseling, careers library, job bank, job interviews.

AFTER GRADUATION 65% of students completing a degree program in 1994–95 went directly on to further study.

ESTIMATED EXPENSES FOR 1996–97 ***Application fee:*** $10. Area resident tuition: $576 full-time, $18 per semester hour part-time. State resident tuition: $896 full-time, $28 per semester hour part-time. Nonresident tuition: $4480 full-time, $140 per semester hour part-time. Part-time mandatory fees: $3 per semester hour. Full-time mandatory fees: $96.

FINANCIAL AID ***College-administered undergrad aid 1995–96:*** need-based scholarships, non-need scholarships, short-term loans, low-interest long-term loans from external sources, Federal Work-Study, part-time jobs. ***Required forms:*** institutional, FAFSA; accepted: CSS Financial Aid PROFILE. ***Priority deadline:*** 4/15.

APPLYING Open admission except for nursing, allied health programs. ***Options:*** early entrance, midyear entrance. ***Required:*** TOEFL for international students, TASP. Test scores used for counseling/placement. ***Application deadline:*** rolling.

APPLYING/TRANSFER ***Application deadline:*** rolling. ***Contact:*** Dr. Cathie Jackson, Director of Admissions and Records, 817-336-7851 Ext. 291.

CONTACT Dr. Cathie Jackson, Director of Admissions and Records, Tarrant County Junior College, 1500 Houston Street, Fort Worth, TX 76102-6599, 817-336-7851 Ext. 291.

TEMPLE COLLEGE
Temple, Texas

UG Enrollment: 2,450	**Tuition & Fees (Area Res): $864**
Application Deadline: 8/23	**Room & Board: $2600**

GENERAL District-supported, 2-year, coed. Part of Texas Higher Education Coordinating Board. Awards certificates, transfer associate, terminal associate degrees. Founded 1926. ***Setting:*** 104-acre small-town campus. ***Total enrollment:*** 2,450. ***Faculty:*** 125 (81 full-time, 44 part-time).

ENROLLMENT PROFILE 2,450 students from 33 states and territories, 4 other countries. 61% women, 39% men, 60% part-time, 97% state residents, 1% live on campus, 6% transferred in, 1% international, 54% 25 or older, 1% Native American, 9% Hispanic, 9% African American, 1% Asian American. ***Areas of study chosen:*** 35% liberal arts/general studies, 5% computer and information sciences.

FIRST-YEAR CLASS 541 total. Of the students who applied, 100% were accepted. 28% from top quarter of their high school class, 39% from top half.

ACADEMIC PROGRAM Calendar: semesters. Academic remediation for entering students, summer session for credit, part-time degree program (daytime, evenings, summer), adult/continuing education programs, internships.

GENERAL DEGREE REQUIREMENTS 64 semester hours; math/science requirements vary according to program; computer course for nursing, business majors; internship (some majors).

MAJORS Art/fine arts, automotive technologies, business administration/commerce/management, computer programming, computer science, criminal justice, data processing, dental services, drafting and design, electrical and electronics technologies, law enforcement/police sciences, liberal arts/general studies, manufacturing technology, medical laboratory technology, medical secretarial studies, medical technology, nursing, practical nursing, respiratory therapy, secretarial studies/office management.

LIBRARY Hubert Dawson Library with 44,326 books, 306 microform titles, 357 periodicals, 1,702 records, tapes, and CDs.

COMPUTERS ON CAMPUS 100 computers for student use in computer center, learning skills lab, library provide access to e-mail, Internet. Staffed computer lab on campus provides training in use of computers, software.

COLLEGE LIFE Drama-theater group. ***Student services:*** personal-psychological counseling. ***Campus security:*** 24-hour emergency response devices and patrols.

HOUSING 126 college housing spaces available; 120 were occupied 1995–96. No special consideration for freshman housing applicants. Off-campus living permitted. ***Option:*** single-sex housing available. Resident assistants live in dorms.

ATHLETICS Member NJCAA. ***Intercollegiate:*** basketball M(s)/W(s), golf M(s), tennis M(s)/W(s). ***Intramural:*** basketball, football, golf, swimming and diving, tennis, volleyball. ***Contact:*** Mr. Danny Scott, Athletic Director, 817-773-9961 Ext. 328.

CAREER PLANNING ***Placement office:*** 2 full-time staff. ***Director:*** Ms. Pat Elliott, Director of Special Support Services, 817-773-9961 Ext. 234. ***Service:*** career counseling. Students must register freshman year.

AFTER GRADUATION 95% of class of 1994 had job offers within 6 months.

EXPENSES FOR 1995–96 Area resident tuition: $864 full-time. State resident tuition: $1280 full-time. Nonresident tuition: $2368 full-time. Part-time tuition per semester hour ranges from $42 to $297 for area residents, $68 to $440 for state residents, $308 to $814 for nonresidents. College room and board: $2600.

FINANCIAL AID ***College-administered undergrad aid 1995–96:*** 50 need-based scholarships (average $600), 100 non-need scholarships (average $500), short-term loans (average $200), low-interest long-term loans from external sources (average $2500), Federal Work-Study, 75 part-time jobs. ***Required forms:*** institutional, FAFSA. ***Priority deadline:*** 7/30.

APPLYING Open admission. ***Option:*** early entrance. ***Required:*** TOEFL for international students. ***Recommended:*** ACT. ***Required for some:*** school transcript, TASP. Test scores used for counseling/placement. ***Application deadline:*** 8/23.

APPLYING/TRANSFER ***Required:*** college transcript. ***Application deadline:*** 8/23.

CONTACT Mr. A. C. Hervey, Director of Admissions and Records, Temple College, Temple, TX 76504-7435, 817-773-9961 Ext. 212. ***E-mail:*** a.c.hervey@templejc.edu.

TEXARKANA COLLEGE
Texarkana, Texas

UG Enrollment: 4,038	**Tuition & Fees (Area Res): $672**
Application Deadline: rolling	**Room & Board: N/Avail**

GENERAL State and locally supported, 2-year, coed. Part of Texas Higher Education Coordinating Board. Awards certificates, transfer associate, terminal associate degrees. Founded 1927. ***Setting:*** 88-acre urban campus. ***Total enrollment:*** 4,038. ***Faculty:*** 196 (126 full-time, 4% with terminal degrees, 70 part-time); student-faculty ratio is 16:1. ***Notable Alumni:*** Ross Perot.

ENROLLMENT PROFILE 4,038 students from 4 states and territories, 7 other countries. 60% women, 40% men, 59% part-time, 52% state residents, 11% transferred in, 2% international, 42% 25 or older, 2% Hispanic, 13% African American. ***Areas of study chosen:*** 20% business management and administrative services, 20% interdisciplinary studies, 15% biological and life sciences, 10% health professions and related sciences, 10% liberal arts/general studies, 10% social sciences, 5% computer and information sciences, 5% education, 5% English language/literature/letters. ***Most popular recent majors:*** nursing, liberal arts/general studies, business administration/commerce/management.

FIRST-YEAR CLASS 1,182 total; 1,182 applied, 100% were accepted, 100% of whom enrolled. 8% from top 10% of their high school class, 12% from top quarter, 66% from top half. 20 class presidents, 45 valedictorians.

ACADEMIC PROGRAM Core, honor code. Calendar: semesters. Academic remediation for entering students, services for LD students, advanced placement, summer session for credit, part-time degree program (daytime, evenings, summer), adult/continuing education programs, co-op programs.

GENERAL DEGREE REQUIREMENTS 62 semester hours; 1 college algebra course; computer course.

MAJORS Agricultural sciences, art/fine arts, automotive technologies, biology/biological sciences, business administration/commerce/management, chemistry, computer programming, computer science, cosmetology, criminal justice, data processing, drafting and design, drug and alcohol/substance abuse counseling, electrical and electronics technologies, emergency medical technology, engineering (general), finance/banking, heating/refrigeration/air conditioning, journalism, law enforcement/police sciences, liberal arts/general studies, mathematics, music, nursing, paper and pulp sciences, physics, practical nursing, real estate, retail management, secretarial studies/office management, theater arts/drama, welding technology.

LIBRARY Palmer Memorial Library with 46,700 books, 1,746 microform titles, 646 periodicals, 3,666 records, tapes, and CDs.

COMPUTERS ON CAMPUS 105 computers for student use in computer center, physical science building, classrooms, library.

COLLEGE LIFE Orientation program (3 days, $77). Drama-theater group, choral group, student-run newspaper, radio station. ***Social organizations:*** 16 open to all. ***Major annual events:*** October Fest, Spring Fest. ***Student services:*** personal-psychological counseling. ***Campus security:*** 24-hour patrols.

HOUSING College housing not available.
ATHLETICS Member NJCAA. ***Intercollegiate:*** baseball M, golf M. ***Intramural:*** badminton, basketball, racquetball, tennis, volleyball. ***Contact:*** Mr. Darreon Clark, Athletic Director, 903-838-4541.
CAREER PLANNING ***Services:*** career counseling, careers library, job bank.
AFTER GRADUATION 25% of students completing a degree program in 1994–95 went directly on to further study.
EXPENSES FOR 1995–96 ***Application fee:*** $10. Area resident tuition: $630 full-time. State resident tuition: $900 full-time. Nonresident tuition: $1400 full-time. Part-time tuition per semester hour ranges from $83 to $231 for area residents, $110 to $330 for state residents, $360 to $572 for nonresidents. Part-time mandatory fees: $1 per semester hour. Full-time mandatory fees: $42.
FINANCIAL AID ***College-administered undergrad aid 1995–96:*** need-based scholarships, non-need scholarships, Federal Work-Study, part-time jobs. ***Required forms:*** institutional, FAFSA. ***Application deadline:*** continuous.
APPLYING Open admission. ***Option:*** early entrance. ***Required:*** TOEFL for international students. ***Recommended:*** 3 years of high school math and science, some high school foreign language. ***Required for some:*** SAT I or ACT. Test scores used for counseling/placement. ***Application deadline:*** rolling.
APPLYING/TRANSFER ***Entrance:*** noncompetitive. ***Application deadline:*** rolling. ***Contact:*** Ms. Georgia A. McFaul, Director of Counseling, 903-838-4541 Ext. 249.
CONTACT Mr. Van Miller, Director of Admissions, Texarkana College, 2500 North Robison Road, Texarkana, TX 75599-0001, 903-838-4541 Ext. 358. ***Fax:*** 903-832-5030. College video available.

TEXAS SOUTHMOST COLLEGE
Brownsville, Texas

UG Enrollment: 6,564 | **Tuition & Fees (Area Res): $772**
Application Deadline: 8/1 | **Room & Board: N/Avail**

GENERAL District-supported, 2-year, coed. Part of Texas Higher Education Coordinating Board. Awards certificates, transfer associate, terminal associate degrees. Founded 1926. ***Setting:*** 65-acre urban campus. ***Total enrollment:*** 6,564. ***Faculty:*** 390 (210 full-time, 180 part-time).
ENROLLMENT PROFILE 6,564 students: 59% women, 47% part-time, 97% state residents, 5% transferred in, 2% international, 32% 25 or older, 1% Native American, 87% Hispanic, 1% African American, 1% Asian American. ***Areas of study chosen:*** 18% social sciences, 14% education, 14% interdisciplinary studies, 3% communications and journalism, 3% engineering and applied sciences, 1% architecture, 1% fine arts, 1% premed.
FIRST-YEAR CLASS 1,100 total. Of the students who applied, 95% were accepted.
ACADEMIC PROGRAM Core. Calendar: semesters. Academic remediation for entering students, English as a second language program offered during academic year, advanced placement, honors program, summer session for credit, part-time degree program (daytime, evenings, weekends, summer), adult/continuing education programs, co-op programs.
GENERAL DEGREE REQUIREMENTS 62 credits; math/science requirements vary according to program; foreign language requirement varies according to program; computer course.
MAJORS Accounting, art/fine arts, automotive technologies, business administration/commerce/management, child care/child and family studies, construction technologies, criminal justice, data processing, drafting and design, drug and alcohol/substance abuse counseling, electrical and electronics technologies, emergency medical technology, finance/banking, fire science, hotel and restaurant management, law enforcement/police sciences, legal secretarial studies, liberal arts/general studies, medical laboratory technology, music, nursing, radiological technology, respiratory therapy, retail management, secretarial studies/office management, social work, word processing.
LIBRARY Arnulfo L. Oliveira Library with 198,728 books, 616,425 microform titles, 2,192 periodicals, 1,246 records, tapes, and CDs. Acquisition spending 1994–95: $774,926.
COMPUTERS ON CAMPUS 30 computers for student use in computer center, library.
COLLEGE LIFE Drama-theater group, student-run newspaper. ***Student services:*** health clinic, personal-psychological counseling. ***Campus security:*** 24-hour emergency response devices and patrols.
HOUSING College housing not available.
ATHLETICS Member NJCAA. ***Intercollegiate:*** baseball M(s), volleyball W(s). ***Intramural:*** badminton, basketball, bowling, football, golf, gymnastics, sailing, soccer, swimming and diving, tennis, volleyball. ***Contact:*** Mr. Arnie Alvarez, Athletic Director, 210-544-8293.
CAREER PLANNING ***Placement office:*** 3 full-time, 1 part-time staff. ***Director:*** Mr. Daniel Montes, Placement Specialist, 210-544-8866. ***Services:*** resume preparation, resume referral, career counseling, careers library, job bank, job interviews.
EXPENSES FOR 1995–96 Area resident tuition: $336 full-time. State resident tuition: $576 full-time. Nonresident tuition: $2256 full-time. Full-time mandatory fees: $436.
FINANCIAL AID ***College-administered undergrad aid 1995–96:*** need-based scholarships, non-need scholarships, short-term loans, low-interest long-term loans from external sources, Federal Work-Study, part-time jobs. ***Required forms:*** institutional, FAFSA. ***Application deadline:*** continuous to 6/1.
APPLYING Open admission. ***Options:*** early entrance, deferred entrance. ***Required:*** TASP. ***Required for some:*** 3 years of high school math and science, some high school foreign language. Test scores used for counseling/placement. ***Application deadline:*** 8/1.
APPLYING/TRANSFER ***Required:*** standardized test scores. ***Entrance:*** noncompetitive. ***Application deadline:*** 8/1.
CONTACT Mr. Ernesto Garcia, Director of Enrollment, Texas Southmost College, 83 Fort Brown, Brownsville, TX 78520-4991, 210-544-8254.

TEXAS STATE TECHNICAL COLLEGE
Sweetwater, Texas

UG Enrollment: 860 | **Tuition & Fees (TX Res): $1553**
Application Deadline: rolling | **Room & Board: $4100**

GENERAL State-supported, 2-year, coed. Part of Texas State Technical College System. Awards certificates, terminal associate degrees. Founded 1970. ***Setting:*** 115-acre rural campus. ***Endowment:*** $50,000. ***Total enrollment:*** 860. ***Faculty:*** 99 (78 full-time, 85% with terminal degrees, 21 part-time); student-faculty ratio is 7:1.
ENROLLMENT PROFILE 860 students: 47% women, 53% men, 24% part-time, 94% state residents, 18% transferred in, 77% have need-based financial aid, 23% have non-need-based financial aid, 1% international, 50% 25 or older, 1% Native American, 17% Hispanic, 5% African American, 1% Asian American. ***Areas of study chosen:*** 23% computer and information sciences, 23% health professions and related sciences, 10% engineering and applied sciences, 8% business management and administrative services. ***Most popular recent majors:*** nursing, emergency medical technology, management information systems.
FIRST-YEAR CLASS 331 total; 465 applied, 100% were accepted, 71% of whom enrolled. 11% from top 10% of their high school class, 14% from top quarter, 33% from top half.
ACADEMIC PROGRAM Core, vocational/technical curriculum. Calendar: quarters. 216 courses offered in 1995–96. Academic remediation for entering students, summer session for credit, part-time degree program (daytime, evenings, summer), adult/continuing education programs, co-op programs and internships.
GENERAL DEGREE REQUIREMENTS 88 credits; computer course for air conditioning, automotive diesel, environmental science majors; internship (some majors).
MAJORS Accounting, computer programming, computer technologies, drafting and design, electrical and electronics technologies, emergency medical technology, environmental sciences, management information systems, nursing, robotics, secretarial studies/office management.
LIBRARY Texas State Technical College Library with 16,680 books, 109 microform titles, 205 periodicals, 23 CD-ROMs, 1,373 records, tapes, and CDs. Acquisition spending 1994–95: $23,518.
COMPUTERS ON CAMPUS 10 computers for student use in library provide access to e-mail, Internet.
COLLEGE LIFE Orientation program (2 days, $38). Student-run newspaper. ***Social organizations:*** 15 open to all. ***Most popular organizations:*** Student Government Association, Data Processing Management Association, Business Professionals of America, Mexican-American Student Club, Vocational Industrial Clubs of America. ***Major annual events:*** Valentine's Dinner and Dance, Halloween Party. ***Student services:*** health clinic, personal-psychological counseling. ***Campus security:*** 24-hour patrols.
HOUSING 96 college housing spaces available; 87 were occupied 1995–96. No special consideration for freshman housing applicants. On-campus residence required in freshman year except if over 21, single parent, married, or living with guardian within 50 miles commuting distance. ***Option:*** single-sex (1 building) housing available. Resident assistants live in dorms.
ATHLETICS ***Intramural:*** football, golf, softball, volleyball.
CAREER PLANNING ***Placement office:*** 2 full-time staff; $46,771 operating expenditure 1994–95. ***Director:*** Ms. Donna Rowland, Placement Officer, 915-235-7444. ***Services:*** job fairs, resume preparation, resume referral, career counseling, careers library, job interviews. 15 organizations recruited on campus 1994–95.
AFTER GRADUATION 95% of class of 1994 had job offers within 6 months.
EXPENSES FOR 1995–96 State resident tuition: $848 full-time. Nonresident tuition: $4240 full-time, $80 per credit part-time. State resident part-time tuition per quarter ranges from $80 to $176. Part-time mandatory fees: $13.30 per credit. Full-time mandatory fees: $705. College room and board: $4100. College room only: $2100.
FINANCIAL AID ***College-administered undergrad aid 1995–96:*** 281 need-based scholarships (average $756), 48 non-need scholarships (average $658), short-term loans (average $475), low-interest long-term loans from external sources (average $2129), 50 Federal Work-Study (averaging $1000), 6 part-time jobs. ***Required forms:*** institutional, FAFSA; accepted: CSS Financial Aid PROFILE. ***Priority deadline:*** 6/1. ***Payment plan:*** installment. ***Waivers:*** full or partial for senior citizens.
APPLYING Open admission. ***Options:*** early entrance, deferred entrance, midyear entrance. ***Required:*** school transcript, TOEFL for international students, CPT. Test scores used for counseling/placement. ***Application deadline:*** rolling. ***Notification:*** continuous.
APPLYING/TRANSFER ***Required:*** standardized test scores, high school transcript, college transcript. ***Entrance:*** noncompetitive. ***Application deadline:*** rolling. ***Notification:*** continuous. ***Contact:*** Ms. Linda L. Graham, Director of Admissions and Records, 915-235-7374.
CONTACT Mr. Jeff Waite, Director of Marketing, Texas State Technical College, Sweetwater, TX 79556-4108, 915-235-7352 or toll-free 800-592-TSTI (in-state). ***Fax:*** 915-235-7416. ***E-mail:*** kshipp@tstc.edu.

TEXAS STATE TECHNICAL COLLEGE–HARLINGEN CAMPUS
Harlingen, Texas

UG Enrollment: 3,056 | **Tuition & Fees (TX Res): $1489**
Application Deadline: rolling | **Room & Board: $2656**

GENERAL State-supported, 2-year, coed. Part of Texas State Technical College System. Awards certificates, terminal associate degrees. Founded 1967. ***Setting:*** 118-acre small-town campus. ***Research spending 1994–95:*** $20,795. ***Total enrollment:*** 3,056. ***Faculty:*** 148 (122 full-time, 4% with terminal degrees, 26 part-time); student-faculty ratio is 24:1.
ENROLLMENT PROFILE 3,056 students: 44% women, 56% men, 44% part-time, 99% state residents, 13% live on campus, 20% transferred in, 78% have need-based financial aid, 10% have non-need-based financial aid, 1% international, 29% 25 or older, 0% Native American, 85% Hispanic, 1% African American, 0% Asian American. ***Areas of study chosen:*** 18% computer and information sciences, 16% engineering and applied sciences, 15% health professions and related sciences, 11% vocational and home economics, 1% agriculture, 1% natural resource sciences. ***Most popular recent majors:*** chemical engineering technology, computer technologies, information science.
FIRST-YEAR CLASS 812 total. Of the students who applied, 100% were accepted, 66% of whom enrolled. 6% from top 10% of their high school class, 13% from top quarter, 24% from top half. 1 valedictorian.
ACADEMIC PROGRAM Core, technical/vocational curriculum, honor code. Calendar: quarters. Academic remediation for entering students, English as a second language program offered during academic year and summer, services for LD students, summer session for credit, part-time degree program (daytime, evenings, weekends, summer), adult/continuing education programs, co-op programs and internships.
GENERAL DEGREE REQUIREMENTS 90 credit hours; math/science requirements vary according to program.
MAJORS Aircraft and missile maintenance, biomedical technologies, chemical engineering technology, computer science, computer technologies, construction technologies, data processing, dental services, drafting and design, electrical and electronics technologies,

Peterson's Guide to Two-Year Colleges 1997 627

Texas State Technical College–Harlingen Campus (continued)
electromechanical technology, electronics engineering technology, environmental health sciences, farm and ranch management, food services technology, heating/refrigeration/air conditioning, information science, instrumentation technology, legal secretarial studies, manufacturing technology, medical records services, secretarial studies/office management, welding technology.
LIBRARY Texas State Technical College Library with 9,400 books, 350 microform titles, 413 periodicals, 35 CD-ROMs, 250 records, tapes, and CDs. Acquisition spending 1994–95: $43,573.
COMPUTERS ON CAMPUS 40 computers for student use in learning resource center, library. Staffed computer lab on campus provides training in use of computers, software. Academic computing expenditure 1994–95: $1.2 million.
COLLEGE LIFE Student-run newspaper. 18% vote in student government elections. ***Most popular organizations:*** Student Congress, Vocational Industrial Clubs of America, Business Professionals of America. ***Major annual events:*** Oktoberfest, Miss TSTC Pageant, Techsan Day. ***Student services:*** health clinic, personal-psychological counseling, women's center. ***Campus security:*** 24-hour emergency response devices and patrols, night watchman for housing area.
HOUSING 483 college housing spaces available; 290 were occupied 1995–96. No special consideration for freshman housing applicants. Off-campus living permitted. ***Option:*** single-sex (8 buildings) housing available.
ATHLETICS ***Intramural:*** badminton, basketball, bowling, cross-country running, football, racquetball, soccer, softball, table tennis (Ping-Pong), tennis, track and field, volleyball, weight lifting. ***Contact:*** Mr. Julian Alvarez, Supervisor of Intramurals, 210-425-0681; Ms. Annette Chavez, Assistant Supervisor of Intramurals, 210-425-0681.
CAREER PLANNING ***Placement office:*** 2 full-time staff; $57,513 operating expenditure 1994–95. ***Director:*** Mr. Hector Cano, Placement Officer, 210-425-0628. ***Services:*** job fairs, career counseling, job bank, job interviews.
EXPENSES FOR 1996–97 State resident tuition: $780 full-time. Nonresident tuition: $3600 full-time, $80 per credit hour (minimum) part-time. State resident part-time tuition per quarter ranges from $80 to $198. Part-time mandatory fees per quarter range from $13.30 to $173.25. Full-time mandatory fees: $709. College room and board: $2656.
FINANCIAL AID ***College-administered undergrad aid 1995–96:*** 1,400 need-based scholarships (averaging $900), 42 non-need scholarships (averaging $475), short-term loans (averaging $100), low-interest long-term loans from external sources (averaging $2625), Federal Work-Study, 300 part-time jobs. ***Required forms:*** institutional, FAFSA; accepted: CSS Financial Aid PROFILE. ***Priority deadline:*** 4/28. ***Payment plan:*** installment.
APPLYING Open admission. ***Options:*** early entrance, deferred entrance, midyear entrance. ***Required:*** school transcript, TOEFL for international students, TASP. ***Recommended:*** SAT I or ACT. Test scores used for counseling/placement. ***Application deadline:*** rolling. ***Notification:*** continuous.
APPLYING/TRANSFER ***Required:*** high school transcript, college transcript, minimum 2.0 college GPA. ***Entrance:*** noncompetitive. ***Application deadline:*** rolling. ***Notification:*** continuous. ***Contact:*** Mr. Agustin V. Rangel, Director of Admissions and Records, 210-425-0665.
CONTACT Miss Cynthia Solis, Admissions Staff Assistant, Texas State Technical College–Harlingen Campus, Harlingen, TX 78550-3697, 210-425-0644. ***Fax:*** 210-425-0698. ***E-mail:*** arangel@tstc.edu. College video available.

TEXAS STATE TECHNICAL COLLEGE–WACO/MARSHALL CAMPUS
Waco, Texas

UG Enrollment: 3,313	**Tuition & Fees (TX Res): $1235**
Application Deadline: rolling	**Room Only: $1806**

GENERAL State-supported, 2-year, coed. Part of Texas State Technical College System. Awards certificates, transfer associate, terminal associate degrees. Founded 1965. ***Setting:*** 200-acre suburban campus. ***Total enrollment:*** 3,313. ***Faculty:*** 323 (223 full-time, 100 part-time); student-faculty ratio is 15:1.
ENROLLMENT PROFILE 3,313 students from 33 states and territories, 2 other countries. 22% women, 78% men, 20% part-time, 97% state residents, 38% transferred in, 1% international, 36% 25 or older, 1% Native American, 11% Hispanic, 11% African American, 1% Asian American. ***Most popular recent majors:*** occupational safety and health, instrumentation technology, automotive technologies.
FIRST-YEAR CLASS 1,292 total; 1,909 applied, 100% were accepted, 68% of whom enrolled.
ACADEMIC PROGRAM Core, hands-on experience curriculum. Calendar: quarters. 959 courses offered in 1995–96. Academic remediation for entering students, services for LD students, summer session for credit, part-time degree program (daytime, evenings, summer), adult/continuing education programs, co-op programs and internships.
GENERAL DEGREE REQUIREMENTS 100 quarter hours; 1 college algebra course.
MAJORS Audio engineering, automotive technologies, aviation technology, biomedical technologies, chemical engineering technology, commercial art, computer programming, computer science, computer technologies, culinary arts, dental services, drafting and design, electrical and electronics technologies, flight training, food services technology, graphic arts, heating/refrigeration/air conditioning, industrial and heavy equipment maintenance, information science, instrumentation technology, machine and tool technologies, manufacturing technology, mechanical engineering technology, nuclear technology, occupational safety and health, ornamental horticulture, printing technologies, welding technology.
LIBRARY Texas State Technical College-Waco/Marshall Campus Library with 62,000 books, 650 periodicals, 20 CD-ROMs, 4,500 records, tapes, and CDs.
COMPUTERS ON CAMPUS Student rooms linked to a campus network. 500 computers for student use in computer center, computer labs, learning resource center, classrooms, library, student center provide access to off-campus computing facilities, e-mail, on-line services, Internet.
COLLEGE LIFE Drama-theater group, student-run newspaper. 25% vote in student government elections. ***Social organizations:*** 25 open to all. ***Most popular organizations:*** Automotive VICA, Society of Mexican-American Engineers and Scientists, Texas Association of Black Persons In Higher Education. ***Major annual events:*** DIA Techsana, Systems Olympics. ***Student services:*** health clinic, personal-psychological counseling, women's center. ***Campus security:*** 24-hour emergency response devices and patrols, late-night transport-escort service, controlled dormitory access.
HOUSING 2,050 college housing spaces available; 1,466 were occupied 1995–96. Freshmen given priority for college housing. On-campus residence required in freshman year except if married or 21 or over. ***Option:*** single-sex housing available. Resident assistants live in dorms.
ATHLETICS ***Intramural:*** basketball, football, golf, racquetball, softball, volleyball, weight lifting.
CAREER PLANNING ***Placement office:*** 1 full-time staff. ***Director:*** Ms. Linda Head, Assistant Placement Officer, 817-867-2220. ***Services:*** job fairs, resume preparation, career counseling, careers library, job bank, job interviews. Students must register sophomore year.
EXPENSES FOR 1995–96 State resident tuition: $720 full-time. Nonresident tuition: $3600 full-time, $80 per quarter hour part-time. State resident part-time tuition per quarter ranges from $80 to $176. Part-time mandatory fees per quarter range from $14.30 to $157.30. Full-time mandatory fees: $515. College room only: $1806 (minimum).
FINANCIAL AID ***College-administered undergrad aid 1995–96:*** need-based scholarships, non-need scholarships, short-term loans, low-interest long-term loans from external sources, 340 Federal Work-Study (averaging $1250), 125 part-time jobs. ***Required forms:*** institutional, FAFSA; accepted: CSS Financial Aid PROFILE. ***Priority deadline:*** 6/1. ***Payment plan:*** installment.
APPLYING Open admission. ***Options:*** Common Application, early entrance. ***Required:*** school transcript, TOEFL for international students, TASP, CPT. Test scores used for counseling/placement. ***Application deadline:*** rolling. ***Notification:*** continuous.
APPLYING/TRANSFER ***Required:*** high school transcript, college transcript. ***Required for some:*** standardized test scores. ***Entrance:*** noncompetitive. ***Application deadline:*** rolling. ***Notification:*** continuous. ***Contact:*** Mr. Charles Reed, Interim Director of Admissions and Records, 817-867-2366.
CONTACT Mr. Charles Reed, Interim Director of Admissions and Records, Texas State Technical College–Waco/Marshall Campus, Waco, TX 76705-1695, 817-867-2366 or toll-free 800-792-8784 (in-state). ***E-mail:*** lrobert@tstc.edu.

TOMBALL COLLEGE
Tomball, Texas

UG Enrollment: 3,641	**Tuition & Fees (Area Res): $828**
Application Deadline: 8/25	**Room & Board: N/Avail**

GENERAL State and locally supported, 2-year, coed. Part of North Harris Montgomery Community College District. Awards certificates, transfer associate, terminal associate degrees. Founded 1988. ***Setting:*** 210-acre suburban campus with easy access to Houston. ***Educational spending 1994–95:*** $1073 per undergrad. ***Total enrollment:*** 3,641. ***Faculty:*** 212 (61 full-time, 29% with terminal degrees, 151 part-time); student-faculty ratio is 24:1.
ENROLLMENT PROFILE 3,641 students: 58% women, 42% men, 65% part-time, 1% international, 46% 25 or older, 1% Native American, 6% Hispanic, 2% African American, 2% Asian American. ***Areas of study chosen:*** 13% fine arts, 11% education, 5% premed.
FIRST-YEAR CLASS 1,119 total. Of the students accepted, 100% enrolled.
ACADEMIC PROGRAM Core, honor code. Calendar: semesters. Academic remediation for entering students, English as a second language program offered during academic year, services for LD students, advanced placement, tutorials, honors program, summer session for credit, part-time degree program (daytime, evenings), adult/continuing education programs, co-op programs and internships.
GENERAL DEGREE REQUIREMENTS 62 credit hours; computer course for accounting, criminal justice, geology majors; internship (some majors).
MAJORS Accounting, aircraft and missile maintenance, applied art, business administration/commerce/management, computer graphics, computer information systems, computer programming, criminal justice, electronics engineering technology, emergency medical technology, geology, heating/refrigeration/air conditioning, human services, legal secretarial studies, liberal arts/general studies, medical secretarial studies, nursing, veterinary technology.
LIBRARY Learning Resource Center with 13,000 books, 219 microform titles, 387 periodicals, 4 CD-ROMs, 217 records, tapes, and CDs. Acquisition spending 1994–95: $323,555.
COMPUTERS ON CAMPUS 92 computers for student use in computer center, computer labs, learning resource center, library provide access to e-mail, on-line services, Internet, campus network. Staffed computer lab on campus provides training in use of computers, software. Academic computing expenditure 1994–95: $135,699.
COLLEGE LIFE ***Social organizations:*** 15 open to all; 1 national fraternity, 1 national sorority. ***Most popular organizations:*** Phi Theta Kappa, Culture Club, Veterinary Technicians Student Organization, Human Services Club, Student Nursing Association. ***Major annual events:*** Bluebonnet DAZE, Lighting of the Commons. ***Campus security:*** 24-hour emergency response devices, late-night transport-escort service, trained security personnel during open hours.
HOUSING College housing not available.
CAREER PLANNING ***Placement office:*** 3 part-time staff; $12,325 operating expenditure 1994–95. ***Director:*** Mr. Larry Middleton, Director of Financial Aid and Student Employment, 713-351-3300. ***Services:*** job fairs, career counseling, careers library, job bank.
AFTER GRADUATION 77% of students completing a degree program in 1994–95 went directly on to further study.
EXPENSES FOR 1996–97 Area resident tuition: $714 full-time, $60 per credit hour part-time. State resident tuition: $1764 full-time, $95 per credit hour part-time. Nonresident tuition: $2064 full-time, $200 per credit hour part-time. Part-time mandatory fees: $15 per semester. Full-time mandatory fees: $114.
FINANCIAL AID ***College-administered undergrad aid 1995–96:*** 210 need-based scholarships (averaging $500), short-term loans (averaging $350), low-interest long-term loans from external sources (averaging $1975), Federal Work-Study, 20 part-time jobs. ***Required forms:*** institutional, FAFSA. ***Priority deadline:*** 4/15. ***Payment plan:*** installment. ***Waivers:*** full or partial for employees or children of employees. ***Notification:*** continuous.
APPLYING Open admission. ***Option:*** early entrance. ***Required:*** school transcript, minimum 3.0 GPA, 3 years of high school math and science. ***Recommended:*** SAT I or ACT, TOEFL for international students, TASP. Test scores used for counseling/placement. ***Application deadline:*** 8/25.
APPLYING/TRANSFER ***Required:*** college transcript. ***Entrance:*** noncompetitive. ***Contact:*** Ms. Mary Shafer, Director of Admissions, 713-351-3310.
CONTACT Ms. Francette Carnahan, Vice President for Student Development, Tomball College, Tomball, TX 77375-4036, 713-357-3758. ***Fax:*** 713-351-3384.

TRINITY VALLEY COMMUNITY COLLEGE
Athens, Texas

UG Enrollment: 4,786 **Tuition & Fees (Area Res): $460**
Application Deadline: rolling **Room & Board: $2682**

GENERAL State and locally supported, 2-year, coed. Part of Texas Higher Education Coordinating Board. Awards certificates, transfer associate, terminal associate degrees. Founded 1946. ***Setting:*** 65-acre small-town campus with easy access to Dallas. ***Total enrollment:*** 4,786. ***Faculty:*** 224 (138 full-time, 86 part-time); student-faculty ratio is 24:1.
ENROLLMENT PROFILE 4,786 students from 19 states and territories, 8 other countries. 46% women, 68% part-time, 94% state residents, 11% transferred in, 3% international, 51% 25 or older, 1% Native American, 4% Hispanic, 18% African American, 1% Asian American. ***Most popular recent majors:*** nursing, computer science, psychology.
FIRST-YEAR CLASS 1,205 total; 1,310 applied, 100% were accepted, 92% of whom enrolled.
ACADEMIC PROGRAM Core. Calendar: semesters. Academic remediation for entering students, English as a second language program offered during academic year, services for LD students, summer session for credit, part-time degree program (daytime, evenings), adult/continuing education programs, co-op programs and internships.
GENERAL DEGREE REQUIREMENTS 65 semester hours; 3 semester hours of math; 8 semester hours of lab science; computer course for business majors; internship (some majors).
MAJORS Accounting, agricultural education, animal sciences, art/fine arts, automotive technologies, biology/biological sciences, business administration/commerce/management, business education, chemistry, child care/child and family studies, child psychology/child development, computer science, corrections, cosmetology, criminal justice, dance, data processing, drafting and design, early childhood education, earth science, education, elementary education, emergency medical technology, (pre)engineering sequence, English, farm and ranch management, fashion merchandising, finance/banking, heating/refrigeration/air conditioning, history, horticulture, insurance, journalism, law enforcement/police sciences, legal secretarial studies, liberal arts/general studies, marketing/retailing/merchandising, mathematics, music, nursing, operating room technology, physical education, physical sciences, political science/government, practical nursing, psychology, range management, real estate, religious studies, sociology, Spanish, speech/rhetoric/public address/debate, theater arts/drama, welding technology.
LIBRARY Main library plus 1 other, with 26,234 books, 6,000 microform titles, 225 periodicals, 2 CD-ROMs, 2,000 records, tapes, and CDs.
COMPUTERS ON CAMPUS 66 computers for student use in labs, library.
COLLEGE LIFE Drama-theater group, choral group, marching band. ***Most popular organizations:*** Student Senate, Phi Theta Kappa, Delta Epsilon Chi. ***Major annual events:*** Homecoming, Cardinal Beauty Pageant, Cardette Spring Show. ***Student services:*** personal-psychological counseling. ***Campus security:*** 24-hour emergency response devices and patrols, controlled dormitory access.
HOUSING 400 college housing spaces available; all were occupied 1995–96. No special consideration for freshman housing applicants. Off-campus living permitted. ***Option:*** single-sex housing available. Resident assistants live in dorms.
ATHLETICS Member NJCAA. ***Intercollegiate:*** basketball M(s)/W(s), football M(s). ***Intramural:*** basketball, football, soccer, table tennis (Ping-Pong), volleyball. ***Contact:*** Mr. Leon Spencer, Athletic Director, 903-675-6218.
CAREER PLANNING ***Placement office:*** 3 full-time, 1 part-time staff. ***Director:*** Mr. Dennis Nolley, Counselor, 903-675-6343. ***Services:*** job fairs, career counseling, careers library, job bank.
EXPENSES FOR 1995–96 Area resident tuition: $460 full-time. State resident tuition: $760 full-time. Nonresident tuition: $2160 full-time. Part-time tuition per semester ranges from $54 to $154 for area residents, $64 to $264 for state residents, $204 to $704 for nonresidents. College room and board: $2682.
FINANCIAL AID ***College-administered undergrad aid 1995–96:*** need-based scholarships, non-need scholarships, short-term loans (average $150), low-interest long-term loans from college funds (average $400), loans from external sources (average $1500), Federal Work-Study, 160 part-time jobs. ***Required forms:*** FAFSA. ***Priority deadline:*** 8/1. ***Payment plan:*** installment.
APPLYING Open admission. ***Options:*** Common Application, early entrance. ***Required:*** TOEFL for international students, TASP. ***Recommended:*** ACT. Test scores used for counseling/placement. ***Application deadline:*** rolling. ***Notification:*** continuous.
APPLYING/TRANSFER ***Entrance:*** noncompetitive. ***Application deadline:*** rolling. ***Notification:*** continuous.
CONTACT Ms. Darlene Magness, Director of School Relations, Trinity Valley Community College, Athens, TX 75751-2765, 903-675-6357. ***Fax:*** 903-675-6316. College video available.

TYLER JUNIOR COLLEGE
Tyler, Texas

UG Enrollment: 7,984 **Tuition & Fees (Area Res): $826**
Application Deadline: rolling **Room & Board: $2400**

GENERAL State and locally supported, 2-year, coed. Part of Texas Higher Education Coordinating Board. Awards transfer associate, terminal associate degrees. Founded 1926. ***Setting:*** 85-acre suburban campus. ***Total enrollment:*** 7,984. ***Faculty:*** 364 (181 full-time, 183 part-time); student-faculty ratio is 20:1.
ENROLLMENT PROFILE 7,984 students from 33 states and territories, 20 other countries. 58% women, 31% part-time, 90% state residents, 8% live on campus, 5% transferred in, 1% international, 38% 25 or older, 1% Native American, 2% Hispanic, 14% African American, 2% Asian American. ***Most popular recent majors:*** computer science, business administration/commerce/management, agricultural education.
FIRST-YEAR CLASS 1,977 total; 2,750 applied, 100% were accepted, 72% of whom enrolled. 10% from top 10% of their high school class, 50% from top half. 1 National Merit Scholar.
ACADEMIC PROGRAM Calendar: semesters. Academic remediation for entering students, English as a second language program offered during academic year, advanced placement, summer session for credit, part-time degree program (daytime, evenings, weekends, summer), adult/continuing education programs, co-op programs and internships.
GENERAL DEGREE REQUIREMENTS 62 semester hours; computer course for allied health majors; internship (some majors).
MAJORS Accounting, agricultural business, agricultural economics, agricultural education, agricultural sciences, art/fine arts, behavioral sciences, business administration/commerce/management, child psychology/child development, computer science, computer technologies, criminal justice, deaf interpreter training, dental services, drafting and design, electrical and electronics technologies, environmental engineering technology, farm and ranch management, fashion merchandising, finance/banking, fire science, graphic arts, health services administration, heating/refrigeration/air conditioning, horticulture, human resources, law enforcement/police sciences, legal secretarial studies, liberal arts/general studies, marketing/retailing/merchandising, medical laboratory technology, medical secretarial studies, modern languages, music, nursing, optometric/ophthalmic technologies, ornamental horticulture, petroleum technology, photography, plastics technology, postal management, practical nursing, printing technologies, psychology, radiological technology, real estate, recreation and leisure services, respiratory therapy, secretarial studies/office management, social science, speech/rhetoric/public address/debate, surveying technology, welding technology.
LIBRARY Vaughn Library and Learning Resource Center with 80,000 books, 340 microform titles, 375 periodicals, 20,000 records, tapes, and CDs.
COMPUTERS ON CAMPUS 60 computers for student use in library.
COLLEGE LIFE Orientation program (2 days, $30). Drama-theater group, choral group, marching band, student-run newspaper. 1% vote in student government elections. ***Social organizations:*** 3 national fraternities, 3 national sororities, 1 local fraternity, 1 local sorority; 5% of eligible men and 5% of eligible women are members. ***Most popular organizations:*** Student Government, Religious Affiliation Clubs. ***Major annual events:*** Homecoming, Annual Career Day. ***Student services:*** health clinic, personal-psychological counseling. ***Campus security:*** 24-hour patrols, controlled dormitory access.
HOUSING 600 college housing spaces available; all were occupied 1995–96. No special consideration for freshman housing applicants. Off-campus living permitted. ***Option:*** single-sex housing available. Resident assistants live in dorms.
ATHLETICS Member NJCAA. ***Intercollegiate:*** baseball M(s), basketball M(s)/W(s), football M(s), golf M, soccer M(s), tennis M(s)/W(s), volleyball W. ***Intramural:*** basketball, racquetball, volleyball, weight lifting. ***Contact:*** Dr. Billy Jack Doggett, Athletic Director, 903-510-2320.
CAREER PLANNING ***Service:*** career counseling.
ESTIMATED EXPENSES FOR 1996–97 Area resident tuition: $465 full-time, $15 per semester hour part-time. State resident tuition: $930 full-time, $30 per semester hour part-time. Nonresident tuition: $1240 full-time, $40 per semester hour part-time. Part-time mandatory fees per semester range from $21 to $131. Full-time mandatory fees: $361. College room and board: $2400. College room only: $1200.
FINANCIAL AID ***College-administered undergrad aid 1995–96:*** 100 need-based scholarships (average $250), 255 non-need scholarships (average $500), short-term loans (average $500), low-interest long-term loans from external sources (average $1750), Federal Work-Study, 200 part-time jobs. ***Required forms:*** institutional, FAFSA; accepted: CSS Financial Aid PROFILE. ***Priority deadline:*** 5/1.
APPLYING Open admission. ***Option:*** early entrance. ***Required:*** TOEFL for international students, TASP. ***Recommended:*** 3 years of high school math and science, SAT I or ACT. Test scores used for counseling/placement. ***Application deadline:*** rolling. Preference given to district residents.
APPLYING/TRANSFER ***Entrance:*** noncompetitive. ***Application deadline:*** rolling.
CONTACT Mr. Kenneth Lewis, Dean of Admissions, Tyler Junior College, Tyler, TX 75711-9020, 903-510-2399. College video available.

VERNON REGIONAL JUNIOR COLLEGE
Vernon, Texas

UG Enrollment: 1,721 **Tuition & Fees (Area Res): $735**
Application Deadline: rolling **Room & Board: $1999**

GENERAL State and locally supported, 2-year, coed. Part of Texas Higher Education Coordinating Board. Awards certificates, transfer associate, terminal associate degrees. Founded 1972. ***Setting:*** 100-acre small-town campus. ***Total enrollment:*** 1,721. ***Faculty:*** 98 (50 full-time, 20% with terminal degrees, 48 part-time); student-faculty ratio is 18:1.
ENROLLMENT PROFILE 1,721 students from 32 states and territories, 4 other countries. 60% women, 64% part-time, 90% state residents, 5% live on campus, 16% transferred in, 1% international, 43% 25 or older, 1% Native American, 10% Hispanic, 7% African American, 2% Asian American. ***Most popular recent majors:*** art/fine arts, science, nursing.
FIRST-YEAR CLASS 208 total. Of the students who applied, 100% were accepted, 12% of whom enrolled.
ACADEMIC PROGRAM Core, honor code. Calendar: semesters. Academic remediation for entering students, services for LD students, advanced placement, summer session for credit, part-time degree program (daytime, evenings, summer), adult/continuing education programs, internships.
GENERAL DEGREE REQUIREMENTS 60 semester hours; computer course; internship (some majors).
MAJORS Accounting, agricultural sciences, art/fine arts, automotive technologies, business administration/commerce/management, child care/child and family studies, computer technologies, cosmetology, criminal justice, drafting and design, farm and ranch management, graphic arts, legal studies, liberal arts/general studies, nursing, practical nursing, science, secretarial studies/office management, theater arts/drama.
LIBRARY Wright Library with 25,000 books, 600 microform titles, 169 periodicals, 397 records, tapes, and CDs.
COMPUTERS ON CAMPUS 80 computers for student use in computer center, classrooms.
COLLEGE LIFE Drama-theater group, choral group. ***Social organizations:*** 3 open to all. ***Most popular organizations:*** Student Government Association, Baptist Student Union. ***Major annual event:*** Sports Day. ***Student services:*** health clinic, personal-psychological counseling. ***Campus security:*** 24-hour patrols.
HOUSING 150 college housing spaces available; all were occupied 1995–96. No special consideration for freshman housing applicants. Off-campus living permitted. ***Option:*** coed housing available. Resident assistants live in dorms.

Vernon Regional Junior College (continued)

ATHLETICS Member NJCAA. ***Intercollegiate:*** baseball M(s), equestrian sports M(s)/W(s), softball W(s), volleyball W(s). ***Intramural:*** archery, basketball, football, tennis, volleyball. ***Contact:*** Mr. Hobie McManigal, Athletic Director, 817-552-6291.
CAREER PLANNING ***Service:*** career counseling.
EXPENSES FOR 1995–96 Area resident tuition: $537 full-time. State resident tuition: $732 full-time. Nonresident tuition: $1057 full-time. Part-time tuition per semester ranges from $53.50 to $214.50 for area residents, $53.50 to $276.50 for state residents, $253.50 to $408.50 for nonresidents. Full-time mandatory fees: $198. College room and board: $1999.
FINANCIAL AID ***College-administered undergrad aid 1995–96:*** 50 need-based scholarships (average $250), 35 non-need scholarships (average $250), Federal Work-Study. ***Required forms:*** institutional, FAFSA. ***Priority deadline:*** 7/1.
APPLYING Open admission. ***Options:*** Common Application, early entrance. ***Required:*** TOEFL for international students, TASP. Test scores used for counseling/placement. ***Application deadline:*** rolling.
APPLYING/TRANSFER ***Application deadline:*** rolling. ***Contact:*** Mr. Joe Hite, Dean of Admissions and Registrar, 817-552-6291.
CONTACT Mr. Joe Hite, Dean of Admissions and Registrar, Vernon Regional Junior College, Vernon, TX 76384-4092, 817-552-6291.

VICTORIA COLLEGE
Victoria, Texas

UG Enrollment: 3,643	**Tuition & Fees (Area Res): $698**
Application Deadline: rolling	**Room & Board: N/Avail**

GENERAL County-supported, 2-year, coed. Part of Texas Higher Education Coordinating Board. Awards transfer associate, terminal associate degrees. Founded 1925. ***Setting:*** 80-acre urban campus. ***Total enrollment:*** 3,643. ***Faculty:*** 120 (80 full-time, 40 part-time); student-faculty ratio is 25:1.
ENROLLMENT PROFILE 3,643 students from 4 states and territories, 2 other countries. 64% women, 61% part-time, 99% state residents, 20% transferred in, 49% 25 or older, 22% Hispanic, 4% African American. ***Most popular recent majors:*** nursing, business administration/commerce/management.
FIRST-YEAR CLASS 770 total; 770 applied, 100% were accepted, 100% of whom enrolled.
ACADEMIC PROGRAM Core. Calendar: semesters. Academic remediation for entering students, services for LD students, advanced placement, summer session for credit, part-time degree program (daytime, evenings, summer), adult/continuing education programs.
GENERAL DEGREE REQUIREMENTS 62 semester hours; computer course for accounting, drafting technology, electronics technology, business administration/management, secretarial studies/office management, nursing majors.
MAJORS Accounting, business administration/commerce/management, computer information systems, drafting and design, electronics engineering technology, law enforcement/police sciences, liberal arts/general studies, medical laboratory technology, nursing, real estate, respiratory therapy, secretarial studies/office management.
LIBRARY University of Houston, Victoria-Victoria College Library with 150,000 books, 1,500 periodicals, 11,000 records, tapes, and CDs.
COMPUTERS ON CAMPUS 225 computers for student use in computer center, computer labs, allied health classroom provide access to main academic computer, off-campus computing facilities, e-mail, Internet. Staffed computer lab on campus provides training in use of computers, software.
COLLEGE LIFE Orientation program (2 days). Drama-theater group, choral group. ***Most popular organization:*** Student Senate. ***Student services:*** personal-psychological counseling.
HOUSING College housing not available.
ATHLETICS ***Intramural:*** basketball, softball.
CAREER PLANNING ***Service:*** career counseling.
EXPENSES FOR 1995–96 Area resident tuition: $680 full-time. State resident tuition: $920 full-time. Nonresident tuition: $2630 full-time. Part-time tuition per semester ranges from $45 to $154 for area residents, $69 to $231 for state residents, $400 to $880 for nonresidents. Part-time mandatory fees: $9 per semester. Full-time mandatory fees: $18.
FINANCIAL AID ***College-administered undergrad aid 1995–96:*** 170 need-based scholarships, 142 non-need scholarships, short-term loans (average $250). ***Required forms:*** institutional, FAFSA. ***Priority deadline:*** 4/15. ***Waivers:*** full or partial for employees or children of employees and senior citizens.
APPLYING Open admission. ***Option:*** early entrance. ***Required:*** TOEFL for international students, TASP. ***Required for some:*** SAT I or ACT. Test scores used for counseling/placement. ***Application deadline:*** rolling.
APPLYING/TRANSFER ***Entrance:*** noncompetitive. ***Application deadline:*** rolling.
CONTACT Mrs. Martha Watts, Registrar, Victoria College, 2200 East Red River, Victoria, TX 77901-4494, 512-572-6407. College video available.

WEATHERFORD COLLEGE
Weatherford, Texas

UG Enrollment: 2,277	**Tuition & Fees (Area Res): $936**
Application Deadline: rolling	**Room & Board: $2646**

GENERAL State and locally supported, 2-year, coed. Part of Texas Higher Education Coordinating Board. Awards certificates, transfer associate, terminal associate degrees. Founded 1869. ***Setting:*** 94-acre small-town campus with easy access to Dallas–Fort Worth. ***Endowment:*** $361,153. ***Research spending 1994–95:*** $58,024. ***Total enrollment:*** 2,277. ***Faculty:*** 94 (42 full-time, 20% with terminal degrees, 52 part-time); student-faculty ratio is 24:1. ***Notable Alumni:*** Jim Wright, Gloria Gilbert Barron, Mary Martin, Hood Simpson.
ENROLLMENT PROFILE 2,277 students: 60% women, 40% men, 50% part-time, 99% state residents, 5% transferred in, 1% international, 56% 25 or older, 1% Native American, 3% Hispanic, 3% African American, 1% Asian American. ***Areas of study chosen:*** 22% business management and administrative services, 16% health professions and related sciences, 11% education, 6% computer and information sciences, 5% agriculture, 4% engineering and applied sciences, 3% premed, 3% psychology, 2% biological and life sciences, 2% performing arts, 2% social sciences, 1% architecture, 1% communications and journalism, 1% English language/literature/letters, 1% fine arts, 1% foreign language and literature, 1% mathematics, 1% physical sciences, 1% predentistry, 1% prelaw, 1% prevet, 1% vocational and home economics. ***Most popular recent majors:*** computer information systems, business administration/commerce/management.
FIRST-YEAR CLASS 1,675 total; 1,675 applied, 100% were accepted, 100% of whom enrolled.
ACADEMIC PROGRAM Core, interdisciplinary curriculum, honor code. Calendar: semesters. Academic remediation for entering students, services for LD students, self-designed majors, Freshman Honors College, tutorials, honors program, summer session for credit, part-time degree program (daytime, evenings, summer), adult/continuing education programs, internships. ROTC: Air Force (c).
GENERAL DEGREE REQUIREMENTS 62 semester hours; 3 semester hours of college algebra; computer course; internship (some majors).
MAJORS Agricultural business, business administration/commerce/management, computer information systems, computer programming, corrections, cosmetology, criminal justice, drafting and design, electronics engineering technology, emergency medical technology, liberal arts/general studies, science, secretarial studies/office management.
LIBRARY Weatherford College Library with 65,710 books, 190 microform titles, 388 periodicals, 2,073 records, tapes, and CDs. Acquisition spending 1994–95: $37,724.
COMPUTERS ON CAMPUS 85 computers for student use in computer center, skills lab provide access to e-mail, on-line services, Internet. Staffed computer lab on campus provides training in use of computers, software. Academic computing expenditure 1994–95: $168,000.
COLLEGE LIFE Drama-theater group, choral group. 15% vote in student government elections. ***Most popular organizations:*** Black Awareness Student Organization, Criminal Justice Club, Phi Theta Kappa. ***Major annual events:*** Homecoming, Halloween Day, Western Day. ***Student services:*** personal-psychological counseling. ***Campus security:*** 24-hour emergency response devices and patrols, late-night transport-escort service.
HOUSING 192 college housing spaces available; 170 were occupied 1995–96. No special consideration for freshman housing applicants. Off-campus living permitted. ***Option:*** coed housing available. Resident assistants live in dorms.
ATHLETICS Member NJCAA. ***Intercollegiate:*** basketball M/W, golf M/W, tennis M/W. ***Contact:*** Mr. Thomas R. McKinley, Athletic Director, 817-594-5471.
CAREER PLANNING ***Placement office:*** 1 full-time staff; $25,000 operating expenditure 1994–95. ***Director:*** Ms. Vicki Smith, Job Placement Coordinator, 817-594-5471. ***Services:*** job fairs, resume preparation, career counseling, careers library, job bank, job interviews.
EXPENSES FOR 1996–97 Area resident tuition: $576 full-time. State resident tuition: $800 full-time. Nonresident tuition: $2560 full-time. Part-time tuition per semester ranges from $60 to $198 for area residents, $81 to $275 for state residents, $240 to $880 for nonresidents. Part-time mandatory fees per semester range from $45 to $110. Full-time mandatory fees: $360. College room and board: $2646.
FINANCIAL AID ***College-administered undergrad aid 1995–96:*** 85 need-based scholarships (average $400), 136 non-need scholarships (average $721), short-term loans (average $246), low-interest long-term loans from external sources (average $1673), 31 Federal Work-Study (averaging $1224). ***Required forms:*** institutional, FAFSA. ***Priority deadline:*** 6/1. ***Waivers:*** full or partial for employees or children of employees and senior citizens. ***Average indebtedness of graduates:*** $2493.
APPLYING Open admission. ***Option:*** early entrance. ***Required:*** TASP. ***Recommended:*** SAT I or ACT, TOEFL for international students. Test scores used for counseling/placement. ***Application deadline:*** rolling. ***Notification:*** continuous.
APPLYING/TRANSFER ***Entrance:*** noncompetitive. ***Application deadline:*** rolling. ***Notification:*** continuous.
CONTACT Mr. Duane Durrett, Director of Admissions, Weatherford College, Weatherford, TX 76086-5699, 817-594-5471 Ext. 249. ***Fax:*** 817-594-0627. College video available.

WESTERN TEXAS COLLEGE
Snyder, Texas

UG Enrollment: 1,200	**Tuition & Fees (Area Res): $626**
Application Deadline: rolling	**Room & Board: $2090**

GENERAL State and locally supported, 2-year, coed. Part of Texas Higher Education Coordinating Board. Awards transfer associate, terminal associate degrees. Founded 1969. ***Setting:*** 165-acre small-town campus. ***Endowment:*** $653,379. ***Research spending 1994–95:*** $27,127. ***Educational spending 1994–95:*** $2575 per undergrad. ***Total enrollment:*** 1,200. ***Faculty:*** 55 (45 full-time, 10 part-time); student-faculty ratio is 20:1. ***Notable Alumni:*** Paul Pressey, professional basketball player; Clarke Dennis, professional golfer; Mike Standly, professional golfer; Dave Appleton, model and world champion cowboy; Steve Carrikes, Texas state senator; Rode Walker, owner of Rode Walker Sportswear Manufacturing.
ENROLLMENT PROFILE 1,200 students from 11 states and territories, 5 other countries. 38% women, 62% men, 54% part-time, 95% state residents, 6% transferred in, 1% international, 45% 25 or older, 1% Native American, 13% Hispanic, 11% African American, 1% Asian American. ***Most popular recent majors:*** business administration/commerce/management, criminal justice.
FIRST-YEAR CLASS 664 total. Of the students who applied, 100% were accepted, 67% of whom enrolled. 15% from top 10% of their high school class, 35% from top quarter, 55% from top half.
ACADEMIC PROGRAM Core, honor code. Calendar: semesters. Academic remediation for entering students, services for LD students, advanced placement, self-designed majors, summer session for credit, part-time degree program (daytime, evenings, summer), adult/continuing education programs, internships.
GENERAL DEGREE REQUIREMENTS 62 semester hours; computer course for all transfer associate degree students; internship (some majors).
MAJORS Accounting, agricultural education, agricultural sciences, art education, art/fine arts, automotive technologies, business administration/commerce/management, communication, computer science, computer technologies, corrections, criminal justice, education, journalism, landscape architecture/design, law enforcement/police sciences, liberal arts/general studies, marketing/retailing/merchandising, parks management, practical nursing, secretarial studies/office management, welding technology.
LIBRARY Western Texas College Resource Center with 43,000 books, 3,500 microform titles, 127 periodicals. Acquisition spending 1994–95: $11,418.
COMPUTERS ON CAMPUS 40 computers for student use in library. Staffed computer lab on campus. Academic computing expenditure 1994–95: $24,938.

COLLEGE LIFE Drama-theater group, choral group, student-run newspaper. 25% vote in student government elections. *Student services:* personal-psychological counseling. *Campus security:* 24-hour emergency response devices and patrols.
HOUSING 232 college housing spaces available; all were occupied 1995–96. On-campus residence required in freshman year. *Options:* coed, international student housing available. Resident assistants live in dorms.
ATHLETICS Member NJCAA. *Intercollegiate:* basketball W(s), golf M(s). *Intramural:* basketball, bowling, football, racquetball, soccer, softball, swimming and diving, tennis, volleyball, weight lifting. *Contact:* Mr. Milton Ham, Athletic Director, 915-573-8511 Ext. 285.
CAREER PLANNING *Placement office:* 3 full-time staff. *Director:* Dr. Mary Hood, Director of Counseling Services, 915-573-8511 Ext. 274. *Services:* resume preparation, career counseling, careers library.
EXPENSES FOR 1995–96 Area resident tuition: $480 full-time. State resident tuition: $600 full-time. Nonresident tuition: $720 full-time. Part-time tuition per semester ranges from $25 to $165 for area residents, $28 to $220 for state residents, $200 to $275 for nonresidents. Part-time mandatory fees per semester range from $19 to $59. Full-time mandatory fees: $146. College room and board: $2090.
FINANCIAL AID *College-administered undergrad aid 1995–96:* 50 need-based scholarships (averaging $300), 150 non-need scholarships (averaging $300), short-term loans (averaging $200), Federal Work-Study, 20 part-time jobs. *Required forms:* institutional, FAFSA. *Priority deadline:* 7/15. *Waivers:* full or partial for senior citizens.
APPLYING Open admission. *Options:* early entrance, deferred entrance. *Required:* school transcript, TASP. *Required for some:* ACT, TOEFL for international students. Test scores used for counseling/placement. *Application deadline:* rolling. *Notification:* continuous.
APPLYING/TRANSFER *Required:* college transcript, minimum 2.0 college GPA. *Recommended:* high school transcript. *Application deadline:* rolling. *Notification:* continuous.
CONTACT Dr. Duane Hood, Dean of Student Services, Western Texas College, Snyder, TX 79549-9502, 915-573-8511 Ext. 204.

WHARTON COUNTY JUNIOR COLLEGE
Wharton, Texas

UG Enrollment: 3,720	Tuition & Fees (Area Res): $864
Application Deadline: 8/15	Room & Board: $2100

GENERAL State and locally supported, 2-year, coed. Part of Texas Higher Education Coordinating Board. Awards transfer associate, terminal associate degrees. Founded 1946. *Setting:* 90-acre rural campus with easy access to Houston. *Total enrollment:* 3,720. *Faculty:* 200 (100 full-time, 100 part-time).
ENROLLMENT PROFILE 3,720 students from 8 states and territories, 5 other countries. 63% women, 37% men, 40% part-time, 98% state residents, 5% live on campus, 16% transferred in, 1% international, 38% 25 or older, 16% Hispanic, 11% African American, 1% Asian American.
FIRST-YEAR CLASS 900 total. Of the students who applied, 100% were accepted. 5% from top 10% of their high school class, 50% from top half.
ACADEMIC PROGRAM Core. Calendar: semesters. Academic remediation for entering students, advanced placement, self-designed majors, summer session for credit, part-time degree program (daytime, evenings, summer), adult/continuing education programs.
GENERAL DEGREE REQUIREMENT 62 semester hours.
MAJORS Agricultural sciences, art/fine arts, automotive technologies, behavioral sciences, biology/biological sciences, business administration/commerce/management, chemistry, computer science, criminal justice, data processing, dental services, drafting and design, electrical and electronics technologies, (pre)engineering sequence, English, farm and ranch management, mathematics, medical laboratory technology, medical records services, music, nursing, ornamental horticulture, physical education, physical therapy, radiological technology, secretarial studies/office management, Spanish, speech/rhetoric/public address/debate, theater arts/drama.
LIBRARY J. M. Hodges Library with 51,478 books, 536 periodicals, 1,352 records, tapes, and CDs.
COMPUTERS ON CAMPUS 250 computers for student use in computer center, department labs provide access to main academic computer, off-campus computing facilities. Staffed computer lab on campus provides training in use of computers, software.
COLLEGE LIFE Drama-theater group. *Student services:* personal-psychological counseling.
HOUSING 135 college housing spaces available; all were occupied 1995–96. No special consideration for freshman housing applicants. Off-campus living permitted. *Option:* single-sex housing available. Resident assistants live in dorms.
ATHLETICS Member NJCAA. *Intercollegiate:* tennis M(s)/W(s), volleyball W(s).
CAREER PLANNING *Service:* career counseling.
EXPENSES FOR 1996–97 Area resident tuition: $834 full-time, $27 per semester hour part-time. State resident tuition: $1423 full-time, $46 per semester hour part-time. Nonresident tuition: $2632 full-time, $85 per semester hour part-time. Part-time mandatory fees: $30 per semester. Full-time mandatory fees: $30. College room and board: $2100.
FINANCIAL AID *College-administered undergrad aid 1995–96:* 725 need-based scholarships (average $356), 560 non-need scholarships (average $150), low-interest long-term loans from college funds (average $1000), loans from external sources (average $2500), Federal Work-Study, part-time jobs. *Required forms:* FAFSA; required for some: state. *Priority deadline:* 7/15.
APPLYING Open admission. *Required:* school transcript, minimum 2.0 GPA, SAT I or ACT, TASP. *Recommended:* 3 years of high school math and science, TOEFL for international students. Test scores used for counseling/placement. *Application deadline:* 8/15.
APPLYING/TRANSFER *Entrance:* noncompetitive. *Application deadline:* 8/15.
CONTACT Mr. Albert Barnes, Dean of Admissions and Registration, Wharton County Junior College, Wharton, TX 77488-3298, 409-532-4560 Ext. 6381.

UTAH

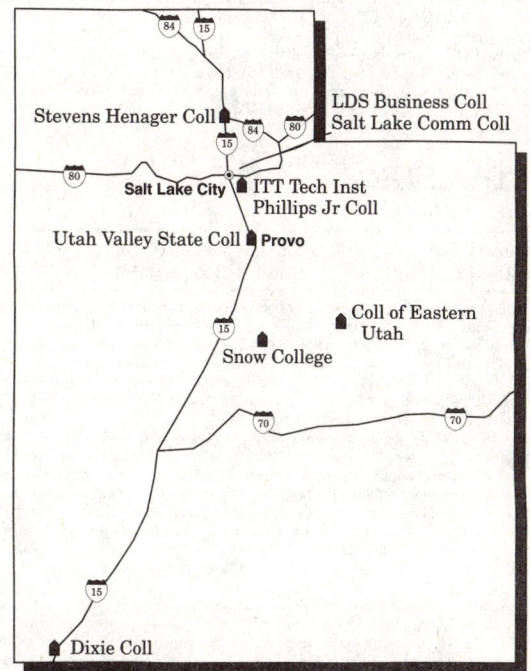

COLLEGE OF EASTERN UTAH
Price, Utah

UG Enrollment: 3,067	Tuition & Fees (UT Res): $1249
Application Deadline: rolling	Room & Board: $2220

GENERAL State-supported, 2-year, coed. Part of Utah System of Higher Education. Awards transfer associate, terminal associate degrees. Founded 1937. *Setting:* 15-acre small-town campus. *Endowment:* $6.4 million. *Total enrollment:* 3,067. *Faculty:* 122 (77 full-time, 45 part-time); student-faculty ratio is 30:1.
ENROLLMENT PROFILE 3,067 students: 48% women, 51% part-time, 98% state residents, 5% transferred in, 1% international, 36% 25 or older, 9% Native American, 3% Hispanic, 1% African American, 1% Asian American. *Most popular recent major:* liberal arts/general studies.
FIRST-YEAR CLASS 1,170 total; 1,500 applied, 100% were accepted, 78% of whom enrolled.
ACADEMIC PROGRAM Core, general education curriculum, honor code. Calendar: quarters. Academic remediation for entering students, English as a second language program offered during academic year, services for LD students, advanced placement, summer session for credit, part-time degree program (daytime, evenings, summer), adult/continuing education programs, co-op programs.
GENERAL DEGREE REQUIREMENTS 93 credits; 1 math course; computer course.
MAJORS Automotive technologies, business administration/commerce/management, carpentry, child care/child and family studies, computer graphics, construction technologies, cosmetology, early childhood education, (pre)engineering sequence, liberal arts/general studies, machine and tool technologies, mining technology, nursing, secretarial studies/office management, welding technology.
LIBRARY 34,413 books, 29 microform titles, 212 periodicals, 812 records, tapes, and CDs. Acquisition spending 1994–95: $18,799.
COMPUTERS ON CAMPUS 150 computers for student use in computer labs, library provide access to Internet. Staffed computer lab on campus.
COLLEGE LIFE Drama-theater group, choral group, student-run newspaper. *Social organizations:* 20 open to all. *Student services:* personal-psychological counseling, women's center. *Campus security:* 24-hour patrols, late-night transport-escort service.
HOUSING 388 college housing spaces available; all were occupied 1995–96. No special consideration for freshman housing applicants. Off-campus living permitted. *Options:* coed, single-sex housing available. Resident assistants live in dorms.
ATHLETICS Member NJCAA. *Intercollegiate:* baseball M(s), basketball M(s)/W(s), volleyball W(s). *Intramural:* basketball, golf, racquetball, soccer, tennis. *Contact:* Mr. Curt Jenson, Athletic Director, 801-637-2120 Ext. 5361.
CAREER PLANNING *Placement office:* 5 full-time staff. *Director:* Ms. Mary Helen Powell, Director of Testing, Advising and Placement, 801-637-2120 Ext. 5324. *Services:* resume preparation, resume referral, career counseling, careers library.
EXPENSES FOR 1995–96 *Application fee:* $20. State resident tuition: $964 full-time. Nonresident tuition: $4033 full-time. Part-time tuition per quarter ranges from $63.25 to $297.85 for state residents, $247 to $1245 for nonresidents. Part-time mandatory fees per quarter range from $9.50 to $95. Full-time mandatory fees: $285. College room and board: $2220 (minimum).
FINANCIAL AID *College-administered undergrad aid 1995–96:* 300 need-based scholarships (average $805), 1,127 non-need scholarships (average $1093), short-term loans (average $335), low-interest long-term loans from external sources (average $3176), Federal

College of Eastern Utah (continued)
Work-Study. ***Required forms:*** institutional, FAFSA; accepted: CSS Financial Aid PROFILE. ***Priority deadline:*** 4/15. ***Waivers:*** full or partial for employees or children of employees and senior citizens.
APPLYING Open admission. ***Option:*** early entrance. ***Required:*** SAT I or ACT, TOEFL for international students, ACT ASSET or ABLE. Test scores used for counseling/placement. ***Application deadline:*** rolling.
APPLYING/TRANSFER ***Application deadline:*** rolling. ***Contact:*** Mrs. Jan L. Young, Director of Admissions and Records, 801-637-2120 Ext. 5205.
CONTACT Mrs. Jan L. Young, Director of Admissions and Records, College of Eastern Utah, Price, UT 84501-2699, 801-637-2120 Ext. 5205. ***Fax:*** 801-637-4102. ***E-mail:*** jyoung@cc.ceu.edu.

DIXIE COLLEGE
St. George, Utah

UG Enrollment: 2,902	Tuition & Fees (UT Res): $1331
Application Deadline: rolling	Room & Board: $2649

GENERAL State-supported, 2-year, coed. Awards certificates, transfer associate, terminal associate degrees. Founded 1911. ***Setting:*** 60-acre small-town campus. ***Endowment:*** $4.9 million. ***Total enrollment:*** 2,902. ***Faculty:*** 152 (78 full-time, 86% with terminal degrees, 74 part-time); student-faculty ratio is 21:1. ***Notable Alumni:*** M. Anthony Burns, president and CEO of Ryder Systems; Nolan Archibald, president and CEO of Black and Decker; M. Kenneth Bowler, vice president of Pfiser Corporation; Garth Milne, vice president of Motorola Corporation.
ENROLLMENT PROFILE 2,902 students from 32 states and territories, 8 other countries. 52% women, 48% men, 23% part-time, 92% state residents, 3% transferred in, 1% international, 16% 25 or older, 2% Native American, 2% Hispanic, 1% African American, 2% Asian American. ***Areas of study chosen:*** 26% liberal arts/general studies, 18% vocational and home economics, 13% business management and administrative services, 9% education, 7% health professions and related sciences, 3% computer and information sciences, 3% foreign language and literature, 3% premed, 3% psychology, 2% biological and life sciences, 2% communications and journalism, 2% engineering and applied sciences, 2% fine arts, 2% performing arts, 2% social sciences, 1% agriculture, 1% English language/literature/letters, 1% predentistry. ***Most popular recent majors:*** liberal arts/general studies, education, business administration/commerce/management.
FIRST-YEAR CLASS 1,160 total; 1,674 applied, 100% were accepted, 69% of whom enrolled. 10% from top 10% of their high school class, 28% from top quarter, 52% from top half.
ACADEMIC PROGRAM Core, general education/vocational curriculum, honor code. Calendar: quarters. 687 courses offered in 1995–96. Academic remediation for entering students, English as a second language program offered during academic year and summer, services for LD students, advanced placement, tutorials, honors program, summer session for credit, part-time degree program (daytime, evenings), adult/continuing education programs, co-op programs.
GENERAL DEGREE REQUIREMENTS 96 credits; 5 credits of math/science; computer course.
MAJORS Accounting, agricultural sciences, aircraft and missile maintenance, architectural technologies, art/fine arts, automotive technologies, aviation administration, aviation technology, biology/biological sciences, botany/plant sciences, business administration/commerce/management, carpentry, chemical engineering technology, chemistry, child care/child and family studies, communication, computer information systems, computer science, construction technologies, consumer services, criminal justice, dance, dental services, drafting and design, early childhood education, economics, education, electrical and electronics technologies, elementary education, emergency medical technology, engineering (general), (pre)engineering sequence, English, environmental sciences, family and consumer studies, family services, fashion merchandising, flight training, food sciences, food services management, forestry, French, geography, geology, German, graphic arts, health science, history, home economics, hotel and restaurant management, humanities, interior design, liberal arts/general studies, library science, marketing/retailing/merchandising, mathematics, mechanical engineering technology, medical technology, music, natural sciences, nursing, nutrition, pharmacy/pharmaceutical sciences, philosophy, physical education, physical sciences, physical therapy, physics, plumbing, political science/government, psychology, range management, respiratory therapy, Russian, science, secretarial studies/office management, social science, sociology, solar technologies, Spanish, speech/rhetoric/public address/debate, theater arts/drama, tourism and travel, veterinary sciences, wildlife management, zoology.
LIBRARY Val A. Browning Library with 61,085 books, 15,536 microform titles, 329 periodicals, 6 on-line bibliographic services, 35 CD-ROMs, 2,398 records, tapes, and CDs. Acquisition spending 1994–95: $47,950.
COMPUTERS ON CAMPUS 450 computers for student use in computer labs, learning resource center, resource center, business department, classrooms, library, student center provide access to off-campus computing facilities, e-mail, on-line services, Internet. Staffed computer lab on campus provides training in use of computers, software.
COLLEGE LIFE Orientation program (2 days, no cost, parents included). Drama-theater group, choral group, student-run newspaper, radio station. ***Social organizations:*** 8 open to all. ***Most popular organizations:*** Dixie Spirit, Outdoors Club, Association of Women Students, Forensics. ***Major annual events:*** Homecoming, D-Week, Student Orientation Week. ***Student services:*** health clinic, personal-psychological counseling. ***Campus security:*** 24-hour patrols.
HOUSING 256 college housing spaces available. No special consideration for freshman housing applicants. Off-campus living permitted. ***Options:*** coed (1 building), single-sex (1 building) housing available. Resident assistants live in dorms.
ATHLETICS Member NJCAA. ***Intercollegiate:*** baseball M(s), basketball M(s)/W(s), football M(s), softball W(s), volleyball W(s). ***Intramural:*** basketball, football, golf, soccer, softball, tennis, volleyball. ***Contact:*** Dr. Karl Brooks, Athletic Director, 801-652-7555.
CAREER PLANNING ***Placement office:*** 2 full-time, 1 part-time staff; $35,666 operating expenditure 1994–95. ***Director:*** Ms. Virginia B. Woodward, Director of Planning and Placement Services, 801-652-7736. ***Services:*** job fairs, resume preparation, career counseling, careers library, job interviews.
EXPENSES FOR 1996–97 ***Application fee:*** $25. State resident tuition: $1040 full-time, $29 per quarter hour part-time. Nonresident tuition: $4548 full-time, $126 per quarter hour part-time. Full-time mandatory fees: $291. College room and board: $2649. College room only: $1050.
FINANCIAL AID ***College-administered undergrad aid 1995–96:*** 333 need-based scholarships (average $500), 500 non-need scholarships (average $900), short-term loans (average $600), 100 Federal Work-Study (averaging $1000), 250 part-time jobs. ***Required forms for some financial aid applicants:*** state; accepted: CSS Financial Aid PROFILE, FAFSA. ***Priority deadline:*** 4/15. ***Payment plan:*** deferred payment. ***Waivers:*** full or partial for employees or children of employees and senior citizens. ***Notification:*** 6/1.
APPLYING Open admission. ***Options:*** early entrance, deferred entrance, midyear entrance. ***Required:*** school transcript, TOEFL for international students. ***Recommended:*** SAT I or ACT, CPT. Test scores used for counseling/placement. ***Application deadline:*** rolling.
APPLYING/TRANSFER ***Required:*** college transcript, minimum 2.0 college GPA. ***Entrance:*** noncompetitive. ***Application deadline:*** rolling.
CONTACT Ms. Darla Rollins, Admissions Coordinator, Dixie College, St. George, UT 84770-3876, 801-652-7706. ***E-mail:*** roos@cc.dixie.edu. College video available.

ITT TECHNICAL INSTITUTE
Murray, Utah

UG Enrollment: 540	Tuition: $15,599/deg prog
Application Deadline: rolling	Room & Board: N/Avail

GENERAL Proprietary, primarily 2-year, coed. Part of ITT Educational Services, Inc. Awards terminal associate, bachelor's degrees. Founded 1984. ***Setting:*** 3-acre suburban campus with easy access to Salt Lake City. ***Total enrollment:*** 540. ***Faculty:*** 30 (24 full-time, 6 part-time); student-faculty ratio is 25:1. ***Notable Alumni:*** Lance Little, draftsman; Bart Burnside, drafter/designer; Robert Horn, designer/drafter; Jason Anderson, electronics technician; James Morrison, electronics instrumentation.
ENROLLMENT PROFILE 540 students from 5 states and territories. 15% women, 0% part-time, 95% state residents, 0% transferred in, 0% international, 48% 25 or older, 5% Native American, 5% Hispanic, 2% African American, 3% Asian American. ***Areas of study chosen:*** 100% engineering and applied sciences. ***Most popular recent major:*** electronics engineering technology.
FIRST-YEAR CLASS 284 total; 324 applied, 98% were accepted, 81% of whom enrolled. 5% from top 10% of their high school class, 15% from top quarter, 25% from top half.
ACADEMIC PROGRAM Core, honor code. Calendar: quarters. 83 courses offered in 1995–96. Academic remediation for entering students, summer session for credit.
GENERAL DEGREE REQUIREMENTS 91 credit hours for associate, 194 credit hours for bachelor's; computer course.
MAJORS Drafting and design, electronics engineering technology (B), industrial design (B).
LIBRARY Learning Resource Center with 1,700 books, 36 periodicals, 2 CD-ROMs.
COMPUTERS ON CAMPUS 65 computers for student use in computer center, learning resource center, student center. Staffed computer lab on campus provides training in use of computers, software.
COLLEGE LIFE ***Campus security:*** 24-hour emergency response devices.
HOUSING College housing not available.
CAREER PLANNING ***Placement office:*** 2 full-time staff. ***Director:*** Ms. Anita J. Booker, Director of Placement, 800-365-2136. ***Services:*** job fairs, resume preparation, resume referral, career counseling, careers library, job interviews. Students must register freshman year.
EXPENSES FOR 1995–96 ***Application fee:*** $100. Tuition per degree program ranges from $15,599 to $17,690 for associate degree, $25,800 to $31,645 for bachelor's degree.
FINANCIAL AID ***College-administered undergrad aid 1995–96:*** need-based scholarships, low-interest long-term loans from external sources, Federal Work-Study. ***Required forms:*** institutional, FAFSA; accepted: CSS Financial Aid PROFILE. ***Priority deadline:*** 9/15. ***Waivers:*** full or partial for employees or children of employees.
APPLYING ***Option:*** deferred entrance. ***Required:*** CPAt. Test scores used for admission. ***Application deadline:*** rolling.
APPLYING/TRANSFER ***Application deadline:*** rolling. ***Contact:*** Mr. Stephen Backman, Director of Education, 801-263-3313.
CONTACT Mr. David Prince, Director of Recruitment, ITT Technical Institute, Murray, UT 84123-2500, 801-263-3313 or toll-free 800-365-2136 (out-of-state). College video available.

LATTER-DAY SAINTS BUSINESS COLLEGE
Utah—See LDS Business College

LDS BUSINESS COLLEGE
Salt Lake City, Utah

UG Enrollment: 830	Tuition & Fees: $1785
Application Deadline: rolling	Room Only: $1422

GENERAL Independent, 2-year, coed, affiliated with Church of Jesus Christ of Latter-day Saints. Part of Latter-day Saints Church Educational System. Awards certificates, transfer associate, terminal associate degrees. Founded 1886. ***Setting:*** 10-acre urban campus. ***Total enrollment:*** 830. ***Faculty:*** 81 (20 full-time, 100% with terminal degrees, 61 part-time).
ENROLLMENT PROFILE 830 students: 73% women, 27% men, 23% part-time, 65% state residents, 15% live on campus, 50% have need-based financial aid, 20% have non-need-based financial aid, 15% international, 28% 25 or older, 1% Native American, 3% Hispanic, 1% African American, 1% Asian American. ***Areas of study chosen:*** 72% business management and administrative services, 15% liberal arts/general studies, 8% computer and information sciences, 5% health professions and related sciences. ***Most popular recent majors:*** accounting, liberal arts/general studies, secretarial studies/office management.
FIRST-YEAR CLASS 330 total; 370 applied, 96% were accepted, 93% of whom enrolled.
ACADEMIC PROGRAM Core, interdisciplinary curriculum, honor code. Calendar: quarters. 198 courses offered in 1995–96. Academic remediation for entering students, advanced placement, summer session for credit, part-time degree program (daytime, evenings), adult/continuing education programs, co-op programs and internships.

GENERAL DEGREE REQUIREMENTS 102 credits; 1 math course; computer course; internship (some majors).
MAJORS Accounting, business administration/commerce/management, computer information systems, fashion merchandising, interior design, legal secretarial studies, liberal arts/general studies, marketing/retailing/merchandising, medical assistant technologies, medical records services, medical secretarial studies, retail management, secretarial studies/office management.
LIBRARY LDS Business College Library with 5,000 books, 130 periodicals, 694 records, tapes, and CDs.
COMPUTERS ON CAMPUS Student rooms linked to a campus network. 210 computers for student use in computer center, computer labs, classrooms, dorms provide access to e-mail, on-line services, Internet. Staffed computer lab on campus provides training in use of computers, software.
COLLEGE LIFE Orientation program (2 days, no cost). Choral group. 40% vote in student government elections. ***Social organizations:*** 1 local sorority; 4% of eligible women are members. ***Most popular organizations:*** International Students Club, Latter-Day Saints Student Association. ***Student services:*** personal-psychological counseling. ***Campus security:*** 24-hour emergency response devices, controlled dormitory access.
HOUSING 112 college housing spaces available; all were occupied 1995–96. No special consideration for freshman housing applicants. Off-campus living permitted. ***Option:*** single-sex housing available. Resident assistants live in dorms.
CAREER PLANNING ***Placement office:*** 1 full-time staff. ***Director:*** Ms. Karen Peterson, Director of Career Services and Cooperative Education, 801-524-8170. ***Services:*** resume preparation, resume referral, career counseling, careers library, job bank, job interviews.
AFTER GRADUATION 98% of class of 1994 had job offers within 6 months.
EXPENSES FOR 1995–96 ***Application fee:*** $20. Tuition: $1785 (minimum) full-time, $52 per credit hour (minimum) part-time. Tuition for non-church members: $2355 full-time, $65 per credit hour part-time. College room only: $1422.
FINANCIAL AID ***College-administered undergrad aid 1995–96:*** need-based scholarships, non-need scholarships, part-time jobs. ***Acceptable forms:*** institutional, FAFSA. ***Priority deadline:*** 8/1. ***Payment plan:*** installment.
APPLYING Open admission. ***Options:*** early entrance, deferred entrance, midyear entrance. ***Required:*** school transcript, interview, TOEFL for international students, Michigan Test of English Language Proficiency. ***Recommended:*** ACT. Test scores used for counseling/placement. ***Application deadline:*** rolling.
APPLYING/TRANSFER ***Required:*** high school transcript, interview. ***Entrance:*** noncompetitive. ***Application deadline:*** rolling. ***Contact:*** Mr. Kevin W. Swenson, Dean of Students, 801-524-8142.
CONTACT Mr. Kevin W. Swenson, Dean of Students, LDS Business College, 411 East South Temple Street, Salt Lake City, UT 84111-1392, 801-524-8142 or toll-free 800-999-5767. ***Fax:*** 801-524-1900. College video and electronic viewbook available.

PHILLIPS JUNIOR COLLEGE
Salt Lake City, Utah

UG Enrollment: 275	**Tuition: $5875/deg prog**
Application Deadline: rolling	**Room & Board: N/Avail**

GENERAL Proprietary, 2-year, coed. Awards certificates, terminal associate degrees. Founded 1989. ***Total enrollment:*** 275. ***Faculty:*** 35.
ENROLLMENT PROFILE 275 students.
FIRST-YEAR CLASS Of the students who applied, 85% were accepted, 80% of whom enrolled.
ACADEMIC PROGRAM Calendar: quarters.
GENERAL DEGREE REQUIREMENTS 90 quarter credit hours; 1 math course; computer course.
MAJORS Accounting, business administration/commerce/management, computer information systems, medical assistant technologies, paralegal studies, secretarial studies/office management, tourism and travel.
HOUSING College housing not available.
EXPENSES FOR 1996–97 ***Application fee:*** $25. Tuition per degree program ranges from $5875 to $10,505.
APPLYING ***Required:*** school transcript. ***Recommended:*** SAT I or ACT. ***Application deadline:*** rolling.
APPLYING/TRANSFER ***Required:*** college transcript. ***Recommended:*** standardized test scores. ***Application deadline:*** rolling.
CONTACT Ms. Gail Benjamin, Director of Admissions, Phillips Junior College, Salt Lake City, UT 84106, 801-485-0221.

SALT LAKE COMMUNITY COLLEGE
Salt Lake City, Utah

UG Enrollment: 19,568	**Tuition & Fees (UT Res): $1446**
Application Deadline: rolling	**Room & Board: N/Avail**

GENERAL State-supported, 2-year, coed. Part of Utah System of Higher Education. Awards certificates, diplomas, transfer associate, terminal associate degrees. Founded 1948. ***Setting:*** 114-acre urban campus. ***Total enrollment:*** 19,568. ***Faculty:*** 1,042 (312 full-time, 15% with terminal degrees, 730 part-time); student-faculty ratio is 20:1.
ENROLLMENT PROFILE 19,568 students from 28 states and territories, 33 other countries. 48% women, 52% men, 63% part-time, 97% state residents, 12% transferred in, 2% international, 39% 25 or older, 1% Native American, 4% Hispanic, 1% African American, 3% Asian American. ***Areas of study chosen:*** 42% liberal arts/general studies, 16% business management and administrative services, 12% vocational and home economics, 7% health professions and related sciences, 4% education, 3% computer and information sciences, 3% engineering and applied sciences, 2% social sciences, 1% architecture, 1% biological and life sciences, 1% communications and journalism, 1% English language/literature/letters. ***Most popular recent majors:*** liberal arts/general studies, business administration/commerce/management.
FIRST-YEAR CLASS 6,151 total; 7,315 applied, 100% were accepted, 84% of whom enrolled.
ACADEMIC PROGRAM Core. Calendar: quarters. 1,640 courses offered in 1995–96. Academic remediation for entering students, English as a second language program offered during academic year, services for LD students, advanced placement, self-designed majors, honors program, summer session for credit, part-time degree program (daytime, evenings, summer), adult/continuing education programs, co-op programs. ROTC: Army (c), Air Force (c).
GENERAL DEGREE REQUIREMENTS 96 credits; math/science requirements vary according to program; computer course for most majors; internship (some majors).
MAJORS Accounting, aircraft and missile maintenance, architectural technologies, art/fine arts, automotive technologies, aviation technology, biology/biological sciences, business administration/commerce/management, carpentry, child care/child and family studies, civil engineering technology, commercial art, communication, computer graphics, computer information systems, computer programming, computer science, computer technologies, construction technologies, cosmetology, criminal justice, culinary arts, data processing, deaf interpreter training, dental services, drafting and design, early childhood education, education, electrical and electronics technologies, electrical engineering technology, electronics engineering technology, elementary education, engineering (general), engineering design, (pre)engineering sequence, engineering technology, English, environmental sciences, finance/banking, flight training, geography, graphic arts, health science, heating/refrigeration/air conditioning, humanities, human services, illustration, industrial administration, industrial and heavy equipment maintenance, international studies, law enforcement/police sciences, liberal arts/general studies, machine and tool technologies, manufacturing technology, marketing/retailing/merchandising, mechanical engineering technology, medical assistant technologies, medical laboratory technology, medical secretarial studies, nursing, occupational therapy, operating room technology, paralegal studies, physical sciences, plumbing, practical nursing, radiological technology, retail management, secretarial studies/office management, social science, surveying technology, transportation technologies, welding technology.
LIBRARY Markosian Library with 61,497 books, 82 microform titles, 653 periodicals, 2 on-line bibliographic services, 21 CD-ROMs, 10,907 records, tapes, and CDs.
COMPUTERS ON CAMPUS Computer purchase plan available. 890 computers for student use in various buildings, library. Staffed computer lab on campus provides training in use of computers, software.
COLLEGE LIFE Drama-theater group, choral group, marching band, student-run newspaper. ***Social organizations:*** 50 open to all; 1 local fraternity, 1 local sorority, coed fraternity. ***Most popular organizations:*** LDSSA, VICA, DECS, PBL. ***Student services:*** health clinic, women's center. ***Campus security:*** 24-hour emergency response devices and patrols, late-night transport-escort service.
HOUSING College housing not available.
ATHLETICS Member NJCAA. ***Intercollegiate:*** basketball M(s)/W(s), softball M, volleyball W. ***Intramural:*** basketball, cross-country running, football, golf, racquetball, riflery, rugby, skiing (downhill), soccer, softball, table tennis (Ping-Pong), tennis, volleyball, weight lifting. ***Contact:*** Ms. Norma Carr, Athletic Director, 801-957-4083.
CAREER PLANNING ***Placement office:*** 14 full-time, 5 part-time staff. ***Director:*** Ms. Tracy Harris-Belnap, Assistant Director of Academic and Career Advising, 801-957-4206. ***Services:*** job fairs, resume preparation, resume referral, career counseling, careers library.
EXPENSES FOR 1995–96 ***Application fee:*** $20. State resident tuition: $1182 full-time, $472 per quarter part-time. Nonresident tuition: $5114 full-time, $1502 per quarter part-time. Part-time mandatory fees: $84 per quarter. Full-time mandatory fees: $264.
FINANCIAL AID ***College-administered undergrad aid 1995–96:*** 6,559 need-based scholarships (average $986), 1,089 non-need scholarships (average $857), short-term loans (average $450), low-interest long-term loans from external sources (average $2209), 124 Federal Work-Study (averaging $1715). ***Required forms:*** institutional, FAFSA; required for some: state; accepted: CSS Financial Aid PROFILE. ***Priority deadline:*** 3/1. ***Payment plan:*** installment. ***Waivers:*** full or partial for minority students and employees or children of employees. ***Average indebtedness of graduates:*** $3686.
APPLYING Open admission except for health science programs. ***Options:*** early entrance, deferred entrance, midyear entrance. ***Required:*** ACT, TOEFL for international students, CPT. ***Required for some:*** 3 years of high school math. Test scores used for counseling/placement. ***Application deadline:*** rolling.
APPLYING/TRANSFER ***Recommended:*** standardized test scores, college transcript. ***Entrance:*** noncompetitive. ***Application deadline:*** rolling. ***Contact:*** Ms. Janet Felker, Transfer Advisor, 801-957-4202.
CONTACT Ms. Amy Aldous Bergerson, Assistant Director of Admissions for School Relations, Salt Lake Community College, PO Box 30808, Salt Lake City, UT 84130-0808, 801-967-4297. ***Fax:*** 801-967-4522.

SNOW COLLEGE
Ephraim, Utah

UG Enrollment: 2,491	**Tuition & Fees (UT Res): $1221**
Application Deadline: 6/1	**Room & Board: $2800**

GENERAL State-supported, 2-year, coed. Part of Utah System of Higher Education. Awards certificates, diplomas, transfer associate degrees. Founded 1888. ***Setting:*** 50-acre rural campus. ***Research spending 1994–95:*** $9576. ***Educational spending 1994–95:*** $2151 per undergrad. ***Total enrollment:*** 2,491. ***Faculty:*** 163 (81 full-time, 35% with terminal degrees, 82 part-time); student-faculty ratio is 19:1. ***Notable Alumni:*** Dee Anderson, owner of Dee's Family Restaurant; Mac Christensen, owner of Mr. Macs clothing; Calvert Therald Larsen, veterinarian; John A. Olsen, plastic surgeon; John Frischknecht, heart specialist.
ENROLLMENT PROFILE 2,491 students from 55 states and territories, 12 other countries. 60% women, 31% part-time, 89% state residents, 25% live on campus, 4% international, 10% 25 or older, 1% Native American, 2% Hispanic, 1% African American, 3% Asian American. ***Areas of study chosen:*** 12% education, 3% business management and administrative services, 3% premed, 2% engineering and applied sciences, 2% English language/literature/letters, 2% psychology, 1% agriculture, 1% biological and life sciences, 1% computer and information sciences, 1% mathematics, 1% natural resource sciences, 1% physical sciences, 1% predentistry, 1% prelaw, 1% prevet, 1% social sciences. ***Most popular recent majors:*** elementary education, business administration/commerce/management.
FIRST-YEAR CLASS 1,182 total; 2,500 applied, 100% were accepted, 47% of whom enrolled.
ACADEMIC PROGRAM Core, interdisciplinary curriculum. Calendar: quarters. 709 courses offered in 1995–96. Academic remediation for entering students, English as a second language program offered during academic year and summer, services for LD

Snow College (continued)
students, tutorials, honors program, summer session for credit, part-time degree program (daytime, evenings, weekends, summer), external degree programs, adult/continuing education programs, co-op programs.
GENERAL DEGREE REQUIREMENTS 96 credits; 1 course in intermediate algebra.
MAJORS Accounting, agricultural business, agricultural economics, agricultural sciences, agronomy/soil and crop sciences, animal sciences, art/fine arts, automotive technologies, biology/biological sciences, botany/plant sciences, business administration/commerce/management, business education, carpentry, chemistry, child care/child and family studies, communication, computer information systems, computer science, construction management, construction technologies, criminal justice, dance, early childhood education, earth science, economics, education, electrical and electronics technologies, elementary education, engineering (general), (pre)engineering sequence, entomology, family services, farm and ranch management, forestry, French, geography, geology, history, home economics, humanities, Japanese, liberal arts/general studies, mathematics, music, music education, music history, natural resource management, natural sciences, nutrition, philosophy, physical education, physical sciences, physics, physiology, political science/government, range management, science education, secretarial studies/office management, sociology, soil conservation, Spanish, theater arts/drama, veterinary sciences, vocational education, voice, wildlife management, zoology.
LIBRARY Lucy Phillips Library with 30,904 books, 466 periodicals, 4 CD-ROMs, 698 records, tapes, and CDs. Acquisition spending 1994–95: $591,519.
COMPUTERS ON CAMPUS 160 computers for student use in computer center, computer labs, classrooms, dorms provide access to e-mail, Internet. Staffed computer lab on campus. Academic computing expenditure 1994–95: $695,741.
COLLEGE LIFE Orientation program (2 days, no cost, parents included). Drama-theater group, choral group, marching band, student-run newspaper. 35% vote in student government elections. ***Social organizations:*** 6 local sororities. ***Most popular organizations:*** Drama Club, Latter-Day Saints Singers, Dead Cats Society. ***Major annual events:*** Homecoming, Snow King/Miss Snow, Earth Day. ***Student services:*** health clinic, personal-psychological counseling. ***Campus security:*** student patrols.
HOUSING 577 college housing spaces available; all were occupied 1995–96. Off-campus living permitted. ***Options:*** coed, single-sex housing available. Resident assistants live in dorms.
ATHLETICS Member NJCAA. ***Intercollegiate:*** baseball M, basketball M(s)/W(s), football M(s), softball W, volleyball W(s). ***Intramural:*** badminton, basketball, bowling, football, racquetball, soccer, softball, tennis, volleyball, wrestling. ***Contact:*** Mr. Ken Beazer, Athletic Director, 801-283-4021 Ext. 206.
CAREER PLANNING ***Placement office:*** 4 full-time, 4 part-time staff; $161,253 operating expenditure 1994–95. ***Director:*** Ms. Mathilda Barreiro, Director, Learning Enrichment Center, 801-283-4021. ***Service:*** career counseling.
EXPENSES FOR 1995–96 ***Application fee:*** $15. State resident tuition: $948 full-time. Nonresident tuition: $4665 full-time. Part-time tuition per quarter ranges from $66 to $331 for state residents, $277 to $1455 for nonresidents. Part-time mandatory fees per quarter range from $7 to $42.50. Full-time mandatory fees: $273. College room and board: $2800.
FINANCIAL AID ***College-administered undergrad aid 1995–96:*** 748 need-based scholarships (averaging $200), 863 non-need scholarships (averaging $903), low-interest long-term loans from external sources (averaging $2625), Federal Work-Study, 175 part-time jobs. ***Required forms:*** institutional, FAFSA. ***Priority deadline:*** 7/1. ***Waivers:*** full or partial for employees or children of employees.
APPLYING Open admission. ***Options:*** early entrance, deferred entrance, midyear entrance. ***Required:*** school transcript, ACT, TOEFL for international students. ***Recommended:*** 3 years of high school math and science, some high school foreign language. Test scores used for counseling/placement. ***Application deadline:*** 6/1. ***Notification:*** continuous.
APPLYING/TRANSFER ***Application deadline:*** 6/1. ***Notification:*** continuous. ***Contact:*** Mr. Mike Anderson, Transfer Counselor, 801-283-4021 Ext. 670.
CONTACT Mr. Brach Schleuter, Coordinator of High School Relations, Snow College, Ephraim, UT 84627-1203, 801-283-4021 Ext. 228.

STEVENS HENAGER COLLEGE
Ogden, Utah

UG Enrollment: 175 | **Tuition: $12,815/deg prog**
Application Deadline: rolling | **Room & Board: N/Avail**

GENERAL Proprietary, 2-year, coed. Part of Bradford Schools, Inc. Awards terminal associate degrees. Founded 1891. ***Setting:*** 1-acre urban campus with easy access to Salt Lake City. ***Total enrollment:*** 175. ***Faculty:*** 17 (8 full-time, 9 part-time).
ENROLLMENT PROFILE 175 students from 12 states and territories, 3 other countries. 65% women, 43% part-time, 80% state residents, 5% transferred in, 50% 25 or older, 1% Native American, 4% Hispanic, 8% African American, 2% Asian American.
FIRST-YEAR CLASS 131 total. Of the students who applied, 90% were accepted, 95% of whom enrolled. 2% from top 10% of their high school class, 10% from top quarter, 68% from top half.
ACADEMIC PROGRAM Core. Calendar: quarters. Academic remediation for entering students, part-time degree program (evenings), adult/continuing education programs.
GENERAL DEGREE REQUIREMENTS 90 quarter hours; 1 math course; computer course.
MAJORS Accounting, business machine technologies, legal secretarial studies, medical secretarial studies, secretarial studies/office management.
LIBRARY 6,500 books, 35 periodicals, 100 records, tapes, and CDs.
HOUSING College housing not available.
CAREER PLANNING ***Service:*** career counseling.
EXPENSES FOR 1996–97 Tuition: $12,815 per degree program. Tuition guaranteed not to increase for student's term of enrollment.
FINANCIAL AID ***College-administered undergrad aid 1995–96:*** need-based scholarships, non-need scholarships, low-interest long-term loans from external sources, Federal Work-Study, part-time jobs. ***Required forms:*** FAFSA. ***Priority deadline:*** 7/31.
APPLYING Open admission. ***Options:*** early entrance, deferred entrance. ***Required:*** school transcript, TOEFL for international students, Wonderlic aptitude test. ***Recommended:*** 3 years of high school math and science, SAT I or ACT. Test scores used for admission and counseling/placement. ***Application deadline:*** rolling.
APPLYING/TRANSFER ***Required:*** college transcript. ***Recommended:*** 3 years of high school math and science. ***Entrance:*** noncompetitive. ***Application deadline:*** rolling.
CONTACT Admissions Office, Stevens Henager College, 2168 Washington Boulevard, Ogden, UT 84401-1420, 801-394-7791 or toll-free 800-371-7791.

UTAH VALLEY STATE COLLEGE
Orem, Utah

UG Enrollment: 14,041 | **Tuition & Fees (UT Res): $1456**
Application Deadline: rolling | **Room & Board: N/Avail**

GENERAL State-supported, primarily 2-year, coed. Part of Utah System of Higher Education. Awards certificates, diplomas, transfer associate, terminal associate, bachelor's degrees. Founded 1941. ***Setting:*** 200-acre suburban campus with easy access to Salt Lake City. ***Endowment:*** $4.4 million. ***Total enrollment:*** 14,041. ***Faculty:*** 536 (158 full-time, 378 part-time); student-faculty ratio is 22:1.
ENROLLMENT PROFILE 14,041 students from 46 states and territories, 66 other countries. 47% women, 55% part-time, 90% state residents, 7% transferred in, 2% international, 23% 25 or older, 1% Native American, 3% Hispanic, 0% African American, 2% Asian American. ***Areas of study chosen:*** 35% interdisciplinary studies, 20% business management and administrative services, 10% engineering and applied sciences, 7% health professions and related sciences, 6% education, 5% computer and information sciences, 5% fine arts, 2% biological and life sciences, 2% mathematics, 1% performing arts, 1% social sciences.
FIRST-YEAR CLASS 9,879 total. Of the students who applied, 100% were accepted.
ACADEMIC PROGRAM Honor code. Calendar: semesters. Academic remediation for entering students, English as a second language program offered during academic year and summer, services for LD students, advanced placement, honors program, summer session for credit, part-time degree program (daytime, evenings, weekends), adult/continuing education programs, co-op programs. ROTC: Army (c), Air Force (c).
GENERAL DEGREE REQUIREMENTS 64 semester hours for associate, 128 semester hours for bachelor's; computer course for business management majors.
MAJORS Accounting, automotive technologies, aviation technology, business administration/commerce/management (B), carpentry, child care/child and family studies, commercial art, computer information systems (B), construction management, construction technologies, drafting and design, early childhood education, electrical and electronics technologies (B), (pre)engineering sequence, fashion merchandising, finance/banking, fire science, graphic arts, hospitality services, hotel and restaurant management, human services, international business, legal secretarial studies, legal studies, liberal arts/general studies, machine and tool technologies, marketing/retailing/merchandising, medical secretarial studies, practical nursing, radiological technology, retail management, secretarial studies/office management, transportation technologies, welding technology.
LIBRARY 86,000 books, 3 microform titles, 486 periodicals, 10 CD-ROMs, 1,064 records, tapes, and CDs. Acquisition spending 1994–95: $161,432.
COMPUTERS ON CAMPUS 90 computers for student use in computer labs, learning resource center, library, student center provide access to main academic computer, off-campus computing facilities, e-mail, Internet. Staffed computer lab on campus provides training in use of computers, software. Academic computing expenditure 1994–95: $978,398.
COLLEGE LIFE Drama-theater group, choral group, student-run newspaper. ***Student services:*** health clinic, personal-psychological counseling. ***Campus security:*** 24-hour patrols.
HOUSING College housing not available.
ATHLETICS Member NJCAA. ***Intercollegiate:*** baseball M(s), basketball M(s)/W(s), softball W(s), tennis M(s), volleyball W(s). ***Intramural:*** basketball, bowling, cross-country running, football, golf, racquetball, skiing (downhill), soccer, tennis, volleyball, water polo, weight lifting. ***Contact:*** Mr. Michael V. Jacobsen, Director of Athletics, 801-222-8000 Ext. 8653.
CAREER PLANNING ***Placement office:*** 3 full-time, 1 part-time staff; $82,794 operating expenditure 1994–95. ***Director:*** Mr. Thomas N. Keele, Director, 801-222-8319. ***Services:*** job fairs, resume preparation, resume referral, career counseling, careers library, job bank, job interviews.
EXPENSES FOR 1995–96 ***Application fee:*** $20. State resident tuition: $1194 full-time. Nonresident tuition: $4329 full-time. Part-time tuition per semester ranges from $62.25 to $573.75 for state residents, $215 to $2080 for nonresidents. Part-time mandatory fees per semester range from $28.15 to $130.85. Full-time mandatory fees: $262.
FINANCIAL AID ***College-administered undergrad aid 1995–96:*** need-based scholarships, 499 non-need scholarships (average $693), short-term loans, low-interest long-term loans from external sources (average $2625), Federal Work-Study. ***Required forms:*** institutional, FAFSA. ***Priority deadline:*** 6/1. ***Waivers:*** full or partial for employees or children of employees and senior citizens.
APPLYING Open admission. ***Option:*** deferred entrance. ***Required:*** TOEFL for international students. ***Recommended:*** school transcript, 3 years of high school math and science, recommendations, ACT. Test scores used for counseling/placement. ***Application deadline:*** rolling.
APPLYING/TRANSFER ***Required:*** college transcript, minimum 2.0 college GPA. ***Recommended:*** standardized test scores, high school transcript, 3 years of high school math and science. ***Entrance:*** noncompetitive. ***Application deadline:*** rolling.
CONTACT Ms. Esther Webster, Registrar, Utah Valley State College, Orem, UT 84058-0001, 801-222-8461. ***E-mail:*** olsensh@uvsc.edu.

VERMONT

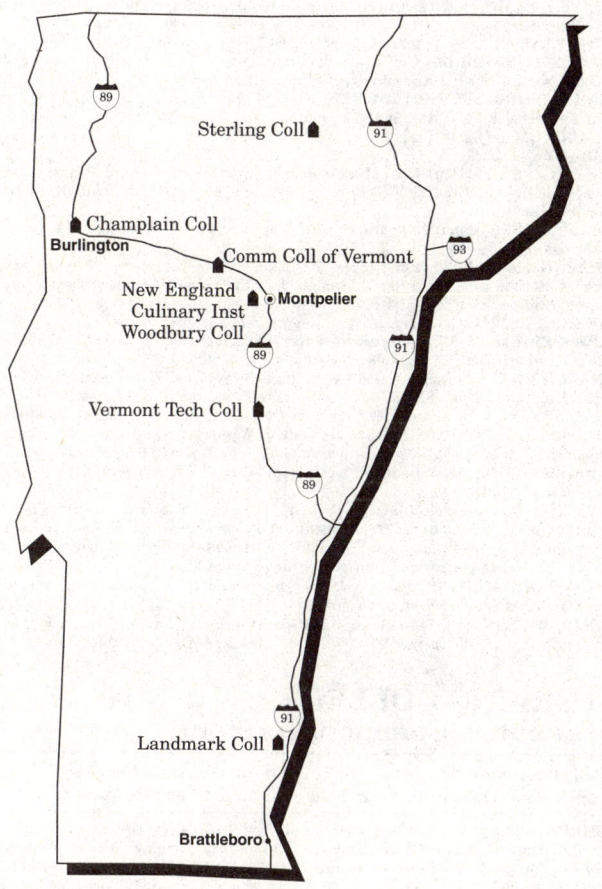

CHAMPLAIN COLLEGE
Burlington, Vermont

UG Enrollment: 2,085	Tuition & Fees: $9325
Application Deadline: rolling	Room & Board: $6285

GENERAL Independent, primarily 2-year, coed. Awards transfer associate, terminal associate, bachelor's degrees. Founded 1878. *Setting:* 19-acre suburban campus. *Endowment:* $2.8 million. *Educational spending 1994–95:* $1736 per undergrad. *Total enrollment:* 2,085. *Faculty:* 128 (60 full-time, 100% with terminal degrees, 68 part-time); student-faculty ratio is 16:1.
ENROLLMENT PROFILE 2,085 students from 19 states and territories, 19 other countries. 60% women, 40% men, 39% part-time, 86% state residents, 21% transferred in, 61% have need-based financial aid, 1% international, 32% 25 or older, 1% Native American, 0% Hispanic, 1% African American, 1% Asian American. *Areas of study chosen:* 30% business management and administrative services, 13% liberal arts/general studies, 6% education, 3% communications and journalism, 3% health professions and related sciences, 3% social sciences, 2% computer and information sciences, 1% engineering and applied sciences. *Most popular recent majors:* human services, accounting, liberal arts/general studies.
FIRST-YEAR CLASS 727 total; 1,392 applied, 91% were accepted, 57% of whom enrolled. 10% from top 10% of their high school class, 55% from top half.
ACADEMIC PROGRAM Core, career-oriented curriculum, honor code. Calendar: semesters. 336 courses offered in 1995–96. Services for LD students, advanced placement, tutorials, summer session for credit, part-time degree program (daytime, evenings, summer), adult/continuing education programs, co-op programs and internships. Off-campus study at Trinity College (VT). ROTC: Army (c).
GENERAL DEGREE REQUIREMENTS 60 credit hours for associate, 120 credit hours for bachelor's; 3 credit hours of math/science for associate degree; computer course for accounting, business management, communications, secretarial, paralegal, law enforcement, hotel-restaurant management, travel-tourism, marketing majors; internship (some majors).
MAJORS Accounting (B), business administration/commerce/management (B), communication (B), computer information systems (B), computer programming (B), criminal justice (B), data processing (B), early childhood education (B), fashion merchandising (B), hotel and restaurant management (B), human services (B), law enforcement/police sciences (B), legal secretarial studies (B), liberal arts/general studies (B), marketing/retailing/merchandising (B), medical secretarial studies (B), occupational therapy, paralegal studies (B), public relations (B), radiological technology (B), respiratory therapy (B), retail management (B), secretarial studies/office management (B), social work (B), sports administration (B), tourism and travel (B).

LIBRARY Champlain College Library plus 1 other, with 36,500 books, 1,200 microform titles, 2,000 periodicals, 12 CD-ROMs, 1,350 records, tapes, and CDs. Acquisition spending 1994–95: $113,978.
COMPUTERS ON CAMPUS Computer purchase plan available. Student rooms linked to a campus network. 150 computers for student use in computer center, computer labs, learning resource center, lab areas, classrooms, library, student center, dorms provide access to main academic computer, e-mail, on-line services, Internet. Staffed computer lab on campus provides training in use of computers, software. Academic computing expenditure 1994–95: $269,436.
COLLEGE LIFE Orientation program (2 days, no cost, parents included). Drama-theater group. *Social organizations:* 7 open to all. *Most popular organizations:* Outing Club, Community Service Dorm Programs, Theater Club, International Club, Snowboarding Club. *Major annual events:* Parents' Weekend, Basketball Classics Weekend. *Student services:* health clinic, personal-psychological counseling. *Campus security:* 24-hour emergency response devices and patrols, late-night transport-escort service.
HOUSING 575 college housing spaces available; 570 were occupied 1995–96. No special consideration for freshman housing applicants. Off-campus living permitted. *Options:* coed (13 buildings), single-sex (2 buildings), international student housing available. Resident assistants live in dorms.
ATHLETICS Member NJCAA. *Intercollegiate:* basketball M(s), soccer M(s)/W(s), softball W(s). *Intramural:* basketball, skiing (downhill), soccer, volleyball, water polo. *Contact:* Ms. Susan Rand, Athletic Director, 802-860-2748.
CAREER PLANNING *Placement office:* 5 full-time, 1 part-time staff; $258,129 operating expenditure 1994–95. *Director:* Ms. Dolly Shaw, Director of Career Planning and Personnel, 802-860-2720. *Services:* job fairs, resume preparation, resume referral, career counseling, careers library, job bank, job interviews.
AFTER GRADUATION 98% of class of 1994 had job offers within 6 months. 30% of students completing transfer associate program went directly to 4-year colleges.
ESTIMATED EXPENSES FOR 1996–97 *Application fee:* $25. Comprehensive fee of $15,610 includes full-time tuition ($9225), mandatory fees ($100), and college room and board ($6285). College room only: $3735. Part-time tuition: $280 per credit hour.
FINANCIAL AID *College-administered undergrad aid 1995–96:* 417 need-based scholarships (average $1777), 37 non-need scholarships (average $5100), low-interest long-term loans from external sources (average $4005), 256 Federal Work-Study (averaging $1535), 15 part-time jobs. *Required forms:* state, institutional, FAFSA; accepted: CSS Financial Aid PROFILE. *Priority deadline:* 5/1. *Payment plan:* installment. *Waivers:* full or partial for employees or children of employees and senior citizens. *Notification:* continuous.
APPLYING *Options:* Common Application, early entrance, deferred entrance, midyear entrance. *Required:* essay, school transcript, TOEFL for international students. *Recommended:* minimum 2.0 GPA, 1 recommendation, interview, SAT I or ACT, SAT II Subject Tests. *Required for some:* minimum 3.0 GPA, 3 years of high school math and science, SAT I or ACT, SAT II Subject Tests. Test scores used for admission and counseling/placement. *Application deadline:* rolling. *Notification:* continuous.
APPLYING/TRANSFER *Required:* essay, high school transcript, college transcript. *Recommended:* standardized test scores, 1 recommendation, interview, minimum 2.0 college GPA, minimum 2.0 high school GPA. *Required for some:* 3 years of high school math and science, minimum 3.0 college GPA, minimum 3.0 high school GPA. *Entrance:* minimally difficult. *Application deadline:* rolling. *Notification:* continuous. *Contact:* Mr. Robert McDermott, Associate Director, 802-860-2727.
CONTACT Ms. Josephine Churchill, Director of Admissions, Champlain College, 163 South Willard Street, Burlington, VT 05401, 802-860-2727 or toll-free 800-570-5858. *Fax:* 802-862-2772. *E-mail:* admission@champlain.edu. College video available.

❖ *See page 720 for a narrative description.* ❖

COMMUNITY COLLEGE OF VERMONT
Waterbury, Vermont

UG Enrollment: 3,024	Tuition & Fees (VT Res): $2907
Application Deadline: rolling	Room & Board: N/Avail

GENERAL State-supported, 2-year, coed. Part of Vermont State Colleges System. Awards certificates, transfer associate, terminal associate degrees. Founded 1970. *Setting:* rural campus. *Total enrollment:* 3,024. *Faculty:* 517 (all part-time); student-faculty ratio is 12:1.
ENROLLMENT PROFILE 3,024 students from 4 states and territories, 3 other countries. 74% women, 26% men, 89% part-time, 95% state residents, 10% transferred in, 85% have need-based financial aid, 75% 25 or older, 0% Native American, 0% Hispanic, 0% African American, 0% Asian American.
FIRST-YEAR CLASS 715 total; 715 applied, 100% were accepted, 100% of whom enrolled.
ACADEMIC PROGRAM Core, general studies curriculum. Calendar: semesters. 1,500 courses offered in 1995–96. Academic remediation for entering students, English as a second language program offered during academic year and summer, self-designed majors, summer session for credit, part-time degree program (daytime, evenings, summer), external degree programs, adult/continuing education programs, co-op programs and internships.
GENERAL DEGREE REQUIREMENTS 60 credits; internship (some majors).
MAJORS Accounting, business administration/commerce/management, child care/child and family studies, child psychology/child development, community services, computer science, education, human services, industrial engineering technology, liberal arts/general studies, manufacturing technology, secretarial studies/office management, social science, teacher aide studies.
COMPUTERS ON CAMPUS Computer purchase plan available. 100 computers for student use in class site offices provide access to main academic computer, e-mail, Internet. Staffed computer lab on campus.
HOUSING College housing not available.
CAREER PLANNING *Service:* career counseling.
EXPENSES FOR 1995–96 State resident tuition: $2730 full-time, $91 per credit part-time. Nonresident tuition: $5460 full-time, $182 per credit part-time. Part-time mandatory fees: $4 per credit. Tuition for nonresidents who are eligible for the New England Regional Student Program: $4140 full-time, $138 per credit part-time. Full-time mandatory fees: $177.
FINANCIAL AID *College-administered undergrad aid 1995–96:* 5 need-based scholarships (averaging $200), low-interest long-term loans from external sources (averag-

Peterson's Guide to Two-Year Colleges 1997

Community College of Vermont (continued)
ing $250), Federal Work-Study. ***Required forms:*** institutional, FAFSA; accepted: CSS Financial Aid PROFILE. ***Priority deadline:*** 8/15. ***Waivers:*** full or partial for employees or children of employees and senior citizens.
APPLYING Open admission. ***Application deadline:*** rolling.
APPLYING/TRANSFER ***Entrance:*** noncompetitive. ***Application deadline:*** rolling. ***Contact:*** Ms. Dianne Maccario, Assistant Director of Student Services, 802-241-3535.
CONTACT Ms. Nancy Severance, Dean of Administration, Community College of Vermont, Waterbury, VT 05676-0120, 802-241-3535.

LANDMARK COLLEGE
Putney, Vermont

UG Enrollment: 240	**Tuition & Fees: $24,450**
Application Deadline: rolling	**Room & Board: $5400**

GENERAL Independent, 2-year, coed. Awards transfer associate, terminal associate degrees (offers degree program for high-potential students with dyslexia, ADHD, or specific learning disabilities). Founded 1983. ***Setting:*** 125-acre rural campus. ***Total enrollment:*** 240. ***Faculty:*** 105 (89 full-time, 16 part-time); student-faculty ratio is 3:1.
ENROLLMENT PROFILE 240 students from 33 states and territories, 10 other countries. 30% women, 70% men, 0% part-time, 2% state residents, 87% transferred in, 40% have need-based financial aid, 0% have non-need-based financial aid, 6% international, 12% 25 or older, 0% Native American, 0% Hispanic, 4% African American, 2% Asian American.
FIRST-YEAR CLASS 87 total.
ACADEMIC PROGRAM Core, liberal arts curriculum, honor code. Calendar: semesters. Academic remediation for entering students, services for LD students, advanced placement, tutorials, honors program, summer session for credit.
GENERAL DEGREE REQUIREMENTS 60 credits; 3 credits of math; 8 credits of science.
MAJOR Liberal arts/general studies.
LIBRARY Landmark College Library with 30,908 books, 117 microform titles, 184 periodicals, 1 on-line bibliographic service, 4 CD-ROMs, 126 records, tapes, and CDs. Acquisition spending 1994–95: $52,460.
COMPUTERS ON CAMPUS Computer purchase plan available. 28 computers for student use in computer center, computer labs, classrooms, library, dorms provide access to on-line services, Internet. Staffed computer lab on campus provides training in use of computers, software. Academic computing expenditure 1994–95: $119,497.
COLLEGE LIFE Orientation program (4 days, no cost, parents included). Drama-theater group, student-run newspaper. 70% vote in student government elections. ***Most popular organizations:*** Student Board of Representatives, Student Residence Coordinators, Student Affairs Committee, International Students Organization. ***Major annual events:*** Holiday Party, Spring Fest. ***Student services:*** health clinic, personal-psychological counseling. ***Campus security:*** 24-hour emergency response devices, controlled dormitory access.
HOUSING 252 college housing spaces available; 240 were occupied 1995–96. Freshmen guaranteed college housing. On-campus residence required through sophomore year except if married. ***Option:*** coed (4 buildings) housing available. Resident assistants live in dorms.
ATHLETICS ***Intercollegiate:*** baseball M, basketball M/W, equestrian sports M/W, skiing (downhill) M/W, soccer M/W, softball W, volleyball M/W, wrestling M. ***Intramural:*** badminton, baseball, basketball, equestrian sports, golf, ice hockey, skiing (cross-country), skiing (downhill), soccer, softball, swimming and diving, table tennis (Ping-Pong), tennis, volleyball, weight lifting, wrestling. ***Contact:*** Mr. Jim Austin, Director of Student Activities and Athletics, 802-387-4767.
CAREER PLANNING ***Placement office:*** 1 full-time staff; $37,566 operating expenditure 1994–95. ***Director:*** Ms. Carole Gaddis, Director of College Placement and Career Preparation, 802-387-4767. ***Services:*** resume preparation, career counseling, careers library.
AFTER GRADUATION 100% of students completing a degree program in 1994–95 went directly on to further study.
EXPENSES FOR 1995–96 ***Application fee:*** $50. Comprehensive fee of $29,850 includes full-time tuition ($24,000), mandatory fees ($450), and college room and board ($5400). Because Landmark College serves only diagnosed learning disabled or ADHD students, tuition, fees, and related expenses may be deductible as a medical expense for federal income tax purposes.
FINANCIAL AID ***College-administered undergrad aid 1995–96:*** 42 need-based scholarships (average $6725), low-interest long-term loans from external sources (average $2457), 60 Federal Work-Study (averaging $1500), 20 part-time jobs. ***Required forms:*** CSS Financial Aid PROFILE, institutional, FAFSA; accepted: state. ***Priority deadline:*** 7/15. ***Payment plan:*** installment.
APPLYING ***Options:*** deferred entrance, midyear entrance. ***Required:*** 3 recommendations, campus interview, Wechsler Adult Intelligence Scale-Revised. Test scores used for counseling/placement. ***Application deadline:*** rolling.
APPLYING/TRANSFER ***Required:*** 3 recommendations, campus interview, college transcript. ***Entrance:*** moderately difficult. ***Application deadline:*** rolling. ***Contact:*** Mr. Francis Sopper, Director of Admissions, 802-387-6718.
CONTACT Mr. Francis Sopper, Director of Admissions, Landmark College, Putney, VT 05346, 802-387-6718. ***Fax:*** 802-387-4779. College video available.

NEW ENGLAND CULINARY INSTITUTE
Montpelier, Vermont

UG Enrollment: 450	**Tuition & Fees: $16,255**
Application Deadline: rolling	**Room & Board: $2860**

Located in Montpelier and Essex, Vermont. Offers an Associate of Occupational Studies degree in culinary arts, a bachelor's degree in service and management, and a certificate program in basic cooking skills with paid, personalized internships. There is a 7:1 student-teacher ratio (lower in production classes) in all 3 programs. Hands-on training in real food service operations. Advanced Placement available in the AOS program.

GENERAL Proprietary, primarily 2-year, specialized, coed. Awards terminal associate, bachelor's degrees. Founded 1980. ***Setting:*** small-town campus. ***Total enrollment:*** 450. ***Faculty:*** 40 (30 full-time, 10 part-time); student-faculty ratio is 7:1.
ENROLLMENT PROFILE 450 students from 35 states and territories, 5 other countries. 33% women, 67% men, 0% part-time, 0% transferred in, 4% international, 53% 25 or older, 1% Hispanic, 1% African American. ***Areas of study chosen:*** 100% vocational and home economics.
FIRST-YEAR CLASS 42 total; 182 applied, 64% were accepted, 36% of whom enrolled.
ACADEMIC PROGRAM Core. Calendar: quarters. Academic remediation for entering students, services for LD students, internships.
GENERAL DEGREE REQUIREMENTS 3684 clock hours for associate, 6387 clock hours for bachelor's; 2 math courses; computer course; internship.
MAJORS Culinary arts, food services management (B).
LIBRARY 800 books.
COMPUTERS ON CAMPUS 14 computers for student use in computer labs provide access to on-line services. Staffed computer lab on campus provides training in use of computers, software.
COLLEGE LIFE ***Social organizations:*** 2 open to all. ***Student services:*** personal-psychological counseling.
HOUSING 180 college housing spaces available; all were occupied 1995–96. Freshmen given priority for college housing. Off-campus living permitted. ***Options:*** coed, single-sex housing available. Resident assistants live in dorms.
CAREER PLANNING ***Services:*** resume preparation, career counseling.
EXPENSES FOR 1996–97 ***Application fee:*** $25. Comprehensive fee of $19,115 includes full-time tuition ($16,255) and college room and board ($2860). College room only: $1490.
FINANCIAL AID ***College-administered undergrad aid 1995–96:*** need-based scholarships (averaging $750), 48 non-need scholarships (averaging $500), short-term loans (averaging $200), low-interest long-term loans from college funds (averaging $3000), loans from external sources (averaging $2625), Federal Work-Study, part-time jobs. ***Required forms:*** CSS Financial Aid PROFILE, institutional, FAFSA; required for some: state. ***Priority deadline:*** 11/1. ***Payment plan:*** installment. ***Waivers:*** full or partial for employees or children of employees.
APPLYING ***Options:*** electronic application, deferred entrance. ***Required:*** essay, school transcript, 3 recommendations. ***Recommended:*** 3 years of high school math and science, some high school foreign language, SAT I, TOEFL for international students. Test scores used for counseling/placement. ***Application deadline:*** rolling.
APPLYING/TRANSFER ***Required:*** essay, high school transcript, 3 recommendations. ***Recommended:*** standardized test scores.
CONTACT Ms. Mary Beth Rowe, Associate Director of Admissions, New England Culinary Institute, Montpelier, VT 05602-9720, 802-223-9261. ***Fax:*** 802-223-0634.

STERLING COLLEGE
Craftsbury Common, Vermont

UG Enrollment: 82	**Comprehensive Fee: $18,582**
Application Deadline: rolling	**Room & Board: N/App**

GENERAL Independent, 2-year, specialized, coed. Awards transfer associate, terminal associate degrees. Founded 1958. ***Setting:*** 150-acre rural campus. ***Research spending 1994–95:*** $3000. ***Educational spending 1994–95:*** $5214 per undergrad. ***Total enrollment:*** 82. ***Faculty:*** 18 (8 full-time, 13% with terminal degrees, 10 part-time); student-faculty ratio is 7:1.
ENROLLMENT PROFILE 82 students from 29 states and territories. 51% women, 49% men, 0% part-time, 17% state residents, 88% live on campus, 9% transferred in, 70% have need-based financial aid, 0% international, 7% 25 or older, 0% Native American, 0% Hispanic, 1% African American, 1% Asian American. ***Areas of study chosen:*** 100% natural resource sciences. ***Most popular recent major:*** natural resource management.
FIRST-YEAR CLASS 60 total; 117 applied, 97% were accepted, 53% of whom enrolled.
ACADEMIC PROGRAM Core, resource management curriculum, honor code. Calendar: quarters. 68 courses offered in 1995–96. Academic remediation for entering students, tutorials, summer session for credit, co-op programs.
GENERAL DEGREE REQUIREMENT Internship (some majors).
MAJORS Agricultural sciences, ecology, environmental sciences, forestry, human ecology, natural resource management, wildlife management.
LIBRARY Brown Library plus 1 other, with 5,500 books, 60 periodicals. Acquisition spending 1994–95: $3000.
COMPUTERS ON CAMPUS 10 computers for student use in computer center.
COLLEGE LIFE Orientation program (2 weeks, $990). ***Student services:*** health clinic, personal-psychological counseling, women's center. ***Campus security:*** student patrols.
HOUSING Freshmen guaranteed college housing. On-campus residence required in freshman year. ***Options:*** freshmen-only, coed, single-sex housing available. Resident assistants live in dorms.
ATHLETICS ***Intramural:*** basketball, skiing (cross-country), table tennis (Ping-Pong), volleyball.
CAREER PLANNING ***Placement office:*** 1 part-time staff. ***Director:*** Ms. Diane Morgan, Director, Career Resource Center, 802-586-7711. ***Services:*** resume preparation, resume referral, career counseling, careers library, job bank. Students must register freshman year.
EXPENSES FOR 1996–97 ***Application fee:*** $35. Comprehensive fee: $18,582.
FINANCIAL AID ***College-administered undergrad aid 1995–96:*** 47 need-based scholarships (average $6437), low-interest long-term loans from external sources (average $3000), Federal Work-Study, 27 part-time jobs. ***Required forms:*** institutional, FAFSA; required for some: CSS Financial Aid PROFILE, state. ***Application deadline:*** continuous. ***Payment plan:*** installment. ***Waivers:*** full or partial for employees or children of employees.
APPLYING ***Options:*** early entrance, deferred entrance. ***Required:*** essay, school transcript, 2 recommendations. ***Recommended:*** minimum 2.0 GPA, 3 years of high school math and science, interview, SAT I or ACT, TOEFL for international students. ***Required for some:*** interview. ***Application deadline:*** rolling. ***Notification:*** continuous until 8/30.
APPLYING/TRANSFER ***Required:*** essay, high school transcript, 2 recommendations. ***Recommended:*** standardized test scores, interview, college transcript, minimum 2.0 high school GPA. ***Required for some:*** interview. ***Entrance:*** moderately difficult. ***Application deadline:*** rolling. ***Notification:*** continuous until 8/30. ***Contact:*** Mr. Edward Houston, Dean of the College, 802-586-7711.

Vermont

CONTACT Ms. Polly W. Russell, Coordinator of Admissions, Sterling College, Craftsbury Common, VT 05827-0072, 802-586-7711 Ext. 46 or toll-free 800-648-3591. College video available.

VERMONT TECHNICAL COLLEGE
Randolph Center, Vermont

UG Enrollment: 746	Tuition & Fees (VT Res): $4760
Application Deadline: rolling	Room & Board: $4854

Vermont Tech offers education for careers in today's technology-driven workplace. Articulation agreements with other regional institutions simplify the transfer process for graduates who want to pursue higher degrees. VTC has averaged 98% placement for every graduating class since 1982. Vermont Tech is a residential coeducational college offering 16 associate and 2 bachelor's degree programs on its 544-acre campus in central Vermont.

GENERAL State-supported, primarily 2-year, coed. Part of Vermont State Colleges System. Awards diplomas, transfer associate, terminal associate, bachelor's degrees. Founded 1866. *Setting:* 544-acre rural campus. *Endowment:* $1.7 million. *Total enrollment:* 746. *Faculty:* 86 (66 full-time, 32% with terminal degrees, 20 part-time); student-faculty ratio is 12:1. *Notable Alumni:* Dr. Craig A. Rogers, director of Intelligent Material Systems and Structures; Dr. A. Z. Soforenzo, president of CSM; Dr. Erwin Small, professor emeritus and associate dean of University of Illinois.
ENROLLMENT PROFILE 746 students from 11 states and territories, 3 other countries. 36% women, 64% men, 9% part-time, 74% state residents, 60% live on campus, 19% transferred in, 62% have need-based financial aid, 1% international, 25% 25 or older, 1% Native American, 1% Hispanic, 0% African American, 0% Asian American. *Areas of study chosen:* 59% engineering and applied sciences, 17% agriculture, 16% health professions and related sciences, 8% business management and administrative services.
FIRST-YEAR CLASS 321 total; 615 applied, 90% were accepted, 58% of whom enrolled. 15% from top 10% of their high school class, 45% from top quarter, 80% from top half. 5 class presidents.
ACADEMIC PROGRAM Core, theoretical and applied technology curriculum, honor code. Calendar: semesters. 215 courses offered in 1995–96. Academic remediation for entering students, English as a second language program, services for LD students, advanced placement, tutorials, honors program, summer session for credit, part-time degree program (daytime), internships.
GENERAL DEGREE REQUIREMENTS 67 credit hours for associate, 132 credit hours for bachelor's; computer course; internship (some majors).
MAJORS Accounting, agricultural business, architectural engineering (B), automotive engineering, biotechnology, business administration/commerce/management, civil engineering technology, computer technologies, construction management, dairy sciences, electrical and electronics technologies, electrical engineering technology, electromechanical technology (B), electronics engineering technology, environmental engineering technology, horticulture, landscape architecture/design, landscaping/grounds maintenance, mechanical engineering technology, practical nursing, rehabilitation therapy, secretarial studies/office management, veterinary technology.
LIBRARY Hartness Library with 53,570 books, 7,720 microform titles, 394 periodicals, 2 on-line bibliographic services, 6 CD-ROMs, 616 records, tapes, and CDs. Acquisition spending 1994–95: $95,944.
COMPUTERS ON CAMPUS Computer purchase plan available. Student rooms linked to a campus network. 175 computers for student use in computer center, computer labs, learning resource center, labs, classrooms, library, student center provide access to main academic computer, e-mail, on-line services, Internet. Staffed computer lab on campus provides training in use of computers, software. Academic computing expenditure 1994–95: $188,893.
COLLEGE LIFE Orientation program (3 days, $60, parents included). Choral group, student-run radio station. 25% vote in student government elections. *Social organizations:* 30 open to all; 85% of eligible men and 100% of eligible women are members. *Most popular organizations:* Weight Lifting Club, Hockey Club, Student Radio Station, American Institute of Architecture Students, Club X. *Major annual events:* Harvest Days, Winter Carnival, Spring Fling. *Student services:* health clinic, personal-psychological counseling. *Campus security:* 24-hour emergency response devices and patrols, controlled dormitory access.
HOUSING 466 college housing spaces available; 420 were occupied 1995–96. Freshmen guaranteed college housing, except by special permission. *Options:* coed (1 building), single-sex (2 buildings) housing available. Resident assistants live in dorms.
ATHLETICS Member NSCAA. *Intercollegiate:* baseball M, basketball M/W, ice hockey M(c)/W(c), soccer M/W, softball W, volleyball M/W. *Intramural:* basketball, bowling, fencing, football, golf, racquetball, riflery, skiing (cross-country), skiing (downhill), soccer, softball, swimming and diving, table tennis (Ping-Pong), tennis, volleyball, water polo, weight lifting. Contact: Mr. Edward Distel, Athletic Director, 802-728-1380.
CAREER PLANNING *Placement office:* 2 full-time staff; $38,794 operating expenditure 1994–95. *Director:* Mr. Brett Chornyak, Director of Career Counseling and Placement, 802-728-1320. *Services:* job fairs, resume preparation, resume referral, career counseling, careers library, job interviews. Students must register freshman year. 100 organizations recruited on campus 1994–95.

AFTER GRADUATION 89% of class of 1994 had job offers within 6 months. 23% of students completing transfer associate program went directly to 4-year colleges.
EXPENSES FOR 1995–96 *Application fee:* $30. State resident tuition: $4152 full-time, $173 per credit hour part-time. Nonresident tuition: $8304 full-time, $346 per credit hour part-time. Part-time mandatory fees: $22.38 per credit hour. Tuition for nonresidents who are eligible for the New England Regional Student Program: $6240 full-time, $260 per credit hour part-time. Full-time mandatory fees: $608. College room and board: $4854. College room only: $2762.
FINANCIAL AID *College-administered undergrad aid 1995–96:* 274 need-based scholarships (average $1352), 9 non-need scholarships (average $4152), low-interest long-term loans from external sources (average $3060), 180 Federal Work-Study (averaging $1000), 110 part-time jobs. *Required forms:* institutional, FAFSA. *Priority deadline:* 3/1. *Payment plans:* installment, deferred payment. *Waivers:* full or partial for employees or children of employees. *Notification:* 4/1.
APPLYING *Options:* early entrance, midyear entrance. *Required:* school transcript, minimum 2.0 GPA, 3 years of high school math, SAT I or ACT, TOEFL for international students. *Recommended:* minimum 3.0 GPA, 3 years of high school science, recommendations, interview. *Required for some:* minimum 3.0 GPA, 3 years of high school science, campus interview. Test scores used for admission and counseling/placement. *Application deadline:* rolling. *Notification:* continuous until 9/1.
APPLYING/TRANSFER *Required:* standardized test scores, high school transcript, 3 years of high school math, college transcript. *Recommended:* 3 years of high school science, interview, minimum 3.0 high school GPA. *Required for some:* 3 years of high school science, campus interview, minimum 3.0 college GPA, minimum 3.0 high school GPA. *Entrance:* moderately difficult. *Application deadline:* rolling. *Notification:* continuous until 9/1. Contact: Ms. Rosemary W. Distel, Director of Admissions, 802-728-1245.
CONTACT Ms. Rosemary W. Distel, Director of Admissions, Vermont Technical College, Randolph Center, VT 05061-0500, 802-728-1245 or toll-free 800-442-VTC1. *Fax:* 802-728-3391 Ext. 390. *E-mail:* admissions@night.vtc.vsc.edu.

❖ *See page 824 for a narrative description.* ❖

WOODBURY COLLEGE
Montpelier, Vermont

UG Enrollment: 140	Tuition & Fees: $8904
Application Deadline: rolling	Room & Board: N/Avail

GENERAL Independent, 2-year, coed. Awards certificates, transfer associate degrees. Founded 1975. *Setting:* 2-acre rural campus. *Total enrollment:* 140. *Faculty:* 35 (10 full-time, 100% with terminal degrees, 25 part-time); student-faculty ratio is 12:1. *Notable Alumni:* Robert Appel, general defender of Vermont.
ENROLLMENT PROFILE 140 students from 5 states and territories, 1 other country. 60% women, 40% men, 20% part-time, 95% state residents, 50% transferred in, 95% have need-based financial aid, 0% have non-need-based financial aid, 1% international, 100% 25 or older, 0% Native American, 1% Hispanic, 2% African American, 0% Asian American. *Areas of study chosen:* 50% prelaw, 20% interdisciplinary studies, 20% social sciences, 10% vocational and home economics. *Most popular recent majors:* paralegal studies, city/community/regional planning.
FIRST-YEAR CLASS 90 total; 100 applied, 100% were accepted, 90% of whom enrolled.
ACADEMIC PROGRAM Competency-based curriculum. Calendar: trimesters. 50 courses offered in 1995–96. Academic remediation for entering students, self-designed majors, part-time degree program (weekends), adult/continuing education programs, internships.
GENERAL DEGREE REQUIREMENTS 60 credits; computer course for all associate degree students; internship.
MAJORS City/community/regional planning, paralegal studies.
COMPUTERS ON CAMPUS 10 computers for student use in computer labs provide access to on-line services, Internet. Staffed computer lab on campus.
COLLEGE LIFE Student-run newspaper. 90% vote in student government elections. *Major annual event:* Community Meeting. *Student services:* personal-psychological counseling.
HOUSING College housing not available.
AFTER GRADUATION 20% of students completing a degree program in 1994–95 went directly on to further study.
ESTIMATED EXPENSES FOR 1996–97 *Application fee:* $20. Tuition: $8904 full-time, $375 per credit part-time.
FINANCIAL AID College-administered undergrad aid 1995–96: need-based scholarships, Federal Work-Study (averaging $300). *Required forms:* FAFSA; required for some: state; accepted: CSS Financial Aid PROFILE, institutional. *Application deadline:* continuous. *Payment plan:* installment.
APPLYING Open admission. *Option:* electronic application. *Required:* essay, school transcript, interview. *Application deadline:* rolling.
APPLYING/TRANSFER *Required:* essay, interview, college transcript. *Entrance:* noncompetitive. *Application deadline:* rolling. Contact: Ms. Kathleen Moore, Admissions Director, 802-229-0516.
CONTACT Ms. Kathleen Moore, Admissions Director, Woodbury College, Montpelier, VT 05602, 802-229-0516. *Fax:* 802-229-2141.

Peterson's Guide to Two-Year Colleges 1997

VIRGINIA

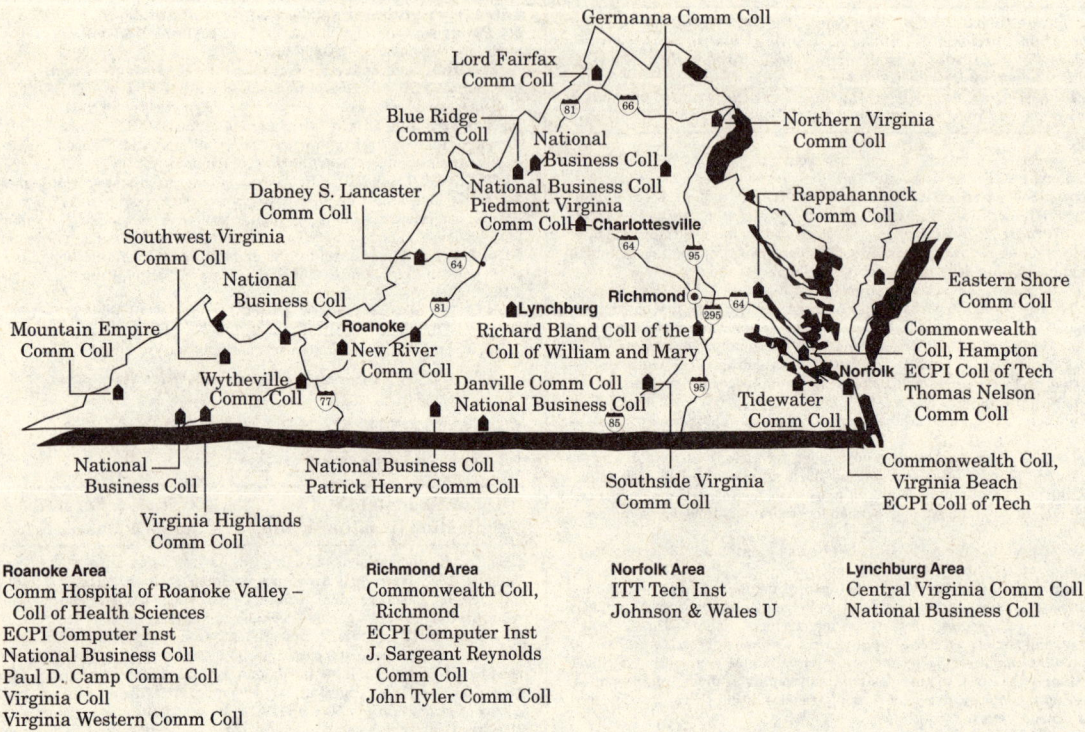

Roanoke Area
Comm Hospital of Roanoke Valley –
   Coll of Health Sciences
ECPI Computer Inst
National Business Coll
Paul D. Camp Comm Coll
Virginia Coll
Virginia Western Comm Coll

Richmond Area
Commonwealth Coll,
   Richmond
ECPI Computer Inst
J. Sargeant Reynolds
   Comm Coll
John Tyler Comm Coll

Norfolk Area
ITT Tech Inst
Johnson & Wales U

Lynchburg Area
Central Virginia Comm Coll
National Business Coll

BLUE RIDGE COMMUNITY COLLEGE
Weyers Cave, Virginia

UG Enrollment: 2,736	Tuition & Fees (VA Res): $1537
Application Deadline: rolling	Room & Board: N/Avail

GENERAL State-supported, 2-year, coed. Part of Virginia Community College System. Awards certificates, diplomas, transfer associate, terminal associate degrees. Founded 1965. *Setting:* 65-acre rural campus. *Endowment:* $195,000. *Educational spending 1994–95:* $970 per undergrad. *Total enrollment:* 2,736. *Faculty:* 145 (41 full-time, 104 part-time); student-faculty ratio is 13:1. *Notable Alumni:* Ray Patterson, physician; Chris Lantz, Harvard Fellow; Rita Wilson, councilperson for Staunton City; Todd Garber, treasurer of Rockingham County.
ENROLLMENT PROFILE 2,736 students from 24 states and territories. 63% women, 37% men, 81% part-time, 99% state residents, 18% transferred in, 2% have need-based financial aid, 0% international, 56% 25 or older, 0% Native American, 1% Hispanic, 3% African American, 1% Asian American. *Areas of study chosen:* 50% liberal arts/general studies, 17% health professions and related sciences, 12% business management and administrative services, 10% engineering and applied sciences, 7% computer and information sciences, 3% prevet. *Most popular recent majors:* liberal arts/general studies, nursing, veterinary technology.
FIRST-YEAR CLASS 635 total; 1,500 applied, 100% were accepted, 42% of whom enrolled.
ACADEMIC PROGRAM Core. Calendar: semesters. Academic remediation for entering students, services for LD students, advanced placement, tutorials, honors program, summer session for credit, part-time degree program (daytime, evenings, summer), adult/continuing education programs, co-op programs and internships.
GENERAL DEGREE REQUIREMENTS 65 semester hours; computer course for drafting and design, electronics technology, management, office systems technology, accounting majors; internship (some majors).
MAJORS Accounting, automotive technologies, business administration/commerce/management, computer information systems, computer technologies, drafting and design, electrical and electronics technologies, finance/banking, liberal arts/general studies, mechanical design technology, mental health/rehabilitation counseling, nursing, secretarial studies/office management, veterinary technology.
LIBRARY Houff Library with 43,775 books, 121 microform titles, 302 periodicals, 14 CD-ROMs, 3,543 records, tapes, and CDs. Acquisition spending 1994–95: $79,042.
COMPUTERS ON CAMPUS 140 computers for student use in computer center, computer labs, classrooms, library provide access to Internet.
COLLEGE LIFE Choral group, student-run newspaper. 10% vote in student government elections. *Student services:* personal-psychological counseling. *Campus security:* 24-hour emergency response devices and patrols, late-night transport-escort service.

HOUSING College housing not available.
ATHLETICS *Intramural:* basketball, softball, tennis, volleyball.
CAREER PLANNING *Placement office:* 2 part-time staff. *Director:* Ms. Elizabeth Hall, Coordinator of Career Services and Student Recruitment, 540-234-9261 Ext. 237. *Services:* resume preparation, resume referral, career counseling, careers library, job bank. 10 organizations recruited on campus 1994–95.
AFTER GRADUATION 86% of students completing a degree program in 1994–95 went directly on to further study.
EXPENSES FOR 1996–97 State resident tuition: $1525 full-time, $47.65 per semester hour part-time. Nonresident tuition: $5024 full-time, $157 per semester hour part-time. Part-time mandatory fees: $6 per semester. Full-time mandatory fees: $12.
FINANCIAL AID College-administered undergrad aid 1995–96: 40 need-based scholarships (averaging $800), short-term loans (averaging $250), low-interest long-term loans from external sources (averaging $1250), Federal Work-Study. *Required forms:* institutional, FAFSA; accepted: CSS Financial Aid PROFILE. *Priority deadline:* 8/1. *Waivers:* full or partial for senior citizens.
APPLYING Open admission except for veterinary technology, nursing programs. *Options:* early entrance, midyear entrance. *Recommended:* SAT I. *Required for some:* 3 years of high school math. Test scores used for counseling/placement. *Application deadline:* rolling. *Notification:* continuous.
APPLYING/TRANSFER *Recommended:* standardized test scores. *Required for some:* 3 years of high school math. *Entrance:* noncompetitive. *Application deadline:* rolling. *Notification:* continuous. *Contact:* Ms. Laura N. Conklin, Admissions and Records Officer, 540-234-9261 Ext. 251.
CONTACT Ms. Laura N. Conklin, Admissions and Records Officer, Blue Ridge Community College, Weyers Cave, VA 24486-0080, 540-234-9261 Ext. 251. *Fax:* 540-234-9066.

CENTRAL VIRGINIA COMMUNITY COLLEGE
Lynchburg, Virginia

UG Enrollment: 4,038	Tuition & Fees (VA Res): $1513
Application Deadline: rolling	Room & Board: N/Avail

GENERAL State-supported, 2-year, coed. Part of Virginia Community College System. Awards certificates, diplomas, transfer associate, terminal associate degrees. Founded 1966. *Setting:* 104-acre suburban campus. *Endowment:* $1.5 million. *Total enrollment:* 4,038. *Faculty:* 200 (60 full-time, 140 part-time); student-faculty ratio is 22:1.
ENROLLMENT PROFILE 4,038 students: 56% women, 44% men, 77% part-time, 99% state residents, 7% transferred in, 1% international, 42% 25 or older, 0% Native American,

0% Hispanic, 13% African American, 0% Asian American. *Most popular recent majors:* business administration/commerce/management, liberal arts/general studies.
FIRST-YEAR CLASS 738 total. Of the students who applied, 100% were accepted, 100% of whom enrolled.
ACADEMIC PROGRAM Core, comprehensive curriculum, honor code. Calendar: semesters. 485 courses offered in 1995–96. Academic remediation for entering students, services for LD students, advanced placement, tutorials, summer session for credit, part-time degree program (daytime, evenings, summer), adult/continuing education programs, co-op programs and internships.
GENERAL DEGREE REQUIREMENTS 65 semester hours; computer course for accounting, management, marketing, office systems technology, banking, electronics engineering technology majors; internship (some majors).
MAJORS Accounting, business administration/commerce/management, civil engineering technology, commercial art, computer information systems, criminal justice, data processing, drafting and design, early childhood education, education, electrical and electronics technologies, (pre)engineering sequence, engineering technology, finance/banking, law enforcement/police sciences, liberal arts/general studies, management information systems, marketing/retailing/merchandising, mechanical engineering technology, medical laboratory technology, radiological technology, retail management, science, secretarial studies/office management.
LIBRARY Bedford Learning Resources Center with 30,000 books, 110 microform titles, 200 periodicals, 4 CD-ROMs, 2,000 records, tapes, and CDs. Acquisition spending 1994–95: $70,000.
COMPUTERS ON CAMPUS 115 computers for student use in computer center, computer labs, learning resource center, classrooms, library provide access to Internet. Staffed computer lab on campus provides training in use of computers, software. Academic computing expenditure 1994–95: $250,000.
COLLEGE LIFE Orientation program (2 days, $47). Student-run newspaper. *Most popular organizations:* Student Government, Data Processing Management Association, Students Together for Environmental Protection, Phi Theta Kappa. *Major annual events:* Semi-Annual Picnic, Graduation Activities. *Student services:* personal-psychological counseling.
HOUSING College housing not available.
ATHLETICS *Intramural:* basketball, bowling.
CAREER PLANNING *Services:* resume preparation, resume referral, career counseling, careers library, job bank.
EXPENSES FOR 1996–97 State resident tuition: $1493 full-time, $46.65 per semester hour part-time. Nonresident tuition: $4992 full-time, $156 per semester hour part-time. Part-time mandatory fees: $10 per semester. Full-time mandatory fees: $20.
FINANCIAL AID *College-administered undergrad aid 1995–96:* 331 need-based scholarships (average $700), 22 non-need scholarships (average $1400), short-term loans (average $300), low-interest long-term loans from external sources (average $1643), 65 Federal Work-Study (averaging $1130). *Required forms:* institutional, FAFSA. *Priority deadline:* 5/1. *Waivers:* full or partial for senior citizens. *Notification:* 6/1.
APPLYING Open admission. *Options:* early entrance, deferred entrance, midyear entrance. *Required:* TOEFL for international students, ACT ASSET or ACT COMPASS. Test scores used for counseling/placement. *Application deadline:* rolling. *Notification:* continuous.
APPLYING/TRANSFER *Entrance:* noncompetitive. *Application deadline:* rolling. *Notification:* continuous.
CONTACT Dr. Robert Bashore, Dean of Students, Central Virginia Community College, Lynchburg, VA 24502-4907, 804-386-4553 or toll-free 800-562-3060 (in-state). College video available.

COMMONWEALTH COLLEGE, HAMPTON
Hampton, Virginia

GENERAL Proprietary, 2-year, coed. Part of Commonwealth Colleges. Awards terminal associate degrees. Founded 1952. *Setting:* 1-acre urban campus with easy access to Norfolk. *Total enrollment:* 272. *Faculty:* 35 (4 full-time, 1% with terminal degrees, 31 part-time).
EXPENSES FOR 1995–96 *Application fee:* $50. Tuition: $6192 full-time, $129 per credit hour part-time. Part-time mandatory fees: $100 per year. Full-time mandatory fees: $100.
CONTACT Mr. Tony Kowalczik, Director of Admissions, Commonwealth College, Hampton, 1120 West Mercury Boulevard, Hampton, VA 23666-3309, 804-838-2122. *Fax:* 804-499-7799.

COMMONWEALTH COLLEGE, RICHMOND
Richmond, Virginia

GENERAL Proprietary, 2-year, coed. Part of Commonwealth Colleges. Awards terminal associate degrees. Founded 1952. *Setting:* suburban campus. *Total enrollment:* 453. *Faculty:* 33 (13 full-time, 1% with terminal degrees, 20 part-time); student-faculty ratio is 18:1.
EXPENSES FOR 1995–96 *Application fee:* $50. Tuition: $6192 full-time, $129 per credit hour part-time. Part-time mandatory fees: $100 per quarter. Full-time mandatory fees: $100.
CONTACT Ms. Tracy Bennington, Director of Admissions, Commonwealth College, Richmond, 8141 Hull Street Road, Richmond, VA 23235-6411, 804-745-2444. *Fax:* 804-499-7799.

COMMONWEALTH COLLEGE, VIRGINIA BEACH
Virginia Beach, Virginia

GENERAL Proprietary, 2-year, coed. Part of Commonwealth Colleges. Awards terminal associate degrees. Founded 1952. *Setting:* suburban campus. *Total enrollment:* 358. *Faculty:* 39 (9 full-time, 1% with terminal degrees, 30 part-time).
EXPENSES FOR 1995–96 *Application fee:* $50. Tuition: $6192 full-time, $129 per credit hour part-time. Part-time mandatory fees: $100 per year. Full-time mandatory fees: $100. College room only: $2475.
CONTACT Mr. Anthony J. Caggiano, Dean of Admissions, Commonwealth College, Virginia Beach, 301 Centre Pointe Drive, Virginia Beach, VA 23462-4417, 804-499-7900. *Fax:* 804-499-7799.

COMMUNITY HOSPITAL OF ROANOKE VALLEY–COLLEGE OF HEALTH SCIENCES
Roanoke, Virginia

UG Enrollment: 561	Tuition & Fees: $4500
Application Deadline: 7/31	Room Only: $1300

GENERAL Independent, primarily 2-year, specialized, coed. Awards certificates, transfer associate, terminal associate, bachelor's degrees. Founded 1982. *Setting:* urban campus. *Total enrollment:* 561. *Faculty:* 49 (34 full-time, 86% with terminal degrees, 15 part-time); student-faculty ratio is 11:1.
ENROLLMENT PROFILE 561 students from 7 states and territories. 76% women, 24% men, 54% part-time, 99% state residents, 15% live on campus, 75% transferred in, 66% 25 or older, 6% African American, 2% Asian American. *Areas of study chosen:* 100% health professions and related sciences. *Most popular recent majors:* nursing, physical therapy, occupational therapy.
FIRST-YEAR CLASS 6 total; 132 applied, 42% were accepted, 11% of whom enrolled.
ACADEMIC PROGRAM Core, honor code. Calendar: semesters. 152 courses offered in 1995–96. Academic remediation for entering students, services for LD students, advanced placement, summer session for credit, part-time degree program (daytime), adult/continuing education programs, internships. Off-campus study at Blue Ridge Community College, Central Virginia Community College.
GENERAL DEGREE REQUIREMENTS 66 credit hours for associate, 121 credit hours for bachelor's; 2 courses in anatomy and physiology; computer course; internship (some majors).
MAJORS Emergency medical technology, medical records services, nursing (B), occupational therapy, physical therapy, respiratory therapy, science.
LIBRARY Learning Resource Center with 7,319 books, 14 microform titles, 170 periodicals, 3 on-line bibliographic services, 9 CD-ROMs, 494 records, tapes, and CDs.
COMPUTERS ON CAMPUS 18 computers for student use in computer labs, learning resource center. Staffed computer lab on campus provides training in use of computers, software.
COLLEGE LIFE 25% vote in student government elections. *Most popular organization:* Student Government Association. *Major annual events:* Health Care Futures, Orientation Picnic, Senior Recognition Dinner. *Student services:* health clinic, personal-psychological counseling. *Campus security:* 24-hour emergency response devices and patrols, late night transport-escort service, controlled dormitory access.
HOUSING 80 college housing spaces available. No special consideration for freshman housing applicants. Off-campus living permitted. *Option:* coed (1 building) housing available. Resident assistants live in dorms.
CAREER PLANNING *Services:* career counseling, careers library.
AFTER GRADUATION 100% of class of 1994 had job offers within 6 months.
ESTIMATED EXPENSES FOR 1996–97 *Application fee:* $25. Tuition: $4500 (minimum) full-time. Part-time tuition per credit hour ranges from $150 to $160. Full-time tuition ranges up to $4800 according to course level. Tuition for summer session ranges from $2250 to $2400 according to course level. College room only for summer session:$475. College room only: $1300.
FINANCIAL AID *College-administered undergrad aid 1995–96:* need-based scholarships, non-need scholarships, short-term loans (averaging $200), low-interest long-term loans from external sources (averaging $6625), 9 Federal Work-Study (averaging $1500), 4 part-time jobs. *Required forms:* institutional, FAFSA; accepted: state. *Priority deadline:* 4/15. *Waivers:* full or partial for employees or children of employees. *Notification:* continuous.
APPLYING *Option:* early decision. *Required:* essay, school transcript, minimum 2.0 GPA, SAT I or ACT, TOEFL for international students. *Recommended:* 3 years of high school math and science. *Required for some:* recommendations, interview, volunteer experience. Test scores used for admission. *Application deadlines:* 7/31, 10/15 for early decision. *Notification:* continuous until 7/31, 12/1 for early decision.
APPLYING/TRANSFER *Required:* essay, standardized test scores, high school transcript, college transcript, minimum 2.0 college GPA, minimum 2.0 high school GPA. *Recommended:* 3 years of high school math and science. *Required for some:* recommendations, interview, volunteer experience. *Entrance:* moderately difficult. *Contact:* Ms. Ruth Robertson, Registrar, 703-985-8481.
CONTACT Ms. Ruth Robertson, Registrar, Community Hospital of Roanoke Valley–College of Health Sciences, PO Box 13186, Roanoke, VA 24031-3186, 703-985-8481.

DABNEY S. LANCASTER COMMUNITY COLLEGE
Clifton Forge, Virginia

UG Enrollment: 1,722	Tuition & Fees (VA Res): $1646
Application Deadline: rolling	Room & Board: N/Avail

GENERAL State-supported, 2-year, coed. Part of Virginia Community College System. Awards certificates, diplomas, transfer associate, terminal associate degrees. Founded 1964. *Setting:* 117-acre rural campus. *Total enrollment:* 1,722. *Faculty:* 160 (38 full-time, 122 part-time); student-faculty ratio is 14:1.
ENROLLMENT PROFILE 1,722 students from 5 states and territories, 1 other country. 60% women, 65% part-time, 96% state residents, 9% transferred in, 1% international, 59% 25 or older, 1% Native American, 0% Hispanic, 6% African American, 1% Asian American. *Most popular recent majors:* liberal arts/general studies, business administration/commerce/management.
FIRST-YEAR CLASS 459 total. Of the students who applied, 100% were accepted, 85% of whom enrolled.

Dabney S. Lancaster Community College (continued)

ACADEMIC PROGRAM Calendar: semesters. Academic remediation for entering students, services for LD students, advanced placement, honors program, summer session for credit, part-time degree program (daytime, evenings), adult/continuing education programs, co-op programs and internships.

GENERAL DEGREE REQUIREMENTS 68 semester hours; math/science requirements vary according to program; computer course.

MAJORS Business administration/commerce/management, computer information systems, computer programming, criminal justice, data processing, drafting and design, education, electrical and electronics technologies, forest technology, legal secretarial studies, liberal arts/general studies, mechanical design technology, medical secretarial studies, nursing, paper and pulp sciences, science, secretarial studies/office management.

LIBRARY 37,716 books, 1,206 microform titles, 376 periodicals, 2,035 records, tapes, and CDs.

COMPUTERS ON CAMPUS Computers for student use in computer center, Achievement Center, library.

COLLEGE LIFE Drama-theater group. ***Social organizations:*** 5 social clubs; 25% of eligible men and 25% of eligible women are members. ***Student services:*** personal-psychological counseling.

HOUSING College housing not available.

ATHLETICS ***Intercollegiate:*** basketball M. ***Intramural:*** basketball, bowling, equestrian sports, football, golf, skiing (downhill), soccer, tennis, volleyball.

CAREER PLANNING ***Director:*** Dr. Robert Goralewicz, Director of Student Services, 540-862-4246. ***Services:*** resume preparation, career counseling, careers library.

AFTER GRADUATION 60% of students completing a degree program in 1994–95 went directly on to further study.

EXPENSES FOR 1996–97 State resident tuition: $1646 full-time, $48.40 per semester hour part-time. Nonresident tuition: $5338 full-time, $157 per semester hour part-time.

FINANCIAL AID ***College-administered undergrad aid 1995–96:*** 67 need-based scholarships (averaging $200), 20 non-need scholarships (averaging $830), short-term loans (averaging $285), low-interest long-term loans from external sources (averaging $1741), Federal Work-Study, part-time jobs. ***Required forms:*** institutional, FAFSA; accepted: CSS Financial Aid PROFILE. ***Priority deadline:*** 5/1. ***Waivers:*** full or partial for senior citizens.

APPLYING Open admission except for nursing program. ***Options:*** early entrance, deferred entrance. ***Required:*** TOEFL for international students, CGP. Test scores used for counseling/placement. ***Application deadline:*** rolling. ***Notification:*** continuous.

APPLYING/TRANSFER ***Required:*** standardized test scores. ***Application deadline:*** rolling. ***Notification:*** continuous.

CONTACT Dr. Robert Goralewicz, Director of Student Services, Dabney S. Lancaster Community College, Clifton Forge, VA 24422, 540-862-4246. College video available.

DANVILLE COMMUNITY COLLEGE
Danville, Virginia

UG Enrollment: 3,869 | **Tuition & Fees (VA Res): $1525**
Application Deadline: rolling | **Room & Board: N/Avail**

GENERAL State-supported, 2-year, coed. Part of Virginia Community College System. Awards transfer associate, terminal associate degrees. Founded 1967. ***Setting:*** 65-acre urban campus. ***Total enrollment:*** 3,869. ***Faculty:*** 149 (54 full-time, 15% with terminal degrees, 95 part-time); student-faculty ratio is 25:1.

ENROLLMENT PROFILE 3,869 students from 7 states and territories, 3 other countries. 60% women, 75% part-time, 98% state residents, 6% transferred in, 56% 25 or older, 1% Native American, 1% Hispanic, 24% African American, 1% Asian American.

FIRST-YEAR CLASS 1,135 total; 1,450 applied, 100% were accepted, 78% of whom enrolled.

ACADEMIC PROGRAM Core, honor code. Calendar: semesters. Academic remediation for entering students, advanced placement, summer session for credit, part-time degree program (daytime, evenings), adult/continuing education programs, co-op programs.

GENERAL DEGREE REQUIREMENT 65 semester hours.

MAJORS Accounting, business administration/commerce/management, computer programming, education, engineering technology, liberal arts/general studies, marketing/retailing/merchandising, science, secretarial studies/office management.

LIBRARY 40,000 books, 6,425 microform titles, 335 periodicals, 1,500 records, tapes, and CDs.

COMPUTERS ON CAMPUS 201 computers for student use in computer center, learning resource center. Staffed computer lab on campus provides training in use of computers, software.

COLLEGE LIFE ***Campus security:*** 24-hour patrols.

HOUSING College housing not available.

ATHLETICS ***Intramural:*** basketball, bowling, football, softball, volleyball.

CAREER PLANNING ***Placement office:*** 1 part-time staff. ***Director:*** Mr. Howard Graves, Placement Director, 804-797-8443. ***Services:*** career counseling, job interviews.

EXPENSES FOR 1996–97 State resident tuition: $1525 full-time, $47.65 per semester hour part-time. Nonresident tuition: $5024 full-time, $157 per semester hour part-time.

FINANCIAL AID ***College-administered undergrad aid 1995–96:*** need-based scholarships, non-need scholarships, low-interest long-term loans from external sources, Federal Work-Study, part-time jobs. ***Required forms:*** CSS Financial Aid PROFILE, FAFSA. ***Application deadline:*** continuous.

APPLYING Open admission. ***Options:*** early entrance, deferred entrance. ***Required:*** school transcript, TOEFL for international students. ***Required for some:*** ACT ASSET. Test scores used for counseling/placement. ***Application deadline:*** rolling. ***Notification:*** continuous. Preference given to district residents.

APPLYING/TRANSFER ***Required:*** high school transcript. ***Required for some:*** standardized test scores. ***Entrance:*** noncompetitive. ***Application deadline:*** rolling. ***Notification:*** continuous.

CONTACT Dr. Grady C. Tuck, Coordinator of Admissions, Danville Community College, 1008 South Main Street, Danville, VA 24541-4088, 804-797-3553 Ext. 220.

EASTERN SHORE COMMUNITY COLLEGE
Melfa, Virginia

UG Enrollment: 684 | **Tuition & Fees (VA Res): $1549**
Application Deadline: rolling | **Room & Board: N/Avail**

GENERAL State-supported, 2-year, coed. Part of Virginia Community College System. Awards transfer associate, terminal associate degrees. Founded 1971. ***Setting:*** 117-acre rural campus. ***Total enrollment:*** 684. ***Faculty:*** 34 (15 full-time, 19 part-time).

ENROLLMENT PROFILE 684 students: 75% women, 65% part-time, 98% state residents, 3% transferred in, 1% international, 45% 25 or older, 0% Native American, 1% Hispanic, 35% African American, 0% Asian American. ***Most popular recent majors:*** nursing, secretarial studies/office management, electrical and electronics technologies.

FIRST-YEAR CLASS 243 total. Of the students who applied, 100% were accepted, 77% of whom enrolled.

ACADEMIC PROGRAM Core, honor code. Calendar: semesters. Academic remediation for entering students, English as a second language program, services for LD students, advanced placement, summer session for credit, part-time degree program (daytime, evenings, summer), adult/continuing education programs. Off-campus study at members of the Virginia Tidewater Consortium for Continuing Higher Education.

GENERAL DEGREE REQUIREMENTS 65 semester hours; math/science requirements vary according to program.

MAJORS Business administration/commerce/management, education, electrical and electronics technologies, liberal arts/general studies, nursing, science, secretarial studies/office management.

LIBRARY 20,479 books, 70 microform titles, 95 periodicals, 334 records, tapes, and CDs.

COMPUTERS ON CAMPUS 33 computers for student use in computer center, library, student center.

COLLEGE LIFE Orientation program (2 days). ***Student services:*** personal-psychological counseling. ***Campus security:*** night security guard.

HOUSING College housing not available.

ATHLETICS ***Intramural:*** basketball, volleyball.

CAREER PLANNING ***Services:*** career counseling, careers library.

AFTER GRADUATION 50% of students completing a degree program in 1994–95 went directly on to further study.

EXPENSES FOR 1996–97 State resident tuition: $1493 full-time, $46.65 per semester hour part-time. Nonresident tuition: $4992 full-time, $156 per semester hour part-time. Part-time mandatory fees: $1.50 per semester hour. Full-time mandatory fees: $56.

FINANCIAL AID ***College-administered undergrad aid 1995–96:*** 15 need-based scholarships (average $400), 30 non-need scholarships (average $500), short-term loans (average $340), low-interest long-term loans from external sources (average $1800), Federal Work-Study. ***Acceptable forms:*** CSS Financial Aid PROFILE, FAFSA. ***Priority deadline:*** 3/15. ***Waivers:*** full or partial for senior citizens.

APPLYING Open admission. ***Option:*** early entrance. ***Required:*** school transcript, TOEFL for international students. Test scores used for counseling/placement. ***Application deadline:*** rolling. ***Notification:*** continuous. Preference given to county residents.

APPLYING/TRANSFER ***Required:*** high school transcript. ***Application deadline:*** rolling. ***Notification:*** continuous.

CONTACT Ms. Faye Wilson, Enrollment Services Specialist, Eastern Shore Community College, Melfa, VA 23410-3000, 804-787-5913. ***Fax:*** 804-787-5919.

ECPI COLLEGE OF TECHNOLOGY
Hampton, Virginia

UG Enrollment: 285 | **Tuition: $13,900/deg prog**
Application Deadline: N/R | **Room & Board: N/Avail**

GENERAL Proprietary, 2-year, coed. Awards certificates, diplomas, terminal associate degrees. Founded 1966. ***Setting:*** suburban campus. ***Total enrollment:*** 285. ***Faculty:*** 23 (9 full-time, 14 part-time); student-faculty ratio is 16:1.

ENROLLMENT PROFILE 285 students from 34 states and territories, 4 other countries. 40% women, 60% men, 40% part-time, 92% state residents, 25% transferred in, 80% have need-based financial aid, 64% 25 or older, 1% Native American, 4% Hispanic, 45% African American, 1% Asian American. ***Areas of study chosen:*** 63% engineering and applied sciences, 37% computer and information sciences.

FIRST-YEAR CLASS 143 total; 340 applied, 58% were accepted, 72% of whom enrolled.

ACADEMIC PROGRAM Core, technical curriculum, honor code. Calendar: trimesters. Average class size 20 in required courses. Advanced placement, Freshman Honors College, tutorials, summer session for credit, part-time degree program (evenings, weekends, summer), adult/continuing education programs, internships.

GENERAL DEGREE REQUIREMENTS 60 credit hours; 1 course each in math and science; computer course; internship (some majors).

MAJORS Accounting, communication equipment technology, computer information systems, computer management, computer science, computer technologies, electrical and electronics technologies, electromechanical technology, electronics engineering technology, engineering technology, health services administration, information science, mechanical engineering technology, medical records services, medical secretarial studies, telecommunications, vocational education, word processing.

LIBRARY ECPI-Virginia Beach Library with 2,500 books, 138 periodicals, 1,267 records, tapes, and CDs.

COMPUTERS ON CAMPUS 100 computers for student use in computer center, computer labs, learning resource center, classrooms, library provide access to main academic computer, on-line services, Internet. Staffed computer lab on campus (open 24 hours a day) provides training in use of computers, software.

COLLEGE LIFE ***Social organizations:*** 6 open to all. ***Most popular organizations:*** SETA, CSI, NVTHS. ***Campus security:*** building and parking lot security.

HOUSING College housing not available.

CAREER PLANNING ***Placement office:*** 1 full-time staff. ***Director:*** Ms. Cindy Loney, Career Advisor, 804-838-9191. ***Services:*** job fairs, resume preparation, resume referral, career counseling, careers library, job bank, job interviews.

EXPENSES FOR 1995–96 ***Application fee:*** $100. Tuition: $13,900 per degree program. Tuition guaranteed not to increase for student's term of enrollment.

FINANCIAL AID *College-administered undergrad aid 1995–96:* need-based scholarships, low-interest long-term loans from external sources, Federal Work-Study. *Required forms:* institutional, FAFSA. *Application deadline:* continuous. *Payment plan:* installment. *Waivers:* full or partial for employees or children of employees. *Notification:* continuous.
APPLYING *Options:* Common Application, deferred entrance, midyear entrance. *Recommended:* SAT I or ACT, SAT II Subject Tests, SAT II: Writing Test. Test scores used for admission. *Notification:* continuous.
APPLYING/TRANSFER *Entrance:* moderately difficult. *Notification:* continuous.
CONTACT Ms. Virginia Whitesel, Director of Admissions, ECPI College of Technology, Hampton, VA 23462, 804-838-9191.

ECPI COLLEGE OF TECHNOLOGY
Virginia Beach, Virginia

UG Enrollment: 720 **Tuition: $13,900/deg prog**
Application Deadline: N/R **Room & Board: N/Avail**

GENERAL Proprietary, 2-year, coed. Awards certificates, diplomas, terminal associate degrees. Founded 1966. *Setting:* 8-acre suburban campus. *Total enrollment:* 720. *Faculty:* 50 (22 full-time, 28 part-time); student-faculty ratio is 16:1.
ENROLLMENT PROFILE 720 students from 34 states and territories, 4 other countries. 48% women, 52% men, 48% part-time, 90% state residents, 35% transferred in, 78% have need-based financial aid, 1% international, 72% 25 or older, 2% Native American, 4% Hispanic, 39% African American, 2% Asian American. *Areas of study chosen:* 55% engineering and applied sciences, 45% computer and information sciences.
FIRST-YEAR CLASS 206 total; 435 applied, 72% were accepted, 65% of whom enrolled.
ACADEMIC PROGRAM Core, technical curriculum, honor code. Calendar: trimesters. Average class size 20 in required courses. Advanced placement, Freshman Honors College, tutorials, summer session for credit, part-time degree program (evenings, weekends, summer), adult/continuing education programs, internships.
GENERAL DEGREE REQUIREMENTS 60 credit hours; 1 course each in math and science; computer course; internship (some majors).
MAJORS Accounting, biomedical technologies, business machine technologies, communication equipment technology, computer information systems, computer management, computer programming, computer science, computer technologies, data processing, electrical and electronics technologies, electromechanical technology, electronics engineering technology, engineering technology, health services administration, information science, mechanical engineering technology, medical records services, medical secretarial studies, telecommunications, vocational education, word processing.
LIBRARY ECPI Virginia Beach Library with 2,500 books, 138 periodicals, 1,267 records, tapes, and CDs.
COMPUTERS ON CAMPUS 200 computers for student use in computer center, computer labs, learning resource center, classrooms, library provide access to main academic computer, on-line services, Internet. Staffed computer lab on campus provides training in use of computers, software.
COLLEGE LIFE *Social organizations:* 6 open to all. *Most popular organizations:* SETA, CSI, NVTHS. *Student services:* personal-psychological counseling. *Campus security:* building and parking lot security.
HOUSING College housing not available.
CAREER PLANNING *Placement office:* 4 full-time, 1 part-time staff. *Director:* Ms. Katie Keene, Manager, 804-490-9090. *Services:* job fairs, resume preparation, resume referral, career counseling, careers library, job bank, job interviews.
EXPENSES FOR 1995–96 *Application fee:* $100. Tuition: $13,900 per degree program. Tuition guaranteed not to increase for student's term of enrollment.
FINANCIAL AID *College-administered undergrad aid 1995–96:* need-based scholarships, low-interest long-term loans from external sources, Federal Work-Study. *Required forms:* institutional, FAFSA. *Application deadline:* continuous. *Payment plan:* installment. *Waivers:* full or partial for employees or children of employees. *Notification:* continuous.
APPLYING *Options:* Common Application, deferred entrance, midyear entrance. *Recommended:* SAT I or ACT, SAT II Subject Tests, SAT II: Writing Test. Test scores used for admission. *Notification:* continuous.
APPLYING/TRANSFER *Entrance:* moderately difficult. *Notification:* continuous.
CONTACT Ms. Frances McNamee, Director of Admissions, ECPI College of Technology, Virginia Beach, VA 23462, 804-490-9090.

ECPI COMPUTER INSTITUTE
Richmond, Virginia

UG Enrollment: 450 **Tuition: $13,900/deg prog**
Application Deadline: rolling **Room & Board: N/Avail**

GENERAL Proprietary, 2-year, coed. Awards certificates, diplomas, terminal associate degrees. Founded 1966. *Setting:* urban campus. *Total enrollment:* 450. *Faculty:* 39 (16 full-time, 23 part-time); student-faculty ratio is 16:1.
ENROLLMENT PROFILE 450 students: 42% women, 58% men, 37% part-time, 93% state residents, 15% transferred in, 76% have need-based financial aid, 52% 25 or older, 2% Native American, 1% Hispanic, 45% African American, 2% Asian American. *Areas of study chosen:* 60% engineering and applied sciences, 40% computer and information sciences.
FIRST-YEAR CLASS 150 total; 265 applied, 79% were accepted, 71% of whom enrolled.
ACADEMIC PROGRAM Core, technical curriculum, honor code. Calendar: trimesters. Average class size 20 in required courses. Advanced placement, Freshman Honors College, tutorials, summer session for credit, part-time degree program (evenings, weekends, summer), adult/continuing education programs, internships.
GENERAL DEGREE REQUIREMENTS 60 semester hours; 1 course each in math and science; computer course; internship (some majors).
MAJORS Accounting, business machine technologies, communication equipment technology, computer information systems, computer management, computer programming, computer science, data processing, electrical and electronics technologies, electromechanical technology, electronics engineering technology, engineering technology, health services administration, information science, mechanical engineering technology, medical records services, medical secretarial studies, telecommunications, vocational education, word processing.
LIBRARY ECPI-Richmond Library with 2,989 books, 81 periodicals, 45 records, tapes, and CDs.
COMPUTERS ON CAMPUS Computers for student use in computer center, computer labs, learning resource center, classrooms, library provide access to main academic computer, on-line services, Internet. Staffed computer lab on campus (open 24 hours a day) provides training in use of computers, software.
COLLEGE LIFE *Campus security:* building and parking lot security.
HOUSING College housing not available.
CAREER PLANNING *Placement office:* 2 full-time staff. *Director:* Ms. Monica Davis, Career Advisor, 804-359-3535. *Services:* job fairs, resume preparation, resume referral, career counseling, careers library, job bank, job interviews.
EXPENSES FOR 1995–96 *Application fee:* $100. Tuition: $13,900 per degree program. Tuition guaranteed not to increase for student's term of enrollment.
FINANCIAL AID *College-administered undergrad aid 1995–96:* need-based scholarships, low-interest long-term loans from external sources, Federal Work-Study. *Required forms:* institutional, FAFSA. *Application deadline:* continuous. *Payment plan:* installment. *Waivers:* full or partial for employees or children of employees. *Notification:* continuous.
APPLYING *Options:* Common Application, deferred entrance, midyear entrance. *Recommended:* SAT I or ACT, SAT II Subject Tests, SAT II: Writing Test. Test scores used for admission. *Application deadline:* rolling. *Notification:* continuous.
APPLYING/TRANSFER *Entrance:* moderately difficult. *Application deadline:* rolling. *Notification:* continuous.
CONTACT Admissions Office, ECPI Computer Institute, 4303 West Broad Street, Richmond, VA 23230, 804-359-3535.

ECPI COMPUTER INSTITUTE
Roanoke, Virginia

UG Enrollment: 180 **Tuition: $13,900/deg prog**
Application Deadline: rolling **Room & Board: N/Avail**

GENERAL Proprietary, 2-year, coed. Awards certificates, diplomas, terminal associate degrees. Founded 1966. *Setting:* suburban campus. *Total enrollment:* 180. *Faculty:* 32 (7 full-time, 25 part-time).
ENROLLMENT PROFILE 180 students: 47% women, 53% men, 35% part-time, 91% state residents, 9% transferred in, 74% have need-based financial aid, 49% 25 or older, 0% Native American, 2% Hispanic, 31% African American, 1% Asian American. *Areas of study chosen:* 60% engineering and applied sciences, 40% computer and information sciences.
FIRST-YEAR CLASS 75 total; 135 applied, 70% were accepted, 79% of whom enrolled.
ACADEMIC PROGRAM Core, technical curriculum, honor code. Calendar: trimesters. Average class size 20 in required courses. Advanced placement, Freshman Honors College, tutorials, summer session for credit, part-time degree program (evenings, weekends, summer), adult/continuing education programs, internships.
GENERAL DEGREE REQUIREMENTS 60 credit hours; 1 course each in math and science; computer course; internship (some majors).
MAJORS Accounting, biomedical technologies, communication equipment technology, computer information systems, computer science, computer technologies, electrical and electronics technologies, electromechanical technology, electronics engineering technology, engineering technology, health services administration, information science, mechanical engineering technology, medical records services, medical secretarial studies, telecommunications, vocational education, word processing.
LIBRARY ECPI-Roanoke Library with 1,500 books, 78 periodicals.
COMPUTERS ON CAMPUS Computers for student use in computer center, computer labs, learning resource center, classrooms, library provide access to main academic computer, on-line services, Internet. Staffed computer lab on campus (open 24 hours a day) provides training in use of computers, software.
COLLEGE LIFE *Campus security:* building and parking lot security.
HOUSING College housing not available.
CAREER PLANNING *Placement office:* 1 full-time, 1 part-time staff. *Director:* Ms. Helen Payne, Career Advisor, 540-342-0043. *Services:* job fairs, resume preparation, resume referral, career counseling, careers library, job bank, job interviews. Students must register freshman year.
EXPENSES FOR 1995–96 *Application fee:* $100. Tuition: $13,900 per degree program. Tuition guaranteed not to increase for student's term of enrollment.
FINANCIAL AID *College-administered undergrad aid 1995–96:* need-based scholarships, low-interest long-term loans from external sources, Federal Work-Study. *Required forms:* institutional, FAFSA. *Application deadline:* continuous. *Payment plan:* installment. *Waivers:* full or partial for employees or children of employees. *Notification:* continuous.
APPLYING *Options:* Common Application, deferred entrance, midyear entrance. *Recommended:* SAT I or ACT, SAT II Subject Tests, SAT II: Writing Test. Test scores used for admission. *Application deadline:* rolling. *Notification:* continuous.
APPLYING/TRANSFER *Entrance:* moderately difficult. *Application deadline:* rolling. *Notification:* continuous.
CONTACT Admissions Office, ECPI Computer Institute, Roanoke, VA 24016, 540-342-0043.

GERMANNA COMMUNITY COLLEGE
Locust Grove, Virginia

UG Enrollment: 2,596 **Tuition & Fees (VA Res): $1514**
Application Deadline: rolling **Room & Board: N/Avail**

GENERAL State-supported, 2-year, coed. Part of Virginia Community College System. Awards certificates, transfer associate, terminal associate degrees. Founded 1970. *Setting:* 100-acre rural campus with easy access to Washington, DC. *Total enrollment:* 2,596. *Faculty:* 135 (38 full-time, 32% with terminal degrees, 97 part-time); student-faculty ratio is 19:1.

Peterson's Guide to Two-Year Colleges 1997

641

Germanna Community College (continued)
ENROLLMENT PROFILE 2,596 students from 5 states and territories, 7 other countries. 67% women, 69% part-time, 99% state residents, 12% transferred in, 25% have need-based financial aid, 14% have non-need-based financial aid, 53% 25 or older, 0% Native American, 1% Hispanic, 9% African American, 1% Asian American. ***Areas of study chosen:*** 31% liberal arts/general studies, 30% business management and administrative services, 10% education, 8% computer and information sciences, 6% biological and life sciences, 5% health professions and related sciences, 4% engineering and applied sciences. ***Most popular recent majors:*** nursing, business administration/commerce/management, science.
FIRST-YEAR CLASS 661 total. Of the students who applied, 100% were accepted, 86% of whom enrolled.
ACADEMIC PROGRAM Core, honor code. Calendar: semesters. 363 courses offered in 1995–96. Academic remediation for entering students, English as a second language program, summer session for credit, part-time degree program (daytime, evenings), adult/continuing education programs. Off-campus study at Mary Washington College, other members of the Virginia Community College System.
GENERAL DEGREE REQUIREMENT 61 semester hours.
MAJORS Accounting, business administration/commerce/management, data processing, education, electrical and electronics technologies, law enforcement/police sciences, liberal arts/general studies, nursing, science, secretarial studies/office management.
LIBRARY 22,412 books, 998 microform titles, 160 periodicals, 1,474 records, tapes, and CDs. Acquisition spending 1994–95: $48,000.
COMPUTERS ON CAMPUS 55 computers for student use in computer labs, learning resource center, library provide access to on-line services. Staffed computer lab on campus provides training in use of computers, software.
COLLEGE LIFE Orientation program (2 days, $17). Student-run newspaper. ***Social organizations:*** 11 open to all. ***Most popular organizations:*** Student Nurses Association, Student Government Association, Phi Theta Kappa, Students Against Substance Abuse. ***Major annual events:*** Germanna Day, Graduation. ***Student services:*** personal-psychological counseling. ***Campus security:*** 24-hour patrols.
HOUSING College housing not available.
ATHLETICS ***Intramural:*** archery, basketball, bowling, football, tennis, volleyball.
CAREER PLANNING ***Placement office:*** 1 part-time staff. ***Director:*** Ms. Pamela Frederick, Counselor, 540-727-3000. ***Services:*** job fairs, career counseling, job bank.
AFTER GRADUATION 80% of students completing a degree program in 1994–95 went directly on to further study.
EXPENSES FOR 1996–97 State resident tuition: $1482 full-time, $46.30 per semester hour part-time. Nonresident tuition: $4800 full-time, $150 per semester hour part-time. Part-time mandatory fees: $1 per semester hour. Full-time mandatory fees: $32.
FINANCIAL AID ***College-administered undergrad aid 1995–96:*** 241 need-based scholarships (average $1000), 50 non-need scholarships (average $500), short-term loans (average $150), low-interest long-term loans from college funds (average $750), loans from external sources (average $2625), Federal Work-Study, 20 part-time jobs. ***Required forms:*** institutional, FAFSA; accepted: CSS Financial Aid PROFILE, state. ***Application deadline:*** continuous to 5/1.
APPLYING Open admission except for nursing program. ***Option:*** early entrance. ***Recommended:*** TOEFL for international students. ***Required for some:*** school transcript, 3 years of high school math. Test scores used for counseling/placement. ***Application deadline:*** rolling. ***Notification:*** continuous.
APPLYING/TRANSFER ***Required for some:*** high school transcript, 3 years of high school math. ***Entrance:*** noncompetitive. ***Application deadline:*** rolling. ***Notification:*** continuous. ***Contact:*** Ms. Pamela Frederick, Counselor, 540-727-3000.
CONTACT Mrs. Linda Crocker, Registrar, Germanna Community College, Locust Grove, VA 22508-0339, 540-727-3000.

ITT TECHNICAL INSTITUTE
Norfolk, Virginia

GENERAL Proprietary, 2-year, coed. Part of ITT Educational Services, Inc. Awards terminal associate degrees. Founded 1988. ***Setting:*** 2-acre suburban campus. ***Total enrollment:*** 266. ***Faculty:*** 17 (15 full-time, 60% with terminal degrees, 2 part-time).
EXPENSES FOR 1995–96 ***Application fee:*** $100. Tuition per degree program ranges from $15,429 to $17,690. Full-time mandatory fees: $540.
CONTACT Ms. Patrice McMillon, Director of Recruitment, ITT Technical Institute, Norfolk, VA 23502-3701, 804-466-1260. College video available.

JOHNSON & WALES UNIVERSITY
Norfolk, Virginia

UG Enrollment: 538	**Tuition & Fees: $11,937**
Application Deadline: rolling	**Room & Board: $4782**

GENERAL Independent, 2-year, coed. Part of Johnson & Wales University. Awards terminal associate degrees. ***Setting:*** urban campus. ***Total enrollment:*** 538. ***Faculty:*** 28 (13 full-time, 15 part-time); student-faculty ratio is 15:1. ***Notable Alumni:*** Emeril Lagesse, owner and executive chef of Emeril's; Edmond Abraim, president and CEO of H&B Powerbilt; Lee Gerovitz, partner at Clever Cleaver Productions; Steve Cassarino, partner at Clever Cleaver Productions; Joel Scanlon, president of Eastern Butcher Block.
ENROLLMENT PROFILE 538 students: 31% women, 69% men, 1% part-time, 70% state residents, 31% transferred in, 95% have need-based financial aid, 5% have non-need-based financial aid, 0% international, 37% 25 or older, 1% Native American, 2% Hispanic, 31% African American, 1% Asian American.
FIRST-YEAR CLASS 201 total; 685 applied, 81% were accepted, 36% of whom enrolled.
ACADEMIC PROGRAM Core, professional culinary curriculum. Calendar: terms. 15 courses offered in 1995–96; average class size 30 in required courses. Academic remediation for entering students, summer session for credit, part-time degree program (daytime), co-op programs and internships.
GENERAL DEGREE REQUIREMENTS 99 quarter hours; internship.
MAJOR Culinary arts.
LIBRARY Johnson & Wales University at Norfolk Library with 2,220 books, 22 periodicals, 2 on-line bibliographic services, 3 CD-ROMs.
COMPUTERS ON CAMPUS 15 computers for student use in computer labs, learning resource center, library provide access to main academic computer, e-mail, Internet. Staffed computer lab on campus provides training in use of computers, software.
COLLEGE LIFE Orientation program (4 days, $65, parents included). ***Social organizations:*** 7 open to all. ***Most popular organizations:*** ACF, Garde Manger, Wine and Beer Club, VICA, Baking and Pastry Club. ***Major annual events:*** Spirit of Norfolk Semiformal, End of Year Blowout, Busch Gardens Trip. ***Student services:*** personal-psychological counseling. ***Campus security:*** trained evening security personnel.
HOUSING 134 in college housing during 1995–96. Freshmen guaranteed college housing. Off-campus living permitted.
CAREER PLANNING ***Placement office:*** 2 full-time staff. ***Director:*** Ms. Torri Butler, Director of Student Services, 804-853-1906. ***Services:*** job fairs, resume preparation, career counseling, careers library, job bank, job interviews. 30 organizations recruited on campus 1994–95.
AFTER GRADUATION 100% of class of 1994 had job offers within 6 months.
EXPENSES FOR 1996–97 Comprehensive fee of $16,719 includes full-time tuition ($11,562), mandatory fees ($375), and college room and board ($4782).
FINANCIAL AID ***College-administered undergrad aid 1995–96:*** 297 need-based scholarships (average $1456), 152 non-need scholarships (average $961), low-interest long-term loans from college funds (average $1422), loans from external sources (average $2561), 66 Federal Work-Study (averaging $1725), 7 part-time jobs. ***Required forms:*** FAFSA. ***Priority deadline:*** 5/1.
APPLYING ***Options:*** Common Application, electronic application, early entrance, deferred entrance, midyear entrance. ***Required:*** school transcript. ***Recommended:*** minimum 2.0 GPA, ACT. ***Required for some:*** recommendations, interview, SAT I. ***Application deadline:*** rolling.
APPLYING/TRANSFER ***Required:*** high school transcript. ***Recommended:*** college transcript, minimum 2.0 college GPA, minimum 2.0 high school GPA. ***Required for some:*** standardized test scores, recommendations, interview, college transcript. ***Entrance:*** minimally difficult. ***Application deadline:*** rolling. ***Contact:*** Ms. Tammy Jaxtheimer, Director of Admissions, 804-853-3508.
CONTACT Ms. Tammy Jaxtheimer, Director of Admissions, Johnson & Wales University, 2428 Almeda Avenue, Suite 316, Norfolk, VA 23513, 804-853-3508. ***E-mail:*** admissions@jwu.edu. College video available.

JOHN TYLER COMMUNITY COLLEGE
Chester, Virginia

UG Enrollment: 5,367	**Tuition & Fees (VA Res): $1545**
Application Deadline: rolling	**Room & Board: N/Avail**

GENERAL State-supported, 2-year, coed. Part of Virginia Community College System. Awards certificates, transfer associate, terminal associate degrees. Founded 1967. ***Setting:*** 62-acre suburban campus with easy access to Richmond. ***Total enrollment:*** 5,367. ***Faculty:*** 227 (67 full-time, 15% with terminal degrees, 160 part-time); student-faculty ratio is 19:1.
ENROLLMENT PROFILE 5,367 students from 39 states and territories, 6 other countries. 61% women, 39% men, 81% part-time, 96% state residents, 14% transferred in, 22% have need-based financial aid, 5% have non-need-based financial aid, 64% 25 or older, 1% Native American, 1% Hispanic, 20% African American, 2% Asian American. ***Areas of study chosen:*** 29% interdisciplinary studies, 15% business management and administrative services, 7% engineering and applied sciences, 7% health professions and related sciences, 7% social sciences, 6% computer and information sciences, 3% education, 1% architecture, 1% fine arts. ***Most popular recent majors:*** nursing, liberal arts/general studies, funeral service.
FIRST-YEAR CLASS 1,450 total; 2,455 applied, 100% were accepted, 59% of whom enrolled.
ACADEMIC PROGRAM Core, interdisciplinary curriculum. Calendar: semesters. 243 courses offered in 1995–96. Academic remediation for entering students, services for LD students, advanced placement, tutorials, summer session for credit, part-time degree program (daytime, evenings, weekends, summer), external degree programs, adult/continuing education programs. ROTC: Army (c).
GENERAL DEGREE REQUIREMENTS 65 semester hours; 6 semester hours of math/science; computer course.
MAJORS Accounting, architectural technologies, automotive technologies, business administration/commerce/management, child psychology/child development, computer information systems, electronics engineering technology, funeral service, human services, instrumentation technology, law enforcement/police sciences, liberal arts/general studies, mechanical engineering technology, nursing, physical therapy, secretarial studies/office management.
LIBRARY 40,685 books, 43,795 microform titles, 138 periodicals, 85 CD-ROMs, 7,564 records, tapes, and CDs. Acquisition spending 1994–95: $397,889.
COMPUTERS ON CAMPUS 500 computers for student use in computer center, academic labs, library. Staffed computer lab on campus provides training in use of computers, software.
COLLEGE LIFE ***Student services:*** personal-psychological counseling. ***Campus security:*** 24-hour patrols.
HOUSING College housing not available.
ATHLETICS ***Intramural:*** football, softball, tennis, volleyball. ***Contact:*** Mr. Steve Fritton, Associate Professor of Physical Education, 804-796-4285.
CAREER PLANNING ***Placement office:*** 1 full-time, 1 part-time staff. ***Director:*** Dr. Charles Garren, Coordinator, College Career Center, 804-796-4167. ***Services:*** job fairs, career counseling, careers library.
EXPENSES FOR 1996–97 State resident tuition: $1525 full-time, $47.65 per semester hour part-time. Nonresident tuition: $5024 full-time, $157 per semester hour part-time. Part-time mandatory fees: $10 per semester. Full-time mandatory fees: $20.
FINANCIAL AID ***College-administered undergrad aid 1995–96:*** need-based scholarships, 249 non-need scholarships (averaging $588), low-interest long-term loans from external sources (averaging $2531), 25 Federal Work-Study (averaging $2000). ***Required forms:*** institutional, FAFSA; accepted: CSS Financial Aid PROFILE. ***Priority deadline:*** 4/15. ***Waivers:*** full or partial for senior citizens. ***Notification:*** 6/15.
APPLYING Open admission. ***Options:*** early entrance, deferred entrance, midyear entrance. ***Recommended:*** school transcript. ***Application deadline:*** rolling. ***Notification:*** continuous. Preference given to district residents.
APPLYING/TRANSFER ***Recommended:*** high school transcript. ***Entrance:*** noncompetitive. ***Contact:*** Ms. Carole Royall, Counselor/Assistant to the Director of Student Services, 804-378-3446.

CONTACT Ms. Judy Wilhelm, Registrar/Enrollment Services Coordinator, John Tyler Community College, Chester, VA 23831, 804-796-4151 or toll-free 800-552-3490 (in-state). ***Fax:*** 804-796-4163.

J. SARGEANT REYNOLDS COMMUNITY COLLEGE
Richmond, Virginia

UG Enrollment: 9,160	**Tuition & Fees (VA Res): $1479**
Application Deadline: rolling	**Room & Board: N/Avail**

GENERAL State-supported, 2-year, coed. Part of Virginia Community College System. Awards certificates, transfer associate, terminal associate degrees. Founded 1972. ***Setting:*** 150-acre urban campus. ***Total enrollment:*** 9,160. ***Faculty:*** 567 (140 full-time, 427 part-time).
ENROLLMENT PROFILE 9,160 students from 30 states and territories, 21 other countries. 62% women, 80% part-time, 98% state residents, 1% international, 67% 25 or older, 1% Native American, 1% Hispanic, 25% African American, 1% Asian American. ***Most popular recent majors:*** business administration/commerce/management, nursing, liberal arts/general studies.
FIRST-YEAR CLASS 1,500 total. Of the students who applied, 100% were accepted.
ACADEMIC PROGRAM Core. Calendar: semesters. Academic remediation for entering students, English as a second language program offered during academic year, services for LD students, honors program, summer session for credit, part-time degree program (daytime, evenings, weekends, summer), adult/continuing education programs, co-op programs and internships. Off-campus study. ROTC: Army (c).
GENERAL DEGREE REQUIREMENTS 61 credit hours; math/science requirements vary according to program; computer course.
MAJORS Accounting, agricultural business, automotive technologies, biology/biological sciences, business administration/commerce/management, civil engineering technology, community services, computer programming, construction technologies, data processing, dental services, education, electrical and electronics technologies, electrical engineering technology, engineering (general), engineering technology, environmental sciences, fashion merchandising, finance/banking, fire science, heating/refrigeration/air conditioning, horticulture, hotel and restaurant management, law enforcement/police sciences, legal secretarial studies, liberal arts/general studies, medical assistant technologies, medical laboratory technology, nursing, optometric/ophthalmic technologies, real estate, recreation and leisure services, respiratory therapy, science, secretarial studies/office management.
LIBRARY 61,129 books, 454 microform titles, 823 periodicals, 594 records, tapes, and CDs.
COMPUTERS ON CAMPUS Computer purchase plan available. 50 computers for student use in labs provide access to main academic computer. Staffed computer lab on campus provides training in use of computers, software.
COLLEGE LIFE Orientation program (2 days, $14, parents included). Drama-theater group. ***Student services:*** personal-psychological counseling, women's center.
HOUSING College housing not available.
ATHLETICS ***Intramural:*** basketball, football, tennis.
CAREER PLANNING ***Director:*** Dr. Claire Robinson, Director of Career Planning and Placement, 804-371-3240. ***Service:*** career counseling.
EXPENSES FOR 1996–97 State resident tuition: $1430 full-time, $47.65 per credit hour part-time. Nonresident tuition: $4710 full-time, $157 per credit hour part-time. Full-time mandatory fees: $49.
FINANCIAL AID ***College-administered undergrad aid 1995–96:*** need-based scholarships, Federal Work-Study, part-time jobs. ***Required forms:*** CSS Financial Aid PROFILE. ***Application deadline:*** continuous to 4/1. ***Waivers:*** full or partial for senior citizens.
APPLYING Open admission except for nursing program. ***Options:*** early entrance, deferred entrance. ***Required:*** school transcript, TOEFL for international students. Test scores used for counseling/placement. ***Application deadline:*** rolling. ***Notification:*** continuous.
APPLYING/TRANSFER ***Required:*** college transcript. ***Application deadline:*** rolling. ***Notification:*** continuous.
CONTACT Ms. Suzan Marshall, Director of Admissions and Records, J. Sargeant Reynolds Community College, PO Box 85622, Richmond, VA 23285-5622, 804-371-3029. College video available.

LORD FAIRFAX COMMUNITY COLLEGE
Middletown, Virginia

UG Enrollment: 3,292	**Tuition & Fees (VA Res): $1426**
Application Deadline: rolling	**Room & Board: N/Avail**

GENERAL State-supported, 2-year, coed. Part of Virginia Community College System. Awards transfer associate, terminal associate degrees. Founded 1969. ***Setting:*** 100-acre rural campus with easy access to Washington, DC. ***Total enrollment:*** 3,292. ***Faculty:*** 148 (39 full-time, 109 part-time); student-faculty ratio is 22:1.
ENROLLMENT PROFILE 3,292 students from 2 states and territories. 66% women, 74% part-time, 96% state residents, 11% transferred in, 59% 25 or older, 1% Hispanic, 4% African American. ***Areas of study chosen:*** 15% liberal arts/general studies, 12% business management and administrative services, 8% education, 5% biological and life sciences, 5% communications and journalism, 5% computer and information sciences, 4% engineering and applied sciences, 2% natural resource sciences, 1% agriculture. ***Most popular recent majors:*** business administration/commerce/management, education, liberal arts/general studies.
FIRST-YEAR CLASS 793 total; 850 applied, 100% were accepted, 93% of whom enrolled.
ACADEMIC PROGRAM Core. Calendar: semesters. Academic remediation for entering students, English as a second language program, services for LD students, advanced placement, honors program, summer session for credit, part-time degree program (daytime, evenings), adult/continuing education programs, co-op programs.
GENERAL DEGREE REQUIREMENTS 61 credits; math/science requirements vary according to program; computer course for business-related majors.
MAJORS Accounting, agricultural business, business administration/commerce/management, civil engineering technology, computer information systems, computer technologies, education, electrical and electronics technologies, horticulture, industrial administration, liberal arts/general studies, mechanical engineering technology, natural resource management, science, secretarial studies/office management.
LIBRARY Learning Resources Center with 40,717 books, 9,000 microform titles, 282 periodicals, 50 CD-ROMs, 5,288 records, tapes, and CDs. Acquisition spending 1994–95: $172,082.
COMPUTERS ON CAMPUS 150 computers for student use in computer center, classrooms, library. Academic computing expenditure 1994–95: $58,516.
COLLEGE LIFE Drama-theater group. 4% vote in student government elections. ***Social organizations:*** 14 open to all; 1 national fraternity; 1% of eligible men are members. ***Most popular organizations:*** Phi Theta Kappa, Phi Beta Lambda, Performing Arts Club, Scientific Society, Ambassadors Club. ***Major annual events:*** Honors Convocation, Fall Activities Day, Spring Fling. ***Student services:*** personal-psychological counseling, women's center. ***Campus security:*** late-night transport-escort service.
HOUSING College housing not available.
ATHLETICS ***Intramural:*** basketball, softball, volleyball.
CAREER PLANNING ***Placement office:*** 1 full-time, 1 part-time staff; $53,058 operating expenditure 1994–95. ***Director:*** Ms. Julie West, Coordinator of Career Development and Placement Assistance, 540-869-1120. ***Services:*** job fairs, resume preparation, resume referral, career counseling, careers library, job interviews.
EXPENSES FOR 1996–97 State resident tuition: $1400 full-time, $46.65 per semester hour part-time. Nonresident tuition: $4680 full-time, $156 per semester hour part-time. Full-time mandatory fees: $26.
FINANCIAL AID ***College-administered undergrad aid 1995–96:*** need-based scholarships, 150 non-need scholarships (average $500), short-term loans (average $500), Federal Work-Study. ***Required forms:*** institutional, FAFSA; accepted: CSS Financial Aid PROFILE. ***Priority deadline:*** 7/1. ***Payment plan:*** deferred payment. ***Waivers:*** full or partial for senior citizens.
APPLYING Open admission. ***Options:*** early entrance, midyear entrance. ***Recommended:*** school transcript, 3 years of high school math. ***Required for some:*** TOEFL for international students. Test scores used for admission and counseling/placement. ***Application deadline:*** rolling. ***Notification:*** continuous. Preference given to district residents.
APPLYING/TRANSFER ***Recommended:*** 3 years of high school math, college transcript. ***Entrance:*** noncompetitive. ***Application deadline:*** rolling. ***Notification:*** continuous. ***Contact:*** Ms. Julie L. West, Coordinator of Career Development/Placement Assistance, 540-869-1120.
CONTACT Mr. Carroll Todd Smith, Coordinator of Admissions and Records, Lord Fairfax Community College, Middletown, VA 22645-0047, 540-869-1120 Ext. 114. ***Fax:*** 540-869-7881.

MOUNTAIN EMPIRE COMMUNITY COLLEGE
Big Stone Gap, Virginia

UG Enrollment: 2,700	**Tuition & Fees (VA Res): $1541**
Application Deadline: rolling	**Room & Board: N/Avail**

GENERAL State-supported, 2-year, coed. Part of Virginia Community College System. Awards certificates, diplomas, transfer associate, terminal associate degrees. Founded 1972. ***Setting:*** small-town campus. ***Endowment:*** $900,000. ***Total enrollment:*** 2,700. ***Faculty:*** 150 (70 full-time, 10% with terminal degrees, 80 part-time); student-faculty ratio is 18:1.
ENROLLMENT PROFILE 2,700 students from 3 states and territories. 64% women, 58% part-time, 99% state residents, 4% transferred in, 30% 25 or older, 2% African American. ***Areas of study chosen:*** 40% liberal arts/general studies, 20% education, 10% business management and administrative services, 5% biological and life sciences, 5% computer and information sciences, 5% engineering and applied sciences, 5% English language/literature/letters, 5% health professions and related sciences, 2% prelaw, 2% premed, 1% predentistry. ***Most popular recent majors:*** criminal justice, secretarial studies/office management, nursing.
FIRST-YEAR CLASS 550 total; 975 applied, 100% were accepted, 56% of whom enrolled. 1 valedictorian.
ACADEMIC PROGRAM Core. Calendar: semesters. 135 courses offered in 1995–96. Academic remediation for entering students, advanced placement, self-designed majors, summer session for credit, part-time degree program (daytime), adult/continuing education programs, co-op programs.
GENERAL DEGREE REQUIREMENTS 65 semester hours; 6 semester hours of math; computer course; internship (some majors).
MAJORS Accounting, architectural technologies, biology/biological sciences, business administration/commerce/management, business education, chemistry, computer information systems, corrections, criminal justice, drafting and design, education, electrical and electronics technologies, electronics engineering technology, elementary education, (pre)engineering sequence, engineering technology, English, environmental sciences, forestry, heating/refrigeration/air conditioning, land use management and reclamation, law enforcement/police sciences, legal secretarial studies, liberal arts/general studies, marketing/retailing/merchandising, mathematics, mechanical design technology, mining technology, nursing, public administration, respiratory therapy, science, secretarial studies/office management, water resources, welding technology.
LIBRARY Robb Hall with 21,500 books, 250 microform titles, 100 periodicals, 200 records, tapes, and CDs. Acquisition spending 1994–95: $200,000.
COMPUTERS ON CAMPUS 150 computers for student use in computer center, computer labs, learning resource center, library provide access to main academic computer, off-campus computing facilities, e-mail, Internet. Staffed computer lab on campus. Academic computing expenditure 1994–95: $800,000.
COLLEGE LIFE Orientation program (3 days, $46). Drama-theater group. 60% vote in student government elections. ***Social organizations:*** 8 open to all. ***Most popular organizations:*** Phi Theta Kappa, Lamda Alpha Epsilon, MECC Group Artists, Phi Beta Lambda, Players On the Mountain. ***Student services:*** personal-psychological counseling. ***Campus security:*** 24-hour patrols.
HOUSING College housing not available.
ATHLETICS ***Intramural:*** basketball, football, tennis, volleyball.
CAREER PLANNING ***Placement office:*** 1 full-time staff; $725,000 operating expenditure 1994–95. ***Director:*** Mr. Allen Duffield, Director, Career Education and Job Placement, 540-523-2400. ***Services:*** job fairs, resume preparation, resume referral, career counseling, careers library, job bank, job interviews.

Mountain Empire Community College (continued)
AFTER GRADUATION 90% of students completing a degree program in 1994–95 went directly on to further study.
EXPENSES FOR 1996–97 State resident tuition: $1493 full-time, $46.65 per semester hour part-time. Nonresident tuition: $4992 full-time, $156 per semester hour part-time. Part-time mandatory fees per semester range from $3 to $9. Full-time mandatory fees: $48.
FINANCIAL AID ***College-administered undergrad aid 1995–96:*** 30 need-based scholarships (average $500), 25 non-need scholarships (average $400), 60 Federal Work-Study (averaging $1200), 5 part-time jobs. ***Required forms:*** institutional, FAFSA. ***Priority deadline:*** 4/15. ***Waivers:*** full or partial for senior citizens. ***Notification:*** 6/15.
APPLYING Open admission except for nursing, respiratory care programs. ***Options:*** early entrance, deferred entrance, midyear entrance. ***Required:*** school transcript, TOEFL for international students. ***Required for some:*** minimum 2.0 GPA, 3 years of high school math and science. Test scores used for counseling/placement. ***Application deadline:*** rolling. ***Notification:*** continuous. Preference given to state residents.
APPLYING/TRANSFER ***Required:*** high school transcript, college transcript. ***Required for some:*** minimum 2.0 high school GPA. ***Application deadline:*** rolling. ***Notification:*** continuous. ***Contact:*** Ms. Debbie Pippin, Assistant to Director of Admissions, 540-523-2400.
CONTACT Mr. Perry Carroll, Director of Admissions, Records, and Financial Aid, Mountain Empire Community College, Big Stone Gap, VA 24219-0700, 540-523-2400 Ext. 209.

NATIONAL BUSINESS COLLEGE
Bluefield, Virginia

UG Enrollment: 165	**Tuition & Fees: $4152**
Application Deadline: rolling	**Room & Board: N/Avail**

GENERAL Proprietary, 2-year, coed. Part of National Business College. Awards terminal associate degrees. Founded 1981. ***Setting:*** small-town campus. ***Total enrollment:*** 165. ***Faculty:*** 15.
ENROLLMENT PROFILE 165 students: 80% women, 18% part-time, 60% state residents, 30% transferred in, 25% 25 or older, 1% Native American, 20% African American.
FIRST-YEAR CLASS 27 total; 33 applied, 100% were accepted, 82% of whom enrolled.
ACADEMIC PROGRAM Core, general education curriculum, honor code. Calendar: quarters. Academic remediation for entering students, advanced placement, summer session for credit, part-time degree program (daytime, evenings, summer), internships.
GENERAL DEGREE REQUIREMENTS 96 quarter hours; math/science requirements vary according to program; computer course; internship (some majors).
MAJORS Accounting, business administration/commerce/management, computer science, data processing, legal secretarial studies, marketing/retailing/merchandising, medical assistant technologies, medical secretarial studies, secretarial studies/office management.
LIBRARY 1,380 books, 12 periodicals.
COMPUTERS ON CAMPUS 16 computers for student use in computer center. Staffed computer lab on campus provides training in use of computers, software.
COLLEGE LIFE ***Campus security:*** 24-hour emergency response devices.
HOUSING College housing not available.
CAREER PLANNING ***Placement office:*** 1 full-time staff. ***Director:*** Ms. Tina Satmary, Career Center Director, 703-326-3621. ***Services:*** job fairs, resume preparation, resume referral, career counseling, careers library, job bank, job interviews. Students must register freshman year.
EXPENSES FOR 1996–97 ***Application fee:*** $20. Tuition: $4122 full-time, $114.50 per quarter hour part-time. Part-time mandatory fees: $30 per year. Full-time mandatory fees: $30.
FINANCIAL AID ***College-administered undergrad aid 1995–96:*** need-based scholarships, 10 non-need scholarships (averaging $2000), low-interest long-term loans from external sources, Federal Work-Study, 3 part-time jobs. ***Required forms:*** FAFSA; accepted: CSS Financial Aid PROFILE. ***Priority deadline:*** 9/15. ***Payment plans:*** installment, deferred payment. ***Waivers:*** full or partial for employees or children of employees.
APPLYING Open admission. ***Option:*** midyear entrance. ***Required:*** school transcript, 3 years of high school math. ***Recommended:*** interview, TOEFL for international students. Test scores used for counseling/placement. ***Application deadline:*** rolling.
APPLYING/TRANSFER ***Required:*** 3 years of high school math. ***Entrance:*** noncompetitive. ***Application deadline:*** rolling. ***Contact:*** Mr. Denver Riffe, Campus Director, 703-326-3621.
CONTACT Mr. Larry W. Steele, Vice President of Admissions, National Business College, Bluefield, VA 24605-1405, 703-986-1800 Ext. 113. ***Fax:*** 703-986-1344. College video available.

NATIONAL BUSINESS COLLEGE
Bristol, Virginia

UG Enrollment: 81	**Tuition & Fees: $4152**
Application Deadline: rolling	**Room & Board: N/Avail**

GENERAL Proprietary, 2-year, coed. Part of National Business College. Awards terminal associate degrees. Founded 1992. ***Setting:*** small-town campus. ***Total enrollment:*** 81. ***Faculty:*** 7 (all part-time); student-faculty ratio is 8:1.
ENROLLMENT PROFILE 81 students: 84% women, 29% part-time, 0% transferred in, 93% have need-based financial aid, 0% international, 40% 25 or older, 0% Native American, 0% Hispanic, 13% African American, 2% Asian American.
FIRST-YEAR CLASS 26 applied, 100% were accepted, 50% of whom enrolled.
ACADEMIC PROGRAM Core, honor code. Calendar: quarters. Academic remediation for entering students, advanced placement, summer session for credit, part-time degree program (daytime, evenings, summer), internships.
GENERAL DEGREE REQUIREMENTS 96 quarter hours; math/science requirements vary according to program; computer course; internship (some majors).
MAJORS Computer science, secretarial studies/office management.
LIBRARY National Business College-Bristol Campus Library with 1,315 books, 15 periodicals.
COMPUTERS ON CAMPUS 20 computers for student use in computer labs, classrooms. Staffed computer lab on campus provides training in use of computers, software.
COLLEGE LIFE ***Campus security:*** 24-hour emergency response devices.
HOUSING College housing not available.
CAREER PLANNING ***Placement office:*** 1 part-time staff. ***Director:*** Ms. Mary Tankersley, Director, Career Center, 703-669-5333. ***Services:*** job fairs, resume preparation, resume referral, career counseling, careers library, job bank, job interviews. Students must register freshman year.
EXPENSES FOR 1996–97 ***Application fee:*** $20. Tuition: $4122 full-time, $114.50 per quarter hour part-time. Part-time mandatory fees: $30 per year. Full-time mandatory fees: $30.
FINANCIAL AID ***College-administered undergrad aid 1995–96:*** need-based scholarships, non-need scholarships, low-interest long-term loans from external sources, Federal Work-Study, 3 part-time jobs. ***Required forms:*** FAFSA; accepted: CSS Financial Aid PROFILE. ***Application deadline:*** continuous. ***Payment plans:*** installment, deferred payment. ***Waivers:*** full or partial for employees or children of employees.
APPLYING Open admission. ***Required:*** school transcript, 3 years of high school math. ***Recommended:*** interview, TOEFL for international students. Test scores used for counseling/placement. ***Application deadline:*** rolling.
APPLYING/TRANSFER ***Entrance:*** noncompetitive. ***Application deadline:*** rolling. ***Contact:*** Ms. Pam Muller, Director, 703-669-5333.
CONTACT Mr. Larry W. Steele, Vice President of Admissions, National Business College, PO Box 6400, Roanoke, VA 24017, 703-986-1800 Ext. 113. ***Fax:*** 703-986-1344. College video available.

NATIONAL BUSINESS COLLEGE
Charlottesville, Virginia

UG Enrollment: 99	**Tuition & Fees: $4152**
Application Deadline: rolling	**Room & Board: N/Avail**

GENERAL Proprietary, 2-year, coed. Part of National Business College. Awards terminal associate degrees. Founded 1975. ***Setting:*** small-town campus with easy access to Richmond. ***Total enrollment:*** 99. ***Faculty:*** 12 part-time.
ENROLLMENT PROFILE 99 students: 70% women, 18% part-time, 90% state residents, 30% transferred in, 25% 25 or older, 1% Native American, 30% African American.
FIRST-YEAR CLASS 15 total; 19 applied, 100% were accepted, 79% of whom enrolled.
ACADEMIC PROGRAM Core, general education curriculum, honor code. Calendar: quarters. Academic remediation for entering students, advanced placement, summer session for credit, part-time degree program (daytime, evenings), internships.
GENERAL DEGREE REQUIREMENTS 96 quarter hours; math/science requirements vary according to program; computer course; internship (some majors).
MAJORS Accounting, business administration/commerce/management, computer science, legal secretarial studies, medical assistant technologies, medical secretarial studies, secretarial studies/office management, tourism and travel.
LIBRARY 1,928 books, 12 periodicals.
COMPUTERS ON CAMPUS 15 computers for student use in computer center, classrooms. Staffed computer lab on campus provides training in use of computers, software.
COLLEGE LIFE ***Campus security:*** 24-hour emergency response devices.
HOUSING College housing not available.
CAREER PLANNING ***Placement office:*** 1 full-time staff. ***Director:*** Ms. Cathy Urichek, Career Center Director, 804-295-0316. ***Services:*** job fairs, resume preparation, resume referral, career counseling, careers library, job bank, job interviews. Students must register freshman year.
EXPENSES FOR 1996–97 ***Application fee:*** $20. Tuition: $4122 full-time, $114.50 per quarter hour part-time. Part-time mandatory fees: $30 per year. Full-time mandatory fees: $30.
FINANCIAL AID ***College-administered undergrad aid 1995–96:*** need-based scholarships, 10 non-need scholarships (average $2000), low-interest long-term loans from external sources, Federal Work-Study, 6 part-time jobs. ***Required forms:*** FAFSA; accepted: CSS Financial Aid PROFILE. ***Priority deadline:*** 9/15. ***Payment plans:*** installment, deferred payment. ***Waivers:*** full or partial for employees or children of employees.
APPLYING Open admission. ***Option:*** midyear entrance. ***Required:*** school transcript, 3 years of high school math. ***Recommended:*** interview, TOEFL for international students. Test scores used for counseling/placement. ***Application deadline:*** rolling.
APPLYING/TRANSFER ***Required:*** 3 years of high school math. ***Entrance:*** noncompetitive. ***Application deadline:*** rolling. ***Contact:*** Ms. Kathy Brewer, Campus Director, 804-295-0136.
CONTACT Mr. Larry W. Steele, Vice President of Admissions, National Business College, 813 East Main Street, Charlottesville, VA 24153, 703-986-1800 Ext. 113. ***Fax:*** 703-986-1344. College video available.

NATIONAL BUSINESS COLLEGE
Danville, Virginia

UG Enrollment: 158	**Tuition & Fees: $4152**
Application Deadline: 9/15	**Room & Board: N/Avail**

GENERAL Proprietary, 2-year, coed. Part of National Business College. Awards terminal associate degrees. Founded 1975. ***Setting:*** small-town campus. ***Total enrollment:*** 158. ***Faculty:*** 18 (1 full-time, 17 part-time).
ENROLLMENT PROFILE 158 students: 80% women, 18% part-time, 90% state residents, 30% transferred in, 70% have need-based financial aid, 0% international, 30% 25 or older, 1% Native American, 20% African American.
FIRST-YEAR CLASS 18 total; 22 applied, 95% were accepted, 86% of whom enrolled.
ACADEMIC PROGRAM Core, general education curriculum, honor code. Calendar: quarters. Academic remediation for entering students, advanced placement, summer session for credit, part-time degree program (daytime, evenings, summer), internships.
GENERAL DEGREE REQUIREMENTS 96 quarter hours; math/science requirements vary according to program; computer course; internship (some majors).
MAJORS Accounting, business administration/commerce/management, computer programming, computer science, fashion merchandising, legal secretarial studies, marketing/retailing/merchandising, medical assistant technologies, medical secretarial studies, secretarial studies/office management.
LIBRARY 3,010 books, 12 periodicals.

Virginia

COMPUTERS ON CAMPUS 14 computers for student use in computer center, word processing area.
COLLEGE LIFE *Campus security:* 24-hour emergency response devices.
HOUSING College housing not available.
CAREER PLANNING *Director:* Mr. William Gardner, Career Center Director, 804-793-6822. *Services:* job fairs, resume preparation, resume referral, career counseling, careers library, job bank, job interviews. Students must register freshman year.
EXPENSES FOR 1996-97 *Application fee:* $25. Tuition: $4122 full-time, $114.50 per quarter hour part-time. Part-time mandatory fees: $30 per year. Full-time mandatory fees: $30.
FINANCIAL AID *College-administered undergrad aid 1995-96:* need-based scholarships, 12 non-need scholarships (average $2400), low-interest long-term loans from external sources (average $500), 3 part-time jobs. *Required forms:* FAFSA; accepted: CSS Financial Aid PROFILE, state. *Priority deadline:* 9/15.
APPLYING Open admission. *Option:* midyear entrance. *Required:* school transcript, 3 years of high school math and science. *Recommended:* recommendations, TOEFL for international students. Test scores used for counseling/placement. *Application deadline:* 9/15. *Notification:* continuous until 10/15.
APPLYING/TRANSFER *Required:* 3 years of high school math and science. *Application deadline:* rolling. *Contact:* Ms. Amy Bracey, Campus Director, 804-793-6822.
CONTACT Mr. Larry W. Steele, Vice President of Admissions, National Business College, Danville, VA 24541-1819, 703-986-1800 Ext. 113. *Fax:* 703-986-1344. College video available.

NATIONAL BUSINESS COLLEGE
Harrisonburg, Virginia

UG Enrollment: 86	Tuition & Fees: $4152
Application Deadline: rolling	Room & Board: N/Avail

GENERAL Proprietary, 2-year, coed. Part of National Business College. Awards terminal associate degrees. Founded 1988. *Setting:* small-town campus. *Total enrollment:* 86. *Faculty:* 18 (all part-time); student-faculty ratio is 8:1.
ENROLLMENT PROFILE 86 students from 2 states and territories. 82% women, 18% part-time, 95% state residents, 25% 25 or older, 18% African American.
FIRST-YEAR CLASS 13 total; 16 applied, 100% were accepted, 81% of whom enrolled.
ACADEMIC PROGRAM Core, general education curriculum, honor code. Calendar: quarters. Academic remediation for entering students, advanced placement, summer session for credit, internships.
GENERAL DEGREE REQUIREMENTS 96 credit hours; math/science requirements vary according to program; computer course; internship (some majors).
MAJORS Accounting, business administration/commerce/management, computer management, data processing, legal secretarial studies, marketing/retailing/merchandising, medical assistant technologies, medical secretarial studies, secretarial studies/office management.
LIBRARY 2,452 books, 19 periodicals.
COMPUTERS ON CAMPUS 20 computers for student use in computer center, classrooms. Staffed computer lab on campus provides training in use of computers, software.
COLLEGE LIFE *Campus security:* 24-hour emergency response devices.
HOUSING College housing not available.
CAREER PLANNING *Director:* Ms. Lynda Blackborn, Career Center Director, 703-432-0943. *Services:* job fairs, resume preparation, resume referral, career counseling, careers library, job bank, job interviews.
EXPENSES FOR 1996-97 *Application fee:* $20. Tuition: $4122 full-time, $114.50 per credit hour part-time. Part-time mandatory fees: $30 per year. Full-time mandatory fees: $30.
FINANCIAL AID *College-administered undergrad aid 1995-96:* need-based scholarships, low-interest long-term loans from external sources, Federal Work-Study. *Required forms:* FAFSA; accepted: CSS Financial Aid PROFILE. *Application deadline:* continuous to 9/15. *Payment plans:* installment, deferred payment. *Waivers:* full or partial for employees or children of employees.
APPLYING Open admission. *Option:* midyear entrance. *Required:* school transcript. *Recommended:* interview, TOEFL for international students. Test scores used for counseling/placement. *Application deadline:* rolling. *Notification:* continuous.
APPLYING/TRANSFER *Entrance:* noncompetitive. *Application deadline:* rolling. *Notification:* continuous. *Contact:* Mr. Ike Stonebergo, Campus Director, 703-432-0943.
CONTACT Mr. Larry W. Steele, Vice President of Admissions, National Business College, Harrisonburg, VA 22801-9709, 703-986-1800 Ext. 113. *Fax:* 703-986-1344. College video available.

NATIONAL BUSINESS COLLEGE
Lynchburg, Virginia

UG Enrollment: 106	Tuition & Fees: $4152
Application Deadline: rolling	Room & Board: N/Avail

GENERAL Proprietary, 2-year, coed. Part of National Business College. Awards terminal associate degrees. Founded 1979. *Setting:* 2-acre small-town campus. *Total enrollment:* 106. *Faculty:* 16 (all part-time).
ENROLLMENT PROFILE 106 students: 72% women, 7% part-time, 100% state residents, 45% transferred in, 0% international, 50% 25 or older, 0% Native American, 0% Hispanic, 28% African American, 0% Asian American.
FIRST-YEAR CLASS 19 total; 23 applied, 100% were accepted, 83% of whom enrolled.
ACADEMIC PROGRAM Core, general education curriculum, honor code. Calendar: quarters. Academic remediation for entering students, advanced placement, summer session for credit, part-time degree program (daytime, evenings, summer), internships.
GENERAL DEGREE REQUIREMENTS 96 quarter hours; math/science requirements vary according to program; computer course; internship (some majors).
MAJORS Accounting, business administration/commerce/management, computer science, fashion merchandising, legal secretarial studies, marketing/retailing/merchandising, medical assistant technologies, medical secretarial studies, secretarial studies/office management.
LIBRARY 1,500 books, 10 periodicals.

COMPUTERS ON CAMPUS 16 computers for student use in computer center, classrooms provide access to main academic computer, on-line services. Staffed computer lab on campus provides training in use of computers, software.
COLLEGE LIFE *Campus security:* 24-hour emergency response devices.
HOUSING College housing not available.
CAREER PLANNING *Director:* Mr. Wade Locy, Career Center Director, 804-239-3500. *Services:* job fairs, resume preparation, resume referral, career counseling, careers library, job bank, job interviews. Students must register freshman year.
EXPENSES FOR 1996-97 *Application fee:* $25. Tuition: $4122 full-time, $114.50 per quarter hour part-time. Part-time mandatory fees: $30 per year. Full-time mandatory fees: $30.
FINANCIAL AID *College-administered undergrad aid 1995-96:* need-based scholarships, 15 non-need scholarships (average $3000), low-interest long-term loans from external sources, 3 part-time jobs. *Required forms:* institutional, FAFSA. *Priority deadline:* 9/15. *Payment plans:* installment, deferred payment. *Waivers:* full or partial for employees or children of employees.
APPLYING Open admission. *Option:* midyear entrance. *Required:* school transcript, 3 years of high school math. *Recommended:* recommendations. Test scores used for counseling/placement. *Application deadline:* rolling.
APPLYING/TRANSFER *Required:* 3 years of high school math. *Entrance:* noncompetitive. *Application deadline:* rolling. *Contact:* Mr. Dave Stephenson, Campus Director, 804-239-3500.
CONTACT Mr. Larry W. Steele, Vice President of Admissions, National Business College, Lynchburg, VA 24502-2653, 703-986-1800 Ext. 113. *Fax:* 703-986-1344. College video available.

NATIONAL BUSINESS COLLEGE
Martinsville, Virginia

UG Enrollment: 148	Tuition & Fees: $4152
Application Deadline: rolling	Room & Board: N/Avail

GENERAL Proprietary, 2-year, coed. Part of National Business College. Awards terminal associate degrees. Founded 1975. *Setting:* small-town campus. *Total enrollment:* 148. *Faculty:* 15 (2 full-time, 13 part-time).
ENROLLMENT PROFILE 148 students from 2 states and territories. 62% women, 5% part-time, 95% state residents, 30% transferred in, 1% international, 25% 25 or older, 1% Native American, 38% African American.
FIRST-YEAR CLASS 18 total; 20 applied, 100% were accepted, 90% of whom enrolled.
ACADEMIC PROGRAM Core, general education curriculum, honor code. Calendar: quarters. Academic remediation for entering students, advanced placement, summer session for credit, part-time degree program (daytime, evenings), internships.
GENERAL DEGREE REQUIREMENTS 96 quarter hours; math/science requirements vary according to program; computer course; internship (some majors).
MAJORS Accounting, business administration/commerce/management, computer science, legal secretarial studies, marketing/retailing/merchandising, medical secretarial studies, secretarial studies/office management.
LIBRARY 1,361 books, 12 periodicals.
COMPUTERS ON CAMPUS 15 computers for student use in computer center, classrooms. Staffed computer lab on campus provides training in use of computers, software.
COLLEGE LIFE Student-run newspaper. *Campus security:* 24-hour emergency response devices.
HOUSING College housing not available.
CAREER PLANNING *Director:* Mr. Michael Martin, Career Center Director, 703-632-5621. *Services:* job fairs, resume preparation, resume referral, career counseling, careers library, job bank, job interviews. Students must register freshman year.
EXPENSES FOR 1996-97 *Application fee:* $25. Tuition: $4122 full-time, $114.50 per quarter hour part-time. Part-time mandatory fees: $30 per year. Full-time mandatory fees: $30.
FINANCIAL AID *College-administered undergrad aid 1995-96:* need-based scholarships, 5 non-need scholarships (average $1000), low-interest long-term loans from external sources, Federal Work-Study, 2 part-time jobs. *Required forms:* FAFSA; accepted: CSS Financial Aid PROFILE. *Priority deadline:* 9/15. *Payment plans:* installment, deferred payment. *Waivers:* full or partial for employees or children of employees.
APPLYING Open admission. *Option:* midyear entrance. *Required:* school transcript, 3 years of high school math. *Recommended:* interview, TOEFL for international students. Test scores used for counseling/placement. *Application deadline:* rolling.
APPLYING/TRANSFER *Required:* 3 years of high school math. *Entrance:* noncompetitive. *Application deadline:* rolling. *Contact:* Ms. June Ford, Campus Director, 703-632-5621.
CONTACT Mr. Larry W. Steele, Vice President for Admissions, National Business College, Martinsville, VA 24114, 703-986-1800 Ext. 113. *Fax:* 703-986-1344. College video available.

NATIONAL BUSINESS COLLEGE
Salem, Virginia

UG Enrollment: 362	Tuition & Fees: $3954
Application Deadline: rolling	Room & Board: $3450

GENERAL Proprietary, primarily 2-year, coed. Part of National Business College. Awards certificates, diplomas, transfer associate, terminal associate, bachelor's degrees. Founded 1886. *Setting:* 3-acre urban campus. *Total enrollment:* 362. *Faculty:* 25 (13 full-time, 60% with terminal degrees, 12 part-time); student-faculty ratio is 10:1.
ENROLLMENT PROFILE 362 students from 10 states and territories, 3 other countries. 80% women, 55% part-time, 85% state residents, 30% transferred in, 70% have need-based financial aid, 3% international, 30% 25 or older, 1% Native American, 1% Hispanic, 20% African American, 1% Asian American.
FIRST-YEAR CLASS 136 total; 150 applied, 95% were accepted, 96% of whom enrolled.
ACADEMIC PROGRAM Core, general education curriculum, honor code. Calendar: quarters. Academic remediation for entering students, advanced placement, summer session for credit, part-time degree program (daytime, evenings), internships.

National Business College (continued)
GENERAL DEGREE REQUIREMENTS 108 quarter hours for associate, 180 quarter hours for bachelor's; 8 quarter hours of math; computer course; internship (some majors).
MAJORS Accounting (B), business administration/commerce/management (B), computer science, fashion merchandising, hospitality services, hotel and restaurant management, legal secretarial studies, marketing/retailing/merchandising, medical assistant technologies, medical secretarial studies, secretarial studies/office management, tourism and travel.
LIBRARY 18,200 books, 40 periodicals, 90 records, tapes, and CDs.
COMPUTERS ON CAMPUS 42 computers for student use in computer center, classrooms. Staffed computer lab on campus provides training in use of computers, software.
COLLEGE LIFE ***Social organizations:*** 1 open to all; local fraternities, local sororities; 10% of eligible men and 20% of eligible women are members. ***Campus security:*** 24-hour emergency response devices.
HOUSING 100 college housing spaces available; 60 were occupied 1995–96. No special consideration for freshman housing applicants. Off-campus living permitted. ***Option:*** coed (1 building) housing available. Resident assistants live in dorms.
CAREER PLANNING ***Placement office:*** 1 full-time staff. ***Director:*** Ms. Judy Steelman, Career Center Director, 540-986-1800. ***Services:*** job fairs, resume preparation, resume referral, career counseling, careers library, job bank, job interviews. Students must register freshman year.
EXPENSES FOR 1995–96 ***Application fee:*** $20. Comprehensive fee of $7404 includes full-time tuition ($3924), mandatory fees ($30), and college room and board ($3450). College room only: $1950. Part-time tuition: $109 per quarter hour. Part-time mandatory fees: $30 per year.
FINANCIAL AID ***College-administered undergrad aid 1995–96:*** need-based scholarships, 50 non-need scholarships (average $200), low-interest long-term loans from external sources, Federal Work-Study, 10 part-time jobs. ***Required forms:*** FAFSA; accepted: CSS Financial Aid PROFILE. ***Priority deadline:*** 9/15. ***Payment plans:*** installment, deferred payment. ***Waivers:*** full or partial for employees or children of employees.
APPLYING Open admission. ***Option:*** midyear entrance. ***Required:*** 3 years of high school math. ***Recommended:*** ACT. Test scores used for counseling/placement. ***Application deadline:*** rolling.
APPLYING/TRANSFER ***Required:*** 3 years of high school math. ***Entrance:*** noncompetitive. ***Application deadline:*** rolling. ***Contact:*** Ms. Anna Counts, Campus Director, 540-986-1800.
CONTACT Mr. Larry W. Steele, Vice President of Admissions, National Business College, PO Box 6400, Roanoke, VA 24017, 540-986-1800 Ext. 113 or toll-free 800-666-6221 (in-state). ***Fax:*** 540-986-1344. College video available.

NEW RIVER COMMUNITY COLLEGE
Dublin, Virginia

UG Enrollment: 1,554 | **Tuition & Fees (VA Res): $1541**
Application Deadline: rolling | **Room & Board: N/Avail**

GENERAL State-supported, 2-year, coed. Part of Virginia Community College System. Awards transfer associate, terminal associate degrees. Founded 1969. ***Setting:*** 100-acre rural campus. ***Total enrollment:*** 1,554. ***Faculty:*** 175 (61 full-time, 12% with terminal degrees, 114 part-time).
ENROLLMENT PROFILE 1,554 students from 21 states and territories, 12 other countries. 53% women, 47% men, 58% part-time, 96% state residents, 16% transferred in, 45% 25 or older, 0% Native American, 1% Hispanic, 4% African American, 2% Asian American. ***Areas of study chosen:*** 12% liberal arts/general studies, 8% business management and administrative services, 5% engineering and applied sciences, 3% biological and life sciences, 3% computer and information sciences, 2% education. ***Most popular recent majors:*** instrumentation technology, liberal arts/general studies, word processing.
FIRST-YEAR CLASS 291 total; 400 applied, 100% were accepted, 73% of whom enrolled.
ACADEMIC PROGRAM Honor code. Calendar: semesters. Academic remediation for entering students, services for LD students, advanced placement, summer session for credit, part-time degree program (daytime, evenings, summer), external degree programs, adult/continuing education programs, co-op programs and internships.
GENERAL DEGREE REQUIREMENTS 65 semester hours; math/science requirements vary according to program; computer course; internship (some majors).
MAJORS Accounting, architectural technologies, automotive technologies, business administration/commerce/management, child care/child and family studies, community services, computer information systems, computer technologies, criminal justice, deaf interpreter training, drafting and design, education, electrical and electronics technologies, fashion merchandising, forensic sciences, instrumentation technology, law enforcement/police sciences, liberal arts/general studies, machine and tool technologies, marketing/retailing/merchandising, medical secretarial studies, paralegal studies, practical nursing, science, secretarial studies/office management, welding technology, word processing.
LIBRARY 31,715 books, 412 microform titles, 258 periodicals, 788 records, tapes, and CDs.
COMPUTERS ON CAMPUS 120 computers for student use in computer center, learning resource center.
COLLEGE LIFE Student-run newspaper. ***Most popular organizations:*** Student Government Association, Phi Beta Lambda, Instrument Society of America, Human Service Organization, Sign Language Club. ***Major annual events:*** Fall Bash, Freaky Friday, Spring Fling. ***Student services:*** personal-psychological counseling. ***Campus security:*** 24-hour patrols.
HOUSING College housing not available.
ATHLETICS ***Intramural:*** archery, basketball, bowling, football, soccer, table tennis (Ping-Pong), tennis, volleyball, weight lifting. ***Contact:*** Mr. Ben Kramer, Activities Counselor, 540-674-3600 Ext. 431.
CAREER PLANNING ***Placement office:*** 2 full-time, 1 part-time staff. ***Director:*** Dr. Dale Conrad, Associate Professor and Counselor, Career Development, 540-674-3600. ***Services:*** job fairs, resume preparation, resume referral, career counseling, careers library, job bank, job interviews.
AFTER GRADUATION 75% of students completing a degree program in 1994–95 went directly on to further study.
EXPENSES FOR 1996–97 State resident tuition: $1493 full-time, $46.65 per semester hour part-time. Nonresident tuition: $4992 full-time, $156 per semester hour part-time. Part-time mandatory fees: $24 per semester. Full-time mandatory fees: $48.
FINANCIAL AID ***College-administered undergrad aid 1995–96:*** 45 need-based scholarships (average $1000), short-term loans (average $700), low-interest long-term loans from external sources (average $2000), Federal Work-Study, 6 part-time jobs. ***Required forms:*** institutional, FAFSA; required for some: state; accepted: CSS Financial Aid PROFILE. ***Priority deadline:*** 4/15. ***Waivers:*** full or partial for senior citizens. ***Notification:*** 5/1. ***Average indebtedness of graduates:*** $3000.
APPLYING Open admission. ***Options:*** early entrance, deferred entrance, midyear entrance. ***Required:*** TOEFL for international students. ***Required for some:*** school transcript. Test scores used for counseling/placement. ***Application deadline:*** rolling. ***Notification:*** continuous. Preference given to local residents.
APPLYING/TRANSFER ***Required for some:*** college transcript. ***Application deadline:*** rolling. ***Notification:*** continuous. ***Contact:*** Mrs. Rita Dixon, Director of Student Development, 540-674-3609.
CONTACT Mrs. Margaret T. Chrisley, Coordinator of Admissions and Records, New River Community College, Dublin, VA 24084-1127, 540-674-3600 Ext. 205. ***Fax:*** 540-674-3634. ***E-mail:*** nrchrim@vccscent.bitnet.

NORTHERN VIRGINIA COMMUNITY COLLEGE
Annandale, Virginia

UG Enrollment: 38,084 | **Tuition & Fees (VA Res): $1584**
Application Deadline: rolling | **Room & Board: N/Avail**

GENERAL State-supported, 2-year, coed. Part of Virginia Community College System. Awards certificates, transfer associate, terminal associate degrees. Founded 1965. ***Setting:*** 435-acre suburban campus with easy access to Washington, DC. ***Endowment:*** $550,000. ***Total enrollment:*** 38,084. ***Faculty:*** 1,387 (502 full-time, 885 part-time).
ENROLLMENT PROFILE 38,084 students: 55% women, 45% men, 75% part-time, 12% transferred in, 8% international, 57% 25 or older, 1% Native American, 7% Hispanic, 13% African American, 13% Asian American. ***Most popular recent majors:*** liberal arts/general studies, business administration/commerce/management.
FIRST-YEAR CLASS 9,561 total; 12,025 applied, 100% were accepted, 80% of whom enrolled.
ACADEMIC PROGRAM Core. Calendar: semesters. 1,300 courses offered in 1995–96. Academic remediation for entering students, English as a second language program offered during academic year and summer, services for LD students, advanced placement, self-designed majors, tutorials, honors program, summer session for credit, part-time degree program (daytime, evenings, weekends, summer), external degree programs, adult/continuing education programs, co-op programs and internships. Off-campus study. Study-abroad program.
GENERAL DEGREE REQUIREMENT 66 credit hours.
MAJORS Accounting, applied art, architectural technologies, art education, art/fine arts, art history, automotive technologies, aviation technology, business administration/commerce/management, civil engineering technology, commercial art, computer information systems, computer science, construction technologies, corrections, dental services, drug and alcohol/substance abuse counseling, early childhood education, electrical and electronics technologies, emergency medical technology, engineering (general), (pre)engineering sequence, fire science, flight training, food services management, gerontology, heating/refrigeration/air conditioning, horticulture, hotel and restaurant management, human services, interior design, international business, law enforcement/police sciences, liberal arts/general studies, marketing/retailing/merchandising, mathematics, mechanical engineering technology, medical laboratory technology, medical records services, mental health/rehabilitation counseling, music, natural sciences, nursing, paralegal studies, photography, physical therapy, purchasing/inventory management, radiological technology, real estate, recreation and leisure services, religious studies, respiratory therapy, sacred music, science, secretarial studies/office management, speech/rhetoric/public address/debate, tourism and travel, veterinary technology.
LIBRARY 295,110 books, 2,066 microform titles, 1,603 periodicals, 3 on-line bibliographic services, 784 CD-ROMs, 2,662 records, tapes, and CDs. Acquisition spending 1994–95: $638,329.
COMPUTERS ON CAMPUS Computer purchase plan available. 1,450 computers for student use in computer labs, learning resource center, labs, classrooms provide access to main academic computer, Internet, software. Staffed computer lab on campus provides training in use of computers, software.
COLLEGE LIFE Student-run newspaper. ***Social organizations:*** 65 open to all. ***Campus security:*** campus police.
HOUSING College housing not available.
ATHLETICS ***Intramural:*** basketball, football, softball, table tennis (Ping-Pong), volleyball.
CAREER PLANNING ***Services:*** job fairs, resume preparation, career counseling, careers library.
EXPENSES FOR 1996–97 State resident tuition: $1584 full-time, $48 per credit hour part-time. Nonresident tuition: $5193 full-time, $157.35 per credit hour part-time.
FINANCIAL AID ***College-administered undergrad aid 1995–96:*** 2,189 need-based scholarships (average $775), 170 non-need scholarships (average $800), short-term loans (average $200), low-interest long-term loans from external sources (average $2694), 233 Federal Work-Study (averaging $1980), 36 part-time jobs. ***Required forms:*** institutional, FAFSA. ***Priority deadline:*** 3/1. ***Waivers:*** full or partial for senior citizens. ***Notification:*** 6/1.
APPLYING Open admission except for veterinary technology, dental hygiene, other health-related programs. ***Options:*** early entrance, deferred entrance. ***Required for some:*** school transcript, TOEFL for international students. Test scores used for counseling/placement. ***Application deadline:*** rolling. ***Notification:*** continuous.
APPLYING/TRANSFER ***Application deadline:*** rolling. ***Notification:*** continuous.
CONTACT Dr. Max L. Bassett, Dean of Academic and Student Services, Northern Virginia Community College, Annandale, VA 22003-3796, 703-323-3195.

Virginia

PATRICK HENRY COMMUNITY COLLEGE
Martinsville, Virginia

UG Enrollment: 2,800	Tuition & Fees (VA Res): $1534
Application Deadline: rolling	Room & Board: N/Avail

GENERAL State-supported, 2-year, coed. Part of Virginia Community College System. Awards transfer associate, terminal associate degrees. Founded 1962. *Setting:* 137-acre rural campus. *Total enrollment:* 2,800. *Faculty:* 88 (38 full-time, 50 part-time).
ENROLLMENT PROFILE 2,800 students from 3 states and territories. 60% women, 69% part-time, 98% state residents, 7% transferred in, 0% international, 52% 25 or older, 1% Native American, 2% Hispanic, 14% African American, 3% Asian American. *Most popular recent majors:* liberal arts/general studies, business administration/commerce/management, nursing.
FIRST-YEAR CLASS Of the students who applied, 100% were accepted, 63% of whom enrolled.
ACADEMIC PROGRAM Calendar: semesters. Academic remediation for entering students, services for LD students, advanced placement, summer session for credit, part-time degree program (daytime, evenings, weekends, summer), adult/continuing education programs, co-op programs.
GENERAL DEGREE REQUIREMENTS 62 semester hours; 3 semester hours of math; computer course.
MAJORS Accounting, business administration/commerce/management, computer programming, data processing, education, electrical and electronics technologies, industrial engineering technology, liberal arts/general studies, nursing, science, secretarial studies/office management.
LIBRARY 32,000 books, 350 periodicals, 2,844 records, tapes, and CDs.
COMPUTERS ON CAMPUS 100 computers for student use in computer center, library.
COLLEGE LIFE Drama-theater group.
HOUSING College housing not available.
ATHLETICS *Intramural:* basketball, table tennis (Ping-Pong), tennis, volleyball.
CAREER PLANNING *Director:* Ms. Cheryl Joyce, Coordinator of Career Development, 540-638-8777 Ext. 310. *Service:* career counseling.
EXPENSES FOR 1996-97 State resident tuition: $1524 full-time, $47.65 per semester hour part-time. Nonresident tuition: $5024 full-time, $157 per semester hour part-time. Part-time mandatory fees: $5 per semester hour. Full-time mandatory fees: $10.
FINANCIAL AID *College-administered undergrad aid 1995-96:* 50 need-based scholarships (averaging $450), 7 non-need scholarships (averaging $300), short-term loans (averaging $100), Federal Work-Study. *Required forms:* CSS Financial Aid PROFILE, institutional, FAFSA. *Priority deadline:* 7/1.
APPLYING Open admission except for nursing program. *Options:* early entrance, deferred entrance. *Required:* school transcript, TOEFL for international students, CGP. *Required for some:* 3 years of high school math and science. Test scores used for counseling/placement. *Application deadline:* rolling. *Notification:* continuous. Preference given to district residents.
APPLYING/TRANSFER *Required:* college transcript. *Application deadline:* rolling. *Notification:* continuous.
CONTACT Mr. Graham Valentine, Coordinator of Admissions and Records, Patrick Henry Community College, Martinsville, VA 24115-5311, 540-638-8777. *Fax:* 540-638-6469.

PAUL D. CAMP COMMUNITY COLLEGE
Franklin, Virginia

UG Enrollment: 1,629	Tuition & Fees (VA Res): $1525
Application Deadline: rolling	Room & Board: N/Avail

GENERAL State-supported, 2-year, coed. Part of Virginia Community College System. Awards certificates, transfer associate, terminal associate degrees. Founded 1971. *Setting:* 99-acre small-town campus. *Endowment:* $15,059. *Educational spending 1994-95:* $1687 per undergrad. *Total enrollment:* 1,629. *Faculty:* 59 (24 full-time, 100% with terminal degrees, 35 part-time).
ENROLLMENT PROFILE 1,629 students from 2 states and territories, 2 other countries. 63% women, 82% part-time, 95% state residents, 11% transferred in, 46% have need-based financial aid, 1% international, 55% 25 or older, 1% Native American, 1% Hispanic, 28% African American, 1% Asian American. *Areas of study chosen:* 40% business management and administrative services, 30% engineering and applied sciences, 20% liberal arts/general studies, 10% computer and information sciences. *Most popular recent majors:* business administration/commerce/management, education, liberal arts/general studies.
FIRST-YEAR CLASS 658 total; 658 applied, 100% were accepted, 100% of whom enrolled.
ACADEMIC PROGRAM Core, interdisciplinary curriculum, honor code. Calendar: semesters. 250 courses offered in 1995-96. Academic remediation for entering students, advanced placement, honors program, summer session for credit, part-time degree program (daytime, evenings, weekends, summer), adult/continuing education programs, co-op programs. Off-campus study at members of the Virginia Tidewater Consortium for Continuing Higher Education.
GENERAL DEGREE REQUIREMENTS 65 semester hours; 6 semester hours of math; computer course for most majors.
MAJORS Business administration/commerce/management, criminal justice, data processing, education, liberal arts/general studies, secretarial studies/office management.
LIBRARY 22,000 books, 200 periodicals, 25 CD-ROMs. Acquisition spending 1994-95: $133,687.
COMPUTERS ON CAMPUS 90 computers for student use in computer center provide access to main academic computer. Staffed computer lab on campus provides training in use of computers, software. Academic computing expenditure 1994-95: $745,602.
COLLEGE LIFE 20% vote in student government elections. *Social organizations:* 2 open to all. *Most popular organizations:* Circle K, Phi Beta Lambda, Phi Theta Kappa, Student Government Association. *Major annual events:* Fall Festival, Christmas Parade, Spring Fling. *Campus security:* night administration/maintenance personnel.
HOUSING College housing not available.
ATHLETICS *Intramural:* basketball, tennis, volleyball.
CAREER PLANNING *Placement office:* 1 full-time staff. *Director:* Mr. Chris Smith, Counselor, 804-569-6721. *Services:* resume preparation, career counseling, careers library, job bank.
EXPENSES FOR 1996-97 State resident tuition: $1525 full-time, $47.65 per semester hour part-time. Nonresident tuition: $5024 full-time, $157 per semester hour part-time.
FINANCIAL AID *College-administered undergrad aid 1995-96:* 5 need-based scholarships (average $250), non-need scholarships, Federal Work-Study. *Required forms:* institutional, FAFSA; accepted: CSS Financial Aid PROFILE. *Priority deadline:* 8/1. *Waivers:* full or partial for senior citizens.
APPLYING Open admission. *Options:* early entrance, deferred entrance. *Required:* school transcript, TOEFL for international students. Test scores used for counseling/placement. *Application deadline:* rolling. *Notification:* continuous. Preference given to state residents.
APPLYING/TRANSFER *Required:* high school transcript, college transcript. *Application deadline:* rolling. *Notification:* continuous. *Contact:* Mr. Walter Biggs, Transfer Coordinator, 804-569-6731.
CONTACT Dr. Jerry J. Standahl, Director of Student Development and Services, Paul D. Camp Community College, Franklin, VA 23851-0737, 804-569-6725. *E-mail:* vccscent@vtbit.cc.vt.edu.

PIEDMONT VIRGINIA COMMUNITY COLLEGE
Charlottesville, Virginia

UG Enrollment: 4,436	Tuition & Fees (VA Res): $1630
Application Deadline: 8/24	Room & Board: N/Avail

GENERAL State-supported, 2-year, coed. Part of Virginia Community College System. Awards transfer associate, terminal associate degrees. Founded 1972. *Setting:* 100-acre suburban campus with easy access to Richmond. *Total enrollment:* 4,436. *Faculty:* 262 (71 full-time, 191 part-time).
ENROLLMENT PROFILE 4,436 students from 11 states and territories, 18 other countries. 61% women, 81% part-time, 96% state residents, 2% transferred in, 60% 25 or older, 1% Hispanic, 11% African American, 1% Asian American. *Most popular recent majors:* nursing, business administration/commerce/management, liberal arts/general studies.
FIRST-YEAR CLASS 845 total. Of the students who applied, 100% were accepted, 98% of whom enrolled. 80% from top half of their high school class.
ACADEMIC PROGRAM Honor code. Calendar: semesters. Academic remediation for entering students, services for LD students, advanced placement, summer session for credit, part-time degree program (daytime, evenings, weekends, summer), adult/continuing education programs, co-op programs. ROTC: Army (c).
GENERAL DEGREE REQUIREMENTS 67 semester hours; 1 math course; computer course.
MAJORS Accounting, art/fine arts, automotive technologies, business administration/commerce/management, computer programming, construction management, criminal justice, data processing, education, electrical and electronics technologies, (pre)engineering sequence, law enforcement/police sciences, liberal arts/general studies, marketing/retailing/merchandising, nursing, science, secretarial studies/office management, theater arts/drama.
LIBRARY 28,000 books, 240 periodicals.
COMPUTERS ON CAMPUS 110 computers for student use in computer center.
COLLEGE LIFE Drama-theater group, student-run newspaper. *Social organizations:* 10 open to all. *Campus security:* 24-hour patrols.
HOUSING College housing not available.
ATHLETICS *Intramural:* baseball, basketball, football, tennis.
CAREER PLANNING *Service:* career counseling.
EXPENSES FOR 1995-96 State resident tuition: $1620 full-time, $47.65 per semester hour part-time. Nonresident tuition: $5338 full-time, $157 per semester hour part-time. Part-time mandatory fees per semester hour range from $3 to $6. Full-time mandatory fees: $10.
FINANCIAL AID *College-administered undergrad aid 1995-96:* need-based scholarships, short-term loans (average $128), low-interest long-term loans from external sources, Federal Work-Study, 200 part-time jobs. *Required forms:* CSS Financial Aid PROFILE, institutional, FAFSA. *Priority deadline:* 7/15. *Waivers:* full or partial for senior citizens.
APPLYING Open admission except for nursing program. *Option:* early entrance. *Required:* TOEFL for international students. *Required for some:* school transcript. *Application deadline:* 8/24. *Notification:* continuous.
APPLYING/TRANSFER *Application deadline:* 8/24. *Notification:* continuous. *Contact:* Ms. Bobbie Potter, Counselor, 804-977-3900 Ext. 430.
CONTACT Ms. Mary Lee Walsh, Director of Student Services, Piedmont Virginia Community College, Charlottesville, VA 22902-7589, 804-961-5400. *Fax:* 804-296-8395.

RAPPAHANNOCK COMMUNITY COLLEGE
Glenns, Virginia

UG Enrollment: 2,129	Tuition & Fees (VA Res): $1509
Application Deadline: rolling	Room & Board: N/Avail

GENERAL State-related, 2-year, coed. Part of Virginia Community College System. Awards certificates, diplomas, transfer associate, terminal associate degrees. Founded 1970. *Setting:* 217-acre rural campus. *Endowment:* $1 million. *Total enrollment:* 2,129. *Faculty:* 132 (30 full-time, 102 part-time); student-faculty ratio is 20:1.
ENROLLMENT PROFILE 2,129 students from 23 states and territories, 3 other countries. 66% women, 81% part-time, 98% state residents, 12% transferred in, 1% international, 68% 25 or older, 0% Native American, 0% Hispanic, 17% African American. *Most popular recent majors:* business administration/commerce/management, nursing.
FIRST-YEAR CLASS 708 total. Of the students who applied, 100% were accepted, 83% of whom enrolled.
ACADEMIC PROGRAM Calendar: semesters. 256 courses offered in 1995-96; average class size 25 in required courses. Academic remediation for entering students, sum-

Peterson's Guide to Two-Year Colleges 1997

Rappahannock Community College (continued)
mer session for credit, part-time degree program (daytime, evenings, summer), adult/continuing education programs. Off-campus study at J. Sargeant Reynolds Community College.
GENERAL DEGREE REQUIREMENTS 6 semester hours; computer course for students without computer competency.
MAJORS Accounting, business administration/commerce/management, computer information systems, engineering technology, law enforcement/police sciences, liberal arts/general studies, nursing, science, secretarial studies/office management.
LIBRARY The Glenns Campus Library with 46,000 books, 102 microform titles, 85 periodicals, 1,900 records, tapes, and CDs.
COMPUTERS ON CAMPUS 32 computers for student use in computer center. Academic computing expenditure 1994–95: $100,000.
COLLEGE LIFE Student-run newspaper. ***Social organizations:*** 21 open to all. ***Most popular organizations:*** Phi Theta Kappa, Culture Club, Poetry Club, Student Government. ***Student services:*** personal-psychological counseling, women's center. ***Campus security:*** 24-hour emergency response devices.
HOUSING College housing not available.
ATHLETICS ***Intramural:*** baseball, football, softball, tennis, volleyball. ***Contact:*** Mr. Wade Johnson, Physical Education Professor, 804-333-6700.
CAREER PLANNING ***Placement office:*** 1 part-time staff. ***Director:*** Dr. Pamela Turner, Director of Student Development, 804-758-6730. ***Services:*** job fairs, resume preparation, resume referral, career counseling, careers library, job bank, job interviews.
EXPENSES FOR 1996–97 State resident tuition: $1493 full-time, $46.65 per semester hour part-time. Nonresident tuition: $4992 full-time, $156 per semester hour part-time. Part-time mandatory fees per semester range from $4.40 to $8.40. Full-time mandatory fees: $16.
FINANCIAL AID ***College-administered undergrad aid 1995–96:*** need-based scholarships (average $500), non-need scholarships (average $400), short-term loans (average $350), low-interest long-term loans from external sources (average $2625), Federal Work-Study. ***Required forms:*** CSS Financial Aid PROFILE, institutional; required for some: state; accepted: FAFSA. ***Priority deadline:*** 5/1.
APPLYING Open admission. ***Option:*** early entrance. ***Required:*** TOEFL for international students, CPT. Test scores used for admission and counseling/placement. ***Application deadline:*** rolling. ***Notification:*** continuous.
APPLYING/TRANSFER ***Required:*** standardized test scores. ***Application deadline:*** rolling. ***Notification:*** continuous.
CONTACT Ms. Wilnet Willis, Admissions and Records Officer, Rappahannock Community College, Glenns Campus, PO Box 287, Glenns, VA 23149-0287, 804-758-6700 Ext. 212.

RICHARD BLAND COLLEGE OF THE COLLEGE OF WILLIAM AND MARY
Petersburg, Virginia

UG Enrollment: 1,205 | **Tuition & Fees (VA Res): $1990**
Application Deadline: 8/15 | **Room & Board: N/Avail**

GENERAL State-supported, 2-year, coed. Part of College of William and Mary. Awards transfer associate degrees. Founded 1961. ***Setting:*** 712-acre rural campus with easy access to Richmond. ***Total enrollment:*** 1,205. ***Faculty:*** 48 (33 full-time, 40% with terminal degrees, 15 part-time); student-faculty ratio is 21:1.
ENROLLMENT PROFILE 1,205 students: 56% women, 44% men, 30% part-time, 93% state residents, 15% transferred in, 5% international, 20% 25 or older, 1% Hispanic, 19% African American, 3% Asian American. ***Areas of study chosen:*** 100% liberal arts/general studies.
FIRST-YEAR CLASS 397 total; 566 applied, 99% were accepted, 71% of whom enrolled. 15% from top 10% of their high school class, 20% from top quarter, 65% from top half.
ACADEMIC PROGRAM Core, honor code. Calendar: semesters. 84 courses offered in 1995–96. Academic remediation for entering students, English as a second language program offered during academic year, advanced placement, honors program, summer session for credit, part-time degree program (daytime, evenings, summer). Study-abroad program. ROTC: Army (c).
GENERAL DEGREE REQUIREMENTS 64 semester hours; 2 semesters each of math and science; computer course.
MAJORS Business administration/commerce/management, liberal arts/general studies, science.
LIBRARY Richard Bland College Library with 61,907 books, 3,213 microform titles, 257 periodicals, 5 CD-ROMs, 3,369 records, tapes, and CDs.
COMPUTERS ON CAMPUS 55 computers for student use in computer center, library. Staffed computer lab on campus provides training in use of computers, software.
COLLEGE LIFE Choral group. ***Social organizations:*** 10 open to all; national fraternities, national sororities; 2% of eligible men and 2% of eligible women are members. ***Most popular organizations:*** Rotaract, Biology Club, Student Government. ***Major annual events:*** Spring Fling, Fall Orientation, International Forum. ***Student services:*** personal-psychological counseling. ***Campus security:*** 24-hour patrols.
HOUSING College housing not available.
ATHLETICS ***Intramural:*** basketball, golf, racquetball, soccer, tennis, volleyball. ***Contact:*** Mr. Cham Pritchard, Athletic Director, 804-862-6235.
CAREER PLANNING ***Service:*** career counseling.
AFTER GRADUATION 88% of students completing a degree program in 1994–95 went directly on to further study.
EXPENSES FOR 1995–96 ***Application fee:*** $20. State resident tuition: $1990 full-time, $80 per semester hour part-time. Nonresident tuition: $5840 full-time, $243 per semester hour part-time.
FINANCIAL AID ***College-administered undergrad aid 1995–96:*** 400 need-based scholarships (average $995), 30 non-need scholarships (average $1000), short-term loans, low-interest long-term loans from external sources, 20 Federal Work-Study (averaging $1500), 20 part-time jobs. ***Required forms:*** CSS Financial Aid PROFILE, institutional, FAFSA. ***Priority deadline:*** 5/1. ***Waivers:*** full or partial for employees or children of employees and senior citizens.
APPLYING ***Option:*** early entrance. ***Required:*** school transcript, TOEFL for international students. ***Recommended:*** SAT I or ACT. Test scores used for admission and counseling/placement. ***Application deadline:*** 8/15. ***Notification:*** continuous.
APPLYING/TRANSFER ***Required:*** high school transcript, college transcript. ***Recommended:*** standardized test scores. ***Entrance:*** minimally difficult. ***Application deadline:*** 8/15. ***Notification:*** continuous. ***Contact:*** Mr. Roger L. Gill, Director of Enrollment Services, 804-862-6225.
CONTACT Mr. Roger L. Gill, Director of Enrollment Services, Richard Bland College of the College of William and Mary, Petersburg, VA 23805-7100, 804-862-6225. ***Fax:*** 804-862-6189.

SOUTHSIDE VIRGINIA COMMUNITY COLLEGE
Alberta, Virginia

UG Enrollment: 1,697 | **Tuition & Fees (VA Res): $1544**
Application Deadline: rolling | **Room & Board: N/Avail**

GENERAL State-supported, 2-year, coed. Part of Virginia Community College System. Awards certificates, diplomas, transfer associate, terminal associate degrees. Founded 1970. ***Setting:*** 207-acre rural campus. ***Endowment:*** $143,571. ***Educational spending 1994–95:*** $2734 per undergrad. ***Total enrollment:*** 1,697. ***Faculty:*** 182 (56 full-time, 10% with terminal degrees, 126 part-time). ***Notable Alumni:*** Robert C. Wrenn, former president of Ruritan International and clerk of the circuit court.
ENROLLMENT PROFILE 1,697 students: 64% women, 36% men, 76% part-time, 99% state residents, 3% transferred in, 52% have need-based financial aid, 1% have non-need-based financial aid, 0% international, 53% 25 or older, 0% Native American, 0% Hispanic, 36% African American, 1% Asian American. ***Most popular recent majors:*** liberal arts/general studies, nursing, secretarial studies/office management.
FIRST-YEAR CLASS 624 total; 1,356 applied, 100% were accepted, 46% of whom enrolled.
ACADEMIC PROGRAM Core, honor code. Calendar: semesters. Academic remediation for entering students, advanced placement, honors program, summer session for credit, part-time degree program (daytime, evenings), adult/continuing education programs. Off-campus study at Hampden-Sydney College, St. Paul's College, Longwood College. Study abroad in England (1% of students participate). ROTC: Army (c).
GENERAL DEGREE REQUIREMENTS 65 semester hours; 1 course each in math and science; computer course for most majors; internship (some majors).
MAJORS Business administration/commerce/management, computer information systems, criminal justice, drafting and design, education, electrical and electronics technologies, human services, liberal arts/general studies, nursing, respiratory therapy, science, secretarial studies/office management.
LIBRARY 28,972 books, 18 microform titles, 266 periodicals, 2 on-line bibliographic services, 24 CD-ROMs, 3,384 records, tapes, and CDs. Acquisition spending 1994–95: $178,316.
COMPUTERS ON CAMPUS 150 computers for student use in computer labs, learning resource center provide access to off-campus computing facilities, e-mail, on-line services, Internet. Staffed computer lab on campus provides training in use of computers, software. Academic computing expenditure 1994–95: $100,949.
COLLEGE LIFE Drama-theater group, choral group. ***Most popular organizations:*** Student Forum, Phi Theta Kappa, Phi Beta Lambda, Alpha Delta Omega. ***Major annual events:*** Women's Festivals, Cultural Events, Kwanza Celebration.
HOUSING College housing not available.
ATHLETICS ***Intramural:*** basketball, softball, table tennis (Ping-Pong), tennis, volleyball.
CAREER PLANNING ***Services:*** resume preparation, resume referral, career counseling, careers library, job interviews.
EXPENSES FOR 1996–97 State resident tuition: $1493 full-time, $46.65 per semester hour part-time. Nonresident tuition: $4992 full-time, $156 per semester hour part-time. Full-time mandatory fees: $51.
FINANCIAL AID ***College-administered undergrad aid 1995–96:*** need-based scholarships, 18 non-need scholarships (averaging $1111), short-term loans, Federal Work-Study, part-time jobs. ***Required forms:*** CSS Financial Aid PROFILE, institutional, FAFSA. ***Priority deadline:*** 5/1. ***Waivers:*** full or partial for senior citizens.
APPLYING Open admission except for nursing program. ***Options:*** early entrance, deferred entrance, midyear entrance. ***Required:*** school transcript, TOEFL for international students. ***Required for some:*** nursing exam. Test scores used for counseling/placement. ***Application deadline:*** rolling. ***Notification:*** continuous. Preference given to district residents.
APPLYING/TRANSFER ***Required:*** college transcript. ***Required for some:*** standardized test scores. ***Application deadline:*** rolling. ***Notification:*** continuous.
CONTACT Dr. John D. Sykes Jr., Director of Admissions, Records, and Institutional Research, Southside Virginia Community College, Alberta, VA 23821-9719, 804-949-1012. ***Fax:*** 804-949-7863.

SOUTHWEST VIRGINIA COMMUNITY COLLEGE
Richlands, Virginia

UG Enrollment: 4,235 | **Tuition & Fees (VA Res): $1551**
Application Deadline: rolling | **Room & Board: N/Avail**

GENERAL State-supported, 2-year, coed. Part of Virginia Community College System. Awards certificates, diplomas, transfer associate, terminal associate degrees. Founded 1968. ***Setting:*** 100-acre rural campus. ***Total enrollment:*** 4,235. ***Faculty:*** 235 (105 full-time, 130 part-time); student-faculty ratio is 20:1.
ENROLLMENT PROFILE 4,235 students from 6 states and territories, 1 other country. 52% women, 61% part-time, 98% state residents, 1% transferred in, 1% international, 57% 25 or older, 1% Native American, 1% Hispanic, 2% African American, 1% Asian American. ***Most popular recent majors:*** liberal arts/general studies, engineering (general), nursing.
FIRST-YEAR CLASS 801 total. Of the students who applied, 99% were accepted.
ACADEMIC PROGRAM Core. Calendar: semesters. Academic remediation for entering students, advanced placement, honors program, summer session for credit, part-time degree program (daytime, evenings, summer), adult/continuing education programs, co-op programs.
GENERAL DEGREE REQUIREMENT 65 semester hours.

MAJORS Accounting, business administration/commerce/management, computer information systems, drafting and design, education, electrical and electronics technologies, engineering (general), human services, land use management and reclamation, law enforcement/police sciences, liberal arts/general studies, mining technology, music, nursing, radiological technology, respiratory therapy, science, secretarial studies/office management.
LIBRARY 58,000 books, 42,000 microform titles, 351 periodicals, 465 records, tapes, and CDs.
COMPUTERS ON CAMPUS 130 computers for student use in computer center, academic division complexes, library.
COLLEGE LIFE Drama-theater group, student-run newspaper. ***Student services:*** personal-psychological counseling, women's center. ***Campus security:*** 24-hour emergency response devices and patrols, student patrols.
HOUSING College housing not available.
ATHLETICS ***Intercollegiate:*** basketball M. ***Intramural:*** basketball, football, tennis, volleyball, weight lifting.
CAREER PLANNING ***Service:*** career counseling.
EXPENSES FOR 1996–97 State resident tuition: $1525 full-time, $47.65 per semester hour part-time. Nonresident tuition: $5024 full-time, $157 per semester hour part-time. Full-time mandatory fees: $26.
FINANCIAL AID ***College-administered undergrad aid 1995–96:*** need-based scholarships, 45 non-need scholarships, low-interest long-term loans, Federal Work-Study. ***Required forms:*** CSS Financial Aid PROFILE, institutional, FAFSA. ***Priority deadline:*** 6/1.
APPLYING Open admission except for allied health, engineering programs. ***Options:*** early entrance, deferred entrance. ***Required:*** school transcript, campus interview, SAT I or ACT, TOEFL for international students. ***Required for some:*** 3 years of high school math and science, ACT ASSET. Test scores used for counseling/placement. ***Application deadline:*** rolling. Preference given to district residents.
APPLYING/TRANSFER ***Required:*** standardized test scores, campus interview, college transcript. ***Required for some:*** 3 years of high school math and science. ***Application deadline:*** rolling.
CONTACT Mr. Roderick B. Moore, Coordinator of Admissions and Records, Southwest Virginia Community College, Richlands, VA 24641, 540-964-2555 Ext. 294 or toll-free 800-822-7822 (in-state). College video available.

THOMAS NELSON COMMUNITY COLLEGE
Hampton, Virginia

UG Enrollment: 7,192	**Tuition & Fees (VA Res): $1546**
Application Deadline: rolling	**Room & Board: N/Avail**

GENERAL State-supported, 2-year, coed. Part of Virginia Community College System. Awards certificates, diplomas, transfer associate, terminal associate degrees. Founded 1968. ***Setting:*** 85-acre suburban campus with easy access to Virginia Beach. ***Total enrollment:*** 7,192. ***Faculty:*** 320 (100 full-time, 21% with terminal degrees, 220 part-time); student-faculty ratio is 24:1.
ENROLLMENT PROFILE 7,192 students from 46 states and territories. 58% women, 73% part-time, 92% state residents, 8% transferred in, 33% have need-based financial aid, 1% have non-need-based financial aid, 0% international, 62% 25 or older, 1% Native American, 2% Hispanic, 28% African American, 3% Asian American.
FIRST-YEAR CLASS 1,274 total; 2,000 applied, 99% were accepted.
ACADEMIC PROGRAM General education curriculum. Calendar: semesters. Academic remediation for entering students, English as a second language program offered during academic year, services for LD students, advanced placement, honors program, summer session for credit, part-time degree program (daytime, evenings, weekends, summer), external degree programs, adult/continuing education programs, co-op programs and internships. Off-campus study at Hampton University, Old Dominion University, Christopher Newport University.
GENERAL DEGREE REQUIREMENTS 65 semester hours; 1 math course; internship (some majors).
MAJORS Accounting, architectural technologies, art/fine arts, automotive technologies, business administration/commerce/management, commercial art, computer information systems, computer science, drafting and design, early childhood education, electrical and electronics technologies, engineering (general), fire science, graphic arts, labor and industrial relations, law enforcement/police sciences, legal secretarial studies, liberal arts/general studies, marketing/retailing/merchandising, mechanical engineering technology, medical laboratory technology, nursing, optometric/ophthalmic technologies, photography, public administration, science, secretarial studies/office management, teacher aide studies.
LIBRARY Learning Resource Center with 66,281 books, 214 microform titles, 467 periodicals, 1 on-line bibliographic service, 6 CD-ROMs, 4,275 records, tapes, and CDs.
COMPUTERS ON CAMPUS 80 computers for student use in computer labs, classroom buildings, library.
COLLEGE LIFE Choral group, student-run newspaper. 5% vote in student government elections. ***Social organizations:*** 9 open to all. ***Most popular organizations:*** Phi Theta Kappa, Black Student Alliance, Circle K International, Student Government Association. ***Major annual events:*** Fall Festival, Spring Fling. ***Student services:*** personal-psychological counseling. ***Campus security:*** 24-hour patrols.
HOUSING College housing not available.
ATHLETICS ***Intramural:*** basketball, sailing, soccer, tennis, volleyball.
CAREER PLANNING ***Placement office:*** 2 full-time, 1 part-time staff. ***Director:*** Dr. Rex Evans, Director of Cooperative Education and Career Services, 804-825-3528. ***Services:*** job fairs, resume preparation, resume referral, career counseling, careers library, job bank, job interviews.
EXPENSES FOR 1996–97 State resident tuition: $1525 full-time, $47.65 per semester hour part-time. Nonresident tuition: $5024 full-time, $157 per semester hour part-time. Part-time mandatory fees: $10.50 per semester. Full-time mandatory fees: $21.
FINANCIAL AID ***College-administered undergrad aid 1995–96:*** 30 need-based scholarships (average $450), 20 non-need scholarships (average $500), short-term loans (average $60), low-interest long-term loans from external sources (average $1800), Federal Work-Study, part-time jobs. ***Required forms:*** institutional, FAFSA; accepted: CSS Financial Aid PROFILE. ***Priority deadline:*** 5/1.
APPLYING Open admission. ***Options:*** early entrance, deferred entrance, midyear entrance. ***Required:*** school transcript. ***Recommended:*** SAT I, TOEFL for international students. Test scores used for counseling/placement. ***Application deadline:*** rolling. ***Notification:*** continuous. Preference given to state residents.
APPLYING/TRANSFER ***Entrance:*** noncompetitive. ***Application deadline:*** rolling. ***Notification:*** continuous. ***Contact:*** Ms. Aileen Girard, Admissions Office Manager, 804-825-2800.
CONTACT Ms. Aileen Girardn, Admissions Office Manager, Thomas Nelson Community College, Hampton, VA 23670-0407, 804-825-2800.

TIDEWATER COMMUNITY COLLEGE
Portsmouth, Virginia

UG Enrollment: 16,780	**Tuition & Fees (VA Res): $1493**
Application Deadline: rolling	**Room & Board: N/Avail**

GENERAL State-supported, 2-year, coed. Part of Virginia Community College System. Awards certificates, diplomas, transfer associate, terminal associate degrees. Founded 1968. ***Setting:*** 520-acre suburban campus. ***Total enrollment:*** 16,780. ***Faculty:*** 805 (255 full-time, 100% with terminal degrees, 550 part-time); student-faculty ratio is 20:1.
ENROLLMENT PROFILE 16,780 students from 53 states and territories, 31 other countries. 58% women, 42% men, 72% part-time, 89% state residents, 9% transferred in, 1% international, 60% 25 or older, 1% Native American, 2% Hispanic, 18% African American, 6% Asian American.
FIRST-YEAR CLASS 3,074 total. Of the students who applied, 100% were accepted, 79% of whom enrolled.
ACADEMIC PROGRAM Core, honor code. Calendar: semesters. Academic remediation for entering students, English as a second language program offered during academic year, services for LD students, advanced placement, tutorials, honors program, summer session for credit, part-time degree program (daytime, evenings, summer), external degree programs, adult/continuing education programs, co-op programs and internships. Off-campus study at members of the Virginia Tidewater Consortium for Continuing Higher Education.
GENERAL DEGREE REQUIREMENTS 65 semester hours; computer course.
MAJORS Accounting, advertising, art/fine arts, automotive technologies, business administration/commerce/management, computer programming, data processing, drafting and design, early childhood education, education, electrical and electronics technologies, engineering (general), finance/banking, graphic arts, industrial administration, liberal arts/general studies, marketing/retailing/merchandising, music, nursing, real estate, science, secretarial studies/office management.
LIBRARY 147,126 books, 525 microform titles, 913 periodicals, 1 on-line bibliographic service, 8,982 records, tapes, and CDs. Acquisition spending 1994–95: $230,000.
COMPUTERS ON CAMPUS Computers for student use in computer labs, learning resource center provide access to main academic computer. Staffed computer lab on campus. Academic computing expenditure 1994–95: $1.2 million.
NOTEWORTHY RESEARCH FACILITIES Center for Innovative Technology.
COLLEGE LIFE Orientation program (2 days, no cost, parents included). Drama-theater group, student-run newspaper. ***Social organizations:*** 1 local fraternity. ***Student services:*** personal-psychological counseling, women's center. ***Campus security:*** 24-hour patrols.
HOUSING College housing not available.
ATHLETICS ***Intramural:*** basketball, tennis.
CAREER PLANNING ***Placement office:*** $1.6 million operating expenditure 1994–95. ***Director:*** Mr. Randy Shannon, Coordinator, Cooperative Education and Placement, 804-484-2121. ***Services:*** resume preparation, career counseling, careers library, job bank, job interviews.
AFTER GRADUATION 65% of students completing a degree program in 1994–95 went directly on to further study.
EXPENSES FOR 1995–96 State resident tuition: $1493 full-time, $46.65 per semester hour part-time. Nonresident tuition: $4992 full-time, $156 per semester hour part-time.
FINANCIAL AID ***College-administered undergrad aid 1995–96:*** 305 need-based scholarships (average $443), 2,194 non-need scholarships (average $1121), low-interest long-term loans from external sources (average $2087), Federal Work-Study. ***Required forms:*** CSS Financial Aid PROFILE, institutional, FAFSA. ***Application deadline:*** continuous. ***Payment plans:*** installment, deferred payment. ***Waivers:*** full or partial for senior citizens.
APPLYING Open admission. ***Options:*** early entrance, deferred entrance, midyear entrance. ***Required:*** TOEFL for international students. Test scores used for counseling/placement. ***Application deadline:*** rolling. ***Notification:*** continuous.
APPLYING/TRANSFER ***Entrance:*** noncompetitive. ***Application deadline:*** rolling. ***Notification:*** continuous. ***Contact:*** Dr. Richard E. Witte, Coordinator of Admissions and Records, 804-484-2121.
CONTACT Dr. Richard E. Witte, Coordinator of Admissions and Records, Tidewater Community College, 7000 College Drive, Portsmouth, VA 23703, 804-484-2121. College video available.

VIRGINIA COLLEGE
Salem, Virginia

UG Enrollment: 80	**Tuition & Fees: $3900**
Application Deadline: rolling	**Room & Board: N/Avail**

GENERAL Proprietary, 2-year, coed. Awards terminal associate degrees. Founded 1982. ***Total enrollment:*** 80. ***Faculty:*** 20 (5 full-time, 15 part-time).
ENROLLMENT PROFILE 80 students.
FIRST-YEAR CLASS 45 total; 60 applied, 100% were accepted, 75% of whom enrolled.
ACADEMIC PROGRAM Core. Calendar: quarters.
GENERAL DEGREE REQUIREMENTS 90 credit hours; 1 course in college algebra; computer course.
MAJORS Computer information systems, electrical and electronics technologies, secretarial studies/office management.
HOUSING College housing not available.
EXPENSES FOR 1996–97 Tuition: $3900 full-time, $130 per credit hour part-time. One-time mandatory fee: $100.

Virginia

Virginia College (continued)
FINANCIAL AID *College-administered undergrad aid 1995–96:* need-based scholarships, low-interest long-term loans from external sources, Federal Work-Study. *Required forms:* FAFSA.
APPLYING *Required:* school transcript, campus interview, CPAt. Test scores used for admission. *Application deadline:* rolling. *Notification:* continuous.
APPLYING/TRANSFER *Required:* standardized test scores, high school transcript, campus interview, college transcript.
CONTACT Ms. Jeanne Richardson, Director of Admissions, Virginia College, Salem, VA 24153-7235, 540-776-0755.

VIRGINIA HIGHLANDS COMMUNITY COLLEGE
Abingdon, Virginia

UG Enrollment: 1,891	Tuition & Fees (VA Res): $1525
Application Deadline: rolling	Room & Board: N/Avail

GENERAL State-supported, 2-year, coed. Part of Virginia Community College System. Awards certificates, diplomas, transfer associate, terminal associate degrees. Founded 1967. *Setting:* 100-acre small-town campus. *Total enrollment:* 1,891. *Faculty:* 131 (47 full-time, 84 part-time); student-faculty ratio is 17:1.
ENROLLMENT PROFILE 1,891 students from 7 states and territories. 60% women, 53% part-time, 96% state residents, 8% transferred in, 75% have need-based financial aid, 5% have non-need-based financial aid, 0% international, 52% 25 or older, 0% Native American, 0% Hispanic, 3% African American, 0% Asian American. *Most popular recent majors:* business administration/commerce/management, education, liberal arts/general studies.
FIRST-YEAR CLASS 499 total; 650 applied, 100% were accepted, 77% of whom enrolled. 15% from top 10% of their high school class, 35% from top quarter, 65% from top half.
ACADEMIC PROGRAM Calendar: semesters. Academic remediation for entering students, services for LD students, advanced placement, summer session for credit, part-time degree program (daytime, evenings), adult/continuing education programs, co-op programs.
GENERAL DEGREE REQUIREMENTS 65 credit hours; math/science requirements vary according to program; computer course for most majors.
MAJORS Accounting, business administration/commerce/management, computer information systems, data processing, drafting and design, education, electrical and electronics technologies, engineering technology, heating/refrigeration/air conditioning, human services, law enforcement/police sciences, liberal arts/general studies, machine and tool technologies, nursing, physical therapy, radiological technology, science, secretarial studies/office management, theater arts/drama.
LIBRARY 29,683 books, 144 microform titles, 174 periodicals, 1,938 records, tapes, and CDs.
COMPUTERS ON CAMPUS 200 computers for student use in computer center, learning lab.
COLLEGE LIFE Orientation program (2 days). Drama-theater group, choral group. *Student services:* personal-psychological counseling.
HOUSING College housing not available.
ATHLETICS *Intramural:* basketball, football, skiing (cross-country), skiing (downhill), tennis, volleyball.
CAREER PLANNING *Service:* career counseling.
AFTER GRADUATION 65% of students completing a degree program in 1994–95 went directly on to further study.
EXPENSES FOR 1996-97 State resident tuition: $1493 full-time, $46.65 per semester hour part-time. Nonresident tuition: $4992 full-time, $156 per semester hour part-time. Part-time mandatory fees: $1 per semester hour. Full-time mandatory fees: $32.
FINANCIAL AID *College-administered undergrad aid 1995–96:* 823 need-based scholarships (average $1500), 25 non-need scholarships (average $1000), Federal Work-Study. *Required forms:* FAFSA; accepted: CSS Financial Aid PROFILE. *Application deadline:* continuous. *Waivers:* full or partial for senior citizens.
APPLYING Open admission except for nursing, radiology, physical therapy programs. *Options:* early entrance, deferred entrance. *Required:* school transcript. *Recommended:* SCAT, ACT ASSET. *Required for some:* 3 years of high school math, SCAT, ACT ASSET. Test scores used for counseling/placement. *Application deadline:* rolling. *Notification:* continuous. Preference given to district and then state residents.
APPLYING/TRANSFER *Required:* high school transcript, college transcript. *Required for some:* 3 years of high school math. *Entrance:* noncompetitive. *Application deadline:* rolling. *Notification:* continuous.
CONTACT Mr. Edward A. Colley, Director of Admissions, Records, and Financial Aid, Virginia Highlands Community College, Abingdon, VA 24212-0828, 540-628-6094 Ext. 260. *Fax:* 540-628-7576.

VIRGINIA WESTERN COMMUNITY COLLEGE
Roanoke, Virginia

UG Enrollment: 6,845	Tuition & Fees (VA Res): $1450
Application Deadline: rolling	Room & Board: N/Avail

GENERAL State-supported, 2-year, coed. Part of Virginia Community College System. Awards transfer associate, terminal associate degrees. Founded 1966. *Setting:* 70-acre urban campus. *Total enrollment:* 6,845. *Faculty:* 202 (102 full-time, 100 part-time).
ENROLLMENT PROFILE 6,845 students from 52 states and territories, 10 other countries. 60% women, 75% part-time, 98% state residents, 20% transferred in, 64% 25 or older, 12% Native American, 1% Hispanic, 7% African American, 1% Asian American. *Most popular recent majors:* liberal arts/general studies, business administration/commerce/management, science.
FIRST-YEAR CLASS 1,499 total. Of the students who applied, 100% were accepted, 66% of whom enrolled. 7% from top 10% of their high school class, 15% from top quarter, 50% from top half.

ACADEMIC PROGRAM Core. Calendar: semesters. Academic remediation for entering students, English as a second language program offered during academic year, services for LD students, advanced placement, summer session for credit, part-time degree program (daytime, evenings, weekends, summer), adult/continuing education programs, co-op programs.
GENERAL DEGREE REQUIREMENTS 60 semester hours; computer course.
MAJORS Accounting, architectural technologies, art/fine arts, automotive technologies, business administration/commerce/management, child care/child and family studies, civil engineering technology, commercial art, computer science, criminal justice, data processing, dental services, early childhood education, education, electrical and electronics technologies, engineering (general), (pre)engineering sequence, liberal arts/general studies, mechanical engineering technology, mental health/rehabilitation counseling, nursing, radio and television studies, radiological technology, science, secretarial studies/office management.
LIBRARY 67,129 books, 125 microform titles, 402 periodicals, 2,638 records, tapes, and CDs.
COMPUTERS ON CAMPUS 110 computers for student use in computer center, engineering building, library provide access to main academic computer. Staffed computer lab on campus (open 24 hours a day) provides training in use of computers, software.
COLLEGE LIFE Drama-theater group, student-run newspaper. *Student services:* personal-psychological counseling.
HOUSING College housing not available.
ATHLETICS *Intramural:* basketball.
CAREER PLANNING *Director:* Ms. Joy Bell, Coordinator of Career Services, 540-857-7298. *Service:* career counseling.
EXPENSES FOR 1996-97 State resident tuition: $1446 full-time, $46.65 per semester hour part-time. Nonresident tuition: $4836 full-time, $156 per semester hour part-time. Part-time mandatory fees: $2 per semester. Full-time mandatory fees: $4.
FINANCIAL AID *College-administered undergrad aid 1995–96:* 13 need-based scholarships (average $700), 13 non-need scholarships (average $492), short-term loans (average $445), low-interest long-term loans from external sources (average $1312), Federal Work-Study, 82 part-time jobs. *Required forms:* FAFSA; accepted: CSS Financial Aid PROFILE. *Application deadline:* continuous to 7/15.
APPLYING Open admission except for health technology programs. *Options:* early entrance, deferred entrance. *Required:* school transcript, TOEFL for international students. *Recommended:* SAT I or ACT. *Required for some:* 3 years of high school math. Test scores used for counseling/placement. *Application deadline:* rolling. *Notification:* continuous. Preference given to local residents.
APPLYING/TRANSFER *Required:* high school transcript, college transcript. *Recommended:* standardized test scores. *Required for some:* 3 years of high school math. *Entrance:* noncompetitive. *Application deadline:* rolling. *Notification:* continuous.
CONTACT Admissions Office, Virginia Western Community College, PO Box 14007, Roanoke, VA 24038, 540-857-7231. *Fax:* 540-857-7204.

WYTHEVILLE COMMUNITY COLLEGE
Wytheville, Virginia

UG Enrollment: 2,600	Tuition & Fees (VA Res): $1445
Application Deadline: rolling	Room & Board: N/Avail

GENERAL State-supported, 2-year, coed. Part of Virginia Community College System. Awards transfer associate, terminal associate degrees. Founded 1967. *Setting:* 141-acre rural campus. *Total enrollment:* 2,600. *Faculty:* 137.
ENROLLMENT PROFILE 2,600 students: 65% women, 35% men, 60% part-time, 100% state residents, 9% transferred in, 58% 25 or older, 3% African American.
FIRST-YEAR CLASS 650 total; 970 applied, 100% were accepted, 67% of whom enrolled.
ACADEMIC PROGRAM Core. Calendar: semesters. Academic remediation for entering students, services for LD students, advanced placement, summer session for credit, part-time degree program (daytime, evenings), external degree programs, adult/continuing education programs.
GENERAL DEGREE REQUIREMENT 62 semester hours.
MAJORS Accounting, business administration/commerce/management, civil engineering technology, communication, computer information systems, corrections, criminal justice, dental services, drafting and design, education, electrical and electronics technologies, law enforcement/police sciences, liberal arts/general studies, machine and tool technologies, mechanical engineering technology, medical laboratory technology, medical secretarial studies, nursing, physical therapy, real estate, science, secretarial studies/office management.
LIBRARY Wytheville Community College Library with 29,000 books, 1,700 microform titles, 261 periodicals, 2,285 records, tapes, and CDs.
COMPUTERS ON CAMPUS 105 computers for student use in computer center. Staffed computer lab on campus provides training in use of computers, software.
COLLEGE LIFE Drama-theater group, student-run newspaper.
HOUSING College housing not available.
ATHLETICS *Intramural:* basketball, football, softball, table tennis (Ping-Pong), tennis, volleyball.
CAREER PLANNING *Service:* career counseling.
EXPENSES FOR 1996-97 State resident tuition: $1400 full-time, $46.65 per credit hour part-time. Nonresident tuition: $4680 full-time, $156 per credit hour part-time. Part-time mandatory fees: $1.50 per credit hour. Full-time mandatory fees: $45.
FINANCIAL AID *College-administered undergrad aid 1995–96:* 50 need-based scholarships (average $300), short-term loans (average $100), low-interest long-term loans from external sources (average $2625), Federal Work-Study. *Required forms:* institutional, FAFSA; accepted: state. *Priority deadline:* 4/15.
APPLYING Open admission. *Option:* early entrance. *Required:* school transcript, TOEFL for international students. *Required for some:* 3 years of high school math, interview. Test scores used for admission. *Application deadline:* rolling. *Notification:* continuous.
APPLYING/TRANSFER *Entrance:* noncompetitive. *Application deadline:* rolling. *Notification:* continuous.
CONTACT Ms. Sherry K. Dix, Registrar, Wytheville Community College, Wytheville, VA 24382-3308, 540-223-4755 or toll-free 800-468-1195 (in-state).

WASHINGTON

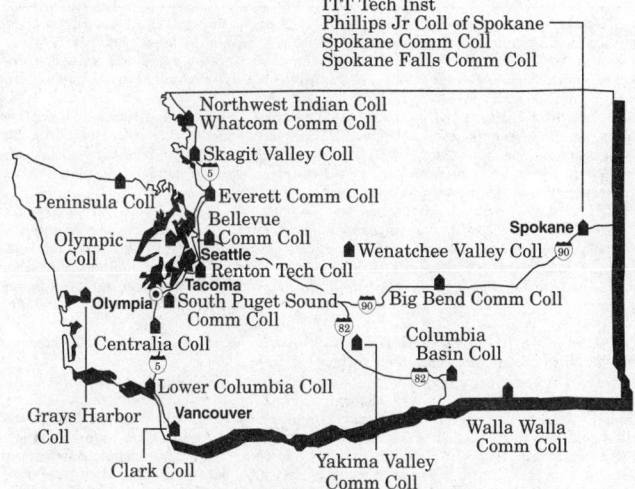

Seattle Area
Art Institute of Seattle
Edmonds Comm Coll
Green River Comm Coll
Highline Comm Coll
ITT Tech Inst

Lake Washington Tech Coll
North Seattle Comm Coll
Pima Medical Inst
Seattle Central Comm Coll
Shoreline Comm Coll
South Seattle Comm Coll

Tacoma Area
Pierce Coll
Tacoma Comm Coll

ART INSTITUTE OF SEATTLE
Seattle, Washington

UG Enrollment: 1,965	Tuition & Fees: $9180
Application Deadline: rolling	Room & Board: $5599

GENERAL Proprietary, 2-year, coed. Part of Education Management Corporation. Awards terminal associate degrees. Founded 1982. *Setting:* urban campus. *Total enrollment:* 1,965. *Faculty:* 147 (44 full-time, 103 part-time).
ENROLLMENT PROFILE 1,965 students from 35 states and territories, 12 other countries. 48% women, 52% men, 6% part-time, 71% state residents, 14% transferred in, 1% international, 26% 25 or older, 1% Native American, 1% Hispanic, 7% African American, 8% Asian American.
FIRST-YEAR CLASS 651 total; 1,302 applied, 100% were accepted, 50% of whom enrolled. 10% from top 10% of their high school class, 21% from top quarter, 79% from top half.
ACADEMIC PROGRAM Concentrated career curriculum. Calendar: quarters. 269 courses offered in 1995–96. Academic remediation for entering students, English as a second language program offered during summer, services for LD students, honors program, summer session for credit, part-time degree program (daytime, evenings), adult/continuing education programs. Off-campus study at 8 members of The Art Institutes, City University.
GENERAL DEGREE REQUIREMENTS 90 credits; 1 math course; computer course.
MAJORS Audio engineering, commercial art, computer graphics, culinary arts, fashion design and technology, fashion merchandising, film and video production, graphic arts, industrial design, interior design, music business, photography, tourism and travel.
LIBRARY 4,000 books, 110 periodicals, 50 records, tapes, and CDs.
COMPUTERS ON CAMPUS Computer purchase plan available. 62 computers for student use in computer center, computer labs, learning resource center, library. Staffed computer lab on campus.
COLLEGE LIFE Orientation program (3 days, parents included). *Most popular organizations:* Multicultural Affairs Organization, American Society of Interior Designers, DECA, Student Advisory Board. *Major annual events:* Student Art Show, Holiday Craft Fair, Holiday Dinner. *Student services:* personal-psychological counseling.
HOUSING 500 college housing spaces available; 162 were occupied 1995–96. No special consideration for freshman housing applicants. Off-campus living permitted. *Option:* coed housing available. Resident assistants live in dorms.
CAREER PLANNING *Placement office:* 6 full-time staff. *Director:* Dr. Barbara Hanna, Director of Student Services, 800-275-2471. *Services:* job fairs, resume preparation, resume referral, career counseling, job bank, job interviews.
EXPENSES FOR 1995–96 *Application fee:* $50. Comprehensive fee of $14,779 includes full-time tuition ($9180) and college room and board ($5599). One-time mandatory fee: $300.
FINANCIAL AID *College-administered undergrad aid 1995–96:* need-based scholarships, 20 non-need scholarships (average $3000), low-interest long-term loans from external sources (average $2625), Federal Work-Study, part-time jobs. *Required forms:* institutional; required for some: CSS Financial Aid PROFILE, state, FAFSA. *Application deadline:* continuous to 7/15. *Payment plan:* installment. *Waivers:* full or partial for employees or children of employees.
APPLYING Open admission. *Option:* deferred entrance. *Recommended:* SAT I or ACT. *Required for some:* TOEFL for international students. Test scores used for admission and counseling/placement. *Application deadline:* rolling. *Notification:* continuous.

CONTACT Mr. Doug Worsley, Director of Admissions, Art Institute of Seattle, 2323 Elliott Avenue, Seattle, WA 98121-1642, 206-448-0900 Ext. 820 or toll-free 800-275-2471. *Fax:* 206-448-2501. College video available.

BELLEVUE COMMUNITY COLLEGE
Bellevue, Washington

UG Enrollment: 10,099	Tuition & Fees (WA Res): $1446
Application Deadline: rolling	Room & Board: N/Avail

GENERAL State-supported, 2-year, coed. Part of Washington State Board for Community and Technical Colleges. Awards transfer associate, terminal associate degrees. Founded 1966. *Setting:* 96-acre suburban campus with easy access to Seattle. *Total enrollment:* 10,099. *Faculty:* 619 (124 full-time, 21% with terminal degrees, 495 part-time).
ENROLLMENT PROFILE 10,099 students: 61% women, 39% men, 47% part-time, 96% state residents, 38% transferred in, 2% international, 47% 25 or older, 1% Native American, 2% Hispanic, 3% African American, 12% Asian American.
FIRST-YEAR CLASS 3,720 total; 5,724 applied, 100% were accepted, 65% of whom enrolled.
ACADEMIC PROGRAM Core. Calendar: quarters. Academic remediation for entering students, English as a second language program offered during academic year and summer, services for LD students, advanced placement, summer session for credit, part-time degree program (daytime, evenings), adult/continuing education programs, co-op programs.
GENERAL DEGREE REQUIREMENTS 90 credits; 1 course each in college algebra and quantitative math.
MAJORS Accounting, business administration/commerce/management, computer information systems, criminal justice, data processing, early childhood education, educational media, fashion merchandising, fire science, interior design, law enforcement/police sciences, liberal arts/general studies, marketing/retailing/merchandising, nursing, radiological technology, real estate, recreation and leisure services, secretarial studies/office management.
LIBRARY Bellevue Community College Library with 42,000 books, 142 microform titles, 485 periodicals, 6,000 records, tapes, and CDs.
COMPUTERS ON CAMPUS 250 computers for student use in computer labs. Staffed computer lab on campus.
COLLEGE LIFE Drama-theater group, student-run newspaper, radio station. *Student services:* health clinic, personal-psychological counseling, women's center.
HOUSING College housing not available.
ATHLETICS *Intercollegiate:* basketball M(s)/W(s), cross-country running M(s)/W(s), golf M(s), soccer M(s), tennis M(s)/W(s), track and field M(s)/W(s), volleyball W(s). *Intramural:* basketball, cross-country running, football, skiing (cross-country), skiing (downhill), soccer, tennis, track and field, volleyball.
CAREER PLANNING *Service:* career counseling.
EXPENSES FOR 1996–97 State resident tuition: $1446 full-time, $48.20 per quarter hour part-time. Nonresident tuition: $5556 full-time, $185 per quarter hour part-time.
FINANCIAL AID *College-administered undergrad aid 1995–96:* 2 need-based scholarships (average $990), 15 non-need scholarships (average $990), low-interest long-term loans from external sources (average $2625), Federal Work-Study, 60 part-time jobs. *Required forms:* institutional, FAFSA; accepted: CSS Financial Aid PROFILE. *Priority deadline:* 4/14.
APPLYING Open admission. *Options:* electronic application, early entrance. *Required:* TOEFL for international students. Test scores used for counseling/placement. *Application deadline:* rolling.
APPLYING/TRANSFER *Application deadline:* rolling.
CONTACT Ms. Theresa Siewert, Director of Admissions and Evaluations, Bellevue Community College, Bellevue, WA 98007-6484, 206-641-2224. College video available.

BIG BEND COMMUNITY COLLEGE
Moses Lake, Washington

UG Enrollment: 1,872	Tuition & Fees (WA Res): $1404
Application Deadline: rolling	Room & Board: $3628

GENERAL State-supported, 2-year, coed. Awards certificates, transfer associate, terminal associate degrees. Founded 1962. *Setting:* 159-acre small-town campus. *Endowment:* $112,241. *Total enrollment:* 1,872. *Faculty:* 148 (48 full-time, 10% with terminal degrees, 100 part-time).
ENROLLMENT PROFILE 1,872 students from 7 states and territories, 6 other countries. 52% women, 48% men, 46% part-time, 96% state residents, 5% live on campus, 5% transferred in, 3% international, 46% 25 or older, 1% Native American, 9% Hispanic, 1% African American, 1% Asian American. *Areas of study chosen:* 55% liberal arts/general studies, 45% vocational and home economics. *Most popular recent majors:* liberal arts/general studies, business administration/commerce/management.
FIRST-YEAR CLASS 586 total. Of the students who applied, 100% were accepted.
ACADEMIC PROGRAM Core. Calendar: quarters. 515 courses offered in 1995–96. Academic remediation for entering students, English as a second language program offered during academic year, services for LD students, advanced placement, summer session for credit, part-time degree program (daytime, evenings, summer), adult/continuing education programs. Off-campus study at Columbia Basin College.
GENERAL DEGREE REQUIREMENTS 93 credit hours; math/science requirements vary according to program; computer course for nursing, automotive technologies majors.
MAJORS Accounting, aircraft and missile maintenance, automotive technologies, aviation technology, business administration/commerce/management, civil engineering technology, computer programming, computer science, data processing, (pre)engineering sequence, flight training, industrial and heavy equipment maintenance, legal secretarial studies, liberal arts/general studies, marketing/retailing/merchandising, medical secretarial studies, nursing, practical nursing, secretarial studies/office management, teacher aide studies, welding technology.
LIBRARY Big Bend Community College Library with 40,000 books, 364 microform titles, 307 periodicals, 1 on-line bibliographic service, 7 CD-ROMs, 3,749 records, tapes, and CDs. Acquisition spending 1994–95: $72,794.
COMPUTERS ON CAMPUS 50 computers for student use in computer center, dorms. Staffed computer lab on campus provides training in use of computers, software.

Peterson's Guide to Two-Year Colleges 1997

Big Bend Community College (continued)

COLLEGE LIFE Drama-theater group, student-run newspaper. ***Major annual events:*** Spring Fling, Winter Carnival. ***Student services:*** personal-psychological counseling. ***Campus security:*** 24-hour emergency response devices.

HOUSING 140 college housing spaces available; 100 were occupied 1995–96. No special consideration for freshman housing applicants. foreign students required to live on campus first quarter. ***Option:*** coed (2 buildings) housing available. Resident assistants live in dorms.

ATHLETICS ***Intercollegiate:*** baseball M(s), basketball M(s)/W(s), volleyball W(s). ***Intramural:*** basketball, racquetball, riflery, softball, volleyball. ***Contact:*** Dr. Mike Lang, Athletic Director, 509-762-6230.

CAREER PLANNING ***Services:*** career counseling, careers library.

EXPENSES FOR 1996–97 ***Application fee:*** $10. State resident tuition: $1404 full-time, $46.80 per credit hour part-time. Nonresident tuition: $5510 full-time, $183.70 per credit hour part-time. College room and board: $3628.

FINANCIAL AID ***College-administered undergrad aid 1995–96:*** 550 need-based scholarships (average $1200), 90 non-need scholarships (average $500), short-term loans (average $150), low-interest long-term loans from college funds (average $2200), loans from external sources (average $2350), 30 Federal Work-Study (averaging $1500), 70 part-time jobs. ***Required forms:*** institutional, FAFSA. ***Priority deadline:*** 7/1. ***Waivers:*** full or partial for employees or children of employees and senior citizens. ***Notification:*** continuous. ***Average indebtedness of graduates:*** $6125.

APPLYING Open admission. ***Options:*** early entrance, deferred entrance, midyear entrance. ***Required:*** TOEFL for international students. ***Required for some:*** school transcript. Test scores used for admission. ***Application deadline:*** rolling. ***Notification:*** continuous.

APPLYING/TRANSFER ***Recommended:*** college transcript. ***Required for some:*** high school transcript. ***Application deadline:*** rolling. ***Notification:*** continuous.

CONTACT Ms. Candis Lacher, Director of Admissions/Registrar, Big Bend Community College, Moses Lake, WA 98837-3299, 509-762-6226. ***Fax:*** 509-762-6329. ***E-mail:*** candyl@bbcc.ctc.edu.

CENTRALIA COLLEGE
Centralia, Washington

UG Enrollment: 1,800 | **Tuition & Fees (WA Res): $1356**
Application Deadline: rolling | **Room & Board: N/Avail**

GENERAL State-supported, 2-year, coed. Part of Washington State Board for Community and Technical Colleges. Awards transfer associate, terminal associate degrees. Founded 1925. ***Setting:*** 12-acre small-town campus. ***Total enrollment:*** 1,800. ***Faculty:*** 112 (55 full-time, 57 part-time); student-faculty ratio is 20:1.

ENROLLMENT PROFILE 1,800 students from 12 states and territories, 7 other countries. 60% women, 5% part-time, 98% state residents, 2% transferred in, 1% international, 69% 25 or older, 1% Native American, 1% Hispanic, 1% African American, 1% Asian American.

FIRST-YEAR CLASS 960 total; 1,200 applied, 100% were accepted, 80% of whom enrolled.

ACADEMIC PROGRAM Core. Calendar: quarters. Academic remediation for entering students, English as a second language program offered during academic year and summer, services for LD students, advanced placement, summer session for credit, part-time degree program (daytime, evenings), external degree programs, adult/continuing education programs, co-op programs. Study abroad in England.

GENERAL DEGREE REQUIREMENTS 93 credits; 1 math course; computer course for engineering majors.

MAJORS Applied art, art/fine arts, biology/biological sciences, broadcasting, business administration/commerce/management, business education, business machine technologies, chemistry, child care/child and family studies, civil engineering technology, commercial art, communication, early childhood education, electrical and electronics technologies, engineering and applied sciences, (pre)engineering sequence, English, forest technology, French, geology, history, humanities, industrial and heavy equipment maintenance, legal secretarial studies, liberal arts/general studies, marketing/retailing/merchandising, medical secretarial studies, music, natural sciences, nursing, physical education, physical sciences, political science/government, practical nursing, psychology, radio and television studies, recreation and leisure services, retail management, science, social science, sociology, theater arts/drama, welding technology.

LIBRARY 31,000 books, 225 periodicals, 500 records, tapes, and CDs.

COMPUTERS ON CAMPUS Computer purchase plan available. 35 computers for student use in learning skills center, instructional labs, library. Staffed computer lab on campus provides training in use of computers, software.

COLLEGE LIFE Drama-theater group, student-run newspaper, radio station. ***Student services:*** personal-psychological counseling, women's center.

HOUSING College housing not available.

ATHLETICS ***Intercollegiate:*** baseball M, basketball M(s)/W(s), volleyball W(s).

CAREER PLANNING ***Service:*** career counseling.

EXPENSES FOR 1995–96 State resident tuition: $1350 full-time, $45 per credit part-time. Nonresident tuition: $5298 full-time, $176.60 per credit part-time. Part-time mandatory fees: $2 per quarter. Full-time mandatory fees: $6.

FINANCIAL AID ***College-administered undergrad aid 1995–96:*** 450 need-based scholarships (averaging $550), 80 non-need scholarships (averaging $570), short-term loans (averaging $200), low-interest long-term loans from college funds (averaging $1000), loans from external sources (averaging $2000), Federal Work-Study, 50 part-time jobs. ***Required forms:*** CSS Financial Aid PROFILE, institutional; accepted: FAFSA. ***Priority deadline:*** 7/15.

APPLYING Open admission except for nursing program. ***Required:*** TOEFL for international students, ACT ASSET. Test scores used for counseling/placement. ***Application deadline:*** rolling.

APPLYING/TRANSFER ***Required:*** standardized test scores. ***Application deadline:*** rolling.

CONTACT Ms. Neena Stoskopf, Admissions Officer, Centralia College, Centralia, WA 98531-4099, 360-736-9391 Ext. 221.

CLARK COLLEGE
Vancouver, Washington

UG Enrollment: 10,300 | **Tuition & Fees (WA Res): $1413**
Application Deadline: 9/5 | **Room & Board: N/Avail**

GENERAL State-supported, 2-year, coed. Part of Washington State Board for Community and Technical Colleges. Awards transfer associate, terminal associate degrees. Founded 1933. ***Setting:*** 100-acre suburban campus with easy access to Portland. ***Total enrollment:*** 10,300. ***Faculty:*** 320 (120 full-time, 10% with terminal degrees, 200 part-time); student-faculty ratio is 30:1.

ENROLLMENT PROFILE 10,300 students from 15 states and territories, 6 other countries. 60% women, 50% part-time, 97% state residents, 15% transferred in, 2% international, 50% 25 or older, 1% Native American, 0% Hispanic, 2% African American, 5% Asian American. ***Most popular recent majors:*** business administration/commerce/management, nursing, secretarial studies/office management.

FIRST-YEAR CLASS 3,000 total. Of the students who applied, 100% were accepted.

ACADEMIC PROGRAM Core. Calendar: quarters. Academic remediation for entering students, English as a second language program offered during academic year and summer, services for LD students, advanced placement, honors program, summer session for credit, part-time degree program (daytime, evenings, weekends, summer), adult/continuing education programs, co-op programs. Study-abroad program. ROTC: Army (c), Air Force (c).

GENERAL DEGREE REQUIREMENTS 90 quarter hours; computer course for accounting, graphics, communications, office technology majors.

MAJORS Accounting, agricultural education, agricultural sciences, anatomy, art/fine arts, automotive technologies, biology/biological sciences, business administration/commerce/management, business education, chemical engineering technology, chemistry, child care/child and family studies, civil engineering technology, commercial art, communication, computer information systems, computer programming, computer science, construction technologies, corrections, criminal justice, culinary arts, data processing, dental services, drug and alcohol/substance abuse counseling, early childhood education, economics, education, electrical and electronics technologies, electromechanical technology, electronics engineering technology, engineering (general), (pre)engineering sequence, engineering technology, English, fashion merchandising, food services management, food services technology, French, geography, geology, German, graphic arts, history, horticulture, humanities, industrial and heavy equipment maintenance, industrial engineering technology, Japanese, journalism, landscaping/grounds maintenance, law enforcement/police sciences, legal secretarial studies, liberal arts/general studies, machine and tool technologies, marketing/retailing/merchandising, materials sciences, mathematics, mechanical design technology, mechanical engineering technology, medical records services, medical secretarial studies, medical technology, music, natural sciences, nursing, ornamental horticulture, paralegal studies, philosophy, physical education, physical sciences, physics, plastics technology, political science/government, practical nursing, printing technologies, psychology, real estate, retail management, science, secretarial studies/office management, social science, sociology, Spanish, speech/rhetoric/public address/debate, teacher aide studies, technical writing, telecommunications, theater arts/drama, welding technology, zoology.

LIBRARY Lewis D. Cannell Library with 50,000 books, 500 periodicals, 1 on-line bibliographic service, 3 CD-ROMs, 500 records, tapes, and CDs.

COMPUTERS ON CAMPUS 250 computers for student use in computer center, library, student center. Staffed computer lab on campus provides training in use of computers, software.

COLLEGE LIFE Drama-theater group, student-run newspaper. ***Major annual events:*** Earth Day, Martin Luther King, Jr. Day. ***Student services:*** legal services, health clinic, personal-psychological counseling, women's center. ***Campus security:*** late-night transport-escort service.

HOUSING College housing not available.

ATHLETICS ***Intercollegiate:*** baseball M, basketball M(s)/W(s), cross-country running M(s)/W(s), fencing M(c)/W(c), track and field M(s)/W(s), volleyball W(s). ***Intramural:*** basketball, fencing, track and field. ***Contact:*** Mr. Roger Daniels, Athletic Director, 360-699-0268.

CAREER PLANNING ***Placement office:*** 3 full-time, 3 part-time staff. ***Director:*** Ms. Jill Anderson, Career Information Specialist, 360-992-2155. ***Services:*** job fairs, resume preparation, resume referral, career counseling, careers library, job interviews. 48 organizations recruited on campus 1994–95.

AFTER GRADUATION 50% of students completing a degree program in 1994–95 went directly on to further study.

EXPENSES FOR 1995–96 State resident tuition: $1413 full-time, $46.75 per quarter hour part-time. Nonresident tuition: $5361 full-time, $178.35 per quarter hour part-time.

FINANCIAL AID ***College-administered undergrad aid 1995–96:*** 25 need-based scholarships (average $150), 20 non-need scholarships (average $250), short-term loans (average $100), Federal Work-Study, 125 part-time jobs. ***Required forms:*** institutional, FAFSA. ***Priority deadline:*** 5/1.

APPLYING Open admission. ***Option:*** early entrance. ***Required:*** TOEFL for international students, ACT ASSET. Test scores used for counseling/placement. ***Application deadline:*** 9/5.

APPLYING/TRANSFER ***Entrance:*** noncompetitive. ***Application deadline:*** 9/5. ***Contact:*** Mrs. Linda Calvert, Director of Admissions, 360-992-2392.

CONTACT Mrs. Linda Calvert, Director of Admissions, Clark College, Vancouver, WA 98663-3598, 360-992-2392.

COLUMBIA BASIN COLLEGE
Pasco, Washington

UG Enrollment: 6,580 | **Tuition & Fees (WA Res): $1414**
Application Deadline: rolling | **Room & Board: N/Avail**

GENERAL State-supported, 2-year, coed. Part of Washington State Board for Community and Technical Colleges. Awards transfer associate, terminal associate degrees. Founded 1955. ***Setting:*** 156-acre small-town campus. ***Total enrollment:*** 6,580. ***Faculty:*** 350 (100 full-time, 10% with terminal degrees, 250 part-time); student-faculty ratio is 18:1.

ENROLLMENT PROFILE 6,580 students from 12 states and territories, 20 other countries. 54% women, 53% part-time, 98% state residents, 30% transferred in, 50% 25 or older, 1% Native American, 3% Hispanic, 1% African American, 2% Asian American. *Most popular recent majors:* liberal arts/general studies, nursing, computer science.
FIRST-YEAR CLASS 920 total; 3,000 applied, 100% were accepted, 31% of whom enrolled.
ACADEMIC PROGRAM Core, honor code. Calendar: quarters. 800 courses offered in 1995–96. Academic remediation for entering students, English as a second language program offered during academic year and summer, services for LD students, advanced placement, summer session for credit, part-time degree program (daytime, evenings, summer), adult/continuing education programs, co-op programs. Off-campus study.
GENERAL DEGREE REQUIREMENT 92 quarter hours.
MAJORS Agricultural business, agricultural technologies, automotive technologies, carpentry, computer science, early childhood education, electrical and electronics technologies, engineering and applied sciences, environmental engineering technology, fire science, law enforcement/police sciences, liberal arts/general studies, machine and tool technologies, marketing/retailing/merchandising, nuclear technology, nursing, paralegal studies, quality control technology, real estate, secretarial studies/office management, welding technology.
LIBRARY Columbia Basin College Library with 55,799 books, 100 microform titles, 539 periodicals, 3,143 records, tapes, and CDs.
COMPUTERS ON CAMPUS 100 computers for student use in computer center, learning resource center, academic buildings, library.
COLLEGE LIFE Drama-theater group, student-run newspaper. *Social organizations:* 38 open to all. *Most popular organizations:* Phi Theta Kappa, Men's Athletic Club, Band Club, Women's Athletic Club, Drama Club. *Major annual events:* Drama Productions, Student Center Entertainment. *Student services:* women's center. *Campus security:* 24-hour patrols.
HOUSING College housing not available.
ATHLETICS *Intercollegiate:* baseball M(s), basketball M(s)/W(s), golf M(s)/W(s), tennis M(s)/W(s), volleyball W(s). *Intramural:* basketball, bowling, football, softball. *Contact:* Mr. Dave Dunterman, Athletic Director, 509-547-0511 Ext. 239.
CAREER PLANNING *Director:* Mr. Theo Dobie, Coordinator of Career and Placement, 509-547-0511 Ext. 224. *Services:* job fairs, resume preparation, resume referral, career counseling, careers library, job interviews.
AFTER GRADUATION 30% of students completing a degree program in 1994–95 went directly on to further study.
EXPENSES FOR 1996-97 State resident tuition: $1401 full-time, $46.70 per quarter hour part-time. Nonresident tuition: $5511 full-time, $183.70 per quarter hour part-time. Part-time mandatory fees: $7 per quarter. Full-time mandatory fees: $13.
FINANCIAL AID *College-administered undergrad aid 1995-96:* 45 need-based scholarships (average $250), 26 non-need scholarships (average $1000), short-term loans (average $100), low-interest long-term loans from external sources (average $2400), Federal Work-Study, 85 part-time jobs. *Required forms:* CSS Financial Aid PROFILE, state, institutional, FAFSA. *Priority deadline:* 5/1.
APPLYING Open admission except for nursing program. *Required:* school transcript, TOEFL for international students. Test scores used for counseling/placement. *Application deadline:* rolling. *Notification:* continuous.
APPLYING/TRANSFER *Entrance:* noncompetitive. *Application deadline:* rolling. *Notification:* continuous.
CONTACT Dr. John Startzel, Associate Dean for Admissions and Registration, Columbia Basin College, Pasco, WA 99301-3397, 509-547-0511 Ext. 300. *Fax:* 509-546-0401.

EDMONDS COMMUNITY COLLEGE
Lynnwood, Washington

UG Enrollment: 9,194	Tuition & Fees (WA Res): $1401
Application Deadline: rolling	Room & Board: $3690

GENERAL State and locally supported, 2-year, coed. Part of Washington State Board for Community and Technical Colleges. Awards certificates, transfer associate, terminal associate degrees. Founded 1967. *Setting:* 115-acre suburban campus with easy access to Seattle. *Total enrollment:* 9,194. *Faculty:* 364 (139 full-time, 225 part-time); student-faculty ratio is 24:1.
ENROLLMENT PROFILE 9,194 students: 61% women, 39% men, 58% part-time, 83% state residents, 36% transferred in, 9% international, 66% 25 or older, 1% Native American, 4% Hispanic, 3% African American, 12% Asian American.
FIRST-YEAR CLASS Of the students who applied, 100% were accepted.
ACADEMIC PROGRAM Core. Calendar: quarters. Academic remediation for entering students, English as a second language program offered during academic year and summer, services for LD students, advanced placement, self-designed majors, honors program, summer session for credit, part-time degree program (daytime, evenings, summer), adult/continuing education programs, co-op programs. Off-campus study at other community colleges in Washington. Study abroad in England, Japan.
GENERAL DEGREE REQUIREMENTS 90 credits; 1 college algebra course.
MAJORS Accounting, business administration/commerce/management, community services, computer information systems, computer technologies, construction management, construction technologies, court reporting, culinary arts, drug and alcohol/substance abuse counseling, early childhood education, electrical and electronics technologies, fashion merchandising, fire science, food services management, food services technology, gerontology, horticulture, human services, information science, international business, international studies, landscape architecture/design, landscaping/grounds maintenance, legal secretarial studies, legal studies, liberal arts/general studies, marketing/retailing/merchandising, medical assistant technologies, medical secretarial studies, mental health/rehabilitation counseling, ornamental horticulture, paralegal studies, public relations, rehabilitation therapy, retail management, secretarial studies/office management, social work, tourism and travel.
LIBRARY 37,540 books, 69 microform titles, 427 periodicals, 1,786 records, tapes, and CDs.
COMPUTERS ON CAMPUS 220 computers for student use in computer center, computer labs, learning resource center, library provide access to on-line services. Staffed computer lab on campus provides training in use of computers, software.
COLLEGE LIFE Choral group, student-run newspaper. *Social organizations:* 40 open to all. *Most popular organizations:* Ski Club, Friendship Groups, Legal Assisting Club, Art Club, Ethnic Clubs. *Major annual events:* Commencement, Campus Bar-B-Q's, Halloween Dance. *Student services:* personal-psychological counseling, women's center. *Campus security:* 24-hour emergency response devices and patrols.
HOUSING 244 college housing spaces available; 240 were occupied 1995–96. No special consideration for freshman housing applicants. Off-campus living permitted. *Options:* coed (4 buildings), international student housing available. Resident assistants live in dorms.
ATHLETICS *Intercollegiate:* basketball M(s)/W(s), soccer M(s), volleyball W(s). *Intramural:* badminton, basketball, bowling, football, golf, table tennis (Ping-Pong), volleyball. *Contact:* Mr. Mark Honey, Athletic Director, 206-640-1507.
CAREER PLANNING *Placement office:* 1 full-time, 3 part-time staff. *Director:* Ms. Laura Enstone, Program Coordinator, 206-640-1462. *Service:* career counseling.
EXPENSES FOR 1996-97 *Application fee:* $15. State resident tuition: $1401 full-time, $46.70 per credit part-time. Nonresident tuition: $5511 full-time, $183.70 per credit part-time. College room and board: $3690.
FINANCIAL AID *College-administered undergrad aid 1995-96:* 275 need-based scholarships (average $550), 144 non-need scholarships (average $550), short-term loans (average $145), low-interest long-term loans from external sources (average $2350), Federal Work-Study, 375 part-time jobs. *Required forms:* institutional, FAFSA. *Priority deadline:* 5/1.
APPLYING Open admission. *Options:* early entrance, deferred entrance. *Required:* TOEFL for international students. *Required for some:* ACT ASSET. Test scores used for counseling/placement. *Application deadline:* rolling.
APPLYING/TRANSFER *Required for some:* standardized test scores. *Entrance:* noncompetitive. *Application deadline:* rolling.
CONTACT Ms. Sharon Bench, Admissions Director, Edmonds Community College, Lynnwood, WA 98036-5999, 206-640-1416. *Fax:* 206-771-3366.

EVERETT COMMUNITY COLLEGE
Everett, Washington

UG Enrollment: 7,788	Tuition & Fees (WA Res): $1382
Application Deadline: rolling	Room & Board: N/Avail

GENERAL State-supported, 2-year, coed. Part of Washington State Board for Community and Technical Colleges. Awards transfer associate, terminal associate degrees. Founded 1941. *Setting:* 25-acre urban campus with easy access to Seattle. *Endowment:* $92,058. *Educational spending 1994-95:* $1718 per undergrad. *Total enrollment:* 7,788. *Faculty:* 230 (113 full-time, 12% with terminal degrees, 117 part-time).
ENROLLMENT PROFILE 7,788 students from 4 states and territories, 12 other countries. 60% women, 40% men, 54% part-time, 98% state residents, 3% transferred in, 1% international, 52% 25 or older, 2% Native American, 3% Hispanic, 1% African American, 5% Asian American. *Areas of study chosen:* 15% business management and administrative services, 3% communications and journalism, 3% engineering and applied sciences, 2% education, 1% architecture, 1% fine arts, 1% library and information studies, 1% natural resource sciences, 1% performing arts, 1% premed, 1% prevet, 1% social sciences. *Most popular recent majors:* liberal arts/general studies, business administration/commerce/management, engineering (general).
FIRST-YEAR CLASS 1,109 total; 1,158 applied, 100% were accepted, 96% of whom enrolled.
ACADEMIC PROGRAM Core, interdisciplinary curriculum, honor code. Calendar: quarters. 1,000 courses offered in 1995–96. Academic remediation for entering students, English as a second language program offered during academic year and summer, services for LD students, advanced placement, summer session for credit, part-time degree program (daytime, evenings, summer), adult/continuing education programs, co-op programs. Off-campus study at 8 members of the Concurrent Enrollment Program.
GENERAL DEGREE REQUIREMENTS 90 quarter credits; computer course for business technology majors.
MAJORS Accounting, American studies, anthropology, architectural technologies, art/fine arts, atmospheric sciences, automotive technologies, aviation technology, biology/biological sciences, botany/plant sciences, business administration/commerce/management, chemistry, child care/child and family studies, civil engineering technology, commercial art, communication, computer science, cosmetology, criminal justice, data processing, drafting and design, early childhood education, earth science, ecology, economics, education, elementary education, engineering (general), engineering and applied sciences, engineering sciences, (pre)engineering sequence, engineering technology, English, environmental health sciences, environmental sciences, film and video production, geography, geology, German, graphic arts, history, human services, industrial arts, Japanese, journalism, law enforcement/police sciences, liberal arts/general studies, manufacturing technology, marketing/retailing/merchandising, mathematics, medical assistant technologies, medical secretarial studies, modern languages, music, nursing, occupational therapy, oceanography, painting/drawing, philosophy, photography, physical education, physics, political science/government, practical nursing, psychology, public administration, retail management, Russian, secretarial studies/office management, sociology, Spanish, speech/rhetoric/public address/debate, theater arts/drama, welding technology, wildlife biology, word processing, zoology.
LIBRARY John Terrey Library-Media Center with 40,578 books, 200 microform titles, 237 periodicals, 3,403 records, tapes, and CDs. Acquisition spending 1994–95: $57,540.
COMPUTERS ON CAMPUS 339 computers for student use in computer center, computer labs, classrooms provide access to e-mail. Staffed computer lab on campus provides training in use of computers, software. Academic computing expenditure 1994–95: $435,487.
COLLEGE LIFE Drama-theater group, student-run newspaper. 1% vote in student government elections. *Student services:* personal-psychological counseling, women's center. *Campus security:* 24-hour patrols.
HOUSING College housing not available.
ATHLETICS Member NJCAA. *Intercollegiate:* basketball M(s)/W(s), soccer M(s), volleyball W(s). *Intramural:* basketball, bowling. *Contact:* Mr. Larry Walker, Coordinator of Health and Physical Activities, 206-388-9508.
CAREER PLANNING *Placement office:* 1 full-time, 1 part-time staff; $193,190 operating expenditure 1994–95. *Director:* Ms. Julie Buchholz, Coordinator/Counselor, 206-388-9267. *Service:* career counseling.
EXPENSES FOR 1995-96 *Application fee:* $20. State resident tuition: $1382 full-time, $46.05 per credit part-time. Nonresident tuition: $5330 full-time, $177.65 per credit part-time.

Everett Community College (continued)

FINANCIAL AID ***College-administered undergrad aid 1995–96:*** 1,223 need-based scholarships, 100 non-need scholarships (average $500), short-term loans (average $250), low-interest long-term loans from external sources (average $1995), Federal Work-Study, 50 part-time jobs. ***Required forms:*** institutional, FAFSA. ***Priority deadline:*** 5/1. ***Waivers:*** full or partial for employees or children of employees and senior citizens. ***Notification:*** 7/31.

APPLYING Open admission. ***Option:*** early entrance. ***Required:*** TOEFL for international students. ***Recommended:*** school transcript. Test scores used for counseling/placement. ***Application deadline:*** rolling. ***Notification:*** continuous.

APPLYING/TRANSFER ***Recommended:*** minimum 2.0 college GPA. ***Entrance:*** noncompetitive. ***Application deadline:*** rolling. ***Notification:*** continuous. ***Contact:*** Ms. Linda Baca, Admissions Manager, 206-388-9219.

CONTACT Ms. Linda Baca, Admissions Manager, Everett Community College, 801 Wetmore Avenue, Everett, WA 98201-1327, 206-388-9219.

GRAYS HARBOR COLLEGE
Aberdeen, Washington

UG Enrollment: 2,815	**Tuition & Fees (WA Res): $1395**
Application Deadline: rolling	**Room & Board: N/Avail**

GENERAL State-supported, 2-year, coed. Part of Washington State Board for Community and Technical Colleges. Awards certificates, diplomas, transfer associate, terminal associate degrees. Founded 1930. ***Setting:*** 125-acre small-town campus with easy access to Seattle. ***Total enrollment:*** 2,815. ***Faculty:*** 87 (47 full-time, 40 part-time); student-faculty ratio is 23:1.

ENROLLMENT PROFILE 2,815 students: 60% women, 23% part-time, 99% state residents, 4% transferred in, 85% have need-based financial aid, 1% international, 29% 25 or older, 1% Native American, 1% Hispanic, 1% African American, 2% Asian American.

FIRST-YEAR CLASS 848 total; 1,200 applied, 100% were accepted, 71% of whom enrolled.

ACADEMIC PROGRAM Core, honor code. Calendar: quarters. 315 courses offered in 1995–96. Academic remediation for entering students, English as a second language program offered during academic year and summer, services for LD students, advanced placement, tutorials, honors program, summer session for credit, part-time degree program (daytime, evenings, summer), adult/continuing education programs, co-op programs and internships.

GENERAL DEGREE REQUIREMENTS 93 credits; math/science requirements vary according to program.

MAJORS Accounting, art/fine arts, automotive technologies, biology/biological sciences, botany/plant sciences, business administration/commerce/management, carpentry, chemistry, child care/child and family studies, criminal justice, data processing, drug and alcohol/substance abuse counseling, early childhood education, ecology, education, engineering (general), (pre)engineering sequence, environmental sciences, fish and game management, geology, home economics, humanities, human services, industrial and heavy equipment maintenance, journalism, law enforcement/police sciences, legal secretarial studies, liberal arts/general studies, machine and tool technologies, marine biology, medical secretarial studies, music, nursing, oceanography, psychology, science, secretarial studies/office management, sociology, theater arts/drama, tourism and travel, water resources, welding technology, wildlife biology, wildlife management, zoology.

LIBRARY Spellman Library with 41,000 books, 401 periodicals, 672 CD-ROMs, 1,325 records, tapes, and CDs.

COMPUTERS ON CAMPUS 200 computers for student use in computer center, computer labs, learning resource center, classrooms, library, student center provide access to Internet. Staffed computer lab on campus provides training in use of computers, software.

COLLEGE LIFE Drama-theater group, choral group, student-run newspaper. ***Social organizations:*** 14 open to all. ***Most popular organizations:*** PTK, Fisheries and Wildlife, Engineering Math Science, Outdoor Club, Student Council. ***Major annual events:*** Sporting Events, Bishop Center, Drama Events. ***Student services:*** personal-psychological counseling, women's center. ***Campus security:*** 24-hour emergency response devices, late-night transport-escort service.

HOUSING College housing not available.

ATHLETICS ***Intercollegiate:*** basketball M(s)/W(s), cross-country running M(s)/W(s), golf M(s)/W(s), soccer M(s), softball W(s), volleyball W(s). ***Intramural:*** soccer, softball. ***Contact:*** Ms. Diane Smith, Athletic Director, 360-532-9020 Ext. 263.

CAREER PLANNING ***Placement office:*** 2 full-time staff. ***Director:*** Mr. Larry Johannes, Career Specialist, 360-532-9020. ***Services:*** job fairs, resume preparation, career counseling, careers library, job bank, job interviews.

EXPENSES FOR 1995–96 State resident tuition: $1350 full-time, $45 per credit part-time. Nonresident tuition: $5298 full-time, $176.60 per credit part-time. Full-time mandatory fees: $45.

FINANCIAL AID ***College-administered undergrad aid 1995–96:*** 699 need-based scholarships (average $900), 50 non-need scholarships (average $520), Federal Work-Study, 50 part-time jobs. ***Required forms:*** institutional, FAFSA. ***Priority deadline:*** 5/1. ***Payment plan:*** deferred payment. ***Waivers:*** full or partial for senior citizens.

APPLYING Open admission. ***Option:*** early entrance. ***Required:*** TOEFL for international students, ACT ASSET, CPT. ***Recommended:*** SAT I, SAT II Subject Tests. Test scores used for counseling/placement. ***Application deadline:*** rolling. ***Notification:*** continuous.

APPLYING/TRANSFER ***Application deadline:*** 9/1. ***Notification:*** continuous. ***Contact:*** Mr. Peter Schmidt, Director of Counseling, 360-532-9020.

CONTACT Ms. Brenda Chadwick, Admissions Officer, Grays Harbor College, Aberdeen, WA 98520-7599, 360-532-9020 Ext. 4026 or toll-free 800-562-4830 (in-state). ***Fax:*** 360-532-6716.

GREEN RIVER COMMUNITY COLLEGE
Auburn, Washington

UG Enrollment: 8,000	**Tuition & Fees (WA Res): $1416**
Application Deadline: rolling	**Room & Board: N/Avail**

GENERAL State-supported, 2-year, coed. Part of Washington State Board for Community and Technical Colleges. Awards certificates, transfer associate, terminal associate degrees. Founded 1965. ***Setting:*** 168-acre rural campus with easy access to Seattle. ***Total enrollment:*** 8,000. ***Faculty:*** 342 (105 full-time, 100% with terminal degrees, 237 part-time); student-faculty ratio is 25:1.

ENROLLMENT PROFILE 8,000 students from 21 states and territories, 30 other countries. 53% women, 47% men, 69% part-time, 94% state residents, 3% transferred in, 51% 25 or older, 1% Native American, 2% Hispanic, 2% African American, 6% Asian American.

FIRST-YEAR CLASS 2,395 total; 5,042 applied, 100% were accepted, 48% of whom enrolled.

ACADEMIC PROGRAM Core. Calendar: quarters. Academic remediation for entering students, English as a second language program offered during academic year and summer, services for LD students, advanced placement, self-designed majors, tutorials, summer session for credit, part-time degree program (daytime, evenings, summer), adult/continuing education programs, co-op programs and internships. Off-campus study at McChord Air Force Base in hazardous materials management program. Study abroad in England.

GENERAL DEGREE REQUIREMENTS 90 quarter hours; 15 quarter hours of math/science including at least 1 lab science course; computer course for most vocational majors.

MAJORS Accounting, air traffic control, automotive technologies, aviation administration, aviation technology, broadcasting, business administration/commerce/management, business education, carpentry, computer information systems, construction technologies, court reporting, criminal justice, drafting and design, early childhood education, electrical and electronics technologies, electronics engineering technology, flight training, forest technology, law enforcement/police sciences, legal secretarial studies, liberal arts/general studies, machine and tool technologies, marketing/retailing/merchandising, medical secretarial studies, music, occupational therapy, physical therapy, pollution control technologies, practical nursing, radio and television studies, real estate, retail management, secretarial studies/office management, transportation technologies, water resources, welding technology.

LIBRARY Holman Library with 26,000 books, 25 microform titles, 325 periodicals, 1 on-line bibliographic service, 15 CD-ROMs, 2,600 records, tapes, and CDs.

COMPUTERS ON CAMPUS Computer purchase plan available. 6 computers for student use in library provide access to Internet. Staffed computer lab on campus (open 24 hours a day) provides training in use of computers, software.

COLLEGE LIFE Drama-theater group, choral group, student-run newspaper, radio station. ***Social organizations:*** 35 open to all. ***Most popular organizations:*** Phi Theta Kappa, Country Dance, Green River Christian Encounter. ***Major annual events:*** Noon-Hour Lecture Series, Noon-Hour Entertainment Programs, Intramural Sports. ***Student services:*** health clinic, personal-psychological counseling, women's center. ***Campus security:*** 24-hour emergency response devices and patrols, student patrols, late-night transport-escort service.

HOUSING College housing not available.

ATHLETICS ***Intercollegiate:*** baseball M(s), basketball M(s)/W(s), golf M(s)/W(s), soccer M(s)/W(s), softball W(s), tennis M(s)/W(s), volleyball W(s). ***Intramural:*** badminton, basketball, football, tennis, volleyball, weight lifting. ***Contact:*** Mr. Michael McGraw, Director of Athletics, 206-833-9111 Ext. 434.

CAREER PLANNING ***Placement office:*** 1 full-time staff. ***Director:*** Dr. Laura Tordenti, Dean of Educational Planning Services, 206-833-9111 Ext. 249. ***Services:*** job fairs, resume preparation, resume referral, career counseling, careers library, job bank, job interviews.

EXPENSES FOR 1996–97 State resident tuition: $1401 full-time, $46.70 per quarter hour part-time. Nonresident tuition: $5511 full-time, $183.70 per quarter hour part-time. Full-time mandatory fees: $15.

FINANCIAL AID ***College-administered undergrad aid 1995–96:*** need-based scholarships, non-need scholarships, low-interest long-term loans from external sources, Federal Work-Study, part-time jobs. ***Required forms:*** CSS Financial Aid PROFILE, institutional, FAFSA. ***Priority deadline:*** 4/15. ***Waivers:*** full or partial for senior citizens. ***Notification:*** continuous.

APPLYING Open admission. ***Options:*** early entrance, deferred entrance, midyear entrance. ***Required:*** ACT ASSET or ACT COMPASS. ***Required for some:*** school transcript, TOEFL for international students. Test scores used for counseling/placement. ***Application deadline:*** rolling. ***Notification:*** continuous.

APPLYING/TRANSFER ***Required for some:*** standardized test scores. ***Entrance:*** noncompetitive. ***Application deadline:*** rolling. ***Notification:*** continuous.

CONTACT Ms. Peggy Morgan, Program Support Supervisor, Green River Community College, 12401 Southeast 320th Street, Auburn, WA 98092-3699, 206-833-9111 Ext. 301. ***Fax:*** 206-939-5135. College video available.

HIGHLINE COMMUNITY COLLEGE
Des Moines, Washington

UG Enrollment: 7,271	**Tuition & Fees (WA Res): $1401**
Application Deadline: rolling	**Room & Board: N/Avail**

GENERAL State-supported, 2-year, coed. Part of Washington State Board for Community and Technical Colleges. Awards transfer associate, terminal associate degrees. Founded 1961. ***Setting:*** 81-acre suburban campus with easy access to Seattle. ***Total enrollment:*** 7,271. ***Faculty:*** 223 (113 full-time, 110 part-time); student-faculty ratio is 28:1. ***Notable Alumni:*** Norm Rice, mayor of Seattle.

ENROLLMENT PROFILE 7,271 students: 66% women, 34% men, 42% part-time, 95% state residents, 40% transferred in, 60% have need-based financial aid, 1% international, 50% 25 or older, 1% Native American, 3% Hispanic, 5% African American, 13% Asian American. ***Most popular recent majors:*** business administration/commerce/management, psychology, education.

FIRST-YEAR CLASS Of the students who applied, 100% were accepted.

ACADEMIC PROGRAM Core, broad-based liberal arts curriculum. Calendar: quarters. Academic remediation for entering students, English as a second language program offered during academic year, services for LD students, advanced placement, self-designed majors, honors program, summer session for credit, part-time degree program (daytime, evenings), co-op programs. Study abroad in England, France, Italy. ROTC: Army (c), Naval (c), Air Force (c).

GENERAL DEGREE REQUIREMENT 90 quarter hours.

MAJORS Accounting, art/fine arts, behavioral sciences, business administration/commerce/management, computer technologies, criminal justice, data processing, dental services, drafting and design, early childhood education, education, engineering (general), engineering and applied sciences, (pre)engineering sequence, engineering technology, English, ethnic

studies, humanities, interior design, jewelry and metalsmithing, journalism, law enforcement/police sciences, legal secretarial studies, library science, marine technology, mathematics, medical assistant technologies, music, natural sciences, nursing, paralegal studies, printing technologies, psychology, respiratory therapy, Romance languages, science, secretarial studies/office management, social science, tourism and travel.
LIBRARY Highline Community College Library with 57,678 books, 70 microform titles, 585 periodicals, 2,200 records, tapes, and CDs. Acquisition spending 1994–95: $849,008.
COMPUTERS ON CAMPUS Computer purchase plan available. 300 computers for student use in lab provide access to e-mail, Internet. Staffed computer lab on campus provides training in use of computers, software.
COLLEGE LIFE Drama-theater group, choral group, student-run newspaper. 1% vote in student government elections. ***Most popular organizations:*** Phi Theta Kappa, Black Student Union, Data Processing Management Association, International Club, Library Technicians Club. ***Student services:*** health clinic, personal-psychological counseling, women's center. ***Campus security:*** 24-hour patrols.
HOUSING College housing not available.
ATHLETICS Member NJCAA. ***Intercollegiate:*** basketball M(s)/W(s), cross-country running M(s), softball W(s), track and field M(s), volleyball W(s), wrestling M(s). ***Contact:*** Mr. Fred Harrison, Athletic Director, 206-878-3710 Ext. 454.
CAREER PLANNING ***Placement office:*** 1 part-time staff. ***Director:*** Ms. Ingrid Gintz, Program Assistant, 206-878-3710 Ext. 563. ***Services:*** resume preparation, career counseling, careers library.
EXPENSES FOR 1996–97 State resident tuition: $1401 full-time, $46.70 per quarter hour part-time. Nonresident tuition: $5511 full-time, $183.70 per quarter hour part-time.
FINANCIAL AID ***College-administered undergrad aid 1995–96:*** 200 need-based scholarships (average $440), 45 non-need scholarships (average $253), low-interest long-term loans from external sources (average $2500), Federal Work-Study, 100 part-time jobs. ***Required forms:*** CSS Financial Aid PROFILE, institutional; accepted: FAFSA. ***Priority deadline:*** 4/1. ***Waivers:*** full or partial for employees or children of employees and senior citizens.
APPLYING Open admission except for allied health, nursing programs. ***Option:*** midyear entrance. ***Required:*** TOEFL for international students. ***Recommended:*** ACT ASSET. Test scores used for counseling/placement. ***Application deadline:*** rolling.
APPLYING/TRANSFER ***Recommended:*** standardized test scores. ***Entrance:*** noncompetitive. ***Application deadline:*** rolling.
CONTACT Mr. Lou Crandall, Highline Community College, Des Moines, WA 98198-9800, 206-878-3710 Ext. 363.

ITT TECHNICAL INSTITUTE
Seattle, Washington

UG Enrollment: 484	**Tuition: $16,239/deg prog**
Application Deadline: rolling	**Room & Board: N/Avail**

GENERAL Proprietary, primarily 2-year, coed. Part of ITT Educational Services, Inc. Awards terminal associate, bachelor's degrees. Founded 1932. ***Setting:*** urban campus. ***Total enrollment:*** 484. ***Faculty:*** 25 (18 full-time, 70% with terminal degrees, 7 part-time).
ENROLLMENT PROFILE 484 students from 4 states and territories, 2 other countries. 11% women, 89% men, 0% part-time, 96% state residents, 2% transferred in, 36% 25 or older, 3% Native American, 6% Hispanic, 10% African American, 11% Asian American. ***Most popular recent major:*** electronics engineering technology.
FIRST-YEAR CLASS 215 total. Of the students accepted, 86% enrolled. 9% from top 10% of their high school class, 20% from top quarter, 49% from top half.
ACADEMIC PROGRAM Core, technical curriculum. Calendar: quarters. Academic remediation for entering students, tutorials.
GENERAL DEGREE REQUIREMENTS 91 credit hours for associate, 180 credit hours for bachelor's; computer course.
MAJORS Drafting and design, electronics engineering technology (B).
LIBRARY Learning Resource Center with 1,032 books, 24 periodicals.
COMPUTERS ON CAMPUS 65 computers for student use in computer labs, learning resource center, classrooms, library.
COLLEGE LIFE ***Social organizations:*** 2 open to all. ***Campus security:*** 24-hour emergency response devices.
HOUSING College housing not available.
CAREER PLANNING ***Placement office:*** 2 full-time staff. ***Director:*** Ms. Laura Nielsen, Director of Placement, 206-244-3300. ***Services:*** resume preparation, resume referral, career counseling, job interviews. Students must register freshman year.
EXPENSES FOR 1996–97 Tuition for associate degree program ranges from $16,239 to $18,510. Tuition for bachelor's degree program: $28,558. Tuition guaranteed not to increase for student's term of enrollment.
FINANCIAL AID ***College-administered undergrad aid 1995–96:*** need-based scholarships, low-interest long-term loans from external sources, Federal Work-Study. ***Required forms:*** institutional, FAFSA; accepted: CSS Financial Aid PROFILE. ***Priority deadline:*** 10/1.
APPLYING ***Option:*** deferred entrance. ***Required:*** CPAt. ***Recommended:*** TOEFL for international students. ***Required for some:*** 3 years of high school math. Test scores used for admission. ***Application deadline:*** rolling. ***Notification:*** continuous.
APPLYING/TRANSFER ***Required for some:*** 3 years of high school math. ***Entrance:*** minimally difficult. ***Application deadline:*** rolling. ***Notification:*** continuous. ***Contact:*** Mr. Don Slayter, Director of Education, 206-244-3300.
CONTACT Mr. Toby Stanley, Director of Recruitment, ITT Technical Institute, 12720 Gateway Drive, Suite 100, Seattle, WA 98168-3333, 206-244-3300. College video available.

ITT TECHNICAL INSTITUTE
Spokane, Washington

UG Enrollment: 241	**Tuition: $15,599/deg prog**
Application Deadline: rolling	**Room & Board: N/Avail**

GENERAL Proprietary, 2-year, coed. Part of ITT Educational Services, Inc. Awards terminal associate degrees. Founded 1985. ***Setting:*** 3-acre suburban campus. ***Total enrollment:*** 241. ***Faculty:*** 18 (14 full-time, 4 part-time).
ENROLLMENT PROFILE 241 students: 0% part-time. ***Most popular recent major:*** electronics engineering technology.
FIRST-YEAR CLASS 117 total; 248 applied.
ACADEMIC PROGRAM Calendar: quarters. Academic remediation for entering students, summer session for credit.
GENERAL DEGREE REQUIREMENTS 90 credit hours; math/science requirements vary according to program; computer course.
MAJORS Drafting and design, electronics engineering technology.
LIBRARY 1,700 books, 6 periodicals, 4 CD-ROMs, 2 records, tapes, and CDs.
COMPUTERS ON CAMPUS 60 computers for student use in computer labs, library. Staffed computer lab on campus.
COLLEGE LIFE ***Campus security:*** 24-hour emergency response devices.
HOUSING College housing not available.
ATHLETICS ***Intramural:*** basketball.
CAREER PLANNING ***Placement office:*** 1 full-time, 1 part-time staff. ***Director:*** Mr. Ray Keevy, Director of Placement, 509-926-2900. ***Services:*** resume preparation, resume referral, career counseling, careers library, job bank, job interviews. Students must register freshman year.
EXPENSES FOR 1996–97 Tuition per degree program ranges from $15,599 to $17,690. Full-time mandatory fees range from $540 to $720. Tuition guaranteed not to increase for student's term of enrollment.
FINANCIAL AID ***College-administered undergrad aid 1995–96:*** need-based scholarships, low-interest long-term loans from external sources, Federal Work-Study. ***Required forms:*** institutional, FAFSA; accepted: CSS Financial Aid PROFILE, state. ***Priority deadline:*** 9/5. ***Waivers:*** full or partial for employees or children of employees.
APPLYING ***Option:*** deferred entrance. ***Required:*** CPAt. ***Recommended:*** 3 years of high school math and science. Test scores used for admission. ***Application deadline:*** rolling.
APPLYING/TRANSFER ***Recommended:*** 3 years of high school math and science. ***Entrance:*** minimally difficult. ***Application deadline:*** rolling. ***Contact:*** Mr. Ken Meronek, Director of Education, 509-926-2900.
CONTACT Mr. Richard Flann, Director of Recruitment, ITT Technical Institute, Spokane, WA 99212-2682, 509-926-2900 Ext. 21 or toll-free 800-777-8324. College video available.

LAKE WASHINGTON TECHNICAL COLLEGE
Kirkland, Washington

UG Enrollment: 2,787	**Tuition & Fees: $1056**
Application Deadline: rolling	**Room & Board: N/Avail**

GENERAL District-supported, 2-year, coed. Part of Washington State Board for Community and Technical Colleges. Awards certificates, transfer associate degrees. ***Setting:*** 57-acre suburban campus with easy access to Seattle. ***Total enrollment:*** 2,787. ***Faculty:*** 310 (60 full-time, 10% with terminal degrees, 250 part-time). ***Notable Alumni:*** Betty Rhynalds, cab and trim clerk specialist at PACCAR Corporation Purchasing Department; Ruth Guilinger, drafter at Boeing; Michael Burley, technician at Microsoft Corporation; Martin Hires, engineer at Boeing; Dick Schubert, technical support at Microsoft Corporation.
ENROLLMENT PROFILE 2,787 students: 51% women, 49% men, 98% state residents, 1% international, 64% 25 or older, 1% Native American, 2% Hispanic, 29% African American, 9% Asian American.
FIRST-YEAR CLASS Of the students who applied, 100% were accepted.
ACADEMIC PROGRAM Interdisciplinary and vocational curriculum. Calendar: quarters. 984 courses offered in 1995–96. Academic remediation for entering students, English as a second language program offered during academic year, services for LD students, advanced placement, summer session for credit, co-op programs and internships.
GENERAL DEGREE REQUIREMENTS 101 credits; math requirement varies according to program; computer course for most majors; internship (some majors).
MAJORS Accounting, automotive technologies, child care/child and family studies, computer technologies, dental services, drafting and design, electrical and electronics technologies, horticulture, hotel and restaurant management, machine and tool technologies, management information systems, medical assistant technologies.
LIBRARY LWTC Library/Media Center with 12,000 books, 300 microform titles, 375 periodicals, 20 CD-ROMs, 2,000 records, tapes, and CDs. Acquisition spending 1994–95: $24,799.
COMPUTERS ON CAMPUS 400 computers for student use in computer labs, learning resource center, classrooms, library, student rooms provide access to Internet. Staffed computer lab on campus. Academic computing expenditure 1994–95: $104,564.
COLLEGE LIFE 30% vote in student government elections. ***Social organizations:*** 1 open to all. ***Most popular organization:*** Associated Student Government. ***Major annual events:*** Summer Party, Christmas Party. ***Student services:*** personal-psychological counseling, women's center. ***Campus security:*** 24-hour emergency response devices, late-night transport-escort service, parking lot security, security cameras.
HOUSING College housing not available.
CAREER PLANNING ***Placement office:*** 1 full-time, 1 part-time staff; $74,292 operating expenditure 1994–95. ***Director:*** Mr. Jeffrey Kuess, Director, Library, 206-803-2212. ***Services:*** job fairs, resume preparation, career counseling, careers library, job bank. 5 organizations recruited on campus 1994–95.
EXPENSES FOR 1996–97 Tuition: $1056 (minimum) full-time. Part-time tuition per credit ranges from $37.45 to $77. Full-time tuition ranges up to$3465 according to program.
FINANCIAL AID ***College-administered undergrad aid 1995–96:*** 153 need-based scholarships (average $1495), 36 non-need scholarships (average $1513), 10 Federal Work-Study (averaging $1475), part-time jobs. ***Required forms:*** institutional, FAFSA; required for some: state income tax form. ***Application deadline:*** continuous. ***Payment plan:*** deferred payment.
APPLYING Open admission except for dental hygiene, nursing programs. ***Option:*** early entrance. ***Required:*** TOEFL for international students. ***Required for some:*** school transcript, ACT ASSET. Test scores used for counseling/placement. ***Application deadline:*** rolling. ***Notification:*** continuous.
APPLYING/TRANSFER ***Required:*** college transcript. ***Required for some:*** standardized test scores, high school transcript, minimum 2.0 college GPA. ***Entrance:*** noncompetitive. ***Application deadline:*** rolling. ***Notification:*** continuous. ***Contact:*** Ms. Suzanne Lawson, Registration Technician, 206-828-5600.
CONTACT Ms. Janet Mandell, Director, Student Services, Lake Washington Technical College, Kirkland, WA 98034, 206-828-5600.

LOWER COLUMBIA COLLEGE
Longview, Washington

UG Enrollment: 4,081	**Tuition & Fees (WA Res): $1445**
Application Deadline: rolling	**Room & Board: N/Avail**

GENERAL State-supported, 2-year, coed. Part of Washington State Board for Community and Technical Colleges. Awards certificates, diplomas, transfer associate, terminal associate degrees. Founded 1934. ***Setting:*** 30-acre small-town campus with easy access to Portland. ***Total enrollment:*** 4,081. ***Faculty:*** 160 (80 full-time, 80 part-time).
ENROLLMENT PROFILE 4,081 students from 6 states and territories, 3 other countries. 62% women, 40% part-time, 97% state residents, 5% transferred in, 1% international, 50% 25 or older, 2% Native American, 5% Hispanic, 1% African American, 4% Asian American.
FIRST-YEAR CLASS 700 total. Of the students who applied, 100% were accepted, 92% of whom enrolled.
ACADEMIC PROGRAM Core. Calendar: quarters. Academic remediation for entering students, English as a second language program offered during academic year, services for LD students, honors program, summer session for credit, part-time degree program (daytime, evenings, summer), adult/continuing education programs, co-op programs. Study abroad in England.
GENERAL DEGREE REQUIREMENTS 90 credits; quantitative reasoning proficiency.
MAJORS Accounting, anthropology, art/fine arts, automotive technologies, biology/biological sciences, business administration/commerce/management, chemical engineering technology, chemistry, child care/child and family studies, computer information systems, computer programming, computer science, computer technologies, data processing, drafting and design, drug and alcohol/substance abuse counseling, early childhood education, earth science, economics, education, electrical and electronics technologies, emergency medical technology, (pre)engineering sequence, engineering technology, English, fire science, history, industrial and heavy equipment maintenance, industrial engineering technology, instrumentation technology, law enforcement/police sciences, legal secretarial studies, liberal arts/general studies, machine and tool technologies, marketing/retailing/merchandising, mathematics, mechanical engineering technology, medical assistant technologies, medical secretarial studies, medical technology, music, nursing, paper and pulp sciences, philosophy, physical education, physics, political science/government, practical nursing, psychology, real estate, secretarial studies/office management, social science, sociology, theater arts/drama, welding technology.
LIBRARY 26,345 books, 2,000 microform titles, 287 periodicals, 1,670 records, tapes, and CDs.
COMPUTERS ON CAMPUS 250 computers for student use in computer center, computer labs, classrooms, library provide access to main academic computer, on-line services. Staffed computer lab on campus provides training in use of computers, software.
COLLEGE LIFE Drama-theater group, student-run newspaper. ***Student services:*** health clinic, personal-psychological counseling.
HOUSING College housing not available.
ATHLETICS ***Intercollegiate:*** basketball M(s)/W(s), golf M(s), soccer M, tennis W(s), volleyball W(s). ***Intramural:*** basketball, soccer.
CAREER PLANNING ***Service:*** career counseling.
EXPENSES FOR 1996–97 State resident tuition: $1445 full-time, $47.10 per credit part-time. Nonresident tuition: $5555 full-time, $184.10 per credit part-time.
FINANCIAL AID ***College-administered undergrad aid 1995–96:*** 40 need-based scholarships (averaging $200), 25 non-need scholarships (averaging $400), low-interest long-term loans from external sources, Federal Work-Study, part-time jobs. ***Required forms:*** CSS Financial Aid PROFILE, state; required for some: FAFSA. ***Priority deadline:*** 5/1.
APPLYING Open admission. ***Options:*** early entrance, deferred entrance. ***Required:*** TOEFL for international students. ***Recommended:*** school transcript. Test scores used for counseling/placement. ***Application deadline:*** rolling. ***Notification:*** continuous.
APPLYING/TRANSFER ***Recommended:*** high school transcript, college transcript. ***Entrance:*** noncompetitive. ***Application deadline:*** rolling.
CONTACT Ms. Mary Harding, Associate Dean of Enrollment Services, Lower Columbia College, Longview, WA 98632-0310, 360-577-2304.

NORTH SEATTLE COMMUNITY COLLEGE
Seattle, Washington

UG Enrollment: 8,199	**Tuition & Fees (WA Res): $1351**
Application Deadline: rolling	**Room & Board: N/Avail**

GENERAL State-supported, 2-year, coed. Part of Seattle Community College District System. Awards transfer associate, terminal associate degrees. Founded 1970. ***Setting:*** 65-acre urban campus. ***Total enrollment:*** 8,199. ***Faculty:*** 290 (110 full-time, 11% with terminal degrees, 180 part-time); student-faculty ratio is 25:1.
ENROLLMENT PROFILE 8,199 students from 50 states and territories, 32 other countries. 58% women, 42% men, 76% part-time, 97% state residents, 21% transferred in, 1% international, 73% 25 or older, 1% Native American, 4% Hispanic, 5% African American, 17% Asian American.
FIRST-YEAR CLASS 3,101 applied, 100% were accepted.
ACADEMIC PROGRAM Core, honor code. Calendar: quarters. Academic remediation for entering students, English as a second language program offered during academic year, advanced placement, summer session for credit, part-time degree program (daytime, evenings, summer), adult/continuing education programs. Off-campus study at 8 institutions in Washington. ROTC: Army (c).
GENERAL DEGREE REQUIREMENTS 90 credits; computer course.
MAJORS Accounting, art/fine arts, business administration/commerce/management, business machine technologies, child care/child and family studies, communication equipment technology, computer programming, computer science, computer technologies, culinary arts, data processing, drafting and design, early childhood education, electrical and electronics technologies, electromechanical technology, electronics engineering technology, food services technology, heating/refrigeration/air conditioning, humanities, liberal arts/general studies, mathematics, medical assistant technologies, medical secretarial studies, music, natural sciences, pharmacy/pharmaceutical sciences, practical nursing, real estate, science, secretarial studies/office management, social science.
LIBRARY 48,477 books, 250 microform titles, 375 periodicals, 14 CD-ROMs, 1,200 records, tapes, and CDs. Acquisition spending 1994–95: $873,076.
COMPUTERS ON CAMPUS 200 computers for student use in computer center, department labs, library provide access to Internet. Academic computing expenditure 1994–95: $281,916.
COLLEGE LIFE Drama-theater group, choral group, student-run newspaper. ***Student services:*** personal-psychological counseling, women's center. ***Campus security:*** late-night transport-escort service, security patrols.
HOUSING College housing not available.
ATHLETICS ***Intramural:*** basketball, skiing (downhill), soccer, tennis, volleyball, weight lifting.
CAREER PLANNING ***Placement office:*** 1 part-time staff; $45,369 operating expenditure 1994–95. ***Director:*** Dr. Gerald B. Schneider, Coordinator, Counseling and Center Services, 206-527-3680. ***Services:*** career counseling, careers library.
AFTER GRADUATION 40% of students completing a degree program in 1994–95 went directly on to further study.
EXPENSES FOR 1995–96 State resident tuition: $1331 full-time, $44.35 per credit part-time. Nonresident tuition: $5279 full-time, $175.95 per credit part-time. Full-time mandatory fees: $20.
FINANCIAL AID ***College-administered undergrad aid 1995–96:*** need-based scholarships (average $700), non-need scholarships (average $500), low-interest long-term loans from college funds (average $700), loans from external sources (average $2000), Federal Work-Study (averaging $600), 30 part-time jobs. ***Required forms:*** institutional, FAFSA. ***Priority deadline:*** 4/1.
APPLYING Open admission. ***Options:*** early entrance, deferred entrance. ***Required:*** TOEFL for international students. Test scores used for counseling/placement. ***Application deadline:*** rolling. ***Notification:*** continuous until 9/24.
APPLYING/TRANSFER ***Entrance:*** noncompetitive. ***Application deadline:*** rolling. ***Notification:*** continuous until 9/24.
CONTACT Ms. June Stacey-Clemons, Associate Dean Enrollment Services, North Seattle Community College, 9600 College Way North, Seattle, WA 98103-3599, 206-527-3773. ***Fax:*** 206-527-3635. College video available.

NORTHWEST INDIAN COLLEGE
Bellingham, Washington

UG Enrollment: 1,500	**Tuition & Fees (WA Res): $930**
Application Deadline: N/R	**Room & Board: N/Avail**

GENERAL Federally supported, 2-year, coed. Awards certificates, transfer associate, terminal associate degrees. Founded 1978. ***Setting:*** 5-acre rural campus. ***Endowment:*** $3 million. ***Total enrollment:*** 1,500. ***Faculty:*** 63 (23 full-time, 1% with terminal degrees, 40 part-time).
ENROLLMENT PROFILE 1,500 students from 6 states and territories, 2 other countries. 55% women, 40% part-time, 95% state residents, 20% transferred in, 90% have need-based financial aid, 10% have non-need-based financial aid, 3% international, 75% 25 or older, 80% Native American, 2% Hispanic, 2% African American, 2% Asian American. ***Areas of study chosen:*** 20% biological and life sciences, 19% education, 14% social sciences, 10% area and ethnic studies, 10% business management and administrative services, 5% communications and journalism, 5% computer and information sciences, 5% engineering and applied sciences, 5% health professions and related sciences, 5% natural resource sciences, 5% physical sciences, 5% psychology, 5% vocational and home economics, 2% liberal arts/general studies, 2% premed, 1% prelaw.
FIRST-YEAR CLASS 75 total; 75 applied, 100% were accepted.
ACADEMIC PROGRAM Core, honor code. Calendar: quarters. 200 courses offered in 1995–96. Academic remediation for entering students, self-designed majors, tutorials, summer session for credit, part-time degree program (daytime, evenings, summer), external degree programs, adult/continuing education programs, co-op programs and internships. Study abroad in Mexico (1% of students participate).
GENERAL DEGREE REQUIREMENTS 92 credits; math/science requirements vary according to program; computer course.
MAJORS Art/fine arts, business administration/commerce/management, construction technologies, early childhood education, education, engineering (general), engineering design, hotel and restaurant management, human services, marine technology, secretarial studies/office management.
COMPUTERS ON CAMPUS 22 computers for student use in computer center, computer labs, learning resource center provide access to main academic computer, e-mail, Internet.
COLLEGE LIFE Choral group. 25% vote in student government elections. ***Student services:*** personal-psychological counseling.
HOUSING College housing not available.
ATHLETICS ***Intramural:*** baseball, basketball, volleyball.
CAREER PLANNING ***Placement office:*** 1 full-time staff. ***Director:*** Ms. Malinda Davidson, Career Specialist, 360-676-2772. ***Services:*** job fairs, resume preparation, career counseling, careers library. 20 organizations recruited on campus 1994–95.
AFTER GRADUATION 40% of students completing a degree program in 1994–95 went directly on to further study.
EXPENSES FOR 1995–96 ***Application fee:*** $25. State resident tuition: $540 full-time, $12 per credit part-time. Nonresident tuition: $2340 full-time, $52 per credit part-time. Full-time mandatory fees: $390.
FINANCIAL AID ***College-administered undergrad aid 1995–96:*** need-based scholarships, non-need scholarships, Federal Work-Study, part-time jobs. ***Required forms:*** CSS Financial Aid PROFILE, state, institutional, FAFSA. ***Application deadline:*** continuous. ***Waivers:*** full or partial for minority students, adult students, and senior citizens.
APPLYING Open admission. ***Option:*** midyear entrance. ***Required:*** school transcript, TABE. Test scores used for counseling/placement. ***Notification:*** continuous. Preference given to Native Americans.
APPLYING/TRANSFER ***Required:*** standardized test scores, college transcript, minimum 2.0 college GPA. ***Entrance:*** noncompetitive. ***Notification:*** continuous. ***Contact:*** Ms. Barbara Lundborg, Transfer Specialist, 360-676-2772.
CONTACT Ms. Lucetta Toby, Admissions Recruiting Officer, Northwest Indian College, Bellingham, WA 98226, 360-676-2772.

OLYMPIC COLLEGE
Bremerton, Washington

UG Enrollment: 7,470	Tuition & Fees (WA Res): $1401
Application Deadline: rolling	Room & Board: N/Avail

GENERAL State-supported, 2-year, coed. Part of Washington State Board for Community and Technical Colleges. Awards transfer associate, terminal associate degrees. Founded 1946. ***Setting:*** 27-acre suburban campus with easy access to Seattle. ***Total enrollment:*** 7,470. ***Faculty:*** 323 (95 full-time, 84% with terminal degrees, 228 part-time).
ENROLLMENT PROFILE 7,470 students: 58% women, 42% men, 52% part-time, 99% state residents, 10% transferred in, 1% international, 75% 25 or older, 2% Native American, 3% Hispanic, 4% African American, 10% Asian American. ***Areas of study chosen:*** 4% health professions and related sciences, 2% computer and information sciences, 1% business management and administrative services. ***Most popular recent majors:*** liberal arts/general studies, business economics, nursing.
FIRST-YEAR CLASS Of the students who applied, 100% were accepted.
ACADEMIC PROGRAM Core, honor code. Calendar: quarters. Academic remediation for entering students, English as a second language program offered during academic year, services for LD students, advanced placement, summer session for credit, part-time degree program (daytime, evenings), adult/continuing education programs, co-op programs. Off-campus study at other community colleges in Washington. Study abroad in England, Wales.
GENERAL DEGREE REQUIREMENTS 90 credits; 1 college algebra course; 4 natural science courses; computer course (varies by major).
MAJORS Accounting, art/fine arts, automotive technologies, business economics, carpentry, civil engineering technology, computer information systems, corrections, cosmetology, criminal justice, drafting and design, early childhood education, electrical and electronics technologies, (pre)engineering sequence, engineering technology, fashion merchandising, fire science, food services technology, legal secretarial studies, liberal arts/general studies, medical assistant technologies, nursing, practical nursing, real estate, science, secretarial studies/office management, welding technology, word processing.
LIBRARY Olympic College Learning Resources Center with 56,763 books, 136 microform titles, 499 periodicals, 25 CD-ROMs, 2,583 records, tapes, and CDs. Acquisition spending 1994–95: $98,464.
COMPUTERS ON CAMPUS Computer purchase plan available. 260 computers for student use in computer center, computer labs, learning resource center provide access to e-mail, Internet. Staffed computer lab on campus provides training in use of computers, software. Academic computing expenditure 1994–95: $590,753.
COLLEGE LIFE Drama-theater group, choral group, student-run newspaper. 10% vote in student government elections. ***Major annual event:*** Commencement. ***Student services:*** personal-psychological counseling, women's center. ***Campus security:*** 24-hour emergency response devices and patrols, student patrols, late-night transport-escort service.
HOUSING College housing not available.
ATHLETICS Member NJCAA. ***Intercollegiate:*** baseball M(s), basketball M(s)/W(s), softball W(s), volleyball W(s). ***Intramural:*** basketball, volleyball. ***Contact:*** Mr. Dick Myers, Athletic Commissioner, 360-478-4709; Ms. Charlotte York, Athletic Commissioner, 360-478-4502.
CAREER PLANNING ***Placement office:*** 1 full-time, 1 part-time staff; $75,000 operating expenditure 1994–95. ***Director:*** Ms. Patricia Triggs, Program Manager, 360-478-4702. ***Services:*** job fairs, resume preparation, resume referral, career counseling, careers library, job bank, job interviews.
EXPENSES FOR 1996–97 State resident tuition: $1401 full-time, $46.70 per credit part-time. Nonresident tuition: $5511 full-time, $183.70 per credit part-time.
FINANCIAL AID ***College-administered undergrad aid 1995–96:*** 887 need-based scholarships (average $1811), 44 non-need scholarships (average $843), short-term loans (average $110), low-interest long-term loans from external sources (average $2282), Federal Work-Study, 187 part-time jobs. ***Required forms:*** institutional, FAFSA. ***Priority deadline:*** 4/15. ***Waivers:*** full or partial for employees or children of employees and senior citizens. ***Notification:*** 6/1.
APPLYING Open admission except for nursing program. ***Options:*** early entrance, deferred entrance. ***Required:*** TOEFL for international students. Test scores used for counseling/placement. ***Application deadline:*** rolling. ***Notification:*** continuous.
APPLYING/TRANSFER ***Application deadline:*** rolling. ***Notification:*** continuous.
CONTACT Dr. Jolene Ramaker, Associate Dean of Students for Enrollment Services, Olympic College, Bremerton, WA 98337-1699, 360-478-4542. ***Fax:*** 360-792-2135. ***E-mail:*** ramaker_jolene/olym_01@ctc.ctc.edu.

PENINSULA COLLEGE
Port Angeles, Washington

UG Enrollment: 3,550	Tuition & Fees (WA Res): $1860
Application Deadline: rolling	Room & Board: $3945

GENERAL State-supported, 2-year, coed. Awards transfer associate, terminal associate degrees. Founded 1961. ***Setting:*** 75-acre small-town campus. ***Total enrollment:*** 3,550. ***Faculty:*** 149 (62 full-time, 87 part-time); student-faculty ratio is 20:1.
ENROLLMENT PROFILE 3,550 students: 51% women, 49% men, 67% part-time, 98% state residents, 2% transferred in, 1% international, 72% 25 or older, 4% Native American, 4% Hispanic, 2% African American, 3% Asian American. ***Most popular recent majors:*** criminal justice, fish and game management, secretarial studies/office management.
FIRST-YEAR CLASS 891 total; 891 applied, 100% were accepted, 100% of whom enrolled.
ACADEMIC PROGRAM Core. Calendar: quarters. Academic remediation for entering students, English as a second language program offered during academic year, services for LD students, advanced placement, honors program, summer session for credit, part-time degree program (daytime, evenings, summer), adult/continuing education programs, internships.
GENERAL DEGREE REQUIREMENTS 90 credits; 1 college algebra course; 3 science courses; computer course (varies by major).
MAJORS Accounting, automotive technologies, business administration/commerce/management, child care/child and family studies, civil engineering technology, criminal justice, data processing, electrical and electronics technologies, fish and game management, liberal arts/general studies, nursing, real estate, secretarial studies/office management.
LIBRARY 33,736 books, 142 microform titles, 383 periodicals, 1,630 records, tapes, and CDs.
COMPUTERS ON CAMPUS 53 computers for student use in computer center, labs provide access to on-line services, Internet. Staffed computer lab on campus.
COLLEGE LIFE Drama-theater group, choral group, student-run newspaper. ***Student services:*** women's center.
HOUSING 85 college housing spaces available; 70 were occupied 1995–96. No special consideration for freshman housing applicants. Off-campus living permitted.
ATHLETICS ***Intramural:*** badminton, basketball, football, tennis, volleyball.
CAREER PLANNING ***Service:*** career counseling.
AFTER GRADUATION 86% of class of 1994 had job offers within 6 months.
EXPENSES FOR 1996–97 ***Application fee:*** $20. State resident tuition: $1860 full-time, $46.50 per credit part-time. Nonresident tuition: $7340 full-time, $183.50 per credit part-time. College room and board: $3945.
FINANCIAL AID ***College-administered undergrad aid 1995–96:*** 361 need-based scholarships (average $743), 140 non-need scholarships (average $848), short-term loans (average $300), low-interest long-term loans from external sources (average $2400), Federal Work-Study, 124 part-time jobs. ***Required forms:*** CSS Financial Aid PROFILE, institutional, FAFSA. ***Priority deadline:*** 6/1. ***Payment plan:*** deferred payment. ***Waivers:*** full or partial for employees or children of employees.
APPLYING Open admission except for nursing, industrial electronics, business computer systems programs. ***Option:*** deferred entrance. ***Required:*** TOEFL for international students, ACT ASSET. ***Recommended:*** SAT I. ***Required for some:*** school transcript. Test scores used for counseling/placement. ***Application deadline:*** rolling. ***Notification:*** continuous.
APPLYING/TRANSFER ***Required:*** standardized test scores, college transcript. ***Required for some:*** high school transcript. ***Application deadline:*** rolling. ***Notification:*** continuous.
CONTACT Mr. Steven Bays, Director of Registration and Continuing Education, Peninsula College, Port Angeles, WA 98362-2779, 360-452-9277 Ext. 208. ***Fax:*** 360-457-8100. ***E-mail:*** sb@ctc.ctc.edu.

PHILLIPS JUNIOR COLLEGE OF SPOKANE
Spokane, Washington

GENERAL Proprietary, 2-year, coed. Part of Phillips Colleges, Inc. Awards transfer associate degrees. Founded 1970. ***Setting:*** 2-acre urban campus. ***Total enrollment:*** 256. ***Faculty:*** 25 (6 full-time, 19 part-time); student-faculty ratio is 19:1.
EXPENSES FOR 1995–96 ***Application fee:*** $25. Tuition: $12,000 per degree program. Tuition guaranteed not to increase for student's term of enrollment.
CONTACT Mr. Terry Edwards, Director of Admissions, Phillips Junior College of Spokane, 1101 North Fancher, Spokane, WA 99212-1275, 509-535-7771 or toll-free 800-284-4306 (out-of-state). College video available.

PIERCE COLLEGE
Tacoma, Washington

UG Enrollment: 10,294	Tuition & Fees (WA Res): $1431
Application Deadline: rolling	Room & Board: N/Avail

GENERAL State-supported, 2-year, coed. Part of Washington State Board for Community and Technical Colleges. Awards transfer associate, terminal associate degrees. Founded 1967. ***Setting:*** 140-acre suburban campus with easy access to Seattle. ***Endowment:*** $4159. ***Total enrollment:*** 10,294. ***Faculty:*** 579 (179 full-time, 400 part-time).
ENROLLMENT PROFILE 10,294 students: 51% women, 49% men, 44% part-time, 85% state residents, 1% international, 56% 25 or older, 2% Native American, 7% Hispanic, 12% African American, 9% Asian American.
FIRST-YEAR CLASS 3,414 total.
ACADEMIC PROGRAM Core, interdisciplinary curriculum, honor code. Calendar: quarters. 250 courses offered in 1995–96. Academic remediation for entering students, English as a second language program offered during academic year and summer, services for LD students, advanced placement, tutorials, summer session for credit, part-time degree program (daytime, evenings, summer), adult/continuing education programs, co-op programs and internships. Off-campus study at Green River Community College, Tacoma Community College, Highline Community College, South Puget Sound Community College. ROTC: Army (c).
GENERAL DEGREE REQUIREMENTS 90 quarter hours; computer course for business, veterinary technology, electronic engineering technology, fashion merchandising majors.
MAJORS Accounting, business administration/commerce/management, computer information systems, computer programming, criminal justice, dental services, drug and alcohol/substance abuse counseling, early childhood education, electronics engineering technology, fashion merchandising, fire science, food services management, legal secretarial studies, liberal arts/general studies, manufacturing technology, marketing/retailing/merchandising, mental health/rehabilitation counseling, paralegal studies, secretarial studies/office management, veterinary technology, word processing.
LIBRARY 55,000 books, 12 microform titles, 425 periodicals, 5 on-line bibliographic services, 10 CD-ROMs, 1,000 records, tapes, and CDs. Acquisition spending 1994–95: $90,853.
COMPUTERS ON CAMPUS 350 computers for student use in computer center, computer labs, learning resource center, library provide access to main academic computer. Staffed computer lab on campus provides training in use of computers, software. Academic computing expenditure 1994–95: $315,932.
COLLEGE LIFE Drama-theater group, choral group, student-run newspaper. 8% vote in student government elections. ***Social organizations:*** 26 open to all. ***Most popular organizations:*** Black Student Union, Phi Theta Kappa, Dental Hygiene Association, Veterinary Technology Association, Latino Student Union. ***Student services:*** women's center. ***Campus security:*** 24-hour emergency response devices and patrols, late-night transport-escort service.
HOUSING College housing not available.

Peterson's Guide to Two-Year Colleges 1997

657

Pierce College (continued)

ATHLETICS ***Intercollegiate:*** baseball M(s), basketball M(s)/W(s), soccer M(s), softball W(s), volleyball W(s). ***Contact:*** Mr. Duncan Stevenson, Athletic Director, 206-964-6612.

CAREER PLANNING ***Placement office:*** 1 part-time staff; $48,518 operating expenditure 1994–95. ***Director:*** Mr. Jorge Ramirez, Director for Student Development, 206-964-6590. ***Services:*** job fairs, resume preparation, career counseling, careers library, job bank, job interviews.

EXPENSES FOR 1996–97 State resident tuition: $1401 full-time, $46.70 per quarter hour part-time. Nonresident tuition: $5511 full-time, $183.70 per quarter hour part-time. Part-time mandatory fees per quarter range from $1 to $10. Full-time mandatory fees: $30.

FINANCIAL AID ***College-administered undergrad aid 1995–96:*** 882 need-based scholarships (average $1398), 298 non-need scholarships (average $485), short-term loans (average $432), low-interest long-term loans from external sources (average $3020), Federal Work-Study. ***Required forms:*** institutional, FAFSA. ***Priority deadline:*** 4/15.

APPLYING Open admission except for international students, veterinary technology, dental hygiene programs. ***Options:*** early entrance, midyear entrance. ***Required:*** TOEFL for international students. ***Recommended:*** ACT ASSET. ***Required for some:*** ACT ASSET. Test scores used for counseling/placement. ***Application deadline:*** rolling.

APPLYING/TRANSFER ***Entrance:*** noncompetitive. ***Application deadline:*** rolling. ***Contact:*** Ms. Cindy Burbank, Coordinator of Admissions, 206-964-6686.

CONTACT Mr. William Ponder, Director of Admissions and Registration, Pierce College, Tacoma, WA 98498-1999, 206-964-6623.

PIMA MEDICAL INSTITUTE
Seattle, Washington

RENTON TECHNICAL COLLEGE
Renton, Washington

UG Enrollment: 810	**Tuition & Fees: $1575**
Application Deadline: rolling	**Room & Board: N/Avail**

GENERAL State-supported, 2-year, coed. Part of Washington State Board for Community and Technical Colleges. Awards certificates, diplomas, terminal associate degrees. Founded 1942. ***Setting:*** 30-acre urban campus with easy access to Seattle. ***Total enrollment:*** 810. ***Faculty:*** 471 (71 full-time, 25% with terminal degrees, 400 part-time).

ENROLLMENT PROFILE 810 students: 50% women, 93% part-time, 98% state residents, 1% transferred in, 1% international, 78% 25 or older, 1% Native American, 1% Hispanic, 8% African American, 13% Asian American.

FIRST-YEAR CLASS 1,801 applied, 100% were accepted, 44% of whom enrolled.

ACADEMIC PROGRAM Calendar: quarters. Academic remediation for entering students, English as a second language program offered during academic year and summer, services for LD students, advanced placement, tutorials, summer session for credit, adult/continuing education programs, co-op programs and internships.

GENERAL DEGREE REQUIREMENTS 100 quarter hours; 5 quarter hours of college math.

MAJORS Accounting, automotive technologies, business administration/commerce/management, civil engineering technology, communication equipment technology, computer science, culinary arts, electrical and electronics technologies, heating/refrigeration/air conditioning, legal secretarial studies, machine and tool technologies, medical assistant technologies, medical secretarial studies, medical technology, musical instrument technology, operating room technology, secretarial studies/office management, surveying technology, teacher aide studies.

LIBRARY Renton Technical College Library with 8,500 books, 73 microform titles, 143 periodicals, 5 on-line bibliographic services, 350 CD-ROMs, 10 records, tapes, and CDs. Acquisition spending 1994–95: $146,896.

COMPUTERS ON CAMPUS Computer purchase plan available. 96 computers for student use in computer labs, learning resource center, classrooms, library. Staffed computer lab on campus provides training in use of computers, software. Academic computing expenditure 1994–95: $32,008.

COLLEGE LIFE ***Social organizations:*** 1 open to all. ***Most popular organization:*** Student Council. ***Major annual event:*** Graduation. ***Campus security:*** security patrols, security system.

HOUSING College housing not available.

CAREER PLANNING ***Placement office:*** $21,600 operating expenditure 1994–95. ***Director:*** Mr. Jon Pozega, Vice President for Student Services, 206-235-5840. ***Services:*** job fairs, resume preparation, resume referral, career counseling, careers library, job bank, job interviews.

AFTER GRADUATION 82% of class of 1994 had job offers within 6 months. 1% of students completing a degree program went directly on to further study.

EXPENSES FOR 1995–96 ***Application fee:*** $25. Tuition: $1575 full-time. Part-time tuition per quarter hour ranges from $50 to $155.

FINANCIAL AID ***College-administered undergrad aid 1995–96:*** need-based scholarships, short-term loans (average $100), Federal Work-Study, part-time jobs. ***Required forms:*** institutional; required for some: CSS Financial Aid PROFILE, FAFSA. ***Application deadline:*** continuous.

APPLYING Open admission. ***Options:*** early entrance, midyear entrance. ***Required:*** ACT ASSET, SLEP. ***Recommended:*** interview. Test scores used for counseling/placement. ***Application deadline:*** rolling. ***Notification:*** continuous.

APPLYING/TRANSFER ***Required:*** standardized test scores. ***Required for some:*** high school transcript, college transcript. ***Contact:*** Mr. Michael J. Crehan, Counselor, 206-235-5840.

CONTACT Mr. Jon Pozega, Vice President for Student Services, Renton Technical College, 3000 Fourth Street, NE, Renton, WA 98056, 206-235-5840. College video available.

SEATTLE CENTRAL COMMUNITY COLLEGE
Seattle, Washington

UG Enrollment: 10,333	**Tuition & Fees (WA Res): $1379**
Application Deadline: rolling	**Room & Board: N/Avail**

GENERAL State-supported, 2-year, coed. Part of Seattle Community College District System. Awards transfer associate, terminal associate degrees. Founded 1966. ***Setting:*** 15-acre urban campus. ***Total enrollment:*** 10,333. ***Faculty:*** 388 (139 full-time, 249 part-time); student-faculty ratio is 25:1.

ENROLLMENT PROFILE 10,333 students: 59% women, 51% part-time, 93% state residents, 8% transferred in, 1% international, 63% 25 or older, 1% Native American, 6% Hispanic, 13% African American, 20% Asian American.

FIRST-YEAR CLASS 2,541 total. Of the students who applied, 100% were accepted, 50% of whom enrolled.

ACADEMIC PROGRAM Core, honor code. Calendar: quarters. Academic remediation for entering students, English as a second language program offered during academic year and summer, services for LD students, summer session for credit, part-time degree program (daytime, evenings, summer), external degree programs, adult/continuing education programs, co-op programs and internships. ROTC: Army (c), Naval (c), Air Force (c).

GENERAL DEGREE REQUIREMENTS 90 credits; 1 college algebra course.

MAJORS Accounting, biotechnology, carpentry, commercial art, cosmetology, culinary arts, deaf interpreter training, drafting and design, drug and alcohol/substance abuse counseling, early childhood education, fashion design and technology, film and video production, graphic arts, hospitality services, hotel and restaurant management, human services, liberal arts/general studies, marine technology, nursing, optometric/ophthalmic technologies, photography, printing technologies, respiratory therapy, science, secretarial studies/office management, word processing.

LIBRARY Main Library with 56,338 books, 82 microform titles, 425 periodicals, 13 CD-ROMs, 4,360 records, tapes, and CDs.

COMPUTERS ON CAMPUS 366 computers for student use in computer center, computer labs, computerized career library, classrooms, library provide access to e-mail. Staffed computer lab on campus provides training in use of computers, software.

COLLEGE LIFE Orientation program (3 days, no cost, parents included). Drama-theater group, choral group, student-run newspaper. 5% vote in student government elections. ***Social organizations:*** 30 open to all. ***Most popular organizations:*** The Triangle Club, African Brothers of Unity, MECHA, Asian/Pacific Islander Student Union, Sea-King Club for the Deaf. ***Major annual events:*** Student Studies Institute, Student Leadership. ***Student services:*** personal-psychological counseling, women's center. ***Campus security:*** 24-hour emergency response devices.

HOUSING College housing not available.

ATHLETICS ***Intramural:*** basketball, softball, tennis, volleyball, weight lifting, wrestling.

CAREER PLANNING ***Service:*** career counseling.

EXPENSES FOR 1996–97 State resident tuition: $1379 full-time, $45.95 per credit part-time. Nonresident tuition: $5489 full-time, $182.95 per credit part-time.

FINANCIAL AID ***College-administered undergrad aid 1995–96:*** 125 need-based scholarships (average $822), 120 non-need scholarships (average $822), short-term loans (average $248), low-interest long-term loans from external sources (average $1500), Federal Work-Study. ***Required forms:*** CSS Financial Aid PROFILE, institutional, FAFSA. ***Priority deadline:*** 6/1. ***Payment plan:*** deferred payment. ***Waivers:*** full or partial for employees or children of employees and senior citizens.

APPLYING Open admission except for nursing program. ***Required for some:*** TOEFL for international students. Test scores used for counseling/placement. ***Application deadline:*** rolling.

APPLYING/TRANSFER ***Entrance:*** noncompetitive. ***Application deadline:*** rolling. ***Contact:*** Ms. Michelle Roddell, Transfer Center Coordinator, 206-587-5469.

CONTACT Admissions Office, Seattle Central Community College, 1701 Broadway, Seattle, WA 98122-2400, 206-587-5450. College video available.

SHORELINE COMMUNITY COLLEGE
Seattle, Washington

UG Enrollment: 8,575	**Tuition & Fees (WA Res): $1337**
Application Deadline: rolling	**Room & Board: N/Avail**

GENERAL State-supported, 2-year, coed. Part of Washington State Board for Community and Technical Colleges. Awards certificates, transfer associate, terminal associate degrees. Founded 1964. ***Setting:*** 80-acre suburban campus. ***Total enrollment:*** 8,575. ***Faculty:*** 333 (150 full-time, 20% with terminal degrees, 183 part-time); student-faculty ratio is 24:1.

ENROLLMENT PROFILE 8,575 students: 60% women, 47% part-time, 96% state residents, 10% transferred in, 12% have need-based financial aid, 3% international, 45% 25 or older, 1% Native American, 1% Hispanic, 3% African American, 10% Asian American. ***Most popular recent majors:*** dental services, nursing, science.

FIRST-YEAR CLASS 2,200 total; 3,000 applied, 100% were accepted, 78% of whom enrolled.

ACADEMIC PROGRAM Core. Calendar: quarters. Academic remediation for entering students, English as a second language program offered during academic year and summer, services for LD students, advanced placement, tutorials, summer session for credit, part-time degree program (daytime, evenings, summer), adult/continuing education programs, co-op programs and internships. Study abroad in England, Ireland.

GENERAL DEGREE REQUIREMENTS 90 credits; math/science requirements vary according to program; internship (some majors).

MAJORS Accounting, audio engineering, automotive technologies, biotechnology, business administration/commerce/management, business machine technologies, chemical engineering technology, child care/child and family studies, civil engineering technology, commercial art, computer graphics, computer information systems, corrections, cosmetology, criminal justice, dental services, dietetics, drafting and design, drug and alcohol/substance abuse counseling, early childhood education, education, (pre)engineering sequence, engineering technology, environmental engineering technology, fashion design and technology, film and video production, graphic arts, human development, industrial arts, industrial engineering technology, information science, international business, laboratory technologies, law enforcement/police sciences, liberal arts/general studies, machine

and tool technologies, manufacturing technology, marine biology, marine technology, marketing/retailing/merchandising, mechanical engineering technology, medical laboratory technology, medical records services, medical secretarial studies, music, nursing, oceanography, photography, printing technologies, purchasing/inventory management, retail management, science, secretarial studies/office management, teacher aide studies.
LIBRARY Ray W. Howard Library/Media Center with 70,000 books, 700 periodicals, 7,000 records, tapes, and CDs. Acquisition spending 1994–95: $116,242.
COMPUTERS ON CAMPUS Computer purchase plan available. 338 computers for student use in computer center, computer labs, classrooms, library. Staffed computer lab on campus provides training in use of computers, software. Academic computing expenditure 1994–95: $270,918.
COLLEGE LIFE Drama-theater group, choral group, student-run newspaper. ***Social organizations:*** 43 open to all. ***Major annual events:*** Robert E. Colbert Lecture Series, The Soulful Sounds of Christmas. ***Student services:*** personal-psychological counseling, women's center. ***Campus security:*** 24-hour emergency response devices and patrols.
HOUSING College housing not available.
ATHLETICS ***Intercollegiate:*** baseball M(s), basketball M(s)/W(s), golf M(s), soccer M(s), softball W(s), tennis W(s), volleyball W(s). ***Intramural:*** archery, badminton, basketball, fencing, gymnastics, racquetball, skiing (cross-country), skiing (downhill), softball, swimming and diving, volleyball. ***Contact:*** Mr. Thomas Heilman, Athletic Director, 206-546-4553.
CAREER PLANNING ***Placement office:*** 2 full-time staff; $70,567 operating expenditure 1994–95. ***Director:*** Ms. Berta Lloyd, Manager, Cooperative Education/Career Employment Services, 206-546-4595. ***Services:*** job fairs, resume preparation, resume referral, career counseling, careers library, job bank, job interviews.
EXPENSES FOR 1995–96 ***Application fee:*** $10. State resident tuition: $1337 full-time, $44.55 per credit part-time. Nonresident tuition: $5285 full-time, $176.15 per credit part-time.
FINANCIAL AID ***College-administered undergrad aid 1995–96:*** need-based scholarships, short-term loans (average $150), low-interest long-term loans from external sources, Federal Work-Study, part-time jobs. ***Required forms:*** institutional, FAFSA; accepted: CSS Financial Aid PROFILE. ***Priority deadline:*** 9/1. ***Payment plan:*** installment. ***Waivers:*** full or partial for employees or children of employees and senior citizens.
APPLYING Open admission. ***Options:*** early entrance, midyear entrance. ***Required for some:*** TOEFL for international students, ACT ASSET. Test scores used for counseling/placement. ***Application deadline:*** rolling.
APPLYING/TRANSFER ***Entrance:*** noncompetitive. ***Application deadline:*** rolling.
CONTACT Mr. David Minger, Director of Admissions/Registrar, Shoreline Community College, Seattle, WA 98133-5696, 206-546-4581. ***Fax:*** 206-546-5826.

SKAGIT VALLEY COLLEGE
Mount Vernon, Washington

UG Enrollment: 7,200	**Tuition & Fees (WA Res): $1401**
Application Deadline: rolling	**Room & Board: N/Avail**

GENERAL State-supported, 2-year, coed. Part of Washington State Board for Community and Technical Colleges. Awards transfer associate, terminal associate degrees. Founded 1926. ***Setting:*** 85-acre small-town campus with easy access to Seattle and Vancouver. ***Total enrollment:*** 7,200. ***Faculty:*** 325 (110 full-time, 215 part-time).
ENROLLMENT PROFILE 7,200 students from 20 states and territories, 10 other countries. 60% women, 54% part-time, 94% state residents, 4% transferred in, 1% international, 68% 25 or older, 2% Native American, 3% Hispanic, 1% African American, 3% Asian American.
FIRST-YEAR CLASS 1,200 total. Of the students who applied, 100% were accepted, 84% of whom enrolled.
ACADEMIC PROGRAM Core. Calendar: quarters. Academic remediation for entering students, English as a second language program offered during academic year, services for LD students, advanced placement, honors program, summer session for credit, part-time degree program (daytime, evenings, summer), adult/continuing education programs, co-op programs and internships. Study abroad in England, Japan, South America.
GENERAL DEGREE REQUIREMENTS 90 credits; 1 intermediate college algebra course; 15 credits of science; computer course for most majors.
MAJORS Accounting, agricultural sciences, agricultural technologies, anthropology, art/fine arts, art history, automotive technologies, biology/biological sciences, business administration/commerce/management, chemistry, child care/child and family studies, civil engineering technology, computer science, computer technologies, construction technologies, culinary arts, earth science, economics, education, electrical and electronics technologies, (pre)engineering sequence, English, ethnic studies, family services, fashion merchandising, food services management, food services technology, geography, graphic arts, history, home economics, hotel and restaurant management, humanities, human services, industrial arts, law enforcement/police sciences, liberal arts/general studies, literature, marine technology, marketing/retailing/merchandising, mathematics, medical secretarial studies, music, natural sciences, nursing, paralegal studies, parks management, philosophy, physical education, political science/government, practical nursing, psychology, recreation and leisure services, retail management, robotics, science, social science, sociology, Spanish, speech/rhetoric/public address/debate.
LIBRARY 56,900 books, 86 microform titles, 528 periodicals, 2,673 records, tapes, and CDs.
COMPUTERS ON CAMPUS 90 computers for student use in computer center. Staffed computer lab on campus provides training in use of computers, software.
COLLEGE LIFE Drama-theater group, student-run newspaper, radio station. ***Student services:*** health clinic, personal-psychological counseling, women's center.
HOUSING College housing not available.
ATHLETICS ***Intercollegiate:*** basketball M(s)/W(s), cross-country running M(s)/W(s), soccer M(s), tennis M(s)/W(s), volleyball W(s). ***Intramural:*** basketball, football, sailing, soccer, tennis, volleyball.
CAREER PLANNING ***Service:*** career counseling.
EXPENSES FOR 1996–97 State resident tuition: $1401 full-time, $46.70 per credit part-time. Nonresident tuition: $5511 full-time, $183.70 per credit part-time.
FINANCIAL AID ***College-administered undergrad aid 1995–96:*** need-based scholarships, 60 non-need scholarships (average $450), short-term loans (average $150), low-interest long-term loans from external sources (average $1850), Federal Work-Study, part-time jobs. ***Required forms:*** CSS Financial Aid PROFILE, institutional, FAFSA. ***Priority deadline:*** 6/1.
APPLYING Open admission. ***Option:*** early entrance. ***Required:*** school transcript, ACT ASSET. ***Recommended:*** TOEFL for international students. Test scores used for counseling/placement. ***Application deadline:*** rolling.
APPLYING/TRANSFER ***Required:*** standardized test scores, college transcript. ***Application deadline:*** rolling.
CONTACT Ms. Robin Thompson, Director of Admissions, Skagit Valley College, Mount Vernon, WA 98273-5899, 360-428-1112.

SOUTH PUGET SOUND COMMUNITY COLLEGE
Olympia, Washington

UG Enrollment: 5,195	**Tuition & Fees (WA Res): $1400**
Application Deadline: rolling	**Room & Board: N/Avail**

GENERAL State-supported, 2-year, coed. Part of Washington State Board for Community and Technical Colleges. Awards certificates, diplomas, transfer associate, terminal associate degrees. Founded 1970. ***Setting:*** 86-acre suburban campus with easy access to Seattle. ***Total enrollment:*** 5,195. ***Faculty:*** 229 (83 full-time, 45% with terminal degrees, 146 part-time); student-faculty ratio is 24:1.
ENROLLMENT PROFILE 5,195 students: 60% women, 40% men, 53% part-time, 95% state residents, 3% transferred in, 100% have need-based financial aid, 1% international, 62% 25 or older, 2% Native American, 3% Hispanic, 2% African American, 10% Asian American. ***Areas of study chosen:*** 50% liberal arts/general studies, 50% vocational and home economics. ***Most popular recent majors:*** liberal arts/general studies, business administration/commerce/management, nursing.
FIRST-YEAR CLASS 1,870 total; 2,850 applied, 100% were accepted, 66% of whom enrolled.
ACADEMIC PROGRAM Core, interdisciplinary curriculum. Calendar: quarters. Academic remediation for entering students, English as a second language program offered during academic year, services for LD students, advanced placement, summer session for credit, part-time degree program (daytime, evenings, summer), adult/continuing education programs, co-op programs and internships.
GENERAL DEGREE REQUIREMENTS 90 credits; math/science requirements vary according to program; computer course for most majors; internship (some majors).
MAJORS Accounting, automotive technologies, business administration/commerce/management, communication equipment technology, computer information systems, computer programming, culinary arts, data processing, deaf interpreter training, dental services, drafting and design, early childhood education, electrical and electronics technologies, fire science, food services management, food services technology, horticulture, information science, landscaping/grounds maintenance, legal secretarial studies, liberal arts/general studies, medical assistant technologies, medical secretarial studies, nursing, paralegal studies, practical nursing, secretarial studies/office management, telecommunications, welding technology.
LIBRARY Media Center with 29,500 books, 220 microform titles, 350 periodicals, 1 on-line bibliographic service, 1 CD-ROM, 3,400 records, tapes, and CDs.
COMPUTERS ON CAMPUS 250 computers for student use in computer center, computer labs, learning resource center, classrooms, library provide access to off-campus computing facilities, on-line services, Internet. Staffed computer lab on campus provides training in use of computers, software.
COLLEGE LIFE Student-run newspaper. 10% vote in student government elections. ***Social organizations:*** 10 open to all. ***Student services:*** personal-psychological counseling. ***Campus security:*** 24-hour emergency response devices and patrols, late-night transport-escort service.
HOUSING College housing not available.
ATHLETICS ***Intercollegiate:*** basketball M(s)/W(s), soccer M(s), softball W(s). ***Intramural:*** basketball, softball. ***Contact:*** Mr. Chris Yates, Director of Student Activities, 360-754-7711.
CAREER PLANNING ***Placement office:*** 1 full-time staff. ***Director:*** Mr. Mark Kenney, Counseling, 360-754-7711 Ext. 261. ***Services:*** job fairs, resume preparation, career counseling, careers library, job bank, job interviews. 485 organizations recruited on campus 1994–95.
AFTER GRADUATION 32% of students completing a degree program in 1994–95 went directly on to further study.
EXPENSES FOR 1996–97 State resident tuition: $1400 full-time, $46.65 per credit part-time. Nonresident tuition: $5510 full-time, $183.65 per credit part-time.
FINANCIAL AID ***College-administered undergrad aid 1995–96:*** 50 need-based scholarships (average $1500), 23 non-need scholarships (average $1000), low-interest long-term loans from external sources (average $926), 30 Federal Work-Study (averaging $2700), 75 part-time jobs. ***Required forms:*** institutional, FAFSA. ***Priority deadline:*** 6/30. ***Waivers:*** full or partial for employees or children of employees. ***Notification:*** 8/15.
APPLYING Open admission except for nursing, fire protection, dental assisting programs. ***Options:*** early entrance, early action, deferred entrance. ***Required:*** TOEFL for international students. ***Recommended:*** SAT I or ACT, ACT ASSET. ***Required for some:*** 3 years of high school math and science. Test scores used for counseling/placement. ***Application deadlines:*** rolling, 5/15 for early action. ***Notification:*** continuous, 6/1 for early action.
APPLYING/TRANSFER ***Required for some:*** 3 years of high school science. ***Application deadline:*** rolling. ***Notification:*** continuous. ***Contact:*** Mr. Joe Townley, Counselor, 360-754-7711 Ext. 261.
CONTACT Mr. Tom Woodnutt, Director of Admissions and Records, South Puget Sound Community College, Olympia, WA 98512-6292, 360-754-7711 Ext. 241. ***E-mail:*** twoodnut@ctc.ctc.edu.

SOUTH SEATTLE COMMUNITY COLLEGE
Seattle, Washington

UG Enrollment: 3,892	**Tuition & Fees (WA Res): $1361**
Application Deadline: rolling	**Room & Board: N/Avail**

Peterson's Guide to Two-Year Colleges 1997

659

South Seattle Community College (continued)
GENERAL State-supported, 2-year, coed. Part of Seattle Community College District System. Awards transfer associate, terminal associate degrees. Founded 1970. ***Setting:*** 65-acre urban campus. ***Total enrollment:*** 3,892. ***Faculty:*** 266 (75 full-time, 191 part-time).
ENROLLMENT PROFILE 3,892 students from 4 states and territories, 24 other countries. 47% women, 53% men, 54% part-time, 91% state residents, 4% transferred in, 4% international, 68% 25 or older, 1% Native American, 3% Hispanic, 10% African American, 24% Asian American. ***Areas of study chosen:*** 10% vocational and home economics, 3% agriculture.
FIRST-YEAR CLASS 1,318 total. Of the students who applied, 100% were accepted.
ACADEMIC PROGRAM Calendar: quarters. Academic remediation for entering students, English as a second language program offered during academic year and summer, services for LD students, advanced placement, summer session for credit, part-time degree program (daytime, evenings, weekends, summer), adult/continuing education programs. Off-campus study at 9 community colleges in the Seattle metropolitan area.
GENERAL DEGREE REQUIREMENTS 90 credits; math/science requirements vary according to degree program; computer course.
MAJORS Accounting, aircraft and missile maintenance, automotive technologies, aviation technology, business administration/commerce/management, computer programming, computer technologies, cosmetology, culinary arts, drafting and design, engineering (general), engineering technology, food sciences, food services management, food services technology, horticulture, hospitality services, industrial and heavy equipment maintenance, landscape architecture/design, landscaping/grounds maintenance, liberal arts/general studies, quality control technology, robotics, science, secretarial studies/office management, vocational education, welding technology.
LIBRARY 29,711 books, 73 microform titles, 650 periodicals, 15 CD-ROMs, 8,674 records, tapes, and CDs.
COMPUTERS ON CAMPUS 256 computers for student use in computer center, library provide access to on-line services. Staffed computer lab on campus provides training in use of computers, software.
COLLEGE LIFE Drama-theater group, choral group, student-run newspaper. ***Most popular organizations:*** Veteran Students Club, Vietnamese Club. ***Major annual events:*** Rainbow Festival, Holiday Dinner. ***Student services:*** personal-psychological counseling, women's center. ***Campus security:*** 24-hour emergency response devices and patrols.
HOUSING College housing not available.
CAREER PLANNING ***Placement office:*** 1 full-time, 5 part-time staff. ***Director:*** Ms. Betsy Hale, Director, Career Information and Employment Center, 206-764-5304. ***Services:*** resume preparation, career counseling, careers library, job bank, job interviews.
EXPENSES FOR 1995–96 State resident tuition: $1331 full-time, $44.35 per credit part-time. Nonresident tuition: $5279 full-time, $175.95 per credit part-time. Full-time mandatory fees: $30.
FINANCIAL AID ***College-administered undergrad aid 1995–96:*** 900 need-based scholarships (averaging $1089), 140 non-need scholarships (averaging $681), short-term loans (averaging $450), low-interest long-term loans from college funds, loans from external sources, Federal Work-Study, 75 part-time jobs. ***Required forms:*** institutional, FAFSA; accepted: CSS Financial Aid PROFILE. ***Priority deadline:*** 5/13. ***Payment plan:*** deferred payment. ***Waivers:*** full or partial for employees or children of employees and senior citizens. ***Notification:*** continuous.
APPLYING Open admission except for international students. ***Option:*** early entrance. ***Required:*** TOEFL for international students. ***Required for some:*** ACT ASSET. Test scores used for counseling/placement. ***Application deadline:*** rolling.
APPLYING/TRANSFER ***Entrance:*** noncompetitive. ***Application deadline:*** rolling.
CONTACT Ms. Kim Manderbach, Director of Admissions and Registration, South Seattle Community College, 6000 16th Avenue, SW, Seattle, WA 98106-1499, 206-764-5378.

SPOKANE COMMUNITY COLLEGE
Spokane, Washington

UG Enrollment: 5,000	**Tuition & Fees (WA Res): $1410**
Application Deadline: rolling	**Room & Board: N/Avail**

GENERAL State-supported, 2-year, coed. Part of Washington State Board for Community and Technical Colleges. Awards certificates, transfer associate, terminal associate degrees. Founded 1963. ***Setting:*** 108-acre urban campus. ***Endowment:*** $33,407. ***Total enrollment:*** 5,000. ***Faculty:*** 342 (184 full-time, 158 part-time); student-faculty ratio is 19:1.
ENROLLMENT PROFILE 5,000 students from 5 states and territories, 16 other countries. 54% women, 46% men, 14% part-time, 96% state residents, 38% transferred in, 40% have need-based financial aid, 8% have non-need-based financial aid, 1% international, 56% 25 or older, 4% Native American, 2% Hispanic, 2% African American, 3% Asian American. ***Areas of study chosen:*** 42% liberal arts/general studies, 22% vocational and home economics, 13% business management and administrative services, 10% health professions and related sciences, 7% engineering and applied sciences, 2% agriculture, 2% computer and information sciences, 2% natural resource sciences. ***Most popular recent majors:*** liberal arts/general studies, nursing, practical nursing.
FIRST-YEAR CLASS 1,000 total. Of the students who applied, 100% were accepted.
ACADEMIC PROGRAM Core, liberal arts/vocational curriculum. Calendar: quarters. 1,400 courses offered in 1995–96. Academic remediation for entering students, English as a second language program, services for LD students, self-designed majors, summer session for credit, part-time degree program (daytime, evenings, summer), adult/continuing education programs, co-op programs and internships. ROTC: Army.
GENERAL DEGREE REQUIREMENTS 90 credits; computer course (varies by major); internship (some majors).
MAJORS Accounting, agricultural business, agricultural technologies, agronomy/soil and crop sciences, architectural technologies, automotive technologies, aviation technology, biomedical technologies, business administration/commerce/management, carpentry, civil engineering technology, computer programming, construction technologies, corrections, cosmetology, culinary arts, data processing, dental services, dietetics, drafting and design, electrical and electronics technologies, electrical engineering technology, electronics engineering technology, fire science, food services technology, forestry, heating/refrigeration/air conditioning, horticulture, hotel and restaurant management, industrial and heavy equipment maintenance, landscaping/grounds maintenance, law enforcement/police sciences, legal secretarial studies, liberal arts/general studies, machine and tool technologies, manufacturing technology, marketing/retailing/merchandising, mechanical design technology, mechanical engineering technology, medical records services, medical secretarial studies, natural resource management, nursing, operating room technology, optometric/ophthalmic technologies, ornamental horticulture, paralegal studies, parks management, practical nursing, respiratory therapy, robotics, secretarial studies/office management, water resources, welding technology, wildlife management, word processing.
LIBRARY Learning Resources Center with 38,967 books, 466 periodicals, 1 on-line bibliographic service, 12 CD-ROMs. Acquisition spending 1994–95: $94,157.
COMPUTERS ON CAMPUS Computer purchase plan available. 400 computers for student use in computer labs, research center, learning resource center, classrooms, library provide access to Internet. Staffed computer lab on campus provides training in use of computers, software. Academic computing expenditure 1994–95: $130,226.
COLLEGE LIFE Drama-theater group, student-run newspaper. 5% vote in student government elections. ***Social organizations:*** 25 open to all. ***Most popular organizations:*** VICA, Delta Epsilon Chi, Intercultural Student Organization, Rho Beta Psi, Student Awareness League. ***Major annual events:*** Spring Fling, Celebration of Cultures, Job Fair. ***Campus security:*** 24-hour emergency response devices and patrols, student patrols, late-night transport-escort service.
HOUSING College housing not available.
ATHLETICS ***Intercollegiate:*** baseball M(s), basketball M(s)/W(s), cross-country running M(s)/W(s), golf M(s)/W(s), soccer M(s)/W(s), softball W(s), tennis M(s)/W(s), track and field M(s)/W(s), volleyball W(s). ***Intramural:*** badminton, basketball, bowling, softball, table tennis (Ping-Pong), tennis, volleyball, water polo. ***Contact:*** Mr. Maurice L. Ray, Director of Athletics, Physical Education and Recreation, 509-533-7220.
CAREER PLANNING ***Placement office:*** 1 full-time, 1 part-time staff; $37,392 operating expenditure 1994–95. ***Director:*** Ms. Alicia Gaskeivicz, Program Coordinator, 509-533-8009. ***Services:*** job fairs, resume preparation, resume referral, career counseling, careers library, job bank, job interviews.
EXPENSES FOR 1996–97 ***Application fee:*** $10. State resident tuition: $1410 full-time, $47 per credit part-time. Nonresident tuition: $5511 full-time, $183.70 per credit part-time.
FINANCIAL AID ***College-administered undergrad aid 1995–96:*** 2,014 need-based scholarships (average $1847), 388 non-need scholarships (average $567), short-term loans (average $380), low-interest long-term loans from external sources (average $3420), 230 Federal Work-Study (averaging $2460), 306 part-time jobs. ***Required forms:*** institutional, FAFSA. ***Priority deadline:*** 2/28. ***Payment plan:*** deferred payment. ***Waivers:*** full or partial for employees or children of employees and senior citizens. ***Notification:*** 8/5.
APPLYING Open admission. ***Options:*** early entrance, deferred entrance, midyear entrance. ***Required:*** SAT I or ACT, TOEFL for international students, ACT ASSET. ***Recommended:*** school transcript. Test scores used for counseling/placement. ***Application deadline:*** rolling.
APPLYING/TRANSFER ***Required:*** standardized test scores. ***Recommended:*** college transcript. ***Application deadline:*** rolling. ***Contact:*** Ms. Pat Erickson, Associate Dean for Student Services, 509-533-8024.
CONTACT Mr. Dan Chacon, Vice President of Student Services, Spokane Community College, North 1810 Greene Street, Spokane, WA 99207-5399, 509-533-7015.

SPOKANE FALLS COMMUNITY COLLEGE
Spokane, Washington

UG Enrollment: 5,300	**Tuition & Fees (WA Res): $1401**
Application Deadline: rolling	**Room & Board: N/Avail**

GENERAL State-supported, 2-year, coed. Part of State Board for Washington Community and Technical Colleges. Awards transfer associate, terminal associate degrees. Founded 1967. ***Setting:*** 125-acre urban campus. ***Endowment:*** $33,407. ***Total enrollment:*** 5,300. ***Faculty:*** 565 (163 full-time, 100% with terminal degrees, 402 part-time).
ENROLLMENT PROFILE 5,300 students from 6 states and territories, 14 other countries. 58% women, 42% men, 22% part-time, 96% state residents, 36% transferred in, 23% have need-based financial aid, 6% have non-need-based financial aid, 1% international, 55% 25 or older, 3% Native American, 3% Hispanic, 2% African American, 6% Asian American. ***Areas of study chosen:*** 71% liberal arts/general studies, 16% vocational and home economics, 6% business management and administrative services, 5% performing arts, 1% computer and information sciences, 1% library and information studies. ***Most popular recent majors:*** liberal arts/general studies, early childhood education.
FIRST-YEAR CLASS 1,100 total. Of the students who applied, 100% were accepted.
ACADEMIC PROGRAM Core. Calendar: quarters. 900 courses offered in 1995–96; average class size 25 in required courses. Academic remediation for entering students, English as a second language program offered during academic year and summer, services for LD students, advanced placement, self-designed majors, summer session for credit, part-time degree program (daytime, evenings), adult/continuing education programs, co-op programs and internships. ROTC: Army (c).
GENERAL DEGREE REQUIREMENTS 90 credit hours; computer course for accounting, business, office administration majors; internship (some majors).
MAJORS Accounting, art/fine arts, business administration/commerce/management, child care/child and family studies, communication, computer information systems, deaf interpreter training, drug and alcohol/substance abuse counseling, early childhood education, (pre)engineering sequence, fashion merchandising, gerontology, graphic arts, interior design, international business, liberal arts/general studies, library science, medical assistant technologies, music, physical fitness/exercise science, physical therapy, real estate, retail management, secretarial studies/office management, social work, teacher aide studies, welding technology, word processing.
LIBRARY Learning Resources Center with 56,286 books, 64 microform titles, 673 periodicals, 1 on-line bibliographic service, 47 CD-ROMs, 2,696 records, tapes, and CDs. Acquisition spending 1994–95: $225,585.
COMPUTERS ON CAMPUS Computer purchase plan available. 250 computers for student use in computer labs, learning resource center, classrooms, library provide access to e-mail, Internet. Staffed computer lab on campus provides training in use of computers, software. Academic computing expenditure 1994–95: $379,818.
COLLEGE LIFE Drama-theater group, choral group, student-run newspaper, radio station. 5% vote in student government elections. ***Social organizations:*** 30 open to all. ***Most popular organizations:*** DECA, Associated Men Students, Associated Women Students, Chorale, Forensics Club. ***Major annual events:*** Spring Fling, Winter Festival,

Club Orientation Week. ***Student services:*** personal-psychological counseling, women's center. ***Campus security:*** late-night transport-escort service, 24-hour emergency dispatch.
HOUSING College housing not available.
ATHLETICS ***Intercollegiate:*** baseball M(s), basketball M(s)/W(s), cross-country running M(s)/W(s), golf M(s)/W(s), soccer M(s)/W(s), softball W(s), tennis M(s)/W(s), track and field M(s)/W(s), volleyball W(s). ***Intramural:*** badminton, basketball, bowling, soccer, softball, table tennis (Ping-Pong), tennis, volleyball. ***Contact:*** Mr. Maurice L. Ray, Director of Athletics, Physical Education, and Recreation, 509-533-7220.
CAREER PLANNING ***Placement office:*** 1 full-time, 3 part-time staff; $42,684 operating expenditure 1994–95. ***Director:*** Ms. Ann Howard, Coordinator of Career/Advising Center, 509-533-3574 Ext. 3. ***Services:*** job fairs, resume preparation, resume referral, career counseling, careers library, job bank, job interviews.
EXPENSES FOR 1996–97 ***Application fee:*** $10. State resident tuition: $1401 full-time. Nonresident tuition: $5511 full-time. State resident part-time tuition: $93.40 for the first 2 credits, $46.70 per credit for the next 8 credits. Nonresident part-time tuition: $367.40 for the first 2 credit, $183.70 per credit for the next 8 credits.
FINANCIAL AID ***College-administered undergrad aid 1995–96:*** 1,210 need-based scholarships (averaging $1745), 320 non-need scholarships (averaging $450), short-term loans (averaging $400), low-interest long-term loans from external sources (averaging $2432), 135 Federal Work-Study (averaging $2600), 328 part-time jobs. ***Required forms:*** institutional, FAFSA. ***Priority deadline:*** 5/30. ***Waivers:*** full or partial for employees or children of employees and senior citizens. ***Notification:*** 8/5.
APPLYING Open admission. ***Options:*** early entrance, deferred entrance, midyear entrance. ***Required:*** SAT I or ACT, TOEFL for international students, ACT ASSET. ***Recommended:*** school transcript. Test scores used for counseling/placement. ***Application deadlines:*** rolling, rolling for nonresidents. ***Notification:*** continuous, continuous for nonresidents.
APPLYING/TRANSFER ***Recommended:*** college transcript. ***Entrance:*** noncompetitive. ***Application deadline:*** rolling. ***Notification:*** continuous. ***Contact:*** Mr. Mike Haberman, Counselor, 509-533-3539.
CONTACT Mr. Larry Owens, Vice President of Student Services, Spokane Falls Community College, 3410 West Fort George Wright Drive, Spokane, WA 99204-5288, 509-533-3520.

TACOMA COMMUNITY COLLEGE
Tacoma, Washington

UG Enrollment: 5,461	Tuition & Fees (WA Res): $1402
Application Deadline: rolling	Room & Board: N/Avail

GENERAL State-supported, 2-year, coed. Part of Washington State Board for Community and Technical Colleges. Awards certificates, diplomas, transfer associate, terminal associate degrees. Founded 1965. ***Setting:*** 150-acre urban campus with easy access to Seattle. ***Total enrollment:*** 5,461. ***Faculty:*** 371 (96 full-time, 275 part-time); student-faculty ratio is 16:1.
ENROLLMENT PROFILE 5,461 students: 64% women, 36% men, 34% part-time, 93% state residents, 10% transferred in, 40% have need-based financial aid, 6% international, 53% 25 or older, 2% Native American, 3% Hispanic, 11% African American, 9% Asian American.
FIRST-YEAR CLASS 2,124 total; 3,925 applied, 100% were accepted, 54% of whom enrolled.
ACADEMIC PROGRAM Core, academic, vocational, and international curriculum, honor code. Calendar: quarters. 633 courses offered in 1995–96. Academic remediation for entering students, English as a second language program offered during academic year and summer, services for LD students, advanced placement, self-designed majors, tutorials, summer session for credit, part-time degree program (daytime, evenings, summer), adult/continuing education programs. Off-campus study at members of the Concurrent Enrollment Program. ROTC: Army (c).
GENERAL DEGREE REQUIREMENTS 90 credits; math/science requirements vary according to program; computer course for all vocational majors.
MAJORS Accounting, anthropology, art/fine arts, behavioral sciences, biology/biological sciences, botany/plant sciences, business administration/commerce/management, business economics, chemistry, computer information systems, computer science, computer technologies, criminal justice, data processing, drug and alcohol/substance abuse counseling, earth science, economics, education, emergency medical technology, engineering (general), (pre)engineering sequence, English, forestry, geology, history, humanities, human services, international business, Japanese, journalism, law enforcement/police sciences, liberal arts/general studies, mathematics, medical records services, medical secretarial studies, music, nursing, occupational therapy, oceanography, paper and pulp sciences, pharmacy/pharmaceutical sciences, philosophy, physical sciences, physical therapy, physics, political science/government, psychology, radiological technology, respiratory therapy, Romance languages, Russian, science, secretarial studies/office management, social science, sociology, Spanish, speech/rhetoric/public address/debate, veterinary sciences, wildlife biology, wildlife management, word processing, zoology.
LIBRARY Pearl Wanamaker Library with 85,961 books, 119 microform titles, 744 periodicals, 2 on-line bibliographic services, 13 CD-ROMs, 3,314 records, tapes, and CDs. Acquisition spending 1994–95: $113,085.
COMPUTERS ON CAMPUS 250 computers for student use in computer center, computer labs, learning resource center, extension centers, library provide access to main academic computer, off-campus computing facilities, e-mail, Internet. Staffed computer lab on campus. Academic computing expenditure 1994–95: $320,924.
COLLEGE LIFE Drama-theater group, student-run newspaper. ***Social organizations:*** 25 open to all. ***Major annual event:*** College Transfer Day. ***Student services:*** personal-psychological counseling, women's center. ***Campus security:*** Sonitrol electronic system.
HOUSING College housing not available.
ATHLETICS ***Intercollegiate:*** baseball M(s), basketball M(s)/W(s), golf M(s)/W(s), soccer M(s)/W(s), volleyball W(s). ***Intramural:*** basketball, bowling, fencing, football, golf, skiing (downhill), soccer, softball, tennis, volleyball. ***Contact:*** Mr. Mike Batt, Athletic Director, 206-566-5097.
CAREER PLANNING ***Placement office:*** 1 full-time, 1 part-time staff; $49,687 operating expenditure 1994–95. ***Director:*** Ms. Kathy Brown, Career Center Coordinator, 206-566-5027. ***Services:*** resume preparation, career counseling, careers library.
EXPENSES FOR 1996–97 State resident tuition: $1402 full-time, $46.48 per credit part-time. Nonresident tuition: $5512 full-time, $183.48 per credit part-time.
FINANCIAL AID ***College-administered undergrad aid 1995–96:*** 2,214 need-based scholarships (averaging $4002), 331 non-need scholarships (averaging $429), short-term loans (averaging $514), 73 Federal Work-Study (averaging $2709), 133 part-time jobs. ***Required forms:*** CSS Financial Aid PROFILE, institutional, FAFSA. ***Priority deadline:*** 4/4. ***Payment plan:*** deferred payment. ***Waivers:*** full or partial for employees or children of employees and senior citizens. ***Notification:*** continuous.
APPLYING Open admission except for some vocational programs. ***Option:*** early entrance. ***Recommended:*** TOEFL for international students, Accuplacer. ***Required for some:*** TOEFL for international students, Accuplacer. Test scores used for counseling/placement. ***Application deadline:*** rolling.
APPLYING/TRANSFER ***Entrance:*** noncompetitive. ***Application deadline:*** rolling. ***Contact:*** Ms. Judy Grantham, College Transfer Advisor, 206-566-5107.
CONTACT Ms. Annette Hayward, Admissions Officer, Tacoma Community College, 5900 South 12th Street, Tacoma, WA 98465-1997, 206-566-5108. ***Fax:*** 206-566-6011. ***E-mail:*** ahayward@msmail.tacoma.ctc.edu.

WALLA WALLA COMMUNITY COLLEGE
Walla Walla, Washington

UG Enrollment: 4,772	Tuition & Fees (WA Res): $1431
Application Deadline: rolling	Room & Board: N/Avail

GENERAL State-supported, 2-year, coed. Part of Washington State Board for Community and Technical Colleges. Awards transfer associate, terminal associate degrees. Founded 1967. ***Setting:*** 125-acre small-town campus. ***Endowment:*** $570,225. ***Total enrollment:*** 4,772. ***Faculty:*** 268 (103 full-time, 5% with terminal degrees, 165 part-time); student-faculty ratio is 20:1.
ENROLLMENT PROFILE 4,772 students: 49% women, 51% men, 50% part-time, 90% state residents, 21% transferred in, 1% international, 48% 25 or older, 2% Native American, 15% Hispanic, 6% African American, 2% Asian American. ***Areas of study chosen:*** 59% liberal arts/general studies, 15% business management and administrative services, 10% health professions and related sciences, 6% agriculture, 6% computer and information sciences, 2% engineering and applied sciences, 2% vocational and home economics. ***Most popular recent majors:*** liberal arts/general studies, business administration/commerce/management, nursing.
FIRST-YEAR CLASS 864 total; 1,320 applied, 100% were accepted, 65% of whom enrolled.
ACADEMIC PROGRAM Core, honor code. Calendar: quarters. 750 courses offered in 1995–96. Academic remediation for entering students, English as a second language program offered during academic year and summer, services for LD students, advanced placement, honors program, summer session for credit, part-time degree program (daytime, evenings), adult/continuing education programs, co-op programs and internships. Off-campus study at other members of the Washington State Board for Community and Technical Colleges.
GENERAL DEGREE REQUIREMENTS 93 credits; math/science requirements vary according to program; computer course for business, agriculture, accounting, office technology, engineering, nursing, respiratory therapy, corrections majors; internship (some majors).
MAJORS Accounting, agricultural business, agricultural sciences, agricultural technologies, automotive technologies, business administration/commerce/management, carpentry, child care/child and family studies, civil engineering technology, computer programming, computer science, computer technologies, corrections, cosmetology, criminal justice, data processing, early childhood education, heating/refrigeration/air conditioning, industrial and heavy equipment maintenance, landscaping/grounds maintenance, legal secretarial studies, liberal arts/general studies, machine and tool technologies, marketing/retailing/merchandising, medical secretarial studies, nursing, practical nursing, recreation and leisure services, respiratory therapy, retail management, secretarial studies/office management, welding technology.
LIBRARY 42,031 books, 138 microform titles, 365 periodicals, 3 on-line bibliographic services, 3,376 records, tapes, and CDs. Acquisition spending 1994–95: $41,000.
COMPUTERS ON CAMPUS 180 computers for student use in computer center, computer labs, writing lab, library provide access to main academic computer, e-mail, Internet. Staffed computer lab on campus provides training in use of computers, software.
COLLEGE LIFE Drama-theater group, choral group, student-run newspaper. 10% vote in student government elections. ***Social organizations:*** 26 open to all. ***Most popular organizations:*** Drama Club, Honors Club, Intramurals Club. ***Major annual events:*** Spring Week, Celebration of Cultures, Family Weekend. ***Student services:*** personal-psychological counseling. ***Campus security:*** late-night transport-escort service.
HOUSING College housing not available.
ATHLETICS Member NJCAA. ***Intercollegiate:*** baseball M(s), basketball M(s)/W(s), equestrian sports M(s)/W(s), football M(s), golf M(s)/W(s), softball W(s), tennis M(s)/W(s), volleyball W(s). ***Intramural:*** basketball, football, racquetball, soccer, softball, table tennis (Ping-Pong), tennis, volleyball, weight lifting. ***Contact:*** Mr. Mike Levens, Athletic Director, 509-527-4312.
CAREER PLANNING ***Placement office:*** 1 full-time, 5 part-time staff. ***Director:*** Mr. Dick Cook, Director of Student Development, 509-527-4262. ***Services:*** job fairs, career counseling, careers library.
AFTER GRADUATION 53% of students completing a degree program in 1994–95 went directly on to further study.
EXPENSES FOR 1996–97 ***Application fee:*** $40. State resident tuition: $1431 full-time, $47.70 per credit part-time. Nonresident tuition: $5541 full-time, $184.70 per credit part-time. Oregon and Idaho residents pay state resident part-time tuition plus a surcharge for 1 to 6 credits.
FINANCIAL AID ***College-administered undergrad aid 1995–96:*** 20 need-based scholarships (averaging $350), 35 non-need scholarships (averaging $867), short-term loans (averaging $300), 100 Federal Work-Study (averaging $1500), 100 part-time jobs. ***Required forms:*** institutional, FAFSA, financial aid transcript (for transfers); accepted: CSS Financial Aid PROFILE. ***Priority deadline:*** 2/15. ***Waivers:*** full or partial for employees or children of employees and senior citizens.
APPLYING Open admission. ***Options:*** Common Application, early entrance, deferred entrance, midyear entrance. ***Required:*** TOEFL for international students, ACT ASSET. ***Recommended:*** school transcript. Test scores used for counseling/placement. ***Application deadline:*** rolling.
APPLYING/TRANSFER ***Recommended:*** high school transcript, college transcript. ***Required for some:*** standardized test scores. ***Entrance:*** noncompetitive. ***Application deadline:*** rolling. ***Contact:*** Ms. Kathy Lindgren, Transfer Advisor, 509-527-4543.

Walla Walla Community College (continued)
CONTACT Mr. Joseph Frostad, Director of Admissions and Records, Walla Walla Community College, Walla Walla, WA 99362-9267, 509-527-4283. ***Fax:*** 509-527-4480. ***E-mail:*** registrarwalla/walladl@ctc.ctc.edu.

WENATCHEE VALLEY COLLEGE
Wenatchee, Washington

UG Enrollment: 3,764	**Tuition & Fees (WA Res): $1407**
Application Deadline: rolling	**Room & Board: $3315**

GENERAL State and locally supported, 2-year, coed. Part of Washington State Board for Community and Technical Colleges. Awards certificates, diplomas, transfer associate, terminal associate degrees. Founded 1939. ***Setting:*** 56-acre rural campus. ***Endowment:*** $358,000. ***Total enrollment:*** 3,764. ***Faculty:*** 203 (67 full-time, 136 part-time).
ENROLLMENT PROFILE 3,764 students: 57% women, 43% men, 39% part-time, 96% state residents, 3% transferred in, 50% have need-based financial aid, 14% have non-need-based financial aid, 1% international, 58% 25 or older, 5% Native American, 5% Hispanic, 1% African American, 1% Asian American. ***Most popular recent majors:*** liberal arts/general studies, nursing, business administration/commerce/management.
FIRST-YEAR CLASS 567 total; 976 applied, 100% were accepted, 58% of whom enrolled.
ACADEMIC PROGRAM Core. Calendar: quarters. Academic remediation for entering students, English as a second language program offered during academic year, services for LD students, advanced placement, honors program, summer session for credit, part-time degree program (daytime, evenings, summer), external degree programs, adult/continuing education programs, co-op programs.
GENERAL DEGREE REQUIREMENTS 93 credits; math/science requirements vary according to program; computer course for health science majors; internship (some majors).
MAJORS Accounting, agricultural technologies, applied art, automotive technologies, biology/biological sciences, business administration/commerce/management, carpentry, chemistry, commercial art, drug and alcohol/substance abuse counseling, early childhood education, economics, education, (pre)engineering sequence, fire science, heating/refrigeration/air conditioning, history, legal secretarial studies, liberal arts/general studies, mathematics, medical assistant technologies, medical laboratory technology, medical secretarial studies, music, music education, nursing, physical education, practical nursing, radiological technology, recreation and leisure services, secretarial studies/office management, sociology, sports medicine, vocational education.
LIBRARY John Brown Library plus 1 other, with 32,000 books, 1,272 microform titles, 282 periodicals, 2,600 records, tapes, and CDs. Acquisition spending 1994–95: $21,597.
COMPUTERS ON CAMPUS 54 computers for student use in computer center, computer labs, labs, classrooms, library provide access to main academic computer. Staffed computer lab on campus provides training in use of computers, software. Academic computing expenditure 1994–95: $100,000.
COLLEGE LIFE Drama-theater group, choral group, student-run newspaper. ***Social organizations:*** 16 open to all. ***Major annual event:*** Cinco de Mayo.
HOUSING 74 college housing spaces available. Off-campus living permitted. ***Option:*** coed (1 building) housing available. Resident assistants live in dorms.
ATHLETICS Member NJCAA. ***Intercollegiate:*** baseball M, basketball M(s)/W(s), softball W(s). ***Intramural:*** badminton, basketball, football, racquetball, skiing (cross-country), skiing (downhill), tennis, volleyball, weight lifting. ***Contact:*** Mr. Sandy Cooprider, Athletic Director, 509-664-2584.
CAREER PLANNING ***Director:*** Mr. John Murio, Counselor, 509-664-2533. ***Services:*** resume preparation, resume referral, career counseling, careers library, job interviews.
EXPENSES FOR 1996–97 State resident tuition: $1401 full-time. Nonresident tuition: $5511 full-time. Part-time tuition per quarter ranges from $93.40 to $420.30 for state residents, $367.40 to $1653 for nonresidents. Part-time mandatory fees: $2 per quarter. Full-time mandatory fees: $6. College room and board: $3315.
FINANCIAL AID ***College-administered undergrad aid 1995–96:*** need-based scholarships (averaging $300), non-need scholarships (averaging $500), low-interest long-term loans from external sources (averaging $2000), Federal Work-Study, 40 part-time jobs. ***Required forms:*** CSS Financial Aid PROFILE, institutional, FAFSA. ***Priority deadline:*** 4/1. ***Payment plan:*** installment. ***Waivers:*** full or partial for employees or children of employees and senior citizens.
APPLYING Open admission except for allied health programs. ***Options:*** Common Application, electronic application, early entrance, deferred entrance. ***Required:*** TOEFL for international students, ACT ASSET. Test scores used for counseling/placement. ***Application deadline:*** rolling.
APPLYING/TRANSFER ***Required for some:*** standardized test scores. ***Entrance:*** noncompetitive.
CONTACT Admissions Office, Wenatchee Valley College, Wenatchee, WA 98801-1799, 509-664-2563. ***Fax:*** 509-664-2538.

WHATCOM COMMUNITY COLLEGE
Bellingham, Washington

UG Enrollment: 2,621	**Tuition & Fees (WA Res): $1365**
Application Deadline: rolling	**Room & Board: N/Avail**

GENERAL State-supported, 2-year, coed. Part of Washington State Board for Community and Technical Colleges. Awards certificates, transfer associate, terminal associate degrees. Founded 1970. ***Setting:*** 20-acre rural campus with easy access to Vancouver. ***Total enrollment:*** 2,621. ***Faculty:*** 166 (33 full-time, 133 part-time).
ENROLLMENT PROFILE 2,621 students from 5 states and territories, 9 other countries. 63% women, 47% part-time, 96% state residents, 10% transferred in, 32% have need-based financial aid, 3% have non-need-based financial aid, 3% international, 31% 25 or older, 2% Native American, 5% Hispanic, 1% African American, 4% Asian American. ***Most popular recent major:*** liberal arts/general studies.
FIRST-YEAR CLASS Of the students who applied, 100% were accepted, 60% of whom enrolled.
ACADEMIC PROGRAM Core, honor code. Calendar: quarters. Academic remediation for entering students, English as a second language program offered during academic year, services for LD students, advanced placement, self-designed majors, tutorials, honors program, summer session for credit, part-time degree program (daytime, evenings, summer), external degree programs, adult/continuing education programs, co-op programs. Study abroad in England.
GENERAL DEGREE REQUIREMENTS 90 quarter credits; math/science requirements vary according to program; computer course for business majors.
MAJORS Accounting, business administration/commerce/management, computer science, computer technologies, early childhood education, law enforcement/police sciences, liberal arts/general studies, medical assistant technologies, medical secretarial studies, nursing, paralegal studies, physical therapy, real estate, secretarial studies/office management.
LIBRARY 13,578 books, 65 microform titles, 528 periodicals, 5 on-line bibliographic services, 13 CD-ROMs, 1,644 records, tapes, and CDs. Acquisition spending 1994–95: $31,482.
COMPUTERS ON CAMPUS 100 computers for student use in computer center. Staffed computer lab on campus provides training in use of computers, software. Academic computing expenditure 1994–95: $63,679.
COLLEGE LIFE Student-run newspaper. 10% vote in student government elections. ***Student services:*** personal-psychological counseling. ***Campus security:*** 24-hour emergency response devices.
HOUSING College housing not available.
CAREER PLANNING ***Placement office:*** 2 part-time staff; $14,488 operating expenditure 1994–95. ***Director:*** Ms. Anne Ziomkowski, Educational Planner, 360-676-2170. ***Services:*** job fairs, resume preparation, resume referral, career counseling, careers library.
EXPENSES FOR 1995–96 State resident tuition: $1365 full-time, $45.50 per credit part-time. Nonresident tuition: $5313 full-time, $177.10 per credit part-time.
FINANCIAL AID ***College-administered undergrad aid 1995–96:*** 960 need-based scholarships (average $1740), 45 non-need scholarships (average $550), short-term loans (average $350), 20 Federal Work-Study (averaging $2000), 65 part-time jobs. ***Required forms:*** institutional, FAFSA. ***Priority deadline:*** 4/15. ***Waivers:*** full or partial for employees or children of employees and senior citizens. ***Notification:*** 7/15.
APPLYING Open admission. ***Required:*** TOEFL for international students, Assessment and Placement Services for Community Colleges. Test scores used for counseling/placement. ***Application deadline:*** rolling.
APPLYING/TRANSFER ***Required for some:*** standardized test scores. ***Entrance:*** noncompetitive.
CONTACT Ms. Laine Johnston, Admissions Coordinator, Whatcom Community College, Bellingham, WA 98226-8003, 360-676-2170 Ext. 217. ***Fax:*** 360-676-2171.

YAKIMA VALLEY COMMUNITY COLLEGE
Yakima, Washington

UG Enrollment: 4,290	**Tuition & Fees (WA Res): $1395**
Application Deadline: 9/15	**Room & Board: $4400**

GENERAL State-supported, 2-year, coed. Part of Washington State Board for Community and Technical Colleges. Awards certificates, transfer associate, terminal associate degrees. Founded 1928. ***Setting:*** 20-acre small-town campus. ***Endowment:*** $1.7 million. ***Total enrollment:*** 4,290. ***Faculty:*** 374 (124 full-time, 250 part-time); student-faculty ratio is 15:1. ***Notable Alumni:*** David Shinn, diplomat; Robert F. Brachtenbac, Washington state supreme court justice; Dr. Penny Hitchcock, chief of the division of microbiology and infectious diseases at the National Institute of Health; Pete Rademacher, 1956 Olympic gold medal-winner.
ENROLLMENT PROFILE 4,290 students: 63% women, 41% part-time, 99% state residents, 1% live on campus, 20% transferred in, 1% international, 50% 25 or older, 5% Native American, 26% Hispanic, 1% African American, 1% Asian American. ***Areas of study chosen:*** 33% liberal arts/general studies, 4% health professions and related sciences, 3% business management and administrative services, 2% education, 1% agriculture, 1% computer and information sciences, 1% engineering and applied sciences. ***Most popular recent majors:*** nursing, dental services, radiological technology.
FIRST-YEAR CLASS 916 total; 1,521 applied, 100% were accepted, 60% of whom enrolled.
ACADEMIC PROGRAM Core, liberal arts and vocational curriculum, honor code. Calendar: quarters. 2,687 courses offered in 1995–96. Academic remediation for entering students, English as a second language program offered during academic year, services for LD students, advanced placement, summer session for credit, part-time degree program (daytime, evenings, weekends, summer), adult/continuing education programs, co-op programs and internships. ROTC: Air Force (c).
GENERAL DEGREE REQUIREMENTS 90 credits; math/science requirements vary according to program; computer course for TV/radio production, business, office occupations, hotel, travel and restaurant management majors.
MAJORS Accounting, agricultural business, agricultural sciences, agricultural technologies, agronomy/soil and crop sciences, animal sciences, automotive technologies, broadcasting, business administration/commerce/management, child care/child and family studies, civil engineering technology, computer graphics, computer science, computer technologies, criminal justice, dental services, drug and alcohol/substance abuse counseling, early childhood education, electrical engineering technology, (pre)engineering sequence, family and consumer studies, fire science, food services management, hotel and restaurant management, industrial and heavy equipment maintenance, instrumentation technology, law enforcement/police sciences, legal secretarial studies, liberal arts/general studies, management information systems, manufacturing technology, marketing/retailing/merchandising, medical secretarial studies, nursing, occupational therapy, radiological technology, secretarial studies/office management, tourism and travel.
LIBRARY Raymond Library with 29,000 books, 1,645 microform titles, 860 periodicals, 5 CD-ROMs, 2,681 records, tapes, and CDs. Acquisition spending 1994–95: $66,558.
COMPUTERS ON CAMPUS 369 computers for student use in computer center, computer labs, learning resource center, classrooms, library, dorms. Staffed computer lab on campus provides training in use of computers, software.
COLLEGE LIFE Drama-theater group, choral group, student-run newspaper. 13% vote in student government elections. ***Social organizations:*** 31 open to all. ***Most popular organizations:*** Veterans with Supporters, Business Management/Marketing Club, Image Makers, Agri-Business Club. ***Major annual events:*** Casino Night, Annual Student/Staff Barbecue, Multi-Cultural Week. ***Student services:*** health clinic, personal-psychological counseling, women's center. ***Campus security:*** 24-hour emergency response devices, late-night transport-escort service, controlled dormitory access.

HOUSING 300 college housing spaces available; 115 were occupied 1995–96. No special consideration for freshman housing applicants. On-campus residence required in freshman year for foreign students. *Option:* coed housing available. Resident assistants live in dorms.
ATHLETICS Member NJCAA. *Intercollegiate:* baseball M(s), basketball M(s)/W(s), softball W(s), tennis M(s)/W(s), volleyball W(s). *Intramural:* badminton, basketball, table tennis (Ping-Pong), tennis, volleyball, wrestling. *Contact:* Mr. Jerry Ward, Athletic Director, 509-575-2393.
CAREER PLANNING *Placement office:* 1 full-time, 1 part-time staff. *Director:* Mr. Tom Mount, Career Counselor, 509-575-2360. *Services:* career counseling, job interviews.
EXPENSES FOR 1995–96 State resident tuition: $1350 full-time, $45 per credit part-time. Nonresident tuition: $5298 full-time, $176.60 per credit part-time. Part-time mandatory fees: $1.50 per credit. Full-time mandatory fees: $45. College room and board: $4400.
FINANCIAL AID *College-administered undergrad aid 1995–96:* 162 need-based scholarships (averaging $800), 150 non-need scholarships (averaging $1000), short-term loans (averaging $100), low-interest long-term loans from external sources (averaging $2625), Federal Work-Study, 400 part-time jobs. *Required forms:* CSS Financial Aid PROFILE, institutional, FAFSA, financial aid transcript (for transfers). *Priority deadline:* 6/1. *Payment plan:* deferred payment. *Waivers:* full or partial for employees or children of employees and senior citizens.
APPLYING Open admission except for nursing, dental hygiene, radiological technology, occupational therapy assistant, early childhood education programs. *Options:* Common Application, electronic application, deferred entrance, midyear entrance. *Required:* TOEFL for international students, ACT ASSET. *Recommended:* school transcript. *Required for some:* school transcript, minimum 2.0 GPA, minimum 3.0 GPA, recommendations, interview. Test scores used for counseling/placement. *Application deadline:* 9/15. *Notification:* continuous until 9/15.
APPLYING/TRANSFER *Recommended:* college transcript. *Required for some:* standardized test scores, high school transcript, recommendations, interview, college transcript, minimum 2.0 college GPA, minimum 3.0 college GPA, minimum 2.0 high school GPA, minimum 3.0 high school GPA. *Entrance:* noncompetitive. *Application deadline:* 9/15. *Notification:* continuous until 9/15. *Contact:* Ms. Maxine Gish, Interim Coordinator for Admissions and Advising, 509-575-2373.
CONTACT Ms. Donna Fulton, Admissions Assistant, Yakima Valley Community College, PO Box 1647, Yakima, WA 98907-1647, 509-575-2373. *Fax:* 509-575-2461.

WEST VIRGINIA

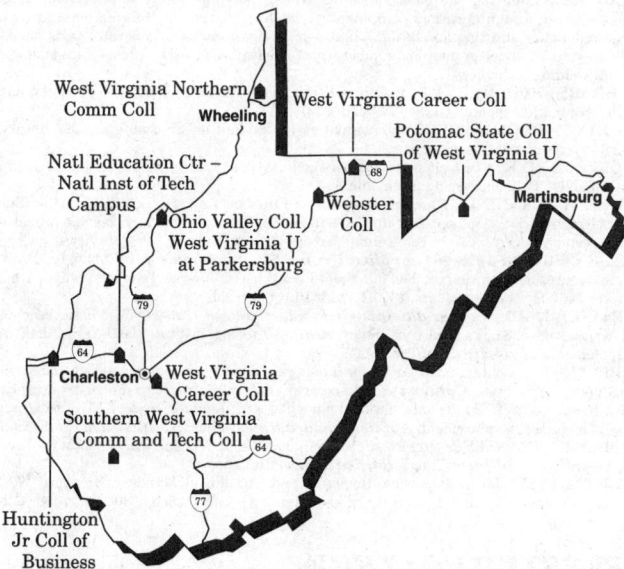

HUNTINGTON JUNIOR COLLEGE OF BUSINESS
Huntington, West Virginia

UG Enrollment: 475	Tuition & Fees: $3600
Application Deadline: rolling	Room & Board: N/Avail

GENERAL Proprietary, 2-year, coed. Awards terminal associate degrees. Founded 1936. *Setting:* urban campus. *Total enrollment:* 475. *Faculty:* 20 (16 full-time, 4 part-time); student-faculty ratio is 20:1.
ENROLLMENT PROFILE 475 students: 60% women, 2% part-time, 90% state residents, 30% transferred in, 0% international, 40% 25 or older.
FIRST-YEAR CLASS 200 total.
ACADEMIC PROGRAM Core. Calendar: quarters. Academic remediation for entering students, services for LD students, summer session for credit, part-time degree program (daytime, evenings).
GENERAL DEGREE REQUIREMENTS 108 credits; computer course.
MAJORS Accounting, business administration/commerce/management, computer programming, computer science, court reporting, dental services, fashion merchandising, legal secretarial studies, medical assistant technologies, medical secretarial studies, secretarial studies/office management.

LIBRARY 1,900 books, 35 periodicals, 100 records, tapes, and CDs.
COMPUTERS ON CAMPUS 60 computers for student use in computer center, classrooms. Staffed computer lab on campus provides training in use of computers, software.
COLLEGE LIFE Orientation program.
HOUSING College housing not available.
CAREER PLANNING *Director:* Ms. Carolyn Smith, Director, 304-697-7550. *Service:* career counseling.
EXPENSES FOR 1996–97 Tuition: $3600 full-time, $375 per course part-time. Tuition guaranteed not to increase for student's term of enrollment.
FINANCIAL AID *College-administered undergrad aid 1995–96:* need-based scholarships, low-interest long-term loans from external sources (average $1500), part-time jobs. *Required forms:* FAFSA. *Application deadline:* continuous. *Waivers:* full or partial for employees or children of employees.
APPLYING Open admission. *Required:* school transcript. Test scores used for counseling/placement. *Application deadline:* rolling.
APPLYING/TRANSFER *Required:* college transcript. *Entrance:* noncompetitive. *Application deadline:* rolling.
CONTACT Mr. James Garrett, Marketing Education Services Director, Huntington Junior College of Business, 900 Fifth Avenue, Huntington, WV 25701-2004, 304-697-7550. *Fax:* 304-697-7554. College video available.

NATIONAL EDUCATION CENTER– NATIONAL INSTITUTE OF TECHNOLOGY CAMPUS
Cross Lanes, West Virginia

UG Enrollment: 380	Tuition: $12,388/deg prog
Application Deadline: rolling	Room & Board: N/Avail

GENERAL Proprietary, 2-year, coed. Part of National Education Corporation. Awards certificates, transfer associate degrees. Founded 1938. *Setting:* small-town campus. *Total enrollment:* 380. *Faculty:* 15 (all full-time); student-faculty ratio is 26:1.
ENROLLMENT PROFILE 380 students from 6 states and territories. 40% women, 0% part-time, 97% state residents, 2% transferred in, 0% international, 10% 25 or older, 0% Native American, 0% Hispanic, 15% African American, 0% Asian American.
ACADEMIC PROGRAM Core. Calendar: quarters.
GENERAL DEGREE REQUIREMENT 15 units.
MAJORS Electronics engineering technology, medical assistant technologies.
COMPUTERS ON CAMPUS 40 computers for student use in classrooms.
COLLEGE LIFE Student-run newspaper.
HOUSING College housing not available.
CAREER PLANNING *Service:* career counseling.
EXPENSES FOR 1996–97 Tuition: $12,388 per degree program.
FINANCIAL AID *College-administered undergrad aid 1995–96:* 280 need-based scholarships (average $4400), short-term loans, low-interest long-term loans from external sources. *Required forms:* institutional, FAFSA. *Application deadline:* continuous.
APPLYING *Option:* deferred entrance. *Required:* school transcript. *Application deadline:* rolling. *Notification:* continuous.
APPLYING/TRANSFER *Required:* high school transcript, college transcript. *Application deadline:* rolling. *Notification:* continuous.
CONTACT Mrs. Karen Wilkinson, Director of Admissions, National Education Center– National Institute of Technology Campus, Cross Lanes, WV 25313-1390, 304-776-6290 Ext. 20.

OHIO VALLEY COLLEGE
Parkersburg, West Virginia

UG Enrollment: 314	Tuition & Fees: $6060
Application Deadline: rolling	Room & Board: $3200

GENERAL Independent, primarily 2-year, coed, affiliated with Church of Christ. Awards transfer associate, terminal associate, bachelor's degrees. Founded 1960. *Setting:* 350-acre small-town campus. *Total enrollment:* 314. *Faculty:* 25 (18 full-time, 7 part-time); student-faculty ratio is 13:1.
ENROLLMENT PROFILE 314 students from 10 states and territories, 4 other countries. 51% women, 49% men, 7% part-time, 45% state residents, 4% transferred in, 4% international, 2% 25 or older, 0% Native American, 0% Hispanic, 5% African American, 0% Asian American.
FIRST-YEAR CLASS 137 total; 365 applied, 91% were accepted, 41% of whom enrolled. 7% from top 10% of their high school class, 28% from top quarter, 59% from top half. 1 National Merit Scholar.
ACADEMIC PROGRAM Core. Calendar: semesters. Academic remediation for entering students, English as a second language program, advanced placement, honors program, summer session for credit, part-time degree program (daytime), co-op programs. ROTC: Air Force (c).
GENERAL DEGREE REQUIREMENTS 68 semester hours for associate, 128 semester hours for bachelor's; 3 semester hours of math; 4 semester hours of science; computer course (varies by major); internship (some majors).
MAJORS Accounting, art education, behavioral sciences, biblical languages, biblical studies (B), business administration/commerce/management (B), communication, computer science, education (B), elementary education (B), (pre)engineering sequence, liberal arts/general studies (B), music education, nursing, physical education, physical sciences, psychology (B), religious studies, secretarial studies/office management, social work, Spanish, speech/rhetoric/public address/debate.
LIBRARY 35,000 books, 1,102 microform titles, 176 periodicals, 4,427 records, tapes, and CDs.
COMPUTERS ON CAMPUS 34 computers for student use in computer center, learning center.
COLLEGE LIFE Orientation program (3 days, no cost, parents included). Drama-theater group, choral group, student-run newspaper. *Social organizations:* 4 local

Ohio Valley College (continued)

fraternities, 4 local sororities; 78% of eligible men and 80% of eligible women are members. ***Student services:*** personal-psychological counseling. ***Campus security:*** 24-hour emergency response devices and patrols, controlled dormitory access.

HOUSING 340 college housing spaces available; 162 were occupied 1995–96. Freshmen guaranteed college housing. On-campus residence required through sophomore year except if living with relatives.

ATHLETICS Member NSCAA. ***Intercollegiate:*** baseball M(s), basketball M(s)/W(s), volleyball W(s). ***Intramural:*** archery, baseball, basketball, bowling, cross-country running, football, tennis, track and field, volleyball.

CAREER PLANNING ***Service:*** career counseling.

EXPENSES FOR 1996–97 Comprehensive fee of $9260 includes full-time tuition ($5600), mandatory fees ($460), and college room and board ($3200). Part-time tuition per semester hour ranges from $175 to $198.

FINANCIAL AID ***College-administered undergrad aid 1995–96:*** need-based scholarships, 190 non-need scholarships (average $300), low-interest long-term loans from external sources (average $2300), Federal Work-Study. ***Required forms:*** CSS Financial Aid PROFILE. ***Priority deadline:*** 8/1. ***Payment plan:*** installment. ***Waivers:*** full or partial for employees or children of employees.

APPLYING ***Options:*** early entrance, early action, deferred entrance. ***Required:*** SAT I or ACT, TOEFL for international students. ***Recommended:*** 3 years of high school science. Test scores used for admission and counseling/placement. ***Application deadlines:*** rolling, 9/1 for early action. ***Notification:*** continuous, continuous until 10/1 for early action.

APPLYING/TRANSFER ***Required:*** standardized test scores. ***Entrance:*** minimally difficult. ***Application deadline:*** rolling. ***Notification:*** continuous.

CONTACT Mr. Robert Crum, Director of Admissions, Ohio Valley College, Parkersburg, WV 26101-8100, 304-485-7384 Ext. 32 or toll-free 800-678-6780 (out-of-state). ***Fax:*** 304-485-8382. College video available.

POTOMAC STATE COLLEGE OF WEST VIRGINIA UNIVERSITY
Keyser, West Virginia

UG Enrollment: 1,163	**Tuition & Fees (WV Res): $1812**
Application Deadline: rolling	**Room & Board: $3636**

GENERAL State-supported, 2-year, coed. Part of University System of West Virginia. Awards transfer associate, terminal associate degrees. Founded 1901. ***Setting:*** 391-acre small-town campus. ***Total enrollment:*** 1,163. ***Faculty:*** 83 (39 full-time, 50% with terminal degrees, 44 part-time); student-faculty ratio is 19:1.

ENROLLMENT PROFILE 1,163 students from 25 states and territories. 49% women, 51% men, 32% part-time, 78% state residents, 35% live on campus, 5% transferred in, 16% 25 or older, 1% Native American, 1% Hispanic, 6% African American. ***Most popular recent majors:*** business administration/commerce/management, (pre)engineering sequence, agricultural sciences.

FIRST-YEAR CLASS 567 total. Of the students who applied, 98% were accepted, 27% of whom enrolled. 13% from top 10% of their high school class, 24% from top quarter, 70% from top half.

ACADEMIC PROGRAM Core. Calendar: semesters. Average class size 25 in required courses. Academic remediation for entering students, services for LD students, advanced placement, tutorials, honors program, summer session for credit, part-time degree program (daytime, evenings, summer), adult/continuing education programs.

GENERAL DEGREE REQUIREMENTS 64 credit hours; math/science requirements vary according to program; computer course for agriculture majors.

MAJORS Accounting, agricultural business, agricultural economics, agricultural education, agricultural sciences, agricultural technologies, agronomy/soil and crop sciences, animal sciences, biology/biological sciences, business administration/commerce/management, business economics, chemistry, civil engineering technology, computer programming, computer science, computer technologies, data processing, early childhood education, economics, education, electrical and electronics technologies, elementary education, engineering (general), (pre)engineering sequence, English, forestry, forest technology, geology, history, horticulture, journalism, liberal arts/general studies, mathematics, mechanical engineering technology, medical secretarial studies, music, music education, parks management, physical education, political science/government, psychology, recreational facilities management, science, secretarial studies/office management, social work, sociology, wildlife management, wood sciences.

LIBRARY Shipper Library with 37,948 books, 15,597 microform titles, 216 periodicals, 1,313 records, tapes, and CDs.

COMPUTERS ON CAMPUS 113 computers for student use in computer center, computer labs, learning resource center, classrooms, library, dorms. Staffed computer lab on campus provides training in use of computers.

COLLEGE LIFE Orientation program (3 days, no cost, parents included). Drama-theater group, choral group, student-run newspaper. 30% vote in student government elections. ***Major annual event:*** Homecoming. ***Student services:*** health clinic, personal-psychological counseling. ***Campus security:*** 24-hour emergency response devices and patrols, controlled dormitory access.

HOUSING 420 college housing spaces available; all were occupied 1995–96. Freshmen guaranteed college housing. On-campus residence required through sophomore year. ***Option:*** single-sex (4 buildings) housing available. Resident assistants live in dorms.

ATHLETICS Member NJCAA. ***Intercollegiate:*** baseball M(s), basketball M(s)/W(s), football M(s), volleyball W(s). ***Intramural:*** basketball, skiing (cross-country), skiing (downhill), tennis, volleyball. ***Contact:*** Mr. Larry Boylard, Director of Athletics, 304-788-6877.

CAREER PLANNING ***Placement office:*** 1 full-time staff. ***Director:*** Ms. Kara Anderson, Counselor, 304-788-6859. ***Services:*** resume preparation, resume referral, career counseling, careers library.

EXPENSES FOR 1995–96 State resident tuition: $1812 full-time, $73.50 per credit hour part-time. Nonresident tuition: $5644 full-time, $233.25 per credit hour part-time. College room and board: $3636.

FINANCIAL AID ***College-administered undergrad aid 1995–96:*** need-based scholarships, 62 non-need scholarships (average $550), short-term loans (average $217), low-interest long-term loans from external sources (average $450), Federal Work-Study, 52 part-time jobs. ***Required forms:*** CSS Financial Aid PROFILE, institutional, FAFSA. ***Priority deadline:*** 3/30. ***Payment plan:*** installment.

APPLYING Open admission for state residents. ***Options:*** early entrance, deferred entrance. ***Required:*** school transcript, SAT I or ACT, TOEFL for international students. Test scores used for counseling/placement. ***Application deadline:*** rolling.

APPLYING/TRANSFER ***Required:*** college transcript, minimum 2.0 college GPA. ***Entrance:*** moderately difficult. ***Application deadline:*** rolling. ***Contact:*** Mr. Charles H. Via, Director of Admissions and Records, 304-788-6820.

CONTACT Mr. Charles H. Via, Director of Admissions and Records, Potomac State College of West Virginia University, Keyser, WV 26726, 304-788-6820. ***Fax:*** 304-788-6939.

❖ ***See page 796 for a narrative description.*** ❖

SOUTHERN WEST VIRGINIA COMMUNITY AND TECHNICAL COLLEGE
Mount Gay, West Virginia

UG Enrollment: 3,097	**Tuition & Fees (WV Res): $1030**
Application Deadline: rolling	**Room & Board: N/Avail**

GENERAL State-supported, 2-year, coed. Part of State College System of West Virginia. Awards transfer associate, terminal associate degrees. Founded 1971. ***Setting:*** 23-acre rural campus. ***Total enrollment:*** 3,097. ***Faculty:*** 192 (60 full-time, 6% with terminal degrees, 132 part-time).

ENROLLMENT PROFILE 3,097 students from 2 states and territories. 68% women, 45% part-time, 99% state residents, 48% transferred in, 80% 25 or older, 1% Native American, 1% Hispanic, 2% African American, 1% Asian American. ***Areas of study chosen:*** 66% interdisciplinary studies, 3% social sciences, 1% communications and journalism, 1% engineering and applied sciences. ***Most popular recent majors:*** liberal arts/general studies, business administration/commerce/management, nursing.

FIRST-YEAR CLASS 839 total; 839 applied, 100% were accepted, 100% of whom enrolled. 1% from top 10% of their high school class, 36% from top half.

ACADEMIC PROGRAM Core, interdisciplinary curriculum. Calendar: semesters. 1,069 courses offered in 1995–96. Academic remediation for entering students, services for LD students, advanced placement, summer session for credit, part-time degree program (daytime, evenings, summer), external degree programs, adult/continuing education programs, co-op programs.

GENERAL DEGREE REQUIREMENTS 63 semester hours; math/science requirements vary according to program; computer course.

MAJORS Accounting, automotive technologies, business administration/commerce/management, communication equipment technology, computer information systems, criminal justice, drafting and design, finance/banking, liberal arts/general studies, medical laboratory technology, nursing, radiological technology, secretarial studies/office management, welding technology.

LIBRARY 70,576 books, 170 microform titles, 233 periodicals, 5,205 records, tapes, and CDs. Acquisition spending 1994–95: $279,000.

COMPUTERS ON CAMPUS 50 computers for student use in computer labs, library. Staffed computer lab on campus.

COLLEGE LIFE ***Student services:*** personal-psychological counseling.

HOUSING College housing not available.

CAREER PLANNING ***Placement office:*** 1 full-time staff. ***Director:*** Ms. Allyn Sue Barker, Career Development Director, 304-792-4384. ***Services:*** job fairs, resume preparation, resume referral, career counseling, careers library, job bank, job interviews.

EXPENSES FOR 1995–96 ***Application fee:*** $10. State resident tuition: $1030 full-time. Nonresident tuition: $2900 full-time. Part-time tuition per semester ranges from $43 to $462 for state residents, $121 to $1331 for nonresidents.

FINANCIAL AID ***College-administered undergrad aid 1995–96:*** need-based scholarships (average $284), Federal Work-Study. ***Required forms:*** institutional, FAFSA, PHEAA supplemental. ***Priority deadline:*** 3/1.

APPLYING Open admission except for nursing, medical laboratory technology, radiologic technology programs. ***Options:*** early entrance, deferred entrance, midyear entrance. ***Required:*** ACT, TOEFL for international students. ***Required for some:*** GED. Test scores used for counseling/placement. ***Application deadline:*** rolling. ***Notification:*** continuous.

APPLYING/TRANSFER ***Required:*** standardized test scores. ***Entrance:*** noncompetitive. ***Application deadline:*** rolling. ***Notification:*** continuous.

CONTACT Mr. James P. Owens, Registrar and Enrollment Manager, Southern West Virginia Community and Technical College, Mount Gay, WV 25637, 304-792-7098. College video available.

WEBSTER COLLEGE
Fairmont, West Virginia

GENERAL Proprietary, 2-year, specialized, coed. Awards transfer associate, terminal associate degrees. Founded 1922. ***Setting:*** 3-acre small-town campus. ***Total enrollment:*** 204. ***Faculty:*** 7 (all full-time).

EXPENSES FOR 1995–96 Tuition: $13,650 per degree program. Tuition guaranteed not to increase for student's term of enrollment.

CONTACT Ms. Cheryl Stickley, Executive Assistant, Webster College, Fairmont, WV 26554-2797, 304-363-8824.

WEST VIRGINIA CAREER COLLEGE
Charleston, West Virginia

UG Enrollment: 200	**Tuition & Fees: $7075**
Application Deadline: rolling	**Room & Board: N/Avail**

GENERAL Proprietary, 2-year, primarily women. Awards terminal associate degrees. Founded 1892. ***Setting:*** urban campus. ***Total enrollment:*** 200. ***Faculty:*** 24 (8 full-time, 16 part-time).

ENROLLMENT PROFILE 200 students from 6 states and territories. 80% women, 2% part-time, 95% state residents, 10% transferred in, 40% 25 or older, 1% Native American, 1% Hispanic, 25% African American, 1% Asian American. ***Most popular recent majors:*** medical assistant technologies, legal studies, accounting.

FIRST-YEAR CLASS 90 total; 130 applied, 100% were accepted, 69% of whom enrolled. 5% from top 10% of their high school class, 10% from top quarter, 20% from top half.
ACADEMIC PROGRAM Calendar: quarters. 50 courses offered in 1995–96. Advanced placement, summer session for credit, part-time degree program (daytime, evenings, summer), adult/continuing education programs.
GENERAL DEGREE REQUIREMENTS 90 quarter hours; 1 business math course; computer course.
MAJORS Accounting, business administration/commerce/management, data processing, legal studies, medical assistant technologies, medical secretarial studies, secretarial studies/office management, word processing.
LIBRARY 1,300 books, 40 periodicals, 100 records, tapes, and CDs.
COMPUTERS ON CAMPUS 75 computers for student use in computer center provide access to main academic computer, on-line services. Staffed computer lab on campus provides training in use of computers, software.
COLLEGE LIFE ***Student services:*** personal-psychological counseling.
HOUSING College housing not available.
CAREER PLANNING ***Service:*** career counseling.
EXPENSES FOR 1996–97 Tuition: $6825 full-time, $142 per quarter hour part-time. Part-time mandatory fees: $50 per quarter hour. Full-time mandatory fees: $250.
FINANCIAL AID ***College-administered undergrad aid 1995–96:*** need-based scholarships, low-interest long-term loans from external sources (average $2500), 25 Federal Work-Study (averaging $1500), 5 part-time jobs. ***Required forms:*** institutional, FAFSA. ***Priority deadline:*** 9/24. ***Payment plan:*** tuition prepayment.
APPLYING Open admission. ***Options:*** Common Application, early entrance, deferred entrance. ***Application deadline:*** rolling.
APPLYING/TRANSFER ***Entrance:*** noncompetitive. ***Application deadline:*** rolling.
CONTACT Admission Department, West Virginia Career College, 1000 Virginia Street East, Charleston, WV 25301-2817, 304-345-2820.

WEST VIRGINIA CAREER COLLEGE
Morgantown, West Virginia

UG Enrollment: 200	**Tuition: $10,800/deg prog**
Application Deadline: rolling	**Room & Board: N/Avail**

GENERAL Proprietary, 2-year, coed. Awards terminal associate degrees (also offers non-degree programs with significant enrollment not reflected in profile). Founded 1922. ***Setting:*** small-town campus with easy access to Pittsburgh. ***Total enrollment:*** 200. ***Faculty:*** 12 (7 full-time, 5 part-time); student-faculty ratio is 22:1.
ENROLLMENT PROFILE 200 students from 2 states and territories, 1 other country. 50% women, 50% men, 0% part-time, 90% state residents, 1% international, 70% 25 or older, 5% African American.
FIRST-YEAR CLASS 85 total. Of the students who applied, 100% were accepted, 80% of whom enrolled.
ACADEMIC PROGRAM Core. Calendar: quarters. Adult/continuing education programs.
GENERAL DEGREE REQUIREMENT 92 quarter hours.
MAJORS Accounting, business administration/commerce/management, legal secretarial studies.
COMPUTERS ON CAMPUS 12 computers for student use in computer center. Staffed computer lab on campus provides training in use of computers, software.
COLLEGE LIFE ***Student services:*** personal-psychological counseling.
HOUSING College housing not available.
CAREER PLANNING ***Service:*** career counseling.
AFTER GRADUATION 5% of students completing a degree program in 1994–95 went directly on to further study.
EXPENSES FOR 1996–97 Tuition: $10,800 per degree program.
FINANCIAL AID ***College-administered undergrad aid 1995–96:*** need-based scholarships, low-interest long-term loans from external sources (averaging $2000). ***Required forms:*** CSS Financial Aid PROFILE, institutional, FAFSA. ***Application deadline:*** continuous.
APPLYING Open admission. ***Required:*** school transcript, interview. ***Recommended:*** 3 years of high school math and science, some high school foreign language, recommendations. ***Application deadline:*** rolling. ***Notification:*** continuous.
CONTACT Admissions Office, West Virginia Career College, Morgantown, WV 26505-5521, 304-296-8282.

WEST VIRGINIA NORTHERN COMMUNITY COLLEGE
Wheeling, West Virginia

UG Enrollment: 2,720	**Tuition & Fees (WV Res): $1438**
Application Deadline: rolling	**Room & Board: N/Avail**

GENERAL State-supported, 2-year, coed. Awards certificates, transfer associate, terminal associate degrees. Founded 1972. ***Setting:*** small-town campus with easy access to Pittsburgh. ***Total enrollment:*** 2,720. ***Faculty:*** 158 (67 full-time, 12% with terminal degrees, 91 part-time); student-faculty ratio is 19:1.
ENROLLMENT PROFILE 2,720 students from 7 states and territories, 3 other countries. 69% women, 61% part-time, 81% state residents, 10% transferred in, 46% have need-based financial aid, 5% have non-need-based financial aid, 1% international, 62% 25 or older, 0% Native American, 1% Hispanic, 2% African American, 1% Asian American. ***Areas of study chosen:*** 37% liberal arts/general studies, 32% health professions and related sciences, 20% business management and administrative services, 5% engineering and applied sciences, 4% computer and information sciences, 2% vocational and home economics. ***Most popular recent majors:*** business administration/commerce/management, nursing, liberal arts/general studies.
FIRST-YEAR CLASS 684 total; 1,400 applied, 100% were accepted, 63% of whom enrolled.
ACADEMIC PROGRAM Calendar: semesters. Academic remediation for entering students, advanced placement, honors program, summer session for credit, part-time degree program (daytime, evenings), adult/continuing education programs, internships.
GENERAL DEGREE REQUIREMENTS 60 credit hours; internship (some majors).
MAJORS Accounting, business administration/commerce/management, computer information systems, criminal justice, culinary arts, data processing, electrical and electronics technologies, emergency medical technology, finance/banking, heating/refrigeration/air conditioning, horticulture, human services, legal secretarial studies, liberal arts/general studies, medical laboratory technology, medical secretarial studies, nursing, operating room technology, radiological technology, respiratory therapy, secretarial studies/office management, social work.
LIBRARY Wheeling B and O Campus Library plus 2 others, with 33,042 books, 135 microform titles, 188 periodicals, 13 CD-ROMs, 1,523 records, tapes, and CDs. Acquisition spending 1994–95: $63,060.
COMPUTERS ON CAMPUS Computer purchase plan available. 130 computers for student use in computer center, computer labs, learning resource center, classrooms, library. Staffed computer lab on campus provides training in use of computers, software. Academic computing expenditure 1994–95: $96,451.
COLLEGE LIFE 2% vote in student government elections. ***Social organizations:*** 1 open to all. ***Student services:*** personal-psychological counseling, women's center. ***Campus security:*** late-night transport-escort service, security personnel during evening and night classes.
HOUSING College housing not available.
ATHLETICS ***Intramural:*** badminton, baseball, basketball, bowling, football, golf, racquetball, soccer, softball, tennis, volleyball, weight lifting. ***Contact:*** Mr. Don Chamberlain, Director of Student Activities, 304-233-5900 Ext. 271.
CAREER PLANNING ***Placement office:*** 2 full-time staff; $53,860 operating expenditure 1994–95. ***Director:*** Mr. Robert Wychlerly, Director of Career and Special Services, 304-233-5900 Ext. 268. ***Services:*** job fairs, resume preparation, resume referral, career counseling, careers library, job bank, job interviews.
EXPENSES FOR 1996–97 State resident tuition: $1416 full-time, $59 per credit hour part-time. Nonresident tuition: $3864 full-time, $161 per credit hour part-time. Part-time mandatory fees: $11 per semester. Full-time mandatory fees: $22.
FINANCIAL AID ***College-administered undergrad aid 1995–96:*** 75 need-based scholarships (average $600), 25 non-need scholarships (average $600), low-interest long-term loans from college funds (average $500), loans from external sources (average $1800), Federal Work-Study. ***Required forms:*** state, institutional, FAFSA, nontaxable income verification. ***Priority deadline:*** 3/15.
APPLYING Open admission except for health science programs. ***Options:*** early entrance, deferred entrance, midyear entrance. ***Required:*** TOEFL for international students, ACT ASSET. ***Required for some:*** school transcript, SAT I or ACT. Test scores used for counseling/placement. ***Application deadline:*** rolling.
APPLYING/TRANSFER ***Entrance:*** noncompetitive. ***Application deadline:*** rolling. ***Contact:*** Ms. Sherry Becker-Gorby, Associate Dean of Academic Affairs/Registrar, 304-233-5900.
CONTACT Ms. Bonnie Ellis, Associate Dean for Student Development, West Virginia Northern Community College, Wheeling, WV 26003, 304-233-5900 Ext. 4218. ***Fax:*** 304-233-5900 Ext. 258.

WEST VIRGINIA UNIVERSITY AT PARKERSBURG
Parkersburg, West Virginia

UG Enrollment: 3,600	**Tuition & Fees (WV Res): $1164**
Application Deadline: N/R	**Room & Board: N/Avail**

GENERAL State-supported, primarily 2-year, coed. Part of University System of West Virginia. Awards certificates, diplomas, transfer associate, terminal associate, bachelor's degrees. Founded 1971. ***Setting:*** 140-acre small-town campus. ***Total enrollment:*** 3,600. ***Faculty:*** 173 (12% of full-time faculty have terminal degrees); student-faculty ratio is 23:1.
ENROLLMENT PROFILE 3,600 students from 3 states and territories, 6 other countries. 63% women, 48% part-time, 97% state residents, 5% transferred in, 1% international, 46% 25 or older, 1% African American.
FIRST-YEAR CLASS 785 total; 963 applied, 100% were accepted, 82% of whom enrolled.
ACADEMIC PROGRAM Core, honor code. Calendar: semesters. 1,420 courses offered in 1995–96. Academic remediation for entering students, services for LD students, advanced placement, summer session for credit, part-time degree program (daytime, evenings, summer), adult/continuing education programs, co-op programs. Study abroad in China. ROTC: Army (c).
GENERAL DEGREE REQUIREMENTS 64 credit hours for associate, 128 credit hours for bachelor's; 3 credit hours of math; 8 credit hours of science; computer course for business, engineering majors.
MAJORS Accounting, automotive technologies, business administration/commerce/management (B), chemical engineering technology, criminal justice, data processing, drafting and design, education, electrical and electronics technologies, electromechanical technology, electronics engineering technology, elementary education (B), (pre)engineering sequence, finance/banking, liberal arts/general studies, machine and tool technologies, marketing/retailing/merchandising, mechanical engineering technology, nursing, secretarial studies/office management, social work, welding technology.
LIBRARY 41,300 books, 397 microform titles, 248 periodicals, 4,267 records, tapes, and CDs.
COMPUTERS ON CAMPUS 96 computers for student use in computer labs provide access to main academic computer, e-mail. Staffed computer lab on campus provides training in use of computers, software.
COLLEGE LIFE Drama-theater group, student-run newspaper. 20% vote in student government elections. ***Student services:*** health clinic, personal-psychological counseling.
HOUSING College housing not available.
ATHLETICS ***Intramural:*** badminton, basketball, bowling, cross-country running, football, golf, table tennis (Ping-Pong), tennis, volleyball, weight lifting.
CAREER PLANNING ***Services:*** resume preparation, resume referral, career counseling, careers library, job bank.
AFTER GRADUATION 20% of students completing transfer associate program in 1994–95 went directly to 4-year colleges.
EXPENSES FOR 1995–96 State resident tuition: $1164 full-time, $48.50 per credit hour part-time. Nonresident tuition: $3636 full-time, $151.50 per credit hour part-time.
FINANCIAL AID ***College-administered undergrad aid 1995–96:*** 390 need-based scholarships (average $582), 206 non-need scholarships (average $582), low-interest long-

West Virginia—Wisconsin

West Virginia University at Parkersburg (continued)
term loans from external sources (average $1895), Federal Work-Study. *Required forms:* CSS Financial Aid PROFILE, institutional, proof of Selective Service registration (for men); accepted: FAFSA. *Priority deadline:* 5/1.
APPLYING Open admission except for nursing, bachelor of science degree programs. *Options:* Common Application, early entrance, deferred entrance. *Required:* ACT, TOEFL for international students. *Required for some:* school transcript. Test scores used for counseling/placement. *Notification:* continuous.
APPLYING/TRANSFER *Required:* standardized test scores, college transcript. *Required for some:* high school transcript. *Entrance:* noncompetitive. *Notification:* continuous. *Contact:* Ms. Robin Ambrozy, Director of Enrollment Retention Management, 304-424-8220.
CONTACT Ms. Robin Ambrozy, Director of Enrollment Retention Management, West Virginia University at Parkersburg, Parkersburg, WV 26101-9577, 304-424-8220.

WEST VIRGINIA UNIVERSITY, POTOMAC STATE COLLEGE
West Virginia—See Potomac State College of West Virginia University

WISCONSIN

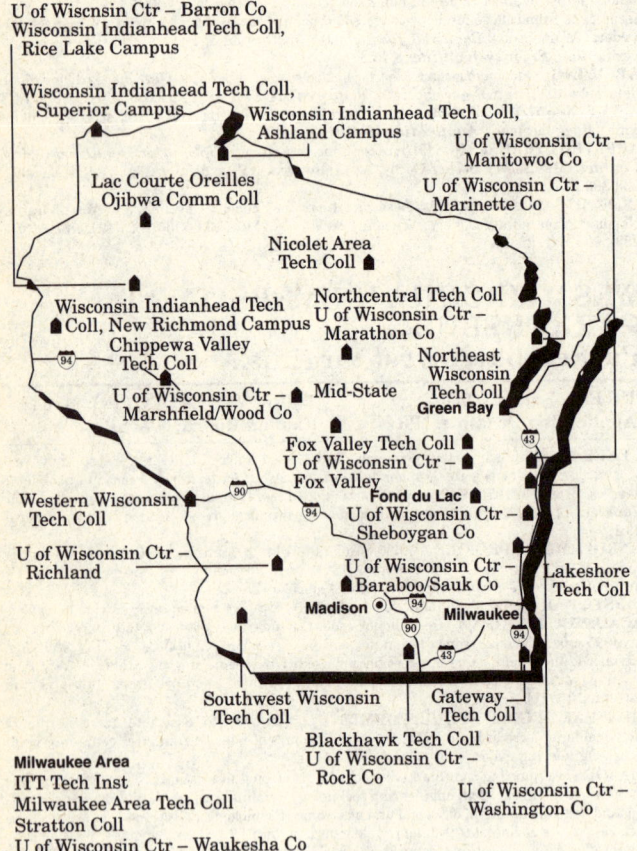

BLACKHAWK TECHNICAL COLLEGE
Janesville, Wisconsin

UG Enrollment: 3,000	**Tuition & Fees (WI Res):** $1596
Application Deadline: rolling	**Room & Board:** N/Avail

GENERAL District-supported, 2-year, coed. Part of Wisconsin Technical College System. Awards transfer associate, terminal associate degrees. Founded 1968. *Setting:* 84-acre rural campus. *Research spending 1994-95:* $119,401. *Total enrollment:* 3,000. *Faculty:* 293 (91 full-time, 2% with terminal degrees, 202 part-time).
ENROLLMENT PROFILE 3,000 students from 4 states and territories. 60% women, 40% men, 61% part-time, 98% state residents, 1% transferred in, 0% international, 60% 25 or older, 1% Native American, 1% Hispanic, 3% African American, 1% Asian American. *Areas of study chosen:* 22% engineering and applied sciences, 8% social sciences, 7% agriculture.
FIRST-YEAR CLASS 1,800 applied, 98% were accepted, 65% of whom enrolled.
ACADEMIC PROGRAM Core. Calendar: semesters. Academic remediation for entering students, English as a second language program offered during academic year and summer, services for LD students, summer session for credit, part-time degree program (daytime, evenings, summer), adult/continuing education programs, co-op programs and internships.
GENERAL DEGREE REQUIREMENTS 65 credits; internship (some majors).
MAJORS Accounting, computer programming, data processing, electrical and electronics technologies, electromechanical technology, fire science, food sciences, food services technology, industrial engineering technology, law enforcement/police sciences, legal secretarial studies, marketing/retailing/merchandising, mechanical design technology, nursing, physical therapy, secretarial studies/office management.
LIBRARY Blackhawk Technical College Library with 25,000 books, 435 periodicals, 1,500 records, tapes, and CDs. Acquisition spending 1994–95: $338,960.
COMPUTERS ON CAMPUS 135 computers for student use in computer center, labs, library. Staffed computer lab on campus provides training in use of computers, software. Academic computing expenditure 1994–95: $300,000.
COLLEGE LIFE Student-run newspaper. *Student services:* personal-psychological counseling, women's center.
HOUSING College housing not available.
CAREER PLANNING *Placement office:* $15,000 operating expenditure 1994–95. *Service:* career counseling. 50 organizations recruited on campus 1994–95.
AFTER GRADUATION 92% of class of 1994 had job offers within 6 months.
EXPENSES FOR 1996-97 *Application fee:* $25. State resident tuition: $1536 full-time, $51.20 per credit part-time. Nonresident tuition: $11,850 full-time, $395 per credit part-time. Part-time mandatory fees: $2 per credit. Full-time mandatory fees: $60.
FINANCIAL AID *College-administered undergrad aid 1995–96:* 32 need-based scholarships (average $80), low-interest long-term loans from external sources (average $2000), Federal Work-Study. *Required forms:* FAFSA; accepted: CSS Financial Aid PROFILE, state. *Priority deadline:* 4/15. *Payment plan:* deferred payment. *Waivers:* full or partial for senior citizens.
APPLYING Open admission. *Option:* early entrance. *Required:* school transcript. *Application deadline:* rolling. *Notification:* continuous. Preference given to district residents.
APPLYING/TRANSFER *Required:* high school transcript, college transcript. *Entrance:* noncompetitive. *Application deadline:* rolling. *Notification:* continuous.
CONTACT Ms. Barbara Erlandson, Student Development and Recruitment Specialist, Blackhawk Technical College, Janesville, WI 53547-5009, 608-757-7713 or toll-free 800-472-0024 (out-of-state). *Fax:* 608-757-9407.

CHIPPEWA VALLEY TECHNICAL COLLEGE
Eau Claire, Wisconsin

UG Enrollment: 3,800	**Tuition & Fees (WI Res):** $1869
Application Deadline: rolling	**Room & Board:** N/Avail

GENERAL District-supported, 2-year, coed. Part of Wisconsin Technical College System. Awards terminal associate degrees. Founded 1912. *Setting:* 160-acre urban campus. *Total enrollment:* 3,800. *Faculty:* 400 (350 full-time, 50% with terminal degrees, 50 part-time); student-faculty ratio is 9:1.
ENROLLMENT PROFILE 3,800 students from 20 states and territories, 7 other countries. 50% women, 10% part-time, 98% state residents, 10% transferred in, 1% international, 50% 25 or older, 1% Native American, 1% Hispanic, 1% African American, 5% Asian American. *Areas of study chosen:* 15% engineering and applied sciences, 7% architecture, 5% agriculture. *Most popular recent majors:* radiological technology, nursing, laboratory technologies.
FIRST-YEAR CLASS 2,350 total; 4,600 applied, 67% of whom enrolled. 10% from top 10% of their high school class, 15% from top quarter, 25% from top half.
ACADEMIC PROGRAM Core. Calendar: semesters. Academic remediation for entering students, English as a second language program offered during academic year and summer, services for LD students, tutorials, summer session for credit, part-time degree program (daytime), adult/continuing education programs, internships.
GENERAL DEGREE REQUIREMENTS 70 credits; math/science requirements vary according to program; computer course; internship (some majors).
MAJORS Accounting, agricultural business, architectural technologies, automotive technologies, business education, child care/child and family studies, civil engineering technology, computer technologies, construction technologies, culinary arts, dairy sciences, data processing, dental services, drafting and design, electrical and electronics technologies, electromechanical technology, fire science, food services management, food services technology, heating/refrigeration/air conditioning, hospitality services, information science, laboratory technologies, law enforcement/police sciences, legal secretarial studies, machine and tool technologies, marketing/retailing/merchandising, mechanical design technology, mechanical engineering technology, medical laboratory technology, medical records services, medical technology, mental health/rehabilitation counseling, nursing, paralegal studies, quality control technology, radiological technology, real estate, secretarial studies/office management, surveying technology, welding technology.
LIBRARY Technical Resource Center with 40,000 books, 997 periodicals, 2,000 records, tapes, and CDs.
COMPUTERS ON CAMPUS 600 computers for student use in computer center, labs, library.
COLLEGE LIFE Drama-theater group, student-run newspaper. 75% vote in student government elections. *Social organizations:* 30 open to all. *Major annual event:* Winter Carnival. *Student services:* health clinic, personal-psychological counseling. *Campus security:* 24-hour emergency response devices, late-night transport-escort service.
HOUSING College housing not available.
ATHLETICS *Intramural:* basketball, bowling, football, golf, skiing (downhill), softball, table tennis (Ping-Pong), volleyball.
CAREER PLANNING *Placement office:* 1 full-time, 1 part-time staff; $250,000 operating expenditure 1994–95. *Director:* Ms. Jeanne Peterson, Counselor, 715-833-6258. *Services:* job fairs, resume preparation, resume referral, career counseling, careers library, job bank, job interviews.

Wisconsin

AFTER GRADUATION 10% of students completing a degree program in 1994–95 went directly on to further study.
EXPENSES FOR 1996–97 *Application fee:* $25. State resident tuition: $1824 full-time, $52.10 per credit part-time. Nonresident tuition: $13,825 full-time, $395 per credit part-time. Part-time mandatory fees: $1.50 per credit. Full-time mandatory fees: $45.
FINANCIAL AID *College-administered undergrad aid 1995–96:* 1,200 need-based scholarships (average $3000), 14 non-need scholarships (average $200), low-interest long-term loans from external sources (average $1351), Federal Work-Study. *Required forms:* institutional; accepted: CSS Financial Aid PROFILE, FAFSA. *Priority deadline:* 3/15. *Waivers:* full or partial for senior citizens.
APPLYING Open admission except for allied health, nursing programs. *Options:* early entrance, deferred entrance. *Required:* school transcript, TOEFL for international students. *Required for some:* interview. Test scores used for counseling/placement. *Application deadline:* rolling. *Notification:* continuous.
APPLYING/TRANSFER *Required:* high school transcript, college transcript. *Required for some:* interview. *Application deadline:* rolling. *Notification:* continuous. *Contact:* Ms. Jeanne Peterson, Counselor, 715-833-6258.
CONTACT Ms. Linda Benedict, Admissions Manager, Chippewa Valley Technical College, 620 West Clairemont Avenue, Eau Claire, WI 54701-6120, 715-833-6246. *Fax:* 715-833-6470. College video available.

FOX VALLEY TECHNICAL COLLEGE
Appleton, Wisconsin

UG Enrollment: 6,370	Tuition & Fees (WI Res): $2337
Application Deadline: rolling	Room & Board: N/Avail

GENERAL State and locally supported, 2-year, coed. Part of Wisconsin Technical College System. Awards certificates, diplomas, transfer associate, terminal associate degrees. Founded 1967. *Setting:* 100-acre suburban campus. *Total enrollment:* 6,370. *Faculty:* 1,241 (244 full-time, 4% with terminal degrees, 997 part-time).
ENROLLMENT PROFILE 6,370 students from 4 states and territories, 20 other countries. 53% women, 35% part-time, 94% state residents, 30% transferred in, 54% 25 or older, 2% Native American, 2% Hispanic, 2% African American, 1% Asian American. *Most popular recent majors:* marketing/retailing/merchandising, nursing, accounting.
FIRST-YEAR CLASS 2,254 total; 4,400 applied, 100% were accepted, 51% of whom enrolled.
ACADEMIC PROGRAM Core, vocational/technical curriculum. Calendar: semesters. Academic remediation for entering students, English as a second language program offered during academic year and summer, services for LD students, advanced placement, summer session for credit, part-time degree program (daytime, evenings, summer), adult/continuing education programs, co-op programs and internships. Study abroad in Holland.
GENERAL DEGREE REQUIREMENTS 74 credits; math/science requirements vary according to program.
MAJORS Accounting, agricultural business, automotive technologies, child care/child and family studies, computer programming, conservation, criminal justice, culinary arts, drafting and design, electrical and electronics technologies, finance/banking, fire science, fish and game management, flight training, food services management, forest technology, graphic arts, hospitality services, industrial administration, industrial engineering technology, insurance, interior design, law enforcement/police sciences, legal secretarial studies, marketing/retailing/merchandising, mechanical design technology, mechanical engineering technology, nursing, occupational therapy, paper and pulp sciences, printing technologies, retail management, secretarial studies/office management, welding technology, word processing.
COMPUTERS ON CAMPUS Computer purchase plan available. 260 computers for student use in computer center, computer labs, learning resource center, library, student center provide access to main academic computer, off-campus computing services, e-mail, on-line services, Internet. Staffed computer lab on campus.
COLLEGE LIFE Student-run newspaper. *Social organizations:* 26 open to all. *Most popular organizations:* Business Professionals of America, Delta Epsilon Chi, Vocational Industrial Clubs of America. *Student services:* health clinic, personal-psychological counseling, women's center. *Campus security:* late-night transport-escort service, 16-hour patrols by trained security personnel.
HOUSING College housing not available.
ATHLETICS *Intramural:* archery, basketball, bowling, golf, skiing (downhill), tennis, volleyball, weight lifting.
CAREER PLANNING *Placement office:* 7 part-time staff. *Director:* Mr. Bob Burdick, Associate Dean, 414-735-5715. *Services:* job fairs, resume referral, career counseling, careers library, job interviews. Students must register sophomore year.
EXPENSES FOR 1996–97 *Application fee:* $25. State resident tuition: $2087 full-time, $56.40 per credit part-time. Nonresident tuition: $14,807 full-time, $400.20 per credit part-time. Full-time mandatory fees: $250.
FINANCIAL AID *College-administered undergrad aid 1995–96:* need-based scholarships, non-need scholarships, low-interest long-term loans from external sources, Federal Work-Study. *Required forms:* FAFSA. *Application deadline:* continuous to 5/15.
APPLYING Open admission. *Options:* early entrance, deferred entrance, midyear entrance. *Required:* ACT or ACT ASSET. Test scores used for counseling/placement. *Application deadline:* rolling.
APPLYING/TRANSFER *Required:* college transcript. *Required for some:* standardized test scores. *Entrance:* noncompetitive. *Application deadline:* rolling.
CONTACT Dr. Michael Schlies, Associate Dean of Student Services, Fox Valley Technical College, Appleton, WI 54913-2277, 414-735-5713. *Fax:* 414-735-2582.

GATEWAY TECHNICAL COLLEGE
Kenosha, Wisconsin

GENERAL State and locally supported, 2-year, coed. Part of Wisconsin Technical College System. Awards terminal associate degrees. Founded 1911. *Setting:* 10-acre urban campus with easy access to Milwaukee and Chicago. *Research spending 1994–95:* $239,486. *Total enrollment:* 10,568. *Faculty:* 850 (231 full-time, 4% with terminal degrees, 619 part-time); student-faculty ratio is 18:1.
EXPENSES FOR 1995–96 State resident tuition: $1542 full-time, $48.20 per credit part-time. Nonresident tuition: $11,854 full-time, $370.45 per credit part-time. Part-time mandatory fees: $1.50 per credit. Full-time mandatory fees: $48.

CONTACT Mr. Kurt Lehrmann, Registrar, Gateway Technical College, 3520 30th Avenue, Kenosha, WI 53144-1690, 414-656-8972. *Fax:* 414-656-8966. College video available.

HERZING COLLEGE OF TECHNOLOGY
Madison, Wisconsin

UG Enrollment: 350	Tuition & Fees: $7440
Application Deadline: rolling	Room & Board: N/Avail

GENERAL Proprietary, 2-year, primarily men. Part of Herzing Institutes, Inc. Awards transfer associate degrees. Founded 1948. *Setting:* suburban campus with easy access to Milwaukee. *Total enrollment:* 350. *Faculty:* 20 (all full-time); student-faculty ratio is 25:1.
ENROLLMENT PROFILE 350 students from 5 states and territories. 8% women, 0% part-time, 95% state residents, 5% transferred in, 0% international, 33% 25 or older, 2% Native American, 3% Hispanic, 3% African American, 2% Asian American.
FIRST-YEAR CLASS 140 total; 225 applied, 85% were accepted, 65% of whom enrolled. 80% from top half of their high school class.
ACADEMIC PROGRAM Core. Calendar: trimesters.
GENERAL DEGREE REQUIREMENTS 100 credit hours; 10 credit hours of math; computer course.
MAJORS Computer technologies, drafting and design, electrical and electronics technologies.
LIBRARY 1,500 books, 15 periodicals.
COMPUTERS ON CAMPUS 45 computers for student use in computer center provide access to e-mail, Internet.
HOUSING College housing not available.
CAREER PLANNING *Service:* career counseling. 45 organizations recruited on campus 1994–95.
AFTER GRADUATION 90% of class of 1994 had job offers within 6 months. 5% of students completing a degree program went directly on to further study.
EXPENSES FOR 1996–97 Tuition: $7440 full-time. One-time mandatory fee: $150.
FINANCIAL AID *College-administered undergrad aid 1995–96:* need-based scholarships, low-interest long-term loans from external sources (average $2500), Federal Work-Study, part-time jobs. *Required forms:* CSS Financial Aid PROFILE, institutional, FAFSA. *Priority deadline:* 10/13.
APPLYING *Option:* early entrance. *Required:* school transcript, 3 years of high school math. *Application deadline:* rolling. *Notification:* continuous.
APPLYING/TRANSFER *Required:* high school transcript. *Application deadline:* rolling. *Notification:* continuous.
CONTACT Mr. William G. Henry, Admissions Director, Herzing College of Technology, 1227 North Sherman Avenue, Madison, WI 53704-4236, 608-249-6611 or toll-free 800-592-1227. College video available.

ITT TECHNICAL INSTITUTE
Greenfield, Wisconsin

UG Enrollment: 418	Tuition: $15,429/deg prog
Application Deadline: rolling	Room & Board: N/Avail

GENERAL Proprietary, 2-year, coed. Part of ITT Educational Services, Inc. Awards terminal associate degrees. Founded 1968. *Setting:* suburban campus with easy access to Milwaukee. *Total enrollment:* 418. *Faculty:* 15 (all full-time, 41% with terminal degrees); student-faculty ratio is 28:1.
ENROLLMENT PROFILE 418 students.
FIRST-YEAR CLASS 219 total; 414 applied, 32% were accepted, 41% of whom enrolled.
ACADEMIC PROGRAM Honor code. Calendar: quarters.
GENERAL DEGREE REQUIREMENTS 91 credits; 1 math course; computer course.
MAJORS Drafting and design, electrical engineering technology.
LIBRARY 100 books, 9 periodicals.
COMPUTERS ON CAMPUS 5 computers for student use in library provide access to Internet. Staffed computer lab on campus provides training in use of computers, software.
COLLEGE LIFE *Campus security:* 24-hour emergency response devices, local police patrol.
HOUSING College housing not available.
CAREER PLANNING *Placement office:* 2 full-time, 1 part-time staff. *Director:* Ms. Sheri Bauer, Director of Placement, 414-282-9494. *Services:* job fairs, resume preparation, resume referral, career counseling, job interviews. 200 organizations recruited on campus 1994–95.
AFTER GRADUATION 94% of class of 1994 had job offers within 6 months.
EXPENSES FOR 1995–96 *Application fee:* $100. Tuition per degree program ranges from $15,429 to $17,690. Tuition guaranteed not to increase for student's term of enrollment.
FINANCIAL AID *College-administered undergrad aid 1995–96:* need-based scholarships, low-interest long-term loans from external sources, Federal Work-Study, part-time jobs. *Required forms:* CSS Financial Aid PROFILE, FAFSA. *Application deadline:* continuous. *Payment plan:* installment.
APPLYING *Option:* deferred entrance. *Required:* CPAt. Test scores used for admission. *Application deadline:* rolling.
APPLYING/TRANSFER *Entrance:* minimally difficult. *Application deadline:* rolling.
CONTACT Mr. David Harris, Director of Recruitment, ITT Technical Institute, Greenfield, WI 53220-4612, 414-282-9494. College video available.

LAC COURTE OREILLES OJIBWA COMMUNITY COLLEGE
Hayward, Wisconsin

UG Enrollment: 488	Tuition & Fees: $2610
Application Deadline: rolling	Room & Board: N/Avail

GENERAL Federally supported, 2-year, coed. Awards transfer associate, terminal associate degrees. Founded 1982. *Setting:* 2-acre rural campus. *Total enrollment:* 488. *Faculty:* 19 (7 full-time, 12 part-time).

Lac Courte Oreilles Ojibwa Community College (continued)
ENROLLMENT PROFILE 488 students: 66% women, 40% part-time, 100% state residents, 4% transferred in, 0% international, 68% 25 or older, 86% Native American, 0% Hispanic, 0% African American, 0% Asian American.
FIRST-YEAR CLASS 178 total; 178 applied, 100% were accepted, 100% of whom enrolled.
ACADEMIC PROGRAM Calendar: semesters. Academic remediation for entering students, part-time degree program (daytime, evenings, weekends).
GENERAL DEGREE REQUIREMENTS 64 credits; math/science requirements vary according to program; computer course.
MAJORS Business administration/commerce/management, carpentry, computer science, drug and alcohol/substance abuse counseling, mental health/rehabilitation counseling, Native American studies, secretarial studies/office management, teacher aide studies.
LIBRARY 8,000 books, 6,000 microform titles, 60 periodicals, 187 records, tapes, and CDs.
COMPUTERS ON CAMPUS 19 computers for student use in computer center.
HOUSING College housing not available.
ATHLETICS ***Intramural:*** basketball, softball, volleyball.
CAREER PLANNING ***Service:*** career counseling.
EXPENSES FOR 1996–97 Tuition: $2560 full-time, $80 per semester hour part-time. Part-time mandatory fees: $25 per semester. Full-time mandatory fees: $50.
FINANCIAL AID ***College-administered undergrad aid 1995–96:*** 143 need-based scholarships (average $650), Federal Work-Study. ***Required forms:*** institutional; required for some: FAFSA. ***Priority deadline:*** 6/1. ***Payment plan:*** installment. ***Waivers:*** full or partial for senior citizens.
APPLYING Open admission. ***Option:*** early entrance. ***Application deadline:*** rolling.
APPLYING/TRANSFER ***Application deadline:*** rolling.
CONTACT Ms. Ann Marie Penzkover, Registrar, Lac Courte Oreilles Ojibwa Community College, Hayward, WI 54843-9419, 715-634-4790.

LAKESHORE TECHNICAL COLLEGE
Cleveland, Wisconsin

UG Enrollment: 2,400 | **Tuition & Fees (WI Res): $1712**
Application Deadline: rolling | **Room & Board: N/Avail**

GENERAL State and locally supported, 2-year, coed. Part of Wisconsin Technical College System. Awards transfer associate, terminal associate degrees. Founded 1967. ***Setting:*** 160-acre rural campus with easy access to Milwaukee. ***Total enrollment:*** 2,400. ***Faculty:*** 336 (104 full-time, 232 part-time).
ENROLLMENT PROFILE 2,400 students from 12 states and territories. 60% women, 40% men, 70% part-time, 99% state residents, 7% transferred in, 0% international, 55% 25 or older, 0% Native American, 1% Hispanic, 0% African American, 3% Asian American. ***Most popular recent majors:*** marketing/retailing/merchandising, nursing, accounting.
FIRST-YEAR CLASS 1,060 total. Of the students who applied, 90% were accepted. 6% from top 10% of their high school class, 30% from top quarter, 65% from top half.
ACADEMIC PROGRAM Core. Calendar: semesters. Academic remediation for entering students, English as a second language program offered during academic year and summer, services for LD students, summer session for credit, part-time degree program (daytime, evenings, weekends), adult/continuing education programs, co-op programs and internships.
GENERAL DEGREE REQUIREMENTS 65 credits; math competence or 1 math course; internship (some majors).
MAJORS Accounting, agricultural sciences, automotive technologies, child care/child and family studies, computer technologies, court reporting, dairy sciences, data processing, dental services, drafting and design, electrical and electronics technologies, electrical engineering technology, electromechanical technology, emergency medical technology, finance/banking, marketing/retailing/merchandising, mechanical design technology, medical assistant technologies, medical secretarial studies, nursing, optical technologies, paralegal studies, pharmacy/pharmaceutical sciences, printing technologies, radiological technology, secretarial studies/office management, teacher aide studies, welding technology.
LIBRARY 32,000 books, 527 periodicals, 3,551 records, tapes, and CDs.
COMPUTERS ON CAMPUS 275 computers for student use in computer center, computer labs, learning resource center, classrooms, library, student center provide access to main academic computer. Staffed computer lab on campus provides training in use of computers, software.
COLLEGE LIFE ***Student services:*** health clinic, personal-psychological counseling. ***Campus security:*** 24-hour patrols.
HOUSING College housing not available.
ATHLETICS ***Intramural:*** basketball, bowling, volleyball.
CAREER PLANNING ***Service:*** career counseling.
EXPENSES FOR 1996–97 ***Application fee:*** $25. State resident tuition: $1638 full-time, $51.20 per credit part-time. Nonresident tuition: $12,640 full-time, $395 per credit part-time. Part-time mandatory fees: $2.30 per credit. Full-time mandatory fees: $74.
FINANCIAL AID ***College-administered undergrad aid 1995–96:*** 760 need-based scholarships (average $1100), low-interest long-term loans from external sources (average $1979), Federal Work-Study, 20 part-time jobs. ***Required forms:*** FAFSA; required for some: state; accepted: CSS Financial Aid PROFILE. ***Application deadline:*** continuous.
APPLYING Open admission. ***Options:*** early entrance, deferred entrance. ***Required:*** ACT, TOEFL for international students, ACT ASSET. ***Required for some:*** school transcript. Test scores used for counseling/placement. ***Application deadline:*** rolling. ***Notification:*** continuous.
APPLYING/TRANSFER ***Required:*** college transcript. ***Required for some:*** standardized test scores, high school transcript. ***Notification:*** continuous.
CONTACT Ms. Corinne Demler, Enrollment Specialist, Lakeshore Technical College, Cleveland, WI 53015-1414, 414-458-4183 Ext. 112.

MADISON AREA TECHNICAL COLLEGE
Madison, Wisconsin

UG Enrollment: 19,050 | **Tuition & Fees (WI Res): $1700**
Application Deadline: 7/1 | **Room & Board: N/Avail**

GENERAL District-supported, 2-year, coed. Part of Wisconsin Technical College System. Awards certificates, diplomas, transfer associate, terminal associate degrees. Founded 1911. ***Setting:*** 150-acre urban campus. ***Research spending 1994–95:*** $195,238. ***Total enrollment:*** 19,050. ***Faculty:*** 1,881 (393 full-time, 1,488 part-time); student-faculty ratio is 8:1.
ENROLLMENT PROFILE 19,050 students from 9 states and territories, 10 other countries. 56% women, 44% men, 65% part-time, 98% state residents, 10% transferred in, 25% have need-based financial aid, 50% 25 or older, 1% Native American, 2% Hispanic, 3% African American, 2% Asian American. ***Areas of study chosen:*** 31% liberal arts/general studies, 26% business management and administrative services, 13% health professions and related sciences, 9% engineering and applied sciences, 5% computer and information sciences, 4% architecture, 4% fine arts, 3% social sciences, 3% vocational and home economics, 1% interdisciplinary studies. ***Most popular recent majors:*** accounting, nursing, marketing/retailing/merchandising.
FIRST-YEAR CLASS 1,614 total; 7,525 applied, 34% of whom enrolled. 1% from top 10% of their high school class, 31% from top half.
ACADEMIC PROGRAM Core, performance-based curriculum, honor code. Calendar: semesters. Academic remediation for entering students, English as a second language program offered during academic year and summer, services for LD students, tutorials, summer session for credit, part-time degree program (daytime, evenings), adult/continuing education programs, co-op programs and internships. Off-campus study at University of Wisconsin Center–Baraboo/Sauk County.
GENERAL DEGREE REQUIREMENTS 64 credits; internship (some majors).
MAJORS Accounting, agricultural technologies, architectural technologies, automotive technologies, biotechnology, business administration/commerce/management, business education, child care/child and family studies, civil engineering technology, commercial art, communication equipment technology, computer programming, computer technologies, court reporting, culinary arts, data processing, dental services, dietetics, electrical and electronics technologies, emergency medical technology, fashion merchandising, finance/banking, fire science, hospitality services, human services, insurance, interior design, laboratory technologies, law enforcement/police sciences, liberal arts/general studies, marketing/retailing/merchandising, mechanical design technology, medical laboratory technology, medical secretarial studies, nursing, occupational therapy, photography, printing technologies, radiological technology, real estate, recreation and leisure services, respiratory therapy, secretarial studies/office management, tourism and travel, veterinary technology, welding technology, word processing.
LIBRARY Truax-Information Resource Center with 66,000 books, 23 microform titles, 657 periodicals, 30 CD-ROMs, 1,430 records, tapes, and CDs. Acquisition spending 1994–95: $69,808.
COMPUTERS ON CAMPUS 1,250 computers for student use in computer labs, learning resource center, library, student center provide access to main academic computer, e-mail, Internet. Staffed computer lab on campus provides training in use of computers, software. Academic computing expenditure 1994–95: $1.4 million.
COLLEGE LIFE Drama-theater group, choral group, student-run newspaper. ***Social organizations:*** 45 open to all. ***Most popular organizations:*** Marketing Club, Minority Networking Groups, Data Processing Management Association, Student Nurses, Business Professionals of America. ***Major annual events:*** Spring Picnic, Celebrate Diversity Series, Service Learning Activities. ***Student services:*** health clinic, personal-psychological counseling, women's center. ***Campus security:*** 24-hour emergency response devices and patrols, late-night transport-escort service.
HOUSING College housing not available.
ATHLETICS Member NJCAA. ***Intercollegiate:*** basketball M/W, bowling M/W, cross-country running M/W, golf M/W, softball W, tennis M/W, track and field M/W, volleyball M/W, wrestling M. ***Intramural:*** basketball, bowling, softball, tennis, volleyball. ***Contact:*** Mr. John Brenegan, Athletic Director, 608-246-6099.
CAREER PLANNING ***Placement office:*** 1 full-time staff; $1.2 million operating expenditure 1994–95. ***Director:*** Ms. Eugenia Best, Education/Career Information Specialist, 608-246-6454. ***Services:*** job fairs, resume preparation, career counseling. 87 organizations recruited on campus 1994–95.
AFTER GRADUATION 38% of class of 1994 had job offers within 6 months.
EXPENSES FOR 1995–96 State resident tuition: $1700 (minimum) full-time. Nonresident tuition: $11,846 (minimum) full-time. Part-time tuition per credit ranges from $48.20 to $59.65 for state residents, $370.20 to $381.65 for nonresidents. Full-time tuition ranges up to $3000 for state residents, $12,212 for nonresidents, acc ording to program.
FINANCIAL AID ***College-administered undergrad aid 1995–96:*** 3,306 need-based scholarships (average $528), 739 non-need scholarships (average $295), short-term loans, low-interest long-term loans from external sources (average $2317), 138 Federal Work-Study (averaging $1269), 645 part-time jobs. ***Required forms:*** institutional, FAFSA. ***Priority deadline:*** 4/15. ***Payment plan:*** deferred payment.
APPLYING Open admission except for data processing, technology, health occupations, quota programs. ***Options:*** early entrance, midyear entrance. ***Required for some:*** school transcript, ACT. Test scores used for admission. ***Application deadline:*** 7/1. ***Notification:*** continuous. Preference given to state residents.
APPLYING/TRANSFER ***Application deadline:*** 7/1. ***Notification:*** continuous. ***Contact:*** Ms. Maureen Menendez, Interim Admissions Administrator, 608-246-6212.
CONTACT Ms. Maureen Menendez, Interim Admissions Administrator, Madison Area Technical College, 3550 Anderson Street, Madison, WI 53704-2599, 608-246-6212. College video available.

MADISON JUNIOR COLLEGE OF BUSINESS
Madison, Wisconsin

UG Enrollment: 99 | **Tuition & Fees: $5940**
Application Deadline: rolling | **Room & Board: N/Avail**

GENERAL Independent, 2-year, coed. Awards certificates, diplomas, terminal associate degrees. Founded 1856. ***Setting:*** urban campus. ***Total enrollment:*** 99. ***Faculty:*** 11 (4 full-time, 7 part-time); student-faculty ratio is 14:1.
ENROLLMENT PROFILE 99 students from 5 states and territories, 2 other countries. 78% women, 22% men, 31% part-time, 92% state residents, 30% transferred in, 2% international, 28% 25 or older, 0% Native American, 0% Hispanic, 0% African American, 0% Asian American. ***Areas of study chosen:*** 100% business management and administrative services. ***Most popular recent majors:*** business administration/commerce/management, secretarial studies/office management, accounting.

FIRST-YEAR CLASS 37 total; 71 applied, 99% were accepted, 53% of whom enrolled.
ACADEMIC PROGRAM Core, business curriculum, honor code. Calendar: trimesters. 47 courses offered in 1995–96. Summer session for credit, part-time degree program (daytime, evenings, summer).
GENERAL DEGREE REQUIREMENTS 63 credits; 1 business math course; computer course.
MAJORS Accounting, business administration/commerce/management, computer programming, legal secretarial studies, marketing/retailing/merchandising, medical secretarial studies, secretarial studies/office management.
LIBRARY 10,158 books, 177 periodicals, 410 records, tapes, and CDs. Acquisition spending 1994–95: $8829.
COMPUTERS ON CAMPUS 33 computers for student use in computer center, classrooms, library. Staffed computer lab on campus provides training in use of computers, software.
COLLEGE LIFE ***Campus security:*** 24-hour emergency response devices.
HOUSING College housing not available.
CAREER PLANNING ***Placement office:*** 1 full-time staff; $32,214 operating expenditure 1994–95. ***Director:*** Ms. Eunice M. Aye, Employment Director, 608-251-6522. ***Services:*** resume preparation, resume referral, career counseling, careers library. Students must register sophomore year.
AFTER GRADUATION 88% of class of 1994 had job offers within 6 months.
EXPENSES FOR 1995–96 ***Application fee:*** $25. Tuition: $5940 full-time, $198 per credit part-time.
FINANCIAL AID ***College-administered undergrad aid 1995–96:*** 53 need-based scholarships (averaging $358), 3 non-need scholarships (averaging $60), low-interest long-term loans from external sources (averaging $3063), part-time jobs. ***Required forms:*** institutional, FAFSA; accepted: CSS Financial Aid PROFILE. ***Application deadline:*** continuous. ***Waivers:*** full or partial for employees or children of employees.
APPLYING Open admission. ***Options:*** deferred entrance, midyear entrance. ***Required:*** school transcript. ***Recommended:*** SAT I or ACT, TOEFL for international students. Test scores used for admission. ***Application deadline:*** rolling. ***Notification:*** continuous.
APPLYING/TRANSFER ***Required:*** high school transcript, college transcript. ***Recommended:*** standardized test scores. ***Entrance:*** noncompetitive. ***Application deadline:*** rolling. ***Notification:*** continuous.
CONTACT Mrs. M. Jeanne Sears, Director of Admissions/Registrar, Madison Junior College of Business, 31 South Henry Street, Madison, WI 53703-3110, 608-251-6522 or toll-free 800-365-5343 (in-state). ***Fax:*** 608-251-6590. ***E-mail:*** madjrcoll@aol.com.

❖ *See page 760 for a narrative description.* ❖

MID-STATE TECHNICAL COLLEGE
Wisconsin Rapids, Wisconsin

UG Enrollment: 3,104	**Tuition & Fees (WI Res): $1718**
Application Deadline: rolling	**Room & Board: N/Avail**

GENERAL State and locally supported, 2-year, coed. Part of Wisconsin Technical College System. Awards diplomas, terminal associate degrees. Founded 1917. ***Setting:*** 155-acre small-town campus. ***Research spending 1994–95:*** $127,090. ***Total enrollment:*** 3,104. ***Faculty:*** 86 (74 full-time, 1% with terminal degrees, 12 part-time); student-faculty ratio is 19:1.
ENROLLMENT PROFILE 3,104 students: 60% women, 64% part-time, 99% state residents, 2% transferred in, 0% international, 51% 25 or older, 1% Native American, 1% Hispanic, 1% African American, 1% Asian American. ***Most popular recent majors:*** accounting, data processing, electrical and electronics technologies.
FIRST-YEAR CLASS 743 total; 1,000 applied, 92% of whom enrolled.
ACADEMIC PROGRAM Core. Calendar: semesters. Academic remediation for entering students, English as a second language program offered during academic year and summer, services for LD students, summer session for credit, part-time degree program (daytime, evenings, summer), adult/continuing education programs, co-op programs.
GENERAL DEGREE REQUIREMENTS 64 credits; computer course for business, technology majors.
MAJORS Accounting, business administration/commerce/management, civil engineering technology, computer technologies, corrections, data processing, drafting and design, electrical and electronics technologies, electronics engineering technology, hotel and restaurant management, instrumentation technology, labor and industrial relations, law enforcement/police sciences, manufacturing technology, marketing/retailing/merchandising, mechanical design technology, nursing, quality control technology, respiratory therapy, retail management, secretarial studies/office management, surveying technology.
LIBRARY Mid-State Technical College Library with 17,412 books, 76 microform titles, 435 periodicals, 10 CD-ROMs, 2,656 records, tapes, and CDs. Acquisition spending 1994–95: $37,270.
COMPUTERS ON CAMPUS 120 computers for student use in computer center, classrooms. Staffed computer lab on campus provides training in use of computers, software. Academic computing expenditure 1994–95: $89,498.
COLLEGE LIFE Student-run newspaper. ***Student services:*** health clinic, personal-psychological counseling, women's center.
HOUSING College housing not available.
ATHLETICS Member NJCAA. ***Intercollegiate:*** basketball M(s), bowling M/W, golf M(s), volleyball W(s). ***Intramural:*** basketball, bowling, football, golf, racquetball, skiing (cross-country), skiing (downhill), table tennis (Ping-Pong), volleyball. ***Contact:*** Mr. Mark Wagner, Athletic Director, 715-422-5430.
CAREER PLANNING ***Placement office:*** 2 full-time staff; $209,535 operating expenditure 1994–95. ***Director:*** Ms. Dana Catalonga, Vocational Evaluator, 715-422-5455. ***Services:*** job fairs, resume preparation, resume referral, career counseling, careers library, job interviews.
EXPENSES FOR 1996–97 ***Application fee:*** $25. State resident tuition: $1638 full-time, $51.20 per credit part-time. Nonresident tuition: $12,640 full-time, $395 per credit part-time. Part-time mandatory fees: $2.50 per credit. Full-time mandatory fees: $80.
FINANCIAL AID ***College-administered undergrad aid 1995–96:*** 298 need-based scholarships (average $200), 103 non-need scholarships (average $531), low-interest long-term loans from external sources (average $1500), 158 Federal Work-Study (averaging $340), 91 part-time jobs. ***Required forms:*** institutional, FAFSA. ***Priority deadline:*** 6/1. ***Payment plan:*** installment. ***Waivers:*** full or partial for senior citizens.
APPLYING Open admission. ***Options:*** early entrance, deferred entrance. ***Required:*** school transcript, TOEFL for international students, ACT ASSET. ***Recommended:*** SAT I or ACT. Test scores used for counseling/placement. ***Application deadline:*** rolling. ***Notification:*** continuous.
APPLYING/TRANSFER ***Required:*** standardized test scores, high school transcript, college transcript. ***Application deadline:*** rolling. ***Notification:*** continuous. ***Contact:*** Ms. Carole Prochnow, Admissions Assistant, 715-422-5444.
CONTACT Ms. Carole Prochnow, Admissions Assistant, Mid-State Technical College, Wisconsin Rapids, WI 54494-5599, 715-422-5444.

MILWAUKEE AREA TECHNICAL COLLEGE
Milwaukee, Wisconsin

UG Enrollment: 23,099	**Tuition & Fees (WI Res): $1158**
Application Deadline: rolling	**Room & Board: N/Avail**

GENERAL District-supported, 2-year, coed. Part of Wisconsin Technical College System. Awards certificates, diplomas, transfer associate, terminal associate degrees. Founded 1912. ***Setting:*** urban campus. ***Total enrollment:*** 23,099. ***Faculty:*** 1,759 (603 full-time, 100% with terminal degrees, 1,156 part-time).
ENROLLMENT PROFILE 23,099 students from 8 states and territories. 56% women, 74% part-time, 98% state residents, 4% transferred in, 1% international, 61% 25 or older, 1% Native American, 4% Hispanic, 19% African American, 2% Asian American. ***Most popular recent majors:*** liberal arts/general studies, human services, nursing.
FIRST-YEAR CLASS 15,000 applied, 100% were accepted, 33% of whom enrolled.
ACADEMIC PROGRAM Core, honor code. Calendar: semesters. 500 courses offered in 1995–96. Academic remediation for entering students, English as a second language program offered during academic year and summer, services for LD students, advanced placement, honors program, summer session for credit, part-time degree program (daytime, evenings), adult/continuing education programs, co-op programs and internships.
GENERAL DEGREE REQUIREMENTS 64 credits; math/science requirements vary according to program; computer course for business majors; internship (some majors).
MAJORS Accounting, agricultural business, automotive technologies, biomedical technologies, broadcasting, business administration/commerce/management, chemical engineering technology, child care/child and family studies, civil engineering technology, commercial art, communication equipment technology, computer information systems, computer programming, computer science, construction technologies, criminal justice, culinary arts, data processing, dental services, dietetics, drafting and design, drug and alcohol/substance abuse counseling, ecology, educational media, electrical and electronics technologies, electrical engineering technology, electromechanical technology, (pre)engineering sequence, environmental health sciences, fashion merchandising, film studies, finance/banking, fire science, food services technology, funeral service, heating/refrigeration/air conditioning, hotel and restaurant management, human services, industrial design, industrial engineering technology, landscaping/grounds maintenance, law enforcement/police sciences, legal secretarial studies, liberal arts/general studies, marketing/retailing/merchandising, mechanical engineering technology, medical laboratory technology, medical secretarial studies, music, nursing, occupational therapy, paralegal studies, photography, physical therapy, pollution control technologies, printing technologies, publishing, radio and television studies, radiological technology, real estate, respiratory therapy, retail management, secretarial studies/office management, surveying technology, transportation technologies, water resources, welding technology.
LIBRARY 65,000 books, 878 periodicals, 300 records, tapes, and CDs.
COMPUTERS ON CAMPUS 1,000 computers for student use in labs, classrooms. Staffed computer lab on campus (open 24 hours a day) provides training in use of computers, software.
COLLEGE LIFE 50% vote in student government elections. ***Student services:*** legal services, personal-psychological counseling, women's center. ***Campus security:*** 24-hour emergency response devices and patrols, student patrols, late-night transport-escort service.
HOUSING College housing not available.
ATHLETICS Member NJCAA. ***Intercollegiate:*** baseball M/W, basketball M/W, bowling M/W, cross-country running M/W, golf M, soccer M, softball M/W, tennis M/W, track and field M/W, volleyball W. ***Intramural:*** badminton, baseball, basketball, bowling, soccer, table tennis (Ping-Pong), tennis, volleyball.
CAREER PLANNING ***Director:*** Ms. Theresa Feldmeier, Manager of Career Planning and Assessment, 414-297-6248. ***Services:*** job fairs, resume preparation, career counseling, careers library, job bank, job interviews.
EXPENSES FOR 1995–96 ***Application fee:*** $25. State resident tuition: $1106 full-time, $46.10 per credit part-time. Nonresident tuition: $8504 full-time, $354.35 per credit part-time. Part-time mandatory fees: $2.15 per credit. Full-time mandatory fees: $52.
FINANCIAL AID ***College-administered undergrad aid 1995–96:*** 504 need-based scholarships (averaging $530), 133 non-need scholarships (averaging $349), short-term loans (averaging $214), low-interest long-term loans from external sources (averaging $1446), Federal Work-Study, 1,188 part-time jobs. ***Required forms:*** institutional, FAFSA, financial aid transcript (for transfers). ***Priority deadline:*** 3/15.
APPLYING Open admission for students satisfying minimum degree requirements (students not meeting these requirements are placed in pre-program curricula). ***Required:*** school transcript, ACT ASSET. ***Recommended:*** essay. ***Required for some:*** TOEFL for international students. Test scores used for counseling/placement. ***Application deadline:*** rolling. ***Notification:*** continuous until 8/20. Preference given to district residents.
APPLYING/TRANSFER ***Required:*** college transcript, minimum 2.0 college GPA. ***Required for some:*** standardized test scores, high school transcript. ***Application deadline:*** rolling. ***Notification:*** continuous until 8/20. ***Contact:*** Dr. Pablo Cardona, Director of Admissions, 414-297-7001.
CONTACT Dr. Pablo Cardona, Director of Admissions, Milwaukee Area Technical College, 700 West State Street, Milwaukee, WI 53233-1443, 414-297-7001. ***Fax:*** 414-271-2195.

MORAINE PARK TECHNICAL COLLEGE
Fond du Lac, Wisconsin

UG Enrollment: 6,670	**Tuition & Fees (WI Res): $1948**
Application Deadline: N/R	**Room & Board: N/Avail**

Moraine Park Technical College (continued)

GENERAL State and locally supported, 2-year, coed. Part of Wisconsin Technical College System. Awards transfer associate, terminal associate degrees. Founded 1967. ***Setting:*** 40-acre small-town campus with easy access to Milwaukee. ***Endowment:*** $15,500. ***Research spending 1994–95:*** $61,836. ***Total enrollment:*** 6,670. ***Faculty:*** 298 (148 full-time, 150 part-time); student-faculty ratio is 19:1.

ENROLLMENT PROFILE 6,670 students: 57% women, 83% part-time, 99% state residents, 1% transferred in, 0% international, 57% 25 or older, 1% Native American, 1% Hispanic, 1% African American, 1% Asian American. ***Areas of study chosen:*** 38% business management and administrative services, 21% vocational and home economics, 19% health professions and related sciences, 14% engineering and applied sciences, 4% agriculture, 3% computer and information sciences, 1% architecture.

FIRST-YEAR CLASS 833 total; 1,200 applied, 100% were accepted, 69% of whom enrolled.

ACADEMIC PROGRAM Core. Calendar: semesters. Academic remediation for entering students, English as a second language program offered during academic year and summer, services for LD students, advanced placement, summer session for credit, part-time degree program (daytime, evenings, weekends, summer), external degree programs, adult/continuing education programs.

GENERAL DEGREE REQUIREMENTS 68 credits; computer course for most majors; internship (some majors).

MAJORS Accounting, agricultural sciences, automotive technologies, civil engineering technology, computer programming, computer technologies, corrections, data processing, drafting and design, electromechanical technology, emergency medical technology, food sciences, graphic arts, hotel and restaurant management, industrial engineering technology, machine and tool technologies, mechanical design technology, medical records services, medical secretarial studies, nursing, secretarial studies/office management, water resources.

LIBRARY Moraine Park Technical College Library/Learning Resource Center with 25,500 books, 547 microform titles, 600 periodicals, 6 CD-ROMs, 4,000 records, tapes, and CDs. Acquisition spending 1994–95: $82,716.

COMPUTERS ON CAMPUS Computers for student use in lab. Academic computing expenditure 1994–95: $694,303.

COLLEGE LIFE ***Social organizations:*** 24 open to all. ***Most popular organizations:*** SMAC, Student Government, Cosmetology Association, Water Quality Association, Food Service Executives. ***Student services:*** personal-psychological counseling, women's center. ***Campus security:*** 24-hour emergency response devices, late-night transport-escort service.

HOUSING College housing not available.

ATHLETICS ***Intramural:*** bowling, golf, volleyball. ***Contact:*** Mr. Glenn Sanville, Manager of Student Life/Athletic Director, 414-924-3103.

CAREER PLANNING ***Director:*** Ms. Mary Cody, Career Center Director, 414-924-3244. ***Services:*** job fairs, resume preparation, resume referral, career counseling, careers library, job interviews. Students must register sophomore year.

AFTER GRADUATION 96% of class of 1994 had job offers within 6 months.

EXPENSES FOR 1996–97 ***Application fee:*** $25. State resident tuition: $1948 full-time, $57.30 per credit part-time. Nonresident tuition: $13,637 full-time, $401.10 per credit part-time.

FINANCIAL AID ***College-administered undergrad aid 1995–96:*** 521 need-based scholarships (average $697), 93 non-need scholarships (average $568), low-interest long-term loans from external sources (average $2211), 50 Federal Work-Study (averaging $1407), 72 part-time jobs. ***Required forms:*** institutional, FAFSA, state income tax form; accepted: CSS Financial Aid PROFILE, state. ***Priority deadline:*** 5/1.

APPLYING Open admission except for nursing program. ***Options:*** early entrance, deferred entrance. ***Required:*** school transcript, ACT ASSET. ***Recommended:*** TOEFL for international students. Test scores used for counseling/placement. ***Notification:*** continuous.

APPLYING/TRANSFER ***Required:*** standardized test scores, high school transcript, college transcript. ***Entrance:*** noncompetitive. ***Application deadline:*** rolling. ***Notification:*** continuous.

CONTACT Mr. Lawrence Pasquini, Dean of Student Services, Moraine Park Technical College, Fond du Lac, WI 54936-1940, 414-924-3193. College video available.

NICOLET AREA TECHNICAL COLLEGE
Rhinelander, Wisconsin

UG Enrollment: 1,433 — **Tuition & Fees (WI Res): $1909**
Application Deadline: rolling — **Room & Board: N/Avail**

GENERAL State and locally supported, 2-year, coed. Part of Wisconsin Technical College System. Awards certificates, diplomas, transfer associate, terminal associate degrees. Founded 1968. ***Setting:*** 280-acre rural campus. ***Total enrollment:*** 1,433. ***Faculty:*** 84 (65 full-time, 19 part-time).

ENROLLMENT PROFILE 1,433 students from 3 states and territories. 68% women, 64% part-time, 99% state residents, 10% transferred in, 0% international, 64% 25 or older, 4% Native American, 1% Hispanic, 1% African American, 0% Asian American. ***Areas of study chosen:*** 30% liberal arts/general studies, 15% business management and administrative services, 9% health professions and related sciences, 4% computer and information sciences. ***Most popular recent majors:*** liberal arts/general studies, accounting, law enforcement/police sciences.

FIRST-YEAR CLASS 560 total; 830 applied, 90% were accepted, 75% of whom enrolled.

ACADEMIC PROGRAM Core. Calendar: semesters. Average class size 30 in required courses. Academic remediation for entering students, English as a second language program offered during academic year, services for LD students, advanced placement, summer session for credit, part-time degree program (daytime, evenings, summer), adult/continuing education programs, co-op programs.

GENERAL DEGREE REQUIREMENTS 64 credits; math/science requirements vary accor; computer course.

MAJORS Accounting, automotive technologies, business administration/commerce/management, child care/child and family studies, computer science, culinary arts, data processing, early childhood education, emergency medical technology, food services management, hotel and restaurant management, information science, law enforcement/police sciences, legal secretarial studies, liberal arts/general studies, machine and tool technologies, marketing/retailing/merchandising, medical secretarial studies, nursing, real estate, secretarial studies/office management, surveying technology.

LIBRARY Richard Brown Library with 38,369 books, 10,822 microform titles, 598 periodicals, 6,813 records, tapes, and CDs.

COMPUTERS ON CAMPUS 50 computers for student use in computer center, classrooms, library provide access to on-line services. Staffed computer lab on campus.

COLLEGE LIFE Drama-theater group, student-run newspaper. ***Student services:*** personal-psychological counseling, women's center.

HOUSING College housing not available.

ATHLETICS Member NJCAA. ***Intramural:*** golf, volleyball.

CAREER PLANNING ***Placement office:*** 1 full-time staff. ***Director:*** Mr. John Seefeld, 715-365-4477. ***Services:*** resume preparation, resume referral, career counseling, careers library. 85 organizations recruited on campus 1994–95.

AFTER GRADUATION 80% of class of 1994 had job offers within 6 months.

EXPENSES FOR 1996–97 ***Application fee:*** $25. State resident tuition: $1909 full-time, $59.65 per credit hour part-time. Nonresident tuition: $6546 full-time, $204.55 per credit hour part-time.

FINANCIAL AID ***College-administered undergrad aid 1995–96:*** need-based scholarships, 112 non-need scholarships (averaging $250), short-term loans (averaging $50), low-interest long-term loans from external sources (averaging $2500), Federal Work-Study. ***Acceptable forms:*** institutional, FAFSA. ***Priority deadline:*** 4/1.

APPLYING Open admission except for nursing program. ***Option:*** early entrance. ***Required:*** school transcript, minimum 2.0 GPA, ACT ASSET, SAT I, or ACT. Test scores used for counseling/placement. ***Application deadline:*** rolling. ***Notification:*** continuous. Preference given to district residents.

APPLYING/TRANSFER ***Required:*** standardized test scores, high school transcript, college transcript, minimum 2.0 high school GPA. ***Entrance:*** noncompetitive. ***Application deadline:*** rolling. ***Notification:*** continuous.

CONTACT Ms. Susan Kordula, Director of Admissions, Nicolet Area Technical College, Rhinelander, WI 54501-0518, 715-365-4451 or toll-free 800-544-3069 (in-state). ***Fax:*** 715-365-4445.

NORTHCENTRAL TECHNICAL COLLEGE
Wausau, Wisconsin

UG Enrollment: 3,500 — **Tuition & Fees (WI Res): $1616**
Application Deadline: rolling — **Room & Board: N/Avail**

GENERAL District-supported, 2-year, coed. Part of Wisconsin Technical College System. Awards transfer associate, terminal associate degrees. Founded 1912. ***Setting:*** 96-acre small-town campus. ***Total enrollment:*** 3,500. ***Faculty:*** 211 (150 full-time, 61 part-time).

ENROLLMENT PROFILE 3,500 students from 3 states and territories, 4 other countries. 58% women, 42% men, 67% part-time, 98% state residents, 69% transferred in, 55% 25 or older, 1% Native American, 1% Hispanic, 1% African American, 6% Asian American.

FIRST-YEAR CLASS 1,600 applied, 99% were accepted, 54% of whom enrolled.

ACADEMIC PROGRAM Calendar: semesters. Academic remediation for entering students, English as a second language program offered during academic year, services for LD students, summer session for credit, part-time degree program (daytime), adult/continuing education programs, internships.

GENERAL DEGREE REQUIREMENTS 64 credits; computer course for business majors; internship (some majors).

MAJORS Accounting, agricultural technologies, architectural technologies, automotive technologies, business administration/commerce/management, computer information systems, deaf interpreter training, dental services, drafting and design, electrical and electronics technologies, electromechanical technology, industrial engineering technology, laser technologies, law enforcement/police sciences, legal secretarial studies, machine and tool technologies, marketing/retailing/merchandising, mechanical design technology, medical secretarial studies, nursing, operating room technology, printing technologies, radiological technology, secretarial studies/office management, welding technology.

LIBRARY 38,000 books, 200 microform titles, 350 periodicals, 15,000 records, tapes, and CDs.

COMPUTERS ON CAMPUS 80 computers for student use in computer center, labs, library provide access to main academic computer, on-line services, Internet. Staffed computer lab on campus provides training in use of computers, software.

COLLEGE LIFE Student-run newspaper. ***Social organizations:*** 3 open to all. ***Major annual events:*** Sno-Fest (Winter Carnival), Career Week Events, Spring Fling. ***Student services:*** health clinic, personal-psychological counseling, women's center.

HOUSING College housing not available.

ATHLETICS ***Intramural:*** badminton, basketball, bowling, football, golf, racquetball, softball, table tennis (Ping-Pong), tennis, volleyball.

CAREER PLANNING ***Placement office:*** 3 full-time, 4 part-time staff. ***Director:*** Ms. Sharon Snyder, Associate Dean, Learning Center, 715-675-3331. ***Services:*** resume preparation, career counseling, careers library. 24 organizations recruited on campus 1994–95.

EXPENSES FOR 1996–97 ***Application fee:*** $25. State resident tuition: $1536 full-time, $51.20 per credit part-time. Nonresident tuition: $11,850 full-time, $395 per credit part-time. Part-time mandatory fees: $2.65 per credit. Full-time mandatory fees: $80.

FINANCIAL AID ***College-administered undergrad aid 1995–96:*** 1,800 need-based scholarships (average $1100), 100 non-need scholarships (average $250), low-interest long-term loans from external sources (average $1900), 210 Federal Work-Study (averaging $1500). ***Required forms:*** institutional; accepted: CSS Financial Aid PROFILE. ***Priority deadline:*** 6/1. ***Payment plan:*** deferred payment.

APPLYING Open admission except for technical nursing, dental hygiene programs. ***Options:*** early entrance, deferred entrance. ***Required:*** school transcript. ***Required for some:*** campus interview, Accuplacer. Test scores used for counseling/placement. ***Application deadline:*** rolling. ***Notification:*** continuous. Preference given to district residents.

APPLYING/TRANSFER ***Required:*** high school transcript, college transcript. ***Required for some:*** campus interview. ***Entrance:*** noncompetitive. ***Application deadline:*** rolling. ***Notification:*** continuous. ***Contact:*** Ms. Lois Wyland, Administrative Assistant, 715-675-3331 Ext. 4014.

CONTACT Mr. Tom Goltz, Dean of Student Services, Northcentral Technical College, Wausau, WI 54401-1880, 715-675-3331 Ext. 4013.

NORTHEAST WISCONSIN TECHNICAL COLLEGE
Green Bay, Wisconsin

GENERAL State and locally supported, 2-year, coed. Part of Wisconsin Technical College System. Awards certificates, diplomas, terminal associate degrees. Founded 1913. ***Setting:*** urban campus. ***Total enrollment:*** 8,594. ***Faculty:*** 310 (235 full-time, 75 part-time).
EXPENSES FOR 1995–96 ***Application fee:*** $10. State resident tuition: $1446 full-time, $48.20 per credit part-time. Nonresident tuition: $11,114 full-time, $370.45 per credit part-time. Part-time mandatory fees: $5.15 per credit. Full-time mandatory fees: $155.
CONTACT Mr. Henry A. Wallace Jr., Dean of Student and Protective Services, Northeast Wisconsin Technical College, 2740 W Mason Street, PO Box 19042, Green Bay, WI 54307-9042, 414-498-5544.

SOUTHWEST WISCONSIN TECHNICAL COLLEGE
Fennimore, Wisconsin

UG Enrollment: 3,870	**Tuition & Fees (WI Res): $1787**
Application Deadline: rolling	**Room & Board: N/Avail**

GENERAL State and locally supported, 2-year, coed. Part of Wisconsin Technical College System. Awards certificates, diplomas, terminal associate degrees. Founded 1967. ***Setting:*** 53-acre rural campus. ***Endowment:*** $205,655. ***Research spending 1994–95:*** $99,064. ***Total enrollment:*** 3,870. ***Faculty:*** 101 (80 full-time, 100% with terminal degrees, 21 part-time).
ENROLLMENT PROFILE 3,870 students from 4 states and territories, 1 other country. 58% women, 42% men, 79% part-time, 98% state residents, 10% transferred in, 70% have need-based financial aid, 4% have non-need-based financial aid, 54% 25 or older, 1% Native American, 1% Hispanic, 1% African American, 1% Asian American. ***Areas of study chosen:*** 29% engineering and applied sciences, 27% business management and administrative services, 26% health professions and related sciences, 11% vocational and home economics, 7% agriculture. ***Most popular recent majors:*** nursing, electromechanical technology, accounting.
FIRST-YEAR CLASS 637 total; 782 applied, 100% were accepted, 70% of whom enrolled. 5% from top 10% of their high school class, 25% from top quarter, 60% from top half.
ACADEMIC PROGRAM Technical curriculum, honor code. Calendar: semesters. 450 courses offered in 1995–96. Academic remediation for entering students, English as a second language program offered during academic year and summer, services for LD students, advanced placement, summer session for credit, part-time degree program (daytime), adult/continuing education programs, internships.
GENERAL DEGREE REQUIREMENTS 64 credits; computer course for most majors; internship (some majors).
MAJORS Accounting, agricultural sciences, agricultural technologies, automotive technologies, child care/child and family studies, computer management, computer programming, cosmetology, dairy sciences, data processing, drafting and design, electrical and electronics technologies, electromechanical technology, finance/banking, food services technology, legal secretarial studies, machine and tool technologies, marketing/retailing/merchandising, mechanical design technology, nursing, practical nursing, secretarial studies/office management, welding technology, word processing.
LIBRARY Southwest Technical College Library plus 1 other, with 25,000 books, 5,500 microform titles, 307 periodicals, 2 on-line bibliographic services, 75 CD-ROMs, 4,300 records, tapes, and CDs. Acquisition spending 1994–95: $42,067.
COMPUTERS ON CAMPUS 187 computers for student use in computer center, labs, classrooms, library. Staffed computer lab on campus provides training in use of computers, software. Academic computing expenditure 1994–95: $201,955.
COLLEGE LIFE Student-run newspaper. ***Social organizations:*** 8 open to all. ***Most popular organizations:*** Business Professionals of America, Vocational Industrial Clubs of America, Health Occupations Students of America, Marketing and Management Association, Post-Secondary Agricultural Students. ***Student services:*** health clinic, personal-psychological counseling, women's center.
HOUSING College housing not available.
ATHLETICS ***Intramural:*** basketball, bowling, softball, volleyball.
CAREER PLANNING ***Placement office:*** 1 full-time, 2 part-time staff; $81,015 operating expenditure 1994–95. ***Director:*** Ms. Sheila Marten, Job Center Specialist, 608-822-3262 Ext. 2335. ***Services:*** resume preparation, resume referral, career counseling, careers library, job bank, job interviews.
AFTER GRADUATION 94% of class of 1994 had job offers within 6 months.
EXPENSES FOR 1996–97 ***Application fee:*** $25. State resident tuition: $1638 full-time, $51.20 per credit part-time. Nonresident tuition: $12,640 full-time, $395 per credit part-time. Part-time mandatory fees: $4.65 per credit. Full-time mandatory fees: $149.
FINANCIAL AID ***College-administered undergrad aid 1995–96:*** 659 need-based scholarships (averaging $1984), 34 non-need scholarships (averaging $359), short-term loans (averaging $85), 89 Federal Work-Study (averaging $961), 5 part-time jobs. ***Required forms:*** institutional; accepted: CSS Financial Aid PROFILE, FAFSA. ***Priority deadline:*** 4/15. ***Payment plans:*** installment, deferred payment.
APPLYING Open admission except for nursing program. ***Options:*** early entrance, midyear entrance. ***Required:*** school transcript, TABE. Test scores used for counseling/placement. ***Application deadline:*** rolling. Preference given to district residents.
APPLYING/TRANSFER ***Required:*** high school transcript, college transcript, minimum 2.0 college GPA. ***Required for some:*** standardized test scores.
CONTACT Ms. Kathy Kreul, Admissions, Southwest Wisconsin Technical College, Fennimore, WI 53809-9778, 608-822-3262 Ext. 2355 or toll-free 800-362-3322 (in-state). ***Fax:*** 608-822-6019.

STRATTON COLLEGE
Milwaukee, Wisconsin

UG Enrollment: 754	**Tuition & Fees: $6720**
Application Deadline: rolling	**Room & Board: N/Avail**

GENERAL Proprietary, 2-year, coed. Part of Bryant and Stratton Business Institute, Inc. Awards diplomas, transfer associate degrees. Founded 1863. ***Setting:*** 2-acre urban campus. ***Educational spending 1994–95:*** $1015 per undergrad. ***Total enrollment:*** 754. ***Faculty:*** 53 (8 full-time, 100% with terminal degrees, 45 part-time); student-faculty ratio is 18:1.
ENROLLMENT PROFILE 754 students from 2 states and territories, 3 other countries. 82% women, 42% part-time, 98% state residents, 6% transferred in, 1% international, 41% 25 or older, 4% Hispanic, 63% African American, 2% Asian American. ***Most popular recent majors:*** medical assistant technologies, accounting, business administration/commerce/management.
FIRST-YEAR CLASS 233 total; 291 applied, 92% were accepted, 87% of whom enrolled. 2% from top 10% of their high school class, 10% from top quarter, 70% from top half.
ACADEMIC PROGRAM Core, vocational curriculum, honor code. Calendar: quarters. 108 courses offered in 1995–96; average class size 20 in required courses. Academic remediation for entering students, advanced placement, summer session for credit, part-time degree program (daytime, evenings), adult/continuing education programs, internships.
GENERAL DEGREE REQUIREMENTS 92 quarter hours; 1 math course; computer course; internship (some majors).
MAJORS Accounting, business administration/commerce/management, computer programming, computer technologies, data processing, hotel and restaurant management, legal secretarial studies, marketing/retailing/merchandising, medical assistant technologies, medical secretarial studies, secretarial studies/office management, tourism and travel, word processing.
LIBRARY Stratton College Library with 7,000 books, 105 periodicals, 6 CD-ROMs, 225 records, tapes, and CDs. Acquisition spending 1994–95: $2500.
COMPUTERS ON CAMPUS 129 computers for student use in computer center, computer labs, classrooms, library. Staffed computer lab on campus provides training in use of computers, software. Academic computing expenditure 1994–95: $135,000.
COLLEGE LIFE Choral group. ***Social organizations:*** 8 open to all. ***Major annual events:*** Professional Day, Career Fair, All School Picnic. ***Student services:*** personal-psychological counseling. ***Campus security:*** 24-hour emergency response devices, patrols by trained security personnel.
HOUSING College housing not available.
CAREER PLANNING ***Placement office:*** 2 full-time, 1 part-time staff; $51,525 operating expenditure 1994–95. ***Director:*** Ms. Diane Kavalauskas, Director of Career Placement Services, 414-276-5200. ***Services:*** job fairs, resume preparation, resume referral, career counseling, careers library, job bank, job interviews. Students must register sophomore year. 30 organizations recruited on campus 1994–95.
AFTER GRADUATION 87% of class of 1994 had job offers within 6 months. 2% of students completing a degree program went directly on to further study.
EXPENSES FOR 1996–97 ***Application fee:*** $30. Tuition: $6720 full-time, $140 per quarter hour part-time.
FINANCIAL AID ***College-administered undergrad aid 1995–96:*** need-based scholarships, 20 non-need scholarships (averaging $2000), low-interest long-term loans from external sources, 40 Federal Work-Study (averaging $2500), 2 part-time jobs. ***Required forms:*** institutional, FAFSA. ***Application deadline:*** continuous.
APPLYING ***Required:*** essay, school transcript, campus interview, CPAt. ***Recommended:*** minimum 2.0 GPA, TOEFL for international students. ***Required for some:*** recommendations. Test scores used for counseling/placement. ***Application deadline:*** rolling.
APPLYING/TRANSFER ***Required:*** essay, high school transcript, campus interview, college transcript. ***Recommended:*** minimum 2.0 college GPA, minimum 2.0 high school GPA. ***Entrance:*** minimally difficult. ***Application deadline:*** rolling. ***Contact:*** Mr. Paul Heidel, Dean of Academic Administration, 414-276-5200.
CONTACT Mr. Jeff Jarmes, Director of Admissions, Stratton College, 1300 North Jackson Street, Milwaukee, WI 53202-2608, 414-276-5200 Ext. 18. College video available.

UNIVERSITY OF WISCONSIN CENTER–BARABOO/SAUK COUNTY
Baraboo, Wisconsin

UG Enrollment: 395	**Tuition & Fees (WI Res): $1818**
Application Deadline: rolling	**Room & Board: N/Avail**

GENERAL State-supported, 2-year, coed. Part of University of Wisconsin System. Awards transfer associate, terminal associate degrees. Founded 1968. ***Setting:*** 68-acre small-town campus. ***Total enrollment:*** 395. ***Faculty:*** 31 (20 full-time, 75% with terminal degrees, 11 part-time); student-faculty ratio is 15:1.
ENROLLMENT PROFILE 395 students: 52% women, 48% men, 33% part-time, 99% state residents, 8% transferred in, 1% international, 30% 25 or older, 1% Native American, 0% Hispanic, 0% African American, 1% Asian American.
FIRST-YEAR CLASS 185 total; 250 applied, 96% were accepted, 77% of whom enrolled. 8% from top 10% of their high school class, 23% from top quarter, 60% from top half. 1 valedictorian.
ACADEMIC PROGRAM Core, liberal studies curriculum. Calendar: semesters. 160 courses offered in 1995–96. Academic remediation for entering students, services for LD students, advanced placement, tutorials, summer session for credit, part-time degree program (daytime, evenings), adult/continuing education programs. Off-campus study at other units of the University of Wisconsin Centers, four-year campuses of the University of Wisconsin. ROTC: Army (c), Naval (c), Air Force (c).
GENERAL DEGREE REQUIREMENT 60 credits.
MAJOR Liberal arts/general studies.
LIBRARY T. N. Savides Library plus 1 other, with 42,330 books, 28,340 microform titles, 120 periodicals, 4 on-line bibliographic services, 5 CD-ROMs, 8,800 records, tapes, and CDs.
COMPUTERS ON CAMPUS 20 computers for student use in computer center, library, student center provide access to main academic computer, e-mail, on-line services, Internet. Staffed computer lab on campus provides training in use of software.
COLLEGE LIFE Drama-theater group, choral group, student-run newspaper. 45% vote in student government elections. ***Social organizations:*** 10 open to all. ***Most popular organizations:*** Student Government Association, Chorus, Wellness Club, Band. ***Major annual events:*** Spring Fling, Welcome Picnic, Drama Productions. ***Student services:*** personal-psychological counseling.
HOUSING College housing not available.

Peterson's Guide to Two-Year Colleges 1997 671

Wisconsin

University of Wisconsin Center–Baraboo/Sauk County *(continued)*
ATHLETICS Member NJCAA. *Intercollegiate:* bowling M/W, golf M/W, tennis M/W. *Intramural:* basketball, gymnastics, soccer, softball, tennis, volleyball. *Contact:* Mr. Steve Rundio, Athletic Director, 608-356-8351.
CAREER PLANNING *Services:* career counseling, careers library.
AFTER GRADUATION 80% of students completing a degree program in 1994–95 went directly on to further study.
EXPENSES FOR 1995-96 *Application fee:* $28. State resident tuition: $1818 full-time, $75.65 per credit part-time. Nonresident tuition: $6090 full-time, $253.65 per credit part-time. Minnesota residents pay tuition at the rate they would pay if attending a comparable state-supported institution in Minnesota.
FINANCIAL AID *College-administered undergrad aid 1995–96:* need-based scholarships, non-need scholarships, low-interest long-term loans from external sources, Federal Work-Study, 2 part-time jobs. *Required forms:* institutional, FAFSA; accepted: CSS Financial Aid PROFILE. *Priority deadline:* 4/15. *Payment plans:* installment, deferred payment.
APPLYING *Options:* early entrance, deferred entrance, midyear entrance. *Required:* school transcript, 3 years of high school math and science, ACT, TOEFL for international students. *Recommended:* some high school foreign language. Test scores used for counseling/placement. *Application deadline:* rolling.
APPLYING/TRANSFER *Required:* college transcript, minimum 2.0 college GPA. *Recommended:* 3 years of high school math and science, some high school foreign language. *Entrance:* moderately difficult. *Application deadline:* rolling. *Contact:* Mr. Thomas Martin, Director of Student Services, 608-356-8724.
CONTACT Ms. Jan Gerlach, Assistant Director of Student Services, University of Wisconsin Center–Baraboo/Sauk County, Baraboo, WI 53913-1015, 608-356-8724.

UNIVERSITY OF WISCONSIN CENTER–BARRON COUNTY
Rice Lake, Wisconsin

UG Enrollment: 518	Tuition & Fees (WI Res): $1906
Application Deadline: 8/27	Room & Board: N/Avail

GENERAL State-supported, 2-year, coed. Part of University of Wisconsin System. Awards transfer associate degrees. Founded 1966. *Setting:* 142-acre small-town campus. *Total enrollment:* 518. *Faculty:* 27 (20 full-time, 7 part-time); student-faculty ratio is 20:1.
ENROLLMENT PROFILE 518 students from 3 states and territories, 1 other country. 56% women, 29% part-time, 97% state residents, 7% transferred in, 1% international, 25% 25 or older, 1% Native American, 3% Asian American.
FIRST-YEAR CLASS 236 total; 298 applied, 100% were accepted, 79% of whom enrolled. 7% from top 10% of their high school class, 27% from top quarter, 53% from top half. 1 National Merit Scholar.
ACADEMIC PROGRAM Core, honor code. Calendar: semesters. Academic remediation for entering students, English as a second language program offered during academic year, services for LD students, advanced placement, tutorials, summer session for credit, part-time degree program (daytime, evenings), adult/continuing education programs. Off-campus study at other units of the University of Wisconsin Centers, four-year campuses of the University of Wisconsin.
GENERAL DEGREE REQUIREMENT 60 credits.
MAJORS Liberal arts/general studies, science.
LIBRARY 39,479 books, 233 periodicals, 6,600 records, tapes, and CDs.
COMPUTERS ON CAMPUS 50 computers for student use in computer center, library, student center.
COLLEGE LIFE Drama-theater group, choral group, student-run newspaper. *Most popular organizations:* Phi Theta Kappa, Student Government, Encore, Explorer Outdoor Club, Delta Psi Omega. *Major annual events:* Humanities Day, Spring Fling. *Student services:* health clinic.
HOUSING College housing not available.
ATHLETICS *Intercollegiate:* basketball M, golf M/W, soccer M/W, tennis M/W, volleyball W. *Intramural:* basketball, bowling, cross-country running, football, golf, ice hockey, softball, table tennis (Ping-Pong), tennis, volleyball. *Contact:* Mr. Ronald Parker, Athletic Director, 715-234-8176.
CAREER PLANNING *Placement office:* 1 part-time staff. *Director:* Dr. Julie Mayrose, Director of Student Services, 715-234-8176. *Services:* resume preparation, career counseling, careers library.
AFTER GRADUATION 92% of students completing a degree program in 1994–95 went directly on to further study.
EXPENSES FOR 1995-96 *Application fee:* $28. State resident tuition: $1670 full-time, $69.50 per credit part-time. Nonresident tuition: $5942 full-time, $247.50 per credit part-time. Part-time mandatory fees: $10.55 per credit. Minnesota residents pay tuition at the rate they would pay if attending a comparable state-supported institution in Minnesota. Full-time mandatory fees: $236.
FINANCIAL AID *College-administered undergrad aid 1995–96:* 230 need-based scholarships (average $1300), 30 non-need scholarships (average $200), low-interest long-term loans from external sources (average $1800), Federal Work-Study, 12 part-time jobs. *Required forms:* CSS Financial Aid PROFILE, institutional, FAFSA. *Priority deadline:* 7/15.
APPLYING *Options:* early entrance, deferred entrance, midyear entrance. *Required:* school transcript, ACT, TOEFL for international students. *Recommended:* SAT I. Test scores used for counseling/placement. *Application deadline:* 8/27. *Notification:* continuous.
APPLYING/TRANSFER *Required:* high school transcript, college transcript. *Entrance:* minimally difficult. *Application deadline:* 8/27. *Notification:* continuous.
CONTACT Ms. June Brunette, Program Assistant, University of Wisconsin Center–Barron County, Rice Lake, WI 54868-2414, 715-234-8176 Ext. 430.

UNIVERSITY OF WISCONSIN CENTER–FOND DU LAC
Fond du Lac, Wisconsin

UG Enrollment: 550	Tuition & Fees (WI Res): $1846
Application Deadline: rolling	Room & Board: N/Avail

GENERAL State-supported, 2-year, coed. Part of University of Wisconsin System. Awards transfer associate degrees. Founded 1968. *Setting:* 182-acre small-town campus with easy access to Milwaukee. *Total enrollment:* 550. *Faculty:* 36.
ENROLLMENT PROFILE 550 students from 3 states and territories. 55% women, 45% men, 33% part-time, 99% state residents, 10% transferred in, 0% international, 27% 25 or older, 1% Native American, 1% Hispanic, 0% African American, 1% Asian American.
FIRST-YEAR CLASS 210 total; 325 applied, 92% were accepted, 70% of whom enrolled. 3% from top 10% of their high school class, 23% from top quarter, 59% from top half.
ACADEMIC PROGRAM Core, honor code. Calendar: semesters. Academic remediation for entering students, advanced placement, summer session for credit, part-time degree program (daytime), adult/continuing education programs. Off-campus study at other units of the University of Wisconsin Centers, four-year campuses of the University of Wisconsin. ROTC: Army (c).
GENERAL DEGREE REQUIREMENTS 60 credits; math/science requirements vary according to program.
MAJOR Liberal arts/general studies.
LIBRARY 41,840 books, 984 microform titles, 153 periodicals, 2,944 records, tapes, and CDs.
COMPUTERS ON CAMPUS 30 computers for student use in computer center, library provide access to e-mail, on-line services, Internet. Staffed computer lab on campus.
COLLEGE LIFE Drama-theater group, choral group, student-run newspaper, radio station. 15% vote in student government elections. *Social organizations:* 8 open to all. *Most popular organizations:* Student Government, Campus Ambassadors. *Student services:* personal-psychological counseling. *Campus security:* 24-hour emergency response devices.
HOUSING College housing not available.
ATHLETICS Member NJCAA. *Intercollegiate:* baseball M, basketball M/W, golf M/W, softball W, tennis M/W, volleyball W. *Intramural:* basketball, bowling, table tennis (Ping-Pong), volleyball. *Contact:* Mr. Craig Schoppe, Acting Athletic Director, 414-929-3663.
CAREER PLANNING *Service:* career counseling.
EXPENSES FOR 1995-96 *Application fee:* $25. State resident tuition: $1846 full-time, $77.55 per credit part-time. Nonresident tuition: $6118 full-time, $255.55 per credit part-time. Minnesota residents pay tuition at the rate they would pay if attending a comparable state-supported institution in Minnesota.
FINANCIAL AID *College-administered undergrad aid 1995–96:* need-based scholarships, 30 non-need scholarships (average $300), Federal Work-Study, 55 part-time jobs. *Required forms:* institutional; accepted: CSS Financial Aid PROFILE, FAFSA. *Priority deadline:* 4/15.
APPLYING *Options:* deferred entrance, midyear entrance. *Required:* school transcript, 3 years of high school math and science, ACT, TOEFL for international students. Test scores used for admission and counseling/placement. *Application deadline:* rolling.
APPLYING/TRANSFER *Required:* college transcript, minimum 2.0 college GPA. *Entrance:* moderately difficult. *Application deadline:* rolling.
CONTACT Mr. John Coffin, Director of Student Services, University of Wisconsin Center–Fond du Lac, 400 Campus Drive, Fond du Lac, WI 54935-2950, 414-929-3606. *E-mail:* bstrande@uwcmail.uwc.edu.

UNIVERSITY OF WISCONSIN CENTER–FOX VALLEY
Menasha, Wisconsin

UG Enrollment: 1,250	Tuition & Fees (WI Res): $1872
Application Deadline: 5/15	Room & Board: N/Avail

GENERAL State-supported, 2-year, coed. Part of University of Wisconsin System. Awards transfer associate degrees. Founded 1933. *Setting:* 33-acre urban campus. *Total enrollment:* 1,250. *Faculty:* 58 (36 full-time, 75% with terminal degrees, 22 part-time); student-faculty ratio is 25:1.
ENROLLMENT PROFILE 1,250 students from 4 states and territories. 52% women, 55% part-time, 99% state residents, 4% transferred in, 0% international, 40% 25 or older, 1% Native American, 1% Hispanic, 1% African American, 1% Asian American.
FIRST-YEAR CLASS 396 total; 640 applied, 86% were accepted, 72% of whom enrolled. 3% from top 10% of their high school class, 13% from top quarter, 45% from top half. 2 valedictorians.
ACADEMIC PROGRAM Core, honor code. Calendar: semesters. Academic remediation for entering students, services for LD students, advanced placement, honors program, summer session for credit, part-time degree program (daytime, evenings, summer), adult/continuing education programs. Off-campus study at other units of the University of Wisconsin Centers, four-year campuses of the University of Wisconsin.
GENERAL DEGREE REQUIREMENTS 60 credit hours; 3 credit hours of math/science.
MAJOR Liberal arts/general studies.
LIBRARY 26,000 books, 20 microform titles, 225 periodicals, 1,300 records, tapes, and CDs.
COMPUTERS ON CAMPUS Computer purchase plan available. 50 computers for student use provide access to main academic computer, e-mail, Internet. Staffed computer lab on campus provides training in use of computers, software.
COLLEGE LIFE Drama-theater group, choral group, student-run newspaper, radio station. *Social organizations:* 29 open to all. *Most popular organizations:* Business Club, Education Club, Earth Science Club, Computer Science Club, Political Science Club. *Major annual events:* Center Activities Board Christmas Party, Honors Convocation, Business Club Stock Exchange Trip to Chicago. *Student services:* personal-psychological counseling.
HOUSING College housing not available.

ATHLETICS Member NJCAA. ***Intercollegiate:*** basketball M/W, golf M/W, soccer M/W, tennis M/W, volleyball W. ***Intramural:*** basketball, volleyball. ***Contact:*** Mr. Mike Spencer, Associate Professor of Athletics, 414-832-2603; Ms. Jill Fogle, Lecturer-Physical Education, 414-832-2643.
CAREER PLANNING ***Services:*** career counseling, careers library.
EXPENSES FOR 1995–96 State resident tuition: $1872 full-time, $78.60 per credit part-time. Nonresident tuition: $6144 full-time, $256.60 per credit part-time. Minnesota residents pay tuition at the rate they would pay if attending a comparable state-supported institution in Minnesota.
FINANCIAL AID ***College-administered undergrad aid 1995–96:*** need-based scholarships, Federal Work-Study, 15 part-time jobs. ***Required forms:*** institutional, FAFSA. ***Priority deadline:*** 4/15.
APPLYING ***Options:*** Common Application, early entrance, deferred entrance. ***Required:*** school transcript, 3 years of high school math and science, ACT, TOEFL for international students. ***Recommended:*** some high school foreign language. Test scores used for admission and counseling/placement. ***Application deadline:*** 5/15. ***Notification:*** continuous.
APPLYING/TRANSFER ***Required:*** college transcript, minimum 2.0 college GPA. ***Entrance:*** minimally difficult. ***Application deadline:*** 5/15. ***Notification:*** continuous.
CONTACT Ms. Rhonda Uschan, Director of Student Services, University of Wisconsin Center–Fox Valley, 1478 Midway Road, PO Box 8002, Menasha, WI 54952-8002, 414-832-2620. ***E-mail:*** foxinfo@uwcmail.uwc.edu. College video available.

UNIVERSITY OF WISCONSIN CENTER–MANITOWOC COUNTY
Manitowoc, Wisconsin

UG Enrollment: 500	**Tuition & Fees (WI Res): $1794**
Application Deadline: N/R	**Room & Board: N/Avail**

GENERAL State-supported, 2-year, coed. Part of University of Wisconsin System. Awards transfer associate degrees. Founded 1935. ***Setting:*** 50-acre small-town campus with easy access to Milwaukee. ***Total enrollment:*** 500. ***Faculty:*** 25 (20 full-time, 75% with terminal degrees, 5 part-time); student-faculty ratio is 20:1.
ENROLLMENT PROFILE 500 students from 3 states and territories, 1 other country. 51% women, 30% part-time, 99% state residents, 15% transferred in, 23% 25 or older, 1% Native American, 1% Hispanic, 0% African American, 2% Asian American.
FIRST-YEAR CLASS 170 total; 220 applied, 95% were accepted, 81% of whom enrolled. 8% from top 10% of their high school class, 25% from top quarter, 51% from top half.
ACADEMIC PROGRAM Core, honor code. Calendar: semesters. 200 courses offered in 1995–96. Academic remediation for entering students, advanced placement, self-designed majors, summer session for credit, part-time degree program (daytime, evenings), adult/continuing education programs. Off-campus study at other units of the University of Wisconsin Centers, four-year campuses of the University of Wisconsin.
GENERAL DEGREE REQUIREMENTS 60 credits; 3 credits of math; 8 credits of science.
MAJOR Liberal arts/general studies.
LIBRARY 25,750 books, 150 periodicals, 2,750 records, tapes, and CDs.
COMPUTERS ON CAMPUS Computer purchase plan available. 30 computers for student use in computer center, computer labs, library. Staffed computer lab on campus provides training in use of computers, software.
COLLEGE LIFE Drama-theater group, student-run newspaper. 20% vote in student government elections. ***Social organizations:*** 3 open to all. ***Most popular organizations:*** Business Club, Drama Club, Music Club. ***Student services:*** personal-psychological counseling.
HOUSING College housing not available.
ATHLETICS Member NAIA. ***Intercollegiate:*** basketball M/W, golf M, tennis M/W, volleyball W. ***Contact:*** Mr. Richard Van Der Vaart, Athletic Director, 414-683-4737.
CAREER PLANNING ***Service:*** career counseling.
AFTER GRADUATION 80% of students completing a degree program in 1994–95 went directly on to further study.
EXPENSES FOR 1995–96 ***Application fee:*** $28. State resident tuition: $1794 full-time, $74.65 per credit part-time. Nonresident tuition: $6066 full-time, $252.65 per credit part-time. Minnesota residents pay tuition at the rate they would pay if attending a comparable state-supported institution in Minnesota.
FINANCIAL AID ***College-administered undergrad aid 1995–96:*** 2 need-based scholarships (average $600), 12 non-need scholarships (average $300), low-interest long-term loans from external sources, Federal Work-Study, part-time jobs. ***Required forms:*** institutional, FAFSA. ***Application deadline:*** continuous.
APPLYING ***Option:*** early entrance. ***Required:*** ACT, TOEFL for international students. ***Recommended:*** 3 years of high school math and science, 2 years of high school foreign language. Test scores used for counseling/placement. ***Notification:*** continuous until 7/1.
APPLYING/TRANSFER ***Recommended:*** 3 years of high school math and science, 2 years of high school foreign language. ***Entrance:*** minimally difficult. ***Notification:*** continuous until 7/1. ***Contact:*** Dr. Michael A. Herrity, Director of Student Services, 414-683-4708.
CONTACT Dr. Michael A. Herrity, Director of Student Services, University of Wisconsin Center–Manitowoc County, 705 Viebahn Street, Manitowoc, WI 54220-6699, 414-683-4708. ***E-mail:*** mherrity@uwcmail.uwc.edu.

UNIVERSITY OF WISCONSIN CENTER–MARATHON COUNTY
Wausau, Wisconsin

UG Enrollment: 1,011	**Tuition & Fees (WI Res): $1839**
Application Deadline: 8/1	**Room & Board: $2516**

GENERAL State-supported, 2-year, coed. Part of University of Wisconsin System. Awards transfer associate degrees. Founded 1933. ***Setting:*** 7-acre small-town campus. ***Educational spending 1994–95:*** $1872 per undergrad. ***Total enrollment:*** 1,011. ***Faculty:*** 71 (49 full-time, 85% with terminal degrees, 22 part-time); student-faculty ratio is 16:1.
ENROLLMENT PROFILE 1,011 students from 3 states and territories, 13 other countries. 55% women, 30% part-time, 97% state residents, 6% transferred in, 44% have need-based financial aid, 9% have non-need-based financial aid, 1% international, 26% 25 or older, 1% Native American, 1% Hispanic, 1% African American, 1% Asian American. ***Areas of study chosen:*** 13% business management and administrative services, 13% education, 13% liberal arts/general studies, 10% health professions and related sciences, 6% engineering and applied sciences, 5% fine arts, 5% natural resource sciences, 5% psychology, 5% social sciences, 3% biological and life sciences, 3% communications and journalism, 3% prelaw, 2% computer and information sciences, 2% English language/literature/letters, 2% premed, 1% agriculture, 1% architecture, 1% foreign language and literature, 1% mathematics, 1% performing arts, 1% philosophy, 1% physical sciences, 1% predentistry, 1% prevet, 1% vocational and home economics.
FIRST-YEAR CLASS 10% from top 10% of their high school class, 28% from top quarter, 63% from top half. 2 National Merit Scholars, 9 valedictorians.
ACADEMIC PROGRAM Honor code. Calendar: semesters. 305 courses offered in 1995–96. Academic remediation for entering students, advanced placement, self-designed majors, honors program, summer session for credit, part-time degree program (daytime, evenings, summer), adult/continuing education programs. Off-campus study at other units of the University of Wisconsin Centers, four-year campuses of the University of Wisconsin. Study abroad in England, Austria, Spain, Portugal. ROTC: Army (c).
GENERAL DEGREE REQUIREMENTS 60 credits; math competence; 12 credits in natural and mathematical science.
MAJORS Agricultural sciences, art/fine arts, behavioral sciences, biology/biological sciences, business administration/commerce/management, communication, computer science, education, elementary education, (pre)engineering sequence, health science, liberal arts/general studies, mathematics, medical technology, music, nursing, occupational therapy, physical sciences, science, social science.
LIBRARY University of Wisconsin-Marathon Library with 37,000 books, 250 microform titles, 150 periodicals, 8 CD-ROMs, 3,000 records, tapes, and CDs. Acquisition spending 1994–95: $23,000.
COMPUTERS ON CAMPUS Computer purchase plan available. 50 computers for student use in computer center, classrooms, library. Staffed computer lab on campus provides training in use of computers, software. Academic computing expenditure 1994–95: $47,938.
COLLEGE LIFE Drama-theater group, choral group, student-run newspaper. ***Social organizations:*** 12 open to all. ***Most popular organizations:*** Fiercely Independent Theatre, Ski Club, Ten Percent Society, Unity, Tempo. ***Major annual events:*** Chorale/Swing Choir Concerts, Educational Assistance Through Scholarships (EATS), Student-Faculty Basketball Game. ***Student services:*** personal-psychological counseling.
HOUSING 162 college housing spaces available; all were occupied 1995–96. No special consideration for freshman housing applicants. Off-campus living permitted. ***Option:*** coed (1 building) housing available. Resident assistants live in dorms.
ATHLETICS Member NJCAA. ***Intercollegiate:*** basketball M/W, golf M/W, soccer M/W, tennis M/W, volleyball W. ***Intramural:*** archery, badminton, basketball, bowling, cross-country running, fencing, football, golf, racquetball, skiing (cross-country), skiing (downhill), soccer, squash, swimming and diving, table tennis (Ping-Pong), tennis, volleyball, water polo, weight lifting. ***Contact:*** Dr. Duane Stremlau, Director of Physical Education and Athletics, 715-845-9602.
CAREER PLANNING ***Services:*** career counseling, careers library.
AFTER GRADUATION 96% of students completing a degree program in 1994–95 went directly on to further study.
EXPENSES FOR 1995–96 ***Application fee:*** $28. State resident tuition: $1839 full-time, $84.20 per credit part-time. Nonresident tuition: $6111 full-time, $262.20 per credit part-time. College room and board: $2516.
FINANCIAL AID ***College-administered undergrad aid 1995–96:*** 484 need-based scholarships (average $1000), 95 non-need scholarships (average $500), short-term loans (average $50), low-interest long-term loans from college funds (average $100), loans from external sources (average $1300), Federal Work-Study, 44 part-time jobs. ***Required forms:*** institutional, FAFSA; accepted: CSS Financial Aid PROFILE. ***Priority deadline:*** 4/15. ***Payment plans:*** installment, deferred payment.
APPLYING ***Options:*** early entrance, deferred entrance, midyear entrance. ***Required:*** 3 years of high school math, ACT, TOEFL for international students. ***Recommended:*** minimum 2.0 GPA, 3 years of high school science, some high school foreign language. Test scores used for counseling/placement. ***Application deadline:*** 8/1.
APPLYING/TRANSFER ***Recommended:*** 3 years of high school math and science, some high school foreign language. ***Entrance:*** minimally difficult. ***Application deadline:*** rolling. ***Contact:*** Mr. Greg Brown, Director of Admissions, 715-845-9602.
CONTACT Mr. Greg Brown, Director of Admissions, University of Wisconsin Center–Marathon County, 518 South Seventh Avenue, Wausau, WI 54401-5396, 715-845-9602 or toll-free 800-442-6459 (in-state). ***Fax:*** 715-848-3568. College video available.

UNIVERSITY OF WISCONSIN CENTER–MARINETTE COUNTY
Marinette, Wisconsin

UG Enrollment: 373	**Tuition & Fees (WI Res): $1793**
Application Deadline: rolling	**Room & Board: N/Avail**

GENERAL State-supported, 2-year, coed. Part of University of Wisconsin System. Awards terminal associate degrees. Founded 1965. ***Setting:*** 36-acre small-town campus. ***Endowment:*** $200,000. ***Total enrollment:*** 373. ***Faculty:*** 25 (15 full-time, 60% with terminal degrees, 10 part-time); student-faculty ratio is 20:1.
ENROLLMENT PROFILE 373 students from 2 states and territories, 8 other countries. 58% women, 37% part-time, 63% state residents, 4% transferred in, 4% international, 32% 25 or older, 1% Native American, 1% Hispanic, 0% African American, 1% Asian American.
FIRST-YEAR CLASS 115 total; 221 applied, 100% were accepted, 52% of whom enrolled. 7% from top 10% of their high school class, 24% from top quarter, 59% from top half. 1 valedictorian.
ACADEMIC PROGRAM Core, liberal arts/transfer curriculum, honor code. Calendar: semesters. 180 courses offered in 1995–96. Academic remediation for entering students, services for LD students, advanced placement, summer session for credit, part-time degree program (daytime), adult/continuing education programs. Off-campus study at other units of the University of Wisconsin Centers, four-year campuses of the University of Wisconsin.
GENERAL DEGREE REQUIREMENTS 60 credits; 12 credits of math/natural science.
MAJORS Accounting, business administration/commerce/management, education, liberal arts/general studies, nursing.

University of Wisconsin Center–Marinette County (continued)
LIBRARY Main library plus 1 other, with 23,000 books, 135 periodicals, 2,600 records, tapes, and CDs.
COMPUTERS ON CAMPUS 45 computers for student use in computer labs, library provide access to e-mail. Staffed computer lab on campus provides training in use of computers, software.
COLLEGE LIFE Drama-theater group, choral group. ***Social organizations:*** 5 open to all. ***Most popular organizations:*** Student Senate, Writers Club/Literature Club, Phi Theta Kappa, Student Ambassadors. ***Major annual events:*** Spring Banquet, End of Year Party, Commencement. ***Student services:*** personal-psychological counseling.
HOUSING College housing not available.
ATHLETICS ***Intercollegiate:*** basketball M, tennis M/W, volleyball W. ***Intramural:*** basketball, football, volleyball. ***Contact:*** Ms. Dorothy Kowalski, Athletic Director, 715-735-4300.
CAREER PLANNING ***Placement office:*** 2 part-time staff. ***Director:*** Mr. Gary Bjordal, Director of Student Services, 715-735-4301. ***Services:*** career counseling, careers library.
AFTER GRADUATION 90% of students completing a degree program in 1994–95 went directly on to further study.
EXPENSES FOR 1995–96 ***Application fee:*** $28. State resident tuition: $1793 full-time, $75.30 per credit part-time. Nonresident tuition: $6065 full-time, $253.30 per credit part-time.
FINANCIAL AID ***College-administered undergrad aid 1995–96:*** need-based scholarships, non-need scholarships, short-term loans (average $75), low-interest long-term loans from external sources, Federal Work-Study, 5 part-time jobs. ***Required forms:*** institutional; accepted: CSS Financial Aid PROFILE, FAFSA. ***Priority deadline:*** 3/1. ***Payment plans:*** installment, deferred payment.
APPLYING Open admission. ***Option:*** midyear entrance. ***Required:*** school transcript, 3 years of high school math and science, ACT, TOEFL for international students. Test scores used for counseling/placement. ***Application deadline:*** rolling. ***Notification:*** continuous.
APPLYING/TRANSFER ***Required:*** high school transcript, 3 years of high school math and science, college transcript, 4 years of high school English, 3 years of high school social science. ***Entrance:*** noncompetitive. ***Application deadline:*** rolling. ***Notification:*** continuous. ***Contact:*** Mr. Gary Bjordal, Director of Student Services, 715-735-4301.
CONTACT Mr. Gary Bjordal, Director of Student Services, University of Wisconsin Center–Marinette County, Marinette, WI 54143-4299, 715-735-4301. ***E-mail:*** sricler@uwcmail.uwc.edu.

UNIVERSITY OF WISCONSIN CENTER–MARSHFIELD/WOOD COUNTY
Marshfield, Wisconsin

UG Enrollment: 579	**Tuition & Fees (WI Res): $1825**
Application Deadline: rolling	**Room & Board: N/Avail**

GENERAL State-supported, 2-year, coed. Part of University of Wisconsin System. Awards transfer associate degrees. Founded 1964. ***Setting:*** 71-acre small-town campus. ***Total enrollment:*** 579. ***Faculty:*** 34 (21 full-time, 10% with terminal degrees, 13 part-time); student-faculty ratio is 17:1.
ENROLLMENT PROFILE 579 students from 6 states and territories, 3 other countries. 61% women, 35% part-time, 99% state residents, 5% transferred in, 25% 25 or older, 1% Native American, 1% Hispanic, 1% African American, 1% Asian American.
FIRST-YEAR CLASS 232 total; 272 applied, 94% were accepted, 91% of whom enrolled. 11% from top 10% of their high school class, 31% from top quarter, 68% from top half.
ACADEMIC PROGRAM Core, liberal arts curriculum, honor code. Calendar: semesters. 143 courses offered in 1995–96. Academic remediation for entering students, services for LD students, advanced placement, tutorials, summer session for credit, part-time degree program (daytime), adult/continuing education programs. Off-campus study at other units of the University of Wisconsin Centers, four-year campuses of the University of Wisconsin. ROTC: Army (c).
GENERAL DEGREE REQUIREMENTS 60 credits; 12 credits of math/science.
MAJOR Liberal arts/general studies.
LIBRARY Learning Resource Center with 30,000 books, 33 microform titles, 160 periodicals, 3,000 records, tapes, and CDs. Acquisition spending 1994–95: $16,000.
COMPUTERS ON CAMPUS 25 computers for student use in computer center, library provide access to off-campus computing facilities, e-mail, on-line services, Internet. Staffed computer lab on campus provides training in use of computers, software.
COLLEGE LIFE Drama-theater group, choral group, student-run newspaper. 20% vote in student government elections. ***Most popular organizations:*** Student Nursing Association, Student Newspaper, Literary Magazine, Computer Club, Phi Theta Kappa. ***Major annual events:*** Fall Picnic, Campus Plays. ***Campus security:*** 24-hour patrols, patrols by city police.
HOUSING College housing not available.
ATHLETICS ***Intercollegiate:*** basketball M/W, golf M/W, soccer M/W, tennis M/W, volleyball W. ***Intramural:*** basketball, bowling, football, skiing (cross-country), skiing (downhill), soccer, swimming and diving, table tennis (Ping-Pong), tennis, volleyball. ***Contact:*** Mr. John Harrington, Athletic Director, 715-389-6557; Ms. Wanda Boldon, Director of Intramurals, 715-389-6504.
CAREER PLANNING ***Service:*** career counseling.
EXPENSES FOR 1995–96 ***Application fee:*** $25. State resident tuition: $1825 full-time, $76.65 per credit part-time. Nonresident tuition: $6097 full-time, $254.65 per credit part-time. Minnesota residents pay tuition at the rate they would pay if attending a comparable state-supported institution in Minnesota.
FINANCIAL AID ***College-administered undergrad aid 1995–96:*** 127 need-based scholarships (average $652), 26 non-need scholarships (average $650), low-interest long-term loans from external sources (average $786), Federal Work-Study, 15 part-time jobs. ***Required forms:*** institutional, FAFSA; accepted: CSS Financial Aid PROFILE. ***Priority deadline:*** 3/15. ***Payment plans:*** installment, deferred payment.
APPLYING ***Options:*** Common Application, early entrance, deferred entrance, midyear entrance. ***Required:*** school transcript, 3 years of high school math and science, ACT, TOEFL for international students. ***Recommended:*** some high school foreign language. ***Required for some:*** essay, recommendations, interview. Test scores used for admission. ***Application deadline:*** rolling.
APPLYING/TRANSFER ***Required:*** college transcript, minimum 2.0 college GPA. ***Required for some:*** essay, interview. ***Entrance:*** moderately difficult. ***Application deadline:*** rolling. ***Contact:*** Mr. James L. Nelson, Director of Student Services, 715-389-6500.
CONTACT Mr. James L. Nelson, Director of Student Services, University of Wisconsin Center–Marshfield/Wood County, Marshfield, WI 54449-0150, 715-389-6500. ***E-mail:*** jnelson@uwcmail.uwc.edu.

UNIVERSITY OF WISCONSIN CENTER–RICHLAND
Richland Center, Wisconsin

UG Enrollment: 375	**Tuition & Fees (WI Res): $1950**
Application Deadline: 8/1	**Room & Board: $2386**

GENERAL State-supported, 2-year, coed. Part of University of Wisconsin System. Awards transfer associate degrees. Founded 1967. ***Setting:*** 135-acre rural campus. ***Total enrollment:*** 375. ***Faculty:*** 33 (19 full-time, 65% with terminal degrees, 14 part-time).
ENROLLMENT PROFILE 375 students: 52% women, 20% part-time, 94% state residents, 8% transferred in, 60% have need-based financial aid, 6% international, 25% 25 or older, 0% Native American, 1% African American.
FIRST-YEAR CLASS 172 total; 275 applied, 95% were accepted, 66% of whom enrolled. 10% from top 10% of their high school class, 25% from top quarter, 60% from top half.
ACADEMIC PROGRAM Core. Calendar: semesters. Academic remediation for entering students, services for LD students, advanced placement, summer session for credit, part-time degree program (daytime, evenings, summer), external degree programs, adult/continuing education programs. Off-campus study at four-year campuses of the University of Wisconsin, other units of the University of Wisconsin Centers.
GENERAL DEGREE REQUIREMENTS 60 credits; 12 credits of math/science.
MAJORS Liberal arts/general studies, science.
LIBRARY Miller Memorial Library with 45,000 books, 200 periodicals, 900 records, tapes, and CDs.
COMPUTERS ON CAMPUS 45 computers for student use in computer center, computer labs, learning resource center, classrooms, library provide access to e-mail, Internet. Staffed computer lab on campus provides training in use of computers, software.
COLLEGE LIFE Drama-theater group, choral group, student-run newspaper. 40% vote in student government elections. ***Social organizations:*** 15 open to all. ***Major annual events:*** Burlap Olympic Games, Roadrunner Road Rallye. ***Student services:*** personal-psychological counseling.
HOUSING 58 college housing spaces available; all were occupied 1995–96. No special consideration for freshman housing applicants. Off-campus living permitted. ***Option:*** coed housing available. Resident assistants live in dorms.
ATHLETICS Member NJCAA. ***Intercollegiate:*** basketball M/W, soccer M, volleyball W. ***Intramural:*** badminton, basketball, cross-country running, football, racquetball, swimming and diving, table tennis (Ping-Pong), tennis, volleyball. ***Contact:*** Ms. Patricia Fellows, Athletic Director, 608-647-6186.
CAREER PLANNING ***Services:*** career counseling, careers library.
AFTER GRADUATION 65% of students completing a degree program in 1994–95 went directly on to further study.
EXPENSES FOR 1995–96 ***Application fee:*** $28. State resident tuition: $1950 full-time, $81.20 per credit part-time. Nonresident tuition: $6222 full-time, $259.20 per credit part-time. Minnesota residents pay tuition at the rate they would pay if attending a comparable state-supported institution in Minnesota. College room and board: $2386 (minimum). College room only: $1530 (minimum).
FINANCIAL AID ***College-administered undergrad aid 1995–96:*** need-based scholarships, 60 non-need scholarships (average $300), short-term loans (average $50), low-interest long-term loans from external sources, Federal Work-Study, part-time jobs. ***Required forms:*** institutional, FAFSA; accepted: CSS Financial Aid PROFILE. ***Priority deadline:*** 4/15. ***Payment plans:*** installment, deferred payment.
APPLYING ***Option:*** early entrance. ***Required:*** school transcript, 3 years of high school math and science, ACT, TOEFL for international students. ***Required for some:*** recommendations, interview. Test scores used for counseling/placement. ***Application deadline:*** 8/1. ***Notification:*** continuous until 8/15.
APPLYING/TRANSFER ***Required:*** college transcript. ***Required for some:*** minimum 2.0 college GPA. ***Entrance:*** noncompetitive. ***Application deadline:*** 8/1. ***Notification:*** continuous until 8/15. ***Contact:*** Mr. John D. Poole, Director of Student Services, 608-647-6186.
CONTACT Mr. John D. Poole, Director of Student Services, University of Wisconsin Center–Richland, Richland Center, WI 53581, 608-647-6186 Ext. 223. ***Fax:*** 608-647-6225. ***E-mail:*** rlninfo@uwcmail.uwc.edu.

UNIVERSITY OF WISCONSIN CENTER–ROCK COUNTY
Janesville, Wisconsin

UG Enrollment: 875	**Tuition & Fees (WI Res): $1825**
Application Deadline: 7/30	**Room & Board: N/Avail**

GENERAL State-supported, 2-year, coed. Part of University of Wisconsin System. Awards transfer associate, terminal associate degrees. Founded 1966. ***Setting:*** 50-acre suburban campus with easy access to Milwaukee. ***Total enrollment:*** 875. ***Faculty:*** 43 (32 full-time, 62% with terminal degrees, 11 part-time); student-faculty ratio is 25:1.
ENROLLMENT PROFILE 875 students from 3 states and territories, 2 other countries. 52% women, 51% part-time, 99% state residents, 11% transferred in, 34% 25 or older, 1% Native American, 1% Hispanic, 5% African American, 1% Asian American.
FIRST-YEAR CLASS 217 total; 307 applied, 86% were accepted, 82% of whom enrolled. 4% from top 10% of their high school class, 18% from top quarter, 52% from top half.
ACADEMIC PROGRAM Core, general studies curriculum. Calendar: semesters. Academic remediation for entering students, services for LD students, advanced placement, summer session for credit, part-time degree program (daytime, evenings, summer), adult/continuing education programs. Off-campus study at other units of the University of Wisconsin Centers, four-year campuses of the University of Wisconsin.

Wisconsin

GENERAL DEGREE REQUIREMENTS 60 credits; 2 science courses, including at least 1 lab science course; 2 math courses.
MAJOR Liberal arts/general studies.
LIBRARY University of Wisconsin-Rock County Library with 60,000 books, 300 periodicals, 2,500 records, tapes, and CDs.
COMPUTERS ON CAMPUS 30 computers for student use in computer center, computer labs, library provide access to main academic computer, e-mail. Staffed computer lab on campus provides training in use of computers, software.
COLLEGE LIFE Orientation program (2 days, $25, parents included). Drama-theater group, choral group, student-run newspaper. *Most popular organizations:* Student Government Association, Multicultural Student Union, U-Rock Players. *Major annual events:* Pow Wow, Fall Fest, May Fest.
HOUSING College housing not available.
ATHLETICS *Intercollegiate:* basketball M, soccer M/W, volleyball W. *Intramural:* basketball, weight lifting. *Contact:* Mr. Peter Mory, Athletic Director, 608-758-6527.
CAREER PLANNING *Service:* career counseling.
EXPENSES FOR 1995-96 *Application fee:* $10. State resident tuition: $1825 full-time, $76.65 per credit part-time. Nonresident tuition: $6095 full-time, $247.50 per credit part-time. Minnesota residents pay tuition at the rate they would pay if attending a comparable state-supported institution in Minnesota.
FINANCIAL AID *College-administered undergrad aid 1995-96:* need-based scholarships, 20 non-need scholarships (average $350), low-interest long-term loans from external sources (average $650), Federal Work-Study, part-time jobs. *Required forms:* institutional, FAFSA. *Application deadline:* continuous to 10/8. *Payment plans:* installment, deferred payment.
APPLYING *Options:* deferred entrance, midyear entrance. *Required:* school transcript, 3 years of high school math and science, ACT, TOEFL for international students. Test scores used for counseling/placement. *Application deadline:* 7/30. *Notification:* continuous until 8/27.
APPLYING/TRANSFER *Required:* high school transcript, college transcript, minimum 2.0 college GPA. *Entrance:* minimally difficult. *Application deadline:* 9/2. *Notification:* continuous until 9/2. *Contact:* Dr. Greg Smith, Director of Student Services, 608-758-6253.
CONTACT Dr. Greg Smith, Director of Student Services, University of Wisconsin Center-Rock County, Janesville, WI 53546-5699, 608-758-6253. *Fax:* 608-755-2732.

UNIVERSITY OF WISCONSIN CENTER-SHEBOYGAN COUNTY
Sheboygan, Wisconsin

UG Enrollment: 458	Tuition & Fees (WI Res): $1827
Application Deadline: rolling	Room & Board: N/Avail

GENERAL State-supported, 2-year, coed. Part of University of Wisconsin System. Awards transfer associate degrees. Founded 1933. *Setting:* 75-acre small-town campus with easy access to Milwaukee. *Total enrollment:* 458. *Faculty:* 32 (25 full-time, 44% with terminal degrees, 7 part-time); student-faculty ratio is 16:1.
ENROLLMENT PROFILE 458 students: 46% women, 54% men, 43% part-time, 99% state residents, 1% transferred in, 1% international, 34% 25 or older, 1% Hispanic, 1% African American, 2% Asian American. *Areas of study chosen:* 22% liberal arts/general studies, 12% education, 11% business management and administrative services, 1% agriculture, 1% architecture, 1% biological and life sciences, 1% communications and journalism, 1% computer and information sciences, 1% engineering and applied sciences, 1% English language/literature/letters, 1% fine arts, 1% health professions and related sciences, 1% prelaw, 1% psychology.
FIRST-YEAR CLASS 153 total; 215 applied, 99% were accepted, 71% of whom enrolled. 6% from top 10% of their high school class, 22% from top quarter, 53% from top half.
ACADEMIC PROGRAM Core, liberal arts curriculum, honor code. Calendar: semesters. 170 courses offered in 1995-96. Academic remediation for entering students, advanced placement, summer session for credit, part-time degree program (daytime, evenings), adult/continuing education programs. Off-campus study at other units of the University of Wisconsin Centers, four-year campuses of the University of Wisconsin.
GENERAL DEGREE REQUIREMENTS 60 credits; math/science requirements vary according to program.
MAJOR Liberal arts/general studies.
LIBRARY Battig Memorial Library with 39,465 books, 39 microform titles, 249 periodicals, 8 CD-ROMs, 2,814 records, tapes, and CDs.
COMPUTERS ON CAMPUS 25 computers for student use in computer labs, physics lab, library provide access to main academic computer, e-mail, on-line services, Internet. Staffed computer lab on campus provides training in use of computers.
COLLEGE LIFE Drama-theater group, choral group, student-run newspaper. *Social organizations:* 5 open to all; 1 coed fraternity; 1% of eligible men and 1% of eligible women are members. *Most popular organizations:* Business Club, Film Committee, Spanish Club, Wellness Club, Zoomers (non-traditional students). *Campus security:* 24-hour patrols by city police.
HOUSING College housing not available.
ATHLETICS Member NJCAA. *Intercollegiate:* basketball M/W, cross-country running M/W, golf M/W, tennis M/W, volleyball W. *Intramural:* basketball, softball, volleyball. *Contact:* Mr. Jack Snyder, Athletic Director, 414-459-6651; Ms. Penny Maletzke, Recreation Specialist, 414-459-6643.
CAREER PLANNING *Service:* career counseling.
EXPENSES FOR 1995-96 *Application fee:* $25. State resident tuition: $1827 full-time, $76.75 per credit hour part-time. Nonresident tuition: $6099 full-time, $254.75 per credit hour part-time. Minnesota residents pay tuition at the rate they would pay if attending a comparable state-supported institution in Minnesota.
FINANCIAL AID *College-administered undergrad aid 1995-96:* need-based scholarships, 11 non-need scholarships (average $300), short-term loans (average $200), low-interest long-term loans, 14 Federal Work-Study (averaging $1600), 15 part-time jobs. *Required forms:* institutional, FAFSA. *Priority deadline:* 4/15. *Payment plan:* installment.
APPLYING Open admission. *Option:* midyear entrance. *Required:* school transcript, ACT. *Required for some:* campus interview, TOEFL for international students. Test scores used for counseling/placement. *Application deadline:* rolling.

APPLYING/TRANSFER *Required:* high school transcript, college transcript. *Required for some:* campus interview. *Application deadline:* rolling. *Contact:* Ms. Linda Gleason, Acting Director of Student Services, 414-459-6633.
CONTACT Ms. Linda Gleason, Acting Director of Student Services, University of Wisconsin Center-Sheboygan County, Sheboygan, WI 53081-4789, 414-459-6633.

UNIVERSITY OF WISCONSIN CENTER-WASHINGTON COUNTY
West Bend, Wisconsin

UG Enrollment: 670	Tuition & Fees (WI Res): $1846
Application Deadline: rolling	Room & Board: N/Avail

GENERAL State-supported, 2-year, coed. Part of University of Wisconsin System. Awards transfer associate degrees. Founded 1968. *Setting:* 87-acre small-town campus with easy access to Milwaukee. *Total enrollment:* 670. *Faculty:* 40 (26 full-time, 58% with terminal degrees, 14 part-time); student-faculty ratio is 18:1.
ENROLLMENT PROFILE 670 students from 3 states and territories. 55% women, 36% part-time, 99% state residents, 5% transferred in, 0% international, 24% 25 or older, 1% Native American, 1% Hispanic, 0% African American, 1% Asian American.
FIRST-YEAR CLASS 231 total; 325 applied, 99% were accepted, 71% of whom enrolled. 4% from top 10% of their high school class, 17% from top quarter, 49% from top half.
ACADEMIC PROGRAM Core, honor code. Calendar: semesters. Academic remediation for entering students, advanced placement, summer session for credit, part-time degree program (daytime, evenings). Off-campus study at other units of the University of Wisconsin Centers, four-year campuses of the University of Wisconsin.
GENERAL DEGREE REQUIREMENTS 60 credits; 12 credits of math/science.
MAJOR Liberal arts/general studies.
LIBRARY 38,631 books, 239 microform titles, 234 periodicals, 6 CD-ROMs, 2,342 records, tapes, and CDs. Acquisition spending 1994-95: $20,428.
COMPUTERS ON CAMPUS Computer purchase plan available. 55 computers for student use in computer center, library provide access to e-mail. Academic computing expenditure 1994-95: $20,487.
COLLEGE LIFE Drama-theater group, choral group, student-run newspaper. *Social organizations:* 10 open to all. *Most popular organizations:* Student Government Association, Environmental Club, Business Club, Phi Theta Kappa. *Major annual events:* Summer Send Off Picnic, Winter Royale, Convocation/Commencement. *Student services:* personal-psychological counseling.
HOUSING College housing not available.
ATHLETICS *Intercollegiate:* basketball M/W, golf M/W, soccer M/W, tennis M/W, volleyball W. *Intramural:* basketball, football, softball, volleyball. *Contact:* Mr. Tom Brigham, 414-335-5252; Ms. Debbie Butschlick, 414-335-5238.
CAREER PLANNING *Service:* career counseling.
AFTER GRADUATION 90% of students completing a degree program in 1994-95 went directly on to further study.
EXPENSES FOR 1995-96 *Application fee:* $28. State resident tuition: $1846 full-time, $76.85 per credit part-time. Nonresident tuition: $6118 full-time, $254.85 per credit part-time. Minnesota residents pay tuition at the rate they would pay if attending a comparable state-supported institution in Minnesota.
FINANCIAL AID *College-administered undergrad aid 1995-96:* need-based scholarships, 35 non-need scholarships (averaging $1000), short-term loans (averaging $200), low-interest long-term loans from external sources (averaging $2000), Federal Work-Study, part-time jobs. *Required forms:* institutional, FAFSA; accepted: CSS Financial Aid PROFILE, state. *Priority deadline:* 4/15. *Payment plans:* installment, deferred payment. *Waivers:* full or partial for senior citizens.
APPLYING Open admission. *Option:* deferred entrance. *Required:* ACT, TOEFL for international students. *Recommended:* school transcript, 3 years of high school math and science, some high school foreign language. *Required for some:* campus interview. Test scores used for counseling/placement. *Application deadline:* rolling.
APPLYING/TRANSFER *Required:* interview. *Recommended:* 3 years of high school math and science, some high school foreign language. *Application deadline:* rolling. *Contact:* Ms. Nancy E. Henderson, Director of Student Services, 414-335-5201.
CONTACT Ms. Nancy E. Henderson, Director of Student Services, University of Wisconsin Center-Washington County, West Bend, WI 53095-3699, 414-335-5201. *Fax:* 414-335-5220.

UNIVERSITY OF WISCONSIN CENTER-WAUKESHA COUNTY
Waukesha, Wisconsin

UG Enrollment: 1,681	Tuition & Fees (WI Res): $1802
Application Deadline: 5/1	Room & Board: N/Avail

GENERAL State-supported, 2-year, coed. Part of University of Wisconsin System. Awards transfer associate degrees. Founded 1966. *Setting:* 86-acre suburban campus with easy access to Milwaukee. *Total enrollment:* 1,681. *Faculty:* 83 (74 full-time, 80% with terminal degrees, 9 part-time); student-faculty ratio is 25:1.
ENROLLMENT PROFILE 1,681 students from 2 states and territories, 4 other countries. 59% women, 41% men, 44% part-time, 98% state residents, 6% transferred in, 1% international, 41% 25 or older, 1% Native American, 2% Hispanic, 1% African American, 1% Asian American.
FIRST-YEAR CLASS 512 total; 980 applied, 82% were accepted, 64% of whom enrolled. 2% from top 10% of their high school class, 13% from top quarter, 38% from top half.
ACADEMIC PROGRAM Core, general studies curriculum, honor code. Calendar: semesters. 400 courses offered in 1995-96. Academic remediation for entering students, services for LD students, advanced placement, self-designed majors, honors program, summer session for credit, part-time degree program (daytime, evenings, summer); adult/continuing education programs. Off-campus study at Carroll College, other units of the University of Wisconsin Centers and 4-year campuses of the University of Wisconsin.
GENERAL DEGREE REQUIREMENTS 60 credits; 18 credits of math/science.
MAJOR Liberal arts/general studies.
LIBRARY 41,000 books, 5,768 microform titles, 300 periodicals, 250 CD-ROMs, 2,000 records, tapes, and CDs.

University of Wisconsin Center–Waukesha County (continued)

COMPUTERS ON CAMPUS 90 computers for student use in computer center, computer labs, classrooms, library provide access to e-mail, on-line services, Internet. Staffed computer lab on campus provides training in use of computers, software.

COLLEGE LIFE Drama-theater group, choral group, student-run newspaper, radio station. 10% vote in student government elections. ***Social organizations:*** 16 open to all. ***Most popular organizations:*** Student Government, Student Activities Committee, Philosophy Club, Phi Theta Kappa, Ski Club. ***Major annual events:*** Fall Fest, Spring Carnival, Honors and Degree Ceremony. ***Campus security:*** late-night transport-escort service, part-time patrols by trained security personnel.

HOUSING College housing not available.

ATHLETICS ***Intercollegiate:*** basketball M/W, golf M/W, soccer M/W, tennis M/W, volleyball W. ***Intramural:*** basketball, bowling, football, skiing (downhill), table tennis (Ping-Pong), volleyball. ***Contact:*** Ms. Mary Ryan, Associate Professor of Physical Education, 414-521-5200.

CAREER PLANNING ***Placement office:*** 1 full-time staff. ***Director:*** Ms. Judy Luedtke, Senior Student Services Coordinator, 414-521-5210. ***Services:*** career counseling, careers library.

EXPENSES FOR 1995–96 ***Application fee:*** $28. State resident tuition: $1802 full-time, $75.05 per credit part-time. Nonresident tuition: $6074 full-time, $253.05 per credit part-time. Minnesota residents pay tuition at the rate they would pay if attending a comparable state-supported institution in Minnesota.

FINANCIAL AID ***College-administered undergrad aid 1995–96:*** need-based scholarships, 25 non-need scholarships (average $400), low-interest long-term loans from external sources (average $2500), 10 Federal Work-Study (averaging $500), 30 part-time jobs. ***Required forms:*** institutional, FAFSA. ***Priority deadline:*** 3/1. ***Payment plan:*** installment.

APPLYING ***Options:*** early entrance, deferred entrance, midyear entrance. ***Required:*** school transcript, 3 years of high school math and science, ACT, TOEFL for international students. ***Recommended:*** some high school foreign language. ***Required for some:*** campus interview, SAT I. Test scores used for admission. ***Application deadline:*** 5/1. ***Notification:*** continuous until 5/1.

APPLYING/TRANSFER ***Required:*** high school transcript, college transcript. ***Recommended:*** minimum 2.0 college GPA. ***Entrance:*** minimally difficult. ***Application deadline:*** 5/1. ***Notification:*** continuous until 5/1. ***Contact:*** Mr. Kurt Eisenmann, Associate Director of Student Services, 414-521-5210.

CONTACT Mr. Kurt Eisenmann, Associate Director of Student Services, University of Wisconsin Center–Waukesha County, Waukesha, WI 53188-2720, 414-521-5210. ***Fax:*** 414-521-5491. ***E-mail:*** tcavallu@uwcmail.uwc.edu. College video available.

WAUKESHA COUNTY TECHNICAL COLLEGE
Pewaukee, Wisconsin

UG Enrollment: 4,700	**Tuition & Fees (WI Res): $1969**
Application Deadline: rolling	**Room & Board: N/Avail**

GENERAL State and locally supported, 2-year, coed. Part of Wisconsin Technical College System. Awards certificates, diplomas, terminal associate degrees. Founded 1923. ***Setting:*** 137-acre small-town campus with easy access to Milwaukee. ***Total enrollment:*** 4,700. ***Faculty:*** 520 (145 full-time, 375 part-time).

ENROLLMENT PROFILE 4,700 students: 65% part-time, 99% state residents, 20% transferred in, 90% 25 or older, 0% Native American, 1% Hispanic, 1% African American, 1% Asian American. ***Most popular recent majors:*** law enforcement/police sciences, marketing/retailing/merchandising, nursing.

FIRST-YEAR CLASS 1,150 total; 2,100 applied, 100% were accepted, 55% of whom enrolled.

ACADEMIC PROGRAM Calendar: semesters. Academic remediation for entering students, English as a second language program offered during academic year, services for LD students, advanced placement, summer session for credit, part-time degree program (daytime, evenings), external degree programs, adult/continuing education programs, co-op programs.

GENERAL DEGREE REQUIREMENTS 66 credits; math/science requirements vary according to program.

MAJORS Accounting, business administration/commerce/management, data processing, drafting and design, electrical and electronics technologies, fashion merchandising, food marketing, industrial engineering technology, insurance, law enforcement/police sciences, machine and tool technologies, marketing/retailing/merchandising, nursing, real estate, secretarial studies/office management.

COMPUTERS ON CAMPUS 50 computers for student use in classrooms, library.

COLLEGE LIFE Student-run newspaper. ***Student services:*** health clinic, personal-psychological counseling, women's center. ***Campus security:*** patrols by police officers 8 am to 10 pm.

HOUSING College housing not available.

ATHLETICS Member NJCAA. ***Intercollegiate:*** basketball M/W, bowling M/W, golf M, soccer M, tennis M, volleyball W, wrestling M. ***Intramural:*** basketball, bowling, fencing, football, soccer, tennis, volleyball. ***Contact:*** Ms. Patti Sykes, Athletic Director, 414-691-5445.

CAREER PLANNING ***Director:*** Dr. Stanley P. Goran, Director of Admissions, 414-691-5271. ***Service:*** career counseling.

ESTIMATED EXPENSES FOR 1996–97 ***Application fee:*** $25. State resident tuition: $1843 full-time, $51.20 per credit part-time. Nonresident tuition: $14,220 full-time, $395 per credit part-time. Part-time mandatory fees: $3.50 per credit. Full-time mandatory fees: $126.

FINANCIAL AID ***College-administered undergrad aid 1995–96:*** need-based scholarships, low-interest long-term loans from external sources, Federal Work-Study. ***Required forms:*** state. ***Application deadline:*** continuous.

APPLYING Open admission. ***Option:*** early entrance. ***Required:*** school transcript. ***Required for some:*** campus interview, ACT ASSET. Test scores used for counseling/placement. ***Application deadline:*** rolling.

APPLYING/TRANSFER ***Required:*** high school transcript, college transcript, minimum 2.0 college GPA. ***Required for some:*** standardized test scores, campus interview. ***Entrance:*** noncompetitive. ***Application deadline:*** rolling.

CONTACT Dr. Stanley P. Goran, Director of Admissions, Waukesha County Technical College, Pewaukee, WI 53072-4601, 414-691-5271.

WESTERN WISCONSIN TECHNICAL COLLEGE
La Crosse, Wisconsin

UG Enrollment: 4,458	**Tuition & Fees (WI Res): $1650**
Application Deadline: rolling	**Room Only: $1150**

GENERAL District-supported, 2-year, coed. Part of Wisconsin Technical College System. Awards certificates, diplomas, terminal associate degrees. Founded 1911. ***Setting:*** 10-acre urban campus. ***Research spending 1994–95:*** $304,094. ***Total enrollment:*** 4,458. ***Faculty:*** 184 (all full-time, 6% with terminal degrees); student-faculty ratio is 24:1.

ENROLLMENT PROFILE 4,458 students: 56% women, 44% men, 60% part-time, 93% state residents, 1% live on campus, 8% transferred in, 63% have need-based financial aid, 0% international, 52% 25 or older, 1% Native American, 1% Hispanic, 1% African American, 1% Asian American. ***Areas of study chosen:*** 39% health professions and related sciences, 25% business management and administrative services, 14% engineering and applied sciences, 8% agriculture, 5% computer and information sciences, 3% vocational and home economics, 1% architecture, 1% communications and journalism. ***Most popular recent majors:*** nursing, accounting, law enforcement/police sciences.

FIRST-YEAR CLASS 1,342 total. Of the students accepted, 66% enrolled.

ACADEMIC PROGRAM Core, honor code. Calendar: semesters. Academic remediation for entering students, English as a second language program offered during academic year and summer, services for LD students, advanced placement, summer session for credit, part-time degree program (daytime, evenings), external degree programs, adult/continuing education programs, co-op programs and internships.

GENERAL DEGREE REQUIREMENTS 68 credits; computer course for most majors except vocational programs; internship (some majors).

MAJORS Accounting, agricultural business, agricultural technologies, automotive technologies, biomedical technologies, business administration/commerce/management, carpentry, child care/child and family studies, commercial art, communication, computer programming, computer technologies, data processing, drafting and design, electrical and electronics technologies, electromechanical technology, emergency medical technology, farm and ranch management, fashion merchandising, finance/banking, food services management, graphic arts, heating/refrigeration/air conditioning, human services, industrial and heavy equipment maintenance, interior design, law enforcement/police sciences, legal secretarial studies, machine and tool technologies, marketing/retailing/merchandising, mechanical design technology, medical assistant technologies, medical laboratory technology, medical records services, medical secretarial studies, medical technology, nursing, occupational therapy, operating room technology, paralegal studies, physical therapy, printing technologies, publishing, radio and television studies, radiological technology, respiratory therapy, retail management, secretarial studies/office management, welding technology, wood sciences.

LIBRARY Western Wisconsin Technical College Library plus 1 other, with 30,329 books, 16 microform titles, 354 periodicals, 4 CD-ROMs, 628 records, tapes, and CDs. Acquisition spending 1994–95: $19,007.

COMPUTERS ON CAMPUS 800 computers for student use in computer center, computer labs, learning resource center, student services department, classrooms provide access to main academic computer, e-mail. Staffed computer lab on campus provides training in use of computers, software.

COLLEGE LIFE Student-run newspaper. 1% vote in student government elections. ***Student services:*** health clinic, personal-psychological counseling, women's center. ***Campus security:*** 24-hour emergency response devices and patrols, student patrols, late-night transport-escort service, controlled dormitory access.

HOUSING 110 college housing spaces available; all were occupied 1995–96. No special consideration for freshman housing applicants. Off-campus living permitted. ***Option:*** coed (1 building) housing available. Resident assistants live in dorms.

ATHLETICS Member NJCAA. ***Intercollegiate:*** basketball M/W, volleyball W. ***Intramural:*** baseball, basketball, volleyball. ***Contact:*** Mr. Dave Fish, Athletic Director/Admissions and Recruitment, 608-785-9442.

CAREER PLANNING ***Placement office:*** 2 full-time, 1 part-time staff. ***Director:*** Ms. Jill Eck, Manager of Student Employment Services, 608-785-9440. ***Services:*** job fairs, resume preparation, resume referral, career counseling, careers library, job bank, job interviews. 45 organizations recruited on campus 1994–95.

EXPENSES FOR 1996–97 ***Application fee:*** $25. State resident tuition: $1650 full-time, $51.20 per credit hour part-time. Nonresident tuition: $12,200 full-time, $395 per credit hour part-time. College room only: $1150.

FINANCIAL AID ***College-administered undergrad aid 1995–96:*** need-based scholarships, non-need scholarships, short-term loans, low-interest long-term loans from external sources, 132 Federal Work-Study (averaging $1010), part-time jobs. ***Required forms:*** institutional; required for some: state; accepted: CSS Financial Aid PROFILE, FAFSA. ***Priority deadline:*** 8/15. ***Payment plan:*** deferred payment. ***Waivers:*** full or partial for senior citizens.

APPLYING Open admission except for health occupations programs. ***Options:*** Common Application, early entrance. ***Required:*** TOEFL for international students, ACT ASSET. ***Required for some:*** 3 years of high school math and science. Test scores used for counseling/placement. ***Application deadline:*** rolling.

APPLYING/TRANSFER ***Required for some:*** 3 years of high school math and science. ***Entrance:*** noncompetitive. ***Application deadline:*** rolling. ***Contact:*** Mr. Richard Markos, Registrar, 608-785-9149.

CONTACT Ms. Kris Anding, Manager of Student Enrollment and Financial Services, Western Wisconsin Technical College, 304 North Sixth Street, PO Box 908, La Crosse, WI 54602-0908, 608-785-9569 or toll-free 800-322-9982 (in-state), 800-248-9982 (out-of-state). ***Fax:*** 608-785-9205. ***E-mail:*** milde@a1.western.tec.wi.us.

WISCONSIN INDIANHEAD TECHNICAL COLLEGE, ASHLAND CAMPUS
Ashland, Wisconsin

UG Enrollment: 474	**Tuition & Fees (WI Res): $1587**
Application Deadline: rolling	**Room & Board: N/Avail**

GENERAL District-supported, 2-year, coed. Part of Wisconsin Technical College System. Awards terminal associate degrees. Founded 1920. *Setting:* 40-acre small-town campus. *Total enrollment:* 474. *Faculty:* 28 (21 full-time, 7 part-time); student-faculty ratio is 18:1.
ENROLLMENT PROFILE 474 students: 65% women, 35% men, 30% part-time, 99% state residents, 3% transferred in, 50% 25 or older, 14% Native American.
FIRST-YEAR CLASS 191 total.
ACADEMIC PROGRAM Core. Calendar: semesters. Academic remediation for entering students, services for LD students, part-time degree program (daytime, evenings, summer), adult/continuing education programs.
GENERAL DEGREE REQUIREMENTS 62 credits; computer course for business majors.
MAJORS Accounting, business administration/commerce/management, food services management, food services technology, hospitality services, nursing, secretarial studies/office management.
LIBRARY 8,046 books, 76 periodicals, 1,823 records, tapes, and CDs.
COMPUTERS ON CAMPUS 73 computers for student use in labs. Staffed computer lab on campus.
COLLEGE LIFE *Student services:* personal-psychological counseling.
HOUSING College housing not available.
CAREER PLANNING *Service:* career counseling.
EXPENSES FOR 1996–97 *Application fee:* $10. State resident tuition: $1587 full-time, $51.20 per credit part-time. Nonresident tuition: $10,658 full-time, $343.80 per credit part-time.
FINANCIAL AID *College-administered undergrad aid 1995–96:* 4 need-based scholarships (averaging $200), low-interest long-term loans from external sources, Federal Work-Study. *Required forms:* institutional, FAFSA; accepted: CSS Financial Aid PROFILE. *Application deadline:* continuous. *Waivers:* full or partial for senior citizens.
APPLYING Open admission except for nursing program. *Option:* early entrance. *Required:* interview, TOEFL for international students. *Required for some:* school transcript. Test scores used for counseling/placement. *Application deadline:* rolling. Preference given to state residents.
APPLYING/TRANSFER *Application deadline:* rolling.
CONTACT Mr. Phil Clark, Educational Services Supervisor, Wisconsin Indianhead Technical College, Ashland Campus, Ashland, WI 54806-3607, 715-682-4591. *Fax:* 715-682-8040.

WISCONSIN INDIANHEAD TECHNICAL COLLEGE, NEW RICHMOND CAMPUS
New Richmond, Wisconsin

UG Enrollment: 1,300	Tuition & Fees (WI Res): $1741
Application Deadline: rolling	Room & Board: N/Avail

GENERAL District-supported, 2-year, coed. Part of Wisconsin Technical College System. Awards terminal associate degrees. Founded 1972. *Setting:* 38-acre small-town campus with easy access to Minneapolis–St. Paul. *Total enrollment:* 1,300. *Faculty:* 65 (41 full-time, 24 part-time); student-faculty ratio is 18:1.
ENROLLMENT PROFILE 1,300 students: 55% women, 45% men, 54% part-time, 96% state residents, 3% transferred in, 55% 25 or older, 1% Native American.
FIRST-YEAR CLASS 400 total; 500 applied, 90% were accepted.
ACADEMIC PROGRAM Core, honor code. Calendar: semesters. Academic remediation for entering students, services for LD students, summer session for credit, part-time degree program (daytime, evenings, summer), adult/continuing education programs, internships.
GENERAL DEGREE REQUIREMENTS 68 credits; computer course for most majors; internship (some majors).
MAJORS Accounting, business administration/commerce/management, computer programming, court reporting, electromechanical technology, marketing/retailing/merchandising, nursing, secretarial studies/office management.
LIBRARY 4,300 books, 164 periodicals, 1,700 records, tapes, and CDs.
COMPUTERS ON CAMPUS 100 computers for student use in computer labs, learning resource center, business department, classrooms. Staffed computer lab on campus.
COLLEGE LIFE *Social organizations:* 9 open to all. *Student services:* personal-psychological counseling. *Campus security:* late-night transport-escort service.
HOUSING College housing not available.
CAREER PLANNING *Placement office:* 1 full-time staff. *Services:* resume preparation, career counseling, careers library, job bank.
EXPENSES FOR 1996–97 *Application fee:* $20. State resident tuition: $1741 full-time, $51.20 per credit part-time. Nonresident tuition: $11,689 full-time, $343.80 per credit part-time.
FINANCIAL AID *College-administered undergrad aid 1995–96:* 18 need-based scholarships (average $270), low-interest long-term loans from external sources, Federal Work-Study. *Required forms:* institutional, FAFSA; accepted: CSS Financial Aid PROFILE. *Application deadline:* continuous. *Waivers:* full or partial for senior citizens.
APPLYING Open admission except for nursing program. *Option:* early entrance. *Required:* school transcript, TOEFL for international students, ACT ASSET. Test scores used for counseling/placement. *Application deadline:* rolling. Preference given to state residents.
APPLYING/TRANSFER *Application deadline:* rolling. *Contact:* Ms. Deborah Hellerud, Educational Services Supervisor, 715-246-6561.
CONTACT Ms. Deborah Hellerud, Educational Services Supervisor, Wisconsin Indianhead Technical College, New Richmond Campus, New Richmond, WI 54017-1738, 715-246-6561 Ext. 4300. *Fax:* 715-246-2777.

WISCONSIN INDIANHEAD TECHNICAL COLLEGE, RICE LAKE CAMPUS
Rice Lake, Wisconsin

UG Enrollment: 1,136	Tuition & Fees (WI Res): $1638
Application Deadline: rolling	Room & Board: N/Avail

GENERAL District-supported, 2-year, coed. Part of Wisconsin Technical College System. Awards terminal associate degrees. Founded 1941. *Setting:* 30-acre small-town campus. *Total enrollment:* 1,136. *Faculty:* 79 (46 full-time, 33 part-time).
ENROLLMENT PROFILE 1,136 students from 2 states and territories. 53% women, 47% men, 32% part-time, 99% state residents, 4% transferred in, 52% 25 or older, 2% Native American, 0% Hispanic, 0% African American, 0% Asian American.
FIRST-YEAR CLASS 590 total. 5% from top 10% of their high school class, 5% from top quarter, 90% from top half.
ACADEMIC PROGRAM Core, honor code. Calendar: semesters. Academic remediation for entering students, services for LD students, tutorials, part-time degree program (daytime, evenings), adult/continuing education programs, internships.
GENERAL DEGREE REQUIREMENTS 64 credits; computer course for most business majors.
MAJORS Accounting, agricultural business, architectural technologies, computer information systems, cosmetology, finance/banking, law enforcement/police sciences, marketing/retailing/merchandising, mechanical engineering technology, nursing, quality control technology, secretarial studies/office management, welding technology.
LIBRARY 3,000 books, 2,550 microform titles, 93 periodicals, 1,700 records, tapes, and CDs.
COMPUTERS ON CAMPUS 78 computers for student use in computer center, classrooms, library.
COLLEGE LIFE Student-run newspaper. *Social organizations:* 9 open to all. *Major annual events:* Fall Fling, Sno Daze, Spring Picnic. *Student services:* personal-psychological counseling. *Campus security:* 24-hour emergency response devices.
HOUSING College housing not available.
ATHLETICS *Intramural:* basketball, football, golf, skiing (cross-country), skiing (downhill), softball, volleyball.
CAREER PLANNING *Placement office:* 1 full-time staff. *Director:* Mr. Steve Feidt, Career Planning Services Counselor, 715-234-7082 Ext. 5258. *Services:* resume preparation, career counseling, careers library.
EXPENSES FOR 1996–97 *Application fee:* $25. State resident tuition: $1638 full-time, $51.20 per credit part-time. Nonresident tuition: $11,002 full-time, $343.80 per credit part-time.
FINANCIAL AID *College-administered undergrad aid 1995–96:* 27 need-based scholarships (average $250), low-interest long-term loans from external sources (average $2625), Federal Work-Study. *Required forms:* state, institutional, FAFSA. *Priority deadline:* 3/15. *Waivers:* full or partial for senior citizens. *Notification:* 6/15. *Average indebtedness of graduates:* $6125.
APPLYING Open admission except for nursing program. *Option:* early entrance. *Required:* TOEFL for international students, ACT ASSET. Test scores used for counseling/placement. *Application deadline:* rolling. Preference given to state residents.
APPLYING/TRANSFER *Application deadline:* rolling.
CONTACT Ms. Charlene Sitenga, Educational Services Specialist, Wisconsin Indianhead Technical College, Rice Lake Campus, Rice Lake, WI 54868-2435, 715-234-7082. *Fax:* 715-234-5172.

WISCONSIN INDIANHEAD TECHNICAL COLLEGE, SUPERIOR CAMPUS
Superior, Wisconsin

UG Enrollment: 800	Tuition & Fees (WI Res): $1741
Application Deadline: rolling	Room & Board: N/Avail

GENERAL District-supported, 2-year, coed. Part of Wisconsin Technical College System. Awards transfer associate degrees. Founded 1912. *Setting:* 6-acre small-town campus. *Total enrollment:* 800. *Faculty:* 76 (41 full-time, 4% with terminal degrees, 35 part-time).
ENROLLMENT PROFILE 800 students from 3 states and territories. 57% women, 43% men, 34% part-time, 88% state residents, 3% transferred in, 0% international, 55% 25 or older, 3% Native American, 0% Hispanic, 0% Asian American.
FIRST-YEAR CLASS Of the students who applied, 80% were accepted.
ACADEMIC PROGRAM Core. Calendar: semesters. Academic remediation for entering students, services for LD students, summer session for credit, part-time degree program (daytime, evenings, summer), adult/continuing education programs, co-op programs and internships.
GENERAL DEGREE REQUIREMENTS 68 credits; computer course.
MAJORS Accounting, computer programming, electrical and electronics technologies, energy management technologies, fashion merchandising, marketing/retailing/merchandising, nursing, secretarial studies/office management.
LIBRARY Learning Resource Center with 8,049 books, 206 periodicals, 1,440 records, tapes, and CDs.
COMPUTERS ON CAMPUS 100 computers for student use in classrooms, library. Staffed computer lab on campus.
COLLEGE LIFE *Student services:* personal-psychological counseling. *Campus security:* 24-hour patrols, student patrols.
HOUSING College housing not available.
EXPENSES FOR 1996–97 *Application fee:* $10. State resident tuition: $1741 full-time, $51.20 per credit part-time. Nonresident tuition: $11,689 full-time, $343.80 per credit part-time. College housing is available through University of Wisconsin-Superior.
FINANCIAL AID *College-administered undergrad aid 1995–96:* 37 need-based scholarships (average $225), low-interest long-term loans from external sources, Federal Work-Study. *Required forms:* institutional, FAFSA. *Application deadline:* continuous. *Waivers:* full or partial for senior citizens.
APPLYING *Option:* early entrance. *Required:* school transcript, TOEFL for international students, ACT ASSET. *Required for some:* SAT II Subject Tests, SAT II: Writing Test. Test scores used for counseling/placement. *Application deadline:* rolling. Preference given to state residents.
APPLYING/TRANSFER *Required:* standardized test scores, high school transcript. *Application deadline:* rolling. *Contact:* Mr. James P. McFaul, Dean of Educational Services, 715-394-6677.

Wisconsin–Wyoming

Wisconsin Indianhead Technical College, Superior Campus (continued)
CONTACT Ms. Nancy O'Neill, Admissions Representative, Wisconsin Indianhead Technical College, Superior Campus, Superior, WI 54880-5207, 715-394-6677 Ext. 6243. *Fax:* 715-394-3771.

WISCONSIN SCHOOL OF ELECTRONICS
Wisconsin—See Herzing College of Technology

WYOMING

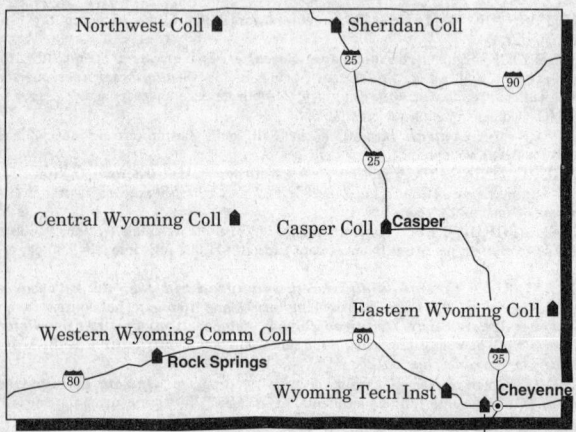

CASPER COLLEGE
Casper, Wyoming

UG Enrollment: 3,743	Tuition & Fees (WY Res): $936
Application Deadline: rolling	Room & Board: $2360

GENERAL District-supported, 2-year, coed. Part of Wyoming Community College Commission. Awards certificates, diplomas, transfer associate, terminal associate degrees. Founded 1945. *Setting:* 175-acre small-town campus. *Endowment:* $50,000. *Educational spending 1994–95:* $2487 per undergrad. *Total enrollment:* 3,743. *Faculty:* 185 (132 full-time, 60% with terminal degrees, 53 part-time); student-faculty ratio is 20:1. *Notable Alumni:* Dick Cheney, former U.S. Secretary of Defense; Dr. Charles Hord, NASA engineer; Dr. Stephen Nicholas, AIDS researcher.
ENROLLMENT PROFILE 3,743 students from 43 states and territories, 13 other countries. 61% women, 20% part-time, 95% state residents, 16% live on campus, 12% transferred in, 1% international, 38% 25 or older, 1% Native American, 1% Hispanic, 1% African American, 1% Asian American. *Most popular recent majors:* business administration/commerce/management, elementary education, nursing.
FIRST-YEAR CLASS 699 total; 900 applied, 99% were accepted, 75% of whom enrolled. 16% from top 10% of their high school class, 37% from top quarter, 68% from top half.
ACADEMIC PROGRAM Core, honor code. Calendar: semesters. 1,128 courses offered in 1995–96. Academic remediation for entering students, English as a second language program offered during academic year, services for LD students, advanced placement, honors program, summer session for credit, part-time degree program (daytime, evenings, summer), adult/continuing education programs, co-op programs and internships. Off-campus study at University of Wyoming–Casper Campus, University of North Dakota. Study abroad in Italy, Costa Rica, Germany (1% of students participate).
GENERAL DEGREE REQUIREMENTS 64 credit hours; computer course for most majors.
MAJORS Accounting, agricultural business, agricultural sciences, agricultural technologies, animal sciences, anthropology, applied art, art/fine arts, automotive technologies, behavioral sciences, biology/biological sciences, botany/plant sciences, business administration/commerce/management, business education, carpentry, ceramic art and design, chemistry, commercial art, communication, computer programming, computer science, computer technologies, construction technologies, corrections, criminal justice, data processing, drafting and design, early childhood education, earth science, ecology, economics, education, electrical and electronics technologies, elementary education, emergency medical technology, engineering (general), engineering and applied sciences, (pre)engineering sequence, English, fire science, flight training, forestry, French, geology, German, history, humanities, industrial arts, Italian, journalism, law enforcement/police sciences, legal secretarial studies, liberal arts/general studies, machine and tool technologies, marketing/retailing/merchandising, mathematics, medical technology, mining technology, music, music education, natural sciences, nursing, occupational therapy, paralegal studies, pharmacy/pharmaceutical sciences, photography, physical education, physical sciences, physical therapy, physics, political science/government, practical nursing, psychology, radiological technology, retail management, science, secretarial studies/office management, social science, social work, sociology, Spanish, speech/rhetoric/public address/debate, theater arts/drama, veterinary sciences, welding technology, wildlife management, zoology.
LIBRARY Goodstein Library with 80,000 books, 117 microform titles, 450 periodicals, 1 on-line bibliographic service, 7 CD-ROMs. Acquisition spending 1994–95: $75,000.

COMPUTERS ON CAMPUS 125 computers for student use in computer center, computer labs, classrooms, library provide access to e-mail, Internet. Staffed computer lab on campus provides training in use of computers, software. Academic computing expenditure 1994–95: $210,000.
COLLEGE LIFE Orientation program (2 days, $15, parents included). Drama-theater group, choral group, student-run newspaper. *Social organizations:* 25 open to all. *Most popular organizations:* Student Senate, Student Activities Board, Agriculture Club, Theater Club, Phi Theta Kappa. *Major annual events:* Casino Night, Back to School Dance, Alumni Banquet. *Student services:* health clinic, personal-psychological counseling. *Campus security:* 24-hour patrols, late-night transport-escort service.
HOUSING 500 college housing spaces available; all were occupied 1995–96. No special consideration for freshman housing applicants. Off-campus living permitted. *Option:* coed (3 buildings) housing available. Resident assistants live in dorms.
ATHLETICS Member NJCAA. *Intercollegiate:* basketball M(s)/W(s), volleyball W(s). *Intramural:* badminton, basketball, bowling, field hockey, football, golf, gymnastics, racquetball, skiing (cross-country), skiing (downhill), soccer, swimming and diving, table tennis (Ping-Pong), tennis, volleyball, water polo, weight lifting, wrestling. *Contact:* Mr. Ed Toohey, Athletic Director, 307-268-2224; Mr. Gary Becker, Women's Coach, 307-268-2627.
CAREER PLANNING *Placement office:* 2 full-time, 2 part-time staff; $100,000 operating expenditure 1994–95. *Director:* Mr. Russ Poppen, Director of Placement Center, 307-268-2662. *Services:* job fairs, resume preparation, resume referral, career counseling, careers library, job bank, job interviews. 9 organizations recruited on campus 1994–95.
EXPENSES FOR 1996–97 State resident tuition: $816 full-time, $34 per credit hour part-time. Nonresident tuition: $2448 full-time, $102 per credit hour part-time. Part-time mandatory fees: $5 per credit hour. Full-time mandatory fees: $120. College room and board: $2360 (minimum).
FINANCIAL AID *College-administered undergrad aid 1995–96:* 550 need-based scholarships (average $550), 1,000 non-need scholarships (average $400), short-term loans (average $100), low-interest long-term loans from external sources (average $2000), Federal Work-Study, 80 part-time jobs. *Required forms:* FAFSA; required for some: institutional; accepted: CSS Financial Aid PROFILE. *Priority deadline:* 4/15. *Payment plans:* installment, deferred payment. *Waivers:* full or partial for children of alumni, employees or children of employees, and senior citizens. *Notification:* 8/1.
APPLYING Open admission for state residents. *Options:* early entrance, midyear entrance. *Required:* school transcript, TOEFL for international students. *Recommended:* 3 years of high school math and science, some high school foreign language, SAT I or ACT. *Required for some:* SAT I or ACT. Test scores used for counseling/placement. *Application deadline:* rolling. *Notification:* continuous until 8/15.
APPLYING/TRANSFER *Required:* high school transcript, college transcript. *Recommended:* standardized test scores, 3 years of high school math and science, some high school foreign language. *Required for some:* standardized test scores. *Entrance:* minimally difficult. *Contact:* Mr. Russ Poppen, Director of Placement Center Director, 307-268-2662.
CONTACT Mrs. Jennifer Black, Admissions Coordinator, Casper College, Casper, WY 82601-4699, 307-268-2491 or toll-free 800-442-2963 (in-state).

CENTRAL WYOMING COLLEGE
Riverton, Wyoming

UG Enrollment: 1,510	Tuition & Fees (WY Res): $1100
Application Deadline: rolling	Room & Board: $2464

GENERAL State and locally supported, 2-year, coed. Part of Wyoming Community College Commission. Awards certificates, diplomas, transfer associate, terminal associate degrees. Founded 1966. *Setting:* 200-acre small-town campus. *Total enrollment:* 1,510. *Faculty:* 110 (50 full-time, 60 part-time); student-faculty ratio is 17:1. *Notable Alumni:* Ken Logge, faculty member at University of Oregon; Clifford Root, general manager at BTI; Diana Clapp, teacher; Avelina Paskett, certified public accountant; Karen J. Spoonhunter, school nurse at Brown University.
ENROLLMENT PROFILE 1,510 students from 22 states and territories, 11 other countries. 65% women, 35% men, 56% part-time, 96% state residents, 15% transferred in, 44% have need-based financial aid, 1% international, 55% 25 or older, 11% Native American, 3% Hispanic, 0% African American, 2% Asian American. *Areas of study chosen:* 13% liberal arts/general studies, 12% health professions and related sciences, 7% business management and administrative services, 6% education, 6% social sciences, 4% agriculture, 3% biological and life sciences, 3% computer and information sciences, 2% fine arts, 2% vocational and home economics, 1% communications and journalism, 1% English language/literature/letters, 1% interdisciplinary studies, 1% performing arts, 1% physical sciences. *Most popular recent majors:* nursing, elementary education, social science.
FIRST-YEAR CLASS 322 total; 455 applied, 100% were accepted, 71% of whom enrolled. 4% from top 10% of their high school class, 15% from top quarter, 51% from top half.
ACADEMIC PROGRAM Core, honor code. Calendar: semesters. 381 courses offered in 1995–96. Academic remediation for entering students, English as a second language program offered during academic year, advanced placement, self-designed majors, honors program, summer session for credit, part-time degree program (daytime), adult/continuing education programs, co-op programs.
GENERAL DEGREE REQUIREMENTS 64 credits; 3 credits of math/science; computer course.
MAJORS Accounting, agricultural business, agricultural sciences, agricultural technologies, animal sciences, art/fine arts, automotive technologies, biology/biological sciences, broadcasting, business administration/commerce/management, business education, business machine technologies, computer information systems, computer science, criminal justice, data processing, economics, education, elementary education, English, equestrian studies, human development, human services, interdisciplinary studies, liberal arts/general studies, management information systems, mathematics, music, Native American studies, natural resource management, nursing, operating room technology, physical education, physical sciences, physical therapy, psychology, radio and television studies, retail management, secretarial studies/office management, social science, telecommunications, theater arts/drama, welding technology.
LIBRARY Central Wyoming College with 34,603 books, 146 microform titles, 348 periodicals, 1 on-line bibliographic service, 250 CD-ROMs, 130 records, tapes, and CDs. Acquisition spending 1994–95: $9526.

COMPUTERS ON CAMPUS 58 computers for student use in computer center, computer labs, classrooms, library provide access to main academic computer, off-campus computing facilities, e-mail, on-line services, Internet. Staffed computer lab on campus provides training in use of computers, software. Academic computing expenditure 1994–95: $91,826.
COLLEGE LIFE Drama-theater group, choral group, student-run newspaper, radio station. ***Student services:*** personal-psychological counseling. ***Campus security:*** 24-hour patrols.
HOUSING 204 college housing spaces available; 122 were occupied 1995–96. No special consideration for freshman housing applicants. Off-campus living permitted. ***Option:*** coed housing available.
ATHLETICS Member NJCAA. ***Intercollegiate:*** equestrian sports M(s)/W(s). ***Intramural:*** badminton, basketball, bowling, equestrian sports, football, skiing (cross-country), skiing (downhill), table tennis (Ping-Pong), tennis, volleyball.
CAREER PLANNING ***Director:*** Ms. Alice Nicol, Counselor, 307-856-9291 Ext. 175. ***Service:*** career counseling. 42 organizations recruited on campus 1994–95.
EXPENSES FOR 1996–97 State resident tuition: $824 full-time, $36 per credit part-time. Nonresident tuition: $2472 full-time, $108 per credit part-time. Part-time mandatory fees: $11.50 per credit. Tuition for nonresidents who are eligible for the Western Undergraduate Exchange Program: $1236 full-time, $54 per credit part-time. Full-time mandatory fees: $276. College room and board: $2464.
FINANCIAL AID ***College-administered undergrad aid 1995–96:*** 153 need-based scholarships (average $500), 403 non-need scholarships (average $1036), short-term loans (average $518), low-interest long-term loans from external sources (average $2625), 38 Federal Work-Study (averaging $2000), 191 part-time jobs. ***Required forms:*** institutional, FAFSA. ***Priority deadline:*** 4/15. ***Payment plans:*** installment, deferred payment. ***Waivers:*** full or partial for employees or children of employees and senior citizens. ***Average indebtedness of graduates:*** $5250.
APPLYING Open admission except for nursing program. ***Options:*** early entrance, deferred entrance. ***Required:*** school transcript, TOEFL for international students. ***Recommended:*** SAT I or ACT. Test scores used for counseling/placement. ***Application deadline:*** rolling.
APPLYING/TRANSFER ***Required:*** college transcript. ***Recommended:*** standardized test scores. ***Entrance:*** noncompetitive. ***Application deadline:*** rolling. ***Contact:*** Ms. Mary Gores, Admissions Officer, 307-856-9291 Ext. 231.
CONTACT Ms. Mary Gores, Admissions Officer, Central Wyoming College, 2660 Peck Avenue, Riverton, WY 82501-2273, 307-856-9291 Ext. 231 or toll-free 800-735-8418 (in-state). ***Fax:*** 307-856-2264. ***E-mail:*** mary@odi.cwc.whecn.edu.

EASTERN WYOMING COLLEGE
Torrington, Wyoming

UG Enrollment: 1,766	**Tuition & Fees (WY Res): $1536**
Application Deadline: rolling	**Room & Board: $2500**

GENERAL State and locally supported, 2-year, coed. Part of Wyoming Community College Commission. Awards certificates, diplomas, transfer associate, terminal associate degrees. Founded 1948. ***Setting:*** 40-acre rural campus. ***Total enrollment:*** 1,766. ***Faculty:*** 136 (39 full-time, 11% with terminal degrees, 97 part-time); student-faculty ratio is 14:1. ***Notable Alumni:*** Carol Clark, James O. Rose, Jack D. Ainsworth.
ENROLLMENT PROFILE 1,766 students from 19 states and territories, 3 other countries. 66% women, 71% part-time, 90% state residents, 8% live on campus, 10% transferred in, 1% international, 55% 25 or older, 1% Native American, 4% Hispanic, 1% African American, 1% Asian American. ***Most popular recent majors:*** education, veterinary technology, criminal justice.
FIRST-YEAR CLASS 160 total; 288 applied, 100% were accepted, 56% of whom enrolled. 10% from top 10% of their high school class, 15% from top quarter, 50% from top half.
ACADEMIC PROGRAM Core, interdisciplinary curriculum. Calendar: semesters. 1,800 courses offered in 1995–96. Academic remediation for entering students, English as a second language program offered during academic year, services for LD students, advanced placement, self-designed majors, summer session for credit, part-time degree program (daytime, evenings, summer), external degree programs, adult/continuing education programs, co-op programs and internships.
GENERAL DEGREE REQUIREMENTS 64 credit hours; computer course for business, agriculture majors; internship (some majors).
MAJORS Accounting, agricultural business, agricultural education, agricultural technologies, animal sciences, art education, biology/biological sciences, business administration/commerce/management, business education, chemistry, child care/child and family studies, child psychology/child development, communication, computer programming, computer science, cosmetology, criminal justice, economics, education, elementary education, English, farm and ranch management, heating/refrigeration/air conditioning, history, humanities, journalism, law enforcement/police sciences, legal secretarial studies, liberal arts/general studies, literature, mathematics, medical secretarial studies, music, music education, physical education, political science/government, psychology, science, secretarial studies/office management, social science, sociology, teacher aide studies, theater arts/drama, veterinary sciences, veterinary technology, welding technology, word processing.
LIBRARY Eastern Wyoming College Library plus 1 other, with 30,000 books, 1,039 microform titles, 150 periodicals, 10 on-line bibliographic services, 1 CD-ROM. Acquisition spending 1994–95: $23,532.
COMPUTERS ON CAMPUS Computer purchase plan available. 71 computers for student use in computer center, computer labs, learning resource center, classrooms, library, student center provide access to main academic computer, Internet. Staffed computer lab on campus provides training in use of computers, software. Academic computing expenditure 1994–95: $51,923.
COLLEGE LIFE Drama-theater group, choral group, student-run newspaper. 33% vote in student government elections. ***Social organizations:*** 1 open to all. ***Most popular organizations:*** Criminal Justice Club, Veterinary Technology Club, Student Senate, Business Club. ***Major annual events:*** Basketball Games, Dances, Volleyball Games. ***Student services:*** health clinic, personal-psychological counseling, women's center. ***Campus security:*** controlled dormitory access.
HOUSING 162 college housing spaces available; 158 were occupied 1995–96. No special consideration for freshman housing applicants. Off-campus living permitted. ***Option:*** coed (2 buildings) housing available. Resident assistants live in dorms.
ATHLETICS Member NJCAA. ***Intercollegiate:*** basketball M(s), equestrian sports M(s)/W(s), volleyball W(s). ***Intramural:*** badminton, basketball, bowling, racquetball, skiing (cross-country), skiing (downhill), softball, table tennis (Ping-Pong), tennis, volleyball. ***Contact:*** Mr. Verl Petsch, Director of Athletics, 307-532-8248.
CAREER PLANNING ***Placement office:*** 1 full-time, 1 part-time staff; $95,882 operating expenditure 1994–95. ***Director:*** Ms. Angie Babcock, Coordinator of Career Center, 307-532-8316. ***Services:*** job fairs, resume preparation, career counseling, careers library, job bank.
AFTER GRADUATION 30% of class of 1994 had job offers within 6 months. 80% of students completing a degree program went directly on to further study.
EXPENSES FOR 1995–96 State resident tuition: $1152 full-time, $36 per credit hour part-time. Nonresident tuition: $3456 full-time, $108 per credit hour part-time. Part-time mandatory fees: $12 per credit hour. Tuition for nonresidents who are eligible for the Western Undergraduate Exchange Program: $1620 full-time, $54 per credit hour part-time. Full-time mandatory fees: $384. College room and board: $2500.
FINANCIAL AID ***College-administered undergrad aid 1995–96:*** 125 need-based scholarships (averaging $760), 155 non-need scholarships (averaging $760), low-interest long-term loans from college funds (averaging $100), loans from external sources (averaging $3062), 72 Federal Work-Study (averaging $1000), 64 part-time jobs. ***Required forms:*** institutional, FAFSA. ***Priority deadline:*** 3/15. ***Payment plan:*** installment. ***Waivers:*** full or partial for minority students, children of alumni, employees or children of employees, adult students, and senior citizens.
APPLYING Open admission. ***Options:*** early entrance, midyear entrance. ***Required:*** TOEFL for international students. ***Recommended:*** minimum 2.0 GPA, 3 years of high school math and science, some high school foreign language, ACT. Test scores used for counseling/placement. ***Application deadline:*** rolling. Preference given to state residents.
APPLYING/TRANSFER ***Recommended:*** 3 years of high school math and science, some high school foreign language, minimum 2.0 high school GPA. ***Entrance:*** moderately difficult. ***Application deadline:*** rolling. ***Contact:*** Ms. Marilyn J. Cotant, Assistant Dean of Students, 307-532-8257.
CONTACT Ms. Marilyn J. Cotant, Assistant Dean of Students, Eastern Wyoming College, Torrington, WY 82240-1699, 307-532-8257 or toll-free 800-658-3195. ***Fax:*** 307-532-8222.

LARAMIE COUNTY COMMUNITY COLLEGE
Cheyenne, Wyoming

UG Enrollment: 4,282	**Tuition & Fees (WY Res): $1160**
Application Deadline: rolling	**Room & Board: $3360**

GENERAL County-supported, 2-year, coed. Part of Wyoming Community College Commission. Awards transfer associate, terminal associate degrees. Founded 1968. ***Setting:*** 270-acre small-town campus. ***Total enrollment:*** 4,282. ***Faculty:*** 255 (80 full-time, 20% with terminal degrees, 175 part-time); student-faculty ratio is 24:1.
ENROLLMENT PROFILE 4,282 students: 59% women, 71% part-time, 90% state residents, 2% live on campus, 25% transferred in, 1% international, 60% 25 or older, 1% Native American, 5% Hispanic, 2% African American, 1% Asian American.
FIRST-YEAR CLASS 1,670 total; 1,974 applied, 100% were accepted, 85% of whom enrolled.
ACADEMIC PROGRAM Core. Calendar: semesters. Academic remediation for entering students, English as a second language program offered during academic year, services for LD students, advanced placement, summer session for credit, part-time degree program (daytime, evenings), adult/continuing education programs, co-op programs and internships.
GENERAL DEGREE REQUIREMENTS 64 credits; 1 course each in college algebra and lab science; computer course for business-related majors; internship (some majors).
MAJORS Accounting, agricultural business, agricultural education, agricultural sciences, anthropology, art/fine arts, automotive technologies, biology/biological sciences, business administration/commerce/management, carpentry, chemistry, child care/child and family studies, child psychology/child development, civil engineering technology, communication, computer information systems, computer science, construction technologies, criminal justice, dental services, early childhood education, economics, education, engineering and applied sciences, (pre)engineering sequence, engineering technology, English, equestrian studies, fire science, hotel and restaurant management, journalism, law enforcement/police sciences, legal secretarial studies, liberal arts/general studies, mathematics, music, nursing, paralegal studies, physical education, political science/government, psychology, public administration, radiological technology, retail management, secretarial studies/office management, sociology, speech/rhetoric/public address/debate, theater arts/drama, wildlife management.
LIBRARY 40,000 books, 350 periodicals.
COMPUTERS ON CAMPUS 600 computers for student use in computer center, computer labs, learning resource center, classrooms provide access to e-mail, on-line services. Staffed computer lab on campus provides training in use of computers, software.
COLLEGE LIFE Drama-theater group, choral group, student-run newspaper. ***Student services:*** personal-psychological counseling. ***Campus security:*** 24-hour patrols, controlled dormitory access.
HOUSING 82 college housing spaces available; all were occupied 1995–96. No special consideration for freshman housing applicants. Off-campus living permitted. ***Option:*** coed housing available. Resident assistants live in dorms.
ATHLETICS ***Intramural:*** basketball, racquetball, soccer, softball, swimming and diving, tennis, track and field, volleyball, water polo.
CAREER PLANNING ***Placement office:*** 1 full-time staff. ***Director:*** Mr. Tom Jones, Counselor, Career Services, 307-778-5222. ***Services:*** job fairs, resume preparation, career counseling, careers library.
AFTER GRADUATION 36% of students completing a degree program in 1994–95 went directly on to further study.
EXPENSES FOR 1996–97 ***Application fee:*** $10. State resident tuition: $992 full-time, $43 per credit hour part-time. Nonresident tuition: $2640 full-time, $115 per credit hour part-time. Part-time mandatory fees: $7 per credit hour. Tuition for nonresidents who are eligible for the Western Undergraduate Exchange Program: $1236 full-time, $61 per credit hour part-time. Full-time mandatory fees: $168. College room and board: $3360.
FINANCIAL AID ***College-administered undergrad aid 1995–96:*** 28 need-based scholarships (averaging $651), 230 non-need scholarships (averaging $442), short-term loans (averaging $100), low-interest long-term loans from external sources (averaging

Laramie County Community College (continued)
$1962), Federal Work-Study, 76 part-time jobs. ***Required forms:*** institutional, FAFSA. ***Priority deadline:*** 4/1. ***Waivers:*** full or partial for employees or children of employees and senior citizens.
APPLYING Open admission except for nursing, radiological technology, equine studies, dental hygiene programs. ***Options:*** early entrance, midyear entrance. ***Required:*** school transcript, TOEFL for international students. ***Required for some:*** interview. Test scores used for counseling/placement. ***Application deadline:*** rolling. ***Notification:*** continuous until 8/31.
APPLYING/TRANSFER ***Required:*** college transcript. ***Recommended:*** high school transcript. ***Required for some:*** interview. ***Entrance:*** noncompetitive. ***Application deadline:*** rolling. ***Notification:*** continuous until 8/31.
CONTACT Ms. Molly Christensen, Admissions Placement Coordinator, Laramie County Community College, Cheyenne, WY 82007-3299, 307-778-5222 Ext. 221 or toll-free 800-522-2993 (in-state). ***Fax:*** 307-778-1399.

NORTHWEST COLLEGE
Powell, Wyoming

UG Enrollment: 2,000	**Tuition & Fees (WY Res): $1304**
Application Deadline: 8/15	**Room & Board: $2764**

GENERAL State and locally supported, 2-year, coed. Part of Wyoming Community College Commission. Awards certificates, transfer associate, terminal associate degrees. Founded 1946. ***Setting:*** 75-acre rural campus. ***Educational spending 1994–95:*** $2675 per undergrad. ***Total enrollment:*** 2,000. ***Faculty:*** 181 (94 full-time, 29% with terminal degrees, 87 part-time); student-faculty ratio is 12:1.
ENROLLMENT PROFILE 2,000 students from 28 states and territories, 10 other countries. 58% women, 34% part-time, 77% state residents, 10% transferred in, 40% have need-based financial aid, 20% have non-need-based financial aid, 1% international, 37% 25 or older, 1% Native American, 3% Hispanic, 1% African American, 1% Asian American. ***Areas of study chosen:*** 20% education, 9% interdisciplinary studies, 8% agriculture, 7% engineering and applied sciences, 6% social sciences, 4% fine arts. ***Most popular recent majors:*** business administration/commerce/management, elementary education.
FIRST-YEAR CLASS 659 total; 1,200 applied, 99% were accepted, 55% of whom enrolled. 15% from top 10% of their high school class, 45% from top quarter, 60% from top half. 2 class presidents, 4 valedictorians.
ACADEMIC PROGRAM Core, general education curriculum, honor code. Calendar: semesters. 670 courses offered in 1995–96. Academic remediation for entering students, English as a second language program offered during academic year, services for LD students, advanced placement, Freshman Honors College, tutorials, honors program, summer session for credit, part-time degree program (daytime, evenings, summer), adult/continuing education programs, co-op programs and internships. Study abroad in England, Canada, Mexico, France (2% of students participate).
GENERAL DEGREE REQUIREMENTS 64 credits; 1 math course.
MAJORS Accounting, agricultural business, agricultural economics, agricultural education, agricultural sciences, agricultural technologies, agronomy/soil and crop sciences, animal sciences, art education, art/fine arts, biology/biological sciences, botany/plant sciences, business administration/commerce/management, business education, ceramic art and design, chemistry, commercial art, communication, computer information systems, computer science, drafting and design, early childhood education, ecology, economics, education, elementary education, engineering (general), (pre)engineering sequence, English, environmental sciences, equestrian studies, farm and ranch management, fish and game management, forestry, graphic arts, health education, history, home economics, home economics education, horticulture, humanities, interior design, jazz, journalism, liberal arts/general studies, marketing/retailing/merchandising, mathematics, modern languages, music, music education, natural resource management, natural sciences, nursing, painting/drawing, parks management, photography, physical education, physical sciences, physical therapy, physics, political science/government, postal management, practical nursing, printing technologies, psychology, public administration, public affairs and policy studies, radiological technology, range management, recreation and leisure services, retail management, science, science education, secretarial studies/office management, social science, social work, sociology, soil conservation, speech/rhetoric/public address/debate, theater arts/drama, tourism and travel, vocational education, welding technology, wildlife biology, wildlife management.
LIBRARY John Taggart Hinckley Library plus 1 other, with 38,000 books, 400 periodicals, 350 CD-ROMs, 400 records, tapes, and CDs. Acquisition spending 1994–95: $43,000.
COMPUTERS ON CAMPUS 150 computers for student use in computer center, computer labs, learning resource center, library, student center, dorms provide access to off-campus computing facilities, e-mail, on-line services. Staffed computer lab on campus provides training in use of computers, software. Academic computing expenditure 1994–95: $187,912.
NOTEWORTHY RESEARCH FACILITIES A.L. Mikelson Field Station.
COLLEGE LIFE Orientation program (3 days, no cost, parents included). Drama-theater group, choral group, student-run newspaper. ***Social organizations:*** 31 open to all. ***Major annual event:*** Homecoming/Alumni Reunion. ***Student services:*** health clinic, personal-psychological counseling. ***Campus security:*** 24-hour patrols, controlled dormitory access.
HOUSING 600 college housing spaces available; 574 were occupied 1995–96. Freshmen guaranteed college housing. On-campus residence required in freshman year except if a parent, 21 or over, or living with married relatives. ***Options:*** coed (8 buildings), single-sex (2 buildings) housing available. Resident assistants live in dorms.
ATHLETICS Member NJCAA. ***Intercollegiate:*** basketball M(s)/W(s), equestrian sports M(s)/W(s), riflery M/W, volleyball W(s), wrestling M(s). ***Intramural:*** archery, badminton, baseball, basketball, bowling, cross-country running, football, golf, gymnastics, racquetball, riflery, sailing, skiing (cross-country), skiing (downhill), soccer, softball, squash, table tennis (Ping-Pong), tennis, volleyball, weight lifting. ***Contact:*** Mr. Ken Rochlitz, Athletic Director, 307-754-6505.
CAREER PLANNING ***Placement office:*** 1 full-time staff; $55,893 operating expenditure 1994–95. ***Director:*** Mr. Dale Jensvold, Director of Career Development, 307-754-6661. ***Service:*** career counseling.
AFTER GRADUATION 59% of students completing a degree program in 1994–95 went directly on to further study.
EXPENSES FOR 1996–97 ***Application fee:*** $10. State resident tuition: $1304 full-time, $54 per credit part-time. Nonresident tuition: $2952 full-time, $126 per credit part-time. Tuition for nonresidents who are eligible for the Western Undergraduate Exchange Program: $1716 full-time, $72 per credit part-time. College room and board: $2764.
FINANCIAL AID ***College-administered undergrad aid 1995–96:*** 160 need-based scholarships (average $750), 400 non-need scholarships (average $400), short-term loans, low-interest long-term loans from external sources (average $1900), Federal Work-Study, 300 part-time jobs. ***Required forms:*** institutional, FAFSA; accepted: CSS Financial Aid PROFILE. ***Priority deadline:*** 3/15. ***Payment plan:*** installment. ***Waivers:*** full or partial for children of alumni, employees or children of employees, and senior citizens. ***Notification:*** 5/1.
APPLYING Open admission for state residents, except for nursing, radiology programs. ***Options:*** early entrance, deferred entrance, midyear entrance. ***Required:*** school transcript, TOEFL for international students. ***Recommended:*** minimum 2.0 GPA, 3 years of high school math and science, some high school foreign language. ***Required for some:*** SAT I or ACT. Test scores used for admission (TOEFL) and counseling/placement (ACT, SAT I). ***Application deadline:*** 8/15. ***Notification:*** continuous.
APPLYING/TRANSFER ***Required:*** high school transcript, college transcript, minimum 2.0 college GPA. ***Required for some:*** standardized test scores. ***Application deadline:*** 8/1. ***Notification:*** continuous. ***Contact:*** Mr. Karl Bear, Director of Admissions, 307-754-6408.
CONTACT Mr. Karl Bear, Director of Admissions, Northwest College, Powell, WY 82435-1898, 307-754-6408 or toll-free 800-442-2946 (in-state). ***Fax:*** 307-754-6700. ***E-mail:*** beark@adm.nwc.whecn.edu.

SHERIDAN COLLEGE
Sheridan, Wyoming

UG Enrollment: 2,555	**Tuition & Fees (WY Res): $940**
Application Deadline: rolling	**Room & Board: $2730**

GENERAL State and locally supported, 2-year, coed. Part of Wyoming Community College Commission. Awards certificates, transfer associate, terminal associate degrees. Founded 1948. ***Setting:*** 64-acre small-town campus. ***Total enrollment:*** 2,555. ***Faculty:*** 215 (73 full-time, 10% with terminal degrees, 142 part-time).
ENROLLMENT PROFILE 2,555 students from 22 states and territories, 10 other countries. 64% women, 36% men, 57% part-time, 94% state residents, 5% live on campus, 10% transferred in, 1% international, 55% 25 or older, 2% Native American, 2% Hispanic, 1% African American, 1% Asian American. ***Areas of study chosen:*** 34% interdisciplinary studies, 13% business management and administrative services, 10% health professions and related sciences, 9% liberal arts/general studies, 8% social sciences, 7% vocational and home economics, 6% education, 2% agriculture, 2% computer and information sciences, 2% fine arts, 2% premed, 1% biological and life sciences, 1% engineering and applied sciences, 1% natural resource sciences, 1% physical sciences, 1% predentistry, 1% prelaw, 1% prevet, 1% psychology. ***Most popular recent majors:*** nursing, business administration/commerce/management, dental sciences.
FIRST-YEAR CLASS 310 total; 700 applied, 86% were accepted, 52% of whom enrolled. 5% from top 10% of their high school class, 12% from top quarter, 46% from top half.
ACADEMIC PROGRAM Core, interdisciplinary curriculum, honor code. Calendar: semesters. 658 courses offered in 1995–96. Academic remediation for entering students, English as a second language program offered during academic year, services for LD students, advanced placement, self-designed majors, summer session for credit, part-time degree program (daytime), adult/continuing education programs, co-op programs and internships. Off-campus study at Western Wyoming Community College in respiratory therapy.
GENERAL DEGREE REQUIREMENTS 64 credit hours; math/science requirements vary according to program; computer course; internship (some majors).
MAJORS Agricultural business, agricultural education, agricultural sciences, art/fine arts, automotive technologies, biology/biological sciences, business administration/commerce/management, computer information systems, criminal justice, dental services, drafting and design, education, elementary education, engineering (general), (pre)engineering sequence, engineering technology, English, history, hospitality services, humanities, industrial and heavy equipment maintenance, law enforcement/police sciences, liberal arts/general studies, machine and tool technologies, music, nursing, physical education, practical nursing, respiratory therapy, science, secretarial studies/office management, social science, Spanish, welding technology.
LIBRARY Griffith Memorial Library with 45,019 books, 4,574 microform titles, 341 periodicals, 2 on-line bibliographic services, 315 CD-ROMs, 187 records, tapes, and CDs. Acquisition spending 1994–95: $53,563.
COMPUTERS ON CAMPUS 200 computers for student use in computer labs, various buildings, library provide access to Internet. Staffed computer lab on campus provides training in use of computers, software. Academic computing expenditure 1994–95: $160,390.
COLLEGE LIFE Choral group, student-run newspaper. 20% vote in student government elections. ***Social organizations:*** 20 open to all. ***Most popular organizations:*** Student Government, Phi Theta Kappa, Art Club, Nursing Club, Police Science Club. ***Major annual events:*** Homecoming, Campus Craze, Christmas Dance. ***Student services:*** personal-psychological counseling. ***Campus security:*** student patrols, patrols by certified officers.
HOUSING 160 college housing spaces available; 155 were occupied 1995–96. No special consideration for freshman housing applicants. Off-campus living permitted. ***Option:*** coed housing available. Resident assistants live in dorms.
ATHLETICS Member NJCAA. ***Intercollegiate:*** basketball M(s)/W(s), volleyball W(s). ***Intramural:*** basketball, bowling, golf, soccer, softball, table tennis (Ping-Pong), tennis, volleyball. ***Contact:*** Mr. Bruce Hoffman, Athletic Director, 307-674-6446.
CAREER PLANNING ***Placement office:*** 3 full-time staff. ***Director:*** Dr. Norma Campbell, Director of Counseling and Advising, 307-674-6446. ***Services:*** resume preparation, career counseling, careers library.
EXPENSES FOR 1996–97 State resident tuition: $760 full-time, $33 per credit hour part-time. Nonresident tuition: $2280 full-time, $99 per credit hour part-time. Part-time mandatory fees: $6 per credit hour. Tuition for nonresidents who are eligible for the Western Undergraduate Exchange Program: $1140 full-time, $50 per credit hour part-time. Full-time mandatory fees: $180. College room and board: $2730.
FINANCIAL AID ***College-administered undergrad aid 1995–96:*** 22 need-based scholarships (average $700), 46 non-need scholarships (average $700), short-term loans (average $100), low-interest long-term loans from college funds, loans from external sources (average $1500), 45 Federal Work-Study (averaging $2040), 40 part-time jobs. ***Required***

forms: institutional, FAFSA; accepted: CSS Financial Aid PROFILE. *Priority deadline:* 3/1. *Payment plans:* installment, deferred payment. *Waivers:* full or partial for employees or children of employees and senior citizens.
APPLYING Open admission except for dental hygiene, nursing programs. *Options:* early entrance, deferred entrance, midyear entrance. *Required:* TOEFL for international students, SAT I or ACT. *Required for some:* school transcript. *Recommended:* school transcript. Test scores used for counseling/placement. *Application deadline:* rolling. *Notification:* continuous.
APPLYING/TRANSFER *Recommended:* high school transcript, college transcript. *Required for some:* high school transcript, college transcript. *Application deadline:* rolling. *Notification:* continuous. *Contact:* Ms. Cindy Mortensen, Registrar, 307-674-6446.
CONTACT Mr. Zane Garstad, Admissions Counselor, Sheridan College, PO Box 1500, Sheridan, WY 82801-1500, 307-674-6446 Ext. 138. *Fax:* 307-674-4293. *E-mail:* ckaiser@generals.sc.whecn.edu.

WESTERN WYOMING COMMUNITY COLLEGE
Rock Springs, Wyoming

UG Enrollment: 3,094	Tuition & Fees (WY Res): $1022
Application Deadline: N/R	Room & Board: $2680

GENERAL State and locally supported, 2-year, coed. Awards certificates, diplomas, transfer associate, terminal associate degrees. Founded 1959. *Setting:* 10-acre small-town campus. *Total enrollment:* 3,094. *Faculty:* 232 (72 full-time, 25% with terminal degrees, 160 part-time); student-faculty ratio is 18:1.
ENROLLMENT PROFILE 3,094 students from 15 states and territories, 11 other countries. 67% women, 61% part-time, 98% state residents, 2% transferred in, 64% 25 or older, 1% Native American, 5% Hispanic, 1% African American, 1% Asian American. *Most popular recent majors:* education, psychology, business administration/commerce/management.
FIRST-YEAR CLASS 1,950 total; 3,000 applied, 100% were accepted, 65% of whom enrolled. 100% from top half of their high school class.
ACADEMIC PROGRAM Core, interdisciplinary curriculum, honor code. Calendar: semesters. 1,900 courses offered in 1995-96; average class size 25 in required courses. Academic remediation for entering students, English as a second language program offered during academic year and summer, services for LD students, advanced placement, Freshman Honors College, tutorials, honors program, summer session for credit, part-time degree program (daytime, evenings, summer), adult/continuing education programs, co-op programs and internships.
GENERAL DEGREE REQUIREMENTS 64 credit hours; 1 course each in math and lab science; computer course; internship (some majors).
MAJORS Accounting, anthropology, art/fine arts, automotive technologies, biology/biological sciences, business administration/commerce/management, chemistry, communication, computer information systems, computer programming, construction technologies, criminal justice, dance, data processing, education, electrical and electronics technologies, electrical engineering technology, engineering (general), (pre)engineering sequence, English, French, geology, German, history, humanities, industrial arts, instrumentation technology, journalism, laboratory technologies, law enforcement/police sciences, legal secretarial studies, liberal arts/general studies, machine and tool technologies, marketing/retailing/merchandising, mathematics, medical assistant technologies, medical secretarial studies, music, natural sciences, nursing, photography, physical education, physical sciences, political science/government, practical nursing, psychology, radiological sciences, radiological technology, respiratory therapy, science, secretarial studies/office management, social science, sociology, Spanish, theater arts/drama, welding technology, word processing.
LIBRARY 32,600 books, 100 periodicals, 500 records, tapes, and CDs. Acquisition spending 1994-95: $14,271.
COMPUTERS ON CAMPUS 120 computers for student use in computer labs, learning resource center, writing lab, classrooms, library provide access to off-campus computing facilities, e-mail, on-line services, Internet. Staffed computer lab on campus provides training in use of computers, software.
COLLEGE LIFE Orientation program (2 days, no cost, parents included). Drama-theater group, choral group, student-run newspaper. 30% vote in student government elections. *Social organizations:* 20 open to all. *Student services:* personal-psychological counseling, women's center. *Campus security:* 24-hour emergency response devices, late-night transport-escort service, controlled dormitory access.

HOUSING 310 college housing spaces available; all were occupied 1995-96. No special consideration for freshman housing applicants. Off-campus living permitted. *Options:* freshmen-only, coed housing available. Resident assistants live in dorms.
ATHLETICS Member NJCAA. *Intercollegiate:* basketball M(s)/W(s), wrestling M(s). *Intramural:* archery, basketball, bowling, cross-country running, football, skiing (downhill), soccer, softball, table tennis (Ping-Pong), tennis, volleyball, weight lifting. *Contact:* Dr. Dick Flores, Athletic Director, 307-382-1600.
CAREER PLANNING *Placement office:* 1 full-time staff. *Director:* Ms. Mickey Lucas, Career Counselor, 307-382-1600. *Services:* resume preparation, resume referral, career counseling, careers library, job interviews. 150 organizations recruited on campus 1994-95.
AFTER GRADUATION 42% of students completing a degree program in 1994-95 went directly on to further study.
EXPENSES FOR 1996-97 State resident tuition: $1022 full-time, $43 per credit hour part-time. Nonresident tuition: $2670 full-time, $115 per credit hour part-time. Full-time tuition for nonresidents who are eligible for the Western Undergraduate Exchange Program: $1434. College room and board: $2680. College room only: $1176.
FINANCIAL AID *College-administered undergrad aid 1995-96:* need-based scholarships (averaging $900), non-need scholarships (averaging $554), short-term loans (averaging $300), low-interest long-term loans from external sources, Federal Work-Study, part-time jobs. *Required forms:* institutional; accepted: FAFSA. *Priority deadline:* 4/1. *Payment plan:* deferred payment. *Waivers:* full or partial for employees or children of employees and senior citizens.
APPLYING Open admission. *Options:* Common Application, early entrance, deferred entrance. *Recommended:* ACT. *Required for some:* TOEFL for international students, ACT ASSET. Test scores used for counseling/placement. *Notification:* continuous.
APPLYING/TRANSFER *Entrance:* noncompetitive. *Notification:* continuous. *Contact:* Ms. Jackie Freeze, Associate Dean of Enrollment Services, 307-382-1637.
CONTACT Ms. Jackie Freeze, Associate Dean of Enrollment Services, Western Wyoming Community College, Rock Springs, WY 82902-0428, 307-382-1637. *Fax:* 307-382-1636. *E-mail:* wwjfreez@antelope.wcc.edu. College video available.

WYOMING TECHNICAL INSTITUTE
Laramie, Wyoming

UG Enrollment: 600	Tuition: $13,900/deg prog
Application Deadline: rolling	Room & Board: N/R

GENERAL Proprietary, 2-year, primarily men. Awards terminal associate degrees. Founded 1966. *Setting:* rural campus. *Total enrollment:* 600. *Faculty:* 47 (44 full-time, 3 part-time).
ENROLLMENT PROFILE 600 students; 1% women, 0% part-time, 10% state residents, 85% have need-based financial aid.
ACADEMIC PROGRAM Core. Calendar: 9-month program. 16 courses offered in 1995-96. Services for LD students.
GENERAL DEGREE REQUIREMENTS 1500 clock hours; computer course for associate of applied science degree students.
MAJOR Automotive technologies.
COMPUTERS ON CAMPUS 42 computers for student use in management department. Staffed computer lab on campus provides training in use of computers, software.
COLLEGE LIFE *Student services:* personal-psychological counseling.
HOUSING Off-campus living permitted.
ATHLETICS *Intercollegiate:* basketball W, bowling W. *Intramural:* softball, volleyball.
CAREER PLANNING *Placement office:* 2 full-time, 1 part-time staff. *Services:* job fairs, resume preparation, resume referral, career counseling, careers library, job bank, job interviews.
AFTER GRADUATION 95% of class of 1994 had job offers within 6 months.
EXPENSES FOR 1995-96 *Application fee:* $100. Tuition: $13,900 per degree program.
FINANCIAL AID *College-administered undergrad aid 1995-96:* 25 non-need scholarships (average $2000), Federal Work-Study. *Application deadline:* continuous.
APPLYING Open admission. *Option:* Common Application. *Required:* school transcript. *Application deadline:* rolling.
APPLYING/TRANSFER *Required:* college transcript.
CONTACT Mr. Pete Schutte, Director of Admissions, Wyoming Technical Institute, Laramie, WY 82070-9519, 307-742-3776 or toll-free 800-521-7158. College video available.

US Territories

US TERRITORIES

AMERICAN SAMOA

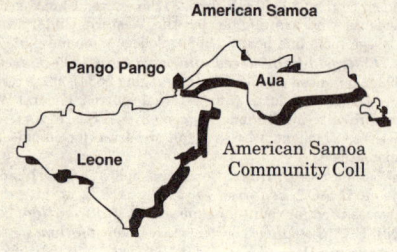

AMERICAN SAMOA COMMUNITY COLLEGE
Pago Pago, American Samoa

CONTACT Mrs. Sina P. Ward, Registrar, American Samoa Community College, Pago Pago, AS 96799-2609, 684-699-1141.

FEDERATED STATES OF MICRONESIA

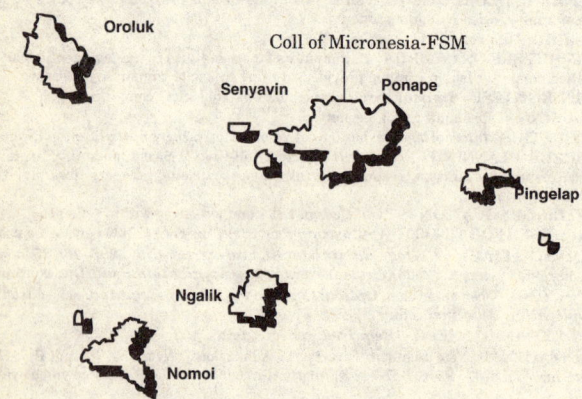

COLLEGE OF MICRONESIA–FSM
Kolonia Pohnpei, Federated States of Micronesia

UG Enrollment: 853	Tuition & Fees: $2210
Application Deadline: 4/15	Room & Board: $2912

GENERAL Territory-supported, 2-year, coed. Founded 1963. *Setting:* 2-acre small-town campus. *Research spending 1994–95:* $129,662. *Total enrollment:* 853. *Faculty:* 37 (all full-time, 8% with terminal degrees); student-faculty ratio is 19:1.
ENROLLMENT PROFILE 853 students: 44% women, 56% men, 15% part-time, 100% territory residents, 20% live on campus, 2% transferred in, 100% have need-based financial aid, 3% 25 or older, 0% Hispanic, 0% African American, 0% Asian American. *Areas of study chosen:* 40% interdisciplinary studies, 1% agriculture.
FIRST-YEAR CLASS 318 total; 331 applied, 96% were accepted, 100% of whom enrolled. 3% from top 10% of their high school class, 10% from top half.
ACADEMIC PROGRAM Core. Calendar: semesters. Average class size 25 in required courses. Academic remediation for entering students, English as a second language program offered during academic year, summer session for credit, adult/continuing education programs, internships.
GENERAL DEGREE REQUIREMENTS 72 semester hours; 1 course each in algebra and trigonometry; computer course for accounting, business, pre-nursing, marine sciences, agriculture, health careers majors.

MAJORS Accounting, agricultural sciences, business administration/commerce/management, education, liberal arts/general studies, marine sciences, nursing, teacher aide studies.
COMPUTERS ON CAMPUS 11 computers for student use in computer center.
COLLEGE LIFE Orientation program (1 week). *Student services:* health clinic, personal-psychological counseling.
HOUSING 148 college housing spaces available; 100 were occupied 1995–96. Freshmen given priority for college housing. Off-campus living permitted. *Option:* coed housing available.
ATHLETICS *Intramural:* basketball, swimming and diving, tennis, track and field, volleyball.
CAREER PLANNING *Service:* career counseling.
EXPENSES FOR 1996–97 *Application fee:* $10. Comprehensive fee of $5122 includes full-time tuition ($2160), mandatory fees ($50), and college room and board ($2912). College room only: $728. Part-time tuition: $60 per semester hour. Part-time mandatory fees: $15 per semester hour. Tuition guaranteed not to increase for student's term of enrollment.
FINANCIAL AID *College-administered undergrad aid 1995–96:* 235 need-based scholarships (average $4000), low-interest long-term loans from college funds (average $500), Federal Work-Study. *Required forms:* CSS Financial Aid PROFILE, FAFSA. *Priority deadline:* 7/1. *Waivers:* full or partial for employees or children of employees.
APPLYING *Options:* deferred entrance, midyear entrance. *Required:* school transcript, minimum 2.0 GPA, TOEFL for international students. *Application deadline:* 4/15. *Notification:* 6/30.
APPLYING/TRANSFER *Required:* high school transcript, college transcript, minimum 2.0 college GPA, minimum 2.0 high school GPA.
CONTACT Ms. Betty Hiesterman, Director of Admissions and Records, College of Micronesia–FSM, Kolonia Pohnpei, FM 96941-0159, 691-320-2480 Ext. 30.

GUAM

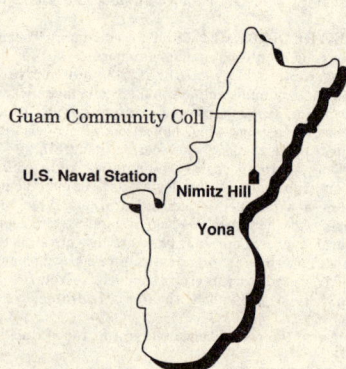

GUAM COMMUNITY COLLEGE
Guam Main Facility, Guam

GENERAL Territory-supported, 2-year, coed. Awards certificates, transfer associate, terminal associate degrees. Founded 1977. *Setting:* 22-acre suburban campus. *Total enrollment:* 723. *Faculty:* 364 (179 full-time, 185 part-time); student-faculty ratio is 2:1.
EXPENSES FOR 1995–96 Tuition: $450 full-time. Part-time mandatory fees: $20 per semester. Full-time mandatory fees: $40.
CONTACT Dr. David G. Watt, Registrar, Guam Community College, Guam Main Facility, GU 96921-3069, 671-734-4311 Ext. 231. *Fax:* 671-734-5238.

US Territories

MARSHALL ISLANDS

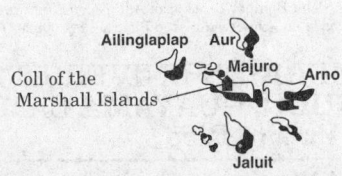

COLLEGE OF THE MARSHALL ISLANDS
Majuro, Marshall Islands

NORTHERN MARIANA ISLANDS

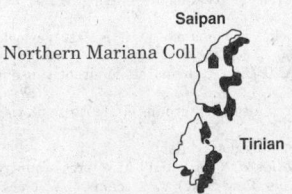

NORTHERN MARIANAS COLLEGE
Saipan, Northern Mariana Islands

UG Enrollment: 954	Tuition & Fees (MP Res): $1815
Application Deadline: rolling	Room & Board: N/Avail

GENERAL Commonwealth-supported, 2-year, coed. Awards certificates, diplomas, transfer associate, terminal associate degrees. Founded 1981. *Setting:* 14-acre rural campus. *Educational spending 1994–95:* $1900 per undergrad. *Total enrollment:* 954. *Faculty:* 82 (62 full-time, 1% with terminal degrees, 20 part-time); student-faculty ratio is 10:1.
ENROLLMENT PROFILE 954 students from 4 states and territories, 4 other countries. 59% women, 41% men, 49% part-time, 77% territory residents, 13% have need-based financial aid, 60% have non-need-based financial aid, 22% international, 36% 25 or older, 63% Native American, 1% Hispanic, 1% African American, 1% Asian American. *Areas of study chosen:* 22% liberal arts/general studies, 17% education, 5% business management and administrative services, 1% agriculture. *Most popular recent majors:* liberal arts/general studies, education, business administration/commerce/management.
FIRST-YEAR CLASS Of the students who applied, 100% were accepted.
ACADEMIC PROGRAM Core. Calendar: semesters. Academic remediation for entering students, English as a second language program offered during academic year and summer, services for LD students, summer session for credit, part-time degree program (daytime, evenings, summer), adult/continuing education programs, co-op programs and internships.
GENERAL DEGREE REQUIREMENTS 61 credits; 1 course each in math and science; computer course for business, office technology, computer science, accounting, sales/marketing, hospitality management majors; internship (some majors).
MAJORS Accounting, agricultural business, agricultural sciences, agricultural technologies, business administration/commerce/management, data processing, education, liberal arts/general studies, marine technology, marketing/retailing/merchandising, nursing, public administration, secretarial studies/office management.
LIBRARY Olympia T. Borja Library plus 1 other, with 25,890 books, 40,000 microform titles, 423 periodicals, 700 records, tapes, and CDs.
COMPUTERS ON CAMPUS 55 computers for student use in computer center. Staffed computer lab on campus provides training in use of computers, software.
COLLEGE LIFE Drama-theater group. 20% vote in student government elections. *Most popular organizations:* Northern Marinas Academy, Korean Association, Micronesion Club, Learning Skills. *Major annual events:* Charter Day, International Night, Haunted House. *Student services:* personal-psychological counseling. *Campus security:* patrols by trained security personnel.
HOUSING College housing not available.
ATHLETICS *Intramural:* basketball, bowling, golf, softball, table tennis (Ping-Pong), tennis, volleyball, weight lifting. *Contact:* Mr. Kurt Barnes, Physical Education Instructor, 670-234-3690 Ext. 1242.
CAREER PLANNING *Placement office:* 2 full-time staff. *Director:* Mr. Victor Mesfa, Director of Student Services, 670-234-3690 Ext. 1511. *Services:* resume preparation, resume referral, career counseling, careers library, job bank, job interviews. 2 organizations recruited on campus 1994–95.
EXPENSES FOR 1995–96 *Application fee:* $15. Territory resident tuition: $1800 full-time, $60 per credit part-time. Nonresident tuition: $3000 full-time, $120 per credit part-time. Full-time mandatory fees: $15.

FINANCIAL AID *College-administered undergrad aid 1995–96:* 376 need-based scholarships (average $772), 24 non-need scholarships (average $828), 20 Federal Work-Study (averaging $709). *Required forms:* FAFSA; required for some: territory, institutional. *Application deadline:* continuous. *Payment plan:* deferred payment. *Waivers:* full or partial for employees or children of employees.
APPLYING Open admission. *Options:* Common Application, early entrance, deferred entrance, midyear entrance. *Required:* school transcript. *Recommended:* SAT I or ACT, TOEFL for international students. Test scores used for counseling/placement. *Application deadline:* rolling.
APPLYING/TRANSFER *Required:* high school transcript, college transcript. *Application deadline:* rolling. *Contact:* Ms. Florine Hofschneider, Director of Admissions and Records, 670-234-3690 Ext. 1440.
CONTACT Ms. Florine Hofschneider, Director of Admissions and Records, Northern Marianas College, P.O. Box 1250, Saipan, MP 96950-1250, 670-234-3690 Ext. 1440. *Fax:* 670-234-0759.

PALAU ISLAND

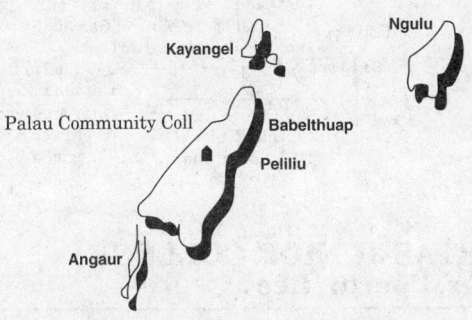

PALAU COMMUNITY COLLEGE
Koror, Palau Island

UG Enrollment: 367	Tuition & Fees: $2610
Application Deadline: 8/29	Room & Board: $2912

GENERAL Territory-supported, 2-year, coed. Awards certificates, transfer associate, terminal associate degrees. Founded 1969. *Setting:* 30-acre small-town campus. *Educational spending 1994–95:* $1482 per undergrad. *Total enrollment:* 367. *Faculty:* 34 (26 full-time, 8 part-time).
ENROLLMENT PROFILE 367 students: 52% women, 48% men, 4% part-time, 20% live on campus, 1% transferred in, 3% international, 8% 25 or older, 0% Native American, 0% Hispanic, 0% African American, 0% Asian American. *Areas of study chosen:* 6% liberal arts/general studies. *Most popular recent majors:* secretarial studies/office management, law enforcement/police sciences.
FIRST-YEAR CLASS 113 total; 183 applied, 82% of whom enrolled. 5% from top 10% of their high school class, 20% from top quarter, 35% from top half.
ACADEMIC PROGRAM Core. Calendar: semesters. 219 courses offered in 1995–96. Academic remediation for entering students, English as a second language program offered during academic year, tutorials, summer session for credit, part-time degree program (daytime, evenings, summer), co-op programs and internships.
GENERAL DEGREE REQUIREMENTS 60 credits; computer course (varies by major); internship (some majors).
MAJORS Accounting, agricultural sciences, automotive technologies, business education, carpentry, construction technologies, electrical and electronics technologies, law enforcement/police sciences, liberal arts/general studies, secretarial studies/office management.
LIBRARY Palau Community College Library with 6,833 books, 27 periodicals, 8 CD-ROMs, 51 records, tapes, and CDs. Acquisition spending 1994–95: $47,687.
COMPUTERS ON CAMPUS 40 computers for student use in computer labs, skill center, library.
COLLEGE LIFE Orientation program (3 days). *Most popular organizations:* Yapese Student Organization, Chuukes Student Organization, Palauans Student Organization. *Major annual event:* Charter Day. *Student services:* health clinic, personal-psychological counseling. *Campus security:* evening patrols by trained security personnel.
HOUSING 228 college housing spaces available; 49 were occupied 1995–96. Freshmen given priority for college housing. off-island students are required to live on campus. *Options:* freshmen-only, single-sex (3 buildings) housing available. Resident assistants live in dorms.
ATHLETICS *Intramural:* archery, badminton, baseball, basketball, cross-country running, softball, table tennis (Ping-Pong), tennis, track and field, volleyball, weight lifting.
CAREER PLANNING *Placement office:* 1 full-time staff; $52,554 operating expenditure 1994–95. *Director:* Ms. Marensia Edward, Director, Student Life and Housing, 680-488-3036. *Services:* resume preparation, resume referral, career counseling, careers library, job interviews. 1 organization recruited on campus 1994–95.
EXPENSES FOR 1995–96 *Application fee:* $10. Comprehensive fee of $5522 includes full-time tuition ($2160), mandatory fees ($450), and college room and board ($2912). College room only: $728. Part-time tuition: $60 per credit.
FINANCIAL AID *College-administered undergrad aid 1995–96:* need-based scholarships, 28 non-need scholarships (averaging $362), 194 Federal Work-Study (averaging $246), part-time jobs. *Required forms:* institutional, FAFSA; accepted: CSS Financial Aid PROFILE. *Priority deadline:* 6/1. *Payment plan:* installment. *Waivers:* full or partial for employees or children of employees.

Peterson's Guide to Two-Year Colleges 1997

US Territories

Palau Community College (continued)
APPLYING Open admission. *Options:* early entrance, deferred entrance, midyear entrance. *Required for some:* TOEFL for international students. Test scores used for admission and counseling/placement. *Application deadlines:* 8/29, rolling for nonresidents. *Notification:* continuous, continuous for nonresidents.
APPLYING/TRANSFER *Entrance:* noncompetitive. *Contact:* Ms. Joyce Ngirachitei, Career and Transfer Counselor, 680-488-3073.
CONTACT Mrs. Dahlia M. Katosang, Director of Admissions and Financial Aid, Palau Community College, PO Box 9, Koror, PW 96940-0009, 680-488-2471 Ext. 04. *Fax:* 680-488-2447.

PUERTO RICO

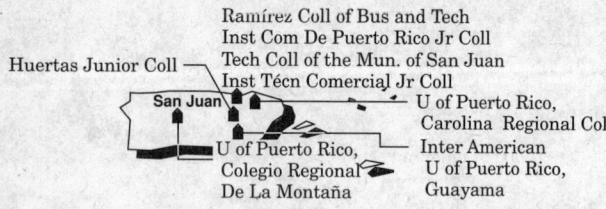

HUERTAS JUNIOR COLLEGE
Caguas, Puerto Rico

UG Enrollment: 2,220	Tuition & Fees: $2520
Application Deadline: rolling	Room & Board: N/Avail

GENERAL Proprietary, 2-year, coed. Awards terminal associate degrees. Founded 1945. *Setting:* 4-acre urban campus with easy access to San Juan. *Educational spending 1994–95:* $570 per undergrad. *Total enrollment:* 2,220. *Faculty:* 91 (25 full-time, 100% with terminal degrees, 66 part-time); student-faculty ratio is 24:1.
ENROLLMENT PROFILE 2,220 students: 61% women, 34% part-time, 100% commonwealth residents, 3% transferred in, 100% Hispanic, 0% African American. *Areas of study chosen:* 37% vocational and home economics, 36% health professions and related sciences, 15% business management and administrative services, 12% computer and information sciences.
FIRST-YEAR CLASS 1,141 total.
ACADEMIC PROGRAM Core. Calendar: trimesters. Academic remediation for entering students, English as a second language program offered during academic year, part-time degree program (daytime, evenings), internships.
GENERAL DEGREE REQUIREMENTS 76 credits; computer course; internship (some majors).
MAJORS Accounting, business administration/commerce/management, computer science, dental services, pharmacy/pharmaceutical sciences, secretarial studies/office management.
LIBRARY Learning Resources Center with 5,524 books, 1,144 periodicals, 200 CD-ROMs, 1,181 records, tapes, and CDs. Acquisition spending 1994–95: $18,000.
COMPUTERS ON CAMPUS 100 computers for student use in computer center. Staffed computer lab on campus provides training in use of computers, software.
COLLEGE LIFE Choral group. *Social organizations:* 1 open to all. *Student services:* health clinic. *Campus security:* 24-hour patrols.
HOUSING College housing not available.
CAREER PLANNING *Placement office:* 2 full-time staff; $30,000 operating expenditure 1994–95. *Director:* Mrs. Lourdes Muñoz, Director of the Occupational Center, 809-743-2156. *Services:* job fairs, resume preparation, resume referral, career counseling, careers library, job bank, job interviews.
EXPENSES FOR 1996–97 *Application fee:* $27. Tuition: $2520 full-time, $70 per credit part-time.
FINANCIAL AID *College-administered undergrad aid 1995–96:* 120 need-based scholarships (averaging $450), Federal Work-Study. *Required forms:* FAFSA. *Application deadline:* continuous.
APPLYING *Options:* Common Application, deferred entrance, midyear entrance. *Required for some:* minimum 2.0 GPA. *Application deadline:* rolling. *Notification:* continuous.
APPLYING/TRANSFER *Required for some:* minimum 2.0 high school GPA. *Contact:* Ms. BarbaraHassim, Director of Admissions, 809-743-2156 Ext. 23.
CONTACT Ms. Barbara Hassim, Director of Admissions, Huertas Junior College, PO Box 8429, Caguas, PR 00625, 809-743-2156 Ext. 23. College video available.

INSTITUTO COMERCIAL DE PUERTO RICO JUNIOR COLLEGE
Hato Rey, Puerto Rico

CONTACT Mr. Pedro Sobrino, Recruiting Official, Instituto Comercial de Puerto Rico Junior College, Hato Rey, PR 00919-0304, 809-763-1010.

INSTITUTO TÉCNICO COMERCIAL JUNIOR COLLEGE
Río Piedras, Puerto Rico

CONTACT Ms. Ana Celia Bonilla, Director of Admissions, Instituto Técnico Comercial Junior College, 806 Ponce de Leon Avenue, Río Piedras, PR 00926, 809-767-4323.

INTER AMERICAN UNIVERSITY OF PUERTO RICO, GUAYAMA CAMPUS
Guayama, Puerto Rico

UG Enrollment: 1,304	Tuition & Fees: $3019
Application Deadline: 8/1	Room & Board: N/Avail

GENERAL Independent, primarily 2-year, coed. Part of Inter American University of Puerto Rico. Awards terminal associate, bachelor's degrees. Founded 1958. *Setting:* 50-acre small-town campus. *Total enrollment:* 1,304. *Faculty:* 89 (40 full-time, 49 part-time).
ENROLLMENT PROFILE 1,304 students: 78% women, 25% part-time, 100% commonwealth residents, 3% transferred in, 100% Hispanic.
FIRST-YEAR CLASS 245 total; 422 applied, 74% were accepted, 79% of whom enrolled. 5% from top 10% of their high school class, 15% from top quarter, 80% from top half.
ACADEMIC PROGRAM Core. Calendar: semesters. Academic remediation for entering students, English as a second language program offered during academic year and summer, services for LD students, summer session for credit, part-time degree program (daytime, evenings), adult/continuing education programs. Off-campus study at other units of the Inter American University of Puerto Rico.
GENERAL DEGREE REQUIREMENTS 60 semester hours for associate; 3 semester hours each of math and science; computer course.
MAJORS Accounting, business administration/commerce/management (B), chemistry (B), computer science, criminal justice (B), elementary education (B), law enforcement/police sciences, marketing/retailing/merchandising, nursing (B), secretarial studies/office management (B).
LIBRARY 16,290 books, 137 microform titles, 212 periodicals, 12 CD-ROMs, 8,352 records, tapes, and CDs.
COMPUTERS ON CAMPUS 70 computers for student use in computer center provide access to Internet.
COLLEGE LIFE Drama-theater group, student-run newspaper. *Student services:* health clinic.
HOUSING College housing not available.
ATHLETICS *Intercollegiate:* basketball M/W, cross-country running M/W, soccer M, softball M/W, table tennis (Ping-Pong) M/W, tennis M/W, track and field M/W, volleyball M/W, weight lifting M. *Intramural:* basketball, cross-country running, softball, table tennis (Ping-Pong), tennis, track and field, volleyball. *Contact:* Mr. Modesto Texidor, Athletic Director, 787-864-2222 Ext. 2261.
CAREER PLANNING *Service:* career counseling.
EXPENSES FOR 1995–96 Tuition: $2790 full-time, $90 per semester hour part-time. Part-time mandatory fees: $114.65 per semester. Full-time mandatory fees: $229.
FINANCIAL AID *College-administered undergrad aid 1995–96:* need-based scholarships, low-interest long-term loans from external sources, Federal Work-Study. *Required forms:* FAFSA. *Application deadline:* continuous to 4/15. *Payment plan:* deferred payment. *Waivers:* full or partial for employees or children of employees.
APPLYING *Options:* early entrance, deferred entrance. *Required:* SAT I, PAA. Test scores used for admission and counseling/placement. *Application deadline:* 8/1.
APPLYING/TRANSFER *Required:* standardized test scores. *Required for some:* high school transcript, minimum 2.0 high school GPA. *Application deadline:* 8/1. *Contact:* Ms. Laura E. Ferrer, Director of Admissions, 787-864-2222 Ext. 220.
CONTACT Mrs. Laura E. Ferrer, Director of Admissions, Inter American University of Puerto Rico, Guayama Campus, Guayama, PR 00785, 787-864-2222 Ext. 220.

RAMÍREZ COLLEGE OF BUSINESS AND TECHNOLOGY
San Juan, Puerto Rico

UG Enrollment: 1,364	Tuition & Fees: $2500
Application Deadline: rolling	Room & Board: N/Avail

GENERAL Proprietary, 2-year, coed. Awards diplomas, transfer associate, terminal associate degrees. Founded 1922. *Setting:* small-town campus with easy access to San Juan. *Total enrollment:* 1,364.
ENROLLMENT PROFILE 1,364 students: 73% women, 0% part-time, 97% commonwealth residents, 6% transferred in, 1% international, 24% 25 or older, 100% Hispanic.
FIRST-YEAR CLASS 850 total; 900 applied, 100% were accepted, 94% of whom enrolled.
ACADEMIC PROGRAM Calendar: trimesters. Academic remediation for entering students, adult/continuing education programs.
GENERAL DEGREE REQUIREMENTS 75 credits; 1 math course; 3 courses in English; computer course.
MAJORS Accounting, business administration/commerce/management, dental services, secretarial studies/office management.
COLLEGE LIFE *Student services:* health clinic, personal-psychological counseling.
HOUSING College housing not available.
CAREER PLANNING *Service:* career counseling.
EXPENSES FOR 1996–97 Tuition: $2500 (minimum) full-time. Part-time tuition per trimester ranges from $98 to $975. Full-time tuition ranges up to $2600 per year according to program.
FINANCIAL AID *College-administered undergrad aid 1995–96:* 381 need-based scholarships (average $300). *Required forms:* institutional, FAFSA; required for some: birth certificate. *Application deadline:* continuous.
APPLYING Open admission. *Required:* minimum 2.0 GPA, campus interview. *Application deadline:* rolling.
APPLYING/TRANSFER *Required:* campus interview, minimum 2.0 high school GPA. *Entrance:* noncompetitive. *Application deadline:* rolling.

US Territories–Republic of Panama

CONTACT Mrs. Evelyn Mercado, Director of Admissions, Ramírez College of Business and Technology, San Juan, PR 00910-0340, 809-763-3120.

TECHNOLOGICAL COLLEGE OF THE MUNICIPALITY OF SAN JUAN
Hato Rey, Puerto Rico

UG Enrollment: 946	Tuition & Fees (PR Res): $1400
Application Deadline: 4/15	Room & Board: N/Avail

GENERAL City-supported, 2-year, coed. Awards diplomas, transfer associate degrees. Founded 1971. *Setting:* 5-acre campus. *Total enrollment:* 946. *Faculty:* 91 (61 full-time, 30 part-time).
ENROLLMENT PROFILE 946 students: 62% women, 13% part-time, 96% commonwealth residents, 5% transferred in, 0% Native American, 100% Hispanic, 0% Asian American.
FIRST-YEAR CLASS 510 total; 630 applied, 81% were accepted, 100% of whom enrolled.
ACADEMIC PROGRAM Core. Calendar: semesters. Academic remediation for entering students, English as a second language program offered during academic year, services for LD students, summer session for credit, part-time degree program (daytime, evenings).
GENERAL DEGREE REQUIREMENTS 72 credits; math/science requirements vary according to program; 1 course in English; computer course.
MAJORS Accounting, computer programming, electronics engineering technology, liberal arts/general studies, medical records services, nursing, secretarial studies/office management, telecommunications.
LIBRARY 10,000 books, 700 periodicals, 300 records, tapes, and CDs.
COMPUTERS ON CAMPUS 38 computers for student use in computer center.
COLLEGE LIFE Student-run newspaper. *Student services:* health clinic, personal-psychological counseling.
HOUSING College housing not available.
ATHLETICS *Intercollegiate:* basketball M/W, cross-country running M/W, tennis M/W, track and field M/W, volleyball M/W, weight lifting M/W. *Intramural:* basketball, cross-country running, tennis, track and field, volleyball, weight lifting.
CAREER PLANNING *Service:* career counseling.
EXPENSES FOR 1996–97 Commonwealth resident tuition: $1400 full-time. Nonresident tuition: $1800 full-time.
FINANCIAL AID *College-administered undergrad aid 1995–96:* 150 need-based scholarships, Federal Work-Study. *Required forms:* commonwealth, FAFSA, affidavit of nonsupport. *Priority deadline:* 9/30.
APPLYING *Required:* SAT I. Test scores used for admission. *Application deadline:* 4/15. *Notification:* continuous until 7/31.
APPLYING/TRANSFER *Required:* standardized test scores. *Entrance:* minimally difficult.
CONTACT Mrs. Ruth E. Vicens, Director of Admissions, Technological College of the Municipality of San Juan, Jose R. Oliver Street, Hato Rey, PR 00918, 809-250-7095 Ext. 249.

UNIVERSITY OF PUERTO RICO, CAROLINA REGIONAL COLLEGE
Carolina, Puerto Rico

CONTACT Mrs. Ivonne Calderon, Admissions Officer, University of Puerto Rico, Carolina Regional College, PO Box 4800, Carolina, PR 00984-4800, 809-257-0000 Ext. 3347.

UNIVERSITY OF PUERTO RICO, COLEGIO REGIONAL DE LA MONTAÑA
Utuado, Puerto Rico

CONTACT Ms. Naidez Casalduc, Admissions Officer, University of Puerto Rico, Colegio Regional de la Montaña, Call Box 2500, Utuado, PR 00641-2500, 809-894-2828 Ext. 264.

REPUBLIC OF PANAMA

PANAMA CANAL COLLEGE
Balboa, Republic of Panama

UG Enrollment: 878	Tuition & Fees: $1920
Application Deadline: N/R	Room & Board: N/Avail

GENERAL Federally supported, 2-year, coed. Part of Department of Defense Dependents Schools. Awards certificates, diplomas, transfer associate, terminal associate degrees. Founded 1933. *Setting:* 10-acre small-town campus. *Total enrollment:* 878. *Faculty:* 48 (10 full-time, 38 part-time).
ENROLLMENT PROFILE 878 students: 54% women, 46% men, 86% part-time, 4% international, 39% 25 or older, 0% Native American, 42% Hispanic, 1% black, 1% Asian. *Most popular recent majors:* liberal arts/general studies, business administration/commerce/management, data processing.
FIRST-YEAR CLASS Of the students who applied, 100% were accepted, 100% of whom enrolled.
ACADEMIC PROGRAM Core, general education curriculum. Calendar: semesters. Average class size 16 in required courses. Academic remediation for entering students, English as a second language program offered during academic year and summer, advanced placement, summer session for credit, part-time degree program (daytime, evenings, summer).
GENERAL DEGREE REQUIREMENTS 64 semester credit hours; 1 lab science course; computer course.
MAJORS Biology/biological sciences, business administration/commerce/management, computer science, data processing, English, liberal arts/general studies, mathematics, social science, Spanish.
LIBRARY Panama Canal College Library plus 1 other, with 50,000 books, 100 periodicals, 1 on-line bibliographic service, 14 CD-ROMs, 20,000 records, tapes, and CDs.
COMPUTERS ON CAMPUS 48 computers for student use in computer labs, learning resource center, library provide access to main academic computer, e-mail, Bulletin Board Service. Staffed computer lab on campus provides training in use of computers, software.
COLLEGE LIFE Student-run newspaper. *Most popular organizations:* Phi Theta Kappa, Student Senate, Ecology Club. *Campus security:* surveillance monitors.
HOUSING College housing not available.
ATHLETICS *Intramural:* archery, badminton, basketball, bowling, football, golf, gymnastics, soccer, swimming and diving, tennis, track and field, volleyball, weight lifting.
CAREER PLANNING *Service:* career counseling.
EXPENSES FOR 1995–96 Full-time tuition: $1920 for U.S. dependents, $6004 for all other students. Part-time tuition per credit: $80 for U.S. dependents, $132 for all other students.
FINANCIAL AID *College-administered undergrad aid 1995–96:* short-term loans (average $300), 16 part-time jobs. *Required forms:* institutional. *Priority deadline:* 8/1.
APPLYING Open admission. *Option:* early entrance. *Required:* Michigan Test of English Language Proficiency. *Recommended:* 3 years of high school math and science, some high school foreign language, SAT I or ACT, TOEFL for international students. Test scores used for counseling/placement.
APPLYING/TRANSFER *Required:* standardized test scores. *Entrance:* minimally difficult.
CONTACT Mrs. Sandra M. Abell, Assistant Dean/Registrar, Panama Canal College, DODDS, Panama, APO Unit #0925, AA 34002, 272-3304.

SWITZERLAND

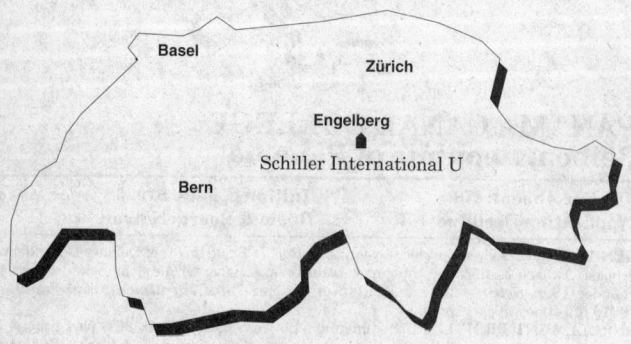

SCHILLER INTERNATIONAL UNIVERSITY
Engelberg, Switzerland

UG Enrollment: 57	Tuition & Fees: $11,300
Application Deadline: rolling	Room & Board: $8500

GENERAL Independent, 2-year, coed. Part of Schiller International University. Awards transfer associate, terminal associate degrees. Founded 1988. *Setting:* urban campus with easy access to Zurich. *Total enrollment:* 57. *Faculty:* 11 (6 full-time, 5 part-time).
ENROLLMENT PROFILE 57 students: 47% women, 53% men, 2% part-time, 87% international. *Areas of study chosen:* 100% business management and administrative services.
ACADEMIC PROGRAM Core, hotel/tourism management curriculum, honor code. Calendar: semesters. English as a second language program offered during academic year and summer, advanced placement, self-designed majors, tutorials, summer session for credit, adult/continuing education programs, co-op programs and internships. Study abroad in Germany, France, Spain, England, United States.
GENERAL DEGREE REQUIREMENTS 62 credits; intermediate competence in a foreign language; computer course; internship (some majors).
MAJORS Hotel and restaurant management, international business.
LIBRARY 1,423 books, 17 periodicals.
COMPUTERS ON CAMPUS 7 computers for student use in computer center.
NOTEWORTHY RESEARCH FACILITIES Hotel Europe, Hotel Bellevue.
COLLEGE LIFE Orientation program (2 days). Student-run newspaper. *Most popular organizations:* Student Government, Student Newspaper. *Major annual event:* Formal Dances. *Student services:* personal-psychological counseling. *Campus security:* 24-hour emergency response devices.
HOUSING 120 college housing spaces available; 57 were occupied 1995–96. *Option:* coed housing available. Resident assistants live in dorms.
ATHLETICS *Intramural:* skiing (cross-country), skiing (downhill), swimming and diving, tennis.
CAREER PLANNING *Services:* resume preparation, career counseling.
EXPENSES FOR 1996–97 *Application fee:* $35. Comprehensive fee of $19,800 includes full-time tuition ($11,100), mandatory fees ($200), and college room and board ($8500). Part-time tuition: $250 per credit. (All figures are in U.S. dollars. Actual costs will vary with the rate of exchange.)
FINANCIAL AID *College-administered undergrad aid 1995–96:* 7 need-based scholarships, low-interest long-term loans from external sources. *Required forms for some financial aid applicants:* institutional, FAFSA; accepted: CSS Financial Aid PROFILE. *Priority deadline:* 3/30. *Payment plan:* deferred payment. *Waivers:* full or partial for employees or children of employees.
APPLYING *Options:* Common Application, deferred entrance, midyear entrance. *Required for some:* English Placement Exam. Test scores used for counseling/placement. *Application deadline:* rolling.
APPLYING/TRANSFER *Entrance:* noncompetitive. *Application deadline:* rolling. *Contact:* Ms. Bella Anand, Associate Director of Admission, 94-4343.
CONTACT Dr. Birgit Black, Director of Studies, Schiller International University, Dorfstrasse 40, Engelberg CH 6390, Switzerland, 94-4343. College video available.

In-Depth Descriptions of the Colleges

An Inside Look

The profiles presented on pages 150–686 provide a wealth of statistics that are crucial components in the college decision-making equation—components such as tuition, financial aid, and major fields of study. This section shifts the focus to a variety of other factors, some of them intangible, that should also be considered.

The following two-page descriptions, prepared exclusively by college officials, are designed to help give students a better sense of the individuality of each institution in terms that include campus environment, student activities, and life-style. Such quality-of-life intangibles can be the deciding factors in the college selection process.

The absence from this section of any college or university does not constitute an editorial decision on the part of Peterson's Guides. In essence, this section is an open forum for colleges and universities, on a voluntary basis, to communicate their particular messages to prospective college students. The descriptions are arranged alphabetically by the official name of the institution.

AMERICAN ACADEMY OF DRAMATIC ARTS
NEW YORK, NEW YORK, AND PASADENA, CALIFORNIA

The College and Its Mission

Founded in New York in 1884, the Academy was the first school in the United States to provide a professional education for actors. Since 1974, the Academy has operated an additional campus in the Los Angeles area, making AADA the only accredited conservatory for actors offering programs in both of the major centers of theatrical activity in the country. Now in its second century, the Academy remains dedicated to a single purpose: training actors. Every activity at the school is directed to that end. The love of acting, as an art and as an occupation, is the spirit that impels the school. For the serious, well-motivated student ready to make a commitment to acting and to concentrated professional training, the Academy offers over a century of success; a well-balanced, carefully structured curriculum; and a vital, dedicated, and caring faculty. Academy training involves the student intellectually, physically, and emotionally. Designed for the individual, it stresses self-discovery and self-discipline. Underlying the training (in California as in New York) are the beliefs that an actor prepared to work on the stage has the best foundation for acting in any medium and that classroom learning must be put to the test in the practical arena of a theater. The soundness of this approach is reflected in the achievements of the alumni, a diverse body of professionals unmatched by the alumni of any other institution. (Academy alumni have been nominated for 93 Oscars, 68 Tonys, and 201 Emmys.) The time spent at the Academy can be an important period of development for those who become professional actors as well as for those who eventually choose other paths. All students are expected to make a commitment to professionalism, excellence, and discipline while enrolled at the Academy. The American Academy of Dramatic Arts is a nonprofit educational institution, chartered in New York by the Board of Regents of the University of the State of New York. In New York the Academy is accredited by the Middle States Association of Colleges and Schools and in California by the Western Association of Schools and Colleges. Both schools are accredited by the National Association of Schools of Theatre.

Academic Program

The Professional Training Program requires two years to complete. Students who meet the requirements of the program receive an associate degree. A third-year performance program is offered to selected graduates. Students who successfully complete this program earn the Certificate of Advanced Studies in Actor training.

The first year consists of two 12-week terms and one 6-week term, providing a total of 30 transferable college credits. Classes include acting, movement, voice and speech, vocal production, acting styles, and theater history. The primary goals of the first-year program are to achieve relaxed, free, and truthful use of oneself in imaginary circumstances; to gain awareness of the body in terms of alignment, flexibility, and strength; to develop an open, well-placed, and well-supported vocal tone; to acquire clearly articulated standard American speech; and to increase understanding of the historical and stylistic backgrounds of drama. Students may enter the first year in mid-September or late January for the course in Pasadena; late October or early February for New York. Admission to the second year is by invitation. Selection is made on the basis of progress, potential, and readiness to benefit from advanced training, as evidenced by the quality of first-year classwork and examination play performances. In 1995, approximately 44 percent of the first-year class was invited to continue into the second year. The second year begins with advanced classwork designed to reinforce and build upon the learning experiences of the first year. Emphasis is gradually shifted to performance opportunities. Additional courses are given in fencing and stage makeup. The second-year course is worth 30 transferable undergraduate credits. Workshops to deal with specific acting problems are set up as needed, and, toward the end of the second year, seminars are scheduled to familiarize students with basic procedures for attaining professional employment. Upon completion of the second year, students graduate from the Professional Training Program with associate degrees. Admission to the third-year program, which emphasizes performance, is also by invitation. Students who undertake a third year of study become members of the Academy Company, the school's performance ensemble. Selection is based on the individual's potential and the overall concept of a balanced acting company. The practical development of the actor is continued through study, rehearsal, and performance of fully-produced plays in Academy theaters over a thirty-week period from late summer to late winter. Agents, casting directors, and other professional personnel are invited to see Academy Company productions, and counseling is offered to assist third-year students in launching professional careers. Students completing the third-year program earn an additional 30 college credits and are awarded a certificate. Guest speakers from the professional world are regularly invited to the Academy to share insights with the students at special assemblies.

The Academy also offers a six-week summer conservatory for those who would like to begin to study, to refresh basic skills, or to test interest and ability in an environment of professional training. Classes begin shortly after the Fourth of July and are open to anyone of high school age or older. Teaching standards are identical to those of the Academy's degree and certificate programs.

Costs

In 1996–97, the total cost of tuition and fees for the full-time program is $9200: $9000 for tuition and $200 for the general fee. (The general fee covers the cost of accident insurance, costume and production costs, use of the library, and student identification.) Students need to budget an additional $400 for purchasing books and scripts, dance attire for movement class, a makeup kit, and other expenses related to the training. The cost of housing varies. It tends to be somewhat higher in New York, while in California, where a car is a virtual necessity, the cost of transportation tends to be higher. On the average, housing, food, transportation, and personal expenses can amount to approximately $7600.

Financial Aid

The Academy makes every effort to assist students in need of financial aid. The Academy participates in various financial aid programs, including government administered grants, loans, and college work-study. Grant awards are determined by financial need. (Only United States citizens and permanent residents are eligible for government-sponsored aid programs.) Payment plans (for those eligible) assist students by extending the payment of tuition over a period of time. Scholarships, awarded on the basis of both need and merit, are available to qualified students, including a limited number of Trustee Awards to first-year students. New York City and Pasadena offer numerous job opportunities for students desiring part-time employment, including on-campus employment (work-study).

Faculty

To achieve its objectives, the Academy requires that its faculty members be well trained in the various performing arts disciplines; seasoned by professional experience; mature, objective, and sympathetic in their relations with students; and exemplars of the commitment to excellence that the Academy hopes to instill in its students. In their own training, the Academy's faculty members represent all of the master teachers and significant systems and philosophies of the performing arts of the past half-century. Their professional experience is diversified, encompassing a variety of positions in film, television, and theater. In selecting faculty members to support its specialized programs, the Academy places more importance on an instructor's professional training and experience and teaching ability than on traditional academic credentials. There are an average of 12 full-time and 8 part-time faculty members at each campus. The student-faculty ratio ranges from 16:1 in classroom instruction, to 4:1 or 3:1 in some performance situations.

Student Body Profile

Academy students reflect a wide diversity of backgrounds and geographical origin; they come from every region of the United States, from Canada, and from many other countries. Fall 1995 enrollment was 208 in Pasadena and 201 in New York, with a combined average of 16 percent members of minority groups and 17 percent international students. The male-female ratio is 45:55. The average age of an entering Academy student is 21. Approximately half of all first-year students come directly after high school; others enroll after a range of experiences, including college, military service, or other careers. The Academy does not maintain living quarters for students at either location. A list of suggested accommodations is provided to all applicants, but students are responsible for securing their own housing.

Student Activities

Students at the American Academy of Dramatic Arts are bonded by their love of acting. A common interest and the collaborative nature of the training contribute to genial social relations among the student body, and, accordingly, school-arranged activities are usually related to the performing arts. Academy students are frequently invited to attend all types of theatrical events for free or given the opportunity to purchase reduced-priced tickets. Every effort is made by the school to facilitate the cultural enrichment of the students.

Facilities and Resources

The Academy in New York is housed in a six-story building that is a registered New York City landmark. It includes classrooms, rehearsal studios, dance studios, a video studio, a student lounge, locker areas, and dressing rooms. A library, made possible by a grant from CBS, is a handsome facility organized to serve the special needs of the actor. Three theaters—a 160-seat proscenium theater, an intimate 160-seat thrust-stage theater, and a semi-arena theater that seats 103—are used for classes, rehearsals, and productions. Production facilities include a prop department, costume department, scene shop, and sound room. AADA/West stands on a five-acre parklike campus with facilities similar to those in New York, including classrooms, studios, a student lounge, full production facilities, a parking lot, and a library. The campus houses two theaters—a 155-seat proscenium house and a 75-seat black-box theater.

Location

Located in midtown Manhattan, the New York home of the Academy is within walking distance of the Grand Central and Pennsylvania train stations, the Port Authority bus terminal, and Broadway and off-Broadway theaters. The West Coast home of the Academy is located near the foothills of the San Gabriel Mountains, approximately 20 minutes by freeway from Los Angeles and Hollywood. At each location, the training at the Academy is enhanced by an exciting variety of nearby cultural and recreational opportunities: theaters, cinemas, concert venues, museums, libraries, restaurants, and sports facilities.

Admission Requirements

AADA seeks talented and highly motivated applicants. An audition/interview is the cornerstone of the admission process. The overall policy is to admit individuals who seem both artistically and academically qualified to undertake a rigorous conservatory program of professional training. Readiness to benefit fully from such training is assessed in the audition/interview. Auditions, whether for entrance into the program in New York City or Pasadena, may be held at either school. In addition, regional auditions are held annually in major cities in the United States and Canada. The audition requires the performance of two contrasting, memorized speeches from published plays, total performance time to be no more than 5 minutes. The audition appointment includes an interview. In the audition/interview, special attention is given to the quality of the applicant's instinctive emotional connection to the audition material. Since good listening is so fundamental to good acting, the auditioner notes how well the applicant listens in the "real world" context of the interview. Other criteria include sensitivity, sense of language, sense of humor, vitality, presence, vocal quality, cultural interests, a realistic sense of self, and the challenge involved in pursuing an acting career.

All entering students must hold a diploma from an accredited secondary school or its equivalent. Transcripts of all previous academic work must be submitted; previous college credits may not be transferred. High school seniors should submit SAT I or ACT scores. Two letters of recommendation and a health certificate are required before an audition is scheduled. International students who are fluent in English are welcome to apply. AADA is approved for the training of veterans.

Application and Information

The Academy operates on a rolling admission basis, but early application is encouraged. There is a nonrefundable application fee of $35. Admission decisions are made within four weeks of the audition. Further information may be obtained from:

For AADA/East:
Jeanne Gosselin
Director of Admission
American Academy of Dramatic Arts
120 Madison Avenue
New York, New York 10016

Telephone: 212-686-9244
800-463-8990 (toll-free)

For AADA/West:
James Wickline
Director of Admission
American Academy of Dramatic Arts
2550 Paloma Street
Pasadena, California 91107

Telephone: 818-798-0777
800-222-2867 (toll-free)

Robert Redford presents fellow AADA alumnus Jason Robards with the Alumni Achievement Award at the Centennial Gala.

AQUINAS COLLEGE AT NEWTON
NEWTON, MASSACHUSETTS

The College and Its Mission

Aquinas College at Newton was founded in 1961 by the Congregation of the Sisters of St. Joseph of Boston. Aquinas is an accredited two-year Catholic college for women. The College offers a curriculum that integrates a liberal arts core with preprofessional and career degree programs. Through degree and certificate programs, Aquinas continues to meet the changing needs of the adult, the traditional, and the nontraditional learner.

Faithful to the unity of ideals fostered among all major religious traditions, Aquinas assumes its character from a commitment to Catholic principles. The College welcomes students of all ethnic and cultural backgrounds and all faiths to its academic and community life.

The goal of Aquinas College is to produce a graduate who is educated to respect self and others, trained to participate in the creation of new worlds in an ever-changing society, and fearless in a commitment to work cooperatively for this postmodern venture.

At Aquinas, students are encouraged to develop their individual potential in an atmosphere of personalized learning and faculty support. In addition to a broad range of academic life, Aquinas students participate in a variety of social activities to promote a balance between their intellectual and personal growth. All students are encouraged to initiate and organize activities that enhance their college experience. Campus Ministry provides an opportunity for students to search, share, and celebrate their values and beliefs. The Legal Association, a professional club for legal students, is sponsored by the Legal Students Chapter of the Southern Middlesex County Legal Secretaries Association. It encourages professional involvement as students attend seminars presented by attorneys, legal secretaries, and paralegals. Phi Theta Kappa is the Alpha Gamma Beta Chapter of the National Honor Society for Junior Colleges. Membership is extended by invitation to students who meet the national Phi Theta Kappa requirements and those of Aquinas. The Society for the Advancement of Management, an international professional association, provides business administration students an opportunity to interact with practicing managers through forums, as well as an opportunity to practice management techniques in organizing and planning events. The Tour Guide Club is designed for women with a strong commitment to the future direction and growth of the College. They explore their strengths by participating in the overall operation of the Admissions Office.

Education at Aquinas means more than acquiring the skills that qualify graduates for employment; it is a total learning experience that is intended to open the mind to the world of ideas, to encourage an awareness of self-worth, and to prepare women to meet challenging opportunities. In addition, Aquinas helps students to discover a life/career path that suits their personality, capabilities, and aspirations.

Aquinas women begin their career or seek further education as qualified professionals prepared for a lifetime of personal growth. Developing marketable skills helps Aquinas graduates enter the career of their choice following graduation.

Aquinas is approved by the Commonwealth of Massachusetts Higher Education Coordinating Council, accredited by the New England Association of Schools and Colleges, and affiliated with the American Association of Community and Junior Colleges, American Association of Medical Assistants, Eastern Business Teachers Association, Massachusetts Association of Business Schools, New England Association of Business Schools, New England Junior College Council, New England Business College Association, National Association for the Education of Young Children, and Massachusetts Association for Children with Learning Disabilities.

Academic Programs

The curriculum at Aquinas serves both the needs of students who are eager to enter the work force upon graduation and the needs of students who want to transfer to a four-year college or university. The Aquinas Counseling Office offers guidance to students who are considering either option, or both.

Aquinas grants the **Associate in Science** degree with majors in business administration (accounting, medical office management, and office management), early childhood education, general business/liberal studies, medical assisting, and office technology (with specialties in executive, human resources, human services, legal, marketing and accounting, medical, and word/information processing).

Aquinas also offers one-year certificate programs, providing necessary skills for immediate employment. Completion of the one-year programs is equivalent to half of the credits needed for an associate degree. Certificates are offered in accounting, biotechnology, customer service, day care, environmental technology, legal research with administrative skills, medical assisting, office administration (executive, legal, medical, and medical insurance), and office technology.

An integral part of the Aquinas experience is the Internship component. Course work is not seen in isolation from the job world. Aquinas students make a smooth transition from school to a career because relationships between school preparation and on-the-job activities have been established.

Costs

The yearly tuition and fees at Aquinas are estimated at $7550 for 1996–97.

Financial Aid

A student's attendance at Aquinas means that she will be able to acquire the special preparation needed for the career of her choice. This requires careful financial planning. The Aquinas Financial Aid program assists as many eligible students as resources permit, with the intention of opening educational opportunities to all qualified students. Ninety percent of the students who applied for financial aid in the 1994–95 academic year received financial aid.

Aquinas participates in federal, state, and private financial aid programs. Federal programs include the Federal Pell Grant, Federal Supplemental Educational Opportunity Grant, Federal Perkins Loan, Federal Stafford Student Loan (subsidized and unsubsidized), Federal PLUS loan, and Federal Work-Study. State programs include the Massachusetts State Scholarship and Gilbert Grant. Private programs include the TERI loan and many Aquinas grants and scholarships. Aquinas offers five full tuition scholarships. Students are required to file the FAFSA.

Faculty

Students entering an Aquinas program are assigned a faculty adviser who meets individually with students to assist them in making sound academic decisions. The student-faculty ratio at Aquinas is 15:1.

Student Body Profile

Aquinas College at Newton is a Catholic women's college, although there is a small percentage of men in the nine-month certificate programs. Approximately half of the students come to Aquinas directly after graduating from high school, while the other half are adults who either graduated from high school several years ago or recently earned their GED. Ninety-two percent of students are enrolled full-time during the day. One hundred percent of students commute. The student body is ethnically and culturally diverse.

Student Activities

The Aquinas Student Association (ASA) is the liaison group for administration, faculty, and students in areas of concern to the student body. ASA officers and representatives are elected by the student body; they coordinate all social activities at the College.

Facilities and Resources

Located on campus are two student lounges, a modern cafeteria, and a spacious and comfortable auditorium with a seating capacity of 850. The chapel, located in the College building, is open to students at all times. Two computer laboratories are equipped with state-of-the-art microcomputers, installed with up-to-date software, and are available for student use during and outside of class for completion of a variety of tasks. The College also provides a well-equipped science laboratory.

The Child Development Center at Aquinas provides early childhood education majors with on-site, hands-on experience in their field.

The Academic Success Center offers support services to help students accelerate and build writing and reading skills, sharpen math skills, gain proficiency in note-taking, and improve the ability to manage time. Individual and group tutoring in all subject areas are available.

Career Services assists in career planning, résumé writing, and interviewing techniques. The career office assists students throughout their working life.

Location

Aquinas is set on a picturesque 14-acre site. The campus is located at 15 Walnut Park, Newton, Massachusetts, a half mile from Exit 17 of the Massachusetts Turnpike. Only a short distance from Newton Corner and the city of Boston, Aquinas is easily accessible from all the greater Boston area communities.

Admission Requirements

Candidates for admission to the College may enter in September, January, or February. All candidates must complete the Aquinas application and submit it with their high school transcript or its equivalent and one letter of recommendation. An interview is required. Applications are evaluated on the basis of the applicant's total record and potential.

Application and Information

There is no specific application deadline at Aquinas. For more information, interested candidates should contact:

Ellen Ronayne
Associate Director of Admissions
Aquinas College at Newton
15 Walnut Park
Newton, Massachusetts 02158
Telephone: 617-969-4400

THE ART INSTITUTE OF DALLAS
DALLAS, TEXAS

The Institute and Its Mission

The mission of the Art Institute of Dallas is to provide postsecondary education programs that will prepare students to successfully enter the highly competitive design- and business-related fields. Graduates are prepared for positions in their chosen fields through curricula that seamlessly integrate new technology into students' lives and emphasize actual job skills needed in the field. The Art Institute of Dallas believes in the worth and potential of each student and strives to provide quality programs and services that foster development of that worth and potential in an environment that encourages free expression, leadership, and responsible decision making. Institute faculty and staff members continually revise curricula that emphasize the actual skills needed in the fields taught, introduce students to working professionals, and work to assist graduates in obtaining first jobs in the field. Since its establishment in 1964, the Institute has trained hundreds of students for entry into the fields of visual communications, computer animation, multimedia, video production, interior design, culinary arts, fashion design, and fashion marketing. Art Institute students mature both personally and professionally by learning to be both individuals and cooperating members of a team, and are provided with instruction in areas of basic skills development, communication, and human relations. Employers consistently turn to the Art Institute of Dallas to employ qualified graduates. This is a testament to the Institute's educational philosophies and how well faculty and staff members analyze industry directions to prepare students for an increasingly high-tech career market. The Art Institute of Dallas began in 1964 as the Dallas Fashion Merchandising College. In 1978, it changed location and became the Fashion and Art Institute of Dallas. In 1979, the Institute was approved to grant associate degrees in each of its programs. In 1984, the Institute changed its name to the Art Institute of Dallas, and, in 1988, moved to its present facilities in north Dallas. The Art Institute of Dallas is a subsidiary of the Art Institutes International, an education company with schools throughout the U.S. In addition to the Art Institute of Dallas, the Art Institutes International include the Art Institutes of Atlanta, Fort Lauderdale, Houston, Philadelphia, Phoenix, Pittsburgh, and Seattle; the Colorado Institute of Art; and the Illinois Institute of Art. The International Board of Advisors of the Art Institutes International comprises world-renowned artists, designers, and entertainment professionals, including film producers Robert Altman and Frank Yablans; sculptor Fernando Botero; illustrators Braldt Bralds, Joe Eula, and David Salle; entertainers Irene Cara and John Denver; interior designers Frederic Mechiche and Juan Montoya; master chefs Michel Rochedy and William Yosses; special effects producer Thomas Smith; and fashion designers Geoffrey Beene, Victor Costa, Hubert de Givenchy, Carolina Herrera, and Phillipe Venet. A local Board of Trustees provides administration, faculty members, and students with regular, ongoing guidance regarding school policies, curriculum, and industry. Individual programs also have Curriculum Advisory Boards. The Art Institute of Dallas is accredited by the Accrediting Commission of Career Schools/Colleges of Technology, and approved and regulated by the Texas Higher Education Coordinating Board and the Texas Education Agency, Division of Proprietary Schools, Veteran's Education, and Driver Training, Austin, Texas. The Art Institute of Dallas is authorized to award the Associate of Applied Arts degree and the Associate of Applied Science degree to graduates of approved programs. The Institute is also approved for the training of veterans and eligible veterans' dependents (certain programs are not eligible until they have been in operation for two years) and authorized under Federal law to enroll nonimmigrant alien students. The Art Institute of Dallas is a member of the Dallas Advertising League, the Art Directors Club of Dallas, and the Public Relations Society of America.

Academic Programs

Each school quarter is eleven weeks and the programs are from 6 to 8 eleven-week quarters in length. All programs are offered on a year-round basis that provides students with strong continuity and the ability to work uninterrupted toward their degrees.

Associate Degree Programs The **Associate of Applied Arts** degree is offered in computer animation (seven quarters/105 credit hours), fashion marketing (six quarters/90 credit hours), fashion design (seven quarters/105 credit hours), interior design (eight quarters/105 credit hours), and visual communications (seven quarters/105 credit hours). The **Associate of Applied Science** degree is offered in culinary arts (six quarters/90 credit hours) and video production (six quarters/90 credit hours). Subject to availability, classes may be scheduled for morning, afternoon, and/or evening.

Transfer Arrangements A credit hour is a unit of measurement, not necessarily an indicator of transferability of credit. The degree-granting programs of the Art Institute of Dallas are, by design, intended to prepare students for an entry-level position in their chosen field, and academic credits earned in a program are not transferable outside the Art Institute system, unless the school to which transfer is sought agrees to accept them. The staff and faculty members of the Art Institute will be happy to assist in any application for credit transfer by supplying transcripts, course descriptions, and the instructor evaluations and recommendations.

Special Programs and Services The Institute offers a developmental studies program designed to help students prepare to succeed in college-level English and math courses, and confidential counseling is available when academic or personal problems create roadblocks to success. Applicants take a placement test upon entering the Institute to facilitate this process. The Institute provides both academic advising and personal counseling for students during their training period. Academic advising is provided by designated faculty academic advisers and the dean of education. The counseling office provides counseling and referrals to students with personal nonacademic needs. Students should contact the career services office for further information. The student and instructor evaluate the student's projects for the purpose of preparing and grooming a professional portfolio. Each student develops techniques and strategies for self-marketing in the chosen field. Emphasis is placed on each student assessing his or her own marketable skills, developing a network of contacts, generating interviews, writing cover letters and résumés, preparing for interviews, developing a professional appearance, closing, and follow up. Students receive instruction in self-confidence, flexibility, and effort required to conduct a successful job search. Special workshops are offered each summer for art teachers and educators and for high school seniors.

Costs

The cost of tuition and fees varies depending on the student's program. Current costs are available from the Art Institute of Dallas Admissions Office. The quarterly tuition is signed to adjustment each academic year, and students are given ninety days notice in the event of an adjustment.

Financial Aid

All students may apply for financial assistance under various federal and state programs, including Federal Stafford Loan (Guaranteed Student Loan), Federal Pell Grant, Federal Supplemental Educational Opportunity Grant, Federal Perkins Loans, Federal College Work-Study, Federal PLUS Loan Program, Vocational Rehabilitation Assistance, and Veterans Administration Benefits. Awards under these programs are based on individual need and the availability of funds. Students should contact the Institute's student financial services office for complete details about financial aid resources. Students receiving financial assistance must maintain satisfactory academic progress standards as outlined in the Institute catalog. The Institute offers scholarships in each of its degree programs. The Art Institutes International Merit Scholarship Program is also available to new and continuing students. One full-tuition Art Institute scholarship is awarded annually through the National Art Education Association (NAEA). Two full-tuition Art Institute scholarships are awarded annually through the National Commercial Art Competition of the Vocational Industrial Clubs of America (VICA). Two full-tuition Art Institute scholarships are awarded annually at the Distributive Education Clubs of America (DECA) Career Development Conference. The Miss National Teenager program awards scholarships to each state winner, who receives a full-tuition scholarship. The winners of the National Scholastic Art Awards Competition may use their full-tuition scholarships at the Institute. For continuing students, the Mildred M. Kelley Scholarship is offered to an outstanding student entering the sixth or seventh quarter of study. Once each quarter, Institute departmental scholarships of $500 are awarded to outstanding continuing students in each degree program. Students attending the Institute on scholarships must maintain at least 2.5 cumulative grade point average in order to retain eligibility. One full-tuition International Board of Advisors Scholarship is offered annually in each of the following areas: visual communications, interior design, fashion design, computer animation, fashion marketing, and video production. Interested students should contact the admissions office for details on any of these scholarships.

Faculty

The faculty includes full- and part-time members. All are experienced professionals with outstanding credentials and reputations in their fields, and many of them have achieved regional and national recognition.

Student Body Profile

Students come to the Art Institute of Dallas from all over the U.S. and abroad and include men and women who have enrolled directly after completing high school, have transferred from colleges and universities, or have left employment situations to prepare for new careers.

Student Activities

The Institute arranges student trips to local cultural and commercial sites. These visits are an integral part of each student's learning experience. In addition to local study trips to support the curriculum, out-of-town seminars and visits are planned in individual programs. The costs related to optional study trips are not included in regular tuition and fees, except for the Paris field trip in the fashion programs.

Facilities and Resources

The Art Institute of Dallas occupies approximately 70,000 square feet of instructional and administrative space situated on four floors. The facility includes lecture classrooms, art/drawing classrooms, drawing/drafting classrooms, life drawing studios, airbrush laboratories, computer science labs, computer graphics/computer-aided design labs, a multimedia production lab, an interior design resource room, a blueprint room, a 4-camera color video studio/control room, a video postproduction lab (including nonlinear Avid and digital audio workstations), and an exhibition gallery. The facility also includes a Learning Resource Center, with a materials collection designed to support the curricula as well as an extensive video collection. For the convenience of students, the Institute also maintains an art supply store. The maximum class size for laboratory classes is approximately 30, and for lecture classes is approximately 40. Classes are as close to professional as possible. What students learn in class, they put to practice in labs and studios, using today's computer technologies. Computer lab facilities at the Institute are exceptionally strong. Students enrolled at the Art Institute of Dallas are given assistance in locating suitable living accommodations. The Housing Coordinator also assists students in finding roommates if it is requested.

Career Planning/Placement Offices The Institute maintains a career services department for graduates and students. Although the school offers no guarantee of employment, considerable effort is put forth to bring together potential employers and graduates who have the skills employers are seeking.

Location

The Art Institute of Dallas is located in the international city of Dallas, which provides a setting of great contrasts for the Institute. Western boots walk beside the latest European fashions. Concert audiences eat barbecue while enjoying a classical symphony. Dallas boasts one of the largest concentrations of corporate headquarters in the country and has been named "the best city for business" by *Fortune* magazine. The fashion, retail, and interior design worlds regularly converge at the World Trade Center and Apparel Mart. The city continues to be one of the leading centers for advertising and graphic design in the Southwest. And the growth of the local film and video production industry has given Dallas the label of the "third coast." Dallas is an engaging and captivating city that is a rewarding place to live, study, and begin a career.

Admission Requirements

High school graduation or a General Education Diploma (GED) is a prerequisite for admission. All applicants are evaluated on the basis of their previous education and their background or stated or demonstrated interest in art, fashion, interior design, multimedia, video production, or visual communications. As part of the evaluation, students must submit a brief essay detailing their interests. Portfolios may also be requested for evaluation. Applicants who have taken the Scholastic Assessment Test (SAT I) or American College Test (ACT) are encouraged to submit scores to the Admissions Office for evaluation. The Institute reserves the right to request any additional information necessary to evaluate an applicant's potential for academic success.

Application and Information

The Institute operates on a rolling admission basis. Applications for admission and/or enrollment agreements must be completed and signed by candidates and their parents or guardians (if applicable) and sent to the Institute with a $50 application fee. A tuition deposit of $100 is due within ten days after the enrollment agreement has been submitted. High school and/or college transcripts should be submitted to the Institute at least a month prior to starting classes. For more information, candidates should contact:

Office of Admissions
The Art Institute of Dallas
Two NorthPark, 8080 Park Lane
Dallas, Texas 75231

Telephone: 214-692-8080
800-275-4243 (toll-free)
Fax: 214-692-6544
World Wide Web: http://www.aii.edu

Today's advanced technologies are integrated into each program of study at the Art Institute of Dallas.

Peterson's Guide to Two-Year Colleges 1997

ART INSTITUTE OF FORT LAUDERDALE
FORT LAUDERDALE, FLORIDA

The Institute and Its Mission
Founded in 1968, the Art Institute of Fort Lauderdale is a member of the Art Institutes International. The other schools in the consortium are the Art Institutes of Atlanta, Dallas, Houston, Illinois, Philadelphia, Phoenix, Pittsburgh, and Seattle and the Colorado Institute of Art in Denver. All member schools share a board of advisers that oversees curriculums and assists in the placement of graduates. This board is made up of some of the most outstanding designers, photographers, and fashion professionals in the country. In 1986, the Art Institute of Fort Lauderdale moved to a new multimillion-dollar high-tech facility. The Institute is accredited by the ACCSCT.

In addition to the associate degree programs, the Institute also offers bachelor's degree programs in business management and marketing, industrial design, and interior design.

Academic Programs
The Institute operates on a quarter calendar. Program length depends on the major selected. All programs begin with basic studies courses. Evening diploma programs run for four quarters. Associate degree programs vary in length. All programs are eighteen or twenty-four months in length. In order to earn a diploma or associate degree, the student must maintain a minimum grade point average of 2.0 (on a 4.0 scale) and pass a portfolio review. The bachelor's degree programs run for six quarters after completion of the associate degree. Program transfer agreements are available with several colleges.

Associate Degree Programs Associate degree programs are available in broadcasting, computer animation, culinary arts, fashion design, fashion marketing, industrial design, interior design (commercial and residential), multimedia, photography, travel and hospitality, video production, and visual communications/advertising design.

Certificate and Diploma Programs Evening diploma programs are available in applied photography, art of cooking, graphic and desktop design, and residential design.

Costs
In 1996–97, the cost of tuition and fees is approximately $9450, with slight variations depending on the student's program. Institute-sponsored housing is $1250 per quarter. An optional meal plan is offered.

Financial Aid
The Art Institute of Fort Lauderdale participates in the Federal Pell Grant, Federal Stafford Student Loan, Federal Perkins Loan, and Federal Work-Study programs and the Florida Student Assistance Grant Program. In addition, the Institute offers many scholarships to both incoming and returning students. Scholarship programs for incoming students include the Art Institute Scholarship Program; the Florida Association of Private Schools Scholarship program, which grants one full scholarship worth more than $20,000; and several scholarships sponsored through high school associations, such as DECA and the National Art Honor Society. Returning students compete for Merit Scholarships, based on a review of submitted artwork, and the Angelo DiVencenzo Scholarship, awarded to the most outstanding student in the field of life drawing.

Students apply for aid by completing the Institute's application and by filing a financial aid form with the Office of Student Financial Services. There is a priority filing date of April 1.

Faculty
The faculty currently numbers 100 full- and part-time members. All are experienced professionals, and many of them have achieved regional and national recognition. Faculty members have outstanding credentials and reputations in the fields of art, design, fashion, and communications. Each student is assigned a faculty adviser. The student-faculty ratio averages 25:1.

Student Body Profile
In fall 1995, enrollment was 1,927. About one fourth of the students come from southern Florida, one fourth from other areas in the state, and one half from other states and countries.

Student Activities
Students participate in many activities both on campus and off campus. Student chapters of the American Society of Magazine Photographers of Florida, National Press Photographers Association, Aquare Circle Club (for the fine arts photographer), and American Society of Interior Designers are available on campus. The fashion division is a member of Distributive Education Clubs of America (DECA), Delta Epsilon Chi chapter.

The Student Advisory Committee gives students a voice in the education process at the Art Institute of Fort Lauderdale. They participate in standing committees established to make policy for the Institute, such as the Student Success Committee, Academic Affairs Committee, and the Curricular Hoc Committee, all of which enhance student life at the Institute and promote interdepartmental interaction as well as community involvement. An active Student Council sponsors many social events, including the Halloween costume contest, a party welcoming new students, picnics, and charity events. The annual student art exhibition is held in the fall.

In 1995, a strong placement assistance program enabled 90 percent of the graduates available for employment to be placed in positions related to their career major. Part-time jobs and freelance work are available through the Employment Assistance Office.

Facilities and Resources
School-sponsored housing provides comfort and security for resident students. The Institute also helps students in finding roommates and locating suitable living arrangements. The director of housing services coordinates all housing arrangements and services. Student housing information is available upon request. The Institute's facility includes the Mark K. Wheeler Art Gallery, a video-graphics computer center, a video equipment checkout center, a technical library, photography darkrooms, an audio recording room, life-drawing

studios, and painting studios. The library is designed to meet the needs of students, with 14,000 volumes and 220 periodicals.

Location

Fort Lauderdale is located 50 miles north of the Miami metropolitan area. Fort Lauderdale has much to offer students of art and fashion. Shows and performances at the Art Museum of Fort Lauderdale, the Broward Center for the Performing Arts, and various theater groups and galleries are just a few of the many cultural activities available to students. Recreational activities abound in southern Florida. Located just minutes from the Institute are some of Fort Lauderdale's well-known beaches and parks. The yearly average temperature is 72 degrees.

Admission Requirements

A high school diploma or successful scores on the General Educational Development (GED) tests are a prerequisite for admission to the Institute's diploma and associate degree programs.

Individuals with a portfolio or previous college education are evaluated during the admissions process for potential advanced placement.

Application and Information

The Institute operates on a rolling admission basis. Applications for admission and/or enrollment agreements must be completed and signed by candidates and their parents or guardians (if applicable) and sent to the Institute with a $50 application fee. A tuition deposit of $100 is due within ten days after the enrollment agreement has been submitted. High school and/or college transcripts should be submitted to the Institute at least a month prior to starting classes.

For more information, candidates should contact:

Office of Admissions
Art Institute of Fort Lauderdale
1799 Southeast 17th Street
Fort Lauderdale, Florida 33316
Telephone: 954-527-1799
800-275-7603 (toll-free)

The Art Institute of Fort Lauderdale.

Peterson's Guide to Two-Year Colleges 1997

THE ART INSTITUTE OF PHILADELPHIA
PHILADELPHIA, PENNSYLVANIA

The Institute and Its Mission

To Art Institute of Philadelphia faculty and staff members, the explosive growth taking place in communications industries is nothing new. For twenty-five years, the Institute has supplied the marketplace with graduates whose skills take creative technologies to the next level. As one of Pennsylvania's most established professional schools for the applied arts, the Institute has trained thousands of talented individuals, seamlessly integrating technology into their lives and teaching the skills employers look for in new hires. Employers consistently return for qualified graduates. This is a testament to the Institute's educational philosophies and how well it analyzes industry directions to prepare students for an increasingly competitive and high-tech career market.

Conveniently located in downtown Philadelphia, the Institute was founded by artist Philip Trachtman in 1971. In 1979, the Art Institutes International acquired the school, which had an enrollment of approximately 275. The Institute moved to its present location in 1982 and today serves approximately 1,400 students in ten major academic programs.

In addition to the Art Institute of Philadelphia, the Art Institutes International include the Art Institutes of Atlanta, Dallas, Fort Lauderdale, Houston, Illinois, Phoenix, Pittsburgh, and Seattle and the Colorado Institute of Art. All member schools share a board of advisers that oversees curricula and assists in the placement of graduates. The International Board of Advisors of the Art Institutes International comprises world-renowned artists, designers, and entertainment professionals, including film producers Robert Altman and Frank Yablans; sculptor Fernando Botero; illustrators Braldt Bralds, Joe Eula, and David Salle; entertainers Irene Cara and John Denver; interior designers Frederic Mechiche and Juan Montoya; master chefs Michel Rochedy and William Yosses; special effects producer Thomas Smith; and fashion designers Geoffrey Beene, Victor Costa, Hubert de Givenchy, Carolina Herrera, and Philippe Venet.

The Art Institute of Philadelphia is licensed by the Pennsylvania Department of Education State Board of Private License Schools and is a member of the Pennsylvania Association of Private School Administrators. The Art Institute of Philadelphia is accredited by the Accrediting Commission of Career Schools/Colleges of Technology, is approved for training veterans and eligible veterans' dependents, and is authorized under federal law to enroll nonimmigrant alien students.

Academic Programs

Each school quarter is eleven weeks long and programs are 6 to 9 eleven-week quarters in length. All programs are offered on a year-round basis that provides students with strong continuity and the ability to work uninterrupted toward their degrees.

Associate Degree Programs The **Associate in Specialized Technology** degree is offered in animation/media arts (eight quarters/120 credits), fashion design (six quarters/97.5 credits), graphic design (eight quarters/120 credits), industrial design technology (eight quarters/120 credits), interior design (nine quarters/135 credits), multimedia studies (eight quarters/120 credits), photography (eight quarters/120 credits), and video production (seven quarters/105 credits). The **Associate in Specialized Business** degree is offered in fashion marketing (six quarters/97.5 credits), music business (seven quarters/105 credits), and visual merchandising (six quarters/97.5 credits).

Transfer Arrangements Graduates of the Art Institute of Philadelphia have the opportunity to apply to colleges and universities to pursue a four-year baccalaureate degree program. Agreements are in effect with a number of four-year institutions that accept credits earned at the Art Institute of Philadelphia. The amount of credit transferred is at the discretion of the accepting institution.

Computer animation, graphic design, multimedia studies, and video production programs are offered both during the day and evening.

Special Programs and Services The Institute offers a skills enhancement program designed to help students prepare to succeed in college-level English and math courses, and confidential counseling is available when academic or personal problems create roadblocks to success.

Academic counseling is provided by faculty members, the academic department director, and the director of education. The student and instructor evaluate the student's projects for the purpose of preparing and grooming a professional portfolio. Each student develops techniques and strategies for self-marketing his or her chosen field. Emphasis is placed on each student assessing his or her own marketable skills, developing a network of contacts, generating interviews, writing cover letters and résumés, preparing for interviews, developing a professional appearance, closing, and following up. Students receive instruction in self-confidence, flexibility, and effort required to conduct a successful job search. Special workshops are offered each summer for art teachers and educators and for high school juniors and seniors.

Off-Campus Programs

The Institute arranges student trips to local cultural and commercial sites. These visits are an integral part of each student's learning experience. In addition to local study trips to support the curriculum, out-of-town seminars and visits are planned in individual programs.

Costs

The cost of tuition and fees varies depending on the student's program. Current costs are available from the Art Institute of Philadelphia Admissions Office. The quarterly tuition is subject to adjustment each academic year, and students are given ninety days' notice in the event of an adjustment.

Financial Aid

All students may apply for financial assistance under various federal and state programs, including Federal Stafford Student Loan (Guaranteed Student Loan), Federal Pell Grant, Federal Supplemental Educational Opportunity Grant (FSEOG), Federal Perkins Loan (FNDSL), Federal College Work-Study (FWS), Federal PLUS (Parent) Loan Program, state-funded assistance programs, vocational rehabilitation assistance, and Veterans Administration Benefits. Awards under these programs are based on individual need and the availability of funds. Students should contact the Institute's Student Financial Services Office for complete details about financial aid resources.

One full-tuition International Board of Advisors Scholarship is offered annually in each of the following: graphic design, interior design, industrial design technology, fashion design, computer animation, photography, fashion marketing, and video production. Merit scholarships are available to incoming students based on previous academic performance and demonstrated financial need. Presidential scholarships are awarded to upper-quarter students based on criteria selected by the program director and the dean of education.

Faculty

The faculty includes full- and part-time members. All are experienced professionals with outstanding credentials and reputations in their fields, and many of them have achieved regional and national recognition. Each student is assigned a faculty adviser. The year-round average class size is 20–25 students.

Student Body Profile

Students come to the Art Institute of Philadelphia from all over the U.S. and abroad and include men and women who have enrolled directly after completing high school, have transferred from colleges and universities, or have left employment situations to prepare for new careers.

Student Activities

Art Institute of Philadelphia students have the opportunity to join professional organizations such as the American Society of Interior Designers (ASID), the American Society of Media Photographers (ASMP), and the Fashion Group of Philadelphia. Students are also encouraged to contribute to the Art Institute student newspaper, *1622*.

Facilities and Resources

Housing an impressive gallery, the Institute occupies nearly 86,000 square feet of space on Chestnut Street in a building originally designed in 1928 as the CBS flagship radio station affiliate. Designated as a historical site by the Philadelphia Historical Commission, the Art Deco building became home to the Art Institute in 1982. In addition to classrooms, studios, laboratories, offices, a learning resource center, and the exhibition gallery, the Institute maintains an art supply store for the convenience of the students. The Institute also provides equipment for student use, including, but not limited to, 4 x 5 cameras, enlargers, a Kreonite color processor, luciographs light tables, a stat camera Ciazo blueprint machine, video editing machines, video cameras, and a Kodak Ektachrome copier. Administration and classroom facilities have been designed to accommodate the special needs of individuals with disabilities. Whether in the student lounge, the gallery, the Institute Supply Store, or the extensive resource center, the daily gathering of students, faculty members, and staff makes it easy to feel the energy, caring, and commitment that underlies education at the Art Institute of Philadelphia.

Students enrolled at the Art Institute of Philadelphia are given assistance in locating housing by members of the Student Services Department. Options include Institute-sponsored dormitory-style housing and independent apartment living.

Classes are structured to be more like life, and the environment is as close to professional as possible. What students learn in class, they put to practice in labs and studios, using today's computer technologies. Computer lab facilities at the Institute are exceptionally strong, including *Lectra* (computerized patternmaking) *Systémes,* as well as Silicon Graphics Indigo 4000, Pentium-based and Macintosh personal computers, and Video Toaster and Adobe Premier computer applications.

Career Planning/Placement Offices The Institute maintains a Career Services Center for graduates and students. Although the school offers no guarantee of employment, considerable effort is put forth to bring together potential employers and graduates who have the skills employers are seeking. Employment assistance is a priority at the Institute. More than 85 percent of graduates are placed within six months of graduation.

Location

The Art Institute is located in Philadelphia, the birthplace of American Democracy, which was founded in 1682. The City of Brotherly Love has grown up around the Liberty Bell and Independence Hall and surrounds the largest municipal landscaped park in the world. With tree-lined streets and elegant blend of contemporary and historic architecture, this fifth-largest city in the U.S. offers the finest in symphony orchestras, theater, film, jazz, and opera. The movie *12 Monkeys* was filmed in Philadelphia, which also claims rights to the original Philly cheesesteak. This city of art, with thirty-two major museums, including the expansive collections at the Museum of Art, also provides some of the finest shopping in the nation, from the Market Street Gallery, one of the nation's largest urban shopping malls, to the European-style Bourse with its fifty international boutiques and restaurants. Sports enthusiasts can follow their favorite teams, often right through league playoffs. Baseball's Phillies, NFL's Eagles, NBA's 76ers, and NHL's Flyers play on Broad Street, at the new CoreStates Center, and at the Vet.

Admission Requirements

High school graduation or a General Education Development (GED) certificate is a prerequisite for admission. All applicants are evaluated on the basis of their previous education and their background or stated or demonstrated interest in animation, fashion design or marketing, graphic design, industrial design technology, interior design, multimedia, photography, video production, or visual merchandising. Portfolios are welcomed but not required. The Institute reserves the right to request any additional information necessary to evaluate an applicant's potential for academic success.

Application and Information

The Institute operates on a rolling admission basis. Applications for admission and/or enrollment agreements must be completed and signed by candidates and their parents or guardians (if applicable) and sent to the Institute with a $50 application fee. A tuition deposit of $100 is due within ten days after the enrollment agreement has been submitted. High school and/or college transcripts should be submitted to the Institute at least a month prior to starting classes. For more information, candidates should contact:

Office of Admissions
The Art Institute of Philadelphia
1622 Chestnut Street
Philadelphia, Pennsylvania 19103-5198

Telephone: 215-567-7080
800-275-2474 (toll-free)
Fax: 215-246-3358
World Wide Web: http://www.aii.edu

The environment at the Art Institute of Philadelphia is conducive to innovation and growth and ensures that graduates have skills that fit the needs of today's competitive marketplace.

Peterson's Guide to Two-Year Colleges 1997

ATLANTIC COMMUNITY COLLEGE
MAYS LANDING, NEW JERSEY

The College and Its Mission

Founded in 1964, ACC held its first classes in fall 1966 in rented facilities in Atlantic City, New Jersey. In February 1968, the College moved to its present main campus location near Mays Landing, the Atlantic County seat. ACC was the second community college organized in the state.

ACC is a comprehensive, two-year public institution serving the residents of Atlantic and Cape May counties, enrolling more than 6,000 students. The College operates nationally recognized casino career and culinary arts programs and is a leader in technology, serving as a member of the Apple Community College Alliance. In addition to the College's main campus in Mays Landing, ACC operates extension centers in Atlantic City and Cape May County.

The Casino Career Institute, located at the Atlantic City Center, was the first casino gaming school in the nation affiliated with a community college and the only licensed slot training school in New Jersey. Opened in 1978, CCI has trained more than 45,000 people for careers in the casino industry. It has provided training for members of several federal governments and many state police forces as other jurisdictions prepare themselves for legalized gaming.

In 1981, as another extension of its role to train workers for the Southern New Jersey hospitality industry, ACC opened the Academy of Culinary Arts, a chefs' training program that has graduated more than 1,400 students. The Academy of Culinary Arts has a full-time enrollment of about 350 students.

Academic Programs

ACC offers 41 transfer and career degree programs as well as noncredit professional development and training services.

Associate Degree Programs Associate in Arts degree programs are designed for students who wish to continue their education at an upper-level institution. The A.A. degree requires a minimum of 46 credits in general education and a minimum of 18 credits in program courses and electives. One basic program of study in liberal arts is available, with options in child development/child care, education, history, humanities, literature, music, prelaw, psychology, social science, social work, sociology, or studio art.

Associate in Science degrees are awarded to students who successfully complete programs which emphasize mathematics, the biological or physical sciences, and business programs intended as prebaccalaureate work. The A.S. degree requires a minimum of 31 credits in general education and a minimum of 33 credits in program courses and electives. Degree programs are available in biology, business administration, chemistry, computer information systems, corrections/juvenile justice, criminal justice, general studies, legal assistant, marine science, mathematics, and science and mathematics.

Associate in Applied Science degree programs emphasize preparation for careers, typically at the technical or semiprofessional level. The A.A.S. degree requires a minimum of 21 credits in general education and a minimum of 43 credits in program courses and electives. Degree programs are available in accounting and finance, business administration, computer integrated manufacturing, computer programming, computer system support, computer system technology, culinary arts, electronics technology, hospitality management, legal assistant, nursing, occupational therapy assistant, office systems technology, physical therapist assistant, respiratory therapy, retailing, and travel and tourism.

In addition, ACC offers several professional series and certificate programs to meet the short-term training needs of the local work force.

The largest cooking school in New Jersey, the Academy of Culinary Arts was founded in 1981 to meet the growing need for highly skilled chefs and food service professionals for the Atlantic City hospitality industry. Facilities include six teaching kitchens with overhead mirrors, a bake shop, and classroom. A $4.6-million facility, constructed in 1991, features more than 28,250 square feet of space, including teaching kitchens, classrooms, a gourmet restaurant, banquet room, administrative and faculty offices, and a retail store. Seventy-five percent of the Academy's training is hands-on. Classes meet five hours a day, Monday through Friday, in a morning or afternoon session from January through May and August/September through December. As part of their training, students operate a gourmet restaurant on the College's campus.

Off-Campus Programs

Cooperative education is an academic program which allows students to receive college credits for working in jobs related to their major while pursuing their studies at ACC. A cooperative education component is required for the culinary arts program, but is optional for all other majors.

Costs

In 1996–97, tuition and general fees for Atlantic County residents or out-of-county New Jersey residents with a chargeback are $62.65 per credit. Out-of-county New Jersey residents without chargebacks pay $116.80 a credit. Out-of-state and out-of-county residents pay $197.40 a credit. The Academy of Culinary Arts requires a nonrefundable deposit of $300 upon application, and a laboratory fee of $220 per credit. There are also parking and mandatory accident and health insurance fees. Some classes require special lab or material costs, or other fees.

Financial Aid

About 65 percent of ACC students who apply receive some form of financial aid, including scholarships, grants, loans, and work-study assistance. Funds are available from federal, state, and private sources for those with a demonstrated need or who meet eligibility requirements. All applicants for aid must complete the Free Application for Federal Student Aid (FAFSA), available from ACC's financial aid office or most high school guidance offices.

Faculty

ACC has 73 full-time and 222 part-time faculty members. All full-time faculty members hold a master's degree, and many also have doctoral degrees in the field of study. Most faculty members also serve as academic advisers. ACC's student-faculty ratio is 20:1.

Student Body Profile

In fall 1995, there were 5,994 students at Atlantic Community College. Atlantic County residents account for 68 percent of the student body. Members of minority groups were as follows: Hispanic, 7 percent; Asian, 5 percent; Native American, .3 percent; and African American, 11 percent. International students make up 4 percent of the total. The average age of students was 25. There is no on-campus housing available.

Student Activities
Every ACC student is a member of the Student Government Association. The main policy-making body of the SGA is the Student Senate, which charters student clubs and organizations, approves budgets, determines student policy and works with faculty and administration to improve the college. There are numerous special interest clubs and organizations open to all students, an on-campus radio station, and a student newspaper.

Facilities and Resources
ACC is built around a quadrangle of lawn. The buildings, designed of split-face brick, natural cedar shakes, and tinted glass, are joined by a system of walkways. A central loop connects buildings and parking areas with the Black Horse Pike (Route 322). ACC's indoor athletic facilities include a gymnasium with a seating capacity of 800 and a weight room with lockers and showers. Outdoor facilities include baseball, softball, and soccer fields; two basketball courts; a nature trail; and an archery range. ACC's housing program assists students in obtaining high-quality living arrangements. Under the program, students have the option of reserved housing or using listings supplied to secure their own.

The College's cultural events are staged in the 444-seat theater located in Walter E. Edge Hall. The resources and facilities of the William Spangler Library are available to the College community and to the residents of Atlantic and Cape May counties. Currently housed in the library are more than 78,000 books, 1,000 phonograph records, and 300 art reproductions, as well as subscriptions to more than 300 periodicals.

Location
Located on 537 acres in the picturesque New Jersey Pinelands, Atlantic Community College is in Atlantic County, New Jersey, 17 miles west of Atlantic City's boardwalk, 45 miles from Philadelphia, and 115 miles from New York City.

Admission Requirements
Admission is available to all applicants who are 18 years of age and older whose high school class has graduated. Applicants who have graduated from an accredited secondary or preparatory school, or those with a state equivalency certificate, are accepted to ACC. Applicants under 18 years of age, not currently enrolled in a high school, and not having a high school diploma or GED, do not qualify for admission to a community college.

Admission to specific programs, such as Culinary Arts or Nursing, is dependent upon students meeting the necessary program requirements and completing course prerequisites.

Application and Information
Applications are reviewed on a continuous basis. The preferred deadline for fall admission is July 1; for spring admission, November 1. There is a $30 application fee, which includes the cost of administering the basic skills placement test, and culinary applicants must pay an additional, nonrefundable $300 deposit.

For an application or additional information, contact:
Admissions Office
Atlantic Community College
5100 Black Horse Pike
Mays Landing, New Jersey 08330-2699
Telephone: 609-343-5000
E-mail: accadmit@nsvm.atlantic.edu/
World Wide Web: http://www.atlantic.edu/

The Academy of Culinary Arts, housed at Atlantic Community College, is New Jersey's largest cooking school, with nearly 400 students.

BALTIMORE INTERNATIONAL CULINARY COLLEGE
BALTIMORE, MARYLAND

The College and Its Mission

The Baltimore International Culinary College, a private, nonprofit two-year college, was founded in 1972 to provide theoretical and technical skills education for individuals seeking careers as hospitality professionals. The College is committed to providing students with the knowledge and ability necessary for employment and success in the hospitality industry.

In 1985, the College was authorized by the state of Maryland to grant associate degrees. In the same year, the College was nationally accredited by what is now the Accrediting Commission for Career Schools and Colleges of Technology. As part of the College's continued growth, restaurant and food service management and innkeeping management were added to its curriculum. In 1987, the European Educational Centre in Ireland was founded, enabling students to study under European chefs and hoteliers in a European environment. In 1989, the College became a candidate for accreditation with the Commission on Higher Education of the Middle States Association of College and Schools and is currently in the final phases of this process. In addition to classrooms and offices, the College's twenty-three-building campus in Baltimore includes a campus bookstore, computer centers, a student union, hotels, inns and restaurants, parking, student dining facilities, Residence Life dormitory and apartments, and a Learning Resource Center comprising a library, an art gallery, and a Career Information Center.

Freshman students who are single, under 21, and live farther than 50 miles from campus are required to live in Residence Life their first year.

Academic Programs

The College provides a comprehensive curriculum, which includes study abroad at the BICC European Educational Centre near Dublin, Ireland.

The College's professional cooking program and the combined program in professional cooking and baking operate throughout the calendar year; new classes begin in the winter, spring, summer, and fall. The professional baking and pastry program begins in the fall and spring semesters. The College's hospitality management programs, which offer associate degrees only, begin in the fall and winter semesters. The culinary arts certificate, which combines cooking and baking, is available evenings and weekends only and begins in the fall and winter semesters.

To earn an associate degree in professional cooking, professional baking and pastry, or professional cooking and baking, the student must complete approximately 70 credits. To earn an associate degree in food and beverage management, hotel/motel/innkeeping management, convention and meeting planning management, or institutional food service management, the student must complete approximately 69 credits. Certificate candidates must complete 52 credits. The certificate program concentrates on technical courses and is intended for students who already have a strong academic background. The associate degree program combines technical hands-on courses with general education courses such as nutrition, sanitation, psychology, English, and mathematics, as well as an internship or externship.

Associate Degree Programs Baltimore International Culinary College awards the associate degree in the following programs: convention and meeting planning management, food and beverage management, hotel/motel/innkeeping management, institutional food service management, professional baking and pastry, professional cooking, and professional cooking and baking. Second-degree options are available for students desiring additional career flexibility. Professional certificates are offered in professional cooking, professional baking and pastry, and culinary arts, which combines cooking and baking.

Off-Campus Programs

All students have the opportunity to study at the College's European Educational Centre in County Cavan, Ireland, which is located 50 miles from Dublin. All students who study in Ireland reside at Bective Court, in fully furnished shared cottages with sleeping, living, and dining areas and kitchens and baths.

Costs

Tuition for 1996–97 is $3197 per semester. Fees range from $856 to $1323, depending on a student's major. Residence Life costs range from $1599 to $2756 per semester and include accommodations in College residence halls and a meal plan.

Financial Aid

Approximately 90 percent of the College's students receive some form of financial aid from federal, state, institutional, and private sources and are employed during their attendance as full-time students. The forms of financial aid available at the College through federal sources include the Federal Pell Grant, the Federal Supplemental Educational Opportunity Grant, the Federal Work-Study Program, the Federal Perkins Loan, the Federal Subsidized and Unsubsidized Stafford Student Loans, FPLUS loans, and veterans' educational benefits. Students are encouraged to investigate the scholarship programs in their home state and apply for state scholarships if the grants can be used in Maryland. The College also offers its own series of scholarships and payment options. Students can request a financial aid application from the Student Financial Planning Office. The College employs the Methodology of Need Analysis, approved by the U.S. Department of Education, as a fair and equitable means of determining the family's ability to contribute to the student's educational expenses, as well as eligibility for other financial aid programs.

Faculty

Baltimore International Culinary College faculty members include 45 chefs and academic instructors of high academic distinction. The student-faculty ratio averages 13:1. Each student is assigned a faculty adviser who oversees the student's progress and answers questions about academic and career concerns. Students are encouraged to discuss program-related issues with and to seek career advice from their faculty adviser.

Student Body Profile

Current enrollment is 850, with 65 percent men and 35 percent women. Approximately 30 percent of students are from out-of-state. Students at the College are eligible to join Alpha Beta Kappa, a national honor society. Students also can join the

Greater Baltimore Chapter of the American Culinary Federation and can participate in a variety of other activities through Student Services.

Student Activities

The Student Council acts as a liaison between the College's administration and the students. The Student Council also works directly with Student Services to plan a variety of activities and events. All students are eligible to participate on the Student Council.

Facilities and Resources

The College offers students the opportunity to study at one of the most progressive, well-equipped international hospitality colleges. The twenty-three-building campus includes kitchens, storerooms, bakeshops, a cooking demonstration theater, academic classrooms, multipurpose rooms, a library, computer centers, a student union, and auxiliary services. There are several public operations that function as in-house training for students, including the Baltimore Baking Company, BICC Harbor Café and Sweet Shoppe, Mount Vernon Hotel and Washington Café, Government House, and the Hopkins Inn.

The European Education Centre is located on 100 acres, with eleven 2-bedroom cottages, laboratory kitchens, and lecture facilities. The complex also comprises the Park Hotel–Deer Park Lodge, with public operations that function as in-house training for students, including the Marquis Dining Room and the Marchioness Ballroom. The Park Hotel has twenty-six guest rooms and the Deer Park Lodge has eight additional rooms. All students enjoy unlimited golf and fishing as well as hiking trails.

Career Planning/Placement Offices The College's Career Information Center offers students access to information about careers in food service and hospitality management. The College's career development services are located in the Career Information Center where coordinators organize on-campus recruiting and offer workshops and assistance in résumé writing and interviewing skills.

Library and Audiovisual Services The College's Library/Learning Resource Center is a member of an interlibrary loan network that enables users to borrow from public, academic, and private libraries throughout Maryland. The library's current core collection has approximately 8,000 volumes, 150 periodicals, and more than 400 audiovisual selections. The library offers students access to the Internet, a worldwide network of electronic information. In-house services include typewriters, computers, and a photocopier.

The College's art gallery is part of the Learning Resource Center and features eight to ten rotating exhibits each year, representing all facets of the art world. Student participation in all exhibits is encouraged.

Location

The College's main campus, located in downtown Baltimore, is just two blocks from the city's famous Inner Harbor, a location that puts the College in the midst of numerous hotels and restaurants. The city offers year-round cultural and entertainment opportunities, such as theater, opera, the Baltimore Symphony Orchestra, museums, sporting events, and festivals. Other attractions in Baltimore, within walking distance of the College, are the National Aquarium, Harborplace, Maryland Science Center, and many historic sites, including Fort McHenry, Mount Vernon, and the Walters Art Gallery. Baltimore also has hundreds of parks and greenways and miles of waterfront for those who enjoy outdoor recreation. Washington, D.C., the nation's capital, is just 30 miles from downtown Baltimore. The city of Baltimore is easily accessed by major highways and bus, rail, and air service. Baltimore/Washington International Airport is a short drive from the campus.

Admission Requirements

Creativity and skill of students must be matched by dedication. The College seeks candidates who desire a professional career in the hospitality industry.

Individuals seeking admission to the College must have earned a high school diploma or have passed the GED. Applicants must either pass the College's placement evaluation, take developmental courses during their first semester, or have one of the following: minimum SAT I scores of 430 verbal and 400 math, a minimum composite ACT score of 15, minimum CLEP scores in the 50th percentile in math and English composition with essay, a secondary degree, or 16 credit hours at the postsecondary level with a minimum average of C in math and English. Transfer students must submit an official college transcript as well as catalog course descriptions for credits they wish to transfer.

The College affords equally to all students the rights, privileges, programs, activities, scholarships and loan programs, and other programs administered by the College without regard to race, color, creed, sex, age, handicap, or national or ethnic origin.

Application and Information

Applicants are required to submit an application form along with a $25 nonrefundable fee. Requests by the College for additional information must be handled in a timely manner. An admission decision is made as soon as a file is complete. Upon acceptance, applicants are asked to submit a $100 tuition deposit.

For additional information, students should contact:

Office of Admissions
Baltimore International Culinary College
17 Commerce Street
Baltimore, Maryland 21202-3230
Telephone: 410-752-4710
            800-624-9926 (toll-free)

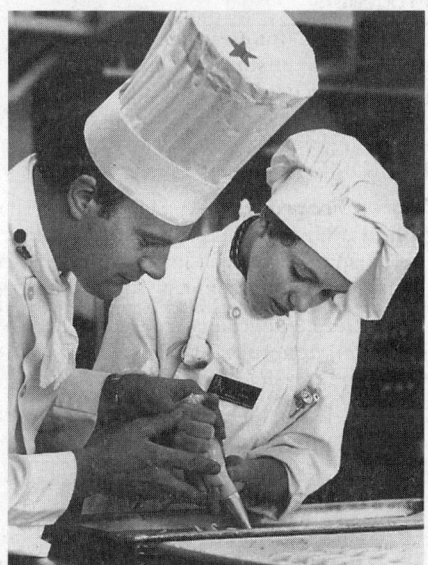

Small classes at Baltimore International Culinary College enable students to receive individual instruction that helps them perfect their skills.

BAY STATE COLLEGE
BOSTON, MASSACHUSETTS

The College and Its Mission

Bay State College, a private, two-year, independent, coeducational institution is located in historic Back Bay Boston. Since 1946, Bay State College has been preparing young men and women with the skills necessary to attain outstanding careers in the business and allied health disciplines.

The College's goal is to prepare and educate students for successful and rewarding professional opportunities. Bay State College accomplishes this by providing the best possible education which enables students to go out in the working world equipped with all the skills needed to professionally succeed or to transfer to a four-year college of his or her choice. Bay State College assists, encourages, supports, and educates students in all their academic, professional, and personal goals and aspirations.

Bay State College is accredited by The New England Association of Schools and Colleges, is authorized to award the Associate in Science and Associate in Applied Science degrees by the Commonwealth of Massachusetts, and is a member of several professional educational associations.

Bay State College's allied health programs are accredited by the Accrediting Bureau of Health Education Schools (ABHES) and Accreditation Council for Occupational Therapy Education (ACOTE) of the American Occupational Therapy Association (AOTA). The physical therapist assistant program is a candidate for accreditation awarded by the Commission on Accreditation in Physical Therapy Education (CAPTE) of the American Physical Therapy Association (APTA). The physical therapist assistant program is in the final stages of completing the full accreditation process.

Academic Programs

Bay State College offers unique courses preparing students for careers in accounting, business, education, fashion, general studies, hospitality, law, medical assisting, office administration, occupational therapy, physical therapy, and travel. In addition, students are exceptionally prepared to transfer to four-year colleges and universities.

Associate Degree Programs Bay State College grants **Associate in Applied Science** degrees in accounting, business administration, hospitality, travel, legal studies, office administration, retail business management, and fashion merchandising.

An **Associate in Science** degree is granted in the areas of early childhood education, general studies, medical assisting, occupational therapy, and physical therapy.

Bay State College's Day and Continuing Education Divisions offer day, evening and weekend classes. A satellite campus is located in Middleborough, MA.

Off-Campus Programs

The internship program, available in all major areas of study, provides practical field experiences so that the students gain the skills and technologies used in the business and medical settings.

Students from Bay State College are among the 250 students participating in the Walt Disney World College Program. During their stay at Walt Disney World, students receive on-the-job training and classroom experience. This is just one of the many internship possibilities for students each year at Bay State College.

Costs

For the 1996–97 academic year, the College's Day Division charges a comprehensive fee of $15,900, which includes full-time tuition ($9200) and room and board ($6700). Tuition for the allied health programs is $9800 per year with an additional $450 lab fee. A student activities fee of $250 is charged to all students. Textbooks are estimated at $500 per year. Bay State College's Continuing Education Division charges $580 per course.

Financial Aid

Personal financial planning and counseling is available for all students and families. Approximately 70 percent of students receive some form of financial assistance. Bay State College requires a completed Free Application for Federal Student Aid (FAFSA) form and signed federal tax forms. The College's institutional financial aid priority deadline is March 1. Financial aid is granted on a rolling basis.

Faculty

There are 45 faculty members, with 53 percent holding advanced degrees and 6 percent who have earned a doctoral degree. The student-faculty ratio is 15:1.

Student Body Profile

There are 674 students in terminal programs. The average age is 18. The student body is ethnically and culturally diverse; 85 percent are state residents, 9 percent are transfer students, 4 percent are international, 78 percent are women, 17 percent are African-American, 9 percent are Hispanic, and 3 percent are Asian-American. In 1995, Bay State College's graduating class had 32 percent who continued on to a four-year college.

There are 221 college housing spaces available. In 1995–96, 221 spaces were occupied. Freshmen are guaranteed college housing. Off-campus living is permitted.

Bay State College's residence halls are located on Commonwealth Avenue. Each residence hall is designed to accommodate from 1 to 5 students per room. One coed building and three single-sex buildings are available. Each hall is staffed by a resident director and resident assistants. Microwaves, washers, dryers, and cable-ready outlets are available in each hall. A campus dining facility is also available. Activities include pizza nights, musicals, discounts to area movies and restaurants, "Blizzard of Bucks," and current social and educational seminars.

Student Activities

Students participate in a multitude of activities offered by the College through student groups. These include the Hospitality Student Association, Travel Club, Fashion Club, Fine Arts Association, Accounting Club, Student Leader Organization, Medical Assisting Society, International Club, drama productions, and Secretarial Science Association.

Sports Intramural athletics are available.

Facilities and Resources

Advisement/Counseling Trained staff members assist students in selecting courses and programs of study to satisfy their educational objectives. A counseling center is available to provide mental and physical health referrals to all Bay State students in need of such services. Referral networks are extensive, within a wide range of geographic areas, and provide access to a variety of public and private health agencies.

Specialized Services A learning center serves as a supplementary learning tool for those individuals wishing to improve their skills through self-paced individualized instruction. The center offers assistance through the use of peer and faculty tutors, individualized learning packets, audio, visual, and other self-study resources. Introductory studies courses are designed for a diverse population of students, workers returning to school, recent high school graduates seeking academic reinforcement, and ESL students. Their individual needs may be met so they can be successful in the traditional course of study leading to an associate degree. A student will register for introductory studies for one semester only, after which he/she may register for courses leading toward the associate degree in his/her chosen field.

Career Planning/Placement Of the number of students seeking assistance from the Career Services Office, there was a 98 percent job placement rate. The primary purpose of the Career Services Office at Bay State College is to see that every graduating senior secures the best possible position in his/her chosen career. The Career Services Office, offering life-long service to all alumni, continually posts job openings for current students and graduates. An average of 10,000 job openings are posted every year. The Career Services Office, under the guidance of the career service director, assists each student through one-on-one career counseling. Services include the Transfer College Fair, placement, job interview counseling, career fairs on campus with over 70 attending companies, résumé preparation, career counseling, career library, and professional dynamics course. Director: Ms. Deborah Walsh, Telephone: 617-236-8030.

Library and Audiovisual Services The library has a combined book collection of approximately 4,000 books. In addition, Bay State College has 250 periodicals, 20 microform titles, and 350 audiovisual titles. There are also more than 60 computers for student use in two computer labs, the learning center, and the library.

Location

The location of Bay State College makes it the perfect place to attend to get a complete education. While the academics are great, students are also within a mile of major league sports, free concerts, museums, the Freedom Trail, Boston Symphony Hall, the Boston Public Library, the Boston Public Gardens, and much more. The city is known for its college atmosphere. Tree-lined streets are mirrored in the skyscrapers of the Back Bay. Major shopping, cultural, and sporting events make college life an experience that students will always remember. The College's location is accessible by public transportation and in proximity to Boston Logan International Airport.

Admissions Requirements

A student must be a high school graduate or a recipient of the GED certificate in order to apply to the College. A personal interview is strongly recommended for all students. Transcripts will be requested once a student has applied, and a decision will be made by the admissions office upon completion of documents.

Application and Information

Applications to Bay State College may be submitted on a rolling basis. A $25 fee is required at the time of application.

Applications should be submitted to:

Director of Admissions
Bay State College
122 Commonwealth Avenue
Boston, Massachusetts 02116

Telephone: 800-81-LEARN (toll-free)
Fax: 617-536-1735

Peterson's Guide to Two-Year Colleges 1997

BEL-REA INSTITUTE OF ANIMAL TECHNOLOGY
DENVER, COLORADO

The Institute and Its Mission

Animal technology is the only subject taught at Bel-Rea. The Institute's program is conducted at its own facility and veterinary hospital in Denver, offering students the advantages of a large city. Both large and small animals are kept on the premises. Accreditation by the American Veterinary Medical Association (AVMA) and the Accrediting Commission of Career Schools/Colleges of Technology (ACCSCT) as well as approval by the Colorado Department of Higher Education, Division of Private Occupational Schools, attests to the standards of excellence strived for in the training program. Students and staff become well acquainted, and much of the learning process is on a one-to-one basis.

Although Bel-Rea's program consists essentially of career preparation and the rate of placement for graduates is high, about 10 percent of the graduates choose to continue their education. Written transfer agreements are available with the University of Denver, Colorado Christian College, New Mexico State University, and Western State College of Colorado in Gunnison, Colorado. Bel-Rea graduates receive offers of jobs from all parts of the United States because of the high quality and thoroughness of their training. In fact, many veterinarians announce to the school placement department their needs for staff members rather than advertise the positions. The careful evaluations that are made of students during their internships also allow the staff to make recommendations to prospective employers, thus broadening placement opportunities for students.

Academic Programs

Bel-Rea Institute of Animal Technology offers a program leading to an **Associate of Applied Science** (A.A.S.) degree in animal technology. The emphasis of the program is on preparing students for a paraprofessional career in veterinary medicine.

Associate Degree Programs The Associate of Applied Science degree is granted upon satisfactory completion of twenty-five courses (114 quarter-credit hours) and a thirteen- or seventeen-week internship. Up to 20 quarter hours of credit may be accepted by transfer from other colleges. However, transferable courses must satisfy the requirements of the general education core, which consists of four courses (20 quarter-credit hours). The rest of a student's program relates directly to veterinary technology.

The Institute's program runs for six consecutive quarters, continuing through the summer, for eighteen/nineteen months. Classes are taken for five quarters, and the internship is done during the sixth. All classes meet between 8 a.m. and 5 p.m., weekdays. During the internship period, students may work between the hours of 6 a.m. and 12 midnight.

Internship and Co-op Programs Internships take place at the Institute's affiliated veterinary hospital and clinic, located 1½ miles from the school; at a Parker, Colorado, large-animal hospital; or at other approved large-animal facilities in the area. A special five-week externship may also be pursued after graduation at Colorado State University's veterinary school. Students interested in working with exotic animals may take a special elective evening course.

Costs

For students entering in the 1996–97 academic year, tuition for the full eighteen/nineteen-month program is $11,650. Books and supplies come to about $1000. Other expenses vary, depending on residence. The Institute does not provide room and board but assists students in finding accommodations in the community. Students who live in apartments or other housing may expect to spend about $4200 for room and board in a twelve-month period. In addition, personal expenditures are likely to run about $800 a year.

Financial Aid

Bel-Rea believes that lack of funds should not keep students from attending the Institute. Thus, admission and financial aid decisions are made separately, and the request for aid has no effect on admission. About 70 percent of Bel-Rea's students receive some form of financial aid. Financial aid packages consist of loans, grants, and jobs. Grant and loan awards are provided on the basis of the analysis of the Free Application for Federal Student Aid (FAFSA). Financial aid applications are accepted on a rolling basis.

Faculty

Bel-Rea prides itself on its faculty. Fourteen members are veterinarians, and the remaining 19 have academic qualifications as well as experience in the field of veterinary medicine. Half of the staff, including members of the core curriculum faculty, have advanced degrees. Most are professionally active and are able to incorporate the most recent advances in the field into classroom work. The ratio of students to faculty (full-time equivalents) is 9:1.

Student Body Profile

The current enrollment is more than 300 women and men. Students come to Bel-Rea from all parts of the United States and generally reside within walking or easy commuting distance of the school. The students range from 18 to 61 years of age. Some students have a previous college background, while others are right out of high school. Sharing housing not only defrays costs but enables students to study and live with people of similar interests.

Student Activities

Bel-Rea Institute believes students should have open-door access to the administration. Student body representatives meet on a regular basis with the Student Services Director. Bel-Rea also has a student chapter of the North American Veterinary Technician Association.

Facilities and Resources

The facilities of the Institute are all housed within one building, which contains five classrooms, a teaching laboratory, three demonstration rooms, a library, a student lounge, administrative offices, and kennel areas for dogs, cats, avian, and laboratory animals. The large-animal facility adjoins the teaching facility. This areas comprises a stable, a tack room, a surgery suite, and a holding area for large animals. The school's facilities are available for student use, both in and out of class, between 7:30 a.m. and 5 p.m, Monday though Friday. Bel-Rea has a trained counselor on staff. There is also placement assistance upon graduation.

Location

Bel-Rea is located in the suburbs of Denver along the eastern border of the city. The downtown center of the city is approximately 8 miles away. Denver is a fast-growing city that offers many cultural and recreational activities. The city has its own symphony and theater center as well as the famous Red Rocks outdoor amphitheater, at which country and rock concerts are presented during the summer months. The Colorado mountains offer some of the finest skiing in the country; many resorts, such as Vail, Copper, Keystone, and Winter Park, are less than 2 hours away.

Admission Requirements

Applicants must hold a high school or equivalency diploma and must have earned an average grade of C or better. High school and college transcripts (if applicable) must be sent to the Institute by the respective schools. Assurance of a desire to work in the veterinary medical profession is required. A health history is also required. Applicants are encouraged to have a personal interview and a tour of the facilities.

Applicants wishing to transfer credits from accredited colleges or universities should submit a transcript immediately following their application. Credits can be accepted only when the courses that have been taken duplicate the Institute's courses and the level of achievement in the courses taken was a grade of C or above. Applicants wishing to transfer college chemistry or math credits must pass the school's proficiency examination.

Application and Information

Classes begin four times each year (every three months), and new students are admitted at the beginning of each quarter. Since the classes in the fall quarter fill rapidly with students who graduate from high school or leave college in the spring, early application for that quarter is advisable. Upon receipt of an application, the Institute will mail a contract to the prospective student. When all application requirements have been met and the Institute has received the signed contract and the required $150 deposit, a letter of acceptance will be mailed. Applicants are admitted on a first-come, first-served basis once the minimum requirements have been met.

Requests for additional information and application forms should be addressed to:

Admissions Department
Bel-Rea Institute of Animal Technology
1681 South Dayton Street
Denver, Colorado 80231
Telephone: 303-751-8700
                800-950-8001 (toll-free)

Bel-Rea students study both large- and small-animal medicine.

Peterson's Guide to Two-Year Colleges 1997

BERGEN COMMUNITY COLLEGE
PARAMUS, NEW JERSEY

The College and Its Mission

For over twenty-five years, Bergen Community College has offered its students a quality educational experience that helps to prepare them for success. The College embraces the concept that a highly developed society that is dynamic and technologically oriented makes it necessary to provide educational opportunities beyond high school to all who can benefit from them. Bergen Community College is a comprehensive, publicly supported two-year college that is fully accredited by the Commission of Higher Education of the Middle States Association of Colleges and Schools. Through its open admissions policy, the College is committed to equal education opportunities for all, regardless of race, sex, religion, age, national origin, or handicap. BCC is a barrier-free facility that is accessible to the handicapped.

BCC offers three types of degree programs in more than 70 fields of study. The College enrolls nearly 13,000 full- and part-time students in its degree and certificate programs. The student body reflects the diversity of the county and this diversity is celebrated on campus. There are more than 20,000 alumni of the College and an additional 1,000 students graduate each year.

Bergen realizes the need to educate students to meet the varied demands of a complex society and to undertake the obligation of intelligent citizenship and family life. To this end, the College offers diverse and useful educational experiences. The variety of programs provides choices and permits flexibility of movement from one curriculum to another, helping the student toward self-discovery and personal self-realization. High academic standards are maintained so that the student can transfer to a four-year college or be prepared for immediate employment.

BCC students can take advantage of special opportunities for learning, including cooperative education, interactive television, honors courses, Freshman Seminar, the College Experience Program, telecourses, and off-campus courses. For students with special needs, the College can arrange for alternate methods of testing and evaluation and provide such important support services as note-taking, tutoring, readers, tape recorders, and front seat placement. Bergen also offers services for the hearing impaired, including interpreting and note-taking.

Over the years, thousands of students from nearly every country in the world have attended BCC. The College provides counseling for international students, which helps make the application process simpler and more efficient and helps to facilitate the adjustment to campus life. For international students, the College offers the American Language Program, a preacademic English as a second language program for individuals whose native language is not English. Some applicants may be eligible to obtain form I-20 to attain or maintain F-1 status.

Academic Programs

The academic programs at Bergen are classified as transfer or career programs. Transfer programs include a course of study that corresponds to the freshman and sophomore offerings at most colleges and universities. After completing their associate degrees at Bergen, many students transfer to a bachelor's degree program at colleges in New Jersey and throughout the United States. The College is also involved in dual-admission programs with four-year colleges in the state. Career programs emphasize training needed to enter a chosen field of employment. They are designed for students planning to begin a career immediately after receiving their associate degree. Graduates of these programs are actively recruited by area employers.

In addition to its programs that prepare students for associate degrees and career certificates, Bergen offers a comprehensive program of noncredit continuing education.

Associate Degree Programs At Bergen, a student can earn an **Associate in Arts (A.A.)**, an **Associate in Science (A.S.)**, or an **Associate in Applied Science (A.A.S.)** degree. The College also offers one-year certificate programs that provide training for specific occupational skills. The A.A. degree is offered in art, communication arts, dance arts, economics, foreign language, history, leisure and recreation, liberal arts, literature, music, philosophy and religion, political science, psychology, sociology, theater arts (acting), and women's studies. The A.S. degree in liberal arts and sciences, with options in natural sciences and mathematics, is offered in biology, chemistry, computer sciences, general curriculum, mathematics, and physics. An A.S. degree in liberal arts and sciences, with options in professional studies, is offered in broadcasting, business administration (business administration, international trade, management, and marketing), education, and general curriculum (professional concentration). There are also A.S. degrees in engineering science and exercise science. The A.A.S. degree is offered in accounting, allied health, banking, business computer programming, business computer programming (microcomputer), commercial art (computer animation, graphic design, illustration, and photography), credit and finance, criminal justice, dental hygiene, diagnostic medical sonography, drafting and design technology, early childhood education, electrical technology, general engineering technology, horticulture therapy technician studies, hotel-restaurant management (catering/banquet management, food service management, and hospitality), legal assistance, manufacturing engineering technology, medical laboratory technology, medical office assistance, nursing, office systems technology (word processing option), ornamental horticulture, physical therapist assistant studies, radiography, real estate, respiratory therapy, and retail business management.

Certificate and Diploma Programs Certificate programs are offered in commercial art, computer-aided drafting technology, computer animation, computer graphics, computer science, culinary arts, data entry (micro-mini computer operations), desktop publishing, exercise science, floral design, food service supervision, illustration, landscaping, media technology, office studies (word processing), photography, real estate sales, small business management, surgical technology, travel studies, and U.S. studies.

Off-Campus Programs

The Adult Learning Center, located at 285 Main Street in Hackensack, provides educational and counseling services for adults who have not completed a formal high school education. Credit and noncredit courses are also offered through the Adult Learning Center. Some of the programs and services offered are in areas such as basic skills, English as a second language, career counseling, precollege remedial courses, employability skills, and high school equivalency. For those students who find it difficult to attend on-campus sessions, telecourses offer a convenient way to learn at home or at work. These courses are fully accredited and have been developed by nationally known educators. Instructors supplement the weekly televised lessons with related materials, written assignments, and on-campus seminars. Students can also take home videocassettes of some courses and return them at the end of the semester.

Credit for Nontraditional Learning Experiences

BCC administers credit by exam for a large number of college-level courses offered at the College. The College also recognizes the CLEP examinations developed by the College Board. In addition, proficiency tests are offered as a method of placement for a variety of college-level courses. Successful scores on these tests allow students to register for a higher level course within the same discipline.

Costs

The 1995–96 tuition for Bergen County residents was $60.50 per credit. Tuition for out-of-county residents was $125.70 per credit, and tuition for out-of-state residents was $242 per credit. There is an additional nonrefundable general fee of $9 per credit.

Financial Aid

There are many ways to finance an education at BCC. The federal government, the state of New Jersey, and BCC itself offer a wide range of financial assistance programs, including scholarships, loans, grants, and part-time employment. The various sources of financial aid include Federal Pell Grants, Federal Supplemental Educational Opportunity Grants, Federal Work-Study, Federal PLUS Loans, Tuition Aid Grants, Garden State Scholarships, and private scholarships.

Faculty

The primary emphasis of the faculty is on effective instruction of students. Research and writing directed toward these goals are encouraged. Faculty members are selected not only for their academic qualifications and experience, but also for their interest in maintaining close student-teacher relationships. They stimulate and guide a variety of activities, including clubs, athletics, and publications. The more than 200 full-time faculty members hold master's degrees, doctorates, or both.

Student Body Profile

Based on fall 1995 enrollments, the student population at Bergen Community College consisted of 71 percent white, 14 percent Hispanic, 9 percent Asian, and 6 percent African American students. The total enrollment for fall 1995 was 13,207. Forty-three percent of students were men, while 57 percent were women. The median age for men was 21, and it was 25 for women. Overall, the median age was 23. Forty-six percent were enrolled in a transfer program; 25 percent in career programs. Of the total enrollment, 71 percent were matriculated and 29 percent were nonmatriculated.

Student Activities

Students at Bergen are encouraged to enrich their college experience through participation in a variety of activities including student government, clubs, student publications and athletics. The student activities programs are a function of the Office of Student Services. The College sponsors numerous lectures, theatrical productions, special events, and excursions that serve as an integral part of campus life. Some of the more popular organizations are Student Government, Student Government Association, and *The Torch*, which is the student newspaper. Many of the clubs and organizations concentrate on academic disciplines and interests while others highlight the various ethnic, racial and cultural aspects of a very diversified student population.

Sports The Department of Athletics sponsors a number of intercollegiate athletic teams for men and women. The men's intercollegiate athletic teams include soccer, cross-country, basketball, baseball, golf wrestling, track and field, and tennis. Women compete on an intercollegiate basis in cross-country, softball, volleyball, track and field, and basketball. There are also intramural sports for those students who enjoy competition. The College is a member of the Garden State Athletic Conference as well as the national Junior College Athletic Association, Region XIX.

All full- and part-time students attending BCC are members of the Student Government. The governing body of the Student Government is the Student Senate. The senate consists of 12 freshman senators and 12 sophomore senators. The Constitution of the Student Government defines its activities. The function of the Student Government Association is to foster student cooperation and student life, to establish and maintain high standards of honor, and to govern the phases of campus life that concern students.

Facilities and Resources

Bergen is proud of the comprehensive facilities and resources that support the academic programs. There are well-equipped labs in allied health, commercial art, drafting and design, horticulture, hotel-restaurant management, robotics, broadcasting, and much more. Some of the facilities, such as the Sidney Silverman Library, the Dental Hygiene Clinic, and the Bergen Room Restaurant, are open to the public. The College recently completed an expansion of its facilities to include a student center, a 300-seat state-of-the-art theater, additional classrooms, and increased library space. The College's master plan is currently under review to determine the need for any additional facilities in the future.

Location

Bergen Community College is located in Paramus, which is the geographic center of Bergen County in northern New Jersey. With more than 300,000 households and nearly 1 million residents, Bergen County is one of the largest counties in the state. The College is located on a 167-acre campus that is bordered by two golf courses and a county park. The county offers convenient transportation to New York City by bus, train, and ferry. The College is approximately 20 minutes from the George Washington Bridge.

Admission Requirements

Bergen maintains an open door policy, which means that most programs are open to anyone with a high school diploma or the equivalent. SAT I scores and high school rank are not criteria for acceptance. Once admitted, students may be accepted into the curriculum of their choice as long as they meet the minimum requirements. Some students may need to take a series of courses to help them prepare for their desired program of study. Allied health programs are competitive and therefore not subject to the open door policy. Admission into these programs is limited to a specific number of candidates because of requirements imposed by accrediting agencies and the availability of faculty, college laboratory, and clinical agency resources. Priority is given to Bergen County residents for admission to these programs.

Application and Information

The application deadline for the spring semester (beginning in January) is November 1 for the nursing day program and for international applicants holding temporary visas and December 1 for all others. The application deadline for the fall semester (beginning in September) is April 1 for dental hygiene, diagnostic medical sonography, nursing (day and evening programs), radiography, respiratory therapy, and surgical technology and July 1 for all other applicants. All academic and/or supporting credentials are due by the application deadline dates or students may not be eligible for consideration.

Director of Admissions and Registration
Bergen Community College
400 Paramus Road
Paramus, New Jersey 07652
Telephone: 201-447-7195

The Bergen Community College Megastructure.

BERKELEY COLLEGE

NEW YORK CITY AND WHITE PLAINS, NEW YORK
WEST PATERSON, WALDWICK, AND WOODBRIDGE, NEW JERSEY

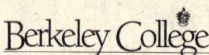

The College and Its Mission

Founded in 1931, Berkeley's coeducational, specialized two-year colleges of business are distinguished in that they offer many of the characteristics of a liberal arts college—campus atmosphere, advisement services, opportunities for personal enrichment, extracurricular activities, and residential facilities—while at the same time retaining the practical aspects of a business school. Recognized nationally for more than 65 years for its academic excellence, Berkeley provides an all-encompassing educational experience. Berkeley's programs are designed to develop professional competencies and awareness for business careers and to provide the knowledge, understanding, and appreciation of culture necessary to meet the demands of an ever-changing society.

All campuses are accredited by the Commission on Higher Education of the Middle States Association of Colleges and Schools. The New York and Westchester campuses are authorized by the New York State Board of Regents to confer the degrees of Associate in Applied Science and Associate in Science and their programs are registered by the New York State Education Department. The New Jersey campuses are licensed as colleges and authorized by the New Jersey Commission on Higher Education to confer the degrees of Associate in Applied Science and Associate in Science. All campuses are approved for the education of veterans and their eligible dependents, for rehabilitative training of handicapped students, and for international students.

Academic Programs

Berkeley College offers educational programs that are designed specifically to meet the needs of students who want to be working in a successful career sooner than four-year college graduates. The College offers many exciting associate degree and certificate programs in dynamic, growing career fields. More intensified programs can be completed in three to twelve months. Berkeley operates on the basis of four quarters beginning in January, April, July, and September. The campuses are closed on legal holidays, during the Thanksgiving recess, and for winter, spring, summer, and fall vacations. An academic year is comprised of three terms totaling thirty-six weeks.

Associate Degree Programs Associate degree programs are offered in business administration (six quarters) with specializations in accounting, customer relations, management, office systems management, retail management, and travel and tourism; fashion marketing and management (six quarters) with specializations in fashion merchandising, fashion production, and international fashion marketing; health information management (six quarters); hotel and restaurant management (seven quarters); interior design (six quarters); international business (six quarters); office administration (six quarters); and paralegal studies (six quarters).

Certificate programs are offered in administrative assistant studies (four quarters), business administration (four quarters), fashion merchandising (four quarters), intensive secretarial/word processing (three quarters), medical records administration (three and four quarters), microcomputer accounting (four quarters), and software management (three quarters).

Berkeley's Professional Series offers intensified programs that can be completed in just three months.

Transfer Arrangements Berkeley programs are designed to develop professional competencies in business careers and provide the understanding necessary to meet the demands of an ever-changing society. Other institutions of higher education will determine how many credits to accept in transfer dependent upon their own policies, comparability of courses, and the requirements of the degree being sought. Each campus has identified a college transfer officer to answer questions and to assist students in transferring credits.

Berkeley College is affiliated by formal agreement with the renowned European Business School, London, and its academic programs have been validated through the EBS London Validation Service by the Open University, the largest university in the United Kingdom. Upon finishing the Berkeley associate degree in international business, students may choose to continue their studies at the London campus and earn a British B.A. (Honours) degree.

Internship and Co-op Programs Berkeley's degree programs provide the best balance of academics and important application of this learning directly in the students' chosen fields via an internship experience. By enhancing a students' education with a professional internship, Berkeley students gain valuable work experience and a network of important business contacts before they graduate. Employers actively seek Berkeley graduates because they can effectively contribute to their respective organizations immediately. Berkeley graduates possess the important analytical ability and critical thinking skills employers require.

Special Programs and Services Counseling and advisement begin at Berkeley as soon as a student applies for admission. The Student Advisement and Counseling Center provides ongoing orientation in addition to Freshman Seminar, and integrates academic, career, and personal counseling. Faculty tutoring and advisement are supplemented by peer tutors. Specialized computer programs can be used to meet individualized needs.

Credit for Nontraditional Learning Experiences

Academic advisers can explore the following options with students: advanced placement sponsored by the College Entrance Examination Board; CLEP (College-Level Examination Program); ACT-PEP (American College Testing Proficiency Examination Program); portfolio assessment, which involves submission of an experiential learning portfolio in the evaluation of credit; DANTES (Defense Activity for Nontraditional Educational Support); challenge exams involve passing specific tests to demonstrate mastery in a subject area. Appropriate credit is given to students who have completed courses approved by the National Program on Non-collegiate Sponsored Instruction.

Costs

In 1996–97, day students pay $3695 per quarter for tuition. Boarding students pay an additional residence fee of $1400 per quarter for a double or $995 per quarter for a triple.

Financial Aid

Sufficient financial aid is available for eligible students. Monies are available in the form of loans, scholarships, grants, and other awards. Berkeley students are eligible for federal and state grants, including Pell Grants, TAP and/or TAG, for which repayment is not required. There are also several low-interest loans designed for students and their parents, offered through the Federal Family Education Loan Program. Berkeley allocates about $2 million annually for student aid, based on need and/or merit. Scholarship assistance is awarded each year by the Alumni Association. Students graduating in the top 10 percent of their high school class, or with a cumulative average of 3.0 automatically qualify for Achievement Awards. Recipients of private scholarships can receive matching grants from Berkeley, and a variety of other grants, scholarships, and institutional loans are available. In addition, through Berkeley's Challenge Program, students who maintain a high GPA can receive loans of up to $3,000 that may be partially or fully cancelled, based on GPA at the time of graduation from Berkeley. Students can beat the rising cost of education by maintaining continuous full-time enrollment status and completing their program at the same tuition rate at which they began.

Faculty

The success of any educational program is determined largely by the character and competence of the faculty members. Berkeley's instructors are chosen for their professional experience as well as their academic credentials. Several of Berkeley's administrators are nationally recognized leaders in business education, authors, lecturers, and consultants.

Student Body Profile

There is a total enrollment of 3,000 students, including day and evening, full-time and part-time, representing twenty-four states and twenty other countries.

Student Activities

While at Berkeley, students have many opportunities to become involved in campus activities and trips. The Student Government Association plans a social calendar that includes theater trips, ski weekends, charity drives, organized sports events, dances, and a College Week trip during spring break. There are a number of on-campus clubs, which plan special events for social as well as professional growth. Phi Beta Lamda sponsors a variety of activities to develop business leadership skills and members of Delta Epsilon Chi participate in school and community projects; and many win awards in local, state, and national competitive events in marketing and distribution. The fashion department has staged fashion shows; and excursions to museums, shows, and cultural centers in New York are part of the arts in contemporary society course. Business administration classes visit the stock exchange and advertising agencies. Students in the office administration program keep abreast of current happenings through speakers from industry and equipment demonstrations as well as field trips. The International Club provides a forum for the special needs and interests of international students. The club organizes social and cultural activities, including field trips that acquaint international students with life in America. The get-acquainted organizational meeting each year often includes a trip to the United Nations. Additional activities, such as international festivals, are organized by international students at individual campuses.

Facilities and Resources

Each campus has its own Learning Resource Center with a cumulative total of 40,000 volumes, 300 periodical subscriptions, and an audiovisual collection of 2,200 items.

A modern dormitory serves the Westchester campus, and attractive apartments are available near the New York City and Garret Mountain campuses.

Career Planning/Placement Offices Berkeley offers a full-service placement division with 15 placement advisers specializing in each major field of study. The placement division provides additional support with résumé writing and personal interview coaching and helps students secure a part-time job while attending class, if needed. Graduates qualify for the free lifetime benefits of job placement assistance and refresher courses.

Location

Life in Berkeley is most profoundly influenced by campus location. All Berkeley campuses enjoy the unparalleled cultural, business, professional, and human resources of the New York metropolitan area. New York includes Broadway, Lincoln Center, the United Nations, Radio City Music Hall, Fifth Avenue, the Metropolitan Museum of Art, the Yankees and the Knicks, the stock exchanges, Fashion Avenue, and Chinatown. Whatever interests a Berkeley student may have, his or her life will be influenced by the dynamic rhythms of the city. The suburban campuses also draw heavily on their own local resources for guest speakers, field trips, and recreational activities. They enjoy the best of both worlds.

Admission Requirements

Graduation from an accredited high school or equivalent, a personal interview, and an entrance exam, are basic requirements for admission to Berkeley College. The following credentials must be submitted as part of the application process: a completed application form and nonrefundable $35 application fee and an unofficial transcript for currently enrolled high school students or high school diploma (or equivalent), plus a high school transcript for high school graduates. Action on application is taken immediately after credential are received.

Application and Information

Applications are accepted on an ongoing basis. All prospective students should contact the director of admissions at the Berkeley College campus most convenient to them.

Berkeley College–New York City Campus
3 East 43rd Street
New York, New York 10017
Telephone: 212-986-4343
800-446-5400 (toll-free)

Berkeley College–Westchester Campus
40 West Red Oak Lane
White Plains, New York 10604
Telephone: 914-694-1122
800-446-5400 (toll-free)

Berkeley College–Garret Mountain Campus
44 Rifle Camp Road
Box 440
West Paterson, New Jersey 07424
Telephone: 201-278-5400
800-446-5400 (toll-free)

Berkeley College–Bergen Campus
100 West Prospect Street
Waldwick, New Jersey 07463
Telephone: 201-652-0388
800-446-5400 (toll-free)

Berkeley College–Middlesex Campus
430 Rahway Avenue
Woodbridge, New Jersey 07095
Telephone: 908-750-1800
800-446-5400 (toll-free)

Peterson's Guide to Two-Year Colleges 1997

BRADLEY ACADEMY FOR THE VISUAL ARTS
YORK, PENNSYLVANIA

The College and Its Mission

Bradley Academy is a tradition of excellence. In 1952, the York Academy of Arts was established by local artists to meet the community's needs for trained visual artists. Thirty years later, the school became part of the Antonelli Institute of Art and Photography group, with headquarters in Philadelphia. In 1988, Bradley Academy once again became an independent school continuing to provide area employers with well-trained graduates.

It is Bradley Academy's mission to be responsive to the needs of employers by teaching, within a supportive environment, the creative, technical, and workplace skills required for a successful career. Bradley's success is measured by the number of students who complete their programs and get jobs in their chosen fields—graphic design, interior design, electronic design, fashion marketing, or electronic pre-press technology. In recent years, 85 to 95 percent of each year's available graduating students are working in their chosen professional fields within ninety days after graduation.

Bradley Academy is people. A staff of dedicated professionals strives to help students realize their full potential and master the skills needed for their first job in their chosen fields. Faculty and staff members believe in their responsibility to provide practical, hands-on career training; develop social skills, good work habits, and technical skills; provide equal opportunity for success based on performance; provide a supportive environment; and prepare students in the classroom for the workplace.

Bradley Academy for the Visual Arts is a private, proprietary institution specializing in career-oriented programs in the visual arts. Most course work is directly related to the student's major field of study. Bradley Academy is accredited by the Accrediting Commission for Career Schools and Colleges of Technology.

Academic Programs

All programs are geared toward career preparation, and general education requirements are held to five courses (communications I and II, psychology, marketing, and professional development) out of the total of twenty-four courses taken in the two-year specialized associate degree programs. Students select their major fields at the time of enrollment, and their courses are block scheduled.

Whenever possible and appropriate, courses are taught in a studio or lab setting providing hands-on instruction. Computer courses are taught with a 1:1 ratio of students to workstations, with a maximum of 16 students per class.

Associate Degree Programs Programs offered for the **Associate in Specialized Technology** degree include electronic design, graphic design, and interior design. Programs for the **Associate in Specialized Business** degree include fashion marketing. A diploma (one-year program) is also offered in electronic pre-press technology.

Specialized associate degree programs require successful completion of 72 credits, taken over four 16-week semesters. The diploma program requires successful completion of 33 credits, including an internship, taken over three 16-week semesters.

Special Programs and Services A variety of continuing education and personal enrichment courses are also offered for high school students and for adults. These generally meet evenings, Saturdays, or during the summer. Topics include drawing and painting, cartooning, computer graphics, and a wide variety of short courses on specific computer software packages. A one-week Summer Studio Program for students who are entering their senior year of high school is held each year in June and August. Students take classes in one of four areas: graphic design, interior design, fashion marketing, or electronic design. There is no tuition charge for Summer Studio. Students buy their own art supplies. Detailed information is available from the Admissions Office.

Credit for Nontraditional Learning Experiences

Advanced standing or academic credit for work done elsewhere is considered on a case-by-case basis by the director of education. A portfolio evaluation is usually part of the process; testing may also be required.

Costs

Tuition for the 1996–97 academic year is $255 per credit. Students in the degree programs usually take 18 credits per semester, making total tuition for the academic year $9180. Costs for art supplies are additional and average $25 to $40 per week. There are no lab fees, and students are not required to own a computer. Starting students can purchase a supply kit that costs $500 to $800, depending on the program.

Bradley Academy does not operate facilities for student housing, but does assist students in finding suitable accommodations and roommates upon request. The neighborhood surrounding Bradley Academy is largely residential, with sufficient rental units available to students at reasonable costs, averaging about $250 per month per student.

Financial Aid

Bradley Academy participates in the Federal Pell Grant, Federal Student Educational Opportunity Grant, Federal College Work-Study, Federal Stafford Student Loan, and PLUS Programs; the Pennsylvania PHEAA grant program; and other sources of aid that may be available to qualified students. Institutional aid is also available and is awarded based on need and merit. The financial affairs manager can assist students in determining eligibility and completing applications and can help families create a personal plan that outlines expenses and identifies financial resources available to students. For the 1994–95 academic year, the average package of grants and loans for first-time students was $4226 per academic year, and 1 out of every 6 students had their full tuition investment covered by grants and loans.

Faculty

Total faculty members number 40. Of these, 9 are full-time and 31 are adjunct. The student-faulty ratio is approximately 15:1. Faculty members are required to have a minimum of three years professional experience in the fields in which they teach, in addition to appropriate academic credentials. Most faculty members have earned bachelor's degrees in their respective fields; approximately one third have earned master's degrees.

Student Body Profile

The average age of students at Bradley Academy is 22. About 55 percent are women, and 45 percent are men. The total number of full-time students enrolled in fall 1996 is about 280, plus about 20 part-time students. Approximately 60 percent of students commute from their homes in south central Pennsylvania and northern Maryland, the other 40 percent rent apartments within a short distance of the school. An additional 50 to 75 students are enrolled in short-term enrichment and self-improvement courses, which usually meet in the evenings or on Saturdays.

Student Activities

Students may get involved with professional organizations such as ASID (American Society of Interior Designers) and the Advertising Club of Central Pennsylvania. The school also has a chapter of Alpha Beta Kappa, a national honor society that promotes and rewards personal integrity and academic excellence. Students maintaining a 3.5 cumulative GPA or higher at the end of the third semester will be considered for induction into ABK. School activities include a school picnic each semester, a Halloween party, and a variety of field trips within each department. Students are also encouraged to get involved with the community through freelance work and frequent community service opportunities.

Facilities and Resources

Bradley Academy is housed in a 25,000-square-foot, turn-of-the-century school building. Twelve spacious classrooms and studios, accommodating an average class size of 25 or fewer, are well suited for studio work as well as lecture classes. The state-of-the-industry computer labs support the computer-based courses in all programs. One lab features sixteen networked PowerMacs; the other has sixteen networked Centris 610 Macintosh computers. They are supported by a Hewlett-Packard Design Jet color printer, scanners, and CD-ROM players. Students routinely work with the current version of industry standard software applications such as Adobe's Dimensions, Illustrator, Photoshop, and Premiere; Microsoft's Excel and Word; and MacroMedia Director; Peachtree; and Quark XPress. Other commonly used applications are also available. The hardware and software in the labs are regularly upgraded to reflect current industry practice. Specialized resource areas such as a graphics lab, display windows, and vignette space allow students to apply the skills learned in the classroom.

Library and Audiovisual Services The library occupies approximately 600 square feet on the lower level of the school. It houses over 1,200 general reference books as well as titles specifically related to the programs offered at the school. It also includes more than 50 periodicals routinely received by the school. Computers with CD-ROM players provide access to the software programs used in the courses as well as general purpose programs and reference sources on CD-ROM. In addition to the library, each program has additional resource areas that contain materials specific to that course of study. For example, the Interior Design Resource Room has catalogs of furniture manufacturers and a wide selection of fabric samples used for window treatments, wall covering or upholstery, tile samples, and paint swatches. The Fashion Marketing Resource Area includes commercial sewing machines, mannequins, and materials used for visual merchandising, as well as industry specific publications. Student artwork is proudly displayed throughout the school. It is used to demonstrate the students' achievements and the nature of their work to prospective employers and students.

Location

The city of York, Pennsylvania, offers a unique blend of small-city convenience, safety, and lifestyle with easy access to the larger population centers of Baltimore, Maryland, (45 minutes); Lancaster; and Harrisburg (each 30 minutes). York was founded in pre-Revolutionary times. It has a rich historic past and a strong commitment to preserving its traditions. York County also offers several major shopping malls and many outlet shopping opportunities. It has a strong manufacturing and industrial base as well, and consistently has one of the lowest unemployment rates in Pennsylvania. Book publishers, furniture manufacturers, and apparel manufacturers are among the many employers in the area. Bradley Academy is located on one of York's main streets, six blocks from the convenience of downtown.

Admission Requirements

Typically, the admissions procedure begins with a visit to Bradley Academy. At that time, prospective students and their families can tour the school and gather the information needed to make a decision. Likewise, the admissions staff will become acquainted with the student's qualifications. To be considered for admission, all applicants must have a high school diploma or hold a GED approved by the state. All applicants are evaluated on their educational backgrounds and demonstrated interest in their chosen fields. Portfolio reviews are required for graphic design and electronic design applicants. Two letters of recommendation are required for all applicants. A school visit is required before the start of classes. High school grade transcripts will be requested for those still enrolled in high school. Bradley Academy reserves the right to request additional information as deemed necessary by the Admissions Committee. Qualified students are accepted at any time. However, early application is strongly encouraged. Bradley Academy is a small school, and some classes fill well in advance of the starting date. An early decision also has the advantage of allowing time for proper processing of financial aid.

Application and Information

Prospective students should contact:

Director of Admissions
Bradley Academy for the Visual Arts
625 East Philadelphia Street
York, Pennsylvania 17403

Telephone: 800-864-7725 (toll-free)
Fax: 717-845-6016
E-mail: bradley@net-works.net
World Wide Web: http://www.bradley-acad.com

BREVARD COLLEGE
BREVARD, NORTH CAROLINA

The College and Its Mission

Brevard College has a beautiful 140-acre campus, on which 89 percent of the students reside. The diverse student body represents over thirty states and fourteen other countries. The College is contemporary in appearance and in educational philosophy. Brevard College evolved through the merger of three institutions: Rutherford College, which was founded in 1853; Weaver College; and Brevard Institute. As a result, Brevard includes among its alumni many honored graduates of each of the three institutions that are a part of the College's rich heritage. Brevard College is approved by the North Carolina Association of Colleges and Universities and the North Carolina State Department of Education, is accredited by the Southern Association of Colleges and Schools, and is a member of the National Association of Schools of Music.

Brevard College's mission has long been to educate worthy young people, regardless of their economic or social background, within a residential liberal arts college setting that fosters respect for truth and beauty, creativity and hard work, tolerance and personal integrity, vigorous activity, and spiritual reflection. At the heart of this mission lies a simple covenant: the College expects all students to commit their hearts and minds to the community of learning at Brevard. In return, the College undertakes to equip them with skills and understanding that will help them to lead lives of achievement and moral purpose. To accomplish this mission, Brevard has gathered a faculty and staff notable for the quality of their academic preparation, their character, and their effectiveness as teachers. Brevard College provides an intensive two-year, university-parallel liberal arts program leading to associate degrees primarily for students intending to transfer to senior colleges. The Brevard difference is that the finest professors are devoted to teaching freshmen and sophomores.

As a result of this commitment, the College has always attracted and welcomed highly motivated students who are already prepared to learn as well as other, less-prepared students who need personal help from faculty members and staff in order to adjust to a rigorous academic program.

Academic Programs

The Brevard College academic program is designed principally for students who plan to go on to a four-year college or university, and the individualized instruction they receive for the first two years is important to Brevard graduates. Since 92 percent of the graduates in the university-parallel program transfer each year, the basic curriculum is composed of courses that are required for transfer credit. Perhaps the College is best described as a working community—teachers and students who believe in the pursuit of knowledge, in creative expression, and in discipline through science, art, theory, and practice. The common goal is intellectual growth. The challenge is a rigorous academic curriculum. Brevard students have a willingness to study hard, practice long, and give of themselves.

Brevard College awards the **Associate in Arts**, the **Associate in Science**, and the **Associate in Fine Arts** degrees and the Junior College Diploma. The College offers a specific curriculum for each of the following areas: accounting, agricultural sciences, art, business administration, communications, computer science, drama, economics, education, English, foreign languages, history, journalism, liberal arts, mathematics, music, philosophy, physical education, political science, pre-engineering, pre-medical sciences, psychology, recreation, religion, and sociology. The College also offers programs in forestry, environmental studies, and wilderness education, and there are opportunities for field studies in the Blue Ridge Mountains and Pisgah National Forest. The College has recently been granted candidacy status by the Southern Association of Colleges and Schools to offer four-year baccalaureate degrees in art and in music.

The core liberal arts curriculum of the College requires each student to build up a strong base in languages and literature, religion, humanities, mathematics and analytical reasoning, history, natural and social sciences, fine arts, and environmental studies, together with exposure to several other cultures and a significant investment in volunteer work in the community. The curriculum utilizes classroom work, tutorials, library and laboratory research, and field studies in the Pisgah national Forest, the Davidson and French Broad River ecosystems, the Great Smoky Mountain National Park, and the Cradle of Forest National Historic Park. Brevard's programs in music and art afford talented students excellent educational and performance opportunities at the College as well as in such off-campus settings as the Brevard Music Center, the Brevard Chamber Orchestra, and the Asheville Museum.

Candidates for the A.A. and A.S. degrees must complete 66 semester hours, and candidates for the A.F.A. degree must complete 66-69 semester hours. The Junior College Diploma requires the completion of 66 semester hours. To be eligible for graduation, students must be in residence for at least two semesters and must complete at least 33 semester hours at Brevard College and have a C (2.0) average or better on all academic work attempted.

Off-Campus Programs

Brevard offers a semester in Austria at Altmunster, which is 45 minutes northeast of Salzburg in the Alps. Curriculum includes German, Austrian studies, music history, and alpine hiking, climbing, and snow skiing. Music majors can arrange for lessons at the world famous "Mozarteum."

Credit for Nontraditional Learning Experiences

Students may be granted credit through successful scores on the CLEP and Advanced Placement examinations of the College Board.

Costs

Estimated costs for 1996–97 are as follows: for students residing out-of-state, the general fee is $625, tuition is $8500, room is $1700, and board is $2200 for a total cost of $13,025. For North Carolina residents, charges are the same, less an automatic North Carolina Legislative Tuition Grant of $1250, for a total cost of $11,775.

Financial Aid

More than half of the present students are receiving financial aid in the form of scholarships or talent awards in art, athletics, drama, music, humanities, social studies, environmental studies, wilderness education, and leadership. All students desiring financial aid are asked to submit the Free Application for

Federal Student Aid (FAFSA); these forms may be secured from high school guidance counselors. Brevard also offers a number of merit awards based on academic performance. All students applying for admission are considered for these scholarships in the Brevard Scholar program.

Faculty

The strength of any college lies in the quality of its instructional staff. Brevard College is fortunate to have experienced faculty members with graduate degrees from fifty-seven universities in the United States and abroad. All of the full-time faculty members hold at least a master's degree. Classes are kept as small as possible, usually numbering 25 to 32 students or fewer, to encourage a close, personal relationship between instructor and student. The faculty-student ratio is 1:14.

Student Body Profile

The student body represents more than thirty states and fourteen other countries. Eighty-nine percent of the students reside on campus. The freshman class of 400 each year typically has an even ratio of men to women, 15 percent minorities, 8 percent international, and an average age of 19 years old.

Student Activities

Sports, music, journalism, student government, or environmental activism—a wide variety of options give students space to discover who they are and what they have to offer. Athletic activities at Brevard College extend from regular fitness programs and intramural sports to national-caliber intercollegiate athletic competition. Whether students choose rock climbing, mountain biking, or tennis, Brevard has facilities to support their interests. Student athletes who want to compete on the intercollegiate level can choose from men's basketball, baseball, cross-country, soccer, track, and golf or women's basketball, cross-country, tennis, track, volleyball, and soccer. Challenging ski slopes, bicycling on the mountain peaks of the Blue Ridge Parkway, white-water rafting, canoeing, camping, hiking, backpacking the Appalachian Trail—all are part of the Brevard College environment.

Facilities and Resources

Facilities on campus include Coltrane Commons, which is the center of campus extracurricular activities; the Boshamer Gymnasium, which has two playing floors; an Olympic-size heated swimming pool; an all-weather track; two soccer fields; and six all-weather tennis courts. Also on campus are the A. G. Myers Dining Hall and five dormitories.

The J. A. Jones Library has 48,000 volumes and a wide variety of computer information systems. The library has seating facilities for 200, a seminar room, individual study carrels, and a record listening facility. A separate listening library for music, which has both tape and disk facilities, is housed in the music building. Other major buildings on campus include the McLarty-Goodson Classroom Building for the humanities, the Bryan Moore Classroom Building for the natural sciences, the Beam Administration Building, the Dunham Music Center, the Sims Art Building, and the Barn Theatre.

Location

Brevard College is located in Brevard, North Carolina, known as the "Land of Waterfalls." Over 100 majestic waterfalls tumble through the nearby national forest. Also awaiting students is the panoramic grandeur of the Great Smoky Mountains National Park.

Brevard is a great college town. In fact, it is rated by Rand McNally as one of the best communities in the U.S. in climate, leisure activity, health care, and safety from crime. Within a thirty minute drive is Asheville, the largest city in Western North Carolina, with a variety of shopping malls, restaurants, theaters, a civic center, and the world-renowned Biltmore House and Gardens.

Admission Requirements

Admission to Brevard College is dependent upon the ability, preparation, character, and motivation of the applicant. Prospective students must show evidence that they can acclimate themselves to the challenge of academic life at the College. Individual assessment is made of each applicant to determine a student's academic maturity. The record of past achievement is considered in conjunction with ability, as measured by the SAT I or ACT. However, more consideration is given to the student's academic record, and test results are used as supplements.

Application and Information

To be considered, students must submit a completed formal application, a recommendation from their high school, official SAT I or ACT scores, and an official high school transcript. Qualified students are accepted as soon as their application has been completed and evaluated.

For more information, students should contact:

Dean of Admissions
Brevard College
Brevard, North Carolina 28712
Telephone: 704–884–8300
Fax: 704–884–3790
E-mail: admissions@lightnin.brevard.edu

Aerial view of the Brevard campus.

Peterson's Guide to Two-Year Colleges 1997

BRIARWOOD COLLEGE
SOUTHINGTON, CONNECTICUT

The College and Its Mission

The mission of Briarwood College is to prepare students for transfer to other colleges and universities and to develop their skills for employment. Briarwood is dedicated to providing an environment in which students can learn to think clearly, reason, and add to their confidence and development. Further, Briarwood College offers counseling and guidance services on a scheduled basis. The Board of Directors, administration, faculty, and staff believe that each individual deserves the dignity and respect entitled to all human beings; and they are committed to assisting students in achieving the highest possible self-worth, self-discipline, and responsible citizenship. Furthermore, Briarwood College encourages students to continue a process of lifelong learning so that they can better serve their families, communities, states, and nations. Briarwood College is convinced that the education students receive will sustain them throughout life and promote greater understanding among people and the trends and forces that will affect their lives.

Academic Programs

Briarwood College is authorized to offer one-year diploma programs and two-year degree programs beyond the high school level in order to qualify students for employment or transfer in various technical and related fields. Subject to this authorization, Briarwood subscribes to the following goals: (1) To aid the student in developing abilities and competence in his or her chosen field of study. To accomplish this end, each curriculum offers sound theoretical instruction along with actual experience in practical phases of work. In addition, Briarwood endeavors to induce its students to develop attitudes and ethics that encourage optimal personal and on-the-job relationships. (2) To assist the student in developing the potential for living a happy, healthy, responsible, and productive life. Briarwood College provides opportunities for students to communicate effectively and to understand and appreciate their own and other cultural and intellectual heritages. (3) To serve businesses, industries, professions, and units of government by providing competent personnel in technical and related fields. Briarwood's faculty keeps abreast of the changing needs of our technological society by continuing educational experiences, among which are professional improvement through graduate study, meetings with other professional groups, visits to business enterprises, consultations with advisory groups, in-service programs, and periodic surveys of graduates. (4) To serve society by stimulating students to develop their respective capacities for participating in and contributing to the democratic way of life; by making them mindful of the fact that all future generations are dependent upon the world's natural resources that are now entrusted to our common stewardship; by encouraging them to exercise restraint, consideration, and justice in individual and group relations with people throughout the world; and by helping them understand that only by making a contribution to the future can a person or a generation pay its debt to the past. (5) To encourage the realization that lifelong learning is a worthy goal, not only for one's personal worth but for living in a constantly changing society.

Education for Life offers qualified graduates an opportunity to return to Briarwood for additional courses tuition-free for the rest of their lives.

Associate Degree Programs The **Associate in Arts** degree (A.A.) is offered in general studies. The **Associate in Applied Science** degree (A.A.S) is offered in accounting, broadcasting, business management, child development, communication, criminal justice, dental administrative assistant studies, dietetic technician studies, executive medical assistant studies, health information technology, hospitality management (hotel and restaurant management and travel and tourism management), legal assistant/paralegal studies, medical office management, mortuary science, occupational therapy assistant studies, office administration (executive), office administration (legal), office administration (medical), office administration (word processing), office management, and retail merchandising (fashion merchandising and retail management).

Costs

For the 1996–97 academic year, costs are as follows: tuition is $9795 for resident and commuter students, part-time students pay $150 per credit. Resident students are also charged a $2296 residency fee. The nonrefundable registration fee for resident and commuter students is $95, part-time students pay $30 per semester. The activity fee is $95 for resident and commuter students and $15 per semester for part-time students. Accident insurance is available to full-time students at a cost of $27. Total costs are $9992 for commuter students and $12,288 for resident students. Food costs are the responsibility of the student. To aid full-time students and their parents in financial planning, Briarwood College guarantees that tuition will not be increased in the second academic year (September to May) of the student's degree program.

Financial Aid

Students requiring assistance in meeting financial obligations to the College should make this known to the director of financial aid and/or the director of admissions.

The following types of financial aid are available individually or in combination. For more information, contact the Financial Aid Office at 860-628-4751 or 800-952-2444 (toll-free). Financial aid includes presidential scholarships, competitive scholarships, state scholarships, and Connecticut Scholastic Achievement Grants. Briarwood College, in conjunction with outside professional associations, also awards several scholarships in the business, health, and office administration fields. As other scholarships become available in specific program fields, they are announced in Briarwood College publications and posted outside the Financial Aid Office. A number of scholarships are awarded annually to students by local civic groups, churches, and fraternal and union organizations. Students are encouraged to explore all outside possibilities, utilizing the assistance of high school guidance officers or the Briarwood College Financial Aid Office. Recipients of the scholarships are usually chosen on the basis of high scholastic achievement, need, and potential for success. Eligible students are encouraged to seek, and are assisted in obtaining, educational benefits from the Veterans Administration, G.I. Bill, and state agencies. There are also grants and loans available, including Connecticut Independent College Student Grants (CICS), Federal Pell Grants, Federal Stafford Student Loans (formerly Guaranteed Student Loans), Federal PLUS loans, and family educational loan programs.

Faculty

The faculty includes 63 professors, 35 associate professors, 30 assistant professors, and 12 other members.

Student Body Profile

There are 565 students currently enrolled. Sixteen percent are members of minority groups, 1 percent are international students, and 60 percent live off campus.

Student Activities

To promote greater student participation in clubs and student government organizations, meetings may be held during counseling periods each week. Students are encouraged to join and participate in clubs, student organizations, and other activities of interest to them. They include Student Government, Hall Council, allied health club, fashion merchandising, Phi Beta Lambda, Psi Beta (a national honor society for the field of psychology), Thomas Jefferson Society, L.O.V.E. (Lending Our Vital Effort, a community volunteer organization), and yearbook staff.

Sports Students may become involved in a wide variety of outdoor/indoor recreational activities such as tennis, basketball, softball, soccer, volleyball, hiking, jogging, golf, and swimming. Skiing is available locally at Mount Southington and on scheduled weekend trips to ski resorts. Briarwood does not participate in a formal athletic conference; however, some intercollegiate competition is available in basketball, softball, and tennis. Indoor activities include weight lifting and exercise machines, aerobics, racquetball, and swimming made available through a special affiliation with the Southington YMCA.

Facilities and Resources

The campus at Briarwood is unique and spacious. The parking lots are well lighted, with ample parking for both commuters and residents. The comfortably furnished classrooms are carpeted and conducive to learning. The specialized laboratories are also well equipped. Briarwood College welcomes students with disabilities; classrooms are fully accessible. The College provides on-campus town-house–style apartments for students living away from home. Administrative offices, the library, the Learning Resource Center, and some classrooms occupy LeConche Hall. Eder Hall houses classrooms and student apartments. Classrooms, labs, and the campus radio station are housed in Ligouri Hall. In addition to classrooms, the large general area in Founders Hall is utilized by the College and various civic organizations for meetings, seminars, and other functions.

Briarwood College has built a fine reputation of academic quality by guiding and assisting students through their college years. To continue this reputation for caring about its students, the College established the Learning Resource Center to assist students who wish to strengthen their basic skills or to develop more effective study skills. The LRC also provides assistance to students who would benefit from additional instruction in some phase of their course work. The Learning Resource Center is staffed by professional instructors and knowledgeable peer tutors.

Career Planning/Placement Offices Briarwood College maintains a Placement and Career Services Office as a service to its graduates. While no college placement office can guarantee employment, graduates are well received by potential employers, and the placement history is excellent. Some off-campus opportunities are available for part-time employment. These positions, which may or may not be related to Briarwood's educational offerings, are posted by the Placement and Career Services Office. In addition, various on-campus positions are processed through the Financial Aid Office.

Library and Audiovisual Services The Dr. Anthony A. Pupillo Library, staffed by a professional librarian, plays an integral part in the education process of the students. A carefully selected collection of books and periodicals is maintained, and new works are acquired regularly. The library is committed to providing support for the various courses and programs of study offered by Briarwood College. Although the library's resources are richest in the curricula taught at the College, a wide variety of works for individual interest and personal growth are also offered. To aid in career decision making and planning, a computerized occupational information system is provided for students. This program, made available through the State Occupational Information Coordinating Committee, is an easy-access, valuable tool for those seeking current data on a particular occupational field. Computer technology and CD-ROM media are available to facilitate student research. Novice users quickly learn to utilize the capabilities of the library's computer system. The library has been expanded and now includes additional areas for study and multimedia computers for student use. Arrangements can also be made for students to use the Elihu Burritt Library at Central Connecticut State University.

Location

Briarwood College is located in Southington, Connecticut, only 2 hours from Boston and New York. Students find skiing and Connecticut beaches readily accessible, and the school is minutes from the Hartford and New Haven Metros. Briarwood serves students from Connecticut, across the nation, and the world. It is a small college with a congenial atmosphere. The picturesque 33-acre campus is nestled at the base of Mt. Southington and provides students the opportunity to take 2-hour daily or weekend excursions to the cultural and entertainment meccas of New York and Boston.

Admission Requirements

Briarwood College welcomes applications from individuals who have satisfactorily completed a recognized high school program or equivalent training as certified by the State Department of Education. Applications are evaluated on a continuous basis, and prospective students are promptly notified regarding their status. Prospective students are encouraged to call the Admissions Office to schedule an appointment to meet with an admissions representative and visit the campus. The College does not require the submission of SAT I or ACT scores. The student's academic performance and class rank, as well as his/her resolve to succeed academically, are viewed as the most reliable indicators of success. An interview may be required for admission. Additional requirements apply to the General Studies Program and the Occupational Therapy Assistant Program. Interested students should contact the Admissions Office for more information on these programs.

Application and Information

For more information, students should contact:

Briarwood College
Admissions Department
2279 Mt. Vernon Road
Southington, Connecticut 06489

CASCO BAY COLLEGE
PORTLAND, MAINE

The College and Its Mission

Casco Bay College is a private, coeducational junior college of business. The College was founded in 1863 by Bryant and Stratton as one of a chain of business schools. It was the first business school established in the state of Maine and is among the oldest in the United States.

The mission of Casco Bay College is to prepare students for successful careers in business and to enhance their lives through an appropriate balance of technical and general education. The College considers students and their needs to be of first importance and strives to maintain a personal and humane organization dedicated to helping students achieve their educational goals. It is the objective of the College to help each student reach his or her potential. For this purpose, the faculty and administration are committed to accepting all students who have graduated from high school or who have earned a general equivalency diploma. The College insists, however, that each student demonstrate a prescribed standard of achievement for each course, certificate, or degree.

Casco Bay College is accredited as a junior college by the Accrediting Council for Independent Colleges and Schools (ACICS), Washington, D.C. It is authorized to award the Associate in Science degree by the legislature of the state of Maine.

One of the outstanding features of Casco Bay College is its placement service for its students and alumni. Casco Bay College maintains a year-round, lifelong placement service. Surveys of classes in past years show that 90 percent of the students who responded were working in their field or were continuing their college education. The director of placement works closely with many of the area and regional employers to facilitate a match of employment needs with an individual graduate's skills and aspirations. Nationwide placement services are available to all Casco Bay graduates through member schools of the ACICS.

Academic Programs

Programs offered at Casco Bay College are carefully planned to meet the needs of beginning and advanced students. Associate degrees are offered in accounting, accounting with a computer application certificate, accounting with an early childhood certificate, accounting with a paralegal certificate, executive administrative assistant studies, general business, legal administrative assistant studies, legal administrative assistant studies with a paralegal certificate, management, management with a computer application certificate, management with a fashion merchandising certificate, management with an early childhood certificate, management with a paralegal certificate, management with a travel and tourism certificate, medical administrative assistant studies, office management, secretarial studies with a computer application certificate, secretarial studies with a fashion merchandising certificate, secretarial studies with an early childhood certificate, and secretarial studies with a travel and tourism certificate. Certificate programs are offered in accounting, office skills, and office technology. Students may enroll part-time in any of the programs, or they may enroll as special students, selecting individual courses.

Casco Bay College is dedicated to providing the highest quality of business education for those students preparing to enter gainful employment as well as for students who wish to continue their college education after receiving the associate degree. Externships provide numerous benefits to each student. Apart from the value represented by the practical experience gained through any externship, the student comes away with enhanced self-confidence rooted in real-world productivity. Another invaluable benefit that cannot be gained inside the classroom is experience working alongside professionals in the student's respective field. This aspect of on-the-job training allows students to personally learn the written and unwritten codes of actual workplace cultures that cannot be replicated in any classroom. Finally, students are able to personally select a professional environment for their externship that is tailored to their own academic progress, personal growth, and future aspirations. Prior to their last semester at Casco Bay College, students are encouraged to meet with their major field classroom instructors and together coordinate externships that match both students' and employers' requirements for mutually advantageous experiences.

Credit for Nontraditional Learning Experiences

Credit for prior learning in college courses, professional training, and life experience is determined by the academic dean.

Costs

The yearly tuition and fees at Casco Bay College are about $5900 in 1996–97.

Financial Aid

Casco Bay College has a comprehensive program for college expense planning. Forms of financial assistance include grants, loans, scholarships, and payment plans. The College also helps students with work-study opportunities and part-time employment.

Faculty

The student-faculty ratio at Casco Bay College is 12:1.

Students entering a Casco Bay College program are assigned a faculty adviser and a senior mentor who meet individually with students to assist them in making sound decisions.

Student Body Profile

Students at Casco Bay College are primarily from towns and cities in Maine. However, a growing number of students come from other areas of New England and from other countries.

Student Activities

In addition to participating in Casco Bay College–sponsored activities, students may become involved with amateur theatrical, dance, and musical groups who advertise for auditions. There are also a number of racquetball, tennis, and physical fitness facilities in the area.

The student senate is the liaison group for administration, faculty, and students in areas of concern to the student body. Student senate officers and representative are elected by the student body; they coordinate all social activities at the College.

Facilities and Resources

Casco Bay College recognizes its responsibility and commitment to the academic success of all its students. It is further recognized that academic success is the result of a joint partnership between students and instructors. Students who are willing to learn find additional assistance available in the Learning and Study Center. The center offers comprehensive support to students in all areas of academic life. Seminars cover a wide variety of study and college survival skills, small study groups are formed, and tutorials are arranged for students needing additional help.

The library is part of the Learning and Study Center. The purpose of the library is to serve the students and faculty members as a resource center of business and other curriculum-related research and as a professional-reading and leisure-reading center. This is accomplished through a small but carefully selected book collection, a well-balanced periodical collection, the nucleus of an audiovisual collection, and an interlibrary loan service. A librarian gives individual attention to each student and faculty member.

In addition to the computer facilities located in the library, the College has three separate computer labs on campus.

Location

Casco Bay College is located in downtown Portland, Maine. Portland is a major financial and cultural center serving more than 500,000 people in the greater Portland area. The College's apartment complex is within walking distance of the College.

Admission Requirements

Candidates for admission to Casco Bay College are evaluated on an individual basis and are encouraged to apply as far in advance of the anticipated starting date as is practical. It is recommended that candidates visit the College for a personal interview, which should be arranged in advance by telephone or letter. The admissions office is open 8 a.m. to 5 p.m. Monday through Friday and by special arrangement. Casco Bay College has a video that describes "College Life/City Style" at Casco Bay College. Students may view the video at their high school guidance office or contact the Director of Admissions for a ten-day at-home viewing of the video. Group visits by students, parents, teachers, and counselors are welcomed. Visitation arrangements may be made by contacting the Director of Admissions.

International students must file a Casco Bay College application of admission, certified transcripts, certificates or diplomas translated into English, proof of English proficiency (a TOEFL score of at least 500), and a notarized affidavit of financial support.

Application and Information

An application processing fee of $25 is required of all applicants. The fee is nonrefundable and must be paid at the time the application is submitted to the Casco Bay College Admissions Office.

Applications should be submitted to:

Director of Admissions
Casco Bay College
477 Congress Street
Portland, Maine 04101-3483

Telephone: 207-772-0196
800-639-1470 (toll-free in Maine only)
E-mail: cbcollege@aol.com

CAZENOVIA COLLEGE
CAZENOVIA, NEW YORK

The College and Its Mission

Cazenovia College was founded in 1824 as a nonsectarian, coeducational Methodist seminary. The College severed its church affiliation in 1942 and today is a private coeducational two-year and four-year institution with a strong emphasis on career-oriented education. Associate and bachelor's degree programs are organized within the Center for Art & Design Studies, the Center for the Humanities & Education, the Center for Natural & Social Sciences, and the Center for Management Studies.

The College is composed of a main campus and two smaller campuses. The main campus is located on a compact 15-acre site in the center of the village of Cazenovia. The main campus contains twenty-one buildings surrounding a quadrangle, with the athletic center located approximately one block from campus. The College's South Campus, located approximately ¼ mile from the main campus, houses the Center for Art & Design. The Equine/Horsemanship programs are located approximately 5 miles from town on their own 20-acre complex. Students find that the smaller classes and limited enrollment (about 1,100 students) offer an opportunity for personal and intellectual growth in an environment free of the pressures sometimes found in large universities. Students can progress with the strong support of concerned faculty members and staff. The residential character of the College favors the development of deep and lasting friendships, while the College's size allows for personal attention, particularly for those needing academic encouragement.

Academic Programs

Associate Degree Programs Cazenovia College offers the A.A., A.A.S., and A.S. degrees in twenty subject areas within four academic centers. In the Center for Art & Design Studies, students can choose programs in advertising/graphic design, commercial illustration, fashion design, fashion illustration, interior environmental design, studio art (photography and studio art), and visual merchandising. Within the Center for Management Studies, programs are available in accounting, business management, equine studies–horsemanship, equine studies–stable and farm management, and retail management. The Center for Humanities & Education houses programs in community/mental health services, criminal justice, social services for children and youth, and social services for the elderly.

Bachelor's Degree Programs Cazenovia College also offers the **Bachelor of Arts** in fine and performing arts, interdisciplinary social science, literature and culture, and science and society; the **Bachelor of Fine Arts** in interior environmental design and visual communications (advertising/graphic design and commercial illustration) the **Bachelor of Professional Studies** in management (business, equine, and retail); and the **Bachelor of Science** in applied arts and sciences (fine and performing arts, interdisciplinary social sciences, literature and culture, human services, and science and society). The bachelor's degree programs are interdisciplinary in curriculum and competency based.

To earn an associate degree at Cazenovia College, a student must complete 61 credits of course work (except where otherwise specified) with a grade point average of not less than 2.0 (C) and must satisfy all additional program requirements. To earn a bachelor's degree at Cazenovia College, a student must complete 127 credits with a grade point average of at least 2.0 and must satisfy all additional program requirements. Arts and sciences credit requirements vary according to the degree sought. Advanced placement and credit by examination are offered to qualified students, and honors courses are offered on selected areas. An independent study arrangement is available to full-time students.

Special Programs and Services Cazenovia offers several special services through its Learning Resources Center, whose programs have been cited by the National Directory of Exemplary Programs. The center tenders support services to all students. Learning acceleration provided by the center includes the Higher Education Opportunity Program and Title IV student-support services. A strong job placement/transfer counseling program is also available on campus. In addition, Cazenovia's Counseling Center offers a wide range of services, including individual counseling by a professional counselor.

Off-Campus Programs

Cazenovia College has affiliations with several institutions outside the continental United States. Students may take a semester abroad in London at the American College in London; in Leysin, Switzerland, at the American College in Switzerland; and in San German, Puerto Rico, at the Inter-American University. Off-campus opportunities closer to home are available through credit-bearing internship programs.

Credit for Nontraditional Learning Experiences

Credit for nontraditional and life experiences may be granted after appropriate portfolio review by the faculty.

Costs

For the academic year 1996–97, tuition is $10,500 per year, room is $2650, and board is $2650. Miscellaneous fees are approximately $150 and books are about $490. Personal and travel expenses average $500, and athletics and other miscellaneous fees specific to the academic concentration or course selection total about $500. Private and group music lessons are available at varying costs.

Financial Aid

Financial aid sources exist at Cazenovia College to bridge the gap between the amount of money a student's family can pay and the cost of attending the institution. Ninety-five percent of the students receive some form of assistance. Need-based federal, state, and institutional sources are available and include grants, loans, and on-campus work-study arrangements. About 40 percent of the students hold work-study jobs. Merit scholarships not based on financial need are also offered in all subject areas. Merit and transfer scholarships vary in amount, averaging between $300 and $3,000 annually and are awarded for two- and four-year periods depending upon the course of study. In 1993 and again in 1995, the College was recognized by *Money* magazine as a top 25 "Best Buy" in the Northeast. Specific details on the various forms of financial aid are available from the director of financial aid.

Faculty

Cazenovia College has 92 faculty members, 47 full-time and 45 part-time. The faculty is more strongly committed to teaching than to research. Many of the part-time faculty members pursue careers outside the College. Their professional experiences enrich the College's programs. The faculty is strongly involved in student life, particularly in program-related student clubs. Faculty members also function as student advisers and academic counselors. The student-faculty ratio is 14:1.

Student Body Profile

The undergraduate student body is 36 percent men and 64 percent women. Eighty-five percent of students come directly from high schools in New York State, while 15 percent transfer in from other colleges. Of the 20 percent from outside the state, about 8 percent are from Middle Atlantic States, 10 percent are from New England, and 2 percent are from states outside these regions and from other countries. Members of minority groups constitute 23 percent of the student body. Eighty-five percent of Cazenovia students live on campus in the five residence halls. Freshmen are assigned housing based on an interest questionnaire; sophomore housing assignments are selected by lottery. Student dining facilities are open seven days a week, up to twelve hours a day, and continuously provide students with meals or snacks. There are no fraternities or sororities. Social life focuses on activities with individual residence halls and campus clubs, as well as dances, theme weekends, student performances, sports events, and intramurals.

Student Activities

The Student Council is an elected body that deals with various aspects of campus life. It consists of presidents of the residence halls and student organizations, class officers, and additional representatives of the freshman class. Six students are also voting members of the 16-member Senate, which governs the College.

Sports In 1995, the College began participation on a provisional basis in Division III of the NCAA and competes in twelve intercollegiate NCAA sports: men's and women's basketball, tennis, soccer, and crew; men's golf and baseball; and women's volleyball and softball. The riding team is an award winning member of the Intercollegiate Horse Show Association. A $5-million athletic facility was completed in 1988.

Facilities and Resources

Library and Audiovisual Services The Witherill Information Resources Center/Library has holdings totaling 70,225 pieces, including 54,778 volumes, 3,415 bound periodicals, 9,328 microfilm reels, and 2,704 audiovisual materials. In addition, the library subscribes to the Interlibrary Loan Subsystem of the OCLC, which provides access to the libraries of other colleges. Cazenovia's Computer Center is equipped with PCs in a local area network, which are all available for student use. For interior/architectural design students, the College offers a computer-aided drafting lab. A Compugraphic computerized typesetting system is available to students in advertising design; a full-color graphics system is available to students in commercial illustration.

Cazenovia College's Learning Resources Center staff of 24 professionals provides workshops and individualized tutoring to help students improve their reading, math, writing, and study skills. The Language Laboratory for the students in the individualized studies program permits students to prepare for credit by examination in modern European languages. The College also has chemistry and biology labs, extensive art studios, and music-practice areas.

The Gertrude T. Chapman Art Center is an on-campus art gallery exhibiting the art of contemporary artists. The Howard and Bess Chapman Cultural Center houses changing exhibitions of regional, historical, and general cultural interest, as well as art exhibits. At the restored Cazenovia College Theater, students produce plays and other entertainments. The theater is also used for film showings and large-group lectures.

The Cazenovia College Nursery School, attended by children from the village, enables students in the child studies programs to learn firsthand about the care and education of children.

Students in the equine studies programs have access to the College's facilities at the Sigety Equine Center in Nelson, New York.

Location

Cazenovia, New York, is a quiet semirural village of 4,000 in the Finger Lakes district of central New York. Many structures in the village are listed in the National Register of Historic Places. The village retains much of its nineteenth-century charm. Cazenovia Lake, less than a mile away, is enjoyed for its beauty and for the opportunities it provides for summer and winter sports. Attractive countryside and numerous ski trails surround the village. In nearby Syracuse, 18 miles away, students can take advantage of a symphony orchestra, a widely acclaimed regional theater, museums, fine restaurants, traveling productions at the Civic Center, and major athletic events at Syracuse University's dome stadium, among other social and cultural offerings.

Admission Requirements

Cazenovia seeks students whose high school and college records, standardized test scores, official recommendations, and qualities of mind and character promise success in college. Prospective students should send in a completed application, a transcript, test scores (where applicable), and a résumé of extracurricular activities. A campus interview is strongly recommended. For freshman applicants to a bachelor's program, the SAT I and ACT are required; SAT I/ACT results are not required for admission to an associate program, although they are strongly recommended. Students who have earned an average of 75 percent or above (on a scale of 0 to 100) in high school and who have a combined SAT I score of at least 900 are most successful at Cazenovia. Freshman applicants should have completed a minimum of six semesters in a regular diploma program in an accredited secondary school. Students may be admitted for deferred entrance or to advanced standing.

Transfer applicants must have a minimum overall GPA of 2.0.

Application and Information

Students can apply to either an associate degree or a bachelor's degree program. Students who have received an associate degree from the lower division may easily make an additional application to pursue baccalaureate studies in the upper division. The College has no application deadlines. Students are accepted on a rolling basis and are notified of a decision within thirty days. However, the College advises candidates to submit all materials before March 1 for admission in September. There is an application fee of $25.

Dean of Admissions and Financial Aid
Cazenovia College
Cazenovia, New York 13035
Telephone: 315-655-8005
800-654-3210 (toll-free)
Fax: 315-655-4860

CHAMPLAIN COLLEGE
BURLINGTON, VERMONT

The College and its Mission

Champlain College is a coeducational, private, nonprofit college founded in 1878. Its 19-acre campus, home to 1,400 students, is nestled among the stately maple trees of Burlington's historic Hill Section. Many of the College's thirty-one buildings, including most of the dormitories, are restored pre-Victorian- and Victorian-era private homes, which give students a unique atmosphere in which to learn and live.

The two-year and four-year educational programs are designed to provide sound professional training for careers in today's complex world, as well as broadening and enriching experiences in humanities and general education. Champlain College is recognized as one of the leading career-building colleges in northern New England, and it has earned the respect of the business, technical, and human services professions for its outstanding skill-building education.

Academic Programs

Associate Degree Programs Champlain College offers the **Associate in Science** degree with majors in accounting, business, business management, communications/public relations, computer information systems, computer programming, early childhood education, executive secretarial studies, hotel-restaurant management, law enforcement, legal secretarial studies, liberal studies, marketing management and retailing, medical secretarial studies, networking systems, occupational therapy assistant studies, office management, paralegal/legal assistant studies, radiography, respiratory therapy, retailing and fashion merchandising, secretarial specialist studies, social services, sport management, and travel/tourism.

Bachelor's Degree Programs Champlain College offers the **Bachelor of Science** degree in accounting, business, and professional studies. The professional studies program offers eighteen career concentrations combining practical liberal arts focus in communications, critical thinking, ethics, and career-centered skills to prepare students for the competitive national and international job market.

Honors Programs Each April, the outstanding first-, second-, third-, and fourth-year male and female students are recognized in each division at the college, along with numerous other recognition awards established over the years by friends and alumni of the College.

Transfer Arrangements As students complete their associate degree requirements, they make their decision to seek employment, continue on at Champlain in their Plus-Two option, or transfer to another institution if their specific needs and interests have changed.

Certificate Programs The College offers Certificates of Concentrated Study to students in specific areas enhancing their opportunities or working toward a career change. These include accounting, networking and systems, computer programming, hospitality services, and management.

Special Programs and Services Army ROTC programs are provided in cooperation with neighboring institutions.

Off-Campus Programs

The College participates in a cooperative education program with major corporations and with early childhood and social service agencies in the Burlington area. Students in retailing and fashion merchandising make local field trips, as well as trips to Montreal and New York City, and participate in off-campus practicums during their freshman and senior years, while students in hotel-restaurant management participate in 180 hours of supervised practica beginning their first year of study. Students in law enforcement, sport management, radiography, respiratory therapy, early childhood education, social services, and legal assistant studies spend varying amounts of time in their respective areas in off-campus practicums with local businesses and agencies. These practica provide valuable firsthand experience for the students. Accounting majors have the opportunity to participate in the Volunteer Income Tax Assistance Program (VITA) or to seek a paid internship with the Financial Aid Office. Marketing and Career Counseling also offer paid internships.

Credit for Nontraditional Learning Experiences

The College gives credit for demonstrated proficiency in areas related to college-level courses as determined by the College Level Examination Program (CLEP) and Advanced Placement program. Associate degree students must complete at least 30 credit hours at Champlain College.

Costs

For the 1995–96 academic year, tuition was $8670 for both in-state and out-of-state residents per year. On-campus room and board costs average $6200 per year. Textbooks and supplies are estimated at $550 per year. There are no hidden lab fees or library fees. The only student fee is a $100 recreation fee for each full-time student.

Financial Aid

The financial aid program at Champlain College includes loans, grants, scholarships, and work-study awards. Its purpose is to help needy students meet the full cost of their education. The College participates in the Federal Perkins Loan Program, Federal Work-Study, Federal Supplemental Educational Opportunity Grant Program, Federal Pell Grant Program, Federal Stafford Student Loan Program, Vermont Student Assistance Corporation, and state loan and grant programs. The College has committed a substantial sum of institutional money to financial need, under its "Support-A-Student" grant program.

Faculty

The College believes its strength lies in its faculty. There are 60 full-time and 68 part-time faculty members whose job it is to teach students, not do research. Most faculty members have completed programs of advanced study, and several have made notable contributions to the business field through lectures, magazine articles, and participation in national and regional conferences.

Student Body Profile

Seventy-five percent of all students complete the two-year associate degree. Eighty-four percent of the entering class plan on completing a four-year degree. Approximately 1,400 students are enrolled in the day college, and the evening division serves 600 additional students. The College is recognized for its high job placement rate. The majority of students secure employment within four months of graduation. Twenty countries and twenty-three states are represented in the 1996 student enrollment.

Student Activities

The Student Activities Board works to sponsor activities of interest to the current student body plus coordinate weekly on-campus movies, ski/snowboarding trips, and special events. The Outing Club, the International Club, the Multi-Cultural Committee, the Literary Club, and the Theatre Program all sponsor events throughout the school year.

Sports Intramural sport nights are Mondays and Wednesdays. Men's and women's nationally ranked soccer teams highlight fall weekend events followed by the men's nationally ranked basketball team throughout the winter months. The varsity cheerleading team is ever-present at the fast-paced basketball games. The College is a member of the National Junior College Athletic Association, Division III.

Facilities and Resources

The three-story William R. Hauke Family Campus Center houses an auditorium, a student lounge, a snack bar, a dining room, educational labs for hotel-restaurant management and communications/public relations majors, and state-of-the-art telecommunications facilities as well as classrooms and faculty offices. Freeman Hall houses the microbiology lab and the hotel management/travel and tourism front desk computer teaching classroom for on-line reservations. Faculty and administrative offices are also located in Freeman.

The Joyce Learning Center contains the College library, word processing laboratories, and classrooms. Six major academic buildings provide classrooms and laboratories. More than 150 computers and terminals are available for students. All campus buildings are linked by fiber-optic cable, enabling students to access the Internet from their dorm rooms and labs. Other technical facilities include the Child Development Center, which serves 25 local children. The Student Resource Center offers students individual tutoring in nearly all courses taught at the College and in general study skills. The writing assistance lab is also available to all students, as is a math/accounting lab.

Advisement/Counseling Academic advising is coordinated through the efforts of department chairpeople, faculty advisers, guidance personnel, and instructors to help students adjust to the academic program. Confidential health and counseling services are provided on campus as well.

Career Planning/Placement Offices The Office of Career Planning and Placement offers individual assistance to students before and after graduation. Over the past five years, Champlain graduates have achieved a 95 percent employment/transfer record. Six full-time career counselors work within specific majors to assist with career counseling and job opportunities or to find the next step match for students. Champlain's service is known as the best within the state, and it is a free, lifetime service.

Location

Burlington is a small city (46,000 people) overlooking majestic Lake Champlain and the Adirondack Mountains of New York to the west. The long and beautiful ridge line of the Green Mountains form the eastern horizon, and, to the north, Montreal, Quebec, is only 90 minutes away. Burlington is one of the nation's most progressive cities, and it is the cultural center of Vermont. Four residential colleges are located in the area, along with one of the leading medical centers on the East Coast. Burlington has an international airport; an Amtrak passenger train route with connections to Montreal, New York City, and Washington; and its own long-distance bus service, Vermont Transit Lines. The Church Street Marketplace, located just a few blocks from campus, attracts people from miles around to its numerous shops and restaurants. Three television stations, fifteen radio stations, and one daily newspaper serve the area.

Vermont is known as the ski capital of the East. The challenging slopes of Stowe, Bolton Valley, Mad River Glen, Smuggler's Notch, and Sugarbush are all less than an hour's drive from Champlain College. The nearby mountains, lakes, and streams also provide opportunities for backpacking, hiking, fishing, hunting, canoeing, sailing, and windsurfing. Great in-line skating and bicycling are just 5 minutes from campus on the 7-mile-long recreation path that follows the spectacular shore of Lake Champlain.

Admission Requirements

The College requires graduation from a recognized secondary school (or an equivalency certificate) as a condition of acceptance. The College also requires a transcript and, if possible, a recommendation from the guidance counselor of the last school attended. A personal interview may be required of applicants to certain programs and is recommended for all candidates. A student with a marginal academic record, but with good potential, may be granted acceptance. The College operates on rolling admissions. Even during the summer months, it may be possible to offer admission to an applicant for the coming fall semester. Students may also start college at midyear.

All candidates for transfer admission who have attended another accredited college are required to file an official transcript of all high school and college work with the director of admissions at Champlain College. A student who transfers from an accredited college may be given transfer credit for all courses completed with a grade of C or better.

Admission requirements for the baccalaureate programs are graduation from a recognized high school or achievement of a high school equivalency certificate plus successful completion of at least 40 credit hours (three semesters) of college course work at Champlain College or another college or university.

Champlain College affirms its commitment to providing equal opportunity in education and employment for qualified persons. Champlain College will make reasonable accommodations to the disability of an otherwise-qualified student, applicant, or employee. Those interested should contact Dolly Shaw, Affirmative Action Officer, with any questions or discrimination complaints or if auxiliary aids or services are needed to participate in Champlain College programs or to apply for admission or employment.

Application and Information

Applicants should fill out the application form and forward it with the application fee of $25 to the Admissions Office. Champlain College operates on a rolling admissions basis for its two-year and four-year degree programs, processing applications as soon as they are received; notification of an admission decision is usually made within three to four weeks.

Mailing Address:

Director of Admissions
Champlain College
P. O. Box 670
Burlington, Vermont 05402-0670
Telephone: 802-860-2727
                800-570-5858 (toll-free)
Fax: 802-860-2775
E-mail: admission@champlain.edu
World Wide Web: http://www.champlain.edu

Street Address:

Admissions Office
Champlain College
163 South Willard Street
Burlington, Vermont 05401

Introduction to Sociology class at Champlain College.

Peterson's Guide to Two-Year Colleges 1997

COCHISE COLLEGE
DOUGLAS, ARIZONA

The College and Its Mission

Cochise College has a national reputation for excellence and offers a commitment to serving students of all backgrounds and abilities. Established in 1961 as the second community college in Arizona, Cochise College believes that today's highly developed society makes it necessary to provide educational opportunities to all who can benefit from them. It is a comprehensive, public institution, fully accredited by the North Central Association of Colleges and Schools.

Each semester, Cochise College enrolls approximately 5,000 credit and noncredit students at two major campuses and a center located in Cochise County, Arizona. The student body is diverse—blending traditional and nontraditional students of varying racial and ethnic backgrounds. Students are encouraged to enrich their college experience through a wide variety of activities sponsored by the College and by student groups.

Academic Programs

Cochise College offers a special blend of courses suitable for students preparing for careers in business and industry, public service, aviation, and nursing or for students planning further study at a four-year institution. In addition, many courses serve to enrich the lives of local residents.

Associate Degree Programs Cochise College grants the degrees of **Associate of Arts, Associate of Science, Associate of General Studies,** and **Associate of Applied Science.** Associate of Arts (A.A.) degrees are offered in a variety of programs of study, including administration of justice, anthropology, art, English, foreign languages, history, journalism, international studies, liberal arts, physical education, political science, pre-education, psychology, and social services. Associate of Science (A.S.) degrees are offered in business administration, computer information systems, computer science, chemistry, electronics technology, life sciences, manufacturing engineering, professional pilot technology, and psychology. Associate of General Studies (A.G.S.) degrees are offered in a variety of programs of study, including agriculture and social services. Associate of Applied Science degrees (A.A.S.) are offered in administration of justice, agriculture, aviation maintenance technology, avionics technology, computer information systems, drafting and design, electronics technology, fire science technology, hospitality administration, media communications, middle management, nursing, power plant operations, professional administrative assistant, professional pilot technology, social services, and welding technology.

Honors Programs The College has chapters of the national two-year college honor society Phi Theta Kappa on each campus.

Transfer Arrangements Cochise College maintains articulation agreements with the University of Arizona, Arizona State University, Northern Arizona University, Western New Mexico University, New Mexico State University, Embry-Riddle Aeronautical University, University of Phoenix, and Western International University to assist the student in preparation for transfer into undergraduate programs. Students who are transferring to Cochise College must have official copies of their academic records sent to the Transcript Clerk's Office. Students must be enrolled before requesting an evaluation of their college transcripts for the purpose of seeking a Cochise College degree. Students who transfer to other institutions should always consult with an academic advisor to discuss their programs well in advance of a transfer date. Cochise College works with major state and area universities to insure that programs will transfer without loss of credits.

Certificate and Diploma Programs In addition to the associate degrees offered, Cochise College offers a number of certificate programs in aviation technology and computer programs in business and medical fields, and in electronics and welding.

Internship and Co-op Programs The College maintains excellent relationships with the business, nonprofit, and government institutions throughout Cochise County and the state of Arizona. These relationships enable the College, through programs like nursing, aviation, and the Career Action Center, to place students in internships and cooperative learning situations which develop employment skills, employer relationships, and extra financial resources.

The College is also a key to the School-to-Work initiative to create even better networks among the schools and businesses of Cochise County. A one-stop career center is located also on the Sierra Vista campus.

Special Programs and Services Language Immersion in the summer is a tremendous program which will enable the student to obtain 4 or 8 credits in either Spanish or English. The courses are intense and encompassing. Students spend time in the classroom and in the community learning and using their new language. Students use traditional and nontraditional materials to experience language and gain new skills. Teachers especially find this program a convenient way to learn necessary skills while earning credits.

Cochise College's location near the Mexican border permits day and weekend travel in Mexico for the Spanish Immersion course for real in-depth language experiences.

Community Programs Cochise College offers a number of programs designed to enrich the community. The Cultural Events Program produces a number of artistic endeavors for the enjoyment of the community. Small Business Development Center, the Center for Professional Development, and Center for Economic Research all provide the business community and government agencies with training, education, and information useful in their operations. The Career Action Center and School-To-Work programs provide employees and interns work experiences. These interns often become the employees of their cooperative institutions. The Conference Center organizes conferences and campus and study tours held on and off campus. The Center's Elderhostel program for older adults provides over fifty-five programs per year throughout Southeastern Arizona and Northwestern Mexico.

Costs

For the 1996–97 academic year, tuition is $26 per unit for state residents, $39 per unit for out-of-state residents up to 6 credits, and $153 per unit if student takes more than 6 units. Professional pilot courses are $127 per unit for in-state students, while out-of-state students pay $153 per unit. On-campus room and board cost $1503 per semester, and apartments are $285 per month.

Financial Aid

The College offers the full array of federal and state government, private and college financial aid resources to students along with help in obtaining the aid for which the student qualifies.

Faculty

Over 400 qualified instructors, both full- and part-time, lead the students toward educational outcomes that will benefit the student in his or her goals. They are certified by the State of Arizona to instruct and often have job-related experience as well as the postbaccalaureate educational degrees that certify their expertise.

Student Body Profile

The average student at Cochise College is about 30 years old. The population is evenly split between men and women students. Cochise College serves a significant minority population who are of Hispanic, African-American, and Asian descent. A wide variety of cultural, religious, and national backgrounds exist in harmony on the campuses. Cochise College serves a number of international students from Mexico, Japan, Europe, Africa, and other parts of the globe.

Student Activities

The College encourages participation in extracurricular activities and campus organizations to promote leadership, student relationships, and social development. Most campus activities are the responsibility of student clubs and organizations. During the year, a full schedule of activities is planned for the student body by the student government and various clubs and organizations.

Sports Cochise College competes with other community colleges in men's and women's basketball, men's and women's rodeo, and men's baseball. The Apache Stronghold Gym is the center for intercollegiate sports, concerts, and a variety of intramural activities.

Facilities and Resources

Cochise College has two campuses. The **Douglas Campus** has residence halls that house men and women students who want to live on campus and enjoy that realm of college experience. Family student housing is also available on a limited basis. The Douglas campus has its own airfield for the aviation program and is a spacious campus with all the amenities of a residential campus. The **Sierra Vista Campus** is located at the corner of Sierra Vista, a city of 40,000, next to the Huachuca Mountains. It is a commuter college which has seen a recent $5-million additional construction of adult education, library, and science buildings, and major renovations to classrooms and laboratories.

Advisement/Counseling An advising program in the Student Development Center on each campus offers students ongoing help with program planning and course placement assessments in writing, reading, and mathematics.

Career Planning/Placement Offices Cochise College has comprehensive career planning and placement services with offices and coordinators on each campus. Most students who wish to work to gain employment experiences and earn extra money and, in some cases, gain extra credit, can do so through the Career Action Center.

Libraries and Audiovisual Services Moving into the twenty-first century, the Cochise College Libraries combine traditional library services with new technologies which include CD-ROM references, faculty/student access to the Internet, a computerized catalog on CD-ROM, and laserdisc technology. The Charles DiPeso Library, located on the Douglas campus, is a modern 18,000-square-foot library complete with an instructional media studio and classroom facilities. The Andrea Cracchiolo Library at the Sierra Vista campus occupies a 22,000 square-foot building, containing state-of-the-art library equipment and materials. The libraries have in excess of 60,000 volumes, 1,200 video titles, and 300 periodical subscriptions.

In compliance with the American Disabilities Act, services are provided for students who have special needs. The contact phone number for the Cochise College ADA coordinator is 520-364-0325.

Location

The College is located in an area rich in history and cultural diversity. The original 540-acre Douglas campus is situated halfway between Douglas and historic Bisbee with panoramic vistas of the Mule and Chiricahua Mountains, as well as neighboring Sonora, Mexico. The Sierra Vista campus opened in 1978, with vistas of the Huachuca and Mule Mountains. Cochise County is located in the further southeast corner of Arizona in the "desert" Southwest. Grasslands with a variety of mesquite trees, yucca plants, and cactus are proud denizens of the region. Location and elevation create a beautiful climate year-round. Clear, blue skies make for great aviation weather as well as outdoor enjoyment virtually all the time.

Admission Requirements

Cochise College operates under the traditional community college open enrollment policies. Any student who has a high school diploma or GED certificate, is over 18 years of age, or is a transfer student in good standing may enroll at Cochise College. In order for an applicant to be admitted to Cochise College, the Admissions Office must receive and approve an application for admission. Out-of-state applicants must include a $10 fee. Official high school or college transcripts are required for applicants applying for financial aid or transfer credit. Applicants wishing to stay in the residence halls and all international applicants must complete the Student Health Record form. International applicants and applicants to the nursing and aviation programs have further requirements. Contact the Admissions Office for further information.

Application and Information

Applications are accepted on an ongoing basis. All prospective students should contact the Admissions Office at the Douglas campus:

Cochise College
4190 West Highway 80
Douglas, Arizona 85607-9724

Telephone: 520-364-0336
800-966-7943 (toll-free)
E-mail: info@tron.cochise.cc.az.us

Students at Cochise College.

Peterson's Guide to Two-Year Colleges 1997

COLLEGE OF ST. CATHERINE–MINNEAPOLIS
MINNEAPOLIS, MINNESOTA

The College and Its Mission

The College of St. Catherine-Minneapolis is a two-year, private, coeducational institution that offers health-care and human service career opportunities through associate degrees and certificate programs. Established in 1902 as St. Mary's Hospital School of Nursing by the Sisters of St. Joseph Carondelet, the institution evolved into St. Mary's Junior College in 1964, then merged with the College of St. Catherine, St. Paul, in 1986 and became St. Mary's Campus of the College of St. Catherine. Known today as the College of St. Catherine-Minneapolis, the College has been providing innovative, professional education programs that respond to the ever-changing needs and technical advancement of society for more than ninety years.

The College provides educational programs for a diverse, coeducational student body. The campus atmosphere and educational philosophy emphasize student development. Students have frequent opportunities for success and receive individualized academic, personal, and financial support. Students are also encouraged to develop leadership abilities, spiritual values, and responsible commitments to society. The mission of the College is to educate competent, technical-level, health-care and human service workers, who have a regard for the whole person.

Academic Program

It is the belief of the College of St. Catherine-Minneapolis that persons holding positions in health-care and human services professions must demonstrate more than a mastery of complex skills. They must also view themselves and the people with whom they work holistically—as multifaceted beings affected by a multitude of spiritual, physical, psychological, and sociological influences. This perspective is strengthened by the development of clear professional ethics, a broad base of liberal knowledge, and interpersonal relationship skills. Individuals educated in a holistic perspective recognize, assess, and work with people's strengths as well as their problems and develop cooperative relationships with both colleagues and clients. They share responsibility for their joint efforts to restore or promote a higher level of health and personal development.

The curriculum therefore combines technical, clinical, and general education components, resulting in well-rounded individuals prepared for immediate employment in their chosen career. Technical courses provide the students with the knowledge, skills, and attitudes necessary to function competently as part of the health-care or human service team. This technical foundation is enhanced through extensive clinical training during internships and fieldwork assignments that often begin as early as a student's first semester. Most programs also require general education courses in the liberal arts and sciences to help students understand and appreciate other important elements of human experience.

The academic calendar includes two semesters that run from September to December and February to May. A four-week term in January is offered between semesters, and there are two summer sessions. Attendance requirements vary with the academic program. Most programs can be completed through either full-time or part-time study, and some evening and weekend programs are available.

Associate Degree Programs The College of St. Catherine-Minneapolis offers two- and three-year programs leading to an **Associate in Applied Science** degree for students preparing to become a chemical dependency family treatment counselor, health-care interpreter, medical records technician/health information specialist, nurse, occupational therapy assistant, physical therapy assistant, radiographer, respiratory therapist, or sonographer.

The **Associate in Arts** degree program offers a two-year liberal arts education in a personal, private-college setting. The program is primarily designed to establish academic success and to prepare students for transfer to a four-year college or university to earn their baccalaureate degree.

Certificate and Diploma Programs The College also offers certificate programs which vary in length from fourteen weeks to three years and are offered for the following career programs: coding specialist, health and wellness counselor, holistic therapist, medical transcription specialist, Montessori teacher, and phlebotomist.

Credit for Nontraditional Learning Experiences

St. Catherine-Minneapolis students who wish to receive college credit for previous knowledge, work, on-the-job training, continuing education, workshops, or military experience may request to take a "challenge examination" and/or skills test which covers the specific content of a required course. Challenge opportunities vary with individual program policies.

Costs

Tuition for the 1996–97 academic year is $328 per credit, or about $9840 per year for a full-time student taking 30 credits. A single room in the residential hall costs approximately $1500 per year. Other estimated yearly costs are $500 for books, $40 for fees, and $1000 for personal expenses.

Financial Aid

More than 75 percent of students at the College of St. Catherine-Minneapolis receive financial assistance through the $7.2-million financial aid program. Students apply for financial aid by completing the Free Application for Federal Student Aid (FAFSA), through which they are considered for all federal, state, and institutional grants and loans available. Students may also apply for work-study assistance. Financial aid eligibility is determined on the basis of need.

Faculty

The student-faculty ratio at the College is 14:1. Technical program instructors are experienced clinical practitioners with required credentials in their field, and the majority of them hold advanced degrees. Faculty members are committed to providing students with personalized assistance and serve as academic advisors to guide students in addressing their academic and professional concerns.

Student Body Profile

Nearly 1,200 students attend the College of St. Catherine-Minneapolis. Some students are recent high school graduates, whereas others are transfer college students or adults returning to the work force or preparing for a career change. Eighty-six percent of the students are women, and students range in age from 18 to the mid-50s. The campus population represents a wide range of racial, ethnic, religious, geographical, socioeconomic, and academic backgrounds.

Campus housing is available and approximately 75 students choose the convenience of Minneapolis campus living. Others commute from many nearby metro areas in Minnesota and Wisconsin. The majority of the students attend college on a part-time basis. Ninety-three percent of the graduates find employment in their field within six months of graduation.

Student Activities

The student life office works with students, staff and faculty to provide a variety of cocurricular activities that encourage cultural, educational, social, and recreational experiences. A number of campus events, workshops, program-related organizations and special interest groups provide opportunities for students to become integrated with others in the campus community. Students may also participate in a wide variety of intramural sports including volleyball, soccer, and basketball.

Facilities and Resources

All academic programs, classrooms, computer labs, two floors of campus housing, the student lounge, cafeteria, and bookstore are housed in two adjacent buildings connected by skyways. The campus library holds an extensive collection of resources in the health-care and human service fields and is affiliated with several local libraries to provide increased access to printed materials.

Each health-care program has its own labs, which are fully furnished with state-of-the-art medical equipment used for hands-on instruction. Clinical and fieldwork experiences are conducted in a wide variety of over 170 metro area hospitals, clinics, long-term care facilities, and other sites providing health-care and human services to the greater community.

Professional counseling services are available to help students with career assessment and exploration and to meet their personal needs. The College also offers additional resources. The staff of the Learning Center offer free, individualized academic assistance to students seeking to improve their reading, writing, math and study skills. Other academic services provided by the Learning Center include tutoring, workshops, assistance for students whose native language is not English, and support and accommodations for students with disabilities. Since 1977, the College has achieved a national reputation for making health-care education accessible to students with vision impairments.

The Access and Success Program is a unique, comprehensive program for single parent students at the College of St. Catherine-Minneapolis. Staff provide advocacy and support in finding affordable housing and child care for single parents. Services available through this program include a weekly support group, newsletter, mentoring programs, and social events for single-parent families.

Location

Located in an urban area on the west bank of the Mississippi and adjacent to Riverside Medical Center, the campus is just minutes from both downtown Minneapolis and the capital city of St. Paul. The Twin Cities are internationally renowned for their high-quality health-care centers, where students pursuing an education in health care will have the opportunity to interact with some of the country's top professionals throughout their clinical experiences.

The St. Paul campus of the College of St. Catherine, a four-year liberal arts college for women, is just 10 minutes away by College shuttle bus or car, and Minneapolis campus students enjoy access to the facilities there, including an expanded library, modern sports and fitness facility, campus housing for women, concert auditorium, and chapel. Students graduating from the Associate in Arts degree program often transfer to the St. Paul campus to pursue their baccalaureate degree.

The Minneapolis-St. Paul metro area also offers an array of cultural and community activities year-round, and its residents take advantage of nearby lakes and parks for a variety of outdoor recreational activities during the four-season climate. In addition, the Twin Cities have one of the finest theater and arts communities in the Midwest.

Admission Requirements

The College of St. Catherine-Minneapolis admits men and women of all races, colors, national and ethnic origins, physical abilities, religions, and ages.

Applicants must have graduated from an accredited secondary school or hold a general equivalency diploma. Candidates are evaluated for admission on the basis of their potential for success, including such achievements as past academic performance, test results, class rank, employment history, communication skills, and letters of recommendation. While interviews are not required, interested students are strongly encouraged to visit the campus and meet with an admission counselor to discuss their educational needs.

Application and Information

Applications are accepted beginning October 1 of each year for admission the following fall, and admission decisions continue until each program reaches its enrollment limit. Early applicants are given priority consideration. To apply to the College, students must submit a completed application form, official high school and/or college transcripts, and a $20 application fee to the Office of Admission. Requests for applications and additional information should be directed to:

The College of St. Catherine-Minneapolis
Office of Admission
601 25th Avenue South
Minneapolis, Minnesota 55454

Telephone: 612-690-7800
Fax: 612-690-7849
E-mail: career-info@admin.stkate.edu

COLORADO MOUNTAIN COLLEGE
GLENWOOD SPRINGS, LEADVILLE, AND STEAMBOAT SPRINGS, COLORADO

The College and Its Mission

There is a different view of the Rocky Mountains at each Colorado Mountain College campus. Learning is personal; classes are small; faculty members are friendly. Colorado Mountain College is a multicampus community college with three residential and twelve commuter locations. This coeducational public institution began operation in fall 1967. Colorado Mountain College is a district-supported college with its own governing board. Colorado Mountain College operates on a semester system with a limited summer session and is fully accredited by the North Central Association of Colleges and Secondary Schools.

The three residential campuses include Alpine Campus in Steamboat Springs, Spring Valley Campus outside of Glenwood Springs, and Timberline Campus in Leadville. At these locations, students still find a traditional college experience, including residence halls, cafeterias, extensive libraries, laboratories, and many opportunities to participate in campus life. The commuter campuses serve primarily local residents, and classes are scheduled for the convenience of working adults. Commuter sites are located in Aspen, Basalt, Breckenridge, Buena Vista, Carbondale, Eagle, Glenwood Springs, Grand County, Rifle, Salida, Siverthorne, and Vail.

Colorado Mountain College offers academic programs for transfer, career training in 16 specialty areas, and courses to enrich the lives and livelihoods of local residents. Students can begin their four-year degree, as the state Core Curriculum project guarantees transfer of academic courses to all public colleges and universities in Colorado. *U.S. News & World Report* has featured Colorado Mountain College for quality and innovation in transfer programs.

Students may also choose to start a career with occupational training programs. In one or two years, students can learn the skills for employment in some unique and exciting programs. The mountain environment gives students many opportunities to learn outside the classroom.

Academic Programs

Colorado Mountain College offers both occupational and transfer programs. Degrees awarded include the **Associate in Arts** degree, **Associate in Science** degree, **Associate in General Studies** degree, **Associate in Applied Science** degree, and a one-year Occupational Proficiency certificate. The Associate in Arts degree is available at all Colorado Mountain College campuses. The state Core Curriculum project guarantees transfer of academic courses to all public colleges and universities in Colorado.

Degrees and programs vary by campus with the residential campuses offering the fullest range of degrees and certificates. Alpine Campus offerings include the Associate in Arts (areas of specialization are business and liberal arts), the Associate in Science (areas of specialization are biology, chemistry, geology, and mathematics), and the Associate in Applied Science and Certificates of Occupational Proficiency (offerings include accounting, business, microcomputer support specialist, resort management, and ski business). Spring Valley Campus offerings include Associate in Arts (areas of specialization are business, liberal arts, outdoor education, and theater), Associate in General Studies in criminal justice, Associate in Science (areas of specialization are biology, chemistry, geology, and mathematics), and Associate in Applied Science and Certificates of Occupational Proficiency (offerings include accounting, business, criminal justice, graphic design, microcomputer support specialist studies, photography, practical nursing, and veterinary technology). Timberline Campus offerings include Associate in Arts (areas of specialization are business, liberal arts, and Outdoor Semester in the Rockies), Associate in General Studies degrees in outdoor recreational leadership, Associate in Science (areas of specialization are biology, chemistry, geology, and mathematics), and Associate in Applied Science and Certificates of Occupational Proficiency (offerings include accounting, business, environmental technology: land rehabilitation or water/wastewater, microcomputer support specialist studies, and ski area operations).

Off-Campus Programs

One of the most popular off-campus programs is the Outdoor Semester in the Rockies. This program blends outdoor adventure with the disciplines of college classes such as science and philosophy. Colorado Mountain College encourages students to take advantage of several study-abroad class tours. The College also offers exciting distance educational opportunities to district and residential campus students through telecourses and a new interactive video system.

Credit for Nontraditional Learning Experiences

Colorado Mountain College awards credit through national standardized exams, challenge exams, and credit for life experience. To be awarded credit, testing options are used if possible and students must be enrolled in a degree or certificate program. Credits posted to a student's academic record through one of these nontraditional methods are noted indicating the method by which they were awarded.

Costs

Colorado Mountain College's tuition for the academic year 1996–97 is $34 per credit hour for in-district students, $63 per credit hour for in-state students, and $200 per credit hour for out-of-state students. Residential campuses have student activity fees of $130 per academic year. Room and board costs average $3700 per year, and the housing reservation deposit is $300. Books average $450 per academic year.

Financial Aid

Colorado Mountain College is approved for participation in all major federal and state financial aid programs, including Federal Pell Grant, Loan Programs, and Work Study. Financial assistance is awarded through a central district office for all Colorado Mountain College campuses and education centers. The application for financial assistance is the Free Application for Federal Student Aid (FAFSA). First priority is given to those students applying on or before March 31. Applications received after this date are processed pending availability of funds. Questions may be addressed to Student Financial Assistance, District Office, P.O. 10001, Glenwood Springs, Colorado 81602.

Faculty

Colorado Mountain College faculty members are accessible to students. They are at Colorado Mountain College because they believe in teaching. There are 75 full-time faculty members and 166 part-time faculty members. The faculty members pride themselves on the high-quality education students receive in the classroom, with classes averaging 15 students. Many faculty members have taught at colleges and universities and have chosen to teach at Colorado Mountain College because of their love for teaching and the blend of invigorating environments and stimulating learning.

Study Body Profile

Colorado Mountain College students are from the local area, forty-eight states, and six other countries. Undergraduate numbers at the residential campuses are 1,262 at the Alpine Campus, 868 at the Spring Valley Campus, and 576 at the Timberline Campus. Approximately 40 percent of students attend full-time. About 50 percent are over 25 years of age. Colorado Mountain College currently houses 150 students each at Alpine and Spring Valley, and about 100 students live on-campus at Timberline. New residence halls are anticipated to be in operation for 1997, in which Alpine and Spring Valley will each be able to accommodate 250 students on-campus, and Timberline will have a 150-bed capacity.

Student Activities

Each residential campus has active Student Government organizations. Each Student Government determines the student activity fee and how the funds are utilized on each campus. Student Government helps to sponsor student activities, clubs and organizations, and guest speakers. Colorado Mountain College's Ski Team holds six national titles. But there is more than snow available for outdoor activities. Students actively participate in hiking, biking, and water sports. Student Activities Offices organize basketball and volleyball intramurals. The soccer clubs compete for the CMC title and with other colleges. Every season brings new activities and celebrations to the mountain resort towns.

Facilities and Resources

The residential campuses offer a full college experience with residence halls, cafeterias, libraries, academic classrooms, learning labs, laboratories, and student center facilities.

The Alpine Campus offers residence halls and classroom buildings. Fall 1992 marked the opening of a new academic building that includes faculty offices, a library, classrooms, instructional and computer laboratories, and recreational space. Spring 1995 saw the opening of a newly remodeled cafeteria, bookstore, and student center. At the Spring Valley Campus, students can enjoy the hot springs pool in Glenwood Springs, the charm of Carbondale, and the culture of Aspen. Spring Valley offers residence halls, a cafeteria, a gymnasium and climbing wall, a student center, a bookstore, classrooms, a working farm, laboratories, and an extensive library. At the Timberline Campus, many students combine their dreams of environmental interests and their college education. Colorado's highest mountain peak is in the backyard, cross-country skiing begins at the edge of campus, and many of Colorado's big name slopes are no more than an hour away. The campus offers classroom facilities, a library and learning lab, a computer lab, and a bookstore. Students enjoy apartment-style housing, a relaxing student center and cafeteria, and have access to Leadville's modern recreation complex.

Location

Like the Rockies that surround it, Colorado Mountain College is wide open and full of possibilities. There are miles of spruce and aspen, wildflowers, backroads, whitewater and bareback ranchland, three national forests, six wilderness areas, and most of Colorado's major ski resorts. There is a spirit among the teachers and students, an atmosphere of encouragement, and an attitude of confidence. **Alpine Campus** is situated above the downtown area on the west end of Steamboat Springs. From there, students look across the rooftops of Steamboat Springs to fresh powder beneath the chairlifts on the other side of town. In Leadville, **Timberline Campus** is surrounded by Colorado's highest peaks and the legends of a town built by silver. High above the Roaring Fork River, **Spring Valley Campus** stretches one's imagination from Aspen to the distant Ragged Mountains. Students look across acres of rolling forests to Mount Sopris and the 14,000-feet summits of the Elk Mountains. The campus is located 10 miles from Glenwood Springs and within 30 miles of several communities. All Colorado Mountain College locations are resort or mountain communities that provide excellent outdoor opportunities.

Admission Requirements

Colorado Mountain College seeks, encourages, and assists all interested students beyond high school-age who demonstrate a desire to learn. With few exceptions, admission follows an open-door policy. Even though Colorado Mountain College has open admission, certain occupational programs have selective admission. Programs with selection requirements and admission deadlines are culinary arts and practical nursing.

To apply for admission, students must complete and return the Colorado Mountain College admissions application and high school and/or college transcripts. There is no application fee. All entering students should submit ACT or SAT I scores for advising and placement purposes.

Transfer students are welcome and should have attained a cumulative grade point average of at least 2.0 on any college work attempted. Non-graduates may take the General Education Development test (GED) to meet graduation equivalence. International students may be considered for admission to the residential campuses. International admission packets are available and must be completed and returned to apply for admission, and a minimum TOEFL score of 500 is required for admission.

Early application is encouraged for students who want to live on campus. Limited on-campus housing fills up quickly. After applying for admission to the residential campuses, students receive housing reservation information.

Application and Information

For more information, students should contact:

Director of Pre-Enrollment Services
P.O. Box 10001 PG
Glenwood Springs, Colorado 81602
Telephone: 970-945-8691
800-621-8559 (toll-free)
Fax: 970-945-7279
E-mail: joinus@coloradomtn.edu
World Wide Web: http://www.coloradomtn.edu

The Colorado Rockies are a textbook for Colorado Mountain College students.

Peterson's Guide to Two-Year Colleges 1997

COLUMBUS STATE COMMUNITY COLLEGE
COLUMBUS, OHIO

The College and Its Mission

Columbus State Community College is a comprehensive, two-year state community college, dedicated to serving central Ohio's changing educational needs. Founded in 1963 as the Columbus Area Technician's School, the College became Columbus Technical Institute (CIT) in 1965 and began offering associate degrees in areas of business, health, public services, and engineering technology. In 1987, it was determined that the community's educational needs would be better served by a comprehensive community college, and the Ohio Board of Regents rechartered CTI as Columbus State Community College.

As a community college, Columbus State has a strong commitment to technical education that prepares graduates for immediate employment and offers a transfer program that meets the freshman and sophomore requirements for a bachelor's degree. Columbus State enrolls more than 16,000 students on its 70-acre main campus near downtown Columbus and at four suburban centers in nearby neighborhoods.

Columbus State is accredited by the North Central Association of Colleges and Schools, and many of the College's degree programs are accredited by professional associations and agencies.

Academic Programs

As a comprehensive community college, Columbus State offers two-year technical and transfer programs. The technical degree programs are designed to prepare students for immediate employment upon graduation. These programs lead to the **Associate of Applied Science** or the **Associate of Technical Studies** degree. Within many of the technical programs, a number of short-term certificate programs (less than two years) are offered to provide students with specific skills and proficiencies. Students may also enroll in individual courses to enhance or add to their existing knowledge or acquire new skills.

The transfer degree programs are designed to enable students to complete the first two years of a bachelor's degree. These programs lead to the **Associate in Arts** and **Associate in Science** degrees. Graduates of these programs can transfer to four-year colleges or universities to complete the last two years of a bachelor's degree program. Formal agreements have been made with colleges and universities in Ohio that allow for course work taken in A.A. or A.S. degree programs at Columbus State to apply to B.A. or B.S. requirements at those institutions. In addition, the core degree requirements at Columbus State constitute the approved "transfer module" of the College, which will transfer to any state-supported institution in Ohio.

The College offers developmental or preparatory courses in composition, reading comprehension, and mathematics for students who need to improve their skills in these areas. These courses are intended to provide students with an opportunity to better prepare themselves for college-level courses and cannot be used to fulfill degree requirements. Students take the College's placement examinations to determine entry-level classes.

Associate Degree Programs Columbus State offers Associate in Applied Science degree programs in arts and sciences (technical communications), business (accounting, business management, computer programming, financial management, hospitality management, law enforcement, legal assisting, marketing, microcomputing, office administration, real estate, and retail management), engineering technology (architecture technology, automotive technology, aviation maintenance, civil engineering technology, construction management technology, electromechanical technology, electronic engineering technology, environmental technology, graphic communications, heating and air conditioning technology, mechanical engineering technology, and quality assurance technology), and health and human services (dental laboratory, early childhood development, emergency medical services, gerontology, health information management, interpreting/transliterating, medical laboratory, mental health/chemical dependency/mental retardation, multi-competency health, nursing, radiographic technology, respiratory care, sports and fitness management, surgical technology, and veterinary technology).

Costs

For Ohio residents, a combined instructional and general fee of $57 per credit hour (up to a maximum of $684 per quarter) is charged for students scheduling 12 to 18 credit hours. Students scheduling more than 18 credit hours are charged an additional $57 per credit hour. Non-Ohio, U.S. residents are charged a combined instructional and general fee of $125 per credit hour (up to a maximum of $1500 per quarter), and international students are charged a fee of $152 per credit hour (up to a maximum of $1824 per quarter) for students scheduling 12 to 18 credit hours. Lab fees are charged to cover the cost of consumable materials used by the student. A one-time matriculation fee of $35 is charged after the twelfth hour of credit is scheduled, and covers the cost of establishing and maintaining a perpetual student record.

Financial Aid

Financial aid is available in four forms: grants, loans, part-time employment, and scholarships. In general, the amount of assistance that a student may receive depends upon the established financial need of the student. This need is determined through the Central Processing Service and is based on the information submitted in the FAFSA. Financial aid is for room, board, fees, books, and commuting expenses.

Faculty

The College employs 191 full-time and 700 adjunct faculty members. As a community college, class sizes are kept low, with a student-faculty ratio of approximately 15:1. The College is proud of the fact that faculty members are experienced workers who subscribe to a very student-centered philosophy.

Student Body Profile

There are more than 16,000 students enrolled at Columbus State, with an average age of 28.7. Ohio residents comprise 97 percent of those attending, and the average credit load per student is 8.7 credit hours. Men make up 41 percent of the students; women, 59 percent. Minority enrollment stands at 20.8 percent. About 35 percent of Columbus State students are attending full-time, with 65 percent attending part-time; 34 percent of part-time students attend night classes only.

Student Activities

Extracurricular activities for students are varied and are coordinated by the Office of Student Activities. There are a number of student organizations, a student newsletter, a literary magazine, and four different student recreation and leisure areas on campus.

Sports Eleven varsity sports are offered for men and women, including men's and women's basketball, men's baseball, women's softball, men's soccer, men's and women's cross-country, women's volleyball, cheerleading, men's golf, and an equestrian team. The College is a member of the National Junior College Athletic Association and competes in Division III. The intramural sports program is also an integral part of campus life. Both team and individual sports are offered to meet the needs of all students.

Facilities and Resources

Columbus State's student services are diverse and award-winning. The Office of Disability Services offers state-of-the-art equipment and services for students with disabilities. The Educational Resources Center provides a multimedia environment to facilitate a wide range of learning experiences. The Bookstore provides all the textbooks and supplies required by the academic departments, as well as software, logowear, gifts, cards, and class rings.

The College's Counseling Center offers comprehensive services to assist students in defining and accomplishing their personal and academic goals. The Placement and Career Services Office provides assistance to enrolled students and alumni of Columbus State who are interested in work while in school and after graduation. The College also has an Office of Minority Affairs, a Health Office, a Wellness Program, extensive tutoring services and a full-service cafeteria.

Location

Columbus State has a modern campus of fifteen buildings located on 70 acres near downtown Columbus, Ohio. Suburban centers are located in Dublin, Westerville, and Gahanna and in southwest Columbus at Bolton Field. The Bolton Field facility, located at a working airport, serves as the aviation maintenance facility during the day and offers a general curriculum during the evening.

Admission Requirements

Regular admission to the College is offered to applicants who are high school graduates or who possess a GED equivalency. Other applicants over 18 years of age may be admitted as regular- or conditional-status students based upon placement test results. Many technologies have established additional requirements that must be fulfilled prior to acceptance into that technology.

Application and Information

To apply to Columbus State Community College, students must complete an application and pay the $10 nonrefundable application fee, submit an official high school transcript and college transcripts (if applicable), and complete the placement tests.

For an application or additional information on admission, financial aid, veterans' benefits, or placement tests, students should contact:

Columbus State Community College
Admissions Office
550 East Spring Street
Columbus, Ohio 43215
Telephone: 614-227-2453
800-621-6407 (toll-free)
Fax: 614-227-5117
E-mail: mdeerwes%cscc@cougar.colstate.cc.oh.us
World Wide Web: http://www.colstate.cc.oh.us

An aerial view of Columbus State's main campus near downtown Columbus.

COMMUNITY COLLEGE OF ALLEGHENY COUNTY

PITTSBURGH, MONROEVILLE, AND WEST MIFFLIN, PENNSYLVANIA

The College and Its Mission

The Community College of Allegheny County has been helping students plan their futures for almost thirty years. CCAC's educational influence extends far beyond the 350 acres that compose its four campuses. The College reaches deep into the communities. Classes are offered at **Allegheny Campus** in Pittsburgh's Northside, **Boyce Campus** in Monroeville, **South Campus** in West Mifflin, and **North Campus** in the North Hills section of Pittsburgh. Classes are also offered at over 400 other locations in Allegheny County. CCAC is the largest community college in Pennsylvania. Its size is a great advantage in terms of the depth and breadth of academic opportunities. However, it is the deep personal commitment that CCAC brings to each student's academic life that makes this College especially effective. High school graduates seeking to begin their college studies find themselves challenged by supporting faculty members who have made a commitment to teaching. Nontraditional students who are returning to school and have family responsibilities can find a wide range of course offerings scheduled at convenient times and locations. CCAC is fully accredited by the Middle States Association of Colleges and Schools.

Academic Programs

CCAC provides a University Parallel Program for students who plan to transfer into baccalaureate degree programs at other colleges and universities. The College also offers career training and technical programs, both full-time and part-time, leading to a diploma, a certificate, or an associate degree. Program requirements vary, but, in general, an associate degree program requires two years of study; a diploma program, one year; and a certificate program, one year or less.

Associate Degree Programs The associate degrees offered by CCAC can be grouped into seven different areas. University Parallel Programs offer associate degrees in accounting; administration of justice; art; biology; business; chemistry; communications/journalism; computer information systems; computer science; economics; engineering science; engineering technology; English/communications; fine arts; fitness, sports, and lifetime recreation; foreign language; health and fitness management; humanities; human services; journalism; liberal arts and sciences; mathematics; mathematics and sciences; music; physics; pre–health professions; psychology; social sciences; sociology/anthropology; speech and theater; teacher education; and theater. Career programs in business offer associate degrees in accounting specialist studies, appraisal science, aviation management, business data processing specialist studies, business management, clerical specialist studies, computer information systems, computer information systems specialist studies, court reporter studies, data-entry technician studies, financial services, food service, health and fitness management, hospitality management, hotel management, hotel-restaurant management, industrial management, information processing (interdisciplinary), labor education, labor studies, legal secretarial specialist studies, management and technologies, marketing management, medical secretarial specialist studies, medical transcriptionist studies, microcomputer systems specialist studies, personnel management, real estate, real estate sales and management, retailing, retail management, retail merchandising, secretarial specialist studies, and word processing specialist studies. Career programs in health offer associate degrees in basic-preparation cook studies; chef's apprentice studies; diagnostic medical sonographer studies; dietary manager studies; dietetics technician studies (food management); dietetics technician studies (nutrition care); electroencephalography (EEG) technologist studies; fitness, sports, and lifetime recreation specialist studies; geriatric assistant studies; health and fitness management; health and image technician studies; health-care assistant studies; health-unit coordinator studies; histologic technician studies; home health-care assistant studies; medical assistant studies; medical assisting; medical insurance specialist studies; medical laboratory technician studies; medical records technician studies; medical transcriptionist studies; nuclear medicine technologist studies; nursing; occupational therapy assistant studies; ophthalmic medical assistant studies; pharmacy technician studies; phlebotomist studies; psychiatric technician studies; radiation therapy technologist studies; radiologic technologist studies; respiratory therapist studies; respiratory therapy technician studies; and surgical technologist studies. Career programs in social service offer associate degrees in administration of criminal justice, child care, corrections administration, fire science and administration, gerontology, human services (infant and child-care option), human services (youth and adult option), interpreter for the deaf training, mental health/mental retardation specialist studies, mental retardation technician studies, paralegal studies, pedology (child development/child care), professional nanny studies, social work specialist studies, social work technician studies, training for special-needs adults (food service), training for special-needs adults (human services aide studies), training for special-needs adults (janitorial/housekeeping studies), and volunteer management. Career programs in applied arts technologies offer associate degrees in commercial art and design, graphics and printing technology, graphics communications, horticulture technology (floriculture), horticulture technology (landscape design), industrial design and art, performing arts, production journalism, and sign painting. Career programs in applied service and trade technologies offer associate degrees in automotive service education, automotive technology, building construction estimating, building construction supervision, building construction technology, carpentry apprenticeship studies, commercial pilot studies, electromechanical technology, electronics (applied) technology, energy management technology, energy management technology (solar energy), flight technology, heating and air-conditioning technology, hospital maintenance technology, ironworker apprenticeship studies, machinist technology, maintenance mechanic technology, plumber apprenticeship studies, sheet-metal worker apprenticeship studies, steamfitter/pipefitter apprenticeship studies, and welding technology. Career programs in engineering and science technologies offer associate degrees in architectural drafting and design technology, chemical science technology, chemical technology, civil engineering technology, computer-aided drafting, computer-aided drafting and design technology, computer electronics, drafting and/or surveying, electrical engineering technology, electronic engineering technology, electronics (advanced), electronics (basic), electronics (digital), industrial model technology, industrial production technology, laboratory technology, mechanical drafting and design technology, mechanical engineering drafting and design technology, microcomputer electronics technology, nondestructive testing technology, quality technology, robotics and automated systems technology, robotics and industrial electronics, science and engineering technology, and telecommunications engineering technology.

Certificate and Diploma Programs CCAC offers the following certificate and diploma programs: administration of security, advanced electronics, applied electronics, basic electronics, carpentry, child care/pedology, clerk-typist studies, dietetics assistant studies, digital electronics, drafting, drafting/surveying, emergency medical services, engineering drafting, food service management, food service training, geriatric assistant studies, graphic design, graphics and printing, health-care assistant studies, health unit coordinator/unit clerk manager studies, heating and air conditioning, hotel/motel management, industrial engineering, ironworking, labor studies, management and personnel administration, medical assistant studies, medical transcription, microcomputer technology, nuclear medicine, photography, plumbing, pre–science technology, radiation therapy, residential construction, respiratory therapy, retail sales management, secretarial science, sheet-metal studies, sign painting, steamfitter/pipefitter studies, stenography, structural drafting, surveying, welding, and word processing.

Costs

For residents of Allegheny County, CCAC's tuition is $68 per credit (1-14 credits) or $1020 per semester (15 credits and above). Residents of other Pennsylvania counties that do not have a community college pay $136 per credit (1-14 credits) or $2040 per semester (15 credits and above). Students living out of state pay $204 per credit (1-14 credits) or $3060 per semester (15 credits and above). A College fee of $50.40 per semester is charged to students taking classes at each campus location. Some courses offered by CCAC require special course or lab fees in addition to the tuition and College fee. All of these costs are estimated for the 1996–97 academic year. CCAC reserves the right to change the tuition and fees at any time and without prior notice.

Financial Aid

Financial aid programs at CCAC are designed to assist students whose ability to contribute toward educational costs is limited. The major factor for most awards is the student's demonstrated need for funds. To be considered for financial aid, a student must be accepted at CCAC on at least a half-time basis (6 credits or more) and submit a completed Pennsylvania State Grant/Free Application for Federal Student Aid, a completed CCAC financial aid application, and a financial aid transcript from each college previously attended (including other CCAC campuses). The availability of funds and the extent of the financial need are primary factors in determining the amount of the assistance offered. There are also a limited number of private scholarships available to CCAC students.

Faculty

CCAC has more than 300 full-time professors and a staff of part-time educators who are experienced, knowledgeable, and committed to teaching. While most faculty members continue their studies and research to remain current in their respective fields, their first commitment is to the students. The student-faculty ratio is 22:1.

Student Body Profile

There are currently over 28,000 students enrolled as full- and part-time credit students. The average age of this student population is 27. In a typical fall semester, the CCAC minority group enrollment is approximately 15 percent. Ninety percent of the students enrolled in credit courses live within Allegheny County. Another 66,577 students are enrolled in noncredit course work.

Student Activities

CCAC student activities include acquiring leadership potential as part of student government or participation in creative endeavors including student publications, drama productions, or art programs. Many cultural clubs and organizations exist as well. Students may also enrich their chosen field of studies as a member of an academically related club or organization. For those who prefer the competitive edge, athletic programs for both men and women are available at designated CCAC campuses. Basketball, baseball, golf, tennis, bowling, softball, volleyball, cross-country, racquetball, and weightlifting are just some of the intramural and intercollegiate athletic programs available at designated campuses.

Facilities and Resources

The Community College of Allegheny County is committed to students' success. The modern facilities available provide the stimulus to enhance the educational experience. Each of the four CCAC campuses provide a developmental child-care center, staffed by professionals, who not only care for each child's physical needs, but provide a stimulating learning environment. CCAC Adult Reentry Services provide educational and emotional support for these students returning to an academic environment after a long absence. Services offered include career and educational planning, basic skills instruction and confidence building. All facilities at the Community College of Allegheny County are designed to accommodate handicapped and disabled students. Paved walkways, accessible building entrances and elevator systems provide easy access to classrooms and laboratories. Reading and brailing for the blind, note-taking, transcribing and counseling services are readily available for physically challenged students. The College maintains excellent computer facilities at each of its four campuses. Students receive hands-on experience on state-of-the-art computers and instructional equipment ranging from a powerful IBM mainframe computer that is used for both instructional and administrative purposes, to microcomputers. Computer labs are available virtually around the clock, providing students the opportunity to direct computer access any time of day or night. CCAC provides valuable job search assistance for its students and graduates. Last year, 1,400 employers posted 2,112 jobs through CCAC Career Services Departments. CCAC's four campus libraries house more than 200,000 volumes and subscribe to more than 1,600 periodicals. Quiet, private reading and study areas are available with knowledgeable librarians who provide the research assistance to help students succeed. Tutorial labs, writing labs, audiovisual aids, international student services and workshops in test taking, study techniques, and basic academic skills are all available at no cost to students through CCAC's learning assistance centers. Supplemental instruction is offered on an individual or small group basis for students who need help outside the classroom.

Location

The College is located in Allegheny County, which surrounds (and includes) the city of Pittsburgh. Pittsburgh is one of the largest corporate headquarters in the United States and has an abundance of cultural activities.

Admission Requirements

The College has an open admission policy. Entrance tests are not required, but applicants are encouraged to participate in these testing programs. To enroll as a full-time student, applicants must have a high school diploma or Pennsylvania GED certificate or must be at least 18 years of age with experience reasonably equivalent to a GED. Students should request an admission application form from the admission office on any CCAC campus and should return the completed application to the admission office. There is no application fee. An applicant is also required to take the College's placement test to determine the level of study suitable for his or her skills and to meet with a College adviser, as scheduled at registration time, to select classes for the coming term.

Application and Information

Application forms and additional information are available at the following CCAC campus locations:

Allegheny Campus (Northside)
Community College of Allegheny County
808 Ridge Avenue
Pittsburgh, Pennsylvania 15212
Telephone: 412-237-2511

North Campus (North Hills)
Community College of Allegheny County
8701 Perry Highway
Pittsburgh, Pennsylvania 15237
Telephone: 412-369-3600

Boyce Campus (Monroeville)
Community College of Allegheny County
595 Beatty Road
Monroeville, Pennsylvania 15146
Telephone: 412-325-6614

South Campus (West Mifflin)
Community College of Allegheny County
1750 Clairton Road and Route 885
West Mifflin, Pennsylvania 15122
Telephone: 412-469-4301

DEAN COLLEGE
FRANKLIN, MASSACHUSETTS

The College and Its Mission

Dean College is committed to being the leader among private, two-year residential colleges, promoting academic success, and building student confidence. The focus of the College is on educating students for transfer to baccalaureate institutions and entry into full-time employment in their major field of study. To support this mission, Dean offers a campus environment that is attractive, safe, and alive with activity. The suburban location near Boston and Providence allows students to take advantage of the cities for recreation, education, and work opportunities. Dean students are part of an academic community that has high expectations of them and a record of helping students achieve success. The academic preparation that students receive enables them to transfer to outstanding private colleges and major state universities across the country. The College is committed to providing personal and academic support, advice and counseling, and the opportunity to discover strengths that may not be evident in high school. Dean students study, work, and play hard. They are part of a vital, active community. This sense of community is evident from the first day on campus. With more than thirty clubs and organizations, it is difficult for anyone to feel left out. Dean provides an outstanding educational value to families. The College will do whatever is in its power to help students meet the cost of attending Dean and provide them with a high-quality education in a student-oriented setting that emphasizes customer service.

Academic Programs

Courses offered in the humanities, communication arts, mathematics, science, and social science areas constitute Dean's programs in the liberal arts and sciences. Students studying in any one of these areas have the option of working toward an **Associate in Arts** or an **Associate in Science** degree. Students studying in the areas of the performing arts, sports/fitness studies, and business generally are considered candidates for the Associate in Science degree. Students gain extensive experience through internships, course work, and independent studies—opportunities that might not be available to them until their junior or senior year at another institution. This experience includes video and radio production, teaching at the Children's Center Preschool on campus, dance, theater and music performances, and an internship in a social service agency. The College operates on a semester plan. Students who achieve honors grades may be inducted into the Upsilon Zeta Chapter of the Phi Theta Kappa Honor Society. Part-time students may be inducted into the Delta Beta Chapter of the Alpha Sigma Lambda Honor Society.

Associate Degree Programs Associate in Arts and Associate in Science degrees are offered in business administration; child studies/education; communication arts; computer information systems; computer science; corrections, probation, and parole; criminal intelligence analysis; dance; fashion merchandising; human services/social work; law enforcement; liberal arts; liberal studies; microcomputer support specialist studies; music; music/theater/dance; pre-engineering; retailing; science; sport/fitness studies (athletic training, health fitness, physical education, recreation leadership, and sports management); and theater arts.

Credit for Nontraditional Learning Experiences

Credit is available through the CLEP program, which is sponsored by the College Board.

Costs

For students entering in September 1996, tuition, room, board, and fees are guaranteed to remain constant for the two years that the student is enrolled at the College. In 1996–97, tuition is $11,880, a room is $4100, and board is $2200, for a total of $18,180. There is a comprehensive fee of $605 for all students. Approximately $1500 is needed to cover other expenses such as books, travel, and personal expenses. The comprehensive fee does not include the cost of optional programs and services such as academic support services, instrumental music and voice instruction, student health insurance, laboratory fees, physical education uniforms, private lessons, field trips, or the cost of materials used in art courses.

Financial Aid

Academic scholarships, athletic scholarships, loans, and part-time jobs are available at Dean, and 70 percent of the student body receives some form of assistance. Students are required to submit the Free Application for Federal Student Aid (FAFSA) and a Dean College financial aid application. To qualify for aid, both forms should be on file in the Financial Aid Office by March 1. Although every effort is made to meet the financial needs of students, campus-based funds are awarded on the basis of demonstrated need, academic promise, and the availability of funds. Students must be admitted before an offer of financial aid can be made. For more information, students should contact the Financial Aid Office (telephone: 508-541-1518).

Faculty

The student-faculty ratio is 14:1. Faculty members are dedicated to teaching and supporting students throughout the academic year. They serve as academic counselors and are available outside of class to assist students. Many faculty members also act as coaches and advisers for student clubs and organizations. Most faculty members hold advanced degrees.

Student Body Profile

Students from more than thirty states represent approximately 92 percent of the student population. International students from more than twenty countries represent 7 percent of the student body. Approximately 74 percent of the student body is white (non-Hispanic), 7 percent is black, 1 percent is Asian, and 1 percent is Hispanic. More than 85 percent of students live on campus.

Student Activities

The Student Government Association, consisting of elected representatives from each residence hall and from the commuter student group, the Student Activities Committee, and the Leadership Council, composed of officers from student organizations, meet frequently to discuss matters of concern to the student body. Students in these groups provide leadership and direction in social activities and programs related to student interests. The president of the College holds informal group discussions with students, and members of the Student Affairs staff meet with residence hall groups and commuting student groups so that each student has an opportunity to be heard. Students are frequently asked to serve on all-College committees that make recommendations to the president.

Facilities and Resources

The E. Ross Anderson Library currently contains over 54,000 volumes, 350 periodical subscriptions, microfilm, and electronic equipment that allows for a full range of teaching and learning aids on tape. A donation from Kersur Technologies connected the library to the World Wide Web in 1996. Also in 1996, an expanded "Writing Center Plus" opened with the addition of fifteen Pentium-based CD-ROM computers. Other facilities include the Campus Center, the Center for the Performing Arts, radio station WGAO, the Telecommunications Center, a language lab, and the Children's Center. The Academic Computer Center, open to all students, includes several computer classrooms equipped with IBM PCs and printers. Pieri Gymnasium includes facilities for basketball and volleyball, a pool, exercise equipment, and training facilities.

Location

The College is located on a 100-acre campus in Franklin, Massachusetts, a suburb of Boston. The College is easily reached from the interstate highway system, and Boston's Logan Airport is less than 30 miles away. Commuter rail service to and from Boston is within a block of the campus. Providence, Rhode Island, and Worcester, Massachusetts, are both within a half-hour's drive. Shopping, restaurants, movie theaters, golf, and many other recreational facilities are within walking distance of the College. The town of Franklin and the College enjoy a friendly relationship, with many local residents attending social and athletic events on campus and Dean students volunteering for various agencies and projects in and around the town.

Admission Requirements

The Office of Admissions accepts students who can reasonably be expected to satisfy the academic requirements established by the College. Students are selected based on their performance in secondary school, the quality of their curriculum, and a recommendation from their guidance counselor, principal, or headmaster. A student's overall grade point average and rank in class are considered in evaluating an application. SAT I scores are optional. A personal interview is highly recommended. During the visit to campus, students will gain a full understanding of the programs, academic expectations, and the support services offered by the College. While on campus for the interview, students have the opportunity to tour with a student guide and to meet with faculty and staff members. International students are encouraged to apply for all academic programs and the summer English as a second language program.

Application and Information

Dean College operates on a rolling admission plan. Applications may be submitted as early in the senior year as a student wishes, usually after first marking period grades are available. Applications are reviewed as soon as an application is complete, and the majority of students are notified in February and March. Applications are accepted as long as there is space available in the College.

Applications can be requested by contacting:

Office of Admissions
Dean College
99 Main Street
Franklin, Massachusetts 02038-1994
Telephone: 800-852-7702 (toll-free)
Fax: 617-541-8726

Students on the campus of Dean College.

Peterson's Guide to Two-Year Colleges 1997

DELAWARE COUNTY COMMUNITY COLLEGE
MEDIA, PENNSYLVANIA

The College and Its Mission

Delaware County Community College is the ninth largest college in the Philadelphia metropolitan area. Established in 1967, DCCC has nearly 10,000 students on its wooded, 123-acre main campus and seven satellite centers in Delaware and Chester counties.

For the past 30 years, community colleges like Delaware County Community College have played a unique role in American higher education. DCCC maintains an open door policy—an opportunity for a high-quality, low-cost college education for all members of the community. Because DCCC is funded by the Commonwealth of Pennsylvania and eleven local school districts, tuition remains affordable.

The College's competency-based curriculum is the basis of DCCC's reputation for academic excellence. Competencies certify to both students and their future employers the skills and knowledge gained in DCCC courses and programs. DCCC provides a supportive environment focused on students' success. Despite its size, DCCC has a personal, small-school atmosphere. Average class size is 24, and faculty members and staff tend to know students by name.

Academic Programs

The **Associate in Arts** and **Associate in Science** degrees are designed for university transfer. The **Associate in Applied Science** degree and certificate programs are designed for students who wish to prepare for specific career goals and employment. The A.A.S. degree will, with planning, also prepare students for transfer to a four-year degree program. There is also a general studies program leading to the Associate in Applied Science degree.

Associate degrees require at least 60 credit hours. Certificates of proficiency require at least 30 credits. Certificates of competency require fewer than 30 credits.

Associate Degree Programs The Associate in Arts (A.A.) and Associate in Science (A.S.) degrees are granted in business administration, behavioral science, communication arts, computer science/management information, engineering, liberal arts, and natural science. The Associate in Applied Science (A.A.S.) degree is granted in the following career fields: administration of justice, allied health management, architectural technology, banking, biomedical-equipment technology, business management, computer-aided drafting and design, computer information systems (programming and network engineering), computer-service technology, construction technology, early childhood education, electronics technology, facility management, fire science technology, general studies, graphic design, hotel and restaurant management, insurance claims adjuster, mechanical technology, medical assistant, nursing*, office administration, paralegal studies, respiratory therapy*, retail management, small-business management, surgical technician*, technical studies, and telecommunications technology. (an * indicates these programs have special admission requirements.)

Certificate and Diploma Programs Certificates of competency or proficiency are awarded in the following career fields: accounting, automated manufacturing, chemical technician, computer-aided drafting and design technology, energy systems technology, health unit clerk, insurance claims adjuster, medical assistant, microcomputers in business, modern office skills, nurse aide/home health aide, office administration, paralegal studies, perioperative nursing, RN first assistant, small-business management, surgical technician, and total quality management. Certificates of competency are awarded in the following occupational fields: auto mechanics, carpentry, electrical, emergency medical technician, hazardous materials technology, heating/ventilating/air conditioning (HVAC&R), machining, municipal police training*, plumbing*, and welding. (an * indicates these programs have special admission requirements.)

DCCC has written transfer agreements with dozens of colleges in the Delaware Valley. Some of these agreements provide for guaranteed acceptance to the four-year institution. DCCC credits transfer easily to colleges and universities across the country. Each year some 1,200 DCCC students transfer to four-year institutions. DCCC operates on a semester schedule and offers two summer sessions.

More than a hundred noncredit courses are offered each semester, including dozens of computer courses and others on career guidance and skills, academic skills, and enrichment topics such as writing, the arts, languages, and finance.

Off-Campus Programs

DCCC offers distance learning through television courses and independent study. Students may participate in the College's summer abroad programs in Germany and Italy.

Credit for Nontraditional Learning Experiences

The Credit for Prior Learning program at DCCC is one of the most active in the region. Students may earn up to 36 credits for noncollege learning through examination or portfolio assessment. The College's cooperative education program allows co-op students to earn up to 6 college credits while gaining hands-on experience in a wide variety of career fields.

Costs

Tuition is based on the number of credit hours and place of residence. In 1995–96, residents of school districts that provide financial support for the College paid $55 per credit hour. Tuition for other Pennsylvania residents was $110 per credit hour. Tuition for out-of-state residents was $165 per credit hour. Fees are separate and several are based on credit hours and type of course. For example, an instructional support fee ranges from $2 to $12 per credit hour, depending on the course. In 1995–96, a full-time student (15 credit hours) could expect to pay total tuition and fees per year of approximately $1800 (sponsors); $3700 (other Pennsylvania residents); $5300 (residents of other states); or $6350 (international students). DCCC is a nonresidential college.

Financial Aid

There are a number of options for financial aid, including federal and state grants, loans, scholarships, and work-study. Approximately 30 percent of DCCC students receive some form of financial aid. Aid is based on financial need. Financial aid programs include Federal Pell Grants, Federal Supplementary Educational Opportunity Grants, Federal Stafford Student Loans, Federal PLUS Loans, state PHEAA grants, federal and institutional work-study, veterans benefits. There are a number of institutional scholarships. Students should apply for financial aid by May 1.

Faculty

DCCC has 132 full-time and about 350 co-adjutant faculty members. About 30 percent of faculty hold doctoral degrees. The student-faculty ratio is 24:1.

Student Body Profile

Total student enrollment for fall 1995 was 9,807, including 3,145 full-time and 6,662 part-time students. The student body is diverse, easily blending older and younger students and different ethnic and racial backgrounds. More than half of students at DCCC attend part-time; the average age is 28. African-American students comprise 9 percent; other members of minority groups make up 4 percent. International students from thirty countries attend DCCC and comprise about 1 percent of the student body. All students live in the community.

Student Activities

Activities on campus include a wide variety of clubs, theater productions, the radio station, the literary magazine, and an active student government association. Each semester there are lectures, concerts, films, and other special programs on campus. Phi Theta Kappa, the national honor society for two-year colleges, has an active chapter at DCCC.

Sports The intercollegiate athletics program includes men's soccer, basketball, and baseball; women's volleyball, basketball, and softball; and coed golf and tennis. DCCC also has a variety of recreational and club sports.

Facilities and Resources

In addition to the main campus, DCCC offers classes at seven satellite locations. There are no residential facilities.

Information technology on campus is state-of-the-art. There are more than 500 computers for student use, and twenty specialized classrooms and computer labs including math/science, graphic design, and automated manufacturing. DCCC's bulletin board system links students and professors, and provides an Internet connection. The library has more than 70,000 volumes and an extensive microform collection. DCCC has a state-of-the-art Learning Center for individualized learning support and a Writing Center which uses a "writing across the curriculum" approach. The College's Career and Counseling Center is the most extensive in the region and has an active job placement center.

Location

DCCC is located in suburban Philadelphia, near the friendly, small town of Media, the county seat of Delaware County. Philadelphia, the nation's fourth-largest city and one of the most historic areas of the United States, offers a wide variety of cultural events, music, sports, films, shopping, and restaurants. DCCC is easily reached by public transit.

Admission Requirements

DCCC has an open admission policy—adults 18 years of age or older are accepted. Before enrolling, students must take placement testing in English and math to ensure that they are placed in appropriate courses.

In general, transfer credits from accredited colleges are readily accepted. Students should request official transcripts be sent to DCCC's Admissions Office.

International students are welcomed. No TOEFL scores are required. Placement tests are given prior to scheduling. DCCC's full- and part-time program in English as a second language prepares students for collegiate courses. DCCC has students from about thirty countries on campus.

Application and Information

Admission is made on a continuous basis. There are special requirements for some programs. International students must complete special application requirements before an I-20 is issued. For an application and complete information, contact:

Admissions Office
Delaware County Community College
901 South Media Line Road
Media, Pennsylvania 19063–1094

Telephone: 610–359–5050
Fax: 610–359–5343
E-mail: admiss@dcccnet.dccc.edu

On the campus of Delaware County Community College.

Peterson's Guide to Two-Year Colleges 1997

FASHION INSTITUTE OF DESIGN AND MERCHANDISING
LOS ANGELES, CALIFORNIA

The Institute and Its Mission

The Fashion Institute of Design and Merchandising (FIDM) provides a dynamic and exciting community of learning in the fashion, retail, and interior design fields. The purpose of the Institute is to provide an educational environment designed to combine student goals with industry needs.

FIDM has a reputation for graduating professionally competent and confident men and women capable of creative thought. It has graduated more than 20,000 students in its twenty-six-year history.

FIDM is accredited by the Accrediting Commission for Community and Junior Colleges of the Western Association of Schools and Colleges (WASC). The interior design program is accredited by the Foundation of Interior Design Education Research (FIDER).

Academic Programs

FIDM operates on a four-quarter academic calendar. New students may begin their studies any quarter throughout the year. The requirement for a two-year Associate of Arts degree is the completion of 90 units.

Associate Degree Programs FIDM offers **Associate of Arts** degrees in apparel manufacturing management, cosmetics and fragrance merchandising, fashion design, interior design, merchandise marketing (fashion merchandising or product development), textile design, and visual presentation and space design. All of these programs offer the highly specialized curriculum of a specific major combined with a core general education/liberal arts foundation.

Transfer Arrangements FIDM accepts course work from other accredited colleges if there is an equivalent course at FIDM and the grade is a C or better. FIDM courses at the 100, 200, and 300 levels are certified by FIDM to be baccalaureate level. FIDM maintains articulation agreements with selected colleges with the intent of enhancing a student's transfer opportunities. Academic counselors will provide assistance to students interested in transferring to other institutions to attain a four-year degree.

Internship and Co-op Programs Internships are available within each of the various majors. Paid and volunteer positions provide work experience for students to gain practical application of classroom skills.

Special Programs and Services FIDM offers Associate of Arts professional designation degrees for individuals with substantial academic and professional experience who wish to add a new field of specialization. These are nine- or twelve-month programs of intensive study in one of the Institute's specialized majors. Students from other regionally accredited programs have the opportunity to complement their previous education by enrolling in a professional designation program. Requirements for completion range from 45 to 66 units, depending on the field of study. FIDM also offers Associate of Arts advanced study programs that develop specialized expertise in the student's unique area of study. These programs are open to students who possess extensive prior academic and professional experience within the discipline area. These areas include fashion design advanced study, interior design advanced study, theater costume advanced study, and international manufacturing and product development. Completion requirements for these programs are 45 units.

In response to student needs, FIDM has established an evening program in addition to the regular daytime courses. The program has been designed to accommodate the time requirements of working students. The entire evening program for the Associate in Arts degree can be completed in 2½ years.

FIDM offers English as a second language (ESL) for students requiring English development to complete their major field of study. The program is concurrent and within FIDM's existing college-level course work. These classes focus on the special needs of students in the areas of oral communication, reading comprehension, and English composition.

Community Programs Community service programs are offered both independently and in cooperation with various community groups. General studies course credit may be awarded to participating students. Each FIDM campus identifies community projects that allow students to support local service agencies.

Off-Campus Programs

FIDM provides the opportunity for students to participate in academic study tours in Europe, Asia, and New York. These tours are specifically designed to broaden and enhance the specialized education offered at the Institute. Study tour participants may earn academic credit under faculty-supervised directed studies. Exchange programs are also available with Esmod, Paris; Instituto Artictico dell' Abbigliamento Marangoni, Milan; Accademia Internazionale d'Alta Mode e d'Arte del Costume Koefia, Rome; St. Martins School of Art, London; College of Distributive Trades, London; and Janette Klein Design School, Mexico City.

Credit for Nontraditional Learning Experiences

The Institute may give credit for demonstrated proficiency in areas related to college-level courses. Sources used to determine proficiency are the College-Level Examination Program (CLEP) and Credit for Academically Relevant Experience (CARE), an Institute-sponsored program.

Costs

For the 1996–97 academic year, tuition starts at $12,115, depending on the major selected by the student. Yearly fees start at $200 for California residents and range up to $500 for international students. Textbooks and supplies start at $1350 per year depending on the major.

Financial Aid

There are several sources of financial funding available to the student, including federal financial aid and education loan programs, California state aid programs, institutional loan programs, and FIDM awards and scholarships.

Faculty

FIDM faculty members are selected as specialists in their fields. Many are actively employed in their respective fields of expertise. They bring daily exposure to their industry into the classroom for the benefit of the students. In pursuit of the best faculty members, consideration is given to both academic excellence as well as practical experience. FIDM has a 16:1 student-instructor ratio.

Student Body Profile

FIDM's ethnically and culturally diverse student body is one of the attractions to the Institute. Nineteen percent of the current student body are international students from more than twenty different countries. Twenty-seven percent of the students are more than 25 years of age. Fifty-five percent of all students complete their associate degree. More than 90 percent find career positions within one year of graduation.

Student Activities

The Student Activities Committee plans and coordinates social activities, cultural events, and community projects, including the ASID Student Chapter, International Club, Delta Epsilon Chi (DEX), Association of Manufacturing Students, Honor Society, and the Alumni Association. The students also produce their own trend newsletter, *The Mode*.

Facilities and Resources

Advisement/Counseling Department Chairs and other trained staff members provide assistance to students in selecting the correct sequence of courses to allow each student to complete degree requirements. The counseling department provides personal guidance and referral to outside counseling services as well as matching peer tutors to specific students' needs. Individual Development and Education Assistance (IDEA) centers at each campus provide students with additional educational assistance to supplement classroom instruction. Services are available in the areas of writing, mathematics, computer competency, study skills, research skills, and reading comprehension.

Career Planning/Placement Offices Career planning and job placement are among the most important services offered by the Institute. Career assistance includes job search techniques, preparation for employment interviews, résumé preparation, and job adjustment assistance. Services provided by the center include undergraduate placement, graduate placement, alumni placement, internships, and industry work/study programs.

Library and Audiovisual Services FIDM's library goes beyond the traditional sources of information. In addition to more than 12,000 books and reference materials, FIDM also features an international video library, subscriptions to major predictive services, international and domestic periodicals, interior design workrooms, textile samples, a trimmings/findings collection, and access to the Internet. FIDM's Costume Museum houses over 4,500 garments from the seventeenth century to present day. The collection includes items from the California Historical Society (First Families), the Hollywood Collection, and the Rudi Gernreich Collection.

State-of-the-art computer labs support and enhance the educational programs of the Institute. Specialized labs offer computerized cutting and marking, graphic and textile design, word processing, and database management.

Location

Established in 1969, FIDM is a private college that now enrolls over 3,000 students a year. The main campus is in the heart of downtown Los Angeles near the garment district. This new campus is adjacent to the beautiful Grand Hope Park. There are additional branch campuses located in San Francisco, San Diego, and Costa Mesa, California.

Admission Requirements

The Institute provides educational opportunities to high school graduates or applicants that meet the Institute's Ability to Benefit (ATB) criteria to pursue a two-year Associate of Arts degree. Qualifications for professional designation programs include students that meet the general education core requirements or who have a U.S. accredited degree. All applicants must have an initial interview with an admission's representative. In addition, students must submit references and specific portfolio projects if applicable to the chosen major. The Institute is on the approved list of the U.S. Department of Justice for non-immigrant students and is authorized to issue Certificates of Eligibility (Form I-20).

Application and Information

Applications are accepted on an ongoing basis. All prospective students should contact:

Director of Admissions
Fashion Institute of Design and Merchandising
919 South Grand Avenue
Los Angeles, California 90015

Telephone: 800-711-7175 (toll-free)
Fax: 213-624-4799
E-mail: info@fidm.com
World Wide Web: http://www.fidm.com/

Debut '96, Beth Herzhaft. Designer: Sonia Kim, FIDM student.

Peterson's Guide to Two-Year Colleges 1997

FISHER COLLEGE
BOSTON, MASSACHUSETTS

The College and Its Mission

Fisher College, a private two-year college for women, was founded in 1903 and has long been a leader in preparing young women for challenging careers. Currently, 400 young women comprise the College's student body. Fisher students come from all parts of the United States and twelve different countries. The College's classroom buildings and dormitories overlook the Charles River and its beautiful esplanade.

Fisher is the first college in the country to include one trip per year as part of its educational process. The Fisher International Research Seminar Trip (F-I-R-S-T) takes students to a new destination each May for one week of international adventure. Students traveled to Athens, Greece, in 1996 and will go to Paris, France, in 1997. Fisher faculty members are there to help students get the most out of this twice-in-a-lifetime opportunity. There is an extraordinary commitment to the students' awareness of global issues. As no textbook can, F-I-R-S-T brings the student face-to-face with new people and their customs. Simply put, Fisher College offers students the world.

Academic Programs

Fisher's programs have been developed with a view to being sensitive to the role of women in high-level careers. The programs are designed to develop marketable skills and to provide students with maximum opportunities to transfer to other colleges and universities.

Associate Degree Programs Fisher College offers associate degree programs in accounting; business administration; criminal justice; early childhood education; fashion merchandising; liberal arts; mass communication assistant studies; medical assistant studies; office administration with executive, international, or legal concentrations; paralegal studies; physical therapist assistant studies; and travel and hospitality management.

The College also offers a certificate program in office administration.

Transfer Arrangements Fisher College's regional accreditation provides full transfer options, and a transfer counselor is available to students who are interested in pursuing a four-year degree. Fisher College has many articulation agreements with colleges and universities.

Internship and Co-op Programs Fisher College's location offers students a wide range of internship choices. All students are encouraged to participate in an internship. Some internship locations include Walt Disney World, Boston Children's Hospital, The Park Plaza Hotel, and Saks Fifth Avenue.

Special Programs and Services Fisher College offers an English as a second language (ESL) program. Students whose native language is not English and whose score on the TOEFL or on the Fisher-administered English placement tests is determined by Fisher faculty members to be insufficient for admission to English I are required to take a cycle of ESL instruction.

Fisher College offers an Academic Support Center that is staffed by a learning skills specialist and Fisher faculty members. It provides a supportive environment where students may receive assistance in reading, writing, and test-taking skills and strategies as well as content tutoring in specific areas.

Costs

For the 1996–97 academic year, tuition for full-time students is $10,900. The annual room and board charge is $6500. There is a comprehensive fee of $1000. The total annual expense for resident students, including fees, is $18,400. The total annual expense for commuting students, including fees, is $11,900.

Financial Aid

A high percentage of students at Fisher receive some form of financial aid. These forms include Fisher Trustee Scholarships, Fisher Honor Scholarships, Federal Pell Grants, Federal Perkins Loans, Federal Stafford Student Loans, Federal Work-Study Program awards, and work-study awards subsidized by Fisher College.

Faculty

The faculty at Fisher is aware of and sensitive to students' needs and aspirations. Faculty members are chosen for their academic qualifications and experience and for their interest in teaching young women in an independent two-year college. Students find that the faculty is involved in promoting the progress and success of each young woman. The student faculty ratio is approximately 20:1, and faculty members and course advisers counsel students both during posted office hours and informally throughout the day. The faculty, students, and administration all share in helping one another, creating the positive atmosphere that is so evident on campus at Fisher.

Student Body Profile

Ninety percent of all students enter Fisher immediately after high school. Students come from fifteen states and twelve countries.

Fifty percent of all students complete a full-time two-year associate degree program and fifty percent transfer to a four-year college. Ninety-eight percent of all students find jobs upon graduation.

Student Activities

The Student Activities Office is the focal point of campus life and offers a full range of extracurricular activities, including Student Government, Yearbook, Volunteer Community Service Club, Fashion Show, Poetry Club, Choir Group, Phi Theta Kappa, and The Women's Issue Support Group.

Sports Fisher College offers intercollegiate basketball and an intramural volleyball club and running club.

Facilities and Resources

Advisement/Counseling A faculty adviser is assigned to each student to assist with the selection of courses.

Career Planning/Placement Offices Fisher College's Placement Office offers students a full range of professional services designed to help guide students along the path to a successful career. Trained staff assist students with developing résumés, interviewing techniques, and identifying specific job opportunities. With a 98 percent–effective placement rate and lifetime assistance, the Placement Office is an invaluable resource.

Library and Audiovisual Services The Fisher College Library contains over 24,000 volumes and 350 periodicals as well as a comprehensive supply of audiovisual materials. Students also have access to the Boston Public Library, located only a few blocks away from the college.

Location

Boston is the "student capital" of the Northeast, a place where numerous educational, cultural, and social opportunities can be found. A particular attraction for Fisher students is the College's proximity to the many points of interest for which Boston is famous. Known for its exciting and stimulating environment, Boston provides a variety of recreational activities seldom found in other large cities. Within walking distance of the College are some of the country's finest facilities for drama, art, and music. Countless schools and colleges are also in Boston, drawing sustenance from one another. At the universities close by, there are plays, lectures, films, concerts, and social activities, which welcome Fisher students.

Excellent transportation facilities link the College to the center of Boston and the surrounding communities. Interstate bus terminals are within walking distance, and Boston's Logan International Airport is only 15 minutes away by taxi. Fisher's accessibility is a great convenience for students living outside New England.

Admission Requirements

The admission process at Fisher may best be described as individualized. The College advocates an admission policy that accentuates positive attributes in a student's record rather than concentrating on negatives. Applicants are evaluated objectively on the basis of their performance in secondary school and their supporting credentials and subjectively on the basis of their character and motivation to attend college. Applicants who have successfully completed the General Educational Development (GED) test are also considered for admission if they present evidence of the potential to perform successfully in collegiate-level courses. The scope of Fisher's program makes it possible for the College to offer an opportunity for admission to students from college-preparatory or business and commercial programs. For this reason, scores on the SAT I are not formally required. International students must present evidence of the ability to speak, read, and write English.

Application and Information

Fisher operates under a rolling admission program that enables the College to take action on an application as soon as a student's credentials have been received and reviewed. To obtain an admission application form and a college catalog, prospective students should contact:

Director of Admissions
Fisher College
118 Beacon Street
Boston, Massachusetts 02116

Telephone: 617-236-8818
800-821-3050 (toll-free in Massachusetts)
800-446-1226 (toll-free outside Massachusetts)
Fax: 617-236-8858

The Administration Building, located on Beacon Street in Boston's Back Bay.

Peterson's Guide to Two-Year Colleges 1997

FRANKLIN INSTITUTE OF BOSTON
BOSTON, MASSACHUSETTS

The Institute and Its Mission

Franklin Institute of Boston is a small, technical college offering a variety of instructional programs based on science, engineering, and technology. Programs of one-, two-, three-, and four-years' duration are provided for various levels of interest, abilities, and objectives. The aim of Franklin Institute is to prepare the students in each program for immediate employment upon graduation in a chosen career field and at the same time give students a technical education upon which they can continue to build. Because of the Institute's student-teacher ratio of 11:1, students receive a great deal of individual attention with a hands-on approach to learning.

The objectives of the Franklin Institute of Boston are threefold: to provide educational opportunities in science and technology for men and women in order that they may better themselves both economically and socially; to provide a sound educational foundation upon which the graduates of the Institute's programs may continue to grow both in personal terms as well as professional and educational terms; and to assess the present and future needs of industry and technology in order to anticipate and respond to those needs through curriculum revisions and the addition of new programs.

The Institute believes that no other educational institution offers more assurance to prospective students than the unique guarantee of the Franklin Institute of Boston. The Franklin Institute makes the following offer to its graduates who may for any reason choose to redirect their career goals: after completing an associate degree program in the regular day school division, any Franklin Institute graduate may return to the Institute to pursue another associate degree in the day division at no tuition charge within five years of completing the first degree. This unusual offer reflects the Institute's confidence in its educational programs and the career success of its graduates.

In addition to associate degrees, Franklin also grants the Bachelor of Science degree in automotive technology.

Academic Programs

Associate Degree Programs Franklin Institute of Boston grants the **Associate in Science** degree in automotive technology. The **Associate in Engineering** degree is awarded in architectural engineering technology, architectural-structural drafting technology, civil engineering technology, computer engineering technology, computer technology, electrical engineering technology, electronic engineering technology, mechanical engineering technology, and medical electronics engineering technology.

The engineering technology associate degree programs require four semesters for completion with a total of 74 semester-hours of credit. Half of the total curriculum in each engineering technology program is devoted to the technical specialty, beginning with elementary subject matter the first semester and progressing to very advanced material by the final semester. One fourth of the total curriculum is devoted to physical science and mathematics, courses in college algebra and trigonometry, analytic geometry, calculus, and college physics. The remaining fourth of the curriculum includes English, humanities, and social studies. Instruction is given in the use of computer applications. Most of the graduates of the engineering technology associate degree programs are employed by industry in various capacities in engineering and scientific fields. A high percentage of graduates continue their education at other colleges and universities.

The architectural engineering technology program provides both basic and advanced courses in architectural drafting and design, structural design, surveying, building methods and materials, estimating, and building services.

The field of civil engineering deals with the planning, design, and construction of structures, highways, and public works. The civil engineering technology program includes both basic and advanced courses in surveying, hydraulics, architecture, engineering mechanics, strength of materials, and structural and concrete designs.

The computer engineering technology program includes both fundamental and advanced courses in digital computer circuits, systems and languages, and electronic devices and circuit theory.

The electrical engineering technology program includes basic and advanced courses in the design and construction of electrical distribution systems for modern commercial and industrial buildings, commercial lighting design, and electrical estimating.

The electronic engineering technology program includes basic and advanced courses in electric and electronic circuit theory, semiconductor devices, principles and design of electrical and electronic equipment, and measurement techniques up to and including microwave frequencies.

The mechanical engineering technology program includes fundamental and advanced courses in applied mechanics, mechanics of materials, thermodynamics, heat transfer, machine design, fluid power, and instrumentation.

The medical electronics engineering technology curriculum incorporates basic and advanced courses in mini- and microcomputers, electronic devices, electric and electronic circuit theory, medical instrumentation, human physiology, medical instrument safety and grounding techniques, semiconductor circuitry, and principles and design of medical electronic instruments.

The industrial technology associate degree programs require four semesters for completion with a total of 70 semester-hours of credit. Over one half of the total curriculum in each industrial technology program is devoted to the technical specialty, beginning with elementary subject matter the first semester and progressing to more advanced material by the final semester. About one fourth of the total curriculum is devoted to basic science and mathematics, including algebra, trigonometry, and precalculus mathematics. The remainder of the curriculum includes English, humanities, and social studies.

Over half of the automotive technology two-year program is devoted to automotive technical specialties, including actual work on vehicles in the student instructional garage. About one third of the program is devoted to basic mathematics, physics, humanities, and social sciences, and the remaining time is devoted to basic mechanical technology studies.

The computer technology program prepares students to meet the rapidly growing demand for technicians who can install, maintain, and repair computer equipment and digital electronic systems.

The architectural-structural drafting technology program is designed to enable its graduates to become skilled and knowledgeable architectural draftspersons, capable of making important contributions to the architectural and/or engineering team that produces the complete working drawings from which buildings, residences, and other structures are erected.

Transfer Arrangements Transfer credit received for courses completed at Franklin is dependent on the policies of the transferring institution. Many graduates receive a full two years' credit toward a baccalaureate degree.

Certificate and Diploma Programs The Certificate of Proficiency programs require two semesters for completion with a total of 34 or 36 semester-hours of credit. Instruction is concentrated in the student's main area of interest. By association with professional practitioners, many students find stimulation and motivation that was lacking in previous school experiences. Graduates of these programs are generally immediately employable in their field of training.

The Computer Technology Certificate of Proficiency program prepares students to meet the rapidly growing demand for technicians who can install, maintain, and repair computer equipment and digital electronic systems.

The Drafting Technology Certificate of Proficiency program is designed for the individual interested in a career as a draftsperson in engineering or architectural firms. Both general and specialized drafting are combined with mathematics to equip the graduate with the necessary preparation for the field of drafting. The faculty for this program offers students a wide variety of practical and invaluable field experience.

The objective of the practical electricity program is to produce qualified technicians capable of assisting licensed electricians or electrical engineers in the layout, installation, maintenance, or testing of electrical equipment or systems. Upon satisfactory completion of the one-year program, students are given credit for apprentice training toward application for the Journeyman Electrician License in Massachusetts or in neighboring states.

Special Programs and Services The Extended Degree Program provides those additional skills that bridge the gap between those that are necessary to receive a high school diploma or its equivalent and those academic skills necessary to succeed in an engineering technology program at the Franklin Institute of Boston. It is a sequence of courses designed to provide an opportunity for highly motivated students to attain an Associate in Engineering degree in five or six semesters. Unique in Boston, the Franklin ESL program focuses upon the acquisition of English as a second language through courses that are based in the English used in engineering and industrial technology. Thus, students can further improve their English acquisition as they are introduced to specific technical language at the same time. It is believed that such an approach will assist students in the particular programs of study to which they have been accepted.

Costs

For the 1996–97 academic year, tuition is $8850. Lab fees range from $100 to $300. Books and supplies average $600. While the Institute does not maintain its own residence halls, various housing options exist within walking distance of the Institute.

Financial Aid

Franklin Institute of Boston offers financial assistance to students on the basis of demonstrated financial need and satisfactory academic progress. All students are encouraged to file the Free Application for Federal Student Aid (FAFSA). The Institute participates in the Federal Pell Grant, Federal Supplemental Educational Opportunity Grant, Federal Direct Loan, Federal Perkins Loan, and Federal Work-Study programs and offers Franklin Institute grants and academic scholarships. State scholarships, VA assistance, rehabilitation funding, and payment plans are available for eligible students.

Faculty

The faculty at Franklin consists of instructors with practical experience in their field of expertise and many years of instruction. Instructors meet annually with the Industrial Advisory Board for each program to review and update the curricula. There are 40 full-time and 5 part-time faculty members.

Student Body Profile

Eighty-five percent of students are state residents, 3 percent are transfer students, and 3 percent are international students. Twenty percent of the student body are 25 years of age or older, and 6 percent are women. The student body is ethnically and culturally diverse: 24 percent are African American, 1 percent are Native American, 7 percent are Hispanic, and 24 percent are Asian American. Thirty percent of students work full-time.

Student Activities

All students are encouraged to participate in the campus environment. Activities include student government, Women's Support Group, engineering week competitions, yearbook, literary magazine, professional honor societies, and athletics.

Sports Franklin offers outdoor recreation programs, including basketball, floor hockey, and volleyball. In addition, students have use of the Blackstone Community Center, which houses a gym, swimming pool, nautilus room, track, and facilities for other activities. The Institute sponsors intercollegiate men's basketball and soccer.

Facilities and Resources

The Union building houses the library, which holds 13,000 bound volumes, 60 periodical subscriptions, 70 computer terminals, and a word processing lab for student use. Other labs associated with individual programs include digital and analog electronics, electrical wiring, computer systems, materials testing, machine tool, CAD, automotive engines, transmissions, drivability, and electrical as well as a full-service garage.

Location

The land on which the Institute stands, at the corner of Berkeley and Appleton Streets in the South End of Boston, was provided by the city in 1906. The Institute complex consists of three buildings, a plaza, a landscaped mall connecting the buildings on Berkeley and Appleton Streets, and a modern underground automotive technology shop. The facilities of the Kendall Administration Building and the Dunham Building are handicapped accessible. The Institute is readily accessible by public transportation and is within close walking distance of many cultural, social, and recreational activities offered in the city of Boston. Franklin students have the opportunity to meet other college students from around the world, as there are over seventy postsecondary institutions in the greater Boston area.

Admission Requirements

All applicants must possess a high school diploma or its equivalent and must have completed four full-year courses in high school English. For associate degrees in engineering technology, satisfactory completion of the following courses in mathematics and science is also required: algebra I, algebra II, geometry, and a laboratory science, preferably physics, although courses in chemistry or biology are acceptable. Additional courses in mathematics, such as trigonometry, math analysis, or precalculus, are helpful but not required.

Admission requirements for associate degree in industrial technology programs include a minimum of two high school courses in mathematics, including the study of elementary algebra, and one course in science. High school courses or practical experience related to an applicant's anticipated program of study are helpful in demonstrating interest and aptitude.

Admission requirements for the Certificate of Proficiency include a minimum of two high school courses in mathematics and one course in science. The study of elementary algebra is recommended and in some cases required. High school courses or practical experience related to an applicant's anticipated program of study are helpful in demonstrating interest and aptitude.

Application and Information

All applicants should complete a Franklin Institute Application for Admission and submit it with the required $35 processing fee to the Office of Admission. Official transcripts of high school records, including first-term senior year grades, should be requested by the student and sent directly from the high school to the Office of Admission. Students are responsible for requesting release of their high school transcripts. Because applications are processed on a rolling basis, applicants are notified of their admission status shortly after all required documents have been received. International applicants are also required to demonstrate English language proficiency and provide a financial statement showing proof of ability to pay the first year's costs. Further information is available through the Office of Admission.

Requests for additional information and application forms should be addressed to:

Office of Admission
Franklin Institute of Boston
41 Berkeley Street
Boston, Massachusetts 02116
Telephone: 617-423-4630
Fax: 617-482-3706

HARCUM COLLEGE
BRYN MAWR, PENNSYLVANIA

The College and Its Mission

Harcum College provides an educational foundation and environment for learning that promotes academic, professional, and personal growth for its students. The College advocates life-long learning as a perpetual process—one with no absolute end.
Harcum is a private, independent, fully-accredited, residential college committed primarily to the education of women. However, Harcum provides both women and men of diverse ages and backgrounds with professional career preparation and a broad liberal arts education. Eighty-seven percent of the students are women.
Harcum's programs, internships, and services promote academic success, professional accomplishment, leadership opportunities, and life-long learning. Harcum's distinction is its emphasis on attention to students' individual needs. Small classes and a faculty committed to teaching enable Harcum to deliver personal attention. Through extracurricular involvement, both on and off campus, students are encouraged to expand and share their knowledge and skills and to serve their communities responsibly.
Harcum was founded in 1915 by Edith Hatcher Harcum who, in that pre-suffrage era, was an extraordinarily farsighted educator. She believed in the abilities of women and she designed curricula which would identify and cultivate the unique talents of each Harcum student. Her curricula combined occupational training with a core of liberal and fine arts studies. After the College's reorganization in 1952 as a nonprofit institution, the board of trustees preserved that tradition by making Harcum the first college in Pennsylvania to award the Associate in Arts and Associate in Science degrees. Today, Harcum is still the only two-year, private, independent women's college to do so.

Academic Programs

Harcum's academic programs are diverse but are divided into three broad categories: health-science programs; liberal arts and sciences; and business and professional studies. Many of the Associate in Science degree programs are designed primarily to prepare students for employment immediately upon graduation. However, many courses taken in these programs will transfer to a four-year college or university as will courses in the Associate in Arts degree programs. The **Associate in Arts** degree is offered in child study/exceptional children, and liberal studies. The **Associate in Science** degree is offered in allied health sciences, which prepares graduates to go on to four-year programs in nursing, pharmacy, and therapy; animal center management; business administration; computer information systems; expanded functions dental assistant; dental hygiene; fashion design and retail merchandising; hospitality and tourism; illustration/graphic design; interior design; medical laboratory technician; occupational therapy assistant; physical therapist assistant; and veterinary technology. The College also offers a one-year certificate program in dental assisting.

Transfer Arrangements Career services staff assist students in preparing for transfer to a four-year institution. Harcum students have been accepted by more than 200 colleges and universities nationwide and abroad. Harcum has close relationships with many colleges and a growing number of articulation agreements with some that enable its students to transfer without loss of academic credit.

Internship and Co-op programs Nearly all of Harcum's programs feature a practicum or internship as an important part of the curriculum. Qualified students spend a period of time gaining valuable work experience in a work place appropriate to their program. There they apply the knowledge they have acquired in the classroom. Many students subsequently receive job offers from their internship sponsors.

Special Programs and Services The College offers a number of special programs to assist students in succeeding at college. Early Entry is a five-week summer program which gives students an opportunity to adjust to college life while strengthening their academic preparation in reading, writing, math and other areas. Achieving Individual Motivation for Success (A.I.M.) develops academic and personal skills, cultural awareness, career plans and life-long learning tools for economically-disadvantaged students. The Personalized Learning Strategies (P.L.U.S.) program assists students with documented learning differences. The English Language Academic offers full- and part-time instruction in English as a Second Language. The Developmental Program provides courses to strengthen skills in English, math, and reading. The Pre-professional Health Track is a one-year program designed to prepare students academically for the occupational therapy assistant, physical therapist assistant, or dental hygiene programs. Students who want to do independent study are encouraged to delve into a topic that deeply interests them. Students are guided in their study, independent of regular classroom attendance, by a qualified, conscientious instructor. Periodic meetings and discussion seminars are held.

Community Programs Students are encouraged to join Harcum's community service program and volunteer their time assisting children and adults with special needs.

Continuing Education Unit Certificate Programs The College's Continuing Education Division offers programs year-round. Courses are offered for professional development and personal enrichment. It is possible to earn an associate degree in the evening in interior design, occupational therapy assistant, physical therapist assistant, and veterinary technology. Short courses awarding a certificate also are offered.

Credit for Nontraditional Learning Experiences

The College awards credit for knowledge acquired outside the usual educational setting by accepting College-Level Examination Program (CLEP) scores for credit toward a degree. The College accepts general and subject examination CLEP scores based on the American Council on Education's recommended cut scores. Students working toward an associate degree may earn a total of 30 credits through challenge exams, CLEP, or transfer credit.

Costs

The 1996–97 tuition for full-time students is $8310; for occupational therapy assistant and physical therapist assistant students it is $8840. Tuition for part-time students is $277 per credit; $294 per credit for occupational therapy assistant and physical therapy assistant students. There is a general fee of $315 per semester for resident students and $249 per semester for commuters, and there are additional miscellaneous fees and deposits. Annual room and board charges are $5080 in 1996–97.

Financial Aid

More than 60 percent of students at Harcum receive some form of financial aid. Available aid includes Harcum grants-in-aid, scholarships, Federal Pell Grants, Federal Supplemental Educational Opportunity Grants, state grants, Federal Perkins Loans, and Federal Work-Study Program awards. Applications for financial aid should be filed before April 15 for September enrollment.

Faculty

All of Harcum's programs are led by full-time directors and have full-time professors. Their expertise is augmented by part-time adjunct instructors who usually are practicing professionals in their fields. There are 38 full-time faculty members. Eighty percent of full-time faculty members have advanced degrees, including 13 percent who hold doctorates. The student-faulty ratio is 9:1.

Student Body Profile

The student body is 87 percent female. The largest age group is between 18 and 21, but nearly as many are between 22 and 29 years of age. The average age is 20–24. Eighty-two percent of students are white; 8 percent are African American; 2 percent are Asian. Full-time students make up 65 percent of the total. Eight percent of the students are enrolled in continuing education. Commuters account for 79 percent. Seventy-eight percent of the students are from Pennsylvania, primarily from the five-county Philadelphia region. The next largest group (7 percent) is from New Jersey. International students make up 10 percent. Sixty-one percent of the students who apply are accepted; 57 percent of those accepted enroll. Of those who enroll, 58 percent graduate. One year after graduation, 64 percent were employed full-time and 8 percent were continuing their educations full-time. Another 28 percent were both employed and attending college.

Student Activities

A variety of team sports, including badminton, softball, tennis, volleyball and field hockey, are offered. The Harcum Bears compete in the Pennsylvania Association of Intercollegiate Athletics for Women. In addition, students can choose from more than 20 clubs such as the Equine Club or the Harcum Singers, join the staffs of the student newspaper or yearbook, or participate in one of the professionally-oriented organizations such as the Organization for Animal Technician Students or the Student American Dental Hygienists Association. The College has a chapter of Phi Theta Kappa, the national honor society for two-year colleges.

Facilities and Resources

Career Planning/Placement Offices All new students take the College's placement test in reading, English, and math to determine if they meet or must do additional work to meet the College's basic skill levels. The Center for Student Development and Counseling provides personal, career, and academic counseling in group and individual settings. Professional and peer tutoring and study groups are available. Career Services staff assist students in selecting and preparing for a career or for transferring to a four-year institution. Seminars in résumé preparation, job hunting, and interviewing are offered and job fairs are held.

Library and Audiovisual Services The library collection has 39,000 volumes, 300 periodicals, and more than 950 audiovisual items. It is a member of the Tri-State College Library Cooperative, a 34-college consortium, which provides access to more than 3 million volumes. Harcum's library also provides connections to the Internet and FirstSearch, an on-line data base, and it is networked with 15 CD-ROM data bases.

Location

Harcum is in Bryn Mawr, Pennsylvania, 12 miles west of Philadelphia and in the heart of the Main Line, a string of attractive suburban communities. The College is in the same area as one of the largest concentrations of educational institutions in the country. There are 55 colleges and universities in the Philadelphia area. The campus is on a parklike 12-acre site next to a commuter railroad station which makes travel to Philadelphia and throughout the area easy. A student at Harcum may take advantage of all the city and its suburbs have to offer. Available in Philadelphia are the world-renowned Philadelphia Orchestra, the Pennsylvania Ballet, the Philadelphia Opera, and the world-famous Philadelphia Museum of Art. The city has major league teams in baseball, football, ice hockey, and basketball. And there are numerous historic sites in and around Philadelphia to visit, including Independence Hall and the Liberty Bell and Valley Forge National Park.

Admission Requirements

All applicants are required to submit secondary school records, results of any standardized tests taken, and a recommendation. SAT I scores are required only for the dental hygiene, medical laboratory technician, occupational therapy assistant, physical therapist assistant, and veterinary technology programs, but SAT I scores are recommended for proper placement in any of Harcum's other programs. An interview is also recommended. The physical therapist assistant program has a March 1 application deadline; the occupational therapy program deadline is March 15. All other programs accept students on a rolling admissions basis.

Application and Information

For more information, students should contact:
Admissions Office
Harcum College
750 Montgomery Avenue
Bryn Mawr, Pennsylvania 19010-3476
Telephone: 610-526-6050
800-345-2600 (toll-free outside Philadelphia)
Fax: 610-526-6147

Library and Academic Center.

HESSER COLLEGE
MANCHESTER, NEW HAMPSHIRE

The College and Its Mission
The primary purpose of Hesser College is to provide a high-quality education that is highly personalized, cost-effective, and employment-oriented. Hesser is committed to preparing and assisting graduates in job placement, successful career entry, and/or the pursuit of further education.

Hesser College was established in 1900 as Hesser Business College, a private nonsectarian junior college. Since 1972, Hesser College has expanded and enriched its curricula in keeping with its tradition of providing an affordable career education of high quality. The physical building encompasses more than fifteen different businesses that all create the Hesser Center of Commerce and Education. This is an unusual and beneficial partnership of business and education.

Academic Programs
The primary goal of the curricula is to prepare students for success in specific career areas. The general education requirements are designed to provide the skills necessary for career growth and lifelong learning. Internships, practicums, and opportunities for part-time work experience are available in all majors.

Associate Degree Programs Hesser College offers the **Associate in Business Science, Associate in Science, Associate in Computer Science, Associate in Arts,** and **Associate in Early Childhood Education** degrees in the following majors: accounting, business administration, business science, communications, computer business applications, computer programming, construction practice management, criminal justice (corrections, law enforcement, and security), early childhood education, executive administrative assistant studies, health-care management, hotel/restaurant management, human services, interior design, legal administrative assistant studies, liberal studies, marketing, medical assistant/certified nurses' assistant studies, medical office management, medical secretary studies, occupational therapist assistant studies, paralegal studies, physical therapist assistant studies, psychology, retail management/fashion merchandising, sales and sales management, small-business management, and travel and tourism. Diploma (one-year) programs are also available.

Off-Campus Programs
The College offers opportunities for cooperative education and internships in most of its academic programs. The early childhood education program includes practicums and supervised fieldwork in the freshman and senior years, utilizing a variety of child-care facilities. The occupational therapist assistant and physical therapist assistant programs require students to participate in at least 265 hours of clinical experience in a health-care setting under the direct supervision of a certified instructor or therapist.

Credit for Nontraditional Learning Experiences
Hesser College offers a variety of options for students to earn college credit by means other than taking traditional college courses. The purpose of these programs is to enable those students who have reached the college level of education in nontraditional ways (e.g., correspondence study, self-study, company, or military training) to assess the level of their achievement and to use the assessment and/or test results in seeking college credit. These programs offer the student the means to shorten the amount of time required in obtaining a degree and to avoid duplication of effort by avoiding inappropriate placement of the student in courses covering materials that have already been learned. These programs cannot be used to erase failing grades or upgrade other grades.

Costs
Part-time students are billed at the rate of $252 per credit for all majors. Lab courses are assessed a $20 lab fee per semester. Field experience, practicums, internships, and externships are assessed a fee of $100 per course. All students taking 9 credits or more must pay the activity fee of $60 per semester and the health fee of $40 per semester.

Current full-time expenses per semester for 1996–97 are as follows: tuition (12–16 credits): $3680; room: $1230; and meal plan (optional/heavy): $850.

Financial Aid
Hesser College offers financial assistance to students on the basis of demonstrated financial need. Sixty percent of students receive some form of aid. More than fifty scholarships are awarded each year to freshman and senior students. The College offers low-interest loans from both internal and external sources. Federal Supplemental Educational Opportunity Grants, Federal Work-Study, Federal Perkins Loans, Federal Stafford Student Loans, and state scholarship programs are available. Eighty-five percent of students work part-time.

Applicants for financial aid must file the CSS financial aid form, a copy of their parents' and/or their own most recent income tax form, state and institutional financial aid applications, and the FAFSA/SAR. The FFS may be submitted in lieu of the CSS form. The priority application deadline is May 1.

Faculty
The faculty of Hesser College consistently receive high student evaluations for their interest in each student's success and for the high quality of their teaching. The majority of the faculty have completed programs of advanced study, and all have practical experience in business or other career fields. Faculty members participate in national and regional conferences and associations and are continually involved with program review and curriculum development. The student-faculty ratio is 18:1.

Student Body Profile
Nearly 85 percent of the students work in the afternoons or evenings while attending Hesser. The 850 men and women currently enrolled represent several states and more than ten countries. A large part of the student population comes from New England, New York, and New Jersey.

Student Activities
Hesser College offers intercollegiate sports in men's and women's basketball, soccer, and volleyball and women's softball and field hockey. The basketball team has consistently been a major power in the Northern New England Small College Conference. Students also participate in a number of intramural sports programs. Extracurricular activities are varied and include social activities, clubs, trips, and educational programs in the residence halls. A freshman orientation program is conducted each fall before classes begin.

Facilities and Resources

The College includes dormitories for approximately 70 percent of the 850 men and women students. A wide range of counseling services are available. Academic advising is coordinated through department chairpersons and the academic support center, and the size of the College allows for individual attention to the financial and career counseling needs of students.

The academic facilities located within the Hesser Commerce and Education Center include two computer labs, an automated office simulation lab, the on-line American Airlines reservation system (SABER) computer lab, the court reporting computer-assisted transcription lab (X-Scribe), a medical assistant lab, and the electronics lab. The College library contains more than 40,000 titles. The Learning Center provides special tutoring and programs in study skills, reading, writing, and math, including computerized instruction.

The College has developed a number of learning assistance programs to help students succeed in their studies. Tutoring and special classes are provided by the faculty throughout each semester. In addition, several departments offer honor programs and special opportunities for independent study. The College also sponsors an active chapter of the national honor society Phi Theta Kappa, which promotes scholarship and service to the College and the community. The transfer counselor, who assists students who wish to continue their education beyond the associate degree level, has developed cooperative transfer agreements with four-year colleges in business, early childhood education, criminal justice, and liberal studies.

Location

Hesser College is located in Manchester, New Hampshire. Manchester has a population of over 100,000 and is a medium-sized city. The College's central location provides easy access to entertainment, shopping, and a wide variety of part-time jobs and academic work experiences.

There is no better place to learn first-hand about business than in the city ranked number one for business in the United States. According to *U.S. News & World Report*, Manchester is "at the hub of things" in the fast-growing, high-tech, financial- and information-oriented businesses of southern New Hampshire. Not only are there outstanding educational opportunities in the nation's best business environment, but the quality of life in Manchester has been cited as one of the best in America.

Manchester is within 1 hour of Boston, and the mountains and major ski resorts are within 1 or 2 hours to the North, as are the beaches of Maine and New Hampshire. The Manchester airport is served by three major carriers, with direct connections to Boston, New York, Pittsburgh, and Washington.

Admission Requirements

Hesser College's freshman class of 609 students was selected by a committee made up of faculty members, administrators, and admission personnel. A high school transcript must be submitted, and international students must also submit TOEFL scores. SAT I scores are not required but may be considered in the admission decision if submitted. Transfer students are required to submit a high school and college transcript, with a minimum of a 2.0 grade point average for college work.

Recommended, but not required, for all applicants are an interview and recommendations from counselors, teachers, and employers. The College operates on a rolling admission basis, and notification is continuous.

Application and Information

Applicants must submit an application form with a $10 nonrefundable fee. Applications are reviewed on a first-come, first-served basis and normally take seven to fourteen days to be fully reviewed.

Requests for additional information and application forms should be addressed to:

Vice President of Enrollment
Hesser College
3 Sundial Avenue
Manchester, New Hampshire 03103
Telephone: 603–668–6660
800–526–9231 (toll-free)
Fax: 603–666–4722

Graduation at Hesser College.

Peterson's Guide to Two-Year Colleges 1997

INDIANA BUSINESS COLLEGE
INDIANAPOLIS, INDIANA

The College and Its Mission

Indiana Business College was founded in 1902 to serve the specific education and career needs and interests of students planning to enter the business community. Indiana Business College consists of ten campuses at convenient locations across the state. Full-time, part-time, and evening classes are available at all locations. The philosophy that underlies the curriculum at the College is one of individual attention, allowing for flexibility and higher achievement in the classroom. The career-oriented emphasis enables course work to be highly specialized. Indiana Business College has a commitment to providing practical education; students are trained by practical application and hands-on experience. This commitment, coupled with a reputation for offering a high-quality education, contributes to the employment opportunities of graduates. The College offers a continuous placement assistance service to its graduates and is continually updating the curriculum to meet the demands of today's business world.

Indiana Business College assists students in locating housing and in finding roommates. There is ample housing available both near the school and in the surrounding areas.

Indiana Business College is accredited by the Accrediting Commission for the Independent Colleges and Schools of the Career College Association and by the Indiana Commission for Postsecondary Proprietary Education.

Academic Programs

Indiana Business College offers the **Associate in Applied Science** degree in accounting; business management; executive, medical, and legal secretarial studies; fashion management; hotel administration; office systems management; travel management; medical assistant studies; and medical records technology.

Indiana Business College also offers diplomas in the areas of accounting, fashion merchandising, hotel operations, medical assisting, medical coding, office specialist studies, secretarial studies, and travel and tourism.

Indiana Business College operates throughout the calendar year; classes begin quarterly in January, April, June, and September. Students must complete a minimum of 107 credit hours to earn an associate degree and a minimum of 73 credit hours for a diploma. (Program requirements vary.) To be awarded a degree or diploma, students must maintain a minimum GPA of 2.0 (on a 4.0 scale).

The accounting programs offered at Indiana Business College include courses in partnership and cost accounting, federal tax, auditing and payroll, and social security taxes. Both diploma and associate degree accounting programs incorporate the courses necessary to prepare students for excellent positions in private business, public accounting, and departments within the government.

The associate degree program in business management includes courses in the areas of computers, accounting, marketing, management, and sales. The College's program helps students to develop the creativity and the supervisory skills needed for managerial positions.

Indiana Business College's secretarial programs include administrative assistant studies and office specialist studies diploma programs and office systems specialist studies and office systems management associate degree programs. The secretarial programs provide students with the necessary foundation in shorthand, typewriting, information processing, and computer technology. Both diploma and associate degree programs in secretarial studies offer an extension for specialization in either the medical or legal field.

The associate degree program in fashion management and the diploma program in fashion merchandising prepare the graduate for a career in the fashion industry. Combining business classes with fashion studies prepares the student to succeed in this competitive field. Included in this curriculum are courses such as textiles, display and design, marketing, and apparel merchandising. The fashion management and fashion merchandising programs are available in Indianapolis only.

The hotel programs are designed to train students for various careers in the hotel and hospitality industry. These programs prepare the student by providing an understanding of business and administrative skills and of travel and hospitality in relation to the hotel industry. The hotel programs are available in Indianapolis and Terre Haute only.

The travel and tourism management programs are the most complete programs offered in this field in the Midwest. The travel industry is fast paced and highly specialized, and, to help students meet the needs of the industry, courses in accounting, information processing, management, and travel and tourism, are included in the curricula. The travel programs are currently offered at the Indianapolis and Muncie campuses only.

Indiana Business College's medical programs include medical assistant studies and medical records technology. The diploma and degree programs in medical assistant studies provide the student with skills to be competent in both front and back office procedures. Both of the diploma and degree programs in medical records technology provide training to analyze medical records, to assign codes to index diagnoses and procedures, and to provide information for reimbursement purposes. Courses in medical science, medical terminology, medical office administration, and medical insurance processing are offered to help students meet the needs of the industry. The medical assistant studies and medical records technology degree programs are offered only at the Indianapolis Medical Annex and Evansville campuses. The medical coding diploma program is offered at all the campuses.

Optional internships are available to students in all associate degree programs.

Costs

For 1996–97, the estimate for full-time tuition is $1895 per quarter. Tuition varies according to the program chosen. Books and supplies average $80 per class.

Financial Aid

Many Indiana Business College students qualify for some form of financial aid. The College participates in the Federal Pell Grant, Federal Supplemental Educational Opportunity Grant, Federal Stafford Student Loan, and Federal PLUS programs. Students' eligibility to participate in these programs is contingent upon demonstration of financial need. In addition, the

College offers scholarships to both graduating high school seniors and nontraditional students.

The placement office assists students in finding part-time jobs as well as Federal Work-Study positions. These employment opportunities help supplement the student's income. Financial planning and financial aid personnel are available to assist the student in the application process.

Students are also encouraged to investigate possibilities for private scholarships.

Faculty

The faculty of Indiana Business College is composed of dedicated professionals who are committed to giving personal attention to every student. The selection of instructors is based not only on their academic credentials, professional training, and business experience, but also on their capacity to develop the student's ability in preparation for the world of work.

Student Body Profile

The student body consists of approximately 1,950 students. Fifty percent of the students are between 19 and 24 years old, and roughly 27 percent are between 25 and 34 years old.

Student Activities

Although there are no official student government bodies on the campuses of Indiana Business College, students may join independent student groups and student councils. (Each campus has various groups or councils.) Coordinating activities with a director or department head, student groups organize a variety of on-campus and off-campus events. Professional organizations are also available for student participation. Intramural sports and group functions vary by campus.

Facilities and Resources

Most campuses include a library and study area for all students. Computer labs are available after scheduled class times. The placement office at each campus is available for advisement, counseling, and career planning.

Location

Situated in the heart of Indianapolis, the main campus of Indiana Business College houses the corporate office for all branches of the College. It is directly across the street from the public library. The excitement of urban living, combined with the cultural and historical sites, makes Indiana Business College's location ideal. Indianapolis' Union Station, Children's Museum, Indiana Repertory Theater, and White River Park Zoo provide a variety of educational and recreational activities. The College is within walking distance of downtown shopping centers and major sports centers such as Market Square Arena and the RCA Dome. It is also readily accessible to many different transportation systems.

In addition to its main campus in Indianapolis, Indiana Business College has campuses located in Anderson, Columbus, Lafayette, Marion, Muncie, Terre Haute, Evansville, and Vincennes. These branches are identical in curriculum and philosophy. The Indianapolis Medical Annex campus specifically offers the medical assisting and medical coding programs. Students many earn credits toward the completion of a program at more than one location. The convenience of having ten locations significantly lessens the cost of an education by eliminating additional housing and transportation expenses.

Admission Requirements

Applicants must be high school graduates or have obtained a General Educational Development (GED) certificate to be considered for admission to Indiana Business College. The College reviews each application for admission and bases the admission decision on academic performance and a personal interview.

The College is open to men and women of any race, faith, or national origin. All students are given equal opportunity to pursue their educational and career goals through the programs offered at Indiana Business College.

Application and Information

All applications must be accompanied by a $30 application fee. High school transcripts are requested directly from the student's school by Indiana Business College. Applicants are notified within two weeks of the completion of all application requirements.

All inquiries should be addressed to:

Admission Office
Indiana Business College
802 North Meridian Street
Indianapolis, Indiana 46204
Telephone: 317-264-5656
800-IBC-GRAD (toll-free)
Fax: 317-634-0471

INTERNATIONAL FINE ARTS COLLEGE
MIAMI, FLORIDA

The College and Its Mission

International Fine Arts College is a small, private, highly specialized degree-granting institution. Founded in 1965, the College is accredited by the Commission on Colleges of the Southern Association of Colleges and Schools. The Interior Design Program is accredited by FIDER, the Foundation for Interior Design Education Research. Students come from around the world to enjoy the warm climate, friendly atmosphere, small classes, frequent field trips, state-of-the-art equipment, and intensive training in business and the arts.

The College staff takes a personal interest in each student's educational, career, and personal development. A College counselor is available for individual or group counseling. The Career Planning and Placement Office assists students in obtaining full- or part-time work during college and after graduation. The formal education and practical training that students receive at International Fine Arts College are designed to prepare them for professional careers into the twenty-first century.

Academic Programs

International Fine Arts College offers **Associate in Arts (A.A.)** degrees in computer animation, digital audio/video, electronic publishing/commercial art, fashion design, fashion merchandising, film and television, interior design, and visual arts. The academic programs of the College are rigorous. Students learn the essentials, enabling them to succeed in exciting, competitive careers. The College operates on a semester system. Either four or six semesters, depending upon the major, of a set curriculum are required for graduation in each of the majors. Depending on the chosen major, the student completes between 70 and 85 credit hours of course work prior to graduation. Internships are an important part of the curriculum in many of the majors. Approximately half of the curriculum is devoted to courses within the students' major areas of study. Academic and business courses are carefully integrated into the remainder of the curriculum in order to promote the development of skills and knowledge essential to the attainment of responsible positions in the business world. Elective courses are available in the fully equipped, state-of-the-art Computer Education Center. Emphasis is placed on the students' participation in a wide array of activities designed to provide exposure to and interaction with top businesses and the people who are industry leaders in the students' chosen fields. Upon graduation, students have the option of either going directly into the workforce to obtain full-time position in their chosen careers or continuing their education at other collegiate institutions.

Off-Campus Programs

Weeklong study tours to New York City and Paris are offered to students in the fashion merchandising and fashion design programs.

Costs

Tuition for the 1996–97 academic year ranges from $9425 to $13,500, depending on the major. Supervised apartment residences cost $2970 per academic year. Each apartment unit is equipped with a full kitchen; no meal plans are offered.

Financial Aid

International Fine Arts College participates in the Federal Pell Grant, Federal Supplemental Educational Opportunity Grant (FSEOG), Florida Student Assistance Grant (FSAG), Federal Perkins Loan, Federal Stafford Student Loan, and Federal PLUS loan Programs. The College also participates in the AMS Fund Management Program, which allows parents and/or students to pay all or any portion of the tuition (exclusive of the $300 tuition deposit) in twelve equal monthly installments with no interest charges. In addition, the College provides its own institutional aid programs, including achievement scholarships, department assistant scholarships, and loans. To be considered for aid, students must submit the institution's financial aid application and additional required documentation. Financial aid is disbursed on a first-come, first-served basis. Approximately 70 percent of the College's students from the United States received financial aid during the 1995–96 school year.

Faculty

Currently, there are 43 full-time and part-time faculty members teaching at the College. All are experienced professionals actively involved in the subject matter they teach. Many have achieved regional and national recognition for their outstanding contributions in their fields. Faculty members are active in advising and counseling students, providing career planning and placement assistance, and supporting and attending student functions.

Student Body Profile

Enrollment for the 1995–96 academic year was 665. Most freshmen are recent high school graduates; the average student is 18 to 22 years old. Approximately 25 percent of the students enrolled at the College are from countries other than the United States. Some of the geographic areas represented are Canada, the Bahamas, the West Indies, Central and South America, Korea, Japan, Thailand, the Republic of Singapore, India, Australia, the Middle East, Africa, and Europe. Nearly 50 percent of the students are from Florida; the remaining 25 percent are from other states within the United States. Elements important to College life at International Fine Arts College are meeting and knowing students from other cultures and learning about different sections of the country and the world.

Approximately 95 percent of the freshmen who come from outside the Miami area reside in the College residences. Spacious, College-owned waterfront apartments are located a few blocks from the College. The Chateau and the Villa feature air-conditioned, carpeted one-bedroom apartments with a private bath and two-bedroom apartments with two private baths. Each apartment has its own self-contained kitchen, dining area, and living room. Students share laundry facilities and swimming pools and other recreation areas. Resident house parents and resident advisers provide care and supervision. Students may request a specific residence and/or a specific roommate. Compatibility surveys are sent to incoming freshmen, and an effort is made to assign students to apartments with others who have expressed similar interests and lifestyles. Applications for housing assignments should be made far in advance of the date of matriculation.

Student Activities

Students lead very active social lives and are encouraged to take advantage of the many exciting College-sponsored events, such as the President's Continental Breakfast and Boat Cruise, trips to Disney World's Magic Kingdom or Epcot Center, the annual Hawaiian Luau and Pool Party, various dances and beach parties, and free movie nights at the residences. Student clubs and organizations include the Students Government Association (SGA), the Internationalites Dance Group, the Caribbean Students Association, and Delta Epsilon Chi, the collegiate affiliate of DECA (a national marketing and management club).

Facilities and Resources

The College is housed within a museum-like building that is named on the National Register of Historic Places. This grand structure provides a comfortable, intimate atmosphere in which students come together to learn, to create, and to succeed. The College's many facilities reflect its desire to stay in touch with the needs of the contemporary students. Amidst the marble-floored ballroom, high ceilings, and stately chandeliers are modern, comfortable drafting tables and chairs, state-of-the-art computers with high-resolution color-graphics monitors and color printers, and additional facilities. The high-end hardware and software used in the computer center are the same equipment used in the worlds of computer animation, digital audio/video, and electronic publishing/commercial art today. The College's extensive library collection contains texts, periodicals, and other published materials related to the varied aspects of fashion, interior design, computer graphics, and visual arts. In addition, International Fine Arts College is a member of the Southeast Florida Library Information Network (SEFLIN). Through this consortium, students are given the privilege of using the library resources and facilities of the fifteen local member colleges and universities.

Location

Miami has been described as the "Magic City," the "Gateway to Latin America and the World," and the "City of the Future." A sophisticated metropolitan area, Miami is a leading center of culture and the arts. International Fine Arts College overlooks the sparkling waters of Biscayne Bay and is close to South Beach and the Art Deco District. A superb Metro-Transit System (including the Metrorail and Metromover) gives students easy access to the bustling downtown area, Miami Beach and other famous Gold Coast beaches, the exclusive shops of Bal Harbour, the spirited festivals of Coconut Grove, Calle Ocho in little Havana, and Miami's own tropical island paradise, Key Biscayne. Cultural facilities, such as the Jackie Gleason Theater of Performing Arts, the Lowe Art Museum, and the Metro-Date Cultural Center, are frequently visited by students both in connection with their studies and in their free time. Recreational facilities, such as Joe Robbie Stadium (home of the Miami Dolphins and Florida Marlins), Miami MetroZoo, Seaquarium, the Orange Bowl, the Miami Arena (home of the Miami Heat and Florida Panthers), and Bayside, downtown Miami's $95-million waterfront shopping and entertainment complex, provide an endless variety of things to do and see.

Admission Requirements

International Fine Arts College seeks to attract students who are interested, enthusiastic, motivated, and who appreciate the educational advantages available in a small, exclusive, private college. The College believes that a high school transcript may not necessarily reflect a student's talents, creativity, and keen interest. Therefore, while the Admissions Committee gives special consideration to applicants who excel in their academic courses as well as in their fashion, design, and art courses, talented students who have difficulty in subjects such as mathematics and science are not penalized.

International Fine Arts College has no admissions formula. Each applicant is reviewed individually in light of his or her experience, achievement, and potential for artistic or creative growth.

In order to be considered for acceptance, students must be graduates of an accredited secondary school, or have received a high school equivalency diploma with satisfactory GED scores. Deferred entrance plans are available to applicants who are being considered for conditional acceptance by the College prior to graduation or in their senior year of high school. Transfer students desiring advanced standing must have completed college-level work that is comparable to courses in International's curriculum.

Application and Information

The College uses a rolling admissions policy. There is a $50 nonrefundable application fee. Once the application, fee, and transcripts have been received, they are reviewed by the Admissions Committee, and the student is notified of the decision usually within one to two weeks. Because major emphasis is placed on individualized instruction, classroom space is limited. Students are urged to apply as early as possible. The Enrollment Agreement must be completed and signed by the prospective student and his or her parents in order for the student to be officially enrolled and have a space reserved in the freshman class. A tuition deposit of $300 is required with the Enrollment Agreement. All tuition fees are refunded upon request before the student enters the College, with the exception of a $100 registration fee.

For further information, students may contact:

Office of Admissions
International Fine Arts College
1737 North Bayshore Drive
Miami, Florida 33132
Telephone: 305-995-5000
800-225-9023 (toll-free)
Fax: 305-374-5933

KEYSTONE COLLEGE
LA PLUME, PENNSYLVANIA

The College and Its Mission

Keystone College has a long and distinguished history dating back to 1868 when it was founded as Keystone Academy. In 1934, the College became Keystone Junior College and in 1994 became Keystone College. However, Keystone College's tradition of providing an educational experience of high quality that is characterized by close student-faculty relationships and individualized counseling has never changed. Keystone is accredited by the Middle States Association of Colleges and Schools.

In addition to the academic facilities, the campus complex consists of ten residence halls, an infirmary, and a Campus Center, which houses dining facilities, book shop, a snack bar, a game room, a post office, study lounges, the radio station, the counseling center, and appropriate administrative offices. Four athletic fields, six tennis courts, and a gymnasium provide the facilities necessary for Keystone's extensive physical education programs, which include intercollegiate baseball, basketball, soccer, softball, and volleyball as well as a strong intramural program. There are also numerous social and service organizations on campus. Keystone College encourages its community of students to sample every aspect of their college campus experiences. Opportunities are available for students to develop into well-rounded individuals.

Academic Programs

Keystone offers career-oriented liberal arts–based educational programs leading to **Associate in Arts, Associate in Fine Arts, Associate in Science,** and **Associate in Applied Science** degrees. Students are offered a wide variety of choices for their fields of study, including allied health (preprofessional programs in cytotechnology, medical technology, nursing, occupational therapy, physical therapy, radiological technology), art, business (accounting/taxation, administration, general business, international business, and microcomputer specialist), criminal justice, communications (corporate, journalism/writing, theater/speech, and pre-TV/radio), early childhood education (early intervention, general, and in-home child care), environmental science and forestry (environmental engineering, environmental studies, forestry/resource management, forest technology, landscape architecture, and wood products/construction), hospitality (culinary arts, hotel/convention and restaurant/food service management, and tourism), human resource management, human services, liberal arts, liberal studies, occupational therapist assistant studies (certified), physical therapist assistant studies, and science (biochemistry, biological science, chemistry/business, and food technology).

The College calendar is based on fall and spring semesters of fifteen weeks each; the fall semester ends before the holiday season.

All students enrolled in Associate in Arts degree programs are required to meet a set of common general education requirements (the core curriculum) in addition to the course requirements particular to each program. The core curriculum is intended to provide students with a broad base of general knowledge and the facility to apply the knowledge in a conceptual framework for further learning.

Keystone has established articulation agreements with many four-year institutions to facilitate transfer procedures for those students who wish to continue their education after graduating from Keystone College.

Sixty-five percent of Keystone graduates transfer to four-year colleges and universities. Others enter into rewarding career opportunities.

Credit for Nontraditional Learning Experiences

The College may give credit for demonstrated proficiency in areas related to college-level courses. Sources used to determine such proficiency are College-Level Examination Program (CLEP); Advanced Placement examination (AP); Tech Prep Articulation (TP); and Defense Activity for Nontraditional Education Support (DANTES). A maximum of 32 credit hours may be earned in this nontraditional manner.

Costs

Tuition for 1995–96 was $8200; room and board were $5240. Keystone College is committed to keeping tuition the same for a student's first two years.

Financial Aid

Every freshman should apply for financial aid. Awards are based on need, in a combination of work-study, loans, and grants. The College's financial aid resources include Keystone Grants, Federal Perkins Loans, state guaranteed loans, Federal Work-Study Program awards, Federal Supplemental Educational Opportunity Grants, Federal Pell Grants, state grants, presidential scholarships, trustee scholarships, and leadership awards. Other scholarships and grants are available through Keystone's private endowments. Nearly 76 percent of Keystone students receive some type of financial assistance.

Faculty

Keystone's faculty consists of 89 full- and part-time members, of whom 25 percent hold doctoral degrees. Faculty members and administrators take an active interest in each student's college life.

Student Body Profile

There are nearly 600 men and women enrolled on a full-time basis; an additional 400 students attend part-time through Keystone's unique Weekender and Mid-Week Programs. The student body is composed of both residents and commuters. A large part of Keystone's enrollment is made up of students from Pennsylvania, New York, and New Jersey, but other parts of the United States and many other countries are also represented.

Sixty-five percent of students earning associate degrees transfer to four-year colleges and universities. Thirty-five percent of students earning associate degrees enter the workforce.

Student Activities

The Student Senate is the central executive and legislative student governing body. It serves as a liaison between students and the administration, allocates student activity funds, supervises student elections, and charters and oversees all student clubs and organizations. The Campus Activity Board coordinates and sponsors, in cooperation with the director of campus life, the majority of the campus social events, including dances, coffeehouses, talent shows, speakers, films, and major weekends. The Interhall Council, whose president is an officer of the Student Senate, comprises elected representatives from each residence hall. This group evaluates and recommends changes in the residence halls and promotes and sponsors campus activities. The Commuter Council, whose president is also an officer of the Student Senate, is open to all commuting students and functions as their official voice. It also sponsors social events for commuting students.

Facilities and Resources

Keystone's principal buildings include Harris Hall, one of the oldest buildings on campus. It accommodates classrooms and administrative and faculty offices. Capwell Hall houses classrooms; laboratories; computer facilities for science, engineering, and mathematics; as well as computer labs open to all students. Studios for ceramics, drawing, sculpture, and painting classes are located in the Art Center, with photographic arts and printmaking laboratories available in the recently renovated Ward Hall.

Keystone College's 28,000-square-foot Gambal Athletic Center houses an NCAA standard-size basketball court, a wellness center, a weight-training room, a classroom/conference room, four locker-room areas, and faculty/coaching staff offices. Additional faculty offices are located in the Social and Behavioral Science Building and the Miller Library. The Miller Library currently holds approximately 38,000 volumes and extensive files of periodicals and audiovisual materials, along with the Linder Art Gallery and the Platt Learning Center. The building also contains several classrooms and conference rooms. Additional facilities include the Early Childhood Education Center, the Poinsard Greenhouse, the Astronomical Observatory, and an environmental center which is run by ECOLOGIA.

Location

People find the wooded foothills of northeastern Pennsylvania to be scenic, safe, and peaceful. The area provides a stimulating and enjoyable backdrop for the College. Students enjoy this refreshing environment in which to live and study. Keystone's 270-acre campus is 15 minutes northwest of Scranton on U.S. Routes 6 and 11. Interstate Routes 380, 80, 81, and 84 and the Northeast Extension of the Pennsylvania Turnpike provide easy access to Keystone from all directions. All the facilities of a modern city are available for Keystone students, yet Keystone College is surrounded by small towns and countryside and has the quiet learning atmosphere of a rural campus.

The area has warm weather from May through September, brisk autumn days with brilliant foliage, and snowy winters pleasing to devotees of cold-weather sports who can take advantage of Keystone's location between the Pocono and Endless Mountains. Opportunities for hunting, fishing, swimming, and skiing are abundant.

Admission Requirements

The College considers applicants who meet the following criteria: graduation from an approved secondary school or completion of a GED program, satisfactory scores on the SAT I or ACT, and evidence of potential for successful college achievement.

In special cases in which students do not appear to have performed up to their potential, and there is some doubt as to their ability to perform successfully in college, students may be admitted on a provisional basis upon completion of a personal interview. Students admitted provisionally will be asked to limit their credit level to 16 credits and participate in a special academic reinforcement program. In addition, to meet the above criteria, all traditional students are encouraged to visit the campus for a personal interview, which may include meeting with a faculty member from the candidate's area of interest. The interview is usually held on the campus. However, an interview with an approved representative of Keystone College may be arranged in the home of the student or at some other mutually convenient location.

Keystone provides an opportunity through its early admission program for a student to be enrolled as a college freshman after his or her junior year of high school. The program is designed for students who desire a college education and who seek challenge in their academic work. To qualify, an applicant must rank high in his or her high school class, have a favorable recommendation from his or her principal or guidance counselor, and equal or surpass minimum scores set by the admission committee on either the SAT I or ACT. Generally, the student's high school will award a high school diploma upon successful completion of either the freshman year at Keystone College or specific course requirements.

Application and Information

All applications are processed on a rolling admission plan. Notification is generally given within three weeks after all credentials have been received. To be considered for admission, a candidate must submit official transcripts of all high school studies, SAT I or ACT scores, and a $25 application fee. In addition, letters of recommendation and a campus interview are highly recommended.

For more information, students should contact:

Office of Admissions
Keystone College
College Avenue
P.O. Box 50
La Plume, Pennsylvania 18440-0200

Telephone: 717–945–5141
800–824–2764 (toll-free)
Fax: 717–945–7916

Students at Keystone College.

Peterson's Guide to Two-Year Colleges 1997

LASELL COLLEGE
NEWTON, MASSACHUSETTS

The College and Its Mission
Founded in 1851, Lasell College, a private college for women, offers associate and bachelor's degree programs. Predominately a residential college, Lasell seeks to provide its 687 students with the experience of living and learning in a community organized around a central educational purpose that Lasell calls "connected" learning. In connected learning, the ideas that students learn in the classroom are reinforced when they are practiced and tested at on-campus training labs and through internships throughout Boston, New England, and the world. Special attention is given to the many opportunities available in the Greater Boston area. Resident students may choose to live in Victorian houses or modern residence halls. Each residence hall plans its own activities and participates in all-College programs. Resident staff members are on hand to provide support when necessary. Special emphasis is placed on the advantage of the College being a close-knit community of women who live, work, and learn together. Lasell College is accredited by the New England Association of Schools and Colleges.

Academic Programs
Candidates earn an associate degree upon successful completion of at least 63 semester hours of academic and technical work. Students then continue and complete between 123 and 128 semester hours to earn a bachelor's degree. Lasell College has selected a primarily integrative approach to a Core Curriculum. Educational research supported by the faculty's experience indicates that the integration of general education skills into all classes will ultimately prove to be effective. Integrative components that are essential parts of the College's Core include a balanced curriculum, written communication, oral communication, critical reasoning, ethical development, quantitative reasoning, and information literacy.

Associate Degree Programs
Lasell College offers **Associate in Arts** degree programs in art, human services, liberal arts, and open studies. **Associate in Science** degree programs are offered in accounting, business management, early childhood education, fashion design, fashion merchandising, health sciences, interior design, marketing, nursing, occupational therapist assistant studies, physical therapist assistant studies, and travel and tourism management.

Honors Program
Lasell College's Honors Program is dedicated to promoting women's growth and development through challenging opportunities provided in students' professional, social, and personal roles. Through guided reflection and analysis, students are encouraged to recognize, enjoy, and appreciate their achievements.

Special Programs and Services
The GATE Program assists students in making a successful transition to college. Students in the GATE Program have the option of enrolling in a lighter course schedule for their first semester. The program does allow students to take the required courses for their major and through academic support services enhance their planning and study skills. Lasell College provides students with the opportunity to earn a minor in women's studies, while simultaneously pursuing a degree in another field. This course of study provides students with the opportunity to develop an understanding and appreciation of their lives as women. Service learning is coordinated through the Center for Women in Public Service and engages a growing number of students each year. Through the integration of services into the curriculum of many courses, Lasell strengthens experiential education by nurturing women's intellectual development and promoting a greater appreciation for the complexities of our society. In 1996, more than 125 Lasell students provided services to more than 1,000 families, working in homeless shelters, tutoring children, repairing the houses of the rural poor in West Virginia, working with children with HIV/AIDS at summer camp and teaching in literacy programs.

Off-Campus Programs
Lasell provides several opportunities for students to gain experience by studying abroad. Lasell students have participated in study-abroad programs in London, Australia, and Japan.

Costs
For the 1996–97 academic year, tuition for full time students is $12,700; room and board charges are $6425; and comprehensive fees are $575.

Financial Aid
Over 88 percent of the students at Lasell receive some form of financial aid. Programs include Lasell grants, Federal Pell Grants, Federal Supplemental Educational Opportunity Grants, Federal Perkins Loans, Federal Stafford Student Loans, Federal Work-Study awards, state scholarships, and Lasell alumnae scholarships. Lasell uses the Free Application for Federal Student Aid (FAFSA) to determine eligibility for federal programs and the Lasell Form to determine a student's eligibility for Lasell scholarship programs. Applicants for aid who wish to enroll in September should mail the FAFSA to the appropriate processing centers as soon as possible after January 1. In 1995–96, the average financial aid package, including loans, grants, and work-study, totaled $11,000.

Faculty
Lasell has a total of 138 faculty members (47 full-time, 91 part-time), many of whom are practicing professionals in their respective fields and bring their experience to the classroom. The student-faculty ratio is 10:1. All full-time faculty members act as academic advisers. Faculty members serve as role models for success, and particular emphasis is placed on their availability for individual and group conferences.

Student Body Profile
Lasell College has a current enrollment of 687 students, with twenty-three states and seven countries being represented. International students represent 6 percent of the total enrollment. Sixteen percent of the enrolled students represent a minority group. The average age of the Lasell student population is 20, although 24 percent of the students are 25 or older. Seventy-five percent of all entering freshmen complete an associate degree within 2 years of study. Of those who graduate with an associate degree, 87 percent continue in a bachelor's degree program at Lasell or another institution. Seventy-two percent of the 1995 graduating class received an associate degree and, on average, 90 percent find jobs within one year.

Student Activities
Lasell students become involved in a variety of campus organizations, including Umoja-Nia (a multicultural organization), the women-in-business club, the student newspaper, The Lasell Crier, the Lasell Community Players and the Commuter Club. Annual events include River Day, the Commencement Ball, and the Torchlight Parade.

Sports
Students participating in Lasell's Athletic Program enjoy NCAA Division III competition and team spirit. Lasell competes in soccer, softball, basketball, and volleyball. In September 1996, the College celebrates the opening of a Recreation Center that will

feature an indoor running track, two volleyball courts, and one basketball court, as well as a fully equipped exercise/weight room and a dance/aerobics studio.

Facilities and Resources

Advisement/Counseling
Each student is assigned to a full-time faculty member who acts as their academic adviser. The adviser assists in selecting classes, arranging a course schedule, and identifying resources to meet specific interests. Advisers and students meet at least twice a year.

Career Planning/Placement Offices
The Career Services Office assists students in exploring career and major options, as well as job opportunities. Interest testing and individual counseling are available to provide information helpful in choosing a major or planning a career. Workshops on résumé writing, job hunting, and interviewing are also available. This office maintains a library of reference materials on job hunting, career possibilities, and employment opportunities. The office sponsors annual on-campus job fairs that bring over 90 employers to campus each year.

Library and Audiovisual Services
The Jessie S. Brennan Library, a modern computerized library, contains more than 50,000 volumes, more than 400 periodical subscriptions, and a large record and video cassette collection. As a member of the Minuteman Library Network, a consortium of over 24 libraries, students and faculty members have easy access to an additional 2 million books and materials using the on-line computer catalog. Many more materials are available through other computer systems in the library.

The Academic Computer Center, a College-wide facility, offers courses and workshops in word-processing, database management, spreadsheets, and desktop publishing. The Computer Center consists of the following four labs: a business application lab, a computer-aided design lab, a writing lab, and a travel and tourism lab. Over 60 computers are available for student use. The Academic Computer Center is open six days a week and five evenings. In September 1996, campuswide networking will be completed, giving students access to e-mail and the Internet. In addition, students may select a residence hall that is equipped with cable television, phone, and personal computer access to the College Network, Library, and Internet. The Learning Center assists students with academic support through free tutorial services on a one-to-one basis, or small group tutorial sessions in the areas of reading, writing, study skills, mathematics, science, and accounting. The Center also conducts workshops and study groups throughout the academic year. The Learning Center is staffed by faculty members and learning instructors. The Health Center is staffed by a nurse and a nurse practitioner. All students are entitled to various services, including consultations with the professional medical staff and ordinary medications. Counseling staff members, including a psychologist, are available for help in special times of need and for various workshops. Students are encouraged to participate in group sessions, workshops, or individual counseling when needed.

Location
The College's 50-acre campus is located in the village of Auburndale, in the suburban city of Newton, 8 miles west of downtown Boston. The campus is 1½ miles from Massachusetts Route 128 at the junction with the Massachusetts Turnpike. Trains, buses, the rapid transit (MBTA), and local taxis provide convenient access to Boston. Students experience both the advantages of a large metropolitan area and the charm and vitality of life in a small New England community. Social and cultural attractions are geared towards the large student population of the area.

Admission Requirements
Applicants are evaluated on the basis of their academic achievement and overall initiative. A high school transcript and letter of recommendation are required of all applicants. SAT I scores are recommended. Prospective students are urged to visit the Lasell campus for a tour and an interview. Appointments may be scheduled Monday through Friday and Saturdays during the academic year by calling the Admission Office. Several open houses and overnight programs are scheduled throughout the year so that prospective students may have an in-depth visit at Lasell. Candidates for admission into the Nursing and Physical Therapist Assistant Programs must have, as a minimum, successfully completed two years of high school math, preferably algebra and geometry, and one year of biology with a lab, with a grade of C or better. Nursing candidates must also successfully complete chemistry with a lab and submit their SAT I scores. Students may earn credit by examination in certain academic subjects through the College-Level Examination Program (CLEP) of the College Entrance Examination Board. CLEP credits are considered transfer credits.

Application and Information
Candidates for admission should submit an application and a $25 fee, a high school transcript, and a letter of recommendation. Lasell has a rolling admission policy, and an applicant will receive a decision shortly after her application has been completed. International students seeking admission should forward an applicant with an academic transcript, one letter of recommendation, and TOEFL scores. Transfer applicants must submit high school and college transcripts and a letter of recommendation.

For further information, students should contact:

Adrienne Franciosi
Director of Admission
Lasell College
1844 Commonwealth Avenue
Newton, Massachusetts 02166

Telephone: 617-243-2225
Fax: 617-243-2326

Lasell's theory of connected learning gives students the opportunity to immediately apply what they have learned in the classroom.

Peterson's Guide to Two-Year Colleges 1997

LINCOLN COLLEGE
LINCOLN, ILLINOIS

The College and Its Mission

The mission of Lincoln College is to assist each student in the development and achievement of personal and educational goals and to ensure that its degree recipients are liberally educated and personally and academically prepared to succeed in four-year colleges. Lincoln College is an excellent beginning for those students with a 15-21 ACT score who desire a residential experience in a supportive atmosphere. Lincoln College has a solid reputation for a high percentage/retention of students who transfer to four-year institutions.

Academic Programs

Associate Degree Programs The majority of students graduate with an **Associate in Arts** degree. This is designed to provide the student with a liberal grounding in the fundamental areas of human knowledge and allow elective selection of courses of general interest or pre-major preparation. This degree is transfer-oriented and fulfills the general education requirements of most four-year colleges and universities nationwide.

A variety of courses and scholarships exist in the performing arts arena. Subjects include dance, music-vocal, music-instrumental, theater, technical theater, visual arts, broadcasting, creative writing, photography, speech and music recording.

Costs

Costs for the 1996–97 academic year include tuition ($8950), room and board ($4150), and fees ($430). Textbooks and supplies are estimated at $350.

Financial Aid

Financial assistance is generally determined by the need of the applicant, along with the availability of funds from federal, state, institutional, and private sources. Lincoln College considers the needs of each individual applicant in creating the financial package. Scholarships are awarded for academic, fine arts, and athletic excellence.

Faculty

The majority of Lincoln College faculty members are full-time. They are directly involved in instruction, advising, and counseling. Of full-time faculty members, 100 percent hold advanced degrees. The student-faculty ratio is 14:1.

Student Body Profile

Twelve different states and five other countries are represented through the Lincoln campus student body. Approximately 88 percent of students are full-time and reside on campus. The average age of the student body is 18.5. Approximately 89 percent of Lincoln College graduates enter immediately into four-year institutions.

Student Activities

Sports Varsity sports for women include basketball, softball, golf, cheerleading, swimming/diving, volleyball, soccer, tennis, and athletic training/management. Varsity sports for men include baseball, basketball, golf, soccer, swimming/diving, wrestling, and athletic training/management.

Facilities and Resources

Lincoln College was established in 1865 and since that time has grown into a 38-acre campus with seven instructional buildings, a library, a swimming pool, a gymnasium, a performing arts center, a student center, two modern computer centers, an art gallery and studio, the Lincoln Museum and Museum of Presidents, administrative offices, a dance studio, a radio station, five residential halls (with a sixth to be constructed), a bookstore, a post office, softball and baseball diamonds, a soccer field, several intramural fields, a weight training center, tennis courts, and several supporting physical plant structures.

The original structure of Lincoln College, University Hall, has been in continuous use since 1866. For both its historic ties to Abraham Lincoln and its Italianate Victorian style of architecture, University Hall is listed on the National Registry of Historical Sites and Places.

Lincoln College is well established in its commitment to a supportive environment. Many programs are designed to assist the student both academically and socially. A very personal approach to education includes the residential component, outstanding faculty and advising, tutorial services, enriched classes, detailed orientation, academic tracking, and a campuswide commitment to student achievement.

Location

The city of Lincoln (population 19,000) is located in the geographic center of Illinois. The city is the hub of six major urban areas: Springfield, Decatur, Bloomington-Normal, Champaign-Urbana, Pekin, and Peoria. There are two airports within an hour's drive, and daily Amtrak service to Chicago and St. Louis is available. The College is located directly off of Interstate 55.

Admission Requirements

For freshman students, acceptance to Lincoln College is based on high school record, standardized test scores, a personal interview, and letters of recommendation. Students with an ACT composite score of 17 or better may be admitted without restriction. Those with an ACT composite score of 16 or lower may be admitted on probationary status. All students entering Lincoln College on probation are required to attend and successfully complete the Academic Development Seminar, which occurs one week prior to the fall semester. Students who are transferring to Lincoln College from another college or university may enter the College at the beginning of any semester. If they were on probation at the previous institution and/or maintained less than a 2.0 GPA (on a 4.0 scale), they may be admitted to Lincoln College on probation as well. Students for whom English is a second language must take the TOEFL examination and have their scores sent to Lincoln College. Any international student with a minimum score of 480 on the Test of English as a Foreign Language (TOEFL) will be granted admission to Lincoln College. Students whose scores are below 480 may be granted conditional acceptance if space is available.

Application and Information

Applications are accepted contingent on the availability of housing. Freshmen are encouraged to apply before August 1. Individuals interested in Lincoln College should contact:

Lincoln College Admissions
300 Keokuk
Lincoln, Illinois 62656

Telephone: 217-732-3155
800-569-0556 (toll-free)
Fax: 217-732-8859

Lincoln College students outside University Hall.

LINCOLN COLLEGE AT NORMAL
NORMAL, ILLINOIS

The College and Its Mission

Lincoln College, a private two-year residential college, has been offering students the opportunity to study and succeed in a highly supportive environment since 1865. Accredited by the North Central Association, Lincoln offers Associate in Arts and Associate in Science degrees.

The mission of Lincoln College is to assist each student in the development and achievement of personal and educational goals and to ensure that degree recipients are liberally educated and personally and academically prepared to succeed in four-year colleges and/or careers. The College is an excellent beginning for those students with a 15–21 ACT score who desire a residential experience in a supportive atmosphere.

Lincoln College has a national reputation for academic achievement, and the College's graduates have continued their studies at more than 200 different four-year colleges and universities in the last decade. Small class sizes, outstanding faculty advisement, free professional tutoring, and a residential experience result in approximately 89 percent of Lincoln College graduates entering immediately into four-year institutions.

Lincoln College at Normal was opened in 1979 as an extension of Lincoln College in Lincoln, Illinois. Today, Lincoln College at Normal has a new modern facility with classrooms, laboratories, and administrative offices. In addition, the College will be constructing a new academic building as well as a new student residence facility on the campus to be in place for the 1996–97 school year. Coexisting in the Bloomington/Normal, Illinois, area with a major state university as well as a private four-year college, Lincoln College at Normal offers students the excitement and diversity of a large university community while still preserving the benefits of a small college atmosphere.

Academic Programs

The college is on a two-semester schedule, with fall and spring components. A limited number of classes are also offered in the summer.

Associate Degree Programs The majority of the College's students graduate with an **Associate in Arts** degree. This is designed to provide the student with a liberal grounding in the fundamental areas of human knowledge and allow a variety of elective selection of courses of general interest or pre-major preparation. This degree is transfer oriented and fulfills the general education requirements of most four-year colleges and universities nationwide. Typical pre-major interests include American studies, art, biology, business administration, chemistry/physics, criminal justice, education, English/literature, environmental science, history/political science, law enforcement, mathematics, media/journalism, music, philosophy and religion, physical education, prenursing, psychology, sociology, speech and theater. The College also offers **Associate in Applied Science** degrees in law enforcement, legal assisting, legal secretarial science, medical secretarial science, office technology, small business administration, securities and investing, and travel/tourism.

Certificate and Diploma Programs These programs are typically completed in one year and include clerical training, legal transcription, managerial training, medical transcription, travel/tourism, and word processing.

Costs

Costs for the 1996–97 academic year include tuition, $8950; room and board, $4150; and fees, $430. Textbooks and supplies are estimated at $350.

Financial Aid

Approximately 82 percent of students at Lincoln College at Normal benefit from some type of financial aid each year. Financial assistance is generally determined by the need of the applicant (from the Free Application for Federal Student Aid) along with the availability of funds from federal, state, institutional, and private sources. Lincoln College considers the needs of each individual applicant in creating the financial aid package. Scholarships are awarded for academic, fine arts, and athletic excellence.

Faculty

The majority of Lincoln College faculty are full-time. Their direct involvement with students includes instruction, advisement, and counseling. Of the full-time faculty, 100 percent hold advanced degrees. The student-faculty ratio is 14:1, and the average class size is 16.

Student Body Profile

Six different states and three other countries are represented through the approximately 500 students enrolled at Lincoln College at Normal. Approximately 70 percent of students are full-time and reside in Lincoln College housing. The average age of the student body is 19. Typically, 75 percent of students graduate on time with a two-year degree, with 89 percent of those students transferring successfully to a four-year university the following semester.

Student Activities

The Student Advisory Committee works to get the student body involved in College and extracurricular activities. This committee also meets with faculty and administration to discuss academic and social policies. Student activities include intramural sports, outdoor activities (camping, canoeing, etc.), music concerts, shopping trips, and athletic events.

Opportunities for course work and scholarships exist in the visual arts at Normal, Illinois. Other areas in the fine arts can be accessed through the campus in Lincoln, and these offerings include broadcasting, dance, music (instrumental and vocal), photography, technical theater, and theater.

Sports Opportunities in varsity athletics are available through the campus in Lincoln, Illinois. Sports for women include athletic training/management, basketball, golf, soccer, softball, swimming/diving, tennis, and volleyball. Sports for men include athletic training/management, baseball, basketball, golf, soccer, swimming/diving, and wrestling.

Facilities and Resources

For the 1996–97 academic year, the College will consist of two modern academic facilities with classrooms, laboratories, an art center, a state-of-the-art lecture hall, and administrative offices. During the 1996–97 academic year, Lincoln College at Normal will be opening new residential housing units on campus. These units will be the primary housing option for students, with Lincoln College–approved off-campus apartment housing available for some students.

Advisement/Counseling Trained full-time faculty members assist students in selecting courses and programs of study to satisfy their educational objectives. The Learning Center provides free professional tutoring to all students in any subject. This takes the form of one-on-one sessions as well as on-line tutorial programs. Students can also make up assignments and do extra credit projects under the direction of the Learning Center personnel.

Dining/Health/Recreation Services Lincoln College students at the campus in Normal may elect to take a number of services from the programs at Illinois State University in Normal. These offerings are available on an a la carte basis and can be arranged with the assistance of the Lincoln College Housing personnel.

Library and Audiovisual Services Lincoln College students at the campus in Normal have library access to the Illinois State University library in Normal, with a combined book collection of 1,659,983 volumes. CD-ROM and on-line databases are available for student use. The College offers three state-of-the-art computer labs for classroom, homework, and project use. These labs have a total of more than 70 computers for the students' use, most with Internet access.

Location

Lincoln College at Normal is located in the city of Normal near the geographic center of Illinois, and with the adjoining city of Bloomington, has a population of over 100,000. The College is situated on 10 acres of land approximately two blocks west of Route 51 (North Main Street) in north Normal, just off Interstate 55. The Bloomington/Normal area is served by three interstate highways, I-55, I-74, and I-39. It also features an airport, bus service, and Amtrak service. Driving time from Chicago and St. Louis is 2½ hours.

Admission Requirements

Acceptance to Lincoln College at Normal is based on a student's high school record, standardized test scores, a personal interview, and letters of recommendation. Students with a minimum ACT composite score of 17 may be admitted without restriction. Those with an ACT composite score of 16 or less may be admitted on provisional status, based on the decision of the Admissions Committee. Students who are transferring to Lincoln College at Normal from another college or university may enter the College at the beginning of any semester. If they have been on academic probation at the previous institution and/or have maintained less than a 2.0 GPA (on a 4.0 scale), they may be admitted to the College on provisional status as well. Students for whom English is a second language must take the TOEFL examination and have their scores sent to the College. Any international student with a minimum score of 480 on the TOEFL will be granted admission to Lincoln College. Students whose scores are below 480 may be granted conditional acceptance if space is available.

Application and Information

Applications are accepted contingent on the availability of housing. Freshmen are encouraged to apply before August 1. Individuals interested in Lincoln College at Normal should contact:

Lincoln College Admissions
715 West Raab Road
Normal, Illinois 61761
Telephone: 309-452-0500
          800-569-0558 (toll-free)
Fax: 309-454-5652

Students enjoy the residential life at Lincoln College at Normal.

Peterson's Guide to Two-Year Colleges 1997

MacCORMAC COLLEGE
CHICAGO AND ELMHURST, ILLINOIS

The College and Its Mission

MacCormac College is an academic community that prepares students to live and work more successfully in a diverse and technologically complex society. To achieve this educational mission, the College provides for the study and exchange of ideas and the acquisition of professional skills so that students think and communicate with greater awareness of themselves and others, gain valuable tools for employment, and develop resources for future opportunities. Serving the individual, the community, and the marketplace, MacCormac College aims to set the standard of excellence in career-oriented education that is both academically and technologically progressive within a personal, supportive environment.

Students who choose MacCormac can expect to pursue academic programs that will lead to good paying jobs upon graduation. They will study in a small environment on either a city or suburban campus where faculty members are able to give attention to students and their needs, and where job placement is of utmost importance. The faculty-student ratio at MacCormac is 1:16. The schedule of classes is planned so that a number of hours each day can be left free for part-time employment. A student generally has either a morning or an afternoon class schedule.

MacCormac College is a private, coeducational, nonprofit nonsectarian institution established to provide educational programs for qualified students preparing for both a career and to further their education. The College is accredited by the Commission on Institutions of Higher Education of the North Central Association of Colleges and Schools. The College grants an associate degree in seven areas and diplomas or certificates in five areas of business, law, travel, and technology.

MacCormac's history dates to 1904 when the College was founded by Dr. Morton C. and Mrs. Mary E. MacCormac, both leaders in business education. The College has successfully maintained its leadership role with programs that include the oldest court reporting program in the United States and the oldest private paralegal studies major in Illinois.

Academic Programs

MacCormac College prepares students for careers in business, law, travel, and technological careers. All of the two-year programs have been developed to give students the academic and technological tools needed for the workplace and to continue their education. With the exception of the court reporting program, all of the majors have a basic core requirement consisting of 48 credits for the first year. In the second year of study, students concentrate in one of the seven major areas to complete a degree with 96 credit hours. The Day Division operates on a quarter system. Students may enter in the autumn, winter, or spring quarter. Court reporting students attend four quarters per year, while students in other majors attend three quarters per year. MacCormac College also has a part-time program in court reporting on both campuses that can be taken two evenings per week and on Saturday mornings. Students in this program may begin in either the autumn or spring semester. On the Elmhurst campus, MacCormac's Evening Division also has an evening paralegal studies program two evenings per week. The Evening Division operates on the semester system. Students may enter the Evening Division paralegal studies program in the autumn, spring, or summer semester.

Associate Degree Programs MacCormac offers the following degree programs: the **Associate in Business Administration** degree in accounting, international business, and tourism management; the **Associate in Paralegal Studies** degree; the **Associate in Applied Science** degree in court reporting, legal secretarial studies, and office systems management.

Certificate and Diploma Programs The College's nine-month diploma programs are offered in computer software specialist studies, executive assistant studies, medical transcriptionist studies, and travel consultant studies. Graduates of the College's part-time court reporting program also earn a diploma. Graduates of the College's evening paralegal studies program earn a paralegal certificate.

Internship and Co-op Programs MacCormac students perform an internship as part of their academic program in the following majors: court reporting, legal secretarial studies, office systems management, computer software specialist studies, executive assistant studies, and medical transcriptionist studies. The internship is performed in the final quarter. Students receive credit for this experience, participate in on-campus seminars, and maintain a journal of their internship experience.

Special Programs and Services MacCormac's English as a second language (ESL) division provides intensive English instruction designed to prepare students whose first language is not English for the pursuit of a college program of study. MacCormac accepts transfer credits from regionally accredited two-year and four-year colleges in both its Day and Evening Divisions.

Continuing Education Unit Certificate Programs Through its Continuing Education Division, the College offers CE units for those taking computer courses and for court reporters taking speedbuilding classes.

Personal Enrichment/Noncredit Programs Noncredit programs are available in a variety of skill development areas and for those seeking retraining or relicensing.

Credit for Nontraditional Learning Experiences

Credit may be given by the College for proficiency in areas related to college-level courses that can be demonstrated. Sources used to determine such proficiency are the College-Level Examination Program (CLEP); Advanced Placement Examination (AP); Defense Activity for Nontraditional Education Support (DANTES); United States Armed Forces Institute (USAFI); and the Office of Education Credit and Credentials of the American Council on Education (ACE). A maximum of 48 credit hours may be earned in this nontraditional manner.

Costs

MacCormac has one of the lowest tuition costs of any private college in Illinois. For the 1996–97 academic year, tuition for students in the Day Division who are full-time is $2500 per quarter. Students in the Evening Division paralegal studies program pay $425 per course per semester. Students in the part-time court reporting program pay $425 per course per semester for the first three quarters and $1875 per semester with the addition of Saturday class after the first year.

Financial Aid

All financial assistance is awarded to students without regard to age, gender, race, creed, national origin, sexual orientation, or disability. Seventy-five percent of students at MacCormac receive some form of financial assistance in the form of grants, loans, or scholarships. Available assistance includes Federal Pell Grants, Federal Supplemental Educational Opportunity Grants, Monetary Award Program (MAP), Federal Family Educational Loan Program for student and parent, Federal Direct Loan for student and parent, Federal Work-Study, and Federal Perkins Loans. In addition, the College offers no-need scholarships on the basis of national standardized tests scores, class rank, or a combination of both. Special scholarships are available for court reporters in their second year, and for students who are members of secondary school business clubs.

Faculty

A college's strength is derived from the quality of its faculty members. MacCormac's instructional staff are seasoned professionals; they are practitioners rather than being research oriented. They pride themselves on their ability to empathize with their students and instill in them a commitment to excellence. There are 25 full-time and 18 part-time faculty members. Of the full-time faculty members, 60 percent hold advanced degrees.

Student Body Profile

MacCormac's Day and Evening Divisions currently enroll 559 students. Ninety-three percent find jobs within six months of graduation, and 15 to 20 percent of MacCormac's graduates continue their education. MacCormac College's students form a diversified group that includes those directly out of high school as well as older, nontraditional students. Many are married and have family responsibilities. Most work part-time to help pay for college costs.

Student Activities

Students are encouraged to participate in social activities and become involved in the worthwhile charitable and cultural activities conducted by the student body and also those sponsored by other departments within the College. Phi Theta Kappa, the international honor society of two-year colleges, has chapters on both campuses. A variety of campus activities both entertaining and service-related, are sponsored by SAC, the Student Activities Council. This organization provides students with the opportunity to gain leadership and organizational skills and to offer direction on student activities. Each campus has its own SAC organization and elected officers.

Facilities and Resources

The College provides a full-service library with ample law resources at its Chicago location, and a satellite Law Resource Center at its suburban Elmhurst location. Both campuses have three computer labs well equipped with IBM compatible computers running DOS- and Windows-based software. A full-time director of placement assists students with part-time job placement during school, and placement in full-time positions after graduation. A director of financial aid assists students with financial planning. Academic advising is available through the Office of the Deans of Students and from faculty advisers. An academic assessment coordinator is charged with maintaining academic programs and support services necessary for all students to achieve success at MacCormac.

Location

The **Downtown Chicago Campus** is located at 506 South Wabash Avenue in what is commonly referred to as the "Education District." Students can extend their learning experience by taking advantage of the many cultural and business resources offered by the city. The Downtown campus is readily accessible from all transportation routes. The **West Suburban Campus** is in Elmhurst at 615 North West Avenue and is situated on 10 acres overlooking a city park with ample free parking.

Admission Requirements

Admission to MacCormac College is open to all students who are academically prepared to succeed in their selected program of study. Applicants are considered on their potential for academic success as determined by academic transcripts, GED scores, and ACT or SAT I scores. Admission to the College is made without respect to age, gender, race, creed, national origin, sexual orientation, or disability. Admission to the College follows a policy of rolling admission although qualified, advanced standing students may be accepted for any quarter throughout the year. Early decision and regular admission applicants must submit the College application form and a $20 nonrefundable application fee; the high school transcript of credits from the school last attended; and, for transfer students, transcripts from all colleges attended; and ACT or SAT I scores (ACT preferred).

Prospective students are encouraged to visit the campus. The admissions office is open on weekdays throughout the year from 8:30 a.m. to 4:30 p.m. and on Saturdays by appointment. Tours of the campus are always available during office hours. Those planning a visit are expected to notify the admissions office in advance.

MacCormac offers the choice of an early decision to students who wish to complete their college application process upon completion of their junior year in high school. Early decision applications and supporting academic credentials must be received by the admissions office no later than November 15. Students accepted are required to submit their advance tuition deposit by January 1.

Application and Information

All applicants will receive written notification of decisions made by the Admissions Office. Upon receipt of an offer of admission, candidates are required to pay a $75 nonrefundable tuition deposit which will be credited toward the tuition for their academic year. Court reporting program candidates (a four-quarter sequence) must submit a $100 nonrefundable deposit.

For more information, students should contact:

Director of Admissions
MacCormac College
615 North West Avenue
Elmhurst, Illinois 60126

Telephone: 708-941-1200
Fax: 708-941-0937

Admissions Office
MacCormac College
506 South Wabash Avenue
Chicago, Illinois 60605

Telephone: 312-922-1884
Fax: 312-922-3196

MADISON JUNIOR COLLEGE OF BUSINESS
MADISON, WISCONSIN

The College and Its Mission
Madison Junior College of Business, founded in 1856, is a private, independent, coeducational two-year institution. It provides a career-oriented business education for those who prefer learning in a friendly, caring, small-college atmosphere that fosters close acquaintance with faculty members as well as with other students.

Madison Junior College of Business is the first and oldest college of its type in Wisconsin and the fifth-oldest college of its type in the United States. Its long tradition of successfully preparing men and women for careers in business has established a reputation for excellence.

Academic Programs
The College's programs are offered on a trimester basis. There are two semesters of study during the school year and a full semester of study during the summer. Attendance during the summer is optional. However, by attending the summer semester, a student may complete degree requirements in as few as sixteen consecutive months. Day classes meet between 7:30 a.m. and 12:20 p.m., Monday through Friday. This leaves afternoons, evenings and weekends free for study and part-time employment. Because of this unusual morning-only class schedule for day students, over half of MJCB's full-time students work in part-time positions that provide them with extra income as well as on-the-job experience. Evening classes meet between 5 and 10 p.m., Monday through Thursday, and are intended to accommodate returning students with full-time work and family obligations.

Associate Degree Programs An associate degree is granted upon satisfactory completion of twenty courses (61 to 68 credit hours). Double majors require twenty-five courses. Degree candidates are required to complete a general education core, which consists of 15 credit hours. All other course work taken relates directly to the student's major field of study. Madison Junior College of Business offers programs leading to the **Associate in Applied Science** (A.A.S.) degree in accounting, business, data systems, executive office administration, general business management, legal office administration, medical office administration, and sales and marketing.

Transfer Arrangements While the emphasis of all programs is on preparing graduates for careers, graduates also have the opportunity to transfer to baccalaureate programs in many colleges and universities across the country. Credit of up to one half the student's program may be accepted in transfer from other colleges.

Certificate and Diploma Programs Diploma programs require satisfactory completion of fifteen courses (46 to 49 credit hours). The certificate program requires ten courses (31 credit hours). All course work taken may also apply toward associate degree programs. Diploma programs are offered in bookkeeping clerical, general clerical, and general secretarial studies. A certificate program is offered in stenographic studies.

Costs
Tuition and fees for 1996–97 are $7440, including the cost of all required books and study materials. Room and board costs are estimated at $4650, while travel and miscellaneous expenses are estimated at $1780.

Financial Aid
Financial aid packages consist of loans, grants, and some small scholarships. Grant and loan awards are provided on the basis of need, as established by the Free Application for Federal Student Aid (FAFSA). Scholarships are awarded on the basis of academic accomplishment.

Faculty
The faculty consists of 16 men and women. Instructors are selection the basis of both academic credentials and work experience in the areas in which they instruct. Most members of the faculty hold advanced degrees, professional designations, or both. The student-faculty ratio is approximately 13:1.

Student Body Profile
The typical MJCB student is not married and is between 17 and 25 years of age (although other age groups are represented). About 30 percent of the 150 students have transferred from other colleges, and about 2 percent are international students. Approximately 32 percent of the students are office administration majors, and 68 percent are business administration majors. Surveys of MJCB students have indicated that they particularly like the College because of the effective employment services, the morning-only schedule of classes, the relevant programs offered, the College's reputation and location, the small size of the College and the classes, and the moderate cost.

Student Activities
The Student Senate is made up of 2 representatives from each major and 1 faculty adviser. It sponsors all student social and recreational activities, which consist of participation in city-league softball, basketball and volleyball for both men and women, as well as dances, parties, picnics, outings and other activities. A portion of the tuition paid by each student is set aside for use by the Student Senate to finance these activities, and most of them are free to MJCB students.

Other activities related to particular career interests are available to MJCB students, such as the Collegiate Secretaries International Club. The College has its own USA/France Exchange Program through which MJCB students may travel to France for specially designed cultural and economic tours.

Facilities and Resources
All academic activities are housed in the MJCB building, which is located at the corner of West Washington Avenue and South Henry Street. Built in 1962, the building contains a library, laboratories, lounges, an auditorium, classrooms, and business academic offices. All facilities are accessible to the physically handicapped. College facilities are available for student use between 7 a.m. and 4 p.m., Monday through Friday, and on Saturday morning.

Advisement/Counseling Each MJCB student is assigned to a faculty adviser who works individually with the student in academic planning and provides other guidance and assistance as needed.

Career Planning/Placement Offices Lifetime employment services are available to graduates through the College Employment Office. Typical of the College's employment effectiveness are statistics for last year's graduates, which verify

97 percent placement of all graduates available for placement, with 88 percent of them employed in positions directly related to their academic majors. Brush-up and review privileges are also available for graduates. There is no additional cost to MJCB graduates for either employment services or review privileges.

Library and Audiovisual Services The MJCB Library holds approximately 5,000 books and maintains approximately 170 magazine and periodical subscriptions. In addition, the College has on-line access to the state library system and the public libraries throughout south-central Wisconsin. Students may use on-line information services, and direct Internet access is available.

Location

Madison Junior College of Business is located in Madison, the state capital of Wisconsin. The population of the urban area is about 200,000, of whom about 50,000 are students attending the University of Wisconsin–Madison and other colleges in the area, including a small church-related college, a college of electronics, a college of broadcasting, a local technical college, and MJCB. Although not a large city, Madison has been designated as an All-America City. It provides the sports, cultural, and social activities usually available only in much larger cities. University athletic teams are of year-round interest to the sports enthusiast, as are the activities and contests involving Madison's internationally famous Olympic athletes. Madison's Civic Center provides a central focus for cultural activities, including theater, music, and art. Dane County Memorial Coliseum offers concerts by popular artists as well as skating and sports facilities. Madison's four in-city lakes offer abundant opportunities for outdoor activities. Madison is located just 77 miles west of Milwaukee and 146 miles north of Chicago, either of which may be reached by interstate highway, bus, or airplane.

The MJCB campus is located within two blocks of the Wisconsin State Capitol in the heart of Madison's thriving downtown business, government, and university district. All lines of the Madison Metro Bus System stop within two blocks of the campus. Ample public parking is available for commuters. The campus is within walking distance of shopping, restaurants, housing, and employment opportunities.

Admission Requirements

MJCB is open to men and women regardless of race, color, religion, handicap, national or ethnic origin, or sexual preference. All students are given an equal opportunity to pursue their educational goals through the programs offered. Admission to the College is based on the applicant's academic history, which must include graduation from high school or equivalent credentials. No college entrance examinations are required, although test scores are considered if available.

Application and Information

Admission to MJCB is on a rolling basis. There is no deadline for applications either for admission or for financial aid. Applications for any semester are considered at any time up to the opening day of classes, unless classes are full. Early application is recommended.

For application forms or further information, students should contact:

Director of Student Services
Madison Junior College of Business
31 South Henry Street
Madison, Wisconsin 53703
Telephone: 608-251-6522
800-365-5343 (toll-free in Wisconsin)
Fax: 608-251-6590
E-mail: madjrcoll@aol.com

An aerial view of the Capitol Square downtown area.

MANOR JUNIOR COLLEGE
JENKINTOWN, PENNSYLVANIA

The College and Its Mission

Manor Junior College is a private, coed Catholic college founded in 1947 by the Ukrainian Sisters of Saint Basil the Great. The College is characterized by its dedication to the education, growth, and self-actualization of the whole person through its personalized and nurturing atmosphere. Upon graduation, 40 percent of Manor's students are employed in their chosen fields; the remaining 60 percent of students transfer to four-year institutions to earn baccalaureate degrees. There are 660 full- and part-time students enrolled at Manor. Extracurricular activities include honor societies, men's intercollegiate soccer and basketball, and women's intercollegiate volleyball and basketball, as well as intramural sports, the yearbook, and special interest and cultural clubs.

Manor provides free counseling and tutoring services through an on-campus learning center. Trained counselors are available to assist students on an individual and confidential basis for academic, career, and personal concerns. Upon entering Manor, students are assigned an academic adviser, who provides guidance and support throughout their Manor experience. Transfer counseling is available for students interested in pursuing a four-year degree.

The College's 35-acre campus includes a modern three-story dormitory, a library/administration building, and an academic building that also houses the bookstore, dining hall, an auditorium-like gymnasium, and a student lounge. The Ukrainian Heritage Studies Center and the Manor Dental Health Center are also located on the campus grounds. Manor is accredited by the Middle States Association of Colleges and Schools.

Academic Programs

Manor offers career-oriented, two-year associate degrees, as well as transfer programs for the purpose of pursuing a bachelor's degree. Internships provide theory with practice, enhancing employment opportunities. The liberal arts core ensures mobility and future advancement. Manor offers fourteen programs with twelve majors leading to associate degrees, six certificate programs, one diploma program, and a transfer program through its three divisions: Liberal Arts, Allied Health/Science/Math, and Business.

The Liberal Arts Division offers **Associate in Arts** degrees in early childhood education, psychology, and liberal arts. In addition, the Liberal Arts Division provides a liberal arts and psychology transfer program as well as an elementary education transfer major, early child care major and human services major. The Allied Health/Science/Math Division offers **Associate in Science** degrees in expanded functions dental assisting, dental hygiene, medical laboratory technology, and veterinary technology. This division also includes allied health transfer programs for students who seek preprofessional programs in animal science, diagnostic imaging, general sciences, nursing, occupational therapy, and physical therapy. The Business Division offers **Associate in Science** degrees in accounting; administrative, legal, and medical secretarial studies; business administration; business administration/computer science; court reporting; health-care management; office technology; and paralegal studies. There are certificate programs in administrative, legal, and medical secretarial studies; health-care management; human resources management; and office technology.

Continuing education at Manor supports the nontraditional student by offering part-time day, evening, and summer classes. In addition, the Office of Continuing Education organizes noncredit workshops and seminars throughout the year in response to community needs. The Human Resources Management Certificate is offered through continuing education.

Off-Campus Programs

Externships are incorporated into the academic studies programs. Students earn credits as they gain practical experience under the supervision of professionals in a specific field of study. Externships are offered in the career-oriented programs of study and in some transfer programs.

Manor's affiliation with several area hospitals enables the allied health program student to fulfill clinical requirements at these sites. Students in other programs of study serve externships in law offices, courtrooms, and day-care centers. Manor has 2+2 and 2+3 articulation agreements with major allied health universities.

Credit for Nontraditional Learning Experiences

Manor Junior College awards credit by examination for college-level learning through the College-Level Examination Program (CLEP). If an individual has knowledge of a particular subject area, via job-related experience or through life experience, there are college-level examinations one can take in order to receive college credit for such knowledge. In addition, Manor administers exemption tests for courses not available through CLEP, provided the respective division chairperson and the Academic Dean have received and accepted an application made by the student.

Costs

Tuition for the 1995–96 academic year was $6790 for full-time studies. Part-time study was $176 per credit hour. Students in certain allied health programs paid an additional $294 per year for full-time study or an additional $85 per credit hour for part-time study. On-campus room and board are available for men and women at $3600 a year. There is an additional $600 fee for a private room. Other fees include a $200 general fee per year and a $100 graduation fee.

Financial Aid

Manor offers a number of options to assist students who need financial aid. Approximately 85 percent of Manor students receive aid through state, federal, and institutional grants, scholarships, or work or loan programs. Loans available to students include the Federal Perkins Loan, subsidized and unsubsidized Federal Stafford and Federal Direct Student Loans, and Federal PLUS programs. Federal aid is available through the Federal Pell Grant, the Federal Supplemental Educational Opportunity Grant, and Federal Work-Study programs. Applicants must submit a Manor Junior College Financial Aid Application, an Early Needs Estimator Form, and copies of 1040 income tax forms.

Special Manor scholarships include the following: The Henry Lewandowski Memorial Scholarship, Manor Allied Health Scholarship, Business Scholarship, Basilian Scholarship, Schlar Athlete Award, Liberal Arts Scholarship, St. Basil Scholarship, Wasyl and Josephine Soroka Scholarship, Joseph and Rose Wawriw Scholarship, Mary Wolchanski Scholarship, Elizabeth A. Stalecker Scholarship, and the Eileen Freedman Memorial Scholarship. Eligibility for these scholarships varies. Applicants should check with the admissions office for details.

Faculty

There are 22 full-time and 70 part-time faculty members at Manor. Forty-six percent of the faculty members have master's degrees and 26 percent possess doctorates in their field. Faculty members spend three fourths of their time teaching and the remainder counseling and advising students. The overall faculty-student ratio is 1:8. Small class size allows for personal attention in an environment conducive to learning.

Student Body Profile

Of the approximately 660 full- and part-time students enrolled at Manor, 215 entered the College as full-time freshman students in 1995. Twenty-two percent of that freshman class live in the on-campus residence hall. Twenty-two percent of the 1995 freshman class are minority students and 6.5 percent are international students from Ukraine, Japan, Vietnam, Jamaica, Russia, Poland, Great Britain, and El Salvador.

Student Activities

Manor encourages students to develop leadership skills through active participation in all aspects of college life. A variety of options for extracurricular participation fall under the umbrella of Manor's student services department, including the Student Senate, athletic teams, and clubs. The Student Senate forms an important art of the College community. The Senate, representing the student population, responds to student interests and concerns and acts as a liaison between the administration and the student body. Other extracurricular activities include intercollegiate men's and women's basketball, intercollegiate men's soccer, and intercollegiate women's volleyball. Manor's sports teams compete in the Eastern Pennsylvania Collegiate Conference. Additional extracurricular activities include the honor societies, intramural sports, the yearbook, the Manor Junior College Chorus, and various special interest and cultural clubs. Student services is also responsible for the campus ministry, the counseling center, the residence hall, and the on-campus security force.

Facilities and Resources

The Academic Building (also called Mother of Perpetual Help Hall) includes classrooms, lecture rooms, laboratories, the chapel, the offices of student services, campus ministry, and counseling. The Academic Building is equipped with up-to-date facilities, including biology, chemistry, and clinical laboratories, as well as modern IBM-compatible microsystems network labs. The Learning Center provides professional and student tutors in all College subjects and conducts workshops in study and research skills. Courses in English as a second language are also offered at the center.

The Basileiad Library has the capacity for 60,000 books, periodicals, and journals. The Library includes a reserve room, reading areas, a micromedia room, and stack areas. The current library collection contains 50,000 volumes, including a special law collection, and subscriptions to 206 periodicals and newspapers. The Library also houses the Small Business Resource Center, which helps local businesses with the solutions to everyday problems.

An on-campus community Manor Dental Health Center was established in 1979 as an adjunct to the Expanded Functions Dental Assisting Program. Located on the lower level of St. Josaphat Hall, the center provides students enrolled in the Expanded Function Dental Assisting (EFDA) Program or the Dental Hygiene Program at Manor with training under the direct supervision of faculty dentists. Currently, over 2,000 patients receive care, including the following services: general dentistry, oral hygiene, orthodontics, prosthodontics, endodontics, and cosmetic dentistry. Because Manor Dental Health Center is a teaching facility, the fees charged for services are lower than those charged by private practitioners. Community residents are welcome as patients.

The Ukrainian Heritage Studies Center, located on campus, preserves and promotes Ukrainian heritage, arts, and culture through four areas: academic programs, a museum collection, a library, and archives. Special events, exhibits, workshops, and seminars are offered throughout the year. Each year, the center sponsors the Ukrainian Festival in the fall and Pysanky Expo in the spring. The center is open to the public for tours and educational presentations by appointment.

Location

Manor is located in Jenkintown, Pennsylvania, 15 miles north of center city, Philadelphia. Manor is accessible via public transportation and is located near the Pennsylvania Turnpike, Route 611, U.S. 1, and Route 232. Centers of cultural and historic interest are found in nearby Philadelphia, Valley Forge, and beautiful Bucks County. Manor's suburban campus is within walking distance of a large shopping mall, medical offices, and a township park.

Admission Requirements

Manor is open to qualified applicants of all races, creeds, and national origins. Candidates are required to have a high school diploma or its equivalent. Admission is based on the applicant's scholastic record, test scores, and interviews. The application procedure involves submission of a completed Manor application form, a high school transcript, SAT I or ACT scores (these scores are not required for students over 21 years old), and completion of Manor's entrance/placement test (waived for candidates who hold the baccalaureate degree). Transfer students must submit transcripts of all college work completed. International students must also submit results of the Test of English as a Foreign Language (TOEFL).

Application and Information

Manor has a rolling admission policy. Students may apply for admission in either the fall or the spring semester. Students interested in attending Manor Junior College are invited to visit the campus and meet with admissions staff, faculty members, program directors, and students. Open houses, career days and nights, and classroom visits are scheduled throughout the year. The Admissions Office is open Monday through Friday, 8:30 a.m. to 6 p.m. (Saturday hours may be arranged). Admissions staff members can schedule visits and answer questions concerning admission, careers, programs, special features, and student life. Application forms, program-of-study bulletins, viewbooks, and catalogs may be received by writing to:

I. Jerry Czenstuch
Dean of Admissions
Manor Junior College
700 Fox Chase Road
Jenkintown, Pennsylvania 19046
Telephone: 215-884-2216

Basileiad Library.

MARIA COLLEGE
ALBANY, NEW YORK

The College and Its Mission

Maria College was established in 1958 by the Religious Sisters of Mercy as an independent two-year, degree-granting institution. The College is career oriented and admits both men and women. The current enrollment is 829, about 89 percent are women. It is accredited by the Middle States Association of Colleges and Schools. Located in a quiet corner of the New York State capital, Albany, Maria College concentrates on preparing its students for productive careers in health, education, and business. Nursing graduates are prepared for the state examination for licensure as registered nurses. The occupational therapy assistant and physical therapist assistant programs lead to certification by the state of New York upon graduation. In addition, following an examination, occupational therapy assistants are certified by the American Occupational Therapy Association. The College's Career Planning and Placement Office is responsible for counseling students and alumni on career development, helping students obtain employment upon graduation, and assisting students in the process of transferring to other institutions. With the cooperation of program chairpersons, this office conducts seminars on résumé preparation, interviewing techniques, and the job search. Individual counseling is available. Placement Office records show full employment for Maria College graduates over the past fifteen years.

Academic Programs

Maria College offers the **Associate in Applied Science (A.A.S.)** degree in allied health (nursing, occupational therapy assistant studies, and physical therapist assistant studies), business sciences (accounting, legal assistant studies, and management), and early childhood education. The **Associate in Arts (A.A.)** degree is offered in liberal arts. The **Associate in Science (A.S.)** degree is offered in general studies. Degrees are conferred on students who have completed at least 64 college credits through courses taken at Maria, transfer credit, credit earned through approved proficiency examinations, or life experience credit. Graduates also must complete the College's requirements of 6 credit hours in religious studies/philosophy and 6 credit hours in English. The required liberal arts core consists of 48 credit hours for an A.A., 32 credit hours for an A.S., and 22 credit hours for an A.A.S. An overall quality point average of at least 2.0 (on a 4.0 scale) is also required. In addition to traditional day classes, Maria College's Evening Division offers degree programs in accounting, general studies, liberal arts, management, nursing, and physical therapist assistant studies. For those who are unable to attend during the day and seek programs for enrichment or a career change, credit-free evening courses, seminars, and workshops are also provided. The first Weekend College to be established in northeastern New York is conducted at Maria. This innovative, degree-granting option allows students to complete degree programs in business, early childhood education, general studies, legal assistant studies, liberal arts, and occupational therapy assistant studies by attending classes every other weekend for two years. Students who wish to continue studies toward a baccalaureate degree may complete the first two years of study at Maria and then transfer to a senior institution for the next two years. To facilitate such a transfer, Maria College has articulation agreements with a wide range of senior colleges. For nursing students, for example, articulation agreements exist with the baccalaureate nursing program at Russell Sage College in Troy, New York, and with the College of Health Related Professions of the State University of New York Health Science Center at Syracuse.

Off-Campus Programs

Clinical laboratory experiences for nursing students are provided at Albany Medical Center, St. Peter's Hospital, and St. Margaret Mary Home. Students in the occupational therapy assistant and physical therapist assistant programs receive clinical training in hospitals, developmental centers, nursing homes, and rehabilitation centers in New York State and at selected sites in other states. Senior students in the early childhood education program are trained in a variety of outside field agencies, which may include day-care centers, home-based centers, Head Start, and centers providing programs for infants and toddlers or for children with special needs.

Credit for Nontraditional Learning Experiences

Maria College recognizes college-level courses taken by students while they are still attending high school. Advanced Placement scores of 5, 4, and 3 normally earn college credit. Maria College grants credit for the Regents College Examinations and the College-Level Examination Programs (CLEP) when these examinations cover comparable material. Proficiency credits are treated as transfer credits. Maria College recognizes that certain adult students may have gained valuable knowledge in their lives from diverse experiences. Some of this learning may qualify as college-level course work. Students requesting credit will be required to substantiate this learning experience. Total credit obtained through life experience is limited to a maximum of 16 nonduplicative transfer credits applied toward a degree, 25 percent of the required 64 credits. The Nursing Program offers advanced placement for licensed practical nurses who may challenge seven credits in nursing. A series of classes is held twice a year to assist licensed practical nurses in meeting the requirements for challenge. Each candidate for advanced placement must be successful in both a written and a skill examination.

Costs

Tuition for the academic year 1996–97 is $5200. Fees are estimated at $50 per academic year (higher for those in the allied health programs). The College does not provide housing, but arrangements for off-campus housing may be made through the Admissions Office.

Financial Aid

Financial aid is available to students through Tuition Assistant Program awards (New York State residents only), Federal Stafford Student Loans, Federal PLUS loans, Federal Perkins Loans, Federal Nursing Loans, Federal Pell Grants, Federal Supplemental Educational Opportunity Grants, and Federal Work-Study awards. Also available to those qualifying are the Regents Awards for Children of Deceased or Disabled Veterans and Disabled Policemen and Firefighters, State Aid to Native Americans, and Veterans Administration educational benefits. Approximately 50 percent of the College's students receive aid. To apply for aid, students must submit both the Free Application for Federal Student Aid (FAFSA) and Maria College's own financial aid application form. The recommended deadline is April 1.

Faculty

Maria College has 66 full- and part-time faculty members. Every freshman is assigned to a faculty adviser, who encourages communication and a strong working relationship. The student-faculty ratio is 14:1.

Student Body Profile

For the entering fall 1995 class, 27 percent were first-time freshmen. Approximately 90 percent of all students are from a radius of 50 miles from the College. Nonresident aliens make up 3 percent of the student body, and approximately 6 percent of full-time enrollees belong to a minority group. Sixty-two percent of students are older than 25. Maria College is a commuter-based institution; less than 10 percent of students seek housing through the Admissions Office. Student government is handled on a departmental basis; each department operates independently of all other departments.

Student Activities

Student government is handled on a departmental basis; each department operates independently of all other departments.

Facilities and Resources

Maria's facilities are located in three buildings. The main building's modern facilities include offices, classrooms, and a working library of 34,000 volumes, a computer center, and a multimedia room. Marian Hall, Maria's allied health facility, has been renovated through grants from the Helene Fuld Foundation and gifts from the College's alumni and friends and includes the Helene Fuld Audio-Visual Laboratory for nursing students, the Bearldean B. Burke Occupational Therapy Teaching Center, the Activities of Daily Living Suite, an auditorium, classrooms, offices, and nursing laboratories. Marian Hall also houses facilities for the physical therapist assistant program. The Campus Nursing School, a fully equipped teaching facility, provides preschool and full-day kindergarten classes and serves as a laboratory school for students majoring in early childhood education.

Location

Maria's urban location makes the many attractions of the capital district readily accessible. City buses provide convenient transportation to the area's sister cities of Schenectady and Troy, to many fine shopping centers, and to the impressive Nelson A. Rockefeller Empire State Plaza, which has the State Museum, indoor and outdoor entertainment areas, and performing arts facilities. Access to the Adirondack Northway—leading to the Saratoga Performing Arts Center and Canada—is minutes away. Amtrak trains are available from Schenectady and Rensselaer. Opportunities for outdoor activities in the area are numerous. The Catskills, the Helderbergs, the Adirondacks, and their many lakes provide four seasons of outdoor enjoyment.

Admission Requirements

Admission to full-time study at Maria College is based on a review of the applicant's high school and/or college performance, SAT I or ACT scores and other objective test data, letters of recommendation, and the applicant's interests, maturity, and objectives. Interviews are required. An early admission program is offered for qualified high school students. Part-time study is also available. Special deadline dates apply to the physical therapist assistant program.

Application and Information

It is recommended that application be made early in the first semester of the last year of high school. Applicants must submit an application form and a nonrefundable $20 fee, offer evidence of completion or anticipated completion of a high school program or its equivalent, present at least 16 units of high school work (as specified by the program selected at the College), and arrange for transcripts and SAT I or ACT scores to be sent to Maria College. All accepted students are required to take placement tests in the basic skills of reading, writing, and mathematics. Inquiries regarding academic programs or admission to Maria College may be directed to:

Director of Admissions
Maria College
700 New Scotland Avenue
Albany, New York 12208
Telephone: 518-438-3111
Fax: 518-438-7170

Students wait in college courtyard for exam doors to open.

Peterson's Guide to Two-Year Colleges 1997

MATER DEI COLLEGE
OGDENSBURG, NEW YORK

The College and Its Mission
Mater Dei College is the first and only private, independent, coeducational liberal arts college founded in the Catholic tradition in northern New York. Established by the Society of the Sisters of St. Joseph in 1960, the College is permanently chartered by the New York State Board of Regents to grant associate degrees in occupational and transfer programs. Mater Dei gained recognition in 1974 when it was accredited by the Middle States Association of Colleges and Schools. Later, the College added the Massena Extension Center in Massena, New York, and the St. Regis Branch Campus on the Akwesasne Mohawk Reservation. Mater Dei College provides postsecondary education for students of any religious faith, aimed at the total development and realization of the individual student's social and spiritual nature. Such an education requires freedom of academic inquiry and respect for each person's worth and dignity. The curriculum at Mater Dei College has expanded and evolved in great measure from the mission statement of the College, which reads as follows: "Mater Dei is a private, coeducational, multicampus college committed to serving people of all backgrounds in their quest for learning. Guided by Catholic Christian principles as articulated in the mission of the Sisters of St. Joseph, this academic community prepares students through programs in the liberal arts and professional studies to pursue excellence in career development, personal growth, and social responsibility."
It is evident that Mater Dei College strives to preserve a sensitive balance between education in the liberal arts and education in career-oriented programs. Although no longer strictly a liberal arts college, the liberal arts program remains at the core of every other program offered. Likewise, strong elements of tradition, academic stability, and the pursuit of excellence continue through emphasis on quality in academic programs, strength in the teaching-learning process, and community service.

Academic Programs
Associate Degree Programs To earn an associate degree at Mater Dei College, a student must complete a minimum of 61 credits of course work with a minimum grade point average of 2.0 (C) and complete all additional program requirements. The academic centers of Arts and Sciences and Professional Studies comprise the two divisions under which Mater Dei College is empowered to confer three degrees: **A.A., A.S.,** and **A.A.S.** Currently, there are ten degree programs available to students: alcohol and chemical dependence studies, court reporting, early childhood studies, liberal arts, opticianry, rehabilitative criminal justice, religious studies, secretarial studies (with options in executive, legal, and medical), small business administration (with options in accounting and management), and social service paraprofessional studies.
Transfer Arrangements Whether a student attends full-time or part-time, the task of the College is to provide the skills graduates need to transfer to a baccalaureate institution or to secure employment. Mater Dei believes that an important part of its job is preparing its students for success in their chosen careers and as members of the community in which they will live. As part of that preparation, field work is required for several programs, and a majority of graduates from all programs go directly into the workforce. Also, many graduates transfer to four-year colleges and are able to take advantage of Mater Dei College's formal articulation agreements with a number of institutions of higher education.
Certificate and Diploma Programs In addition to the ten degree programs, Mater Dei has a two-semester certificate program providing entry-level skills in the general secretarial field.
Special Programs and Services The College also offers credit/noncredit summer session courses, time-shortened courses, and weekend courses for enrichment, acceleration, or remedial work.

Off-Campus Programs
Mater Dei College is a member of the Sisters of St. Joseph's Consortium of Colleges Student Exchange Program. Students are allowed to study for a semester or a full year at a member campus located in such places as Massachusetts, Montana, Pennsylvania, California, Michigan, Kansas, Minnesota, and New York. The College coordinates travel to many exciting places. During the 1995–96 school year for example, groups traveled to Spain, Morocco, Germany, Ireland, and London. The trip to London allowed students to combine study with travel and receive academic credit as well.

Credit for Nontraditional Learning Experiences
Incoming students may earn credit toward a Mater Dei College program from the following options: Advanced Placement Examinations, the College-Level Examination Program, The New York State College Proficiency Examination Program, the Regents External Degree Program, transfer credit from colleges and universities, nontraditional and noncollegiate-sponsored programs, and credit by evaluation.

Costs
For the 1995–96 academic year, tuition was $5900 for full-time students and $246 per credit hour for part-time degree students, room was $1980, board was $2040 (twenty meals per week), miscellaneous fees were about $325, books and supplies were approximately $700, and personal costs were about $800.

Financial Aid
Financial aid sources exist at Mater Dei College to assist students and their families in contributing toward educational costs. Eighty-five percent of students receive some form of assistance. The College participates in the following programs: the Pell Grant, Federal Supplemental Educational Opportunity Grant, Federal Work-Study, Veterans Administration Educational Assistance, U.S. Bureau of Indian Affairs Aid to Native Americans, Federal Family Education Loan Programs, New York State Tuition Assistance Program (TAP), New York State Higher Education Opportunity Program (HEOP), and other federal and state programs. Also attainable are other institutional scholarships and grants. Financial aid applications for fall enrollment should be filed with the director of financial aid on or before the April 1 priority date.

Faculty
Mater Dei College has 23 full-time and approximately 10 part-time faculty members. Most of the part-time faculty members are active practitioners outside the College in careers related to the courses they teach. Their professional experiences enrich the College's programs and provide valuable network opportunities to the "real world" for students. All are experienced, knowledgeable, and committed to teaching. The student-faculty ratio is about 15:1.

Student Body Profile
Mater Dei enjoys a diverse group of individuals who make up the student body. Of approximately 400 students from a variety of religious faiths currently enrolled at the College, 80 percent commute. The average age of the total group is 27. Information by campus location shows that approximately 60 percent of students attend the main campus in Ogdensburg, 30 percent attend the Massena Extension Center, and 10 percent of students attend the St. Regis Branch Campus on the Akwesasne Mohawk Reservation. Students belonging to minority groups are estimated as follows: Pacific/Asian, .5 percent; Hispanic, .3 percent; African American, .5 percent; and Native American, 10 percent.

Mater Dei gathers a majority of its students (about 81 percent) from the St. Lawrence River Valley.

Student Activities

Students at Mater Dei have a wide variety of choices when determining their social outlets. Clubs or groups available to join include Concern Club, "Making Miracles Happen" Committee, Ski Club, Environmental Action Club, Student Government Association, SHAPERS, Optical Students Club, Hall Council, Phi Theta Kappa, Liberal Arts Club, and the Horseback Riding Club. Other activities exist in many different areas, which are sponsored by the groups on campus, such as weekend retreats, hiking trips to the Adirondack Mountains, "Making Miracles Happen" Benefit Dance Marathon, St. Lawrence University hockey games, skiing trips, Crop Walk, Fall fest, soccer and basketball games, optical fair, shopping trips, tree planting, Immaculata Literary Magazine, current-issue group discussions, Movies with Meaning, student art exhibits, and free theater tickets. These are a few examples of what is available to Mater Dei students.

Sports Intramural sports provide recreational releases to supplement academic learning. They provide an outlet to relieve stress, a time for exercise, an opportunity to meet new friends, or just a time for fun. The coed activities scheduled reflect the interests of the current students, but usually include volleyball, soccer, Ping-Pong, and basketball. Throughout the year, activities are scheduled in a tournament format and are open to students from all Mater Dei sites. Mater Dei is a member of Region III of the National Junior College Athletic Association. The intercollegiate sports program provides competition with other colleges in women's basketball and soccer. The basketball program began in 1990, quickly followed by soccer in 1991. In these few years, Mater Dei has had several students named Soccer and Basketball Academic All Americans, a Basketball Coach of the Year for the division and region, and a Basketball MVP of the division and region.

Facilities and Resources

Mater Dei's **Main Campus** in Ogdensburg, New York, supports several academic buildings. Immaculata Hall is named after the founder of Mater Dei College and its first president, Mother Immaculata. Facilities here include classrooms, a computer lab, new science laboratories, a model courtroom, student lounges, the cafeteria, and faculty and staff offices. Avila Hall, besides being the residence hall, also contains a computer lab, classrooms, student services staff offices, the Academic Success Center, the Student Recreation Center, a new fitness facility, and sauna.
Massena Extension Center is located in downtown Massena, New York. Its facilities include an Academic Success Center, a computer lab/classroom, a science laboratory, three classrooms, a student lounge, and office space. St. Regis Branch Campus is located in the Community Building on the Akwesasne Mohawk Reservation. The facilities here include four classrooms, a computer lab, and the tribal lounge. As with the academic facilities, recreational facilities on campus are open to all students. Trails for cross-country skiing leave directly from the back of school property. In spring 1995, a regulation soccer field with electronic scoreboard and a multipurpose field used for a variety of sporting events were completed.

Advisement/Counseling Mater Dei meets the needs of its students through many offices. Special areas of interest encompass counseling services for the disabled, career development, and academic success. Counseling services are available for all students to assist with personal concerns, academic and financial matters, transfer situations, and vocational choices. The Office of Disability Services serves the identified needs of students with handicapping conditions and/or learning disabilities.

Career Planning/Placement Offices Within each academic program and with each student lies the responsibility to develop and explore job potential and job placement strategies. Many resources for assistance can be found in the Career Development Office. Résumé preparation, correspondence techniques, and interview skills instruction are offered. Registered alumni also receive appropriate current job listings. For those students interested in furthering their education beyond the associate degree level, assistance in the selection and application to appropriate educational institutions is readily available. The specific purpose of the Academic Success Centers is to strengthen and develop basic reading, writing, math, and study skills for those students needing review and/or reinforcement or for those who are returning to classes after an extended period of time. This goal is achieved through placement testing, extensive tutoring, a flexible program of developmental courses, the use of individualized instructional methods and materials, and regularly scheduled academic counseling sessions.

Library and Audiovisual Services Augsbury Memorial Library houses approximately 60,000 catalogued print and nonprint items and 290 periodicals. The Alcohol and Chemical Dependency Collection of more than 1,100 volumes, along with several specialized journals, audiovisual materials, and vertical file materials, is the second-largest ACDS collection in New York State. The library receives interlibrary loan requests in this collection from across the U.S. and from Canada.

Location

Mater Dei is located in St. Lawrence County on the St. Lawrence Seaway in upstate New York. The main campus lies on Route 37, near the city of Ogdensburg. Ogdensburg offers many attractions such as the home and museum of artist Fredric Remington and the Ogdensburg-Prescott International Bridge. After the opening of the bridge linking the U.S. and Canada, Ogdensburg has developed an industrial park, shopping centers, several excellent motels and restaurants, and two marinas. Recreational facilities for skiing, bowling, horseback riding, swimming, and golf are available at nearby locations. Concerts, plays, films, and other cultural and special events are offered regularly at the many colleges, theaters, and community facilities located throughout the northern New York region. Ottawa, Ontario, Canada's capitol, is less than an hour away and provides a stylish and cosmopolitan center brimming with year-round activity. Concerts, shopping, skating for miles on the canal during "Winterlude," and many cultural and historical sites and events make up only a few of the social functions available.

Admission Requirements

Applicants do not have to be Catholic to attend Mater Dei; however, in order to be considered for admissions into the College, an applicant must submit a complete application form, available from the director of admission services, accompanied by a nonrefundable fee of $25; submit an official copy of the high school transcript that verifies graduation from high school with a minimum academic average of 75 percent; or submit a copy of the GED diploma and complete the College's placement testing. Transfer students must also submit official transcripts from all colleges previously attended. Interviews, SAT I scores, and ACT scores are not required but are strongly recommended.

Application and Information

Mater Dei College operates on a rolling admissions basis for its two-year associate degree programs. Applications are processed as soon as they are received. Notification of an admission decision is usually made within three to four weeks. Completed application forms or requests for additional information should be directed to the following address:

Mater Dei College
Admissions Services
5428 State Highway 37
Ogdensburg, New York 13669
Telephone: 315-393-5030 Ext. 434
800-724-4080 (toll-free in New York)
Fax: 315-393-5056

McINTOSH COLLEGE
DOVER, NEW HAMPSHIRE

The College and Its Mission
For the residential or commuting student seeking the intimate personal experience of a small college and the technical training in practical skills needed to compete in today's computer-oriented job market, McIntosh College is the answer. For over 100 years, McIntosh has provided an exciting variety of business and professional opportunities to recent high school graduates and adults seeking career changes or re-entry into the job market. McIntosh is a two-year degree-granting institution fully accredited by the New England Association of Schools and Colleges. The College currently enrolls over 1,000 students at its campus in Dover, New Hampshire, and at its off-campus center in Stoneham, Massachusetts.

The Mission of the College combines a clearly defined educational philosophy with a profound understanding of the present and future role of the College in combining effective business-oriented associate degree and certificate programs with a fully equipped learning facility in order to enhance the quality of personal and professional life of the business and academic communities which it serves.

McIntosh is a career-oriented institution dedicated to the personal, intellectual, and professional growth of its students. The College has a century-long tradition of providing academic programs which integrate the acquisition of job-related skills with the development of clear, critical thinking and effective reasoning. While McIntosh recognizes its obligation to provide the specific skills necessary for the student to function in a contemporary work environment, it operates under the philosophy that a college is more than a training facility. Students must leave the college experience with a sense of competence in their chosen fields, a belief in themselves as individuals, and an enhanced critical awareness of the world around them.

Academic Programs
McIntosh College offers a unique blend of courses and programs of study designed to prepare students for careers in business, industry, public service, allied health, paralegalism, travel, tourism, criminal justice, and culinary arts. All programs of study provide students with academic credit which will allow them to continue their studies at four-year institutions.

Associate Degree Programs McIntosh College is authorized by the Postsecondary Education Commission of the State of New Hampshire to offer associate degree programs with major areas of concentration in accounting, accounting and taxation, administrative information systems, business management, computer systems management, computers and telecommunications, computer applications, criminal justice, general business studies, legal office systems, medical assisting, medical office systems, paralegal studies, and tourism management.

Honors Programs The McIntosh College Beta Gamma Gamma Chapter of the Phi Theta Kappa Honor Society supports a number of scholarship opportunities and activities for honor students.

Transfer Arrangements McIntosh students can earn an associate degree and a fully articulated bachelor of art degree in one continuous program of study at the Dover campus through the uniquely structured McIntosh/New England College 2+2 Program. Academic counseling is available and full support is provided for students wishing to continue their education at other institutions of higher learning.

Certificate and Diploma Programs McIntosh offers a variety of professional one-year certificate programs designed to provide students with a number of specialized career change options. Professional certificates are available in accounting, bookkeeping, business management, CPA preparatory studies, criminal justice, culinary arts, information systems, medical assisting, medical records management, office support, paralegal studies, taxation, and travel and tourism.

Internship and Co-op Programs All academic departments supporting degree programs support for-credit internship opportunities for qualified students. The Office of Career Development will assist students in finding appropriate internships in accounting, business, computer studies, criminal justice, information systems, medical assisting, paralegal studies, taxation, or tourism.

Off-Campus Programs
McIntosh students enrolled in the CPA-TRAK career change program may earn credit for course work completed at the College's alternative site in Stoneham, Massachusetts.

Credit for Nontraditional Learning Experiences
The College will grant credit to students who have passed authorized advanced placement courses in high school with grades of B or better or who present evidence of having received scores of 460 or better on CLEP examinations in subject areas which directly correspond to the content of individual McIntosh courses.

Costs
The tuition for a standard McIntosh College course is $125 per credit. Tourism management courses include prepayment for a Caribbean and a European tour and are charged at $175 per credit. Culinary arts courses are $220 per credit. College-authorized internships are $125 per credit. The College charges a nonrefundable $15 application fee and a $35 per-term registration fee. There is a $50 graduation fee and an optional $5 student ID fee. The cost of books is about $40 per course. The cost of room and board in the dormitory ranges from $2900 to $3300 per academic year, depending on the choice of meal plan.

The typical annual cost (including tuition, fees and books) for a full-time, two-year degree candidate not enrolled in culinary arts, tourism management, or the CPA-TRAK Program would be approximately $4740. The cost of the Culinary Arts Certificate Program (including tuition, fees, books, knives, and uniforms) is $8980.

Financial Aid
The Office of Financial Aid provides information and personal counseling with respect to the various federal grant and loan programs and institutional scholarships available to students attending McIntosh College. McIntosh College believes that every student should have access to the financial resources needed to pursue academic or career interests. Pell Grants, Supplemental Educational Opportunity Grants, Federal Work-Study, Stafford Loans, and State Incentive Programs are all available to students attending McIntosh College.

Faculty

There are 20 full-time faculty members at McIntosh College. Of these, 85 percent hold advanced degrees and specialized certifications.

Student Body Profile

McIntosh College attracts students from a wide age spectrum. Because the College offers parallel day and evening programs, there is a substantial mix of recent high school graduates and older students returning to school. The average age of a McIntosh student is 26, slightly higher at night and slightly lower during the day program. About 83 percent of the students are directly enrolled in a degree or a certificate program. The remainder are taking individual classes for career enhancement or personal enrichment. Students are generally career oriented. More than 50 percent of graduates continue their studies at the bachelor's degree level.

Student Activities

The College supports a variety of social clubs, organizations, sports teams and other extracurricular activities designed to enhance and enrich the student's educational experience at McIntosh. The Student Activities Committee provides a forum for students interested in planning and implementing social and cultural events at the College. There is a chapter of Delta Epsilon Chi on campus. There are clubs focusing on skiing, drama, and travel. Departmental associations include the McIntosh Paralegal Association, the Law and Order Society, and Collegiate Secretaries International. In addition, there are active men's and women's softball teams.

Facilities and Resources

In recent years, McIntosh has anticipated changes in the business environment and the need for a newly oriented work force by establishing a superior computer facility consisting of five computer labs housing more than 130 individual and networked stations. An integrated curriculum provides specific computer instruction related to each major field of study. In addition, McIntosh students can roam the Internet, explore on-line services such as WestLaw, or browse through an extensive CD-ROM collection in the newly constructed McIntosh academic and paralegal library facilities. A fully equipped medical lab and a real-world operative teaching kitchen provide hands-on working environments for medical assisting and culinary arts majors. At McIntosh, emphasis is placed on the practical aspects of career development. Internships are available in all departments. Degree and certificate programs in tourism management feature travel seminars in such places as Mexico, Europe, and the Caribbean. These tours are built into the curriculum and the tuition structure to provide future professionals with a firsthand look at the travel industry.

On-campus student housing facilities at McIntosh College have been carefully designed to provide a warm, supportive living and learning environment that will serve to nurture students' personal development and to enhance their opportunities for academic and professional success. The Sherwood Hall facility includes spacious furnished living units that have cable TV, air-conditioning, a full bath, and access to a computer lab. Residential students may choose from a variety of meal plans. Initial inquiries about eligibility requirements and the availability of on-campus housing should be directed to the Office of Admissions. Room assignments are made on a first-come, first-served basis, depending on eligibility.

Advisement/Counseling

The faculty and administration of the College are committed to the principle that students should be given every possible opportunity to achieve academic and professional success. For this reason, the College offers extensive academic and career counseling to its students. In addition, the College provides free tutorial assistance in accounting, computer applications, English, and math.

Career Planning/Placement Offices

The College provides free career counseling and placement referral services to its students and graduates through the Office of Career Development.

Location

McIntosh College consists of two separate facilities situated next to the Spaulding Turnpike in Dover, New Hampshire. Dover is a city of about 26,000 located in the Seacoast area of New Hampshire about one hour north of Boston. The College is conveniently located just a short drive from coastal beaches and world class skiing. The academic center is located on a 13-acre tract of land on Cataract Avenue. Residential housing, the Culinary Arts Center, and the corporate training facilities occupy the grounds of the McIntosh College Inn and Conference Center, located on Silver Street. There is an off-campus center at 92 Montvale Avenue in Stoneham, Massachusetts, where a section of CPA-TRAK is offered.

Admission Requirements

A high school diploma or its equivalent (GED) is required of all students accepted for admission at McIntosh College with matriculated student status. Students can apply and can be admitted at any time during the year. Classes begin every eight weeks. A student taking two or more courses each term can expect to graduate in two years or less.

Application and Information

Applications for admission are accepted on an ongoing basis. Students may begin classes during any six 8-week terms scheduled throughout the year. For application materials, students should contact:

McIntosh College Office of Admissions
23 Cataract Avenue
Dover, New Hampshire 03820

Telephone: 800-MCINTOSH (toll-free)
Fax: 603-742-7292

Students at McIntosh College.

Peterson's Guide to Two-Year Colleges 1997

MIAMI-DADE COMMUNITY COLLEGE
MIAMI, FLORIDA

The College and Its Mission

Miami-Dade Community College is nationally and internationally recognized as one of the largest and best community colleges in the country. At Miami-Dade student success is the priority. The mission of the College is to provide accessible, affordable, high-quality education by keeping the learner's needs at the center of decision making and working in partnership with its dynamic, multicultural community.

Miami-Dade Community College is accredited by the Southern Association of Colleges and Schools and offers undergraduate study in over 120 areas and professions. More than 123,000 credit and noncredit students are enrolled at five major campuses and numerous outreach centers.

Academic Programs

The instructional program at Miami-Dade Community College is designed to prepare students to transfer to the upper division of senior colleges and universities or for immediate job entry into career fields. The Associate in Arts degree, offered for students planning to transfer to a university, can be earned in 60 credits, including 36 credits of required general education and 24 credits of electives. The state of Florida is developing a set of common program prerequisites for each program to facilitate student transfer. A variety of Associate in Science degrees, college credit certificate programs, vocational credit certificate programs, and supplemental courses are offered to prepare students to enter the job market or upgrade skills. These programs vary in length. The Associate in Science degree includes 18 credits of general education requirements. A few Associate in Science degree programs include courses that have articulation agreements for transfer to one or more universities; others offer advanced certificate training. The Medical Center Campus offers a wide range of allied health and nursing programs with clinicals in major local hospitals and health-care centers. Courses are offered year-round in two major terms of sixteen weeks each and two summer terms of six weeks each. Vocational credit certificate programs and supplemental courses generally do not follow the academic calendar.

Associate Degree Programs Miami-Dade offers the **Associate in Arts** degree, which prepares students for transfer to upper-division programs. The following **Associate in Science** degree programs are available at one or more campuses: air-conditioning, refrigeration, and heating systems technology; architectural design and construction technology; automotive service management; aviation administration; aviation maintenance management; building construction technology; business administration/management; child development and education; civil engineering technology; computer information systems analysis; computer-integrated manufacturing technology; court reporting; criminal justice technology; dietetic technician studies; drafting and design technology; electrical power technology; environmental science technology; fashion marketing management; film production technology; financial services; fire science technology; funeral services; graphic arts technology; graphic design technology; hospitality management; industrial management technology; interpreter training program for hearing impaired; land surveying; landscape technology; legal assisting; office systems technology; photographic technology; professional pilot technology; radio and television broadcast programming; and travel industry management.

Allied health and nursing Associate in Science degree programs offered at the Medical Center Campus include dental hygiene, dental laboratory technology management, diagnostic medical sonography specialist studies, emergency medical services, health information management, health services management, medical laboratory technology, midwifery, nursing-ADN, nursing-ADN (accelerated option), nursing-ADN (transition), physical therapist assisting, radiation therapy technology, radiography, respiratory care, and vision care technology/opticianry. Paramedic and radiation therapy specialist college credit certificates are also offered at the Medical Center Campus.

Honors Programs The honors programs are part of a comprehensive effort by the College to reward excellence and provide intellectual challenge through scholarships, honors courses, academic programs, and special recognition.

Transfer Arrangements A statewide articulation agreement among all Florida institutions of higher education facilitates transfers and ensures that a student who is awarded the Associate in Arts degree at Miami-Dade has met general education requirements for admission to the upper division in public state universities. In addition, Miami-Dade has negotiated articulation agreements with many colleges and universities in Florida and other states.

Certificate and Diploma Programs Vocational credit certificate programs are offered at one or more campuses in accounting operations, apparel design for industry, architectural drafting, bail bonding, basic X-ray machine operator studies, bookkeeping, business administration operations, business administration operations (food industry management option), business software applications, child-care supervision, coder specialist studies, commercial art, computer programming, correctional officer–Dade County studies, correctional officer–state of Florida studies, correctional probation officer studies, criminal justice assisting, data entry operations, elderly and disabled care services, electrocardiography technology technician studies, electronic technology, fashion marketing, fire fighting, general office clerk studies, general studies (no program intention), home and family management, import/export marketing, infant/toddler supervision, insurance marketing, law enforcement, legal secretarial studies, mechanical drafting, medical assisting, medical record transcribing, occupational safety and health technology, office support service, optometric assisting, pharmacy technician studies, phlebotomy technician studies, printing and graphic arts, private security guard studies, public administration supervision, radio broadcasting, real estate marketing, respiratory care technician studies, secretarial studies, television production operations, ticket agent/reservationist studies, travel agency operations, and word processing.

Internship and Co-op Programs Co-op programs provide an opportunity for students to obtain career-related work experience while earning academic credit. Work experience may be paid or voluntary.

Special Programs and Services New World School of the Arts (NWSA) is a unique cooperative venture of Dade County Public Schools, Miami-Dade Community College, and the University of Florida. Through its sponsoring institutions, NWSA awards high school diplomas, Associate in Arts degrees, and Bachelor of Music and Bachelor of Fine Arts degrees. Students are admitted through audition or portfolio presentation. Other special programs and services include academic remediation for entering students, English as a second language, services for disabled students (including learning disabled), study abroad, and advanced placement.

Community Programs Community programs are offered both independently and in cooperation with community organizations. Workshops and seminars are held throughout the year in response to community needs.

Continuing Education Unit Certificate Programs Miami-Dade provides students the opportunity to obtain Continuing Education Units (CEUs) for certain courses. Transcripts designating CEUs are provided.

Personal Enrichment/Noncredit Courses A wide array of noncredit courses and programs are offered both on and off campus.

Off-Campus Programs

Study-abroad programs, both short-term and full semester, are available in many countries. Internships and clinicals may be scheduled off campus. In addition, distance-learning opportunities exist in several formats.

Credit for Nontraditional Learning Experiences

The College may award credit for demonstrated proficiency in areas related to college-level courses. Sources used to determine such proficiency are College-Level Examination Program (CLEP), Advanced Placement Program (AP), Proficiency Examination Program (PEP), International Baccalaureate Program (I.B.), Dual Enrollment (DE), Tech Prep Articulation (TP), Defense Activity for Nontraditional Education Support (DANTES), United States Armed Forces Institute (USAFI), Institutional Credit by Exam, and internal Miami-Dade procedures for awarding credit related to specific programs for approval licensures.

Costs

For the 1996–97 academic year, tuition costs are $41.25 per credit for Florida residents and $145 per credit for nonresidents. Textbooks and supplies for full-time students are estimated at $700. On-campus housing is not available; room and board costs will vary depending upon the type of off-campus housing desired.

Financial Aid

The amounts and types of financial aid that a student receives are determined through federal, state, and institutional guidelines and are offered to students in packages, which may consist of grants, loans, employment, and scholarships. Financial aid is based upon financial need as determined by the federal government's system of needs analysis. Available assistance includes Federal Pell Grants, Federal Supplemental Educational Opportunity Grants, Florida Student Assistance Grant Program, Florida Undergraduate Scholars Program, Federal Work-Study Program, Florida Work Experience Program (FWEP), Federal Perkins Loan, Federal Family Education Loan Programs, and Federal PLUS loans. In addition, the College offers grants, scholarships, loans, and employment to students as well as funding for the purchase of special equipment and services for disabled students.

Faculty

There are 901 full-time faculty members and 765 part-time faculty members. Of the full-time faculty members, 93 percent hold advanced degrees; 22 percent have earned doctorate degrees.

Student Body Profile

More than 123,000 credit and noncredit students are enrolled at Miami-Dade, including over 1,000 international students from 100 countries. Ninety percent of students with an Associate in Arts degree continue their education at a four-year college. Eighteen percent of the upper-division students in the Florida State University System started college at Miami-Dade. Thirty-eight percent of all students are enrolled in noncredit/continuing education programs for personal enrichment or career training. The average age of students is 26, although about 28 percent of students are between 21 and 25 years old. More than 67 percent attend on a part-time basis. Fifty-seven percent are female. The student body is ethnically and culturally diverse. Miami-Dade enrolls more black and Hispanic students than any other college or university in the United States.

Student Activities

More than 100 organizations offer opportunities to participate in student government, student publications, music ensembles, dramatic productions (in English and Spanish), religious activities, service and political clubs, national and local fraternities and sororities, professional organizations, and honor societies.

Sports Miami-Dade is a member of NJCAA. Intercollegiate and intramural athletics play an important role; teams include women's basketball, swimming and diving, tennis, and volleyball and men's baseball, basketball, golf, swimming and diving, tennis, and track and field. In addition, sports facilities such as wellness centers; racquet, tennis, and handball courts; swimming pools; and a track field are available to students and the community.

Facilities and Resources

Career Planning/Placement Offices Trained staff members assist students in selecting courses and programs of study to satisfy their educational objectives. Each campus has a career center where students who are uncertain about their future careers may obtain career counseling and vocational interest testing and may review a variety of career materials. The campus Job Placement Centers provide part-time or full-time job referral services to actively enrolled students or graduates. The centers also provide training that prepares students for job search, résumé writing, and effective job interviews. In addition, Career Fairs are scheduled on the campuses.

Library and Audiovisual Services The campus libraries have a combined book collection of more than 300,000 titles and more than 4,000 periodicals. Numerous CD-ROM and on-line databases are available. Computers for student use are available in computer labs, learning resource centers, labs, classrooms, and the library.

Location

Blessed with a sunny, subtropical climate, beautiful beaches, and an international flavor, Miami has been a mecca for students and tourists for decades. A variety of exciting cultural, sporting, and intellectual activities take place each week. Opportunities to explore unique settings such as the historic Art Deco District and Little Havana or the Everglades National Park abound. Miami is a gateway city with easy access to most countries. Five campuses and numerous outreach centers are located throughout the greater Miami area. **North Campus** is located on a 245-acre, fully landscaped site with free, lighted parking areas and a lake around which the buildings are clustered. **Kendall Campus** is situated 23 miles southwest of the North Campus on a 185-acre site. Focal points of the campus' award-winning landscape designs are the lakes and lush tropical growth. **Wolfson Campus**, the only urban campus, is located in the heart of Miami's business community and has two award-winning buildings. **Medical Center Campus** is located in Miami's medical/civic center complex. **Homestead Campus**, the newest campus, is located on an 8-acre site in the historic business district of Homestead. Off-campus commuter sites are located in the major suburbs.

Admission Requirements

Miami-Dade has an open-door admission policy. The College provides educational opportunities to all high school graduates, including those who have a state high school equivalency diploma, and to transfer students from other colleges and universities. Students 18 years of age and older who do not have a high school diploma or equivalency diploma may enroll in occupational courses. In addition to the application to the College, which carries a $15 application fee, students must have official transcripts from high school, college, university, or other postsecondary educational institutions sent directly to the Admission Office from the institutions. High school equivalency diploma or certificate holders must provide the original document and score report (which will be returned) or an exact copy of the documents. Florida residents must complete a Florida residency statement. Test scores such as SAT I, ACT, or TOEFL should be sent directly to the Admissions Office by the testing board. Students not presenting test scores will be tested for placement purposes upon acceptance to the College.

Application and Information

Applications are accepted on an ongoing basis. All prospective students should contact:

District Office of Admissions
300 N.E. 2 Avenue
Miami, Florida 33132-2296

Telephone: 305-237-7534
Fax: 305-237-7460
World Wide Web: http://www.mdcc.edu

MIDDLESEX COUNTY COLLEGE
EDISON, NEW JERSEY

The College and Its Mission

Middlesex County College is one of the largest and among the oldest county colleges in New Jersey. The College, a two-year publicly supported coeducational institution, is committed to serving all those who can benefit from postsecondary learning, and the student body reflects this belief. Over 550 courses are offered during the day, evening, and on weekends. Students have the opportunity to prepare academically and through cooperative work placements, clinical experience, and laboratory work for careers in business, health, social science, and science technologies.

Middlesex County College offers modern, well-equipped facilities located on a beautiful 200-acre campus, together with excellent learning resources and dedicated faculty members. Most students commute to the College from Middlesex County, although a growing number commute from out of county. Each year, more and more students from outside the United States enroll in the International Student Program. All students have the opportunity to add to their collegiate experience through participation in a variety of student activities and clubs. Many students participate in intercollegiate sports. The College has a recreational facility with a 25-meter pool, dance studio, wrestling and weight rooms, and racquetball courts. The College philosophy is directed toward assisting each individual in reaching his or her maximum potential, and counselors work with students to ensure this goal.

Academic Programs

More than seventy different degree and certificate programs, either transfer or career oriented, may be taken full-time or part-time during the days, evening, and weekends. Courses are offered during the fall and spring semesters, a January winter session, and summer sessions. The College offers **Associate in Arts (A.A.)** and **Associate in Science (A.S.)** degree programs designed specifically to transfer to four-year colleges and universities in the fields of arts, business education, engineering, and sciences. Students interested in preparing for careers in medicine and law begin study at MCC with courses in science and liberal arts. Graduates have an excellent success rate in transferring to colleges and universities nationwide. In selected programs there is a formal credit transfer agreement with four-year institutions such as Rutgers, The State University of New Jersey; New Jersey Institute of Technology; and New York University.

MCC has dual-degree programs with Rutgers University. MCC students who complete the designated transfer associate degree program and fulfill the necessary criteria are guaranteed admission with full junior status at Camden, Newark, and New Brunswick campuses of Rutgers University.

MCC also has a joint admission program with New Jersey Institute of Technology (NJIT). Under the terms of the agreement, MCC offers students who apply for admission to designated associate degree programs the opportunity to be admitted simultaneously to the related baccalaureate program at NJIT. Jointly admitted students who successfully complete the specified associate degree program at MCC and receive the recommendation of their program dean may then enroll in the third year of study in the designated program at NJIT without further admission review.

MCC has an agreement with Thomas Edison College in Trenton that allows students to attain a four-year degree without leaving the community college campus in Edison.

Many challenging programs and options designed to prepare students for entry into the job market are available in business education, engineering technologies, health technologies, and science. MCC has one of the few professional culinary arts programs in the state. MCC has the only Psychosocial Rehabilitation and Treatment Program in the state. Graduates of career programs receive an **Associate in Applied Science (A.A.S.)** degree. Many graduates holding the A.A.S. degree transfer to four-year colleges, which may accept all or part of the credits earned at MCC. Certificate programs are available in the evenings through the Division of Continuing Students.

In addition to associate degree and certificate curricula, the College offers students the opportunity to enroll in a plan of study through the Open College Program. Open College serves students who want to try out an individualized academic program prior to formally enrolling in a specific degree or certificate program. The College offers Project Connections, a nationally recognized program for students with learning disabilities. Students interested in military education may participate in the Army or Air Force ROTC program through cross-registration at Rutgers University.

Degree and certificate programs are offered in accounting; automotive technology; biological laboratory technology; biology; business administration; chemical technology; chemistry; civil/construction engineering technology; communication; computer-integrated manufacturing engineering technology; computer programming; computer science; criminal justice (correction administration and police science); culinary arts; dental hygiene; dietetic technology; education technology (assistant in early childhood education, assistant in special education, teacher aide, and teacher assistant studies); electrical engineering technology (computer electronics technology); English; environmental technology; fashion merchandising; fire science technology; graphic arts; heating, ventilating, and air-conditioning design technology; history; hotel, restaurant, and institution management (hotel/motel management, professional food preparation, and restaurant food service management); industrial technology; journalism; legal assistant studies; liberal arts; management (credit and financial management and management support services); marketing; marketing art and design (advertising graphics design and professional commercial photography); mathematics; mechanical engineering technology; medical laboratory technology; modern languages; music; nursing; office administration; pharmacy assistant studies; physical education/recreation; physics; political science; psychology; psychosocial rehabilitation and treatment; radiography education; respiratory care; retail management; social and rehabilitation services; social services; sociology; surveying technology; theater; and visual arts.

Off-Campus Programs

In addition to the main campus in Edison, MCC offers classes at fourteen sites throughout the county in industry and schools. There are two outreach centers in New Brunswick and Perth Amboy. Both centers offer a comprehensive English as a Second

Language Program. The College offers credit courses through a network of public adult schools, public libraries, corporations, and hospitals.

MCC offers a special program in a Pueblo Indian village in New Mexico and study-abroad programs in England, France, Spain, and other countries.

Credit for Nontraditional Learning Experiences

There are several programs at the College through which applicants may earn credit for knowledge learned in nontraditional ways. Both Credit by Examination and the College-Level Examination Program (CLEP) are available. College credit can be awarded to students who have taken the Defense Activity for Non-Traditional Education Support (DANTES) courses and/or tests in college-level subjects.

Costs

The 1996–97 tuition is $62.50 per credit hour for in-county residents and $125 per credit hour for out-of-county residents. There are also mandatory accident and health insurance fees and parking and technology fees. Some classes require special lab or material costs or other fees.

Financial Aid

Through its financial aid programs, MCC makes every effort to overcome economic barriers. Funds from federal, state, and private sources are available to those who have need and meet the eligibility requirements. To be considered for financial aid, a student must complete the Free Application for Federal Student Aid (FAFSA) and the MCC Financial Aid Form. The priority deadline for the fall semester is May 1 and November 1 for the spring semester. Before a financial aid application can be reviewed, the student must be accepted to a degree program and be matriculated for a minimum of 6 credits.

Faculty

There are 192 full-time and 346 part-time members of the faculty. The student-faculty ratio is 21:1. Of the full-time faculty, nearly 90 percent are teaching faculty members and serve as academic advisers.

Student Body Profile

There are about 12,000 students on campus, including 5,000 full-time and 7,000 part-time. The campus population is diverse, with students from over sixty countries in attendance. Approximately half of the students come directly from high school with an average age of 25 for the entire student body.

Student Activities

There are more than sixty chartered clubs and organizations, a College Center Program Board, College Assembly, national honor societies, special minority student activities, and a College newspaper, radio station, and literary magazine. The College offers intercollegiate and intramural competition through membership in Region XIX of the National Junior College Athletic Association and Garden State Athletic Conference.

Facilities and Resources

The campus is composed of twenty-five buildings, including a state-of-the-art Technical Services Center, a fully equipped Recreation Center, and a 440-seat Performing Arts Center. The Career Counseling and Placement Center provides students with assistance in making decisions about career choices, education programs, college transfer, job placement, and other personal concerns. Bilingual counseling is available to Spanish-speaking students.

Location

The College is located just 15 minutes away from New Brunswick, New Jersey. The College is conveniently located near numerous restaurants and shopping centers. The New Jersey shore is less than 30 minutes away. Mass transit to the College is available from many surrounding areas and easy transportation is available to New York City and Philadelphia.

Admission Requirements

The admission policy is based on the premise that the College should provide an opportunity for further education to all citizens of the community. Enrollment is open to anyone who holds a high school diploma or any non–high school graduates 18 years of age or older who can demonstrate an ability to benefit from a college education. Applicants to most programs are not required to submit any standardized test scores.

Admission to programs that specify additional selective criteria may require a review of prior educational performance, standardized test scores, the completion of an appropriate developmental program, or, when suitable, an assessment of an applicant's aptitude and interest, as determined during an admission counseling interview.

Application and Information

Completed applications are reviewed on a continuous basis, with the exception of the limited-seat programs in dental hygiene, nursing, and radiography education. A completed application form, a required $25 nonrefundable application fee, and all supporting materials should be sent to the director of admissions.

For application forms or additional information, students should contact:

Admissions Office
Middlesex County College
155 Mill Road
Edison, New Jersey 08818-3050
Telephone: 908-906-2510

MITCHELL COLLEGE
NEW LONDON, CONNECTICUT

The College and its Mission

Mitchell College is a private, coeducational, two-year residential college specializing in developing the untapped potential of students. With only 500 full-time students and a 12:1 student-faculty ratio, Mitchell College is dedicated to one thing—creating an environment where each student can achieve academic, personal, and career success. Mitchell provides the personal support and encouragement that large universities and community colleges sometimes cannot. With a foundation grounded in the liberal arts tradition, Mitchell is committed to the philosophy that each student has the potential for unlimited success.

The Mitchell College experience is called "Educating for Success." In two years, student potential is developed through the College's unwavering commitment toward individual asset development. This philosophy comes to life through the Mitchell College community: a faculty that embraces the task of developing students' intellectual capabilities, a staff specifically trained for programs and services that encourage academic and personal growth, and fellow students who are also exploring their own potential.

Many of today's high school graduates are not ready to make the commitment to enroll at a four-year college or university. For these students, full of potential, a two-year college is the perfect start. Mitchell specializes in bridging the gap between high school and a four-year college. Students have the opportunity to earn a degree in two years in a small campus environment where they never will get lost in the crowd. Small classes give every student individualized attention from faculty members, and Mitchell's academic reputation makes transferring credits easy after graduation.

Academic Programs

There are nineteen academic degree programs offered, each designed to match similar programs at four-year colleges and universities. Students earn associate degrees in two years in semesters that run from September to December and January to May. Summer Sessions are also available with limited course offerings. All programs build a foundation for further study at four-year colleges and universities. More than 90 percent of Mitchell graduates transfer to earn their bachelor's degrees.

Students with diagnosed learning disabilities may enroll in the Learning Resources Center, which provides supplemental instruction and support along with a student's regular academic program. Students who need additional instruction in English as a second language may enroll in the Intensive English Program, which prepares them to enroll in Mitchell's regular academic program.

The Mitchell academic experience is organized with distinct goals in mind. The first of these goals is that students will be able to demonstrate a minimum level of competency in certain areas vital to success as a student and as a participant in society in general. The Mitchell faculty has decided that a student should possess skills in writing, mathematics, computer information technology, and wellness. The core curriculum and minimum grade requirements in certain courses make sure students meet these competency levels before they graduate. The second academic goal deals with the specific courses each student must take. Regardless of students' majors at Mitchell, they are required to take a core selection of courses that help them reach a predetermined level of competency and make sure their first two years of college are broad in content. Students in every major must take an expository writing course, a literature course, two mathematics courses, an introductory computer information systems course, an introductory psychology course, a communications course, a lab science course, and a wellness course.

The nineteen academic programs offered at Mitchell are athletic training, business administration (accounting, business administration management), criminal justice, early childhood education, engineering studies, graphic design, health fitness, human services, information systems, liberal arts, life science, marine science, public administration/political studies, physical education, physical science, recreation, sports management, and therapeutic recreation.

Students undecided about their academic majors are enrolled in the Discovery Program, specially designed to provide special courses, additional advising and services to explore their full potential, and assistance in choosing an academic major. Students in all academic majors are supported by the Tutoring Center, which offers unlimited free professional assistance in all disciplines.

Off-Campus Programs

Out-of-classroom learning experiences are an increasingly important element of a Mitchell education. Nearly all academic programs require or encourage students to participate in internships or practicum experiences as part of their two-year curriculum.

Mitchell students may remain on campus for two years following graduation to earn a bachelor's degree from the University of New Haven in classes offered on the Mitchell campus. This partnership, established in 1995, offers bachelor's degrees in accounting, business administration, criminal justice, engineering, liberal arts, sports management, and tourism and travel administration. Mitchell also has articulation agreements with more than 20 four-year colleges and universities so that graduates transfer easily as juniors in specific four-year programs.

Costs

Tuition, room, board, and fees for the 1996–97 year are $18,435. Additional annual miscellaneous expenses, including books, are estimated at $1500 per year. Students enrolled in the Learning Resource Center pay an additional $1976 per semester. Students enrolled in the English as a second language program pay regular tuition and room and board costs.

Financial Aid

Mitchell annually awards more than $2 million in financial aid, both in need-based scholarships and in programs designed to recognize academic, athletic, and leadership abilities. Accepted students may qualify for grants and scholarships that do not need to be repaid. They include Connecticut Independent College Student Grant Program, Federal Pell Grants, Federal Supplemental Educational Opportunity Grants, Mitchell Grants, or Mitchell Scholarships. Self-help aid in the forms of loans also are available. They include Federal Stafford Student Loan, Unsubsidized Stafford Loan, Federal PLUS Loan, and Federal

Perkins Loan programs. On-campus job opportunities are plentiful for students, regardless of their financial aid status.

MVP (Mitchell Valued Potential) scholarships are awarded based on an individual student's ability to contribute to the College. They may be given to students who demonstrate potential in leadership, volunteerism, and involvement in school activities. Athletic scholarships are available to students who participate in field hockey, soccer, basketball, baseball, softball, women's volleyball, and men's lacrosse.

Faculty
Twenty-one full-time and 15 part-time faculty members teach in Mitchell's classrooms. The student-faculty ratio is 12:1.

Student Body Profile
The Mitchell College community is diverse, with about 500 full-time students from throughout the country and across the globe. Mitchell is primarily a residential college, with more than 90 percent of full-time students living in campus residence halls. Nearly all full-time students are traditional college age, 18–22. About 150 part-time students, many of whom are adults commuting from nearby towns, add to the Mitchell College classroom experience. Most students come from New England states, with about 50 percent from Connecticut, 30 percent from other New England states, and the remaining 20 percent from other states. Each year about fifteen to twenty other countries are represented by students on the Mitchell campus. Members of minority groups comprise about 10 percent of the campus population.

Student Activities
Faculty-led clubs for students interested in biking, community service, choir, music, the yearbook, skiing, multicultural affairs, psychology, and history bring together students with similar interests. Spirit Weekends are filled with guest comedians, bands, formal and casual dances, lectures, and organized trips to Boston and New York City. Rolling lawns, the 26-acre Mitchell Woods, and the riverfront beach offer plenty of opportunities to outdoor enthusiasts.

Mitchell College is a member of the National Junior College Athletic Association and fields twelve intercollegiate teams. Men play baseball, basketball, lacrosse, and soccer; women play basketball, field hockey, soccer, softball, and volleyball; men and women compete together in golf, sailing, and tennis teams. The College has a history of athletic excellence, winning many national and New England championships. A full schedule of intramural sports is organized for students of all athletic experience and ability.

Facilities and Resources
Mitchell is nationally recognized for its C.A.R.E.S. model of student services. C.A.R.E.S. stands for Careering, Advising, Retaining, Educating, and Supporting, the five areas Mitchell has determined critical to student academic success. The C.A.R.E.S. program offers active support in all areas of a student's life at Mitchell, from orientation to graduation two years later. The Tutoring Center, the Discovery Program, the Learning Resource Center, the Career and Transfer Center, and the Center for Student Academic Success are part of the C.A.R.E.S. model.

The campus includes a 40,000-volume library, two primary classroom instruction buildings, seven residence halls, a fully equipped gymnasium, a fitness center, and indoor recreational areas. Of special note are three new computer labs featuring high-level Macintosh and PC-based networked systems.

Location
New London, Connecticut, where Mitchell College makes its home, is a major center of activity in southeastern Connecticut, a region rich in historic significance. This small but sophisticated city, also home to Connecticut College and the U.S. Coast Guard Academy, is a maritime and resort center located midway between Boston and New York City on the main railroad line.

The Mitchell College campus is located in the city's most scenic residential section. Bordered by a long stretch of sandy beach, the campus consists of approximately 65 acres of gently sloping hillside and forest.

Places for shopping, banking, dining, and fun are within easy walking distance, or accessed by buses that pass by the College entrance. A major shopping mall, factory outlet centers, and fine and casual dining establishments are located minutes from campus. The region is also home to major tourist attractions, such as the U.S.S. Nautilus Museum, Mystic Marinelife Aquarium, Mystic Seaport, Olde Mystick Village, Ocean Beach Park, Stonington vineyards, Foxwoods Resort and Casino, and Essex Steam Train.

Admission Requirements
Each applicant is treated individually; no strict guidelines are imposed in the admissions process. A student's potential for success is far more important than what he or she has accomplished in the past. The SAT I or ACT are recommended but not required. An on-campus interview and attendance at an open house event are recommended but not required.

Application and Information
Applications should be accompanied by an official transcript, sent directly from the student's high school. Mitchell uses a rolling admissions policy. Students can expect to be notified of decisions within three weeks of sending an application.

For more information, students should contact:

Dr. Arthur Forst
Dean of Enrollment Management
Mitchell College
New London, Connecticut 06320
Telephone: 800-443-2811 (toll-free)
Fax: 860-444-1209

Mitchell's riverfront campus and beach offer students many opportunities for outdoor activities after class.

MOUNT IDA COLLEGE
NEWTON CENTRE, MASSACHUSETTS

The College and Its Mission

Founded in 1899, Mount Ida has become one of the Northeast's most innovative postsecondary institutions. All freshman students begin in Mount Ida's renowned Junior College Division, which features eight schools that offer thirty-seven two- and three-year associate degree programs. After earning an associate degree, students may choose to enter employment or to continue in one of the Mount Ida Senior College Division's two-year bachelor's degree programs. The associate degree guarantees that a student may enter the junior year of at least one of Mount Ida's bachelor degree programs. This flexible system allows students to exercise educational options one step at a time as they gain knowledge and experience.

Mount Ida's beautiful 85-acre campus was once an elegant country estate. Academic, administrative, and residential buildings are surrounded by playing fields, ponds, and wooded areas in a comfortable, self-contained environment. Over the last eight years more than $16 million of new construction has been completed, providing new dormitories, classrooms, buildings, and an expansion of the Learning Resource Center. In 1994, construction was completed on a $2.5-million student center. This facility accommodates the bookstore, a food court, a radio station, student lounges, a fitness room, an auditorium seating over 200, and offices for organizations such as the student government, the yearbook, the school newspaper, and much more.

Academic Programs

Associate Degree Programs The eight schools of Mount Ida's Junior College Division offer the A.A.A., A.A.S., A.A., or A.S. degrees in the following fields of study: accounting, advertising/sales, business administration, canine science, child study, communications, computer systems management, criminal justice, dental assisting/office management, education, equine studies, facilities management, fashion design, fashion merchandising, funeral service management, graphic design, hotel/restaurant management, human services, individualized studies, interior design, interior management, liberal arts, marketing, occupational therapy assistant studies, opticianry, paralegal studies, pharmacy technician studies, physical education, pre-engineering, prepharmacy, public administration, science, technical electricity, travel/tourism, veterinary technician studies, and visual merchandising.

The Senior College Division's bachelor degree programs are designed for students who have completed associate degree programs at Mount Ida or at other accredited institutions and choose to continue study to earn a baccalaureate degree. The Liberal Studies Program accepts all credits earned by associate degree graduates or 60 credits earned by students during the first two years of college, regardless of course content, provided that a quality point average (QPA) of at least 2.0 has been achieved. The senior-year core curriculum includes interdisciplinary courses covering liberal arts, humanities, and sciences in addition to an independent study project. Students entering any other senior college program must have their transcripts evaluated on a course-by-course basis to determine what they will earn in transfer credit. Every effort is made to allow maximum credit transfer.

Mount Ida's Senior College Division offers the Bachelor of Science degree in bereavement counseling, business administration, criminal justice, equine studies, fashion design, fashion merchandising/fashion marketing, funeral home management, graphic design, hotel administration, interior design, journalism/writing, management, media production, public administration, retail management, veterinary technology, and visual merchandising. The College also offers baccalaureate degrees in legal studies, liberal studies, and teacher certification (N–3).

Mount Ida's Bachelor of Science in veterinary technology provides a framework on which students can develop individually customized portfolios of experience in the animal research, medical, and veterinary fields. Seniors participate in six 5-week, off-campus externship rotations at a variety of facilities, including the Tufts University School of Veterinary Medicine Teaching Hospital, Massachusetts Institute of Technology, Harvard Primate Center, New England Aquarium, and approximately seventy other sites.

Mount Ida offers Intensive English courses at three levels: introductory, intermediate, and advanced. Students with TOEFL scores below 425 take a special Intensive English course 12 hours a week with an additional 3-hour language laboratory. They may not take other courses until achieving a TOEFL score of at least 425.

The Learning Opportunities Program was designed and developed to provide additional academic support for students with learning disabilities. The program focuses on developing and strengthening individual learning styles that create successful, independent learning. Students are mainstreamed in a regular degree curriculum. Services and accommodations for participants in the Learning Opportunities Program (LOP) include the following: individual tutoring by professional learning specialists, reduced course load (from four to three the first semester), 2-credit study skills course required for students with a reduced course load, special accommodations such as extra time on tests, taping lectures, provisions for taped texts or oral tests, diagnostic testing and outside service referral, and substitute courses where needed.

Costs

Tuition for the 1996–97 academic year is $11,590. Courses for the New England Institute of Applied Arts and Sciences are $266 per credit. Room and board charges are $8150, and books and supplies range from $300 to $500, depending on the program of study.

Financial Aid

Mount Ida supplements federal, state, and private funding with a substantial commitment of College funds. As a result, about 70 percent of Mount Ida's students received financial assistance during the academic year 1995–96. Grants, scholarships, campus employment, and loans are utilized to enable students to afford the College's opportunities. Mount Ida does not have a financial aid application deadline.

Faculty

Mount Ida's faculty consists of approximately 200 members, 75 percent of whom hold a masters or higher degree in their field of concentration. The student-faculty ratio is 10:1. Most classes at Mount Ida have fewer than 25 students; such smaller classes are conducive to the individual attention to students for which Mount Ida is renowned.

Student Body Profile

Approximately 2,000 full-time students form as diverse a population as can be found on any college campus. They reflect different national, cultural, ethnic, educational, and economic backgrounds. Ninety percent of the students represent New England, New York, New Jersey, and Pennsylvania. Students from Bermuda, Columbia, Venezuela, Peru, Ireland, England, Sweden, India, Japan, Australia, and South Africa make up the international population.

Student Activities

At Mount Ida College, where each student is known by name and recognized as an individual, students find it easy to become involved. Students are encouraged to start new positive groups on campus that will enrich the College community. Campus organizations and clubs reflect the diversity of the student body and afford wonderful opportunities for creative expression and leadership development. Some of these are the Commuter Council, the Residence Hall Council, the Judicial Board, the Multicultural Council, Phi Theta Kappa Honor Society, Tau Epsilon Phi, the International Student Club, the Drama Club, the student newspaper, the yearbook, a literary magazine, the Veterinary Technology Club, A.S.I.D., the Fashion and Design Club, and the Communications Club. A wide variety of social, cultural, and recreational activities are also an important part of student life. These include intercollegiate mixers, Parents' Weekend, international dinners, a faculty lecture series, Winter Carnival, a Spring Semiformal, the Spring Fling Weekend, the Annual Fashion Show, and Senior Week.

Sports Various intercollegiate sports are offered during the school year including basketball, lacrosse, and soccer for men and soccer, softball, and volleyball for women. There is also a coed equestrian team. Mount Ida College is a member of the National Junior College Athletic Association (NJCAA). Many of Mount Ida's teams have enjoyed national rank and tournament action in recent years.

Facilities and Resources

The Learning Resource Center and the National Center for Death Education house approximately 62,000 volumes, 530 periodicals, and a variety of media, including videodiscs and educational software programs. Other on-campus facilities include a nursery school, a dental laboratory, computer laboratories, art studios, a communications laboratory, and facilities for the programs in veterinary technician studies and veterinary technology, including animal kennels, laboratories, and a surgical operating theater.

In January 1993, the College purchased a farm in Dover, Massachusetts, only 4 miles from campus. The Mount Ida College Equestrian Center is a 4-acre facility that backs up to miles of trails abutting conservation land. The Equestrian Center consists of several barns, outdoor arenas, and turnout areas, as well as stalls for 32 horses and a 120-foot by 60-foot indoor arena with an observation area. The instructional activities at the facility include community riding lessons, children's equestrian summer camp, and the Collegiate Equestrian Team. Teaching emphasis is on hunters, jumpers, dressage, and combined training, and a number of horses at the facility compete effectively on various regional circuits. There is a home on the property where the director of the equine program resides. Transportation is provided for students traveling to the facility. The size and flexibility of the Equestrian Center is conducive to continued expansion of the Equine Studies Program.

Each student is assigned a faculty adviser in their major field of study. Freshman and transfer students are also assigned Personal Advisors for Leadership (PAL) who meet with them throughout the year to discuss issues ranging from student life to career goals. The Career Services Office, the Health Center, the Counseling Center, and the Residence Life departments are all professionally staffed.

Location

Newton, a city of 90,000, is located only 8 miles from the center of Boston. College shuttle buses connect students with the Newton Centre business district, where there is MBTA subway service to Boston. The Boston metropolitan area is home to more than sixty other institutions of higher learning, numerous historic sites, a wide variety of shops, and diverse cultural and social opportunities. Local industrial parks, business districts, and shopping malls provide a wide variety of easily accessible employment opportunities.

Admission Requirements

A composite evaluation is made of each applicant. Official college and high school transcripts are required; recommendations, a personal statement, and SAT I scores are recommended. Students applying to the Senior Division for fashion design, graphic design, and interior design must submit a portfolio for review.

Application and Information

Mount Ida uses a rolling admission policy, so there is no deadline for the submission of applications. Applications are considered as long as there is space in the desired program of study. Applicants are notified within three to four weeks after all credentials have been received.

All correspondence should be directed to:

Judy Kaufman or Harold Duvall
Codirectors of Admissions
Mount Ida College
777 Dedham Street
Newton Centre, Massachusetts 02159

Telephone: 617-928-4553 or 4535
World Wide Web: http://www.mountida.edu

Shaw Hall.

NAVAJO COMMUNITY COLLEGE
TSAILE, ARIZONA, AND SHIPROCK, NEW MEXICO

The College and Its Mission

Navajo Community College, the first tribally-controlled college to be established in the United States and the first to be fully accredited, was founded in 1968 to meet the educational needs of the Navajo people. It is chartered by the Navajo Nation Council and authority for its direction lies with a 10-member Board of Regents. The mission of Navajo Community College is to strengthen personal foundations for responsible learning and living consistent with Sa'ah Naagháí Bike'eh Hózhóón, which is the educational philosophy of the College—the Dine traditional living system, which places life in harmony with the natural world and universe. The College offers academically challenging and transferable college-level courses, prepares students for entry into the job market, and provides courses that develop and upgrade college-level skills. One unique function of Navajo Community College is to promote, nurture, and enrich the language, culture, and history of the Navajo people. It also provides educational programs, research, leadership, and consulting services to address the Navajo Nation and community needs.

College facilities include a residential campus at Tsaile, Arizona, and a branch campus at Shiprock, New Mexico. The College provides off-campus centers in Arizona in Chinle, Ganado, Tuba City, and Window Rock and in New Mexico at Crownpoint. The College enrolls an average of 2,200 students.

Navajo Community College is fully accredited by the Commission on Institutions of Higher Education of the North Central Association of Colleges and Schools. The College holds memberships in the American Association of Community and Junior Colleges; the Arizona, American, and Pacific Associations of Collegiate Registrars and Admissions Officers; the American Indian Higher Education Consortium; and the Association of American Colleges.

Academic Programs

Navajo Community College's programs and facilities are open to all, regardless of race, sex, creed, or national origin. It is dedicated to providing a sound, basic education in a familiar environment for students who plan to transfer to a four-year college or university or who plan to complete a program of study leading directly to employment. The College operates on a sixteen-week, two-semester calendar system and summer sessions. All credits are expressed in terms of semester hours. A minimum of 64 credit hours must be earned in an academic program of study designed to meet general education and program requirements. Academic degrees which can be earned include the **Associate of Arts**, the **Associate of Science**, and the **Associate of Applied Sciences** degrees. Certificate programs designed for employment opportunities are also available. As part of its curriculum, the College teaches the history, language, and culture of the Navajo people. Navajo history and philosophy are integrated into the traditional academic subjects of the College curricula to enhance student respect for Navajo heritage and to develop an appreciation of basic universal concepts and principles.

Associate Degree Programs The Associate of Arts degree is offered in business, computer information systems, elementary education, fine arts, liberal arts, Navajo bilingual-bicultural education, Navajo culture, Navajo history and Indian studies, Navajo language, psychology, social science, and social work. The Associate of Science degree is offered in computer science, earth/environmental sciences, life sciences, and pre-engineering. Preprofessional programs are offered in forestry, medicine, nursing, physical therapy, resource science, and veterinary science. The Associate of Applied Science is offered in business administration, educational assistant studies, and office administration.

Certificate and Diploma Programs Certificate programs include bicultural specialist, clerical, and instructional assistant studies.

Special Programs and Services The Continuing Education Program is designed to meet the professional educational needs of registered nurses, educators, administrators, and other professionals and paraprofessionals employed in or near the Navajo Nation. The program builds upon strengths inherent in the Navajo culture and lifestyles and takes those beliefs and practices into the work setting to help individuals provide more sensitive care and services to those they serve. This program is located in Tuba City; however, programs are offered through the Navajo Nation and are specifically developed to meet the training needs of requesting agencies. For more information on available programs, contact the coordinator, Tuba City, Arizona (telephone: 520-283-6321 or -6322).

Off-Campus Programs

NCC Centers are located in Tuba City (telephone: 520-283-5113), Window Rock (telephone: 520-871-2230), Chinle (telephone: 520-674-3319), Ganado (telephone: 520-755-3555), and Crownpoint (telephone: 505-786-7391). The centers make it possible for residents of the Navajo Nation and others in these areas to take classes to fulfill general education requirements, work on a certificate, an associate degree program, or enroll in classes for personal interest and enjoyment.

Credit for Nontraditional Learning Experiences

Students currently enrolled at Navajo Community College may apply for credit by examination in certain courses by contacting the respective campus Deans of Instruction. Each division has qualifications in order for a course to be challenged. Students must pay the cost of the examination and the per-credit-hour tuition fees. NCC credit by examination is not necessarily transferable to other colleges and universities.

Costs

The total cost per semester in 1996–97, including tuition, room and board, and other incidental fees, is estimated at $2105. The tuition is $25 per credit hour. A refundable housing deposit of $50 is required at Tsaile Campus. Students living in the dorms are also required to purchase meal tickets under a five-day meal plan or a seven-day meal plan.

Financial Aid

Navajo Community College attempts to make it possible for potential students to enroll. Most types of financial help are available to citizens of the United States who are high school graduates. No scholarship or other financial assistance is available for international students. The forms of financial aid available are Federal Pell Grants, Federal Supplemental Educational Opportunity Grants (FSEOG), Federal Work-Study Program, Bureau of Indian Affairs Grants, Navajo Tribal Scholarships, sponsored scholarships, Arizona State Student Incentive Grants, and New Mexico State Student Incentive Grants.

Faculty

Navajo Community College has 52 full-time faculty members on its Tsaile, Shiprock, and community campuses. Of these, 19 percent have doctorates, 60 percent have master's degrees, and 21 percent have baccalaureate degrees. Of the full-time faculty members, 15 percent are authorities on Navajo history, culture, language, or arts. An additional 107 adjunct instructors teach at locations throughout the Navajo Nation.

Student Body Profile

The distinctiveness of each campus is reflective of the needs of the community it serves together with the special characteristics of its students. There are approximately 2,200 students campuswide. Tsaile Campus is unique within the NCC system in serving a large residential student population as well as commuting students with an average age of 19. Shiprock Campus, with students of an average age of 24, has developed strengths in scientific research programs involving faculty and students. A significant number of the community campus students are adults around 33 years of age with established households and values. The students enrolled at Navajo community campus account for half of the total student headcount. The enrollment is predominantly Navajo, with 10 percent other Native Americans and another 10 percent other ethnic groups, including international students.

Student Activities

All campuses have organized student government associations to create a more cohesive relationship among students. All registered students are members of the Associated Students of Navajo Community College. ASNCC handles all administrative tasks and coordinates all clubs, organizations, and programs that are under its charter. Its activities are coordinated through the Student Programs Office at Tsaile, by the student activities coordinator at Shiprock, and by the academic adviser at community campuses. The president of the Tsaile student body serves as a voting member of the Board of Regents.

Facilities and Resources

At the Tsaile Campus, the design of the buildings reflects the strength and dignity of the rich Navajo culture and heritage. The administrative, instructional, housing, recreational, cafeteria, and library facilities are accurately placed in reverence to traditional Navajo beliefs and paralleling education with Navajo ceremonial life.

Institutional support services and additional facilities include postal service, the computer center, the Navajo Community College Museum and Gallery, and a bookstore.

The Shiprock Campus is set in a 500-acre compound with its own accommodations for student, athletic, administrative, instructional, dining, and research services.

Advisement/Counseling Academic advisers provide vital services to students concerning their program of study and career options. Each student is assigned an adviser to provide guidance on academic programs and enrollment. They also assist students in making appropriate decisions concerning long-range educational goals.

Library and Audiovisual Services The NCC Library, known as Naaltoos Ba'Hoogan ("House of Papers"), contains a complete college-level collection of print and nonprint materials. The library provides books, magazines, newspapers, microfilm, pamphlets, and microfiche for student and faculty use. In keeping with the philosophy of the College, the library houses the Moses-Donner collection of Indian materials. This reference section includes books, periodicals, newspapers, phonograph records, maps, and films.

Location

Navajo Community College's **Tsaile Campus** is located in the Navajo Nation at an altitude of approximately 7,000 feet. It has an abundance of semidesert vegetation as well as sagebrush, and piñon and juniper trees. The Lukachukai Cliffs of the Chuska Mountain Range with an altitude of 7,900 feet lie to the east and historic Canyon de Chelly National Monument begins 3 miles to the southwest. Spring and summer weather is generally mild. Winters are cold and snowy, but there is ample sunshine on the snow-covered landscape. The air is fragrant with evergreens and remarkably clear of pollution. The campus is an expression of the Navajo's desire for harmony between humanity and nature. The **Shiprock Campus** is part of the community of Shiprock, New Mexico, situated in the Four Corners area. Shiprock is surrounded by distant mountains with the majestic and legendary Shiprock standing in isolated grandeur on the western horizon. Students can expect long Indian summers with short periods of wind and rain and pleasantly warm winters with occasional light rain.

Admission Requirements

All qualified students of sufficient maturity are admitted without regard to race, sex, creed, or national origin. To be eligible for Title IV, Federal Financial Aid, students must have a high school diploma or its recognized equivalent or demonstrate the ability to benefit from the education or training offered. International students must have a score of 500 or above on the Test of English as a Foreign Language (TOEFL) and have sufficient financial resources to support themselves while attending Navajo Community College. Navajo Community College does not provide any scholarships or financial assistance to international students.

Application and Information

Applicants must supply the Office of Admissions with a formal application and official high school/college transcripts at least thirty days prior to the intended date of arrival. For international students, all documents must be submitted at least six months prior to date of expected enrollment. All Native American students are required to provide a Certificate of Indian Blood.

For inquiries, correspondence, and information, students should contact:

Office of Admissions
Navajo Community College
P.O. Box 67
Tsaile, Arizona 86556
Telephone: 520-724-6633

Office of Admissions
Navajo Community College
P.O. Box 580
Shiprock, New Mexico 87420
Telephone: 505-368-3529

The Ned A. Hatathli Center on the Tsaile campus.

Peterson's Guide to Two-Year Colleges 1997

NEWBURY COLLEGE
BROOKLINE, MASSACHUSETTS

The College and Its Mission

Newbury College is proud to have one of the largest two- to four-year (2+2) enrollments of any private college in New England. More than 1,050 men and women are currently enrolled as full-time day students, and the total College enrollment is more than 5,400. Students come to Newbury from more than twenty states and forty countries. The College provides housing for men and women on campus. Residence halls differ in age and design, providing a variety of styles. Approximately 30 percent of the students live in the College's residence halls.

Founded in 1962, Newbury College has grown and changed dramatically in the past thirty-five years. However, Newbury College remains committed to promoting the intellectual and personal growth of a diverse population of traditional and nontraditional students. As a community of learners, the College places a strong emphasis on effective teaching and the professional development of faculty and staff members who are dedicated to students' inquiry and discovery in the classroom, curricular, and extracurricular activities. Newbury College's eight academic departments combine hands-on training with rigorous course work to sharpen job skills. The College strives to graduate students who are professionally competent, ethically aware, socially responsible, prepared for lifelong learning, and share a sense of independence derived from knowledge, experience, and reflection.

The College is accredited by the New England Association of Schools and Colleges, the American Physical Therapy Association, and the American Medical Association Joint Review Committee for Respiratory Therapy Education.

In addition to its associate degree programs, the College also offers bachelor's programs in accounting, business managment, criminal justice, health-care administration, information systems, international business management, legal studies, and retail managment.

Academic Programs

Newbury College offers bachelor's and associate degrees across eight academic departments. The College observes a two-semester academic calendar, with first-semester examinations falling before the December holiday break. There is also an extensive summer session.

Bachelor's Degree Programs Bachelor's degree programs are offered in accounting, business management, criminal justice*, health care administration*, information systems*, international business management, legal studies, and retail management*. (Majors with an * are scheduled to be available in fall 1997.)

Associate Degree Programs Associate degrees are offered in twenty-one majors, including accounting, business management, computer application systems, computer information systems, environmental science, fashion design, fashion merchandising, finance, food service and restaurant management, graphic design, hotel and resort management, humanities, interior design, marketing, medical assistant studies, physical therapy assistant studies, psychology, retail management, respiratory care, sociology/social science, and travel and convention management.

Working with an adviser, students plan their courses of study around a prescribed major core. Program requirements establish a framework that includes course work in general education and intensive study in the major area where hands-on training is stressed. For most associate degree programs, at least 60 credits are required, with a schedule averaging five courses per semester.

Internship and Co-op Programs Student internships or clinical affiliations are an integral part of the college curriculum. Students experience "real world" situations through their internships or affiliations, which provide them with on-the-job experience in their chosen fields.

Credit for Nontraditional Learning Experiences

Newbury College accepts transfer credits from fully accredited postsecondary institutions, from the College-Level Examination Program (CLEP); and the United States Armed Forces Institute. The College will accept the transfer of credits for courses that meet the College's academic standards and requirements and in which the student received a grade of C or better.

Costs

For 1996–97, the total cost of a year in most programs at Newbury is $11,320 for tuition, $6670 for room and board (based on double occupancy), and approximately $300 for books and academic supplies. There is an annual $500 comprehensive student fee. All fees are subject to change. For up-to-date information, students should contact the Admissions Office.

Financial Aid

It is the College's hope that all qualified and motivated students should have the opportunity to pursue a college degree. To this end, Newbury endeavors to meet the financial need of all students. A brochure describing financial planning, scholarships, grant aid, and loan programs may be obtained from the Financial Aid Office. The College offers students a variety of need-based and non-need-based scholarship programs. The College also sponsors several academically based scholarship programs. These include the Presidential Scholarships and a series of Recognition Scholarships which are awarded on the basis of a student's academic record, extracurricular activities, and motivation to succeed. Applications for these programs are given to interested students as part of the admission application. Also available to students is work-study, through which eligible students can gain experience with a job on campus as well as earn money for expenses.

Faculty

Newbury has a total faculty of more than 515 members, 54 of whom are full-time. A low student-faculty ratio of 17:1 strongly encourages interaction between faculty members and students. Faculty members are skilled professionals with years of experience and expertise in their fields. They also serve as academic advisers, helping students explore career options outside of the classroom.

Student Body Profile

Newbury College has 1,054 students currently enrolled. Their average age is 23 years old. The number of international students at Newbury College is 23 percent. The student population at Newbury College is 7 percent Hispanic, 3 percent Asian/Pacific Islander, and 13 percent African American. Twenty-five percent of the College's students live off campus. Eighty-nine percent of the students at Newbury are from a New England state.

Student Activities

Students are encouraged to become active participants in the programs that supplement their academic work. Some of the clubs and organizations offered at Newbury are the Aerobics Club, Black Student Union, Drama Club, Design Guild, Innkeepers Club, International Club, Professional Convention Management Association, Pineapple Club, Physical Therapy Club, Radio Club, Respiratory Therapy Club, Student Government Association, and Yearbook Club.

Sports As a member of Region XXI of the National Junior College Athletic Association, Newbury College offers eight varsity sports. Men compete in soccer, basketball, baseball, and golf. Women compete in golf, basketball, softball, and volleyball. In addition to the intercollegiate athletic teams, Newbury also sponsors a variety of recreational activities for both men and women. This intramural program is student oriented in every respect and includes basketball, volleyball, baseball, softball, floor hockey, aerobics, and flag football.

Facilities and Resources

The Hospitality Center is equipped with state-of-the-art airline and hotel reservation systems. Other resources on campus include the respiratory and physical therapy laboratories, two science laboratories, and seven fully equipped kitchens.

Career Planning/Placement Offices The Career Planning and Placement Center offers students practical guidance and career counseling throughout their education by means of individual conferences and group workshops. The Career Center also maintains a job bank which can be utilized by students conducting a job search or seeking an internship.

Library and Audiovisual Services The Newbury College Library, staffed by professionals, houses 30,000 volumes and subscribes to 1,010 printed and electronic periodicals. The library is a member of the Minuteman Library Network, a consortium of 32 libraries, and extends its services to all members of the Newbury community, including graduates. The Academic Resource Center offers learning support services for all students. Professional staff members and trained peer tutors provide both individual and group tutorial sessions in all subject areas. There are three computer laboratories equipped with Macintosh and IBM-compatible computers and a variety of software. The Media Resource Center provides a diversity of services to support, supplement, and enrich the academic and study needs of the Newbury community. Available in the Media Resource Center are a TV studio, a radio studio (WNBY), a darkroom, and a production/preview room in which slide shows, overhead transparencies, and other audiovisual materials are produced, edited, and presented.

Location

Situated only four miles from downtown Boston, Newbury College's Brookline campus is located in an affluent neighborhood within easy walking distance to public transportation, first-run cinemas, and prestigious shopping centers. A shuttle bus provides transportation to and from campus.

Boston is the cultural, business, and education capital of New England. The city provides students with important educational resources and the opportunity to bring career goals into focus through internships and field trips. Equally important is the fact that Boston is the home of the world's largest and most diverse population of college students.

Admission Requirements

The Admission Committee considers each full-time, day-division candidate on an individual basis. The committee requires an official transcript of all previous secondary and applicable college study. SAT I scores are strongly recommended and TOEFL scores are required for all international students. Emphasis is placed upon the candidate's secondary school record, breadth of interest, school recommendations, and other qualifications. The Admission Committee selects not only those applicants whose past academic endeavors are of high quality, but also those who show promise of future academic achievement.

Application and Information

Applications for admission should be filed well in advance of the proposed entrance date, especially if the applicant intends to seek financial aid. However, students submitting applications as late as August are considered for admission on a space-available basis. A nonrefundable application fee of $30 must accompany the application for all day school applicants. In addition, international students need to submit an affidavit of financial support.

For more information, students should contact:

Admission Center
Newbury College
129 Fisher Avenue
Brookline, Massachusetts 02146

Telephone: 617-730–7007 (admission)
            617-730–7100 (financial aid)
Fax: 617-731–9618

An aerial view of the Newbury College campus.

Peterson's Guide to Two-Year Colleges 1997

NEW HAMPSHIRE TECHNICAL INSTITUTE
CONCORD, NEW HAMPSHIRE

The Institute and Its Mission

New Hampshire Technical Institute was established in 1961 by the state legislature as a statewide postsecondary facility. It is a division of the New Hampshire Department of Postsecondary Technical Education. The system includes the Institute, six regional technical colleges, the Police Standards and Training Council, and the Christa McAuliffe Planetarium. Information on the system's educational programs may be obtained from any of its units.

The Institute, which opened in 1965 with 256 students, emphasizes technical education of high quality. Its mission is to serve the entire state of New Hampshire.

Each academic program reflects contemporary technical principles and practices. Math, science, communication, and social science courses enhance the curriculum and help graduates to achieve career goals and personal fulfillment as enlightened, productive members of society. Graduates of the Institute are paraprofessionals equipped with the knowledge, skills, habits, attitudes, and ideas for success in initial employment and for advancement. NHTI graduates find that they are in high demand in today's competitive job market, due in part to the solid reputation the Institute has gained. Most recent reports show that 78 percent of NHTI's graduates opted for immediate employment in the field in which they studied; 18 percent transferred to such four-year colleges as the University of New Hampshire, Plymouth State College, and Rochester Institute of Technology, in most cases with full junior status; 3 percent are employed in an area other than their field of study; and less than 1 percent were not employed. New Hampshire Technical Institute has institutional accreditation from the New England Association of Schools and Colleges. Specialized accreditations include the following: engineering technology programs are accredited by the Technology Accreditation Commission of the Accreditation Board for Engineering and Technology (ABET); the dental assisting and dental hygiene programs are fully accredited by the Commission on Dental Accreditation of the American Dental Association; the nursing program is fully accredited by the National League for Nursing (NLN) and fully approved by the New Hampshire Board of Nurse Education and Nurse Registration; the radiologic technology program is fully accredited by the Joint Review Committee on Education in Radiologic Technology; the Paralegal Studies Program is accredited by the American Bar Association; the paramedic program is accredited by the Joint Review committee on Educational programs for the EMT-Paramedic; and the Human Services programs are accredited by the National Organization for Human Services Education.

Academic Programs

Several of NHTI's programs cannot be found anywhere else in New Hampshire. These include the associate degree programs in dental hygiene, radiologic technology, and paramedic studies and diploma programs in dental assisting and diagnostic medical sonography.

All students at the Institute are required to take courses in the arts and sciences that provide the sound general background that is a necessary foundation for a complete education. Among the offerings are courses in the physical sciences, the biological sciences, mathematics, English composition and literature, sociology, economics, psychology, and history.

Associate Degree Programs The New Hampshire Technical Institute awards **Associate in Science** (A.S.) degrees. Majors include business administration (accounting, banking and finance, human resource management, management, and marketing), computer information systems, criminal justice, dental hygiene, early childhood education, engineering technology (architectural, computer, electronic, industrial/manufacturing, and mechanical), health sciences, hotel management, human services (alcoholism counseling and mental health), nursing, paramedic studies, radiologic technology, and travel and tourism.

Certificate and Diploma Programs One-year diploma programs are offered in dental assisting and diagnostic medical sonography. A variety of certificate programs are available in accounting, community social services, computer information systems, computer technology programming, conflict resolution and mediation, early childhood education, entrepreneurship/small business management, gerontology, hotel administration, human resource management, landscape design, management, marketing, medical transcription, office assistant, paralegal studies, and travel and tourism.

New Hampshire Technical Institute also offers developmental courses for students who wish to pursue an associate degree program but lack the English, math, science, or study skills needed to complete a program in two years. Instruction is offered in a classroom setting, supplemented by seminars, labs, special needs groups, and tutoring.

Costs

For 1995–96, basic academic-year costs for full-time students who are New Hampshire residents were as follows: tuition, $2410; room and board, $3966; books and supplies, $500 (estimated); fees, $156; and personal expenses, $2300 (estimated). Tuition for out-of-state students was $5678 for the academic year; other costs were the same. Some programs have specialized equipment requirements that involve additional expenditure. New England residents may qualify for the New England Regional student plan, which has a tuition of $3616.

Financial Aid

NHTI participates in the major financial aid programs, including Federal Pell Grants, Federal Stafford Student Loan, Federal PLUS, Alternative Loans for Parents and Students, Institute and Governor's Success grants, the Higher Education Loans, and veterans' assistance. NHTI provides some form of financial assistance to 60 percent of its students. NHTI's priority deadline is May 1 for receipt of the following: electronic receipt of the Free Application for Federal Student Aid (FAFSA), NHTI application for financial aid, appropriate tax returns, and acceptance into a program. Students applying for financial aid after this date will receive financial aid on a funds available basis only. NHTI's financial aid office encourages all students who are interested in receiving aid to apply for admission to NHTI before January 1 in order to ensure prompt processing for financial aid.

In addition to these sources, financial aid sometimes is available in the student's hometown. Local agencies provide low-cost loans or scholarships ranging from $50 to $1000.

Listings of such sources are usually available through high school guidance counselors. The New Hampshire Higher Education Assistance Foundation has a free computerized scholarship search. Applications are available by writing to the Foundation at 44 Warren Street, Concord, New Hampshire 03301, or by calling 800-525-2577, Ext. 119 (toll-free).

Federal regulations and New Hampshire Technical Institute policy require that a student must continue satisfactory academic progress and remain in good standing to receive federal or state financial aid.

Faculty

NHTI's faculty members know what skills are needed for success beyond the classroom. They possess a broad spectrum of knowledge and experience. Many have earned both advanced academic degrees and top credentials in their professional fields. On the Institute's faculty there are members with Ph.D. degrees, registered professional engineers, certified clinical mental health counselors, registered radiologic technicians, certified family nurse practitioners, registered nurses, registered dental hygienists, certified dental assistants, and computer analysts. NHTI has a low student-faculty ratio of 14:1.

Student Activities

Campus life at NHTI includes more than classroom study. More than thirty student activities, intercollegiate and intramural athletics, recreational activities, and social events are regularly available.

Student Senate, whose members are elected by the student body, is responsible for most of the social events, while the Residence Hall Council plans activities for each of the residence halls.

Facilities and Resources

There are five major administrative academic buildings and three modern residence halls on the 225-acre campus. The residence halls house 350 students.

Modern classroom buildings house some of the most up-to-date technical and clinical laboratories available anywhere in New Hampshire. The computer laboratories are equipped with the latest in microcomputer systems. Engineering technology students have access to the latest facilities for robotics and computer-aided design. The Paul E. Farnum Library contains approximately 30,000 volumes. The Christa McAuliffe Planetarium opened in February 1990. The Dr. Goldie Crocker Wellness Center, opened in 1995, is the new home for many student activities, including student government, intramural and intercollegiate sports, concerts, dances and academic functions. The Learning and Career Center provides academic support services in tutoring, disabilities, computer-assisted instruction, English as a second language (ESL), and career counseling.

Location

The Institute is built on the site of a Mohawk Indian encampment, and the Merrimack River gracefully surrounds part of campus. The three residence halls overlook the 10-acre Fort Eddy Pond. The capital city of Concord, New Hampshire, is nearby. Concord, a city of 35,000, offers exceptional entertainment as well as excellent dining, recreational, and shopping opportunities. The campus is located within easy commuting distance of the White Mountains and the lake and seacoast regions of New Hampshire. Boston is only a 90-minute drive away.

Admission Requirements

Each program of study has specific requirements for admission which are listed in the Institute catalog. All applicants to the Institute must be high school graduates or the equivalent. A candidate must submit an application for admission and have official transcripts forwarded by high schools and colleges previously attended. It is strongly recommended that applicants submit either SAT I or ACT scores. A response is sent within four weeks of receiving all required materials. It is strongly recommended that students submit an application by March 1 to be considered for the fall semester. Applications received after that date are considered on a space-available basis. Campus tours and interviews can be arranged by calling the Admissions Office.

Application and Information

Candidates must submit the New Hampshire Technical Candidates application form, which is available directly from the NHTI Admissions Office or from the applicant's high school guidance office. Requests for information and application forms for candidates should be addressed to:

Frank Meyer, Director
Admissions Office
New Hampshire Technical Institute
11 Institute Drive
Concord, New Hampshire 03301-7412

Telephone: 603-225-1865
800-247-0179 Ext. 865 (toll-free)
Fax: 603-225-1809

NEW MEXICO MILITARY INSTITUTE
ROSWELL, NEW MEXICO

The College and Its Mission

New Mexico Military Institute was established in 1891 and became a State (Territorial) School in 1893. Its purpose then and now was "for the education and training of the youth of this country with a mandate by law to be of as high a standard as like institutions in other states and territories of the United States." New Mexico Military Institute is primarily an academic institution operating within the framework of a military environment. NMMI is accredited by the North Central Association of Colleges and Schools, the State of New Mexico Department of Education, and by the Department of the Army as a Military Junior college offering Junior and Senior ROTC (Honor School with Distinction or its equivalent since 1909).

Academic Programs

New Mexico Military Institute provides a comprehensive liberal arts curriculum including such disciplines as English, foreign language (Spanish, German, French), history, sociology, philosophy, political science, psychology, business administration, economics, computer science, chemistry, physics, biology, math through college calculus, geology, art, music, and physical education.

Associate Degree Programs The school awards an **Associate in Arts** degree, which requires 68 hours (6 in English, 6 to 8 in the humanities, 9 in social science/history, 8 in laboratory science, 6 to 10 in military science, 3 in mathematics, 2 in physical education, with the balance in electives). A normal load is 17 hours per semester. A cadet may choose to concentrate in a particular area while pursuing the Associate in Arts degree.

Many cadets are interested in pursuing a military career through the ROTC Basic Camp (Camp Challenge) approach. In order to qualify for the two-year commissioning program, a student must successfully complete a six-week training program conducted by the U.S. Army. This course occurs the summer before cadets enter their freshman (second class) year at New Mexico Military Institute. In special cases, students who have three or more years of high school ROTC or prior military service may apply for advanced placement credit. If accepted, they need not attend the Basic Camp. All eligible camp cadets can compete for a two-year scholarship that is awarded upon completion of the Basic Camp. For the 1995 Camp Challenge, there were 1,400 scholarships available. Two years of advanced military science (MS III and MS IV), are required during the freshman and sophomore years, respectively. An advanced ROTC camp is required during the summer between MS II and MS IV. This camp is also six weeks long. Upon successful completion of all phases; two years of college, Basic Camp, MS III, advanced camp, and MS IV, the cadet is commissioned as a second lieutenant in the United States Army Reserve.

Costs

For the academic year 1996–97, in-state tuition is $677, out-of-state tuition is $2428, room is $1000, board is $1800, and the matriculation fee is $5. Accident insurance costs $128. Other fixed fees are $760. Uniforms, books, and supplies cost $1700. This includes all uniform purchases. Additional funds will be necessary for personal expenses. The amount needed varies depending on a cadet's spending habits. New Mexico Military Institute offers a deferred payment plan requiring an initial deposit of $2200. All costs are subject to change.

Financial Aid

Federal financial aid is available to all eligible college students. New Mexico Military Institute participates in the Federal Pell Grant, Federal Supplemental Educational Opportunity Grant, Federal Perkins Loan, Federal Work Study program, Stafford Loan, Parent Loan for Undergraduate Students program and specialized programs for New Mexico residents. New Mexico Military Institute offers a varied scholarship program for merit-based and need-based considerations. The New Mexico Legislator Scholarship Program is available only to New Mexico residents. Scholarships are renewable based on the continued eligibility of the recipient. In 1994–95 over 80 percent of the College student body received either federal or scholarship assistance amounting to more than $1 million. Currently 379 students receive $1,424,764 in assistance, ranging from $500 scholarships to $7,000 in federal financial aid. A full-time financial aid officer is available.

Faculty

NMMI has 75 full-time faculty members, many with terminal degrees, and all are required to have at least a master's degree. The student-faculty ratio is 18:1.

Student Body Profile

The junior college population of 450 at New Mexico Military Institute generally includes cadets from more than forty-two different states and ten other countries. In 1994–95, the ethnic breakdown included 15.9 percent Hispanic, 5.2 percent African American, 3.8 percent Asian, and 3.5 percent Native American students. There were 44 cadets representing ten different nations. Eighteen percent of the corps of cadets were female. Over one third of College students are pursuing an Army commission. College cadets entering the corps of cadets for the first time are new cadets for one semester. New cadets receive yearling status at the completion of one semester and old cadet status with the completion of one year. The new cadet environment is stressful, formal, strict, and just. All cadets are held strictly accountable for their actions. NMMI operates with a Cadet Honor Code that states a cadet will not lie, cheat, or steal, or tolerate those who do. Every cadet is obligated to support and enforce the honor system. NMMI maintains a strict policy regarding the possession, use, or sale of alcoholic beverages and illegal drugs. All cadets live on campus.

Student Activities

Students enjoy video games, pool, bowling, and the snack bar during their free time. Movies on Friday and Saturday nights also contribute to weekend fun. Informal dances are held almost every weekend. Recorded music is provided by students and professional disc jockeys. Two formal balls are held each year, the Homecoming Ball in the fall and the Final Ball in the spring. Escorts from all over the country attend. NMMI students can participate in outdoor activities at the nearby ski resort area of Ruidoso and the Mescalero Apache Indian Reservation. Other attractions include Carlsbad Caverns, Lincoln National Forest, Bottomless Lakes, Living Desert State Park, and the historical town of Lincoln, famous for the exploits of Billy the Kid, Pat Garrett, and John Chisum. Rounding out the Institute's extracurricular activities, students enjoy marching and concert bands, soccer, judo and karate clubs, color guards, and rifle and drill teams. Students may also participate in Saunders Cavalry, Hunter/Jumper, Drama, or Phi Theta Kappa clubs. Student publications include *The Maverick* and the Bronco yearbook.

Facilities and Resources

NMMI's campus encompasses over 40 acres and has some of the finest academic facilities in the country. The yellow brick buildings reflect a military style traditional to the campus since 1909. The Toles Learning Center houses the library and its 68,000-volume collection, TV/communication studio, academic computer center, 200-seat lecture hall, classrooms, and the Student Assistance Center. Available to cadets is an on-line catalog. Also located in the Toles Learning Center is the Computer Services Center. College faculty academic advisers are available to provide students with assistance in college exploration and selection. A computerized college scholarship search program is available in the center for cadet use. NMMI is a regional test center for the ACT, SAT I, TOEFL, and GRE. College-Level Entrance Proficiency (CLEP) exams are available to those cadets wishing to challenge a course. A liaison officer is available whose duties include working with and assisting students interested in attending the national service academies. The Student Assistance Center (SAC) provides professional advisers who offer academic, career, and personal counseling. Transfer guidance on colleges and service academy admission is also available. More specifically, SAC works closely with teaching faculty, guiding their students through the academic program and supporting and encouraging good study habits, proper behavior, and overall academic achievement and growth. Approximately $15 million in cadet room renovations have allowed each cadet access to a state-of the-art computer network, cable TV, and telephones. New Mexico Military Institute has excellent athletic facilities and athletic playing fields. They include a physical education building with four regulation basketball courts, four handball/racquetball courts, an Olympic-size swimming pool with sunning decks, Nautilus exercise equipment and Universal exercise machines. A separate building houses the varsity team locker and weight rooms and a gymnasium for varsity basketball games. The playing fields include twelve tennis courts, a baseball diamond, running tracks (quarter-mile and half-mile), football and soccer fields, and an eighteen-hole golf course.

Location

New Mexico Military Institute is located in the city of Roswell in the southeastern part of New Mexico. It is within sixty miles of skiing in the mountains of Ruidoso and within 200 miles of El Paso to the south and Albuquerque and Santa Fe to the north. The nearest regional airport is Albuquerque International Airport.

Admission Requirements

The minimum standards for normal admission to the college are graduation from high school with at least a 2.0 GPA (on a 4.0 scale) or equivalent and a composite score of 17 on the ACT, or a combined verbal/mathematics score of 800 on the recentered SAT I and a 2.0 GPA. Prospective students for the Army Commissioning program will need a composite score of 19 on the ACT, or a combined verbal/mathematics score of 950 on the recentered SAT I. Applicants and members of the corps of cadets must have never been married, have no dependent children, be in good physical condition, able to participate in athletic and leadership development activities, and cannot be over the age of 23 at the time of admission. The admissions policy of New Mexico Military Institute is nondiscriminatory with respect to race, color, creed, or national or ethnic origin and is in compliance with federal laws with respect to sex and the handicapped. Priority of admission is given to New Mexico residents.

Application and Information

An initial inquiry is welcome at any time. Campus tours are conducted weekdays. Interested students should call to schedule an appointment at any time except for school holidays. Applications are accepted through July into all classes. Notification of acceptance is made on a rolling admissions basis.

For more information, students should contact:

Director of Admissions
New Mexico Military Institute
101 West College Boulevard
Roswell, New Mexico 88201-5173
Telephone: 505-624-8050
800-421-5376 (toll-free)
Fax: 505-624-8058
E-mail: admissions@yogi.nmmi.cc.nm.us

Peterson's Guide to Two-Year Colleges 1997

NORTHWESTERN BUSINESS COLLEGE
CHICAGO, ILLINOIS

The College and Its Mission

Northwestern Business College was established in 1902 as Chicago's first private business college, and for nearly a century it has been helping ambitious students get started on the path to success. As business needs have changed over the years, so have the College's programs of study. Students will find today's NBC is much different from the traditional "business college" of years past. Just like its students, NBC is diversified, career-oriented, and right in step with the times. More than 1,200 students attend classes at the College's two easily-accessible campuses—one in Jefferson Park, just northwest of the Chicago Loop, the other in suburban Hickory Hills.

The College believes in its mission: "The professionals of Northwestern Business College, an institution of higher education, empower students to realize their full personal and career potential. NBC's commitment, integrity, and personal attention provide a thriving workforce through quality educational programs." These educational programs provide hands-on knowledge and training in many of today's most sought-after professions. A highly-focused curriculum and career-relevant courses make it possible for students to earn an associate degree in only eighteen months.

Northwestern Business College is accredited by the Accrediting Council for Independent Colleges and Schools and is a candidate for accreditation with the North Central Association of Colleges and Schools.

Academic Programs

The academic calendar year is divided into four quarters: fall, winter, spring, and summer. Each term is approximately twelve weeks in length. Three terms constitute the academic year; however, students who wish to graduate early attend all four quarters.

Northwestern Business College is committed to providing students with both a foundation and the essential tools necessary for continued personal and intellectual growth. To that end, the College requires that a minimum of 30 percent of a student's course work be in general education. This general education core requirement includes courses in communications and humanities, the sciences, mathematics and technology, and life skills and is intended to help students build a foundation for learning through study and exploration.

Associate Degree Programs Associate in Applied Science degree programs are offered in accounting, allied health (health information technology or medical assisting), business administration (with an optional emphasis in advertising/public relations, business management, finance and investment management, marketing management, or retailing), computer science (business computer programming or business information systems), hospitality management, office technology (with an emphasis in executive, general, information processing, legal, or medical), paralegal, retail merchandising, and travel and tourism (with an emphasis in accounting, computer applications, hospitality management, office technology, or business management).

In order to graduate with an Associate in Applied Science degree, each student must successfully complete a minimum of 100 quarter hours of credit, with a cumulative GPA of at least 2.0.

Certificate and Diploma Programs The College offers an advanced certificate in senior accounting, which requires that the student complete an additional 80 hours beyond the executive accounting Associate in Applied Science degree program or its equivalent. This program qualifies graduates to sit for the Illinois CPA examinations.

Internship and Co-op Programs NBC's renowned externship program puts students on site with one of the area's major employers. Students work in their field of study, earn college credit, and gain valuable business skills at the same time, while also opening doors to potential full-time employment. Externship participants are not remunerated and should be prepared to assume the costs of transportation, lunch, appropriate wardrobe, and other related expenses.

Credit for Nontraditional Learning Experiences

The College will evaluate life experience credits through written examination. Northwestern Business College offers two types of proficiency examinations to determine a student's prior knowledge of a subject. Advanced Status Examinations are given to determine advanced class placement, but do not provide college credit. Credit By Examination (CBE) is a comprehensive exam that relates specifically to the subject matter for which credit is sought, and students who pass the CBE will receive credit for that course. Students should contact the Student Services Department for the list of classes for which proficiency examinations may be taken.

Costs

For the 1996–97 academic year, tuition is $140 per credit hour and $200 per credit hour for computer classes.

Financial Aid

Northwestern Business College recognizes that many students need financial assistance. The College's Financial Assistance Office is available to assist those students and families requiring financial assistance in addition to their own contributions to cover the cost of their NBC education. Financial assistance is available to eligible students who are declared majors in degree or advanced certificate programs and enrolled for 7 or more credit hours. Available assistance includes Federal Work-Study, Pell Grants, Supplemental Educational Opportunity Grants, PLUS Loans, Stafford Loans, Federal Direct Loans, and Veteran's Benefits. In addition, the College offers scholarships and a payment plan. All students applying for financial aid must complete and submit the FAFSA, as well as any other required forms, depending upon the type of aid sought.

Faculty

Because NBC's faculty is made up of working professionals who have built successful careers in the same fields in which they teach, they are able to share insights and perspectives that give meaning to the "real world" outside of the classroom. The approximately 75 faculty members at Northwestern include practicing lawyers, certified public accountants, travel agents, computer programmers, and medical personnel. Small class size (the College has a student-faculty ratio of 16:1) and a comfortable atmosphere allow faculty members and students to work together on a more personal level. Whether students are working in hotel management, business, computer, travel, medical, or retail operations, NBC's faculty members have been there and are ready and eager to pass along the benefits of their experience.

Student Body Profile

The caliber of NBC's faculty members is matched by the quality of the students who enroll. The commitment, creativity, and seriousness of the student body is one of the school's greatest strengths. NBC's enrollment includes approximately 1,200 students. Seventy percent reside within Chicago city limits; others travel from neighboring suburbs, and some from as far away as Indiana. Several hundred of these students attend part-time in the College's evening program.

Nearly twenty countries are represented in the student body. NBC's international students come from diverse ethnic heritages and pride themselves on their bilingual expertise. The College encourages and welcomes economic, racial, ethnic, and religious diversity in its student body.

Student Activities

NBC believes that college is about more than simply attending classes. It's also about participating in activities, sharing interests, helping others succeed, and building lasting friendships. The College's numerous career organizations, which encourage students to explore their career interests outside of the classroom, include Business, Inc.; Hospitality International; Medical Assisting Students Association (MASA); Northwestern Secretaries Association (NSA); Passport; the Paralegal Club; and the Retailing Club. NBC also sponsors a chapter of Alpha Beta Gamma, a national business society established in 1970 to recognize and encourage scholarship among college students in business curricula. In addition, the College offers Student Ambassadors, a service organization of students responsible for representing NBC at special community and college events; Students Helping Students, a peer tutoring program; and an externship program, which offers students the opportunity to gain practical experience in their field of study during their last quarter at NBC.

Facilities and Resources

Advisement/Counseling All new students are assigned a faculty adviser, who is available throughout the school year to provide advice and assistance with scheduling classes and other academic matters. Students who are admitted conditionally are assigned a second adviser in addition to their major area adviser, who will monitor their progress and with whom they must meet regularly. The College provides limited personal counseling to help students with school-related problems and/or to provide referral assistance to appropriate outside agencies.

Career Planning/Placement Offices Because the majority of NBC students are interested in gaining work experience while attending college, job placement is available after their first quarter. The NBC Career Development Office also serves as an active liaison between employers and graduates. More than 90 percent of NBC's graduates have been successfully placed in the field of their choice. The College offers a lifetime placement assistance program that NBC graduates may use at any time in the future. In addition to on-campus recruitment and career fairs, NBC offers guidance in résumé writing, interviewing, and job search techniques, which build the confidence of students and enhance their professional images.

Library and Audiovisual Services Each campus has a special interest library/resource center with current books, periodicals, and reference material for students' use in classroom research and recreational reading. The resource center has an on-line computer service and also houses video- and audiotapes for student use.

Location

The **North Campus** of Northwestern Business College is conveniently located at 4829 North Lipps Avenue, 7 miles northwest of Chicago's Loop in a residential/commercial area. It is easily accessible by bus, rapid transit, commuter train, and car and is convenient to both the Kennedy and Edens Expressways. There is ample parking available. The North Campus provides a comfortable base of operations within the wider world of the city and includes its own array of buildings and environments to support students' learning.

The suburban **South Campus** moved into its new quarters at 8020 West 87th Street in Hickory Hills in the fall of 1992. This one-story building is conveniently located near the intersection of 87th Street, Roberts Road, and the Tri-State Tollway.

Admission Requirements

Northwestern Business College seeks students who have the desire for practical career preparation in their chosen fields and have the ability to achieve academic success. To be admitted to the College, a prospective student must be a high school graduate or hold a General Equivalency Development (GED) certificate and have the minimum required SAT I or ACT scores (minimum conditional scores are 550–700 on the SAT I and 15–17 on the ACT). If SAT I or ACT scores are not available, the CPAt exam administered on campus may be used for admission. Transfer applicants must be in good standing at their previous institution and should submit ACT or SAT I scores as well as official transcripts from previous institutions to the registrar's office at the NBC campus they plan to attend. The College will typically accept transfer credits for courses taken within the last five years for which a grade of C or better has been earned that are comparable to its own courses and fulfill graduation requirements. All transfer applicants are required to take the CPAt examination administered on campus.

International applicants are expected to meet the same admissions requirements as all other students. In addition, applicants whose native language is not English are requested to take the Test of English as a Foreign Language (TOEFL) and must achieve a minimum score of 500 (international students may use the CPAt exam administered on campus in lieu of the TOEFL).

Application and Information

Applications are accepted on a rolling basis, and should be made as far in advance as possible. All prospective students should contact:

North Campus
Director of Admissions
Northwestern Business College
4839 North Milwaukee Avenue
Chicago, Illinois 60630
Telephone: 800-396-5613 (toll-free)

Suburban South Campus
Director of Admissions
Northwestern Business College
8020 West 87th Street
Hickory Hills, Illinois 60457
Telephone: 800-682-9113 (toll-free)

PAUL SMITH'S COLLEGE
PAUL SMITHS, NEW YORK

The College and Its Mission
Paul Smith's College was named for an entrepreneur whose famous resort on Lower St. Regis Lake was synonymous with Adirondack hospitality. Many of the rich and famous of the late nineteenth and early twentieth centuries gathered at the resort to enjoy the mountain wilderness and the comfortable accommodations provided by Paul Smith and his wife, Lydia. Vast land holdings, acquired over the years, were passed on to Smith's son Phelps, who, upon his death in 1937, bequeathed the bulk of the estate to the establishment of a college in his father's name. Paul Smith's College was chartered as a college of the arts and sciences; however, in the tradition of Paul Smith, who believed in "learning by doing", the school provides students with the opportunity to gain practical experience in a chosen field, while obtaining the academic background necessary for a well-rounded education. Today, the College-owned Hotel Saranac, in nearby Saranac Lake, provides students of hotel and restaurant management, culinary arts, and travel and tourism with experience in many aspects of the hospitality industry. Furthermore, the immense expanse of woodlands, lakes, and streams surrounding the campus offers students of forestry, ecology and environmental technology, and environmental studies a large-scale laboratory in which to practice. The combination of "hands-on" and classroom learning that Paul Smith's prescribes has attracted students from twenty-eight states and nine other countries to the campus.

Paul Smith's College of Arts and Sciences is approved and chartered by the Regents of the University of the State of New York and the Commissioner of Education of New York State. The College is accredited by the Commission on Higher Education of the Middle States Association of Colleges and Schools. Paul Smith's is accredited additionally by the Society of American Foresters (forest recreation and forest technician); the Technology Accreditation Commission of the Accreditation Board for Engineering and Technology (surveying technology); and the American Culinary Federation Educational Institute Accrediting Commission (culinary arts).

Academic Programs
Associate Degree Programs Paul Smith's College offers two-year programs leading to **Associate in Applied Science** (A.A.S.), **Associate in Arts** (A.A.), and **Associate in Science** (A.S.) degrees. Courses of study include business administration, culinary arts, ecology and environmental technology, environmental studies, forest recreation, forest technology, hotel and restaurant management, liberal arts, preprofessional forestry, surveying technology, tourism and travel, and urban tree management. Paul Smith's also offers a one-year certificate program in baking. Programs are designed to combine liberal studies with the specific course work and work experience necessary to prepare students either for a particular occupation or for further study at a four-year institution.

The Forestry Division grants A.A.S. degrees in all concentrations. The preprofessional forestry program is comparable to the first two years of a four-year curriculum, and credits earned are readily acceptable by most forestry schools. The forest technician program is designed to prepare students for employment in the forest industry in land and timber management. The forest recreation program teaches the design, development, and operation of recreational facilities. The urban tree management program teaches the planning, planting, and maintenance of trees and plants in the urban environment. Students in this program work for a tree expert company as a requirement for graduation. The surveying technology program gives students valuable technical and work experience while offering credit for two years of the admission requirements for the licensing examination for land surveyor.

The Hospitality Division grants A.A.S. and A.S. degrees as well as certificates (baking). The hotel and restaurant management, culinary arts, and tourism and travel programs are five-semester programs; three semesters are spent in the classroom and lab study at the main campus, one semester is spent training at the College-owned Hotel Saranac, and one is spent on externship working in the field at sites around the country. Students in the culinary arts, hotel and restaurant management, and tourism and travel programs may choose to continue their education at a four-year institution or begin work immediately. Students in the business administration program receive an A.S. degree and are ready to transfer to a four-year business program at another college or university. Students in the baking program are finished after two academic semesters in an intensive, hands-on curriculum and a one-semester externship at a commercial or retail bakery outlet. This training prepares a graduate to be a journeyman baker.

The ecology and environmental technology and environmental studies programs at Paul Smith's are designed to give students a broad background in the environmental field, with a specific focus on the Adirondack lakes, streams, and forests where the school is located. Students in environmental studies are prepared to enter a four-year college to finish their degree, while students in the ecology and environmental technology program have the option of beginning a career as a lab/environmental technician upon graduation or entering a four-year college or university in a range of majors from wildlife biology to environmental engineering.

The Liberal Arts Division awards an A.A. degree upon completion of two years of study. Concentrations are offered in American studies, general studies, mathematics, science, and technical communications. Students may then transfer to a number of prestigious four-year colleges and universities.

Off-Campus Programs
Cooperative work experiences for credit are required in the following programs: baking, culinary arts, hotel and restaurant management, surveying technology, tourism and travel, and urban tree management. Students in these programs have the opportunity to practice what they have learned at locations throughout the country.

Costs
For each of the fall and spring terms in 1996–97, tuition is $5500, board is $1240, and room is $1245. Summer sessions are required for some programs, and the costs vary by program. Additional fees to cover lab charges, student activities, and other costs vary from $155 to $575 per semester, depending on the program. The cost of books and supplies is estimated at $250 to $500 per semester.

Financial Aid
Federal programs available at the College include the Federal Pell Grant, Federal Supplemental Educational Opportunity Grant (FSEOG), Federal Stafford Student Loan, Federal Perkins Loan, and Federal Work-Study programs. The Federal Work-Study awards provide work for more than 70 percent of the student body, and more than 80 percent of the students receive some form of financial aid. The Financial Aid Office encourages students to apply for aid with the Free Application for Federal Student Aid (FAFSA) by the end of January to be processed by March 15. A financial aid brochure is available. State programs processed through the College include New York State Tuition

Assistance Program (TAP), Vermont State Assistance Program, and Rhode Island Educational Assistance Program. College scholarship programs include the Presidential Scholarship, a non-need-based scholarship awarded to outstanding first-year students; the Paul Smith's Scholarship, which has been established to defray costs for prospective students who demonstrate financial need and academic ability; Vocational Scholarships for students who have been recommended by their vocational high school programs; Alumni "Pass it On" Scholarships for students recommended by Paul Smith's College graduates; special Achievement Awards for leadership in athletics; and the Adirondack Scholarship, which is offered to eligible prospective students who have graduated from a high school located within the Adirondack Park.

Faculty

Paul Smith's College faculty is composed of 74 full-time and part-time members. Most faculty members live on or near the campus and participate in all phases of academic life. The student-faculty ratio is approximately 14:1.

Student Body Profile

In fall 1995, Paul Smith's enrolled a total of 771 students from the United States (primarily the Northeast) and nine other countries. The average age of enrolled students was 22, with a range from 17 to 56. Four percent were international students, and another 6 percent belonged to minority groups. Less than 10 percent of students live off campus. Many students enter Paul Smith's soon after high school, although an increasing number of students enroll at Paul Smith's after years in the work force.

Student Activities

Student activities are an important part of life at Paul Smith's. The Student Government is primarily responsible for the sponsorship and funding of a variety of campuswide activities, such as freshman orientation, concerts, dances, talent nights, and weekly movies. Other popular organizations include the Forestry Club, Adirondack Experience Club, Travel Club, American Junior Culinary Federation, yearbook, campus radio station, and Emergency Wilderness Response Team.

Sports For those interested in athletics, Paul Smith's has two gymnasiums, which house a swimming pool, basketball courts, a fitness center with Universal and free weights, an archery and rifle range, a padded aerobics room, a rock-climbing wall, and a multiple-use court for badminton, volleyball, and other indoor sports. Outside, the College has tennis courts, sand volleyball courts, and miles of wooded trails for the cross-country runner or mountain biking enthusiast. Paul Smith's participates at the intercollegiate level in men's and women's Alpine and Nordic skiing, basketball, soccer, and woodsmen's competitions.

Facilities and Resources

Thousands of acres of College-owned lands and waterways in the Adirondack Mountains provide the natural laboratories for students in the forestry and environmental programs. The ninety-two-room Hotel Saranac, with its restaurants, banquet and catering facilities, lounge, gift shop, and travel agency, offers occupational experience for hotel and restaurant management, culinary arts, and tourism and travel students. Located in the College's more traditional classroom buildings are state-of-the-art laboratories for chemistry, biology, physics, computers, graphic arts, photography, mechanical drawing, travel, and culinary arts. The Forestry Division's resources are augmented by a permanent Lane sawmill complex, a mechanical skidder, recreational campsites, and a sugar bush. Paul Smith's library houses 56,000 volumes, 430 periodicals, a computer lab, audiovisual equipment, and four study rooms. Paul Smith's also provides for its students a Student Health Center, 24-hour campus security, a job placement and college transfer office, personal counseling, and campus ministry.

Location

The College is located in the midst of approximately 13,400 acres of College-owned forests and lakes on the shore of Lower St. Regis Lake in the Adirondack Mountains of northern New York State. Students have access to 23 miles of navigable water for boating and fishing, while nearby forests and mountains provide sites for hiking, climbing, and more. The campus is located 22 miles from Lake Placid, site of the 1932 and 1980 Winter Olympics. Students go there to shop or to watch athletes train in luge, bobsled, ski jumping, and other winter sports. Whiteface Mountain, Big Tupper Ski Area, and Titus Mountain provide skiing venues for the beginner as well as the expert.

Admission Requirements

Admission requirements vary by program. The minimum admission requirements for the preprofessional forestry and ecology and environmental technology programs are 3 years of math, including algebra II, and 3 years of science, including biology and chemistry. The minimum requirements for admission to the forest recreation, forest technician, and surveying technology programs are 3 years of math, including algebra II, and 2 years of science, including one lab science. For the hotel and restaurant management, culinary arts, tourism and travel, business administration, liberal arts, and urban tree management programs, the minimum admission requirements are 2 years of math, including 1 year of algebra, and 2 years of science, including one lab science. Assuming all course prerequisites have been fulfilled, admissions decisions are based on academic performance, extracurricular activities, and a personal interview.

Application and Information

Applicants must submit a formal application for admission, a $25 application fee, SAT I and/or ACT scores, and an official high school transcript. Transfer students must submit an official copy of their college transcript. Recommendations, a personal interview, and an essay are all highly recommended but not required. International students are required to submit scores from the TOEFL examination. Because the College operates on a continuing admissions systems, applicants are urged to apply as early as possible. Prospective students normally receive a decision within three to five weeks of the receipt of all application materials.

For more information, students should contact:

Duncan S. Adamson
Director of Admissions
Paul Smith's College
Paul Smiths, New York 12970

Telephone: 518-327-6227
800-421-2605 (toll-free)
(Monday through Friday, 8 a.m. to 5 p.m.)
Fax: 518-327-6161

Students learning in Paul Smith's outdoor classroom.

Peterson's Guide to Two-Year Colleges 1997

PEIRCE COLLEGE
PHILADELPHIA, PENNSYLVANIA

The College and Its Mission

Peirce College is a nonprofit, independent, coeducational two-year college that was founded in 1865. Peirce's mission is to provide high-quality business and career education to a diverse student community in an academic environment that supports the professional excellence of faculty members, staff, alumni, and the business community. Peirce is committed to the philosophy that education should be practical and useful, that each student's ambitions are important, and that personal relationships between students and College faculty members and staff must be maintained. Each year, 30 percent of the graduates transfer to four-year colleges and universities, but most seek immediate employment. Peirce offers a free lifetime placement service to all graduates.

The College campus has an eight-story academic building and six adjacent buildings and facilities used for classrooms, offices, the Student/Faculty Center, and residence halls. The Student/Faculty Center gives individual students and student activity groups space for meetings, recreation, and informal gatherings. All faculty members have offices in this facility, which also includes a lounge and a game room.

Student development programs include a series of Awareness Weeks, a Martin Luther King Day celebration, Women's Month, and organized trips. Student activities include service and cultural organizations, fraternities, sororities, and clubs.

The College is accredited by the Commission on Higher Education of the Middle States Association of Colleges and Schools to award associate degrees. Peirce is approved by the Veterans Administration for educational benefit obtainable under the G.I. bill. The Court Reporting Program is approved by the National Court Reporters Association. The Paralegal Studies Program is approved by the American Bar Association.

Academic Programs

While Peirce's curriculum is business oriented, it is more than just vocational training. The strongly career-oriented programs give students a firm foundation in general education. In all degree programs, students must take general education core courses in English, humanities, social science, and math. All degree programs include training in microcomputers. Word processing is an integral component of the office technologies program. Supervised cooperative education is available in all programs except business transfer and general studies.

A minimum of 60 credits is required for the associate degrees. Certificates of proficiency require 18-24 credits.

Peirce College offers eleven programs leading to associate degrees and five programs leading to certificates of proficiency. Most programs may be pursued in full- or part-time day or evening classes.

Peirce offers associate degrees in accounting, business administration, business transfer, computer network technologies, court reporting, general studies, hospitality management, medical practice management, microcomputing, office technologies, and paralegal studies.

Certificates of proficiency are offered in accounting, computer network technologies, microcomputing, office technologies, and paralegal studies. The accounting certificate program requires an earned associate or bachelor's degree for acceptance.

The Division of Continuing Education offers all programs except court reporting during evening and Saturday classes.

Costs

In 1995-96, tuition and fees were $6500 per year for full-time day students. Books and supplies averaged $50 per course. Evening and summer courses were $181 per credit. College housing was available at $3470 per year. Two or three students may share a housekeeping apartment. Off-campus accommodations are also available. (Costs are subject to change.)

Financial Aid

During the 1995-96 academic year, about 93 percent of the College's students received approximately $4 million in financial aid. Financial assistance includes scholarships, grants, loans, and on-campus employment. Peirce College participates in most federal and state aid programs. Scholarships and grants from College sources are available for both new and returning students. Many opportunities for part-time employment are available in Philadelphia. Applicants for aid must submit both a College financial aid application (available from the Financial Aid Office) and the Pennsylvania State Grant/Federal Aid Application (available from the College's Financial Aid Office or from Pennsylvania high school guidance offices).

Faculty

Peirce College has 30 full-time and 65 adjunct faculty members with broad and diverse professional backgrounds. Most of the faculty members have advanced degrees, and many are practitioners in their fields. Attorneys, certified public accountants, psychologists, market analysts, computer experts, healthcare professionals, business managers, and other professionals are among the teaching staff at Peirce. An overall student-faculty ratio of 19:1 ensures that faculty members are readily available to provide personal guidance to individual students. Faculty members also serve as career and academic advisers.

Student Body Profile

There are currently 746 men and women enrolled as day students and 398 men and women enrolled as evening students. The student body includes both recent high school graduates and adult learners. Ninety percent of the students are from the Philadelphia area, while 8 percent are from other countries. Ninety-five percent of Peirce students live off campus.

Student Activities

The College Activities Board is composed of all officially recognized student representatives and sponsors of all officially recognized student organizations. Through cooperative efforts with the director of student activities, the board is responsible for the planning, coordinating, and budgeting process for educational, cultural, social, and charitable activities. This body works to promote a sense of community at the College.

Facilities and Resources

Peirce has seven microcomputer classrooms to simplify learning and enhance instruction. Each includes printer support with dot matrix and/or laser printers.

Each of the general computer classrooms are configured with 24 Zenith Data Systems 386SX microcomputers with super VGA color monitors, running current versions of MS-DOS and Microsoft Windows applications on Novell Netware 3.11, networked via 10BASE-T and fiber optic. Also included in each classroom is an instructor workstation with a VGA-compatible projection system.

One of the computer classrooms is equipped with Zenith Data Systems 486DX2 microcomputers and three classrooms are equipped with Pentium microcomputers with color monitors. These classrooms run Microsoft Windows for Workgroups over Novell. One of these classrooms has a dedicated Novell Netware 3.12 file server and a Novell Netware 4.1 server, which provide hands-on experience with Novell's operating system. A classroom is dedicated to the developmental education needs of Peirce students. This classroom is configured with Zenith Data Systems 486DX microcomputers with super VGA color monitors and operates on the same Novell Ethernet network. A comprehensive package of instructional and tutorial software can be accessed through the network.

Peirce also has a Hewlett-Packard 3C color scanner and a Hewlett-Packard 1200C color printer. Peirce students can enhance the look of professional business documents using this equipment. In addition, Peirce has five portable multimedia CD-ROM centers equipped with a Dell Pentium microcomputer with super VGA color monitor and a CD-ROM, overhead projector with a VCR, and a Hewlett-Packard 4L laser printer or a Hewlett Packard 650C color printer. Students have the opportunity to experience the multimedia CD-ROM technology.

All microcomputer classrooms are available for student use during nonclass hours. A drop-in microcomputer laboratory is available to students throughout the day and evening hours to work on projects, complete writing assignments, or to further develop computing skills. The laboratory is equipped with fifteen Zenith Data Systems 386SX microcomputers with the exact configuration as in the classrooms, along with printers. These computers are also connected to the main academic computer network for access to the complete range of instructional software.

Location

Because the College is located in the center of Philadelphia, one half block from the Avenue of the Arts, all of the distinctive business, educational, historical, and cultural features of one of the nation's largest and most diversified metropolitan areas are available to Peirce students. All sections of the city and suburban areas are easily accessible to the College community by public transportation.

Admission Requirements

It is the policy of Peirce College to offer admission to applicants without regard to sex, sexual orientation, ancestry, age, race, creed, color, national origin, or an individual's handicap. Admission is based on the student's academic record, personal qualifications, and aptitude for the program selected. Requirements include a high school diploma or general equivalency diploma and a high school transcript. SAT I scores are not required, but are recommended. Admission interviews are strongly recommended. The Admissions Office encourages phone calls and visits to the College. Transfer credits may be accepted up to a maximum of 30 semester credit hours in which a grade of C or better is earned.

Application and Information

Applications, transcripts, testing results, and high school recommendations should be forwarded to the Admissions Office. Applicants are notified of the admission decision shortly after all necessary credentials have been received.

Admissions Office
Peirce College
1420 Pine Street
Philadelphia, Pennsylvania 19102-4699
Telephone: 215-545-6400

Students relax in front of the main entrance of Peirce College.

Peterson's Guide to Two-Year Colleges 1997

PENNSYLVANIA COLLEGE OF TECHNOLOGY
WILLIAMSPORT, PENNSYLVANIA

The College and Its Mission

Pennsylvania College of Technology is Pennsylvania's premier technical college. As an affiliate of The Pennsylvania State University, Penn College enjoys a national reputation for the high quality and diversity of its educational programs in traditional and advanced technologies. Rich opportunities for success in careers based on the new generation of technology are available to graduates of Penn College. More than 90 percent of graduates in recent years have been successful in achieving job placement or pursuing advanced degrees. Among the keys to graduate success is Penn College's emphasis on personal attention and hands-on experience using the latest technology. Campus facilities are state-of-the-art and feature industry-standard equipment. Small classes provide individualized, personal attention from faculty members who are experienced both in teaching and in applying their skills in business and industry. The history of Penn College can be traced back to the former Williamsport Technical Institute—founded in 1941 and nationally renowned as a premier training facility. Today, Penn College continues a tradition of excellence as a modern, comprehensive college emphasizing education in advanced and emerging technologies—and committed to education that meets the needs of a modern workplace.

The Penn College experience focuses on excellence and individual attention from faculty experienced in technology-based training. Student projects reflect real working situations. In fact, a number of campus buildings—the Professional Development Center, Victorian House, and a rustic retreat used for professional gatherings—were designed and constructed by students. State-of-the-art laboratories make a walk through the campus seem like a walk through the future. A fine dining restaurant, child-care center, aviation hangar, dental clinic, and fully automated "factory of the future" are just a sample of the diverse laboratories utilized by Penn College students. The top four reasons students apply to Penn College are program choice, convenience, quality, and affordable cost. The classroom may be a computer lab, a health-care clinic, an airplane hangar, a machine shop, or a forest. It is a campus that truly simulates the modern world of work. Penn College's hands-on learning environment gives students the opportunity to use the most modern tools available to develop their knowledge and skills. Many students participate in internships and cooperative education experiences earning academic credit for real work experiences. The College offers programs leading to associate degrees and certificates in vocational and technical fields and in the liberal arts and sciences, as well as programs for college and university transfer, and unique Bachelor of Science degrees. Programs are housed on four campuses: the main campus in Williamsport, the Earth Science Center located 12 miles south of Williamsport, the Aviation Center at the Williamsport-Lycoming County Airport, and the north campus in Wellsboro.

Academic Programs

Associate Degree Programs "Degrees that Work" best describes Penn College's portfolio of program offerings. Penn College awards associate degrees that are designed to help prepare students for employment or to serve as the basis for additional education. Associate degree programs require a minimum of 60 credits. **Associate degrees (A.A.S., A.A.A., A.A., or A.S.)** are offered in accounting, advertising art, architectural technology, auto body technology, automated manufacturing technology, automotive engineering technology, automotive service management, automotive technology (including programs that emphasize Ford and Toyota training), aviation technology, avionics technology, baking and pastry arts, biology, broadcast communications, building construction technology, business management, civil engineering technology, computer-aided drafting, computer information systems (with emphasis in business programming, computer science, microcomputer applications development, or microcomputer specialist), culinary arts technology, dental hygiene, diesel technology, early childhood education, electrical technology, electronics technology (with emphasis in biomedical electronics, communications/fiber optics, computer-automation maintenance, electronics engineering technology, industrial laser/optics, or industrial process control), environmental technology, food and hospitality management, forest technology, general studies, graphic communication, health arts (with emphasis in cardiovascular technology, emergency medical services/paramedic, general, practical nursing, or surgical technology), heavy construction equipment technology, human services, HVAC (heating, ventilation, and air conditioning) technology, individual studies, industrial maintenance technology, interior plantscape/floral design, landscape/nursery technology, legal assistant studies, mass communications, nursing, occupational therapy assisting, office information systems, office technology (with emphasis in executive assistant, communication specialist, medical office assistant, or office administration specialist), physical sciences, plastics and polymer technology, pre-engineering, quality assurance technology, radiography, surveying technology, toolmaking technology, vocational teacher education, welding technology, and wood products manufacturing.

Bachelor Degree Programs Unique Bachelor of Science (B.S.) degrees focus on the College's "centers of excellence" in such diverse career areas as applied human services, automotive technology management, aviation maintenance technology, business administration, computer-aided product and systems design, computer information technology: analysis and design concentration or data communications and networking concentration, construction management, dental hygiene: health policy and administration concentration or special populations care concentration, electronics engineering technology, graphic design, HVAC technology, legal assistant studies, manufacturing engineering technology, nursing, physician assistant studies, plastics and polymer engineering technology, technical and professional communication, technology management, and welding and fabrication engineering technology.

Transfer Arrangements The A.A.A. programs offer students the opportunity to gain the technical and professional skills needed for employment and to prepare for transfer to a four-year college. The A.A.S. degree programs offer students the technical and occupational skills needed for employment and also can help prepare students for transfer to a four-year college. The A.A. degree programs are designed to parallel the first two years of a liberal arts education at a four-year college. Credits can usually be transferred toward the first two years of a bachelor's degree program.

Certificate Programs Certificate programs are not primarily designed for transfer but, in certain cases, can be used to transfer to some colleges. They vary in length but do not exceed two years of course work. A feature of these programs is the elective. Students have the option of selecting elective courses to broaden the basic academic work required in order to enrich their educational experience. Certificate programs are offered in auto body technician, automotive service technician, aviation maintenance technician, building construction carpentry, cabinetmaking and millwork, computer applications technology, diesel technician, electrical occupations, heavy construction equipment technician, machinist general, plumbing, practical nursing, surgical technology, and welding.

Off-Campus Programs

Cooperative education (co-op) offers Penn College students the opportunity to participate in off-campus, real-life work situations. On co-op assignment, students earn academic credit while they work as regular employees of the co-op employer. Students have worked in co-op assignments throughout Pennsylvania, as well as in eighteen other states, the District of Columbia, Canada, and Puerto Rico. The College also participates in a cross-registration program with Lycoming College, a four-year private institution. Full-time students may cross-register at Lycoming for courses not offered at Penn College.

Credit for Nontraditional Learning Experiences

Penn College offers opportunities for students to transfer course credit earned at other institutions, college credit earned before high school graduation, service credit, DANTES credit, and credit earned through the College-Level Examination Program. A maximum of 30 credits may be transferred.

Costs

Tuition and related fees are based on a per-credit-hour charge. Annual tuition and fees for 1995–96 were approximately $6200 for in-state students and $7200 for out-of-state students. Meal plans are offered by the College dining facility.

Financial Aid

In a typical year, more than 70 percent of students receive financial assistance, with total awards for Penn College students equal to more than $18 million a year. Types of aid available include Federal Pell Grants, Pennsylvania Higher Education Assistance Agency grants, Federal Supplemental Educational Opportunity Grants, Federal Work-Study awards, Federal Stafford Student Loans, Federal PLUS, veterans benefits, Bureau of Vocational Rehabilitation benefits, and emergency loans. The College also has ways to help students budget their money and stretch their dollars. A deferred-payment plan is available in which students can spread their tuition cost over two payments each semester.

Faculty

Penn College has a student-teacher ratio of about 18:1, and the average class size is 18. The College encourages staff development activities among all faculty members to keep instructional methods current with rapidly emerging technologies. Advisory committees made up of faculty members and representatives of business and industry also help ensure that programs meet current workplace needs.

Student Body Profile

There are 4,728 students enrolled. Of these, 3,572 are full-time students and 1,156 are part-time. There is a wide range of ages in the student population—from 16 to more than 60.

Student Activities

The Student Government Association and the Campus Activities Board represent the student body in matters related to College policy and activities. Participation offers students the opportunity to develop leadership skills while contributing to the well-being of the College and the student body. In addition, over twenty active student organizations are recognized on campus.

Facilities and Resources

The hands-on experience offered at Penn College creates a need for a variety of special academic facilities. The main campus includes such facilities as computer and word processing labs (twenty-seven instructional computer labs with over 800 computer systems), an entire printing operation, a dental clinic that is open to the public, an automotive-trades center, a diesel center, a working machine shop, a sophisticated welding facility, a building-trades center dedicated to the construction technologies, a broadcasting studio, modern science laboratories, an architectural studio, computer-aided drafting facilities, and a restaurant that is open to the public. Off-campus facilities include one of the nation's finest aviation/avionics instructional facilities, located at the local airport, and the Earth Science Center, which is dedicated to natural resources management and features greenhouses, a working sawmill, and a diesel technology center.

Library Services The College library is located on the main campus in the Learning Resources Center. The library is open every day during the academic semesters and offers over 60,000 volumes and 900 periodical subscriptions and multiple CD-ROM databases. All material in the general collection may be borrowed, except periodicals and reference materials. Services available through the College library include reference—a skilled, friendly staff is available to assist individual students and to provide classroom instruction in research techniques; interlibrary loan—materials not available in the College library may be borrowed from other libraries; reserves—instructors may set aside specific materials for use for their class; computer searches—on-line and CD-ROM computer searching of databases is available, usually without a fee, for students and staff; and computer minilab—both IBM and Macintosh computers, with printers and resident applications software, are available for students.

Location

The main campus is in the city of Williamsport, known internationally as the home of Little League baseball. Williamsport is the county seat of Lycoming County, which has a population of over 121,000. Williamsport, with a population of over 32,500, offers the advantages of a city situated in a rural environment. The surrounding area is an outdoor-lover's paradise, with ample opportunity for hunting, fishing, hiking, camping, backpacking, and other outdoor activities.

Admission Requirements

It is the intention of Penn College to offer educational opportunities to anyone who has the interest, desire, and ability to pursue advanced study. Because of the wide variety of program offerings, admission criteria vary according to the program offering. At a minimum, applicants must have a high school diploma or its equivalent. Some programs are restricted to students who meet certain academic skills and prerequisites, who have attained certain levels of academic achievement, and who have earned an acceptable score on the SAT I. Questions regarding admission standards for specific programs should be directed to the Office of Admissions. The College offers equal opportunity for admission without regard to age, race, color, creed, sex, national origin, handicap, veteran status, or political affiliation. To ensure that applicants have the necessary entry-level skills, all students are required to take the College's placement examinations, which are used to assess skills in math, English, and reading. When the placement tests indicate that such help is needed, the College provides opportunities for students to develop the basic skills necessary for associate degree and certificate programs. International students whose native language is not English are required to take the TOEFL, submit an affidavit of support, and comply with test regulations of the Immigration and Naturalization Service, along with meeting all other admission requirements.

Application and Information

Office of Admissions
Pennsylvania College of Technology
One College Avenue
Williamsport, Pennsylvania 17701
Telephone: 717-327-4761
800-367-9222 (toll-free)
World Wide Web: http://www.pct.edu/

PIMA COMMUNITY COLLEGE
TUCSON, ARIZONA

The College and Its Mission
Since 1966, Pima Community College has been committed to equal access, quality learning experiences, and equitable opportunity for student success. PCC is the fifth-largest community college in the United States and among the top 25 chosen by international students from all over the world. Students have chosen to take advantage of the low cost, smaller classes, and transferability to such prominent universities like the University of Arizona, also in Tucson.

Five campuses, located throughout the incredible desert landscaped city, offer degrees and certificates in over 70 fields of study. General education and college transfer courses are taught at all campuses; however, specialized programs are taught only in certain locations. Computer labs, libraries, Student Unions, student publications, sports teams, activities, a Center for the Arts, and a full range of student services and resources make the educational experience a complete one. Pima constantly strives to bring the most up-to-date and innovative programs to its students.

Academic Programs
Degrees and certificates in a variety of disciplines are offered, each with different program requirements. PCC has an Honors Program, a Cooperative Education Program, and bilingual courses. An intensive English program is also available. Pima operates year-round, including evenings and weekends.

Associate degrees are granted upon completing a program. A minimum of 60 credit hours of course work at the 100 level or higher is required to earn to an associate degree; however, completion of some programs extend beyond the 60 credit hour minimum. At least 15 semester hours of the total required must be earned at Pima Community College.

Basic, advanced, and technical certificates are awarded in many short-term study program areas, and are granted upon completing a prescribed program curriculum. At least six semester hours of the total required must be earned at Pima.

Associate Degree Programs Students must complete the general education and other requirements outlined, and keep informed of changes that may occur at PCC or a transfer institution. Degree programs include administration of justice, American Indian studies, anthropology, archaeology, Asian studies, automotive technology, business administration, computer science, construction, drama, education, electronics technology, engineering, fine arts, fitness and sport sciences, geology, hospitality, interdisciplinary sciences, liberal arts and sciences, manufacturing technology, mathematics, music, political science, pre–optical sciences, public administration, social services, sociology, speech communication, and youth care rehabilitation.

Certificate and Diploma Programs Certificate programs include some of the same areas of study as degree programs as well as accounting; advertising art and computer graphics; air-conditioning; applied arts; apprentice-related instruction; archaeology; automotive technology; aviation technology; bilingual business administration; construction drafting; construction technology; court administration; dental assisting education; dental hygiene; dental laboratory technology; design; drafting technology; early childhood education; emergency medical technology; environmental technology; finance; fire science; foods, clothing, family, and consumer resources; graphic technology; international business studies; interpreter training; landscape technician studies; legal assistant studies; media communications; mental health technician studies; microcomputer technician studies; nursing; office education; pharmacy technology; radiologic technology; real estate; Reserve Officer Training Corps (ROTC); respiratory therapy; welding; and youth care.

Off-Campus Programs
Students may participate in exchange programs in Mexico and Canada. Telecourses, Internet courses, and distance-learning programs are also offered.

Credit for Nontraditional Learning Experiences
Students have the opportunity to officially earn and record advanced placement in the College through examinations, including advanced placement examinations from high school, College-Level Examination Program (CLEP), Defense Activity for Non-Traditional Education Support (DANTES), and special examinations for credit. Students cannot receive credit by examination for a course that is lower than that in which they are currently enrolled or for which they have already received credit. A maximum of 30 credit hours by examination may be earned by students currently or previously enrolled at PCC.

Costs
For fall or summer semester, Arizona residents pay $31 per credit hour, plus a $5 per-student, per-semester processing fee. For fall semester, out-of-state and international students pay $53 per credit hour for the first 6 credit hours and $160 per credit hour for 7 or more credit hours, in addition to the $5 processing fee (per student, per semester). For summer semester, students pay $160 per credit hour plus the $5 per-student, per-semester processing fee. Additional special and miscellaneous fees may apply to laboratories, music lessons, and special programs. Complete details are available in the College catalog. Tuition and fees are subject to change. Students should estimate approximately $500 per year for books, supplies, etc. Room and board costs vary between $6500 and $9000 per year.

Financial Aid
A full range of student financial aid is offered through the Financial Aid Office. The financial aid program funds are from federal and state programs and private donors. Funds are awarded to students based on financial need, academic achievement, and program of study. Completing the Free Application for Federal Student Aid is the first step in the application process. A separate application may be required for certain scholarships. Priority consideration for assistance is given to students who complete the entire application process prior to May 12 for the fall semester that begins in August. It is important to note that May 12 is a priority date, not an application deadline. All students are encouraged to apply for financial aid. Students who do not have financial need may still qualify for scholarships, temporary short-term loans, or other programs.

Faculty
Pima Community College employs more than 1,500 full- and part-time faculty members, offering students a low student-

faculty ratio of 20:1. Many instructors have advanced degrees and teach courses both at PCC and the University of Arizona. A number of instructors are respected professionals in their field of expertise.

Student Body Profile

Approximately 26,000 students attend Pima Community College. Minority enrollment accounts for more than 35 percent of the total enrollment, and international students make up 2 percent. The average age of a PCC student is 28 and the median age is 25; less than 20 percent of the students are under the age of 20. More than one third of students are enrolled in university transfer programs.

Student Activities

There are various PCC student publications, including the *Aztec Press*, a weekly newspaper; the *SandScript*, an award-winning magazine published by the West Campus; or the *Cababi*, which is published by the graphic technology students at the Downtown Campus. Clubs and activities designed to promote student leadership are also sponsored by the College.

Sports The College is a member of the Arizona Community College Athletic Association and the National Junior College Athletic Association (NJCAA Region 1). Intercollegiate and intramural teams compete in soccer, baseball, golf, cross-country, basketball, tennis, track, volleyball, softball, flag football, and racquetball. Recreational sports such as karate, ice hockey, rodeo, Tae Kwon Do, judo, indoor track, marathon, and wrestling are also offered.

Facilities and Resources

Computer labs, Student Unions, cafeterias, a Center for the Arts complete with a gallery, two theaters and classrooms, bookstores, a gymnasium, student orientation programs, tutoring and advising services, free parking, and convenient bus service to all campuses are available. Assistance is given to international students in locating housing, orientation to PCC and Tucson, and all other aspects of making the experience at Pima a good one.

The Student Development staff provides a number of services to students, including human development education courses, special programs designed to assist minority students, women re-entering college, international students, veterans, and physically impaired or limited-mobility students, career centers, job placement services, and Disabled Student Resources (DSR).

PIMAINFO gives students access to several services either through screen computer kiosks located at each campus and in locations throughout Tucson and the surrounding areas or through a personal computer. Information on registration, academic calendars, campus maps, services for international students, admission requirements, student orientation, a college catalog, schedule of classes, and an interactive schedule planner is accessible. Individual student data can be viewed, as well as PIMA LINK, the PCC Library Information Network.

Library and Audiovisual Services Library services are available at the **Desert Vista, Downtown, East,** and **West Campuses.** Resources are listed in a single computerized catalog and shared through courier and telefacsimile services, which include thousands of books and journals, videos, audio tapes, CDs, microforms, and several CD-ROM databases.

Location

Tucson, a city of about 700,000, lies in the spectacular Arizona-Sonora Desert—the only place in the world where the saguaro cactus grows. Five mountain ranges, blue skies, lots of sunshine, and stunning sunsets surround the Old Pueblo, as it is called. Students can explore any one of many museums or historical site like the Spanish-built Mission of San Xavier del Bac or the O.K. Corral in Tombstone; enjoy many outdoor activities like golfing, tennis, hiking, and even snow skiing atop Mount Lemmon; or visit the Kitt Peak Observatory, the Titan missile silo, or Biosphere 2, a space-age enclosed ecological project. Just hours away are the beaches of Mexico, lakes and skiing in northern Arizona, and the magnificent Grand Canyon.

Admission Requirements

The Pima County Community College District is open to students if they fall within one of the following categories; however, accessibility may be limited because of certain curriculum requirements, fiscal constraints, and/or facility limitations. Students may be accepted if they are a graduate from an accredited high school, a recipient of a GED certificate of high school equivalency, a transfer student from an accredited college, a non–high school graduate who is 18 years of age or older who can benefit from instruction, a non–high school graduate between the ages of 16 and 18 who has officially withdrawn from high school and who can benefit from instruction, a student currently enrolled in high school who presents written approval from his/her principal and parents or legal guardians, a student currently enrolled in high school who presents a combined score of 930 or more on the verbal and math portions of the SAT I or a composite score of 22 or more on the ACT and written approval from his/her parents or guardians, an international student planning to enroll for 12 credit hours or more who has completed an academic program equivalent to an American secondary school and has a score of 450 or better on the TOEFL or whose native language is English, or an international student planning to enroll for less that 12 credit hours who must demonstrate English proficiency if enrolling in courses other that ESL or courses offered bilingually. For all programs, preference in admission may be given to Pima and Santa Cruz county residents. No person shall be denied admission to the College on the basis of sex, race, creed, color, national origin, age, or handicap. Admissions offices are open year-round at each of the College campuses to receive applications and to provide information on curriculum programs, class schedules, and registration procedures.

Application and Information

Admission is made on a continuous basis. International students must complete special application requirements before an I-20 is issued. For an application and complete information, please contact:

Pima Community College
2200 West Anklam Road, Room SC236
Tucson, Arizona 85709-0001
Telephone: 520-748-4964
Fax: 520-748-4965
E-mail: lnutt@pimacc.pima.edu
World Wide Web: http://www.pima.edu

Peterson's Guide to Two-Year Colleges 1997

POTOMAC STATE COLLEGE OF WEST VIRGINIA UNIVERSITY
KEYSER, WEST VIRGINIA

The College and Its Mission

Since 1901, Potomac State College has provided a setting for serious academic thought and reflection. Here young men and women have found an environment that fosters individual growth, a dedicated faculty, personalized attention, and an opportunity for self-direction. As the only residential branch of West Virginia University, Potomac State College provides the advantages of attending a major university on a small-college campus. With an enrollment of approximately 1,100 students, Potomac State College is large enough to offer a variety of majors, but small enough not to lose sight of its commitment: the student is the College's most important concern. The College has maintained full and continuous accreditation as an associate degree–granting institution since first accredited by the North Central Association in 1926. Potomac State's accreditation was recently extended for ten years, the maximum allowable time period between accreditation visits. Small junior colleges are not for everyone. They are for individuals who want professors to call them by name, who enjoy the freedom to express themselves in class, and who like the feeling of belonging that a small campus can offer. Potomac State College, with its small enrollment, allows each student to become a full member of the college community, not just a number. The educational experience at Potomac State is designed to allow students to become an integral part of the College, to develop their maximum potential, and to go forth with confidence as they pursue a baccalaureate degree at West Virginia University or another college or university or seek employment in their chosen field.

Four residence halls, accommodating 60 to 100 students each, are available for living on campus. Two halls are for men, one is for women, and one is a privileged living residence hall for qualified men and women students. Each residence hall is served by a full-time resident director and several student resident assistants. Each facility comfortably houses two to a room and is within easy walking distance of the library, academic buildings, and dining facilities. Residence halls are air-conditioned, have cable television, and each room is equipped with a private telephone for each occupant.

Academic Programs

The breadth of educational offerings at Potomac State College can best be seen in the diversity of its transfer majors. Potomac State offers thirty-five programs leading to an **Associate in Arts (A.A.)** degree, including agriculture, biology, business administration, chemistry, civil engineering, computer science, economics, electrical engineering, elementary education, English, foreign languages, forestry, general program (nonscience majors), general program (science majors), geology, history, journalism, mathematics, mechanical engineering, music, physical education, physics, political science, preprofessional programs (dentistry, law, medical technology, medicine, nursing, pharmacy, physical therapy, social work, and veterinary medicine), psychology, secondary education, and sociology.

Twelve two-year career/technical programs are offered, leading to an **Associate in Applied Science (A.A.S.)** degree, including accounting technology, agriculture technology, electronics technology, general business technology, horticulture technology, industrial supervision and management technology, microcomputer application specialization, microcomputer programming specialization, office systems technology (options in executive secretarial, medical secretarial, and information processing), and small business administration technology.

Program requirements may vary, but, in general, students are required to complete a minimum of 64 prescribed credit hours and maintain at least a 2.0 grade-point average in order to graduate with an Associate in Arts or an Associate in Applied Science degree. Potomac State College's academic calendar is based on two semesters and two 5-week summer terms.

Credit for Nontraditional Learning Experiences

Applicants who have gained a significant level of maturity through their life experiences may gain college credit for their educationally related experiences through the College-Level Examination Program (CLEP) of the CEEB. The policy of the West Virginia Board of Trustees allows credit to be awarded for successful completion of any of the CLEP Subject Examinations, except English composition and freshman English, as well as allowing up to 34 hours of general education credit for successful performance on the CLEP General Examinations.

Costs

Potomac State College is committed to maintaining relatively low costs without compromising high-quality instruction. In fact, Potomac State's costs have consistently been below those of other West Virginia colleges and the College is considered by many to be an educational bargain—not only by West Virginians, but by out-of-state students as well. Yearly tuition and fees for West Virginia residents in 1995–96 averaged $1812 and for nonresidents, $5644. Room costs are $1772 per year and board costs are $1844 per year for both residents and nonresidents.

Financial Aid

Potomac State College has numerous scholarships available and the Financial Aid Office works diligently to ensure that no qualified student is denied an education because of limited financial resources. Approximately 85 percent of all students receive some form of financial assistance—scholarships, Pell grants, loans, and college work-study, with awards averaging $2200 per academic year. An institutional application for financial aid as well as the FAFSA must be completed in order to be considered for assistance. Interested students should contact the Financial Aid Office at 304-788-6852.

Faculty

The faculty at Potomac State is primarily a teaching faculty, geared toward fostering a positive relationship with students. With 40 full-time faculty members and 30 part-time members, the ratio of students to faculty is about 14:1. Since a high priority is placed on individual interaction between instructors and students, faculty members also act as students' academic advisers. Potomac State takes pride in its small class sizes and its commitment to provide students more personal attention than they would generally receive at large universities.

Student Body Profile

A regional branch of West Virginia University, Potomac State College is a public, coeducational, junior college attracting students from twenty-six states and several other countries. Its

1,163 students primarily come from high schools ranging in size from 150 to 2,500 in the states of West Virginia, Maryland, Pennsylvania, and Virginia. Approximately 80 percent of the students at Potomac State are between the ages of 18 and 21 and 8 percent of all students belong to a minority population. Potomac State's male-female ratio is approximately 51:49 with one-third of its students living in college residential housing.

Student Activities

The executive and legislative arm of the student body, the student government organization, works in cooperation with the College administration to advance the interests of students. It represents the students' concerns and issues, budgets the student activity funds, and plans activities for the students. Members of the student government are elected officers, and all students are encouraged to participate. In addition to student government, students are encouraged to participate in Sigma Phi Omega honor society, to become involved with various clubs and performing groups, or to become a staff member of the student newspaper at Potomac State, the *Pasquino*.

Sports For those with well-developed athletic skills, Potomac State provides an opportunity to participate in intercollegiate team sports. The college is a member of Region XX of the National Junior College Athletic Association (NJCAA). Varsity sports in volleyball and basketball are available for women. For men, football, basketball, and baseball are options in the sports arena.

Facilities and Resources

Library and Audiovisual Services The heart of any academic institution is its library, and Potomac State is justly proud of the resources available in the Mary F. Shipper Library. Under the expert guidance of professional librarians, students may research a report or simply browse through our 43,000-volume, open-stack library. Potomac State also has a Learning Resource Center that utilizes the latest in media technology and houses a 24,000-piece collection of nonprint materials to assist students in their studies. CD-ROM and on-line databases are available for student, faculty, and staff use.

As a complement to its library's resources, Potomac State also provides students with ample access to state-of-the-art computer facilities. Located in Academy Hall, the Computer Center utilizes a Digital Equipment VAX 4000. In addition to 140 personal computers available for student use, Potomac State College is a member of WVNET. WVNET is a statewide computer network that provides students, faculty, and staff access to a wide variety of hardware and software systems.

Tutoring/Counseling Student Support Services is a program at Potomac State that was designed to help the student. An expert student support services staff provides academic tutoring; study and reading skill development; academic, personal, and social counseling; career counseling; and assistance with the transfer process to the main campus or to other colleges and universities. The student support services staff is committed to provide any service that will assist the student toward a more successful college career.

Location

Situated in West Virginia's's eastern panhandle, the 16-acre campus is ideally located for the enjoyment of the state's proud mountain heritage. Located in Keyser, West Virginia, a quiet community of about 8,000 residents, Potomac State College's campus is within leisurely walking distance of local shopping and community facilities. The College is accessible by U.S. Route 220 and I-68, Amtrak, and regional air service through Cumberland, Maryland.

Admission Requirements

Potomac State College of West Virginia University endeavors to admit students who show reasonable promise of successful academic performance. For West Virginia residents, the principal qualification for admission is graduation from an accredited high school or a high school diploma through the General Education Development (GED) tests. Non–West Virginia residents must meet one of the following criteria to qualify for admission: graduation from an accredited high school with a high school GPA of 2.5 or above, graduation from an accredited high school with an ACT composite score of 16 (SAT I combined score of 760) or above, or graduation from an accredited high school with a GPA of 2.0 or above and an ACT composite score of 14 (SAT I combined score of 660) or above.

Application and Information

Students should submit an official transcript as well as copies of ACT or SAT I scores when applying for admission to Potomac State. All prospective students should contact:

Office of Admissions and Records
Potomac State College of West Virginia
Keyser, West Virginia 26726

Telephone: 304-788-6820
Fax: 304-788-6939

Campus life at Potomac State College.

Peterson's Guide to Two-Year Colleges 1997

ROBERT MORRIS COLLEGE
CHICAGO, ORLAND PARK, AND SPRINGFIELD, ILLINOIS

The College and Its Mission

Robert Morris College is a private nonprofit college dedicated to providing students from diverse socioeconomic and academic backgrounds the foundation necessary to meet the expectations of business and society. The College meets the needs of each student through a distinctive step-by-step approach to academic achievement combined with a high degree of guidance and faculty involvement. Robert Morris College is accredited by the North Central Association of Colleges and Schools. Its history dates to 1913. The College provides students with a choice of three campuses—Chicago, Orland Park, and Springfield, Illinois.

The College recognizes diversity among its student body and offers choices that include three levels of academic achievement: a diploma in ten months, an associate degree in as little as fifteen months, and the Bachelor of Business Administration degree in three years or less.

The records of the College's students and graduates are the best indicators of what a prospective student can expect from RMC. Eighty-four percent of Robert Morris College students graduate from the programs they begin. The Placement Department, which has offices at each of the College's three campuses, continuously cultivates employment opportunities for Robert Morris graduates among personnel representatives in business, industry, and professional offices. Over the years, 95 percent of all Robert Morris College graduates requesting job placement assistance successfully secured employment in their chosen field.

Academic Programs

The College's academic calendar consists of five quarters, each of which is ten weeks long. The year-round calendar enables students to earn a diploma in ten months, an associate degree in five additional months, and a bachelor's degree in fifteen additional months.

By concentrating on the specialized subjects related to the student's chosen career field, the College's diploma curricula provide students with the skills and knowledge necessary to enter the job market. A diploma requires 64 quarter hours of credit with core requirements dependent on the student's major. Diplomas can be earned in the following areas: accounting, administrative secretarial, business administration, CAD/drafting, computerized business systems, computer systems technician, executive secretarial, graphic design, health information technology, interior design, legal secretarial, medical assisting, multimedia and computer imaging, and travel and tourism. All credits earned toward a diploma can be applied toward meeting associate and bachelor's degree requirements.

Associate Degree Programs An associate degree requires at least 100 quarter hours of credit with a minimum of 32 hours of credit in general education in the areas of communications, humanities, math/science, and social/behavioral science. A minimum of 52 quarter hours of credit is required in major course work, and the remaining hours are electives split between general education and major course work. The **Associate in Applied Science** degree is awarded in accounting, allied health, business administration, CAD/drafting, computers, graphic design, secretarial science, and travel and tourism.

The bachelor's degree requires a minimum of 180 quarter hours of credit. A minimum of 76 hours of credit is required in general education courses and 104 hours in major course work. The Bachelor of Business Administration degree offers concentrations in accounting, business administration, computer information systems, health-care management, and sports management. More than 26 transfer agreements have been established between Robert Morris College and community colleges, allowing students who have earned associate degrees elsewhere to complete their bachelor's degree at RMC by transferring in as a junior.

Degrees vary among campuses. Both peer tutoring and faculty tutoring are available to students at no additional cost and hours are targeted to meet individual students' schedules and needs.

Off Campus Arrangements

The College has well-established cooperative education programs for all majors. Major area corporations and professional offices are among participating co-op employers. In addition, Robert Morris College offers students the opportunity to study abroad at the Institute of European Studies in Vienna, Austria. Students are able to earn 16 quarter hours of credit while studying abroad.

Credit for Nontraditional Learning Experiences

Robert Morris College does not grant credit for nontraditional learning experiences.

Costs

Robert Morris College has one of the lowest tuition rates of any baccalaureate degree–granting private college in the state. Tuition for 1996–97 is $3250 per quarter. The cost of books and supplies varies by major from $200 to $300 per quarter.

Financial Aid

Robert Morris College participates in the following federal and state financial aid programs: the Federal Pell Grant, Illinois Monetary Award (SSIG/IMA), Federal Supplemental Educational Opportunity Grant (FSEOG), Federal Stafford Student Loan, Federal Perkins Loan, Federal PLUS loan, and Federal Work-Study (FWS) programs. In addition, the College awards institutional grants on the basis of need, scholarship, residence, academic major, or a combination of these factors. All students must complete a financial-planning interview with their admission counselor, and all are urged to complete the Free Application for Federal Student Aid (FAFSA). Approximately 90 percent of the student body receives some financial assistance. In the 1995–96 academic year the College awarded over $5 million in institutional aid.

Faculty

The faculty members at Robert Morris College are selected on the basis of their academic credentials, career experience in their field, and dedication to giving special attention to every student. All faculty members possess a master's degree in their chosen field and many possess a Ph.D. or professional certification in their area of specialization. The student-faculty ratio is approximately 20:1.

Student Body Profile

The student body of just over 3,400 is a multicultural, ethnic, and racial mix representative of the communities served. For the 1995–96 academic year, the institutional demographics were as follows: 29 percent Caucasian, 28 percent Hispanic, 40 percent African American, and 3 percent Asian. Twenty-four percent of students are men, while 76 percent are women. Breaking down age groups, 38 percent of students were between the ages of 18 and 21, 33 percent between 21 and 25, and 29 percent were 26 or older.

Robert Morris College is recognized as awarding more associate degrees to minorities than any other Illinois institution and ranks seventeenth in the nation. Robert Morris College is also recognized as a Hispanic Serving Institution by the Hispanic Association of Colleges and Universities (HACU).

Student Activities

Robert Morris College offers students a wide range of student organizations, including RMC Student Ambassadors, Alpha Beta Gamma (International Honor Society), American Center for Design, The Eagle Newspaper, the Ecology Club, and Collegiate Secretaries International. Robert Morris College offers students several intercollegiate sports programs, including men's and women's basketball, women's soccer, women's volleyball, men's baseball, and track and field. The College is a member of the National Association of Intercollegiate Athletics (NAIA) and the Chicagoland Collegiate Athletic Conference (CCAC) Division II.

Facilities and Resources

The College provides general purpose classrooms, specialized laboratories, and study/leisure lounges at each campus. The technology-based library has on-line capability connecting the College's three campuses. Multimedia CD-ROM, as well as on-line access to the Internet, offer students advanced research capabilities along with sizeable collections of reference and resource volumes, as well as periodical subscriptions and vertical file information. State-of-the-art computer laboratories are used for in-class instruction and out-of-class practice.

Location

Located in Chicago's Loop, the College's main campus is in the heart of the downtown business and financial district. The cultural and business activities in the area are easily accessible to students and are often incorporated into the students' learning experience. The **Chicago Campus** is located at 180 North LaSalle Street and is readily accessible from all parts of the city and suburbs by bus or train. Parking is available in the immediate vicinity. The **Orland Park Campus** is located at 43 Orland Square Drive, adjacent to the Orland Square Mall. Situated approximately 30 miles southwest of Chicago, the campus is accessible via bus and train and interstates 80 and 55, which run parallel on the south and north of the campus, respectively. Known as the "Golf Center of the World," Orland Park is also becoming a corporate center of the southwest Chicago suburbs, offering students ample opportunity for professional growth through externships and employment. The **Springfield Campus** is located at 3101 Montvale Drive (Montvale Drive and Wabash Avenue), just east of White Oaks Mall. Located in the capital city of Illinois, students have at their fingertips a variety of governmental, historical, and cultural opportunities that enhance their educational experience. In addition, these activities further students' professional growth through externships and employment opportunities. The College is accessible by bus and ample parking is also available.

Admission Requirements

The individualized admissions process consists of the evaluation of the student's high school transcript or GED test scores by the Admissions Review Board and an interview with an admissions counselor. The College offers a tuition-free College Prep Program to applicants whose high school records indicate a need for strengthening communications and study skills before beginning career programs. College Prep concentrates students' efforts on study skills, grammar, word usage, oral communications, basic math skills, time management, and personal development through counseling regarding attitudes and attendance. Upon successful completion of College Prep, applicants may enter diploma or degree programs.

Robert Morris College admits students of any race, color, sex, national origin, or with any disabilities and grants them all rights and privileges accorded to Robert Morris College students. It does not discriminate on any of these bases in administration of its admission or educational policies, loan programs, placement service, housing, or other College-administered programs.

Application and Information

Applications can be obtained by contacting the Admissions Office at any of the College's three campuses. The completed application and the $20 application fee should be sent to the Admissions Office. The College operates on a rolling admission basis, and the students can enroll at any of the five times. For further information, prospective students should contact:

Admissions Office
Robert Morris College
180 North LaSalle Street
Chicago, Illinois 60601
Telephone: 312-836-4608
800-225-1520 (toll-free)

Admissions Office
Robert Morris Office
43 Orland Square Drive
Orland Park, Illinois 60462
Telephone: 708-460-8000
800-225-1520 (toll-free)

Admissions Office
Robert Morris Office
3101 Montvale Drive
Springfield, Illinois 62704
Telephone: 217-793-2500
800-445-7271 (toll-free)

SAGE JUNIOR COLLEGE OF ALBANY
ALBANY, NEW YORK

The College and Its Mission
Sage Junior College of Albany is a private coeducational two-year college offering over twenty associate degree programs. Founded in 1957, the College provides a solid liberal arts foundation regardless of the major of study. Sage JCA is part of the Sage Colleges, which is a federation of four distinct colleges. The others are Russell Sage College, which offers bachelor's degrees for women; Sage Evening College, which offers associate and bachelor's degrees in the evening, and Sage Graduate School, which offers ten master's degree programs.

Academic Programs
Associate degree programs at Sage JCA generally require the completion of two years of full-time academic study. More than twenty programs are offered. Students can pursue degrees that lead either directly to careers or to eventual transfer to a four-year college. The College provides comprehensive academic and career development advisement, so students who are undecided can distinguish and develop their interests.

Associate Degree Programs Sage JCA offers associate degree programs in accounting, chemical dependency studies, child-care management, communication, computer information systems, criminal justice, elementary education preparation, English, fine arts, graphic design, history, individual studies, intercultural and global studies, interior design, legal assistant studies, liberal arts, marketing and management, math/science (physical science, pre-health/medical professions, prenutrition, and pre–physical therapy), office information management, philosophy, photography, psychology, social work, and sociology.

Internship and Co-op Programs Sage JCA internships assist students in sharpening skills and clarifying goals while gaining marketable experience. Field placements in business, communications, interior design, legal assistance, graphic design, and social science are offered throughout the Capital Region at such locations as the New York State Assembly, major retail stores, law firms, advertising and public relations agencies, banks, newspapers and magazines, television and radio stations, New York State offices, hospitals and health centers, and community and nonprofit agencies.

Off-Campus Programs
Each year, Sage Junior College of Albany students may spend a semester abroad at the American College in Paris or may participate in Sage College's residency program with Oxford University, England.

Costs
Undergraduate full-time tuition is $7700 per year in 1996–97. The residence programs for Sage JCA students costs approximately $5960, including room and board.

Financial Aid
Sage Junior College of Albany has a long-standing commitment to assisting students and their families in meeting the costs of a private college education. The College works to meet this need on an individual basis through a combined package of scholarships, awards, and loans from federal, state, and private sources. More than 85 percent of Sage JCA students receive financial assistance. New students should apply for financial aid by March 15.

Faculty
A 12:1 student-faculty ratio and an average class size of 20 allow faculty members to give close personal attention to each student's educational goals. Sage JCA professors are recognized for excellent teaching and for the friendly and supportive relationships they have with their students. Every Sage JCA student is assigned a faculty adviser and receives special attention right from the start.

Student Body Profile
Students from throughout the Northeast and ten countries attend Sage JCA. Students start on paths to success by focusing on their talents, interests, and goals while experiencing the rich diversity of a collegiate community. The full-time student enrollment at Sage JCA is 700, and the College serves many part-time students as well.

Student Activities
Students at Sage Junior College of Albany can strengthen and complement their educational experience by getting involved in campus activities; participation in student organizations enables them to meet new people and develop valuable leadership and team building skills. Available activities include the Student Senate, men's basketball, women's volleyball, *Phoenix* (the student newspaper), cheerleading, the Sage Junior College Activities Board, Phi Theta Kappa (the honor fraternity), the Art Club, the Black and Latin Student Alliance, student advisers, travel-abroad programs, the paralegal Club, *Vernacular* (the art and literary magazine), Amnesty International, the Paint and Sketch Club, Delta Epsilom Chi, the marketing club, Off-the-Shelf (a speaker's series), drama club, Residence Hall Council, and JCAB (the activities board).

The Student Senate is a group of representatives, elected from the student body at Sage Junior College of Albany, who serve as a legislative advisory body for the consideration of problems and policies affecting all students. The Student Senate is the official liaison between the students and the College's administration. In areas of student affairs, the senate serves as a legislative body, and it also has the responsibility of approving all funds that organizations request from the student body. These funds are used to promote students projects and student activities so as to better serve the campus as a whole.

Facilities and Resources
The campus consists of nearly 15 acres. In addition to the academic facilities and residence hall, there is a campus center, a gymnasium, and an art gallery. Sage JCA offers a variety of residence opportunities for students. A new coeducational residence hall is now available. Students are housed there on a first-come, first-served basis. Women at Sage JCA also have the opportunity to reside at Russell Sage College. Many women choose to become part of the four-year college environment, which broadens the Sage JCA student's experience. Students can also receive assistance with finding nearby apartments.

Sage JCA has an Academic Computer Center, an AT&T Computerized Classroom and Electronic Classroom Training Center. All Sage JCA students have an e-mail address with access to the Internet.

The Sage JCA library houses over 125,0000 volumes and owns a growing collection of approximately 25,000 art slides. Automated retrieval systems link students to more than 6,000 other libraries and 500 different databases.

Location

Sage JCA is located in the existing Capital Region of New York State. Within this area there are fourteen colleges and universities, and a rich variety of cultural, educational, and recreational opportunities are available. The Sage Colleges incorporates a campus in Troy as well as Albany.

Admission Requirements

Each applicant's potential for success at Sage Junior College in Albany is considered on an individual basis. The College's goal is to admit students who will benefit from the collegial environment and contribute to the Sage JCA community.

Application and Information

The Admissions Committee makes its decision concerning each freshman candidate after receiving his or her completed application form with a $20 nonrefundable fee, an official high school transcript to date, and at least one recommendation from teachers, administrators, and/or counselors. Transfer students should also submit the application form, the $20 fee, and their high school transcript. In addition, they must send official college transcripts to date. International students should specifically request an international application and also must achieve a score of at least 500 on the Test of English as a Foreign Language (TOEFL), administered by the Education Testing Service. An interview with a member of the admission staff is strongly recommended to enable the candidate and the College to become acquainted with one another.

Students may obtain application forms and further information by contacting:

Office of Admission
Sage Junior College of Albany
140 New Scotland Avenue
Albany, New York 12208
Telephone: 518-445-1730
800-999-9522 (toll-free)
E-mail: jcaadm@sage.edu

Sage JCA fine arts student at work on campus.

SANTA MONICA COLLEGE
SANTA MONICA, CALIFORNIA

The College and Its Mission

Santa Monica College is a two-year community college, founded in 1929. The College is supported by the state of California and is accredited by the Western Association of Schools and Colleges. It has an enrollment of 21,585 students, including 2,262 students from ninety-nine other countries.

Santa Monica College welcomes students from all countries in the world and provides special assistance to them through the International Student Center. New incoming students are given an orientation that includes an introduction to the College and its services. In addition, information on immigration issues, housing, and registration are also covered in these sessions.

Santa Monica College ranks first among the 107 community colleges in California in transferring students to the University of California. The College also has articulation agreements with the California State Universities as well as with outstanding private universities, including the University of Southern California and Pepperdine and Loyola Marymount Universities. To a great extent, the reputation of Santa Monica as one of the leading community colleges in America is based on the quality of its teaching faculty. Unlike some universities that place more emphasis on research, Santa Monica College chooses its professors for their ability to teach as well as their expertise in their fields.

A high priority is placed on individual interaction between instructors and students. Smaller classes give students the opportunity to receive more personal attention than they would in introductory courses at large universities.

The College radio station, KCRW, is the leading public radio station in southern California, providing both local and national news and entertainment programs. The Santa Monica Associates, a community-based foundation, enables the College to bring some of the world's outstanding scientists, writers, and artists to the campus for lectures and interaction with students. Santa Monica College students also present symphony concerts, plays, and operas.

Academic Programs

Graduation from Santa Monica College with the **Associate in Arts** degree is granted upon successful completion of a program of studies that includes the mastery of minimum skill requirements in English and mathematics; a selection of courses from the natural sciences, social sciences, and humanities; and prescribed courses in the major field. Graduating students are required to complete a minimum of 60 units with at least a C (2.0) average. A unit is based on the number of hours of classroom instruction. Most courses offer 3 units of credit for classes that meet 3 hours a week for a semester. Full-time students take a minimum of 12 units per semester.

Santa Monica College offers programs of courses that parallel the lower division, or the first two years, of four-year universities and colleges. Students wishing to transfer must complete a minimum of 56 transfer-level units in fields including English, mathematics, humanities, the physical sciences, and the social sciences. Requirements vary among universities, and it is to the student's advantage to choose the university to which he or she plans to transfer as soon as possible.

All nine campuses of the University of California, including UCLA and Berkeley, give preference to California's community college students over all other applicants for third-year transfer; however, students must complete the required courses with at least a 2.8 grade point average. In some majors, such as engineering and economics, a higher grade point average may be necessary for acceptance at high-demand campuses such as UCLA.

The nineteen campuses of the California State University also give preference to community college students who have completed a prescribed program of lower-division courses with 56 transfer-level units and a minimum grade point average of 2.5. Campuses and majors in high demand by students may require higher grade point averages.

Associate Degree Programs Santa Monica College offers courses in seventy-six academic major fields of study, including accounting, administration of justice, anatomy, anthropology, architecture, art, astronomy, automotive technology, bilingual education, biological sciences, botany, broadcasting, business administration, chemistry, child development, Chinese, cinema, communication, computer information systems, construction technology, economics, electronics, engineering, English, fashion merchandising, fire science, French, geography, geology, German, graphic design, history, home economics, interior design, Italian, Japanese, journalism, management, mathematics, merchandising, philosophy, photography, physical education, physics, physiology, political science, printing, real estate, respiratory therapy, Russian, sociology, Spanish, speech, theater arts, and zoology. Courses for preprofessional study in such fields as chiropractic studies, medicine, optometry, pharmacy, physical therapy, and veterinary science are also offered.

Students who complete their first two years of undergraduate requirements may receive an Associate in Arts degree before transferring to a four-year university to complete their bachelor's degree. Occupational certificates are also granted in certain two-year programs including accounting, administration of justice, architecture, automotive technology, child development, computer information systems, cosmetology, electronics, fashion design, management, office information systems, photography, printing, real estate, recreational leadership, and supervision.

Credit for Nontraditional Learning Experiences

The cooperative work experience program at Santa Monica College makes it possible for students to earn College credit for work experience in technical, business, or professional settings. The program is a joint effort of the College and the community to combine on-the-job training with classroom instruction, enabling the student to acquire knowledge, skills, and attitudes necessary to enter into or progress in a chosen occupation.

Costs

For the 1996–97 academic year, California residents pay an enrollment fee of $13 per unit. Nonresidents pay an enrollment fee of $13 per unit plus $140 per unit in tuition. It is estimated that room and board in a homestay or apartment for this period will cost $8400. Other costs include sickness and accident insurance, $500, and textbooks and supplies, $490. International students should have a minimum of $15,000 available to them to cover all of their costs for the year.

Financial Aid

U.S. students receive government support in the form of grants and loans based on their financial need. International students do not qualify for government support, but they are eligible to compete for 200 non-need scholarships (averaging $500) given by private donors.

Faculty

Santa Monica has 227 full-time faculty members and 664 part-time faculty members. All hold the equivalent of a master's degree or higher and are certified by the state of California. Although faculty members are chosen on the basis of their teaching ability, many of the professors hold doctoral degrees, particularly in the sciences. The student-faculty ratio is 40:1, although some classes are larger or smaller than 40, depending on the subject. Many faculty members maintain office hours to advise students on an individual basis. In addition, counselors on the faculty help students plan their schedules and provide special assistance for personal learning problems.

Student Body Profile

Santa Monica College has a total enrollment of 21,737 students, of whom 44 percent are men and 56 percent are women. The average age is 25. The racial breakdown of the student group includes Asian, 19.5 percent; African American, 11.1 percent; Filipino, 2.3 percent; Hispanic, 18.5 percent; Native American, .8 percent; other (nonwhites), 1.6 percent; and white (non-Hispanic), 40.9 percent. Thirty percent of students are enrolled full-time; part-time enrollment is 70 percent. Of the full-time students enrolled, 65 percent plan to transfer to a four-year college or university, 13 percent are undecided, 6 percent are taking classes for personal interest, 4 percent enroll for professional development, 3 percent enroll for a vocational certificate or an associate degree, and 9 percent enroll for other reasons. The international student population numbers 2,140.

Student Activities

All students are encouraged to join a variety of clubs supported by the Associated Students. The clubs are organized by students with special interests such as ecology, geology, biology, skiing, karate, dance, music, and drama. There is also an international club and clubs organized by students from Hong Kong, Indonesia, and India. The clubs normally meet once a week and conduct activities on and off campus throughout the year.

Sports Sports facilities at the College include off-site tennis courts, a gymnasium, a swimming pool, and the track built for the 1984 Olympics in Los Angeles. The College competes on the varsity level in men's football and men's and women's basketball, tennis, track, and volleyball. All students have access to the sports facilities for classes and individual training.

Facilities and Resources

Santa Monica College has excellent teaching facilities, including laboratories for science, electronics, computers, and nursing. It also has a large library with 103,392 bound volumes, and a learning resources center provides media-assisted individual instruction and free tutoring. There are 160 terminals/PCs available for student use at various locations throughout the campus. Other facilities include an amphitheater, a music room and auditorium, a little theater, an art gallery, a planetarium, a media center, and a student activities building. The Associated Student Center provides study areas and a computer laboratory with free use of Macintosh computers to all students. The Student Center also includes a cafeteria, conference center, and bookstore.

The Santa Monica College Transfer Center assists students who are seeking to continue their studies at a four-year college or university. Its services include workshops on the application process, opportunities to meet with representatives from the four-year institutions, and tours of the campuses throughout California.

A Mentor Program in the arts gives exceptionally talented students in the performing and applied arts an opportunity to further develop their abilities through individual instruction. Mentor programs exist in architecture, art, dance, fashion design, music, photography, and theater arts. Students wishing to be part of the Mentor Program must demonstrate exceptional abilities and commitment. The program of study is tailored to the goals of the individual and will often result in a one-person show of the student's work or a public performance.

Location

Santa Monica College is located on the beautiful coast of Southern California in the city of Santa Monica. Because of the nearness to the ocean, Santa Monica has clean air and a mild climate throughout the year. It is just to the west of Los Angeles, one of the most cosmopolitan cities in the world. The campus provides easy access to outstanding theater, music, and museum facilities in Los Angeles as well as to Universal Studios and other centers of the entertainment industry. Santa Monica College is less than 10 miles from UCLA, USC, Pepperdine University, Loyola Marymount University, and other fine institutions of higher education in the Los Angeles area.

Admission Requirements

Santa Monica College has an open admission policy. Math and English tests are given upon entry in order to counsel students and place them at the proper course levels. International students who are below the university level in English are able to take pre-university courses in ESL while they are taking university transfer-level courses, such as mathematics, that are not as dependent on English skills. International students are required to have an English level equivalent to a TOEFL score of 450.

Application and Information

Applications are accepted on an ongoing basis prior to the beginning of each semester. For the 1996–97 academic year, the fall semester begins August 26, the winter session begins January 6, the spring semester begins February 18, and the summer session begins June 17. All students should apply a month prior to the beginning of a semester or session in order to have the best selection of classes. International students must submit the documents required by the U.S. government for issuing I-20 student visas two months in advance. These documents include transcripts from high school and other colleges or universities attended, verification of financial support and a certification of the minimum English level. International student applications will be processed within three days, and notification of acceptance can be made by fax or express mail when necessary.

For more information, students should contact:

Mr. Gordon Newman
Dean of Admissions
Santa Monica College
1900 Pico Boulevard
Santa Monica, California 90405-1628
Telephone: 310–452–9380

International students should contact:

Dr. Elena Garate Eskey
Dean of International Education
International Student Center
Santa Monica College
1900 Pico Boulevard
Santa Monica, California 90405-1628
Telephone: 310-452-9217
Fax: 310-452-4186

STATE UNIVERSITY OF NEW YORK COLLEGE OF AGRICULTURE AND TECHNOLOGY AT COBLESKILL

COBLESKILL, NEW YORK

The College and Its Mission

SUNY Cobleskill is a fully accredited, residential college of the State University of New York. About 2,500 men and women are enrolled in one of nearly forty associate degree programs or the upper-division Bachelor of Technology degree program in four specialized areas of agriculture. Courses in the applied sciences and technologies are complemented by strong liberal arts and sciences and business programs.

Diversity is the key to the Cobleskill experience. Nontraditional students and the general public are offered night courses, workshops, mini-courses, and summer programs. An academic support center, child-care program, and other services help support an increasing enrollment of adult students seeking new career skills.

In addition to its associate degree programs, SUNY Cobleskill also offers the Bachelor of Technology degree.

Academic Programs

Associate Degree Programs SUNY Cobleskill offers the **Associate in Arts, Associate in Science,** and **Associate in Applied Science** degrees. Two-year associate degree programs are offered in accounting, agricultural business, agricultural engineering technology, agricultural equipment technology, agricultural science, agronomy, animal science, biological technology, business, chemical technology, commercial cooking, communications/telecommunications, computer information systems, computer science, culinary arts, diesel technology, early childhood studies, environmental studies, fisheries and wildlife technology, hotel technology, institutional foods, liberal arts and sciences, medical career transfer studies, medical laboratory technology, ornamental horticulture (plant science), restaurant management, and travel and resort marketing. A one- or two-semester undeclared major program is available for students who are undecided about the choice of a particular degree program.

Academic program highlights include the agricultural program, which is one of the strongest of its kind in the United States; the business programs, which prepare students to compete in the highly competitive world of business; and the early childhood program, whose diversity has resulted in its strong reputation for excellence. The College has one of the most comprehensive two-year culinary, hospitality, and tourism programs in the Northeast. The liberal arts and sciences programs offer students a chance to explore alternatives as well as to build a strong educational background in the humanities, social sciences, sciences, and mathematics.

The College calendar consists of a fall and spring semester. SUNY Cobleskill is fully accredited by the Middle States Association of Colleges and Schools. All programs are approved by the New York State Department of Education.

Honors Programs The Honors Program offers an opportunity for high-achievement students to work individually and collectively with faculty members at an advanced academic level. The program is designed to provide challenges, opportunities, and flexibility to Cobleskill's best scholars in their courses of study.

Transfer Arrangements The Transfer Center is available for students interested in transferring to other institutions. The College has many articulation agreements with other SUNY schools and public and private colleges both within and outside New York State.

Internship and Co-op Programs Work experiences range from grooming a golf course to working with adolescents in a social service agency. Previous professional experience may qualify some students for partial internship credit.

Special Programs and Services Special programs and services include academic remediation for entering students, English as a second language, services for learning-disabled students, and advanced placement.

The College offers associate degrees in business administration and microcomputer support that can be earned by attending classes only on Saturdays.

The Educational Opportunity Program (EOP) provides an opportunity to attend college to New York State residents who are both educationally and economically disadvantaged. To meet students' developmental needs, the program offers tutorial assistance and developmental courses in mathematics, reading, and study skills, along with intensive individual and group counseling. Additionally, EOP offers a five-week summer program to ease the transition from high school to college for newly-entering EOP students. Financial aid is provided to assist with educational costs. Students should refer to the current application guidebook for eligibility guidelines.

SUNY Cobleskill complies strictly with the Americans With Disabilities Act. Services include, but are not limited to, assistance with registration, advisement, financial aid, readers for blind persons, interpreters for deaf students, notetakers, special equipment, and tutoring.

Personal Enrichment/Noncredit Programs More than 500 noncredit programs are available in a variety of areas.

Off-Campus Programs

Qualified students in the culinary, hospitality, and tourism program may spend their third semester in England at Birmingham College.

Costs

For 1995–96, annual costs for full-time attendance at Cobleskill for New York State residents were tuition: $3200; room and board: approximately $5300; fees: $600; and books and supplies: approximately $600. Tuition for out-of-state students was $8300 per year in 1995–96. (Tuition and fees are subject to change.)

Financial Aid

Almost 70 percent of Cobleskill's students receive some kind of financial aid. Cobleskill participates in the Federal Pell Grant, Federal Work-Study, Federal Perkins Loan, Federal PLUS loan, Federal Stafford Student Loan, and Federal Unsubsidized Stafford Loan programs. The College also participates in New York State's Tuition Assistance Program (TAP), Regents Award for Children of Deceased Police Officers or Firefighters, Scholarship for Children of Deceased or Disabled Veterans, and U.S. Bureau of Indian Affairs Aid to Native Americans, as well as other state grant and scholarship programs. Students are encouraged to apply for private scholarships from the Cobleskill College Foundation, Cobleskill Alumni Association, and other organizations and companies. Emergency loans are available from the Faculty Student Association and the Financial Aid Office. Approximately $8 million is awarded annually through these programs.

To apply for financial aid, students must file the Free Application for Federal Student Aid as early as possible. March 15 is the preferred and recommended filing date for the College's financial aid application.

Faculty

There are 120 full-time faculty members. A significant number of Cobleskill faculty members come to the classroom from business, industry, and the service professions. They bring their students the benefit of their work and personal experiences. Cobleskill students work side by side in small classes with faculty members who are world-renowned lecturers, authors, and award winners.

Student Body Profile

Ninety-eight percent of all graduates find jobs within one year of graduation or transfer to a four-year institution. Approximately 52 percent of the student population is 18 to 19 years of age; 14 percent are older than 25. About 49 percent of the students are women. The student body is ethnically and culturally diverse.

Student Activities

Students participate in on-campus activities throughout the year, including films, concerts, theater productions, lectures, and art exhibitions. More than fifty clubs and organizations respond to a variety of interests, ranging from agriculture to an outing club. More than forty organizations offer opportunities to participate in student government, student publications, music ensembles, dramatic productions, religious activities, social and service clubs, professional organizations, and an honor society. At the beginning of each term, a club fair helps students get acquainted with the groups that interest them. Many films, art exhibits, dance programs, musical concerts, and theatrical productions are offered each year.

Sports Intercollegiate competition for men is sponsored in baseball, basketball, cross-country, golf, track, lacrosse, soccer, tennis, and wrestling. Women's intercollegiate sports are basketball, cross-country, soccer, softball, tennis, track, and volleyball. An extensive intramural program is also available. Physical education classes stress lifetime sports such as archery, bowling, golf, swimming, and tennis.

Facilities and Resources

Fifty-seven buildings are located on the 750-acre campus. Cobleskill's facilities include modern classrooms and laboratories, a multimedia learning resources center, state-of-the-art computing networks, a farm, modern food preparation kitchens and a student-operated restaurant, an art gallery, a theater, ski trails and a lodge, and outstanding physical education facilities. Ten residence halls accommodate about 80 percent of Cobleskill's students. A special residence hall is being offered to upperclass students enrolled in the Bachelor of Technology degree program or those who have independent student status. This mature students' living community emphasizes a strong academic focus and independent lifestyle. Special amenities such as room refrigerator/microwave units, single or double room options, flexible guest policies, meal plan flexibility, conference space, computer lab, and kitchen area for floor or individual meals are all part of this special option. The hall is open for all vacation and recess periods, August through May.

Ten residence halls feature lounges, study rooms equipped with computers, recreation rooms, and laundry facilities. The Beard Health Infirmary is equipped and staffed for both inpatient and outpatient care. Bouck Hall houses a theater, gymnasium, bowling alley, swimming pool, snackbar, bookstore, state-of-the-art exercise room, and weight room. The Career Development Center offers career counseling, career-planning seminars, job interviews, résumé writing, job placement for the disabled, and opportunities for permanent, part-time, and summer jobs.

SUNY Cobleskill has an outstanding 98 percent placement/transfer rate. Of those employed, 95 percent are working in the area in which they were prepared. Sixty-six percent of the respondents in last year's graduating class transferred to public and private colleges and universities throughout the nation.

Advisement/Counseling All faculty members assist students in selecting courses and programs of study to satisfy their educational objectives. Each student has an adviser assigned from his/her area of study.

The Academic Support Center assists students in overcoming problems with studies. The professional staff helps students improve reading, writing, math, and study skills and develops computer software programs designed to meet students' learning needs.

Career Planning/Placement Offices The Career Development Center provides counseling to develop educational and career plans; conducts numerous seminars in career planning, transfer topics, job search, and life skills; and assists students in the use of a computer-based career planning system. Placement services are also provided at the Center and include on-campus recruitment by industry representatives.

Library and Audiovisual Services The Learning Resources Center (Library) helps students learn how to use the resources needed to reach their academic and professional goals. In addition to books, magazines, newspapers, pamphlets, videos, slides, and filmstrips, the library has an automated catalog, microcomputers, media production facilities, a learning lab for self-paced instruction, and a study lounge.

Location

SUNY Cobleskill is located in the village of Cobleskill, set in scenic and historic Schoharie County. The county, with a population of only 30,000, offers the rare combination of a rural quality of life and close proximity to metropolitan areas. State and private parks, streams, lakes, mountain trails, and ski areas provide a full range of outdoor activities. North of the county lies the great Mohawk Valley and the Adirondacks; to the south and west stretch the Catskills. Schoharie County is abundant in cultural, recreational, historic, and tourist attractions, including Minekill State Park, the Old Stone Fort, the Iroquois Indian Museum, and internationally known Howe Caverns and Secret Caverns. The village of Cobleskill is a small, friendly college town with 5,300 residents. Convenient shopping, entertainment, fast food restaurants, fine dining, a movie theater, and health services are located near the College. Cobleskill is midway between Oneonta and Albany, about 160 miles northwest of New York City. It is less than a one-hour drive from the Albany-Schenectady-Troy area.

Admission Requirements

Applicants to associate degree programs must have graduated from high school or hold a high school equivalency diploma. Students apply and are accepted to a specific curriculum. Admission requirements vary according to the program selected. Decisions are based primarily on grades earned in academic courses, including the specific high school prerequisite courses of each curriculum. The review process takes into account the applicant's individual overall background, including available data such as test scores, rank in class, and teacher/counselor recommendations. A personal interview is not required but may be beneficial to the candidate and is strongly recommended. Applicants with subject deficiencies are encouraged to make up work prior to registration. When necessary, remedial programs are recommended.

A limited number of high school seniors are admitted to Cobleskill under an early admission program.

Application and Information

Cobleskill operates on a rolling admission system, admitting students on a first-come, first-served basis. Applicants are encouraged to submit applications as early as possible. Candidates must submit the State University of New York Application form, available in all New York State high school guidance offices and college transfer offices.

Requests for further information should be addressed to:

Admissions Office
SUNY Cobleskill
Cobleskill, New York 12043

Telephone: 518-234-5525
800-295-8988 (toll-free)
Fax: 518-234-5333
E-mail: admissions@snycob.cobleskill.edu
World Wide Web: http://www.cobleskill.edu

STATE UNIVERSITY OF NEW YORK COLLEGE OF AGRICULTURE AND TECHNOLOGY AT MORRISVILLE

MORRISVILLE, NEW YORK

The College and Its Mission

At SUNY Morrisville, one of the two-year colleges of agriculture and technology, students can choose from a wide range of programs in agriculture, business, health, hospitality, engineering technologies, liberal arts, natural resources, and other technologies. Upon graduation, students are prepared for transfer to a four-year college or university or direct entry into the job market.

Centrally located in New York State, SUNY Morrisville attracts students not only from every county in the state but also from out of state and other nations as well. The campus is surrounded by rolling hills, and the area is rich with recreational activities that can't be found in an urban setting.

As a residential campus, SUNY Morrisville is a home away from home for most students. Living on campus is comfortable, convenient, and fun. Students can live in one of nine residence halls and choose from a variety of living arrangements. Living away from home with peers is exciting; students make many friends, develop new interests, and become responsible and independent members of the campus community.

Academic Programs

SUNY Morrisville students can choose from more than 80 majors and options ranging from liberal arts to the technologies. Graduates can transfer as juniors within SUNY and to private institutions or pursue their career goals.

The College operates on a semester basis. More than 600 courses were offered in 1995–96; average class size is 35 in required courses. Academic remediation is available for entering students. English as a second language courses are offered during the academic year, with an intensive ESL program offered during the summer. Services for learning disabled students are provided through the College Skills Center. Army ROTC is offered in conjunction with Syracuse University.

Associate Degree Programs Associate in Arts degree programs are available in individual studies, liberal arts/humanities, and liberal arts/social science. **Associate in Science** degree programs are available in accounting, architectural technology, biological technology, biology, business administration, chemistry, computer science, nutrition and dietetics, engineering science, individual studies, liberal arts/math, and physics. **Associate in Applied Science** degree programs are available in accounting, agricultural business, agricultural engineering, agricultural science, animal science–dairy, aquaculture and aquatic science, automotive technology, business administration, computer information systems, computer systems technology, design and drafting, dietetic technician studies, electrical engineering technology, environmental technology, equine science and management, equine racing management, food service administration, forest technology, horticulture, individual studies, information processing, journalism, mechanical engineering technology, medical laboratory technology, natural resources conservation, nursing, office management, office technology, plastics technology, pre–environmental science and forestry, restaurant management, ski area technology, travel and tourism/hospitality management, and wood products technology. **Associate in Occupational Studies** degree programs are available in agricultural mechanics, automotive service specialist, diesel technology, and residential construction.

Honors Programs More than $200,000 in academic scholarships are offered annually to top applicants to the College, with awards up to $6000 for the two years. At the conclusion of each semester, the names of all full-time students whose academic performance was at the A level (4.0 grade point average) are included on an honor roll called the President's List. Full-time students at the B level (3.0 grade point average or better) are included on the Dean's List.

Certificate and Diploma Programs Certificate programs are available in agricultural mechanics, automotive mechanics, casino management, and word processing.

Internship and Co-op Programs Internships and co-op programs are available in some selected academic programs. Interested students should contact the Admissions Office for more information.

Special Programs and Services The focus of the International Studies Program is to foster a better understanding of the world among the campus community through a wide variety of activities. Some of these activities include coordination of services for international students to assure that their stay is enjoyable and rewarding, exploration of opportunities for and encouragement of student/faculty participation in travel and study-abroad programs, exploration of exchange programs, and assistance in grant development focused at raising funds in support of an expanded international studies program.

Community Programs The SUNY Morrisville Center for Business and Community Programs enhances the College's public service mission by providing research, training, and technical assistance to business, community, and governmental organizations. The center incorporates the Business and Industry Center, the Rural Services Institute, Conferencing, and the Skilled Worker Emeritus Program.

Off-Campus Programs

The College offers courses and degree programs at the Norwich Campus and part-time courses at the extension site in Oneida to better serve the educational needs of people in those areas. Most continuing education courses are offered in Norwich and Oneida, but satellite sites operate in other locations when demand is evidenced.

Costs

Tuition for the 1996–97 academic year is $3200 for full-time students from New York State. Nonresident tuition is $8300. Tuition is $128 on a per-credit basis. On-campus room and board costs average $5200 per year. Room and board costs remain the same for a student's two years of study.

Financial Aid

SUNY Morrisville does everything possible to help make an education affordable for students. Financial need is calculated by estimating what a family can contribute from income and assets and subtracting this amount from the total annual budget. Federal financial assistance includes Pell Grants, Federal Supplemental Educational Opportunity Grants (FSEOG), Subsidized and Unsubsidized Direct Loans, PLUS Loans, Perkins Loans, and work-study. New York State financial assistance includes the Tuition Assistance Program (TAP) and Aid for Part-Time Study (APTS). Interested students should contact the Financial Aid Office (telephone: 315–684–6289) for more information.

Faculty

There are 126 full-time and 45 part-time faculty members. Of the full-time faculty members, 90 percent hold advanced degrees and 17 percent have earned doctorates.

Student Body Profile

The College enrollment features 3,151 students from fourteen states and territories and eleven other countries. Forty-nine percent are women; 18 percent attend on a part-time basis; and 98 percent are New York State residents. Sixty percent live on campus and 19 percent of students are 25 years of age or older. Forty-four percent of students transferred directly to a four-year college or university.

Student Activities

There is a wide range of clubs and organizations at SUNY Morrisville to get involved in, including the African Student Union Black Alliance (ASUBA), agriculture club, agricultural engineering club, Alpha Delta Mu, the American Marketing Association of SUNY Morrisville, the Arcadian, architectural club, Asian Students International Association (ASIA), Campus Activities Board (CAB), the Chimes, conservation club, dairy club, Delta Lambda Mu, Delta Psi Omega, the Engineering Science Society, Friars' drama club, horticulture club, the Inter-Greek Council, Jazz Singers, and Latino American Student Organization (LASO).

Sports The College is a member of the National Junior College Athletic Association, Division III. Teams compete in Region III of the NJCAA. The College is also a member of the Mountain Valley Collegiate Conference. Intercollegiate sports offered for men include baseball, basketball, cross-country, equestrian sports, lacrosse, riflery, skiing (downhill), swimming and diving, track and field, and wrestling. Intercollegiate sports offered for women include basketball, cross-country, equestrian sports, riflery, skiing (downhill), softball, swimming and diving, track and field, and volleyball. Intramural sports offered include badminton, basketball, bowling, cross-country running, equestrian sports, football, riflery, skiing (cross-country and downhill), soccer, softball, swimming and diving, tennis, track and field, volleyball, and water polo.

Facilities and Resources

Advisement/Counseling The College maintains a counseling center staffed by professional counselors. Counseling services assists students in exploring their social, emotional, career, and academic development. Professional counselors work with individuals or groups of students to help them better understand themselves, resolve problems, and deal with important decisions.

Career Planning/Placement Offices The Career Planning and Placement Center provides students with transfer counseling and job placement assistance. Services provided include job fairs, résumé preparation, résumé referral, career counseling, careers library, job bank, and job interviews.

Library and Audiovisual Services The campus library has a collection of 99,258 bound volumes; 320 microform titles; 568 periodical subscriptions; and 2,330 records, tapes, and CDs. Two CD-ROMs are available for student use as well as on-line biographical services.

The College maintains two state-of-the-art academic computing centers for general student use. They contain IBM-compatible and Macintosh computers and terminals connected to a centralized campus computer. The College also has 13 specialized computer laboratories supporting specific academic programs. The College computers give students access to e-mail, Internet information, the World Wide Web, and a variety of other academic resources. Every Morrisville student receives a user code and password to the centralized computer on campus. A computer room in each residence hall provides extended student access to the centralized computer. Commuter students can enjoy 24-hour remote access from home using the campus dial-in lines.

Location

The College is located in Morrisville, New York, on Route 20; 30 miles southeast of Syracuse; 30 miles southwest of Utica; and a half-hour drive from the Thruway, Exit 34 at Canastota. The area features many great places to find shopping, entertainment, and cultural opportunities. Travel connections by air are made at Hancock International Airport in Syracuse, or at Oneida County Airport (Utica-Rome) in Oriskany. Train connections are made in Syracuse or Utica. Morrisville is serviced directly from Binghamton and Utica on a daily basis by Chenango Valley Bus Lines.

Admission Requirements

A candidate for admission to a regular two-year curriculum at SUNY Morrisville should be a high school graduate or the equivalent with grades acceptable to the curriculum in which admission is sought. Applicants are admitted without regard to race, color, religion, national origin, sex, age, handicap, sexual orientation, or marital or parental status. The credentials of each applicant are evaluated on an individual basis, and admission is granted to those who have the potential for success in the curriculum of their choice. Students are admitted to specific programs of study rather than to a general freshman program. Although an interview is not required for admission to the College, students are encouraged to visit the campus during the admissions process. A recommendation is not required; however, if a student feels that a recommendation from a guidance counselor, faculty member, or employer would provide beneficial information to the admissions committee, that recommendation should be sent directly to the Admissions Office. ACT and SAT I scores are recommended, but not required for admission to the College. If an applicant has already have taken, or is planning to take the SAT I or ACT examinations, they should submit scores with the application for admission or have the examining agency send the scores directly to the Admissions Office. Transfer applicants should submit high school and college transcripts. A minimum college grade point average (GPA) of 2.0 is recommended.

Application Information

For further information, all prospective students should contact:

Director of Admissions
State University of New York
College of Agriculture and Technology at Morrisville
Morrisville, New York 13408

Telephone: 315-684-6046
800-258-0111 (toll-free)
Fax: 315-684-6116
E-mail: admitmor@snymorva.cs.snymor.edu
World Wide Web: http://www.snymor.edu/

On the campus of SUNY Morrisville.

Peterson's Guide to Two-Year Colleges 1997

STATE UNIVERSITY OF NEW YORK COLLEGE OF ENVIRONMENTAL SCIENCE AND FORESTRY, RANGER SCHOOL

WANAKENA, NEW YORK

The College and Its Mission

The Forest Technology Program is offered through the State University of New York College of Environmental Science and Forestry (ESF), Ranger School. Throughout its history, the College has focused on the environmental issues of the time in each of its three mission areas: instruction, research, and public service. The College is dedicated to educating future scientists and managers who, through specialized skills, will be able to use a holistic approach to solving the environmental and resource problems facing society.

More than 3,200 students have graduated from the program over the past eighty-three years, including 180 women since 1974. Established in 1912 with the gift of 1,800 acres of land in the Adirondack Mountains, the ESF Forest Technology Program is the oldest in the nation. The Ranger School's managed forest includes both hardwood and coniferous trees and is bounded on two sides by the New York State Forest Preserve. It is also adjacent to several acres of virgin timber in the Adirondack Forest preserve.

The main campus building houses the central academic, dining, and recreational facilities. Dormitory wings are located on either side of the main campus building. Each dorm room is designed to accommodate 2 people. All second-year students live on campus, with the exception of married students accompanied by their families. These students should arrange for rental accommodations well before the start of the academic year.

Academic Programs

Associate Degree Programs Students who complete the program earn an **Associate in Applied Science (A.A.S.)** degree in forest technology.

The two-year curriculum prepares students for work as forest or surveying technicians or as forestry aides. Students may fulfill the program's freshman liberal arts and sciences requirements at any accredited college. The second year of study takes place on the Wanakena campus where classes meet from 8 a.m. to 5 p.m., Monday through Friday. Time is equally divided between classroom and laboratory work and experience in the field. Students must also devote several hours to evening and weekend study. Forestry agencies and the wood industry employ graduates as forest technicians, and approximately one quarter of the program's graduates join surveying firms.

The ESF Ranger School's 1+1 plan requires 30 credit hours of course work in general studies at an accredited college during the freshman year and an additional 45 credit hours at the Wanakena campus in the second year of the program. Field study is a large component of the curriculum. Several short field trips, made at no additional expense to the student, take place as part of the second year of study. The trips enhance courses in dendrology, silviculture, forest management and recreation, wildlife ecology, and surveying. Students who are considering later transfer to a baccalaureate program should follow the suggestions for freshman course selection outlined in the ESF catalog.

Transfer Arrangements Counseling is available for students interested in pursuing a four-year degree on the main campus in Syracuse. Students should contact the ESF admissions office.

Costs

The cost of the first year varies according to the institution attended. Estimated tuition and fees for the 1996–97 academic year at the Wanakena campus total $3433 for residents of New York State and $8300 for out-of-state residents. Room and board at the Wanakena campus are $5820 and the estimated cost of books, personal expenses, and travel is $2200. (Books and supplies are sold on campus.)

Financial Aid

More than 80 percent of Ranger School students receive some form of financial aid, including grants and scholarships, low-interest loans, and student employment. ESF mails the College Aid Application to all applicants to the Forest Technology Program and encourages them to submit that form as well as the Free Application for Federal Student Aid.

Faculty

Five full-time faculty members and 1 part-time instructor teach at the Wanakena campus. The student-faculty ratio is approximately 10:1. Students have ready access to faculty members for consultations. Faculty members are housed on campus, and faculty offices are located near student living quarters. There is close contact between student and faculty members in the classroom and at fieldwork sites.

Student Body Profile

Ninety percent of all students complete the Forest Technology Program. About 50 percent go on to careers as forest technicians or aides with private companies or government agencies; some 30 percent become surveyors. Many graduates of the Forest Technology Program go on to receive Bachelor of Science and even graduate-level degrees at ESF's main campus in Syracuse or at other colleges and universities.

Student Activities

ESF has a representative Undergraduate Student Association. The association sponsors the Woodsmen Team and many social and recreational events. Students in the second year of the Forest Technology Program live under ESF regulations and follow the house rules of the Wanakena campus.

Location

The 1,800-acre campus is situated on the banks of the Oswegatchie River near the Adirondack Mountain hamlet of Wanakena, approximately 65 miles east of Watertown, New York, and 35 miles west of Tupper Lake on New York State's Route 3. At the Wanakena campus, social and recreational activities utilize the area's year-round opportunities for outdoor enjoyment. An excellent hospital, located in Star Lake, New York, serves the community.

Admission Requirements

Students may apply to ESF for admission to the Ranger School's Forest Technology Program during their senior year in high school for guaranteed transfer admission or during their freshman year of college for transfer admission. Prospective students should consult the current catalog for specific information concerning the application process. ESF cooperates with more than fifty colleges in New York, Alabama, Connecticut, Maryland, Massachusetts, New Jersey, Pennsylvania, and Rhode Island in pre-ESF transfer programs. Acceptance to the Ranger School is contingent upon satisfactory completion of first-year courses. While in high school, applicants must complete at least 3 years of science and mathematics (including courses in biology and trigonometry), units in English and social studies, and electives, such as computer science and mechanical drawing. Transfer students are considered on the basis of college course work and interest in forestry. Students are required to have a minimum 2.0 GPA in the prerequisite college-level course work. In addition to academic requirements, applicants must be able to meet the physical requirements of the Ranger School program and must submit a full medical report. Parents of applicants under 18 years old should be aware of the field nature of the program and its rigorous study-work regimen.

Application and Information

The Forest Technology Program accepts students for fall admission only. Fall admission decisions are made beginning around the middle of January and continue on a rolling basis until the class is filled. Application forms for New York State residents are available at all high schools in the state and at all colleges in the state university system. Out-of-state students should request application forms from the Office of Undergraduate Admissions at ESF. Students should address requests for information to:

Office of Undergraduate Admissions
106 Bray Hall
State University of New York
College of Environmental Science and Forestry
1 Forestry Drive
Syracuse, New York 13210–2779
Telephone: 315–470–6600
　　　　　800–7777–ESF (toll-free)
Fax: 315–470–6933
E-mail: esfinfo@mailbox.syr.edu
World Wide Web: http://www.esf.edu

STATE UNIVERSITY OF NEW YORK COLLEGE OF TECHNOLOGY AT CANTON

CANTON, NEW YORK

The College and Its Mission

The State University of New York College of Technology at Canton is the oldest two-year college in New York State and the only college of technology north of the New York State Thruway. It is a two-year, coeducational, residential college located on 555 acres along the banks of the Grasse River. SUNY Canton shares the commitment of the University as a whole to provide educational opportunities for New York State residents.

Dedicated to providing varied educational opportunities in the technologies, SUNY Canton offers twenty-five programs leading to an associate degree, seven programs leading to a one-year certificate, and a 1+1 program with SUNY Environmental Science and Forestry at Syracuse. Enrollment is about 2,000.

Associate degree programs in construction management, early childhood studies, human services, and office technology–medical and a joint baccalaureate degree program in business/economics with SUNY Potsdam have been added for the 1995–96 academic year. Two other associate degree programs, physical therapy assistant studies and occupational therapy assistant studies, are currently being reviewed for registration by SUNY and the State Education Department.

The College has articulation agreements in several areas with four-year colleges, including SUNY Potsdam, SUNY Plattsburgh, SUNY Oswego, and SUNY Oneonta. These agreements facilitate transfers to the four-year colleges, enabling students to pursue and complete the baccalaureate degree in two years following graduation from Canton. Approximately one third of the College's graduates transfer to baccalaureate institutions following completion of degree requirements at SUNY Canton. New linkages with area schools, such as the Liberty Partnership Program and the Tech Prep Initiative with northern New York two-year colleges and BOCES (Board of Cooperative Education Services), are ongoing.

Academic Programs

Associate Degree Programs SUNY Canton grants **Associate in Arts, Associate in Science,** and **Associate in Applied Science** degrees in the following curricula: accounting, air conditioning engineering technology, apprentice training–industrial trades, automotive technology, business administration, business economics, civil engineering technology, computer information systems, construction engineering technology, criminal justice, early childhood studies, electrical engineering technology, engineering science, human services, individual studies, industrial technology, liberal arts–humanities, liberal arts–science, liberal arts–social science, mechanical engineering technology, medical laboratory technology, mortuary science, nursing, office technology, and veterinary science technology.

Certificate Programs The College offers one-year certificates in the following programs: automotive mechanics, building construction, computer-aided drafting, early childhood studies, electrical construction and maintenance, heating and plumbing service, and individual studies.

Special Programs and Services At the heart of SUNY Canton are four Centers of Excellence—in Business and Public Service, Engineering and Technology, Health and Medical Technologies, and Liberal Arts and Science—that operate as links between the worlds of work and academia. With the support of the business community, these centers assess the needs of employers in areas most vital to the economy. In turn, the centers provide up-to-date, hands-on training to students and other constituencies.

The work of these centers is no longer confined to the SUNY Canton campus. Using the wide array of information technologies available to the College, the centers provide education where and when the customer needs it. Academic courses and programs that respond to the ever-changing economy are developed and marketed. The enterprise partnerships that are being formed with the business community ensure the continued strength of these centers. Financial support for new and improved facilities, new equipment, programming, in-service education, and future needs is available to the centers. These Centers of Excellence, rather than creating something new, actually build upon a rich heritage of technological, business, and health education.

Off-Campus Programs

SUNY Canton is a member of the Associated Colleges of the St. Lawrence Valley, a four-college consortium that also includes Clarkson University, the SUNY College of Arts and Sciences at Potsdam, and St. Lawrence University. The Associated Colleges, with nearly 12,500 students in two villages 10 miles apart, expands opportunities through such activities as cross-registration for courses at the other three campuses, coordination of social events, and privileges at all four college libraries.

Credit for Nontraditional Learning Experiences

SUNY Canton has a proficiency examination program to serve students who seek recognition for achievement acquired outside the conventional college classroom.

Costs

SUNY Canton's tuition was $3200 per year for New York State residents and $8300 for nonresidents in 1995–96. On-campus housing was $2900 per year, and fourteen meals a week cost $1900. Books, fees, and other expenses are approximately $1900 per year.

Financial Aid

SUNY Canton offers a comprehensive program of financial assistance to help students and their families meet the costs of a high-quality two-year education. Approximately 85 percent of students receive some form of financial aid. Traditional federal and state financial aid programs are available, including Federal Pell Grant, FSEOG, Federal Perkins Loan, Federal Stafford Student Loan, Federal Work-Study, Tuition Assistance Program, Educational Opportunity Program, and Empire State Minority Scholarships. The College Foundation also provides more than $81,000 in scholarships to some 120 students. To apply for aid, students must complete the Free Application for Federal Student Aid (FAFSA) and the SUNY Canton Financial Aid Supplemental Form. New York State residents must also complete the NYS Tuition Assistance Program application. SUNY Canton is a participant in the William D. Ford Direct Loan Program.

Faculty

Faculty members at SUNY Canton are genuinely interested in each student's welfare and have high expectations that students will succeed academically. They truly believe that a SUNY Canton education prepares its graduates to become successfully employed or to pursue a baccalaureate degree. Most faculty members have on-the-job professional experience, are licensed in their fields, or are current practitioners in their professions. The student-faculty ratio is 22:1.

Student Body Profile
SUNY Canton has a total population of about 2,000 students, 1,600 of whom are full-time. The average age of the students is 20. SUNY Canton draws students from all over the Northeast, with the majority coming from within New York State. Minority students make up 15 percent of the student population, and half of the students live on campus.

Student Activities
SUNY Canton has more than fifty student organizations to join. Some of them are the Aerobics Club, Computer Club, Construction Club, Greek Council, Outing Club, Sign Language Club, and Student Cooperative Alliance (SCA). The SCA is the student government, and it provides a means of cooperation and unity among students, faculty, and administration. Students sit on many campuswide committees, including Commencement, the College Council, and the Student-Faculty Judicial Board. The College Union Board is the major programming group for entertainment and activities.

Sports Intercollegiate and intramural athletics play an important role; teams include women's basketball, soccer, and softball and men's basketball, football, lacrosse, soccer, and hockey (twelve-time national champions).

Facilities and Resources
Academic facilities include the Academic Computing Center, which features Digital Equipment Corporation mainframe and terminals and three classrooms containing seventy-five PCs; a computer classroom in the School of Engineering and Technology containing forty PCs; two college farms; an Educational Communications Center featuring a six-channel, closed-circuit television distribution system and a production studio; and seven major instructional buildings. Approximately 70 percent of the campus's instructional space is composed of laboratories.

SUNY Canton has broken ground for a new Student Union that is set to be completed for the beginning of the 1996–97 academic year.

Library and Audiovisual Services Southworth Library, with a fully automated card catalog system, houses more than 50,000 volumes, more than 400 periodical subscriptions, and 1,500 tapes and recordings. A separate Bibliographic Instruction Room with a seating capacity of 40 is equipped with video projection and provides a place for library instruction as well as a reading room. The library also provides open access to the periodical collection as well as word processing facilities on the lower level. A CD-ROM local area network with six computer workstations for the periodical and newspaper index has also been provided through construction/rehabilitation funds. The approximate cost of the construction/rehabilitation project was $3 million.

As a result of SUNY's Library Automation Implementation Project (LAIP), Canton now has a fully automated library with an on-line public access catalog named SLEUTH and an automated circulation system.

Location
Canton lies in the St. Lawrence River valley at the foothills of the Adirondack Mountains. The gentle rolling hills of this agricultural heartland are an hour's drive from Ottawa, Canada, and 2 hours from Montreal, the second-largest French-speaking city in the world. The winter playground of Lake Placid (site of the 1932 and 1980 Olympics) is just 2 hours to the south. Canton and the neighboring towns are Smalltown U.S.A. in the best sense. People are friendly and neighbors are always ready to lend a helping hand, and they extend that hospitality to the students who come to the region's four colleges.

Admission Requirements
Admission to SUNY Canton is based on the student's academic background, personal experience, and potential for success. Incoming freshmen must meet the following minimum requirements: be a graduate of an accredited secondary school or hold a high school equivalency diploma; have completed, with a satisfactory level of achievement, the minimum course prerequisites for their selected curriculum; and demonstrate evidence of the potential for success in the selected curriculum. For candidates not applying directly from high school, additional criteria include work experience, special skills, or unusual circumstances interfering with past performance. The College does not require the SAT I or ACT exams for admission. However, all new students (except transfers) must take the ACT Assessment and have the results on file before the start of classes.

Application and Information
For more information, students should contact:

Dean of Enrollment Management
SUNY College of Technology at Canton
Cornell Drive
Canton, New York 13617
Telephone: 315-386-7123
           800-388-7123 (toll-free)
Fax: 315-386-7309

Students on the Canton campus.

Peterson's Guide to Two-Year Colleges 1997

STATE UNIVERSITY OF NEW YORK COLLEGE OF TECHNOLOGY AT FARMINGDALE

FARMINGDALE, NEW YORK

The College and Its Mission

Founded in 1912, the State University of New York at Farmingdale is the oldest public college on Long Island. Originally intended to serve a largely agrarian community, Farmingdale emerged in the 1980s as a leader in technical higher education, offering two-year associate degree programs in engineering technologies, health sciences, business, and arts and sciences. Since the first baccalaureate degrees were awarded in 1987, the College has expanded its Bachelor of Science and Bachelor of Technology degree offerings. Farmingdale is located in Long Island's equivalent to California's Silicon Valley (an area on Long Island's Route 110 containing a multitude of headquarters and branch offices of high-tech companies).

SUNY Farmingdale is fully accredited by the Middle States Association of Colleges and Schools. All programs are approved by the New York State Department of Education. All applicable programs are registered with and accredited by the requisite professional accrediting bodies.

In addition to its associate degree programs, SUNY Farmingdale offers the Bachelor of Science and the Bachelor of Technology. Upper-division baccalaureate degrees are awarded in aeronautical science–professional pilot studies, aviation administration, construction management technology, electrical engineering technology, industrial technology, manufacturing engineering technology, and visual communications.

Academic Programs

The curricula are organized into four schools: Arts and Sciences, Engineering Technologies, Health Sciences and Human Services, and Business. Graduation credit requirements vary from program to program. Students must maintain a minimum GPA of 2.0. The College calendar consists of fall and spring semesters and a three-part summer session.

Associate Degree Programs Farmingdale offers **Associate in Arts, Associate in Science,** and **Associate in Applied Science** degrees. Two-year associate degree programs are offered in advertising art and design, aerospace technology, aircraft maintenance technology, automotive engineering technology, biomedical engineering technology, business administration, computer information systems, computer science, construction/architectural engineering technology, criminal justice, computer systems technology, dental hygiene, electrical engineering technology, food and nutrition, liberal arts and sciences, mechanical engineering technology, medical laboratory technology, nursing, and ornamental horticulture.

Transfer Arrangements Transfer opportunities for degree recipients include a number of articulation and joint-admissions agreements designed to accommodate incoming transfers at the junior-year level as well as Farmingdale graduating seniors.

Certificate and Diploma Programs The College offers a one-year certificate program in pretechnical studies and a college-preparatory program called pathways. A one- or two-semester undeclared major program is available for students who are undecided about the choice of a particular program.

Special Programs and Services The College offers evening and summer courses for degree and certificate programs, credit-free programs, and other activities for nontraditional students. In addition, the College also provides the Tutoring Center, Institute for Learning in Retirement, and Office for Public Service and Continuing Education.

The Educational Opportunity Center (EOC) of Long Island, based at the Farmingdale campus, is designed to provide a tuition-free, nondegree education for economically and educationally disadvantaged persons. Farmingdale's Educational Opportunity Program (EOP) provides tutorial assistance, developmental courses in mathematics and reading, special work in study skills, and intensive counseling for students who meet the program's economic and educational criteria.

Costs

For 1996–97, annual costs for full-time attendance at Farmingdale for New York State residents are tuition, $3200 (associate degree), as well as nominal fees; room and board, approximately $5290; and books and supplies, approximately $600. Tuition for out-of-state students is $8300 per year. Tuition and fees are subject to change.

Financial Aid

Almost 70 percent of Farmingdale's students receive some kind of financial aid. Farmingdale participates in the Federal Pell Grant, Federal Supplemental Educational Opportunity Grant (FSEOG), Federal Work-Study, Federal Perkins Loan, Federal PLUS loan, Federal Stafford Student Loan, and Federal Unsubsidized Stafford Loan programs. The College also participates in New York State's Tuition Assistance Program (TAP), Regents Award for Children of Deceased Police Officers or Firefighters, Scholarship for Children of Deceased or Disabled Veterans, and U.S. Bureau of Indian Affairs Aid to Native Americans, as well as other state grant and scholarship programs. Students are encouraged to apply for private scholarships from the Farmingdale College Foundation, Farmingdale Alumni Association, and other organizations and companies. Emergency loans are available from the Student Government Association and Alumni Association. Approximately $8 million is awarded annually through these programs. To apply for financial aid, students must file the Free Application for Federal Student Aid as early as possible. In addition, May 1 is the preferred and recommended filing date for the College's financial aid application.

Faculty

There are 265 full-time faculty members. A significant number of Farmingdale faculty members come to the classroom from business, industry, and the service professions. They bring to their students the benefit of their work and personal experiences. Farmingdale students work side by side in small classes with faculty members who are world-renowned lecturers, authors, award winners, and inventors.

Student Body Profile

The College has a population of approximately 6,200 students. Of that total, 2,800 are part-time, and 3,400 are full-time. Twenty-three percent are members of minority groups. About 8 percent live on campus. The majority of students are from New York State, with less than 1 percent from out of state. The average age of all students is 21, while the average age of freshmen is 18.

Student Activities

The Student Government Association has authority over all student organizations and elects officers on an annual basis.

Sixteen senators and 7 executive board members make up the governing board, which acts in matters promoting the interests of the College and its students.

Students participate in on-campus activities throughout the year, including films, concerts, theater productions, lectures, art exhibitions, and all-College theme weekends; there are also opportunities to become involved in the campus radio station. Dozens of clubs and organizations respond to a variety of interests, ranging from skydiving to philosophy.

While the Farmingdale student body numbers more than 6,200, more than 22,000 people utilize the campus each year, attending workshops, seminars, summer sessions, sports events, the Festival of the Arts, and the circus.

Sports Intercollegiate competition for men is sponsored in baseball, basketball, cross-country, golf, indoor and outdoor track, lacrosse, soccer, tennis, and wrestling. Women's intercollegiate sports are basketball, cheerleading, cross-country, soccer, softball, tennis, track, and volleyball. An extensive intramural program is also available.

Facilities and Resources

Five residence halls feature lounges, study rooms, recreation rooms, and laundry facilities. The Cohen Infirmary is equipped and staffed for both inpatient and outpatient care. The Student Union houses a theater, gymnasium, weight room, and billiards room.

An on-campus Child Care Center provides child care for the children of students, faculty members, and alumni. Other academic facilities include a technology transfer and utilization center, a modern physical education facility, health-care facilities, abundant state-of-the-art technical equipment, a fleet of single- and twin-engine airplanes, an impressive greenhouse complex, modern classrooms, and many laboratories for engineering, biology, chemistry, and physics.

Advisement/Counseling Counseling and support services include academic, financial aid, career, psychological, and residence-life counseling.

Career Planning/Placement Offices The Career Development Center offers career counseling, career-planning seminars, job interviews, résumé writing, job placement for the disabled, and opportunities for permanent, part-time, and summer jobs. A reference library of occupational and educational information is open daily.

Recent reports show that Farmingdale graduates experience a high job placement and transfer rate. Of those employed, 76 percent are working in the area in which they were prepared at Farmingdale. Fifty-five percent of the respondents in last year's graduating class transferred to public and private colleges and universities throughout the nation.

Library and Audiovisual Services The Greenley Library has a collection of more than 125,000 volumes, 25,000 pamphlets, and microforms and other materials. Tutoring services in all disciplines taught at the College are available, as are evaluations to detect learning disabilities and assess problems in reading, writing, and mathematics. Computer facilities include a multinode DEC cluster computer system, numerous on-line video monitor terminals, hundreds of microcomputers, and a computer graphics center.

Location

The picturesque 380-acre Farmingdale campus is located 1 mile north of the village of Farmingdale on Melville Road, just off Route 110 and midway between the Southern State Parkway and Long Island Expressway. Farmingdale is on the border between Nassau and Suffolk Counties. New York City is 45 minutes away by car, and some of the world's best beaches (including Jones Beach and Fire Island) are minutes away to the south of the campus.

Admission Requirements

Applicants to associate degree programs must have graduated from high school or hold a high school equivalency diploma. Students apply and are accepted to a specific curriculum. Admission requirements vary according to the program selected. Decisions are based primarily on grades earned in academic courses, including the specific high school prerequisite courses of each curriculum. The review process takes into account the applicant's individual overall background, including available data such as test scores, rank in class, and teacher/counselor recommendations. A personal interview is not required but may be beneficial to the candidate. Applicants with subject deficiencies can make up work prior to registration. When necessary, remedial programs are recommended.

A limited number of high school seniors are admitted to Farmingdale under an early admission program.

Application and Information

Farmingdale operates on a rolling admission system, admitting students on a first-come, first-served basis. Applicants are encouraged to submit applications as early as possible. Applicants to the associate degree programs in dental hygiene and nursing are urged to submit their application materials by January 15. Candidates must submit the State University of New York Application Form, available in all New York State high school guidance offices and college transfer offices.

Requests for further information should be addressed to:

Admissions Office
SUNY Farmingdale
Route 110
Farmingdale, New York 11735
Telephone: 516-420-2200
Fax: 516-420-2633
World Wide Web: http://www.farmingdale.edu

SUOMI COLLEGE
HANCOCK, MICHIGAN

The College and Its Mission

Founded by Finnish immigrants in 1896, Suomi College is the only private college in Michigan's Upper Peninsula. It is one of only 28 colleges in the United States that are affiliated with the Evangelical Lutheran Church in America, and remains the only college founded by Finns in the United States. Suomi College provides a college education in a Christian environment, but is nonsectarian in its instruction, counseling, and campus religious services. The College offers personalized educational opportunities to men and women seeking a quality postsecondary education rooted in the liberal arts and an education designed to foster the abilities necessary for responsible citizenship, academic competence, and career success. Suomi College offers programs in liberal education, career education, talent development, and continuing/lifelong learning. The College is fully accredited by the North Central Association of Colleges and Secondary Schools, the Michigan Commission on College Accreditation, and the Michigan Department of Public Instruction. In addition, the College holds membership in the Lutheran Education Conference of North America, the Michigan Association of Independent Colleges and Universities, and the American Council on Education. Suomi College is expanding with plans to build a new chapel, renovate the library and other existing structures, and acquire a six-story building four blocks from campus to be utilized for classrooms and offices beginning in 1998.

Academic Programs

The educational experience at Suomi College focuses on providing students with a broad academic experience with courses taken both inside and outside their major concentration. Graduation from Suomi College at the associate level requires students to have earned a cumulative grade point of 2.0, to have completed at least 30 semester hours at the college, and to have completed a program approved by the college. To earn an associate degree students must complete a minimum of 60 semester hours. As a liberal arts college, Suomi believes that the attainment of certain skills is essential to leading an aware, productive, healthy, and satisfying life. The College, therefore, requires a core curriculum, approved by MACRAO, for all A.A. degrees. Within the core curriculum areas, students have an element of choice. Many programs offer the opportunity to gain work experience and to put classroom knowledge into practice through internships. One to 6 credits can be earned, depending on the program. Students who believe they have already learned the content of a course may request an examination for credit. A maximum of 16 hours of credit may be earned in this fashion and applied toward degree requirements. Students may also earn credits through advanced placement. Suomi College awards associate degrees in the liberal education division and the career education division. Majors in the liberal education division include English, fine arts, Finnish studies, health sciences, history, liberal studies, pre-education, pre-engineering, prelaw, and social science. Majors in the career education division include business administration, criminal justice, human services, nursing, physical therapist assistant studies, and travel services. Suomi College also has a talent development division. This division offers a learning disabilities program that provides close individual attention for students with learning disabilities, a pro-college program for students who need remedial or special academic support, and an English as a second language (ESL) program for international students.

Off-Campus Programs

Suomi College offers credit courses in Baraga, Michigan, at the Keewenaw Bay Tribal Center (located 30 miles south of Hancock). Students in the nursing and physical therapist assisting program receive clinical experience in community health-care facilities. Students in the travel service program may elect to participate in an exchange program at a number of Finnish colleges. This study-abroad opportunity offers students the advantages of an international experience and education, without compromising projected graduation dates.

Costs

Tuition for the 1996–97 school year is $9500; room is $2000; and board is $1700. About $1000 should be allowed for other costs, such as books, supplies, application and tuition/housing fees, and personal expenses. Incoming freshmen in the learning disabilities program attend a one-week orientation session prior to the fall semester at a cost of $650 (residents) and $420 (commuters). International students in the ESL program attend a two-week orientation program prior to the fall semester at a cost of $1625.

Financial Aid

Suomi College supports the philosophy that every student should have the opportunity to attend college, regardless of their family's financial circumstances. Approximately 92 percent of Suomi students receive financial aid. This aid includes grants, scholarships, loans, and on-campus employment (work-study). All students are encouraged to apply for aid. Last year, in addition to federal, state, and private financial aid, Suomi awarded over $800,000 in need- and merit-based institutional grants. This institutional aid is awarded not only to students from lower-income families, but also to students from middle- and upper-middle-income families. With such excellent financial aid packages, the cost of attending Suomi may be less than or equal to the cost of attending a public university. All accepted students may be considered for federal and Suomi-funded assistance. Michigan residents may apply for state-funded programs. Students must apply for aid by submitting the Free Application for Federal Student Aid (FAFSA) by May 1 to receive priority consideration for need-based aid. Michigan residents are urged to submit these forms by February 15 to maximize state-funded aid.

Faculty

Suomi's 31 faculty members hold degrees from over twenty different universities creating a diverse and dynamic academic atmosphere. Faculty members at Suomi College are committed to excellence in teaching and to a personalized focus on the students. There are no graduate assistants at Suomi and with a student-faculty ratio of 15:1, professors are available to work closely with students, providing academic and personal support. Many members of the faculty have worked in their chosen fields, but are now dedicated to teaching. Because of their work experience, the faculty is knowledgeable not only about theories, but also about how these theories are used in the workplace. Faculty members serve as academic advisers and maintain generous office hours.

Student Body Profile

The College currently serves approximately 350 students. The small size of the College allows for each student to receive personalized attention in the classroom and throughout the campus. The student body represents at least twelve states and six other countries. Diversity is welcomed at Suomi, and the College currently has a 12 percent minority representation and 6 percent international representation. The College's residential halls offer a traditional college experience through its coeducational programs and activities. The College also offers opportunities for involvement for commuter students, who make up 40 percent of the student population.

Student Activities

Activities are provided for students to develop their individual talents and interests. Activities include the student senate, the campus choir, the annual drama production, the Concert-Lecture Series, convocations (featuring regionally known speakers, artists, and performers), and a variety of student organizations. Students are invited to participate in the religious life on campus. While chapel attendance is not mandatory, interested students are encouraged to participate in weekly worship and special events coordinated by the Campus Chaplain. The College has a strong intramural and club sports program for men and women. Sports activities include basketball, volleyball, skiing (downhill and cross-country), golf, swimming, tennis, floor hockey, bowling, and softball.

Facilities and Resources

The Suomi College library contains a carefully selected collection of over 27,500 books, 350 magazines titles, and 16,300 audiovisual materials. The library has access to a regional computerized system and interlibrary loan. Other facilities include two academic computing labs for student use, a nursing center, science labs and music rooms, and the Finnish American Heritage Center, which holds facilities for the visual arts, performing arts, lectures, and interactive exhibits. Suomi College recognizes that students come to college with varying academic needs and abilities. To help all students reach their optimum potential, the College offers peer and professional tutoring, a teaching/learning center, student support services, the pro-college program, the English as a second language program, and the learning disabilities program. Suomi College also offers personal counseling and career planning.

Location

Suomi College is located in the pristine and beautifully rugged Upper Peninsula town of Hancock, Michigan. Northern Upper Michigan, also called the Copper Country, was once the single greatest supplier of copper in the world. The area is rich in history and culture ready to be explored. Much of Suomi's campus was built on a hillside allowing for panoramic views of the beautiful scenery that is especially breathtaking in the fall. Centrally located in downtown Hancock and only 2 miles from its neighboring city of Houghton, Suomi students enjoy the benefits of both cities, including shopping, restaurants, theaters, and recreational activities. Suomi College is easily accessible by car, and is a 4-hour drive from Green Bay, Wisconsin; 2 hours from Marquette, Michigan; 6 hours from Minneapolis, Minnesota; and 8 hours from Chicago, Illinois. Hancock is serviced by the Houghton County Airport located just 5 miles away and the Greyhound Bus Line. Suomi's proximity to Lake Superior and to several national parks allows for unlimited outdoor activities. Students enjoy hiking, camping, picnicking, fishing, swimming, canoeing, ice skating, ice hockey, and the viewing of over 150 waterfalls in the Upper Peninsula. With more than 200 inches of snow each year, there is excellent skiing and snowmobiling. Suomi has excellent relations with the community and with Michigan Technological University located in Houghton. Students are often invited to participate in community music and drama groups and together with M.T.U., Suomi presents a Concert-Lecture Series featuring internationally know lecturers, soloists, and ensembles several times each year. Suomi students are fortunate to have the Finnish American Heritage Center located on campus. The center houses a museum, art gallery, theater, and the Finnish American Historical Archives, which are the oldest and most valuable of their kind in North America.

Admission Requirements

To be accepted as a student at Suomi College, an applicant must have the academic ability and background for work on the college level. In order to be considered for acceptance, students must provide the completed application, transcripts from all high schools and colleges attended (or an official copy of their GED equivalency exam), the $20 application fee and ACT or SAT I scores. Students who have a 2.0 grade point average in high school college-preparatory courses and who provide acceptable ACT or SAT I scores are considered for regular admission. Those with lower grade point averages or ACT/SAT I scores are required to take institutional testing and submit letters of recommendation in order to determine admission status. The above listed requirements will satisfy most associate degree-level programs with the exception of the nursing and physical therapist assistant programs. These programs require a 2.5 grade point average or better, and students must have completed one year of both high school algebra and chemistry with a minimum grade of C.

Application and Information

While applications are accepted on a rolling basis, May 30 is the priority filing date. Those students interested in the nursing program are encouraged to apply by early March, since the nursing class for the next year is chosen in mid-March. Students should submit all materials for their files as soon as possible. Admission decisions will be made within 10 working days upon completion of the student's file.

For an application or further information on programs or financial aid, please contact:

Suomi College Admissions
601 Quincy Street
Hancock, Michigan 49930-1882
Telephone: 906-487-7274
800-682-7604 (toll-free)

Built in 1896, Old Main was the first building on Suomi's campus.

Peterson's Guide to Two-Year Colleges 1997

THE SWISS HOSPITALITY INSTITUTE, CÉSAR RITZ
WASHINGTON, CONNECTICUT

The Institute and Its Mission

The Swiss Hospitality Institute, *César Ritz,* is the only Swiss College of Hospitality Management in the United States. The Institute prepares students to be managers in the international hospitality industry, the fastest growing industry in the world. The Institute is a private college and is accredited by the State of Connecticut and by ACICS.

The Institute is a small exclusive institution, with a maximum enrollment of 120 students. Classes are small, and each student receives individual attention. The faculty-student ratio is 7:1. All students are trained in the Swiss art of hotelerie combined with American techniques of management.

Swiss professionalism is apparent in the curriculum, the high standards of service, and the system of professional assessment which measures the professional performance of each student. Many student activities are connected with hospitality, such as planning social events, organizing trips to New York City and Boston, designing and managing banquets and international galas, and planning and managing events for individuals and community groups. Students are expected to perform professionally and to undertake responsibilities in several areas of the Institute, just as they will do in a hotel, resort, or restaurant.

The Institute's international standing rests on the highest professional standards which were first established in Switzerland. Like other organizations of proven leadership, and like César Ritz, the Swiss Hospitality Institute, *César Ritz,* has achieved a defining role in its field through uncompromising adherence to excellence.

The Swiss Hospitality Institute, *César Ritz,* is the American College of Hotelconsult Colleges in Switzerland. There are two Hotelconsult colleges in Switzerland. The Institut Hôtelier, *César Ritz,* in Le Bouveret on the shores of Lake Geneva, offers a Swiss Diploma in Hospitality Management. The International College of Hospitality Administration in Brig, Switzerland, offers the B.A. degree through Washington State University. The newest Hotelconsult program opens at the International College of Tourism and Hotel Management in Sydney, Australia, in August 1996. Students in the two-year Associate of Science Degree Program at the Swiss Hospitality Institute, *César Ritz,* in Washington, Connecticut, may take one of their two years in Switzerland or in Australia. These students would be eligible for a Swiss Diploma and an American Associate of Science degree, and they would have internship opportunities in Switzerland, in Australia, and in the United States.

Academic Programs

Associate Degree Programs The Associate of Science degree in hospitality management is a two-year program. The curriculum combines the art of European hotellerie, emphasizing service and practical professionalism, with American management techniques that include computer technology, marketing strategies, and business. There is a strong liberal arts component that includes the humanities, science, and social science. The program includes two paid internships at the finest hotels and restaurants in the United States and abroad. The director of internships arranges up to three interviews with prospective employers for each student and oversees the internship. In contrast to the experience of many college graduates, students obtain good positions in their chosen field. Three quarters of the graduates are working in the hospitality industry; the remainder are continuing their studies for the baccalaureate degree. Graduates of the program who want to continue their education for a baccalaureate degree may have the best of both worlds. They will have the intense, practical experience at the highest professional level for their associate degree at the Institute and then the final two years of education in the major for their bachelor's degree. The associate degree in hospitality management enables them to gain experience in the industry, if they wish, before continuing their education.

Transfer Arrangements The Swiss Hospitality Institute accepts transfers of up to 30 credits for the Associate of Science Degree from another accredited institution for those courses that are comparable to the courses at the Institute and those in which the student earned a grade of C (2.0) or better. Students with prior college experience who wish to have their previous academic work reviewed for possible transfer credit must arrange to have an official transcript mailed directly to the Admissions Office from each college or university attended.

Certificate and Diploma Programs The certificate program in hospitality management is designed for students who already have a college degree and who want to work in the hospitality industry. This program is also available for students who have extensive experience in hospitality, but who have not been to college. During the one-year program, students will study at the Institute for six months and then do an internship of 800 hours at an excellent hotel or resort.

Special Programs and Services The City and Guilds of London is a prestigious organization representing the highest standards for professionals in all industries. The organization has training centers in 85 countries. Swiss Hospitality Institute is the only training center for the hospitality industry in the United States. Students are offered the opportunity to achieve international recognition and can earn a certificate or diploma from City and Guilds of London while attending the Institute. Other special programs and services include English as a second language, a Learning Center with peer tutorials, and study-abroad opportunities.

Off-Campus Programs

Students with appropriate GPAs and professional attitude scores may chose to spend their second year of study at the Institute's sister campus, Institut Hôtelier *César Ritz* (IHCR) in Le Bouveret, on Lake Geneva in Switzerland. Students who complete the requirements of both institutions earn an A.S. in hospitality management from the Swiss Hospitality Institute and a Swiss Diploma from IHCR.

Credit for Nontraditional Learning Experiences

Credit may be awarded for prior noncollegiate, professional experience in the hospitality industry. For details and required criteria, students should consult the registrar.

Costs

Expenses for the 1996–97 academic year include tuition, $13,000, and room and board, $4250. Each student is required to have an operating account of $1500 which covers books, uniforms, and supplies.

Financial Aid

The Institute has several types of financial assistance programs, scholarships and grants, low-interest loans, and employment opportunities, to assist all eligible part-time or full-time students in meeting their educational expenses. In many cases, the Institute's financial aid officer will award a qualified student a financial aid package which may include all three types of financial aid. Assistance with financial planning is available for families on an individual basis to help them determine how they can best utilize their own resources and other funds to meet the cost of education.

Faculty

The student-faculty ratio at the Institute is 7:1. All full-time faculty members have student advising responsibilities, and all faculty members have earned appropriate advanced degrees and European hospitality experience. To support its mission, the Institute has a faculty composed of American and international members.

Student Body Profile

The Institute attracts students from twenty-three countries around the world. Forty percent of the students are American. The average age of the students is in the early 20s. Some students seeking second careers or a postbaccalaureate certificate already have a bachelor's or graduate degree.

Student Activities

The Student Association is the student government of the Institute. All students are members. The elected officers have the responsibility of identifying concerns of fellow students, organizing activities, and serving as student representatives. The Student Association has four standing committees: the social committee, the recreational sports committee, the college store committee, and the yearbook committee. Recreational activities and volunteer and community service opportunities are available to students.

Facilities and Resources

Most students live on campus. Student rooms are designed for double occupancy. Each residence hall has a spacious lounge equipped with cable television, a VCR, and a microwave oven. There is also a Student Club. The campus was completely renovated prior to its opening in 1992. All equipment is state-of-the-art. The library's present collection consists of 9,000 bound volumes, 200 periodical subscriptions, and 200 videotapes. The library uses OCLC (Online Computer Library Center) as a national on-line catalog utility. Four CD-ROMs support the library's services, as well as Internet access.

Computer facilities include two computer laboratories with IBM-compatible machines. Career planning, health services, and counseling and personal support services are available to all students.

Location

The Institute is situated on 27 wooded acres in Washington, Connecticut, a charming, historic New England village of 3,000 residents. The rolling hills of Northwestern Connecticut provide a perfect setting for outdoor recreational pursuits such as hiking, cycling, skiing, and water sports. The campus is within easy reach of the cultural advantages of such major cities as Hartford, 45 miles away, New York City, 85 miles away, and Boston, 90 miles away. Many students hold part-time jobs in the area. Students are actively involved in community events.

Admission Requirements

The Institute requires national applicants to submit a completed application form, $25 application fee, official high school transcripts or GED scores, and two letters of recommendation. SAT I scores are not required but are highly recommended. Factors such as courses taken, grades earned, absence and tardiness figures, and class rank are considered. Students for whom English is not a native language are required to show proof of English competency. Because of the unusual nature of the campus and the program, applicants are strongly encouraged to schedule an on-campus interview. Interviews can be arranged off-campus if necessary. Admission is determined by a committee primarily composed of faculty members. The Institute seeks to maintain its 50-50 mix of American and international students. The Institute seeks students who are motivated to succeed in a management career in the international hospitality industry.

Application and Information

The Institute accepts applications throughout the year for its May, August, October, and January starting dates. Applicants are notified of their admission status shortly after their files are complete, usually within two weeks. For application materials and additional information, students should contact:

Karen Lambert
Director of Admissions
Swiss Hospitality Institute, *César Ritz*
101 Wykeham Road
Washington, Connecticut
Telephone: 860-868-9555 (outside the U.S.)
800-955-0809 (toll-free)
Fax: 860-868-2114

The elegant grounds of Swiss Hospitality Institute.

Peterson's Guide to Two-Year Colleges 1997

UNIVERSITY OF THE STATE OF NEW YORK, REGENTS COLLEGE

ALBANY, NEW YORK

The College and Its Mission

A recognized leader in the field of nontraditional college education for twenty-five years, Regents College of the University of the State of New York has enabled more than 72,000 individuals—primarily working adults—to earn fully accredited associate and bachelor's degrees in liberal arts, business, nursing, and technology. Believing that what individuals know is more valuable than where or how they learned it, the College pioneered the process of knowledge evaluation and assessment. The College has no residency requirement, and its programs are available worldwide. Most Regents College students are returning to college to complete an education begun elsewhere. The College accepts the broadest possible array of prior college-level credit in transfer, including classroom and distance courses from accredited colleges, proficiency examinations, and accredited on-the-job or military training. Although the College itself does not offer courses, Regents College faculty members, drawn from other colleges and universities, design the curiculum and determine how credit can be earned. Professional academic advisers help students design an individualized study plan using college courses, examinations, and other sources of credit to complete their degree requirements. Students work at their own pace while maintaining a full-time work schedule and family and civic responsibilities.

Regents College is accredited by the Middle States Association of Colleges and Schools, the Commission on Higher Education, and by the New York State Board of Regents. The nursing degrees are also accredited by the National League for Nursing.

Academic Programs

Regents College has demanding academic requirements, but the programs are self-paced and highly flexible. Faculty members establish and monitor academic policies and standards and determine degree requirements, including the ways in which credit can be earned. Most students bring prior college-level credit with them when they enroll. They receive an initial evaluation of this credit and then work with professional academic advisers by phone, mail, and computer bulletin board to plan how they will complete their degrees. They use not only both classroom and distance college courses, but also performance examinations, portfolio assessments, and special assessments. The academic advisers can search DistanceLearn, a Regents College database of over 7,000 college-level courses and proficiency examinations available at a distance, for courses that enrolled students may use to complete their degree requirements. Students in the nursing program may also contact nurse educators for advice and guidance about preparing for the clinical performance examinations.

The Regents College Bulletin Board gives students access to a wide variety of information 24 hours a day and allows them to communicate with advisers at times convenient to them.

The College offers twenty-six associate and baccalaureate degrees in liberal arts, business, nursing, and technology. The associate degrees articulate with the appropriate bachelor's degrees.

Associate Degree Programs The most flexible degrees are those in the liberal arts. The College offers both an **Associate in Arts** and an **Associate in Science**. Of the total 60 credits, students must earn 48 arts and sciences credits in the A.A. degree and 30 arts and sciences credits in the A.S. degree. Both degrees include a written English requirement.

In business, the College offers an **Associate in Science** in business. Of the 60 total credits, 33 must be in the arts and sciences. Students must fulfill a written English requirement and requirements in macroeconomics, microeconomics, mathematics, and statistics. Required core business courses include introduction to accounting I and II, introduction to business law, computers, principles of management, and principles of marketing. There is a time limit of twenty years on courses applied to the business component.

The nursing program offers two associate degrees in nursing, an **Associate in Science** and an **Associate in Applied Science**. The associate degree nursing programs are 66 semester hours in credit, 30 in general education and 36 in nursing. The nursing component is composed of six written nursing examinations and one clinical performance examination. To test the clinical competencies of its nursing students, Regents College pioneered in the creation of rigorous performance examinations. College courses in nursing and nursing examinations must have been completed within five years prior to enrollment.

In technology, the College offers **Associate in Science** degrees in computer software (60 credits), electronics technology (64 credits), nuclear technology (60 credits), and technology with specialty (60 credits). Of the total, 30 credits must be earned in the arts and sciences component and the remainder in the technology component. As part of the arts and sciences component, students must complete a written English requirement and different specific sciences and mathematics, depending on the degree program. The technology component requirements also vary with the degree program. Time limits apply to courses in the technology component. Laboratories are required in some degrees.

Off-Campus Programs

To facilitate the academic work of their employees, some employers enter into agreements with Regents College to form study and advisement groups. The College also assists businesses that would like to have their training evaluated for college-level credit as part of the American Council on Education (ACE) or New York State (NYS) Program for Noncollegiate-Sponsored Instruction (PONSI). In addition, the College has formed collaborations with some community colleges to help students to continue using the community college facilities while pursuing a baccalaureate degree.

Credit for Nontraditional Learning Experiences

Students may earn credit for regionally accredited college course work that they have earned in the classroom or by distance study such as correspondence, video, or computer courses. They may also bring in credit earned through proficiency examinations such as the College-Level Examination Program (CLEP), the Graduate Record Examination (GRE), DANTES examinations, and Regents College Examinations, which are offered worldwide by American College Testing as ACT PEP: Regents College Examinations. Other credit sources include military and corporate training evaluated by the

American Council on Education as college-level and certain certificate and licensure programs.

Thousands of people take and pass Regents College Examinations every year, using the results to obtain credit or advanced placement at colleges and universities, toward Regents College degree requirements, and for other purposes. Examinations are available in the arts and sciences, business, education, and nursing. Several carry upper-level credit and others are accompanied by expended study guides to help students prepare for an exam.

Costs

Regents College charges a $565 fee for enrollment (which covers initial evaluation and advisement services for one year), a $270 annual advisement fee (for each year after the first), and a $340 (associate programs) or $370 (baccalaureate programs) fee for program completion and graduation. The College also offers a credit review in the liberal arts and business programs. For $115 students receive an evaluation based on student copies of academic documents prior to enrollment. If they enroll within three months in the program for which they received the evaluation and if their official documents are the same as the student copies, they may deduct $75 from the enrollment fee. Time to degree completion differs among programs: liberal arts programs take between one and one and one half years on average, business programs take about two years, technology programs take about two and one half years, and nursing programs take about one and one half years for the associate degree and about three and one half for the bachelor's degree. Additional costs depend on the amount of credit that students need to earn and what credit sources they choose. Proficiency examinations are the least expensive mode of earning credit. Regents College keeps college costs as low as possible in part by accepting the broadest possible array of prior-earned nonduplicative credit. Students should also figure in costs for books, travel (if necessary), and communication with the College.

Financial Aid

Some financial aid is available, particularly the College's own Access to Learning Scholarships and aid connected with Veterans Affairs benefits. The College participates in the PLATO and TERI supplemental loan programs. Because of the nontraditional nature of Regents College, students seeking financial aid should contact the Regents College Financial Aid Office before enrolling.

Faculty

The 300 faculty members of Regents College are drawn from many colleges and universities, mostly in New York State, and from industries and health-care facilities. Faculty members establish and monitor academic policies and standards, determine degree requirements, including the ways in which credit can be earned, develop the content for all examinations, review the records of students to verify their degree completion, and recommend degree conferral to the Board of Regents.

Student Body Profile

Regents College has over 20,000 students currently enrolled. Approximately 4,500 graduate each year, many going directly to graduate school. Students live in every state in the United States and many other countries. The average student age is 39, but it can range up to 80. Over 81 percent are working adults employed full-time. Over 20 percent of currently enrolled students belong to groups historically underserved by higher education.

Facilities and Resources

Regents College, as an assessment institution, does not offer classes itself. The College helps students to locate appropriate credit sources either in their local communities or through distance providers.

Location

Regents College is located wherever students seek a degree. Because its program is totally portable, the College moves with students whenever and wherever they move. The administrative offices of Regents College are located in Albany, New York, the capital of New York State. Once a year the College holds a formal commencement ceremony to recognize all who have completed a degree that year. Proud of their accomplishments, many students travel great distances to attend.

Admission Requirements

Regents College has open admissions except in the nursing program. The nursing degrees are specifically designed to serve individuals with significant background or experience in a clinically oriented health-care discipline. Therefore, admission to the program is open only to registered nurses, licensed practical/vocational nurses, paramedics, emergency medical technicians, military service corpsmen, individuals who hold a degree in a clinically oriented health-care field in which they have had the opportunity to provide direct patient care (i.e., physicians, respiratory therapists, chiropractors, and physicians' assistants), or individuals who have completed 50 percent or more of the clinical nursing courses in a registered nursing education program. Exceptions may be made for individuals who do not meet these qualifications but who can document significant clinical background.

Application and Information

Students may apply at any time during the year. For information, students should contact:

Regents College
7 Columbia Circle
Albany, New York 12203-5159
Telephone: 518-464-8500

VALLEY FORGE MILITARY COLLEGE
WAYNE, PENNSYLVANIA

The College and Its Mission

Valley Forge Military College is a private, residential nonsectarian college offering the freshman and sophomore years of college. The primary mission of the College is to prepare students for transfer to competitive senior colleges and universities. The College, established in 1935, has a long tradition of providing opportunities for personal growth in academics, character, self-discipline, and leadership to all students, regardless of race, creed, or national origin. Slightly more than 15 percent of the approximately 200 students who comprise the College are members of minority groups. The diverse student body represents more than thirty states and ten countries. The College fosters each student's academic and intellectual development through personalized instruction and close student-faculty relationships within the structure of a military environment that emphasizes self-discipline and traditional values. More than 90 percent of the students transfer to competitive colleges and universities throughout the United States upon completion of their associate degree.

Valley Forge Military College is the only college in the northeastern United States that offers qualified freshmen the opportunity to participate in an Early Commissioning Program, leading to a commission as a second lieutenant in the U.S. Army Reserves at the end of their sophomore year. This program, offered through the Reserve Officers' Training Corps (ROTC) Department and involving approximately 28 percent of the student body, provides qualified students with two-year, full-tuition scholarships and liberal financial assistance for room and board. Students interested in Air Force ROTC may select this option through a host campus agreement with a local college. All eligible cadets participate in military science training at the introductory level.

A distinctive feature of the Corps of Cadets and the College is their self-governing nature. The majority of the Corps of Cadets are housed in Younghusband Hall, under the supervision of the Commandant of Cadets and the Company Tactical Officer. Cadets dine together in the Regimental Mess. Nondenominational chapel services are held on a weekly basis in the Chapel of Saint Cornelius the Centurion for all members of the Corps of Cadets. Catholic mass is held on campus on Sunday evening. Jewish cadets are provided the opportunity to participate in religious services in one of the local synagogues.

The College is accredited by the Middle States Association of Colleges and Schools and is approved by the Pennsylvania State Council of Education and the Commission on Higher Education of the Pennsylvania State Department of Education. The College is a member of the National Association of Independent Colleges and Universities, the Commission on Independent Colleges and Universities, and the Association of Military Colleges and Schools in the United States.

Academic Programs

All students are required to complete a core program of approximately 45 credits designed to establish the essential competence necessary for continued intellectual development and to facilitate the transfer process. Included in the core program are two semesters of English, emphasizing composition and research; one semester of literature; two semesters of Western civilization; two semesters of mathematics; two semesters of science; and one semester of computer science. Qualified cadets must also complete four semesters of military science. In addition, all sophomores participate in the sophomore writing seminar, a guided research experience. To satisfy the requirement for an associate degree, cadets must complete an additional six to eight courses related to their selected major. Associate degrees are awarded upon completion of the degree requirements with a quality point average of 2.0 or better.

Associate Degree Programs Valley Forge Military College offers programs leading to the associate degree in business, criminal justice, engineering, liberal arts, and science. An associate degree in general studies is also awarded.

Transfer Arrangements Transfer of academic credits and completion of the baccalaureate degree is facilitated by articulation agreements with a number of outstanding colleges and universities. Currently agreements are in place with Widner University, the University of Pittsburgh's School of Engineering, Drexel University, Clarkson University, the Philadelphia College of Pharmacy and Science, and Cabrini College.

Credit for Nontraditional Learning Experiences

Valley Forge Military College may give credit for demonstrated proficiency in areas related to college-level courses. Sources used to determine such proficiency are College-Level Examination Program (CLEP), Advanced Placement Examination (AP), Tech Prep Articulation (TP), Defense Activity for Nontraditional Education Support (DANTES), United States Armed Forces Institute (USAFI), Office of Education Credit and Credentials of the American Council on Education (ACE), and National Cryptologic School (NCS).

Costs

The annual charge for 1996–97 is estimated at $18,800. This charge includes tuition, room and board, uniforms, maintenance, haircuts, and other fees. Optional expenses may include fee-based courses, such as SCUBA, aviation, and driver's education or membership in the cavalry troop or artillery battery. A fee is charged for Health Center confinement over 24 hours' duration. For information on the payment plan, contact the Finance Office.

Financial Aid

The College operates an extensive program of financial assistance. Part of this program involves the federal and state student loan and grant programs, including Federal Pell Grants and Pennsylvania Higher Education Assistance Agency (PHEAA) Grants. Moreover, many states have a reciprocal agreement with Pennsylvania for state assistance. A cadet may also participate in the Federal Work-Study Program, through which he will be assigned work on campus at the federal minimum wage rate. In addition, qualified cadets in the advanced ROTC commissioning program are eligible for two-year, full-tuition scholarships. These scholarships are supplemented by assistance for room and board provided by the College.

The second area of student aid is the Valley Forge scholarship program, administered by the College's financial aid officer, which includes academic, athletic, music, and work scholarships as well as scholarships for merit and leadership.

Faculty

There are 14 full-time and 17 part-time faculty members holding the academic rank of professor, associate professor, assistant professor, or instructor. These faculty members are deeply dedicated to teaching as a lifelong profession and have strong personal leadership qualities. The Military Science Department has 4 active-duty Army officers and 3 noncommissioned officers assigned as full-time faculty members for the ROTC program. The faculty-student ratio is approximately 1:10. Classes are small, and the classroom atmosphere contributes to a harmonious relationship between faculty members and the students. Funds for professional development are available to all faculty members.

Student Body Profile

The Corps of Cadets is self-administered through a tactical officer and a cadet chain of command. The College's cadets are appointed to major command positions in the Corps. The first captain is generally a sophomore in the College. The tactical officer is responsible for administration, training, and disciplinary advice and acts in the role of counselor in all phases of cadet life, except academic matters. Minor breaches of conduct are handled within each company. More serious offenses are handled by the Regimental Disciplinary Committee, composed of faculty members and cadets, or by the Academy Board, composed of senior members of the faculty and staff. Through their representatives, cadets cooperate with the administration in enforcing regulations and exert a strong impact on student conduct. A Student Advisory Council, consisting of cadets elected by their fellow cadets, represents the cadets to the College administration. The Dean's Council meets monthly to discuss aspects of academic life.

Student Activities

A renowned band, drill team, and cavalry troop, as well as glee club, choir, and other club activities, attract students to Valley Forge. The band and glee club have traveled widely, appearing in London and Washington, D.C., and at the Philadelphia Academy of Music. Cadet honor units have assisted local communities in ceremonial functions involving national and international celebrities and dignitaries.

Sports Athletics and physical training play an important part in a cadet's life. Cadets are expected to participate in sports and physical conditioning at some level as a means to developing a competitive spirit, teamwork, and sense of fair play. For students aspiring to compete in intercollegiate football at the Division I-A or Division I-AA level, Valley Forge's intercollegiate football program offers a distinctive opportunity. One of the few residential junior college–level programs in the Northeast, Valley Forge's program combines the strong academic transfer focus of the military college with the highly successful experience of a fifteen-year preparatory program that has routinely placed players on national levels in basketball, cross-country, lacrosse, soccer, wrestling, and tennis. Club and interscholastic teams are available in golf, polo, and riflery.

Facilities and Resources

Campus buildings are modern and well equipped to meet student needs. College classrooms are located in two buildings and contain chemistry, biology, and physics laboratories. A recently renovated computer laboratory supports the computer science curriculum and student requirements through a local area network.

Library and Audiovisual Services The Mary H. Baker Memorial Library is a learning resource center for independent study and research. There are more than 60,000 volumes and audio-visual materials, microfilm, and periodicals. The library provides on-line database access and membership in the Tri-State Library Consortium supports the College requirements.

Location

Valley Forge Military College is on a magnificently landscaped 115-acre campus in the Main Line community of Wayne, 15 miles west of Philadelphia and close to the Valley Forge National Historic Park. Ample opportunities exist for cadets to enjoy cultural and entertainment resources and activities in the Philadelphia area.

Admission Requirements

Admission to the College is based upon review of an applicant's SAT I or ACT scores, high school transcript, recommendations from a guidance counselor, and personal interview. Students may be accepted for mid-year admission. Minimum requirements for admission on a nonprobational status are a high school diploma or equivalency diploma with a minimum 2.0 average, rank in the upper half of the class, and a minimum combined SAT I score of 800 or the equivalent on the ACT. International students for whom English is a second language must have a minimum score of 500 on the Test of English as a Foreign Language (TOEFL). Up to 20 percent of an entering class may be admitted on a conditional or probationary status, and individual entrance requirements may be waived by the dean of the College for students who display a sincere commitment to pursuing a college degree.

Application and Information

Valley Forge Military College follows a program of rolling admissions. Applicants are notified of the admission decision as soon as their files are complete. A nonrefundable registration fee of $25, applied toward tuition, is required of all applicants.

For application forms and further information, students should contact:

Major Kelly M. DeShane
College Admissions Coordinator
Valley Forge Military College
1001 Eagle Road
Wayne, Pennsylvania 19087
Telephone: 800-234-VFMC (toll-free)

The Corps of Cadets on parade.

Peterson's Guide to Two-Year Colleges 1997

VENTURA COUNTY COMMUNITY COLLEGE DISTRICT
MOORPARK, OXNARD, AND VENTURA, CALIFORNIA

The College and Its Mission
The Ventura County Community College District, founded in 1925, has a rich tradition of strong academic and vocational programs. The colleges at Moorpark, Oxnard, and Ventura are funded by the State of California and are fully accredited by the Western Association of Colleges and Schools.

Academic Programs
Associate Degree Programs Students completing a two-year program can earn an **Associate of Arts (A.A.)** or **Associate of Science (A.S.)** degree from the Ventura Colleges. Those completing certain vocational programs can also earn a certificate of achievement.

Among the three schools, programs are available in accounting, agricultural business management (concentrations in animal science management and landscape horticultural management, agronomy and plant sciences, alcohol and drug studies, anthropology, archaeology, art, astronomy, astrophysics, automotive technology (body and fender repair), behavioral science (concentrations in anthropology, psychology, and sociology), bilingual and cross-cultural studies, biology, business, business/logistics, business information systems, business management (concentrations in management, marketing, and merchandising), ceramics, clerical studies, child development, commercial art, communications (concentrations in print media, public relations, and television), computer information systems, computer science, configuration/data management, construction technology (concentrations in building inspection and construction management), criminal justice, dance, diesel mechanics, drafting technology (concentrations in architectural and civil drafting and construction, electronic drafting and manufacturing, and mechanical design and manufacturing), economics, electronics and applied electronics, electronic technology, engineering, English, environmental hazardous materials technology, environmental science, environmental studies, exotic animal training and management, fashion design (design and merchandising), fine arts, fire technology (preservice, in-service, and administrative services), fitness management specialist studies, general liberal arts and sciences, geology, graphic communication (concentrations in computerized composition, graphic design, and printing technology), graphic design, history, home economics, hotel and restaurant management (concentrations in culinary arts, hotel management, and restaurant management), industrial safety, information processing, interior design, international and intercultural studies, international business, journalism, landscape horticulture (concentrations in landscape architecture and city and regional planning, landscape construction and management, nursery and greenhouse management, and turfgrass and park management), legal assisting, liberal studies, machine technology, mathematics, medical assisting, music, natural resources, network engineer studies, nursing science, philosophy, political science, photography, photojournalism, physical education, physical science (engineering technology), physics, psychiatric technology and apprenticeship, psychology, radio and television studies, radiologic technology, real estate (concentration in escrow and sales), recreation, secretarial studies, social science (concentrations in geography, history, philosophy, and political science), sociology, Spanish, supervision (concentrations in marketing, office microcomputer, office technician studies, and word processing), theater arts (concentrations in acting and directing), water science (wastewater and water), and welding technology.

Transfer Arrangements All of the Ventura Colleges offer all of the general education courses necessary to transfer to the University of California and other public and private universities throughout the U.S. Because the colleges are part of the California State system of higher education, both the University of California and the California State universities accept transfer courses from the Ventura Colleges exactly as their own courses. The University of California also give priority consideration to community college students as third-year transfer students.

Certificate and Diploma Programs Certificates are offered for programs of study in child development (school-age child care and early childhood education), drafting technology/CAD, environmental technology, and microcomputer applications.

Special Programs and Services While business management, computer science, and engineering are among the most popular majors at all three of the schools, each College features different programs. The Colleges have special English programs for students who need additional preparation before entering university-level courses requiring high English proficiency. The Ventura Colleges also offer a full range of vocational courses for students who need specific training to start a career.

Costs
For the academic year 1996–97, California residents pay an enrollment fee of $13 per unit; nonresidents pay $141 per unit in tuition and enrollment fees. The total tuition cost for a two-semester college year is $3432. International students living in a homestay or apartment can estimate costs between $3800 and $7700 for two semesters, making an estimated total between $10,000 and $13,000 for costs including tuition, living expenses, health insurance, and books and supplies.

Financial Aid
Resident students may receive government grants and loans for support when there is proof of financial need. Applications are accepted on a continuous basis.

Faculty
The Ventura Colleges have a total of 394 full-time professors. All faculty members have the equivalent of a master's degree and many have doctoral degrees. They are all dedicated to teaching students on a personal level. Small classes give students the opportunity to interact with faculty members in an ideal academic setting.

Student Activities
All students are encouraged to participate in campus-shared governance. Student Government assumes major responsibility

of coordinating student activities and expressing student concerns, interests, and views to the College administration.

Facilities and Resources

All of the Ventura Colleges have modern library facilities, computers, centers for performing arts, and athletic facilities that include gymnasiums, swimming pools, tracks, playing fields, and tennis courts.

Location

The Ventura Colleges of Moorpark, Oxnard, and Ventura are located on Southern California's Gold Coast between Santa Barbara and Malibu. The three campuses, each more than 100 acres, are in Ventura County, extending from the mountains to the sea. It is a peaceful, family environment, only an hour away from the cultural center of Los Angeles.

Admission Requirements

The admission policy is based on the premise that the Colleges provide the opportunity for further education to the community and international students. The Ventura Colleges have an open-door admissions policy. Educational opportunities are given to all high school graduates, students with GED equivalency diplomas, and international students with proof of equivalent education. International students need to submit a minimum score of 450 on the TOEFL with their application. ESL courses are available for those who are at the pre-university English level.

Application and Information

For more information, U.S. students should contact:

Ms. Kathy Colborn, Registrar
Moorpark College
Moorpark, California 93021-2899
Telephone: 805-378-1410

Ms. Delores Tabor-King, Registrar
Oxnard College
4000 South Rose Avenue
Oxnard, California 93033-6699
Telephone: 805-986-5843

Ms. Joan Halk, Registrar
Ventura College
4667 Telegraph Road
Ventura, California 93003
Telephone: 805-378-1500

International students should contact:

Dr. Elise D. Schneider, Provost
International Student Program
71 Day Road
Ventura, California 93003
Telephone: 805-648-8945

VERMONT TECHNICAL COLLEGE
RANDOLPH CENTER, VERMONT

The College and Its Mission

From its hilltop vantage point in a picturesque New England village, Vermont Technical College looks out on a changing world—a high-tech world. More and more, career success in this world depends on our ability to understand, use, and even master the technologies that shape our lives. Vermont Tech is equipping students with the technical, communication, and problem-solving skills they will need to succeed in the high-tech world of the 21st century. The College was founded in 1866 as Vermont's first teacher training institution. It became the Vermont School of Agriculture in 1910, reflecting the educational needs of the agrarian society of the time. Technical courses were added to the College mission in 1957, and a long-term institutional commitment to technical education was reflected in a name change to Vermont Technical College in 1962. Today, students choose Vermont Tech for a multitude of reasons, but those most frequently given include the College's academic reputation, the fact that graduates get good jobs, the academic programs offered, and the small college atmosphere. For more than a decade, Vermont Tech has maintained a remarkable placement record—98 percent of each year's graduates have been either employed or attending college within four months of graduation. Of those taking jobs, 90 percent were working in fields directly related to their majors at VTC. A public, residential, coeducational college, Vermont Tech is the only technical college among the five institutions that make up the Vermont State Colleges system. Most of the 821 students live on campus. The College is accredited by the New England Association of Schools and Colleges. In addition, the following associate's degree programs are accredited by the Technology Accreditation Commission of the Accreditation Board for Engineering and Technology (TAC of ABET): architectural and building engineering technology; civil engineering technology; computer engineering technology; electrical and electronics engineering technology; and mechanical engineering technology. The veterinary technology program is accredited by the American Veterinary Medical Association as a program for educating veterinary technicians. Practical nursing programs are approved by the Vermont Board of Nursing and accredited by the National League for Nursing (NLN).

Academic Programs

Vermont Technical College offers 16 associate degree programs and two bachelor's degree programs in a wide range of technical and related fields. Graduates are prepared to work effectively in positions that support the activities of engineers, scientists, architects, management specialists, and other professionals. Whether preparing for associate's or bachelor's degrees, students receive a rigorous and broad-based education centered on a core curriculum that includes both technical and general education electives. The number of credits required for graduation ranges from 65 to 72 for the associate's degree and from 133 to 142 for the baccalaureate, depending on the major. Most degree programs offer project courses in which students work as teams on real-world assignments. The academic calendar is divided into two semesters, with the fall semester beginning in late August and finals ending just before the holiday break in December. The spring semester begins in mid-January, with finals ending in the middle of May. For students seeking the bachelor's degree, a two-year program at Vermont Tech is excellent preparation for baccalaureate programs offered either at Vermont Tech or at other colleges and universities. VTC's own bachelor's curricula are "two-plus-two" programs, allowing for a seamless transition between associate's and bachelor's programs. For students who want to transfer to other institutions after two years, the process is simplified by formal articulation agreements with a number of excellent schools throughout the Northeast. These include the University of Vermont, Northeastern University, Norwich University, Rochester Institute of Technology, SUNY Institute of Technology, the University of New Hampshire, and the College of Agriculture and Life Sciences at Cornell University. Vermont Tech graduates are routinely accepted as transfers to many other outstanding colleges and universities nationwide. There are five programs leading to the **Associate in Engineering** degree: civil engineering technology; computer engineering technology; electrical and electronics engineering technology; mechanical engineering technology; and rehabilitation engineering technology. Dual majors are possible in several areas. Programs leading to the **Associate in Applied Science** degree are accounting; agribusiness management technology; architectural and building engineering technology; automotive technology; biotechnology; business technology and management, construction practice and management (one-year certificate also offered in construction practice); daily farm management technology; landscape development and ornamental horticulture; occupational therapy assistant; and veterinary technology. VTC also offers three-year options in its associate's degree programs for students whose math, science, or English skills need some strengthening. The **Bachelor of Science** degree is offered in architectural engineering technology and in electro-mechanical engineering technology. Practical nursing programs are offered in Bennington, Brattleboro, or Colchester, Vermont, as well as on the main campus. Graduates of these programs are eligible to apply for licensure as licensed practical nurses (LPNs).

Off-Campus Programs

Several academic programs offer opportunity for off-campus externships that provide real-world experience in the student's field of study. These are typically a required part of the curriculum. They take place in the summer between the first and second years and usually earn one academic credit over a ten-week period. Externships are a required part of the automotive technology, biotechnology, and veterinary technology programs. Rehabilitation engineering technology students have optional summer internship opportunities at regional rehabilitation facilities.

Credit for Nontraditional Learning Experiences

Students seeking transfer credit for nontraditional learning experiences should send a written request for credit evaluation to the registrar, along with all available documentation. Credit may be awarded to satisfactory scores on CLEP exams, and students who can document previous experience that the College evaluates as equivalent to a course required in their VTC major may receive credit by equivalency examination.

Costs

Tuition for 1995–1996 was $4152 per year for Vermont residents and $8304 for out-of-state students. The yearly room rate was $2762, and the meal plan was $2092 per year. Other required annual fees totaled $888. Many of VTC's programs are available at reduced tuition to New England students through the New England Regional Student Program, sponsored by the New England Board of Higher Education.

Financial Aid

About 78 percent of VTC's students receive financial aid from federal, state, and campus-based sources. There are a number of institutional scholarships available, as well as work-study opportunities. An Institutional Application for Financial Aid is required. All funds are awarded on the basis of financial need, and prospective students seeking aid must file the Free Application for Federal Student Aid (FAFSA). Some state agencies may require additional information. Students are urged to apply for financial aid by the March 1 priority deadline so that awards may be announced by May. However, applications are reviewed on a rolling basis after March 1 until available funds are exhausted.

Faculty

Excellence in instruction is a direct result of the quality of the faculty at Vermont Tech. The 55 full-time faculty members bring to the College a special blend of industrial experience and teaching expertise. Almost all have advanced degrees. Students are assured individual attention as a result of the 12:1 student-faculty ratio.

Student Body Profile

Total enrollment at Vermont Technical College in fall 1995 was 821 students, 519 men and 302 women. Of the 321 new students enrolling on the main campus in fall 1995, 68 percent were Vermont residents and 32 percent were from nine other states and three foreign nations; 25 percent were women; and the average age was 22. About 75 percent of new students reside in the campus residence halls.

Student Activities

Vermont Tech students can participate in a variety of clubs, sports, activities, and special events for social interaction and the occasional diversion from academic demands. There are seven varsity and more than twenty intramural sports for both men and women. Varsity teams have won several conference championships in recent years, including women's softball and volleyball and men's baseball, soccer, volleyball, and basketball. The men's basketball and women's volleyball teams advanced to the national championship tournaments in 1995. Campus life also includes recreation, social events, and community service learning opportunities. A student activities board arranges weekly activities and social events and provides students with support and counseling. Over thirty student clubs provide outlets for student creativity, from radio station WVTC-FM to the yearbook and student chapters of professional organizations. The College's well-maintained residence halls are fully "wired" for the information age. Every student room has data connections for direct access to the campuswide computer network and Internet, as well as telephone service and cable television lines.

Facilities and Resources

Vermont Tech students learn in modern laboratories with state-of-the-art equipment. There are twenty-one buildings on the 544-acre campus. Facilities housed in the three main academic buildings include three computer-aided design and drafting labs (9-station and 21-station Pentium and 21-station 486 labs); four general academic computing labs (three 386 and one 486, including a 24-hour lab, making sixty-five stations total); an 8-station Pentium electrical/electronics lab; a 16-station Pentium business technology lab; recently renovated mechanical engineering technology labs, including computer-numerically-controlled equipment and computer-aided manufacturing software; first-rate veterinary technology facilities, including a 12-station lab area, radiography suite and darkroom, and surgery suite; two civil engineering technology labs; a biotechnology lab with instrumentation typical of the most modern research labs; architectural drafting studios; a campuswide microcomputer network with Internet access; four instrumented electronics labs; a fully equipped automotive technology center with the latest in computerized diagnostics; and rehabilitation engineering technology laboratory with assistive technology such as voice-recognition computer software and twelve Pentium and LCII Macintosh stations. Agriculture students gain practical experience at the College dairy facility. A newly-renovated main freestall barn houses a 90-registered-Holstein milking herd. Students learn to work with a computerized herd management system. Veterinary technology students also work with the horses, sheep, and calves in the livestock facility on the farm. The Student Health and Physical Education facility houses a double-court gymnasium, a six-lane indoor pool, and two racquetball courts. There are also weight and exercise rooms on campus. Academic support services are provided by the Judd Support Center and include paraprofessional and peer tutoring, a TRIO Student Support Services program offering individualized academic, personal, career, and college transfer counseling for students from disadvantages backgrounds, and special support services for students with disabilities. A Learning Center offers tutoring, study groups, and review sessions. Hartness Library, which is computer-linked to other state and national libraries, currently has a 53,000-volume collection and receives over 300 on-line periodicals. Optical disk reference services offer rapid-search capabilities. Library resources are accessible through any networked-terminal on campus. The four residence halls house 560 students.

Location

VTC's location is rural but far from isolated (exit 4 of Interstate 89 is just a mile away). For day-to-day needs, the nearby village of Randolph offers a variety of shops and restaurants, movie theater, bowling alley, and the Chandler Music Hall. For special shopping and events, Burlington and Montpelier, Vermont, and Hanover, New Hampshire, are within an hour's drive. Boston and Montreal are just 3 hours away. Amtrak's Vermonter stops twice daily in downtown Randolph, and there is also convenient bus service through Vermont Transit. Students enjoy the rich variety of recreational activities available in Vermont. Some of the top ski resorts in the East are less than an hour from campus. There is also hiking on the Appalachian Trail, canoeing on numerous lakes and rivers, camping in the Green Mountain National Forest, and biking on the miles of scenic country roads.

Admission Requirements

Each applicant receives individual consideration for admission based on receipt and review of the official secondary school transcript, letters of recommendation, proof of high school graduation or a high school equivalency diploma, and SAT I scores. A personal interview is required only for the veterinary technology program, although an interview and campus visit are strongly recommended for all applicants as the best way to get the "feel" of campus life. Because of the technical nature of the curriculum, applicants should have strong math and science aptitude. The college offers deferred admission and advanced placement for transfer students.

Application and Information

VTC follows a rolling admission policy, but timely application is recommended. Applicants are notified of their status within two weeks of receipt of their completed application and supporting documents. For more information on Vermont Technical college, students should contact:

Director of Admissions
Vermont Technical College
Randolph Center, Vermont 05061
Telephone: 802-728-1000 (voice/TDD)
800-442-VTC-1 (toll-free in New England;
voice/TDD)
Fax: 800-442-1390
E-mail: admissions@night.vtc.vsc.edu
World Wide Web: http://www.vtc.vsc.edu

The high-tech campus of Vermont Technical College is situated in a scenic New England village in the heart of Vermont.

Peterson's Guide to Two-Year Colleges 1997

VIRGINIA MARTI COLLEGE OF FASHION AND ART
LAKEWOOD, OHIO

The College and Its Mission

The Virginia Marti College of Fashion and Art was founded in 1966 and offers two-year associate degrees. The College offers a skills-based curriculum, special student services, financial aid opportunities, and flexible scheduling with day and evening class times. Students at the Virginia Marti College of Fashion and Art receive firsthand experience via seminars, speakers, and field trips to the fashion capitals of the world.

Academic Programs

The Virginia Marti College of Fashion and Art is a private college accredited by the Accrediting Commission of Career Schools and Colleges of Technology. The College offers two-year **Associate in Business** degrees in commercial art, fashion design, fashion merchandising, and interior design and certificate programs in jewelry design and repair and haute couture—dressmaking/tailoring. The programs are based on current trends and changes in the various fields. The school stresses hands-on skills within quality programs/curricula and simulated work conditions. The College operates on three 11-week quarters and a summer quarter of eight weeks. Having approximately one month off before the fall quarter gives students time to participate in College-sponsored field trips to Paris, Italy, and New York.

Associate Degree Programs The Associate in Business degree in fashion retail merchandising prepares women and men for the retail field by offering broad studies in merchandising and general business. All work in the fashion marketplace is studied. The instructors are retail and business professionals who provide hands-on experience and know the latest trends and technology in the fashion retail business. Students are also required to complete an internship in their final quarter. This provides the unique opportunity to apply classroom studies to the workplace. The Associate in Business degree in fashion retail merchandising is eight quarters long and can be completed in two years by attending full-time year-round. To qualify for the associate degree, students are required to complete 108 credit hours of acceptable academic work. Career opportunities include buyer, specialty store manager, field representative, importer/exporter, retail advertiser, merchandise manager, fashion consultant, bridal consultant, visual merchandiser, and fashion editor.

The Virginia Marti College specializes in teaching couture sewing and the European method of design and pattern making. The Associate in Business degree in fashion design is for students interested in creating original styles from the sketch through the finished garment. The European method of design and pattern making teaches students how to measure and draft a custom fit block for each individual client. The students' art skills are developed from basic art through fashion illustration to the development of a collection of their own original fashions. To meet current industry skill standards, students also have the opportunity to learn computer-aided pattern making and design. Fashion design students experience critiques at the end of every quarter. The art faculty critiques the students' artwork from basic drawing through their final portfolio. The sewing projects, fashion design interpretations, and original designs are critiqued by guests, both designers and merchandisers from the fashion industry, and Mrs. Virginia Marti Veith. Career opportunities include couture designer, pattern maker, draper, grader, marker, freelance specialty line designer, and costume designer. The Associate in Business degree in fashion design is eight quarters and can be completed in two years by attending full-time year-round. To qualify for the degree, students are required to complete a minimum of 110 credit hours of acceptable academic work.

A professional interior designer must understand three-dimensional space (design) in order to create a pleasing environment. This eight-quarter program teaches students the basic processes of design and its applications, which, upon completion, enables them to access the interior design field as an entry-level professional. The students learn the techniques and theory necessary to fulfill a useful position in any design-related business. This is achieved through a series of lab-type classes (studios) taught by practicing professionals. The Associate in Business degree in interior design can be completed in two years by attending full-time year-round. To qualify, students are required to complete a minimum of 105 credit hours of acceptable academic work. Career opportunities include interior designer, residential or commercial specialization within interior design, computer-aided design applications, historic preservation/restoration adaptive use, home furnishing consultant, specification writing, exhibition display work, and craft specialist.

The Associate in Business degree in commercial art is specifically designed to create a studio atmosphere whereby working professionals from the commercial art industry provide the instruction. Small classes are the norm for this major—thoroughly preparing students to be complete professional artists at graduation. Except for basics, all commercial art courses employ both MAC and PC graphic software programs. Continuous computer software updating allows students to employ the latest in graphic applications in the industry. The Associate in Business degree in commercial art is eight quarters long and can be completed in two years by attending full-time year-round. To qualify, students are required to complete a minimum of 105 credit hours of acceptable academic work. Career opportunities include package designer, typographer, portrait artist, fashion illustrator, technical illustrator, graphic designer, animator, greeting card illustrator, computer graphic designer, commercial artist, television and movie graphics, and set designer.

Certificate and Diploma Programs The Virginia Marti College of Fashion and Art offers a jewelry design and repair certificate program to provide training in this special field. The course curriculum offers hands-on experience and basic skills provided by instructors from the industry and so necessary for entry into the jewelry design/repair field. In addition to gemology and diamond grading, the program includes jewelry repair, wax carving and casting (lost wax process), and an internship phase. The jewelry design and repair program can be completed in nine months on a full-time basis. To qualify for the certificate, students are required to complete a minimum of 38 credit hours of acceptable academic work. Career opportunities include jewelry repair, jewelry designer, wax modeler/caster, gemologist, jewelry sales, and jewelry display artist.

The College specializes in teaching couture sewing. This certificate program is for those interested in creating styles from commercial patterns. Coupled with the couture sewing techniques are three quarters of classes on alterations, a class in millinery (hat making), and the reconstruction/preservation of historic clothing. Since graduates of this program often go into business for themselves, a course in entrepreneurship (small business management) is also included. As with the fashion design program, students' work is critiqued at the end of the quarter. The haute couture—dressmaking/tailoring program can be completed in twelve months attending on a full-time basis. Career opportunities include couture dressmaker, alterations specialist, tailor, bridal and bridesmaid's dressmaker, and haute couture/French dressmaker.

Transfer Arrangements Virginia Marti College accepts credits earned at other colleges and universities when the subjects apply to the program chosen at Virginia Marti College and the applicant has completed all entrance requirements for enrollment. The courses must coincide with VMC courses and have an equal or greater number of credits. For course credits to transfer, students must have earned a grade no lower than a C (or a GPA no lower than a 2.0). The College is authorized to accept and transfer up to 45 credits from other institutions. All applicants must have official academic transcripts sent directly to the registrar. Applicants are expected to provide course descriptions (catalogs) to aid in evaluation of transfer credits. Interested students should contact the registrar at 216-221-8584.

Costs

Degree and certificate tuition is $175 per credit hour for full-time attendance; books and supplies average $200 per quarter; general fees are $60 (maximum); and lab fees are in accordance with the subjects taken.

Financial Aid

The College is interested in helping deserving students obtain advantages of an education in fashion, art, and design careers, and therefore offers access to various forms of financial aid. Students are encouraged to fill out financial aid applications. The College participates in federal and state programs, including Pell grants, SEOG grants, OIG (state), Perkins loans, direct Stafford loans, and PLUS (parent) loans. Applications and/or information on financial aid may be obtained from financial aid officers at the College. Advisers help students complete all necessary paperwork, as well as plan course schedules that meet individual needs.

Faculty

Instructors at Virginia Marti College of Fashion and Art use their own experiences to help students understand the intricacies of careers in the fashion and design fields. All instructors of general subjects have master's degrees and years of practical experience. The College curriculum is constantly updated by advisory boards made up of industry professionals who look at current and future job/career trends and their associated skills.

Student Body Profile

The enrollment of approximately 250 students is made up of 85 percent women and 15 percent men whose average age is between the early twenties and thirties. Five percent of the total are from other countries. Students come from a radius of approximately 100 miles, from some states outside of Ohio, and from other countries. A surprising number of students have had some college experience prior to attending Virginia Marti College, including some with four-year bachelor's degrees. The College has no dormitories and therefore all students live off campus.

Student Activities

The College offers seminars, guest speakers, field trips (local, out-of-state, and out-of-country), and opportunities to interact with local and national professional organizations. The interior design program sponsors a student chapter of the American Society of Interior Designers (ASID).

Facilities and Resources

Advisement/Counseling Trained staff members assist students in scheduling and course selection to satisfy educational objectives. Additional free services include tutoring, open computer lab hours, and continuous career planning.

Career Planning/Placement Offices The College has aggressive placement services that work to match graduates with jobs and internships at a successful rate. As graduation approaches, placement and job skills seminars are presented. Free lifetime job placement is available to all graduates.

Location

The College is based in Lakewood, Ohio, located on the shores of Lake Erie, 6 miles west of downtown Cleveland in Cuyahoga County. Lakewood has a population of 59,718 and is primarily a vintage residential community offering diversity in housing from modest single homes to luxury "Gold Coast" condominiums. The community has twenty-two parks and playgrounds, an indoor ice rink, twenty-seven tennis courts, two swimming pools, a boat launch, a soccer field, and many other noted recreational programs. Special attractions include Beck Center for the Cultural Arts, Summer Band Concerts, and Old Stone House Historical Museum and Library.

Admission Requirements

Applicants who wish to enroll in a program of study at Virginia Marti College of Fashion and Art must have earned a high school diploma or have successfully completed the General Education Development (GED) test. Applicants must submit official transcripts from high school and from any college previously attended. A personal interview and a tour of the College are recommended. Some programs ask for submission of a portfolio. Students without a portfolio are expected to take one or two art fundamental classes. The College reserves the right to request any background information necessary in evaluating an applicant's potential for academic success. Applicants should have proficiency in writing and speaking English and in basic mathematics. An admission test is required to determine deficiencies in the language arts and math areas. Failure to attain minimum scores may result in enrollment in developmental classes or denial of admission.

International students seeking admission must have a score of at least 450 on the TOEFL. Such students are provided English language support tutors for as long as necessary while in attendance.

Application and Information

Applications are accepted on an ongoing basis. All prospective students should contact:

Director of Admissions
Virginia Marti College of Fashion and Art
11724 Detroit Avenue
Lakewood, Ohio 44107
Telephone: 216-221-8584
800-473-4350 (toll-free)

On the campus of Virginia Marti College of Fashion and Art.

Peterson's Guide to Two-Year Colleges 1997

WAYNE COUNTY COMMUNITY COLLEGE
DETROIT, MICHIGAN

The College and Its Mission

Wayne County Community College has served as a leader in providing education services and training to residents of southeast Michigan. Distinctive in its purpose and history, WCCC was established by a public mandate and chartered in 1967. In 1969, the first classes were offered by the institution known as the "college without walls" in that WCCC had no buildings or facilities of its own. By 1982, the College had constructed five campuses within its 550–square–mile service district. As a two-year "open door" institution, WCCC is committed to providing an affordable high-quality education in an atmosphere of friendly support and encouragement.

Academic Program

The College operates on a two-semester system and also offers a summer term.

WCCC offers **Associate of Arts, Associate of Applied Science,** and **Associate of Science** degrees plus one-year and two-year certificates.

The certificate and degree programs offered at Wayne County Community College include the following: accounting; automotive service technology; aviation mechanics (options in airframe and power plant); business administration; child-care training; computer graphic technology; computer information systems; criminal justice (options in law enforcement administration and corrections); dental assisting; dental hygiene; dietetic technology; electrical/electronics technology (options in computer technology, electronics engineering technology, industrial electronics and control technology, and telecommunications technology); emergency medical technology; environmental and natural resources; environmental, health, and safety technology; general studies; gerontology; heating, ventilating, and air-conditioning; heavy equipment maintenance technology; honors program; interior design; lawn and ornamental plant maintenance; machine tool technology/numerical control; manufacturing technology; mental health; Muslim world studies; nursing; occupational therapy assistant studies; office information systems (options in administrative assistant studies, general office clerical, legal secretarial, medical secretarial, and word/information processing); pre-engineering (transfer); pharmacy assistant technology; substance abuse counseling; telecommunications technology; urban teacher studies (options in special education, elementary education, secondary education, and special education); and veterinary technology.

WCCC offers a combination of programs oriented toward general education, transfer to baccalaureate institutions, and career preparation. All degree programs require the completion of at least 60 credit hours, including the last 15 at WCCC, and specific program or academic group requirements; a varying number of credit hours in U.S. government; and a final grade point average of at least 2.0. Requirements for the Associate of Arts and Associate of Science degrees include a specified number of credit hours in English, humanities, mathematics/sciences, and natural and social sciences. Associate of Applied Science degree requirements include specified credit hours in general education, specific courses, and occupational support courses.

Several associate degree programs are linked to four-year degree programs at senior-level institutions. WCCC honors program and environmental and natural resources graduates may transfer to the University of Michigan in Ann Arbor to complete baccalaureate studies. Graduates of the computer information systems program can transfer all credits and earn a Bachelor of Business Administration degree at Detroit College of Business in Dearborn. Eight WCCC allied health programs may lead to the University of Detroit Mercy's Bachelor of Science in Health Services degree. Graduates of some vocational education programs can transfer to Detroit Mercy and earn a degree in the innovative field of plastics manufacturing technology. Graduates of the business administration program can transfer to Cleary College in Ypsilanti and Howell. The urban teacher program is a cooperative venture of WCCC and Detroit-area school districts. Students can earn an associate degree and then complete a baccalaureate degree at Wayne State University in the teacher education program.

Certificate programs are designed for students seeking job-entry skills and those aiming to improve job performance or to qualify for advancement. Specific program requirements vary by program.

Costs

Tuition in 1996–97 is $54 per credit hour for Wayne County residents who live in WCCC's service district. Average fees for the academic year are $90. Estimated costs per academic year for a full-time in-district student who is a dependent include $1506 for tuition and fees, $2200 for room and board, $600 for books, $800 for transportation, and $675 for personal expenses.

Financial Aid

A student must apply to be considered for financial aid, which is granted based on need. Available assistance includes Federal Pell Grants, Federal Supplemental Educational Opportunity Grants, Federal Work-Study awards, Federal Stafford Student Loans, Michigan Part-time Student Grants, Michigan College Work-Study awards, and Michigan Educational Opportunity Grants. Michigan's Tuition Incentive Program (TIP) provides free community-college tuition for two years to eligible high school graduates. Though applications are accepted on an ongoing basis, students are encouraged to apply early. The priority date for fall semester enrollment is June 1.

Faculty

The WCCC faculty includes 150 full-time and 250 part-time instructors.

Student Body Profile

WCCC has a rich and diverse student population; approximately 70 percent are women and more than 50 percent are members of minority groups. While some 85 percent are Michigan residents, citizens from more than thirty countries are also enrolled in programs of study at the College. Nearly half of the students are freshmen, and nearly 70 percent of all WCCC students attend part-time. There are no on-campus housing facilities. Excellent child-care facilities in a safe and caring educational environment are available for a limited number of students at four of the campuses.

Student Activities

Student government, clubs, publications, films, lectures, performing arts events, and other activities offer opportunities for students beyond the classroom.

There is a Student Government Association on each campus. Each has three branches of government: the executive, the legislative, and the judicial.

Facilities and Resources

WCCC offers a wide range of support services to help students have a meaningful and productive educational experience.

The Career Planning and Placement Office offers aid that includes computerized career information and exploration resources, such as the Michigan Occupational Information System, Sigi-Plus, and the Perfect Résumé Service. A computer job-sharing network lists a variety of opportunities.

Multi-Learning Laboratories have filmstrips, slides, programmed texts, tapes, reading machines, and textbooks at varying levels of difficulty to help students improve academically.

The Project Gold helps new students by means of one-on-one instruction and monitoring, special seminars on study techniques and time management, and specially designed entry-level courses in math, English, reading, speech, and basic technical areas. The Institute for Human Resources helps students to strengthen their academic and social skills through tutoring and other services.

The Access College Careers and Educational Supportive Services (ACCESS) helps such students as displaced homemakers, people who speak English as a second language, and those who are physically handicapped. This department can provide tutors, note takers, braille and taped materials, and interpreters for the deaf.

The Learning Resource Center at each campus is a library and more. Features include the Detroit Area Library Network (DALNET), a computer link between all WCCC libraries and the libraries of several local colleges, universities, and hospitals.

Location

Wayne County Community College's five facilities are located in suburban, urban, and rural areas of Wayne County.

Metropolitan Detroit offers a broad choice of cultural institutions and recreational activities, including major sports teams. In addition to being the world's automotive capital, Detroit is host to leading medical institutions, high-technology manufacturers, and international-class financial institutions.

Three facilities are located in Detroit. The **Downtown Campus** is at the edge of Detroit's convention center. The **Eastern Campus** is part of a medical/retail/residential corridor on the east side of the city. The **Northwest Campus** is located in a business hub and near a diverse residential community in northwest Detroit.

The **Downriver Campus** is located in suburban Taylor (an industrial and residential community), and the **Western Center** sits on more than 100 acres in the growing industrial community of Belleville.

All College facilities are easily accessible via freeways.

Admission Requirements

WCCC has an open admission policy—acceptance is automatic for those who are age 18 or older. Admission is granted on a nonselective basis. However, all students are assessed upon entry in English and math for placement into appropriate courses.

Students at other colleges or universities who wish to transfer credits to WCCC should request that official copies of their transcripts be forwarded to WCCC's Office of Admissions. Generally, credit earned from regionally accredited institutions and from all publicly supported junior and community colleges is readily accepted if it has been earned with a grade of C or better and is appropriate to the student's planned curriculum. Students should note that grades are not transferable; only credit hours can be transferred.

WCCC welcomes applications from international students who have completed secondary education and are eligible for admission to college-level studies. International applicants should begin the admission process at the earliest possible date: from three to six months before a semester begins is recommended. In addition to meeting other admission criteria, international students must score 500 or above on the Test of English as a Foreign Language (TOEFL) or score at least 70 on the Michigan Test. The TOEFL is given in countries throughout the world. Testing information is available from TOEFL, Box 6151, Princeton, New Jersey 08541, and from the U.S. embassies or consulates. Michigan Test information is available from the English Language Institute, University of Michigan, Ann Arbor, Michigan 48109 (telephone: 313-764-2416).

Application and Information

Applications are accepted on an ongoing basis. For international students, correspondence concerning admission and all credentials and support of the application must be on file in the Office of Admissions prior to its issuance of an I-20 A-B.

For an application form and additional information, students should contact:

Office of Admissions
Wayne County Community College
801 West Fort Street
Detroit, Michigan 48226-2539
Fax: 313-961-2791

Peterson's Guide to Two-Year Colleges 1997

WHITE PINES COLLEGE
CHESTER, NEW HAMPSHIRE

The College and Its Mission

White Pines College is a private, nonprofit, two-year liberal arts college that specializes in providing a highly personalized environment for living and learning. Students from around the world attend WPC to get a solid start in pursuit of a bachelor's degree in various fields. The student body is intentionally kept small to encourage interaction among this highly diversified group. An important part of the educational experience at White Pines College is the exchange of ideas among young men and women from different cultures and backgrounds. The members of the current freshman class, which number 60, represent four continents. Students come from eight states and eleven countries. Their ages range from 17 to 55. Yet all of the differences among the student body only serve to complement each other.

There is an honors society, whose members function primarily as tutors for students who need additional assistance. Tennis, volleyball, and basketball are commonly played at the intramural level. Other sports are also available, depending on the level of interest of the students.

The campus sits on the main street of the town. Many of the buildings on this street date back to the eighteenth century, some with important historical significance. Douglas Hall, currently one of the men's dormitories, was the home of three of New Hampshire's governors in the late 1700s. The founders of White Pines College picked this setting because of the ideal educational atmosphere the town offers.

Academic Programs

Associate Degree Programs White Pines College grants the **Associate in Arts** degree in the fields of advertising design, communications and media (concentrations in broadcast journalism, photojournalism, and print journalism), early childhood education, general studies, insurance and risk management, professional photography, and social work (concentrations in child welfare/child care and gerontology).

The general studies curriculum concentrates on developing the students' understanding of the intellectual and cultural heritage of American society. The program is specifically designed for those students who wish to transfer to four-year colleges and universities throughout the United States. It offers a broad range of studies that fulfill most other colleges' core curriculum and electives. This core of liberal arts courses is an integral part of all programs at White Pines College.

The advertising design program is for students who choose to enter the market immediately upon graduation from White Pines and seek positions in the advertising and design field and for those who plan to transfer to a four-year institution as design majors. All students in the advertising design program take a common core of courses, aimed at providing the students with a sound background and the skills necessary for success. As advertising design majors, students gain an appreciation of design and the many ways it can influence one's view.

The program in communications and media prepares students for immediate entry into positions after graduation or for transfer to a four-year program for further study. Instruction is given in general newswriting, newswriting for radio and television, newspaper layout, graphics, and copyediting. Internships are available with newspapers and broadcasting studios.

The major in professional photography is designed both for students who wish to pursue a photography career in a studio, business, or industry immediately after completion of the two-year program and for those who plan to transfer to a four-year institution for further study. Students in the professional photography program learn to apply creative thinking and contemporary techniques to the art of effective photographic communications. Extensive training in the areas of portraiture and commercial photography is provided as well. Emphasis is placed on the development of a working portfolio.

Students in the social work program take a common core of courses in order to learn the theories, concepts, and skills basic to social work practice. During their second year, students work with faculty members in choosing a specialized field placement that best meets their interests and needs. The field placement is required and is supervised. Students also have a selection of other courses to complement their main field of interest. Specializations are offered in child welfare and gerontology.

Students in the early childhood education program qualify for a position in a nursery school, preschool, or child-care center. In a career that combines the skills of teaching and social work, students learn the fundamental human needs of young children. Students learn to identify problems and develop and implement solutions. The program includes 20 hours of observation in an early childhood setting and a semester of a hands-on internship. Graduates are prepared for a position working with children or for further study for a bachelor's degree in education.

Special Programs and Services The College has a new English as a second language program. The placement of international students depends upon their TOEFL scores. Students with advanced skills in English enroll directly into degree-granting academic programs. Scores below 500 indicate the need for intensive work in English language courses and language labs. Depending on their level of proficiency, first-year students may take two or more academic credit courses toward graduation in their major.

The academic year is divided into two 15-week semesters.

Costs

For the 1996–97 academic year, tuition is $8000. Room and board are $4200. An additional $500 per semester is charged for a private room (if available). The average cost of books and supplies is $600 per academic year; photography students should allow approximately $600 more over a two-year period for film and photo supplies. All costs are subject to change.

Financial Aid

Any student may apply for financial aid by filing the Free Application for Federal Student Aid (FAFSA) and the White Pines College financial aid form. Financial aid is awarded to qualified applicants and is based on financial need, academic promise, and personal recommendations.

Faculty

There are 19 members on the White Pines College faculty. All full-time faculty members hold master's degrees, and 60 percent hold doctorates from a recognized college or university. Selected members of the faculty assist students in directed and independent studies, with approval from the academic dean.

Student Body Profile

There were 55 students enrolled in 1995–96; their average age was 24 years old. Six were international students, and 10 percent were members of minority groups. Fifty percent of the student body was from New Hampshire, the other 50 percent were from the other New England states, as well as New York and New Jersey. Thirty-five percent were commuters, and 65 percent lived in College housing.

Student Activities

The Dalrymple Student Center has a snack bar, ping-pong and pool tables, and an air hockey table. Students participate in the Student Senate, College Activities Committee, and the Resident Life Council. Recreational activities vary with the season; outdoor opportunities include cross-country skiing, jogging, ice skating, canoeing, tennis, and camping. The College also provides equipment for basketball, badminton, softball, and volleyball.

Facilities and Resources

The Powers Building contains an art studio, classrooms, faculty offices, and the College cafeteria. The Lane Building, an adjoining structure, houses classrooms, administrative offices, and the admissions reception area. The photography laboratory has well-equipped darkrooms and expanded studios for professional photography and photojournalism students. Dalrymple Center houses a biology laboratory, classrooms, faculty offices, and the student center.

Library and Audiovisual Services The Wadleigh Library (1986), a learning resource center, incorporates reference services and an audiovisual center and has room to allow the present collection of 20,000 volumes to double in size. Individual study carrels and a meeting room for lectures and other programs promote the informational, educational, cultural, and recreational needs of the College community.

A modern, state-of-the-art Macintosh computer laboratory is equipped with the most current design software, including Quark Express, Adobe Illustrator/Adobe Photoshop, and Pagemaker.

Location

The town of Chester, established in 1722, is located in southern New Hampshire, just minutes from Manchester, New Hampshire's largest city. The college is situated on Route 121, just north of Route 102. Boston is 1 hour south, and the Atlantic Ocean is 45 minutes to the east. Some of New Hampshire's famed ski resorts are within 1 hour's drive, and most, within 2 hours.

Admission Requirements

White Pines College welcomes applications for admission from men and women of any race, religion, creed, or ethnic background. The Admissions Committee of the College seeks a diversified student body and considers applications from students from all sections of this country and from abroad. The Admissions Committee meets throughout the year to consider applications for admission in the fall. Students may also be accepted for admission at the beginning of the second semester in January.

Acceptance for admission is based not only on satisfactory academic preparation but also on teacher and counselor recommendations and the personal interview. It is the student's overall ability to benefit from attending White Pines College that is the paramount criterion in the selection process. Candidates must hold a diploma from a secondary school or provide equivalent credentials. It is recommended that all candidates take either the Scholastic Assessment Test (SAT I) of the College Board or the ACT examination of American College Testing.

Students who wish to transfer credits from other colleges must make formal application for admission to White Pines College. Up to 30 credits can be accepted in transfer. These credits must carry a grade of C or better, and the courses should correspond to those offered at White Pines. The applicant for transfer admission should follow the same procedure for admission as the freshman applicant.

A visit to the campus is strongly recommended. An appointment for a personal interview and a tour of the campus may be arranged by telephoning or writing directly to the director of admissions.

Application and Information

Applicants should complete an application form and forward it to the director of admissions with a check or money order in the amount of $25 to cover the application fee. (Checks should be made payable to White Pines College.) They should request that their high school counselor forward their academic transcript and three letters of recommendation to the director of admissions. The submission of SAT I or ACT scores is recommended for all applicants and is essential for students who wish to transfer after graduation from White Pines.

For further information, students should contact:

Director of Admissions
White Pines College
40 Chester Street
Chester, New Hampshire 03036
Telephone: 603-887-4401
800-974-6372 (toll-free)

Front entrance of the Wadleigh Library at White Pines.

Peterson's Guide to Two-Year Colleges 1997

INDEX OF COLLEGES AND UNIVERSITIES

This index gives the page locations of various entries for all the colleges and universities in this book. The page numbers for the college profiles are printed in regular type, those for profiles with special announcements in italic type, and those for in-depth descriptions in boldface type. When there is more than one number in boldface type, it indicates that the institution has more than one in-depth message; in most such cases, the first of the series is a general institutional description.

College	Page
Abraham Baldwin Agricultural College	264
Academy of Business College	165
Adirondack Community College	*453*
Aiken Technical College	582
Aims Community College	228
Alabama Aviation and Technical College	150
Alabama Southern Community College (Monroeville, AL)	150
Alabama Southern Community College (Thomasville, AL)	151
Alamance Community College	488
Albuquerque Technical Vocational Institute	446
Alexandria Technical College	389
Allan Hancock College	182
Allen County Community College	326
Allentown Business School	552
Alpena Community College	375
Alvin Community College	603
Amarillo College	604
American Academy McAllister Institute of Funeral Service	454
American Academy of Art	282
American Academy of Dramatic Arts	454, **688**
American Academy of Dramatic Arts/West	182, **688**
American Academy of Nutrition	593
American Flyers College	246
American Institute of Business	317
American Institute of Commerce	317
American Institute of Design	553
American River College	182
American Samoa Community College	682
Ancilla College	308
Andover College	*347*
Andrew College	265
Angelina College	604
Anne Arundel Community College	352
Anoka-Ramsey Community College	*389*
Anson Community College	488
Antelope Valley College	183
Antonelli College (OH)	515
Antonelli Institute (PA)	553
Apollo College–Phoenix, Inc.	165
Apollo College–Tri-City, Inc.	165
Apollo College–Tucson, Inc.	165
Apollo College–Westside, Inc.	165
Aquinas College at Milton	361
Aquinas College at Newton	361, **690**
Aquinas College (TN)	593
Arapahoe Community College	229
Arizona Western College	166
Arkansas State University–Beebe Branch	174
Art Institute of Atlanta	265
Art Institute of Dallas	*604*, **692**
Art Institute of Fort Lauderdale	*246*, **694**
The Art Institute of Houston	605
The Art Institute of Philadelphia	553, **696**
Art Institute of Pittsburgh	*553*
Art Institute of Seattle	651
Asheville-Buncombe Technical Community College	489
Asnuntuck Community-Technical College	237
Assumption College for Sisters	436
Athens Area Technical Institute	266
ATI Health Education Center	247
Atlanta Metropolitan College	266
Atlantic Community College	437, **698**
Augusta Technical Institute	266
Austin Community College (MN)	390
Austin Community College (TX)	605
Bacone College	538
Bainbridge College	267
Baker College of Jackson	376
Bakersfield College	183
Baltimore City Community College	353
Baltimore International Culinary College	353, **700**
Barstow College	183
Barton County Community College	327
Bauder College	267
Bay de Noc Community College	376
Bay Mills Community College	376
Bay Path College	*362*
Bay State College	*362*, **702**
Beal College	348
Beaufort County Community College	489
Bee County College	605
Belleville Area College	283
Bellevue Community College	651
Belmont Technical College	515
Bel-Rea Institute of Animal Technology	229, **704**
Berean Institute	554
Bergen Community College	*437*, **706**
Berkeley College (NJ)	438, **708**
Berkeley College (New York, NY)	454
Berkeley College (White Plains, NY)	455
Berkshire Community College	363
Bessemer State Technical College	151
Bethany Lutheran College	*390*
Bevill State Community College	151
Big Bend Community College	651
Bishop State Community College	151
Bismarck State College	511
Blackfeet Community College	420
Black Hawk College (Kewanee, IL)	283
Black Hawk College (Moline, IL)	283
Blackhawk Technical College	666
Black River Technical College	174
Bladen Community College	489
Blair Junior College	229
Blinn College	606
Blue Mountain Community College	546
Blue Ridge Community College (NC)	490
Blue Ridge Community College (VA)	638
Borough of Manhattan Community College of the City University of New York	455
Bossier Parish Community College	344
Bowling Green State University–Firelands College	516
Bradford School	516
Bradley Academy for the Visual Arts	554, **710**
Brainerd Community College	390
Bramson ORT Technical Institute	455
Brazosport College	606
Brevard College	*490*, **712**
Brevard Community College	247
Briarcliffe–The College for Business and Technology	456
Briarwood College	238, **714**
Bristol Community College	363
Bronx Community College of the City University of New York	456
Brookdale Community College	438
Brookhaven College	606
Brooks College	183
Broome Community College	456
Broward Community College	247
Brown Institute	390
The Brown Mackie College	327
The Brown Mackie College-Olathe Campus	327
Brunswick College	267
Brunswick Community College	491
Bryant and Stratton Business Institute, Eastern Hills Campus	459
Bryant and Stratton Business Institute (Albany, NY)	457
Bryant and Stratton Business Institute (Buffalo, NY)	457
Bryant and Stratton Business Institute (Cicero, NY)	457
Bryant and Stratton Business Institute (Lackawanna, NY)	458
Bryant and Stratton Business Institute (Rochester, NY)	458
Bryant and Stratton Business Institute (Rochester, NY)	459
Bryant and Stratton Business Institute (Syracuse, NY)	459
Bryant and Stratton College (Parma, OH)	516
Bryant and Stratton College (Richmond Heights, OH)	517
Bucks County Community College	554
Bunker Hill Community College	363
Burlington County College	438
Butler County Community College (KS)	328
Butler County Community College (PA)	555
Butte College	184
Cabrillo College	184
Cañada College	184
Caldwell Community College and Technical Institute	491
Cambria-Rowe Business College	555
Camden County College	439
Cape Cod Community College	364
Cape Fear Community College	491
Capital Community Technical College	238
The Career Center	248
Carl Albert State College	539
Carl Sandburg College	284
Carroll Community College	354
Carteret Community College	492
Casco Bay College	348, **716**
Casper College	678
Castle College	*432*
Catawba Valley Community College	492
Catholic Medical Center of Brooklyn and Queens School of Nursing	460
Catonsville Community College	354
Cayuga County Community College	460
Cazenovia College	*460*, **718**
Cecil Community College	354
Cecils Junior College of Business	492
Cedar Valley College	607
Central Alabama Community College	152
Central Arizona College	166
Central Carolina Community College	493
Central Carolina Technical College	583
Central City Business Institute	461
Central College (KS)	328
Central Community College–Grand Island Campus	423
Central Community College–Hastings Campus	424
Central Community College–Platte Campus	424
Central Florida Community College	248
Centralia College	652
Central Indian Bible College	591
Central Lakes College	391
Central Maine Medical Center School of Nursing	348
Central Maine Technical College	349
Central Ohio Technical College	517
Central Oregon Community College	*546*
Central Pennsylvania Business School	555
Central Piedmont Community College	493
Central Texas College	607
Central Virginia Community College	638
Central Wyoming College	678
Cerritos College	185
Cerro Coso Community College	185
Chabot College	185
Chaffey College	186
Champlain College	635, **720**
Chandler-Gilbert Community College	166
Chaparral Career College	166
Charles County Community College	355
Charles Stewart Mott Community College	376
Charter College	162
Chatfield College	517
Chattahoochee Technical Institute	268
Chattahoochee Valley State Community College	152
Chattanooga State Technical Community College	594
Chemeketa Community College	547
Chesapeake College	355
Chesterfield-Marlboro Technical College	583
Chicago College of Commerce	284
CHI Institute	556
CHI Institute, RETS Campus	556
Chipola Junior College	248
Chippewa Valley Technical College	666
Churchman Business School	556
Cincinnati State Technical and Community College	518
Cisco Junior College	607
Citrus College	186
City College of San Francisco	187
City Colleges of Chicago, Harold Washington College	284
City Colleges of Chicago, Harry S Truman College	285
City Colleges of Chicago, Kennedy-King College	285

Peterson's Guide to Two-Year Colleges 1997

Index of Colleges and Universities

City Colleges of Chicago, Malcolm X College 286
City Colleges of Chicago, Olive-Harvey College 286
City Colleges of Chicago, Richard J. Daley College 286
City Colleges of Chicago, Wilbur Wright College 287
Clackamas Community College 547
Clarendon College 608
Clark College 652
Clark State Community College 518
Clatsop Community College 548
Clermont College 519
Cleveland Community College 493
Cleveland Institute of Electronics 519
Cleveland State Community College 594
Clinton Community College (IA) 317
Clinton Community College (NY) 461
Cloud County Community College 328
Clovis Community College 446
Coahoma Community College 402
Coastal Carolina Community College 494
Coastline Community College 187
Cochise College (Douglas, AZ) *167*, **722**
Cochise College (Sierra Vista, AZ) 167
Cochran School of Nursing 461
Coconino County Community College 168
Coffeyville Community College 329
Colby Community College *329*
College of Alameda 187
College of DuPage 287
College of Eastern Utah 631
College of Lake County 288
College of Marin 188
College of Micronesia–FSM 682
College of Oceaneering 188
College of St. Catherine–Minneapolis 391, **724**
The College of Saint Thomas More 608
College of San Mateo 188
College of Southern Idaho 279
College of The Albemarle 494
College of the Canyons 189
College of the Desert 189
College of the Mainland 608
College of the Marshall Islands 683
College of the Redwoods 189
College of the Sequoias 190
College of the Siskiyous *190*
Collin County Community College 609
Colorado Institute of Art 230
Colorado Mountain College, Alpine Campus 230, **726**
Colorado Mountain College, Roaring Fork Campus-Spring Valley Center *230*, **726**
Colorado Mountain College, Timberline Campus 231, **726**
Colorado Northwestern Community College 231
Columbia Basin College 652
Columbia College (CA) 191
Columbia-Greene Community College 462
Columbia Junior College of Business 583
Columbia State Community College 595
Columbus State Community College 519, **728**
Columbus Technical Institute 268
Commonwealth Business College 308
Commonwealth Business College 308
Commonwealth College, Hampton 639
Commonwealth College, Richmond 639
Commonwealth College, Virginia Beach 639
Commonwealth Institute of Funeral Service 609
Community College of Allegheny County Allegheny Campus *557*, **730**
Community College of Allegheny County Boyce Campus 557, **730**
Community College of Allegheny County North Campus 557, **730**
Community College of Allegheny County South Campus 558, **730**
Community College of Aurora 232
Community College of Beaver County 558
Community College of Denver 232
Community College of Philadelphia 559
Community College of Rhode Island 581
Community College of Southern Nevada *430*
Community College of the Air Force 152
Community College of Vermont 635
Community Hospital of Roanoke Valley–College of Health Sciences 639
Compton Community College 191
Computer Career Center 609
Connors State College 539
Contra Costa College 191
Copiah-Lincoln Community College 403
Copiah-Lincoln Community College–Natchez Campus 403
Corning Community College 462
Cossatot Technical College 174
Cosumnes River College 191
Cottey College 409
County College of Morris 439
Cowley County Community College and Vocational-Technical School 330
Crafton Hills College 192
Craven Community College 494
Crowder College 410
Cuesta College 192
Culinary Institute of America 462
Cumberland County College 440
Cumberland School of Technology (LA) 345
Cumberland School of Technology (TN) 595
Cuyahoga Community College, Eastern Campus 519
Cuyahoga Community College, Metropolitan Campus 520
Cuyahoga Community College, Western Campus 520
Cuyamaca College 193
Cypress College 193
Dabney S. Lancaster Community College 639
Daley College 288
Dallas Institute of Funeral Service 609
Dalton College 268
Danville Area Community College 288
Danville Community College 640
Darton College 268
Davidson County Community College 495
Davis College 521
Dawson Community College 420
Daytona Beach Community College 249
Dean College *364*, **732**
Dean Institute of Technology 559
De Anza College 193
Deep Springs College 194
DeKalb College 269
DeKalb Technical Institute 269
Delaware County Community College *560*, **734**
Delaware Technical & Community College, Jack F. Owens Campus 244
Delaware Technical & Community College, Stanton/Wilmington Campus 244
Delaware Technical & Community College, Terry Campus 245
Delgado Community College 345
Del Mar College 609
Delta College 377
Denmark Technical College 584
Denver Automotive and Diesel College 232
Des Moines Area Community College 318
DeVry Technical Institute 440
Diablo Valley College 194
Dixie College 632
Dodge City Community College 330
Doña Ana Branch Community College 447
Don Bosco Technical Institute 194
Donnelly College 331
Douglas MacArthur State Technical College 153
D-Q University 194
Draughons Junior College (AL) 153
Draughons Junior College (Clarksville, TN) 595
Draughons Junior College (Nashville, TN) 595
DuBois Business College 560
Duff's Business Institute 560
Dull Knife Memorial College 420
Dundalk Community College 355
Dunwoody Institute 391
Durham Technical Community College 495
Dutchess Community College 463
Dyersburg State Community College 596
East Arkansas Community College 175
East Central College 410
East Central Community College 403
Eastern Arizona College 168
Eastern Idaho Technical College 279
Eastern Maine Technical College 349
Eastern New Mexico University–Roswell 447
Eastern Oklahoma State College 539
Eastern Shore Community College 640
Eastern Wyoming College 679
Eastfield College 610
East Georgia College 269
East Los Angeles College 195
East Mississippi Community College 404
ECPI College of Technology (Hampton, VA) 640
ECPI College of Technology (Virginia Beach, VA) 641
ECPI Computer Institute (Richmond, VA) 641
ECPI Computer Institute (Roanoke, VA) 641
Edgecombe Community College 496
Edison Community College 249
Edison State Community College 521
Edmonds Community College 653
Education America–Tampa Technical Institute Campus 249
Elaine P. Nunez Community College 345
El Camino College 195
El Centro College 610
Electronic Institute 561
Electronic Institutes 561
Elgin Community College 289
Elizabethtown Community College 337
Ellsworth Community College 318
El Paso Community College 611
Emory University, Oxford College 270
Endicott College *365*
Enterprise State Junior College 153
Erie Business Center, Main 561
Erie Business Center South 561
Erie Community College, City Campus 463
Erie Community College, North Campus 464
Erie Community College, South Campus 464
Essex Community College 356
Essex County College 440
ETI Technical College 521
Eugenio María de Hostos Community College of the City University of New York 464
Everett Community College 653
Evergreen Valley College 195
Fairleigh Dickinson University, Edward Williams College 441
Fashion Institute of Design and Merchandising, Los Angeles Campus *196*, **736**
Fashion Institute of Design and Merchandising, San Diego Campus 196
Fashion Institute of Design and Merchandising, San Francisco Campus 196
Fayetteville Technical Community College 496
Feather River Community College District 197
Fergus Falls Community College 392
Finger Lakes Community College 465
Fiorello H. LaGuardia Community College of the City University of New York *465*
Fisher College *365*, **738**
Flagler Career Institute 250
Flathead Valley Community College 421
Florence-Darlington Technical College 584
Florida College 250
Florida Community College at Jacksonville 250
Florida Hospital College of Health Sciences 251
Florida Keys Community College 251
Florida National College 251
Floyd College 270
Fond du Lac Tribal and Community College 392
Foothill College 197
Forrest Junior College 584
Forsyth Technical Community College 496
Fort Belknap College 421
Fort Berthold Community College 511
Fort Peck Community College 421
Fort Scott Community College 331
Fox Valley Technical College 667
Franklin Institute of Boston 366, **740**
Frank Phillips College 611
Frederick Community College 356
Fresno City College 197
Front Range Community College 232
Fugazzi College (KY) 337
Fugazzi College (TN) 596
Fullerton College 198
Full Sail Center for the Recording Arts 251
Fulton-Montgomery Community College 466
Gadsden State Community College 154
Gainesville College 270
Galveston College 611
Garden City Community College 331
Garland County Community College 175
Garrett Community College 356
Gaston College 497
Gateway College 425
Gateway Community College 168
Gateway Community-Technical College 238
Gateway Technical College 667
Gavilan College 198
Gem City College 289
Genesee Community College 466
George Corley Wallace State Community College 154
George C. Wallace State Community College 154
Georgia Military College 271
Germanna Community College 641
Glendale Community College (AZ) 169
Glendale Community College (CA) 199
Glen Oaks Community College 377
Gloucester County College 441
Gogebic Community College 378
Golden West College 199
Gordon College (GA) 271
Grand Rapids Community College 378
Grays Harbor College 654
Grayson County College 612
Great Basin College 431
Great Lakes Junior College of Business 378
Greenfield Community College 366
Green River Community College 654
Greenville Technical College 585
Grossmont College 199
Guam Community College 682
Guilford Technical Community College 497
Gulf Coast Community College 252
Gupton-Jones College of Funeral Service 272
Gwinnett Technical Institute 272
Hagerstown Business College 357
Hagerstown Junior College 357
Halifax Community College 497
Hamilton Business College 319
Harcum College *562*, **742**
Harford Community College 358
Harold Washington College 289
Harrisburg Area Community College 562
Harry M. Ayers State Technical College 155
Hartnell College 200
Haskell Indian Nations University 332
Hawaii Tokai International College 276
Hawkeye Community College 319
Haywood Community College 498
Hazard Community College 337
Heald Business College (Concord, CA) 200
Heald Business College (Fresno, CA) 200
Heald Business College (Hayward, CA) 200
Heald Business College (Oakland, CA) 201
Heald Business College (Rancho Cordova, CA) 201

Index of Colleges and Universities

Heald Business College (Salinas, CA) 201
Heald Business College (San Francisco, CA) 201
Heald Business College (San Jose, CA) 201
Heald Business College (Santa Rosa, CA) 201
Heald Business College (Stockton, CA) 201
Heald Business College (HI) 276
Heald Institute of Technology (Hayward, CA) 201
Heald Institute of Technology (Martinez, CA) 201
Heald Institute of Technology (Milpitas, CA) 202
Heald Institute of Technology (Sacramento, CA) 202
Heald Institute of Technology (San Francisco, CA) 202
Heartland Community College 289
Heart of the Ozarks Technical Community College 411
Helena College of Technology of The University of Montana 421
Helene Fuld College of Nursing of North General Hospital 466
Henderson Community College 337
Henry Ford Community College 379
Herkimer County Community College 467
Herzing College of Business and Technology (AL) 155
Herzing College of Business and Technology (GA) 272
Herzing College of Technology 667
Hesser College 433, **744**
Hesston College 332
Hibbing Community College 392
Highland Community College (IL) 290
Highland Community College (KS) 332
Highland Park Community College 379
Highline Community College 654
Hill College of the Hill Junior College District 612
Hillsborough Community College 252
Hinds Community College 404
Hiwassee College 596
Hocking College 521
Holmes Community College 404
Holy Cross College *309*
Holyoke Community College 366
Hopkinsville Community College 337
Horry-Georgetown Technical College 585
Hostos Community College 467
Housatonic Community-Technical College 239
Houston Community College System 613
Howard College 613
Howard Community College 358
Hudson County Community College 441
Hudson Valley Community College 467
Huertas Junior College 684
Huntington Junior College of Business 663
Hussian School of Art 563
Hutchinson Community College and Area Vocational School 333
ICM School of Business 563
ICS Center for Degree Studies 563
Allegany Community College 352
Ashland Community College 336
Draughons Junior College (KY) 336
Illinois Central College 290
Illinois Eastern Community Colleges, Frontier Community College 290
Illinois Eastern Community Colleges, Lincoln Trail College 291
Illinois Eastern Community Colleges, Olney Central College 291
Illinois Eastern Community Colleges, Wabash Valley College 291
Illinois Valley Community College 292
Imperial Valley College 202
Independence Community College 333
Indiana Business College 309, **746**
Indiana Vocational Technical Colleges 309
Indian Hills Community College 319
Indian River Community College 252
Institute of American Indian Arts 447
Institute of Career Education 253
Institute of Design and Construction 468
Institute of Electronic Technology 337
Instituto Comercial de Puerto Rico Junior College 684
Instituto Técnico Comercial Junior College 684
Inter American University of Puerto Rico, Guayama Campus 684
Interboro Institute 468
International Business College 309
International Fine Arts College *253*, **748**
Inver Hills Community College 393
Iowa Central Community College 320
Iowa Lakes Community College 320
Iowa Western Community College 321
Irvine Valley College 202
Isothermal Community College 498
Itasca Community College 393
Itawamba Community College 405
ITT Technical Institute (AL) 155
ITT Technical Institute (AR) 175
ITT Technical Institute (Phoenix, AZ) 169
ITT Technical Institute (Tucson, AZ) 169
ITT Technical Institute (Anaheim, CA) 203
ITT Technical Institute (Carson, CA) 203
ITT Technical Institute (Oxnard, CA) 203
ITT Technical Institute (Sacramento, CA) 203
ITT Technical Institute (San Bernardino, CA) 204
ITT Technical Institute (San Diego, CA) 204
ITT Technical Institute (Van Nuys, CA) 204
ITT Technical Institute (West Covina, CA) 204
ITT Technical Institute (CO) 233
ITT Technical Institute (Fort Lauderdale, FL) 253
ITT Technical Institute (Jacksonville, FL) 254
ITT Technical Institute (Tampa, FL) 254
ITT Technical Institute (ID) 279
ITT Technical Institute (Hoffman Estates, IL) 292
ITT Technical Institute (Matteson, IL) 292
ITT Technical Institute (Evansville, IN) 310
ITT Technical Institute (Fort Wayne, IN) 310
ITT Technical Institute (Indianapolis, IN) 310
ITT Technical Institute (KY) 337
ITT Technical Institute (MA) 367
ITT Technical Institute (MO) 411
ITT Technical Institute (NE) 425
ITT Technical Institute (Dayton, OH) 522
ITT Technical Institute (Youngstown, OH) 522
ITT Technical Institute (OR) 548
ITT Technical Institute (Knoxville, TN) 597
ITT Technical Institute (Memphis, TN) 597
ITT Technical Institute (Nashville, TN) 597
ITT Technical Institute (Arlington, TX) 613
ITT Technical Institute (Austin, TX) 614
ITT Technical Institute (Garland, TX) 614
ITT Technical Institute (Houston, TX) 614
ITT Technical Institute (Houston, TX) 614
ITT Technical Institute (San Antonio, TX) 615
ITT Technical Institute (UT) 632
ITT Technical Institute (VA) 642
ITT Technical Institute (Seattle, WA) 655
ITT Technical Institute (Spokane, WA) 655
ITT Technical Institute (WI) 667
Ivy Tech State College–Central Indiana 310
Ivy Tech State College–Columbus 311
Ivy Tech State College–Eastcentral 311
Ivy Tech State College–Kokomo 311
Ivy Tech State College–Lafayette 312
Ivy Tech State College–Northcentral 312
Ivy Tech State College–Northeast 312
Ivy Tech State College–Northwest 313
Ivy Tech State College–Southcentral 313
Ivy Tech State College–Southeast 313
Ivy Tech State College–Southwest 314
Ivy Tech State College–Wabash Valley 314
Ivy Tech State College–Whitewater 314
Jackson Community College 380
Jackson State Community College 597
Jacksonville College 615
James H. Faulkner State Community College 155
James Sprunt Community College 498
Jamestown Business College 468
Jamestown Community College 468
Jefferson College 411
Jefferson Community College (KY) 337
Jefferson Community College (NY) 469
Jefferson Community College (OH) 522
Jefferson Davis Community College 156
Jefferson State Community College 156
Jewish Hospital College of Nursing and Allied Health 411
J. F. Drake State Technical College 157
John A. Gupton College 598
John A. Logan College 293
John C. Calhoun State Community College 157
John M. Patterson State Technical College 157
Johnson & Wales University (CO) 233
Johnson & Wales University (VA) 642
Johnson County Community College 334
Johnson Technical Institute 563
Johnston Community College 499
John Tyler Community College 642
John Wood Community College 293
Joliet Junior College 293
Jones County Junior College 405
J. Sargeant Reynolds Community College 643
Junior College of Albany 469
Kalamazoo Valley Community College 380
Kankakee Community College 294
Kansas City Kansas Community College 334
Kaskaskia College 294
Katharine Gibbs School (CT) 239
Katharine Gibbs School (MA) 367
Katharine Gibbs School (NJ) 442
Katharine Gibbs School (Melville, NY) 469
Katharine Gibbs School (New York, NY) 470
KD Studio 615
Keiser College of Technology (Daytona Beach, FL) 254
Keiser College of Technology (Fort Lauderdale, FL) 254
Keiser College of Technology (Melbourne, FL) 255
Keiser College of Technology (Sarasota, FL) 255
Keiser College of Technology (Tallahassee, FL) 255
Kellogg Community College 380
Kelsey Jenney College 205
Kemper Military Junior College 412
Kennebec Valley Technical College 349
Kennedy-King College 294
Kent State University, Ashtabula Campus 523
Kent State University, East Liverpool Campus 523
Kent State University, Geauga Campus 523
Kent State University, Salem Campus 524
Kent State University, Stark Campus 524
Kent State University, Trumbull Campus 525
Kent State University, Tuscarawas Campus 525
Kentucky College of Business (Danville, KY) 337
Kentucky College of Business (Florence, KY) 337
Kentucky College of Business (Lexington, KY) 337
Kentucky College of Business (Louisville, KY) 338
Kentucky College of Business (Pikeville, KY) 338
Kentucky College of Business (Richmond, KY) 338
Kettering College of Medical Arts 525
Keystone College *564*, **750**
Kilgore College 615
Kilian Community College 591
Kingsborough Community College of the City University of New York 470
Kings River Community College 205
Kingwood College 616
Kirkwood Community College 321
Kirtland Community College 381
Kishwaukee College 295
Knoxville Business College 598
Labette Community College 335
Labouré College *367*
Lac Courte Oreilles Ojibwa Community College 667
Lackawanna Junior College 564
LaGuardia Community College 470
Lake Area Vocational-Technical Institute 591
Lake City Community College 255
Lake Land College 295
Lakeland Community College 526
Lakeland Medical-Dental Academy 393
Lake Michigan College 381
Lakeshore Technical College 668
Lake-Sumter Community College 255
Lake Tahoe Community College 205
Lake Washington Technical College 655
Lakewood Community College 393
Lamar Community College 233
Lamar University–Orange 616
Lamar University–Port Arthur 616
Lamson Junior College 170
Landmark College 636
Lane Community College 548
Laney College 206
Lansdale School of Business 565
Lansing Community College 381
Laramie County Community College 679
Laredo Community College 616
Lasell College *368*, **752**
Las Positas College 206
Lassen College 206
Latter-Day Saints Business College 632
Lawson State Community College 158
LDS Business College 632
Lee College (TX) 617
Lehigh Carbon Community College 565
Lenoir Community College 499
Lewis and Clark Community College 296
Lewis College of Business 382
Lexington College 296
Lexington Community College 338
Lima Technical College *526*
Lincoln College (Lincoln, IL) 296, **754**
Lincoln College (Normal, IL) 297, **756**
Lincoln Land Community College 297
Lincoln School of Commerce 425
Lincoln Technical Institute (IN) 315
Lincoln Technical Institute (Allentown, PA) 565
Lincoln Technical Institute (Philadelphia, PA) 565
Linn-Benton Community College 549
Little Big Horn College 422
Little Hoop Community College 512
Long Beach City College 207
Long Island College Hospital School of Nursing 470
Longview Community College 412
Lon Morris College 617
Lorain County Community College 527
Lord Fairfax Community College 643
Los Angeles City College 207
Los Angeles Harbor College 208
Los Angeles Mission College 208
Los Angeles Pierce College 208
Los Angeles Southwest College 209
Los Angeles Trade-Technical College 209
Los Angeles Valley College 209
Los Medanos College 210
Louisburg College 499
Louise Harkey School of Nursing –Cabarrus Memorial Hospital 500
Louisiana State University at Alexandria 346
Louisiana State University at Eunice 346
Louisville Technical Institute 338
Lower Columbia College 656
Lowthian College 394
Luna Vocational Technical Institute 448
Lurleen B. Wallace State Junior College 158
Lutheran College of Health Professions 315
Luzerne County Community College 566
MacCormac Junior College 297, **758**
Macomb Community College 382
Macon College 272
Macon Technical Institute 273
Madison Area Technical College 668
Madison Junior College of Business 668, **760**
Madisonville Community College 338
Malcolm X College 298

Peterson's Guide to Two-Year Colleges 1997 835

Index of Colleges and Universities

Manatee Community College 256
Manchester Community-Technical College 239
Manor Junior College *566*, **762**
Maple Woods Community College 413
Maria College *470*, **764**
Marian Court College 368
Maric College of Medical Careers 210
Marion Military Institute 158
Marion Technical College 527
Marshalltown Community College 321
Martin Community College 500
Mary Holmes College 405
Maryland College of Art and Design 359
Marymount College, Palos Verdes, California 210
Massachusetts Bay Community College 368
Massasoit Community College 369
Massey College of Business and Technology 273
Mater Dei College *471*, **766**
Mayland Community College 501
Maysville Community College 338
McCann School of Business 567
McCarrie Schools of Health Sciences and Technology 567
McCook Community College 425
McDowell Technical Community College 501
McHenry County College 298
McIntosh College 433, **768**
McLennan Community College 617
Meadows College of Business 273
Median School of Allied Health Careers 567
Medical Institute of Minnesota *394*
Mendocino College 211
Merced College 211
Mercer County Community College 442
Mercy College of Northwest Ohio 527
Meridian Community College 406
Merritt College 211
Mesabi Community College 394
Mesa Community College 170
Metropolitan Community College 426
Miami-Dade Community College *256*, **770**
Miami-Jacobs College 528
Miami University–Hamilton Campus 528
Miami University–Middletown Campus 528
Michiana College 315
Mid-America Baptist Theological Seminary 598
Mid-America College of Funeral Service 315
Middle Georgia College *273*
Middlesex Community College (MA) 369
Middlesex Community– Technical College (CT) 240
Middlesex County College *442*, **772**
Midland College 618
Midlands Technical College 585
Mid Michigan Community College 383
Mid-Plains Community College 426
Mid-State College *350*
Midstate College 298
Mid-State Technical College 669
Miles Community College 422
Milwaukee Area Technical College 669
Mineral Area College 413
Minneapolis Community College 395
Minnesota Riverland Technical College 395
MiraCosta College 212
Mission College 212
Mississippi County Community College 176
Mississippi Delta Community College 406
Mississippi Gulf Coast Community College 407
Miss Wade's Fashion Merchandising College 618
Mitchell College 240, **774**
Mitchell Community College 501
Mitchell Technical Institute 591
Moberly Area Community College 413
Modesto Junior College 212
Mohave Community College 170
Mohawk Valley Community College 471
Monroe College (Bronx, NY) 472
Monroe College (New Rochelle, NY) 472
Monroe Community College 472
Monroe County Community College 383
Montana State University College of Technology–Great Falls 422
Montcalm Community College 383
Monterey Peninsula College 213
Montgomery College–Germantown Campus 359
Montgomery College 619
Montgomery College–Rockville Campus 359
Montgomery College–Takoma Park Campus 360
Montgomery Community College 502
Montgomery County Community College 567
Moorpark College 213, **822**
Moraine Park Technical College 669
Moraine Valley Community College 299
Morgan Community College 234
Morrison Institute of Technology *299*
Morton College 299
Motlow State Community College 598
Mountain Empire Community College 643
Mountain View College 619
Mount Ida College 370, **776**
Mount Wachusett Community College 370
Mt. Hood Community College 549
Mt. San Antonio College 213
Mt. San Jacinto College 214
Murray State College 540
Muscatine Community College 322
Muskegon Community College 384
Muskingum Area Technical College 529
Napa Valley College 214
Nash Community College 502
Nashville State Technical Institute 599
Nassau Community College 473
National Business College (Bluefield, VA) 644
National Business College (Bristol, VA) 644
National Business College (Charlottesville, VA) 644
National Business College (Danville, VA) 644
National Business College (Harrisonburg, VA) 645
National Business College (Lynchburg, VA) 645
National Business College (Martinsville, VA) 645
National Business College (Roanoke, VA) 645
National Education Center–National Institute of Technology Campus (WV) 663
National Education Center–Spartan School of Aeronautics Campus 540
National Education Center–Tampa Technical Institute Campus 257
National Education Center–Vale Technical Institute Campus 568
National Institute for Paralegal Arts and Sciences 257
National School of Technology, Inc. 257
Naugatuck Valley Community–Technical College 240
Navajo Community College 171, **778**
Navarro College 619
Nebraska College of Business 427
Nebraska College of Technical Agriculture 427
Nebraska Indian Community College 427
NEI College of Technology 395
Neosho County Community College 335
Nettleton Career College 592
Newbury College *371*, **780**
The New England Banking Institute 371
New England Culinary Institute *636*
New England Institute of Applied Arts and Sciences 371
New England Institute of Technology and Florida Culinary Institute 257
New England Institute of Technology 582
New Hampshire Technical College (Berlin, NH) 434
New Hampshire Technical College (Claremont, NH) 434
New Hampshire Technical College (Laconia, NH) 434
New Hampshire Technical College (Manchester, NH) 435
New Hampshire Technical College (Nashua, NH) 435
New Hampshire Technical College (Stratham, NH) 435
New Hampshire Technical Institute 435, **782**
New Kensington Commercial School 568
New Mexico Junior College 448
New Mexico Military Institute *448*, **784**
New Mexico State University–Alamogordo 449
New Mexico State University–Carlsbad 449
New Mexico State University–Grants 449
Newport Business Institute 568
New River Community College 646
New York City Technical College of the City University of New York 473
Niagara County Community College 474
Nicolet Area Technical College 670
Nielsen Electronics Institute 586
Normandale Community College 396
Northampton County Area Community College 568
North Arkansas Community/Technical College 176
North Central Michigan College 384
North Central Missouri College 414
North Central Technical College 529
Northcentral Technical College 670
North Central Texas College 620
North Country Community College 474
North Dakota State College of Science 512
North Dakota State University–Bottineau 512
Northeast Alabama State Community College 159
Northeast Community College 428
Northeastern Junior College 234
Northeastern Oklahoma Agricultural and Mechanical College 541
Northeast Iowa Community College, Calmar Campus 322
Northeast Iowa Community College, Peosta Campus 323
Northeast Metro Technical College 396
Northeast Mississippi Community College 407
Northeast State Technical Community College 599
Northeast Texas Community College 620
Northeast Wisconsin Technical College 671
Northern Essex Community College 371
Northern Maine Technical College 350
Northern Marianas College 683
Northern Nevada Community College 431
Northern New Mexico Community College 449
Northern Oklahoma College 541
Northern Virginia Community College 646
North Florida Community College 257
North Harris College 620
North Hennepin Community College 396
North Idaho College 280
North Iowa Area Community College 323
North Lake College 621
Northland Community and Technical College 397
Northland Pioneer College 171
North Seattle Community College 656
North Shore Community College 372
NorthWest Arkansas Community College 176
Northwest College 680
Northwestern Business College 300, **786**
Northwestern College (OH) 529
Northwestern Connecticut Community-Technical College 241
Northwestern Michigan College 385
Northwest Indian College 656
Northwest Iowa Community College 323
Northwest Mississippi Community College 408
Northwest-Shoals Community College 159
Northwest State Community College 530
Northwest Technical Institute 397
Norwalk Community-Technical College 241
Oakland Community College 385
Oakton Community College 300
Ocean County College 443
Odessa College 621
Ohio Institute of Photography and Technology 530
Ohio State University Agricultural Technical Institute 530
Ohio University–Southern Campus 531
Ohio Valley College 663
Ohlone College 215
Okaloosa-Walton Community College 258
Oklahoma City Community College 541
Oklahoma State University, Oklahoma City 542
Oklahoma State University, Okmulgee 542
Olean Business Institute 474
Olive-Harvey College 300
Olympic College 657
Omaha College of Health Careers 428
Onondaga Community College 475
Orangeburg-Calhoun Technical College 586
Orange Coast College 215
Orange County Community College 475
Oregon Polytechnic Institute 549
Otero Junior College 235
Ouachita Technical College 177
Our Lady of the Lake College 346
Owensboro Community College 338
Owensboro Junior College of Business 339
Owens Community College 531
Owens Community College 531
Oxford College 273
Oxnard College 215, **822**
Ozarka Technical College 177
Ozarks Technical Community College 414
Paducah Community College 339
Palau Community College 683
Palm Beach Community College 258
Palo Alto College 621
Palomar College 216
Palo Verde College 216
Pamlico Community College 502
Panama Canal College 685
Panola College 622
Paradise Valley Community College 171
Paralegal Institute, Inc. 172
Paris Junior College 622
Parkland College 301
Parks College 450
Parks Junior College 235
Pasadena City College 216
Pasco-Hernando Community College 259
Passaic County Community College 443
Patrick Henry Community College 647
Paul D. Camp Community College 647
Paul Smith's College *476*, **788**
Peace College 503
Pearl River Community College 408
Peirce College *569*, **790**
Pellissippi State Technical Community College 599
Peninsula College 657
Penn Commercial, Inc. 569
Pennco Tech 569
Pennsylvania College of Technology *569*, **792**
Pennsylvania Institute of Technology 570
Pennsylvania State University Abington–Ogontz Campus 570
Pennsylvania State University Allentown Campus 571
Pennsylvania State University Altoona Campus 571
Pennsylvania State University Beaver Campus 571
Pennsylvania State University Berks Campus 572
Pennsylvania State University Delaware County Campus 572
Pennsylvania State University DuBois Campus 572
Pennsylvania State University Fayette Campus 573
Pennsylvania State University Hazleton Campus 573
Pennsylvania State University McKeesport Campus 573
Pennsylvania State University Mont Alto Campus 574
Pennsylvania State University New Kensington Campus 574
Pennsylvania State University Schuylkill Campus 574
Pennsylvania State University Shenango Campus 575
Pennsylvania State University Wilkes-Barre Campus 575
Pennsylvania State University Worthington Scranton Campus 575

Index of Colleges and Universities

Pennsylvania State University York Campus 576
Penn Technical Institute 576
Penn Valley Community College 415
Pensacola Junior College 259
Peoples College 259
Petit Jean Technical College 177
Phillips Beth Israel School of Nursing 476
Phillips County Community College 177
Phillips Junior College (CA) 217
Phillips Junior College, Condie Campus 217
Phillips Junior College (LA) 347
Phillips Junior College of Business 259
Phillips Junior College of Jackson 408
Phillips Junior College of Spokane 657
Phillips Junior College of Springfield 415
Phillips Junior College (UT) 633
Phoenix College 172
Piedmont Community College 503
Piedmont Technical College 586
Piedmont Virginia Community College 647
Pierce College 657
Pikes Peak Community College 235
Pima Community College 172, **794**
Pima Medical Institute (Mesa, AZ) 172
Pima Medical Institute (Tucson, AZ) 172
Pima Medical Institute (CO) 236
Pima Medical Institute (NM) 450
Pima Medical Institute (WA) 658
Pines Technical College 178
Pine Technical College 397
Pitt Community College 503
Pittsburgh Institute of Aeronautics 576
Pittsburgh Institute of Mortuary Science, Incorporated 576
Pittsburgh Technical Institute 576
Plaza Business Institute 476
Polk Community College 260
Porterville College 217
Portland Community College 550
Potomac State College of West Virginia University 664, **796**
PPI Health Careers School 236
Prairie State College 301
Pratt Community College and Area Vocational School 335
Prestonsburg Community College 339
Prince George's Community College 360
Professional Skills Institute 532
Prospect Hall 260
Pueblo College of Business and Technology 236
Pueblo Community College 236
Pulaski Technical College 178
Queen of the Holy Rosary College 218
Queensborough Community College of the City University of New York 476
Quincy College 372
Quinebaug Valley Community-Technical College 242
Quinsigamond Community College 373
Rainy River Community College 398
Ramírez College of Business and Technology 684
Rancho Santiago College 218
Randolph Community College 504
Ranger College 622
Ranken Technical College 415
Rappahannock Community College 647
Raritan Valley Community College 444
Rasmussen College Eagan 398
Rasmussen College Mankato 398
Rasmussen College Minnetonka 399
Rasmussen College St. Cloud 399
Raymond Walters College 532
Reading Area Community College 577
Redlands Community College 543
Red River Technical College 178
Red Rocks Community College 236
Reid State Technical College 159
Remington Education Center–Vale Campus 577
Rend Lake College 301
Renton Technical College 658
RETS Electronic Institute 339
RETS Medical and Business Institute 339
RETS Tech Center 532
Richard Bland College of the College of William and Mary 648
Richland College 622
Richland Community College 302
Richmond Community College 504
Rich Mountain Community College 178
Ricks College 280
Rio Hondo College 218
Rio Salado Community College 172
Riverside Community College 218
Roane State Community College 600
Roanoke-Chowan Community College 504
Robert Morris College *302*, **798**
Robeson Community College 504
Rochester Business Institute 477
Rochester Community College 399
Rockingham Community College 505
Rockland Community College 477
Rock Valley College 302
Rogers State College 543
Rogue Community College 550
Rose State College 543
Rowan-Cabarrus Community College 505
Roxbury Community College 373
Sacramento City College 219
Saddleback College 219
Sage Junior College of Albany *477*, **800**
Saint Augustine College 303
St. Catharine College 339
Saint Charles County Community College 416
St. Clair County Community College 385
St. Cloud Technical College 400
St. Gregory's College 544
St. Hyacinth College and Seminary 373
St. Johns River Community College 260
St. Louis Community College at Florissant Valley 416
St. Louis Community College at Forest Park 416
St. Louis Community College at Meramec 417
Saint Mary's College (NC) 505
St. Paul Technical College 400
St. Petersburg Junior College 260
St. Philip's College 623
St. Vincent's College 242
Salem Community College 444
Salish Kootenai College 423
Salt Lake Community College 633
Salvation Army College for Officer Training 220
Sampson Community College 506
San Antonio College 623
San Bernardino Valley College 220
Sandhills Community College 506
San Diego City College 220
San Diego Mesa College 220
San Diego Miramar College 221
Sanford-Brown College (Des Peres, MO) 417
Sanford-Brown College (Hazelwood, MO) 417
Sanford-Brown College (N. Kansas City, MO) 418
Sanford-Brown College (St. Charles, MO) 418
San Francisco College of Mortuary Science 221
San Jacinto College–Central Campus 623
San Jacinto College–North Campus 624
San Jacinto College–South Campus 624
San Joaquin Delta College 221
San Joaquin Valley College 222
San Jose City College 222
San Juan College 450
Santa Barbara City College 222
Santa Fe Community College (FL) 261
Santa Fe Community College (NM) 450
Santa Monica College 223, **802**
Santa Rosa Junior College 223
Sauk Valley Community College 303
Savannah Technical Institute 274
Sawyer College of Business (Cleveland, OH) 532
Sawyer College of Business (Cleveland Heights, OH) 533
Schenectady County Community College 478
Schiller International University 686
Schoolcraft College 386
Scott Community College 324
Scottsdale Community College 173
Seattle Central Community College 658
Seminole Community College 261
Seminole Junior College 544
Seward County Community College 336
Shasta College 224
Shawnee Community College 303
Shelby State Community College 600
Shelton State Community College 160
Sheridan College 680
Shoreline Community College 658
Shorter College (AR) 179
Sierra College 224
Simmons Institute of Funeral Service 478
Sinclair Community College 533
Sisseton-Wahpeton Community College 592
Skagit Valley College 659
Skyline College 224
Snead State Community College 160
Snow College 633
Solano Community College 225
Somerset Community College 340
South Arkansas Community College 179
South College (FL) 262
South College (GA) 274
Southeast Community College, Beatrice Campus 428
Southeast Community College (KY) 340
Southeast Community College, Lincoln Campus 429
Southeast Community College, Milford Campus 429
Southeastern Baptist Theological Seminary 507
Southeastern Community College (NC) 507
Southeastern Community College, North Campus 324
Southeastern Community College, South Campus 324
Southeastern Illinois College 304
Southeast Technical Institute 592
Southern Arkansas University Tech 179
Southern College 262
Southern Maine Technical College 350
Southern Ohio College, Cincinnati Campus 533
Southern Ohio College, Northeast Campus 534
Southern Ohio College, Northern Kentucky Campus 340
Southern State Community College 534
Southern Union State Community College 160
Southern University at Shreveport–Bossier City Campus 347
Southern West Virginia Community and Technical College 664
South Florida Community College 262
South Georgia College 274
South Mountain Community College 173
South Plains College 625
South Puget Sound Community College 659
South Seattle Community College 659
Southside Virginia Community College 648
South Suburban College 304
SouthWest Collegiate Institute for the Deaf 625
Southwestern College (CA) 225
Southwestern College of Business (Cincinnati, OH) 534
Southwestern College of Business (Cincinnati, OH) 535
Southwestern College of Business (Dayton, OH) 535
Southwestern College of Business (Middletown, OH) 535
Southwestern Community College (IA) 325
Southwestern Community College (NC) 507
Southwestern Indian Polytechnic Institute 451
Southwestern Michigan College 386
Southwestern Oklahoma State University at Sayre 545
Southwestern Oregon Community College 550
Southwestern Technical College 400
Southwest Florida College of Business 262
Southwest Mississippi Community College 408
Southwest Missouri State University– West Plains 418
Southwest Texas Junior College 625
Southwest Virginia Community College 648
Southwest Wisconsin Technical College 671
Spartanburg Methodist College 587
Spartanburg Technical College 587
Spencer School of Business 429
Spokane Community College 660
Spokane Falls Community College 660
Spoon River College 305
Springfield College in Illinois 305
Springfield Technical Community College 373
Standing Rock College 513
Stanly Community College 508
Stark Technical College 535
State Community College of East St. Louis 305
State Fair Community College 418
State Technical Institute at Memphis 601
State University of New York College of Agriculture and Technology at Cobleskill 478, **804**
State University of New York College of Agriculture and Technology at Morrisville 479, **806**
State University of New York College of Environmental Science & Forestry, Ranger School 480, **808**
State University of New York College of Technology at Alfred 480
State University of New York College of Technology at Canton *480*, **810**
State University of New York College of Technology at Delhi 481
State University of New York College of Technology at Farmingdale 481, **812**
Stenotype Academy 482
Sterling College (VT) 636
Stevens Henager College 634
Stone Child College 423
Stratton College 671
Suffolk County Community College–Ammerman Campus 482
Suffolk County Community College–Eastern Campus 483
Suffolk County Community College–Western Campus 483
Sullivan County Community College *483*
Suomi College *387*, **814**
Surry Community College 508
Sussex County Community College 445
Swiss Hospitality Institute "César Ritz" *242*, **816**
Tacoma Community College 661
Taft College 225
Tallahassee Community College 263
Tarrant County Junior College 626
Taylor Business Institute 484
Technical Career Institutes 484
Technical College of the Lowcountry 587
Technological College of the Municipality of San Juan 685
Temple College 626
Tennessee Institute of Electronics 601
Terra State Community College 536
Texarkana College 626
Texas Southmost College 627
Texas State Technical College–Harlingen Campus 627
Texas State Technical College 627
Texas State Technical College–Waco/Marshall Campus 628
Thaddeus Stevens State School of Technology 577
Thomas Nelson Community College 649
Thomas Technical Institute 274
Thompson Institute 578
Three Rivers Community College 419
Three Rivers Community-Technical College 243
Tidewater Community College 649

Peterson's Guide to Two-Year Colleges 1997 837

Index of Colleges and Universities

Tokai International College	276
Tomball College	628
Tompkins Cortland Community College	484
Treasure Valley Community College	551
Trenholm State Technical College	161
Triangle Tech, Inc.–DuBois School	578
Triangle Tech, Inc.–Erie School	578
Triangle Tech, Inc.–Greensburg Center	579
Triangle Tech, Inc.	578
Tri-County Community College	508
Tri-County Technical College	587
Trident Technical College	588
Trinidad State Junior College	237
Trinity Valley Community College	629
Triton College	306
Trocaire College	485
Truckee Meadows Community College	431
Truett-McConnell College	274
Truman College	306
Tulsa Junior College	545
Tunxis Community Technical College	243
Turtle Mountain Community College	513
Tyler Junior College	629
UAB Walker College	161
Ulster County Community College	485
Umpqua Community College	551
Union County College	445
United Tribes Technical College	513
The University of Akron–Wayne College	536
University of Alaska Anchorage, Kenai Peninsula College	162
University of Alaska Anchorage, Kodiak College	163
University of Alaska Anchorage, Matanuska-Susitna College	163
University of Alaska, Prince William Sound Community College	163
University of Alaska Southeast, Ketchikan Campus	164
University of Alaska Southeast, Sitka Campus	164
University of Cincinnati Clermont College	536
University of Cincinnati Raymond Walters College	537
University of Hawaii–Hawaii Community College	276
University of Hawaii–Honolulu Community College	276
University of Hawaii–Kapiolani Community College	277
University of Hawaii–Kauai Community College	277
University of Hawaii–Leeward Community College	277
University of Hawaii–Maui Community College	278
University of Hawaii–Windward Community College	278
University of Kentucky, Ashland Community College	340
University of Kentucky, Elizabethtown Community College	340
University of Kentucky, Hazard Community College	341
University of Kentucky, Henderson Community College	341
University of Kentucky, Hopkinsville Community College	341
University of Kentucky, Jefferson Community College	342
University of Kentucky, Lexington Community College	342
University of Kentucky, Madisonville Community College	342
University of Kentucky, Maysville Community College	343
University of Kentucky, Paducah Community College	343
University of Kentucky, Prestonsburg Community College	343
University of Kentucky, Somerset Community College	344
University of Kentucky, Southeast Community College	344
University of Maine at Augusta	351
University of New Mexico–Gallup Branch	451
University of New Mexico–Los Alamos Branch	451
University of New Mexico–Valencia Campus	452
University of North Dakota–Lake Region	514
University of North Dakota–Williston	514
University of Pittsburgh–Titusville	579
University of Puerto Rico, Carolina Regional College	685
University of Puerto Rico, Colegio Regional de la Montaña	685
University of South Carolina at Beaufort	588
University of South Carolina at Lancaster	589
University of South Carolina at Sumter	589
University of South Carolina at Union	589
University of South Carolina Salkehatchie Regional Campus	589
University of the State of New York, Regents College	485, **818**
University of Wisconsin Center–Baraboo/Sauk County	671
University of Wisconsin Center–Barron County	672
University of Wisconsin Center–Fond du Lac	672
University of Wisconsin Center–Fox Valley	672
University of Wisconsin Center–Manitowoc County	673
University of Wisconsin Center–Marathon County	673
University of Wisconsin Center–Marinette County	673
University of Wisconsin Center–Marshfield/Wood County	674
University of Wisconsin Center–Richland	674
University of Wisconsin Center–Rock County	674
University of Wisconsin Center–Sheboygan County	675
University of Wisconsin Center–Washington County	675
University of Wisconsin Center–Waukesha County	675
Utah Valley State College	634
Utica School of Commerce	486
Valencia Community College	263
Valley Forge Military College	*579*, **820**
Vance-Granville Community College	509
Ventura College	226, **822**
Vermilion Community College	400
Vermont Technical College	*637*, **824**
Vernon Regional Junior College	629
Victoria College	630
Victor Valley College	226
Villa Maria College of Buffalo	486
Vincennes University	316
Vincennes University–Jasper Center	316
Virginia College at Birmingham	161
Virginia College at Huntsville	162
Virginia College	649
Virginia Highlands Community College	650
Virginia Marti College of Fashion and Art	537, **826**
Virginia Western Community College	650
Vista Community College	227
Volunteer State Community College	601
Wake Technical Community College	509
Waldorf College	*325*
Wallace State Community College	162
Walla Walla Community College	661
Walters State Community College	602
Ward Stone College	263
Warren County Community College	445
Washington County Technical College	351
Washington State Community College	537
Washtenaw Community College	*387*
Watkins Institute of Interior Design	602
Waubonsee Community College	306
Waukesha County Technical College	676
Waycross College	275
Wayne Community College	509
Wayne County Community College	388, **828**
Weatherford College	630
Webster College (Fort Pierce, FL)	263
Webster College (Gainesville, FL)	263
Webster College (New Port Richey, FL)	264
Webster College (Ocala, FL)	264
Webster College (WV)	664
Welder Training and Testing Institute	580
Wenatchee Valley College	662
Wentworth Military Academy and Junior College	419
Westark Community College	180
Westchester Business Institute	486
Westchester Community College	487
Western Dakota Technical Institute	592
Western Iowa Tech Community College	326
Western Nebraska Community College	430
Western Nevada Community College	432
Western Oklahoma State College	545
Western Piedmont Community College	510
Western Texas College	630
Western Wisconsin Technical College	676
Western Wyoming Community College	681
West Hills Community College	227
West Los Angeles College	227
Westmoreland County Community College	580
West Shore Community College	388
West Side Institute of Technology	538
West Valley College	227
West Virginia Career College	664
West Virginia Career College	665
West Virginia Northern Community College	665
West Virginia University at Parkersburg	665
West Virginia University, Potomac State College	664, **796**
Wharton County Junior College	631
Whatcom Community College	662
White Pines College	436, **830**
Wilkes Community College	510
William Rainey Harper College	307
Williamsburg Technical College	590
The Williamson Free School of Mechanical Trades	580
Williamsport School of Commerce	581
Willmar Community College	401
Willmar Technical College	401
Wilson Technical Community College	510
Wisconsin Indianhead Technical College, Ashland Campus	676
Wisconsin Indianhead Technical College, New Richmond Campus	677
Wisconsin Indianhead Technical College, Rice Lake Campus	677
Wisconsin Indianhead Technical College, Superior Campus	677
Wisconsin School of Electronics	678
Woodbury College	637
Wood College	409
Wood Tobe–Coburn School	487
Worthington Community College	402
Wor-Wic Community College	360
Wright College	307
Wright State University, Lake Campus	538
Wyoming Technical Institute	681
Wytheville Community College	650
Yakima Valley Community College	662
Yavapai College	173
York Technical College	590
Young Harris College	275
Yuba College	*228*

To find the *very best* college for *you*—get these *Peterson's* guides

The #1 Bestselling College Guide

Available at Fine Bookstores Near You

Or Order Direct
Call: 800-338-3282
Fax: 609-243-9150

ISBN Prefix: 1-56079-

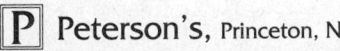
Peterson's, Princeton, NJ

Peterson's Guide to Four-Year Colleges 1997

"... the ultimate dream catalog for students...."
—*The Tennessean*

Gives you details on over 2,000 colleges with more than 900 two-page narrative descriptions. Plus—contains guidance for you on selecting the right school, getting in, and financial aid. It also includes *QuickFind*, a software disk to help you select and apply to colleges.
ISBN 604-9, 3,180 pp., 8½ x 11, $24.95 pb, 27th edition

College Money Handbook 1997

The most complete directory available of financial aid programs offered by more than 1,600 colleges. Covering more than $36 billion in institutional, state, and federal aid, it has a free software disk that estimates costs and helps find the right payment plan for you.
ISBN 697-9, 720 pp., 8½ x 11, $26.95 pb, 14th edition

Peterson's Guide to Scholarships, Grants & Prizes 1997

Provides details on more than $2 billion in aid available to students from nearly 2,000 private sources. Plus—a free software disk allows you to search data according to your own criteria and then print out a list of matching awards.
ISBN 696-0, 550 pp., 8½ x 11, $24.95 pb

USA TODAY Financial Aid for College

Pat Ordovensky

"... could save you thousands." —*College Preview*

A quick guide to determine what your financial aid options are, how to calculate your ability to pay, how and when to apply—and how to fill out the forms.
ISBN 568-9, 160 pp., 6 x 9, $8.95 pb

USA TODAY Getting into College

Pat Ordovensky

"A good starting point for all students of any age." —*VOYA*

Provides you—and your parents—with a concise overview of the entire selection, application, and admission process. Plus—it answers the most commonly asked questions from *USA TODAY's* annual "Financial Aid and Admissions Hotline."
ISBN 463-1, 160 pp., 6 x 9, $8.95 pb

Writing a Winning College Application Essay

Wilma Davidson and Susan McCloskey

Break the tough task of college essay writing into manageable steps and write a practically painless application essay that will help you stand out. Here's a quick read with plenty of humor and fun features such as the "Writer's Survival Kit" for avoiding common errors.
ISBN 601-4, 120 pp., 6 x 9, $9.95 pb

Visit Peterson's on the Internet
http://www.petersons.com

Learn about colleges, financial aid, language studies, summer and leisure-time activities, internships—and much more.